Food & Beverage Market Place

Volume 1

2021

Twentieth Edition

Food & Beverage Market Place

Volume 1

Food & Beverage Manufacturers

Product Categories

Company Profiles

Grey House Publishing

AMENIA, NY 12501

PRESIDENT: Richard Gottlieb
PUBLISHER: Leslie Mackenzie
EDITORIAL DIRECTOR: Laura Mars

PRODUCTION MANAGER: Kristen Hayes
RESEARCH ASSISTANTS: Olivia Parsonson; Sarah Reside
COMPOSITION: David Garoogian

MARKETING DIRECTOR: Jessica Moody

Grey House Publishing, Inc.
4919 Route 22
Amenia, NY 12501
518.789.8700
FAX 845.373.6390
www.greyhouse.com
e-mail: books @greyhouse.com

First edition published 2001
Twentieth edition published 2020
Printed in Canada

Food & beverage market place. — 20th ed. (2021) —
3 v. ; 27.5 cm. Annual
Includes index.
ISSN: 1554-6334

1. Food industry and trade—United States—Directories. 2. Food industry and trade—Canada—Directories. 3. Beverage industry—United States—Directories. 4. Beverage industry—Canada—Directories. I. Grey House Publishing, Inc. II. Title: Food & beverage market place.

HD9003.T48
338-dc21

3-Volume Set ISBN: 978-1-64265-464-6
Volume 1 ISBN: 978-1-64265-465-3
Volume 2 ISBN: 978-1-64265-466-0
Volume 3 ISBN: 978-1-64265-467-7

Table of Contents

VOLUME 1

VOLUME 2

VOLUME 3

Introduction

This 2021 edition of *Food & Beverage Market Place* represents the largest, most comprehensive resource of food and beverage manufacturers and service suppliers on the market today. These three volumes include over 45,000 company profiles that address all sectors of the industry—finished goods and ingredients manufacturers, equipment manufacturers, and third-party logistics providers, including transportation, warehousing, wholesalers, brokers, importers and exporters.

While the food and beverage industry generally continues to grow, the reality of the COVID-19 pandemic has presented many challenges to this truly essential industry. At the time of this writing, out of home consumption, with its high margin of profit, has been reduced nearly to a standstill for several months. Mandated quarantines have disrupted supply chains. Consumers are shifing to digital shopping and home delivery. The industry is redefining its work force and finding new ways to connect with customers.

One segment has found a silver lining in the cloud of COVID-19, and that is meal-kit companies. As consumers adapt to cooking and eating at home, meal kits, delivered to your door with conveniently packaged food and easy-to-follow recipes, have a huge appeal. Time will tell if they can sustain and build on the momentum created by the current quarantine.

Another interesting consequence of the current environment is the kinds of foods that people are eating. While certain long-standing food trends are well entrenched in our society, especially now, including natural and organic food, like those with antioxidants for healthy aging, and foods with good bacteria that promote digestive health, there is a significant uptick in online searches for cinammon roll and hot cross buns recipes, and a shortage of yeast on supermarket shelves. The growth in plant-based food is significant and, experts say, a trend that is likely to continue. While that would be a good thing, hopefully another trend—quarantine snacking—is temporary, as people start to spend less time around the house. In addition, following this Introduction in Volume 1 are two items that offer more information related to COVID-19 and the food and beverage industry: *Best Practices for Retail Food Stores, Restaurants & Food Pick Up and Delivery Services;* and *The Impact of COVID-19 on Shopping Behavior.*

Other industry trends are likely to continue, as consumers focus on foods that encourage sustainability, foods that are convenient and healthy, foods that are processed in secure and safe environments, and foods with complex world flavors.

As food and beverage consumers' needs evolve, *Food & Beverage Market Place* continues to keep pace. The research for this edition focused on ingredient, nutrition and health food manufacturers. You'll find packaging that is mindful of the environment, and processing systems that are safe and secure. Whatever slice of the market you cater to, you will find your buyers, sellers, and users in this comprehensive, three-volume reference tool containing the complete coverage our subscribers have come to expect. Our extensive indexing makes quick work of locating exactly the company, product or service you are looking for.

Data Statistics

Each of the eight chapters in *Food & Beverage Market Place* reflects a massive update effort. This 2021 edition includes hundreds of new company profiles and thousands of updates throughout the three volumes. You will find 83,214 key executives, 22,668 web sites, and 15,869 e-mails. The volumes break down as follows:

Volume 1 Food, Beverage & Ingredient Manufacturers - 14,086

Volume 2 Equipment, Supply & Service Providers - 13,465

Volume 3 Third Party Logistics
Brokers - 1,287
Importers & Exporters - 8,818
Transportation Firms - 707
Warehouse Companies - 1,044
Wholesalers & Distributors - 5,904

Arrangement

The product category sections for both food and beverage products in Volume 1 and equipment and supplies in Volume 2 begin with Product Category Lists. These include over 6,000 alphabetical terms for everything from Abalone to Zinc Citrate, from Adhesive Tapes to Zipper Application Systems. Use the detailed cross-references to find the full entry in the Product Category sections that immediately follow. Here you will find up to three levels of detail, for example—*Fish & Seafood: Fish: Abalone* or *Ingredients, Flavors & Additives: Vitamins & Supplements: Zinc Citrate*—with the name, location, phone number and packaging format of companies who manufacturer/process the product you are looking for. Organic and Gluten-Free categories make it easy to locate those manufacturers who focus on these food types.

In addition to company profiles, this edition has 17 indexes, 15 chapter-specific, arranged by geographic region, product or company type, and two—All Brands and All Companies—that comprise all three volumes. See the Table of Contents for a complete list of specific indexes. Plus, chapters include User Guides that help you navigate chapter-specific data.

We are confident that this reference is the foremost research tool in the food and beverage industry. It will prove invaluable to manufacturers, buyers, specifiers, market researchers, consultants, and anyone working in food and beverage—one of the largest industries in the country.

Praise for previous editions:

> *"...This set can be used to find basic information or to track trends in a dynamic industry.... Recommended for large public or academic libraries."*
>
> *"...Each volume contains helpful user guides and key that describes the field of data that appear in that chapter.... This publication is essential for researchers in the food industry, and large academic and public libraries."*
>
> —American Reference Books Annual

Online Database & Mailing Lists

Food & Beverage Market Place is also available for subscription on https://gold.greyhouse.com for even faster, easier access to this wealth of information. Subscribers can search by product category, state, sales volume, employee size, personnel name, title and much more. Plus, users can print out prospect sheets or download data into their own spreadsheet or database. This database is a must for anyone marketing a product or service to this vast industry. Visit the site, or call 800-562-2139 for a free trial.

Summary of Best Practices for Retail Food Stores, Restaurants, and Food Pick-Up/Delivery Services During the COVID-19 Pandemic

FDA U.S. FOOD & DRUG ADMINISTRATION

BE HEALTHY, BE CLEAN

- Employees - Stay home or leave work if sick; consult doctor if sick, and contact supervisor
- Employers - Instruct sick employees to stay home and send home immediately if sick
- Employers - Pre-screen employees exposed to COVID-19 for temperature and other symptoms

- Wash your hands often with soap and water for at least 20 seconds
- If soap and water are not available, use a 60% alcohol-based hand sanitizer per CDC
- Avoid touching your eyes, nose, and mouth with unwashed hands
- Wear mask/face covering per CDC & FDA

- Never touch Ready-to-Eat foods with bare hands
- Use single service gloves, deli tissue, or suitable utensils
- Wrap food containers to prevent cross contamination
- Follow 4 steps to food safety Clean, Separate, Cook, and Chill

CLEAN & DISINFECT

- Train employees on cleaning and disinfecting procedures, and protective measures, per CDC and FDA
- Have and use cleaning products and supplies
- Follow protective measures

- Disinfect high-touch surfaces frequently
- Use EPA-registered disinfectant
- Ensure food containers and utensils are cleaned and sanitized

- Prepare and use sanitizers according to label instructions
- Offer sanitizers and wipes to customers to clean grocery cart/basket handles, or utilize store personnel to conduct cleaning/sanitizing

SOCIAL DISTANCE

- Help educate employees and customers on importance of social distancing:
  - Signs
  - Audio messages
  - Consider using every other check-out lane to aid in distancing

- Avoid displays that may result in customer gatherings; discontinue self-serve buffets and salad bars; discourage employee gatherings
- Place floor markings and signs to encourage social distancing

- Shorten customer time in store by encouraging them to:
  - Use shopping lists
  - Order ahead of time, if offered
- Set up designated pick-up areas inside or outside retail establishments

PICK-UP & DELIVERY

- If offering delivery options:
  - Ensure coolers and transport containers are cleaned and sanitized
  - Maintain time and temperature controls
  - Avoid cross contamination; for example, wrap food during transport

- Encourage customers to use "no touch" deliveries
- Notify customers as the delivery is arriving by text message or phone call

- Establish designated pick-up zones for customers
- Offer curb-side pick-up
- Practice social distancing by offering to place orders in vehicle trunks

For more information, see **Best Practices for Retail Food Stores, Restaurants, and Food Pick-Up/Delivery Services During the COVID-19 Pandemic**

April 2020

blue chip
the
impact of
COVID-19
on shopping
behavior
© 2020 blue chip. All rights reserved.

introduction

At the onset of the coronavirus pandemic in the U.S., we saw grocery shopping behavior change seemingly overnight. With social distancing and safety in mind, many have turned to online grocery and click-and-collect to fulfill their shopping needs. Others have continued to rely on trips to physical grocery stores, often struggling to navigate the disruption in that experience brought on by the crisis. With these shifting dynamics in mind, the question for many retailers and manufacturers is how the current crisis, and the changes it has brought, will impact future shopping behavior once the country returns to a new normal.

From April 4–5, 2020, Blue Chip fielded a national survey among 500 primary grocery shoppers across the U.S. to better understand how their grocery shopping behavior has changed due to the coronavirus pandemic, what their impressions are of the new shopping environment, and what they predict their shopping behavior will be like in the future. The results paint a picture of what retailers and brands should be thinking about now to win with shoppers later.

FROM emotion to transaction in-store

The coronavirus crisis has highlighted the central importance of the in-store grocery shopping experience in modern American lives.

Even as the virus spread through the U.S. in March, 9 out of 10 shoppers still chose to get their groceries in a physical store. Three times as many people still shopped in a physical store compared to online.

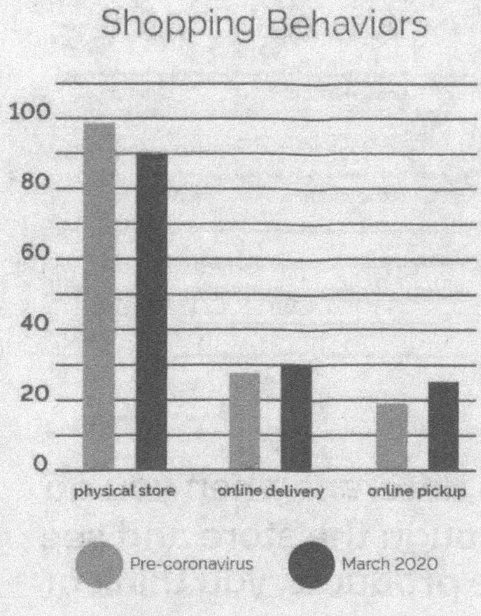

FROM emotion to transaction in-store

What do you enjoy about shopping in-store?

83% picking from products that are on sale

69% broad selection of products

Key drivers for choosing to shop in-store:
DISCOVERY
INDEPENDENCE
EXPLORATION

69% ability to discover new products

64% comparing prices

20% interaction with store personnel

20% seeing friends or neighbors

Source: Blue Chip survey of 500 U.S. grocery shoppers conducted from April 4 – 5, 2020

Respondents noted **discovery, independence** and **exploration** as key motivators driving this choice. The experience of going into a grocery store and picking their own foods gives consumers a sense of control. This is even more true now, when so much of their life feels out of their control.

> **"I don't think the person picking your food would use the same care as you would picking your own."**

> **"It's different when you go through the store and see the products, you think of things not on your list."**

THE changing in-store experience

Although 90% of surveyed shoppers still make in-store trips, those shopping experiences are nearly unrecognizable compared to pre-pandemic times. Everything from social distancing measures to one-way aisles, capacity limits to inventory challenges—it is entirely unfamiliar. Self-serve areas of the store, such as sampling areas, hot bars, bakeries and delis, have closed. Prepared foods in many stores are likewise on temporary hiatus. The in-store experience that retailers spent years building has begun dissolving, and the pendulum has swung back toward a fundamentally transactional experience. Shoppers are being retrained to treat the visit as such.

from browsing to sprinting

Shoppers are going through stores with *purpose*, planning with clear intention to get in and out with what they need quickly, in order to limit exposure. This has been compounded by retailers managing shopper traffic flow in their stores with measures like traffic-controlled checkout queues, one-way aisle flow, one-in-one-out policies and more.

Walmart recently implemented a one-in-one-out policy.

Source: Field Agent

THE changing in-store experience

In this environment, shoppers appear to be forming strategies for their limited stock-up trips, driven by the simple goal of acquiring each item on their list. There is less browsing, less consideration between brands and less discovery.

Adding to that, brands and grocery merchandisers have reduced in-store promotions, which, pre-pandemic, would have affected in-store shopping behaviors. Given that shopping is more mission driven today, pre-store planning and list-making are more important than ever, providing opportunities for both retailers and brands to reach shoppers. Going forward, it will be important to observe the nature and behaviors of the in-store trip that endure as shoppers adapt to a new normal, which may be driven more by efficiency and offer fewer experiences, like sampling.

from "my brand" to "any brand"

Brands in commodity categories that shoppers consider essential have been in high demand and susceptible to frantic buying and out-of-stocks. As a result, these brands have faced difficult challenges in maintaining inventories—a fact that will affect their brand strategies during the crisis and beyond. Shoppers now make purchase decisions based upon what is available and whether they need to stock up.

Leading brands in essential categories like toilet paper had, up until recently, loyal shoppers that led on differentiated positioning, but out-of-stock issues have forced shoppers to try competitors that they may be unfamiliar with. Those less familiar brands will now forever be in shopper consideration sets in future trips after the crisis has passed. Once we reach that new normal, leading brands in essential categories will need to reestablish their dominance in the shopper consideration set and potentially reevaluate their value proposition.

THE changing in-store experience

Once we reach that new normal, leading brands in essential categories will need to reestablish their dominance in the shopper consideration set. On the flip side, those brands gaining trial due to their availability should think about how to stay top-of-mind and turn new triers into future buyers.

looking ahead

Once the pandemic subsides and Americans once again feel safe and welcome shopping in-store, the experience may still be fundamentally different. Learned shopping behaviors are likely to stay. A heightened concern over cleanliness and sanitation will certainly remain, potentially disrupting long-held practices of food and beverage sampling. The store, the aisle and the category will be shopped differently.

So what should brands and retailers be thinking about *now* to have real impact *later?*

implications

- Sampling—once a key discovery and trial driver for food and beverage—will not come back immediately, if at all. Rethink in-store sampling strategy (e.g., individually wrapped, single serve packages).
- While in-store activity has stalled, price and promotion will play a big part in brands getting back in front of shoppers and easing the squeeze felt during the pandemic period.
- Brands will need to rebuild loyalty with consumers who may have temporarily switched to other brands. Premium brands will need to lean into their value proposition and rebuild those relationships.
- Retailers will need to reevaluate how to bring back experience elements within the boundaries of the new normal.

FROM transaction to emotion online

Facing the new reality of social distancing and the potential health risks of going to the grocery store, many consumers turned to e-commerce solutions to fulfill their needs. While 90% of shoppers were making in-store trips, online and click-and-collect increased 32% during March 2020 compared to before the pandemic. Additionally, our survey showed that half of people who haven't shopped online yet are open to doing so in the future.

Why shop online?

Pre-coronavirus	March 2020
86% convenience	**89%** minimize exposure to health risk
79% good prices	**85%** convenience
75% saves me time	**84%** reduces stress

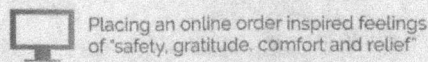

Placing an online order inspired feelings of "safety, gratitude, comfort and relief"

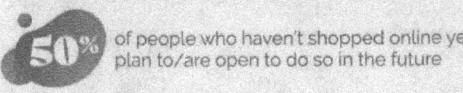

50% of people who haven't shopped online yet plan to/are open to do so in the future

Source: Blue Chip survey of 500 U.S. grocery shoppers conducted from April 4 – 5, 2020

Before the coronavirus pandemic, consumers valued e-commerce because it was convenient, saving them time and money. However, as external motivators pushed people online, there was a shift in the value equation. Safety, convenience and stress reduction emerged as key factors to shop online. "Reducing stress" increased 20 points alone during this time period. Online grocery shopping inspired feelings of safety, relief, comfort and gratitude.

THE spectrum of satisfaction

While heightened emotions surround the e-commerce experience, only 4 in 10 surveyed noted they were "very satisfied" with the actual online shopping experience itself.

Those who were satisfied with the experience noted emotional associations of safety, relief and comfort, along with a new recognition of the practical aspects of convenience and time-saving.

"It makes my life easier. I feel safer being at home instead of having to go our and shop."

"I am less intimidated by the process; the ease and convenience of it was a revelation."

For others, out-of-stock items, product substitutions, lengthy delivery windows and inflated prices soured the experience.

"Prices were extremely marked up. They would substitute store brand when possible, but the price was the same as name brand."

"Not always having what I need in stock and not finding out until after I attempt to place an order."

THE spectrum of satisfaction

the missing link

Until now, online grocery shopping has, for most shoppers, been largely functional and transactional. The convenience it provides rises to the top of shopper needs and imparts a higher-level benefit of control over one's time, which is critical for many. But for many others, it hasn't risen to the level of true *shopping*. It lacks the *feel* of shopping, the *visceral reward* of shopping, the *personal touch* of shopping. It has been the red-haired stepchild of *real shopping*. It lacks the feelings of trust, humanity and control that are inherent in the in-store experience.

Looking ahead, when going to the grocery store is no longer a life or death situation and the heightened emotions around health and safety subside, the pre-crisis e-commerce selling points of convenience and time-saving alone will not be enough to keep some shoppers in the e-commerce environment.

How can retailers and brands evolve the online experience on the other end of this crisis to fill the emotional voids of trust, humanity and control in the current online grocery environment?

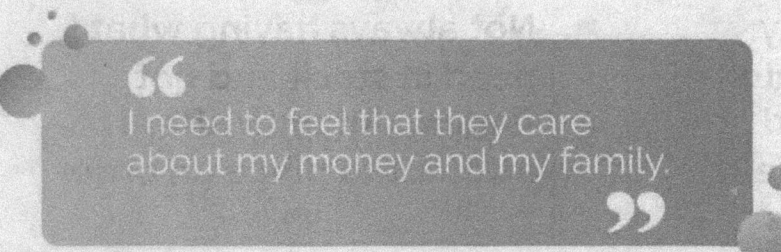

> "I need to feel that they care about my money and my family."

> "I need to trust the person selecting my order."

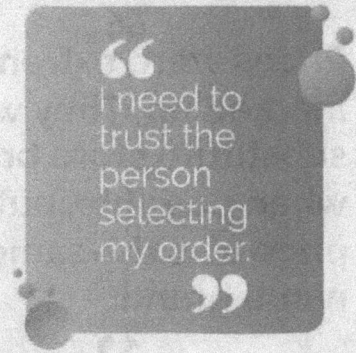

THE spectrum of satisfaction

immediate implications

- Brands and retailers should implement shopper offers to entice repeat purchase online.
- Surprise and delight in delivery orders to keep margins but 'sweeten the deal' on some of the price disparity. Brands can also consider incentives to help offset delivery fees.
- Brands must show up meaningfully and consistently online. If you don't already have an e-commerce strategy in place, plan for it now. Invest in e-commerce but as a brand equity builder.
- Take the time now to reevaluate your e-commerce content to not only ensure there are guideposts for size comparison and product variations but to inspire further exploration and discovery.

longer term

- Online customer service for brand and retailers will be more important than ever. It will no longer be about just providing technical support; it will require human interaction, advice and guidance.
- In the e-commerce space, retailers must examine how to translate those distinct elements of brand personality cultivated in the in-store environment via associates, atmosphere, interaction and selection that shoppers *trust*.
- Humanizing the person fulfilling the order will build trust and affirm that they care about the order as much the shopper who placed it.
- Additionally, show the precautionary measures they use to handle their order with care.

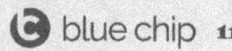

finding the balance

Shopping as we know it has most likely changed forever. At the end of this pandemic, the pendulum may fall back to rest in the middle (or slightly left or right of center) for in-store and online shopping. In all likelihood, the in-store experience won't fully return to what shoppers once considered normal, given the new level of purpose and intention they have brought to the experience and their learned behaviors around "sprint" shopping and heightened safety. At the same time, many who shifted at least some of their shopping to e-commerce, motivated by emotional drivers that emerged in the crisis, may continue to shop more frequently online—especially if retailers and brands deliver emotions that transform the experience from one that is strictly transactional to one that is about building ongoing relationships with shoppers.

Further, as the crisis subsides, we may see the emergence of a Brave New Shopper in the U.S. One with new adaptability, a sharpened set of shopping skills and higher expectations for their shopping experience. To incite discovery and rebuild loyalty in-store, brands will need to reteach shoppers how to navigate categories and find ways to encourage them to shop the aisles. In e-commerce, retailers must develop a richer shopping experience. By instilling emotions like trust, control and humanity into online shopping, they can boost the consumer-retailer relationship and inspire online loyalty.

In the end, the coronavirus crisis has accelerated the appearance of a new omnichannel reality born of uncertainty but fed by the need for action and a spirit of adaptability. This new reality defines a bright, promising future for the brands and retailers who choose to embrace it.

"The impact of COVID-19 on shopping behavior." Blue Chip, 2020. Reprinted with permission, May 2020. The full report can be found online: https://www2.smartbrief.com/rest/lp-proxy/landing-pages/ce9cde09-910e-42db-a5e3-5baa26fb454f.

MANUFACTURERS

Manufacturer User Guide

The **Food & Beverage Manufacturers Chapter** of *Food & Beverage Market Place* includes companies that manufacture food and beverage products, both finished goods and ingredients. The chapter begins with a **Product Category Listing** of food and beverage products that are manufactured by companies in this chapter. This category list is followed by a **Product Category Index**, organized by product. Each company listing includes packaging type, city and phone number.

Following the **Product Category Index** are the descriptive listings, which are organized alphabetically. Following the A – Z Food and Beverage Manufacturers listings are four indexes: **Brand Index**, which lists food and beverage brand names; **Ethnic Food Index**, which lists companies by ethnic type of food they manufacture; **Geographic Index**, which lists all companies by state, and **Parent Company Index**; which lists companies by their corporate parent. These Indexes refers to listing numbers, not page numbers.

Below is a sample listing illustrating the kind of information that is or might be included in a Food and Beverage Manufacturer listing. Each numbered item of information is described in the User Key on the following page.

---

1 → 100000

2 → **(HQ) AFF Specialties**

3 → 555 Maplewood Drive

Cordova, TN 38016

4 → 001-381-3222

5 → 001-381-3223

6 → 888-381-324

7 → info@AFF.com

8 → www.AFF.com

9 → Manufacturer of Italian cheese and dried pasta and cooking oils. Exporter of olive oil.

10 → President: Brian Miller
CFO: Philip George
COO: Blakeny Pinschell
Vice President: Kristin Rolls
Marketing: Melissa Backwith

11 → *Estimated Sales*: $65 Million

12 → *Number Employees*: 80

13 → *Sq. Footage*: 30000

14 → *Parent Co.*: Associated Foods

15 → *Type of Packaging:* Consumer, Food Service, Bulk

16 → *Company is also listed in the following section(s)*: Exporter

17 → *Other Locations*: AFF Specialties, Atlanta, GA

18 → *Brands:* Unique, Fiesta, Baking Rite, Carruso, Golden Dairy

Manufacturer User Key

1 → **Record Number:** Entries are listed alphabetically within each category and numbered sequentially. The entry number, rather than the page number, is used in the indexes to refer to listings.

2 → **Company Name:** Formal name of company. HQ indicates headquarter location. If names are completely capitalized, the listing will appear at the beginning of the alphabetized section.

3 → **Address:** Location or permanent address of the company. If the mailing address differs from the street address, it will appear second. Companies are indexed by state.

4 → **Phone Number:** The listed phone number is usually for the main office, but may also be for the sales, marketing, or public relations office as provided.

5 → **Fax Number:** This is listed when provided by the company.

6 → **Toll-Free Number:** This is listed when provided by the company.

7 → **E-Mail:** This is listed when provided, and is generally the main office e-mail.

8 → **Web Site:** This is listed when provided by the company and is also referred to as an URL address. These web sites are accessed through the Internet by typing http:// before the URL address.

9 → **Description**: This paragraph contains a brief description of the food and beverages manufactured by the company, as well as other services they provide. Companies are indexed by the ethnic food they manufacture.

10 → **Key Personnel:** Names and titles of company executives.

11 → **Estimated Sales:** This is listed when provided by the company.

12 → **Number of Employees:** Total number of employees within the company.

13 → **Sq. Footage:** Size of facility.

14 → **Parent Co.:** If the listing is a division of another company, the parent is listed here. Companies are indexed by the ethnic foods they manufacture.

15 → **Type of Packaging:** Indicates the market that the food or beverage products are packaged for.

16 → Indicates what other section in ***Food & Beverage Market Place*** this company is listed: Volume 1: Manufacturers. Volume 2: Equipment, Supplies & Services; Transportation; Warehouse; Wholesalers/Distributors. Volume 3: Brokers; Importers/Exporters.

17 → **Other locations:** Indicates other company locations.

18 → **Brands:** Listing of brand names that the company manufactures. Companies are indexed by brand names.

A

Abalone Fish *See Fish & Seafood: Fish: Abalone*
Arborio Rice *See Cereals, Grains, Rice & Flour: Rice: Aborio*
Acacia Gum *See Ingredients, Flavors & Additives: Gums: Acacia Gum*
Acetic Acidulants *See Ingredients, Flavors & Additives: Acidulants: Acetic*
Acidophilus Cultures *See Ingredients, Flavors & Additives: Cultures & Yeasts: Acidophilus Cultures*
Acids *See Ingredients, Flavors & Additives: Acids*
Acidulants *See Ingredients, Flavors & Additives: Acidulants*
Acorn Squash *See Fruits & Vegetables: Squash: Acorn*
Active Salt *See Spices, Seasonings & Seeds: Salt: Active*
Additives *See Ingredients, Flavors & Additives: Additives*
Additives Enzymes *See Ingredients, Flavors & Additives: Enzymes: Additives*
Ade Juices *See Beverages: Juices: Ade*
Adipic Acids *See Ingredients, Flavors & Additives: Acids: Adipic*
Adjuncts *See Ingredients, Flavors & Additives: Adjuncts*
Adobo Powders *See Ingredients, Flavors & Additives: Powders: Adobo*
Adzuki Beans *See Fruits & Vegetables: Beans: Adzuki*
Agar-Agar *See Ingredients, Flavors & Additives: Gums: Agar-Agar*
Agents *See Ingredients, Flavors & Additives: Agents*
Agnolotti *See Pasta & Noodles: Agnolotti*
Albacore Tuna Fish *See Fish & Seafood: Fish: Tuna: Albacore*
Albumen Solids *See Eggs & Egg Products: Solids: Albumen*
Alcoholic Beverages *See Beverages: Alcoholic Beverages*
Alcohols *See Ingredients, Flavors & Additives: Alcohols*
Alfalfa *See Cereals, Grains, Rice & Flour: Alfalfa*
Alfalfa Seeds *See Spices, Seasonings & Seeds: Seeds: Alfalfa*
Alfalfa Sprouts *See Fruits & Vegetables: Sprouts: Alfalfa*
Alfredo Sauces *See Sauces, Dips & Dressings: Sauces: Alfredo*
Algae *See Fruits & Vegetables: Algae*
Algin & Alginates *See Ingredients, Flavors & Additives: Gums: Algin & Alginates*
All Purpose Flour *See Cereals, Grains, Rice & Flour: Flour: All Purpose*
All Purpose Herbs Blends *See Ingredients, Flavors & Additives: Blends: Herbs: All Purpose*
Alligator Game *See Meats & Meat Products: Game: Alligator*
Allspice *See Spices, Seasonings & Seeds: Spices: Allspice*
Almond Biscotti *See Baked Goods: Cookies & Bars: Biscotti: Almond*
Almond Cookies *See Baked Goods: Cookies & Bars: Almond Cookies*
Almond Flavors *See Ingredients, Flavors & Additives: Flavors: Almond*
Almond Flour *See Cereals, Grains, Rice & Flour: Flour: Almond*
Almond Nut Butters *See Nuts & Nut Butters: Nut Butters: Almond*
Almond Nut Pastes *See Nuts & Nut Butters: Nut Pastes: Almond*
Almond Oils *See Oils, Shortening & Fats: Oils: Almond*
Almond Pastes *See Ingredients, Flavors & Additives: Pastes: Almond*
Almonds *See Nuts & Nut Butters: Nuts: Almonds*
Aloe Juices *See Beverages: Juices: Aloe*
Aloe Vera *See Fruits & Vegetables: Aloe Vera*
Amaranth *See Cereals, Grains, Rice & Flour: Grains: Amaranth*
Amaretto Cookies *See Baked Goods: Cookies & Bars: Amaretto Cookies*
Amaretto Flavors *See Ingredients, Flavors & Additives: Flavors: Amaretto*
Amaretto Liqueurs & Cordials *See Beverages: Spirits & Liqueurs: Liqueurs & Cordials: Amaretto*
Amber Ale *See Beverages: Beers: American & British Ale: Amber Ale*
Amber Jack *See Fish & Seafood: Fish: Amber Jack*
Amber Lager *See Beverages: Beers: Lager: Amber Lager*
American & British Ale *See Beverages: Beers: American & British Ale*
American Cheese *See Cheese & Cheese Products: Cheese: American*
American Cheese Imitations *See Cheese & Cheese Products: Imitation Cheeses & Substitutes: Imitation: American*
American Cheese Powders *See Ingredients, Flavors & Additives: Powders: Cheese: American*
American Cheese Substitutes *See Cheese & Cheese Products: Imitation Cheeses & Substitutes: Substitutes: American*
American/Skim Milk Cheese, Sliced Blend *See Cheese & Cheese Products: Cheese: Blend - American/Skim Milk: Sliced*
Aminoacetic Acids *See Ingredients, Flavors & Additives: Acids: Aminoacetic*
Ammonium Carbonate *See Ingredients, Flavors & Additives: Ammonium Carbonate*
Ammonium Phosphates *See Ingredients, Flavors & Additives: Phosphates: Ammonium Phosphates*
Analogs *See Ingredients, Flavors & Additives: Analogs*
Ancho Ground Chile Pepper *See Spices, Seasonings & Seeds: Spices: Chile Pepper: Ancho Ground*
Ancho Peppers *See Fruits & Vegetables: Peppers: Ancho*
Anchovies *See Fish & Seafood: Fish: Anchovies*
Anchovies Paste *See Fish & Seafood: Fish: Anchovies: Paste*
Andouille Sausage Seasonings *See Spices, Seasonings & Seeds: Seasonings: Sausage: Andouille*
Andouille Sausages *See Meats & Meat Products: Smoked, Cured & Deli Meats: Sausages: Andouille*
Angel Food Cake *See Baked Goods: Cakes & Pastries: Angel Food Cake*
Angel Hair *See Pasta & Noodles: Angel Hair*
Animal Crackers *See Baked Goods: Cookies & Bars: Animal Crackers*
Anise Flavors *See Ingredients, Flavors & Additives: Flavors: Anise; See also Spices/Anise Seed*
Anise Liqueur *See Beverages: Spirits & Liqueurs: Liqueurs & Cordials: Anise Liqueur*
Anise or Aniseed Oils *See Oils, Shortening & Fats: Oils: Anise or Aniseed*
Anise or Aniseed Seeds *See Spices, Seasonings & Seeds: Seeds: Anise or Aniseed*
Anise, Star *See Spices, Seasonings & Seeds: Spices: Anise - Star*
Annatto Colors *See Ingredients, Flavors & Additives: Colors: Annatto*
Annatto Natural Colors *See Ingredients, Flavors & Additives: Colors: Natural: Annatto*
Annatto Seeds *See Spices, Seasonings & Seeds: Seeds: Annatto*
Anthocyanins Grape Skin *See Ingredients, Flavors & Additives: Colors: Natural: Anthocyanins Grape Skin*
Anticaking Additives *See Ingredients, Flavors & Additives: Additives: Anticaking*
Anticaking Agents *See Ingredients, Flavors & Additives: Agents: Anticaking*
Antimicrobial Agents *See Ingredients, Flavors & Additives: Agents: Antimicrobial*
Antioxidants *See Specialty & Organic Foods: Organic Foods: Natural: Antioxidants; See also Organic Foods; See also Ingredients, Flavors & Additives: Antioxidants*
Antipasto *See Prepared Foods: Antipasto*
Antipasto Salads *See Prepared Foods: Prepared Salads: Antipasto*
Appaloosa Beans *See Fruits & Vegetables: Beans: Appaloosa*
Appetizers *See Prepared Foods: Appetizers; See also Prepared Foods: Appetizers: Fresh, Canned & Frozen*
Apple *See Fruits & Vegetables: Apple*
Apple Boysin Berry Juices *See Beverages: Juices: Apple Boysin Berry*
Apple Butter *See Jams, Jellies & Spreads: Spreads: Apple Butter*
Apple Cider Juices *See Beverages: Juices: Apple Cider*
Apple Cider Vinegar *See Sauces, Dips & Dressings: Vinegar: Apple Cider*
Apple Cobbler *See Baked Goods: Cakes & Pastries: Apple Cobbler*
Apple Cranberry Juices *See Beverages: Juices: Apple Cranberry*
Apple Flavors *See Ingredients, Flavors & Additives: Flavors: Apple*
Apple Grape Juices *See Beverages: Juices: Apple Grape*
Apple Juices *See Beverages: Juices: Apple*
Apple Pectins *See Ingredients, Flavors & Additives: Pectins: Apple*
Apple Pies *See Baked Goods: Pies: Apple*
Apple Rings *See Fruits & Vegetables: Apple: Rings*
Apple Sauces *See Fruits & Vegetables: Sauces: Apple*
Apple Sauces with Other Fruit or Spices *See Fruits & Vegetables: Sauces: Apple: with Other Fruit or Spices*
Apple Slices *See Fruits & Vegetables: Apple: Slices*
Apricot *See Fruits & Vegetables: Apricot*
Apricot Jams *See Jams, Jellies & Spreads: Jams: Apricot*
Apricot Juices *See Beverages: Juices: Apricot*
Apricot Kernals *See Fruits & Vegetables: Apricot: Kernals*
Aquaculture *See Specialty & Organic Foods: Aquaculture; See also Organic Foods*
Arabic *See Ingredients, Flavors & Additives: Gums: Arabic*
Arctic Charr *See Fish & Seafood: Fish: Arctic Charr*
Ardouille Sausage *See Meats & Meat Products: Pork & Pork Products: Sausage: Ardouille*
Aroma Chemicals & Materials *See Ingredients, Flavors & Additives: Aroma Chemicals & Materials; See also See Ingredients, Flavors & Additives: Aroma Chemicals; See also See Ingredients, Flavors & Additives: Aroma Chemicals & Materials: Materials*
Arrowroot Flour *See Cereals, Grains, Rice & Flour: Flour: Arrowroot*
Arrowroot Starches *See Ingredients, Flavors & Additives: Starches: Arrowroot*
Arrowroot Thickening Agents *See Ingredients, Flavors & Additives: Agents: Thickening: Arrowroot*
Artichoke *See Fruits & Vegetables: Artichoke*
Artificial Flavors *See Ingredients, Flavors & Additives: Flavors: Artificial*
Artificial Sweeteners *See Sugars, Syrups & Sweeteners: Artificial*
Ascorbic Acid *See Ingredients, Flavors & Additives: Antioxidants: Ascorbic Acid; See also Flavors & Additives: Vitamins & Supplements: C: Ascorbic Acid*
Aseptic Packed Capsicums Peppers *See Fruits & Vegetables: Peppers: Capsicums: Aseptic Packed*
Asiago Cheese *See Cheese & Cheese Products: Cheese: Asiago*
Asian *See Ethnic Foods: Asian*
Asian Pear *See Fruits & Vegetables: Pear: Asian*
Asparagus *See Fruits & Vegetables: Asparagus*
Aspartame *See Sugars, Syrups & Sweeteners: Sugar Substitutes: Aspartame*
Au Gratin Potatoes *See Fruits & Vegetables: Potatoes: Au Gratin*
Autolysates Yeast *See Ingredients, Flavors & Additives: Cultures & Yeasts: Yeast: Autolysates*
Avocado *See Fruits & Vegetables: Avocado*
Avocado Oils *See Oils, Shortening & Fats: Oils: Avocado*
Avocado Products *See Fruits & Vegetables: Avocado: Avocado Products*

B

Babka *See Baked Goods: Cakes & Pastries: Babka*
Baby Carrot *See Fruits & Vegetables: Carrot: Baby*
Baby Spinach *See Fruits & Vegetables: Spinach: Baby*
Bacillus Cultures *See Ingredients, Flavors & Additives: Cultures & Yeasts: Bacillus*
Bacon *See Meats & Meat Products: Smoked, Cured & Deli Meats: Bacon*
Bacon Pork Rinds *See Snack Foods: Pork Rinds: Bacon*
Bacon Slices *See Meats & Meat Products: Smoked, Cured & Deli Meats: Bacon: Slices*
Bacteria *See Ingredients, Flavors & Additives: Cultures & Yeasts: Bacteria*
Bacterial Cultures, Starter Media & Culture Replacements *See Ingredients, Flavors & Additives: Cultures & Yeasts: Bacterial Cultures, Starter Media & Culture Replacements*
Bacteriological Cultures & Yeasts *See Ingredients, Flavors & Additives: Cultures & Yeasts: Bacteriological*
Bagel Chips *See Snack Foods: Chips: Bagel Chips*
Bagels *See Baked Goods: Breads: Bagels*
Bagged Parboiled Rice *See Cereals, Grains, Rice & Flour: Rice: Parboiled: Bagged*
Bagged Specialty-Packaged Candy *See Candy & Confectionery: Specialty-Packaged Candy: Bagged*
Bagged Wheat *See Cereals, Grains, Rice & Flour: Wheat: Bagged*
Baguettes *See Baked Goods: Breads: Baguettes*
Baita Fruli Cheese *See Cheese & Cheese Products: Cheese: Baita Fruli*
Baked & Stuffed Potatoes *See Fruits & Vegetables: Potatoes: Baked & Stuffed*

EXAMPLE: **Canadian Style Bacon** *See Meats & Meat Products: Smoked, Cured & Deli Meats: Bacon: Canadian Style* (1 = Canadian Style Bacon; 2 = Meats & Meat Products; 3 = Smoked, Cured & Deli Meats; 4 = Bacon; 5 = Canadian Style)

1. Product or Service you are looking for
2. Main Category, in alphabetical order, located in the page headers starting on page 27
3. Category Description, located in black bars and in page headers
4. Product Category, located in gray bars
5. Product Type, located under gray bars, centered in bold

Product Category List

Baked Beans *See Prepared Foods: Baked Beans (see also Pork & Beans); See also Fruits & Vegetables: Beans: Baked*

Baked Chips *See Snack Foods: Chips: Baked*

Baked Goods *See Baked Goods*

Baked Potato Chips *See Snack Foods: Chips: Potato: Baked*

Bakers Active Yeast *See Ingredients, Flavors & Additives: Cultures & Yeasts: Yeast: Bakers Active*

Bakers Cheese Powders *See Ingredients, Flavors & Additives: Powders: Cheese: Bakers*

Bakers' & Confectioners' Supplies *See Ingredients, Flavors & Additives: Confectionery: Bakers' & Confectioners' Supplies*

Bakers' Yeast *See Ingredients, Flavors & Additives: Cultures & Yeasts: Yeast: Bakers'*

Bakery Ingredients *See Ingredients, Flavors & Additives: Ingredients: Bakery*

Bakery Mix Flour *See Cereals, Grains, Rice & Flour: Flour: Bakery Mix*

Baking Bits *See Ingredients, Flavors & Additives: Bits: Baking*

Baking Chocolate *See Candy & Confectionery: Chocolate Products: Baking Chocolate*

Baking Decorations *See Candy & Confectionery: Decorations & Icings: Decorations: Baking*

Baking Doughs *See Doughs, Mixes & Fillings: Doughs: Baking*

Baking Fillings *See Doughs, Mixes & Fillings: Fillings: Baking*

Baking Mixes *See Doughs, Mixes & Fillings: Mixes: Baking*

Baking Mixes Flour *See Cereals, Grains, Rice & Flour: Flour: Baking Mixes*

Baking Powders *See Ingredients, Flavors & Additives: Powders: Baking*

Baking Seasonings *See Spices, Seasonings & Seeds: Seasonings: Baking*

Baking Shells *See Baked Goods: Pies: Baking Shells*

Baking Soda *See Ingredients, Flavors & Additives: Leaveners: Baking Soda*

Baklava *See Baked Goods: Cakes & Pastries: Baklava*

Balsamic Vinegar *See Sauces, Dips & Dressings: Vinegar: Balsamic*

Balsamic Vinegar Salad Dressings *See Sauces, Dips & Dressings: Salad Dressings: Balsamic Vinegar*

Bamboo Shoots *See Fruits & Vegetables: Bamboo Shoots*

Banana *See Fruits & Vegetables: Banana*

Banana Chips *See Snack Foods: Chips: Banana*

Banana Flakes *See Ingredients, Flavors & Additives: Flakes: Banana*

Banana Flavors *See Ingredients, Flavors & Additives: Flavors: Banana*

Banana Peppers *See Fruits & Vegetables: Peppers: Banana*

Banana Products *See Fruits & Vegetables: Banana: Banana Products*

Bar Mixers *See Beverages: Mixers: Bar Mixers*

Bar Syrups *See Sugars, Syrups & Sweeteners: Syrups: Bar*

Barbecue Potato Chips *See Snack Foods: Chips: Potato: Barbecue*

Barbecue Products *See Specialty Processed Foods: Barbecue Products (See also Specific Foods)*

Barbecue Sauces *See Sauces, Dips & Dressings: Sauces: Barbecue*

Barbecue Seasonings *See Spices, Seasonings & Seeds: Seasonings: Barbecue*

Barbecued Beef *See Meats & Meat Products: Beef & Beef Products: Barbecued*

Barbecued Chicken *See Meats & Meat Products: Poultry: Chicken: Barbecued*

Barbecued Chicken, Frozen *See Meats & Meat Products: Poultry: Chicken: Barbecued Frozen*

Barbecued Pork *See Meats & Meat Products: Pork & Pork Products: Barbecued*

Barley *See Cereals, Grains, Rice & Flour: Barley*

Barley Bran Fiber *See Cereals, Grains, Rice & Flour: Fiber: Barley Bran*

Barley Flour *See Cereals, Grains, Rice & Flour: Flour: Barley*

Bars, Cereal *See Cereals, Grains, Rice & Flour: Cereal: Bars*

Bars, Cookies *See Baked Goods: Cookies & Bars: Bars*

Bartlett Pear *See Fruits & Vegetables: Pear: Bartlett*

Bases *See Ingredients, Flavors & Additives: Bases*

Bases, Ice Cream *See Dairy Products: Ice Cream: Bases*

Basil Leaf *See Spices, Seasonings & Seeds: Spices: Basil Leaf*

Basil Spices *See Spices, Seasonings & Seeds: Spices: Basil*

Basmati Rice *See Cereals, Grains, Rice & Flour: Rice: Basmati*

Bass *See Fish & Seafood: Fish: Bass*

Batters *See Doughs, Mixes & Fillings: Batters*

Bay Leaves *See Spices, Seasonings & Seeds: Spices: Bay Leaves*

Bean Dips *See Sauces, Dips & Dressings: Dips: Bean*

Bean Flour *See Cereals, Grains, Rice & Flour: Flour: Bean*

Bean Oils *See Oils, Shortening & Fats: Oils: Bean*

Bean Sprouts *See Fruits & Vegetables: Sprouts: Bean*

Beans *See Fruits & Vegetables: Beans*

Bearnaise Sauces *See Sauces, Dips & Dressings: Sauces: Bearnaise*

Bee Pollen & Propolis *See Sugars, Syrups & Sweeteners: Honey: Bee Pollen & Propolis*

Beech Mushrooms *See Fruits & Vegetables: Mushrooms: Beech*

Beef & Beef Products *See Meats & Meat Products: Beef & Beef Products*

Beef & Beef Products, Sliced *See Meats & Meat Products: Beef & Beef Products: Sliced*

Beef & Beef Products, Special Trim *See Meats & Meat Products: Beef & Beef Products: Special Trim*

Beef Bases *See Ingredients, Flavors & Additives: Bases: Beef*

Beef Bouillon *See Ingredients, Flavors & Additives: Bases: Bouillon: Beef*

Beef Casings *See Meats & Meat Products: Smoked, Cured & Deli Meats: Sausages: Casings: Sausage, Pork, Beef*

Beef Certified Organic *See Specialty & Organic Foods: Organic Foods: Certified: Beef; See also Organic Foods*

Beef Dinners *See Meats & Meat Products: Beef & Beef Products: Dinners*

Beef Dinners, Prepared Meals *See Prepared Foods: Prepared Meals: Beef Dinner*

Beef Extracts *See Ingredients, Flavors & Additives: Extracts: Beef*

Beef Frankfurters *See Meats & Meat Products: Frankfurters: Beef*

Beef Jerky *See Meats & Meat Products: Smoked, Cured & Deli Meats: Beef Jerky*

Beef Marinades *See Sauces, Dips & Dressings: Marinades: Beef*

Beef Soup *See Prepared Foods: Soups & Stews: Beef Soup*

Beef Stew *See Meats & Meat Products: Beef & Beef Products: Stew; See also See Prepared Foods: Soups & Stews: Beef Stew*

Beef Stock Powders *See Ingredients, Flavors & Additives: Powders: Beef Stock*

Beef, Frozen Rolls *See Meats & Meat Products: Beef & Beef Products: Rolls - Frozen*

Beer Flavors *See Ingredients, Flavors & Additives: Flavors: Beer*

Beers *See Beverages: Beers*

Bees Wax *See Sugars, Syrups & Sweeteners: Honey: Bees Wax*

Beet Jellies *See Jams, Jellies & Spreads: Jellies: Beets*

Beet Juices *See Beverages: Juices: Beet*

Beet Powder *See Fruits & Vegetables: Dried & Dehydrated Vegetables: Beet Powder*

Beet Relishes *See Relishes & Pickled Products: Relishes: Beets*

Beets *See Fruits & Vegetables: Beets*

Belgian & French Ale *See Beverages: Beers: Belgian & French Ale*

Bell Peppers *See Fruits & Vegetables: Peppers: Bell*

Bell Peppers, Dehydrated *See Fruits & Vegetables: Dried & Dehydrated Vegetables: Bell Peppers*

Benzoate of Soda *See Ingredients, Flavors & Additives: Benzoate of Soda*

Benzoic Acids *See Ingredients, Flavors & Additives: Acids: Benzoic*

Berries *See Fruits & Vegetables: Berries*

Berries, Frozen *See Fruits & Vegetables: Frozen Fruit: Berries*

Beta Carotene *See Ingredients, Flavors & Additives: Vitamins & Supplements: Beta Carotene*

Betaine Beet *See Ingredients, Flavors & Additives: Colors: Natural: Betaine Beet*

Beverage Bases *See Ingredients, Flavors & Additives: Bases: Beverage*

Beverage Extracts *See Ingredients, Flavors & Additives: Extracts: Beverages*

Beverage Flavors *See Ingredients, Flavors & Additives: Flavors: Beverage*

Beverage Mixes *See Doughs, Mixes & Fillings: Mixes: Beverage*

Beverage Powders *See Ingredients, Flavors & Additives: Powders: Beverage*

Beverage Syrups *See Sugars, Syrups & Sweeteners: Syrups: Beverages*

Beverages *See Beverages*

Bialys *See Baked Goods: Breads: Bialys*

Binders *See Ingredients, Flavors & Additives: Binders*

Binders for Meat Products *See Ingredients, Flavors & Additives: Binders: for Meat Products*

Bing Cherries *See Fruits & Vegetables: Cherries: Bing*

Bioflavinoids *See Ingredients, Flavors & Additives: Bioflavinoids*

Biopolymers *See Ingredients, Flavors & Additives: Biopolymers*

Biotin *See Ingredients, Flavors & Additives: Vitamins & Supplements: Biotin*

Biscotti *See Baked Goods: Cookies & Bars: Biscotti*

Biscuit Mixes *See Doughs, Mixes & Fillings: Mixes: Biscuit*

Biscuits *See Baked Goods: Breads: Biscuits*

Bits *See Ingredients, Flavors & Additives: Bits*

Bits, Imitation Bacon *See Meats & Meat Products: Smoked, Cured & Deli Meats: Bacon: Bits Imitation*

Bits, Real Bacon *See Meats & Meat Products: Smoked, Cured & Deli Meats: Bacon: Bits Real*

Bitters *See Beverages: Bitters*

Black & Tan Ale *See Beverages: Beers: American & British Ale: Black & Tan*

Black Bean Sauces *See Sauces, Dips & Dressings: Sauces: Black Bean*

Black Beans *See Fruits & Vegetables: Beans: Black*

Black Cod Fish *See Fish & Seafood: Fish: Cod: Black*

Black Currant Tea *See Beverages: Coffee & Tea: Tea: Black Currant*

Black Forest Ham *See Meats & Meat Products: Smoked, Cured & Deli Meats: Ham: Black Forest*

Black Olives *See Fruits & Vegetables: Olives: Black*

Black Pepper *See Spices, Seasonings & Seeds: Spices: Pepper: Black - White - Red; See also See Spices, Seasonings & Seeds: Spices: Black Pepper - Ground*

Black Pepper Oils *See Oils, Shortening & Fats: Oils: Black Pepper*

Black Puinoa Rice *See Cereals, Grains, Rice & Flour: Rice: Black Puinoa*

Black Sesame Seeds *See Spices, Seasonings & Seeds: Seeds: Sesame: Black*

Black Sliced Truffles *See Fruits & Vegetables: Mushrooms: Truffles: Black Sliced*

Black Tea *See Beverages: Coffee & Tea: Tea: Black*

Black Thai Rice *See Cereals, Grains, Rice & Flour: Rice: Black Thai*

Black Tiger Shrimp *See Fish & Seafood: Shellfish: Shrimp: Black Tiger*

Black Trumpet Mushrooms *See Fruits & Vegetables: Mushrooms: Black Trumpet*

Black Trumpet Mushrooms, Dehydrated *See Fruits & Vegetables: Dried & Dehydrated Vegetables: Mushrooms: Black Trumpets*

Black Walnuts *See Nuts & Nut Butters: Nuts: Walnuts: Black*

Black Whole Truffles *See Fruits & Vegetables: Mushrooms: Truffles: Black Whole*

Black-eyed Peas *See Fruits & Vegetables: Peas: Black-eyed*

Blackberry *See Fruits & Vegetables: Berries: Blackberry*

Blackberry Flavors *See Ingredients, Flavors & Additives: Flavors: Blackberry*

Blackening Seasonings *See Spices, Seasonings & Seeds: Seasonings: Blackening*

Blackeye Beans *See Fruits & Vegetables: Beans: Blackeye (Cowpeas)*

Blended Scotch Whiskey *See Beverages: Spirits & Liqueurs: Scotch Whiskey: Blended*

Blends *See Ingredients, Flavors & Additives: Blends*

Blends, Butter *See Dairy Products: Butter: Blends*

Blends, Corn Syrups *See Sugars, Syrups & Sweeteners: Syrups: Corn: Blends*

Blintzes *See Baked Goods: Cakes & Pastries: Blintzes*

Blood Orange *See Fruits & Vegetables: Orange: Blood*

Blood Orange Juice *See Beverages: Juices: Orange: Blood*

Blood Sausages *See Meats & Meat Products: Smoked, Cured & Deli Meats: Sausages: Blood*

Blue Cheese *See Cheese & Cheese Products: Cheese: Blue*

Blue Cheese Salad Dressings *See Sauces, Dips & Dressings: Salad Dressings: Blue Cheese*

Blue Cheese Salad Dressings, Mixes *See Sauces, Dips & Dressings: Salad Dressings: Mixes: Blue Cheese*

Blue Crab *See Fish & Seafood: Shellfish: Crab: Blue*

Blue Lake Beans *See Fruits & Vegetables: Beans: Blue Lake*

Blueberry *See Fruits & Vegetables: Berries: Blueberry*

Blueberry Flavors *See Ingredients, Flavors & Additives: Flavors: Blueberry*

Blueberry Juices *See Beverages: Juices: Blueberry*

Blueberry Pies *See Baked Goods: Pies: Blueberry*

Bluefish *See Fish & Seafood: Fish: Bluefish*

Boar *See Meats & Meat Products: Game: Boar*

Bock Lager *See Beverages: Beers: Lager: Bock*

Bockwurst Sausages *See Meats & Meat Products: Smoked, Cured & Deli Meats: Sausages: Bockwurst*

Boiled Eggs *See Eggs & Egg Products: Boiled*

Bok Choy Cabbage *See Fruits & Vegetables: Cabbage: Bok Choy*
Boletes Mushrooms *See Fruits & Vegetables: Mushrooms: Boletes*
Bologna Smoked, Cured & Deli Meats *See Meats & Meat Products: Smoked, Cured & Deli Meats: Bologna*
Bon Bons *See Candy & Confectionery: Candy: Bon Bons*
Boned Herring *See Fish & Seafood: Fish: Herring: Boned*
Borage Oils *See Oils, Shortening & Fats: Oils: Borage*
Bordeaux Vinegar *See Sauces, Dips & Dressings: Vinegar: Bordeaux*
Boric/Boracic Acids *See Ingredients, Flavors & Additives: Acids: Boric/Boracic*
Borscht *See Prepared Foods: Soups & Stews: Borscht*
Bosc Pear *See Fruits & Vegetables: Pear: Bosc*
Boston Butterhead Lettuce *See Fruits & Vegetables: Lettuce: Butterhead: Boston*
Botanical Extracts *See Ingredients, Flavors & Additives: Extracts: Botanical*
Bottled Apple Juices *See Beverages: Juices: Apple: Bottled*
Bottled Beers *See Beverages: Beers: Bottled*
Bottled Cherry Juices *See Beverages: Juices: Cherry: Bottled*
Bottled Cranberry Juices *See Beverages: Juices: Cranberry: Bottled*
Bottled Fruit & Vegetable Juices *See Beverages: Juices: Fruit & Vegetable: Bottled*
Bottled Fruit Juices *See Beverages: Juices: Fruit: Bottled*
Bottled Grape Juices *See Beverages: Juices: Grape: Bottled*
Bottled Grapefruit Juices *See Beverages: Juices: Grapefruit: Bottled*
Bottled Lemon Juices *See Beverages: Juices: Lemon: Bottled*
Bottled Water *See Beverages: Water: Bottled*
Bottomfish *See Fish & Seafood: Fish: Bottomfish*
Boudin Sausages *See Meats & Meat Products: Smoked, Cured & Deli Meats: Sausages: Boudin*
Bouillon Bases *See Ingredients, Flavors & Additives: Bases: Bouillon*
Bourbon Whiskey *See Beverages: Spirits & Liqueurs: Whiskey, American: Bourbon*
Bows *See Pasta & Noodles: Bows*
Boxed Apple Juices *See Beverages: Juices: Apple: Boxed*
Boxed Cherry Juices *See Beverages: Juices: Cherry: Boxed*
Boxed Chocolate *See Candy & Confectionery: Chocolate Products: Boxed Chocolate*
Boxed Cranberry Juices *See Beverages: Juices: Cranberry: Boxed*
Boxed Grape Juices *See Beverages: Juices: Grape: Boxed*
Boxed Grapefruit Juices *See Beverages: Juices: Grapefruit: Boxed*
Boxed Pineapple Juices *See Beverages: Juices: Pineapple: Boxed*
Boxed Specialty-Packaged Candy *See Candy & Confectionery: Specialty-Packaged Candy: Boxed*
Boxed Specialty-Packaged Candy, Non-Chocolate *See Candy & Confectionery: Specialty-Packaged Candy: Non-Chocolate - Boxed*
Boxed Tomato Juices *See Beverages: Juices: Tomato: Boxed*
Boysenberry *See Fruits & Vegetables: Berries: Boysenberry*
Bra Cheese *See Cheese & Cheese Products: Cheese: Bra*
Bran *See Cereals, Grains, Rice & Flour: Bran*
Brandied Fruits *See Fruits & Vegetables: Brandied Fruits*
Brandy *See Beverages: Spirits & Liqueurs: Brandy*
Brandy Liqueur *See Beverages: Spirits & Liqueurs: Liqueurs & Cordials: Brandy Liqueur*
Bratwurst *See Meats & Meat Products: Smoked, Cured & Deli Meats: Bratwurst*
Bratwurst Sausages *See Meats & Meat Products: Smoked, Cured & Deli Meats: Sausages: Bratwurst*
Braunschweiger Sausages *See Meats & Meat Products: Smoked, Cured & Deli Meats: Sausages: Braunschweiger*
Brazil Nuts *See Nuts & Nut Butters: Nuts: Brazil*
Bread Crumbs & Croutons *See Baked Goods: Bread Crumbs & Croutons; See also Baked Goods: Bread Crumbs & Croutons: Bread Crumbs*
Bread Doughs *See Doughs, Mixes & Fillings: Doughs: Bread*
Bread Mixes *See Doughs, Mixes & Fillings: Mixes: Bread*
Bread Sticks *See Baked Goods: Bread Sticks*
Bread Stuffing *See Baked Goods: Stuffing: Bread*
Bread, Wheat *See Cereals, Grains, Rice & Flour: Wheat: Bread*
Breaded Chicken *See Meats & Meat Products: Poultry: Chicken: Breaded*
Breaded Clam Strips *See Fish & Seafood: Shellfish: Clam: Breaded Strips*
Breaded Frozen Veal *See Meats & Meat Products: Beef & Beef Products: Veal: Breaded Frozen*
Breaded Pork *See Meats & Meat Products: Pork & Pork Products: Breaded*
Breaded Shrimp *See Fish & Seafood: Shellfish: Shrimp: Breaded*
Breaded Vegetables *See Prepared Foods: Breaded Vegetables*
Breading *See Doughs, Mixes & Fillings: Breading*
Breading Batters *See Doughs, Mixes & Fillings: Batters: Breading*
Breading Mixes *See Doughs, Mixes & Fillings: Mixes: Breading*
Breads *See Baked Goods: Breads*
Breakfast Cereal *See Cereals, Grains, Rice & Flour: Cereal: Breakfast*
Breakfast, Instant *See Prepared Foods: Breakfast Foods: Instant*
Breakfast, Prepared Meals *See Prepared Foods: Prepared Meals: Breakfast*
Breast Turkey *See Meats & Meat Products: Poultry: Turkey: Breast*
Breath Tablets *See Candy & Confectionery: Candy: Breath Tablets*
Brewers' Active Yeast *See Ingredients, Flavors & Additives: Cultures & Yeasts: Yeast: Brewers Active*
Brewers' Rice *See Cereals, Grains, Rice & Flour: Rice: Brewers'*
Brewers' Yeast *See Ingredients, Flavors & Additives: Cultures & Yeasts: Yeast: Brewers'*
Brewing Adjuncts *See Ingredients, Flavors & Additives: Adjuncts: Brewing*
Brie *See Cheese & Cheese Products: Cheese: Brie*
Brisket of Beef *See Meats & Meat Products: Beef & Beef Products: Brisket*
Brittles *See Candy & Confectionery: Candy: Brittles*
Broad Beans *See Fruits & Vegetables: Beans: Broad*
Broccoli *See Fruits & Vegetables: Broccoli*
Broccoli & Cauliflower Mixed Vegetables *See Fruits & Vegetables: Vegetables Mixed: Broccoli & Cauliflower*
Broccoli, Dried *See Fruits & Vegetables: Dried & Dehydrated Vegetables: Broccoli*
Broccoli, Peas & Carrots Mixed Vegetables *See Fruits & Vegetables: Vegetables Mixed: Broccoli, Peas & Carrots*
Broilers *See Meats & Meat Products: Poultry: Chicken: Broilers*
Brook Trout *See Fish & Seafood: Fish: Trout: Brook*
Broth *See Prepared Foods: Broth*
Broth Powders *See Ingredients, Flavors & Additives: Powders: Broth*
Brown Bettys *See Baked Goods: Cakes & Pastries: Brown Bettys*
Brown Breads *See Baked Goods: Breads: Brown*
Brown Mustard *See Sauces, Dips & Dressings: Mustard: Brown*
Brown Rice *See Cereals, Grains, Rice & Flour: Rice: Brown*
Brown Rice Crisps *See Cereals, Grains, Rice & Flour: Crisps: Brown Rice*
Brown Sugar *See Sugars, Syrups & Sweeteners: Sugar: Brown*
Brownie Mixes *See Doughs, Mixes & Fillings: Mixes: Brownie*
Brownie Pies *See Baked Goods: Pies: Brownie*
Brownies with Nuts *See Baked Goods: Cookies & Bars: Brownies: with Nuts*
Brownies, Baking Mixes *See Doughs, Mixes & Fillings: Mixes: Baking: Brownies*
Brownies, Cookies & Bars *See Baked Goods: Cookies & Bars: Brownies*
Brussel Sprouts *See Fruits & Vegetables: Brussel Sprouts*
Buckwheat Flour *See Cereals, Grains, Rice & Flour: Flour: Buckwheat*
Buffalo *See Meats & Meat Products: Game: Buffalo*
Bulgar Wheat *See Cereals, Grains, Rice & Flour: Wheat: Bulgar*
Bulk Wines *See Beverages: Wines: Bulk*
Bulking Additives *See Ingredients, Flavors & Additives: Additives: Bulking*
Bulking Agents *See Ingredients, Flavors & Additives: Agents: Bulking*
Buns *See Baked Goods: Breads: Buns*
Burgers, Veal *See Meats & Meat Products: Beef & Beef Products: Veal: Burgers*
Burgers, Vegetarian *See Specialty & Organic Foods: Vegetarian Products: Burgers; See also Organic Foods*
Burnt Sugar Colors *See Ingredients, Flavors & Additives: Colors: Burnt Sugar*
Burritos *See Ethnic Foods: Burritos*
Burritos, Prepared Meals *See Prepared Foods: Prepared Meals: Burritos*
Butter *See Dairy Products: Butter*
Butter & Cheese Colors *See Ingredients, Flavors & Additives: Colors: Butter & Cheese*
Butter Beans *See Fruits & Vegetables: Beans: Butter*
Butter, Flavors *See Ingredients, Flavors & Additives: Flavors: Butter*
Butter, Honey *See Sugars, Syrups & Sweeteners: Honey: Butter*
Butter, Maple Flavors *See Ingredients, Flavors & Additives: Flavors: Maple: Butter*
Butter, Maple Sugar *See Sugars, Syrups & Sweeteners: Sugar: Maple: Butter*
Butter, Milk Flavors *See Ingredients, Flavors & Additives: Flavors: Milk: Butter*
Butter, Snack Seasonings *See Spices, Seasonings & Seeds: Seasonings: Snack: Butter*
Butter, Toffee Rum Flavors *See Ingredients, Flavors & Additives: Flavors: Rum: Butter Toffee*
Butterfish *See Fish & Seafood: Fish: Butterfish*
Butterhead Lettuce *See Fruits & Vegetables: Lettuce: Butterhead*
Buttermilk *See Dairy Products: Buttermilk & Buttermilk Products: Buttermilk*
Buttermilk & Buttermilk Products *See Dairy Products: Buttermilk & Buttermilk Products*
Buttermilk Bacteria *See Ingredients, Flavors & Additives: Cultures & Yeasts: Bacteria: Buttermilk*
Buttermilk Flavors *See Ingredients, Flavors & Additives: Flavors: Buttermilk*
Buttermilk Powders *See Ingredients, Flavors & Additives: Powders: Buttermilk*
Buttermilk Products *See Dairy Products: Buttermilk & Buttermilk Products: Buttermilk Products*
Butterscotch Candy *See Candy & Confectionery: Candy: Butterscotch*
Butterscotch Flavors *See Ingredients, Flavors & Additives: Flavors: Butterscotch*

C

Cabbage *See Fruits & Vegetables: Cabbage*
Cabbage Flakes *See Fruits & Vegetables: Dried & Dehydrated Vegetables: Cabbage Flakes*
Cabbage Seeds *See Spices, Seasonings & Seeds: Seeds: Cabbage*
Cabernet Sauvignon *See Beverages: Wines: Red Grape Wines: Cabernet Sauvignon*
Cacciatore Sausages *See Meats & Meat Products: Smoked, Cured & Deli Meats: Sausages: Cacciatore*
Caciotta Cheese *See Cheese & Cheese Products: Cheese: Caciotta*
Cactus *See Fruits & Vegetables: Cactus*
Caffeine *See Ingredients, Flavors & Additives: Caffeine*
Cajeta Flavors *See Ingredients, Flavors & Additives: Flavors: Cajeta*
Cajun Fried Porkskins *See Prepared Foods: Porkskins: Fried: Cajun*
Cajun Sausages *See Meats & Meat Products: Smoked, Cured & Deli Meats: Sausages: Cajun*
Cajun Spice Snack Seasonings *See Spices, Seasonings & Seeds: Seasonings: Snack: Cajun Spice*
Cajun Style Seasonings *See Spices, Seasonings & Seeds: Seasonings: Cajun Style*
Cake Batters *See Doughs, Mixes & Fillings: Batters: Cake*
Cake Decorations *See Candy & Confectionery: Decorations & Icings: Decorations: Cake*
Cake Fillings *See Doughs, Mixes & Fillings: Fillings: Cake*
Cake Flour *See Cereals, Grains, Rice & Flour: Flour: Cake*
Cake Icings *See Candy & Confectionery: Decorations & Icings: Icings: Cake*
Cake Mixes *See Doughs, Mixes & Fillings: Mixes: Cake*
Cakes *See Baked Goods: Cakes & Pastries: Cakes*
Cakes & Donut Toppings *See Ingredients, Flavors & Additives: Toppings: Cakes & Donuts*
Cakes & Pastries *See Baked Goods: Cakes & Pastries*
Cakes, Crab *See Fish & Seafood: Shellfish: Crab: Cakes*
Cakes, Fish *See Fish & Seafood: Fish: Cakes*

EXAMPLE: **Canadian Style Bacon** (1) *See Meats & Meat Products:* (2) *Smoked, Cured & Deli Meats:* (3) *Bacon:* (4) *Canadian Style* (5)

1. Product or Service you are looking for
2. Main Category, in alphabetical order, located in the page headers starting on page 27
3. Category Description, located in black bars and in page headers
4. Product Category, located in gray bars
5. Product Type, located under gray bars, centered in bold

Caraway Seeds *See Spices, Seasonings & Seeds: Seeds: Caraway*
Carboxymethylcellulose *See Ingredients, Flavors & Additives: Gums: Carboxymethylcellulose*
Cardamom Oils *See Oils, Shortening & Fats: Oils: Cardamom*
Cardamom Seeds *See Spices, Seasonings & Seeds: Seeds: Cardamom*
Cardamom Spices *See Spices, Seasonings & Seeds: Spices: Cardamom*
Caribou *See Meats & Meat Products: Game: Caribou*
Carmine *See Ingredients, Flavors & Additives: Colors: Natural: Carmine*
Carob Candy *See Candy & Confectionery: Candy: Carob*
Carob Candy Coatings *See Candy & Confectionery: Candy Coatings: Carob*
Carob Ingredients *See Candy & Confectionery: Chocolate Products: Carob Ingredients*
Carob Powder Spices *See Spices, Seasonings & Seeds: Spices: Carob Powder*
Carob Powders *See Ingredients, Flavors & Additives: Powders: Carob*
Carotenoids *See Ingredients, Flavors & Additives: Colors: Natural: Carotenoids*
Carp *See Fish & Seafood: Fish: Carp*
Carrageenan *See Ingredients, Flavors & Additives: Gums: Carrageenan*
Carrot *See Fruits & Vegetables: Carrot*
Carrot Cake *See Baked Goods: Cakes & Pastries: Carrot Cake*
Carrot Juices *See Beverages: Juices: Carrot*
Cascabel Peppers *See Fruits & Vegetables: Peppers: Cascabel*
Casein *See Ingredients, Flavors & Additives: Casein & Caseinates; See also Ingredients, Flavors & Additives: Casein & Caseinates: Casein*
Cashews *See Nuts & Nut Butters: Nuts: Cashews*
Casings *See Meats & Meat Products: Smoked, Cured & Deli Meats: Sausages: Casings: Sausage, Pork, Beef*
Cassava Chips *See Snack Foods: Chips: Cassava*
Cassava Powders *See Ingredients, Flavors & Additives: Powders: Cassava*
Cassava Starches *See Ingredients, Flavors & Additives: Starches: Cassava*
Cassava Tapioca *See Cereals, Grains, Rice & Flour: Tapioca: Cassava*
Casseroles, Prepared Meals *See Prepared Foods: Prepared Meals: Casseroles*
Cassia *See Spices, Seasonings & Seeds: Spices: Cassia (Cinnamon); See also Spices, Seasonings & Seeds: Spices: Cinnamon: Cassia*
Cassia Oils *See Oils, Shortening & Fats: Oils: Cassia*
Castor Oils *See Oils, Shortening & Fats: Oils: Castor*
Catfish *See Fish & Seafood: Fish: Catfish*
Cauliflower *See Fruits & Vegetables: Cauliflower*
Cauliflower, Pickled *See Relishes & Pickled Products: Pickled Products: Cauliflower*
Cavatappi *See Pasta & Noodles: Cavatappi*
Cavatelli *See Pasta & Noodles: Cavatelli*
Caviar *See Fish & Seafood: Caviar (Roe)*
Cayenne Pepper *See Spices, Seasonings & Seeds: Spices: Cayenne Pepper*
Cayenne Spices *See Spices, Seasonings & Seeds: Spices: Cayenne*
Ceasar Salad Dressings *See Sauces, Dips & Dressings: Salad Dressings: Ceasar*
Ceasar Salad Dressings, Mixes *See Sauces, Dips & Dressings: Salad Dressings: Mixes: Ceasar*
Celery *See Fruits & Vegetables: Celery*
Celery Flakes *See Fruits & Vegetables: Dried & Dehydrated Vegetables: Celery Flakes; See also Spices, Seasonings & Seeds: Spices: Celery Flakes*
Celery Oils *See Oils, Shortening & Fats: Oils: Celery*
Celery Powders *See Ingredients, Flavors & Additives: Powders: Celery*
Celery Salt *See Spices, Seasonings & Seeds: Salt: Celery*
Celery Seeds *See Spices, Seasonings & Seeds: Seeds: Celery*
Celery Sticks *See Fruits & Vegetables: Celery: Sticks*
Cellulose Fiber *See Cereals, Grains, Rice & Flour: Fiber: Cellulose*
Cellulose Gel *See Ingredients, Flavors & Additives: Cellulose Gel*
Cereal *See Cereals, Grains, Rice & Flour: Cereal*
Cereal Bars *See Cereals, Grains, Rice & Flour: Cereal: Bars*
Cereal Binders *See Ingredients, Flavors & Additives: Binders: Cereal*
Cereal Crisps *See Cereals, Grains, Rice & Flour: Crisps: Cereal*
Cereal Solids Hydrolyzed Anticaking Agents *See Ingredients, Flavors & Additives: Agents: Anticaking: Cereal Solids Hydrolyzed*
Cereal Solids Hydrolyzed Products *See Ingredients, Flavors & Additives: Hydrolyzed Products: Cereal Solids*
Certified Dyes *See Ingredients, Flavors & Additives: Colors: Dyes: Certified*
Certified Organic Foods *See Specialty & Organic Foods: Organic Foods: Certified; See also Organic Foods*
Chai Tea *See Beverages: Coffee & Tea: Tea: Chai*
Challah *See Baked Goods: Breads: Challah*
Chalupa Shells *See Ethnic Foods: Shells: Chalupa*
Chamomile Tea *See Beverages: Coffee & Tea: Tea: Chamomile*
Champagne *See Beverages: Wines: French: Champagne*
Champagne Vinegar *See Sauces, Dips & Dressings: Vinegar: Champagne*
Chanterelle *See Fruits & Vegetables: Mushrooms: Chanterelle*
Chardonnay *See Beverages: Wines: White Grape Varieties: Chardonnay*
Cheddar Cheese *See Cheese & Cheese Products: Cheese: Cheddar*
Cheddar Cheese, Imitation *See Cheese & Cheese Products: Imitation Cheeses & Substitutes: Imitation: Cheddar*
Cheddar Cheese, Powders *See Ingredients, Flavors & Additives: Powders: Cheese: Cheddar*
Cheddar Snack Seasonings *See Spices, Seasonings & Seeds: Seasonings: Snack: Cheddar*
Cheese *See Cheese & Cheese Products; See also Cheese & Cheese Products: Cheese*
Cheese Bacteria *See Ingredients, Flavors & Additives: Cultures & Yeasts: Bacteria: Cheese*
Cheese Blends *See Ingredients, Flavors & Additives: Blends: Cheese*
Cheese Cake *See Baked Goods: Cakes & Pastries: Cheese Cake*
Cheese Curls *See Snack Foods: Cheese Curls*
Cheese Dips *See Sauces, Dips & Dressings: Dips: Cheese*
Cheese Flavors *See Ingredients, Flavors & Additives: Flavors: Cheese*
Cheese Foods & Substitutes *See Cheese & Cheese Products: Imitation Cheeses & Substitutes: Cheese Foods & Substitutes*
Cheese Loaves, Yellow Process *See Cheese & Cheese Products: Cheese: Process Loaves: Yellow*
Cheese Pizza *See Prepared Foods: Pizza & Pizza Products: Pizza: Cheese*
Cheese Powders *See Ingredients, Flavors & Additives: Powders: Cheese*
Cheese Ravioli *See Pasta & Noodles: Ravioli: Cheese*
Cheese Sauces *See Sauces, Dips & Dressings: Sauces: Cheese*
Cheese Seasonings *See Spices, Seasonings & Seeds: Seasonings: Cheese*
Cheese Starter Media *See Ingredients, Flavors & Additives: Starter Media: Cheese*
Cheese Substitutes *See Cheese & Cheese Products: Imitation Cheeses & Substitutes: Substitutes*
Cheese Twists *See Snack Foods: Cheese Twists*
Cheese, Blend - American/Skim Milk *See Cheese & Cheese Products: Cheese: Blend - American/Skim Milk*
Cheese, No-Fat *See Cheese & Cheese Products: Cheese: No-Fat*
Cheese, White/Yellow Process Sliced *See Cheese & Cheese Products: Cheese: Process Sliced: White/Yellow*
Cheesecake Flavors *See Ingredients, Flavors & Additives: Flavors: Cheesecake*
Chelating Agents *See Ingredients, Flavors & Additives: Chelating Agents*
Chemicals *See Ingredients, Flavors & Additives: Chemicals*
Chemicals, Aroma *See Ingredients, Flavors & Additives: Aroma Chemicals & Materials: Chemicals*
Cherries *See Fruits & Vegetables: Cherries*
Cherry Flavors *See Ingredients, Flavors & Additives: Flavors: Cherry*
Cherry Juices *See Beverages: Juices: Cherry*
Cherry Peppers *See Fruits & Vegetables: Peppers: Cherry*
Cherry Pies *See Baked Goods: Pies: Cherry*
Cherry Tomato *See Fruits & Vegetables: Tomato: Cherry*
Chervil *See Spices, Seasonings & Seeds: Spices: Chervil*
Chestnut Flower Flour *See Cereals, Grains, Rice & Flour: Flour: Chestnut Flower*
Chestnuts *See Nuts & Nut Butters: Nuts: Chestnuts*
Chewing Gum *See Candy & Confectionery: Candy: Chewing Gum*
Chianti *See Beverages: Wines: Italian: Chianti*
Chick Beans *See Fruits & Vegetables: Beans: Chick*
Chicken *See Meats & Meat Products: Poultry: Chicken*
Chicken & Dumplings Soups & Stews *See Prepared Foods: Soups & Stews: Chicken & Dumplings*
Chicken & Noodles Soups & Stews *See Prepared Foods: Soups & Stews: Chicken & Noodles*
Chicken Bases *See Ingredients, Flavors & Additives: Bases: Chicken*
Chicken Broth *See Prepared Foods: Broth: Chicken*
Chicken Bulk *See Meats & Meat Products: Poultry: Chicken: Bulk (Leg Quarters, Legs, Thighs)*
Chicken Extenders *See Ingredients, Flavors & Additives: Extenders: Chicken*
Chicken Extracts *See Ingredients, Flavors & Additives: Extracts: Chicken*
Chicken Fats & Lard *See Oils, Shortening & Fats: Fats & Lard: Chicken*
Chicken Frankfurters *See Meats & Meat Products: Frankfurters: Chicken*
Chicken Marinades *See Sauces, Dips & Dressings: Marinades: Chicken*
Chicken Nuggets *See Meats & Meat Products: Poultry: Chicken: Nuggets*
Chicken Sausages *See Meats & Meat Products: Smoked, Cured & Deli Meats: Sausages: Chicken*
Chicken, Cut-Up Frozen *See Meats & Meat Products: Poultry: Chicken: Cut-Up Frozen*
Chicken, Cut-Up IQF *See Meats & Meat Products: Poultry: Chicken: Cut-Up IQF (Individually Quick Frozen)*
Chicken, Prepared Meals *See Prepared Foods: Prepared Meals: Chicken*
Chicken, Prepared Salads *See Prepared Foods: Prepared Salads: Chicken*
Chicks Hatcheries *See Eggs & Egg Products: Hatcheries: Chicks*
Chicory *See Fruits & Vegetables: Chicory*
Chile Pepper Spices *See Spices, Seasonings & Seeds: Spices: Chile Pepper*
Chile Peppers *See Fruits & Vegetables: Peppers: Chile*
Chili *See Prepared Foods: Chili*
Chili Beans *See Fruits & Vegetables: Beans: Chili*
Chili Crush *See Spices, Seasonings & Seeds: Spices: Chili Crush*
Chili Dips *See Sauces, Dips & Dressings: Dips: Chili*
Chili Mixes *See Doughs, Mixes & Fillings: Mixes: Chili*
Chili Pods *See Spices, Seasonings & Seeds: Spices: Chili Pods*
Chili Powder *See Spices, Seasonings & Seeds: Spices: Chili Powder; See also Ingredients, Flavors & Additives: Powders: Chili*
Chili Sauces *See Sauces, Dips & Dressings: Sauces: Chili*
Chili with Cheese *See Prepared Foods: Chili: with Cheese*
Chilled Apple Juices *See Beverages: Juices: Apple: Chilled*
Chilled Cherry Juices *See Beverages: Juices: Cherry: Chilled*
Chilled Grape Juices *See Beverages: Juices: Grape: Chilled*
Chimichangas *See Prepared Foods: Prepared Meals: Burritos: Chimichangas*
Chinese *See Ethnic Foods: Chinese*
Chinese Black Rice *See Cereals, Grains, Rice & Flour: Rice: Chinese Black*
Chinese Cabbage *See Fruits & Vegetables: Cabbage: Chinese*
Chinese Spices *See Spices, Seasonings & Seeds: Spices: Chinese*
Chinese Style Seasonings *See Spices, Seasonings & Seeds: Seasonings: Chinese Style*
Chip Dips *See Sauces, Dips & Dressings: Dips: Chip*
Chipotle Peppers *See Fruits & Vegetables: Peppers: Chipotle*
Chipped Beef *See Meats & Meat Products: Beef & Beef Products: Chipped*
Chips *See Snack Foods: Chips*
Chives *See Spices, Seasonings & Seeds: Spices: Chives; See also Fruits & Vegetables: Chives*
Chlorophyll *See Ingredients, Flavors & Additives: Chlorophyll*

EXAMPLE: **Canadian Style Bacon** (1) *See Meats & Meat Products:* (2) *Smoked, Cured & Deli Meats:* (3) *Bacon:* (4) *Canadian Style* (5)

1. Product or Service you are looking for
2. Main Category, in alphabetical order, located in the page headers starting on page 27
3. Category Description, located in black bars and in page headers
4. Product Category, located in gray bars
5. Product Type, located under gray bars, centered in bold

Chocolate Almond Biscotti *See Baked Goods: Cookies & Bars: Biscotti: Chocolate Almond*

Chocolate Bars *See Candy & Confectionery: Chocolate Products: Chocolate Bars*

Chocolate Bases *See Ingredients, Flavors & Additives: Bases: Chocolate*

Chocolate Candy *See Candy & Confectionery: Chocolate Products: Chocolate Candy*

Chocolate Candy Coatings *See Candy & Confectionery: Candy Coatings: Chocolate*

Chocolate Cherries *See Candy & Confectionery: Chocolate Products: Chocolate Cherries*

Chocolate Chip Compound for Ice Cream *See Ingredients, Flavors & Additives: Chocolate Products: Chocolate Chip Compound for Ice Cream*

Chocolate Chip Cookies *See Baked Goods: Cookies & Bars: Chocolate Chip Cookies*

Chocolate Chips *See Candy & Confectionery: Chocolate Products: Chocolate Chips; See also Snack Foods: Chips: Chocolate*

Chocolate Chunks *See Candy & Confectionery: Chocolate Products: Chocolate Chunks*

Chocolate Coated Nuts *See Nuts & Nut Butters: Nuts: Coated: Chocolate*

Chocolate Coated Raisins *See Fruits & Vegetables: Raisins: Chocolate Coated*

Chocolate Covered Apple *See Fruits & Vegetables: Apple: Covered: Chocolate*

Chocolate Dessert Fillings *See Doughs, Mixes & Fillings: Fillings: Dessert: Chocolate*

Chocolate Dipped Biscotti *See Baked Goods: Cookies & Bars: Biscotti: Chocolate Dipped*

Chocolate Drinks *See Beverages: Cocoa & Chocolate Drinks: Chocolate Drinks*

Chocolate Fillings *See Doughs, Mixes & Fillings: Fillings: Chocolate*

Chocolate Flavors *See Ingredients, Flavors & Additives: Flavors: Chocolate*

Chocolate Liqueur *See Beverages: Spirits & Liqueurs: Liqueurs & Cordials: Chocolate Liqueur*

Chocolate Milk *See Dairy Products: Milk & Milk Products: Milk: Chocolate*

Chocolate Products *See Candy & Confectionery: Chocolate Products; See also Ingredients, Flavors & Additives: Chocolate Products*

Chocolate Pudding *See Dairy Products: Pudding: Chocolate*

Chop Suey *See Ethnic Foods: Chop Suey*

Chopped Broccoli *See Fruits & Vegetables: Broccoli: Chopped*

Chopped Broccoli, Dehydrated *See Fruits & Vegetables: Dried & Dehydrated Vegetables: Broccoli: Chopped*

Chopped Celery *See Fruits & Vegetables: Celery: Chopped*

Chopped Clam *See Fish & Seafood: Shellfish: Clam: Chopped*

Chopped Garlic *See Spices, Seasonings & Seeds: Spices: Garlic: Chopped*

Chopped Onion *See Spices, Seasonings & Seeds: Spices: Onion: Chopped*

Chopped Shellfish *See Fish & Seafood: Shellfish: Chopped*

Chorizo Sausages *See Meats & Meat Products: Smoked, Cured & Deli Meats: Sausages: Chorizo*

Chourico Sausages *See Meats & Meat Products: Smoked, Cured & Deli Meats: Sausages: Chourico*

Chow Chow *See Ethnic Foods: Chow Chow*

Chow Fun Noodles *See Pasta & Noodles: Noodles: Chow Fun*

Chow Mein *See Ethnic Foods: Chow Mein*

Chow Mein Noodles *See Pasta & Noodles: Noodles: Chow Mein*

Chowder *See Fish & Seafood: Fish: Chowder; See also Prepared Foods: Soups & Stews: Chowder; See also Prepared Foods: Chowder*

Christmas Specialty-Packaged Candy *See Candy & Confectionery: Specialty-Packaged Candy: Christmas*

Chub *See Fish & Seafood: Fish: Chub*

Chum Salmon *See Fish & Seafood: Fish: Salmon: Chum*

Chunky Salsa *See Sauces, Dips & Dressings: Salsa: Chunky*

Churros *See Baked Goods: Cakes & Pastries: Churros*

Chutney *See Prepared Foods: Chutney*

Cider & Vinegar Colors *See Ingredients, Flavors & Additives: Colors: Cider & Vinegar*

Cinnamon Flavors *See Ingredients, Flavors & Additives: Flavors: Cinnamon*

Cinnamon Leaf & Bark Oils *See Oils, Shortening & Fats: Oils: Cinnamon - Leaf & Bark*

Cinnamon Rolls *See Baked Goods: Breads: Rolls: Cinnamon*

Cinnamon Spices *See Spices, Seasonings & Seeds: Spices: Cinnamon*

Cinnamon Toast *See Baked Goods: Breads: Cinnamon Toast*

Cinnamon Toast, Snack Seasonings *See Spices, Seasonings & Seeds: Seasonings: Snack: Cinnamon Toast*

Citric Acidulants *See Ingredients, Flavors & Additives: Acidulants: Citric*

Citron *See Spices, Seasonings & Seeds: Spices: Citron*

Citrus Blends Juices *See Beverages: Juices: Citrus Blends*

Citrus Flavors *See Ingredients, Flavors & Additives: Flavors: Citrus*

Citrus Fruits *See Fruits & Vegetables: Citrus Fruits*

Citrus Oils *See Oils, Shortening & Fats: Oils: Citrus*

Citrus Pectins *See Ingredients, Flavors & Additives: Pectins: Citrus*

Citrus Peel Products *See Fruits & Vegetables: Citrus Peel Products*

Citrus Pulps & Purees *See Fruits & Vegetables: Pulps & Purees: Citrus*

Clam *See Fish & Seafood: Shellfish: Clam*

Clam & Fish Chowder *See Prepared Foods: Chowder: Clam & Fish*

Clam Juice *See Fish & Seafood: Shellfish: Clam: Juice*

Clam Sauces *See Sauces, Dips & Dressings: Sauces: Clam*

Clarifying Agents *See Ingredients, Flavors & Additives: Agents: Clarifying*

Cloudear Mushrooms *See Fruits & Vegetables: Mushrooms: Cloudear*

Clove Oils *See Oils, Shortening & Fats: Oils: Clove*

Cloves *See Spices, Seasonings & Seeds: Spices: Cloves*

Club Soda *See Beverages: Soft Drinks & Sodas: Club Soda*

Coagulants *See Ingredients, Flavors & Additives: Coagulants*

Coarse Frozen Ground Beef *See Meats & Meat Products: Beef & Beef Products: Ground: Coarse Frozen*

Coated Candy Bars *See Candy & Confectionery: Candy: Candy Bars: Coated*

Coated Nuts *See Nuts & Nut Butters: Nuts: Coated*

Coated Popcorn *See Snack Foods: Popcorn: Coated*

Coatings *See Ingredients, Flavors & Additives: Coatings*

Cocktail Fruit *See Fruits & Vegetables: Fruit: Cocktail*

Cocktail Mixes *See Doughs, Mixes & Fillings: Mixes: Cocktail*

Cocktail Onion *See Fruits & Vegetables: Onion: Cocktail*

Cocktail Sauces *See Sauces, Dips & Dressings: Sauces: Cocktail*

Cocktail Seafood *See Fish & Seafood: Seafood: Cocktail*

Cocktail Shrimp *See Fish & Seafood: Shellfish: Shrimp: Cocktail*

Cocktail Tomato *See Fruits & Vegetables: Tomato: Cocktail*

Cocktail Tomato Juices *See Beverages: Juices: Tomato: Cocktail*

Cocoa & Chocolate Drinks *See Beverages: Cocoa & Chocolate Drinks*

Cocoa & Cocoa Products *See Candy & Confectionery: Chocolate Products: Cocoa & Cocoa Products*

Cocoa & Rice Pellets *See Ingredients, Flavors & Additives: Half-Products: Cocoa & Rice Pellets*

Cocoa Butter *See Ingredients, Flavors & Additives: Cocoa Butter*

Cocoa Flavors *See Ingredients, Flavors & Additives: Flavors: Cocoa*

Cocoa Powders *See Ingredients, Flavors & Additives: Powders: Cocoa*

Cocoa Replacers *See Ingredients, Flavors & Additives: Replacers: Cocoa*

Cocoa Rice Crisps *See Cereals, Grains, Rice & Flour: Crisps: Cocoa Rice*

Cocoa Soy Crisps *See Cereals, Grains, Rice & Flour: Crisps: Cocoa Soy*

Coconut & Coconut Products *See Fruits & Vegetables: Coconut & Coconut Products*

Coconut Candy *See Candy & Confectionery: Candy: Coconut*

Coconut Flavors *See Ingredients, Flavors & Additives: Flavors: Coconut*

Coconut Juices *See Beverages: Juices: Coconut*

Coconut Oils *See Oils, Shortening & Fats: Oils: Coconut*

Cod *See Fish & Seafood: Fish: Cod*

Cod Liver Oils *See Oils, Shortening & Fats: Oils: Cod Liver*

Coffee *See Beverages: Coffee & Tea: See also Beverages: Coffee & Tea: Coffee*

Coffee Cake *See Baked Goods: Cakes & Pastries: Coffee Cake*

Coffee Creamers *See Dairy Products: Creamers: Coffee*

Coffee Extenders *See Ingredients, Flavors & Additives: Extenders: Coffee*

Coffee Extracts *See Ingredients, Flavors & Additives: Extracts: Coffee*

Coffee Flavors *See Ingredients, Flavors & Additives: Flavors: Coffee*

Coffee Liqueur *See Beverages: Spirits & Liqueurs: Liqueurs & Cordials: Coffee Liqueur*

Coho Salmon *See Fish & Seafood: Fish: Salmon: Coho*

Cola Soft Drinks *See Beverages: Soft Drinks & Sodas: Soft Drinks: Cola*

Colby *See Cheese & Cheese Products: Cheese: Colby*

Cold Smoked Seafood *See Fish & Seafood: Seafood: Smoked: Cold*

Cole Slaw *See Prepared Foods: Prepared Salads: Cole Slaw*

Collard Greens *See Fruits & Vegetables: Collard Greens*

Colloids Stabilizers *See Ingredients, Flavors & Additives: Stabilizers: Colloids*

Colored Crisps *See Cereals, Grains, Rice & Flour: Crisps: Colored*

Colored Pellets *See Ingredients, Flavors & Additives: Half-Products: Colored Pellets*

Colored Starch Bits *See Ingredients, Flavors & Additives: Toppings: Colored Starch Bits; See also Ingredients, Flavors & Additives: Bits: Colored Starch*

Colors *See Ingredients, Flavors & Additives: Colors*

Compacting Agents *See Ingredients, Flavors & Additives: Agents: Compacting*

Compound Coatings *See Ingredients, Flavors & Additives: Coatings: Compound*

Compounds *See Ingredients, Flavors & Additives: Compounds*

Concentrate Ade Juices *See Beverages: Juices: Ade: Concentrate*

Concentrate Apple Juices *See Beverages: Juices: Apple: Concentrate*

Concentrate Apricot Juices *See Beverages: Juices: Apricot: Concentrate*

Concentrate Cherry Juices *See Beverages: Juices: Cherry: Concentrate*

Concentrate Cranberry Juices *See Beverages: Juices: Cranberry: Concentrate*

Concentrate Drink Juices *See Beverages: Juices: Drink: Concentrate*

Concentrate Fruit & Vegetable Juices *See Beverages: Juices: Fruit & Vegetable: Concentrate*

Concentrate Fruit Juices *See Beverages: Juices: Fruit: Concentrate*

Concentrate Fruit Punch Juices *See Beverages: Juices: Fruit Punch: Concentrate*

Concentrate Fruit Puree Juices *See Beverages: Juices: Vegetable: Concentrates - Fruit Puree*

Concentrate Grape Juices *See Beverages: Juices: Grape: Concentrate*

Concentrate Grapefruit Juices *See Beverages: Juices: Grapefruit: Concentrate*

Concentrate Lemon Juices *See Beverages: Juices: Lemon: Concentrate*

Concentrate Lemonade Juices *See Beverages: Juices: Lemonade: Concentrate*

Concentrate Orange Juices *See Beverages: Juices: Orange: Concentrate*

Concentrate Orange Juices, Frozen *See Beverages: Juices: Orange: Concentrate - Frozen*

Concentrate Pineapple Juices *See Beverages: Juices: Pineapple: Concentrate*

Concentrate Soy Protein *See Fruits & Vegetables: Soy: Soy Protein: Concentrate*

Concentrates *See Ingredients, Flavors & Additives: Concentrates*

Conch Fish *See Fish & Seafood: Fish: Conch*

Conch Shellfish *See Fish & Seafood: Shellfish: Conch*

Conchigite Rigate *See Pasta & Noodles: Conchigite Rigate*

Condensed Buttermilk *See Dairy Products: Buttermilk & Buttermilk Products: Buttermilk Products: Condensed*

Condensed Milk *See Dairy Products: Milk & Milk Products: Milk: Condensed*

Condensed Milk, Bulk Only *See Dairy Products: Milk & Milk Products: Milk: Condensed - Bulk Only*

Condiments *See Sauces, Dips & Dressings: Condiments*

Cones *See Baked Goods: Cones*

Confectioners Crunch *See Candy & Confectionery: Confectionery: Confectioners Crunch*

Confectioners Dipping Fruit *See Fruits & Vegetables: Dipping Fruit: Confectioners'*

Confectionery *See Candy & Confectionery: Confectionery: Confectionery; See also Candy & Confectionery: Confectionery; See also Ingredients, Flavors & Additives: Confectionery*

Confectionery Candy Coatings *See Candy & Confectionery: Candy Coatings: Confectionery*

Confectionery Toppings *See Ingredients, Flavors & Additives: Toppings: Confectionery*

Convenience Food *See Prepared Foods: Convenience Food*

Convenience Prepared Meals *See Prepared Foods: Prepared Meals: Convenience*

Cooked *See Eggs & Egg Products: Cooked*

Cooked Chicken, Breaded - Frozen *See Meats & Meat Products: Poultry: Chicken: Cooked - Breaded - Frozen*

Cooked Corn-on-the-Cob *See Fruits & Vegetables: Corn: Corn-on-the-Cob: Cooked*

Cooked Crab *See Fish & Seafood: Shellfish: Crab: Cooked*
Cooked Frozen Hamburger *See Meats & Meat Products: Beef & Beef Products: Hamburger: Cooked Frozen*
Cooked Frozen Patties *See Meats & Meat Products: Beef & Beef Products: Patties: Cooked Frozen*
Cooked Ham, Water-added Chilled *See Meats & Meat Products: Smoked, Cured & Deli Meats: Ham: Cooked - Water-added Chilled*
Cooked Oysters *See Fish & Seafood: Shellfish: Oysters: Cooked*
Cooked Shrimp *See Fish & Seafood: Shellfish: Shrimp: Cooked*
Cookie Batters *See Doughs, Mixes & Fillings: Batters: Cookie*
Cookie Bits *See Ingredients, Flavors & Additives: Bits: Cookie*
Cookie Doughs *See Doughs, Mixes & Fillings: Doughs: Cookie*
Cookie Fillings *See Doughs, Mixes & Fillings: Fillings: Cookie*
Cookie Mixes *See Doughs, Mixes & Fillings: Mixes: Cookie*
Cookies *See Baked Goods: Cookies & Bars: Cookies*
Cookies & Bars *See Baked Goods: Cookies & Bars*
Cookies & Biscuits *See Baked Goods: Cookies & Bars: Cookies & Biscuits*
Cookies Bars *See Baked Goods: Cookies & Bars: Bars*
Cooking Compounds *See Ingredients, Flavors & Additives: Compounds: Cooking*
Cooking Compounds, Fats & Lard *See Oils, Shortening & Fats: Fats & Lard: Lard: Cooking Compounds*
Cooking Oils *See Oils, Shortening & Fats: Oils: Cooking*
Cooking Wines *See Beverages: Wines: Cooking*
Coriander *See Spices, Seasonings & Seeds: Spices: Coriander (Cilantro)*
Coriander Seed Oils *See Oils, Shortening & Fats: Oils: Coriander Seed*
Coriander Seeds *See Spices, Seasonings & Seeds: Seeds: Coriander*
Corn *See Fruits & Vegetables: Corn*
Corn Bran Fiber *See Cereals, Grains, Rice & Flour: Fiber: Corn Bran*
Corn Breads *See Baked Goods: Breads: Corn*
Corn Candy *See Candy & Confectionery: Candy: Corn*
Corn Chips *See Snack Foods: Chips: Corn*
Corn Dogs *See Meats & Meat Products: Frankfurters: Corn Dogs*
Corn Flour *See Cereals, Grains, Rice & Flour: Flour: Corn*
Corn Fritters *See Prepared Foods: Prepared Meals: Corn Fritters*
Corn Meal *See Cereals, Grains, Rice & Flour: Corn Meal*
Corn Nuts *See Snack Foods: Corn Nuts*
Corn Oils *See Oils, Shortening & Fats: Oils: Corn*
Corn Starches *See Ingredients, Flavors & Additives: Starches: Corn*
Corn Syrups *See Sugars, Syrups & Sweeteners: Syrups: Corn*
Corn-Based Cereal *See Cereals, Grains, Rice & Flour: Cereal: Corn-Based*
Corn-on-the-Cob *See Fruits & Vegetables: Corn: Corn-on-the-Cob*
Corned Beef *See Meats & Meat Products: Smoked, Cured & Deli Meats: Corned Beef*
Cornish Game Hens *See Meats & Meat Products: Poultry: Cornish Game Hens*
Corsignano *See Cheese & Cheese Products: Cheese: Corsignano*
Cottage Cheese *See Cheese & Cheese Products: Cheese: Cottage*
Cotton Candy *See Candy & Confectionery: Candy: Cotton*
Cottonseed Oils *See Oils, Shortening & Fats: Oils: Cottonseed*
Couscous *See Ethnic Foods: Couscous*
Covered Apple *See Fruits & Vegetables: Apple: Covered*
Crab *See Fish & Seafood: Shellfish: Crab; See also Prepared Foods: Prepared Meals: Crab*
Crab Extracts *See Ingredients, Flavors & Additives: Extracts: Crab*
Crab Meat *See Fish & Seafood: Shellfish: Crab: Meat*
Crackers *See Baked Goods: Crackers; See also Baked Goods: Crackers: Crackers*
Cranberry *See Fruits & Vegetables: Berries: Cranberry*
Cranberry Juices *See Beverages: Juices: Cranberry*
Cranberry Orange Biscotti *See Baked Goods: Cookies & Bars: Biscotti: Cranberry Orange*
Cranberry Sauces *See Fruits & Vegetables: Sauces: Cranberry*
Crayfish *See Fish & Seafood: Shellfish: Crayfish*
Cream *See Dairy Products: Cream*
Cream Ale *See Beverages: Beers: American & British Ale: Cream Ale*
Cream Cheese *See Cheese & Cheese Products: Cheese: Cream*
Cream Cheese Powders *See Ingredients, Flavors & Additives: Powders: Cheese: Cream*
Cream Dessert Fillings *See Doughs, Mixes & Fillings: Fillings: Dessert: Cream*
Cream from Milk *See Dairy Products: Cream: from Milk*
Cream of Broccoli Soups & Stews *See Prepared Foods: Soups & Stews: Cream of Broccoli*
Cream of Mushroom Soups & Stews *See Prepared Foods: Soups & Stews: Cream of Mushroom*
Cream of Potato Soups & Stews *See Prepared Foods: Soups & Stews: Cream of Potato*
Cream of Tartar *See Spices, Seasonings & Seeds: Spices: Tartar: Cream*
Cream Puff *See Baked Goods: Cakes & Pastries: Cream Puff*
Cream Soda *See Beverages: Soft Drinks & Sodas: Soft Drinks: Cream Soda - Vanilla; See also Beverages: Soft Drinks & Sodas: Soft Drinks: Cream Soda*
Creamers *See Dairy Products: Creamers*
Creamy Dijon Salad Dressings *See Sauces, Dips & Dressings: Salad Dressings: Mixes: Creamy Dijon; See also Sauces, Dips & Dressings: Salad Dressings: Creamy Dijon*
Creme Fillings *See Doughs, Mixes & Fillings: Fillings: Creme*
Cremes Candy *See Candy & Confectionery: Candy: Cremes*
Creole Chicken *See Prepared Foods: Prepared Meals: Chicken: Creole*
Crepes *See Prepared Foods: Crepes*
Criminis Mushrooms *See Fruits & Vegetables: Mushrooms: Criminis*
Crisp Rice Toppings *See Ingredients, Flavors & Additives: Toppings: Crisp Rice*
Crisped Bran Crisps *See Cereals, Grains, Rice & Flour: Crisps: Crisped Bran*
Crisped Corn Crisps *See Cereals, Grains, Rice & Flour: Crisps: Crisped Corn*
Crisped Oat Crisps *See Cereals, Grains, Rice & Flour: Crisps: Crisped Oat*
Crisped Rice Crisps *See Cereals, Grains, Rice & Flour: Crisps: Crisped Rice*
Crisped Soy Crisps *See Cereals, Grains, Rice & Flour: Crisps: Crisped Soy*
Crisped Wheat Crisps *See Cereals, Grains, Rice & Flour: Crisps: Crisped Wheat*
Crisps *See Cereals, Grains, Rice & Flour: Crisps*
Criterion Apple *See Fruits & Vegetables: Apple: Criterion*
Croaker *See Fish & Seafood: Fish: Croaker*
Croissant Sesame Crackers *See Baked Goods: Crackers: Croissant Sesame Crackers*
Croissants *See Baked Goods: Breads: Croissants*
Croquettes *See Prepared Foods: Croquettes*
Croutons *See Baked Goods: Bread Crumbs & Croutons: Croutons; See also Baked Goods: Bread Crumbs & Croutons: Crumbs*
Crumpets *See Baked Goods: Cakes & Pastries: Crumpets*
Crunch Toppings *See Ingredients, Flavors & Additives: Toppings: Crunch*
Crunches *See Baked Goods: Crunches*
Crunchy Peanut Butter *See Nuts & Nut Butters: Nut Butters: Peanut Butter: Crunchy*
Crushed Canned Tomato *See Fruits & Vegetables: Tomato: Canned: Crushed*
Crushed Fruits & Vegetables *See Fruits & Vegetables: Crushed*
Crushed Onion *See Fruits & Vegetables: Onion: Crushed*
Crushed Red Pepper *See Spices, Seasonings & Seeds: Spices: Red Pepper: Crushed*
Crysanthemums *See Fruits & Vegetables: Crysanthemums*
Crystalline Fructose *See Sugars, Syrups & Sweeteners: Fructose: Crystalline*
Crystallized Ginger *See Spices, Seasonings & Seeds: Spices: Ginger: Crystallized; See also Fruits & Vegetables: Ginger: Crystallized*
Crystallized, Glace Candied Fruits *See Fruits & Vegetables: Candied Fruits: Crystallized, Glace*
Cucumber *See Fruits & Vegetables: Cucumber*
Cucumber for Pickling *See Fruits & Vegetables: Cucumber: for Pickling*
Cultured Flavors *See Ingredients, Flavors & Additives: Flavors: Cultured*
Cultures *See Ingredients, Flavors & Additives: Cultures & Yeasts: Cultures*
Cultures & Yeasts *See Ingredients, Flavors & Additives: Cultures & Yeasts*
Cumin Seeds *See Spices, Seasonings & Seeds: Seeds: Cumin*
Cumin Spices *See Spices, Seasonings & Seeds: Spices: Cumin*
Cupcake *See Baked Goods: Cakes & Pastries: Cupcakes*
Curd Seasonings *See Spices, Seasonings & Seeds: Seasonings: Curd*
Cured Smoked Seafood *See Fish & Seafood: Seafood: Smoked: Cured*
Curing Preparations *See Ingredients, Flavors & Additives: Curing Preparations*
Currants Berries *See Fruits & Vegetables: Berries: Currants*
Curry Powder *See Spices, Seasonings & Seeds: Spices: Curry Powder; See also Ingredients, Flavors & Additives: Powders: Curry*
Curry Sauces *See Sauces, Dips & Dressings: Sauces: Curry*
Cusk *See Fish & Seafood: Fish: Cusk*
Custard *See Dairy Products: Custard*
Custard Dessert Fillings *See Doughs, Mixes & Fillings: Fillings: Dessert: Custard*
Custard Powders *See Ingredients, Flavors & Additives: Powders: Custard*
Custom Blends *See Ingredients, Flavors & Additives: Blends: Custom*
Custom Designed Colloid Stabilizers *See Ingredients, Flavors & Additives: Stabilizers: Colloids: Custom Designed*

D

D'Anjou/Bosc Pear *See Fruits & Vegetables: Pear: D'Anjou/Bosc*
Dairy Bases *See Ingredients, Flavors & Additives: Bases: Dairy*
Dairy Butter *See Dairy Products: Butter: Dairy*
Dairy Coagulants *See Ingredients, Flavors & Additives: Coagulants: Dairy*
Dairy Drinks *See Dairy Products: Dairy Drinks*
Dairy Flavors *See Ingredients, Flavors & Additives: Flavors: Dairy*
Dairy Ingredients *See Ingredients, Flavors & Additives: Ingredients: Dairy*
Dairy Products *See Dairy Products*
Dairy Seasonings *See Spices, Seasonings & Seeds: Seasonings: Dairy Products*
Dairy Whipped Toppings *See Ingredients, Flavors & Additives: Toppings: Whipped: Dairy*
Danish *See Baked Goods: Cakes & Pastries: Danish*
Darjeeling Tea *See Beverages: Coffee & Tea: Tea: Darjeeling*
Dark Green Zucchini *See Fruits & Vegetables: Zucchini: Dark Green*
Dark Red Kidney Beans *See Fruits & Vegetables: Beans: Kidney: Dark Red*
Dark Rum *See Beverages: Spirits & Liqueurs: Rum: Dark*
DarkLager/Dunkel Lager *See Beverages: Beers: Lager: DarkLager/Dunkel*
Dates *See Fruits & Vegetables: Dates*
De Arbol Peppers *See Fruits & Vegetables: Peppers: De Arbol*
Decaffeinated Coffee *See Beverages: Coffee & Tea: Coffee: Decaffeinated*
Decaffeinated Coffee, Naturally *See Beverages: Coffee & Tea: Coffee: Decaffeinated Naturally*
Decaffeinated Espresso *See Beverages: Coffee & Tea: Espresso: Decaffeinated*
Decaffeinated Tea *See Beverages: Coffee & Tea: Tea: Decaffeinated*
Decorations *See Candy & Confectionery: Decorations & Icings; See also Candy & Confectionery: Decorations & Icings: Decorations*
Decorative Items *See Ingredients, Flavors & Additives: Decorative Items*
Defatted Wheat Germ *See Cereals, Grains, Rice & Flour: Wheat: Germ: Defatted*
Defoamers *See Ingredients, Flavors & Additives: Defoamers*
Dehydrated Capsicums Peppers *See Fruits & Vegetables: Peppers: Capsicums: Dehydrated*

1 2 3 4 5
EXAMPLE: **Canadian Style Bacon** *See Meats & Meat Products: Smoked, Cured & Deli Meats: Bacon: Canadian Style*

1. Product or Service you are looking for
2. Main Category, in alphabetical order, located in the page headers starting on page 27
3. Category Description, located in black bars and in page headers
4. Product Category, located in gray bars
5. Product Type, located under gray bars, centered in bold

Dehydrated Carrot *See Fruits & Vegetables: Carrot: Dehydrated*
Dehydrated Celery *See Fruits & Vegetables: Celery: Dehydrated*
Dehydrated Egg *See Eggs & Egg Products: Dehydrated*
Dehydrated Food *See Specialty Processed Foods: Dehydrated Food (See also Specific Foods)*
Dehydrated Fruit *See Fruits & Vegetables: Dried & Dehydrated Fruits: Dehydrated Fruit; See also Fruits & Vegetables: Dehydrated*
Dehydrated Mushrooms *See Fruits & Vegetables: Mushrooms: Dehydrated*
Dehydrated Onion *See Fruits & Vegetables: Dried & Dehydrated Vegetables: Onion: Dehydrated*
Dehydrated Parsley *See Spices, Seasonings & Seeds: Spices: Parsley: Dehydrated*
Dehydrated Potatoes *See Fruits & Vegetables: Potatoes: Dehydrated*
Dehydrated Shellfish *See Fish & Seafood: Shellfish: Dehydrated*
Dehydrated Soup *See Prepared Foods: Soups & Stews: Dehydrated Soup*
Dehydrated Vegetables *See Fruits & Vegetables: Dried & Dehydrated Vegetables: Dehydrated Vegetables; See also Fruits & Vegetables: Dehydrated*
Deli Foods *See Meats & Meat Products: Smoked, Cured & Deli Meats: Deli Foods*
Deli Meats *See Meats & Meat Products: Smoked, Cured & Deli Meats: Deli Meats*
Deli Meats, Fresh Turkey Breast *See Meats & Meat Products: Smoked, Cured & Deli Meats: Turkey: Deli Breast - Fresh*
Deli Meats, Frozen Turkey Breast *See Meats & Meat Products: Smoked, Cured & Deli Meats: Turkey: Deli Breast - Frozen*
Deli Meats, Smoked Turkey Breast *See Meats & Meat Products: Smoked, Cured & Deli Meats: Turkey: Deli Breast - Smoked*
Desiccated & Shredded Coconut *See Fruits & Vegetables: Coconut & Coconut Products: Desiccated & Shredded*
Desiccated Egg *See Eggs & Egg Products: Dried: Desiccated*
Desiccated Fruit *See Fruits & Vegetables: Dried & Dehydrated Fruits: Desiccated Fruit*
Desiccated Vegetables *See Fruits & Vegetables: Dried & Dehydrated Vegetables: Desiccated Vegetables*
Dessert Fillings *See Doughs, Mixes & Fillings: Fillings: Dessert*
Dessert Mixes *See Doughs, Mixes & Fillings: Mixes: Dessert*
Dessert Mixes, Frozen *See Doughs, Mixes & Fillings: Mixes: Frozen: Dessert*
Dessert Sauces *See Sauces, Dips & Dressings: Sauces: Dessert*
Dessert Tarts *See Baked Goods: Cakes & Pastries: Dessert Tarts*
Dessert Toppings *See Ingredients, Flavors & Additives: Toppings: Dessert*
Desserts *See Baked Goods: Desserts*
Dextrin Starches *See Ingredients, Flavors & Additives: Starches: Dextrin*
Dextrose Corn Syrups *See Sugars, Syrups & Sweeteners: Syrups: Corn: Dextrose*
Dextrose Sweeteners *See Ingredients, Flavors & Additives: Sweeteners: Dextrose*
Diced & Cooked Chicken *See Meats & Meat Products: Poultry: Chicken: Diced & Cooked*
Diced Canned Pear *See Fruits & Vegetables: Pear: Canned: Diced*
Diced Frozen Chicken *See Meats & Meat Products: Poultry: Chicken: Diced Frozen*
Diced Tomato *See Fruits & Vegetables: Tomato: Diced*
Diet & Weight Loss Aids *See Specialty & Organic Foods: Dietary Products: Diet & Weight Loss Aids; See also Organic Foods*
Dietary Products *See Specialty & Organic Foods: Dietary Products; See also Organic Foods*
Dietary Supplements *See Specialty & Organic Foods: Dietary Products: Dietary Supplements; See also Organic Foods*
Dietetic Candy *See Candy & Confectionery: Candy: Dietetic*
Dietetic Juices *See Beverages: Juices: Dietetic*
Digestive Aids *See Ingredients, Flavors & Additives: Digestive Aids*
Dijon Mixes *See Sauces, Dips & Dressings: Salad Dressings: Mixes: Dijon*
Dill Pickles *See Relishes & Pickled Products: Pickled Products: Pickles: Dill*
Dill Seeds *See Spices, Seasonings & Seeds: Seeds: Dill*
Dill Spices *See Spices, Seasonings & Seeds: Spices: Dill*
Dill Weed Spices *See Spices, Seasonings & Seeds: Spices: Dill Weed*
Dillweed Oils *See Oils, Shortening & Fats: Oils: Dillweed*
Dim Sum *See Ethnic Foods: Dim Sum*
Dip Mixes *See Doughs, Mixes & Fillings: Mixes: Dip*
Dipping Fruit *See Fruits & Vegetables: Dipping Fruit*
Dips *See Sauces, Dips & Dressings: Dips*
Distilled Water *See Beverages: Water: Distilled*
Divinity Candy *See Candy & Confectionery: Candy: Divinity*
Dogfish *See Fish & Seafood: Fish: Dogfish*
Dolcetto *See Beverages: Wines: Red Grape Wines: Dolcetto*
Dolphin *See Fish & Seafood: Fish: Dolphin*
Donut Mixes *See Doughs, Mixes & Fillings: Mixes: Donut*
Doughnut Doughs *See Doughs, Mixes & Fillings: Doughs: Doughnuts*
Doughnut Fillings *See Doughs, Mixes & Fillings: Fillings: Doughnuts*
Doughnuts *See Baked Goods: Cakes & Pastries: Doughnuts*
Doughs *See Doughs, Mixes & Fillings: Doughs*
Dressing Flavors *See Ingredients, Flavors & Additives: Flavors: Flavors: Dressing*
Dried & Dehydrated Fruits *See Fruits & Vegetables: Dried & Dehydrated Fruits*
Dried & Dehydrated Vegetables *See Fruits & Vegetables: Dried & Dehydrated Vegetables*
Dried Apple *See Fruits & Vegetables: Apple: Dried*
Dried Apricot *See Fruits & Vegetables: Apricot: Dried*
Dried Banana *See Fruits & Vegetables: Banana: Dried*
Dried Beans *See Fruits & Vegetables: Beans: Dried*
Dried Beet Pulp *See Fruits & Vegetables: Pulps & Purees: Pulp: Dried Beet*
Dried Blueberry *See Fruits & Vegetables: Berries: Blueberry: Dried*
Dried Cantaloupe *See Fruits & Vegetables: Melon: Cantaloupe: Dried*
Dried Cayenne Pepper *See Spices, Seasonings & Seeds: Spices: Cayenne Pepper: Dried*
Dried Cherries *See Fruits & Vegetables: Cherries: Dried*
Dried Chicken Fats *See Oils, Shortening & Fats: Fats & Lard: Chicken: Dried*
Dried Chile Peppers *See Fruits & Vegetables: Peppers: Chile: Dried Pods*
Dried Chives *See Fruits & Vegetables: Dried & Dehydrated Vegetables: Dried Chives*
Dried Coconut *See Fruits & Vegetables: Coconut & Coconut Products: Dried*
Dried Cranberry *See Fruits & Vegetables: Berries: Cranberry: Dried*
Dried Cream *See Dairy Products: Cream: Dried*
Dried Egg *See Eggs & Egg Products: Dried*
Dried Fruit *See Fruits & Vegetables: Dried & Dehydrated Fruits: Dried Fruit*
Dried Honey *See Sugars, Syrups & Sweeteners: Honey: Dried*
Dried Mango *See Fruits & Vegetables: Mango: Dried*
Dried Molasses *See Sugars, Syrups & Sweeteners: Molasses: Dried*
Dried Papaya *See Fruits & Vegetables: Papaya: Dried*
Dried Peach *See Fruits & Vegetables: Peach: Dried*
Dried Pear *See Fruits & Vegetables: Pear: Dried*
Dried Pineapple *See Fruits & Vegetables: Pineapple: Dried*
Dried Plums *See Fruits & Vegetables: Plums: Dried*
Dried Prunes *See Fruits & Vegetables: Prunes: Dried*
Dried Raisins *See Fruits & Vegetables: Raisins: Dried*
Dried Refried Beans *See Fruits & Vegetables: Beans: Refried: Dried*
Dried Sliced Beef *See Meats & Meat Products: Beef & Beef Products: Sliced: Dried*
Dried Spices *See Spices, Seasonings & Seeds: Spices: Dried*
Dried Strawberry *See Fruits & Vegetables: Berries: Strawberry: Dried*
Dried Tomato *See Fruits & Vegetables: Tomato: Dried*
Drink Mixes *See Doughs, Mixes & Fillings: Mixes: Drink*
Dry Beans *See Fruits & Vegetables: Beans: Dry*
Dry Buttermilk *See Dairy Products: Buttermilk & Buttermilk Products: Buttermilk Products: Dry*
Dry Malt *See Cereals, Grains, Rice & Flour: Malt: Dry*
Dry Pancake Batters *See Doughs, Mixes & Fillings: Batters: Pancake: Dry*
Dry Peas *See Fruits & Vegetables: Peas: Dry*
Dry Raisin Juice *See Ingredients, Flavors & Additives: Replacers: Raisin Juice: Dry*
Dry Sweetcream Buttermilk *See Dairy Products: Buttermilk & Buttermilk Products: Buttermilk Products: Dry Sweetcream*
Duck *See Meats & Meat Products: Poultry: Duck*
Duck Sauces *See Sauces, Dips & Dressings: Sauces: Duck*
Dumpling Mixes *See Doughs, Mixes & Fillings: Mixes: Dumplings*
Dumplings *See Baked Goods: Cakes & Pastries: Dumplings*
Dungeness Crab *See Fish & Seafood: Shellfish: Crab: Dungeness*
Dusting Starches *See Ingredients, Flavors & Additives: Starches: Dusting*
Dutch *See Ethnic Foods: Dutch*
Dyes *See Ingredients, Flavors & Additives: Colors: Dyes*

E

E - Tocopherol *See Ingredients, Flavors & Additives: Vitamins & Supplements: E - Tocopherol*
Earl Grey Tea *See Beverages: Coffee & Tea: Tea: Earl Grey*
Earl Grey Tea, Decaffeinated *See Beverages: Coffee & Tea: Tea: Earl Grey Decaffeinated*
Easter Specialty-Packaged Candy *See Candy & Confectionery: Specialty-Packaged Candy: Easter*
Eastern Oregon Dry Bulb Onion *See Fruits & Vegetables: Onion: Eastern Oregon Dry Bulb Onion*
Echinacea Purpurea Powders *See Ingredients, Flavors & Additives: Powders: Echinacea Purpurea*
Eclairs *See Baked Goods: Cakes & Pastries: Eclairs*
Edam *See Cheese & Cheese Products: Cheese: Edam*
Edible Coatings *See Ingredients, Flavors & Additives: Coatings: Edible*
Edible Dry Beans *See Fruits & Vegetables: Beans: Dry: Edible*
Edible Oils *See Oils, Shortening & Fats: Oils: Edible*
Edible Release, Grease Agents *See Ingredients, Flavors & Additives: Agents: Release,Grease: Edible*
Eel *See Fish & Seafood: Fish: Eel*
Egg Drop Soup *See Prepared Foods: Soups & Stews: Egg Drop Soup*
Egg Nog *See Dairy Products: Egg Nog*
Egg Noodles *See Pasta & Noodles: Noodles: Egg*
Egg Powders *See Ingredients, Flavors & Additives: Powders: Egg*
Egg Replacers *See Ingredients, Flavors & Additives: Replacers: Egg*
Egg Rolls *See Ethnic Foods: Egg Rolls*
Egg Substitutes *See Eggs & Egg Products: Substitutes*
Egg Tomato *See Fruits & Vegetables: Tomato: Roma (Egg)*
Eggplant *See Fruits & Vegetables: Eggplant*
Eggplant Parmigiana *See Prepared Foods: Prepared Meals: Eggplant Parmigiana*
Eggplant, Dried & Dehydrated *See Fruits & Vegetables: Dried & Dehydrated Vegetables: Eggplant*
Eggs & Egg Products *See Eggs & Egg Products*
Eggs, Pickled Products *See Relishes & Pickled Products: Pickled Products: Eggs*
Eggs, Prepared Meals *See Prepared Foods: Prepared Meals: Eggs*
Elbow Macaroni *See Pasta & Noodles: Elbow Macaroni*
Emu *See Meats & Meat Products: Game: Emu*
Emulsifiers *See Ingredients, Flavors & Additives: Emulsifiers*
Enchiladas *See Ethnic Foods: Enchiladas*
Endive *See Spices, Seasonings & Seeds: Spices: Endive*
Energy Bars *See Specialty & Organic Foods: Health & Dietary: Energy Bars; See also Organic Foods*
English Breakfast Tea *See Beverages: Coffee & Tea: Tea: English Breakfast*
English Breakfast Tea, Decaffeinated *See Beverages: Coffee & Tea: Tea: English Breakfast Decaffeinated*
English Muffins *See Baked Goods: Breads: English Muffins*
English Style B Ale *See Beverages: Beers: American & British Ale: English Style B*
Enhancers *See Ingredients, Flavors & Additives: Enhancers*
Enokis Mushrooms *See Fruits & Vegetables: Mushrooms: Enokis*
Enrichment & Nutrient Additives *See Ingredients, Flavors & Additives: Additives: Enrichment & Nutrient*
Enrichment Blends *See Ingredients, Flavors & Additives: Blends: Enrichment*
Entrees Prepared Meals *See Prepared Foods: Prepared Meals: Entrees*
Enzymes *See Ingredients, Flavors & Additives: Enzymes*
Enzymes Additives *See Ingredients, Flavors & Additives: Additives: Enzymes*
Epazote Herb *See Spices, Seasonings & Seeds: Spices: Epazote Herb*
Escargot *See Prepared Foods: Prepared Meals: Escargot*
Escarole *See Spices, Seasonings & Seeds: Spices: Escarole*
Espresso *See Beverages: Coffee & Tea: Espresso*
Essential Fatty Acids *See Ingredients, Flavors & Additives: Fatty Acids: Essential*
Essential Oils *See Oils, Shortening & Fats: Oils: Essential*
Ethnic Foods *See Ethnic Foods*
Ethyleneamines *See Ingredients, Flavors & Additives: Ethyleneamines*
Etoufee *See Prepared Foods: Prepared Meals: Etoufee*

Evaporated Milk *See Dairy Products: Milk & Milk Products: Milk: Evaporated*
Extenders *See Ingredients, Flavors & Additives: Extenders*
Extra Virgin Olive Oils *See Oils, Shortening & Fats: Oils: Olive: Extra Virgin*
Extract Flavors *See Ingredients, Flavors & Additives: Flavors: Extract*
Extracts *See Ingredients, Flavors & Additives: Extracts*
Extracts, Spices *See Spices, Seasonings & Seeds: Spices: Extracts*
Extracts, Yeast *See Ingredients, Flavors & Additives: Cultures & Yeasts: Yeast: Extracts*

F

Fair-Trade Tea *See Beverages: Coffee & Tea: Tea: Fair-Trade*
Fajita Chicken Strips *See Meats & Meat Products: Poultry: Chicken: Fajita Strips*
Fajita Marinades *See Sauces, Dips & Dressings: Marinades: Fajita*
Fajita Seasonings *See Spices, Seasonings & Seeds: Seasonings: Fajita*
Farfalle *See Pasta & Noodles: Farfalle*
Farina Cereal *See Cereals, Grains, Rice & Flour: Cereal: Farina*
Farm-Raised Game *See Meats & Meat Products: Game: Farm-Raised*
Fat & Cholesterol Free *See Eggs & Egg Products: Fat & Cholesterol Free*
Fat Flavors *See Ingredients, Flavors & Additives: Flavors: Fat*
Fat Replacers *See Ingredients, Flavors & Additives: Replacers: Fat*
Fat-Free Ice Cream *See Dairy Products: Ice Cream: Fat-Free*
Fat-Free Milk *See Dairy Products: Milk & Milk Products: Milk: Fat-Free*
Fats *See Oils, Shortening & Fats*
Fats & Lard *See Oils, Shortening & Fats: Fats & Lard*
Fatty Acids *See Ingredients, Flavors & Additives: Fatty Acids*
Fava Beans *See Fruits & Vegetables: Beans: Fava*
Fennel Seeds *See Spices, Seasonings & Seeds: Seeds: Fennel*
Fennel Spices *See Spices, Seasonings & Seeds: Spices: Fennel*
Fenugreek Seeds *See Spices, Seasonings & Seeds: Seeds: Fenugreek*
Fenugreek Spices *See Spices, Seasonings & Seeds: Spices: Fenugreek*
Fermented Products *See Specialty Processed Foods: Fermented Products (See also Specific Foods)*
Feta Cheese *See Cheese & Cheese Products: Cheese: Feta*
Fettuccine *See Pasta & Noodles: Fettuccine*
Feverfew Powders *See Ingredients, Flavors & Additives: Powders: Feverfew*
Fiber *See Cereals, Grains, Rice & Flour: Fiber*
Fig Pastes *See Ingredients, Flavors & Additives: Pastes: Fig*
Fig, Dried *See Fruits & Vegetables: Dried & Dehydrated Fruits: Fig*
Figs *See Fruits & Vegetables: Figs*
Filberts *See Nuts & Nut Butters: Nuts: Filberts*
Filet Mignon *See Meats & Meat Products: Beef & Beef Products: Filet Mignon*
Filled Candy *See Candy & Confectionery: Candy: Filled*
Filled Doughnuts *See Baked Goods: Cakes & Pastries: Doughnuts: Filled*
Fillers *See Ingredients, Flavors & Additives: Fillers*
Fillets, Chicken *See Meats & Meat Products: Poultry: Chicken: Fillets*
Fillets, Fish *See Fish & Seafood: Fish: Fillets*
Fillets, Herring *See Fish & Seafood: Fish: Herring: Fillets*
Fillets, Turkey *See Meats & Meat Products: Poultry: Turkey: Fillets*
Fillings *See Doughs, Mixes & Fillings: Fillings*
Finfish *See Fish & Seafood: Fish: Finfish*
Fire Roasted Vegetables *See Fruits & Vegetables: Fire Roasted Vegetables*
Firming Agents *See Ingredients, Flavors & Additives: Agents: Firming*
Fish *See Fish & Seafood: Fish; See also Prepared Foods: Prepared Meals: Fish*
Fish & Chips *See Prepared Foods: Prepared Meals: Fish & Chips*
Fish Oils *See Oils, Shortening & Fats: Oils: Fish*
Fish Paste *See Fish & Seafood: Fish: Paste*
Fish Patties *See Prepared Foods: Prepared Meals: Fish Patties*
Fish Powders *See Ingredients, Flavors & Additives: Powders: Fish*
Fish Sauces *See Sauces, Dips & Dressings: Sauces: Fish*
Fish Steaks *See Fish & Seafood: Fish: Steaks*
Fish Sticks *See Prepared Foods: Prepared Meals: Fish Sticks; See also See Fish & Seafood: Fish: Sticks*
Flakes *See Ingredients, Flavors & Additives: Flakes*
Flat Breads *See Baked Goods: Breads: Flat*
Flavor Bases *See Ingredients, Flavors & Additives: Bases: Flavor*
Flavor Bits *See Ingredients, Flavors & Additives: Bits: Flavor*
Flavor Enhancers *See Ingredients, Flavors & Additives: Flavors: Flavors: Enhancers; See also See Ingredients, Flavors & Additives: Flavor Enhancers*
Flavored Cheese Cake *See Baked Goods: Cakes & Pastries: Cheese Cake: Flavored*
Flavored Coffee *See Beverages: Coffee & Tea: Coffee: Flavored*
Flavored Ice Cream *See Dairy Products: Ice Cream: Flavored*
Flavored Liquid Vinegar *See Sauces, Dips & Dressings: Vinegar: Liquid: Flavored*
Flavored Milk *See Dairy Products: Milk & Milk Products: Milk: Flavored*
Flavored Pellets *See Ingredients, Flavors & Additives: Half-Products: Flavored Pellets*
Flavored Popcorn *See Snack Foods: Popcorn: Flavored*
Flavored Pretzels *See Snack Foods: Pretzels: Flavored*
Flavored Stout *See Beverages: Beers: Stout & Porter: Flavored Stout*
Flavored Sugar Bits *See Ingredients, Flavors & Additives: Bits: Flavored Sugar*
Flavored Tea *See Beverages: Coffee & Tea: Tea: Flavored*
Flavored Water *See Beverages: Water: Flavored*
Flavored Wraps *See Baked Goods: Wraps: Flavored*
Flavoring Extracts *See Ingredients, Flavors & Additives: Extracts: Flavoring*
Flavors *See Ingredients, Flavors & Additives: Flavors; See also Ingredients, Flavors & Additives: Flavors: Flavors*
Flax Crisps *See Cereals, Grains, Rice & Flour: Crisps: Flax*
Flax Seeds *See Spices, Seasonings & Seeds: Seeds: Flax*
Flounder *See Fish & Seafood: Fish: Flounder*
Flour *See Cereals, Grains, Rice & Flour: Flour*
Flour, Rice Starch, Organic *See Specialty & Organic Foods: Organic Foods: Rice Starch: Flour; See also Organic Foods*
Flowers, Edible *See Fruits & Vegetables: Flowers - Edible*
Fluid Shortening *See Oils, Shortening & Fats: Shortening: Fluid*
Fluke *See Fish & Seafood: Fish: Fluke*
Foaming & Whipping Agents *See Ingredients, Flavors & Additives: Agents: Foaming & Whipping*
Focaccia *See Baked Goods: Breads: Focaccia*
Foie Gras *See Meats & Meat Products: Pates & Foie Gras: Foie Gras*
Fondant *See Sugars, Syrups & Sweeteners: Sugar: Fondant*
Fondants *See Candy & Confectionery: Candy: Fondants*
Fontina Cheese *See Cheese & Cheese Products: Cheese: Fontina*
Food Bases *See Ingredients, Flavors & Additives: Bases: Food*
Food Ingredients *See Ingredients, Flavors & Additives: Ingredients: Food*
Food Preservatives *See Ingredients, Flavors & Additives: Preservatives: Food*
Food Releases *See Ingredients, Flavors & Additives: Releases: Food*
Foodservice, Individual Packets *See Prepared Foods: Individual Packets: Foodservice*
Formula *See Baby Foods: Formula*
Fortification Protein *See Ingredients, Flavors & Additives: Vitamins & Supplements: Protein Supplements: Fortification Protein*
Fortified Refined Vegetable Oils *See Oils, Shortening & Fats: Oils: Vegetable: Fortified Refined*
Fortune Cookies *See Baked Goods: Cookies & Bars: Fortune Cookies*
Fra Diavolo Sauces *See Sauces, Dips & Dressings: Sauces: Fra Diavolo*
Fragrances *See Ingredients, Flavors & Additives: Aroma Chemicals & Materials: Fragrances*
Frankfurters *See Meats & Meat Products: Frankfurters*
Frankfurters, Mini *See Meats & Meat Products: Frankfurters: Mini*
Free Flow Additives *See Ingredients, Flavors & Additives: Additives: Free Flow*
Freeze-Dried Food *See Specialty Processed Foods: Freeze Dried Food (See also Specific Foods)*
Freeze-Dried Fruits & Vegetables *See Fruits & Vegetables: Dehydrated: Freeze Dried; See also Fruits & Vegetables: Dried & Dehydrated Fruits: Freeze Dried; See also Fruits & Vegetables: Dried & Dehydrated Vegetables: Freeze Dried*
Freeze-Dried Mushrooms *See Fruits & Vegetables: Dried & Dehydrated Vegetables: Mushrooms: Freeze Dried*
Freeze-Dried Seafood *See Fish & Seafood: Seafood: Freeze-Dried*
French Breads *See Baked Goods: Breads: French*
French Fries *See Prepared Foods: French Fries*
French Salad Dressings *See Sauces, Dips & Dressings: Salad Dressings: French; See also See Sauces, Dips & Dressings: Salad Dressings: Mixes: French*
French Toast *See Prepared Foods: French Toast*
French Wines *See Beverages: Wines: French*
Fresh Apple *See Fruits & Vegetables: Apple: Fresh*
Fresh Bagels *See Baked Goods: Breads: Bagels: Fresh*
Fresh Bakes Goods *See Baked Goods: Fresh*
Fresh Beef *See Meats & Meat Products: Beef & Beef Products: Fresh*
Fresh Biscuits *See Baked Goods: Breads: Biscuits: Fresh*
Fresh Breads *See Baked Goods: Breads: Fresh*
Fresh Chicken *See Meats & Meat Products: Poultry: Chicken: Fresh*
Fresh Clam *See Fish & Seafood: Shellfish: Clam: Fresh*
Fresh Crab *See Fish & Seafood: Shellfish: Crab: Fresh*
Fresh Cream *See Dairy Products: Cream: Fresh*
Fresh Eggs *See Eggs & Egg Products: Fresh*
Fresh Fish *See Fish & Seafood: Fish: Fresh*
Fresh Fish Cakes *See Fish & Seafood: Fish: Cakes: Fresh*
Fresh Fruit *See Fruits & Vegetables: Fresh Fruit*
Fresh Ham *See Meats & Meat Products: Smoked, Cured & Deli Meats: Ham: Fresh*
Fresh Herring *See Fish & Seafood: Fish: Herring: Fresh*
Fresh Lamb *See Meats & Meat Products: Lamb: Fresh*
Fresh Lobster *See Fish & Seafood: Shellfish: Lobster: Fresh*
Fresh Milk *See Dairy Products: Milk & Milk Products: Milk: Fresh*
Fresh Mushrooms *See Fruits & Vegetables: Mushrooms: Fresh*
Fresh Oysters *See Fish & Seafood: Shellfish: Oysters: Fresh*
Fresh Peas *See Fruits & Vegetables: Peas: Fresh*
Fresh Pies *See Baked Goods: Pies: Fresh*
Fresh Pork *See Meats & Meat Products: Pork & Pork Products: Fresh*
Fresh Potatoes *See Fruits & Vegetables: Potatoes: Fresh*
Fresh Prepared Foods *See Prepared Foods: Fresh*
Fresh Rolls *See Baked Goods: Breads: Rolls: Fresh*
Fresh Sardines *See Fish & Seafood: Fish: Sardines: Fresh*
Fresh Seafood *See Fish & Seafood: Seafood: Fresh*
Fresh Shellfish *See Fish & Seafood: Shellfish: Fresh*
Fresh Shrimp *See Fish & Seafood: Shellfish: Shrimp: Fresh*
Fresh Soy *See Fruits & Vegetables: Soy: Fresh*
Fresh Stew *See Prepared Foods: Soups & Stews: Fresh Stew*
Fresh Succotash *See Fruits & Vegetables: Succotash: Fresh*
Fresh Tomato *See Fruits & Vegetables: Tomato: Fresh*
Fresh Turkey *See Meats & Meat Products: Poultry: Turkey: Fresh*
Fresh Veal *See Meats & Meat Products: Beef & Beef Products: Veal: Fresh*
Fresh Vegetables *See Fruits & Vegetables: Fresh Vegetables*
Fresh Yeast *See Ingredients, Flavors & Additives: Cultures & Yeasts: Yeast: Fresh*
Freshwater Fish *See Fish & Seafood: Fish: Freshwater*
Fried Chips *See Snack Foods: Chips: Fried*
Fried Oysters *See Fish & Seafood: Shellfish: Oysters: Fried*
Fried Porkskins *See Prepared Foods: Porkskins: Fried*
Fried Rice, Prepared Meals *See Prepared Foods: Prepared Meals: Fried Rice*
Fried Rice, Seasonings *See Spices, Seasonings & Seeds: Seasonings: Fried Rice*
Frozen Appetizers *See Prepared Foods: Appetizers: Frozen*
Frozen Apple *See Fruits & Vegetables: Apple: Frozen*
Frozen Apple Juices *See Beverages: Juices: Apple: Frozen*
Frozen Apricot *See Fruits & Vegetables: Apricot: Frozen*
Frozen Apricot Juices *See Beverages: Juices: Apricot: Frozen*

1	2	3	4	5
EXAMPLE: **Canadian Style Bacon**	*See Meats & Meat Products:*	*Smoked, Cured & Deli Meats:*	*Bacon:*	*Canadian Style*

1. Product or Service you are looking for
2. Main Category, in alphabetical order, located in the page headers starting on page 27
3. Category Description, located in black bars and in page headers
4. Product Category, located in gray bars
5. Product Type, located under gray bars, centered in bold

Frozen Artichoke *See Fruits & Vegetables: Artichoke: Frozen*
Frozen Asparagus *See Fruits & Vegetables: Asparagus: Frozen*
Frozen Au Gratin Potatoes *See Fruits & Vegetables: Potatoes: Au Gratin: Frozen*
Frozen Bagels *See Baked Goods: Breads: Bagels: Frozen*
Frozen Baked & Stuffed Potatoes *See Fruits & Vegetables: Potatoes: Baked & Stuffed: Frozen*
Frozen Baked Goods *See Baked Goods: Frozen*
Frozen Baking Doughs *See Doughs, Mixes & Fillings: Doughs: Baking: Frozen*
Frozen Barbecued Beef *See Meats & Meat Products: Beef & Beef Products: Barbecued: Frozen*
Frozen Barbecued Pork *See Meats & Meat Products: Pork & Pork Products: Barbecued: Frozen*
Frozen Beans *See Fruits & Vegetables: Beans: Frozen*
Frozen Beef & Beef Products *See Meats & Meat Products: Beef & Beef Products: Frozen*
Frozen Beef Stew *See Meats & Meat Products: Beef & Beef Products: Stew: Frozen*
Frozen Beets *See Fruits & Vegetables: Beets: Frozen*
Frozen Berries *See Fruits & Vegetables: Berries: Frozen*
Frozen Beverage Mixes *See Doughs, Mixes & Fillings: Mixes: Beverage: Frozen*
Frozen Biscuits *See Baked Goods: Breads: Biscuits: Frozen*
Frozen Black-eyed Peas *See Fruits & Vegetables: Peas: Black-eyed: Frozen*
Frozen Blackberry *See Fruits & Vegetables: Berries: Blackberry: Frozen*
Frozen Blintzes *See Baked Goods: Cakes & Pastries: Blintzes: Frozen*
Frozen Blue Lake Beans *See Fruits & Vegetables: Beans: Blue Lake: Frozen*
Frozen Blueberry *See Fruits & Vegetables: Berries: Blueberry: Frozen*
Frozen Boysenberry *See Fruits & Vegetables: Berries: Boysenberry: Frozen*
Frozen Breads *See Baked Goods: Breads: Frozen*
Frozen Broccoli *See Fruits & Vegetables: Broccoli: Frozen*
Frozen Broth *See Prepared Foods: Broth: Frozen*
Frozen Brussel Sprouts *See Fruits & Vegetables: Brussel Sprouts: Frozen*
Frozen Buns *See Baked Goods: Breads: Buns: Frozen*
Frozen Butter Beans *See Fruits & Vegetables: Beans: Butter: Frozen*
Frozen Cabbage *See Fruits & Vegetables: Cabbage: Frozen*
Frozen Cake Batters *See Doughs, Mixes & Fillings: Batters: Cake: Frozen*
Frozen Cakes *See Baked Goods: Cakes & Pastries: Frozen Cakes*
Frozen Cappuccino Mixes *See Doughs, Mixes & Fillings: Mixes: Cappuccino: Frozen*
Frozen Capsicums Peppers *See Fruits & Vegetables: Peppers: Capsicums: Frozen*
Frozen Carrot *See Fruits & Vegetables: Carrot: Frozen*
Frozen Cauliflower *See Fruits & Vegetables: Cauliflower: Frozen*
Frozen Celery *See Fruits & Vegetables: Celery: Frozen*
Frozen Cheese Cake *See Baked Goods: Cakes & Pastries: Cheese Cake: Frozen*
Frozen Cherries *See Fruits & Vegetables: Cherries: Frozen*
Frozen Cherry Juices *See Beverages: Juices: Cherry: Frozen*
Frozen Chicken *See Meats & Meat Products: Poultry: Chicken: Frozen*
Frozen Chicken Fats & Lard *See Oils, Shortening & Fats: Fats & Lard: Chicken: Frozen*
Frozen Chili *See Prepared Foods: Chili: Frozen*
Frozen Chop Suey *See Ethnic Foods: Chop Suey: Frozen*
Frozen Clam *See Fish & Seafood: Shellfish: Clam: Frozen*
Frozen Clam Strips *See Fish & Seafood: Shellfish: Clam: Frozen Strips*
Frozen Coconut & Coconut Products *See Fruits & Vegetables: Coconut & Coconut Products: Frozen*
Frozen Convenience Food *See Prepared Foods: Convenience Food: Frozen*
Frozen Cookies *See Baked Goods: Cookies & Bars: Frozen Cookies*
Frozen Corn *See Fruits & Vegetables: Corn: Frozen*
Frozen Corn-on-the-Cob *See Fruits & Vegetables: Corn: Corn-on-the-Cob: Frozen*
Frozen Crab *See Fish & Seafood: Shellfish: Crab: Frozen; See also See Prepared Foods: Prepared Meals: Crab: Frozen*
Frozen Crab Meat *See Fish & Seafood: Shellfish: Crab: Meat Frozen*
Frozen Cranberry *See Fruits & Vegetables: Berries: Cranberry: Frozen*
Frozen Cranberry Juices *See Beverages: Juices: Cranberry: Frozen*
Frozen Crayfish *See Fish & Seafood: Shellfish: Crayfish: Frozen*
Frozen Crepes *See Prepared Foods: Crepes: Frozen*
Frozen Dehydrated Potatoes *See Fruits & Vegetables: Potatoes: Dehydrated: Frozen*
Frozen Doughnuts *See Baked Goods: Cakes & Pastries: Doughnuts: Frozen*
Frozen Doughs *See Doughs, Mixes & Fillings: Doughs: Frozen*
Frozen Eggs *See Eggs & Egg Products: Frozen*
Frozen Enchiladas *See Ethnic Foods: Enchiladas: Frozen*
Frozen Entrees *See Prepared Foods: Prepared Meals: Entrees: Frozen*
Frozen Figs *See Fruits & Vegetables: Figs: Frozen*
Frozen Fish *See Fish & Seafood: Fish: Frozen*
Frozen Fish Cakes *See Fish & Seafood: Fish: Cakes: Frozen*
Frozen Fish Sticks *See Prepared Foods: Prepared Meals: Fish Sticks: Frozen*
Frozen Foods *See Specialty Processed Foods: Frozen Foods (See also Specific Foods)*
Frozen French Fries *See Prepared Foods: French Fries: Frozen*
Frozen French Toast *See Prepared Foods: French Toast: Frozen*
Frozen Fruit *See Fruits & Vegetables: Frozen Fruit*
Frozen Fruit & Vegetable Juices *See Beverages: Juices: Fruit & Vegetable: Frozen*
Frozen Fruit Juices *See Beverages: Juices: Fruit: Frozen*
Frozen Fruit Pies *See Baked Goods: Pies: Fruit: Frozen*
Frozen Garlic Breads *See Baked Goods: Breads: Garlic: Frozen*
Frozen Gnocchi *See Pasta & Noodles: Gnocchi: Frozen*
Frozen Grape Juices *See Beverages: Juices: Grape: Frozen*
Frozen Grapefruit Juices *See Beverages: Juices: Grapefruit: Frozen*
Frozen Green Beans *See Fruits & Vegetables: Beans: Green: Frozen*
Frozen Ground Beef & Beef Products *See Meats & Meat Products: Beef & Beef Products: Ground: Frozen*
Frozen Ham *See Meats & Meat Products: Smoked, Cured & Deli Meats: Ham: Frozen*
Frozen Herring *See Fish & Seafood: Fish: Herring: Frozen*
Frozen Kale *See Fruits & Vegetables: Kale: Frozen*
Frozen Kidney Beans *See Fruits & Vegetables: Beans: Kidney: Frozen*
Frozen Lamb *See Meats & Meat Products: Lamb: Frozen*
Frozen Lasagna *See Pasta & Noodles: Lasagna: Frozen*
Frozen Lemon Juices *See Beverages: Juices: Lemon: Frozen*
Frozen Lima Beans *See Fruits & Vegetables: Beans: Lima: Frozen*
Frozen Lobster *See Fish & Seafood: Shellfish: Lobster: Frozen*
Frozen Mashed Sweet Potatoes *See Fruits & Vegetables: Sweet Potatoes: Mashed: Frozen*
Frozen Meat Balls *See Prepared Foods: Meat Balls: Frozen*
Frozen Meat Pies *See Baked Goods: Pies: Meat: Frozen*
Frozen Melon Balls *See Fruits & Vegetables: Melon: Balls: Frozen*
Frozen Mixes *See Doughs, Mixes & Fillings: Mixes: Frozen*
Frozen Mozzarella Cheese, Lite Shredded *See Cheese & Cheese Products: Cheese: Mozzarella: Lite Shredded - Frozen*
Frozen Muffins *See Baked Goods: Cakes & Pastries: Muffins: Frozen*
Frozen Mushrooms *See Fruits & Vegetables: Mushrooms: Frozen*
Frozen Non-Dairy Desserts *See Baked Goods: Desserts: Non-Dairy: Frozen*
Frozen Non-Fruit Pies *See Baked Goods: Pies: Non-Fruit: Frozen*
Frozen Okra *See Fruits & Vegetables: Okra: Frozen*
Frozen Onion *See Fruits & Vegetables: Onion: Frozen*
Frozen Onion Rings *See Prepared Foods: Onion Rings: Frozen*
Frozen Oven Type Potatoes *See Fruits & Vegetables: Potatoes: Oven Type: Frozen*
Frozen Oysters *See Fish & Seafood: Shellfish: Oysters: Frozen*
Frozen Pancakes *See Prepared Foods: Pancakes: Frozen*
Frozen Pasta *See Pasta & Noodles: Pasta: Frozen*
Frozen Patties Beef & Beef Products *See Meats & Meat Products: Beef & Beef Products: Patties: Frozen*
Frozen Peach *See Fruits & Vegetables: Peach: Frozen*
Frozen Pear *See Fruits & Vegetables: Pear: Frozen*
Frozen Peas *See Fruits & Vegetables: Peas: Frozen*
Frozen Peas & Carrots *See Fruits & Vegetables: Vegetables Mixed: Peas & Carrots: Frozen*
Frozen Peppers *See Fruits & Vegetables: Peppers: Frozen*
Frozen Pineapple *See Fruits & Vegetables: Pineapple: Frozen*
Frozen Pineapple Juices *See Beverages: Juices: Pineapple: Frozen*
Frozen Pizza *See Prepared Foods: Pizza & Pizza Products: Pizza: Frozen*
Frozen Pizza Doughs *See Doughs, Mixes & Fillings: Doughs: Pizza: Frozen*
Frozen Pizza Shells *See Prepared Foods: Pizza & Pizza Products: Shells: Frozen*
Frozen Plums *See Fruits & Vegetables: Plums: Frozen*
Frozen Pork & Pork Products *See Meats & Meat Products: Pork & Pork Products: Frozen*
Frozen Potato Rounds *See Fruits & Vegetables: Potatoes: Frozen: Rounds*
Frozen Potatoes *See Fruits & Vegetables: Potatoes: Frozen*
Frozen Prepared Foods *See Prepared Foods: Frozen*
Frozen Prepared Meals *See Prepared Foods: Prepared Meals: Frozen*
Frozen Prepared Pork & Pork Products *See Meats & Meat Products: Pork & Pork Products: Prepared: Frozen*
Frozen Prunes *See Fruits & Vegetables: Prunes: Frozen*
Frozen Pumpkin *See Fruits & Vegetables: Pumpkin: Frozen*
Frozen Rabbit *See Meats & Meat Products: Game: Rabbit: Frozen*
Frozen Raspberries *See Fruits & Vegetables: Berries: Raspberries: Frozen*
Frozen Ravioli *See Pasta & Noodles: Ravioli: Frozen*
Frozen Rhubarb *See Fruits & Vegetables: Rhubarb: Frozen*
Frozen Rice *See Cereals, Grains, Rice & Flour: Rice: Frozen*
Frozen Rolls *See Baked Goods: Breads: Rolls: Frozen*
Frozen Rutabaga *See Fruits & Vegetables: Rutabaga: Frozen*
Frozen Sauces *See Sauces, Dips & Dressings: Sauces: Frozen*
Frozen Scampi *See Fish & Seafood: Shellfish: Scampi: Frozen*
Frozen Seafood *See Fish & Seafood: Seafood: Frozen*
Frozen Shellfish *See Fish & Seafood: Shellfish: Frozen*
Frozen Shrimp *See Fish & Seafood: Shellfish: Shrimp: Frozen*
Frozen Sliced Beef & Beef Products *See Meats & Meat Products: Beef & Beef Products: Sliced: Frozen*
Frozen Slices Apple *See Fruits & Vegetables: Apple: Slices: Frozen*
Frozen Soup *See Prepared Foods: Soups & Stews: Frozen Soup*
Frozen Spaghetti *See Pasta & Noodles: Spaghetti: Frozen*
Frozen Special Trim Beef & Beef Products *See Meats & Meat Products: Beef & Beef Products: Special Trim: Frozen*
Frozen Spinach *See Fruits & Vegetables: Spinach: Frozen*
Frozen Squash *See Fruits & Vegetables: Squash: Frozen*
Frozen Stew *See Prepared Foods: Soups & Stews: Frozen Stew*
Frozen Strawberry *See Fruits & Vegetables: Berries: Strawberry: Frozen*
Frozen Stuffed Cabbage *See Prepared Foods: Prepared Meals: Stuffed Cabbage: Frozen*
Frozen Substitutes *See Eggs & Egg Products: Substitutes: Frozen*
Frozen Succotash *See Fruits & Vegetables: Succotash: Frozen*
Frozen Sweet Potatoes *See Fruits & Vegetables: Sweet Potatoes: Frozen*
Frozen Tamales *See Ethnic Foods: Tamales: Frozen*
Frozen Tomato *See Fruits & Vegetables: Tomato: Frozen*
Frozen Tomato Juices *See Beverages: Juices: Tomato: Frozen*
Frozen Tomato Sauces *See Sauces, Dips & Dressings: Sauces: Tomato: Frozen*
Frozen Tuna *See Fish & Seafood: Fish: Tuna: Frozen*
Frozen Turkey *See Meats & Meat Products: Poultry: Turkey: Frozen*
Frozen Turnip *See Fruits & Vegetables: Turnip: Frozen*
Frozen Veal *See Meats & Meat Products: Beef & Beef Products: Veal: Frozen*
Frozen Vegetables *See Fruits & Vegetables: Frozen Vegetables*
Frozen Vegetables Mixed *See Fruits & Vegetables: Vegetables Mixed: Frozen*
Frozen Venison *See Meats & Meat Products: Game: Venison: Frozen*
Frozen Waffles *See Baked Goods: Waffles: Frozen*
Frozen Wax Beans *See Fruits & Vegetables: Beans: Wax: Frozen*
Frozen Yams *See Fruits & Vegetables: Yams: Frozen*
Frozen Yogurt *See Dairy Products: Yogurt: Frozen*
Frozen Yogurt Powders *See Ingredients, Flavors & Additives: Powders: Yogurt: Frozen*
Fructose *See Sugars, Syrups & Sweeteners: Fructose*

Fruit *See Fruits & Vegetables: Fruit*
Fruit & Vegetable Coating Waxes *See Ingredients, Flavors & Additives: Waxes: Fruit & Vegetable Coating*
Fruit & Vegetable Juices *See Beverages: Juices: Fruit & Vegetable*
Fruit & Vegetable Pulps & Purees *See Fruits & Vegetables: Pulps & Purees: Fruit & Vegetable*
Fruit & Vegetable Puree *See Fruits & Vegetables: Pulps & Purees: Puree: Fruit & Vegetable*
Fruit Bases *See Ingredients, Flavors & Additives: Bases: Fruit*
Fruit Butter Spreads *See Jams, Jellies & Spreads: Spreads: Fruit Butter*
Fruit Cake *See Baked Goods: Cakes & Pastries: Fruit Cake*
Fruit Cobbler *See Baked Goods: Cakes & Pastries: Fruit Cobbler*
Fruit Cocktail *See Fruits & Vegetables: Fruit Cocktail*
Fruit Concentrates *See Ingredients, Flavors & Additives: Concentrates: Fruit*
Fruit Extracts *See Ingredients, Flavors & Additives: Extracts: Fruit*
Fruit Fillings *See Doughs, Mixes & Fillings: Fillings: Fruit*
Fruit Flavors *See Ingredients, Flavors & Additives: Flavors: Fruit*
Fruit Juices *See Beverages: Juices: Fruit*
Fruit Oils *See Oils, Shortening & Fats: Oils: Fruit*
Fruit Pastes *See Ingredients, Flavors & Additives: Pastes: Fruit*
Fruit Pectins *See Ingredients, Flavors & Additives: Pectins: Fruit*
Fruit Pies *See Baked Goods: Pies: Fruit*
Fruit Powders *See Ingredients, Flavors & Additives: Powders: Fruit*
Fruit Pulp *See Fruits & Vegetables: Pulps & Purees: Pulp: Fruit*
Fruit Pulps & Purees *See Fruits & Vegetables: Pulps & Purees: Fruit*
Fruit Punch Juices *See Beverages: Juices: Fruit Punch*
Fruit Puree *See Fruits & Vegetables: Pulps & Purees: Puree: Fruit*
Fruit Puree Concentrates *See Ingredients, Flavors & Additives: Concentrates: Fruit Puree*
Fruit Salad *See Fruits & Vegetables: Fruit: Salad*
Fruit Syrups *See Sugars, Syrups & Sweeteners: Syrups: Fruit*
Fruit Toppings *See Ingredients, Flavors & Additives: Toppings: Fruit*
Fruit, Certified Organic *See Specialty & Organic Foods: Organic Foods: Certified: Fruit; See also Organic Foods*
Fruits & Vegetables *See Fruits & Vegetables*
Fruits, Organic *See Specialty & Organic Foods: Organic Foods: Fruits; See also Organic Foods*
Fryer Rabbit *See Meats & Meat Products: Game: Rabbit: Fryer*
Fudge Candy *See Candy & Confectionery: Candy: Fudge*
Fudge Chocolate Products *See Candy & Confectionery: Chocolate Products: Fudge*
Fudge Sauces *See Sauces, Dips & Dressings: Sauces: Fudge*
Fudgesicles *See Dairy Products: Ice Cream: Fudgesicles*
Fumaric Acidulants *See Ingredients, Flavors & Additives: Acidulants: Fumaric*
Fund Raising Specialty-Packaged Candy *See Candy & Confectionery: Specialty-Packaged Candy: Fund Raising*
Funnel Cake *See Baked Goods: Cakes & Pastries: Funnel Cake*

G

Galangal *See Fruits & Vegetables: Galangal*
Game Meat & Poultry *See Meats & Meat Products: Game: Meat & Poultry; See also See Meats & Meat Products: Game*
Garbanzo Beans *See Fruits & Vegetables: Beans: Garbanzo*
Garlic *See Fruits & Vegetables: Garlic*
Garlic Bread Sticks *See Baked Goods: Bread Sticks: Garlic*
Garlic Breads *See Baked Goods: Breads: Garlic*
Garlic Juices *See Beverages: Juices: Garlic*
Garlic Oils *See Oils, Shortening & Fats: Oils: Garlic*
Garlic Powders *See Ingredients, Flavors & Additives: Powders: Garlic (See also Spices/Garlic Powder)*
Garlic Salt *See Spices, Seasonings & Seeds: Salt: Garlic; See also See Spices, Seasonings & Seeds: Spices: Garlic Salt*
Garlic Sauces *See Sauces, Dips & Dressings: Sauces: Garlic*
Garlic Spices *See Spices, Seasonings & Seeds: Spices: Garlic*
Gefilte Fish *See Fish & Seafood: Fish: Gefilte*
Gelatin Thickeners *See Ingredients, Flavors & Additives: Thickeners: Gelatin*
Gelato *See Dairy Products: Ice Cream: Gelato*
Gellan *See Ingredients, Flavors & Additives: Gums: Gellan*
General Grocery *See General Grocery*
Geoduck Clams *See Fish & Seafood: Shellfish: Geoduck Clams*
Gewurztraminer *See Beverages: Wines: White Grape Varieties: Gewurztraminer*
Ghatti *See Ingredients, Flavors & Additives: Gums: Ghatti*
Gherkins Pickles *See Relishes & Pickled Products: Pickled Products: Pickles: Gherkins*
Giardiniera *See Prepared Foods: Giardiniera*
Gin *See Beverages: Spirits & Liqueurs: Gin*
Ginger *See Fruits & Vegetables: Ginger*
Ginger Ale *See Beverages: Soft Drinks & Sodas: Soft Drinks: Ginger Ale*
Ginger Oils *See Oils, Shortening & Fats: Oils: Ginger*
Ginger Pieces *See Spices, Seasonings & Seeds: Spices: Ginger: Pieces*
Ginger Sauces *See Sauces, Dips & Dressings: Sauces: Ginger*
Ginger Snaps *See Baked Goods: Cookies & Bars: Ginger Snaps*
Ginger Spices *See Spices, Seasonings & Seeds: Spices: Ginger*
Gingko Powders *See Ingredients, Flavors & Additives: Powders: Gingko*
Ginseng Powders *See Ingredients, Flavors & Additives: Powders: Ginseng*
Ginseng Spices *See Spices, Seasonings & Seeds: Spices: Ginseng*
Glace *See Fruits & Vegetables: Glace*
Glandulars *See Ingredients, Flavors & Additives: Glandulars*
Glass-Packed Apple Juices *See Beverages: Juices: Apple: Glass-Packed*
Glass-Packed Apricot Juices *See Beverages: Juices: Apricot: Glass-Packed*
Glass-Packed Cherry Juices *See Beverages: Juices: Cherry: Glass-Packed*
Glass-Packed Chilled Tomato Juices *See Beverages: Juices: Tomato: Glass-Packed Chilled*
Glass-Packed Cranberry Juices *See Beverages: Juices: Cranberry: Glass-Packed*
Glass-Packed Fish *See Fish & Seafood: Fish: Packed: Glass*
Glass-Packed Fruit & Vegetable Juices *See Beverages: Juices: Fruit & Vegetable: Glass-Packed*
Glass-Packed Fruit Juices *See Beverages: Juices: Fruit: Glass-Packed*
Glass-Packed Grape Juices *See Beverages: Juices: Grape: Glass-Packed*
Glass-Packed Grapefruit Juices *See Beverages: Juices: Grapefruit: Glass-Packed*
Glass-Packed Lemon Juices *See Beverages: Juices: Lemon: Glass-Packed*
Glass-Packed Pineapple Juices *See Beverages: Juices: Pineapple: Glass-Packed*
Glazed & Coated Nuts *See Nuts & Nut Butters: Nuts: Glazed & Coated*
Glazes *See Sauces, Dips & Dressings: Glazes*
Gluconates *See Ingredients, Flavors & Additives: Flavor Enhancers: Gluconates*
Gluconic Acids (Gluconolactone) *See Ingredients, Flavors & Additives: Acids: Gluconic (Gluconolactone)*
Glucose *See Sugars, Syrups & Sweeteners: Syrups: Corn: Glucose - Etc.*
Glutamic Acids *See Ingredients, Flavors & Additives: Acids: Glutamic*
Gluten Flour *See Cereals, Grains, Rice & Flour: Flour: Gluten*
Gluten Wheat *See Cereals, Grains, Rice & Flour: Wheat: Glutten*
Glycine *See Ingredients, Flavors & Additives: Glycine*
Gnocchi *See Pasta & Noodles: Gnocchi*
Goat *See Meats & Meat Products: Goat*
Goat Milk *See Dairy Products: Milk & Milk Products: Milk: Goat*
Goat's Cheese *See Cheese & Cheese Products: Cheese: Goat's*
Gold Kiwi *See Fruits & Vegetables: Kiwi: Gold*
Golden Delicious Apple *See Fruits & Vegetables: Apple: Golden Delicious*
Golden Scallopino Squash *See Fruits & Vegetables: Squash: Golden Scallopino*
Golden Trout *See Fish & Seafood: Fish: Trout: Golden*
Goose Berries *See Fruits & Vegetables: Berries: Goose*
Goose Poultry *See Meats & Meat Products: Poultry: Goose*
Gorgonzola Cheese *See Cheese & Cheese Products: Cheese: Gorgonzola*
Gotu Kola Powders *See Ingredients, Flavors & Additives: Powders: Gotu Kola*
Gouda Cheese *See Cheese & Cheese Products: Cheese: Gouda*
Gourmet & Specialty Foods *See Specialty & Organic Foods: Gourmet & Specialty Foods; See also Organic Foods major cateory; See also Specialty & Organic Foods: Gourmet & Specialty Foods: Gourmet & Specialty Foods*
Gourmet Flavored Lollypops *See Candy & Confectionery: Candy: Lollypops: Gourmet Flavored*
Gourmet Potato Chips *See Snack Foods: Chips: Potato: Gourmet*
Gourmet Salad Dressings *See Sauces, Dips & Dressings: Salad Dressings: Gourmet*
Graham Toppings *See Ingredients, Flavors & Additives: Toppings: Graham*
Grain Flavors *See Ingredients, Flavors & Additives: Flavors: Grain*
Grain-Based Ingredients *See Ingredients, Flavors & Additives: Grain-Based*
Grains *See Cereals, Grains, Rice & Flour: Grains*
Granita Ice Cream *See Dairy Products: Ice Cream: Granita*
Granita Mixes *See Doughs, Mixes & Fillings: Mixes: Granita*
Granny Smith Apple *See Fruits & Vegetables: Apple: Granny Smith*
Granola *See Cereals, Grains, Rice & Flour: Granola*
Granola Toppings *See Ingredients, Flavors & Additives: Toppings: Granola*
Granulated Garlic *See Fruits & Vegetables: Garlic: Granulated; See also Spices, Seasonings & Seeds: Spices: Garlic: Granulated*
Granulated Onion *See Fruits & Vegetables: Dried & Dehydrated Vegetables: Onion: Granulated; See also Spices, Seasonings & Seeds: Spices: Onion: Granulated*
Granulated Peanuts *See Nuts & Nut Butters: Nuts: Peanuts: Granulated*
Granulated Starch Pearl Tapioca *See Cereals, Grains, Rice & Flour: Tapioca: Pearl: Granulated, Starch*
Granulated Sugar *See Sugars, Syrups & Sweeteners: Sugar: Granulated*
Granules Honey *See Sugars, Syrups & Sweeteners: Honey: Granules*
Grape *See Fruits & Vegetables: Grape*
Grape Ade Juices *See Beverages: Juices: Ade: Grape*
Grape Jams *See Jams, Jellies & Spreads: Jams: Grape*
Grape Juices *See Beverages: Juices: Grape*
Grape Leaves *See Fruits & Vegetables: Grape: Leaves*
Grape Skin Extract Color *See Ingredients, Flavors & Additives: Colors: Grape Skin Extract Color*
Grapefruit *See Fruits & Vegetables: Grapefruit*
Grapefruit Juices *See Beverages: Juices: Grapefruit*
Grapefruit Oils *See Oils, Shortening & Fats: Oils: Grapefruit*
Grapeseed Oils *See Oils, Shortening & Fats: Oils: Grapeseed*
Grated Cheese *See Cheese & Cheese Products: Cheese: Grated*
Gravy *See Sauces, Dips & Dressings: Gravy*
Gravy Bases *See Ingredients, Flavors & Additives: Bases: Gravy*
Gravy Mixes *See Doughs, Mixes & Fillings: Mixes: Gravy*
Great Northern Beans *See Fruits & Vegetables: Beans: Great Northern*
Greek Beans *See Fruits & Vegetables: Beans: Greek*
Greek Olives *See Fruits & Vegetables: Olives: Greek*
Greek Oregano *See Spices, Seasonings & Seeds: Spices: Oregano: Greek*
Greek Style Seasonings *See Spices, Seasonings & Seeds: Seasonings: Greek Style*
Green & Yellow Split Peas, Dried *See Fruits & Vegetables: Peas: Green & Yellow Split - Dried*
Green Beans *See Fruits & Vegetables: Beans: Green*
Green Bell Peppers, Dried *See Fruits & Vegetables: Dried & Dehydrated Vegetables: Bell Peppers: Green*

EXAMPLE: **Canadian Style Bacon** (1) *See Meats & Meat Products* (2)*: Smoked, Cured & Deli Meats* (3)*: Bacon* (4)*: Canadian Style* (5)

1. Product or Service you are looking for
2. Main Category, in alphabetical order, located in the page headers starting on page 27
3. Category Description, located in black bars and in page headers
4. Product Category, located in gray bars
5. Product Type, located under gray bars, centered in bold

H

I

Individually Packaged Cookies & Bars *See Baked Goods: Cookies & Bars: Individually Packaged*
Ingredients *See Ingredients, Flavors & Additives: Ingredients; See also Baked Goods: Ingredients*
Ingredients, Flavors & Additives *See Ingredients, Flavors & Additives*
Ingredients, Flavors & Additives, Almond Pastes *See Ingredients, Flavors & Additives: Pastes: Almond*
Ingredients, Organic Foods *See Specialty & Organic Foods: Organic Foods: Ingredients; See also Organic Foods*
Ink Squid *See Fish & Seafood: Shellfish: Squid: Ink*
Inositol *See Ingredients, Flavors & Additives: Vitamins & Supplements: Inositol*
Instant Cereal *See Cereals, Grains, Rice & Flour: Cereal: Instant*
Instant Coffee *See Beverages: Coffee & Tea: Coffee: Instant*
Instant Coffee, Decaffeinated *See Beverages: Coffee & Tea: Coffee: Instant - Decaffeinated*
Instant Potatoes *See Fruits & Vegetables: Potatoes: Instant*
Instant Rice *See Cereals, Grains, Rice & Flour: Rice: Instant*
Instant Tea *See Beverages: Coffee & Tea: Tea: Instant*
Instantized Flour *See Cereals, Grains, Rice & Flour: Flour: Instantized*
Invert Sugar *See Sugars, Syrups & Sweeteners: Sugar: Invert*
IQF Frozen Cherries *See Fruits & Vegetables: Cherries: Frozen: IQF (Individually Quick Frozen)*
IQF Rice *See Cereals, Grains, Rice & Flour: Rice: IQF (Individual Quick Frozen)*
IQF Vegetables *See Fruits & Vegetables: Vegetables: IQF (Individual Quick Frozen)*
Irish Breakfast Tea *See Beverages: Coffee & Tea: Tea: Irish Breakfast*
Irish Creme Flavors *See Ingredients, Flavors & Additives: Flavors: Irish Creme*
Irish Whiskey *See Beverages: Spirits & Liqueurs: Irish Whiskey*
Isolate Soy Protein *See Fruits & Vegetables: Soy: Soy Protein: Isolate*
Italian *See Ethnic Foods: Italian*
Italian Beans *See Fruits & Vegetables: Beans: Italian*
Italian Beef & Beef Products *See Meats & Meat Products: Beef & Beef Products: Italian*
Italian Breads *See Baked Goods: Breads: Italian*
Italian Herbs Seasonings *See Spices, Seasonings & Seeds: Seasonings: Italian Herbs*
Italian Olives *See Fruits & Vegetables: Olives: Italian*
Italian Style Salad Dressings *See Sauces, Dips & Dressings: Salad Dressings: Italian Style*
Italian Style Salad Dressings, Mixes *See Sauces, Dips & Dressings: Salad Dressings: Mixes: Italian Style*
Italian Style Seasonings *See Spices, Seasonings & Seeds: Seasonings: Italian Style*
Italian Wines *See Beverages: Wines: Italian*

J

Jalapeno & Chiles Peppers *See Fruits & Vegetables: Peppers: Jalapeno & Chiles*
Jalapeno Peppers *See Fruits & Vegetables: Peppers: Jalapeno*
Jamacain Beef Patties *See Meats & Meat Products: Beef & Beef Products: Patties: Jamacain*
Jambalaya *See Ethnic Foods: Jambalaya*
Jambalaya Mixes *See Doughs, Mixes & Fillings: Mixes: Jambalaya*
Jams *See Jams, Jellies & Spreads: Jams*
Japanese *See Ethnic Foods: Japanese*
Japanese Wines *See Beverages: Wines: Japanese*
Japones Peppers *See Fruits & Vegetables: Peppers: Japones*
Jarred or Cupped Fruit *See Fruits & Vegetables: Fruit: Jarred or Cupped*
Jasmati Rice *See Cereals, Grains, Rice & Flour: Rice: Jasmati*
Jasmine Rice *See Cereals, Grains, Rice & Flour: Rice: Jasmine*
Jasmine Tea *See Beverages: Coffee & Tea: Tea: Jasmine*
Jellied Cranberry Sauces *See Fruits & Vegetables: Sauces: Cranberry: Jellied*
Jellies *See Jams, Jellies & Spreads: Jellies*
Jelly Beans *See Candy & Confectionery: Candy: Jelly Beans*
Jelly Powders *See Ingredients, Flavors & Additives: Powders: Jelly*
Jerk Sauces *See Sauces, Dips & Dressings: Sauces: Jerk*
Juice Bases *See Ingredients, Flavors & Additives: Bases: Juice*
Juice Concentrates *See Beverages: Juices: Concentrates*
Juice Drinks *See Beverages: Juices: Drink*
Juice, Tropical Fruit *See Beverages: Juices: Tropical Fruits*
Juices *See Beverages: Juices*
Juniper Berries *See Fruits & Vegetables: Berries: Juniper; See also Spices, Seasonings & Seeds: Spices: Juniper Berries*

K

Kale *See Fruits & Vegetables: Kale*
Karaya Gum *See Ingredients, Flavors & Additives: Gums: Karaya Gum*
Kasmati Rice *See Cereals, Grains, Rice & Flour: Rice: Kasmati*
Kefir *See Dairy Products: Milk & Milk Products: Kefir*
Kegged Beers *See Beverages: Beers: Kegged*
Kelp Products *See Fruits & Vegetables: Kelp Products*
Ketchup *See Sauces, Dips & Dressings: Ketchup*
Key Lime Juices *See Beverages: Juices: Key Lime*
Key Lime Pies *See Baked Goods: Pies: Key Lime*
Kidney Beans *See Fruits & Vegetables: Beans: Kidney*
Kielbasa Sausage Seasonings *See Spices, Seasonings & Seeds: Seasonings: Sausage: Kielbasa*
Kielbasa Sausages *See Meats & Meat Products: Smoked, Cured & Deli Meats: Sausages: Kielbasa*
Kiev Chicken *See Prepared Foods: Prepared Meals: Chicken: Kiev*
King Cod *See Fish & Seafood: Fish: King Cod*
King Crab *See Fish & Seafood: Shellfish: Crab: King*
King Salmon *See Fish & Seafood: Fish: Salmon: King*
Kingfish *See Fish & Seafood: Fish: Kingfish*
Kisses *See Candy & Confectionery: Candy: Kisses*
Kiwi *See Fruits & Vegetables: Kiwi*
Klingstone Peach *See Fruits & Vegetables: Peach: Klingstone*
Knishes *See Prepared Foods: Knishes*
Knockwurst *See Meats & Meat Products: Smoked, Cured & Deli Meats: Knockwurst*
Knockwurst Sausages *See Meats & Meat Products: Smoked, Cured & Deli Meats: Sausages: Knockwurst*
Kohlrabi *See Fruits & Vegetables: Kohlrabi*
Kolsch Belgian & French Ale *See Beverages: Beers: Belgian & French Ale: Kolsch*
Kosher Foods *See Ethnic Foods: Kosher Foods*
Kosher Frankfurters *See Meats & Meat Products: Frankfurters: Kosher*
Kosher Pickles *See Relishes & Pickled Products: Pickled Products: Pickles: Kosher*
Kumquat *See Fruits & Vegetables: Kumquat*

L

Lactic Acidulants *See Ingredients, Flavors & Additives: Acidulants: Lactic*
Lactobacillus Acidophilus *See Ingredients, Flavors & Additives: Cultures & Yeasts: Lactobacillus Acidophilus*
Lactoferrin *See Ingredients, Flavors & Additives: Lactoferrin*
Lactose Sweeteners *See Ingredients, Flavors & Additives: Sweeteners: Lactose*
Lactose-Free Milk *See Dairy Products: Milk & Milk Products: Milk: Lactose-Free*
Lady Fingers *See Baked Goods: Cookies & Bars: Lady Fingers; See also Baked Goods: Cakes & Pastries: Ladyfingers*
Lager Beers *See Beverages: Beers: Lager*
Lamb *See Meats & Meat Products: Lamb*
Lamb Marinades *See Sauces, Dips & Dressings: Marinades: Lamb*
Langostinos *See Fish & Seafood: Shellfish: Langostinos*
Lard *See Oils, Shortening & Fats: Fats & Lard: Lard*
Lasagna *See Pasta & Noodles: Lasagna; See also Prepared Foods: Prepared Meals: Lasagna*
Latte Coffee *See Beverages: Coffee & Tea: Coffee: Latte*
Lavender *See Spices, Seasonings & Seeds: Spices: Lavender*
Lavender Flowers *See Spices, Seasonings & Seeds: Spices: Lavender Flowers*
Leaveners *See Ingredients, Flavors & Additives: Leaveners*
Lecithin Emulsifiers *See Ingredients, Flavors & Additives: Emulsifiers: Lecithin*
Lecithinated Stabilizers *See Ingredients, Flavors & Additives: Stabilizers: Lecithinated*
Leek *See Fruits & Vegetables: Leek*
Leeks, Chopped Dried *See Fruits & Vegetables: Dried & Dehydrated Vegetables: Leeks - Chopped*
Leg of Lamb *See Meats & Meat Products: Lamb: Leg of*
Lemon *See Fruits & Vegetables: Lemon*
Lemon & Basil Seasonings *See Spices, Seasonings & Seeds: Seasonings: Lemon & Basil*
Lemon & Dill Seasonings *See Spices, Seasonings & Seeds: Seasonings: Lemon & Dill*
Lemon Ade Juices *See Beverages: Juices: Ade: Lemon*
Lemon Flavors *See Ingredients, Flavors & Additives: Flavors: Lemon*
Lemon Grass Oils *See Oils, Shortening & Fats: Oils: Lemon Grass*
Lemon Grass Spices *See Spices, Seasonings & Seeds: Spices: Lemon Grass*
Lemon Juices *See Beverages: Juices: Lemon*
Lemon Oils *See Oils, Shortening & Fats: Oils: Lemon*
Lemon Peel *See Spices, Seasonings & Seeds: Spices: Lemon Peel*
Lemon Pepper Seasonings *See Spices, Seasonings & Seeds: Seasonings: Lemon Pepper*
Lemon Sauces *See Sauces, Dips & Dressings: Sauces: Lemon*
Lemon Tea *See Beverages: Coffee & Tea: Tea: Lemon*
Lemon-Lime Soda *See Beverages: Soft Drinks & Sodas: Soft Drinks: Lemon-Lime Soda*
Lemon-Meringue Pies *See Baked Goods: Pies: Lemon-Meringue*
Lemonade Juices *See Beverages: Juices: Lemonade*
Lentil Beans *See Fruits & Vegetables: Beans: Lentil; See also Fruits & Vegetables: Beans: Dried: Lentil Blend*
Lentil Soup *See Prepared Foods: Soups & Stews: Lentil Soup*
Lettuce *See Fruits & Vegetables: Lettuce*
Licorice Candy *See Candy & Confectionery: Candy: Licorice*
Licorice Flavors *See Ingredients, Flavors & Additives: Flavors: Licorice*
Light Red Kidney Beans *See Fruits & Vegetables: Beans: Kidney: Light Red*
Lima Beans *See Fruits & Vegetables: Beans: Lima*
Limburger Cheese *See Cheese & Cheese Products: Cheese: Limburger*
Lime *See Fruits & Vegetables: Lime*
Lime Flavors *See Ingredients, Flavors & Additives: Flavors: Lime*
Lime Juices *See Beverages: Juices: Lime*
Lime Oils *See Oils, Shortening & Fats: Oils: Lime*
Lingonberries *See Fruits & Vegetables: Berries: Lingonberries*
Linguica Sausages *See Meats & Meat Products: Smoked, Cured & Deli Meats: Sausages: Linguica*
Link Sausages *See Meats & Meat Products: Smoked, Cured & Deli Meats: Sausages: Link*
Liqueur Cake *See Baked Goods: Cakes & Pastries: Liqueur Cake*
Liqueur Flavors *See Ingredients, Flavors & Additives: Flavors: Liqueur*
Liqueurs & Cordials *See Beverages: Spirits & Liqueurs: Liqueurs & Cordials*
Liquid *See Eggs & Egg Products: Liquid*
Liquid & Granulated Sugar *See Sugars, Syrups & Sweeteners: Sugar: Liquid & Granulated*
Liquid Beverage Mixes *See Doughs, Mixes & Fillings: Mixes: Beverage: Liquid*
Liquid Chicken Fats & Lard *See Oils, Shortening & Fats: Fats & Lard: Chicken: Liquid*
Liquid Egg Whites *See Eggs & Egg Products: Liquid: Whites*
Liquid Honey *See Sugars, Syrups & Sweeteners: Honey: Liquid*
Liquid Mixes *See Doughs, Mixes & Fillings: Mixes: Liquid*
Liquid Spices *See Spices, Seasonings & Seeds: Spices: Liquid*
Liquid Sugar *See Sugars, Syrups & Sweeteners: Sugar: Liquid*
Liquid Vegetable Shortening *See Oils, Shortening & Fats: Shortening: Vegetable: Liquid*
Liquid Vinegar *See Sauces, Dips & Dressings: Vinegar: Liquid*
Live Crab *See Fish & Seafood: Shellfish: Crab: Live*

EXAMPLE: **Canadian Style Bacon**[1] *See Meats & Meat Products:*[2] *Smoked, Cured & Deli Meats:*[3] *Bacon:*[4] *Canadian Style*[5]

1. Product or Service you are looking for
2. Main Category, in alphabetical order, located in the page headers starting on page 27
3. Category Description, located in black bars and in page headers
4. Product Category, located in gray bars
5. Product Type, located under gray bars, centered in bold

M

Mixed Nuts *See Nuts & Nut Butters: Nuts: Mixed Nuts*
Mixers *See Beverages: Mixers*
Mixes *See Doughs, Mixes & Fillings: Mixes*
Mixes, Salad Dressings *See Sauces, Dips & Dressings: Salad Dressings: Mixes*
Mixes, Sauces *See Sauces, Dips & Dressings: Sauces: Mixes*
Mocha Biscotti *See Baked Goods: Cookies & Bars: Biscotti: Mocha*
Mocha Coffee & Tea *See Beverages: Coffee & Tea: Mocha*
Modified Food Starches *See Ingredients, Flavors & Additives: Agents: Anticaking: Modified Food Starch*
Modified Rice Starches *See Ingredients, Flavors & Additives: Starches: Rice: Modified*
Modified Starches *See Ingredients, Flavors & Additives: Starches: Modified*
Modifiers Agents *See Ingredients, Flavors & Additives: Agents: Modifiers*
Molasses *See Sugars, Syrups & Sweeteners: Molasses*
Molasses Flakes *See Ingredients, Flavors & Additives: Flakes: Molasses*
Molasses Powders *See Ingredients, Flavors & Additives: Powders: Molasses*
Molding Starches *See Ingredients, Flavors & Additives: Starches: Molding*
Mole Sauces *See Sauces, Dips & Dressings: Sauces: Mole*
Monkfish *See Fish & Seafood: Fish: Monkfish*
Montasio *See Cheese & Cheese Products: Cheese: Montasio*
Monte Veronese *See Cheese & Cheese Products: Cheese: Monte Veronese*
Monterey Jack *See Cheese & Cheese Products: Cheese: Monterey Jack*
Morel Mushrooms *See Fruits & Vegetables: Mushrooms: Morel; See alsoFruits & Vegetables: Dried & Dehydrated Vegetables: Mushrooms: Morels Whole*
Mortadella Sausages *See Meats & Meat Products: Smoked, Cured & Deli Meats: Sausages: Mortadella*
Mousse Candy *See Candy & Confectionery: Candy: Mousse*
Mousseron *See Fruits & Vegetables: Mushrooms: Mousseron*
Mozzarella *See Cheese & Cheese Products: Cheese: Mozzarella*
Mozzarella Cheese, Low Moisture Part Skim *See Cheese & Cheese Products: Cheese: Mozzarella: Low Moisture Part Skim*
Mozzarella Cheese, Low Moisture Part Skim, Shredded - Frozen *See Cheese & Cheese Products: Cheese: Mozzarella: Low Moisture Part Skim Shredded - Frozen*
Mozzarella Sticks *See Prepared Foods: Prepared Meals: Mozzarella Sticks*
Mozzarella, Imitation *See Cheese & Cheese Products: Imitation Cheeses & Substitutes: Imitation: Mozzarella*
MSG & Salt Mixture *See Spices, Seasonings & Seeds: Salt: MSG & Salt Mixture*
Muenster *See Cheese & Cheese Products: Cheese: Muenster*
Muesli Cereal *See Cereals, Grains, Rice & Flour: Cereal: Muesli*
Muffin Batters *See Doughs, Mixes & Fillings: Batters: Muffin*
Muffin Loaves *See Baked Goods: Cakes & Pastries: Muffin Loaves*
Muffin Mixes *See Doughs, Mixes & Fillings: Mixes: Muffin*
Muffins *See Baked Goods: Cakes & Pastries: Muffins*
Mulato Peppers *See Fruits & Vegetables: Peppers: Mulato*
Mulberries *See Fruits & Vegetables: Berries: Mulberries*
Mulled Wine Spice *See Spices, Seasonings & Seeds: Spices: Mulled Wine Spice*
Mullet *See Fish & Seafood: Fish: Mullet*
Mulling *See Spices, Seasonings & Seeds: Spices: Mulling*
Multi-Grain Breads *See Baked Goods: Breads: Multi-Grain*
Multi-Packs Specialty-Packaged Candy *See Candy & Confectionery: Specialty-Packaged Candy: Multi-Packs*
Mung Bean Noodles *See Pasta & Noodles: Noodles: Mung Bean*
Mung Bean Sprouts *See Fruits & Vegetables: Sprouts: Mung Bean*
Mung Beans *See Fruits & Vegetables: Beans: Mung*
Muscovy Duck *See Meats & Meat Products: Game: Muscovy Duck*
Mushroom Sauces *See Sauces, Dips & Dressings: Sauces: Mushroom*
Mushrooms *See Fruits & Vegetables: Dried & Dehydrated Vegetables: Mushrooms; See also Fruits & Vegetables: Mushrooms*
Muskox *See Meats & Meat Products: Game: Muskox*
Mussels *See Fish & Seafood: Shellfish: Mussels*
Mustard *See Sauces, Dips & Dressings: Mustard; See also Fruits & Vegetables: Mustard*
Mustard Bran *See Cereals, Grains, Rice & Flour: Bran: Mustard*
Mustard Flour *See Cereals, Grains, Rice & Flour: Flour: Mustard*
Mustard Oils *See Oils, Shortening & Fats: Oils: Mustard*
Mustard Powder *See Spices, Seasonings & Seeds: Spices: Mustard Powder; See also Ingredients, Flavors & Additives: Powders: Mustard*
Mustard Seeds *See Spices, Seasonings & Seeds: Seeds: Mustard*
Mustard Spices *See Spices, Seasonings & Seeds: Spices: Mustards; See also Spices, Seasonings & Seeds: Spices: Mustard*
Mustard Spices, Dry - Prepared *See Spices, Seasonings & Seeds: Spices: Mustard: Dry - Prepared*
Mutton *See Meats & Meat Products: Mutton*

N

Nacho Cheese Sauces *See Sauces, Dips & Dressings: Sauces: Cheese: Nacho*
Nacho Cheese Snack Seasonings *See Spices, Seasonings & Seeds: Seasonings: Snack: Nacho Cheese*
Nacho Chips *See Snack Foods: Chips: Nacho*
Napoli Salami *See Meats & Meat Products: Smoked, Cured & Deli Meats: Salami: Napoli*
Natural Chemicals *See Ingredients, Flavors & Additives: Chemicals: Natural*
Natural Colors *See Ingredients, Flavors & Additives: Colors: Natural; See also See Ingredients, Flavors & Additives: Colors: Natural: Others*
Natural Flavorings Spices *See Spices, Seasonings & Seeds: Spices: Natural Flavorings*
Natural Granules Honey *See Sugars, Syrups & Sweeteners: Honey: Granules: Natural*
Natural Gums *See Ingredients, Flavors & Additives: Gums: Natural*
Natural Organic Foods *See Specialty & Organic Foods: Organic Foods: Natural; See also Organic Foods*
Natural Sweeteners *See Sugars, Syrups & Sweeteners: Natural Sweeteners*
Naval Orange *See Fruits & Vegetables: Orange: Naval*
Navy Beans *See Fruits & Vegetables: Beans: Navy*
Nectar *See Fruits & Vegetables: Nectar*
Nectarines *See Fruits & Vegetables: Nectarines*
Neutral Spirits & Liqueurs *See Beverages: Spirits & Liqueurs: Neutral*
New England Chowder *See Prepared Foods: Soups & Stews: Chowder: New England*
New York Style Cheese Cake *See Baked Goods: Cakes & Pastries: Cheese Cake: New York Style*
Niacin *See Ingredients, Flavors & Additives: Vitamins & Supplements: Niacin*
No Salt Potato Chips *See Snack Foods: Chips: Potato: No Salt*
No-Fat Cheese *See Cheese & Cheese Products: Cheese: No-Fat*
No-Fat Yogurt *See Dairy Products: Yogurt: No-Fat*
Non-Alcoholic Beers *See Beverages: Beers: Non-Alcoholic*
Non-Alcoholic Beverages *See Beverages: Non-Alcoholic Beverages*
Non-Alcoholic Wines *See Beverages: Wines: Non-Alcoholic*
Non-Dairy & Imitation Dairy Bases *See Ingredients, Flavors & Additives: Bases: Dairy: Non-Dairy & Imitation*
Non-Dairy Coffee Creamers *See Dairy Products: Creamers: Coffee: Non-Dairy*
Non-Dairy Cream *See Dairy Products: Cream: Non-Dairy*
Non-Dairy Desserts *See Baked Goods: Desserts: Non-Dairy*
Non-Dairy Ice Cream *See Dairy Products: Ice Cream: Non-Dairy*
Non-Dairy Whipped Toppings *See Ingredients, Flavors & Additives: Toppings: Whipped: Non-Dairy*
Non-Fat Cheese Cake *See Baked Goods: Cakes & Pastries: Cheese Cake: Non-Fat*
Non-Fat Milk Solids *See Dairy Products: Milk & Milk Products: Milk Solids: Non-Fat*
Non-Fat Salad Dressings *See Sauces, Dips & Dressings: Salad Dressings: Non-Fat*
Non-Fruit Pies *See Baked Goods: Pies: Non-Fruit*
Non-Fruit Toppings *See Ingredients, Flavors & Additives: Toppings: Non-Fruit*
Non-Stick Coatings *See Ingredients, Flavors & Additives: Coatings: Non-Stick*
Nonpareils *See Candy & Confectionery: Candy: Nonpareils*
Noodles *See Pasta & Noodles: Noodles*
Nougats *See Candy & Confectionery: Candy: Nougats*
Novelties, Candy *See Candy & Confectionery: Candy: Novelties*
Novelties, Ice Cream *See Dairy Products: Ice Cream: Novelties*
Nut Breads *See Baked Goods: Breads: Nut*
Nut Butters *See Nuts & Nut Butters: Nut Butters*
Nut Flavors *See Ingredients, Flavors & Additives: Flavors: Nut*
Nut Flour *See Cereals, Grains, Rice & Flour: Flour: Nut*
Nut Meats *See Nuts & Nut Butters: Nuts: Nut Meats*
Nut Pastes *See Nuts & Nut Butters: Nut Pastes*
Nutmeg *See Spices, Seasonings & Seeds: Spices: Nutmeg (See also Mace)*
Nutmeg Oils *See Oils, Shortening & Fats: Oils: Nutmeg*
Nutraceuticals *See Ingredients, Flavors & Additives: Vitamins & Supplements: Nutraceuticals*
Nutritional Supplements *See Ingredients, Flavors & Additives: Vitamins & Supplements: Nutritional Supplements*
Nuts *See Nuts & Nut Butters: Nuts*
NY Strip Steak *See Meats & Meat Products: Beef & Beef Products: NY Strip Steak*

O

Oat Bran *See Cereals, Grains, Rice & Flour: Oats & Oat Products: Oat Bran*
Oat Bran Fiber *See Cereals, Grains, Rice & Flour: Fiber: Oat Bran*
Oat Fiber Crisps *See Cereals, Grains, Rice & Flour: Crisps: Oat Fiber*
Oat Flour *See Cereals, Grains, Rice & Flour: Flour: Oat*
Oatmeal *See Cereals, Grains, Rice & Flour: Oats & Oat Products: Oatmeal*
Oatmeal & Chocolate Chip Cookies *See Baked Goods: Cookies & Bars: Oatmeal & Chocolate Chip Cookies*
Oatmeal Cereal *See Cereals, Grains, Rice & Flour: Cereal: Oatmeal*
Oatmeal Cookies *See Baked Goods: Cookies & Bars: Oatmeal Cookies*
Oatmeal Raisin Cookies *See Baked Goods: Cookies & Bars: Oatmeal Raisin Cookies*
Oats & Oat Products *See Cereals, Grains, Rice & Flour: Oats & Oat Products*
Oats Fiber *See Cereals, Grains, Rice & Flour: Fiber: Oats*
Oats Flakes *See Ingredients, Flavors & Additives: Flakes: Oats*
Ocean Perch *See Fish & Seafood: Fish: Perch: Ocean*
Octopus *See Fish & Seafood: Shellfish: Octopus*
Oil & Vinegar Salad Dressings *See Sauces, Dips & Dressings: Salad Dressings: Oil & Vinegar*
Oil & Vinegar Salad Dressings, Mixes *See Sauces, Dips & Dressings: Salad Dressings: Mixes: Oil & Vinegar*
Oils *See Oils, Shortening & Fats; See also See Oils, Shortening & Fats: Oils*
Okra *See Fruits & Vegetables: Okra*
Olive Loaf *See Meats & Meat Products: Smoked, Cured & Deli Meats: Olive Loaf*
Olive Oil Anchovies *See Fish & Seafood: Fish: Anchovies: Olive Oil*
Olive Oil Bread Sticks *See Baked Goods: Bread Sticks: Olive Oil*
Olive Oils *See Oils, Shortening & Fats: Oils: Olive*
Olive Spreads *See Jams, Jellies & Spreads: Spreads: Olive*
Olives *See Fruits & Vegetables: Olives*
One Percent Milk *See Dairy Products: Milk & Milk Products: Milk: 1 Percent*
Onion *See Fruits & Vegetables: Onion*
Onion Bread Sticks *See Baked Goods: Bread Sticks: Onion*
Onion for Dehydration *See Fruits & Vegetables: Dried & Dehydrated Vegetables: Onion: for Dehydration*
Onion Juices *See Beverages: Juices: Onion*
Onion Oils *See Oils, Shortening & Fats: Oils: Onion*
Onion Powders *See Ingredients, Flavors & Additives: Powders: Onion (See also Spices/Onion Powder)*
Onion Rings *See Prepared Foods: Onion Rings*
Onion Salt *See Spices, Seasonings & Seeds: Salt: Onion*
Onion Spices *See Spices, Seasonings & Seeds: Spices: Onion*
Onion, Dried & Dehydrated *See Fruits & Vegetables: Dried & Dehydrated Vegetables: Onion*

1 2 3 4 5

EXAMPLE: **Canadian Style Bacon** *See Meats & Meat Products: Smoked, Cured & Deli Meats: Bacon: Canadian Style*

1. Product or Service you are looking for
2. Main Category, in alphabetical order, located in the page headers starting on page 27
3. Category Description, located in black bars and in page headers
4. Product Category, located in gray bars
5. Product Type, located under gray bars, centered in bold

P

Q

EXAMPLE: **Canadian Style Bacon** *See Meats & Meat Products: Smoked, Cured & Deli Meats: Bacon: Canadian Style* (1 = Canadian Style Bacon; 2 = See Meats & Meat Products:; 3 = Smoked, Cured & Deli Meats:; 4 = Bacon:; 5 = Canadian Style)

1. Product or Service you are looking for
2. Main Category, in alphabetical order, located in the page headers starting on page 27
3. Category Description, located in black bars and in page headers
4. Product Category, located in gray bars
5. Product Type, located under gray bars, centered in bold

R

Rabbit *See Meats & Meat Products: Game: Rabbit*
Radish *See Fruits & Vegetables: Radish*
Rainbow Trout *See Fish & Seafood: Fish: Trout: Rainbow*
Raisin Breads *See Baked Goods: Breads: Raisin*
Raisin Juice Replacers *See Ingredients, Flavors & Additives: Replacers: Raisin Juice*
Raisin Juices *See Beverages: Juices: Raisin*
Raisins *See Fruits & Vegetables: Raisins*
Ramen Noodles *See Pasta & Noodles: Noodles: Ramen*
Ranch Salad Dressing *See Sauces, Dips & Dressings: Salad Dressings: Ranch*
Ranch Salad Dressing Mixes *See Sauces, Dips & Dressings: Salad Dressings: Mixes: Ranch*
Ranch Snack Seasonings *See Spices, Seasonings & Seeds: Seasonings: Snack: Ranch*
Rape Seeds *See Spices, Seasonings & Seeds: Seeds: Rape*
Raschera *See Cheese & Cheese Products: Cheese: Raschera*
Raspberries *See Fruits & Vegetables: Berries: Raspberries*
Raspberry Flavors *See Ingredients, Flavors & Additives: Flavors: Raspberry*
Raspberry Juices *See Beverages: Juices: Raspberry*
Raspberry Vinegar *See Sauces, Dips & Dressings: Vinegar: Raspberry*
Raspberry Vinegrette Salad Dressing *See Sauces, Dips & Dressings: Salad Dressings: Raspberry Vinegrette*
Raspberry Vinegrette Salad Dressing Mixes *See Sauces, Dips & Dressings: Salad Dressings: Mixes: Raspberry Vinegrette*
Ravioli *See Pasta & Noodles: Ravioli*
Raw & Shelled Peanuts *See Nuts & Nut Butters: Nuts: Peanuts: Raw & Shelled*
Raw Beef & Beef Products *See Meats & Meat Products: Beef & Beef Products: Raw*
Raw Chicken *See Meats & Meat Products: Poultry: Chicken: Raw*
Raw Crayfish *See Fish & Seafood: Shellfish: Crayfish: Raw*
Raw Peanuts *See Nuts & Nut Butters: Nuts: Peanuts: Raw*
Raw Pork & Pork Products *See Meats & Meat Products: Pork & Pork Products: Raw*
Raw Turkey *See Meats & Meat Products: Poultry: Turkey: Raw*
Raw Veal *See Meats & Meat Products: Beef & Beef Products: Veal: Raw*
Ready to Use Icings *See Candy & Confectionery: Decorations & Icings: Icings: Ready to Use*
Red Bell Peppers, Dried *See Fruits & Vegetables: Dried & Dehydrated Vegetables: Bell Peppers: Red*
Red Bordeaux *See Beverages: Wines: French: Red Bordeaux*
Red Burgundy *See Beverages: Wines: French: Red Burgundy*
Red Cabbage *See Fruits & Vegetables: Cabbage: Red*
Red Currants *See Fruits & Vegetables: Berries: Currants: Red*
Red Delicious Apple *See Fruits & Vegetables: Apple: Red Delicious*
Red Grape Wines *See Beverages: Wines: Red Grape Wines; See also Beverages: Wines: Red Grapes*
Red Looseleaf Lettuce *See Fruits & Vegetables: Lettuce: Looseleaf: Red*
Red Meritage/Bordeaux *See Beverages: Wines: Red Grape Wines: Red Meritage/Bordeaux*
Red Onion *See Fruits & Vegetables: Onion: Red*
Red Pear *See Fruits & Vegetables: Pear: Red*
Red Pepper *See Spices, Seasonings & Seeds: Spices: Red Pepper; See also Spices, Seasonings & Seeds: Spices: Pepper: Black - White - Red*
Red Potatoes *See Fruits & Vegetables: Potatoes: Red*
Reduced-Calorie Beer *See Beverages: Beers: Specialty &Cider: Reduced Calorie Beer*
Reduced-Calorie Salad Dressing Mixes *See Sauces, Dips & Dressings: Salad Dressings: Mixes: Reduced-Calorie*
Reduced-Fat Cheddar Cheese *See Cheese & Cheese Products: Cheese: Cheddar: Reduced Fat*
Reduced-Fat Milk *See Dairy Products: Milk & Milk Products: Milk: Reduced-Fat*
Reduced-Fat Shredded Cheddar Cheese *See Cheese & Cheese Products: Cheese: Cheddar: Reduced Fat - Shredded*
Refried Beans *See Fruits & Vegetables: Beans: Refried*
Refrigerated Appetizers *See Prepared Foods: Appetizers: Refrigerated*
Refrigerated Apple Juices *See Beverages: Juices: Apple: Refrigerated*
Refrigerated Apricot Juices *See Beverages: Juices: Apricot: Refrigerated*
Refrigerated Buns *See Baked Goods: Breads: Buns: Refrigerated*
Refrigerated Cherry Juices *See Beverages: Juices: Cherry: Refrigerated*
Refrigerated Cranberry Juices *See Beverages: Juices: Cranberry: Refrigerated*
Refrigerated Egg Substitutes *See Eggs & Egg Products: Substitutes: Refrigerated*
Refrigerated Fruit Juices *See Beverages: Juices: Fruit: Refrigerated*
Refrigerated Grape Juices *See Beverages: Juices: Grape: Refrigerated*
Refrigerated Grapefruit Juices *See Beverages: Juices: Grapefruit: Refrigerated*
Refrigerated Juices *See Beverages: Juices: Refrigerated*
Refrigerated Lemon Juices *See Beverages: Juices: Lemon: Refrigerated*
Refrigerated Pancakes *See Prepared Foods: Pancakes: Refrigerated*
Refrigerated Pineapple Juices *See Beverages: Juices: Pineapple: Refrigerated*
Regular & Lowfat Bakery Mix *See Cereals, Grains, Rice & Flour: Flour: Bakery Mix: Regular & Lowfat*
Regular Chili Powders *See Ingredients, Flavors & Additives: Powders: Chili: Regular*
Release, Grease Agents *See Ingredients, Flavors & Additives: Agents: Release, Grease*
Releases *See Ingredients, Flavors & Additives: Releases*
Relishes *See Relishes & Pickled Products: Relishes*
Relishes & Condiments *See Relishes & Pickled Products: Relishes: Relishes & Condiments*
Replacers *See Ingredients, Flavors & Additives: Replacers*
Replacers, Milk Solids *See Dairy Products: Milk & Milk Products: Milk Solids: Replacers*
Resistant Starch Fiber *See Cereals, Grains, Rice & Flour: Fiber: Resistant Starch*
Rhubarb *See Fruits & Vegetables: Rhubarb*
Rhubarb Pie *See Baked Goods: Pies: Rhubarb Pie*
Rib Center Cut Pork *See Meats & Meat Products: Pork & Pork Products: Rib Center Cut*
Rib Chop Lamb *See Meats & Meat Products: Lamb: Rib Chop*
Rib Chop Veal *See Meats & Meat Products: Beef & Beef Products: Veal: Rib Chop*
Rib Eye Roast Beef *See Meats & Meat Products: Beef & Beef Products: Rib Eye Roast*
Rib Eye Steak *See Meats & Meat Products: Beef & Beef Products: Rib Eye Steak*
Rib Rub Seasonings *See Spices, Seasonings & Seeds: Seasonings: Rib Rub*
Rib Steak *See Meats & Meat Products: Beef & Beef Products: Rib Steak*
Rice *See Cereals, Grains, Rice & Flour: Rice*
Rice Bran *See Cereals, Grains, Rice & Flour: Bran: Rice*
Rice Bran Oils *See Oils, Shortening & Fats: Oils: Rice Bran*
Rice Cakes *See Snack Foods: Rice Cakes*
Rice Crisps *See Cereals, Grains, Rice & Flour: Crisps: Rice*
Rice Flour *See Cereals, Grains, Rice & Flour: Flour: Rice*
Rice Mixes *See Doughs, Mixes & Fillings: Mixes: Rice*
Rice Pilaf *See Cereals, Grains, Rice & Flour: Rice: Pilaf*
Rice Powders *See Ingredients, Flavors & Additives: Powders: Rice*
Rice Pudding *See Dairy Products: Pudding: Rice*
Rice Starches *See Ingredients, Flavors & Additives: Starches: Rice*
Rice Starches, Organic *See Specialty & Organic Foods: Organic Foods: Rice Starch; See also Organic Foods*
Rice, Bagged Parboiled *See Cereals, Grains, Rice & Flour: Rice: Parboiled: Bagged*
Rice, Parboiled, US #1 Long Grain *See Cereals, Grains, Rice & Flour: Rice: Parboiled: US #1 Long Grain*
Rice, Prepared Meals *See Prepared Foods: Prepared Meals: Rice*
Rice-Based Cereal *See Cereals, Grains, Rice & Flour: Cereal: Rice-Based*
Ricotta *See Cheese & Cheese Products: Cheese: Ricotta*
Riesling *See Beverages: Wines: White Grape Varieties: Riesling*
Rigatoni *See Pasta & Noodles: Rigatoni*
Riso *See Pasta & Noodles: Riso*
Risotto Rice *See Cereals, Grains, Rice & Flour: Rice: Risotto*
Roast Beef *See Meats & Meat Products: Beef & Beef Products: Roast Beef*
Roast Pork Tenderloin *See Meats & Meat Products: Pork & Pork Products: Tenderloin Roast*
Roasted Coffee *See Beverages: Coffee & Tea: Coffee: Roasted*
Roasted Garlic & Herb Crackers *See Baked Goods: Crackers: Roasted Garlic & Herb Crackers*
Roasted Nuts *See Nuts & Nut Butters: Nuts: Roasted*
Roasted Peanuts *See Nuts & Nut Butters: Nuts: Peanuts: Roasted*
Roasted Peppers *See Fruits & Vegetables: Peppers: Roasted*
Roasted Vegetables *See Fruits & Vegetables: Roasted Vegetables*
Rock Candy *See Candy & Confectionery: Candy: Rock*
Rock Fish *See Fish & Seafood: Fish: Rock Fish*
Rock Salt *See Spices, Seasonings & Seeds: Salt: Rock*
Rolled Oats *See Cereals, Grains, Rice & Flour: Oats & Oat Products: Rolled*
Rolls *See Baked Goods: Breads: Rolls*
Roma Tomato *See Fruits & Vegetables: Tomato: Roma (Egg)*
Romaine Lettuce *See Fruits & Vegetables: Lettuce: Romaine*
Romano *See Cheese & Cheese Products: Cheese: Romano*
Rome Beauty *See Fruits & Vegetables: Apple: Rome Beauty*
Root Beer Extracts *See Ingredients, Flavors & Additives: Extracts: Root Beer*
Root Beer Flavors *See Ingredients, Flavors & Additives: Flavors: Root Beer*
Roots & Tubers *See Fruits & Vegetables: Roots & Tubers*
Roquefort *See Cheese & Cheese Products: Cheese: Roquefort*
Rosellino *See Cheese & Cheese Products: Cheese: Rosellino*
Rosemary *See Spices, Seasonings & Seeds: Spices: Rosemary*
Rosemary Spices, Cut *See Spices, Seasonings & Seeds: Spices: Rosemary: Cut*
Rotelle *See Pasta & Noodles: Rotelle*
Rotini *See Pasta & Noodles: Rotini*
Royal Jellies *See Jams, Jellies & Spreads: Jellies: Royal*
Rubbed Sage *See Spices, Seasonings & Seeds: Spices: Sage: Rubbed*
Rugulach *See Baked Goods: Cakes & Pastries: Rugulach*
Rum *See Beverages: Spirits & Liqueurs: Rum*
Rum Cake *See Baked Goods: Cakes & Pastries: Rum Cake*
Rum Flavors *See Ingredients, Flavors & Additives: Flavors: Rum*
Rusk *See Baked Goods: Cakes & Pastries: Rusk*
Russet Potatoes, Fresh *See Fruits & Vegetables: Potatoes: Fresh: Russet*
Rutabaga *See Fruits & Vegetables: Rutabaga*
Rye *See Cereals, Grains, Rice & Flour: Rye*
Rye Breads *See Baked Goods: Breads: Rye*
Rye Flour *See Cereals, Grains, Rice & Flour: Flour: Rye*

S

Sablefish *See Fish & Seafood: Fish: Sablefish*
Saccharin *See Sugars, Syrups & Sweeteners: Sugar Substitutes: Saccharin*
Safflower Oils *See Oils, Shortening & Fats: Oils: Safflower*
Saffron *See Spices, Seasonings & Seeds: Spices: Saffron*
Sage *See Spices, Seasonings & Seeds: Spices: Sage*
Sage Leaves *See Spices, Seasonings & Seeds: Spices: Sage: Leaves*
Sage Oils *See Oils, Shortening & Fats: Oils: Sage*
Sake *See Beverages: Wines: Japanese: Sake*
Salad Dressings *See Sauces, Dips & Dressings: Salad Dressings*
Salad Greens *See Fruits & Vegetables: Salad Greens*
Salad Oils *See Oils, Shortening & Fats: Oils: Salad*
Salad, Prepared Meals *See Prepared Foods: Prepared Meals: Salad*
Salami *See Meats & Meat Products: Smoked, Cured & Deli Meats: Salami*
Salmon *See Fish & Seafood: Fish: Salmon*
Salmon Caviar *See Fish & Seafood: Caviar (Roe): Salmon*
Salmon Sausages *See Meats & Meat Products: Smoked, Cured & Deli Meats: Sausages: Salmon*
Salmon Steak *See Fish & Seafood: Fish: Salmon: Steak*
Salmon, Prepared Salads *See Prepared Foods: Prepared Salads: Salmon*
Salsa *See Sauces, Dips & Dressings: Salsa*
Salsa Dips *See Sauces, Dips & Dressings: Dips: Salsa*
Salsa with Cheese *See Sauces, Dips & Dressings: Salsa: with Cheese*
Salt *See Spices, Seasonings & Seeds: Salt*
Salt Anchovies *See Fish & Seafood: Fish: Anchovies: Salt*
Salt Substitutes *See Spices, Seasonings & Seeds: Salt: Substitutes*
Salt-free Chili Powders *See Ingredients, Flavors & Additives: Powders: Chili: Salt-free*
Salted & Marinated Herring *See Fish & Seafood: Fish: Herring: Salted & Marinated*
Salted Almonds *See Nuts & Nut Butters: Nuts: Almonds: Salted*
Salted Butter *See Dairy Products: Butter: Salted*
Salted Fish *See Fish & Seafood: Fish: Salted*
Salted Peanuts *See Nuts & Nut Butters: Nuts: Peanuts: Salted*
Salted Pecans *See Nuts & Nut Butters: Nuts: Pecan: Salted*

Salted Potato Chips *See Snack Foods: Chips: Potato: Salted*
Sandwich Creme Cookies *See Baked Goods: Cookies & Bars: Sandwich Creme Cookies*
Sandwiches, Prepared Meals *See Prepared Foods: Prepared Meals: Sandwiches*
Sangiovese *See Beverages: Wines: Red Grape Wines: Sangiovese*
Sardines *See Fish & Seafood: Fish: Sardines*
Sarsaparilla *See Beverages: Soft Drinks & Sodas: Soft Drinks: Sarsaparilla*
Sassafras Oils *See Oils, Shortening & Fats: Oils: Sassafras*
Sauce Bases *See Ingredients, Flavors & Additives: Bases: Sauce*
Sauces *See Fruits & Vegetables: Sauces; See also Sauces, Dips & Dressings: Sauces*
Sauerkraut *See Relishes & Pickled Products: Sauerkraut*
Sauerkraut Juice *See Relishes & Pickled Products: Sauerkraut: Juice*
Sausage Binders *See Ingredients, Flavors & Additives: Binders: Sausage*
Sausage Casings *See Meats & Meat Products: Smoked, Cured & Deli Meats: Sausages: Casings: Sausage, Pork, Beef*
Sausage Seasonings *See Spices, Seasonings & Seeds: Seasonings: Sausage*
Sausage, Pork *See Meats & Meat Products: Pork & Pork Products: Sausage*
Sausage, Smoked *See Meats & Meat Products: Smoked, Cured & Deli Meats: Sausages*
Sausage, Turkey *See Meats & Meat Products: Poultry: Turkey: Sausage*
Sauvignon Blanc *See Beverages: Wines: White Grape Varieties: Sauvignon Blanc*
Savory *See Spices, Seasonings & Seeds: Spices: Savory*
Saw Palmetto Berry Powders *See Ingredients, Flavors & Additives: Powders: Saw Palmetto Berry*
Scallions *See Fruits & Vegetables: Scallions*
Scallops *See Fish & Seafood: Shellfish: Scallops*
Scampi *See Fish & Seafood: Shellfish: Scampi*
Scampi, Prepared Meals *See Prepared Foods: Prepared Meals: Scampi*
Schnapps Liqueur *See Beverages: Spirits & Liqueurs: Liqueurs & Cordials: Schnapps Liqueur*
Scones *See Baked Goods: Breads: Scones*
Scotch Whiskey *See Beverages: Spirits & Liqueurs: Scotch Whiskey*
Scrapple *See Meats & Meat Products: Pork & Pork Products: Scrapple*
Sea Bass *See Fish & Seafood: Fish: Sea Bass*
Sea Salt *See Spices, Seasonings & Seeds: Salt: Sea*
Sea Trout *See Fish & Seafood: Fish: Sea Trout*
Seafood *See Fish & Seafood: Seafood*
Seafood Bases *See Ingredients, Flavors & Additives: Bases: Seafood*
Seafood Extracts *See Ingredients, Flavors & Additives: Extracts: Seafood*
Seafood Flavors *See Ingredients, Flavors & Additives: Flavors: Seafood*
Seafood Powders *See Ingredients, Flavors & Additives: Powders: Seafood*
Seafood Ravioli *See Pasta & Noodles: Ravioli: Seafood*
Seafood Salad *See Fish & Seafood: Seafood: Salad*
Seafood Sauces *See Sauces, Dips & Dressings: Sauces: Seafood*
Seafood Soup Bases *See Ingredients, Flavors & Additives: Bases: Soup: Seafood*
Seafood, Prepared Meals *See Prepared Foods: Prepared Meals: Seafood*
Seafood, Prepared Salads *See Prepared Foods: Prepared Salads: Seafood*
Seasoning Powders *See Ingredients, Flavors & Additives: Powders: Seasoning*
Seasonings *See Spices, Seasonings & Seeds: Seasonings*
Seasonings for Corned Beef *See Spices, Seasonings & Seeds: Seasonings: for Corned Beef*
Seasonings for Tacos *See Spices, Seasonings & Seeds: Seasonings: for Tacos*
Seaweeds & Sea Vegetables *See Fruits & Vegetables: Seaweeds & Sea Vegetables*
Seedless Watermelon *See Fruits & Vegetables: Melon: Watermelon: Seedless*
Seeds *See Spices, Seasonings & Seeds: Seeds*
Self-Rising Flour *See Cereals, Grains, Rice & Flour: Flour: Self-Rising*
Semolina *See Pasta & Noodles: Semolina*
Semolina Flour *See Cereals, Grains, Rice & Flour: Flour: Semolina*
Serrano Peppers *See Fruits & Vegetables: Peppers: Serrano*
Sesame Bread Sticks *See Baked Goods: Bread Sticks: Sesame*
Sesame Oils *See Oils, Shortening & Fats: Oils: Sesame*
Sesame Seeds *See Spices, Seasonings & Seeds: Seeds: Sesame*
Shad *See Fish & Seafood: Fish: Shad*
Shad Caviar *See Fish & Seafood: Caviar (Roe): Shad*
Shallot *See Fruits & Vegetables: Shallot*
Shallots *See Spices, Seasonings & Seeds: Spices: Shallots*
Shallots, Freeze-Dried *See Fruits & Vegetables: Dried & Dehydrated Vegetables: Shallots - Freeze Dried*
Shark *See Fish & Seafood: Fish: Shark*
Sheephead *See Fish & Seafood: Fish: Sheephead*
Shelf Stable Entrees *See Prepared Foods: Prepared Meals: Entrees: Shelf Stable*
Shelled Nuts *See Nuts & Nut Butters: Nuts: Shelled*
Shellfish *See Fish & Seafood: Shellfish: Shellfish; See also Fish & Seafood: Shellfish*
Shells *See Ethnic Foods: Shells; See also Pasta & Noodles: Shells*
Sherbet *See Dairy Products: Ice Cream: Sherbet*
Sherry *See Beverages: Wines: Spanish: Sherry*
Sherry Vinegar *See Sauces, Dips & Dressings: Vinegar: Sherry*
Shiitake *See Fruits & Vegetables: Mushrooms: Shiitake; See also See Fruits & Vegetables: Dried & Dehydrated Vegetables: Mushrooms: Shiitake Whole*
Shoestring French Fries *See Prepared Foods: French Fries: Shoestring*
Shoofly Mixes *See Doughs, Mixes & Fillings: Mixes: Shoofly*
Shoofly Pie *See Baked Goods: Pies: Shoofly Pie*
Short Breads *See Baked Goods: Breads: Short*
Shortening *See Oils, Shortening & Fats; See also See Oils, Shortening & Fats: Shortening*
Shredded Cheddar Cheese *See Cheese & Cheese Products: Cheese: Cheddar: Shredded*
Shrimp *See Fish & Seafood: Shellfish: Shrimp*
Shrimp, Frozen Scampi *See Prepared Foods: Prepared Meals: Scampi: Shrimp Frozen*
Sicilian Style Sausages *See Meats & Meat Products: Smoked, Cured & Deli Meats: Sausages: Sicilian Style (with Cheese)*
Siciliano Salami *See Meats & Meat Products: Smoked, Cured & Deli Meats: Salami: Siciliano*
Single & Blended Enrichment & Nutrient Additives *See Ingredients, Flavors & Additives: Additives: Enrichment & Nutrient: Single & Blended*
Sirloin Cubes *See Meats & Meat Products: Beef & Beef Products: Sirloin Cubes*
Skim Milk *See Dairy Products: Milk & Milk Products: Milk: Skim*
Sliced Beef & Beef Products *See Meats & Meat Products: Beef & Beef Products: Sliced*
Sliced Blend, American/Skim Milk Cheese *See Cheese & Cheese Products: Cheese: Blend - American/Skim Milk: Sliced*
Sliced Peaches *See Fruits & Vegetables: Peach: Sliced*
Slushes *See Dairy Products: Ice Cream: Slushes*
Small Red Beans *See Fruits & Vegetables: Beans: Small Red*
Smelt *See Fish & Seafood: Fish: Smelt*
Smoke Flavors *See Ingredients, Flavors & Additives: Flavors: Smoke*
Smoked & Cured Fish *See Fish & Seafood: Fish: Smoked & Cured*
Smoked Ham *See Meats & Meat Products: Smoked, Cured & Deli Meats: Ham: Smoked*
Smoked Meat *See Meats & Meat Products: Smoked, Cured & Deli Meats: Smoked Meat*
Smoked Salmon *See Fish & Seafood: Fish: Salmon: Smoked*
Smoked Sausages *See Meats & Meat Products: Smoked, Cured & Deli Meats: Sausages: Smoked*
Smoked Seafood *See Fish & Seafood: Seafood: Smoked*
Smoked Shellfish *See Fish & Seafood: Shellfish: Smoked*
Smoked Turkey *See Meats & Meat Products: Smoked, Cured & Deli Meats: Turkey: Smoked*
Smoked, Cured & Deli Meats *See Meats & Meat Products: Smoked, Cured & Deli Meats*
Smooth Peanut Butter *See Nuts & Nut Butters: Nut Butters: Peanut Butter: Smooth*
Smoothie Powder Mixes *See Doughs, Mixes & Fillings: Mixes: Smoothie Powder*
Smoothie Powders *See Ingredients, Flavors & Additives: Powders: Smoothie*
Smoothies *See Beverages: Smoothies*
Snack Foods *See Snack Foods*
Snack Pellets *See Snack Foods: Snack Pellets*
Snack Seasonings *See Spices, Seasonings & Seeds: Seasonings: Snack*
Snails *See Fish & Seafood: Shellfish: Snails*
Snake Beans *See Fruits & Vegetables: Beans: Snake*
Snap Peas *See Fruits & Vegetables: Peas: Snap*
Snapper *See Fish & Seafood: Fish: Snapper*
Snow Crab *See Fish & Seafood: Shellfish: Crab: Snow*
Sockeye Salmon *See Fish & Seafood: Fish: Salmon: Sockeye*
Soda Water *See Beverages: Soft Drinks & Sodas: Soda Water*
Sodium *See Ingredients, Flavors & Additives: Sodium*
Sodium Alginates *See Ingredients, Flavors & Additives: Sodium Alginates*
Sodium Benzoate *See Ingredients, Flavors & Additives: Sodium Benzoate*
Sodium Citrate *See Ingredients, Flavors & Additives: Sodium Citrate*
Sodium Phosphate *See Ingredients, Flavors & Additives: Phosphates: Sodium Phosphate*
Soft Cookies *See Baked Goods: Cookies & Bars: Soft Cookies*
Soft Drinks & Sodas *See Beverages: Soft Drinks & Sodas; See also Beverages: Soft Drinks & Sodas: Soft Drinks*
Soft Pretzels *See Snack Foods: Pretzels: Soft*
Soft Shell Crab *See Fish & Seafood: Shellfish: Crab: Soft Shell*
Sole *See Fish & Seafood: Fish: Sole*
Solids *See Eggs & Egg Products: Solids*
Solubilizers *See Ingredients, Flavors & Additives: Surfactants & Solubilizers: Solubilizers*
Sorbet *See Dairy Products: Ice Cream: Sorbet*
Sorbic Acidulants *See Ingredients, Flavors & Additives: Acidulants: Sorbic*
Sorbitol *See Ingredients, Flavors & Additives: Sweeteners: Sorbitol*
Sorghum *See Cereals, Grains, Rice & Flour: Sorghum*
Sorrel *See Spices, Seasonings & Seeds: Spices: Sorrel*
Soup Bases *See Ingredients, Flavors & Additives: Bases: Soup*
Soup Blend *See Fruits & Vegetables: Dried & Dehydrated Vegetables: Soup Blend*
Soup Mixes *See Doughs, Mixes & Fillings: Mixes: Soup*
Soups & Stews *See Prepared Foods: Soups & Stews*
Sour Cream *See Dairy Products: Sour Cream*
Sour Cream & Onion Potato Chips *See Snack Foods: Chips: Potato: Sour Cream & Onion*
Sour Cream & Onion Snack Seasonings *See Spices, Seasonings & Seeds: Seasonings: Snack: Sour Cream & Onion*
Sour Cream Flavors *See Ingredients, Flavors & Additives: Flavors: Sour: Cream*
Sour Flavors *See Ingredients, Flavors & Additives: Flavors: Sour*
Sourdough Breads *See Baked Goods: Breads: Sourdough*
Southern Peas *See Fruits & Vegetables: Peas: Southern*
Southwest Seasonings *See Spices, Seasonings & Seeds: Seasonings: Southwest*
Soy *See Fruits & Vegetables: Soy*
Soy Bean *See Fruits & Vegetables: Soy: Soy Bean*
Soy Bean Meal *See Cereals, Grains, Rice & Flour: Soy Bean Meal*
Soy Bran Fiber *See Cereals, Grains, Rice & Flour: Fiber: Soy Bran*
Soy Crisps *See Cereals, Grains, Rice & Flour: Crisps: Soy*
Soy Crumbs Toppings *See Ingredients, Flavors & Additives: Toppings: Soy Crumbs*
Soy Flakes *See Ingredients, Flavors & Additives: Flakes: Soy*
Soy Frankfurters *See Meats & Meat Products: Frankfurters: Soy*
Soy Milk *See Fruits & Vegetables: Soy: Soy Milk*
Soy Milk Powders *See Ingredients, Flavors & Additives: Powders: Soy Milk*
Soy Nuts *See Nuts & Nut Butters: Nuts: Soy*
Soy Powders *See Ingredients, Flavors & Additives: Powders: Soy*
Soy Protein *See Fruits & Vegetables: Soy: Soy Protein*

EXAMPLE: **Canadian Style Bacon** (1) *See Meats & Meat Products* (2)*: Smoked, Cured & Deli Meats* (3)*: Bacon* (4)*: Canadian Style* (5)

1. Product or Service you are looking for
2. Main Category, in alphabetical order, located in the page headers starting on page 27
3. Category Description, located in black bars and in page headers
4. Product Category, located in gray bars
5. Product Type, located under gray bars, centered in bold

T

Tart Cherries *See Fruits & Vegetables: Cherries: Tart*
Tartar *See Spices, Seasonings & Seeds: Spices: Tartar*
Tartar Sauces *See Sauces, Dips & Dressings: Sauces: Tartar*
Tartaric Acidulants *See Ingredients, Flavors & Additives: Acidulants: Tartaric*
Tarts *See Baked Goods: Cakes & Pastries: Tarts*
Tartufo *See Fruits & Vegetables: Tartufo*
Tasso *See Meats & Meat Products: Smoked, Cured & Deli Meats: Tasso*
Tater Tots *See Prepared Foods: French Fries: Tater Tots*
Tea *See Beverages: Coffee & Tea: Tea*
Tea Bags *See Beverages: Coffee & Tea: Tea: Bags*
Tea Cookies *See Baked Goods: Cookies & Bars: Tea Cookies*
Tea Extracts *See Ingredients, Flavors & Additives: Extracts: Tea*
Tea Flavors *See Ingredients, Flavors & Additives: Flavors: Tea*
Tea, Fair-Trade *See Beverages: Coffee & Tea: Tea: Fair-Trade*
Teas *See Spices, Seasonings & Seeds: Spices: Teas*
Tempeh *See Ethnic Foods: Tempeh*
Tenderizers *See Ingredients, Flavors & Additives: Tenderizers*
Tenderizing Compounds *See Ingredients, Flavors & Additives: Compounds: Tenderizing*
Tequila and Mezcal *See Beverages: Spirits & Liqueurs: Tequila and Mezcal*
Teriyaki Sauces *See Sauces, Dips & Dressings: Sauces: Teriyaki*
Texture Modifiers Agents *See Ingredients, Flavors & Additives: Agents: Modifiers: Texture*
Textured Vegetable Protein *See Fruits & Vegetables: Textured Vegetable Protein*
Texturized Soy Protein *See Fruits & Vegetables: Soy: Protein: Texturized; See also Fruits & Vegetables: Soy: Soy Protein: Texturized*
Thick Bacon Slices *See Meats & Meat Products: Smoked, Cured & Deli Meats: Bacon: Slices Thick*
Thickeners *See Ingredients, Flavors & Additives: Thickeners*
Thickening Agents *See Ingredients, Flavors & Additives: Agents: Thickening*
Thin Boiling Starches *See Ingredients, Flavors & Additives: Starches: Thin Boiling*
Thousand Island Salad Dressing *See Sauces, Dips & Dressings: Salad Dressings: Thousand Island*
Thousand Island Salad Dressing Mixes *See Sauces, Dips & Dressings: Salad Dressings: Mixes: Thousand Island*
Thyme *See Spices, Seasonings & Seeds: Spices: Thyme*
Thyme Oils *See Oils, Shortening & Fats: Oils: Thyme*
Tilapia *See Fish & Seafood: Fish: Tilapia*
Tiramisu *See Baked Goods: Cakes & Pastries: Tiramisu*
Toasted Breads *See Baked Goods: Breads: Toasted*
Toffee *See Candy & Confectionery: Candy: Toffee*
Tofu Powders *See Ingredients, Flavors & Additives: Powders: Tofu*
Tomatillos *See Fruits & Vegetables: Tomatillos*
Tomato *See Fruits & Vegetables: Tomato*
Tomato Concentrates *See Ingredients, Flavors & Additives: Concentrates: Tomato*
Tomato Juices *See Beverages: Juices: Tomato*
Tomato Pastes *See Ingredients, Flavors & Additives: Pastes: Tomato*
Tomato Pesto Seasonings *See Spices, Seasonings & Seeds: Seasonings: Tomato Pesto*
Tomato Powder *See Fruits & Vegetables: Dried & Dehydrated Vegetables: Tomatoes: Tomato Powder; See also Ingredients, Flavors & Additives: Powders: Tomato*
Tomato Pulps & Purees *See Fruits & Vegetables: Pulps & Purees: Tomato; See also Fruits & Vegetables: Pulps & Purees: Puree: Tomato*
Tomato Sauce with Spices *See Sauces, Dips & Dressings: Sauces: Tomato: with Spices*
Tomato Sauces *See Sauces, Dips & Dressings: Sauces: Tomato*
Tomatoes, Dried *See Fruits & Vegetables: Dried & Dehydrated Vegetables: Tomatoes*
Tomatoes, Dried Halves *See Fruits & Vegetables: Dried & Dehydrated Vegetables: Tomatoes: Halves*
Tongue *See Meats & Meat Products: Beef & Beef Products: Tongue*
Toppings *See Sugars, Syrups & Sweeteners: Syrups: Toppings; See also Ingredients, Flavors & Additives: Toppings*
Tortellini *See Pasta & Noodles: Tortellini*
Tortes *See Baked Goods: Cakes & Pastries: Tortes*
Tortilla & Tortilla Products *See Ethnic Foods: Tortilla & Tortilla Products*
Tortilla Chips *See Snack Foods: Chips: Tortilla*
Tortillas *See Ethnic Foods: Tortilla & Tortilla Products: Tortillas*
Tortoni *See Dairy Products: Ice Cream: Tortoni*
Torula *See Ingredients, Flavors & Additives: Cultures & Yeasts: Yeast: Torula Dried*
Toscano Salami *See Meats & Meat Products: Smoked, Cured & Deli Meats: Salami: Toscano*
Tostadas *See Ethnic Foods: Tostadas*
Tragacanth *See Ingredients, Flavors & Additives: Gums: Tragacanth*
Trail Mix *See Snack Foods: Trail Mix*
Trail Mixes *See Doughs, Mixes & Fillings: Mixes: Trail*
Tricalcium Phosphate *See Ingredients, Flavors & Additives: Agents: Anticaking: Tricalcium Phosphate*
Tripe *See Meats & Meat Products: Tripe*
Tropical & Exotic Fruit *See Fruits & Vegetables: Tropical & Exotic Fruit*
Tropical Fruit Juices *See Beverages: Juices: Tropical Fruits*
Trout *See Fish & Seafood: Fish: Trout*
Truffles, Candy *See Candy & Confectionery: Candy: Truffles*
Truffles, Mushrooms *See Fruits & Vegetables: Mushrooms: Truffles*
Tubetti *See Pasta & Noodles: Tubetti*
Tuffoli *See Pasta & Noodles: Tuffoli*
Tuna *See Fish & Seafood: Fish: Tuna*
Tuna, Prepared Salads *See Prepared Foods: Prepared Salads: Tuna*
Turbot *See Fish & Seafood: Fish: Turbot*
Turkey *See Meats & Meat Products: Poultry: Turkey*
Turkey Dinner, Prepared Meals *See Prepared Foods: Prepared Meals: Turkey Dinner*
Turkey Frankfurters *See Meats & Meat Products: Frankfurters: Turkey*
Turkey Leg *See Meats & Meat Products: Poultry: Turkey: Leg*
Turkey Sausages *See Meats & Meat Products: Smoked, Cured & Deli Meats: Sausages: Turkey*
Turkey, Game *See Meats & Meat Products: Game: Turkey*
Turkey, Prepared Salads *See Prepared Foods: Prepared Salads: Turkey*
Turkey, Smoked *See Meats & Meat Products: Smoked, Cured & Deli Meats: Turkey*
Turmeric Natural Colors *See Ingredients, Flavors & Additives: Colors: Natural: Turmeric*
Turmeric Spices *See Spices, Seasonings & Seeds: Spices: Turmeric*
Turnip *See Fruits & Vegetables: Turnip*
Turnip Greens *See Fruits & Vegetables: Turnip: Turnip Greens: Canned*
Turnovers *See Baked Goods: Cakes & Pastries: Turnovers*
Turtle Seafood *See Fish & Seafood: Seafood: Turtle*
Twists Pretzels *See Snack Foods: Pretzels: Twists*
Two Percent Milk *See Dairy Products: Milk & Milk Products: Milk: 2 Percent*

U

Uncompounded Aroma Materials *See Ingredients, Flavors & Additives: Aroma Chemicals & Materials: Materials: Uncompounded*
Uncooked Frozen Hamburger *See Meats & Meat Products: Beef & Beef Products: Hamburger: Uncooked Frozen*
Unsalted Butter *See Dairy Products: Butter: Unsalted*

V

V.S. Cognac Three Star Brandy *See Beverages: Spirits & Liqueurs: Brandy: V.S. Cognac Three Star*
V.S.O.P. Cognac Brandy *See Beverages: Spirits & Liqueurs: Brandy: V.S.O.P. Cognac*
Vacuum Packed Coffee *See Beverages: Coffee & Tea: Coffee: Vacuum Packed*
Valencia Orange *See Fruits & Vegetables: Orange: Valencia*
Valentine Specialty-Packaged Candy *See Candy & Confectionery: Specialty-Packaged Candy: Valentine*
Valerian Root Powders *See Ingredients, Flavors & Additives: Powders: Valerian Root*
Vanilla Beans *See Spices, Seasonings & Seeds: Spices: Vanilla Beans*
Vanilla Butter Flavors *See Ingredients, Flavors & Additives: Flavors: Butter: Vanilla*
Vanilla Extracts *See Ingredients, Flavors & Additives: Extracts: Vanilla*
Vanilla Flavors *See Ingredients, Flavors & Additives: Flavors: Vanilla*
Vanilla Powders *See Ingredients, Flavors & Additives: Powders: Vanilla*
Vanilla Pudding *See Dairy Products: Pudding: Vanilla*
Vanilla Spices *See Spices, Seasonings & Seeds: Spices: Vanilla*
Vanillin Flavors *See Ingredients, Flavors & Additives: Flavors: Vanillin*
Variegates Flavors *See Ingredients, Flavors & Additives: Flavors: Variegates*
Veal *See Meats & Meat Products: Beef & Beef Products: Veal*
Veal Cutlet *See Meats & Meat Products: Beef & Beef Products: Veal: Cutlet*
Veal Sausages *See Meats & Meat Products: Smoked, Cured & Deli Meats: Sausages: Veal*
Vegetable Bases *See Ingredients, Flavors & Additives: Bases: Vegetable*
Vegetable Colors *See Ingredients, Flavors & Additives: Colors: Vegetable*
Vegetable Concentrates *See Ingredients, Flavors & Additives: Concentrates: Vegetable*
Vegetable Extracts *See Ingredients, Flavors & Additives: Extracts: Vegetable*
Vegetable Flavors *See Ingredients, Flavors & Additives: Flavors: Vegetable*
Vegetable Gum *See Ingredients, Flavors & Additives: Gums: Vegetable Gum*
Vegetable Juices *See Beverages: Juices: Vegetable*
Vegetable Mixes *See Doughs, Mixes & Fillings: Mixes: Vegetable*
Vegetable Oils *See Oils, Shortening & Fats: Oils: Vegetable*
Vegetable Proteins *See Ingredients, Flavors & Additives: Hydrolyzed Products: Vegetable Proteins*
Vegetable Pulp *See Fruits & Vegetables: Pulps & Purees: Pulp: Vegetable*
Vegetable Puree *See Fruits & Vegetables: Pulps & Purees: Puree: Vegetable*
Vegetable Ravioli *See Pasta & Noodles: Ravioli: Vegetable*
Vegetable Seeds *See Spices, Seasonings & Seeds: Seeds: Vegetable*
Vegetable Shortening *See Oils, Shortening & Fats: Shortening: Vegetable*
Vegetable Stuffing *See Prepared Foods: Stuffing: Vegetable*
Vegetables *See Fruits & Vegetables: Vegetables*
Vegetables, Mixed *See Fruits & Vegetables: Vegetables Mixed*
Vegetables, Organic *See Specialty & Organic Foods: Organic Foods: Vegetables; See also Organic Foods*
Vegetables, Pickled *See Relishes & Pickled Products: Pickled Products: Vegetables*
Vegetarian Products *See Specialty & Organic Foods: Vegetarian Products; See also Organic Foods*
Vegetarian, Prepared Meals *See Prepared Foods: Prepared Meals: Vegetarian*
Veggie & Rice Pellets *See Ingredients, Flavors & Additives: Half-Products: Veggie & Rice Pellets*
Vending Specialty-Packaged Candy *See Candy & Confectionery: Specialty-Packaged Candy: Vending*
Venison *See Meats & Meat Products: Game: Venison*
Venison Sausages *See Meats & Meat Products: Smoked, Cured & Deli Meats: Sausages: Venison*
Vermicelli *See Pasta & Noodles: Vermicelli*
Vinegar *See Sauces, Dips & Dressings: Vinegar*
Viognier *See Beverages: Wines: White Grape Varieties: Viognier*
Vitamin A *See Ingredients, Flavors & Additives: Vitamins & Supplements: A*
Vitamin C *See Ingredients, Flavors & Additives: Vitamins & Supplements: C*
Vitamin E *See Ingredients, Flavors & Additives: Vitamins & Supplements: E - Tocopherol*
Vitamin Oils *See Oils, Shortening & Fats: Oils: Vitamin*
Vitamins & Supplements *See Ingredients, Flavors & Additives: Vitamins & Supplements; See also Ingredients, Flavors & Additives: Vitamins & Supplements: Supplements: Vitamins; See also Ingredients, Flavors & Additives: Vitamins & Supplements: Vit*
Vodka *See Beverages: Spirits & Liqueurs: Vodka*

EXAMPLE: **Canadian Style Bacon**[1] *See Meats & Meat Products*[2]*: Smoked, Cured & Deli Meats*[3]*: Bacon*[4]*: Canadian Style*[5]

1. Product or Service you are looking for
2. Main Category, in alphabetical order, located in the page headers starting on page 27
3. Category Description, located in black bars and in page headers
4. Product Category, located in gray bars
5. Product Type, located under gray bars, centered in bold

Baby Foods

Cereal

Gerber Products Co
Arlington, VA 800-284-9488
Hain Celestial Group Inc
Lake Success, NY 800-434-4246
Happy Family
New York, NY 855-644-2779
Healthy Times Baby Food
San Diego, CA 858-513-1550

Formula

Abbott Laboratories
Abbott Park, IL 847-938-3887
Gerber Products Co
Arlington, VA 800-284-9488
Hain Celestial Group Inc
Lake Success, NY 800-434-4246

Organic

Amara Organic Baby Food
San Francisco, CA 267-981-6411
Ella's Kitchen
New Castle, DE 800-685-7799
Fresh Bellies
White Plains, NY 866-888-0467
Gerber Products Co
Arlington, VA 800-284-9488
Hain Celestial Group Inc
Lake Success, NY 800-434-4246
Happy Family
New York, NY 855-644-2779
Healthy Times Baby Food
San Diego, CA 858-513-1550
J M Swank Co
North Liberty, IA 800-593-6375
Little Duck Organics
New York, NY 877-458-1321
Oh Baby Foods, Inc.
Fayetteville, AR 800-788-1451
Plum Organics
Emeryville, CA 877-914-7586
Sprout Nutrition
Montvale, NJ 877-704-8777
Square One Organics
River Forest, IL 866-771-7138
Stonyfield Organic
Londonderry, NH 800-776-2697
Tastybaby
Malibu, CA 866-588-8278

Puree

Gerber Products Co
Arlington, VA 800-284-9488
Hain Celestial Group Inc
Lake Success, NY 800-434-4246
Happy Family
New York, NY 855-644-2779
Little Duck Organics
New York, NY 877-458-1321
Oh Baby Foods, Inc.
Fayetteville, AR 800-788-1451
Once Upon a Farm
San Diego, CA 888-983-1606
Square One Organics
River Forest, IL 866-771-7138

Whole

Gerber Products Co
Arlington, VA 800-284-9488
Hain Celestial Group Inc
Lake Success, NY 800-434-4246
Happy Family
New York, NY 855-644-2779

Baked Goods

General

A Southern Season
Hillsborough, NC 800-253-3663
Adam Matthews Inc
Jeffersontown, KY 502-499-1244
Adams Foods & Milling
Dothan, AL 334-983-4233
Ak Mak Bakeries
Sanger, CA 559-875-5511
Aladdin Bakers
Brooklyn, NY 718-499-1818
Alati-Caserta Desserts
Montr,al, QC 877-377-5680
Alfred & Sam's Italian Bakery
Lancaster, PA 717-392-6311
Allegria Italian Bakers
Sunnyvale, CA 800-467-8648
Alois J Binder Bakery
New Orleans, LA 504-947-1111
Alpha Baking Company
South Bend, IN 773-261-6000
Amalfitano's Italian Bakery
New Castle, DE 302-324-9005
Amcan Industries
Elmsford, NY 914-347-4838
American Copak Corporation
Chatsworth, CA 818-576-1000
Ames International Inc
Fife, WA 888-469-2637
Amoroso's Baking Co
Bellmawr, NJ 215-471-4740
Andre-Boudin Bakeries
San Francisco, CA 415-882-1849
Anthony & Sons Italian Bakery
Fairfield, NJ 973-575-5865
April Hill Inc
Grand Rapids, MI 616-245-0595
Arturo's Spinella's Bakery
Waterbury, CT 203-754-3056
Artuso Pastry
Bronx, NY 718-367-2515
Aryzta
Los Angeles, CA 855-427-9982
Athens Baking Company
Fresno, CA 800-775-2867
Athens Foods Inc
Brookpark, OH 843-916-2000
Atkinson Milling Co.
Selma, NC 800-948-5707
Atlanta Bread Co.
Smyrna, GA 800-398-3728
August Foods LTD
Lubbock, TX 806-744-1918
Aunt Gussie Cookies & Crackers
Garfield, NJ 800-422-6654
Aunt Heddy's Bakery
Brooklyn, NY 718-782-0582
Aunt Millie's Bakeries
Fort Wayne, IN 855-755-2253
Automatic Rolls Of New Jersey
Edison, NJ 877-222-2867
Award Baking Intl
New Germany, MN 800-333-3523
Awrey Bakeries
Livonia, MI 800-950-2253
Azteca Foods Inc
Chicago, IL 708-563-6600
B&A Bakery
Toronto, ON 800-263-2878
Bagel Guys
Brooklyn, NY 718-222-4361
Bagels By Bell
Brooklyn, NY 718-272-2780
Bake City
Atlanta, GA 855-336-4777
Bake Rite Rolls Inc
Bensalem, PA 800-949-5623
BakeMark USA
Schaumburg, IL 847-519-3135
Baker Boy Bake Shop Inc
Dickinson, ND 800-437-2008
Baker Boys
Calgary, AB 877-246-6036
Baker's Dozen & Cafe
Herkimer, NY 315-866-6770
Bakerhaus Veit Limited
Woodbridge, ON 800-387-8860
Bakers of Paris
Brisbane, CA 415-468-9100
BakeryCorp
Miami, FL 305-623-3838
Baking Leidenheimer
New Orleans, LA 800-259-9099
Baldinger Baking Co
St Paul, MN 651-224-5761
Balticshop.Com LLC
Glastonbury, CT 800-506-2312
Bama Foods LTD
Tulsa, OK 800-756-2262
Banquet Schusters Bakery
Pueblo, CO 719-544-1062
Baptista's Bakery
Franklin, WI 414-409-2000
Barbara's Bakery
Lakeville, MN 800-343-0590
Barbero Bakery, Inc.
Trenton, NJ 609-394-5122
Barker System Bakery
Mt Carmel, PA 570-339-3380
Base Culture
Clearwater, FL
Basque French Bakery
Fresno, CA 559-268-7088
Bays English Muffin Corporation
Chicago, IL 800-367-2297
BBU Bakeries
Horsham, PA 800-984-0989
Beanitos
Austin, TX 512-609-8017
Beatrice Bakery Co
Beatrice, NE 800-228-4030
Beck's Waffles of Oklahoma
Shawnee, OK 800-646-6254
Beckmann's Old World Bakery
Santa Cruz, CA 831-423-9242
Bella-Napoli Italian Bakery
Troy, NY 888-800-0103
Berkshire Mountain Bakery
Housatonic, MA 866-274-6124
Berlin Natural Bakery
Berlin, OH 800-686-5334
Best Harvest Bakeries
Kansas City, KS 800-811-5715
Best Maid Cookie Co
River Falls, WI 888-444-0322
Beth's Fine Desserts
Mill Valley, CA 415-383-3991
Better Bagel Bakery
Sarasota, FL 941-924-0393
Better Bites Bakery
Austin, TX
Betty Lou's
McMinnville, OR 800-242-5205
Bien Cuit
Brooklyn, NY 718-852-0200
Bindi North America
Kearny, NJ 973-812-8118
Birkholm's Solvang Bakery
Solvang, CA 800-377-4253
Bite Size Bakery
Rio Rancho, NM 505-994-3093
Blue Dog Bakery
Seattle, WA 888-749-7229
Blue Planet Foods
Collegedale, TN 877-396-3145
Bluepoint Bakery
Denver, CO 303-298-1100
Boboli Intl. Inc.
Stockton, CA 209-473-3507
Bodacious Foods
Jasper, GA 800-391-1979
Bonert's Pies Inc
Santa Ana, CA 714-540-3535
Bonnie Baking Company
La Porte, IN 219-362-4561
Borinquen Biscuit Corporation
Yauco, PR 787-856-3030
Boudreaux's Foods
New Orleans, LA 504-733-8440
BP Gourmet
Hauppauge, NY 631-234-8200
Bread Box Cafe
Astoria, NY 718-389-9703
Breadworks
Charlottesville, VA 434-296-4663
Brooklyn Bagel Company
Staten Island, NY 800-349-3055
Brooklyn Baking Company
Waterbury, CT 203-574-9198
Brookshire Grocery Company
Tyler, TX 888-937-3776
Bruce Baking Company
New Rochelle, NY 914-636-0808
Bubbles Baking Co
Van Nuys, CA 800-777-4970
Bunny Bread
Evansville, IN
Buns & Roses Organic Wholegrain Bakery
Edmonton, AB 780-438-0098
Buonitalia
New York, NY 212-633-9090
Burnham & Morrill Co
Portland, ME 800-813-2165
Busken Bakery
Cincinnati, OH 513-871-2114
Byrnes & Kiefer Co
Callery, PA 724-538-5200
C W Resources Inc
New Britain, CT 860-229-7700
Calgary Italian Bakery
Calgary, AB 800-661-6868
California Smart Foods
San Francisco, CA 415-826-0449
Calise & Sons Bakery Inc
Lincoln, RI 800-225-4737
Calmar Bakery
Calmar, AB 780-985-3583
Campbell Soup Co.
Camden, NJ 800-257-8443
Canada Bread Co, Ltd
Etobicoke, ON 800-465-5515
Canaf Foods International
Bolton, ON 905-362-0524
Caribbean Food Delights Inc
Tappan, NY 845-398-3000
Carmine's Bakery
Sanford, FL 407-328-4141
Carole's Cheesecake Company
Toronto, ON 416-256-0000
Carolina Foods Inc
Charlotte, NC 800-234-0441
Case Side Holdings Company
Kensington, PE 902-836-4214
Casino Bakery
Tampa, FL 813-242-0311
Catania Bakery
Washington, DC 202-332-5135
Cateraid Inc
Howell, MI 800-508-8217
CBC Foods
Little River, KS 800-276-4770
Cedarlane Foods
Carson, CA 800-826-3322
Celebrity Cheesecake
Davie, FL 877-986-2253
Cellone Bakery Inc
Pittsburgh, PA 800-334-8438
Central Bakery
Fall River, MA 508-675-7620
Charlie's Specialties Inc
Hermitage, PA 724-346-2350
Chattanooga Bakery Inc
Chattanooga, TN 800-251-3404
Cheesecake Etc Desserts
Miami Springs, FL 305-887-0258
Cheesecake Factory Inc.
Calabasas Hills, CA 818-871-3000
Chella's Dutch Delicacies
Lake Oswego, OR 800-458-3331
Chelsea Flower Market
New York, NY 888-727-7887
Cheri's Desert Harvest
Tucson, AZ 800-743-1141
Chewys Rugulach
San Diego, CA 800-241-3456
Chex Finer Foods Inc
Mansfield, MA 800-227-8114

Chicago Pastry
Bloomingdale, IL 630-529-6391
Chisholm Bakery
Chisholm, MN 218-254-4006
Chmura's Bakery
Indian Orchard, MA 413-543-2521
Chocolate Chix
Waxahachie, TX 214-744-2442
Chudleigh's
Milton, ON 800-387-4028
Cinderella Cheese Cake Co
Riverside, NJ 800-521-1171
City Cafe & Bakery
Fayetteville, GA 770-461-6800
Clarkson Scottish Bakery
Mississauga, ON 905-823-1500
Claxton Bakery Inc
Claxton, GA 800-841-4211
Clement's Pastry Shops Inc
Hyattsville, MD 301-277-6300
Cloverhill Bakery-Vend Corporation
Chicago, IL 773-745-9800
Clyde's Delicious Donuts
Addison, IL 630-628-6555
Coby's Cookies
Toronto, ON 416-633-1567
Cohen's Bakery
Ellenville, NY 845-647-2200
Colchester Bakery
Colchester, CT 860-537-2415
Cold Spring Bakery Inc
Cold Spring, MN 320-685-8681
Cole's Quality Foods
Grand Rapids, MI 616-975-0081
Collin Street Bakery
Corsicana, TX 800-267-4657
Colombo Bakery
Sacramento, CA 916-648-1011
Colonial Cookies, Ltd
Kitchener, ON 800-265-6508
Colors Gourmet Pizza
Vista, CA 760-597-1400
Community Bakeries
Downers Grove, IL 800-952-5754
Community Orchards
Fort Dodge, IA 888-573-8212
Cookie Factory
Bronx, NY 718-379-6223
Cookie Kingdom
Oglesby, IL 815-883-3331
Cookie Specialties Inc
Wheeling, IL 847-537-3888
Cookie Tree Bakeries
Salt Lake City, UT 801-268-2253
Cookies United
Islip, NY 631-581-4000
Cookiezen, LLC
Falls Church, VA 703-389-9274
Corfu Foods Inc
Bensenville, IL 630-595-2510
Cotton Baking Company
Alexandria, LA 318-448-6600
Cougar Mountain Baking Co
Seattle, WA 877-328-2622
Country Club Bakery
Fairmont, WV 304-363-5690
Creative Spices
Union City, CA 510-471-4956
Creme Curls
Hudsonville, MI 800-466-1219
Crum Creek Mils
Springfield, PA 888-607-3500
Crusty Bakery Inc
New York, NY 917-733-6396
Culinar Canada
Baie-Comeau, QC 418-296-4395
Culinary Masters Corporation
Alpharetta, GA 800-261-5261
Cupoladua Oven
Wexford, PA 412-592-5378
Cusano's Baking Company
Hallandale, FL 954-458-1010
Cutie Pie Corp
Salt Lake City, UT 800-453-4575
Dairy State Foods Inc
Milwaukee, WI 800-435-4499
Dakota Brands Intl
Jamestown, ND 800-844-5073
Dancing Deer Baking Company
Boston, MA 888-699-3337
Daniel's Bagel & Baguette Corporation
Calgary, AB 403-243-3207
Davis Bakery & Delicatessen
Cleveland, OH 216-292-3060
Davis Bread & Desserts
Davis, CA 530-220-4375
DeBeukelaer Cookie Co
Madison, MS 601-856-7454
Deerfield Bakery
Buffalo Grove, IL 847-520-0068
Del's Pastry
Toronto, ON 800-461-0663
Delia's Food Co
Cincinnati, OH 513-221-4322
Delicious Frookie
Des Plaines, IL 847-699-3200
Denny's 5th Avenue Bakery
Bloomington, MN 952-881-4445
Desserts by David Glass
South Windsor, CT 860-462-7520
Desserts Of Distinction
Tigard, OR 503-654-8370
Desserts On Us Inc
Arcata, CA 707-822-0160
Dewey's Bakery
Winston-Salem, NC 877-339-3974
Di Camillo Baking Co
Niagara Falls, NY 800-634-4363
Dimitria Delights Baking Co
North Grafton, MA 800-763-1113
Dimpflmeier Bakery
Toronto, ON 800-268-2421
Dinkel's Bakery Inc
Chicago, IL 800-822-8817
Dipaolo Baking Co Inc
Rochester, NY 585-232-3510
Divine Foods
Elizabethtown, NC 910-862-2576
Dong Kee Company
Chicago, IL 312-225-6340
Doral International
Bayside, NY 718-224-7413
Dough-To-Go
Santa Clara, CA 408-727-4094
Drader Manufacturing Industries
Edmonton, AB 800-661-4122
Dufflet Pastries
Toronto, ON 866-238-0899
Dunford Bakers
West Jordan, UT 800-748-4335
Dunkin' Brands Inc.
Canton, MA 800-859-5339
Dutch Ann Foods Company
Natchez, MS 601-445-5566
Dutch Girl Donut Co
Detroit, MI 313-368-3020
Dutchess Bakery
Charleston, WV 304-346-4237
DWC Specialities
Horicon, WI 800-383-8808
Dynamic Foods
Lubbock, TX 806-723-5600
Eddy's Bakery
Boise, ID 208-377-8100
Edelweiss Patisserie
Medford, MA 781-628-0225
Eden Vineyards Winery
Alva, FL 239-728-9463
Edner Corporation
Hayward, CA 510-441-8504
Edwards Baking Company
Marshall, MN 866-739-2328
El Charro Mexican Food Ind
Roswell, NM 575-622-8590
El Peto Products
Cambridge, ON 800-387-4064
Elegant Desserts
Lyndhurst, NJ 201-933-0770
Eli's Cheesecake
Chicago, IL 800-354-2253
Ellison Bakery, Inc.
Fort Wayne, IN
Elmwood Pastry Shop
West Hartford, CT 860-233-2029
Ener-G Foods
Seattle, WA 800-331-5222
Engel's Bakeries
Calgary, AB 403-250-9560
Entenmann's
Totowa, NJ 973-785-7601
Erba Food Products
Brooklyn, NY 718-272-7700
Ericas Rugelach & Baking Co
Brooklyn, NY 718-965-3657
Esco Foods Inc
San Francisco, CA 415-864-2147
Euroam Importers Inc
Auburn, WA 888-839-2702
European Bakers
Tucker, GA 770-723-6180
European Style Bakery
Beverly Hills, CA 818-368-6876
Falcone's Cookie Land LTD
Brooklyn, NY 718-236-4200
Fancy Lebanese Bakery
Halifax, NS 902-429-0400
Fantasia
Sedalia, MO 660-827-1172
Fantasy Cookie Company
Sylmar, CA 800-354-4488
Fantini Baking Co Inc
Haverhill, MA 800-343-2110
Fantis Foods Inc
Carlstadt, NJ 201-933-6200
Farrell Baking Company
West Middlesex, PA 724-342-7906
Father Sam's Bakery
Buffalo, NY 800-521-6719
Fayes Bakery Products
Dexter, MO 573-624-4920
Fazio's Bakery
St Louis, MO 314-645-6239
Federal Pretzel Baking Company
Bridgeport, NJ 215-467-0505
Felix Roma & Son Inc
Endicott, NY 607-748-3336
Ferrara Bakery & Cafe
New York, NY 212-226-6150
Field's Pies
Pauls Valley, OK 800-286-7501
Fiera Foods
Toronto, ON 800-675-6356
Finkemeier Bakery
Kansas City, KS 913-831-3103
Firehook Bakery & Coffeehouse
Chantilly, VA 703-263-2253
Fireside Kitchen
Halifax, NS 902-454-7387
Flamin' Red's Woodfired
Pawlet, VT 802-325-3641
Flax4Life
Bellingham, WA 877-352-9487
Fleischer's Bagels
Macedon, NY 315-986-9999
Flowers Baking Co
Birmingham, AL 205-252-1161
Flowers Baking Co
Tuscaloosa, AL 205-752-5586
Flowers Baking Co
El Paso, TX 800-328-6111
Flowers Foods Inc.
Thomasville, GA 229-226-9110
Food Mill
Oakland, CA 510-482-3848
Food of Our Own Design
Maplewood, NJ 973-762-0985
Fortella Fortune Cookies
Chicago, IL 312-567-9000
Fortune Cookie Factory
Oakland, CA 510-832-5552
Forty Second Street Bagel Cafe
Upland, CA 909-949-7334
Foxtail Foods
Fairfield, OH 800-487-2253
France Delices
Montreal, QC 800-663-1365
Franklin Baking Company
Kinston, NC 800-248-7494
Frankly Natural Bakers
San Diego, CA 800-727-7229
Franz Bakery Outlet Store
Portland, OR 503-232-2191
Freedman's Bakery
Belmar, NJ 732-681-2334
Freedom Foods LLC
Randolph, VM 802-728-0070
Fresh Start Bakeries
Brea, CA 714-256-8900
Frisco Baking Co Inc
Los Angeles, CA 323-225-6111
Future Bakery & Cafe
Toronto, ON 416-231-1491
G Debbas Chocolatier
Fresno, CA 559-294-2071
Gabila's Knishes
Copiague, NY 631-789-2220

Gadoua Bakery
Napierville, QC....800-661-7246
GAF Seelig Inc
Flushing, NY....718-899-5000
Galasso's Bakery
Mira Loma, CA....951-360-1211
Gambino's Bakeries Inc
Kenner, LA....504-712-0809
Gardner Pie Co
Akron, OH....330-245-2030
Gartner Studios Inc
Stillwater, MN....651-351-7700
George's Candy Shop Inc
Mobile, AL....800-633-1306
Georgia Fruitcake Co
Claxton, GA....912-739-2683
German Bakery at Village Corner
Stone Mountain, GA....866-476-6443
GH Bent Company
Milton, MA....617-322-9287
Giant Food
Landover, MD....888-469-4426
Ginny Bakes
Miami, FL....305-638-5103
Glamorgan Bakery
Calgary, AB....403-232-2800
Global Bakeries Inc
Pacoima, CA....818-896-0525
Glutino
Laval, QC....800-363-3438
Gold Coast Bakeries
Santa Ana, CA....714-545-2253
Gold Coast Baking Co Inc
Santa Ana, CA....714-545-2253
Gold Crust Baking Co Inc
Landover, MD....301-364-3320
Gold Medal Bakery Inc
Fall River, MA....508-674-5766
Gold Standard Baking Inc
Chicago, IL....800-648-7904
Golden Brown Bakery Inc
South Haven, MI....269-637-3418
Golden Edibles LLC
Davie, FL....866-779-7781
Goldilocks USA
Hayward, CA....510-476-0700
Goll's Bakery
Havre De Grace, MD....410-939-4321
Good Old Days Foods
Little Rock, AR....501-565-1257
Gould's Maple Sugarhouse
Shelburne Falls, MA....413-625-6170
Gourmet Croissant
Brooklyn, NY....718-499-4911
Grandma Beth's Cookies
Alliance, NE....308-762-8433
Granello Bakery
Las Vegas, NV....702-361-0311
Granny Roddy's LLC
Annandale, VA....703-503-3431
Grebe's Bakery
Milwaukee, WI....800-833-3158
Grecian Delight Foods Inc
Elk Grove Village, IL....800-621-4387
Greenhills Irish Bakery
Dorchester Ctr, MA....617-825-8187
Gregory's Foods, Inc.
St Paul, MN....800-231-4734
Greyston Bakery Inc
Yonkers, NY....800-289-2253
Grossingers Home Bakery
New York, NY....800-479-6996
Guttenplan's Frozen Dough
Middletown, NJ....888-422-4357
GWB Foods Corporation
Brooklyn, NY....877-977-7610
H Cantin
Beauport, QC....800-463-5268
H&S Bakery
Baltimore, MD....800-959-7655
H-E-B Grocery Co. LP
San Antonio, TX....800-432-3113
Haby's Alsatian Bakery
Castroville, TX....830-538-2118
Hafner USA
Stone Mountain, GA....888-725-4605
Hahn's Old Fashioned Cake Co
Farmingdale, NY....631-249-3456
Handy Pax
Randolph, MA....781-963-8300
Harbar LLC
Canton, MA....800-881-7040
Harlan Bakeries
Avon, IN....800-435-2738
Harold Food Company
Charlotte, NC....704-588-8061
Harting's Bakery
Bowmansville, PA....717-445-5644
Harvest Bakery
Central Islip, NY....631-232-1709
Harvest Valley Bakery Inc
La Salle, IL....815-224-9030
Havi Food Services Worldwide
Oak Park, IL....708-445-1700
Hawaii Candy Inc
Honolulu, HI....800-303-2507
Hawaii Star Bakery
Honolulu, HI....808-841-3602
Hawaiian Bagel
Honolulu, HI....808-596-0638
Health Valley Company
Irwindale, CA....800-334-3204
Heidi's Gourmet Desserts
Tucker, GA....800-241-4166
Heltzman Bakery
Louisville, KY....502-447-3515
Herman's Bakery
Cambridge, MN....763-689-1515
Heyerly Bakery
Ossian, IN....260-622-4196
Highlandville Packing
Highlandville, MO....417-443-3365
Holsum Bakery Inc
Phoenix, AZ....602-252-2351
Holt's Bakery Inc
Douglas, GA....912-384-2202
Home Bakery
Rochester, MI....248-651-4830
Home Maid Bakery
Wailuku, HI....808-244-7015
Home Style Bakery Of Grand Junction
Grand Junction, CO....970-243-1233
Homestead Baking Co
Rumford, RI....800-556-7216
Homestyle Bread Bakery
Phoenix, AZ....602-268-0676
Horizon Snack Foods
Livermore, CA....800-229-2552
Hostess Brands
Kansas City, MO....816-701-4600
Hunt Country Foods Inc
Marshall, VA....540-364-2622
Hye Quality Bakery
Fresno, CA....877-445-1778
Il Gelato
Astoria, NY....800-899-9299
Il Giardino Del Dolce Inc
Chicago, IL....773-889-2388
Immaculate Consumption
Columbia, SC....888-826-6567
Independent Bakers Association
Washington, DC....202-333-8190
Ingles Markets
Black Mountain, NC....828-669-2941
Interbake Foods
Richmond, VA....800-221-1002
International Brownie
East Weymouth, MA....800-230-1588
Irresistible Cookie Jar
Hayden Lake, ID....208-664-1261
Italian Bakery of Virginia
Virginia, MN....218-741-3464
Italian Peoples Bakery Inc
Ewing, NJ....609-771-1369
J & J Wall Bakery Co
Sacramento, CA....916-381-1410
J J Gandy's Pies Inc
Palm Harbor, FL....727-938-7437
J M Swank Co
North Liberty, IA....800-593-6375
J.P. Sunrise Bakery
Edmonton, AB....780-454-5797
Jacques Pastries
Suncook, NH....603-485-4035
Jacquet Bakery
New York, NY
Jamae Natural Foods
Los Angeles, CA....800-343-0052
James Skinner Company
Omaha, NE....800-358-7428
Jerabek's New Bohemian Coffee House
Saint Paul, MN....651-228-1245
Jerusalem House
Eugene, OR....541-485-1012
Jewel Bakery
Melrose Park, IL....708-531-6000
Jim's Cheese Pantry
Waterloo, WI....800-345-3571
Jimmys Cookies
Clifton, NJ....973-779-8500
Joey's Fine Foods
Newark, NJ....973-482-1400
John J. Nissen Baking Company
Brewer, ME....207-989-7654
John W Macy's Cheesesticks Inc
Elmwood Park, NJ....800-643-0573
Jon Donaire Desserts
Santa Fe Springs, CA....877-366-2473
Jonathan Lord Cheesecakes
Bohemia, NY....800-814-7517
Jubelt Variety Bakeries
Litchfield, IL....217-324-5314
Jubilations
West Point, MS....800-530-7808
Julian's Recipe
Brooklyn, NY....888-640-8880
Just Desserts
Fairfield, CA....415-780-6860
Just Off Melrose
Palm Springs, CA....760-320-7414
K & S Cakes
Leesburg, VA....910-265-6779
Kangaroo Brands
Omaha, NE....877-266-2472
Kapaa Bakery
Kapaa, HI....808-821-0060
Keebler Company
Battlecreek, MI....800-962-1413
Keller's Bakery
Lafayette, LA....337-235-1568
Kemach Food Products
Brooklyn, NY....718-272-5655
Keystone Pretzel Bakery
Lititz, PA....888-572-4500
Kids Kookie Company
San Clemente, CA....800-350-7577
Kim & Scott's Gourmet Pretzels
Chicago, IL....800-578-9478
Kim and Jake's
Boulder, CO....303-499-9126
King's Hawaiian Holding Co Inc.
Torrance, CA....877-695-4227
Koffee Kup Bakery
Burlington, VT....802-863-2696
Kollar Cookies
Long Branch, NJ....732-343-4217
Korbs Baking Company
Pawtucket, RI....401-726-4422
Kosher French Baguettes
Brooklyn, NY....718-633-4994
Kossar's Bagels & Bialys
New York, NY....877-424-2597
Krispy Kreme Doughnuts Inc
Charlotte, NC
Kroger Bakery
Clackamas, OR....503-650-2000
Kupris Home Bakery
Bolton, CT....860-649-4746
Kyger Bakery Products
Lafayette, IN....765-447-1252
L & M Bakery
Riverside, NJ....888-887-1335
LA Boulangerie
San Diego, CA....858-578-4040
La Brea Bakery Inc
San Leandro, CA....855-427-9982
La Buena Mexican Foods Products
Tucson, AZ....520-624-1796
La Moderna
Toluca, MX
LA Patisserie Bakery
Cupertino, CA....408-446-4744
La Piccolina
Decatur, GA....800-626-1624
La Tempesta
S San Francisco, CA....800-762-8330
LA Torilla Factory
Santa Rosa, CA....800-446-1516
Lake States Yeast
Rhinelander, WI....715-369-4949
Lakeview Bakery
Calgary, AB....403-246-6127
Lamonaca Bakery
Windber, PA....814-467-4909
Landolfi's Food Products
Trenton, NJ....609-392-1830

Lanthier Bakery
Alexandria, ON....................613-525-2435
Lark Fine Foods
Essex, MA....................978-768-0012
Laronga Bakery
Somerville, MA....................617-625-8600
Larosa Bakery Inc
Shrewsbury, NJ....................800-527-6722
Latonia Bakery
Covington, KY....................859-491-8855
Laura's French Baking Co
Los Angeles, CA....................888-353-5144
Lavash Corp
Los Angeles, CA....................323-663-5249
Lavoi Corporation
Atlanta, GA....................404-325-1016
Lax & Mandel Bakery
South Euclid, OH....................216-382-8877
Le Chic French Bakery
Miami Beach, FL....................305-673-5522
Le Donne Brothers Bakery
Roseto, PA....................610-588-0423
Lefse House
Camrose, AB....................780-672-7555
Leidenheimer Baking Co
New Orleans, LA....................800-259-9099
Lenchner Bakery
Concord, ON....................905-738-8811
Leo's Bakery
Marshfield, MA....................781-837-3300
Lepage Bakeries
Auburn, ME....................207-783-9161
Lewis Bakeries Inc
Evansville, IN....................812-425-4642
Linden Cookies Inc
Congers, NY....................845-268-5050
Livermore Falls Baking Company
Livermore Falls, ME....................207-897-3442
Loafin' Around
Madison, AL....................301-570-4513
Loghouse Foods
Minneapolis, MN....................763-546-8395
Lombardi's Bakery
Torrington, CT....................860-489-4766
Lone Star Bakery
Round Rock, TX....................512-255-7268
Longo's Bakery Inc
Hazleton, PA....................570-454-5825
Lotus Bakery
Santa Rosa, CA....................800-875-6887
Louis Swiss Pastry
Aspen, CO....................970-925-8592
Love Quiches Desserts
Freeport, NY....................516-623-8800
Love's Bakery
Honolulu, HI....................808-841-0397
Lowcountry Produce
Raleigh, NC....................800-935-2792
Lucerne Foods
Pleasanton, CA....................877-232-4271
Lucy's Sweet Surrender
Beachwood, OH....................216-752-0828
Ludwick's Frozen Donuts
Grand Rapids, MI....................800-366-8816
Luna's Tortillas
Dallas, TX....................214-747-2661
Lupi-Marchigiano Bakery
New Haven, CT....................203-562-9491
Mac Farms Of Hawaii Inc
Captain Cook, HI....................808-328-2435
Mac's Donut Shop
Aliquippa, PA....................724-375-6776
Maggiora Baking Co
Richmond, CA....................510-235-0274
Magna Foods Corporation
City of Industry, CA....................800-995-4394
Main Street Gourmet
Cuyahoga Falls, OH....................800-678-6246
Mancuso Cheese Co
Joliet, IL....................815-722-2475
Manderfield's Home Bakery
Menasha, WI....................920-882-6500
Maple Leaf Bakery
Montreal, QC....................800-268-3708
Marika's Kitchen
Hancock, ME....................800-694-9400
Marin Food Specialties
Byron, CA....................925-634-6126
Marshall's Biscuit Company
Westerville, OH....................251-679-6226
Martino's Bakery
Burbank, CA....................818-842-0715

Mary Ann's Baking Co Inc
Sacramento, CA....................916-681-7444
Mary of Puddin Hill
Palestine, TX....................800-545-8889
Matthew's Bakery
Stamford, CT....................203-316-9392
Maui Bagel
Kahului, HI....................808-270-7561
Mayer's Cider Mill
Webster, NY....................800-543-0043
Mazelle's Cheesecakes Concoctions Creations
Dallas, TX....................214-328-9102
McKee Foods Corp.
Collegedale, TN....................800-522-4499
Mediterranean Gyro Products
Long Island City, NY....................718-786-3399
Mehaffies Pies
Dayton, OH....................800-289-7437
Meijer Inc
Grand Rapids, MI....................616-453-6711
Mememe Inc
Toronto, ON....................416-972-0973
Metropolitan Baking Co
Hamtramck, MI....................313-875-7246
Meyer's Bakeries
Casa Grande, AZ....................800-528-5770
Michel's Bakery
Philadelphia, PA....................267-345-7914
Mikawaya LLC
Vernon, CA....................323-587-5504
Mikey's
Scottsdale, AZ
Milano Bakery Inc
Joliet, IL....................815-727-2253
Millie's Pierogi
Chicopee Falls, MA....................800-743-7641
Modern Italian Bakery of West Babylon
Oakdale, NY....................631-589-7300
Molinaro's Fine Italian Foods Ltd.
Mississauga, ON....................905-281-0352
Mom's Bakery
Sherman, TX....................903-893-7585
Mom's Famous
Boca Raton, FL....................561-750-1903
Monaco Baking Company
Santa Fe Springs, CA....................800-569-4640
Monastery Fruitcake
Martinsburg, WV....................304-596-2024
Monks' Specialty Bakery
Piffard, NY
Monster Cone
Montreal, QC....................800-542-9801
Montione's Biscotti & Baked Goods
Norton, MA....................800-559-1010
Moon Rabbit Foods
Savannah, NY....................828-273-6649
Morabito Baking Co Inc
Norristown, PA....................800-525-7747
Morrison Meat Pies
West Valley, UT....................801-977-0181
Mozzicato De Pasquale Bakery
Hartford, CT....................860-296-0426
Mrs Baird's
Horsham, PA....................800-984-0989
Mrs. Fly's Bakery
Collegeville, PA....................610-489-7288
Mt. View Bakery
Mountain View, HI....................808-968-6353
Multi Marques
Montreal, QC....................514-934-1866
My Cup of Cake™
Port Washington, NY....................516-767-5137
My Grandma's Coffee Cake
Hyde Park, MA....................800-847-2636
Nabisco
Parsippany, NJ....................973-682-5000
Naji's Pita Gourmet Restaurant
Birmingham, AL....................205-945-6001
Najla's Specialty Foods Inc
Louisville, KY....................877-962-5527
Naleway Foods
Winnipeg, MB....................800-665-7448
Nancy's Specialty Foods
Newark, CA....................510-494-1100
Nardi Breads
South Windsor, CT....................860-289-5458
Natural Food Mill
Corona, CA....................800-797-5090
Naturally Delicious Inc
Oakland Park, FL....................888-221-7352
Nature's Hilights
Chico, CA....................800-313-6454

Nature's Path Foods
Blaine, WA....................888-808-9505
Ne-Mo's Bakery Inc
Escondido, CA....................800-325-2692
Neuman Bakery Specialties
Addison, IL....................800-253-5298
Nevada Baking Company
Las Vegas, NV....................702-384-8950
New Bakery Company of Ohio
Zanesville, OH....................800-848-9845
New England Country Bakers
Watertown, CT....................800-225-3779
New England Muffin Co Inc
Fall River, MA....................508-675-2833
New Horizons Baking Co
Fremont, IN....................260-495-7055
New Salem Tea-Bread Company
New Salem, MA....................800-897-5910
New York Bakeries Inc
Hialeah, FL....................305-883-0790
New York Frozen Foods Inc
Bedford, OH....................216-292-5655
New York Intl Bread Co
Orlando, FL....................407-843-9744
Nicole's Divine Crackers
Chicago, IL....................312-640-8883
Nikki's Cookies
Milwaukee, WI....................800-776-7107
Nikola's Foods
Bloomington, MN....................888-645-6527
Nonni's Foods LLC
Tulsa, OK....................877-295-9604
North American Enterprises
Tucson, AZ....................800-817-8666
Northeast Foods Inc
Baltimore, MD....................800-769-2867
Northside Bakery
Brooklyn, NY....................718-782-2700
Northwoods Candy Emporium
Branson, MO....................417-332-1010
Notre Dame Bakery
Conception Harbour, NL....................709-535-2738
Nustef Foods
Mississauga, ON....................877-306-7562
Nutri-Bake Inc
Laval, QC....................450-933-5936
Nutrilicious Natural Bakery
Countryside, IL....................800-835-8097
O'Doughs
Toronto, ON....................855-636-8447
Oak State Products Inc
Wenona, IL....................815-853-4348
Oakhurst Industries
Commerce, CA....................818-502-1400
Oakrun Farm Bakery
Ancaster, ON....................800-263-6422
OH Chocolate
Seattle, WA....................206-329-8777
Ohta Wafer Factory
Honolulu, HI....................808-949-2775
Old Country Bakery
North Hollywood, CA....................818-838-2302
Old Fashioned Kitchen Inc
Lakewood, NJ....................732-364-4100
Olivia's Croutons
New Haven, VT....................888-425-3080
Orange Bakery
Irvine, CA....................949-863-1377
Orwasher's Bakery
New York, NY....................212-288-6569
Otis Spunkmeyer
Brockport, NY....................855-427-9982
Ottenberg's Bakers
Sykesville, MD....................800-334-7264
Our Farms To You, LLC
Middletown, VA....................703-507-7604
Outer Aisle
Galeta, CA....................805-242-9265
Oven Fresh Baking Company
Chicago, IL....................773-638-1234
Ozark Empire
Rogers, AR....................479-636-3313
Ozery Bakery Inc
Vaughan, ON....................905-265-1143
PDEQ
Fresno, CA....................559-490-4412
P&H Milling Group
Cambridge, ON....................519-650-6400
Pacific Ocean Produce
Santa Cruz, CA....................831-423-2654
Palermo Bakery
Seaside, CA....................831-394-8212

Pan Pepin
Bayamon, PR 787-787-1717
Pan-O-Gold Baking Co.
St. Cloud, MN.................... 800-444-7005
Panera Bread
Saint Louis, MO 314-984-1000
Pantry Shelf/Mixxm
Hutchinson, KS.................. 800-968-3346
Paris Pastry
Van Nuys, CA 805-487-2227
Park Avenue Bakery
Helena, MT...................... 406-449-8424
Pasta Shoppe
Nashville, TN 800-247-0188
Pastry Chef
Pawtucket, RI 800-639-8606
Pati-Petite Cookies Inc
Bridgeville, PA 800-253-5805
Patisserie Wawel
Montreal, QC 614-524-3348
Peggy Lawton Kitchens
East Walpole, MA................ 800-843-7325
Peking Noodle Co Inc
Los Angeles, CA.................. 323-223-0897
Pellman Foods Inc
New Holland, PA 717-354-8070
Pete & Joy's Bakery
Little Falls, MN................... 320-632-6388
Petrofsky's Bakery Products
Chesterfield, MO 636-519-1613
Phipps Desserts
North York, ON................... 416-391-5800
Piantedosi Baking Co Inc
Malden, MA 800-339-0080
Pie Piper Products
Wheeling, IL...................... 800-621-8183
Piemonte Bakery Co
Rockford, IL 815-962-4833
Pierre's French Bakery
Portland, OR 503-233-8871
Pioneer Frozen Foods
Duncanville, TX 972-298-4281
Pita King Bakery
Everett, WA...................... 425-258-4040
Pittsfield Rye Bakery
Pittsfield, MA 413-443-9141
Plaidberry Company
Vista, CA......................... 760-727-5403
Plehn's Bakery Inc
Louisville, KY 502-896-4438
Pocono Cheesecake Factory
Swiftwater, PA 570-839-6844
Pollman's Bake Shop
Mobile, AL 251-438-1511
Poppies International
Battleboro, NC 252-442-4309
Portuguese Baking Company
Newark, NJ....................... 973-589-8875
Positively 3rd St Bakery
Duluth, MN....................... 218-724-8619
Powers Baking Company
Miami, FL......................... 305-381-7000
President's Choice
Brampton, ON.................... 888-495-5111
Priester's Pecans
Fort Deposit, AL.................. 866-477-4736
Primos Northgate
Flowood, MS 601-936-3398
Prince of Peace
Hayward, CA 800-732-2328
Productos Del Plata
Miami, FL......................... 786-357-8261
Protano's Bakery
Hollywood, FL 954-925-3474
Publix Super Market
Lakeland, FL...................... 800-242-1227
Pure's Food Specialties
Broadview, IL 708-344-8884
Purity Factories
St. John's, NL 800-563-3411
Quality Bakery
Invermere, BC.................... 888-681-9977
Quality Bakery Products
Houston, TX 866-449-4977
Quality Croutons
Chicago, IL....................... 800-334-2796
Quality Naturally Foods
City Of Industry, CA.............. 888-498-6986
Quinzani Bakery
Boston, MA....................... 800-999-1062
R.M. Palmer Co.
West Reading, PA................. 610-372-8971

R.W. Frookies
Sag Harbor, NY................... 800-913-3663
Ranaldi Bros. Frozen Food Products
Warwick, RI 401-737-5130
Ranieri Fine Foods
Brooklyn, NY 718-599-9520
Real Food Marketing
Kansas City, MO.................. 816-221-4100
Real Torino
Brookside, NJ 973-895-5420
Red Plate Foods
Bend, OR......................... 541-550-7676
Rich Products Corp
Buffalo, NY....................... 800-828-2021
Rich's Ice Cream Co Inc
West Palm Beach, FL 561-833-7585
Richmond Baking Co
Richmond, IN 765-962-8535
Rising Dough Bakery
Sacramento, CA 916-387-9700
Robert's Bakery
Minnetonka, MN.................. 612-473-9719
Rockland Bakery
Nanuet, NY....................... 800-734-4376
Rolling Pin Bakery
Bow Island, AB................... 403-545-2434
Rolling Pin Bakery
Great Bend, KS................... 620-793-5381
Roma & Ray's Italian Bakery
Valley Stream, NY 516-825-7610
Roma Bakeries
Rockford, IL 815-964-6737
Romero's Food Products Inc
Santa Fe Springs, CA 800-719-2690
Rondo Specialty Foods LTD
New Castle, DE................... 800-724-6636
Rosemark Bakery
St Paul, MN...................... 651-698-3838
Rotella's Italian Bakery Inc.
La Vista, NE 402-592-6600
Rothbury Farms
Grand Rapids, MI 877-684-2879
Rovira Biscuit Corporation
Ponce, PR 787-844-8585
Rowena
Norfolk, VA...................... 800-627-8699
Royal Home Bakery
Newmarket, ON 905-715-7044
Rubschlager Baking Corp
.... 800-661-7246
Rudolph's Specialty Bakery
Toronto, ON 800-268-1589
Ruiz Flour Tortillas
Riverside, CA 909-947-7811
Run-A-Ton Group Inc
Chester, NJ 800-247-6580
Russell & Kohne Inc
Newport Beach, CA 949-645-8441
Ruth Ashbrook Bakery
Portland, OR 503-240-7437
Ryals Bakery
Milledgeville, GA................. 478-452-0321
Ryke's Bakery
Muskegon, MI.................... 231-726-2253
S & M Communion Bread Co
Nashville, TN 615-292-1969
Sacramento Baking Co
Sacramento, CA 916-361-2000
Salem Baking Company
Winston Salem, NC............... 800-274-2994
San Anselmo's Cookies & Biscotti
San Anselmo, CA 800-229-1249
San Francisco Fine Bakery
Redwood City, CA 650-369-8573
San Francisco French Bread
Oakland, CA 510-729-6232
San-J International Inc
Henrico, VA 800-446-5500
Sanborn Sourdough Bakery
Las Vegas, NV 702-795-1030
Sandors Bakeries
Miami, FL........................ 305-642-8484
Sanitary Bakery
Nanticoke, PA.................... 570-735-6630
Sara Lee Frozen Bakery
Kings Mountain, NC............. 800-323-7117
Sarabeth's Office
Bronx, NY........................ 800-773-7378
SASIB Biscuits and Snacks Division
Hudson, OH 330-656-3317
Saxby Foods
Edmonton, AB 780-440-4179

Schadel's Bakery
Silver City, NM................... 505-538-3031
Schaller's Bakery Inc
Greensburg, PA................... 800-241-1777
Schat's Dutch Bakeries
Bishop, CA 866-323-5854
Schulze & Burch Biscuit Co
Chicago, IL....................... 773-927-6622
Schwan's Food Service Inc.
Marshall, MN 877-302-7426
Schwebel Baking Co.
Youngstown, OH.................. 800-860-2867
Scialo Brothers Bakery
Providence, RI 877-421-0986
Scotty Wotty's Creamy Cheesecake
Hillsborough, NJ.................. 908-281-9720
Seaver's Bakery
Kingsport, TN.................... 423-245-2441
Sedona Baking Company
Gardena, CA 323-770-2674
Shamrock Foods Co
Phoenix, AZ 800-289-3663
Shashy's Bakery & Fine Foods
Montgomery, AL.................. 334-263-7341
Shaw Baking Company
Thunder Bay, ON 807-345-7327
Sheila's Select Gourmet Recipe
Heber City, UT 800-516-7286
Sheryl's Chocolate Creations
Hicksville, NY 888-882-2462
Siljans Crispy Cup Company
Calgary, AB....................... 403-275-0135
Silver Tray Cookies
Fort Lauderdale, FL 305-883-0800
Simit + Smith
Ridgefield, NJ.................... 201-699-0320
Simon Hubig Company
New Orleans, LA 504-945-2181
Sinbad Sweets
Madera, CA....................... 866-746-2232
SJR Foods
New Bedford, MA 617-500-4516
Slingshot Foods
San Francisco, CA 415-423-2444
Smart Baking Co.
Sanford, FL....................... 407-915-5519
Smith's Bakery
Hattiesburg, MS 601-288-7000
Smoak's Bakery & Catering Service
Augusta, GA 706-738-1792
Solana Beach Baking Company
Carlsbad, CA..................... 760-444-9800
Soloman Baking Company
Denver, CO 303-371-2777
Sophia Foods
Brooklyn, NY 718-272-1110
Southern Season
Chapel Hill, NC 877-929-7133
Southwest Foods
Tyler, TX......................... 888-937-3776
Spanish Gardens Food Manufacturing
Kansas City, KS 913-831-4242
Specialty Bakers
Marysville, PA 800-233-0778
Specialty Food Association
New York, NY 646-878-0301
Spilke's Baking Company
Moosic, PA 570-457-2400
Spohrers Bakeries
Collingdale, PA................... 610-532-9959
Spring Glen Fresh Foods
Ephrata, PA 800-641-2853
St Armands Baking Co
Bradenton, FL.................... 941-753-7494
St-Germain Bakery
Honolulu, HI..................... 808-847-5396
St. Amour Inc/French Cookies
Costa Mesa, CA 714-754-1900
Stacy's Pita Chip Co
Randolph, MA 888-332-4477
Standard Bakery Inc
Kealakekua, HI................... 808-322-3688
Stangl's Bakery
Ambridge, PA 724-266-5675
Starbucks
Seattle, WA 800-782-7282
Stauffer's
Cuba, NY 585-968-2700
Stella D'oro
Charlotte, NC 800-995-2623
Sterling Foods LLC
San Antonio, TX.................. 210-490-1669

Steve's Authentic Key Lime Pies
Brooklyn, NY 888-450-5463
Steve's Mom
Bronx, NY 800-362-4545
Sticky Fingers Bakeries
Spokane, WA 800-458-5826
Strauss Bakery
Brooklyn, NY 718-851-7728
Strossner's Bakery & Cafe
Greenville, SC 864-233-2990
Sugar Bowl Bakery
Hayward, CA 888-688-1380
Summerfield Foods
Santa Rosa, CA 707-579-3938
Sun Pac Foods
Brampton, ON 905-792-2700
Sunset Specialty Foods
Lake Arrowhead, CA 909-337-7643
Super Mom's LLC
St Paul Park, MN 800-944-7276
Superior Bakery Inc
N Grosvenordale, CT 860-923-9555
Superior Cake Products
Southbridge, MA 508-764-3276
Svenhard's Swedish Bakery Inc
Oakland, CA 800-705-3379
Swatt Baking Co
Olean, NY 800-370-6656
Sweet Endings Inc
West Palm Beach, FL 888-635-1177
Sweet Gallery Exclusive Pastry
Toronto, ON 416-766-0289
Sweet Life Enterprises
Santa Ana, CA 714-256-8900
Sweet Sams Baking Corp
Bronx, NY 718-822-0599
Sweetery
Anderson, SC 800-752-1188
T. Marzetti Company
Westerville, OH 800-999-1835
Table De France
Ontario, CA 909-923-5205
Tasty Mix Quality Foods
Brooklyn, NY 718-855-7680
Teeny Foods Inc
Portland, OR 503-252-3006
Tennessee Bun Company
Nashville, TN 888-486-2867
Terranettis Italian Bakery
Mechanicsburg, PA 717-697-5434
Teti Bakery
Etobicoke, ON 800-465-0123
Texas Crumb & Food Products
Farmers Branch, TX 800-522-7862
The Great San Saba River Pecan Company
San Saba, TX 800-621-8121
The Konery
Brooklyn, NY 917-750-4147
The Pillsbury Company
Chelsea, MA 800-370-7834
Thyme Garden Herb Co
Alsea, OR 800-482-4372
Tom Cat Bakery Inc
Queens, NY 718-786-7659
Tomanetti Food Products Inc
Oakmont, PA 800-875-3040
Tomaro's Bakery
Clarksburg, WV 304-622-0691
Traditional Baking Inc
Bloomington, CA 909-877-8471
Treasure Foods
West Valley, UT 801-974-0911
Tripoli Bakery Inc
Lawrence, MA 978-682-7754
Troppers
Santa Barbara, CA 805-969-4054
Trumps Food Interest
Vancouver, BC 604-732-8473
Turano Baking
Berwyn, IL 708-788-9220
Turnbull Bakeries
New Orleans, LA 504-581-5383
Tuscan Bakery
Portland, OR 800-887-2261
Twin City Bagels
South St Paul, MN 651-554-0200
Twin Marquis
Brooklyn, NY 800-367-6868
Two Chefs on a Roll
Carson, CA 800-842-3025
ULDO USA
Lexington, MA 781-860-7800
Ultimate Biscotti
Eugene, OR 541-344-8220
Uncle Andy's Cafe
South Portland, ME 207-799-7199
Uncle Ralph's Cookies
Frederick, MD 800-422-0626
United Noodle Manufacturing Company
Salt Lake City, UT 801-485-0951
United Pies Of Elkhart Inc
Elkhart, IN 574-294-3419
Upper Crust Bakery USA
Phoenix, AZ 602-255-0464
Upper Crust Biscotti
Pismo Beach, CA 866-972-6879
Uptown Bakers
Hyattsville, MD 301-864-1500
Valley Bakery
Burnaby, BC 604-291-0674
Valley Lahvosh
Fresno, CA 800-480-2704
Vallos Baking Co
Bethlehem, PA 610-866-1012
Van de Kamps
Peoria, IL 800-798-3318
Vande Walle's Candies Inc
Appleton, WI 800-738-1020
Venus Wafers Inc
Hingham, MA 800-545-4538
Verdant Kitchen
Norcross, GA 912-349-2958
Vie De France Yamazaki Inc
Vienna, VA 800-446-4404
Vigneri Chocolate Inc.
Rochester, NY 877-844-6374
Vocatura Bakery Inc
Norwich, CT 860-887-2220
Wally Biscotti
Denver, CO 866-659-2559
Wedding Cake Studio
Williamsfield, OH 440-667-1765
Wedemeyer's Bakery
S San Francisco, CA 650-873-1000
Wegmans Food Markets Inc.
Rochester, NY 800-934-6267
WEIS Markets Inc.
Sunbury, PA 866-999-9347
Wendysue & Tobey's
Gardena, CA 310-516-9705
Wenger's Bakery
Reading, PA 610-372-6545
Wenner Bakery
Bayport, NY 800-869-6262
Wenzel's Bakery
Tamaqua, PA 570-668-2360
Weston Foods
Etobicoke, ON 416-252-7323
Wheat Montana Farms Inc
Three Forks, MT 800-535-2798
Whole Earth Bakery
New York, NY 212-677-7597
Wick's Pies Inc
Winchester, IN 800-642-5880
Widoffs Modern Bakery
Worcester, MA 508-752-7200
William Poll Inc
New York, NY 800-993-7655
Williamsburg Chocolatier
Williamsburg, VA 757-253-1474
Willmar Cookie & Nut Company
Willmar, MN 800-426-7845
Willmark Sales Company
Brooklyn, NY 718-388-7141
Wisconsin Cheeseman
Madison, WI 800-693-0834
Wolferman's
Medford, OR 800-798-6241
Wonton Food
Brooklyn, NY 800-776-8889
Woodie Pie Company
Artesia, NM 575-746-2132
World Of Chantilly
Brooklyn, NY 718-859-1110
Wow! Factor Desserts
Sherwood Park, AB 800-604-2253
Wuollet Bakery
Minneapolis, MN 612-922-4341
Y Z Enterprises Inc
Maumee, OH 800-736-8779
Ya-Hoo Baking Co
Sherman, TX 888-869-2466
Young's Bakery
Uniontown, PA 724-437-6361
Zoelsmann's Bakery & Deli
Pueblo, CO 719-543-0407

Bread Crumbs & Croutons

H&S Edible Products Corporation
Mount Vernon, NY 800-253-3364
Just Off Melrose
Palm Springs, CA 760-320-7414
Lecoq Cuisine Corp
Bridgeport, CT 203-334-1010
Lesley Stowe Fine Foods
Richmond, BC 604-238-2180
Mignardise
Chambly, QC 450-447-0777
Olivia's Croutons
New Haven, VT 888-425-3080
Quality Bakery Products
Houston, TX 866-449-4977
Quality Croutons
Chicago, IL 800-334-2796
Rothbury Farms
Grand Rapids, MI 877-684-2879
Sugar Foods Corp
New York, NY
Sun Pac Foods
Brampton, ON 905-792-2700

Bread Crumbs

4C Foods Corp
Brooklyn, NY 718-272-4242
Colonna Brothers Inc
North Bergen, NJ 201-864-1115
Duval Bakery Products
Jacksonville, FL 904-354-7878
Lakeview Bakery
Calgary, AB 403-246-6127
Newly Weds Foods Inc
Chicago, IL 800-621-7521
Quality Bakery Products
Houston, TX 866-449-4977
Richmond Baking Co
Richmond, IN 765-962-8535
Sun Pac Foods
Brampton, ON 905-792-2700
Texas Crumb & Food Products
Farmers Branch, TX 800-522-7862
Turnbull Bakeries
New Orleans, LA 504-581-5383
Vigo Importing Co
Tampa, FL 800-282-4130

Croutons

Ace Bakery
North York, ON 800-443-7929
Aladdin Bakers
Brooklyn, NY 718-499-1818
Eco-Planet Cookies
Santa Monica, CA 310-829-9050
Icco Cheese Co
Orangeburg, NY 845-680-2436
Just Off Melrose
Palm Springs, CA 760-320-7414
Lakeview Bakery
Calgary, AB 403-246-6127
Live A Little Gourmet Foods
Oakland, CA 888-744-2300
Natural Food Mill
Corona, CA 800-797-5090
Olivia's Croutons
New Haven, VT 888-425-3080
Progresso Quality Foods
Vineland, NJ 856-691-1565
Quality Bakery Products
Houston, TX 866-449-4977
Quality Croutons
Chicago, IL 800-334-2796
Rothbury Farms
Grand Rapids, MI 877-684-2879
San Francisco French Bread
Oakland, CA 510-729-6232
Sugar Foods Corp
Sun Valley, CA 818-768-7900
Sun Pac Foods
Brampton, ON 905-792-2700

Crumbs

Aladdin Bakers
Brooklyn, NY 718-499-1818
Eco-Planet Cookies
Santa Monica, CA 310-829-9050

Icco Cheese Co
Orangeburg, NY 845-680-2436
Newly Weds Foods Inc
Chicago, IL 800-621-7521
Progresso Quality Foods
Vineland, NJ 856-691-1565
Quality Bakery Products
Houston, TX 866-449-4977
Richmond Baking Co
Richmond, IN 765-962-8535
Sun Pac Foods
Brampton, ON. 905-792-2700
Texas Crumb & Food Products
Farmers Branch, TX 800-522-7862
Vigo Importing Co
Tampa, FL. 800-282-4130

Bread Sticks

Andre-Boudin Bakeries
San Francisco, CA 415-882-1849
Bake Crafters Food Company
McDonald, TN 423-396-3392
Clown Global Brands
Northbrook, IL 800-323-5778
Colonna Brothers Inc
North Bergen, NJ 201-864-1115
Dwayne Keith Brooks Company
Orangevale, CA 916-988-1030
Falcone's Cookie Land LTD
Brooklyn, NY 718-236-4200
Good Groceries
Brooklyn, NY 347-853-7462
John W Macy's Cheesesticks Inc
Elmwood Park, NJ 800-643-0573
Kemach Food Products
Brooklyn, NY 718-272-5655
La Piccolina
Decatur, GA 800-626-1624
Nature's Hilights
Chico, CA 800-313-6454
Real Food Marketing
Kansas City, MO. 816-221-4100
Stella D'oro
Charlotte, NC 800-995-2623
Teeny Foods Inc
Portland, OR 503-252-3006
Tomanetti Food Products
Oakmont, PA. 800-875-3040
Tropical Nut Fruit & Bulk Cndy
Lithia Springs, GA 800-544-3762
Turnbull Bakeries
New Orleans, LA 504-581-5383

Garlic

Djerdan Burek Corp
South Hackensack, NJ 888-462-8735

Sesame

Nature's Legacy Inc.
Hudson, MI. 517-448-2050

Breads

Angelic Bakehouse
Cudahy, WI
Arctic Beverages
Winnipeg, MB. 866-503-1270
Aunt Millie's Bakeries
Fort Wayne, IN 855-755-2253
Bake Crafters Food Company
McDonald, TN 423-396-3392
BakeMark Ingredients Canada
Richmond, BC 800-665-9441
BakeryCorp
Miami, FL. 305-623-3838
Bakkavor USA
Charlotte, NC 800-842-3025
Barely Bread
Beckmann's Old World Bakery
Santa Cruz, CA. 831-423-9242
Beer Bakers Inc.
Nashville, TN 615-775-3329
Bella Chi-Cha Products
Santa Cruz, CA. 831-423-1851
Berkshire Mountain Bakery
Housatonic, MA 866-274-6124
Bien Cuit
Brooklyn, NY 718-852-0200
Bimbo Bakeries USA Inc.
Horsham, PA. 800-984-0989
Bluepoint Bakery
Denver, CO 303-298-1100
Boboli Intl. Inc.
Stockton, CA. 209-473-3507
Brazi Bites
Portland, OR. 503-303-2272
Butter Krust Baking Company
Thomasville, GA. 800-282-8093
California Lavash
Gilroy, CA. 408-846-7705
Chatila's
Salem, NH. 603-898-5459
Chella's Dutch Delicacies
Lake Oswego, OR. 800-458-3331
Clarmil Manufacturing Corp
Hayward, CA 888-252-7645
Colchester Bakery
Colchester, CT 860-537-2415
Cotton Baking Company
Alexandria, LA. 318-448-6600
Cyrils Bakery
Fort Lauderdale, FL 800-929-7457
Dole & Bailey Inc
Woburn, MA. 781-935-1234
East Balt Commissary Inc
Chicago, IL 800-621-8555
Essential Baking Co, The
Seattle, WA 206-545-3804
Flowers Baking Co
El Paso, TX 800-328-6111
Flowers Foods Inc.
Thomasville, GA. 229-226-9110
Food for Life Baking
Corona, CA. 800-797-5090
Franklin Baking Co.
Goldsboro, NC 919-735-0344
French Meadow Bakery & Cafe
Minneapolis, MN 612-870-7855
Frisco Baking Co Inc
Los Angeles, CA. 323-225-6111
Fullbloom Baking Co
Newark, CA 800-201-9909
GAF Seelig Inc
Flushing, NY. 718-899-5000
Gold Coast Baking Co Inc
Santa Ana, CA 714-545-2253
Goldilocks USA
Hayward, CA 510-476-0700
Grace Baking Company
Richmond, CA 510-231-7200
Granello Bakery
Las Vegas, NV. 702-361-0311
Greenhills Irish Bakery
Dorchester Ctr, MA 617-825-8187
H&S Bakery
Baltimore, MD 800-959-7655
Haby's Alsatian Bakery
Castroville, TX 830-538-2118
Happy Campers
Portland, OR
Holsum Bakery Inc
Phoenix, AZ 602-252-2351
Hybread
Marina del Ray, CA 310-312-1200
Jacquet Bakery
New York, NY
Julian Bakery
Oceanside, CA 760-721-5200
Kim and Jake's
Boulder, CO 303-499-9126
King's Hawaiian Holding Co Inc.
Torrance, CA. 877-695-4227
Klosterman Baking Co.
Cincinnati, OH 877-301-1004
Koffee Kup Bakery
Burlington, VT 802-863-2696
La Brea Bakery Inc
San Leandro, CA. 855-427-9982
Lakeview Bakery
Calgary, AB. 403-246-6127
Lavoi Corporation
Atlanta, GA. 404-325-1016
Love's Bakery
Honolulu, HI. 808-841-0397
Martins Famous Pastry Shoppe
Chambersburg, PA 800-548-1200
Metropolitan Bakery
Philadelphia, PA. 877-412-7323
Metropolitan Baking Co
Hamtramck, MI. 313-875-7246
Mikey's
. 480-696-2483
Morabito Baking Co Inc
Norristown, PA 800-525-7747
Morse's Sauerkraut
Waldoboro, ME. 866-832-5569
Mrs Baird's
Horsham, PA. 800-984-0989
Natural Food Mill
Corona, CA. 800-797-5090
Natural Ovens Bakery Inc
Manitowoc, WI. 800-558-3535
Naturally Delicious Inc
Oakland Park, FL 888-221-7352
Nature's Hilights
Chico, CA. 800-313-6454
Nema Food Distribution
Fairfield, NJ 973-256-4415
Neuman Bakery Specialties
Addison, IL. 800-253-5298
New Horizon Foods
Union City, CA 510-489-8600
O'Doughs
Toronto, ON 855-636-8447
Oasis Breads
Escondido, CA 760-747-7390
Old World Bakery
Cincinnati, OH 513-931-1411
One Degree Organic Foods
Abbotsford, BC. 855-834-2642
Orlando Baking Co
Cleveland, OH 800-362-5504
Orwasher's Bakery
New York, NY 212-288-6569
Pepperidge Farm Inc.
Norwalk, CT. 888-737-7374
Plehn's Bakery Inc
Louisville, KY 502-896-4438
Rockland Bakery
Nanuet, NY. 800-734-4376
Royal Caribbean Bakery
Mt Vernon, NY 888-818-0971
Sanborn Sourdough Bakery
Las Vegas, NV 702-795-1030
Sandors Bakeries
Miami, FL. 305-642-8484
Simit + Smith
Ridgefield, NJ. 201-699-0320
Southern Baking
Greer, SC. 864-627-1380
Spelt Right Foods, LLC
Brooklyn, NY 877-773-5801
Sterling Foods LLC
San Antonio, TX. 210-490-1669
Superior Baking Co
Brockton, MA. 800-696-2253
T. Marzetti Company
Westerville, OH. 800-999-1835
Taste Maker Foods
Memphis, TN 800-467-1407
The Lancaster Food Company
Lancaster, PA
The Perfect Pita
Springfield, VA. 703-644-0004
Turano Baking
Berwyn, IL 708-788-9220
Upper Crust Bakery USA
Phoenix, AZ 602-255-0464
Vermont Bread Co
Brattleboro, VT. 802-254-4600
Vie De France Yamazaki Inc
Vienna, VA 800-446-4404
Whipped Pastry Boutique
Brooklyn, NY 718-858-8088
Wuollet Bakery
Minneapolis, MN 612-922-4341

Bagels

Ace Bakery
North York, ON. 800-443-7929
Aladdin Bakers
Brooklyn, NY 718-499-1818
Alpha Baking Company
South Bend, IN 773-261-6000
Amoroso's Baking Co
Bellmawr, NJ. 215-471-4740
Andre-Boudin Bakeries
San Francisco, CA 415-882-1849
Awrey Bakeries
Livonia, MI. 800-950-2253
Bagel Factory
Los Angeles, CA. 310-836-9865
Bagel Guys
Brooklyn, NY 718-222-4361

Bagelworks
New York, NY 212-744-6444
Bake Crafters Food Company
McDonald, TN 423-396-3392
Barely Bread
BBU Bakeries
Horsham, PA 800-984-0989
Better Bagel Bakery
Sarasota, FL 941-924-0393
Boca Bagelworks
Boca Raton, FL....................561-852-8992
Brooklyn Bagel Company
Staten Island, NY 800-349-3055
Buckhead Gourmet
Atlanta, GA....................800-673-6338
Bylada Foods
Moonachie, NJ 201-933-7474
California Smart Foods
San Francisco, CA 415-826-0449
Century Blends LLC
Hunt Valley, MD....................410-771-6606
Chatila's
Salem, NH....................603-898-5459
Dakota Brands Intl
Jamestown, ND....................800-844-5073
Enjoy Life Foods
Chicago, IL....................888-503-6569
Felix Roma & Son Inc
Endicott, NY....................607-748-3336
Fleischer's Bagels
Macedon, NY 315-986-9999
French Meadow Bakery & Cafe
Minneapolis, MN 612-870-7855
Global Bakeries Inc
Pacoima, CA....................818-896-0525
Greater Knead, The
Bensalem, PA 267-522-8523
H&S Bakery
Baltimore, MD 800-959-7655
Harlan Bakeries
Avon, IN 800-435-2738
Lakeview Bakery
Calgary, AB....................403-246-6127
Lenchner Bakery
Concord, ON....................905-738-8811
Maui Bagel
Kahului, HI....................808-270-7561
O'Doughs
Toronto, ON 855-636-8447
Otis Spunkmeyer
Brockport, NY 855-427-9982
Ottenberg's Bakers
Sykesville, MD....................800-334-7264
Pan-O-Gold Baking Co.
St. Cloud, MN....................800-444-7005
Petrofsky's Bakery Products
Chesterfield, MO 636-519-1613
Positively 3rd St Bakery
Duluth, MN....................218-724-8619
Prairie Malt
Biggar, SK....................306-948-3500
Quality Naturally Foods
City Of Industry, CA....................888-498-6986
Rudi's Organic Bakery
Boulder, CO 877-293-0876
Schwebel Baking Co.
Youngstown, OH....................800-860-2867
SJR Foods
New Bedford, MA 617-500-4516
Spelt Right Foods, LLC
Brooklyn, NY 877-773-5801
Twin City Bagels
South St Paul, MN 651-554-0200
Ultimate Bagel
Santa Barbara, CA 805-845-2511
Wenner Bakery
Bayport, NY 800-869-6262
Western Bagel Baking Corp
Van Nuys, CA....................818-786-5847

Fresh

Bagel Guys
Brooklyn, NY 718-222-4361
Bantam Bagels
New York, NY 646-852-6320
Felix Roma & Son Inc
Endicott, NY....................607-748-3336
Fleischer's Bagels
Macedon, NY 315-986-9999
Harlan Bakeries
Avon, IN 800-435-2738
Rockland Bakery
Nanuet, NY....................800-734-4376
Russ & Daughters
New York, NY 800-787-7229
Western Bagel Baking Corp
Van Nuys, CA....................818-786-5847

Frozen

Aladdin Bakers
Brooklyn, NY 718-499-1818
Andre-Boudin Bakeries
San Francisco, CA 415-882-1849
Awrey Bakeries
Livonia, MI....................800-950-2253
Brooklyn Bagel Company
Staten Island, NY 800-349-3055
Bylada Foods
Moonachie, NJ 201-933-7474
Fleischer's Bagels
Macedon, NY 315-986-9999
Guttenplan's Frozen Dough
Middletown, NJ 888-422-4357
Harlan Bakeries
Avon, IN 800-435-2738
Petrofsky's Bakery Products
Chesterfield, MO 636-519-1613
Quality Naturally Foods
City Of Industry, CA....................888-498-6986
Wenner Bakery
Bayport, NY 800-869-6262
Western Bagel Baking Corp
Van Nuys, CA....................818-786-5847

Baguettes

Ace Bakery
North York, ON....................800-443-7929
Epi De France Bakery
Atlanta, GA....................800-325-1014
Frisco Baking Co Inc
Los Angeles, CA....................323-225-6111
Julian's Recipe
Brooklyn, NY 888-640-8880
Kosher French Baguettes
Brooklyn, NY 718-633-4994
Lavoi Corporation
Atlanta, GA....................404-325-1016
Tom Cat Bakery Inc
Queens, NY....................718-786-7659

Bialys

Harlan Bakeries
Avon, IN 800-435-2738
Russ & Daughters
New York, NY 800-787-7229

Biscuits

American Vintage Wine Biscuits
Long Island City, NY 718-361-1003
Awrey Bakeries
Livonia, MI....................800-950-2253
Bake Crafters Food Company
McDonald, TN 423-396-3392
Baker Boy Bake Shop Inc
Dickinson, ND 800-437-2008
Bama Foods LTD
Tulsa, OK 800-756-2262
Bluechip Group
Salt Lake City, UT 800-878-0099
Borinquen Biscuit Corporation
Yauco, PR....................787-856-3030
Bremner Biscuit Company
Denver, CO....................866-972-6879
Bridgford Foods Corp
Anaheim, CA 800-527-2105
Buonitalia
New York, NY 212-633-9090
Byrd Cookie
Savannah, GA....................800-291-2973
Callie's Charleston Biscuits
North Charleston, SC 843-577-1198
Chelsea Flower Market
New York, NY 888-727-7887
Chelsea Milling Co.
Chelsea, MI....................800-727-2460
Chex Finer Foods Inc
Mansfield, MA 800-227-8114
Damascus Bakery
Brooklyn, NY 718-855-1456
Del's Pastry
Toronto, ON 800-461-0663
Di Camillo Baking Co
Niagara Falls, NY....................800-634-4363
Ener-G Foods
Seattle, WA 800-331-5222
Falcone's Cookie Land LTD
Brooklyn, NY 718-236-4200
Fresh Start Bakeries
Brea, CA 714-256-8900
Frisco Baking Co Inc
Los Angeles, CA....................323-225-6111
Grebe's Bakery
Milwaukee, WI 800-833-3158
GWB Foods Corporation
Brooklyn, NY 877-977-7610
Heltzman Bakery
Louisville, KY 502-447-3515
Hostess Brands
Kansas City, MO....................816-701-4600
Keebler Company
Battlecreek, MI....................800-962-1413
Le Chef Bakery
Montebello, CA 323-888-2929
Lone Star Bakery
Round Rock, TX....................512-255-7268
Mason Dixie Biscuit Co.
Washington, DC 202-880-2315
Merlino Italian Baking Company
Kent, WA....................800-800-9490
Mom's Bakery
Sherman, TX....................903-893-7585
Pacific Ocean Produce
Santa Cruz, CA....................831-423-2654
Pett Spice Products Inc
Atlanta, GA....................404-691-5235
Pioneer Frozen Foods
Duncanville, TX 972-298-4281
Purity Factories
St. John's, NL 800-563-3411
Quality Naturally Foods
City Of Industry, CA....................888-498-6986
Rovira Biscuit Corporation
Ponce, PR....................787-844-8585
Royal Home Bakery
Newmarket, ON 905-715-7044
Schulze & Burch Biscuit Co
Chicago, IL....................773-927-6622
Stella D'oro
Charlotte, NC 800-995-2623
Sterling Foods LLC
San Antonio, TX....................210-490-1669
Superior Bakery Inc
N Grosvenordale, CT 860-923-9555
Ultimate Biscotti
Eugene, OR....................541-344-8220
Wedemeyer's Bakery
S San Francisco, CA....................650-873-1000
Y Z Enterprises Inc
Maumee, OH....................800-736-8779

Fresh

Automatic Rolls Of New Jersey
Edison, NJ....................877-222-2867
Ener-G Foods
Seattle, WA....................800-331-5222
Mrs. Kavanagh's English Muffins
Rumford, RI 800-556-7216
New Bakery Company of Ohio
Zanesville, OH 800-848-9845
Quinzani Bakery
Boston, MA....................800-999-1062

Frozen

Awrey Bakeries
Livonia, MI....................800-950-2253
Bake Crafters Food Company
McDonald, TN 423-396-3392
Bama Foods LTD
Tulsa, OK 800-756-2262
Callie's Charleston Biscuits
North Charleston, SC 843-577-1198
Dynamic Foods
Lubbock, TX....................806-723-5600
Fresh Start Bakeries
Brea, CA 714-256-8900
Lone Star Bakery
Round Rock, TX....................512-255-7268
Pacific Ocean Produce
Santa Cruz, CA....................831-423-2654

Brown

Burnham & Morrill Co
Portland, ME....................800-813-2165
Naji's Pita Gourmet Restaurant
Birmingham, AL..................205-945-6001
Terranettis Italian Bakery
Mechanicsburg, PA................717-697-5434

Buns

Ace Bakery
North York, ON..................800-443-7929
Alois J Binder Bakery
New Orleans, LA..................504-947-1111
Aryzta
Los Angeles, CA..................855-427-9982
Athens Baking Company
Fresno, CA......................800-775-2867
Aunt Millie's Bakeries
Fort Wayne, IN..................855-755-2253
Baldinger Baking Co
St Paul, MN......................651-224-5761
Best Harvest Bakeries
Kansas City, KS..................800-811-5715
Bimbo Bakeries USA Inc.
Horsham, PA......................800-984-0989
Bread Box Cafe
Astoria, NY......................718-389-9703
Calgary Italian Bakery
Calgary, AB......................800-661-6868
Caribbean Food Delights Inc
Tappan, NY......................845-398-3000
Colombo Bakery
Sacramento, CA..................916-648-1011
Country Club Bakery
Fairmont, WV....................304-363-5690
Dimpflmeier Bakery
Toronto, ON......................800-268-2421
El Peto Products
Cambridge, ON...................800-387-4064
European Bakers
Tucker, GA......................770-723-6180
Fancy Lebanese Bakery
Halifax, NS......................902-429-0400
Flowers Baking Co
Birmingham, AL..................205-252-1161
Flowers Baking Co
Tuscaloosa, AL...................205-752-5586
Food for Life Baking
Corona, CA......................800-797-5090
Frisco Baking Co Inc
Los Angeles, CA..................323-225-6111
Gadoua Bakery
Napierville, QC...................800-661-7246
Gold Coast Bakeries
Santa Ana, CA...................714-545-2253
Gold Coast Baking Co Inc
Santa Ana, CA...................714-545-2253
H&S Bakery
Baltimore, MD...................800-959-7655
Harting's Bakery
Bowmansville, PA.................717-445-5644
Holsum Bakery Inc
Phoenix, AZ.....................602-252-2351
Hostess Brands
Kansas City, MO.................816-701-4600
J.P. Sunrise Bakery
Edmonton, AB....................780-454-5797
Kim and Jake's
Boulder, CO.....................303-499-9126
Klosterman Baking Co.
Cincinnati, OH...................877-301-1004
Lakeview Bakery
Calgary, AB......................403-246-6127
Lavoi Corporation
Atlanta, GA......................404-325-1016
Metropolitan Baking Co
Hamtramck, MI...................313-875-7246
Mrs Baird's
Horsham, PA.....................800-984-0989
Nardi Breads
South Windsor, CT...............860-289-5458
Natural Food Mill
Corona, CA......................800-797-5090
New Horizons Baking Co
Fremont, IN......................260-495-7055
O'Doughs
Toronto, ON......................855-636-8447
Ottenberg's Bakers
Sykesville, MD...................800-334-7264
Ozark Empire
Rogers, AR......................479-636-3313
Ozery Bakery
Vaughan, ON.....................888-556-5560
Pan-O-Gold Baking Co.
St. Cloud, MN....................800-444-7005
Pepperidge Farm Inc.
Norwalk, CT.....................888-737-7374
Red Plate Foods
Bend, OR........................541-550-7676
Rotella's Italian Bakery Inc.
La Vista, NE.....................402-592-6600
Royal Home Bakery
Newmarket, ON...................905-715-7044
Rudi's Organic Bakery
Boulder, CO.....................877-293-0876
Schwan's Food Service Inc.
Marshall, MN....................877-302-7426
Schwebel Baking Co.
Youngstown, OH..................800-860-2867
Smart Baking Co.
Sanford, FL......................407-915-5519
Tennessee Bun Company
Nashville, TN....................888-486-2867
Twin Marquis
Brooklyn, NY.....................800-367-6868
Wenger's Bakery
Reading, PA.....................610-372-6545

Sticky

Bluepoint Bakery
Denver, CO......................303-298-1100
Cinnamon Bakery
Braintree, MA....................800-886-2867
Keller's Bakery
Lafayette, LA....................337-235-1568

Challah

Atlanta Bread Co.
Smyrna, GA......................800-398-3728
Orwasher's Bakery
New York, NY....................212-288-6569

Cinnamon Toast

Happy Campers
Portland, OR
Loghouse Foods
Minneapolis, MN.................763-546-8395

Corn

Bake Crafters Food Company
McDonald, TN....................423-396-3392
Dynamic Foods
Lubbock, TX.....................806-723-5600
Legacy Bakehouse
Waukesha, WI....................800-967-2447
Sara Lee Frozen Bakery
Kings Mountain, NC...............800-323-7117
Tova Industries LLC
Louisville, KY....................888-532-8682

Croissants

Andre-Boudin Bakeries
San Francisco, CA................415-882-1849
Bake Crafters Food Company
McDonald, TN....................423-396-3392
BakeMark Canada
Laval, QC.......................800-361-4998
Bluepoint Bakery
Denver, CO......................303-298-1100
California Smart Foods
San Francisco, CA................415-826-0449
Edner Corporation
Hayward, CA.....................510-441-8504
GAF Seelig Inc
Flushing, NY.....................718-899-5000
Galaxy Desserts
Richmond, CA....................800-225-3523
Global Bakeries Inc
Pacoima, CA.....................818-896-0525
Nikola's Foods
Bloomington, MN.................888-645-6527
Sara Lee Frozen Bakery
Kings Mountain, NC...............800-323-7117
Vie De France Yamazaki Inc
Vienna, VA......................800-446-4404

English Muffins

Aryzta
Los Angeles, CA..................855-427-9982
Aunt Millie's Bakeries
Fort Wayne, IN...................855-755-2253
Bimbo Bakeries USA Inc.
Horsham, PA.....................800-984-0989
Food for Life Baking
Corona, CA......................800-797-5090
Fresh Start Bakeries
Brea, CA.......................714-256-8900
H&S Bakery
Baltimore, MD...................800-959-7655
Homestead Baking Co
Rumford, RI.....................800-556-7216
Meyer's Bakeries
Casa Grande, AZ.................800-528-5770
Mikey's
Scottsdale, AZ
Mikey's
...............................480-696-2483
Mrs. Kavanagh's English Muffins
Rumford, RI.....................800-556-7216
Natural Food Mill
Corona, CA......................800-797-5090
New Horizons Baking Co
Fremont, IN......................260-495-7055
Oakrun Farm Bakery
Ancaster, ON.....................800-263-6422
Ottenberg's Bakers
Sykesville, MD...................800-334-7264
Rudi's Organic Bakery
Boulder, CO.....................877-293-0876
Weston Foods
Etobicoke, ON...................416-252-7323
Wolferman's
Medford, OR.....................800-798-6241

Flat

Ak Mak Bakeries
Sanger, CA......................559-875-5511
Aladdin Bakers
Brooklyn, NY....................718-499-1818
American Flatbread
Pittsfield, NH....................603-435-5119
California Lavash
Gilroy, CA.......................408-846-7705
Di Camillo Baking Co
Niagara Falls, NY.................800-634-4363
Falcone's Cookie Land LTD
Brooklyn, NY....................718-236-4200
Flatout Inc
Saline, MI.......................866-944-5445
Good Wives
Wilmington, MA..................800-521-8160
Just Off Melrose
Palm Springs, CA.................760-320-7414
Kemach Food Products
Brooklyn, NY....................718-272-5655
Klosterman Baking Co.
Cincinnati, OH...................877-301-1004
Kronos
Glendale Heights, IL...............800-621-0099
Molinaro's Fine Italian Foods Ltd.
Mississauga, ON..................905-281-0352
Nita Crisp Crackers LLC
Fort Collins, CO..................866-493-4609
Nu-World Amaranth Inc
Naperville, IL....................630-369-6851
O'Doughs
Toronto, ON.....................855-636-8447
Old London Foods
Yadkinville, NC
Real Food Marketing
Kansas City, MO.................816-221-4100
Rudolph's Specialty Bakery
Toronto, ON.....................800-268-1589
Rustic Bakery Inc.
San Rafael, CA...................415-479-5600
Rustic Crust Inc
Pittsfield, NH....................603-435-5119
Schwebel Baking Co.
Youngstown, OH..................800-860-2867
Sonoma Flatbreads
Columbus, OH
Teeny Foods Inc
Portland, OR.....................503-252-3006
Teti Bakery
Etobicoke, ON...................800-465-0123
Valley Lahvosh
Fresno, CA......................800-480-2704
Vicky's Artisan Bakery
Markham, ON....................905-944-0940

Focaccia

Company	Location	Phone
Atlanta Bread Co.	Smyrna, GA	800-398-3728
Clarmil Manufacturing Corp	Hayward, CA	888-252-7645
Colors Gourmet Pizza	Vista, CA	760-597-1400
Epi De France Bakery	Atlanta, GA	800-325-1014
Molinaro's Fine Italian Foods Ltd.	Mississauga, ON	905-281-0352
Real Food Marketing	Kansas City, MO	816-221-4100
Teeny Foods Inc	Portland, OR	503-252-3006
Tomanetti Food Products Inc	Oakmont, PA	800-875-3040

French

Company	Location	Phone
Atlanta Bread Co.	Smyrna, GA	800-398-3728
Frisco Baking Co Inc	Los Angeles, CA	323-225-6111
Galasso's Bakery	Mira Loma, CA	951-360-1211
Gold Coast Bakeries	Santa Ana, CA	714-545-2253
Hawaii Star Bakery	Honolulu, HI	808-841-3602
Le Donne Brothers Bakery	Roseto, PA	610-588-0423
Leidenheimer Baking Co	New Orleans, LA	800-259-9099
Metropolitan Baking Co	Hamtramck, MI	313-875-7246
Orlando Baking Co	Cleveland, OH	800-362-5504
Piemonte Bakery Co	Rockford, IL	815-962-4833
Quinzani Bakery	Boston, MA	800-999-1062
The Pillsbury Company	Chelsea, MA	800-370-7834
Tom Cat Bakery Inc	Queens, NY	718-786-7659

Fresh

Company	Location	Phone
Ace Bakery	North York, ON	800-443-7929
Alfred & Sam's Italian Bakery	Lancaster, PA	717-392-6311
Alois J Binder Bakery	New Orleans, LA	504-947-1111
Alpha Baking Company	South Bend, IN	773-261-6000
Amoroso's Baking Co	Bellmawr, NJ	215-471-4740
Andre-Boudin Bakeries	San Francisco, CA	415-882-1849
Baldinger Baking Co	St Paul, MN	651-224-5761
Brooklyn Baking Company	Waterbury, CT	203-574-9198
Casino Bakery	Tampa, FL	813-242-0311
Chicago Pastry	Bloomingdale, IL	630-529-6391
Cole's Quality Foods	Grand Rapids, MI	616-975-0081
Colombo Bakery	Sacramento, CA	916-648-1011
Ener-G Foods	Seattle, WA	800-331-5222
Epi De France Bakery	Atlanta, GA	800-325-1014
Father Sam's Bakery	Buffalo, NY	800-521-6719
Felix Roma & Son Inc	Endicott, NY	607-748-3336
Galasso's Bakery	Mira Loma, CA	951-360-1211
Glamorgan Bakery	Calgary, AB	403-232-2800
Gold Coast Bakeries	Santa Ana, CA	714-545-2253
Gold Standard Baking Inc	Chicago, IL	800-648-7904
Gonnella Baking Company	Schamburg, IL	800-322-8829
Harlan Bakeries	Avon, IN	800-435-2738
Highlandville Packing	Highlandville, MO	417-443-3365
Homestead Baking Co	Rumford, RI	800-556-7216
Jubelt Variety Bakeries	Litchfield, IL	217-324-5314
Kosher French Baguettes	Brooklyn, NY	718-633-4994
L & M Bakery	Riverside, NJ	888-887-1335
Landolfi's Food Products	Trenton, NJ	609-392-1830
Lanthier Bakery	Alexandria, ON	613-525-2435
Leidenheimer Baking Co	New Orleans, LA	800-259-9099
Lucerne Foods	Pleasanton, CA	877-232-4271
Multi Marques	Montreal, QC	514-934-1866
Naji's Pita Gourmet Restaurant	Birmingham, AL	205-945-6001
Natural Food Mill	Corona, CA	800-797-5090
Natural Ovens Bakery Inc	Manitowoc, WI	800-558-3535
Nevada Baking Company	Las Vegas, NV	702-384-8950
Ottenberg's Bakers	Sykesville, MD	800-334-7264
Piantedosi Baking Co Inc	Malden, MA	800-339-0080
Piemonte Bakery Co	Rockford, IL	815-962-4833
Pittsfield Rye Bakery	Pittsfield, MA	413-443-9141
Positively 3rd St Bakery	Duluth, MN	218-724-8619
Quinzani Bakery	Boston, MA	800-999-1062
Real Food Marketing	Kansas City, MO	816-221-4100
Rudi's Organic Bakery	Boulder, CO	877-293-0876
San Francisco French Bread	Oakland, CA	510-729-6232
Schwebel Baking Co.	Youngstown, OH	800-860-2867
Shaw Baking Company	Thunder Bay, ON	807-345-7327
St Armands Baking Co	Bradenton, FL	941-753-7494
Superior Bakery Inc	N Grosvenordale, CT	860-923-9555
Swatt Baking Co	Olean, NY	800-370-6656
Teeny Foods Inc	Portland, OR	503-252-3006
Terranettis Italian Bakery	Mechanicsburg, PA	717-697-5434
Weston Foods	Etobicoke, ON	416-252-7323
Wolferman's	Medford, OR	800-798-6241

Frozen

Company	Location	Phone
Ace Bakery	North York, ON	800-443-7929
Alpha Baking Company	South Bend, IN	773-261-6000
American Flatbread	Pittsfield, NH	603-435-5119
Andre-Boudin Bakeries	San Francisco, CA	415-882-1849
Awrey Bakeries	Livonia, MI	800-950-2253
Caribbean Food Delights Inc	Tappan, NY	845-398-3000
Cedarlane Foods	Carson, CA	800-826-3322
Cole's Quality Foods	Grand Rapids, MI	616-975-0081
Epi De France Bakery	Atlanta, GA	800-325-1014
Guttenplan's Frozen Dough	Middletown, NJ	888-422-4357
Harlan Bakeries	Avon, IN	800-435-2738
Leidenheimer Baking Co	New Orleans, LA	800-259-9099
New York Frozen Foods Inc	Bedford, OH	216-292-5655
Piantedosi Baking Co Inc	Malden, MA	800-339-0080
Positively 3rd St Bakery	Duluth, MN	218-724-8619
Real Food Marketing	Kansas City, MO	816-221-4100
Rhodes International Inc	Salt Lake City, UT	800-876-7333
Rubschlager Baking Corp		800-661-7246
Rudi's Organic Bakery	Boulder, CO	877-293-0876
The Pillsbury Company	Chelsea, MA	800-370-7834
Wenner Bakery	Bayport, NY	800-869-6262
Wolferman's	Medford, OR	800-798-6241

Garlic

Company	Location	Phone
Cole's Quality Foods	Grand Rapids, MI	616-975-0081
Dabruzzi's Italian Foods	Hudson, WI	715-386-3653
Landolfi's Food Products	Trenton, NJ	609-392-1830
Piemonte Bakery Co	Rockford, IL	815-962-4833
Real Food Marketing	Kansas City, MO	816-221-4100

Frozen

Company	Location	Phone
Better Baked Foods Inc	North East, PA	814-725-8778

Honey Buns

Company	Location	Phone
Maple Donuts	York, PA	800-627-5348

Italian

Company	Location	Phone
Armanino Foods of Distinction	Hayward, CA	800-255-8588
Butter Krust Baking Company	Thomasville, GA	800-282-8093
Cusano's Baking Company	Hallandale, FL	954-458-1010
Epi De France Bakery	Atlanta, GA	800-325-1014
Frisco Baking Co Inc	Los Angeles, CA	323-225-6111
Le Donne Brothers Bakery	Roseto, PA	610-588-0423
Metropolitan Baking Co	Hamtramck, MI	313-875-7246
Milano Bakery Inc	Joliet, IL	815-727-2253
Orlando Baking Co	Cleveland, OH	800-362-5504
Piemonte Bakery Co	Rockford, IL	815-962-4833
Quinzani Bakery	Boston, MA	800-999-1062
Schwebel Baking Co.	Youngstown, OH	800-860-2867
Scialo Brothers Bakery	Providence, RI	877-421-0986
Teeny Foods Inc	Portland, OR	503-252-3006
Tom Cat Bakery Inc	Queens, NY	718-786-7659
Wenner Bakery	Bayport, NY	800-869-6262

Melba Toast

Company	Location	Phone
Old London Foods	Yadkinville, NC	
Turnbull Bakeries	New Orleans, LA	504-581-5383
Turnbull Cone Baking Company	Chattanooga, TN	423-265-4551

Multi-Grain

Company	Location	Phone
Beckmann's Old World Bakery	Santa Cruz, CA	831-423-9242
French Meadow Bakery & Cafe	Minneapolis, MN	612-870-7855
Harvest Innovations	Indianola, IA	515-962-5063
Mother Nature's Goodies	Yucaipa, CA	909-795-6018

Multigrains Bread Co
Lawrence, MA 978-691-6100
Natural Food Mill
Corona, CA. 800-797-5090
Rudi's Organic Bakery
Boulder, CO 877-293-0876

Nut

L & M Bakery
Riverside, NJ. 888-887-1335

Pita

Bake Crafters Food Company
McDonald, TN 423-396-3392
Byblos Bakery
Calgary, AB. 403-250-3711
Corfu Foods Inc
Bensenville, IL 630-595-2510
Fancy Lebanese Bakery
Halifax, NS 902-429-0400
Father Sam's Bakery
Buffalo, NY. 800-521-6719
Food for Life Baking
Corona, CA. 800-797-5090
Global Bakeries Inc
Pacoima, CA. 818-896-0525
Kangaroo Brands
Omaha, NE 877-266-2472
Klosterman Baking Co.
Cincinnati, OH 877-301-1004
Konto's Foods
Patterson, NJ. 973-278-2800
Kronos
Glendale Heights, IL. 800-621-0099
Mediterranean Gyro Products
Long Island City, NY 718-786-3399
Mediterranean Pita Bakery
Edmonton, AB 780-476-6666
Naji's Pita Gourmet Restaurant
Birmingham, AL. 205-945-6001
Ozery Bakery
Vaughan, ON. 888-556-5560
Pita King Bakery
Everett, WA. 425-258-4040
Pita Products
Farmington Hills, MI 800-600-7482
Schwebel Baking Co.
Youngstown, OH. 800-860-2867
Soloman Baking Company
Denver, CO 303-371-2777
Stacy's Pita Chip Co
Randolph, MA 888-332-4477
Teeny Foods Inc
Portland, OR 503-252-3006
The Perfect Pita
Springfield, VA. 703-644-0004
Toufayan Bakeries
Ridgefield, NJ. 201-861-4131

Pumpernickel

Atlanta Bread Co.
Smyrna, GA 800-398-3728
Colchester Bakery
Colchester, CT 860-537-2415
Dimpflmeier Bakery
Toronto, ON 800-268-2421
Orwasher's Bakery
New York, NY 212-288-6569

Raisin

Clarmil Manufacturing Corp
Hayward, CA 888-252-7645
French Meadow Bakery & Cafe
Minneapolis, MN 612-870-7855
Natural Food Mill
Corona, CA. 800-797-5090
Nature's Path Foods
Blaine, WA 888-808-9505
Orwasher's Bakery
New York, NY 212-288-6569
Ottenberg's Bakers
Sykesville, MD 800-334-7264
Schwebel Baking Co.
Youngstown, OH. 800-860-2867

Reduced-Fat

Schwebel Baking Co.
Youngstown, OH. 800-860-2867

Rolls

Ace Bakery
North York, ON. 800-443-7929
Alois J Binder Bakery
New Orleans, LA. 504-947-1111
Alpha Baking Company
South Bend, IN 773-261-6000
Amoroso's Baking Co
Bellmawr, NJ. 215-471-4740
April Hill Inc
Grand Rapids, MI 616-245-0595
Atlanta Bread Co.
Smyrna, GA 800-398-3728
Aunt Millie's Bakeries
Fort Wayne, IN 855-755-2253
Automatic Rolls Of New Jersey
Edison, NJ. 877-222-2867
Awrey Bakeries
Livonia, MI. 800-950-2253
B&A Bakery
Toronto, ON 800-263-2878
Bake Rite Rolls Inc
Bensalem, PA 800-949-5623
Baker Boy Bake Shop Inc
Dickinson, ND 800-437-2008
Baker's Dozen & Cafe
Herkimer, NY 315-866-6770
Bakers of Paris
Brisbane, CA. 415-468-9100
BakeryCorp
Miami, FL. 305-623-3838
Baking Leidenheimer
New Orleans, LA 800-259-9099
Baldinger Baking Co
St Paul, MN. 651-224-5761
Basque French Bakery
Fresno, CA 559-268-7088
Beckmann's Old World Bakery
Santa Cruz, CA. 831-423-9242
Berlin Natural Bakery
Berlin, OH. 800-686-5334
Best Harvest Bakeries
Kansas City, KS 800-811-5715
Better Bagel Bakery
Sarasota, FL 941-924-0393
Bluepoint Bakery
Denver, CO 303-298-1100
Bonnie Baking Company
La Porte, IN. 219-362-4561
Busken Bakery
Cincinnati, OH 513-871-2114
Butter Krust Baking Company
Thomasville, GA. 800-282-8093
California Smart Foods
San Francisco, CA 415-826-0449
Cellone Bakery Inc
Pittsburgh, PA. 800-334-8438
Clarmil Manufacturing Corp
Hayward, CA 888-252-7645
Clyde's Delicious Donuts
Addison, IL. 630-628-6555
Cohen's Bakery
Ellenville, NY. 845-647-2200
Colombo Bakery
Sacramento, CA 916-648-1011
Country Club Bakery
Fairmont, WV. 304-363-5690
Dakota Brands Intl
Jamestown, ND. 800-844-5073
Dimpflmeier Bakery
Toronto, ON 800-268-2421
Dipaolo Baking Co Inc
Rochester, NY. 585-232-3510
Eden Vineyards Winery
Alva, FL 239-728-9463
Egypt Star Bakery Inc
Allentown, PA. 610-434-8516
Ener-G Foods
Seattle, WA. 800-331-5222
Epi De France Bakery
Atlanta, GA. 800-325-1014
Felix Roma & Son Inc
Endicott, NY. 607-748-3336
Flowers Baking Co
Tuscaloosa, AL 205-752-5586
Forty Second Street Bagel Cafe
Upland, CA. 909-949-7334
French Meadow Bakery & Cafe
Minneapolis, MN 612-870-7855
Fresh Start Bakeries
Brea, CA 714-256-8900
Galasso's Bakery
Mira Loma, CA. 951-360-1211
German Bakery at Village Corner
Stone Mountain, GA. 866-476-6443
Giant Food
Landover, MD. 888-469-4426
Global Bakeries Inc
Pacoima, CA. 818-896-0525
Gold Coast Bakeries
Santa Ana, CA 714-545-2253
Gold Medal Bakery Inc
Fall River, MA 508-674-5766
Golden Brown Bakery Inc
South Haven, MI. 269-637-3418
Grebe's Bakery
Milwaukee, WI 800-833-3158
Guttenplan's Frozen Dough
Middletown, NJ 888-422-4357
H&S Bakery
Baltimore, MD 800-959-7655
Havi Food Services Worldwide
Oak Park, IL 708-445-1700
Hawaii Star Bakery
Honolulu, HI. 808-841-3602
Heltzman Bakery
Louisville, KY 502-447-3515
Holsum Bakery Inc
Phoenix, AZ 602-252-2351
Homestead Baking Co
Rumford, RI 800-556-7216
Hostess Brands
Kansas City, MO. 816-701-4600
James Skinner Company
Omaha, NE 800-358-7428
John J. Nissen Baking Company
Brewer, ME. 207-989-7654
Julian's Recipe
Brooklyn, NY 888-640-8880
Kim and Jake's
Boulder, CO 303-499-9126
King's Hawaiian Holding Co Inc.
Torrance, CA. 877-695-4227
Klosterman Baking Co.
Cincinnati, OH 877-301-1004
Koffee Kup Bakery
Burlington, VT 802-863-2696
Lake States Yeast
Rhinelander, WI 715-369-4949
Lanthier Bakery
Alexandria, ON. 613-525-2435
Lavoi Corporation
Atlanta, GA. 404-325-1016
Leidenheimer Baking Co
New Orleans, LA 800-259-9099
Lepage Bakeries
Auburn, ME 207-783-9161
Livermore Falls Baking Company
Livermore Falls, ME. 207-897-3442
Longo's Bakery Inc
Hazleton, PA. 570-454-5825
Lucerne Foods
Pleasanton, CA 877-232-4271
Maggiora Baking Co
Richmond, CA 510-235-0274
Marshall's Biscuit Company
Westerville, OH. 251-679-6226
Martins Famous Pastry Shoppe
Chambersburg, PA 800-548-1200
Mary Ann's Baking Co Inc
Sacramento, CA 916-681-7444
Maui Bagel
Kahului, HI. 808-270-7561
Metropolitan Baking Co
Hamtramck, MI. 313-875-7246
Milano Bakery Inc
Joliet, IL 815-727-2253
Morabito Baking Co Inc
Norristown, PA 800-525-7747
Mrs Baird's
Horsham, PA. 800-984-0989
Mrs. Kavanagh's English Muffins
Rumford, RI 800-556-7216
Mt. View Bakery
Mountain View, HI 808-968-6353
Multi Marques
Montreal, QC 514-934-1866
Nevada Baking Company
Las Vegas, NV 702-384-8950
New Bakery Company of Ohio
Zanesville, OH 800-848-9845
New York Bakeries Inc
Hialeah, FL. 305-883-0790

New York Frozen Foods Inc
Bedford, OH 216-292-5655
Orlando Baking Co
Cleveland, OH 800-362-5504
Orwasher's Bakery
New York, NY 212-288-6569
Oven Ready Products
Guelph, ON. 519-767-2415
Pan-O-Gold Baking Co.
St. Cloud, MN. 800-444-7005
Pepperidge Farm Inc.
Norwalk, CT 888-737-7374
Piemonte Bakery Co
Rockford, IL 815-962-4833
Pittsfield Rye Bakery
Pittsfield, MA 413-443-9141
Portuguese Baking Company
Newark, NJ. 973-589-8875
Powers Baking Company
Miami, FL. 305-381-7000
Quinzani Bakery
Boston, MA. 800-999-1062
Roma Bakeries
Rockford, IL 815-964-6737
Rudi's Organic Bakery
Boulder, CO 877-293-0876
Ryals Bakery
Milledgeville, GA. 478-452-0321
San Francisco French Bread
Oakland, CA 510-729-6232
Schwebel Baking Co.
Youngstown, OH. 800-860-2867
Shaw Baking Company
Thunder Bay, ON 807-345-7327
Simon Hubig Company
New Orleans, LA 504-945-2181
St Armands Baking Co
Bradenton, FL. 941-753-7494
St-Germain Bakery
Honolulu, HI. 808-847-5396
Sterling Foods LLC
San Antonio, TX. 210-490-1669
Superior Bakery Inc
N Grosvenordale, CT 860-923-9555
Swatt Baking Co
Olean, NY. 800-370-6656
Terranettis Italian Bakery
Mechanicsburg, PA. 717-697-5434
Tom Cat Bakery Inc
Queens, NY. 718-786-7659
Tomaro's Bakery
Clarksburg, WV 304-622-0691
Tripoli Bakery Inc
Lawrence, MA 978-682-7754
Turano Baking
Berwyn, IL 708-788-9220
Upper Crust Bakery USA
Phoenix, AZ 602-255-0464
Valley Bakery
Burnaby, BC 604-291-0674
Vallos Baking Co
Bethlehem, PA 610-866-1012
Wedemeyer's Bakery
S San Francisco, CA. 650-873-1000
Wenner Bakery
Bayport, NY 800-869-6262
Weston Foods
Etobicoke, ON 416-252-7323
Zoelsmann's Bakery & Deli
Pueblo, CO 719-543-0407

Cinnamon

Chef's Pride Gifts LLC
Taylor, MI. 800-878-1800
Cinnamon Bakery
Braintree, MA. 800-886-2867
Clarmil Manufacturing Corp
Hayward, CA 888-252-7645
James Skinner Company
Omaha, NE 800-358-7428
Lone Star Bakery
Round Rock, TX. 512-255-7268
Lone Star Consolidated Foods Inc.
Dallas, TX. 800-658-5637
Maple Donuts
York, PA 800-627-5348
Mrs Baird's
Horsham, PA. 800-984-0989
Pacific Ocean Produce
Santa Cruz, CA. 831-423-2654
Sara Lee Frozen Bakery
Kings Mountain, NC. 800-323-7117
Schwan's Food Service Inc.
Marshall, MN 877-302-7426
Svenhard's Swedish Bakery Inc
Oakland, CA. 800-705-3379

Fresh

Best Harvest Bakeries
Kansas City, KS 800-811-5715
Felix Roma & Son Inc
Endicott, NY. 607-748-3336
Galasso's Bakery
Mira Loma, CA. 951-360-1211
Homestead Baking Co
Rumford, RI 800-556-7216
Lanthier Bakery
Alexandria, ON. 613-525-2435
Leidenheimer Baking Co
New Orleans, LA 800-259-9099
Lucerne Foods
Pleasanton, CA 877-232-4271
Multi Marques
Montreal, QC 514-934-1866
New York Frozen Foods Inc
Bedford, OH 216-292-5655
Ottenberg's Bakers
Sykesville, MD 800-334-7264
Quinzani Bakery
Boston, MA. 800-999-1062
Schwebel Baking Co.
Youngstown, OH. 800-860-2867
Shaw Baking Company
Thunder Bay, ON 807-345-7327
Terranettis Italian Bakery
Mechanicsburg, PA. 717-697-5434
Weston Foods
Etobicoke, ON 416-252-7323

Frozen

Awrey Bakeries
Livonia, MI. 800-950-2253
Bake Crafters Food Company
McDonald, TN 423-396-3392
Dwayne Keith Brooks Company
Orangevale, CA 916-988-1030
Dynamic Foods
Lubbock, TX. 806-723-5600
Fresh Start Bakeries
Brea, CA 714-256-8900
Guttenplan's Frozen Dough
Middletown, NJ 888-422-4357
J & J Wall Bakery Co
Sacramento, CA 916-381-1410
James Skinner Company
Omaha, NE 800-358-7428
Leidenheimer Baking Co
New Orleans, LA 800-259-9099
Lone Star Bakery
Round Rock, TX. 512-255-7268
Pacific Ocean Produce
Santa Cruz, CA. 831-423-2654

Sweet

Awrey Bakeries
Livonia, MI. 800-950-2253
Baker Boy Bake Shop Inc
Dickinson, ND 800-437-2008
Clyde's Delicious Donuts
Addison, IL. 630-628-6555
King's Hawaiian Holding Co Inc.
Torrance, CA. 877-695-4227
Lone Star Consolidated Foods Inc.
Dallas, TX. 800-658-5637
McKee Foods Corp.
Collegedale, TN 800-522-4499
St Armands Baking Co
Bradenton, FL. 941-753-7494
Zoelsmann's Bakery & Deli
Pueblo, CO 719-543-0407

Rye

Alfred & Sam's Italian Bakery
Lancaster, PA. 717-392-6311
Alpha Baking Company
South Bend, IN 773-261-6000
Amest Food
Stony Point, NY 718-360-0886
Amoroso's Baking Co
Bellmawr, NJ. 215-471-4740
Atlanta Bread Co.
Smyrna, GA 800-398-3728
Chicago Pastry
Bloomingdale, IL 630-529-6391
Chmura's Bakery
Indian Orchard, MA 413-543-2521
Colchester Bakery
Colchester, CT 860-537-2415
Cybros
Waukesha, WI. 800-876-2253
Dimpflmeier Bakery
Toronto, ON 800-268-2421
French Meadow Bakery & Cafe
Minneapolis, MN 612-870-7855
Hawaii Star Bakery
Honolulu, HI. 808-841-3602
Highlandville Packing
Highlandville, MO 417-443-3365
Metropolitan Baking Co
Hamtramck, MI. 313-875-7246
Orlando Baking Co
Cleveland, OH 800-362-5504
Orwasher's Bakery
New York, NY 212-288-6569
Patisserie Wawel
Montreal, QC 614-524-3348
Piemonte Bakery Co
Rockford, IL. 815-962-4833
Pyrenees French Bakery
Bakersfield, CA 888-898-7159
Quality Bakery
Invermere, BC. 888-681-9977
Rubschlager Baking Corp
. 800-661-7246
Rudi's Organic Bakery
Boulder, CO 877-293-0876
Rudolph's Specialty Bakery
Toronto, ON 800-268-1589
Terranettis Italian Bakery
Mechanicsburg, PA. 717-697-5434
Tribeca Oven
Carlstadt, NJ 201-935-8800

Scones

Bette's Oceanview Diner
Berkeley, CA. 510-644-3230
Bluepoint Bakery
Denver, CO 303-298-1100
Butter Baked Goods
Vancouver, BC 604-221-4333
California Smart Foods
San Francisco, CA 415-826-0449
Case Side Holdings Company
Kensington, PE. 902-836-4214
Conifer Foods
Medina, WA 800-588 9160
Davis Bread & Desserts
Davis, CA 530-220-4375
Dere Street
Danbury, CT 203-797-9386
Immaculate Consumption
Columbia, SC 888-826-6567
Moon Rabbit Foods
Savannah, NY. 828-273-6649
Nikola's Foods
Bloomington, MN. 888-645-6527
Sticky Fingers Bakeries
Spokane, WA. 800-458-5826
Treasure Foods
West Valley, UT. 801-974-0911
Uptown Bakers
Hyattsville, MD 301-864-1500

Short

Biscottea
Issaquah, WA 425-313-1993
Merlino Italian Baking Company
Kent, WA. 800-800-9490
R.M. Palmer Co.
West Reading, PA 610-372-8971
Vermont Chocolatiers
Northfield, VT 877-485-4226
Walkers Shortbread
Hauppauge, NY 800-521-0141

Soda

Greenhills Irish Bakery
Dorchester Ctr, MA 617-825-8187

Sourdough

Atlanta Bread Co.
Smyrna, GA 800-398-3728

Beckmann's Old World Bakery
Santa Cruz, CA 831-423-9242
Berkshire Mountain Bakery
Housatonic, MA 866-274-6124
French Meadow Bakery & Cafe
Minneapolis, MN 612-870-7855
Frisco Baking Co Inc
Los Angeles, CA 323-225-6111
Gold Coast Bakeries
Santa Ana, CA 714-545-2253
Gold Coast Baking Co Inc
Santa Ana, CA 714-545-2253
H&S Bakery
Baltimore, MD 800-959-7655
Hawaii Star Bakery
Honolulu, HI 808-841-3602
Kim and Jake's
Boulder, CO 303-499-9126
Morabito Baking Co Inc
Norristown, PA 800-525-7747
Orwasher's Bakery
New York, NY 212-288-6569
Ottenberg's Bakers
Sykesville, MD 800-334-7264
Rudi's Organic Bakery
Boulder, CO 877-293-0876
Schwebel Baking Co.
Youngstown, OH 800-860-2867

Wheat

Alpha Baking Company
South Bend, IN 773-261-6000
Atlanta Bread Co.
Smyrna, GA 800-398-3728
Beckmann's Old World Bakery
Santa Cruz, CA 831-423-9242
Butter Krust Baking Company
Thomasville, GA 800-282-8093
Highlandville Packing
Highlandville, MO 417-443-3365
Klosterman Baking Co.
Cincinnati, OH 877-301-1004
Metropolitan Baking Co
Hamtramck, MI 313-875-7246
Naji's Pita Gourmet Restaurant
Birmingham, AL 205-945-6001
Orlando Baking Co
Cleveland, OH 800-362-5504
Orwasher's Bakery
New York, NY 212-288-6569
Pyrenees French Bakery
Bakersfield, CA 888-898-7159
Rudi's Organic Bakery
Boulder, CO 877-293-0876
Schwebel Baking Co.
Youngstown, OH 800-860-2867
Shaw Baking Company
Thunder Bay, ON 807-345-7327
Tribeca Oven
Carlstadt, NJ 201-935-8800

White

Alpha Baking Company
South Bend, IN 773-261-6000
Arctic Beverages
Winnipeg, MB 866-503-1270
Beckmann's Old World Bakery
Santa Cruz, CA 831-423-9242
Highlandville Packing
Highlandville, MO 417-443-3365
Klosterman Baking Co.
Cincinnati, OH 877-301-1004
Metropolitan Baking Co
Hamtramck, MI 313-875-7246
Orwasher's Bakery
New York, NY 212-288-6569
Pan-O-Gold Baking Co.
St. Cloud, MN 800-444-7005
Pyrenees French Bakery
Bakersfield, CA 888-898-7159
Rudi's Organic Bakery
Boulder, CO 877-293-0876
Schwebel Baking Co.
Youngstown, OH 800-860-2867
Shaw Baking Company
Thunder Bay, ON 807-345-7327
Terranettis Italian Bakery
Mechanicsburg, PA 717-697-5434

Cakes & Pastries

BakeMark Canada
Laval, QC 800-361-4998

Angel Food Cake

Kyger Bakery Products
Lafayette, IN 765-447-1252
Specialty Bakers
Marysville, PA 800-233-0778

Babka

Aunt Heddy's Bakery
Brooklyn, NY 718-782-0582
Morse's Sauerkraut
Waldoboro, ME 866-832-5569

Baklava

Athens Baking Company
Fresno, CA 800-775-2867
Athens Foods Inc
Brookpark, OH 843-916-2000
Fillo Factory, The
Northvale, NJ 800-653-4556
Marika's Kitchen
Hancock, ME 800-694-9400
Sinbad Sweets
Madera, CA 866-746-2232

Blintzes

Frozen

Echo Lake Foods, Inc.
Burlington, WI 262-763-9551
Old Fashioned Kitchen Inc
Lakewood, NJ 732-364-4100

Brown Bettys

Euro Chocolate Fountain
San Diego, CA 800-423-9303

Cakes

Adams Foods & Milling
Dothan, AL 334-983-4233
Alati-Caserta Desserts
Montr,al, QC 877-377-5680
Angel's Bakeries
Brooklyn, NY 718-389-1400
Aryzta
Los Angeles, CA 855-427-9982
Atkins Elegant Desserts
Fishers, IN 800-887-8808
Awrey Bakeries
Livonia, MI 800-950-2253
BakeMark Canada
Laval, QC 800-361-4998
Baker Boy Bake Shop Inc
Dickinson, ND 800-437-2008
BakeryCorp
Miami, FL 305-623-3838
Balboa Dessert Co Inc
Santa Ana, CA 800-974-9699
Banquet Schusters Bakery
Pueblo, CO 719-544-1062
Bauducco Foods Inc.
Miami, FL 305-477-9270
BBU Bakeries
Horsham, PA 800-984-0989
Beatrice Bakery Co
Beatrice, NE 800-228-4030
Berke-Blake Fancy Foods, Inc.
Longwood, FL 888-386-2253
Big Fatty's Flaming Foods
Valley View, TX 888-248-6332
Bimbo Bakeries USA Inc.
Horsham, PA 800-984-0989
Birkholm's Solvang Bakery
Solvang, CA 800-377-4253
Bittersweet Pastries
Norwood, NJ 800-217-2938
Bluepoint Bakery
Denver, CO 303-298-1100
Breadworks
Charlottesville, VA 434-296-4663
Brownie Baker Inc
Fresno, CA 800-598-6501
Busken Bakery
Cincinnati, OH 513-871-2114
C'est Gourmet
Framingham, MA 508-877-0000
Cal-Java International Inc
Northridge, CA 800-207-2750
Calamondin Cafe
Fort Myers, FL 239-288-5535
California Smart Foods
San Francisco, CA 415-826-0449
Calmar Bakery
Calmar, AB 780-985-3583
Caribbean Food Delights Inc
Tappan, NY 845-398-3000
Carole's Cheesecake Company
Toronto, ON 416-256-0000
Carolina Foods Inc
Charlotte, NC 800-234-0441
Case Side Holdings Company
Kensington, PE 902-836-4214
Cateraid Inc
Howell, MI 800-508-8217
Celebrity Cheesecake
Davie, FL 877-986-2253
Chattanooga Bakery Inc
Chattanooga, TN 800-251-3404
Cheesecake Etc Desserts
Miami Springs, FL 305-887-0258
Cheesecake Factory Inc.
Calabasas Hills, CA 818-871-3000
Cheryl's Cookies
Westerville, OH 800-443-8124
Chocolate Chix
Waxahachie, TX 214-744-2442
Cinderella Cheese Cake Co
Riverside, NJ 800-521-1171
City Bakery Cafe
Asheville, NC 877-328-3687
Clarmil Manufacturing Corp
Hayward, CA 888-252-7645
Cloverhill Bakery-Vend Corporation
Chicago, IL 773-745-9800
Clyde's Delicious Donuts
Addison, IL 630-628-6555
Collin Street Bakery
Corsicana, TX 800-267-4657
Comanzo & Company Specialty Bakers
Smithfield, RI 888-352-5455
Cookie Factory
Bronx, NY 718-379-6223
Crane's Pie Pantry Restaurant
Fennville, MI 269-561-2297
Culinar Canada
Baie-Comeau, QC 418-296-4395
Dancing Deer Baking Company
Boston, MA 888-699-3337
David's Cookies
Cedar Grove, NJ 800-500-2800
Davis Bakery & Delicatessen
Cleveland, OH 216-292-3060
Decadent Desserts
Calgary, AB 403-245-5535
Deerfield Bakery
Buffalo Grove, IL 847-520-0068
Del's Pastry
Toronto, ON 800-461-0663
Denny's 5th Avenue Bakery
Bloomington, MN 952-881-4445
Desserts by David Glass
South Windsor, CT 860-462-7520
Di Camillo Baking Co
Niagara Falls, NY 800-634-4363
Dinkel's Bakery Inc
Chicago, IL 800-822-8817
Dr. Cookie
Seattle, WA 206-389-9321
Dufflet Pastries
Toronto, ON 866-238-0899
Dutch Kitchen Bake Shop & Deli
Fitchburg, MA 978-345-1393
DWC Specialities
Horicon, WI 800-383-8808
Dynamic Foods
Lubbock, TX 806-723-5600
Eddy's Bakery
Boise, ID 208-377-8100
Edelweiss Patisserie
Medford, MA 781-628-0225
Effies Homemade
Hyde Park, MA 617-364-9300
Eilenberger Bakeries
Palestine, TX 800-831-2544
El Peto Products
Cambridge, ON 800-387-4064
Elmwood Pastry Shop
West Hartford, CT 860-233-2029

Entenmann's
Totowa, NJ 973-785-7601
European Style Bakery
Beverly Hills, CA 818-368-6876
Fantasia
Sedalia, MO 660-827-1172
Farm & Oven Snacks
Boulder, CO
Ferrara Bakery & Cafe
New York, NY 212-226-6150
Firehook Bakery & Coffeehouse
Chantilly, VA 703-263-2253
Fireside Kitchen
Halifax, NS 902-454-7387
Flowers Baking Co
El Paso, TX 800-328-6111
Flowers Foods Inc.
Thomasville, GA 229-226-9110
Food of Our Own Design
Maplewood, NJ 973-762-0985
Foxtail Foods
Fairfield, OH 800-487-2253
France Delices
Montreal, QC 800-663-1365
Franklin Baking Co.
Goldsboro, NC 919-735-0344
Fruit of the Boot
Gaineswillve, FL 352-376-3643
Future Bakery & Cafe
Toronto, ON 416-231-1491
Georgia Fruitcake Co
Claxton, GA 912-739-2683
Giant Food
Landover, MD 888-469-4426
Golden Brown Bakery Inc
South Haven, MI 269-637-3418
Golden Kernel Pecan Co
Cameron, SC 803-823-2311
Golden Walnut Specialty Foods
Wayzata, MN 800-843-3645
Goldilocks USA
Hayward, CA 510-476-0700
Gourmet Treats
Torrance, CA 800-444-9549
Great Western Co LLC
Hollywood, AL 256-259-3578
Grebe's Bakery
Milwaukee, WI 800-833-3158
Greyston Bakery Inc
Yonkers, NY 800-289-2253
Grossingers Home Bakery
New York, NY 800-479-6996
GWB Foods Corporation
Brooklyn, NY 877-977-7610
Haby's Alsatian Bakery
Castroville, TX 830-538-2118
Hahn's Old Fashioned Cake Co
Farmingdale, NY 631-249-3456
Harrington's of Vermont
Richmond, VT
Hawaii Candy Inc
Honolulu, HI 800-303-2507
Haydel's Bakery
New Orleans, LA 800-442-1342
Heidi's Gourmet Desserts
Tucker, GA 800-241-4166
Heltzman Bakery
Louisville, KY 502-447-3515
Holton Food Products
La Grange, IL 708-352-5599
Hot Cakes-Molten Chocolate
Seattle, WA 206-453-3792
Hudson River Foods
Castleton, NY 888-417-9343
Hunt Country Foods Inc
Marshall, VA 540-364-2622
Ivy Cottage Scone Mixes
S Pasadena, CA 626-441-2761
Jacquet Bakery
New York, NY
James Skinner Company
Omaha, NE 800-358-7428
JC's Pie Pops
Chatsworth, CA 818-349-1880
Jennies Gluten-Free Bakery
Moosic, PA 570-457-2400
Joey's Fine Foods
Newark, NJ 973-482-1400
John J. Nissen Baking Company
Brewer, ME 207-989-7654
Jon Donaire Desserts
Santa Fe Springs, CA 877-366-2473

Just Desserts
Fairfield, CA 415-780-6860
K & S Cakes
Leesburg, VA 910-265-6779
Keller's Bakery
Lafayette, LA 337-235-1568
Kennedy Gourmet
Glendale Heights, IL 800-729-8116
Kyger Bakery Products
Lafayette, IN 765-447-1252
L & M Bakery
Riverside, NJ 888-887-1335
Laura's French Baking Co
Los Angeles, CA 888-353-5144
Lax & Mandel Bakery
South Euclid, OH 216-382-8877
Le Chef Bakery
Montebello, CA 323-888-2929
Little Miss Muffin
Chicago, IL 800-456-9328
Lone Star Bakery
Round Rock, TX 512-255-7268
Lone Star Consolidated Foods Inc.
Dallas, TX 800-658-5637
Love Quiches Desserts
Freeport, NY 516-623-8800
M/S Smears
Chadbourn, NC 910-654-5163
Mac's Donut Shop
Aliquippa, PA 724-375-6776
Martino's Bakery
Burbank, CA 818-842-0715
Mary of Puddin Hill
Palestine, TX 800-545-8889
Matthews 1812 House
Cornwall Bridge, CT 800-662-1812
Maurice French Pastries
Metairie, LA 888-285-8261
McKee Foods Corp.
Collegedale, TN 800-522-4499
Mchaffies Pies
Dayton, OH 800-289-7437
Michel's Bakery
Philadelphia, PA 267-345-7914
Mid-Atlantic Foods Inc
Easton, MD 800-922-4688
Milano Bakery Inc
Joliet, IL 815-727-2253
Moon Rabbit Foods
Savannah, NY 828-273-6649
Moravian Cookies Shop
Winston Salem, NC 800-274-2994
Mortgage Apple Cake
Teaneck, NJ 201-692-9538
Mozzicato De Pasquale Bakery
Hartford, CT 860-296-0426
Multi Marques
Montreal, QC 514-934-1866
My Cup of Cake™
Port Washington, NY 516-767-5137
My Daddy's Cheesecake
Cape Girardeau, MO 800-735-6765
My Grandma's Coffee Cake
Hyde Park, MA 800-847-2636
Naturally Delicious Inc
Oakland Park, FL 888-221-7352
New Glarus Bakery & Tea Room
New Glarus, WI 866-805-5536
New York Bakeries Inc
Hialeah, FL 305-883-0790
Northside Bakery
Brooklyn, NY 718-782-2700
O & H Danish Bakery Inc
Racine, WI 262-637-8895
Ohta Wafer Factory
Honolulu, HI 808-949-2775
Old Country Bakery
North Hollywood, CA 818-838-2302
Our Lady of Guadalupe Trappist Abbey
Carlton, OR 503-852-0103
Pacific Ocean Produce
Santa Cruz, CA 831-423-2654
Pastry Chef
Pawtucket, RI 800-639-8606
Patti's Plum Puddings
Lawndale, CA 310-376-1463
Pearl River Pastry & Chocolate
Pearl River, NY 800-632-2639
Pellman Foods Inc
New Holland, PA 717-354-8070
Pepperidge Farm Inc.
Norwalk, CT 888-737-7374

Pie Piper Products
Wheeling, IL 800-621-8183
Plaza Sweets Bakery
Mamaroneck, NY 800-816-8416
Plehn's Bakery Inc
Louisville, KY 502-896-4438
Pocono Cheesecake Factory
Swiftwater, PA 570-839-6844
Quality Bakery Products
Houston, TX 866-449-4977
Real Food Marketing
Kansas City, MO 816-221-4100
Rich's Ice Cream Co Inc
West Palm Beach, FL 561-833-7585
Rising Dough Bakery
Sacramento, CA 916-387-9700
Rockland Bakery
Nanuet, NY 800-734-4376
Rolling Pin Bakery
Bow Island, AB 403-545-2434
Rowena
Norfolk, VA 800-627-8699
Royal Caribbean Bakery
Mt Vernon, NY 888-818-0971
Royal Home Bakery
Newmarket, ON 905-715-7044
Rudolph's Specialty Bakery
Toronto, ON 800-268-1589
Ruth Ashbrook Bakery
Portland, OR 503-240-7437
Ryals Bakery
Milledgeville, GA 478-452-0321
Ryke's Bakery
Muskegon, MI 231-726-2253
Sacramento Baking Co
Sacramento, CA 916-361-2000
Safeway Inc.
Pleasanton, CA 877-723-3929
Samadi Sweets Cafe
Falls Church, VA 703-578-0606
Sara Lee Frozen Bakery
Kings Mountain, NC 800-323-7117
Saxby Foods
Edmonton, AB 780-440-4179
Scialo Brothers Bakery
Providence, RI 877-421-0986
Silver Tray Cookies
Fort Lauderdale, FL 305-883-0800
Silverland Bakery
Forest Park, IL 708-488-0800
Smart Baking Co.
Sanford, FL 407-915-5519
Smoak's Bakery & Catering Service
Augusta, GA 706-738-1792
Southeast Dairy Processors Inc
Tampa, FL 813-620-1516
Specialty Bakers
Marysville, PA 800-233-0778
Spilke's Baking Company
Moosic, PA 570-457-2400
Standard Bakery Inc
Kealakekua, HI 808-322-3688
Sterling Foods LLC
San Antonio, TX 210-490-1669
Steve's Mom
Bronx, NY 800-362-4545
Strossner's Bakery & Cafe
Greenville, SC 864-233-2990
Sugar Plum LLC
Houma, LA 985-872-9524
Superior Cake Products
Southbridge, MA 508-764-3276
Swagger Foods Corp
Vernon Hills, IL 847-913-1200
Sweet Endings Inc
West Palm Beach, FL 888-635-1177
Sweet Gallery Exclusive Pastry
Toronto, ON 416-766-0289
Sweet Lady Jane
Los Angeles, CA 323-653-7145
Tasty Baking Company
Philadelphia, PA 800-248-2789
The Great San Saba River Pecan Company
San Saba, TX 800-621-8121
Trumps Food Interest
Vancouver, BC 604-732-8473
Two Chicks and a Ladle
New York, NY 212-251-0025
Uncle Ralph's Cookies
Frederick, MD 800-422-0626
Uniquely Together
Chicago, IL 800-613-7276

Upper Crust Bakery USA
Phoenix, AZ 602-255-0464
Uptown Bakers
Hyattsville, MD 301-864-1500
Vickey's Vittles
North Hills, CA. 818-841-1944
Vigneri Chocolate Inc.
Rochester, NY. 877-844-6374
Warwick Ice Cream
Warwick, RI 401-821-8403
Wedding Cake Studio
Williamsfield, OH. 440-667-1765
Weiss Homemade Kosher Bakery
Brooklyn, NY 800-498-3477
Wenger's Bakery
Reading, PA 610-372-6545
Whipped Pastry Boutique
Brooklyn, NY 718-858-8088
White Oak Farms Inc
Sandown, NH 800-473-8869
Wholesome Bakery
San Francisco, CA 415-343-5414
Williamsburg Chocolatier
Williamsburg, VA 757-253-1474
World Of Chantilly
Brooklyn, NY 718-859-1110
Wow! Factor Desserts
Sherwood Park, AB 800-604-2253
Ya-Hoo Baking Co
Sherman, TX. 888-869-2466
Young's Bakery
Uniontown, PA 724-437-6361
Zoelsmann's Bakery & Deli
Pueblo, CO 719-543-0407

Cannoli

Artuso Pastry
Bronx, NY. 718-367-2515
Golden Cannoli
Chelsea, MA 617-868-2826

Carrot Cake

Clarmil Manufacturing Corp
Hayward, CA 888-252-7645
Eli's Cheesecake
Chicago, IL 800-354-2253
Nush Foods
Salt Lake City, UT 801-953-1370

Cheese Cake

American Quality Foods
Mills River, NC. 828-890-8344
Aryzta
Los Angeles, CA. 855-427-9982
Atkins Elegant Desserts
Fishers, IN. 800-887-8808
Balboa Dessert Co Inc
Santa Ana, CA 800-974-9699
Berke-Blake Fancy Foods, Inc.
Longwood, FL 888-386-2253
Bindi North America
Kearny, NJ. 973-812-8118
Brownie Baker Inc
Fresno, CA 800-598-6501
California Smart Foods
San Francisco, CA 415-826-0449
Carole's Cheesecake Company
Toronto, ON 416-256-0000
Cateraid Inc
Howell, MI 800-508-8217
Celebrity Cheesecake
Davie, FL 877-986-2253
Chatila's
Salem, NH. 603-898-5459
Cheesecake Etc Desserts
Miami Springs, FL 305-887-0258
Cheesecake Factory Inc.
Calabasas Hills, CA 818-871-3000
Cheesecake Momma
Ukiah, CA. 707-462-2253
Cinderella Cheese Cake Co
Riverside, NJ. 800-521-1171
Collin Street Bakery
Corsicana, TX. 800-267-4657
D-Liteful Baking Company
Medley, FL 305-883-6449
Desserts by David Glass
South Windsor, CT 860-462-7520
Eli's Cheesecake
Chicago, IL 800-354-2253
Future Bakery & Cafe
Toronto, ON 416-231-1491
Golden Walnut Specialty Foods
Wayzata, MN 800-843-3645
Heidi's Gourmet Desserts
Tucker, GA 800-241-4166
Hoff's Bakery
Medford, MA 888-871-5100
Holey Moses Cheesecake
Westhampton Beach, NY 800-225-2253
Jon Donaire Desserts
Santa Fe Springs, CA 877-366-2473
Jubilations
West Point, MS 800-530-7808
Love Quiches Desserts
Freeport, NY. 516-623-8800
Mazelle's Cheesecakes Concoctions Creations
Dallas, TX. 214-328-9102
Mehaffies Pies
Dayton, OH. 800-289-7437
New England Country Bakers
Watertown, CT 800-225-3779
Pellman Foods Inc
New Holland, PA 717-354-8070
Pie Piper Products
Wheeling, IL. 800-621-8183
Pocono Cheesecake Factory
Swiftwater, PA 570-839-6844
Scotty Wotty's Creamy Cheesecake
Hillsborough, NJ. 908-281-9720
Steve's Mom
Bronx, NY. 800-362-4545
Sweet Lady Jane
Los Angeles, CA. 323-653-7145
Tolteca Foodservice
Norcross, GA 800-541-6835
Trumps Food Interest
Vancouver, BC 604-732-8473
Two Chicks and a Ladle
New York, NY 212-251-0025
Wow! Factor Desserts
Sherwood Park, AB 800-604-2253

Flavored

Jon Donaire Desserts
Santa Fe Springs, CA 877-366-2473
Junior's Cheesecake
Maspeth, NY. 800-458-6467
Pellman Foods Inc
New Holland, PA 717-354-8070
Sugarplum Desserts
Langley, BC 604-534-2282

Frozen

Balboa Dessert Co Inc
Santa Ana, CA 800-974-9699
Cateraid Inc
Howell, MI 800-508-8217
Cinderella Cheese Cake Co
Riverside, NJ. 800-521-1171
Desserts Of Distinction
Tigard, OR 503-654-8370
Galaxy Desserts
Richmond, CA 800-225-3523
Heidi's Gourmet Desserts
Tucker, GA 800-241-4166
Lawler Foods LTD
Humble, TX 800-541-8285
Love Quiches Desserts
Freeport, NY. 516-623-8800
Mehaffies Pies
Dayton, OH. 800-289-7437
Pellman Foods Inc
New Holland, PA 717-354-8070
Sugarplum Desserts
Langley, BC 604-534-2282

Low-Fat

American Quality Foods
Mills River, NC. 828-890-8344

NewYork Style

Cannoli Factory
Wyandanch, NY 631-643-2700

Non-Fat

Two Chicks and a Ladle
New York, NY 212-251-0025

Churros

Tolteca Foodservice
Norcross, GA 800-541-6835

Coffee Cake

Awrey Bakeries
Livonia, MI. 800-950-2253
Boston Coffee Cake
North Andover, MA 800-434-0500
Clyde's Delicious Donuts
Addison, IL. 630-628-6555
DWC Specialities
Horicon, WI 800-383-8808
Homefree LLC
Windham, NH. 800-552-7172
James Skinner Company
Omaha, NE 800-358-7428
L & M Bakery
Riverside, NJ. 888-887-1335
Nikola's Foods
Bloomington, MN. 888-645-6527
Sedona Baking Company
Gardena, CA 323-770-2674
Wholesome Bakery
San Francisco, CA 415-343-5414

Cream Puff

Boboli Intl. Inc.
Stockton, CA. 209-473-3507
Creme Curls
Hudsonville, MI 800-466-1219
Hafner USA
Stone Mountain, GA. 888-725-4605
Irene's Bakery & Gourmet
Bensalem, PA 215-244-6200
McKee Foods Corp.
Collegedale, TN 800-522-4499
Rich's Ice Cream Co Inc
West Palm Beach, FL. 561-833-7585

Crumpets

Aryzta
Los Angeles, CA. 855-427-9982
Wolferman's
Medford, OR. 800-798-6241

Cupcakes

Better Bites Bakery
Austin, TX
Butter Baked Goods
Vancouver, BC 604-221-4333
Crumbs Bake Shop
New York, NY 877-278-6270
Lucky Spoon Bakery LLC
Salt Lake City, UT 801-824-0624
Magnolia Bakery
New York, NY 855-622-5379
Mrs Baird's
Horsham, PA. 800-984-0989
Red Plate Foods
Bend, OR. 541-550-7676
Sweet Lady Jane
Los Angeles, CA. 323-653-7145
Tasty Baking Company
Philadelphia, PA 800-248-2789
Veronica's Treats
Middleboro, MA. 866-576-1122
Wholesome Bakery
San Francisco, CA 415-343-5414

Danish

Aryzta
Los Angeles, CA. 855-427-9982
Atlanta Bread Co.
Smyrna, GA 800-398-3728
Awrey Bakeries
Livonia, MI. 800-950-2253
BakeMark Canada
Laval, QC 800-361-4998
Brownie Baker Inc
Fresno, CA 800-598-6501
California Smart Foods
San Francisco, CA 415-826-0449
Chicago Pastry
Bloomingdale, IL 630-529-6391
Clyde's Delicious Donuts
Addison, IL. 630-628-6555
Davis Bread & Desserts
Davis, CA 530-220-4375

Del's Pastry
Toronto, ON 800-461-0663
Dimitria Delights Baking Co
North Grafton, MA 800-763-1113
Entenmann's
Totowa, NJ 973-785-7601
Fiera Foods
Toronto, ON 800-675-6356
Gourmet Croissant
Brooklyn, NY 718-499-4911
Heltzman Bakery
Louisville, KY 502-447-3515
James Skinner Company
Omaha, NE 800-358-7428
Joey's Fine Foods
Newark, NJ 973-482-1400
Laura's French Baking Co
Los Angeles, CA 888-353-5144
Mary Ann's Baking Co Inc
Sacramento, CA 916-681-7444
Michel's Bakery
Philadelphia, PA 267-345-7914
Roma Bakeries
Rockford, IL 815-964-6737
Shaw Baking Company
Thunder Bay, ON 807-345-7327
Strossner's Bakery & Cafe
Greenville, SC 864-233-2990
Svenhard's Swedish Bakery Inc
Oakland, CA 800-705-3379
Uptown Bakers
Hyattsville, MD 301-864-1500
Vie De France Yamazaki Inc
Vienna, VA 800-446-4404

Dessert Tarts

Birkholm's Solvang Bakery
Solvang, CA 800-377-4253

Doughnuts

All Round Foods Bakery Prod
Westbury, NY 800-428-8802
Annette's Donuts Ltd.
Toronto, ON 888-839-7857
Awrey Bakeries
Livonia, MI 800-950-2253
Bake Crafters Food Company
McDonald, TN 423-396-3392
Baker Boy Bake Shop Inc
Dickinson, ND 800-437-2008
Baker's Dozen & Cafe
Herkimer, NY 315-866-6770
BBU Bakeries
Horsham, PA 800-984-0989
Busken Bakery
Cincinnati, OH 513-871-2114
Butter Krust Baking Company
Thomasville, GA 800-282-8093
California Smart Foods
San Francisco, CA 415-826-0449
Carolina Foods Inc
Charlotte, NC 800-234-0441
Case Side Holdings Company
Kensington, PE 902-836-4214
Chatila's
Salem, NH 603-898-5459
Cloverhill Bakery-Vend Corporation
Chicago, IL 773-745-9800
Clyde's Delicious Donuts
Addison, IL 630-628-6555
Davis Bakery & Delicatessen
Cleveland, OH 216-292-3060
Denny's 5th Avenue Bakery
Bloomington, MN 952-881-4445
Donut Farm
Oakland, CA 510-338-6319
Dunford Bakers
West Jordan, UT 800-748-4335
Dutch Girl Donut Co
Detroit, MI 313-368-3020
Elmwood Pastry Shop
West Hartford, CT 860-233-2029
Entenmann's
Totowa, NJ 973-785-7601
Giant Food
Landover, MD 888-469-4426
Grebe's Bakery
Milwaukee, WI 800-833-3158
Harting's Bakery
Bowmansville, PA 717-445-5644
Heltzman Bakery
Louisville, KY 502-447-3515
Jubelt Variety Bakeries
Litchfield, IL 217-324-5314
Keller's Bakery
Lafayette, LA 337-235-1568
Koffee Kup Bakery
Burlington, VT 802-863-2696
Lepage Bakeries
Auburn, ME 207-783-9161
Lone Star Consolidated Foods Inc.
Dallas, TX 800-658-5637
Ludwick's Frozen Donuts
Grand Rapids, MI 800-366-8816
Mac's Donut Shop
Aliquippa, PA 724-375-6776
Madyson's Marshmallows
Heber City, UT 435-315-0045
Maple Donuts
York, PA 800-627-5348
Maui Bagel
Kahului, HI 808-270-7561
Mrs. Willman's Baking
Burnaby, BC 604-434-0027
Mt. View Bakery
Mountain View, HI 808-968-6353
Nutrilicious Natural Bakery
Countryside, IL 800-835-8097
Pan-O-Gold Baking Co.
St. Cloud, MN 800-444-7005
Parmenter's Northville Cider Mill
Northville, MI 248-349-3181
Plehn's Bakery Inc
Louisville, KY 502-896-4438
Quality Naturally Foods
City Of Industry, CA 888-498-6986
Rolling Pin Bakery
Bow Island, AB 403-545-2434
Ruth Ashbrook Bakery
Portland, OR 503-240-7437
Sara Lee Frozen Bakery
Kings Mountain, NC 800-323-7117
Shaw Baking Company
Thunder Bay, ON 807-345-7327
Steve's Doughnut Shop
Somerset, MA 508-672-0865
Vallos Baking Co
Bethlehem, PA 610-866-1012
Yum Yum Donut Shops Inc
City Of Industry, CA 626-964-1478

Frozen

All Round Foods Bakery Prod
Westbury, NY 800-428-8802
Awrey Bakeries
Livonia, MI 800-950-2253
Bake Crafters Food Company
McDonald, TN 423-396-3392
Carolina Foods Inc
Charlotte, NC 800-234-0441
Clyde's Delicious Donuts
Addison, IL 630-628-6555
Ludwick's Frozen Donuts
Grand Rapids, MI 800-366-8816
Mel-O-Cream Donuts Intl
Springfield, IL 217-483-7272

Dumplings

Atkinson Milling Co.
Selma, NC 800-948-5707
Byrnes & Kiefer Co
Callery, PA 724-538-5200
Chang Food Company
Garden Grove, CA 714-265-9990
Chateau Food Products Inc
Cicero, IL 708-863-4207
Chinese Spaghetti Factory
Boston, MA 617-445-7714
Community Orchards
Fort Dodge, IA 888-573-8212
Dimitria Delights Baking Co
North Grafton, MA 800-763-1113
Harvest Food Products Co Inc
Hayward, CA 510-675-0383
Harvest Time Foods
Ayden, NC 252-746-6675
Jewel Date Co
Thermal, CA 760-399-4474
La Tang Cuisine Manufacturing
Houston, TX 713-780-4876
Mando Inc
Englewood, NJ 201-568-9337
Mayfield Farms and Nursery
Athens, TN 423-746-9859
Millie's Pierogi
Chicopee Falls, MA 800-743-7641
Naleway Foods
Winnipeg, MB 800-665-7448
Prime Food Processing Corp
Brooklyn, NY 718-963-2323
Shine Foods Inc
Torrance, CA 310-533-6010
Sweet Sue Kitchens
Athens, AL 256-216-0500
Twin Marquis
Brooklyn, NY 800-367-6868
Wei-Chuan USA Inc
Bell Gardens, CA 562-372-2020

Eclairs

Boboli Intl. Inc.
Stockton, CA 209-473-3507
Creme Curls
Hudsonville, MI 800-466-1219
Rich's Ice Cream Co Inc
West Palm Beach, FL 561-833-7585

Frozen Cakes

Alati-Caserta Desserts
Montr,al, QC 877-377-5680
Andros Foods North America
Mount Jackson, VA 844-426-3767
Awrey Bakeries
Livonia, MI 800-950-2253
Bodega Chocolates
Fountain Valley, CA 888-326-3342
Carolina Foods Inc
Charlotte, NC 800-234-0441
Carousel Cakes
Nanuet, NY 800-659-2253
Cinderella Cheese Cake Co
Riverside, NJ 800-521-1171
Dynamic Foods
Lubbock, TX 806-723-5600
Fantasia
Sedalia, MO 660-827-1172
French Patisserie
Pacifica, CA 800-300-2253
Grossingers Home Bakery
New York, NY 800-479-6996
Heidi's Gourmet Desserts
Tucker, GA 800-241-4166
James Skinner Company
Omaha, NE 800-358-7428
Kyger Bakery Products
Lafayette, IN 765-447-1252
Little Miss Muffin
Chicago, IL 800-456-9328
Lone Star Bakery
Round Rock, TX 512-255-7268
Love Quiches Desserts
Freeport, NY 516-623-8800
McCain Foods Ltd.
Toronto, ON 416-955-1700
Mehaffies Pies
Dayton, OH 800-289-7437
My Grandma's Coffee Cake
Hyde Park, MA 800-847-2636
Pacific Ocean Produce
Santa Cruz, CA 831-423-2654
Pastry Chef
Pawtucket, RI 800-639-8606
Pellman Foods Inc
New Holland, PA 717-354-8070
Real Food Marketing
Kansas City, MO 816-221-4100
Rowena
Norfolk, VA 800-627-8699
Saxby Foods
Edmonton, AB 780-440-4179
Schwan's Company
Marshall, MN 800-533-5290
The Daphne Baking Company, LLC
New York, NY 212-517-7626
Uncle Ralph's Cookies
Frederick, MD 800-422-0626
Warwick Ice Cream
Warwick, RI 401-821-8403

Fruit Cake

Beatrice Bakery Co
Beatrice, NE 800-228-4030
Caribbean Food Delights Inc
Tappan, NY...................... 845-398-3000
Claxton Bakery Inc
Claxton, GA 800-841-4211
Collin Street Bakery
Corsicana, TX...................... 800-267-4657
Fireside Kitchen
Halifax, NS 902-454-7387
Milano Bakery Inc
Joliet, IL 815-727-2253
Multi Marques
Montreal, QC 514-934-1866
Neuman Bakery Specialties
Addison, IL...................... 800-253-5298
Old Cavendish Products
Cavendish, VT 800-536-7899

Fruit Cobbler

Good Old Days Foods
Little Rock, AR...................... 501-565-1257
Harold Food Company
Charlotte, NC 704-588-8061
Lone Star Bakery
Round Rock, TX...................... 512-255-7268
Pacific Ocean Produce
Santa Cruz, CA...................... 831-423-2654
Quality Bakery Products
Houston, TX 866-449-4977
Spring Glen Fresh Foods
Ephrata, PA...................... 800-641-2853
Ya-Hoo Baking Co
Sherman, TX...................... 888-869-2466

Ladyfingers

Specialty Bakers
Marysville, PA 800-233-0778

Liqueur Cake

Beatrice Bakery Co
Beatrice, NE 800-228-4030
Dinkel's Bakery Inc
Chicago, IL...................... 800-822-8817

Muffins

Abe's Vegan Muffins
NY...................... 845-735-5100
American Quality Foods
Mills River, NC...................... 828-890-8344
Andre-Boudin Bakeries
San Francisco, CA 415-882-1849
Angel's Bakeries
Brooklyn, NY 718-389-1400
Aryzta
Los Angeles, CA...................... 855-427-9982
Atlanta Bread Co.
Smyrna, GA 800-398-3728
Awrey Bakeries
Livonia, MI...................... 800-950-2253
Bake Crafters Food Company
McDonald, TN 423-396-3392
Bake Rite Rolls Inc
Bensalem, PA 800-949-5623
BakeMark Canada
Laval, QC 800-361-4998
BakeMark Ingredients Canada
Richmond, BC 800-665-9441
Baker Boy Bake Shop Inc
Dickinson, ND 800-437-2008
BakeryCorp
Miami, FL...................... 305-623-3838
BBU Bakeries
Horsham, PA...................... 800-984-0989
Bluepoint Bakery
Denver, CO...................... 303-298-1100
Brownie Baker Inc
Fresno, CA 800-598-6501
Busken Bakery
Cincinnati, OH 513-871-2114
Calgary Italian Bakery
Calgary, AB...................... 800-661-6868
California Smart Foods
San Francisco, CA 415-826-0449
Case Side Holdings Company
Kensington, PE...................... 902-836-4214
Central Bakery
Fall River, MA 508-675-7620
Chatila's
Salem, NH...................... 603-898-5459
Cloverhill Bakery-Vend Corporation
Chicago, IL...................... 773-745-9800
Community Bakeries
Downers Grove, IL...................... 800-952-5754
Continental Mills Inc
Tukwila, WA...................... 206-816-7000
Del's Pastry
Toronto, ON 800-461-0663
Denny's 5th Avenue Bakery
Bloomington, MN...................... 952-881-4445
DWC Specialities
Horicon, WI 800-383-8808
Edelweiss Patisserie
Medford, MA 781-628-0225
Edner Corporation
Hayward, CA 510-441-8504
El Peto Products
Cambridge, ON...................... 800-387-4064
Entenmann's
Totowa, NJ 973-785-7601
Enterprises Pates et Croutes
Boucherville, QC 800-265-7790
Farm & Oven Snacks
Boulder, CO
Fireside Kitchen
Halifax, NS...................... 902-454-7387
Foxtail Foods
Fairfield, OH...................... 800-487-2253
Fresh Start Bakeries
Brea, CA...................... 714-256-8900
Gourmet Croissant
Brooklyn, NY 718-499-4911
Greyston Bakery Inc
Yonkers, NY 800-289-2253
Hawaii Star Bakery
Honolulu, HI...................... 808-841-3602
Heltzman Bakery
Louisville, KY 502-447-3515
Homestead Baking Co
Rumford, RI 800-556-7216
Hudson River Foods
Castleton, NY 888-417-9343
International Brownie
East Weymouth, MA...................... 800-230-1588
Irresistible Cookie Jar
Hayden Lake, ID...................... 208-664-1261
James Skinner Company
Omaha, NE 800-358-7428
Joey's Fine Foods
Newark, NJ...................... 973-482-1400
Lavoi Corporation
Atlanta, GA...................... 404-325-1016
Lenny & Larry's
Panorama City, CA
Lone Star Bakery
Round Rock, TX...................... 512-255-7268
Lucky Spoon Bakery LLC
Salt Lake City, UT 801-824-0624
Mac's Donut Shop
Aliquippa, PA 724-375-6776
Magnificent Muffin
Farmingdale, NY 631-454-8022
Main Street Gourmet
Cuyahoga Falls, OH 800-678-6246
Meyer's Bakeries
Casa Grande, AZ...................... 800-528-5770
Michel's Bakery
Philadelphia, PA 267-345-7914
Mikey's
.... 480-696-2483
Mt. View Bakery
Mountain View, HI 808-968-6353
Muffin Revolution
Richmond, CA 510-859-7655
New England Muffin Co Inc
Fall River, MA 508-675-2833
New Horizons Baking Co
Fremont, IN...................... 260-495-7055
Nikola's Foods
Bloomington, MN...................... 888-645-6527
North Coast Farms
Santa Cruz, CA...................... 831-426-3733
Notre Dame Bakery
Conception Harbour, NL 709-535-2738
Oakrun Farm Bakery
Ancaster, ON...................... 800-263-6422
Otis Spunkmeyer
Norcross, GA 855-427-9982
Oven Fresh Baking Company
Chicago, IL...................... 773-638-1234
Pacific Ocean Produce
Santa Cruz, CA...................... 831-423-2654
Pan-O-Gold Baking Co.
St. Cloud, MN...................... 800-444-7005
Plaidberry Company
Vista, CA...................... 760-727-5403
Red Plate Foods
Bend, OR...................... 541-550-7676
Rising Dough Bakery
Sacramento, CA 916-387-9700
Sara Lee Frozen Bakery
Kings Mountain, NC...................... 800-323-7117
Shaw Baking Company
Thunder Bay, ON 807-345-7327
Soozy's Grain-Free
New York, NY
Sterling Foods LLC
San Antonio, TX...................... 210-490-1669
Upper Crust Bakery USA
Phoenix, AZ 602-255-0464
Uptown Bakers
Hyattsville, MD 301-864-1500
Vitalicious
New York, NY 877-848-2877
Weston Foods
Etobicoke, ON 416-252-7323

Frozen

Dynamic Foods
Lubbock, TX...................... 806-723-5600
Main Street Gourmet
Cuyahoga Falls, OH 800-678-6246

Whole Grain

Main Street Gourmet
Cuyahoga Falls, OH 800-678-6246

Panettones

Vigneri Chocolate Inc.
Rochester, NY...................... 877-844-6374

Pastries

Alessi Bakery
Tampa, FL...................... 813-879-4544
Artuso Pastry
Bronx, NY...................... 718-367-2515
Aryzta
Los Angeles, CA...................... 855-427-9982
Athens Foods Inc
Brookpark, OH 843-916-2000
Atlanta Bread Co.
Smyrna, GA 800-398-3728
BakeryCorp
Miami, FL...................... 305-623-3838
Banquet Schusters Bakery
Pueblo, CO 719-544-1062
Big Fatty's Flaming Foods
Valley View, TX 888-248-6332
Bimbo Bakeries USA Inc.
Horsham, PA...................... 800-984-0989
Boboli Intl. Inc.
Stockton, CA...................... 209-473-3507
Bodega Chocolates
Fountain Valley, CA 888-326-3342
Byrnes & Kiefer Co
Callery, PA 724-538-5200
Calgary Italian Bakery
Calgary, AB...................... 800-661-6868
Caribbean Food Delights Inc
Tappan, NY...................... 845-398-3000
Case Side Holdings Company
Kensington, PE 902-836-4214
Castella Imports Inc
Brentwood, NY...................... 631-231-5500
Chatila's
Salem, NH...................... 603-898-5459
Chella's Dutch Delicacies
Lake Oswego, OR...................... 800-458-3331
Chicago Pastry
Bloomingdale, IL 630-529-6391
Clarkson Scottish Bakery
Mississauga, ON...................... 905-823-1500
Clement's Pastry Shops Inc
Hyattsville, MD 301-277-6300
Cohen's Bakery
Ellenville, NY...................... 845-647-2200
Cookie Factory
Bronx, NY...................... 718-379-6223
Creme Curls
Hudsonville, MI 800-466-1219

Crepini & The Crepe Team
Brooklyn, NY 718-372-0505
Cyrils Bakery
Fort Lauderdale, FL 800-929-7457
Denny's 5th Avenue Bakery
Bloomington, MN. 952-881-4445
Dimitria Delights Baking Co
North Grafton, MA 800-763-1113
Dipaolo Baking Co Inc
Rochester, NY. 585-232-3510
Dufour Pastry Kitchens Inc
Bronx, NY. 800-439-1282
Edelweiss Patisserie
Medford, MA 781-628-0225
Elegant Desserts
Lyndhurst, NJ 201-933-0770
Ferrara Bakery & Cafe
New York, NY 212-226-6150
Fiera Foods
Toronto, ON 800-675-6356
Fillo Factory, The
Northvale, NJ 800-653-4556
Food of Our Own Design
Maplewood, NJ. 973-762-0985
Future Bakery & Cafe
Toronto, ON 416-231-1491
Glamorgan Bakery
Calgary, AB. 403-232-2800
Hafner USA
Stone Mountain, GA. 888-725-4605
Holt's Bakery Inc
Douglas, GA 912-384-2202
James Skinner Company
Omaha, NE 800-358-7428
John J. Nissen Baking Company
Brewer, ME. 207-989-7654
Just Desserts
Fairfield, CA. 415-780-6860
Keller's Bakery
Lafayette, LA 337-235-1568
Laura's French Baking Co
Los Angeles, CA. 888-353-5144
Lax & Mandel Bakery
South Euclid, OH 216-382-8877
Lenchner Bakery
Concord, ON. 905-738-8811
Let Them Eat Cake
Tampa, FL. 813-837-6888
Little Miss Muffin
Chicago, IL 800-456-9328
Lucy's Sweet Surrender
Beachwood, OH 216-752-0828
Mac's Donut Shop
Aliquippa, PA 724-375-6776
Mary Ann's Baking Co Inc
Sacramento, CA 916-681-7444
Michel's Bakery
Philadelphia, PA 267-345-7914
Mikawaya LLC
Vernon, CA 323-587-5504
Moravian Cookies Shop
Winston Salem, NC. 800-274-2994
Morse's Sauerkraut
Waldoboro, ME. 866-832-5569
Mrs. Willman's Baking
Burnaby, BC 604-434-0027
Nancy's Specialty Foods
Newark, CA 510-494-1100
Northside Bakery
Brooklyn, NY 718-782-2700
Oakrun Farm Bakery
Ancaster, ON. 800-263-6422
Old Country Bakery
North Hollywood, CA 818-838-2302
Pauline's Pastries
Vaughan, ON. 877-292-6826
Pepperidge Farm Inc.
Norwalk, CT 888-737-7374
Poppies International
Battleboro, NC 252-442-4309
Prime Pastries
Concord, ON. 905-669-5883
Quaker Bonnet
Buffalo, NY. 800-283-2447
Quality Naturally Foods
City Of Industry, CA. 888-498-6986
Ranaldi Bros. Frozen Food Products
Warwick, RI 401-737-5130
Ravico USA
Riderwood, MD 443-921-8025
Rockland Bakery
Nanuet, NY 800-734-4376
Rolling Pin Bakery
Bow Island, AB. 403-545-2434
Royal Caribbean Bakery
Mt Vernon, NY 888-818-0971
Ryke's Bakery
Muskegon, MI. 231-726-2253
Scialo Brothers Bakery
Providence, RI 877-421-0986
Shaw Baking Company
Thunder Bay, ON 807-345-7327
Simit + Smith
Ridgefield, NJ 201-699-0320
Solana Beach Baking Company
Carlsbad, CA. 760-444-9800
Spohrers Bakeries
Collingdale, PA. 610-532-9959
St-Germain Bakery
Honolulu, HI. 808-847-5396
Standard Bakery Inc
Kealakekua, HI 808-322-3688
Strossner's Bakery & Cafe
Greenville, SC. 864-233-2990
Svenhard's Swedish Bakery Inc
Oakland, CA 800-705-3379
Sweet Gallery Exclusive Pastry
Toronto, ON 416-766-0289
Taste It Presents Inc
Kenilworth, NJ 908-241-0672
Tasty Baking Company
Philadelphia, PA 800-248-2789
Turano Baking
Berwyn, IL 708-788-9220
Uptown Bakers
Hyattsville, MD 301-864-1500
Valley Bakery
Burnaby, BC 604-291-0674
Vie De France Yamazaki Inc
Vienna, VA 800-446-4404
Vienna Bakery
Barrington, RI. 401-245-2355
Vigneri Chocolate Inc.
Rochester, NY. 877-844-6374
Weiss Homemade Kosher Bakery
Brooklyn, NY 800-498-3477
Wenger's Bakery
Reading, PA 610-372-6545

Pecan Log

Golden Kernel Pecan Co
Cameron, SC. 803-823-2311

Petit Fours

Cookies United
Islip, NY 631-581-4000
Ferrara Bakery & Cafe
New York, NY 212-226-6150
Mazelle's Cheesecakes Concoctions Creations
Dallas, TX. 214-328-9102

Pound Cake

Abe's Vegan Muffins
NY. 845-735-5100
Adams Foods & Milling
Dothan, AL 334-983-4233
Brownie Baker Inc
Fresno, CA 800-598-6501
Clarmil Manufacturing Corp
Hayward, CA 888-252-7645
McDuffies Bakery
Clarence, NY. 800-875-1598
New England Country Bakers
Watertown, CT 800-225-3779
Rowena
Norfolk, VA. 800-627-8699
Silver Tray Cookies
Fort Lauderdale, FL 305-883-0800

Pudding Cake

Sticky Toffee Pudding Company
Austin, TX. 512-472-0039

Puff Pastry

Aryzta
Los Angeles, CA. 855-427-9982
BakeMark USA
Schaumburg, IL. 847-519-3135
Dutchland Frozen Foods
Lester, IA. 888-497-7243

Rugulach

Byrnes & Kiefer Co
Callery, PA 724-538-5200
Chewys Rugulach
San Diego, CA 800-241-3456
Ericas Rugelach & Baking Co
Brooklyn, NY 718-965-3657
Morse's Sauerkraut
Waldoboro, ME. 866-832-5569
Neuman Bakery Specialties
Addison, IL 800-253-5298
Steve's Mom
Bronx, NY. 800-362-4545
Suzanne's Sweets
Katonah, NY

Rum Cake

Cassandra's Gourmet Classics/Island Treasures Gourmet
Manassas, VA 703-590-7900

Sponge Cake

Clarmil Manufacturing Corp
Hayward, CA 888-252-7645
Multi Marques
Montreal, QC 514-934-1866
Patisserie Wawel
Montreal, QC 614-524-3348
Specialty Bakers
Marysville, PA 800-233-0778
Sticky Toffee Pudding Company
Austin, TX. 512-472-0039
Sweet Gallery Exclusive Pastry
Toronto, ON 416-766-0289

Strudel

Aryzta
Los Angeles, CA. 855-427-9982
Athens Foods Inc
Brookpark, OH 843-916-2000
Creme Curls
Hudsonville, MI 800-466-1219
Culinary Institute Lenotre
Houston, TX 888-536-6873
Dimitria Delights Baking Co
North Grafton, MA 800-763-1113
Fillo Factory, The
Northvale, NJ 800-653-4556
Rising Dough Bakery
Sacramento, CA 916-387-9700
Sinbad Sweets
Madera, CA. 866-746-2232
Svenhard's Swedish Bakery Inc
Oakland, CA 800-705-3379

Tarts

Bluepoint Bakery
Denver, CO 303-298-1100
California Smart Foods
San Francisco, CA 415-826-0449
City Bakery
New York, NY 212-366-1414
Clarmil Manufacturing Corp
Hayward, CA 888-252-7645
Denny's 5th Avenue Bakery
Bloomington, MN. 952-881-4445
Dufflet Pastries
Toronto, ON 866-238-0899
Dufour Pastry Kitchens Inc
Bronx, NY. 800-439-1282
Elegant Desserts
Lyndhurst, NJ 201-933-0770
Firehook Bakery & Coffeehouse
Chantilly, VA. 703-263-2253
Galaxy Desserts
Richmond, CA 800-225-3523
Granello Bakery
Las Vegas, NV. 702-361-0311
Greyston Bakery Inc
Yonkers, NY 800-289-2253
Hail Merry
Dallas, TX. 214-905-5005
Health Valley Company
Irwindale, CA 800-334-3204
J.P. Sunrise Bakery
Edmonton, AB 780-454-5797
Joey's Fine Foods
Newark, NJ 973-482-1400
Love Quiches Desserts
Freeport, NY 516-623-8800

Royal Home Bakery
Newmarket, ON 905-715-7044
Sinbad Sweets
Madera, CA 866-746-2232
Sweet Lady Jane
Los Angeles, CA 323-653-7145
The Daphne Baking Company, LLC
New York, NY 212-517-7626
Trumps Food Interest
Vancouver, BC 604-732-8473

Tiramisu

Bindi North America
Kearny, NJ 973-812-8118
Vigneri Chocolate Inc.
Rochester, NY 877-844-6374

Tortes

Alessi Bakery
Tampa, FL 813-879-4544
Aryzta
Los Angeles, CA 855-427-9982
Balboa Dessert Co Inc
Santa Ana, CA 800-974-9699
Dufflet Pastries
Toronto, ON 866-238-0899
Heidi's Gourmet Desserts
Tucker, GA 800-241-4166
Hoff's Bakery
Medford, MA 888-871-5100
Strossner's Bakery & Cafe
Greenville, SC 864-233-2990
Sweet Endings Inc
West Palm Beach, FL 888-635-1177
Sweet Gallery Exclusive Pastry
Toronto, ON 416-766-0289
Vigneri Chocolate Inc.
Rochester, NY 877-844-6374

Turnovers

BakeMark Canada
Laval, QC 800-361-4998
BakeMark USA
Schaumburg, IL 847-519-3135
Creme Curls
Hudsonville, MI 800-466-1219
Del's Pastry
Toronto, ON 800-461-0663
Fiera Foods
Toronto, ON 800-675-6356
Oven Ready Products
Guelph, ON 519-767-2415

Cones

Great Western Co LLC
Hollywood, AL 256-259-3578
Joy Cone Co
Hermitage, PA 724-962-5747
Kemach Food Products
Brooklyn, NY 718-272-5655
Monster Cone
Montreal, QC 800-542-9801
O'Boyle's Ice Cream Company
Bristol, PA 215-788-3882
Olde Tyme Food Corporation
East Longmeadow, MA 800-356-6533
Ono Cones of Hawaii LLC
Pearl City, HI 808-487-8690
Table De France
Ontario, CA 909-923-5205
Turnbull Cone Baking Company
Chattanooga, TN 423-265-4551

Cookies & Bars

Almond Cookies

Andre-Boudin Bakeries
San Francisco, CA 415-882-1849
Balticshop.Com LLC
Glastonbury, CT 800-506-2312
Bindi North America
Kearny, NJ 973-812-8118
Dong Kee Company
Chicago, IL 312-225-6340
Erba Food Products
Brooklyn, NY 718-272-7700
Fortella Fortune Cookies
Chicago, IL 312-567-9000
Mamma Says
Butler, NJ 877-283-6282

Y Z Enterprises Inc
Maumee, OH 800-736-8779

Animal Crackers

Good Zebra
. 512-698-7907
Old Colony Baking Co Inc
Northbrook, IL 847-498-5434

Bars

18 Rabbits Inc.
San Francisco, CA 415-922-6006
AMT Labs Inc
North Salt Lake, UT 801-294-3126
Aryzta
Los Angeles, CA 855-427-9982
Bake Crafters Food Company
McDonald, TN 423-396-3392
Bakeology
Torrance, CA
Barbara's Bakery
Lakeville, MN 800-343-0590
Betty Lou's
McMinnville, OR 800-242-5205
Big Spoon Roasters
Durham, NC 919-309-9100
California Smart Foods
San Francisco, CA 415-826-0449
Cambridge Food
Monterey, CA 800-433-2584
Carrie's Chocolates
Edmonton, AB 877-778-2462
Chase & Poe Candy Co
St Joseph, MO 800-786-1625
CHS Sunprairie
Minot, ND 800-556-6807
Cream Of The West
Harlowton, MT 800-477-2383
Edner Corporation
Hayward, CA 510-441-8504
Ethel's Baking Co.
St. Clair Shores, MI 586-552-5110
Fieldbrook Foods Corp.
Dunkirk, NY 800-333-0805
Food of Our Own Design
Maplewood, NJ 973-762-0985
Frankly Natural Bakers
San Diego, CA 800-727-7229
Frozfruit Corporation
Gardena, CA 310-217-1034
Fullbloom Baking Co
Newark, CA 800-201-9909
Genisoy
San Francisco, CA 866-972-6879
Global Health Laboratories
Amityville, NY 631-777-2134
Govadinas Fitness Foods
San Diego, CA 800-900-0108
Hain Celestial Group Inc
Lake Success, NY 800-434-4246
Health Valley Company
Irwindale, CA 800-334-3204
Jamae Natural Foods
Los Angeles, CA 800-343-0052
JSL Foods
Los Angeles, CA 800-745-3236
Kashi Company
Solana Beach, CA 877-747-2467
L & M Bakery
Riverside, NJ 888-887-1335
Lotus Bakery
Santa Rosa, CA 800-875-6887
Magnolia Bakery
New York, NY 855-622-5379
Marin Food Specialties
Byron, CA 925-634-6126
Matt's Cookies
Wheeling, IL 847-537-3888
Merlino Italian Baking Company
Kent, WA 800-800-9490
Nana's Cookie Co.
San Diego, CA 800-836-7534
Naturally Clean Eats
Manhattan Beach, CA
Nature's Bakery
Reno, NV
Nature's Plus
Melville, NY 800-645-9500
Nellson Candies Inc
Irwindale, CA 626-334-4508

No Cow
Denver, CO
Nothin' But Foods
Elmwood Park, NJ 203-557-8637
Oberweis Dairy Inc
North Aurora, IL 866-623-7934
Oven Arts
Hackensack, NJ 855-354-4070
Premier Protein
Emeryville, CA 888-836-8977
Redd Superfood Energy Bars
Portland, ME 207-370-4433
Sam Mills USA
Boynton Beach, FL 561-572-0510
Santa Barbara Bar
Santa Barbara, CA 855-722-2701
Schulze & Burch Biscuit Co
Chicago, IL 773-927-6622
Sheffa Foods
New York, NY 800-494-1956
Sucesores de Pedro Cortes
Hato Rey, PR 787-754-7040
Sweety Novelty
Monterey Park, CA 626-282-4482
Tate's Bake Shop
Southampton, NY 631-283-9830
That's It Nutrition
Los Angeles, CA 888-862-5235
Thinkthin, LLC
Los Angeles, CA 866-988-4465
Tram Bar LLC
Victor, ID 208-354-4790
Tribe 9 Foods
Madison, WI 608-257-7216
Ultimate Nutrition
Farmington, CT 860-409-7100
Wai Lana Snacks
Sacramento, CA 888-924-5262
Weaver Nut Co. Inc.
Ephrata, PA 800-473-2688
Wella Bar
East Lockhart, TX 877-725-7289
Wholesome Bakery
San Francisco, CA 415-343-5414
Your Bar Factory
LaSalle, QC 888-366-0258
Zego Foods
San Francisco, CA 415-706-8094

Big Cookies

Buff Bake
Santa Ana, CA 949-274-9464

Biscotti

Award Baking Intl
New Germany, MN 800-333-3523
Be-Bop Biscotti
Bend, OR 888-545-7487
Bernadette Baking Company
Medford, MA 781-393-8700
Big Island Candies Inc
Hilo, HI 800-935-5510
Biscoti Di Suzy
Oakland, CA 800-211-5903
Biscotti Goddess
Richmond, VA 804-745-9490
Di Camillo Baking Co
Niagara Falls, NY 800-634-4363
Elliott Bay Baking Co.
Seattle, WA 206-545-3804
Euro Cafe
Rochester, NY 800-298-9410
Ferrara Bakery & Cafe
New York, NY 212-226-6150
G Debbas Chocolatier
Fresno, CA 559-294-2071
Grain-Free JK Gourmet, Inc.
Toronto, ON 800-608-0465
Healing Home Foods
Pound Ridge, NY 914-764-1303
Immaculate Consumption
Columbia, SC 888-826-6567
Irene's Bakery & Gourmet
Bensalem, PA 215-244-6200
Just Off Melrose
Palm Springs, CA 760-320-7414
La Tempesta
S San Francisco, CA 800-762-8330
Larosa Bakery Inc
Shrewsbury, NJ 800-527-6722

Mamma Says
Butler, NJ 877-283-6282
Merlino Italian Baking Company
Kent, WA. 800-800-9490
Mikaela's Simply Divine
Dover, NJ 866-659-1553
Montione's Biscotti & Baked Goods
Norton, MA. 800-559-1010
Moon Dance Baking
Rohnert Park, CA 707-588-0800
My Boy's Baking LLC
Allentown, PA. 610-759-4552
Nikola's Foods
Bloomington, MN. 888-645-6527
Nonni's Foods LLC
Tulsa, OK 877-295-9604
North American Enterprises
Tucson, AZ 800-817-8666
Spring Street Bake Shop
Pottstown, PA 484-624-8201
Sweet Mavens, LLC
Glastonbury, CT 860-490-1407
The Bites Company
Westport, CT. 203-296-2482
Thyme Garden Herb Co
Alsea, OR 800-482-4372
Touche Bakery
London, ON 518-455-0044
Tuscan Bakery
Portland, OR 800-887-2261
Tutti Gourmet
Hudson, QC. 450-458-0911
Ultimate Biscotti
Eugene, OR. 541-344-8220
Upper Crust Biscotti
Pismo Beach, CA 866-972-6879
Wally Biscotti
Denver, CO 866-659-2559

Almond

Sweet Mavens, LLC
Glastonbury, CT 860-490-1407

Chocolate Almond

Nonni's Foods LLC
Tulsa, OK 877-295-9604

Chocolate Dipped

Sweet Mavens, LLC
Glastonbury, CT 860-490-1407

Brownies

American Quality Foods
Mills River, NC. 828-890-8344
Andre-Boudin Bakeries
San Francisco, CA 415-882-1849
Bake Crafters Food Company
McDonald, TN 423-396-3392
BakeMark Canada
Laval, QC 800-361-4998
Bakers Breakfast Cookie
Bellingham, WA 877-889-1090
Better Bites Bakery
Austin, TX
Big Island Candies Inc
Hilo, HI. 800-935-5510
Boca Bons East
Greenacres, FL 800-314-2835
Brownie Baker Inc
Fresno, CA 800-598-6501
Browniepops LLC
Leawood, KS. 816-797-0715
Byrnes & Kiefer Co
Callery, PA 724-538-5200
Cheryl's Cookies
Westerville, OH. 800-443-8124
Chris's Cookies
Teterboro, NJ. 201-288-8881
Christie Cookie
Nashville, TN 800-458-2447
Cisse Trading Co
Mamaroneck, NY 914-381-5555
Coby's Cookies
Toronto, ON 416-633-1567
Dufflet Pastries
Toronto, ON 866-238-0899
DWC Specialities
Horicon, WI 800-383-8808
Dynamic Foods
Lubbock, TX. 806-723-5600
Eilenberger Bakeries
Palestine, TX. 800-831-2544
Fairytale Brownies
Phoenix, AZ 800-324-7982
Farm & Oven Snacks
Boulder, CO
Food of Our Own Design
Maplewood, NJ. 973-762-0985
Frankly Natural Bakers
San Diego, CA 800-727-7229
Handy Pax
Randolph, MA 781-963-8300
Harvest Valley Bakery Inc
La Salle, IL 815-224-9030
Heavenscent Edibles
New York, NY 212-369-0310
Heidi's Gourmet Desserts
Tucker, GA 800-241-4166
Hudson River Foods
Castleton, NY 888-417-9343
Lavoi Corporation
Atlanta, GA. 404-325-1016
Lawler Foods LTD
Humble, TX 800-541-8285
Lone Star Bakery
Round Rock, TX. 512-255-7268
Mac's Donut Shop
Aliquippa, PA 724-375-6776
Magnolia Bakery
New York, NY 855-622-5379
Mari's New York
New York, NY
McDuffies Bakery
Clarence, NY. 800-875-1598
Michel's Bakery
Philadelphia, PA 267-345-7914
Mrs Sullivan's Pies
Jackson, TN 731-427-2101
Mrs. Fields Original Cookies
Bloomfield, CO. 800-266-2547
Otis Spunkmeyer
Norcross, GA 855-427-9982
Oven Arts
Hackensack, NJ. 855-354-4070
Pacific Ocean Produce
Santa Cruz, CA. 831-423-2654
Peggy Lawton Kitchens
East Walpole, MA. 800-843-7325
Pie Piper Products
Wheeling, IL. 800-621-8183
Rule Breaker
Brooklyn, NY 646-820-8074
Salt of the Earth Bakery
Brooklyn, NY 646-330-5089
Selma's Cookies
Apopka, FL. 800-992-6654
Sheila G Brands LLC
West Palm Beach, FL 561-688-1890
Sheila Gs Brownie Brittle Co
West Palm Beach, FL 561-557-1178
Silverland Bakery
Forest Park, IL 708-488-0800
Sterling Foods LLC
San Antonio, TX. 210-490-1669
Sweet Lady Jane
Los Angeles, CA. 323-653-7145
Tasty Baking Company
Philadelphia, PA 800-248-2789
Veronica's Treats
Middleboro, MA 866-576-1122
Vitalicious
New York, NY 877-848-2877
Wholesome Bakery
San Francisco, CA 415-343-5414
William Poll Inc
New York, NY 800-993-7655

Individually Wrapped

French Meadow Bakery & Cafe
Minneapolis, MN 612-870-7855
Lenny & Larry's
Panorama City, CA
Nature's Bakery
Reno, NV

with Nuts

Dinkel's Bakery Inc
Chicago, IL 800-822-8817

Chocolate Chip Cookies

Abimar Foods Inc
Abilene, TX. 325-691-5425
Belgian Boys
Farmingdale, NY
Carve Nutrition
Marina Del Rey, CA 310-905-8100
Chris's Cookies
Teterboro, NJ. 201-288-8881
Christie Cookie
Nashville, TN 800-458-2447
Country Choice Organic
Eden Prairie, MN 952-829-8824
Dinkel's Bakery Inc
Chicago, IL 800-822-8817
Erba Food Products
Brooklyn, NY 718-272-7700
Homefree LLC
Windham, NH 800-552-7172
Linden Cookies Inc
Congers, NY 845-268-5050
Mary's Gone Crackers
Gridley, CA. 888-258-1250
Mississippi Cheese Straw
Yazoo City, MS. 800-530-7496
Peggy Lawton Kitchens
East Walpole, MA. 800-843-7325
Sugar & Plumm
New York, NY 212-787-8778
Sunset Specialty Foods
Lake Arrowhead, CA 909-337-7643

Cookies

A La Carte
Chicago, IL 800-722-2370
A Southern Season
Hillsborough, NC 800-253-3663
Abimar Foods Inc
Abilene, TX. 325-691-5425
Abraham's Natural Foods
Long Branch, NJ. 800-327-9903
Alessi Bakery
Tampa, FL. 813-879-4544
All Wrapped Up
Plantation, FL 800-891-2194
Alpendough
Ames International Inc
Fife, WA 888-469-2637
Andre-Boudin Bakeries
San Francisco, CA 415-882-1849
Angel's Bakeries
Brooklyn, NY 718-389-1400
Arcor USA
Coral Gables, FL. 800-572-7267
Arturo's Spinella's Bakery
Waterbury, CT. 203-754-3056
Aunt Gussie Cookies & Crackers
Garfield, NJ. 800-422-6654
Austin Special Foods Company
Austin, TX. 512-372-8665
Authentic Marotti Biscotti
Lewisville, TX 972-221-7295
Back to Nature Foods
. 855-346-2225
Bake Crafters Food Company
McDonald, TN 423-396-3392
BakeMark Canada
Laval, QC 800-361-4998
BakeMark Ingredients Canada
Richmond, BC 800-665-9441
BakeMark USA
Schaumburg, IL. 847-519-3135
Baker Boy Bake Shop Inc
Dickinson, ND 800-437-2008
Bakers Breakfast Cookie
Bellingham, WA 877-889-1090
Bama Foods LTD
Tulsa, OK 800-756-2262
Barbara's Bakery
Lakeville, MN. 800-343-0590
Bavarian Specialty Foods, LLC
Los Angeles, CA. 626-856-3188
Beckmann's Old World Bakery
Santa Cruz, CA. 831-423-9242
Berkshire Mountain Bakery
Housatonic, MA 866-274-6124
Best Maid Cookie Co
River Falls, WI. 888-444-0322
Beth's Fine Desserts
Mill Valley, CA. 415-383-3991

Betty Lou's
McMinnville, OR 800-242-5205
Big Fatty's Flaming Foods
Valley View, TX 888-248-6332
Big Island Candies Inc
Hilo, HI 800-935-5510
Biscomerica Corporation
Rialto, CA 909-877-5997
Biscotti & Co.
White Plains, NY 914-682-2165
Bite Size Bakery
Rio Rancho, NM 505-994-3093
Bitsy's Brainfood
New York, NY 212-461-1572
Bloomfield Bakers
Los Alamitos, CA 800-594-4111
Blue Chip Cookies
Milford, OH 800-888-9866
Bluechip Group
Salt Lake City, UT 800-878-0099
Bluepoint Bakery
Denver, CO 303-298-1100
Borinquen Biscuit Corporation
Yauco, PR 787-856-3030
Boston America Corporation
Woburn, MA 781-933-3535
Botanical Bakery, LLC
Napa, CA 707-344-8103
BP Gourmet
Hauppauge, NY 631-234-8200
Brimhall Foods
Bartlett, TN 800-628-6559
Brooklyn Baking Company
Waterbury, CT 203-574-9198
Brooklyn Cookie Company
Brooklyn, NY 347-973-0568
Brownie Baker Inc
Fresno, CA 800-598-6501
Buckeye Pretzel Company
Williamsport, PA 800-257-6029
Buonitalia
New York, NY 212-633-9090
Busken Bakery
Cincinnati, OH 513-871-2114
Byrd Cookie
Savannah, GA 800-291-2973
Byrnes & Kiefer Co
Callery, PA 724-538-5200
California Smart Foods
San Francisco, CA 415-826-0449
Carolina Cookie Co
Greensboro, NC 800-447-5797
Case Side Holdings Company
Kensington, PE 902-836-4214
Charlie's Specialties Inc
Hermitage, PA 724-346-2350
Chatila's
Salem, NH 603-898-5459
Chelsea Flower Market
New York, NY 888-727-7887
Chip'n Dipped Cookie Co
Huntington, NY 631-470-2579
Chocoholics Divine Desserts
Linden, CA 800-760-2462
Chocolate Chix
Waxahachie, TX 214-744-2442
Chocolate Moon
Asheville, NC 800-723-1236
Chocolates a La Carte
Valencia, CA 800-818-2462
Chris's Cookies
Teterboro, NJ 201-288-8881
Christie Cookie
Nashville, TN 800-458-2447
City Bakery
New York, NY 212-366-1414
Clarmil Manufacturing Corp
Hayward, CA 888-252-7645
Collin Street Bakery
Corsicana, TX 800-267-4657
Colonial Cookies, Ltd
Kitchener, ON 800-265-6508
Commercial Bakeries
Toronto, ON 416-247-5478
Consolidated Biscuit Company
McComb, OH
Cookie Factory
Bronx, NY 718-379-6223
Cookie Kingdom
Oglesby, IL 815-883-3331
Cookie Specialties Inc
Wheeling, IL 847-537-3888

Cookie Tree Bakeries
Salt Lake City, UT 801-268-2253
Cookies United
Islip, NY 631-581-4000
Cooperstown Cookie Company
Cooperstown, NY 888-269-7315
Country Choice Organic
Eden Prairie, MN 952-829-8824
Cybele's Free To Eat
Los Angeles, CA 877-895-3729
Cybros
Waukesha, WI 800-876-2253
Dainty Confections
Windsor, ON 800-268-0222
Dairy State Foods Inc
Milwaukee, WI 800-435-4499
Dancing Deer Baking Company
Boston, MA 888-699-3337
Dare Foods
Spartanburg, SC 800-668-3273
Dare Foods Incorporated
Kitchener, ON 800-668-3273
David's Cookies
Cedar Grove, NJ 800-500-2800
DeBeukelaer Cookie Co
Madison, MS 601-856-7454
Delicious Frookie
Des Plaines, IL 847-699-3200
DeLuscious Cookies
Los Angeles, CA 323-460-2370
Di Camillo Baking Co
Niagara Falls, NY 800-634-4363
Diamond Bakery Co LTD
Honolulu, HI 808-847-3551
DiBella Baking Company
Oceanside, CA 888-857-6151
Dinkel's Bakery Inc
Chicago, IL 800-822-8817
DO, Cookie Dough Confections
New York, NY 646-892-3600
Dong Kee Company
Chicago, IL 312-225-6340
Donsuemor Madeleines
Alameda, CA 888-420-4441
Dr. Lucy's LLC
Norfolk, VA 757-233-9495
Dufflet Pastries
Toronto, ON 866-238-0899
Dutchess Bakery
Charleston, WV 304-346-4237
Eco-Planet Cookies
Santa Monica, CA 310-829-9050
Edelweiss Patisserie
Medford, MA 781-628-0225
Eleni's Cookies
New York, NY 888-435-3647
Elliott Bay Baking Co.
Seattle, WA 206-545-3804
Ellison Bakery, Inc.
Fort Wayne, IN
Elmwood Pastry Shop
West Hartford, CT 860-233-2029
Ener-G Foods
Seattle, WA 800-331-5222
Enjoy Life Foods
Chicago, IL 888-503-6569
Entenmann's
Totowa, NJ 973-785-7601
Erba Food Products
Brooklyn, NY 718-272-7700
Ericas Rugelach & Baking Co
Brooklyn, NY 718-965-3657
Ethel's Baking Co.
St. Clair Shores, MI 586-552-5110
Ethnic Edibles
New York, NY 718-320-0147
Falcone's Cookie Land LTD
Brooklyn, NY 718-236-4200
Fancypants Bakery
Walpole, MA 508-660-1140
Fantasy Cookie Company
Sylmar, CA 800-354-4488
Fantis Foods Inc
Carlstadt, NJ 201-933-6200
Federal Pretzel Baking Company
Bridgeport, NJ 215-467-0505
Fernando C Pujals & Bros
Guaynabo, PR 787-792-3080
Ferrara Bakery & Cafe
New York, NY 212-226-6150
Firefly Fandango
Seattle, WA 206-760-3700

Fireside Kitchen
Halifax, NS 902-454-7387
Flathau's Fine Foods
Hattiesburg, MS 888-263-1299
FNI Group LLC
Sherborn, MA 508-655-4175
Food Mill
Oakland, CA 510-482-3848
Fortella Fortune Cookies
Chicago, IL 312-567-9000
Fortunate Cookie
Stowe, VT 866-266-5337
Fortune Cookie Factory
Oakland, CA 510-832-5552
Foxtail Foods
Fairfield, OH 800-487-2253
Frankly Natural Bakers
San Diego, CA 800-727-7229
GH Bent Company
Milton, MA 617-322-9287
Giant Food
Landover, MD 888-469-4426
Ginny Bakes
Miami, FL 305-638-5103
Gladder's Gourmet Cookies
Lockhart, TX 888-398-4523
Glennys
Brooklyn, NY 888-864-1243
Glow Gluten Free
New York, NY 800-497-7434
Glutino
Laval, QC 800-363-3438
Golden Kernel Pecan Co
Cameron, SC 803-823-2311
Golden Walnut Specialty Foods
Wayzata, MN 800-843-3645
Goodie Girl
Ridgefield, NJ
Gourmet Treats
Torrance, CA 800-444-9549
Grandma Beth's Cookies
Alliance, NE 308-762-8433
Granello Bakery
Las Vegas, NV 702-361-0311
Grey Ghost Bakery
Charleston, SC 803-238-1123
Greyston Bakery Inc
Yonkers, NY 800-289-2253
GWB Foods Corporation
Brooklyn, NY 877-977-7610
H-E-B Grocery Co. LP
San Antonio, TX 800-432-3113
H.B. Trading
Totowa, NJ 973-812-1022
Haby's Alsatian Bakery
Castroville, TX 830-538-2118
Handy Pax
Randolph, MA 781-963-8300
Hannah Max Baking
Gardena, CA 310-324-9871
Harvest Valley Bakery Inc
La Salle, IL 815-224-9030
Hawaii Candy Inc
Honolulu, HI 800-303-2507
Hawaiian King Candies
Honolulu, HI 800-570-1902
Health Valley Company
Irwindale, CA 800-334-3204
Heavenscent Edibles
New York, NY 212-369-0310
Heltzman Bakery
Louisville, KY 502-447-3515
HempNut
Henderson, NV 707-576-7050
Heritage Short Bread
Hilton Head Isle, SC 843-422-3458
Heyerly Bakery
Ossian, IN 260-622-4196
Hollandia Bakeries Limited
Mt Brydges, ON 800-265-3480
Holt's Bakery Inc
Douglas, GA 912-384-2202
Holton Food Products
La Grange, IL 708-352-5599
Homefree LLC
Windham, NH 800-552-7172
Hudson River Foods
Castleton, NY 888-417-9343
Hunt Country Foods Inc
Marshall, VA 540-364-2622
Immaculate Baking Company
Wakefield, MA 888-826-6567

Immaculate Consumption
Columbia, SC 888-826-6567
Indianola Pecan House Inc
Indianola, MS 800-541-6252
Interbake Foods
Richmond, VA. 800-221-1002
Irene's Bakery & Gourmet
Bensalem, PA 215-244-6200
Irresistible Cookie Jar
Hayden Lake, ID. 208-664-1261
J & M Foods Inc
Little Rock, AR. 800-264-2278
Jamae Natural Foods
Los Angeles, CA. 800-343-0052
Jimmys Cookies
Clifton, NJ. 973-779-8500
Joey's Fine Foods
Newark, NJ 973-482-1400
Joseph's Lite Cookies
Deming, NM. 800-373-3726
Jovial Foods
North Stonington, CT 877-642-0644
JSL Foods
Los Angeles, CA. 800-745-3236
Jubelt Variety Bakeries
Litchfield, IL. 217-324-5314
Just Desserts
Fairfield, CA 415-780-6860
K & F Select Fine Coffees
Portland, OR 800-558-7788
Kashi Company
Solana Beach, CA. 877-747-2467
Kauai Kookie
Eleele, HI 800-361-1126
Keebler Company
Battlecreek, MI 800-962-1413
Keller's Bakery
Lafayette, LA 337-235-1568
Kelsen, Inc.
Melville, NY. 888-253-5736
Kemach Food Products
Brooklyn, NY 718-272-5655
Kerri Kreations
Santa Cruz, CA. 831-429-5129
Kids Kookie Company
San Clemente, CA. 800-350-7577
Kim and Jake's
Boulder, CO 303-499-9126
Klara's Gourmet Cookies
Lee, MA 413-243-3370
Kollar Cookies
Long Branch, NJ. 732-343-4217
LA Boulangerie
San Diego, CA 858-578-4040
Larosa Bakery Inc
Shrewsbury, NJ 800-527-6722
Lavoi Corporation
Atlanta, GA. 404-325-1016
Lazzaroni USA
Saddle Brook, NJ 201-368-1240
Lenny & Larry's
Panorama City, CA
Leo's Bakery & Deli
East Rochester, NY. 585-249-1000
Linden Cookies Inc
Congers, NY 845-268-5050
Liz Lovely Inc
Waitsfield, VT. 802-496-6390
Lotte USA Inc
Battle Creek, MI 269-963-6664
Lotus Bakery
Santa Rosa, CA. 800-875-6887
Lovin Oven Cakery
Round Lake Beach, IL 888-775-0099
Lucky Spoon Bakery LLC
Salt Lake City, UT 801-824-0624
Ludwick's Frozen Donuts
Grand Rapids, MI 800-366-8816
Luv Yu Bakery
Louisville, KY. 502-451-4511
LWC Brands Inc.
Dallas, TX. 800-552-8006
Mac Farms Of Hawaii Inc
Captain Cook, HI 808-328-2435
Mac's Donut Shop
Aliquippa, PA 724-375-6776
Madrona Specialty Foods LLC
Seattle, WA 425-656-2997
Magna Foods Corporation
City of Industry, CA 800-995-4394
Magnolia Bakery
New York, NY 855-622-5379
Mamma Says
Butler, NJ 877-283-6282
Marin Food Specialties
Byron, CA. 925-634-6126
Mary's Gone Crackers
Gridley, CA. 888-258-1250
Matt's Cookies
Wheeling, IL. 847-537-3888
Maxine's Heavenly
Los Angeles, CA
McDuffies Bakery
Clarence, NY. 800-875-1598
McKee Foods Corp.
Collegedale, TN 800-522-4499
Mctavish Shortbread
Portland, OR 800-256-9844
Merlino Italian Baking Company
Kent, WA. 800-800-9490
Michael's Cookies
Clear Lake, IA. 800-822-5384
Miss Meringue
San Marcos, CA 800-561-6516
Monaco Baking Company
Santa Fe Springs, CA 800-569-4640
Moon Dance Baking
Rohnert Park, CA 707-588-0800
Moon Rabbit Foods
Savannah, NY. 828-273-6649
Moravian Cookies Shop
Winston Salem, NC. 800-274-2994
Mozzicato De Pasquale Bakery
Hartford, CT 860-296-0426
Mrs. Denson's Cookie Company
Ukiah, CA. 800-219-3199
Mrs. Fields Original Cookies
Bloomfield, CO. 800-266-2547
Mt. View Bakery
Mountain View, HI 808-968-6353
My Boy's Baking LLC
Allentown, PA. 610-759-4552
Nabisco
Parsippany, NJ. 973-682-5000
Nana's Cookie Co.
San Diego, CA 800-836-7534
Natural Nectar
Huntington, NY 631-367-7280
Nikki's Cookies
Milwaukee, WI 800-776-7107
Northwoods Candy Emporium
Branson, MO. 417-332-1010
Nothin' But Foods
Elmwood Park, NJ 203-557-8637
Notre Dame Bakery
Conception Harbour, NL 709-535-2738
Nui Foods
Anaheim, CA
Nustef Foods
Mississauga, ON. 877-306-7562
Nutrilicious Natural Bakery
Countryside, IL. 800-835-8097
Oak State Products Inc
Wenona, IL 815-853-4348
Oh, Sugar! LLC
Roswell, GA 866-557-8427
Old Colony Baking Co Inc
Northbrook, IL 847-498-5434
Olde Colony Bakery
Mt Pleasant, SC. 800-722-9932
Otis Spunkmeyer
Norcross, GA 855-427-9982
Our Cookie
Miami, FL. 877-885-2715
Oven Arts
Hackensack, NJ. 855-354-4070
Pamela's Products
Ukiah, CA. 707-462-6605
Paris Pastry
Van Nuys, CA. 805-487-2227
Partners: A Tasteful Choice
Kent, WA. 800-632-7477
Pati-Petite Cookies Inc
Bridgeville, PA 800-253-5805
Peggy Lawton Kitchens
East Walpole, MA. 800-843-7325
Peking Noodle Co Inc
Los Angeles, CA. 323-223-0897
Pepperidge Farm Inc.
Norwalk, CT. 888-737-7374
Plehn's Bakery Inc
Louisville, KY 502-896-4438
Poppie's Dough
Chicago, IL. 888-767-7431
Poppies International
Battleboro, NC 252-442-4309
Positively 3rd St Bakery
Duluth, MN. 218-724-8619
Pure Batch
Hillsborough, NJ. 609-373-2015
Pure's Food Specialties
Broadview, IL 708-344-8884
Quaker Bonnet
Buffalo, NY. 800-283-2447
Quality Naturally Foods
City Of Industry, CA. 888-498-6986
R.W. Frookies
Sag Harbor, NY. 800-913-3663
Real Cookies
Merrick, NY 800-822-5113
Rene Rey Chocolates Ltd
North Vancouver, BC 888-985-0949
Richmond Baking Co
Richmond, IN 765-962-8535
Rip Van
Brooklyn, NY 415-529-5403
Rose Randolph Cookies, LLC
Wappingers Falls, NY. 917-834-2310
Rustic Bakery Inc.
San Rafael, CA 415-479-5600
Ryke's Bakery
Muskegon, MI. 231-726-2253
Sacramento Cookie Factory
Sacramento, CA 877-877-2646
Salem Baking Company
Winston Salem, NC. 800-274-2994
Salt of the Earth Bakery
Brooklyn, NY 646-330-5089
San Anselmo's Cookies & Biscotti
San Anselmo, CA 800-229-1249
Sandusky Filling & Brittle
Sandusky, OH 800-274-8853
Sanitary Bakery
Nanticoke, PA. 570-735-6630
Sara Snacker Cookie Company
Rye, NY. 914-305-6363
Schulze & Burch Biscuit Co
Chicago, IL 773-927-6622
Scialo Brothers Bakery
Providence, RI 877-421-0986
Sejoyia Foods
Louisville, CO. 855-293-5577
Selma Good Company
Selma, AL. 334-412-4214
Selma's Cookies
Apopka, FL. 800-992-6654
Shepherdsfield Bakery
Fulton, MO 573-642-0009
Sherwood Brands
New Brunswick, NJ 973-249-8200
Sheryl's Chocolate Creations
Hicksville, NY 888-882-2462
Shur-Good Biscuit Co.
Cincinnati, OH 513-458-6200
Silver Tray Cookies
Fort Lauderdale, FL 305-883-0800
Simit + Smith
Ridgefield, NJ. 201-699-0320
Simple Mills
Chicago, IL. 312-600-6196
Simply Gourmet Confections
Irvine, CA 714-505-3955
Simply Shari's Gluten Free
Thousand Oaks, CA 805-241-5676
Sister's Gourmet
Winder, GA. 877-338-1388
Skipping Stone Productions
Paso Robles, CA. 805-226-2998
Smoak's Bakery & Catering Service
Augusta, GA 706-738-1792
Snyder's-Lance Inc.
Charlotte, NC 800-438-1880
Sorbee Intl.
Philadelphia, PA 800-654-3997
Soupergirl
Washington, DC 202-609-7177
Spilke's Baking Company
Moosic, PA 570-457-2400
Sporting Colors LLC
St. Louis, MO 888-394-2292
Spring Street Bake Shop
Pottstown, PA 484-624-8201
Spruce Foods
San Clemente, CA. 800-326-3612
Sprucewood Handmade Cookie Company
Warkworth, ON. 877-632-1300

St. Amour Inc/French Cookies
Costa Mesa, CA 714-754-1900
Stauffer Biscuit Co
York, PA 888-480-1988
Stauffer's
Cuba, NY 585-968-2700
Stella D'oro
Charlotte, NC 800-995-2623
Sterling Foods LLC
San Antonio, TX 210-490-1669
Steve & Andy's Organics
Brooklyn, NY 718-499-7933
Steve's Mom
Bronx, NY 800-362-4545
Sucre
New Orleans, LA 504-708-4366
Sugar & Plumm
New York, NY 212-787-8778
Suity Confections Co
Miami, FL 305-639-3300
Sunset Specialty Foods
Lake Arrowhead, CA 909-337-7643
Susie's Smart Cookie
Katonah, NY 914-740-1007
Sweet Loren's
New York, NY 646-257-5700
Sweet Pillar
Newport Beach, CA 310-913-7261
Table De France
Ontario, CA 909-923-5205
Taste of Nature Inc.
Santa Monica, CA 310-396-4433
Tasty Baking Company
Philadelphia, PA 800-248-2789
Tasty Brand Inc
Calabasas, CA 818-225-9000
Tate's Bake Shop
Southampton, NY 631-283-9830
Tea Aura
Toronto, ON 416-225-8868
That's How We Roll, LLC
Fairfield, NJ 973-602-3011
Thyme Garden Herb Co
Alsea, OR 800-482-4372
Todd's
Vernon, CA 800-938-6337
Torn Ranch
Novato, CA 707-796-7800
Touche Bakery
London, ON 518-455-0044
Tribe 9 Foods
Madison, WI 608-257-7216
Trumps Food Interest
Vancouver, BC 604-732-8473
Turkey Hill Sugarbush
Waterloo, QC 450-539-4822
Uncle Ralph's Cookies
Frederick, MD 800-422-0626
United Noodle Manufacturing Company
Salt Lake City, UT 801-485-0951
Unna Bakery
New York, NY 917-543-8133
Uptown Bakers
Hyattsville, MD 301-864-1500
V L Foods
White Plains, NY 914-697-4851
Valley Bakery
Burnaby, BC 604-291-0674
Veronica's Treats
Middleboro, MA 866-576-1122
Vickey's Vittles
North Hills, CA 818-841-1944
Voortman Bakery
Burlington, ON 800-808-5950
Wackym's Kitchen
Dallas, TX 214-327-7667
Walkers Shortbread
Hauppauge, NY 800-521-0141
Wenger's Bakery
Reading, PA 610-372-6545
Westbrae Natural Foods
Melville, NY 800-434-4246
Whipped Pastry Boutique
Brooklyn, NY 718-858-8088
Wholesome Bakery
San Francisco, CA 415-343-5414
Wildlife Cookies Co
St Charles, IL 630-377-6196
Williams & Bennett
Orlando, FL 561-276-9007
Willmar Cookie & Nut Company
Willmar, MN 800-426-7845
Wonton Food
Brooklyn, NY 800-776-8889
Y Z Enterprises Inc
Maumee, OH 800-736-8779
Ya-Hoo Baking Co
Sherman, TX 888-869-2466
Yohay Baking Co
Lindenhurst, NY 631-225-0300
Young's Bakery
Uniontown, PA 724-437-6361
Zazi Baking Company
Petaluma, CA 707-778-1635

Cookies & Biscuits

A Southern Season
Hillsborough, NC 800-253-3663
Abimar Foods Inc
Abilene, TX 325-691-5425
Ames International Inc
Fife, WA 888-469-2637
Arcor USA
Coral Gables, FL 800-572-7267
Arturo's Spinella's Bakery
Waterbury, CT 203-754-3056
Aunt Gussie Cookies & Crackers
Garfield, NJ 800-422-6654
Bama Foods LTD
Tulsa, OK 800-756-2262
Barbara's Bakery
Lakeville, MN 800-343-0590
Best Maid Cookie Co
River Falls, WI 888-444-0322
Betty Lou's
McMinnville, OR 800-242-5205
Bite Size Bakery
Rio Rancho, NM 505-994-3093
Blendco Inc
Hattiesburg, MS 888-253-6326
Blue Dog Bakery
Seattle, WA 888-749-7229
Bluechip Group
Salt Lake City, UT 800-878-0099
Borinquen Biscuit Corporation
Yauco, PR 787-856-3030
Bremner Biscuit Company
Denver, CO 866-972-6879
Brimhall Foods
Bartlett, TN 800-628-6559
Brooklyn Baking Company
Waterbury, CT 203-574-9198
Buckeye Pretzel Company
Williamsport, PA 800-257-6029
Buonitalia
New York, NY 212-633-9090
Busken Bakery
Cincinnati, OH 513-871-2114
Byrd Cookie
Savannah, GA 800-291-2973
Case Side Holdings Company
Kensington, PE 902-836-4214
Charlie's Specialties Inc
Hermitage, PA 724-346-2350
Chelsea Flower Market
New York, NY 888-727-7887
Chicago Pastry
Bloomingdale, IL 630-529-6391
Chocolate Chix
Waxahachie, TX 214-744-2442
Colonial Cookies, Ltd
Kitchener, ON 800-265-6508
Cookie Factory
Bronx, NY 718-379-6223
Cookie Specialties Inc
Wheeling, IL 847-537-3888
Cookie Tree Bakeries
Salt Lake City, UT 801-268-2253
Cooper Street Cookies
Birmingham, MI 248-283-7700
Dairy State Foods Inc
Milwaukee, WI 800-435-4499
Dancing Deer Baking Company
Boston, MA 888-699-3337
Dare Foods
Spartanburg, SC 800-668-3273
DeBeukelaer Cookie Co
Madison, MS 601-856-7454
Di Camillo Baking Co
Niagara Falls, NY 800-634-4363
Diamond Bakery Co LTD
Honolulu, HI 808-847-3551
Dinkel's Bakery Inc
Chicago, IL 800-822-8817
Dong Kee Company
Chicago, IL 312-225-6340
Dufflet Pastries
Toronto, ON 866-238-0899
Dutchess Bakery
Charleston, WV 304-346-4237
DWC Specialities
Horicon, WI 800-383-8808
Edelweiss Patisserie
Medford, MA 781-628-0225
Edward & Sons Trading Co
Carpinteria, CA 805-684-8500
Ellison Bakery, Inc.
Fort Wayne, IN
Elmwood Pastry Shop
West Hartford, CT 860-233-2029
Erba Food Products
Brooklyn, NY 718-272-7700
Ericas Rugelach & Baking Co
Brooklyn, NY 718-965-3657
Falcone's Cookie Land LTD
Brooklyn, NY 718-236-4200
Fantasy Cookie Company
Sylmar, CA 800-354-4488
Federal Pretzel Baking Company
Bridgeport, NJ 215-467-0505
Fernando C Pujals & Bros
Guaynabo, PR 787-792-3080
Ferrara Bakery & Cafe
New York, NY 212-226-6150
Fireside Kitchen
Halifax, NS 902-454-7387
Food Mill
Oakland, CA 510-482-3848
Forever Green Food Inc.
Commerce, CA 323-721-9928
Fortella Fortune Cookies
Chicago, IL 312-567-9000
Fortune Cookie Factory
Oakland, CA 510-832-5552
Foxtail Foods
Fairfield, OH 800-487-2253
Frankly Natural Bakers
San Diego, CA 800-727-7229
G Debbas Chocolatier
Fresno, CA 559-294-2071
GH Bent Company
Milton, MA 617-322-9287
Giant Food
Landover, MD 888-469-4426
Grandma Beth's Cookies
Alliance, NE 308-762-8433
Granowska's
Toronto, ON 416-533-7755
Greyston Bakery Inc
Yonkers, NY 800-289-2253
GWB Foods Corporation
Brooklyn, NY 877-977-7610
H-E-B Grocery Co. LP
San Antonio, TX 800-432-3113
Hain Celestial Group Inc
Lake Success, NY 800-434-4246
Handy Pax
Randolph, MA 781-963-8300
Harvest Valley Bakery Inc
La Salle, IL 815-224-9030
Hawaii Candy Inc
Honolulu, HI 800-303-2507
Health Valley Company
Irwindale, CA 800-334-3204
Heyerly Bakery
Ossian, IN 260-622-4196
Holt's Bakery Inc
Douglas, GA 912-384-2202
Hunt Country Foods Inc
Marshall, VA 540-364-2622
Hye Quality Bakery
Fresno, CA 877-445-1778
Immaculate Consumption
Columbia, SC 888-826-6567
Interbake Foods
Richmond, VA 800-221-1002
Irresistible Cookie Jar
Hayden Lake, ID 208-664-1261
Jamae Natural Foods
Los Angeles, CA 800-343-0052
James Candy Company
Atlantic City, NJ 800-441-1404
Jim's Cheese Pantry
Waterloo, WI 800-345-3571
Joey's Fine Foods
Newark, NJ 973-482-1400

Jubelt Variety Bakeries
Litchfield, IL . . . 217-324-5314
Just Desserts
Fairfield, CA . . . 415-780-6860
Kedem
Bayonne, NJ . . . 718-369-4600
Keebler Company
Battlecreek, MI . . . 800-962-1413
Kemach Food Products
Brooklyn, NY . . . 718-272-5655
Kids Kookie Company
San Clemente, CA . . . 800-350-7577
Kinnikinnick Foods
Edmonton, AB . . . 877-503-4466
Kollar Cookies
Long Branch, NJ . . . 732-343-4217
LA Boulangerie
San Diego, CA . . . 858-578-4040
Larosa Bakery Inc
Shrewsbury, NJ . . . 800-527-6722
Le Chef Bakery
Montebello, CA . . . 323-888-2929
Linden Cookies Inc
Congers, NY . . . 845-268-5050
Loc Maria Biscuits
Philadelphia, PA
Loghouse Foods
Minneapolis, MN . . . 763-546-8395
Lotus Bakery
Santa Rosa, CA . . . 800-875-6887
Ludwick's Frozen Donuts
Grand Rapids, MI . . . 800-366-8816
Mac Farms Of Hawaii Inc
Captain Cook, HI . . . 808-328-2435
Mac's Donut Shop
Aliquippa, PA . . . 724-375-6776
Magna Foods Corporation
City of Industry, CA . . . 800-995-4394
Marin Food Specialties
Byron, CA . . . 925-634-6126
Merlino Italian Baking Company
Kent, WA . . . 800-800-9490
Mozzicato De Pasquale Bakery
Hartford, CT . . . 860-296-0426
Mt. View Bakery
Mountain View, HI . . . 808-968-6353
Nabisco
Parsippany, NJ . . . 973-682-5000
Nicole's Divine Crackers
Chicago, IL . . . 312-640-8883
Nikki's Cookies
Milwaukee, WI . . . 800-776-7107
Northwoods Candy Emporium
Branson, MO . . . 417-332-1010
Notre Dame Bakery
Conception Harbour, NL . . . 709-535-2738
Nustef Foods
Mississauga, ON . . . 877-306-7562
Nutrilicious Natural Bakery
Countryside, IL . . . 800-835-8097
Oak State Products Inc
Wenona, IL . . . 815-853-4348
Ohta Wafer Factory
Honolulu, HI . . . 808-949-2775
Paris Pastry
Van Nuys, CA . . . 805-487-2227
Pati-Petite Cookies Inc
Bridgeville, PA . . . 800-253-5805
Peggy Lawton Kitchens
East Walpole, MA . . . 800-843-7325
Peking Noodle Co Inc
Los Angeles, CA . . . 323-223-0897
Pioneer Frozen Foods
Duncanville, TX . . . 972-298-4281
Positively 3rd St Bakery
Duluth, MN . . . 218-724-8619
Pure's Food Specialties
Broadview, IL . . . 708-344-8884
Purity Factories
St. John's, NL . . . 800-563-3411
R.M. Palmer Co.
West Reading, PA . . . 610-372-8971
R.W. Frookies
Sag Harbor, NY . . . 800-913-3663
Richmond Baking Co
Richmond, IN . . . 765-962-8535
Rose Randolph Cookies, LLC
Wappingers Falls, NY . . . 917-834-2310
Rovira Biscuit Corporation
Ponce, PR . . . 787-844-8585
Ryke's Bakery
Muskegon, MI . . . 231-726-2253

S & M Communion Bread Co
Nashville, TN . . . 615-292-1969
Salem Baking Company
Winston Salem, NC . . . 800-274-2994
San Anselmo's Cookies & Biscotti
San Anselmo, CA . . . 800-229-1249
Sandusky Filling & Brittle
Sandusky, OH . . . 800-274-8853
Sanitary Bakery
Nanticoke, PA . . . 570-735-6630
Schulze & Burch Biscuit Co
Chicago, IL . . . 773-927-6622
Scialo Brothers Bakery
Providence, RI . . . 877-421-0986
Sheryl's Chocolate Creations
Hicksville, NY . . . 888-882-2462
Silver Tray Cookies
Fort Lauderdale, FL . . . 305-883-0800
Smoak's Bakery & Catering Service
Augusta, GA . . . 706-738-1792
Snyder's-Lance Inc.
Charlotte, NC . . . 800-438-1880
Spilke's Baking Company
Moosic, PA . . . 570-457-2400
Sporting Colors LLC
St. Louis, MO . . . 888-394-2292
St. Amour Inc/French Cookies
Costa Mesa, CA . . . 714-754-1900
Stauffer's
Cuba, NY . . . 585-968-2700
Stella D'oro
Charlotte, NC . . . 800-995-2623
Sunset Specialty Foods
Lake Arrowhead, CA . . . 909-337-7643
Table De France
Ontario, CA . . . 909-923-5205
Thyme Garden Herb Co
Alsea, OR . . . 800-482-4372
Treasure Foods
West Valley, UT . . . 801-974-0911
Triple-C
Hamilton, ON . . . 800-263-9105
Turnbull Cone Baking Company
Chattanooga, TN . . . 423-265-4551
Tuscan Bakery
Portland, OR . . . 800-887-2261
Ultimate Biscotti
Eugene, OR . . . 541-344-8220
Uncle Ralph's Cookies
Frederick, MD . . . 800-422-0626
United Noodle Manufacturing Company
Salt Lake City, UT . . . 801-485-0951
Uptown Bakers
Hyattsville, MD . . . 301-864-1500
UTZ Quality Foods Inc.
Hanover, PA . . . 800-367-7629
V L Foods
White Plains, NY . . . 914-697-4851
Venus Wafers Inc
Hingham, MA . . . 800-545-4538
Wenger's Bakery
Reading, PA . . . 610-372-6545
Westbrae Natural Foods
Melville, NY . . . 800-434-4246
Willmar Cookie & Nut Company
Willmar, MN . . . 800-426-7845
Wonton Food
Brooklyn, NY . . . 800-776-8889
Y Z Enterprises Inc
Maumee, OH . . . 800-736-8779
Ya-Hoo Baking Co
Sherman, TX . . . 888-869-2466
Young's Bakery
Uniontown, PA . . . 724-437-6361

Fortune Cookies

Dong Kee Company
Chicago, IL . . . 312-225-6340
Fortella Fortune Cookies
Chicago, IL . . . 312-567-9000
Fortune Cookie Factory
Oakland, CA . . . 510-832-5552
Hawaii Candy Inc
Honolulu, HI . . . 800-303-2507
Ohta Wafer Factory
Honolulu, HI . . . 808-949-2775
Peking Noodle Co Inc
Los Angeles, CA . . . 323-223-0897
United Noodle Manufacturing Company
Salt Lake City, UT . . . 801-485-0951
Wings Foods of Alberta Ltd
Edmonton, AB . . . 780-433-6406

Wonton Food
Brooklyn, NY . . . 800-776-8889

Frozen Cookies

Bama Foods LTD
Tulsa, OK . . . 800-756-2262
GWB Foods Corporation
Brooklyn, NY . . . 877-977-7610
Orange Bakery
Irvine, CA . . . 949-863-1377
RoRo's Baking Company
Dallas, TX . . . 972-897-2315
Sugarplum Desserts
Langley, BC . . . 604-534-2282
Sunset Specialty Foods
Lake Arrowhead, CA . . . 909-337-7643

Ginger Snaps

Country Choice Organic
Eden Prairie, MN . . . 952-829-8824
Mary's Gone Crackers
Gridley, CA . . . 888-258-1250

Individually Packaged

Biscomerica Corporation
Rialto, CA . . . 909-877-5997
Boulder Cookie
Boulder, CO
Munk Pack
Greenwich, CT
No Cow
Denver, CO
Paleo Prime Foods
Chicago, IL . . . 312-659-6596

Macaroons

Abimar Foods Inc
Abilene, TX . . . 325-691-5425
Duverger
Oxnard, CA
Emmy's Organics
Ithaca, NY . . . 855-463-6697
Erba Food Products
Brooklyn, NY . . . 718-272-7700
Jennies Gluten-Free Bakery
Moosic, PA . . . 570-457-2400
L & M Bakery
Riverside, NJ . . . 888-887-1335
Macaron Paris LLC
New York, NY . . . 212-465-0510
Northern Valley Baking Co
Dumont, NJ . . . 201-338-2812
Poppies International
Battleboro, NC . . . 252-442-4309
St. Julien Macaroons
Sandown, NH . . . 800-473-8869
Steve's Mom
Bronx, NY . . . 800-362-4545
Sucre
New Orleans, LA . . . 504-708-4366
Sugar & Plumm
New York, NY . . . 212-787-8778

Mini Cookies

Bakeology
Torrance, CA
Bauducco Foods Inc.
Miami, FL . . . 305-477-9270
Biscomerica Corporation
Rialto, CA . . . 909-877-5997
Ginny Bakes
Miami, FL . . . 305-638-5103

Oatmeal & Chocolate Chip Cookies

Klara's Gourmet Cookies
Lee, MA . . . 413-243-3370
Olivia's Kitchen
New York, NY . . . 917-374-0077
Sweet Street Desserts
Reading, PA . . . 800-793-3897

Oatmeal Cookies

Abimar Foods Inc
Abilene, TX . . . 325-691-5425
Country Choice Organic
Eden Prairie, MN . . . 952-829-8824
Homefree LLC
Windham, NH . . . 800-552-7172

Kashi Company
Solana Beach, CA 877-747-2467
Mississippi Cheese Straw
Yazoo City, MS 800-530-7496
Olivia's Kitchen
New York, NY 917-374-0077
Peggy Lawton Kitchens
East Walpole, MA 800-843-7325

Oatmeal Raisin Cookies

Linden Cookies Inc
Congers, NY 845-268-5050

Sandwich Creme Cookies

Abimar Foods Inc
Abilene, TX 325-691-5425
Biscomerica Corporation
Rialto, CA 909-877-5997
Country Choice Organic
Eden Prairie, MN 952-829-8824
Tasty Brand Inc
Calabasas, CA 818-225-9000

Soft Cookies

Biscomerica Corporation
Rialto, CA 909-877-5997
Jack's Paleo Kitchen
Ferndale, WA
Oak State Products Inc
Wenona, IL 815-853-4348

Sugar Cookies

Falcone's Cookie Land LTD
Brooklyn, NY 718-236-4200
Young's Bakery
Uniontown, PA 724-437-6361

Tea Cookies

Botanical Bakery, LLC
Napa, CA 707-344-8103
Hawaii Candy Inc
Honolulu, HI 800-303-2507
J & M Foods Inc
Little Rock, AR 800-264-2278
Klara's Gourmet Cookies
Lee, MA 413-243-3370
Ohta Wafer Factory
Honolulu, HI 808-949-2775
Simply Scruptious Confections
Irvine, CA 714-505-3955

Wafers

Arcor USA
Coral Gables, FL 800-572-7267
Castella Imports Inc
Brentwood, NY 631-231-5500
DeBeukelaer Corp
Madison, MS 601-856-7454
Fernando C Pujals & Bros
Guaynabo, PR 787-792-3080
Functional Foods
Roseville, MI 877-372-0550
Honey Wafer Baking Co
Crestwood, IL 800-977-9012
Kitchen Table
Syosset, NY 800-486-4582
Loacker USA
New York, NY 212-742-8510
Pez Candy Inc
Orange, CT 203-795-0531
Q Bell Foods
Nyack, NY 845-358-1475
Ruger LLC
Bethesda, MD 301-675-2398
Smarties
Union, NJ 800-631-7968
Snyder's-Lance Inc.
Charlotte, NC 800-438-1880
Table De France
Ontario, CA 909-923-5205
V L Foods
White Plains, NY 914-697-4851
Yohay Baking Co
Lindenhurst, NY 631-225-0300

Sugar

ADM Wild Flavors & Specialty
Erlanger, KY 859-342-3600

Alfred L. Wolff, Inc.
Park Ridge, IL 847-759-8888
American Culinary Garden
Springfield, MO 888-831-2433
Annie's Frozen Yogurt
Minneapolis, MN 800-969-9648
BakeMark Canada
Laval, QC 800-361-4998
Bouchard Family Farm
Fort Kent, ME 800-239-3237
Brookside Foods
Abbotsford, BC 800-468-1714
Calico Cottage
Amityville, NY 800-645-5345
California Cereal Products
Oakland, CA 510-452-4500
Canada Bread Co, Ltd
Etobicoke, ON 800-465-5515
Chelsea Milling Co.
Chelsea, MI 800-727-2460
Country Choice Organic
Eden Prairie, MN 952-829-8824
Crown Processing Company
Cerritos, CA 562-865-0293
Dutch Ann Foods Company
Natchez, MS 601-445-5566
Ellison Milling Company
Lethbridge, AB 403-328-6622
Embassy Flavours Ltd.
Brampton, ON 800-334-3371
Flavormatic Industries
Wappingers Falls, NY 845-297-9100
Foley's Chocolates & Candies
Richmond, BC 888-236-5397
Great Recipes
Beaverton, OR 800-273-2331
Gregory's Foods, Inc.
St Paul, MN 800-231-4734
GWB Foods Corporation
Brooklyn, NY 877-977-7610
JER Creative Food Concepts, Inc.
Commerce, CA 800-350-2462
La Cookie
Burbank, CA 818-495-5732
Marie Callender's Gourmet Products/Goldrush Products
San Jose, CA 800-729-5428
Martha Olson's Great Foo
Sutter Creek, CA 800-973-3966
Mimac Glaze
Brampton, ON 877-990-9975
Natrium Products Inc
Cortland, NY 800-962-4203
Ottens Flavors
Philadelphia, PA 800-523-0767
Paradise Island Foods
Nanaimo, BC 800-889-3370
Petra International
Mississauga, ON 800-261-7226
Pillsbury
Minneapolis, MN 800-775-4777
Produits Alimentaire
St Lambert De Lauzon, QC 800-463-1787
Sanford Milling Co Inc
Henderson, NC 866-438-4526
Southern Brown Rice
Weiner, AR 800-421-7423
Southern Style Nuts
Denison, TX 903-463-3161
Sugar Flowers Plus
Glendale, CA 800-972-2935
Tasty Selections
Concord, ON 905-760-2353
Teff Co
Nampa, ID 888-822-2221
Westco-BakeMark
Pico Rivera, CA 562-949-1054
Yorktown Baking Company
Yorktown Heights, NY 800-235-3961

Crackers

Crackers

34-Degrees
Denver, CO 303-861-4818
Abimar Foods Inc
Abilene, TX 325-691-5425
American Vintage Wine Biscuits
Long Island City, NY 718-361-1003
Aunt Gussie Cookies & Crackers
Garfield, NJ 800-422-6654
Back to Nature Foods
. 855-346-2225
Bake Crafters Food Company
McDonald, TN 423-396-3392
Bama Foods LTD
Tulsa, OK 800-756-2262
Bespoke Provisions
Boulder, CO 646-963-1245
Bite Size Bakery
Rio Rancho, NM 505-994-3093
Bitsy's Brainfood
New York, NY 212-461-1572
Blue Dog Bakery
Seattle, WA 888-749-7229
Borinquen Biscuit Corporation
Yauco, PR 787-856-3030
Christie-Brown
East Hanover, NJ 973-503-4000
Consolidated Biscuit Company
McComb, OH
Dairyfood USA Inc
Blue Mounds, WI 800-236-3300
Dan-D Foods Ltd
Richmond, BC 800-633-4788
Dare Foods Incorporated
Kitchener, ON 800-668-3273
Delicious Frookie
Des Plaines, IL 847-699-3200
Diamond Bakery Co LTD
Honolulu, HI 808-847-3551
Earth Balance
Boulder, CO 866-234-6429
Ella's Flats
Naples, FL
Falcone's Cookie Land LTD
Brooklyn, NY 718-236-4200
Flackers
Minneapolis, MN
Flax4Life
Bellingham, WA 877-352-9487
Foods Alive
Angola, IN 260-488-4497
Fortitude Brands LLC
Coral Gables, FL 305-661-8198
Gilda Industries Inc
Hialeah, FL 305-887-8286
Glutino
Laval, QC 800-363-3438
Good Groceries
Brooklyn, NY 347-853-7462
Grains of Health LLC
Fremont, CA 510-516-2556
GWB Foods Corporation
Brooklyn, NY 877-977-7610
Handy Pax
Randolph, MA 781-963-8300
Healing Home Foods
Pound Ridge, NY 914-764-1303
Health Valley Company
Irwindale, CA 800-334-3204
Hye Quality Bakery
Fresno, CA 877-445-1778
Interbake Foods
Richmond, VA 800-221-1002
J & M Foods Inc
Little Rock, AR 800-264-2278
Jilz Gluten Free
Ventura, CA 805-585-5297
Jim's Cheese Pantry
Waterloo, WI 800-345-3571
Jovial Foods
North Stonington, CT 877-642-0644
Kameda USA Inc.
Torrance, CA 310-944-9639
Kapow Now!
North Vancouver, BC 604-726-6391
Kashi Company
Solana Beach, CA 877-747-2467
Keebler Company
Battlecreek, MI 800-962-1413
Kemach Food Products
Brooklyn, NY 718-272-5655
La Piccolina
Decatur, GA 800-626-1624
Legacy Bakehouse
Waukesha, WI 800-967-2447
Magna Foods Corporation
City of Industry, CA 800-995-4394
Manischewitz Co
Newark, NJ 201-553-1100
Mary's Gone Crackers
Gridley, CA 888-258-1250
Nabisco
Parsippany, NJ 973-682-5000

Nicole's Divine Crackers
Chicago, IL 312-640-8883
Nonni's Foods LLC
Tulsa, OK 877-295-9604
Oberweis Dairy Inc
North Aurora, IL. 866-623-7934
Panorama Foods Inc.
Braintree, MA 781-592-1069
Partners: A Tasteful Choice
Kent, WA. 800-632-7477
Pepperidge Farm Inc.
Norwalk, CT 888-737-7374
Richmond Baking Co
Richmond, IN 765-962-8535
Rovira Biscuit Corporation
Ponce, PR 787-844-8585
San-J International Inc
Henrico, VA 800-446-5500
Schulze & Burch Biscuit Co
Chicago, IL 773-927-6622
Simple Mills
Chicago, IL 312-600-6196
Small Planet Foods
Minneapolis, MN 800-624-4123
Snyder's-Lance Inc.
Charlotte, NC 800-438-1880
Stauffer Biscuit Co
York, PA 888-480-1988
TH Foods, Inc.
Loves Park, IL. 815-636-9500
That's How We Roll, LLC
Fairfield, NJ 973-602-3011
Urban Accents
Chicago, IL. 877-872-7742
Urban Oven
Chandler, AZ. 866-770-6836
Venus Wafers Inc
Hingham, MA. 800-545-4538
Vision Pack Brands
El Segundo, CA 877-477-8500
Way Better Snacks
Minneapolis, MN 612-314-2060
Willmar Cookie & Nut Company
Willmar, MN. 800-426-7845

Meal

Newly Weds Foods Inc
Chicago, IL 800-621-7521
Richmond Baking Co
Richmond, IN 765-962-8535
Sugar Foods Corp
New York, NY

Oyster Crackers

Panorama Foods Inc.
Braintree, MA. 781-592-1069

Poppy & Sesame Crackers

Ella's Flats
Naples, FL

Saltines

Abimar Foods Inc
Abilene, TX. 325-691-5425

Crunches

Rustic Bakery Inc.
San Rafael, CA 415-479-5600
Sweet Street Desserts
Reading, PA 800-793-3897

Desserts

Adams Foods & Milling
Dothan, AL 334-983-4233
Aglamesis Bros Ice Cream
Cincinnati, OH 513-531-5196
Agropur
Granby, QC. 800-363-5686
Al Gelato Bornay
Franklin Park, IL. 847-455-5355
Alati-Caserta Desserts
Montr,al, QC. 877-377-5680
Alexian Pâtés
Neptune, NJ 800-927-9473
Alpenrose Dairy
Portland, OR 503-244-1133
American Classic Ice Cream Company
Bay Shore, NY 800-736-4100
Andre-Boudin Bakeries
San Francisco, CA 415-882-1849
Aryzta
Los Angeles, CA. 855-427-9982
ASK Foods Inc
Palmyra, PA. 800-879-4275
Athens Foods Inc
Brookpark, OH 843-916-2000
Awrey Bakeries
Livonia, MI. 800-950-2253
BakeryCorp
Miami, FL. 305-623-3838
Balboa Dessert Co Inc
Santa Ana, CA 800-974-9699
Bama Foods LTD
Tulsa, OK 800-756-2262
Banquet Schusters Bakery
Pueblo, CO 719-544-1062
Barnes Ice Cream Company
Manchester, ME 207-622-0827
Baskin-Robbins LLC
Canton, MA 800-859-5339
BBU Bakeries
Horsham, PA. 800-984-0989
Beatrice Bakery Co
Beatrice, NE 800-228-4030
Best Maid Cookie Co
River Falls, WI 888-444-0322
Beth's Fine Desserts
Mill Valley, CA. 415-383-3991
Birdsall Ice Cream Company
Mason City, IA 641-423-5365
Birkholm's Solvang Bakery
Solvang, CA 800-377-4253
Bittersweet Pastries
Norwood, NJ. 800-217-2938
Black's Barbecue
Lockhart, TX. 888-632-8225
Blue Bell Creameries LP
Brenham, TX. 800-327-8135
Bluepoint Bakery
Denver, CO 303-298-1100
Boboli Intl. Inc.
Stockton, CA. 209-473-3507
Bonnie Doon LLC
Elkhart, IN. 574-264-3390
Brighams
Arlington, MA 800-242-2423
Brown's Ice Cream Co
Minneapolis, MN 612-378-1075
Brownie Brittle, LLC
West Palm Beach, FL 561-688-1890
Browns' Ice Cream Company
Minneapolis, MN 612-378-1075
Bubbies Homemade Ice Cream
Aiea, HI. 808-487-7218
Buck's Spumoni Company
Milford, CT. 888-222-8257
Busken Bakery
Cincinnati, OH 513-871-2114
Calmar Bakery
Calmar, AB 780-985-3583
Cannoli Factory
Wyandanch, NY 631-643-2700
Caprine Estates
Bellbrook, OH. 937-848-7406
Caribbean Food Delights Inc
Tappan, NY. 845-398-3000
Carole's Cheesecake Company
Toronto, ON 416-256-0000
Carolina Foods Inc
Charlotte, NC 800-234-0441
Carousel Cakes
Nanuet, NY. 800-659-2253
Cascadian Farm Inc
Sedro Woolley, WA. 360-855-0542
Case Side Holdings Company
Kensington, PE 902-836-4214
Cateraid Inc
Howell, MI 800-508-8217
CBC Foods
Little River, KS. 800-276-4770
Cedar Crest Specialties
Cedarburg, WI. 800-877-8341
Celebrity Cheesecake
Davie, FL 877-986-2253
Centreside Dairy
Renfrew, ON. 800-889-9974
Chattanooga Bakery Inc
Chattanooga, TN. 800-251-3404
Cheesecake Etc Desserts
Miami Springs, FL 305-887-0258
Cheesecake Factory Inc.
Calabasas Hills, CA 818-871-3000
Chef Hans' Gourmet Foods
Monroe, LA. 800-890-4267
Chef's Pride Gifts LLC
Taylor, MI 800-878-1800
Chella's Dutch Delicacies
Lake Oswego, OR. 800-458-3331
Chelsea Milling Co.
Chelsea, MI. 800-727-2460
Chewys Rugulach
San Diego, CA 800-241-3456
Chicago Pastry
Bloomingdale, IL 630-529-6391
Chocolaterie Bernard Callebaut
Calgary, AB. 800-661-8367
Chudleigh's
Milton, ON 800-387-4028
Ciao Bella Gelato Company
Irvington, NJ. 800-435-2863
Clarkson Scottish Bakery
Mississauga, ON. 905-823-1500
Claxton Bakery Inc
Claxton, GA 800-841-4211
Clement's Pastry Shops Inc
Hyattsville, MD 301-277-6300
Cloverhill Bakery-Vend Corporation
Chicago, IL 773-745-9800
Clyde's Delicious Donuts
Addison, IL. 630-628-6555
Coby's Cookies
Toronto, ON 416-633-1567
Cold Fusion Foods
West Hollywood, CA 310-287-3244
Collin Street Bakery
Corsicana, TX. 800-267-4657
Community Orchards
Fort Dodge, IA 888-573-8212
Conifer Specialties Inc
Woodinville, WA. 800-588-9160
Cookie Factory
Bronx, NY. 718-379-6223
Country Choice Organic
Eden Prairie, MN 952-829-8824
Creme Curls
Hudsonville, MI 800-466-1219
Crystal Creamery
Modesto, CA. 866-225-4821
Culinar Canada
Baie-Comeau, QC. 418-296-4395
Cummings Studio Chocolates
Salt Lake City, UT 800-537-3957
Dancing Deer Baking Company
Boston, MA. 888-699-3337
Dannon Yo Cream
Portland, OR 800-962-7326
David's Cookies
Cedar Grove, NJ 800-500-2800
Davis Bakery & Delicatessen
Cleveland, OH 216-292-3060
Davis Bread & Desserts
Davis, CA 530-220-4375
Deep Foods Inc
Union, NJ 908-810-7500
Deerfield Bakery
Buffalo Grove, IL 847-520-0068
Del's Pastry
Toronto, ON 800-461-0663
Delicious Desserts
Brooklyn, NY 718-680-1156
Desserts by David Glass
South Windsor, CT 860-462-7520
Desserts Of Distinction
Tigard, OR 503-654-8370
Di Camillo Baking Co
Niagara Falls, NY. 800-634-4363
Dimitria Delights Baking Co
North Grafton, MA 800-763-1113
Dinkel's Bakery Inc
Chicago, IL. 800-822-8817
Dipaolo Baking Co Inc
Rochester, NY. 585-232-3510
Divine Delights
Petaluma, CA 800-443-2836
Don's Food Products
Schwenksville, PA 888-321-3667
Dufflet Pastries
Toronto, ON 866-238-0899
DWC Specialities
Horicon, WI 800-383-8808
Dynamic Foods
Lubbock, TX. 806-723-5600

Eddy's Bakery
Boise, ID . . . 208-377-8100
Edelweiss Patisserie
Medford, MA . . . 781-628-0225
Edwards Baking Company
Marshall, MN . . . 866-739-2328
Elegant Desserts
Lyndhurst, NJ . . . 201-933-0770
Eli's Cheesecake
Chicago, IL . . . 800-354-2253
Elmwood Pastry Shop
West Hartford, CT . . . 860-233-2029
European Style Bakery
Beverly Hills, CA . . . 818-368-6876
Fairview Dairy Inc
Latrobe, PA . . . 724-537-7111
Fantasia
Sedalia, MO . . . 660-827-1172
Farr Candy Company
Idaho Falls, ID . . . 208-522-8215
Fendall Ice Cream Company
Salt Lake City, UT . . . 801-355-3583
Field's Pies
Pauls Valley, OK . . . 800-286-7501
Fieldbrook Foods Corp.
Dunkirk, NY . . . 800-333-0805
Fiera Foods
Toronto, ON . . . 800-675-6356
Fillo Factory, The
Northvale, NJ . . . 800-653-4556
Fireside Kitchen
Halifax, NS . . . 902-454-7387
Flavor Right Foods Group
St Phoenix, AZ . . . 888-464-3734
Flavors from Florida
Bartow, FL . . . 800-888-0409
Flowers Baking Co
El Paso, TX . . . 800-328-6111
FNI Group LLC
Sherborn, MA . . . 508-655-4175
Food of Our Own Design
Maplewood, NJ . . . 973-762-0985
Foxtail Foods
Fairfield, OH . . . 800-487-2253
France Delices
Montreal, QC . . . 800-663-1365
Frankly Natural Bakers
San Diego, CA . . . 800-727-7229
French Patisserie
Pacifica, CA . . . 800-300-2253
Frozfruit Corporation
Gardena, CA . . . 310-217-1034
FrutStix
Santa Barbara, CA . . . 805-965-1656
Future Bakery & Cafe
Toronto, ON . . . 416-231-1491
Galliker Dairy Co
Johnstown, PA . . . 800-477-6455
Garber Ice Cream Co Inc
Winchester, VA . . . 800-662-5422
Gardner Pie Co
Akron, OH . . . 330-245-2030
Gelato Fresco
Toronto, ON . . . 416-785-5415
Georgia Fruitcake Co
Claxton, GA . . . 912-739-2683
GH Bent Company
Milton, MA . . . 617-322-9287
Giant Food
Landover, MD . . . 888-469-4426
Gifford's Ice Cream
Skowhegan, ME . . . 800-950-2604
Gimbals Fine Candies
S San Francisco, CA . . . 800-344-6225
Glover's Ice Cream Inc
Frankfort, IN . . . 800-686-5163
GoBio!
Action, ON . . . 519-853-2958
Golden Brown Bakery Inc
South Haven, MI . . . 269-637-3418
Good Old Days Foods
Little Rock, AR . . . 501-565-1257
Gourmet Croissant
Brooklyn, NY . . . 718-499-4911
Govatos Chocolates
Wilmington, DE . . . 888-799-5252
Grace Baking Company
Richmond, CA . . . 510-231-7200
Grainaissance
Emeryville, CA . . . 800-472-4697
Granowska's
Toronto, ON . . . 416-533-7755
Great American Dessert Co
Flushing, NY . . . 800-458-6467
Great Northern Maple Products
Saint Honor, De Shenley, QC . . . 418-485-7777
Grebe's Bakery
Milwaukee, WI . . . 800-833-3158
Grecian Delight Foods Inc
Elk Grove Village, IL . . . 800-621-4387
Greyston Bakery Inc
Yonkers, NY . . . 800-289-2253
Grossingers Home Bakery
New York, NY . . . 800-479-6996
Gumpert's Canada
Mississauga, ON . . . 800-387-9324
H-E-B Grocery Co. LP
San Antonio, TX . . . 800-432-3113
Haby's Alsatian Bakery
Castroville, TX . . . 830-538-2118
Hafner USA
Stone Mountain, GA . . . 888-725-4605
Hahn's Old Fashioned Cake Co
Farmingdale, NY . . . 631-249-3456
Handy Pax
Randolph, MA . . . 781-963-8300
Hanover Foods Corp
Hanover, PA . . . 717-632-6000
Happy & Healthy Products Inc
Boca Raton, FL . . . 561-367-0739
Harold Food Company
Charlotte, NC . . . 704-588-8061
Harry & David
Medford, OR . . . 877-322-1200
Harvest Bakery
Central Islip, NY . . . 631-232-1709
Harvest Valley Bakery Inc
La Salle, IL . . . 815-224-9030
Health Valley Company
Irwindale, CA . . . 800-334-3204
Hearthy Foods
Los Angeles, CA . . . 213-372-5093
Heidi's Gourmet Desserts
Tucker, GA . . . 800-241-4166
Heltzman Bakery
Louisville, KY . . . 502-447-3515
HFI Foods
Redmond, WA . . . 425-883-1320
Holt's Bakery Inc
Douglas, GA . . . 912-384-2202
Holton Food Products
La Grange, IL . . . 708-352-5599
Homer's Ice Cream
Wilmette, IL . . . 847-251-0477
Hormel Foods Corp.
Austin, MN . . . 507-437-5611
Hostess Brands
Kansas City, MO . . . 816-701-4600
Hunt Country Foods Inc
Marshall, VA . . . 540-364-2622
Hunter Farms - High Point Division
High Point, NC . . . 800-446-8035
Ice Cream Bowl
Zanesville, OH . . . 740-452-5267
Ice Cream Club Inc
Boynton Beach, FL . . . 800-535-7711
Ice Cream Specialties Inc
St Louis, MO . . . 800-662-7550
Il Gelato
Astoria, NY . . . 800-899-9299
Incredible Cheesecake
San Diego, CA . . . 619-563-9722
It's It Ice Cream Co
Burlingame, CA . . . 800-345-1928
Italian Bakery of Virginia
Virginia, MN . . . 218-741-3464
J.A.M.B. Low Carb Distributor
Pompano Beach, FL . . . 800-708-6738
J.P. Sunrise Bakery
Edmonton, AB . . . 780-454-5797
J.W. Haywood & Sons Dairy
Louisville, KY . . . 502-774-2311
Jack & Jill Ice Cream
Moorestown, NJ . . . 856-813-2300
James Skinner Company
Omaha, NE . . . 800-358-7428
Jaxon's Ice Cream Parlor
Dania Beach, FL . . . 954-923-4445
Joey's Fine Foods
Newark, NJ . . . 973-482-1400
John J. Nissen Baking Company
Brewer, ME . . . 207-989-7654
Johnson's Real Ice Cream
Columbus, OH . . . 614-231-0014
Jon Donaire Desserts
Santa Fe Springs, CA . . . 877-366-2473
Josh & John's Ice Cream
Colorado Springs, CO . . . 800-530-2855
Joyva Corp
Brooklyn, NY . . . 718-497-0170
Jubelt Variety Bakeries
Litchfield, IL . . . 217-324-5314
Just Desserts
Fairfield, CA . . . 415-780-6860
Kan-Pak
Arkansas City, KS . . . 800-378-1265
Kapaa Poi Factory
Kapaa, HI . . . 808-822-5426
Katrina's Tartufo
Port Jeffrsn Sta, NY . . . 800-480-8836
Klinke Brothers Ice Cream Co
Memphis, TN . . . 901-322-6640
KOZY Shack Enterprises Inc
St Paul, MN . . . 855-716-1555
Kyger Bakery Products
Lafayette, IN . . . 765-447-1252
L & M Bakery
Riverside, NJ . . . 888-887-1335
Larosa Bakery Inc
Shrewsbury, NJ . . . 800-527-6722
Lax & Mandel Bakery
South Euclid, OH . . . 216-382-8877
Leader Candies
Brooklyn, NY . . . 718-366-6900
Lenchner Bakery
Concord, ON . . . 905-738-8811
Lone Star Bakery
Round Rock, TX . . . 512-255-7268
Love Quiches Desserts
Freeport, NY . . . 516-623-8800
Lucy's Sweet Surrender
Beachwood, OH . . . 216-752-0828
M&L Gourmet Ice Cream
Baltimore, MD . . . 410-276-4880
Mac's Donut Shop
Aliquippa, PA . . . 724-375-6776
Mack's Bill Ice Cream
Dover, PA . . . 717-292-1931
Mackie International, Inc.
Riverside, CA . . . 800-733-9762
Maple Island
Saint Paul, MN . . . 800-369-1022
Mar-Key Foods
Vidalia, GA . . . 912-537-4204
Marie Callender's
Mission Viejo, CA . . . 800-776-7437
Mario's Gelati
Vancouver, BC . . . 604-879-9411
Martino's Bakery
Burbank, CA . . . 818-842-0715
Mary Ann's Baking Co Inc
Sacramento, CA . . . 916-681-7444
Matador Processors
Blanchard, OK . . . 800-847-0797
Mayer's Cider Mill
Webster, NY . . . 800-543-0043
Mazelle's Cheesecakes Concoctions Creations
Dallas, TX . . . 214-328-9102
McCain Foods Ltd.
Toronto, ON . . . 416-955-1700
McConnell's Fine Ice Cream
Santa Barbara, CA . . . 805-963-8813
Meadows Country Products
Hollidaysburg, PA . . . 888-499-1001
Mehaffies Pies
Dayton, OH . . . 800-289-7437
Mia Products
Scranton, PA . . . 570-207-5328
Michel's Bakery
Philadelphia, PA . . . 267-345-7914
Michele's Family Bakery
York, PA . . . 717-741-2027
Michelle Chocolatiers
Colorado Springs, CO . . . 888-447-3654
Michigan Dairy LLC
Livonia, MI . . . 734-367-5390
Mikawaya LLC
Vernon, CA . . . 323-587-5504
Miles of Chocolate
Austin, TX
Millie's Pierogi
Chicopee Falls, MA . . . 800-743-7641
Mississippi Cheese Straw
Yazoo City, MS . . . 800-530-7496
Mister Cookie Face
Dunkirk, NY . . . 800-333-0305

Model Dairy LLC
Reno, NV 800-433-2030
Monaco Baking Company
Santa Fe Springs, CA 800-569-4640
Moonlight Gourmet
Tyler, TX........................903-581-1228
Mozzicato De Pasquale Bakery
Hartford, CT 860-296-0426
Mrs Baird's
Horsham, PA......................800-984-0989
Mrs Sullivan's Pies
Jackson, TN 731-427-2101
Mt. View Bakery
Mountain View, HI................808-968-6353
Multi Marques
Montreal, QC 514-934-1866
Multiflex Company
Hawthorne, NJ 973-636-9700
My Daddy's Cheesecake
Cape Girardeau, MO...............800-735-6765
My Grandma's Coffee Cake
Hyde Park, MA....................800-847-2636
Najila's
Binghamton, NY...................607-722-4287
Natural Fruit Corp
Hialeah, FL......................305-887-7525
Naturally Delicious Inc
Oakland Park, FL.................888-221-7352
Nature's Hilights
Chico, CA........................800-313-6454
New York Bakeries Inc
Hialeah, FL......................305-883-0790
Nikki's Cookies
Milwaukee, WI....................800-776-7107
Northside Bakery
Brooklyn, NY.....................718-782-2700
Notre Dame Bakery
Conception Harbour, NL 709-535-2738
O'Boyle's Ice Cream Company
Bristol, PA......................215-788-3882
Oak Leaf Confections
.................................877-261-7887
OH Chocolate
Seattle, WA......................206-329-8777
Old Country Bakery
North Hollywood, CA 818-838-2302
Old Fashioned Kitchen Inc
Lakewood, NJ.....................732-364-4100
Omaha Steaks Inc
.................................800-960-8400
Out of a Flower
Lancaster, TX....................800-743-4696
Pacific Ocean Produce
Santa Cruz, CA...................831-423-2654
Parker Products
Fort Worth, TX...................817-336-7441
Pasta Factory
Melrose Park, IL.................800-615-6951
Pastry Chef
Pawtucket, RI....................800-639-8606
Patisserie Wawel
Montreal, QC.....................614-524-3348
Pearl River Pastry & Chocolate
Pearl River, NY..................800-632-2639
Peggy Lawton Kitchens
East Walpole, MA.................800-843-7325
Pellman Foods Inc
New Holland, PA..................717-354-8070
Perry's Ice Cream Co Inc
Akron, NY........................800-873-7797
Petersen Ice Cream Company
Oak Park, IL.....................708-386-6130
Phipps Desserts
North York, ON...................416-391-5800
Pie Piper Products
Wheeling, IL.....................800-621-8183
Piedmont Candy Co
Lexington, NC....................336-248-2477
Pinocchio Italian Ice Cream Company
Edmonton, AB.....................780-455-1905
Platte Valley Creamery
Scottsbluff, NE..................308-632-4225
Plehn's Bakery Inc
Louisville, KY...................502-896-4438
Pocono Cheesecake Factory
Swiftwater, PA...................570-839-6844
Poppies International
Battleboro, NC...................252-442-4309
Price Co
Yakima, WA.......................509-966-4110
Pride Dairies
Bottineau, ND....................701-228-2216

Priester's Pecans
Fort Deposit, AL.................866-477-4736
Puritan/ATZ Ice Cream
Kendallville, IN.................260-347-2700
Purity Dairies LLC
Nashville, TN....................615-244-1900
Purity Ice Cream Co
Ithaca, NY.......................607-272-1545
Quality Naturally Foods
City Of Industry, CA.............888-498-6986
Real Food Marketing
Kansas City, MO..................816-221-4100
Reinhold Ice Cream Company
Pittsburgh, PA...................412-321-7600
Reiter Dairy
Newport, KY......................800-544-6455
Reiter Dairy LLC
Springfield, OH..................937-323-5777
Rhino Foods Inc
Burlington, VT...................802-862-0252
Rich's Ice Cream Co Inc
West Palm Beach, FL..............561-833-7585
Rising Dough Bakery
Sacramento, CA...................916-387-9700
Rolling Pin Bakery
Bow Island, AB...................403-545-2434
Roma Bakeries
Rockford, IL.....................815-964-6737
Rosati Italian Water Ice
Clifton Heights, PA..............855-476-7284
Roselani Tropics Ice Cream
Wailuku, HI......................808-244-7951
Rowena
Norfolk, VA......................800-627-8699
Royal Home Bakery
Newmarket, ON....................905-715-7044
RW Delights
Millington, NJ...................866-892-1096
Ryals Bakery
Milledgeville, GA................478-452-0321
Ryke's Bakery
Muskegon, MI.....................231-726-2253
Sacramento Baking Co
Sacramento, CA...................916-361-2000
Sara Lee Frozen Bakery
Kings Mountain, NC...............800-323-7117
Sarabeth's Office
Bronx, NY........................800-773-7378
Savino's Italian Ices
Deerfield Beach, FL..............954-426-4119
Saxby Foods
Edmonton, AB.....................780-440-4179
Schneider's Dairy Inc
Pittsburgh, PA...................412-881-3525
Schneider-Valley Farms Inc
Williamsport, PA.................570-326-2021
Schwan's Food Service Inc.
Marshall, MN.....................877-302-7426
Scialo Brothers Bakery
Providence, RI...................877-421-0986
Scotty Wotty's Creamy Cheesecake
Hillsborough, NJ.................908-281-9720
Seaver's Bakery
Kingsport, TN....................423-245-2441
Serv-Agen Corporation
Cherry Hill, NJ..................856-663-6966
Shaw Baking Company
Thunder Bay, ON..................807-345-7327
Silver Tray Cookies
Fort Lauderdale, FL..............305-883-0800
Sinbad Sweets
Madera, CA.......................866-746-2232
Sisler's Ice & Ice Cream
Ohio, IL.........................888-891-3856
Smoak's Bakery & Catering Service
Augusta, GA......................706-738-1792
Snelgrove Ice Cream Company
Salt Lake City, UT...............800-569-0005
So Delicious Dairy Free
Springfield, OR..................866-388-7853
Solana Beach Baking Company
Carlsbad, CA.....................760-444-9800
Southern Ice Cream Specialties
Marietta, GA.....................770-428-0452
Specialty Bakers
Marysville, PA...................800-233-0778
Spilke's Baking Company
Moosic, PA.......................570-457-2400
Spohrers Bakeries
Collingdale, PA..................610-532-9959
Spring Glen Fresh Foods
Ephrata, PA......................800-641-2853

Standard Bakery Inc
Kealakekua, HI...................808-322-3688
Stewart's Shops Corp
Ballston Spa, NY.................518-581-1200
Stone's Home Made Candy Shop
Oswego, NY.......................888-223-3928
Strossner's Bakery & Cafe
Greenville, SC...................864-233-2990
SugarCreek
Cincinnati, OH...................800-445-2715
Super Stores Industries
Turlock, CA......................209-668-2100
Superior Cake Products
Southbridge, MA..................508-764-3276
Svenhard's Swedish Bakery Inc
Oakland, CA......................800-705-3379
Sweenors Chocolates
Wakefield, RI....................800-834-3123
Sweet Endings Inc
West Palm Beach, FL..............888-635-1177
Sweet Gallery Exclusive Pastry
Toronto, ON......................416-766-0289
Sweet Lady Jane
Los Angeles, CA..................323-653-7145
Sweet Street Desserts
Reading, PA......................800-793-3897
Sweetaly
Oceanside, CA....................760-539-2196
Sweety Novelty
Monterey Park, CA................626-282-4482
Table De France
Ontario, CA......................909-923-5205
Taste It Presents Inc
Kenilworth, NJ...................908-241-0672
Tasty Baking Company
Philadelphia, PA.................800-248-2789
Tebay Dairy Company
Parkersburg, WV..................304-863-3705
Terrapin Ridge
Clearwater, FL...................800-999-4052
The Great San Saba River Pecan Company
San Saba, TX.....................800-621-8121
The Piping Gourmets
.................................786-233-8660
The Valpo Velvet Shoppe
Valparaiso, IN...................219-464-4141
Tillamook County Creamery Association
Tillamook, OR....................503-842-4481
Tipiak Inc
Stamford, CT.....................203-961-9117
Tirawisu
Sherman Oaks, CA.................818-906-2640
Toft Dairy Inc
Sandusky, OH.....................800-521-4606
Tofutti Brands Inc
Cranford, NJ.....................908-272-2400
Tony's Ice Cream Co
Gastonia, NC.....................704-867-7085
Top Hat Co Inc
Wilmette, IL.....................847-256-6565
Treat Ice Cream Co
San Jose, CA.....................408-292-9321
Tropical Treets
North York, ON...................888-424-8229
Turkey Hill Dairy Inc
Conestoga, PA....................800-693-2479
Two Chefs on a Roll
Carson, CA.......................800-842-3025
Two Chicks and a Ladle
New York, NY.....................212-251-0025
TyRy Inc
Rocklin, CA......................800-322-6325
Umpqua Dairy
Roseburg, OR.....................888-672-6455
Uncle Ralph's Cookies
Frederick, MD....................800-422-0626
United Pies Of Elkhart Inc
Elkhart, IN......................574-294-3419
Uptown Bakers
Hyattsville, MD..................301-864-1500
Van de Kamps
Peoria, IL.......................800-798-3318
Varda Chocolatier
Elizabeth, NJ....................800-448-2732
Vickey's Vittles
North Hills, CA..................818-841-1944
Vie De France Yamazaki Inc
Vienna, VA.......................800-446-4404
Vigneri Chocolate Inc.
Rochester, NY....................877-844-6374
VIP Foods
Flushing, NY.....................718-821-5330

Vitamilk Dairy
Bellingham, WA 206-529-4128
Warwick Ice Cream
Warwick, RI 401-821-8403
Wedding Cake Studio
Williamsfield, OH.................. 440-667-1765
Welch Foods Inc.
Concord, MA 800-340-6870
Weldon Ice Cream Co
Millersport, OH.................. 740-467-2400
Welsh Farms
Clifton, NJ.................. 973-772-2388
Wenger's Bakery
Reading, PA 610-372-6545
White Coffee Corporation
Long Island City, NY 800-221-0140
Whitey's Ice Cream Inc
Moline, IL.................. 888-594-4839
Wick's Pies Inc
Winchester, IN 800-642-5880
Williamsburg Chocolatier
Williamsburg, VA.................. 757-253-1474
Winmix/Natural Care Products
Englewood, FL 941-475-7432
Woodie Pie Company
Artesia, NM.................. 575-746-2132
Wright's Ice Cream Co
Cayuga, IN 800-686-9561
Wuollet Bakery
Minneapolis, MN 612-922-4341
Ya-Hoo Baking Co
Sherman, TX.................. 888-869-2466
Young's Bakery
Uniontown, PA 724-437-6361
Zoelsmann's Bakery & Deli
Pueblo, CO 719-543-0407

Low Carb

Real Food Marketing
Kansas City, MO.................. 816-221-4100

Low-Calorie

Cedar Crest Specialties
Cedarburg, WI.................. 800-877-8341
Fendall Ice Cream Company
Salt Lake City, UT 801-355-3583
Health Valley Company
Irwindale, CA 800-334-3204
Jaxon's Ice Cream Parlor
Dania Beach, FL 954-923-4445
Master Mix
Placentia, CA 714-524-1698
O'Boyle's Ice Cream Company
Bristol, PA.................. 215-788-3882
Price Co
Yakima, WA 509-966-4110
Real Food Marketing
Kansas City, MO.................. 816-221-4100
Tova Industries LLC
Louisville, KY 888-532-8682

Fresh

Botanical Bakery, LLC
Napa, CA.................. 707-344-8103
Fresh Start Bakeries
Brea, CA 714-256-8900
Super Mom's LLC
St Paul Park, MN 800-944-7276

Frozen

Aladdin Bakers
Brooklyn, NY 718-499-1818
Alati-Caserta Desserts
Montr,al, QC 877-377-5680
All Round Foods Bakery Prod
Westbury, NY 800-428-8802
Andre-Boudin Bakeries
San Francisco, CA 415-882-1849
Aphrodite Divine Confections
Garland, TX 972-485-1005
Athens Foods Inc
Brookpark, OH 843-916-2000
Atkins Elegant Desserts
Fishers, IN.................. 800-887-8808
Awrey Bakeries
Livonia, MI.................. 800-950-2253
Bake Crafters Food Company
McDonald, TN 423-396-3392
Baker Boy Bake Shop Inc
Dickinson, ND 800-437-2008
Bama Foods LTD
Tulsa, OK 800-756-2262
Beck's Waffles of Oklahoma
Shawnee, OK 800-646-6254
Best Maid Cookie Co
River Falls, WI 888-444-0322
Boboli Intl. Inc.
Stockton, CA.................. 209-473-3507
Bodega Chocolates
Fountain Valley, CA 888-326-3342
Brooklyn Bagel Company
Staten Island, NY 800-349-3055
Caribbean Food Delights Inc
Tappan, NY.................. 845-398-3000
Carolina Foods Inc
Charlotte, NC 800-234-0441
CBC Foods
Little River, KS.................. 800-276-4770
Cedarlane Foods
Carson, CA 800-826-3322
Chewys Rugulach
San Diego, CA 800-241-3456
Cinderella Cheese Cake Co
Riverside, NJ.................. 800-521-1171
Cole's Quality Foods
Grand Rapids, MI 616-975-0081
Cookie Tree Bakeries
Salt Lake City, UT 801-268-2253
Culinary Institute Lenotre
Houston, TX 888-536-6873
Desserts Of Distinction
Tigard, OR 503-654-8370
Dimitria Delights Baking Co
North Grafton, MA 800-763-1113
Dutch Ann Foods Company
Natchez, MS 601-445-5566
Dynamic Foods
Lubbock, TX.................. 806-723-5600
Edner Corporation
Hayward, CA 510-441-8504
Edwards Baking Company
Marshall, MN 866-739-2328
Eli's Cheesecake
Chicago, IL.................. 800-354-2253
Engel's Bakeries
Calgary, AB.................. 403-250-9560
English Bay Batter Us Inc
Columbus, OH 800-253-6844
Fantasia
Sedalia, MO 660-827-1172
Fantis Foods Inc
Carlstadt, NJ 201-933-6200
Field's Pies
Pauls Valley, OK.................. 800-286-7501
Fiera Foods
Toronto, ON 800-675-6356
Fleischer's Bagels
Macedon, NY 315-986-9999
France Delices
Montreal, QC 800-663-1365
Fresh Start Bakeries
Brea, CA 714-256-8900
Gabila's Knishes
Copiague, NY 631-789-2220
Gardner Pie Co
Akron, OH.................. 330-245-2030
Good Old Days Foods
Little Rock, AR.................. 501-565-1257
Gourmet Croissant
Brooklyn, NY 718-499-4911
Grecian Delight Foods Inc
Elk Grove Village, IL 800-621-4387
Gregory's Foods, Inc.
St Paul, MN.................. 800-231-4734
Grossingers Home Bakery
New York, NY 800-479-6996
Guttenplan's Frozen Dough
Middletown, NJ 888-422-4357
GWB Foods Corporation
Brooklyn, NY 877-977-7610
Harlan Bakeries
Avon, IN 800-435-2738
Harold Food Company
Charlotte, NC 704-588-8061
J & J Wall Bakery Co
Sacramento, CA 916-381-1410
James Skinner Company
Omaha, NE 800-358-7428
Kyger Bakery Products
Lafayette, IN.................. 765-447-1252
Leidenheimer Baking Co
New Orleans, LA 800-259-9099
Lenchner Bakery
Concord, ON.................. 905-738-8811
Lone Star Bakery
Round Rock, TX.................. 512-255-7268
Love Quiches Desserts
Freeport, NY.................. 516-623-8800
Ludwick's Frozen Donuts
Grand Rapids, MI 800-366-8816
Main Street Gourmet
Cuyahoga Falls, OH 800-678-6246
Mehaffies Pies
Dayton, OH.................. 800-289-7437
Mother Nature's Goodies
Yucaipa, CA 909-795-6018
Mrs Sullivan's Pies
Jackson, TN 731-427-2101
Mrs. Kavanagh's English Muffins
Rumford, RI 800-556-7216
My Grandma's Coffee Cake
Hyde Park, MA.................. 800-847-2636
Naleway Foods
Winnipeg, MB.................. 800-665-7448
Nancy's Specialty Foods
Newark, CA 510-494-1100
New England Muffin Co Inc
Fall River, MA 508-675-2833
Old Fashioned Kitchen Inc
Lakewood, NJ.................. 732-364-4100
Orange Bakery
Irvine, CA.................. 949-863-1377
PDEQ
Fresno, CA 559-490-4412
Pacific Ocean Produce
Santa Cruz, CA.................. 831-423-2654
Pastry Chef
Pawtucket, RI 800-639-8606
Pellman Foods Inc
New Holland, PA 717-354-8070
Petrofsky's Bakery Products
Chesterfield, MO 636-519-1613
Poppies International
Battleboro, NC 252-442-4309
Positively 3rd St Bakery
Duluth, MN.................. 218-724-8619
Prairie City Bakery
Vernon Hills, IL 800-338-5122
Ramona's Mexican Foods
Gardena, CA 310-323-1950
Ranaldi Bros. Frozen Food Products
Warwick, RI 401-737-5130
Real Food Marketing
Kansas City, MO.................. 816-221-4100
Rhodes International Inc
Salt Lake City, UT 800-876-7333
Rich Products Corp
Buffalo, NY.................. 800-828-2021
RoRo's Baking Company
Dallas, TX.................. 972-897-2315
Rowena
Norfolk, VA.................. 800-627-8699
Sara Lee Frozen Bakery
Kings Mountain, NC.................. 800-323-7117
Saxby Foods
Edmonton, AB 780-440-4179
Spelt Right Foods, LLC
Brooklyn, NY 877-773-5801
Sunset Specialty Foods
Lake Arrowhead, CA 909-337-7643
Super Mom's LLC
St Paul Park, MN 800-944-7276
Table De France
Ontario, CA.................. 909-923-5205
Tasty Mix Quality Foods
Brooklyn, NY 718-855-7680
The Pillsbury Company
Chelsea, MA 800-370-7834
Two Chefs on a Roll
Carson, CA 800-842-3025
Uncle Ralph's Cookies
Frederick, MD.................. 800-422-0626
Wenner Bakery
Bayport, NY 800-869-6262
Wick's Pies Inc
Winchester, IN 800-642-5880
Wolferman's
Medford, OR.................. 800-798-6241

Ingredients

1-2-3 Gluten Free
Chagrin Falls, OH.................. 216-378-9233
Al-Rite Fruits & Syrups Co
Miami, FL.................. 305-652-2540

AnaCon Foods Company
Atchison, KS 800-328-0291
BakeMark USA
Pico Rivera, CA 866-232-8575
Brolite Products Inc
Streamwood, IL 888-276-5483
California Blending Co
El Monte, CA 626-448-1918
Castella Imports Inc
Brentwood, NY 631-231-5500
Caulipower
Encino, CA 844-422-8544
Cherrybrook Kitchen
Burlington, MA 866-458-8225
Clara Foods
San Francisco, CA
Clofine Dairy Products Inc
Linwood, NJ 609-653-1000
Creme Curls
Hudsonville, MI 800-466-1219
Deer Creek Honey Farms LTD
London, OH 740-852-0899
Dorothy Dawson Food Products
Jackson, MI 517-788-9830
Dufour Pastry Kitchens Inc
Bronx, NY 800-439-1282
Eden Processing
Poplar Grove, IL 815-765-2000
Flavorchem Corp
Downers Grove, IL 800-435-2867
Fleischmann's Yeast
Chesterfield, MO 800-777-4959
GAF Seelig Inc
Flushing, NY 718-899-5000
Holton Food Products
La Grange, IL 708-352-5599
Hulman & Co
Terre Haute, IN 812-232-9446
Indiana Sugars
Lemont, IL 630-986-9150
Lake States Yeast
Rhinelander, WI 715-369-4949
Lucas Meyer
Decatur, IL 800-769-3660
Lyoferm & Vivolac Cultures
Indianapolis, IN 317-356-8460
Main Street Ingredients
La Crosse, WI 800-359-2345
Meli's Monster Cookies
Austin, TX
Pacific Westcoast Foods
Beaverton, OR 800-874-9333
Roland Machinery
Springfield, IL 800-325-1183
Watson Inc
West Haven, CT 800-388-3481

Pies

American Quality Foods
Mills River, NC 828-890-8344
Bake Crafters Food Company
McDonald, TN 423-396-3392
Bear Creek Smokehouse Inc
Marshall, TX 800-950-2327
Beckmann's Old World Bakery
Santa Cruz, CA 831-423-9242
Berke-Blake Fancy Foods, Inc.
Longwood, FL 888-386-2253
Bluepoint Bakery
Denver, CO 303-298-1100
Bonert's Pies Inc
Santa Ana, CA 714-540-3535
Chatila's
Salem, NH 603-898-5459
Chattanooga Bakery Inc
Chattanooga, TN 800-251-3404
Cheryl's Cookies
Westerville, OH 800-443-8124
Clarmil Manufacturing Corp
Hayward, CA 888-252-7645
Collin Street Bakery
Corsicana, TX 800-267-4657
Davis Bread & Desserts
Davis, CA 530-220-4375
Entenmann's
Totowa, NJ 973-785-7601
Golden Kernel Pecan Co
Cameron, SC 803-823-2311
Goldilocks USA
Hayward, CA 510-476-0700
Granello Bakery
Las Vegas, NV 702-361-0311
JC's Pie Pops
Chatsworth, CA 818-349-1880
Keller's Bakery
Lafayette, LA 337-235-1568
Lowcountry Produce
Raleigh, NC 800-935-2792
Moon Rabbit Foods
Savannah, NY 828-273-6649
Mrs Baird's
Horsham, PA 800-984-0989
Primos Northgate
Flowood, MS 601-936-3398
Rockland Bakery
Nanuet, NY 800-734-4376
Shawnee Canning Co
Cross Junction, VA 800-713-1414
Sweet Lady Jane
Los Angeles, CA 323-653-7145
Table Talk Pies Inc
Worcester, MA 508-798-8811
Tasty Baking Company
Philadelphia, PA 800-248-2789
Willamette Valley Pie Co
Salem, OR 503-362-8857

Apple

Bama Foods LTD
Tulsa, OK 800-756-2262
Cheryl's Cookies
Westerville, OH 800-443-8124
Davis Bread & Desserts
Davis, CA 530-220-4375
Gould's Maple Sugarhouse
Shelburne Falls, MA 413-625-6170
Mayer's Cider Mill
Webster, NY 800-543-0043
Mehaffies Pies
Dayton, OH 800-289-7437

Baking Shells

American Quality Foods
Mills River, NC 828-890-8344
Bama Foods LTD
Tulsa, OK 800-756-2262
Calise & Sons Bakery Inc
Lincoln, RI 800-225-4737
Canada Bread Co, Ltd
Etobicoke, ON 800-465-5515
Dessert Innovations Inc
Atlanta, GA 800-359-7351
Dufour Pastry Kitchens Inc
Bronx, NY 800-439-1282
Dutch Ann Foods Company
Natchez, MS 601-445-5566
Father Sam's Bakery
Buffalo, NY 800-521-6719
Hafner USA
Stone Mountain, GA 888-725-4605
Hong Kong Noodle Company
Chicago, IL 312-842-0480
Lamonaca Bakery
Windber, PA 814-467-4909
Livermore Falls Baking Company
Livermore Falls, ME 207-897-3442
Lone Star Bakery
Round Rock, TX 512-255-7268
Maple Donuts
York, PA 800-627-5348
Molinaro's Fine Italian Foods Ltd.
Mississauga, ON 905-281-0352
Pacific Ocean Produce
Santa Cruz, CA 831-423-2654
Pasta Factory
Melrose Park, IL 800-615-6951
Richmond Baking Co
Richmond, IN 765-962-8535
Specialty Bakers
Marysville, PA 800-233-0778
Tomaro's Bakery
Clarksburg, WV 304-622-0691
Wick's Pies Inc
Winchester, IN 800-642-5880

Blueberry

Mehaffies Pies
Dayton, OH 800-289-7437

Brownie

Bama Foods LTD
Tulsa, OK 800-756-2262
Sweet Street Desserts
Reading, PA 800-793-3897

Cherry

Bama Foods LTD
Tulsa, OK 800-756-2262
Davis Bread & Desserts
Davis, CA 530-220-4375
Mehaffies Pies
Dayton, OH 800-289-7437

Fresh

Aryzta
Los Angeles, CA 855-427-9982
August Foods LTD
Lubbock, TX 806-744-1918
Banquet Schusters Bakery
Pueblo, CO 719-544-1062
BBU Bakeries
Horsham, PA 800-984-0989
Busken Bakery
Cincinnati, OH 513-871-2114
Carole's Cheesecake Company
Toronto, ON 416-256-0000
Case Side Holdings Company
Kensington, PE 902-836-4214
Celebrity Cheesecake
Davie, FL 877-986-2253
Clarkson Scottish Bakery
Mississauga, ON 905-823-1500
Del's Pastry
Toronto, ON 800-461-0663
Dufflet Pastries
Toronto, ON 866-238-0899
El Peto Products
Cambridge, ON 800-387-4064
Foxtail Foods
Fairfield, OH 800-487-2253
Giant Food
Landover, MD 888-469-4426
Greyston Bakery Inc
Yonkers, NY 800-289-2253
Horizon Snack Foods
Livermore, CA 800-229-2552
Italian Bakery of Virginia
Virginia, MN 218-741-3464
L & M Bakery
Riverside, NJ 888-887-1335
Love Quiches Desserts
Freeport, NY 516-623-8800
Mehaffies Pies
Dayton, OH 800-289-7437
Michel's Bakery
Philadelphia, PA 267-345-7914
Mrs Sullivan's Pies
Jackson, TN 731-427-2101
Mt. View Bakery
Mountain View, HI 808-968-6353
New England Country Bakers
Watertown, CT 800-225-3779
Northside Bakery
Brooklyn, NY 718-782-2700
Notre Dame Bakery
Conception Harbour, NL 709-535-2738
Plaidberry Company
Vista, CA 760-727-5403
Priester's Pecans
Fort Deposit, AL 866-477-4736
Rising Dough Bakery
Sacramento, CA 916-387-9700
Roma Bakeries
Rockford, IL 815-964-6737
Ryke's Bakery
Muskegon, MI 231-726-2253
Scialo Brothers Bakery
Providence, RI 877-421-0986
Seaver's Bakery
Kingsport, TN 423-245-2441
Sinbad Sweets
Madera, CA 866-746-2232
Spring Glen Fresh Foods
Ephrata, PA 800-641-2853
Standard Bakery Inc
Kealakekua, HI 808-322-3688
Sweet Endings Inc
West Palm Beach, FL 888-635-1177
The Great San Saba River Pecan Company
San Saba, TX 800-621-8121
United Pies Of Elkhart Inc
Elkhart, IN 574-294-3419

Van de Kamps
Peoria, IL....800-798-3318
Wenger's Bakery
Reading, PA....610-372-6545
Zoelsmann's Bakery & Deli
Pueblo, CO....719-543-0407

Fruit

Bonert's Pies Inc
Santa Ana, CA....714-540-3535
Table Talk Pies Inc
Worcester, MA....508-798-8811

Frozen

Bama Foods LTD
Tulsa, OK....800-756-2262
Cutie Pie Corp
Salt Lake City, UT....800-453-4575
Dynamic Foods
Lubbock, TX....806-723-5600
Edwards Baking Company
Marshall, MN....866-739-2328
Field's Pies
Pauls Valley, OK....800-286-7501
Gardner Pie Co
Akron, OH....330-245-2030
Harold Food Company
Charlotte, NC....704-588-8061
Mehaffies Pies
Dayton, OH....800-289-7437
Pastry Chef
Pawtucket, RI....800-639-8606

Key Lime

Cheesecake Etc Desserts
Miami Springs, FL....305-887-0258

Lemon-Meringue

D-Liteful Baking Company
Medley, FL....305-883-6449
Kyger Bakery Products
Lafayette, IN....765-447-1252
Mehaffies Pies
Dayton, OH....800-289-7437

Meat

Goldilocks USA
Hayward, CA....510-476-0700
Mexi-Frost Specialties Company
Brooklyn, NY....718-625-3324
Morrison Lamothe
Toronto, ON....877-677-6533
Mortimer's Fine Foods
Burlington, ON....905-336-0000
The Van Cleve Seafood Company
Spotsylvania, VA....800-628-5202

Frozen

Mexi-Frost Specialties Company
Brooklyn, NY....718-625-3324

Non-Fruit

Le Donne Brothers Bakery
Roseto, PA....610-588-0423
MacEwan's Meats
Calgary, AB....403-228-9999
Snyder Foods
Port Perry, ON....905-985-7373

Frozen

Bama Foods LTD
Tulsa, OK....800-756-2262
Dimitria Delights Baking Co
North Grafton, MA....800-763-1113
Dynamic Foods
Lubbock, TX....806-723-5600
Edwards Baking Company
Marshall, MN....866-739-2328
Field's Pies
Pauls Valley, OK....800-286-7501
Gardner Pie Co
Akron, OH....330-245-2030
Kyger Bakery Products
Lafayette, IN....765-447-1252
Nancy's Specialty Foods
Newark, CA....510-494-1100
Pastry Chef
Pawtucket, RI....800-639-8606
Wick's Pies Inc
Winchester, IN....800-642-5880

Peach

Bama Foods LTD
Tulsa, OK....800-756-2262
Davis Bread & Desserts
Davis, CA....530-220-4375
Mehaffies Pies
Dayton, OH....800-289-7437

Rhubarb Pie

Bear Stewart Corp
Chicago, IL....800-697-2327

Stuffing

Amalgamated Produce
Bridgeport, CT....800-358-3808
Bodin Foods
New Iberia, LA....337-367-1344
Coastal Seafoods
Ridgefield, CT....203-431-0453
Good Old Days Foods
Little Rock, AR....501-565-1257
Quality Bakery Products
Houston, TX....866-449-4977
Rothbury Farms
Grand Rapids, MI....877-684-2879
Texas Crumb & Food Products
Farmers Branch, TX....800-522-7862

for Meat

Bluechip Group
Salt Lake City, UT....800-878-0099
Leelanau Fruit Co
Peshawbestown, MI....231-271-3514
Savoie's Sausage and Food Products
Opelousas, LA....337-942-7241
Texas Crumb & Food Products
Farmers Branch, TX....800-522-7862
World Flavors Inc
Warminster, PA....215-672-4400

for Poultry

Leelanau Fruit Co
Peshawbestown, MI....231-271-3514
Savoie's Sausage and Food Products
Opelousas, LA....337-942-7241
World Flavors Inc
Warminster, PA....215-672-4400

Waffles

Augustin's Waffles
Long Valley, NJ....908-684-0830
Bake Crafters Food Company
McDonald, TN....423-396-3392
Continental Mills Inc
Tukwila, WA....206-816-7000
Eat Dutch Waffles, LLC
Orem, UT....801-319-4788
Food for Life Baking
Corona, CA....800-797-5090
Jacquet Bakery
New York, NY
Julian's Recipe
Brooklyn, NY....888-640-8880
Kloss Manufacturing Co Inc
Allentown, PA....800-445-7100
Natural Food Mill
Corona, CA....800-797-5090
Nature's Path Foods
Blaine, WA....888-808-9505
Poppies International
Battleboro, NC....252-442-4309
Shepherdsfield Bakery
Fulton, MO....573-642-0009
Swapples
Washington, DC
The Stroopie
Lancaster, PA....717-875-3426
Van's International Foods
Torrance, CA....310-320-8611
WaffleWaffle
Nutley, NJ....201-559-1286

Frozen

Bake Crafters Food Company
McDonald, TN....423-396-3392
Beck's Waffles of Oklahoma
Shawnee, OK....800-646-6254
Continental Mills Inc
Tukwila, WA....206-816-7000
Echo Lake Foods, Inc.
Burlington, WI....262-763-9551
Van's International Foods
Torrance, CA....310-320-8611

Wraps

LA Torilla Factory
Santa Rosa, CA....800-446-1516
Maria and Ricardo's
Canton, MA....800-881-7040
Nanka Seimen Company
Vernon, CA....323-585-9967
Scott Adams Foods
Newton, NJ....973-300-2091
Valley Lahvosh
Fresno, CA....800-480-2704
Wrawp
Pomona, CA....855-972-9748

Flavored

LA Torilla Factory
Santa Rosa, CA....800-446-1516

Beverages

General

A Hill of Beans Coffee Roasters
Omaha, NE ... 402-333-6048

A. Lassonde Inc.
Rougemont, QC ... 866-552-7643

ABC Tea House
Baldwin Park, CA ... 888-220-3988

Abita Brewing Co
Covington, LA ... 800-737-2311

Absopure Water Company
Plymouth, MI ... 800-422-7678

Abunda Life
Asbury Park, NJ ... 732-775-9338

Acacia Vineyard
Napa, CA ... 877-226-1700

Ace Farm USA Inc
Bronx, NY ... 718-991-3816

Acqua Blox LLC
Santa Fe Springs, CA ... 562-693-9599

Adirondack Beverages Inc
Scotia, NY ... 800-316-6096

Admiral Beverage Corp
Worland, WY ... 307-347-4201

Agri-Mark Inc
West Springfield, MA ... 978-552-5500

Aimonetto and Sons
Renton, WA ... 866-823-2777

Ajiri Tea Company
Upper Black Eddy, PA ... 610-982-5075

Al-Rite Fruits & Syrups Co
Miami, FL ... 305-652-2540

Alacer Corp
Carlisle, PA ... 888-425-2362

Alfer Laboratories
Chatsworth, CA ... 818-709-0737

All American Foods Inc
Mankato, MN ... 800-833-2661

All Juice Food & Beverage
Ankeny, IA ... 800-736-5674

Allegro Coffee Co
Thornton, CO ... 800-666-4869

Aloe Farms Inc
Harlingen, TX ... 800-262-6771

Aloe Laboratories
Harlingen, TX ... 800-258-5380

Aloha Distillers
Honolulu, HI ... 808-841-5787

Alpenglow Beverage Company
Linden, VA ... 540-635-2118

Alpine Valley Water
Harvey, IL ... 708-333-3910

Alternative Health & Herbs
Albany, OR ... 800-345-4152

Ambootia Tea Estate
Chicago, IL ... 312-661-1550

Amcan Beverages Inc
American Canyon, CA ... 800-972-5962

Amcan Industries
Elmsford, NY ... 914-347-4838

American Soy Products Inc
Saline, MI ... 734-429-2310

Andalusia Distributing Co Inc
Andalusia, AL ... 334-222-3671

Andrew Peller Limited
Grimsby, ON ... 905-643-4131

Apple & Eve LLC
Port Washington, NY ... 800-969-8018

Aqua Clara Bottling & Distribution
Clearwater, FL ... 727-446-2999

Arbuckle Coffee Roasters
Tucson, AZ ... 800-533-8278

Arcadian Estate Winery
Rock Stream, NY ... 800-298-1346

Ariel Vineyards
Napa, CA ... 800-456-9472

Arizona Beverage Company
Cincinnati, OH ... 800-832-3775

Asiamerica Ingredients
Westwood, NJ ... 201-497-5531

Aspire
Chicago, OH

Atlanta Coffee Roasters
Atlanta, GA ... 800-252-8211

August Schell Brewing Co
New Ulm, MN ... 800-770-5020

Austrian Trade Commission
New York, NY ... 212-421-5250

B.M. Lawrence & Company
San Francisco, CA ... 415-981-2926

Bacardi Canada, Inc.
Toronto, ON ... 905-451-6100

Barrows Tea Company
New Bedford, MA ... 800-832-5024

Batavia Wine Cellars
Canandaigua, NY ... 585-396-7600

Baywood Cellars
Lodi, CA ... 800-214-0445

BCGA Concept Corporation
New York, NY ... 212-488-0661

Bean Forge
Coos Bay, OR ... 888-292-1632

Beckmen Vineyards
Los Olivos, CA ... 805-688-8664

Belton Foods Inc
Dayton, OH ... 800-443-2266

Benmarl Wine Co
Marlboro, NY ... 845-236-4265

Berkeley Farms
Hayward, CA ... 800-395-7004

Best Foods
Englewood Cliffs, NJ ... 201-894-4000

Bevco Sales International Inc.
Surrey, BC ... 800-663-0090

Beverage Capital Corporation
Baltimore, MD ... 410-242-7404

Bianchi Winery
Paso Robles, CA ... 805-226-9922

Big Red Bottling
Austin, TX ... 254-772-7791

Birdseye Dairy-Morning Glory
Green Bay, WI ... 920-494-5388

Black Prince Distillery Inc
Clifton, NJ ... 973-365-2050

Blk Enterprises
New York, NY ... 212-764-3331

Blossom Water, LLC
Westwood, MA ... 855-325-5777

Blue Sky Beverage Company
Corona, CA ... 800-426-7367

Bolt House Farms-Shipping Dept
Bakersfield, CA ... 800-467-4683

Borden Dairy
Dallas, TX ... 855-311-1583

Boston's Best Coffee Roasters
South Easton, MA ... 800-898-8393

Boulder Beer
Boulder, CO ... 303-444-8448

Brander Vineyard
Santa Ynez, CA ... 800-970-9979

Brick Brewery
Kitchener, ON ... 800-505-8971

Brimstone Hill Vineyard
Pine Bush, NY ... 845-744-2231

British Aisles, LTD.
Nashua, NH ... 800-520-8565

Brookshire Grocery Company
Tyler, TX ... 888-937-3776

Buckmaster Coffee Co
Hillsboro, OR ... 800-962-9148

Buena Vista Historic Tstng Rm
Sonoma, CA ... 800-926-1266

Buffalo Trace Distillery
Frankfort, KY ... 800-654-8471

Bully Hill Vineyards
Hammondsport, NY ... 607-868-3610

Cadillac Coffee Co
Ft. Wayne, IN ... 800-438-6900

Cafe Altura
Santa Paula, CA ... 800-526-8328

Cafe Du Monde Coffee Stand
New Orleans, LA ... 800-772-2927

Cafe Yaucono/Jimenez & Fernandez
San Juan, PR ... 787-721-3337

California Natural Products
Lathrop, CA ... 209-858-2525

Callaway Vineyards & Winery
Temecula, CA ... 800-472-2377

Canadian Mist Distillers
Collingwood, ON ... 705-445-4690

Canoe Ridge Vineyard
Walla Walla, WA ... 509-527-0885

Cappo Drinks
Baldwin Park, CA ... 626-813-1006

Capri Sun
Granite City, IL

Caracolillo Coffee Mills
Tampa, FL ... 800-682-0023

Caravan Company
Worcester, MA ... 508-752-3777

Carmenet Winery
Sonoma, CA ... 707-996-3526

Carolina Products
Tampa, FL ... 813-313-1800

Carolina Treet
Wilmington, NC ... 800-616-6344

Cascade Mountain Winery
Amenia, NY ... 845-373-9021

Cass-Clay Creamery
Fargo, ND ... 701-293-6455

Castello di Borghese Vineyard
Cutchogue, NY ... 631-734-5111

Cawy Bottling Co
Miami, FL ... 877-917-2299

CB Beverage Corporation
Hopkins, MN ... 952-935-9905

Cecchetti Sebastiani Cellar
Sonoma, CA ... 707-933-3230

Cedar Creek Winery
Cedarburg, WI ... 800-827-8020

Cedar Lake Foods
Cedar Lake, MI ... 800-246-5039

Central Dairies
St Johns, NL ... 800-563-6455

Chalone Vineyard
Soledad, CA ... 831-678-1717

Chase Brothers Dairy
Oxnard, CA ... 800-438-6455

Chateau des Charmes Wines
St. Davids, ON ... 800-263-2541

Chateau Julien Winery
Carmel, CA ... 831-624-2600

Chateau St Jean Winery
Kenwood, CA ... 707-833-4134

Cheribundi
Geneva, NY ... 800-699-0460

Chestnut Mountain Winery
Hoschton, GA ... 770-867-6914

Chicago Coffee Roastery
Huntley, IL ... 800-762-5402

Chicama Vineyards
West Tisbury, MA ... 888-244-2262

Chimere Winery
Santa Maria, CA ... 805-928-5611

Chocolat
Bellevue, WA ... 800-808-2462

Chouinard Vineyards & Winery
Castro Valley, CA ... 510-582-9900

Christine Woods Winery
Philo, CA ... 707-895-2115

Christopher Creek Winery
Healdsburg, CA ... 707-433-2001

Cienega Valley Winery/DeRose
Hollister, CA ... 831-636-9143

Cimarron Cellars
Caney, OK ... 580-889-5997

Cinnabar Winery
Saratoga, CA ... 408-867-1010

Citrosuco North America Inc
Lake Wales, FL ... 800-356-4592

Citrus International
Winter Park, FL ... 407-629-8037

Citrus Service
Winter Garden, FL ... 407-656-4999

City Bean
Los Angeles, CA ... 888-248-9232

City Brewing Company
La Crosse, WI ... 608-785-4200

Claiborne & Churchill Vintners
San Luis Obispo, CA ... 805-544-4066

Classic Tea
Libertyville, IL ... 630-680-9934

Clayton Coffee & Tea
Modesto, CA ... 209-576-1120

Clear Creek Distillery
Portland, OR ... 503-248-9470

Clear Mountain Coffee Company
Silver Spring, MD ... 301-587-2233

Clearwater Coffee Company
Lake Zurich, IL 847-540-7711
Cline Cellars
Sonoma, CA 800-543-2070
Clinton Vineyards Inc
Clinton Corners, NY 845-266-5372
Clos Du Bois Winery
Geyserville, CA 800-222-3189
Clos Du Lac Cellars
Ione, CA 209-274-2238
Clos Du Val Co LTD
Napa, CA. 707-261-5200
Clos Pegase Winery
Calistoga, CA 800-866-8583
Cloudstone Vineyards
Los Altos Hills, CA 650-948-8621
Clover Hill Vineyards & Winery
Breinigsville, PA. 800-256-8374
Coastal Goods
Barnstable, MA. 508-375-1050
Coastlog Industries
Novi, MI 248-344-9556
Cobraz Brazilian Coffee
New York, NY 212-759-7700
Coca-Cola Beverages Northeast
Bedford, NH 844-619-3388
Cocolalla Winery
Cocolalla, ID. 208-263-3774
Coffee Associates
Edgewater, NJ. 201-945-1060
Coffee Barrel
Holt, MI. 517-694-9000
Coffee Bean
Englewood, CO. 303-922-1238
Coffee Bean & Tea Leaf
Bloomington, MN. 952-853-1148
Coffee Bean Intl
Portland, OR 800-877-0474
Coffee Bean of Leesburg
Leesburg, VA 800-232-6872
Coffee Beanery LTD
Flushing, MI 800-441-2255
Coffee Butler Service
Alexandria, VA 703-823-0028
Coffee Culture-A House
Lincoln, NE. 402-438-8456
Coffee Holding Co Inc
Staten Island, NY 800-458-2233
Coffee Masters
Spring Grove, IL. 800-334-6485
Coffee Mill Roastery
Elon, NC 800-729-1727
Coffee Millers & Roasting
Cape Coral, FL 239-573-6800
Coffee People
Beaverton, OR 800-354-5282
Coffee Process
Houston, TX 713-695-8483
Coffee Reserve
Phoenix, AZ 888-755-6789
Coffee Roasters Inc
Oakland, NJ 800-285-2445
Coffee Roasters Of New Orleans
Kenner, LA 800-737-5464
Coffee Roasters of New Orleans
New Orleans, LA 800-737-5464
Coffee Up
Chicago, IL 847-288-9330
Coffee Works
Sacramento, CA 800-275-3335
Cold Hollow Cider Mill
Waterbury Center, VT. 800-327-7537
College Coffee Roaster
Mountville, PA 717-285-9561
Coloma Frozen Foods Inc
Coloma, MI. 800-642-2723
Colonial Coffee Roasters Inc
Miami, FL. 305-638-0885
Colorado Cellars
Palisade, CO 970-464-7921
Colorado Spice Co
Boulder, CO 800-677-7423
Columbia Winery
Woodinville, WA. 425-488-2776
Commodities Marketing Inc
Clarksburg, NJ 732-516-0700
Community Coffee Co.
Baton Rouge, LA 800-884-5282
Concannon Vineyard
Livermore, CA 800-258-9866
Conneaut Cellars Winery LLC
Conneaut Lake, PA 877-229-9463
Conrotto A. Winery
Gilroy, CA. 408-847-2233
Continental Coffee Products Company
Houston, TX 800-323-6178
Cool
Richardson, TX. 972-437-9352
Coon Creek Winery
St Helena, CA 800-793-7960
Cooper Mountain Vineyards
Beaverton, OR 503-649-0027
Corim Industries Inc
Brick, NJ. 800-942-4201
Cosentino Winery
Napa, CA. 800-764-1220
Cotswold Cottage Foods
Arvada, CO 800-208-1977
Country Pure Foods Inc
Akron, OH. 877-995-8423
Cowie Wine Cellars & Vineyards
Paris, AR 479-963-3990
Crescini Wines
Soquel, CA 831-462-1466
Cristom Vineyards
Salem, OR. 503-375-3068
Criveller California Corp
Healdsburg, CA 888-849-2266
Cronin Vineyards
Woodside, CA. 650-851-1452
Crown Regal Wine Cellars
Brooklyn, NY 718-604-1430
Cruse Vineyards
Chester, SC 803-377-3944
Crystal & Vigor Beverages
Kearny, NJ. 201-991-2342
Crystal Springs Bottled Water
Lakeland, FL. 800-728-5508
Crystal Springs Water Company
Lakeland, FL. 800-728-5508
CTL Foods
Colfax, WI. 800-962-5227
Culligan International Company
Rosemont, IL. 847-205-6000
Cuneo Cellars
Amity, OR 503-835-2782
Cutrale Citrus Juices
Auburndale, FL. 863-965-5000
Cutting Edge Beverages
Boca Raton, FL. 561-347-5860
Cuvaison Winery
Calistoga, CA 707-942-6266
Cygnet Cellars
Hollister, CA. 831-637-7559
Dairy Fresh Foods Inc
Taylor, MI 313-299-0735
Dairy Maid Dairy LLC
Frederick, MD. 301-663-5114
Dalla Valle Vineyards
Napa, CA. 707-944-2676
Dallis Brothers
Long Island City, NY 718-845-3010
Damron Corp
Chicago, IL 800-333-1860
David Rio
San Francisco, CA 800-454-9605
Davis Bynum Winery
Healdsburg, CA 800-826-1073
Daybreak Coffee Roasters
Glastonbury, CT 800-882-5282
Daymar Select Fine Coffees
El Cajon, CA. 800-466-7590
De Coty Coffee Co
San Angelo, TX 800-588-8001
Deaver Vineyards
Plymouth, CA 209-245-4099
Deer Park Spring Water Co
Chesapeake, VA 800-832-0271
Del's Lemonade & Refreshments
Cranston, RI 401-463-6190
Delicato Family Vineyards
Napa, CA. 707-265-1700
DeLima Coffee
Liverpool, NY. 800-962-8864
Deloach Vineyards
Santa Rosa, CA. 707-755-3300
Delorimier Winery
Geyserville, CA 800-546-7718
Denatale Vineyards
Healdsburg, CA 707-431-8460
Denning's Point Distillery, LLC
Beacon, NY. 845-476-8413
Destileria Serralles Inc
Mercedita, PR 787-840-1000
Devansoy Farms
Carroll, IA. 800-747-8605
Devine Foods
Elwyn, PA 888-338-4631
Devlin Wine Cellars
Soquel, CA 831-476-7288
DG Yuengling & Son, Inc.
Pottsville, PA. 570-628-4890
Diageo Canada Inc.
Toronto, ON 416-626-2000
Diamond Creek Vineyards
Calistoga, CA 707-942-6926
Diamond Water Bottling Fclty
Hot Springs, AR 501-623-1251
Diehl Food Ingredients
Defiance, OH 800-251-3033
Digrazia Vineyards
Brookfield, CT 800-230-8853
Distant Lands Coffee Roaster
Renton, WA. 800-758-4437
Distillata
Cleveland, OH 800-999-2906
Divine Foods
Elizabethtown, NC 910-862-2576
DMH Ingredients Inc
Libertyville, IL 847-362-9977
Domaine Chandon
Yountville, CA 888-242-6366
Domaine St George Winery
Healdsburg, CA 707-433-5508
Don Hilario Estate Coffee
Oldsmar, FL 800-799-1903
Don Jose Foods
Scottsdale, AZ. 480-443-1000
Donatoni Winery
Inglewood, CA 310-645-5445
Door Peninsula Winery
Sturgeon Bay, WI 800-551-5049
Douwe Egberts
Worthington, OH 800-582-6617
Downeast Coffee Roasters
Pawtucket, RI 800-345-2007
Dr Konstantin Frank's Vinifera
Hammondsport, NY 800-320-0735
Dream Foods Intl
Santa Monica, CA. 310-315-5739
DreamPak LLC
Alexandria, VA 877-687-4662
Dreyer Sonoma
Woodside, CA. 650-851-9448
Droubi's Imports
Houston, TX 713-334-1829
Dry Creek Vineyard
Healdsburg, CA 800-864-9463
DS Services of America
Lakeland, FL. 800-728-5508
Duck Pond Cellars
Dundee, OR. 800-437-3213
Duckhorn Vineyards
St Helena, CA 888-354-8885
Duncan Peak Vineyards
Lafayette, CA 925-283-3632
Dundee Wine Company
Dundee, OR. 888-427-4953
Dunn Vineyards
Angwin, CA 707-965-3642
Duplin Wine Cellars
Rose Hill, NC 800-774-9634
Dutch Henry Winery
Calistoga, CA. 888-224-5879
E & J Gallo Winery
Modesto, CA. 877-687-9463
E L K Run Vineyards
Mt Airy, MD 800-414-2513
Eagle Coffee Co Inc
Baltimore, MD 410-685-5893
Eagle Crest Vineyards LLC
Conesus, NY. 800-977-7117
Easley Winery
Indianapolis, IN 317-636-4516
East Side Winery/Oak Ridge Vineyards
Lodi, CA 209-369-4758
Eastern Tea Corp
Monroe Twp, NJ. 800-221-0865
Eastrise Trading Corp.
Baldwin Park, CA
Eberle Winery
Paso Robles, CA. 805-238-9607
Ed Oliveira Winery
Arcata, CA 707-822-3023
Eden Foods Inc
Clinton, MI 888-424-3336

Edgewood Estate Winery
Napa, CA........................800-755-2374
Edmunds St. John
Berkeley, CA....................510-981-1510
Edna Valley Vineyard
San Luis Obispo, CA.............866-979-8477
Eight O'Clock Coffee Company
North Bergen, NJ................800-299-2739
El Paso Winery
Ulster Park, NY.................845-331-8642
Eldorado Artesian Springs Inc
Louisville, CO..................303-499-1316
Elk Cove Vineyards
Gaston, OR......................877-355-2683
Ellis Coffee Co
Philadelphia, PA................800-822-3984
Elliston Vineyards
Sunol, CA.......................925-862-2377
Elmhurst Milked
Elma, NY........................888-356-1925
Empire Tea Svc
Columbus, IN....................800-790-0246
Empresas La Famosa
Toa Baja, PR....................787-251-0060
Ener-G Foods
Seattle, WA.....................800-331-5222
Enz Vineyards
Hollister, CA...................831-637-6443
Eola Hills Wine Cellars
Rickreall, OR...................800-291-6730
EOS Estate Winery
Paso Robles, CA.................800-249-9463
Erath Vineyards Winery
Dundee, OR......................800-539-5463
Erba Food Products
Brooklyn, NY....................718-272-7700
Espresso Vivace
Seattle, WA.....................206-860-5869
Essentia Water
Bothell, WA.....................877-293-2239
Eureka Water Co
Oklahoma City, OK...............800-310-8474
Eurobubblies
Ashland, MA.....................800-273-0750
European Coffee
Clearwater, FL..................888-635-4882
European Roasterie
Le Center, MN...................888-588-5282
Evensen Vineyards
Oakville, CA....................707-944-2396
Everfresh Beverages
Warren, MI......................800-323-3416
Ex Drinks
Henderson, NV...................866-753-4929
Eyrie Vineyards
Mcminnville, OR.................888-440-4970
Fall Creek Vineyards
Austin, TX......................512-476-4477
Far Niente Winery
Oakville, CA....................707-944-2861
Farella-Park Vineyards
Napa, CA........................707-254-9489
Farfelu Vineyards
Flint Hill, VA..................540-364-2930
Farmland Dairies
Wallington, NJ..................888-727-6252
Fee Brothers
Rochester, NY...................800-961-3337
Fenestra Winery
Livermore, CA...................800-789-9463
Fenn Valley Vineyards
Fennville, MI...................269-561-2396
Fenn Valley Vineyards
Fennville, MI...................800-432-6265
Ferolito Vultaggio & Sons
Woodbury, NY....................800-832-3775
Ferrante Winery & Ristorante
Geneva, OH......................440-466-6046
Ferrara Bakery & Cafe
New York, NY....................212-226-6150
Ferrara Winery
Escondido, CA...................760-745-7632
Ferrari-Carano
Healdsburg, CA..................800-831-0381
Ferrigno Vineyards & Wine
St James, MO....................573-265-7742
Fess Parker Winery
Los Olivos, CA..................800-841-1104
Ficklin Vineyards Winery
Madera, CA......................559-674-4598
Fidalgo Bay Roasting Co
Burlington, WA..................800-310-5540
Field Coffee
Norcross, GA....................844-343-5326
Field Stone Winery
Healdsburg, CA..................800-544-7273
Fieldbrook Valley Winery
Mckinleyville, CA...............707-839-4140
Fife Vineyards
Redwood Valley, CA..............707-485-0323
Filsinger Vineyards & Winery
Temecula, CA....................951-302-6363
Finlay Extracts & Ingredients USA, Inc.
Florham Park, NJ................800-288-6272
Fiore Winery
Pylesville, MD..................410-452-0132
Firelands Winery
Sandusky, OH....................800-548-9463
Firestone Vineyard
Los Olivos, CA..................805-688-3940
First Colony Coffee & Tea Company
Norfolk, VA.....................800-446-8555
First Roasters of Central Florida
Longwood, FL....................407-699-6364
Fisher Ridge Wine Co Inc
Charleston, WV..................304-342-8702
Fisher Vineyards
Santa Rosa, CA..................707-539-7511
Fitzpatrick Winery & Lodge
Somerset, CA....................800-245-9166
Fizz-O Water Co
Tulsa, OK.......................918-834-3691
Flavouressence Products
Mississauga, ON.................866-209-7778
Flora Springs Winery
St Helena, CA...................707-963-5711
Florida Caribbean Distillers
Lake Alfred, FL.................863-956-2002
Florida Food Products Inc
Eustis, FL......................800-874-2331
Florida Fruit Juices
Chicago, IL.....................773-586-6200
Florida Key West
Fort Myers, FL..................239-694-8787
Flynn Vineyards Winery
Rickreall, OR...................888-427-4953
Fmali Herb
Santa Cruz, CA..................831-423-7913
Foley Estates Vineyard
Lompoc, CA......................805-737-6222
Folgers Coffee Co
Orrville, OH....................800-937-9745
Folie _ Deux Winery
Oakville, CA....................800-535-6400
Folklore Foods
Selby, SD.......................605-649-1144
Foppiano Vineyards
Healdsburg, CA..................707-433-7272
Foris Vineyards
Cave Junction, OR...............541-592-3752
Forman Vineyard
St Helena, CA...................707-963-3900
Fortino Winery
Gilroy, CA......................888-617-6606
Fortuna Cellars
Davis, CA.......................530-756-6686
Fortunes International Teas
Mc Kees Rocks, PA...............412-771-7767
Four Chimneys Farm Winery Trust
Himrod, NY......................607-243-7502
Four Sisters Winery
Belvidere, NJ...................908-475-3671
Fox Vineyards & Winery
Social Circle, GA...............770-787-5402
Foxen Foxen 7200
Santa Maria, CA.................805-937-4251
Franco's Cocktail Mixes
Pompano Beach, FL...............800-782-4508
Frank Family Vineyards
Calistoga, CA...................880-574-9463
Frank-Lin Distributors
Fairfield, CA...................800-922-9363
Franklin Hill Vineyards
Bangor, PA......................888-887-2839
Franzia Winery
Ripon, CA.......................209-599-4111
Fratelli Perata
Paso Robles, CA.................805-238-2809
Frederick Wildman & Sons LTD
New York, NY....................800-733-9463
Freed, Teller & Freed
South San Francisco, CA.........800-370-7371
Freemark Abbey Winery
St Helena, CA...................800-963-9698
Freixenet USA Inc
Sonoma, CA......................707-996-4981
Frey Vineyards
Redwood Valley, CA..............800-760-3739
Frick Winery
Geyserville, CA.................707-857-1980
Frisinger Cellars
Napa, CA........................707-255-3749
Frog's Leap Winery
Rutherford, CA..................800-959-4704
Frontenac Point Vineyard
Trumansburg, NY.................607-387-9619
Gadsden Coffee/Caffe
Arivaca, AZ.....................888-514-5282
Gainey Vineyard
Santa Ynez, CA..................805-688-0558
Galante Vineyards
Carmel Valley, CA...............800-425-2683
Galena Cellars Winery
Galena, IL......................800-397-9463
Galleano Winery
Mira Loma, CA...................951-685-5376
Galliker Dairy Co
Johnstown, PA...................800-477-6455
Gary Farrell Vineyards-Winery
Healdsburg, CA..................866-277-9463
Gehl Foods, Inc.
Germantown, WI..................800-521-2873
George A Dickel & Company
Tullahoma, TN...................888-342-5352
Georgia Wines Inc
Ringgold, GA....................706-937-2177
Georis Winery
Carmel Valley, CA...............831-659-1050
Germanton Winery
Germanton, NC...................800-322-2894
Ginseng Up Corp
Worcester, MA...................800-446-7364
Girard Spring Water
North Providence, RI............800-477-9287
Girardet Wine Cellar
Roseburg, OR....................541-679-7252
Glen Summit Springs Water Company
Mountain Top, PA................800-621-7596
Glenora Wine Cellars
Dundee, NY......................800-243-5513
Global Beverage Company
Rochester, NY...................585-381-3560
Global Food Industries
Townville, SC...................800-225-4152
Global Health Laboratories
Amityville, NY..................631-777-2134
Globus Coffee LLC
Manhasset, NY...................516-304-5780
Gloria Ferrer Champagne
Sonoma, CA......................707-933-1917
Gloria Jean's Gourmet Coffees
Irvine, CA......................877-320-5282
Gloria Winery & Vineyard
Springfield, MO.................417-926-6263
Glunz Family Winery & Cellars
Grayslake, IL...................847-548-9463
Golden Moon Tea
Bristow, VA.....................877-327-5473
Golden Town Apple Products
Rougemont, QC...................866-552-7643
Good Earth Company
New Providence, NJ..............888-625-8227
Good Harbor Vineyards & Winery
Lake Leelanau, MI...............231-256-7165
Good-O-Beverages Inc
Bronx, NY.......................718-328-6400
Goodson Brothers Coffee
Knoxville, TN...................800-737-1519
Goosecross Cellars Inc
Yountville, CA..................800-276-9210
Gourmet Mondiale
Ste-Catherine, QC...............450-638-6380
Goya Foods Inc.
Jersey City, NJ.................201-348-4900
Grace Tea Co
Acton, MA.......................978-635-9500
Grainaissance
Emeryville, CA..................800-472-4697
Grand River Cellars
Madison, OH.....................440-298-9838
Grande River Vineyards
Palisade, CO....................800-264-7696
Granite Springs Winery
Somerset, CA....................800-638-6041
Great Eastern Sun Trading Co
Asheville, NC...................800-334-5809

Great Western Juice Co
Maple Heights, OH . . . 800-321-9180
Green Mountain Chocolate Inc
Franklin, MA . . . 508-520-7160
Green Mountain Cidery
Middlebury, VT. . . . 802-388-0700
Green Spot Packaging
Claremont, CA . . . 800-456-3210
Greenfield Wine Company
Vallejo, CA . . . 707-552-5199
Greenwood Ridge Vineyards
Philo, CA. . . . 707-895-2002
Groth Vineyards & Winery
Oakville, CA. . . . 707-944-0290
Groupe Paul Masson
Longueuil, QC . . . 514-878-3050
Gruet Winery
Albuquerque, NM. . . . 888-857-9463
Guenoc & Langtry Estate
Middletown, CA. . . . 707-995-7501
Guglielmo Winery
Morgan Hill, CA. . . . 408-779-2145
Guilliams Winery
St Helena, CA. . . . 707-963-9059
Guinness Import Co
Stamford, CT. . . . 800-521-1591
Gundlach-Bundschu Winery
Sonoma, CA . . . 707-939-3015
GWB Foods Corporation
Brooklyn, NY. . . . 877-977-7610
H & H Products Co
Orlando, FL. . . . 800-678-8448
H Coturri & Sons Winery
Glen Ellen, CA . . . 866-268-8774
H R Nicholson Co
Baltimore, MD . . . 800-638-3514
Habersham Vineyards & Winery
Helen, GA. . . . 706-878-9463
Hafner Vineyard
Healdsburg, CA . . . 707-433-4606
Hahn Family Wines
Soledad, CA . . . 831-678-4555
Haight Brown Vineyard
Litchfield, CT . . . 800-577-9463
Hallcrest Vineyards
Felton, CA. . . . 831-335-4441
Handley Cellars
Philo, CA. . . . 800-733-3151
Hanks Beverage Co
Feasterville-Trevose, PA. . . . 800-289-4722
Hanover Foods Corp
Hanover, PA . . . 717-632-6000
Hanzell Vineyards
Sonoma, CA . . . 707-996-3860
Harbor Winery
West Sacramento, CA. . . . 916-371-6776
Harmony Bay Coffee
North Andover, MA . . . 800-514-3663
Harmony Cellars
Harmony, CA . . . 800-432-9239
Harney & Sons Tea Co.
Millerton, NY. . . . 800-832-8463
Harold L King & Co Inc
Redwood City, CA . . . 888-368-2233
Harpersfield Vineyard
Geneva, OH. . . . 440-466-4739
Harrisburg Dairies Inc
Harrisburg, PA . . . 800-692-7429
Hart Winery
Temecula, CA . . . 877-638-8788
Hartford Family Winery
Forestville, CA . . . 707-887-8030
Has Beans Coffee & Tea Co
Chico, CA . . . 800-427-2326
Hastings Co-Op Creamery-Dairy
Hastings, MN . . . 651-437-9414
Hathaway Coffee Co Inc
Summit Argo, IL. . . . 708-458-7666
Hawaii Coffee Company
Honolulu, HI. . . . 800-338-8353
Hawaiian Isles Kona Coffee Co
Honolulu, HI. . . . 800-657-7716
Hawaiian Natural Water Company
Pearl City, HI . . . 808-483-0520
Haydenergy Health
Valley Stream, NY . . . 800-255-1660
Hazlitt 1852 Vineyards
Hector, NY . . . 888-750-0494
Health-Ade LLC
Los Angeles, CA. . . . 844-337-6368
Heartland Vinyards
Westlake, OH . . . 440-871-0701
Heaven Hill Distilleries Inc.
Bardstown, KY . . . 502-337-1000
Heck Cellars
Arvin, CA . . . 661-854-6120
Hecker Pass Winery
Gilroy, CA. . . . 408-842-8755
Hegy's South Hills Vineyard & Winery
Twin Falls, ID . . . 208-599-0074
Heineman Winery
Put In Bay, OH . . . 419-285-2811
Heitz Wine Cellars
St Helena, CA . . . 707-963-3542
Helena View/Johnston Vineyard
Calistoga, CA . . . 707-942-4956
Heller Estates
Carmel Valley, CA . . . 800-625-8466
Hells Canyon Winery
Caldwell, ID . . . 800-318-7873
Henry Estate Winery
Umpqua, OR. . . . 800-782-2686
Henry Hill & Co
Napa, CA. . . . 707-253-1663
Heritage Books & Gifts
Virginia Beach, VA. . . . 800-862-2923
Heritage Coffee Co & Cafe
Juneau, AK . . . 800-478-5282
Heritage Farms Dairy
Murfreesboro, TN. . . . 615-895-2790
Heritage Wine Cellars
North East, PA. . . . 800-747-0083
Hermann J. Wiemer Vineyard
Dundee, NY . . . 800-371-7971
Hermannhof Vineyards
Hermann, MO. . . . 800-393-0100
Heron Hill Winery
Hammondsport, NY . . . 800-441-4241
Hess Collection
Napa, CA. . . . 707-255-1144
Hi-Country Foods Corporation
Selah, WA . . . 509-697-7292
HiBix Corporation
Pleasanton, CA. . . . 925-225-0800
High Grade Beverage
Monmouth Jct, NJ. . . . 887-327-4277
High Rise Coffee Roasters
Colorado Springs, CO. . . . 719-633-1833
Highland Manor Winery
Jamestown, TN . . . 931-879-9519
Highwood Distillers
High River, AB. . . . 403-652-3202
Hiland Dairy Foods Co
Springfield, MO . . . 800-492-4022
Hillcrest Vineyards
Roseburg, OR . . . 541-673-3709
Hillsboro Coffee Company
Tampa, FL. . . . 813-877-2126
Hinckley Springs Bottled Water
. . . 800-201-6218
Hinzerling Winery
Prosser, WA. . . . 800-727-6702
Home Roast Coffee
Lutz, FL. . . . 813-949-0807
Homewood Winery
Sonoma, CA . . . 707-996-6353
Honest Tea Inc
Atlanta, GA. . . . 800-520-2653
Honeywood Winery
Salem, OR. . . . 800-726-4101
Honig Vineyard and Winery
Rutherford, CA. . . . 800-929-2217
Hood River Coffee Co
Hood River, OR . . . 800-336-2954
Hood River Distillers Inc
Hood River, OR . . . 541-386-1588
Hood River Vineyards and Winery
Hood River, OR . . . 541-386-3772
Hoodsport Winery
Hoodsport, WA . . . 800-580-9894
Hop Kiln Winery
Healdsburg, CA . . . 707-433-6491
Hopkins Vineyard
Warren, CT . . . 860-868-7954
Horizon Cellars Winery
Siler City, NC . . . 919-742-1404
House of Coffee Beans
Houston, TX . . . 800-422-1799
Hubers Orchard Winery-Vineyards
Borden, IN. . . . 800-345-9463
Hudson Valley Brewery
Beacon, NY. . . . 845-218-9156
Hudson Valley Farmhouse Cider
Staatsburg, NY . . . 845-266-3979
Hudson Valley Fruit Juice
Highland, NY . . . 845-691-8061
Hunter Farms - High Point Division
High Point, NC . . . 800-446-8035
Husch Vineyards & Winery
Philo, CA. . . . 800-554-8724
Hyde Park Brewing Company
Hyde Park, NY . . . 845-229-8277
Hygeia Dairy Company
Corpus Christi, TX . . . 361-854-4561
Ideal Distributing Company
Bothell, WA. . . . 425-488-6121
ILHWA American Corporation
Belleville, NJ . . . 800-446-7364
Imperial Foods, Inc.
Long Island City, NY . . . 718-784-3400
Indian Hollow Farms
Richland Center, WI. . . . 800-236-3944
Indian Rock Vineyards
Murphys, CA. . . . 209-728-8514
Indian Springs Vineyards
Penn Vally, CA . . . 800-375-9311
Indigo Coffee Roasters
Florence, MA . . . 800-447-5450
Inglenook
Rutherford, CA . . . 707-968-1100
Ingleside Vineyards
Colonial Beach, VA . . . 804-224-8687
Inn Foods Inc
Watsonville, CA . . . 800-708-7836
Inniskillin Wines
Niagara-On-The-Lake, ON. . . . 888-466-4754
Intense Milk
Buffalo, NY. . . . 716-892-3156
Inter-American Products
Cincinnati, OH . . . 800-645-2233
Inter-Continental Imports Company
Newington, CT . . . 800-424-4422
Iron Horse Vineyards
Sebastopol, CA . . . 707-887-1507
Ironstone Vineyards
Murphys, CA. . . . 209-728-1251
Island Sweetwater Beverage Company
Bryn Mawr, PA . . . 610-525-7444
J Filippi Winery
Rancho Cucamonga, CA . . . 909-899-5755
J. Fritz Winery
Cloverdale, CA. . . . 800-418-9463
J. Stonestreet & Sons Vineyard
Healdsburg, CA . . . 800-355-8008
J.B. Peel Coffee Roasters
Red Hook, NY . . . 800-231-7372
J.G. British Imports
Bradenton, FL. . . . 888-965-1700
Jack Daniel Distillery
Lynchburg, TN . . . 888-551-5225
Jamaica John Inc
Franklin Park, IL. . . . 847-451-1730
Java Sun Coffee Roasters
Marblehead, MA. . . . 781-631-7788
Jayone Foods Inc
Paramount, CA . . . 562-633-7400
Jenny's Country Kitchen
Dover, MN . . . 800-357-3497
Jeremiah's Pick Coffee Co
San Francisco, CA . . . 877-537-3642
Jodar Vineyard & Winery
Placerville, CA . . . 530-644-3474
Jodyana Corporation
Miami, FL. . . . 888-563-5282
Jogue Inc
Northville, MI. . . . 800-531-3888
Johlin Century Winery
Oregon, OH. . . . 419-693-6288
John A Vassilaros & Son Inc
Flushing, NY. . . . 718-886-4140
John Conti Coffee Co
Louisville, KY . . . 800-928-5282
Johnson Estate Winery
Westfield, NY . . . 800-374-6569
Johnston's Winery Inc
Ballston Spa, NY . . . 518-882-6310
Jones Brewing Company
Smithton, PA. . . . 724-483-2400
Joseph Phelps Vineyards
St Helena, CA . . . 800-707-5789
Joseph Swan Vineyards
Forestville, CA . . . 707-573-3747
Josuma Coffee Co
Menlo Park, CA . . . 650-366-5453
Joullian Vineyards
Carmel Valley, CA . . . 866-659-8101

Juice Mart
West Hills, CA 877-888-1011
Juicy Whip Inc
La Verne, CA 909-392-7500
Justin Vineyards & Winery LLC
Paso Robles, CA 800-237-4152
Kaffe Magnum Opus
Millville, NJ 800-652-5282
Kalin Cellars
Novato, CA 415-883-3543
Kan-Pak
Arkansas City, KS 800-378-1265
Kate's Vineyard
Napa, CA 707-255-2644
Kathryn Kennedy Winery
Saratoga, CA 408-867-4170
Kauai Coffee Co Inc
Kalaheo, HI 800-545-8605
Kava King
Ormond Beach, FL 800-638-0082
Kelley's Island Wine Company
Kelleys Island, OH 419-746-2678
Kemach Food Products
Brooklyn, NY 718-272-5655
Kendall-Jackson
Fulton, CA 866-287-9818
Kenwood Vineyards
Kenwood, CA 707-833-5891
KeVita
Oxnard, CA 888-310-6106
Kicking Horse Coffee
Invermere, BC 888-287-5282
King Brewing Company
Pontiac, MI 248-745-5900
King Estate Winery
Eugene, OR 800-884-4441
King Juice Co
Milwaukee, WI 414-482-0303
Kiona Vineyards Winery
Benton City, WA 509-588-6716
Kirigin Cellars
Gilroy, CA 408-847-8827
Kistler Vineyards
Sebastopol, CA 707-823-5603
Kittling Ridge Estate Wines & Spirits
Vaughan, ON 800-461-9463
Kittridge & Fredrickson LTD
Portland, OR 800-558-7788
Klingshirn Winery
Avon Lake, OH 440-933-6666
Knapp Vineyards
Romulus, NY 800-869-9271
Knouse Foods Co-Op Inc.
Peach Glen, PA 717-677-8181
Kobricks Coffee Company
Jersey City, NJ 800-562-7491
Kona Coffee Council
Kealakekua, HI 808-323-2911
Koryo Winery Company
Gardena, CA 310-532-9616
Kramer Vineyards
Gaston, OR 800-619-4637
Krier Foods
Random Lake, WI 920-994-2469
Kunde Estate Winery
Kenwood, CA 707-833-5501
Kusmi Tea
New York, NY 646-346-1756
L.A. Libations
El Segundo, CA
La Abra Farm & Winery
Lovingston, VA 434-263-5392
LA Buena Vida Vineyards
Grapevine, TX 817-481-9463
LA Chiripada Winery
Dixon, NM 800-528-7801
LA Costa Coffee Roasting Co
Carlsbad, CA 760-438-8160
LA Jota Vineyard Co
Angwin, CA 877-222-0292
LA Rocca Vineyards & Winery
Forest Ranch, CA 800-808-9463
La Rochelle Winery
Livermore, CA 888-647-7768
La Vans Coffee Company
Bordentown, NJ 609-298-0688
LA Vina Winery
Anthony, NM 575-882-7632
Labatt Brewing Company
Toronto, ON 800-268-2337
Lacas Coffee Co Inc
Pennsauken, NJ 800-220-1133

Laetitia Vineyard & Winery
Arroyo Grande, CA 888-809-8463
Lafollette Vineyard & Winery
Sebastopol, CA 707-395-3902
Laird & Company
Scobeyville, NJ 877-438-5247
Lake Sonoma Winery
Glen Ellen, CA 877-586-2796
Lakeridge Winery & Vineyards
Clermont, FL 800-768-9463
Lakeshore Winery
Romulus, NY 315-549-7075
Lakewood Juice Co.
Miami, FL 866-324-5900
Lakewood Vineyards Inc
Watkins Glen, NY 877-535-9252
Lambert Bridge Winery
Healdsburg, CA 800-975-0555
Lamoreaux Landing Wine Cellars
Lodi, NY 607-582-6011
Lancaster County Winery LTD
Willow Street, PA 717-464-3555
Land O'Lakes Inc
Arden Hills, MN 800-328-9680
Landmark Vineyards
Kenwood, CA 707-833-0053
Lange Estate Winery & Vineyard
Dundee, OR 503-538-6476
Larry's Vineyards & Winery
Altamont, NY 518-355-7365
Latah Creek Wine Cellar
Spokane Valley, WA 509-926-0164
Latcham Vineyards
Somerset, CA 800-750-5591
Laurel Glen Vineyard
Glen Ellen, CA 707-933-9877
Lava Cap Winery
Placerville, CA 800-475-0175
Lavazza Premium Coffees
New York, NY 800-466-3287
Layman Distributing
Salem, VA 800-237-1319
Lazy Creek Vineyards
Philo, CA 888-529-9275
Le Bleu Corp
Advance, NC 800-854-4471
Leaves Pure Teas
Scottsdale, AZ 800-242-8807
Leelanau Cellars
Omena, MI 800-782-8128
Leeward Winery
Oxnard, CA 805-656-5054
Leidenfrost Vineyards
Hector, NY 607-546-2800
Lemon Creek Winery
Berrien Springs, MI 269-471-1321
Lemon-X Corporation
Huntington Station, NY 800-220-1061
Lenox-Martell Inc
Boston, MA 877-325-2489
Leonetti Cellar
Walla Walla, WA 509-525-1670
Leroy Hill Coffee Co Inc
Mobile, AL 800-866-5282
Les Bourgeois Vineyards
Rocheport, MO 800-690-1830
Les Mouts De P.O.M.
Sain-Francois-Xavier, QC 819-845-5555
Lewis Cellars
Napa, CA 707-255-3400
Lexington Coffee & Tea
Lexington, KY 859-277-1102
LiDestri Food & Drink
Fairport, NY 585-377-7700
Lifeway
Morton Grove, IL 877-281-3874
Light Rock Beverage Company
Danbury, CT 203-743-3410
Lincourt Vineyards
Solvang, CA 805-688-8554
Lindsay's Teas
Petaluma, CA 800-624-7031
Lingle Brothers Coffee
Bell Gardens, CA 562-927-3317
Lion Brewery Inc
Wilkes Barre, PA 888-295-2337
Lipsey Mountain Spring Water
Norcross, GA 770-449-0001
Little Amana Winery
Amana, IA 319-668-9664
Live Oaks Winery
Gilroy, CA 408-842-2401

Lockcoffee
Larchmont, NY 914-273-7838
Lola Savannah
Houston, TX 888-663-9166
Lorina, Inc.
Coral Gables, FL 305-779-3085
Lost Trail Root Beer
Louisburg, KS 800-748-7765
Louis Dreyfus Company Citrus Inc
Winter Garden, FL 407-656-1000
Louis Dreyfus Company LLC
Wilton, CT 203-761-2000
Louisburg Cider Mill
Louisburg, KS 800-748-7765
Love Creek Orchards
Medina, TX 800-449-0882
Lowcountry Produce
Raleigh, NC 800-935-2792
Lucas Vineyards & Winery
Interlaken, NY 800-682-9463
Lucas Winery
Lodi, CA 209-368-2006
Lucerne Foods
Pleasanton, CA 877-232-4271
Luxco Inc
St Louis, MO 314-772-2626
Lynfred Winery Inc
Roselle, IL 630-529-9463
Lyons Magnus
Fresno, CA 800-344-7130
M S Walker Inc
Somerville, MA 617-776-6700
M.E. Swing Company
Alexandria, VA 800-485-4019
Mackie International, Inc.
Riverside, CA 800-733-9762
MacKinlay Teas
Ann Arbor, MI 734-846-0966
Maddalena Restaurant-Sn
Los Angeles, CA 800-626-7722
Madison Foods
Saint Paul, MN 651-265-8212
Madys Company
San Francisco, CA 415-822-2227
Magnetic Springs
Columbus, OH 800-572-2990
Magnum Coffee Roastery
Nunica, MI 888-937-5282
Majestic Coffee & Tea Inc
San Carlos, CA 650-591-5678
Makana Beverages Inc.
Oxnard, CA
Manhattan Special Bottling
Brooklyn, NY 718-388-4144
Mar-Key Foods
Vidalia, GA 912-537-4204
Marie Brizard Wines & Spirits
St. Helena, CA 800-878-1123
Markham Vineyards
St Helena, CA 707-963-5292
Martin Ray Winery
Santa Rosa, CA 707-823-2404
Marva Maid Dairy
Newport News, VA 800-768-6243
Masala Chai Company
Santa Cruz, CA 831-475-8881
Master Brew
Northbrook, IL 847-564-3600
Matilija Water Company
Santa Barbara, CA 805-963-7873
Maui Gold Pineapple Company
Pukalani, HI 808-877-3805
Maxwell House & Post
Rye Brook, NY 914-335-2500
Mayacamas Vineyards & Winery
Napa, CA 707-224-4030
Mayer Bros
Buffalo, NY 800-696-2928
Mayer's Cider Mill
Webster, NY 800-543-0043
Mayfield Farms and Nursery
Athens, TN 423-746-9859
McArthur Dairy LLC
Miami, FL 561-659-4811
Mccutcheon Apple Products
Frederick, MD 800-888-7537
Mcgregor Vineyard Winery
Dundee, NY 800-272-0192
McSteven's
Vancouver, WA 800-838-1056
Meadow Brook Dairy Co
Erie, PA 800-352-4010

Meier's Wine Cellars Inc
Cincinnati, OH 800-346-2941
Melitta USA Inc
Clearwater, FL 888-635-4880
Meramec Vineyards
St James, MO 877-216-9463
Merci Spring Water
Maryland Heights, MO.......... 314-872-9323
Meridian Beverage Company
Atlanta, GA.................. 800-728-1481
Merlinos
Canon City, CO.................. 719-275-5558
Merritt Estate Winery Inc
Forestville, NY.................. 888-965-4800
Michigan Dairy LLC
Livonia, MI.................. 734-367-5390
Mike's Beverage Company
Toronto, ON 647-428-3123
Milsolv Corporation
Butler, WI.................. 800-558-8501
Minnehaha Spring Water Company
Cleveland, OH 216-431-0243
Mogen David Wine Corp
Westfield, NY 716-326-3151
Monarch Beverage Company
Atlanta, GA.................. 800-241-3732
Mondial Foods Company
Los Angeles, CA.................. 213-383-3531
Monster Beverage Corp.
Corona, CA.................. 800-426-7367
Mother Parker's Tea & Coffee
Mississauga, ON.................. 800-387-9398
Mount Olympus Waters
.... 800-782-5508
Mountain Valley Products Inc
Sunnyside, WA.................. 509-837-8084
Mountain Valley Spring Water
Asheville, NC.................. 800-627-1062
Murray Cider Co Inc
Roanoke, VA.................. 540-977-9000
Music Mountain Water Company
Shreveport, LA.................. 800-349-6555
Natalie's Orchid Island Juice Co.
Ft. Pierce, FL.................. 800-373-7444
Natrel
St. Laurent, QC.................. 800-501-1150
Natural Spring Water Company
Johnson City, TN 423-926-7905
Nature's Plus
Melville, NY.................. 800-645-9500
Neenah Springs
Oxford, WI 608-586-5696
Nehalem Bay Winery
Nehalem, OR.................. 888-368-9463
Nestle USA Inc
Glendale, CA 800-225-2270
New Age Beverages
Denver, CO.................. 303-289-8655
Niche W&S
Cedar Knolls, NJ.................. 973-993-8450
North Country Natural Spring Water
Port Kent, NY.................. 518-834-9400
Northland Cranberries
Jackson, WI.................. 866-719-5215
Northwest Naturals LLC
Bothell, WA.................. 425-881-2200
Northwestern Coffee Mills
Washburn, WI.................. 800-243-5283
Northwestern Foods
Arden Hills, MN.................. 800-236-4937
Ntc Marketing
Williamsville, NY.................. 800-333-1637
Nutritional Counselors of America
Spencer, TN 931-946-3600
O-At-Ka Milk Prods Co-Op Inc.
Batavia, NY.................. 800-828-8152
Ocean Spray International
Lakeville-Middleboro, MA 800-662-3263
Octavia Tea LLC
Batavia, IL.................. 866-505-6387
Office General des Eaux Minerales
Montreal, QC 514-482-7221
Old Dutch Mustard Company
Great Neck, NY 516-466-0522
Old Fashioned Natural Products
Santa Ana, CA 800-552-9045
Old Orchard Brands, LLC
Sparta, MI.................. 800-330-2173
Omar Coffee Co
Newington, CT 800-394-6627
One World Enterprises
Los Angeles, CA.................. 888-663-2626
Opa! Originals
Rochester, NY.................. 585-368-5623
Orchid Island Juice Co
Fort Pierce, FL 800-373-7444
Organic Gemini
Brooklyn, NY 347-662-2900
Orientex Foods
Pittsburg, CA 800-660-0962
Ormand Peugeog Corporation
Miami, FL.................. 305-624-6834
Pappy's Sassafras Tea
Columbus Grove, OH.................. 877-659-5110
Paramount Distillers
Cleveland, OH 800-821-2989
Parducci Wine Cellars
Ukiah, CA.................. 888-362-9463
Partners Coffee LLC
Atlanta, GA.................. 800-341-5282
Pearl Coffee Co
Akron, OH.................. 800-822-5282
Peerless Coffee & Tea
Oakland, CA 800-310-5662
Perfect Foods Inc
Goshen, NY.................. 800-933-3288
Pernod Ricard USA
New York, NY 212-372-5400
Perricone Juices
Beaumont, CA.................. 951-769-7171
Perry Creek Winery
Somerset, CA 800-880-4026
Personal Edge Nutrition
Ballwin, MO 514-636-4512
Pete's Brewing Company
San Antonio, TX.................. 800-877-7383
Pfefferkorn's Coffee Inc
Baltimore, MD 800-682-4665
Phamous Phloyd's Barbecue
Denver, CO.................. 800-497-3281
Phillips Beverage Company
Minneapolis, MN 612-362-7500
Phillips Syrup Corp
Cleveland, OH 800-350-8443
Pleasant Valley Wine Co
Hammondsport, NY 607-569-6111
Pleasant View Dairy
Highland, IN.................. 219-838-0155
Polar Beverages Inc.
Worcester, MA 800-734-9800
Polar Water Company
Carnegie, PA.................. 412-429-5550
Pontiac Coffee Break
Waterford, MI.................. 248-332-6333
Porto Rico Importing
New York, NY 212-477-5421
Post Familie Vineyards
Altus, AR 800-275-8423
Postum
Charlotte, NC 704-221-5587
Powell & Mahoney Ltd.
Salem, MA 978-745-4332
Premier Juices
Clearwater, FL 727-533-8200
Premium Water
Kansas City, MO.................. 800-332-3332
Pride Dairies
Bottineau, ND.................. 701-228-2216
Prince of Peace
Hayward, CA 800-732-2328
Productos Del Plata
Miami, FL.................. 786-357-8261
Progenix Corporation
Wausau, WI.................. 800-233-3356
Promised Land Dairy
Colorado Springs, CO.................. 877-520-2479
Purity Dairies LLC
Nashville, TN 615-244-1900
Q.E. Tea
Bridgeville, PA 800-622-8327
Quality Kitchen Corporation
Wyoming, DE 302-697-3118
Quality Naturally Foods
City Of Industry, CA.................. 888-498-6986
R.J. Corr Naturals
Posen, IL.................. 708-389-4200
RC Bottling Company
Evenasville, IN 812-424-7978
REBBL
Emeryville, CA.................. 855-732-2500
Rebound
Newburgh, NY 845-562-5400
Red Diamond Coffee & Tea
Moody, AL 800-292-4651
Reggie's Roast
Linden, NJ.................. 908-862-3700
Rejuvila
Boulder, CO 877-480-4402
Renault Winery
Egg Harbor City, NJ 609-965-2111
Revive Kombucha
Petaluma, CA 707-536-1193
Richland Beverage Association
Carrollton, TX.................. 214-357-0248
Robert Keenan Winery
St Helena, CA.................. 707-963-9177
Robert Mondavi Winery
Oakville, CA.................. 888-766-6328
Rondo Specialty Foods LTD
New Castle, DE.................. 800-724-6636
Roos Foods
Kenton, DE.................. 800-343-3642
Roselani Tropics Ice Cream
Wailuku, HI.................. 808-244-7951
Rosenberger's Dairies
Hatfield, PA.................. 800-355-9074
Royal Cup Coffee
Birmingham, AL.................. 800-366-5836
Russo Farms
Vineland, NJ.................. 856-692-5942
Rutherford Hill Winery
Rutherford, CA.................. 707-963-1871
Safeway Milk Plant
Tempe, AZ 480-894-4391
San Francisco Bay Coffee
Lincoln, CA 800-829-1300
San-Ei Gen FFI
New York, NY 212-315-7850
Sandstone Winery
Amana, IA.................. 319-622-3081
Sara Lee Foodservice
Peoria, IL.................. 800-641-4025
Saranac Brewery
Utica, NY 800-765-6288
Saratoga Spring Water Co
Saratoga Springs, NY.................. 888-426-8642
Sazerac Company, Inc.
Metairie, LA 866-729-3722
Schirf Brewing Company
Park City, UT 435-649-0900
Schneider's Dairy Inc
Pittsburgh, PA.................. 412-881-3525
Schramsberg Vineyards
Calistoga, CA 800-877-3623
Scotian Gold
Coldbrook, NS 888-726-8426
Sea Breeze Fruit Flavors
Towaco, NJ.................. 800-732-2733
Sesinco Foods
New York, NY 212-243-1306
Shasta Beverages Inc
Baltimore, MS.................. 800-834-9980
Sherbrooke OEM Ltd
Sherbrooke, QC 866-851-2579
Silvan Ridge Winery
Eugene, OR.................. 541-345-1945
Silver Springs Citrus Inc
Howey-in-the-Hills, FL 800-940-2277
Simi Winery
Healdsburg, CA 707-433-3686
Simpson & Vail
Brookfield, CT 800-282-8327
Skjodt-Barrett Foods
Brampton, ON.................. 877-600-1200
Smeltzer Orchard Co
Frankfort, MI 231-882-4421
Smith Dairy
Orrville, OH 800-776-7076
SnowBird Corporation
Bayonne, NJ 800-576-1616
Solana Gold Organics
Sebastopol, CA.................. 800-459-1121
Somerset Syrup & Concessions
Edison, NJ.................. 800-526-8865
Southern Beverage Packers Inc
Appling, GA 800-326-2469
Spangler Vineyards
Roseburg, OR 541-679-9654
Specialty Coffee Roasters
Delray Beach, FL 800-253-9363
SPI West Port, Inc
South San Fancisco, CA
Spoetzl Brewery
Shiner, TX.................. 361-594-3383
St Arnold Brewing Co
Houston, TX 800-801-6402

St Julian Winery
Paw Paw, MI . . . 800-732-6002
Stash Tea Co
Portland, OR . . . 800-547-1514
STE Michelle Wine Estates
Woodinville, WA . . . 800-267-6793
Sterling Vineyards
Calistoga, CA . . . 707-942-3344
Stevens Point Brewery
Stevens Point, WI . . . 800-369-4911
Stevens Tropical Plantation
West Palm Beach, FL . . . 561-683-4701
Stewart's Private Blend Foods
Chicago, IL . . . 800-654-2862
Stockton Graham & Co
Raleigh, NC . . . 800-835-5943
Stone Hill Winery
Hermann, MO . . . 573-486-2221
Stop & Shop Manufacturing
Readville, MA . . . 508-977-5132
Straub Brewery Inc
St Marys, PA . . . 814-834-2875
Sturm Foods Inc
Manawa, WI . . . 800-347-8876
Summit Brewing Company
Saint Paul, MN . . . 651-265-7800
Sun Orchard INC
Haines City, FL . . . 877-875-8423
Sun Pac Foods
Brampton, ON . . . 905-792-2700
Sunlike Juice
Rougemont, QC . . . 866-552-7643
Sunshine Farms
Portage, WI . . . 608-742-2016
Sunsweet Growers Inc.
Yuba City, CA . . . 800-417-2253
Suntory International
New York, NY . . . 212-891-6600
Super Stores Industries
Turlock, CA . . . 209-668-2100
Superbrand Dairies
Miami, FL . . . 305-769-6600
Sutter Home Winery
St Helena, CA . . . 800-967-4663
SVB Food & Beverage Company
Martinsburg, WV . . . 304-267-8500
Swiss Premium Dairy Inc
Lebanon, PA . . . 800-222-2129
SYFO Beverage Company of Florida
Ponte Vedra Beach, FL . . . 904-381-9002
Tamarack Farms Dairy
Newark, OH . . . 866-221-4141
Tatra Herb Co
Morrisville, PA . . . 888-828-7248
Taylor Wine Company
Hammondsport, NY . . . 607-868-3245
Templar Food Products
New Providence, NJ . . . 800-883-6752
Terrace At J Vineyards
Healdsburg, CA . . . 800-885-9463
Tetley USA
Marietta, GA . . . 770-428-5555
Tetley USA
Edison, NJ . . . 800-728-0084
Texas Coffee Co
Beaumont, TX . . . 800-259-3400
Texas Coffee Traders Inc
Austin, TX . . . 800-343-4875
The Humphrey Co
Lockport, NY . . . 716-597-1974
The Kroger Co.
Murray, KY . . . 800-632-6900
The Water Kefir People
Bend, OR
Thomas Canning/Maidstone
Maidstone, ON . . . 519-737-1531
Thomas Kruse Winery
Gilroy, CA . . . 408-842-7016
Three Lakes Winery
Three Lakes, WI . . . 800-944-5434
Todhunter Foods
Lake Alfred, FL . . . 863-956-1116
Toft Dairy Inc
Sandusky, OH . . . 800-521-4606
Tone Products Inc
Melrose Park, IL . . . 800-536-8663
Traditional Medicinals Inc
Sebastopol, CA . . . 800-543-4372
Tree Top Inc
Selah, WA . . . 509-697-7251
Trefethen Family Vineyards
Napa, CA . . . 707-255-7700
Trigo Corporation
Toa Baja, PR . . . 787-794-1300
Triple Springs Spring Water Co
Meriden, CT . . . 203-235-8374
Tropicana Products Inc.
Chicago, IL . . . 800-237-7799
TruBrain
Santa Monica, CA . . . 650-241-8372
True Organic Product Inc
Helm, CA . . . 800-487-0379
Tumericalive Healing Enterprise
New York, NY . . . 347-559-6760
Turkey Hill Dairy Inc
Conestoga, PA . . . 800-693-2479
Turkey Hill Sugarbush
Waterloo, QC . . . 450-539-4822
United Dairy Inc.
Martins Ferry, OH . . . 800-252-1542
United Dairymen of Arizona
Tempe, AZ . . . 480-966-7211
Universal Impex Corporation
Toronto, ON . . . 416-743-7778
Up Mountain Switchel
Brooklyn, NY . . . 315-939-3085
Uptime Energy, Inc.
Canoga Park, CA
V Sattui Winery
St Helena, CA . . . 707-963-7774
Valley Fig Growers
Fresno, CA . . . 559-237-3893
Valley View Packing Co
Yuba City, CA . . . 530-673-7356
Van Roy Coffee Co
Cleveland, OH . . . 877-826-7669
Vancouver Island Brewing Company
Victoria, BC . . . 800-663-6383
Varni Brothers/7-Up Bottling
Modesto, CA . . . 209-521-1777
Vegetable Juices Inc
Chicago, IL . . . 888-776-9752
Ventura Coastal LLC
Ventura, CA . . . 805-653-7000
Venture Vineyards
Lodi, NY . . . 888-635-6277
Vie-Del Co
Fresno, CA . . . 559-834-2525
Viking Distillery
Albany, GA . . . 866-729-3722
Villa Mt. Eden Winery
Saint Helena, CA . . . 866-931-1624
Vincor Canada
Mississauga, ON . . . 800-265-9463
Vintage Wine Estates
Santa Rosa, CA . . . 877-289-9463
Vita Food Products Inc
Chicago, IL . . . 800-989-8482
Vitamilk Dairy
Bellingham, WA . . . 206-529-4128
Von Stiehl Winery
Algoma, WI . . . 800-955-5208
W.J. Stearns & Sons/Mountain Dairy
Storrs Mansfield, CT . . . 860-423-9289
Wagner Vineyards
Lodi, NY . . . 866-924-6378
Wah Yet Group
Hayward, CA . . . 800-229-3392
Water Concepts
East Dundee, IL . . . 847-699-9797
Wayne Dairy Products Inc
Richmond, IN . . . 765-935-7521
Weaver Nut Co. Inc.
Ephrata, PA . . . 800-473-2688
Wechsler Coffee Corporation
Teterboro, NJ . . . 800-800-2633
WEIS Markets Inc.
Sunbury, PA . . . 866-999-9347
Welch Foods Inc
Concord, MA . . . 800-340-6870
Welch Foods Inc.
Concord, MA . . . 800-340-6870
Welsh Farms
Wallington, NJ . . . 800-221-0663
Westbrae Natural Foods
Melville, NY . . . 800-434-4246
Wheeling Coffee & Spice Co
Wheeling, WV . . . 800-500-0141
Whitaker & Assoc Architects
Atlanta, GA . . . 404-266-1265
White Coffee Corporation
Long Island City, NY . . . 800-221-0140
White Rock Products Corp
Flushing, NY . . . 800-969-7625
WhiteWave Foods
Denver, CO . . . 800-488-9283
Whole Herb Co
Sonoma, CA . . . 707-935-1077
Widmers Wine Cellars
Canandaigua, NY . . . 585-374-6311
Wild Aseptics, LLC
Erlanger, KY . . . 877-787-7221
Winchester Farms Dairy
Winchester, KY . . . 859-745-5500
Windmill Water Inc
Edgewood, NM . . . 505-281-9287
Winmix/Natural Care Products
Englewood, FL . . . 941-475-7432
Woodbury Vineyards
Fredonia, NY . . . 866-691-9463
World Citrus West
Fullerton, CA . . . 714-870-6171
Yakima Craft Brewing Company
Yakima, WA . . . 509-654-7357
Yoder Dairies
Chesapeake, VA . . . 757-482-4068
Yoo-Hoo Chocolate Beverage Company
Carlstadt, NJ . . . 201-933-0070
York Mountain Winery
Templeton, CA . . . 805-237-7575
Young Winfield
Hamilton, ON . . . 905-893-2536
Zd Wines
Napa, CA . . . 800-487-7757
Zeigler's
Lansdale, PA . . . 215-855-5161
Zephyrhills Bottled Water Company
Tampa, FL . . . 800-950-9398

Alcoholic Beverages

A. Nonini Winery
Fresno, CA . . . 559-275-1936
A. Rafanelli Winery
Healdsburg, CA . . . 707-433-1385
Abita Brewing Co
Covington, LA . . . 800-737-2311
Acacia Vineyard
Napa, CA . . . 877-226-1700
Ackerman Winery
Amana, IA . . . 319-622-3379
Adair Vineyards
New Paltz, NY . . . 845-255-1377
Adam Puchta Winery
Hermann, MO . . . 573-486-5596
Adams County Winery
Orrtanna, PA . . . 877-601-7936
Adelaida Cellars Inc
Paso Robles, CA . . . 800-676-1232
Adelsheim Vineyard
Newberg, OR . . . 503-538-3652
Adler Fels Winery
Santa Rosa, CA . . . 707-539-3123
Afton Mountain Vineyards Inc
Afton, VA . . . 540-456-8667
Ahlgren Vineyard
Boulder Creek, CA . . . 800-338-6071
Airlie Winery
Monmouth, OR . . . 503-838-6013
Alba Vineyard & Winery
Milford, NJ . . . 908-995-7800
Alexis Bailly Vineyard
Hastings, MN . . . 651-437-1413
Allegro Winery & Vineyards
Brogue, PA . . . 717-927-9148
Almarla Vineyards & Winery
Shubuta, MS . . . 601-687-5548
Aloha Distillers
Honolulu, HI . . . 808-841-5787
Alpen Cellars
Trinity Center, CA . . . 530-266-9513
Alpine Vineyards
Monroe, OR . . . 541-424-5851
Alta Vineyard Cellar
Calistoga, CA . . . 707-942-6708
Altamura Winery
Napa, CA . . . 707-253-2000
Alto Vineyards & Winery
Alto Pass, IL . . . 618-893-4898
Amador Foothill Winery
Plymouth, CA . . . 800-778-9463
Amalthea Cellars Farm Winery
Atco, NJ . . . 856-768-8585
Amberg Wine Cellars
Clifton Springs, NY . . . 315-462-3455
Americana Vineyards & Winery
Interlaken, NY . . . 888-600-8067

Amity Vineyards
Amity, OR........................888-264-8966
Amizetta Vineyards
St Helena, CA....................707-963-1460
Amwell Valley Vineyard
Ringoes, NJ......................908-788-5852
Anchor Brewing Company
San Francisco, CA................415-863-8350
Ancient Peaks Winery
Santa Margarita, CA..............805-365-7045
Anderson Valley Brewing Co
Boonville, CA....................800-207-2237
Anderson's Conn Valley Vineyards
St Helena, CA....................800-946-3497
Andrew Peller Limited
Grimsby, ON......................905-643-4131
Angry Orchard Cider Company, LLC
Walden, NY.......................888-845-3311
Annapolis Winery
Annapolis, CA....................707-886-5460
Antelope Valley Winery
Lancaster, CA....................800-282-8332
Anthony Road Wine Co
Penn Yan, NY.....................800-559-2182
Applewood Winery
Warwick, NY......................845-988-9292
Arbor Crest Wine Cellars
Spokane, WA......................509-927-9463
Arbor Hill Grapery & Winery
Naples, NY.......................800-554-7553
Argyle Winery
Dundee, OR.......................888-427-4953
Arizona Vineyards
Nogales, AZ......................520-287-7972
Arns Winery
St Helena, CA....................707-963-3429
Arrowood Winery
Glen Ellen, CA...................800-938-5170
Artesa Vineyards & Winery
Napa, CA.........................707-224-1668
Ashland Vineyards & Winery
Ashland, OR......................541-488-0088
ASV Wines
Delano, CA.......................661-792-3159
Au Bon Climat Winery
Los Olivos, CA...................805-937-9801
August Schell Brewing Co
New Ulm, MN......................800-770-5020
Augusta Winery
Augusta, MO......................888-667-9463
Autumn Wind Vineyard
Newberg, OR......................503-538-6931
B R Cohn Winery & Olive Oil Co
Glen Ellen, CA...................800-330-4064
Babcock Winery & Vineyards
Lompoc, CA.......................805-736-1455
Bacardi Canada, Inc.
Toronto, ON......................905-451-6100
Bacardi USA Inc
Coral Gables, FL.................800-222-2734
Bad Seed Cider Company, LLC
Highland, NY.....................845-236-0956
Bagley's
Hector, NY.......................607-582-6421
Baileyana Winery
San Luis Obispo, CA..............805-544-9080
Baily Vineyard & Winery
Temecula, CA.....................951-676-9463
Balagna Winery Company
Los Alamos, NM...................505-672-3678
Baldwin Vineyards
Pine Bush, NY....................845-744-2226
Balic Winery
Mays Landing, NJ.................609-625-2166
Banfi Vintners
Old Brookville, NY...............800-645-6511
Barca Wine Cellars
Roseville, CA....................916-786-0770
Bargetto Winery
Soquel, CA.......................800-422-7438
Baron Vineyards
Paso Robles, CA..................805-239-3313
Basignani Winery
Sparks Glencoe, MD...............410-472-0703
Baxters Vineyards & Winery
Nauvoo, IL.......................800-854-1396
Baywood Cellars
Lodi, CA.........................800-214-0445
Beachaven Vineyards & Winery
Clarksville, TN..................931-645-8867
Beam Suntory
Chicago, IL......................312-964-6999
Bear Creek Winery
Cave Junction, OR................877-273-4843
Beaucanon Estate Wines
Napa, CA.........................800-660-3520
Beckmen Vineyards
Los Olivos, CA...................805-688-8664
Bedell Northfork LLC
Cutchogue, NY....................631-734-7537
Bell Mountain Vineyards
Willow City, TX..................830-685-3297
Bellerose Vineyard
Healdsburg, CA...................707-433-1637
Benziger Family Winery
Glen Ellen, CA...................888-490-2739
Bernardo Winery
San Diego, CA....................858-487-1866
Bernardus Winery Tasting Rm
Carmel Valley, CA................800-223-2533
Bernheim Distilling Company
Louisville, KY...................800-303-0053
Berryessa Gap Tasting Room
Winters, CA......................530-795-3201
Bethel Heights Vineyard
Salem, OR........................503-399-9588
Bianchi Winery
Paso Robles, CA..................805-226-9922
Bias Vineyards & Winery
Berger, MO.......................800-905-2427
Bidwell Vineyard
Cutchogue, NY....................631-734-5200
Biltmore Estate Wine Company
Asheville, NC....................800-411-3812
Binns Vineyards & Winery
Las Cruces, NM...................575-526-6738
Bishop Farms Winery
Cheshire, CT.....................203-272-8243
Bittermilk LLC
Charleston, SC...................843-641-0455
Black Mesa Winery
Velarde, NM......................800-852-6372
Black Prince Distillery Inc
Clifton, NJ......................973-365-2050
Black Sheep Vintners
Murphys, CA......................209-728-2157
Blumenhof Vineyards-Winery
Dutzow, MO.......................800-419-2245
Boeger Winery
Placerville, CA..................800-655-2634
Bogle Vineyards Inc
Clarksburg, CA...................916-744-1030
Bohemian Brewery
Midvale, UT......................801-566-5474
Boisset Family Estates
St Helena, CA....................800-878-1123
Bonny Doon Vineyard
Santa Cruz, CA...................888-819-6789
Boordy Vineyards Inc
Hydes, MD........................410-592-5015
Bordoni Vineyards
Vallejo, CA......................707-642-1504
Boskydel Vineyard
Lake Leelanau, MI................231-256-7272
Bouchaine Vineyards
Napa, CA.........................800-654-9463
Boulder Beer
Boulder, CO......................303-444-8448
Brander Vineyard
Santa Ynez, CA...................800-970-9979
Braren Pauli Winery
Redwood Valley, CA...............800-423-6519
Braswell's Winery
Dora, AL.........................205-648-8335
Bravard Vineyards & Winery
Hopkinsville, KY.................270-269-2583
Breitenbach Wine Cellars
Dover, OH........................330-343-3603
Briceland Vineyards
Redway, CA.......................707-923-2429
Brick Brewery
Kitchener, ON....................800-505-8971
Brimstone Hill Vineyard
Pine Bush, NY....................845-744-2231
Bristle Ridge Vineyards
Knob Noster, MO..................800-994-9463
Broad Run Vineyards
Louisville, KY...................502-231-0372
Broadhead Brewing Co
Orl,ans, ON......................613-830-3944
Broadley Vineyards
Monroe, OR.......................541-847-5934
Bronco Wine Co
Ceres, CA........................855-874-2394
Brooklyn Cider House
Brooklyn, NY.....................347-295-0308
Brookmere Wine & Vineyard
Belleville, PA...................717-935-5380
Brotherhood Winery
Washingtonville, NY..............845-496-3661
Brown County Winery
Nashville, IN....................888-298-2984
Brutocao Cellars
Hopland, CA......................800-433-3689
Bryant Vineyard
Talladega, AL....................256-268-2638
Buccia Vineyard
Conneaut, OH.....................440-593-5976
Buckingham Valley Vineyards
Buckingham, PA...................215-794-7188
Buehler Vineyards
St Helena, CA....................707-963-2155
Bull and Barrel Brewpub
Brewster, NY.....................845-278-2855
Burnley Vineyards
Barboursville, VA................540-832-2828
Butler Winery
Bloomington, IN..................812-332-6660
Butterfly Creek Winery
Mariposa, CA.....................209-742-4567
Buttonwood Farm Winery & Vineyard
Solvang, CA......................800-715-1404
Byington Vineyard & Winery
Los Gatos, CA....................408-354-1111
Byron Vineyard & Winery
Santa Maria, CA..................805-938-7365
Cache Cellars
Davis, CA........................530-756-6068
Cain Vineyard & Winery
St Helena, CA....................707-963-1616
Cakebread Cellars
Rutherford, CA...................800-588-0298
Calafia Cellars
St Helena, CA....................707-963-0114
Calera Wine Co
Hollister, CA....................831-637-9170
Callaway Vineyards & Winery
Temecula, CA.....................800-472-2377
Camas Prairie Winery
Moscow, ID.......................800-616-0214
Cambria Winery
Santa Maria, CA..................888-339-9463
Campari
New York, NY.....................212-891-3600
Canoe Ridge Vineyard
Walla Walla, WA..................509-527-0885
Caparone Winery LLC
Paso Robles, CA..................805-610-5308
Caporale Winery
Napa, CA.........................707-253-9230
Caprock Winery Inc
Lubbock, TX......................800-546-9463
Cardinale Winery
Oakville, CA.....................800-588-0279
Carlson Vineyards Winery
Palisade, CO.....................888-464-5554
Carmenet Winery
Sonoma, CA.......................707-996-3526
Carneros Creek Winery
Napa, CA.........................707-253-9464
Carrousel Cellars
Gilroy, CA.......................408-847-2060
Casa Larga Vineyards
Fairport, NY.....................585-223-4210
Casa Nuestra Winery & Vineyard
St Helena, CA....................866-844-9463
Castello di Borghese Vineyard
Cutchogue, NY....................631-734-5111
Catoctin Vineyards
Brookeville, MD..................301-774-2310
Catskill Distilling Company
Bethel, NY.......................845-583-3141
Cavender Castle Winery
Atlanta, GA......................706-864-4759
Caymus Vineyards
Rutherford, CA...................707-967-3010
Cayuga Ridge Estate Winery
Ovid, NY.........................800-598-9463
Cedar Creek Winery
Cedarburg, WI....................800-827-8020
Cedar Mountain Winery
Livermore, CA....................925-373-6636
Chacewater Winery and Olive Mill
Kelseyville, CA..................707-279-2995
Chaddsford Winery
Chadds Ford, PA..................610-388-6221

Chalet Debonne Vineyards
Madison, OH. 440-466-3485
Chalk Hill Estate Winery
Healdsburg, CA 707-657-4839
Chalone Vineyard
Soledad, CA 831-678-1717
Chambord
Louisville, KY. 800-523-3811
Champoeg Wine Cellars Inc
Aurora, OR 503-678-2144
Channing Rudd Cellars
Middletown, CA. 707-987-2209
Chappellet Winery
St Helena, CA. 800-494-6379
Charles B. Mitchell Vineyards
Somerset, CA 800-704-9463
Charles Spinetta Winery
Plymouth, CA. 209-245-3384
Chateau Anne Marie
Carlton, OR. 503-864-2991
Chateau Boswell Winery
St Helena, CA. 707-963-5472
Chateau Chevre Winery
Napa, CA. 707-944-2184
Chateau des Charmes Wines
St. Davids, ON 800-263-2541
Chateau Diana Winery
Healdsburg, CA 707-433-6992
Chateau Grand Traverse Winery
Traverse City, MI 231-938-6120
Chateau Julien Winery
Carmel, CA. 831-624-2600
Chateau LA Fayette Reneau
Hector, NY. 800-469-9463
Chateau Montelena Winery
Calistoga, CA 707-942-5105
Chateau Morrisette Winery
Floyd, VA 540-593-2865
Chateau Potelle Winery
St Helena, CA. 707-255-9440
Chateau Ra-Ha
Jerseyville, IL 866-639-4832
Chateau Souverain
Cloverdale, CA 877-687-9463
Chateau St Jean Winery
Kenwood, CA. 707-833-4134
Chatom Vineyards Inc
San Andreas, CA. 800-435-8852
Chestnut Mountain Winery
Hoschton, GA. 770-867-6914
Chicama Vineyards
West Tisbury, MA. 888-244-2262
Chimere Winery
Santa Maria, CA 805-928-5611
Chouinard Vineyards & Winery
Castro Valley, CA 510-582-9900
Christine Woods Winery
Philo, CA. 707-895-2115
Christopher Creek Winery
Healdsburg, CA 707-433-2001
Cienega Valley Winery/DeRose
Hollister, CA. 831-636-9143
Cimarron Cellars
Caney, OK. 580-889-5997
Cinnabar Winery
Saratoga, CA. 408-867-1010
City Brewing Company
La Crosse, WI. 608-785-4200
Claiborne & Churchill Vintners
San Luis Obispo, CA 805-544-4066
Clear Creek Distillery
Portland, OR. 503-248-9470
Cline Cellars
Sonoma, CA 800-543-2070
Clos Du Bois Winery
Geyserville, CA 800-222-3189
Clos Du Lac Cellars
Ione, CA 209-274-2238
Clos Du Val Co LTD
Napa, CA. 707-261-5200
Clos Pegase Winery
Calistoga, CA 800-866-8583
Cloudstone Vineyards
Los Altos Hills, CA 650-948-8621
Clover Hill Vineyards & Winery
Breinigsville, PA. 800-256-8374
Cocktail Kits 2 Go LLC
New York, NY 917-750-3998
Cocolalla Winery
Cocolalla, ID. 208-263-3774
Colorado Cellars
Palisade, CO 970-464-7921

Columbia Winery
Woodinville, WA. 425-488-2776
Concannon Vineyard
Livermore, CA 800-258-9866
Conneaut Cellars Winery LLC
Conneaut Lake, PA 877-229-9463
Conrotto A. Winery
Gilroy, CA. 408-847-2233
Coon Creek Winery
St Helena, CA. 800-793-7960
Cooper Mountain Vineyards
Beaverton, OR 503-649-0027
Corby Distilleries
Toronto, ON 800-367-9079
Cosentino Winery
Napa, CA. 800-764-1220
Cowie Wine Cellars & Vineyards
Paris, AR. 479-963-3990
Crescini Wines
Soquel, CA 831-462-1466
Cribari Vineyard Inc
Fresno, CA 800-277-9095
Cristom Vineyards
Salem, OR. 503-375-3068
Criveller California Corp
Healdsburg, CA 888-849-2266
Cronin Vineyards
Woodside, CA. 650-851-1452
Crooked Vine/Stony Ridge Wnry
Livermore, CA 925-449-0458
Crossings Winery
Glenns Ferry, ID 208-366-2539
Crown Regal Wine Cellars
Brooklyn, NY 718-604-1430
Cruse Vineyards
Chester, SC 803-377-3944
Cuneo Cellars
Amity, OR. 503-835-2782
Cuvaison Winery
Calistoga, CA 707-942-6266
Cygnet Cellars
Hollister, CA. 831-637-7559
Dalla Valle Vineyards
Napa, CA. 707-944-2676
Davis Bynum Winery
Healdsburg, CA 800-826-1073
Deaver Vineyards
Plymouth, CA 209-245-4099
Deloach Vineyards
Santa Rosa, CA. 707-755-3300
Delorimier Winery
Geyserville, CA 800-546-7718
Denatale Vineyards
Healdsburg, CA 707-431-8460
Denning's Point Distillery, LLC
Beacon, NY. 845-476-8413
Devlin Wine Cellars
Soquel, CA 831-476-7288
DG Yuengling & Son, Inc.
Pottsville, PA. 570-628-4890
Diageo Canada Inc.
Toronto, ON 416-626-2000
Diageo North America Inc
Norwalk, CT 203-229-2100
Diamond Creek Vineyards
Calistoga, CA 707-942-6926
Diamond Water Bottling Fclty
Hot Springs, AR 501-623-1251
Digrazia Vineyards
Brookfield, CT 800-230-8853
Domaine St George Winery
Healdsburg, CA 707-433-5508
Donatoni Winery
Inglewood, CA 310-645-5445
Door Peninsula Winery
Sturgeon Bay, WI 800-551-5049
Dreyer Sonoma
Woodside, CA. 650-851-9448
Dry Creek Vineyard
Healdsburg, CA 800-864-9463
Duck Pond Cellars
Dundee, OR. 800-437-3213
Duckhorn Vineyards
St Helena, CA. 888-354-8885
Duncan Peak Vineyards
Lafayette, CA 925-283-3632
Dundee Wine Company
Dundee, OR. 888-427-4953
Dunn Vineyards
Angwin, CA 707-965-3642
Duplin Wine Cellars
Rose Hill, NC 800-774-9634

Dutch Henry Winery
Calistoga, CA 888-224-5879
E L K Run Vineyards
Mt Airy, MD 800-414-2513
Eagle Crest Vineyards LLC
Conesus, NY 800-977-7117
East Side Winery/Oak Ridge Vineyards
Lodi, CA 209-369-4758
Eberle Winery
Paso Robles, CA. 805-238-9607
Ed Oliveira Winery
Arcata, CA 707-822-3023
Edgewood Estate Winery
Napa, CA. 800-755-2374
Edmunds St. John
Berkeley, CA. 510-981-1510
Edna Valley Vineyard
San Luis Obispo, CA 866-979-8477
El Molino Winery
St Helena, CA 707-963-3632
Elk Cove Vineyards
Gaston, OR 877-355-2683
Elliston Vineyards
Sunol, CA 925-862-2377
Enz Vineyards
Hollister, CA. 831-637-6443
Eola Hills Wine Cellars
Rickreall, OR 800-291-6730
EOS Estate Winery
Paso Robles, CA. 800-249-9463
Erath Vineyards Winery
Dundee, OR. 800-539-5463
Esterlina Vineyard & Winery
Healdsburg, CA 888-474-7456
Evensen Vineyards
Oakville, CA. 707-944-2396
Eyrie Vineyards
Mcminnville, OR 888-440-4970
Fall Creek Vineyards
Austin, TX. 512-476-4477
Far Niente Winery
Oakville, CA. 707-944-2861
Farella-Park Vineyards
Napa, CA. 707-254-9489
Farfelu Vineyards
Flint Hill, VA 540-364-2930
Farmstead At Long Meadow Ranch
St Helena, CA 877-627-2645
Fenestra Winery
Livermore, CA 800-789-9463
Fenn Valley Vineyards
Fennville, MI 800-432-6265
Ferrante Winery & Ristorante
Geneva, OH. 440-466-6046
Ferrara Winery
Escondido, CA 760-745-7632
Ferrari-Carano
Healdsburg, CA 800-831-0381
Ferrigno Vineyards & Wine
St James, MO 573-265-7742
Fess Parker Winery
Los Olivos, CA. 800-841-1104
Ficklin Vineyards Winery
Madera, CA. 559-674-4598
Field Stone Winery
Healdsburg, CA 800-544-7273
Fieldbrook Valley Winery
Mckinleyville, CA 707-839-4140
Fife Vineyards
Redwood Valley, CA. 707-485-0323
Filsinger Vineyards & Winery
Temecula, CA 951-302-6363
Fiore Winery
Pylesville, MD 410-452-0132
Firelands Winery
Sandusky, OH 800-548-9463
Firestone Vineyard
Los Olivos, CA. 805-688-3940
Fisher Ridge Wine Co Inc
Charleston, WV 304-342-8702
Fisher Vineyards
Santa Rosa, CA. 707-539-7511
Fitzpatrick Winery & Lodge
Somerset, CA 800-245-9166
Flora Springs Winery
St Helena, CA. 707-963-5711
Florida Caribbean Distillers
Lake Alfred, FL 863-956-2002
Flying Embers
Ventura, CA
Flynn Vineyards Winery
Rickreall, OR 888-427-4953

Foley Estates Vineyard
Lompoc, CA 805-737-6222
Folie _ Deux Winery
Oakville, CA 800-535-6400
Foris Vineyards
Cave Junction, OR 541-592-3752
Forman Vineyard
St Helena, CA 707-963-3900
Fortino Winery
Gilroy, CA 888-617-6606
Fortuna Cellars
Davis, CA 530-756-6686
Four Sisters Winery
Belvidere, NJ 908-475-3671
Fox Vineyards & Winery
Social Circle, GA 770-787-5402
Foxen Foxen 7200
Santa Maria, CA 805-937-4251
Frank Family Vineyards
Calistoga, CA 880-574-9463
Frank-Lin Distributors
Fairfield, CA 800-922-9363
Franklin Hill Vineyards
Bangor, PA 888-887-2839
Franzia Winery
Ripon, CA 209-599-4111
Fratelli Perata
Paso Robles, CA 805-238-2809
Frederick Wildman & Sons LTD
New York, NY 800-733-9463
Freemark Abbey Winery
St Helena, CA 800-963-9698
Freixenet USA Inc
Sonoma, CA 707-996-4981
Frey Vineyards
Redwood Valley, CA 800-760-3739
Frick Winery
Geyserville, CA 707-857-1980
Frisinger Cellars
Napa, CA 707-255-3749
Frog's Leap Winery
Rutherford, CA 800-959-4704
Frontenac Point Vineyard
Trumansburg, NY 607-387-9619
Gainey Vineyard
Santa Ynez, CA 805-688-0558
Galante Vineyards
Carmel Valley, CA 800-425-2683
Galena Cellars Winery
Galena, IL 800-397-9463
Gallup Sales Company
Gallup, NM 505-863-5241
Gary Farrell Vineyards-Winery
Healdsburg, CA 866-277-9463
George A Dickel & Company
Tullahoma, TN 888-342-5352
Georgia Wines Inc
Ringgold, GA 706-937-2177
Georis Winery
Carmel Valley, CA 831-659-1050
Germanton Winery
Germanton, NC 800-322-2894
Girardet Wine Cellar
Roseburg, OR 541-679-7252
Gloria Ferrer Champagne
Sonoma, CA 707-933-1917
Gloria Winery & Vineyard
Springfield, MO 417-926-6263
Glunz Family Winery & Cellars
Grayslake, IL 847-548-9463
Golden City Brewery
Golden, CO 303-279-8092
Good Harbor Vineyards & Winery
Lake Leelanau, MI 231-256-7165
Goodson Brothers Coffee
Knoxville, TN 800-737-1519
Grand River Cellars
Madison, OH 440-298-9838
Grand Teton Brewing Co
Victor, ID 888-899-1656
Grande River Vineyards
Palisade, CO 800-264-7696
Granite Springs Winery
Somerset, CA 800-638-6041
Great Divide Brewing Co
Denver, CO 303-296-9460
Greenfield Wine Company
Vallejo, CA 707-552-5199
Greenwood Ridge Vineyards
Philo, CA 707-895-2002
Groth Vineyards & Winery
Oakville, CA 707-944-0290
Groupe Paul Masson
Longueuil, QC 514-878-3050
Gruet Winery
Albuquerque, NM 888-857-9463
Guenoc & Langtry Estate
Middletown, CA 707-995-7501
Guglielmo Winery
Morgan Hill, CA 408-779-2145
Guilliams Winery
St Helena, CA 707-963-9059
Gundlach-Bundschu Winery
Sonoma, CA 707-939-3015
H Coturri & Sons Winery
Glen Ellen, CA 866-268-8774
Habersham Vineyards & Winery
Helen, GA 706-878-9463
Hafner Vineyard
Healdsburg, CA 707-433-4606
Hahn Family Wines
Soledad, CA 831-678-4555
Haight Brown Vineyard
Litchfield, CT 800-577-9463
Hallcrest Vineyards
Felton, CA 831-335-4441
Handley Cellars
Philo, CA 800-733-3151
Hanzell Vineyards
Sonoma, CA 707-996-3860
Harbor Winery
West Sacramento, CA 916-371-6776
Harmony Cellars
Harmony, CA 800-432-9239
Harpersfield Vineyard
Geneva, OH 440-466-4739
Hart Winery
Temecula, CA 877-638-8788
Hartford Family Winery
Forestville, CA 707-887-8030
Hazlitt 1852 Vineyards
Hector, NY 888-750-0494
Heartland Vinyards
Westlake, OH 440-871-0701
Heck Cellars
Arvin, CA 661-854-6120
Hecker Pass Winery
Gilroy, CA 408-842-8755
Hegy's South Hills Vineyard & Winery
Twin Falls, ID 208-599-0074
Heineman Winery
Put In Bay, OH 419-285-2811
Helena View/Johnston Vineyard
Calistoga, CA 707-942-4956
Hells Canyon Winery
Caldwell, ID 800-318-7873
Henry Estate Winery
Umpqua, OR 800-782-2686
Henry Hill & Co
Napa, CA 707-253-1663
Heritage Wine Cellars
North East, PA 800-747-0083
Hermann J. Wiemer Vineyard
Dundee, NY 800-371-7971
Hermannhof Vineyards
Hermann, MO 800-393-0100
Heron Hill Winery
Hammondsport, NY 800-441-4241
Hess Collection
Napa, CA 707-255-1144
Hidden Mountain Ranch Winery
Paso Robles, CA 805-226-9907
Highland Manor Winery
Jamestown, TN 931-879-9519
Highwood Distillers
High River, AB 403-652-3202
Hillcrest Vineyards
Roseburg, OR 541-673-3709
Hinzerling Winery
Prosser, WA 800-727-6702
Hiram Walker & Sons
Windsor, ON 519-254-5171
Homewood Winery
Sonoma, CA 707-996-6353
Honeywood Winery
Salem, OR 800-726-4101
Honig Vineyard and Winery
Rutherford, CA 800-929-2217
Hood River Distillers Inc
Hood River, OR 541-386-1588
Hood River Vineyards and Winery
Hood River, OR 541-386-3772
Hoodsport Winery
Hoodsport, WA 800-580-9894
Hop Kiln Winery
Healdsburg, CA 707-433-6491
Hopkins Vineyard
Warren, CT 860-868-7954
Horizon Cellars Winery
Siler City, NC 919-742-1404
Hubers Orchard Winery-Vineyards
Borden, IN 800-345-9463
Hudson Valley Brewery
Beacon, NY 845-218-9156
Hudson Valley Farmhouse Cider
Staatsburg, NY 845-266-3979
Hunt Country Vineyards
Branchport, NY 800-946-3289
Husch Vineyards & Winery
Philo, CA 800-554-8724
Hyde Park Brewing Company
Hyde Park, NY 845-229-8277
Ingleside Vineyards
Colonial Beach, VA 804-224-8687
Inniskillin Wines
Niagara-On-The-Lake, ON 888-466-4754
Ipswich Ale Brewery
Ipswich, MA 978-356-3329
Iron Horse Vineyards
Sebastopol, CA 707-887-1507
Ironstone Vineyards
Murphys, CA 209-728-1251
J Filippi Winery
Rancho Cucamonga, CA 909-899-5755
J Lohr Vineyards & Wines
San Jose, CA 408-288-5057
J. Fritz Winery
Cloverdale, CA 800-418-9463
J. Stonestreet & Sons Vineyard
Healdsburg, CA 800-355-8008
Jack Daniel Distillery
Lynchburg, TN 888-551-5225
Jodar Vineyard & Winery
Placerville, CA 530-644-3474
Johlin Century Winery
Oregon, OH 419-693-6288
Johnson's Alexander Valley Wines
Healdsburg, CA 800-888-5532
Johnston's Winery Inc
Ballston Spa, NY 518-882-6310
Jones Brewing Company
Smithton, PA 724-483-2400
Joseph Swan Vineyards
Forestville, CA 707-573-3747
Joullian Vineyards
Carmel Valley, CA 866-659-8101
Justin Vineyards & Winery LLC
Paso Robles, CA 800-237-4152
Kalin Cellars
Novato, CA 415-883-3543
Kate's Vineyard
Napa, CA 707-255-2644
Kathryn Kennedy Winery
Saratoga, CA 408-867-4170
Kelley's Island Wine Company
Kelleys Island, OH 419-746-2678
Kelson Creek Winery
Plymouth, CA 209-245-4700
Kendall-Jackson
Fulton, CA 866-287-9818
King Brewing Company
Pontiac, MI 248-745-5900
King Estate Winery
Eugene, OR 800-884-4441
Kiona Vineyards Winery
Benton City, WA 509-588-6716
Kirigin Cellars
Gilroy, CA 408-847-8827
Kistler Vineyards
Sebastopol, CA 707-823-5603
Kittling Ridge Estate Wines & Spirits
Vaughan, ON 800-461-9463
Klingshirn Winery
Avon Lake, OH 440-933-6666
Knapp Vineyards
Romulus, NY 800-869-9271
Koryo Winery Company
Gardena, CA 310-532-9616
Kramer Vineyards
Gaston, OR 800-619-4637
Kunde Estate Winery
Kenwood, CA 707-833-5501
L Mawby Vineyards
Peshawbestown, MI 231-271-3522
La Abra Farm & Winery
Lovingston, VA 434-263-5392

LA Buena Vida Vineyards
Grapevine, TX 817-481-9463
LA Chiripada Winery
Dixon, NM 800-528-7801
LA Rocca Vineyards & Winery
Forest Ranch, CA 800-808-9463
LA Vina Winery
Anthony, NM 575-882-7632
Labatt Brewing Company
Toronto, ON 800-268-2337
Laetitia Vineyard & Winery
Arroyo Grande, CA....................888-809-8463
Lafollette Vineyard & Winery
Sebastopol, CA....................707-395-3902
Laird & Company
Scobeyville, NJ....................877-438-5247
Lake Sonoma Winery
Glen Ellen, CA 877-586-2796
Lakeridge Winery & Vineyards
Clermont, FL....................800-768-9463
Lakeshore Winery
Romulus, NY 315-549-7075
Lakewood Vineyards Inc
Watkins Glen, NY....................877-535-9252
Lambert Bridge Winery
Healdsburg, CA 800-975-0555
Lamoreaux Landing Wine Cellars
Lodi, NY 607-582-6011
Lancaster County Winery LTD
Willow Street, PA 717-464-3555
Landmark Vineyards
Kenwood, CA....................707-833-0053
Lange Estate Winery & Vineyard
Dundee, OR....................503-538-6476
Larry's Vineyards & Winery
Altamont, NY 518-355-7365
Latah Creek Wine Cellar
Spokane Valley, WA 509-926-0164
Latcham Vineyards
Somerset, CA 800-750-5591
Laurel Glen Vineyard
Glen Ellen, CA 707-933-9877
Lava Cap Winery
Placerville, CA 800-475-0175
Lazy Creek Vineyards
Philo, CA....................888-529-9275
Le Vigne Winery
Paso Robles, CA....................800-891-6055
Leelanau Cellars
Omena, MI 800-782-8128
Leidenfrost Vineyards
Hector, NY 607-546-2800
Lemon Creek Winery
Berrien Springs, MI 269-471-1321
Leonetti Cellar
Walla Walla, WA....................509-525-1670
Les Bourgeois Vineyards
Rocheport, MO....................800-690-1830
Lewis Cellars
Napa, CA....................707-255-3400
Lincourt Vineyards
Solvang, CA 805-688-8554
Little Amana Winery
Amana, IA....................319-668-9664
Little Hills Winery
St Charles, MO 877-584-4557
Live Oaks Winery
Gilroy, CA....................408-842-2401
Livermore Valley Cellars
Livermore, CA 925-454-9463
Livingston Moffett Winery
Saint Helena, CA 800-788-0370
Llano Estacado Winery
Lubbock, TX....................800-634-3854
Lockwood Vineyards
St. Helena, CA 707-963-6925
Loew Vineyards
Mt Airy, MD....................301-831-5464
Lolonis Winery
Walnut Creek, CA....................925-938-8066
Long Vineyards
St Helena, CA....................707-963-2496
Lost Mountain Winery
Sequim, WA 888-683-5229
Louis M Martini Winery
St Helena, CA....................800-321-9463
Lucas Winery
Lodi, CA 209-368-2006
Luxco Inc
St Louis, MO....................314-772-2626
Lve & Raymond Vineyards
St Helena, CA....................800-525-2659

Lynfred Winery Inc
Roselle, IL....................630-529-9463
M S Walker Inc
Somerville, MA 617-776-6700
Madison Foods
Saint Paul, MN 651-265-8212
Madison Vineyard
Ribera, NM....................575-421-8028
Madonna Estate Winery
Napa, CA....................866-724-2993
Madrona Vineyards
Camino, CA 530-644-5948
Magnanini Farm Winery
Wallkill, NY 845-895-2767
Magnotta Winery Corporation
Vaughan, ON....................800-461-9463
Mama Rap's & Winery
Gilroy, CA....................800-842-6262
Marie Brizard Wines & Spirits
St. Helena, CA 800-878-1123
Marietta Cellars
Geyservill, CA 707-433-2747
Marimar Torres Estates
Sebastopol, CA....................707-823-4365
Marin Brewing Co
Larkspur, CA....................415-461-4677
Markham Vineyards
St Helena, CA....................707-963-5292
Markko Vineyard
Conneaut, OH....................800-252-3197
Marlow Wine Cellars
Monteagle, TN 931-924-2120
Martin & Weyrich Winery
Templeton, CA 805-239-1640
Mastantuono Winery
Templeton, CA 805-238-0676
Matanzas Creek Winery
Santa Rosa, CA....................800-500-6464
Matson Vineyards
Redding, CA....................530-222-2833
Maui Wine
Kula, HI....................877-878-6058
Maurice Carrie Winery
Temecula, CA 800-716-1711
Mayacamas Vineyards & Winery
Napa, CA....................707-224-4030
Mazzocco Vineyards
Healdsburg, CA 800-501-8466
McCormick Distilling Co
Weston, MO 888-640-3082
McDowell Valley Vineyards & Cellars
Hopland, CA....................707-744-1774
McHenry Vineyard
Davis, CA 530-756-3202
McIntosh's Ohio Valley Wines
Bethel, OH 937-379-1159
Menghini Winery
Julian, CA....................760-765-2072
Meredyth Vineyard
Middleburg, VA 540-687-6277
Meridian Vineyards
Napa, CA....................800-226-7133
Merryvale Vineyards
St Helena, CA....................800-326-6069
Messina Hof Winery & Resort
Bryan, TX....................979-778-9463
Michael David Winery
Lodi, CA 888-707-9463
Michel-Schlumberger Wine Est
Healdsburg, CA 800-447-3060
Mike's Beverage Company
Toronto, ON 647-428-3123
Milat Vineyards Winery
St Helena, CA....................800-546-4528
Mill Creek Vineyards
Healdsburg, CA 877-349-2121
Millbrook Vineyards
Millbrook, NY 800-662-9463
Milliaire Winery
Murphys, CA....................209-728-1658
Mission Mountain Winery
Dayton, MT....................406-849-5524
Mon Ami Restaurant
Port Clinton, OH....................800-777-4266
Montelle Winery
Augusta, MO....................888-595-9463
Monterey Vineyard
Gonzales, CA 831-675-4000
Montevina Winery
Plymouth, CA....................209-245-6942
Montmorenci Vineyards
Aiken, SC 803-649-4870

Moonlight Brewing Company
Windsor, CA 707-528-2537
Moss Creek Winery
Napa, CA....................707-252-1295
Mount Palomar Winery
Temecula, CA 800-854-5177
Mt Bethel Winery
Altus, AR 479-468-2444
Mt Eden Vineyards
Saratoga, CA....................408-867-9587
Mt Nittany Vineyard & Winery
Centre Hall, PA....................814-466-6373
Mt Pleasant Winery
Branson, MO....................800-467-9463
Murphy Goode Estate Winery
Geyserville, CA 707-431-7644
Nahmias et Fils
Yonkers, NY....................914-294-0055
Naked Mountain Winery Vineyard
Markham, VA 540-364-1609
Nalle Winery
Healdsburg, CA 707-433-1040
Nantucket Vineyard
Nantucket, MA 508-228-9235
Napa Cellars
Napa, CA....................800-535-6400
Napa Wine Company
Oakville, CA....................800-848-9630
Nashoba Valley Winery
Bolton, MA....................978-779-5521
National Wine & Spirits
Indianapolis, IN
Navarro Vineyards
Philo, CA....................707-895-3686
Naylor Wine Cellars Inc
Stewartstown, PA 800-292-3370
Nevada City Winery
Nevada City, CA....................800-203-9463
Nevada County Wine Guild
Nevada City, CA....................855-494-7025
New Belgium Brewing Co
Fort Collins, CO 888-622-4044
New Hope Winery
New Hope, PA....................800-592-9463
New Land Vineyard
Geneva, NY....................315-585-4432
Newport Vineyards & Winery
Middletown, RI....................401-848-5161
Newton Vineyard
St Helena, CA....................707-204-7423
Nicasio Vineyards
Soquel, CA 831-423-1073
Niche W&S
Cedar Knolls, NJ....................973-993-8450
Nichelini Family Winery Inc
St Helena, CA....................707-963-0717
Niebaum-Coppola Estate Winery
Rutherford, CA....................800-782-4266
Nissley Vineyards & Winery
Bainbridge, PA 800-522-2387
Nordman Of California
Sanger, CA 559-638-9923
Northern Lights Brewing Company
Airway Heights, WA....................509-242-2739
Northern Vineyards Winery
Stillwater, MN....................651-430-1032
Northville Winery & Brewing Co
Northville, MI....................248-320-6507
Nutmeg Vineyard
Andover, CT....................860-742-8402
Oak Grove Orchards Winery
Rickreall, OR 541-364-7052
Oak Knoll Winery
Hillsboro, OR 800-625-5665
Oak Ridge Winery LLC
Lodi, CA 209-369-4758
Oak Spring Winery
Altoona, PA....................814-946-3799
Oasis Winery
Hume, VA 800-304-7656
Obester Winery
Half Moon Bay, CA 650-726-9463
Ocena Winery & Vineyards
New Era, MI 231-861-4657
Ogeki Sake USA Inc
Hollister, CA....................831-637-9217
Ojai Vineyard
Oak View, CA....................805-649-1674
Old Creek Ranch Winery
Ventura, CA....................805-649-4132
Old Mill Winery
Geneva, OH....................440-466-5560

Old Rip Van Winkle Distillery
Frankfort, KY 502-897-9113
Old South Winery
Natchez, MS 601-445-9924
Old Wine Cellar
Amana, IA. 319-622-3116
Olde Heurich Brewing Company
Washington, DC 202-333-2313
Olympic Cellars
Port Angeles, WA 360-452-0160
One Vineyard and Winery
Saint Helena, CA 707-963-1123
Optima Wine Cellars
Healdsburg, CA 707-431-8222
Opus One
Oakville, CA. 800-292-6787
Orange County Distillery
Goshen, NY. 845-651-2929
Orchard Heights Winery
Salem, OR. 503-391-7308
Orfila Vineyards
Escondido, CA 760-738-6500
Organic Wine Co Inc
San Francisco, CA 888-326-9463
Ormand Peugeog Corporation
Miami, FL. 305-624-6834
Orr Mountain Winery
Madisonville, TN 423-442-5340
Pabst Brewing Company
San Antonio, TX. 800-947-2278
Pacheco Ranch Winery
Novato, CA. 415-883-5583
Pacific Echo Cellars
Philo, CA. 707-895-2065
Pacific Hop Exchange Brewing Company
Novato, CA. 415-884-2820
Page Mill Winery
Livermore, CA 925-456-7676
Pahlmeyer Winery
St Helena, CA. 707-255-2321
Pahrump Valley Winery
Pahrump, NV 800-368-9463
Palmer Vineyards Inc
Riverhead, NY 800-901-8783
Panther Creek Cellars
Dundee, OR. 503-472-8080
Pantry Shelf/Mixxm
Hutchinson, KS. 800-968-3346
Paper City Brewery
Holyoke, MA 413-535-1588
Paradise Valley Vineyards
Phoenix, AZ 602-233-8727
Paraiso Vineyards
Soledad, CA 831-678-0300
Pastori Winery
Cloverdale, CA. 707-857-3418
Paumanok Vineyards
Aquebogue, NY 631-722-8800
Peaceful Bend Winery
Steelville, MO. 573-775-3000
Peconic Bay Winery
Cutchogue, NY 631-734-7361
Pedrizzetti Winery
Morgan Hill, CA. 408-779-7389
Pedroncelli J Winery
Geyserville, CA 800-836-3894
Peju Province Winery
Rutherford, CA. 800-446-7358
Pellegrini Wine Co
Santa Rosa, CA. 800-891-0244
Penn Shore Winery Vineyards
North East, PA. 814-725-8688
Pennsylvania Renaissance Faire
Manheim, PA 717-664-0476
Pernod Ricard USA
New York, NY 212-372-5400
Perry Creek Winery
Somerset, CA 800-880-4026
Pete's Brewing Company
San Antonio, TX. 800-877-7383
Peter Michael Winery
Calistoga, CA 800-354-4459
Peterson & Sons Winery
Kalamazoo, MI. 269-626-9755
Pharmco Aaper
Brookfield, CT 203-740-3471
Pheasant Ridge Winery
Lubbock, TX. 806-746-6033
Philip Togni Vineyard
St Helena, CA. 707-963-3731
Phillips Beverage Company
Minneapolis, MN 612-362-7500
Piedmont Vineyards & Winery
Middleburg, VA 540-687-5528
Piedra Creek Winery
San Luis Obispo, CA 805-541-1281
Pikes Peak Vineyards
Colorado Springs, CO. 719-576-0075
Pindar Vineyards
Peconic, NY 631-734-6200
Pine Ridge Vineyards
Napa, CA. 800-575-9777
Plainfield Winery & Tasting Rm
Plainfield, IN. 888-761-9463
Plam Vineyards & Winery
La Quinta, CA. 760-972-4465
Plum Creek Winery
Palisade, CO 970-464-7586
Plymouth Colony Winery
Plymouth, MA. 508-747-3334
Pommeraie Winery
Sebastopol, CA 707-823-9463
Ponderosa Valley Vineyard
Ponderosa, NM 800-946-3657
Ponzi Vineyards
Sherwood, OR. 503-628-1227
Porter Creek Vineyards
Healdsburg, CA 707-433-6321
Prager Winery & Port Works
St Helena, CA 800-969-7678
Presque Isle Wine Cellars
North East, PA. 800-488-7492
Preston Premium Wines
Pasco, WA. 509-545-1990
Preston Vineyards & Winery
Healdsburg, CA 800-305-9707
Prince Michel
Leon, VA. 800-869-8242
Prohibition Distillery, LLC
Roscoe, NY. 917-685-8989
Quady Winery
Madera, CA. 800-733-8068
Quail Ridge Cellars & Vineyards
Saint Helena, CA 800-706-9463
Quilceda Creek Vintners
Snohomish, WA 360-568-2389
Quivira Vineyards & Winery
Healdsburg, CA 800-292-8339
R.H. Phillips
Esparto, CA. 530-662-3504
Rabbit Ridge Winery
Paso Robles, CA. 805-467-3331
Radanovich Vineyards & Winery
Mariposa, CA 209-966-3187
Rainbow Hills Vineyards
Newcomerstown, OH 740-545-9305
Rancho De Philo Winery
Rancho Cucamonga, CA 909-987-4208
Rancho Sisquoc Winery
Santa Maria, CA. 805-934-4332
Rapazzini Winery
Gilroy, CA. 800-842-6262
Ravenswood Winery
Sonoma, CA 866-568-3946
Rebec Vineyards
Amherst, VA 434-946-5168
Redhawk Vineyard & Winery
Salem, OR. 503-362-1596
Reeve Wines
Healdsburg, CA 707-235-6345
Refresco Beverages US Inc.
Tampa, FL. 888-260-3776
Renaissance Vineyard & Winery
Oregon House, CA 800-655-3277
Renault Winery
Egg Harbor City, NJ 609-965-2111
Renwood Winery
Plymouth, CA 800-348-8466
Retzlaff Vineyards
Livermore, CA 925-447-8941
Richard L. Graeser Winery
Calistoga, CA 707-942-4437
Richardson Vineyards
Sonoma, CA 707-938-2610
Richland Beverage Association
Carrollton, TX. 214-357-0248
Ridge Vineyards Inc
Cupertino, CA. 408-867-3233
Ritchie Creek Vineyard
St Helena, CA 707-963-4661
River Run Vintners
Watsonville, CA 831-726-3112
Roberian Vineyards
Forestville, NY 716-679-1620
Robert F Pliska & Company Winery
Purgitsville, WV 877-747-2737
Robert Keenan Winery
St Helena, CA 707-963-9177
Robert Mondavi Winery
Oakville, CA. 888-766-6328
Robert Mueller Cellars
Windsor, CA 707-837-7399
Robert Pecota Winery
Calistoga, CA 707-479-7770
Robert Sinskey Vineyards Inc
Napa, CA. 800-869-2030
Robller Vineyard Winery
New Haven, MO. 573-237-3986
Roche Caneros Estate Winery
Sonoma, CA 800-825-9475
Rodney Strong Vineyards
Healdsburg, CA 800-474-9463
Rogue Ales Brewery
Newport, OR. 541-265-3188
Rombauer Vineyards
St Helena, CA. 800-622-2206
Rose Creek Vineyards
Hagerman, ID 208-837-4353
Rosenblum Cellars
Alameda, CA. 510-865-7007
Roudon-Smith Vineyards
Saratoga, CA. 831-438-1244
Round Hill Vineyards
St Helena, CA. 800-778-0424
Rudd Winery
Oakville, CA. 707-944-8577
Rutherford Hill Winery
Rutherford, CA 707-963-1871
Saddleback Cellars
Oakville, CA. 707-944-1305
Sainte Genevieve Winery
Ste Genevieve, MO. 800-398-1298
Saintsbury
Napa, CA. 707-252-0592
Sakeone Corp
Forest Grove, OR 800-550-7253
Salamandre Wine Cellars
Aptos, CA 831-685-0321
Salishan Vineyards
La Center, WA. 360-263-2713
San Dominique Winery
Camp Verde, AZ 480-945-8583
Sand Castle Winery
Erwinna, PA 800-722-9463
Sandia Shadows Vineyard & Winery
Albuquerque, NM. 505-856-1006
Sanford Winery
Lompoc, CA 800-426-9463
Santa Barbara Winery
Santa Barbara, CA 805-963-3633
Santa Cruz Mountain Vineyard
Felton, CA. 831-426-6209
Santa Fe Vineyards
Espanola, NM 505-753-8100
Santa Ynez Wine Corp
Los Olivos, CA. 800-824-8584
Sarah's Vineyard
Gilroy, CA. 408-842-4278
Saranac Brewery
Utica, NY 800-765-6288
Satiety Winery & Cafe
Davis, CA. 530-757-2699
Saucilito Canyon Vineyard
San Luis Obispo, CA 805-543-2111
Sausal Winery
Healdsburg, CA 800-500-2285
Savannah Chanelle Vineyards
Saratoga, CA. 408-741-2934
Sawtooth Winery
Nampa, ID. 208-467-1200
Sazerac Co Inc
New Orleans, LA 504-831-9450
Sazerac Company, Inc.
Metairie, LA 866-729-3722
Scenic Valley Winery
Lanesboro, MN. 507-259-4981
Schirf Brewing Company
Park City, UT 435-649-0900
Schloss Doepken Winery
Ripley, NY 716-326-3636
Schoppaul Hill Winery atIvanhoe
Denton, TX. 940-380-9463
Schramsberg Vineyards
Calistoga, CA 800-877-3623
Schug Carneros Estate Winery
Sonoma, CA 800-966-9365

Sea Ridge Winery
Occidental, CA 800-692-5780
Seavey Vineyard
St Helena, CA 707-963-8339
Seghesio Family Vineyards
Healdsburg, CA 707-433-0545
Sequoia Grove
Napa, CA. 800-851-7841
Serendipity Cellars
Monmouth, OR. 503-838-4284
Seven Hills Winery
Walla Walla, WA. 877-777-7870
Seven Lakes Vineyard & Winery
Fenton, MI 810-373-6081
Shafer Vineyards
Napa, CA. 707-944-2877
Shallon Winery
Astoria, OR. 503-325-5978
Sharon Mill Winery
Manchester, MI. 734-971-6337
Shenandoah Vineyards
Plymouth, CA. 209-245-4455
Sierra Vista Winery
Placerville, CA 800-946-3916
Signore Winery
Brooktondale, NY. 607-539-7935
Signorello Vineyards
Napa, CA. 707-255-5990
Silvan Ridge Winery
Eugene, OR. 541-345-1945
Silver Creek Distillers
Rigby, ID. 208-754-0042
Silver Fox Vineyards
Mariposa, CA. 209-966-4800
Silver Mountain Vineyards
Santa Cruz, CA 408-353-2278
Silverado Vineyards Inc
Napa, CA. 800-997-1770
Simi Winery
Healdsburg, CA 707-433-3686
Simon Levi Cellars
Kenwood, CA. 888-315-0040
Six Mile Creek Vineyard
Ithaca, NY. 800-260-0612
Sky Vineyards
Glen Ellen, CA 707-935-1391
Slate Quarry Winery
Nazareth, PA 610-746-3900
Smith Vineyard & Winery
Grass Valley, CA. 530-273-7032
Smith-Madrone Vineyards & Winery
St Helena, CA. 707-963-2283
Smothers Brothers Tasting Room
Glen Ellen, CA 800-795-9463
Sobon Estate
Plymouth, CA. 209-333-6275
Sokol Blosser Winery
Dayton, OR. 800-582-6668
Solis Winery
Gilroy, CA. 888-838-6427
Sonoita Vineyards
Elgin, AZ. 520-455-5893
Sonoma Wine Services
Vineburg, CA 707-996-9773
Sonoma-Cutrer Vineyards
Windsor, CA 707-528-1181
Southern California Brewing Company
Los Angeles, CA. 213-622-1261
Sow's Ear Winery
Brooksville, ME 207-326-4649
Spangler Vineyards
Roseburg, OR 541-679-9654
Spoetzl Brewery
Shiner, TX. 361-594-3383
Spottswoode
St Helena, CA. 707-963-0134
Spring Mountain Vineyard
St Helena, CA. 877-769-4637
Springhill Cellars
Albany, OR 541-928-1009
Spurgeon Vineyards & Winery
Highland, WI 800-236-5555
St Arnold Brewing Co
Houston, TX 800-801-6402
St Francis Winery & Vineyards
Santa Rosa, CA. 707-833-4668
St Innocent Winery
Salem, OR. 503-378-1526
St Julian Winery
Paw Paw, MI. 800-732-6002
St. James Winery
Saint James, MO. 800-280-9463

Stags' Leap Winery
Napa, CA. 707-944-1303
Starr & Brown
Portland, OR 503-287-1775
Starr Hill Winery & Vineyard
Curwensville, PA 814-236-0910
Ste Chapelle Winery
Caldwell, ID 877-783-2427
Stearns Wharf Vintners
Santa Barbara, CA 805-966-6624
Steltzner Vineyards
Napa, CA. 800-707-9463
Sterling Vineyards
Calistoga, CA 707-942-3344
Steuk's Country Market &Winery
Sandusky, OH 419-625-8324
Stevenot Winery
Murphys, CA. 209-728-3485
Stevens Point Brewery
Stevens Point, WI 800-369-4911
Stone Hill Winery
Hermann, MO. 573-486-2221
Stonegate
St Helena, CA. 707-603-2203
Stoneridge Winery
Sutter Creek, CA. 209-223-1761
Stonington Vineyards
Stonington, CT 800-421-9463
Stony Hill Vineyard
St Helena, CA. 707-963-2636
Stonybrook Mountain Winery
Calistoga, CA 707-942-5282
Storrs Winery
Santa Cruz, CA. 831-458-5030
Story Winery
Plymouth, CA 800-712-6390
Stoutridge Vineyard
Marlboro, NY
Straub Brewery Inc
St Marys, PA 814-834-2875
Streblow Vineyards
Saint Helena, CA 707-963-5892
Stryker Sonoma
Geyserville, CA 800 433-1944
Sudwerk Privatbrauerei Hubsch
Davis, CA. 530-758-8700
Sugar Creek Winery
Defiance, MO 636-987-2400
Sullivan Vineyards
St Helena, CA. 877-244-7337
Summit Brewing Company
Saint Paul, MN 651-265-7800
Summit Lake Vineyards
Angwin, CA 707-965-2488
Sunrise Winery
San Jose, CA. 408-741-1310
Sutter Home Winery
St Helena, CA. 800-967-4663
Sweet Traders
Huntington Beach, CA 714-903-6800
Sycamore Vineyards
Saint Helena, CA 800-963-9698
Takara Sake USA Inc
Berkeley, CA. 510-540-8250
Talbott Vineyards
Salinas, CA. 831-675-3000
Talley Vineyards
Arroyo Grande, CA. 805-489-2508
Tamuzza Vineyards
Hope, NJ. 856-896-0619
Taos Brewing Supply
El Prado, NM 575-779-0449
Tarara Winery
Leesburg, VA 703-771-7100
Taylor Wine Company
Hammondsport, NY 607-868-3245
Terrace At J Vineyards
Healdsburg, CA 800-885-9463
The Boisset Collection
St. Helena, CA 707-967-7667
The Meeker Vineyard
Healdsburg, CA 707-431-2148
The Rubin Family of Wines
Sebastopol, CA. 707-887-8130
Thoma Vineyards
Dallas, OR. 800-884-1927
Thomas Fogarty Winery
Woodside, CA. 800-247-4163
Thomas Kruse Winery
Gilroy, CA. 408-842-7016
Thornton Winery
Temecula, CA 951-699-0099

Thorpe Vineyard
Wolcott, NY 315-594-2502
Three Meadows Spirits LLC
Millerton, NY 845-702-3903
Tkc Vineyards
Plymouth, CA. 888-627-2356
Tomasello Winery
Hammonton, NJ 800-666-9463
Topolos at Russian River Vine
Forestville, CA 707-887-3344
Transamerica Wine Corporation
Brooklyn, NY 718-875-4017
Trefethen Family Vineyards
Napa, CA. 707-255-7700
Trentadue Winery
Geyserville, CA 888-332-3032
Triple Rock Brewing Co Brkly
Berkeley, CA. 510-843-2739
Truchard Vineyards
Napa, CA. 707-253-7153
Truckee River Winery
Truckee, CA 530-587-4626
Tucker Cellars
Sunnyside, WA 509-837-8701
Tudal Winery
St Helena, CA. 707-963-3947
Tularosa Vineyards
Tularosa, NM 800-687-4467
Tuthilltown Spirits
Gardiner, NY. 845-255-1527
Tyee Wine Cellars
Corvallis, OR 541-753-8754
Uinta Brewing Co
Salt Lake City, UT 801-467-0909
US Distilled Products Co
Princeton, MN. 763-389-4903
Val Verde Winery
Del Rio, TX. 830-775-9714
Valhalla Winery
Veneta, OR 541-935-9711
Valley of the Moon Winery
Glen Ellen, CA 707-996-6941
Valley View Winery
Jacksonville, OR. 800-781-9463
Van Der Heyden Vineyards
Napa, CA. 800-948-9463
Vancouver Island Brewing Company
Victoria, BC 800-663-6383
Varni Brothers/7-Up Bottling
Modesto, CA. 209-521-1777
Ventana Vineyards Winery
Monterey, CA 800-237-8846
Vetter Vineyards Winery
Westfield, NY 716-326-3100
Via Della Chiesa Vineyards
Raynham, MA. 508-822-7775
Viader Vineyards & Winery
Deer Park, CA. 707-963-3816
Viano Vineyards
Martinez, CA 925-228-6465
Viansa Winery
Sonoma, CA 800-995-4740
Vie-Del Co
Fresno, CA 559-834-2525
Villa Helena/Arger-Martucci Winery
St Helena, CA. 707-963-4334
Villa Milan Vineyard
Milan, IN. 812-654-3419
Villa Mt. Eden Winery
Saint Helena, CA 866-931-1624
Villar Vintners of Valdese
Valdese, NC. 828-879-3202
Vincent Arroyo Winery
Calistoga, CA 707-942-6995
Vincor Canada
Mississauga, ON. 800-265-9463
Vinoklet Winery
Cincinnati, OH 513-385-9309
Von Stiehl Winery
Algoma, WI. 800-955-5208
Von Strasser
Calistoga, CA 888-359-9463
Vynecrest Winery
Breinigsville, PA. 800-361-0725
Wachusett Brewing Co
Westminster, MA 978-874-9965
Warner Vineyards
Paw Paw, MI. 800-756-5357
Warwick Valley Winery & Distillery
Warwick, NY 845-258-4858
Wasson Brothers Winery
Sandy, OR 503-668-3124

Weibel Vineyards
Lodi, CA . . . 800-932-9463
Wente Family Estates
Livermore, CA . . . 925-456-2305
Wermuth Winery
Calistoga, CA . . . 707-942-5924
West Park Wine Cellars
West Park, NY. . . . 845-384-6709
Westbend Vinyards
Lewisville, NC . . . 866-901-5032
Westport Rivers Vineyard
Westport, MA . . . 800-993-9695
Westwood Winery
Sonoma, CA . . . 707-933-7837
Whaler Vineyard
Ukiah, CA . . . 707-462-6355
Whitcraft Winery
Santa Barbara, CA . . . 805-730-1086
White Oak Vineyards & Winery
Healdsburg, CA . . . 707-433-8429
White Rock Vineyards
Napa, CA. . . . 707-257-7922
Whitecliff Vineyard & Winery
Gardiner, NY. . . . 845-255-4613
Whitehall Lane Winery
St Helena, CA . . . 707-963-9454
Whitford Cellars
Napa, CA. . . . 707-942-0840
Widmers Wine Cellars
Canandaigua, NY . . . 585-374-6311
Wiederkehr Wine Cellars Inc
Altus, AR . . . 800-622-9463
Wild Hog Vineyard
Cazadero, CA . . . 707-847-3687
Wild Horse Winery & Vineyards
Templeton, CA . . . 805-434-2541
Wildhurst Vineyards
Kelseyville, CA. . . . 800-595-9463
William Grant & Sons
Irvine, CA
William Harrison Winery LLC
St Helena, CA . . . 707-963-8762
William Hill Estate Winery
Napa, CA. . . . 707-265-3024
Williams Selyem Winery
Healdsburg, CA . . . 707-433-6425
Williamsburg Winery LTD
Williamsburg, VA . . . 757-229-0999
Wimberley Valley Winery
Driftwood, TX . . . 512-847-2592
Windwalker Vineyards & Winery
Somerset, CA . . . 530-620-4054
Witness Tree Vineyard LTD
Salem, OR. . . . 888-478-8766
Wolf Creek Winery
Barberton, OH. . . . 800-436-0426
Wollersheim Winery
Prairie Du Sac, WI . . . 800-847-9463
Wooden Valley Winery
Fairfield, CA . . . 707-864-0730
Woodside Vineyards
Menlo Park, CA . . . 650-851-3144
Woodward Canyon
Touchet, WA . . . 509-525-4129
Worden
Spokane, WA. . . . 509-455-7835
Wyandotte Winery LLC
Gahanna, OH. . . . 877-906-7464
Yakima Craft Brewing Company
Yakima, WA . . . 509-654-7357
Yakima River Winery
Prosser, WA. . . . 509-786-2805
Yamhill Valley Vineyards
Mcminnville, OR . . . 800-825-4845
York Mountain Winery
Templeton, CA . . . 805-237-7575
Zaca Mesa Winery
Los Olivos, CA . . . 800-350-7972
Zayante Vineyards
Felton, CA. . . . 831-335-7992
Zd Wines
Napa, CA. . . . 800-487-7757

Beers

AB InBev
St. Louis, MO . . . 314-577-7427
Abita Brewing Co
Covington, LA . . . 800-737-2311
Alaskan Brewing Company
Juneau, AK . . . 907-780-5866
AleSmith Brewing Company
San Diego, CA . . . 858-549-9888
Alley Kat Brewing Co, Ltd
Edmonton, AB . . . 780-436-8922
Amstell Holding
New Bedford, MA . . . 508-995-6100
Amsterdam Brewing Company
Toronto, ON . . . 416-504-6882
Anchor Brewing Company
San Francisco, CA . . . 415-863-8350
Anderson Valley Brewing Co
Boonville, CA. . . . 800-207-2237
Andrews Brewing Co
Andrews, NC. . . . 828-321-2006
Anheuser-Busch
St. Louis, MO . . . 800-342-5283
Apani Southwest
Abilene, TX. . . . 325-690-1550
Arnold Foods Company
Horsham, PA. . . . 800-984-0989
Assets Grille & Southwest Brewing Company
Albuquerque, NM. . . . 505-889-6400
Atwater Block Brewing Company
Detroit, MI . . . 313-877-9205
August Schell Brewing Co
New Ulm, MN. . . . 800-770-5020
Avery Brewing Company
Boulder, CO . . . 877-844-5679
Bad Frog Brewery Co
St Augustine, FL. . . . 888-223-3764
Baltimore Brewing Company
Baltimore, MD . . . 410-837-5000
Bar Harbor Brewing Company
Bar Harbor, ME. . . . 207-288-4592
Bay Hawk Ales
Irvine, CA . . . 949-442-7565
Beaver Street Brewery
Flagstaff, AZ. . . . 928-779-0079
Bell's Brewery Inc
Kalamazoo, MI . . . 269-382-2338
Belmont Brewing Co
Long Beach, CA . . . 562-433-3891
Berghoff Brewery
Chicago, IL . . . 608-358-4992
Berkshire Brewing Co Inc
South Deerfield, MA . . . 877-222-7468
Big Bucks Brewery & Steakhouse
Gaylord, MI. . . . 989-731-0401
Big Rock Brewery
Calgary, AB. . . . 800-242-3107
Big Sky Brewing Co
Missoula, MT . . . 800-559-2774
Bison Brewing Company
Berkeley, CA. . . . 510-697-1537
BJ's Restaurants Inc.
Huntington Beach, CA . . . 714-500-2400
Bloomington Brewing Co
Bloomington, IN . . . 812-323-2112
Blue Point Brewing Co
Patchogue, NY . . . 631-475-6944
Bluegrass Brewing Company
Louisville, KY . . . 502-899-7070
Bohemian Brewery
Midvale, UT . . . 801-566-5474
Boston Beer Co Inc.
Boston, MA. . . . 888-661-2337
Boston Stoker
Vandalia, OH. . . . 937-890-6401
Boulder Beer
Boulder, CO . . . 303-444-8448
Boulder Creek Brewing Company
Boulder Creek, CA . . . 831-338-7882
Boulevard Brewing
Kansas City, MO. . . . 816-474-7095
Bow Valley Brewing Company
Canmore, AB . . . 403-678-2739
Brasserie Brasel Brewery
Lasalle, QC . . . 800-463-2728
Breckenridge Brewery
Denver, CO . . . 800-328-6723
Brewers Association
Boulder, CO . . . 888-822-6273
Brewery Ommegang
Cooperstown, NY . . . 800-544-1809
Brick Brewery
Kitchener, ON. . . . 800-505-8971
Bristol Brewing Co
Colorado Springs, CO. . . . 719-368-6120
Broadhead Brewing Co
Orl,ans, ON. . . . 613-830-3944
Broken Bow Brewery
Tuckahoe, NY. . . . 914-268-0900
Brooklyn Brew Shop
Brooklyn, NY . . . 718-874-0119
Brooklyn Brewery
Brooklyn, NY . . . 718-486-7422
Browns Brewing Co
Troy, NY . . . 518-273-2337
Buffalo Bill Brewing Company
Hayward, CA . . . 510-886-9823
Bull and Barrel Brewpub
Brewster, NY . . . 845-278-2855
Calapooia Brewing Co
Albany, OR . . . 541-928-1931
Capalbo's Fruit Baskets
Clifton, NJ. . . . 800-252-6262
Capital Brewery & Beer Garden
Middleton, WI. . . . 608-836-7100
Captain Lawrence Brewing Co
Elmsford, NY . . . 914-741-2337
Carolina Brewery
Chapel Hill, NC . . . 919-942-1800
Carta Blanca
El Paso, TX. . . . 915-544-6367
Catskill Brewery
Livingston Manor, NY . . . 845-439-1232
Champion Beverages
Darien, CT. . . . 203-655-9026
Christopher Joseph Brewing Company
Paradise Valley, AZ. . . . 480-948-7882
Cisco Brewers
Nantucket, MA . . . 508-325-5929
City Brewing Company
La Crosse, WI . . . 608-785-4200
Clemson Bros. Brewery
Middletown, NY . . . 845-775-4638
Clipper City Brewing
Halethorpe, MD . . . 410-247-7822
Columbus Brewing Co
Columbus, OH . . . 614-464-2739
Copper Tank Brewing Company
Austin, TX. . . . 512-854-9380
Craft Brew Alliance
Portland, OR . . . 503-331-7270
Creemore Springs Brewery
Creemore, ON. . . . 800-267-2240
Criveller California Corp
Healdsburg, CA . . . 888-849-2266
Crooked River Brewing Company
Cleveland, OH . . . 216-771-2337
Crowley Beverage Corporation
Wayland, MA . . . 800-997-3337
Dempsey's Restaurant & Brewery
Petaluma, CA . . . 707-765-9694
Deschutes Brewery
Bend, OR. . . . 541-385-8606
DG Yuengling & Son, Inc.
Pottsville, PA. . . . 570-628-4890
Dl Geary Brewing
Portland, ME. . . . 207-878-2337
Dogfish Head Craft Brewery
Lewes, DE. . . . 888-834-3474
Dogwood Brewing Company
Atlanta, GA. . . . 404-367-0500
Drakes Brewing Co
San Leandro, CA. . . . 510-568-2739
Durango Brewing Co
Durango, CO. . . . 970-247-3396
Eastern Brewing Corporation
Hammonton, NJ . . . 609-561-2700
El Toro Brew Pub
Morgan Hill, CA. . . . 408-782-2739
Etna Brewing Co
Etna, CA . . . 530-467-5277
Falla Imports
Greenville, ME . . . 609-476-4106
Flagstaff Brewing Co
Flagstaff, AZ. . . . 928-773-1442
Florida Brewery
Auburndale, FL. . . . 863-965-1825
Flying Dog Brewery
Frederick, MD. . . . 301-694-7899
Fort Garry Brewing Company
Winnipeg, MB. . . . 204-487-3678
Fox N Hare Brewing Co.
Port Jervis, NY . . . 845-672-0100
French's Coffee
Walnut Creek, CA. . . . 925-932-5901
Full Sail Brewing Co
Hood River, OR . . . 888-244-2337
Gambrinus Co
San Antonio, TX. . . . 210-490-9128
Garrison Brewing
Halifax, NS . . . 902-453-5343
Genesee Brewing Company
Rochester, NY. . . . 585-263-9200

Gentle Ben's Brewing Co
Tucson, AZ 520-624-4177
Golden City Brewery
Golden, CO 303-279-8092
Goose Island Beer Co
Chicago, IL 800-466-7363
Gordon Biersch Brewery Restaurant
San Jose, CA 408-278-1008
Grain Belt
New Ulm, MN 800-770-5020
Grand Teton Brewing Co
Victor, ID 888-899-1656
Gray's Brewing Co
Janesville, WI 608-752-3552
Great Divide Brewing Co
Denver, CO 303-296-9460
Great Lakes Brewing Co.
Cleveland, OH 216-771-4404
Great Lakes Wine & Spirits
Highland Park, MI 313-453-2200
Great Northern Brewing Co
Whitefish, MT 406-863-1000
Great Western Brewing Company
Saskatoon, SK 800-764-4492
Guinness Import Co
Stamford, CT 800-521-1591
Hair Of The Dog Brewing
Portland, OR 503-232-6585
Hale's Brewery
Seattle, WA 206-782-0737
Harpoon Brewery
Boston, MA 800-427-7666
Heartland Brewery
New York, NY 212-400-2300
Hog Haus Brewing Company
Fayetteville, AR 479-521-2739
Hogtown Brewing Company
Mississauga, ON 905-855-9065
Hornell Brewing Company
New Hyde Park, NY 516-812-0300
Humboldt Brews LLC
Arcata, CA 707-826-2739
Hyde Park Brewing Company
Hyde Park, NY 845-229-8277
Ipswich Ale Brewery
Ipswich, MA 978-356-3329
Jacob Leinenkugel Brewing Co
Chippewa Falls, WI 715-723-5557
Jones Brewing Company
Smithton, PA 724-483-2400
Karl Strauss Brewing Co
San Diego, CA 858-273-2739
Keegan Ales
Kingston, NY 845-331-2739
Kevton Gourmet Tea
Streetman, TX 888-538-8668
Kirin Brewery
Los Angeles, CA 310-381-3040
Kona Brewing
Kailua Kona, HI 808-334-1133
Krinos Foods
Bronx, NY 718-729-9000
La Brasserie McAuslan Brewing
Montreal, QC 514-939-3060
Labatt Brewing Company
Toronto, ON 800-268-2337
Lafayette Brewing Co
Lafayette, IN 765-742-2591
Laguna Beach Brewing Company
Laguna Beach, CA 949-497-3381
Lakefront Brewery Inc
Milwaukee, WI 414-372-8800
Lakeport Brewing Corporation
Moncton, NB 800-268-2337
Lang Creek Brewery
Marion, MT 406-858-2200
Left Hand Brewing Co
Longmont, CO 303-772-0258
Legend Brewing Co
Richmond, VA 804-232-8871
Leinenkugel's
Chippewa Falls, WI 888-534-6437
Les Brasseurs Du Nord
Blainville, QC 800-378-3733
Les Brasseurs GMT
Montreal, QC 888-253-8330
Lion Brewery Inc
Wilkes Barre, PA 888-295-2337
Long Trail Brewing Co Inc
Bridgewater Cors, VT 802-672-5011
Los Gatos Brewing Company
Los Gatos, CA 408-395-9929

Lost Coast Brewery
Eureka, CA 707-267-9651
M J Barleyhoppers Sports Bar
Lewiston, ID 800-232-6730
Magnotta Winery Corporation
Vaughan, ON 800-461-9463
Manhattan Beach Brewing Company
Manhattan Beach, CA 310-798-2744
Marin Brewing Co
Larkspur, CA 415-461-4677
Maritime Pacific Brewing Co
Seattle, WA 206-782-6181
Mayer's Cider Mill
Webster, NY 800-543-0043
Mendocino Brewing Co Inc
Ukiah, CA 707-463-2627
Mike's Beverage Company
Toronto, ON 647-428-3123
Millrose Restaurant
South Barrington, IL 800-464-5576
Millstream Brewing Co
Amana, IA 319-622-3672
Mishawaka Brewing Company
Granger, IN 574-256-9993
Moet Hennessy USA
New York, NY 212-251-8200
Molson Coors Beverage Company
Chicago, IL 800-645-5376
Molson Coors North America
Chicago, IL 800-645-5376
Moonlight Brewing Company
Windsor, CA 707-528-2537
Moosehead Breweries Ltd.
St. John, NB
Mountain Sun Pubs & Breweries
Boulder, CO 303-546-0886
Nevada City Brewing
Nevada City, CA 530-265-2446
New Belgium Brewing Co
Fort Collins, CO 888-622-4044
New Glarus Brewing CompaNy
New Glarus, WI 608-527-5850
New Holland Brewing Co
Holland, MI 616-355-6422
Newburgh Brewing Company
Newburgh, NY 845-569-2337
North American Breweries Inc.
Rochester, NY 585-546-1030
Northampton Brewing Company
Northampton, MA 413-584-9903
Northern Breweries
Marie, ON 514-908-7545
Northern Lights Brewing Company
Airway Heights, WA 509-242-2739
Northville Winery & Brewing Co
Northville, MI 248-320-6507
Nutfield Brewing Company
Derry, NH 603-434-9678
Oak Creek Brewing Company
Sedona, AZ 928-204-1300
Odell Brewing Co
Fort Collins, CO 970-498-9070
Okanagan Spring Brewery
Vernon, BC 800-652-0755
Oland Breweries
Halifax, NS 800-268-2337
Old Credit Brewing Co. Ltd.
Toronto, ON 416-494-2766
Olde Heurich Brewing Company
Washington, DC 202-333-2313
Onalaska Brewing
Onalaska, WA 360-978-4253
Oskar Blues Brewery
Longmont, CO 303-776-1914
Pabst Brewing Company
San Antonio, TX 800-947-2278
Pacific Coast Brewing
Oakland, CA 510-836-2739
Pacific Hop Exchange Brewing Company
Novato, CA 415-884-2820
Pacific Western Brewing Company
Prince George, BC 250-562-2424
Palmetto Brewing Co
Charleston, SC 843-937-0903
Paper City Brewery
Holyoke, MA 413-535-1588
Peekskill Brewery
Peekskill, N7 914-734-2337
Pennsylvania Brewing Company
Pittsburgh, PA 412-237-9400
Pete's Brewing Company
San Antonio, TX 800-877-7383

Pike Brewing Co
Seattle, WA 206-622-6044
Pittsburgh Brewing Co
Pittsburgh, PA 412-682-7400
Prescott Brewing Co
Prescott, AZ 928-771-2795
Pyramid Alehouse-Seattle
Seattle, WA 206-682-3377
Red Brick Brewing Company
Atlanta, GA 800-475-5417
Red White & Brew
Redding, CA 530-222-5891
Redhook Brewery
Portland, OR 503-331-7270
Remarkable Liquids
Altamont, NY 518-861-5351
Richland Beverage Association
Carrollton, TX 214-357-0248
River Market Brewing Company
Kansas City, MO 816-471-6300
Rock Bottom Restaurant & Brewery
Denver, CO 303-534-7616
Rogue Ales Brewery
Newport, OR 541-265-3188
Rohrbach Brewing Co
Rochester, NY 585-594-9800
Russell Breweries, Inc.
Surrey, BC 604-599-1190
Santa Cruz Mountain Brewing
Santa Cruz, CA 831-425-4900
Santa Fe Brewing Co
Santa Fe, NM 505-424-3333
Sapporo USA, Inc.
New York, NY 212-922-9165
Saranac Brewery
Utica, NY 800-765-6288
Schirf Brewing Company
Park City, UT 435-649-0900
Schlafly Tap Room
St Louis, MO 314-241-2337
Sea Dog Brewing Company
Topsham, ME 207-725-0162
Sequoia Brewing Co
Fresno, CA 559-264-5521
Seven Barrel Brewery
West Lebanon, NH 603-298-5566
Shipyard Brewing Co
Portland, ME 207-761-0807
Shipyard Brewing Co
Portland, ME 800-789-0684
Short's Brewing Co
Bellaire, MI 231-498-2300
Sierra Nevada Taproom & Rstrnt
Chico, CA 530-893-3520
Sleeman Breweries, Ltd.
Guelph, ON 800-268-8537
Smuttynose Brewing Co
Portsmouth, NH 603-436-4026
Snake River Brewing Company
Jackson, WY 307-739-2337
Southern California Brewing Company
Los Angeles, CA 213-622-1261
Spoetzl Brewery
Shiner, TX 361-594-3383
Sprecher Brewing Co
Milwaukee, WI 888-650-2739
St Arnold Brewing Co
Houston, TX 800-801-6402
St. Croix Beer Company
Saint Paul, MN 651-387-0708
St. Stan's Brewing Company
Modesto, CA 209-284-0170
Stevens Point Brewery
Stevens Point, WI 800-369-4911
Stone Brewing
Escondido, CA 760-294-7899
StoneHammer Brewing
Guelph, ON 519-824-1194
Stoudt Brewing Co
Adamstown, PA 717-484-4386
Straub Brewery Inc
St Marys, PA 814-834-2875
Stroh Brewery
Detroit, MI 313-446-2000
Stroh's Beer
Detroit, MI
Sudwerk Privatbrauerei Hubsch
Davis, CA 530-758-8700
Summit Brewing Company
Saint Paul, MN 651-265-7800
Sweet Water Brewing Co
Atlanta, GA 404-691-2537

Taos Brewing Supply
El Prado, NM 575-779-0449
Taos Mesa Brewing Co
El Prado, NM 575-758-1900
The Roscoe NY Beer Company, Inc.
Roscoe, NY 607-290-5002
Tin Whistle Brewing Co
Penticton, BC 250-770-1122
Trafalgar Brewing Company
Oakville, ON 905-337-0133
Triple Rock Brewing Co Brkly
Berkeley, CA 510-843-2739
Triumph Brewing Co
Princeton, NJ 609-924-7855
Uinta Brewing Co
Salt Lake City, UT 801-467-0909
Unibroue/Unibrew
Chambly, QC 450-658-7658
Vancouver Island Brewing Company
Victoria, BC 800-663-6383
Vino's Brew Pub
Little Rock, AR 501-375-8466
Wachusett Brewing Co
Westminster, MA 978-874-9965
Wagner Vineyards
Lodi, NY 866-924-6378
Wellington Brewery
Guelph, ON 800-576-3853
Westtown Brew Works
Westtown, NY
What's Brewing
San Antonio, TX 877-262-7311
Whistler Brewing Company
Whistler, BC 604-731-2900
Whistler Brewing Company
Whistler, BC 604-962-8889
Yakima Craft Brewing Company
Yakima, WA 509-654-7357
Yonkers Brewing Company LLC
Yonkers, NY 914-226-8327

American & British Ale

Amber Ale

Alaskan Brewing Company
Juneau, AK 907-780-5866
Bull and Barrel Brewpub
Brewster, NY 845-278-2855
Genesee Brewing Company
Rochester, NY 585-263-9200
Grand Teton Brewing Co
Victor, ID 888-899-1656
Keegan Ales
Kingston, NY 845-331-2739
Pete's Brewing Company
San Antonio, TX 800-877-7383
St Arnold Brewing Co
Houston, TX 800-801-6402
Unibroue/Unibrew
Chambly, QC 450-658-7658

American Ale

Bull and Barrel Brewpub
Brewster, NY 845-278-2855
Fox N Hare Brewing Co.
Port Jervis, NY 845-672-0100
Newburgh Brewing Company
Newburgh, NY 845-569-2337
Westtown Brew Works
Westtown, NY
Yonkers Brewing Company LLC
Yonkers, NY 914-226-8327

Black & Tan

DG Yuengling & Son, Inc.
Pottsville, PA 570-628-4890
Stevens Point Brewery
Stevens Point, WI 800-369-4911

Cream Ale

Genesee Brewing Company
Rochester, NY 585-263-9200
Northern Lights Brewing Company
Airway Heights, WA 509-242-2739

India Pale Ale

Broken Bow Brewery
Tuckahoe, NY 914-268-0900
Bull and Barrel Brewpub
Brewster, NY 845-278-2855
Catskill Brewery
Livingston Manor, NY 845-439-1232
Clemson Bros. Brewery
Middletown, NY 845-775-4638
Fox N Hare Brewing Co.
Port Jervis, NY 845-672-0100
Golden City Brewery
Golden, CO 303-279-8092
Hudson Valley Brewery
Beacon, NY 845-218-9156
Keegan Ales
Kingston, NY 845-331-2739
Newburgh Brewing Company
Newburgh, NY 845-569-2337
Peekskill Brewery
Peekskill, N7 914-734-2337
St Arnold Brewing Co
Houston, TX 800-801-6402
The Roscoe NY Beer Company, Inc.
Roscoe, NY 607-290-5002
Yonkers Brewing Company LLC
Yonkers, NY 914-226-8327

Mild Ale

Hudson Valley Brewery
Beacon, NY 845-218-9156

Pale Ale

Clemson Bros. Brewery
Middletown, NY 845-775-4638
Deschutes Brewery
Bend, OR 541-385-8606
DG Yuengling & Son, Inc.
Pottsville, PA 570-628-4890
Northern Lights Brewing Company
Airway Heights, WA 509-242-2739
Pete's Brewing Company
San Antonio, TX 800-877-7383
Stevens Point Brewery
Stevens Point, WI 800-369-4911

Scottish Style

Genesee Brewing Company
Rochester, NY 585-263-9200

Belgian & French Ale

Belgian Style Blo

Newburgh Brewing Company
Newburgh, NY 845-569-2337

Kolsch

St Arnold Brewing Co
Houston, TX 800-801-6402

Bottled

Alaskan Brewing Company
Juneau, AK 907-780-5866
Arizona Beverage Company
Cincinnati, OH 800-832-3775
August Schell Brewing Co
New Ulm, MN 800-770-5020
Big Rock Brewery
Calgary, AB 800-242-3107
Brooklyn Brewery
Brooklyn, NY 718-486-7422
Buffalo Bill Brewing Company
Hayward, CA 510-886-9823
DG Yuengling & Son, Inc.
Pottsville, PA 570-628-4890
Jones Brewing Company
Smithton, PA 724-483-2400
Spaten North America Inc
Little Neck, NY 718-281-1912
Stevens Point Brewery
Stevens Point, WI 800-369-4911
Straub Brewery Inc
St Marys, PA 814-834-2875

Canned

Arizona Beverage Company
Cincinnati, OH 800-832-3775
Jones Brewing Company
Smithton, PA 724-483-2400
Patagonia Provisions
Sausalito, CA 888-221-8208
Stevens Point Brewery
Stevens Point, WI 800-369-4911

Kegged

Bohemian Brewery
Midvale, UT 801-566-5474
DG Yuengling & Son, Inc.
Pottsville, PA 570-628-4890
Golden City Brewery
Golden, CO 303-279-8092
Jones Brewing Company
Smithton, PA 724-483-2400

Lager

Amber Lager

Broken Bow Brewery
Tuckahoe, NY 914-268-0900
Catskill Brewery
Livingston Manor, NY 845-439-1232
DG Yuengling & Son, Inc.
Pottsville, PA 570-628-4890
Grain Belt
New Ulm, MN 800-770-5020
Hyde Park Brewing Company
Hyde Park, NY 845-229-8277
Karl Strauss Brewing Co
San Diego, CA 858-273-2739
Stevens Point Brewery
Stevens Point, WI 800-369-4911
Unibroue/Unibrew
Chambly, QC 450-658-7658
Yonkers Brewing Company LLC
Yonkers, NY 914-226-8327

Black Beer

Brooklyn Brewery
Brooklyn, NY 718-486-7422
Hyde Park Brewing Company
Hyde Park, NY 845-229-8277

Bock

St Arnold Brewing Co
Houston, TX 800-801-6402

DarkLager/Dunkel

Brick Brewery
Kitchener, ON 800-505-8971

Malt Liquor

Bad Frog Brewery Co
St Augustine, FL 888-223-3764
Jones Brewing Company
Smithton, PA 724-483-2400
Mike's Beverage Company
Toronto, ON 647-428-3123

PaleLager

Deschutes Brewery
Bend, OR 541-385-8606
Hyde Park Brewing Company
Hyde Park, NY 845-229-8277

Pilsner

Anderson Valley Brewing Co
Boonville, CA 800-207-2237
Big Rock Brewery
Calgary, AB 800-242-3107
Catskill Brewery
Livingston Manor, NY 845-439-1232
Hyde Park Brewing Company
Hyde Park, NY 845-229-8277
St Arnold Brewing Co
Houston, TX 800-801-6402

Non-Alcoholic

Athletic Brewing Co.
Stratford, CT 203-273-0422
B.M. Lawrence & Company
San Francisco, CA 415-981-2926
Jones Brewing Company
Smithton, PA 724-483-2400
Lion Brewery Inc
Wilkes Barre, PA 888-295-2337
Richland Beverage Association
Carrollton, TX 214-357-0248

Specialty &Cider

Draft Cider

Angry Orchard Cider Company, LLC
Walden, NY....................888-845-3311
Applewood Winery
Warwick, NY....................845-988-9292
Bad Seed Cider Company, LLC
Highland, NY....................845-236-0956
Brooklyn Cider House
Brooklyn, NY....................347-295-0308
Graft Cider
Newburgh, NY....................410-967-1926
Gravity Ciders, Inc.
Sydney, NY
Hudson Valley Farmhouse Cider
Staatsburg, NY....................845-266-3979
Northville Winery & Brewing Co
Northville, MI....................248-320-6507
Warwick Valley Winery & Distillery
Warwick, NY....................845-258-4858

Fruit Beer

Brooklyn Brewery
Brooklyn, NY....................718-486-7422
Buffalo Bill Brewing Company
Hayward, CA....................510-886-9823
Clemson Bros. Brewery
Middletown, NY....................845-775-4638
Downeast Cider House
East Boston, MA....................857-301-8881
Hudson Valley Brewery
Beacon, NY....................845-218-9156
Unibroue/Unibrew
Chambly, QC....................450-658-7658

Herb & Spice Beer

Remarkable Liquids
Altamont, NY....................518-861-5351

Reduced Calorie Beer

DG Yuengling & Son, Inc.
Pottsville, PA....................570-628-4890

Stout & Porter

Dry Stout

Alaskan Brewing Company
Juneau, AK....................907-780-5866
Catskill Brewery
Livingston Manor, NY....................845-439-1232
Keegan Ales
Kingston, NY....................845-331-2739
Newburgh Brewing Company
Newburgh, NY....................845-569-2337
The Roscoe NY Beer Company, Inc.
Roscoe, NY....................607-290-5002

Flavored Porter

Deschutes Brewery
Bend, OR....................541-385-8606
Westtown Brew Works
Westtown, NY

Flavored Stout

Broken Bow Brewery
Tuckahoe, NY....................914-268-0900
Brooklyn Brewery
Brooklyn, NY....................718-486-7422
Buffalo Bill Brewing Company
Hayward, CA....................510-886-9823
Deschutes Brewery
Bend, OR....................541-385-8606
Hyde Park Brewing Company
Hyde Park, NY....................845-229-8277
St Arnold Brewing Co
Houston, TX....................800-801-6402

Imperial Stout

Clemson Bros. Brewery
Middletown, NY....................845-775-4638

Porter

Brooklyn Brewery
Brooklyn, NY....................718-486-7422
Clemson Bros. Brewery
Middletown, NY....................845-775-4638
DG Yuengling & Son, Inc.
Pottsville, PA....................570-628-4890
Hyde Park Brewing Company
Hyde Park, NY....................845-229-8277

Sweet Stout

Pete's Brewing Company
San Antonio, TX....................800-877-7383

Wheat

Flavored Wheat

Broken Bow Brewery
Tuckahoe, NY....................914-268-0900
Clemson Bros. Brewery
Middletown, NY....................845-775-4638

Wheat Ale

Alley Kat Brewing Co, Ltd
Edmonton, AB....................780-436-8922
Grand Teton Brewing Co
Victor, ID....................888-899-1656
Hudson Valley Brewery
Beacon, NY....................845-218-9156
Yonkers Brewing Company LLC
Yonkers, NY....................914-226-8327

Bitters

Fee Brothers
Rochester, NY....................800-961-3337
Flora Inc
Lynden, WA....................800-446-2110
Hella Cocktail
Long Island City, NY....................646-854-8004
Improper Goods
Portland, OR....................503-662-7147
King Floyd's
Novato, CA....................415-475-7811
Kittling Ridge Estate Wines & Spirits
Vaughan, ON....................800-461-9463
Stirrings
New Bedford, MA....................866-646-4266

Cocoa & Chocolate Drinks

Chocolate Drinks

B&D Food Corporation
New York, NY....................212-937-8456
Cacoco
Coca-Cola Beverages Northeast
Bedford, NH....................844-619-3388
Fermalife
North American Beverage Co
Ocean City, NJ....................609-399-1486
Richard's Gourmet Coffee
West Bridgewater, MA....................800-370-2633
Sucre
New Orleans, LA....................504-708-4366
Yoo-Hoo Chocolate Beverage Company
Carlstadt, NJ....................201-933-0070

Hot Chocolate

City Bakery
New York, NY....................212-366-1414
Gourmet du Village
Morin-Heights, QC....................800-668-2314
Know Brainer
Lafayette, CO....................303-475-0456
Lacas Coffee Co Inc
Pennsauken, NJ....................800-220-1133
Madrona Specialty Foods LLC
Seattle, WA....................425-656-2997
Mars Inc.
McLean, VA....................703-821-4900
Tea Room
San Leandro, CA....................510-567-8868

Hot Cocoa

Blue Marble Brands
Providence, RI....................888-534-0246
Caffe D'Amore Gourmet Beverages
Pittsburgh, PA....................800-999-0171
Chatz Roasting Co
Ceres, CA....................209-541-1100
Chicago Coffee Roastery
Huntley, IL....................800-762-5402
Cisse Trading Co
Mamaroneck, NY....................914-381-5555
Coffee Masters
Spring Grove, IL....................800-334-6485
Conifer Foods
Medina, WA....................800-588-9160
Country Choice Organic
Eden Prairie, MN....................952-829-8824
Gloria Jean's Gourmet Coffees
Irvine, CA....................877-320-5282
Indulgent Foods
Farmington, UT....................801-939-9100
Jenny's Country Kitchen
Dover, MN....................800-357-3497
Keurig, Inc
Reading, MA....................866-901-2739
Kittridge & Fredrickson LTD
Portland, OR....................800-558-7788
Nantucket Tea Traders
Nantucket, MA....................508-325-0203
Neighbors Coffee
Oklahoma City, OK....................800-299-9016
Northwestern Foods
Arden Hills, MN....................800-236-4937
Omanhene Cocoa Bean Co
Milwaukee, WI....................800-588-2462
Swagger Foods Corp
Vernon Hills, IL....................847-913-1200
Utah Coffee Roasters
South Salt Lake, UT....................888-486-3334
White Coffee Corporation
Long Island City, NY....................800-221-0140

with Marshmallows

Todd's
Des Moines, IA....................800-247-5363

Coffee & Tea

Ajiri Tea Company
Upper Black Eddy, PA....................610-982-5075
Alvita
Amherst, NY....................833-258-4821
Amelia Bay
Suwanee, GA....................770-772-6360
Aroma Coffee Company
Forest Park, IL....................708-488-8340
Atlanta Bread Co.
Smyrna, GA....................800-398-3728
Bellocq
Brooklyn, NY....................347-463-9231
Bhakti
Boulder, CO....................303-484-8770
Burke Brands
Miami, FL....................877-436-7225
Captain Cook Coffee Company
Kealakekua, HI....................650-766-9149
Fairwinds Gourmet Coffee
Lincoln, CA....................800-829-1300
Farmer Brothers Company
Northlake, TX....................682-549-6600
GH Ford Tea Company
Shokan, NY....................845-464-6755
Groundwork Coffee Co.
North Hollywood, CA....................818-506-6020
Ingenuity Beverages
Brooklyn, NY....................800-611-7434
Javo Beverage Co., Inc.
Vista, CA....................760-330-1141
JFG Coffee
New Orleans, LA....................800-535-1961
Kohana Coffee
Austin, TX....................512-904-1174
La Crema Coffee Company
West Chester, OH....................513-779-6278
Lowcountry Produce
Raleigh, NC....................800-935-2792
North River Roasters
Poughkeepsie, NY....................845-418-2739
Onnit Labs
Austin, TX....................855-666-4899
Orinoco Coffee & Tea
Jessup, MD....................410-312-5292
Point Group
Satellite Beach, FL....................888-272-1249
Queen City Coffee Company
West Chester, OH....................800-487-7460
Sara Lee Coffee & Tea
Suffolk, VA....................757-538-8083
Southern Season
Chapel Hill, NC....................877-929-7133
Stevens Creative Enterprises, Inc.
New York, NY....................646-558-6336

Stonewall Kitchen
York, ME........800-826-1752
Sun Opta Inc.
Mississauga, ON........952-820-2518
Teeccino
Carpinteria, CA........800-498-3434
Tetley Tea
New Providence, NJ........800-728-0084
Texas Spice Co
Round Rock, TX........800-880-8007
TMI Trading Co
Brooklyn, NY........718-821-5052
Torke Coffee Co
Sheboygan, WI........800-242-7671
TreeHouse Foods, Inc.
Oak Brook, IL........708-483-1300
UBF Food Solutions
Lisle, IL........630-955-5394
Zephyr Hills
Tampa, FL........800-950-9398

Cappuccino

Agropur
Granby, QC........800-363-5686
Aloe'Ha Drink Products
Houston, TX........713-978-6359
American Instants Inc
Flanders, NJ........973-584-8811
Arcadia Dairy Farms Inc
Arden, NC........828-684-3556
Arctic Beverages
Winnipeg, MB........866-503-1270
Baltimore Brewing Company
Baltimore, MD........410-837-5000
Beacon Drive Inn
Spartanburg, SC........864-585-9387
Beaver Street Brewery
Flagstaff, AZ........928-779-0079
Belmar Spring Water
Glen Rock, NJ........201-444-1010
Better Beverages Inc
Cerritos, CA........800-344-5219
Bigelow Tea
Fairfield, CT........888-244-3569
Blenheim Bottling Company
Hamer, SC........800-270-9344
Bluechip Group
Salt Lake City, UT........800-878-0099
Boissons Miami Pomor
Longueuil, QC........877-977-3744
Bottle Green Drinks Company
Mississauga, ON........905-273-6137
Bow Valley Brewing Company
Canmore, AB........403-678-2739
Brasserie Brasel Brewery
Lasalle, QC........800-463-2728
Caffe D'Oro
Chino, CA........800-200-5005
Caffe D'Vita
Chino, CA........800-200-5005
Campbell Soup Co.
Camden, NJ........800-257-8443
Chicago Coffee Roastery
Huntley, IL........800-762-5402
Clipper City Brewing
Halethorpe, MD........410-247-7822
Creemore Springs Brewery
Creemore, ON........800-267-2240
Creme D'Lite
Irving, TX........972-255-7255
De Coty Coffee Co
San Angelo, TX........800-588-8001
Dogfish Head Craft Brewery
Lewes, DE........888-834-3474
Ensemble Beverages
Montgomery, AL........334-324-7719
Faygo Beverages Inc
Detroit, MI........313-925-1600
Finlays
Lincoln, RI........800-288-6272
Flora Inc
Lynden, WA........800-446-2110
Florida Natural Flavors
Casselberry, FL........800-872-5979
Florida's Natural Growers
Lake Wales, FL........888-657-6600
Fresh Juice Delivery
Beverly Hills, CA........310-271-7373
Fresh Samantha
Saco, ME........800-658-4635
Gedney Foods Co
Sun Valley, CA........888-244-0653
Great Lakes Brewing Co.
Cleveland, OH........216-771-4404
Great Northern Brewing Co
Whitefish, MT........406-863-1000
Great Western Brewing Company
Saskatoon, SK........800-764-4492
Halifax Group
Washington, DC........202-530-8300
Healthmate Products
Highland Park, IL........847-579-1051
Hobarama Corporation
Miami, FL........880-439-2295
Hogtown Brewing Company
Mississauga, ON........905-855-9065
Honickman Affiliates
Pennsauken, NJ........800-573-7745
Ideal Dairy Farms
Hudson Falls, NY........518-747-5059
Indian River Select® LLC
Stuart, FL........888-373-7426
Indulgent Foods
Farmington, UT........801-939-9100
Jianlibao America
New York, NY........800-526-1688
Key Colony Red Parrot Juice
Lemont, IL........844-783-8572
King Cupboard
Red Lodge, MT........800-962-6555
Kola
New York, NY........212-688-1895
Lake Country Foods Inc
Oconomowoc, WI........262-567-5521
Lakefront Brewery Inc
Milwaukee, WI........414-372-8800
Left Hand Brewing Co
Longmont, CO........303-772-0258
Magic Valley Quality Milk
Jerome, ID........208-324-7519
Martin Coffee Co
Jacksonville, FL........904-355-9661
Mendocino Brewing Co Inc
Ukiah, CA........707-463-2627
Millstream Brewing Co
Amana, IA........319-622-3672
Monticello Vineyards-Corley
Napa, CA........707-253-2802
Moosehead Breweries Ltd.
St. John, NB
Mrs Clark's Foods
Ankeny, IA........800-736-5674
Nature's First Inc
Orange, CT........800-523-3752
Neighbors Coffee
Oklahoma City, OK........800-299-9016
Noel Corp
Yakima, WA........509-248-1313
North American Breweries Inc.
Rochester, NY........585-546-1030
Northumberland Dairy
Miramichi, NB........800-501-1150
Northwestern Foods
Arden Hills, MN........800-236-4937
Oak Farms
El Paso, TX........800-395-7004
Ojai Cook
Los Angeles, CA........886-571-1551
Olympic Foods
Spokane, WA........509-455-8059
Pennsylvania Brewing Company
Pittsburgh, PA........412-237-9400
Quality Naturally Foods
City Of Industry, CA........888-498-6986
Reiter Dairy
Newport, KY........800-544-6455
Richard's Gourmet Coffee
West Bridgewater, MA........800-370-2633
Royale Brands
Davenport, IA........563-386-5222
San Marco Coffee, Inc.
Charlotte, NC........800-715-9298
Santa Cruz Mountain Brewing
Santa Cruz, CA........831-425-4900
Sebastiani Vineyards
Sonoma, CA........855-232-2338
Shipyard Brewing Co
Portland, ME........800-789-0684
Southern Gardens Citrus
Clewiston, FL........863-983-3030
Southern Heritage Coffee Company
Indianapolis, IN........800-486-1198
Stewart's Beverages
rye Brook, NY........800-762-7753
Swiss Dairy
Riverside, CA........951-898-9427
Taos Brewing Supply
El Prado, NM........575-779-0449
Thyme Garden Herb Co
Alsea, OR........800-482-4372
Tonex
Wallington, NJ........973-773-5135
Tova Industries LLC
Louisville, KY........888-532-8682
Triple H Food Processors Inc
Riverside, CA........951-352-5700
True Beverages
O Fallon, MO........800-325-6152
Ultra Seal
New Paltz, NY........845-255-2490
Unilever Canada
Toronto, ON........416-415-3000
Virgil's Root Beer
Norwalk, CT........800-997-3337
Warren Laboratories LLC
Abbott, TX........800-421-2563
Whistler Brewing Company
Whistler, BC........604-962-8889

Coffee

A Hill of Beans Coffee Roasters
Omaha, NE........402-333-6048
Afineur
Brooklyn, NY........617-480-1340
Ajiri Tea Company
Upper Black Eddy, PA........610-982-5075
Alakef Coffee Roasters Inc
Duluth, MN........800-438-9228
All Goode Organics
Santa Barbara, CA........805-683-3370
Allann Brothers Coffee Roasters
Albany, OR........800-926-6886
Allegro Coffee Co
Thornton, CO........800-666-4869
Alpen Sierra Coffee Company
Minden, NV........800-531-1405
Alpine Coffee Roasters
Leavenworth, WA........800-246-2761
Amcan Beverages Inc
American Canyon, CA........800-972-5962
Ancora Coffee Roasters
Madison, WI........800-260-0217
Arbuckle Coffee Roasters
Tucson, AZ........800-533-8278
ARCO Coffee
Superior, WI........800-283-2726
Armenia Coffee Corporation
Purchase, NY........914-694-6100
Armeno Coffee Roasters LTD
Northborough, MA........508-393-2821
Aroma Coffee Roasters Inc
Hoboken, NJ........201-792-1730
Aroma Ridge
Marietta, GA........800-528-2123
Artist Coffee
Londonderry, NH........866-440-4511
Atlanta Coffee & Tea Co
........800-426-4781
Atlanta Coffee Roasters
Atlanta, GA........800-252-8211
Atlantic Natural Foods
Nashville, NC........888-491-0524
Austin Chase Coffee
Seattle, WA........888-502-2333
Avalon Organic Coffees
Albuquerque, NM........800-662-2575
B&D Food Corporation
New York, NY........212-937-8456
B&K Coffee
Oneonta, NY........800-432-1499
B.B. Bean, Coffee
Monument, CO........719-481-1170
Baby's Coffee
Key West, FL........800-523-2326
Back Bay Trading
Alpharetta, GA........800-650-8327
Baltimore Coffee & Tea Co Inc
Lutherville, MD........800-823-1408
Barefoot Contessa Pantry
York, ME........800-826-1752
Barnie's Coffee and Tea
Orlando, FL........800-284-1416
Barrie House Gourmet Coffee
Elmsford, NY........800-876-2233
Barrington Coffee Roasting
Lee, MA........800-528-0998

Batdorf & Bronson
Olympia, WA . . . 800-955-5282
Bay View Farm
Honaunau, HI . . . 800-662-5880
Bean Forge
Coos Bay, OR . . . 888-292-1632
Benbow's Coffee Roasters
Bar Harbor, ME. . . 207-288-2552
Berardi's Fresh Roast
Cleveland, OH . . . 800-876-9109
Big Shoulders Coffee
Chicago, IL . . . 312-846-1883
Big Train Inc
Lake Forest, CA . . . 800-244-8724
Big Watt Coffee
Minneapolis, MN
Blackbear Coffee Company
Hendersonville, NC . . . 828-692-6333
Boston's Best Coffee Roasters
South Easton, MA. . . 800-898-8393
Bountiful Pantry
Nantucket, MA . . . 617-487-8019
Boyd's Coffee Co
Portland, OR . . . 800-735-2878
Boyer's Coffee
Denver, CO. . . 800-452-5282
Bridgetown Coffee
Portland, OR . . . 800-726-0320
Brisk Coffee Co
Tampa, FL. . . 800-899-5282
Brooklyn Bean Roastery
Brooklyn, NY . . . 908-205-0018
Brown & Jenkins Trading Company
Cambridge, VT . . . 800-456-5282
Bruce Coffee Svc Plan USA
Hartford, CT . . . 800-227-6638
Buckmaster Coffee Co
Hillsboro, OR . . . 800-962-9148
Buywell Coffee
Colorado Springs, CO. . . 877-294-6246
Cadillac Coffee Co
Ft. Wayne, IN . . . 800-438-6900
Cafe Altura
Santa Paula, CA . . . 800-526-8328
Cafe Bustelo
Miami, FL. . . 800-990-9039
Cafe Cartago
Denver, CO . . . 800-443-8666
Cafe Del Mundo
Anchorage, AK. . . 800-770-2326
Cafe Descafeinado de Chiapas
Doral, FL. . . 305-499-9775
Cafe Du Monde Coffee Stand
New Orleans, LA . . . 800-772-2927
Cafe Kreyol
Manassas, VA
Cafe La Semeuse
Brooklyn, NY . . . 800-242-6333
Cafe Moak
Rockford, MI . . . 616-866-7625
Cafe Moto
San Diego, CA . . . 800-818-3363
Cafe Society Coffee Company
Dallas, TX. . . 800-717-6000
Cafe Yaucono/Jimenez & Fernandez
San Juan, PR. . . 787-721-3337
Caffe Appassionato Coffee
Seattle, WA . . . 888-502-2333
Caffe D'Oro
Chino, CA. . . 800-200-5005
Caffe Darte
Federal Way, WA . . . 800-999-5334
Caffe Ibis Gallery Deli
Logan, UT. . . 888-740-4777
Caffe Luca Coffee Roaste
Seattle, WA . . . 800-728-9116
Caffe Trieste
San Francisco, CA . . . 415-550-1107
Cajun Creole Products Inc
New Iberia, LA. . . 800-946-8688
Cape Cod Coffee Roasters
Mashpee, MA. . . 508-477-2400
Cappuccine
Corona, CA. . . 800-511-3127
Capricorn Coffees Inc
San Francisco, CA . . . 800-541-0758
Captain Cook Coffee Company
Kealakekua, HI. . . 650-766-9149
Caracolillo Coffee Mills
Tampa, FL. . . 800-682-0023
Caravan Company
Worcester, MA . . . 508-752-3777
Caribbean Coffee Co
Goleta, CA . . . 800-932-5282
Caribou Coffee Co Inc
Minneapolis, MN . . . 888-227-4268
Carrabassett Coffee Roasters
Kingfield, ME . . . 888-292-2326
Cascade Coffee
Everett, WA. . . 800-995-9655
Chatz Roasting Co
Ceres, CA . . . 209-541-1100
Chauvin Coffee Corporation
Saint Louis, MO . . . 800-455-5282
Chicago Coffee Roastery
Huntley, IL . . . 800-762-5402
Chock Full O'Nuts
. . . 888-246-2598
City Bean
Los Angeles, CA. . . 888-248-9232
Clayton Coffee & Tea
Modesto, CA. . . 209-576-1120
Clear Mountain Coffee Company
Silver Spring, MD. . . 301-587-2233
Clearwater Coffee Company
Lake Zurich, IL. . . 847-540-7711
Cobraz Brazilian Coffee
New York, NY . . . 212-759-7700
Coffee Associates
Edgewater, NJ. . . 201-945-1060
Coffee Barrel
Holt, MI. . . 517-694-9000
Coffee Bean
Englewood, CO. . . 303-922-1238
Coffee Bean & Tea Leaf
Bloomington, MN. . . 952-853-1148
Coffee Bean Intl
Portland, OR . . . 800-877-0474
Coffee Bean of Leesburg
Leesburg, VA. . . 800-232-6872
Coffee Beanery LTD
Flushing, MI . . . 800-441-2255
Coffee Brothers Inc
Colton, CA . . . 888-443-5282
Coffee Butler Service
Alexandria, VA . . . 703-823-0028
Coffee Culture-A House
Lincoln, NE. . . 402-438-8456
Coffee Exchange
Providence, RI . . . 877-263-3334
Coffee Express Roasting Co
Plymouth, MI . . . 800-466-9000
Coffee Holding Co Inc
Staten Island, NY . . . 800-458-2233
Coffee Masters
Spring Grove, IL. . . 800-334-6485
Coffee Mill Roastery
Elon, NC . . . 800-729-1727
Coffee Mill Roasting Company
Sudbury, ON . . . 705-525-2700
Coffee Millers & Roasting
Cape Coral, FL . . . 239-573-6800
Coffee People
Beaverton, OR . . . 800-354-5282
Coffee Process
Houston, TX . . . 713-695-8483
Coffee Reserve
Phoenix, AZ . . . 888-755-6789
Coffee Roasters Inc
Oakland, NJ . . . 800-285-2445
Coffee Roasters Of New Orleans
Kenner, LA . . . 800-737-5464
Coffee Roasters of New Orleans
New Orleans, LA . . . 800-737-5464
Coffee Up
Chicago, IL . . . 847-288-9330
Coffee Works
Sacramento, CA . . . 800-275-3335
College Coffee Roaster
Mountville, PA . . . 717-285-9561
Colonial Coffee Roasters Inc
Miami, FL. . . 305-638-0885
Community Coffee Co.
Baton Rouge, LA . . . 800-884-5282
Continental Coffee Products Company
Houston, TX . . . 800-323-6178
Copper Moon Coffee LLC
Lafayette, IN. . . 317-541-9000
Corim Industries Inc
Brick, NJ. . . 800-942-4201
Counter Culture Coffee
Durham, NC . . . 888-238-5282
Cupper's Coffee Company
Lethbridge, AB . . . 403-380-4555
Custom Coffee Plan
Torrance, CA. . . 800-841-5949
Dallis Brothers
Long Island City, NY . . . 718-845-3010
David Rio
San Francisco, CA . . . 800-454-9605
Daybreak Coffee Roasters
Glastonbury, CT . . . 800-882-5282
Daymar Select Fine Coffees
El Cajon, CA. . . 800-466-7590
Dazbog Coffee Co
Denver, CO . . . 303-892-9999
De Coty Coffee Co
San Angelo, TX . . . 800-588-8001
Dean & De Luca Inc
Honolulu, HI. . . 808-729-9720
Deep Valley
New York, NY . . . 917-673-5121
DeLima Coffee
Liverpool, NY. . . 800-962-8864
Diedrich Coffee
Irvine, CA. . . 800-354-5282
Dillanos Coffee Roasters
Sumner, WA . . . 800-234-5282
Distant Lands Coffee Roaster
Renton, WA. . . 800-758-4437
DMH Ingredients Inc
Libertyville, IL . . . 847-362-9977
Don Hilario Estate Coffee
Oldsmar, FL . . . 800-799-1903
Downeast Coffee Roasters
Pawtucket, RI . . . 800-345-2007
Droubi's Imports
Houston, TX . . . 713-334-1829
Dunkin' Brands Inc.
Canton, MA . . . 800-859-5339
Eagle Coffee Co Inc
Baltimore, MD . . . 410-685-5893
East Indies Coffee & Tea Co
Lebanon, PA . . . 800-220-2326
ECOM Agroindustrial Corporation Ltd
Pully,
Eight O'Clock Coffee Company
North Bergen, NJ . . . 800-299-2739
Eldorado Coffee Distributors
Flushing, NY. . . 800-635-2566
Ellis Coffee Co
Philadelphia, PA . . . 800-822-3984
Equal Exchange Inc
West Bridgewater, MA . . . 774-776-7400
Erba Food Products
Brooklyn, NY . . . 718-272-7700
Espresso Vivace
Seattle, WA . . . 206-860-5869
European Coffee
Clearwater, FL . . . 888-635-4882
European Roasterie
Le Center, MN . . . 888-588-5282
F. Gavina & Sons
Vernon, CA. . . 800-428-4627
Fama Sales Co
New York, NY . . . 800-682-0425
Fenn Valley Vineyards
Fennville, MI . . . 269-561-2396
Ferrara Bakery & Cafe
New York, NY . . . 212-226-6150
Fidalgo Bay Roasting Co
Burlington, WA. . . 800-310-5540
Field Coffee
Norcross, GA . . . 844-343-5326
Finlays
Lincoln, RI . . . 800-288-6272
First Colony Coffee & Tea Company
Norfolk, VA. . . 800-446-8555
First Roasters of Central Florida
Longwood, FL . . . 407-699-6364
Flat Tire Bike Shop
Cave Creek, AZ . . . 480-488-5261
Folgers Coffee Co
Orrville, OH . . . 800-937-9745
Four Sigmatic
Venice, CA
Fratello Coffee Roasters
Calgary, AB. . . 800-465-7227
Freed, Teller & Freed
South San Francisco, CA . . . 800-370-7371
French Market Coffee
New Orleans, LA . . . 800-535-1961
Gadsden Coffee/Caffe
Arivaca, AZ. . . 888-514-5282
Gardner's Gourmet
Fremont, CA . . . 800-676-8558

Gerhart Coffee Co
Lancaster, PA 800-536-4310
Global Food Industries
Townville, SC 800-225-4152
Globus Coffee LLC
Manhasset, NY 516-304-5780
Gloria Jean's Gourmet Coffees
Irvine, CA 877-320-5282
GoBio!
Action, ON 519-853-2958
Godiva Chocolatier
New York, NY 800-946-3482
Green Mountain Chocolate Inc
Franklin, MA 508-520-7160
Greene Brothers Specialty Coffee Roaster
Hackettstown, NJ 908-979-0022
Greenwell Farms Inc
Kealakekua, HI 888-592-5662
Grounds for Change
Poulsbo, WA 800-796-6820
Harmony Bay Coffee
North Andover, MA 800-514-3663
Harold L King & Co Inc
Redwood City, CA 888-368-2233
Has Beans Coffee & Tea Co
Chico, CA 800-427-2326
Hathaway Coffee Co Inc
Summit Argo, IL 708-458-7666
Hawaii Coffee Company
Honolulu, HI 800-338-8353
Hawaiian Isles Kona Coffee Co
Honolulu, HI 800-657-7716
Heartland Sweeteners
Carmel, IN 317-566-9750
Hena Inc
Brooklyn, NY 718-272-8237
Heritage Coffee Co & Cafe
Juneau, AK 800-478-5282
Heyday Beverage Co.
Austin, TX 512-443-9876
High Brew Coffee
Austin, TX
High Rise Coffee Roasters
Colorado Springs, CO 719-633-1833
Hillsboro Coffee Company
Tampa, FL 813-877-2126
Home Roast Coffee
Lutz, FL 813-949-0807
Hood River Coffee Co
Hood River, OR 800-336-2954
House of Coffee Beans
Houston, TX 800-422-1799
House of Tsang
San Francisco, CA 415-282-9952
Humboldt Bay Coffee Co.
Eureka, CA 707-444-3969
Ideal Distributing Company
Bothell, WA 425-488-6121
Immordl
San Clemente, CA 844-466-6735
Indigo Coffee Roasters
Florence, MA 800-447-5450
Innovative Beverage Concepts
Irvine, CA 949-831-8656
Instant Products of America
Columbus, IN 812-372-9100
Inter-American Products
Cincinnati, OH 800-645-2233
Inter-Continental Imports Company
Newington, CT 800-424-4422
Ito En USA Inc
Brooklyn, NY 808-847-4477
J.B. Peel Coffee Roasters
Red Hook, NY 800-231-7372
J.M. Smucker Co.
Orrville, OH 888-550-9555
Jaguar Yerba Company
Ashland, OR 800-839-0775
Jamaica John Inc
Franklin Park, IL 847-451-1730
Jamaican Gourmet Coffee Company
Philadelphia, PA 800-261-2859
Jasper Products Corp
Joplin, MO 417-206-3877
Java Beans and Joe Coffee
Petaluma, CA 800-624-7031
Java Cabana
Miami, FL 305-592-7302
Java Sun Coffee Roasters
Marblehead, MA 781-631-7788
Java-Gourmet/Keuka Lake Coffee Roaster
Penn Yan, NY 888-478-2739

Javalution Coffee Company
Chula Vista, CA 800-982-3197
Javo Beverage Co., Inc.
Vista, CA 760-330-1141
Jelks Coffee Roasters
Shreveport, LA 800-235-7361
Jenny's Country Kitchen
Dover, MN 800-357-3497
Jeremiah's Pick Coffee Co
San Francisco, CA 877-537-3642
Jodyana Corporation
Miami, FL 888-563-5282
John A Vassilaros & Son Inc
Flushing, NY 718-886-4140
John Conti Coffee Co
Louisville, KY 800-928-5282
Josuma Coffee Co
Menlo Park, CA 650-366-5453
Juice Tyme, Inc.
Chicago, IL 800-236-5823
Kaffe Magnum Opus
Millville, NJ 800-652-5282
Kauai Coffee Co Inc
Kalaheo, HI 800-545-8605
Keurig Dr Pepper
Plano, TX 800-696-5891
Keurig, Inc
Reading, MA 866-901-2739
Keystone Coffee Co
San Jose, CA 408-998-2221
Kicking Horse Coffee
Invermere, BC 888-287-5282
Kittridge & Fredrickson LTD
Portland, OR 800-558-7788
Kobricks Coffee Company
Jersey City, NJ 800-562-7491
Kohana Coffee
Austin, TX 512-904-1174
Kona Coffee Council
Kealakekua, HI 808-323-2911
Kona Premium Coffee Company
Holualoa, HI 888-322-9550
Kraft Heinz Canada
North York, ON 416-441-5000
LA Costa Coffee Roasting Co
Carlsbad, CA 760-438-8160
La Societe
Montreal, QC 514-507-9223
La Vans Coffee Company
Bordentown, NJ 609-298-0688
Lacas Coffee Co Inc
Pennsauken, NJ 800-220-1133
Laird Superfood
Sisters, OR 888-670-6796
Larry's Beans
Raleigh, NC 919-828-1234
Lavazza Premium Coffees
New York, NY 800-466-3287
Leavenworth Coffee Roast
Leavenworth, WA 800-246-2761
Lenson Coffee & Tea Company
Pleasantville, NJ 609-646-3003
Leona's Restaurante
Chimayo, NM 888-561-5569
Leroy Hill Coffee Co Inc
Mobile, AL 800-866-5282
Lexington Coffee & Tea
Lexington, KY 859-277-1102
Limitless
Chicago, IL
Lindsay's Teas
Petaluma, CA 800-624-7031
Lingle Brothers Coffee
Bell Gardens, CA 562-927-3317
Lockcoffee
Larchmont, NY 914-273-7838
Lola Savannah
Houston, TX 888-663-9166
Longbottom Coffee & Tea Inc
Hillsboro, OR 800-288-1271
Lost Coast Roast
Arcata, CA
Louis Dreyfus Company LLC
Wilton, CT 203-761-2000
Love Creek Orchards
Medina, TX 800-449-0882
Lowcountry Produce
Raleigh, NC 800-935-2792
Lowery's Premium Roast Gourmet Coffee
Snohomish, WA 800-767-1783
M.E. Swing Company
Alexandria, VA 800-485-4019

Madrinas Coffee
St. Louis, MO
Magnum Coffee Roastery
Nunica, MI 888-937-5282
Majestic Coffee & Tea Inc
San Carlos, CA 650-591-5678
Massimo Zanetti Beverage USA
Suffolk, VA 888-246-2598
Master Brew
Northbrook, IL 847-564-3600
Maui Coffee Roasters Wholesale
Kahului, HI 800-645-2877
Maxwell House & Post
Rye Brook, NY 914-335-2500
Mayorga Coffee
Rockville, MD 877-526-3322
Mccullagh Coffee Roasters
Buffalo, NY 800-753-3473
Melitta USA Inc
Clearwater, FL 888-635-4880
Mercon Coffee Group.ÿ
Miami, FL 786-254-2300
Michael's Gourmet Coffee
Ft. Lauderdale, FL 888-346-4646
Mills Coffee Roasting Co
Providence, RI 888-781-5282
Milone Brothers Coffee Co
Modesto, CA 800-974-8500
Mokk-a
Rotterdam,
Monarch Beverage Company
Atlanta, GA 800-241-3732
Montana Coffee Traders
Whitefish, MT 800-345-5282
MorningStar Coffee Company
West Chester, PA 888-854-2233
Mother Parker's Tea & Coffee
Mississauga, ON 800-387-9398
Mountain City Coffee Roasters
Enka, NC 888-730-0869
Mountanos Family Coffee & Tea Co.
Petaluma, CA 800-624-7031
Moutanos Brothers Coffee Company
South San Francisco, CA 800-624-7031
Mr Espresso
Oakland, CA 510-287-5200
Muqui Coffee Company
San Jose, CA 408-272-8471
Mystic Coffee Roasters
Mystic, CT 860-536-2999
Nantucket Tea Traders
Nantucket, MA 508-325-0203
Native American Herbal Tea
Aberdeen, SD 888-291-8517
Nature's First Inc
Orange, CT 800-523-3752
NeuRoast
New York, NY
New Barn Organics
Rohnert Park, CA 888-635-7102
New England Tea & Coffee Co
Malden, MA 800-225-3537
New Harmony Coffee & Tea Co.
New Harmony, IN 812-682-4563
New Jamaican Gold
Hayward, CA 800-672-9956
Nobletree Coffee
Brooklyn, NY 718-643-6080
North American Coffees
Morriston, NJ 973-359-0300
Northwest Naturals LLC
Bothell, WA 425-881-2200
Northwestern Coffee Mills
Washburn, WI 800-243-5283
NuZee, Inc.
Vista, CA 844-696-8933
O'Neill Coffee Co
West Middlesex, PA 724-528-2244
Oasis Coffee Co Inc
Norwalk, CT 203-847-0554
Olam Spices
Fresno, CA 559-447-1390
Olympic Coffee & Roasting
Bellevue, WA 888-244-8313
Omar Coffee Co
Newington, CT 800-394-6627
Oskri Corporation
Lake Mills, WI 920-648-8300
Pan American Coffee Co
Hoboken, NJ 800-229-1883
Paramount Coffee
Lansing, MI 800-968-1222

Partners Coffee LLC
Atlanta, GA . . . 800-341-5282
Pascal Coffee
Yonkers, NY . . . 914-969-7933
Peaberry's Coffee & Tea
Oakland, CA . . . 510-653-0450
Pear's Coffee
Bellevue, NE . . . 800-828-7688
Pearl Coffee Co
Akron, OH . . . 800-822-5282
Peerless Coffee & Tea
Oakland, CA . . . 800-310-5662
Peet's Coffee
Berkeley, CA . . . 800-999-2132
PepsiCo.
Purchase, NY . . . 914-253-2000
Pfefferkorn's Coffee Inc
Baltimore, MD . . . 800-682-4665
Picnik
Austin, TX
PJ's Coffee & Tea
Covington, LA . . . 800-527-1055
Plaza House Coffee
Staten Island, NY . . . 718-979-9555
Polly's Gourmet Coffee
Long Beach, CA . . . 562-433-2996
Pontiac Coffee Break
Waterford, MI . . . 248-332-6333
Pontiac Foods
Columbia, SC . . . 803-699-1600
Porto Rico Importing
New York, NY . . . 212-477-5421
Puroast Coffee Co Inc
Woodland, CA . . . 877-569-2243
Q.E. Tea
Bridgeville, PA . . . 800-622-8327
Queen Anne Coffee Roaster
Seattle, WA . . . 206-284-2530
Reading Coffee Roasters
Birdsboro, PA . . . 800-331-6713
Red Diamond Coffee & Tea
Moody, AL . . . 800-292-4651
Rethemeyer Coffee Company
St Louis, MO . . . 314-231-0990
Richard's Gourmet Coffee
West Bridgewater, MA . . . 800-370-2633
Riffel's Coffee Company
Wichita, KS . . . 888-399-4567
RISE Brewing Co.
Cos Cob, CT
River Road Coffee
Lake Clear, NY . . . 315-769-9941
Roasterie Inc
Kansas City, MO . . . 800-376-0245
Rocky Mountain Coffee Roasters
Jasper, Alberta T0E 1E0, AB . . . 800 666-3465
Rodda Coffee Company
Yachats, OR . . . 541-547-4132
Ronnoco Coffee Co
St Louis, MO . . . 800-428-2287
Rostov's Coffee & Tea Co
Richmond, VA . . . 800-637-6772
Rowland Coffee Roasters Inc.
Miami, FL . . . 866-318-0422
Royal Cup Coffee
Birmingham, AL . . . 800-366-5836
S & D Coffee Inc
Concord, NC . . . 800-933-2210
Sahara Coffee
Reno, NV . . . 775-825-5033
Sambets Cajun Deli
Austin, TX . . . 800-472-6238
San Francisco Bay Coffee
Lincoln, CA . . . 800-829-1300
San Francisco Bay Coffee Company
Lincoln, CA . . . 800-829-1300
San Jose Apartments
San Jose, CA . . . 408-347-8209
San Juan Coffee Roasting Co
Friday Harbor, WA . . . 800-624-4119
San Marco Coffee, Inc.
Charlotte, NC . . . 800-715-9298
SANGARIA USA
Torrance, CA . . . 310-530-2202
Santa Barbara Roasting Co
Santa Barbara, CA . . . 800-321-5282
Santa Elena Coffee Company
Hutto, TX . . . 512-846-2908
Sappore Coffee Co Of Alaska
Anchorage, AK . . . 907-333-3626
Schuil Coffee Co
Grand Rapids, MI . . . 616-956-6815
Seattle's Best Coffee
Seattle, WA . . . 800-611-7793
Seven Hills Coffee Co
Blue Ash, OH . . . 513-489-5220
Shamrock Foods Co
Phoenix, AZ . . . 800-289-3663
Shelburne Falls Coffee Roaster
Shelburne Falls, MA . . . 413-625-2123
Sierra Madre Coffee
Denver, CO . . . 303-446-0050
Simpson & Vail
Brookfield, CT . . . 800-282-8327
Sivetz Coffee
Corvallis, OR . . . 541-753-9713
Slo Roasted Coffee
Los Osos, CA . . . 800-382-6837
South Beach Coffee Company
Miami Beach, FL . . . 305-576-9696
Southern Heritage Coffee Company
Indianapolis, IN . . . 800-486-1198
Specialty Coffee Roasters
Delray Beach, FL . . . 800-253-9363
Specialty Food Association
New York, NY . . . 646-878-0301
Spices of Life Gourmet Coffee
Fort Myers, FL . . . 239-334-8004
Spinelli Coffee Company
Seattle, WA . . . 415-821-7100
Starbucks
Seattle, WA . . . 800-782-7282
Stasero International
Kent, WA . . . 888-929-2378
Steep & Brew
Monona, WI . . . 800-876-1986
Stevens Creative Enterprises, Inc.
New York, NY . . . 646-558-6336
Stewart's Private Blend Foods
Chicago, IL . . . 800-654-2862
Stockton Graham & Co
Raleigh, NC . . . 800-835-5943
Sugai Kona Coffee
Holualoa, HI . . . 808-322-7717
Sunup Green Coffee
New York, NY . . . 212-842-9767
Sweeney's Gourmet Coffee Roast
Henderson, NV . . . 702-558-0505
Tadin Herb & Tea Co
Vernon, CA . . . 800-838-2346
Teeccino
Carpinteria, CA . . . 800-498-3434
Texas Coffee Co
Beaumont, TX . . . 800-259-3400
Texas Coffee Traders Inc
Austin, TX . . . 800-343-4875
Thanksgiving Coffee Co
Fort Bragg, CA . . . 800-462-1999
The Coffee Bean & Tea Leaf
Los Angeles, CA . . . 877-653-1963
Thrive Farmers
Roswell, GA . . . 855-553-2763
Tierra Farm
Valatie, NY . . . 519-392-8300
TMI Trading Co
Brooklyn, NY . . . 718-821-5052
Toddy Products Inc
Midland, TX . . . 713-225-2066
Tom & Dave's Coffee
San Rafael, CA . . . 800-249-5050
Torke Coffee Co
Sheboygan, WI . . . 800-242-7671
Torrefazione Italia
Seattle, WA . . . 800-827-2333
Torreo Coffee Company
Philadelphia, PA . . . 888-286-7736
Tradewinds Coffee Company
Raleigh, NC . . . 800-457-0406
Tristao Trading
New York, NY . . . 212-285-8120
Uncommon Grounds Coffee
Berkeley, CA . . . 800-567-9183
United Intratrade
Houston, TX . . . 713-827-7799
Utah Coffee Roasters
South Salt Lake, UT . . . 888-486-3334
Valley Tea & Coffee
Alhambra, CA . . . 626-281-5799
Van Roy Coffee Co
Cleveland, OH . . . 877-826-7669
Vermont Coffee Co
Middlebury, VT . . . 888-308-5099
Victor Allen Coffee Company
Albuquerque, NM . . . 800-662-2575
Victor Allen's Coffee and Tea
Little Chute, WI . . . 800-394-5282
Village Roaster
Lakewood, CO . . . 800-237-3822
Wallingford Coffee Co Inc
Cincinnati, OH . . . 800-533-3690
Walsh's Coffee Roasters
San Mateo, CA . . . 650-347-5112
Wandering Bear Coffee
New York, NY . . . 929-251-3752
Weaver Nut Co. Inc.
Ephrata, PA . . . 800-473-2688
Wechsler Coffee Corporation
Teterboro, NJ . . . 800-800-2633
West Coast Specialty Coffee
Campbell, CA . . . 650-259-9308
What's Brewing
San Antonio, TX . . . 877-262-7311
Wheeling Coffee & Spice Co
Wheeling, WV . . . 800-500-0141
White Cloud Coffee
Boise, ID . . . 888-229-3249
White Coffee Corporation
Long Island City, NY . . . 800-221-0140
Willoughby's Coffee & Tea
Branford, CT . . . 800-388-8400
World Cup Coffee & Tea
Portland, OR . . . 503-228-5503
World Of Coffee
Stirling, NJ . . . 800-543-0062
Young Winfield
Hamilton, ON . . . 905-893-2536

Americano

NeuRoast
New York, NY

Cappuccino

B&D Food Corporation
New York, NY . . . 212-937-8456
Caffe D'Amore
Beloit, WI . . . 800-999-0171
Caffe D'Amore Gourmet Beverages
Pittsburgh, PA . . . 800-999-0171
High Brew Coffee
Austin, TX
Instant Products of America
Columbus, IN . . . 812-372-9100
Sherwood Brands
New Brunswick, NJ . . . 973-249-8200
Wild Aseptics, LLC
Erlanger, KY . . . 877-787-7221

Decaffeinated

Arbuckle Coffee Roasters
Tucson, AZ . . . 800-533-8278
Atlanta Coffee & Tea Co
. . . 800-426-4781
Caffe Darte
Federal Way, WA . . . 800-999-5334
Caffe Luca Coffee Roaste
Seattle, WA . . . 800-728-9116
Chock Full O'Nuts
. . . 888-246-2598
Coffee Exchange
Providence, RI . . . 877-263-3334
Coffee Roasters Of New Orleans
Kenner, LA . . . 800-737-5464
Folgers Coffee Co
Orrville, OH . . . 800-937-9745
French Market Coffee
New Orleans, LA . . . 800-535-1961
Grounds for Change
Poulsbo, WA . . . 800-796-6820
Hawaii Coffee Company
Honolulu, HI . . . 800-338-8353
Heritage Coffee Co & Cafe
Juneau, AK . . . 800-478-5282
Jelks Coffee Roasters
Shreveport, LA . . . 800-235-7361
Kaffe Magnum Opus
Millville, NJ . . . 800-652-5282
Kohana Coffee
Austin, TX . . . 512-904-1174
Mccullagh Coffee Roasters
Buffalo, NY . . . 800-753-3473
Puroast Coffee Co Inc
Woodland, CA . . . 877-569-2243
San Francisco Bay Coffee Company
Lincoln, CA . . . 800-829-1300

Stewart's Private Blend Foods
Chicago, IL 800-654-2862
Thanksgiving Coffee Co
Fort Bragg, CA 800-462-1999
Utah Coffee Roasters
South Salt Lake, UT 888-486-3334
Van Roy Coffee Co
Cleveland, OH 877-826-7669
Weaver Nut Co. Inc.
Ephrata, PA 800-473-2688
Wechsler Coffee Corporation
Teterboro, NJ. 800-800-2633

Flavored

A Hill of Beans Coffee Roasters
Omaha, NE 402-333-6048
Arbuckle Coffee Roasters
Tucson, AZ 800-533-8278
ARCO Coffee
Superior, WI 800-283-2726
Aroma Coffee Company
Forest Park, IL 708-488-8340
Atlanta Coffee & Tea Co
.... 800-426-4781
Cafe Society Coffee Company
Dallas, TX 800-717-6000
Coffee Roasters Of New Orleans
Kenner, LA 800-737-5464
Daymar Select Fine Coffees
El Cajon, CA 800-466-7590
De Coty Coffee Co
San Angelo, TX 800-588-8001
Distant Lands Coffee Roaster
Renton, WA 800-758-4437
East Indies Coffee & Tea Co
Lebanon, PA 800-220-2326
Empire Coffee Company
Port Chester, NY 800-642-1100
Folgers Coffee Co
Orrville, OH 800-937-9745
Forto Coffee
New York, NY 844-450-7575
French Market Coffee
New Orleans, LA 800-535-1961
Greene Brothers Specialty Coffee Roaster
Hackettstown, NJ 908-979-0022
Harold L King & Co Inc
Redwood City, CA 888-368-2233
Hawaii Coffee Company
Honolulu, HI 800-338-8353
Heritage Coffee Co & Cafe
Juneau, AK 800-478-5282
Java Beans and Joe Coffee
Petaluma, CA 800-624-7031
Jelks Coffee Roasters
Shreveport, LA 800-235-7361
Jodyana Corporation
Miami, FL 888-563-5282
Kaffe Magnum Opus
Millville, NJ 800-652-5282
Kauai Coffee Co Inc
Kalaheo, HI 800-545-8605
Lexington Coffee & Tea
Lexington, KY 859-277-1102
Longbottom Coffee & Tea Inc
Hillsboro, OR 800-288-1271
Love Creek Orchards
Medina, TX 800-449-0882
Lowery's Premium Roast Gourmet Coffee
Snohomish, WA 800-767-1783
Magnum Coffee Roastery
Nunica, MI 888-937-5282
Mccullagh Coffee Roasters
Buffalo, NY 800-753-3473
New Age Beverages
Denver, CO 303-289-8655
Pearl Coffee Co
Akron, OH 800-822-5282
Puroast Coffee Co Inc
Woodland, CA 877-569-2243
Riffel's Coffee Company
Wichita, KS 888-399-4567
San Francisco Bay Coffee Company
Lincoln, CA 800-829-1300
San Juan Coffee Roasting Co
Friday Harbor, WA 800-624-4119
Stewart's Private Blend Foods
Chicago, IL 800-654-2862
Thanksgiving Coffee Co
Fort Bragg, CA 800-462-1999
Utah Coffee Roasters
South Salt Lake, UT 888-486-3334
Weaver Nut Co. Inc.
Ephrata, PA 800-473-2688
Wechsler Coffee Corporation
Teterboro, NJ 800-800-2633

Iced

Arizona Beverage Company
Cincinnati, OH 800-832-3775
Bossen
Hayward, CA 510-324-0168
Cold Brew EvyTea
Boston, MA 617-429-5229
Grady's Cold Brew
Bronx, NY 718-860-1600
Kohana Coffee
Austin, TX 512-904-1174

Instant

Alpine Start Foods
Boulder, CO
Chameleon Cold Brew
Austin, TX
Chock Full O'Nuts
.... 888-246-2598
Coffee Globe LLC
Huntington Beach, CA 587-966-1171
Coffee Holding Co Inc
Staten Island, NY 800-458-2233
Daymar Select Fine Coffees
El Cajon, CA 800-466-7590
Folgers Coffee Co
Orrville, OH 800-937-9745
Instant Products of America
Columbus, IN 812-372-9100
Know Brainer
Lafayette, CO 303-475-0456
Kuju Coffee
San Francisco, CA 415-634-5858
LonoLife
Oceanside, CA 855-843-8566
NeuRoast
New York, NY
Tonex
Wallington, NJ 973-773-5135

Instant - Decaffeinated

Swagger Foods Corp
Vernon Hills, IL 847-913-1200

Latte

Navitas Naturals
Novato, CA 888-645-4282
NeuRoast
New York, NY
Pop & Bottle Inc.
San Francisco, CA

Roasted

A Hill of Beans Coffee Roasters
Omaha, NE 402-333-6048
Alakef Coffee Roasters Inc
Duluth, MN 800-438-9228
Allegro Coffee Co
Thornton, CO 800-666-4869
Arbuckle Coffee Roasters
Tucson, AZ 800-533-8278
Armeno Coffee Roasters LTD
Northborough, MA 508-393-2821
Atlanta Coffee & Tea Co
.... 800-426-4781
Boyd's Coffee Co
Portland, OR 800-735-2878
Brisk Coffee Co
Tampa, FL 800-899-5282
Buckmaster Coffee Co
Hillsboro, OR 800-962-9148
Cafe Bustelo
Miami, FL 800-990-9039
Cafe Grumpy
Brooklyn, NY 718-383-0748
Cafe Moto
San Diego, CA 800-818-3363
Caffe Darte
Federal Way, WA 800-999-5334
Caffe Ibis Gallery Deli
Logan, UT 888-740-4777
Captain Cook Coffee Company
Kealakekua, HI 650-766-9149
Clear Mountain Coffee Company
Silver Spring, MD 301-587-2233
Coffee Bean Intl
Portland, OR 800-877-0474
Coffee Reserve
Phoenix, AZ 888-755-6789
Colonial Coffee Roasters Inc
Miami, FL 305-638-0885
Daymar Select Fine Coffees
El Cajon, CA 800-466-7590
Di Lusso & Be Bop Baskote LLC
Redmond, OR 888-545-7487
Distant Lands Coffee Roaster
Renton, WA 800-758-4437
Eldorado Coffee Distributors
Flushing, NY 800-635-2566
Ethical Bean Coffee
Vancouver, BC 877-431-3830
Finger Lakes Coffee Roasters
Victor, NY 800-420-6154
Folgers Coffee Co
Orrville, OH 800-937-9745
Generous Coffee
Denver, CO
Grounds for Change
Poulsbo, WA 800-796-6820
Grounds For Thought
Bowling Green, OH 419-354-3266
Heritage Coffee Co & Cafe
Juneau, AK 800-478-5282
House of Coffee Beans
Houston, TX 800-422-1799
Indigo Coffee Roasters
Florence, MA 800-447-5450
Jeremiah's Pick Coffee Co
San Francisco, CA 877-537-3642
Kauai Coffee Co Inc
Kalaheo, HI 800-545-8605
Kohana Coffee
Austin, TX 512-904-1174
KonaRed Corp.
Carlsbad, CA 949-682-4700
Lexington Coffee & Tea
Lexington, KY 859-277-1102
Lola Savannah
Houston, TX 888-663-9166
Lucile's
Boulder, CO 800-727-3653
M.E. Swing Company
Alexandria, VA 800-485-4019
Magnum Coffee Roastery
Nunica, MI 888-937-5282
Maui Coffee Roasters Wholesale
Kahului, HI 800-645-2877
Mccullagh Coffee Roasters
Buffalo, NY 800-753-3473
Milone Brothers Coffee Co
Modesto, CA 800-974-8500
Montana Coffee Traders
Whitefish, MT 800-345-5282
MorningStar Coffee Company
West Chester, PA 888-854-2233
New Harmony Coffee & Tea Co.
New Harmony, IN 812-682-4563
North River Roasters
Poughkeepsie, NY 845-418-2739
Oasis Coffee Co Inc
Norwalk, CT 203-847-0554
Olympic Coffee & Roasting
Bellevue, WA 888-244-8313
Pan American Coffee Co
Hoboken, NJ 800-229-1883
Pfefferkorn's Coffee Inc
Baltimore, MD 800-682-4665
Puroast Coffee Co Inc
Woodland, CA 877-569-2243
San Francisco Bay Coffee
Lincoln, CA 800-829-1300
San Juan Coffee Roasting Co
Friday Harbor, WA 800-624-4119
Sara Lee Foodservice
Peoria, IL 800-641-4025
Southern Heritage Coffee Company
Indianapolis, IN 800-486-1198
Steep & Brew
Monona, WI 800-876-1986
Stewart's Private Blend Foods
Chicago, IL 800-654-2862
Texas Coffee Co
Beaumont, TX 800-259-3400
Torke Coffee Co
Sheboygan, WI 800-242-7671
U Roast Em Inc
Hayward, WI 715-634-6255

Utah Coffee Roasters
South Salt Lake, UT 888-486-3334
Van Roy Coffee Co
Cleveland, OH 877-826-7669
Weaver Nut Co. Inc.
Ephrata, PA 800-473-2688
Wheeling Coffee & Spice Co
Wheeling, WV 800-500-0141
White Cloud Coffee
Boise, ID 888-229-3249
Young Winfield
Hamilton, ON 905-893-2536

Vacuum Packed

Folgers Coffee Co
Orrville, OH 800-937-9745

Espresso

A Hill of Beans Coffee Roasters
Omaha, NE 402-333-6048
Arel Group Wine & Spirits Inc
Atlanta, GA 404-869-4387
Aroma Coffee Company
Forest Park, IL 708-488-8340
B&K Coffee
Oneonta, NY 800-432-1499
Bluechip Group
Salt Lake City, UT 800-878-0099
Caffe Darte
Federal Way, WA 800-999-5334
Caffe Luca Coffee Roaste
Seattle, WA 800-728-9116
Chock Full O'Nuts
.... 888-246-2598
Dallis Brothers
Long Island City, NY 718-845-3010
Distant Lands Coffee Roaster
Renton, WA 800-758-4437
Fama Sales Co
New York, NY 800-682-0425
Folklore Foods
Selby, SD 605-649-1144
Fratelli Mantova
Naperville, IL 630-904-0002
Heritage Coffee Co & Cafe
Juneau, AK 800-478-5282
High Brew Coffee
Austin, TX
Ideal Dairy Farms
Hudson Falls, NY 518-747-5059
Kobricks Coffee Company
Jersey City, NJ 800-562-7491
Martin Coffee Co
Jacksonville, FL 904-355-9661
Monticello Vineyards-Corley
Napa, CA 707-253-2802
Oak Farms
El Paso, TX 800-395-7004
Puroast Coffee Co Inc
Woodland, CA 877-569-2243
Reiter Dairy
Newport, KY 800-544-6455
San Marco Coffee, Inc.
Charlotte, NC 800-715-9298
Sebastiani Vineyards
Sonoma, CA 855-232-2338
Sopralco
Plantation, FL 954-584-2225
Southern Heritage Coffee Company
Indianapolis, IN 800-486-1198
Ultra Seal
New Paltz, NY 845-255-2490
Unilever Canada
Toronto, ON 416-415-3000

Mocha

Jones Brewing Company
Smithton, PA 724-483-2400
REBBL
Emeryville, CA 855-732-2500

Tea

8th Wonder
Denver, CO 303-868-6296
Abunda Life
Asbury Park, NJ 732-775-9338
Ahmad Tea
Deer Park, TX 800-637-7704
Ajiri Tea Company
Upper Black Eddy, PA 610-982-5075
Al-Rite Fruits & Syrups Co
Miami, FL 305-652-2540
Alaska Herb & Tea Co
Anchorage, AK 800-654-2764
Alexander Gourmet Beverages
Bolton, ON 800-265-5081
Allen Flavors Inc
Edison, NJ 908-561-5995
Alpine Pure USA
Falls River, MA 888-332-3392
Alternative Health & Herbs
Albany, OR 800-345-4152
Amazon Trading, Ltd.
Colombo,
Amcan Beverages Inc
American Canyon, CA 800-972-5962
American Instants Inc
Flanders, NJ 973-584-8811
American Soy Products Inc
Saline, MI 734-429-2310
Argo Tea
Chicago, IL 612-553-1550
Artist Coffee
Londonderry, NH 866-440-4511
Atlanta Coffee & Tea Co
.... 800-426-4781
B&K Coffee
Oneonta, NY 800-432-1499
Bagai Tea Company
San Marcos, CA 760-591-3084
Baily Tea USA Inc
Rockville, MD 301-704-1739
Barnes & Watson Fine Teas
Seattle, WA 800-447-8832
Barrows Tea Company
New Bedford, MA 800-832-5024
Beacon Drive Inn
Spartanburg, SC 864-585-9387
Bellocq
Brooklyn, NY 347-463-9231
Bhakti
Boulder, CO 303-484-8770
Bigelow Tea
Fairfield, CT 888-241 3569
Blue Willow Tea Co
Berkeley, CA 800-328-0353
Boston Tea Company
Hackensack, NJ 800-495-9026
Bountiful Pantry
Nantucket, MA 617-487-8019
Boyd's Coffee Co
Portland, OR 800-735-2878
Bread & Chocolate Inc
Wells River, VT 800-524-6715
Brew Dr. Kombucha
Portland, OR 760-487-8895
Bruce Tea
Buddha Teas
Carlsbad, CA 800-642-3754
Busy Bee Yerba Mate
Cadillac Coffee Co
Ft. Wayne, IN 800-438-6900
Caribbean Coffee Co
Goleta, CA 800-932-5282
Carolina Treet
Wilmington, NC 800-616-6344
Celebrity Tea, LLC
Tampa, FL 813-600-3317
Cham Cold Brew Tea
New York, NY 646-926-0206
Charleston Tea Plantation
Wadmalaw Island, SC 800-443-5987
Chartreuse Organic Tea
Trenton, MI 866-315-7832
Chicago Coffee Roastery
Huntley, IL 800-762-5402
China Mist Brands
Scottsdale, AZ 800-242-8807
Choice Organic Teas
Seattle, WA 866-972-6879
City Bean
Los Angeles, CA 888-248-9232
Clayton Coffee & Tea
Modesto, CA 209-576-1120
Clear Mountain Coffee Company
Silver Spring, MD 301-587-2233
Clearly Kombucha
San Francisco, CA
Coca-Cola Beverages Northeast
Bedford, NH 844-619-3388
Coffee Bean & Tea Leaf
Bloomington, MN 952-853-1148
Coffee Bean Intl
Portland, OR 800-877-0474
Coffee Beanery LTD
Flushing, MI 800-441-2255
Coffee Mill Roastery
Elon, NC 800-729-1727
Coffee Roasters Of New Orleans
Kenner, LA 800-737-5464
Colorado Spice Co
Boulder, CO 800-677-7423
Community Coffee Co.
Baton Rouge, LA 800-884-5282
Company of a Philadelphia Gentleman
Philadelphia, PA 215-427-2827
Continental Coffee Products Company
Houston, TX 800-323-6178
Cora Italian Specialties
Countryside, IL 800-696-2672
Cotswold Cottage Foods
Arvada, CO 800-208-1977
Custom Coffee Plan
Torrance, CA 800-841-5949
Damron Corp
Chicago, IL 800-333-1860
David Rio
San Francisco, CA 800-454-9605
Davidson's Organics
Reno, NV 800-882-5888
Davinci Gourmet LTD
Seattle, WA 800-640-6779
De Coty Coffee Co
San Angelo, TX 800-588-8001
DMH Ingredients Inc
Libertyville, IL 847-362-9977
Dried Ingredients, LLC.
Miami, FL 786-999-8499
Droubi's Imports
Houston, TX 713-334-1829
East Indies Coffee & Tea Co
Lebanon, PA 800-220-2326
Eastern Tea Corp
Monroe Twp, NJ 800-221-0865
Eastrise Trading Corp.
Baldwin Park, CA
Eden Foods Inc
Clinton, MI 888-424-3336
Empire Tea Svc
Columbus, IN 800-790-0246
Equal Exchange Inc
West Bridgewater, MA 774-776-7400
Evy Tea
Boston, MA
Farmtrue
North Stonington, CT 860-495-2231
Fat Snax
Brooklyn, NY 347-496-5834
Father's Country Hams
Bremen, KY 270-525-3554
Fee Brothers
Rochester, NY 800-961-3337
Field Coffee
Norcross, GA 844-343-5326
Finlay Extracts & Ingredients USA, Inc.
Florham Park, NJ 800-288-6272
Finlays
Lincoln, RI 800-288-6272
Flora Inc
Lynden, WA 800-446-2110
Flying Embers
Ventura, CA
Fmali Herb
Santa Cruz, CA 831-423-7913
Fortunes International Teas
Mc Kees Rocks, PA 412-771-7767
Generation Tea
Monsey, NY 866-742-5668
GH Ford Tea Company
Shokan, NY 845-464-6755
Gloria Jean's Gourmet Coffees
Irvine, CA 877-320-5282
Golden Moon Tea
Bristow, VA 877-327-5473
Good Earth Company
New Providence, NJ 888-625-8227
Grace Tea Co
Acton, MA 978-635-9500
Great Eastern Sun Trading Co
Asheville, NC 800-334-5809
H & H Products Co
Orlando, FL 800-678-8448
Hain Celestial Group Inc
Lake Success, NY 800-434-4246

Harney & Sons Tea Co.
Millerton, NY 800-832-8463
Harris Tea Company
Moorestown, NJ 856-793-0290
Has Beans Coffee & Tea Co
Chico, CA 800-427-2326
Herbs Etc
Santa Fe, NM 888-694-3727
Heritage Books & Gifts
Virginia Beach, VA 800-862-2923
Holy Kombucha
Dallas, TX 855-694-6595
House of Coffee Beans
Houston, TX 800-422-1799
Humm Kombucha
Bend, OR 541-306-6329
Ideal Distributing Company
Bothell, WA 425-488-6121
IGZU
ILHWA American Corporation
Belleville, NJ 800-446-7364
Ineeka Inc
Chicago, IL 312-733-8327
Innovative Beverage Concepts
Irvine, CA 949-831-8656
International Tea Importers
Pico Rivera, CA 877-832-5263
J.G. British Imports
Bradenton, FL 888-965-1700
Javo Beverage Co., Inc.
Vista, CA 760-330-1141
John A Vassilaros & Son Inc
Flushing, NY 718-886-4140
Juice Tyme, Inc.
Chicago, IL 800-236-5823
Kasira
Buena Park, CA 800-220-6131
Keurig, Inc
Reading, MA 866-901-2739
KeVita
Oxnard, CA 888-310-6106
Kobricks Coffee Company
Jersey City, NJ 800-562-7491
KOE Organic Kombucha
Vernon, CA
Kombucha Wonder Drink
Portland, OR 877-224-7331
Kuli Kuli, Inc.
Oakland, CA 510-350-8325
LA Lifestyle Nutritional Products
Santa Ana, CA 800-387-4786
Lacas Coffee Co Inc
Pennsauken, NJ 800-220-1133
Leaves Pure Teas
Scottsdale, AZ 800-242-8807
Lexington Coffee & Tea
Lexington, KY 859-277-1102
LIVE Soda
Austin, TX
Lowcountry Produce
Raleigh, NC 800-935-2792
Lyons Magnus
Fresno, CA 800-344-7130
MacKinlay Teas
Ann Arbor, MI 734-846-0966
Madys Company
San Francisco, CA 415-822-2227
Marin Kombucha
Novato, CA 415-496-5441
Mars Inc.
McLean, VA 703-821-4900
Martin Bauer Group
Sacaucus, NJ 201-659-3100
Masala Chai Company
Santa Cruz, CA 831-475-8881
Master Brew
Northbrook, IL 847-564-3600
Metropolitan Tea Company
Cheektowaga, NY 800-388-0351
Mighty Leaf Tea
San Rafael, CA 877-698-5323
MindFull, Inc.
Hutto, TX
Miracle Tree
Miami, FL 888-590-1555
Miss Tea Brooklyn Inc
Brooklyn, NY 718-389-9090
Montana Coffee Traders
Whitefish, MT 800-345-5282
Mother Parker's Tea & Coffee
Mississauga, ON 800-387-9398
Mountanos Family Coffee & Tea Co.
Petaluma, CA 800-624-7031
Mr. Mak's
New York, NY 888-953-9209
New Age Beverages
Denver, CO 303-289-8655
Newby Teas
East Lansing, MI 517-999-0590
Nirwana Foods
Jersey City, NJ 201-659-2200
Northwestern Foods
Arden Hills, MN 800-236-4937
Numi Organic Tea
Oakland, CA 888-404-6864
O'Neil's Distributors
Goodland, IN 219-297-4521
O'Neill Coffee Co
West Middlesex, PA 724-528-2244
Pappy's Sassafras Tea
Columbus Grove, OH 877-659-5110
PepsiCo.
Purchase, NY 914-253-2000
Piper & Leaf
Huntsville, AL 256-929-9404
Pocas International
South Hackensack, NJ 201-941-7900
Prince of Peace
Hayward, CA 800-732-2328
Progenix Corporation
Wausau, WI 800-233-3356
Q.E. Tea
Bridgeville, PA 800-622-8327
Refresco Beverages US Inc.
Tampa, FL 888-260-3776
Republic of Tea
Novato, CA 800-298-4832
Richard's Gourmet Coffee
West Bridgewater, MA 800-370-2633
Rooibee Red Tea
Louisville, KY 502-749-0800
Royal Pacific Coffee Co
Scottsdale, AZ 480-951-8251
S & D Coffee Inc
Concord, NC 800-933-2210
Sampac Enterprises
S San Francisco, CA 650-876-0808
Schneider's Dairy Inc
Pittsburgh, PA 412-881-3525
Secret Tea Garden
Vancouver, BC 604-261-3070
Serendipitea
Manhasset, NY 888-832-5433
Sherwood Brands
New Brunswick, NJ 973-249-8200
Simpson & Vail
Brookfield, CT 800-282-8327
SpecialTeas
Norwalk, CT 888-365-6983
Starbucks
Seattle, WA 800-782-7282
Stevens Creative Enterprises, Inc.
New York, NY 646-558-6336
Stewart's Private Blend Foods
Chicago, IL 800-654-2862
Sturm Foods Inc
Manawa, WI 800-347-8876
Sunfood
El Cajon, CA 888-729-3663
Sunlike Juice
Rougemont, QC 866-552-7643
Takeiya USA
Huntington Beach, CA 714-374-9900
Tata Tea
Plant City, FL 813-754-2602
Tatra Herb Co
Morrisville, PA 888-828-7248
Tazo Tea
Kent, WA 855-829-6832
Tea Beyond
West Caldwell, NJ 973-226-0327
Tea Forte
Concord, MA 978-369-1598
Tea Needs Inc
Boca Raton, FL 877-832-8289
Tea Room
San Leandro, CA 510-567-8868
Teeccino
Carpinteria, CA 800-498-3434
Templar Food Products
New Providence, NJ 800-883-6752
Ten Ren Tea & Ginseng Co Inc
New York, NY 800-292-2049
Tetley USA
Marietta, GA 770-428-5555
Tetley USA
Edison, NJ 800-728-0084
The Tea Spot, Inc.
Boulder, CO 303-444-8324
Thirs-Tea Corp
Boca Raton, FL 561-948-5600
Thrive Farmers
Roswell, GA 855-553-2763
Thyme Garden Herb Co
Alsea, OR 800-482-4372
TMI Trading Co
Brooklyn, NY 718-821-5052
Traditional Medicinals Inc
Sebastopol, CA 800-543-4372
Two Leaves & A Bud Inc
Basalt, CO 866-631-7973
U Roast Em Inc
Hayward, WI 715-634-6255
Ultra Seal
New Paltz, NY 845-255-2490
Uncle Lee's Tea Inc
South El Monte, CA 800-732-8830
Unilever Canada
Toronto, ON 416-415-3000
Unilever Food Solutions
Englewood Cliffs, NJ
Van Roy Coffee Co
Cleveland, OH 877-826-7669
VIP Foods
Flushing, NY 718-821-5330
Weaver Nut Co. Inc.
Ephrata, PA 800-473-2688
Wechsler Coffee Corporation
Teterboro, NJ 800-800-2633
White Coffee Corporation
Long Island City, NY 800-221-0140
White Rock Products Corp
Flushing, NY 800-969-7625
Whole Herb Co
Sonoma, CA 707-935-1077
Wild Hibiscus Flower Company
Richford, VT 800-499-8490
Wild Zora Foods
Loveland, CO 970-541-9672
Wise Mouth
Warren, RI
World Ginseng Ctr Inc
San Francisco, CA 800-747-8808
Yaupon Tea
Savannah, GA 912-596-1506
Yellow Emperor Inc
Eugene, OR 877-485-6664
Yogi® Tea
Springfield, OR 800-964-4832
Zest Tea LLC
Baltimore, MD 636-579-1809
Zhena's Gypsy Tea
Commerce, CA 800-448-0803

Bags

ABC Tea House
Baldwin Park, CA 888-220-3988
Barrows Tea Company
New Bedford, MA 800-832-5024
Blue Ridge Tea & Herb Co
Brooklyn, NY 718-625-3100
Carrington Tea Co.
Closter, NJ 800-505-9546
Choice Organic Teas
Seattle, WA 866-972-6879
Eastern Shore Tea
Lutherville, MD 800-823-1408
Eastern Tea Corp
Monroe Twp, NJ 800-221-0865
Empire Tea Svc
Columbus, IN 800-790-0246
Modern Tea Packers
Brooklyn, NY 718-417-1060
Newby Teas
East Lansing, MI 517-999-0590
Numi Organic Tea
Oakland, CA 888-404-6864
Tetley Tea
New Providence, NJ 800-728-0084

Black

Alpine Pure USA
Falls River, MA 888-332-3392

Atlanta Coffee & Tea Co
. . . . 800-426-4781
Bellocq
Brooklyn, NY 347-463-9231
Frontier Co-op
Norway, IA 844-550-6200
GH Ford Tea Company
Shokan, NY 845-464-6755
Harney & Sons Tea Co.
Millerton, NY 800-832-8463
Harris Tea Company
Moorestown, NJ 856-793-0290
MindFull, Inc.
Hutto, TX
Nourishtea
Toronto, ON 416-539-9299
SpecialTeas
Norwalk, CT 888-365-6983
Stash Tea Co
Portland, OR 800-547-1514
Talbott Teas
Emeryville, CA 855-850-6309

Chai

Alpine Pure USA
Falls River, MA 888-332-3392
Bhakti
Boulder, CO 303-484-8770
Chai Diaries
Mission Viejo, CA 917-460-6828
Choice Organic Teas
Seattle, WA 866-972-6879
David Rio
San Francisco, CA 800-454-9605
Davinci Gourmet LTD
Seattle, WA 800-640-6779
Father's Country Hams
Bremen, KY 270-525-3554
Gray Duck
Minneapolis, MN
Harris Tea Company
Moorestown, NJ 856-793-0290
Know Brainer
Lafayette, CO 303-475-0456
Masala Chai Company
Santa Cruz, CA 831-475-8881
Nature's Guru
Cerritos, CA 949-478-4878
Oregon Chai
Portland, OR 888-874-2424
Pacific Chai
Farmington, UT 888-882-4248
Sattwa Chai
Newberg, OR 503-538-4715
Stash Tea Co
Portland, OR 800-547-1514
Templar Food Products
New Providence, NJ 800-883-6752
Third Street Inc
Louisville, CO 800-636-3790
Toddy Products Inc
Midland, TX 713-225-2066

Chamomile

Castella Imports Inc
Brentwood, NY 631-231-5500
Cham Cold Brew Tea
New York, NY 646-926-0206
Choice Organic Teas
Seattle, WA 866-972-6879
The Poseidon Group
New York, NY 646-926-0206

Darjeeling

Choice Organic Teas
Seattle, WA 866-972-6879
GH Ford Tea Company
Shokan, NY 845-464-6755

Decaffeinated

Alexander Gourmet Beverages
Bolton, ON 800-265-5081
Ancora Coffee Roasters
Madison, WI 800-260-0217
Boston Tea Company
Hackensack, NJ 800-495-9026
Castella Imports Inc
Brentwood, NY 631-231-5500
Choice Organic Teas
Seattle, WA 866-972-6879
GH Ford Tea Company
Shokan, NY 845-464-6755
Harney & Sons Tea Co.
Millerton, NY 800-832-8463
Martin Bauer Group
Sacaucus, NJ 201-659-3100
Masala Chai Company
Santa Cruz, CA 831-475-8881
Mother Parker's Tea & Coffee
Mississauga, ON 800-387-9398
SpecialTeas
Norwalk, CT 888-365-6983
Weaver Nut Co. Inc.
Ephrata, PA 800-473-2688

Earl Grey

Alpine Pure USA
Falls River, MA 888-332-3392
Blue Willow Tea Co
Berkeley, CA 800-328-0353
Choice Organic Teas
Seattle, WA 866-972-6879
GH Ford Tea Company
Shokan, NY 845-464-6755
Harris Tea Company
Moorestown, NJ 856-793-0290

Earl Grey Decaffeinated

Choice Organic Teas
Seattle, WA 866-972-6879

English Breakfast

Choice Organic Teas
Seattle, WA 866-972-6879
Harris Tea Company
Moorestown, NJ 856-793-0290

Fair-Trade

Flying Bird Botanicals LLC
Bellingham, WA 360-366-8013
North River Roasters
Poughkeepsie, NY 845-418-2739

Flavored

Alaska Herb & Tea Co
Anchorage, AK 800-654-2764
Aqua Vie Beverage Corporation
Ketchum, ID 800-744-7500
Arbuckle Coffee Roasters
Tucson, AZ 800-533-8278
Belmar Spring Water
Glen Rock, NJ 201-444-1010
Best Foods
Englewood Cliffs, NJ 201-894-4000
Boston Tea Company
Hackensack, NJ 800-495-9026
Cafe Society Coffee Company
Dallas, TX 800-717-6000
Celebrity Tea, LLC
Tampa, FL 813-600-3317
Choice Organic Teas
Seattle, WA 866-972-6879
Coca-Cola Beverages Northeast
Bedford, NH 844-619-3388
Daymar Select Fine Coffees
El Cajon, CA 800-466-7590
Dr. B's Beverages, LLC
Inwood, WV 304-283-2257
East Indies Coffee & Tea Co
Lebanon, PA 800-220-2326
Empire Tea Svc
Columbus, IN 800-790-0246
Father's Country Hams
Bremen, KY 270-525-3554
First Colony Coffee & Tea Company
Norfolk, VA 800-446-8555
Fortunes International Teas
Mc Kees Rocks, PA 412-771-7767
Harney & Sons Tea Co.
Millerton, NY 800-832-8463
Harris Tea Company
Moorestown, NJ 856-793-0290
Houston Tea & Beverage
Houston, TX 800-585-4549
LemonKind
New York, NY 954-678-1700
Martin Bauer Group
Sacaucus, NJ 201-659-3100
Masala Chai Company
Santa Cruz, CA 831-475-8881
Mother Parker's Tea & Coffee
Mississauga, ON 800-387-9398
Pappy's Sassafras Tea
Columbus Grove, OH 877-659-5110
Rooibee Red Tea
Louisville, KY 502-749-0800
San Francisco Bay Coffee Company
Lincoln, CA 800-829-1300
SpecialTeas
Norwalk, CT 888-365-6983
Stewart's Private Blend Foods
Chicago, IL 800-654-2862
Weaver Nut Co. Inc.
Ephrata, PA 800-473-2688

Green

360 Nutrition
Los Angeles, CA 213-805-3015
Aiya America Inc
Torrance, CA 310-212-1395
Alexander Gourmet Beverages
Bolton, ON 800-265-5081
Alpine Pure USA
Falls River, MA 888-332-3392
Ancora Coffee Roasters
Madison, WI 800-260-0217
AOI Tea Company
Huntington Beach, CA 877-264-0877
Baycliff Co Inc
Garwood, NJ 866-772-7569
Bellocq
Brooklyn, NY 347-463-9231
Boston Tea Company
Hackensack, NJ 800-495-9026
China Mist Brands
Scottsdale, AZ 800-242-8807
Choice Organic Teas
Seattle, WA 866-972-6879
Davinci Gourmet LTD
Seattle, WA 800-640-6779
Eden Foods Inc
Clinton, MI 888-424-3336
Empire Tea Svc
Columbus, IN 800-790-0246
Fmali Herb
Santa Cruz, CA 831-423-7913
Fortunes International Teas
Mc Kees Rocks, PA 412-771-7767
Frontier Co-op
Norway, IA 844-550-6200
Fuzz East Coast
Englewood Cliffs, NJ 866-438-3893
GH Ford Tea Company
Shokan, NY 845-464-6755
Harney & Sons Tea Co.
Millerton, NY 800-832-8463
Harris Tea Company
Moorestown, NJ 856-793-0290
Healthy Beverage LLC
Doylestown, PA 800-295-1388
Jade Leaf Matcha
San Francisco, CA
Limitless
Chicago, IL
Martin Bauer Group
Sacaucus, NJ 201-659-3100
MindFull, Inc.
Hutto, TX
Motto
Milton, MA 617-848-9248
Nourishtea
Toronto, ON 416-539-9299
Nu Naturals Inc
Eugene, OR 800-753-4372
REBBL
Emeryville, CA 855-732-2500
RFi Ingredients
Blauvelt, NY 800-962-7663
Sencha Naturals
Los Angeles, CA 888-473-6242
SpecialTeas
Norwalk, CT 888-365-6983
Stash Tea Co
Portland, OR 800-547-1514
Talbott Teas
Emeryville, CA 855-850-6309
Teapigs
Brooklyn, NY 212-705-8723
Templar Food Products
New Providence, NJ 800-883-6752
The Healthy Beverage Company
Doylestown, PA 800-295-1388

The Long Life Beverage Company
Mission Hills, CA 800-848-7331

Herbal

Abunda Life
Asbury Park, NJ 732-775-9338
Algonquin Tea
Eganville, ON 800-292-6671
Alternative Health & Herbs
Albany, OR 800-345-4152
Ancora Coffee Roasters
Madison, WI 800-260-0217
Bellocq
Brooklyn, NY 347-463-9231
Berardi's Fresh Roast
Cleveland, OH 800-876-9109
Best Foods
Englewood Cliffs, NJ 201-894-4000
Body Breakthrough Inc
Deer Park, NY 800-924-3343
Boston Spice & Tea Company
Boston, VA 800-966-4372
Boston Tea Company
Hackensack, NJ 800-495-9026
Chartreuse Organic Tea
Trenton, MI 866-315-7832
China Mist Brands
Scottsdale, AZ 800-242-8807
Choice Organic Teas
Seattle, WA 866-972-6879
Coffee Bean Intl
Portland, OR 800-877-0474
Common Folk Farm
Naples, ME 207-787-2764
Empire Tea Svc
Columbus, IN 800-790-0246
Fmali Herb
Santa Cruz, CA 831-423-7913
Fortunes International Teas
Mc Kees Rocks, PA 412-771-7767
Frontier Co-op
Norway, IA 844-550-6200
GH Ford Tea Company
Shokan, NY 845-464-6755
Harris Tea Company
Moorestown, NJ 856-793-0290
Health & Wholeness Store
Fairfield, IA 800-255-8332
Herb Tea Company
Oxnard, CA 805-486-6477
HerbaSway Laboratories
Wallingford, CT 800-672-7322
Heritage Books & Gifts
Virginia Beach, VA 800-862-2923
Hobe Laboratories Inc
Tempe, AZ 800-528-4482
ILHWA American Corporation
Belleville, NJ 800-446-7364
Madys Company
San Francisco, CA 415-822-2227
Martin Bauer Group
Sacaucus, NJ 201-659-3100
Montana Tea & Spice Trading
Missoula, MT 406-721-4882
Mother Parker's Tea & Coffee
Mississauga, ON 800-387-9398
Native Scents
Taos, NM 800-645-3471
Nourishtea
Toronto, ON 416-539-9299
NOW Foods
Bloomingdale, IL 888-669-3663
Nutritional Counselors of America
Spencer, TN 931-946-3600
Old Fashioned Natural Products
Santa Ana, CA 800-552-9045
Organic India USA
Boulder, CO 888-550-8332
P C Teas Co
Burlingame, CA 800-423-8728
Progenix Corporation
Wausau, WI 800-233-3356
San Francisco Bay Coffee Company
Lincoln, CA 800-829-1300
Stash Tea Co
Portland, OR 800-547-1514
Sugai Kona Coffee
Holualoa, HI 808-322-7717
Tatra Herb Co
Morrisville, PA 888-828-7248
Templar Food Products
New Providence, NJ 800-883-6752
Traditional Medicinals Inc
Sebastopol, CA 800-543-4372
Triple Leaf Tea Inc
S San Francisco, CA 800-552-7448
Vermont Liberty Tea
Waterbury, VT 802-244-6102
Wah Yet Group
Hayward, CA 800-229-3392
Whole Herb Co
Sonoma, CA 707-935-1077

Iced

4C Foods Corp
Brooklyn, NY 718-272-4242
Al-Rite Fruits & Syrups Co
Miami, FL 305-652-2540
Amcan Beverages Inc
American Canyon, CA 800-972-5962
Arizona Beverage Company
Cincinnati, OH 800-832-3775
Arteasans Beverages LLC
North Miami Beach, FL 305-363-5410
Bay Pac Beverages
Walnut Creek, CA 925-279-0800
Best Foods
Englewood Cliffs, NJ 201-894-4000
Better Beverages Inc
Cerritos, CA 800-344-5219
Bhakti
Boulder, CO 303-484-8770
Bigelow Tea
Fairfield, CT 888-244-3569
Boyd's Coffee Co
Portland, OR 800-735-2878
China Mist Brands
Scottsdale, AZ 800-242-8807
Clover Farms Dairy Co Inc
Reading, PA 800-323-0123
Coca-Cola Beverages Northeast
Bedford, NH 844-619-3388
Dr. B's Beverages, LLC
Inwood, WV 304-283-2257
Droubi's Imports
Houston, TX 713-334-1829
Ensemble Beverages
Montgomery, AL 334-324-7719
Farmland Dairies
Wallington, NJ 888-727-6252
Galliker Dairy Co
Johnstown, PA 800-477-6455
Global Beverage Company
Rochester, NY 585-381-3560
Good-O-Beverages Inc
Bronx, NY 718-328-6400
Harney & Sons Tea Co.
Millerton, NY 800-832-8463
Harris Tea Company
Moorestown, NJ 856-793-0290
Hearttea Inc.
Brooklyn, NY 917-725-3164
Honest Tea Inc
Atlanta, GA 800-520-2653
Inko's Tea
Willowbrook, IL
Ito En USA Inc
Brooklyn, NY 808-847-4477
Joe Tea and Joe Chips
Upper Montclair, NJ 973-744-7502
Keurig Dr Pepper
Plano, TX 800-696-5891
Lassonde Pappas & Company, Inc.
Carneys Point, NJ 800-257-7019
Leroy Hill Coffee Co Inc
Mobile, AL 800-866-5282
Marburger Farm Dairy
Evans City, PA 800-331-1295
Moonshine Sweet Tea
Austin, TX 888-793-3883
Motto
Milton, MA 617-848-9248
Northwestern Foods
Arden Hills, MN 800-236-4937
PR Bar
Chandler, AZ 800-397-5556
Purity Organic
Oakland, CA 415-440-7777
Rosenberger's Dairies
Hatfield, PA 800-355-9074
Schneider's Dairy Inc
Pittsburgh, PA 412-881-3525
Schneider-Valley Farms Inc
Williamsport, PA 570-326-2021
Serengeti Tea Co
Gardena, CA 888-604-2040
Stash Tea Co
Portland, OR 800-547-1514
Sturm Foods Inc
Manawa, WI 800-347-8876
Sunlike Juice
Rougemont, QC 866-552-7643
Sweet Leaf Tea Company
Austin, TX 512-328-7775
Swiss Premium Dairy Inc
Lebanon, PA 800-222-2129
The Healthy Beverage Company
Doylestown, PA 800-295-1388
Third Street Inc
Louisville, CO 800-636-3790
Tradewinds
Austin, TX
Turkey Hill Dairy Inc
Conestoga, PA 800-693-2479
United Dairy Inc.
Martins Ferry, OH 800-252-1542
White Rock Products Corp
Flushing, NY 800-969-7625
Zeigler's
Lansdale, PA 215-855-5161

Instant

American Instants Inc
Flanders, NJ 973-584-8811
Best Foods
Englewood Cliffs, NJ 201-894-4000
Castella Imports Inc
Brentwood, NY 631-231-5500
Cusa Tea
Boulder, CO
Daymar Select Fine Coffees
El Cajon, CA 800-466-7590
Finlay Extracts & Ingredients USA, Inc.
Florham Park, NJ 800-288-6272
Harris Tea Company
Moorestown, NJ 856-793-0290
Martin Bauer Group
Sacaucus, NJ 201-659-3100
Northwestern Foods
Arden Hills, MN 800-236-4937
Pappy's Sassafras Tea
Columbus Grove, OH 877-659-5110
Prince of Peace
Hayward, CA 800-732-2328
VIP Foods
Flushing, NY 718-821-5330
Weaver Nut Co. Inc.
Ephrata, PA 800-473-2688
Whole Herb Co
Sonoma, CA 707-935-1077

Irish Breakfast

Choice Organic Teas
Seattle, WA 866-972-6879
Harris Tea Company
Moorestown, NJ 856-793-0290

Jasmine

Alpine Pure USA
Falls River, MA 888-332-3392
Blue Willow Tea Co
Berkeley, CA 800-328-0353
Choice Organic Teas
Seattle, WA 866-972-6879

Lemon

Davinci Gourmet LTD
Seattle, WA 800-640-6779
Father's Country Hams
Bremen, KY 270-525-3554

Loose Leaf

Bigelow Tea
Fairfield, CT 888-244-3569
Choice Organic Teas
Seattle, WA 866-972-6879
David Rio
San Francisco, CA 800-454-9605
Great Lakes Tea & Spice
Glen Arbor, MI 877-645-9363
Newby Teas
East Lansing, MI 517-999-0590
Numi Organic Tea
Oakland, CA 888-404-6864

Rishi Tea
Milwaukee, WI 866-747-4483
Takeiya USA
Huntington Beach, CA 714-374-9900
Tea Room
San Leandro, CA. 510-567-8868
The Tao of Tea
Portland, OR 503-736-0119
Thrive Farmers
Roswell, GA 855-553-2763
Tiesta Tea
Chicago, IL 312-202-6800
Vermont Tea & Trading Co Inc
Middlebury, VT. 888-255-9327
Wild Leaf Active Tea
Sparta, NJ 888-605-7564

Mint

Choice Organic Teas
Seattle, WA 866-972-6879
Father's Country Hams
Bremen, KY 270-525-3554
GH Ford Tea Company
Shokan, NY. 845-464-6755
Harris Tea Company
Moorestown, NJ 856-793-0290

Mint Herb

Choice Organic Teas
Seattle, WA 866-972-6879
REBBL
Emeryville, CA. 855-732-2500

Oolong

Astral Extracts
Syosset, NY. 516-496-2505
Bellocq
Brooklyn, NY 347-463-9231
Choice Organic Teas
Seattle, WA 866-972-6879
Harney & Sons Tea Co.
Millerton, NY 800-832-8463
Martin Bauer Group
Sacaucus, NJ. 201-659-3100
SpecialTeas
Norwalk, CT 888-365-6983
Stash Tea Co
Portland, OR 800-547-1514
Templar Food Products
New Providence, NJ 800-883-6752
Whole Herb Co
Sonoma, CA 707-935-1077

Orange Pekoe

Choice Organic Teas
Seattle, WA 866-972-6879

Peppermint Leaf

Choice Organic Teas
Seattle, WA. 866-972-6879
Martin Bauer Group
Sacaucus, NJ. 201-659-3100
Whole Herb Co
Sonoma, CA 707-935-1077

Sun

American Instants Inc
Flanders, NJ 973-584-8811
Atlanta Coffee & Tea Co
. 800-426-4781
Thirs-Tea Corp
Boca Raton, FL. 561-948-5600
Unilever Canada
Toronto, ON 416-415-3000

Juices

Alamance Foods
Burlington, NC
Alfer Laboratories
Chatsworth, CA 818-709-0737
All Juice Food & Beverage
Ankeny, IA 800-736-5674
Aloe Farms Inc
Harlingen, TX. 800-262-6771
Aloe Laboratories
Harlingen, TX. 800-258-5380
Amcan Beverages Inc
American Canyon, CA 800-972-5962
Amcan Industries
Elmsford, NY 914-347-4838
American Soy Products Inc
Saline, MI 734-429-2310
Arctic Beverages
Winnipeg, MB. 866-503-1270
Aseltine Cider Company
Comstock Park, MI. 616-784-6615
Back to Nature Foods
. 855-346-2225
Berkeley Farms
Hayward, CA 800-395-7004
Beverage Capital Corporation
Baltimore, MD 410-242-7404
Birdseye Dairy-Morning Glory
Green Bay, WI. 920-494-5388
Bully Hill Vineyards
Hammondsport, NY 607-868-3610
Cadbury Beverages Canada
Mississauga, ON. 905-712-4121
California Custom Fruits
Baldwin Park, CA. 877-558-0056
Carolina Products
Tampa, FL. 813-313-1800
Cascadian Farm Inc
Sedro Woolley, WA. 360-855-0542
Cell-Nique
Norwalk, CT 888-417-9343
Chase Brothers Dairy
Oxnard, CA. 800-438-6455
Citrosuco North America Inc
Lake Wales, FL 800-356-4592
Citrus International
Winter Park, FL. 407-629-8037
Citrus Service
Winter Garden, FL 407-656-4999
Clover Farms Dairy Co Inc
Reading, PA 800-323-0123
Coastlog Industries
Novi, MI 248-344-9556
Coca-Cola Bottling Co. Consolidated
Charlotte, NC 800-866-2653
Coca-Cola Bottling Company UNITED, Inc.
Birmingham, AB. 800-844-2653
Coca-Cola Co.
Atlanta, GA. 800-438-2653
Coca-Cola European Partners
Uxbridge, Middx, ... 800-418-4223
Cold Hollow Cider Mill
Waterbury Center, VT. 800-327-7537
Commodities Marketing Inc
Clarksburg, NJ 732-516-0700
Conoley Citrus Packers Inc
Winter Garden, FL 407-656-3300
Country Life
Hauppauge, NY 800-645-5768
Country Pure Foods Inc
Akron, OH. 877-995-8423
Crown Regal Wine Cellars
Brooklyn, NY 718-604-1430
Cumberland Dairy
Rosenhayn, NJ 800-257-8484
Cutting Edge Beverages
Boca Raton, FL. 561-347-5860
Cyclone Enterprises Inc
Houston, TX 281-872-0087
Daily Greens LLC
Austin, TX. 512-524-1500
Dairy Maid Dairy LLC
Frederick, MD. 301-663-5114
Damon Industries
Sparks, NV 800-225-3046
Del Monte Fresh Produce Inc.
Coral Gables, FL. 800-950-3683
Del's Lemonade & Refreshments
Cranston, RI 401-463-6190
Empresa La Famosa
Toa Baja, PR 787-251-0060
Empresas La Famosa
Toa Baja, PR 787-251-0060
Everfresh Beverages
Warren, MI 800-323-3416
Farmland Dairies
Wallington, NJ 888-727-6252
Flavouressence Products
Mississauga, ON. 866-209-7778
Florida Key West
Fort Myers, FL 239-694-8787
Four Chimneys Farm Winery Trust
Himrod, NY 607-243-7502
Fuzz East Coast
Englewood Cliffs, NJ 866-438-3893
GLCC Co
Paw Paw, MI. 269-657-3167
Global Beverage Company
Rochester, NY. 585-381-3560
Good-O-Beverages Inc
Bronx, NY. 718-328-6400
Green Spot Packaging
Claremont, CA 800-456-3210
Hallcrest Vineyards
Felton, CA. 831-335-4441
Happy Planet Foods
Burnaby, BC 800-811-3213
Harrisburg Dairies Inc
Harrisburg, PA 800-692-7429
Heck Cellars
Arvin, CA 661-854-6120
Helthe Brands
Austin, TX. 888-311-2157
Heritage Farms Dairy
Murfreesboro, TN. 615-895-2790
Hi-Country Foods Corporation
Selah, WA 509-697-7292
Honest Tea Inc
Atlanta, GA. 800-520-2653
Howard Foods Inc
Danvers, MA. 978-774-6207
Hudson Valley Fruit Juice
Highland, NY 845-691-8061
Hygeia Dairy Company
Corpus Christi, TX 361-854-4561
Inn Foods Inc
Watsonville, CA 800-708-7836
IQ Juice
Bayville, NY. 516-864-0034
Island Aseptics
Byesville, OH 740-685-2548
IZZE Beverage
Boulder, CO 877-476-7380
Jin+Ja
New York, NY 215-690-1470
Johanna Foods Inc.
Flemington, NJ 800-727-6700
Juice Mart
West Hills, CA 877-888-1011
Juice Tyme, Inc.
Chicago, IL 800-236-5823
Juicy Whip Inc
La Verne, CA 909-392-7500
Kan-Pak
Arkansas City, KS. 800-378-1265
Kemach Food Products
Brooklyn, NY 718-272-5655
Keurig Dr Pepper
Plano, TX 800-696-5891
KidsLuv
San Francisco, CA 855-543-7588
King Juice Co
Milwaukee, WI. 414-482-0303
Kleinpeter Farms Dairy LLC
Baton Rouge, LA 225-753-2121
Knouse Foods Co-Op Inc.
Peach Glen, PA. 717-677-8181
Kobu Beverages, LLC,
Brooklyn, NY 718-566-2739
Krier Foods
Random Lake, WI. 920-994-2469
Lakewood Juice Company
Miami, FL. 866-324-5900
Legacy Juice Works
Saratoga Springs, NY 518-583-1108
Lemon-X Corporation
Huntington Station, NY 800-220-1061
Lenox-Martell Inc
Boston, MA. 877-325-2489
Louis Dreyfus Company Citrus Inc
Winter Garden, FL 407-656-1000
Lyons Magnus
Fresno, CA 800-344-7130
M & B Products Inc
Tampa, FL. 800-899-7255
Magnotta Winery Corporation
Vaughan, ON. 800-461-9463
Mamma Chia
Carlsbad, CA. 855-588-2442
Marburger Farm Dairy
Evans City, PA 800-331-1295
Marquis
Los Angeles, CA. 213-250-7414
Marva Maid Dairy
Newport News, VA. 800-768-6243
Maui Gold Pineapple Company
Pukalani, HI 808-877-3805

Mayer Bros
Buffalo, NY....800-696-2928
Mayer's Cider Mill
Webster, NY....800-543-0043
Mayfield Dairy Farms LLC
Athens, TN....800-362-9546
Mayfield Farms and Nursery
Athens, TN....423-746-9859
Mccutcheon Apple Products
Frederick, MD....800-888-7537
Meduri Farms
Dallas, OR....877-388-8800
Meier's Wine Cellars Inc
Cincinnati, OH....800-346-2941
Meramec Vineyards
St James, MO....877-216-9463
Misfit Juicery
Washington, DC....703-465-5355
Mott's
Plano, TX....800-426-4891
Mott's LLP
Plano, TX....800-426-4891
Mountain Valley Products Inc
Sunnyside, WA....509-837-8084
Naked Juice Company
Monrovia, CA....877-858-4237
Nana Mae's Organics
Sebastopol, CA....707-829-7359
Natalie's Orchid Island Juice Co.
Ft. Pierce, FL....800-373-7444
National Grape Co-Op
Westfield, NY....800-340-6870
Nootra Life
Northland Cranberries
Jackson, WI....866-719-5215
Northland Juices
Port Washington, NY....866-719-5215
Northwest Naturals LLC
Bothell, WA....425-881-2200
Oakhurst Dairy
Portland, ME....800-482-0718
Oberweis Dairy Inc
North Aurora, IL....866-623-7934
Odwalla
Sugar Land, TX....800-639-2552
Patience Fruit & Co.
Villeroy, QC
Peace Mountain Natural Beverages
Springfield, MA....413-567-4942
Perfect Foods Inc
Goshen, NY....800-933-3288
Pilgrim Foods
Great Neck, NY....516-466-0522
POM Wonderful LLC
Los Angeles, CA....866-976-6999
Premier Juices
Clearwater, FL....727-533-8200
Pressery
Denver, CO
Purity Dairies LLC
Nashville, TN....615-244-1900
Purity Organic
Oakland, CA....415-440-7777
Pyramid Juice Company
Ashland, OR....541-482-2292
R.J. Corr Naturals
Posen, IL....708-389-4200
Rapunzel Pure Organics
Bloomfield, NJ....800-225-1449
Refresco Beverages US Inc.
Tampa, FL....888-260-3776
Reiter Dairy LLC
Springfield, OH....937-323-5777
SANGARIA USA
Torrance, CA....310-530-2202
Saratoga Spring Water Co
Saratoga Springs, NY....888-426-8642
Scally's Imperial Importing Company Inc
Staten Island, NY....718-983-1938
Schneider's Dairy Inc
Pittsburgh, PA....412-881-3525
Schneider-Valley Farms Inc
Williamsport, PA....570-326-2021
Sherrill Orchards
Arvin, CA....661-858-2035
Shonan USA Inc
Grandview, WA....509-882-5583
Silver Springs Citrus Inc
Howey-in-the-Hills, FL....800-940-2277
Sir Real Foods
White Plains, NY....914-948-9342
Skimpy Cocktails LLC
Carrollton, TX....469-892-7988
Smeltzer Orchard Co
Frankfort, MI....231-882-4421
SoBe Beverages
Norwalk, CT....800-588-0548
Solana Gold Organics
Sebastopol, CA....800-459-1121
St Julian Winery
Paw Paw, MI....800-732-6002
St. James Winery
Saint James, MO....800-280-9463
Starbucks
Seattle, WA....800-782-7282
Stevens Tropical Plantation
West Palm Beach, FL....561-683-4701
Stop & Shop Manufacturing
Readville, MA....508-977-5132
Suja Juice
Oceanside, CA....855-879-7852
Sun Orchard Inc
Miami, FL....800-505-8423
Sun Pac Foods
Brampton, ON....905-792-2700
Sun Tropics Inc
San Ramon, CA....925-380-6324
Sunco & Frenchie
Clifton, NJ....973-478-1011
Sundance Industries
Newburgh, NY....845-565-6065
Sunfresh Beverages Inc.
Birmingham, AL....706-324-0040
Sunlike Juice
Rougemont, QC....866-552-7643
Sunny Avocado
Jamul, CA....800-999-2862
Sunny Delight Beverage Company
Cincinnati, OH
Super Stores Industries
Turlock, CA....209-668-2100
Superbrand Dairies
Miami, FL....305-769-6600
Switch Beverage
Darien, CT....203-202-7383
Tamarack Farms Dairy
Newark, OH....866-221-4141
Tazo Tea
Kent, WA....855-829-6832
Thomas Canning/Maidstone
Maidstone, ON....519-737-1531
Titusville Dairy Products Co
Titusville, PA....800-352-0101
Todhunter Foods
Lake Alfred, FL....863-956-1116
Toft Dairy Inc
Sandusky, OH....800-521-4606
Tradewinds
Austin, TX
Trailblazer Foods
Portland, OR....800-777-7179
Tree Top Inc
Selah, WA....509-697-7251
Treesweet Products
Houston, TX....281-876-3759
Tri-Boro Fruit Co
Fresno, CA....559-486-4141
Triple D Orchards Inc
Empire, MI....231-326-5174
True Organic Product Inc
Helm, CA....800-487-0379
Uncle Matt's Organic
Clermont, FL....833-729-8625
United Juice Companies of America
Vero Beach, FL....772-562-5442
Valley Fig Growers
Fresno, CA....559-237-3893
Valley View Packing Co
Yuba City, CA....530-673-7356
Vegetable Juices Inc
Chicago, IL....888-776-9752
Ventura Coastal LLC
Ventura, CA....805-653-7000
Veryfine Products Inc
Mason, OH
Vive Organic
Venice, CA....877-774-9291
Washington State Juice
Pacoima, CA....818-899-1195
Welch Foods Inc.
Concord, MA....800-340-6870
Welsh Farms
Wallington, NJ....800-221-0663
White House Foods
Winchester, VA....540-662-3401
White Rock Products Corp
Flushing, NY....800-969-7625
Winmix/Natural Care Products
Englewood, FL....941-475-7432
Yoder Dairies
Chesapeake, VA....757-482-4068

Ade

Honest Tea Inc
Atlanta, GA....800-520-2653
Optimal Nutrients
Foster City, CA....707-528-1800
PepsiCo.
Purchase, NY....914-253-2000
Sunfresh Beverages Inc.
Birmingham, AL....706-324-0040

Concentrate

California Custom Fruits
Baldwin Park, CA....877-558-0056
Garden of Flavor LLC
Cleveland, OH....216-702-7991
Wild Aseptics, LLC
Erlanger, KY....877-787-7221

Grape

Arizona Beverage Company
Cincinnati, OH....800-832-3775

Lemon

Arizona Beverage Company
Cincinnati, OH....800-832-3775
Borden Dairy
Dallas, TX....855-311-1583
Natalie's Orchid Island Juice Co.
Ft. Pierce, FL....800-373-7444
Perricone Juices
Beaumont, CA....951-769-7171
Sun Orchard INC
Haines City, FL....877-875-8423
Sunfresh Beverages Inc.
Birmingham, AL....706-324-0040

Orange

Arizona Beverage Company
Cincinnati, OH....800-832-3775
Sunfresh Beverages Inc.
Birmingham, AL....706-324-0040

Aloe

Alfer Laboratories
Chatsworth, CA....818-709-0737
Aloe Farms Inc
Harlingen, TX....800-262-6771
Aloe Laboratories
Harlingen, TX....800-258-5380
Detoxwater
Brooklyn, NY....888-887-4318
Emerling International Foods
Buffalo, NY....716-833-7381
JJ Martin Group
Newark, NJ....862-240-1813
Lakewood Juice Co.
Miami, FL....866-324-5900
Pocas International
South Hackensack, NJ....201-941-7900
Superbrand Dairies
Miami, FL....305-769-6600
Vink & Beri
Montgomeryville, PA....215-654-5252

Apple

All Juice Food & Beverage
Ankeny, IA....800-736-5674
Apple & Eve LLC
Port Washington, NY....800-969-8018
Aseltine Cider Company
Comstock Park, MI....616-784-6615
Birdseye Dairy-Morning Glory
Green Bay, WI....920-494-5388
Cal India Foods Inc
Chino, CA....909-613-1660
Carolina Products
Tampa, FL....813-313-1800
Cherry Central Cooperative, Inc.
Traverse City, MI....231-946-1860

Citrosuco North America Inc
Lake Wales, FL 800-356-4592
Cold Hollow Cider Mill
Waterbury Center, VT 800-327-7537
Coloma Frozen Foods Inc
Coloma, MI 800-642-2723
Country Pure Foods Inc
Akron, OH 877-995-8423
Erba Food Products
Brooklyn, NY 718-272-7700
Florida Fruit Juices
Chicago, IL 773-586-6200
Golden Town Apple Products
Rougemont, QC 866-552-7643
Green Spot Packaging
Claremont, CA 800-456-3210
Hazel Creek Orchards
Mt Airy, GA 706-754-4899
Heritage Farms Dairy
Murfreesboro, TN 615-895-2790
Hi-Country Foods Corporation
Selah, WA 509-697-7292
Knouse Foods Co-Op Inc.
Peach Glen, PA 717-677-8181
Lakewood Juice Co.
Miami, FL 866-324-5900
Lassonde Pappas & Company, Inc.
Carneys Point, NJ 800-257-7019
Legacy Juice Works
Saratoga Springs, NY 518-583-1108
M & B Products Inc
Tampa, FL 800-899-7255
Madera Enterprises Inc
Madera, CA 800-507-9555
Materne North America
New York, NY 212-675-7881
Mayer Bros
Buffalo, NY 800-696-2928
Mayfield Farms and Nursery
Athens, TN 423-746-9859
Mccutcheon Apple Products
Frederick, MD 800-888-7537
Merlinos
Canon City, CO 719-275-5558
Mott's
Plano, TX 800-426-4891
Mott's LLP
Plano, TX 800-426-4891
Mountain Valley Products Inc
Sunnyside, WA 509-837-8084
Murray Cider Co Inc
Roanoke, VA 540-977-9000
Nana Mae's Organics
Sebastopol, CA 707-829-7359
Nestle USA Inc
Glendale, CA 800-225-2270
Old Dutch Mustard Company
Great Neck, NY 516-466-0522
Old Orchard Brands, LLC
Sparta, MI 800-330-2173
Perricone Juices
Beaumont, CA 951-769-7171
Rosenberger's Dairies
Hatfield, PA 800-355-9074
Smeltzer Orchard Co
Frankfort, MI 231-882-4421
Solana Gold Organics
Sebastopol, CA 800-459-1121
Sunlike Juice
Rougemont, QC 866-552-7643
Tree Top Inc
Selah, WA 509-697-7251
Triple D Orchards Inc
Empire, MI 231-326-5174
True Organic Product Inc
Helm, CA 800-487-0379
Valley View Packing Co
Yuba City, CA 530-673-7356
White House Foods
Winchester, VA 540-662-3401
Yoder Dairies
Chesapeake, VA 757-482-4068

Bottled

Apple & Eve LLC
Port Washington, NY 800-969-8018
Aseltine Cider Company
Comstock Park, MI 616-784-6615
Broughton Foods LLC
El Paso, TX 800-395-7004
Carolina Products
Tampa, FL 813-313-1800
Northland Juices
Port Washington, NY 866-719-5215

Boxed

Cloverland/Green Spring Dairy
Baltimore, MD 800-876-6455
Emerling International Foods
Buffalo, NY 716-833-7381

Canned

Emerling International Foods
Buffalo, NY 716-833-7381
Florida's Natural Growers
Lake Wales, FL 888-657-6600
Greenwood Associates
Niles, IL 847-579-5500
Langer Juice Co Inc
City of Industry, CA 626-336-3100
Manzana Products Co.
Sebastopol, CA 707-823-5313
Mason County Fruit Packers Cooperative
Hart, MI 231-873-7504
Mccutcheon Apple Products
Frederick, MD 800-888-7537
Mrs Clark's Foods
Ankeny, IA 800-736-5674
Noel Corp
Yakima, WA 509-248-1313
Old Dutch Mustard Company
Great Neck, NY 516-466-0522
Sunlike Juice
Rougemont, QC 866-552-7643
Triple D Orchards Inc
Empire, MI 231-326-5174

Chilled

Emerling International Foods
Buffalo, NY 716-833-7381

Concentrate

Citrosuco North America Inc
Lake Wales, FL 800-356-4592
GLCC Co
Paw Paw, MI 269-657-3167
Green Spot Packaging
Claremont, CA 800-456-3210
Mountain Valley Products Inc
Sunnyside, WA 509-837-8084
Pacific Coast Fruit Co
Portland, OR 503-234-6411
Small Planet Foods
Minneapolis, MN 800-624-4123
Sun Pac Foods
Brampton, ON 905-792-2700
Tree Top Inc
Selah, WA 509-697-7251
Valley View Packing Co
Yuba City, CA 530-673-7356

Frozen

Greenwood Associates
Niles, IL 847-579-5500
Old Dutch Mustard Company
Great Neck, NY 516-466-0522
Old Orchard Brands, LLC
Sparta, MI 800-330-2173
Smeltzer Orchard Co
Frankfort, MI 231-882-4421
Triple D Orchards Inc
Empire, MI 231-326-5174

Glass-Packed

Emerling International Foods
Buffalo, NY 716-833-7381

Apple Cider

CideRoad, LLC
Mendham, NJ 973-543-9003
Five Star Foodies
Cincinnati, OH
Lassonde Pappas & Company, Inc.
Carneys Point, NJ 800-257-7019
Lost Trail Root Beer
Louisburg, KS 800-748-7765
Parmenter's Northville Cider Mill
Northville, MI 248-349-3181
Shawnee Canning Co
Cross Junction, VA 800-713-1414
Shire City Herbals
Pittsfield, MA 413-213-6702
Spotted Tavern Winery & Dodd's Cider Mill
Hartwood, VA 540-752-4453
Talbott Farms
Palisade, CO 970-464-5656
Wild Aseptics, LLC
Erlanger, KY 877-787-7221
Zeigler's
Lansdale, PA 215-855-5161

Sparkling

Clos Saint-Denis
Richelieu, QC 450-645-9777
Lost Trail Root Beer
Louisburg, KS 800-748-7765

Apricot

Valley View Packing Co
Yuba City, CA 530-673-7356

Canned

Emerling International Foods
Buffalo, NY 716-833-7381
Greenwood Associates
Niles, IL 847-579-5500

Concentrate

Valley View Packing Co
Yuba City, CA 530-673-7356

Frozen

Greenwood Associates
Niles, IL 847-579-5500

Glass-Packed

Emerling International Foods
Buffalo, NY 716-833-7381
Greenwood Associates
Niles, IL 847-579-5500

Beet

Emerling International Foods
Buffalo, NY 716-833-7381
Legacy Juice Works
Saratoga Springs, NY 518-583-1108
Vegetable Juices Inc
Chicago, IL 888-776-9752

Blueberry

Blueberry Store
Grand Junction, MI 877-654-2400
Hazel Creek Orchards
Mt Airy, GA 706-754-4899
Jasper Wyman & Son
Topsfield, MA 978-887-7472
Lakewood Juice Co.
Miami, FL 866-324-5900
Lassonde Pappas & Company, Inc.
Carneys Point, NJ 800-257-7019
Patience Fruit & Co.
Villeroy, QC

Carrot

Emerling International Foods
Buffalo, NY 716-833-7381
Lakewood Juice Co.
Miami, FL 866-324-5900
Post Familie Vineyards
Altus, AR 800-275-8423
Vegetable Juices Inc
Chicago, IL 888-776-9752

Cherry

Erba Food Products
Brooklyn, NY 718-272-7700
Greenwood Associates
Niles, IL 847-579-5500
Hazel Creek Orchards
Mt Airy, GA 706-754-4899
Lakewood Juice Co.
Miami, FL 866-324-5900
Langer Juice Co Inc
City of Industry, CA 626-336-3100
M & B Fruit Juice Co
Akron, OH 330-253-7465
Manzana Products Co.
Sebastopol, CA 707-823-5313

Merlinos
Canon City, CO 719-275-5558
Sunlike Juice
Rougemont, QC 866-552-7643

Canned

Emerling International Foods
Buffalo, NY 716-833-7381

Concentrate

GLCC Co
Paw Paw, MI 269-657-3167

Frozen

Emerling International Foods
Buffalo, NY 716-833-7381
Milne Fruit Products Inc
Prosser, WA 509-786-2611

Glass-Packed

Emerling International Foods
Buffalo, NY 716-833-7381
Greenwood Associates
Niles, IL 847-579-5500
Minute Maid Company
Atlanta, GA 800-520-2653

Citrus Blends

Apac Chemical Corporation
Arcadia, CA 866-849-2722
Apple & Eve LLC
Port Washington, NY 800-969-8018
Citrus International
Winter Park, FL 407-629-8037
Citrus Service
Winter Garden, FL 407-656-4999
Conoley Citrus Packers Inc
Winter Garden, FL 407-656-3300
Emerling International Foods
Buffalo, NY 716-833-7381
Florida's Natural Growers
Lake Wales, FL 888-657-6600
Fresh Juice Delivery
Beverly Hills, CA 310-271-7373
Galliker Dairy Co
Johnstown, PA 800-477-6455
Green Spot Packaging
Claremont, CA 800-456-3210
Island Aseptics
Byesville, OH 740-685-2548
Johanna Foods Inc.
Flemington, NJ 800-727-6700
Kennesaw Fruit & Juice
Pompano Beach, FL 800-949-0371
Key Colony Red Parrot Juice
Lemont, IL 844-783-8572
Minute Maid Company
Atlanta, GA 800-520-2653
Sales USA
Salado, TX 800-766-7344
Saratoga Spring Water Co
Saratoga Springs, NY 888-426-8642
Silver Springs Citrus Inc
Howey-in-the-Hills, FL 800-940-2277
Southern Gardens Citrus
Clewiston, FL 863-983-3030
Sun Orchard INC
Haines City, FL 877-875-8423
Sunlike Juice
Rougemont, QC 866-552-7643
Superbrand Dairies
Miami, FL 305-769-6600
T G Lee Dairy
Orlando, FL 800-432-4872
Ventura Coastal LLC
Ventura, CA 805-653-7000
World Citrus West
Fullerton, CA 714-870-6171

Coconut

Amy & Brian Naturals
Buena Park, CA
Buddha Brands
Montreal, QC 514-382-3805
C2O Pure Coconut Water
Long Beach, CA 877-295-0873
Coco Lopez Inc
Miramar, FL 800-341-2242
Commodities Marketing Inc
Clarksburg, NJ 732-516-0700
Genius Juice
Torrance, CA 800-682-7790
Lakewood Juice Co.
Miami, FL 866-324-5900
Pocas International
South Hackensack, NJ 201-941-7900
Pure Life Organic Foods
Las Vegas, NV 708-990-5817
Vink & Beri
Montgomeryville, PA 215-654-5252

Concentrates

Chase Brothers Dairy
Oxnard, CA 800-438-6455
Citrosuco North America Inc
Lake Wales, FL 800-356-4592
Citrus Service
Winter Garden, FL 407-656-4999
Del's Lemonade & Refreshments
Cranston, RI 401-463-6190
Delano Growers Grape Products
Delano, CA 661-725-3255
Fee Brothers
Rochester, NY 800-961-3337
GLCC Co
Paw Paw, MI 269-657-3167
Green Spot Packaging
Claremont, CA 800-456-3210
Imperial Flavors Beverage Co
Milwaukee, WI 414-536-7788
Juice Tyme, Inc.
Chicago, IL 800-236-5823
KERR Concentrates Inc
Salem, OR 800-910-5377
Lemon-X Corporation
Huntington Station, NY 800-220-1061
Louis Dreyfus Company Citrus Inc
Winter Garden, FL 407-656-1000
Main Squeeze
Columbia, MO 573-817-5616
Maui Gold Pineapple Company
Pukalani, HI 808-877-3805
Merci Spring Water
Maryland Heights, MO 314-872-9323
Minute Maid Company
Atlanta, GA 800-520-2653
Mountain Valley Products Inc
Sunnyside, WA 509-837-8084
Northwest Naturals LLC
Bothell, WA 425-881-2200
Ntc Marketing
Williamsville, NY 800-333-1637
Orange Bang Inc
Sylmar, CA 818-833-1000
Pacific Coast Fruit Co
Portland, OR 503-234-6411
RFi Ingredients
Blauvelt, NY 800-962-7663
Rocket Products Company
Fenton, MO 800-325-9567
Sea Breeze Fruit Flavors
Towaco, NJ 800-732-2733
Silver Springs Citrus Inc
Howey-in-the-Hills, FL 800-940-2277
Sun Pac Foods
Brampton, ON 905-792-2700
Sunsweet Growers Inc.
Yuba City, CA 800-417-2253
Tastepoint
Philadelphia, PA 800-363-5286
Tone Products Inc
Melrose Park, IL 800-536-8663
Tova Industries LLC
Louisville, KY 888-532-8682
Tropicana Products Inc.
Chicago, IL 800-237-7799
Valley Fig Growers
Fresno, CA 559-237-3893
Valley View Packing Co
Yuba City, CA 530-673-7356
Vegetable Juices Inc
Chicago, IL 888-776-9752
Vie-Del Co
Fresno, CA 559-834-2525
Welch Foods Inc
Concord, MA 800-340-6870
Welch Foods Inc.
Concord, MA 800-340-6870

Cranberry

Apple & Eve LLC
Port Washington, NY 800-969-8018
Atoka Cranberries, Inc.
Manseau, Quebec, QC 819-356-2001
Delectable Gourmet LLC
Deer Park, NY 800-696-1350
Erba Food Products
Brooklyn, NY 718-272-7700
Key Colony Red Parrot Juice
Lemont, IL 844-783-8572
Lakewood Juice Co.
Miami, FL 866-324-5900
Langer Juice Co Inc
City of Industry, CA 626-336-3100
Lassonde Pappas & Company, Inc.
Carneys Point, NJ 800-257-7019
Mccutcheon Apple Products
Frederick, MD 800-888-7537
Northland Juices
Port Washington, NY 866-719-5215
Old Orchard Brands, LLC
Sparta, MI 800-330-2173
Patience Fruit & Co.
Villeroy, QC
Sunlike Juice
Rougemont, QC 866-552-7643
Welch Foods Inc.
Concord, MA 800-340-6870

Bottled

Apple & Eve LLC
Port Washington, NY 800-969-8018
Northland Juices
Port Washington, NY 866-719-5215

Boxed

Emerling International Foods
Buffalo, NY 716-833-7381

Canned

Emerling International Foods
Buffalo, NY 716-833-7381
Mccutcheon Apple Products
Frederick, MD 800-888-7537

Concentrate

GLCC Co
Paw Paw, MI 269-657-3167
Pacific Coast Fruit Co
Portland, OR 503-234-6411
Sea Breeze Fruit Flavors
Towaco, NJ 800-732-2733
Simply Incredible Foods
Port Edwards, WI 715-697-6232
Small Planet Foods
Minneapolis, MN 800-624-4123

Frozen

Milne Fruit Products Inc
Prosser, WA 509-786-2611
Old Orchard Brands, LLC
Sparta, MI 800-330-2173

Glass-Packed

Emerling International Foods
Buffalo, NY 716-833-7381

Dietetic

Boissons Miami Pomor
Longueuil, QC 877-977-3744
Florida Natural Flavors
Casselberry, FL 800-872-5979
Healthmate Products
Highland Park, IL 847-579-1051
Southern Gardens Citrus
Clewiston, FL 863-983-3030

Drink

Concentrate

Beverage Flavors Intl
Chicago, IL 773-248-3860
Commodities Marketing Inc
Clarksburg, NJ 732-516-0700
Wild Aseptics, LLC
Erlanger, KY 877-787-7221

Fruit

3V Company
Brooklyn, NY 718-858-7333
A. Lassonde Inc.
Rougemont, QC 866-552-7643
Alca Trading Co.
Miami, FL. 305-265-8331
All American Seasonings
Denver, CO 303-623-2320
All Juice Food & Beverage
Ankeny, IA 800-736-5674
ALO Drink
South San Francisco, CA 650-616-7777
Amcan Beverages Inc
American Canyon, CA 800-972-5962
Andros Foods North America
Mount Jackson, VA. 844-426-3767
Apple & Eve LLC
Port Washington, NY 800-969-8018
Aseltine Cider Company
Comstock Park, MI. 616-784-6615
B.M. Lawrence & Company
San Francisco, CA 415-981-2926
Batavia Wine Cellars
Canandaigua, NY 585-396-7600
Birdseye Dairy-Morning Glory
Green Bay, WI. 920-494-5388
Brothers International Food Corporation
Rochester, NY. 585-343-3007
Bully Hill Vineyards
Hammondsport, NY 607-868-3610
Cal India Foods Inc
Chino, CA. 909-613-1660
Carolina Products
Tampa, FL. 813-313-1800
Century Foods Intl LLC
Sparta, WI. 800-269-1901
Ceres Fruit Juices
San Diego, CA 800-778-6498
Chase Brothers Dairy
Oxnard, CA. 800-438-6455
Chiquita Brands LLC.
Fort Lauderdale, FL 954-924-5700
Citrosuco North America Inc
Lake Wales, FL. 800-356-4592
Cold Hollow Cider Mill
Waterbury Center, VT. 800-327-7537
Country Pure Foods Inc
Akron, OH. 877-995-8423
Crown Regal Wine Cellars
Brooklyn, NY 718-604-1430
Cutrale Citrus Juices
Auburndale, FL. 863-965-5000
Del's Lemonade & Refreshments
Cranston, RI 401-463-6190
Erba Food Products
Brooklyn, NY 718-272-7700
Everfresh Beverages
Warren, MI 800-323-3416
Faribault Foods, Inc.
Fairbault, MN 507-331-1400
Fizzy Lizzy
Jersey City, NJ 800-203-9336
Florida Fruit Juices
Chicago, IL 773-586-6200
Florida Key West
Fort Myers, FL 239-694-8787
Four Chimneys Farm Winery Trust
Himrod, NY 607-243-7502
Fruigees
Los Angeles, CA
Galliker Dairy Co
Johnstown, PA. 800-477-6455
Global Beverage Company
Rochester, NY. 585-381-3560
Golden Town Apple Products
Rougemont, QC 866-552-7643
Great Western Juice Co
Maple Heights, OH. 800-321-9180
Hale Indian River Groves
Vero Beach, FL. 800-562-4502
Harrisburg Dairies Inc
Harrisburg, PA 800-692-7429
Healthee
Arcadia, CA 626-574-1719
Heck Cellars
Arvin, CA. 661-854-6120
Heineman Winery
Put In Bay, OH 419-285-2811
Heritage Farms Dairy
Murfreesboro, TN. 615-895-2790
Hi-Country Foods Corporation
Selah, WA 509-697-7292
Hudson Valley Fruit Juice
Highland, NY 845-691-8061
Hygeia Dairy Company
Corpus Christi, TX 361-854-4561
Inn Foods Inc
Watsonville, CA 800-708-7836
IQ Juice
Bayville, NY. 516-864-0034
Island Aseptics
Byesville, OH 740-685-2548
Lakewood Juice Co.
Miami, FL. 866-324-5900
Leeward Resources
Baltimore, MD 410-837-9003
Leonard Fountain Specialties
Detroit, MI 313-891-4141
Louis Dreyfus Company Citrus Inc
Winter Garden, FL 407-656-1000
Ludfords
Riverside, CA 951-823-0306
Madera Enterprises Inc
Madera, CA. 800-507-9555
Malibu Beach Beverage
Roswell, GA 877-825-0655
Mamma Chia
Carlsbad, CA. 855-588-2442
Maui Gold Pineapple Company
Pukalani, HI 808-877-3805
Mayer Bros
Buffalo, NY. 800-696-2928
Mayer's Cider Mill
Webster, NY 800-543-0043
Mayfield Farms and Nursery
Athens, TN 423-746-9859
Mccutcheon Apple Products
Frederick, MD. 800-888-7537
Meduri Farms
Dallas, OR. 877-388-8800
Meramec Vineyards
St James, MO 877-216-9463
Merlinos
Canon City, CO. 719-275-5558
Monarch Beverage Company
Atlanta, GA. 800-241-3732
Mott's LLP
Plano, TX 800-426-4891
Mountain Valley Products Inc
Sunnyside, WA 509-837-8084
Mrs. Denson's Cookie Company
Ukiah, CA. 800-219-3199
Murray Cider Co Inc
Roanoke, VA. 540-977-9000
Nana Mae's Organics
Sebastopol, CA 707-829-7359
Natalie's Orchid Island Juice Co.
Ft. Pierce, FL. 800-373-7444
National Grape Co-Op
Westfield, NY 800-340-6870
Nectar Island
St Paul, MN. 651-292-9963
Northland Cranberries
Jackson, WI. 866-719-5215
Northland Juices
Port Washington, NY 866-719-5215
Northwest Naturals LLC
Bothell, WA. 425-881-2200
Ntc Marketing
Williamsville, NY. 800-333-1637
Oatworks
New York, NY 646-624-2400
Old Orchard Brands, LLC
Sparta, MI 800-330-2173
PepsiCo.
Purchase, NY 914-253-2000
Point Group
Satellite Beach, FL 888-272-1249
Prairie Farms Dairy Inc.
Edwardsville, IL 618-659-5700
Premier Juices
Clearwater, FL 727-533-8200
Purity Dairies LLC
Nashville, TN 615-244-1900
Quality Kitchen Corporation
Wyoming, DE 302-697-3118
R.J. Corr Naturals
Posen, IL. 708-389-4200
Reiter Dairy LLC
Springfield, OH. 937-323-5777
River Hills Harvest
Minneapolis, MN 855-662-3779
Rosenberger's Dairies
Hatfield, PA. 800-355-9074
Sambazon
San Clemente, CA. 877-726-2296
SANGARIA USA
Torrance, CA. 310-530-2202
Saratoga Spring Water Co
Saratoga Springs, NY 888-426-8642
Schneider's Dairy Inc
Pittsburgh, PA 412-881-3525
Schneider-Valley Farms Inc
Williamsport, PA. 570-326-2021
Shoreline Fruit
Traverse City, MI 800-836-3972
Silver Springs Citrus Inc
Howey-in-the-Hills, FL 800-940-2277
Smart Juice
Whitehall, PA 610-443-1506
Smeltzer Orchard Co
Frankfort, MI 231-882-4421
Smith Dairy
Orrville, OH 800-776-7076
Solana Gold Organics
Sebastopol, CA 800-459-1121
St Julian Winery
Paw Paw, MI. 800-732-6002
St. James Winery
Saint James, MO. 800-280-9463
Stevens Tropical Plantation
West Palm Beach, FL 561-683-4701
Stone Hill Winery
Hermann, MO 573-486-2221
Sun Opta Inc.
Mississauga, ON. 952-820-2518
Sun Pac Foods
Brampton, ON. 905-792-2700
Sun Tropics Inc
San Ramon, CA 925-380-6324
Sunlike Juice
Rougemont, QC 866-552-7643
Sunny Avocado
Jamul, CA. 800-999-2862
Sunsweet Growers Inc.
Yuba City, CA. 800-417-2253
Super Stores Industries
Turlock, CA 209-668-2100
Superbrand Dairies
Miami, FL. 305-769-6600
Swiss Premium Dairy Inc
Lebanon, PA 800-222-2129
Tamarack Farms Dairy
Newark, OH 866-221-4141
Titusville Dairy Products Co
Titusville, PA 800-352-0101
Todhunter Foods
Lake Alfred, FL. 863-956-1116
Toft Dairy Inc
Sandusky, OH. 800-521-4606
Tree Top Inc
Selah, WA 509-697-7251
Treesweet Products
Houston, TX. 281-876-3759
Tri-Boro Fruit Co
Fresno, CA 559-486-4141
Triple D Orchards Inc
Empire, MI 231-326-5174
True Organic Product Inc
Helm, CA 800-487-0379
Valley Fig Growers
Fresno, CA 559-237-3893
Valley View Packing Co
Yuba City, CA. 530-673-7356
Ventura Coastal LLC
Ventura, CA. 805-653-7000
Venture Vineyards
Lodi, NY. 888-635-6277
Veryfine Products Inc
Mason, OH
Welch Foods Inc
Concord, MA 800-340-6870
Welch Foods Inc.
Concord, MA 800-340-6870
White Rock Products Corp
Flushing, NY. 800-969-7625
Wild Poppy
Los Angeles, CA. 310-384-1004
Winmix/Natural Care Products
Englewood, FL 941-475-7432
World Citrus West
Fullerton, CA 714-870-6171
Yoder Dairies
Chesapeake, VA 757-482-4068

Bottled

Apple & Eve LLC
Port Washington, NY 800-969-8018
Aseltine Cider Company
Comstock Park, MI 616-784-6615
Bully Hill Vineyards
Hammondsport, NY 607-868-3610
Carolina Products
Tampa, FL 813-313-1800
Lakewood Juice Co.
Miami, FL 866-324-5900

Canned

B.M. Lawrence & Company
San Francisco, CA 415-981-2926
Blue Monkey
Long Beach, CA
Mccutcheon Apple Products
Frederick, MD 800-888-7537
Northland Cranberries
Jackson, WI 866-719-5215
SANGARIA USA
Torrance, CA 310-530-2202
Silver Springs Citrus Inc
Howey-in-the-Hills, FL 800-940-2277
Sun Pac Foods
Brampton, ON 905-792-2700
Triple D Orchards Inc
Empire, MI 231-326-5174

Concentrate

American Fruits & Flavors
Pacoima, CA 818-899-9574
Citrosuco North America Inc
Lake Wales, FL 800-356-4592
Felbro Food Products
Los Angeles, CA 323-936-5266
GLCC Co
Paw Paw, MI 269-657-3167
Green Spot Packaging
Claremont, CA 800-456-3210
Lakewood Juice Co.
Miami, FL 866-324-5900
Louis Dreyfus Company Citrus Inc
Winter Garden, FL 407-656-1000
Mountain Valley Products Inc
Sunnyside, WA 509-837-8084
Pacific Coast Fruit Co
Portland, OR 503-234-6411
Sea Breeze Fruit Flavors
Towaco, NJ 800-732-2733
Shoreline Fruit
Traverse City, MI 800-836-3972
Tree Top Inc
Selah, WA 509-697-7251
Valley Fig Growers
Fresno, CA 559-237-3893
Valley View Packing Co
Yuba City, CA 530-673-7356
Ventura Coastal LLC
Ventura, CA 805-653-7000

Frozen

Citrosuco North America Inc
Lake Wales, FL 800-356-4592
Del's Lemonade & Refreshments
Cranston, RI 401-463-6190
Emerling International Foods
Buffalo, NY 716-833-7381
Florida Natural Flavors
Casselberry, FL 800-872-5979
Florida's Natural Growers
Lake Wales, FL 888-657-6600
Greenwood Associates
Niles, IL 847-579-5500
Harrisburg Dairies Inc
Harrisburg, PA 800-692-7429
Inn Foods Inc
Watsonville, CA 800-708-7836
Lt Blender's Frozen Concoctions
Galveston, TX 409-765-5666
Minute Maid Company
Atlanta, GA 800-520-2653
Old Orchard Brands, LLC
Sparta, MI 800-330-2173
Saratoga Spring Water Co
Saratoga Springs, NY 888-426-8642
Smeltzer Orchard Co
Frankfort, MI 231-882-4421
Triple D Orchards Inc
Empire, MI 231-326-5174
Unique Ingredients LLC
Gold Canyon, AZ 480-983-2498
Wild Fruitz Beverages
Ambler, PA 888-688-7632

Glass-Packed

Lakewood Juice Co.
Miami, FL 866-324-5900
Lorina, Inc.
Coral Gables, FL 305-779-3085
Northland Cranberries
Jackson, WI 866-719-5215

Refrigerated

Silver Springs Citrus Inc
Howey-in-the-Hills, FL 800-940-2277

Fruit & Vegetable

Aileen Quirk & Sons Inc
Kansas City, MO 816-471-4580
Apple & Eve LLC
Port Washington, NY 800-969-8018
Arcadia Dairy Farms Inc
Arden, NC 828-684-3556
Astral Extracts
Syosset, NY 516-496-2505
Barsotti Family Juice Co.
Camino, CA 530-622-4629
Beckman & Gast Co
St Henry, OH 419-678-4195
Bevco Sales International Inc.
Surrey, BC 800-663-0090
Beverage Capital Corporation
Baltimore, MD 410-242-7404
Blue Moon Foods
White River Junction, VT 802-295-1165
Cal-Tex Citrus Juice LP
Houston, TX 800-231-0133
Campbell Soup Co.
Camden, NJ 800-257-8443
Citrosuco North America Inc
Lake Wales, FL 800-356-4592
Community Orchards
Fort Dodge, IA 888-573-8212
Florida's Natural Growers
Lake Wales, FL 888-657-6600
Fresh Juice Delivery
Beverly Hills, CA 310-271-7373
Fresh Samantha
Saco, ME 800-658-4635
Great Western Juice Co
Maple Heights, OH 800-321-9180
Greenwood Associates
Niles, IL 847-579-5500
H R Nicholson Co
Baltimore, MD 800-638-3514
Hanover Foods Corp
Hanover, PA 717-632-6000
Hudson Valley Fruit Juice
Highland, NY 845-691-8061
Indian River Select® LLC
Stuart, FL 888-373-7426
Island Aseptics
Byesville, OH 740-685-2548
Jel Sert
West Chicago, IL 800-323-2592
Key Colony Red Parrot Juice
Lemont, IL 844-783-8572
Lakewood Juice Co.
Miami, FL 866-324-5900
Lakewood Juice Company
Miami, FL 866-324-5900
Lane's Dairy
El Paso, TX 915-772-6700
Langer Juice Co Inc
City of Industry, CA 626-336-3100
Lenox-Martell Inc
Boston, MA 877-325-2489
M & B Fruit Juice Co
Akron, OH 330-253-7465
Manzana Products Co.
Sebastopol, CA 707-823-5313
Mayfield Farms and Nursery
Athens, TN 423-746-9859
Meier's Wine Cellars Inc
Cincinnati, OH 800-346-2941
Minute Maid Company
Atlanta, GA 800-520-2653
Mrs Clark's Foods
Ankeny, IA 800-736-5674
Noel Corp
Yakima, WA 509-248-1313
Ocean Spray International
Lakeville-Middleboro, MA 800-662-3263
Old Dutch Mustard Company
Great Neck, NY 516-466-0522
Olympic Foods
Spokane, WA 509-455-8059
Paw Paw Grape Juice Company
Paw Paw, MI 800-756-5357
Plaidberry Company
Vista, CA 760-727-5403
Post Familie Vineyards
Altus, AR 800-275-8423
Reiter Dairy
Newport, KY 800-544-6455
RFi Ingredients
Blauvelt, NY 800-962-7663
Sales USA
Salado, TX 800-766-7344
Schepps Dairy
Dallas, TX 800-395-7004
Seneca Juice
Marion, NY 315-926-3228
Southern Gardens Citrus
Clewiston, FL 863-983-3030
Tamarack Farms Dairy
Newark, OH 866-221-4141
Ultra Seal
New Paltz, NY 845-255-2490
Unique Ingredients LLC
Gold Canyon, AZ 480-983-2498
Vegetable Juices Inc
Chicago, IL 888-776-9752

Bottled

Apple & Eve LLC
Port Washington, NY 800-969-8018
Beverage Capital Corporation
Baltimore, MD 410-242-7404
Lassonde Pappas & Company, Inc.
Carneys Point, NJ 800-257-7019
Polar Beverages Inc.
Worcester, MA 800-734-9800

Canned

B.M. Lawrence & Company
San Francisco, CA 415-981-2926
Beverage Capital Corporation
Baltimore, MD 410-242-7404
Polar Beverages Inc.
Worcester, MA 800-734-9800

Concentrate

Astral Extracts
Syosset, NY 516-496-2505
Citrosuco North America Inc
Lake Wales, FL 800-356-4592
Emerling International Foods
Buffalo, NY 716-833-7381
Wild Aseptics, LLC
Erlanger, KY 877-787-7221

Frozen

Citrosuco North America Inc
Lake Wales, FL 800-356-4592
Ludfords
Riverside, CA 951-823-0306

Refrigerated

Lakewood Juice Co.
Miami, FL 866-324-5900

Fruit Punch

Arizona Beverage Company
Cincinnati, OH 800-832-3775
Borden Dairy
Dallas, TX 855-311-1583
Erba Food Products
Brooklyn, NY 718-272-7700
Reilly Dairy & Food Company
Tampa, FL 813-839-8458
Rocket Products Company
Fenton, MO 800-325-9567
Sunfresh Beverages Inc.
Birmingham, AL 706-324-0040
Sunlike Juice
Rougemont, QC 866-552-7643

Trailblazer Foods
Portland, OR 800-777-7179
Triple H Food Processors Inc
Riverside, CA 951-352-5700
United Dairy Inc.
Martins Ferry, OH 800-252-1542

Concentrate

Better Beverages Inc
Cerritos, CA 800-344-5219
Mayer Bros
Buffalo, NY 800-696-2928

Garlic

Emerling International Foods
Buffalo, NY 716-833-7381
Howard Foods Inc
Danvers, MA 978-774-6207
Vegetable Juices Inc
Chicago, IL 888-776-9752

Grape

A.W. Jantzi & Sons
Wellesley, ON 519-656-2400
Arcadia Dairy Farms Inc
Arden, NC 828-684-3556
Bully Hill Vineyards
Hammondsport, NY 607-868-3610
Country Pure Foods Inc
Akron, OH 877-995-8423
Crown Regal Wine Cellars
Brooklyn, NY 718-604-1430
Everfresh Beverages
Warren, MI 800-323-3416
Florida Fruit Juices
Chicago, IL 773-586-6200
Florida's Natural Growers
Lake Wales, FL 888-657-6600
Four Chimneys Farm Winery Trust
Himrod, NY 607-243-7502
Green Spot Packaging
Claremont, CA 800-456-3210
Greenwood Associates
Niles, IL 847-579-5500
Growers Cooperative Juice Co
Westfield, NY 716-326-3161
Hillcrest Orchard
Lake Placid, FL 865-397-5273
Kayco
Bayonne, NJ 718-369-4600
Kedem
Bayonne, NJ 718-369-4600
Lakewood Juice Co.
Miami, FL 866-324-5900
Langer Juice Co Inc
City of Industry, CA 626-336-3100
Lassonde Pappas & Company, Inc.
Carneys Point, NJ 800-257-7019
M & B Fruit Juice Co
Akron, OH 330-253-7465
Madera Enterprises Inc
Madera, CA 800-507-9555
Manzana Products Co.
Sebastopol, CA 707-823-5313
Mayer Bros
Buffalo, NY 800-696-2928
Mayer's Cider Mill
Webster, NY 800-543-0043
Mccutcheon Apple Products
Frederick, MD 800-888-7537
Meier's Wine Cellars Inc
Cincinnati, OH 800-346-2941
Meramec Vineyards
St James, MO 877-216-9463
Merlinos
Canon City, CO 719-275-5558
Minute Maid Company
Atlanta, GA 800-520-2653
Paklab Products
Boucherville, QC 888-946-3233
Post Familie Vineyards
Altus, AR 800-275-8423
Royal Wine Corp
Bayonne, NJ 718-384-2400
St Julian Winery
Paw Paw, MI 800-732-6002
St. James Winery
Saint James, MO 800-280-9463
Sunlike Juice
Rougemont, QC 866-552-7643
Tree Top Inc
Selah, WA 509-697-7251
True Organic Product Inc
Helm, CA 800-487-0379
Venture Vineyards
Lodi, NY 888-635-6277
Welch Foods Inc.
Concord, MA 800-340-6870

Bottled

Broughton Foods LLC
El Paso, TX 800-395-7004
Manischewitz Co
Newark, NJ 201-553-1100
Northland Juices
Port Washington, NY 866-719-5215
Sunlike Juice
Rougemont, QC 866-552-7643

Boxed

Cloverland/Green Spring Dairy
Baltimore, MD 800-876-6455
Wild Aseptics, LLC
Erlanger, KY 877-787-7221

Canned

Emerling International Foods
Buffalo, NY 716-833-7381
Growers Cooperative Juice Co
Westfield, NY 716-326-3161
Mccutcheon Apple Products
Frederick, MD 800-888-7537
Unique Ingredients LLC
Gold Canyon, AZ 480-983-2498
Wild Aseptics, LLC
Erlanger, KY 877-787-7221

Chilled

Emerling International Foods
Buffalo, NY 716-833-7381
Wild Aseptics, LLC
Erlanger, KY 877-787-7221

Concentrate

GLCC Co
Paw Paw, MI 269-657-3167
Green Spot Packaging
Claremont, CA 800-456-3210
Louis Dreyfus Company Citrus Inc
Winter Garden, FL 407-656-1000
Mayer Bros
Buffalo, NY 800-696-2928
Mountain Valley Products Inc
Sunnyside, WA 509-837-8084
Paklab Products
Boucherville, QC 888-946-3233
Small Planet Foods
Minneapolis, MN 800-624-4123
Sun Pac Foods
Brampton, ON 905-792-2700
Tree Top Inc
Selah, WA 509-697-7251
Welch's Global Ingredients Group
Concord, MA 978-371-3692

Frozen

Emerling International Foods
Buffalo, NY 716-833-7381
Growers Cooperative Juice Co
Westfield, NY 716-326-3161
Louis Dreyfus Company Citrus Inc
Winter Garden, FL 407-656-1000
Milne Fruit Products Inc
Prosser, WA 509-786-2611
Wild Aseptics, LLC
Erlanger, KY 877-787-7221

Glass-Packed

Emerling International Foods
Buffalo, NY 716-833-7381
Growers Cooperative Juice Co
Westfield, NY 716-326-3161
Unique Ingredients LLC
Gold Canyon, AZ 480-983-2498
Wild Aseptics, LLC
Erlanger, KY 877-787-7221

Grapefruit

Cutrale Citrus Juices
Auburndale, FL 863-965-5000
Florida Fruit Juices
Chicago, IL 773-586-6200
Gene's Citrus Ranch
Palmetto, FL 888-723-2006
Greenwood Associates
Niles, IL 847-579-5500
Indian River Select® LLC
Stuart, FL 888-373-7426
Kennesaw Fruit & Juice
Pompano Beach, FL 800-949-0371
Lakewood Juice Co.
Miami, FL 866-324-5900
Lassonde Pappas & Company, Inc.
Carneys Point, NJ 800-257-7019
Louis Dreyfus Company Citrus Inc
Winter Garden, FL 407-656-1000
Mayer Bros
Buffalo, NY 800-696-2928
Minute Maid Company
Atlanta, GA 800-520-2653
Natalie's Orchid Island Juice Co.
Ft. Pierce, FL 800-373-7444
Ocean Spray International
Lakeville-Middleboro, MA 800-662-3263
Perricone Juices
Beaumont, CA 951-769-7171
Quality Kitchen Corporation
Wyoming, DE 302-697-3118
Saratoga Spring Water Co
Saratoga Springs, NY 888-426-8642
Silver Springs Citrus Inc
Howey-in-the-Hills, FL 800-940-2277
Sun Orchard INC
Haines City, FL 877-875-8423
Sun Orchard Inc
Miami, FL 800-505-8423
Sunlike Juice
Rougemont, QC 866-552-7643
Superbrand Dairies
Miami, FL 305-769-6600
Tropicana Products Inc.
Chicago, IL 800-237-7799
United Juice Companies of America
Vero Beach, FL 772-562-5442
World Citrus West
Fullerton, CA 714-870-6171
Yoder Dairies
Chesapeake, VA 757-482-4068

Bottled

Northland Juices
Port Washington, NY 866-719-5215

Boxed

Emerling International Foods
Buffalo, NY 716-833-7381
Wild Aseptics, LLC
Erlanger, KY 877-787-7221

Canned

Emerling International Foods
Buffalo, NY 716-833-7381
Ocean Spray International
Lakeville-Middleboro, MA 800-662-3263
Wild Aseptics, LLC
Erlanger, KY 877-787-7221

Concentrate

Sea Breeze Fruit Flavors
Towaco, NJ 800-732-2733
Sun Pac Foods
Brampton, ON 905-792-2700

Frozen

Emerling International Foods
Buffalo, NY 716-833-7381
Ocean Spray International
Lakeville-Middleboro, MA 800-662-3263
Wild Aseptics, LLC
Erlanger, KY 877-787-7221

Glass-Packed

Emerling International Foods
Buffalo, NY 716-833-7381
Ocean Spray International
Lakeville-Middleboro, MA 800-662-3263

Wild Aseptics, LLC
Erlanger, KY....................877-787-7221

Refrigerated

Ocean Spray International
Lakeville-Middleboro, MA..........800-662-3263
Wild Aseptics, LLC
Erlanger, KY....................877-787-7221

Guava

Stevens Tropical Plantation
West Palm Beach, FL..............561-683-4701

Key Lime

Florida Key West
Fort Myers, FL...................239-694-8787

Lemon

Agrocan
Ville St Laurent, QC..............877-247-6226
Castella Imports Inc
Brentwood, NY...................631-231-5500
Erba Food Products
Brooklyn, NY....................718-272-7700
Florida Key West
Fort Myers, FL...................239-694-8787
Greenwood Associates
Niles, IL.......................847-579-5500
Jus-Made
Dallas, TX......................800-969-3746
Lakewood Juice Co.
Miami, FL.......................866-324-5900
Lassonde Pappas & Company, Inc.
Carneys Point, NJ................800-257-7019
Louis Dreyfus Company Citrus Inc
Winter Garden, FL................407-656-1000
Minute Maid Company
Atlanta, GA.....................800-520-2653
Natalie's Orchid Island Juice Co.
Ft. Pierce, FL...................800-373-7444
Nielsen Citrus Products Inc
Huntington Beach, CA.............714-892-5586
Perricone Juices
Beaumont, CA....................951-769-7171
Sophia Foods
Brooklyn, NY....................718-272-1110
Sun Orchard Inc
Miami, FL.......................800-505-8423
Wild Aseptics, LLC
Erlanger, KY....................877-787-7221

Canned

Emerling International Foods
Buffalo, NY.....................716-833-7381
Wild Aseptics, LLC
Erlanger, KY....................877-787-7221

Concentrate

Citrico
Northbrook, IL...................800-445-2171
Citromax Flavors Inc
Carlstadt, NJ....................201-933-8405
Louis Dreyfus Company Citrus Inc
Winter Garden, FL................407-656-1000

Frozen

Emerling International Foods
Buffalo, NY.....................716-833-7381
Louis Dreyfus Company Citrus Inc
Winter Garden, FL................407-656-1000
Nielsen Citrus Products Inc
Huntington Beach, CA.............714-892-5586
Wild Aseptics, LLC
Erlanger, KY....................877-787-7221

Glass-Packed

Emerling International Foods
Buffalo, NY.....................716-833-7381
Wild Aseptics, LLC
Erlanger, KY....................877-787-7221

Refrigerated

Wild Aseptics, LLC
Erlanger, KY....................877-787-7221

Lemonade

4Pure
ME..............................207-831-1030
Anderson Erickson Dairy
Des Moines, IA..................515-265-2521
Anderson Erickson Dairy
Kansas City, KS.................913-621-4801
Calvert's
El Paso, TX.....................888-472-5727
Del's Lemonade & Refreshments
Cranston, RI....................401-463-6190
Fermenting Fairy
Santa Monica, CA
Happy Planet Foods
Burnaby, BC.....................800-811-3213
Hubert's Lemonade
Tustin, CA......................877-265-3286
Joe Tea and Joe Chips
Upper Montclair, NJ..............973-744-7502
Jones Soda Company
Seattle, WA.....................800-656-6050
Lakewood Juice Co.
Miami, FL.......................866-324-5900
Lassonde Pappas & Company, Inc.
Carneys Point, NJ................800-257-7019
Lorina, Inc.
Coral Gables, FL.................305-779-3085
M & B Fruit Juice Co
Akron, OH.......................330-253-7465
Me & the Bees Lemonade
Austin, TX
Natrel
St. Laurent, QC..................800-501-1150
Newman's Own
Westport, CT....................203-222-0136
Poppilu
Chicago, IL
Rocket Products Company
Fenton, MO......................800-325-9567
Sunlike Juice
Rougemont, QC...................866-552-7643
Sweet Leaf Tea Company
Austin, TX......................512-328-7775
Third Street Inc
Louisville, CO...................800-636-3790
United Juice Companies of America
Vero Beach, FL...................772-562-5442
Zeigler's
Lansdale, PA....................215-855-5161

Concentrate

Baltimore Brewing Company
Baltimore, MD...................410-837-5000
Beaulieu Vineyard
Rutherford, CA...................707-257-5749
Beaver Street Brewery
Flagstaff, AZ....................928-779-0079
Bow Valley Brewing Company
Canmore, AB.....................403-678-2739
Brasserie Brasel Brewery
Lasalle, QC.....................800-463-2728
Bravard Vineyards & Winery
Hopkinsville, KY.................270-269-2583
Clipper City Brewing
Halethorpe, MD..................410-247-7822
Creemore Springs Brewery
Creemore, ON....................800-267-2240
Dogfish Head Craft Brewery
Lewes, DE.......................888-834-3474
Great Lakes Brewing Co.
Cleveland, OH...................216-771-4404
Great Northern Brewing Co
Whitefish, MT....................406-863-1000
Great Western Brewing Company
Saskatoon, SK....................800-764-4492
Hogtown Brewing Company
Mississauga, ON..................905-855-9065
Lakefront Brewery Inc
Milwaukee, WI....................414-372-8800
Left Hand Brewing Co
Longmont, CO....................303-772-0258
Mayer Bros
Buffalo, NY.....................800-696-2928
Mendocino Brewing Co Inc
Ukiah, CA.......................707-463-2627
Millstream Brewing Co
Amana, IA.......................319-622-3672
Minute Maid Company
Atlanta, GA.....................800-520-2653
Monticello Vineyards-Corley
Napa, CA........................707-253-2802
Moosehead Breweries Ltd.
St. John, NB
Pennsylvania Brewing Company
Pittsburgh, PA...................412-237-9400
Santa Cruz Mountain Brewing
Santa Cruz, CA...................831-425-4900
Sebastiani Vineyards
Sonoma, CA......................855-232-2338
Shipyard Brewing Co
Portland, ME.....................800-789-0684
Small Planet Foods
Minneapolis, MN..................800-624-4123
Whistler Brewing Company
Whistler, BC.....................604-962-8889

Lime

Castella Imports Inc
Brentwood, NY...................631-231-5500
Emerling International Foods
Buffalo, NY.....................716-833-7381
Florida's Natural Growers
Lake Wales, FL...................888-657-6600
Greenwood Associates
Niles, IL.......................847-579-5500
Lassonde Pappas & Company, Inc.
Carneys Point, NJ................800-257-7019
M & B Fruit Juice Co
Akron, OH.......................330-253-7465
Mott's LLP
Plano, TX.......................800-426-4891
Natalie's Orchid Island Juice Co.
Ft. Pierce, FL...................800-373-7444
Nielsen Citrus Products Inc
Huntington Beach, CA.............714-892-5586
Perricone Juices
Beaumont, CA....................951-769-7171
Sun Orchard Inc
Miami, FL.......................800-505-8423
Sunfresh Beverages Inc.
Birmingham, AL...................706-324-0040
True Organic Product Inc
Helm, CA........................800-487-0379
United Juice Companies of America
Vero Beach, FL...................772-562-5442
Wild Aseptics, LLC
Erlanger, KY....................877-787-7221

Mango

Lakewood Juice Co.
Miami, FL.......................866-324-5900
Stevens Tropical Plantation
West Palm Beach, FL..............561-683-4701
Sunlike Juice
Rougemont, QC...................866-552-7643

Onion

Emerling International Foods
Buffalo, NY.....................716-833-7381
Howard Foods Inc
Danvers, MA.....................978-774-6207
Vegetable Juices Inc
Chicago, IL.....................888-776-9752

Orange

Alta Dena Certified Dairy LLC
City Of Industry, CA..............800-535-1369
Anderson Erickson Dairy
Des Moines, IA..................515-265-2521
Anderson Erickson Dairy
Kansas City, KS.................913-621-4801
Arcadia Dairy Farms Inc
Arden, NC.......................828-684-3556
Birdseye Dairy-Morning Glory
Green Bay, WI....................920-494-5388
Borden Dairy
Dallas, TX......................855-311-1583
Broughton Foods LLC
El Paso, TX.....................800-395-7004
Byrne Dairy, Inc.
Syracuse, NY....................800-899-1535
Cass-Clay Creamery
Fargo, ND.......................701-293-6455
Chase Brothers Dairy
Oxnard, CA......................800-438-6455
Citrosuco North America Inc
Lake Wales, FL...................800-356-4592
Cloverland/Green Spring Dairy
Baltimore, MD...................800-876-6455
Country Pure Foods Inc
Akron, OH.......................877-995-8423
Cutrale Citrus Juices
Auburndale, FL...................863-965-5000
Emerling International Foods
Buffalo, NY.....................716-833-7381

Erba Food Products
Brooklyn, NY 718-272-7700
Everfresh Beverages
Warren, MI 800-323-3416
Evolution Fresh
Seattle, WA 800-794-9986
Florida Fruit Juices
Chicago, IL 773-586-6200
Florida's Natural Growers
Lake Wales, FL 888-657-6600
Galliker Dairy Co
Johnstown, PA 800-477-6455
Gene's Citrus Ranch
Palmetto, FL 888-723-2006
Green Spot Packaging
Claremont, CA 800-456-3210
Greenwood Associates
Niles, IL 847-579-5500
Harrisburg Dairies Inc
Harrisburg, PA 800-692-7429
Heritage Farms Dairy
Murfreesboro, TN 615-895-2790
Hygeia Dairy Company
Corpus Christi, TX 361-854-4561
Indian River Select® LLC
Stuart, FL 888-373-7426
Inn Foods Inc
Watsonville, CA 800-708-7836
Jus-Made
Dallas, TX 800-969-3746
Key Colony Red Parrot Juice
Lemont, IL 844-783-8572
Lakewood Juice Co.
Miami, FL 866-324-5900
Lassonde Pappas & Company, Inc.
Carneys Point, NJ 800-257-7019
Leonard Fountain Specialties
Detroit, MI 313-891-4141
Lorina, Inc.
Coral Gables, FL 305-779-3085
Louis Dreyfus Company Citrus Inc
Winter Garden, FL 407-656-1000
M & B Fruit Juice Co
Akron, OH 330-253-7465
M & B Products Inc
Tampa, FL 800-899-7255
Marva Maid Dairy
Newport News, VA 800-768-6243
Mayer Bros
Buffalo, NY 800-696-2928
Minute Maid Company
Atlanta, GA 800-520-2653
Natalie's Orchid Island Juice Co.
Ft. Pierce, FL 800-373-7444
Noel Corp
Yakima, WA 509-248-1313
Northland Juices
Port Washington, NY 866-719-5215
Perricone Juices
Beaumont, CA 951-769-7171
Prairie Farms Dairy Inc.
Edwardsville, IL 618-659-5700
Quality Kitchen Corporation
Wyoming, DE 302-697-3118
Reilly Dairy & Food Company
Tampa, FL 813-839-8458
Reiter Dairy
Newport, KY 800-544-6455
Reiter Dairy LLC
Springfield, OH 937-323-5777
Rocket Products Company
Fenton, MO 800-325-9567
Saratoga Spring Water Co
Saratoga Springs, NY 888-426-8642
Sun Orchard INC
Haines City, FL 877-875-8423
Sun Orchard Inc
Miami, FL 800-505-8423
Sunlike Juice
Rougemont, QC 866-552-7643
Super Stores Industries
Turlock, CA 209-668-2100
Superbrand Dairies
Miami, FL 305-769-6600
Swiss Premium Dairy Inc
Lebanon, PA 800-222-2129
Toft Dairy Inc
Sandusky, OH 800-521-4606
Treesweet Products
Houston, TX 281-876-3759
Tropicana Products Inc.
Chicago, IL 800-237-7799
True Organic Product Inc
Helm, CA 800-487-0379
United Dairy Farmers Inc.
Cincinnati, OH 866-837-4833
United Dairy Inc.
Martins Ferry, OH 800-252-1542
United Juice Companies of America
Vero Beach, FL 772-562-5442
US Sugar Company
Clewiston, FL 863-983-8121
Wild Aseptics, LLC
Erlanger, KY 877-787-7221
World Citrus West
Fullerton, CA 714-870-6171
Yoder Dairies
Chesapeake, VA 757-482-4068

Concentrate

California Citrus Producers
Lindsay, CA 559-562-5169
Chase Brothers Dairy
Oxnard, CA 800-438-6455
Country Pure Foods Inc
Ellington, CT 877-995-8423
Green Spot Packaging
Claremont, CA 800-456-3210
Greenwood Associates
Niles, IL 847-579-5500
Louis Dreyfus Company Citrus Inc
Winter Garden, FL 407-656-1000
Mayer Bros
Buffalo, NY 800-696-2928
Minute Maid Company
Atlanta, GA 800-520-2653
Sea Breeze Fruit Flavors
Towaco, NJ 800-732-2733
Small Planet Foods
Minneapolis, MN 800-624-4123
Sun Pac Foods
Brampton, ON 905-792-2700

Concentrate - Frozen

Louis Dreyfus Company Citrus Inc
Winter Garden, FL 407-656-1000

Not Concentrated

Broughton Foods LLC
El Paso, TX 800-395-7004
Citrosuco North America Inc
Lake Wales, FL 800-356-4592
Greenwood Associates
Niles, IL 847-579-5500
Minute Maid Company
Atlanta, GA 800-520-2653
Silver Springs Citrus Inc
Howey-in-the-Hills, FL 800-940-2277

Papaya

Lakewood Juice Co.
Miami, FL 866-324-5900
Stevens Tropical Plantation
West Palm Beach, FL 561-683-4701
Sunlike Juice
Rougemont, QC 866-552-7643

Peach

Green Spot Packaging
Claremont, CA 800-456-3210
Hazel Creek Orchards
Mt Airy, GA 706-754-4899
Sunlike Juice
Rougemont, QC 866-552-7643
Valley View Packing Co
Yuba City, CA 530-673-7356

Pear

Valley View Packing Co
Yuba City, CA 530-673-7356

Pineapple

Cal India Foods Inc
Chino, CA 909-613-1660
Commodities Marketing Inc
Clarksburg, NJ 732-516-0700
Country Pure Foods Inc
Akron, OH 877-995-8423
Emerling International Foods
Buffalo, NY 716-833-7381
Florida Fruit Juices
Chicago, IL 773-586-6200
Greenwood Associates
Niles, IL 847-579-5500
Lakewood Juice Co.
Miami, FL 866-324-5900
Langer Juice Co Inc
City of Industry, CA 626-336-3100
Lassonde Pappas & Company, Inc.
Carneys Point, NJ 800-257-7019
M & B Products Inc
Tampa, FL 800-899-7255
Maui Gold Pineapple Company
Pukalani, HI 808-877-3805
Mondial Foods Company
Los Angeles, CA 213-383-3531
Ntc Marketing
Williamsville, NY 800-333-1637
Sunlike Juice
Rougemont, QC 866-552-7643
True Organic Product Inc
Helm, CA 800-487-0379
Wild Aseptics, LLC
Erlanger, KY 877-787-7221

Boxed

Wild Aseptics, LLC
Erlanger, KY 877-787-7221

Canned

Ntc Marketing
Williamsville, NY 800-333-1637
Wild Aseptics, LLC
Erlanger, KY 877-787-7221

Concentrate

Maui Gold Pineapple Company
Pukalani, HI 808-877-3805
Pacific Coast Fruit Co
Portland, OR 503-234-6411
Sun Pac Foods
Brampton, ON 905-792-2700
Transpacific Foods Inc
Irvine, CA 949-975-9900

Frozen

Wild Aseptics, LLC
Erlanger, KY 877-787-7221

Glass-Packed

Wild Aseptics, LLC
Erlanger, KY 877-787-7221

Refrigerated

Wild Aseptics, LLC
Erlanger, KY 877-787-7221

Portioned

Arcadia Dairy Farms Inc
Arden, NC 828-684-3556

Powdered Fruit

American Fruits & Flavors
Pacoima, CA 818-899-9574
Energy Foods Intl.
Miami, FL 844-772-6622

Prune

Emerling International Foods
Buffalo, NY 716-833-7381
Erba Food Products
Brooklyn, NY 718-272-7700
Lakewood Juice Co.
Miami, FL 866-324-5900
Lassonde Pappas & Company, Inc.
Carneys Point, NJ 800-257-7019
Madera Enterprises Inc
Madera, CA 800-507-9555
Sunsweet Growers Inc.
Yuba City, CA 800-417-2253
Valley View Packing Co
Yuba City, CA 530-673-7356
Wild Aseptics, LLC
Erlanger, KY 877-787-7221

Raisin

Lion Raisins Inc
Selma, CA 559-834-6677

Victor Packing
Madera, CA....................559-673-5908

Raspberry

Hazel Creek Orchards
Mt Airy, GA....................706-754-4899
Meduri Farms
Dallas, OR....................877-388-8800
Merlinos
Canon City, CO....................719-275-5558
Stone Hill Winery
Hermann, MO....................573-486-2221

Refrigerated

Apple & Eve LLC
Port Washington, NY....................800-969-8018
Perfect Foods Inc
Goshen, NY....................800-933-3288
Swiss Premium Dairy Inc
Lebanon, PA....................800-222-2129
World Citrus West
Fullerton, CA....................714-870-6171

Strawberry

Green Spot Packaging
Claremont, CA....................800-456-3210
Madera Enterprises Inc
Madera, CA....................800-507-9555
Merlinos
Canon City, CO....................719-275-5558

Tangerine

Emerling International Foods
Buffalo, NY....................716-833-7381
Greenwood Associates
Niles, IL....................847-579-5500
Louis Dreyfus Company Citrus Inc
Winter Garden, FL....................407-656-1000
Minute Maid Company
Atlanta, GA....................800-520-2653
Perricone Juices
Beaumont, CA....................951-769-7171
True Organic Product Inc
Helm, CA....................800-487-0379
United Juice Companies of America
Vero Beach, FL....................772-562-5442
Wild Aseptics, LLC
Erlanger, KY....................877-787-7221

Tomato

Alimentaire Whyte's Inc
Laval, QC....................866-420-9520
Beckman & Gast Co
St Henry, OH....................419-678-4195
Cal-Tex Citrus Juice LP
Houston, TX....................800-231-0133
Dei Fratelli
Toledo, OH....................800-837-1631
Erba Food Products
Brooklyn, NY....................718-272-7700
Natalie's Orchid Island Juice Co.
Ft. Pierce, FL....................800-373-7444
Ocean Spray International
Lakeville-Middleboro, MA....................800-662-3263
Sun Pac Foods
Brampton, ON....................905-792-2700
Thomas Canning/Maidstone
Maidstone, ON....................519-737-1531
Welch Foods Inc.
Concord, MA....................800-340-6870
Wild Aseptics, LLC
Erlanger, KY....................877-787-7221

Boxed

Wild Aseptics, LLC
Erlanger, KY....................877-787-7221

Canned

Agrocan
Ville St Laurent, QC....................877-247-6226
Emerling International Foods
Buffalo, NY....................716-833-7381
Hirzel Canning Co & Farms
Luckey, OH....................419-419-7525
Wild Aseptics, LLC
Erlanger, KY....................877-787-7221

Cocktail

Emerling International Foods
Buffalo, NY....................716-833-7381
Vegetable Juices Inc
Chicago, IL....................888-776-9752

Frozen

Vegetable Juices Inc
Chicago, IL....................888-776-9752
Wild Aseptics, LLC
Erlanger, KY....................877-787-7221

Glass-Packed Chilled

Emerling International Foods
Buffalo, NY....................716-833-7381
Wild Aseptics, LLC
Erlanger, KY....................877-787-7221

Tropical Fruits

Care Foods International
Long Island, NY....................718-392-3355
Emerling International Foods
Buffalo, NY....................716-833-7381
Green Spot Packaging
Claremont, CA....................800-456-3210
Hawaiian Sun Products
Honolulu, HI....................808-845-3211
Healthmate Products
Highland Park, IL....................847-579-1051
International Trade Impact Inc
Lawrenceville, NJ....................800-223-5484
Lakewood Juice Co.
Miami, FL....................866-324-5900
Langer Juice Co Inc
City of Industry, CA....................626-336-3100
Lassonde Pappas & Company, Inc.
Carneys Point, NJ....................800-257-7019
Mondial Foods Company
Los Angeles, CA....................213-383-3531
Rubicon Food Products
Richmond Hill, ON....................905-883-1112
Stevens Tropical Plantation
West Palm Beach, FL....................561-683-4701
Sunlike Juice
Rougemont, QC....................866-552-7643
True Organic Product Inc
Helm, CA....................800-487-0379
Wild Aseptics, LLC
Erlanger, KY....................877-787-7221

Vegetable

Apple & Eve LLC
Port Washington, NY....................800-969-8018
B.M. Lawrence & Company
San Francisco, CA....................415-981-2926
Beckman & Gast Co
St Henry, OH....................419-678-4195
Campbell Soup Co.
Camden, NJ....................800-257-8443
Century Foods Intl LLC
Sparta, WI....................800-269-1901
Evolution Fresh
Seattle, WA....................800-794-9986
Florida Food Products Inc
Eustis, FL....................800-874-2331
Greenwood Associates
Niles, IL....................847-579-5500
Howard Foods Inc
Danvers, MA....................978-774-6207
Hudson Valley Fruit Juice
Highland, NY....................845-691-8061
Island Aseptics
Byesville, OH....................740-685-2548
Ludfords
Riverside, CA....................951-823-0306
Rapunzel Pure Organics
Bloomfield, NJ....................800-225-1449
RFi Ingredients
Blauvelt, NY....................800-962-7663
Tamarack Farms Dairy
Newark, OH....................866-221-4141
Thomas Canning/Maidstone
Maidstone, ON....................519-737-1531
Vegetable Juices Inc
Chicago, IL....................888-776-9752

Concentrates - Fruit Puree

GLCC Co
Paw Paw, MI....................269-657-3167
Greenwood Associates
Niles, IL....................847-579-5500
RFi Ingredients
Blauvelt, NY....................800-962-7663

Mixers

Bar Mixers

Better Beverages Inc
Cerritos, CA....................800-344-5219
Callie's Charleston Biscuits
North Charleston, SC....................843-577-1198
Coastal Promotions, Inc.
Destin, FL....................850-460-2328
Davis & Davis Gourmet Foods
Allison Park, PA....................412-487-7770
Hella Cocktail
Long Island City, NY....................646-854-8004
Improper Goods
Portland, OR....................503-662-7147
LA Jota Vineyard Co
Angwin, CA....................877-222-0292
Mixallogy
Ponte Vedra Beach, FL
Nimble Nectar
....................951-775-9543
Panorama Foods Inc.
Braintree, MA....................781-592-1069
Q Mixers
Brooklyn, NY....................718-398-6642
Refresco Beverages US Inc.
Tampa, FL....................888-260-3776
Regatta Craft Mixers
Locust Valley, NY
Stirrings
New Bedford, MA....................866-646-4266
The Murphs Famous Inc.
Henrietta, NY....................888-281-6400
United Juice Companies of America
Vero Beach, FL....................772-562-5442

Prepared Cocktail Mixes

A.C. Calderoni
Brisbane, CA....................866-468-1897
Al-Rite Fruits & Syrups Co
Miami, FL....................305-652-2540
American Beverage Marketers
New Albany, IN....................812-944-3585
Bacardi Canada, Inc.
Toronto, ON....................905-451-6100
Bacardi USA Inc
Coral Gables, FL....................800-222-2734
Bartush Schnitzius Foods Co
Lewisville, TX....................972-219-1270
Beam Suntory
Chicago, IL....................312-964-6999
Blue Crab Bay
Melfa, VA....................800-221-2722
Callie's Charleston Biscuits
North Charleston, SC....................843-577-1198
Carolina Treet
Wilmington, NC....................800-616-6344
Century Blends LLC
Hunt Valley, MD....................410-771-6606
Circle B Ranch
Seymour, MO....................417-683-0271
Coastal Cocktails
Irvine, CA....................949-250-8951
Cocktail Crate
Long Island City, NY....................718-316-2033
Commodities Marketing Inc
Clarksburg, NJ....................732-516-0700
Davis & Davis Gourmet Foods
Allison Park, PA....................412-487-7770
Demitri's Bloody Mary Seasonings
Seattle, WA....................800-627-9649
Fee Brothers
Rochester, NY....................800-961-3337
Fentimans North America
Burnaby, BC....................877-326-3248
Ficks & Co.
San Francisco, CA
Finest Call
New Albany, IN....................812-944-3585
Flavouressence Products
Mississauga, ON....................866-209-7778
Franco's Cocktail Mixes
Pompano Beach, FL....................800-782-4508
Frank & Dean's Cocktail Mixes
Pasadena, CA....................626-351-4272

Glossop's Syrup
Los Angeles, CA....424-832-7266
Great Western Juice Co
Maple Heights, OH....800-321-9180
Hella Cocktail
Long Island City, NY....646-854-8004
Island Aseptics
Byesville, OH....740-685-2548
Island Oasis Frozen Cocktail
Beloit, WI....800-777-4752
Jus-Made
Dallas, TX....800-969-3746
Key Colony Red Parrot Juice
Lemont, IL....844-783-8572
Kittling Ridge Estate Wines & Spirits
Vaughan, ON....800-461-9463
LA Paz Products Inc
Brea, CA....714-990-0982
Lemate Of New England Inc
Foxboro, MA....508-543-9035
Lemon-X Corporation
Huntington Station, NY....800-220-1061
Main Squeeze
Columbia, MO....573-817-5616
Margarita Man
San Antonio, TX....800-950-8149
Mele-Koi Farms
Newport Beach, CA....949-660-9000
Miramar Fruit Trading Company
Doral, FL....305-883-4774
Misty's Restaurant & Lounge
Lincoln, NE....402-466-7222
Morris Kitchen
Brooklyn, NY....347-457-6994
Mott's LLP
Plano, TX....800-426-4891
Mr. C's
Kent, WA....888-929-2378
Owl's Brew
New York, NY....212-564-0218
Prima Foods International
Silver Springs, FL....800-774-8751
Royale Brands
Davenport, IA....563-386-5222
Ruffner's
Wayne, PA....610-687-9800
Sea Breeze Fruit Flavors
Towaco, NJ....800-732-2733
Sirocco Enterprises Inc
New Orleans, LA....504-834-1549
Skinny Mixes LLC
Clearwater, FL....727-826-0306
Southern Twist Cocktail
Folly Beach, SC....843-343-9577
St Julian Winery
Paw Paw, MI....800-732-6002
Stirrings
New Bedford, MA....866-646-4266
Stonewall Kitchen
York, ME....800-826-1752
SuckerPunch Gourmet
Bridgeview, IL....708-784-3000
Texas Beach
Richmond, VA....757-403-3598
Trader Vic's Food Products
Emeryville, CA....877-762-4824
Tree Ripe Products
Whippany, NJ....800-873-3747
Tropical Illusions
Trenton, MO....660-359-5422
Ubons Sauce LLC
Yazoo City, MS....662-716-7100
Uncle Dougie's
Chicago, IL
Vegetable Juices Inc
Chicago, IL....888-776-9752
Wagner Excello Food Products
Broadview, IL....708-338-4488
Wild Aseptics, LLC
Erlanger, KY....877-787-7221

Non-Alcoholic Beverages

American Instants Inc
Flanders, NJ....973-584-8811
Ariel Vineyards
Napa, CA....800-456-9472
Atlanta Coffee & Tea Co
....800-426-4781
B.M. Lawrence & Company
San Francisco, CA....415-981-2926
Ex Drinks
Henderson, NV....866-753-4929
Fee Brothers
Rochester, NY....800-961-3337
Finlays
Lincoln, RI....800-288-6272
Florida Caribbean Distillers
Lake Alfred, FL....863-956-2002
Franco's Cocktail Mixes
Pompano Beach, FL....800-782-4508
Ipswich Ale Brewery
Ipswich, MA....978-356-3329
Kristian Regale
Hudson, WI....715-386-8388
Lion Brewery Inc
Wilkes Barre, PA....888-295-2337
Martin Coffee Co
Jacksonville, FL....904-355-9661
Meier's Wine Cellars Inc
Cincinnati, OH....800-346-2941
Natural Group
Oxnard, CA....805-485-3420
Pok Pok Som
Portland, OR....503-235-0004
Richland Beverage Association
Carrollton, TX....214-357-0248
Skimpy Cocktails LLC
Carrollton, TX....469-892-7988
Sweet Traders
Huntington Beach, CA....714-903-6800
TOST Beverages LLC
Red Hook, NY

Smoothies

Blendtopia
Nashville, TN
Bluechip Group
Salt Lake City, UT....800-878-0099
Bright Greens
Portland, OR....760-487-8895
Broughton Foods LLC
El Paso, TX....800-395-7004
Caffe D'Amore Gourmet Beverages
Pittsburgh, PA....800-999-0171
Cascade Fresh
Seattle, WA....800-511-0057
Dr. Smoothie Brands
Fullerton, CA....888-466-9941
Essential Living Foods
Torrance, CA....310-319-1555
Evolution Fresh
Seattle, WA....800-794-9986
Foods Alive
Angola, IN....260-488-4497
Gardner's Gourmet
Fremont, CA....800-676-8558
Genius Juice
Torrance, CA....800-682-7790
GPI USA LLC.
Mokena, IL....800-929-4248
Hain Celestial Group Inc
Lake Success, NY....800-434-4246
Happy Family
New York, NY....855-644-2779
Happy Planet Foods
Burnaby, BC....800-811-3213
Hunter Farms - High Point Division
High Point, NC....800-446-8035
Ideal Dairy Farms
Hudson Falls, NY....518-747-5059
Jus-Made
Dallas, TX....800-969-3746
K & F Select Fine Coffees
Portland, OR....800-558-7788
Lane's Dairy
El Paso, TX....915-772-6700
Maola Milk & Ice Cream Co.
....844-287-1970
Navitas Naturals
Novato, CA....888-645-4282
NOKA
Pacific Palisades, CA
Oak Farms
El Paso, TX....800-395-7004
Odwalla
Sugar Land, TX....800-639-2552
Saratoga Spring Water Co
Saratoga Springs, NY....888-426-8642
Scally's Imperial Importing Company Inc
Staten Island, NY....718-983-1938
Sheila's Select Gourmet Recipe
Heber City, UT....800-516-7286
Soylent
Los Angeles, CA
Stonyfield Organic
Londonderry, NH....800-776-2697
Sunshine Dairy Foods Inc
Portland, OR....503-234-7526
Victor Packing
Madera, CA....559-673-5908

Soft Drinks & Sodas

51 Fifty Enterprises
Livingston, CA....855-513-4389
Arctic Beverages
Winnipeg, MB....866-503-1270
Beverage Capital Corporation
Baltimore, MD....410-242-7404
Big Red Bottling
Austin, TX....254-772-7791
BN Soda
Brookline, MA....617-782-7888
Cadbury Beverages Canada
Mississauga, ON....905-712-4121
Cawston Press
Pittsburgh, PA
Cool
Richardson, TX....972-437-9352
Fentimans North America
Burnaby, BC....877-326-3248
Grand Teton Brewing Co
Victor, ID....888-899-1656
Grown-up Soda
New York, NY....212-355-7454
High Grade Beverage
Monmouth Jct, NJ....887-327-4277
Honest Tea Inc
Atlanta, GA....800-520-2653
Ipswich Ale Brewery
Ipswich, MA....978-356-3329
J.M. Smucker Co.
Orrville, OH....888-550-9555
Jones Soda Company
Seattle, WA....800-656-6050
PepsiCo.
Purchase, NY....914-253-2000
Reed's, Inc.
Los Angeles, CA
Refresco Beverages US Inc.
Tampa, FL....888-260-3776
Safeway Inc.
Pleasanton, CA....877-723-3929
Sipp
Stamford, CT....866-222-4735
Smith & Salmon
Burlington, VT....802-578-8242
Snow Beverages
New York, NY....212-353-3270
Stevens Point Brewery
Stevens Point, WI....800-369-4911
Tincture Distillers
Arlington, VA....888-658-6899
Universal Impex Corporation
Toronto, ON....416-743-7778
Zevia
Culver City, CA....855-469-3842

Club Soda

Ipswich Ale Brewery
Ipswich, MA....978-356-3329
Joia All Natural Soda
Minneapolis, MN....612-308-2056
Regatta Craft Mixers
Locust Valley, NY

Soda Water

Coca-Cola Beverages Northeast
Bedford, NH....844-619-3388

Soft Drinks

1642
Montreal, QC....800-774-4907
A-Treat Bottling Co
Allentown, PA....800-220-1531
Abita Brewing Co
Covington, LA....800-737-2311
Admiral Beverage Corp
Worland, WY....307-347-4201
Arctic Beverages
Winnipeg, MB....866-503-1270
Aspire
Chicago, OH
B.M. Lawrence & Company
San Francisco, CA....415-981-2926

Beverage Capital Corporation
Baltimore, MD 410-242-7404
Blue Sky Beverage Company
Corona, CA 800-426-7367
BN Soda
Brookline, MA 617-782-7888
Catawissa Bottling Co
Catawissa, PA 800-892-4419
Cawy Bottling Co
Miami, FL 877-917-2299
Coca-Cola Beverages Northeast
Bedford, NH 844-619-3388
Coca-Cola Co.
Atlanta, GA 800-438-2653
Cool Mountain Beverages Inc
Des Plaines, IL 888-838-7632
Crystal & Vigor Beverages
Kearny, NJ 201-991-2342
CTL Foods
Colfax, WI 800-962-5227
Everfresh Beverages
Warren, MI 800-323-3416
Ginseng Up Corp
Worcester, MA 800-446-7364
Global Beverage Company
Rochester, NY 585-381-3560
Good-O-Beverages Inc
Bronx, NY 718-328-6400
Hanks Beverage Co
Feasterville-Trevose, PA 800-289-4722
Haydenergy Health
Valley Stream, NY 800-255-1660
Island Sweetwater Beverage Company
Bryn Mawr, PA 610-525-7444
Krier Foods
Random Lake, WI 920-994-2469
Lenox-Martell Inc
Boston, MA 877-325-2489
Leonard Fountain Specialties
Detroit, MI 313-891-4141
Lost Trail Root Beer
Louisburg, KS 800-748-7765
Manhattan Special Bottling
Brooklyn, NY 718-388-4144
Mar-Key Foods
Vidalia, GA 912-537-4204
Monarch Beverage Company
Atlanta, GA 800-241-3732
Moon Shot Energy
Austin, TX 512-387-4703
Mt Claire Beverages
Torrington, CT 888-525-2473
National Beverage Corporation
Fort Lauderdale, FL 877-622-3499
Original American Beverage Company
North Stonington, CT 800-625-3767
Polar Beverages Inc.
Worcester, MA 800-734-9800
Q Drinks
Brooklyn, NY 718-398-6642
R.J. Corr Naturals
Posen, IL 708-389-4200
RC Bottling Company
Evenasville, IN 812-424-7978
Roselani Tropics Ice Cream
Wailuku, HI 808-244-7951
SANGARIA USA
Torrance, CA 310-530-2202
Saranac Brewery
Utica, NY 800-765-6288
Shasta Beverages Inc
Baltimore, MS 800-834-9980
Signature Beverage
Merrick, NY 800-277-2755
Soho Beverages
Vienna, VA 703-689-2800
Southern Beverage Packers Inc
Appling, GA 800-326-2469
Stop & Shop Manufacturing
Readville, MA 508-977-5132
The Veri Soda Company
New York, NY 203-409-3995
Todhunter Foods
Lake Alfred, FL 863-956-1116
Varni Brothers/7-Up Bottling
Modesto, CA 209-521-1777
Vermont Sweetwater Bottling Co
Poultney, VT 800-974-9877
Wet Planet Beverage
Monachie, NJ 201-288-1999
White Label Yerba Mate Soda
New York, NY
White Rock Products Corp
Flushing, NY 800-969-7625
Wild Poppy
Los Angeles, CA 310-384-1004
Zevia
Culver City, CA 855-469-3842

Cola

1642
Montreal, QC 800-774-4907
A-Treat Bottling Co
Allentown, PA 800-220-1531
Adirondack Beverages Inc
Scotia, NY 800-316-6096
Al's Beverage Company
East Windsor, CT 888-257-7632
Aloe'Ha Drink Products
Houston, TX 713-978-6359
American Bottling & Beverage
Walterboro, SC 843-538-7937
Bar Harbor Brewing Company
Bar Harbor, ME 207-288-4592
Better Beverages Inc
Cerritos, CA 800-344-5219
Beverage America
Holland, MI 616-396-1281
Beverage House Inc
Cartersville, GA 888-367-8327
Boylan Bottling Company
Haledon, NJ 800-289-7978
Cable Car Beverage Corporation
Denver, CO 303-298-9038
Castle Beverages Inc
Ansonia, CT 203-734-0883
Catawissa Bottling Co
Catawissa, PA 800-892-4419
Champion Beverages
Darien, CT 203-655-9026
Coca-Cola Beverages Northeast
Bedford, NH 844-619-3388
Coca-Cola Bottling Co. Consolidated
Charlotte, NC 800-866-2653
Coca-Cola Bottling Company UNITED, Inc.
Birmingham, AB 800-844-2653
Coca-Cola Co.
Atlanta, GA 800-438-2653
Coca-Cola European Partners
Uxbridge, Middx, ... 800-418-4223
Cornell Beverages Inc
Brooklyn, NY 718-381-3000
Crowley Beverage Corporation
Wayland, MA 800-997-3337
Double-Cola Company
Chattanooga, TN 423-267-5691
Dr Pepper Snapple Group
Plano, TX 800-696-5891
Egg Cream America Inc
Northbrook, IL 847-559-2703
Faygo Beverages Inc
Detroit, MI 313-925-1600
Gulf States Canners Inc
Clinton, MS 601-924-0511
Hampton Associates & Sons
Fairfax, VA 703-968-5847
Honickman Affiliates
Pennsauken, NJ 800-573-7745
Hosmer Mountain Bottling Co
Willimantic, CT 800-763-2445
Jones Soda Company
Seattle, WA 800-656-6050
Kennebec Fruit Company
Lisbon Falls, ME 207-353-8173
Keurig Dr Pepper
Plano, TX 800-696-5891
Kola
New York, NY 212-688-1895
Lenox-Martell Inc
Boston, MA 877-325-2489
Leonard Fountain Specialties
Detroit, MI 313-891-4141
Millstream Brewing Co
Amana, IA 319-622-3672
Moceri South Western
San Diego, CA 619-297-7900
New York Bottling Co Inc
Bronx, NY 718-842-7416
Noel Corp
Yakima, WA 509-248-1313
North Shore Bottling Co
Brooklyn, NY 718-272-8900
Northern Neck
Montross, VA 804-493-8051
Pennsylvania Dutch: Birch Beer
Doylestown, PA 856-662-1869
Pocono Mountain Bottling Company
Wilkes Barre, PA 570-822-7695
Premier Beverages
Plano, TX 972-547-6295
REED'S Inc
Los Angeles, CA 800-997-3337
Rivella USA
Boca Raton, FL 561-417-5810
Sarum Tea Company
Lakeville, CT 860-435-2086
Shabazz Fruit Cola Company
Newark, NJ 973-230-4641
Shasta Beverages Inc
Baltimore, MS 800-834-9980
SoBe Beverages
Norwalk, CT 800-588-0548
Stewart's Beverages
rye Brook, NY 800-762-7753
Sun State Beverage
Atlanta, GA 770-451-3990
Thomas Kemper Soda Company
Austin, TX 206-381-8712
Triple XXX Root Beer Co.
West Lafayette, IN 765-743-5373
USA Beverage
Warrenton, MO 636-456-5468
Virgil's Root Beer
Norwalk, CT 800-997-3337

Cream Soda

Catawissa Bottling Co
Catawissa, PA 800-892-4419
Coca-Cola Beverages Northeast
Bedford, NH 844-619-3388
Cool Mountain Beverages Inc
Des Plaines, IL 888-838-7632
Dr Pepper Snapple Group
Plano, TX 800-696-5891
Ipswich Ale Brewery
Ipswich, MA 978-356-3329
Jones Soda Company
Seattle, WA 800-656-6050
Keurig Dr Pepper
Plano, TX 800-696-5891
Signature Beverage
Merrick, NY 800-277-2755

Cream Soda - Vanilla

Thomas Kemper Soda Company
Austin, TX 206-381-8712

Ginger Ale

1642
Montreal, QC 800-774-4907
Adirondack Beverages Inc
Scotia, NY 800-316-6096
Bruce Cost Ginger Ale
Brooklyn, NY 212-488-0661
Bull's Head
Richmond, QC 819-212-1583
Coca-Cola Beverages Northeast
Bedford, NH 844-619-3388
Cool Mountain Beverages Inc
Des Plaines, IL 888-838-7632
Dr Pepper Snapple Group
Plano, TX 800-696-5891
Grand Teton Brewing Co
Victor, ID 888-899-1656
Keurig Dr Pepper
Plano, TX 800-696-5891
Leonard Fountain Specialties
Detroit, MI 313-891-4141
Regatta Craft Mixers
Locust Valley, NY
Thomas Kemper Soda Company
Austin, TX 206-381-8712
Verdant Kitchen
Norcross, GA 912-349-2958

Lemon-Lime Soda

Cool Mountain Beverages Inc
Des Plaines, IL 888-838-7632
Ipswich Ale Brewery
Ipswich, MA 978-356-3329
Manhattan Special Bottling
Brooklyn, NY 718-388-4144
Shasta Beverages Inc
Baltimore, MS 800-834-9980

Sarsaparilla

Manhattan Special Bottling
Brooklyn, NY 718-388-4144

Sparkling Water

Arctic Beverages
Winnipeg, MB.................... 866-503-1270
Bevco Sales International Inc.
Surrey, BC........................ 800-663-0090
Blue Sky Beverage Company
Corona, CA........................ 800-426-7367
Coca-Cola Bottling Co. Consolidated
Charlotte, NC 800-866-2653
Coca-Cola Bottling Company UNITED, Inc.
Birmingham, AB.................. 800-844-2653
Coca-Cola European Partners
Uxbridge, Middx,................. 800-418-4223
Crystal Geyser Water Co.
Burlingame, CA 800-443-9737
Crystal Rock LLC
Watertown, CT 800-525-0070
Dr Pepper Snapple Group
Plano, TX 800-696-5891
DRY Soda Co.
Seattle, WA.......................... 888-379-7632
Eternal Water
Walnut Creek, CA................. 877-854-5494
Hinckley Springs Bottled Water
.... 800-201-6218
Kalena
Chicago, IL
Keurig Dr Pepper
Plano, TX 800-696-5891
LaCroix
Ft. Lauderdale, FL 888-241-7360
Make It Simple
Woodbury, MN
Matilija Water Company
Santa Barbara, CA 805-963-7873
Mount Olympus Waters
.... 800-782-5508
Polar Beverages Inc.
Worcester, MA 800-734-9800
Polar Water Company
Carnegie, PA 412-429-5550
R.J. Corr Naturals
Posen, IL 708-389-4200
Saratoga Spring Water Co
Saratoga Springs, NY 888-426-8642
Signature Beverage
Merrick, NY 800-277-2755
Southern Beverage Packers Inc
Appling, GA 800-326-2469
Sparkletts
Lakeland, FL......................... 800-728-5508
Spindrift Beverage
Waltham, MA 617-391-0356
Sweet Earth Foods
Moss Landing, CA 800-737-3311
Topo Chico Mineral Water
Plano, TX 888-456-4357
TOST Beverages LLC
Red Hook, NY
Universal Beverages Inc
Ponte Vedra Bch, FL............. 904-280-7795

Tonic Water

1642
Montreal, QC 800-774-4907
Regatta Craft Mixers
Locust Valley, NY

Spirits & Liqueurs

Brandy

Corby Distilleries
Toronto, ON 800-367-9079
Craft Distillers
Ukiah, CA............................. 800-782-8145
Denning's Point Distillery, LLC
Beacon, NY........................... 845-476-8413
E & J Gallo Winery
Modesto, CA......................... 877-687-9463
Heaven Hill Distilleries Inc.
Bardstown, KY 502-337-1000
Heck Cellars
Arvin, CA 661-854-6120
Hood River Distillers Inc
Hood River, OR 541-386-1588
Ironstone Vineyards
Murphys, CA......................... 209-728-1251
Kittling Ridge Estate Wines & Spirits
Vaughan, ON......................... 800-461-9463
Laird & Company
Scobeyville, NJ..................... 877-438-5247
M S Walker Inc
Somerville, MA 617-776-6700
Marie Brizard Wines & Spirits
St. Helena, CA 800-878-1123
Pernod Ricard USA
New York, NY 212-372-5400
Stoutridge Vineyard
Marlboro, NY
Todhunter Foods
West Palm Beach, FL 800-336-9463
US Distilled Products Co
Princeton, MN....................... 763-389-4903
Vie-Del Co
Fresno, CA 559-834-2525

Grappa

Catskill Distilling Company
Bethel, NY 845-583-3141

Luxury Cognac

Heaven Hill Distilleries Inc.
Bardstown, KY 502-337-1000

V.S. Cognac Three Star

Corby Distilleries
Toronto, ON 800-367-9079

V.S.O.P. Cognac

Corby Distilleries
Toronto, ON 800-367-9079

X.O. Cognac

Corby Distilleries
Toronto, ON 800-367-9079

Gin

A. Smith Bowman Distillery
Fredericksburg, VA............... 540-373-4555
Beam Suntory
Chicago, IL........................... 312-964-6999
Catskill Distilling Company
Bethel, NY 845-583-3141
Corby Distilleries
Toronto, ON 800-367-9079
Denning's Point Distillery, LLC
Beacon, NY........................... 845-476-8413
Destileria Serralles Inc
Mercedita, PR 787-840-1000
Diageo Canada Inc.
Toronto, ON 416-626-2000
E & J Gallo Winery
Modesto, CA......................... 877-687-9463
Heaven Hill Distilleries Inc.
Bardstown, KY 502-337-1000
Hiram Walker & Sons
Windsor, ON......................... 519-254-5171
Hood River Distillers Inc
Hood River, OR 541-386-1588
Laird & Company
Scobeyville, NJ..................... 877-438-5247
Marie Brizard Wines & Spirits
St. Helena, CA 800-878-1123
Orange County Distillery
Goshen, NY........................... 845-651-2929
Pernod Ricard USA
New York, NY 212-372-5400
Prohibition Distillery, LLC
Roscoe, NY........................... 917-685-8989
Stoutridge Vineyard
Marlboro, NY
Tuthilltown Spirits
Gardiner, NY......................... 845-255-1527
Union Square Wines & Spirits
New York, NY 212-675-8100
Viking Distillery
Albany, GA........................... 866-729-3722
Vincor Canada
Mississauga, ON................... 800-265-9463
Warwick Valley Winery & Distillery
Warwick, NY 845-258-4858

Irish Whiskey

Beam Suntory
Chicago, IL........................... 312-964-6999
Corby Distilleries
Toronto, ON 800-367-9079
George A Dickel & Company
Tullahoma, TN 888-342-5352
Heaven Hill Distilleries Inc.
Bardstown, KY 502-337-1000
Hiram Walker & Sons
Windsor, ON......................... 519-254-5171
Jack Daniel Distillery
Lynchburg, TN 888-551-5225
Kittling Ridge Estate Wines & Spirits
Vaughan, ON......................... 800-461-9463
Laird & Company
Scobeyville, NJ..................... 877-438-5247
Pernod Ricard USA
New York, NY 212-372-5400

Liqueurs & Cordials

Aloha Distillers
Honolulu, HI......................... 808-841-5787
Bacardi Canada, Inc.
Toronto, ON 905-451-6100
Beam Suntory
Chicago, IL........................... 312-964-6999
Black Prince Distillery Inc
Clifton, NJ............................ 973-365-2050
Chambord
Louisville, KY...................... 800-523-3811
Clear Creek Distillery
Portland, OR......................... 503-248-9470
Destileria Serralles Inc
Mercedita, PR 787-840-1000
Diageo North America Inc
Norwalk, CT......................... 203-229-2100
Florida Caribbean Distillers
Lake Alfred, FL 863-956-2002
Heaven Hill Distilleries Inc.
Bardstown, KY 502-337-1000
Highwood Distillers
High River, AB..................... 403-652-3202
Hiram Walker & Sons
Windsor, ON......................... 519-254-5171
Kittling Ridge Estate Wines & Spirits
Vaughan, ON......................... 800-461-9463
M S Walker Inc
Somerville, MA 617-776-6700
Marie Brizard Wines & Spirits
St. Helena, CA 800-878-1123
Paramount Distillers
Cleveland, OH 800-821-2989
Pernod Ricard USA
New York, NY 212-372-5400
Phillips Beverage Company
Minneapolis, MN 612-362-7500
Renault Winery
Egg Harbor City, NJ 609-965-2111
Sakeone Corp
Forest Grove, OR 800-550-7253
Todhunter Foods
West Palm Beach, FL 800-336-9463
Union Square Wines & Spirits
New York, NY 212-675-8100
US Distilled Products Co
Princeton, MN....................... 763-389-4903

Amaretto

Heaven Hill Distilleries Inc.
Bardstown, KY 502-337-1000

Anise Liqueur

Pernod Ricard USA
New York, NY 212-372-5400

Chocolate Liqueur

Aloha Distillers
Honolulu, HI......................... 808-841-5787

Coffee Liqueur

Aloha Distillers
Honolulu, HI......................... 808-841-5787
Heaven Hill Distilleries Inc.
Bardstown, KY 502-337-1000

Fruit Liqueur

KAS Spirits
Mahopac, NY 845-750-6000

Nahmias et Fils
Yonkers, NY 914-294-0055
Warwick Valley Winery & Distillery
Warwick, NY 845-258-4858

Herbal Liqueur

KAS Spirits
Mahopac, NY 845-750-6000
Tuthilltown Spirits
Gardiner, NY 845-255-1527

Schnapps Liqueuer

Marie Brizard Wines & Spirits
St. Helena, CA 800-878-1123

Neutral

Buffalo Trace Distillery
Frankfort, KY 800-654-8471
M S Walker Inc
Somerville, MA 617-776-6700
Paramount Distillers
Cleveland, OH 800-821-2989
Royal Wine Corp
Bayonne, NJ 718-384-2400

Rum

A. Smith Bowman Distillery
Fredericksburg, VA 540-373-4555
Bacardi Canada, Inc.
Toronto, ON 905-451-6100
Bacardi USA Inc
Coral Gables, FL 800-222-2734
Beam Suntory
Chicago, IL 312-964-6999
Buffalo Trace Distillery
Frankfort, KY 800-654-8471
Corby Distilleries
Toronto, ON 800-367-9079
Destileria Serralles Inc
Mercedita, PR 787-840-1000
Florida Caribbean Distillers
Lake Alfred, FL 863-956-2002
Heaven Hill Distilleries Inc.
Bardstown, KY 502-337-1000
Highwood Distillers
High River, AB 403-652-3202
Hiram Walker & Sons
Windsor, ON 519-254-5171
Hood River Distillers Inc
Hood River, OR 541-386-1588
Kittling Ridge Estate Wines & Spirits
Vaughan, ON 800-461-9463
Marie Brizard Wines & Spirits
St. Helena, CA 800-878-1123
Terressentia Corp.
Ladson, SC 843-225-3100
Trigo Corporation
Toa Baja, PR 787-794-1300
Union Square Wines & Spirits
New York, NY 212-675-8100

Dark

Bacardi Canada, Inc.
Toronto, ON 905-451-6100
Corby Distilleries
Toronto, ON 800-367-9079

White Silver

Corby Distilleries
Toronto, ON 800-367-9079

Scotch Whiskey

A. Smith Bowman Distillery
Fredericksburg, VA 540-373-4555
Bacardi Canada, Inc.
Toronto, ON 905-451-6100
Beam Suntory
Chicago, IL 312-964-6999
Brown-Forman Corp
Louisville, KY 502-585-1100
Canadian Mist Distillers
Collingwood, ON 705-445-4690
George A Dickel & Company
Tullahoma, TN 888-342-5352
Heaven Hill Distilleries Inc.
Bardstown, KY 502-337-1000
Hiram Walker & Sons
Windsor, ON 519-254-5171
Hood River Distillers Inc
Hood River, OR 541-386-1588
Jack Daniel Distillery
Lynchburg, TN 888-551-5225
Kittling Ridge Estate Wines & Spirits
Vaughan, ON 800-461-9463
Laird & Company
Scobeyville, NJ 877-438-5247
Maker's Mark Distillery Inc
Loretto, KY 270-865-2881
Marie Brizard Wines & Spirits
St. Helena, CA 800-878-1123
Pernod Ricard USA
New York, NY 212-372-5400

Blended

Maker's Mark Distillery Inc
Loretto, KY 270-865-2881

Highland Malt

Maker's Mark Distillery Inc
Loretto, KY 270-865-2881

Tequila and Mezcal

A. Smith Bowman Distillery
Fredericksburg, VA 540-373-4555
Beam Suntory
Chicago, IL 312-964-6999
Brown-Forman Corp
Louisville, KY 502-585-1100
Corby Distilleries
Toronto, ON 800-367-9079
Heaven Hill Distilleries Inc.
Bardstown, KY 502-337-1000
Highwood Distillers
High River, AB 403-652-3202
Hood River Distillers Inc
Hood River, OR 541-386-1588
Luxco Inc
St Louis, MO 314-772-2626
Marie Brizard Wines & Spirits
St. Helena, CA 800-878-1123
McCormick Distilling Co
Weston, MO 888-640-3082
Union Square Wines & Spirits
New York, NY 212-675-8100
Vincor Canada
Mississauga, ON 800-265-9463

Vodka

A. Smith Bowman Distillery
Fredericksburg, VA 540-373-4555
Bacardi Canada, Inc.
Toronto, ON 905-451-6100
Bacardi USA Inc
Coral Gables, FL 800-222-2734
Barber's Farm Distillery LLC
Middleburgh, NY
Beam Suntory
Chicago, IL 312-964-6999
Boisset Family Estates
St Helena, CA 800-878-1123
Brown-Forman Corp
Louisville, KY 502-585-1100
Capalbo's Fruit Baskets
Clifton, NJ 800-252-6262
Catskill Distilling Company
Bethel, NY 845-583-3141
Corby Distilleries
Toronto, ON 800-367-9079
Crillon Importers LTD
Paramus, NJ 201-368-8878
Denning's Point Distillery, LLC
Beacon, NY 845-476-8413
Destileria Serralles Inc
Mercedita, PR 787-840-1000
Florida Caribbean Distillers
Lake Alfred, FL 863-956-2002
Heaven Hill Distilleries Inc.
Bardstown, KY 502-337-1000
Highwood Distillers
High River, AB 403-652-3202
Hiram Walker & Sons
Windsor, ON 519-254-5171
Hood River Distillers Inc
Hood River, OR 541-386-1588
Kittling Ridge Estate Wines & Spirits
Vaughan, ON 800-461-9463
Laird & Company
Scobeyville, NJ 877-438-5247
Luxco Inc
St Louis, MO 314-772-2626
Marie Brizard Wines & Spirits
St. Helena, CA 800-878-1123
McCormick Distilling Co
Weston, MO 888-640-3082
Orange County Distillery
Goshen, NY 845-651-2929
Pernod Ricard USA
New York, NY 212-372-5400
Prohibition Distillery, LLC
Roscoe, NY 917-685-8989
R&A Imports
Pacific Palisades, CA 310-454-2247
Stoutridge Vineyard
Marlboro, NY
Terressentia Corp.
Ladson, SC 843-225-3100
Three Meadows Spirits LLC
Millerton, NY 845-702-3903
Trigo Corporation
Toa Baja, PR 787-794-1300
Tuthilltown Spirits
Gardiner, NY 845-255-1527
Union Square Wines & Spirits
New York, NY 212-675-8100
Viking Distillery
Albany, GA 866-729-3722
Vincor Canada
Mississauga, ON 800-265-9463

Whiskey, American

Beam Suntory
Chicago, IL 312-964-6999
Catskill Distilling Company
Bethel, NY 845-583-3141
Corby Distilleries
Toronto, ON 800-367-9079
Denning's Point Distillery, LLC
Beacon, NY 845-476-8413
Florida Caribbean Distillers
Lake Alfred, FL 863-956-2002
George A Dickel & Company
Tullahoma, TN 888-342-5352
Heaven Hill Distilleries Inc.
Bardstown, KY 502-337-1000
Hiram Walker & Sons
Windsor, ON 519-254-5171
Jack Daniel Distillery
Lynchburg, TN 888-551-5225
Kittling Ridge Estate Wines & Spirits
Vaughan, ON 800-461-9463
Laird & Company
Scobeyville, NJ 877-438-5247
McCormick Distilling Co
Weston, MO 888-640-3082
Nahmias et Fils
Yonkers, NY 914-294-0055
Prohibition Distillery, LLC
Roscoe, NY 917-685-8989
Sazerac Company, Inc.
Metairie, LA 866-729-3722
Stoutridge Vineyard
Marlboro, NY
US Distilled Products Co
Princeton, MN 763-389-4903

Bourbon

A. Smith Bowman Distillery
Fredericksburg, VA 540-373-4555
Brown-Forman Corp
Louisville, KY 502-585-1100
Buffalo Trace Distillery
Frankfort, KY 800-654-8471
Catskill Distilling Company
Bethel, NY 845-583-3141
Corby Distilleries
Toronto, ON 800-367-9079
Heaven Hill Distilleries Inc.
Bardstown, KY 502-337-1000
Laird & Company
Scobeyville, NJ 877-438-5247
Marie Brizard Wines & Spirits
St. Helena, CA 800-878-1123
Old Rip Van Winkle Distillery
Frankfort, KY 502-897-9113
Orange County Distillery
Goshen, NY 845-651-2929
Pernod Ricard USA
New York, NY 212-372-5400

Sazerac Company, Inc.
Metairie, LA 866-729-3722
Tuthilltown Spirits
Gardiner, NY. 845-255-1527
Viking Distillery
Albany, GA 866-729-3722

Rye Whiskey

Catskill Distilling Company
Bethel, NY 845-583-3141
Tuthilltown Spirits
Gardiner, NY. 845-255-1527

Tennessee Whiskey

Brown-Forman Corp
Louisville, KY. 502-585-1100

Whiskey, Canadian

Beam Suntory
Chicago, IL 312-964-6999
Brown-Forman Corp
Louisville, KY. 502-585-1100
Corby Distilleries
Toronto, ON 800-367-9079

Sports Drinks

Asiamerica Ingredients
Westwood, NJ. 201-497-5531
Berri Pro
Santa Monica, CA
Bonk Breaker
Santa Monica, CA. 310-315-4129
Captiva Limited Inc
Augusta, NJ. 973-579-7883
Cell-Nique
Norwalk, CT 888-417-9343
Celsius
Boca Raton, FL. 866-423-5748
Century Foods Intl LLC
Sparta, WI. 800-269-1901
Coca-Cola Beverages Northeast
Bedford, NH 844-619-3388
Cool
Richardson, TX. 972-437-9352
Crystal Star Herbal Nutrition
Salinas, CA 831-422-7500
GREEN Energy
Kailua, HI 808-396-9454
Hiball, Inc.
San Francisco, CA 833-442-2553
I Rice & Co Inc
Philadelphia, PA 800-232-6022
Ito En USA Inc
Brooklyn, NY 808-847-4477
Kill Cliff
Atlanta, GA. 855-552-5433
Lassonde Pappas & Company, Inc.
Carneys Point, NJ 800-257-7019
LifeAID
Santa Cruz, CA 888-558-1113
Masala Chai Company
Santa Cruz, CA. 831-475-8881
MODe Sports Nutrition
Costa Mesa, CA 949-274-9948
Monarch Beverage Company
Atlanta, GA. 800-241-3732
Nature's Best Inc
Hauppauge, NY 800-345-2378
Nhs Labs Inc
Star, ID 888-546-8694
Nutrisciences Labs
Farmingdale, NY 855-492-7388
Nutriwest
Douglas, WY. 800-443-3333
Nuun Active Hydration
Seattle, WA 855-426-6886
Optimum Nutrition
Aurora, IL 800-763-3444
Pitbull Energy Products
Carson, CA 800-686-3697
PowerBar
Kings Mountain, NC. 800-587-6937
Pyure Brands
Naples, FL. 305-509-5096
Queen of America
Belleview, FL 352-245-3600
Refresco Beverages US Inc.
Tampa, FL. 888-260-3776
Sherbrooke OEM Ltd
Sherbrooke, QC 866-851-2579
The Pickle Juice Company
Mesquite, TX 972-755-0289
Tigo+
FL 786-207-4772
Tova Industries LLC
Louisville, KY 888-532-8682
Ultima Health Products Inc.
Cortland, OH. 888-663-8584
Uptime Energy, Inc.
Canoga Park, CA
Wild Aseptics, LLC
Erlanger, KY. 877-787-7221

Water

3 Springs Water Co
Laurel Run, PA 800-332-7873
3 Water
Huntington, NY 877-371-8704
Absopure Water Company
Plymouth, MI 800-422-7678
Acqua Blox LLC
Santa Fe Springs, CA 562-693-9599
Adobe Springs
Patterson, CA 408-897-3023
Alamance Foods
Burlington, NC
Alpine Valley Water
Harvey, IL. 708-333-3910
Aqua Clara Bottling & Distribution
Clearwater, FL 727-446-2999
Arbor Springs Water Co
Ferndale, MI 248-543-7151
Ax Water
Fargo, ND
Blossom Water, LLC
Westwood, MA. 855-325-5777
Blue Hills Spring Water Company
Quincy, MA. 614-715-3900
Blue Sky Beverage Company
Corona, CA. 800-426-7367
Captiva Limited Inc
Augusta, NJ. 973-579-7883
Cascade Clear Water
Portland, OR. 800-888-3879
Clearly Canadian Beverage Corporation
Vaughan, ON. 866-414-2326
Crystal Springs
Mississauga, ON. 800-822-5889
Crystal Springs Bottled Water
Lakeland, FL. 800-728-5508
Crystal Springs Water Company
Lakeland, FL. 800-728-5508
Culligan International Company
Rosemont, IL. 847-205-6000
Distillata
Cleveland, OH 800-999-2906
DS Services of America
Lakeland, FL. 800-728-5508
Eldorado Artesian Springs Inc
Louisville, CO. 303-499-1316
Essentia Water
Bothell, WA. 877-293-2239
Eureka Water Co
Oklahoma City, OK 800-310-8474
Fantis Foods Inc
Carlstadt, NJ 201-933-6200
Fizz-O Water Co
Tulsa, OK 918-834-3691
Fizzy Lizzy
Jersey City, NJ 800-203-9336
Girard Spring Water
North Providence, RI 800-477-9287
Glen Summit Springs Water Company
Mountain Top, PA. 800-621-7596
Global Beverage Company
Rochester, NY. 585-381-3560
Green-Go Cactus Water
Oakville, CA. 707-944-2039
GWB Foods Corporation
Brooklyn, NY 877-977-7610
Harrisburg Dairies Inc
Harrisburg, PA 800-692-7429
Hawaiian Natural Water Company
Pearl City, HI 808-483-0520
Heck Cellars
Arvin, CA 661-854-6120
Herbal Water, Inc.
Yuba City, CA. 610-668-4000
Holly Camp Springs Inc
Hudgins, VA 804-795-2096
Island Sweetwater Beverage Company
Bryn Mawr, PA 610-525-7444
Kentwood Springs
Lakeland, FL. 800-728-5508
Le Bleu Corp
Advance, NC. 800-854-4471
Light Rock Beverage Company
Danbury, CT 203-743-3410
Lipsey Mountain Spring Water
Norcross, GA 770-449-0001
Lynn Springs Water LLC
Tucker, GA 770-572-5928
Maverick Brands, LLC
Palo Alto, CA 424-571-7230
Mayer Bros
Buffalo, NY. 800-696-2928
Metro Mint
San Francisco, CA 415-979-0781
Minnehaha Spring Water Company
Cleveland, OH 216-431-0243
Monarch Beverage Company
Atlanta, GA. 800-241-3732
Mountain Valley Spring Company
Hot Springs, AR. 800-643-1501
Mountain Valley Spring Water
Asheville, NC 800-627-1062
Mt Claire Beverages
Torrington, CT 888-525-2473
Music Mountain Water Company
Shreveport, LA 800-349-6555
Nantze Springs Inc
Dothan, AL. 800-239-7873
Natural Group
Oxnard, CA. 805-485-3420
Natural Spring Water Company
Johnson City, TN 423-926-7905
Naya
Montreal, QC 450-562-7911
Neenah Springs
Oxford, WI 608-586-5696
North American Water Group
Overland Park, KS 913-469-1156
North Country Natural Spring Water
Port Kent, NY. 518-834-9400
Northern Falls
Rockford, MI 616-915-0970
Oakhurst Dairy
Portland, ME. 800-482-0718
Office General des Eaux Minerales
Montreal, QC 514-482-7221
Ozarka Drinking Water
Dallas, TX. 817-354-9526
Peace Mountain Natural Beverages
Springfield, MA 413-567-4942
Penta Water
Colton, CA 800-531-5088
Pocono Spring Company
Mt Pocono, PA 800-634-4584
Premium Water
Kansas City, MO. 800-332-3332
Primo Water Corporation
Winston-Salem, NC 844-237-7466
Private Spring Water
San Martin, CA. 877-664-1500
Pure Flo Water Co
Santee, CA 800-787-3356
Q Mixers
Brooklyn, NY 718-398-6642
Quibell Spring Water Beverage
Martinsville, VA 540-632-0100
R.J. Corr Naturals
Posen, IL. 708-389-4200
Rebound
Newburgh, NY 845-562-5400
Refresco Beverages US Inc.
Tampa, FL. 888-260-3776
Sand Springs
Williamstown, MA 413-458-8281
Saratoga Spring Water Co
Saratoga Springs, NY 888-426-8642
Schneider's Dairy Inc
Pittsburgh, PA. 412-881-3525
SnowBird Corporation
Bayonne, NJ 800-576-1616
Something Natural LLC
Boston, MA. 617-315-7169
St. Clair Industries
Ft Lauderdale, FL. 954-491-0400
Talking Rain Beverage Co
Preston, WA 800-734-0748
TRC Corp
Tulsa, OK 800-258-5028
Triple Springs Spring Water Co
Meriden, CT 203-235-8374

Universal Beverages Inc
Leesburg, FL....................352-315-1010
Varni Brothers/7-Up Bottling
Modesto, CA....................209-521-1777
Vichy Springs Mineral Water
Ukiah, CA....................707-462-9515
Water Concepts
East Dundee, IL....................847-699-9797
White Rock Products Corp
Flushing, NY....................800-969-7625
Windmill Water Inc
Edgewood, NM....................505-281-9287
Winterbrook Beverage Group
Greendale, IN....................812-537-7348
Zephyrhills Bottled Water Company
Tampa, FL....................800-950-9398

Bottled

Absopure Water Company
Plymouth, MI....................800-422-7678
Alamance Foods
Burlington, NC
Alpine Valley Water
Harvey, IL....................708-333-3910
Aqua Clara Bottling & Distribution
Clearwater, FL....................727-446-2999
Arbor Springs Water Co
Ferndale, MI....................248-543-7151
Arctic Beverages
Winnipeg, MB....................866-503-1270
Asarasi
Danbury, CT
Belmar Spring Water
Glen Rock, NJ....................201-444-1010
Bevco Sales International Inc.
Surrey, BC....................800-663-0090
Bio-Hydration Research Lab
Carlsbad, CA....................800-531-5088
Brands Within Reach
Mamaroneck, NY....................847-720-9090
Broughton Foods LLC
El Paso, TX....................800-395-7004
Calcium Springs Water Company
Park City, UT....................435-615-7600
Captiva Limited Inc
Augusta, NJ....................973-579-7883
Clark Spring Water Co
Pueblo, CO....................719-543-1594
Coca-Cola Beverages Northeast
Bedford, NH....................844-619-3388
Coca-Cola Co.
Atlanta, GA....................800-438-2653
Country Pure Foods Inc
Akron, OH....................877-995-8423
Crystal Rock LLC
Watertown, CT....................800-525-0070
Crystal Springs
Mississauga, ON....................800-822-5889
Crystal Springs Bottled Water
Lakeland, FL....................800-728-5508
Crystal Springs Water Company
Lakeland, FL....................800-728-5508
Deer Park Spring Water Co
Chesapeake, VA....................800-832-0271
Distillata
Cleveland, OH....................800-999-2906
DS Services of America
Lakeland, FL....................800-728-5508
Eldorado Artesian Springs Inc
Louisville, CO....................303-499-1316
Eureka Water Co
Oklahoma City, OK....................800-310-8474
Figuerola Laboratories
Santa Ynez, CA....................800-219-1147
Fiji Water Co LLC
Los Angeles, CA....................888-426-3454
Girard Spring Water
North Providence, RI....................800-477-9287
Glen Summit Springs Water Company
Mountain Top, PA....................800-621-7596
Global Beverage Company
Rochester, NY....................585-381-3560
GWB Foods Corporation
Brooklyn, NY....................877-977-7610
H3O
Beckley, WV....................888-436-9287
Hawaiian Natural Water Company
Pearl City, HI....................808-483-0520
Heck Cellars
Arvin, CA....................661-854-6120
Hi-Country Foods Corporation
Selah, WA....................509-697-7292
Hinckley Springs Bottled Water
....................800-201-6218
Holly Camp Springs Inc
Hudgins, VA....................804-795-2096
Island Sweetwater Beverage Company
Bryn Mawr, PA....................610-525-7444
Le Bleu Corp
Advance, NC....................800-854-4471
Light Rock Beverage Company
Danbury, CT....................203-743-3410
Lipsey Mountain Spring Water
Norcross, GA....................770-449-0001
Matilija Water Company
Santa Barbara, CA....................805-963-7873
Merci Spring Water
Maryland Heights, MO....................314-872-9323
Mount Olympus Waters
....................800-782-5508
Mountain Valley Spring Company
Hot Springs, AR....................800-643-1501
Mountain Valley Spring Water
Asheville, NC....................800-627-1062
Music Mountain Water Company
Shreveport, LA....................800-349-6555
Natural Spring Water Company
Johnson City, TN....................423-926-7905
Naya
Montreal, QC....................450-562-7911
Neo North America Inc.
San Francisco, CA....................800-604-7051
New Age Beverages
Denver, CO....................303-289-8655
Nirvana Natural Spring Water
Forestport, NY....................888-463-5675
North American Water Group
Overland Park, KS....................913-469-1156
Peace Mountain Natural Beverages
Springfield, MA....................413-567-4942
Pocono Mountain Bottling Company
Wilkes Barre, PA....................570-822-7695
Pocono Spring Company
Mt Pocono, PA....................800-634-4584
Polar Beverages Inc.
Worcester, MA....................800-734-9800
Polar Water Company
Carnegie, PA....................412-429-5550
Premium Water
Kansas City, MO....................800-332-3332
Primo Water Corporation
Winston-Salem, NC....................844-237-7466
Private Spring Water
San Martin, CA....................877-664-1500
Pure Flo Water Co
Santee, CA....................800-787-3356
Quibell Spring Water Beverage
Martinsville, VA....................540-632-0100
SnowBird Corporation
Bayonne, NJ....................800-576-1616
Southern Beverage Packers Inc
Appling, GA....................800-326-2469
Sparkletts
Lakeland, FL....................800-728-5508
Tanzamaji USA
Fairview, TX
Titusville Dairy Products Co
Titusville, PA....................800-352-0101
Universal Beverages Inc
Leesburg, FL....................352-315-1010
Universal Beverages Inc
Ponte Vedra Bch, FL....................904-280-7795
Varni Brothers/7-Up Bottling
Modesto, CA....................209-521-1777
Vichy Springs Mineral Water
Ukiah, CA....................707-462-9515
Virginia Artesian Bottling Company
Mechanicsville, VA....................804-779-7500
Water Concepts
East Dundee, IL....................847-699-9797
Windmill Water Inc
Edgewood, NM....................505-281-9287
Winterbrook Beverage Group
Greendale, IN....................812-537-7348
Zephyrhills Bottled Water Company
Tampa, FL....................800-950-9398

Distilled

Alacer Corp
Carlisle, PA....................888-425-2362
Alpine Valley Water
Harvey, IL....................708-333-3910
Arcadia Dairy Farms Inc
Arden, NC....................828-684-3556
Belmar Spring Water
Glen Rock, NJ....................201-444-1010
Bevco Sales International Inc.
Surrey, BC....................800-663-0090
Broughton Foods LLC
El Paso, TX....................800-395-7004
Clark Spring Water Co
Pueblo, CO....................719-543-1594
Crystal Rock LLC
Watertown, CT....................800-525-0070
Crystal Springs Water Company
Lakeland, FL....................800-728-5508
Deer Park Spring Water Co
Chesapeake, VA....................800-832-0271
Distillata
Cleveland, OH....................800-999-2906
Energy Brands/Haute Source
Flushing, NY....................800-746-0087
Fizz-O Water Co
Tulsa, OK....................918-834-3691
Hinckley Springs Bottled Water
....................800-201-6218
Le Bleu Corp
Advance, NC....................800-854-4471
Matilija Water Company
Santa Barbara, CA....................805-963-7873
Merci Spring Water
Maryland Heights, MO....................314-872-9323
Mount Olympus Waters
....................800-782-5508
Mountain Valley Spring Company
Hot Springs, AR....................800-643-1501
Polar Beverages Inc.
Worcester, MA....................800-734-9800
Polar Water Company
Carnegie, PA....................412-429-5550
Premium Water
Kansas City, MO....................800-332-3332
Reiter Dairy
Newport, KY....................800-544-6455
SnowBird Corporation
Bayonne, NJ....................800-576-1616
Southern Beverage Packers Inc
Appling, GA....................800-326-2469
Sparkletts
Lakeland, FL....................800-728-5508
Zephyr Hills
Tampa, FL....................800-950-9398

Flavored

Avitae
Cleveland, OH....................888-228-4823
Bitter Love
Portland, ME
Blossom Water, LLC
Westwood, MA....................855-325-5777
Blume Honey Water
Pittsburgh, PA....................412-406-7391
Captiva Limited Inc
Augusta, NJ....................973-579-7883
Clearly Canadian Beverage Corporation
Vanghan, ON....................866-414-2326
Ex Drinks
Henderson, NV....................866-753-4929
Flurowater, Inc.
Los Angeles, CA
Harmless Harvest
San Francisco, CA
Heritage Short Bread
Hilton Head Isle, SC....................843-422-3458
Hiball, Inc.
San Francisco, CA....................833-442-2553
Hinckley Springs Bottled Water
....................800-201-6218
Hint Water
San Francisco, CA....................415-513-4050
Hubble
Manhattan Beach, CA
Keurig Dr Pepper
Plano, TX....................800-696-5891
KidsLuv
San Francisco, CA....................855-543-7588
Northern Falls
Rockford, MI....................616-915-0970
Pervida
Blacksburg, VA....................540-808-0800
Sapp Birch Water
Chicago, IL....................708-351-7777
Saratoga Spring Water Co
Saratoga Springs, NY....................888-426-8642
Sun Opta Inc.
Mississauga, ON....................952-820-2518

Treo Brands
Harrison, NY....................914-341-1850
True Nopal Cactus Water
Scottsdale, AZ....................480-636-8044
Tu Me Beverage Company
CA....................818-237-5105
Unique Beverage Company
Everett, WA....................425-267-0959
Varni Brothers/7-Up Bottling
Modesto, CA....................209-521-1777
Verday
New York, NY
Watermark Innovation
Southampton, NY....................631-259-2329

Mineral

3 Springs Water Co
Laurel Run, PA....................800-332-7873
Adobe Springs
Patterson, CA....................408-897-3023
Beaulieu Vineyard
Rutherford, CA....................707-257-5749
Clearly Canadian Beverage Corporation
Vanghan, ON....................866-414-2326
Matilija Water Company
Santa Barbara, CA....................805-963-7873
Monticello Vineyards-Corley
Napa, CA....................707-253-2802
Office General des Eaux Minerales
Montreal, QC....................514-482-7221
R.J. Corr Naturals
Posen, IL....................708-389-4200
SD Watersboten
Ardmore, PA....................610-645-7572
Seawater Food & Beverage
Dallas, TX....................214-537-5070
Sebastiani Vineyards
Sonoma, CA....................855-232-2338

Spring

Amanda Hills Spring Water
Etna, OH....................800-375-0885
Arizona Beverage Company
Cincinnati, OH....................800-832-3775
Belmar Spring Water
Glen Rock, NJ....................201-444-1010
Bevco Sales International Inc.
Surrey, BC....................800-663-0090
Clark Spring Water Co
Pueblo, CO....................719-543-1594
Country Pure Foods Inc
Akron, OH....................877-995-8423
Crystal Geyser Water Co.
Burlingame, CA....................800-443-9737
Crystal Rock LLC
Watertown, CT....................800-525-0070
Crystal Springs Water Company
Lakeland, FL....................800-728-5508
Deer Park Spring Water Co
Chesapeake, VA....................800-832-0271
Eternal Water
Walnut Creek, CA....................877-854-5494
Fizz-O Water Co
Tulsa, OK....................918-834-3691
Garelick Farms
Dallas, TX....................800-343-4982
Girard Spring Water
North Providence, RI....................800-477-9287
Glen Summit Springs Water Company
Mountain Top, PA....................800-621-7596
Harford Glen Water
Harford, NY....................866-844-8351
Harrisburg Dairies Inc
Harrisburg, PA....................800-692-7429
Hawaiian Natural Water Company
Pearl City, HI....................808-483-0520
Hinckley Springs Bottled Water
....................800-201-6218
Holly Camp Springs Inc
Hudgins, VA....................804-795-2096
Kentwood Springs
Lakeland, FL....................800-728-5508
Matilija Water Company
Santa Barbara, CA....................805-963-7873
Mayer Bros
Buffalo, NY....................800-696-2928
Merci Spring Water
Maryland Heights, MO....................314-872-9323
Meridian Beverage Company
Atlanta, GA....................800-728-1481
Minnehaha Spring Water Company
Cleveland, OH....................216-431-0243
Mount Olympus Waters
....................800-782-5508
Mountain Valley Spring Company
Hot Springs, AR....................800-643-1501
Music Mountain Water Company
Shreveport, LA....................800-349-6555
National Beverage Corporation
Fort Lauderdale, FL....................877-622-3499
Natural Spring Water Company
Johnson City, TN....................423-926-7905
Naya
Montreal, QC....................450-562-7911
North Country Natural Spring Water
Port Kent, NY....................518-834-9400
Northern Falls
Rockford, MI....................616-915-0970
Polar Beverages Inc.
Worcester, MA....................800-734-9800
Polar Water Company
Carnegie, PA....................412-429-5550
Premium Water
Kansas City, MO....................800-332-3332
Private Spring Water
San Martin, CA....................877-664-1500
Sand Springs
Williamstown, MA....................413-458-8281
Saratoga Spring Water Co
Saratoga Springs, NY....................888-426-8642
Signature Beverage
Merrick, NY....................800-277-2755
SnowBird Corporation
Bayonne, NJ....................800-576-1616
Southern Beverage Packers Inc
Appling, GA....................800-326-2469
Triple Springs Spring Water Co
Meriden, CT....................203-235-8374
Tumai Water
Martinsburg, WV....................866-948-8624
Varni Brothers/7-Up Bottling
Modesto, CA....................209-521-1777
White Rock Products Corp
Flushing, NY....................800-969-7625
Windmill Water Inc
Edgewood, NM....................505-281-9287
Yoder Dairies
Chesapeake, VA....................757-482-4068
Zephyr Hills
Tampa, FL....................800-950-9398

Wines

A to Z Wineworks
Newburg, OR....................800-739-4455
A. Nonini Winery
Fresno, CA....................559-275-1936
A. Rafanelli Winery
Healdsburg, CA....................707-433-1385
Abingdon Vineyard & Winery
Abingdon, VA....................276-623-1255
Acacia Vineyard
Napa, CA....................877-226-1700
Ackerman Winery
Amana, IA....................319-622-3379
Adair Vineyards
New Paltz, NY....................845-255-1377
Adam Puchta Winery
Hermann, MO....................573-486-5596
Adams County Winery
Orrtanna, PA....................877-601-7936
Adelaida Cellars Inc
Paso Robles, CA....................800-676-1232
Adelsheim Vineyard
Newberg, OR....................503-538-3652
Adler Fels Winery
Santa Rosa, CA....................707-539-3123
Afton Mountain Vineyards Inc
Afton, VA....................540-456-8667
Ahlgren Vineyard
Boulder Creek, CA....................800-338-6071
Airlie Winery
Monmouth, OR....................503-838-6013
Alba Vineyard & Winery
Milford, NJ....................908-995-7800
Alexis Bailly Vineyard
Hastings, MN....................651-437-1413
Allegro Winery & Vineyards
Brogue, PA....................717-927-9148
Allied Wine Corporation
Ellenville, NY....................800-796-4100
Almarla Vineyards & Winery
Shubuta, MS....................601-687-5548
Alpen Cellars
Trinity Center, CA....................530-266-9513
Alpine Vineyards
Monroe, OR....................541-424-5851
Alta Vineyard Cellar
Calistoga, CA....................707-942-6708
Altamura Winery
Napa, CA....................707-253-2000
Alto Vineyards & Winery
Alto Pass, IL....................618-893-4898
Amador Foothill Winery
Plymouth, CA....................800-778-9463
Amalthea Cellars Farm Winery
Atco, NJ....................856-768-8585
Amavi Cellars
Walla Walla, WA....................509-525-3541
Amberg Wine Cellars
Clifton Springs, NY....................315-462-3455
AmByth Estate
Templeton, CA....................805-319-6967
Americana Vineyards & Winery
Interlaken, NY....................888-600-8067
Amity Vineyards
Amity, OR....................888-264-8966
Amizetta Vineyards
St Helena, CA....................707-963-1460
Amrhein's Wine Cellars
Bent Mountain, VA....................540-929-4632
Amwell Valley Vineyard
Ringoes, NJ....................908-788-5852
Anchor Brewing Company
San Francisco, CA....................415-863-8350
Ancient Peaks Winery
Santa Margarita, CA....................805-365-7045
Anderson's Conn Valley Vineyards
St Helena, CA....................800-946-3497
Andrew Peller Limited
Grimsby, ON....................905-643-4131
Annapolis Winery
Annapolis, CA....................707-886-5460
Antelope Valley Winery
Lancaster, CA....................800-282-8332
Anthony Road Wine Co
Penn Yan, NY....................800-559-2182
Arbor Crest Wine Cellars
Spokane, WA....................509-927-9463
Arbor Hill Grapery & Winery
Naples, NY....................800-554-7553
Arbor Mist Winery
Canandaigua, NY....................866-396-7394
Arcadian Estate Winery
Rock Stream, NY....................800-298-1346
Arel Group Wine & Spirits Inc
Atlanta, GA....................404-869-4387
Argyle Winery
Dundee, OR....................888-427-4953
Ariel Vineyards
Napa, CA....................800-456-9472
Arizona Vineyards
Nogales, AZ....................520-287-7972
Arns Winery
St Helena, CA....................707-963-3429
Arrowood Winery
Glen Ellen, CA....................800-938-5170
Artesa Vineyards & Winery
Napa, CA....................707-224-1668
Ashland Vineyards & Winery
Ashland, OR....................541-488-0088
ASV Wines
Delano, CA....................661-792-3159
Atlas Peak Vineyards
Napa, CA....................707-252-7971
Atwater Block Brewing Company
Detroit, MI....................313-877-9205
Au Bon Climat Winery
Los Olivos, CA....................805-937-9801
Augusta Winery
Augusta, MO....................888-667-9463
Autumn Hill Vineyards/Blue Ridge Wine
Stanardsville, VA....................434-985-6100
Autumn Wind Vineyard
Newberg, OR....................503-538-6931
Avalon Organic Coffees
Albuquerque, NM....................800-662-2575
B R Cohn Winery & Olive Oil Co
Glen Ellen, CA....................800-330-4064
Babcock Winery & Vineyards
Lompoc, CA....................805-736-1455
Bagley's
Hector, NY....................607-582-6421
Baileyana Winery
San Luis Obispo, CA....................805-544-9080

Baily Vineyard & Winery
Temecula, CA 951-676-9463
Balagna Winery Company
Los Alamos, NM.................. 505-672-3678
Baldwin Vineyards
Pine Bush, NY 845-744-2226
Balic Winery
Mays Landing, NJ................ 609-625-2166
Banfi Vintners
Old Brookville, NY.............. 800-645-6511
Barboursville Vineyards
Barboursville, VA 540-832-3824
Barca Wine Cellars
Roseville, CA 916-786-0770
Bargetto Winery
Soquel, CA 800-422-7438
Baron Vineyards
Paso Robles, CA 805-239-3313
Basignani Winery
Sparks Glencoe, MD.............. 410-472-0703
Batavia Wine Cellars
Canandaigua, NY 585-396-7600
Baxters Vineyards & Winery
Nauvoo, IL 800-854-1396
Baywood Cellars
Lodi, CA 800-214-0445
Beachaven Vineyards & Winery
Clarksville, TN 931-645-8867
Bear Creek Winery
Cave Junction, OR 877-273-4843
Beaucanon Estate Wines
Napa, CA........................ 800-660-3520
Beaulieu Vineyard
Rutherford, CA 707-257-5749
Beckmen Vineyards
Los Olivos, CA 805-688-8664
Bedell Northfork LLC
Cutchogue, NY 631-734-7537
Bell Mountain Vineyards
Willow City, TX 830-685-3297
Bellerose Vineyard
Healdsburg, CA 707-433-1637
Benmarl Wine Co
Marlboro, NY 845-236-4265
Benziger Family Winery
Glen Ellen, CA 888-490-2739
Bernardo Winery
San Diego, CA 858-487-1866
Bernardus Winery Tasting Rm
Carmel Valley, CA 800-223-2533
Berryessa Gap Tasting Room
Winters, CA 530-795-3201
Bethel Heights Vineyard
Salem, OR....................... 503-399-9588
Bianchi Winery
Paso Robles, CA 805-226-9922
Bias Vineyards & Winery
Berger, MO 800-905-2427
Bidwell Vineyard
Cutchogue, NY 631-734-5200
Biltmore Estate Wine Company
Asheville, NC 800-411-3812
Binns Vineyards & Winery
Las Cruces, NM 575-526-6738
Bishop Farms Winery
Cheshire, CT 203-272-8243
Black Bear Farm Winery
Chenango Forks, NY 607-656-9863
Black Mesa Winery
Velarde, NM 800-852-6372
Black Sheep Vintners
Murphys, CA..................... 209-728-2157
Blalock Seafood & Specialty
Orange Beach, AL 251-974-5811
Blue Hills Spring Water Company
Quincy, MA...................... 614-715-3900
Blue Mountain Vineyards
New Tripoli, PA 610-298-3068
Blumenhof Vineyards-Winery
Dutzow, MO 800-419-2245
Boeger Winery
Placerville, CA 800-655-2634
Bogle Vineyards Inc
Clarksburg, CA.................. 916-744-1030
Boisset Family Estates
St Helena, CA 800-878-1123
Bonny Doon Vineyard
Santa Cruz, CA.................. 888-819-6789
Bonterra Vineyard
Hopland, CA..................... 707-744-7575
Boordy Vineyards Inc
Hydes, MD 410-592-5015
Bordoni Vineyards
Vallejo, CA 707-642-1504
Borra Vineyards
Lodi, CA 209-368-2446
Boskydel Vineyard
Lake Leelanau, MI 231-256-7272
Bouchaine Vineyards
Napa, CA........................ 800-654-9463
Brandborg Cellars
Elkton, OR 510-215-9553
Brander Vineyard
Santa Ynez, CA.................. 800-970-9979
Braren Pauli Winery
Redwood Valley, CA.............. 800-423-6519
Braswell's Winery
Dora, AL 205-648-8335
Bravard Vineyards & Winery
Hopkinsville, KY 270-269-2583
Breaux Vineyards
Purcellville, VA................ 800-492-9961
Breitenbach Wine Cellars
Dover, OH....................... 330-343-3603
Briceland Vineyards
Redway, CA 707-923-2429
Bridgeview Vineyards Winery
Cave Junction, OR 877-273-4843
Brimstone Hill Vineyard
Pine Bush, NY 845-744-2231
Bristle Ridge Vineyards
Knob Noster, MO 800-994-9463
Broad Run Vineyards
Louisville, KY 502-231-0372
Broadley Vineyards
Monroe, OR 541-847-5934
Bronco Wine Co
Ceres, CA 855-874-2394
Brookmere Wine & Vineyard
Belleville, PA 717-935-5380
Brotherhood Winery
Washingtonville, NY 845-496-3661
Brothers International Food Corporation
Rochester, NY................... 585-343-3007
Brown County Winery
Nashville, IN................... 888-298-2984
Brown-Forman Corp
Louisville, KY.................. 502-585-1100
Brutocao Cellars
Hopland, CA..................... 800-433-3689
Bryant Vineyard
Talladega, AL 256-268-2638
Buccia Vineyard
Conneaut, OH 440-593-5976
Buckingham Valley Vineyards
Buckingham, PA 215-794-7188
Buehler Vineyards
St Helena, CA 707-963-2155
Buena Vista Historic Tstng Rm
Sonoma, CA 800-926-1266
Buffalo Trace Distillery
Frankfort, KY 800-654-8471
Bully Hill Vineyards
Hammondsport, NY 607-868-3610
Burnley Vineyards
Barboursville, VA 540-832-2828
Butler Winery
Bloomington, IN................. 812-332-6660
Butterfly Creek Winery
Mariposa, CA 209-742-4567
Buttonwood Farm Winery & Vineyard
Solvang, CA..................... 800-715-1404
Byington Vineyard & Winery
Los Gatos, CA................... 408-354-1111
Byron Vineyard & Winery
Santa Maria, CA 805-938-7365
Cache Cellars
Davis, CA 530-756-6068
Cain Vineyard & Winery
St Helena, CA 707-963-1616
Cakebread Cellars
Rutherford, CA 800-588-0298
Calafia Cellars
St Helena, CA 707-963-0114
Calera Wine Co
Hollister, CA................... 831-637-9170
California Olive Oil Council
Berkeley, CA.................... 888-718-9830
Callaway Vineyards & Winery
Temecula, CA 800-472-2377
Camas Prairie Winery
Moscow, ID...................... 800-616-0214
Cambria Winery
Santa Maria, CA 888-339-9463
Campagana Winery
Redwood Valley, CA.............. 707-485-1221
Campari
New York, NY 212-891-3600
Canoe Ridge Vineyard
Walla Walla, WA................. 509-527-0885
Capalbo's Fruit Baskets
Clifton, NJ..................... 800-252-6262
Caparone Winery LLC
Paso Robles, CA 805-610-5308
Caporale Winery
Napa, CA........................ 707-253-9230
Caprock Winery Inc
Lubbock, TX..................... 800-546-9463
Cardinale Winery
Oakville, CA.................... 800-588-0279
Carlson Vineyards Winery
Palisade, CO 888-464-5554
Carmenet Winery
Sonoma, CA 707-996-3526
Carneros Creek Winery
Napa, CA........................ 707-253-9464
Carrousel Cellars
Gilroy, CA...................... 408-847-2060
Casa Larga Vineyards
Fairport, NY 585-223-4210
Casa Nuestra Winery & Vineyard
St Helena, CA 866-844-9463
Cascade Mountain Winery
Amenia, NY 845-373-9021
Castello di Borghese Vineyard
Cutchogue, NY 631-734-5111
Catoctin Vineyards
Brookeville, MD................. 301-774-2310
Cavender Castle Winery
Atlanta, GA..................... 706-864-4759
Caymus Vineyards
Rutherford, CA 707-967-3010
Cayuga Ridge Estate Winery
Ovid, NY........................ 800-598-9463
Cecchetti Sebastiani Cellar
Sonoma, CA 707-933-3230
Cedar Creek Winery
Cedarburg, WI................... 800-827-8020
Cedar Mountain Winery
Livermore, CA 925-373-6636
Chacewater Winery and Olive Mill
Kelseyville, CA................. 707-279-2995
Chaddsford Winery
Chadds Ford, PA................. 610-388-6221
Chalet Debonne Vineyards
Madison, OH..................... 440-466-3485
Chalk Hill Estate Winery
Healdsburg, CA 707-657-4839
Chalone Vineyard
Soledad, CA 831-678-1717
Chambord
Louisville, KY.................. 800-523-3811
Champoeg Wine Cellars Inc
Aurora, OR 503-678-2144
Channing Rudd Cellars
Middletown, CA.................. 707-987-2209
Chappellet Winery
St Helena, CA 800-494-6379
Charles B. Mitchell Vineyards
Somerset, CA 800-704-9463
Charles Krug Winery
St Helena, CA 707-967-2200
Charles Spinetta Winery
Plymouth, CA 209-245-3384
Chateau Anne Marie
Carlton, OR..................... 503-864-2991
Chateau Boswell Winery
St Helena, CA 707-963-5472
Chateau Chevre Winery
Napa, CA........................ 707-944-2184
Chateau des Charmes Wines
St. Davids, ON 800-263-2541
Chateau Diana Winery
Healdsburg, CA 707-433-6992
Chateau Grand Traverse Winery
Traverse City, MI 231-938-6120
Chateau Julien Winery
Carmel, CA...................... 831-624-2600
Chateau LA Fayette Reneau
Hector, NY 800-469-9463
Chateau Montelena Winery
Calistoga, CA 707-942-5105
Chateau Morrisette Winery
Floyd, VA 540-593-2865
Chateau Potelle Winery
St Helena, CA 707-255-9440

Chateau Ra-Ha
Jerseyville, IL 866-639-4832
Chateau Souverain
Cloverdale, CA 877-687-9463
Chateau St Jean Winery
Kenwood, CA 707-833-4134
Chatom Vineyards Inc
San Andreas, CA. 800-435-8852
Chestnut Mountain Winery
Hoschton, GA 770-867-6914
Chicama Vineyards
West Tisbury, MA 888-244-2262
Chimere Winery
Santa Maria, CA 805-928-5611
Chouinard Vineyards & Winery
Castro Valley, CA 510-582-9900
Christensen Ridge Winery
Madison, VA 540-923-4800
Christine Woods Winery
Philo, CA. 707-895-2115
Christopher Creek Winery
Healdsburg, CA 707-433-2001
Cienega Valley Winery/DeRose
Hollister, CA. 831-636-9143
Cimarron Cellars
Caney, OK. 580-889-5997
Cinnabar Winery
Saratoga, CA. 408-867-1010
Claiborne & Churchill Vintners
San Luis Obispo, CA 805-544-4066
Clear Creek Distillery
Portland, OR 503-248-9470
Cliff Lede Vineyards
Yountville, CA 800-428-2259
Cline Cellars
Sonoma, CA 800-543-2070
Clinton Vineyards Inc
Clinton Corners, NY. 845-266-5372
Clos Du Bois Winery
Geyserville, CA 800-222-3189
Clos Du Lac Cellars
Ione, CA 209-274-2238
Clos Du Val Co LTD
Napa, CA. 707-261-5200
Clos Pegase Winery
Calistoga, CA 800-866-8583
Cloudstone Vineyards
Los Altos Hills, CA 650-948-8621
Clover Hill Vineyards & Winery
Breinigsville, PA. 800-256-8374
Cocolalla Winery
Cocolalla, ID. 208-263-3774
Colorado Cellars
Palisade, CO 970-464-7921
Columbia Winery
Woodinville, WA. 425-488-2776
Concannon Vineyard
Livermore, CA 800-258-9866
Conneaut Cellars Winery LLC
Conneaut Lake, PA 877-229-9463
Conrotto A. Winery
Gilroy, CA. 408-847-2233
Coon Creek Winery
St Helena, CA. 800-793-7960
Cooper Mountain Vineyards
Beaverton, OR 503-649-0027
Cooper Vineyards
Louisa, VA 540-894-5474
Cosentino Winery
Napa, CA. 800-764-1220
Country Life
Hauppauge, NY 800-645-5768
Cowie Wine Cellars & Vineyards
Paris, AR. 479-963-3990
Crescini Wines
Soquel, CA 831-462-1466
Cribari Vineyard Inc
Fresno, CA 800-277-9095
Cristom Vineyards
Salem, OR. 503-375-3068
Cronin Vineyards
Woodside, CA. 650-851-1452
Crooked Vine/Stony Ridge Wnry
Livermore, CA 925-449-0458
Crossings Winery
Glenns Ferry, ID 208-366-2539
Crown Regal Wine Cellars
Brooklyn, NY 718-604-1430
Cruse Vineyards
Chester, SC 803-377-3944
Cuneo Cellars
Amity, OR. 503-835-2782

Cuvaison Winery
Calistoga, CA 707-942-6266
Cygnet Cellars
Hollister, CA. 831-637-7559
Dalla Valle Vineyards
Napa, CA. 707-944-2676
Damiani Wine Cellars LLC
Burdett, NY. 607-546-5557
Davis Bynum Winery
Healdsburg, CA 800-826-1073
Deaver Vineyards
Plymouth, CA 209-245-4099
Delicato Family Vineyards
Napa, CA. 707-265-1700
Deloach Vineyards
Santa Rosa, CA. 707-755-3300
Delorimier Winery
Geyserville, CA 800-546-7718
Denatale Vineyards
Healdsburg, CA 707-431-8460
Destileria Serralles Inc
Mercedita, PR. 787-840-1000
Devlin Wine Cellars
Soquel, CA 831-476-7288
Diageo Canada Inc.
Toronto, ON 416-626-2000
Diageo North America Inc
Norwalk, CT 203-229-2100
Diamond Creek Vineyards
Calistoga, CA 707-942-6926
Diamond Water Bottling Fclty
Hot Springs, AR 501-623-1251
Digrazia Vineyards
Brookfield, CT 800-230-8853
Domaine Chandon
Yountville, CA 888-242-6366
Domaine St George Winery
Healdsburg, CA 707-433-5508
Dominion Wine Cellars
Culpeper, VA. 540-825-8772
Don Sebastiani & Sons
Sonoma, CA 707-224-0410
Donatoni Winery
Inglewood, CA 310-645-5445
Door Peninsula Winery
Sturgeon Bay, WI 800-551-5049
Douknie Winery
Purcellville, VA. 540-668-6464
Dr Konstantin Frank's Vinifera
Hammondsport, NY 800-320-0735
Dreyer Sonoma
Woodside, CA. 650-851-9448
Dry Creek Vineyard
Healdsburg, CA 800-864-9463
Duck Pond Cellars
Dundee, OR. 800-437-3213
Duckhorn Vineyards
St Helena, CA. 888-354-8885
Duncan Peak Vineyards
Lafayette, CA 925-283-3632
Dundee Wine Company
Dundee, OR. 888-427-4953
Dunn Vineyards
Angwin, CA 707-965-3642
Duplin Wine Cellars
Rose Hill, NC 800-774-9634
Dutch Henry Winery
Calistoga, CA 888-224-5879
E & J Gallo Winery
Modesto, CA. 877-687-9463
E L K Run Vineyards
Mt Airy, MD 800-414-2513
Eagle Crest Vineyards LLC
Conesus, NY 800-977-7117
Easley Winery
Indianapolis, IN 317-636-4516
East Side Winery/Oak Ridge Vineyards
Lodi, CA 209-369-4758
Ed Oliveira Winery
Arcata, CA 707-822-3023
Edgewood Estate Winery
Napa, CA. 800-755-2374
Edmunds St. John
Berkeley, CA. 510-981-1510
Edna Valley Vineyard
San Luis Obispo, CA 866-979-8477
El Molino Winery
St Helena, CA. 707-963-3632
El Paso Winery
Ulster Park, NY. 845-331-8642
Elk Cove Vineyards
Gaston, OR 877-355-2683

Elliston Vineyards
Sunol, CA 925-862-2377
Enz Vineyards
Hollister, CA. 831-637-6443
Eola Hills Wine Cellars
Rickreall, OR 800-291-6730
EOS Estate Winery
Paso Robles, CA 800-249-9463
Erath Vineyards Winery
Dundee, OR. 800-539-5463
Esterlina Vineyard & Winery
Healdsburg, CA 888-474-7456
Evensen Vineyards
Oakville, CA. 707-944-2396
Evergreen Juices Inc.
Don Mills, ON 877-915-8423
Eyrie Vineyards
Mcminnville, OR 888-440-4970
Fall Creek Vineyards
Austin, TX. 512-476-4477
Fantis Foods Inc
Carlstadt, NJ 201-933-6200
Far Niente Winery
Oakville, CA. 707-944-2861
Farella-Park Vineyards
Napa, CA. 707-254-9489
Farfelu Vineyards
Flint Hill, VA 540-364-2930
Farmstead At Long Meadow Ranch
St Helena, CA. 877-627-2645
Fenestra Winery
Livermore, CA 800-789-9463
Fenn Valley Vineyards
Fennville, MI 800-432-6265
Ferrante Winery & Ristorante
Geneva, OH. 440-466-6046
Ferrara Winery
Escondido, CA 760-745-7632
Ferrari-Carano
Healdsburg, CA 800-831-0381
Ferrigno Vineyards & Wine
St James, MO 573-265-7742
Fess Parker Winery
Los Olivos, CA. 800-841-1104
Fetzer Vineyards
Hopland, CA. 707-744-1250
Ficklin Vineyards Winery
Madera, CA. 559-674-4598
Field Stone Winery
Healdsburg, CA 800-544-7273
Fieldbrook Valley Winery
Mckinleyville, CA 707-839-4140
Fife Vineyards
Redwood Valley, CA. 707-485-0323
Filsinger Vineyards & Winery
Temecula, CA 951-302-6363
Fiore Winery
Pylesville, MD 410-452-0132
Firelands Winery
Sandusky, OH 800-548-9463
Firestone Vineyard
Los Olivos, CA. 805-688-3940
First Colony Winery
Charlottesville, VA. 877-979-7105
Fisher Ridge Wine Co Inc
Charleston, WV 304-342-8702
Fisher Vineyards
Santa Rosa, CA. 707-539-7511
Fitzpatrick Winery & Lodge
Somerset, CA 800-245-9166
Flora Springs Winery
St Helena, CA 707-963-5711
Flynn Vineyards Winery
Rickreall, OR 888-427-4953
Foley Estates Vineyard
Lompoc, CA 805-737-6222
Folie _ Deux Winery
Oakville, CA. 800-535-6400
Foppiano Vineyards
Healdsburg, CA 707-433-7272
Foris Vineyards
Cave Junction, OR 541-592-3752
Forman Vineyard
St Helena, CA 707-963-3900
Fortino Winery
Gilroy, CA. 888-617-6606
Fortuna Cellars
Davis, CA 530-756-6686
Four Sisters Winery
Belvidere, NJ 908-475-3671
Fox Run Vineyards
Penn Yan, NY 800-636-9786

Fox Vineyards & Winery
Social Circle, GA 770-787-5402
Foxen Foxen 7200
Santa Maria, CA 805-937-4251
Franciscan Estate
St. Helena, CA 707-967-3830
Frank Family Vineyards
Calistoga, CA 880-574-9463
Franklin Hill Vineyards
Bangor, PA 888-887-2839
Franzia Winery
Ripon, CA 209-599-4111
Fratelli Perata
Paso Robles, CA 805-238-2809
Frederick Wildman & Sons LTD
New York, NY 800-733-9463
Freemark Abbey Winery
St Helena, CA 800-963-9698
Freixenet USA Inc
Sonoma, CA 707-996-4981
Frey Vineyards
Redwood Valley, CA 800-760-3739
Frick Winery
Geyserville, CA 707-857-1980
Frisinger Cellars
Napa, CA 707-255-3749
Frog's Leap Winery
Rutherford, CA 800-959-4704
Frontenac Point Vineyard
Trumansburg, NY 607-387-9619
Gainey Vineyard
Santa Ynez, CA 805-688-0558
Galante Vineyards
Carmel Valley, CA 800-425-2683
Galena Cellars Winery
Galena, IL 800-397-9463
Galleano Winery
Mira Loma, CA 951-685-5376
Gary Farrell Vineyards-Winery
Healdsburg, CA 866-277-9463
Georgia Wines Inc
Ringgold, GA 706-937-2177
Georis Winery
Carmel Valley, CA 831-659-1050
Germanton Winery
Germanton, NC 800-322-2894
Geyser Peak Winery
Healdsburg, CA 800-255-9463
Girardet Wine Cellar
Roseburg, OR 541-679-7252
Glenora Wine Cellars
Dundee, NY 800-243-5513
Gloria Ferrer Champagne
Sonoma, CA 707-933-1917
Gloria Winery & Vineyard
Springfield, MO 417-926-6263
Glunz Family Winery & Cellars
Grayslake, IL 847-548-9463
Gold Digger Cellars
Oroville, WA 509-476-4887
Good Harbor Vineyards & Winery
Lake Leelanau, MI 231-256-7165
Goodson Brothers Coffee
Knoxville, TN 800-737-1519
Goosecross Cellars Inc
Yountville, CA 800-276-9210
Grand River Cellars
Madison, OH 440-298-9838
Grand View Winery
East Calais, VT 802-456-7012
Grande River Vineyards
Palisade, CO 800-264-7696
Granite Springs Winery
Somerset, CA 800-638-6041
Great Lakes Wine & Spirits
Highland Park, MI 313-453-2200
Greenfield Wine Company
Vallejo, CA 707-552-5199
Greenwood Ridge Vineyards
Philo, CA 707-895-2002
Groth Vineyards & Winery
Oakville, CA 707-944-0290
Groupe Paul Masson
Longueuil, QC 514-878-3050
Gruet Winery
Albuquerque, NM 888-857-9463
Guenoc & Langtry Estate
Middletown, CA 707-995-7501
Guglielmo Winery
Morgan Hill, CA 408-779-2145
Guilliams Winery
St Helena, CA 707-963-9059
Gundlach-Bundschu Winery
Sonoma, CA 707-939-3015
H Coturri & Sons Winery
Glen Ellen, CA 866-268-8774
Habersham Vineyards & Winery
Helen, GA 706-878-9463
Hafner Vineyard
Healdsburg, CA 707-433-4606
Hahn Family Wines
Soledad, CA 831-678-4555
Haight Brown Vineyard
Litchfield, CT 800-577-9463
Hallcrest Vineyards
Felton, CA 831-335-4441
Handley Cellars
Philo, CA 800-733-3151
Hanzell Vineyards
Sonoma, CA 707-996-3860
Harbor Winery
West Sacramento, CA 916-371-6776
Harmony Cellars
Harmony, CA 800-432-9239
Harpersfield Vineyard
Geneva, OH 440-466-4739
Hart Winery
Temecula, CA 877-638-8788
Hartford Family Winery
Forestville, CA 707-887-8030
Hazlitt 1852 Vineyards
Hector, NY 888-750-0494
Heartland Vinyards
Westlake, OH 440-871-0701
Heaven Hill Distilleries Inc.
Bardstown, KY 502-337-1000
Heck Cellars
Arvin, CA 661-854-6120
Hecker Pass Winery
Gilroy, CA 408-842-8755
Hegy's South Hills Vineyard & Winery
Twin Falls, ID 208-599-0074
Heineman Winery
Put In Bay, OH 419-285-2811
Heitz Wine Cellars
St Helena, CA 707-963-3542
Helena View/Johnston Vineyard
Calistoga, CA 707-942-4956
Heller Estates
Carmel Valley, CA 800-625-8466
Hells Canyon Winery
Caldwell, ID 800-318-7873
Henry Estate Winery
Umpqua, OR 800-782-2686
Henry Hill & Co
Napa, CA 707-253-1663
Heritage Wine Cellars
North East, PA 800-747-0083
Hermann J. Wiemer Vineyard
Dundee, NY 800-371-7971
Hermannhof Vineyards
Hermann, MO 800-393-0100
Heron Hill Winery
Hammondsport, NY 800-441-4241
Hess Collection
Napa, CA 707-255-1144
Hickory Farms
Maumee, OH 800-753-8558
Hidden Mountain Ranch Winery
Paso Robles, CA 805-226-9907
Highland Manor Winery
Jamestown, TN 931-879-9519
Hill Top Berry Farm & Winery
Nellysford, VA 434-361-1266
Hillcrest Vineyards
Roseburg, OR 541-673-3709
Hinzerling Winery
Prosser, WA 800-727-6702
Homewood Winery
Sonoma, CA 707-996-6353
Honeywood Winery
Salem, OR 800-726-4101
Honig Vineyard and Winery
Rutherford, CA 800-929-2217
Hood River Vineyards and Winery
Hood River, OR 541-386-3772
Hoodsport Winery
Hoodsport, WA 800-580-9894
Hop Kiln Winery
Healdsburg, CA 707-433-6491
Hopkins Vineyard
Warren, CT 860-868-7954
Horizon Cellars Winery
Siler City, NC 919-742-1404
Horton Vineyards
Gordonsville, VA 800-829-4633
Houdini Inc
Fullerton, CA 714-525-0325
Hubers Orchard Winery-Vineyards
Borden, IN 800-345-9463
Hunt Country Vineyards
Branchport, NY 800-946-3289
Husch Vineyards & Winery
Philo, CA 800-554-8724
Indian Rock Vineyards
Murphys, CA 209-728-8514
Indian Springs Vineyards
Penn Vally, CA 800-375-9311
Inglenook
Rutherford, CA 707-968-1100
Ingleside Vineyards
Colonial Beach, VA 804-224-8687
Inniskillin Wines
Niagara-On-The-Lake, ON 888-466-4754
Iron Horse Vineyards
Sebastopol, CA 707-887-1507
Ironstone Vineyards
Murphys, CA 209-728-1251
J Filippi Winery
Rancho Cucamonga, CA 909-899-5755
J Lohr Vineyards & Wines
San Jose, CA 408-288-5057
J. Fritz Winery
Cloverdale, CA 800-418-9463
J. Stonestreet & Sons Vineyard
Healdsburg, CA 800-355-8008
Jamaican Gourmet Coffee Company
Philadelphia, PA 800-261-2859
Jefferson Vineyards
Charlottesville, VA 800-272-3042
Jodar Vineyard & Winery
Placerville, CA 530-644-3474
Johlin Century Winery
Oregon, OH 419-693-6288
Johnson Estate Winery
Westfield, NY 800-374-6569
Johnson's Alexander Valley Wines
Healdsburg, CA 800-888-5532
Johnston's Winery Inc
Ballston Spa, NY 518-882-6310
Joseph Phelps Vineyards
St Helena, CA 800-707-5789
Joseph Swan Vineyards
Forestville, CA 707-573-3747
Joullian Vineyards
Carmel Valley, CA 866-659-8101
Justin Vineyards & Winery LLC
Paso Robles, CA 800-237-4152
Kalin Cellars
Novato, CA 415-883-3543
Kate's Vineyard
Napa, CA 707-255-2644
Kathryn Kennedy Winery
Saratoga, CA 408-867-4170
Kelley's Island Wine Company
Kelleys Island, OH 419-746-2678
Kelson Creek Winery
Plymouth, CA 209-245-4700
Kendall-Jackson
Fulton, CA 866-287-9818
Kenwood Vineyards
Kenwood, CA 707-833-5891
King Brewing Company
Pontiac, MI 248-745-5900
King Estate Winery
Eugene, OR 800-884-4441
Kiona Vineyards Winery
Benton City, WA 509-588-6716
Kirigin Cellars
Gilroy, CA 408-847-8827
Kistler Vineyards
Sebastopol, CA 707-823-5603
Kittling Ridge Estate Wines & Spirits
Vaughan, ON 800-461-9463
Klingshirn Winery
Avon Lake, OH 440-933-6666
Knapp Vineyards
Romulus, NY 800-869-9271
Konzelmann Estate Winery
Niagara on the Lake, ON 905-935-2866
Koryo Winery Company
Gardena, CA 310-532-9616
Kramer Vineyards
Gaston, OR 800-619-4637
Krinos Foods
Bronx, NY 718-729-9000

Kristin Hill Winery
Amity, OR........503-835-4012
Kunde Estate Winery
Kenwood, CA........707-833-5501
L Mawby Vineyards
Peshawbestown, MI........231-271-3522
La Abra Farm & Winery
Lovingston, VA........434-263-5392
LA Buena Vida Vineyards
Grapevine, TX........817-481-9463
LA Chiripada Winery
Dixon, NM........800-528-7801
LA Jota Vineyard Co
Angwin, CA........877-222-0292
LA Rocca Vineyards & Winery
Forest Ranch, CA........800-808-9463
La Rochelle Winery
Livermore, CA........888-647-7768
LA Vina Winery
Anthony, NM........575-882-7632
Laetitia Vineyard & Winery
Arroyo Grande, CA........888-809-8463
Lafollette Vineyard & Winery
Sebastopol, CA........707-395-3902
Laird & Company
Scobeyville, NJ........877-438-5247
Lake Sonoma Winery
Glen Ellen, CA........877-586-2796
Lakeridge Winery & Vineyards
Clermont, FL........800-768-9463
Lakeshore Winery
Romulus, NY........315-549-7075
Lakewood Vineyards Inc
Watkins Glen, NY........877-535-9252
Lambert Bridge Winery
Healdsburg, CA........800-975-0555
Lamoreaux Landing Wine Cellars
Lodi, NY........607-582-6011
Lancaster County Winery LTD
Willow Street, PA........717-464-3555
Landmark Vineyards
Kenwood, CA........707-833-0053
Lange Estate Winery & Vineyard
Dundee, OR........503-538-6476
Larry's Vineyards & Winery
Altamont, NY........518-355-7365
Latah Creek Wine Cellar
Spokane Valley, WA........509-926-0164
Latcham Vineyards
Somerset, CA........800-750-5591
Laurel Glen Vineyard
Glen Ellen, CA........707-933-9877
Lava Cap Winery
Placerville, CA........800-475-0175
Lazy Creek Vineyards
Philo, CA........888-529-9275
Le Vigne Winery
Paso Robles, CA........800-891-6055
Leelanau Cellars
Omena, MI........800-782-8128
Leeward Winery
Oxnard, CA........805-656-5054
Leidenfrost Vineyards
Hector, NY........607-546-2800
Lemon Creek Winery
Berrien Springs, MI........269-471-1321
Leonetti Cellar
Walla Walla, WA........509-525-1670
Les Bourgeois Vineyards
Rocheport, MO........800-690-1830
Lewis Cellars
Napa, CA........707-255-3400
Life Force Specialty Foods
Moscow, ID........877-657-9471
Lincourt Vineyards
Solvang, CA........805-688-8554
Little Amana Winery
Amana, IA........319-668-9664
Little Hills Winery
St Charles, MO........877-584-4557
Live Oaks Winery
Gilroy, CA........408-842-2401
Livermore Valley Cellars
Livermore, CA........925-454-9463
Livingston Moffett Winery
Saint Helena, CA........800-788-0370
Llano Estacado Winery
Lubbock, TX........800-634-3854
Lockwood Vineyards
St. Helena, CA........707-963-6925
Loew Vineyards
Mt Airy, MD........301-831-5464
Lolonis Winery
Walnut Creek, CA........925-938-8066
Long Vineyards
St Helena, CA........707-963-2496
Lost Mountain Winery
Sequim, WA........888-683-5229
Louis M Martini Winery
St Helena, CA........800-321-9463
Lucas Vineyards & Winery
Interlaken, NY........800-682-9463
Lucas Winery
Lodi, CA........209-368-2006
Luxco Inc
St Louis, MO........314-772-2626
Lve & Raymond Vineyards
St Helena, CA........800-525-2659
Lynfred Winery Inc
Roselle, IL........630-529-9463
M S Walker Inc
Somerville, MA........617-776-6700
Maddalena Restaurant-Sn
Los Angeles, CA........800-626-7722
Madison Foods
Saint Paul, MN........651-265-8212
Madison Vineyard
Ribera, NM........575-421-8028
Madonna Estate Winery
Napa, CA........866-724-2993
Madrona Vineyards
Camino, CA........530-644-5948
Magnanini Farm Winery
Wallkill, NY........845-895-2767
Mama Rap's & Winery
Gilroy, CA........800-842-6262
Manischewitz Wine Co.
Brooklyn, NY........718-339-0547
Marie Brizard Wines & Spirits
St. Helena, CA........800-878-1123
Marietta Cellars
Geyservill, CA........707-433-2747
Marimar Torres Estates
Sebastopol, CA........707-823-4365
Markham Vineyards
St Helena, CA........707-963-5292
Markko Vineyard
Conneaut, OH........800-252-3197
Marlow Wine Cellars
Monteagle, TN........931-924-2120
Martin & Weyrich Winery
Templeton, CA........805-239-1640
Martin Ray Winery
Santa Rosa, CA........707-823-2404
Mastantuono Winery
Templeton, CA........805-238-0676
Matanzas Creek Winery
Santa Rosa, CA........800-500-6464
Matson Vineyards
Redding, CA........530-222-2833
Maui Wine
Kula, HI........877-878-6058
Maurice Carrie Winery
Temecula, CA........800-716-1711
Mayacamas Vineyards & Winery
Napa, CA........707-224-4030
Mazzocco Vineyards
Healdsburg, CA........800-501-8466
McDowell Valley Vineyards & Cellars
Hopland, CA........707-744-1774
Mcgregor Vineyard Winery
Dundee, NY........800-272-0192
McHenry Vineyard
Davis, CA........530-756-3202
McIntosh's Ohio Valley Wines
Bethel, OH........937-379-1159
Meier's Wine Cellars Inc
Cincinnati, OH........800-346-2941
Menghini Winery
Julian, CA........760-765-2072
Meredyth Vineyard
Middleburg, VA........540-687-6277
Meridian Vineyards
Napa, CA........800-226-7133
Merritt Estate Winery Inc
Forestville, NY........888-965-4800
Merryvale Vineyards
St Helena, CA........800-326-6069
Messina Hof Winery & Resort
Bryan, TX........979-778-9463
Michael David Winery
Lodi, CA........888-707-9463
Michel-Schlumberger Wine Est
Healdsburg, CA........800-447-3060
Milat Vineyards Winery
St Helena, CA........800-546-4528
Milea Estate Vineyard
Staatsburg, NY........845-264-0403
Mill Creek Vineyards
Healdsburg, CA........877-349-2121
Millbrook Vineyards
Millbrook, NY........800-662-9463
Milliaire Winery
Murphys, CA........209-728-1658
Mission Mountain Winery
Dayton, MT........406-849-5524
Mogen David Wine Corp
Westfield, NY........716-326-3151
Montelle Winery
Augusta, MO........888-595-9463
Monterey Vineyard
Gonzales, CA........831-675-4000
Montevina Winery
Plymouth, CA........209-245-6942
Monticello Vineyards-Corley
Napa, CA........707-253-2802
Montmorenci Vineyards
Aiken, SC........803-649-4870
Morgan Winery
Salinas, CA........831-751-7777
Mosby Winery
Buellton, CA........800-706-6729
Moss Creek Winery
Napa, CA........707-252-1295
Mosti Mondiale/Gourmet Mondiale
Ste-Catherine, QC........450-638-6380
Mount Palomar Winery
Temecula, CA........800-854-5177
Mountain Cove Vineyards
Lovingston, VA........434-263-5392
Mt Baker Vineyards
Everson, WA........360-592-2300
Mt Bethel Winery
Altus, AR........479-468-2444
Mt Eden Vineyards
Saratoga, CA........408-867-9587
Mt Nittany Vineyard & Winery
Centre Hall, PA........814-466-6373
Mt Pleasant Winery
Branson, MO........800-467-9463
Murphy Goode Estate Winery
Geyserville, CA........707-431-7644
Naked Mountain Winery Vineyard
Markham, VA........540-364-1609
Nalle Winery
Healdsburg, CA........707-433-1040
Nantucket Vineyard
Nantucket, MA........508-228-9235
Napa Cellars
Napa, CA........800-535-6400
Napa Wine Company
Oakville, CA........800-848-9630
Nashoba Valley Winery
Bolton, MA........978-779-5521
National Wine & Spirits
Indianapolis, IN
Navarro Vineyards
Philo, CA........707-895-3686
Naylor Wine Cellars Inc
Stewartstown, PA........800-292-3370
Nevada City Winery
Nevada City, CA........800-203-9463
Nevada County Wine Guild
Nevada City, CA........855-494-7025
New Hope Winery
New Hope, PA........800-592-9463
New Land Vineyard
Geneva, NY........315-585-4432
Newman's Own
Westport, CT........203-222-0136
Newport Vineyards & Winery
Middletown, RI........401-848-5161
Newton Vineyard
St Helena, CA........707-204-7423
Nicasio Vineyards
Soquel, CA........831-423-1073
Niche W&S
Cedar Knolls, NJ........973-993-8450
Nichelini Family Winery Inc
St Helena, CA........707-963-0717
Niebaum-Coppola Estate Winery
Rutherford, CA........800-782-4266
Nissley Vineyards & Winery
Bainbridge, PA........800-522-2387
Nordman Of California
Sanger, CA........559-638-9923

Northern Vineyards Winery
Stillwater, MN. 651-430-1032
Northville Winery & Brewing Co
Northville, MI 248-320-6507
Nutmeg Vineyard
Andover, CT 860-742-8402
Oak Grove Orchards Winery
Rickreall, OR 541-364-7052
Oak Knoll Winery
Hillsboro, OR 800-625-5665
Oak Ridge Winery LLC
Lodi, CA 209-369-4758
Oak Spring Winery
Altoona, PA. 814-946-3799
Oasis Winery
Hume, VA 800-304-7656
Obester Winery
Half Moon Bay, CA 650-726-9463
Ocena Wineary & Vineyards
New Era, MI 231-861-4657
Ojai Vineyard
Oak View, CA 805-649-1674
Old Creek Ranch Winery
Ventura, CA. 805-649-4132
Old Firehouse Winery
Geneva, OH. 800-362-6751
Old House Vineyards
Culpeper, VA. 540-423-1032
Old Mill Winery
Geneva, OH. 440-466-5560
Old South Winery
Natchez, MS 601-445-9924
Old Wine Cellar
Amana, IA. 319-622-3116
Oliver Winery
Bloomington, IN 800-258-2783
Olympic Cellars
Port Angeles, WA 360-452-0160
One Vineyard and Winery
Saint Helena, CA 707-963-1123
Optima Wine Cellars
Healdsburg, CA 707-431-8222
Opus One
Oakville, CA 800-292-6787
Orchard Heights Winery
Salem, OR. 503-391-7308
Orfila Vineyards
Escondido, CA 760-738-6500
Organic Wine Co Inc
San Francisco, CA 888-326-9463
Ormand Peugeog Corporation
Miami, FL. 305-624-6834
Orr Mountain Winery
Madisonville, TN 423-442-5340
Pacheco Ranch Winery
Novato, CA 415-883-5583
Pacific Echo Cellars
Philo, CA. 707-895-2065
Page Mill Winery
Livermore, CA 925-456-7676
Pahlmeyer Winery
St Helena, CA 707-255-2321
Pahrump Valley Winery
Pahrump, NV 800-368-9463
Palmer Vineyards Inc
Riverhead, NY 800-901-8783
Panther Creek Cellars
Dundee, OR. 503-472-8080
Paradise Valley Vineyards
Phoenix, AZ 602-233-8727
Paraiso Vineyards
Soledad, CA 831-678-0300
Parducci Wine Cellars
Ukiah, CA 888-362-9463
Pastori Winery
Cloverdale, CA 707-857-3418
Paumanok Vineyards
Aquebogue, NY 631-722-8800
Pazdar Winery
Scotchtown Branch, NY 845-695-1903
Peaceful Bend Winery
Steelville, MO 573-775-3000
Peconic Bay Winery
Cutchogue, NY 631-734-7361
Pedrizzetti Winery
Morgan Hill, CA. 408-779-7389
Pedroncelli J Winery
Geyserville, CA 800-836-3894
Peju Province Winery
Rutherford, CA 800-446-7358
Pellegrini Wine Co
Santa Rosa, CA. 800-891-0244

Penn Shore Winery Vineyards
North East, PA. 814-725-8688
Pennsylvania Renaissance Faire
Manheim, PA 717-664-0476
Pernod Ricard USA
New York, NY 212-372-5400
Perry Creek Winery
Somerset, CA 800-880-4026
Peter Michael Winery
Calistoga, CA 800-354-4459
Peterson & Sons Winery
Kalamazoo, MI 269-626-9755
Pheasant Ridge Winery
Lubbock, TX. 806-746-6033
Philip Togni Vineyard
St Helena, CA 707-963-3731
Piedmont Vineyards & Winery
Middleburg, VA 540-687-5528
Piedra Creek Winery
San Luis Obispo, CA 805-541-1281
Pikes Peak Vineyards
Colorado Springs, CO. 719-576-0075
Pindar Vineyards
Peconic, NY 631-734-6200
Pine Ridge Vineyards
Napa, CA. 800-575-9777
Plainfield Winery & Tasting Rm
Plainfield, IN. 888-761-9463
Plam Vineyards & Winery
La Quinta, CA. 760-972-4465
Pleasant Valley Wine Co
Hammondsport, NY 607-569-6111
Plum Creek Winery
Palisade, CO 970-464-7586
Plymouth Colony Winery
Plymouth, MA. 508-747-3334
Pommeraie Winery
Sebastopol, CA. 707-823-9463
Ponderosa Valley Vineyard
Ponderosa, NM 800-946-3657
Ponzi Vineyards
Sherwood, OR. 503-628-1227
Porter Creek Vineyards
Healdsburg, CA 707-433-6321
Post Familie Vineyards
Altus, AR 800-275-8423
Prager Winery & Port Works
St Helena, CA. 800-969-7678
Presque Isle Wine Cellars
North East, PA. 800-488-7492
Preston Premium Wines
Pasco, WA. 509-545-1990
Preston Vineyards & Winery
Healdsburg, CA 800-305-9707
Prince Michel
Leon, VA. 800-869-8242
Quady Winery
Madera, CA. 800-733-8068
Quail Ridge Cellars & Vineyards
Saint Helena, CA 800-706-9463
Quilceda Creek Vintners
Snohomish, WA 360-568-2389
Quivira Vineyards & Winery
Healdsburg, CA 800-292-8339
R.H. Phillips
Esparto, CA. 530-662-3504
Rabbit Ridge Winery
Paso Robles, CA. 805-467-3331
Radanovich Vineyards & Winery
Mariposa, CA 209-966-3187
Rainbow Hills Vineyards
Newcomerstown, OH 740-545-9305
Rancho De Philo Winery
Rancho Cucamonga, CA 909-987-4208
Rancho Sisquoc Winery
Santa Maria, CA 805-934-4332
Rapazzini Winery
Gilroy, CA. 800-842-6262
Rebec Vineyards
Amherst, VA 434-946-5168
Redhawk Vineyard & Winery
Salem, OR. 503-362-1596
Reeve Wines
Healdsburg, CA 707-235-6345
Renaissance Vineyard & Winery
Oregon House, CA 800-655-3277
Renault Winery
Egg Harbor City, NJ 609-965-2111
Renwood Winery
Plymouth, CA 800-348-8466
Retzlaff Vineyards
Livermore, CA 925-447-8941

Richard L. Graeser Winery
Calistoga, CA 707-942-4437
Richardson Vineyards
Sonoma, CA 707-938-2610
Ridge Vineyards Inc
Cupertino, CA. 408-867-3233
Ritchie Creek Vineyard
St Helena, CA 707-963-4661
River Run Vintners
Watsonville, CA 831-726-3112
Roberian Vineyards
Forestville, NY 716-679-1620
Robert F Pliska & Company Winery
Purgitsville, WV 877-747-2737
Robert Keenan Winery
St Helena, CA 707-963-9177
Robert Mondavi Winery
Oakville, CA 888-766-6328
Robert Mueller Cellars
Windsor, CA 707-837-7399
Robert Pecota Winery
Calistoga, CA 707-479-7770
Robert Sinskey Vineyards Inc
Napa, CA. 800-869-2030
Robller Vineyard Winery
New Haven, MO 573-237-3986
Roche Caneros Estate Winery
Sonoma, CA 800-825-9475
Rockbridge Vineyard
Raphine, VA 540-377-6204
Rodney Strong Vineyards
Healdsburg, CA 800-474-9463
Rogue Ales Brewery
Newport, OR. 541-265-3188
Rombauer Vineyards
St Helena, CA 800-622-2206
Rose Creek Vineyards
Hagerman, ID 208-837-4353
Rosenblum Cellars
Alameda, CA. 510-865-7007
Roudon-Smith Vineyards
Saratoga, CA. 831-438-1244
Round Hill Vineyards
St Helena, CA 800-778-0424
Royal Wine Corp
Bayonne, NJ 718-384-2400
Rudd Winery
Oakville, CA. 707-944-8577
Rutherford Hill Winery
Rutherford, CA. 707-963-1871
Saddleback Cellars
Oakville, CA. 707-944-1305
Sainte Genevieve Winery
Ste Genevieve, MO. 800-398-1298
Saintsbury
Napa, CA. 707-252-0592
Salamandre Wine Cellars
Aptos, CA 831-685-0321
Salishan Vineyards
La Center, WA. 360-263-2713
San Dominique Winery
Camp Verde, AZ. 480-945-8583
Sand Castle Winery
Erwinna, PA 800-722-9463
Sandia Shadows Vineyard & Winery
Albuquerque, NM 505-856-1006
Sandstone Winery
Amana, IA. 319-622-3081
Sanford Winery
Lompoc, CA 800-426-9463
Santa Barbara Winery
Santa Barbara, CA 805-963-3633
Santa Cruz Mountain Vineyard
Felton, CA. 831-426-6209
Santa Fe Vineyards
Espanola, NM 505-753-8100
Santa Ynez Wine Corp
Los Olivos, CA 800-824-8584
Sarah's Vineyard
Gilroy, CA. 408-842-4278
Satiety Winery & Cafe
Davis, CA 530-757-2699
Saucilito Canyon Vineyard
San Luis Obispo, CA 805-543-2111
Sausal Winery
Healdsburg, CA 800-500-2285
Savannah Chanelle Vineyards
Saratoga, CA. 408-741-2934
Sawtooth Winery
Nampa, ID. 208-467-1200
Scenic Valley Winery
Lanesboro, MN. 507-259-4981

Schloss Doepken Winery
Ripley, NY 716-326-3636
Schoppaul Hill Winery atIvanhoe
Denton, TX 940-380-9463
Schramsberg Vineyards
Calistoga, CA 800-877-3623
Schug Carneros Estate Winery
Sonoma, CA 800-966-9365
Sea Ridge Winery
Occidental, CA 800-692-5780
Seavey Vineyard
St Helena, CA 707-963-8339
Sebastiani Vineyards
Sonoma, CA 855-232-2338
Seghesio Family Vineyards
Healdsburg, CA 707-433-0545
Sequoia Grove
Napa, CA. 800-851-7841
Serendipity Cellars
Monmouth, OR 503-838-4284
Seven Hills Winery
Walla Walla, WA. 877-777-7870
Seven Lakes Vineyard & Winery
Fenton, MI 810-373-6081
Shafer Vineyards
Napa, CA. 707-944-2877
Shallon Winery
Astoria, OR 503-325-5978
Sharon Mill Winery
Manchester, MI. 734-971-6337
Sharp Rock Farm B & B
Sperryville, VA 540-987-8020
Shenandoah Vineyards
Plymouth, CA 209-245-4455
Sierra Vista Winery
Placerville, CA 800-946-3916
Signore Winery
Brooktondale, NY. 607-539-7935
Signorello Vineyards
Napa, CA. 707-255-5990
Silvan Ridge Winery
Eugene, OR. 541-345-1945
Silver Fox Vineyards
Mariposa, CA 209-966-4800
Silver Mountain Vineyards
Santa Cruz, CA. 408-353-2278
Silverado Vineyards Inc
Napa, CA. 800-997-1770
Simi Winery
Healdsburg, CA 707-433-3686
Simon Levi Cellars
Kenwood, CA 888-315-0040
Six Mile Creek Vineyard
Ithaca, NY. 800-260-0612
Sky Vineyards
Glen Ellen, CA 707-935-1391
Slate Quarry Winery
Nazareth, PA 610-746-3900
Smith Vineyard & Winery
Grass Valley, CA. 530-273-7032
Smith-Madrone Vineyards & Winery
St Helena, CA 707-963-2283
Smokehouse Winery
Sperryville, VA 540-987-3194
Smothers Brothers Tasting Room
Glen Ellen, CA 800-795-9463
Sobon Estate
Plymouth, CA 209-333-6275
Sokol Blosser Winery
Dayton, OR. 800-582-6668
Solis Winery
Gilroy, CA. 888-838-6427
Sonoita Vineyards
Elgin, AZ. 520-455-5893
Sonoma Wine Services
Vineburg, CA 707-996-9773
Sonoma-Cutrer Vineyards
Windsor, CA 707-528-1181
Sow's Ear Winery
Brooksville, ME 207-326-4649
Spangler Vineyards
Roseburg, OR 541-679-9654
Spottswoode
St Helena, CA. 707-963-0134
Spring Mountain Vineyard
St Helena, CA. 877-769-4637
Springhill Cellars
Albany, OR 541-928-1009
Spurgeon Vineyards & Winery
Highland, WI 800-236-5555
St Francis Winery & Vineyards
Santa Rosa, CA. 707-833-4668

St Innocent Winery
Salem, OR. 503-378-1526
St Julian Winery
Paw Paw, MI. 800-732-6002
St. James Winery
Saint James, MO. 800-280-9463
Stags' Leap Winery
Napa, CA. 707-944-1303
Starr & Brown
Portland, OR. 503-287-1775
Starr Hill Winery & Vineyard
Curwensville, PA 814-236-0910
Ste Chapelle Winery
Caldwell, ID 877-783-2427
STE Michelle Wine Estates
Woodinville, WA. 800-267-6793
Stearns Wharf Vintners
Santa Barbara, CA 805-966-6624
Steltzner Vineyards
Napa, CA. 800-707-9463
Sterling Vineyards
Calistoga, CA 707-942-3344
Steuk's Country Market &Winery
Sandusky, OH 419-625-8324
Stevenot Winery
Murphys, CA. 209-728-3485
Stone Hill Winery
Hermann, MO 573-486-2221
Stonegate
St Helena, CA 707-603-2203
Stoneridge Winery
Sutter Creek, CA. 209-223-1761
Stonington Vineyards
Stonington, CT 800-421-9463
Stony Hill Vineyard
St Helena, CA 707-963-2636
Stonybrook Mountain Winery
Calistoga, CA 707-942-5282
Storrs Winery
Santa Cruz, CA. 831-458-5030
Story Winery
Plymouth, CA 800-712-6390
Stoutridge Vineyard
Marlboro, NY
Streblow Vineyards
Saint Helena, CA 707-963-5892
Stryker Sonoma
Geyserville, CA 800-433-1944
Sugar Creek Winery
Defiance, MO 636-987-2400
Sullivan Vineyards
St Helena, CA. 877-244-7337
Summit Lake Vineyards
Angwin, CA 707-965-2488
Sunrise Winery
San Jose, CA. 408-741-1310
Sunstone Vineyards & Winery
Santa Ynez, CA. 800-313-9463
Susquehanna Valley Winery
Danville, PA 570-275-2364
Sutter Home Winery
St Helena, CA. 800-967-4663
Swanson Vineyards & Winery
Rutherford, CA. 800-942-0809
Swedish Hill Vineyard & Winery
Romulus, NY 888-549-9463
Sweet Traders
Huntington Beach, CA 714-903-6800
Sycamore Vineyards
Saint Helena, CA 800-963-9698
Sylvin Farms Winery
Egg Harbor City, NJ 609-965-1548
Tabor Hill Winery & Restaurant
Buchanan, MI. 800-283-3363
Talbott Vineyards
Salinas, CA. 831-675-3000
Talley Vineyards
Arroyo Grande, CA. 805-489-2508
Tamuzza Vineyards
Hope, NJ. 856-896-0619
Tarara Winery
Leesburg, VA 703-771-7100
Taylor Wine Company
Hammondsport, NY 607-868-3245
Terrace At J Vineyards
Healdsburg, CA 800-885-9463
The Boisset Collection
St. Helena, CA 707-967-7667
The Meeker Vineyard
Healdsburg, CA 707-431-2148
The Rubin Family of Wines
Sebastopol, CA. 707-887-8130

Thoma Vineyards
Dallas, OR. 800-884-1927
Thomas Fogarty Winery
Woodside, CA. 800-247-4163
Thomas Kruse Winery
Gilroy, CA. 408-842-7016
Thornton Winery
Temecula, CA 951-699-0099
Thorpe Vineyard
Wolcott, NY 315-594-2502
Three Lakes Winery
Three Lakes, WI 800-944-5434
Tkc Vineyards
Plymouth, CA 888-627-2356
Todhunter Foods
West Palm Beach, FL 800-336-9463
Todhunter Foods
Lake Alfred, FL. 863-956-1116
Tomasello Winery
Hammonton, NJ 800-666-9463
Topolos at Russian River Vine
Forestville, CA 707-887-3344
Transamerica Wine Corporation
Brooklyn, NY 718-875-4017
Treasury Wine Estates
Napa, CA. 707-259-4500
Trefethen Family Vineyards
Napa, CA. 707-255-7700
Trentadue Winery
Geyserville, CA 888-332-3032
Trigo Corporation
Toa Baja, PR 787-794-1300
Truchard Vineyards
Napa, CA. 707-253-7153
Truckee River Winery
Truckee, CA 530-587-4626
Tucker Cellars
Sunnyside, WA 509-837-8701
Tudal Winery
St Helena, CA 707-963-3947
Tularosa Vineyards
Tularosa, NM 800-687-4467
Twenty Rows
Napa, CA 800-620-7697
Tyee Wine Cellars
Corvallis, OR 541-753-8754
Union Square Wines & Spirits
New York, NY 212-675-8100
Union Wine Co
Tualatin, OR
V Sattui Winery
St Helena, CA. 707-963-7774
Val Verde Winery
Del Rio, TX. 830-775-9714
Valhalla Winery
Veneta, OR 541-935-9711
Valley of the Moon Winery
Glen Ellen, CA 707-996-6941
Valley View Winery
Jacksonville, OR. 800-781-9463
Van Der Heyden Vineyards
Napa, CA. 800-948-9463
Ventana Vineyards Winery
Monterey, CA 800-237-8846
Veramar Vineyard
Berryville, VA. 540-955-5510
Vetter Vineyards Winery
Westfield, NY 716-326-3100
Via Della Chiesa Vineyards
Raynham, MA. 508-822-7775
Viader Vineyards & Winery
Deer Park, CA. 707-963-3816
Viano Vineyards
Martinez, CA 925-228-6465
Viansa Winery
Sonoma, CA 800-995-4740
Vie-Del Co
Fresno, CA 559-834-2525
Villa Helena/Arger-Martucci Winery
St Helena, CA. 707-963-4334
Villa Milan Vineyard
Milan, IN. 812-654-3419
Villa Mt. Eden Winery
Saint Helena, CA 866-931-1624
Villar Vintners of Valdese
Valdese, NC. 828-879-3202
Vincent Arroyo Winery
Calistoga, CA 707-942-6995
Vinoklet Winery
Cincinnati, OH 513-385-9309
Vintage Wine Estates
Santa Rosa, CA. 877-289-9463

Vista D'Oro Farms
Langley, BC 855-514-3539
Von Stiehl Winery
Algoma, WI....................800-955-5208
Von Strasser
Calistoga, CA 888-359-9463
Vynecrest Winery
Breinigsville, PA....................800-361-0725
Wagner Vineyards
Lodi, NY....................866-924-6378
Wagshal's Imports
Washington, DC 202-363-5698
Warner Vineyards
Paw Paw, MI....................800-756-5357
Wasson Brothers Winery
Sandy, OR....................503-668-3124
Weibel Vineyards
Lodi, CA....................800-932-9463
Wente Family Estates
Livermore, CA 925-456-2305
Wermuth Winery
Calistoga, CA 707-942-5924
West Park Wine Cellars
West Park, NY....................845-384-6709
Westbend Vinyards
Lewisville, NC 866-901-5032
Westport Rivers Vineyard
Westport, MA 800-993-9695
Westwood Winery
Sonoma, CA 707-933-7837
Whaler Vineyard
Ukiah, CA....................707-462-6355
Whitcraft Winery
Santa Barbara, CA 805-730-1086
White Hall Vineyards
Crozet, VA....................434-823-8615
White Oak Vineyards & Winery
Healdsburg, CA 707-433-8429
White Rock Vineyards
Napa, CA....................707-257-7922
Whitecliff Vineyard & Winery
Gardiner, NY....................845-255-4613
Whitehall Lane Winery
St Helena, CA....................707-963-9454
Whitford Cellars
Napa, CA....................707-942-0840
Widmers Wine Cellars
Canandaigua, NY 585-374-6311
Wiederkehr Wine Cellars Inc
Altus, AR 800-622-9463
Wild Hog Vineyard
Cazadero, CA 707-847-3687
Wild Horse Winery & Vineyards
Templeton, CA 805-434-2541
Wildhurst Vineyards
Kelseyville, CA....................800-595-9463
William Grant & Sons
Irvine, CA
William Harrison Winery LLC
St Helena, CA....................707-963-8762
William Hill Estate Winery
Napa, CA....................707-265-3024
Williams Selyem Winery
Healdsburg, CA 707-433-6425
Williamsburg Winery LTD
Williamsburg, VA....................757-229-0999
Willowcroft Farm Vineyards
Leesburg, VA 703-777-8161
Wimberley Valley Winery
Driftwood, TX 512-847-2592
Windwalker Vineyards & Winery
Somerset, CA 530-620-4054
Wine Group
San Francisco, CA 415-986-8700
Wine-A-Rita
Texarkana, TX....................903-832-7309
Wintergreen Winery
Nellysford, VA 434-361-2519
Wishnev Wine Management
Walnut Creek, CA....................925-930-6374
Witness Tree Vineyard LTD
Salem, OR....................888-478-8766
Wolf Creek Winery
Barberton, OH....................800-436-0426
Wollersheim Winery
Prairie Du Sac, WI 800-847-9463
Woodbury Vineyards
Fredonia, NY 866-691-9463
Wooden Valley Winery
Fairfield, CA....................707-864-0730
Woodside Vineyards
Menlo Park, CA 650-851-3144
Woodward Canyon
Touchet, WA....................509-525-4129
Worden
Spokane, WA....................509-455-7835
Wyandotte Winery LLC
Gahanna, OH....................877-906-7464
Yakima River Winery
Prosser, WA....................509-786-2805
Yamhill Valley Vineyards
Mcminnville, OR 800-825-4845
York Mountain Winery
Templeton, CA 805-237-7575
Zaca Mesa Winery
Los Olivos, CA....................800-350-7972
Zayante Vineyards
Felton, CA....................831-335-7992
Zd Wines
Napa, CA....................800-487-7757

Bulk

Brothers International Food Corporation
Rochester, NY....................585-343-3007
Cribari Vineyard Inc
Fresno, CA 800-277-9095

Cooking

Batavia Wine Cellars
Canandaigua, NY 585-396-7600
California Olive Oil Council
Berkeley, CA....................888-718-9830
Cribari Vineyard Inc
Fresno, CA 800-277-9095
Emerling International Foods
Buffalo, NY....................716-833-7381
Four Chimneys Farm Winery Trust
Himrod, NY 607-243-7502
KARI-Out Co
White Plains, NY 800-433-8799
Mizkan Americas Inc
Mount Prospect, IL....................800-323-4358
Rapazzini Winery
Gilroy, CA....................800-842-6262
Todhunter Foods
West Palm Beach, FL 800-336-9463
Todhunter Foods
Lake Alfred, FL....................863-956-1116

Marsala

Cribari Vineyard Inc
Fresno, CA 800-277-9095
Pernod Ricard USA
New York, NY 212-372-5400

French

Beaulieu Vineyard
Rutherford, CA....................707-257-5749
Boisset Family Estates
St Helena, CA....................800-878-1123

Champagne

Briceland Vineyards
Redway, CA 707-923-2429
Brimstone Hill Vineyard
Pine Bush, NY 845-744-2231
Brotherhood Winery
Washingtonville, NY 845-496-3661
Buena Vista Historic Tstng Rm
Sonoma, CA 800-926-1266
Bully Hill Vineyards
Hammondsport, NY 607-868-3610
Chateau des Charmes Wines
St. Davids, ON 800-263-2541
Chicama Vineyards
West Tisbury, MA....................888-244-2262
Chouinard Vineyards & Winery
Castro Valley, CA 510-582-9900
Clinton Vineyards Inc
Clinton Corners, NY....................845-266-5372
Domaine Chandon
Yountville, CA 888-242-6366
Dr Konstantin Frank's Vinifera
Hammondsport, NY 800-320-0735
Fenn Valley Vineyards
Fennville, MI 800-432-6265
Frontenac Point Vineyard
Trumansburg, NY....................607-387-9619
Glenora Wine Cellars
Dundee, NY 800-243-5513
Marie Brizard Wines & Spirits
St. Helena, CA 800-878-1123
Meier's Wine Cellars Inc
Cincinnati, OH 800-346-2941
Mon Ami Restaurant
Port Clinton, OH....................800-777-4266
Schramsberg Vineyards
Calistoga, CA 800-877-3623
St Julian Winery
Paw Paw, MI....................800-732-6002
Stone Hill Winery
Hermann, MO....................573-486-2221
Thornton Winery
Temecula, CA....................951-699-0099
Vintage Wine Estates
Santa Rosa, CA....................877-289-9463
Westport Rivers Vineyard
Westport, MA 800-993-9695
Woodbury Vineyards
Fredonia, NY 866-691-9463
York Mountain Winery
Templeton, CA 805-237-7575

Red

Callaway Vineyards & Winery
Temecula, CA....................800-472-2377
Union Square Wines & Spirits
New York, NY 212-675-8100
Warwick Valley Winery & Distillery
Warwick, NY 845-258-4858
Whitecliff Vineyard & Winery
Gardiner, NY....................845-255-4613

Red Bordeaux

Babcock Winery & Vineyards
Lompoc, CA 805-736-1455
Pahlmeyer Winery
St Helena, CA....................707-255-2321

Red Burgundy

Bristle Ridge Vineyards
Knob Noster, MO 800-994-9463
Cribari Vineyard Inc
Fresno, CA 800-277-9095
Heineman Winery
Put In Bay, OH 419-285-2811

White

Firelands Winery
Sandusky, OH....................800-548-9463
Frey Vineyards
Redwood Valley, CA....................800-760-3739
Warwick Valley Winery & Distillery
Warwick, NY 845-258-4858
Whitecliff Vineyard & Winery
Gardiner, NY....................845-255-4613

White Burgundy

Buena Vista Historic Tstng Rm
Sonoma, CA 800-926-1266

Italian

Boisset Family Estates
St Helena, CA....................800-878-1123
Buena Vista Historic Tstng Rm
Sonoma, CA 800-926-1266
E & J Gallo Winery
Modesto, CA....................877-687-9463
V Sattui Winery
St Helena, CA....................707-963-7774

Chianti

E & J Gallo Winery
Modesto, CA....................877-687-9463

Moscato d' Asti

Fetzer Vineyards
Hopland, CA....................707-744-1250

Red

E & J Gallo Winery
Modesto, CA....................877-687-9463
Frey Vineyards
Redwood Valley, CA....................800-760-3739
Seghesio Family Vineyards
Healdsburg, CA 707-433-0545

White

Callaway Vineyards & Winery
Temecula, CA....................800-472-2377

Seghesio Family Vineyards
Healdsburg, CA 707-433-0545

Japanese

Sake

Ogeki Sake USA Inc
Hollister, CA. 831-637-9217
Takara Sake USA Inc
Berkeley, CA. 510-540-8250

Non-Alcoholic

Ariel Vineyards
Napa, CA. 800-456-9472
Black Bear Farm Winery
Chenango Forks, NY 607-656-9863
Cedar Creek Winery
Cedarburg, WI. 800-827-8020
Kedem
Bayonne, NJ 718-369-4600
Royal Wine Corp
Bayonne, NJ 718-384-2400
Tabor Hill Winery & Restaurant
Buchanan, MI 800-283-3363
Wiederkehr Wine Cellars Inc
Altus, AR 800-622-9463

Portuguese

Port

Alto Vineyards & Winery
Alto Pass, IL 618-893-4898
Chateau Grand Traverse Winery
Traverse City, MI 231-938-6120
Chouinard Vineyards & Winery
Castro Valley, CA 510-582-9900
Cienega Valley Winery/DeRose
Hollister, CA. 831-636-9143
Fenestra Winery
Livermore, CA 800-789-9463
Fenn Valley Vineyards
Fennville, MI 800-432-6265
Ficklin Vineyards Winery
Madera, CA. 559-674-4598

Red Grape Wines

Hazlitt 1852 Vineyards
Hector, NY 888-750-0494
Hermannhof Vineyards
Hermann, MO 800-393-0100
Heron Hill Winery
Hammondsport, NY 800-441-4241

Cabernet Sauvignon

A. Rafanelli Winery
Healdsburg, CA 707-433-1385
Amrhein's Wine Cellars
Bent Mountain, VA. 540-929-4632
Applewood Winery
Warwick, NY 845-988-9292
Autumn Hill Vineyards/Blue Ridge Wine
Stanardsville, VA 434-985-6100
Babcock Winery & Vineyards
Lompoc, CA 805-736-1455
Barboursville Vineyards
Barboursville, VA 540-832-3824
Black Mesa Winery
Velarde, NM 800-852-6372
Breaux Vineyards
Purcellville, VA. 800-492-9961
Burnley Vineyards
Barboursville, VA 540-832-2828
Cardinale Winery
Oakville, CA 800-588-0279
Catoctin Vineyards
Brookeville, MD. 301-774-2310
Cedar Creek Winery
Cedarburg, WI. 800-827-8020
Chateau Morrisette Winery
Floyd, VA 540-593-2865
Chatom Vineyards Inc
San Andreas, CA. 800-435-8852
Chicama Vineyards
West Tisbury, MA. 888-244-2262
Chouinard Vineyards & Winery
Castro Valley, CA 510-582-9900
Cienega Valley Winery/DeRose
Hollister, CA. 831-636-9143
Columbia Winery
Woodinville, WA. 425-488-2776
Cooper Vineyards
Louisa, VA 540-894-5474
Cosentino Winery
Napa, CA. 800-764-1220
Cribari Vineyard Inc
Fresno, CA 800-277-9095
Cuvaison Winery
Calistoga, CA 707-942-6266
Delicato Family Vineyards
Napa, CA. 707-265-1700
Douknie Winery
Purcellville, VA. 540-668-6464
E & J Gallo Winery
Modesto, CA. 877-687-9463
Farfelu Vineyards
Flint Hill, VA 540-364-2930
Fenestra Winery
Livermore, CA 800-789-9463
Fetzer Vineyards
Hopland, CA. 707-744-1250
Ficklin Vineyards Winery
Madera, CA. 559-674-4598
First Colony Winery
Charlottesville, VA 877-979-7105
Foris Vineyards
Cave Junction, OR 541-592-3752
Freemark Abbey Winery
St Helena, CA 800-963-9698
Frog's Leap Winery
Rutherford, CA 800-959-4704
Georgia Wines Inc
Ringgold, GA 706-937-2177
Greenwood Ridge Vineyards
Philo, CA. 707-895-2002
Groth Vineyards & Winery
Oakville, CA 707-944-0290
Hahn Family Wines
Soledad, CA 831-678-4555
Hazlitt 1852 Vineyards
Hector, NY 888-750-0494
Heineman Winery
Put In Bay, OH 419-285-2811
Honig Vineyard and Winery
Rutherford, CA 800-929-2217
Le Vigne Winery
Paso Robles, CA. 800-891-6055
Mayacamas Vineyards & Winery
Napa, CA. 707-224-4030
Oasis Winery
Hume, VA 800-304-7656
Obester Winery
Half Moon Bay, CA 650-726-9463
Old House Vineyards
Culpeper, VA. 540-423-1032
Pahlmeyer Winery
St Helena, CA 707-255-2321
Piedmont Vineyards & Winery
Middleburg, VA 540-687-5528
Plum Creek Winery
Palisade, CO 970-464-7586
Retzlaff Vineyards
Livermore, CA 925-447-8941
Ritchie Creek Vineyard
St Helena, CA 707-963-4661
Robert Pecota Winery
Calistoga, CA 707-479-7770
Rodney Strong Vineyards
Healdsburg, CA 800-474-9463
Seven Hills Winery
Walla Walla, WA. 877-777-7870
Shafer Vineyards
Napa, CA. 707-944-2877
Signorello Vineyards
Napa, CA. 707-255-5990
Silver Fox Vineyards
Mariposa, CA 209-966-4800
Silver Oak
Oakville, CA. 707-944-8808
Smith Vineyard & Winery
Grass Valley, CA. 530-273-7032
Smothers Brothers Tasting Room
Glen Ellen, CA 800-795-9463
Sonoita Vineyards
Elgin, AZ. 520-455-5893
Spottswoode
St Helena, CA 707-963-0134
Stone Mountain Vineyards
Dyke, VA. 434-990-9463
Sycamore Vineyards
Saint Helena, CA 800-963-9698
Tularosa Vineyards
Tularosa, NM 800-687-4467
Veramar Vineyard
Berryville, VA. 540-955-5510
Veritas Vineyard
Afton, VA 540-456-8000
Vincent Arroyo Winery
Calistoga, CA 707-942-6995
Von Stiehl Winery
Algoma, WI. 800-955-5208
Wente Family Estates
Livermore, CA 925-456-2305
Westbend Vinyards
Lewisville, NC 866-901-5032
White Hall Vineyards
Crozet, VA. 434-823-8615
White Oak Vineyards & Winery
Healdsburg, CA 707-433-8429
Whitehall Lane Winery
St Helena, CA. 707-963-9454
Willowcroft Farm Vineyards
Leesburg, VA 703-777-8161
Wintergreen Winery
Nellysford, VA 434-361-2519
Woodside Vineyards
Menlo Park, CA 650-851-3144
York Mountain Winery
Templeton, CA 805-237-7575
Zd Wines
Napa, CA. 800-487-7757

Dolcetto

Cosentino Winery
Napa, CA. 800-764-1220
Firelands Winery
Sandusky, OH 800-548-9463
Witness Tree Vineyard LTD
Salem, OR. 888-478-8766

Malbec

Brotherhood Winery
Washingtonville, NY 845-496-3661
E & J Gallo Winery
Modesto, CA. 877-687-9463

Merlot

A. Rafanelli Winery
Healdsburg, CA 707-433-1385
Applewood Winery
Warwick, NY 845-988-9292
Autumn Hill Vineyards/Blue Ridge Wine
Stanardsville, VA 434-985-6100
Babcock Winery & Vineyards
Lompoc, CA 805-736-1455
Barboursville Vineyards
Barboursville, VA. 540-832-3824
Breaux Vineyards
Purcellville, VA. 800-492-9961
Brotherhood Winery
Washingtonville, NY 845-496-3661
Cain Vineyard & Winery
St Helena, CA 707-963-1616
Chateau Grand Traverse Winery
Traverse City, MI 231-938-6120
Chateau Morrisette Winery
Floyd, VA 540-593-2865
Chateau Souverain
Cloverdale, CA 877-687-9463
Chicama Vineyards
West Tisbury, MA. 888-244-2262
Cienega Valley Winery/DeRose
Hollister, CA. 831-636-9143
Columbia Winery
Woodinville, WA. 425-488-2776
Cooper Vineyards
Louisa, VA 540-894-5474
Cosentino Winery
Napa, CA. 800-764-1220
Cribari Vineyard Inc
Fresno, CA 800-277-9095
Cuvaison Winery
Calistoga, CA 707-942-6266
Delicato Family Vineyards
Napa, CA. 707-265-1700
Douknie Winery
Purcellville, VA. 540-668-6464
E & J Gallo Winery
Modesto, CA. 877-687-9463
Fenestra Winery
Livermore, CA 800-789-9463
Fetzer Vineyards
Hopland, CA. 707-744-1250

Firelands Winery
Sandusky, OH … 800-548-9463
First Colony Winery
Charlottesville, VA … 877-979-7105
Foris Vineyards
Cave Junction, OR … 541-592-3752
Frog's Leap Winery
Rutherford, CA … 800-959-4704
Gainey Vineyard
Santa Ynez, CA … 805-688-0558
Georgia Wines Inc
Ringgold, GA … 706-937-2177
Greenwood Ridge Vineyards
Philo, CA … 707-895-2002
Groth Vineyards & Winery
Oakville, CA … 707-944-0290
Gundlach-Bundschu Winery
Sonoma, CA … 707-939-3015
Hahn Family Wines
Soledad, CA … 831-678-4555
Hazlitt 1852 Vineyards
Hector, NY … 888-750-0494
Henry Estate Winery
Umpqua, OR … 800-782-2686
Heron Hill Winery
Hammondsport, NY … 800-441-4241
Jefferson Vineyards
Charlottesville, VA … 800-272-3042
Le Vigne Winery
Paso Robles, CA … 800-891-6055
Nevada City Winery
Nevada City, CA … 800-203-9463
Oasis Winery
Hume, VA … 800-304-7656
Old House Vineyards
Culpeper, VA … 540-423-1032
Plum Creek Winery
Palisade, CO … 970-464-7586
Retzlaff Vineyards
Livermore, CA … 925-447-8941
Robert Pecota Winery
Calistoga, CA … 707-479-7770
Rodney Strong Vineyards
Healdsburg, CA … 800-474-9463
Seven Hills Winery
Walla Walla, WA … 877-777-7870
Shafer Vineyards
Napa, CA … 707-944-2877
Signorello Vineyards
Napa, CA … 707-255-5990
Silver Fox Vineyards
Mariposa, CA … 209-966-4800
Smith Vineyard & Winery
Grass Valley, CA … 530-273-7032
Smothers Brothers Tasting Room
Glen Ellen, CA … 800-795-9463
Sycamore Vineyards
Saint Helena, CA … 800-963-9698
Tularosa Vineyards
Tularosa, NM … 800-687-4467
Veritas Vineyard
Afton, VA … 540-456-8000
Vincent Arroyo Winery
Calistoga, CA … 707-942-6995
Von Stiehl Winery
Algoma, WI … 800-955-5208
Westbend Vinyards
Lewisville, NC … 866-901-5032
White Hall Vineyards
Crozet, VA … 434-823-8615
White Oak Vineyards & Winery
Healdsburg, CA … 707-433-8429
Whitehall Lane Winery
St Helena, CA … 707-963-9454
York Mountain Winery
Templeton, CA … 805-237-7575

Pinot Noir

A to Z Wineworks
Newburg, OR … 800-739-4455
Babcock Winery & Vineyards
Lompoc, CA … 805-736-1455
Barboursville Vineyards
Barboursville, VA … 540-832-3824
Brotherhood Winery
Washingtonville, NY … 845-496-3661
Buena Vista Historic Tstng Rm
Sonoma, CA … 800-926-1266
Byron Vineyard & Winery
Santa Maria, CA … 805-938-7365
Cambria Winery
Santa Maria, CA … 888-339-9463
Chateau Grand Traverse Winery
Traverse City, MI … 231-938-6120
Columbia Winery
Woodinville, WA … 425-488-2776
Cosentino Winery
Napa, CA … 800-764-1220
Cristom Vineyards
Salem, OR … 503-375-3068
Cuvaison Winery
Calistoga, CA … 707-942-6266
E & J Gallo Winery
Modesto, CA … 877-687-9463
Edna Valley Vineyard
San Luis Obispo, CA … 866-979-8477
Fenestra Winery
Livermore, CA … 800-789-9463
Fess Parker Winery
Los Olivos, CA … 800-841-1104
Fetzer Vineyards
Hopland, CA … 707-744-1250
Firelands Winery
Sandusky, OH … 800-548-9463
Flynn Vineyards Winery
Rickreall, OR … 888-427-4953
Foris Vineyards
Cave Junction, OR … 541-592-3752
Fox Run Vineyards
Penn Yan, NY … 800-636-9786
Frontenac Point Vineyard
Trumansburg, NY … 607-387-9619
Gainey Vineyard
Santa Ynez, CA … 805-688-0558
Greenwood Ridge Vineyards
Philo, CA … 707-895-2002
Gundlach-Bundschu Winery
Sonoma, CA … 707-939-3015
Hahn Family Wines
Soledad, CA … 831-678-4555
Handley Cellars
Philo, CA … 800-733-3151
Hanzell Vineyards
Sonoma, CA … 707-996-3860
Hartford Family Winery
Forestville, CA … 707-887-8030
Henry Estate Winery
Umpqua, OR … 800-782-2686
Hermann J. Wiemer Vineyard
Dundee, NY … 800-371-7971
Heron Hill Winery
Hammondsport, NY … 800-441-4241
Mark West Wines
Forestville, CA … 707-544-4813
Mayacamas Vineyards & Winery
Napa, CA … 707-224-4030
Mcgregor Vineyard Winery
Dundee, NY … 800-272-0192
Milea Estate Vineyard
Staatsburg, NY … 845-264-0403
Nalle Winery
Healdsburg, CA … 707-433-1040
Nehalem Bay Winery
Nehalem, OR … 888-368-9463
Pahlmeyer Winery
St Helena, CA … 707-255-2321
Ritchie Creek Vineyard
St Helena, CA … 707-963-4661
Rodney Strong Vineyards
Healdsburg, CA … 800-474-9463
Sonoma-Cutrer Vineyards
Windsor, CA … 707-528-1181
Taste Wine Co
New York, NY … 212-461-1708
Tualatin Estate Vineyards
Forest Grove, OR … 503-357-5005
Westwood Winery
Sonoma, CA … 707-933-7837
Whitford Cellars
Napa, CA … 707-942-0840
Williams Selyem Winery
Healdsburg, CA … 707-433-6425
Witness Tree Vineyard LTD
Salem, OR … 888-478-8766
Woodside Vineyards
Menlo Park, CA … 650-851-3144
York Mountain Winery
Templeton, CA … 805-237-7575
Zd Wines
Napa, CA … 800-487-7757

Red Meritage/Bordeaux

Fenn Valley Vineyards
Fennville, MI … 800-432-6265

Sangiovese

Babcock Winery & Vineyards
Lompoc, CA … 805-736-1455
Columbia Winery
Woodinville, WA … 425-488-2776
Cosentino Winery
Napa, CA … 800-764-1220
E & J Gallo Winery
Modesto, CA … 877-687-9463
Fenestra Winery
Livermore, CA … 800-789-9463
Le Vigne Winery
Paso Robles, CA … 800-891-6055
Nevada City Winery
Nevada City, CA … 800-203-9463
Plum Creek Winery
Palisade, CO … 970-464-7586
Tularosa Vineyards
Tularosa, NM … 800-687-4467
Vincent Arroyo Winery
Calistoga, CA … 707-942-6995

Syrah

Babcock Winery & Vineyards
Lompoc, CA … 805-736-1455
Black Mesa Winery
Velarde, NM … 800-852-6372
Brotherhood Winery
Washingtonville, NY … 845-496-3661
Cambria Winery
Santa Maria, CA … 888-339-9463
Cedar Creek Winery
Cedarburg, WI … 800-827-8020
Chouinard Vineyards & Winery
Castro Valley, CA … 510-582-9900
Columbia Winery
Woodinville, WA … 425-488-2776
Cooper Vineyards
Louisa, VA … 540-894-5474
Cosentino Winery
Napa, CA … 800-764-1220
Cuvaison Winery
Calistoga, CA … 707-942-6266
Fenestra Winery
Livermore, CA … 800-789-9463
Fess Parker Winery
Los Olivos, CA … 800-841-1104
Gainey Vineyard
Santa Ynez, CA … 805-688-0558
Handley Cellars
Philo, CA … 800-733-3151
Le Vigne Winery
Paso Robles, CA … 800-891-6055
Nevada City Winery
Nevada City, CA … 800-203-9463
Plum Creek Winery
Palisade, CO … 970-464-7586
Signorello Vineyards
Napa, CA … 707-255-5990
Sky Vineyards
Glen Ellen, CA … 707-935-1391
Tularosa Vineyards
Tularosa, NM … 800-687-4467
Westwood Winery
Sonoma, CA … 707-933-7837
Whitford Cellars
Napa, CA … 707-942-0840

Zinfandel

A. Nonini Winery
Fresno, CA … 559-275-1936
A. Rafanelli Winery
Healdsburg, CA … 707-433-1385
Brotherhood Winery
Washingtonville, NY … 845-496-3661
Chateau Souverain
Cloverdale, CA … 877-687-9463
Chatom Vineyards Inc
San Andreas, CA … 800-435-8852
Chouinard Vineyards & Winery
Castro Valley, CA … 510-582-9900
Cienega Valley Winery/DeRose
Hollister, CA … 831-636-9143
Columbia Winery
Woodinville, WA … 425-488-2776
Cosentino Winery
Napa, CA … 800-764-1220
Cribari Vineyard Inc
Fresno, CA … 800-277-9095
Cuvaison Winery
Calistoga, CA … 707-942-6266

Delicato Family Vineyards
Napa, CA........................707-265-1700
E & J Gallo Winery
Modesto, CA....................877-687-9463
Fenestra Winery
Livermore, CA..................800-789-9463
Fess Parker Winery
Los Olivos, CA.................800-841-1104
Fetzer Vineyards
Hopland, CA....................707-744-1250
Frog's Leap Winery
Rutherford, CA.................800-959-4704
Gundlach-Bundschu Winery
Sonoma, CA.....................707-939-3015
Handley Cellars
Philo, CA......................800-733-3151
Hartford Family Winery
Forestville, CA................707-887-8030
Le Vigne Winery
Paso Robles, CA................800-891-6055
Livermore Valley Cellars
Livermore, CA..................925-454-9463
Nalle Winery
Healdsburg, CA.................707-433-1040
Nevada City Winery
Nevada City, CA................800-203-9463
Old Wine Cellar
Amana, IA......................319-622-3116
Ravenswood Winery
Sonoma, CA.....................866-568-3946
Rodney Strong Vineyards
Healdsburg, CA.................800-474-9463
Seghesio Family Vineyards
Healdsburg, CA.................707-433-0545
Silver Fox Vineyards
Mariposa, CA...................209-966-4800
Sky Vineyards
Glen Ellen, CA.................707-935-1391
Stonybrook Mountain Winery
Calistoga, CA..................707-942-5282
Vincent Arroyo Winery
Calistoga, CA..................707-942-6995
Von Stiehl Winery
Algoma, WI.....................800-955-5208
Wente Family Estates
Livermore, CA..................925-456-2305
White Oak Vineyards & Winery
Healdsburg, CA.................707-433-8429
Williams Selyem Winery
Healdsburg, CA.................707-433-6425
Woodside Vineyards
Menlo Park, CA.................650-851-3144
York Mountain Winery
Templeton, CA..................805-237-7575

Red Grapes

Alto Vineyards & Winery
Alto Pass, IL..................618-893-4898
Babcock Winery & Vineyards
Lompoc, CA.....................805-736-1455
Chateau Grand Traverse Winery
Traverse City, MI..............231-938-6120
Chicama Vineyards
West Tisbury, MA...............888-244-2262
Chouinard Vineyards & Winery
Castro Valley, CA..............510-582-9900
Cienega Valley Winery/DeRose
Hollister, CA..................831-636-9143
Columbia Winery
Woodinville, WA................425-488-2776
Cosentino Winery
Napa, CA.......................800-764-1220
Cribari Vineyard Inc
Fresno, CA.....................800-277-9095
E & J Gallo Winery
Modesto, CA....................877-687-9463
Fess Parker Winery
Los Olivos, CA.................800-841-1104
Galleano Winery
Mira Loma, CA..................951-685-5376
Heineman Winery
Put In Bay, OH.................419-285-2811
Mt Baker Vineyards
Everson, WA....................360-592-2300
Newport Vineyards & Winery
Middletown, RI.................401-848-5161
Oliver Winery
Bloomington, IN................800-258-2783
Ravenswood Winery
Sonoma, CA.....................866-568-3946
Steltzner Vineyards
Napa, CA.......................800-707-9463

Swedish Hill Vineyard & Winery
Romulus, NY....................888-549-9463
Tabor Hill Winery & Restaurant
Buchanan, MI...................800-283-3363
Wiederkehr Wine Cellars Inc
Altus, AR......................800-622-9463
Wild Horse Winery & Vineyards
Templeton, CA..................805-434-2541
Wildhurst Vineyards
Kelseyville, CA................800-595-9463
Wooden Valley Winery
Fairfield, CA..................707-864-0730

Spanish

Sherry

Brotherhood Winery
Washingtonville, NY............845-496-3661
Cribari Vineyard Inc
Fresno, CA.....................800-277-9095
Pleasant Valley Wine Co
Hammondsport, NY...............607-569-6111

Sparkling (See also French/Champagne)

A to Z Wineworks
Newburg, OR....................800-739-4455
Brimstone Hill Vineyard
Pine Bush, NY..................845-744-2231
Brown-Forman Corp
Louisville, KY.................502-585-1100
Buena Vista Historic Tstng Rm
Sonoma, CA.....................800-926-1266
Bully Hill Vineyards
Hammondsport, NY...............607-868-3610
Clinton Vineyards Inc
Clinton Corners, NY............845-266-5372
Diamond Water Bottling Fclty
Hot Springs, AR................501-623-1251
Domaine Chandon
Yountville, CA.................888-242-6366
Dr Konstantin Frank's Vinifera
Hammondsport, NY...............800-320-0735
E & J Gallo Winery
Modesto, CA....................877-687-9463
Glenora Wine Cellars
Dundee, NY.....................800-243-5513
Gloria Ferrer Champagne
Sonoma, CA.....................707-933-1917
Hazlitt 1852 Vineyards
Hector, NY.....................888-750-0494
Hermannhof Vineyards
Hermann, MO....................800-393-0100
Heron Hill Winery
Hammondsport, NY...............800-441-4241
La Rochelle Winery
Livermore, CA..................888-647-7768
Meier's Wine Cellars Inc
Cincinnati, OH.................800-346-2941
Milea Estate Vineyard
Staatsburg, NY.................845-264-0403
Mon Ami Restaurant
Port Clinton, OH...............800-777-4266
Mt Baker Vineyards
Everson, WA....................360-592-2300
Oliver Winery
Bloomington, IN................800-258-2783
Schramsberg Vineyards
Calistoga, CA..................800-877-3623
St Innocent Winery
Salem, OR......................503-378-1526
Swedish Hill Vineyard & Winery
Romulus, NY....................888-549-9463
Tabor Hill Winery & Restaurant
Buchanan, MI...................800-283-3363
Tualatin Estate Vineyards
Forest Grove, OR...............503-357-5005
V Sattui Winery
St Helena, CA..................707-963-7774
Vintage Wine Estates
Santa Rosa, CA.................877-289-9463
Wiederkehr Wine Cellars Inc
Altus, AR......................800-622-9463
Woodbury Vineyards
Fredonia, NY...................866-691-9463

White Grape Varieties

Alto Vineyards & Winery
Alto Pass, IL..................618-893-4898
Babcock Winery & Vineyards
Lompoc, CA.....................805-736-1455

Cienega Valley Winery/DeRose
Hollister, CA..................831-636-9143
Hazlitt 1852 Vineyards
Hector, NY.....................888-750-0494
Hermannhof Vineyards
Hermann, MO....................800-393-0100
Heron Hill Winery
Hammondsport, NY...............800-441-4241

Chardonnay

A to Z Wineworks
Newburg, OR....................800-739-4455
Amrhein's Wine Cellars
Bent Mountain, VA..............540-929-4632
Applewood Winery
Warwick, NY....................845-988-9292
Autumn Hill Vineyards/Blue Ridge Wine
Stanardsville, VA..............434-985-6100
Babcock Winery & Vineyards
Lompoc, CA.....................805-736-1455
Barboursville Vineyards
Barboursville, VA..............540-832-3824
Benmarl Wine Co
Marlboro, NY...................845-236-4265
Breaux Vineyards
Purcellville, VA...............800-492-9961
Brotherhood Winery
Washingtonville, NY............845-496-3661
Buena Vista Historic Tstng Rm
Sonoma, CA.....................800-926-1266
Burnley Vineyards
Barboursville, VA..............540-832-2828
Byron Vineyard & Winery
Santa Maria, CA................805-938-7365
Cambria Winery
Santa Maria, CA................888-339-9463
Catoctin Vineyards
Brookeville, MD................301-774-2310
Cedar Creek Winery
Cedarburg, WI..................800-827-8020
Chateau Grand Traverse Winery
Traverse City, MI..............231-938-6120
Chateau Morrisette Winery
Floyd, VA......................540-593-2865
Chateau Souverain
Cloverdale, CA.................877-687-9463
Chicama Vineyards
West Tisbury, MA...............888-244-2262
Chouinard Vineyards & Winery
Castro Valley, CA..............510-582-9900
Cienega Valley Winery/DeRose
Hollister, CA..................831-636-9143
Columbia Winery
Woodinville, WA................425-488-2776
Cooper Vineyards
Louisa, VA.....................540-894-5474
Cosentino Winery
Napa, CA.......................800-764-1220
Cribari Vineyard Inc
Fresno, CA.....................800-277-9095
Cristom Vineyards
Salem, OR......................503-375-3068
Cuvaison Winery
Calistoga, CA..................707-942-6266
Delicato Family Vineyards
Napa, CA.......................707-265-1700
Douknie Winery
Purcellville, VA...............540-668-6464
E & J Gallo Winery
Modesto, CA....................877-687-9463
Edna Valley Vineyard
San Luis Obispo, CA............866-979-8477
Fenestra Winery
Livermore, CA..................800-789-9463
Fenn Valley Vineyards
Fennville, MI..................800-432-6265
Fess Parker Winery
Los Olivos, CA.................800-841-1104
Fetzer Vineyards
Hopland, CA....................707-744-1250
Firelands Winery
Sandusky, OH...................800-548-9463
First Colony Winery
Charlottesville, VA............877-979-7105
Flynn Vineyards Winery
Rickreall, OR..................888-427-4953
Foris Vineyards
Cave Junction, OR..............541-592-3752
Fox Run Vineyards
Penn Yan, NY...................800-636-9786
Freemark Abbey Winery
St Helena, CA..................800-963-9698

Frog's Leap Winery
Rutherford, CA 800-959-4704
Frontenac Point Vineyard
Trumansburg, NY 607-387-9619
Gainey Vineyard
Santa Ynez, CA. . . . 805-688-0558
Georgia Wines Inc
Ringgold, GA 706-937-2177
Groth Vineyards & Winery
Oakville, CA. . . . 707-944-0290
Gundlach-Bundschu Winery
Sonoma, CA 707-939-3015
Hahn Family Wines
Soledad, CA 831-678-4555
Handley Cellars
Philo, CA. . . . 800-733-3151
Hanzell Vineyards
Sonoma, CA 707-996-3860
Hartford Family Winery
Forestville, CA 707-887-8030
Hazlitt 1852 Vineyards
Hector, NY 888-750-0494
Heineman Winery
Put In Bay, OH 419-285-2811
Hermann J. Wiemer Vineyard
Dundee, NY 800-371-7971
Heron Hill Winery
Hammondsport, NY 800-441-4241
Kistler Vineyards
Sebastopol, CA. . . . 707-823-5603
Le Vigne Winery
Paso Robles, CA. . . . 800-891-6055
Maui Wine
Kula, HI. . . . 877-878-6058
Mayacamas Vineyards & Winery
Napa, CA. . . . 707-224-4030
Mcgregor Vineyard Winery
Dundee, NY 800-272-0192
Milea Estate Vineyard
Staatsburg, NY 845-264-0403
Nalle Winery
Healdsburg, CA 707-433-1040
Nehalem Bay Winery
Nehalem, OR. . . . 888-368-9463
Nevada City Winery
Nevada City, CA. . . . 800-203-9463
Oasis Winery
Hume, VA 800-304-7656
Obester Winery
Half Moon Bay, CA 650-726-9463
Old House Vineyards
Culpeper, VA. . . . 540-423-1032
Pahlmeyer Winery
St Helena, CA. . . . 707-255-2321
Plum Creek Winery
Palisade, CO 970-464-7586
Retzlaff Vineyards
Livermore, CA 925-447-8941
Rodney Strong Vineyards
Healdsburg, CA 800-474-9463
Shafer Vineyards
Napa, CA. . . . 707-944-2877
Signorello Vineyards
Napa, CA. . . . 707-255-5990
Sky Vineyards
Glen Ellen, CA 707-935-1391
Smith Vineyard & Winery
Grass Valley, CA. . . . 530-273-7032
Sonoma-Cutrer Vineyards
Windsor, CA 707-528-1181
Stone Mountain Vineyards
Dyke, VA. . . . 434-990-9463
Stonington Vineyards
Stonington, CT 800-421-9463
Tularosa Vineyards
Tularosa, NM 800-687-4467
Veramar Vineyard
Berryville, VA. . . . 540-955-5510
Veritas Vineyard
Afton, VA 540-456-8000
Vincent Arroyo Winery
Calistoga, CA 707-942-6995
Wente Family Estates
Livermore, CA 925-456-2305
White Hall Vineyards
Crozet, VA. . . . 434-823-8615
White Oak Vineyards & Winery
Healdsburg, CA 707-433-8429
Whitehall Lane Winery
St Helena, CA. . . . 707-963-9454
Whitford Cellars
Napa, CA. . . . 707-942-0840
Williams Selyem Winery
Healdsburg, CA 707-433-6425
Willowcroft Farm Vineyards
Leesburg, VA 703-777-8161
Wintergreen Winery
Nellysford, VA 434-361-2519
Witness Tree Vineyard LTD
Salem, OR. . . . 888-478-8766
Woodside Vineyards
Menlo Park, CA 650-851-3144
Zd Wines
Napa, CA. . . . 800-487-7757

Gewurztraminer

Babcock Winery & Vineyards
Lompoc, CA 805-736-1455
Chouinard Vineyards & Winery
Castro Valley, CA 510-582-9900
Columbia Winery
Woodinville, WA. . . . 425-488-2776
Cosentino Winery
Napa, CA. . . . 800-764-1220
Fenn Valley Vineyards
Fennville, MI 800-432-6265
Fetzer Vineyards
Hopland, CA. . . . 707-744-1250
Foris Vineyards
Cave Junction, OR 541-592-3752
Fox Run Vineyards
Penn Yan, NY 800-636-9786
Gundlach-Bundschu Winery
Sonoma, CA 707-939-3015
Hazlitt 1852 Vineyards
Hector, NY 888-750-0494
Mcgregor Vineyard Winery
Dundee, NY 800-272-0192
Nevada City Winery
Nevada City, CA. . . . 800-203-9463
Stonington Vineyards
Stonington, CT 800-421-9463
Tualatin Estate Vineyards
Forest Grove, OR 503-357-5005
White Hall Vineyards
Crozet, VA. . . . 434-823-8615

Pinot Blanc

Foris Vineyards
Cave Junction, OR 541-592-3752
Handley Cellars
Philo, CA. . . . 800-733-3151
Nehalem Bay Winery
Nehalem, OR. . . . 888-368-9463
Tualatin Estate Vineyards
Forest Grove, OR 503-357-5005
Witness Tree Vineyard LTD
Salem, OR. . . . 888-478-8766

Pinot Gris

A to Z Wineworks
Newburg, OR 800-739-4455
Babcock Winery & Vineyards
Lompoc, CA 805-736-1455
Cambria Winery
Santa Maria, CA 888-339-9463
Columbia Winery
Woodinville, WA. . . . 425-488-2776
Cosentino Winery
Napa, CA. . . . 800-764-1220
Cristom Vineyards
Salem, OR. . . . 503-375-3068
Flynn Vineyards Winery
Rickreall, OR 888-427-4953
Foris Vineyards
Cave Junction, OR 541-592-3752
Hahn Family Wines
Soledad, CA 831-678-4555
Handley Cellars
Philo, CA. . . . 800-733-3151
Hazlitt 1852 Vineyards
Hector, NY 888-750-0494
Heineman Winery
Put In Bay, OH 419-285-2811
Henry Estate Winery
Umpqua, OR. . . . 800-782-2686
Jefferson Vineyards
Charlottesville, VA 800-272-3042
Kistler Vineyards
Sebastopol, CA. . . . 707-823-5603
Seven Hills Winery
Walla Walla, WA. . . . 877-777-7870
White Hall Vineyards
Crozet, VA. . . . 434-823-8615

Riesling

A to Z Wineworks
Newburg, OR 800-739-4455
Abingdon Vineyard & Winery
Abingdon, VA. . . . 276-623-1255
Applewood Winery
Warwick, NY 845-988-9292
Autumn Hill Vineyards/Blue Ridge Wine
Stanardsville, VA 434-985-6100
Barboursville Vineyards
Barboursville, VA. . . . 540-832-3824
Brotherhood Winery
Washingtonville, NY 845-496-3661
Catoctin Vineyards
Brookeville, MD. . . . 301-774-2310
Chateau Grand Traverse Winery
Traverse City, MI 231-938-6120
Chouinard Vineyards & Winery
Castro Valley, CA 510-582-9900
Columbia Winery
Woodinville, WA. . . . 425-488-2776
Douknie Winery
Purcellville, VA. . . . 540-668-6464
E & J Gallo Winery
Modesto, CA. . . . 877-687-9463
Fenestra Winery
Livermore, CA 800-789-9463
Fenn Valley Vineyards
Fennville, MI 800-432-6265
Fess Parker Winery
Los Olivos, CA 800-841-1104
Fetzer Vineyards
Hopland, CA. . . . 707-744-1250
Firelands Winery
Sandusky, OH 800-548-9463
Fox Run Vineyards
Penn Yan, NY 800-636-9786
Freemark Abbey Winery
St Helena, CA 800-963-9698
Frontenac Point Vineyard
Trumansburg, NY 607-387-9619
Greenwood Ridge Vineyards
Philo, CA. . . . 707-895-2002
Gundlach-Bundschu Winery
Sonoma, CA 707-939-3015
Handley Cellars
Philo, CA. . . . 800-733-3151
Hazlitt 1852 Vineyards
Hector, NY 888-750-0494
Heineman Winery
Put In Bay, OH 419-285-2811
Hermann J. Wiemer Vineyard
Dundee, NY 800-371-7971
Heron Hill Winery
Hammondsport, NY 800-441-4241
Jefferson Vineyards
Charlottesville, VA 800-272-3042
Mcgregor Vineyard Winery
Dundee, NY 800-272-0192
Milea Estate Vineyard
Staatsburg, NY 845-264-0403
Oasis Winery
Hume, VA 800-304-7656
Obester Winery
Half Moon Bay, CA 650-726-9463
Plum Creek Winery
Palisade, CO 970-464-7586
Seven Hills Winery
Walla Walla, WA. . . . 877-777-7870
Tualatin Estate Vineyards
Forest Grove, OR 503-357-5005
Veramar Vineyard
Berryville, VA. . . . 540-955-5510
Westbend Vinyards
Lewisville, NC 866-901-5032
Willowcroft Farm Vineyards
Leesburg, VA 703-777-8161
Wintergreen Winery
Nellysford, VA 434-361-2519

Sauvignon Blanc

Babcock Winery & Vineyards
Lompoc, CA 805-736-1455
Brotherhood Winery
Washingtonville, NY 845-496-3661
Chateau Souverain
Cloverdale, CA 877-687-9463

Chicama Vineyards
West Tisbury, MA.................. 888-244-2262
Chouinard Vineyards & Winery
Castro Valley, CA.................. 510-582-9900
Cosentino Winery
Napa, CA.......................... 800-764-1220
Delicato Family Vineyards
Napa, CA.......................... 707-265-1700
E & J Gallo Winery
Modesto, CA....................... 877-687-9463
Fenestra Winery
Livermore, CA..................... 800-789-9463
Fetzer Vineyards
Hopland, CA....................... 707-744-1250
Frog's Leap Winery
Rutherford, CA.................... 800-959-4704
Gainey Vineyard
Santa Ynez, CA.................... 805-688-0558
Groth Vineyards & Winery
Oakville, CA...................... 707-944-0290
Handley Cellars
Philo, CA......................... 800-733-3151
Honig Vineyard and Winery
Rutherford, CA.................... 800-929-2217
Mayacamas Vineyards & Winery
Napa, CA.......................... 707-224-4030
Nalle Winery
Healdsburg, CA.................... 707-433-1040
Nevada City Winery
Nevada City, CA................... 800-203-9463
Plum Creek Winery
Palisade, CO...................... 970-464-7586
Retzlaff Vineyards
Livermore, CA..................... 925-447-8941
Rodney Strong Vineyards
Healdsburg, CA.................... 800-474-9463
Signorello Vineyards
Napa, CA.......................... 707-255-5990
Spottswoode
St Helena, CA..................... 707-963-0134

Wente Family Estates
Livermore, CA..................... 925-456-2305
Westbend Vinyards
Lewisville, NC.................... 866-901-5032
White Oak Vineyards & Winery
Healdsburg, CA.................... 707-433-8429
Whitehall Lane Winery
St Helena, CA..................... 707-963-9454

Viognier

Amrhein's Wine Cellars
Bent Mountain, VA................. 540-929-4632
Breaux Vineyards
Purcellville, VA.................. 800-492-9961
Brotherhood Winery
Washingtonville, NY............... 845-496-3661
Cambria Winery
Santa Maria, CA................... 888-339-9463
Chicama Vineyards
West Tisbury, MA.................. 888-244-2262
Cienega Valley Winery/DeRose
Hollister, CA..................... 831-636-9143
Columbia Winery
Woodinville, WA................... 425-488-2776
Cosentino Winery
Napa, CA.......................... 800-764-1220
Cristom Vineyards
Salem, OR......................... 503-375-3068
Fenestra Winery
Livermore, CA..................... 800-789-9463
Fess Parker Winery
Los Olivos, CA.................... 800-841-1104
Seven Hills Winery
Walla Walla, WA................... 877-777-7870
Signorello Vineyards
Napa, CA.......................... 707-255-5990
Tularosa Vineyards
Tularosa, NM...................... 800-687-4467
Witness Tree Vineyard LTD
Salem, OR......................... 888-478-8766

White Grapes

Chateau Grand Traverse Winery
Traverse City, MI................. 231-938-6120
Chicama Vineyards
West Tisbury, MA.................. 888-244-2262
Chouinard Vineyards & Winery
Castro Valley, CA................. 510-582-9900
Columbia Winery
Woodinville, WA................... 425-488-2776
Cribari Vineyard Inc
Fresno, CA........................ 800-277-9095
Galleano Winery
Mira Loma, CA..................... 951-685-5376
Heineman Winery
Put In Bay, OH.................... 419-285-2811
Maui Wine
Kula, HI.......................... 877-878-6058
Mt Baker Vineyards
Everson, WA....................... 360-592-2300
Newport Vineyards & Winery
Middletown, RI.................... 401-848-5161
Oliver Winery
Bloomington, IN................... 800-258-2783
Steltzner Vineyards
Napa, CA.......................... 800-707-9463
Swedish Hill Vineyard & Winery
Romulus, NY....................... 888-549-9463
Tabor Hill Winery & Restaurant
Buchanan, MI...................... 800-283-3363
V Sattui Winery
St Helena, CA..................... 707-963-7774
Wiederkehr Wine Cellars Inc
Altus, AR......................... 800-622-9463
Wild Horse Winery & Vineyards
Templeton, CA..................... 805-434-2541
Wildhurst Vineyards
Kelseyville, CA................... 800-595-9463
Wooden Valley Winery
Fairfield, CA..................... 707-864-0730

Candy & Confectionery

Candy

21st Century Snack Foods
Ronkonkoma, NY....631-588-8000
A La Carte
Chicago, IL....800-722-2370
A Southern Season
Hillsborough, NC....800-253-3663
Abbott's Candy Shop
Hagerstown, IN....877-801-1200
Abdallah Candies & Gifts
Burnsville, MN....952-890-0859
Across Foods, LLC
New Hope, PA....215-693-6274
Adirondack Maple Farms
Fonda, NY....518-853-4022
Aglamesis Bros Ice Cream
Cincinnati, OH....513-531-5196
Alaska Jacks
Anchorage, AK....888-660-2257
All Wrapped Up
Plantation, FL....800-891-2194
Ameri-Suisse Group
South Plainfield, NJ....908-222-1001
American Food Products Inc
Methuen, MA....978-682-1855
American Licorice
La Porte, IL....866-442-2783
American Mint
New York, NY....800-401-6468
American Specialty Confections
Saint Paul, MN....800-776-2085
AmeriGift
Oxnard, CA....800-421-9039
Amy's Candy Bar
Chicago, IL....773-942-6386
Andre Prost Inc
Old Saybrook, CT....800-243-0897
Andre's Confiserie Suisse
Kansas City, MO....800-892-1234
Ann Hemyng Candy Inc
Trumbauersville, PA....800-779-7004
Annabelle Candy Co Inc
Hayward, CA....510-783-2900
Arcor USA
Coral Gables, FL....800-572-7267
Arizona Cowboy
Phoenix, AZ....800-529-8627
Art CoCo Chocolate Company
Geneva, IL....877-232-9901
Artesian Honey Producers
Artesian, SD....605-527-2423
Artisan Confections
Hershey, PA....866-237-0152
Arway Confections Inc
Chicago, IL....800-695-0612
Asher's Chocolates
Kulpsville, PA....855-827-4377
Asti Holdings Ltd
New Westminster, BC....604-523-6866
Atkinson Candy Co
Lufkin, TX....936-639-2333
Aunt Aggie De's Pralines
Sinton, TX....800-333-9354
Aunt Sally's Praline Shops
New Orleans, LA....800-642-7257
Aurora Products
Orange, CT....800-398-1048
Azar Nut Co
El Paso, TX....800-351-8178
B & R Classics LLC
Huntington, NY....631-427-5675
B. Nutty
Oakland, CA....510-374-4658
Bacci Chocolate Design
Swampscott, MA....888-725-2877
Baker Candy Company
Snohomish, WA....425-422-6331
Baker Maid Products, Inc.
New Orleans, LA....800-664-7882
Baker's Candies Factory Store
Greenwood, NE....800-804-7330
Balticshop.Com LLC
Glastonbury, CT....800-506-2312
Banner Candy Manufacturing Company
Brooklyn, NY....718-647-4747
Barcelona Nut Co
Baltimore, MD....800-296-6887
Bari & Gail
Walpole, MA....800-828-9318
Bazaar Inc
River Grove, IL....800-736-1888
Bee International
Chula Vista, CA....800-421-6465
Beehive Botanicals
Hayward, WI....800-233-4483
Belly Treats, Inc.
Toronto, ON....416-418-3285
Ben Heggy's Candy Co
Canton, OH....330-455-7703
Bergen Marzipan & Chocolate
Bergenfield, NJ....201-385-8343
Betty Jane Homemade Candy
Dubuque, IA....800-642-1254
Betty Lou's
McMinnville, OR....800-242-5205
Bidwell Candies
Mattoon, IL....217-234-3858
Birnn Chocolates of Vermont
South Burlington, VT....800-338-3141
Biscomerica Corporation
Rialto, CA....909-877-5997
Bissinger's Handcrafted Chocolatier
St. Louis, MO....314-615-2400
Black Forest Organic
Oakbrook Terrace, IL....800-323-1768
Black Hound New York
Brooklyn, NY....800-344-4417
Blanton's
Frankfort, KY....502-223-9874
Blommer Chocolate Co
Chicago, IL....800-621-1606
Blommer Chocolate Co
East Greenville, PA....800-825-8181
Bluebird Restaurant
Logan, UT....435-752-3155
Boca Bons East
Greenacres, FL....800-314-2835
Boston America Corporation
Woburn, MA....781-933-3535
Boston Fruit Slice & Confectionery Corporation
Lawrence, MA....978-686-2699
Bread & Chocolate Inc
Wells River, VT....800-524-6715
British Aisles, LTD.
Nashua, NH....800-520-8565
Brittle Kittle
· Tigard, OR....800-447-2128
Buonitalia
New York, NY....212-633-9090
Burke Candy Ingredients Inc
Milwaukee, WI....888-287-5350
Butterfields
Nashville, NC....800-945-5957
C Howard Co
Bellport, NY....631-286-7940
Cadbury Adams
Toronto, ON....416-590-5000
Cadbury Trebor Allan
Granby, QC....800-387-3267
Calif Snack Foods
South El Monte, CA....626-454-4099
Cambridge Brands Inc
Cambridge, MA....617-491-2500
Cameo Confections
Bay Village, OH....440-871-5732
Cameron Birch Syrup & Confections
Wasilla, AK....800-962-4724
Campbell Soup Co.
Camden, NJ....800-257-8443
Candy Bouquet of Elko
Elko, NV....888-855-3391
Candy Central
East Hanover, NJ
Candy Mountain Sweets & Treats
Atlanta, GA....800-621-1954
Canelake's Candy
Virginia, MN....888-928-8889
Capco Enterprises
East Hanover, NJ....800-252-1011
Cape Cod Sweets, LLC
Pocasset, MA....508-564-5840
Caprine Estates
Bellbrook, OH....937-848-7406
Caribbean Cookie Company
Virginia Beach, VA....800-326-5200
Carolyn's Gourmet
Concord, MA....800-656-2940
Carrie's Chocolates
Edmonton, AB....877-778-2462
Catoris Candies Inc
New Kensington, PA....724-335-4371
Charlotte's Confections
Millbrae, CA....800-798-2427
Chase & Poe Candy Co
St Joseph, MO....800-786-1625
Cheese Straws & More
Monroe, LA....800-997-1921
Cheri's Desert Harvest
Tucson, AZ....800-743-1141
Chevalier Chocolates
Enfield, CT....860-741-3330
Chex Finer Foods Inc
Mansfield, MA....800-227-8114
Chocoholics Divine Desserts
Linden, CA....800-760-2462
Chocolat Belge Heyez
St-Lazare-De-Bellechasse, QC....450-653-5616
Chocolat Jean Talon
Montreal, QC....888-333-8540
Chocolat Michel Cluizel
New York, NY....646-415-9126
Chocolate By Design Inc
Ronkonkoma, NY....631-737-0082
Chocolate Moon
Asheville, NC....800-723-1236
Chocolate Smith
Santa Fe, NM....505-473-2111
Chocolate Soup
Steamboat Springs, CO....970-870-0224
Chocolate Street of Hartville
Hartville, OH....888-853-5904
Chocolate Studio
Norristown, PA....610-272-3872
Chocolaterie Stam
Des Moines, IA....877-782-6246
Chocolates by Mark
Houston, TX....832-736-2626
Chocolates By Mr Roberts
Boca Raton, FL....561-392-3007
Chocolati Handmade Chocolates
Seattle, WA....206-784-5212
Chocolatier
Exeter, NH....888-246-5528
Chris Candies Inc
Pittsburgh, PA....412-322-9400
Clasen Quality Chocolate
Madison, WI....877-459-4500
Classic Confectionery
Fort Worth, TX....800-674-4435
Clear-Vu Industries
Ashland, MA....508-881-9100
Cloud Nine
Claremont, CA....909-624-3147
CNS Confectionery Products
Bayonne, NJ....888-823-4330
Cocomels by JJ's Sweets
Boulder, CO....303-800-6492
Colts Chocolates
Nashville, TN....615-251-0100
Confectionately Yours LTD
Buffalo Grove, IL....800-875-6978
ConSup North America
Lincoln Park, NJ....973-628-7330
Cowgirl Chocolates
Moscow, ID....888-882-4098
Cranberry Sweets Co
Coos Bay, OR....800-527-5748
Creative Cotton
Northbrook, IL....847-291-4128
Creme Curls
Hudsonville, MI....800-466-1219
Croft's Crackers
Monroe, WI....608-325-1223
Crown Candy Corp
Macon, GA....800-241-3529
Crystal Temptations
North Arlington, NJ....201-246-7990

CTC Manufacturing
Calgary, AB....800-668-7677
Cummings Studio Chocolates
Salt Lake City, UT....800-537-3957
Cupid Candies
Chicago, IL....773-925-8191
Custom Confections & More
Algonquin, IL....832-420-5944
Cyclone Enterprises Inc
Houston, TX....281-872-0087
Daprano & Company
Charlotte, NC....877-365-2337
Dare Foods
Spartanburg, SC....800-668-3273
Das Foods
Chicago, IL....312-224-8590
David Bradley Chocolatier
Windsor, NJ....877-289-7933
Day Spring Enterprises
Cheektowaga, NY....800-879-7677
Daymar Select Fine Coffees
El Cajon, CA....800-466-7590
Dayton Nut Specialties
Springboro, OH....937-743-4377
Debrand Chocolatier
Fort Wayne, IN....260-969-8333
Decko Products Inc
Sandusky, OH....800-537-6143
Delancey Dessert Company
New York, NY....800-254-5254
Dessert Innovations Inc
Atlanta, GA....800-359-7351
Di Camillo Baking Co
Niagara Falls, NY....800-634-4363
Dilettante Chocolates
Kent, WA....800-800-9490
Dillon Candy Co
Boston, GA....800-382-8338
Dipasa USA Inc
Brownsville, TX....956-831-4072
Divine Delights
Petaluma, CA....800-443-2836
Donaldson's Finer Chocolates
Lebanon, IN....800-975-7236
Donells Candies
Casper, WY....877-461-2009
Donna & Company
Cranford, NJ....908-272-4380
Donnelly Fine Chocolates
Santa Cruz, CA....888-685-1871
Dorothy Timberlake Candies
Madison, NH....603-447-2221
Doscher's Candies Co.
Cincinnati, OH....513-381-8656
Doumak Inc
Elk Grove Village, IL....800-323-0318
Downeast Candies
Boothbay Harbor, ME....207-633-5178
Dundee Brandied Fruit Co
Dundee, OR....503-537-2500
Dundee Candy Shop
Louisville, KY....866-877-9266
Dundee Groves
Dundee, FL....800-294-2266
Dynamic Confections
Salt Lake City, UT....801-355-4422
Eclat Chocolate
West Chester, PA....610-692-5206
EcoNatural Solutions
Boulder, CO....303-357-5682
Ed & Don's Of Hawaii Inc
Honolulu, HI....808-423-8200
Eda's Sugar Free
Philadelphia, PA....215-324-3412
Edner Corporation
Hayward, CA....510-441-8504
Elaine's Toffee Co.
Clayton, CA....800-883-3050
Elegant Edibles
Houston, TX....800-227-3226
Elmer Chocolate®
Ponchatoula, LA....800-843-9537
Emmy's Candy from Belgium
Charlotte, NC....866-879-1901
Enstrom Candies, Inc.
Grand Junction, CO....800-367-8766
Esther Price Candies & Gifts
Dayton, OH....855-337-8437
Euphoria Chocolate Company
Eugene, OR....541-344-4914
Evans Creole Candy
New Orleans, LA....800-637-6675

F B Washburn Candy Corp
Brockton, MA....508-588-0820
Fabio Imports
Oceanside, CA....760-726-7040
Family Sweets Candy Company
Elk Grove Village, IL....800-334-1607
Faroh Candies
Middleburg Heights, OH....440-888-9866
Farr Candy Company
Idaho Falls, ID....208-522-8215
Fernando C Pujals & Bros
Guaynabo, PR....787-792-3080
Ferrara Bakery & Cafe
New York, NY....212-226-6150
Ferrara Candy Co Inc
Chicago, IL....800-323-1768
Ficon
St Louis, MO....888-569-4099
Fieldbrook Foods Corp.
Dunkirk, NY....800-333-0805
Fitzkee's Candies Inc
York, PA....717-741-1031
Flix Candy
Niles, IL....847-647-1370
Foley's Chocolates & Candies
Richmond, BC....888-236-5397
Forbes Candies
Virginia Beach, VA....800-626-5898
Foreign Candy Company
Hull, IA....800-831-8541
Fralinger's
Atlantic City, NJ....800-938-2339
Frankford Candy & Chocolate Co
Philadelphia, PA....800-523-9090
Freed, Teller & Freed
South San Francisco, CA....800-370-7371
G Debbas Chocolatier
Fresno, CA....559-294-2071
G Scaccianoce & Co
Bronx, NY....718-991-4462
Gardners Candies Inc
Tyrone, PA....800-242-2639
Gearharts Fine Chocolates
Charlottesville, VA....800-625-0595
Gene & Boots Candies Inc
Perryopolis, PA....800-864-4222
Georgia Nut Co
Skokie, IL....877-674-2993
Germack Pistachio Co
Detroit, MI....800-872-4006
Gia Michaels Confections Inc
Elmont, NY....516-354-3905
Gifford's Ice Cream & Candy Co
Silver Spring, MA....800-708-1938
Gimbals Fine Candies
S San Francisco, CA....800-344-6225
Gingerhaus, LLC
Norfolk, VA....757-348-4274
GKI Foods
Brighton, MI....248-486-0055
Glee Gum
Providence, RI....401-351-6415
GNS Foods
Arlington, TX....817-795-4671
Godiva Chocolatier
New York, NY....800-946-3482
Goetze's Candy Co
Baltimore, MD....410-342-2010
Golden Edibles LLC
Davie, FL....866-779-7781
Golden Fluff Popcorn Co
Lakewood, NJ....732-367-5448
Goodart Candy Inc
Lubbock, TX....806-747-2600
Govadinas Fitness Foods
San Diego, CA....800-900-0108
Govatos Chocolates
Wilmington, DE....888-799-5252
Graeter's Mfg. Co.
Cincinnati, OH....800-721-3323
Grandpops Lollipops
Kansas City, MO....800-255-7873
Gray & Company
Hart, MI....800-551-6009
Great Expectations Confectionery Gourmet Foods
Chicago, IL....773-525-4865
Green County Foods
Monroe, WI....800-233-3564
Green Mountain Chocolate Inc
Franklin, MA....508-520-7160
Greenwell Farms Inc
Kealakekua, HI....888-592-5662

Groovy Candies
Cleveland, OH....888-729-1960
Gurley's Foods
Willmar, MN....800-426-7845
GWB Foods Corporation
Brooklyn, NY....877-977-7610
H.B. Trading
Totowa, NJ....973-812-1022
Haby's Alsatian Bakery
Castroville, TX....830-538-2118
Happy Goat
Boston, MA....617-549-2776
Hauser Chocolates
Westerly, RI....888-599-8231
Haven's Candies
Westbrook, ME....800-639-6309
Hawaii Candy Inc
Honolulu, HI....800-303-2507
Hawaiian Host Inc
Honolulu, HI....888-414-4678
Healthy Food Brands LLC
Brooklyn, NY....212-444-9909
Heavenly Organics, LLC
Longmont, CO....641-636-2095
Hebert Candies
Shrewsbury, MA....866-609-6533
Helms Candy Co., Inc
Bristol, VA....276-669-2533
Hernan
Del Rio, TX....646-263-3598
Hershey Co.
Hershey, PA....800-468-1714
Hialeah Products Co
Hollywood, FL....800-923-3379
Hickory Farms
Maumee, OH....800-753-8558
Hickory Harvest Foods
Akron, OH....800-448-6887
Holistic Products Corporation
Englewood, NJ....800-221-0308
Hospitality Mints LLC
Boone, NC....800-334-5181
House of Spices
Flushing, NY....718-507-4600
Humphrey Co
Cleveland, OH....800-486-3739
Hyde Candy Company
Seattle, WA....206-322-5743
Imani Chimani Chocolate
Brooklyn, NY....718-484-1011
Imperial Nougat Co
Santa Fe Springs, CA....562-693-8423
Indianola Pecan House Inc
Indianola, MS....800-541-6252
International Home Foods
Parsippany, NJ....973-359-9920
Issimo Food Group
La Jolla, CA....619-260-1900
Jakeman's Maple Products
Beachville, ON....800-382-9795
James Candy Company
Atlantic City, NJ....800-441-1404
Jason & Son Specialty Foods
Rancho Cordova, CA....800-810-9093
Jed's Maple Products
Derby, VT....802-766-2700
Jerry's Nut House
Denver, CO....303-861-2262
Jeryl's Jems
Tappan, NY....201-236-8372
Jo's Candies
Torrance, CA....800-770-1946
Joe Clark Fund Raising Candies
Tarentum, PA....888-459-9520
Joray Candy
Brooklyn, NY....718-871-6300
Josh Early Candies
Allentown, PA....610-395-4321
Joyva Corp
Brooklyn, NY....718-497-0170
Judy's Cream Caramels
Sherwood, OR....503-625-7161
Just Born Inc
Bethlehem, PA....800-445-5787
K & F Select Fine Coffees
Portland, OR....800-558-7788
Kara Chocolates
Orem, UT....800-284-5272
Kastner's Pastry Shop & Grocery
Surfside, FL....305-866-6993
Kate Latter Candy Company
New Orleans, LA....800-825-5359

Kateri Foods
Hopkins, MN 800-330-8351
Kehr's candies
Milwaukee, WI 414-344-4305
Kemach Food Products
Brooklyn, NY 718-272-5655
Kencraft, Inc.
Alpine, UT 800-377-4368
Kenny's Candy & Confections
Perham, MN
Kerr Brothers
Toronto, ON 416-252-7341
Key III Candies
Fort Wayne, IN 800-752-2382
Kidsmania
Santa Fe Springs, CA 562-946-8822
King Nut Co
Solon, OH 800-860-5464
Kloss Manufacturing Co Inc
Allentown, PA 800-445-7100
Knudsen Candy
Hayward, CA 800-736-6887
Koeze Company
Grand Rapids, MI 800-555-9688
Koppers Chocolate
Cranford, NJ 800-325-0026
Krema Nut Co
Columbus, OH 800-222-4132
L C Good Candy Company
Allentown, PA 610-432-3290
Lagomarcino's Confectionery
Moline, IL 309-764-1814
Lake Champlain Chocolates
Burlington, VT 800-634-8105
Lammes Candies
Austin, TX 800-252-1885
Lanco
Hauppauge, NY 800-938-4500
Landies Candies Co
Buffalo, NY 800-955-2634
Larosa Bakery Inc
Shrewsbury, NJ 800-527-6722
Laura Paige Candy Company
Newburgh, NY 845-566-4209
Layman Distributing
Salem, VA 800-237-1319
Le Grand Confectionary
Sacramento, CA 888-361-2125
Leader Candies
Brooklyn, NY 718-366-6900
Len Libby Chocolatier-Maine
Scarborough, ME 207-883-4897
Lerro Candy Company
Darby, PA 610-461-8886
Loghouse Foods
Minneapolis, MN 763-546-8395
Long Grove Confectionery
Buffalo Grove, IL 800-373-3102
Longford-Hamilton Company
Beaverton, OR 503-642-5661
Loretta's Authentic Pralines
New Orleans, LA 504-529-6170
Lotte USA Inc
Battle Creek, MI 269-963-6664
Lou-Retta's Custom Chocolates
Buffalo, NY 716-833-7111
Louis J Rheb Candy Co
Baltimore, MD 800-514-8293
Lowery's Home Made Candies
Muncie, IN 800-541-3340
Lucille's Own Make Candies
Manahawkin, NJ 800-426-9168
Lucky You
San Diego, CA 619-450-6700
Ludo LLC
Solon, OH 440-542-6000
Ludwick's Frozen Donuts
Grand Rapids, MI 800-366-8816
Lukas Confections
York, PA 717-843-0921
Lynard Company
Stamford, CT 203-323-0231
Mac Farms Of Hawaii Inc
Captain Cook, HI 808-328-2435
Madrona Specialty Foods LLC
Seattle, WA 425-656-2997
Magna Foods Corporation
City of Industry, CA 800-995-4394
Manhattan Food Brands, LLC
Metuchen, NJ 732-906-2168
Maple Grove Farms Of Vermont
St Johnsbury, VT 802-748-5141
Mari's Candy
Chicago, IL 773-254-3351
Marich Confectionery
Hollister, CA 800-624-7055
Maries Candies
West Liberty, OH 866-465-5781
Marin Food Specialties
Byron, CA 925-634-6126
Marlow Candy & Nut Co
Englewood, NJ 201-569-3725
Mars Inc.
McLean, VA 703-821-4900
Mary of Puddin Hill
Palestine, TX 800-545-8889
MarySue.com
Baltimore, MD 800-662-2639
Marzipan Specialties Inc
Nashville, TN 615-226-4800
Matangos Candies
Harrisburg, PA 717-234-0882
Maxfield Candy
Salt Lake City, UT 800-288-8002
Menehune Mac
Honolulu, HI 808-841-3344
Merb's Candies
St Louis, MO 314-832-7117
Merlin Candies
Harahan, LA 800-899-1549
Michelle Chocolatiers
Colorado Springs, CO 888-447-3654
Midwest Nut Co
Minneapolis, MN 800-328-5502
Miesse Candies
Lancaster, PA 717-392-6011
Mister Snacks Inc
Amherst, NY 800-333-6393
Mitch Chocolate
Melville, NY 631-777-2400
Mom N' Pops Inc
New Windsor, NY 845-567-0640
Monastery Fruitcake
Martinsburg, WV 304-596-2024
Monterrey Products
San Antonio, TX 210-435-2872
Moo Chocolate/Organic Children's Chocolate LLC
Cos Cob, CT 203-561-8864
Moonlight Gourmet
Tyler, TX 903-581-1228
Moore's Candies
Baltimore, MD 410-836-8840
Mother Nature's Goodies
Yucaipa, CA 909-795-6018
Mount Franklin Foods
El Paso, TX 800-351-8178
Mrs Annie's Peanut Patch
Floresville, TX 830-393-7845
Multiflex Company
Hawthorne, NJ 973-636-9700
Munson's Chocolates
Bolton, CT 888-686-7667
Muth's Candy Store
Louisville, KY 502-582-2639
Naron Mary Sue Candies
Baltimore, MD 800-662-2639
Nassau Candy Distributors
Hicksville, NY 516-433-7100
National Importers
Richmond, BC 888-894-6464
Natural Foods Inc
Toledo, OH 419-537-1711
Natural Rush
San Francisco, CA 415-863-2503
Nature's Candy
Fredericksburg, TX 800-729-0085
Naylor Candies Inc
Mt Wolf, PA 717-266-2706
Neal's Chocolates
Salt Lake City, UT 801-521-6500
New Century Snacks
City of Commerce, CA 800-688-6887
Newton Candy Company
Houston, TX 713-691-6969
Niagara Chocolates
Buffalo, NY 877-261-7887
Nora's Candy Shop
Rome, NY 888-544-8224
Northwest Chocolate Factory
Salem, OR 503-362-1340
Northwoods Candy Emporium
Branson, MO 417-332-1010
Nutty Bavarian
Sanford, FL 800-382-4788
Oak Leaf Confections
.... 877-261-7887
OH Chocolate
Seattle, WA 206-329-8777
Oh, Sugar! LLC
Roswell, GA 866-557-8427
Old Dominion Peanut Corp
Norfolk, VA 800-368-6887
Old Monmouth Candies
Freehold, NJ 732-462-1311
Old Time Candy Co
Lagrange, OH 440-355-4345
Olde Tyme Food Corporation
East Longmeadow, MA 800-356-6533
Olde Tyme Mercantile
Arroyo Grande, CA 805-489-7991
Ole Smoky Candy Kitchen
Gatlinburg, TN 865-436-4716
Olivier's Candies
Calgary, AB 403-266-6028
Ooh La La Candy
.... 855-817-1896
Pacific Gold Marketing
Arlington, TX 817-795-4671
Palmer Candy Co
Sioux City, IA 800-831-0828
Pangburn Candy Company
Fort Worth, TX 817-332-8856
Pantry Shelf/Mixxm
Hutchinson, KS 800-968-3346
Papas Chris A & Son Co
Covington, KY 859-431-0499
Parker Products
Fort Worth, TX 817-336-7441
Parkside Candy Co
Buffalo, NY 716-833-7540
Patsy's Candy
Colorado Springs, CO 866-372-8797
Paul's Candy Factory
Salt Lake City, UT 800-825-9912
Paulaur Corp
Cranbury, NJ 609-395-8844
Peanut Patch Gift Shop
Courtland, VA 800-544-0896
Pearl River Pastry & Chocolate
Pearl River, NY 800-632-2639
Pearson Candy Co
St Paul, MN 651-698-0356
Pease's Candy
Springfield, IL 217-523-3721
Pecan Deluxe Candy Co
Dallas, TX 800-733-3589
Perfetti Van Melle USA Inc
Erlanger, KY 859-283-1234
Pez Candy Inc
Orange, CT 203-795-0531
Pfizer
New York, NY 800-879-3477
Phillip's Candy House
Dorchester, MA 617-282-2090
Phillips Candies
Seaside, OR 503-738-5402
Piedmont Candy Co
Lexington, NC 336-248-2477
Pine River Pre-Pack Inc
Newton, WI 920-726-4216
Pippin Snack Pecans
Albany, GA 800-554-6887
Plantation Candies
Telford, PA 888-678-6468
Plyley's Candy
Lagrange, IN 877-665-2778
Popcorn Connection
North Hollywood, CA 800-852-2676
Poppers Supply Company
Allentown, PA 800-457-9810
Poppingfun Inc
Neenah, WI 920-486-7210
Priester's Pecans
Fort Deposit, AL 866-477-4736
Prifti Candy Company
Worcester, MA 800-447-7438
Primrose Candy Co
Chicago, IL 800-268-9522
Prince of Peace
Hayward, CA 800-732-2328
Produits Alimentaire
St Lambert De Lauzon, QC 800-463-1787
Project 7
San Clemente, CA 949-891-0729
Promotion in Motion Companies
Closter, NJ 800-369-7391

Pulakos 926 Chocolate
Erie, PA 814-452-4026
Pure Dark
Hackettstown, NJ 973-856-1899
Purity Candy Co
Lewisburg, PA. 800-821-4748
Quality Candy Company
Walnut, CA 909-444-1025
Queen Bee Gardens
Lovell, WY 800-225-7553
Queensway Foods Company
Burlingame, CA 650-871-7770
Quigley Industries Inc
Farmington, MI. 800-367-2441
Quintessential Chocolates
Fredericksburg, TX. 800-842-3382
R.L. Albert & Son
Stamford, CT. 203-622-8655
R.M. Palmer Co.
West Reading, PA 610-372-8971
Ragold Confections
Wilton Manors, FL 954-566-9092
Realsalt
Heber City, UT 800-367-7258
Rebecca-Ruth Candy Factory
Frankfort, KY 800-444-3866
Red Rocker Candy
Troy, VA 434-589-2011
Republica Del Cacao LLC
Long Beach, CA 932-256-1320
Richards Maple Products
Chardon, OH. 800-352-4052
Richardson Brands Co
Canajoharie, NY. 518-673-3553
Ricos Candy Snack & Bakery
Hialeah, FL 305-885-7392
Riddles' Sweet Impressions
Edmonton, AB 780-465-8085
Rigoni Di Asiago
Miami, FL. 305-470-7583
Rito Mints
Trois Rivieres, QC 819-379-1449
Rivard Popcorn Products
Lancaster, PA 717-898-7131
Riverdale Fine Foods
Dayton, OH. 800-548-1304
Rosalind Candy Castle Inc
New Brighton, PA. 724-843-1144
Rosetti's Fine Foods Biscotti
Clovis, CA 559-323-6450
Ross Fine Candies
Waterford, MI 248-682-5640
Ruger LLC
Bethesda, MD 301-675-2398
Runk Candy Company
Cincinnati, OH 800-641-8551
Russell Stover Candies Inc.
Kansas City, MO. 800-777-4004
Ruth Hunt Candy Co
Mt Sterling, KY 800-927-0302
S P Enterprises
Las Vegas, NV 800-746-4774
S Zitner Co
Philadelphia, PA 215-229-9828
S.L. Kaye Company
New York, NY 212-683-5600
Sahagian & Associates
Oak Park, IL 800-327-9273
Salem Old Fashioned Candies
Salem, MA 978-744-3242
Sally Lane's Candy Farm
Paris, TN. 731-642-5801
Sambets Cajun Deli
Austin, TX. 800-472-6238
Sanders Candy Inc
Clinton Twp, MI 800-852-2253
Sandy Candy
Chester Springs, PA 800-386-7263
Sconza Candy Co
Oakdale, CA 877-568-8137
Scott's Candy
Glennville, GA 800-356-2100
Scott-Bathgate
Winnipeg, MB. 800-216-2990
Scripture Candy
Birmingham, AL. 888-317-7333
Seattle Bar Company
Seattle, WA 206-601-4301
Seattle Gourmet Foods
Tukwila, WA. 800-800-9490
See's Candies
Carson, CA 800-347-7337

Senor Murphy Candymaker
Santa Fe, NM 877-988-4311
Shaker Country Meadowsweets
Hillside, NJ. 800-524-1304
Shane Candy Co
Philadelphia, PA 215-922-1048
Sherbrooke OEM Ltd
Sherbrooke, QC 866-851-2579
Sherm Edwards Candies
Trafford, PA 800-436-5424
Sifers Valomilk Candy Co
Shawnee, KS. 913-722-0991
Silver Sweet Candies
Lawrence, MA 978-688-0474
Silverland Bakery
Forest Park, IL 708-488-0800
Simply Scruptious Confections
Irvine, CA 714-505-3955
SmartSweets
Vancouver, BC
Snackerz
Commerce, CA. 888-576-2253
Sole Grano LLC
Fair Lawn, NJ 201-797-7100
Sorbee Intl.
Philadelphia, PA 800-654-3997
South Beach Novelties & Confectionery
Staten Island, NY 718-727-4500
Southern Style Nuts
Denison, TX 903-463-3161
Spangler Candy Co
Bryan, OH. 888-636-4221
Specialty Food Association
New York, NY 646-878-0301
Spokandy
Spokane, WA. 509-624-1969
Squirrel Brand Company
McKinney, TX 800-624-8242
St Laurent Brothers
Bay City, MI 800-289-7688
Standard Functional Foods Grp
Nashville, TN 800-226-4340
Star Kay White Inc
Congers, NY 800-874-8518
Stark Candy Company
Revere, MA. 800-225-5508
Startupcandy Co
Provo, UT 801-373-8673
Stevens Creative Enterprises, Inc.
New York, NY 646-558-6336
Stewart Candies
Waycross, GA 912-283-1970
Stichler Products Inc
Reading, PA. 610-921-0211
Stone's Home Made Candy Shop
Oswego, NY 888-223-3928
Storck Canada
Mississauga, ON. 905-272-4480
Storck U.S.A.
Chicago, IL 800-852-5542
Stutz Candy Company
Philadelphia, PA 888-692-2639
Sucesores de Pedro Cortes
Hato Rey, PR. 787-754-7040
Sugar Plum LLC
Houma, LA 985-872-9524
Sunridge Farms
Royal Oaks, CA 831-786-7000
Sweenors Chocolates
Wakefield, RI 800-834-3123
Sweet Candy Company
Salt Lake City, UT 855-772-7720
Sweet City Supply
Virginia Beach, VA 888-793-3824
Sweet Sensations
Labrador City, NL. 709-944-2660
Sweetcraft Candies
Timonium, MD 410-252-0684
SweetWorks Inc
Buffalo, NY. 716-634-0880
Tastee Apple
Newcomerstown, OH 800-262-7753
Tasty Brand Inc
Calabasas, CA. 818-225-9000
Temo Candy
Akron, OH. 330-376-7229
Terri Lynn Inc
Elgin, IL 800-323-0775
Testamints Sales-Distribution
Hopatcong, NJ 888-879-0400
Texas Coffee Traders Inc
Austin, TX. 800-343-4875

Texas Toffee
Odessa, TX 800-599-2133
The Great San Saba River Pecan Company
San Saba, TX 800-621-8121
Todd's
Vernon, CA 800-938-6337
Toffee Co
Houston, TX 713-688-5531
Tom & Sally's Handmade Chocolates
Brattleboro, VT. 800-827-0800
Tony Vitrano Company
Jessup, MD 800-481-3784
Tootsie Roll Industries Inc.
Chicago, IL 866-972-6879
Torie & Howard LLC
New Milford, CT 860-799-7772
Torn & Glasser
Los Angeles, CA. 800-282-6887
Totally Chocolate
Blaine, WA 800-255-5506
Toucan Chocolates
Waban, MA. 617-964-8696
Trappistine Quality Candy
Wrentham, MA 866-549-8929
Tremblay's Sweet Shop
Hayward, WI. 715-634-2785
Triple-C
Hamilton, ON 800-263-9105
Tropical Foods
Charlotte, NC 800-438-4470
Tropical Foods
Lithia Springs, GA 800-544-3762
Tropical Nut & Fruit Co
Orlando, FL. 800-749-8869
Tropical Nut Fruit & Bulk Cndy
Lithia Springs, GA 800-544-3762
Truan's Candies
Detroit, MI 800-584-3004
Truffle Treasures
Ottawa, ON 613-761-3859
Turkey Hill Sugarbush
Waterloo, QC 450-539-4822
Twenty First Century Snacks
Ronkonkoma, NY. 800-975-2883
Tyler Candy Co LLC
Tyler, TX. 903-561-3046
Ultimate Nut & Candy Company
Los Angeles, CA. 800-767-5259
Valhrona
Los Angeles, CA. 310-277-0401
Van Leer Chocolate Corporation
Chicago, IL 800-225-1418
Van Otis Chocolates
Manchester, NH 800-826-6847
Vande Walle's Candies Inc
Appleton, WI 800-738-1020
Varda Chocolatier
Elizabeth, NJ. 800-448-2732
Vaughn-Russell Candy Kitchen
Greenville, SC. 864-271-7786
Velatis
Silver Spring, MD. 888-483-5284
Velvet Creme Popcorn Co
Westwood, KS. 888-553-6708
Verdant Kitchen
Norcross, GA 912-349-2958
Vigneri Chocolate Inc.
Rochester, NY. 877-844-6374
Vitality Life Choice
Carson City, NV 800-423-8365
Warner-Lambert Confections
Cambridge, MA 617-491-2500
Warrell Corp
Camp Hill, PA. 800-233-7082
Warrell Corp
Camp Hill, PA. 844-234-3217
Waymouth Farms Inc
Minneapolis, MN 800-527-0094
Weaver Nut Co. Inc.
Ephrata, PA 800-473-2688
Webb's Candy
Davenport, FL. 800-289-9322
Wedding Cake Studio
Williamsfield, OH. 440-667-1765
Westbrae Natural Foods
Melville, NY. 800-434-4246
Westdale Foods Company
Orland Park, IL 708-458-7774
Whetstone Candy Company
St. Augustine, FL 904-825-1700
White-Stokes Company
Chicago, IL 800-978-6537

Whitley Peanut Factory Inc
Hayes, VA 800-470-2244
Widman's Candy Shop
Crookston, MN 218-281-1487
Wilkinson-Spitz
Yonkers, NY 914-237-5000
Williams & Bennett
Orlando, FL 561-276-9007
Williams Candy Co
Chesapeake, VA 757-545-9311
Williams Candy Company
Somerville, MA 617-776-0814
Williamsburg Chocolatier
Williamsburg, VA 757-253-1474
Wilson Candy Co
Jeannette, PA 724-523-3151
Wilson's Fantastic Candy
Memphis, TN 901-767-1900
Winans Chocolates & Coffees
Piqua, OH 937-381-0247
Windmill Candies
Granite Falls, MN 877-771-8892
Windsor Confections
Oakland, CA 800-860-0021
Winfrey Fudge & Candy
Rowley, MA 888-946-3739
Wisconsin Dairyland Fudge Company
Wisconsin Dells, WI 608-254-7771
Wisteria Candy Cottage
Boulevard, CA 800-458-8246
Woodstock Farms Manufacturing
Edison, NJ 800-526-4349
World Confections Inc
South Orange, NJ 718-768-8100
Wright's Ice Cream Co
Cayuga, IN 800-686-9561
Wrigley
Chicago, IL 312-794-6000
Yost Candy Co Inc
Dalton, OH 800-750-1976
Z Specialty Food, LLC
Woodland, CA 800-678-1226
Zachary Confections Inc
Frankfort, IN 800-445-4222

Bon Bons

Delaviuda USA Inc
Coral Gables, FL 786-599-9814
Ferrara Bakery & Cafe
New York, NY 212-226-6150
Kerr Brothers
Toronto, ON 416-252-7341
Knudsen Candy
Hayward, CA 800-736-6887
Tony Vitrano Company
Jessup, MD 800-481-3784

Breath Tablets

Ferrero USA Inc
Somerset, NJ 800-337-7376
Hershey Co.
Hershey, PA 800-468-1714
Liberty Natural Products Inc
Oregon City, OR 800-289-8427
Pfizer
New York, NY 800-879-3477
Sherbrooke OEM Ltd
Sherbrooke, QC 866-851-2579

Brittles

Arway Confections Inc
Chicago, IL 800-695-0612
B & B Pecan Processors
Turkey, NC 866-328-7322
Bazzini Holdings LLC
Allentown, PA 610-366-1606
Brittle Kittle
Tigard, OR 800-447-2128
Buddy Squirrel LLC
St Francis, WI 800-972-2658
Charlotte's Confections
Millbrae, CA 800-798-2427
Chase & Poe Candy Co
St Joseph, MO 800-786-1625
Cheese Straws & More
Monroe, LA 800-997-1921
Claeys Candy Inc
South Bend, IN 574-287-1818
Crickle Company
Thomasville, GA 800-237-8689
Crown Candy Corp
Macon, GA 800-241-3529
Dillon Candy Co
Boston, GA 800-382-8338
Elegant Edibles
Houston, TX 800-227-3226
Enstrom Candies, Inc.
Grand Junction, CO 800-367-8766
Georgia Nut Co
Skokie, IL 877-674-2993
GKI Foods
Brighton, MI 248-486-0055
GNS Foods
Arlington, TX 817-795-4671
Gurley's Foods
Willmar, MN 800-426-7845
Hialeah Products Co
Hollywood, FL 800-923-3379
Idaho Candy Co
Boise, ID 800-898-6986
Kay Foods Co
Detroit, MI 313-393-1100
La Piccolina
Decatur, GA 800-626-1624
Layman Distributing
Salem, VA 800-237-1319
Maries Candies
West Liberty, OH 866-465-5781
Michele's Chocolate Truffles
Clackamas, OR 800-656-7112
Mrs Annie's Peanut Patch
Floresville, TX 830-393-7845
Muth's Candy Store
Louisville, KY 502-582-2639
Old Dominion Peanut Corp
Norfolk, VA 800-368-6887
Olde Tyme Mercantile
Arroyo Grande, CA 805-489-7991
Olivier's Candies
Calgary, AB 403-266-6028
Palmer Candy Co
Sioux City, IA 800-831-0828
Patsy's Candy
Colorado Springs, CO 866-372-8797
Roger's Recipe
Glover, VT 802-525-3050
Sally Lane's Candy Farm
Paris, TN 731-642-5801
Sconza Candy Co
Oakdale, CA 877-568-8137
Snackerz
Commerce, CA 888-576-2253
Squirrel Brand Company
McKinney, TX 800-624-8242
St. Jacobs Candy Co.
Waterloo, ON 519-884-3505
Susie's South Forty Confection
Midland, TX 800-221-4442
Sweet Jubilee Gourmet
Mechanicsburg, PA 877-691-9732
Trophy Nut Co
Tipp City, OH 800-219-9004
Vande Walle's Candies Inc
Appleton, WI 800-738-1020
Warrell Corp
Camp Hill, PA 800-233-7082

Butterscotch

Ferrara Candy Co Inc
Chicago, IL 800-323-1768
Sole Grano LLC
Fair Lawn, NJ 201-797-7100
Weaver Nut Co. Inc.
Ephrata, PA 800-473-2688

Candy Bars

Alcove Chocolate
Los Angeles, CA 323-284-2229
Ameri Candy
Louisville, KY 502-583-1776
Ann Hemyng Candy Inc
Trumbauersville, PA 800-779-7004
Arctic Beverages
Winnipeg, MB 866-503-1270
Bertie County Peanuts
Windsor, NC 800-457-0005
Blommer Chocolate Co
Chicago, IL 800-621-1606
Cambridge Brands Inc
Cambridge, MA 617-491-2500
Carrie's Chocolates
Edmonton, AB 877-778-2462
Chase & Poe Candy Co
St Joseph, MO 800-786-1625
Chocolate Street of Hartville
Hartville, OH 888-853-5904
Chris Candies Inc
Pittsburgh, PA 412-322-9400
Cloud Nine
Claremont, CA 909-624-3147
Doscher's Candies Co.
Cincinnati, OH 513-381-8656
Eda's Sugar Free
Philadelphia, PA 215-324-3412
Edner Corporation
Hayward, CA 510-441-8504
Ferrara Bakery & Cafe
New York, NY 212-226-6150
G Debbas Chocolatier
Fresno, CA 559-294-2071
Gardners Candies Inc
Tyrone, PA 800-242-2639
Go Max Go Foods
Good Stuff Cacao
Metamora, MI 248-690-5114
Hershey Co.
Hershey, PA 800-468-1714
Joyva Corp
Brooklyn, NY 718-497-0170
Long Grove Confectionary
Buffalo Grove, IL 800-373-3102
Lukas Confections
York, PA 717-843-0921
Mars Inc.
McLean, VA 703-821-4900
Niagara Chocolates
Buffalo, NY 877-261-7887
Nikki's Coconut Butter
Hudson, WI
NuGo Nutrition
Oakmont, PA 888-421-2032
Papas Chris A & Son Co
Covington, KY 859-431-0499
Raaka Chocolate
Brooklyn, NY 855-255-3354
Ruth Hunt Candy Co
Mt Sterling, KY 800-927-0302
RXBAR
Chicago, IL 312-624-8200
Sucesores de Pedro Cortes
Hato Rey, PR 787-754-7040
Vande Walle's Candies Inc
Appleton, WI 800-738-1020
Weaver Nut Co. Inc.
Ephrata, PA 800-473-2688
World Confections Inc
South Orange, NJ 718-768-8100

Coated

Alcove Chocolate
Los Angeles, CA 323-284-2229

Caramel

Amella
El Segundo, CA 800-205-0080
Asti Holdings Ltd
New Westminster, BC 604-523-6866
Becky's Blissful Bakery
Pewaukee, WI 262-327-4111
Bequet Confections
Bozeman, MT 877-423-7838
Big Picture Farm LLC
Townshend, VT 802-221-0547
Cambridge Brands Inc
Cambridge, MA 617-491-2500
Carousel Candies
Geneva, IL 888-656-1552
Charlotte's Confections
Millbrae, CA 800-798-2427
Chocolate Signatures LP
Toronto, ON 416-234-8528
Cocomels by JJ's Sweets
Boulder, CO 303-800-6492
Das Foods
Chicago, IL 312-224-8590
Davinci Gourmet LTD
Seattle, WA 800-640-6779
Double Premium Confections
McLean, VA 202-495-1884
Ferrara Candy Co Inc
Chicago, IL 800-323-1768

Gene & Boots Candies Inc
Perryopolis, PA ... 800-864-4222

GKI Foods
Brighton, MI ... 248-486-0055

Goetze's Candy Co
Baltimore, MD ... 410-342-2010

J Morgan's Confections
Ogden, UT ... 801-399-3007

Jason & Son Specialty Foods
Rancho Cordova, CA ... 800-810-9093

Judy's Cream Caramels
Sherwood, OR ... 503-625-7161

Key III Candies
Fort Wayne, IN ... 800-752-2382

Knudsen Candy
Hayward, CA ... 800-736-6887

Kohler Original Recipe Chocolates
Kohler, WI ... 920-208-4930

Leader Candies
Brooklyn, NY ... 718-366-6900

Lowery's Home Made Candies
Muncie, IN ... 800-541-3340

Lukas Confections
York, PA ... 717-843-0921

Matangos Candies
Harrisburg, PA ... 717-234-0882

Mccreas Candies
Hyde Park, MA ... 617-276-3388

Moonstruck Chocolate Co
Portland, OR ... 800-557-6666

Moore's Candies
Baltimore, MD ... 410-836-8840

Mrs Prindables
Niles, IL ... 888-215-1100

Muth's Candy Store
Louisville, KY ... 502-582-2639

Nunes Farms Marketing
Gustine, CA ... 209-862-3033

Ruth Hunt Candy Co
Mt Sterling, KY ... 800-927-0302

S Zitner Co
Philadelphia, PA ... 215-229-9828

St. Jacobs Candy Co.
Waterloo, ON ... 519-884-3505

Suss Sweets
Nashua, NH ... 603-864-8563

Sweet Designs Chocolatier Inc
Lakewood, OH ... 216-226-4888

Tahana Confections LLC
Portsmouth, NH ... 603-498-6246

Tastee Apple
Newcomerstown, OH ... 800-262-7753

The Lovely Candy Company LLC
Woodstock, IL ... 801-824-0624

Tropical Nut Fruit & Bulk Cndy
Lithia Springs, GA ... 800-544-3762

Vande Walle's Candies Inc
Appleton, WI ... 800-738-1020

Weaver Nut Co. Inc.
Ephrata, PA ... 800-473-2688

White-Stokes Company
Chicago, IL ... 800-978-6537

World Confections Inc
South Orange, NJ ... 718-768-8100

Carob

Clasen Quality Chocolate
Madison, WI ... 877-459-4500

Famarco Limited
Virginia Beach, VA ... 757-460-3573

GKI Foods
Brighton, MI ... 248-486-0055

Setton International Foods
Commack, NY ... 800-227-4397

Chewing Gum

Adams USA Inc.
Cookeville, TN ... 800-251-6857

American Food Products Inc
Methuen, MA ... 978-682-1855

Arcor USA
Coral Gables, FL ... 800-572-7267

Beehive Botanicals
Hayward, WI ... 800-233-4483

C Howard Co
Bellport, NY ... 631-286-7940

Candyrific
Louisville, KY ... 502-893-3626

Fernando C Pujals & Bros
Guaynabo, PR ... 787-792-3080

Ford Gum & Mach Co Inc
Akron, NY ... 716-542-4561

Foreign Candy Company
Hull, IA ... 800-831-8541

Glee Gum
Providence, RI ... 401-351-6415

Golden Fluff Popcorn Co
Lakewood, NJ ... 732-367-5448

Hershey Co.
Hershey, PA ... 800-468-1714

Lotte USA Inc
Battle Creek, MI ... 269-963-6664

Mars Inc.
McLean, VA ... 703-821-4900

Oak Leaf Confections
... 877-261-7887

Perfetti Van Melle USA Inc
Erlanger, KY ... 859-283-1234

Pfizer
New York, NY ... 800-879-3477

Simply Gum
New York, NY

SP Enterprises, Inc.
Las Vegas, NV ... 800-746-4774

Sweet Breath
New York, NY ... 877-673-9777

SweetWorks Inc
Buffalo, NY ... 716-634-0880

Whetstone Chocolates
St Augustine, FL ... 877-261-7887

World Confections Inc
South Orange, NJ ... 718-768-8100

Wrigley
Chicago, IL ... 312-794-6000

Chocolate Substitutes

Blommer Chocolate Co
Chicago, IL ... 800-621-1606

Cocoa Drops

Blommer Chocolate Co
Chicago, IL ... 800-621-1606

Hershey Co.
Hershey, PA ... 800-468-1714

Coconut

Chase & Poe Candy Co
St Joseph, MO ... 800-786-1625

Crown Candy Corp
Macon, GA ... 800-241-3529

David Bradley Chocolatier
Windsor, NJ ... 877-289-7933

Dundee Groves
Dundee, FL ... 800-294-2266

GKI Foods
Brighton, MI ... 248-486-0055

Island Delights, Inc.
Seville, OH ... 866-877-4100

Mari's Candy
Chicago, IL ... 773-254-3351

Olde Tyme Mercantile
Arroyo Grande, CA ... 805-489-7991

Papas Chris A & Son Co
Covington, KY ... 859-431-0499

Sally Lane's Candy Farm
Paris, TN ... 731-642-5801

Corn

American Food Products Inc
Methuen, MA ... 978-682-1855

El Brands
Ozark, AL ... 334-445-2828

Fernando C Pujals & Bros
Guaynabo, PR ... 787-792-3080

Frankford Candy & Chocolate Co
Philadelphia, PA ... 800-523-9090

Gurley's Foods
Willmar, MN ... 800-426-7845

Hyde & Hyde Inc
Corona, CA ... 951-279-5239

Jelly Belly Candy Co.
Fairfield, CA ... 800-522-3267

New Century Snacks
City of Commerce, CA ... 800-688-6887

Rogers' Chocolates Ltd
Victoria, BC ... 800-663-2220

Seattle Bar Company
Seattle, WA ... 206-601-4301

Setton International Foods
Commack, NY ... 800-227-4397

Snackerz
Commerce, CA ... 888-576-2253

Sweet Candy Company
Salt Lake City, UT ... 855-772-7720

Sweet City Supply
Virginia Beach, VA ... 888-793-3824

Todd's
Vernon, CA ... 800-938-6337

Triple-C
Hamilton, ON ... 800-263-9105

Trophy Nut Co
Tipp City, OH ... 800-219-9004

Cotton

Barcelona Nut Co
Baltimore, MD ... 800-296-6887

Brennan Snacks Manufacturing
Bogalusa, LA ... 800-290-7486

Fare Foods Corp
Du Quoin, IL ... 618-542-2155

Great Western Co LLC
Hollywood, AL ... 256-259-3578

Kloss Manufacturing Co Inc
Allentown, PA ... 800-445-7100

Olde Tyme Food Corporation
East Longmeadow, MA ... 800-356-6533

Taste of Nature Inc.
Santa Monica, CA ... 310-396-4433

Cremes

Blommer Chocolate Co
Chicago, IL ... 800-621-1606

Brown & Haley
Fife, WA ... 800-426-8400

Chocolates a La Carte
Valencia, CA ... 800-818-2462

De Fluri's Fine Chocolate
Martinsburg, WV ... 304-264-3698

Fannie May Fine Chocolate
Oakdale, MN ... 800-999-3629

Fernando C Pujals & Bros
Guaynabo, PR ... 787-792-3080

Goetze's Candy Co
Baltimore, MD ... 410-342-2010

Lammes Candies
Austin, TX ... 800-252-1885

Layman Distributing
Salem, VA ... 800-237-1319

Lowery's Home Made Candies
Muncie, IN ... 800-541-3340

Maramor Chocolates
Columbus, OH ... 800-843-7722

Moore's Candies
Baltimore, MD ... 410-836-8840

New Century Snacks
City of Commerce, CA ... 800-688-6887

Palmer Candy Co
Sioux City, IA ... 800-831-0828

Patsy's Candy
Colorado Springs, CO ... 866-372-8797

Rene Rey Chocolates Ltd
North Vancouver, BC ... 888-985-0949

Sanders Candy Inc
Clinton Twp, MI ... 800-852-2253

Sweet City Supply
Virginia Beach, VA ... 888-793-3824

V L Foods
White Plains, NY ... 914-697-4851

Z Specialty Food, LLC
Woodland, CA ... 800-678-1226

Dietetic

Balanced Health Products
New York, NY ... 212-794-9878

Bidwell Candies
Mattoon, IL ... 217-234-3858

GKI Foods
Brighton, MI ... 248-486-0055

Hillside Candy Co
Hillside, NJ ... 800-524-1304

Lowery's Home Made Candies
Muncie, IN ... 800-541-3340

Lukas Confections
York, PA ... 717-843-0921

Olde Tyme Mercantile
Arroyo Grande, CA ... 805-489-7991

Sally Lane's Candy Farm
Paris, TN ... 731-642-5801

Setton International Foods
Commack, NY ... 800-227-4397

Divinity

Ludwick's Frozen Donuts
Grand Rapids, MI . . . 800-366-8816

Filled

American Food Products Inc
Methuen, MA . . . 978-682-1855
Andre's Confiserie Suisse
Kansas City, MO . . . 800-892-1234
Arcor USA
Coral Gables, FL . . . 800-572-7267
Bissinger's Handcrafted Chocolatier
St. Louis, MO . . . 314-615-2400
Brockmann's Chocolates
Delta, BC . . . 888-494-2270
Brown & Haley
Fife, WA . . . 800-426-8400
Cadbury Trebor Allan
Granby, QC . . . 800-387-3267
Chocolate By Design Inc
Ronkonkoma, NY . . . 800-536-3618
Chocolate House
Milwaukee, WI . . . 800-236-2022
Chocolates a La Carte
Valencia, CA . . . 800-818-2462
Chocolove
Boulder, CO . . . 888-246-2656
Double Play Foods
New York, NY . . . 212-682-4611
El Brands
Ozark, AL . . . 334-445-2828
Empress Chocolate Company
Brooklyn, NY . . . 800-793-3809
Fannie May Fine Chocolate
Oakdale, MN . . . 800-999-3629
Fernando C Pujals & Bros
Guaynabo, PR . . . 787-792-3080
Ferrero USA Inc
Somerset, NJ . . . 800-337-7376
Frankford Candy & Chocolate Co
Philadelphia, PA . . . 800-523-9090
Goetze's Candy Co
Baltimore, MD . . . 410-342-2010
Hagensborg Chocolates LTD.
Burnaby, BC . . . 877-554-7763
Harbor Sweets
Salem, MA . . . 800-243-2115
Hyde & Hyde Inc
Corona, CA . . . 951-279-5239
Idaho Candy Co
Boise, ID . . . 800-898-6986
Knudsen Candy
Hayward, CA . . . 800-736-6887
Leader Candies
Brooklyn, NY . . . 718-366-6900
Lowery's Home Made Candies
Muncie, IN . . . 800-541-3340
Nature's Candy
Fredericksburg, TX . . . 800-729-0085
New Century Snacks
City of Commerce, CA . . . 800-688-6887
Plantation Candies
Telford, PA . . . 888-678-6468
Primrose Candy Co
Chicago, IL . . . 800-268-9522
Rebecca-Ruth Candy Factory
Frankfort, KY . . . 800-444-3866
Richardson Brands Co
Canajoharie, NY . . . 518-673-3553
Setton International Foods
Commack, NY . . . 800-227-4397
Snackerz
Commerce, CA . . . 888-576-2253
Sweet Candy Company
Salt Lake City, UT . . . 855-772-7720
Todd's
Vernon, CA . . . 800-938-6337
V L Foods
White Plains, NY . . . 914-697-4851
Warner Candy
El Paso, TX . . . 847-928-7200
Webb's Candy
Davenport, FL . . . 800-289-9322

Fudge

Amcan Industries
Elmsford, NY . . . 914-347-4838
Bear Creek Smokehouse Inc
Marshall, TX . . . 800-950-2327
Betty Lou's
McMinnville, OR . . . 800-242-5205
Blommer Chocolate Co
Chicago, IL . . . 800-621-1606
Bodega Chocolates
Fountain Valley, CA . . . 888-326-3342
Calico Cottage
Amityville, NY . . . 800-645-5345
Cambridge Brands Inc
Cambridge, MA . . . 617-491-2500
Charlotte's Confections
Millbrae, CA . . . 800-798-2427
Country Fresh Food & Confections, Inc.
Oliver Springs, TN . . . 800-545-8782
Crown Candy Corp
Macon, GA . . . 800-241-3529
Donells Candies
Casper, WY . . . 877-461-2009
Downeast Candies
Boothbay Harbor, ME . . . 207-633-5178
Enstrom Candies, Inc.
Grand Junction, CO . . . 800-367-8766
Fieldbrook Foods Corp.
Dunkirk, NY . . . 800-333-0805
Fudge Fatale
Studio City, CA . . . 800-809-8298
Gene & Boots Candies Inc
Perryopolis, PA . . . 800-864-4222
Giambri's Quality Sweets Inc
Clementon, NJ . . . 866-238-0169
Haven's Candies
Westbrook, ME . . . 800-639-6309
Hershey Co.
Hershey, PA . . . 800-468-1714
J Morgan's Confections
Ogden, UT . . . 801-399-3007
James Candy Company
Atlantic City, NJ . . . 800-441-1404
JER Creative Food Concepts, Inc.
Commerce, CA . . . 800-350-2462
Kelly's Candies
Pooler, GA . . . 800-523-3051
Layman Distributing
Salem, VA . . . 800-237-1319
Maple Leaf Cheesemakers
New Glarus, WI . . . 888-624-1234
McJak Candy Company LLC
Medina, OH . . . 800-424-2942
Nancy's Candy
Meadows Of Dan, VA . . . 800-328-3834
Olde Tyme Mercantile
Arroyo Grande, CA . . . 805-489-7991
Phenomenal Fudge Inc
Shoreham, VT . . . 800-430-5442
Phillip's Candy House
Dorchester, MA . . . 617-282-2090
Rocky Top Country Store
Sevierville, TN . . . 866-260-0670
St. Jacobs Candy Co.
Waterloo, ON . . . 519-884-3505
Sweenors Chocolates
Wakefield, RI . . . 800-834-3123
The Lovely Candy Company LLC
Woodstock, IL . . . 801-824-0624
Tony Vitrano Company
Jessup, MD . . . 800-481-3784
Vande Walle's Candies Inc
Appleton, WI . . . 800-738-1020
Webb's Candy
Davenport, FL . . . 800-289-9322

Gums & Jellies

Albanese Confectionery Group
Merrillville, IN . . . 800-536-0581
Amazing Candy Craft Company
Hollis, NY . . . 800-429-9368
American Food Products Inc
Methuen, MA . . . 978-682-1855
Andros Foods North America
Mount Jackson, VA . . . 844-426-3767
Arcor USA
Coral Gables, FL . . . 800-572-7267
Au'some Candies
Monmouth Junction, NJ . . . 877-287-6649
Barcelona Nut Co
Baltimore, MD . . . 800-296-6887
Beehive Botanicals
Hayward, WI . . . 800-233-4483
Boston Fruit Slice & Confectionery Corporation
Lawrence, MA . . . 978-686-2699
C Howard Co
Bellport, NY . . . 631-286-7940
Cadbury Trebor Allan
Granby, QC . . . 800-387-3267
Cambridge Brands Inc
Cambridge, MA . . . 617-491-2500
Diamond Foods
Santa Cruz, CA . . . 831-457-3200
El Brands
Ozark, AL . . . 334-445-2828
Extreme Creations
El Dorado Hills, CA . . . 916-941-0444
Fannie May Fine Chocolate
Oakdale, MN . . . 800-999-3629
Fernando C Pujals & Bros
Guaynabo, PR . . . 787-792-3080
Ferrara Candy Co Inc
Chicago, IL . . . 800-323-1768
Foreign Candy Company
Hull, IA . . . 800-831-8541
Frankford Candy & Chocolate Co
Philadelphia, PA . . . 800-523-9090
Ganong Bros Ltd
St. Stephen, NB . . . 888-270-8222
Gene & Boots Candies Inc
Perryopolis, PA . . . 800-864-4222
GNS Foods
Arlington, TX . . . 817-795-4671
Golden Fluff Popcorn Co
Lakewood, NJ . . . 732-367-5448
Gurley's Foods
Willmar, MN . . . 800-426-7845
Haribo of America
Baltimore, MD . . . 847-260-0580
Healthy Food Brands LLC
Brooklyn, NY . . . 212-444-9909
Hershey Co.
Hershey, PA . . . 800-468-1714
Hyde & Hyde Inc
Corona, CA . . . 951-279-5239
Island Snacks
Buena Park, CA . . . 714-994-1228
Jelly Belly Candy Co.
Fairfield, CA . . . 800-522-3267
Joyva Corp
Brooklyn, NY . . . 718-497-0170
Kenny's Candy & Confections
Perham, MN
Kolatin Real Kosher Gelatin
Lakewood, NJ . . . 732-364-8700
Koppers Chocolate
Cranford, NJ . . . 800-325-0026
Leader Candies
Brooklyn, NY . . . 718-366-6900
Liberty Orchards Co Inc
Cashmere, WA . . . 800-231-3242
Little I
Blaine, WA . . . 360-332-3258
Mt Franklin Foods
El Paso, TX . . . 800-685-1475
New Century Snacks
City of Commerce, CA . . . 800-688-6887
Oak Leaf Confections
. . . 877-261-7887
Original Foods
Dunnville, ON . . . 888-440-8880
Palmer Candy Co
Sioux City, IA . . . 800-831-0828
Richardson Brands Co
Canajoharie, NY . . . 518-673-3553
Roseville Corporation
Mountain View, CA . . . 888-247-9338
Ruger LLC
Bethesda, MD . . . 301-675-2398
SmartSweets
Vancouver, BC
Snackerz
Commerce, CA . . . 888-576-2253
Sole Grano LLC
Fair Lawn, NJ . . . 201-797-7100
Sorbee Intl.
Philadelphia, PA . . . 800-654-3997
Standard Functional Foods Grp
Nashville, TN . . . 800-226-4340
Stevens Creative Enterprises, Inc.
New York, NY . . . 646-558-6336
Suity Confections Co
Miami, FL . . . 305-639-3300
Sweet Blessings
Malibu, CA . . . 310-317-1172
Sweet City Supply
Virginia Beach, VA . . . 888-793-3824
SWELL Philadelphia Chewing Gum Corporation
Havertown, PA . . . 610-449-1700
Taste of Nature Inc.
Santa Monica, CA . . . 310-396-4433

Tasty Brand Inc
Calabasas, CA....818-225-9000
The Pur Company
Toronto, ON....416-941-7557
Toe-Food Chocolates and Candy
Berkeley, CA....888-863-3663
Triple-C
Hamilton, ON....800-263-9105
Trophy Nut Co
Tipp City, OH....800-219-9004
Warner Candy
El Paso, TX....847-928-7200
Weaver Nut Co. Inc.
Ephrata, PA....800-473-2688
World Confections Inc
South Orange, NJ....718-768-8100

Hard

A La Carte
Chicago, IL....800-722-2370
Adams & Brooks Inc
Los Angeles, CA....213-749-3226
American Food Products Inc
Methuen, MA....978-682-1855
Anastasia Confections Inc
Orlando, FL....800-329-7100
Arcor USA
Coral Gables, FL....800-572-7267
Artek USA
Westlake Village, CA....866-278-3501
Baker Candy Company
Snohomish, WA....425-422-6331
Barcelona Nut Co
Baltimore, MD....800-296-6887
Bidwell Candies
Mattoon, IL....217-234-3858
Blanton's
Frankfort, KY....502-223-9874
Brother's Trading LLC
San Gabriel, CA....626-378-9323
Butterfields
Nashville, NC....800-945-5957
C Howard Co
Bellport, NY....631-286-7940
Cadbury Trebor Allan
Granby, QC....800-387-3267
Cambridge Brands Inc
Cambridge, MA....617-491-2500
Cap Candy
Napa, CA....707-251-9321
Claeys Candy Inc
South Bend, IN....574-287-1818
Cloud Nine
Claremont, CA....909-624-3147
Day Spring Enterprises
Cheektowaga, NY....800-879-7677
Doscher's Candies Co.
Cincinnati, OH....513-381-8656
Eda's Sugar Free
Philadelphia, PA....215-324-3412
El Brands
Ozark, AL....334-445-2828
Enstrom Candies, Inc.
Grand Junction, CO....800-367-8766
F B Washburn Candy Corp
Brockton, MA....508-588-0820
Fannie May Fine Chocolate
Oakdale, MN....800-999-3629
Fernando C Pujals & Bros
Guaynabo, PR....787-792-3080
Ferrara Candy Co Inc
Chicago, IL....800-323-1768
Foreign Candy Company
Hull, IA....800-831-8541
Frankford Candy & Chocolate Co
Philadelphia, PA....800-523-9090
Giambri's Quality Sweets Inc
Clementon, NJ....866-238-0169
Gimbals Fine Candies
S San Francisco, CA....800-344-6225
Grumpe's Specialties
Baird, TX....866-854-1106
Gurley's Foods
Willmar, MN....800-426-7845
Hawaii Candy Inc
Honolulu, HI....800-303-2507
Helms Candy Co., Inc
Bristol, VA....276-669-2533
Hillside Candy Co
Hillside, NJ....800-524-1304
Hyde & Hyde Inc
Corona, CA....951-279-5239
Ice Chips Candy
Olympia, WA....866-202-6623
Idaho Candy Co
Boise, ID....800-898-6986
Karma Candy
Hamilton, ON....905-527-6222
Kencraft, Inc.
Alpine, UT....800-377-4368
Kerr Brothers
Toronto, ON....416-252-7341
Leader Candies
Brooklyn, NY....718-366-6900
Lotte USA Inc
Battle Creek, MI....269-963-6664
Mitch Chocolate
Melville, NY....631-777-2400
Moore's Candies
Baltimore, MD....410-836-8840
Mt Franklin Foods
El Paso, TX....800-685-1475
Nassau Candy Distributors
Hicksville, NY....516-433-7100
New Century Snacks
City of Commerce, CA....800-688-6887
New Hope Natural Media
Boulder, CO....303-939-8440
Oak Leaf Confections
....877-261-7887
Old Dominion Peanut Corp
Norfolk, VA....800-368-6887
Olivier's Candies
Calgary, AB....403-266-6028
Original Foods
Dunnville, ON....888-440-8880
Palmer Candy Co
Sioux City, IA....800-831-0828
Perfetti Van Melle USA Inc
Erlanger, KY....859-283-1234
Pez Candy Inc
Orange, CT....203-795-0531
Piedmont Candy Co
Lexington, NC....336-248-2477
Plantation Candies
Telford, PA....888-678-6468
Primrose Candy Co
Chicago, IL....800-268-9522
Produits Alimentaire
St Lambert De Lauzon, QC....800-463-1787
Quigley Industries Inc
Farmington, MI....800-367-2441
Rainbow Pops
Cheektowaga, NY....800-879-7677
Richardson Brands Co
Canajoharie, NY....518-673-3553
Ricos Candy Snack & Bakery
Hialeah, FL....305-885-7392
Salem Old Fashioned Candies
Salem, MA....978-744-3242
Sconza Candy Co
Oakdale, CA....877-568-8137
Scripture Candy
Birmingham, AL....888-317-7333
Setton International Foods
Commack, NY....800-227-4397
Smarties
Union, NJ....800-631-7968
Snackerz
Commerce, CA....888-576-2253
SP Enterprises, Inc.
Las Vegas, NV....800-746-4774
Spangler Candy Co
Bryan, OH....888-636-4221
St. Jacobs Candy Co.
Waterloo, ON....519-884-3505
Sweenors Chocolates
Wakefield, RI....800-834-3123
Sweet Candy Company
Salt Lake City, UT....855-772-7720
Sweet City Supply
Virginia Beach, VA....888-793-3824
SWELL Philadelphia Chewing Gum Corporation
Havertown, PA....610-449-1700
Todd's
Vernon, CA....800-938-6337
Tootsie Roll Industries Inc.
Chicago, IL....866-972-6879
Torie & Howard LLC
New Milford, CT....860-799-7772
Trophy Nut Co
Tipp City, OH....800-219-9004
Turkey Hill Sugarbush
Waterloo, QC....450-539-4822
V L Foods
White Plains, NY....914-697-4851
Warner Candy
El Paso, TX....847-928-7200
Weaver Nut Co. Inc.
Ephrata, PA....800-473-2688
Webb's Candy
Davenport, FL....800-289-9322
Williams Candy Co
Chesapeake, VA....757-545-9311
Wrigley
Chicago, IL....312-794-6000

Jelly Beans

American Food Products Inc
Methuen, MA....978-682-1855
Arcor USA
Coral Gables, FL....800-572-7267
Cambridge Brands Inc
Cambridge, MA....617-491-2500
Cap Candy
Napa, CA....707-251-9321
El Brands
Ozark, AL....334-445-2828
Fannie May Fine Chocolate
Oakdale, MN....800-999-3629
Fernando C Pujals & Bros
Guaynabo, PR....787-792-3080
Ferrara Candy Co Inc
Chicago, IL....800-323-1768
Ganong Bros Ltd
St. Stephen, NB....888-270-8222
Gimbals Fine Candies
S San Francisco, CA....800-344-6225
GNS Foods
Arlington, TX....817-795-4671
Gurley's Foods
Willmar, MN....800-426-7845
Jelly Belly Candy Co.
Fairfield, CA....800-522-3267
Just Born Inc
Bethlehem, PA....800-445-5787
Leader Candies
Brooklyn, NY....718-366-6900
Mt Franklin Foods
El Paso, TX....800-685-1475
New Century Snacks
City of Commerce, CA....800-688-6887
Palmer Candy Co
Sioux City, IA....800-831-0828
Setton International Foods
Commack, NY....800-227-4397
Snackerz
Commerce, CA....888-576-2253
Stevens Creative Enterprises, Inc.
New York, NY....646-558-6336
Sweet Candy Company
Salt Lake City, UT....855-772-7720
Sweet City Supply
Virginia Beach, VA....888-793-3824
Todd's
Vernon, CA....800-938-6337
Triple-C
Hamilton, ON....800-263-9105
Warner Candy
El Paso, TX....847-928-7200
Weaver Nut Co. Inc.
Ephrata, PA....800-473-2688

Kisses

Cadbury Trebor Allan
Granby, QC....800-387-3267
Setton International Foods
Commack, NY....800-227-4397

Licorice

American Food Products Inc
Methuen, MA....978-682-1855
American Licorice
La Porte, IL....866-442-2783
Andros Foods North America
Mount Jackson, VA....844-426-3767
Buddy Squirrel LLC
St Francis, WI....800-972-2658
Cadbury Trebor Allan
Granby, QC....800-387-3267
Cambridge Brands Inc
Cambridge, MA....617-491-2500
Capco Enterprises
East Hanover, NJ....800-252-1011

El Brands
Ozark, AL 334-445-2828
Fannie May Fine Chocolate
Oakdale, MN 800-999-3629
Ferrara Candy Co Inc
Chicago, IL 800-323-1768
Fiesta Candy Company
Rochester, NH 800-285-9735
Foreign Candy Company
Hull, IA 800-831-8541
G Scaccianoce & Co
Bronx, NY 718-991-4462
Ganong Bros Ltd
St. Stephen, NB 888-270-8222
Gimbals Fine Candies
S San Francisco, CA 800-344-6225
Groovy Candies
Cleveland, OH 888-729-1960
Gurley's Foods
Willmar, MN 800-426-7845
Haribo of America
Baltimore, MD 847-260-0580
Jelly Belly Candy Co.
Fairfield, CA 800-522-3267
Kenny's Candy & Confections
Perham, MN
Kookaburra
Monroe, WA 360-805-6858
Morre-Tec Ind Inc
Union, NJ 908-686-0307
Morris National
Azusa, CA 626-385-2000
New Century Snacks
City of Commerce, CA 800-688-6887
Palmer Candy Co
Sioux City, IA 800-831-0828
Patsy's Candy
Colorado Springs, CO 866-372-8797
Sahagian & Associates
Oak Park, IL 800-327-9273
Snackerz
Commerce, CA 888-576-2253
Sorbee Intl.
Philadelphia, PA 800-654-3997
Sweet Candy Company
Salt Lake City, UT 855-772-7720
Sweet City Supply
Virginia Beach, VA 888-793-3824
The Lovely Candy Company LLC
Woodstock, IL 801-824-0624
Todd's
Vernon, CA 800-938-6337
Triple-C
Hamilton, ON 800-263-9105
Warner Candy
El Paso, TX 847-928-7200
Westbrae Natural Foods
Melville, NY 800-434-4246

Lollypops

Adams & Brooks Inc
Los Angeles, CA 213-749-3226
Amazing Candy Craft Company
Hollis, NY 800-429-9368
American Food Products Inc
Methuen, MA 978-682-1855
Andros Foods North America
Mount Jackson, VA 844-426-3767
Ann Hemyng Candy Inc
Trumbauersville, PA 800-779-7004
Arcor USA
Coral Gables, FL 800-572-7267
Artek USA
Westlake Village, CA 866-278-3501
Au'some Candies
Monmouth Junction, NJ 877-287-6649
Baraboo Candy Co LLC
Baraboo, WI 800-967-1690
Browniepops LLC
Leawood, KS 816-797-0715
Cadbury Trebor Allan
Granby, QC 800-387-3267
Cap Candy
Napa, CA 707-251-9321
Carrie's Chocolates
Edmonton, AB 877-778-2462
CTC Manufacturing
Calgary, AB 800-668-7677
Das Foods
Chicago, IL 312-224-8590
David Bradley Chocolatier
Windsor, NJ 877-289-7933
Day Spring Enterprises
Cheektowaga, NY 800-879-7677
El Brands
Ozark, AL 334-445-2828
Extreme Creations
El Dorado Hills, CA 916-941-0444
Fernando C Pujals & Bros
Guaynabo, PR 787-792-3080
Ferrara Candy Co Inc
Chicago, IL 800-323-1768
Foreign Candy Company
Hull, IA 800-831-8541
Frankford Candy & Chocolate Co
Philadelphia, PA 800-523-9090
Fun Factory
Milwaukee, WI 877-894-6767
Glennys
Brooklyn, NY 888-864-1243
Groovy Candies
Cleveland, OH 888-729-1960
Grumpe's Specialties
Baird, TX 866-854-1106
Gurley's Foods
Willmar, MN 800-426-7845
Hand Made Lollies
Maitland, FL 877-784-2724
Helms Candy Co., Inc
Bristol, VA 276-669-2533
Impact Confections
Janesville, WI 800-535-4401
James Candy Company
Atlantic City, NJ 800-441-1404
Jed's Maple Products
Derby, VT 802-766-2700
Kencraft, Inc.
Alpine, UT 800-377-4368
Kendon Candies Inc
San Jose, CA 800-332-2639
Kerr Brothers
Toronto, ON 416-252-7341
Laura Paige Candy Company
Newburgh, NY 845-566-4209
Leader Candies
Brooklyn, NY 718-366-6900
Light Vision Confections
Cincinnati, OH 513-351-9444
Linda's Lollies Company
Mahwan, NJ 800-347-1545
McIlhenny Company
Avery Island, LA 800-634-9599
McJak Candy Company LLC
Medina, OH 800-424-2942
Melville Candy Corp
Weymouth, MA 781-331-2005
Mitch Chocolate
Melville, NY 631-777-2400
Mom N' Pops Inc
New Windsor, NY 845-567-0640
Multiflex Company
Hawthorne, NJ 973-636-9700
New Century Snacks
City of Commerce, CA 800-688-6887
Original Foods
Dunnville, ON 888-440-8880
Original Gourmet Food Co
Salem, NH 603-894-1200
Parkside Candy Co
Buffalo, NY 716-833-7540
Perfetti Van Melle USA Inc
Erlanger, KY 859-283-1234
Plymouth Lollipop Company
Westford, MA 800-777-0115
Primrose Candy Co
Chicago, IL 800-268-9522
Produits Alimentaire
St Lambert De Lauzon, QC 800-463-1787
Rainbow Pops
Cheektowaga, NY 800-879-7677
Richardson Brands Co
Canajoharie, NY 518-673-3553
Riddles' Sweet Impressions
Edmonton, AB 780-465-8085
Roseville Corporation
Mountain View, CA 888-247-9338
Salem Old Fashioned Candies
Salem, MA 978-744-3242
Scripture Candy
Birmingham, AL 888-317-7333
Setton International Foods
Commack, NY 800-227-4397
Smarties
Union, NJ 800-631-7968
Sorbee Intl.
Philadelphia, PA 800-654-3997
SP Enterprises, Inc.
Las Vegas, NV 800-746-4774
Spangler Candy Co
Bryan, OH 888-636-4221
Strawberry Hill Grand Delights
Everett, MA 617-319-3557
Suity Confections Co
Miami, FL 305-639-3300
Tom & Sally's Handmade Chocolates
Brattleboro, VT 800-827-0800
Tootsie Roll Industries Inc.
Chicago, IL 866-972-6879
Triple-C
Hamilton, ON 800-263-9105
Turkey Hill Sugarbush
Waterloo, QC 450-539-4822
Williamsburg Chocolatier
Williamsburg, VA 757-253-1474
World Confections Inc
South Orange, NJ 718-768-8100
Wrigley
Chicago, IL 312-794-6000
Yost Candy Co Inc
Dalton, OH 800-750-1976

Gourmet Flavored

Das Foods
Chicago, IL 312-224-8590
Hand Made Lollies
Maitland, FL 877-784-2724
Kendon Candies Inc
San Jose, CA 800-332-2639

Lozenges

Adams USA Inc.
Cookeville, TN 800-251-6857
Bestco Inc
Mooresville, NC 704-664-4300
Cadbury Trebor Allan
Granby, QC 800-387-3267
Ganong Bros Ltd
St. Stephen, NB 888-270-8222
Holistic Products Corporation
Englewood, NJ 800-221-0308
Kerr Brothers
Toronto, ON 416-252-7341
MYNTZ!
Kent, WA 800-800-9490
Rito Mints
Trois Rivieres, QC 819-379-1449
Snackerz
Commerce, CA 888-576-2253
Sorbee Intl.
Philadelphia, PA 800-654-3997

Maple

Butternut Mountain Farm
Morrisville, VT 800-828-2376
D & D Sugarwoods Farm
Glover, VT 800-245-3718
Finding Home Farms
Middletown, NY 845-355-4335
Jed's Maple Products
Derby, VT 802-766-2700
Key III Candies
Fort Wayne, IN 800-752-2382
Maple Grove Farms Of Vermont
St Johnsbury, VT 802-748-5141
Maple Valley Cooperative
Cashton, WI 608-654-7319
Nature's Candy
Fredericksburg, TX 800-729-0085
Richards Maple Products
Chardon, OH 800-352-4052
Swisser Sweet Maple
Castorland, NY 315-346-1034

Marshmallow

Charlotte's Confections
Millbrae, CA 800-798-2427
Clown Global Brands
Northbrook, IL 800-323-5778
Doumak Inc
Elk Grove Village, IL 800-323-0318
Durkee-Mower
Lynn, MA 781-593-8007
EIWA America Inc.
Torrance, CA 310-327-7222

Gimbals Fine Candies
S San Francisco, CA 800-344-6225
Glatech Productions LLC
Lakewood, NJ 732-364-8700
Golden Fluff Popcorn Co
Lakewood, NJ 732-367-5448
Kolatin Real Kosher Gelatin
Lakewood, NJ 732-364-8700
Madyson's Marshmallows
Heber City, UT 435-315-0045
Philadelphia Candies Inc
Hermitage, PA 724-981-6341
Plush Puffs Marshmallows
Burbank, CA 818-784-2931
S Zitner Co
Philadelphia, PA 215-229-9828
Solo Foods
Countryside, IL 800-328-7656
The Crispery
Portsmouth, VA 501-224-8947
White-Stokes Company
Chicago, IL 800-978-6537

Marshmallow Creme

Solo Foods
Countryside, IL 800-328-7656

Marshmallows

Annabelle Candy Co Inc
Hayward, CA 510-783-2900
Charlotte's Confections
Millbrae, CA 800-798-2427
Chicago Vegan Foods
Lombard, IL 630-629-9667
David Bradley Chocolatier
Windsor, NJ 877-289-7933
Doumak Inc
Elk Grove Village, IL 800-323-0318
Ferrara Candy Co Inc
Chicago, IL 800-323-1768
Frankford Candy & Chocolate Co
Philadelphia, PA 800-523-9090
Ganong Bros Ltd
St. Stephen, NB 888-270-8222
Golden Fluff Popcorn Co
Lakewood, NJ 732-367-5448
Joyva Corp
Brooklyn, NY 718-497-0170
Just Born Inc
Bethlehem, PA 800-445-5787
Michele's Chocolate Truffles
Clackamas, OR 800-656-7112
Papas Chris A & Son Co
Covington, KY 859-431-0499
Patsy's Candy
Colorado Springs, CO 866-372-8797
Richardson Brands Co
Canajoharie, NY 518-673-3553
Roseville Corporation
Mountain View, CA 888-247-9338
S Zitner Co
Philadelphia, PA 215-229-9828
Smashmallow
Sonoma, CA 707-512-0605
Spangler Candy Co
Bryan, OH 888-636-4221
Strawberry Hill Grand Delights
Everett, MA 617-319-3557
Sucre
New Orleans, LA 504-708-4366
Suity Confections Co
Miami, FL 305-639-3300
Sweet City Supply
Virginia Beach, VA 888-793-3824
Warrell Corp
Camp Hill, PA 800-233-7082

Marzipan

American Almond Products Co
Brooklyn, NY 800-825-6663
Amoretti
Oxnard, CA 800-266-7388
B. Nutty
Oakland, CA 510-374-4658
Snackerz
Commerce, CA 888-576-2253
Sweet Swiss Confections Inc
Spokane, WA 509-838-1334

Miniatures

Foreign Candy Company
Hull, IA 800-831-8541
Hershey Co.
Hershey, PA 800-468-1714

Mints

Adams USA Inc.
Cookeville, TN 800-251-6857
Ameri Candy
Louisville, KY 502-583-1776
American Mint
New York, NY 800-401-6468
Art CoCo Chocolate Company
Geneva, IL 877-232-9901
Big Sky Brands
Mississauga, ON 416-599-5415
Boston America Corporation
Woburn, MA 781-933-3535
Brown & Haley
Fife, WA 800-426-8400
Cadbury Trebor Allan
Granby, QC 800-387-3267
Chocolati Handmade Chocolates
Seattle, WA 206-784-5212
Cloud Nine
Claremont, CA 909-624-3147
Cracked Candy LLC
Brooklyn, NY 646-543-1405
Ferrara Candy Co Inc
Chicago, IL 800-323-1768
Foley's Chocolates & Candies
Richmond, BC 888-236-5397
Ford Gum & Mach Co Inc
Akron, NY 716-542-4561
Fun Factory
Milwaukee, WI 877-894-6767
G Scaccianoce & Co
Bronx, NY 718-991-4462
Helms Candy Co., Inc
Bristol, VA 276-669-2533
Hillside Candy Co
Hillside, NJ 800-524-1304
Hint Mint
Los Angeles, CA 800-991-6468
Hospitality Mints LLC
Boone, NC 800-334-5181
IFive Brands
Seattle, WA 800-882-5615
Joe Clark Fund Raising Candies
Tarentum, PA 888-459-9520
Kerr Brothers
Toronto, ON 416-252-7341
Koppers Chocolate
Cranford, NJ 800-325-0026
Landies Candies Co
Buffalo, NY 800-955-2634
Little I
Blaine, WA 360-332-3258
Marich Confectionery
Hollister, CA 800-624-7055
Matangos Candies
Harrisburg, PA 717-234-0882
Maxfield Candy
Salt Lake City, UT 800-288-8002
MYNTZ!
Kent, WA 800-800-9490
Naylor Candies Inc
Mt Wolf, PA 717-266-2706
New Century Snacks
City of Commerce, CA 800-688-6887
Palmer Candy Co
Sioux City, IA 800-831-0828
Perfetti Van Melle USA Inc
Erlanger, KY 859-283-1234
Pfizer
New York, NY 800-879-3477
Piedmont Candy Co
Lexington, NC 336-248-2477
Plantation Candies
Telford, PA 888-678-6468
Rebecca-Ruth Candy Factory
Frankfort, KY 800-444-3866
Reutter Candy & Chocolates
Baltimore, MD 800-392-0870
Rito Mints
Trois Rivieres, QC 819-379-1449
Salem Old Fashioned Candies
Salem, MA 978-744-3242
Schuster Marketing Corporation
Milwaukee, WI 888-254-8948
Scripture Candy
Birmingham, AL 888-317-7333
Sencha Naturals
Los Angeles, CA 888-473-6242
Setton International Foods
Commack, NY 800-227-4397
Sherbrooke OEM Ltd
Sherbrooke, QC 866-851-2579
SP Enterprises, Inc.
Las Vegas, NV 800-746-4774
Sweenors Chocolates
Wakefield, RI 800-834-3123
Sweet Breath
New York, NY 877-673-9777
Todd's
Vernon, CA 800-938-6337
Tootsie Roll Industries Inc.
Chicago, IL 866-972-6879
Unica
Glen Ellyn, IL 630-790-8107
VerMints Inc.
Braintree, VT 800-367-4442
VitaThinQ Inc.
Davie, FL
Weaver Nut Co. Inc.
Ephrata, PA 800-473-2688
Webb's Candy
Davenport, FL 800-289-9322
Wrench Mints
Chicago, IL 312-496-3690
Wrigley
Chicago, IL 312-794-6000

Mousse

Abel & Schafer Inc
Ronkonkoma, NY 800-443-1260
Alati-Caserta Desserts
Montr,al, QC 877-377-5680
Alexian Pâtés
Neptune, NJ 800-927-9473
Blommer Chocolate Co
Chicago, IL 800-621-1606
Century Blends LLC
Hunt Valley, MD 410-771-6606
Desserts by David Glass
South Windsor, CT 860-462-7520
Granowska's
Toronto, ON 416-533-7755
HFI Foods
Redmond, WA 425-883-1320
Hormel Foods Corp.
Austin, MN 507-437-5611
Jon Donaire Desserts
Santa Fe Springs, CA 877-366-2473
Love Quiches Desserts
Freeport, NY 516-623-8800
Paris Pastry
Van Nuys, CA 805-487-2227
Tova Industries LLC
Louisville, KY 888-532-8682
World Of Chantilly
Brooklyn, NY 718-859-1110

Nougats

Asti Holdings Ltd
New Westminster, BC 604-523-6866
Ferrara Bakery & Cafe
New York, NY 212-226-6150
Ferrara Candy Co Inc
Chicago, IL 800-323-1768
Joe Clark Fund Raising Candies
Tarentum, PA 888-459-9520
Lukas Confections
York, PA 717-843-0921
Webb's Candy
Davenport, FL 800-289-9322
White-Stokes Company
Chicago, IL 800-978-6537

Novelties

Ann Hemyng Candy Inc
Trumbauersville, PA 800-779-7004
Carrie's Chocolates
Edmonton, AB 877-778-2462
Chocolate Street of Hartville
Hartville, OH 888-853-5904
Chocolates by Mark
Houston, TX 832-736-2626
Chris Candies Inc
Pittsburgh, PA 412-322-9400

David Bradley Chocolatier
Windsor, NJ 877-289-7933
Doscher's Candies Co.
Cincinnati, OH 513-381-8656
Ferrara Bakery & Cafe
New York, NY 212-226-6150
Gourmet du Village
Morin-Heights, QC 800-668-2314
Hershey Co.
Hershey, PA 800-468-1714
Laura Paige Candy Company
Newburgh, NY 845-566-4209
Leader Candies
Brooklyn, NY 718-366-6900
Long Grove Confectionary
Buffalo Grove, IL 800-373-3102
Maxfield Candy
Salt Lake City, UT 800-288-8002
Merb's Candies
St Louis, MO 314-832-7117
Merlin Candies
Harahan, LA 800-899-1549
Niagara Chocolates
Buffalo, NY 877-261-7887
Papas Chris A & Son Co
Covington, KY 859-431-0499
Sherbrooke OEM Ltd
Sherbrooke, QC 866-851-2579
Stichler Products Inc
Reading, PA 610-921-0211
Weaver Nut Co. Inc.
Ephrata, PA 800-473-2688
World Confections Inc
South Orange, NJ 718-768-8100
Yost Candy Co Inc
Dalton, OH 800-750-1976
Zachary Confections Inc
Frankfort, IN 800-445-4222

Peanut Brittle

B & B Pecan Processors
Turkey, NC 866-328-7322
Maxwell's Gourmet Food
Raleigh, NC 800-952-6887
Moore's Candies
Baltimore, MD 410-836-8840
Muth's Candy Store
Louisville, KY 502-582-2639
Sally Lane's Candy Farm
Paris, TN 731-642-5801
Virginia Diner Inc
Wakefield, VA 888-823-4637

Popcorn Specialties

Cloud Nine
Claremont, CA 909-624-3147
Eda's Sugar Free
Philadelphia, PA 215-324-3412
Faroh Candies
Middleburg Heights, OH 440-888-9866
Fun City Popcorn
Las Vegas, NV 800-423-1710
GKI Foods
Brighton, MI 248-486-0055
Golden Kernel Pecan Co
Cameron, SC 803-823-2311
Humphrey Co
Cleveland, OH 800-486-3739
Kenny's Candy & Confections
Perham, MN
Koeze Company
Grand Rapids, MI 800-555-9688
Midwest Nut Co
Minneapolis, MN 800-328-5502
Olympia Candies
Strongsville, OH 800-574-7747
Pop Art Snacks
Salt Lake City, UT 801-983-7470
Popcorn Connection
North Hollywood, CA 800-852-2676
Poppers Supply Company
Allentown, PA 800-457-9810
Popsalot
Beverly Hills, CA 213-761-0156
Rygmyr Foods
South Saint Paul, MN 800-545-3903
Vande Walle's Candies Inc
Appleton, WI 800-738-1020
Weaver Popcorn Co Inc
Van Buren, IN

Rock

Salem Old Fashioned Candies
Salem, MA 978-744-3242
Setton International Foods
Commack, NY 800-227-4397

Taffy

Adams & Brooks Inc
Los Angeles, CA 213-749-3226
Alaska Jacks
Anchorage, AK 888-660-2257
Anastasia Confections Inc
Orlando, FL 800-329-7100
Annabelle Candy Co Inc
Hayward, CA 510-783-2900
Bidwell Candies
Mattoon, IL 217-234-3858
Cadbury Trebor Allan
Granby, QC 800-387-3267
Charlotte's Confections
Millbrae, CA 800-798-2427
Downeast Candies
Boothbay Harbor, ME 207-633-5178
El Brands
Ozark, AL 334-445-2828
Ferrara Candy Co Inc
Chicago, IL 800-323-1768
Forbes Candies
Virginia Beach, VA 800-626-5898
Foreign Candy Company
Hull, IA 800-831-8541
Gurley's Foods
Willmar, MN 800-426-7845
Haven's Candies
Westbrook, ME 800-639-6309
Humphrey Co
Cleveland, OH 800-486-3739
James Candy Company
Atlantic City, NJ 800-441-1404
Jelly Belly Candy Co.
Fairfield, CA 800-522-3267
Kencraft, Inc.
Alpine, UT 800-377-4368
Lammes Candies
Austin, TX 800-252-1885
Layman Distributing
Salem, VA 800-237-1319
Lowery's Home Made Candies
Muncie, IN 800-541-3340
Lukas Confections
York, PA 717-843-0921
Maxfield Candy
Salt Lake City, UT 800-288-8002
Merb's Candies
St Louis, MO 314-832-7117
New Century Snacks
City of Commerce, CA 800-688-6887
Original Foods
Dunnville, ON 888-440-8880
Patsy's Candy
Colorado Springs, CO 866-372-8797
Phillip's Candy House
Dorchester, MA 617-282-2090
Primrose Candy Co
Chicago, IL 800-268-9522
Queen Bee Gardens
Lovell, WY 800-225-7553
Sahagian & Associates
Oak Park, IL 800-327-9273
Salem Old Fashioned Candies
Salem, MA 978-744-3242
Salty Road
Brooklyn, NY 929-250-2615
Seattle Gourmet Foods
Tukwila, WA 800-800-9490
Setton International Foods
Commack, NY 800-227-4397
Snackerz
Commerce, CA 888-576-2253
Squirrel Brand Company
McKinney, TX 800-624-8242
St. Jacobs Candy Co.
Waterloo, ON 519-884-3505
Sweet Candy Company
Salt Lake City, UT 855-772-7720
Sweet City Supply
Virginia Beach, VA 888-793-3824
Taffy Town Inc
Salt Lake City, UT 800-765-4770
Todd's
Vernon, CA 800-938-6337

Warrell Corp
Camp Hill, PA 800-233-7082
Webb's Candy
Davenport, FL 800-289-9322

Toffee

Blissfully Better
Chester, NJ
Bt. McElrath Chocolatier
Minneapolis, MN 612-331-8800
Cadbury Trebor Allan
Granby, QC 800-387-3267
Cary's of Oregon
Grants Pass, OR 888-822-9300
Chocolate Signatures LP
Toronto, ON 416-234-8528
Columbine Confections LLC
Windsor, CO 970-377-2293
Confectionately Yours LTD
Buffalo Grove, IL 800-875-6978
Creative Cotton
Northbrook, IL 847-291-4128
Double Premium Confections
McLean, VA 202-495-1884
Elegant Edibles
Houston, TX 800-227-3226
Enstrom Candies, Inc.
Grand Junction, CO 800-367-8766
Fancy's Candy's
Rougemont, NC 888-403-2629
Ferncreek Confections LLC
Fort Collins, CO 970-377-2293
Ferrara Candy Co Inc
Chicago, IL 800-323-1768
Georgia Nut Co
Skokie, IL 877-674-2993
Kohler Original Recipe Chocolates
Kohler, WI 920-208-4930
Landies Candies Co
Buffalo, NY 800-955-2634
Laurie & Sons
New York, NY 212-866-6600
Leader Candies
Brooklyn, NY 718-366-6900
Lukas Confections
York, PA 717-843-0921
Madrona Specialty Foods LLC
Seattle, WA 425-656-2997
Manhattan Food Brands, LLC
Metuchen, NJ 732-906-2168
Marich Confectionery
Hollister, CA 800-624-7055
Maries Candies
West Liberty, OH 866-465-5781
Moonstruck Chocolate Co
Portland, OR 800-557-6666
Northern Flair Foods
Mound, MN 888-530-4453
Nunes Farms Marketing
Gustine, CA 209-862-3033
Old Dominion Peanut Corp
Norfolk, VA 800-368-6887
Pecan Deluxe Candy Co
Dallas, TX 800-733-3589
Perfetti Van Melle USA Inc
Erlanger, KY 859-283-1234
Poco Dolce
San Francisco, CA 415-255-1443
Praim Co
Salem, MA 800-970-9646
Quigley Industries Inc
Farmington, MI 800-367-2441
Sticky Toffee Pudding Company
Austin, TX 512-472-0039
Sweet Shop USA
Mt Pleasant, TX 888-957-9338
Tall Grass Toffee Co
Lenexa, KS 877-344-0442
Texas Toffee
Odessa, TX 800-599-2133
Toffee Boutique
Rancho Cordova, CA 916-638-8462
Toffee Co
Houston, TX 713-688-5531
Vande Walle's Candies Inc
Appleton, WI 800-738-1020
Weaver Nut Co. Inc.
Ephrata, PA 800-473-2688
Webb's Candy
Davenport, FL 800-289-9322

Truffles

Anette's Chocolate & Ice Cream
Napa, CA....707-252-4228
Birnn Chocolates of Vermont
South Burlington, VT....800-338-3141
Boca Bons East
Greenacres, FL....800-314-2835
Bodega Chocolates
Fountain Valley, CA....888-326-3342
Bt. McElrath Chocolatier
Minneapolis, MN....612-331-8800
Candy Basket Inc
Portland, OR....800-864-1924
Chocoholics Divine Desserts
Linden, CA....800-760-2462
Chocolate Signatures LP
Toronto, ON....416-234-8528
Chocolati Handmade Chocolates
Seattle, WA....206-784-5212
De Fluri's Fine Chocolate
Martinsburg, WV....304-264-3698
Double Premium Confections
McLean, VA....202-495-1884
Fine & Raw Chocolate
Brooklyn, NY....718-366-3633
G Debbas Chocolatier
Fresno, CA....559-294-2071
GKI Foods
Brighton, MI....248-486-0055
J Morgan's Confections
Ogden, UT....801-399-3007
Just Truffles
St Paul, MN....877-977-9177
Kohler Original Recipe Chocolates
Kohler, WI....920-208-4930
Moonstruck Chocolate Co
Portland, OR....800-557-6666
Moore's Candies
Baltimore, MD....410-836-8840
Morris National
Azusa, CA....626-385-2000
No Whey Foods
Lakewood, NJ....732-806-5218
Noble Chocolates NV
Veurne,
Poco Dolce
San Francisco, CA....415-255-1443
Praim Co
Salem, MA....800-970-9646
Premium Chocolatiers LLC
Lakewood, NJ....732-806-5218
Sabatino Truffles USA
West Haven, CT....888-444-9971
Sugar & Plumm
New York, NY....212-787-8778
Sweet Designs Chocolatier Inc
Lakewood, OH....216-226-4888
Sweet Shop USA
Mt Pleasant, TX....888-957-9338
Tea Room
San Leandro, CA....510-567-8868
Two Friends Chocolates
Boxborough, MA....978-264-1949
Veritas Chocolatier
Glenview, IL....800-555-8331
Vosges Haut-Chocolat
Chicago, IL....888-301-9866

Candy Coatings

Caramel

Abdallah Candies & Gifts
Burnsville, MN....952-890-0859
Calico Cottage
Amityville, NY....800-645-5345
Sapore della Vita
Sarasota, FL....941-914-4256
Sweet Shop USA
Mt Pleasant, TX....888-957-9338
The Ardent Homesteader
Arden, NY

Carob

Clasen Quality Chocolate
Madison, WI....877-459-4500

Chocolate

Anette's Chocolate & Ice Cream
Napa, CA....707-252-4228
Blommer Chocolate Co
Chicago, IL....800-621-1606
Clasen Quality Chocolate
Madison, WI....877-459-4500
Laurie & Sons
New York, NY....212-866-6600
Madyson's Marshmallows
Heber City, UT....435-315-0045
Michael Mootz Candies
Hanover Twp, PA....570-823-8272
Pacific Gold Marketing
Arlington, TX....817-795-4671
Sole Grano LLC
Fair Lawn, NJ....201-797-7100
Sucesores de Pedro Cortes
Hato Rey, PR....787-754-7040
Sweet Pillar
Newport Beach, CA....310-913-7261
US Chocolate Corp
Brooklyn, NY....718-788-8555
Williams & Bennett
Orlando, FL....561-276-9007

Confectionery

Cache Creek Foods LLC
Woodland, CA....530-662-1764
Paulsen Foods
Atlanta, GA....404-873-1804

Chocolate Products

A La Carte
Chicago, IL....800-722-2370
Abdallah Candies & Gifts
Burnsville, MN....952-890-0859
Adams & Brooks Inc
Los Angeles, CA....213-749-3226
Aglamesis Bros Ice Cream
Cincinnati, OH....513-531-5196
Al Richard's Chocolates
Bayonne, NJ....888-777-6964
Al-Rite Fruits & Syrups Co
Miami, FL....305-652-2540
Alaska Jacks
Anchorage, AK....888-660-2257
Alati-Caserta Desserts
Montr,al, QC....877-377-5680
Albanese Confectionery Group
Merrillville, IN....800-536-0581
Alcove Chocolate
Los Angeles, CA....323-284-2229
Ameri Candy
Louisville, KY....502-583-1776
American Nut & Chocolate Co
Boston, MA....800-797-6887
Ames International Inc
Fife, WA....888-469-2637
Andre-Boudin Bakeries
San Francisco, CA....415-882-1849
Baker Candy Company
Snohomish, WA....425-422-6331
Barkeater Chocolates
North Creek, NY....518-251-4438
Barkthins Snacking Chocolate
Congers, NY....845-770-5802
Barry Callebaut USA
Chicago, IL....866-443-0460
Betty Lou's
McMinnville, OR....800-242-5205
Big Island Candies Inc
Hilo, HI....800-935-5510
Bissinger's Handcrafted Chocolatier
St. Louis, MO....314-615-2400
Bixby & Co., LLC
Rockland, ME....207-691-1778
Blackberry Patch
Thomasville, GA....800-853-5598
Blanton's
Frankfort, KY....502-223-9874
Blommer Chocolate Co
Chicago, IL....800-621-1606
Blommer Chocolate Co
East Greenville, PA....800-825-8181
Bloomsberry LLC
Salem, MA....800-745-5154
Bridge Brands Chocolate
San Francisco, CA....888-732-4626
Brighams
Arlington, MA....800-242-2423
Brix Chocolates
Youngstown, OH....866-613-2749
Cacao Prieto
Brooklyn, NY....347-225-0130
Cachafaz US
Miami, FL....305-779-6340
Calico Cottage
Amityville, NY....800-645-5345
Campbell Soup Co.
Camden, NJ....800-257-8443
Candy Cottage Company
Huntingdon Valley, PA....215-953-8288
Canelake's Candy
Virginia, MN....888-928-8889
Cape Cod Provisions
Pocasset, MA....508-564-5840
Charles Chocolates
San Francisco, CA
Chase & Poe Candy Co
St Joseph, MO....800-786-1625
Chelsea Milling Co.
Chelsea, MI....800-727-2460
Cherry Moon Farms
San Diego, CA....800-580-2913
Chic Naturals
Lahaina, HI....808-463-7878
Chip'n Dipped Cookie Co
Huntington, NY....631-470-2579
Choclatique
Los Angeles, CA....310-479-3849
Chocolat Michel Cluizel
New York, NY....646-415-9126
Chocolat Moderne, LLC.
New York, NY....212-229-4797
Chocolate Chocolate Chocolate
St Louis, MO....314-338-3501
Chocolate Fantasies
Burr Ridge, IL....630-572-0045
Chocolate Works
Freeport, NY
ChocoME US LLC
Laguna Hills, CA....949-500-8837
Chocomize
Long Island City, NY....800-621-3294
Chocopologie By Knipschildt
Norwalk, CT....203-854-4754
Chris Candies Inc
Pittsburgh, PA....412-322-9400
Chuao Chocolatier
Carlsbad, CA....888-635-1444
Chukar Cherries
Prosser, WA....800-624-9544
Claeys Candy Inc
South Bend, IN....574-287-1818
Clasen Quality Chocolate
Madison, WI....877-459-4500
Clear Mountain Coffee Company
Silver Spring, MD....301-587-2233
Coca-Cola Beverages Northeast
Bedford, NH....844-619-3388
Cocomira Confections
Toronto, ON....866-413-9049
Colorado Nut Co
Denver, CO....800-876-1625
Columbine Confections LLC
Windsor, CO....970-377-2293
Confection Art Inc
Portland, OR....503-505-0481
Crown Candy Corp
Macon, GA....800-241-3529
Cummings Studio Chocolates
Salt Lake City, UT....800-537-3957
Dandelion Chocolate
San Francisco, CA....800-785-2301
Davinci Gourmet LTD
Seattle, WA....800-640-6779
Daymar Select Fine Coffees
El Cajon, CA....800-466-7590
Dessert Innovations Inc
Atlanta, GA....800-359-7351
Desserts by David Glass
South Windsor, CT....860-462-7520
Dipasa USA Inc
Brownsville, TX....956-831-4072
Donaldson's Finer Chocolates
Lebanon, IN....800-975-7236
Droga Chocolates
Fort Lauderdale, FL....800-213-0754
East Shore Specialty Foods
Hartland, WI....800-236-1069
Eda's Sugar Free
Philadelphia, PA....215-324-3412
Edward Marc Brands
Pittsburgh, PA....877-488-1808

Elmer Chocolate®
Ponchatoula, LA 800-843-9537
Enstrom Candies, Inc.
Grand Junction, CO 800-367-8766
Euro Chocolate Fountain
San Diego, CA 800-423-9303
Fabio Imports
Oceanside, CA 760-726-7040
Faroh Candies
Middleburg Heights, OH 440-888-9866
Figamajigs
San Mateo, CA 650-227-3830
Fitzkee's Candies Inc
York, PA 717-741-1031
Fran's Chocolates
Seattle, WA 800-422-3726
Free2b Foods
Boulder, CO
Gardners Candies Inc
Tyrone, PA 800-242-2639
GEM Berry Products
Orofino, ID 888-231-1699
Gene & Boots Candies Inc
Perryopolis, PA 800-864-4222
Gertrude Hawk Chocolates
Dunmore, PA 800-822-2032
GH Bent Company
Milton, MA 617-322-9287
Ghirardelli Chocolate Co
San Leandro, CA 800-877-9338
Gloria Jean's Gourmet Coffees
Irvine, CA 877-320-5282
Golden Moon Tea
Bristow, VA 877-327-5473
Gorant Chocolatier
Youngstown, OH 330-726-8821
Gourmedas Inc
Quebec, QC 418-210-3703
Gourmet Nut
Brooklyn, NY 347-413-5180
Govadinas Fitness Foods
San Diego, CA 800-900-0108
Gray & Company
Hart, MI 800-551-6009
Green & Black's Organic Chocolate
Plano, TX 877-299-1254
Green Mountain Chocolate Inc
Franklin, MA 508-520-7160
H B Taylor Co
Chicago, IL 773-254-4805
H Fox & Co Inc
Brooklyn, NY 718-385-4600
Haven's Candies
Westbrook, ME 800-639-6309
Hershey Co.
Hershey, PA 800-468-1714
Hialeah Products Co
Hollywood, FL 800-923-3379
Hickory Farms
Maumee, OH 800-753-8558
Hnina Gourmet
Los Angeles, CA 323-876-2609
Home Bakery
Rochester, MI 248-651-4830
Hope Foods
Boulder, CO 303-248-7019
Humboldt Chocolate
Eureka, CA 707-630-5355
Hunt Country Foods Inc
Marshall, VA 540-364-2622
Imani Chimani Chocolate
Brooklyn, NY 718-484-1011
Island Princess
Honolulu, HI 866-872-8601
Jason & Son Specialty Foods
Rancho Cordova, CA 800-810-9093
Jer's Chocolates
Solana Beach, CA 800-540-7265
Joe Clark Fund Raising Candies
Tarentum, PA 888-459-9520
John Kelly Chocolates
Los Angeles, CA 800-609-4243
Jomart Chocolates
Brooklyn, NY 718-375-1277
Justin's Nut Butter
Boulder, CO 844-448-0302
Kamish Food Products
Chicago, IL 773-725-6959
Karma Candy
Hamilton, ON 905-527-6222
Kemach Food Products
Brooklyn, NY 718-272-5655

Key III Candies
Fort Wayne, IN 800-752-2382
Knudsen Candy
Hayward, CA 800-736-6887
Koeze Company
Grand Rapids, MI 800-555-9688
Kohler Original Recipe Chocolates
Kohler, WI 920-208-4930
Koppers Chocolate
Cranford, NJ 800-325-0026
KOZY Shack Enterprises Inc
St Paul, MN 855-716-1555
La Cure Gourmande USA
New York, NY 646-935-9329
Landies Candies Co
Buffalo, NY 800-955-2634
Layman Distributing
Salem, VA 800-237-1319
Lerro Candy Company
Darby, PA 610-461-8886
Lily's Sweets
Boulder, CO 877-587-0557
Loghouse Foods
Minneapolis, MN 763-546-8395
Long Grove Confectionary
Buffalo Grove, IL 800-373-3102
Lou-Retta's Custom Chocolates
Buffalo, NY 716-833-7111
Louis J Rheb Candy Co
Baltimore, MD 800-514-8293
Lowery's Home Made Candies
Muncie, IN 800-541-3340
Lukas Confections
York, PA 717-843-0921
Lynch Foods
North York, ON 416-449-5464
Lyons Magnus
Fresno, CA 800-344-7130
Maple Leaf Cheesemakers
New Glarus, WI 888-624-1234
MarySue.com
Baltimore, MD 800-662-2639
Matangos Candies
Harrisburg, PA 717-234-0882
Maxfield Candy
Salt Lake City, UT 800-288-8002
Merb's Candies
St Louis, MO 314-832-7117
Mont Blanc Gourmet
Denver, CO 800-877-3811
Morse's Sauerkraut
Waldoboro, ME 866-832-5569
Munson's Chocolates
Bolton, CT 888-686-7667
My Sweet
Brooklyn, NY 347-689-4402
NibMor
Kennebunk, ME 207-502-7541
No Whey Foods
Lakewood, NJ 732-806-5218
Noble Chocolates NV
Veurne,
Northwest Chocolate Factory
Salem, OR 503-362-1340
Northwestern Foods
Arden Hills, MN 800-236-4937
Oak Leaf Confections
.... 877-261-7887
Old Time Candy Co
Lagrange, OH 440-355-4345
Olde Tyme Mercantile
Arroyo Grande, CA 805-489-7991
Organic Nectars LLC
Malden On Hudson, NY 845-246-0506
Pacari Organic Chocolate
Boca Raton, FL
Parkside Candy Co
Buffalo, NY 716-833-7540
Pascha Chocolate
Toronto, Ontario, ... 855-472-7242
Paulaur Corp
Cranbury, NJ 609-395-8844
Pecan Deluxe Candy Co
Dallas, TX 800-733-3589
Pez Candy Inc
Orange, CT 203-795-0531
Philadelphia Candies Inc
Hermitage, PA 724-981-6341
Phillip's Candy House
Dorchester, MA 617-282-2090
Phillips Syrup Corp
Cleveland, OH 800-350-8443

Pied-Mont/Dora
Anne Des Plaines, QC 800-363-8003
Plantation Candies
Telford, PA 888-678-6468
Praim Co
Salem, MA 800-970-9646
Premium Chocolatiers LLC
Lakewood, NJ 732-806-5218
Pretzel Perfection
Vancouver, WA 360-635-3886
Priester's Pecans
Fort Deposit, AL 866-477-4736
Prince of Peace
Hayward, CA 800-732-2328
Pulakos 926 Chocolate
Erie, PA 814-452-4026
Puratos Canada
Mississauga, ON 905-362-3668
Q Bell Foods
Nyack, NY 845-358-1475
Rapunzel Pure Organics
Bloomfield, NJ 800-225-1449
Ravico USA
Riderwood, MD 443-921-8025
Raw Rev
Hawthorne, NY 914-326-4095
Rawmantic Chocolate
New York, NY 212-247-2229
Rich's Ice Cream Co Inc
West Palm Beach, FL 561-833-7585
Ripple Brand Collective
Congers, NY 845-353-1251
Rocky Mountain Chocolate Factory
Durango, CO 888-525-2462
Roland Machinery
Springfield, IL 800-325-1183
Rosalind Candy Castle Inc
New Brighton, PA 724-843-1144
S Zitner Co
Philadelphia, PA 215-229-9828
SAPNA Foods
Atlanta, GA 404-589-0977
Sapore della Vita
Sarasota, FL 941-914-4256
Saxon Chocolates
Toronto, ON 416-675-6363
Scharffen Berger Chocolate Maker
San Francisco, CA 866-608-6944
Scott's Candy
Glennville, GA 800-356-2100
Sea Breeze Fruit Flavors
Towaco, NJ 800-732-2733
See's Candies
Carson, CA 800-347-7337
Seth Ellis Chocolatier
Boulder, CO 720-565-2462
Shakespeare's
Davenport, IA 800-664-4114
Shane Candy Co
Philadelphia, PA 215-922-1048
Sherwood Brands
New Brunswick, NJ 973-249-8200
Shoreline Chocolates
Alburg, VT 800-310-3730
Sibu Sura Chocolates, LLC
Myersville, MD 877-642-7872
Sjaak's Organic Chocolates
Petaluma, CA 707-775-2434
Snack Works/Metrovox Snacks
Orange, CA 800-783-9870
Sole Grano LLC
Fair Lawn, NJ 201-797-7100
Somebody's Mother's Chocolate
Houston, TX 713-627-3055
Southern Season
Chapel Hill, NC 877-929-7133
Spice Rack Chocolates
Fredericksburg, VA 540-847-2063
Strawberry Hill Grand Delights
Everett, MA 617-319-3557
Stutz Candy Company
Philadelphia, PA 888-692-2639
Sucesores de Pedro Cortes
Hato Rey, PR 787-754-7040
Sucre
New Orleans, LA 504-708-4366
Sugar & Plumm
New York, NY 212-787-8778
Sulpice Chocolate
Barrington, IL 630-301-2345
Sunridge Farms
Royal Oaks, CA 831-786-7000

Sweet Designs Chocolatier Inc
Lakewood, OH ... 216-226-4888

Sweet Traders
Huntington Beach, CA ... 714-903-6800

Swerseys Chocolate
Brooklyn, NY ... 718-497-8800

Taza Chocolate
Somerville, MA ... 617-623-0804

TCHO Ventures
San Francisco, CA ... 415-981-0189

Tea Room
San Leandro, CA ... 510-567-8868

Terri Lynn Inc
Elgin, IL ... 800-323-0775

Texas Coffee Traders Inc
Austin, TX ... 800-343-4875

Theo Chocolate
Seattle, WA ... 206-632-5100

Tonex
Wallington, NJ ... 973-773-5135

Tropical Nut & Fruit Co
Orlando, FL ... 800-749-8869

Tumbador Chocolate
Brooklyn, NY ... 718-788-0200

UnReal Brands
Boston, MA

US Chocolate Corp
Brooklyn, NY ... 718-788-8555

V Chocolates
Salt Lake City, UT ... 801-269-8444

Valley View Blueberries
Vancouver, WA ... 360-892-2839

Vermont Confectionery
Bennington, VT ... 800-545-9243

Vigneri Chocolate Inc.
Rochester, NY ... 877-844-6374

Vintage Plantations Cho colates
Newark, NJ ... 800-207-7058

Vivoo
Verona,

Weaver Nut Co. Inc.
Ephrata, PA ... 800-473-2688

Webb's Candy
Davenport, FL ... 800-289-9322

Western Syrup Company
Santa Fe Springs, CA ... 562-921-4485

Wild Things Snacks
Seattle, WA ... 720-231-9196

William Bounds
Torrance, CA ... 800-473-0504

Wilson Candy Co
Jeannette, PA ... 724-523-3151

Windy City Organics
Northbrook, IL ... 800-925-0577

World Confections Inc
South Orange, NJ ... 718-768-8100

World's Finest Chocolate Inc
Chicago, IL ... 888-821-8452

Yoo-Hoo Chocolate Beverage Company
Carlstadt, NJ ... 201-933-0070

Z Specialty Food, LLC
Woodland, CA ... 800-678-1226

Zachary Confections Inc
Frankfort, IN ... 800-445-4222

Zotter Chocolates
Cape Coral, FL ... 239-214-7883

Baking Chocolate

Artisan Kettle
... 833-605-6929

Blommer Chocolate Co
Chicago, IL ... 800-621-1606

Ghirardelli Chocolate Co
San Leandro, CA ... 800-877-9338

Hershey Co.
Hershey, PA ... 800-468-1714

Jomart Chocolates
Brooklyn, NY ... 718-375-1277

King Arthur Flour
Norwich, VT ... 800-827-6836

Taza Chocolate
Somerville, MA ... 617-623-0804

Boxed Chocolate

Abdallah Candies & Gifts
Burnsville, MN ... 952-890-0859

Ameri Candy
Louisville, KY ... 502-583-1776

Ann Hemyng Candy Inc
Trumbauersville, PA ... 800-779-7004

Astor Chocolate Corp
Lakewood, NJ ... 732-901-1001

Berkshire Bark Inc
Sheffield, MA ... 413-229-8120

Bissinger's Handcrafted Chocolatier
St Louis, MO ... 800-325-8881

Blommer Chocolate Co
Chicago, IL ... 800-621-1606

Boca Bons East
Greenacres, FL ... 800-314-2835

Brockmann's Chocolates
Delta, BC ... 888-494-2270

Brown & Haley
Fife, WA ... 800-426-8400

Buddy Squirrel LLC
St Francis, WI ... 800-972-2658

Charlotte's Confections
Millbrae, CA ... 800-798-2427

Chocolates a La Carte
Valencia, CA ... 800-818-2462

Chocolates by Mark
Houston, TX ... 832-736-2626

Chocolates Turin
Plano, TX ... 972-731-6771

Claudia B Chocolates
San Antonio, TX ... 800-725-4602

Daniel Le Chocolat Belge
Vancouver, BC ... 604-879-7782

David Bradley Chocolatier
Windsor, NJ ... 877-289-7933

Davinci Gourmet LTD
Seattle, WA ... 800-640-6779

Double Premium Confections
McLean, VA ... 202-495-1884

Elmer Chocolate®
Ponchatoula, LA ... 800-843-9537

Empress Chocolate Company
Brooklyn, NY ... 800-793-3809

Fannie May Fine Chocolate
Oakdale, MN ... 800-999-3629

Faroh Candies
Middleburg Heights, OH ... 440-888-9866

Fenton & Lee Chocolatiers
Eugene, OR ... 800-336-8661

Frankford Candy & Chocolate Co
Philadelphia, PA ... 800-523-9090

Functional Foods
Roseville, MI ... 877-372-0550

Ganong Bros Ltd
St. Stephen, NB ... 888-270-8222

Godiva Chocolatier
New York, NY ... 800-946-3482

Gorant Chocolatier
Youngstown, OH ... 330-726-8821

Guylian USA Inc.
Englewood Cliffs, NJ ... 201-871-4144

Hagensborg Chocolates LTD.
Burnaby, BC ... 877-554-7763

Harbor Sweets
Salem, MA ... 800-243-2115

Harry London Candies Inc
Melrose Park, IL ... 800-333-3629

Hawaiian King Candies
Honolulu, HI ... 800-570-1902

Hibiscus Aloha Corporation
Honolulu, HI ... 808-591-8826

Imagine Chocolate
Burnank, CA ... 916-837-5772

Jer's Chocolates
Solana Beach, CA ... 800-540-7265

Joe Clark Fund Raising Candies
Tarentum, PA ... 888-459-9520

Joyva Corp
Brooklyn, NY ... 718-497-0170

Koeze Company
Grand Rapids, MI ... 800-555-9688

Kohler Original Recipe Chocolates
Kohler, WI ... 920-208-4930

Lammes Candies
Austin, TX ... 800-252-1885

Liberty Orchards Co Inc
Cashmere, WA ... 800-231-3242

Lindt & Sprungli USA
Stratham, NH ... 603-778-8100

Long Grove Confectionary
Buffalo Grove, IL ... 800-373-3102

Maggie Lyon Chocolatiers
Norcross, GA ... 800-969-3500

Maramor Chocolates
Columbus, OH ... 800-843-7722

MarySue.com
Baltimore, MD ... 800-662-2639

Maxfield Candy
Salt Lake City, UT ... 800-288-8002

Michele's Chocolate Truffles
Clackamas, OR ... 800-656-7112

Munson's Chocolates
Bolton, CT ... 888-686-7667

Niagara Chocolates
Buffalo, NY ... 877-261-7887

NibMor
Kennebunk, ME ... 207-502-7541

Papas Chris A & Son Co
Covington, KY ... 859-431-0499

Patsy's Candy
Colorado Springs, CO ... 866-372-8797

Peanut Patch
Yuma, AZ ... 800-872-7688

Piedmont Candy Co
Lexington, NC ... 336-248-2477

Queen Bee Gardens
Lovell, WY ... 800-225-7553

R.M. Palmer Co.
West Reading, PA ... 610-372-8971

Rene Rey Chocolates Ltd
North Vancouver, BC ... 888-985-0949

Reutter Candy & Chocolates
Baltimore, MD ... 800-392-0870

Rogers' Chocolates Ltd
Victoria, BC ... 800-663-2220

Russell Stover Candies Inc.
Kansas City, MO ... 800-777-4004

Ruth Hunt Candy Co
Mt Sterling, KY ... 800-927-0302

S Zitner Co
Philadelphia, PA ... 215-229-9828

Sanders Candy Inc
Clinton Twp, MI ... 800-852-2253

Scott's Candy
Glennville, GA ... 800-356-2100

Seattle Chocolates
Tukwila, WA ... 800-334-3600

Sjaak's Organic Chocolates
Petaluma, CA ... 707-775-2434

Stutz Candy Company
Philadelphia, PA ... 888-692-2639

Sugar & Plumm
New York, NY ... 212-787-8778

Susie's South Forty Confection
Midland, TX ... 800-221-4442

Sweet Blessings
Malibu, CA ... 310-317-1172

Sweet Designs Chocolatier Inc
Lakewood, OH ... 216-226-4888

Sweet Shop USA
Mt Pleasant, TX ... 888-957-9338

Swerseys Chocolate
Brooklyn, NY ... 718-497-8800

Tootsie Roll Industries Inc.
Chicago, IL ... 866-972-6879

Trophy Nut Co
Tipp City, OH ... 800-219-9004

Vande Walle's Candies Inc
Appleton, WI ... 800-738-1020

Whetstone Chocolates
St Augustine, FL ... 877-261-7887

Wilson Candy Co
Jeannette, PA ... 724-523-3151

World Confections Inc
South Orange, NJ ... 718-768-8100

Candy & Confectionery:Chocolate Products:White

Candy Basket Inc
Portland, OR ... 800-864-1924

Sjaak's Organic Chocolates
Petaluma, CA ... 707-775-2434

Chocolate Bars

Amano Artisan Chocolate
Orem, UT ... 801-655-1996

B. Nutty
Oakland, CA ... 510-374-4658

Blommer Chocolate Co
Chicago, IL ... 800-621-1606

Chocomize
Long Island City, NY ... 800-621-3294

Chris Candies Inc
Pittsburgh, PA ... 412-322-9400

Dina's Organic Chocolate
Mt Kisco, NY ... 888-625-2008

Divine Chocolate
Washington, DC ... 202-332-8913

Earth Source Organics
Vista, CA....760-734-1867
Eating Evolved
Setauket, NY....631-675-2440
Eda's Sugar Free
Philadelphia, PA....215-324-3412
Elements Truffles
Kearny, NJ....917-836-2819
Equal Exchange Inc
West Bridgewater, MA....774-776-7400
Fine & Raw Chocolate
Brooklyn, NY....718-366-3633
Funkychunky Inc.
Edina, MN....888-473-8659
Good Stuff Cacao
Metamora, MI....248-690-5114
Greenwell Farms Inc
Kealakekua, HI....888-592-5662
Gutsii
Los Angeles, CA
Hershey Co.
Hershey, PA....800-468-1714
Honey Acres
Neosho, WI....920-474-4411
Hu Kitchen
New York, NY....212-510-8919
Jer's Chocolates
Solana Beach, CA....800-540-7265
JoJo's Chocolate
Mesa, AZ....805-395-6567
Jomart Chocolates
Brooklyn, NY....718-375-1277
Joyfuls
Fairfield, NJ....888-989-9050
Justin's Nut Butter
Boulder, CO....844-448-0302
Kiss My Keto
Los Angeles, CA....310-765-1553
Kohler Original Recipe Chocolates
Kohler, WI....920-208-4930
Lily's Sweets
Boulder, CO....877-587-0557
Loacker USA
New York, NY....212-742-8510
Madecasse
Brooklyn, NY....917-382-2020
Malie Kai Hawaiian Chocolates
Honolulu, HI....808-599-8600
MilkBoy Swiss Chocolate
Brooklyn, NY
Moonstruck Chocolate Co
Portland, OR....800-557-6666
Munson's Chocolates
Bolton, CT....888-686-7667
Olive & Sinclair Chocolate Co
Nashville, TN....615-262-3007
Pascha Chocolate
Toronto, Ontario,....855-472-7242
Poco Dolce
San Francisco, CA....415-255-1443
Praim Co
Salem, MA....800-970-9646
Pure7 Chocolate
Lynn, MA....844-547-8737
Raaka Chocolate
Brooklyn, NY....855-255-3354
Rawmantic Chocolate
New York, NY....212-247-2229
Sjaak's Organic Chocolates
Petaluma, CA....707-775-2434
Sucre
New Orleans, LA....504-708-4366
Sulpice Chocolate
Barrington, IL....630-301-2345
Sweet Designs Chocolatier Inc
Lakewood, OH....216-226-4888
Taza Chocolate
Somerville, MA....617-623-0804
Tony's Chocolonely
Portland, OR....503-388-5990
Travel Chocolate
New York, NY....718-841-7030
Videri Chocolate Factory
Raleigh, NC....919-755-5053
Vivra Chocolate
Walpole, MA....800-359-8950
Zazubean
Vancouver, BC....604-801-5488

Chocolate Candy

21st Century Snack Foods
Ronkonkoma, NY....631-588-8000
Abbott's Candy Shop
Hagerstown, IN....877-801-1200
Aglamesis Bros Ice Cream
Cincinnati, OH....513-531-5196
Alexandra & Nicolay Chocolate Company
Portaland, PA....570-897-6223
All American Snacks
Midland, TX....800-840-2455
All Wrapped Up
Plantation, FL....800-891-2194
Ameri-Suisse Group
South Plainfield, NJ....908-222-1001
American Nut & Chocolate Co
Boston, MA....800-797-6887
AmeriGift
Oxnard, CA....800-421-9039
Andre Prost Inc
Old Saybrook, CT....800-243-0897
Andre's Confiserie Suisse
Kansas City, MO....800-892-1234
Ann Hemyng Candy Inc
Trumbauersville, PA....800-779-7004
Anthony Thomas Candy Co
Columbus, OH....877-226-3921
Art CoCo Chocolate Company
Geneva, IL....877-232-9901
Artisan Confections
Hershey, PA....866-237-0152
Aunt Sally's Praline Shops
New Orleans, LA....800-642-7257
B & B Pecan Processors
Turkey, NC....866-328-7322
Baker Candy Company
Snohomish, WA....425-422-6331
Baker Maid Products, Inc.
New Orleans, LA....800-664-7882
Baker's Candies Factory Store
Greenwood, NE....800-804-7330
Banner Candy Manufacturing Company
Brooklyn, NY....718-647-4747
Baraboo Candy Co LLC
Baraboo, WI....800-967-1690
Bari & Gail
Walpole, MA....800-828-9318
Bee International
Chula Vista, CA....800-421-6465
Ben Heggy's Candy Co
Canton, OH....330-455-7703
Bergen Marzipan & Chocolate
Bergenfield, NJ....201-385-8343
Best Chocolate In Town
Indianapolis, IN....888-294-2378
Bidwell Candies
Mattoon, IL....217-234-3858
Birnn Chocolates of Vermont
South Burlington, VT....800-338-3141
Biscomerica Corporation
Rialto, CA....909-877-5997
Bissinger's Handcrafted Chocolatier
St. Louis, MO....314-615-2400
Black Hound New York
Brooklyn, NY....800-344-4417
Blanton's
Frankfort, KY....502-223-9874
Blommer Chocolate Co
Chicago, IL....800-621-1606
Blommer Chocolate Co
East Greenville, PA....800-825-8181
Bluebird Restaurant
Logan, UT....435-752-3155
Boca Bons East
Greenacres, FL....800-314-2835
Boyer Candy Co Inc
Altoona, PA....814-944-9401
Bread & Chocolate Inc
Wells River, VT....800-524-6715
Brockmann's Chocolates
Delta, BC....888-494-2270
Bt. McElrath Chocolatier
Minneapolis, MN....612-331-8800
Buddy Squirrel LLC
St Francis, WI....800-972-2658
Byrne & Carlson
Portsmouth, NH....888-559-9778
Cambridge Brands Inc
Cambridge, MA....617-491-2500
Cameo Confections
Bay Village, OH....440-871-5732
Campbell Soup Co.
Camden, NJ....800-257-8443
Candy Central
East Hanover, NJ
Candy Flowers
Mentor, OH....440-974-1333
Canelake's Candy
Virginia, MN....888-928-8889
Caribbean Cookie Company
Virginia Beach, VA....800-326-5200
Carousel Candies
Geneva, IL....888-656-1552
Carrie's Chocolates
Edmonton, AB....877-778-2462
Charlotte's Confections
Millbrae, CA....800-798-2427
Chase & Poe Candy Co
St Joseph, MO....800-786-1625
Chevalier Chocolates
Enfield, CT....860-741-3330
Chocoholics Divine Desserts
Linden, CA....800-760-2462
Chocolat Belge Heyez
St-Lazare-De-Bellechasse, QC....450-653-5616
Chocolat Jean Talon
Montreal, QC....888-333-8540
Chocolate By Design Inc
Ronkonkoma, NY....631-737-0082
Chocolate Chocolate Chocolate
St Louis, MO....314-338-3501
Chocolate Creations
Monaca, PA....724-774-7675
Chocolate House
Milwaukee, WI....800-236-2022
Chocolate Moon
Asheville, NC....800-723-1236
Chocolate Smith
Santa Fe, NM....505-473-2111
Chocolate Street of Hartville
Hartville, OH....888-853-5904
Chocolate Studio
Norristown, PA....610-272-3872
Chocolaterie Bernard Callebaut
Calgary, AB....800-661-8367
Chocolaterie Stam
Des Moines, IA....877-782-6246
Chocolates a La Carte
Valencia, CA....800-818-2462
Chocolates by Mark
Houston, TX....832-736-2626
Chocolates By Mr Roberts
Boca Raton, FL....561-392-3007
Chocolates El Rey, Inc
Houston, TX....800-357-3999
Chocolati Handmade Chocolates
Seattle, WA....206-784-5212
Chocolatier
Exeter, NH....888-246-5528
Chocolove
Boulder, CO....888-246-2656
Chris Candies Inc
Pittsburgh, PA....412-322-9400
Christopher Norman Chocolates
Hudson, NY....518-822-0300
Clasen Quality Chocolate
Madison, WI....877-459-4500
Classic Confectionery
Fort Worth, TX....800-674-4435
Clear-Vu Industries
Ashland, MA....508-881-9100
Cloud Nine
Claremont, CA....909-624-3147
CNS Confectionery Products
Bayonne, NJ....888-823-4330
Colts Chocolates
Nashville, TN....615-251-0100
ConSup North America
Lincoln Park, NJ....973-628-7330
Cora Italian Specialties
Countryside, IL....800-696-2672
Cowgirl Chocolates
Moscow, ID....888-882-4098
Creative Cotton
Northbrook, IL....847-291-4128
Criterion Chocolates Inc
Eatontown, NJ....800-804-6060
Croft's Crackers
Monroe, WI....608-325-1223
Crown Candy Corp
Macon, GA....800-241-3529
Cummings Studio Chocolates
Salt Lake City, UT....800-537-3957
DAGOBA Organic Chocolate
Ashland, OR....866-972-6879
Dairy Management Inc
Rosemont, IL....800-853-2479

Daprano & Company
Charlotte, NC 877-365-2337
David Bradley Chocolatier
Windsor, NJ. . . . 877-289-7933
Daymar Select Fine Coffees
El Cajon, CA. . . . 800-466-7590
Dayton Nut Specialties
Springboro, OH. . . . 937-743-4377
Delancey Dessert Company
New York, NY 800-254-5254
Dessert Innovations Inc
Atlanta, GA. . . . 800-359-7351
DGZ Chocolate
Houston, TX 877-949-9444
Dilettante Chocolates
Kent, WA. . . . 800-800-9490
Dipasa USA Inc
Brownsville, TX 956-831-4072
Divine Delights
Petaluma, CA 800-443-2836
Dolphin Natural Chocolates
Cambria, CA. . . . 800-236-5744
Donaldson's Finer Chocolates
Lebanon, IN 800-975-7236
Donells Candies
Casper, WY. . . . 877-461-2009
Donnelly Fine Chocolates
Santa Cruz, CA. . . . 888-685-1871
Doscher's Candies Co.
Cincinnati, OH 513-381-8656
Double Play Foods
New York, NY. . . . 212-682-4611
Dundee Brandied Fruit Co
Dundee, OR. . . . 503-537-2500
Dundee Candy Shop
Louisville, KY 866-877-9266
Dundee Groves
Dundee, FL. . . . 800-294-2266
Ed & Don's Of Hawaii Inc
Honolulu, HI. . . . 808-423-8200
Eda's Sugar Free
Philadelphia, PA 215-324-3412
Emmy's Candy from Belgium
Charlotte, NC 866-879-1901
Endangered Species Chocolate
Indianapolis, IN 800-293-0160
Esther Price Candies & Gifts
Dayton, OH. . . . 855-337-8437
Ethel M Chocolates
Henderson, NV. . . . 800-438-4356
Euphoria Chocolate Company
Eugene, OR. . . . 541-344-4914
Euro Cafe
Rochester, NY. . . . 800-298-9410
Evans Creole Candy
New Orleans, LA 800-637-6675
Fairytale Brownies
Phoenix, AZ 800-324-7982
Fancy's Candy's
Rougemont, NC 888-403-2629
Fantasy Chocolates
Boynton Beach, FL. . . . 800-804-4962
Faroh Candies
Middleburg Heights, OH 440-888-9866
Fenton & Lee Chocolatiers
Eugene, OR. . . . 800-336-8661
Ferrara Candy Co Inc
Chicago, IL. . . . 800-323-1768
Ferrero USA Inc
Somerset, NJ. . . . 800-337-7376
Ficon
St Louis, MO. . . . 888-569-4099
Fitzkee's Candies Inc
York, PA 717-741-1031
Foley's Chocolates & Candies
Richmond, BC 888-236-5397
Fralinger's
Atlantic City, NJ 800-938-2339
Frankford Candy & Chocolate Co
Philadelphia, PA 800-523-9090
Functional Foods
Roseville, MI 877-372-0550
G Debbas Chocolatier
Fresno, CA 559-294-2071
Ganong Bros Ltd
St. Stephen, NB. . . . 888-270-8222
Gardners Candies Inc
Tyrone, PA. . . . 800-242-2639
Gene & Boots Candies Inc
Perryopolis, PA. . . . 800-864-4222
Georgia Nut Co
Skokie, IL 877-674-2993

Germack Pistachio Co
Detroit, MI 800-872-4006
Ghirardelli Chocolate Co
San Leandro, CA. . . . 800-877-9338
Ghyslain Chocolatier
Union City, IN. . . . 866-449-7524
GKI Foods
Brighton, MI 248-486-0055
Godiva Chocolatier
New York, NY 800-946-3482
Goldenberg's Peanut Chews
Bethlehem, PA 888-645-3453
Gorant Chocolatier
Youngstown, OH. . . . 330-726-8821
Govatos Chocolates
Wilmington, DE 888-799-5252
Great Expectations Confectionery Gourmet Foods
Chicago, IL 773-525-4865
Green County Foods
Monroe, WI. . . . 800-233-3564
Green Mountain Chocolate Inc
Franklin, MA 508-520-7160
Greenwell Farms Inc
Kealakekua, HI 888-592-5662
Gurley's Foods
Willmar, MN. . . . 800-426-7845
Hagensborg Chocolates LTD.
Burnaby, BC 877-554-7763
Harbor Sweets
Salem, MA 800-243-2115
Hauser Chocolates
Westerly, RI. . . . 888-599-8231
Haven's Candies
Westbrook, ME. . . . 800-639-6309
Hawaiian Host Inc
Honolulu, HI. . . . 888-414-4678
Hawaiian King Candies
Honolulu, HI. . . . 800-570-1902
Healthy Food Brands LLC
Brooklyn, NY 212-444-9909
Hebert Candies
Shrewsbury, MA. . . . 866-609-6533
Helms Candy Co., Inc
Bristol, VA 276-669-2533
Hershey Co.
Hershey, PA. . . . 800-468-1714
Hialeah Products Co
Hollywood, FL 800-923-3379
Hibiscus Aloha Corporation
Honolulu, HI. . . . 808-591-8826
Huppen Bakery
Los Angeles, CA. . . . 323-656-7501
Hyde Candy Company
Seattle, WA. . . . 206-322-5743
Idaho Candy Co
Boise, ID. . . . 800-898-6986
Imperial Nougat Co
Santa Fe Springs, CA 562-693-8423
Issimo Food Group
La Jolla, CA 619-260-1900
Jason & Son Specialty Foods
Rancho Cordova, CA 800-810-9093
Jeryl's Jems
Tappan, NY. . . . 201-236-8372
Jo's Candies
Torrance, CA. . . . 800-770-1946
Joe Clark Fund Raising Candies
Tarentum, PA. . . . 888-459-9520
Josh Early Candies
Allentown, PA. . . . 610-395-4321
Just Born Inc
Bethlehem, PA 800-445-5787
Kara Chocolates
Orem, UT 800-284-5272
Kastner's Pastry Shop & Grocery
Surfside, FL 305-866-6993
Kate Latter Candy Company
New Orleans, LA 800-825-5359
Kelly's Candies
Pooler, GA 800-523-3051
Kemach Food Products
Brooklyn, NY 718-272-5655
Kennedy Gourmet
Glendale Heights, IL. . . . 800-729-8116
Key III Candies
Fort Wayne, IN 800-752-2382
Knudsen Candy
Hayward, CA 800-736-6887
Koeze Company
Grand Rapids, MI 800-555-9688
Koppers Chocolate
Cranford, NJ 800-325-0026

L C Good Candy Company
Allentown, PA. . . . 610-432-3290
Lake Champlain Chocolates
Burlington, VT 800-634-8105
Lanco
Hauppauge, NY 800-938-4500
Landies Candies Co
Buffalo, NY. . . . 800-955-2634
Lang's Chocolates
Williamsport, PA. . . . 570-323-6320
Layman Distributing
Salem, VA. . . . 800-237-1319
Lazzaroni USA
Saddle Brook, NJ 201-368-1240
Len Libby Chocolatier-Maine
Scarborough, ME 207-883-4897
Les Chocolats Vadeboncoeur Inc.
Montreal, QC 800-276-8504
Lindt & Sprungli USA
Stratham, NH 603-778-8100
Long Grove Confectionary
Buffalo Grove, IL 800-373-3102
Longford-Hamilton Company
Beaverton, OR 503-642-5661
Loretta's Authentic Pralines
New Orleans, LA 504-529-6170
Lou-Retta's Custom Chocolates
Buffalo, NY. . . . 716-833-7111
Louis J Rheb Candy Co
Baltimore, MD 800-514-8293
Lowery's Home Made Candies
Muncie, IN 800-541-3340
Lucille's Own Make Candies
Manahawkin, NJ. . . . 800-426-9168
Lukas Confections
York, PA 717-843-0921
Lynard Company
Stamford, CT. . . . 203-323-0231
Madelaine Chocolate Company
Rockaway Beach, NY. . . . 800-322-1505
Madrona Specialty Foods LLC
Seattle, WA. . . . 425-656-2997
Maggie Lyon Chocolatiers
Norcross, GA 800-969-3500
Maramor Chocolates
Columbus, OH 800-843-7722
Marich Confectionery
Hollister, CA. . . . 800-624-7055
Marlow Candy & Nut Co
Englewood, NJ 201-569-3725
Mary of Puddin Hill
Palestine, TX. . . . 800-545-8889
MarySue.com
Baltimore, MD 800-662-2639
Maxfield Candy
Salt Lake City, UT 800-288-8002
Menehune Mac
Honolulu, HI. . . . 808-841-3344
Merb's Candies
St Louis, MO. . . . 314-832-7117
Merlin Candies
Harahan, LA 800-899-1549
Michele's Chocolate Truffles
Clackamas, OR. . . . 800-656-7112
Michelle Chocolatiers
Colorado Springs, CO. . . . 888-447-3654
Miesse Candies
Lancaster, PA. . . . 717-392-6011
Mom N' Pops Inc
New Windsor, NY. . . . 845-567-0640
Mona Lisa Foods
Chicago, IL 866-443-0460
Moore's Candies
Baltimore, MD 410-836-8840
Munson's Chocolates
Bolton, CT 888-686-7667
Muth's Candy Store
Louisville, KY 502-582-2639
Nancy's Candy
Meadows Of Dan, VA. . . . 800-328-3834
Naron Mary Sue Candies
Baltimore, MD 800-662-2639
Nassau Candy Distributors
Hicksville, NY 516-433-7100
Natural Rush
San Francisco, CA 415-863-2503
Neal's Chocolates
Salt Lake City, UT 801-521-6500
Neuchatel Chocolatier
Oxford, PA 800-597-0759
Newton Candy Company
Houston, TX 713-691-6969

Niagara Chocolates
Buffalo, NY....877-261-7887
Nora's Candy Shop
Rome, NY....888-544-8224
Northern Flair Foods
Mound, MN....888-530-4453
Northwest Chocolate Factory
Salem, OR....503-362-1340
Nunes Farms Marketing
Gustine, CA....209-862-3033
OH Chocolate
Seattle, WA....206-329-8777
Old Dominion Peanut Corp
Norfolk, VA....800-368-6887
Old Monmouth Candies
Freehold, NJ....732-462-1311
Old Time Candy Co
Lagrange, OH....440-355-4345
Olde Tyme Mercantile
Arroyo Grande, CA....805-489-7991
Olivier's Candies
Calgary, AB....403-266-6028
Omanhene Cocoa Bean Co
Milwaukee, WI....800-588-2462
Oregon Bark
Portland, OR
Pacific Gold Marketing
Arlington, TX....817-795-4671
Palmer Candy Co
Sioux City, IA....800-831-0828
Pangburn Candy Company
Fort Worth, TX....817-332-8856
Papas Chris A & Son Co
Covington, KY....859-431-0499
Patsy's Candy
Colorado Springs, CO....866-372-8797
Paul's Candy Factory
Salt Lake City, UT....800-825-9912
Paulaur Corp
Cranbury, NJ....609-395-8844
Peanut Patch
Yuma, AZ....800-872-7688
Pearl River Pastry & Chocolate
Pearl River, NY....800-632-2639
Pease's Candy
Springfield, IL....217-523-3721
Pecan Deluxe Candy Co
Dallas, TX....800-733-3589
Phillip's Candy House
Dorchester, MA....617-282-2090
Pine River Pre-Pack Inc
Newton, WI....920-726-4216
Pippin Snack Pecans
Albany, GA....800-554-6887
Plantation Candies
Telford, PA....888-678-6468
Plyley's Candy
Lagrange, IN....877-665-2778
Prifti Candy Company
Worcester, MA....800-447-7438
Prince of Peace
Hayward, CA....800-732-2328
Pulakos 926 Chocolate
Erie, PA....814-452-4026
Purity Candy Co
Lewisburg, PA....800-821-4748
Queen Bee Gardens
Lovell, WY....800-225-7553
Quintessential Chocolates
Fredericksburg, TX....800-842-3382
R.L. Albert & Son
Stamford, CT....203-622-8655
Ragold Confections
Wilton Manors, FL....954-566-9092
Rebecca-Ruth Candy Factory
Frankfort, KY....800-444-3866
Rene Rey Chocolates Ltd
North Vancouver, BC....888-985-0949
Reutter Candy & Chocolates
Baltimore, MD....800-392-0870
Riddles' Sweet Impressions
Edmonton, AB....780-465-8085
Riverdale Fine Foods
Dayton, OH....800-548-1304
Rogers' Chocolates Ltd
Victoria, BC....800-663-2220
Rosalind Candy Castle Inc
New Brighton, PA....724-843-1144
Rosetti's Fine Foods Biscotti
Clovis, CA....559-323-6450
Roseville Corporation
Mountain View, CA....888-247-9338
Royal Baltic LTD
Brooklyn, NY....718-385-8300
Runk Candy Company
Cincinnati, OH....800-641-8551
S P Enterprises
Las Vegas, NV....800-746-4774
S Zitner Co
Philadelphia, PA....215-229-9828
S.L. Kaye Company
New York, NY....212-683-5600
Sahagian & Associates
Oak Park, IL....800-327-9273
Sanders Candy Inc
Clinton Twp, MI....800-852-2253
Scott's Candy
Glennville, GA....800-356-2100
Seattle Bar Company
Seattle, WA....206-601-4301
Seattle Chocolates
Tukwila, WA....800-334-3600
Seattle Gourmet Foods
Tukwila, WA....800-800-9490
Setton International Foods
Commack, NY....800-227-4397
Shakespeare's
Davenport, IA....800-664-4114
Shane Candy Co
Philadelphia, PA....215-922-1048
Sherm Edwards Candies
Trafford, PA....800-436-5424
Sherwood Brands of Rhode Island Inc
Rumford, RI....401-726-4500
Sifers Valomilk Candy Co
Shawnee, KS....913-722-0991
Silver Sweet Candies
Lawrence, MA....978-688-0474
Silverland Bakery
Forest Park, IL....708-488-0800
Sjaak's Organic Chocolates
Petaluma, CA....707-775-2434
Sorbee Intl.
Philadelphia, PA....800-654-3997
South Beach Novelties & Confectionery
Staten Island, NY....718-727-4500
South Bend Chocolate Co
South Bend, IN....800-301-4961
SP Enterprises, Inc.
Las Vegas, NV....800-746-4774
Spangler Candy Co
Bryan, OH....888-636-4221
Spokandy
Spokane, WA....509-624-1969
Sporting Colors LLC
St. Louis, MO....888-394-2292
Squirrel Brand Company
McKinney, TX....800-624-8242
St. Jacobs Candy Co.
Waterloo, ON....519-884-3505
Stanchfield Farms
Milo, ME....207-732-5173
Standard Functional Foods Grp
Nashville, TN....800-226-4340
Stewart Candies
Waycross, GA....912-283-1970
Stutz Candy Company
Philadelphia, PA....888-692-2639
Sucesores de Pedro Cortes
Hato Rey, PR....787-754-7040
Sucre
New Orleans, LA....504-708-4366
Suity Confections Co
Miami, FL....305-639-3300
Sun Empire Foods
Kerman, CA....800-252-4786
Supreme Chocolatier
Staten Island, NY....718-761-9600
Susie's South Forty Confection
Midland, TX....800-221-4442
Sweenors Chocolates
Wakefield, RI....800-834-3123
Sweet Blessings
Malibu, CA....310-317-1172
Sweet Candy Company
Salt Lake City, UT....855-772-7720
Testamints Sales-Distribution
Hopatcong, NJ....888-879-0400
Toe-Food Chocolates and Candy
Berkeley, CA....888-863-3663
Tom & Sally's Handmade Chocolates
Brattleboro, VT....800-827-0800
Tootsie Roll Industries Inc.
Chicago, IL....866-972-6879
Totally Chocolate
Blaine, WA....800-255-5506
Toucan Chocolates
Waban, MA....617-964-8696
Trappistine Quality Candy
Wrentham, MA....866-549-8929
Tremblay's Sweet Shop
Hayward, WI....715-634-2785
Triple-C
Hamilton, ON....800-263-9105
Trophy Nut Co
Tipp City, OH....800-219-9004
Tropical Nut & Fruit Co
Orlando, FL....800-749-8869
Truan's Candies
Detroit, MI....800-584-3004
Ultimate Nut & Candy Company
Los Angeles, CA....800-767-5259
US Chocolate Corp
Brooklyn, NY....718-788-8555
V L Foods
White Plains, NY....914-697-4851
Valhrona
Los Angeles, CA....310-277-0401
Van Leer Chocolate Corporation
Chicago, IL....800-225-1418
Van Otis Chocolates
Manchester, NH....800-826-6847
Vande Walle's Candies Inc
Appleton, WI....800-738-1020
Varda Chocolatier
Elizabeth, NJ....800-448-2732
Vaughn-Russell Candy Kitchen
Greenville, SC....864-271-7786
Vermont Nut Free Chocolates
Grand Isle, VT....888-468-8373
Vigneri Chocolate Inc.
Rochester, NY....877-844-6374
Vitality Life Choice
Carson City, NV....800-423-8365
Warner-Lambert Confections
Cambridge, MA....617-491-2500
Warrell Corp
Camp Hill, PA....800-233-7082
Weaver Nut Co. Inc.
Ephrata, PA....800-473-2688
Webb's Candy
Davenport, FL....800-289-9322
Westdale Foods Company
Orland Park, IL....708-458-7774
Whetstone Candy Company
St. Augustine, FL....904-825-1700
Whetstone Chocolates
St Augustine, FL....877-261-7887
Widman's Candy Shop
Crookston, MN....218-281-1487
Wilbur Chocolate Candy
Lititz, PA....888-294-5287
Wilkinson-Spitz
Yonkers, NY....914-237-5000
Williams Candy Co
Chesapeake, VA....757-545-9311
Williams Candy Company
Somerville, MA....617-776-0814
Williamsburg Chocolatier
Williamsburg, VA....757-253-1474
Wilson Candy Co
Jeannette, PA....724-523-3151
Windmill Candies
Granite Falls, MN....877-771-8892
Windsor Confections
Oakland, CA....800-860-0021
Winfrey Fudge & Candy
Rowley, MA....888-946-3739
Wisconsin Dairyland Fudge Company
Wisconsin Dells, WI....608-254-7771
Wisteria Candy Cottage
Boulevard, CA....800-458-8246
World Confections Inc
South Orange, NJ....718-768-8100
Yamate Chocolatier
Highland Park, NJ....800-433-2462
Z Specialty Food, LLC
Woodland, CA....800-678-1226
Zenobia Co
Bronx, NY....866-936-6242

Chocolate Cherries

Bissinger's Handcrafted Chocolatier
St. Louis, MO....314-615-2400
Cambridge Brands Inc
Cambridge, MA....617-491-2500

Faroh Candies
Middleburg Heights, OH 440-888-9866
Farr Candy Company
Idaho Falls, ID 208-522-8215
GKI Foods
Brighton, MI 248-486-0055
Godiva Chocolatier
New York, NY 800-946-3482
Gray & Company
Hart, MI. 800-551-6009
Hialeah Products Co
Hollywood, FL 800-923-3379
Lerro Candy Company
Darby, PA 610-461-8886
Lowery's Home Made Candies
Muncie, IN 800-541-3340
Marich Confectionery
Hollister, CA. 800-624-7055
Maxfield Candy
Salt Lake City, UT 800-288-8002
Moore's Candies
Baltimore, MD 410-836-8840
Papas Chris A & Son Co
Covington, KY 859-431-0499
Terri Lynn Inc
Elgin, IL 800-323-0775
Truan's Candies
Detroit, MI 800-584-3004

Chocolate Chips

Blommer Chocolate Co
Chicago, IL. 800-621-1606
Hershey Co.
Hershey, PA. 800-468-1714
Homefree LLC
Windham, NH. 800-552-7172
King Arthur Flour
Norwich, VT. 800-827-6836
Lily's Sweets
Boulder, CO 877-587-0557
Loghouse Foods
Minneapolis, MN 763-546-8395
Pascha Chocolate
Toronto, Ontario, ... 855-472-7242
Setton International Foods
Commack, NY 800-227-4397
Tea Room
San Leandro, CA. 510-567-8868

Chocolate Chunks

Blommer Chocolate Co
Chicago, IL. 800-621-1606
Chocomize
Long Island City, NY 800-621-3294
Fine & Raw Chocolate
Brooklyn, NY 718-366-3633
JC's Pie Pops
Chatsworth, CA 818-349-1880
Michael Mootz Candies
Hanover Twp, PA 570-823-8272

Cocoa & Cocoa Products

Al-Rite Fruits & Syrups Co
Miami, FL. 305-652-2540
Alaska Herb & Tea Co
Anchorage, AK. 800-654-2764
Alexander Gourmet Beverages
Bolton, ON 800-265-5081
American Key Food Products Inc
Closter, NJ. 877-263-7539
American Nut & Chocolate Co
Boston, MA. 800-797-6887
American Yeast
Memphis, TN 866-920-9885
Andre's Confiserie Suisse
Kansas City, MO. 800-892-1234
Andre-Boudin Bakeries
San Francisco, CA 415-882-1849
Ann Hemyng Candy Inc
Trumbauersville, PA 800-779-7004
Aunt Aggie De's Pralines
Sinton, TX. 800-333-9354
BakeMark Canada
Laval, QC 800-361-4998
Barkeater Chocolates
North Creek, NY. 518-251-4438
Barry Callebaut USA
Chicago, IL. 866-443-0460
Blommer Chocolate Co
Chicago, IL. 800-621-1606
Blommer Chocolate Co
East Greenville, PA. 800-825-8181
Blue Marble Brands
Providence, RI 888-534-0246
Boyd's Coffee Co
Portland, OR 800-735-2878
Bread & Chocolate Inc
Wells River, VT 800-524-6715
Brookema Company
West Chicago, IL 630-562-2290
Calico Cottage
Amityville, NY 800-645-5345
Cambridge Brands Inc
Cambridge, MA 617-491-2500
Campbell Soup Co.
Camden, NJ. 800-257-8443
Caprine Estates
Bellbrook, OH. 937-848-7406
Carrie's Chocolates
Edmonton, AB 877-778-2462
Chatz Roasting Co
Ceres, CA 209-541-1100
Chocolat Belge Heyez
St-Lazare-De-Bellechasse, QC. 450-653-5616
Chocolat Jean Talon
Montreal, QC 888-333-8540
Chocolate Street of Hartville
Hartville, OH 888-853-5904
Chocolaterie Bernard Callebaut
Calgary, AB. 800-661-8367
Chocolates by Mark
Houston, TX 832-736-2626
Cloud Nine
Claremont, CA 909-624-3147
CocoaPlanet Inc.
Sonoma, CA 650-454-0757
Consolidated Mills Inc
Houston, TX 713-896-4196
Creative Cotton
Northbrook, IL 847-291-4128
Crown Candy Corp
Macon, GA 800-241-3529
Davidson's Organics
Reno, NV 800-882-5888
Donells Candies
Casper, WY. 877-461-2009
Doscher's Candies Co.
Cincinnati, OH 513-381-8656
ECOM Agroindustrial Corporation Ltd
Pully,
Equal Exchange Inc
West Bridgewater, MA 774-776-7400
Erba Food Products
Brooklyn, NY 718-272-7700
Foley's Chocolates & Candies
Richmond, BC 888-236-5397
Forbes Chocolate BP
Broadview Hts, OH. 440-838-4400
G Debbas Chocolatier
Fresno, CA 559-294-2071
Gel Spice Co LLC
Bayonne, NJ 800-922-0230
Georgia Nut Co
Skokie, IL. 877-674-2993
Germack Pistachio Co
Detroit, MI 800-872-4006
Ghirardelli Chocolate Co
San Leandro, CA. 800-877-9338
GKI Foods
Brighton, MI 248-486-0055
Godiva Chocolatier
New York, NY 800-946-3482
Govatos Chocolates
Wilmington, DE 888-799-5252
Hauser Chocolates
Westerly, RI. 888-599-8231
Hebert Candies
Shrewsbury, MA 866-609-6533
Herb Patch of Vermont
Bellows Falls, VT. 800-282-4372
Hershey Co.
Hershey, PA. 800-468-1714
Hialeah Products Co
Hollywood, FL 800-923-3379
Home Bakery
Rochester, MI 248-651-4830
Homefree LLC
Windham, NH. 800-552-7172
Jason & Son Specialty Foods
Rancho Cordova, CA 800-810-9093
Jenny's Country Kitchen
Dover, MN 800-357-3497
JER Creative Food Concepts, Inc.
Commerce, CA 800-350-2462
King Arthur Flour
Norwich, VT. 800-827-6836
King Cupboard
Red Lodge, MT. 800-962-6555
Koeze Company
Grand Rapids, MI 800-555-9688
Loghouse Foods
Minneapolis, MN 763-546-8395
Magna Foods Corporation
City of Industry, CA 800-995-4394
Marich Confectionery
Hollister, CA. 800-624-7055
Martha Olson's Great Foo
Sutter Creek, CA. 800-973-3966
Mc Steven's Coca Factory Store
Vancouver, WA 800-547-2803
Merlin Candies
Harahan, LA 800-899-1549
Michelle Chocolatiers
Colorado Springs, CO. 888-447-3654
Monster Cone
Montreal, QC 800-542-9801
Nantucket Tea Traders
Nantucket, MA 508-325-0203
Natra US
Chula Vista, CA 800-262-6216
New Organics
Kenwood, CA 734-677-5570
Niagara Chocolates
Buffalo, NY. 877-261-7887
Nora's Candy Shop
Rome, NY. 888-544-8224
OH Chocolate
Seattle, WA 206-329-8777
Olam Spices
Fresno, CA 559-447-1390
Olivier's Candies
Calgary, AB. 403-266-6028
Paulaur Corp
Cranbury, NJ. 609-395-8844
Phillips Syrup Corp
Cleveland, OH 800-350-8443
Pine River Pre-Pack Inc
Newton, WI. 920-726-4216
Plantation Candies
Telford, PA 888-678-6468
Quality Naturally Foods
City Of Industry, CA. 888-498-6986
R.M. Palmer Co.
West Reading, PA 610-372-8971
Rapunzel Pure Organics
Bloomfield, NJ 800-225-1449
Riddles' Sweet Impressions
Edmonton, AB 780-465-8085
Service Packing Company
Vancouver, BC 604-681-0264
Setton International Foods
Commack, NY 800-227-4397
Stevens Creative Enterprises, Inc.
New York, NY 646-558-6336
Sturm Foods Inc
Manawa, WI 800-347-8876
Sucesores de Pedro Cortes
Hato Rey, PR. 787-754-7040
Sweenors Chocolates
Wakefield, RI 800-834-3123
Taza Chocolate
Somerville, MA 617-623-0804
Terri Lynn Inc
Elgin, IL 800-323-0775
Timber Peaks Gourmet
Parker, CO. 800-982-7687
Tom & Sally's Handmade Chocolates
Brattleboro, VT. 800-827-0800
Top Hat Co Inc
Wilmette, IL 847-256-6565
Tova Industries LLC
Louisville, KY 888-532-8682
Vande Walle's Candies Inc
Appleton, WI 800-738-1020
Varda Chocolatier
Elizabeth, NJ. 800-448-2732
Vigneri Chocolate Inc.
Rochester, NY. 877-844-6374
White Coffee Corporation
Long Island City, NY 800-221-0140
Wilbur Chocolate Candy
Lititz, PA. 888-294-5287
Williamsburg Chocolatier
Williamsburg, VA 757-253-1474

Wisconsin Cheeseman
Madison, WI 800-693-0834

Cocoa Bean

Blommer Chocolate Co
Chicago, IL 800-621-1606
Ghirardelli Chocolate Co
San Leandro, CA 800-877-9338

Fudge

BakeMark Ingredients Canada
Richmond, BC 800-665-9441
Blommer Chocolate Co
Chicago, IL 800-621-1606
Calico Cottage
Amityville, NY 800-645-5345
Original Herkimer Cheese
Ilion, NY 315-895-7428
Solo Foods
Countryside, IL 800-328-7656

Confectionery

Confectioners Crunch

Bon Courage Gourmet
Durham, NC 888-865-5841
Cocomira Confections
Toronto, ON 866-413-9049
Island Princess
Honolulu, HI 866-872-8601
Plush Puffs Marshmallows
Burbank, CA 818-784-2931

Confectionery

1000 Islands River Rat Cheese
Clayton, NY 800-752-1341
Aglamesis Bros Ice Cream
Cincinnati, OH 513-531-5196
Amcan Industries
Elmsford, NY 914-347-4838
American Almond Products Co
Brooklyn, NY 800-825-6663
American Food Products Inc
Methuen, MA 978-682-1855
American Key Food Products Inc
Closter, NJ 877-263-7539
American Licorice
La Porte, IL 866-442-2783
Ames International Inc
Fife, WA 888-469-2637
Andre's Confiserie Suisse
Kansas City, MO 800-892-1234
Andrews Caramel Apples
Chicago, IL 800-305-3004
Andros Foods North America
Mount Jackson, VA 844-426-3767
Ann Hemyng Candy Inc
Trumbauersville, PA 800-779-7004
Arway Confections Inc
Chicago, IL 800-695-0612
Aunt Aggie De's Pralines
Sinton, TX 800-333-9354
Baker Candy Company
Snohomish, WA 425-422-6331
Bazzini Holdings LLC
Allentown, PA 610-366-1606
Beehive Botanicals
Hayward, WI 800-233-4483
Bestco Inc
Mooresville, NC 704-664-4300
Betty Jane Homemade Candy
Dubuque, IA 800-642-1254
Betty Lou's
McMinnville, OR 800-242-5205
Bissinger's Handcrafted Chocolatier
St. Louis, MO 314-615-2400
Blanton's
Frankfort, KY 502-223-9874
Blommer Chocolate Co
East Greenville, PA 800-825-8181
Boca Bons East
Greenacres, FL 800-314-2835
Bodega Chocolates
Fountain Valley, CA 888-326-3342
Brennan Snacks Manufacturing
Bogalusa, LA 800-290-7486
Brittle Kittle
Tigard, OR 800-447-2128
Brookside Foods
Abbotsford, BC 800-468-1714
Burke Candy Ingredients Inc
Milwaukee, WI 888-287-5350
Byrne & Carlson
Portsmouth, NH 888-559-9778
Byrnes & Kiefer Company
Callery, PA 724-538-5200
C Howard Co
Bellport, NY 631-286-7940
Cambridge Brands Inc
Cambridge, MA 617-491-2500
Campbell Soup Co.
Camden, NJ 800-257-8443
Canelake's Candy
Virginia, MN 888-928-8889
Caprine Estates
Bellbrook, OH 937-848-7406
Carrie's Chocolates
Edmonton, AB 877-778-2462
Casani Candy Company
Pennsauken, NJ 856-488-0045
Catoris Candies Inc
New Kensington, PA 724-335-4371
Charlotte's Confections
Millbrae, CA 800-798-2427
Chase & Poe Candy Co
St Joseph, MO 800-786-1625
Cheese Straws & More
Monroe, LA 800-997-1921
Chex Finer Foods Inc
Mansfield, MA 800-227-8114
Chocolat Belge Heyez
St-Lazare-De-Bellechasse, QC 450-653-5616
Chocolat Jean Talon
Montreal, QC 888-333-8540
Chocolate Street of Hartville
Hartville, OH 888-853-5904
Chocolates by Mark
Houston, TX 832-736-2626
Chocolati Handmade Chocolates
Seattle, WA 206-784-5212
Chris Candies Inc
Pittsburgh, PA 412-322-9400
Christopher Norman Chocolates
Hudson, NY 518-822-0300
Clasen Quality Chocolate
Madison, WI 877-459-4500
Cloud Nine
Claremont, CA 909-624-3147
Concord Foods, LLC
Brockton, MA 508-580-1700
Confectionately Yours LTD
Buffalo Grove, IL 800-875-6978
Creative Cotton
Northbrook, IL 847-291-4128
Creme Curls
Hudsonville, MI 800-466-1219
Creole Delicacies Gourmet Shop
New Orleans, LA 504-525-9508
Crown Candy Corp
Macon, GA 800-241-3529
CTC Manufacturing
Calgary, AB 800-668-7677
Cummings Studio Chocolates
Salt Lake City, UT 800-537-3957
Cupid Candies
Chicago, IL 773-925-8191
David Bradley Chocolatier
Windsor, NJ 877-289-7933
Day Spring Enterprises
Cheektowaga, NY 800-879-7677
Daymar Select Fine Coffees
El Cajon, CA 800-466-7590
Decko Products Inc
Sandusky, OH 800-537-6143
Dessert Innovations Inc
Atlanta, GA 800-359-7351
Dillon Candy Co
Boston, GA 800-382-8338
Dipasa USA Inc
Brownsville, TX 956-831-4072
DMH Ingredients Inc
Libertyville, IL 847-362-9977
Dolphin Natural Chocolates
Cambria, CA 800-236-5744
Donaldson's Finer Chocolates
Lebanon, IN 800-975-7236
Donells Candies
Casper, WY 877-461-2009
Doscher's Candies Co.
Cincinnati, OH 513-381-8656
Doumak Inc
Elk Grove Village, IL 800-323-0318
Downeast Candies
Boothbay Harbor, ME 207-633-5178
Dyna Tabs LLC
Brooklyn, NY 718-376-6084
EcoNatural Solutions
Boulder, CO 303-357-5682
Eda's Sugar Free
Philadelphia, PA 215-324-3412
Edison Grainery
Benicia, CA 510-382-0202
Edward & Sons Trading Co
Carpinteria, CA 805-684-8500
El Brands
Ozark, AL 334-445-2828
Elmer Chocolate®
Ponchatoula, LA 800-843-9537
Enstrom Candies, Inc.
Grand Junction, CO 800-367-8766
Fantazzmo Fun Stuff
Schaumburg, IL 847-413-4036
Faroh Candies
Middleburg Heights, OH 440-888-9866
Farr Candy Company
Idaho Falls, ID 208-522-8215
Fernando C Pujals & Bros
Guaynabo, PR 787-792-3080
Ferrara Bakery & Cafe
New York, NY 212-226-6150
Ferrara Candy Co Inc
Chicago, IL 800-323-1768
Fitzkee's Candies Inc
York, PA 717-741-1031
FNI Group LLC
Sherborn, MA 508-655-4175
Forbes Candies
Virginia Beach, VA 800-626-5898
Frankford Candy & Chocolate Co
Philadelphia, PA 800-523-9090
FrutStix
Santa Barbara, CA 805-965-1656
Fudge Farms
Buchanan, MI 800-874-0261
G Debbas Chocolatier
Fresno, CA 559-294-2071
G Scaccianoce & Co
Bronx, NY 718-991-4462
Gardners Candies Inc
Tyrone, PA 800-242-2639
Gene & Boots Candies Inc
Perryopolis, PA 800-864-4222
Georgia Nut Co
Skokie, IL 877-674-2993
Germack Pistachio Co
Detroit, MI 800-872-4006
Gimbals Fine Candies
S San Francisco, CA 800-344-6225
GKI Foods
Brighton, MI 248-486-0055
Godiva Chocolatier
New York, NY 800-946-3482
Golden Fluff Popcorn Co
Lakewood, NJ 732-367-5448
Goodart Candy Inc
Lubbock, TX 806-747-2600
Govatos Chocolates
Wilmington, DE 888-799-5252
Gray & Company
Hart, MI 800-551-6009
Green Mountain Chocolate Inc
Franklin, MA 508-520-7160
Greenwell Farms Inc
Kealakekua, HI 888-592-5662
Groovy Candies
Cleveland, OH 888-729-1960
Gurley's Foods
Willmar, MN 800-426-7845
GWB Foods Corporation
Brooklyn, NY 877-977-7610
H.B. Trading
Totowa, NJ 973-812-1022
Haby's Alsatian Bakery
Castroville, TX 830-538-2118
Happy Hive
Dearborn Heights, MI 313-562-3707
Harlow House Company
Atlanta, GA 404-325-1270
Hauser Chocolates
Westerly, RI 888-599-8231
Haven's Candies
Westbrook, ME 800-639-6309
Hawaii Candy Inc
Honolulu, HI 800-303-2507

Hebert Candies
Shrewsbury, MA 866-609-6533
Hershey Co.
Hershey, PA 800-468-1714
Hialeah Products Co
Hollywood, FL 800-923-3379
Hillside Candy Co
Hillside, NJ 800-524-1304
Holistic Products Corporation
Englewood, NJ 800-221-0308
Hospitality Mints LLC
Boone, NC 800-334-5181
Imuraya USA
Irvine, CA 949-251-9205
J.A.M.B. Low Carb Distributor
Pompano Beach, FL 800-708-6738
James Candy Company
Atlantic City, NJ 800-441-1404
Jason & Son Specialty Foods
Rancho Cordova, CA 800-810-9093
JER Creative Food Concepts, Inc.
Commerce, CA 800-350-2462
Joe Clark Fund Raising Candies
Tarentum, PA 888-459-9520
Jomart Chocolates
Brooklyn, NY 718-375-1277
Joyva Corp
Brooklyn, NY 718-497-0170
Judy's Cream Caramels
Sherwood, OR 503-625-7161
Kay Foods Co
Detroit, MI 313-393-1100
Kemach Food Products
Brooklyn, NY 718-272-5655
Key III Candies
Fort Wayne, IN 800-752-2382
Kloss Manufacturing Co Inc
Allentown, PA 800-445-7100
Knudsen Candy
Hayward, CA 800-736-6887
Koeze Company
Grand Rapids, MI 800-555-9688
Kolatin Real Kosher Gelatin
Lakewood, NJ 732-364-8700
Koppers Chocolate
Cranford, NJ 800-325-0026
Lanco
Hauppauge, NY 800-938-4500
Landies Candies Co
Buffalo, NY 800-955-2634
Lang's Chocolates
Williamsport, PA 570-323-6320
Laura Paige Candy Company
Newburgh, NY 845-566-4209
Layman Distributing
Salem, VA 800-237-1319
Leader Candies
Brooklyn, NY 718-366-6900
Lerro Candy Company
Darby, PA 610-461-8886
Loghouse Foods
Minneapolis, MN 763-546-8395
Long Grove Confectionary
Buffalo Grove, IL 800-373-3102
Lou-Retta's Custom Chocolates
Buffalo, NY 716-833-7111
Louis J Rheb Candy Co
Baltimore, MD 800-514-8293
Lowery's Home Made Candies
Muncie, IN 800-541-3340
Lukas Confections
York, PA 717-843-0921
Mac Farms Of Hawaii Inc
Captain Cook, HI 808-328-2435
Magna Foods Corporation
City of Industry, CA 800-995-4394
Manhattan Food Brands, LLC
Metuchen, NJ 732-906-2168
Maple Grove Farms Of Vermont
St Johnsbury, VT 802-748-5141
Mari's Candy
Chicago, IL 773-254-3351
Marich Confectionery
Hollister, CA 800-624-7055
Maries Candies
West Liberty, OH 866-465-5781
Mary of Puddin Hill
Palestine, TX 800-545-8889
MarySue.com
Baltimore, MD 800-662-2639
Marzipan Specialties Inc
Nashville, TN 615-226-4800

Matangos Candies
Harrisburg, PA 717-234-0882
Maxfield Candy
Salt Lake City, UT 800-288-8002
Merb's Candies
St Louis, MO 314-832-7117
Merlin Candies
Harahan, LA 800-899-1549
Michael Mootz Candies
Hanover Twp, PA 570-823-8272
Michelle Chocolatiers
Colorado Springs, CO 888-447-3654
Midwest Nut Co
Minneapolis, MN 800-328-5502
Milsolv Corporation
Butler, WI 800-558-8501
Milton A. Klein Company
New York, NY 800-221-0248
Mitch Chocolate
Melville, NY 631-777-2400
Mitsubishi Chemical Holdings
New York, NY 212-672-9400
Moore's Candies
Baltimore, MD 410-836-8840
Mrs Annie's Peanut Patch
Floresville, TX 830-393-7845
Multiflex Company
Hawthorne, NJ 973-636-9700
Munson's Chocolates
Bolton, CT 888-686-7667
Muth's Candy Store
Louisville, KY 502-582-2639
My Daddy's Cheesecake
Cape Girardeau, MO 800-735-6765
MYNTZ!
Kent, WA 800-800-9490
Nature's Candy
Fredericksburg, TX 800-729-0085
Naylor Candies Inc
Mt Wolf, PA 717-266-2706
New Century Snacks
City of Commerce, CA 800-688-6887
Niagara Chocolates
Buffalo, NY 877-261-7887
Nora's Candy Shop
Rome, NY 888-544-8224
Northwest Chocolate Factory
Salem, OR 503-362-1340
Northwoods Candy Emporium
Branson, MO 417-332-1010
Nunes Farms Marketing
Gustine, CA 209-862-3033
OCG Cacao
Whitinsville, MA 888-482-2226
OH Chocolate
Seattle, WA 206-329-8777
Old Time Candy Co
Lagrange, OH 440-355-4345
Olde Tyme Food Corporation
East Longmeadow, MA 800-356-6533
Olde Tyme Mercantile
Arroyo Grande, CA 805-489-7991
Ole Smoky Candy Kitchen
Gatlinburg, TN 865-436-4716
Olivier's Candies
Calgary, AB 403-266-6028
Palmer Candy Co
Sioux City, IA 800-831-0828
Parker Products
Fort Worth, TX 817-336-7441
Parkside Candy Co
Buffalo, NY 716-833-7540
Paulaur Corp
Cranbury, NJ 609-395-8844
Peanut Patch Gift Shop
Courtland, VA 800-544-0896
Pecan Deluxe Candy Co
Dallas, TX 800-733-3589
Pez Candy Inc
Orange, CT 203-795-0531
Pfizer
New York, NY 800-879-3477
Philadelphia Candies Inc
Hermitage, PA 724-981-6341
Phillip's Candy House
Dorchester, MA 617-282-2090
Pine River Pre-Pack Inc
Newton, WI 920-726-4216
Pioneer Marketing International
Los Gatos, CA 408-356-4990
Plaidberry Company
Vista, CA 760-727-5403

Plantation Candies
Telford, PA 888-678-6468
Popcorn Connection
North Hollywood, CA 800-852-2676
Poppers Supply Company
Allentown, PA 800-457-9810
Priester's Pecans
Fort Deposit, AL 866-477-4736
Prince of Peace
Hayward, CA 800-732-2328
Produits Alimentaire
St Lambert De Lauzon, QC 800-463-1787
Pulakos 926 Chocolate
Erie, PA 814-452-4026
Quigley Industries Inc
Farmington, MI 800-367-2441
R.M. Palmer Co.
West Reading, PA 610-372-8971
Rebecca-Ruth Candy Factory
Frankfort, KY 800-444-3866
Richards Maple Products
Chardon, OH 800-352-4052
Ricos Candy Snack & Bakery
Hialeah, FL 305-885-7392
Riddles' Sweet Impressions
Edmonton, AB 780-465-8085
Rito Mints
Trois Rivieres, QC 819-379-1449
Rivard Popcorn Products
Lancaster, PA 717-898-7131
Rosalind Candy Castle Inc
New Brighton, PA 724-843-1144
Ross Fine Candies
Waterford, MI 248-682-5640
Ruth Hunt Candy Co
Mt Sterling, KY 800-927-0302
S Zitner Co
Philadelphia, PA 215-229-9828
Salem Old Fashioned Candies
Salem, MA 978-744-3242
Sally Lane's Candy Farm
Paris, TN 731-642-5801
Scott's Candy
Glennville, GA 800-356-2100
See's Candies
Carson, CA 800-347-7337
Senor Murphy Candymaker
Santa Fe, NM 877-988-4311
Sensational Sweets
Lewisburg, PA 570-524-4361
Shane Candy Co
Philadelphia, PA 215-922-1048
Sherm Edwards Candies
Trafford, PA 800-436-5424
Signature Brands LLC
Ocala, FL 800-456-9573
Simply Gourmet Confections
Irvine, CA 714-505-3955
Smarties
Union, NJ 800-631-7968
Snackerz
Commerce, CA 888-576-2253
Somerset Syrup & Concessions
Edison, NJ 800-526-8865
Southern Style Nuts
Denison, TX 903-463-3161
Splendid Specialties
Petaluma, CA 707-796-7800
Star Kay White Inc
Congers, NY 800-874-8518
Stark Candy Company
Revere, MA 800-225-5508
Startupcandy Co
Provo, UT 801-373-8673
Stichler Products Inc
Reading, PA 610-921-0211
Stone's Home Made Candy Shop
Oswego, NY 888-223-3928
Stutz Candy Company
Philadelphia, PA 888-692-2639
Sucesores de Pedro Cortes
Hato Rey, PR 787-754-7040
Sweenors Chocolates
Wakefield, RI 800-834-3123
Sweet City Supply
Virginia Beach, VA 888-793-3824
Taste of Nature Inc.
Santa Monica, CA 310-396-4433
Taste Teasers
Dallas, TX 800-526-1840
Temo Candy
Akron, OH 330-376-7229

Texas Toffee
Odessa, TX 800-599-2133
Todd's
Vernon, CA 800-938-6337
Tom & Sally's Handmade Chocolates
Brattleboro, VT 800-827-0800
Torn & Glasser
Los Angeles, CA 800-282-6887
Torn Ranch
Novato, CA 707-796-7800
Tropical Foods
Charlotte, NC 800-438-4470
Tropical Foods
Lithia Springs, GA 800-544-3762
Tropical Nut & Fruit Co
Orlando, FL 800-749-8869
Tropical Nut Fruit & Bulk Cndy
Lithia Springs, GA 800-544-3762
Vande Walle's Candies Inc
Appleton, WI 800-738-1020
Varda Chocolatier
Elizabeth, NJ 800-448-2732
Vigneri Chocolate Inc.
Rochester, NY 877-844-6374
Virginia Diner Inc
Wakefield, VA 888-823-4637
Warner Candy
El Paso, TX 847-928-7200
Warrell Corp
Camp Hill, PA 844-234-3217
Weaver Nut Co. Inc.
Ephrata, PA 800-473-2688
Weaver Popcorn Co Inc
Van Buren, IN
Webb's Candy
Davenport, FL 800-289-9322
Wedding Cake Studio
Williamsfield, OH 440-667-1765
Westbrae Natural Foods
Melville, NY 800-434-4246
Whetstone Chocolates
St Augustine, FL 877-261-7887
White-Stokes Company
Chicago, IL 800-978-6537
Wilbur Chocolate Candy
Lititz, PA 888-294-5287
Williamsburg Chocolatier
Williamsburg, VA 757-253-1474
Wilson Candy Co
Jeannette, PA 724-523-3151
Wilson's Fantastic Candy
Memphis, TN 901-767-1900
Winans Chocolates & Coffees
Piqua, OH 937-381-0247
Wisconsin Cheeseman
Madison, WI 800-693-0834
World Confections Inc
South Orange, NJ 718-768-8100
Wright's Ice Cream Co
Cayuga, IN 800-686-9561
Yamate Chocolatier
Highland Park, NJ 800-433-2462
Yost Candy Co Inc
Dalton, OH 800-750-1976
Z Specialty Food, LLC
Woodland, CA 800-678-1226

Decorations & Icings

Decorations

Baking

Byrnes & Kiefer Company
Callery, PA 724-538-5200
Jomart Chocolates
Brooklyn, NY 718-375-1277
King Arthur Flour
Norwich, VT 800-827-6836
L&M Bakers Supply Company
Toronto, ON 800-465-7361
Satin Fine Foods
Chester, NY
Signature Brands LLC
Ocala, FL 800-456-9573

Cake

Adams Foods & Milling
Dothan, AL 334-983-4233
American Key Food Products Inc
Closter, NJ 877-263-7539
BakeMark Canada
Laval, QC 800-361-4998
Byrnes & Kiefer Company
Callery, PA 724-538-5200
Decko Products Inc
Sandusky, OH 800-537-6143
Erba Food Products
Brooklyn, NY 718-272-7700
Jomart Chocolates
Brooklyn, NY 718-375-1277
King Arthur Flour
Norwich, VT 800-827-6836
L&M Bakers Supply Company
Toronto, ON 800-465-7361
Multiflex Company
Hawthorne, NJ 973-636-9700
Paulaur Corp
Cranbury, NJ 609-395-8844
Petra International
Mississauga, ON 800-261-7226
Signature Brands LLC
Ocala, FL 800-456-9573
Sugar Flowers Plus
Glendale, CA 800-972-2935

Icings

BakeMark Canada
Laval, QC 800-361-4998
BakeMark Ingredients Canada
Richmond, BC 800-665-9441
Byrnes & Kiefer Company
Callery, PA 724-538-5200
Chelsea Milling Co.
Chelsea, MI 800-727-2460
Creme Unlimited
Matteson, IL 800-227-3637
Erba Food Products
Brooklyn, NY 718-272-7700
Lawrence Foods Inc
Elk Grove Village, IL 847-437-2400
Louisiana Gourmet Enterprises
Houma, LA 800-328-5586
Mimac Glaze
Brampton, ON 877-990-9975
Newport Flavours & Fragrances
Orange, CA 714-744-3700
Parrish's Cake Decorating
Gardena, CA 800-736-8443
Quality Naturally Foods
City Of Industry, CA 888-498-6986
Ribus Inc.
St. Louis, MO 314-727-4287
Snelgrove Ice Cream Company
Salt Lake City, UT 800-569-0005
Solo Foods
Countryside, IL 800-328-7656
Warwick Ice Cream
Warwick, RI 401-821-8403
Westco-BakeMark
Pico Rivera, CA 562-949-1054

Ready to Use

Presto Avoset Group
Claremont, CA 909-399-0062

Specialty-Packaged Candy

Bagged

American Licorice
La Porte, IL 866-442-2783
Ann Hemyng Candy Inc
Trumbauersville, PA 800-779-7004
Blommer Chocolate Co
Chicago, IL 800-621-1606
Cambridge Brands Inc
Cambridge, MA 617-491-2500
Chase & Poe Candy Co
St Joseph, MO 800-786-1625
Crown Candy Corp
Macon, GA 800-241-3529
David Bradley Chocolatier
Windsor, NJ 877-289-7933
Eda's Sugar Free
Philadelphia, PA 215-324-3412
Ganong Bros Ltd
Moncton, NB 506-389-7898
GKI Foods
Brighton, MI 248-486-0055
Hialeah Products Co
Hollywood, FL 800-923-3379
Hillside Candy Co
Hillside, NJ 800-524-1304
Joyva Corp
Brooklyn, NY 718-497-0170
Kerr Brothers
Toronto, ON 416-252-7341
Leader Candies
Brooklyn, NY 718-366-6900
Ludwick's Frozen Donuts
Grand Rapids, MI 800-366-8816
Lukas Confections
York, PA 717-843-0921
Olde Tyme Mercantile
Arroyo Grande, CA 805-489-7991
Papas Chris A & Son Co
Covington, KY 859-431-0499
Piedmont Candy Co
Lexington, NC 336-248-2477
Quigley Industries Inc
Farmington, MI 800-367-2441
Salem Old Fashioned Candies
Salem, MA 978-744-3242
Suity Confections Co
Miami, FL 305-639-3300
Weaver Nut Co. Inc.
Ephrata, PA 800-473-2688
Webb's Candy
Davenport, FL 800-289-9322
World Confections Inc
South Orange, NJ 718-768-8100
Yost Candy Co Inc
Dalton, OH 800-750-1976

Boxed

Anastasia Confections Inc
Orlando, FL 800-329-7100
Anthony Thomas Candy Co
Columbus, OH 877-226-3921
Arcor USA
Coral Gables, FL 800-572-7267
Astor Chocolate Corp
Lakewood, NJ 732-901-1001
Baraboo Candy Co LLC
Baraboo, WI 800-967-1690
Best Chocolate In Town
Indianapolis, IN 888-294-2378
Blanton's
Frankfort, KY 502-223-9874
Blommer Chocolate Co
East Greenville, PA 800-825-8181
Boyer Candy Co Inc
Altoona, PA 814-944-9401
Calico Cottage
Amityville, NY 800-645-5345
Chocolate House
Milwaukee, WI 800-236-2022
Ghirardelli Chocolate Co
San Leandro, CA 800-877-9338
GKI Foods
Brighton, MI 248-486-0055
MarySue.com
Baltimore, MD 800-662-2639
Ruth Hunt Candy Co
Mt Sterling, KY 800-927-0302
Scott's Candy
Glennville, GA 800-356-2100
Terri Lynn Inc
Elgin, IL 800-323-0775

Christmas

Bee International
Chula Vista, CA 800-421-6465
Blanton's
Frankfort, KY 502-223-9874
Charlotte's Confections
Millbrae, CA 800-798-2427
Chase & Poe Candy Co
St Joseph, MO 800-786-1625
Chocolat Jean Talon
Montreal, QC 888-333-8540
David Bradley Chocolatier
Windsor, NJ 877-289-7933
Day Spring Enterprises
Cheektowaga, NY 800-879-7677
Doscher's Candies Co.
Cincinnati, OH 513-381-8656
Ferrara Bakery & Cafe
New York, NY 212-226-6150
Gimbals Fine Candies
S San Francisco, CA 800-344-6225

GKI Foods
Brighton, MI 248-486-0055
Groovy Candies
Cleveland, OH 888-729-1960
Haven's Candies
Westbrook, ME 800-639-6309
Kerr Brothers
Toronto, ON 416-252-7341
Landies Candies Co
Buffalo, NY 800-955-2634
Leader Candies
Brooklyn, NY 718-366-6900
Lukas Confections
York, PA 717-843-0921
Madrona Specialty Foods LLC
Seattle, WA 425-656-2997
Old Dominion Peanut Corp
Norfolk, VA 800-368-6887
Papas Chris A & Son Co
Covington, KY 859-431-0499
Piedmont Candy Co
Lexington, NC 336-248-2477
R.M. Palmer Co.
West Reading, PA 610-372-8971
Setton International Foods
Commack, NY 800-227-4397
Shane Candy Co
Philadelphia, PA 215-922-1048
World Confections Inc
South Orange, NJ 718-768-8100
Zachary Confections Inc
Frankfort, IN 800-445-4222

Easter

Bee International
Chula Vista, CA 800-421-6465
Blanton's
Frankfort, KY 502-223-9874
Charlotte's Confections
Millbrae, CA 800-798-2427
Chase & Poe Candy Co
St Joseph, MO 800-786-1625
Chocolat Jean Talon
Montreal, QC 888-333-8540
David Bradley Chocolatier
Windsor, NJ 877-289-7933
Day Spring Enterprises
Cheektowaga, NY 800-879-7677
Doscher's Candies Co.
Cincinnati, OH 513-381-8656
Ferrara Bakery & Cafe
New York, NY 212-226-6150
Gimbals Fine Candies
S San Francisco, CA 800-344-6225
GKI Foods
Brighton, MI 248-486-0055
Golden Fluff Popcorn Co
Lakewood, NJ 732-367-5448
Groovy Candies
Cleveland, OH 888-729-1960
Leader Candies
Brooklyn, NY 718-366-6900
Madrona Specialty Foods LLC
Seattle, WA 425-656-2997
Multiflex Company
Hawthorne, NJ 973-636-9700
Papas Chris A & Son Co
Covington, KY 859-431-0499
Piedmont Candy Co
Lexington, NC 336-248-2477
R.M. Palmer Co.
West Reading, PA 610-372-8971
S Zitner Co
Philadelphia, PA 215-229-9828
Vande Walle's Candies Inc
Appleton, WI 800-738-1020
Vigneri Chocolate Inc.
Rochester, NY 877-844-6374
World Confections Inc
South Orange, NJ 718-768-8100
Zachary Confections Inc
Frankfort, IN 800-445-4222

Fund Raising

Chase & Poe Candy Co
St Joseph, MO 800-786-1625
David Bradley Chocolatier
Windsor, NJ 877-289-7933
Hillside Candy Co
Hillside, NJ 800-524-1304
Joe Clark Fund Raising Candies
Tarentum, PA 888-459-9520
Joyva Corp
Brooklyn, NY 718-497-0170
Koeze Company
Grand Rapids, MI 800-555-9688
Leader Candies
Brooklyn, NY 718-366-6900
Lukas Confections
York, PA 717-843-0921
Old Dominion Peanut Corp
Norfolk, VA 800-368-6887
Papas Chris A & Son Co
Covington, KY 859-431-0499
Quigley Industries Inc
Farmington, MI 800-367-2441
Terri Lynn Inc
Elgin, IL 800-323-0775
Vande Walle's Candies Inc
Appleton, WI 800-738-1020

Halloween

Astor Chocolate Corp
Lakewood, NJ 732-901-1001
Bee International
Chula Vista, CA 800-421-6465
Blanton's
Frankfort, KY 502-223-9874
Charlotte's Confections
Millbrae, CA 800-798-2427
Chase & Poe Candy Co
St Joseph, MO 800-786-1625
Chocolat Jean Talon
Montreal, QC 888-333-8540
David Bradley Chocolatier
Windsor, NJ 877-289-7933
Day Spring Enterprises
Cheektowaga, NY 800-879-7677
Ferrara Bakery & Cafe
New York, NY 212-226-6150
Gimbals Fine Candies
S San Francisco, CA 800-344-6225
GKI Foods
Brighton, MI 248-486-0055
Groovy Candies
Cleveland, OH 888-729-1960
Joyva Corp
Brooklyn, NY 718-497-0170
Kerr Brothers
Toronto, ON 416-252-7341
Leader Candies
Brooklyn, NY 718-366-6900
Lukas Confections
York, PA 717-843-0921
Madrona Specialty Foods LLC
Seattle, WA 425-656-2997
Piedmont Candy Co
Lexington, NC 336-248-2477
R.M. Palmer Co.
West Reading, PA 610-372-8971
Shane Candy Co
Philadelphia, PA 215-922-1048
World Confections Inc
South Orange, NJ 718-768-8100
Yost Candy Co Inc
Dalton, OH 800-750-1976
Zachary Confections Inc
Frankfort, IN 800-445-4222

Multi-Packs

World Confections Inc
South Orange, NJ 718-768-8100

Non-Chocolate - Boxed

Hillside Candy Co
Hillside, NJ 800-524-1304

Leader Candies
Brooklyn, NY 718-366-6900
Moore's Candies
Baltimore, MD 410-836-8840
Ozone Confectioners & Bakers Supplies
Elmwood Park, NJ 201-791-4444
Webb's Candy
Davenport, FL 800-289-9322

Packaged for Racks

American Licorice
La Porte, IL 866-442-2783
David Bradley Chocolatier
Windsor, NJ 877-289-7933
Jason & Son Specialty Foods
Rancho Cordova, CA 800-810-9093
Joyva Corp
Brooklyn, NY 718-497-0170
Setton International Foods
Commack, NY 800-227-4397
Sherbrooke OEM Ltd
Sherbrooke, QC 866-851-2579
Weaver Nut Co. Inc.
Ephrata, PA 800-473-2688

Packaged for Theaters

American Licorice
La Porte, IL 866-442-2783
Joyva Corp
Brooklyn, NY 718-497-0170

Valentine

Arway Confections Inc
Chicago, IL 800-695-0612
Astor Chocolate Corp
Lakewood, NJ 732-901-1001
Bee International
Chula Vista, CA 800-421-6465
Blanton's
Frankfort, KY 502-223-9874
Charlotte's Confections
Millbrae, CA 800-798-2427
Chase & Poe Candy Co
St Joseph, MO 800-786-1625
David Bradley Chocolatier
Windsor, NJ 877-289-7933
Day Spring Enterprises
Cheektowaga, NY 800-879-7677
Ferrara Bakery & Cafe
New York, NY 212-226-6150
Gimbals Fine Candies
S San Francisco, CA 800-344-6225
Groovy Candies
Cleveland, OH 888-729-1960
Leader Candies
Brooklyn, NY 718-366-6900
R.M. Palmer Co.
West Reading, PA 610-372-8971
Rito Mints
Trois Rivieres, QC 819-379-1449
Shane Candy Co
Philadelphia, PA 215-922-1048
Vande Walle's Candies Inc
Appleton, WI 800-738-1020
World Confections Inc
South Orange, NJ 718-768-8100
Zachary Confections Inc
Frankfort, IN 800-445-4222

Vending

Chase & Poe Candy Co
St Joseph, MO 800-786-1625
GKI Foods
Brighton, MI 248-486-0055
Joyva Corp
Brooklyn, NY 718-497-0170
Lukas Confections
York, PA 717-843-0921
Papas Chris A & Son Co
Covington, KY 859-431-0499
Sherbrooke OEM Ltd
Sherbrooke, QC 866-851-2579

Cereals, Grains, Rice & Flour

Alfalfa

Christopher's Herb Shop
Springville, UT 888-372-4372
Enray, Inc
Livermore, CA 800-288-3637
International Specialty Supply
Cookeville, TN 931-526-1106
Julie Anne's
Las Vegas, NV 702-767-4765
New Organics
Kenwood, CA 734-677-5570
S & E Organic Farms Inc
Bakersfield, CA 661-325-2644
Verhoff Alfalfa Mill Inc
Ottawa, OH 800-834-8563

Barley

Agricore United
St Louis Park, MN 877-509-5865
Christopher's Herb Shop
Springville, UT 888-372-4372
Ferris Organic Farms
Eaton Rapids, MI 800-628-8736
Fizzle Flat Farm, L.L.C.
Yale, IL 618-793-2060
Grain Millers Inc
Eden Prairie, MN 800-232-6287
Graysmarsh Berry Farm
Sequim, WA 800-683-4367
Great River Organic Milling
Arcadia, WI. 608-687-9580
Green Foods Corp.
Oxnard, CA. 800-777-4430
J M Swank Co
North Liberty, IA 800-593-6375
La Crosse Milling Company
Cochrane, WI 800-441-5411
Natural Way Mills Inc
Middle River, MN. 218-222-3677
Ottawa Valley Grain Products
Renfrew, ON 613-432-3614
Pines International
Lawrence, KS 800-697-4637
Prairie Malt
Biggar, SK. 306-948-3500
Raymond-Hadley Corporation
Spencer, NY 800-252-5220
T.S. Smith & Sons
Bridgeville, DE. 302-337-8271
Terra Ingredients
Minneapolis, MN 888-497-3308
Timeless Seeds
Ulm, MT 406-866-3340
Wallace Grain & Pea Company
Pullman, WA. 509-878-1561

Bran

Bluechip Group
Salt Lake City, UT 800-878-0099
Bunge North America Inc.
Chesterfield, MO 314-292-2000
Canadian Harvest-U.S.A.
Edina, MN. 888-689-5800
Cereal Food Processors Inc
Mcpherson, KS 800-835-2067
Chef Hans' Gourmet Foods
Monroe, LA. 800-890-4267
Great Grains Milling Company
Scobey, MT 406-783-5581
GS Dunn & Company
Hamilton, ON 905-522-0833
Healthy Food Ingredients
Fargo, ND 844-275-3443
J M Swank Co
North Liberty, IA 800-593-6375
J.R. Short Canadian Mills
Toronto, ON 416-421-3463
Kerry Foodservice
Mansfield, OH 800-533-2722
Knappen Milling Co
Augusta, MI 800-562-7736
New Organics
Kenwood, CA 734-677-5570
Ohta Wafer Factory
Honolulu, HI 808-949-2775
Raymond-Hadley Corporation
Spencer, NY 800-252-5220
Ricex Company
El Dorado Hills, CA 916-933-3000
Riviana Foods Inc.
Houston, TX 713-529-3251
SJH Enterprises
Middleton, WI. 888-745-3845
Southern Brown Rice
Weiner, AR 800-421-7423
Star of the West Milling Co.
Frankenmuth, MI 989-652-9971

Mustard

GS Dunn & Company
Hamilton, ON 905-522-0833

Rice

Beaumont Rice Mills
Beaumont, TX. 409-832-2521
Bunge North America Inc.
Chesterfield, MO 314-292-2000
Farmers Rice Milling Co
Lake Charles, LA 337-433-5205
Louis Dreyfus Corporation
Rotterdam,
RiceBran Technologies
Scottsdale, AZ. 602-522-3000
Ricex Company
El Dorado Hills, CA 916-933-3000
Riviana Foods Inc.
Houston, TX 713-529-3251
Sahara Natural Foods
San Leandro, CA. 510-352-5111
Southern Brown Rice
Weiner, AR 800-421-7423

Wheat

Bluechip Group
Salt Lake City, UT 800-878-0099
Canadian Harvest-U.S.A.
Edina, MN. 888-689-5800
Cereal Food Processors Inc
Mcpherson, KS 800-835-2067
New Organics
Kenwood, CA 734-677-5570

Cereal

Amcan Industries
Elmsford, NY 914-347-4838
B & G Foods Inc.
Parsippany, NJ. 973-401-6500
Back to Nature Foods
. 855-346-2225
Barbara's Bakery
Lakeville, MN. 800-343-0590
Batory Foods
Des Plaines, IL 847-299-1999
Bob's Red Mill Natural Foods
Milwaukie, OR 800-349-2173
Cambridge Food
Monterey, CA 800-433-2584
Clara Foods
Clara City, MN 888-844-8518
Coach's Oats
Yorba Linda, CA. 714-692-6885
Continental Mills Inc
Tukwila, WA. 206-816-7000
Earnest Eats
Solana Beach, CA. 858-299-4238
Earth Song Whole Foods
Fair Oaks, CA 877-327-8476
Edison Grainery
Benicia, CA. 510-382-0202
Fiddlers Green Farm
North Vassalboro, ME 800-729-7935
Freekehlicious
Norwood, NJ. 201-297-7957
Grain Place Foods Inc
Marquette, NE. 888-714-7246
Grain Process Enterprises Ltd.
Scarborough, ON 800-387-5292
Great River Organic Milling
Arcadia, WI. 608-687-9580
Hain Celestial Group Inc
Lake Success, NY 800-434-4246
Harvest Innovations
Indianola, IA. 515-962-5063
Hearthside Food Solutions
Downers Grove, IL. 630-967-3600
InfraReady Products Ltd.
Saskatoon, SK. 800-510-1828
Ingles Markets
Black Mountain, NC. 828-669-2941
Inn Maid Food
Lenox, MA 413-637-2732
Kashi Company
Solana Beach, CA. 877-747-2467
Kay's Naturals, Inc.
Clara City, MN 866-873-5499
KAYS Processing LLC
Clara City, MN 320-847-3220
Kemach Food Products
Brooklyn, NY 718-272-5655
McKee Foods Corp.
Collegedale, TN 800-522-4499
Meijer Inc
Grand Rapids, MI 616-453-6711
Nature's Path Foods
Blaine, WA 888-808-9505
Newman's Own
Westport, CT. 203-222-0136
Nu-World Amaranth Inc
Naperville, IL 630-369-6851
Prairie Mills Products LLC
Rochester, IN 574-223-3177
Publix Super Market
Lakeland, FL. 800-242-1227
Raymond-Hadley Corporation
Spencer, NY 800-252-5220
SBK Preserves
Bronx, NY. 800-773-7378
Specialty Food Association
New York, NY 646-878-0301
Sunridge Farms
Royal Oaks, CA 831-786-7000
Sunridge Farms Inc
Salinas, CA 831-755-1530
TMI Trading Co
Brooklyn, NY 718-821-5052
Two Moms In The Raw
Longmont, CO 720-221-8555
Wegmans Food Markets Inc.
Rochester, NY. 800-934-6267
WEIS Markets Inc.
Sunbury, PA. 866-999-9347
Wildtime Foods
Eugene, OR. 800-356-4458
Winn-Dixie Stores
Jacksonville, FL 800-967-9105

Bars

Bobo's Oat Bars
Boulder, CO 303-938-1977
Budi Products LLC
Marblehead, MA. 781-990-3411
Coco International
Wayne, NJ. 973-694-1200
Don't Go Nuts
Salida, CO. 855-666-8826
Earnest Eats
Solana Beach, CA. 858-299-4238
FreeYumm
Vancouver, BC
Kashi Company
Solana Beach, CA. 877-747-2467
Kellogg Canada Inc.
Mississauga, ON. 888-876-3750
Kuli Kuli, Inc.
Oakland, CA. 510-350-8325
Quaker Oats Company
Chicago, IL 312-821-1000
The Good Bean
Berkeley, CA. 561-243-7773
Two Moms In The Raw
Longmont, CO 720-221-8555

Breakfast

Back to the Roots
Oakland, CA 510-922-9758
Bake Crafters Food Company
McDonald, TN 423-396-3392
Barbara's Bakery
Lakeville, MN.......... 800-343-0590
Bede Inc
Haledon, NJ 866-239-6565
Birkett Mills
Penn Yan, NY 315-536-3311
Black Ranch Organic Grains
Etna, CA 916-467-3387
Blue Marble Brands
Providence, RI 888-534-0246
Blue Planet Foods
Collegedale, TN 877-396-3145
Bluechip Group
Salt Lake City, UT 800-878-0099
Bob's Red Mill Natural Foods
Milwaukie, OR 800-349-2173
C H Guenther & Son Inc
San Antonio, TX.......... 210-227-1401
California Cereal Products
Oakland, CA 510-452-4500
Carlisle Cereal Company
Bismarck, ND 800-809-6018
Christine & Rob's Inc
Stayton, OR.......... 503-769-2993
CHS Sunprairie
Minot, ND.......... 800-556-6807
Cook Natural Products
Lafayette, CA 800-537-7589
Cook-In-The-Kitchen
Hampden, ME.......... 207-848-4900
Country Choice Organic
Eden Prairie, MN 952-829-8824
Cream Of The West
Harlowton, MT 800-477-2383
Dakota Specialty Milling, Inc.
Fargo, ND 844-633-2746
Edwards Mill
Hollister, MO 800-222-0525
Efco Products Inc
Poughkeepsie, NY 800-284-3326
Ener-G Foods
Seattle, WA 800-331-5222
Fry Krisp Food Products
Jackson, MI.......... 877-854-5440
General Mills
Minneapolis, MN 800-248-7310
GFA Brands Inc
Paramus, NJ 201-568-9300
Gilster-Mary Lee Corp
Chester, IL.......... 618-826-2361
GKI Foods
Brighton, MI 248-486-0055
Grain Craft
Chattanooga, TN.......... 423-265-2313
Grain Process Enterprises Ltd.
Scarborough, ON 800-387-5292
Health Valley Company
Irwindale, CA 800-334-3204
Hodgson Mill Inc
Effingham, IL 800-347-0198
Homestead Mills
Cook, MN 800-652-5233
I Heart Keenwah
Chicago, IL
Indiana Grain Company
Baltimore, MD 410-685-6410
International Home Foods
Parsippany, NJ.......... 973-359-9920
Julian Bakery
Oceanside, CA 760-721-5200
Kashi Company
Solana Beach, CA.......... 877-747-2467
Kellogg Canada Inc.
Mississauga, ON.......... 888-876-3750
Kellogg Co.
Battle Creek, MI 800-962-1413
Knappen Milling Co
Augusta, MI 800-562-7736
Lima Grain Cereal Seeds LLC
Fort Collins, CO 970-498-2200
Little Crow Foods
Warsaw, IN 800-288-2769
Luban International
Doral, FL.......... 305-629-8730
Lundberg Family Farms
Richvale, CA.......... 530-538-3500
Martha Olson's Great Foo
Sutter Creek, CA.......... 800-973-3966
Mills Brothers Intl
Seattle, WA 206-575-3000
Mixes by Danielle
Warren, OH.......... 800-537-6499
Morrison Milling Co
Denton, TX 800-531-7912
Native State Foods
Santa Monica, CA.......... 866-647-2291
Natural Food Mill
Corona, CA.......... 800-797-5090
Natural Way Mills Inc
Middle River, MN.......... 218-222-3677
Nestle USA Inc
Glendale, CA 800-225-2270
Nutri Base
Phoenix, AZ 877-223-5459
One Degree Organic Foods
Abbotsford, BC.......... 855-834-2642
Organic Milling
San Dimas, CA.......... 909-599-0961
Pacific Ethanol Inc.
Sacramento, CA 916-403-2123
Patagonia Provisions
Sausalito, CA 888-221-8208
PepsiCo.
Purchase, NY 914-253-2000
Post Consumer Brands
Lakeville, MN.......... 800-431-7678
Quaker Oats Company
Chicago, IL 312-821-1000
Quaker Oats Company
Peterborough, ON.......... 800-267-6287
Senor Pinos de Santa Fe
Santa Fe, NM 505-473-3437
Silver Palate Kitchens
Cresskill, NJ 201-568-0110
Small Planet Foods
Minneapolis, MN 800-624-4123
Stafford County Flour Mills Company
Hudson, KS.......... 800-530-5640
Star of the West Milling Co.
Frankenmuth, MI 989-652-9971
Sturm Foods Inc
Manawa, WI 800-347-8876
Teeccino
Carpinteria, CA.......... 800-498-3434
The Soulfull Project
Camden, NJ
TyRy Inc
Rocklin, CA 800-322-6325
US Mills
Bala Cynwyd, PA 800-422-1125
Wanda's Nature Farm
Lincoln, NE.......... 800-735-6828
Weetabix Canada
Cobourg, ON.......... 888-933-8249
Weetabix Food Co.
Marlborough, MA.......... 800-343-0590

Corn-Based

Kellogg Canada Inc.
Mississauga, ON.......... 888-876-3750
Terra Ingredients
Minneapolis, MN 888-497-3308

Farina

Bob's Red Mill Natural Foods
Milwaukie, OR 800-349-2173
Sturm Foods Inc
Manawa, WI 800-347-8876

Instant

Nature's Legacy Inc.
Hudson, MI.......... 517-448-2050
Quaker Oats Company
Chicago, IL.......... 312-821-1000
San Francisco Spice Co.
Woodland, CA.......... 866-972-6879
TMI Trading Co
Brooklyn, NY 718-821-5052

Muesli

Bliss Gourmet Foods
St. Paul, MN
Bob's Red Mill Natural Foods
Milwaukie, OR 800-349-2173
GrandyOats
Hiram, ME 207-935-7415
Seven Sundays, LLC
Minneapolis, MN 612-562-5316
Zego Foods
San Francisco, CA 415-706-8094

Mueslix

Hodgson Mill Inc
Effingham, IL 800-347-0198
Kellogg Canada Inc.
Mississauga, ON.......... 888-876-3750

Oatmeal

Bob's Red Mill Natural Foods
Milwaukie, OR 800-349-2173
Earnest Eats
Solana Beach, CA.......... 858-299-4238
Inviting Foods
Chicago, IL 844-782-5374
Maker Oats
.... 844-782-5374
MUSH Foods
Vista, CA
Mylk Labs
City of Industry, CA
Natierra
Van Nuys, CA.......... 310-559-0259
New Organics
Kenwood, CA.......... 734-677-5570
Quaker Oats Company
Chicago, IL 312-821-1000
Sturm Foods Inc
Manawa, WI 800-347-8876

Rice-Based

Bob's Red Mill Natural Foods
Milwaukie, OR 800-349-2173
Fantastic World Foods
Providence, RI
Kashi Company
Solana Beach, CA.......... 877-747-2467
Kellogg Canada Inc.
Mississauga, ON.......... 888-876-3750
Lundberg Family Farms
Richvale, CA.......... 530-538-3500
Post Consumer Brands
Lakeville, MN.......... 800-431-7678

Rolled Oats

Bob's Red Mill Natural Foods
Milwaukie, OR 800-349-2173
GF Harvest
Powell, WY.......... 888-941-9922
GloryBee
Eugene, OR.......... 800-456-7923
Hodgson Mill Inc
Effingham, IL 800-347-0198
Innovative Beverage Concepts
Irvine, CA.......... 949-831-8656
La Crosse Milling Company
Cochrane, WI 800-441-5411
New Organics
Kenwood, CA.......... 734-677-5570
Terra Ingredients
Minneapolis, MN 888-497-3308
Umpqua Oats
Henderson, NV.......... 877-303-8107
Zego Foods
San Francisco, CA 415-706-8094

Wheat-Based

Bob's Red Mill Natural Foods
Milwaukie, OR 800-349-2173
H Fox & Co Inc
Brooklyn, NY 718-385-4600
Hodgson Mill Inc
Effingham, IL.......... 800-347-0198
Weetabix Canada
Cobourg, ON.......... 888-933-8249

Corn Germ

Aussie Crunch
Nashville, TN 800-401-6534
Kreher Family Farms
Clarence, NY.......... 716-759-6802

Corn Meal

Adluh Flour
Columbia, SC 800-692-3584

Agricor Inc
Marion, IN. 765-662-0606
American Key Food Products Inc
Closter, NJ. 877-263-7539
Ashland Milling
Ashland, VA 888-897-3336
Atkinson Milling Co.
Selma, NC. 800-948-5707
Bob's Red Mill Natural Foods
Milwaukie, OR 800-349-2173
Bunge
Chesterfield, MO 314-292-2000
California Oils Corp
Richmond, CA 800-225-6457
Hodgson Mill Inc
Effingham, IL 800-347-0198
Homestead Mills
Cook, MN. 800-652-5233
Hoople Country Kitchen Inc
Rockport, IN 877-466-7537
House-Autry Mills Inc
Four Oaks, NC 800-849-0802
J P Green Milling Co
Mocksville, NC. 336-751-2126
King Arthur Flour
Norwich, VT. 800-827-6836
Lakeside Mills
Rutherfordton, NC 828-286-4866
Maysville Milling Company
Maysville, NC. 606-759-8789
Mills Brothers Intl
Seattle, WA 206-575-3000
Nustef Foods
Mississauga, ON. 877-306-7562
Renwood Mills
Newton, NC 828-464-1611
Scott's Auburn Mills
Russellville, KY 270-726-2080
Shawnee Milling Co
Shawnee, OK 405-273-7000
Shenandoah Mills
Lebanon, TN. 615-444-0841
SJH Enterprises
Middleton, WI. 888-745-3845
Southeastern Mills Inc
Rome, GA. 800-334-4468
UNOI Grainmill
Seaford, DE. 302-629-4083
War Eagle Mill
Rogers, AR 866-492-7324
Wilkins Rogers Inc
Ellicott City, MD. 410-465-5800

Crisps

Bran

Ace Bakery
North York, ON. 800-443-7929
Flat Cracker Inc.
Lawrence, NY. 347-223-2587

Cereal

Kii Naturals Inc
Vaughan, ON. 905-738-8887
Post Consumer Brands
Lakeville, MN. 800-431-7678

Flax

Harvest Innovations
Indianola, IA. 515-962-5063
Terra Ingredients
Minneapolis, MN 888-497-3308

Rice

Kameda USA Inc.
Torrance, CA. 310-944-9639
Victoria Amory & Co LLC
Greenwich, CT 203-220-6454

Fiber

Alfred L. Wolff, Inc.
Park Ridge, IL. 847-759-8888
Batory Foods
Des Plaines, IL 847-299-1999
Brenntag North America
Reading, PA 610-926-6100
Bunge Loders Croklaan
Channahon, IL 800-621-4710
Canadian Harvest-U.S.A.
Edina, MN. 888-689-5800
Cereal Ingredients, Inc.
Leavenworth, KS 913-727-3434
Crea Fill Fibers Corp
Chestertown, MD 800-832-4662
Eckhart Corporation
Novato, CA. 800-200-4201
Functional Foods
Englishtown, NJ 800-442-9524
Garuda International
Exeter, CA. 559-594-4380
Grain Millers Inc
Eden Prairie, MN 800-232-6287
Great Grains Milling Company
Scobey, MT. 406-783-5581
Gum Technology Corporation
Tucson, AZ 800-369-4867
Healthy Food Ingredients
Fargo, ND 844-275-3443
N D Labs
Lynbrook, NY 888-263-5227
Nellson Nutraceutical LLC
Anaheim, CA 844-635-5766
Ricex Company
El Dorado Hills, CA 916-933-3000
San-Ei Gen FFI
New York, NY 212-315-7850
Solvaira Specialties
North Tonawanda, NY 888-698-1936
Southern Brown Rice
Weiner, AR 800-421-7423
TIC Gums
Belcamp, MD 800-899-3953
Unique Ingredients LLC
Gold Canyon, AZ 480-983-2498
Weetabix Canada
Cobourg, ON. 888-933-8249
World Flavors Inc
Warminster, PA 215-672-4400
Yerba Prima
Ashland, OR 800-488-4339

Cellulose

Gum Technology Corporation
Tucson, AZ 800-369-4867

Corn Bran

Canadian Harvest-U.S.A.
Edina, MN. 888-689-5800

Nuts

Post Consumer Brands
Lakeville, MN. 800-431-7678

Oat Bran

Canadian Harvest-U.S.A.
Edina, MN. 888-689-5800
La Crosse Milling Company
Cochrane, WI 800-441-5411
New Organics
Kenwood, CA. 734-677-5570

Oats

Canadian Harvest-U.S.A.
Edina, MN. 888-689-5800
La Crosse Milling Company
Cochrane, WI 800-441-5411
New Organics
Kenwood, CA. 734-677-5570
Organic Planet
San Francisco, CA 415-765-5590

Pea Bran

Best Cooking Pulses, Inc.
Portage la Prairie, MB 204-857-4451

Psyllium

Psyllium Labs
Schaumburg, IL. 888-851-6667

Soy Bran

Fibred
Cumberland, MD 800-598-8894

Supplements

Abunda Life
Asbury Park, NJ 732-775-9338
Southern Brown Rice
Weiner, AR 800-421-7423

Wheat Bran

Canadian Harvest-U.S.A.
Edina, MN. 888-689-5800
Cereal Ingredients, Inc.
Leavenworth, KS 913-727-3434

Flour

Adluh Flour
Columbia, SC 800-692-3584
AG Processing Inc
Omaha, NE 800-247-1345
Agri-Dairy Products
Purchase, NY 914-697-9580
Agricore United
St Louis Park, MN 877-509-5865
American Almond Products Co
Brooklyn, NY 800-825-6663
Arcadia Biosciences
Davis, CA 530-756-7077
Ardent Mills Corp
Denver, CO 800-851-9618
Ashland Milling
Ashland, VA 888-897-3336
Atlantic Seasonings
Kinston, NC 800-433-5261
Attala Development Corporation
Kosciusko, MS 662-289-2981
Azteca Milling
Irving, TX 800-364-0040
Bakery Essentials Inc
Vernon Hills, IL 847-573-0844
Bartlett Milling Co.
Statesville, NC 800-438-6016
Bay State Milling Co.
Quincy, MA. 800-553-5687
Beta Pure Foods
Santa Cruz, CA. 831-685-6565
Big J Milling Co
Brigham City, UT 435-723-3459
Birkett Mills
Penn Yan, NY 315-536-3311
Blend Pak Inc
Bloomfield, KY 502-252-8000
Bluechip Group
Salt Lake City, UT 800-878-0099
Bob's Red Mill Natural Foods
Milwaukie, OR 800-349-2173
Bouchard Family Farm
Fort Kent, ME. 800-239-3237
Brandt Mills
Mifflinville, PA. 570-752-4271
Byrd Mill Co
Ashland, VA 888-897-3336
California Cereal Products
Oakland, CA 510-452-4500
Centennial Mills
Cheney, WA 509-235-6216
Central Milling Co
Logan, UT. 435-752-6625
Cereal Food Processors
Salt Lake City, UT 801-355-2981
Cereal Food Processors Inc
Mcpherson, KS. 800-835-2067
Cereal Food Processors Inc
Mission Woods, KS 913-890-6300
Champlain Valley Milling Corp
Westport, NY. 518-962-4711
CHS Inc.
Inver Grove Hts., MN. 800-328-6539
CHS Sunprairie
Minot, ND. 800-556-6807
Clofine Dairy Products Inc
Linwood, NJ 609-653-1000
Community Mill & Bean
Savannah, NY. 800-755-0554
Continental Grain Company
New York, NY 212-207-5100
Cup 4 Cup LLC
Yountville, CA 833-287-4287
Dakota Specialty Milling, Inc.
Fargo, ND 844-633-2746
Devansoy Farms
Carroll, IA. 800-747-8605
Dillman Farm Inc
Bloomington, IN. 800-359-1362
Dipasa USA Inc
Brownsville, TX 956-831-4072
Eden Foods Inc
Clinton, MI 888-424-3336
Edison Grainery
Benicia, CA. 510-382-0202

El Peto Products
Cambridge, ON....................800-387-4064
Ellison Milling Company
Lethbridge, AB....................403-328-6622
Ener-G Foods
Seattle, WA....................800-331-5222
Erba Food Products
Brooklyn, NY....................718-272-7700
Fairhaven Cooperative Flour Mill
Bellingham, WA....................360-757-9947
Farmers Way
Food & Vine Inc.
Napa, CA....................707-251-3900
Fresh Hemp Foods
Winnipeg, NB....................800-665-4367
Gilt Edge Flour Mills
Richmond, UT....................435-258-2425
Giusto's Specialty Foods Inc
S San Francisco, CA....................650-873-6566
Glean, LLC
Snow Hill, NC
Grain Process Enterprises Ltd.
Scarborough, ON....................800-387-5292
Great Grains Milling Company
Scobey, MT....................406-783-5581
Great River Organic Milling
Arcadia, WI....................608-687-9580
Greenfield Mills
North Howe, IN....................260-367-2394
GS Dunn & Company
Hamilton, ON....................905-522-0833
H Nagel & Son Co
Cincinnati, OH....................513-665-4550
Healthy Food Ingredients
Fargo, ND....................844-275-3443
Heartland Mills Shipping
Marienthal, KS....................800-232-8533
Hialeah Products Co
Hollywood, FL....................800-923-3379
Hodgson Mill Inc
Effingham, IL....................800-347-0198
Homestead Mills
Cook, MN....................800-652-5233
Hudson Valley Hops
Beacon, NY....................845-202-2398
Idaho Frank Association Inc
Pleasant Hill, CA....................925-609-8458
Idaho Pacific Holdings Inc
Rigby, ID....................800-238-5503
Inca Gold Organics
Scarborough, ON....................416-264-4622
Iya Foods LLC
North Aurora, IL....................630-854-7107
J P Green Milling Co
Mocksville, NC....................336-751-2126
J.M. Smucker Co.
Orrville, OH....................888-550-9555
J.R. Short Canadian Mills
Toronto, ON....................416-421-3463
Jovial Foods
North Stonington, CT....................877-642-0644
Kemach Food Products
Brooklyn, NY....................718-272-5655
King Arthur Flour
Norwich, VT....................800-827-6836
King Milling Co Inc
Lowell, MI....................616-897-9264
Knappen Milling Co
Augusta, MI....................800-562-7736
Lacey Milling Company
Hanford, CA....................559-584-6634
Lehi Mills
Lehi, UT....................877-311-3566
Lucas Meyer
Decatur, IL....................800-769-3660
Mennel Milling Company
Fostoria, OH....................800-688-8151
Mex America Foods LLC
St Marys, PA....................814-781-1447
Mills Brothers Intl
Seattle, WA....................206-575-3000
Minn-Dak Growers LTD
Grand Forks, ND....................701-746-7453
Montana Flour & Grains
Fort Benton, MT....................800-622-5790
Morris J Golombeck Inc
Brooklyn, NY....................718-284-3505
Mother Earth Enterprises
New York, NY....................866-436-7688
Natural Products Inc
Grinnell, IA....................641-236-0852
Natural Way Mills Inc
Middle River, MN....................218-222-3677
Nature's Legacy Inc.
Hudson, MI....................517-448-2050
New Hope Mills Mfg Inc
Auburn, NY....................315-252-2676
New Organics
Kenwood, CA....................734-677-5570
Newly Weds Foods Inc
Chicago, IL....................800-621-7521
North Dakota Mill & Elevator Assn.
Grand Forks, ND....................800-538-7721
Northwestern Foods
Arden Hills, MN....................800-236-4937
NutraSun
Regina, SK....................306-751-2040
Old Dutch Mustard Company
Great Neck, NY....................516-466-0522
One Degree Organic Foods
Abbotsford, BC....................855-834-2642
Oregon Potato Co
Boardman, OR....................800-336-6311
Organic Gemini
Brooklyn, NY....................347-662-2900
Orlinda Milling Company
Orlinda, TN....................615-654-3633
Pacific Grain & Foods
Fresno, CA....................559-276-2580
Panhandle Milling
Dawn, TX....................800-897-5226
Particle Control
Albertville, MN....................763-497-3075
Pillsbury
Minneapolis, MN....................800-775-4777
Prairie Mills Products LLC
Rochester, IN....................574-223-3177
Produits Alimentaire
St Lambert De Lauzon, QC....................800-463-1787
Quality Naturally Foods
City Of Industry, CA....................888-498-6986
R&J Farms
West Salem, OH....................419-846-3179
Raymond-Hadley Corporation
Spencer, NY....................800 252-5220
Renwood Mills
Newton, NC....................828-464-1611
Research Products Co
Salina, KS....................800-234-7174
Sanford Milling Co Inc
Henderson, NC....................866-438-4526
Scott's Auburn Mills
Russellville, KY....................270-726-2080
SFP Food Products
Conway, AR....................800-654-5329
Shawnee Milling Co
Shawnee, OK....................405-273-7000
Shawnee Milling Co
Shawnee, OK....................800-654-2600
Shepherdsfield Bakery
Fulton, MO....................573-642-0009
SJH Enterprises
Middleton, WI....................888-745-3845
Solnuts
Hudson, IA....................800-648-3503
Southeastern Mills Inc
Rome, GA....................800-334-4468
Southern Brown Rice
Weiner, AR....................800-421-7423
Star of the West Milling Co.
Frankenmuth, MI....................989-652-9971
Teff Co
Nampa, ID....................888-822-2221
To Your Health Sprouted Flour Co., Inc.
Floyd, VA....................540-283-9589
Uhlmann Co
Kansas City, MO....................866-866-8627
War Eagle Mill
Rogers, AR....................866-492-7324
Wheat Montana Farms Inc
Three Forks, MT....................800-535-2798
Wilkins Rogers Inc
Ellicott City, MD....................410-465-5800

All Purpose

Ardent Mills Corp
Denver, CO....................800-851-9618
Bob's Red Mill Natural Foods
Milwaukie, OR....................800-349-2173
Cereal Food Processors Inc
Mcpherson, KS....................800-835-2067
King Arthur Flour
Norwich, VT....................800-827-6836
Orlinda Milling Company
Orlinda, TN....................615-654-3633
Uhlmann Co
Kansas City, MO....................866-866-8627
UNOI Grainmill
Seaford, DE....................302-629-4083

Almond

Bob's Red Mill Natural Foods
Milwaukie, OR....................800-349-2173
NOW Foods
Bloomingdale, IL....................888-669-3663

Amaranth

Bob's Red Mill Natural Foods
Milwaukie, OR....................800-349-2173

Arrowroot

American Key Food Products Inc
Closter, NJ....................877-263-7539

Bakery Mix

Regular & Lowfat

1-2-3 Gluten Free
Chagrin Falls, OH....................216-378-9233
Mennel Milling Company
Fostoria, OH....................800-688-8151

Baking Mixes

1-2-3 Gluten Free
Chagrin Falls, OH....................216-378-9233
Cereal Food Processors Inc
Mcpherson, KS....................800-835-2067
Cup 4 Cup LLC
Yountville, CA....................833-287-4287
Harvest Innovations
Indianola, IA....................515-962-5063
Hodgson Mill Inc
Effingham, IL....................800-347-0198
Homefree LLC
Windham, NH....................800-552-7172
Hudson River Foods
Castleton, NY....................888-417-9343
NOW Foods
Bloomingdale, IL....................888-669-3663
Shawnee Milling Co
Shawnee, OK....................800-654-2600
Southern Culture Foods
Peachtree Corners, GA

Barley

Bob's Red Mill Natural Foods
Milwaukie, OR....................800-349-2173
CHS Inc.
Inver Grove Hts., MN....................800-328-6539
Eden Foods Inc
Clinton, MI....................888-424-3336
Ettlinger Corp
Lincolnshire, IL....................847-564-5020
Grain Millers Inc
Eden Prairie, MN....................800-232-6287
Great River Organic Milling
Arcadia, WI....................608-687-9580
Heartland Mills Shipping
Marienthal, KS....................800-232-8533
Hodgson Mill Inc
Effingham, IL....................800-347-0198
Homefree LLC
Windham, NH....................800-552-7172
Homestead Mills
Cook, MN....................800-652-5233
La Crosse Milling Company
Cochrane, WI....................800-441-5411
New Organics
Kenwood, CA....................734-677-5570
SJH Enterprises
Middleton, WI....................888-745-3845

Bean

Besco Grain Ltd
Brunkild, MB....................204-736-3570
Bob's Red Mill Natural Foods
Milwaukie, OR....................800-349-2173
BRAMI Snacks
New York, NY....................917-291-1945
Love Grown Foods
Denver, CO....................855-328-5683

Bleached

Hodgson Mill Inc
Effingham, IL 800-347-0198

Buckwheat

Bob's Red Mill Natural Foods
Milwaukie, OR 800-349-2173
Bouchard Family Farm
Fort Kent, ME 800-239-3237
Byrd Mill Co
Ashland, VA 888-897-3336
Eden Foods Inc
Clinton, MI 888-424-3336
Ener-G Foods
Seattle, WA 800-331-5222
Fairhaven Cooperative Flour Mill
Bellingham, WA 360-757-9947
Great River Organic Milling
Arcadia, WI 608-687-9580
Greenfield Mills
North Howe, IN 260-367-2394
Homestead Mills
Cook, MN 800-652-5233
King Arthur Flour
Norwich, VT 800-827-6836
Minn-Dak Growers LTD
Grand Forks, ND 701-746-7453
New Hope Mills Mfg Inc
Auburn, NY 315-252-2676
New Organics
Kenwood, CA 734-677-5570
Terra Ingredients
Minneapolis, MN 888-497-3308
UNOI Grainmill
Seaford, DE 302-629-4083

Cake

Byrd Mill Co
Ashland, VA 888-897-3336
Cereal Food Processors Inc
Mission Woods, KS 913-890-6300
H Nagel & Son Co
Cincinnati, OH 513-665-4550
King Arthur Flour
Norwich, VT 800-827-6836
Pillsbury
Minneapolis, MN 800-775-4777

Cassava

Otto's Naturals
Clinton, NJ 732-654-6886

Corn

Adluh Flour
Columbia, SC 800-692-3584
Agricor Inc
Marion, IN 765-662-0606
Ardent Mills Corp
Denver, CO 800-851-9618
Attala Development Corporation
Kosciusko, MS 662-289-2981
Azteca Milling
Irving, TX 800-364-0040
Bob's Red Mill Natural Foods
Milwaukie, OR 800-349-2173
Byrd Mill Co
Ashland, VA 888-897-3336
Ener-G Foods
Seattle, WA 800-331-5222
Fairhaven Cooperative Flour Mill
Bellingham, WA 360-757-9947
Great River Organic Milling
Arcadia, WI 608-687-9580
Mex America Foods LLC
St Marys, PA 814-781-1447
Mills Brothers Intl
Seattle, WA 206-575-3000
Minsa Corp
Lubbock, TX 800-852-8291
Shenandoah Mills
Lebanon, TN 615-444-0841
Tom Farms
Leesburg, IN 574-453-3300

Masa

Bob's Red Mill Natural Foods
Milwaukie, OR 800-349-2173

Gluten

Bluechip Group
Salt Lake City, UT 800-878-0099
Clofine Dairy Products Inc
Linwood, NJ 609-653-1000
North Dakota Mill & Elevator Assn.
Grand Forks, ND 800-538-7721
NOW Foods
Bloomingdale, IL 888-669-3663
Organic Planet
San Francisco, CA 415-765-5590
SJH Enterprises
Middleton, WI 888-745-3845

Graham

Bob's Red Mill Natural Foods
Milwaukie, OR 800-349-2173
Great River Organic Milling
Arcadia, WI 608-687-9580

Hazelnut

Bob's Red Mill Natural Foods
Milwaukie, OR 800-349-2173
King Arthur Flour
Norwich, VT 800-827-6836

Instantized

TyRy Inc
Rocklin, CA 800-322-6325

Millet

Bob's Red Mill Natural Foods
Milwaukie, OR 800-349-2173
Heartland Mills Shipping
Marienthal, KS 800-232-8533
New Organics
Kenwood, CA 734-677-5570

Mustard

GS Dunn & Company
Hamilton, ON 905-522-0833
Harvest Innovations
Indianola, IA 515-962-5063
Minn-Dak Growers LTD
Grand Forks, ND 701-746-7453
Montana Specialty Mills LLC
Great Falls, MT 800-332-2024
Tova Industries LLC
Louisville, KY 888-532-8682

Nut

American Almond Products Co
Brooklyn, NY 800-825-6663
Amoretti
Oxnard, CA 800-266-7388
Harvest Innovations
Indianola, IA 515-962-5063
Hialeah Products Co
Hollywood, FL 800-923-3379
Mother Earth Enterprises
New York, NY 866-436-7688
Santa Barbara Pistachio Co
Maricopa, CA 800-896-1044

Oat

Ardent Mills Corp
Denver, CO 800-851-9618
Bob's Red Mill Natural Foods
Milwaukie, OR 800-349-2173
Eden Foods Inc
Clinton, MI 888-424-3336
GF Harvest
Powell, WY 888-941-9922
Grain Millers Inc
Eden Prairie, MN 800-232-6287
Healthy Food Ingredients
Fargo, ND 844-275-3443
Heartland Mills Shipping
Marienthal, KS 800-232-8533
Homefree LLC
Windham, NH 800-552-7172
La Crosse Milling Company
Cochrane, WI 800-441-5411
New Organics
Kenwood, CA 734-677-5570
Particle Control
Albertville, MN 763-497-3075

SJH Enterprises
Middleton, WI 888-745-3845

Pancake

Bette's Oceanview Diner
Berkeley, CA 510-644-3230
Bouchard Family Farm
Fort Kent, ME 800-239-3237
Byrd Mill Co
Ashland, VA 888-897-3336
Carbon's Golden Malted
South Bend, IN 800-253-0590
Champlain Valley Milling Corp
Westport, NY 518-962-4711
Foxtail Foods
Fairfield, OH 800-487-2253
Great River Organic Milling
Arcadia, WI 608-687-9580
Gust John Foods & Products
Batavia, IL 800-756-5886
Homestead Mills
Cook, MN 800-652-5233
Little Crow Foods
Warsaw, IN 800-288-2769
Marie Callender's Gourmet Products/Goldrush Products
San Jose, CA 800-729-5428
Martha Olson's Great Foo
Sutter Creek, CA 800-973-3966
New Hope Mills Mfg Inc
Auburn, NY 315-252-2676
Northwestern Foods
Arden Hills, MN 800-236-4937
Quality Naturally Foods
City Of Industry, CA 888-498-6986
SFP Food Products
Conway, AR 800-654-5329
Shenandoah Mills
Lebanon, TN 615-444-0841
Southern Culture Foods
Peachtree Corners, GA
Wanda's Nature Farm
Lincoln, NE 800-735-6828

Pastry

Bob's Red Mill Natural Foods
Milwaukie, OR 800-349-2173
Brandt Mills
Mifflinville, PA 570-752-4271
Cereal Food Processors Inc
Mission Woods, KS 913-890-6300
Champlain Valley Milling Corp
Westport, NY 518-962-4711
Eden Foods Inc
Clinton, MI 888-424-3336
Ellison Milling Company
Lethbridge, AB 403-328-6622
H Nagel & Son Co
Cincinnati, OH 513-665-4550
King Arthur Flour
Norwich, VT 800-827-6836
Natural Way Mills Inc
Middle River, MN 218-222-3677
New Organics
Kenwood, CA 734-677-5570
SJH Enterprises
Middleton, WI 888-745-3845

Pea

Best Cooking Pulses, Inc.
Portage la Prairie, MB 204-857-4451

Potato

AgraWest Foods
Prince Edward Island, NS 877-687-1400
Ardent Mills Corp
Denver, CO 800-851-9618
Bob's Red Mill Natural Foods
Milwaukie, OR 800-349-2173
Emerling International Foods
Buffalo, NY 716-833-7381
Ener-G Foods
Seattle, WA 800-331-5222
Ettlinger Corp
Lincolnshire, IL 847-564-5020
Hodgson Mill Inc
Effingham, IL 800-347-0198
Idaho Pacific Holdings Inc
Rigby, ID 800-238-5503
King Arthur Flour
Norwich, VT 800-827-6836

Oregon Potato Co
Boardman, OR 800-336-6311

Pancake

Linda's Gourmet Latkes
Los Angeles, CA........ 888-452-8537

Quinoa

Ardent Mills Corp
Denver, CO........ 800-851-9618
Bob's Red Mill Natural Foods
Milwaukie, OR........ 800-349-2173
Inca Gold Organics
Scarborough, ON........ 416-264-4622

Rice

Affiliated Rice Milling
Alvin, TX........ 281-331-6176
Ardent Mills Corp
Denver, CO........ 800-851-9618
Axiom Foods, Inc.
Los Angeles, CA........ 800-711-3587
Bob's Red Mill Natural Foods
Milwaukie, OR........ 800-349-2173
California Cereal Products
Oakland, CA........ 510-452-4500
Eden Foods Inc
Clinton, MI........ 888-424-3336
Ener-G Foods
Seattle, WA........ 800-331-5222
Far West Rice Inc
Nelson, CA........ 530-891-1339
Harvest Innovations
Indianola, IA........ 515-962-5063
J M Swank Co
North Liberty, IA........ 800-593-6375
King Arthur Flour
Norwich, VT........ 800-827-6836
KODA Farms Inc
South Dos Palos, CA........ 209-392-2191
Lundberg Family Farms
Richvale, CA........ 530-538-3500
Sage V Foods
Boulder, CO........ 303-449-5626

Rye

Ardent Mills Corp
Denver, CO........ 800-851-9618
Bob's Red Mill Natural Foods
Milwaukie, OR........ 800-349-2173
Champlain Valley Milling Corp
Westport, NY........ 518-962-4711
Ellison Milling Company
Lethbridge, AB........ 403-328-6622
Fairhaven Cooperative Flour Mill
Bellingham, WA........ 360-757-9947
Great River Organic Milling
Arcadia, WI........ 608-687-9580
Heartland Mills Shipping
Marienthal, KS........ 800-232-8533
Homestead Mills
Cook, MN........ 800-652-5233
King Arthur Flour
Norwich, VT........ 800-827-6836
SJH Enterprises
Middleton, WI........ 888-745-3845

Self-Rising

Cereal Food Processors Inc
Mcpherson, KS........ 800-835-2067
Orlinda Milling Company
Orlinda, TN........ 615-654-3633

Semolina

Bob's Red Mill Natural Foods
Milwaukie, OR........ 800-349-2173
CHS Inc.
Inver Grove Hts., MN........ 800-328-6539
Heartland Mills Shipping
Marienthal, KS........ 800-232-8533
Howson Mills
Blyth, ON........ 866-422-7522
King Arthur Flour
Norwich, VT........ 800-827-6836
North Dakota Mill & Elevator Assn.
Grand Forks, ND........ 800-538-7721

Sorghum

Bob's Red Mill Natural Foods
Milwaukie, OR........ 800-349-2173

Soy Protein

Champlain Valley Milling Corp
Westport, NY........ 518-962-4711

Soybean

Acatris USA
Edina, MN........ 952-920-7700
AG Processing Inc
Omaha, NE........ 800-247-1345
Besco Grain Ltd
Brunkild, MB........ 204-736-3570
Bob's Red Mill Natural Foods
Milwaukie, OR........ 800-349-2173
Clofine Dairy Products Inc
Linwood, NJ........ 609-653-1000
Devansoy Farms
Carroll, IA........ 800-747-8605
Healthy Food Ingredients
Fargo, ND........ 844-275-3443
IOM Grain
Portland, IN........ 877-283-8882
Lucas Meyer
Decatur, IL........ 800-769-3660
Modern Macaroni Co LTD
Honolulu, HI........ 808-845-6841
New Organics
Kenwood, CA........ 734-677-5570
Solnuts
Hudson, IA........ 800-648-3503
Spectrum Foods Inc
Springfield, IL........ 217-528-5301
Tom Farms
Leesburg, IN........ 574-453-3300

Spelt

Bob's Red Mill Natural Foods
Milwaukie, OR........ 800-349-2173
Heartland Mills Shipping
Marienthal, KS........ 800-232-8533
King Arthur Flour
Norwich, VT........ 800-827-6836
Nature's Legacy Inc.
Hudson, MI........ 517-448-2050

Tapioca

American Key Food Products Inc
Closter, NJ........ 877-263-7539
Bob's Red Mill Natural Foods
Milwaukie, OR........ 800-349-2173
Ener-G Foods
Seattle, WA........ 800-331-5222
Kinnikinnick Foods
Edmonton, AB........ 877-503-4466
NOW Foods
Bloomingdale, IL........ 888-669-3663
Tipiak Inc
Stamford, CT........ 203-961-9117

Triticale

Bob's Red Mill Natural Foods
Milwaukie, OR........ 800-349-2173

Wheat

Arcadia Biosciences
Davis, CA........ 530-756-7077
King Milling Co Inc
Lowell, MI........ 616-897-9264
New Organics
Kenwood, CA........ 734-677-5570
Shawnee Milling Co
Shawnee, OK........ 800-654-2600
Siemer Milling Co
Teutopolis, IL........ 800-826-1065

White Unbleached

Bob's Red Mill Natural Foods
Milwaukie, OR........ 800-349-2173
Champlain Valley Milling Corp
Westport, NY........ 518-962-4711
Ener-G Foods
Seattle, WA........ 800-331-5222
Great Grains Milling Company
Scobey, MT........ 406-783-5581
Heartland Mills Shipping
Marienthal, KS........ 800-232-8533
King Arthur Flour
Norwich, VT........ 800-827-6836
King Milling Co Inc
Lowell, MI........ 616-897-9264
Lehi Mills
Lehi, UT........ 877-311-3566
Natural Way Mills Inc
Middle River, MN........ 218-222-3677
Tolteca Foodservice
Norcross, GA........ 800-541-6835
Uhlmann Co
Kansas City, MO........ 866-866-8627

Whole wheat

Brandt Mills
Mifflinville, PA........ 570-752-4271
Cereal Food Processors Inc
Mission Woods, KS........ 913-890-6300
Great Grains Milling Company
Scobey, MT........ 406-783-5581
Great River Organic Milling
Arcadia, WI........ 608-687-9580
Hodgson Mill Inc
Effingham, IL........ 800-347-0198
Homestead Mills
Cook, MN........ 800-652-5233
Keynes Brothers Inc
Logan, OH........ 800-282-5627
King Arthur Flour
Norwich, VT........ 800-827-6836
Lehi Mills
Lehi, UT........ 877-311-3566
Montana Specialty Mills LLC
Great Falls, MT........ 800-332-2024
New Organics
Kenwood, CA........ 734-677-5570
Panhandle Milling
Dawn, TX........ 800-897-5226
Siemer Milling Co
Teutopolis, IL........ 800-826-1065
SJH Enterprises
Middleton, WI........ 888-745-3845
Terra Botanica Products
Dahlonega, GA........ 770-718-9340
Uhlmann Co
Kansas City, MO........ 866-866-8627
War Eagle Mill
Rogers, AR........ 866-492-7324

Pastry

Brandt Mills
Mifflinville, PA........ 570-752-4271
George's Candy Shop Inc
Mobile, AL........ 800-633-1306
New Organics
Kenwood, CA........ 734-677-5570
SJH Enterprises
Middleton, WI........ 888-745-3845

Grains

Acharice Specialties
Greenville, MS........ 800-432-4901
Agfinity Inc
Eaton, CO........ 800-433-4688
Aliments Trigone
St-Francois-De-La-Rivier, QC........ 877-259-7491
Ancient Harvest
Boulder, CO........ 310-217-8125
Ardent Mills Corp
Denver, CO........ 800-851-9618
Attala Development Corporation
Kosciusko, MS........ 662-289-2981
Azteca Milling
Irving, TX........ 800-364-0040
Bakery Essentials Inc
Vernon Hills, IL........ 847-573-0844
Baptista's Bakery
Franklin, WI........ 414-409-2000
Beaumont Rice Mills
Beaumont, TX........ 409-832-2521
Besco Grain Ltd
Brunkild, MB........ 204-736-3570
Beta Pure Foods
Santa Cruz, CA........ 831-685-6565
Big J Milling Co
Brigham City, UT........ 435-723-3459
Black Ranch Organic Grains
Etna, CA........ 916-467-3387

Blue Planet Foods
Collegedale, TN 877-396-3145
Briess Malt & Ingredients Co.
Chilton, WI 800-657-0806
Bunge North America Inc.
Chesterfield, MO 314-292-2000
California Cereal Products
Oakland, CA 510-452-4500
Canadian Harvest-U.S.A.
Edina, MN. 888-689-5800
Caribbean Food Delights Inc
Tappan, NY 845-398-3000
Cayuga Pure Organics
Brooktondale, NY. 607-273-2621
Central Milling Co
Logan, UT 435-752-6625
Champlain Valley Milling Corp
Westport, NY. 518-962-4711
Chef Hans' Gourmet Foods
Monroe, LA. 800-890-4267
CHS Inc.
Inver Grove Hts., MN. 800-328-6539
CHS Sunflower
Grandin, ND 701-484-5313
Cinnabar Specialty Foods Inc
Prescott, AZ 866-293-6433
Coach's Oats
Yorba Linda, CA. 714-692-6885
Conrad Rice Mill Inc
New Iberia, LA. 800-551-3245
Continental Grain Company
New York, NY 212-207-5100
Cormier Rice Milling Co Inc
De Witt, AR 870-946-3561
Dakota Specialty Milling, Inc.
Fargo, ND 844-633-2746
Devansoy Farms
Carroll, IA. 800-747-8605
DMH Ingredients Inc
Libertyville, IL 847-362-9977
Ellison Milling Company
Lethbridge, AB 403-328-6622
Everspring Farms
Seaforth, ON. 519-527-0990
Fairhaven Cooperative Flour Mill
Bellingham, WA 360-757-9947
Falcon Rice Mill Inc
Crowley, LA 800-738-7423
Fall River Wild Rice
Fall River Mills, CA. 800-626-4366
Farmer Direct Organic
Regina, SK 306-563-7815
Farmers Rice Milling Co
Lake Charles, LA 337-433-5205
Farmers Way
Ferris Organic Farms
Eaton Rapids, MI 800-628-8736
Fizzle Flat Farm, L.L.C.
Yale, IL. 618-793-2060
Freeland Bean & Grain Inc
Freeland, MI 800-447-9131
Fresh Ideas
Las Vegas, NV 702-701-4272
Garber Farms
Iota, LA. 800-824-2284
Grain Place Foods Inc
Marquette, NE. 888-714-7246
Grain Process Enterprises Ltd.
Scarborough, ON 800-387-5292
Great Western Malting Co
Vancouver, WA 360-693-3661
Grey Owl Foods
Grand Rapids, MN 800-527-0172
Hall Grain Company
Akron, CO. 970-345-2206
Harvest Innovations
Indianola, IA. 515-962-5063
HealthBest
San Marcos, CA 760-752-5230
Healthy Food Ingredients
Fargo, ND 844-275-3443
Heartland Gourmet LLC
Lincoln, NE. 800-735-6828
Heartland Mills Shipping
Marienthal, KS 800-232-8533
High Quality Organics
Reno, NV 775-971-8550
Highland Family Farms
Mapleton, MN. 507-524-3797
Homegrown Naturals
Napa, CA. 800-288-1089

Homestead Mills
Cook, MN. 800-652-5233
Honeyville Grain Inc
Brigham City, UT 435-494-4200
In Harvest Inc
Bemidji, MN. 800-346-7032
Inn Maid Food
Lenox, MA 413-637-2732
J & L Grain Processing
Riceville, IA 800-244-9211
J M Swank Co
North Liberty, IA 800-593-6375
J. R. Simplot Co.
Boise, ID 208-336-2110
J.R. Short Canadian Mills
Toronto, ON 416-421-3463
Kashi Company
Solana Beach, CA. 877-747-2467
Knappen Milling Co
Augusta, MI 800-562-7736
La Crosse Milling Company
Cochrane, WI 800-441-5411
LaCrosse Milling Company
Cochrane, WI 800-441-5411
Landreth Wild Rice
Norman, OK 800-333-3533
Leech Lake Wild Rice
Cass Lake, MN 218-335-8200
Legumex Walker, Inc.
Winnipeg, MB. 204-808-0448
Lone Pine Enterprise Inc
Carlisle, AR 870-552-3217
Louisiana Rice Mill
Crowley, LA 337-783-9777
Lowell Farms
El Campo, TX. 888-484-9213
Luxor California Exports Corp.
San Diego, CA 619-465-7777
Maple Leaf Foods International
North York, ON. 800-268-3708
Marubeni America Corp.
New York, NY 212-450-0100
McKnight Milling Company
Hickory Ridge, AR. 800-287-2383
Mid Kansas Co-Op Assn
Moundridge, KS 800-864-4428
Mille Lacs Wild Rice Corp
Aitkin, MN 800-626-3809
Mills Brothers Intl
Seattle, WA 206-575-3000
Minn-Dak Growers LTD
Grand Forks, ND. 701-746-7453
Minnestalgia Foods LLC
Mcgregor, MN 800-328-6731
Montana Flour & Grains
Fort Benton, MT. 800-622-5790
Montana Specialty Mills LLC
Great Falls, MT. 800-332-2024
Mosher Products Inc
Cheyenne, WY 307-632-1492
Mountain High Organics
New Milford, CT 860-210-7805
Mustard Seed
Central, SC 877-621-2591
Natural Food Mill
Corona, CA. 800-797-5090
Natural Way Mills Inc
Middle River, MN. 218-222-3677
Nature's Legacy Inc.
Hudson, MI. 517-448-2050
New Organics
Kenwood, CA. 734-677-5570
Northwestern Extract
Germantown, WI. 800-466-3034
Olam Spices
Fresno, CA 559-447-1390
Osowski Farms
Minto, ND. 701-248-3341
Ottawa Valley Grain Products
Renfrew, ON 613-432-3614
Perfect Foods Inc
Goshen, NY. 800-933-3288
Pines International
Lawrence, KS 800-697-4637
Pizzey's Milling & Baking Company
Twin Falls, ID 208-733-7555
Pleasant Grove Farms
Pleasant Grove, CA 916-655-3391
R&J Farms
West Salem, OH 419-846-3179
Raymond-Hadley Corporation
Spencer, NY 800-252-5220

Rice Hull Specialty Products
Stuttgart, AR. 870-673-8507
Riviana Foods Inc.
Houston, TX 713-529-3251
Roberts Seed
Axtell, NE. 308-743-2565
S & E Organic Farms Inc
Bakersfield, CA 661-325-2644
Scott's Auburn Mills
Russellville, KY 270-726-2080
SJH Enterprises
Middleton, WI. 888-745-3845
Sole Grano LLC
Fair Lawn, NJ 201-797-7100
Sorrenti Family Farms
Escalon, CA 888-435-9490
Southeastern Mills Inc
Rome, GA. 800-334-4468
Southern Brown Rice
Weiner, AR 800-421-7423
Specialty Commodities Inc
Fargo, ND 701-282-8222
Specialty Rice Inc
Brinkley, AR. 800-467-1233
Stan-Mark Food Products Inc
Chicago, IL. 800-651-0994
Star of the West Milling Co.
Frankenmuth, MI 989-652-9971
Stengel Seed & Grain Co
Milbank, SD 605-432-6030
Sun West Foods
Davis, CA 530-758-8550
Sunnyland Mills
Fresno, CA 800-501-8017
SunWest Foods, Inc.
Davis, CA 530-758-8550
T.S. Smith & Sons
Bridgeville, DE. 302-337-8271
Teff Co
Nampa, ID. 888-822-2221
Terra Ingredients LLC
Minneapolis, MN 855-497-3308
Timeless Seeds
Ulm, MT 406-866-3340
Trinidad Benham Corporation
Denver, CO 303-220-1400
Tundra Wild Rice
Pine Falls, NB. 204-367-8651
TyRy Inc
Rocklin, CA 800-322-6325
Uhlmann Co
Kansas City, MO. 866-866-8627
Vitamins
Chicago, IL. 312-861-0700
Wagner Gourmet Foods
Lenexa, KS 913-469-5411
Weisenberger Mills
Midway, KY 800-643-8678
WG Thompson & Sons
Blenheim, ON. 800-265-5225
Wheat Montana Farms Inc
Three Forks, MT. 800-535-2798
Wild Rice Exchange
Woodland, CA. 800-223-7423
World Nutrition, Inc.
Scottsdale, AZ. 800-548-2710

Granola

18 Rabbits Inc.
San Francisco, CA 415-922-6006
Ace Bakery
North York, ON. 800-443-7929
Alvarado Street Bakery
Petaluma, CA 707-789-6700
Ambrosial Granola
Brooklyn, NY 718-491-1335
Barbara's Bakery
Lakeville, MN. 800-343-0590
Bear Naked, Inc.
Solana Beach, CA. 866-374-4442
Beaujolais Panforte
Santa Rosa, CA. 800-776-1778
Big Boss Baking Co
High Point, NC 336-861-1212
Bliss Gourmet Foods
St. Paul, MN
Blue Planet Foods
Collegedale, TN 877-396-3145
Bob's Red Mill Natural Foods
Milwaukie, OR 800-349-2173
Boulder Granola
Boulder, CO 303-443-1136

Chappaqua Crunch
Marblehead, MA 781-631-8118
Cream Of The West
Harlowton, MT 800-477-2383
Edner Corporation
Hayward, CA 510-441-8504
EFFi Foods
Los Angeles, CA 310-582-5938
Enjoy Life Foods
Chicago, IL 888-503-6569
GKI Foods
Brighton, MI 248-486-0055
Grain Process Enterprises Ltd.
Scarborough, ON 800-387-5292
Grain-Free JK Gourmet, Inc.
Toronto, ON 800-608-0465
Grandma Emily
Montreal, QC 877-943-3661
GrandyOats
Hiram, ME 207-935-7415
Healing Home Foods
Pound Ridge, NY 914-764-1303
Health Valley Company
Irwindale, CA 800-334-3204
Hialeah Products Co
Hollywood, FL 800-923-3379
Hudson Henry Baking Co.
Palmyra, VA 817-733-0709
Inn Maid Food
Lenox, MA 413-637-2732
Julie's Real
Dallas, TX 877-659-4375
Lehi Valley Trading Company
Mesa, AZ 480-684-1402
Lola Granola Bar Corporation
Croton Falls, NY 914-617-8833
Lowcountry Produce
Raleigh, NC 800-935-2792
McKee Foods Corp.
Collegedale, TN 800-522-4499
Michaelene's Gourmet Granola
Clarkston, MI 248-625-0156
Mother Nature's Goodies
Yucaipa, CA 909-795-6018
Nature's Habit Brand. Inc.
Washago, ON 707-712-2826
Nature's Path Foods
Blaine, WA 888-808-9505
New Century Snacks
City of Commerce, CA 800-688-6887
New England Natural Bakers
Greenfield, MA 800-910-2884
Nuts About Granola
York, PA 717-814-9648
Orchard Pond
Tallahassee, FL 850-894-0154
Organic Milling
San Dimas, CA 909-599-0961
Partners: A Tasteful Choice
Kent, WA 800-632-7477
Poppa's Granola
Perkinsville, VT 802-263-5342
Positively 3rd St Bakery
Duluth, MN 218-724-8619
Purely Pecans
Valdosta, GA 800-627-6630
Red Rose Trading Company
Lancaster, PA 717-293-7833
Riverside Natural Foods
Vaughan, ON 416-360-8200
San Franola Granola
San Francisco, CA 415-506-9582
SBK Preserves
Bronx, NY 800-773-7378
Schulze & Burch Biscuit Co
Chicago, IL 773-927-6622
Small Batch Organics
Manchester Center, VT 802-367-1054
Small Planet Foods
Minneapolis, MN 800-624-4123
Snackerz
Commerce, CA 888-576-2253
Sole Grano LLC
Fair Lawn, NJ 201-797-7100
The Safe + Fair Food Company
Chicago, IL
The Toasted Oat Bakehouse
Columbus, OH
Torn & Glasser
Los Angeles, CA 800-282-6887
Two Moms In The Raw
Longmont, CO 720-221-8555
Udi's Granola
Denver, CO 303-657-6366
US Mills
Bala Cynwyd, PA 800-422-1125
Vikis Foods
Bethpage, NY 516-767-8700
Viktoria's Gourmet Foods, LLC
Bethpage, NY 516-767-8700
Well Dressed Food Company
Tupper Lake, NY 518-359-5280
WholeMe
Minneapolis, MN 612-247-9728
Wildway
San Antonio, TX 512-677-9965

Grits

Callie's Charleston Biscuits
North Charleston, SC 843-577-1198
Healthy Food Ingredients
Fargo, ND 844-275-3443
J P Green Milling Co
Mocksville, NC 336-751-2126
Minn-Dak Growers LTD
Grand Forks, ND 701-746-7453
Natural Products Inc
Grinnell, IA 641-236-0852
Natural Way Mills Inc
Middle River, MN 218-222-3677
Sturm Foods Inc
Manawa, WI 800-347-8876

Corn White & Yellow

Agricor Inc
Marion, IN 765-662-0606
House-Autry Mills Inc
Four Oaks, NC 800-849-0802
Mills Brothers Intl
Seattle, WA 206-575-3000

Hominy

Cateraid Inc
Howell, MI 800-508-8217
Juanita's Foods
Wilmington, CA 800-303-2965

Canned

Juanita's Foods
Wilmington, CA 800-303-2965

Hops

Andean Naturals LLC
Foster City, CA 650-303-1780
Hops Extract Corporation of America
Yakima, WA 800-339-8410
Hudson Valley Hops
Beacon, NY 845-202-2398
John I. Haas
Washington, DC
Northwestern Extract
Germantown, WI 800-466-3034
S S Steiner Inc
New York, NY 212-838-8901
Watson Inc
West Haven, CT 800-388-3481
Yakima Chief-Hopunion LLC
Yakima, WA 509-453-4792

Hummus

Banzos
Denver, CO 303-447-2133
Haig's Delicacies
Hayward, CA 510-782-6285
Helen's Pure Foods
Cheltenham, PA 215-379-6433
Hope Foods
Boulder, CO 303-248-7019
Hungry Sultan
Lake Forest, CA 949-215-0000
Ithaca Craft Hummus
Escondido, CA 855-979-6751
Pita Pal
Houston, TX 713-777-7482
Quong Hop & Company
S San Francisco, CA 650-553-9900
Tribe Mediterranean
Taunton, MA 800-848-6687

Malt

Briess Malt & Ingredients Co.
Chilton, WI 800-657-0806
Great Western Malting Co
Vancouver, WA 360-693-3661
Hudson Valley Malt
Germantown, NY 845-489-3450
Jones Brewing Company
Smithton, PA 724-483-2400
Lake Country Foods Inc
Oconomowoc, WI 262-567-5521
Lion Brewery Inc
Wilkes Barre, PA 888-295-2337
Malt Diastase Co
Saddle Brook, NJ 800-526-0180
Malteurop North America
Milwaukee, WI 414-671-1166
Northwestern Extract
Germantown, WI 800-466-3034
Prairie Malt
Biggar, SK 306-948-3500
Premier Malt Products Inc
Warren, MI 800-521-1057
Rahr Malting Co
Shakopee, MN 952-445-1431
United Canadian Malt
Peterborough, ON 800-461-6400
Watson Inc
West Haven, CT 800-388-3481

Syrup

Briess Malt & Ingredients Co.
Chilton, WI 800-657-0806
Malt Diastase Co
Garfield, NJ 800-772-0416
Schiff Food Products Co Inc
Totowa, NJ 973-237-1990
United Canadian Malt
Peterborough, ON 800-461-6400

Millet

American Key Food Products Inc
Closter, NJ 877-263-7539
CHS Sunflower
Grandin, ND 701-484-5313
Great River Organic Milling
Arcadia, WI 608-687-9580
Healthy Food Ingredients
Fargo, ND 844-275-3443
Hialeah Products Co
Hollywood, FL 800-923-3379
Mills Brothers Intl
Seattle, WA 206-575-3000
Natural Way Mills Inc
Middle River, MN 218-222-3677
Organic Planet
San Francisco, CA 415-765-5590
Red River Commodities Inc
Fargo, ND 800-437-5539

Oats & Oat Products

Agricore United
St Louis Park, MN 877-509-5865
Anna's Oatcakes
Weston, VT 802-824-3535
Avena Foods Ltd.
Regina, SK 306-757-3663
Barbara's Bakery
Lakeville, MN 800-343-0590
Blue Planet Foods
Collegedale, TN 877-396-3145
Fizzle Flat Farm, L.L.C.
Yale, IL 618-793-2060
GF Harvest
Powell, WY 888-941-9922
Giusto's Specialty Foods Inc
S San Francisco, CA 650-873-6566
Grain Millers Inc
Eden Prairie, MN 800-232-6287
Healthy Food Ingredients
Fargo, ND 844-275-3443
Heartland Mills Shipping
Marienthal, KS 800-232-8533
Honeyville Grain Inc
Brigham City, UT 435-494-4200
J M Swank Co
North Liberty, IA 800-593-6375
Oatworks
New York, NY 646-624-2400

Particle Control
Albertville, MN. 763-497-3075
Richardson International
Winnipeg, MB. 866-217-6211
SJH Enterprises
Middleton, WI. 888-745-3845
West Thomas Partners, LLC
Grand Rapids, MI 616-755-8432

Oat Bran

Foley's Chocolates & Candies
Richmond, BC 888-236-5397
Grain Millers Inc
Eden Prairie, MN 800-232-6287
Natural Foods Inc
Toledo, OH 419-537-1711
SJH Enterprises
Middleton, WI. 888-745-3845

Oatmeal

Grain Millers Inc
Eden Prairie, MN 800-232-6287
Honeyville Grain Inc
Brigham City, UT 435-494-4200
LaCrosse Milling Company
Cochrane, WI 800-441-5411
Nature's Path Foods
Blaine, WA 888-808-9505
Oats Overnight
Tempe, AZ
Silver Palate Kitchens
Cresskill, NJ 201-568-0110
The Kroger Co.
Murray, KY. 800-632-6900

Quick

Modern Oats
Irvine, CA 888-662-2334

Rolled

Grain Millers Inc
Eden Prairie, MN 800-232-6287
Heartland Mills Shipping
Marienthal, KS 800-232-8533
Honeyville Grain Inc
Brigham City, UT 435-494-4200

Steel Cut

King Arthur Flour
Norwich, VT. 800-827-6836

Poi

Aloha Poi Factory Inc
Wailuku, HI. 808-244-3536
Pueo Poi Shop
Hilo, HI. 808-935-8435

Quinoa

Alter Eco
San Francisco, CA 415-701-1214
EatKeenwa, Inc.
Jersey City, NJ 855-453-3692
Highland Farm Foods
Rock Hill, SC 803-396-1439
I Heart Keenwah
Chicago, IL
Nature's Earthly Choice
Eagle, ID. 208-898-4004
Terra Ingredients
Minneapolis, MN 888-497-3308
Tiny Hero Foods
San Francisco, CA 855-778-4662
Top Tier Foods Inc.
Vancouver, BC 778-628-0015

Rice

Acharice Specialties
Greenville, MS 800-432-4901
Affiliated Rice Milling
Alvin, TX 281-331-6176
Agrusa
Leonia, NJ. 201-592-5950
Ankeny Lake Wild Rice
Salem, OR. 800-555-5380
Baycliff Co Inc
Garwood, NJ. 866-772-7569
Beaumont Rice Mills
Beaumont, TX. 409-832-2521
Berberian Nut Company
Chico, CA 530-981-4900
Bgreen Food
San Diego, CA 619-825-9330
Bluechip Group
Salt Lake City, UT 800-878-0099
Bunge
Chesterfield, MO 314-292-2000
Bunge North America Inc.
Chesterfield, MO 314-292-2000
Buonitalia
New York, NY 212-633-9090
California Cereal Products
Oakland, CA 510-452-4500
California Natural Products
Lathrop, CA 209-858-2525
Caribbean Food Delights Inc
Tappan, NY. 845-398-3000
Castor River Farms
Dexter, MO
Chef Hans' Gourmet Foods
Monroe, LA. 800-890-4267
Chef Merito Inc
Van Nuys, CA 800-637-4861
Chieftain Wild Rice
Spooner, WI 800-262-6368
Cinnabar Specialty Foods Inc
Prescott, AZ 866-293-6433
Commodities Marketing Inc
Clarksburg, NJ 732-516-0700
Conrad Rice Mill Inc
New Iberia, LA 800-551-3245
Cormier Rice Milling Co Inc
De Witt, AR 870-946-3561
Country Cupboard
Lewisburg, PA. 570-523-3211
Crunchy Rollers
Dallas, TX
Dalian Xinfeng International Industry & Trade Co.
Golden Valley, MN 612-964-7391
Deerwood Rice & Grain Procng
Deerwood, MN 218-534-3762
Dixie Rice
Gueydan, LA. 337-536-9276
Eden Foods Inc
Clinton, MI 888-424-3336
Falcon Rice Mill Inc
Crowley, LA 800-738-7423
Fall River Wild Rice
Fall River Mills, CA 800-626-4366
Fantastic World Foods
Providence, RI
Farmers Rice Milling Co
Lake Charles, LA 337-433-5205
Garber Farms
Iota, LA. 800-824-2284
Genki USA
Torrance, CA
Giusto's Specialty Foods Inc
S San Francisco, CA. 650-873-6566
Gourmet House
Allentown, PA. 800-226-9522
Goya Foods Inc.
Jersey City, NJ 201-348-4900
Green Valley Foods
Salem, OR. 844-588-3535
Grey Owl Foods
Grand Rapids, MN 800-527-0172
Hung's Noodle House
Calgary, AB. 403-250-1663
In Harvest Inc
Bemidji, MN. 800-346-7032
Kalustyan
New York, NY 800-352-3451
KODA Farms Inc
South Dos Palos, CA 209-392-2191
Kohinoor Foods
Edison, NJ. 888-440-7423
Landreth Wild Rice
Norman, OK 800-333-3533
Leech Lake Wild Rice
Cass Lake, MN. 218-335-8200
Lone Pine Enterprise Inc
Carlisle, AR 870-552-3217
Lotus Foods
Richmond, CA 510-525-3137
Louis Dreyfus Corporation
Rotterdam,
Louisiana Gourmet Enterprises
Houma, LA 800-328-5586
Louisiana Rice Mill
Crowley, LA 337-783-9777
Lowell Farms
El Campo, TX. 888-484-9213
Lundberg Family Farms
Richvale, CA. 530-538-3500
McKnight Milling Company
Hickory Ridge, AR 800-287-2383
Mermaid Spice Corporation
Fort Myers, FL 239-693-1986
Mille Lacs Wild Rice Corp
Aitkin, MN 800-626-3809
Mills Brothers Intl
Seattle, WA 206-575-3000
Minnestalgia Foods LLC
Mcgregor, MN 800-328-6731
Miracle Noodle
Los Angeles, CA. 800-948-4205
Mountain High Organics
New Milford, CT 860-210-7805
Natural Way Mills Inc
Middle River, MN. 218-222-3677
North Bay Trading Co
Brule, WI. 800-348-0164
Oak Grove Smoke House Inc
Prairieville, LA 225-673-6857
Olam Spices
Fresno, CA 559-447-1390
Pleasant Grove Farms
Pleasant Grove, CA 916-655-3391
Primo Foods
Toronto, ON 800-377-6945
Producers Rice Mill Inc.
Stuttgart, AR 870-673-4444
Raymond-Hadley Corporation
Spencer, NY 800-252-5220
Ribus Inc.
St. Louis, MO 314-727-4287
Rice Company
Fair Oaks, CA 916-784-7745
Rice Foods
Mount Vernon, IL 618-242-0026
Rice Hull Specialty Products
Stuttgart, AR 870-673-8507
Riceland Foods Inc.
Stuttgart, AR 855-742-3929
Ricetec
Alvin, TX 800-580-7423
Riviana Foods Inc.
Houston, TX 713-529-3251
Royal Caribbean Bakery
Mt Vernon, NY 888-818-0971
Sage V Foods
Boulder, CO 303-449-5626
Shah Trading Company
Scarborough, ON 416-292-6927
Sorrenti Family Farms
Escalon, CA 888-435-9490
Southern Brown Rice
Weiner, AR 800-421-7423
Specialty Rice Inc
Brinkley, AR. 800-467-1233
Sun West
Torrance, CA. 310-320-4000
SunWest Foods, Inc.
Davis, CA 530-758-8550
SunWest Organics
Davis, CA 530-758-8550
Tipiak Inc
Stamford, CT. 203-961-9117
Torn & Glasser
Los Angeles, CA. 800-282-6887
Trinidad Benham Corporation
Denver, CO 303-220-1400
Tropical Foods
Lithia Springs, GA 800-544-3762
Tundra Wild Rice
Pine Falls, NB. 204-367-8651
Vigo Importing Co
Tampa, FL. 800-282-4130
Wagner Gourmet Foods
Lenexa, KS 913-469-5411
Wild Rice Exchange
Woodland, CA. 800-223-7423
Wildly Organic
Silver Bay, MN. 800-945-3801
Willow Foods
Beaverton, OR 800-338-3609
Wysong Corp
Midland, MI 800-748-0188

Arborio

Gourmet House
Allentown, PA. 800-226-9522

Lundberg Family Farms
Richvale, CA. 530-538-3500

Basmati

Commodities Marketing Inc
Clarksburg, NJ 732-516-0700
Gourmet House
Allentown, PA. 800-226-9522
In Harvest Inc
Bemidji, MN. 800-346-7032
Kalustyan
New York, NY 800-352-3451
Lone Pine Enterprise Inc
Carlisle, AR 870-552-3217
Lundberg Family Farms
Richvale, CA. 530-538-3500
McKnight Milling Company
Hickory Ridge, AR. 800-287-2383
New Organics
Kenwood, CA 734-677-5570
Ricetec
Alvin, TX 800-580-7423
Southern Brown Rice
Weiner, AR 800-421-7423
Specialty Rice Inc
Brinkley, AR. 800-467-1233
Wild Rice Exchange
Woodland, CA. 800-223-7423

Brewers'

Beaumont Rice Mills
Beaumont, TX. 409-832-2521
Commodities Marketing Inc
Clarksburg, NJ 732-516-0700

Brown

Bunge North America Inc.
Chesterfield, MO 314-292-2000
California Natural Products
Lathrop, CA 209-858-2525
Castor River Farms
Dexter, MO
Cormier Rice Milling Co Inc
De Witt, AR 870-946-3561
Gourmet House
Allentown, PA. 800-226-9522
Healthee
Arcadia, CA 626-574-1719
Lone Pine Enterprise Inc
Carlisle, AR 870-552-3217
Louisiana Rice Mill
Crowley, LA 337-783-9777
Lundberg Family Farms
Richvale, CA. 530-538-3500
McKnight Milling Company
Hickory Ridge, AR. 800-287-2383
New Organics
Kenwood, CA 734-677-5570
Ricetec
Alvin, TX 800-580-7423
Sobaya
Cowansville, QC. 800-319-8808
Southern Brown Rice
Weiner, AR 800-421-7423
Wild Rice Exchange
Woodland, CA. 800-223-7423

Frozen

Sage V Foods
Boulder, CO 303-449-5626

Hulls

Farmers Rice Milling Co
Lake Charles, LA 337-433-5205
Rice Hull Specialty Products
Stuttgart, AR. 870-673-8507

IQF (Individual Quick Frozen)

Emerling International Foods
Buffalo, NY. 716-833-7381
Sage V Foods
Boulder, CO 303-449-5626

Instant

Mars Inc.
McLean, VA 703-821-4900
Sage V Foods
Boulder, CO 303-449-5626

Jasmine

Commodities Marketing Inc
Clarksburg, NJ 732-516-0700
Falcon Rice Mill Inc
Crowley, LA 800-738-7423
Gourmet House
Allentown, PA. 800-226-9522
In Harvest Inc
Bemidji, MN. 800-346-7032
KP USA Trading
Los Angeles, CA. 323-881-9871
Lowell Farms
El Campo, TX. 888-484-9213
Lundberg Family Farms
Richvale, CA. 530-538-3500
New Organics
Kenwood, CA 734-677-5570
Ricetec
Alvin, TX 800-580-7423

Milled

Besco Grain Ltd
Brunkild, MB 204-736-3570
Cormier Rice Milling Co Inc
De Witt, AR 870-946-3561
Farmers Rice Milling Co
Lake Charles, LA 337-433-5205

Organic

Gourmet House
Allentown, PA. 800-226-9522
Koda Farms
South Dos Palos, CA 209-392-2191
Sage V Foods
Boulder, CO 303-449-5626

Parboiled

US #1 Long Grain

McKnight Milling Company
Hickory Ridge, AR. 800-287-2383

Pilaf

Chef Hans' Gourmet Foods
Monroe, LA. 800-890-4267
Country Cupboard
Lewisburg, PA. 570-523-3211
Kashi Company
Solana Beach, CA. 877-747-2467
Lundberg Family Farms
Richvale, CA. 530-538-3500
Wild Rice Exchange
Woodland, CA. 800-223-7423

Precooked

Riviana Foods Inc.
Houston, TX 713-529-3251
Sage V Foods
Boulder, CO 303-449-5626

Risotto

Agrusa
Leonia, NJ. 201-592-5950
Italian Foods Corporation
Raleigh, NC 888-516-7262
Lundberg Family Farms
Richvale, CA. 530-538-3500

Spanish

Country Cupboard
Lewisburg, PA. 570-523-3211

Canned

Conrad Rice Mill Inc
New Iberia, LA. 800-551-3245

Wehani

Lundberg Family Farms
Richvale, CA. 530-538-3500

White

Castor River Farms
Dexter, MO
Falcon Rice Mill Inc
Crowley, LA 800-738-7423
Gourmet House
Allentown, PA. 800-226-9522

Wild

Ankeny Lake Wild Rice
Salem, OR. 800-555-5380
Chef Hans' Gourmet Foods
Monroe, LA. 800-890-4267
Chieftain Wild Rice
Spooner, WI 800-262-6368
Conrad Rice Mill Inc
New Iberia, LA 800-551-3245
Country Cupboard
Lewisburg, PA. 570-523-3211
Deerwood Rice & Grain Procng
Deerwood, MN 218-534-3762
Fall River Wild Rice
Fall River Mills, CA 800-626-4366
Floating Leaf Fine Foods
Winnipeg, MB. 866-989-7696
Gourmet House
Allentown, PA. 800-226-9522
Grey Owl Foods
Grand Rapids, MN 800-527-0172
In Harvest Inc
Bemidji, MN. 800-346-7032
Landreth Wild Rice
Norman, OK 800-333-3533
Leech Lake Wild Rice
Cass Lake, MN 218-335-8200
Lundberg Family Farms
Richvale, CA. 530-538-3500
Mille Lacs Wild Rice Corp
Aitkin, MN 800-626-3809
Minnestalgia Foods LLC
Mcgregor, MN 800-328-6731
North Bay Trading Co
Brule, WI. 800-348-0164
Secret Garden
Park Rapids, MN. 800-950-4409
Sorrenti Family Farms
Escalon, CA 888-435-9490
Southern Brown Rice
Weiner, AR 800-421-7423
Sun West Foods
Davis, CA 530-758-8550
SunWest Foods, Inc.
Davis, CA 530-758-8550
Tundra Wild Rice
Pine Falls, NB. 204-367-8651
Wild Rice Exchange
Woodland, CA. 800-223-7423

Rye

Alfred & Sam's Italian Bakery
Lancaster, PA. 717-392-6311
Fizzle Flat Farm, L.L.C.
Yale, IL 618-793-2060
Healthy Food Ingredients
Fargo, ND 844-275-3443
Montana Specialty Mills LLC
Great Falls, MT. 800-332-2024
Natural Way Mills Inc
Middle River, MN. 218-222-3677

Sorghum

DuPont Pioneer
Johnston, IA 515-535-5954
Healthy Food Ingredients
Fargo, ND 844-275-3443
Nu Life Market
Scott City, KS 866-962-5236
Webbpak Inc
Trussville, AL. 800-655-3500

Bagged & Bulk

Nu Life Market
Scott City, KS 866-962-5236

Grain

Nu Life Market
Scott City, KS 866-962-5236

Soy Bean Meal

Clofine Dairy Products Inc
Linwood, NJ 609-653-1000
International Service Group
Alpharetta, GA 770-518-0988

Tapioca

American Key Food Products Inc
Closter, NJ....877-263-7539
Commodities Marketing Inc
Clarksburg, NJ....732-516-0700
Heartline Foods
Westport, CT....203-222-0381
Organic Planet
San Francisco, CA....415-765-5590

Wheat

Agri-Dairy Products
Purchase, NY....914-697-9580
Agricore United
St Louis Park, MN....877-509-5865
Aliments Trigone
St-Francois-De-La-Rivier, QC....877-259-7491
Bakery Essentials Inc
Vernon Hills, IL....847-573-0844
Bluechip Group
Salt Lake City, UT....800-878-0099
Briess Malt & Ingredients Co.
Chilton, WI....800-657-0806
Bunge
Chesterfield, MO....314-292-2000
DuPont Pioneer
Johnston, IA....515-535-5954
El Peto Products
Cambridge, ON....800-387-4064
Ferris Organic Farms
Eaton Rapids, MI....800-628-8736
Fizzle Flat Farm, L.L.C.
Yale, IL....618-793-2060
Florence Macaroni Manufacturing
Chicago, IL....800-647-2782
Healthy Food Ingredients
Fargo, ND....844-275-3443
Knappen Milling Co
Augusta, MI....800-562-7736
Knight Seed Company
Burnsville, MN....800-328-2999
Kreher Family Farms
Clarence, NY....716-759-6802
Lone Pine Enterprise Inc
Carlisle, AR....870-552-3217
Louis Dreyfus Corporation
Rotterdam,
Manildra Milling Corporation
Fairway, KS....800-323-8435
Montana Specialty Mills LLC
Great Falls, MT....800-332-2024
Natural Way Mills Inc
Middle River, MN....218-222-3677
Nature's Legacy Inc.
Hudson, MI....517-448-2050
New Organics
Kenwood, CA....734-677-5570
Perfect Foods Inc
Goshen, NY....800-933-3288
Pines International
Lawrence, KS....800-697-4637
Pleasant Grove Farms
Pleasant Grove, CA....916-655-3391
Roberts Seed
Axtell, NE....308-743-2565
SJH Enterprises
Middleton, WI....888-745-3845
Sunnyland Mills
Fresno, CA....800-501-8017
T.S. Smith & Sons
Bridgeville, DE....302-337-8271
Viterra, Inc
Regina, SK....866-647-4090
Wysong Corp
Midland, MI....800-748-0188
Zinda Products
Candiac, QC....888-867-6664

Bread

Chicago Pastry
Bloomingdale, IL....630-529-6391

Flakes

Attala Development Corporation
Kosciusko, MS....662-289-2981
King Arthur Flour
Norwich, VT....800-827-6836

Germ

Ardent Mills Corp
Denver, CO....800-851-9618
Canadian Harvest-U.S.A.
Edina, MN....888-689-5800
Garuda International
Exeter, CA....559-594-4380
Green Foods Corp.
Oxnard, CA....800-777-4430
New Organics
Kenwood, CA....734-677-5570
Norac Technologies
Edmonton, AB....780-414-9595
Star of the West Milling Co.
Frankenmuth, MI....989-652-9971
Viobin USA
Monticello, IL....888-473-9645
Vitamins
Chicago, IL....312-861-0700

Defatted

Vitamins
Chicago, IL....312-861-0700

Gluten

Ardent Mills Corp
Denver, CO....800-851-9618
Bluechip Group
Salt Lake City, UT....800-878-0099
Clofine Dairy Products Inc
Linwood, NJ....609-653-1000
El Peto Products
Cambridge, ON....800-387-4064
Manildra Milling Corporation
Fairway, KS....800-323-8435

Winter

Natural Way Mills Inc
Middle River, MN....218-222-3677

Whey & Whey Products

Agri-Dairy Products
Purchase, NY....914-697-9580
Anderson Custom Processing
New Ulm, MN....877-588-4950
Berkshire Dairy
Wyomissing, PA....877-696-6455
Blossom Farm Products
Ridgewood, NJ....800-729-1818
Bongard's Creameries
Chanhassen, MN....952-277-5500
Brewster Dairy Inc
Brewster, OH....800-874-8874
Calpro Ingredients
Corona, CA....909-493-4890
Century Foods Intl LLC
Sparta, WI....800-269-1901
Clofine Dairy Products Inc
Linwood, NJ....609-653-1000
Con Yeager Spice Co
Zelienople, PA....800-222-2460
CP Kelco
Atlanta, GA....800-535-2687
Crest Foods Inc
Ashton, IL....877-273-7893
Davisco Foods International
Eden Prairie, MN....800-757-7611
Farmdale Creamery Inc
San Bernardino, CA....800-346-7306
First District Association
Litchfield, MN....320-693-3236
Grande Cheese Company
Fond du Lac, WI....800-678-3122
Grande Custom Ingredients Group
Fond du Lac, WI....800-772-3210
Great Lakes Cheese Company, Inc.
Hiram, OH....440-834-2500
Hilmar Cheese Company
Hilmar, CA....800-577-5772
Holmes Cheese Co
Millersburg, OH....330-674-6451
Honeyville Grain Inc
Brigham City, UT....435-494-4200
Kantner Group
Wapakoneta, OH....877-738-3448
Lactalis USA Inc
Belmont, WI....608-762-5136
Land O'Lakes Inc
Arden Hills, MN....800-328-9680
Leprino Foods Co.
Denver, CO....800-537-7466
Main Street Ingredients
La Crosse, WI....800-359-2345
Minerva Cheese Factory
Minerva, OH....330-868-4196
Mt Capra Products
Chehalis, WA....800-574-1961
Particle Control
Albertville, MN....763-497-3075
Plainview Milk Products
Plainview, MN....800-356-5606
Quality Ingredients
Burnsville, MN....952-898-4002
Saputo Cheese USA Inc.
Lincolnshire, IL....847-267-1100
Tillamook County Creamery Association
Tillamook, OR....503-842-4481
Valley Queen Cheese Factory
Milbank, SD....605-432-4563
Westin Foods
Omaha, NE....800-228-6098

Cheese & Cheese Products

General

Advanced Food Products LLC
New Holland, PA 800-732-5373
Agri-Mark Inc
West Springfield, MA 978-552-5500
Agropur
Appleton, WI 920-687-2489
Asiago PDO & Speck Alto Adige PGI
New York, NY 646-624-2885
Austrian Trade Commission
New York, NY 212-421-5250
Bletsoe's Cheese Inc
Marathon, WI 715-443-2526
Blue Marble Brands
Providence, RI 888-534-0246
Brazos Valley Cheese
Waco, TX 254-230-2535
Brookshire Grocery Company
Tyler, TX 888-937-3776
Capalbo's Fruit Baskets
Clifton, NJ 800-252-6262
Caputo Cheese
Melrose Park, IL 708-450-0074
Cheese Merchants of America
Carol Stream, IL 630-768-0317
Comte Cheese Association
New York, NY 646-515-9209
Couturier Na Inc
Hudson, NY 518-851-2570
Dairiconcepts
Springfield, MO 877-596-4374
Dairyfood USA Inc
Blue Mounds, WI 800-236-3300
Di Bruno Bros
Philadelphia, PA 215-922-2876
Farms For City Kids Foundation, Inc.
Reading, VT 802-484-1236
GAF Seelig Inc
Flushing, NY 718-899-5000
Golden Valley Dairy Products
Tulare, CA 559-687-1188
Good PLANeT Foods
Bellevue, WA 425-449-8134
Green Dirt Farm
Weston, MO 816-386-2156
Hilmar Ingredients
Hilmar, CA 888-300-4465
Hormel Foods Corp.
Austin, MN 507-437-5611
Ingles Markets
Black Mountain, NC 828-669-2941
J & M Foods Inc
Little Rock, AR 800-264-2278
Kantner Group
Wapakoneta, OH 877-738-3448
Liuzzi Angeloni Cheese
Hamden, CT 203-287-8477
Maplebrook Farm
Bennington, VT 802-440-9950
Marwood Sales, Inc
Overland Park, KS 800-745-2881
Meijer Inc
Grand Rapids, MI 616-453-6711
Minerva Dairy Inc
Minerva, OH 330-868-4196
Old Tavern Food Products Inc
Waukesha, WI 888-542-5317
Parmela Creamery
Torrance, CA 310-584-7541
Point Reyes Farmstead Cheese Co.
Point Reyes Station, CA 800-591-6787
Pondini Imports
Somerset, NJ 732-545-1255
Publix Super Market
Lakeland, FL 800-242-1227
Reilly Dairy & Food Company
Tampa, FL 813-839-8458
Rogue Creamery
Central Point, OR 866-396-4704
Shaker Valley Foods
Cleveland, OH 216-961-8600
Swiss Heritage Cheese Inc
Monticello, WI 608-938-4455
T. Marzetti Company
Westerville, OH 800-999-1835
Twin County Dairy
Kalona, IA 319-656-2776
Tyson Foods Inc.
Springdale, AR 479-290-4000
Wegmans Food Markets Inc.
Rochester, NY 800-934-6267
WEIS Markets Inc.
Sunbury, PA 866-999-9347
Winn-Dixie Stores
Jacksonville, FL 800-967-9105

Cheese

1000 Islands River Rat Cheese
Clayton, NY 800-752-1341
350 Cheese Straws
Beaufort, NC 252-838-9080
4C Foods Corp
Brooklyn, NY 718-272-4242
Advanced Food Products LLC
New Holland, PA 800-732-5373
Agri-Dairy Products
Purchase, NY 914-697-9580
Agropur
Granby, QC 800-363-5686
Agropur
Appleton, WI 920-687-2489
AgSource Milk Analysis Laboratory
Bonduel, WI 715-758-2178
Al Pete Meats
Muncie, IN 765-288-8817
Alberta Cheese Company
Calgary, AB 403-279-4353
Alpine Cheese Company
Winesburg, OH 330-359-6291
Alta Dena Certified Dairy LLC
City Of Industry, CA 800-535-1369
Ambrosi Cheese USA
Maspeth, NY
American Cheesemen
Clear Lake, IA 641-357-7176
Anchor Appetizer Group
Appleton, WI 920-997-2200
Anco Foods
Miami, FL 866-343-1108
Annie's Homegrown
Berkeley, CA 800-288-1089
Applegate Farms
Bridgewater, NJ 866-587-5858
Ardmore Cheese Company
Ardmore, TN 931-427-2191
Ariza Cheese Co
Paramount, CA 800-762-4736
Arla Foods Inc
Concord, ON 905-669-9393
Associated Milk Producers Inc.
New Ulm, MN 800-533-3580
Astro Dairy Products
Toronto, ON 416-622-2811
Atwood Cheese Company
Atwood, ON 519-356-2271
Avanti Foods Co
Walnut, IL 800-243-3739
B & D Foods
Boise, ID 208-344-1183
Bang & Soderlund Inc
Bonita Springs, FL 239-498-0600
Bartlett Dairy & Food Service
Jamaica, NY 718-658-2299
Bass Lake Cheese Factory
Somerset, WI 800-368-2437
Beecher's Handmade Cheese
Seattle, WA 206-956-1964
Bel Brands USA
Chicago, IL 312-462-1500
Bel Cheese USA
Leitchfield, KY 270-259-4071
BelGioioso Cheese Inc.
Green Bay, WI 920-863-2123
Belle Plaine Cheese Factory
Shawano, WI 866-245-5924
Bellwether Farms
Valley Ford, CA 707-478-8067
Berner Food & Beverage LLC
Dakota, IL 800-819-8199
Biazzo Dairy Products Inc
Ridgefield, NJ 201-941-6800
Bieri's Jackson Cheese
Jackson, WI 800-321-6077
Biery Cheese Co
Louisville, OH 330-875-3381
Big Picture Farm LLC
Townshend, VT 802-221-0547
Big Russ Beer Cheese
Beaver Dam, KY 270-485-6544
Blakely Freezer Locker
Blakeley, GA 229-723-3622
Blaser's USA, Inc.
Comstock, WI 866-570-2439
Bletsoe's Cheese Inc
Marathon, WI 715-443-2526
Blue Harbour Cheese
Halifax, NS 902-240-0305
Boar's Head
Sarasota, FL 800-352-6277
Bongard's Creameries
Chanhassen, MN 952-277-5500
Borden Dairy
Dallas, TX 855-311-1583
Boulder Vegans LLC
Morrison, CO 303-667-5628
Brewster Dairy Inc
Brewster, OH 800-874-8874
Brunkow Cheese Of Wisconsin
Darlington, WI 608-776-3716
Brunnett Dairy Co-Op
Grantsburg, WI 715-689-2748
Bunker Hill Cheese Co Inc
Millersburg, OH 800-253-6636
Buonitalia
New York, NY 212-633-9090
Byrne Dairy, Inc.
Syracuse, NY 800-899-1535
CA Fortune & Company
Bloomingdale, IL 630-539-3100
Cabot Creamery Co-Op
Waitsfield, VT 888-792-2268
Cady Cheese Factory
Wilson, WI 715-772-4218
Calabro Cheese Corp
East Haven, CT 203-469-1311
Callie's Charleston Biscuits
North Charleston, SC 843-577-1198
Capalbo's Fruit Baskets
Clifton, NJ 800-252-6262
Caprine Estates
Bellbrook, OH 937-848-7406
Carr Cheese Factory/GileCheese Company
Cuba City, WI 608-744-8455
Carr Valley Cheese
Fennimore, WI 800-462-7258
Carr Valley Cheese Company
La Valle, WI 800-462-7258
Cascade Cheese Co
Cascade, WI 920-528-8221
Castle Cheese
Slippery Rock, PA 800-252-4373
Caves Of Faribault/SwissValley
Faribault, MN 507-334-5260
Cedar Grove Cheese Inc
Plain, WI 800-200-6020
Cedar Valley Cheese Store
Belgium, WI 920-994-9500
Chalet Cheese Co-Op
Monroe, WI 608-325-4343
Cheddar Box Cheese House
Shawano, WI 715-526-5411
Cheese Factory
Buffalo, NY 716-828-0178
CheeseLand
Seattle, WA 206-709-1220
Chicago 58 Food Products
Woodbridge, ON 416-603-4244
Chicopee Provision Co Inc
Chicopee, MA 800-924-6328
Churny Company
Waupaca, WI 715-258-4040
Churny Company
Glenview, IL 847-646-5500
Clofine Dairy Products Inc
Linwood, NJ 609-653-1000
Clover Leaf Cheese
Calgary, AB 888-835-0126

Clover Stornetta Farms Inc
Petaluma, CA 800-237-3315
Cobb Hill Cheese
Hartland, VT 802-436-4360
Colonna Brothers Inc
North Bergen, NJ 201-864-1115
Colony Brands Inc
Monroe, WI. 800-544-9036
Commercial Creamery Co
Spokane, WA. 509-747-4131
Cooper Lake Farm LLC
Bearsville, NY 845-679-7822
Corfu Foods Inc
Bensenville, IL 630-595-2510
Creamland Dairies Inc
Albuquerque, NM. 505-247-0721
Crowley Cheese Inc
Mt Holly, VT. 800-683-2606
Crystal Farms Dairy Company
Minnetonka, MN. 800-672-8260
Curran's Cheese Plant Inc
Browntown, WI 608-966-3361
Cyclone Enterprises Inc
Houston, TX 281-872-0087
Cypress Grove
Arcata, CA 707-825-1100
Dairy Farmers Of America
Kansas City, KS 888-332-6455
Dairy Fresh Foods Inc
Taylor, MI 313-299-0735
Dairy Group
Jericho, NY 516-433-0080
Dan Carter
Richfield, WI 800-782-0741
Dean Foods Co.
Dallas, TX. 800-395-7004
Deca & Otto Farms
Miami, FL 305-629-9335
Decatur Dairy
Brodhead, WI 608-897-8661
Deppeler Cheese Factory
Monroe, WI. 608-325-6311
Deseret Dairy Products
Salt Lake City, UT 801-240-7350
Dexpa
Cumming, GA. 770-887-7412
Dimock Dairy Products
Dimock, SD. 605-928-3833
Dole & Bailey Inc
Woburn, MA 781-935-1234
Drangle Foods
Gilman, WI 715-447-8241
Dulce de Leche Delcampo Products
Miami, FL. 877-472-9408
Dupont Cheese
Marion, WI 800-895-2873
Dutch Cheese Makers Corp
Garden City, NY 631-533-9202
Dutch Farms Inc
Chicago, IL 800-637-3447
Eatem Foods Co
Vineland, NJ 800-683-2836
Eau Galle Cheese Factory Shop
Durand, WI 715-283-4211
Ellsworth Cooperative Creamery
Ellsworth, WI 715-273-4311
Elm City Cheese Co Inc
Hamden, CT 203-865-5768
Emkay Trading Corporation
Elmsford, NY 914-592-9000
F & A Dairy Products Inc
Dresser, WI 800-657-8582
Fairview Swiss Cheese
Fredonia, PA 724-475-4154
Fantis Foods Inc
Carlstadt, NJ 201-933-6200
Farmdale Creamery Inc
San Bernardino, CA 800-346-7306
Farmers Cooperative Dairy
Saint-Hubert, QC 800-501-1150
Farmgate Cheese LLC
Los Angelse, CA. 310-733-6853
Father's Country Hams
Bremen, KY 270-525-3554
Finlandia Cheese
Parsippany, NJ. 973-316-6609
First District Association
Litchfield, MN 320-693-3236
Fleur De Lait Foods Inc
New Holland, PA 800-322-2743
Floron Food Services
Edmonton, AB 780-438-9300
Food Matters Again
Brooklyn, NY 718-361-3183
Foremost Farms USA
Baraboo, WI 800-362-9196
Frank Brunckhorst Company
Sarasota, FL 804-722-4100
Frankfort Cheese
Edgar, WI 715-352-2345
Franklin's Cheese
Los Banos, CA 209-826-6259
Fried Provisions Company
Evans City, PA 724-538-3160
Friendship Dairies LLC
Friendship, NY 800-854-3243
Frog City Cheese
Plymouth Notch, VT. 802-672-3650
Froma-Dar
St. Boniface, QC. 819-535-3946
Fry Foods Inc
Tiffin, OH 800-626-2294
Gad Cheese Retail Store
Medford, WI 715-748-4273
GAF Seelig Inc
Flushing, NY. 718-899-5000
Galaxy Dairy Products
Ramsey, NJ 201-818-2030
GFA Brands Inc
Paramus, NJ 201-568-9300
Gibbsville Cheese Company
Sheboygan Falls, WI. 920-564-3242
Gile Cheese Store
Cuba City, WI 608-744-3456
Gossner Foods Inc.
Logan, UT. 800-944-0454
GPI USA LLC.
Mokena, IL 800-929-4248
Grafton Village Cheese Co LLC
Brattleboro, VT. 800-472-3866
Graham Cheese Corporation
Elnora, IN 800-472-9178
Grande Cheese Company
Fond du Lac, WI. 800-678-3122
Great American Appetizers
Nampa, ID. 800-282-4834
Great Lakes Cheese Company
Wausau, WI. 715-842-3214
Great Lakes Cheese Company, Inc.
Hiram, OH. 440-834-2500
Green Bay Cheese
Lincolnshire, IL 800-824-3373
Green Valley Food Corp
Dallas, TX. 800-853-8399
Greenberg Cheese Co
Commerce, CA 800-301-4507
Guggisberg Cheese
Millersburg, OH 800-262-2505
H B Taylor Co
Chicago, IL. 773-254-4805
H-E-B Grocery Co. LP
San Antonio, TX. 800-432-3113
Harrington's of Vermont
Richmond, VT
Heluva Good Cheese
Lynnfield, MA 800-644-5473
Henning Cheese Factory
Kiel, WI. 920-894-3032
Heritage Farms Dairy
Murfreesboro, TN. 615-895-2790
Hickory Farms
Maumee, OH. 800-753-8558
Hidden Villa Ranch
Fullerton, CA 800-326-3220
High Ridge Foods LLC
White Plains, NY 914-761-2900
Hiland Dairy Foods Co
Springfield, MO 800-492-4022
Hilmar Cheese Company
Hilmar, CA 800-577-5772
Hilmar Ingredients
Hilmar, CA 888-300-4465
Hollow Road Farms
Stuyvesant, NY 518-758-1881
Holmes Cheese Co
Millersburg, OH 330-674-6451
Hooks Cheese Co
Mineral Point, WI. 608-987-3259
Icco Cheese Co
Orangeburg, NY 845-680-2436
Idaho Milk Products
Jerome, ID. 208-644-2882
IMAC
Oklahoma City, OK 888-878-7827
Imperial Foods, Inc.
Long Island City, NY 718-784-3400
Inter-American Products
Cincinnati, OH 800-645-2233
International Cheese Company
Toronto, ON 416-769-3547
International Trading Company
Houston, TX 713-224-5901
Ito Cariani Sausage Company
Hayward, CA 510-887-0882
Ivanhoe Cheese Inc
Madoc, ON 613-473-4269
J B & Son LTD
Yonkers, NY 914-963-5192
J G Noble Cheese Company
Etiwanda, CA 909-899-2603
Jim's Cheese Pantry
Waterloo, WI. 800-345-3571
John Koller & Son Inc
Fredonia, PA 724-475-4154
Joseph Farms
Atwater, CA 209-394-7984
JVM Sales Corp.
Linden, NJ. 908-862-4866
Kantner Group
Wapakoneta, OH. 877-738-3448
Karoun Dairies Inc
San Fernando, CA. 888-767-0778
Keller's Creamery
Kansas City, MO. 800-535-5371
Kirby Holloway Provision Co
Harrington, DE 800-995-4729
Klondike Cheese Factory
Monroe, WI. 608-325-3021
Kolb-Lena Bresse Bleu Inc
Lena, IL. 815-369-4577
Kraemer Wisconsin Cheese LTD
Watertown, WI 800-236-8033
LA Grander Hillside Dairy Inc
Stanley, WI 715-644-2275
Lactalis American Group Inc
Buffalo, NY. 877-522-8254
Lactalis Ingredients Inc
Buffalo, NY
Lactalis USA Inc
Belmont, WI 608-762-5136
Lake Erie Frozen Foods Co
Ashland, OH 800-766-8501
Lakeview Banquit Cheese
Salt Lake City, UT 801-364-3607
Lamagna Cheese Co
Verona, PA. 412-828-6112
Land O'Lakes Inc
Arden Hills, MN. 800-328-9680
Laura Chenel's Chevre
Sonoma, CA 707-996-1252
Layman Distributing
Salem, VA. 800-237-1319
Le Sueur Cheese Co
Le Sueur, MN 800-757-7611
Lebanon Cheese Co
Lebanon, NJ 908-236-2611
Lengacher's Cheese House
Kinzers, PA 717-355-6490
Leprino Foods Co.
Denver, CO 800-537-7466
Leraysville Cheese Factory
Le Raysville, PA. 800-595-5196
LFI Inc
Fairfield, NJ 973-882-0550
Lifeline Food Company, Inc.
Seaside, CA. 831-899-5040
Lifeway
Morton Grove, IL 877-281-3874
Linden Cheese Factory
Linden, WI 800-660-5051
Lioni Latticini Inc
Union, NJ 908-624-9450
Lisanatti Foods
Oregon City, OR. 866-864-3922
Liuzzi Angeloni Cheese
Hamden, CT 203-287-8477
Los Altos Food Products
City Of Industry, CA. 626-330-6555
Lynn Dairy Inc
Granton, WI 715-238-7129
M.H. Greenebaum
Airmont, NY. 973-538-9200
Mahoning Swiss Cheese Cooperative
Smicksburg, PA. 814-257-8884
Maison Riviera
Varennes, QC 800-363-0092

Mancuso Cheese Co
Joliet, IL 815-722-2475
Maple Leaf Cheesemakers
New Glarus, WI 888-624-1234
Maplehill Creamery
Stuyvesant, NY 518-758-7777
Marathon Cheese
Medford, WI 715-748-4500
Marathon Cheese Corp
Marathon, WI 715-443-2211
Marin French Cheese Co
Petaluma, CA 800-292-6001
Marshallville Packing Co
Marshallville, OH 330-855-2871
Marva Maid Dairy
Newport News, VA 800-768-6243
Marwood Sales, Inc
Overland Park, KS 800-745-2881
Masters Gallery Foods Inc
Plymouth, WI 800-236-8431
Matador Processors
Blanchard, OK 800-847-0797
Mccadam Cheese Co Inc
Chateaugay, NY 800-639-4031
Meister Cheese Company
Muscoda, WI 800-634-7837
Michael Granese & Company
Norristown, PA 610-272-5099
Michigan Dairy LLC
Livonia, MI 734-367-5390
Michigan Farm Cheese Dairy
Fountain, MI 877-624-3373
Middlebury Cheese Company
Middlebury, IN 800-262-2505
Middlefield Cheese House
Middlefield, OH 800-327-9477
Mille Lacs Gourmet Foods
Madison, WI 800-843-1381
Miller's Cheese Corp
Brooklyn, NY 718-965-1840
Milsolv Corporation
Butler, WI 800-558-8501
Minerva Cheese Factory
Minerva, OH 330-868-4196
Morningland Dairy Cheese Company
Mountain View, MO 417-855-0588
Mossholder's Farm Cheese Factory
Appleton, WI 920-734-7575
Mozzarella Co
Dallas, TX 800-798-2954
Mt Sterling Co-Op Creamery
Highland, WI 866-289-4628
Nasonville Dairy
Marshfield, WI 715-676-2177
Nema Food Distribution
Fairfield, NJ 973-256-4415
Network Food Brokers
Haverford, PA 610-649-7210
Newburg Corners Cheese Factory
Bangor, WI 608-452-3636
Nodine's Smokehouse Inc
Torrington, CT 800-222-2059
Noon Hour Food Products Inc
Chicago, IL 800-621-6636
Nor-Tech Dairy Advisors
Sioux Falls, SD 605-338-2404
Northern Utah Manufacturing
Wellsville, UT 435-245-4542
Northern WIS Produce Co
Manitowoc, WI 920-684-4461
Old Chatham Sheepherding Co
Old Chatham, NY 888-743-3760
Old Country Cheese
Cashton, WI 888-320-9469
Old Europe Cheese Inc
Benton Harbor, MI 269-925-5003
Old Fashioned Foods
Mayville, WI 920-387-7924
Old Wisconsin Food Products
Homewood, IL 888-633-5684
Olde Tyme Food Corporation
East Longmeadow, MA 800-356-6533
ORB Weaver Farm
New Haven, VT 802-877-3755
Original Herkimer Cheese
Ilion, NY 315-895-7428
Oscar's Wholesale Meats
Ogden, UT 801-621-5655
Oshkosh Cold Storage
Oshkosh, WI 800-580-4680
Pacific Cheese Co
Hayward, CA 510-784-8800
Park Cheese Company Inc
Fond Du Lac, WI 800-752-7275
Parker Farm
Minneapolis, MN 800-869-6685
Parkers Farm
Coon Rapids, MN 800-869-6685
Parmalat Canada
Toronto, ON 800-563-1515
Pastorelli Food Products
Chicago, IL 800-767-2829
Pearl Valley Cheese Inc
Fresno, OH 740-545-6002
Pecoraro Dairy Products
Brooklyn, NY 718-388-2379
Penn Cheese
Winfield, PA 570-524-7700
Pine River Cheese & Butter Company
Ripley, ON 800-265-1175
Pine River Pre-Pack Inc
Newton, WI 920-726-4216
Plumrose USA
Chicago, IL 800-526-4909
Plymouth Cheese Counter
Plymouth, WI 888-607-9477
Pollio Dairy Products
Campbell, NY 607-527-3621
Prairie Farms Dairy Inc.
Edwardsville, IL 618-659-5700
Prima Kase
Monticello, WI 608-938-4227
Providence Cheese
Johnston, RI 401-421-5653
Purity Dairies LLC
Nashville, TN 615-244-1900
Queensboro Farm Products
Canastota, NY 315-687-6133
Queensboro Farm Products
Jamica, NY 718-658-5000
Ragersville Swiss Cheese
Sugarcreek, OH 330-897-3055
Raven Creamery Company
Portland, OR 503-288-5101
REDCLAY Gourmet
Winston-Salem, NC 336-575-3360
Redwood Hill Farm
Sebastopol, CA 877-238-3543
Regez Cheese & Paper Supply
Monroe, WI 608-325-3417
Renard's Cheese
Algoma, WI 920-487-2825
RM Heagy Foods
Lancaster, PA 717-569-1032
Roberto A Cheese Factory
East Canton, OH 330-488-1551
Rochester Cheese
Rochester, MN 888-288-6678
Roelli Cheese Co
Shullsburg, WI 800-575-4372
Rogue Creamery
Central Point, OR 866-396-4704
Ron's Wisconsin Cheese LLC
Luxemburg, WI 920-845-5330
Roos Foods
Kenton, DE 800-343-3642
Rosenberger's Dairies
Hatfield, PA 800-355-9074
Roth Cheese USA
Fitchburg, WI 608-285-9800
Royal Baltic LTD
Brooklyn, NY 718-385-8300
Rumiano Cheese Co.
Crescent City, CA 866-328-2433
Rumiano Cheese Factory
Willows, CA 866-328-2433
Safeway Inc.
Pleasanton, CA 877-723-3929
Salemville Cheese
Cambria, WI 920-394-3431
Salmans & Assoc
Chicago, IL 312-226-1820
Saputo Cheese USA Inc.
Lincolnshire, IL 847-267-1100
Saputo Inc.
Montreal, QC 800-672-8866
Sardinia Cheese
Seymour, CT 203-735-3374
Sargento Foods Inc
Plymouth, WI 800-243-3737
Sartori Co
Plymouth, WI 920-893-6061
Saxon Creamery
Cleveland, WI 920-693-8500
Schneider Cheese
Waldo, WI 920-467-3351
Schneider's Dairy Inc
Pittsburgh, PA 412-881-3525
Schobert's Cottage Cheese Corporation
Akron, OH 216-733-6876
Schreiber Foods Inc.
Green Bay, WI 920-437-7601
Schuman Cheese
Fairfield, NJ 800-888-2433
Scott's of Wisconsin
Sun Prairie, WI 800-693-0834
Scray's Cheese
De Pere, WI 920-336-8359
Sea Stars Goat Cheese
Santa Cruz, CA 831-423-7200
Sequoia Specialty Cheese Company
Visalia, CA 559-752-4106
Shenk's Foods
Lancaster, PA 717-393-4240
Sierra Cheese Mfg Co
Compton, CA 800-266-4270
Sierra Nevada Cheese Co.
Willows, CA 530-934-8660
Silani Sweet Cheese
Woodbridge, ON 905-792-3811
Simon's Specialty Cheese
Appleton, WI 800-444-0374
Sini Fulvi U.S.A.
Newark, NJ 973-274-0822
Sisler's Ice & Ice Cream
Ohio, IL 888-891-3856
Sofo Foods
Toledo, OH 800-447-4211
Sommer Maid Creamery Inc
Pipersville, PA 215-345-6160
Sonoma Creamery
Sonoma, CA 707-996-1000
Sparboe Foods Corp
New Hampton, IA 641-394-3040
Spaulding & Assoc
Brighton, MI 810-229-4166
Specialities Importers & Distributers
Millington, NJ 800-899-6689
Specialty Cheese Co Inc
Reeseville, WI 800-367-1711
Spring Grove Foods
Miamisburg, OH 937-866-4311
Springbank Cheese Company
Woodstock, ON 800-265-1973
Springdale Cheese Factory
Richland Center, WI 608-538-3213
Sprout Creek Farm
Poughkeepsie, NY 845-485-8432
St. Maurice Laurent
St-Bruno-Lac-St-Jean, QC 418-343-3655
Stallings Head Cheese Co
Houston, TX 713-523-1751
State Of Maine Cheese Co
Rockport, ME 800-762-8895
Steiner Cheese
Baltic, OH 888-897-5505
Stella Foods
Hinesburg, VT 802-482-2121
Stella Reedsburg
Reedsburg, WI 608-524-8244
Stremick's Heritage Foods
Santa Ana, CA 800-371-9010
Sugarbush Farm
Woodstock, VT 800-281-1757
Sun States
Charlotte, NC 704-821-0615
Sun-Re Cheese Co
Sunbury, PA 570-286-1511
Sunnyrose Cheese
Diamond City, AB 403-381-4024
Sunshine Farms
Portage, WI 608-742-2016
Super Stores Industries
Turlock, CA 209-668-2100
Suprema Specialties
Manteca, CA 209-858-9696
Supreme Artisan Foods
San Diego, CA 844-278-3663
Supreme Dairy Farms Co
Warwick, RI 401-739-8180
Swiss American Inc
St Louis, MO 800-325-8150
Swiss Way Cheese
Berne, IN 260-589-3531
T Sterling Assoc
Jamestown, NY 716-483-0769

Taftsville Country Store
Taftsville, VT 800-854-0013
Tall Talk Dairy
Canby, OR 503-266-1644
Taylor Cheese Corp
Weyauwega, WI 920-867-2337
The Worlds Best Cheese
Armonk, NY 800-922-4337
Thiel Cheese & Ingredients
Hilbert, WI 920-989-1440
Tholstrup Cheese
Muskegon, MI 800-426-0938
Tillamook County Creamery Association
Tillamook, OR 503-842-4481
Timber Lake Cheese Company
Timber Lake, SD 605-865-3605
Tomanetti Food Products Inc
Oakmont, PA 800-875-3040
Torkelson Cheese Co
Lena, IL 815-369-4265
Trega Foods
Weyauwega, WI 920-867-2137
Tropical Cheese
Perth Amboy, NJ 888-874-4928
Twin County Dairy
Kalona, IA 319-656-2776
Umpqua Dairy
Roseburg, OR 888-672-6455
V & V Supremo
Chicago, IL 888-887-8773
Valley Grain Products
Fresno, CA 559-675-3400
Valley Queen Cheese Factory
Milbank, SD 605-432-4563
Valley View Cheese Co Inc
Conewango Valley, NY 716-296-5821
Vella Cheese Co
Sonoma, CA 800-848-0505
Vermont Creamery
Websterville, VT 800-884-6287
Vern's Cheese
Chilton, WI 920-849-7717
VOD Gourmet
Greenwich, CT 203-531-5172
Wagshal's Imports
Washington, DC 202-363-5698
Wapsie Creamery
Independence, IA 319-334-7193
Weaver Brothers
Berne, IN 219-589-2869
Wenger Spring Brook Cheese Inc
Davis, IL 815-865-5612
West Point Dairy Products
West Point, NE 402-372-5551
Western Creamery
Brampton, ON 800-265-3230
Weyauwega Star Dairy
Weyauwega, WI 888-813-9720
Whitehall Specialties Inc
Whitehall, WI 888-755-9900
WhiteWave Foods
Denver, CO 800-488-9283
Widmer's Cheese Cellars Inc
Theresa, WI 888-878-1107
Williams-R J
Linwood, MI 800-968-4462
Williams-R J
Linwood, MI 800-968-4492
Winger Cheese
Towner, ND 701-537-5463
Winona Foods
Green Bay, WI 920-662-2184
Wisconsin Cheeseman
Madison, WI 800-693-0834
Wisconsin Farmers Union
Chippewa Falls, WI 800-272-5531
Wisconsin Milk Mktng Board Inc
Madison, WI 800-589-5127
Wohlt Cheese Corp
New London, WI 920-982-9000
Woolwich Dairy
Orangeville, ON 877-438-3499
World Cheese Inc
Brooklyn, NY 718-965-1700
Yerba Santa Goat Dairy
Lakeport, CA 707-263-8131
Zimmerman Cheese Inc
South Wayne, WI 608-968-3414

American

Crystal Farms Dairy Company
Minnetonka, MN 800-672-8260
Reilly Dairy & Food Company
Tampa, FL 813-839-8458
Sargento Foods Inc
Plymouth, WI 800-243-3737

Asiago

BelGioioso Cheese Inc.
Green Bay, WI 920-863-2123
JVM Sales Corp.
Linden, NJ 908-862-4866
Kantner Group
Wapakoneta, OH 877-738-3448
Lactalis American Group Inc
Buffalo, NY 877-522-8254
Park Cheese Company Inc
Fond Du Lac, WI 800-752-7275
Sargento Foods Inc
Plymouth, WI 800-243-3737
Sartori Co
Plymouth, WI 920-893-6061
Vella Cheese Co
Sonoma, CA 800-848-0505
Weyauwega Star Dairy
Weyauwega, WI 888-813-9720

Blend - American/Skim Milk

Sliced

Kantner Group
Wapakoneta, OH 877-738-3448

Blue

Bletsoe's Cheese Inc
Marathon, WI 715-443-2526
Clofine Dairy Products Inc
Linwood, NJ 609-653-1000
Great Hill Dairy Inc
Marion, MA 888-748-2208
Lactalis American Group Inc
Buffalo, NY 877-522-8254
Marathon Cheese Corp
Marathon, WI 715-443-2211
Reilly Dairy & Food Company
Tampa, FL 813-839-8458
Roth Cheese USA
Fitchburg, WI 608-285-9800
Sargento Foods Inc
Plymouth, WI 800-243-3737

Brie

Daphne's Creamery
.... 707-762-1760
Kolb-Lena Bresse Bleu Inc
Lena, IL 815-369-4577
Lactalis American Group Inc
Buffalo, NY 877-522-8254
Marin French Cheese Co
Petaluma, CA 800-292-6001
Old Europe Cheese Inc
Benton Harbor, MI 269-925-5003
Reilly Dairy & Food Company
Tampa, FL 813-839-8458
Supreme Artisan Foods
San Diego, CA 844-278-3663
Woolwich Dairy
Orangeville, ON 877-438-3499

Camembert

Kolb-Lena Bresse Bleu Inc
Lena, IL 815-369-4577
Lakeview Banquit Cheese
Salt Lake City, UT 801-364-3607
Marin French Cheese Co
Petaluma, CA 800-292-6001
Old Europe Cheese Inc
Benton Harbor, MI 269-925-5003
Reilly Dairy & Food Company
Tampa, FL 813-839-8458

Cheddar

Advanced Food Products LLC
New Holland, PA 800-732-5373
Alberta Cheese Company
Calgary, AB 403-279-4353
Alta Dena Certified Dairy LLC
City Of Industry, CA 800-535-1369
Ardmore Cheese Company
Ardmore, TN 931-427-2191
Bass Lake Cheese Factory
Somerset, WI 800-368-2437
Bletsoe's Cheese Inc
Marathon, WI 715-443-2526
Cady Cheese Factory
Wilson, WI 715-772-4218
Crystal Farms Dairy Company
Minnetonka, MN 800-672-8260
Daphne's Creamery
.... 707-762-1760
Father's Country Hams
Bremen, KY 270-525-3554
Foremost Farms USA
Baraboo, WI 800-362-9196
Golden Valley Dairy Products
Tulare, CA 559-687-1188
Guggisberg Cheese
Millersburg, OH 800-262-2505
Hilmar Cheese Company
Hilmar, CA 800-577-5772
Kantner Group
Wapakoneta, OH 877-738-3448
Kraft Heinz Canada
North York, ON 416-441-5000
Lactalis USA Inc
Belmont, WI 608-762-5136
Reilly Dairy & Food Company
Tampa, FL 813-839-8458
Saputo Cheese USA Inc.
Lincolnshire, IL 847-267-1100
Sargento Foods Inc
Plymouth, WI 800-243-3737
Trega Foods
Weyauwega, WI 920-867-2137
Twin County Dairy
Kalona, IA 319-656-2776

Reduced Fat

Kantner Group
Wapakoneta, OH 877-738-3448
Whitehall Specialties Inc
Whitehall, WI 888-755-9900

Reduced Fat - Shredded

Crowley Cheese Inc
Mt Holly, VT 800-683-2606
Kantner Group
Wapakoneta, OH 877-738-3448

Shredded

Horizon Organic Dairy
Broomfield, CO 888-494-3020
Kantner Group
Wapakoneta, OH 877-738-3448
WhiteWave Foods
Denver, CO 800-488-9283

Colby

Bass Lake Cheese Factory
Somerset, WI 800-368-2437
Belle Plaine Cheese Factory
Shawano, WI 866-245-5924
Bletsoe's Cheese Inc
Marathon, WI 715-443-2526
Brunkow Cheese Of Wisconsin
Darlington, WI 608-776-3716
Brunnett Dairy Co-Op
Grantsburg, WI 715-689-2748
Cady Cheese Factory
Wilson, WI 715-772-4218
Dupont Cheese
Marion, WI 800-895-2873
Finlandia Cheese
Parsippany, NJ 973-316-6609
Graham Cheese Corporation
Elnora, IN 800-472-9178
Guggisberg Cheese
Millersburg, OH 800-262-2505
Heluva Good Cheese
Lynnfield, MA 800-644-5473
Henning Cheese Factory
Kiel, WI 920-894-3032
Middlebury Cheese Company
Middlebury, IN 800-262-2505
Pine River Cheese & Butter Company
Ripley, ON 800-265-1175
Reilly Dairy & Food Company
Tampa, FL 813-839-8458
Reiter Dairy
Newport, KY 800-544-6455

Saputo Cheese USA Inc.
Lincolnshire, IL....847-267-1100
Sargento Foods Inc
Plymouth, WI....800-243-3737
Swiss American Inc
St Louis, MO....800-325-8150
Wapsie Creamery
Independence, IA....319-334-7193
Widmer's Cheese Cellars Inc
Theresa, WI....888-878-1107

Cottage

Aimonetto and Sons
Renton, WA....866-823-2777
Alpina
Batavia, NY....855-886-1914
Alta Dena Certified Dairy LLC
City Of Industry, CA....800-535-1369
Anderson Dairy Inc
Las Vegas, NV....702-642-7507
Anderson Erickson Dairy
Des Moines, IA....515-265-2521
Anderson Erickson Dairy
Kansas City, KS....913-621-4801
Astro Dairy Products
Toronto, ON....416-622-2811
Berkeley Farms
Hayward, CA....800-395-7004
Borden Dairy
Dallas, TX....855-311-1583
Broughton Foods LLC
El Paso, TX....800-395-7004
Byrne Dairy, Inc.
Syracuse, NY....800-899-1535
Clofine Dairy Products Inc
Linwood, NJ....609-653-1000
Cloverland/Green Spring Dairy
Baltimore, MD....800-876-6455
Darigold
Seattle, WA....800-333-6455
Friendship Dairies LLC
Friendship, NY....800-854-3243
GAF Seelig Inc
Flushing, NY....718 899-5000
Good Culture
Irvine, CA....844-899-8884
H-E-B Grocery Co. LP
San Antonio, TX....800-432-3113
Heritage Farms Dairy
Murfreesboro, TN....615-895-2790
Hiland Dairy Foods Co
Springfield, MO....800-492-4022
Horizon Organic Dairy
Broomfield, CO....888-494-3020
HP Hood LLC
Lynnfield, MA....800-343-6592
Kemps LLC
St Paul, MN
Marva Maid Dairy
Newport News, VA....800-768-6243
Michigan Dairy LLC
Livonia, MI....734-367-5390
Nancy's Probiotic Foods
Eugene, OR
Oakhurst Dairy
Portland, ME....800-482-0718
Old Home Foods Inc
New Brighton, MN....651-312-8900
Plains Dairy Products
Amarillo, TX....800-365-5608
Prairie Farms Dairy Inc.
Edwardsville, IL....618-659-5700
Purity Dairies LLC
Nashville, TN....615-244-1900
Queensboro Farm Products
Canastota, NY....315-687-6133
Queensboro Farm Products
Jamica, NY....718-658-5000
Reilly Dairy & Food Company
Tampa, FL....813-839-8458
Rockview Farms
Downey, CA....800-423-2479
Schepps Dairy
Dallas, TX....800-395-7004
Sisler's Ice & Ice Cream
Ohio, IL....888-891-3856
Smith Dairy
Orrville, OH....800-776-7076
Springfield Creamery Inc
Eugene, OR....541-689-2911
Super Stores Industries
Turlock, CA....209-668-2100

Umpqua Dairy
Roseburg, OR....888-672-6455
WhiteWave Foods
Denver, CO....800-488-9283

Cream

Alouette Cheese USA
New Holland, PA....800-322-2743
Astro Dairy Products
Toronto, ON....416-622-2811
Clofine Dairy Products Inc
Linwood, NJ....609-653-1000
Don's Food Products
Schwenksville, PA....888-321-3667
Emkay Trading Corporation
Elmsford, NY....914-592-9000
Franklin Foods
Enosburg Falls, VT....800-933-6114
GAF Seelig Inc
Flushing, NY....718-899-5000
Horizon Organic Dairy
Broomfield, CO....888-494-3020
Kite Hill
Hayward, CA....888-588-0994
Kraft Heinz Canada
North York, ON....416-441-5000
Marburger Farm Dairy
Evans City, PA....800-331-1295
Original Herkimer Cheese
Ilion, NY....315-895-7428
Queensboro Farm Products
Jamica, NY....718-658-5000
Rachael's Smoked Fish
Springfield, MA....800-327-3412
Reilly Dairy & Food Company
Tampa, FL....813-839-8458
Schepps Dairy
Dallas, TX....800-395-7004
Schneider's Dairy Inc
Pittsburgh, PA....412-881-3525
Schreiber Foods Inc.
Green Bay, WI....920-437-7601
Sierra Nevada Cheese Co.
Willows, CA....530-934-8660
Springfield Creamery Inc
Eugene, OR....541-689-2911
Tofutti Brands Inc
Cranford, NJ....908-272-2400
WhiteWave Foods
Denver, CO....800-488-9283
Woolwich Dairy
Orangeville, ON....877-438-3499

Edam

Old Europe Cheese Inc
Benton Harbor, MI....269-925-5003
Saputo Cheese USA Inc.
Lincolnshire, IL....847-267-1100

Feta

Advanced Food Products LLC
New Holland, PA....800-732-5373
Alberta Cheese Company
Calgary, AB....403-279-4353
Atwood Cheese Company
Atwood, ON....519-356-2271
Blue Marble Brands
Providence, RI....888-534-0246
Castella Imports Inc
Brentwood, NY....631-231-5500
FAGE USA Dairy Ind Inc
Johnstown, NY....866-962-5912
Kolb-Lena Bresse Bleu Inc
Lena, IL....815-369-4577
Lactalis American Group Inc
Buffalo, NY....877-522-8254
Lamagna Cheese Co
Verona, PA....412-828-6112
Michigan Farm Cheese Dairy
Fountain, MI....877-624-3373
Mt Capra Products
Chehalis, WA....800-574-1961
Mt Sterling Co-Op Creamery
Highland, WI....866-289-4628
Pecoraro Dairy Products
Brooklyn, NY....718-388-2379
Reilly Dairy & Food Company
Tampa, FL....813-839-8458
Sierra Cheese Mfg Co
Compton, CA....800-266-4270

Stickney Hill Dairy Inc
Kimball, MN....320-398-5360
Trega Foods
Weyauwega, WI....920-867-2137
Vermont Creamery
Websterville, VT....800-884-6287
Woolwich Dairy
Orangeville, ON....877-438-3499

Fontina

Atwood Cheese Company
Atwood, ON....519-356-2271
BelGioioso Cheese Inc.
Green Bay, WI....920-863-2123
Lactalis American Group Inc
Buffalo, NY....877-522-8254
Old Europe Cheese Inc
Benton Harbor, MI....269-925-5003
Park Cheese Company Inc
Fond Du Lac, WI....800-752-7275
Prima Kase
Monticello, WI....608-938-4227
Sartori Co
Plymouth, WI....920-893-6061

Goat's

Alta Dena Certified Dairy LLC
City Of Industry, CA....800-535-1369
Bass Lake Cheese Factory
Somerset, WI....800-368-2437
Daphne's Creamery
....707-762-1760
Epic Source Food
Frisco, TX....214-407-7154
Lactalis American Group Inc
Buffalo, NY....877-522-8254
Laura Chenel's Chevre
Sonoma, CA....707-996-1252
Mackenzie Creamery
Hiram, OH....330-569-3368
Montchevre-Betin, Inc
Rolling Hills Estates, CA....310-541-3520
Mozzarella Co
Dallas, TX....800-798-2954
Mt Capra Products
Chehalis, WA....800-574-1961
Mt Sterling Co-Op Creamery
Highland, WI....866-289-4628
Quillisascut Cheese Co
Rice, WA....509-738-2011
Rollingstone Chevre
Parma, ID....208-722-6460
Sierra Nevada Cheese Co.
Willows, CA....530-934-8660
Sprout Creek Farm
Poughkeepsie, NY....845-485-8432
Stickney Hill Dairy Inc
Kimball, MN....320-398-5360
Swiss American Inc
St Louis, MO....800-325-8150
Vermont Creamery
Websterville, VT....800-884-6287
Vermont Creamery
Websterville, VT....802-479-9371
Westfield Farm
Hubbardston, MA....877-777-3900

Gorgonzola

BelGioioso Cheese Inc.
Green Bay, WI....920-863-2123
Lactalis American Group Inc
Buffalo, NY....877-522-8254
Reilly Dairy & Food Company
Tampa, FL....813-839-8458

Gouda

Bass Lake Cheese Factory
Somerset, WI....800-368-2437
Bel Brands USA
Chicago, IL....312-462-1500
Cady Cheese Factory
Wilson, WI....715-772-4218
Finlandia Cheese
Parsippany, NJ....973-316-6609
Old Europe Cheese Inc
Benton Harbor, MI....269-925-5003
Prima Kase
Monticello, WI....608-938-4227
Roth Cheese USA
Fitchburg, WI....608-285-9800

Winchester Cheese Company
Winchester, CA....951-926-4239
Woolwich Dairy
Orangeville, ON....877-438-3499

Grated

Calabro Cheese Corp
East Haven, CT....203-469-1311
Clofine Dairy Products Inc
Linwood, NJ....609-653-1000
Colonna Brothers Inc
North Bergen, NJ....201-864-1115
Elm City Cheese Co Inc
Hamden, CT....203-865-5768
Icco Cheese Co
Orangeburg, NY....845-680-2436
JVM Sales Corp.
Linden, NJ....908-862-4866
Kantner Group
Wapakoneta, OH....877-738-3448
Mancuso Cheese Co
Joliet, IL....815-722-2475
Park Cheese Company Inc
Fond Du Lac, WI....800-752-7275
Pastene Co LTD
Canton, MA....781-298-3397
Sargento Foods Inc
Plymouth, WI....800-243-3737
Sun-Re Cheese Co
Sunbury, PA....570-286-1511

Gruyere

Castella Imports Inc
Brentwood, NY....631-231-5500
Roth Cheese USA
Fitchburg, WI....608-285-9800

Havarti

Finlandia Cheese
Parsippany, NJ....973-316-6609
Prima Kase
Monticello, WI....608-938-4227
Roth Cheese USA
Fitchburg, WI....608-285-9800

Low-Fat

Cabot Creamery Co-Op
Waitsfield, VT....888-792-2268
Froma-Dar
St. Boniface, QC....819-535-3946
Lactalis American Group Inc
Buffalo, NY....877-522-8254
Le Sueur Cheese Co
Le Sueur, MN....800-757-7611

Mascarpone

BelGioioso Cheese Inc.
Green Bay, WI....920-863-2123
GAF Seelig Inc
Flushing, NY....718-899-5000
Lactalis American Group Inc
Buffalo, NY....877-522-8254
Miceli Dairy Products Co
Cleveland, OH....216-791-6222
Pecoraro Dairy Products
Brooklyn, NY....718-388-2379
Reilly Dairy & Food Company
Tampa, FL....813-839-8458
Vermont Creamery
Websterville, VT....800-884-6287
Vermont Creamery
Websterville, VT....802-479-9371

Monterey Jack

Alberta Cheese Company
Calgary, AB....403-279-4353
Alta Dena Certified Dairy LLC
City Of Industry, CA....800-535-1369
Avanti Foods Co
Walnut, IL....800-243-3739
Bass Lake Cheese Factory
Somerset, WI....800-368-2437
Belle Plaine Cheese Factory
Shawano, WI....866-245-5924
Bletsoe's Cheese Inc
Marathon, WI....715-443-2526
Brunkow Cheese Of Wisconsin
Darlington, WI....608-776-3716
Cabot Creamery Co-Op
Waitsfield, VT....888-792-2268
Cady Cheese Factory
Wilson, WI....715-772-4218
Henning Cheese Factory
Kiel, WI....920-894-3032
Hilmar Cheese Company
Hilmar, CA....800-577-5772
Horizon Organic Dairy
Broomfield, CO....888-494-3020
Lakeview Banquit Cheese
Salt Lake City, UT....801-364-3607
Pine River Cheese & Butter Company
Ripley, ON....800-265-1175
Reilly Dairy & Food Company
Tampa, FL....813-839-8458
Rumiano Cheese Factory
Willows, CA....866-328-2433
Sargento Foods Inc
Plymouth, WI....800-243-3737
Suprema Specialties
Manteca, CA....209-858-9696
Swiss American Inc
St Louis, MO....800-325-8150
Vella Cheese Co
Sonoma, CA....800-848-0505
Wapsie Creamery
Independence, IA....319-334-7193
WhiteWave Foods
Denver, CO....800-488-9283

Mozzarella

Angelo & Franco U.S.A.
Hawthorne, CA....310-263-0506
Antonio Mozzarella Factory
Springfield, NJ....973-379-0033
Atwood Cheese Company
Atwood, ON....519-356-2271
B & D Foods
Boise, ID....208-344-1183
BelGioioso Cheese Inc.
Green Bay, WI....920-863-2123
Biazzo Dairy Products Inc
Ridgefield, NJ....201-941-6800
Bletsoe's Cheese Inc
Marathon, WI....715-443-2526
Brunnett Dairy Co-Op
Grantsburg, WI....715-689-2748
Cacique
Monrovia, CA....800-521-6987
Calabro Cheese Corp
East Haven, CT....203-469-1311
Clofine Dairy Products Inc
Linwood, NJ....609-653-1000
Crystal Farms Dairy Company
Minnetonka, MN....800-672-8260
Daphne's Creamery
....707-762-1760
Deca & Otto Farms
Miami, FL....305-629-9335
Floron Food Services
Edmonton, AB....780-438-9300
Foremost Farms USA
Baraboo, WI....800-362-9196
Fry Foods Inc
Tiffin, OH....800-626-2294
Golden Valley Dairy Products
Tulare, CA....559-687-1188
Great Lakes Cheese Company, Inc.
Hiram, OH....440-834-2500
Henning Cheese Factory
Kiel, WI....920-894-3032
J B & Son LTD
Yonkers, NY....914-963-5192
Kantner Group
Wapakoneta, OH....877-738-3448
Lactalis American Group Inc
Buffalo, NY....877-522-8254
Lactalis USA Inc
Belmont, WI....608-762-5136
Lakeview Banquit Cheese
Salt Lake City, UT....801-364-3607
Lamagna Cheese Co
Verona, PA....412-828-6112
Leprino Foods Co.
Denver, CO....800-537-7466
Liuzzi Angeloni Cheese
Hamden, CT....203-287-8477
Mancuso Cheese Co
Joliet, IL....815-722-2475
Marathon Cheese Corp
Marathon, WI....715-443-2211
Miceli Dairy Products Co
Cleveland, OH....216-791-6222
Michael Granese & Company
Norristown, PA....610-272-5099
Mozzarella Co
Dallas, TX....800-798-2954
Pecoraro Dairy Products
Brooklyn, NY....718-388-2379
Pine River Cheese & Butter Company
Ripley, ON....800-265-1175
Pollio Dairy Products
Campbell, NY....607-527-3621
Reilly Dairy & Food Company
Tampa, FL....813-839-8458
Sargento Foods Inc
Plymouth, WI....800-243-3737
Sierra Cheese Mfg Co
Compton, CA....800-266-4270
Sun-Re Cheese Co
Sunbury, PA....570-286-1511
Suprema Specialties
Manteca, CA....209-858-9696
Supreme Dairy Farms Co
Warwick, RI....401-739-8180
Trega Foods
Weyauwega, WI....920-867-2137
WhiteWave Foods
Denver, CO....800-488-9283
Wisconsin Milk Mktng Board Inc
Madison, WI....800-589-5127
Woolwich Dairy
Orangeville, ON....877-438-3499

Lite Shredded - Frozen

Kantner Group
Wapakoneta, OH....877-738-3448

Low Moisture Part Skim

Kantner Group
Wapakoneta, OH....877-738-3448

Low Moisture Part Skim Shredded - Frozen

Kantner Group
Wapakoneta, OH....877-738-3448

Muenster

Finlandia Cheese
Parsippany, NJ....973-316-6609
Heluva Good Cheese
Lynnfield, MA....800-644-5473
Reilly Dairy & Food Company
Tampa, FL....813-839-8458
Roth Cheese USA
Fitchburg, WI....608-285-9800
Sargento Foods Inc
Plymouth, WI....800-243-3737
Springdale Cheese Factory
Richland Center, WI....608-538-3213
Wenger Spring Brook Cheese Inc
Davis, IL....815-865-5612

Natural American

Barrel

Arla Foods Inc
Concord, ON....905-669-9393

No-Fat

Le Sueur Cheese Co
Le Sueur, MN....800-757-7611
Shenk's Foods
Lancaster, PA....717-393-4240

Parmesan

Atwood Cheese Company
Atwood, ON....519-356-2271
BelGioioso Cheese Inc.
Green Bay, WI....920-863-2123
Castella Imports Inc
Brentwood, NY....631-231-5500
Cheese Merchants of America
Carol Stream, IL....630-768-0317
Clofine Dairy Products Inc
Linwood, NJ....609-653-1000
Colonna Brothers Inc
North Bergen, NJ....201-864-1115
Crystal Farms Dairy Company
Minnetonka, MN....800-672-8260

Icco Cheese Co
Orangeburg, NY 845-680-2436
JVM Sales Corp.
Linden, NJ. 908-862-4866
Kantner Group
Wapakoneta, OH. 877-738-3448
Lactalis American Group Inc
Buffalo, NY. 877-522-8254
Mancuso Cheese Co
Joliet, IL 815-722-2475
Miceli Dairy Products Co
Cleveland, OH 216-791-6222
Park Cheese Company Inc
Fond Du Lac, WI 800-752-7275
Parmx
Calgary, AB. 403-237-0707
Reilly Dairy & Food Company
Tampa, FL. 813-839-8458
Sargento Foods Inc
Plymouth, WI 800-243-3737
Sartori Co
Plymouth, WI 920-893-6061
Suprema Specialties
Manteca, CA. 209-858-9696
Valley Grain Products
Fresno, CA 559-675-3400
Weyauwega Star Dairy
Weyauwega, WI 888-813-9720

Pecorino

Kantner Group
Wapakoneta, OH. 877-738-3448

Pepatello

Rumiano Cheese Factory
Willows, CA 866-328-2433

Process Loaves

Yellow

Arla Foods Inc
Concord, ON. 905-669-9393
Kantner Group
Wapakoneta, OH. 877-738-3448
Wohlt Cheese Corp
New London, WI 920-982-9000

Process Sliced

White/Yellow

Kantner Group
Wapakoneta, OH. 877-738-3448
Kraft Heinz Canada
North York, ON. 416-441-5000

Processed American

Finlandia Cheese
Parsippany, NJ. 973-316-6609
Kantner Group
Wapakoneta, OH. 877-738-3448
Schreiber Foods Inc.
Green Bay, WI. 920-437-7601
Welcome Dairy Inc
Colby, WI 715-223-2874
Wohlt Cheese Corp
New London, WI 920-982-9000

Processed Swiss

Finlandia Cheese
Parsippany, NJ. 973-316-6609

Provolone

Alberta Cheese Company
Calgary, AB. 403-279-4353
BelGioioso Cheese Inc.
Green Bay, WI. 920-863-2123
Brunnett Dairy Co-Op
Grantsburg, WI 715-689-2748
Crystal Farms Dairy Company
Minnetonka, MN. 800-672-8260
Golden Valley Dairy Products
Tulare, CA. 559-687-1188
Kantner Group
Wapakoneta, OH. 877-738-3448
Lactalis American Group Inc
Buffalo, NY. 877-522-8254
Lamagna Cheese Co
Verona, PA. 412-828-6112
Mancuso Cheese Co
Joliet, IL 815-722-2475
Park Cheese Company Inc
Fond Du Lac, WI 800-752-7275
Reilly Dairy & Food Company
Tampa, FL. 813-839-8458
Sargento Foods Inc
Plymouth, WI 800-243-3737
Trega Foods
Weyauwega, WI 920-867-2137

Ricotta

Alberta Cheese Company
Calgary, AB. 403-279-4353
BelGioioso Cheese Inc.
Green Bay, WI. 920-863-2123
Biazzo Dairy Products Inc
Ridgefield, NJ. 201-941-6800
Calabro Cheese Corp
East Haven, CT. 203-469-1311
Castella Imports Inc
Brentwood, NY. 631-231-5500
Crystal Farms Dairy Company
Minnetonka, MN. 800-672-8260
J B & Son LTD
Yonkers, NY 914-963-5192
Kantner Group
Wapakoneta, OH. 877-738-3448
Kite Hill
Hayward, CA 888-588-0994
Lactalis American Group Inc
Buffalo, NY. 877-522-8254
Lamagna Cheese Co
Verona, PA. 412-828-6112
Liuzzi Angeloni Cheese
Hamden, CT 203-287-8477
Losurdo Creamery
Hackensack, NJ. 888-567-8736
Mancuso Cheese Co
Joliet, IL 815-722-2475
Miceli Dairy Products Co
Cleveland, OH 216-791-6222
Michael Granese & Company
Norristown, PA 610-272-5099
Pecoraro Dairy Products
Brooklyn, NY 718-388-2379
Pollio Dairy Products
Campbell, NY. 607-527-3621
Reilly Dairy & Food Company
Tampa, FL. 813-839-8458
Sargento Foods Inc
Plymouth, WI 800-243-3737
Schneider's Dairy Inc
Pittsburgh, PA. 412-881-3525
Sierra Cheese Mfg Co
Compton, CA 800-266-4270
Sun-Re Cheese Co
Sunbury, PA. 570-286-1511
Supreme Dairy Farms Co
Warwick, RI 401-739-8180
Tofutti Brands Inc
Cranford, NJ 908-272-2400

Romano

Advanced Food Products LLC
New Holland, PA 800-732-5373
BelGioioso Cheese Inc.
Green Bay, WI. 920-863-2123
Brunnett Dairy Co-Op
Grantsburg, WI. 715-689-2748
Castella Imports Inc
Brentwood, NY. 631-231-5500
Clofine Dairy Products Inc
Linwood, NJ 609-653-1000
Colonna Brothers Inc
North Bergen, NJ 201-864-1115
JVM Sales Corp.
Linden, NJ. 908-862-4866
Kantner Group
Wapakoneta, OH. 877-738-3448
Mancuso Cheese Co
Joliet, IL 815-722-2475
Miceli Dairy Products Co
Cleveland, OH 216-791-6222
Park Cheese Company Inc
Fond Du Lac, WI 800-752-7275
Reilly Dairy & Food Company
Tampa, FL. 813-839-8458
Sargento Foods Inc
Plymouth, WI 800-243-3737
Sartori Co
Plymouth, WI 920-893-6061
Suprema Specialties
Manteca, CA. 209-858-9696
Valley Grain Products
Fresno, CA 559-675-3400
Weyauwega Star Dairy
Weyauwega, WI 888-813-9720

String

Aunt Lizzie's Inc
Memphis, TN 800-993-7788
Baker Cheese Factory Inc
St Cloud, WI. 920-477-7871
Bletsoe's Cheese Inc
Marathon, WI 715-443-2526
Horizon Organic Dairy
Broomfield, CO 888-494-3020
Parmalat Canada
Toronto, ON 800-563-1515
Weyauwega Star Dairy
Weyauwega, WI 888-813-9720
WhiteWave Foods
Denver, CO. 800-488-9283

Swiss

Bletsoe's Cheese Inc
Marathon, WI 715-443-2526
Brewster Dairy Inc
Brewster, OH 800-874-8874
Clofine Dairy Products Inc
Linwood, NJ 609-653-1000
Crystal Farms Dairy Company
Minnetonka, MN. 800-672-8260
Emmi Roth USA
Monroe, WI. 608-845-5796
Finlandia Cheese
Parsippany, NJ. 973-316-6609
Guggisberg Cheese
Millersburg, OH 800-262-2505
Heluva Good Cheese
Lynnfield, MA 800-644-5473
Holmes Cheese Co
Millersburg, OH 330-674-6451
Kolb-Lena Bresse Bleu Inc
Lena, IL. 815-369-4577
Los Altos Food Products
City Of Industry, CA. 626-330-6555
Marathon Cheese Corp
Marathon, WI 715-443-2211
Middlebury Cheese Company
Middlebury, IN 800-262-2505
Middlefield Cheese House
Middlefield, OH 800-327-9477
Penn Cheese
Winfield, PA 570-524-7700
Ragersville Swiss Cheese
Sugarcreek, OH. 330-897-3055
Sargento Foods Inc
Plymouth, WI 800-243-3737
Steiner Cheese
Baltic, OH. 888-897-5505
Wenger Spring Brook Cheese Inc
Davis, IL 815-865-5612

Imitation Cheeses & Substitutes

Cheese Foods & Substitutes

A Southern Season
Hillsborough, NC 800-253-3663
Al Pete Meats
Muncie, IN 765-288-8817
Arla Foods Inc
Concord, ON. 905-669-9393
B & D Foods
Boise, ID 208-344-1183
Baker Cheese Factory Inc
St Cloud, WI. 920-477-7871
Bel Brands USA
Chicago, IL 312-462-1500
Bernardi Italian Foods Company
Bloomsburg, PA 570-389-5500
Castle Cheese
Slippery Rock, PA. 800-252-4373
Century Foods Intl LLC
Sparta, WI. 800-269-1901
Cheese Straws & More
Monroe, LA. 800-997-1921
Clofine Dairy Products Inc
Linwood, NJ 609-653-1000

Earth Island
Chatsworth, CA 888-394-3949
Galaxy Nutritional Foods Inc
North Kingstown, RI 800-441-9419
Great American Appetizers
Nampa, ID.......................... 800-282-4834
Hormel Foods Corp.
Austin, MN 507-437-5611
Ingretec
Lebanon, PA 717-273-0711
John W Macy's Cheesesticks Inc
Elmwood Park, NJ 800-643-0573
Kantner Group
Wapakoneta, OH.................... 877-738-3448
Matador Processors
Blanchard, OK 800-847-0797
Mehaffies Pies
Dayton, OH.......................... 800-289-7437
Nuts For Cheese
London, ON 519-601-5070
Parkers Farm
Coon Rapids, MN................... 800-869-6685
Parmela Creamery
Torrance, CA........................ 310-584-7541
Pine River Pre-Pack Inc
Newton, WI.......................... 920-726-4216
Pocono Cheesecake Factory
Swiftwater, PA 570-839-6844
Sierra Cheese Mfg Co
Compton, CA 800-266-4270
Texas Heat
San Antonio, TX.................... 800-656-5916
Tomanetti Food Products Inc
Oakmont, PA........................ 800-875-3040
Vtopian Artisan Cheeses
Portland, OR
Whitehall Specialties Inc
Whitehall, WI 888-755-9900
Wisconsin Milk Mktng Board Inc
Madison, WI 800-589-5127

Imitation

American

Kantner Group
Wapakoneta, OH.................... 877-738-3448

Cheddar

Kantner Group
Wapakoneta, OH.................... 877-738-3448

Mozzarella

Kantner Group
Wapakoneta, OH.................... 877-738-3448

Parmesan

Kantner Group
Wapakoneta, OH.................... 877-738-3448

Substitutes

Chicago Vegan Foods
Lombard, IL 630-629-9667
Earth Island
Chatsworth, CA 888-394-3949
Hormel Foods Corp.
Austin, MN 507-437-5611
Kantner Group
Wapakoneta, OH.................... 877-738-3448
Parmela Creamery
Torrance, CA........................ 310-584-7541

American

Kantner Group
Wapakoneta, OH.................... 877-738-3448

Dairy Products

Butter

Agri-Mark Inc
West Springfield, MA . . . 978-552-5500
Ahara Ghee
Portland, OR . . . 503-997-5050
Allfresh Food Products
Evanston, IL . . . 847-869-3100
American Almond Products Co
Brooklyn, NY . . . 800-825-6663
Ancient Organics
Berkeley, CA . . . 510-280-5043
Associated Milk Producers Inc.
New Ulm, MN . . . 800-533-3580
Bartlett Dairy & Food Service
Jamaica, NY . . . 718-658-2299
Borden Dairy
Dallas, TX . . . 855-311-1583
Butterball Farms
Grand Rapids, MI . . . 888-828-8837
Byrne Dairy, Inc.
Syracuse, NY . . . 800-899-1535
California Dairies Inc.
Visalia, CA . . . 559-625-2200
Carr Valley Cheese Company
La Valle, WI . . . 800-462-7258
Cass-Clay Creamery
Fargo, ND . . . 701-293-6455
Challenge Dairy Products, Inc.
Dublin, CA . . . 800-733-2479
Chef Shamy Gourmet
Salt Lake City, UT
Clover Sonoma
Petaluma, CA . . . 800-237-3315
Cloverland Dairy
Saint Clairsville, OH . . . 740-699-0509
Crush Foods Service
Westlake Village, CA . . . 818-699-6381
Crystal Farms Dairy Company
Minnetonka, MN . . . 800-672-8260
Dairy Farmers Of America
Kansas City, KS . . . 888-332-6455
Daphne's Creamery
. . . 707-762-1760
Darigold
Seattle, WA . . . 800-333-6455
Epicurean Butter
Federal Heights, CO . . . 303-427-5527
Farmdale Creamery Inc
San Bernardino, CA . . . 800-346-7306
Farmtrue
North Stonington, CT . . . 860-495-2231
Foothills Creamery
Calgary, AB . . . 800-661-4909
Foremost Farms USA
Baraboo, WI . . . 800-362-9196
GAF Seelig Inc
Flushing, NY . . . 718-899-5000
Gossner Foods Inc.
Logan, UT . . . 800-944-0454
Gourmet Ghee
Lynbrook, NY . . . 516-744-0770
Graf Creamery Co
Bonduel, WI . . . 715-758-2137
Grassland Dairy Products Inc
Greenwood, WI . . . 800-428-8837
Green River Chocolates
Hinesburg, VT . . . 802-482-6727
Grouse Hunt Farm Inc
Tamaqua, PA . . . 570-467-2850
H B Taylor Co
Chicago, IL . . . 773-254-4805
Hidden Villa Ranch
Fullerton, CA . . . 800-326-3220
Hope Creamery
Hope, MN . . . 507-451-2029
Horizon Organic Dairy
Broomfield, CO . . . 888-494-3020
Houlton Farms Dairy
Houlton, ME . . . 207-532-3170
J M Swank Co
North Liberty, IA . . . 800-593-6375
Kozlowski Farms
Forestville, CA . . . 800-473-2767
Land O'Lakes Inc
Arden Hills, MN . . . 800-328-9680
Lost Trail Root Beer
Louisburg, KS . . . 800-748-7765
Maison Riviera
Varennes, QC . . . 800-363-0092
Marburger Farm Dairy
Evans City, PA . . . 800-331-1295
Maryland & Virginia Milk Producers Cooperative
Reston, VA . . . 703-742-6800
Minerva Cheese Factory
Minerva, OH . . . 330-868-4196
Minerva Dairy Inc
Minerva, OH . . . 330-868-4196
Natrel
St. Laurent, QC . . . 800-501-1150
O-At-Ka Milk Prods Co-Op Inc.
Batavia, NY . . . 800-828-8152
Oakhurst Dairy
Portland, ME . . . 800-482-0718
Oasis Food Co
Hillside, NJ . . . 800-275-0477
OMGhee
Cedar Grove, NJ . . . 973-931-3476
Plainview Milk Products
Plainview, MN . . . 800-356-5606
Prairie Farms Dairy Inc.
Edwardsville, IL . . . 618-659-5700
Pride Dairies
Bottineau, ND . . . 701-228-2216
Producers Dairy Foods Inc
Fresno, CA . . . 559-264-6583
Pure Indian
Princeton Jct., NJ . . . 877-588-4433
Purity Farms
La Farge, WI . . . 877-211-4819
Queensboro Farm Products
Canastota, NY . . . 315-687-6133
Reilly Dairy & Food Company
Tampa, FL . . . 813-839-8458
Rockview Farms
Downey, CA . . . 800-423-2479
Schepps Dairy
Dallas, TX . . . 800-395-7004
Schneider's Dairy Inc
Pittsburgh, PA . . . 412-881-3525
Shenk's Foods
Lancaster, PA . . . 717-393-4240
Sisler's Ice & Ice Cream
Ohio, IL . . . 888-891-3856
Sommer Maid Creamery Inc
Pipersville, PA . . . 215-345-6160
Sparboe Foods Corp
New Hampton, IA . . . 641-394-3040
Tin Star Foods
Austin, TX
Turner & Pease Company
Seattle, WA . . . 206-282-9535
Umpqua Dairy
Roseburg, OR . . . 888-672-6455
United Dairymen of Arizona
Tempe, AZ . . . 480-966-7211
Ventura Foods LLC
Brea, CA . . . 800-421-6257
Vermont Creamery
Websterville, VT . . . 800-884-6287
Westin Foods
Omaha, NE . . . 800-228-6098
WhiteWave Foods
Denver, CO . . . 800-488-9283
Whitewave Foods Company
Broomfield, CO . . . 303-635-4000

Blends

Chef Shamy Gourmet
Salt Lake City, UT
Medlee Foods
Chicago, IL . . . 312-442-0406

Dairy

Agropur
Granby, QC . . . 800-363-5686
Allfresh Food Products
Evanston, IL . . . 847-869-3100
Alliston Creamery
Alliston, ON . . . 705-435-6751
Century Foods Intl LLC
Sparta, WI . . . 800-269-1901
Clofine Dairy Products Inc
Linwood, NJ . . . 609-653-1000
Crystal Creamery
Modesto, CA . . . 866-225-4821
Danish Maid Butter Co
Chicago, IL . . . 773-731-8787
F C C
Mcminnville, OR . . . 503-472-2157
Grassland Dairy Products Inc
Greenwood, WI . . . 800-428-8837
Keller's Creamery
Kansas City, MO . . . 800-535-5371
Larosa Bakery Inc
Shrewsbury, NJ . . . 800-527-6722
Mt Sterling Co-Op Creamery
Highland, WI . . . 866-289-4628
St. Maurice Laurent
St-Bruno-Lac-St-Jean, QC . . . 418-343-3655
Swagger Foods Corp
Vernon Hills, IL . . . 847-913-1200
Tillamook County Creamery Association
Tillamook, OR . . . 503-842-4481
United Dairymen of Arizona
Tempe, AZ . . . 480-966-7211
Vermont Creamery
Websterville, VT . . . 800-884-6287
WhiteWave Foods
Denver, CO . . . 800-488-9283

Low Fat

Dixie USA
Tomball, TX . . . 800-233-3668

Salted

Grassland Dairy Products Inc
Greenwood, WI . . . 800-428-8837
Reilly Dairy & Food Company
Tampa, FL . . . 813-839-8458

Unsalted

Grassland Dairy Products Inc
Greenwood, WI . . . 800-428-8837
Keller's Creamery
Kansas City, MO . . . 800-535-5371
Reilly Dairy & Food Company
Tampa, FL . . . 813-839-8458

Buttermilk & Buttermilk Products

Buttermilk

Agri-Dairy Products
Purchase, NY . . . 914-697-9580
Alta Dena Certified Dairy LLC
City Of Industry, CA . . . 800-535-1369
Anderson Dairy Inc
Las Vegas, NV . . . 702-642-7507
Associated Milk Producers Inc.
New Ulm, MN . . . 800-533-3580
Barber Dairies
Birmingham, AL . . . 205-942-2351
Borden Dairy
Dallas, TX . . . 855-311-1583
Broughton Foods LLC
El Paso, TX . . . 800-395-7004
California Dairies Inc.
Visalia, CA . . . 559-625-2200
Century Foods Intl LLC
Sparta, WI . . . 800-269-1901
Chase Brothers Dairy
Oxnard, CA . . . 800-438-6455
Clofine Dairy Products Inc
Linwood, NJ . . . 609-653-1000
Cloverland Dairy
Saint Clairsville, OH . . . 740-699-0509
Dairy Maid Dairy LLC
Frederick, MD . . . 301-663-5114
Friendship Dairies LLC
Friendship, NY . . . 800-854-3243
Graf Creamery Co
Bonduel, WI . . . 715-758-2137
J M Swank Co
North Liberty, IA . . . 800-593-6375

Kleinpeter Farms Dairy LLC
Baton Rouge, LA 225-753-2121
Ludwig Dairy Product
Elk Grove Vlg, IL.................847-860-8646
Marburger Farm Dairy
Evans City, PA 800-331-1295
McArthur Dairy LLC
Miami, FL.........................561-659-4811
Mom's Bakery
Sherman, TX.......................903-893-7585
Plains Dairy Products
Amarillo, TX......................800-365-5608
Plainview Milk Products
Plainview, MN 800-356-5606
Pleasant View Dairy
Highland, IN 219-838-0155
Promised Land Dairy
Colorado Springs, CO..............877-520-2479
Queensboro Farm Products
Jamica, NY 718-658-5000
Reilly Dairy & Food Company
Tampa, FL.........................813-839-8458
Schepps Dairy
Dallas, TX........................800-395-7004
Schneider-Valley Farms Inc
Williamsport, PA..................570-326-2021
United Dairy Farmers Inc.
Cincinnati, OH 866-837-4833
Welsh Farms
Wallington, NJ 800-221-0663
Winchester Farms Dairy
Winchester, KY....................859-745-5500
Yoder Dairies
Chesapeake, VA 757-482-4068

Buttermilk Products

Graf Creamery Co
Bonduel, WI 715-758-2137

Condensed

Graf Creamery Co
Bonduel, WI 715-758-2137

Dry

Kantner Group
Wapakoneta, OH....................877-738-3448

Dry Sweetcream

Kantner Group
Wapakoneta, OH....................877-738-3448

Cream

Alta Dena Certified Dairy LLC
City Of Industry, CA..............800-535-1369
Anastasia Confections Inc
Orlando, FL.......................800-329-7100
Anderson Dairy Inc
Las Vegas, NV 702-642-7507
Arcor USA
Coral Gables, FL..................800-572-7267
Barber Dairies
Birmingham, AL....................205-942-2351
Bartlett Dairy & Food Service
Jamaica, NY 718-658-2299
Berkeley Farms
Hayward, CA 800-395-7004
Berkshire Dairy
Wyomissing, PA 877-696-6455
Bluechip Group
Salt Lake City, UT 800-878-0099
Broughton Foods LLC
El Paso, TX.......................800-395-7004
Byrne Dairy, Inc.
Syracuse, NY 800-899-1535
C F Burger Creamery Co
Detroit, MI.......................313-584-4040
Cass-Clay Creamery
Fargo, ND 701-293-6455
Clover Farms Dairy Co Inc
Reading, PA 800-323-0123
Clover Sonoma
Petaluma, CA 800-237-3315
Clover Stornetta Farms Inc
Petaluma, CA 800-237-3315
Country Fresh
Grand Rapids, MI..................616-243-0173
D & D Sugarwoods Farm
Glover, VT 800-245-3718
Fairlife
Chicago, IL
Farmdale Creamery Inc
San Bernardino, CA 800-346-7306
First District Association
Litchfield, MN 320-693-3236
GAF Seelig Inc
Flushing, NY......................718-899-5000
GPI USA LLC.
Mokena, IL 800-929-4248
H B Taylor Co
Chicago, IL 773-254-4805
Horizon Organic Dairy
Broomfield, CO 888-494-3020
HP Hood LLC
Lynnfield, MA 800-343-6592
Ideal Dairy Farms
Hudson Falls, NY 518-747-5059
Jasper Products Corp
Joplin, MO 417-206-3877
Kleinpeter Farms Dairy LLC
Baton Rouge, LA 225-753-2121
Marburger Farm Dairy
Evans City, PA 800-331-1295
Maryland & Virginia Milk Producers Cooperative
Reston, VA 703-742-6800
Muller-Pinehurst Dairy
Rockford, IL 815-968-0441
Natural By Nature
Newark, DE........................302-455-1261
Oak Farms
El Paso, TX.......................800-395-7004
Oakhurst Dairy
Portland, ME......................800-482-0718
Pioneer Dairy
Southwick, MA.....................413-569-6132
Plains Dairy Products
Amarillo, TX......................800-365-5608
Price's Creameries
El Paso, TX.......................915-565-2711
Producers Dairy Foods Inc
Fresno, CA 559-264-6583
Purity Dairies LLC
Nashville, TN 615-244-1900
Queensboro Farm Products
Jamica, NY 718-658-5000
Reilly Dairy & Food Company
Tampa, FL.........................813-839-8458
Reiter Dairy LLC
Springfield, OH...................937-323-5777
Rosenberger's Dairies
Hatfield, PA......................800-355-9074
Sabatino Truffles USA
West Haven, CT 888-444-9971
Saint Albans Cooperative Creamery
Saint Albans, VT..................802-524-6581
Schepps Dairy
Dallas, TX........................800-395-7004
Schneider's Dairy Inc
Pittsburgh, PA....................412-881-3525
Stonyfield Organic
Londonderry, NH 800-776-2697
Turner Dairy Farms Inc
Pittsburgh, PA....................800-892-1039
United Dairy Inc.
Martins Ferry, OH.................800-252-1542
Velda Farms
Orlando, FL.......................800-795-4649
Vermont Creamery
Websterville, VT..................800-884-6287
W.J. Stearns & Sons/Mountain Dairy
Storrs Mansfield, CT 860-423-9289
WhiteWave Foods
Denver, CO 800-488-9283

Dried

Agri-Dairy Products
Purchase, NY 914-697-9580
Batory Foods
Des Plaines, IL 847-299-1999
Blossom Farm Products
Ridgewood, NJ 800-729-1818
Century Foods Intl LLC
Sparta, WI........................800-269-1901
Clofine Dairy Products Inc
Linwood, NJ 609-653-1000
Kantner Group
Wapakoneta, OH....................877-738-3448
Quality Ingredients
Burnsville, MN....................952-898-4002

Fresh

Agri-Dairy Products
Purchase, NY 914-697-9580
Agropur
Granby, QC........................800-363-5686
Auburn Dairy Products Inc
Auburn, WA 800-950-9264
Brum's Dairy
Pembroke, ON......................613-735-2325
Clofine Dairy Products Inc
Linwood, NJ 609-653-1000
Larosa Bakery Inc
Shrewsbury, NJ....................800-527-6722
Northumberland Dairy
Miramichi, NB 800-501-1150
O-At-Ka Milk Prods Co-Op Inc.
Batavia, NY.......................800-828-8152
Stremick's Heritage Foods
Santa Ana, CA 800-371-9010

Non-Dairy

Bay Valley Foods
El Paso, TX.......................800-236-1119
New Barn Organics
Rohnert Park, CA 888-635-7102
Nutpods
Bellevue, WA 800-977-6094
Siggi's Dairy
..................................855-860-6683
Sugar Foods Corp
Sun Valley, CA 818-768-7900

Whipped

Alamance Foods
Burlington, NC
Berkeley Farms
Hayward, CA 800-395-7004
Brighams
Arlington, MA 800-242-2423
Broughton Foods LLC
El Paso, TX.......................800-395-7004
C F Burger Creamery Co
Detroit, MI 313-584-4040
Cass-Clay Creamery
Fargo, ND 701-293-6455
Caughman's Meat Plant
Lexington, SC.....................803-356-0076
Clofine Dairy Products Inc
Linwood, NJ 609-653-1000
Crave Natural Foods
Los Angeles, CA...................877-425-2599
Crystal Farms Dairy Company
Minnetonka, MN....................800-672-8260
Erba Food Products
Brooklyn, NY 718-272-7700
Jasper Products Corp
Joplin, MO 417-206-3877
Marva Maid Dairy
Newport News, VA..................800-768-6243
Mayfield Dairy Farms LLC
Athens, TN 800-362-9546
Prairie Farms Dairy Inc.
Edwardsville, IL..................618-659-5700
Schepps Dairy
Dallas, TX........................800-395-7004
Schneider's Dairy Inc
Pittsburgh, PA....................412-881-3525
Tiller Foods Company
Dayton, OH........................937-435-4601
Yoder Dairies
Chesapeake, VA 757-482-4068

from Milk

Auburn Dairy Products Inc
Auburn, WA 800-950-9264
DairyPure
El Paso, TX.......................800-395-7004
Trickling Springs Creamery
Chambersburg, PA 717-709-0711

Creamers

Auburn Dairy Products Inc
Auburn, WA 800-950-9264
Broughton Foods LLC
El Paso, TX.......................800-395-7004
DairyPure
El Paso, TX.......................800-395-7004
H B Taylor Co
Chicago, IL.......................773-254-4805

Kan-Pak
Arkansas City, KS . . . 800-378-1265
Mccullagh Coffee Roasters
Buffalo, NY . . . 800-753-3473
Nature's First Inc
Orange, CT . . . 800-523-3752
Nulaid Foods Inc
Ripon, CA . . . 209-599-2121
Promised Land Dairy
Colorado Springs, CO . . . 877-520-2479
Schepps Dairy
Dallas, TX . . . 800-395-7004
Schneider's Dairy Inc
Pittsburgh, PA . . . 412-881-3525
Smith Dairy
Orrville, OH . . . 800-776-7076
Tiller Foods Company
Dayton, OH . . . 937-435-4601
Utah Coffee Roasters
South Salt Lake, UT . . . 888-486-3334
W.J. Stearns & Sons/Mountain Dairy
Storrs Mansfield, CT . . . 860-423-9289

Coffee

Agri-Dairy Products
Purchase, NY . . . 914-697-9580
Baldwin Richardson Foods
Oakbrook Terrace, IL . . . 866-644-2732
Boston's Best Coffee Roasters
South Easton, MA . . . 800-898-8393
Byrne Dairy, Inc.
Syracuse, NY . . . 800-899-1535
C F Burger Creamery Co
Detroit, MI . . . 313-584-4040
Califia Farms
Pasadena, CA . . . 844-237-4779
Danone North America
Broomfield, CO . . . 303-635-4000
H B Taylor Co
Chicago, IL . . . 773-254-4805
Hanan Products Co
Hicksville, NY . . . 516-938-1000
Kiss My Keto
Los Angeles, CA . . . 310-765-1553
Know Brainer
Lafayette, CO . . . 303-475-0456
Natural Bliss
. . . 800-637-8534
Safeway Milk Plant
Tempe, AZ . . . 480-894-4391
Tova Industries LLC
Louisville, KY . . . 888-532-8682
WhiteWave Foods
Denver, CO . . . 800-488-9283

Non-Dairy

Bay Valley Foods
El Paso, TX . . . 800-236-1119
Broughton Foods LLC
El Paso, TX . . . 800-395-7004
Diehl Food Ingredients
Defiance, OH . . . 800-251-3033
Erba Food Products
Brooklyn, NY . . . 718-272-7700
Golden 100
Deland, FL . . . 386-734-0113
Laird Superfood
Sisters, OR . . . 888-670-6796
Lake City Foods
Mississauga, ON . . . 905-625-8244
Leaner Creamer
Beverly Hills, CA . . . 866-739-2298
Mccullagh Coffee Roasters
Buffalo, NY . . . 800-753-3473
NeuRoast
New York, NY
New Barn Organics
Rohnert Park, CA . . . 888-635-7102
Oatly
New York, NY
Quality Ingredients
Burnsville, MN . . . 952-898-4002
Stickney & Poor Company
Peterborough, NH . . . 603-924-2259
Tiller Foods Company
Dayton, OH . . . 937-435-4601
Tonex
Wallington, NJ . . . 973-773-5135

Custard

Artuso Pastry
Bronx, NY . . . 718-367-2515
BakeMark Ingredients Canada
Richmond, BC . . . 800-665-9441
Dreyer's Grand Ice Cream Inc.
Oakland, CA . . . 877-437-3937
Schoep's Ice Cream
Madison, WI . . . 800-236-4050

Dairy

1000 Islands River Rat Cheese
Clayton, NY . . . 800-752-1341
A B Munroe Dairy Inc
East Providence, RI . . . 401-438-4450
Abbott Laboratories
Abbott Park, IL . . . 847-938-3887
Advanced Food Products LLC
New Holland, PA . . . 800-732-5373
Aglamesis Bros Ice Cream
Cincinnati, OH . . . 513-531-5196
Agri-Dairy Products
Purchase, NY . . . 914-697-9580
Agri-Mark Inc
West Springfield, MA . . . 978-552-5500
Agropur
Granby, QC . . . 800-363-5686
Al Gelato Bornay
Franklin Park, IL . . . 847-455-5355
Al Pete Meats
Muncie, IN . . . 765-288-8817
Al's Beverage Company
East Windsor, CT . . . 888-257-7632
All American Foods Inc
Mankato, MN . . . 800-833-2661
Allfresh Food Products
Evanston, IL . . . 847-869-3100
Alliston Creamery
Alliston, ON . . . 705-435-6751
Alpenrose Dairy
Portland, OR . . . 503-244-1133
Alpina
Batavia, NY . . . 855-886-1914
American Classic Ice Cream Company
Bay Shore, NY . . . 800-736-4100
American Lecithin Company
Oxford, CT . . . 800-364-4416
Ammerland America
Hallandale Beach, FL . . . 954-350-0325
Anderson Dairy Inc
Las Vegas, NV . . . 702-642-7507
Anderson Erickson Dairy
Des Moines, IA . . . 515-265-2521
Anderson Erickson Dairy
Kansas City, KS . . . 913-621-4801
APC Inc
Ankeny, IA . . . 800-369-2672
Ariza Cheese Co
Paramount, CA . . . 800-762-4736
Arla Foods Inc
Concord, ON . . . 905-669-9393
Astro Dairy Products
Toronto, ON . . . 416-622-2811
Atwood Cheese Company
Atwood, ON . . . 519-356-2271
Auburn Dairy Products Inc
Auburn, WA . . . 800-950-9264
Avanti Foods Co
Walnut, IL . . . 800-243-3739
B & D Foods
Boise, ID . . . 208-344-1183
Baird Dairy LLC
Clarksville, IN . . . 812-283-3345
Baker Cheese Factory Inc
St Cloud, WI . . . 920-477-7871
Barber Dairies
Birmingham, AL . . . 205-942-2351
Barnes Ice Cream Company
Manchester, ME . . . 207-622-0827
Bartlett Dairy & Food Service
Jamaica, NY . . . 718-658-2299
Bartolini Ice Cream
Bronx, NY . . . 718-589-5151
BCFoods
Santa Rosa, CA . . . 707-547-1776
Bel Brands USA
Chicago, IL . . . 312-462-1500
Belle Plaine Cheese Factory
Shawano, WI . . . 866-245-5924
Berkeley Farms
Hayward, CA . . . 800-395-7004
Bernardi Italian Foods Company
Bloomsburg, PA . . . 570-389-5500
Berner Food & Beverage LLC
Dakota, IL . . . 800-819-8199
Bernie's Foods
Brooklyn, NY . . . 718-417-6677
Biazzo Dairy Products Inc
Ridgefield, NJ . . . 201-941-6800
Bio-K + International Inc.
Laval, QC . . . 800-593-2465
Birdsall Ice Cream Company
Mason City, IA . . . 641-423-5365
Bliss Brothers Dairy, Inc.
Attleboro, MA . . . 800-622-8789
Bloomfield Bakers
Los Alamitos, CA . . . 800-594-4111
Blossom Farm Products
Ridgewood, NJ . . . 800-729-1818
Blue Bell Creameries LP
Brenham, TX . . . 800-327-8135
Blue Ribbon Farm Dairy Fresh
Exeter, PA . . . 570-655-5579
Bluechip Group
Salt Lake City, UT . . . 800-878-0099
Bongard's Creameries
Chanhassen, MN . . . 952-277-5500
Bonnie Doon LLC
Elkhart, IN . . . 574-264-3390
Borden Dairy
Dallas, TX . . . 855-311-1583
Boston's Best Coffee Roasters
South Easton, MA . . . 800-898-8393
Braum's Inc
Oklahoma City, OK . . . 800-327-6455
Brewster Dairy Inc
Brewster, OH . . . 800-874-8874
Brighams
Arlington, MA . . . 800-242-2423
Brookshire Grocery Company
Tyler, TX . . . 888-937-3776
Brookside Foods
Abbotsford, BC . . . 800-468-1714
Brown Dairy Inc
Coalville, UT . . . 435-336-5952
Brown Produce Company
Farina, IL . . . 618-245-3301
Brown's Ice Cream Co
Minneapolis, MN . . . 612-378-1075
Browns' Ice Cream Company
Minneapolis, MN . . . 612-378-1075
Brum's Dairy
Pembroke, ON . . . 613-735-2325
Brunkow Cheese Of Wisconsin
Darlington, WI . . . 608-776-3716
Bubbies Homemade Ice Cream
Aiea, HI . . . 808-487-7218
Buck's Spumoni Company
Milford, CT . . . 888-222-8257
Bunker Hill Cheese Co Inc
Millersburg, OH . . . 800-253-6636
Buonitalia
New York, NY . . . 212-633-9090
Bush Brothers Provision Co
West Palm Beach, FL . . . 800-327-1345
Butter Buds Food Ingredients
Racine, WI . . . 800-426-1119
Butterball Farms
Grand Rapids, MI . . . 888-828-8837
Byrne Dairy, Inc.
Syracuse, NY . . . 800-899-1535
Cabot Creamery Co-Op
Waitsfield, VT . . . 888-792-2268
Calabro Cheese Corp
East Haven, CT . . . 203-469-1311
California Dairies Inc.
Visalia, CA . . . 559-625-2200
Calpro Ingredients
Corona, CA . . . 909-493-4890
Caprine Estates
Bellbrook, OH . . . 937-848-7406
Cascade Fresh
Seattle, WA . . . 800-511-0057
Casper's Ice Cream
Richmond, UT . . . 800-772-4182
Cass-Clay Creamery
Fargo, ND . . . 701-293-6455
Castle Cheese
Slippery Rock, PA . . . 800-252-4373
Cedar Crest Specialties
Cedarburg, WI . . . 800-877-8341
Central Dairies
St Johns, NL . . . 800-563-6455

Central Dairy
Jefferson City, MO 573-635-6148
Centreside Dairy
Renfrew, ON 800-889-9974
Century Foods Intl LLC
Sparta, WI 800-269-1901
Challenge Dairy Products, Inc.
Dublin, CA 800-733-2479
Chase Brothers Dairy
Oxnard, CA 800-438-6455
Cheese Straws & More
Monroe, LA 800-997-1921
Chester Dairy Co
Chester, IL 618-826-2394
Chicago 58 Food Products
Woodbridge, ON 416-603-4244
Chocolaterie Bernard Callebaut
Calgary, AB 800-661-8367
Chozen Ice Cream
New York, NY 212-675-4191
Churny Company
Waupaca, WI 715-258-4040
Ciao Bella Gelato Company
Irvington, NJ 800-435-2863
Circus Man Ice Cream Corporation
Farmingdale, NY 516-249-4400
Clofine Dairy Products Inc
Linwood, NJ 609-653-1000
Clover Farms Dairy Co Inc
Reading, PA 800-323-0123
Clover Sonoma
Petaluma, CA 800-237-3315
Clover Stornetta Farms Inc
Petaluma, CA 800-237-3315
Cloverland Dairy
Saint Clairsville, OH 740-699-0509
Cloverland/Green Spring Dairy
Baltimore, MD 800-876-6455
Coastlog Industries
Novi, MI 248-344-9556
Colchester Foods
Bozrah, CT 800-243-0469
Colonna Brothers Inc
North Bergen, NJ 201-864-1115
Colteryahn Dairy
Pittsburgh, PA 412-881-1408
Compton Dairy
Shelbyville, IN 317-398-8621
Cordon Bleu International
Anjou, QC 800-363-1182
Corfu Foods Inc
Bensenville, IL 630-595-2510
Country Delite Farms LLC
Nashville, TN 800-232-4791
Cream Crock Distributors
Sterling, MA 800-423-2736
Creamland Dairies Inc
Albuquerque, NM 505-247-0721
Crescent Ridge Dairy
Sharon, MA 800-660-2740
Crowley Cheese Inc
Mt Holly, VT 800-683-2606
Crystal Creamery
Modesto, CA 866-225-4821
Crystal Farms Dairy Company
Minnetonka, MN 800-672-8260
Crystal Lake LLC
Warsaw, IN 574-858-2514
Culture Systems Inc
Mishawaka, IN 574-258-0602
Cumberland Dairy
Rosenhayn, NJ 800-257-8484
Cyclone Enterprises Inc
Houston, TX 281-872-0087
Czepiel Millers Dairy
Ludlow, MA 413-589-0828
D F Ingredients Inc
Washington, MO 888-583-0802
Dairy Fresh Foods Inc
Taylor, MI 313-299-0735
Dairy King Milk Farms/Foodservice
Whitter, CA 800-900-6455
Dairy Maid Dairy LLC
Frederick, MD 301-663-5114
Dairy-Mix Inc
St Petersburg, FL 800-955-6101
Dairytown Products Ltd
Sussex, NB 800-561-5598
Daisy Brand
Dallas, TX 877-292-9830
Danish Maid Butter Co
Chicago, IL 773-731-8787
Dannon Yo Cream
Portland, OR 800-962-7326
Danone North America
Broomfield, CO 303-635-4000
Darifair Foods
Jacksonville, FL 904-268-9916
Daybreak Foods Inc
Long Prairie, MN 320-732-2966
Dean Foods Co.
Dallas, TX 800-395-7004
Debel Food Products
Elizabeth, NJ 800-421-3447
Deep Foods Inc
Union, NJ 908-810-7500
Deseret Dairy Products
Salt Lake City, UT 801-240-7350
Dimock Dairy Products
Dimock, SD 605-928-3833
Dixie Egg Co
Jacksonville, FL 800-394-3447
Double B Foods Inc
Arlington, TX 800-679-0349
Driftwood Dairy
El Monte, CA 626-444-9591
Dupont Cheese
Marion, WI 800-895-2873
Dutch Farms Inc
Chicago, IL 800-637-3447
Eagle Family Foods
Richfield, OH 888-656-3245
Eatem Foods Co
Vineland, NJ 800-683-2836
Eberhard Creamery
Redmond, OR 541-548-5181
Echo Spring Dairy
Eugene, OR 541-342-1291
Eggland's Best Eggs
Malvern, PA 800-922-3447
Elm City Cheese Co Inc
Hamden, CT 203-865-5768
Emkay Trading Corporation
Elmsford, NY 914-592-9000
Erie Foods Intl Inc
Erie, IL 309-659-2233
Erivan Dairy
Oreland, PA 215-887-2009
Everything Yogurt
Washington, DC 202-842-2990
F C C
Mcminnville, OR 503-472-2157
Fairview Dairy Inc
Latrobe, PA 724-537-7111
Fairview Swiss Cheese
Fredonia, PA 724-475-4154
Farbest-Tallman Foods Corp
Montvale, NJ 201-573-4900
Farmdale Creamery Inc
San Bernardino, CA 800-346-7306
Farmer's Hen House
Kalona, IA 319-683-2206
Farmers Dairies
El Paso, TX 915-772-2736
Farmers Seafood Co Wholesale
Shreveport, LA 800-874-0203
Farmland Dairies
Wallington, NJ 888-727-6252
Farmland Fresh Dairies
Newark, NJ 973-961-2500
Farr Candy Company
Idaho Falls, ID 208-522-8215
Feature Foods
Brampton, ON 905-452-7741
Fendall Ice Cream Company
Salt Lake City, UT 801-355-3583
Fieldbrook Foods Corp.
Dunkirk, NY 800-333-0805
First District Association
Litchfield, MN 320-693-3236
Flavors from Florida
Bartow, FL 800-888-0409
Fleur De Lait Foods Inc
New Holland, PA 800-322-2743
Foothills Creamery
Calgary, AB 800-661-4909
Foremost Farms USA
Baraboo, WI 800-362-9196
Freeman Industries
Tuckahoe, NY 800-666-6454
Fried Provisions Company
Evans City, PA 724-538-3160
Friendship Dairies LLC
Friendship, NY 800-854-3243
Frog City Cheese
Plymouth Notch, VT 802-672-3650
Froma-Dar
St. Boniface, QC 819-535-3946
Frozfruit Corporation
Gardena, CA 310-217-1034
Gad Cheese Retail Store
Medford, WI 715-748-4273
GAF Seelig Inc
Flushing, NY 718-899-5000
Galliker Dairy Co
Johnstown, PA 800-477-6455
Gamay Flavors
New Berlin, WI 888-345-4560
Garber Ice Cream Co Inc
Winchester, VA 800-662-5422
Gelato Fresco
Toronto, ON 416-785-5415
GFA Brands Inc
Paramus, NJ 201-568-9300
Gibbsville Cheese Company
Sheboygan Falls, WI 920-564-3242
Gifford's Ice Cream
Skowhegan, ME 800-950-2604
Global Food Industries
Townville, SC 800-225-4152
Glover's Ice Cream Inc
Frankfort, IN 800-686-5163
Golden Valley Dairy Products
Tulare, CA 559-687-1188
Grace Foods International
Astoria, NY 718-433-4789
Graf Creamery Co
Bonduel, WI 715-758-2137
Graham Cheese Corporation
Elnora, IN 800-472-9178
Grande Cheese Company
Fond du Lac, WI 800-678-3122
Grassland Dairy Products Inc
Greenwood, WI 800-428-8837
Great American Appetizers
Nampa, ID 800-282-4834
Great Lakes Cheese Company, Inc.
Hiram, OH 440-834-2500
Great Valley Mills
Barto, PA 800-688-6455
Green Dirt Farm
Weston, MO 816-386-2156
Grossingers Home Bakery
New York, NY 800-479-6996
Guers Dairy
Tamaqua, PA 570-277-6611
Guida's Dairy
New Britain, CT 800-832-8929
H B Taylor Co
Chicago, IL 773-254-4805
H-E-B Grocery Co. LP
San Antonio, TX 800-432-3113
Harrisburg Dairies Inc
Harrisburg, PA 800-692-7429
Harvest Direct
Norwell, MA 800-733-2106
Hastings Co-Op Creamery-Dairy
Hastings, MN 651-437-9414
Heartland Farms Dairy & Food Products, LLC
St. Louis, MO 888-633-6455
Heartland Ingredients LLC
Troy, MO 800-557-2621
Heluva Good Cheese
Lynnfield, MA 800-644-5473
HempNut
Henderson, NV 707-576-7050
Henning Cheese Factory
Kiel, WI 920-894-3032
Henningsen Foods Inc
Omaha, NE 800-228-2769
Heritage's Dairy Stores
West Deptford, NJ 856-845-2855
High Road Craft Ice Cream, Inc.
Atlanta, GA 678-701-7623
Highland Dairies
Wichita, KS 800-336-0765
Hiland Dairy Foods Co
Springfield, MO 800-492-4022
Hillandale
Lake City, FL 386-397-1300
Holmes Cheese Co
Millersburg, OH 330-674-6451
Holton Food Products
La Grange, IL 708-352-5599
Homer's Ice Cream
Wilmette, IL 847-251-0477

Homestead Dairy
Plymouth, IN … 574-936-6126

Honeyville Grain Inc
Brigham City, UT … 435-494-4200

Hope Creamery
Hope, MN … 507-451-2029

Horizon Organic Dairy
Broomfield, CO … 888-494-3020

Hormel Foods Corp.
Austin, MN … 507-437-5611

Houlton Farms Dairy
Houlton, ME … 207-532-3170

Hudsonville Ice Cream
Holland, MI … 616-546-4005

Humboldt Creamery
Modesto, CA … 888-316-6064

Hunter Farms - High Point Division
High Point, NC … 800-446-8035

Hygeia Dairy Company
Corpus Christi, TX … 361-854-4561

Icco Cheese Co
Orangeburg, NY … 845-680-2436

Ice Cream Bowl
Zanesville, OH … 740-452-5267

Ice Cream Club Inc
Boynton Beach, FL … 800-535-7711

Ice Cream Specialties Inc
St Louis, MO … 800-662-7550

Ideal Dairy Farms
Hudson Falls, NY … 518-747-5059

IMAC
Oklahoma City, OK … 888-878-7827

Imperial Foods, Inc.
Long Island City, NY … 718-784-3400

Independent Dairy Inc
Monroe, MI … 734-241-6016

Ingles Markets
Black Mountain, NC … 828-669-2941

Ingredia Inc
Wapakoneta, OH … 419-738-4060

Ingretec
Lebanon, PA … 717-273-0711

Instantwhip Foods Inc
Columbus, OH … 800-544-9447

International Cheese Company
Toronto, ON … 416-769-3547

International Farmers Market
Chamblee, GA … 770-455-1777

International Food Products
Fenton, MO … 800-227-8427

Inverness Dairy
Cheboygan, MI … 231-627-4655

Ise America Inc
Galena, MD … 410-755-6300

Island Farms Dairies Cooperative Association
Victoria, BC … 250-360-5200

It's It Ice Cream Co
Burlingame, CA … 800-345-1928

Ito Cariani Sausage Company
Hayward, CA … 510-887-0882

J B & Son LTD
Yonkers, NY … 914-963-5192

J M Swank Co
North Liberty, IA … 800-593-6375

J.W. Haywood & Sons Dairy
Louisville, KY … 502-774-2311

Jack & Jill Ice Cream
Moorestown, NJ … 856-813-2300

Jaxon's Ice Cream Parlor
Dania Beach, FL … 954-923-4445

Jim's Cheese Pantry
Waterloo, WI … 800-345-3571

John W Macy's Cheesesticks Inc
Elmwood Park, NJ … 800-643-0573

Johnson's Real Ice Cream
Columbus, OH … 614-231-0014

Johnson, Nash & Sons Farms
Warsaw, NC … 910-289-6842

Joseph Farms
Atwater, CA … 209-394-7984

Josh & John's Ice Cream
Colorado Springs, CO … 800-530-2855

Kalamazoo Creamery
Kalamazoo, MI … 616-343-2558

Kan-Pak
Arkansas City, KS … 800-378-1265

Katrina's Tartufo
Port Jeffrsn Sta, NY … 800-480-8836

Kauai Producers
Lihue, HI … 800-262-1400

Keller's Creamery
Kansas City, MO … 800-535-5371

Kemps LLC
St Paul, MN

Kent Foods Inc
Gonzales, TX … 830-672-7993

Kentucky Beer Cheese
Nicholasville, KY … 859-887-1645

Kirby Holloway Provision Co
Harrington, DE … 800-995-4729

Kleinpeter Farms Dairy LLC
Baton Rouge, LA … 225-753-2121

Klinke Brothers Ice Cream Co
Memphis, TN … 901-322-6640

Klondike Cheese Factory
Monroe, WI … 608-325-3021

Kolb-Lena Bresse Bleu Inc
Lena, IL … 815-369-4577

LA Grander Hillside Dairy Inc
Stanley, WI … 715-644-2275

Lake Country Foods Inc
Oconomowoc, WI … 262-567-5521

Lake Erie Frozen Foods Co
Ashland, OH … 800-766-8501

Lakeview Banquit Cheese
Salt Lake City, UT … 801-364-3607

Lakeview Farms
Delphos, OH … 800-755-9925

Lancaster Packing Company
Myerstown, PA … 717-397-9727

Land O'Lakes Inc
Arden Hills, MN … 800-328-9680

Lane's Dairy
El Paso, TX … 915-772-6700

Larkin Cold Storage
Long Island City, NY … 718-937-2007

Larosa Bakery Inc
Shrewsbury, NJ … 800-527-6722

Layman Distributing
Salem, VA … 800-237-1319

Leprino Foods Co.
Denver, CO … 800-537-7466

Lewes Dairy Inc
Lewes, DE … 302-645-6281

Lifeway
Morton Grove, IL … 877-281-3874

Longacres Modern Dairy Inc
Barto, PA … 610-845-7551

Lowell-Paul Dairy
Greeley, CO … 970-353-0278

Lubbers Family Farm
Grand Rapids, MI … 616-453-4257

Ludwig Dairy Product
Elk Grove Vlg, IL … 847-860-8646

Lyoferm & Vivolac Cultures
Indianapolis, IN … 317-356-8460

M.E. Franks Inc.
Wayne, PA … 610-989-9688

Mack's Bill Ice Cream
Dover, PA … 717-292-1931

Magic Valley Quality Milk
Jerome, ID … 208-324-7519

Main Street Ingredients
La Crosse, WI … 800-359-2345

Mancuso Cheese Co
Joliet, IL … 815-722-2475

Maola Milk & Ice Cream Co.
… 844-287-1970

Maple Hill Farms
Bloomfield, CT … 800-842-7304

Maple Leaf Foods International
North York, ON … 800-268-3708

Marantha Natural Foods
San Francisco, CA … 866-972-6879

Marathon Cheese Corp
Marathon, WI … 715-443-2211

Marburger Farm Dairy
Evans City, PA … 800-331-1295

Marin French Cheese Co
Petaluma, CA … 800-292-6001

Mario's Gelati
Vancouver, BC … 604-879-9411

Marshallville Packing Co
Marshallville, OH … 330-855-2871

Marva Maid Dairy
Newport News, VA … 800-768-6243

Marwood Sales, Inc
Overland Park, KS … 800-745-2881

Master Mix
Placentia, CA … 714-524-1698

Matador Processors
Blanchard, OK … 800-847-0797

Mayfield Dairy Farms LLC
Athens, TN … 800-362-9546

Maytag Dairy Farms Inc
Newton, IA … 800-247-2458

McAnally Enterprises
Lakeview, CA … 800-726-2002

McArthur Dairy LLC
Miami, FL … 561-659-4811

Mccadam Cheese Co Inc
Chateaugay, NY … 800-639-4031

McConnell's Fine Ice Cream
Santa Barbara, CA … 805-963-8813

Meadow Brook Dairy Co
Erie, PA … 800-352-4010

Meadowbrook Farm
Bronx, NY … 718-828-6400

Meijer Inc
Grand Rapids, MI … 616-453-6711

Mercer's Dairy
Boonville, NY … 866-637-2377

Meyer Brothers Dairy
Maple Plain, MN … 952-473-7343

Micalizzi Italian Ice
Bridgeport, CT … 203-366-2353

Michael Granese & Company
Norristown, PA … 610-272-5099

Michele's Family Bakery
York, PA … 717-741-2027

Michelle Chocolatiers
Colorado Springs, CO … 888-447-3654

Michigan Dairy LLC
Livonia, MI … 734-367-5390

Michigan Farm Cheese Dairy
Fountain, MI … 877-624-3373

Michigan Milk Producers Assn
Novi, MI … 248-474-6672

Mikawaya LLC
Vernon, CA … 323-587-5504

Milk Specialties Global
Eden Prairie, MN … 952-942-7310

Milky Way Jersey Farm Inc
Starr, SC … 864-352-2014

Miller's Cheese Corp
Brooklyn, NY … 718-965-1840

Milnot Company
Orrville, OH … 888-656-3245

Milsolv Corporation
Butler, WI … 800-558-8501

Minerva Cheese Factory
Minerva, OH … 330-868-4196

Minerva Dairy Inc
Minerva, OH … 330-868-4196

Mister Cookie Face
Dunkirk, NY … 800-333-0305

Mitchel Dairies
Bronx, NY … 718-994-6655

Model Dairy LLC
Reno, NV … 800-433-2030

Monument Farms Dairy
Middlebury, VT … 802-545-2119

Mooresville Ice Cream Co
Mooresville, NC … 800-304-7172

Morning Star Foods
East Brunswick, NJ … 800-237-5320

Morningland Dairy Cheese Company
Mountain View, MO … 417-855-0588

Mountain High Yogurt
Minneapolis, MN … 866-964-4878

Mountainside Farms Inc
Roxbury, NY … 607-326-4161

Mt Sterling Co-Op Creamery
Highland, WI … 866-289-4628

Muller-Pinehurst Dairy
Rockford, IL … 815-968-0441

Mulligan Sales
City of Industry, CA … 626-968-9621

Murdock Farm Dairy
Winchendon, MA … 978-297-2196

Mystic Lake Dairy
Sammamish, WA … 425-868-2029

Natrel
St. Laurent, QC … 800-501-1150

Natural By Nature
Newark, DE … 302-455-1261

Natural Fruit Corp
Hialeah, FL … 305-887-7525

Nature's Dairy
Roswell, NM … 575-623-9640

Ninth Avenue Foods
CA … 626-364-8722

Nodine's Smokehouse Inc
Torrington, CT … 800-222-2059

Noon Hour Food Products Inc
Chicago, IL … 800-621-6636

Nor-Tech Dairy Advisors
Sioux Falls, SD....605-338-2404
Northumberland Dairy
Miramichi, NB....800-501-1150
Norwalk Dairy
Santa Fe Springs, CA....562-921-5712
O'Boyle's Ice Cream Company
Bristol, PA....215-788-3882
O-At-Ka Milk Prods Co-Op Inc.
Batavia, NY....800-828-8152
Oak Farm's Dairy
Waco, TX....254-756-5421
Oak Farms
El Paso, TX....800-395-7004
Oak Grove Dairy
Clintonville, WI....715-823-6226
Oakhurst Dairy
Portland, ME....800-482-0718
Oberweis Dairy Inc
North Aurora, IL....866-623-7934
OCG Cacao
Whitinsville, MA....888-482-2226
Old Home Foods Inc
New Brighton, MN....651-312-8900
Olde Tyme Food Corporation
East Longmeadow, MA....800-356-6533
Oregon Hill Farms
St Helens, OR....800-243-4541
Organic Pastures
Fresno, CA....877-729-6455
Orientex Foods
Pittsburg, CA....800-660-0962
Oskaloosa Food Products
Oskaloosa, IA....800-477-7239
Out of a Flower
Lancaster, TX....800-743-4696
Park Cheese Company Inc
Fond Du Lac, WI....800-752-7275
Parkers Farm
Coon Rapids, MN....800-869-6685
Pascobel Inc
Longueuil, QC....450-677-2443
Pastorelli Food Products
Chicago, IL....800-767-2829
Pearl Valley Cheese Inc
Fresno, OH....740-545-6002
Pecoraro Dairy Products
Brooklyn, NY....718-388-2379
Penn Cheese
Winfield, PA....570-524-7700
Perry's Ice Cream Co Inc
Akron, NY....800-873-7797
PET Dairy
Winston Salem, NC....800-735-2050
Petersen Ice Cream Company
Oak Park, IL....708-386-6130
Philip R's Frozen Desserts
Winchester, MA....781-721-6330
Pierz Cooperative Association
Pierz, MN....320-468-6655
Pine River Cheese & Butter Company
Ripley, ON....800-265-1175
Pine River Pre-Pack Inc
Newton, WI....920-726-4216
Pioneer Dairy
Southwick, MA....413-569-6132
Plains Dairy Products
Amarillo, TX....800-365-5608
Plainview Milk Products
Plainview, MN....800-356-5606
Platte Valley Creamery
Scottsbluff, NE....308-632-4225
Pleasant View Dairy
Highland, IN....219-838-0155
Plehn's Bakery Inc
Louisville, KY....502-896-4438
Plymouth Cheese Counter
Plymouth, WI....888-607-9477
Pocono Cheesecake Factory
Swiftwater, PA....570-839-6844
Pollio Dairy Products
Campbell, NY....607-527-3621
Pon Food Corp
Ponchatoula, LA....985-386-6941
Potomac Farms Dairy Inc
Cumberland, MD....301-722-4410
Potter Siding Creamery Company
Tripoli, IA....319-882-4444
Prairie Farms Dairy Inc.
Edwardsville, IL....618-659-5700
Prestige Proteins
Boca Raton, FL....561-997-8770
Price's Creameries
El Paso, TX....915-565-2711
Pride Dairies
Bottineau, ND....701-228-2216
Primo Foods
Oceanside, CA....760-439-8711
Producers Dairy Foods Inc
Fresno, CA....559-264-6583
Promised Land Dairy
Colorado Springs, CO....877-520-2479
Protient
St Paul, MN....800-328-9680
Publix Super Market
Lakeland, FL....800-242-1227
Pure Gourmet
Glenside, PA....215-609-4219
Puritan/ATZ Ice Cream
Kendallville, IN....260-347-2700
Purity Dairies LLC
Nashville, TN....615-244-1900
Purity Farms
La Farge, WI....877-211-4819
Purity Ice Cream Co
Ithaca, NY....607-272-1545
Quality Dairy Co
East Lansing, MI....517-319-4114
Quality Ingredients
Burnsville, MN....952-898-4002
Queensboro Farm Products
Canastota, NY....315-687-6133
Queensboro Farm Products
Jamica, NY....718-658-5000
Rachael's Smoked Fish
Springfield, MA....800-327-3412
Ragersville Swiss Cheese
Sugarcreek, OH....330-897-3055
Ramsen Inc
Lakeville, MN....952-431-0400
Ranieri Fine Foods
Brooklyn, NY....718-599-9520
Ratners Retail Foods
New York, NY....212-677-5588
Red Smith Foods Inc
Davie, FL....954-581-1996
Rehemond Farm Inc
Minot, ME....207-345-5611
Reinhold Ice Cream Company
Pittsburgh, PA....412-321-7600
Reiter Dairy
Newport, KY....800-544-6455
Reiter Dairy LLC
Springfield, OH....937-323-5777
Rich's Ice Cream Co Inc
West Palm Beach, FL....561-833-7585
Ritchey's Dairy
Martinsburg, PA....800-296-2157
RM Heagy Foods
Lancaster, PA....717-569-1032
Rockview Farms
Downey, CA....800-423-2479
Rocky Top Farms
Ellsworth, MI....800-862-9303
Ronny Brook Farm Dairy
Ancramdale, NY....800-772-6455
Ronzoni
Largo, FL....800-730-5957
Roos Foods
Kenton, DE....800-343-3642
Rosa Brothers Milk Co Inc
Hanford, CA....559-685-8825
Rose Acre Farms
Wolcott, IN....765-258-4015
Rosebud Creamery
Plattsburgh, NY....518-561-5160
Roselani Tropics Ice Cream
Wailuku, HI....808-244-7951
Rosenberger's Dairies
Hatfield, PA....800-355-9074
Royal Crest Dairy
Denver, CO....888-226-6455
Rutter's Dairy
York, PA....800-840-1664
S.T. Jerrell Company
Bessemer, AL....205-426-8930
Safeway Milk Plant
Tempe, AZ....480-894-4391
Saint Albans Cooperative Creamery
Saint Albans, VT....802-524-6581
Sapore della Vita
Sarasota, FL....941-914-4256
Saputo Cheese USA Inc.
Lincolnshire, IL....847-267-1100
Saputo Dairy Division (Canada)
Saint-Laurent, QC....800-672-8866
Schepps Dairy
Dallas, TX....800-395-7004
Schneider's Dairy Inc
Pittsburgh, PA....412-881-3525
Schneider-Valley Farms Inc
Williamsport, PA....570-326-2021
Seger Egg Corporation
Farina, IL....618-245-3301
Sequoia Specialty Cheese Company
Visalia, CA....559-752-4106
Sesinco Foods
New York, NY....212-243-1306
Shenk's Foods
Lancaster, PA....717-393-4240
Siegel Egg Co
North Billerica, MA....978-528-2010
Sierra Cheese Mfg Co
Compton, CA....800-266-4270
Siggi's Dairy
....855-860-6683
Silani Sweet Cheese
Woodbridge, ON....905-792-3811
Sisler's Ice & Ice Cream
Ohio, IL....888-891-3856
Skim Delux Mendenhall Laboratories
Paris, TN....800-642-9321
Skinners' Dairy
Ponte Vedra Beach, FL....904-733-5440
Smith Dairy
Orrville, OH....800-776-7076
Smith Packing Regional Meat
Utica, NY....315-732-5125
Snelgrove Ice Cream Company
Salt Lake City, UT....800-569-0005
Snow Dairy Inc
Springville, UT....801-489-6081
Sommer Maid Creamery Inc
Pipersville, PA....215-345-6160
Source Food Technology
Durham, NC....866-277-3849
Southeast Dairy Processors Inc
Tampa, FL....813-620-1516
Southern Ice Cream Specialties
Marietta, GA....770-428-0452
Sparboe Foods Corp
New Hampton, IA....641-394-3040
Specialty Food Association
New York, NY....646-878-0301
Specialty Ingredients
Buffalo Grove, IL....847-419-9595
Spring Grove Foods
Miamisburg, OH....937-866-4311
Spring Hill Pure Water
Haverhill, MA....978-373-3481
Springbank Cheese Company
Woodstock, ON....800-265-1973
Springdale Cheese Factory
Richland Center, WI....608-538-3213
Springfield Creamery Inc
Eugene, OR....541-689-2911
St. Maurice Laurent
St-Bruno-Lac-St-Jean, QC....418-343-3655
Steiner Cheese
Baltic, OH....888-897-5505
Stewart's Shops Corp
Ballston Spa, NY....518-581-1200
Stone's Home Made Candy Shop
Oswego, NY....888-223-3928
Stop & Shop Manufacturing
Readville, MA....508-977-5132
Straus Family Creamery
Petaluma, CA....800-572-7783
Stremick's Heritage Foods
Santa Ana, CA....800-371-9010
Sturm Foods Inc
Manawa, WI....800-347-8876
SugarCreek
Cincinnati, OH....800-445-2715
Sunny Fresh Foods
Monticello, MN....800-872-3447
Sunshine Dairy
Middletown, CT....860-346-6644
Sunshine Dairy Foods Inc
Portland, OR....503-234-7526
Sunshine Farms
Portage, WI....608-742-2016
Super Stores Industries
Turlock, CA....209-668-2100
Superbrand Dairies
Miami, FL....305-769-6600

Superior Dairy
Wauseon, OH 419-335-3553
Supreme Dairy Farms Co
Warwick, RI 401-739-8180
Swagger Foods Corp
Vernon Hills, IL 847-913-1200
Sweety Novelty
Monterey Park, CA.................... 626-282-4482
Swiss American Inc
St Louis, MO.................... 800-325-8150
Swiss Dairy
Riverside, CA 951-898-9427
Swiss Premium Dairy Inc
Lebanon, PA 800-222-2129
T. Marzetti Company
Westerville, OH.................... 800-999-1835
Tamarack Farms Dairy
Newark, OH 866-221-4141
Tanglewood Farms
Warsaw, VA.................... 804-394-4505
Tebay Dairy Company
Parkersburg, WV.................... 304-863-3705
Texas Heat
San Antonio, TX.................... 800-656-5916
The Valpo Velvet Shoppe
Valparaiso, IN 219-464-4141
Thomas Dairy
Rutland, VT 802-773-6788
Thornton Foods Company
Eden Prairie, MN 952-944-1735
Tillamook County Creamery Association
Tillamook, OR 503-842-4481
Tiller Foods Company
Dayton, OH.................... 937-435-4601
Titusville Dairy Products Co
Titusville, PA 800-352-0101
Toft Dairy Inc
Sandusky, OH 800-521-4606
Tolteca Foodservice
Norcross, GA 800-541-6835
Tomanetti Food Products Inc
Oakmont, PA.................... 800-875-3040
Tony's Ice Cream Co
Gastonia, NC.................... 704-867-7085
Trickling Springs Creamery
Chambersburg, PA 717-709-0711
Tropical Treets
North York, ON.................... 888-424-8229
Turner & Pease Company
Seattle, WA.................... 206-282-9535
Turner Dairy Farms Inc
Pittsburgh, PA.................... 800-892-1039
Twin County Dairy
Kalona, IA.................... 319-656-2776
Umpqua Dairy
Roseburg, OR 888-672-6455
United Dairy Farmers Inc.
Cincinnati, OH 866-837-4833
United Dairy Inc.
Martins Ferry, OH.................... 800-252-1542
United Dairymen of Arizona
Tempe, AZ.................... 480-966-7211
United Valley Bell Dairy
Charleston, WV.................... 304-344-2511
Upstate Farms
Buffalo, NY.................... 716-896-3156
Upstate Niagara Co-Op Inc.
Buffalo, NY.................... 716-892-3156
US Foods & Pharmaceuticals Inc
Madison, WI.................... 800-362-8294
Valley Grain Products
Fresno, CA 559-675-3400
Valley Milk Products
Strasburg, VA 540-465-5113
Valley Queen Cheese Factory
Milbank, SD 605-432-4563
Van Peenans Dairy
Wayne, NJ.................... 973-694-2551
Vance's Foods
San Francisco, CA 415-621-1171
Velda Farms
Orlando, FL.................... 800-795-4649
Vella Cheese Co
Sonoma, CA 800-848-0505
Velvet Ice Cream Co Inc
Utica, OH 800-589-5000
Vermont Creamery
Websterville, VT.................... 800-884-6287
Vita Plus Corp
Madison, WI 608-256-1988
Vitamilk Dairy
Bellingham, WA 206-529-4128
Vitarich Ice Cream
Fortuna, CA 707-725-6182
W.J. Stearns & Sons/Mountain Dairy
Storrs Mansfield, CT 860-423-9289
Wabash Valley Produce Inc
Dubois, IN.................... 812-678-3131
Wapsie Creamery
Independence, IA 319-334-7193
Warwick Ice Cream
Warwick, RI 401-821-8403
Waugh Foods Inc
East Peoria, IL.................... 309-427-8000
Wawa Inc
Wawa, PA 800-444-9292
Wayne Dairy Products Inc
Richmond, IN 765-935-7521
Wegmans Food Markets Inc.
Rochester, NY.................... 800-934-6267
WEIS Markets Inc.
Sunbury, PA.................... 866-999-9347
Weldon Ice Cream Co
Millersport, OH.................... 740-467-2400
Welsh Farms
Wallington, NJ 800-221-0663
Welsh Farms
Clifton, NJ.................... 973-772-2388
Wenger Spring Brook Cheese Inc
Davis, IL 815-865-5612
Wenk Foods Inc
Madison, SD 605-256-4569
Wessanan
Minneapolis, MN 612-331-3775
Westin Foods
Omaha, NE 800-228-6098
WhiteWave Foods
Denver, CO 800-488-9283
Whitewave Foods Company
Broomfield, CO 303-635-4000
Whitey's Ice Cream Inc
Moline, IL.................... 888-594-4839
Whitney Foods Inc
Jamaica, NY 718-291-3333
Widmer's Cheese Cellars Inc
Theresa, WI.................... 888-878-1107
Winchester Farms Dairy
Winchester, KY.................... 859-745-5500
Winmix/Natural Care Products
Englewood, FL 941-475-7432
Winn-Dixie Stores
Jacksonville, FL 800-967-9105
Winsor SB Dairy
Johnston, RI 401-231-7832
Wisconsin Milk Mktng Board Inc
Madison, WI.................... 800-589-5127
Wolf Canyon Foods
Carmel, CA.................... 831-626-1323
Woolwich Dairy
Orangeville, ON 877-438-3499
World Cheese Inc
Brooklyn, NY 718-965-1700
Wright's Ice Cream Co
Cayuga, IN 800-686-9561
Wurth Dairy
Caseyville, IL 217-271-7580
Yoder Dairies
Chesapeake, VA 757-482-4068
Yoplait
Mississauga, ON.................... 800-516-7780
Young's Jersey Dairy
Yellow Springs, OH 937-325-0629
Ziegenfelder Ice Cream Co
Wheeling, WV 800-322-3642
Zuccaro Produce
Columbia Heights, MN.................... 612-333-1122

Dehydrated

Cheeses, Buttermilk, Milk

Associated Milk Producers Inc.
New Ulm, MN.................... 800-533-3580
Fleur De Lait Foods Inc
New Holland, PA 800-322-2743
Florence Pasta & Cheese
Marshall, MN 800-533-5290
Tolteca Foodservice
Norcross, GA 800-541-6835

Dairy Alternatives

Annabella
Longmont, CO
CO YO
Albuquerque, NM.................... 505-247-0012
Culina
Austin, TX
Danone North America
Broomfield, CO 303-635-4000
Elmhurst Milked
Elma, NY 888-356-1925
Fora Foods
Brooklyn, NY
Forager Project
San Francisco, CA
Galaxy Nutritional Foods Inc
North Kingstown, RI 800-441-9419
Global Gardens Group Inc.
Richmond, BC 855-409-4365
Goat Partners Intl.
Rolling Meadows, IL 833-872-4628
Good Karma Foods
Boulder, CO 800-550-6731
Good PLANeT Foods
Bellevue, WA 425-449-8134
Happy Planet Foods
Burnaby, BC 800-811-3213
Jasper Products Corp
Joplin, MO 417-206-3877
Killer Creamery
Boise, ID
LAVVA
Warwick, NY
Leaner Creamer
Beverly Hills, CA 866-739-2298
MALK Organics
Houston, TX 281-974-3251
Mooala
Dallas, TX.................... 214-206-1902
New Barn
.... 888-635-7102
New Barn Organics
Rohnert Park, CA 888-635-7102
Oatly
New York, NY
Planet Oat
Lynnfield, MA 800-242-2423
Ripple
Berkeley, CA
Three Trees Almondmilk
San Mateo, CA 855-863-8733
Violife
Thessaloniki,
Vixen Kitchen
Santa Cruz, CA.................... 707-223-5627
WhiteWave Foods
Denver, CO 800-488-9283

Dairy Drinks

Alpina
Batavia, NY.................... 855-886-1914
Baskin-Robbins LLC
Canton, MA 800-859-5339
Dahlicious
Leominster, MA
Danone North America
Broomfield, CO 303-635-4000
McArthur Dairy LLC
Miami, FL.................... 561-659-4811
Ninth Avenue Foods
CA.................... 626-364-8722
PowerBar
Kings Mountain, NC.................... 800-587-6937
Smith Dairy
Orrville, OH 800-776-7076

Egg Nog

Alta Dena Certified Dairy LLC
City Of Industry, CA.................... 800-535-1369
Anderson Dairy Inc
Las Vegas, NV 702-642-7507
Broughton Foods LLC
El Paso, TX.................... 800-395-7004
C F Burger Creamery Co
Detroit, MI 313-584-4040
Cass-Clay Creamery
Fargo, ND.................... 701-293-6455
Chase Brothers Dairy
Oxnard, CA.................... 800-438-6455
HP Hood LLC
Lynnfield, MA 800-343-6592
Kleinpeter Farms Dairy LLC
Baton Rouge, LA 225-753-2121

Plains Dairy Products
Amarillo, TX. 800-365-5608
Rockview Farms
Downey, CA 800-423-2479
Smith Dairy
Orrville, OH 800-776-7076
United Dairy Inc.
Martins Ferry, OH. 800-252-1542
WhiteWave Foods
Denver, CO 800-488-9283
Yoder Dairies
Chesapeake, VA 757-482-4068

Ice Cream

Agave Dream
La Canada, CA 310-619-1575
Aglamesis Bros Ice Cream
Cincinnati, OH 513-531-5196
Agropur
Granby, QC. 800-363-5686
Al Gelato Bornay
Franklin Park, IL. 847-455-5355
Al-Rite Fruits & Syrups Co
Miami, FL. 305-652-2540
Alpenrose Dairy
Portland, OR 503-244-1133
American Classic Ice Cream Company
Bay Shore, NY 800-736-4100
Anderson Dairy Inc
Las Vegas, NV 702-642-7507
Anderson Erickson Dairy
Des Moines, IA. 515-265-2521
Anderson Erickson Dairy
Kansas City, KS 913-621-4801
Archibald Frozen Desserts
New Albany, IN 812-941-8267
Arctic Beverages
Winnipeg, MB. 866-503-1270
Arctic Ice Cream Co
Ewing, NJ 800-858-8966
Arctic Zero
San Diego, CA 888-272-1715
Asael Farr & Sons Co
Salt Lake City, UT 877-553-2777
B&M Enterprises
Greenfield, WI 414-399-7402
Barnes Ice Cream Company
Manchester, ME 207-622-0827
Bartolini Ice Cream
Bronx, NY. 718-589-5151
Baskin-Robbins LLC
Canton, MA 800-859-5339
Bassett's
Philadelphia, PA 888-999-6314
Beck's Ice Cream
York, PA 717-764-4585
Ben & Jerry's Homemade Inc
South Burlington, VT. 866-258-6877
Berkeley Farms
Hayward, CA 800-395-7004
Bernie's Foods
Brooklyn, NY 718-417-6677
Birdsall Ice Cream Company
Mason City, IA 641-423-5365
Black Market Gelato
North Hollywood, CA 818-983-6040
Blue Bell Creameries LP
Brenham, TX. 800-327-8135
Bonnie Doon LLC
Elkhart, IN. 574-264-3390
Bonnie's Ice Cream
Paradise, PA 717-687-9301
Boulder Homemade Inc
Boulder, CO 800-691-5002
Brighams
Arlington, MA 800-242-2423
Brookside Foods
Abbotsford, BC. 800-468-1714
Brothers Desserts
Santa Ana, CA 949-655-0080
Brothers International Desserts
Santa Ana, CA 949-655-0080
Broughton Foods LLC
El Paso, TX. 800-395-7004
Brown's Ice Cream Co
Minneapolis, MN 612-378-1075
Browns' Ice Cream Company
Minneapolis, MN 612-378-1075
Bubbies Homemade Ice Cream
Aiea, HI. 808-487-7218
Buck's Spumoni Company
Milford, CT. 888-222-8257

Byrne Dairy, Inc.
Syracuse, NY 800-899-1535
Casper's Ice Cream
Richmond, UT. 800-772-4182
Cass-Clay Creamery
Fargo, ND 701-293-6455
Cedar Crest Specialties
Cedarburg, WI. 800-877-8341
Central Dairy
Jefferson City, MO 573-635-6148
Centreside Dairy
Renfrew, ON. 800-889-9974
Chino Valley Dairy
Chino, CA. 800-324-7948
Chocolate Shoppe Ice Cream Co
Madison, WI 800-466-8043
Chocolaterie Bernard Callebaut
Calgary, AB. 800-661-8367
Choctal
Pasadena, CA 626-798-1351
Circus Man Ice Cream Corporation
Farmingdale, NY 516-249-4400
Clemmy's
Randcho Mirage, CA 877-253-6698
Clover Sonoma
Petaluma, CA 800-237-3315
Cookie Kingdom
Oglesby, IL 815-883-3331
Cool Brands International
Ronkonkoma, NY. 631-737-9700
Coolhaus
Culver City, CA 310-853-8995
Country Clubs Famous Desserts
Feasterville Trevose, PA. 800-843-2253
Country Fresh
Grand Rapids, MI 616-243-0173
Crave Natural Foods
Los Angeles, CA. 877-425-2599
Creamland Dairies Inc
Albuquerque, NM. 505-247-0721
Crystal Creamery
Modesto, CA. 866-225-4821
Culture Republick
Englewood Cliffs, NJ 800-662-0348
Dannon Yo Cream
Portland, OR 800-962-7326
Deconna Ice Cream
Reddick, FL 800-824-8254
Dippin' Dots LLC
Paducah, KY 270-443-8994
Dolci Gelati
Washington, DC 202-257-5323
Double Rainbow Gourmet Ice Cream
San Francisco, CA 800-489-3580
Dreyer's Grand Ice Cream Inc.
Oakland, CA 877-437-3937
Dunkin' Brands Inc.
Canton, MA 800-859-5339
Eagle Ice Cream Company
Cleveland, OH 440-232-0085
Eden Creamery
Los Angeles, CA
Elgin Dairy Foods
Chicago, IL 800-786-9900
Enlightened
Bronx, NY. 212-888-1120
Fairview Dairy Inc
Latrobe, PA 724-537-7111
Farmers Cooperative Dairy
Saint-Hubert, QC 800-501-1150
Farmland Dairies
Wallington, NJ 888-727-6252
Farr Candy Company
Idaho Falls, ID 208-522-8215
Feeding the Turkeys, Inc.
Boston, MA. 207-712-4034
Fendall Ice Cream Company
Salt Lake City, UT 801-355-3583
Fieldbrook Foods Corp.
Dunkirk, NY 800-333-0805
Flavors from Florida
Bartow, FL 800-888-0409
Foothills Creamery
Calgary, AB. 800-661-4909
Fosselman's Ice Cream Co
Alhambra, CA. 626-282-6533
Frozfruit Corporation
Gardena, CA. 310-217-1034
Galliker Dairy Co
Johnstown, PA. 800-477-6455
Garber Ice Cream Co Inc
Winchester, VA. 800-662-5422

Gelato Fresco
Toronto, ON 416-785-5415
Getchell Brothers Inc
Brewer, ME. 800-949-4423
Gifford's Ice Cream
Skowhegan, ME 800-950-2604
Gifford's Ice Cream & Candy Co
Silver Spring, MA. 800-708-1938
Glover's Ice Cream Inc
Frankfort, IN. 800-686-5163
Good Humor-Breyers Ice Cream
Englewood Cliffs, NJ 800-931-2854
Gossner Foods Inc.
Logan, UT 800-944-0454
Graeter's Mfg. Co.
Cincinnati, OH 800-721-3323
Grays Ice Cream
Tiverton, RI. 401-624-4500
Green Dirt Farm
Weston, MO 816-386-2156
Green River Chocolates
Hinesburg, VT. 802-482-6727
Greenwood Ice Cream Co
Atlanta, GA. 800-678-6166
Haagen-Dazs
Wilkes-Barre, PA 800-767-0120
Herrell's Ice Cream
Northampton, MA. 413-586-9700
Hershey Creamery Co
Harrisburg, PA 888-240-1905
Homer's Ice Cream
Wilmette, IL 847-251-0477
Honey Hut
Brecksville, OH 440-526-0606
Hood Home Service
Burlington, VT 802-864-0941
Houlton Farms Dairy
Houlton, ME. 207-532-3170
House of Flavors Inc
Ludington, MI. 800-930-7740
House of Spices
Flushing, NY. 718-507-4600
HP Hood LLC
Lynnfield, MA 800-343-6592
Hudsonville Ice Cream
Holland, MI. 616-546-4005
Humboldt Creamery
Modesto, CA. 888-316-6064
Humphry Slocombe
San Francisco, CA 415-550-6971
Hunt-Wesson Foods
Chicago, IL 877-266-2472
Hunter Farms - High Point Division
High Point, NC 800-446-8035
Ice Cream Bowl
Zanesville, OH 740-452-5267
Ice Cream Club Inc
Boynton Beach, FL. 800-535-7711
Ice Cream Specialties Inc
St Louis, MO. 800-662-7550
Ideal Dairy Farms
Hudson Falls, NY 518-747-5059
Il Gelato
Astoria, NY. 800-899-9299
Independent Dairy Inc
Monroe, MI. 734-241-6016
It's It Ice Cream Co
Burlingame, CA 800-345-1928
J.W. Haywood & Sons Dairy
Louisville, KY. 502-774-2311
Jack & Jill Ice Cream
Moorestown, NJ 856-813-2300
Jaxon's Ice Cream Parlor
Dania Beach, FL. 954-923-4445
Jeni's Splendid Ice Creams
Columbus, OH 614-488-3224
Johnson's Real Ice Cream
Columbus, OH 614-231-0014
Josh & John's Ice Cream
Colorado Springs, CO. 800-530-2855
Kan-Pak
Arkansas City, KS. 800-378-1265
Katies Korner Inc
Girard, OH 330-539-4140
Katrina's Tartufo
Port Jeffrsn Sta, NY 800-480-8836
Kemps LLC
St Paul, MN
Killer Creamery
Boise, ID
Kith Treats
New York, NY 646-648-6285

Klinke Brothers Ice Cream Co
Memphis, TN 901-322-6640
Lee's Ice Cream
Scottsdale, AZ. 888-669-5337
Leiby's Premium Ice Cream
Tamaqua, PA. 877-453-4297
Living Harvest Foods
Portland, OR 888-690-3958
Louis Sherry Premium Chocolate and Tins
Chicago, IL 212-849-2862
Lucerne Foods
Pleasanton, CA 877-232-4271
M&L Gourmet Ice Cream
Baltimore, MD 410-276-4880
Mack's Bill Ice Cream
Dover, PA 717-292-1931
Mack's Homemade Ice Cream
York, PA 717-741-2027
MacKay's Cochrane Ice Cream
Cochrane, AB 403-932-2455
Mama Tish's Italian Specialties
Chicago, IL 708-929-2023
Mammoth Creameries
Austin, TX
Maola Milk & Ice Cream Co
New Bern, NC. 800-476-1021
Maola Milk & Ice Cream Co.
. 844-287-1970
Maple Island
Saint Paul, MN 800-369-1022
Mario's Gelati
Vancouver, BC 604-879-9411
Mayfield Dairy Farms LLC
Athens, TN. 800-362-9546
McConnell's Fine Ice Cream
Santa Barbara, CA 805-963-8813
Micalizzi Italian Ice
Bridgeport, CT 203-366-2353
Michele's Family Bakery
York, PA 717-741-2027
Michelle Chocolatiers
Colorado Springs, CO. 888-447-3654
Michigan Dairy LLC
Livonia, MI. 734-367-5390
Mikawaya LLC
Vernon, CA 323-587-5504
Minus the Moo
Dorchester, MA. 703-999-7183
Mister Cookie Face
Dunkirk, NY 800-333-0305
Model Dairy LLC
Reno, NV 800-433-2030
Mooresville Ice Cream Co
Mooresville, NC. 800-304-7172
Mozzicato De Pasquale Bakery
Hartford, CT 860-296-0426
Mr. Green Tea Ice Cream
Keyport, NJ. 732-446-9800
Muller-Pinehurst Dairy
Rockford, IL 815-968-0441
My/Mo Mochi Ice Cream
Vernon, CA 323-587-5504
Natural Fruit Corp
Hialeah, FL 305-887-7525
Nelson Ice Cream
Stillwater, MN. 651-430-1103
Nestle USA Inc
Glendale, CA 800-225-2270
New Direction Foods
Huntington Beach, CA 888-393-5590
New Horizon Foods
Union City, CA. 510-489-8600
O'Boyle's Ice Cream Company
Bristol, PA. 215-788-3882
O'Danny Boy Ice Cream
Trotwood, OH. 937-837-2100
Oberweis Dairy Inc
North Aurora, IL. 866-623-7934
Oregon Ice Cream Co.
Vancouver, WA 360-713-6800
Out of a Flower
Lancaster, TX 800-743-4696
Perry's Ice Cream Co Inc
Akron, NY. 800-873-7797
Petersen Ice Cream Company
Oak Park, IL 708-386-6130
Phin & Phebes
Brooklyn, NY 718-383-4300
Pierre's French Ice Cream Inc
Cleveland, OH 800-837-7342
Platte Valley Creamery
Scottsbluff, NE 308-632-4225
Plehn's Bakery Inc
Louisville, KY 502-896-4438
Pony Boy Ice Cream
Acushnet, MA. 508-994-4422
Prairie Farms Dairy Inc.
Edwardsville, IL 618-659-5700
Price's Creameries
El Paso, TX. 915-565-2711
Pride Dairies
Bottineau, ND. 701-228-2216
Producers Dairy Foods Inc
Fresno, CA 559-264-6583
Puritan/ATZ Ice Cream
Kendallville, IN 260-347-2700
Purity Dairies LLC
Nashville, TN 615-244-1900
Purity Ice Cream Co
Ithaca, NY. 607-272-1545
Reinhold Ice Cream Company
Pittsburgh, PA 412-321-7600
Reiter Dairy
Newport, KY. 800-544-6455
Reiter Dairy LLC
Springfield, OH. 937-323-5777
Rhino Foods Inc
Burlington, VT 802-862-0252
Rich's Ice Cream Co Inc
West Palm Beach, FL 561-833-7585
Richardson's Ice Cream
Middleton, MA. 978-774-5450
Ronny Brook Farm Dairy
Ancramdale, NY. 800-772-6455
Roselani Tropics Ice Cream
Wailuku, HI. 808-244-7951
Safeway Inc.
Pleasanton, CA 877-723-3929
San Bernardo Ice Cream
Miramar, FL 954-322-2668
Schneider's Dairy Inc
Pittsburgh, PA 412-881-3525
Schneider-Valley Farms Inc
Williamsport, PA. 570-326-2021
Schoep's Ice Cream
Madison, WI 800-236-4050
Scotsburn Ice Cream Co.
Saint-Hubert, QC 800-501-1150
Seaside Ice Cream
Pelham, NY. 914-636-2751
Sebastiano's
Toledo, OH 419-382-0615
Shaner's Family Restaurant
South Paris, ME 207-743-6367
Sisler's Ice & Ice Cream
Ohio, IL. 888-891-3856
Smith Dairy
Orrville, OH 800-776-7076
Snelgrove Ice Cream Company
Salt Lake City, UT 800-569-0005
Snow Monkey
Santa Monica, CA
Snow's Ice Cream Co Inc
Greenfield, MA. 413-774-7438
South County Creamery
Great Barrington, MA. 413-528-8400
Southern Ice Cream Specialties
Marietta, GA. 770-428-0452
Springdale Ice Cream & Bev
Cincinnati, OH 513-671-2790
St Clair Ice Cream Co
Norwalk, CT. 203-853-4774
Steve's Ice Cream, Craft Collective
Brooklyn, NY 888-782-7688
Stewart's Shops Corp
Ballston Spa, NY 518-581-1200
Stone's Home Made Candy Shop
Oswego, NY 888-223-3928
SugarCreek
Cincinnati, OH 800-445-2715
Super Stores Industries
Turlock, CA 209-668-2100
Sweet Mountain Magic
Chicago, IL. 773-755-4539
Sweety Novelty
Monterey Park, CA. 626-282-4482
Tearrific Ice Cream
Bridgeport, CT 203-354-9805
Tebay Dairy Company
Parkersburg, WV. 304-863-3705
Ted Drewes Frozen Custard
St Louis, MO. 314-481-2652
The Valpo Velvet Shoppe
Valparaiso, IN 219-464-4141
Three Twins Ice Cream
Petaluma, CA 707-763-8946
Tillamook County Creamery Association
Tillamook, OR 503-842-4481
Toft Dairy Inc
Sandusky, OH 800-521-4606
Tony's Ice Cream Co
Gastonia, NC. 704-867-7085
Too Cool Chix
New York, NY 929-244-3022
Treat Ice Cream Co
San Jose, CA. 408-292-9321
Tropical Treets
North York, ON. 888-424-8229
Turkey Hill Dairy Inc
Conestoga, PA. 800-693-2479
Umpqua Dairy
Roseburg, OR 888-672-6455
Unilever US
Englewood Cliffs, NJ 800-298-5018
United Dairy Farmers Inc.
Cincinnati, OH 866-837-4833
United Dairy Inc.
Martins Ferry, OH. 800-252-1542
Van Dyke Ice Cream
Ridgewood, NJ 201-444-1429
Van Leeuwen
Brooklyn, NY 718-701-1630
Velda Farms
Orlando, FL. 800-795-4649
Velvet Ice Cream Co Inc
Utica, OH 800-589-5000
Vitamilk Dairy
Bellingham, WA 206-529-4128
Vitarich Ice Cream
Fortuna, CA 707-725-6182
Warwick Ice Cream
Warwick, RI 401-821-8403
Wayne Dairy Products Inc
Richmond, IN 765-935-7521
Weldon Ice Cream Co
Millersport, OH. 740-467-2400
Wells Enterprises Inc.
Le Mars, IA. 712-546-4000
Welsh Farms
Wallington, NJ 800-221-0663
Welsh Farms
Clifton, NJ. 973-772-2388
Whitey's Ice Cream Inc
Moline, IL. 888-594-4839
Winmix/Natural Care Products
Englewood, FL 941-475-7432
World's Greatest Ice Cream
Miami Beach, FL 305-538-0207
Wright's Ice Cream Co
Cayuga, IN 800-686-9561
WSU Creamery
Pullman, WA. 800-457-5442
Ziegenfelder Ice Cream Co
Wheeling, WV 800-322-3642
Zurheide Ice Cream Company
Sheboygan, WI 920-458-4581

Bases

Boulder Homemade Inc
Boulder, CO 800-691-5002
GPI USA LLC.
Mokena, IL 800-929-4248
Solo Foods
Countryside, IL. 800-328-7656
Turner Dairy Farms Inc
Pittsburgh, PA. 800-892-1039

Cones

Sugar

Kith Treats
New York, NY 646-648-6285
Three Twins Ice Cream
Petaluma, CA 707-763-8946

Wafer

Foothills Creamery
Calgary, AB. 800-661-4909
Kith Treats
New York, NY 646-648-6285

Fat-Free

Cedar Crest Specialties
Cedarburg, WI. 800-877-8341

Clay Center Locker Plant
Clay Center, KS 800-466-5543
Perry's Ice Cream Co Inc
Akron, NY. 800-873-7797

Flavored

Boulder Homemade Inc
Boulder, CO 800-691-5002
Byrne Dairy, Inc.
Syracuse, NY 800-899-1535
DF Mavens
Astoria, NY. 347-813-4705
Hershey Creamery Co
Harrisburg, PA 888-240-1905
Mack's Bill Ice Cream
Dover, PA 717-292-1931
Penny Lick Ice Cream Company
Hastings, NY. 914-525-1580
Petersen Ice Cream Company
Oak Park, IL 708-386-6130
San Bernardo Ice Cream
Miramar, FL 954-322-2668

Gelato

Boulder Homemade Inc
Boulder, CO 800-691-5002
Casper's Ice Cream
Richmond, UT. 800-772-4182
Ciao Bella Gelato Company
Irvington, NJ. 800-435-2863
Forte Gelato
Greens Farms, CT. 203-764-1826
Gelateria Naia
Hercules, CA. 510-724-2479
Gelato Fiasco
Brunswick, ME. 207-607-4262
Gelato Giuliana
New Haven, CT 203-772-0607
Good Humor-Breyers Ice Cream
Englewood Cliffs, NJ 800-931-2854
Graeter's Mfg. Co.
Cincinnati, OH 800-721-3323
Maple's Organics
Yarmouth, ME. 207-846-1000
Revel, Gelato
Huntington Beach, CA 866-203-9145
Snelgrove Ice Cream Company
Salt Lake City, UT 800-569-0005
Talenti Gelato e Sorbetto
Dallas, CA
Unilever US
Englewood Cliffs, NJ 800-298-5018
Weldon Ice Cream Co
Millersport, OH. 740-467-2400

Granita

Folklore Foods
Selby, SD. 605-649-1144

Ice Milk

Kith Treats
New York, NY 646-648-6285
Perry's Ice Cream Co Inc
Akron, NY. 800-873-7797
Whitey's Ice Cream Inc
Moline, IL. 888-594-4839

Ices

Cappola Foods
Toronto, ON 416-633-0389
Chill & Moore
Fort Worth, TX 800-676-3055
Dippin' Dots LLC
Paducah, KY. 270-443-8994
Gelato Fresco
Toronto, ON 416-785-5415
Helados Mexico
Chino, CA
Kemach Food Products
Brooklyn, NY 718-272-5655
Mackie International, Inc.
Riverside, CA 800-733-9762
Mama Tish's Italian Specialties
Chicago, IL. 708-929-2023
Mar-Key Foods
Vidalia, GA. 912-537-4204
Rosati Italian Water Ice
Clifton Heights, PA. 855-476-7284
Tova Industries LLC
Louisville, KY 888-532-8682

Low-Fat

Eden Creamery
Los Angeles, CA
Good Humor-Breyers Ice Cream
Englewood Cliffs, NJ 800-931-2854
Hudsonville Ice Cream
Holland, MI. 616-546-4005
Mayfield Dairy Farms LLC
Athens, TN 800-362-9546
Perry's Ice Cream Co Inc
Akron, NY. 800-873-7797
Stewart's Shops Corp
Ballston Spa, NY 518-581-1200
Vitarich Ice Cream
Fortuna, CA 707-725-6182
Wink Frozen Desserts
Stamford, CT. 516-323-5283

Non-Dairy

Low-Calorie

Chicago Vegan Foods
Lombard, IL 630-629-9667
Coconut Bliss
Eugene, OR. 844-305-5441
Eden Creamery
Los Angeles, CA
Hakuna Banana
Los Angeles, CA. 323-736-1630
Luna & Larry's Coconut Bliss
Eugene, OR. 541-345-0020
NadaMoo
Austin, TX
New Barn Organics
Rohnert Park, CA 888-635-7102
Vixen Kitchen
Santa Cruz, CA. 707-223-5627
Wink Frozen Desserts
Stamford, CT. 516-323-5283

Novelties

Broughton Foods LLC
El Paso, TX. 800-395-7004
Country Fresh
Grand Rapids, MI 616-243-0173
Del's Lemonade & Refreshments
Cranston, RI 401-463-6190
Dreyer's Grand Ice Cream Inc.
Oakland, CA 877-437-3937
Fieldbrook Foods Corp.
Dunkirk, NY. 800-333-0805
Foothills Creamery
Calgary, AB. 800-661-4909
Frozfruit Corporation
Gardena, CA. 310-217-1034
Glover's Ice Cream Inc
Frankfort, IN. 800-686-5163
Grossingers Home Bakery
New York, NY 800-479-6996
Hershey Creamery Co
Harrisburg, PA 888-240-1905
Ice Cream Specialties Inc
St Louis, MO. 800-662-7550
It's It Ice Cream Co
Burlingame, CA 800-345-1928
Natural Fruit Corp
Hialeah, FL. 305-887-7525
Nestle USA Inc
Glendale, CA 800-225-2270
Perry's Ice Cream Co Inc
Akron, NY. 800-873-7797
Schneider's Dairy Inc
Pittsburgh, PA. 412-881-3525
Schoep's Ice Cream
Madison, WI. 800-236-4050
Southern Ice Cream Specialties
Marietta, GA. 770-428-0452
Sweety Novelty
Monterey Park, CA. 626-282-4482
Unilever US
Englewood Cliffs, NJ 800-298-5018
Vitarich Ice Cream
Fortuna, CA 707-725-6182
Weldon Ice Cream Co
Millersport, OH. 740-467-2400
Wells Enterprises Inc.
Le Mars, IA. 712-546-4000
Whitey's Ice Cream Inc
Moline, IL. 888-594-4839
Wright's Ice Cream Co
Cayuga, IN 800-686-9561

Ziegenfelder Ice Cream Co
Wheeling, WV 800-322-3642

Popsicles

Brewla Inc.
Brooklyn, NY 855-543-7677
Broughton Foods LLC
El Paso, TX. 800-395-7004
Chill Pop
Cleveland, OH
Chloe's Fruit
New York, NY 646-442-8000
DeeBee's Organics
Victoria, BC 855-515-8327
Hershey Co.
Hershey, PA. 800-468-1714
Hershey Creamery Co
Harrisburg, PA 888-240-1905
Ice Cream Specialties Inc
St Louis, MO. 800-662-7550
Iris Brands
St. Louis Park, MN
JonnyPops
Minneapolis, MN 651-243-0705
Leader Candies
Brooklyn, NY 718-366-6900
Mackie International, Inc.
Riverside, CA 800-733-9762
Mar-Key Foods
Vidalia, GA. 912-537-4204
Modern Pop
Laguna Beach, CA
Natural Ice Fruits
Orlando, FL. 407-270-9194
Ruby Rockets
New York, NY 855-543-7677
Scotsburn Ice Cream Co.
Saint-Hubert, QC 800-501-1150
Unilever US
Englewood Cliffs, NJ 800-298-5018
Welch Foods Inc.
Concord, MA 800-340-6870
Ziegenfelder Ice Cream Co
Wheeling, WV 800-322-3642

Ribbons

Solo Foods
Countryside, IL. 800-328-7656

Roll

Grossingers Home Bakery
New York, NY 800-479-6996

Sherbet

Byrne Dairy, Inc.
Syracuse, NY 800-899-1535
Cedar Crest Specialties
Cedarburg, WI. 800-877-8341
Dippin' Dots LLC
Paducah, KY. 270-443-8994
Fieldbrook Foods Corp.
Dunkirk, NY 800-333-0805
Flavors from Florida
Bartow, FL 800-888-0409
Gelato Fresco
Toronto, ON 416-785-5415
Hudsonville Ice Cream
Holland, MI. 616-546-4005
Jel Sert
West Chicago, IL 800-323-2592
Johnson's Real Ice Cream
Columbus, OH 614-231-0014
Mayfield Dairy Farms LLC
Athens, TN 800-362-9546
Perry's Ice Cream Co Inc
Akron, NY. 800-873-7797
Pierre's French Ice Cream Inc
Cleveland, OH 800-837-7342
Schneider-Valley Farms Inc
Williamsport, PA. 570-326-2021
Schoep's Ice Cream
Madison, WI. 800-236-4050
The Valpo Velvet Shoppe
Valparaiso, IN. 219-464-4141
Tova Industries LLC
Louisville, KY 888-532-8682
Wayne Dairy Products Inc
Richmond, IN 765-935-7521

Slushes

Al-Rite Fruits & Syrups Co
Miami, FL....305-652-2540
Fee Brothers
Rochester, NY....800-961-3337
Flavouressence Products
Mississauga, ON....866-209-7778
Royale Brands
Davenport, IA....563-386-5222
Tropical Illusions
Trenton, MO....660-359-5422
Wayne Dairy Products Inc
Richmond, IN....765-935-7521

Sorbet

Açaí Roots
San Diego, CA....866-401-2224
Agave Dream
La Canada, CA....310-619-1575
Ben & Jerry's Homemade Inc
South Burlington, VT....866-258-6877
Bernie's Foods
Brooklyn, NY....718-417-6677
Boulder Homemade Inc
Boulder, CO....800-691-5002
Brothers Desserts
Santa Ana, CA....949-655-0080
Ciao Bella Gelato Company
Irvington, NJ....800-435-2863
Coolhaus
Culver City, CA....310-853-8995
Dannon Yo Cream
Portland, OR....800-962-7326
Fieldbrook Foods Corp.
Dunkirk, NY....800-333-0805
Gelateria Naia
Hercules, CA....510-724-2479
Gelati Celesti
Redondo Beach, CA....800-550-7550
Gelato Fresco
Toronto, ON....416-785-5415
GoodPop
Austin, TX....888-840-0188
Gourmet Sorbet Corporation
New York, NY....646-243-9868
Graeter's Mfg. Co.
Cincinnati, OH....800-721-3323
Green Dirt Farm
Weston, MO....816-386-2156
Homer's Ice Cream
Wilmette, IL....847-251-0477
Jolly Llama
Richmond, UT
MacKay's Cochrane Ice Cream
Cochrane, AB....403-932-2455
Mama Tish's Italian Specialties
Chicago, IL....708-929-2023
Penny Lick Ice Cream Company
Hastings, NY....914-525-1580
Pierre's French Ice Cream Inc
Cleveland, OH....800-837-7342
Royal Ice Cream Co
Manchester, CT....800-246-2958
Sun Tropics Inc
San Ramon, CA....925-380-6324
Talenti Gelato e Sorbetto
Dallas, CA
Twenty-Two Desserts
Brooklyn, NY....917-979-3438
Unilever US
Englewood Cliffs, NJ....800-298-5018
Winmix/Natural Care Products
Englewood, FL....941-475-7432

Tortoni

Royal Ice Cream Co
Manchester, CT....800-246-2958

Milk & Milk Products

Ingredia Inc
Wapakoneta, OH....419-738-4060

Kefir

Clover Sonoma
Petaluma, CA....800-237-3315
Clover Stornetta Farms Inc
Petaluma, CA....800-237-3315
Emerling International Foods
Buffalo, NY....716-833-7381
Fermenting Fairy
Santa Monica, CA
Jamieson Laboratories
Windsor, ON....800-265-5088
Latta USA
Fair Lawn, NJ....201-512-8400
Lifeway
Morton Grove, IL....877-281-3874
Nancy's Probiotic Foods
Eugene, OR
Redwood Hill Farm
Sebastopol, CA....877-238-3543
Wallaby Yogurt Co
Broomfield, CO....855-925-4636

Milk

A2 Milk Company
Boulder, CO....844-422-6455
Agri-Mark Inc
West Springfield, MA....978-552-5500
Aimonetto and Sons
Renton, WA....866-823-2777
All American Foods Inc
Mankato, MN....800-833-2661
Alpenrose Dairy
Portland, OR....503-244-1133
Alta Dena Certified Dairy LLC
City Of Industry, CA....800-535-1369
Anderson Dairy Inc
Las Vegas, NV....702-642-7507
Anderson Erickson Dairy
Des Moines, IA....515-265-2521
Anderson Erickson Dairy
Kansas City, KS....913-621-4801
Aurora Organic Dairy
Boulder, CO....303-284-3313
Barber Dairies
Birmingham, AL....205-942-2351
Berkeley Farms
Hayward, CA....800-395-7004
Borden Dairy
Dallas, TX....855-311-1583
Broughton Foods LLC
El Paso, TX....800-395-7004
Byrne Dairy, Inc.
Syracuse, NY....800-899-1535
Cass-Clay Creamery
Fargo, ND....701-293-6455
Cedar Lake Foods
Cedar Lake, MI....800-246-5039
Chase Brothers Dairy
Oxnard, CA....800-438-6455
Chino Valley Dairy
Chino, CA....800-324-7948
Clover Sonoma
Petaluma, CA....800-237-3315
Coastlog Industries
Novi, MI....248-344-9556
Country Fresh
Grand Rapids, MI....616-243-0173
Cumberland Dairy
Rosenhayn, NJ....800-257-8484
Dairy Farmers Of America
Kansas City, KS....888-332-6455
Dairy Maid Dairy LLC
Frederick, MD....301-663-5114
DairyAmerica
Fresno, CA....800-722-3110
DairyPure
El Paso, TX....800-395-7004
Darigold
Seattle, WA....800-333-6455
Devansoy Farms
Carroll, IA....800-747-8605
Fairlife
Chicago, IL
Farmland Dairies
Wallington, NJ....888-727-6252
Five Acre Farms
Brooklyn, NY....718-522-3819
Fonterra Co-operative Group Limited
Chicago, IL....888-869-6455
Foremost Farms USA
Baraboo, WI....800-362-9196
GAF Seelig Inc
Flushing, NY....718-899-5000
Galliker Dairy Co
Johnstown, PA....800-477-6455
Garelick Farms
Dallas, TX....800-343-4982
Gossner Foods Inc.
Logan, UT....800-944-0454
GPI USA LLC.
Mokena, IL....800-929-4248
Green Dirt Farm
Weston, MO....816-386-2156
H-E-B Grocery Co. LP
San Antonio, TX....800-432-3113
Happy Planet Foods
Burnaby, BC....800-811-3213
Harrisburg Dairies Inc
Harrisburg, PA....800-692-7429
Hastings Co-Op Creamery-Dairy
Hastings, MN....651-437-9414
Heritage Farms Dairy
Murfreesboro, TN....615-895-2790
Hiland Dairy Foods Co
Springfield, MO....800-492-4022
Horizon Organic Dairy
Broomfield, CO....888-494-3020
HP Hood LLC
Lynnfield, MA....800-343-6592
Hygeia Dairy Company
Corpus Christi, TX....361-854-4561
Ingredia Inc
Wapakoneta, OH....419-738-4060
Intense Milk
Buffalo, NY....716-892-3156
J M Swank Co
North Liberty, IA....800-593-6375
Jasper Products Corp
Joplin, MO....417-206-3877
Keller's Creamery
Kansas City, MO....800-535-5371
Lafleur Dairy Products,
New Orleans, LA....504-729-3330
Land O'Lakes Inc
Arden Hills, MN....800-328-9680
Marva Maid Dairy
Newport News, VA....800-768-6243
Maryland & Virginia Milk Producers Cooperative
Reston, VA....703-742-6800
Mayfield Dairy Farms LLC
Athens, TN....800-362-9546
McArthur Dairy LLC
Miami, FL....561-659-4811
Mead Johnson Nutrition
Chicago, IL....312-466-5800
Meadow Brook Dairy Co
Erie, PA....800-352-4010
Meijer Inc
Grand Rapids, MI....616-453-6711
Michigan Dairy LLC
Livonia, MI....734-367-5390
Milnot Company
Orrville, OH....888-656-3245
Muller-Pinehurst Dairy
Rockford, IL....815-968-0441
Natrel
St. Laurent, QC....800-501-1150
Natural By Nature
Newark, DE....302-455-1261
Ninth Avenue Foods
CA....626-364-8722
Norwalk Dairy
Santa Fe Springs, CA....562-921-5712
Oakhurst Dairy
Portland, ME....800-482-0718
Olam Spices
Fresno, CA....559-447-1390
Parmalat Canada
Toronto, ON....800-563-1515
Plains Dairy Products
Amarillo, TX....800-365-5608
Pleasant View Dairy
Highland, IN....219-838-0155
Prairie Farms Dairy Inc.
Edwardsville, IL....618-659-5700
Price's Creameries
El Paso, TX....915-565-2711
Pride Dairies
Bottineau, ND....701-228-2216
Promised Land Dairy
Colorado Springs, CO....877-520-2479
Purity Dairies LLC
Nashville, TN....615-244-1900
Queensboro Farm Products
Canastota, NY....315-687-6133
Queensboro Farm Products
Jamica, NY....718-658-5000
Reilly Dairy & Food Company
Tampa, FL....813-839-8458
Reiter Dairy LLC
Springfield, OH....937-323-5777

Roland Machinery
Springfield, IL....................800-325-1183
Rosa Brothers Milk Co Inc
Hanford, CA....................559-685-8825
Rosenberger's Dairies
Hatfield, PA....................800-355-9074
Rye Fresh
Piscataway, NJ....................732-855-0008
Safeway Inc.
Pleasanton, CA....................877-723-3929
Safeway Milk Plant
Tempe, AZ....................480-894-4391
Santini Foods
San Lorenzo, CA....................800-835-6888
Saputo Inc.
Montreal, QC....................800-672-8866
Schepps Dairy
Dallas, TX....................800-395-7004
Schneider's Dairy Inc
Pittsburgh, PA....................412-881-3525
Schneider-Valley Farms Inc
Williamsport, PA....................570-326-2021
Smith Dairy
Orrville, OH....................800-776-7076
Stewart's Shops Corp
Ballston Spa, NY....................518-581-1200
Stonyfield Organic
Londonderry, NH....................800-776-2697
Stop & Shop Manufacturing
Readville, MA....................508-977-5132
Sunshine Farms
Portage, WI....................608-742-2016
Super Stores Industries
Turlock, CA....................209-668-2100
Superbrand Dairies
Miami, FL....................305-769-6600
Swiss Premium Dairy Inc
Lebanon, PA....................800-222-2129
Swissland Milk
Berne, IN....................260-589-2761
Tamarack Farms Dairy
Newark, OH....................866-221-4141
Toft Dairy Inc
Sandusky, OH....................800-521-4606
Trickling Springs Creamery
Chambersburg, PA....................717-709-0711
Turkey Hill Dairy Inc
Conestoga, PA....................800-693-2479
Umpqua Dairy
Roseburg, OR....................888-672-6455
United Dairy Inc.
Martins Ferry, OH....................800-252-1542
United Dairymen of Arizona
Tempe, AZ....................480-966-7211
Valley Farms LLC
Williamsport, PA....................570-326-2021
Velda Farms
Orlando, FL....................800-795-4649
Vitamilk Dairy
Bellingham, WA....................206-529-4128
W.J. Stearns & Sons/Mountain Dairy
Storrs Mansfield, CT....................860-423-9289
Wayne Dairy Products Inc
Richmond, IN....................765-935-7521
Welsh Farms
Wallington, NJ....................800-221-0663
WhiteWave Foods
Denver, CO....................800-488-9283
Whitewave Foods Company
Broomfield, CO....................303-635-4000
Winchester Farms Dairy
Winchester, KY....................859-745-5500
Yoder Dairies
Chesapeake, VA....................757-482-4068

1 Percent

A2 Milk Company
Boulder, CO....................844-422-6455
Alta Dena Certified Dairy LLC
City Of Industry, CA....................800-535-1369
Berkeley Farms
Hayward, CA....................800-395-7004
Borden Dairy
Dallas, TX....................855-311-1583
Broughton Foods LLC
El Paso, TX....................800-395-7004
Chase Brothers Dairy
Oxnard, CA....................800-438-6455
Cumberland Dairy
Rosenhayn, NJ....................800-257-8484
Dairy Maid Dairy LLC
Frederick, MD....................301-663-5114
Meadow Brook Dairy Co
Erie, PA....................800-352-4010
Pleasant View Dairy
Highland, IN....................219-838-0155
Promised Land Dairy
Colorado Springs, CO....................877-520-2479
Safeway Milk Plant
Tempe, AZ....................480-894-4391
Schneider's Dairy Inc
Pittsburgh, PA....................412-881-3525
Valley Farms LLC
Williamsport, PA....................570-326-2021
Yoder Dairies
Chesapeake, VA....................757-482-4068

2 Percent

A2 Milk Company
Boulder, CO....................844-422-6455
Alta Dena Certified Dairy LLC
City Of Industry, CA....................800-535-1369
Berkeley Farms
Hayward, CA....................800-395-7004
Borden Dairy
Dallas, TX....................855-311-1583
Broughton Foods LLC
El Paso, TX....................800-395-7004
Cumberland Dairy
Rosenhayn, NJ....................800-257-8484
Dairy Maid Dairy LLC
Frederick, MD....................301-663-5114
Meadow Brook Dairy Co
Erie, PA....................800-352-4010
Oak Knoll Dairy, Inc.
Windsor, VT....................802-674-5426
Pleasant View Dairy
Highland, IN....................219-838-0155
Promised Land Dairy
Colorado Springs, CO....................877-520-2479
Safeway Milk Plant
Tempe, AZ....................480-894-4391
Schneider's Dairy Inc
Pittsburgh, PA....................412-881-3525
Stewart's Shops Corp
Ballston Spa, NY....................518-581-1200
Swiss Premium Dairy Inc
Lebanon, PA....................800-222-2129
T G Lee Dairy
Orlando, FL....................800-432-4872
Valley Farms LLC
Williamsport, PA....................570-326-2021
Winchester Farms Dairy
Winchester, KY....................859-745-5500

Chocolate

A2 Milk Company
Boulder, CO....................844-422-6455
Alta Dena Certified Dairy LLC
City Of Industry, CA....................800-535-1369
Barber Dairies
Birmingham, AL....................205-942-2351
Berkeley Farms
Hayward, CA....................800-395-7004
Borden Dairy
Dallas, TX....................855-311-1583
Broughton Foods LLC
El Paso, TX....................800-395-7004
Chase Brothers Dairy
Oxnard, CA....................800-438-6455
Clover Sonoma
Petaluma, CA....................800-237-3315
Cloverland/Green Spring Dairy
Baltimore, MD....................800-876-6455
Cocoa Metro
St. George, UT....................888-676-1527
Happy Planet Foods
Burnaby, BC....................800-811-3213
Harrisburg Dairies Inc
Harrisburg, PA....................800-692-7429
Hygeia Dairy Company
Corpus Christi, TX....................361-854-4561
Intense Milk
Buffalo, NY....................716-892-3156
Kleinpeter Farms Dairy LLC
Baton Rouge, LA....................225-753-2121
Marburger Farm Dairy
Evans City, PA....................800-331-1295
McArthur Dairy LLC
Miami, FL....................561-659-4811
Natrel
St. Laurent, QC....................800-501-1150
Norwalk Dairy
Santa Fe Springs, CA....................562-921-5712
Oak Knoll Dairy, Inc.
Windsor, VT....................802-674-5426
Plains Dairy Products
Amarillo, TX....................800-365-5608
Promised Land Dairy
Colorado Springs, CO....................877-520-2479
Swiss Dairy
Riverside, CA....................951-898-9427
TruMoo
El Paso, TX....................800-395-7004
Valley Farms LLC
Williamsport, PA....................570-326-2021
Winchester Farms Dairy
Winchester, KY....................859-745-5500
Yoder Dairies
Chesapeake, VA....................757-482-4068
Yoo-Hoo Chocolate Beverage Company
Carlstadt, NJ....................201-933-0070

Condensed

Abbott Laboratories
Abbott Park, IL....................847-938-3887
Agri-Mark Inc
West Springfield, MA....................978-552-5500
All American Foods Inc
Mankato, MN....................800-833-2661
Berkshire Dairy
Wyomissing, PA....................877-696-6455
Blossom Farm Products
Ridgewood, NJ....................800-729-1818
Eagle Family Foods
Richfield, OH....................888-656-3245
Galloway Co
Neenah, WI....................800-722-8903
Graf Creamery Co
Bonduel, WI....................715-758-2137
J.M. Smucker Co.
Orrville, OH....................888-550-9555
Milnot Company
Orrville, OH....................888-656-3245
O-At-Ka Milk Prods Co-Op Inc.
Batavia, NY....................800-828-8152
Queensboro Farm Products
Jamica, NY....................718-658-5000
Ronzoni
Largo, FL....................800-730-5957
Saint Albans Cooperative Creamery
Saint Albans, VT....................802-524-6581

Condensed - Bulk Only

Agri-Dairy Products
Purchase, NY....................914-697-9580
Clofine Dairy Products Inc
Linwood, NJ....................609-653-1000
Maryland & Virginia Milk Producers Cooperative
Reston, VA....................703-742-6800

Evaporated

Abbott Laboratories
Abbott Park, IL....................847-938-3887
Agri-Dairy Products
Purchase, NY....................914-697-9580
Clofine Dairy Products Inc
Linwood, NJ....................609-653-1000
Meyenberg Goat Milk
Turlock, CA....................800-891-4628
Milnot Company
Orrville, OH....................888-656-3245

Fat-Free

Agri-Mark Inc
West Springfield, MA....................978-552-5500
Alta Dena Certified Dairy LLC
City Of Industry, CA....................800-535-1369
Berkeley Farms
Hayward, CA....................800-395-7004
Broughton Foods LLC
El Paso, TX....................800-395-7004
California Dairies Inc.
Visalia, CA....................559-625-2200
Chase Brothers Dairy
Oxnard, CA....................800-438-6455
Clofine Dairy Products Inc
Linwood, NJ....................609-653-1000
First District Association
Litchfield, MN....................320-693-3236
Humboldt Creamery
Modesto, CA....................888-316-6064

IMAC
Oklahoma City, OK 888-878-7827
Main Street Ingredients
La Crosse, WI 800-359-2345
Meadow Brook Dairy Co
Erie, PA 800-352-4010
Norwalk Dairy
Santa Fe Springs, CA 562-921-5712
Plainview Milk Products
Plainview, MN 800-356-5606
Promised Land Dairy
Colorado Springs, CO 877-520-2479
Quality Ingredients
Burnsville, MN 952-898-4002
Ramsen Inc
Lakeville, MN 952-431-0400
Saint Albans Cooperative Creamery
Saint Albans, VT 802-524-6581
Schneider's Dairy Inc
Pittsburgh, PA 412-881-3525
Swiss Dairy
Riverside, CA 951-898-9427
Valley Farms LLC
Williamsport, PA 570-326-2021

Flavored

Berkeley Farms
Hayward, CA 800-395-7004
Borden Dairy
Dallas, TX 855-311-1583
Broughton Foods LLC
El Paso, TX 800-395-7004
Chase Brothers Dairy
Oxnard, CA 800-438-6455
Coco Lopez Inc
Miramar, FL 800-341-2242
Country Fresh
Grand Rapids, MI 616-243-0173
Fairlife
Chicago, IL
Intense Milk
Buffalo, NY 716-892-3156
Marburger Farm Dairy
Evans City, PA 800-331-1295
Norwalk Dairy
Santa Fe Springs, CA 562-921-5712
Schepps Dairy
Dallas, TX 800-395-7004
Schneider's Dairy Inc
Pittsburgh, PA 412-881-3525
Schneider-Valley Farms Inc
Williamsport, PA 570-326-2021
TruMoo
El Paso, TX 800-395-7004
Winchester Farms Dairy
Winchester, KY 859-745-5500

Fresh

A B Munroe Dairy Inc
East Providence, RI 401-438-4450
Agropur
Granby, QC 800-363-5686
Al's Beverage Company
East Windsor, CT 888-257-7632
Alpenrose Dairy
Portland, OR 503-244-1133
Anderson Dairy Inc
Las Vegas, NV 702-642-7507
Bartlett Dairy & Food Service
Jamaica, NY 718-658-2299
Berkeley Farms
Hayward, CA 800-395-7004
Bliss Brothers Dairy, Inc.
Attleboro, MA 800-622-8789
Blue Ribbon Farm Dairy Fresh
Exeter, PA 570-655-5579
Borden Dairy
Dallas, TX 855-311-1583
Braum's Inc
Oklahoma City, OK 800-327-6455
Brown Dairy Inc
Coalville, UT 435-336-5952
Brum's Dairy
Pembroke, ON 613-735-2325
Caprine Estates
Bellbrook, OH 937-848-7406
Central Dairy
Jefferson City, MO 573-635-6148
Chase Brothers Dairy
Oxnard, CA 800-438-6455
Chester Dairy Co
Chester, IL 618-826-2394
Clover Farms Dairy Co Inc
Reading, PA 800-323-0123
Clover Stornetta Farms Inc
Petaluma, CA 800-237-3315
Cloverland/Green Spring Dairy
Baltimore, MD 800-876-6455
Coastlog Industries
Novi, MI 248-344-9556
Colteryahn Dairy
Pittsburgh, PA 412-881-1408
Compton Dairy
Shelbyville, IN 317-398-8621
Country Delite Farms LLC
Nashville, TN 800-232-4791
Cream Crock Distributors
Sterling, MA 800-423-2736
Crescent Ridge Dairy
Sharon, MA 800-660-2740
Cumberland Creamery
Antioch, TN 615-641-1027
Czepiel Millers Dairy
Ludlow, MA 413-589-0828
Dairy Management Inc
Rosemont, IL 800-853-2479
Darifair Foods
Jacksonville, FL 904-268-9916
Daybreak Foods Inc
Long Prairie, MN 320-732-2966
Dean Foods Co.
Dallas, TX 800-395-7004
Deseret Dairy Products
Salt Lake City, UT 801-240-7350
Eagle Family Foods
Richfield, OH 888-656-3245
Everything Yogurt
Washington, DC 202-842-2990
Farmers Dairies
El Paso, TX 915-772-2736
Farmland Dairies
Wallington, NJ 888-727-6252
Gandy's Dairies LLC
Lubbock, TX 800-338-6841
Garelick Farms
Lynn, MA 781-599-1300
Guers Dairy
Tamaqua, PA 570-277-6611
H-E-B Grocery Co. LP
San Antonio, TX 800-432-3113
Harrisburg Dairies Inc
Harrisburg, PA 800-692-7429
Hastings Co-Op Creamery-Dairy
Hastings, MN 651-437-9414
Heritage Farms Dairy
Murfreesboro, TN 615-895-2790
Heritage's Dairy Stores
West Deptford, NJ 856-845-2855
Highland Dairies
Wichita, KS 800-336-0765
Homestead Dairy
Plymouth, IN 574-936-6126
Hood Sterile Division
Oneida, NY 315-363-3870
Houlton Farms Dairy
Houlton, ME 207-532-3170
Humboldt Creamery
Modesto, CA 888-316-6064
Hygeia Dairy Company
Corpus Christi, TX 361-854-4561
Inverness Dairy
Cheboygan, MI 231-627-4655
Kalamazoo Creamery
Kalamazoo, MI 616-343-2558
Kemps LLC
St Paul, MN
Kleinpeter Farms Dairy LLC
Baton Rouge, LA 225-753-2121
Land O'Lakes Inc
Arden Hills, MN 800-328-9680
Land-O-Sun Dairies Inc
O Fallon, IL 314-436-6820
Lehigh Valley Dairy Farms
Lansdale, PA 800-395-7004
Longacres Modern Dairy Inc
Barto, PA 610-845-7551
Louisville Dairy
Louisville, KY 502-451-9111
Lowell-Paul Dairy
Greeley, CO 970-353-0278
Lubbers Family Farm
Grand Rapids, MI 616-453-4257
Ludwig Dairy Product
Elk Grove Vlg, IL 847-860-8646
Magic Valley Quality Milk
Jerome, ID 208-324-7519
Maple Hill Farms
Bloomfield, CT 800-842-7304
Maplehurst Farms
Rochelle, IL 815-562-8723
Marburger Farm Dairy
Evans City, PA 800-331-1295
McArthur Dairy LLC
Miami, FL 561-659-4811
Meadow Brook Dairy Co
Erie, PA 800-352-4010
Meadowbrook Farm
Bronx, NY 718-828-6400
Meyenberg Goat Milk
Turlock, CA 800-891-4628
Meyer Brothers Dairy
Maple Plain, MN 952-473-7343
Michigan Milk Producers Assn
Novi, MI 248-474-6672
Milky Way Jersey Farm Inc
Starr, SC 864-352-2014
Mitchel Dairies
Bronx, NY 718-994-6655
Monument Farms Dairy
Middlebury, VT 802-545-2119
Morning Glory Dairy
De Pere, WI 920-336-4206
Morning Star Foods
East Brunswick, NJ 800-237-5320
Mountainside Farms Inc
Roxbury, NY 607-326-4161
Muller-Pinehurst Dairy
Rockford, IL 815-968-0441
Murdock Farm Dairy
Winchendon, MA 978-297-2196
Mystic Lake Dairy
Sammamish, WA 425-868-2029
Nature's Dairy
Roswell, NM 575-623-9640
Northern Dairy
Franklin Park, IL 847-671-2697
Northumberland Dairy
Miramichi, NB 800-501-1150
Norwalk Dairy
Santa Fe Springs, CA 562-921-5712
Oak Farm's Dairy
Waco, TX 254-756-5421
Oak Grove Dairy
Clintonville, WI 715-823-6226
Oberweis Dairy Inc
North Aurora, IL 866-623-7934
Peeler's Jersey Farms
Athens, GA 706-543-7383
Pierz Cooperative Association
Pierz, MN 320-468-6655
Pioneer Dairy
Southwick, MA 413-569-6132
Potomac Farms Dairy Inc
Cumberland, MD 301-722-4410
Potter Siding Creamery Company
Tripoli, IA 319-882-4444
Producers Dairy Foods Inc
Fresno, CA 559-264-6583
Pure Milk & Ice Cream Company
Austin, TX 512-837-2685
Purity Dairies LLC
Nashville, TN 615-244-1900
Quality Dairy Co
East Lansing, MI 517-319-4114
Queensboro Farm Products
Jamica, NY 718-658-5000
Rehemond Farm Inc
Minot, ME 207-345-5611
Reiter Dairy LLC
Springfield, OH 937-323-5777
Richardson's Ice Cream
Middleton, MA 978-774-5450
Ritchey's Dairy
Martinsburg, PA 800-296-2157
Rockview Farms
Downey, CA 800-423-2479
Ronny Brook Farm Dairy
Ancramdale, NY 800-772-6455
Rosebud Creamery
Plattsburgh, NY 518-561-5160
Royal Crest Dairy
Denver, CO 888-226-6455
Rutter's Dairy
York, PA 800-840-1664

S.T. Jerrell Company
Bessemer, AL 205-426-8930
Safeway Milk Plant
Tempe, AZ 480-894-4391
Saint Albans Cooperative Creamery
Saint Albans, VT. 802-524-6581
Santini Foods
San Lorenzo, CA. 800-835-6888
Schneider's Dairy Inc
Pittsburgh, PA. 412-881-3525
Seger Egg Corporation
Farina, IL. 618-245-3301
Shedd Food Products
Dallas, TX. 214-374-4751
Skinners' Dairy
Ponte Vedra Beach, FL. 904-733-5440
Snow Dairy Inc
Springville, UT. 801-489-6081
Southeast Dairy Processors Inc
Tampa, FL. 813-620-1516
Spring Hill Pure Water
Haverhill, MA. 978-373-3481
Stop & Shop Manufacturing
Readville, MA. 508-977-5132
Stremick's Heritage Foods
Santa Ana, CA 800-371-9010
Suiza Dairy Corporation
San Juan, PR. 787-707-6500
Sunshine Dairy
Middletown, CT. 860-346-6644
Sunshine Dairy Foods Inc
Portland, OR. 503-234-7526
Super Stores Industries
Turlock, CA 209-668-2100
Superbrand Dairies
Miami, FL. 305-769-6600
Swiss Dairy
Riverside, CA 951-898-9427
Swiss Premium Dairy Inc
Lebanon, PA 800-222-2129
Tamarack Farms Dairy
Newark, OH 866-221-4141
Tanglewood Farms
Warsaw, VA. 804-394-4505
Thomas Dairy
Rutland, VT 802-773-6788
Toft Dairy Inc
Sandusky, OH. 800-521-4606
Tri-State Dairy
Fort Wayne, IN 256-534-8464
Turner Dairy Farms Inc
Pittsburgh, PA. 800-892-1039
Ultra Dairy
Delhi, NY 607-746-2141
Umpqua Dairy
Roseburg, OR. 888-672-6455
United Dairy Farmers Inc.
Cincinnati, OH 866-837-4833
United Dairymen of Arizona
Tempe, AZ. 480-966-7211
United Valley Bell Dairy
Charleston, WV. 304-344-2511
Valley Milk Products
Strasburg, VA 540-465-5113
Van Peenans Dairy
Wayne, NJ. 973-694-2551
Verifine Dairy
Sheboygan, WI 920-457-7733
Vitamilk Dairy
Bellingham, WA 206-529-4128
W.J. Stearns & Sons/Mountain Dairy
Storrs Mansfield, CT 860-423-9289
Wawa Inc
Wawa, PA 800-444-9292
Wessanan
Minneapolis, MN 612-331-3775
Whitney Foods Inc
Jamaica, NY 718-291-3333
Winchester Farms Dairy
Winchester, KY. 859-745-5500
Winsor SB Dairy
Johnston, RI 401-231-7832
Wurth Dairy
Caseyville, IL 217-271-7580
Young's Jersey Dairy
Yellow Springs, OH 937-325-0629

Goat

Abunda Life
Asbury Park, NJ 732-775-9338
C F Burger Creamery Co
Detroit, MI 313-584-4040
Coach Farm Enterprises
Pine Plains, NY. 800-999-4628
Fat Toad Farm
Brookfield, VT 802-279-0098
Maison Riviera
Varennes, QC 800-363-0092
Meyenberg Goat Milk
Turlock, CA 800-891-4628
Oak Knoll Dairy, Inc.
Windsor, VT 802-674-5426
Sunshine Farms
Portage, WI. 608-742-2016
Woolwich Dairy
Orangeville, ON 877-438-3499

Half & Half

C F Burger Creamery Co
Detroit, MI 313-584-4040
Cass-Clay Creamery
Fargo, ND 701-293-6455
Central Dairy
Jefferson City, MO 573-635-6148
Chase Brothers Dairy
Oxnard, CA. 800-438-6455
Clover Farms Dairy Co Inc
Reading, PA 800-323-0123
Horizon Organic Dairy
Broomfield, CO 888-494-3020
Oak Knoll Dairy, Inc.
Windsor, VT 802-674-5426
Prairie Farms Dairy Inc.
Edwardsville, IL. 618-659-5700
Rockview Farms
Downey, CA 800-423-2479
Safeway Milk Plant
Tempe, AZ 480-894-4391
Stonyfield Organic
Londonderry, NH 800-776-2697
Tiller Foods Company
Dayton, OH. 937-435-4601
WhiteWave Foods
Denver, CO. 800-488-9283
Whitewave Foods Company
Broomfield, CO 303-635-4000
Yoder Dairies
Chesapeake, VA 757-482-4068

Lactose-Free

DairyPure
El Paso, TX. 800-395-7004

Low-Fat

Anderson Erickson Dairy
Des Moines, IA. 515-265-2521
Anderson Erickson Dairy
Kansas City, KS 913-621-4801
Berkeley Farms
Hayward, CA 800-395-7004
Borden Dairy
Dallas, TX. 855-311-1583
Chase Brothers Dairy
Oxnard, CA. 800-438-6455
Cloverland/Green Spring Dairy
Baltimore, MD 800-876-6455
Country Fresh Farms
Salt Lake City, UT 800-878-0099
Dairy Maid Dairy LLC
Frederick, MD. 301-663-5114
DairyPure
El Paso, TX. 800-395-7004
Humboldt Creamery
Modesto, CA. 888-316-6064
Intense Milk
Buffalo, NY. 716-892-3156
Marva Maid Dairy
Newport News, VA. 800-768-6243
McArthur Dairy LLC
Miami, FL. 561-659-4811
Meadow Brook Dairy Co
Erie, PA. 800-352-4010
Pleasant View Dairy
Highland, IN. 219-838-0155
Safeway Milk Plant
Tempe, AZ 480-894-4391
Schneider's Dairy Inc
Pittsburgh, PA. 412-881-3525
Schneider-Valley Farms Inc
Williamsport, PA. 570-326-2021
Swiss Dairy
Riverside, CA 951-898-9427
Swiss Premium Dairy Inc
Lebanon, PA 800-222-2129
T G Lee Dairy
Orlando, FL. 800-432-4872
Valley Farms LLC
Williamsport, PA. 570-326-2021
Winchester Farms Dairy
Winchester, KY. 859-745-5500
Yoder Dairies
Chesapeake, VA 757-482-4068

Reduced-Fat

Berkeley Farms
Hayward, CA 800-395-7004
Borden Dairy
Dallas, TX. 855-311-1583
Dairy Maid Dairy LLC
Frederick, MD. 301-663-5114
Humboldt Creamery
Modesto, CA. 888-316-6064
Marva Maid Dairy
Newport News, VA. 800-768-6243
McArthur Dairy LLC
Miami, FL. 561-659-4811
Meadow Brook Dairy Co
Erie, PA. 800-352-4010
Norwalk Dairy
Santa Fe Springs, CA 562-921-5712
Pleasant View Dairy
Highland, IN 219-838-0155
Safeway Milk Plant
Tempe, AZ 480-894-4391
Schneider's Dairy Inc
Pittsburgh, PA. 412-881-3525
Schneider-Valley Farms Inc
Williamsport, PA. 570-326-2021
Swiss Dairy
Riverside, CA 951-898-9427
Swiss Premium Dairy Inc
Lebanon, PA 800-222-2129
WhiteWave Foods
Denver, CO. 800-488-9283
Winchester Farms Dairy
Winchester, KY. 859-745-5500
Yoder Dairies
Chesapeake, VA 757-482-4068

Skim

Agri-Mark Inc
West Springfield, MA. 978-552-5500
Berkeley Farms
Hayward, CA 800-395-7004
Borden Dairy
Dallas, TX. 855-311-1583
Chase Brothers Dairy
Oxnard, CA. 800-438-6455
Cloverland/Green Spring Dairy
Baltimore, MD 800-876-6455
Country Fresh Farms
Salt Lake City, UT 800-878-0099
Cumberland Dairy
Rosenhayn, NJ 800-257-8484
Dairy Maid Dairy LLC
Frederick, MD. 301-663-5114
IMAC
Oklahoma City, OK 888-878-7827
Kleinpeter Farms Dairy LLC
Baton Rouge, LA 225-753-2121
Marva Maid Dairy
Newport News, VA. 800-768-6243
McArthur Dairy LLC
Miami, FL. 561-659-4811
Meadow Brook Dairy Co
Erie, PA 800-352-4010
Pleasant View Dairy
Highland, IN. 219-838-0155
Safeway Milk Plant
Tempe, AZ 480-894-4391
Saint Albans Cooperative Creamery
Saint Albans, VT. 802-524-6581
Schneider's Dairy Inc
Pittsburgh, PA. 412-881-3525
Schneider-Valley Farms Inc
Williamsport, PA. 570-326-2021
Stewart's Shops Corp
Ballston Spa, NY 518-581-1200
Swiss Premium Dairy Inc
Lebanon, PA 800-222-2129
Valley Farms LLC
Williamsport, PA. 570-326-2021

WhiteWave Foods
Denver, CO 800-488-9283
Winchester Farms Dairy
Winchester, KY 859-745-5500
Yoder Dairies
Chesapeake, VA 757-482-4068

Strawberry

Berkeley Farms
Hayward, CA 800-395-7004
DairyPure
El Paso, TX 800-395-7004
Hygeia Dairy Company
Corpus Christi, TX 361-854-4561
Intense Milk
Buffalo, NY 716-892-3156
Kleinpeter Farms Dairy LLC
Baton Rouge, LA 225-753-2121
TruMoo
El Paso, TX 800-395-7004

Sweetened

All American Foods Inc
Mankato, MN 800-833-2661
Gateway Food Products Co
Dupo, IL 877-220-1963
Milnot Company
Orrville, OH 888-656-3245

Sweetened & Condensed

Arnhem Group
Cranford, NJ 800-851-1052
Reilly Dairy & Food Company
Tampa, FL 813-839-8458
Suprema Specialties
Manteca, CA 209-858-9696

Vanilla Flavored

Intense Milk
Buffalo, NY 716-892-3156

Whole

A2 Milk Company
Boulder, CO 844-422-6455
Berkeley Farms
Hayward, CA 800-395-7004
Borden Dairy
Dallas, TX 855-311-1583
Cloverland/Green Spring Dairy
Baltimore, MD 800-876-6455
Cumberland Dairy
Rosenhayn, NJ 800-257-8484
DairyAmerica
Fresno, CA 800-722-3110
GAF Seelig Inc
Flushing, NY 718-899-5000
Happy Planet Foods
Burnaby, BC 800-811-3213
Kleinpeter Farms Dairy LLC
Baton Rouge, LA 225-753-2121
Marva Maid Dairy
Newport News, VA 800-768-6243
McArthur Dairy LLC
Miami, FL 561-659-4811
Meadow Brook Dairy Co
Erie, PA 800-352-4010
Plainview Milk Products
Plainview, MN 800-356-5606
Pleasant View Dairy
Highland, IN 219-838-0155
Safeway Milk Plant
Tempe, AZ 480-894-4391
Saint Albans Cooperative Creamery
Saint Albans, VT 802-524-6581
Schneider's Dairy Inc
Pittsburgh, PA 412-881-3525
Schneider-Valley Farms Inc
Williamsport, PA 570-326-2021
Stewart's Shops Corp
Ballston Spa, NY 518-581-1200
T G Lee Dairy
Orlando, FL 800-432-4872
Trickling Springs Creamery
Chambersburg, PA 717-709-0711
WhiteWave Foods
Denver, CO 800-488-9283
Winchester Farms Dairy
Winchester, KY 859-745-5500
Yoder Dairies
Chesapeake, VA 757-482-4068

Milk Products

Milk & Milk Fat: Enzyme

Brown's Dairy
New Orleans, LA 800-680-6455
Farmers Cooperative Dairy
Saint-Hubert, QC 800-501-1150
Garden Spot Distributors
New Holland, PA 800-829-5100
Idaho Milk Products
Jerome, ID 208-644-2882
Maple Island
Saint Paul, MN 800-369-1022

Milk Proteins

Austrade
Palm Beach Gdns, FL 561-209-2447
Clofine Dairy Products Inc
Linwood, NJ 609-653-1000
Erie Foods Intl Inc
Erie, IL 309-659-2233
Kantner Group
Wapakoneta, OH 877-738-3448
Lactalis USA Inc
Belmont, WI 608-762-5136
Main Street Ingredients
La Crosse, WI 800-359-2345
Rosa Brothers Milk Co Inc
Hanford, CA 559-685-8825

Modified - Dry Blends

Kantner Group
Wapakoneta, OH 877-738-3448
King Arthur Flour
Norwich, VT 800-827-6836

Non-Dairy Milk - Imitation

Ripple
Berkeley, CA

Milk Solids

Non-Fat

California Dairies Inc.
Visalia, CA 559-625-2200
Kantner Group
Wapakoneta, OH 877-738-3448
Main Street Ingredients
La Crosse, WI 800-359-2345
Ramsen Inc
Lakeville, MN 952-431-0400

Replacers

APC Inc
Ankeny, IA 800-369-2672
Kantner Group
Wapakoneta, OH 877-738-3448

Whole

Kantner Group
Wapakoneta, OH 877-738-3448
Lactalis USA Inc
Belmont, WI 608-762-5136
Meyenberg Goat Milk
Turlock, CA 800-891-4628

Pudding

Advanced Food Products LLC
New Holland, PA 800-732-5373
Aryzta
Los Angeles, CA 855-427-9982
Dufflet Pastries
Toronto, ON 866-238-0899
Echo Farms Puddings
Hinsdale, NH 866-488-3246
Gehl Foods, Inc.
Germantown, WI 800-521-2873
Good Old Days Foods
Little Rock, AR 501-565-1257
GPI USA LLC.
Mokena, IL 800-929-4248
Grainaissance
Emeryville, CA 800-472-4697
Hormel Foods Corp.
Austin, MN 507-437-5611
Hudson River Foods
Castleton, NY 888-417-9343
Inter-American Products
Cincinnati, OH 800-645-2233
Kosto Food Products Co
Wauconda, IL 847-487-2600
KOZY Shack Enterprises Inc
St Paul, MN 855-716-1555
Michigan Desserts
Oak Park, MI 800-328-8632
Rodgers' Puddings
Chesapeake, VA 757-543-9290
Serv-Agen Corporation
Cherry Hill, NJ 856-663-6966
Spring Glen Fresh Foods
Ephrata, PA 800-641-2853
Terrapin Ridge
Clearwater, FL 800-999-4052

Chocolate

EJZ Foods
Winston-Salem, NC
Knouse Foods Co-Op Inc.
Peach Glen, PA 717-677-8181
KOZY Shack Enterprises Inc
St Paul, MN 855-716-1555

Plum

Patti's Plum Puddings
Lawndale, CA 310-376-1463

Rice

Knouse Foods Co-Op Inc.
Peach Glen, PA 717-677-8181
KOZY Shack Enterprises Inc
St Paul, MN 855-716-1555
Lakeview Farms
Delphos, OH 800-755-9925
Petit Pot
Emeryville, CA 650-488-7432

Tapioca

Knouse Foods Co-Op Inc.
Peach Glen, PA 717-677-8181
KOZY Shack Enterprises Inc
St Paul, MN 855-716-1555

Vanilla

Knouse Foods Co-Op Inc.
Peach Glen, PA 717-677-8181
KOZY Shack Enterprises Inc
St Paul, MN 855-716-1555

Sour Cream

Aimonetto and Sons
Renton, WA 866-823-2777
Alta Dena Certified Dairy LLC
City Of Industry, CA 800-535-1369
Anderson Erickson Dairy
Des Moines, IA 515-265-2521
Anderson Erickson Dairy
Kansas City, KS 913-621-4801
Astro Dairy Products
Toronto, ON 416-622-2811
Auburn Dairy Products Inc
Auburn, WA 800-950-9264
Berkeley Farms
Hayward, CA 800-395-7004
Bison Foods
Buffalo, NY 716-892-3156
Borden Dairy
Dallas, TX 855-311-1583
Broughton Foods LLC
El Paso, TX 800-395-7004
Byrne Dairy, Inc.
Syracuse, NY 800-899-1535
Campbell Soup Co.
Camden, NJ 800-257-8443
Cascade Fresh
Seattle, WA 800-511-0057
Central Dairy
Jefferson City, MO 573-635-6148
Chino Valley Dairy
Chino, CA 800-324-7948
Clofine Dairy Products Inc
Linwood, NJ 609-653-1000
Clover Farms Dairy Co Inc
Reading, PA 800-323-0123
Clover Sonoma
Petaluma, CA 800-237-3315

Clover Stornetta Farms Inc
Petaluma, CA 800-237-3315
Cloverland/Green Spring Dairy
Baltimore, MD 800-876-6455
Country Fresh
Grand Rapids, MI 616-243-0173
Creamland Dairies Inc
Albuquerque, NM 505-247-0721
Dairy Maid Dairy LLC
Frederick, MD 301-663-5114
DairyPure
El Paso, TX 800-395-7004
Daisy Brand
Dallas, TX 877-292-9830
Darigold
Seattle, WA 800-333-6455
Elgin Dairy Foods
Chicago, IL 800-786-9900
Farmers Cooperative Dairy
Saint-Hubert, QC 800-501-1150
Foremost Farms USA
Baraboo, WI 800-362-9196
Friendship Dairies LLC
Friendship, NY 800-854-3243
GAF Seelig Inc
Flushing, NY 718-899-5000
Good Culture
Irvine, CA 844-899-8884
HP Hood LLC
Lynnfield, MA 800-343-6592
Hunter Farms - High Point Division
High Point, NC 800-446-8035
Kemps LLC
St Paul, MN
Lakeview Farms
Delphos, OH 800-755-9925
Ludwig Dairy Product
Elk Grove Vlg, IL 847-860-8646
Marburger Farm Dairy
Evans City, PA 800-331-1295
Marquez Brothers International
Hanford, CA 800-858-1119
Marva Maid Dairy
Newport News, VA 800-768-6243
Mayfield Dairy Farms LLC
Athens, TN 800-362-9546
Nancy's Probiotic Foods
Eugene, OR
Natural By Nature
Newark, DE 302-455-1261
Oakhurst Dairy
Portland, ME 800-482-0718
Old Home Foods Inc
New Brighton, MN 651-312-8900
Parmalat Canada
Toronto, ON 800-563-1515
Plains Dairy Products
Amarillo, TX 800-365-5608
Pleasant View Dairy
Highland, IN 219-838-0155
Prairie Farms Dairy Inc.
Edwardsville, IL 618-659-5700
Purity Dairies LLC
Nashville, TN 615-244-1900
Queensboro Farm Products
Canastota, NY 315-687-6133
Queensboro Farm Products
Jamica, NY 718-658-5000
Reilly Dairy & Food Company
Tampa, FL 813-839-8458
Roos Foods
Kenton, DE 800-343-3642
Rosenberger's Dairies
Hatfield, PA 800-355-9074
Schepps Dairy
Dallas, TX 800-395-7004
Schneider-Valley Farms Inc
Williamsport, PA 570-326-2021
Sisler's Ice & Ice Cream
Ohio, IL 888-891-3856
Smith Dairy
Orrville, OH 800-776-7076
Springfield Creamery Inc
Eugene, OR 541-689-2911
Sterzing Food Co
Burlington, IA 800-754-8467
Tiller Foods Company
Dayton, OH 937-435-4601
Umpqua Dairy
Roseburg, OR 888-672-6455
United Dairy Inc.
Martins Ferry, OH 800-252-1542
Upstate Farms
Buffalo, NY 716-896-3156
Upstate Niagara Co-Op Inc.
Buffalo, NY 716-892-3156
Vitamilk Dairy
Bellingham, WA 206-529-4128
Wallaby Yogurt Co
Broomfield, CO 855-925-4636

Yogurt

Agro Farma Inc.
New Berlin, NY 877-847-6181
Aimonetto and Sons
Renton, WA 866-823-2777
Alta Dena Certified Dairy LLC
City Of Industry, CA 800-535-1369
Anderson Erickson Dairy
Des Moines, IA 515-265-2521
Anderson Erickson Dairy
Kansas City, KS 913-621-4801
Anita's Yogurt
Brooklyn, NY
Astro Dairy Products
Toronto, ON 416-622-2811
Auburn Dairy Products Inc
Auburn, WA 800-950-9264
Bartlett Dairy & Food Service
Jamaica, NY 718-658-2299
Ben & Jerry's Homemade Inc
South Burlington, VT 866-258-6877
Berkeley Farms
Hayward, CA 800-395-7004
Blue Hill Yogurt
Pocantico Hills, NY 914-366-9600
Broughton Foods LLC
El Paso, TX 800-395-7004
Brown Cow Farm
Londonderry, NH 888-429-5459
Byrne Dairy, Inc.
Syracuse, NY 800-899-1535
Cascade Fresh
Seattle, WA 800-511-0057
Cass-Clay Creamery
Fargo, ND 701-293-6455
Cedar Crest Specialties
Cedarburg, WI 800-877-8341
Chino Valley Dairy
Chino, CA 800-324-7948
Chobani, Inc.
Norwich, NY
Clio Snacks
Roselle, NJ
Clofine Dairy Products Inc
Linwood, NJ 609-653-1000
Clover Sonoma
Petaluma, CA 800-237-3315
Clover Stornetta Farms Inc
Petaluma, CA 800-237-3315
Cloverland/Green Spring Dairy
Baltimore, MD 800-876-6455
CO YO
Albuquerque, NM 505-247-0012
Coach Farm Enterprises
Pine Plains, NY 800-999-4628
Coconut Collaborative
Continental Yogurt
Glendale, CA 818-240-7400
Culina
Austin, TX
Culture
New York, NY 718-499-0207
Dairy Maid Dairy LLC
Frederick, MD 301-663-5114
Dannon Company
Allentown, PA 877-326-6668
Danone North America
Broomfield, CO 303-635-4000
Darigold
Seattle, WA 800-333-6455
Deca & Otto Farms
Miami, FL 305-629-9335
Dreaming Cow
GA
Ellenos
Seattle, WA 206-535-7562
FAGE USA Dairy Ind Inc
Johnstown, NY 866-962-5912
Farmers Cooperative Dairy
Saint-Hubert, QC 800-501-1150
Farmland Dairies
Wallington, NJ 888-727-6252
Fieldbrook Foods Corp.
Dunkirk, NY 800-333-0805
Franklin Foods
Enosburg Falls, VT 800-933-6114
General Mills
Minneapolis, MN 800-248-7310
Glover's Ice Cream Inc
Frankfort, IN 800-686-5163
GPI USA LLC.
Mokena, IL 800-929-4248
Green Dirt Farm
Weston, MO 816-386-2156
Green Mountain Creamery
Brattleboro, VT 855-996-4946
Heritage Farms Dairy
Murfreesboro, TN 615-895-2790
Horizon Organic Dairy
Broomfield, CO 888-494-3020
Hudson River Foods
Castleton, NY 888-417-9343
Icelandic Milk and Skyr Corporation
New York, NY 212-966-6950
Icelandic Provisions
New York, NY 866-991-7597
Imperial Foods, Inc.
Long Island City, NY 718-784-3400
Jason & Son Specialty Foods
Rancho Cordova, CA 800-810-9093
Jaxon's Ice Cream Parlor
Dania Beach, FL 954-923-4445
Katies Korner Inc
Girard, OH 330-539-4140
Kemps LLC
St Paul, MN
Kite Hill
Hayward, CA 888-588-0994
Klinke Brothers Ice Cream Co
Memphis, TN 901-322-6640
Krinos Foods
Bronx, NY 718-729-9000
LAVVA
Warwick, NY
Lifeway
Morton Grove, IL 877-281-3874
Ludwig Dairy Product
Elk Grove Vlg, IL 847-860-8646
Lyo-San
Lachute, QC 800-363-3697
Maison Riviera
Varennes, QC 800-363-0092
Maple Hill Creamery
Kinderhook, NY 518-758-7777
Maplehill Creamery
Stuyvesant, NY 518-758-7777
Marburger Farm Dairy
Evans City, PA 800-331-1295
Master Mix
Placentia, CA 714-524-1698
Michigan Dairy LLC
Livonia, MI 734-367-5390
Mister Snacks Inc
Amherst, NY 800-333-6393
Mountain High Yogurt
Minneapolis, MN 866-964-4878
Nancy's Probiotic Foods
Eugene, OR
Natural By Nature
Newark, DE 302-455-1261
Old Chatham Sheepherding Co
Old Chatham, NY 888-743-3760
Old Home Foods Inc
New Brighton, MN 651-312-8900
Parmalat Canada
Toronto, ON 800-563-1515
Pavel's Yogurt
San Leandro, CA 510-352-1474
Pecoraro Dairy Products
Brooklyn, NY 718-388-2379
Pioneer Dairy
Southwick, MA 413-569-6132
Plains Dairy Products
Amarillo, TX 800-365-5608
Powerful Foods
Miami, FL 305-779-2449
Prairie Farms Dairy Inc.
Edwardsville, IL 618-659-5700
Purity Dairies LLC
Nashville, TN 615-244-1900
Queensboro Farm Products
Jamica, NY 718-658-5000
Redwood Hill Farm
Sebastopol, CA 877-238-3543

Reilly Dairy & Food Company
Tampa, FL 813-839-8458
Restaurant Systems International
Staten Island, NY 718-494-8888
Rockview Farms
Downey, CA 800-423-2479
Schreiber Foods Inc.
Green Bay, WI. 920-437-7601
Siggi's Dairy
New York, NY 212-966-6950
Siggi's Dairy
. . . . 855-860-6683
Springfield Creamery Inc
Eugene, OR. 541-689-2911
Stonyfield Organic
Londonderry, NH 800-776-2697
Super Stores Industries
Turlock, CA 209-668-2100
The Valpo Velvet Shoppe
Valparaiso, IN 219-464-4141
Toft Dairy Inc
Sandusky, OH 800-521-4606
Tropical Illusions
Trenton, MO 660-359-5422
United Dairy Farmers Inc.
Cincinnati, OH 866-837-4833
Upstate Farms
Buffalo, NY. 716-896-3156
Wallaby Yogurt Co
Broomfield, CO 855-925-4636
WhiteWave Foods
Denver, CO. 800-488-9283
Yoplait
Mississauga, ON. 800-516-7780

Bases, Flavors, Stabilizers

California Custom Fruits
Baldwin Park, CA. 877-558-0056
Chobani, Inc.
Norwich, NY
Idaho Milk Products
Jerome, ID. 208-644-2882
Nature's Godfather
Lexington, MA 339-970-9888

Frozen

Brighams
Arlington, MA 800-242-2423
Byrne Dairy, Inc.
Syracuse, NY 800-899-1535
Cedar Crest Specialties
Cedarburg, WI. 800-877-8341
Chino Valley Dairy
Chino, CA. 800-324-7948
Cloud Top
Pasadena, CA 888-263-1778
Dannon Yo Cream
Portland, OR. 800-962-7326
Elgin Dairy Foods
Chicago, IL 800-786-9900
Fieldbrook Foods Corp.
Dunkirk, NY 800-333-0805
Foothills Creamery
Calgary, AB. 800-661-4909
Glover's Ice Cream Inc
Frankfort, IN. 800-686-5163
Hudsonville Ice Cream
Holland, MI. 616-546-4005
Jack & Jill Ice Cream
Moorestown, NJ 856-813-2300
Jaxon's Ice Cream Parlor
Dania Beach, FL. 954-923-4445
Kemps LLC
St Paul, MN
Klinke Brothers Ice Cream Co
Memphis, TN 901-322-6640
Lafleur Dairy Products,
New Orleans, LA 504-729-3330
MacKay's Cochrane Ice Cream
Cochrane, AB 403-932-2455
Mayfield Dairy Farms LLC
Athens, TN 800-362-9546
O'Boyle's Ice Cream Company
Bristol, PA. 215-788-3882
Perry's Ice Cream Co Inc
Akron, NY. 800-873-7797
Petersen Ice Cream Company
Oak Park, IL 708-386-6130
Rainbow Valley Frozen Yogurt
White Lake, MI. 800-979-8669
Reinhold Ice Cream Company
Pittsburgh, PA 412-321-7600
Restaurant Systems International
Staten Island, NY 718-494-8888
Stonyfield Organic
Londonderry, NH 800-776-2697
The Valpo Velvet Shoppe
Valparaiso, IN. 219-464-4141
Toft Dairy Inc
Sandusky, OH 800-521-4606
Turkey Hill Dairy Inc
Conestoga, PA. 800-693-2479
Vitarich Ice Cream
Fortuna, CA 707-725-6182
Welsh Farms
Clifton, NJ. 973-772-2388
Whitey's Ice Cream Inc
Moline, IL. 888-594-4839

Low-Fat

Alta Dena Certified Dairy LLC
City Of Industry, CA. 800-535-1369
Auburn Dairy Products Inc
Auburn, WA 800-950-9264
Broughton Foods LLC
El Paso, TX. 800-395-7004
Bunker Hill Cheese Co Inc
Millersburg, OH 800-253-6636
Cascade Fresh
Seattle, WA 800-511-0057
Dannon Company
Allentown, PA. 877-326-6668
FAGE USA Dairy Ind Inc
Johnstown, NY 866-962-5912
Natren Inc
Thousand Oaks, CA 800-992-3323
Perry's Ice Cream Co Inc
Akron, NY. 800-873-7797
Siggi's Dairy
. . . . 855-860-6683
Upstate Niagara Co-Op Inc.
Buffalo, NY. 716-892-3156
Vitarich Ice Cream
Fortuna, CA 707-725-6182
Wunder Creamery
New York, NY 844-986-3371

No-Fat

Agro Farma Inc.
New Berlin, NY 877-847-6181
Broughton Foods LLC
El Paso, TX. 800-395-7004
Cascade Fresh
Seattle, WA 800-511-0057
Cedar Crest Specialties
Cedarburg, WI. 800-877-8341
FAGE USA Dairy Ind Inc
Johnstown, NY 866-962-5912
Gifford's Ice Cream
Skowhegan, ME 800-950-2604
O'Boyle's Ice Cream Company
Bristol, PA. 215-788-3882
Perry's Ice Cream Co Inc
Akron, NY. 800-873-7797
Vitarich Ice Cream
Fortuna, CA 707-725-6182

with Fruit

Alpina
Batavia, NY. 855-886-1914
Broughton Foods LLC
El Paso, TX. 800-395-7004
Byrne Dairy, Inc.
Syracuse, NY 800-899-1535
Chobani, Inc.
Norwich, NY
Dannon Company
Allentown, PA. 877-326-6668
Green Mountain Creamery
Brattleboro, VT. 855-996-4946
Noosa Yoghurt
Bellvue, CO 844-800-4329
Petersen Ice Cream Company
Oak Park, IL 708-386-6130
Stonyfield Organic
Londonderry, NH 800-776-2697
Yoplait
Mississauga, ON. 800-516-7780

Doughs, Mixes & Fillings

Batters

Breading

Beneficial Blends
Tampa, FL 800-230-5952
Blend Pak Inc
Bloomfield, KY 502-252-8000
Chef Merito Inc
Van Nuys, CA 800-637-4861
Concord Foods, LLC
Brockton, MA 508-580-1700
Dorothy Dawson Food Products
Jackson, MI 517-788-9830
Drum Rock Specialty Co Inc
Warwick, RI 401-737-5165
Fry Krisp Food Products
Jackson, MI 877-854-5440
Griffith Foods Inc.
Alsip, IL 708-371-0900
Hydroblend Limited
Nampa, ID 208-467-7441
Louisiana Fish Fry Products
Baton Rouge, LA 800-356-2905
Quality Naturally Foods
City Of Industry, CA 888-498-6986
Richmond Baking Co
Richmond, IN 765-962-8535
Richmond Baking Co
Alma, GA 912-632-7213
Shenandoah Mills
Lebanon, TN 615-444-0841
Specialty Products
Gloucester, MA 800-222-6846
Texas Crumb & Food Products
Farmers Branch, TX 800-522-7862
Tova Industries LLC
Louisville, KY 888-532-8682
UFL Foods
Mississauga, ON 905-670-7776
Wilkins Rogers Inc
Ellicott City, MD 410-465-5800
World Flavors Inc
Warminster, PA 215-672-4400
Yorktown Baking Company
Yorktown Heights, NY 800-235-3961

Cake

Frozen

BakeMark USA
Schaumburg, IL 847-519-3135

Cookie

BakeMark USA
Schaumburg, IL 847-519-3135
French Meadow Bakery & Cafe
Minneapolis, MN 612-870-7855

Muffin

Bagelworks
New York, NY 212-744-6444
BakeMark USA
Schaumburg, IL 847-519-3135
Coby's Cookies
Toronto, ON 416-633-1567

Tempora

Andy's Seasoning
St Louis, MO 800-305-3004

Breading

Andy's Seasoning
St Louis, MO 800-305-3004
Atkinson Milling Co.
Selma, NC 800-948-5707
Blend Pak Inc
Bloomfield, KY 502-252-8000
Blendex Co
Louisville, KY 800-626-6325
Chef Hans' Gourmet Foods
Monroe, LA 800-890-4267
Colonna Brothers Inc
North Bergen, NJ 201-864-1115
Dorothy Dawson Food Products
Jackson, MI 517-788-9830
Drum Rock Specialty Co Inc
Warwick, RI 401-737-5165
Drusilla Seafood
Baton Rouge, LA 800-364-8844
Griffith Foods Inc.
Alsip, IL 708-371-0900
House-Autry Mills Inc
Four Oaks, NC 800-849-0802
Hydroblend Limited
Nampa, ID 208-467-7441
Lakeside Mills
Rutherfordton, NC 828-286-4866
Louisiana Fish Fry Products
Baton Rouge, LA 800-356-2905
Newly Weds Foods Inc
Chicago, IL 800-621-7521
Oak Grove Smoke House Inc
Prairieville, LA 225-673-6857
Quality Bakery Products
Houston, TX 866-449-4977
Richmond Baking Co
Richmond, IN 765-962-8535
Roland Machinery
Springfield, IL 800-325-1183
Shenandoah Mills
Lebanon, TN 615-444-0841
Southeastern Mills Inc
Rome, GA 800-334-4468
Specialty Products
Gloucester, MA 800-222-6846
Taste Maker Foods
Memphis, TN 800-467-1407
Texas Crumb & Food Products
Farmers Branch, TX 800-522-7862
Tova Industries LLC
Louisville, KY 888-532-8682
United Supermarkets
Lubbock, TX 806-745-9667
Wilkins Rogers Inc
Ellicott City, MD 410-465-5800
World Flavors Inc
Warminster, PA 215-672-4400

Doughs

American Ingredients Co
Lenexa, KS 800-669-4092
Athens Baking Company
Fresno, CA 800-775-2867
Athens Foods Inc
Brookpark, OH 843-916-2000
Batory Foods
Des Plaines, IL 847-299-1999
Bridgford Foods Corp
Anaheim, CA 800-527-2105
Carolina Foods Inc
Charlotte, NC 800-234-0441
Cohen's Bakery
Ellenville, NY 845-647-2200
Creme Curls
Hudsonville, MI 800-466-1219
D I Mfg LLC
Omaha, NE 402-330-5650
Dimitria Delights Baking Co
North Grafton, MA 800-763-1113
EFCO Products Inc
Poughkeepsie, NY 800-284-3326
Fillo Factory, The
Northvale, NJ 800-653-4556
Lentia Enterprises Ltd.
Surrey, BC 888-768-7368
Leon's Bakery
North Haven, CT 800-223-6844
Northwestern Foods
Arden Hills, MN 800-236-4937
Ranaldi Bros. Frozen Food Products
Warwick, RI 401-737-5130
Rhodes International Inc
Salt Lake City, UT 800-876-7333
Spelt Right Foods, LLC
Brooklyn, NY 877-773-5801
Teeny Foods Inc
Portland, OR 503-252-3006
TNT Crust
Green Bay, WI 920-431-7240

Baking

Bridgford Foods Corp
Anaheim, CA 800-527-2105
Clofine Dairy Products Inc
Linwood, NJ 609-653-1000
Creme Curls
Hudsonville, MI 800-466-1219
Dufour Pastry Kitchens Inc
Bronx, NY 800-439-1282
EFCO Products Inc
Poughkeepsie, NY 800-284-3326
Northwestern Foods
Arden Hills, MN 800-236-4937

Frozen

Callie's Charleston Biscuits
North Charleston, SC 843-577-1198
Creme Curls
Hudsonville, MI 800-466-1219
Dufour Pastry Kitchens Inc
Bronx, NY 800-439-1282
Sugarplum Desserts
Langley, BC 604-534-2282

Bread

Baker Boy Bake Shop Inc
Dickinson, ND 800-437-2008
Country Home Bakers
Atlanta, GA 800-241-6445
J & J Wall Bakery Co
Sacramento, CA 916-381-1410
Lone Star Bakery
Round Rock, TX 512-255-7268
Lora Brody Products Inc
Waltham, MA 781-899-3910
Pacific Ocean Produce
Santa Cruz, CA 831-423-2654
Pyrenees French Bakery
Bakersfield, CA 888-898-7159
Rhodes International Inc
Salt Lake City, UT 800-876-7333
Senape's Bakery Inc
Hazleton, PA 570-454-0839
Spelt Right Foods, LLC
Brooklyn, NY 877-773-5801

Cookie

Austin Special Foods Company
Austin, TX 512-372-8665
Best Maid Cookie Co
River Falls, WI 888-444-0322
Cappello's
Denver, CO 844-353-2863
CBC Foods
Little River, KS 800-276-4770
Coby's Cookies
Toronto, ON 416-633-1567
David's Cookies
Cedar Grove, NJ 800-500-2800
Edoughble
Los Angeles, CA
Gladder's Gourmet Cookies
Lockhart, TX 888-398-4523
JUST Inc
San Francisco, CA 844-423-6637
Lone Star Bakery
Round Rock, TX 512-255-7268
Michael's Cookies
Clear Lake, IA 800-822-5384
Otis Spunkmeyer
Brockport, NY 855-427-9982
Pacific Ocean Produce
Santa Cruz, CA 831-423-2654
The Cookie Dough Cafe
Bloomington, IL 309-539-4585
Touche Bakery
London, ON 519-455-0044

Doughnuts

BakeMark Canada
Laval, QC 800-361-4998
Baker Boy Bake Shop Inc
Dickinson, ND 800-437-2008

Country Home Bakers
Atlanta, GA........800-241-6445
EFCO Products Inc
Poughkeepsie, NY........800-284-3326

Frozen

Annie's Frozen Yogurt
Minneapolis, MN........800-969-9648
Austin Special Foods Company
Austin, TX........512-372-8665
Baker Boy Bake Shop Inc
Dickinson, ND........800-437-2008
Best Maid Cookie Co
River Falls, WI........888-444-0322
Bridgford Foods Corp
Anaheim, CA........800-527-2105
Carolina Foods Inc
Charlotte, NC........800-234-0441
Coby's Cookies
Toronto, ON........416-633-1567
Cookie Tree Bakeries
Salt Lake City, UT........801-268-2253
Country Home Bakers
Atlanta, GA........800-241-6445
Creme Curls
Hudsonville, MI........800-466-1219
Dakota Brands Intl
Jamestown, ND........800-844-5073
De Iorio's Foods Inc
Utica, NY........800-649-7612
Dimitria Delights Baking Co
North Grafton, MA........800-763-1113
Dough-To-Go
Santa Clara, CA........408-727-4094
Dufour Pastry Kitchens Inc
Bronx, NY........800-439-1282
English Bay Batter Us Inc
Columbus, OH........800-253-6844
Enterprises Pates et Croutes
Boucherville, QC........800-265-7790
Famous Specialties Co
Island Park, NY........800-894-9218
Gonnella Baking Company
Schamburg, IL........800-322-8829
Guttenplan's Frozen Dough
Middletown, NJ........888-422-4357
Harlan Bakeries
Avon, IN........800-435-2738
J & J Wall Bakery Co
Sacramento, CA........916-381-1410
La Cookie
Burbank, CA........818-495-5732
Leon's Bakery
North Haven, CT........800-223-6844
Lone Star Bakery
Round Rock, TX........512-255-7268
Mel-O-Cream Donuts Intl
Springfield, IL........217-483-7272
Michael's Cookies
Clear Lake, IA........800-822-5384
Morrison Meat Pies
West Valley, UT........801-977-0181
Orange Bakery
Irvine, CA........949-863-1377
Otis Spunkmeyer
Brockport, NY........855-427-9982
Quality Naturally Foods
City Of Industry, CA........888-498-6986
Ranaldi Bros. Frozen Food Products
Warwick, RI........401-737-5130
Rhodes International Inc
Salt Lake City, UT........800-876-7333
Rich Products Corp
Buffalo, NY........800-828-2021
Sinbad Sweets
Madera, CA........866-746-2232
Tasty Mix Quality Foods
Brooklyn, NY........718-855-7680
TNT Crust
Green Bay, WI........920-431-7240
Ya-Hoo Baking Co
Sherman, TX........888-869-2466

Improvers

California Blending Co
El Monte, CA........626-448-1918

Pizza

A Tavola Together
Stockton, CA........209-608-5455
Baker Boy Bake Shop Inc
Dickinson, ND........800-437-2008
BBU Bakeries
Horsham, PA........800-984-0989
Cohen's Bakery
Ellenville, NY........845-647-2200
De Iorio's Foods Inc
Utica, NY........800-649-7612
French Meadow Bakery & Cafe
Minneapolis, MN........612-870-7855
Northwestern Foods
Arden Hills, MN........800-236-4937
Senape's Bakery Inc
Hazleton, PA........570-454-0839
Spelt Right Foods, LLC
Brooklyn, NY........877-773-5801
TNT Crust
Green Bay, WI........920-431-7240
Weisenberger Mills
Midway, KY........800-643-8678

Frozen

TNT Crust
Green Bay, WI........920-431-7240

Puff Pastry

Dufour Pastry Kitchens Inc
Bronx, NY........800-439-1282
Fillo Factory, The
Northvale, NJ........800-653-4556
VLR Food Corporation
Vaughan, ON........800-387-7437

Fillings

Abel & Schafer Inc
Ronkonkoma, NY........800-443-1260
Bake N Joy Foods
North Andover, MA........800-666-4937
Calico Cottage
Amityville, NY........800-645-5345
Frank Korinek & Co
Cicero, IL........708-652-2870
Lyons Magnus
Fresno, CA........800-344-7130
Newport Flavours & Fragrances
Orange, CA........714-744-3700
Pacific Westcoast Foods
Beaverton, OR........800-874-9333
Patisserie Wawel
Montreal, QC........614-524-3348
Puratos Canada
Mississauga, ON........905-362-3668
Skjodt-Barrett Foods
Brampton, ON........877-600-1200
Ya-Hoo Baking Co
Sherman, TX........888-869-2466

Baking

Bear Stewart Corp
Chicago, IL........800-697-2327
Century Blends LLC
Hunt Valley, MD........410-771-6606
Clements Foods Co
Oklahoma City, OK........800-654-8355

Cake

Abel & Schafer Inc
Ronkonkoma, NY........800-443-1260
American Key Food Products Inc
Closter, NJ........877-263-7539
Bear Stewart Corp
Chicago, IL........800-697-2327
Belcolade
Pennsauken, NJ........856-661-9123
Brookside Foods
Abbotsford, BC........800-468-1714
California Custom Fruits
Baldwin Park, CA........877-558-0056
Erba Food Products
Brooklyn, NY........718-272-7700
Golden West Fruit Company
Commerce, CA........323-726-9419
JER Creative Food Concepts, Inc.
Commerce, CA........800-350-2462
Lawrence Foods Inc
Elk Grove Village, IL........847-437-2400
Pacific Westcoast Foods
Beaverton, OR........800-874-9333
Plaidberry Company
Vista, CA........760-727-5403
Quality Naturally Foods
City Of Industry, CA........888-498-6986
Skjodt-Barrett Foods
Brampton, ON........877-600-1200
Solo Foods
Countryside, IL........800-328-7656
Westco-BakeMark
Pico Rivera, CA........562-949-1054
Ya-Hoo Baking Co
Sherman, TX........888-869-2466

Chocolate

Erba Food Products
Brooklyn, NY........718-272-7700

Creme

Galaxy Desserts
Richmond, CA........800-225-3523

Dessert

Chocolate

Century Blends LLC
Hunt Valley, MD........410-771-6606

Cream

Flavor Right Foods Group
St Phoenix, AZ........888-464-3734

Meringue

Bear Stewart Corp
Chicago, IL........800-697-2327

Doughnuts

BakeMark USA
Schaumburg, IL........847-519-3135
Pamlico Packing Company
Grantsboro, NC........800-682-1113
Skjodt-Barrett Foods
Brampton, ON........877-600-1200

Fruit

EFCO Products Inc
Poughkeepsie, NY........800-284-3326

Meringue

Jada Foods LLC
Hallandale Beach, FL........855-936-3746
Sweet Whispers
Mclean, VA........954-328-5079

Pie

Abel & Schafer Inc
Ronkonkoma, NY........800-443-1260
American Almond Products Co
Brooklyn, NY........800-825-6663
American Key Food Products Inc
Closter, NJ........877-263-7539
BakeMark Canada
Laval, QC........800-361-4998
BakeMark Ingredients Canada
Richmond, BC........800-665-9441
Baldwin Richardson Foods
Oakbrook Terrace, IL........866-644-2732
Bear Stewart Corp
Chicago, IL........800-697-2327
Brookside Foods
Abbotsford, BC........800-468-1714
California Custom Fruits
Baldwin Park, CA........877-558-0056
Carriere Foods Inc
Saint-Denis-Sur-Richelie, QC........450-787-3411
Clements Foods Co
Oklahoma City, OK........800-654-8355
Country Cupboard
Lewisburg, PA........570-523-3211
Eden Processing
Poplar Grove, IL........815-765-2000
Erba Food Products
Brooklyn, NY........718-272-7700
Frank Korinek & Co
Cicero, IL........708-652-2870
Fruit Fillings Inc
Fresno, CA........800-995-4514
Golden West Fruit Company
Commerce, CA........323-726-9419
Grandma Hoerner's Inc
Alma, KS........785-765-2300

H Cantin
Beauport, QC 800-463-5268
Indian Bay Frozen Foods
Centreville, NL....................709-678-2844
JER Creative Food Concepts, Inc.
Commerce, CA....................800-350-2462
Knouse Foods Co-Op Inc.
Peach Glen, PA....................717-677-8181
Lawrence Foods Inc
Elk Grove Village, IL....................847-437-2400
Leahy Orchards
Franklin Centre, QC....................800-667-7380
Lynch Foods
North York, ON....................416-449-5464
Michigan Desserts
Oak Park, MI....................800-328-8632
Nation Wide Canning Ltd.
Cottam, ON....................519-839-4831
Pacific Westcoast Foods
Beaverton, OR....................800-874-9333
Pearson's Berry Farm
Bowden, AB....................403-224-3011
Pied-Mont/Dora
Anne Des Plaines, QC....................800-363-8003
Plaidberry Company
Vista, CA....................760-727-5403
Reinhart Foods
Toronto, ON....................416-645-4910
Schmidt Bros Inc
Swanton, OH....................800-200-7318
Skjodt-Barrett Foods
Brampton, ON....................877-600-1200
Steel's Gourmet Foods, Ltd.
Bridgeport, PA....................800-678-3357
Steve's Authentic Key Lime Pies
Brooklyn, NY....................888-450-5463
Valley View Blueberries
Vancouver, WA....................360-892-2839
White-Stokes Company
Chicago, IL....................800-978-6537
Ya-Hoo Baking Co
Sherman, TX....................888-869-2466

Mixes

1-2-3 Gluten Free
Chagrin Falls, OH....................216-378-9233
Bountiful Pantry
Nantucket, MA....................617-487-8019
Boyd's Coffee Co
Portland, OR....................800-735-2878
Calico Cottage
Amityville, NY....................800-645-5345
Cherryvale Farms
....................310-910-1124
De Iorio's Foods Inc
Utica, NY....................800-649-7612
Gluten-Free Heaven
Pleasant Grove, UT....................801-380-6478
Golden Malted
South Bend, IN....................888-596-4040
Lehi Mills
Lehi, UT....................877-311-3566
Ontario Foods
Guelph, ON....................888-466-2372
Paradigm Foodworks Inc
Lake Oswego, OR....................800-234-0250
Phoenix Foods
Canton, TX....................903-287-9166
Shawnee Canning Co
Cross Junction, VA....................800-713-1414
Sister's Gourmet
Winder, GA....................770-338-1388
Smart Flour Foods, LLC
Austin, TX....................512-706-1775
VCPB Transportation
Secaucus, NJ....................201-770-0070

Baking

1-2-3 Gluten Free
Chagrin Falls, OH....................216-378-9233
Abel & Schafer Inc
Ronkonkoma, NY....................800-443-1260
Advanced Food Services
Lenexa, KS....................913-888-8088
Adventure Foods
Whittier, NC....................828-497-4113
America's Classic Foods
Cambria, CA....................805-927-0745
Annie's Frozen Yogurt
Minneapolis, MN....................800-969-9648
Arnel's Originals, Inc
Ventura, CA....................805-322-6900
Bake N Joy Foods
North Andover, MA....................800-666-4937
BakeMark Ingredients Canada
Richmond, BC....................800-665-9441
Bear Stewart Corp
Chicago, IL....................800-697-2327
Bernard Food Industries Inc
Evanston, IL....................800-323-3663
Beth's Fine Desserts
Mill Valley, CA....................415-383-3991
Bette's Oceanview Diner
Berkeley, CA....................510-644-3230
Big Steer
Houston, TX....................800-421-4951
Blend Pak Inc
Bloomfield, KY....................502-252-8000
Bluechip Group
Salt Lake City, UT....................800-878-0099
Bob's Red Mill Natural Foods
Milwaukie, OR....................800-349-2173
Brass Ladle Products
Concordville, PA....................800-955-2353
Brookema Company
West Chicago, IL....................630-562-2290
Byrd Mill Co
Ashland, VA....................888-897-3336
Byrnes & Kiefer Company
Callery, PA....................724-538-5200
C W Resources Inc
New Britain, CT....................860-229-7700
Cafe Du Monde Coffee Stand
New Orleans, LA....................800-772-2927
Calhoun Bend Mill
Libuse, LA....................800-519-6455
Calico Cottage
Amityville, NY....................800-645-5345
Carol Lee Donuts
Salina, KS....................785-827-2402
Century Foods Intl LLC
Sparta, WI....................800-269-1901
Cereal Food Processors Inc
Mcpherson, KS....................800-835-2067
Chelsea Milling Co.
Chelsea, MI....................800-727-2460
Chimayo To Go / Cibolo Junction
Albuquerque, NM....................800-683-9628
Choice Food Distributors LLC
Nashville, TN....................615-350-6070
Chukar Cherries
Prosser, WA....................800-624-9544
Cinnabar Specialty Foods Inc
Prescott, AZ....................866-293-6433
Cisse Trading Co
Mamaroneck, NY....................914-381-5555
Clabber Girl Corporation
Terre Haute, IN....................812-232-9446
CMA Global Partners/German Foods LLC
NW Washington, DC....................800-881-6419
Commodities Marketing Inc
Clarksburg, NJ....................732-516-0700
Continental Mills Inc
Tukwila, WA....................206-816-7000
Cook-In-The-Kitchen
Hampden, ME....................207-848-4900
Cotswold Cottage Foods
Arvada, CO....................800-208-1977
Country Home Creations Inc
Flint, MI....................800-457-3477
Cowboy Food & Drink
Chagrin Falls, OH....................800-759-5489
Cream Of The West
Harlowton, MT....................800-477-2383
Creation Nation
Calabasas, CA....................424-234-5800
Crown Maple Syrup
Dover Plains, NY....................845-877-0640
Crum Creek Mils
Springfield, PA....................888-607-3500
Dakota Specialty Milling, Inc.
Fargo, ND....................844-633-2746
Dawn Food Products, Inc
Jackson, MI....................800-248-1144
De Iorio's Foods Inc
Utica, NY....................800-649-7612
Dorothy Dawson Food Products
Jackson, MI....................517-788-9830
Dowd & Rogers
San Clemente, CA....................800-232-8619
Dr. Pete's
Savannah, GA....................912-233-3035
Drusilla Seafood
Baton Rouge, LA....................800-364-8844
EFCO Products Inc
Poughkeepsie, NY....................800-284-3326
El Peto Products
Cambridge, ON....................800-387-4064
Ellison Milling Company
Lethbridge, AB....................403-328-6622
Embassy Flavours Ltd.
Brampton, ON....................800-334-3371
Ener-G Foods
Seattle, WA....................800-331-5222
English Bay Batter Us Inc
Columbus, OH....................800-253-6844
Fiera Foods
Toronto, ON....................800-675-6356
Food Concentrate Corporation
Oklahoma City, OK....................405-840-5633
Foodstirs
Santa Monica, CA....................844-250-3332
Frank Korinek & Co
Cicero, IL....................708-652-2870
French Feast Inc.
Englewood, NJ....................201-731-3102
Fry Krisp Food Products
Jackson, MI....................877-854-5440
Galloway Co
Neenah, WI....................800-722-8903
Gilster-Mary Lee Corp
Chester, IL....................618-826-2361
Global Food Industries
Townville, SC....................800-225-4152
Good Food Inc
Honey Brook, PA....................800-327-4406
Grain Millers Inc
Eden Prairie, MN....................800-232-6287
Grain Process Enterprises Ltd.
Scarborough, ON....................800-387-5292
Great Grains Milling Company
Scobey, MT....................406-783-5581
Great Recipes
Beaverton, OR....................800-273-2331
Gregory's Foods, Inc.
St Paul, MN....................800-231-4734
Gust John Foods & Products
Batavia, IL....................800-756-5886
H Nagel & Son Co
Cincinnati, OH....................513-665-4550
HC Brill Company
Tucker, GA....................800-241-8526
Heartland Food Products
Westwood, KS....................866-571-0222
Heidi's Gourmet Desserts
Tucker, GA....................800-241-4166
Highland Sugarworks
Websterville, VT....................800-452-4012
Hodgson Mill Inc
Effingham, IL....................800-347-0198
Hollman Foods
Des Moines, IA....................888-926-2879
Homestead Mills
Cook, MN....................800-652-5233
House-Autry Mills Inc
Four Oaks, NC....................800-849-0802
Inn Maid Food
Lenox, MA....................413-637-2732
Iveta Gourmet Inc
Santa Cruz, CA....................831-423-5149
J.M. Smucker Co.
Orrville, OH....................888-550-9555
Johnson's Food Products
Dorchester, MA....................617-265-3400
Kamish Food Products
Chicago, IL....................773-725-6959
Little Crow Foods
Warsaw, IN....................800-288-2769
Louisiana Gourmet Enterprises
Houma, LA....................800-328-5586
Lynch Foods
North York, ON....................416-449-5464
Manischewitz Co
Newark, NJ....................201-553-1100
Maple Grove Farms Of Vermont
St Johnsbury, VT....................802-748-5141
Marie Callender's Gourmet Products/Goldrush Products
San Jose, CA....................800-729-5428
Martha Olson's Great Foo
Sutter Creek, CA....................800-973-3966
Minnestalgia Foods LLC
Mcgregor, MN....................800-328-6731
Miss Jones Baking Co.
Emeryville, CA

Modern Products Inc
Mequon, WI 800-877-8935
Nantucket Tea Traders
Nantucket, MA 508-325-0203
New Hope Mills Mfg Inc
Auburn, NY 315-252-2676
No Pudge! Foods
Wolfeboro Falls, NH 888-667-8343
Northwestern Foods
Arden Hills, MN 800-236-4937
Old Tyme Mill Company
Chicago, IL 773-521-9484
Paradise Island Foods
Nanaimo, BC 800-889-3370
Pelican Bay Ltd.
Dunedin, FL 800-826-8982
Pett Spice Products Inc
Atlanta, GA 404-691-5235
Pillsbury
Minneapolis, MN 800-775-4777
Puratos Canada
Mississauga, ON 905-362-3668
Quality Naturally Foods
City Of Industry, CA 888-498-6986
Real Cookies
Merrick, NY 800-822-5113
Red Rose Trading Company
Lancaster, PA 717-293-7833
Reimann Food Classics
Palatine, IL 847-991-1366
Renwood Mills
Newton, NC 828-464-1611
Richmond Baking Co
Alma, GA 912-632-7213
Roland Machinery
Springfield, IL 800-325-1183
Rose Randolph Cookies, LLC
Wappingers Falls, NY 917-834-2310
Rothbury Farms
Grand Rapids, MI 877-684-2879
S&N Food Company
Mesquite, TX 972-222-1184
Sells Best
Mishawaka, IN 800-837-8368
SFP Food Products
Conway, AR 800-654-5329
Shenandoah Mills
Lebanon, TN 615-444-0841
Sister's Gourmet
Winder, GA 770-338-1388
Sofo Foods
Toledo, OH 800-447-4211
SOUPerior Bean & Spice Company
Vancouver, WA 800-878-7687
Southeastern Mills Inc
Rome, GA 800-334-4468
Stevens Creative Enterprises, Inc.
New York, NY 646-558-6336
Strossner's Bakery & Cafe
Greenville, SC 864-233-2990
Subco Foods Inc
Sheboygan, WI 800-473-0757
Sundial Herb Garden
Higganum, CT 860-345-4290
Swagger Foods Corp
Vernon Hills, IL 847-913-1200
Sweetstacks LLC
San Diego, CA 619-997-1097
Tait Farm Foods
Centre Hall, PA 800-787-2716
Tarazi Specialty Foods
Chino, CA 909-628-3601
Taste Maker Foods
Memphis, TN 800-467-1407
Taste of Gourmet
Indianola, MS 800-833-7731
Tasty Mix Quality Foods
Brooklyn, NY 718-855-7680
Tasty Selections
Concord, ON 905-760-2353
Texas Crumb & Food Products
Farmers Branch, TX 800-522-7862
The Invisible Chef
Canton, OH 330-880-5223
The Lollipop Tree, Inc
Auburn, NY 800-842-6691
Timber Peaks Gourmet
Parker, CO 800-982-7687
Tova Industries LLC
Louisville, KY 888-532-8682
Valley View Blueberries
Vancouver, WA 360-892-2839
VIP Foods
Flushing, NY 718-821-5330
Wanda's Nature Farm
Lincoln, NE 800-735-6828
War Eagle Mill
Rogers, AR 866-492-7324
Weisenberger Mills
Midway, KY 800-643-8678
West Pac
Idaho Falls, ID 800-973-7407
Westco-BakeMark
Pico Rivera, CA 562-949-1054
Wilkins Rogers Inc
Ellicott City, MD 410-465-5800
Wisconsin Wilderness Food Products
Lake Bluff, IL 800-359-3039
World Flavors Inc
Warminster, PA 215-672-4400
Yorktown Baking Company
Yorktown Heights, NY 800-235-3961

Brownies

Bluechip Group
Salt Lake City, UT 800-878-0099
Chelsea Milling Co.
Chelsea, MI 800-727-2460
Hodgson Mill Inc
Effingham, IL 800-347-0198
Sister's Gourmet
Winder, GA 770-338-1388
Sisters' Gourmet
Dacula, GA 216-292-7700

Beverage

Abunda Life
Asbury Park, NJ 732-775-9338
Al-Rite Fruits & Syrups Co
Miami, FL 305-652-2540
Alexander International (USA)
Brightwaters, NY 866-965-0143
Alkinco
New York, NY 800-424-7118
Atlantic Seasonings
Kinston, NC 800-433-5261
Bacardi Canada, Inc.
Toronto, ON 905-451-6100
Bainbridge Festive Foods
Farmington, TN 800-545-9205
Baldwin Richardson Foods
Oakbrook Terrace, IL 866-644-2732
Bartush Schnitzius Foods Co
Lewisville, TX 972-219-1270
Bede Inc
Haledon, NJ 866-239-6565
Best Foods
Englewood Cliffs, NJ 201-894-4000
Blue Crab Bay
Melfa, VA 800-221-2722
Boissons Miami Pomor
Longueuil, QC 877-977-3744
Boyd's Coffee Co
Portland, OR 800-735-2878
Brookema Company
West Chicago, IL 630-562-2290
Cappuccine
Corona, CA 800-511-3127
Carborator Rental Svc
Philadelphia, PA 800-220-3556
Carolina Treet
Wilmington, NC 800-616-6344
Century Blends LLC
Hunt Valley, MD 410-771-6606
Century Foods Intl LLC
Sparta, WI 800-269-1901
Chase Brothers Dairy
Oxnard, CA 800-438-6455
Citrus Service
Winter Garden, FL 407-656-4999
Consolidated Mills Inc
Houston, TX 713-896-4196
Creative Foodworks Inc
San Antonio, TX 210-212-4761
Dairy-Mix Inc
St Petersburg, FL 800-955-6101
Devansoy Farms
Carroll, IA 800-747-8605
Diamond Crystal Brands Inc
Savannah, GA 800-654-5115
Erba Food Products
Brooklyn, NY 718-272-7700
Fair Scones
Medina, WA 800-588-9160
Fine Foods Intl
St Louis, MO 314-842-4473
Finest Call
New Albany, IN 812-944-3585
Finlays
Lincoln, RI 800-288-6272
Flavor Systems Intl.
Cincinnati, OH 800-498-2783
Fountain Shakes/MS Foods
Minnetonka, MN 952-988-6940
Four Percent Company
Highland Park, MI 313-345-5880
Franco's Cocktail Mixes
Pompano Beach, FL 800-782-4508
Frank & Dean's Cocktail Mixes
Pasadena, CA 626-351-4272
Genisoy
San Francisco, CA 866-972-6879
Gilly's Hot Vanilla
Lenox, MA 413-637-1515
Gilster-Mary Lee Corp
Chester, IL 618-826-2361
GLCC Co
Paw Paw, MI 269-657-3167
Great Western Juice Co
Maple Heights, OH 800-321-9180
Green Foods Corp.
Oxnard, CA 800-777-4430
H Fox & Co Inc
Brooklyn, NY 718-385-4600
Hena Inc
Brooklyn, NY 718-272-8237
Highwood Distillers
High River, AB 403-652-3202
Instant Products of America
Columbus, IN 812-372-9100
J. Crow Company
New Ipswich, NH 800-878-1965
Jel Sert
West Chicago, IL 800-323-2592
Jogue Inc
Northville, MI 800-531-3888
Jus-Made
Dallas, TX 800-969-3746
K & F Select Fine Coffees
Portland, OR 800-558-7788
Kemach Food Products
Brooklyn, NY 718-272-5655
Kittling Ridge Estate Wines & Spirits
Vaughan, ON 800-461-9463
LA Paz Products Inc
Brea, CA 714-990-0982
Lake City Foods
Mississauga, ON 905-625-8244
Land O'Lakes Inc
Arden Hills, MN 800-328-9680
Lasco Foods Inc
St Louis, MO 314-832-1906
Lemate Of New England Inc
Foxboro, MA 508-543-9035
Lynch Foods
North York, ON 416-449-5464
Main Street Ingredients
La Crosse, WI 800-359-2345
Mar-Key Foods
Vidalia, GA 912-537-4204
Margarita Man
San Antonio, TX 800-950-8149
Mc Steven's Coca Factory Store
Vancouver, WA 800-547-2803
Mccullagh Coffee Roasters
Buffalo, NY 800-753-3473
Melchers Flavors of America
Indianapolis, IN 800-235-2867
Mele-Koi Farms
Newport Beach, CA 949-660-9000
Mingo Bay Beverages
Myrtle Beach, SC 843-448-5320
Minute Maid Company
Atlanta, GA 800-520-2653
Natural Formulas
Hayward, CA 510-372-1800
Northwestern Foods
Arden Hills, MN 800-236-4937
Paca Foods Inc
Tampa, FL 800-388-7419
Phillips Syrup Corp
Cleveland, OH 800-350-8443
Pied-Mont/Dora
Anne Des Plaines, QC 800-363-8003

Plainview Milk Products
Plainview, MN 800-356-5606
PR Bar
Chandler, AZ. 800-397-5556
Pro Form Labs
Orinda, CA 707-752-9010
Quality Instant Teas
Morristown, NJ. 888-283-8327
Quality Naturally Foods
City Of Industry, CA. 888-498-6986
Robertet Flavors
Piscataway, NJ 732-981-8300
Roos Foods
Kenton, DE. 800-343-3642
Ruffner's
Wayne, PA. 610-687-9800
Schlotterbeck & Foss Company
Portland, ME. 800-777-4666
Sea Breeze Fruit Flavors
Towaco, NJ. 800-732-2733
Skim Delux Mendenhall Laboratories
Paris, TN. 800-642-9321
Skinny Mixes LLC
Clearwater, FL 727-826-0306
Southern Gardens Citrus
Clewiston, FL 863-983-3030
Sturm Foods Inc
Manawa, WI 800-347-8876
Subco Foods Inc
Sheboygan, WI 800-473-0757
SugarCreek
Cincinnati, OH 800-445-2715
Swagger Foods Corp
Vernon Hills, IL 847-913-1200
Tex-Mex Gourmet
Brenham, TX. 888-345-8467
The Peanut Butter Shop of Williamsburg
Toano, VA. 800-831-1828
Thirs-Tea Corp
Boca Raton, FL. 561-948-5600
Tova Industries LLC
Louisville, KY 888-532-8682
Trader Vic's Food Products
Emeryville, CA. 877-762-4824
Tree Ripe Products
Whippany, NJ 800-873-3747
Ultra Seal
New Paltz, NY 845-255-2490
United Citrus
Norwood, MA. 800-229-7300
VIP Foods
Flushing, NY. 718-821-5330
Wayne Dairy Products Inc
Richmond, IN 765-935-7521
Webbpak Inc
Trussville, AL 800-655-3500
Wechsler Coffee Corporation
Teterboro, NJ. 800-800-2633
Welsh Farms
Wallington, NJ 800-221-0663
World Flavors Inc
Warminster, PA 215-672-4400

Frozen

Al-Rite Fruits & Syrups Co
Miami, FL. 305-652-2540
Baldwin Richardson Foods
Oakbrook Terrace, IL 866-644-2732
J. Crow Company
New Ipswich, NH 800-878-1965
Jogue Inc
Northville, MI. 800-531-3888

Liquid

Baldwin Richardson Foods
Oakbrook Terrace, IL 866-644-2732
Hummingbird Kitchens
Whitehouse, TX 800-921-9470
J. Crow Company
New Ipswich, NH 800-878-1965
Jogue Inc
Northville, MI. 800-531-3888
Pestano Foods
New Rochelle, NY

Biscuit

Atkinson Milling Co.
Selma, NC. 800-948-5707
Blackberry Patch
Thomasville, GA. 800-853-5598
Bob's Red Mill Natural Foods
Milwaukie, OR 800-349-2173
Bountiful Pantry
Nantucket, MA 617-487-8019
Byrd Mill Co
Ashland, VA 888-897-3336
Country Cupboard
Lewisburg, PA. 570-523-3211
Father's Country Hams
Bremen, KY 270-525-3554
House-Autry Mills Inc
Four Oaks, NC 800-849-0802
Iveta Gourmet Inc
Santa Cruz, CA 831-423-5149
J.M. Smucker Co.
Orrville, OH 888-550-9555
Mennel Milling Company
Fostoria, OH 800-688-8151
Weisenberger Mills
Midway, KY 800-643-8678

Bread

Abel & Schafer Inc
Ronkonkoma, NY. 800-443-1260
Aunt Millie's Bakeries
Fort Wayne, IN 855-755-2253
BakeMark USA
Schaumburg, IL. 847-519-3135
Bob's Red Mill Natural Foods
Milwaukie, OR 800-349-2173
Bountiful Pantry
Nantucket, MA 617-487-8019
Byrd Mill Co
Ashland, VA 888-897-3336
Chester's International , LLC
Mountain Brook, AL 800-288-1555
Chimayo To Go / Cibolo Junction
Albuquerque, NM. 800-683-9628
Cotswold Cottage Foods
Arvada, CO. 800-208-1977
Drusilla Seafood
Baton Rouge, LA 800-364-8844
Grain Process Enterprises Ltd.
Scarborough, ON 800-387-5292
Hollman Foods
Des Moines, IA. 888-926-2879
Kokopelli's Kitchen
Phoenix, AZ 888-943-9802
Lehi Mills
Lehi, UT 877-311-3566
Lentia Enterprises Ltd.
Surrey, BC. 888-768-7368
Leonard Mountain Inc
Bixby, OK. 800-822-7700
Marie Callender's
Mission Viejo, CA 800-776-7437
Old Tyme Mill Company
Chicago, IL 773-521-9484
Pamela's Products
Ukiah, CA. 707-462-6605
Pett Spice Products Inc
Atlanta, GA. 404-691-5235
Phoenix Foods
Canton, TX 903-287-9166
Puratos Canada
Mississauga, ON. 905-362-3668
Rabbit Creek
Louisburg, KS. 800-837-3073
Rill Specialty Foods
Thorp, WA. 509-964-2520
Sambets Cajun Deli
Austin, TX. 800-472-6238
Sassafras Enterprises Inc
Chicago, IL 800-537-4941
Sells Best
Mishawaka, IN 800-837-8368
Smart Flour Foods, LLC
Austin, TX. 512-706-1775
SOUPerior Bean & Spice Company
Vancouver, WA 800-878-7687
Southeastern Mills Inc
Rome, GA. 800-334-4468
Strossner's Bakery & Cafe
Greenville, SC. 864-233-2990
The Lollipop Tree, Inc
Auburn, NY. 800-842-6691
Timber Peaks Gourmet
Parker, CO. 800-982-7687
Valley View Blueberries
Vancouver, WA 360-892-2839

Low Carb

Dixie USA
Tomball, TX 800-233-3668

Breading

Blend Pak Inc
Bloomfield, KY 502-252-8000
Chef Hans' Gourmet Foods
Monroe, LA. 800-890-4267
Dorothy Dawson Food Products
Jackson, MI. 517-788-9830
Griffith Foods Inc.
Alsip, IL 708-371-0900
Newly Weds Foods Inc
Chicago, IL 800-621-7521
Roland Machinery
Springfield, IL. 800-325-1183
Specialty Products
Gloucester, MA. 800-222-6846
Texas Crumb & Food Products
Farmers Branch, TX 800-522-7862

Brownie

BakeMark USA
Schaumburg, IL. 847-519-3135
Cherryvale Farms
. 310-910-1124
Country Cupboard
Lewisburg, PA. 570-523-3211
Dawn Food Products, Inc
Jackson, MI. 800-248-1144
Lehi Mills
Lehi, UT 877-311-3566
No Pudge! Foods
Wolfeboro Falls, NH. 888-667-8343
Pamela's Products
Ukiah, CA 707-462-6605
Rabbit Creek
Louisburg, KS. 800-837-3073
Touche Bakery
London, ON 519-455-0044

Cake

Abel & Schafer Inc
Ronkonkoma, NY. 800-443-1260
Atkinson Milling Co.
Selma, NC. 800-948-5707
BakeMark Ingredients Canada
Richmond, BC 800-665-9441
BakeMark USA
Schaumburg, IL. 847-519-3135
Bear Stewart Corp
Chicago, IL 800-697-2327
Beth's Fine Desserts
Mill Valley, CA. 415-383-3991
Brass Ladle Products
Concordville, PA. 800-955-2353
Brookema Company
West Chicago, IL 630-562-2290
Butternut Mountain Farm
Morrisville, VT. 800-828-2376
Byrd Mill Co
Ashland, VA 888-897-3336
Byrnes & Kiefer Company
Callery, PA 724-538-5200
Chelsea Milling Co.
Chelsea, MI. 800-727-2460
Country Cupboard
Lewisburg, PA. 570-523-3211
Dawn Food Products, Inc
Jackson, MI. 800-248-1144
Dr. Oetker Canada Ltd.
Mississauga, ON. 800-387-6939
Embassy Flavours Ltd.
Brampton, ON. 800-334-3371
Good Food Inc
Honey Brook, PA 800-327-4406
Halladay's Harvest Barn
Bellows Falls, VT. 802-463-3471
Kiki's Gluten-Free
Park Ridge, IL
Kingly Heirs
Elkhart, IN. 574-596-3763
Kodiak Cakes
Park City, UT 801-328-4067
Little Crow Foods
Warsaw, IN 800-288-2769
Louisiana Gourmet Enterprises
Houma, LA 800-328-5586

Martha Olson's Great Foo
Sutter Creek, CA . . . 800-973-3966
Meadowvale Inc
Yorkville, IL . . . 800-953-0201
Northwestern Foods
Arden Hills, MN . . . 800-236-4937
Pillsbury
Minneapolis, MN . . . 800-775-4777
Quality Naturally Foods
City Of Industry, CA . . . 888-498-6986
Royal Resources
New Orleans, LA . . . 800-888-9932
Sells Best
Mishawaka, IN . . . 800-837-8368
Sundial Herb Garden
Higganum, CT . . . 860-345-4290
Tasty Selections
Concord, ON . . . 905-760-2353
Tova Industries LLC
Louisville, KY . . . 888-532-8682
VIP Foods
Flushing, NY . . . 718-821-5330
Wanda's Nature Farm
Lincoln, NE . . . 800-735-6828
West Pac
Idaho Falls, ID . . . 800-973-7407

Cappuccino

Mc Steven's Coca Factory Store
Vancouver, WA . . . 800-547-2803
Mont Blanc Gourmet
Denver, CO . . . 800-877-3811
Utah Coffee Roasters
South Salt Lake, UT . . . 888-486-3334

Chili

Chili Dude
Dallas, TX . . . 214-354-9906
Fernandez Chili Co
Alamosa, CO . . . 719-589-6043
Monterrey Products
San Antonio, TX . . . 210-435-2872
Red Lion Spicy Foods Company
Red Lion, PA . . . 717-309-8303
Texas Heat
San Antonio, TX . . . 800-656-5916
Tova Industries LLC
Louisville, KY . . . 888-532-8682
Westfield Foods
Greenville, RI . . . 401-949-3558

Cocktail

Al-Rite Fruits & Syrups Co
Miami, FL . . . 305-652-2540
Bacardi USA Inc
Coral Gables, FL . . . 800-222-2734
Demitri's Bloody Mary Seasonings
Seattle, WA . . . 800-627-9649
Franco's Cocktail Mixes
Pompano Beach, FL . . . 800-782-4508
Frank & Dean's Cocktail Mixes
Pasadena, CA . . . 626-351-4272
Great Western Juice Co
Maple Heights, OH . . . 800-321-9180
Island Aseptics
Byesville, OH . . . 740-685-2548
LA Paz Products Inc
Brea, CA . . . 714-990-0982
Lemon-X Corporation
Huntington Station, NY . . . 800-220-1061
Leonard Fountain Specialties
Detroit, MI . . . 313-891-4141
Main Squeeze
Columbia, MO . . . 573-817-5616
Natural Fruit Corp
Hialeah, FL . . . 305-887-7525
Ruffner's
Wayne, PA . . . 610-687-9800
Skinny Mixes LLC
Clearwater, FL . . . 727-826-0306
Tree Ripe Products
Whippany, NJ . . . 800-873-3747
Wagner Excello Food Products
Broadview, IL . . . 708-338-4488

Cookie

BakeMark USA
Schaumburg, IL . . . 847-519-3135
Big Dipper Dough Co.
Traverse City, MI . . . 231-883-6035
Cherryvale Farms
. . . 310-910-1124
FatBoy's Cookie Company
Fair Lawn, NJ . . . 888-328-2690
FlapJacked
Westminster, CO . . . 720-476-4758
Jimmys Cookies
Clifton, NJ . . . 973-779-8500
Lehi Mills
Lehi, UT . . . 877-311-3566
Zemas Madhouse Foods Inc.
Highland Park, IL . . . 847-910-4512

Dessert

Abel & Schafer Inc
Ronkonkoma, NY . . . 800-443-1260
All American Seasonings
Denver, CO . . . 303-623-2320
American Key Food Products Inc
Closter, NJ . . . 877-263-7539
Baird Dairy LLC
Clarksville, IN . . . 812-283-3345
Bear Stewart Corp
Chicago, IL . . . 800-697-2327
Blend Pak Inc
Bloomfield, KY . . . 502-252-8000
Brass Ladle Products
Concordville, PA . . . 800-955-2353
Byrd Mill Co
Ashland, VA . . . 888-897-3336
Byrnes & Kiefer Company
Callery, PA . . . 724-538-5200
Calico Cottage
Amityville, NY . . . 800-645-5345
California Custom Fruits
Baldwin Park, CA . . . 877-558-0056
Carolina Foods Inc
Charlotte, NC . . . 800-234-0441
Century Blends LLC
Hunt Valley, MD . . . 410-771-6606
Chelsea Milling Co.
Chelsea, MI . . . 800-727-2460
Clofine Dairy Products Inc
Linwood, NJ . . . 609-653-1000
Creme Curls
Hudsonville, MI . . . 800-466-1219
Dairy-Mix Inc
St Petersburg, FL . . . 800-955-6101
Dutch Ann Foods Company
Natchez, MS . . . 601-445-5566
Embassy Flavours Ltd.
Brampton, ON . . . 800-334-3371
Famous Specialties Co
Island Park, NY . . . 800-894-9218
First Food Co
Dallas, TX . . . 800-527-1866
Galliker Dairy Co
Johnstown, PA . . . 800-477-6455
Galloway Co
Neenah, WI . . . 800-722-8903
Golden Fluff Popcorn Co
Lakewood, NJ . . . 732-367-5448
Great Recipes
Beaverton, OR . . . 800-273-2331
Gumpert's Canada
Mississauga, ON . . . 800-387-9324
Heidi's Gourmet Desserts
Tucker, GA . . . 800-241-4166
Kent Precision Foods Group Inc
Muscatine, IA . . . 800-442-5242
Kosto Food Products Co
Wauconda, IL . . . 847-487-2600
Limpert Bros Inc
Vineland, NJ . . . 800-691-1353
Lloyd's
Exton, PA . . . 610-647-3144
Louisiana Gourmet Enterprises
Houma, LA . . . 800-328-5586
Lynch Foods
North York, ON . . . 416-449-5464
Maple Island
Saint Paul, MN . . . 800-369-1022
Master Mix
Placentia, CA . . . 714-524-1698
Meadowvale Inc
Yorkville, IL . . . 800-953-0201
Mennel Milling Company
Fostoria, OH . . . 800-688-8151
Michigan Desserts
Oak Park, MI . . . 800-328-8632
Nanci's Frozen Yogurt
Mesa, AZ . . . 800-788-0808
Natrel
St. Laurent, QC . . . 800-501-1150
Nature's Hand Inc
Nog Incorporated
Dunkirk, NY . . . 800-332-2664
Northwestern Foods
Arden Hills, MN . . . 800-236-4937
Pasta Factory
Melrose Park, IL . . . 800-615-6951
Paulaur Corp
Cranbury, NJ . . . 609-395-8844
Quality Naturally Foods
City Of Industry, CA . . . 888-498-6986
Rio Syrup Co
St Louis, MO . . . 800-325-7666
S&N Food Company
Mesquite, TX . . . 972-222-1184
Schneider's Dairy Inc
Pittsburgh, PA . . . 412-881-3525
Sells Best
Mishawaka, IN . . . 800-837-8368
Serv-Agen Corporation
Cherry Hill, NJ . . . 856-663-6966
Sno Shack Inc
Rexburg, ID . . . 888-766-7425
Specialty Bakers
Marysville, PA . . . 800-233-0778
SugarCreek
Cincinnati, OH . . . 800-445-2715
Swagger Foods Corp
Vernon Hills, IL . . . 847-913-1200
Timber Peaks Gourmet
Parker, CO . . . 800-982-7687
Tova Industries LLC
Louisville, KY . . . 888-532-8682
Tropical Illusions
Trenton, MO . . . 660-359-5422
VIP Foods
Flushing, NY . . . 718-821-5330
Welch Foods Inc.
Concord, MA . . . 800-340-6870
Wisconsin Wilderness Food Products
Lake Bluff, IL . . . 800 359 3039

Low Carb

Dixie USA
Tomball, TX . . . 800-233-3668

Dip

Advanced Food Products LLC
New Holland, PA . . . 800-732-5373
Amberland Foods
Harvey, ND . . . 800-950-4558
Au Printemps Gourmet
Saint-Jerome, QC . . . 800-438-6676
Big Steer
Houston, TX . . . 800-421-4951
C W Resources Inc
New Britain, CT . . . 860-229-7700
Chugwater Chili
Chugwater, WY . . . 800-972-4454
Country Home Creations Inc
Flint, MI . . . 800-457-3477
Erba Food Products
Brooklyn, NY . . . 718-272-7700
Fountain Valley Foods
Colorado Springs, CO . . . 719-573-6012
Heluva Good Cheese
Lynnfield, MA . . . 800-644-5473
Hollman Foods
Des Moines, IA . . . 888-926-2879
Jodie's Kitchen
Pinellas Park, FL . . . 800-728-3704
Just Delicious Gourmet Foods
Seal Beach, CA . . . 800-871-6085
Lesley Elizabeth Inc
Lapeer, MI . . . 800-684-3300
Limited Edition
Midland, TX . . . 432-686-2008
Olde Tyme Food Corporation
East Longmeadow, MA . . . 800-356-6533
Rabbit Creek
Louisburg, KS . . . 800-837-3073
Spice Hunter Inc
Richmond, VA . . . 800-444-3061
Swagger Foods Corp
Vernon Hills, IL . . . 847-913-1200
The Pantry Club
Clearwater, FL . . . 877-335-8842

Donut

BakeMark USA
Schaumburg, IL.................847-519-3135

Drink

American Instants Inc
Flanders, NJ.................973-584-8811
Bread & Chocolate Inc
Wells River, VT.................800-524-6715
Desert Pepper Trading Co
El Paso, TX.................888-472-5727
Frontera Foods
Chicago, IL.................800-509-4441
Granny Blossom Specialty Foods
Wells, VT.................802-645-0507
Leonard Mountain Inc
Bixby, OK.................800-822-7700
Nature's Hand Inc

Dumplings

Tova Industries LLC
Louisville, KY.................888-532-8682

Frozen

Bama Frozen Dough
Tulsa, OK.................800-756-2262
Best Foods
Englewood Cliffs, NJ.................201-894-4000
Pro Form Labs
Orinda, CA.................707-752-9010

Granita

Nanci's Frozen Yogurt
Mesa, AZ.................800-788-0808

Gravy

Dorothy Dawson Food Products
Jackson, MI.................517-788-9830
Griffith Foods Inc.
Alsip, IL.................708-371-0900
Lawry's Foods
Hunt Valley, MD.................800-952-9797
Morgan Foods Inc
Austin, IN.................888-430-1780
R C Fine Foods Inc
Hillsborough, NJ.................800-526-3953

Hot Chocolate

Mrs. Field's Hot Cocoas
Farmington, UT.................800-845-2400
Utah Coffee Roasters
South Salt Lake, UT.................888-486-3334

Ice Cream

Agri-Dairy Products
Purchase, NY.................914-697-9580
Al-Rite Fruits & Syrups Co
Miami, FL.................305-652-2540
America's Classic Foods
Cambria, CA.................805-927-0745
Baird Dairy LLC
Clarksville, IN.................812-283-3345
Blue Bell Creameries LP
Brenham, TX.................800-327-8135
Clofine Dairy Products Inc
Linwood, NJ.................609-653-1000
Cumberland Dairy
Rosenhayn, NJ.................800-257-8484
Dairy-Mix Inc
St Petersburg, FL.................800-955-6101
Galliker Dairy Co
Johnstown, PA.................800-477-6455
Kosto Food Products Co
Wauconda, IL.................847-487-2600
Leiby's Premium Ice Cream
Tamaqua, PA.................877-453-4297
Master Mix
Placentia, CA.................714-524-1698
Natrel
St. Laurent, QC.................800-501-1150
Nog Incorporated
Dunkirk, NY.................800-332-2664
Quality Naturally Foods
City Of Industry, CA.................888-498-6986
Queensboro Farm Products
Canastota, NY.................315-687-6133
Queensboro Farm Products
Jamica, NY.................718-658-5000
Reiter Dairy LLC
Springfield, OH.................937-323-5777
Schneider's Dairy Inc
Pittsburgh, PA.................412-881-3525
Titusville Dairy Products Co
Titusville, PA.................800-352-0101
Tova Industries LLC
Louisville, KY.................888-532-8682
Vitarich Ice Cream
Fortuna, CA.................707-725-6182

Jambalaya

Reggie Balls Cajun Foods
Lake Charles, LA.................337-436-0291

Liquid

Best Foods
Englewood Cliffs, NJ.................201-894-4000
National Fruit Flavor Co Inc
New Orleans, LA.................800-966-1123
Pro Form Labs
Orinda, CA.................707-752-9010

Muffin

Abel & Schafer Inc
Ronkonkoma, NY.................800-443-1260
Atkinson Milling Co.
Selma, NC.................800-948-5707
Aunt Millie's Bakeries
Fort Wayne, IN.................855-755-2253
Bake N Joy Foods
North Andover, MA.................800-666-4937
Dr. Oetker Canada Ltd.
Mississauga, ON.................800-387-6939
EFCO Products Inc
Poughkeepsie, NY.................800-284-3326
Fiera Foods
Toronto, ON.................800-675-6356
FlapJacked
Westminster, CO.................720-476-4758
Food Concentrate Corporation
Oklahoma City, OK.................405-840-5633
Grain Process Enterprises Ltd.
Scarborough, ON.................800-387-5292
Gust John Foods & Products
Batavia, IL.................800-756-5886
Hodgson Mill Inc
Effingham, IL.................800-347-0198
Iveta Gourmet Inc
Santa Cruz, CA.................831-423-5149
J.M. Smucker Co.
Orrville, OH.................888-550-9555
Kodiak Cakes
Park City, UT.................801-328-4067
Kokopelli's Kitchen
Phoenix, AZ.................888-943-9802
Marie Callender's
Mission Viejo, CA.................800-776-7437
Mennel Milling Company
Fostoria, OH.................800-688-8151
Pemberton's Foods Inc
Gray, ME.................800-255-8401
Rill Specialty Foods
Thorp, WA.................509-964-2520
Sells Best
Mishawaka, IN.................800-837-8368
Shepherdsfield Bakery
Fulton, MO.................573-642-0009
Sorrenti Family Farms
Escalon, CA.................888-435-9490

Pancake

Atkinson Milling Co.
Selma, NC.................800-948-5707
Bette's Oceanview Diner
Berkeley, CA.................510-644-3230
Birch Benders
Denver, CO.................855-572-6225
Blackberry Patch
Thomasville, GA.................800-853-5598
Bob's Red Mill Natural Foods
Milwaukie, OR.................800-349-2173
Byrd Mill Co
Ashland, VA.................888-897-3336
Casually Gourmet
New Haven, VT.................800-639-7604
Cereal Food Processors Inc
Mcpherson, KS.................800-835-2067
CHS Sunprairie
Minot, ND.................800-556-6807
Country Cupboard
Lewisburg, PA.................570-523-3211
Cream Of The West
Harlowton, MT.................800-477-2383
D & D Sugarwoods Farm
Glover, VT.................800-245-3718
FlapJacked
Westminster, CO.................720-476-4758
Golden Malted
South Bend, IN.................888-596-4040
Greenfield Mills
North Howe, IN.................260-367-2394
Gust John Foods & Products
Batavia, IL.................800-756-5886
Heartland Food Products
Westwood, KS.................866-571-0222
Highland Sugarworks
Websterville, VT.................800-452-4012
Hodgson Mill Inc
Effingham, IL.................800-347-0198
Homestead Mills
Cook, MN.................800-652-5233
Inn Maid Food
Lenox, MA.................413-637-2732
J.M. Smucker Co.
Orrville, OH.................888-550-9555
Kamish Food Products
Chicago, IL.................773-725-6959
Kodiak Cakes
Park City, UT.................801-328-4067
Kokopelli's Kitchen
Phoenix, AZ.................888-943-9802
Lehi Mills
Lehi, UT.................877-311-3566
Little Crow Foods
Warsaw, IN.................800-288-2769
Maple Grove Farms Of Vermont
St Johnsbury, VT.................802-748-5141
Mennel Milling Company
Fostoria, OH.................800-688-8151
Minnestalgia Foods LLC
Mcgregor, MN.................800-328-6731
Nature's Path Foods
Blaine, WA.................888-808-9505
North Coast Farms
Santa Cruz, CA.................831-426-3733
Northwestern Foods
Arden Hills, MN.................800-236-4937
Old Tyme Mill Company
Chicago, IL.................773-521-9484
Pemberton's Foods Inc
Gray, ME.................800-255-8401
Reimann Food Classics
Palatine, IL.................847-991-1366
SFP Food Products
Conway, AR.................800-654-5329
Smart Flour Foods, LLC
Austin, TX.................512-706-1775
Sweetstacks LLC
San Diego, CA.................619-997-1097
Tait Farm Foods
Centre Hall, PA.................800-787-2716
Turkey Hill Sugarbush
Waterloo, QC.................450-539-4822
Valley View Blueberries
Vancouver, WA.................360-892-2839
Weisenberger Mills
Midway, KY.................800-643-8678

Pie Crust

Country Cupboard
Lewisburg, PA.................570-523-3211
Smart Flour Foods, LLC
Austin, TX.................512-706-1775

Powdered

1-2-3 Gluten Free
Chagrin Falls, OH.................216-378-9233
Crystal Star Herbal Nutrition
Salinas, CA.................831-422-7500
Northwestern Foods
Arden Hills, MN.................800-236-4937
Pro Form Labs
Orinda, CA.................707-752-9010

Punch

Four Percent Company
Highland Park, MI.................313-345-5880
Quality Naturally Foods
City Of Industry, CA.................888-498-6986

Tova Industries LLC
Louisville, KY 888-532-8682

Rice

Manischewitz Co
Newark, NJ 201-553-1100

Shoofly

Good Food Inc
Honey Brook, PA 800-327-4406

Smoothie Powder

Farmers Way
Monin Inc.
Clearwater, FL 855-352-8671
Nanci's Frozen Yogurt
Mesa, AZ 800-788-0808

Soup

Amalgamated Produce
Bridgeport, CT 800-358-3808
Amberland Foods
Harvey, ND 800-950-4558
Bernard Food Industries Inc
Evanston, IL 800-323-3663
Best Foods
Englewood Cliffs, NJ 201-894-4000
Bob's Red Mill Natural Foods
Milwaukie, OR 800-349-2173
Boston Spice & Tea Company
Boston, VA 800-966-4372
Bountiful Pantry
Nantucket, MA 617-487-8019
Brookema Company
West Chicago, IL 630-562-2290
Campbell Soup Co.
Camden, NJ 800-257-8443
Commodities Marketing Inc
Clarksburg, NJ 732-516-0700
Cook-In-The-Kitchen
Hampden, ME 207 848 4900
Country Home Creations Inc
Flint, MI 800-457-3477
Crazy Jerrys Inc Kahuna-Sauces
Woodstock, GA 800-347-2823
Diamond Crystal Brands Inc
Savannah, GA 800-654-5115
Dismat Corporation
Toledo, OH 419-531-8963
Dorothy Dawson Food Products
Jackson, MI 517-788-9830
Edward & Sons Trading Co
Carpinteria, CA 805-684-8500
Fair Scones
Medina, WA 800-588-9160
Flavor House, Inc.
Adelanto, CA 760-246-9131
Halladay's Harvest Barn
Bellows Falls, VT 802-463-3471
High Country Gourmet
Orem, UT 801-426-4383
Hummingbird Kitchens
Whitehouse, TX 800-921-9470
Idaho Pacific Holdings Inc
Rigby, ID 800-238-5503
Kemach Food Products
Brooklyn, NY 718-272-5655
Kent Precision Foods Group Inc
Muscatine, IA 800-442-5242
Lake City Foods
Mississauga, ON 905-625-8244
Lynch Foods
North York, ON 416-449-5464
Magic Seasoning Blends
New Orleans, LA 800-457-2857
Nor-Cliff Farms
Port Colborne, ON 905-835-0808
North Bay Trading Co
Brule, WI 800-348-0164
R C Fine Foods Inc
Hillsborough, NJ 800-526-3953
Rabbit Creek
Louisburg, KS 800-837-3073
Rill Specialty Foods
Thorp, WA 509-964-2520
Sheila's Select Gourmet Recipe
Heber City, UT 800-516-7286
Sorrenti Family Farms
Escalon, CA 888-435-9490
Spice Hunter Inc
Richmond, VA 800-444-3061
Swagger Foods Corp
Vernon Hills, IL 847-913-1200
Tova Industries LLC
Louisville, KY 888-532-8682
Tropical Nut Fruit & Bulk Cndy
Lithia Springs, GA 800-544-3762
Vogue Cuisine Foods
Sunnyvale, CA 888-236-4144
Westfield Foods
Greenville, RI 401-949-3558
White Coffee Corporation
Long Island City, NY 800-221-0140

Trail

Aurora Products
Orange, CT 800-398-1048
Bazzini Holdings LLC
Allentown, PA 610-366-1606
Chukar Cherries
Prosser, WA 800-624-9544
Dave's Gourmet
San Rafael, CA 800-758-0372
Durey-Libby Edible Nuts
Carlstadt, NJ 800-332-6887
Hialeah Products Co
Hollywood, FL 800-923-3379
Inn Maid Food
Lenox, MA 413-637-2732
Jason & Son Specialty Foods
Rancho Cordova, CA 800-810-9093
King Nut Co
Solon, OH 800-860-5464
Marantha Natural Foods
San Francisco, CA 866-972-6879
Midwest Nut Co
Minneapolis, MN 800-328-5502
Nature Kist Snacks
Commerce, CA 323-278-9578
New England Natural Bakers
Greenfield, MA 800-910-2884
Nspired Natural Foods
Boulder, CO 800-434-4246
Nut Factory
Spokane Valley, WA 888-239-5288
Sonne
Wahpeton, ND 800-727-6663
Sunridge Farms
Royal Oaks, CA 831-786-7000
Superior Nut & Candy
Chicago, IL 800-843-2238
Timber Peaks Gourmet
Parker, CO 800-982-7687
Tova Industries LLC
Louisville, KY 888-532-8682
Tropical Foods
Charlotte, NC 800-438-4470
Valley View Blueberries
Vancouver, WA 360-892-2839
Waymouth Farms Inc
Minneapolis, MN 800-527-0094
Weaver Nut Co. Inc.
Ephrata, PA 800-473-2688
Wysong Corp
Midland, MI 800-748-0188

Waffle

Bountiful Pantry
Nantucket, MA 617-487-8019
Byrd Mill Co
Ashland, VA 888-897-3336
Cereal Food Processors Inc
Mcpherson, KS 800-835-2067
Country Cupboard
Lewisburg, PA 570-523-3211
Cream Of The West
Harlowton, MT 800-477-2383
Eat My Waffles
Cardiff By The Sea, CA
Golden Malted
South Bend, IN 888-596-4040
Great Grains Milling Company
Scobey, MT 406-783-5581
Gust John Foods & Products
Batavia, IL 800-756-5886
Heartland Food Products
Westwood, KS 866-571-0222
Inn Maid Food
Lenox, MA 413-637-2732
J.M. Smucker Co.
Orrville, OH 888-550-9555
Kamish Food Products
Chicago, IL 773-725-6959
Kodiak Cakes
Park City, UT 801-328-4067
Maple Grove Farms Of Vermont
St Johnsbury, VT 802-748-5141
Mennel Milling Company
Fostoria, OH 800-688-8151
North Coast Farms
Santa Cruz, CA 831-426-3733
Old Tyme Mill Company
Chicago, IL 773-521-9484
Reimann Food Classics
Palatine, IL 847-991-1366
SFP Food Products
Conway, AR 800-654-5329
Smart Flour Foods, LLC
Austin, TX 512-706-1775
WaffleWaffle
Nutley, NJ 201-559-1286

Yogurt Powder

Kantner Group
Wapakoneta, OH 877-738-3448

Eggs & Egg Products

General

Almark Foods
Gainesville, GA 800-849-3447
Alta Dena Certified Dairy LLC
City Of Industry, CA. 800-535-1369
Bartolini Ice Cream
Bronx, NY. 718-589-5151
Brookshire Grocery Company
Tyler, TX. 888-937-3776
Brown Produce Company
Farina, IL. 618-245-3301
Burn Brae Farms
Mississauga, ON. 905-624-3600
Cal-Maine Foods Inc.
Jackson, MS 601-948-6813
Cargill Kitchen Solutions Inc.
Wayzata, MN 833-535-5205
Cordon Bleu International
Anjou, QC. 800-363-1182
Creighton Brothers
Warsaw, IN 574-267-3101
Crystal Lake LLC
Warsaw, IN 574-858-2514
Davidson's Safest Choice Eggs
Lansing, IL 800-410-7619
Debel Food Products
Elizabeth, NJ. 800-421-3447
Dutch Farms Inc
Chicago, IL. 800-637-3447
Eggland's Best Eggs
Malvern, PA 800-922-3447
Farbest-Tallman Foods Corp
Montvale, NJ. 201-573-4900
Golden Valley Foods Ltd.
Abbotsford, BC. 888-299-8855
Henningsen Foods Inc
Omaha, NE 800-228-2769
Hidden Villa Ranch
Fullerton, CA 800-326-3220
Hillandale
Lake City, FL 386-397-1300
Hormel Foods Corp.
Austin, MN. 507-437-5611
Ingles Markets
Black Mountain, NC. 828-669-2941
J M Swank Co
North Liberty, IA 800-593-6375
Kreher Family Farms
Clarence, NY. 716-759-6802
Lubbers Family Farm
Grand Rapids, MI 616-453-4257
Meijer Inc
Grand Rapids, MI 616-453-6711
MFI Food Canada
Winnipeg, MB. 204-992-8200
National Food Corporation
Everett, WA. 425-349-4257
NestFresh
Denver, CO 877-241-8385
Nulaid Foods Inc
Ripon, CA. 209-599-2121
Oliver Egg Products
Crewe, VA. 800-525-3447
Publix Super Market
Lakeland, FL. 800-242-1227
Rembrandt Foods
Spirit Lake, IA 877-344-4055
Rose Acre Farms
Wolcott, IN 765-258-4015
Rosenberger's Dairies
Hatfield, PA. 800-355-9074
Sauder's Eggs
Lititz, PA 800-233-0413
Smith Packing Regional Meat
Utica, NY 315-732-5125
T. Marzetti Company
Westerville, OH. 800-999-1835
Turner Dairy Farms Inc
Pittsburgh, PA. 800-892-1039
Vital Farms
Austin, TX. 877-455-3063
Wegmans Food Markets Inc.
Rochester, NY. 800-934-6267
WEIS Markets Inc.
Sunbury, PA. 866-999-9347
Wenk Foods Inc
Madison, SD 605-256-4569
WhiteWave Foods
Denver, CO 800-488-9283
Wilcox Farms
Roy, WA 360-458-7774
Winn-Dixie Stores
Jacksonville, FL 800-967-9105
Yoder Dairies
Chesapeake, VA 757-482-4068

Boiled

Agri-Dairy Products
Purchase, NY 914-697-9580

Cooked

Cargill Kitchen Solutions Inc.
Wayzata, MN 833-535-5205
Crystal Lake LLC
Warsaw, IN 574-858-2514
Egg Low Farms
Sherburne, NY 607-674-4653

Dehydrated

Ballas Egg Products Corp
Zanesville, OH 740-453-0386
Oskaloosa Food Products
Oskaloosa, IA 800-477-7239

Dried

Ballas Egg Products Corp
Zanesville, OH 740-453-0386
Century Blends LLC
Hunt Valley, MD. 410-771-6606
Double B Foods Inc
Arlington, TX 800-679-0349
Henningsen Foods Inc
Omaha, NE 800-228-2769
Kelly Flour Company
Addison, IL 630-678-5300
King Arthur Flour
Norwich, VT. 800-827-6836
MFI Food Canada
Winnipeg, MB. 204-992-8200
Oskaloosa Food Products
Oskaloosa, IA 800-477-7239
Wenk Foods Inc
Madison, SD 605-256-4569

Desiccated

Agri-Dairy Products
Purchase, NY 914-697-9580
Clofine Dairy Products Inc
Linwood, NJ 609-653-1000
New Organics
Kenwood, CA 734-677-5570

Fat & Cholesterol Free

Cargill Kitchen Solutions Inc.
Wayzata, MN 833-535-5205
Hormel Foods Corp.
Austin, MN. 507-437-5611
Tofutti Brands Inc
Cranford, NJ 908-272-2400

Fresh

Agri-Dairy Products
Purchase, NY 914-697-9580
Broughton Foods LLC
El Paso, TX. 800-395-7004
Byrne Dairy, Inc.
Syracuse, NY 800-899-1535
Creighton Brothers
Warsaw, IN 574-267-3101
Davidson's Safest Choice Eggs
Lansing, IL 800-410-7619
Dixie Egg Co
Jacksonville, FL 800-394-3447
Egg Innovations
Warsaw, IN 800-337-1951
Egg Low Farms
Sherburne, NY 607-674-4653
Feature Foods
Brampton, ON. 905-452-7741
Golden Valley Foods Ltd.
Abbotsford, BC. 888-299-8855
Great Valley Mills
Barto, PA. 800-688-6455
Happy Egg Dealers
Tampa, FL. 813-248-2362
Horizon Organic Dairy
Broomfield, CO 888-494-3020
Ise America Inc
Galena, MD. 410-755-6300
Mountainside Farms Inc
Roxbury, NY. 607-326-4161
National Food Corporation
Everett, WA. 425-349-4257
Oskaloosa Food Products
Oskaloosa, IA 800-477-7239
Pete and Gerry's Organic Eggs
Monroe, NH 800-210-6657
Radlo Foods
Watertown, MA. 800-370-1439
Rose Acre Farms Inc
Seymour, IN 800-356-3447
Schepps Dairy
Dallas, TX. 800-395-7004
Siegel Egg Co
North Billerica, MA 978-528-2010
Sommer Maid Creamery Inc
Pipersville, PA. 215-345-6160
Sparboe Foods Corp
New Hampton, IA. 641-394-3040
Sunny Fresh Foods
Monticello, MN 800-872-3447
Suter Co Inc
Sycamore, IL. 800-435-6942

Frozen

Agri-Dairy Products
Purchase, NY 914-697-9580
Almark Foods
Gainesville, GA 800-849-3447
Ballas Egg Products Corp
Zanesville, OH 740-453-0386
Brown Produce Company
Farina, IL. 618-245-3301
Cargill Kitchen Solutions Inc.
Wayzata, MN 833-535-5205
Century Blends LLC
Hunt Valley, MD. 410-771-6606
Creighton Brothers
Warsaw, IN 574-267-3101
Crystal Lake LLC
Warsaw, IN 574-858-2514
Dixie Egg Co
Jacksonville, FL 800-394-3447
Global Egg Corporation
Toronto, ON 416-231-2309
Great Valley Mills
Barto, PA. 800-688-6455
Ise America Inc
Galena, MD. 410-755-6300
Kent Foods Inc
Gonzales, TX 830-672-7993
Land O'Lakes Inc
Arden Hills, MN. 800-328-9680
McAnally Enterprises
Lakeview, CA 800-726-2002
MFI Food Canada
Winnipeg, MB. 204-992-8200
Michael Foods, Inc.
Minnetonka, MN. 952-258-4000
Oliver Egg Products
Crewe, VA. 800-525-3447
Oskaloosa Food Products
Oskaloosa, IA 800-477-7239
Siegel Egg Co
North Billerica, MA 978-528-2010
Sparboe Foods Corp
New Hampton, IA. 641-394-3040
Wenk Foods Inc
Madison, SD 605-256-4569

Hard-Boiled

Almark Foods
Gainesville, GA 800-849-3447
Cargill Kitchen Solutions Inc.
Wayzata, MN 833-535-5205
Creighton Brothers
Warsaw, IN 574-267-3101
Dixie Egg Co
Jacksonville, FL 800-394-3447
Eggland's Best Eggs
Malvern, PA 800-922-3447
Feature Foods
Brampton, ON.................. 905-452-7741
Ise America Inc
Galena, MD.................. 410-755-6300
Pete and Gerry's Organic Eggs
Monroe, NH 800-210-6657
Radlo Foods
Watertown, MA.................. 800-370-1439
Sunny Fresh Foods
Monticello, MN 800-872-3447
Suter Co Inc
Sycamore, IL.................. 800-435-6942

Hatcheries

Amick Farms LLC
Batesburg, SC.................. 800-926-4257
Hickory Baked Ham Co
Castle Rock, CO 303-688-2633
Norfolk Hatchery
Norfolk, NE.................. 800-345-2449

Chicks

Turkey

Hickory Baked Ham Co
Castle Rock, CO 303-688-2633

Liquid

Ballas Egg Products Corp
Zanesville, OH 740-453-0386
Brown Produce Company
Farina, IL.................. 618-245-3301
Cargill Kitchen Solutions Inc.
Wayzata, MN 833-535-5205
Crystal Lake LLC
Warsaw, IN 574-858-2514
Eggology
Canoga Park, CA 818-610-2222
Global Egg Corporation
Toronto, ON 416-231-2309
Golden Valley Foods Ltd.
Abbotsford, BC.................. 888-299-8855
Kent Foods Inc
Gonzales, TX 830-672-7993
McAnally Enterprises
Lakeview, CA.................. 800-726-2002
MFI Food Canada
Winnipeg, MB.................. 204-992-8200
Michael Foods, Inc.
Minnetonka, MN.................. 952-258-4000
National Food Corporation
Everett, WA.................. 425-349-4257
Nulaid Foods Inc
Ripon, CA.................. 209-599-2121
Oskaloosa Food Products
Oskaloosa, IA 800-477-7239
Primer Foods Corporation
Cameron, WI.................. 800-365-2409
Sunny Fresh Foods
Monticello, MN 800-872-3447
Wilcox Farms
Roy, WA 360-458-7774

Whites

Eggland's Best Eggs
Malvern, PA 800-922-3447
Eggology
Canoga Park, CA 818-610-2222
Golden Valley Foods Ltd.
Abbotsford, BC.................. 888-299-8855
Horizon Organic Dairy
Broomfield, CO 888-494-3020
MFI Food Canada
Winnipeg, MB.................. 204-992-8200
Michael Foods, Inc.
Minnetonka, MN.................. 952-258-4000
National Food Corporation
Everett, WA.................. 425-349-4257
Pete and Gerry's Organic Eggs
Monroe, NH 800-210-6657
WhiteWave Foods
Denver, CO 800-488-9283

Whole

Golden Valley Foods Ltd.
Abbotsford, BC.................. 888-299-8855
Michael Foods, Inc.
Minnetonka, MN.................. 952-258-4000
National Food Corporation
Everett, WA.................. 425-349-4257

Yolk

Golden Valley Foods Ltd.
Abbotsford, BC.................. 888-299-8855
Michael Foods, Inc.
Minnetonka, MN.................. 952-258-4000
National Food Corporation
Everett, WA.................. 425-349-4257

Low-Cholesterol

Cargill Kitchen Solutions Inc.
Wayzata, MN 833-535-5205

Mix

Cargill Kitchen Solutions Inc.
Wayzata, MN 833-535-5205
National Food Corporation
Everett, WA.................. 425-349-4257
Oliver Egg Products
Crewe, VA.................. 800-525-3447
Primer Foods Corporation
Cameron, WI.................. 800-365-2409
Sunny Fresh Foods
Monticello, MN 800-872-3447

Peeled

Agri-Dairy Products
Purchase, NY 914-697-9580
Dixie Egg Co
Jacksonville, FL 800-394-3447
Eggland's Best Eggs
Malvern, PA 800-922-3447
Feature Foods
Brampton, ON.................. 905-452-7741
Great Valley Mills
Barto, PA.................. 800-688-6455
Ise America Inc
Galena, MD.................. 410-755-6300
MFI Food Canada
Winnipeg, MB.................. 204-992-8200

Prepared

Agri-Dairy Products
Purchase, NY 914-697-9580
Almark Foods
Gainesville, GA 800-849-3447
Cargill Kitchen Solutions Inc.
Wayzata, MN 833-535-5205
Clofine Dairy Products Inc
Linwood, NJ 609-653-1000
Eggland's Best Eggs
Malvern, PA 800-922-3447
Primer Foods Corporation
Cameron, WI.................. 800-365-2409

Quail

Squab Producers of California
Modesto, CA.................. 209-537-4744

Solids

Albumen

Brown Produce Company
Farina, IL.................. 618-245-3301
Holton Food Products
La Grange, IL 708-352-5599
Wabash Valley Produce Inc
Dubois, IN.................. 812-678-3131

Whole Egg

Oliver Egg Products
Crewe, VA.................. 800-525-3447
Primer Foods Corporation
Cameron, WI.................. 800-365-2409

Fortified

Cargill Kitchen Solutions Inc.
Wayzata, MN 833-535-5205

Substitutes

Bay Valley Foods
El Paso, TX.................. 800-236-1119
Cargill Kitchen Solutions Inc.
Wayzata, MN 833-535-5205
JUST Inc
San Francisco, CA 844-423-6637
Michael Foods, Inc.
Minnetonka, MN.................. 952-258-4000

Frozen

Cargill Kitchen Solutions Inc.
Wayzata, MN 833-535-5205
Clofine Dairy Products Inc
Linwood, NJ 609-653-1000

Refrigerated

Cargill Kitchen Solutions Inc.
Wayzata, MN 833-535-5205
Clofine Dairy Products Inc
Linwood, NJ 609-653-1000
Michael Foods, Inc.
Minnetonka, MN.................. 952-258-4000

Yolk

Clofine Dairy Products Inc
Linwood, NJ 609-653-1000
Global Egg Corporation
Toronto, ON 416-231-2309
MFI Food Canada
Winnipeg, MB.................. 204-992-8200
Michael Foods, Inc.
Minnetonka, MN.................. 952-258-4000
National Food Corporation
Everett, WA.................. 425-349-4257
Norac Technologies
Edmonton, AB 780-414-9595
Wabash Valley Produce Inc
Dubois, IN.................. 812-678-3131

Ethnic Foods

General

Afia Foods
Austin, TX. 512-698-8448
Amy's Kitchen Inc
Santa Rosa, CA. 707-781-6600
Ayara Products
Los Angeles, CA. 310-410-8848
Bayou Crab
Grand Bay, AL 251-824-2076
Blansh International
Turlock, CA 209-250-1237
Blue Marble Brands
Providence, RI 888-534-0246
British Aisles, LTD.
Nashua, NH. 800-520-8565
Bruce Foods Corporation
Lafayette, LA 800-299-9082
Burke Corp
Nevada, IA 800-654-1152
C&J Trading
San Francisco, CA 415-822-8910
Calidad Foods
Grand Prairie, TX 214-521-7999
Casablanca Market
Newark, CA 650-964-3000
Chong Mei Trading
East Point, GA 404-768-3838
CJ Omni
South Gate, CA. 323-567-8171
Cocina De Mino
Oklahoma City, OK 405-632-1036
Corfu Foods Inc
Bensenville, IL 800-874-9767
Deluxe Delight
Lost Angeles, CA 424-230-3664
Discovery Foods
Hayward, CA 510-780-9238
Don Jose Foods
Scottsdale, AZ. 480-443-1000
El Perico Charro
Garden City, KS 620-275-6454
Elena's Food Specialties
S San Francisco, CA. 800-376-5368
Ethnic Gourmet Foods
Boulder, CO 800-434-4246
Falafel Republic
Needham Heights, MA 781-878-6027
Frontera Foods
Chicago, IL. 800-509-4441
Gharana Foods
Edison, NJ. 732-985-9331
Goldilocks USA
Hayward, CA 510-476-0700
Gringo Jack's
Manchester Ctr, VT 802-362-0836
H & W Foods
Kapolei, HI 808-682-8300
Hong Kong Supermarket
Norcross, GA 770-582-6800
Houston Calco, Inc
Houston, TX 713-236-8668
India's Rasoi
St Louis, MO. 314-361-6911
JaynRoss Creations LLC
Whitmore Lake, MI 734-657-5852
Juanita's Foods
Wilmington, CA 800-303-2965
Kyong Hae Kim Company
Honolulu, HI. 808-926-8720
LA Mexicana Tortilla
Seattle, WA 206-763-1488
M&M Food Distributors/Oriental Pride
Virginia Beach, VA. 757-499-5676
Manischewitz Co
Newark, NJ 201-553-1100
Maria & Son
St Louis, MO. 866-481-9009
Marjie's Plantain Foods, Inc.
New York, NY 908-627-5627
Marukai Market
Gardena, CA 310-660-6300
Marukan Vinegar USA Inc.
Paramount, CA 562-630-6060
Marukome USA Inc.
Irvine, CA 949-863-0110
Maya Kaimal
Rhinebeck, NY 845-876-8200
Mayakaimal Fine Indian Foods
Rhinebeck, NY 845-876-8200
Mercado Latino
City Of Industry, CA. 800-432-7266
Mishrun
Edison, NJ. 347-495-4320
Mission Foods Corp.
Irving, TX 214-583-5113
Monsoon Kitchens
Shrewsbury, MA. 508-842-0070
Morii Foods, Inc.
Tualatin, OR 503-691-7007
My Own Meals Inc
Deerfield, IL 847-948-1118
National Importers
Richmond, BC 888-894-6464
Natural Quick Foods
Seattle, WA. 206-365-5757
Oriental Foods
Alhambra, CA. 626-293-1994
Preferred Brands Inc
Stamford, CT. 800-827-8900
Rancho Sierra
Salinas, CA 800-398-2929
Rico Foods Inc
Paterson, NJ 973-278-0589
Rokeach Food Corp
Newark, NJ. 973-589-1472
Rothman's Food Inc
St Louis, MO. 314-367-5448
Salonika Imports Inc
Pittsburgh, PA 800-794-2256
Sanchez Distributors
San Antonio, TX. 210-341-1682
Santini Foods
San Lorenzo, CA. 800-835-6888
Shell Ridge Jalapeno Project
Rockport, TX 512-790-8028
Snapdragon Foods
Oakland, CA 877-881-7627
Squair Food Company
Los Angeles, CA. 213-749-7041
Steve Mendez
Woodland, CA. 530-662-0512
Sukhi's Gourmet Indian Food
Hayward, CA 888-478-5447
Sun Sun Food Products
Edmonton, AB 780-454-4261
T. Marzetti Company
Westerville, OH. 800-999-1835
Taj Gourmet Foods
Boulder, CO 800-434-4246
Tamashiro Market Inc
Honolulu, HI. 808-841-8047
Taqueria El Milagro
Chicago, IL. 773-579-2410
Tekita House Foods
El Paso, TX. 915-779-2181
Tropical Cheese
Perth Amboy, NJ. 888-874-4928
Universal Impex Corporation
Toronto, ON 416-743-7778
VIP Sales Company
Hayward, CA 866-536-8008
Wing Seafood Company
Chicago, IL. 312-421-8686
Wing Sing Chong Company
S San Francisco, CA. 415-552-1234
Wong Wing
Florenceville-Bristol, NB 866-622-2461
Y.M.C. Corp.
Chicago, IL. 312-842-4900
Yamasho Inc
Elk Grove Village, IL 847-981-9342
Ying Leong Look Funn Factory
Honolulu, HI. 808-537-4304
Zippy's Inc
Honolulu, HI. 808-973-0880

Asian

99 Ranch Market
Hacienda Heights, CA 626-839-2899
Ajinomoto Foods North America, Inc.
Ontario, CA. 909-477-4700
Ajinomoto Frozen Foods USA, Inc.
Ontario, CA. 866-536-8008
Amy Food Inc
Houston, TX 713-910-5860
Asian Foods Inc
St Paul, MN. 651-558-2400
Chungs Gourmet Foods
Houston, TX 713-741-2118
CJ Foods
La Palma, CA 714-367-7200
CJ Omni
South Gate, CA. 323-567-8171
Discovery Foods
Hayward, CA 510-780-9238
Feel Good Foods
Brooklyn, NY 800-638-8949
House of Tsang
San Francisco, CA 415-282-9952
JMAC Trading, Inc.
Torrance, CA. 877-566-4569
Kahiki Foods Inc
Columbus, OH 855-524-4540
Lucky Foods
Tualatin, OR 503-612-1300
McCormick & Company
Hunt Valley, MD. 410-527-6189
Naughty Noah's
La Jolla, CA
San-J International Inc
Henrico, VA 800-446-5500
Sempio Foods
Cerritos, CA 562-207-9540
Snapdragon Foods
Oakland, CA 877-881-7627
Star Anise Foods
San Francisco, CA
Suji's Korean Cuisine
Seattle, WA 206-985-6640
Superior Foods
Watsonville, CA 831-728-3691
We Rub You
Brooklyn, NY 718-387-9797
Yai's Thai
Denver, CO
Ying's Kitchen
Lake Villa, IL 847-403-7078

Burritos

Baja Foods LLC
Chicago, IL. 773-376-9030
Bakkavor USA
Charlotte, NC 800-842-3025
Camino Real Foods Inc
Vernon, CA 800-421-6201
Cedarlane Foods
Carson, CA 800-826-3322
Elena's Food Specialties
S San Francisco, CA. 800-376-5368
La Tang Cuisine Manufacturing
Houston, TX 713-780-4876
Manuel's Odessa Tortilla
Odessa, TX 800-753-2445
Mexi-Frost Specialties Company
Brooklyn, NY 718-625-3324
Pepe's Mexican Restaurant
Anaheim, CA 714-952-9410
Queen International Foods
Monterey Park, CA. 800-423-4414
Ramona's Mexican Foods
Gardena, CA 310-323-1950
Ruiz Food Products Inc.
Dinuba, CA. 800-477-6474
Supreme Frozen Products
Chicago, IL. 773-622-3777
Sweet Earth Foods
Moss Landing, CA 800-737-3311
The Food Collective
Irvine, CA. 866-328-8638

Chinese

Amy Food Inc
Houston, TX. 713-910-5860
Asian Foods Inc
St Paul, MN. 651-558-2400

First Oriental Market
Decatur, GA 404-377-6950
Hong Kong Supermarket
Norcross, GA 770-582-6800
La Choy
Chicago, IL 312-549-5000
National Importers
Richmond, BC 888-894-6464
P & S Food & Liquor
Chicago, IL 773-685-0088
Wei-Chuan USA Inc
Bell Gardens, CA 562-372-2020
Wong Wing
Florenceville-Bristol, NB 866-622-2461

Chop Suey

Canned

Young's Noodle Factory Inc
Honolulu, HI 808-533-6478

Frozen

Nanka Seimen Company
Vernon, CA 323-585-9967

Chow Chow

Golding Farms Foods
Winston Salem, NC 336-766-6161
Lancaster Packing Company
Myerstown, PA 717-397-9727
United Pickles
Bronx, NY 718-933-6060

Chow Mein

C&J Trading
San Francisco, CA 415-822-8910
Willow Foods
Beaverton, OR 800-338-3609
Y.M.C. Corp.
Chicago, IL 312-842-4900

Couscous

Bob's Red Mill Natural Foods
Milwaukie, OR 800-349-2173
Hodgson Mill Inc
Effingham, IL 800-347-0198
Lundberg Family Farms
Richvale, CA 530-538-3500
Organic Planet
San Francisco, CA 415-765-5590
Setton International Foods
Commack, NY 800-227-4397

Dim Sum

Calco of Calgary
Calgary, AB 403-295-3578
Fine Choice Foods
Richmond, BC 866-760-0888
Shine Foods Inc
Torrance, CA 310-533-6010

Egg Rolls

Amy Food Inc
Houston, TX 713-910-5860
Asian Foods Inc
St Paul, MN 651-558-2400
Cathay Foods Corporation
Boston, MA 617-427-1507
Chang Food Company
Garden Grove, CA 714-265-9990
Chinese Spaghetti Factory
Boston, MA 617-445-7714
Chungs Gourmet Foods
Houston, TX 713-741-2118
Dong Kee Company
Chicago, IL 312-225-6340
Egg Roll Fantasy
Auburn, CA 530-887-9197
Fine Choice Foods
Richmond, BC 866-760-0888
Frozen Specialties Inc
Perrysburg, OH 419-867-2005
Harvest Food Products Co Inc
Hayward, CA 510-675-0383
Health is Wealth Foods
Moonachie, NJ 201-933-7474
Kubla Khan Food Company
Portland, OR 503-234-7494
La Tang Cuisine Manufacturing
Houston, TX 713-780-4876
Mexi-Frost Specialties Company
Brooklyn, NY 718-625-3324
Nanka Seimen Company
Vernon, CA 323-585-9967
Passport Food Group
Ontario, CA 310-463-0954
Peking Noodle Co Inc
Los Angeles, CA 323-223-0897
Prime Food Processing Corp
Brooklyn, NY 718-963-2323
Shine Foods Inc
Torrance, CA 310-533-6010
Spring Kitchen
Houston, TX 713-222-0598
Valdez Food Inc
Philadelphia, PA 215-634-6106
Wei-Chuan USA Inc
Bell Gardens, CA 562-372-2020
Willow Foods
Beaverton, OR 800-338-3609
Wong Wing
Florenceville-Bristol, NB 866-622-2461
Wonton Food
Brooklyn, NY 800-776-8889

Spring Rolls

Calco of Calgary
Calgary, AB 403-295-3578
Chang Food Company
Garden Grove, CA 714-265-9990
Chungs Gourmet Foods
Houston, TX 713-741-2118
Clarmil Manufacturing Corp
Hayward, CA 888-252-7645
Health is Wealth Foods
Moonachie, NJ 201-933-7474
Spring Kitchen
Houston, TX 713-222-0598
Willow Foods
Beaverton, OR 800-338-3609

Wrappers

Delta Food Products
Edmonton, AB 780-424-3636
International Noodle Co
Madison Heights, MI 248-583-2479
Mandarin Noodle Manufacturing Company
Calgary, AB 403-265-1383
Wing's Food Products
Toronto, ON 416-259-2662

Enchiladas

Canned & Frozen

Baja Foods LLC
Chicago, IL 773-376-9030
Queen International Foods
Monterey Park, CA 800-423-4414

Frozen

Cedarlane Foods
Carson, CA 800-826-3322
Elena's Food Specialties
S San Francisco, CA 800-376-5368
Ruiz Food Products Inc.
Dinuba, CA 800-477-6474

Filafel

Kronos
Glendale Heights, IL 800-621-0099

Guacamole

Avo-King Internatl
Orange, CA 800-286-5464
Diversified Avocado Products
Mission Viejo, CA 800-879-2555
Frontera Foods
Chicago, IL 800-509-4441
Sunny Avocado
Jamul, CA 800-999-2862

Halal Foods

Al Safa Halal
New York City, NY 800-268-8147
Burke Corp
Nevada, IA 800-654-1152
Butterball Farms
Grand Rapids, MI 888-828-8837
Crescent Foods
Chicago, IL 800-939-6268
Foremost Farms USA
Baraboo, WI 800-362-9196
Global Food Industries
Townville, SC 800-225-4152
Halal Fine Foods
Toronto, ON 416-679-8000
J&M Food Products Co
Deerfield, IL 847-948-1290
Javed & Sons
Houston, TX 713-835-6850
Madani Halal
Ozone Park, NY 718-323-9732
Midamar
Cedar Rapids, IA 800-362-3711
My Own Meals Inc
Deerfield, IL 847-948-1118
National Fruit Flavor Co Inc
New Orleans, LA 800-966-1123
Nema Food Distribution
Fairfield, NJ 973-256-4415
Northwestern Foods
Arden Hills, MN 800-236-4937
Saad Wholesale Meats
Detroit, MI 313-831-8126
Salwa Foods
Lawrenceville, GA 770-263-8207
Zabiha Halal Meat Processors
Addison, IL 630-620-5000

Italian

Amanida USA Corp
Coral Gables, FL
Boscoli Foods Inc
Kenner, LA 504-469-5500
Fratelli Mantova
Naperville, IL 630-904-0002
Italian Connection
Dumont, NJ 201-385-2226
Joe Fazio's Famous Italian
Charleston, WV 304-344-3071
Marconi Italian Specialty Foods
Chicago, IL 312-421-0485
Sapore della Vita
Sarasota, FL 941-914-4256
Shamrock Foods Co
Phoenix, AZ 800-289-3663
Sidari's Italian Foods
Cleveland, OH 216-431-3344
Stella D'oro
Charlotte, NC 800-995-2623
Superior Foods
Watsonville, CA 831-728-3691

Jambalaya

Chef Hans' Gourmet Foods
Monroe, LA 800-890-4267
Mama Amy's Quality Foods
Mississauga, ON 905-456-0056

Japanese

Ajinomoto Frozen Foods USA, Inc.
Ontario, CA 866-536-8008
Genki USA
Torrance, CA
House Foods America Corp
Garden Grove, CA 877-333-7077
Imuraya USA
Irvine, CA 949-251-9205
Japan Gold USA
Poway, CA 858-486-1707
Marukai Market
Gardena, CA 310-660-6300
Marukome USA Inc.
Irvine, CA 949-863-0110
Otafuku Foods
Santa Fe Springs, CA 562-404-4700
Sun Noodle
Honolulu, HI 808-841-5808
Yamasho Inc
Elk Grove Village, IL 847-981-9342

Kosher Foods

A-1 Eastern-Homemade Pickle Co
Los Angeles, CA 323-223-1141
Abraham's Natural Foods
Long Branch, NJ 800-327-9903

Adrienne's Gourmet Foods
Santa Barbara, CA 800-937-7010
Al-Rite Fruits & Syrups Co
Miami, FL 305-652-2540
All American Foods Inc
Mankato, MN 800-833-2661
Alle Processing Corp
Flushing, NY 718-894-2000
Allied Wine Corporation
Ellenville, NY 800-796-4100
Alta Dena Certified Dairy LLC
City Of Industry, CA 800-535-1369
Annie Chun's
Los Angeles, CA 415-479-8272
Arbre Farms Inc
Walkerville, MI 231-873-3337
Aunt Gussie Cookies & Crackers
Garfield, NJ 800-422-6654
Avatar Corp
University Park, IL 800-255-3181
Bake Crafters Food Company
McDonald, TN 423-396-3392
Bascom Family Farms Inc
Brattleboro, VT 888-266-6271
Beatrice Bakery Co
Beatrice, NE 800-228-4030
Bella Viva Orchards
Hughson, CA 800-552-8218
Benson's Gourmet Seasonings
Azusa, CA 800-325-5619
Bernie's Foods
Brooklyn, NY 718-417-6677
Biazzo Dairy Products Inc
Ridgefield, NJ 201-941-6800
Blue Planet Foods
Collegedale, TN 877-396-3145
Bluechip Group
Salt Lake City, UT 800-878-0099
Boca Bons East
Greenacres, FL 800-314-2835
Briess Malt & Ingredients Co.
Chilton, WI 800-657-0806
Bruno Specialty Foods
West Sayville, NY 631-589-1700
Butterball Farms
Grand Rapids, MI 888-828-8837
Cache Creek Foods LLC
Woodland, CA 530-662-1764
Calhoun Bend Mill
Libuse, LA 800-519-6455
California Custom Fruits
Baldwin Park, CA 877-558-0056
Campbell Soup Co.
Camden, NJ 800-257-8443
Capalbo's Fruit Baskets
Clifton, NJ 800-252-6262
Carmi Flavor & Fragrance Company
Commerce, CA 800-421-9647
Casa Visco
Schenectady, NY 888-607-2823
Catch Up Logistics
Pittsburgh, PA 412-441-9512
Champlain Valley Milling Corp
Westport, NY 518-962-4711
Chewys Rugulach
San Diego, CA 800-241-3456
Chris Candies Inc
Pittsburgh, PA 412-322-9400
Christopher's Herb Shop
Springville, UT 888-372-4372
Coach's Oats
Yorba Linda, CA 714-692-6885
Coffee Masters
Spring Grove, IL 800-334-6485
Commissariat Imports
Los Angeles, CA 310-475-5628
Cookies United
Islip, NY 631-581-4000
Country Choice Organic
Eden Prairie, MN 952-829-8824
Crosby Molasses Company
Saint John, NB 800-561-2206
Deer Creek Honey Farms LTD
London, OH 740-852-0899
Delicious Frookie
Des Plaines, IL 847-699-3200
Dr Praeger's Sensible Foods
Elmwood Park, NJ 877-772-3437
Dynamic Health Laboratories Inc.
Brooklyn, NY 800-396-2114
Eatem Foods Co
Vineland, NJ 800-683-2836
Ed Roller Inc
Rochester, NY 585-458-8020
Eggology
Canoga Park, CA 818-610-2222
Elan Vanilla Co
Newark, NJ 973-344-8014
Enrico's/Ventre Packing
Syracuse, NY 888-472-8237
Erba Food Products
Brooklyn, NY 718-272-7700
FNI Group LLC
Sherborn, MA 508-655-4175
Foremost Farms USA
Baraboo, WI 800-362-9196
Fratelli Beretta USA
Mount Olive, NJ 201-438-0723
Freeda Vitamins Inc
Long Island City, NY 800-777-3737
Fresh Roasted Almond Company
Warren, MI 877-478-6887
Georgia Spice Company
Atlanta, GA 800-453-9997
Gerber Products Co
Arlington, VA 800-284-9488
Gimbals Fine Candies
S San Francisco, CA 800-344-6225
GKI Foods
Brighton, MI 248-486-0055
GoBio!
Action, ON 519-853-2958
Gold Pure Food Products Co. Inc.
Hempstead, NY 800-422-4681
Golden Fluff Popcorn Co
Lakewood, NJ 732-367-5448
Hanan Products Co
Hicksville, NY 516-938-1000
Happy & Healthy Products Inc
Boca Raton, FL 561-367-0739
Harbar LLC
Canton, MA 800-881-7040
Harvest Valley Bakery Inc
La Salle, IL 815-224-9030
Hausbeck Pickle Co
Saginaw, MI 866-754-4721
Helen's Pure Foods
Cheltenham, PA 215-379-6433
Hermann Pickle Co
Garrettsville, OH 800-245-2696
Hialeah Products Co
Hollywood, FL 800-923-3379
Honey Run Winery
Chico, CA 530-345-6405
Honeywood Winery
Salem, OR 800-726-4101
House of Flavors Inc
Ludington, MI 800-930-7740
Imagine Foods
Boulder, CO 800-434-4246
International Glatt Kosher
Brooklyn, NY 718-630-5555
Joe Jurgielewicz & Sons
Hamburg, PA 800-543-8257
Joyva Corp
Brooklyn, NY 718-497-0170
Kaplan & Zubrin
Camden, NJ 856-964-1083
Kayco
Bayonne, NJ 718-369-4600
KD Canners Inc
Mississauga, ON 905-602-1825
Kedem
Bayonne, NJ 718-369-4600
Kemach Food Products
Brooklyn, NY 718-272-5655
Klein's Kosher Pickles
Phoenix, AZ 800-437-4255
L & S Packing Co
Farmingdale, NY 800-286-6487
Lee Kum Kee USA Inc
City Of Industry, CA 800-654-5082
Lenchner Bakery
Concord, ON 905-738-8811
Lifeway
Morton Grove, IL 877-281-3874
Loriva Culinary Oils
San Francisco, CA 866-972-6879
Losurdo Creamery
Hackensack, NJ 888-567-8736
M&L Gourmet Ice Cream
Baltimore, MD 410-276-4880
Macabee Foods
West Nyack, NY 845-623-1300
Mada'n Kosher Foods
Dania, FL 954-925-0077
Magic Seasoning Blends
New Orleans, LA 800-457-2857
Main Street Gourmet
Cuyahoga Falls, OH 800-678-6246
Mancini Packing Co
Zolfo Springs, FL 800-741-1778
Manischewitz Co
Newark, NJ 201-553-1100
Maple Products
Sherbrooke, QC 819-569-5161
Marie Callender's Gourmet Products/Goldrush Products
San Jose, CA 800-729-5428
Marion-Kay Spice Co
Brownstown, IN 800-627-7423
Martin Farms
Brockport, NY 877-838-7369
Marukan Vinegar USA Inc.
Paramount, CA 562-630-6060
Mendocino Mustard
Fort Bragg, CA 800-964-2270
Mille Lacs Wild Rice Corp
Aitkin, MN 800-626-3809
Miller's Cheese Corp
Brooklyn, NY 718-965-1840
Milmar Food Group
Goshen, NY 845-294-5400
Mogen David Wine Corp
Westfield, NY 716-326-3151
Mona Lisa Foods
Chicago, IL 866-443-0460
Mrs. Leeper's Pasta
Excelsior Springs, MO 800-848-5266
Mushroom Co
Cambridge, MD 410-221-8971
Musicon Deer Farm
Goshen, NY 845-294-6378
My Brother Bobby's Salsa
Poughkeepsie, NY 845-462-6227
My Grandma's Coffee Cake
Hyde Park, MA 800-847-2636
National Fruit Flavor Co Inc
New Orleans, LA 800-966-1123
Nature's Products Inc
Sunrise, FL 800-752-7873
Navarro Pecan Co
Corsicana, TX 800-333-9507
Northwestern Foods
Arden Hills, MN 800-236-4937
Norwalk Dairy
Santa Fe Springs, CA 562-921-5712
Nu-World Amaranth Inc
Naperville, IL 630-369-6851
Old Fashioned Kitchen Inc
Lakewood, NJ 732-364-4100
Pacific Salmon Company
Edmonds, WA 425-774-1315
Palmieri Food Products
New Haven, CT 800-845-5447
Preferred Brands Inc
Stamford, CT 800-827-8900
Price Co
Yakima, WA 509-966-4110
Primo Foods
Oceanside, CA 760-439-8711
Quality Naturally Foods
City Of Industry, CA 888-498-6986
Rachael's Smoked Fish
Springfield, MA 800-327-3412
Ranaldi Bros. Frozen Food Products
Warwick, RI 401-737-5130
Real Kosher Sausage Company
Newark, NJ 973-690-5394
Redmond Minerals Inc
Heber City, UT 866-312-7258
Rogers Sugar Inc.
Montreal, QC 514-527-8686
Royal Palate Foods
Inglewood, CA 310-330-7701
Russian Chef
New York, NY 212-249-1550
Sandt's Honey Co
Easton, PA 800-935-3960
Seabrook Brothers & Sons
Seabrook, NJ 856-455-8080
Setton International Foods
Commack, NY 800-227-4397
Simply Divine
New York, NY 212-541-7300
Solana Gold Organics
Sebastopol, CA 800-459-1121

Spilke's Baking Company
Moosic, PA . . . 570-457-2400
Steve's Mom
Bronx, NY. . . 800-362-4545
Strub Pickles
Brantford, ON . . . 519-751-1717
Sun Harvest Foods Inc
San Diego, CA . . . 619-661-0909
Sunergia Soyfoods
Charlottesville, VA . . . 800-693-5134
Sure-Fresh Produce Inc
Santa Maria, CA . . . 888-423-5379
Thomas Canning/Maidstone
Maidstone, ON . . . 519-737-1531
Todhunter Foods
West Palm Beach, FL . . . 800-336-9463
Top Hat Co Inc
Wilmette, IL . . . 847-256-6565
Touche Bakery
London, ON . . . 518-455-0044
Tova Industries LLC
Louisville, KY . . . 888-532-8682
Umanoff & Parsons
Bronx, NY. . . 800-248-9993
US Chocolate Corp
Brooklyn, NY . . . 718-788-8555
Vacaville Fruit Co
Vacaville, CA . . . 707-447-1085
Vermont Country Naturals
Charlotte, VT . . . 800-528-7021
Weaver Nut Co. Inc.
Ephrata, PA . . . 800-473-2688
Weinberg Foods
Kirkland, WA . . . 800-866-3447
Weiss Homemade Kosher Bakery
Brooklyn, NY . . . 800-498-3477
Wenner Bakery
Bayport, NY . . . 800-869-6262
World Cheese Inc
Brooklyn, NY . . . 718-965-1700
World Harbors
Auburn, ME . . . 800-355-6221
World Of Chantilly
Brooklyn, NY . . . 718-859-1110
World's Finest Chocolate Inc
Chicago, IL . . . 888-821-8452
Y Z Enterprises Inc
Maumee, OH. . . 800-736-8779
Your Bar Factory
LaSalle, QC. . . 888-366-0258

Matzo

Erba Food Products
Brooklyn, NY . . . 718-272-7700
Manischewitz Co
Newark, NJ . . . 201-553-1100
Streit's
Orangeburg, NY . . . 845-359-9203

Meal

Manischewitz Co
Newark, NJ . . . 201-553-1100

Mexican

Alamo Tamale Corporation
Houston, TX . . . 800-252-0586
Amy Food Inc
Houston, TX . . . 713-910-5860
Art's Mexican Products
Kansas City, KS . . . 913-371-2163
Cacique
Monrovia, CA. . . 800-521-6987
Feel Good Foods
Brooklyn, NY . . . 800-638-8949
Fiesta Mexican Foods
Brawley, CA . . . 760-344-3580
Flying Burrito Co
Fayetteville, AR . . . 479-527-0400
Fresca Mexican Foods LLC
Boise, ID. . . 208-376-6922
Frontera Foods
Chicago, IL. . . 800-509-4441
Gladstone Food Products Company
Kansas City, MO. . . 816-436-1255
Intermex Products USA LTD
Grand Prairie, TX . . . 972-660-2071
J & J Snack Foods Corp
Pennsauken, NJ. . . 800-486-9533
JJ's Tamales & Barbacoa
San Antonio, TX. . . 210-737-1300
LA Chapalita Inc
South El Monte, CA . . . 626-443-8556
La Preferida, Inc.
Chicago, IL . . . 773-254-7200
Leona's Restaurante
Chimayo, NM. . . 888-561-5569
Los Pericos Food Products
Pomona, CA . . . 909-623-5625
McCormick & Company
Hunt Valley, MD. . . 410-527-6189
Mission Foodservice
Oldsmar, FL . . . 800-443-7994
Molli
Dallas, TX
National Importers
Richmond, BC . . . 888-894-6464
Palacios & Sons
Irving, TX . . . 469-449-2060
Patricia Quintana
Los Angeles, CA
PepsiCo.
Purchase, NY . . . 914-253-2000
Red's All Natural
North Sioux City, SD . . . 605-956-7337
Sabor Mexicano
Berkeley, CA
San Antonio Farms
Platteville, WI . . . 800-236-1119
Shamrock Foods Co
Phoenix, AZ . . . 800-289-3663
Superior Foods
Watsonville, CA . . . 831-728-3691
T.W. Garner Food Company
Winston Salem, NC. . . 800-476-7383
Teasdale Quality Foods Inc
Atwater, CA . . . 209-358-5616
Truco Enterprises
Carrollton, TX. . . 972-869-4600
Tyson Foods Inc.
Springdale, AR . . . 479-290-4000

Oriental

Cafe Spice
New Windsor, NY. . . 845-863-0910
Hanmi Inc
Chicago, IL . . . 773-271-0730
Koha Food
Honolulu, HI. . . 808-845-4232
M&M Food Distributors/Oriental Pride
Virginia Beach, VA. . . 757-499-5676
Mah Chena Company
Chicago, IL. . . 312-226-5100

Paella

Conrad Rice Mill Inc
New Iberia, LA. . . 800-551-3245
Cuizina Food Company
Woodinville, WA. . . 425-486-7000

Parve Foods

Bruno Specialty Foods
West Sayville, NY. . . 631-589-1700
Coach's Oats
Yorba Linda, CA. . . 714-692-6885
Country Choice Organic
Eden Prairie, MN . . . 952-829-8824
Delicious Frookie
Des Plaines, IL . . . 847-699-3200
Dr Praeger's Sensible Foods
Elmwood Park, NJ . . . 877-772-3437
Dynamic Health Laboratories Inc.
Brooklyn, NY . . . 800-396-2114
Eggology
Canoga Park, CA . . . 818-610-2222
Enrico's/Ventre Packing
Syracuse, NY . . . 888-472-8237
FNI Group LLC
Sherborn, MA . . . 508-655-4175
GoBio!
Action, ON . . . 519-853-2958
Happy & Healthy Products Inc
Boca Raton, FL. . . 561-367-0739
Honey Run Winery
Chico, CA . . . 530-345-6405
KD Canners Inc
Mississauga, ON. . . 905-602-1825
Marukan Vinegar USA Inc.
Paramount, CA . . . 562-630-6060
Mrs. Leeper's Pasta
Excelsior Springs, MO . . . 800-848-5266
New World Pasta Co
Harrisburg, PA . . . 800-730-5957
Northwestern Foods
Arden Hills, MN. . . 800-236-4937
Touche Bakery
London, ON . . . 518-455-0044
US Chocolate Corp
Brooklyn, NY . . . 718-788-8555
Y Z Enterprises Inc
Maumee, OH. . . 800-736-8779

Shells

Chalupa

Rudy's Tortillas
Carrollton, TX. . . 800-878-2401

Taco

Abuelita Mexican Foods
Manassas Park, VA . . . 703-369-0232
Amigos Canning Company
San Antonio, TX. . . 210-798-5360
Anita's Mexican Foods Corporation
San Bernardino, CA . . . 909-884-8706
Azteca Foods Inc
Chicago, IL . . . 708-563-6600
El Rancho Tortilla
San Antonio, TX. . . 210-922-8411
La Buena Mexican Foods Products
Tucson, AZ . . . 520-624-1796
La Preferida, Inc.
Chicago, IL . . . 773-254-7200
Las Cruces Brand Products
El Paso, TX. . . 915-779-5709
Las Cruces Foods
Las Cruces, NM . . . 575-526-2352
Li'l Guy Foods
Kansas City, MO. . . 800-886-8226
Luna's Tortillas
Dallas, TX. . . 214-747-2661
Manuel's Odessa Tortilla
Odessa, TX . . . 800 753 2445
Mission Foodservice
Oldsmar, FL . . . 800-443-7994
Perez Food Products
Kansas City, MO. . . 816-931-8761
Puebla Foods Inc
Passaic, NJ . . . 973-473-0201
Rudy's Tortillas
Carrollton, TX. . . 800-878-2401
Sam's Leon Mexican Food
Omaha, NE . . . 402-733-3809
Spanish Gardens Food Manufacturing
Kansas City, KS . . . 913-831-4242

Tabbouleh

Bishop Brothers
Bristow, OK . . . 800-859-8304
Tarazi Specialty Foods
Chino, CA. . . 909-628-3601

Tacos

Amigos Canning Company
San Antonio, TX. . . 210-798-5360
Flying Burrito Co
Fayetteville, AR . . . 479-527-0400
La Preferida, Inc.
Chicago, IL. . . 773-254-7200
Mission Foods Corp.
Irving, TX . . . 214-583-5113
Queen International Foods
Monterey Park, CA. . . 800-423-4414
R & S Mexican Food
Glendale, AZ. . . 602-272-2727
Ruiz Food Products Inc.
Dinuba, CA. . . 800-477-6474

Fillings

Burke Corp
Nevada, IA . . . 800-654-1152
First Original Texas Chili Company
Fort Worth, TX . . . 800-507-0009
Ready Foods Inc
Denver, CO. . . 800-748-1218
Texas Chili Co
Fort Worth, TX . . . 800-507-0009

Tamales

Abuelita Mexican Foods
Manassas Park, VA 703-369-0232
Alamo Tamale Corporation
Houston, TX 800-252-0586
Art's Tamales
Metamora, IL 309-367-2850
Baja Foods LLC
Chicago, IL 773-376-9030
Comanche Tortilla Factory
Fort Stockton, TX 432-336-3245
El Rey Cooked Meats
St Louis, MO 314-521-3113
Grande Tortilla Factory
Tucson, AZ 520-622-8338
Kelly Foods
Jackson, TN 731-424-2255
La Buena Mexican Foods Products
Tucson, AZ 520-624-1796
Luna's Tortillas
Dallas, TX 214-747-2661
Mama Maria's Tortillas
Midvale, UT 801-566-5150
Manuel's Odessa Tortilla
Odessa, TX 800-753-2445
Mexi-Frost Specialties Company
Brooklyn, NY 718-625-3324
Mi Ranchito Foods
Phoenix, AZ 602-272-3949
Mr Jay's Tamales & Chili
Lynwood, CA 310-537-3932
R & S Mexican Food
Glendale, AZ 602-272-2727
Ramona's Mexican Foods
Gardena, CA 310-323-1950
Ruiz Food Products Inc.
Dinuba, CA 800-477-6474
Supreme Frozen Products
Chicago, IL 773-622-3777
Supreme Frozen Products
Elk Grove Village, IL 847-979-8480
Texas Tamale Co
Houston, TX 713-795-5500
Tom Tom Tamale & Bakery Co
Chicago, IL 773-523-5675

Frozen

Art's Tamales
Metamora, IL 309-367-2850
Baja Foods LLC
Chicago, IL 773-376-9030
Edmond's Chile Co
St Louis, MO 314-772-1499
El Rey Cooked Meats
St Louis, MO 314-521-3113
Mexi-Frost Specialties Company
Brooklyn, NY 718-625-3324
Mi Ranchito Foods
Phoenix, AZ 602-272-3949
Ramona's Mexican Foods
Gardena, CA 310-323-1950
Ruiz Food Products Inc.
Dinuba, CA 800-477-6474
Tom Tom Tamale & Bakery Co
Chicago, IL 773-523-5675

Taquitos

Queen International Foods
Monterey Park, CA 800-423-4414
Ruiz Food Products Inc.
Dinuba, CA 800-477-6474

Tempeh

Twenty-First Century Foods
Jamaica Plain, MA 617-522-7595

Tortilla & Tortilla Products

Anita's Mexican Foods Corporation
San Bernardino, CA 909-884-8706
Cabo Chips
Cypress, CA
Calidad Foods
Grand Prairie, TX 214-521-7999
Comanche Tortilla Factory
Fort Stockton, TX 432-336-3245
El Matador Foods
Baytown, TX 800-470-2447
Fresca Mexican Foods LLC
Boise, ID 208-376-6922
Frontera Foods
Chicago, IL 800-509-4441
Good Wives
Wilmington, MA 800-521-8160
Harbar LLC
Canton, MA 800-881-7040
La Bonita Ole Inc
Tampa, FL 800-522-6648
La Preferida, Inc.
Chicago, IL 773-254-7200
LA Torilla Factory
Santa Rosa, CA 800-446-1516
Los Pericos Food Products
Pomona, CA 909-623-5625
Mama Maria's Tortillas
Midvale, UT 801-566-5150
Maria and Ricardo's
Canton, MA 800-881-7040
Masienda
Los Angeles, CA
Mi Rancho
San Leandro, CA 510-553-0444
Mission Foods
Tempe, AZ 480-491-2511
Mission Foods Corp.
Irving, TX 214-583-5113
Mrs Rios Corn Products
San Angelo, TX 325-653-5640
One Degree Organic Foods
Abbotsford, BC 855-834-2642
Rudolph's Specialty Bakery
Toronto, ON 800-268-1589
Siete Family Foods
Austin, TX
Tolteca Foodservice
Norcross, GA 800-541-6835

Tortillas

Abuelita Mexican Foods
Manassas Park, VA 703-369-0232
Azteca Foods Inc
Chicago, IL 708-563-6600
Azteca Milling
Irving, TX 800-364-0040
Bien Padre Foods Inc
Eureka, CA 707-442-4585
Blue Marble Brands
Providence, RI 888-534-0246
Bueno Foods
Albuquerque, NM 800-888-7336
Casa Valdez Inc
Caldwell, ID 208-459-6461
Cedarlane Foods
Carson, CA 800-826-3322
Comanche Tortilla Factory
Fort Stockton, TX 432-336-3245
Custom Ingredients Inc
New Braunfels, TX 800-457-8935
Delicious Popcorn
Waupaca, WI 715-258-7683
El Charro Mexican Food Ind
Roswell, NM 575-622-8590
El Milagro
Chicago, IL 773-579-6120
El Rancho Tortilla
San Antonio, TX 210-922-8411
Father Sam's Bakery
Buffalo, NY 800-521-6719
Fiesta Mexican Foods
Brawley, CA 760-344-3580
Flowers Foods Inc.
Thomasville, GA 229-226-9110
Food Products Corporation
Phoenix, AZ 602-273-7139
French Meadow Bakery & Cafe
Minneapolis, MN 612-870-7855
Frontera Foods
Chicago, IL 800-509-4441
Grande Tortilla Factory
Tucson, AZ 520-622-8338
Great Western Tortilla
Denver, CO 303-298-0705
Harbar LLC
Canton, MA 800-881-7040
La Buena Mexican Foods Products
Tucson, AZ 520-624-1796
LA Canasta Mexican Foods
Phoenix, AZ 855-269-7721
LA Chapalita Inc
South El Monte, CA 626-443-8556
La Chiquita Tortilla Manufacturing
Atlanta, GA 800-486-3942
LA Colonial
San Jose, CA 408-436-5551
LA Mexicana Tortilla Factory
Duncanville, TX 214-943-7770
LA Reina Inc
Los Angeles, CA 800-367-7522
LA Tapatia Tortilleria Inc
Fresno, CA 559-441-1030
LA Torilla Factory
Santa Rosa, CA 800-446-1516
La Tortilla Factory
Santa Rosa, CA 800-446-1516
Lago Tortillas International
Austin, TX 800-369-9017
Laredo Tortilleria & Mexican
Fort Wayne, IN 800-252-7336
Las Cruces Brand Products
El Paso, TX 915-779-5709
Las Cruces Foods
Las Cruces, NM 575-526-2352
Li'l Guy Foods
Kansas City, MO 800-886-8226
Lone Star Bakery
Round Rock, TX 512-255-7268
Los Amigo Tortilla Mfg Co
Atlanta, GA 800-969-8226
Luna's Tortillas
Dallas, TX 214-747-2661
Manuel's Mexican-American Fine Foods
Salt Lake City, UT 800-748-5072
Manuel's Odessa Tortilla
Odessa, TX 800-753-2445
Metzger Popcorn Co
Delphos, OH 800-819-6072
Mexi-Frost Specialties Company
Brooklyn, NY 718-625-3324
Mexican Accent
New Berlin, WI 262-784-4422
Mi Mama's Tortilla Factory Inc
Omaha, NE 402-345-2099
Mi Ranchito Foods
Phoenix, AZ 602-272-3949
Mikey's
. 480-696-2483
Mission Foods Corp.
Irving, TX 214-583-5113
Mission Foodservice
Oldsmar, FL 800-443-7994
Natural Food Mill
Corona, CA 800-797-5090
Ozuna Food Products Corporation
Sunnyvale, CA 408-400-0495
Pacific Ocean Produce
Santa Cruz, CA 831-423-2654
Pepe's Mexican Restaurant
Anaheim, CA 714-952-9410
Perez Food Products
Kansas City, MO 816-931-8761
Puebla Foods Inc
Passaic, NJ 973-473-0201
R & S Mexican Food
Glendale, AZ 602-272-2727
Ramona's Mexican Foods
Gardena, CA 310-323-1950
Ready Foods Inc
Denver, CO 800-748-1218
Rudi's Organic Bakery
Boulder, CO 877-293-0876
Rudolph's Specialty Bakery
Toronto, ON 800-268-1589
Rudy's Tortillas
Carrollton, TX 800-878-2401
Ruiz Flour Tortillas
Riverside, CA 909-947-7811
Ruiz Food Products Inc.
Dinuba, CA 800-477-6474
Sabor Mexicano
Berkeley, CA
Sam's Leon Mexican Food
Omaha, NE 402-733-3809
Sanitary Tortilla Manufacturing Company
San Antonio, TX 210-226-9209
Selecto Sausage Co
Houston, TX 713-926-1626
Severance Foods Inc
Hartford, CT 860-724-7063
Shirley Foods
Shirley, IN 800-560-2908
Soloman Baking Company
Denver, CO 303-371-2777
Spanish Gardens Food Manufacturing
Kansas City, KS 913-831-4242

Sweet Corn Products Co
Bloomfield, NE 877-628-6115
Tolteca Foodservice
Norcross, GA 800-541-6835
Tortillas Inc
North Las Vegas, NV 702-399-3300
Vermont Tortilla Company
Shelburne, VT 802-999-4823

Tostadas

Delicious Popcorn
Waupaca, WI 715-258-7683
El Rancho Tortilla
San Antonio, TX 210-922-8411
Happy's Potato Chip Co
Minneapolis, MN 612-781-3121
La Buena Mexican Foods Products
Tucson, AZ 520-624-1796
LA Tapatia Tortilleria Inc
Fresno, CA 559-441-1030
Las Cruces Brand Products
El Paso, TX 915-779-5709
Luna's Tortillas
Dallas, TX 214-747-2661
Manuel's Mexican-American Fine Foods
Salt Lake City, UT 800-748-5072
Mission Foodservice
Oldsmar, FL 800-443-7994
Rudy's Tortillas
Carrollton, TX 800-878-2401

Wonton Chips

Maebo Noodle Factory Inc
Hilo, HI 877-663-8667

Wontons

Chang Food Company
Garden Grove, CA 714-265-9990
Delta Food Products
Edmonton, AB 780-424-3636
Harvest Food Products Co Inc
Hayward, CA 510-675-0383
La Tang Cuisine Manufacturing
Houston, TX 713-780-4876
Mandarin Noodle Manufacturing Company
Calgary, AB 403-265-1383
Montreal Chop Suey Company
Montreal, QC 514-522-3134
Nanka Seimen Company
Vernon, CA 323-585-9967
Passport Food Group
Ontario, CA 310-463-0954
Peking Noodle Co Inc
Los Angeles, CA 323-223-0897
Wan Hua Foods
Seattle, WA 206-622-8417
Wonton Food
Brooklyn, NY 800-776-8889

Fish & Seafood

Canned

American Tuna
Bonita, CA 866-817-0497
Crusoe Seafood LLC
Sun Valley, CA 866-343-7629
King Oscar
San Diego, CA
Season Brand
Newark, NJ 201-553-1100
Vital Choice
Bellingham, WA 800-608-4825

General

Lamex Foods Inc.
Bloomington, MN 952-844-0585
Omega Pure
Irvine, CA 562-429-3335
Sofina Foods Inc
Markham, ON 855-763-4621

Caviar (Roe)

Angy's Food Products Inc
Westfield, MA 413-572-1010
Black River Caviar
Breckenridge, CO 888-315-0575
Calvisius Caviar
New York, NY 212-207-8222
Castella Imports Inc
Brentwood, NY 631-231-5500
Ferroclad Fishery
Batchawana Bay, ON 705-882-2295
Fine Foods Trading Company
Union City, NJ 973-772-2221
Fulton Fish Market
New York, NY 718-842-8908
High Liner Foods Inc.
Lunenburg, NS 902-634-8811
Kelley's Katch Caviar
Savannah, TN 888-681-8565
Newell Lobsters
Yarmouth, NS 902-742-6272
Notre Dame Seafoods Inc.
Comfort Cove, NL 709-244-5511
Paramount Caviar
Long Island City, NY 800-992-2842
Produits Belle Baie
Caraquet, NB 506-727-4414
Raffield Fisheries Inc
Port St Joe, FL 850-229-8494
Royal Caviar Inc
Glendale, CA 818-546-5858
Royal Gourmet Caviar
Lynbrook, NY 516-612-7407
Russ & Daughters
New York, NY 800-787-7229
Russian Chef
New York, NY 212-249-1550
Sterling Caviar LLC
Sacramento, CA 800-525-0333
Warbucks Seafood
Brooklyn, NY 718-998-4900

Herring

Cowart Seafood Corp
Lottsburg, VA 804-529-6101

Salmon

Captain Little Seafood
Queens County, NS 902-947-2087
Crown Prince Inc
City Of Industry, CA 626-912-3700
Haines Packing Company
Haines, AK 907-766-2883
Johns Cove Fisheries
Yarmouth, NS 902-742-8691
Vital Choice
Bellingham, WA 800-608-4825

Shad

Calise & Sons Bakery Inc
Lincoln, RI 800-225-4737
Flowers Baking Co
El Paso, TX 800-328-6111

Fish

A&C Quinlin Fisheries
Centreville, NS 902-745-2742
Ace Development
Bruneau, ID 208-845-2487
Acme Smoked Fish Corporation
Brooklyn, NY 718-383-8585
Acme Steak & Seafood
Youngstown, OH 800-686-2263
Acushnet Fish Corporation
Fairhaven, MA 508-997-7482
Agger Fish Corp
Brooklyn, NY 718-855-1717
Al Safa Halal
New York City, NY 800-268-8147
Alaska Sausage & Seafood
Anchorage, AK 800-798-3636
Alaskan Gourmet Seafoods
Anchorage, AK 800-288-3740
Alpine Butcher
Lowell, MA 978-256-7771
Amano Fish Cake Factory
Hilo, HI 808-935-5555
Amcan Industries
Elmsford, NY 914-347-4838
Annabelle Lee
Kennebunkport, ME 207-967-4611
Aquatec Seafoods Ltd.
Comox, BC 250-339-6412
Arrowac Fisheries
Seattle, WA 206-282-5655
Asian Foods Inc
St Paul, MN 651-558-2400
Atlantic Capes Fisheries
Cape May, NJ 609-884-3000
Atlantic Fish Specialties
Charlottetown, PE 902-894-7005
Atlantic Sea Pride
Boston, MA 617-269-7700
B.M. Lawrence & Company
San Francisco, CA 415-981-2926
Baensch Food Products Co
Milwaukee, WI 414-562-4643
Bakalars Sausage Co
La Crosse, WI 608-784-0384
Baker's Point Fisheries
Oyster Pond Jeddore, NS 902-845-2347
Basin Crawfish Processors
Breaux Bridge, LA 337-332-6655
Bay Haven Lobster Pound
York, ME 207-363-5265
Bayou Food Distributors
Kenner, LA 800-516-8283
Bayou Land Seafood
Breaux Bridge, LA 337-667-6118
Beaver Street Fisheries
Jacksonville, FL 800-874-6426
Becker Foods
Westminster, CA 714-891-9474
Belle River Enterprises
Belle River, PE 902-962-2248
Billingsgate Fish Company
Calgary, AB 403-571-7700
Birch Street Seafoods
Digby, NS 902-245-6551
Blalock Seafood & Specialty
Orange Beach, AL 251-974-5811
Blue Harvest Foods
New Bedford, MA 508-993-5700
Blue Lakes Trout Farm
Jerome, ID 208-734-7151
BlueWater Seafoods
Gloucester, MA 888-560-2539
Bornstein Seafoods
Bellingham, WA 360-734-7990
Bos Smoked Fish Inc
Woodstock, ON 519-537-5000
Boston Seafarms
Boston, MA 617-784-4777
Boundary Fish Company
Blaine, WA 360-332-6715
Boutique Seafood Brokers
Atlanta, GA 404-752-8852
Breakwater Fisheries
St John's, NL 709-754-1999
Brookshire Grocery Company
Tyler, TX 888-937-3776
Brucepac
Woodburn, OR 800-899-3629
Burleigh Brothers Seafoods
Ellerslie, PE 902-831-2349
Caito Fisheries Inc
Fort Bragg, CA 707-964-6368
Caleb Haley & Co LLC
Bronx, NY 718-617-7474
California Shellfish Company
San Francisco, CA 415-923-7400
Canadian Fish Exporters
Auburndale, MA 800-225-4215
Captain Alex Seafoods
Niles, IL 847-803-8833
Carrington Foods Co Inc
Saraland, AL 251-675-9700
Certi Fresh Foods Inc
Wilmington, CA 310-221-6262
Channel Fish Processing
Gloucester, MA 800-457-0054
Channel Fish Processing Co Inc
Boston, MA 800-536-3474
Charlton Charters
Warrenton, OR 503-338-0569
Chicago Food Market
Chicago, IL 312-842-4361
Chicken Of The Sea
El Segundo, CA 844-267-8862
Chuck's Seafoods
Charleston, OR 541-888-5525
Clear Springs Foods Inc.
Buhl, ID 800-635-8211
Connors Aquaculture
Eastport, ME 207-853-6081
Consolidated Sea Products
Mobile, AL 251-433-3240
Cook Inlet Processing
Anchorage, AK 907-243-1166
Cooke Aguaculture
Blacks Harbour, NB 506-456-6600
Cowart Seafood Corp
Lottsburg, VA 804-529-6101
Crest International Corporation
San Diego, CA 800-548-1232
Crown Prince Inc
City Of Industry, CA 626-912-3700
Cuizina Food Company
Woodinville, WA 425-486-7000
Culver Fish Farm
Mcpherson, KS 800-241-5205
Cushner Seafoods Inc
Baltimore, MD 410-358-5564
Dave's Gourmet Albacore
Watsonville, CA 206-999-5517
Deep Creek Custom Packing
Ninilchik, AK 800-764-0078
Delaware Valley Fish Co
Norristown, PA 610-277-4900
Delta Pride Catfish
Indianola, MS 800-228-3474
Dixon's Fisheries
East Peoria, IL 800-373-1457
Dole & Bailey Inc
Woburn, MA 781-935-1234
Dressel Collins Fish Company
Seattle, WA 206-725-0121
Dynamic Foods
Lubbock, TX 806-723-5600
Ed's Kasilof Seafoods
Kasilof, AK 800-982-2377
Edelman Meats Inc
Antigo, WI 715-623-7686
Emery Smith Fisheries Limited
Shag Harbour, NS 902-723-2115
Erba Food Products
Brooklyn, NY 718-272-7700
Feature Foods
Brampton, ON 905-452-7741
Ferroclad Fishery
Batchawana Bay, ON 705-882-2295
Finestkind Fish Market
York, ME 800-288-8154
First Oriental Market
Decatur, GA 404-377-6950

Fish Brothers
Blue Lake, CA 800-244-0583
Fishermens Net
Portland, ME.................... 207-772-3565
Fishpeople
Portland, OR 503-342-2424
Flavor House, Inc.
Adelanto, CA 760-246-9131
Fleet Fisheries Inc
New Bedford, MA 508-910-2100
Fresh Island Fish
Kahului, HI 808-871-1111
Freshwater Fish Market
Winnipeg, MB.................... 800-345-3113
Fulton Fish Market
New York, NY 718-842-8908
Garden & Valley Isle Seafood
Honolulu, HI...................... 800-689-2733
George Robberecht Seafood
Montross, VA 804-472-3556
Giovanni's Appetizing Food Co
Richmond, MI.................... 586-727-9355
Glenn Sales Company
Atlanta, GA...................... 770-952-9292
Gold Star Smoked Fish Inc
Brooklyn, NY 718-522-1545
Gorton's Inc.
Gloucester, MA.................. 800-222-6846
Great Glacier Salmon
Prince Rupert, BC................ 250-627-4955
Great Northern Products Inc
Cranston, RI 401-490-4590
Hallmark Fisheries
Charleston, OR 541-888-3253
Hamilos Bros Inspected Meat
Madison, IL...................... 618-876-3710
Handy International Inc
Salisbury, MD.................... 800-426-3977
Harbor Fish Market
Portland, ME..................... 800-370-1790
Harbor Seafood
New Hyde Park, NY.............. 800-645-2211
Harbour Lobster Ltd
Shag Harbour, NS................ 902-723-2500
Hawaii International Seafood
Kailua, HI 808-839-5010
Henry Davis Company
Gary, IN.......................... 219-949-8555
HFI Foods
Redmond, WA.................... 425-883-1320
High Liner Foods Inc.
Lunenburg, NS 902-634-8811
Homer's Wharf Seafood Company
New Bedford, MA 508-997-0766
Idaho Trout Company
Buhl, ID.......................... 866-878-7688
Independent Packers Corporation
Seattle, WA...................... 206-285-6000
Indian Bay Frozen Foods
Centreville, NL 709-678-2844
Indian Valley Meats
Indian, AK....................... 907-653-7511
Ingles Markets
Black Mountain, NC.............. 828-669-2941
Inshore Fisheries
Middle West Pubnico, NS........... 902-762-2522
International Seafoods - Alaska
Kodiak, AK...................... 907-486-4768
Isaacson & Stein Fish Company
Chicago, IL...................... 312-421-2444
Island Marine Products
Clarks Harbour, NS............... 902-745-2222
J Deluca Fish Co Inc
San Pedro, CA.................... 310-684-5180
J Moniz Co Inc
Fall River, MA 508-674-8451
J Turner Seafood
Gloucester, MA.................. 978-281-8535
J. Matassini & Sons Fish Company
Tampa, FL........................ 813-229-0829
J.S. McMillan Fisheries
North Vancouver, BC.............. 604-981-4000
James L. Mood Fisheries
Nova Scotia, NS 902-723-2360
Jessie's Ilwaco Fish Company
San Francisco, CA 360-642-3773
Joe Patti's Seafood Co
Pensacola, FL 800-500-9929
John B. Wright Fish Company
Gloucester, MA.................. 978-283-4205
K&N Fisheries
Upper Port La Tour, NS 902-768-2478

Key Largo Fisheries
Key Largo, FL.................... 800-432-4358
King Fish Restaurants
Louisville, KY 502-339-0565
Kodiak Salmon Packers
Larsen Bay, AK.................. 907-847-2250
Kwikpak Fisheries
Anchorage, AK.................. 800-509-3332
L&M Evans
Conyers, GA.................... 770-483-9373
LEF McLean Brothers International
Wheatley, ON 519-825-4656
Leo G. Atkinson Fisheries
Clarks Harbor, NS................ 902-745-3047
Les Trois Petits Cochons
Brooklyn, NY 800-537-7283
LLJ's Sea Products
Round Pond, ME 207-529-4224
Lougheed Fisheries
Owen Sound, ON 519-376-1586
Lowland Seafood
Lowland, NC.................... 252-745-3751
Lund's Fisheries
Cape May, NJ 609-884-7600
Mada'n Kosher Foods
Dania, FL 954-925-0077
Manischewitz Co
Newark, NJ 201-553-1100
Mariner Seafood LLC
New Bedford, MA 774-202-4121
Martin Brothers Seafood Co
Westwego, LA.................. 504-341-2251
Maxim's Import Corporation
Miami, FL...................... 800-331-6652
Meijer Inc
Grand Rapids, MI 616-453-6711
Menemsha Fish Market
Chilmark, MA.................. 508-645-2282
Mid-South Fish Company
Aubrey, AR 870-295-5600
Mill Cove Lobster Pound
Trevett, ME.................... 207-633-3340
Millen Fish
Millen, GA 478-982-4988
Minor Fisheries
Port Colborne, ON 905-834-9232
Mutual Fish Co
Seattle, WA 206-322-4368
Nelson Crab Inc
Tokeland, WA.................. 800-262-0069
Neptune Foods
Vernon, CA 323-232-8300
Nodine's Smokehouse Inc
Torrington, CT 800-222-2059
Noon Hour Food Products Inc
Chicago, IL 800-621-6636
Nordic Group Inc
Boston, MA.................... 800-486-4002
North Atlantic Inc
Portland, ME.................... 207-774-6025
North Atlantic Seafood
Portland, ME.................... 800-774-6025
Northern Products Corporation
Seattle, WA 888-599-6290
Notre Dame Seafoods Inc.
Comfort Cove, NL 709-244-5511
Ocean Beauty Seafoods Inc
Seattle, WA 800-365-8950
Ocean Fresh Seafoods
Seattle, WA 206-285-2412
Okuhara Foods Inc
Honolulu, HI.................... 808-848-0581
Omaha Steaks Inc
.... 800-960-8400
Ore-Cal Corp
Los Angeles, CA.................. 800-827-7474
Pacific American Fish Co Inc
Vernon, CA 800-625-2525
Pacific Salmon Company
Edmonds, WA.................. 425-774-1315
Pacific Seafoods International
Port Hardy, BC 250-949-8781
Paramount Caviar
Long Island City, NY 800-992-2842
Park 100 Foods Inc
Tipton, IN 800-854-6504
Paul Piazza & Son Inc
New Orleans, LA 800-969-6011
Penguin Frozen Foods Inc
Northbrook, IL 800-323-1485
Peter Pan Seafoods Inc.
Bellevue, WA 206-728-6000

Premier Smoked Fish Company
Bensalem, PA 800-654-6682
Proacec USA
Santa Monica, CA................ 310-996-7770
Produits Belle Baie
Caraquet, NB 506-727-4414
Protica Inc
Whitehall, PA 800-776-8422
Publix Super Market
Lakeland, FL.................... 800-242-1227
QualiGourmet
Boisbriand, QC 514-287-3530
Quinault Pride
Taholah, WA 360-276-4431
Rachael's Smoked Fish
Springfield, MA 800-327-3412
Raffield Fisheries Inc
Port St Joe, FL.................. 850-229-8494
Rego Smoked Fish Company
Flushing, NY.................... 718-894-1400
Roland Seafood Co
Atlantic Beach, FL 904-246-9443
Roman Sausage Company
Santa Clara, CA 800-497-7462
Royal Seafood Inc
Brooklyn, NY 718-769-1517
Russian Chef
New York, NY 212-249-1550
S.A.S. Foods
Norcross, GA 770-263-9312
Salmon River Smokehouse
Gustavus, AK 907-697-2330
Salt River Lobster Inc
Boothbay, ME.................... 207-633-5357
Santa Monica Seafood Co.
Rancho Dominguez, CA............ 800-969-8862
Sau-Sea Foods
Tarrytown, NY 914-631-1717
SC Enterprises
Owen Sound, ON 519-371-0456
Scandia Seafood Company
Rockland, ME.................... 207-596-7102
Schafer Fisheries Inc
Thomson, IL 800-291-3474
Sea Bear Smokehouse
Anacortes, WA 800-645-3474
Sea Best Corporation
Ipswich, MA 978-768-7475
Sea Farm & Farm Fresh Importing Company
Monterey Park, CA................ 323-265-7075
Sea Fresh USA Inc
North Kingstown, RI 401-583-0200
Sea Horse Wharf
Phippsburg, ME 207-389-2312
Sea Lyons
Spanish Fort, AL.................. 251-626-2841
Sea Safari
Belhaven, NC 800-688-6174
Sea-Fresh Seafood Market
Mobile, AL 251-634-8650
Seabreeze Fish
Bakersfield, CA 661-323-7936
Seafood Connection
Honolulu, HI.................... 808-591-8550
Seafood Express
Brunswick, ME.................... 207-729-0887
Seafood Hawaii Inc
Honolulu, HI.................... 808-597-1971
Seafood International
Henderson, LA 337-228-7568
Seafood Packaging Inc
New Orleans, LA 800-949-9656
Seafood Plus Corporation
Orland Park, IL.................. 708-795-4820
Seafood Producers Co-Op
Bellingham, WA 360-733-0120
Seafood Services
Newburyport, MA.................. 508-999-6785
Seaway Company
Fairhaven, MA 508-992-1221
Seven Seas Seafoods
Alhambra, CA.................... 626-570-9129
Sewell's Seafood & Fish Market
Rogersville, AL.................. 256-247-1378
Seymour & Sons Seafoods Inc
Diberville, MS 228-392-4020
Sharkco's
Venice, LA 504-534-9577
Shore Trading Co
Alpharetta, GA 770-998-0566
Shuckman's Fish Co & Smokery
Louisville, KY 502-775-6478

Silver Streak Bass Co
El Campo, TX 979-543-6343
SOPAKCO Foods
Mullins, SC 800-276-9678
Sorrento Lobster
Sorrento, ME 207-422-9082
South Shores Seafood
Anaheim, CA 714-956-2722
Southern Fish & Oyster Company
Mobile, AL 251-438-2408
Southern Pride Catfish Company
Seattle, WA 800-343-8046
Spence & Company
Brockton, MA 508-427-5577
Sportsman's Paradise Whites Ranch
Paradise, UT 435-245-3053
Sportsmen's Cannery & Smokehouse
Winchester Bay, OR 800-457-8048
Sportsmens Seafoods
San Diego, CA 619-224-3551
St. Simons Seafood
Brunswick, GA 912-265-5225
State Fish Distributors
Chicago, IL 312-451-0800
Stavis Seafoods
Boston, MA 800-390-5103
Sterling Caviar LLC
Elverta, CA 800-525-0333
Stoller Fisheries
Spirit Lake, IA 800-831-5174
Strub Pickles
Brantford, ON 519-751-1717
Sunshine Food Sales
Miami, FL 305-696-2885
Sunshine Seafood
Stonington, ME 207-367-2955
Super Snooty Sea Food Corporation
Boston, MA 617-426-6390
Superior Seafood
New Orleans, LA 504-293-3474
Sweet Water Seafood
Carlstadt, NJ 201-939-6622
Taku Smokehouse
Juneau, AK 800-582-5122
Tampa Maid Foods Inc
Lakeland, FL 800-237-7637
Tempest Fisheries LTD
New Bedford, MA 508-997-0720
Tenth & M Seafoods
Anchorage, AK 800-770-2722
Thompson Seafood
Darien, GA 912-437-4649
Three Rivers Fish Company
Simmesport, LA 318-941-2467
Tichon Sea Food Corp
New Bedford, MA 508-999-5607
Trident Seafoods Corp
Wrangell, AK 907-874-3346
Tropic Fish Hawaii LLC
Honolulu, HI 808-591-2936
True World Foods LLC
Rockleigh, NJ 201-750-0024
Ungars Food
Elmwood Park, NJ 201-773-6846
Union Fisheries Corp
Chicago, IL 773-738-0448
United Fishing Agency LTD
Honolulu, HI 808-536-2148
Valdez Food Inc
Philadelphia, PA 215-634-6106
Van de Kamps
Peoria, IL 800-798-3318
Viking Seafoods Inc
Malden, MA 800-225-3020
Vinalhaven Fishermens Co-op
Camden, ME 207-236-0092
Virginia Trout Co
Monterey, VA 540-468-2280
Vita Food Products Inc
Chicago, IL 800-989-8482
Wabash Seafood Co
Chicago, IL 312-733-5070
Wanchese Fish Co Inc
Suffolk, VA 757-673-4500
Waterfield Farms
Amherst, MA 413-549-3558
Wegmans Food Markets Inc.
Rochester, NY 800-934-6267
West Coast Seafood Processors Association
Portland, OR 503-227-5076
Weyand's Fishery
Wyandotte, MI 800-521-9815
White Cap Fish Market
Islip, NY 631-277-6577
Yamasa Fish Cake Co
Los Angeles, CA 213-626-2211

Abalone

Crown Prince Inc
City Of Industry, CA 626-912-3700
North Pacific Seafoods Inc
Seattle, WA 206-726-9900

Amber Jack

Griffin's Seafood
Golden Meadow, LA 985-396-2453

Anchovies

Chicken Of The Sea
El Segundo, CA 844-267-8862
Crown Prince Inc
City Of Industry, CA 626-912-3700
Northwest Wild Products
Astoria, OR 503-791-1907

Canned

Ron Son Foods Inc
Swedesboro, NJ 856-241-7333
Vital Choice
Bellingham, WA 800-608-4825

Olive Oil

Castella Imports Inc
Brentwood, NY 631-231-5500

Paste

Giovanni's Appetizing Food Co
Richmond, MI 586-727-9355

Arctic Charr

Fumoir Grizzly
St Augustin, QC 418-878-8941

Bass

Culver Fish Farm
Mcpherson, KS 800-241-5205
Louisiana Seafood Exchange
Jefferson, LA 800-969-9394
Minor Fisheries
Port Colborne, ON 905-834-9232
North Atlantic Seafood
Portland, ME 800-774-6025
Wanchese Fish Co Inc
Suffolk, VA 757-673-4500

Striped

Advanced Aquaculture Systems
Brandon, FL 800-994-7599

Bluefish

Menemsha Fish Market
Chilmark, MA 508-645-2282
Raffield Fisheries Inc
Port St Joe, FL 850-229-8494

Bottomfish

Charlton Charters
Warrenton, OR 503-338-0569

Butterfish

Atlantic Capes Fisheries
Cape May, NJ 609-884-3000
Okuhara Foods Inc
Honolulu, HI 808-848-0581
Raffield Fisheries Inc
Port St Joe, FL 850-229-8494

Cakes

Amano Fish Cake Factory
Hilo, HI 808-935-5555
LA Monica Fine Foods
Millville, NJ
Valdez Food Inc
Philadelphia, PA 215-634-6106
Viking Seafoods Inc
Malden, MA 800-225-3020
Yamasa Fish Cake Co
Los Angeles, CA 213-626-2211

Canned

Cuizina Food Company
Woodinville, WA 425-486-7000
LA Monica Fine Foods
Millville, NJ

Fresh

Cuizina Food Company
Woodinville, WA 425-486-7000
Valdez Food Inc
Philadelphia, PA 215-634-6106
Yamasa Fish Cake Co
Los Angeles, CA 213-626-2211

Frozen

Amano Fish Cake Factory
Hilo, HI 808-935-5555
Cuizina Food Company
Woodinville, WA 425-486-7000
Gorton's Inc.
Gloucester, MA 800-222-6846
Viking Seafoods Inc
Malden, MA 800-225-3020
Yamasa Fish Cake Co
Los Angeles, CA 213-626-2211

Canned

Alaskan Gourmet Seafoods
Anchorage, AK 800-288-3740
Amano Fish Cake Factory
Hilo, HI 808-935-5555
B.M. Lawrence & Company
San Francisco, CA 415-981-2926
Chicken Of The Sea
El Segundo, CA 844-267-8862
Chuck's Seafoods
Charleston, OR 541-888-5525
Cook Inlet Processing
Anchorage, AK 907-243-1166
Cowart Seafood Corp
Lottsburg, VA 804-529-6101
Deep Creek Custom Packing
Ninilchik, AK 800-764-0078
Dressel Collins Fish Company
Seattle, WA 206-725-0121
Fishhawk Fisheries
Astoria, OR 503-325-5252
IMO Foods
Yarmouth, NS 902-742-3519
Indian Valley Meats
Indian, AK 907-653-7511
J Moniz Co Inc
Fall River, MA 508-674-8451
J Turner Seafood
Gloucester, MA 978-281-8535
J.S. McMillan Fisheries
North Vancouver, BC 604-981-4000
Kodiak Salmon Packers
Larsen Bay, AK 907-847-2250
LLJ's Sea Products
Round Pond, ME 207-529-4224
Monterey Fish Company
Salinas, CA 831-771-9221
Nelson Crab Inc
Tokeland, WA 800-262-0069
Noon Hour Food Products Inc
Chicago, IL 800-621-6636
Notre Dame Seafoods Inc.
Comfort Cove, NL 709-244-5511
Ocean Fresh Seafoods
Seattle, WA 206-285-2412
Pacific Salmon Company
Edmonds, WA 425-774-1315
Pastene Co LTD
Canton, MA 781-298-3397
Quinault Pride
Taholah, WA 360-276-4431
Ron Son Foods Inc
Swedesboro, NJ 856-241-7333
S&D Bait Company
Morgan City, LA 504-252-3500
Shafer-Haggart
Vancouver, BC 604-669-5512
Sportsman's Paradise Whites Ranch
Paradise, UT 435-245-3053
Sportsmen's Cannery & Smokehouse
Winchester Bay, OR 800-457-8048
Sportsmens Seafoods
San Diego, CA 619-224-3551

Trident Seafoods Corp
Wrangell, AK 907-874-3346

Carp

Culver Fish Farm
Mcpherson, KS 800-241-5205
Stoller Fisheries
Spirit Lake, IA 800-831-5174

Catfish

America's Catch
Itta Bena, MS 800-242-0041
Carolina Classics Catfish Inc
Ayden, NC 252-746-2818
Catfish Wholesale
Abbeville, LA 800-334-7292
Channel Fish Processing
Gloucester, MA 800-457-0054
CJ's Seafood
Des Allemands, LA 985-758-1237
Consolidated Catfish Co LLC
Isola, MS 662-962-3101
Culver Fish Farm
Mcpherson, KS 800-241-5205
Delta Catfish Products
Eudora, AR 870-355-4192
Delta Pride Catfish
Indianola, MS 800-228-3474
Fish Breeders of Idaho
Hagerman, ID 208-837-6114
Great American Foods Commissary
Hughes Springs, TX 903-639-1482
Guidry's Catfish Inc
Breaux Bridge, LA 337-228-7546
Haring Catfish
Wisner, LA 800-467-3474
Harvest Select
Northport, AL 800-816-7426
Inshore Fisheries
Middle West Pubnico, NS 902-762-2522
J. Matassini & Sons Fish Company
Tampa, FL 813-229-0829
New Orleans Fish House II LLC
New Orleans, LA 800-839-3474
Pickwick Catfish Farm
Counce, TN 731-689-3805
Pond Pure Catfish
Moulton, AL 256-974-6698
Roadrunner Seafood Inc
Colquitt, GA 229-758-6098
Roy Dick Company
Griffin, GA 770-227-3916
Seymour & Sons Seafoods Inc
Diberville, MS 228-392-4020
Southern Farms Fish Processors
Kansas City, MO 800-264-2594
Southern Pride Catfish Company
Seattle, WA 800-343-8046

Chowder

LA Monica Fine Foods
Millville, NJ

Chub

Raffield Fisheries Inc
Port St Joe, FL 850-229-8494
Russ & Daughters
New York, NY 800-787-7229

Cod

Alaska Pacific Seafoods
Kodiak, AK 907-486-3234
Angy's Food Products Inc
Westfield, MA 413-572-1010
Arrowac Fisheries
Seattle, WA 206-282-5655
BlueWater Seafoods
Gloucester, MA 888-560-2539
Breakwater Fisheries
St John's, NL 709-754-1999
C.L. Deveau & Son
Salmon River, NS 902-649-2812
Canadian Fish Exporters
Auburndale, MA 800-225-4215
Castella Imports Inc
Brentwood, NY 631-231-5500
Ceilidh Fisherman's Cooperative
Port Hood, NS 902-787-2666
Certi Fresh Foods Inc
Wilmington, CA 310-221-6262
Channel Fish Processing
Gloucester, MA 800-457-0054
D Waybret & Sons Fisher ies
Shelburne, NS 902-745-3477
Davis Strait Fisheries
Halifax, NS 902-450-5115
DB Kenney Fisheries
Westport, NS 902-839-2023
Deep Creek Custom Packing
Ninilchik, AK 800-764-0078
Dorset Fisheries
St Josephs, NL 709-739-7147
Felix Custom Smoking
Monroe, WA 425-485-2439
Harbor Seafood
New Hyde Park, NY 800-645-2211
Helshiron Fisheries
Grand Manan, NB 506-662-3696
High Liner Foods Inc.
Lunenburg, NS 902-634-8811
Independent Packers Corporation
Seattle, WA 206-285-6000
Inshore Fisheries
Middle West Pubnico, NS 902-762-2522
K&N Fisheries
Upper Port La Tour, NS 902-768-2478
La Have Seafoods
La Have, NS 902-688-2773
Lund's Fisheries
Cape May, NJ 609-884-7600
Menemsha Fish Market
Chilmark, MA 508-645-2282
MG Fisheries
Grand Manan, NB 506-662-3471
Mutual Fish Co
Seattle, WA 206-322-4368
Neptune Foods
Vernon, CA 323-232-8300
Nordic Group Inc
Boston, MA 800-486-4002
North Atlantic Seafood
Portland, ME 800-774-6025
Northern Products Corporation
Seattle, WA 888-599-6290
Northwest Fisheries
Hubbards, NS 902-228-2232
Northwest Wild Products
Astoria, OR 503-791-1907
Notre Dame Seafoods Inc.
Comfort Cove, NL 709-244-5511
Ocean Pride Fisheries
Lower Wedgeport, NS 902-663-4579
Paul Piazza & Son Inc
New Orleans, LA 800-969-6011
Peter Pan Seafoods Inc.
Bellevue, WA 206-728-6000
Produits Belle Baie
Caraquet, NB 506-727-4414
Royal Seafood Inc
Brooklyn, NY 718-769-1517
Seafood Producers Co-Op
Bellingham, WA 360-733-0120
Spruce Lane Investments
Stratford, PE 902-892-2600
Taku Smokehouse
Juneau, AK 800-582-5122
Tampa Bay Fisheries Inc
Dover, FL 800-732-3663
Viking Seafoods Inc
Malden, MA 800-225-3020
Vital Choice
Bellingham, WA 800-608-4825

Black

Alaska Pacific Seafoods
Kodiak, AK 907-486-3234
Dragnet Fisheries
Anchorage, AK 907-276-4551
Fishhawk Fisheries
Astoria, OR 503-325-5252
North Pacific Seafoods Inc
Seattle, WA 206-726-9900
Pacific Salmon Company
Edmonds, WA 425-774-1315
Royal Seafood Inc
Brooklyn, NY 718-769-1517
Seafood Producers Co-Op
Bellingham, WA 360-733-0120

Conch

Anchor Frozen Foods
Westbury, NY 800-566-3474
Roadrunner Seafood Inc
Colquitt, GA 229-758-6098

Croaker

Glenn Sales Company
Atlanta, GA 770-952-9292
Griffin's Seafood
Golden Meadow, LA 985-396-2453
Raffield Fisheries Inc
Port St Joe, FL 850-229-8494
Roadrunner Seafood Inc
Colquitt, GA 229-758-6098

Cusk

Canadian Fish Exporters
Auburndale, MA 800-225-4215

Dehydrated

Oregon Freeze Dry, Inc.
Albany, OR 541-926-6001

Eel

George Robberecht Seafood
Montross, VA 804-472-3556
Ocean Union Company
Lawrenceville, GA 770-995-1957

Fillets

Arrowac Fisheries
Seattle, WA 206-282-5655
Barry Group
Corner Brook, NL 709-785-7387
Bayou Food Distributors
Kenner, LA 800-516-8283
Cozy Harbor Seafood Inc
Portland, ME 800-225-2586
Ducktrap River Of Maine
Belfast, ME 800-434-8727
Erba Food Products
Brooklyn, NY 718-272-7700
Good Harbor Fillet Company
New Bedford, MA 800-343-8046
Jessie's Ilwaco Fish Company
San Francisco, CA 360-642-3773
Neptune Foods
Vernon, CA 323-232-8300
Nordic Group Inc
Boston, MA 800-486-4002
Ocean Beauty Seafoods Inc
Seattle, WA 800-365-8950
Pacific American Fish Co Inc
Vernon, CA 800-625-2525
Pacific Seafoods International
Port Hardy, BC 250-949-8781
Penguin Frozen Foods Inc
Northbrook, IL 800-323-1485
Roman Sausage Company
Santa Clara, CA 800-497-7462
Super Snooty Sea Food Corporation
Boston, MA 617-426-6390
Taku Smokehouse
Juneau, AK 800-582-5122
Ungars Food
Elmwood Park, NJ 201-773-6846

Finfish

Arrowac Fisheries
Seattle, WA 206-282-5655
Bold Coast Smokehouse
Lubec, ME 888-733-0807
Highland Fisheries
Glace Bay, NS 902-849-6016

Flounder

Bon Secour Fisheries Inc
Bon Secour, AL 251-949-7411
Carrington Foods Co Inc
Saraland, AL 251-675-9700
Catfish Wholesale
Abbeville, LA 800-334-7292
Glenn Sales Company
Atlanta, GA 770-952-9292
Gorton's Inc.
Gloucester, MA 800-222-6846

Griffin's Seafood
Golden Meadow, LA. 985-396-2453
Gulf City Marine Supply
Bayou La Batre, AL 251-824-2516
Inshore Fisheries
Middle West Pubnico, NS. 902-762-2522
Lund's Fisheries
Cape May, NJ 609-884-7600
Menemsha Fish Market
Chilmark, MA. 508-645-2282
Mirasco
Atlanta, GA. 770-956-1945
North Atlantic Seafood
Portland, ME. 800-774-6025
Northern Products Corporation
Seattle, WA 888-599-6290
Pamlico Packing Company
Grantsboro, NC. 800-682-1113
Roadrunner Seafood Inc
Colquitt, GA 229-758-6098
Royal Seafood Inc
Brooklyn, NY 718-769-1517
Tampa Maid Foods Inc
Lakeland, FL. 800-237-7637
Thompson Seafood
Darien, GA 912-437-4649
Wanchese Fish Co Inc
Suffolk, VA. 757-673-4500

Fluke

Agger Fish Corp
Brooklyn, NY 718-855-1717

Fresh

Arrowac Fisheries
Seattle, WA. 206-282-5655
Atlantic Salmon of Maine
Belfast, ME. 800-508-7861
Baker's Point Fisheries
Oyster Pond Jeddore, NS 902-845-2347
Bama Fish Atlanta
East Point, GA 404-765-9896
Bayou Land Seafood
Breaux Bridge, LA 337-667-6118
Birch Street Seafoods
Digby, NS 902-245-6551
Blue Circle Foods
Washington, DC 202-232-5282
Bon Secour Fisheries Inc
Bon Secour, AL. 251-949-7411
Cleanfish Inc
San Francisco, CA 415-626-3500
Cook Inlet Processing
Anchorage, AK. 907-243-1166
Crest International Corporation
San Diego, CA 800-548-1232
Deep Creek Custom Packing
Ninilchik, AK 800-764-0078
Ferroclad Fishery
Batchawana Bay, ON 705-882-2295
Galilean Seafood Inc
Bristol, RI 401-253-3030
Harbor Fish Market
Portland, ME. 800-370-1790
HFI Foods
Redmond, WA. 425-883-1320
High Liner Foods Inc.
Lunenburg, NS 902-634-8811
Inshore Fisheries
Middle West Pubnico, NS. 902-762-2522
International Seafoods - Alaska
Kodiak, AK. 907-486-4768
Island Marine Products
Clarks Harbour, NS. 902-745-2222
J. Matassini & Sons Fish Company
Tampa, FL. 813-229-0829
Jessie's Ilwaco Fish Company
San Francisco, CA 360-642-3773
King Food Service
Rock Island, IL 309-787-4488
Kyler's Catch Seafood Market
New Bedford, MA 888-859-5377
LA Monica Fine Foods
Millville, NJ
Lougheed Fisheries
Owen Sound, ON 519-376-1586
Mac Knight Smoke House Inc
Miami, FL. 305-651-3323
Mariner Seafood LLC
New Bedford, MA 774-202-4121
Menemsha Fish Market
Chilmark, MA. 508-645-2282
Minor Fisheries
Port Colborne, ON 905-834-9232
Morey's Seafood Intl LLC
Motley, MN. 800-808-3474
Mutual Fish Co
Seattle, WA 206-322-4368
North Atlantic Seafood
Portland, ME. 800-774-6025
Ocean Beauty Seafoods Inc
Seattle, WA 800-365-8950
Ocean Fresh Seafoods
Seattle, WA. 206-285-2412
Pacific American Fish Co Inc
Vernon, CA 800-625-2525
Pacific Seafoods International
Port Hardy, BC 250-949-8781
Paul Piazza & Son Inc
New Orleans, LA 800-969-6011
QualiGourmet
Boisbriand, QC 514-287-3530
Royal Seafood Inc
Brooklyn, NY 718-769-1517
Sportsman's Paradise Whites Ranch
Paradise, UT 435-245-3053
Sunshine Food Sales
Miami, FL. 305-696-2885
Tampa Bay Fisheries Inc
Dover, FL 800-732-3663
Trident Seafoods Corp
Wrangell, AK 907-874-3346
Union Fisheries Corp
Chicago, IL 773-738-0448
Virginia Trout Co
Monterey, VA 540-468-2280
Wanchese Fish Co Inc
Suffolk, VA. 757-673-4500
Weyand's Fishery
Wyandotte, MI 800-521-9815
Yamasa Fish Cake Co
Los Angeles, CA. 213-626-2211

Freshwater

Hamilos Bros Inspected Meat
Madison, IL. 618-876-3710

Frozen

Alaskan Gourmet Seafoods
Anchorage, AK. 800-288-3740
Alpine Butcher
Lowell, MA. 978-256-7771
Amano Fish Cake Factory
Hilo, HI 808-935-5555
Arrowac Fisheries
Seattle, WA. 206-282-5655
Baker's Point Fisheries
Oyster Pond Jeddore, NS 902-845-2347
Bama Fish Atlanta
East Point, GA 404-765-9896
Barry Group
Corner Brook, NL. 709-785-7387
Bayou Land Seafood
Breaux Bridge, LA 337-667-6118
Beaver Street Fisheries
Jacksonville, FL 800-874-6426
Big Al's Seafood
Bozman, MD. 410-745-2637
Birch Street Seafoods
Digby, NS 902-245-6551
Birdie Pak Products
Chicago, IL 773-247-5293
Blue Circle Foods
Washington, DC 202-232-5282
Bon Secour Fisheries Inc
Bon Secour, AL. 251-949-7411
Breakwater Fisheries
St John's, NL. 709-754-1999
Buedel Food Products
Bridgeview, IL 708-496-3500
Carrington Foods Co Inc
Saraland, AL. 251-675-9700
Certi Fresh Foods Inc
Wilmington, CA 310-221-6262
Channel Fish Processing
Gloucester, MA. 800-457-0054
Clear Springs Foods Inc.
Buhl, ID. 800-635-8211
Cook Inlet Processing
Anchorage, AK. 907-243-1166
Cozy Harbor Seafood Inc
Portland, ME. 800-225-2586
Crest International Corporation
San Diego, CA 800-548-1232
Cuizina Food Company
Woodinville, WA. 425-486-7000
DB Kenney Fisheries
Westport, NS. 902-839-2023
Deep Creek Custom Packing
Ninilchik, AK 800-764-0078
Delta Pride Catfish
Indianola, MS 800-228-3474
Ferroclad Fishery
Batchawana Bay, ON 705-882-2295
George Robberecht Seafood
Montross, VA 804-472-3556
Glacier Fish Company
Seattle, WA 206-298-1200
Great Glacier Salmon
Prince Rupert, BC. 250-627-4955
Great Northern Products Inc
Cranston, RI 401-490-4590
Hamilos Bros Inspected Meat
Madison, IL. 618-876-3710
Handy International Inc
Salisbury, MD 800-426-3977
HFI Foods
Redmond, WA. 425-883-1320
High Liner Foods Inc.
Lunenburg, NS 902-634-8811
Hook Line and Savor
Gloucester, MA. 833-457-2867
Independent Packers Corporation
Seattle, WA 206-285-6000
Inshore Fisheries
Middle West Pubnico, NS. 902-762-2522
International Seafoods - Alaska
Kodiak, AK. 907-486-4768
Island Marine Products
Clarks Harbour, NS. 902-745-2222
J. Matassini & Sons Fish Company
Tampa, FL. 813-229-0829
Jessie's Ilwaco Fish Company
San Francisco, CA 360-642-3773
Key Largo Fisheries
Key Largo, FL. 800-432-4358
Kodiak Salmon Packers
Larsen Bay, AK. 907-847-2250
Kyler's Catch Seafood Market
New Bedford, MA 888-859-5377
Lougheed Fisheries
Owen Sound, ON 519-376-1586
Lund's Fisheries
Cape May, NJ 609-884-7600
Mada'n Kosher Foods
Dania, FL 954-925-0077
Martin Brothers Seafood Co
Westwego, LA. 504-341-2251
Menemsha Fish Market
Chilmark, MA. 508-645-2282
Mill Cove Lobster Pound
Trevett, ME. 207-633-3340
Minor Fisheries
Port Colborne, ON 905-834-9232
Monterey Fish Company
Salinas, CA 831-771-9221
Morey's Seafood Intl LLC
Motley, MN. 800-808-3474
Mutual Fish Co
Seattle, WA 206-322-4368
Nelson Crab Inc
Tokeland, WA 800-262-0069
Nordic Group Inc
Boston, MA. 800-486-4002
North Atlantic Seafood
Portland, ME. 800-774-6025
Notre Dame Seafoods Inc.
Comfort Cove, NL 709-244-5511
Ocean Beauty Seafoods Inc
Seattle, WA. 800-365-8950
Ocean Fresh Seafoods
Seattle, WA 206-285-2412
Okuhara Foods Inc
Honolulu, HI. 808-848-0581
Pacific American Fish Co Inc
Vernon, CA 800-625-2525
Pacific Salmon Company
Edmonds, WA. 425-774-1315
Pacific Seafoods International
Port Hardy, BC 250-949-8781
Pamlico Packing Company
Grantsboro, NC. 800-682-1113

Paul Piazza & Son Inc
New Orleans, LA 800-969-6011
Penguin Frozen Foods Inc
Northbrook, IL 800-323-1485
Peter Pan Seafoods Inc.
Bellevue, WA 206-728-6000
Quinault Pride
Taholah, WA 360-276-4431
Royal Seafood Inc
Brooklyn, NY 718-769-1517
Santa Monica Seafood Co.
Rancho Dominguez, CA 800-969-8862
Sea Safari
Belhaven, NC 800-688-6174
Seymour & Sons Seafoods Inc
Diberville, MS 228-392-4020
Spruce Lane Investments
Stratford, PE 902-892-2600
Sterling Caviar LLC
Elverta, CA 800-525-0333
Sunshine Food Sales
Miami, FL 305-696-2885
Super Snooty Sea Food Corporation
Boston, MA 617-426-6390
Taku Smokehouse
Juneau, AK 800-582-5122
Tampa Bay Fisheries Inc
Dover, FL 800-732-3663
Tampa Maid Foods Inc
Lakeland, FL 800-237-7637
Tichon Sea Food Corp
New Bedford, MA 508-999-5607
Trident Seafoods Corp
Wrangell, AK 907-874-3346
Union Fisheries Corp
Chicago, IL 773-738-0448
Viking Seafoods Inc
Malden, MA 800-225-3020
Virginia Trout Co
Monterey, VA 540-468-2280
Wanchese Fish Co Inc
Suffolk, VA 757-673-4500
Weyand's Fishery
Wyandotte, MI 800-521-9815
White Cap Fish Market
Islip, NY 631-277-6577
Yamasa Fish Cake Co
Los Angeles, CA 213-626-2211

Gefilte

Erba Food Products
Brooklyn, NY 718-272-7700
Manischewitz Co
Newark, NJ 201-553-1100

Grouper

Griffin's Seafood
Golden Meadow, LA 985-396-2453
Mirasco
Atlanta, GA 770-956-1945
North Atlantic Seafood
Portland, ME 800-774-6025
Ocean Union Company
Lawrenceville, GA 770-995-1957
Poseidon Enterprises
Charlotte, NC 800-863-7886

Haddock

Adams Fisheries Ltd
Shag Harbour, NS 902-723-2435
BlueWater Seafoods
Gloucester, MA 888-560-2539
Canadian Fish Exporters
Auburndale, MA 800-225-4215
Davis Strait Fisheries
Halifax, NS 902-450-5115
DB Kenney Fisheries
Westport, NS 902-839-2023
High Liner Foods Inc.
Lunenburg, NS 902-634-8811
I. Deveau Fisheries LTD
Barrington Passage, NS 902-745-2877
Inshore Fisheries
Middle West Pubnico, NS 902-762-2522
Island Marine Products
Clarks Harbour, NS 902-745-2222
La Have Seafoods
La Have, NS 902-688-2773
Leo G. Atkinson Fisheries
Clarks Harbor, NS 902-745-3047
Menemsha Fish Market
Chilmark, MA 508-645-2282
MG Fisheries
Grand Manan, NB 506-662-3471
Nordic Group Inc
Boston, MA 800-486-4002
North Atlantic Seafood
Portland, ME 800-774-6025
Ocean Pride Fisheries
Lower Wedgeport, NS 902-663-4579
W.A. Beans & Sons
Bangor, ME 800-649-1958

Hake

Canadian Fish Exporters
Auburndale, MA 800-225-4215
Helshiron Fisheries
Grand Manan, NB 506-662-3696
Mirasco
Atlanta, GA 770-956-1945
North Atlantic Seafood
Portland, ME 800-774-6025

Halibut

Alaska Pacific Seafoods
Kodiak, AK 907-486-3234
Alaskan Gourmet Seafoods
Anchorage, AK 800-288-3740
Angy's Food Products Inc
Westfield, MA 413-572-1010
Arrowac Fisheries
Seattle, WA 206-282-5655
Boundary Fish Company
Blaine, WA 360-332-6715
California Shellfish Company
San Francisco, CA 415-923-7400
Calkins & Burke
Vancouver, BC 800-669-7992
Captain Little Seafood
Queens County, NS 902-947-2087
Certi Fresh Foods Inc
Wilmington, CA 310-221-6262
Channel Fish Processing
Gloucester, MA 800-457-0054
Charlton Charters
Warrenton, OR 503-338-0569
D Waybret & Sons Fisher ies
Shelburne, NS 902-745-3477
Deep Creek Custom Packing
Ninilchik, AK 800-764-0078
Felix Custom Smoking
Monroe, WA 425-485-2439
Fishhawk Fisheries
Astoria, OR 503-325-5252
Glacier Fish Company
Seattle, WA 206-298-1200
Haines Packing Company
Haines, AK 907-766-2883
High Liner Foods Inc.
Lunenburg, NS 902-634-8811
Independent Packers Corporation
Seattle, WA 206-285-6000
Indian Valley Meats
Indian, AK 907-653-7511
Island Marine Products
Clarks Harbour, NS 902-745-2222
Menemsha Fish Market
Chilmark, MA 508-645-2282
Neptune Foods
Vernon, CA 323-232-8300
North Atlantic Seafood
Portland, ME 800-774-6025
North Pacific Seafoods Inc
Seattle, WA 206-726-9900
Northwest Fisheries
Hubbards, NS 902-228-2232
Northwest Wild Products
Astoria, OR 503-791-1907
Ocean Beauty Seafoods Inc
Seattle, WA 800-365-8950
Pacific Salmon Company
Edmonds, WA 425-774-1315
Peter Pan Seafoods Inc.
Bellevue, WA 206-728-6000
Santa Monica Seafood Co.
Rancho Dominguez, CA 800-969-8862
Seafood Producers Co-Op
Bellingham, WA 360-733-0120
Taku Smokehouse
Juneau, AK 800-582-5122
Tampa Bay Fisheries Inc
Dover, FL 800-732-3663
Tenth & M Seafoods
Anchorage, AK 800-770-2722
Trident Seafoods Corp
Wrangell, AK 907-874-3346
Viking Seafoods Inc
Malden, MA 800-225-3020
Vital Choice
Bellingham, WA 800-608-4825

Herring

Acme Smoked Fish Corporation
Brooklyn, NY 718-383-8585
Alimentaire Whyte's Inc
Laval, QC 866-420-9520
Angy's Food Products Inc
Westfield, MA 413-572-1010
Baensch Food Products Co
Milwaukee, WI 414-562-4643
Barry Group
Corner Brook, NL 709-785-7387
Bos Smoked Fish Inc
Woodstock, ON 519-537-5000
Breakwater Fisheries
St John's, NL 709-754-1999
Canadian Fish Exporters
Auburndale, MA 800-225-4215
Castella Imports Inc
Brentwood, NY 631-231-5500
Chicago 58 Food Products
Woodbridge, ON 416-603-4244
Comeau's Seafoods
Saulnierville, NS 902-769-2101
Cowart Seafood Corp
Lottsburg, VA 804-529-6101
Delta Pacific Seafoods
Delta, BC 604-946-5160
Dragnet Fisheries
Anchorage, AK 907-276-4551
Duguay Fish Packers
Cap-Pele, NB 506-577-2287
Feature Foods
Brampton, ON 905-452-7741
Ferroclad Fishery
Batchawana Bay, ON 705-882-2295
Flaum Appetizing
Brooklyn, NY 718-821-1970
Gaudet & Ouellette
Cap-Pele, NB 506-577-4016
Great Northern Products Inc
Cranston, RI 401-490-4590
Island Marine Products
Clarks Harbour, NS 902-745-2222
Leslie Leger & Sons
Cap-Pele, NB 506-577-4730
Lund's Fisheries
Cape May, NJ 609-884-7600
Menemsha Fish Market
Chilmark, MA 508-645-2282
Newell Lobsters
Yarmouth, NS 902-742-6272
North Pacific Seafoods Inc
Seattle, WA 206-726-9900
Premier Smoked Fish Company
Bensalem, PA 800-654-6682
Produits Belle Baie
Caraquet, NB 506-727-4414
Rachael's Smoked Fish
Springfield, MA 800-327-3412
Raffield Fisheries Inc
Port St Joe, FL 850-229-8494
Royal Seafood Inc
Brooklyn, NY 718-769-1517
Russ & Daughters
New York, NY 800-787-7229
Salmolux Inc
Federal Way, WA 253-874-6570
Spruce Lane Investments
Stratford, PE 902-892-2600
Strub Pickles
Brantford, ON 519-751-1717
Trident Seafoods Corp
Wrangell, AK 907-874-3346
Vita Food Products Inc
Chicago, IL 800-989-8482

Boned

Feature Foods
Brampton, ON 905-452-7741

Fillets
Angy's Food Products Inc
Westfield, MA....................413-572-1010

Fresh
Angy's Food Products Inc
Westfield, MA....................413-572-1010
Bella Coola Fisheries
Surrey, BC....................604-541-0339
Feature Foods
Brampton, ON....................905-452-7741
Ferroclad Fishery
Batchawana Bay, ON....................705-882-2295
Royal Seafood Inc
Brooklyn, NY....................718-769-1517
Trident Seafoods Corp
Wrangell, AK....................907-874-3346

Frozen
Angy's Food Products Inc
Westfield, MA....................413-572-1010
Bella Coola Fisheries
Surrey, BC....................604-541-0339
Breakwater Fisheries
St John's, NL....................709-754-1999
Ferroclad Fishery
Batchawana Bay, ON....................705-882-2295
Great Northern Products Inc
Cranston, RI....................401-490-4590
Island Marine Products
Clarks Harbour, NS....................902-745-2222
Lund's Fisheries
Cape May, NJ....................609-884-7600
Menemsha Fish Market
Chilmark, MA....................508-645-2282
Peter Pan Seafoods Inc.
Bellevue, WA....................206-728-6000
Royal Seafood Inc
Brooklyn, NY....................718-769-1517
Trident Seafoods Corp
Wrangell, AK....................907-874-3346

Salted & Marinated
Feature Foods
Brampton, ON....................905-452-7741
High Liner Foods Inc.
Lunenburg, NS....................902-634-8811
Island Marine Products
Clarks Harbour, NS....................902-745-2222

Spiced
Baensch Food Products Co
Milwaukee, WI....................414-562-4643
Feature Foods
Brampton, ON....................905-452-7741

Imitation
Flavor House, Inc.
Adelanto, CA....................760-246-9131
HFI Foods
Redmond, WA....................425-883-1320
Ocean Food Co. Ltd.
Toronto, ON....................416-285-6487
Peter Pan Seafoods Inc.
Bellevue, WA....................206-728-6000
Shining Ocean Inc
Sumner, WA....................800-935-6464
Trans-Ocean Products Inc
Bellingham, WA....................800-290-2722

King Cod
Deep Creek Custom Packing
Ninilchik, AK....................800-764-0078
Minor Fisheries
Port Colborne, ON....................905-834-9232

Kingfish
Sunshine Food Sales
Miami, FL....................305-696-2885

Lumpfish
Notre Dame Seafoods Inc.
Comfort Cove, NL....................709-244-5511
Russian Chef
New York, NY....................212-249-1550

Mackerel
Atlantic Capes Fisheries
Cape May, NJ....................609-884-3000
Atlantic Fish Specialties
Charlottetown, PE....................902-894-7005
Bold Coast Smokehouse
Lubec, ME....................888-733-0807
Bos Smoked Fish Inc
Woodstock, ON....................519-537-5000
Breakwater Fisheries
St John's, NL....................709-754-1999
Canadian Fish Exporters
Auburndale, MA....................800-225-4215
Castella Imports Inc
Brentwood, NY....................631-231-5500
Chicken Of The Sea
El Segundo, CA....................844-267-8862
Crown Prince Inc
City Of Industry, CA....................626-912-3700
Ducktrap River Of Maine
Belfast, ME....................800-434-8727
Erba Food Products
Brooklyn, NY....................718-272-7700
Griffin's Seafood
Golden Meadow, LA....................985-396-2453
J Deluca Fish Co Inc
San Pedro, CA....................310-684-5180
Lund's Fisheries
Cape May, NJ....................609-884-7600
Menemsha Fish Market
Chilmark, MA....................508-645-2282
Northwest Wild Products
Astoria, OR....................503-791-1907
Notre Dame Seafoods Inc.
Comfort Cove, NL....................709-244-5511
Ocean Union Company
Lawrenceville, GA....................770-995-1957
Royal Seafood Inc
Brooklyn, NY....................718-769-1517
Russ & Daughters
New York, NY....................800-787-7229
Spruce Lane Investments
Stratford, PE....................902-892-2600
Sunshine Food Sales
Miami, FL....................305-696-2885
Vital Choice
Bellingham, WA....................800-608-4825

Mahi-Mahi
Griffin's Seafood
Golden Meadow, LA....................985-396-2453
North Atlantic Seafood
Portland, ME....................800-774-6025
Ocean Beauty Seafoods Inc
Seattle, WA....................800-365-8950
Omega Foods
Mississauga, ON....................877-212-9484
Peter Pan Seafoods Inc.
Bellevue, WA....................206-728-6000

Marlin
Mid-Pacific Hawaii Fishery
Hilo, HI....................808-935-6110
Sportsmens Seafoods
San Diego, CA....................619-224-3551

Meal
Acatris USA
Edina, MN....................952-920-7700
Barry Group
Corner Brook, NL....................709-785-7387

Monkfish
Agger Fish Corp
Brooklyn, NY....................718-855-1717
Atlantic Capes Fisheries
Cape May, NJ....................609-884-3000
North Atlantic Seafood
Portland, ME....................800-774-6025

Mullet
Griffin's Seafood
Golden Meadow, LA....................985-396-2453
Raffield Fisheries Inc
Port St Joe, FL....................850-229-8494
Roadrunner Seafood Inc
Colquitt, GA....................229-758-6098

Orange Roughy
Neptune Foods
Vernon, CA....................323-232-8300

Packed
Ore-Cal Corp
Los Angeles, CA....................800-827-7474

Glass
Indian Valley Meats
Indian, AK....................907-653-7511
Noon Hour Food Products Inc
Chicago, IL....................800-621-6636

Pouch
Cook Inlet Processing
Anchorage, AK....................907-243-1166
Haines Packing Company
Haines, AK....................907-766-2883
Indian Valley Meats
Indian, AK....................907-653-7511
Noon Hour Food Products Inc
Chicago, IL....................800-621-6636
Seajoy
Miami, FL....................877-537-1717

Paste
Giovanni's Appetizing Food Co
Richmond, MI....................586-727-9355

Patties
CBS Food Products Corporation
Franklin, TN....................800-216-9605
Roman Sausage Company
Santa Clara, CA....................800-497-7462

Perch
A&A Marine & Drydock Company
Blenheim, ON....................519-676-2030
High Liner Foods Inc.
Lunenburg, NS....................902-634-8811
Inshore Fisheries
Middle West Pubnico, NS....................902-762-2522
Kingsville Fisherman's Company
Kingsville, ON....................519-733-6534
Minor Fisheries
Port Colborne, ON....................905-834-9232
Mutual Fish Co
Seattle, WA....................206-322-4368
North Atlantic Seafood
Portland, ME....................800-774-6025
Paul Piazza & Son Inc
New Orleans, LA....................800-969-6011
Royal Seafood Inc
Brooklyn, NY....................718-769-1517
Viking Seafoods Inc
Malden, MA....................800-225-3020

Ocean
DB Kenney Fisheries
Westport, NS....................902-839-2023
Mill Cove Lobster Pound
Trevett, ME....................207-633-3340

Pickerel
A&A Marine & Drydock Company
Blenheim, ON....................519-676-2030
Kingsville Fisherman's Company
Kingsville, ON....................519-733-6534
Minor Fisheries
Port Colborne, ON....................905-834-9232

Pollack
Alaska Pacific Seafoods
Kodiak, AK....................907-486-3234
BlueWater Seafoods
Gloucester, MA....................888-560-2539
Glacier Fish Company
Seattle, WA....................206-298-1200
Glenn Sales Company
Atlanta, GA....................770-952-9292
Harbor Seafood
New Hyde Park, NY....................800-645-2211
Inshore Fisheries
Middle West Pubnico, NS....................902-762-2522
K&N Fisheries
Upper Port La Tour, NS....................902-768-2478

Neptune Foods
Vernon, CA 323-232-8300
North Atlantic Seafood
Portland, ME...................... 800-774-6025
Peter Pan Seafoods Inc.
Bellevue, WA 206-728-6000

Pompano

Griffin's Seafood
Golden Meadow, LA................ 985-396-2453

Red Snapper

Northwest Wild Products
Astoria, OR....................... 503-791-1907

Rock Fish

Deep Creek Custom Packing
Ninilchik, AK..................... 800-764-0078
North Pacific Seafoods Inc
Seattle, WA 206-726-9900
Seafood Producers Co-Op
Bellingham, WA 360-733-0120
Vital Choice
Bellingham, WA 800-608-4825

Sablefish

Rego Smoked Fish Company
Flushing, NY...................... 718-894-1400
Russ & Daughters
New York, NY 800-787-7229
Vital Choice
Bellingham, WA 800-608-4825

Salmon

Alaska General Seafoods
Kenmore, WA 425-485-7755
Alaska Pacific Seafoods
Kodiak, AK....................... 907-486-3234
Alaskan Gourmet Seafoods
Anchorage, AK.................... 800-288-3740
Alaskan Smoked Salmon & Seafood
Anchorage, AK.................... 907-349-8234
Alder Springs Smoked Salmon
Sequim, WA 360-683-2829
Angy's Food Products Inc
Westfield, MA.................... 413-572-1010
Aquatec Seafoods Ltd.
Comox, BC........................ 250-339-6412
Arrowac Fisheries
Seattle, WA 206-282-5655
Atlantic Salmon of Maine
Belfast, ME....................... 800-508-7861
Barry Group
Corner Brook, NL................. 709-785-7387
Bella Coola Fisheries
Surrey, BC........................ 604-541-0339
Bering Sea Fisheries
Snohomish, WA 425-334-1498
Blue Marble Brands
Providence, RI 888-534-0246
BlueWater Seafoods
Gloucester, MA................... 888-560-2539
Blundell Seafoods
Richmond, BC 604-270-3300
Bos Smoked Fish Inc
Woodstock, ON................... 519-537-5000
Brucepac
Woodburn, OR 800-899-3629
Caito Fisheries Inc
Fort Bragg, CA................... 707-964-6368
California Shellfish Company
San Francisco, CA 415-923-7400
Calkins & Burke
Vancouver, BC 800-669-7992
Casey Fisheries
Digby, NS 902-245-5801
Certi Fresh Foods Inc
Wilmington, CA 310-221-6262
Charlton Charters
Warrenton, OR 503-338-0569
Chicken Of The Sea
El Segundo, CA 844-267-8862
Chuck's Seafoods
Charleston, OR................... 541-888-5525
Dave's Gourmet Albacore
Watsonville, CA 206-999-5517
Dear North
Juneau, AK....................... 907-789-8500
Deep Creek Custom Packing
Ninilchik, AK..................... 800-764-0078
Delta Pacific Seafoods
Delta, BC......................... 604-946-5160
Dragnet Fisheries
Anchorage, AK.................... 907-276-4551
Dressel Collins Fish Company
Seattle, WA 206-725-0121
Ducktrap River Of Maine
Belfast, ME....................... 800-434-8727
FDI Inc
Berkeley, IL...................... 708-544-1880
Fiddlers Green Farm
North Vassalboro, ME 800-729-7935
Fishhawk Fisheries
Astoria, OR....................... 503-325-5252
Giovanni's Appetizing Food Co
Richmond, MI..................... 586-727-9355
Glacier Fish Company
Seattle, WA 206-298-1200
Great Glacier Salmon
Prince Rupert, BC................ 250-627-4955
Great Pacific Seafoods
Seattle, WA 206-764-7180
Haines Packing Company
Haines, AK 907-766-2883
Handy International Inc
Salisbury, MD..................... 800-426-3977
Heritage Salmon Company
Richmond, BC 604-277-3093
High Liner Foods Inc.
Lunenburg, NS.................... 902-634-8811
High Tide Seafoods Inc
Port Angeles, WA 360-452-8488
Independent Packers Corporation
Seattle, WA 206-285-6000
Indian Valley Meats
Indian, AK........................ 907-653-7511
J.S. McMillan Fisheries
North Vancouver, BC 604-981-4000
Jessie's Ilwaco Fish Company
San Francisco, CA 360-642-3773
Kodiak Salmon Packers
Larsen Bay, AK................... 907-847-2250
Maine Coast Nordic
Mahiasport, ME 207-255-6714
Menemsha Fish Market
Chilmark, MA..................... 508-645-2282
Morey's Seafood Intl LLC
Motley, MN....................... 800-808-3474
Mutual Fish Co
Seattle, WA 206-322-4368
Nelson Crab Inc
Tokeland, WA 800-262-0069
Neptune Foods
Vernon, CA....................... 323-232-8300
Nordic Group Inc
Boston, MA....................... 800-486-4002
North Atlantic Seafood
Portland, ME...................... 800-774-6025
North Pacific Seafoods Inc
Seattle, WA 206-726-9900
Northern Products Corporation
Seattle, WA 888-599-6290
Northwest Wild Products
Astoria, OR....................... 503-791-1907
Ocean Beauty Seafoods Inc
Seattle, WA 800-365-8950
Ocean Food Co. Ltd.
Toronto, ON 416-285-6487
Okuhara Foods Inc
Honolulu, HI...................... 808-848-0581
Omega Foods
Mississauga, ON.................. 877-212-9484
Pacific Salmon Company
Edmonds, WA..................... 425-774-1315
Pacific Seafoods International
Port Hardy, BC 250-949-8781
Paramount Caviar
Long Island City, NY 800-992-2842
Patagonia Provisions
Sausalito, CA 888-221-8208
Perona Farms
Andover, NJ 800-750-6190
Peter Pan Seafoods Inc.
Bellevue, WA 206-728-6000
Poseidon Enterprises
Charlotte, NC 800-863-7886
Premier Smoked Fish Company
Bensalem, PA 800-654-6682
QualiGourmet
Boisbriand, QC 514-287-3530
Quinault Pride
Taholah, WA 360-276-4431
Rachael's Smoked Fish
Springfield, MA 800-327-3412
Rego Smoked Fish Company
Flushing, NY...................... 718-894-1400
Roman Sausage Company
Santa Clara, CA 800-497-7462
Royal Seafood Inc
Brooklyn, NY..................... 718-769-1517
Russian Chef
New York, NY 212-249-1550
Salmolux Inc
Federal Way, WA 253-874-6570
Salty Girl Seafood
Santa Barbara, CA 805-699-5025
Santa Monica Seafood Co.
Rancho Dominguez, CA........... 800-969-8862
Seafood Producers Co-Op
Bellingham, WA 360-733-0120
Shafer-Haggart
Vancouver, BC 604-669-5512
Splendid Spreads
Eagan, MN 877-773-2374
Sportsmen's Cannery & Smokehouse
Winchester Bay, OR 800-457-8048
Taku Smokehouse
Juneau, AK....................... 800-582-5122
Tampa Bay Fisheries Inc
Dover, FL 800-732-3663
Tenth & M Seafoods
Anchorage, AK.................... 800-770-2722
Trident Seafoods Corp
Wrangell, AK 907-874-3346
Verlasso
FL 786-522-8418
Vita Food Products Inc
Chicago, IL....................... 800-989-8482
Vital Choice
Bellingham, WA 800-608-4825
Walcan Seafood
Heroit Bay, BC 250-285-3361
Woodsmoke Provisions
Atlanta, GA....................... 404-355-5125

Chum

Haines Packing Company
Haines, AK 907-766-2883

Coho

Haines Packing Company
Haines, AK 907-766-2883

King

Haines Packing Company
Haines, AK 907-766-2883

Pink

Chicken Of The Sea
El Segundo, CA 844-267-8862
Crown Prince Inc
City Of Industry, CA.............. 626-912-3700
Haines Packing Company
Haines, AK 907-766-2883

Smoked

Alaska Bounty Seafoods & Smokery
Sitka, AK......................... 907-747-3730
Alaska Jacks
Anchorage, AK.................... 888-660-2257
Alaska Seafood Co
Juneau, AK....................... 800-451-1400
Alaska Smokehouse
Woodinville, WA.................. 800-422-0852
Alaskan Gourmet Seafoods
Anchorage, AK.................... 800-288-3740
Alaskan Smoked Salmon & Seafood
Anchorage, AK.................... 907-349-8234
Alder Springs Smoked Salmon
Sequim, WA 360-683-2829
Bold Coast Smokehouse
Lubec, ME........................ 888-733-0807
California Shellfish Company
San Francisco, CA 415-923-7400
Comeau's Seafoods
Saulnierville, NS.................. 902-769-2101
Dollar Food Manufacturing
Vancouver, BC 604-253-1422
Dressel Collins Fish Company
Seattle, WA 206-725-0121
E-Fish-Ent Fish Company
Sooke, BC........................ 250-642-4007

Felix Custom Smoking
Monroe, WA 425-485-2439
Fish Brothers
Blue Lake, CA 800-244-0583
Fish King Processors
Brunswick, GA 800-841-0205
Fumoir Grizzly
St Augustin, QC 418-878-8941
Giovanni's Appetizing Food Co
Richmond, MI 586-727-9355
Haines Packing Company
Haines, AK 907-766-2883
Homarus Inc
Long Island City, NY 917-832-0333
Imperial Salmon House
Vancouver, BC 604-251-1114
Jensen's Old Fashioned Smokehouse
Seattle, WA 206-364-5569
Kasilof Fish Company
Everett, WA 800-322-7552
Katy's Smokehouse
Trinidad, CA 707-677-0151
Nordic Group Inc
Boston, MA 800-486-4002
Ocean Pride Fisheries
Lower Wedgeport, NS 902-663-4579
Oceanfood Sales
Vancouver, BC 877-255-1414
Oven Head Salmon Smokers
Bethel, NB 877-955-2507
Pacific Seafoods International
Port Hardy, BC 250-949-8781
Paramount Caviar
Long Island City, NY 800-992-2842
Pickwick Catfish Farm
Counce, TN 731-689-3805
Portier Fine Foods
Mamaroneck, NY 800-272-9463
Premier Smoked Fish Company
Bensalem, PA 800-654-6682
Rego Smoked Fish Company
Flushing, NY 718-894-1400
Rier Smoked Salmon
Lubec, ME 888-733-0807
Russ & Daughters
New York, NY 800-787-7229
Russian Chef
New York, NY 212-249-1550
SeaBear Wild Salmon
Anacortes, WA 800-645-3474
Sullivan Harbor Farm
Hancock Village, ME 800-422-4014

Sockeye

Alaska Smokehouse
Woodinville, WA 800-422-0852
Haines Packing Company
Haines, AK 907-766-2883

Steak

Arrowac Fisheries
Seattle, WA 206-282-5655
Nelson Crab Inc
Tokeland, WA 800-262-0069
Neptune Foods
Vernon, CA 323-232-8300

Salted

Canadian Fish Exporters
Auburndale, MA 800-225-4215
DB Kenney Fisheries
Westport, NS 902-839-2023
Island Marine Products
Clarks Harbour, NS 902-745-2222
Taku Smokehouse
Juneau, AK 800-582-5122

Sardines

Castella Imports Inc
Brentwood, NY 631-231-5500
Crown Prince Inc
City Of Industry, CA 626-912-3700
Erba Food Products
Brooklyn, NY 718-272-7700
J Deluca Fish Co Inc
San Pedro, CA 310-684-5180
Jessie's Ilwaco Fish Company
San Francisco, CA 360-642-3773
Northwest Wild Products
Astoria, OR 503-791-1907
Raffield Fisheries Inc
Port St Joe, FL 850-229-8494

Canned

Ardy Fisher
. 877-699-5066
Blue Marble Brands
Providence, RI 888-534-0246
Chicken Of The Sea
El Segundo, CA 844-267-8862
Crown Prince Inc
City Of Industry, CA 626-912-3700
Pastene Co LTD
Canton, MA 781-298-3397
Season Brand
Newark, NJ 201-553-1100
Vital Choice
Bellingham, WA 800-608-4825

Fresh

Jessie's Ilwaco Fish Company
San Francisco, CA 360-642-3773

Sea Bass

Arrowac Fisheries
Seattle, WA 206-282-5655
North Atlantic Seafood
Portland, ME 800-774-6025
Ocean Beauty Seafoods Inc
Seattle, WA 800-365-8950
Santa Monica Seafood Co.
Rancho Dominguez, CA 800-969-8862
Tampa Bay Fisheries Inc
Dover, FL 800-732-3663

Sea Trout

Glenn Sales Company
Atlanta, GA 770-952-9292

Shad

Fishhawk Fisheries
Astoria, OR 503-325-5252
Lund's Fisheries
Cape May, NJ 609-884-7600
Nelson Crab Inc
Tokeland, WA 800-262-0069

Shark

Agger Fish Corp
Brooklyn, NY 718-855-1717
Arrowac Fisheries
Seattle, WA 206-282-5655
Caito Fisheries Inc
Fort Bragg, CA 707-964-6368
Louisiana Seafood Exchange
Jefferson, LA 800-969-9394
Mid-Pacific Hawaii Fishery
Hilo, HI 808-935-6110
New Orleans Fish House II LLC
New Orleans, LA 800-839-3474
Ocean Beauty Seafoods Inc
Seattle, WA 800-365-8950
Pacific Salmon Company
Edmonds, WA 425-774-1315
Scandinavian Laboratories
Belvidere, PA 866-623-2650

Sheephead

Griffin's Seafood
Golden Meadow, LA 985-396-2453
New Orleans Fish House II LLC
New Orleans, LA 800-839-3474
Stoller Fisheries
Spirit Lake, IA 800-831-5174

Smelt

Burleigh Brothers Seafoods
Ellerslie, PE 902-831-2349
Certi Fresh Foods Inc
Wilmington, CA 310-221-6262
Channel Fish Processing
Gloucester, MA 800-457-0054
Fishhawk Fisheries
Astoria, OR 503-325-5252
Jessie's Ilwaco Fish Company
San Francisco, CA 360-642-3773
Minor Fisheries
Port Colborne, ON 905-834-9232
Pacific Salmon Company
Edmonds, WA 425-774-1315

Smoked & Cured

Acme Smoked Fish Corporation
Brooklyn, NY 718-383-8585
Alaska Jacks
Anchorage, AK 888-660-2257
Alaska Sausage & Seafood
Anchorage, AK 800-798-3636
Alaskan Gourmet Seafoods
Anchorage, AK 800-288-3740
Bos Smoked Fish Inc
Woodstock, ON 519-537-5000
Buedel Food Products
Bridgeview, IL 708-496-3500
California Shellfish Company
San Francisco, CA 415-923-7400
Chuck's Seafoods
Charleston, OR 541-888-5525
Deep Creek Custom Packing
Ninilchik, AK 800-764-0078
Dressel Collins Fish Company
Seattle, WA 206-725-0121
Ducktrap River Of Maine
Belfast, ME 800-434-8727
Fish Brothers
Blue Lake, CA 800-244-0583
Gold Star Smoked Fish Inc
Brooklyn, NY 718-522-1545
High Liner Foods Inc.
Lunenburg, NS 902-634-8811
Homarus Inc
Long Island City, NY 917-832-0333
J Moniz Co Inc
Fall River, MA 508-674-8451
J Turner Seafood
Gloucester, MA 978-281-8535
Mac Knight Smoke House Inc
Miami, FL 305-651-3323
Menemsha Fish Market
Chilmark, MA 508-645-2282
Mutual Fish Co
Seattle, WA 206-322-4368
Nelson Crab Inc
Tokeland, WA 800-262-0069
Nordic Group Inc
Boston, MA 800-486-4002
Ocean Fresh Seafoods
Seattle, WA 206-285-2412
Paramount Caviar
Long Island City, NY 800-992-2842
Premier Smoked Fish Company
Bensalem, PA 800-654-6682
Quinault Pride
Taholah, WA 360-276-4431
Rego Smoked Fish Company
Flushing, NY 718-894-1400
Russ & Daughters
New York, NY 800-787-7229
Russian Chef
New York, NY 212-249-1550
Sea Bear Smokehouse
Anacortes, WA 800-645-3474
Sterling Caviar LLC
Elverta, CA 800-525-0333
Taku Smokehouse
Juneau, AK 800-582-5122

Snapper

Bon Secour Fisheries Inc
Bon Secour, AL 251-949-7411
California Shellfish Company
San Francisco, CA 415-923-7400
Griffin's Seafood
Golden Meadow, LA 985-396-2453
North Atlantic Seafood
Portland, ME 800-774-6025
Northern Products Corporation
Seattle, WA 888-599-6290
Ocean Union Company
Lawrenceville, GA 770-995-1957
Poseidon Enterprises
Charlotte, NC 800-863-7886

Sole

BlueWater Seafoods
Gloucester, MA 888-560-2539
DB Kenney Fisheries
Westport, NS 902-839-2023

Gorton's Inc.
Gloucester, MA.......................800-222-6846
High Liner Foods Inc.
Lunenburg, NS.......................902-634-8811
Northwest Wild Products
Astoria, OR.......................503-791-1907
Penguin Frozen Foods Inc
Northbrook, IL.......................800-323-1485
Royal Seafood Inc
Brooklyn, NY.......................718-769-1517
Vital Choice
Bellingham, WA.......................800-608-4825

Steaks

Ocean Beauty Seafoods Inc
Seattle, WA.......................800-365-8950

Sticks

High Liner Foods Inc.
Lunenburg, NS.......................902-634-8811
Viking Seafoods Inc
Malden, MA.......................800-225-3020

Sturgeon

Charlton Charters
Warrenton, OR.......................503-338-0569
Fiddlers Green Farm
North Vassalboro, ME.......................800-729-7935
Fish Breeders of Idaho
Hagerman, ID.......................208-837-6114
Fish Brothers
Blue Lake, CA.......................800-244-0583
Fishhawk Fisheries
Astoria, OR.......................503-325-5252
Great Northern Products Inc
Cranston, RI.......................401-490-4590
Homarus Inc
Long Island City, NY.......................917-832-0333
Jessie's Ilwaco Fish Company
San Francisco, CA.......................360-642-3773
Lund's Fisheries
Cape May, NJ.......................609-884-7600
Menemsha Fish Market
Chilmark, MA.......................508-645-2282
Northwest Wild Products
Astoria, OR.......................503-791-1907
Rego Smoked Fish Company
Flushing, NY.......................718-894-1400
Russ & Daughters
New York, NY.......................800-787-7229
Russian Chef
New York, NY.......................212-249-1550
Sportsmen's Cannery & Smokehouse
Winchester Bay, OR.......................800-457-8048
Sterling Caviar LLC
Elverta, CA.......................800-525-0333

Swordfish

Arrowac Fisheries
Seattle, WA.......................206-282-5655
Caito Fisheries Inc
Fort Bragg, CA.......................707-964-6368
Griffin's Seafood
Golden Meadow, LA.......................985-396-2453
James L. Mood Fisheries
Nova Scotia, NS.......................902-723-2360
Menemsha Fish Market
Chilmark, MA.......................508-645-2282
North Atlantic Seafood
Portland, ME.......................800-774-6025
Ocean Beauty Seafoods Inc
Seattle, WA.......................800-365-8950
Peter Pan Seafoods Inc.
Bellevue, WA.......................206-728-6000
Poseidon Enterprises
Charlotte, NC.......................800-863-7886
Santa Monica Seafood Co.
Rancho Dominguez, CA.......................800-969-8862
Tampa Bay Fisheries Inc
Dover, FL.......................800-732-3663

Steak

North Atlantic Seafood
Portland, ME.......................800-774-6025

Tilapia

BlueWater Seafoods
Gloucester, MA.......................888-560-2539
Fish Breeders of Idaho
Hagerman, ID.......................208-837-6114

North Atlantic Seafood
Portland, ME.......................800-774-6025
Pots de Creme
Lexington, KY.......................859-299-2254
Vince's Seafoods
Gretna, LA.......................504-368-1544
Waterfield Farms
Amherst, MA.......................413-549-3558

Trout

Alleghany's Fish Farm
Saint Philemon, QC.......................418-469-2823
Atlantic Fish Specialties
Charlottetown, PE.......................902-894-7005
Blue Lakes Trout Farm
Jerome, ID.......................208-734-7151
Bold Coast Smokehouse
Lubec, ME.......................888-733-0807
Bos Smoked Fish Inc
Woodstock, ON.......................519-537-5000
Burleigh Brothers Seafoods
Ellerslie, PE.......................902-831-2349
Caito Fisheries Inc
Fort Bragg, CA.......................707-964-6368
Catfish Wholesale
Abbeville, LA.......................800-334-7292
Certi Fresh Foods Inc
Wilmington, CA.......................310-221-6262
Culver Fish Farm
Mcpherson, KS.......................800-241-5205
Dave's Gourmet Albacore
Watsonville, CA.......................206-999-5517
Ducktrap River Of Maine
Belfast, ME.......................800-434-8727
Ferroclad Fishery
Batchawana Bay, ON.......................705-882-2295
Fiddlers Green Farm
North Vassalboro, ME.......................800-729-7935
Fish Breeders of Idaho
Hagerman, ID.......................208-837-6114
Fish Brothers
Blue Lake, CA.......................800-244-0583
Fumoir Grizzly
St Augustin, QC.......................418-878-8941
Griffin's Seafood
Golden Meadow, LA.......................985-396-2453
Homarus Inc
Long Island City, NY.......................917-832-0333
Idaho Trout Company
Buhl, ID.......................866-878-7688
J. Matassini & Sons Fish Company
Tampa, FL.......................813-229-0829
Lenny's Bee Productions
Bearsville, NY.......................845-679-4514
Louisiana Seafood Exchange
Jefferson, LA.......................800-969-9394
Morey's Seafood Intl LLC
Motley, MN.......................800-808-3474
Pamlico Packing Company
Grantsboro, NC.......................800-682-1113
Portier Fine Foods
Mamaroneck, NY.......................800-272-9463
Pots de Creme
Lexington, KY.......................859-299-2254
Rego Smoked Fish Company
Flushing, NY.......................718-894-1400
Russian Chef
New York, NY.......................212-249-1550
SC Enterprises
Owen Sound, ON.......................519-371-0456
Sunburst Trout Farms
Waynesville, NC.......................800-673-3051
Thompson Seafood
Darien, GA.......................912-437-4649
Vince's Seafoods
Gretna, LA.......................504-368-1544
Virginia Trout Co
Monterey, VA.......................540-468-2280
Wanchese Fish Co Inc
Suffolk, VA.......................757-673-4500
Woodsmoke Provisions
Atlanta, GA.......................404-355-5125

Brook

Russ & Daughters
New York, NY.......................800-787-7229

Golden

Idaho Trout Company
Buhl, ID.......................866-878-7688

Rainbow

Blue Lakes Trout Farm
Jerome, ID.......................208-734-7151
Clear Springs Foods Inc.
Buhl, ID.......................800-635-8211
Dave's Gourmet Albacore
Watsonville, CA.......................206-999-5517
Idaho Trout Company
Buhl, ID.......................866-878-7688
Sportsman's Paradise Whites Ranch
Paradise, UT.......................435-245-3053

Tuna

Brucepac
Woodburn, OR.......................800-899-3629
Captain Little Seafood
Queens County, NS.......................902-947-2087
Charlton Charters
Warrenton, OR.......................503-338-0569
Chicken Of The Sea
El Segundo, CA.......................844-267-8862
Chuck's Seafoods
Charleston, OR.......................541-888-5525
Crown Prince Inc
City Of Industry, CA.......................626-912-3700
Dave's Gourmet Albacore
Watsonville, CA.......................206-999-5517
Erba Food Products
Brooklyn, NY.......................718-272-7700
Great Northern Products Inc
Cranston, RI.......................401-490-4590
Griffin's Seafood
Golden Meadow, LA.......................985-396-2453
Hallmark Fisheries
Charleston, OR.......................541-888-3253
Homarus Inc
Long Island City, NY.......................917-832-0333
Independent Packers Corporation
Seattle, WA.......................206-285-6000
Island Marine Products
Clarks Harbour, NS.......................902-745-2222
James L. Mood Fisheries
Nova Scotia, NS.......................902-723-2360
Jessie's Ilwaco Fish Company
San Francisco, CA.......................360-642-3773
Lund's Fisheries
Cape May, NJ.......................609-884-7600
Menemsha Fish Market
Chilmark, MA.......................508-645-2282
Mid-Pacific Hawaii Fishery
Hilo, HI.......................808-935-6110
Neptune Foods
Vernon, CA.......................323-232-8300
New Orleans Fish House II LLC
New Orleans, LA.......................800-839-3474
North Atlantic Seafood
Portland, ME.......................800-774-6025
Northwest Wild Products
Astoria, OR.......................503-791-1907
Ocean Beauty Seafoods Inc
Seattle, WA.......................800-365-8950
Ocean Union Company
Lawrenceville, GA.......................770-995-1957
Omega Foods
Mississauga, ON.......................877-212-9484
Pastene Co LTD
Canton, MA.......................781-298-3397
Peter Pan Seafoods Inc.
Bellevue, WA.......................206-728-6000
Poseidon Enterprises
Charlotte, NC.......................800-863-7886
Roman Sausage Company
Santa Clara, CA.......................800-497-7462
Royal Seafood Inc
Brooklyn, NY.......................718-769-1517
Russ & Daughters
New York, NY.......................800-787-7229
Russian Chef
New York, NY.......................212-249-1550
Sportsmen's Cannery & Smokehouse
Winchester Bay, OR.......................800-457-8048
Sportsmens Seafoods
San Diego, CA.......................619-224-3551
Stavis Seafoods
Boston, MA.......................800-390-5103
Triangle Seafood
Louisville, KY.......................502-561-0055
Tuna Fresh
Gretna, LA.......................504-363-2744
Vince's Seafoods
Gretna, LA.......................504-368-1544

Vital Choice
Bellingham, WA 800-608-4825
Wanchese Fish Co Inc
Suffolk, VA 757-673-4500
White Cap Fish Market
Islip, NY 631-277-6577

Albacore

Caito Fisheries Inc
Fort Bragg, CA 707-964-6368
Chicken Of The Sea
El Segundo, CA 844-267-8862
Crown Prince Inc
City Of Industry, CA 626-912-3700
Dave's Gourmet Albacore
Watsonville, CA 206-999-5517
Fish Brothers
Blue Lake, CA 800-244-0583
Royal Seafood Inc
Brooklyn, NY 718-769-1517
Sportsmens Seafoods
San Diego, CA 619-224-3551

Canned

Blue Marble Brands
Providence, RI 888-534-0246
Bumble Bee
San Diego, CA 858-715-4000
Chicken Of The Sea
El Segundo, CA 844-267-8862
Chuck's Seafoods
Charleston, OR 541-888-5525
Crown Prince Inc
City Of Industry, CA 626-912-3700
Hallmark Fisheries
Charleston, OR 541-888-3253
Safe Catch
Sausalito, CA 888-568-4211
Season Brand
Newark, NJ 201-553-1100
Shafer-Haggart
Vancouver, BC 604-669-5512
Sportsmen's Cannery & Smokehouse
Winchester Bay, OR 800-457-8048
Sportsmens Seafoods
San Diego, CA 619-224-3551
Starkist Co
Pittsburgh, PA 412-231-0361
Vital Choice
Bellingham, WA 800-608-4825

Canned - Chunk Light in Oil

Chicken Of The Sea
El Segundo, CA 844-267-8862

Canned - Chunk Light in Water

Chicken Of The Sea
El Segundo, CA 844-267-8862

Canned - Chunk Solid in Oil

Chicken Of The Sea
El Segundo, CA 844-267-8862

Canned - Chunk Solid in Water

Chicken Of The Sea
El Segundo, CA 844-267-8862

Frozen

Cuizina Food Company
Woodinville, WA 425-486-7000
Great Northern Products Inc
Cranston, RI 401-490-4590
Hallmark Fisheries
Charleston, OR 541-888-3253
Independent Packers Corporation
Seattle, WA 206-285-6000
Jessie's Ilwaco Fish Company
San Francisco, CA 360-642-3773
Lund's Fisheries
Cape May, NJ 609-884-7600
Menemsha Fish Market
Chilmark, MA 508-645-2282
Royal Seafood Inc
Brooklyn, NY 718-769-1517
Wanchese Fish Co Inc
Suffolk, VA 757-673-4500
White Cap Fish Market
Islip, NY 631-277-6577

Pouch-Packed

Chicken Of The Sea
El Segundo, CA 844-267-8862
Safe Catch
Sausalito, CA 888-568-4211
Season Brand
Newark, NJ 201-553-1100

Yellowfin

Russ & Daughters
New York, NY 800-787-7229

Turbot

Breakwater Fisheries
St John's, NL 709-754-1999
North Atlantic Seafood
Portland, ME 800-774-6025
Notre Dame Seafoods Inc.
Comfort Cove, NL 709-244-5511
Penguin Frozen Foods Inc
Northbrook, IL 800-323-1485
Spruce Lane Investments
Stratford, PE 902-892-2600
Stavis Seafoods
Boston, MA 800-390-5103

Whitefish

Bos Smoked Fish Inc
Woodstock, ON 519-537-5000
Ferroclad Fishery
Batchawana Bay, ON 705-882-2295
Flaum Appetizing
Brooklyn, NY 718-821-1970
Homarus Inc
Long Island City, NY 917-832-0333
Minor Fisheries
Port Colborne, ON 905-834-9232
Rachael's Smoked Fish
Springfield, MA 800-327-3412
Rego Smoked Fish Company
Flushing, NY 718-894-1400
Russ & Daughters
New York, NY 800-787-7229
Russian Chef
New York, NY 212-249-1550

Whiting

Arrowac Fisheries
Seattle, WA 206-282-5655
Bon Secour Fisheries Inc
Bon Secour, AL 251-949-7411
Certi Fresh Foods Inc
Wilmington, CA 310-221-6262
Channel Fish Processing
Gloucester, MA 800-457-0054
Glenn Sales Company
Atlanta, GA 770-952-9292
Jessie's Ilwaco Fish Company
San Francisco, CA 360-642-3773
Mirasco
Atlanta, GA 770-956-1945
Morey's Seafood Intl LLC
Motley, MN 800-808-3474
Pamlico Packing Company
Grantsboro, NC 800-682-1113
Stavis Seafoods
Boston, MA 800-390-5103

Seafood

A&C Quinlin Fisheries
Centreville, NS 902-745-2742
Acadian Fine Foods
New Orleans, LA 504-581-2355
Acme Steak & Seafood
Youngstown, OH 800-686-2263
Agger Fish Corp
Brooklyn, NY 718-855-1717
Ah Dor Kosher Fish Corporation
Monsey, NY 845-425-2060
Alabama Gulf Seafood
Bayou La Batre, AL 251-824-4396
Alaska Aquafarms
Moose Pass, AK 907-288-3667
Alaska General Seafoods
Kenmore, WA 425-485-7755
Alaska Ocean Trading
Anchorage, AK 907-243-4399
Alaska Pacific Seafoods
Kodiak, AK 907-486-3234
Alaska Sausage & Seafood
Anchorage, AK 800-798-3636
Alaskan Gourmet Seafoods
Anchorage, AK 800-288-3740
Alaskan Leader Fisheries
Lynden, WA 360-318-1280
Aliotti Wholesale Fish Company
Monterey, CA 408-722-4597
Alyeska Seafoods
Unalaska, AK 907-581-1211
Amcan Industries
Elmsford, NY 914-347-4838
American Canadian Fisheries
Bellingham, WA 800-344-7942
American Seafoods
Seattle, WA 206-448-0300
Ameripure Processing Co
Franklin, LA 800-328-6729
Anchor Frozen Foods
Westbury, NY 800-566-3474
Annette Island Packing Company
Metlakatla, AK 907-886-4441
AquaCuisine
Portland, OR 208-323-2782
Aquatec Seafoods Ltd.
Comox, BC 250-339-6412
Aquatech
Anchorage, AK 877-938-2722
Arista Industries Inc
Wilton, CT 800-255-6457
Arizona Sunland Foods
Tucson, AZ 520-624-7068
Arrowac Fisheries
Seattle, WA 206-282-5655
ASC Seafood Inc
Largo, FL 800-876-3474
Atka Pride Seafoods Inc
Juneau, AK 888-927-4232
Atlanta Fish Market
Atlanta, GA 404-262-3165
Atlantic Aqua Farms
Orwell Cove, PE 902-651-2563
Atlantic Foods
Scotch Plains, NJ 908-889-8182
Atlantic Mussel Growers Corporation
Murray Harbour, PE 800-838-3106
Atlantic Sea Pride
Boston, MA 617-269-7700
Atlantic Seacove Inc
Boston, MA 617-442-6206
Atlantic Seafood Direct
Portland, ME 800-774-6025
Aurora Alaska Premium Smoked Salmon & Seafood
Anchorage, AK 800-653-3474
Axelsson & Johnson Fish Company
Cape May, NJ 609-884-8426
B & C Riverside
Vacherie, LA 225-265-8356
B & J Seafood
New Bern, NC 252-637-0483
B G Smith & Sons Oyster Co
Sharps, VA 877-483-8279
B&M Fisheries
Georgetown, MA 978-352-6663
B.C. Fisheries
Hancock, ME 207-422-8205
B.M. Lawrence & Company
San Francisco, CA 415-981-2926
Baensch Food Products Co
Milwaukee, WI 414-562-4643
Bailey's Basin Seafood
Morgan City, LA 985-384-4926
Bakalars Sausage Co
La Crosse, WI 608-784-0384
Bandon Bay Fisheries
Bandon, OR 541-347-4454
Basin Crawfish Processors
Breaux Bridge, LA 337-332-6655
Bay Hundred Seafood Inc
St Michaels, MD 410-745-9329
Bay Oceans Sea Foods
Garibaldi, OR 503-322-3316
Bayley's Lobster Pound
Scarborough, ME 800-932-6456
Bayou Crab
Grand Bay, AL 251-824-2076
Bayou Food Distributors
Kenner, LA 800-516-8283
Bayou Land Seafood
Breaux Bridge, LA 337-667-6118
Beaver Street Fisheries
Jacksonville, FL 800-874-6426

Becker Foods
Westminster, CA 714-891-9474
Belle River Enterprises
Belle River, PE 902-962-2248
Benton's Seafood Ctr
Tifton, GA 229-382-4976
Big Easy Foods
Lake Charles, LA 855-477-9296
Big Island Seafood, LLC
Atlanta, GA 404-366-8943
Bill's Seafood
Baltimore, MD 410-256-9520
Billingsgate Fish Company
Calgary, AB 403-571-7700
Billy's Seafood Inc
Bon Secour, AL 888-424-5597
Biloxi Freezing Processing Inc.
Biloxi, MS 228-436-0017
Blakely Freezer Locker
Blakeley, GA 229-723-3622
Blalock Seafood & Specialty
Orange Beach, AL 251-974-5811
Blau Oyster Co Inc
Bow, WA 360-766-6171
Blount Fine Foods
Fall River, MA 774-888-1300
Blue Star Food Products
Doral, FL 305-836-6858
BlueWater Seafoods
Gloucester, MA 888-560-2539
Bodin Foods
New Iberia, LA 337-367-1344
Bon Secour Fisheries Inc
Bon Secour, AL 251-949-7411
Bornstein Seafoods
Bellingham, WA 360-734-7990
Boston Seafarms
Boston, MA 617-784-4777
Boundary Fish Company
Blaine, WA 360-332-6715
Boutique Seafood Brokers
Atlanta, GA 404-752-8852
Bradye P. Todd & Son
Cambridge, MD 410-228-8633
Braun Seafood Co
Cutchogue, NY 631-734-6700
Breakwater Fisheries
St John's, NL 709-754-1999
Breakwater Seafoods & Chowder
Aberdeen, WA 360-532-5693
Byrd's Seafood
Crisfield, MD 410-968-0990
C C Conway Seafoods
Wicomico, VA 804-642-2853
C F Gollott & Son Seafood
Diberville, MS 228-392-2747
C. Gould Seafoods
Scottsdale, AZ 480-314-9250
C.E. Fish Company
Jonesboro, ME 207-434-2631
Cajun Crawfish Distributors
Branch, LA 888-254-8626
Cajun Seafood Enterprises
Murrayville, GA 706-864-9688
Caleb Haley & Co LLC
Bronx, NY 718-617-7474
California Shellfish Company
San Francisco, CA 415-923-7400
Callis Seafood
Lancaster, VA 804-462-7634
Cameron Seafood Processors
Cameron, LA 318-775-5510
Can Am Seafood
Lubec, ME 207-733-2267
Canadian Fish Exporters
Auburndale, MA 800-225-4215
Cantrell's Seafood
Bath, ME 207-442-7261
Cape Ann Seafood
Gloucester, MA 978-283-0687
Capt Collier Seafood
Coden, AL 251-824-4925
Captain Alex Seafoods
Niles, IL 847-803-8833
Captain's Choice
Federal Way, WA 253-941-1184
Carrington Foods Co Inc
Saraland, AL 251-675-9700
Cathay Foods Corporation
Boston, MA 617-427-1507
Cedar Valley Fish Market
Waterloo, IA 319-236-2965
Centennial Food Corporation
Calgary, AB 403-214-0044
Central Coast Seafood
Atascadero, CA 800-273-4741
Certi Fresh Foods Inc
Wilmington, CA 310-221-6262
Certi-Fresh Foods, Inc
Wilmington, CA 910-221-6262
Channel Fish Processing
Gloucester, MA 800-457-0054
Channel Fish Processing Co Inc
Boston, MA 800-536-3474
Charles H. Parks & Company
Fishing Creek, MD 410-397-3400
Charlton Charters
Warrenton, OR 503-338-0569
Chases Lobster Pound
Port Howe, NS 902-243-2408
Chef Hans' Gourmet Foods
Monroe, LA 800-890-4267
Cherbogue Fisheries
Yarmouth, NS 902-742-9157
Chester W. Howeth & Brother
Crisfield, MD 410-968-1398
Chris Hansen Seafood
Port Sulphur, LA 504-564-2888
Chuck's Seafoods
Charleston, OR 541-888-5525
City Market
Brunswick, GA 912-265-4430
Clarke J F Corp
Franklin Square, NY 800-229-7474
Clayton's Crab Co
Rockledge, FL 321-636-6673
Clearwater Fine Foods
Bedford, NS 902-443-0550
Clem's Seafood & Specialties
Buckner, KY 502-222-7571
Coast Seafoods Company
Bellevue, WA 800-423-2303
Coastal Seafood Partners
Chicago, IL 773-235-4000
Coastal Seafood Processors
Harahan, LA 504-734-9444
Cobscook Bay Seafood
Perry, ME 207-853-2890
Cohen's Original Tasty Coddie
Baltimore, MD 410-539-0111
Coldwater Fish Farms
Lisco, NE 800-658-4450
Collins Cavier Co
Michigan City, IN 219-809-8100
Comeaux's
Lafayette, LA 888-264-5460
Conroy Foods
Pittsburgh, PA 412-781-0977
Consolidated Catfish Co LLC
Isola, MS 662-962-3101
Cowart Seafood Corp
Lottsburg, VA 804-529-6101
Cozy Harbor Seafood Inc
Portland, ME 800-225-2586
Craby's Fish Market
Blackwood, NJ 856-227-9743
Cranberry Isles Fisherman's
Islesford, ME 207-244-5438
Craven Crab Company
New Bern, NC 252-637-3562
Crest International Corporation
San Diego, CA 800-548-1232
Crevettes Du Nord
Gaspe, QC 418-368-1414
Cuizina Food Company
Woodinville, WA 425-486-7000
Cushner Seafoods Inc
Baltimore, MD 410-358-5564
Custom House Seafoods
Portland, ME 207-773-2778
D Seafood
Chicago, IL 312-808-1086
D&M Seafood
Honolulu, HI 808-531-0687
Dave's Gourmet Albacore
Watsonville, CA 206-999-5517
Davis Street Fish Market
Evanston, IL 847-869-3474
DB Kenney Fisheries
Westport, NS 902-839-2023
De Maria's Seafood
Newport News, VA 757-930-3474
Deep Creek Custom Packing
Ninilchik, AK 800-764-0078
Del's Seaway Shrimp & Oyster Company
Biloxi, MS 228-432-2604
Denzer's Food Products
Baltimore, MD 410-889-1500
Di Cola's Seafood
Chicago, IL 773-238-7071
Diamond Seafood
Wood Dale, IL 630-787-1100
DIP Seafood Mudbugs
Mobile, AL 251-479-0123
Dixon's Fisheries
East Peoria, IL 800-373-1457
Don's Dock Seafood Market
Des Plaines, IL 847-827-1817
Door County Fish Market
Northbrook, IL 847-559-9229
Dorchester Crab Co
Wingate, MD 410-397-8103
Doug Hardy Company
Deer Isle, ME 207-348-6604
Dow Distribution
Honolulu, HI 808-836-3511
Down East Specialty Products/Cape Bald Packers
Portland, ME 800-369-6327
Dressel Collins Fish Company
Seattle, WA 206-725-0121
Drusilla Seafood
Baton Rouge, LA 800-364-8844
Dubois Seafood
Houma, LA 985-876-2514
Ducktrap River Of Maine
Belfast, ME 800-434-8727
Duxbury Mussel & Seafood Corporation
Kingston, MA 781-585-5517
E. Gagnon & Fils
St Therese-De-Gaspe, QC 418-385-3011
Eagle Seafood Producers
Brooklyn, NY 718-963-0939
East Point Seafood Company
Raymond, WA 888-317-8459
Eastern Fish Company
Teaneck, NJ 800-526-9066
Eastern Sea Products
Scoudouc, NB 800-565-6364
Eastern Seafood Co
Chicago, IL 312-243-2090
Eastside Seafood
Macon, GA 478-743-1888
Ed's Kasilof Seafoods
Kasilof, AK 800-982-2377
Eldorado Seafood Inc
Burlington, MA 800-416-5656
Elliott Seafood Company
Cushing, ME 207-354-2533
Emery Smith Fisheries Limited
Shag Harbour, NS 902-723-2115
Errol's Cajun Foods
Belle Rose, LA 866-746-6003
Eschete's Seafood
Houma, LA 985-872-4120
Eskimo Candy Inc
Kihei, HI 808-879-5686
Faidley Seafood
Baltimore, MD 410-727-4898
Fantis Foods Inc
Carlstadt, NJ 201-933-6200
Farm 2 Market
San Francisco, CA 800-447-2967
Farmers Seafood Co Wholesale
Shreveport, LA 800-874-0203
Feature Foods
Brampton, ON 905-452-7741
Ferme Ostreicole Dugas
Caraquet, NB 506-727-3226
Fine Line Seafood
Newtown, PA 215-598-3359
First Oriental Market
Decatur, GA 404-377-6950
Fish Breeders of Idaho
Hagerman, ID 208-837-6114
Fish Brothers
Blue Lake, CA 800-244-0583
Fish Express
Lihue, HI 808-245-9918
Fish King
Glendale, CA 818-244-2161
Fish Market Inc
Louisville, KY 502-587-7474
Fishermens Net
Portland, ME 207-772-3565
Fishhawk Fisheries
Astoria, OR 503-325-5252

Fishland Market
Honolulu, HI 808-523-6902
Flavor House, Inc.
Adelanto, CA 760-246-9131
Fleet Fisheries Inc
New Bedford, MA 508-910-2100
Fortune Seas
Gloucester, MA......................978-281-6666
Fournier R & Sons Seafood
Biloxi, MS......................228-392-4293
Frank Mattes & Sons Reliable Seafood
Bel Air, MD 410-879-5444
Frank Pagano Company
Lockport, IL 815-838-0303
French Market Foods
Lake Charles, LA 337-477-9296
French Quarter Seafood
Chalmette, LA......................504-277-1679
Fresh Island Fish
Kahului, HI 808-871-1111
Fresh Pack Seafood
Waldoboro, ME......................207-832-7720
Fresh Seafood Distrib
Daphne, AL......................251-626-1106
Freshwater Farms Of Ohio
Urbana, OH......................800-634-7434
Friendship International
Rockland, ME 207-594-1111
Frozen Specialties Inc
Perrysburg, OH......................419-867-2005
Fulcher's Point Pride Seafood
Oriental, NC 252-249-0123
Fulton Fish Market
New York, NY 718-842-8908
FW Thurston
Bernard, ME......................207-244-3320
G & J Land & Marine Food Distr
Morgan City, LA......................800-256-9187
Galilean Seafood Inc
Bristol, RI 401-253-3030
Garden & Valley Isle Seafood
Honolulu, HI......................800-689-2733
George Robberecht Seafood
Montross, VA 804-472-3556
Georgia Seafood Wholesale
Chamblee, GA......................770-936-0483
Gerard & Dominique Seafoods
Harbor, OR 800-858-0449
Gesco ENR
Gaspe, QC......................418-368-1414
Gilmore's Seafoods
Bath, ME......................800-849-9667
Giovanni's Appetizing Food Co
Richmond, MI......................586-727-9355
Glenn Sales Company
Atlanta, GA......................770-952-9292
Gold Star Seafoods
Chicago, IL 773-376-8080
Golden Alaska Seafoods LLC
Seattle, WA......................206-441-1990
Golden Eye Seafood
Tall Timbers, MD 301-994-2274
Golden Gulf Coast Packing Co
Biloxi, MS......................228-374-6121
Good Harbor Fillet Company
New Bedford, MA 800-343-8046
Gorton's Inc.
Gloucester, MA......................800-222-6846
Graham & Rollins Inc
Hampton, VA 800-272-2728
Graham Fisheries
Bayou La Batre, AL 251-824-7370
Great American Seafood Company
Champaigne, IL 217-352-0986
Great American Smokehouse & Seafood Company
Brookings, OR 800-828-3474
Great Glacier Salmon
Prince Rupert, BC......................250-627-4955
Great Midwest Seafood Company
Davenport, IA......................563-388-4770
Great Northern Products Inc
Cranston, RI 401-490-4590
Green Turtle Cannery & Seafood
Islamorada, FL 305-664-9595
Griffin's Seafood
Golden Meadow, LA......................985-396-2453
Gulf Atlantic Freezers
Gretna, LA 504-392-3590
Gulf Central Seafood
Biloxi, MS......................228-436-6346
Gulf Crown Seafood Co
Delcambre, LA 337-685-4722
Gulf Food Products Co Inc
New Orleans, LA 504-733-1516
Gulf Marine & Industrial Supplies Inc
Houston, TX 800-886-6252
Gulf Pride Enterprises
Biloxi, MS......................888-689-0560
Gulf Shrimp, Inc.
Fort Myers Beach, FL......................239-463-8788
H&H Fisheries Limited
Eastern Passage, NS 866-773-4400
H.Gass Seafood
Hollywood, MD 301-373-6882
Hallmark Fisheries
Charleston, OR 541-888-3253
Hama Hama Oyster® Company
Lilliwaup, WA......................888-877-5844
Hamilton Marine
Rockland, ME......................207-594-8181
Handy International Inc
Salisbury, MD......................800-426-3977
Hansen Caviar Company
Kingston, NY 800-735-0441
Harbor Fish Market
Portland, ME......................800-370-1790
Harbor Seafood
New Hyde Park, NY 800-645-2211
Harbour Lobster Ltd
Shag Harbour, NS......................902-723-2500
Haring Catfish
Wisner, LA 800-467-3474
Harlon's LA Fish
Kenner, LA 504-467-3809
Harpers Seafood Market
Thomasville, GA......................229-226-7525
Harvard Seafood Company
Grand Bay, AL 251-865-0558
Hawaii International Seafood
Kailua, HI 808-839-5010
Heritage Salmon
Eastport, ME......................877-407-5577
HFI Foods
Redmond, WA......................425-883-1320
Higgins Seafood
Lafitte, LA......................504-689-3577
High Liner Foods Inc.
Lunenburg, NS 902-634-8811
Hillard Bloom Packing Co Inc
Port Norris, NJ 856-785-0120
Hillmans Shrimp & Oyster
Port Lavaca, TX 800-582-4416
Hilo Fish Company
Hilo, HI......................808-961-0877
Homer's Wharf Seafood Company
New Bedford, MA 508-997-0766
Hong Kong Supermarket
Norcross, GA 770-582-6800
Honolulu Fish Company
Honolulu, HI......................808-833-1123
Horst Seafood
Juneau, AK 877-518-4300
Hosford & Wood Fresh Seafood Providers
Tucson, AZ 520-795-1920
Huck's Seafood
Easton, MD......................410-770-9211
Hue's Seafood
Baton Rouge, LA 225-383-0809
Idaho Trout Company
Buhl, ID......................866-878-7688
Imaex Trading Company
Suwanee, GA 678-541-0234
Independent Packers Corporation
Seattle, WA......................206-285-6000
Indian Bay Frozen Foods
Centreville, NL......................709-678-2844
Indian Ridge Shrimp Co
Chauvin, LA 800-594-0920
Indian Valley Meats
Indian, AK......................907-653-7511
Inland Seafood Inc
Atlanta, GA......................800-883-3474
Inlet Salmon
Fort Lauderdale, FL 954-525-9777
Inny's Wholesale
Honolulu, HI......................808-841-3172
Inshore Fisheries
Middle West Pubnico, NS......................902-762-2522
Interior Alaska Fish Processors
Fairbanks, AK......................800-478-3885
International Seafoods - Alaska
Kodiak, AK......................907-486-4768
International Seafoods of Chicago
Chicago, IL 312-243-2330
Ipswich Maritime Product Company
Ipswich, MA 978-356-9866
Ipswich Shellfish Co Inc
Ipswich, MA 800-477-9424
ISF Trading
Portland, ME......................207-879-1575
Island Marine Products
Clarks Harbour, NS......................902-745-2222
Island Scallops
Qualicum Beach, BC 250-757-9811
Island Seafood
Eliot, ME......................207-439-8508
Island Seafoods
Kodiak, AK......................800-355-8575
J & B Seafood
Coden, AL......................251-824-4512
J & L Seafood
Bayou La Batre, AL 251-824-2371
J Bernard Seafood
Cottonport, LA 318-876-2716
J Deluca Fish Co Inc
San Pedro, CA......................310-684-5180
J M Clayton Co
Cambridge, MD 800-652-6931
J Moniz Co Inc
Fall River, MA 508-674-8451
J P's Shellfish Co
Eliot, ME......................207-439-6018
J Turner Seafood
Gloucester, MA......................978-281-8535
J&R Fisheries
Seward, AK......................907-224-5584
J. Matassini & Sons Fish Company
Tampa, FL......................813-229-0829
J.R. Fish Company
Wrangell, AK 907-874-2399
J.R.'s Seafood
Oak Lawn, IL 708-422-4555
J.S. McMillan Fisheries
North Vancouver, BC 604-981-4000
Ja-Ca Seafood Products
Boston, MA......................978-281-8848
James L. Mood Fisheries
Nova Scotia, NS 902-723-2360
Janes Family Foods
Mississauga, ON......................800-565-2637
JBS Packing Inc
Port Arthur, TX......................409-982-3216
Jessie's Ilwaco Fish Company
San Francisco, CA 360-642-3773
Jim Foley Company
Marietta, GA......................770-427-5102
Joe Fazio's Famous Italian
Charleston, WV 304-344-3071
Joe Patti's Seafood Co
Pensacola, FL 800-500-9929
John B. Wright Fish Company
Gloucester, MA......................978-283-4205
Johns Cove Fisheries
Yarmouth, NS 902-742-8691
Johnson Sea Products Inc
AL......................251-824-2693
Jubilee Foods
Bayou La Batre, AL 251-824-2110
K Horton Specialty Foods
Portland, ME......................207-228-2056
K.S.M. Seafood Corporation
Baton Rouge, LA 225-383-1517
Kachemak Bay Seafood
Homer, AK......................907-235-2799
Karla's Smokehouse
Rockaway Beach, OR......................503-355-2362
Kent's Wharf
Swans Island, ME......................207-526-4186
Kettle Master
Hillsville, VA 276-728-7571
Key Largo Fisheries
Key Largo, FL......................800-432-4358
Keys Fisheries Market & Marina
Marathon, FL 866-743-4353
Keyser Brothers
Lottsburg, VA 804-529-6837
Kibun Foods
Seattle, WA......................206-467-6287
King & Prince Seafood
Brunswick, GA 888-391-5223
King & Prince Seafood Corp
Brunswick, GA......................800-841-0205
Kings Seafood Co
Costa Mesa, CA 800-269-8425
Kitchens Seafood
Plant City, FL 800-327-0132

Kodiak Salmon Packers
Larsen Bay, AK....................907-847-2250
Kona Fish Co Inc
Kailua Kona, HI..................808-326-7708
KOOL Ice & Seafood Co
Cambridge, MD..................800-437-2417
L & M Lockers
Belt, MT........................406-277-3522
L&C Fisheries
Kensington, PE...................902-886-2770
L&M Evans
Conyers, GA.....................770-483-9373
L.H. Rodriguez Wholesale Seafood
Tucson, AZ......................520-623-1931
LA Monica Fine Foods
Millville, NJ
Lady Gale Seafood
Baldwin, LA.....................337-923-2060
Landlocked Seafoods
Carroll, IA.......................712-792-9599
Larry J. Williams Company
Jesup, GA.......................912-427-7729
Lartigue Seafood
Orange Beach, AL................251-948-2644
Leblanc Seafood
Lafitte, LA.......................504-689-2631
LEF McLean Brothers International
Wheatley, ON.....................519-825-4656
Les Trois Petits Cochons
Brooklyn, NY....................800-537-7283
Lisbon Seafood Co
Fall River, MA...................508-672-3617
Little River Seafood Inc
Reedville, VA....................804-453-3670
Livingston's Bulls Bay Seafood
Mc Clellanville, SC...............843-887-3519
LLJ's Sea Products
Round Pond, ME..................207-529-4224
Lombardi's Seafood
Winter Park, FL..................800-879-8411
Lombardi's Seafood Inc
Winter Park, FL..................407-628-3474
Long Food Industries
Fripp Island, SC..................843-838-3205
Los Angeles Smoking & Curing Company
Seattle, WA.....................213-628-1246
Louisiana Oyster Processors
Baton Rouge, LA.................225-291-6923
Louisiana Packing Company
Westwego, LA...................800-666-1293
Louisiana Pride Seafood
New Orleans, LA.................504-286-8736
Louisiana Seafoods
New Orleans, LA.................504-286-8736
Lowcountry Shellfish Inc
Charleston, SC..................800-999-2503
Lowland Seafood
Lowland, NC.....................252-745-3751
Lucky Seafood Corporation
Morrow, GA.....................770-960-9889
Lumar Lobster
Lawrence, NY...................516-371-0083
Lund's Fisheries
Cape May, NJ...................609-884-7600
Lusty Lobster
Portland, ME....................207-773-2829
Luxury Crab
St John's, NL....................709-739-6668
MacGregors Meat & Seafood
Toronto, ON.....................888-383-3663
Machias Bay Seafood
Machias, ME.....................207-255-8671
Maloney Seafood Corporation
Quincy, MA.....................800-566-2837
Manchac Seafood Market
Ponchatoula, LA.................985-370-7070
Maple Leaf Foods International
North York, ON..................800-268-3708
Marine MacHines
Bar Harbor, ME..................207-288-0107
Market Fisheries
Chicago, IL.....................773-483-3233
Martin Brothers Seafood Co
Westwego, LA...................504-341-2251
Martin Seafood Company
Jessup, MD.....................410-799-5822
Maxim's Import Corporation
Miami, FL.......................800-331-6652
Mazzetta Company
Highland Park, IL.................847-433-1150
McCoy Matt Frontier International
Pismo Beach, CA.................805-773-2994
Mcfarling Foods Inc
Indianapolis, IN..................317-635-2633
Mclaughlin Seafood
Bangor, ME......................800-222-9107
McNasby's Seafood Market
Annapolis, MD...................410-295-9022
Meat & Fish Fellas
Glendale, AZ.....................623-931-6190
Menemsha Fish Market
Chilmark, MA....................508-645-2282
Meredith & Meredith
Toddville, MD....................410-397-8151
Merrill Seafood Center
Jacksonville, FL.................904-744-3132
Metafoods LLC
Brookhaven, GA..................404-843-2400
Metompkin Bay Oyster Company, Inc
Crisfield, MD....................410-968-0662
Mid-Atlantic Foods Inc
Easton, MD......................800-922-4688
Midwest Seafood
Indianapolis, IN..................317-466-1027
Mill Cove Lobster Pound
Trevett, ME......................207-633-3340
Miller Johnson Seafood
Coden, AL.......................251-873-4444
Mills Seafood Ltd.
Bouctouche, NB..................506-743-2444
Milsolv Corporation
Butler, WI.......................800-558-8501
Mister Fish Inc.
Baltimore, MD...................410-288-2722
Misty Islands Seafoods
Dipper Harbour, NB...............506-659-2781
Mobile Bay Seafood
Coden, AL.......................251-973-0410
Mobile Processing
Mobile, AL......................251-438-6944
Mohn's Fisheries
Harpers Ferry, IA.................563-586-2269
Monarch Seafoods Inc
Honolulu, HI.....................808-841-7877
Moon's Seafood Company
Melbourne, FL...................800-526-5624
Morey's Seafood Intl LLC
Motley, MN......................800-808-3474
Morgan Mill
Cherokee, NC....................828-497-9227
Mortillaro Lobster Company
Gloucester, MA...................978-282-4621
Mutual Fish Co
Seattle, WA.....................206-322-4368
N.B.J. Enterprises
Mobile, AL......................251-661-2285
N.Y.K. Line (North America)
Lombard, IL.....................888-695-7447
Nagasako Fish
Wailuku, HI.....................808-242-4073
Nan Sea Enterprises of Wisconsin
Waukesha, WI...................262-542-8841
Nancy's Shellfish
Falmouth, ME....................207-774-3411
National Fish & Seafood Inc
Gloucester, MA...................800-229-1750
National Fish & Seafood Inc
Gloucester, MA...................800-229-1750
Nelson Crab Inc
Tokeland, WA....................800-262-0069
Neptune Fisheries
Newport News, VA.................800-545-7474
New Ocean
Doraville, GA....................770-458-5235
New Orleans Gulf Seafood
New Orleans, LA.................504-733-1516
New Wave Cuisine
Mount Holly, NJ..................800-486-0276
Newfound Resources
St Josephs, NL...................709-579-7676
Newmeadows Lobster Inc
Portland, ME....................800-668-1612
Nisbet Oyster Company
Bay Center, WA..................888-875-6629
Noon Hour Food Products Inc
Chicago, IL.....................800-621-6636
Nordic Group Inc
Boston, MA......................800-486-4002
Norpac Fisheries Inc
Honolulu, HI.....................808-528-3474
North Atlantic Inc
Portland, ME....................207-774-6025
North Atlantic Products
South Thomaston, ME.............207-596-0331
North Atlantic Seafood
Portland, ME....................800-774-6025
North Pacific Seafoods Inc
Seattle, WA.....................206-726-9900
Northern Discovery Seafoods
Grapeview, WA...................800-843-6921
Northern Keta Caviar
Juneau, AK......................907-586-6095
Northern Ocean Marine
Gloucester, MA...................978-283-0222
Northern Products Corporation
Seattle, WA.....................888-599-6290
Northern Wind Inc
New Bedford, MA.................888-525-2525
Northwest Natural Foods
Olympia, WA.....................360-866-9661
Notre Dame Seafoods Inc.
Comfort Cove, NL.................709-244-5511
Ntc Marketing
Williamsville, NY.................800-333-1637
O'Donnell-Usen
Tampa, FL.......................813-241-9200
O'Hara Corp
Rockland, ME....................207-594-4444
Oak Island Seafood Company
Portland, ME....................207-594-9250
Ocean Beauty Seafoods Inc
Seattle, WA.....................800-365-8950
Ocean Crest Seafoods
Gloucester, MA...................800-259-4769
Ocean Food Co. Ltd.
Toronto, ON.....................416-285-6487
Ocean Fresh Seafoods
Seattle, WA.....................206-285-2412
Ocean King International
Alhambra, CA....................626-289-9399
Ocean Select Seafood
Delcambre, LA...................337-685-5315
Ocean Springs Seafood
Ocean Springs, MS................228-875-0104
Ocean Union Company
Lawrenceville, GA................770-995-1957
Oceanledge Seafoods
Rockland, ME....................207-594-4955
Oceans Prome Distributi ng
Glenview, IL.....................847-998-5813
Offshore Seafood Co
St Petersburg, FL.................727-329-8848
Offshore Systems Inc
Dutch Harbor, AK.................907-581-1827
Ohana Seafood, LLC
Honolulu, HI.....................808-843-1844
Okuhara Foods Inc
Honolulu, HI.....................808-848-0581
Olsen Fish Co
Minneapolis, MN.................800-882-0212
Orca Bay Foods
Seattle, WA.....................800-932-6722
Oregon Seafoods
Coos Bay, OR....................541-267-3474
Oversea Fishery & Investment
Honolulu, HI.....................808-847-2500
P & J Oyster Co
New Orleans, LA.................504-523-2651
P & T Flannery Seafood Inc
San Francisco, CA................415-346-1303
P&E Foods
Honolulu, HI.....................808-839-9094
P&L Seafood of Venice
Gretna, LA......................504-363-2744
P. Janes & Sons
Hant's Harbor, NL.................709-586-2252
P.J. Markos Seafood Company
Ipswich, MA.....................978-356-4347
P.J. Merrill Seafood Inc
Portland, ME....................207-773-1321
P.M. Innis Lobster Company
Biddeford Pool, ME...............207-284-5000
P.T. Fish
Portland, ME....................207-772-0239
Pacific American Fish Co Inc
Vernon, CA......................800-625-2525
Pacific Gourmet Seafood
Bakersfield, CA..................661-533-1260
Pacific Salmon Company
Edmonds, WA....................425-774-1315
Pacific Seafoods International
Port Hardy, BC...................250-949-8781
Pacific Valley Foods Inc
Bellevue, WA....................425-643-1805
Pacsea Corporation
Aiea, HI.........................808-836-8888

Pamlico Packing Company
Grantsboro, NC....................800-682-1113
Parker Fish Company
Wrightsville, GA..................478-864-3406
Paul Piazza & Son Inc
New Orleans, LA..................800-969-6011
PEI Mussel King
Morrell, PE.......................800-673-2767
Pelican Seafoods
Pelican, AK.......................907-735-2211
Pemaquid Seafood
Pemaquid, ME.....................866-864-2897
Penguin Frozen Foods Inc
Northbrook, IL...................800-323-1485
Perino's Inc
Marrero, LA......................504-347-5410
Perona Farms
Andover, NJ......................800-750-6190
Peter Pan Seafoods Inc.
Bellevue, WA.....................206-728-6000
Phillips Foods
Baltimore, MD....................888-234-2722
Phillips Seafood
Townsend, GA.....................912-832-4423
Piazza's Seafood World LLC
St Rose, LA......................504-602-5050
Pilot Meat & Sea Food Company
Galena, IL.......................319-556-0760
Pine Point Seafood
Scarborough, ME..................207-883-4701
Pioneer Live Shrimp
Oak Brook, IL....................630-789-1133
Point Judith Fisherman's Company
Narragansett, RI.................401-782-1500
Point Saint George Fisheries
Santa Rosa, CA...................707-542-9490
Pon Food Corp
Ponchatoula, LA..................985-386-6941
Pond Pure Catfish
Moulton, AL......................256-974-6698
Pontchartrain Blue Crab
Slidell, LA......................985-649-6645
POP Fishing & Marine
Honolulu, HI.....................808-537-2905
Port Royal Seafood
St. Helena, SC...................843-812-0257
Portland Shellfish Company
Portland, ME.....................207-799-9290
Portland Specialty Seafoods
Portland, ME.....................207-775-5765
Portsmouth Chowder Co
Portsmouth, NH...................877-616-7631
Poseidon Enterprises
Charlotte, NC....................800-863-7886
Poteet Seafood Co
Brunswick, GA....................912-264-5340
Premier Pacific Seafoods Inc
Seattle, WA......................206-286-8584
Premiere Seafood
Lexington, KY....................606-259-3474
Price Seafood
Havre De Grace, MD...............410-939-2782
Prime Cut Meat & Seafood Company
Phoenix, AZ......................800-277-1054
Primo Foods
Oceanside, CA....................760-439-8711
Produits Belle Baie
Caraquet, NB.....................506-727-4414
Quality Crab Co Inc
Elizabeth City, NC...............252-338-0808
Quality Fisheries
Niota, IL........................217-448-4241
Quality Meats & Seafood
West Fargo, ND...................800-342-4250
Quality Seafood
Apalachicola, FL.................850-653-9696
R & R Seafood
Tybee Island, GA.................912-786-5504
R&J Seafoods
Ninilchik, AK....................907-567-3222
Raffield Fisheries Inc
Port St Joe, FL..................850-229-8494
Rainbow Seafood Market
Baldwin Park, CA.................626-962-6888
Rainbow Seafoods
Topsfield, MA....................978-887-9121
Red Chamber Co
Vernon, CA.......................323-234-9000
Registry Steak & Seafood
Bridgeview, IL...................708-458-3100
Rego Smoked Fish Company
Flushing, NY.....................718-894-1400

Reilly's Sea Products
South Bristol, ME.................207-644-1400
Resource Trading Company
Portland, ME.....................207-772-2299
Rippons Seafood
Ocean City, MD...................410-723-0056
Roadrunner Seafood Inc
Colquitt, GA.....................229-758-6098
Robin & Cohn Seafood Distributors
Chalmette, LA....................504-277-1679
Rock Point Oyster Company
Quilcene, WA.....................360-765-3765
Rockport Lobster Co
Gloucester, MA...................978-281-0225
Rocky Point Shrimp Association
Phoenix, AZ......................602-254-8041
Roland Seafood Co
Atlantic Beach, FL...............904-246-9443
Rose Hill Seafood
Columbus, GA.....................706-322-1269
Roy Dick Company
Griffin, GA......................770-227-3916
Royal Atlantic Seafood
Gloucester, MA...................978-281-6373
Royal Baltic LTD
Brooklyn, NY.....................718-385-8300
Royal Lagoon Seafood Inc
Theodore, AL.....................800-844-6972
Royal Pacific Fisheries
Kenai, AK........................907-283-9370
Royal Seafood Inc
Brooklyn, NY.....................718-769-1517
Ruark & Ashton
Woolford, MD.....................800-725-5032
Rubino's Seafood Company
Chicago, IL......................312-258-0020
Ruggiero Seafood
Newark, NJ.......................866-225-2627
Russo's Seafood
Savannah, GA.....................866-234-5196
Rymer Seafood
Chicago, IL......................312-236-3266
S S Lobster LTD
Fitchburg, MA....................978-342-6135
Sahalee of Alaska
Anchorage, AK....................800-349-4151
Salamatof Seafoods
Kenai, AK........................907-283-7000
Salmolux Inc
Federal Way, WA..................253-874-6570
Santa Monica Seafood Co.
Rancho Dominguez, CA.............800-969-8862
SC Enterprises
Owen Sound, ON...................519-371-0456
Sea Bear Smokehouse
Anacortes, WA....................800-645-3474
Sea Fresh USA Inc
North Kingstown, RI..............401-583-0200
Sea Pac Of Idaho Inc
Filer, ID........................208-326-3100
Sea Pearl Seafood
Bayou La Batre, AL...............800-872-8804
Sea Safari
Belhaven, NC.....................800-688-6174
Sea Snack Foods Inc
Los Angeles, CA..................213-622-2204
Sea View Fillet Company
New Bedford, MA..................508-984-1406
Sea Watch Intl
Easton, MD.......................410-822-7500
Seafare Market Wholesale
Moody, ME........................207-646-5160
Seafood Merchants LTD
Vernon Hills, IL.................847-634-0900
Seafood Producers Co-Op
Bellingham, WA...................360-733-0120
Seafood Specialties
Anna, IL.........................618-833-6083
Sealaska Corp
Juneau, AK.......................907-586-1512
SeaPerfect Atlantic Farms
Charleston, SC...................800-728-0099
SeaSpecialties
Miami, FL........................800-654-6682
Seatech Corporation
Lynnwood, WA.....................425-487-3231
Seatrade Corporation
Hoboken, NJ......................201-963-5700
Seaview Lobster Co
Kittery, ME......................800-245-4997
Seymour & Sons Seafoods Inc
Diberville, MS...................228-392-4020

Shamrock Foods Co
Phoenix, AZ......................800-289-3663
Shaw's Southern Belle Frozen, Inc.
Jacksonville, FL.................888-742-9772
Shawmut Fishing Company
Anchorage, AK....................709-334-2559
Shemper Seafood Co
Biloxi, MS.......................228-435-2703
Shining Ocean Inc
Sumner, WA.......................800-935-6464
Shore Seafood Distr
Saxis, VA........................757-824-5517
Signature Seafoods Inc
Seattle, WA......................206-285-2815
Silver Lining Seafood
Seattle, WA......................800-426-5490
Silverston Fisheries
Superior, WI.....................715-392-5551
Singleton Seafood Company
Plant City, FL...................813-241-1500
Sonoma Seafoods
Sonoma, CA.......................800-411-2123
Southern Pride Catfish Company
Seattle, WA......................800-343-8046
Southern Shell Fish Company
Harvey, LA.......................504-341-5631
Southern Shellfish
Savannah, GA.....................912-897-3650
Southside Seafood Inc
Scranton, PA.....................570-969-9726
Spinney Creek Shellfish
Eliot, ME........................877-778-6727
Sportsmen's Cannery
Winchester Bay, OR...............800-457-8048
Sportsmen's Cannery & Smokehouse
Winchester Bay, OR...............800-457-8048
Sportsmens Seafoods
San Diego, CA....................619-224-3551
St. Ours & Company
East Weymouth, MA................781-331-8520
St. Simons Seafood
Brunswick, GA....................912-265-5225
Stacey's Famous Foods
Hayden, ID.......................800-782-2395
Stanley's Best Seafood
Coden, AL........................251-824-2801
Star Seafood
Bayou La Batre, AL...............251-824-3110
Starich
Daphne, AL.......................251-626-5037
Steve Connolly Seafood Co Inc
Boston, MA.......................800-225-5595
Stewarts Seafood
Coden, AL........................251-824-7368
Stone Crabs Inc
Miami Beach, FL..................800-260-2722
Straub's
Clayton, MO......................888-725-2121
Sunshine Food Sales
Miami, FL........................305-696-2885
Sunshine Seafood
Stonington, ME...................207-367-2955
Super Snooty Sea Food Corporation
Boston, MA.......................617-426-6390
Superior Ocean Produce
Chicago, IL......................773-283-8400
Superior Seafood & Meat Company
South Bend, IN...................574-289-0511
T&T Seafood
Baker, LA........................225-261-5438
T.B. Seafood
Portland, ME.....................207-871-2420
T.J. Kraft
Honolulu, HI.....................808-842-3474
Taku Smokehouse
Juneau, AK.......................800-582-5122
Tampa Maid Foods Inc
Lakeland, FL.....................800-237-7637
Tempest Fisheries LTD
New Bedford, MA..................508-997-0720
Terry Brothers, Inc
Willis Wharf, VA.................757-442-6251
Tex-Mex Cold Storage
Brownsville, TX..................956-831-9433
Tichon Sea Food Corp
New Bedford, MA..................508-999-5607
Tideland Seafood Company
Dulac, LA........................985-563-4516
Tony's Seafood LTD
Baton Rouge, LA..................800-356-2905
Triangle Seafood
Louisville, KY...................502-561-0055

Trident Seafoods Corp
Seattle, WA......800-426-5490
Trident Seafoods Corp
Wrangell, AK......907-874-3346
Triton Seafood Co
Medley, FL......305-888-0051
Tsar Nicoulai Caviar LLC
San Francisco, CA......800-952-2842
Turk Brothers Custom Meats Inc
Ashland, OH......800-789-1051
Union Fisheries Corp
Chicago, IL......773-738-0448
Union Seafoods
Phoenix, AZ......602-254-4114
United Provision Meat Company
Columbus, OH......614-252-1126
Upcountry Fisheries
Makawao, HI......808-871-8484
Val's Seafood
Mobile, AL......251-639-2570
Valdez Food Inc
Philadelphia, PA......215-634-6106
Van de Kamps
Peoria, IL......800-798-3318
Viking Seafoods Inc
Malden, MA......800-225-3020
Viking Trading
Atlanta, GA......770-455-8630
Vinalhaven Fishermens Co-op
Camden, ME......207-236-0092
Vince's Seafoods
Gretna, LA......504-368-1544
Vincent Piazza Jr & Sons
Harahan, LA......800-259-5016
Virginia Trout Co
Monterey, VA......540-468-2280
Vision Seafood Partners
Kingston, MA......781-585-2000
W. Forrest Haywood Seafood Company
Poquoson, VA......757-868-6748
W.O. Sasser
Savannah, GA......912-897-1154
W.T. Ruark & Company
Fishing Creek, MD......410-397-3133
Wabash Seafood Co
Chicago, IL......312-733-5070
Wabi Fishing Company
Marysville, WA......888-536-7696
Wagner Seafood
Oak Lawn, IL......708-636-2646
Wagshal's Imports
Washington, DC......202-363-5698
Wainani Kai Seafood
Honolulu, HI......808-847-7435
Walden Foods
Winchester, VA......800-648-7688
Walker Meats
Carrollton, GA......800-741-3601
Walker's Seafood
Jonesboro, AR......870-932-0375
Wallace Fisheries
Gulf Shores, AL......251-986-7211
Wallace Plant Company
Bath, ME......207-443-2640
Walsh's Seafood
Gouldsboro, ME......207-963-2578
Wanchese Fish Co Inc
Suffolk, VA......757-673-4500
Waterfront Seafood
Bayou La Batre, AL......251-824-2185
Waterfront Seafood Market
West Des Moines, IA......515-223-5106
WEIS Markets Inc.
Sunbury, PA......866-999-9347
West Bay Fishing
Gouldsboro, ME......207-963-2392
Weyand's Fishery
Wyandotte, MI......800-521-9815
Wharton Seafood Sales
Paauilo, HI......800-352-8507
White Cap Fish Market
Islip, NY......631-277-6577
Wichita Fish Co
Wichita, KS......316-265-3474
Wiegardt Brothers
Nahcotta, WA......360-665-4111
Wild Planet Foods
McKinleyville, CA......800-998-9945
Winn-Dixie Stores
Jacksonville, FL......800-967-9105
Winter Harbor Co-Op Inc
Winter Harbor, ME......207-963-5857
WK Eckerd & Sons
Brunswick, GA......912-265-0332
Wolverton Seafood
Houlton, ME......506-276-4629
Woodfield Fish & Oyster Company
Galesville, MD......410-897-1093
World Flavors Inc
Warminster, PA......215-672-4400
Wright Brand Oysters
Coden, AL......251-824-7880
Y&W Shellfish
Woodbine, GA......912-729-4814
Yarmer Boys Catfish International
Beaumont, TX......409-842-1962
Yeomen Seafoods Inc
Gloucester, MA......978-283-7422
Zabiha Halal Meat Processors
Addison, IL......630-620-5000

Canned

Alaska Pacific Seafoods
Kodiak, AK......907-486-3234
Charles H. Parks & Company
Fishing Creek, MD......410-397-3400
Chuck's Seafoods
Charleston, OR......541-888-5525
Cowart Seafood Corp
Lottsburg, VA......804-529-6101
Crown Prince Inc
City Of Industry, CA......626-912-3700
Dressel Collins Fish Company
Seattle, WA......206-725-0121
J Moniz Co Inc
Fall River, MA......508-674-8451
J Turner Seafood
Gloucester, MA......978-281-8535
Kodiak Salmon Packers
Larsen Bay, AK......907-847-2250
LA Monica Fine Foods
Millville, NJ
LLJ's Sea Products
Round Pond, ME......207-529-4224
Mid-Atlantic Foods Inc
Easton, MD......800-922-4688
Noon Hour Food Products Inc
Chicago, IL......800-621-6636
Notre Dame Seafoods Inc.
Comfort Cove, NL......709-244-5511
Ocean Fresh Seafoods
Seattle, WA......206-285-2412
Safe Catch
Sausalito, CA......888-568-4211
Sea Watch Intl
Easton, MD......410-822-7500
Seatech Corporation
Lynnwood, WA......425-487-3231
Southern Shell Fish Company
Harvey, LA......504-341-5631
Sportsmens Seafoods
San Diego, CA......619-224-3551
Tideland Seafood Company
Dulac, LA......985-563-4516
Trident Seafoods Corp
Wrangell, AK......907-874-3346

Cocktail

Sea Snack Foods Inc
Los Angeles, CA......213-622-2204

Freeze-Dried

Haines Packing Company
Haines, AK......907-766-2883
Wolf Canyon Foods
Carmel, CA......831-626-1323

Fresh

Anderson Seafood
Anaheim, CA......714-777-7100
Aquatec Seafoods Ltd.
Comox, BC......250-339-6412
Arrowac Fisheries
Seattle, WA......206-282-5655
Atlantic Capes Fisheries
Cape May, NJ......609-884-3000
Atlantic Sea Pride
Boston, MA......617-269-7700
Atlantic Seacove Inc
Boston, MA......617-442-6206
B G Smith & Sons Oyster Co
Sharps, VA......877-483-8279
Bayou Land Seafood
Breaux Bridge, LA......337-667-6118
BlueWater Seafoods
Gloucester, MA......888-560-2539
Boundary Fish Company
Blaine, WA......360-332-6715
Briney Sea Delicaseas
Tumwater, WA......888-772-5666
Buzzards Bay Trading Company
Fairhaven, MA......508-996-0242
Caraquet Ice Company
Caraquet, NB......506-727-7211
Carolina Classics Catfish Inc
Ayden, NC......252-746-2818
Charles H. Parks & Company
Fishing Creek, MD......410-397-3400
Coast Seafoods Company
Bellevue, WA......800-423-2303
Cowart Seafood Corp
Lottsburg, VA......804-529-6101
Cozy Harbor Seafood Inc
Portland, ME......800-225-2586
Crest International Corporation
San Diego, CA......800-548-1232
DB Kenney Fisheries
Westport, NS......902-839-2023
French Creek Seafood
Parksville, BC......250-248-7100
Granville Gates & Sons
Hubbards, NS......902-228-2559
Great Atlantic Trading Company
Brentwood, TN......888-268-8780
Gulf Crown Seafood Co
Delcambre, LA......337-685-4722
Hallmark Fisheries
Charleston, OR......541-888-3253
Harbor Fish Market
Portland, ME......800-370-1790
Hillard Bloom Packing Co Inc
Port Norris, NJ......856-785-0120
Hillmans Shrimp & Oyster
Port Lavaca, TX......800-582-4416
Hilo Fish Company
Hilo, HI......808-961-0877
Independent Packers Corporation
Seattle, WA......206-285-6000
International Seafoods - Alaska
Kodiak, AK......907-486-4768
Island Marine Products
Clarks Harbour, NS......902-745-2222
J. Matassini & Sons Fish Company
Tampa, FL......813-229-0829
Jessie's Ilwaco Fish Company
San Francisco, CA......360-642-3773
Keyser Brothers
Lottsburg, VA......804-529-6837
LA Monica Fine Foods
Millville, NJ
Little River Seafood Inc
Reedville, VA......804-453-3670
Menemsha Fish Market
Chilmark, MA......508-645-2282
Minterbrook Oyster Co
Gig Harbor, WA......253-857-5251
National Fish & Oyster
Olympia, WA......360-491-5550
Nordic Group Inc
Boston, MA......800-486-4002
North Pacific Seafoods Inc
Seattle, WA......206-726-9900
Ocean Beauty Seafoods Inc
Seattle, WA......800-365-8950
Ocean Fresh Seafoods
Seattle, WA......206-285-2412
Pacific American Fish Co Inc
Vernon, CA......800-625-2525
Pacific Salmon Company
Edmonds, WA......425-774-1315
Pacific Seafoods International
Port Hardy, BC......250-949-8781
Pamlico Packing Company
Grantsboro, NC......800-682-1113
Paul Piazza & Son Inc
New Orleans, LA......800-969-6011
Portland Shellfish Company
Portland, ME......207-799-9290
Quality Seafood
Apalachicola, FL......850-653-9696
Red Chamber Co
Vernon, CA......323-234-9000
Rippons Seafood
Ocean City, MD......410-723-0056

Royal Seafood Inc
Brooklyn, NY 718-769-1517
Ruggiero Seafood
Newark, NJ 866-225-2627
Stone Crabs Inc
Miami Beach, FL 800-260-2722
Sunshine Food Sales
Miami, FL 305-696-2885
Tampa Bay Fisheries Inc
Dover, FL 800-732-3663
Taylor Shellfish Farms
Shelton, WA 360-426-6178
Terry Brothers, Inc
Willis Wharf, VA 757-442-6251
Trident Seafoods Corp
Wrangell, AK 907-874-3346
Ultimate Foods
Linden, NJ 908-486-0800
Union Fisheries Corp
Chicago, IL 773-738-0448
Wanchese Fish Co Inc
Suffolk, VA 757-673-4500
Weyand's Fishery
Wyandotte, MI 800-521-9815
Wiegardt Brothers
Nahcotta, WA 360-665-4111

Frozen

Acme Steak & Seafood
Youngstown, OH 800-686-2263
Alaskan Gourmet Seafoods
Anchorage, AK 800-288-3740
Aliotti Wholesale Fish Company
Monterey, CA 408-722-4597
American Seafoods
Seattle, WA 206-448-0300
Anderson Seafood
Anaheim, CA 714-777-7100
Aquatec Seafoods Ltd.
Comox, BC 250-339-6412
Arista Industries Inc
Wilton, CT 800-255-6457
Arrowac Fisheries
Seattle, WA 206-282-5655
ASC Seafood Inc
Largo, FL 800-876-3474
Atlantic Capes Fisheries
Cape May, NJ 609-884-3000
Azuma Foods Intl Inc USA
Hayward, CA 510-782-1112
B G Smith & Sons Oyster Co
Sharps, VA 877-483-8279
Bandon Bay Fisheries
Bandon, OR 541-347-4454
Bay Oceans Sea Foods
Garibaldi, OR 503-322-3316
Bayou Land Seafood
Breaux Bridge, LA 337-667-6118
Beaver Street Fisheries
Jacksonville, FL 800-874-6426
Biloxi Freezing Processing Inc.
Biloxi, MS 228-436-0017
Blount Fine Foods
Fall River, MA 774-888-1300
BlueWater Seafoods
Gloucester, MA 888-560-2539
Bon Secour Fisheries Inc
Bon Secour, AL 251-949-7411
Boundary Fish Company
Blaine, WA 360-332-6715
Buzzards Bay Trading Company
Fairhaven, MA 508-996-0242
C F Gollott & Son Seafood
Diberville, MS 228-392-2747
Callis Seafood
Lancaster, VA 804-462-7634
Caraquet Ice Company
Caraquet, NB 506-727-7211
Carolina Atlantic Seafood Enterprises
Beaufort, NC 252-504-2663
Carolina Classics Catfish Inc
Ayden, NC 252-746-2818
Carrington Foods Co Inc
Saraland, AL 251-675-9700
Cathay Foods Corporation
Boston, MA 617-427-1507
Certi Fresh Foods Inc
Wilmington, CA 310-221-6262
Channel Fish Processing
Gloucester, MA 800-457-0054
Chases Lobster Pound
Port Howe, NS 902-243-2408
Cherbogue Fisheries
Yarmouth, NS 902-742-9157
Chester W. Howeth & Brother
Crisfield, MD 410-968-1398
Clearwater Fine Foods
Bedford, NS 902-443-0550
Cowart Seafood Corp
Lottsburg, VA 804-529-6101
Cozy Harbor Seafood Inc
Portland, ME 800-225-2586
Crest International Corporation
San Diego, CA 800-548-1232
Crevettes Du Nord
Gaspe, QC 418-368-1414
Cuizina Food Company
Woodinville, WA 425-486-7000
Czimer's Game & Seafoods
Homer Glen, IL 888-294-6377
DB Kenney Fisheries
Westport, NS 902-839-2023
Deep Creek Custom Packing
Ninilchik, AK 800-764-0078
Del's Seaway Shrimp & Oyster Company
Biloxi, MS 228-432-2604
E. Gagnon & Fils
St Therese-De-Gaspe, QC 418-385-3011
Eastern Fish Company
Teaneck, NJ 800-526-9066
F W Bryce Inc
Gloucester, MA 978-283-7080
Fish Breeders of Idaho
Hagerman, ID 208-837-6114
Fish King
Glendale, CA 818-244-2161
Fish Market Inc
Louisville, KY 502-587-7474
French Creek Seafood
Parksville, BC 250-248-7100
Frozen Specialties Inc
Perrysburg, OH 419-867-2005
Galilean Seafood Inc
Bristol, RI 401-253-3030
George Robberecht Seafood
Montross, VA 804-472-3556
Gerard & Dominique Seafoods
Harbor, OR 800-858-0449
Gesco ENR
Gaspe, QC 418-368-1414
Golden Gulf Coast Packing Co
Biloxi, MS 228-374-6121
Good Harbor Fillet Company
New Bedford, MA 800-343-8046
Gorton's Inc.
Gloucester, MA 800-222-6846
Great Atlantic Trading Company
Brentwood, TN 888-268-8780
Great Glacier Salmon
Prince Rupert, BC 250-627-4955
Great Northern Products Inc
Cranston, RI 401-490-4590
Gulf Pride Enterprises
Biloxi, MS 888-689-0560
H&H Fisheries Limited
Eastern Passage, NS 866-773-4400
Hallmark Fisheries
Charleston, OR 541-888-3253
Handy International Inc
Salisbury, MD 800-426-3977
HFI Foods
Redmond, WA 425-883-1320
Higgins Seafood
Lafitte, LA 504-689-3577
High Liner Foods Inc.
Lunenburg, NS 902-634-8811
Hillard Bloom Packing Co Inc
Port Norris, NJ 856-785-0120
Hillmans Shrimp & Oyster
Port Lavaca, TX 800-582-4416
Hilo Fish Company
Hilo, HI 808-961-0877
Independent Packers Corporation
Seattle, WA 206-285-6000
Indian Ridge Shrimp Co
Chauvin, LA 800-594-0920
International Seafoods - Alaska
Kodiak, AK 907-486-4768
Island Marine Products
Clarks Harbour, NS 902-745-2222
Island Scallops
Qualicum Beach, BC 250-757-9811
J. Matassini & Sons Fish Company
Tampa, FL 813-229-0829
Janes Family Foods
Mississauga, ON 800-565-2637
JBS Packing Inc
Port Arthur, TX 409-982-3216
Jessie's Ilwaco Fish Company
San Francisco, CA 360-642-3773
Jubilee Foods
Bayou La Batre, AL 251-824-2110
Key Largo Fisheries
Key Largo, FL 800-432-4358
Keyser Brothers
Lottsburg, VA 804-529-6837
Kitchens Seafood
Plant City, FL 800-327-0132
Kodiak Salmon Packers
Larsen Bay, AK 907-847-2250
L&C Fisheries
Kensington, PE 902-886-2770
LA Monica Fine Foods
Millville, NJ
Lady Gale Seafood
Baldwin, LA 337-923-2060
Lombardi's Seafood
Winter Park, FL 800-879-8411
Louisiana Packing Company
Westwego, LA 800-666-1293
Lund's Fisheries
Cape May, NJ 609-884-7600
Luxury Crab
St John's, NL 709-739-6668
Maple Leaf Foods International
North York, ON 800-268-3708
Martin Seafood Company
Jessup, MD 410-799-5822
Maxim's Import Corporation
Miami, FL 800-331-6652
Menemsha Fish Market
Chilmark, MA 508-645-2282
Mid-Atlantic Foods Inc
Easton, MD 800-922-4688
Minterbrook Oyster Co
Gig Harbor, WA 253-857-5251
Mobile Processing
Mobile, AL 251-438-6944
Morey's Seafood Intl LLC
Motley, MN 800-808-3474
Mutual Fish Co
Seattle, WA 206-322-4368
Nan Sea Enterprises of Wisconsin
Waukesha, WI 262-542-8841
National Fish & Oyster
Olympia, WA 360-491-5550
Nelson Crab Inc
Tokeland, WA 800-262-0069
Neptune Fisheries
Newport News, VA 800-545-7474
Newfound Resources
St Josephs, NL 709-579-7676
Nordic Group Inc
Boston, MA 800-486-4002
North Pacific Seafoods Inc
Seattle, WA 206-726-9900
Northern Wind Inc
New Bedford, MA 888-525-2525
Notre Dame Seafoods Inc.
Comfort Cove, NL 709-244-5511
Ocean Beauty Seafoods Inc
Seattle, WA 800-365-8950
Ocean Food Co. Ltd.
Toronto, ON 416-285-6487
Ocean Fresh Seafoods
Seattle, WA 206-285-2412
Ocean Springs Seafood
Ocean Springs, MS 228-875-0104
Okuhara Foods Inc
Honolulu, HI 808-848-0581
Orca Bay Foods
Seattle, WA 800-932-6722
P. Janes & Sons
Hant's Harbor, NL 709-586-2252
Pacific American Fish Co Inc
Vernon, CA 800-625-2525
Pacific Seafoods International
Port Hardy, BC 250-949-8781
Pacific Valley Foods Inc
Bellevue, WA 425-643-1805
Pamlico Packing Company
Grantsboro, NC 800-682-1113
Paul Piazza & Son Inc
New Orleans, LA 800-969-6011
PEI Mussel King
Morrell, PE 800-673-2767

Peter Pan Seafoods Inc.
Bellevue, WA 206-728-6000
Portland Shellfish Company
Portland, ME 207-799-9290
Prairie Cajun Wholesale
Eunice, LA 337-546-6195
Quality Seafood
Apalachicola, FL 850-653-9696
Resource Trading Company
Portland, ME 207-772-2299
Royal Seafood Inc
Brooklyn, NY 718-769-1517
Ruggiero Seafood
Newark, NJ 866-225-2627
Santa Monica Seafood Co.
Rancho Dominguez, CA 800-969-8862
Sea Pearl Seafood
Bayou La Batre, AL 800-872-8804
Sea Safari
Belhaven, NC 800-688-6174
Sea Snack Foods Inc
Los Angeles, CA 213-622-2204
Sea Watch Intl
Easton, MD 410-822-7500
Seafood Producers Co-Op
Bellingham, WA 360-733-0120
Seajoy
Miami, FL 877-537-1717
Seatech Corporation
Lynnwood, WA 425-487-3231
Seymour & Sons Seafoods Inc
Diberville, MS 228-392-4020
Shawmut Fishing Company
Anchorage, AK 709-334-2559
Silver Lining Seafood
Seattle, WA 800-426-5490
Spruce Lane Investments
Stratford, PE 902-892-2600
St. Ours & Company
East Weymouth, MA 781-331-8520
Stacey's Famous Foods
Hayden, ID 800-782-2395
Stone Crabs Inc
Miami Beach, FL 800-260-2722
Sunshine Food Sales
Miami, FL 305-696-2885
Super Snooty Sea Food Corporation
Boston, MA 617-426-6390
Sweet Water Seafood
Carlstadt, NJ 201-939-6622
Taku Smokehouse
Juneau, AK 800-582-5122
Tampa Bay Fisheries Inc
Dover, FL 800-732-3663
Tampa Maid Foods Inc
Lakeland, FL 800-237-7637
Taylor Shellfish Farms
Shelton, WA 360-426-6178
Tex-Mex Cold Storage
Brownsville, TX 956-831-9433
Tichon Sea Food Corp
New Bedford, MA 508-999-5607
Trident Seafoods Corp
Wrangell, AK 907-874-3346
Triton Seafood Co
Medley, FL 305-888-0051
Ultimate Foods
Linden, NJ 908-486-0800
Union Fisheries Corp
Chicago, IL 773-738-0448
Viking Seafoods Inc
Malden, MA 800-225-3020
Vince's Seafoods
Gretna, LA 504-368-1544
Vincent Piazza Jr & Sons
Harahan, LA 800-259-5016
Virginia Trout Co
Monterey, VA 540-468-2280
Wanchese Fish Co Inc
Suffolk, VA 757-673-4500
Weyand's Fishery
Wyandotte, MI 800-521-9815
White Cap Fish Market
Islip, NY 631-277-6577

Smoked

Anderson Seafood
Anaheim, CA 714-777-7100
Blount Fine Foods
Fall River, MA 774-888-1300
Cooke Aguaculture
Blacks Harbour, NB 506-456-6600
Dressel Collins Fish Company
Seattle, WA 206-725-0121
Indian Valley Meats
Indian, AK 907-653-7511
Salmolux Inc
Federal Way, WA 253-874-6570
Sea Bear Smokehouse
Anacortes, WA 800-645-3474

Cold

Tonex
Wallington, NJ 973-773-5135

Cured

J Moniz Co Inc
Fall River, MA 508-674-8451
J Turner Seafood
Gloucester, MA 978-281-8535
Ocean Fresh Seafoods
Seattle, WA 206-285-2412
Tideland Seafood Company
Dulac, LA 985-563-4516

Lox

Bold Coast Smokehouse
Lubec, ME 888-733-0807
Homarus Inc
Long Island City, NY 917-832-0333
Vita Food Products Inc
Chicago, IL 800-989-8482

Nova Style

Vita Food Products Inc
Chicago, IL 800-989-8482
Vital Choice
Bellingham, WA 800-608-4825

Turtle

Bayou Land Seafood
Breaux Bridge, LA 337-667-6118

Shellfish

Canned

Channel Fish Processing
Gloucester, MA 800-457-0054
Charles H. Parks & Company
Fishing Creek, MD 410-397-3400
Chicken Of The Sea
El Segundo, CA 844-267-8862
Chuck's Seafoods
Charleston, OR 541-888-5525
Crown Prince Inc
City Of Industry, CA 626-912-3700
Cuizina Food Company
Woodinville, WA 425-486-7000
Gulf City Marine Supply
Bayou La Batre, AL 251-824-2516
Hallmark Fisheries
Charleston, OR 541-888-3253
Mid-Atlantic Foods Inc
Easton, MD 800-922-4688
Nelson Crab Inc
Tokeland, WA 800-262-0069
Notre Dame Seafoods Inc.
Comfort Cove, NL 709-244-5511
Ntc Marketing
Williamsville, NY 800-333-1637
Pacific Salmon Company
Edmonds, WA 425-774-1315
Peter Pan Seafoods Inc.
Bellevue, WA 206-728-6000
Sea Safari
Belhaven, NC 800-688-6174
Southern Shell Fish Company
Harvey, LA 504-341-5631
Sweet Water Seafood
Carlstadt, NJ 201-939-6622
Trident Seafoods Corp
Wrangell, AK 907-874-3346

Chopped

S & M Fisheries Inc
Kennebunkport, ME 207-985-3456

Clam

Atlantic Aqua Farms
Orwell Cove, PE 902-651-2563
Atlantic Capes Fisheries
Cape May, NJ 609-884-3000
Big Al's Seafood
Bozman, MD 410-745-2637
Biloxi Freezing Processing Inc.
Biloxi, MS 228-436-0017
Blount Fine Foods
Fall River, MA 774-888-1300
Bon Secour Fisheries Inc
Bon Secour, AL 251-949-7411
C.E. Fish Company
Jonesboro, ME 207-434-2631
Caito Fisheries Inc
Fort Bragg, CA 707-964-6368
Cajun Crawfish Distributors
Branch, LA 888-254-8626
Certi Fresh Foods Inc
Wilmington, CA 310-221-6262
Chases Lobster Pound
Port Howe, NS 902-243-2408
Chester River Clam Co
Centreville, MD 410-758-3810
Chuck's Seafoods
Charleston, OR 541-888-5525
Clearwater Fine Foods
Bedford, NS 902-443-0550
Coast Seafoods Company
Bellevue, WA 800-423-2303
Comeaux's
Lafayette, LA 888-264-5460
Crevettes Du Nord
Gaspe, QC 418-368-1414
Crown Prince Inc
City Of Industry, CA 626-912-3700
Cuizina Food Company
Woodinville, WA 425-486-7000
Davis Strait Fisheries
Halifax, NS 902-450-5115
Del's Seaway Shrimp & Oyster Company
Biloxi, MS 228-432-2604
E. Gagnon & Fils
St Therese-De-Gaspe, QC 418-385-3011
Frozen Specialties Inc
Perrysburg, OH 419-867-2005
Fulton Fish Market
New York, NY 718-842-8908
Gerard & Dominique Seafoods
Harbor, OR 800-858-0449
Gesco ENR
Gaspe, QC 418-368-1414
Gulf Pride Enterprises
Biloxi, MS 888-689-0560
H&H Fisheries Limited
Eastern Passage, NS 866-773-4400
Hillard Bloom Packing Co Inc
Port Norris, NJ 856-785-0120
Hillmans Shrimp & Oyster
Port Lavaca, TX 800-582-4416
Huck's Seafood
Easton, MD 410-770-9211
Innovative Fishery Products
Belliveau Cove, NS 902-837-5163
International Enterprises
Herring Neck, NL 709-628-7406
Island Scallops
Qualicum Beach, BC 250-757-9811
JBS Packing Inc
Port Arthur, TX 409-982-3216
Jubilee Foods
Bayou La Batre, AL 251-824-2110
L&C Fisheries
Kensington, PE 902-886-2770
L&M Evans
Conyers, GA 770-483-9373
LA Monica Fine Foods
Millville, NJ
Lady Gale Seafood
Baldwin, LA 337-923-2060
Louisiana Packing Company
Westwego, LA 800-666-1293
Menemsha Fish Market
Chilmark, MA 508-645-2282
Mid-Atlantic Foods Inc
Easton, MD 800-922-4688
Mill Cove Lobster Pound
Trevett, ME 207-633-3340
Mobile Processing
Mobile, AL 251-438-6944
Mutual Fish Co
Seattle, WA 206-322-4368
Nan Sea Enterprises of Wisconsin
Waukesha, WI 262-542-8841

New Orleans Fish House II LLC
New Orleans, LA 800-839-3474
Newfound Resources
St Josephs, NL 709-579-7676
North Atlantic Seafood
Portland, ME 800-774-6025
Northern Wind Inc
New Bedford, MA 888-525-2525
Northwest Wild Products
Astoria, OR 503-791-1907
Ocean Springs Seafood
Ocean Springs, MS 228-875-0104
PEI Mussel King
Morrell, PE 800-673-2767
Pine Point Seafood
Scarborough, ME 207-883-4701
Price Seafood
Havre De Grace, MD 410-939-2782
Resource Trading Company
Portland, ME 207-772-2299
SeaPerfect Atlantic Farms
Charleston, SC 800-728-0099
Shawmut Fishing Company
Anchorage, AK 709-334-2559
St. Ours & Company
East Weymouth, MA 781-331-8520
Stavis Seafoods
Boston, MA 800-390-5103
Tampa Bay Fisheries Inc
Dover, FL 800-732-3663
Terry Brothers, Inc
Willis Wharf, VA 757-442-6251
Vincent Piazza Jr & Sons
Harahan, LA 800-259-5016
Vital Choice
Bellingham, WA 800-608-4825
Young's Lobster Pound
Belfast, ME 207-338-1160

Breaded Strips

LA Monica Fine Foods
Millville, NJ

Canned

Blount Fine Foods
Fall River, MA 774-888-1300
Chicken Of The Sea
El Segundo, CA 844-267-8862
Chuck's Seafoods
Charleston, OR 541-888-5525
Cuizina Food Company
Woodinville, WA 425-486-7000
LA Monica Fine Foods
Millville, NJ
Mid-Atlantic Foods Inc
Easton, MD 800-922-4688
Mutual Fish Co
Seattle, WA 206-322-4368
New Orleans Food Co-op
New Orleans, LA 800-628-4900
Stavis Seafoods
Boston, MA 800-390-5103

Chopped

LA Monica Fine Foods
Millville, NJ

Fresh

Coast Seafoods Company
Bellevue, WA 800-423-2303
Cuizina Food Company
Woodinville, WA 425-486-7000
LA Monica Fine Foods
Millville, NJ
Menemsha Fish Market
Chilmark, MA 508-645-2282
Mutual Fish Co
Seattle, WA 206-322-4368
Sweet Water Seafood
Carlstadt, NJ 201-939-6622
Taylor Shellfish Farms
Shelton, WA 360-426-6178
Terry Brothers, Inc
Willis Wharf, VA 757-442-6251

Frozen

Cedar Key Aquaculture Farms
Riverview, FL 888-252-6735
Certi Fresh Foods Inc
Wilmington, CA 310-221-6262
Clearwater Fine Foods
Bedford, NS 902-443-0550
Cuizina Food Company
Woodinville, WA 425-486-7000
Gorton's Inc.
Gloucester, MA 800-222-6846
Harbor Seafood
New Hyde Park, NY 800-645-2211
Hillard Bloom Packing Co Inc
Port Norris, NJ 856-785-0120
LA Monica Fine Foods
Millville, NJ
Menemsha Fish Market
Chilmark, MA 508-645-2282
Mid-Atlantic Foods Inc
Easton, MD 800-922-4688
Minterbrook Oyster Co
Gig Harbor, WA 253-857-5251
Mutual Fish Co
Seattle, WA 206-322-4368
St. Ours & Company
East Weymouth, MA 781-331-8520
Taylor Shellfish Farms
Shelton, WA 360-426-6178

Frozen Strips

LA Monica Fine Foods
Millville, NJ

Juice

Chincoteague Seafood Co Inc
Parsonsburg, MD 443-260-4800
Crown Prince Inc
City Of Industry, CA 626-912-3700
Flavor House, Inc.
Adelanto, CA 760-246-9131

Minced

LA Monica Fine Foods
Millville, NJ

Whole

LA Monica Fine Foods
Millville, NJ

Conch

Denzer's Food Products
Baltimore, MD 410-889-1500
Fulton Fish Market
New York, NY 718-842-8908
Harbor Seafood
New Hyde Park, NY 800-645-2211
LA Monica Fine Foods
Millville, NJ
Sweet Water Seafood
Carlstadt, NJ 201-939-6622
Triton Seafood Co
Medley, FL 305-888-0051

Crab

Arrowac Fisheries
Seattle, WA 206-282-5655
Bandon Bay Fisheries
Bandon, OR 541-347-4454
Barry Group
Corner Brook, NL 709-785-7387
Bay Hundred Seafood Inc
St Michaels, MD 410-745-9329
Bayou Food Distributors
Kenner, LA 800-516-8283
Bayou Land Seafood
Breaux Bridge, LA 337-667-6118
Beaver Street Fisheries
Jacksonville, FL 800-874-6426
Big Al's Seafood
Bozman, MD 410-745-2637
Blue Star Food Products
Doral, FL 305-836-6858
Bradye P. Todd & Son
Cambridge, MD 410-228-8633
Caito Fisheries Inc
Fort Bragg, CA 707-964-6368
California Shellfish Company
San Francisco, CA 415-923-7400
Callis Seafood
Lancaster, VA 804-462-7634
Captain Little Seafood
Queens County, NS 902-947-2087
Carrington Foods Co Inc
Saraland, AL 251-675-9700
Catfish Wholesale
Abbeville, LA 800-334-7292
Cathay Foods Corporation
Boston, MA 617-427-1507
Ceilidh Fisherman's Cooperative
Port Hood, NS 902-787-2666
Certi Fresh Foods Inc
Wilmington, CA 310-221-6262
Charles H. Parks & Company
Fishing Creek, MD 410-397-3400
Clearwater Fine Foods
Bedford, NS 902-443-0550
Crab Quarters
Baltimore, MD 410-686-2222
Crown Prince Inc
City Of Industry, CA 626-912-3700
Cuizina Food Company
Woodinville, WA 425-486-7000
Dave's Gourmet Albacore
Watsonville, CA 206-999-5517
Dorchester Crab Co
Wingate, MD 410-397-8103
Fisherman's Market International
Halifax, NS 902-445-3474
Fishhawk Fisheries
Astoria, OR 503-325-5252
Fulton Fish Market
New York, NY 718-842-8908
Goldcoast Salads
Naples, FL 239-513-0430
Great Northern Products Inc
Cranston, RI 401-490-4590
Gulf Stream Crab Company
Bayou La Batre, AL 251-824-4717
H.Gass Seafood
Hollywood, MD 301-373-6882
Hallmark Fisheries
Charleston, OR 541-888-3253
Handy International Inc
Salisbury, MD 800-426-3977
Harris Crab House
Grasonville, MD 410-827-9500
Huck's Seafood
Easton, MD 410-770-9211
Independent Packers Corporation
Seattle, WA 206-285-6000
J. Matassini & Sons Fish Company
Tampa, FL 813-229-0829
JBS Packing Inc
Port Arthur, TX 409-982-3216
Jessie's Ilwaco Fish Company
San Francisco, CA 360-642-3773
Keyser Brothers
Lottsburg, VA 804-529-6837
Kitchens Seafood
Plant City, FL 800-327-0132
LA Monica Fine Foods
Millville, NJ
Larry J. Williams Company
Jesup, GA 912-427-7729
Little River Seafood Inc
Reedville, VA 804-453-3670
Lowland Seafood
Lowland, NC 252-745-3751
Luxury Crab
St John's, NL 709-739-6668
Martin Brothers Seafood Co
Westwego, LA 504-341-2251
McGraw Seafood
Tracadie Sheila, NB 506-395-3374
Menemsha Fish Market
Chilmark, MA 508-645-2282
Mercer Processing
Modesto, CA 209-529-0150
Mutual Fish Co
Seattle, WA 206-322-4368
Nelson Crab Inc
Tokeland, WA 800-262-0069
New Orleans Fish House II LLC
New Orleans, LA 800-839-3474
North Atlantic Seafood
Portland, ME 800-774-6025
Northwest Wild Products
Astoria, OR 503-791-1907
Notre Dame Seafoods Inc.
Comfort Cove, NL 709-244-5511
Ocean Food Co. Ltd.
Toronto, ON 416-285-6487
Ocean Union Company
Lawrenceville, GA 770-995-1957
Pamlico Packing Company
Grantsboro, NC 800-682-1113

Peter Pan Seafoods Inc.
Bellevue, WA 206-728-6000
Phillips Foods
Baltimore, MD 888-234-2722
Price Seafood
Havre De Grace, MD 410-939-2782
Produits Belle Baie
Caraquet, NB 506-727-4414
Red Chamber Co
Vernon, CA 323-234-9000
Rippons Seafood
Ocean City, MD 410-723-0056
Sea Safari
Belhaven, NC 800-688-6174
Sea Watch Intl
Easton, MD 410-822-7500
Silver Lining Seafood
Seattle, WA 800-426-5490
Southern Shell Fish Company
Harvey, LA 504-341-5631
St. Ours & Company
East Weymouth, MA 781-331-8520
Stone Crabs Inc
Miami Beach, FL 800-260-2722
Sunshine Food Sales
Miami, FL 305-696-2885
Taku Smokehouse
Juneau, AK 800-582-5122
Trident Seafoods Corp
Wrangell, AK 907-874-3346
Vince's Seafoods
Gretna, LA 504-368-1544
Vital Choice
Bellingham, WA 800-608-4825
W.T. Ruark & Company
Fishing Creek, MD 410-397-3133
Waverly Crabs
Baltimore, MD 410-243-1181
Young's Lobster Pound
Belfast, ME 207-338-1160

Blue

Casey's Seafood Inc
Newport News, VA 757-928-1979
J M Clayton Co
Cambridge, MD 800-652-6931
Little River Seafood Inc
Reedville, VA 804-453-3670
Price Seafood
Havre De Grace, MD 410-939-2782
Sea Safari
Belhaven, NC 800-688-6174

Cakes

Bradley Creek Seafood
Savannah, GA 912-484-3510
Casey's Seafood Inc
Newport News, VA 757-928-1979
Chesapeake Bay Crab Cakes & More
Owings Mills, MD 800-282-2722
Handy International Inc
Salisbury, MD 800-426-3977
J. Matassini & Sons Fish Company
Tampa, FL 813-229-0829
LA Monica Fine Foods
Millville, NJ
Tampa Bay Fisheries Inc
Dover, FL 800-732-3663
The Van Cleve Seafood Company
Spotsylvania, VA 800-628-5202

Cakes Frozen

Chincoteague Seafood Co Inc
Parsonsburg, MD 443-260-4800
Coastal Seafoods
Ridgefield, CT 203-431-0453
Cuizina Food Company
Woodinville, WA 425-486-7000
Handy International Inc
Salisbury, MD 800-426-3977
J. Matassini & Sons Fish Company
Tampa, FL 813-229-0829

Canned

Cathay Foods Corporation
Boston, MA 617-427-1507
Charles H. Parks & Company
Fishing Creek, MD 410-397-3400
Chicken Of The Sea
El Segundo, CA 844-267-8862

Cuizina Food Company
Woodinville, WA 425-486-7000
Mutual Fish Co
Seattle, WA 206-322-4368
Sea Safari
Belhaven, NC 800-688-6174
Southern Shell Fish Company
Harvey, LA 504-341-5631
Trident Seafoods Corp
Wrangell, AK 907-874-3346
Vital Choice
Bellingham, WA 800-608-4825

Claws Stone

Luxury Crab
St John's, NL 709-739-6668

Cooked

Bayou Food Distributors
Kenner, LA 800-516-8283

Dungeness

Arrowac Fisheries
Seattle, WA 206-282-5655
Dave's Gourmet Albacore
Watsonville, CA 206-999-5517
Glacier Fish Company
Seattle, WA 206-298-1200
Jessie's Ilwaco Fish Company
San Francisco, CA 360-642-3773

Fresh

Arrowac Fisheries
Seattle, WA 206-282-5655
Bayou Land Seafood
Breaux Bridge, LA 337-667-6118
Cathay Foods Corporation
Boston, MA 617-427-1507
Charles H. Parks & Company
Fishing Creek, MD 410-397-3400
Cuizina Food Company
Woodinville, WA 425-486-7000
Daley Brothers ltd.
St John's, NL 709-364-8844
Dave's Gourmet Albacore
Watsonville, CA 206-999-5517
J. Matassini & Sons Fish Company
Tampa, FL 813-229-0829
Jessie's Ilwaco Fish Company
San Francisco, CA 360-642-3773
Keyser Brothers
Lottsburg, VA 804-529-6837
Little River Seafood Inc
Reedville, VA 804-453-3670
Lowland Seafood
Lowland, NC 252-745-3751
Menemsha Fish Market
Chilmark, MA 508-645-2282
Mutual Fish Co
Seattle, WA 206-322-4368
Nelson Crab Inc
Tokeland, WA 800-262-0069
Phillips Foods
Baltimore, MD 888-234-2722
Portland Shellfish Company
Portland, ME 207-799-9290
Rippons Seafood
Ocean City, MD 410-723-0056
Sea Watch Intl
Easton, MD 410-822-7500
Stone Crabs Inc
Miami Beach, FL 800-260-2722
Sunshine Food Sales
Miami, FL 305-696-2885
Taylor Shellfish Farms
Shelton, WA 360-426-6178
Trident Seafoods Corp
Wrangell, AK 907-874-3346

Frozen

Arrowac Fisheries
Seattle, WA 206-282-5655
Bandon Bay Fisheries
Bandon, OR 541-347-4454
Bayou Land Seafood
Breaux Bridge, LA 337-667-6118
Beaver Street Fisheries
Jacksonville, FL 800-874-6426
Callis Seafood
Lancaster, VA 804-462-7634

Carrington Foods Co Inc
Saraland, AL 251-675-9700
Cathay Foods Corporation
Boston, MA 617-427-1507
Certi Fresh Foods Inc
Wilmington, CA 310-221-6262
Clearwater Fine Foods
Bedford, NS 902-443-0550
Cowart Seafood Corp
Lottsburg, VA 804-529-6101
Cuizina Food Company
Woodinville, WA 425-486-7000
Daley Brothers ltd.
St John's, NL 709-364-8844
Dave's Gourmet Albacore
Watsonville, CA 206-999-5517
Fogo Island Cooperative Society
Seldom Fogo Island, NL 709-627-3452
Great Northern Products Inc
Cranston, RI 401-490-4590
Higgins Seafood
Lafitte, LA 504-689-3577
Independent Packers Corporation
Seattle, WA 206-285-6000
J. Matassini & Sons Fish Company
Tampa, FL 813-229-0829
Jessie's Ilwaco Fish Company
San Francisco, CA 360-642-3773
Keyser Brothers
Lottsburg, VA 804-529-6837
Kitchens Seafood
Plant City, FL 800-327-0132
Luxury Crab
St John's, NL 709-739-6668
Menemsha Fish Market
Chilmark, MA 508-645-2282
Mutual Fish Co
Seattle, WA 206-322-4368
Notre Dame Seafoods Inc.
Comfort Cove, NL 709-244-5511
Pamlico Packing Company
Grantsboro, NC 800-682-1113
Portland Shellfish Company
Portland, ME 207-799-9290
Sea Safari
Belhaven, NC 800-688-6174
Sea Watch Intl
Easton, MD 410-822-7500
Silver Lining Seafood
Seattle, WA 800-426-5490
Spruce Lane Investments
Stratford, PE 902-892-2600
St. Ours & Company
East Weymouth, MA 781-331-8520
Stone Crabs Inc
Miami Beach, FL 800-260-2722
Sunshine Food Sales
Miami, FL 305-696-2885
Taku Smokehouse
Juneau, AK 800-582-5122
Taylor Shellfish Farms
Shelton, WA 360-426-6178
Trident Seafoods Corp
Wrangell, AK 907-874-3346

Imitation

Harbor Seafood
New Hyde Park, NY 800-645-2211

King

Arrowac Fisheries
Seattle, WA 206-282-5655
Harbor Seafood
New Hyde Park, NY 800-645-2211
New Ocean
Doraville, GA 770-458-5235
North Pacific Seafoods Inc
Seattle, WA 206-726-9900
Tenth & M Seafoods
Anchorage, AK 800-770-2722

Live

Dorchester Crab Co
Wingate, MD 410-397-8103

Meat

Bandon Bay Fisheries
Bandon, OR 541-347-4454
Bay Hundred Seafood Inc
St Michaels, MD 410-745-9329

Bayou Food Distributors
Kenner, LA 800-516-8283
Bayou Land Seafood
Breaux Bridge, LA 337-667-6118
Beaver Street Fisheries
Jacksonville, FL 800-874-6426
Blalock Seafood & Specialty
Orange Beach, AL 251-974-5811
Blue Crab Bay
Melfa, VA 800-221-2722
Boja's Foods Inc
Bayou La Batre, AL 251-824-4186
Certi Fresh Foods Inc
Wilmington, CA 310-221-6262
Charles H. Parks & Company
Fishing Creek, MD 410-397-3400
Dave's Gourmet Albacore
Watsonville, CA 206-999-5517
Dorchester Crab Co
Wingate, MD 410-397-8103
Hallmark Fisheries
Charleston, OR 541-888-3253
Harmon's Original Clam Cakes
Kennebunkport, ME 207-967-4100
Harvest Time Seafood Inc
Abbeville, LA 337-893-9029
Keyser Brothers
Lottsburg, VA 804-529-6837
Little River Seafood Inc
Reedville, VA 804-453-3670
Luxury Crab
St John's, NL 709-739-6668
Martin Brothers Seafood Co
Westwego, LA 504-341-2251
Nelson Crab Inc
Tokeland, WA 800-262-0069
Pamlico Packing Company
Grantsboro, NC 800-682-1113
Penguin Frozen Foods Inc
Northbrook, IL 800-323-1485
Peter Pan Seafoods Inc.
Bellevue, WA 206-728-6000
Phillips Foods
Baltimore, MD 888-234-2722
Rippons Seafood
Ocean City, MD 410-723-0056
Sea Safari
Belhaven, NC 800-688-6174
Sea Watch Intl
Easton, MD 410-822-7500
Southern Shell Fish Company
Harvey, LA 504-341-5631
W.T. Ruark & Company
Fishing Creek, MD 410-397-3133

Meat Canned

Bayou Land Seafood
Breaux Bridge, LA 337-667-6118
Cathay Foods Corporation
Boston, MA 617-427-1507
Charles H. Parks & Company
Fishing Creek, MD 410-397-3400
Martin Brothers Seafood Co
Westwego, LA 504-341-2251
Miami Crab Corporation
Miami, FL 800-269-8395
New Orleans Food Co-op
New Orleans, LA 800-628-4900
Peter Pan Seafoods Inc.
Bellevue, WA 206-728-6000
Phillips Foods
Baltimore, MD 888-234-2722
Sea Safari
Belhaven, NC 800-688-6174
Southern Shell Fish Company
Harvey, LA 504-341-5631

Meat Frozen

Alpine Butcher
Lowell, MA 978-256-7771
Bandon Bay Fisheries
Bandon, OR 541-347-4454
Bayou Land Seafood
Breaux Bridge, LA 337-667-6118
Beaver Street Fisheries
Jacksonville, FL 800-874-6426
Cathay Foods Corporation
Boston, MA 617-427-1507
Certi Fresh Foods Inc
Wilmington, CA 310-221-6262
Harvest Time Seafood Inc
Abbeville, LA 337-893-9029
Keyser Brothers
Lottsburg, VA 804-529-6837
Luxury Crab
St John's, NL 709-739-6668
Martin Brothers Seafood Co
Westwego, LA 504-341-2251
Miami Crab Corporation
Miami, FL 800-269-8395
Nelson Crab Inc
Tokeland, WA 800-262-0069
Penguin Frozen Foods Inc
Northbrook, IL 800-323-1485
Peter Pan Seafoods Inc.
Bellevue, WA 206-728-6000
Phillips Foods
Baltimore, MD 888-234-2722

Snow

Arrowac Fisheries
Seattle, WA 206-282-5655
Breakwater Fisheries
St John's, NL 709-754-1999
Harbor Seafood
New Hyde Park, NY 800-645-2211
New Ocean
Doraville, GA 770-458-5235
North Pacific Seafoods Inc
Seattle, WA 206-726-9900
Spruce Lane Investments
Stratford, PE 902-892-2600
Taku Smokehouse
Juneau, AK 800-582-5122

Soft Shell

Bayou Food Distributors
Kenner, LA 800-516-8283
Cowart Seafood Corp
Lottsburg, VA 804-529-6101
Handy International Inc
Salisbury, MD 800-426-3977
Rippons Seafood
Ocean City, MD 410-723-0056
W.T. Ruark & Company
Fishing Creek, MD 410-397-3133

Stone

Stone Crabs Inc
Miami Beach, FL 800-260-2722

Stuffed

Belle River Enterprises
Belle River, PE 902-962-2248
Bon Secour Fisheries Inc
Bon Secour, AL 251-949-7411
Clayton's Crab Co
Rockledge, FL 321-636-6673
Dave's Gourmet Albacore
Watsonville, CA 206-999-5517
E. Gagnon & Fils
St Therese-De-Gaspe, QC 418-385-3011
Gerard & Dominique Seafoods
Harbor, OR 800-858-0449
Handy International Inc
Salisbury, MD 800-426-3977
Lowland Seafood
Lowland, NC 252-745-3751
Menemsha Fish Market
Chilmark, MA 508-645-2282
Nan Sea Enterprises of Wisconsin
Waukesha, WI 262-542-8841
Pamlico Packing Company
Grantsboro, NC 800-682-1113
Rippons Seafood
Ocean City, MD 410-723-0056
Shawmut Fishing Company
Anchorage, AK 709-334-2559

Crayfish

Basin Crawfish Processors
Breaux Bridge, LA 337-332-6655
Bayou Land Seafood
Breaux Bridge, LA 337-667-6118
Gulf Marine
Westwego, LA 504-436-2682
Natchitoches Crawfish Company
Natchitoches, LA 318-352-2194
Northwest Wild Products
Astoria, OR 503-791-1907
Ocean Pride Seafood
Delcambre, LA 337-685-2336
Raffield Fisheries Inc
Port St Joe, FL 850-229-8494
Vince's Seafoods
Gretna, LA 504-368-1544

Frozen

Bayou Land Seafood
Breaux Bridge, LA 337-667-6118

Live

Belle River Enterprises
Belle River, PE 902-962-2248

Raw

Bayou Land Seafood
Breaux Bridge, LA 337-667-6118

Dehydrated

Mercer Processing
Modesto, CA 209-529-0150

Fresh

Acme Steak & Seafood
Youngstown, OH 800-686-2263
Arrowac Fisheries
Seattle, WA 206-282-5655
B G Smith & Sons Oyster Co
Sharps, VA 877-483-8279
Bay Oceans Sea Foods
Garibaldi, OR 503-322-3316
Bayou Land Seafood
Breaux Bridge, LA 337-667-6118
Blount Fine Foods
Fall River, MA 774-888-1300
BlueWater Seafoods
Gloucester, MA 888-560-2539
Bon Secour Fisheries Inc
Bon Secour, AL 251-949-7411
C F Gollott & Son Seafood
Diberville, MS 228-392-2747
Channel Fish Processing
Gloucester, MA 800-457-0054
Charles H. Parks & Company
Fishing Creek, MD 410-397-3400
Coast Seafoods Company
Bellevue, WA 800-423-2303
Cowart Seafood Corp
Lottsburg, VA 804-529-6101
Cozy Harbor Seafood Inc
Portland, ME 800-225-2586
Delaware Valley Fish Co
Norristown, PA 610-277-4900
Fisherman's Market International
Halifax, NS 902-445-3474
Gulf City Marine Supply
Bayou La Batre, AL 251-824-2516
Gulf Pride Enterprises
Biloxi, MS 888-689-0560
Hallmark Fisheries
Charleston, OR 541-888-3253
Hillard Bloom Packing Co Inc
Port Norris, NJ 856-785-0120
Hillmans Shrimp & Oyster
Port Lavaca, TX 800-582-4416
Independent Packers Corporation
Seattle, WA 206-285-6000
Intervest Trading Company Inc.
Halifax, NS 902-425-2018
IOE Atlanta
Galena, MD 410-755-6300
Island Marine Products
Clarks Harbour, NS 902-745-2222
J. Matassini & Sons Fish Company
Tampa, FL 813-229-0829
Jessie's Ilwaco Fish Company
San Francisco, CA 360-642-3773
Keyser Brothers
Lottsburg, VA 804-529-6837
LA Monica Fine Foods
Millville, NJ
Little River Seafood Inc
Reedville, VA 804-453-3670
Minterbrook Oyster Co
Gig Harbor, WA 253-857-5251
National Fish & Oyster
Olympia, WA 360-491-5550
Nelson Crab Inc
Tokeland, WA 800-262-0069

Pacific Salmon Company
Edmonds, WA....................425-774-1315
Paul Piazza & Son Inc
New Orleans, LA................800-969-6011
Peter Pan Seafoods Inc.
Bellevue, WA....................206-728-6000
Portland Shellfish Company
Portland, ME....................207-799-9290
Quality Seafood
Apalachicola, FL................850-653-9696
Rippons Seafood
Ocean City, MD..................410-723-0056
Royal Seafood Inc
Brooklyn, NY....................718-769-1517
Ruggiero Seafood
Newark, NJ......................866-225-2627
Seafood Producers Co-Op
Bellingham, WA..................360-733-0120
Sportsmen's Cannery & Smokehouse
Winchester Bay, OR..............800-457-8048
Stone Crabs Inc
Miami Beach, FL.................800-260-2722
Sweet Water Seafood
Carlstadt, NJ...................201-939-6622
Taylor Shellfish Farms
Shelton, WA.....................360-426-6178
Terry Brothers, Inc
Willis Wharf, VA................757-442-6251
Tichon Sea Food Corp
New Bedford, MA.................508-999-5607
Trident Seafoods Corp
Wrangell, AK....................907-874-3346
Wanchese Fish Co Inc
Suffolk, VA.....................757-673-4500
Wiegardt Brothers
Nahcotta, WA....................360-665-4111
Young's Lobster Pound
Belfast, ME.....................207-338-1160

Frozen

A.C. Inc.
Beals, ME.......................207-497-2261
Arista Industries Inc
Wilton, CT......................800-255-6457
Arrowac Fisheries
Seattle, WA.....................206-282-5655
B G Smith & Sons Oyster Co
Sharps, VA......................877-483-8279
Bandon Bay Fisheries
Bandon, OR......................541-347-4454
Bayou Land Seafood
Breaux Bridge, LA...............337-667-6118
Beaver Street Fisheries
Jacksonville, FL................800-874-6426
Bon Secour Fisheries Inc
Bon Secour, AL..................251-949-7411
Breakwater Fisheries
St John's, NL...................709-754-1999
Callis Seafood
Lancaster, VA...................804-462-7634
Carrington Foods Co Inc
Saraland, AL....................251-675-9700
Cathay Foods Corporation
Boston, MA......................617-427-1507
Certi Fresh Foods Inc
Wilmington, CA..................310-221-6262
Channel Fish Processing
Gloucester, MA..................800-457-0054
Clearwater Fine Foods
Bedford, NS.....................902-443-0550
Cowart Seafood Corp
Lottsburg, VA...................804-529-6101
Cozy Harbor Seafood Inc
Portland, ME....................800-225-2586
Cuizina Food Company
Woodinville, WA.................425-486-7000
Eastern Fish Company
Teaneck, NJ.....................800-526-9066
Fish King
Glendale, CA....................818-244-2161
Glacier Fish Company
Seattle, WA.....................206-298-1200
Golden Gulf Coast Packing Co
Biloxi, MS......................228-374-6121
Great Northern Products Inc
Cranston, RI....................401-490-4590
Gulf City Marine Supply
Bayou La Batre, AL..............251-824-2516
Hallmark Fisheries
Charleston, OR..................541-888-3253
Handy International Inc
Salisbury, MD...................800-426-3977
Hillard Bloom Packing Co Inc
Port Norris, NJ.................856-785-0120
Hillmans Shrimp & Oyster
Port Lavaca, TX.................800-582-4416
Independent Packers Corporation
Seattle, WA.....................206-285-6000
Indian Ridge Shrimp Co
Chauvin, LA.....................800-594-0920
Intervest Trading Company Inc.
Halifax, NS.....................902-425-2018
Island Marine Products
Clarks Harbour, NS..............902-745-2222
J. Matassini & Sons Fish Company
Tampa, FL.......................813-229-0829
Janes Family Foods
Mississauga, ON.................800-565-2637
Jessie's Ilwaco Fish Company
San Francisco, CA...............360-642-3773
Key Largo Fisheries
Key Largo, FL...................800-432-4358
Keyser Brothers
Lottsburg, VA...................804-529-6837
Lund's Fisheries
Cape May, NJ....................609-884-7600
Luxury Crab
St John's, NL...................709-739-6668
Maxim's Import Corporation
Miami, FL.......................800-331-6652
Menemsha Fish Market
Chilmark, MA....................508-645-2282
Mid-Atlantic Foods Inc
Easton, MD......................800-922-4688
Minterbrook Oyster Co
Gig Harbor, WA..................253-857-5251
National Fish & Oyster
Olympia, WA.....................360-491-5550
Nelson Crab Inc
Tokeland, WA....................800-262-0069
Neptune Fisheries
Newport News, VA................800-545-7474
O'Hara Corp
Rockland, ME....................207-594-4444
Okuhara Foods Inc
Honolulu, HI....................808-848-0581
Pacific American Fish Co Inc
Vernon, CA......................800-625-2525
Pacific Salmon Company
Edmonds, WA.....................425-774-1315
Paul Piazza & Son Inc
New Orleans, LA.................800-969-6011
Penguin Frozen Foods Inc
Northbrook, IL..................800-323-1485
Portland Shellfish Company
Portland, ME....................207-799-9290
Quality Seafood
Apalachicola, FL................850-653-9696
Royal Seafood Inc
Brooklyn, NY....................718-769-1517
Ruggiero Seafood
Newark, NJ......................866-225-2627
Sea Pearl Seafood
Bayou La Batre, AL..............800-872-8804
Sea Snack Foods Inc
Los Angeles, CA.................213-622-2204
Seafood Producers Co-Op
Bellingham, WA..................360-733-0120
Seymour & Sons Seafoods Inc
Diberville, MS..................228-392-4020
Silver Lining Seafood
Seattle, WA.....................800-426-5490
Spruce Lane Investments
Stratford, PE...................902-892-2600
St. Ours & Company
East Weymouth, MA...............781-331-8520
Stone Crabs Inc
Miami Beach, FL.................800-260-2722
Taku Smokehouse
Juneau, AK......................800-582-5122
Tampa Maid Foods Inc
Lakeland, FL....................800-237-7637
Taylor Shellfish Farms
Shelton, WA.....................360-426-6178
Tichon Sea Food Corp
New Bedford, MA.................508-999-5607
Trident Seafoods Corp
Wrangell, AK....................907-874-3346
Triton Seafood Co
Medley, FL......................305-888-0051
Viking Seafoods Inc
Malden, MA......................800-225-3020
Vince's Seafoods
Gretna, LA......................504-368-1544
Wanchese Fish Co Inc
Suffolk, VA.....................757-673-4500
Young's Lobster Pound
Belfast, ME.....................207-338-1160

Geoduck Clams

Peter Pan Seafoods Inc.
Bellevue, WA....................206-728-6000

Langostinos

Kitchens Seafood
Plant City, FL..................800-327-0132

Live

A.C. Inc.
Beals, ME.......................207-497-2261

Lobster

Acme Steak & Seafood
Youngstown, OH..................800-686-2263
Adams Fisheries Ltd
Shag Harbour, NS................902-723-2435
Arista Industries Inc
Wilton, CT......................800-255-6457
Barry Group
Corner Brook, NL................709-785-7387
Bay Haven Lobster Pound
York, ME........................207-363-5265
Bay Shore Chowders & Bisques
Fall River, MA..................888-675-6892
BBS Lobster Co
Machiasport, ME.................207-255-8888
Beal's Lobster Pier
SW Harbor, ME...................800-244-7178
Bickford Daniel Lobster Company
Vinalhaven, ME..................207-863-4688
Blount Fine Foods
Fall River, MA..................774-888-1300
Bon Secour Fisheries Inc
Bon Secour, AL..................251-949-7411
Boothbay Lobster Wharf
Boothbay Harbor, ME.............207-633-4900
Boston Direct Lobsters
Jefferson, LA...................504-834-6404
C.B.S. Lobster Company
Portland, ME....................207-775-2917
Captain Little Seafood
Queens County, NS...............902-947-2087
Castle Hill Lobster
Ipswich, MA.....................978-356-3947
Ceilidh Fisherman's Cooperative
Port Hood, NS...................902-787-2666
Certi Fresh Foods Inc
Wilmington, CA..................310-221-6262
Chases Lobster Pound
Port Howe, NS...................902-243-2408
Clearwater Fine Foods
Bedford, NS.....................902-443-0550
Coastside Lobster Company
Stonington, ME..................207-367-2297
Corea Lobster Cooperative
Corea, ME.......................207-963-7936
Cranberry Isles Fisherman's
Islesford, ME...................207-244-5438
D Waybret & Sons Fisher ies
Shelburne, NS...................902-745-3477
DB Kenney Fisheries
Westport, NS....................902-839-2023
Dorset Fisheries
St Josephs, NL..................709-739-7147
Dunham's Lobster Pot
Avon, ME........................207-639-2815
Fisherman's Market International
Halifax, NS.....................902-445-3474
Fulton Fish Market
New York, NY....................718-842-8908
FW Thurston
Bernard, ME.....................207-244-3320
Gerard & Dominique Seafoods
Harbor, OR......................800-858-0449
Giovanni's Appetizing Food Co
Richmond, MI....................586-727-9355
Goldcoast Salads
Naples, FL......................239-513-0430
Gouldsboro Enterprises
Gouldsboro, ME..................207-963-2203
Graffam Brothers
Rockport, ME....................800-535-5358
Great Northern Products Inc
Cranston, RI....................401-490-4590

Greg's Lobster Company
Harwich Port, MA. 508-432-8080
H&H Fisheries Limited
Eastern Passage, NS 866-773-4400
Hancock Gourmet Lobster Co
Topsham, ME 207-725-1855
Harbor Seafood
New Hyde Park, NY. 800-645-2211
Howard Turner & Son
Marie Joseph, NS 902-347-2616
I. Deveau Fisheries LTD
Barrington Passage, NS 902-745-2877
Innovative Fishery Products
Belliveau Cove, NS 902-837-5163
International Enterprises
Herring Neck, NL. 709-628-7406
Island Lobster
Matinicus, ME 207-366-3937
Island Marine Products
Clarks Harbour, NS. 902-745-2222
J. Matassini & Sons Fish Company
Tampa, FL. 813-229-0829
Kitchens Seafood
Plant City, FL 800-327-0132
Kona Cold Lobsters
Kailua Kona, HI 808-329-4332
L&C Fisheries
Kensington, PE. 902-886-2770
Little River Lobster Company
East Boothbay, ME. 207-633-2648
Lobster Gram
Chicago, IL. 800-548-3562
Look Lobster Co
Jonesport, ME. 207-497-2353
Lusty Lobster
Portland, ME. 207-773-2829
Luxury Crab
St John's, NL. 709-739-6668
Maine Lobster Outlet
York, ME. 207-363-4449
McGraw Seafood
Tracadie Sheila, NB 506-395-3374
Menemsha Fish Market
Chilmark, MA. 508-645-2282
Mill Cove Lobster Pound
Trevett, ME. 207-633-3340
Nan Sea Enterprises of Wisconsin
Waukesha, WI. 262-542-8841
New Harbor Fisherman's Cooperative
New Harbor, ME. 866-883-2922
Newell Lobsters
Yarmouth, NS 902-742-6272
North Atlantic Seafood
Portland, ME. 800-774-6025
North Lake Fish Cooperative
Elmira, PE. 902-357-2572
Northern Wind Inc
New Bedford, MA 888-525-2525
Northwest Wild Products
Astoria, OR 503-791-1907
Notre Dame Seafoods Inc.
Comfort Cove, NL 709-244-5511
P.M. Innis Lobster Company
Biddeford Pool, ME 207-284-5000
Paul Piazza & Son Inc
New Orleans, LA 800-969-6011
Paul Stevens Lobster
Hingham, MA. 781-740-8001
Penguin Frozen Foods Inc
Northbrook, IL 800-323-1485
Pine Point Seafood
Scarborough, ME 207-883-4701
Point Lobster Co
Point Pleasant Beach, NJ 732-892-1729
Port Lobster Co Inc
Kennebunkport, ME 800-486-7029
Produits Belle Baie
Caraquet, NB 506-727-4414
Red Chamber Co
Vernon, CA 323-234-9000
Resource Trading Company
Portland, ME. 207-772-2299
Rockport Lobster Co
Gloucester, MA. 978-281-0225
Sealand Lobster Corporation
Tenants Harbor, ME 207-372-6247
Seymour & Sons Seafoods Inc
Diberville, MS 228-392-4020
St. Ours & Company
East Weymouth, MA. 781-331-8520
Stavis Seafoods
Boston, MA. 800-390-5103
Stone Crabs Inc
Miami Beach, FL 800-260-2722
Stonington Lobster Co-Op
Stonington, ME. 207-367-2286
Straub's
Clayton, MO 888-725-2121
Sunshine Food Sales
Miami, FL. 305-696-2885
Taylor Lobster Co
Kittery, ME 207-439-1350
Thomas Lobster Co
Islesford, ME 207-244-5876
Three Rivers Fish Company
Simmesport, LA 318-941-2467
Trenton Bridge Lobster Pound
Trenton, ME 207-667-2977
Vital Choice
Bellingham, WA 800-608-4825
West Brothers Lobster
Steuben, ME 207-546-3622
Young's Lobster Pound
Belfast, ME. 207-338-1160

Fresh

Capt Joe & Sons Inc
Gloucester, MA. 978-283-1454
Clearwater Fine Foods
Bedford, NS 902-443-0550
J. Matassini & Sons Fish Company
Tampa, FL. 813-229-0829
Menemsha Fish Market
Chilmark, MA. 508-645-2282
Paul Piazza & Son Inc
New Orleans, LA 800-969-6011
Portland Shellfish Company
Portland, ME. 207-799-9290
Poseidon Enterprises
Charlotte, NC 800-863-7886
St. Ours & Company
East Weymouth, MA. 781-331-8520
Stone Crabs Inc
Miami Beach, FL 800-260-2722
Sunshine Food Sales
Miami, FL. 305-696-2885

Frozen

Acme Steak & Seafood
Youngstown, OH. 800-686-2263
Arista Industries Inc
Wilton, CT 800-255-6457
Certi Fresh Foods Inc
Wilmington, CA 310-221-6262
Great Northern Products Inc
Cranston, RI 401-490-4590
Island Marine Products
Clarks Harbour, NS. 902-745-2222
J. Matassini & Sons Fish Company
Tampa, FL. 813-229-0829
Kitchens Seafood
Plant City, FL 800-327-0132
Luxury Crab
St John's, NL. 709-739-6668
Menemsha Fish Market
Chilmark, MA. 508-645-2282
North Bay Fisherman's Cooperative
Ballantyne's Cove, NS 902-863-4988
Notre Dame Seafoods Inc.
Comfort Cove, NL 709-244-5511
Paul Piazza & Son Inc
New Orleans, LA 800-969-6011
Penguin Frozen Foods Inc
Northbrook, IL 800-323-1485
Portland Shellfish Company
Portland, ME. 207-799-9290
Seymour & Sons Seafoods Inc
Diberville, MS 228-392-4020
Stone Crabs Inc
Miami Beach, FL 800-260-2722
Sunshine Food Sales
Miami, FL. 305-696-2885

Live

Bay Shore Chowders & Bisques
Fall River, MA 888-675-6892
Chases Lobster Pound
Port Howe, NS 902-243-2408
DB Kenney Fisheries
Westport, NS. 902-839-2023
H&H Fisheries Limited
Eastern Passage, NS 866-773-4400
Harbour Lobster Ltd
Shag Harbour, NS. 902-723-2500
Island Marine Products
Clarks Harbour, NS. 902-745-2222
James L. Mood Fisheries
Nova Scotia, NS 902-723-2360
Johns Cove Fisheries
Yarmouth, NS 902-742-8691
Lumar Lobster
Lawrence, NY. 516-371-0083
Menemsha Fish Market
Chilmark, MA. 508-645-2282

Meat

Acme Steak & Seafood
Youngstown, OH. 800-686-2263
Island Marine Products
Clarks Harbour, NS. 902-745-2222
Luxury Crab
St John's, NL. 709-739-6668

Tails

Anchor Frozen Foods
Westbury, NY 800-566-3474
Arista Industries Inc
Wilton, CT 800-255-6457
King & Prince Seafood Corp
Brunswick, GA 800-841-0205
Neptune Fisheries
Newport News, VA. 800-545-7474
New Ocean
Doraville, GA 770-458-5235
Stone Crabs Inc
Miami Beach, FL 800-260-2722
Tampa Bay Fisheries Inc
Dover, FL 800-732-3663

Mussels

Atlantic Aqua Farms
Orwell Cove, PE. 902-651-2563
Atlantic Mussel Growers Corporation
Murray Harbour, PE 800-838-3106
Bay Shore Chowders & Bisques
Fall River, MA 888-675-6892
Blount Fine Foods
Fall River, MA 774-888-1300
Harbor Seafood
New Hyde Park, NY. 800-645-2211
Hillmans Shrimp & Oyster
Port Lavaca, TX 800-582-4416
L&C Fisheries
Kensington, PE. 902-886-2770
Minterbrook Oyster Co
Gig Harbor, WA 253-857-5251
North Atlantic Seafood
Portland, ME. 800-774-6025
Northwest Wild Products
Astoria, OR. 503-791-1907
Olympia Oyster Co
Shelton, WA 877-427-3193
Patagonia Provisions
Sausalito, CA 888-221-8208
PEI Mussel King
Morrell, PE 800-673-2767
Stavis Seafoods
Boston, MA. 800-390-5103
Sweet Water Seafood
Carlstadt, NJ 201-939-6622
Tampa Bay Fisheries Inc
Dover, FL 800-732-3663
Taylor Shellfish Farms
Shelton, WA 360-426-6178
Vital Choice
Bellingham, WA 800-608-4825

Octopus

Anchor Frozen Foods
Westbury, NY 800-566-3474
Arista Industries Inc
Wilton, CT 800-255-6457
Fish King
Glendale, CA 818-244-2161
Fulton Fish Market
New York, NY 718-842-8908

Oysters

Ameripure Processing Co
Franklin, LA 800-328-6729
Aquatec Seafoods Ltd.
Comox, BC 250-339-6412

Atlantic Aqua Farms
Orwell Cove, PE....902-651-2563
Atlantic Capes Fisheries
Cape May, NJ....609-884-3000
B G Smith & Sons Oyster Co
Sharps, VA....877-483-8279
Barry Group
Corner Brook, NL....709-785-7387
Bay Hundred Seafood Inc
St Michaels, MD....410-745-9329
Blalock Seafood & Specialty
Orange Beach, AL....251-974-5811
Blau Oyster Co Inc
Bow, WA....360-766-6171
Bon Secour Fisheries Inc
Bon Secour, AL....251-949-7411
Callis Seafood
Lancaster, VA....804-462-7634
Canoe Lagoon Oyster Company
Coffman Cove, AK....907-329-2253
Coast Seafoods Company
Bellevue, WA....800-423-2303
Cowart Seafood Corp
Lottsburg, VA....804-529-6101
Crown Prince Inc
City Of Industry, CA....626-912-3700
Dave's Gourmet Albacore
Watsonville, CA....206-999-5517
Farm 2 Market
San Francisco, CA....800-447-2967
Ferme Ostreicole Dugas
Caraquet, NB....506-727-3226
Fish Breeders of Idaho
Hagerman, ID....208-837-6114
Great Northern Products Inc
Cranston, RI....401-490-4590
Gulf City Marine Supply
Bayou La Batre, AL....251-824-2516
H.Gass Seafood
Hollywood, MD....301-373-6882
Harpers Seafood Market
Thomasville, GA....229-226-7525
Harris Crab House
Grasonville, MD....410-827-9500
Higgins Seafood
Lafitte, LA....504-689-3577
Hillard Bloom Packing Co Inc
Port Norris, NJ....856-785-0120
Hillmans Shrimp & Oyster
Port Lavaca, TX....800-582-4416
Huck's Seafood
Easton, MD....410-770-9211
J. Matassini & Sons Fish Company
Tampa, FL....813-229-0829
Louisiana Oyster Processors
Baton Rouge, LA....225-291-6923
McGraw Seafood
Tracadie Sheila, NB....506-395-3374
Mill Cove Lobster Pound
Trevett, ME....207-633-3340
Neptune Foods
Vernon, CA....323-232-8300
New Orleans Fish House II LLC
New Orleans, LA....800-839-3474
Nisbet Oyster Company
Bay Center, WA....888-875-6629
North Atlantic Seafood
Portland, ME....800-774-6025
Northwest Wild Products
Astoria, OR....503-791-1907
Pamlico Packing Company
Grantsboro, NC....800-682-1113
PEI Mussel King
Morrell, PE....800-673-2767
Rippons Seafood
Ocean City, MD....410-723-0056
Roadrunner Seafood Inc
Colquitt, GA....229-758-6098
Roy Dick Company
Griffin, GA....770-227-3916
Sea Pearl Seafood
Bayou La Batre, AL....800-872-8804
Southern Shell Fish Company
Harvey, LA....504-341-5631
Tampa Bay Fisheries Inc
Dover, FL....800-732-3663
Tampa Maid Foods Inc
Lakeland, FL....800-237-7637
Terry Brothers, Inc
Willis Wharf, VA....757-442-6251
Vital Choice
Bellingham, WA....800-608-4825
W.T. Ruark & Company
Fishing Creek, MD....410-397-3133
Wiegardt Brothers
Nahcotta, WA....360-665-4111
Wilsons Oysters
Houma, LA....985-857-8855

Canned

Chicken Of The Sea
El Segundo, CA....844-267-8862
New Orleans Food Co-op
New Orleans, LA....800-628-4900
Olympia Oyster Co
Shelton, WA....877-427-3193
Southern Shell Fish Company
Harvey, LA....504-341-5631

Fresh

B G Smith & Sons Oyster Co
Sharps, VA....877-483-8279
Blau Oyster Co Inc
Bow, WA....360-766-6171
Boquet's Oyster House
Chauvin, LA....504-594-5574
Coast Seafoods Company
Bellevue, WA....800-423-2303
Cowart Seafood Corp
Lottsburg, VA....804-529-6101
Great Northern Products Inc
Cranston, RI....401-490-4590
Hillmans Shrimp & Oyster
Port Lavaca, TX....800-582-4416
J. Matassini & Sons Fish Company
Tampa, FL....813-229-0829
Mac's Oysters
Fanny Bay, BC....250-335-2233
Minterbrook Oyster Co
Gig Harbor, WA....253-857-5251
National Fish & Oyster
Olympia, WA....360-491-5550
Olympia Oyster Co
Shelton, WA....877-427-3193
Rippons Seafood
Ocean City, MD....410-723-0056
Taylor Shellfish Farms
Shelton, WA....360-426-6178
Terry Brothers, Inc
Willis Wharf, VA....757-442-6251
Wiegardt Brothers
Nahcotta, WA....360-665-4111

Fried

J. Matassini & Sons Fish Company
Tampa, FL....813-229-0829

Frozen

B G Smith & Sons Oyster Co
Sharps, VA....877-483-8279
Big Al's Seafood
Bozman, MD....410-745-2637
Bon Secour Fisheries Inc
Bon Secour, AL....251-949-7411
Boquet's Oyster House
Chauvin, LA....504-594-5574
Callis Seafood
Lancaster, VA....804-462-7634
Cowart Seafood Corp
Lottsburg, VA....804-529-6101
Dave's Gourmet Albacore
Watsonville, CA....206-999-5517
Great Northern Products Inc
Cranston, RI....401-490-4590
Hillard Bloom Packing Co Inc
Port Norris, NJ....856-785-0120
Hillmans Shrimp & Oyster
Port Lavaca, TX....800-582-4416
Minterbrook Oyster Co
Gig Harbor, WA....253-857-5251
National Fish & Oyster
Olympia, WA....360-491-5550
Olympia Oyster Co
Shelton, WA....877-427-3193
Pamlico Packing Company
Grantsboro, NC....800-682-1113
Sea Pearl Seafood
Bayou La Batre, AL....800-872-8804
Tampa Maid Foods Inc
Lakeland, FL....800-237-7637

Prawns

Caito Fisheries Inc
Fort Bragg, CA....707-964-6368
Pots de Creme
Lexington, KY....859-299-2254
Vital Choice
Bellingham, WA....800-608-4825

Scallops

Arista Industries Inc
Wilton, CT....800-255-6457
Atlantic Capes Fisheries
Cape May, NJ....609-884-3000
Blue Harvest Foods
New Bedford, MA....508-993-5700
Bold Coast Smokehouse
Lubec, ME....888-733-0807
Bon Secour Fisheries Inc
Bon Secour, AL....251-949-7411
Captain Little Seafood
Queens County, NS....902-947-2087
Casey Fisheries
Digby, NS....902-245-5801
Centennial Food Corporation
Calgary, AB....403-214-0044
Certi Fresh Foods Inc
Wilmington, CA....310-221-6262
Clearwater Fine Foods
Bedford, NS....902-443-0550
DB Kenney Fisheries
Westport, NS....902-839-2023
Ducktrap River Of Maine
Belfast, ME....800-434-8727
Farm 2 Market
San Francisco, CA....800-447-2967
Fish King
Glendale, CA....818-244-2161
Fulton Fish Market
New York, NY....718-842-8908
Georgia Seafood Wholesale
Chamblee, GA....770-936-0483
Great Northern Products Inc
Cranston, RI....401-490-4590
Hillmans Shrimp & Oyster
Port Lavaca, TX....800-582-4416
Homarus Inc
Long Island City, NY....917-832-0333
Innovative Fishery Products
Belliveau Cove, NS....902-837-5163
Island Scallops
Qualicum Beach, BC....250-757-9811
J. Matassini & Sons Fish Company
Tampa, FL....813-229-0829
LA Monica Fine Foods
Millville, NJ
Lowland Seafood
Lowland, NC....252-745-3751
Menemsha Fish Market
Chilmark, MA....508-645-2282
Mill Cove Lobster Pound
Trevett, ME....207-633-3340
Mills Seafood Ltd.
Bouctouche, NB....506-743-2444
Neptune Fisheries
Newport News, VA....800-545-7474
Neptune Foods
Vernon, CA....323-232-8300
New Ocean
Doraville, GA....770-458-5235
North Bay Fisherman's Cooperative
Ballantyne's Cove, NS....902-863-4988
North Lake Fish Cooperative
Elmira, PE....902-357-2572
Northern Wind Inc
New Bedford, MA....888-525-2525
Northwest Wild Products
Astoria, OR....503-791-1907
O'Hara Corp
Rockland, ME....207-594-4444
Pamlico Packing Company
Grantsboro, NC....800-682-1113
Portier Fine Foods
Mamaroneck, NY....800-272-9463
Resource Trading Company
Portland, ME....207-772-2299
Tampa Bay Fisheries Inc
Dover, FL....800-732-3663
Tampa Maid Foods Inc
Lakeland, FL....800-237-7637
Taylor Shellfish Farms
Shelton, WA....360-426-6178

Tenth & M Seafoods
Anchorage, AK....................800-770-2722
Tichon Sea Food Corp
New Bedford, MA....................508-999-5607
Viking Seafoods Inc
Malden, MA....................800-225-3020
Vital Choice
Bellingham, WA....................800-608-4825
Wanchese Fish Co Inc
Suffolk, VA....................757-673-4500
Young's Lobster Pound
Belfast, ME....................207-338-1160

Sea Cucumber

Captain Little Seafood
Queens County, NS....................902-947-2087

Shellfish

Acme Steak & Seafood
Youngstown, OH....................800-686-2263
Anglo American Trading
Harvey, LA....................504-341-5631
Aquatec Seafoods Ltd.
Comox, BC....................250-339-6412
Arista Industries Inc
Wilton, CT....................800-255-6457
Arrowac Fisheries
Seattle, WA....................206-282-5655
B G Smith & Sons Oyster Co
Sharps, VA....................877-483-8279
Badger Island Shell-Fish & Lobster
Kittery, ME....................207-703-0431
Bandon Bay Fisheries
Bandon, OR....................541-347-4454
Bay Hundred Seafood Inc
St Michaels, MD....................410-745-9329
Bay Oceans Sea Foods
Garibaldi, OR....................503-322-3316
Bayou Food Distributors
Kenner, LA....................800-516-8283
Bayou Land Seafood
Breaux Bridge, LA....................337-667-6118
Beaver Street Fisheries
Jacksonville, FL....................800-874-6426
Blount Fine Foods
Fall River, MA....................774-888-1300
BlueWater Seafoods
Gloucester, MA....................888-560-2539
Boyton Shellfish
Ellsworth, ME....................207-667-8580
Bradye P. Todd & Son
Cambridge, MD....................410-228-8633
Breakwater Fisheries
St John's, NL....................709-754-1999
C F Gollott & Son Seafood
Diberville, MS....................228-392-2747
Caleb Haley & Co LLC
Bronx, NY....................718-617-7474
California Shellfish Company
San Francisco, CA....................415-923-7400
Callis Seafood
Lancaster, VA....................804-462-7634
Carrington Foods Co Inc
Saraland, AL....................251-675-9700
Cathay Foods Corporation
Boston, MA....................617-427-1507
Centennial Food Corporation
Calgary, AB....................403-214-0044
Certi Fresh Foods Inc
Wilmington, CA....................310-221-6262
Charles H. Parks & Company
Fishing Creek, MD....................410-397-3400
Chuck's Seafoods
Charleston, OR....................541-888-5525
Clearwater Fine Foods
Bedford, NS....................902-443-0550
Coast Seafoods Company
Bellevue, WA....................800-423-2303
Cooke Aguaculture
Blacks Harbour, NB....................506-456-6600
Cowart Seafood Corp
Lottsburg, VA....................804-529-6101
Cozy Harbor Seafood Inc
Portland, ME....................800-225-2586
Crown Prince Inc
City Of Industry, CA....................626-912-3700
Cuizina Food Company
Woodinville, WA....................425-486-7000
Dave's Gourmet Albacore
Watsonville, CA....................206-999-5517
DB Kenney Fisheries
Westport, NS....................902-839-2023
Denzer's Food Products
Baltimore, MD....................410-889-1500
Dorchester Crab Co
Wingate, MD....................410-397-8103
Ducktrap River Of Maine
Belfast, ME....................800-434-8727
Eastern Fish Company
Teaneck, NJ....................800-526-9066
Fish King
Glendale, CA....................818-244-2161
Fishhawk Fisheries
Astoria, OR....................503-325-5252
French Market Foods
Lake Charles, LA....................337-477-9296
Frozen Specialties Inc
Perrysburg, OH....................419-867-2005
Golden Gulf Coast Packing Co
Biloxi, MS....................228-374-6121
Gorton's Inc.
Gloucester, MA....................800-222-6846
Great Northern Products Inc
Cranston, RI....................401-490-4590
Gulf Pride Enterprises
Biloxi, MS....................888-689-0560
H.B. Dawe
Cupids, NL....................709-528-4347
H.Gass Seafood
Hollywood, MD....................301-373-6882
Handy International Inc
Salisbury, MD....................800-426-3977
Henry H. Misner Ltd.
Simcoe, ON....................519-426-5546
Hillard Bloom Packing Co Inc
Port Norris, NJ....................856-785-0120
Hillmans Shrimp & Oyster
Port Lavaca, TX....................800-582-4416
Huck's Seafood
Easton, MD....................410-770-9211
Independent Packers Corporation
Seattle, WA....................206-285-6000
Indian Ridge Shrimp Co
Chauvin, LA....................800-594-0920
Island Marine Products
Clarks Harbour, NS....................902-745-2222
J M Clayton Co
Cambridge, MD....................800-652-6931
J. Matassini & Sons Fish Company
Tampa, FL....................813-229-0829
Jessie's Ilwaco Fish Company
San Francisco, CA....................360-642-3773
Key Largo Fisheries
Key Largo, FL....................800-432-4358
Keyser Brothers
Lottsburg, VA....................804-529-6837
King & Prince Seafood Corp
Brunswick, GA....................800-841-0205
Kitchens Seafood
Plant City, FL....................800-327-0132
LA Monica Fine Foods
Millville, NJ
Little River Seafood Inc
Reedville, VA....................804-453-3670
Long Food Industries
Fripp Island, SC....................843-838-3205
Lowland Seafood
Lowland, NC....................252-745-3751
Lund's Fisheries
Cape May, NJ....................609-884-7600
Luxury Crab
St John's, NL....................709-739-6668
Maine Mahogony Shellfish
Addison, ME....................207-483-2865
Martin Brothers Seafood Co
Westwego, LA....................504-341-2251
Maxim's Import Corporation
Miami, FL....................800-331-6652
Menemsha Fish Market
Chilmark, MA....................508-645-2282
Mercer Processing
Modesto, CA....................209-529-0150
Mid-Atlantic Foods Inc
Easton, MD....................800-922-4688
Nancy's Shellfish
Falmouth, ME....................207-774-3411
Neptune Fisheries
Newport News, VA....................800-545-7474
Notre Dame Seafoods Inc.
Comfort Cove, NL....................709-244-5511
Ntc Marketing
Williamsville, NY....................800-333-1637
Ocean Harvest
Dennysville, ME....................207-726-0609
Okuhara Foods Inc
Honolulu, HI....................808-848-0581
Pacific American Fish Co Inc
Vernon, CA....................800-625-2525
Pacific Salmon Company
Edmonds, WA....................425-774-1315
Pamlico Packing Company
Grantsboro, NC....................800-682-1113
Paul Piazza & Son Inc
New Orleans, LA....................800-969-6011
Penguin Frozen Foods Inc
Northbrook, IL....................800-323-1485
Produits Belle Baie
Caraquet, NB....................506-727-4414
Quality Seafood
Apalachicola, FL....................850-653-9696
Raffield Fisheries Inc
Port St Joe, FL....................850-229-8494
Rippons Seafood
Ocean City, MD....................410-723-0056
Roland Seafood Co
Atlantic Beach, FL....................904-246-9443
Royal Seafood Inc
Brooklyn, NY....................718-769-1517
Ruggiero Seafood
Newark, NJ....................866-225-2627
Sea Pearl Seafood
Bayou La Batre, AL....................800-872-8804
Sea Safari
Belhaven, NC....................800-688-6174
Sea Snack Foods Inc
Los Angeles, CA....................213-622-2204
SeaPerfect Atlantic Farms
Charleston, SC....................800-728-0099
Seymour & Sons Seafoods Inc
Diberville, MS....................228-392-4020
Silver Lining Seafood
Seattle, WA....................800-426-5490
Southern Shell Fish Company
Harvey, LA....................504-341-5631
Sportsmen's Cannery & Smokehouse
Winchester Bay, OR....................800-457-8048
St. Ours & Company
East Weymouth, MA....................781-331-8520
Stone Crabs Inc
Miami Beach, FL....................800-260-2722
Sunshine Food Sales
Miami, FL....................305-696-2885
Sunshine Seafood
Stonington, ME....................207-367-2955
Taku Smokehouse
Juneau, AK....................800-582-5122
Tampa Maid Foods Inc
Lakeland, FL....................800-237-7637
Terry Brothers, Inc
Willis Wharf, VA....................757-442-6251
Thompson Seafood
Darien, GA....................912-437-4649
Trident Seafoods Corp
Wrangell, AK....................907-874-3346
Triton Seafood Co
Medley, FL....................305-888-0051
Valdez Food Inc
Philadelphia, PA....................215-634-6106
Viking Seafoods Inc
Malden, MA....................800-225-3020
Vince's Seafoods
Gretna, LA....................504-368-1544
W.T. Ruark & Company
Fishing Creek, MD....................410-397-3133
Wanchese Fish Co Inc
Suffolk, VA....................757-673-4500
Wiegardt Brothers
Nahcotta, WA....................360-665-4111

Shrimp

Anchor Frozen Foods
Westbury, NY....................800-566-3474
Arista Industries Inc
Wilton, CT....................800-255-6457
Bandon Bay Fisheries
Bandon, OR....................541-347-4454
Barry Group
Corner Brook, NL....................709-785-7387
Bay Oceans Sea Foods
Garibaldi, OR....................503-322-3316
Bayou Food Distributors
Kenner, LA....................800-516-8283
Bayou Land Seafood
Breaux Bridge, LA....................337-667-6118

Beaver Street Fisheries
Jacksonville, FL 800-874-6426
Big Easy Foods
Lake Charles, LA 855-477-9296
Biloxi Freezing Processing Inc.
Biloxi, MS. 228-436-0017
Blalock Seafood & Specialty
Orange Beach, AL 251-974-5811
BlueWater Seafoods
Gloucester, MA. 888-560-2539
Bon Secour Fisheries Inc
Bon Secour, AL. 251-949-7411
Breakwater Fisheries
St John's, NL. 709-754-1999
C F Gollott & Son Seafood
Diberville, MS 228-392-2747
Callis Seafood
Lancaster, VA 804-462-7634
Captain Little Seafood
Queens County, NS. 902-947-2087
Carrington Foods Co Inc
Saraland, AL. 251-675-9700
Catfish Wholesale
Abbeville, LA 800-334-7292
Certi Fresh Foods Inc
Wilmington, CA 310-221-6262
Channel Fish Processing
Gloucester, MA. 800-457-0054
Chuck's Seafoods
Charleston, OR 541-888-5525
Clearwater Fine Foods
Bedford, NS 902-443-0550
Cozy Harbor Seafood Inc
Portland, ME. 800-225-2586
Crevettes Du Nord
Gaspe, QC. 418-368-1414
Crown Prince Inc
City Of Industry, CA. 626-912-3700
Del's Seaway Shrimp & Oyster Company
Biloxi, MS. 228-432-2604
Diazteca Inc
Rio Rico, AZ. 520-761-4621
Ducktrap River Of Maine
Belfast, ME. 800-434-8727
Eastern Fish Company
Teaneck, NJ. 800-526-9066
Eldorado Seafood Inc
Burlington, MA. 800-416-5656
Farm 2 Market
San Francisco, CA 800-447-2967
Fish Breeders of Idaho
Hagerman, ID 208-837-6114
Fish King
Glendale, CA 818-244-2161
Fishhawk Fisheries
Astoria, OR. 503-325-5252
French Market Foods
Lake Charles, LA 337-477-9296
Georgia Seafood Wholesale
Chamblee, GA. 770-936-0483
Gerard & Dominique Seafoods
Harbor, OR 800-858-0449
Gesco ENR
Gaspe, QC. 418-368-1414
Golden Gulf Coast Packing Co
Biloxi, MS. 228-374-6121
Great Northern Products Inc
Cranston, RI 401-490-4590
Gulf City Marine Supply
Bayou La Batre, AL 251-824-2516
Gulf Crown Seafood Co
Delcambre, LA 337-685-4722
Gulf Marine
Westwego, LA. 504-436-2682
Gulf Pride Enterprises
Biloxi, MS. 888-689-0560
Hallmark Fisheries
Charleston, OR 541-888-3253
Harbor Seafood
New Hyde Park, NY 800-645-2211
Hi Seas
Dulac, LA 985-563-7155
Homarus Inc
Long Island City, NY 917-832-0333
Imaex Trading Company
Suwanee, GA 678-541-0234
Indian Ridge Shrimp Co
Chauvin, LA 800-594-0920
J. Matassini & Sons Fish Company
Tampa, FL. 813-229-0829
JBS Packing Inc
Port Arthur, TX. 409-982-3216
Jessie's Ilwaco Fish Company
San Francisco, CA 360-642-3773
Joe Patti's Seafood Co
Pensacola, FL 800-500-9929
Jubilee Foods
Bayou La Batre, AL 251-824-2110
King & Prince Seafood Corp
Brunswick, GA. 800-841-0205
Kitchens Seafood
Plant City, FL 800-327-0132
LA Monica Fine Foods
Millville, NJ
Lady Gale Seafood
Baldwin, LA 337-923-2060
Larry J. Williams Company
Jesup, GA 912-427-7729
Louisiana Packing Company
Westwego, LA. 800-666-1293
Louisiana Seafood Promotion & Marketing Board
Baton Rouge, LA 225-342-0552
Lowland Seafood
Lowland, NC. 252-745-3751
Luxury Crab
St John's, NL. 709-739-6668
Maxim's Import Corporation
Miami, FL. 800-331-6652
Mill Cove Lobster Pound
Trevett, ME. 207-633-3340
Mobile Processing
Mobile, AL. 251-438-6944
Nelson Crab Inc
Tokeland, WA. 800-262-0069
Neptune Fisheries
Newport News, VA. 800-545-7474
Neptune Foods
Vernon, CA 323-232-8300
New Ocean
Doraville, GA. 770-458-5235
New Orleans Fish House II LLC
New Orleans, LA 800-839-3474
Newfound Resources
St Josephs, NL 709-579-7676
Northwest Wild Products
Astoria, OR. 503-791-1907
Ntc Marketing
Williamsville, NY. 800-333-1637
Ocean Pride Seafood
Delcambre, LA 337-685-2336
Ocean Springs Seafood
Ocean Springs, MS 228-875-0104
Ore-Cal Corp
Los Angeles, CA. 800-827-7474
Pacific American Fish Co Inc
Vernon, CA 800-625-2525
Pamlico Packing Company
Grantsboro, NC. 800-682-1113
Paul Piazza & Son Inc
New Orleans, LA 800-969-6011
Penguin Frozen Foods Inc
Northbrook, IL 800-323-1485
Pioneer Live Shrimp
Oak Brook, IL. 630-789-1133
Price Seafood
Havre De Grace, MD 410-939-2782
Produits Belle Baie
Caraquet, NB 506-727-4414
Quality Seafood
Apalachicola, FL. 850-653-9696
Red Chamber Co
Vernon, CA. 323-234-9000
Resource Trading Company
Portland, ME. 207-772-2299
Rocky Point Shrimp Association
Phoenix, AZ 602-254-8041
Roland Seafood Co
Atlantic Beach, FL 904-246-9443
Roy Dick Company
Griffin, GA 770-227-3916
Sau-Sea Foods
Tarrytown, NY 914-631-1717
Sea Pearl Seafood
Bayou La Batre, AL 800-872-8804
Sea Snack Foods Inc
Los Angeles, CA. 213-622-2204
Seafood Producers Co-Op
Bellingham, WA 360-733-0120
Seajoy
Miami, FL. 877-537-1717
Singleton Seafood
Tampa, FL. 800-732-3663
Smith & Sons Seafood
Darien, GA 912-437-6471
Southern Shell Fish Company
Harvey, LA 504-341-5631
Stavis Seafoods
Boston, MA. 800-390-5103
Tampa Bay Fisheries Inc
Dover, FL 800-732-3663
Tampa Maid Foods Inc
Lakeland, FL. 800-237-7637
Tenth & M Seafoods
Anchorage, AK. 800-770-2722
Tex-Mex Cold Storage
Brownsville, TX 956-831-9433
Thompson Seafood
Darien, GA 912-437-4649
Tideland Seafood Company
Dulac, LA 985-563-4516
Trident Seafoods Corp
Wrangell, AK 907-874-3346
Valdez Food Inc
Philadelphia, PA 215-634-6106
Viking Seafoods Inc
Malden, MA 800-225-3020
Vincent Piazza Jr & Sons
Harahan, LA 800-259-5016
Vital Choice
Bellingham, WA 800-608-4825
Wayne Estay Shrimp Company
Grand Isle, LA 877-787-2166
Young's Lobster Pound
Belfast, ME. 207-338-1160

Black Tiger

Bay Oceans Sea Foods
Garibaldi, OR 503-322-3316
Biloxi Freezing Processing Inc.
Biloxi, MS. 228-436-0017
BlueWater Seafoods
Gloucester, MA. 888-560-2539
Crevettes Du Nord
Gaspe, QC. 418-368-1414
Del's Seaway Shrimp & Oyster Company
Biloxi, MS. 228-432-2604
Gerard & Dominique Seafoods
Harbor, OR 800-858-0449
Gesco ENR
Gaspe, QC. 418-368-1414
Gulf Pride Enterprises
Biloxi, MS. 888-689-0560
JBS Packing Inc
Port Arthur, TX. 409-982-3216
Jubilee Foods
Bayou La Batre, AL 251-824-2110
Lady Gale Seafood
Baldwin, LA 337-923-2060
Louisiana Packing Company
Westwego, LA. 800-666-1293
Mobile Processing
Mobile, AL 251-438-6944
Newfound Resources
St Josephs, NL 709-579-7676
Ocean Springs Seafood
Ocean Springs, MS 228-875-0104
Price Seafood
Havre De Grace, MD 410-939-2782
Resource Trading Company
Portland, ME. 207-772-2299
Stavis Seafoods
Boston, MA. 800-390-5103
Vincent Piazza Jr & Sons
Harahan, LA 800-259-5016

Breaded

Eldorado Seafood Inc
Burlington, MA. 800-416-5656
Fish King
Glendale, CA 818-244-2161
Golden Gulf Coast Packing Co
Biloxi, MS. 228-374-6121
J. Matassini & Sons Fish Company
Tampa, FL. 813-229-0829
King & Prince Seafood Corp
Brunswick, GA 800-841-0205
LA Monica Fine Foods
Millville, NJ
Neptune Foods
Vernon, CA 323-232-8300
Ocean Springs Seafood
Ocean Springs, MS 228-875-0104
Pacific American Fish Co Inc
Vernon, CA 800-625-2525

Penguin Frozen Foods Inc
Northbrook, IL 800-323-1485
Sea Pearl Seafood
Bayou La Batre, AL 800-872-8804
Seajoy
Miami, FL 877-537-1717
Tampa Bay Fisheries Inc
Dover, FL 800-732-3663
Tampa Maid Foods Inc
Lakeland, FL 800-237-7637

Canned

Bayou Land Seafood
Breaux Bridge, LA 337-667-6118
Channel Fish Processing
Gloucester, MA 800-457-0054
Chicken Of The Sea
El Segundo, CA 844-267-8862
Chuck's Seafoods
Charleston, OR 541-888-5525
Nelson Crab Inc
Tokeland, WA 800-262-0069
New Orleans Food Co-op
New Orleans, LA 800-628-4900
Ntc Marketing
Williamsville, NY 800-333-1637
Ore-Cal Corp
Los Angeles, CA 800-827-7474
Seafood Producers Co-Op
Bellingham, WA 360-733-0120
Southern Shell Fish Company
Harvey, LA 504-341-5631
Trident Seafoods Corp
Wrangell, AK 907-874-3346
Vital Choice
Bellingham, WA 800-608-4825

Cooked

King & Prince Seafood Corp
Brunswick, GA 800-841-0205
Neptune Fisheries
Newport News, VA 800-545-7474
Neptune Foods
Vernon, CA 323-232-8300
Pacific American Fish Co Inc
Vernon, CA 800-625-2525
Tampa Bay Fisheries Inc
Dover, FL 800-732-3663

Fresh

Cozy Harbor Seafood Inc
Portland, ME 800-225-2586
Davis Strait Fisheries
Halifax, NS 902-450-5115
Great Northern Products Inc
Cranston, RI 401-490-4590
J. Matassini & Sons Fish Company
Tampa, FL 813-229-0829
Jessie's Ilwaco Fish Company
San Francisco, CA 360-642-3773
Nelson Crab Inc
Tokeland, WA 800-262-0069
Paul Piazza & Son Inc
New Orleans, LA 800-969-6011
Quality Seafood
Apalachicola, FL 850-653-9696
Trident Seafoods Corp
Wrangell, AK 907-874-3346

Frozen

Alpine Butcher
Lowell, MA 978-256-7771
Arista Industries Inc
Wilton, CT 800-255-6457
Bandon Bay Fisheries
Bandon, OR 541-347-4454
Bayou Land Seafood
Breaux Bridge, LA 337-667-6118
Beaver Street Fisheries
Jacksonville, FL 800-874-6426
Bon Secour Fisheries Inc
Bon Secour, AL 251-949-7411
Breakwater Fisheries
St John's, NL 709-754-1999
C F Gollott & Son Seafood
Diberville, MS 228-392-2747
Callis Seafood
Lancaster, VA 804-462-7634
Carrington Foods Co Inc
Saraland, AL 251-675-9700
Certi Fresh Foods Inc
Wilmington, CA 310-221-6262
Channel Fish Processing
Gloucester, MA 800-457-0054
Clearwater Fine Foods
Bedford, NS 902-443-0550
Cozy Harbor Seafood Inc
Portland, ME 800-225-2586
Eastern Fish Company
Teaneck, NJ 800-526-9066
Fisherman's Reef Shrimp Company
Beaumont, TX 409-842-9520
Golden Gulf Coast Packing Co
Biloxi, MS 228-374-6121
Great Northern Products Inc
Cranston, RI 401-490-4590
Indian Ridge Shrimp Co
Chauvin, LA 800-594-0920
J. Matassini & Sons Fish Company
Tampa, FL 813-229-0829
Jessie's Ilwaco Fish Company
San Francisco, CA 360-642-3773
Kitchens Seafood
Plant City, FL 800-327-0132
Luxury Crab
St John's, NL 709-739-6668
Maxim's Import Corporation
Miami, FL 800-331-6652
Neptune Fisheries
Newport News, VA 800-545-7474
Pacific American Fish Co Inc
Vernon, CA 800-625-2525
Paul Piazza & Son Inc
New Orleans, LA 800-969-6011
Penguin Frozen Foods Inc
Northbrook, IL 800-323-1485
Portland Shellfish Company
Portland, ME 207-799-9290
Quality Seafood
Apalachicola, FL 850-653-9696
Sea Pearl Seafood
Bayou La Batre, AL 800-872-8804
Sea Snack Foods Inc
Los Angeles, CA 213-622-2204
Seafood Producers Co-Op
Bellingham, WA 360-733-0120
Spruce Lane Investments
Stratford, PE 902-892-2600
Suram Trading Corporation
Coral Gables, FL 305-448-7165
Tampa Maid Foods Inc
Lakeland, FL 800-237-7637
Tex-Mex Cold Storage
Brownsville, TX 956-831-9433
Trident Seafoods Corp
Wrangell, AK 907-874-3346
Viking Seafoods Inc
Malden, MA 800-225-3020

Jumbo

Davis Strait Fisheries
Halifax, NS 902-450-5115

Peeled

Bayou Food Distributors
Kenner, LA 800-516-8283
Neptune Fisheries
Newport News, VA 800-545-7474
Seajoy
Miami, FL 877-537-1717
Tampa Bay Fisheries Inc
Dover, FL 800-732-3663
Tampa Maid Foods Inc
Lakeland, FL 800-237-7637

Rock

Caito Fisheries Inc
Fort Bragg, CA 707-964-6368
Davis Strait Fisheries
Halifax, NS 902-450-5115

Smoked

Menemsha Fish Market
Chilmark, MA 508-645-2282

Squid

Aliotti Wholesale Fish Company
Monterey, CA 408-722-4597
Anchor Frozen Foods
Westbury, NY 800-566-3474
Atlantic Capes Fisheries
Cape May, NJ 609-884-3000
Blue Gold Mussels
New Bedford, MA 508-993-2635
Breakwater Fisheries
St John's, NL 709-754-1999
Caito Fisheries Inc
Fort Bragg, CA 707-964-6368
Channel Fish Processing
Gloucester, MA 800-457-0054
Fulton Fish Market
New York, NY 718-842-8908
Great Northern Products Inc
Cranston, RI 401-490-4590
Harbor Seafood
New Hyde Park, NY 800-645-2211
J Deluca Fish Co Inc
San Pedro, CA 310-684-5180
LA Monica Fine Foods
Millville, NJ
Lund's Fisheries
Cape May, NJ 609-884-7600
Menemsha Fish Market
Chilmark, MA 508-645-2282
Northwest Wild Products
Astoria, OR 503-791-1907
Notre Dame Seafoods Inc.
Comfort Cove, NL 709-244-5511
Pacific American Fish Co Inc
Vernon, CA 800-625-2525
Pacific Salmon Company
Edmonds, WA 425-774-1315
Royal Seafood Inc
Brooklyn, NY 718-769-1517
Ruggiero Seafood
Newark, NJ 866-225-2627
Sea Watch Intl
Easton, MD 410-822-7500
Spruce Lane Investments
Stratford, PE 902-892-2600
Stavis Seafoods
Boston, MA 800-390-5103
Sweet Water Seafood
Carlstadt, NJ 201-939-6622
Tampa Bay Fisheries Inc
Dover, FL 800-732-3663
Tichon Sea Food Corp
New Bedford, MA 508-999-5607
Vital Choice
Bellingham, WA 800-608-4825

Urchins

Captain Little Seafood
Queens County, NS 902-947-2087

Whelk

Captain Little Seafood
Queens County, NS 902-947-2087

Sushi

Azuma Foods Intl Inc USA
Hayward, CA 510-782-1112
Baycliff Company
New York, NY 212-772-6078
IOE Atlanta
Galena, MD 410-755-6300

Fruits & Vegetables

General

Alfred Louie Inc
Bakersfield, CA 661-831-2520
Arbre Farms Inc
Walkerville, MI. 231-873-3337
Black's Barbecue
Lockhart, TX. 888-632-8225
Brooklyn Whatever LLC
Brooklyn, NY 917-669-5525
Brookshire Grocery Company
Tyler, TX. 888-937-3776
Capalbo's Fruit Baskets
Clifton, NJ. 800-252-6262
Coco Lopez Inc
Miramar, FL 800-341-2242
Colavita USA
Edison, NJ. 888-265-2848
Country Fresh Inc
Spring, TX. 281-453-3300
Crop One
Oakland, CA
Diazteca Inc
Rio Rico, AZ. 520-761-4621
Duda Farm Fresh Foods Inc
Oviedo, FL 407-365-2111
Farm Fresh to You
Anaheim, CA 800-796-6009
Five Ponds Farm
Lineville, AL. 256-396-5217
Five Star Home Foods, Inc.
King of Prussia, PA. 800-246-5405
Four Seasons Produce Inc
Ephrata, PA. 800-422-8384
Fresh Origins
San Marcos, CA 760-736-4072
Frieda's Inc
Los Alamitos, CA. 714-826-6100
Fruvemex
Calexico, CA. 760-203-1896
G. Banis Company
Wilmington, DE 617-516-9092
GAF Seelig Inc
Flushing, NY. 718-899-5000
Grace & I
Los Angeles, CA. 800-584-1736
Gulf Pecan Company
Mobile, AL 251-661-2931
Highland Family Farms
Mapleton, MN. 507-524-3797
Ingles Markets
Black Mountain, NC. 828-669-2941
J M Swank Co
North Liberty, IA 800-593-6375
Jain Americas Inc
Columbus, OH 888-473-7539
Kingsburg Orchards
Kingsburg, CA 559-897-5132
La Morena
Huamantla, ... 222-211-0515
Lamex Foods Inc.
Bloomington, MN. 952-844-0585
Local Roots Farms
Burt, NY 716-946-3198
Made In Nature
Boulder, CO 800-906-7426
Manassero Farms
Irvine, CA. 949-554-5103
Meijer Inc
Grand Rapids, MI 616-453-6711
NAR
Nashua, NH. 603-888-5420
North Bay Produce Inc
Traverse City, MI 231-946-1941
Oak Hill Farm
Glen Ellen, CA 800-878-7808
Oberweis Dairy Inc
North Aurora, IL. 866-623-7934
Oneonta Starr Ranch Growers
Wenatchee, WA. 509-663-2191
ORB Weaver Farm
New Haven, VT 802-877-3755
Patsy's Italian Restaurant
New York, NY 212-247-3491
Peterson Farms Inc
Shelby, MI. 231-861-0119
Plenty
San Francisco, CA 650-735-3737
Prairie Thyme LTD
Santa Fe, NM 800-869-0009
Primo Foods
Oceanside, CA 760-439-8711
Publix Super Market
Lakeland, FL. 800-242-1227
Root Cellar Preserves
Wellesley, MA. 781-864-7440
Safeway Inc.
Pleasanton, CA 877-723-3929
Seneca Foods Corp
Marion, NY. 315-926-8100
Shamrock Foods Co
Phoenix, AZ 800-289-3663
Smirk's
Fort Morgan, CO. 970-762-0202
Steckel Produce
Jerseyville, IL 618-498-4274
The Power of Fruit
Lebanon, NJ 908-450-9806
Tolteca Foodservice
Norcross, GA 800-541-6835
Tropical Açaí LLC
Pompano Beach, FL 855-550-2224
Tru Fru, LLC
Salt Lake City, UT 888-437-2497
Veggie Grill
Irvine, CA
Wegmans Food Markets Inc.
Rochester, NY. 800-934-6267
WEIS Markets Inc.
Sunbury, PA. 866-999-9347
Western Pacific Produce
Santa Barbara, CA 800-963-4451
Winn-Dixie Stores
Jacksonville, FL 800-967-9105
Wish Farms
Plant City, FL 813-752-5111
Wonderful Citrus
Mission, TX 956-205-7300
Z&S Distributing
Fresno, CA 800-467-0788

Algae

New Earth
Klamath Falls, OR 541-882-5406
Sea Veggies
Commerce, CA 323-728-4762
Vitarich Laboratories
Naples, FL. 800-817-9999

Aloe Vera

Alfer Laboratories
Chatsworth, CA 818-709-0737
Aloe Commodities International
Carrollton, TX. 800-701-2563
Aloe Farms Inc
Harlingen, TX. 800-262-6771
Aloe Laboratories
Harlingen, TX. 800-258-5380
Christopher's Herb Shop
Springville, UT 888-372-4372
Emerling International Foods
Buffalo, NY. 716-833-7381
Florida Food Products Inc
Eustis, FL 800-874-2331
Real Aloe Company
Las Vegas, NV 800-541-7809
Russo Farms
Vineland, NJ 856-692-5942
Universal Preservachem Inc
Somerset, NJ. 732-568-1266
Warren Laboratories LLC
Abbott, TX 800-421-2563
Winning Solutions Inc
Irving, TX. 800-899-2563

Apple

A. Gagliano Co Inc
Milwaukee, WI 800-272-1516
AgroCepia
Miami, FL. 305-704-3488
Agvest
Cleveland, OH 216-464-3737
Allan Bros. Inc.
Naches, WA. 509-653-2625
Apple Acres
La Fayette, NY 603-893-8596
Applewood Orchards Inc
Deerfield, MI 800-447-3854
Baker Produce
Kennewick, WA 800-624-7553
Ballantine Produce Company
Reedley, CA 559-875-2583
Belleharvest Sales Inc
Belding, MI. 800-452-7753
Ben B. Schwartz & Sons
Detroit, MI 313-841-8300
Bennett's Apples & Cider
Ancaster, ON. 905-648-6878
Bridenbaugh Orchards
Martinsburg, PA 814-793-2364
Brothers International Food Corporation
Rochester, NY. 585-343-3007
Burnette Foods
Elk Rapids, MI 231-264-8116
Cahoon Farms
Wolcott, NY 315-594-9610
Cal Harvest Marketing Inc
Hanford, CA 559-582-4494
Chazy Orchards
Chazy, NY. 518-846-7171
Chelan Fresh Marketing
Chelan, WA. 509-682-2591
Chief Wenatchee
Wenatchee, WA. 509-662-5197
Citrosuco North America Inc
Lake Wales, FL. 800-356-4592
Clements Foods Co
Oklahoma City, OK 800-654-8355
Coloma Frozen Foods Inc
Coloma, MI. 800-642-2723
Congdon Orchards Inc.
Yakima, WA 509-966-4440
Country Fresh Inc
Spring, TX. 281-453-3300
Crane & Crane Inc
Brewster, WA 509-689-3447
Del Mar Food Products Corp
Watsonville, CA 831-722-3516
Diamond Fruit Growers
Hood River, OR 541-354-5300
Earthbound Farm
San Jn Bautista, CA 800-690-3200
Ever Fresh Fruit Co
Boring, OR 800-239-8026
Flippin-Seaman Inc
Tyro, VA 434-277-5828
Fowler Farms
Wolcott, NY 800-836-9537
Fruit Growers Supply Company
Valencia, CA. 888-997-4855
George W Saulpaugh & Son
Germantown, NY 518-537-6500
Giumarra Companies
Los Angeles, CA. 213-627-2900
Golden Town Apple Products
Rougemont, QC 866-552-7643
Harner Farms
State College, PA 814-237-7919
Hazel Creek Orchards
Mt Airy, GA 706-754-4899
Henggeler Packing Company
Fruitland, ID 208-452-4212
HH Dobbins Inc
Lyndonville, NY 877-362-2467
Hillcrest Orchard
Lake Placid, FL. 865-397-5273
Indian Hollow Farms
Richland Center, WI. 800-236-3944
International Home Foods
Parsippany, NJ. 973-359-9920
J C Watson Co
Parma, ID 208-722-5141
Knight's Appleden Fruit LTD
Colborne, ON 905-349-2521
Kozlowski Farms
Forestville, CA 800-473-2767

Leroux Creek
Hotchkiss, CO....877-970-5670
Love Creek Orchards
Medina, TX....800-449-0882
Mariani Packing Co.
Vacaville, CA....707-452-2800
Marley Orchards Corporation
Yakima, WA....509-248-5231
Mason County Fruit Packers Cooperative
Hart, MI....231-873-7504
Matson Fruit Co
Selah, WA....509-697-7100
Mayer's Cider Mill
Webster, NY....800-543-0043
Mayfield Farms and Nursery
Athens, TN....423-746-9859
Mrs Prindables
Niles, IL....888-215-1100
Naraghi Group
Escalon, CA....209-579-5253
National Fruit Product Co Inc
Winchester, VA....540-723-9614
Natural Foods Inc
Toledo, OH....419-537-1711
Naumes, Inc.
Medford, OR....541-772-6268
New Era Canning Company
New Era, MI....231-861-2151
New Organics
Kenwood, CA....734-677-5570
New York Apple Sales Inc
Glenmont, NY....888-477-6770
Niagara Foods
Middleport, NY....716-735-7722
North Bay Produce Inc
Traverse City, MI....231-946-1941
Northern Orcharad Co Inc
Peru, NY....518-643-2367
Nuchief Sales Inc
Wenatchee, WA....888-269-4638
Oneonta Starr Ranch Growers
Wenatchee, WA....509-663-2191
P R Farms Inc
Clovis, CA....559-299-0201
Pacific Coast Fruit Co
Portland, OR....503-234-6411
Pandol Brothers Inc
Delano, CA....661-725-3755
Park 100 Foods Inc
Tipton, IN....800-854-6504
Pastor Chuck Orchards
Portland, ME....207-773-1314
Pavero Cold Storage
Highland, NY....800-435-2994
Peterson Farms Inc
Shelby, MI....231-861-0119
Reinhart Foods
Toronto, ON....416-645-4910
Rice Fruit Co
Gardners, PA....800-627-3359
Roche Fruit LLC
Yakima, WA....509-248-7200
S Zitner Co
Philadelphia, PA....215-229-9828
Scotian Gold
Coldbrook, NS....888-726-8426
Shafer Lake Fruit Inc
Hartford, MI....269-621-3194
Shawnee Canning Co
Cross Junction, VA....800-713-1414
Smeltzer Orchard Co
Frankfort, MI....231-882-4421
Snowcrest Packer
Abbotsford, BC....800-265-3686
Solana Gold Organics
Sebastopol, CA....800-459-1121
Stadelman Fruit LLC
Zillah, WA....509-829-5145
Stanley Orchards Sales, Inc.
Modena, NY....845-883-7351
Sunshine Farm & Garden
Renick, WV....304-497-2208
Symms Fruit Ranch Inc
Caldwell, ID....208-459-4821
T.S. Smith & Sons
Bridgeville, DE....302-337-8271
Tastee Apple
Newcomerstown, OH....800-262-7753
Timber Crest Farms
Healdsburg, CA....888-766-4233
Tom Ringhausen Orchards
Hardin, IL....800-258-6645
Tony Vitrano Company
Jessup, MD....800-481-3784
Trinity Fruit Sale Co
Fresno, CA....559-433-3777
Triple D Orchards Inc
Empire, MI....231-326-5174
United Apple Sales
New Paltz, NY....585-765-2460
Vermont Village
Barre, VT
Viva Tierra
Mt Vernon, WA....360-855-0566
White House Foods
Winchester, VA....540-662-3401
Wiards Orchards Inc
Ypsilanti, MI....734-390-9211
Yakima Fresh
Yakima, WA....509-248-5770

Canned

Burnette Foods
Elk Rapids, MI....231-264-8116
Emerling International Foods
Buffalo, NY....716-833-7381
New Era Canning Company
New Era, MI....231-861-2151
New Organics
Kenwood, CA....734-677-5570
Setton International Foods
Commack, NY....800-227-4397
Terri Lynn Inc
Elgin, IL....800-323-0775
Unique Ingredients LLC
Gold Canyon, AZ....480-983-2498

Caramel

Andrews Caramel Apples
Chicago, IL....800-305-3004
S Zitner Co
Philadelphia, PA....215-229-9828
Tastee Apple
Newcomerstown, OH....800-262-7753

Covered

Candied

Calif Snack Foods
South El Monte, CA....626-454-4099

Caramel

Carousel Candies
Geneva, IL....888-656-1552
DGZ Chocolate
Houston, TX....877-949-9444
Parmenter's Northville Cider Mill
Northville, MI....248-349-3181
S Zitner Co
Philadelphia, PA....215-229-9828

Criterion

Natural Foods Inc
Toledo, OH....419-537-1711
Weaver Nut Co. Inc.
Ephrata, PA....800-473-2688

Dried

AgroCepia
Miami, FL....305-704-3488
American Importing Co.
Minneapolis, MN....855-273-0466
Atwater Foods
Lyndonville Orleans, NY....585-765-2639
Bedemco Inc
White Plains, NY....914-683-1119
Emerling International Foods
Buffalo, NY....716-833-7381
Golden Town Apple Products
Rougemont, QC....866-552-7643
Golden Valley Natural
Shelley, ID....888-270-7147
Green Earth Orchards
Salt Lake City, UT....801-888-7161
Just Tomatoes
Westley, CA....800-537-1985
Kozlowski Farms
Forestville, CA....800-473-2767
Leroux Creek
Hotchkiss, CO....877-970-5670
Made In Nature
Boulder, CO....800-906-7426
Mariani Packing Co.
Vacaville, CA....707-452-2800
Mayfield Farms and Nursery
Athens, TN....423-746-9859
New Organics
Kenwood, CA....734-677-5570
Niagara Foods
Middleport, NY....716-735-7722
Setton International Foods
Commack, NY....800-227-4397
Solana Gold Organics
Sebastopol, CA....800-459-1121
Terri Lynn Inc
Elgin, IL....800-323-0775
ThreeWorks Snacks
259 Niagara St., ON
Timber Crest Farms
Healdsburg, CA....888-766-4233
Unique Ingredients LLC
Gold Canyon, AZ....480-983-2498

Fresh

Belleharvest Sales Inc
Belding, MI....800-452-7753
Bridenbaugh Orchards
Martinsburg, PA....814-793-2364
Chazy Orchards
Chazy, NY....518-846-7171
Ever Fresh Fruit Co
Boring, OR....800-239-8026
Golden Town Apple Products
Rougemont, QC....866-552-7643
Naraghi Group
Escalon, CA....209-579-5253
Peterson Farms Inc
Shelby, MI....231-861-0119
Price Co
Yakima, WA....509-966-4110
Unique Ingredients LLC
Gold Canyon, AZ....480-983-2498

Frozen

Agvest
Cleveland, OH....216-464-3737
Cahoon Farms
Wolcott, NY....315-594-9610
Citrosuco North America Inc
Lake Wales, FL....800-356-4592
Emerling International Foods
Buffalo, NY....716-833-7381
Ever Fresh Fruit Co
Boring, OR....800-239-8026
Mason County Fruit Packers Cooperative
Hart, MI....231-873-7504
New Organics
Kenwood, CA....734-677-5570
Pacific Coast Fruit Co
Portland, OR....503-234-6411
Paris Foods Corporation
Trappe, MD....410-200-9595
Peterson Farms Inc
Shelby, MI....231-861-0119
Setton International Foods
Commack, NY....800-227-4397
Smeltzer Orchard Co
Frankfort, MI....231-882-4421
Snowcrest Packer
Abbotsford, BC....800-265-3686
Terri Lynn Inc
Elgin, IL....800-323-0775
Triple D Orchards Inc
Empire, MI....231-326-5174
Unique Ingredients LLC
Gold Canyon, AZ....480-983-2498

Golden Delicious

Allan Bros. Inc.
Naches, WA....509-653-2625
Baker Produce
Kennewick, WA....800-624-7553
Belleharvest Sales Inc
Belding, MI....800-452-7753

Pomace

Emerling International Foods
Buffalo, NY....716-833-7381
Unique Ingredients LLC
Gold Canyon, AZ....480-983-2498

Red Delicious

Allan Bros. Inc.
Naches, WA....509-653-2625
Baker Produce
Kennewick, WA....800-624-7553
Belleharvest Sales Inc
Belding, MI....800-452-7753

Rings

AgroCepia
Miami, FL....305-704-3488
Timber Crest Farms
Healdsburg, CA....888-766-4233

Slices

Boskovich Farms Inc
Oxnard, CA....805-487-2299
Bridenbaugh Orchards
Martinsburg, PA....814-793-2364
Chiquita Brands LLC.
Fort Lauderdale, FL....954-924-5700
Ever Fresh Fruit Co
Boring, OR....800-239-8026
Golden Town Apple Products
Rougemont, QC....866-552-7643
Mayfield Farms and Nursery
Athens, TN....423-746-9859
Naraghi Group
Escalon, CA....209-579-5253
National Fruit Product Co Inc
Winchester, VA....540-723-9614
New Era Canning Company
New Era, MI....231-861-2151
White House Foods
Winchester, VA....540-662-3401

Canned

Mayfield Farms and Nursery
Athens, TN....423-746-9859
New Era Canning Company
New Era, MI....231-861-2151

Frozen

Ever Fresh Fruit Co
Boring, OR....800-239-8026
Mayfield Farms and Nursery
Athens, TN....423-746-9859

Apricot

American Key Food Products Inc
Closter, NJ....877-263-7539
Ballantine Produce Company
Reedley, CA....559-875-2583
Brandt Farms Inc
Reedley, CA....559-638-6961
California Fruit
San Diego, CA....877-378-4811
Copper Hills Fruit Sales
Fresno, CA....559-432-5400
Custom Produce Sales
Parlier, CA....559-254-5800
Del Mar Food Products Corp
Watsonville, CA....831-722-3516
Fowler Packing Co
Fresno, CA....559-834-5911
HMC Farms
Kingsburg, CA....559-897-1025
Kalustyan
New York, NY....800-352-3451
Kings Canyon
Reedley, CA....559-638-3571
Miss Scarlett's Flowers
Juneau, AK....800-345-6734
Muirhead Canning Co
The Dalles, OR....541-298-1660
Natural Foods Inc
Toledo, OH....419-537-1711
P R Farms Inc
Clovis, CA....559-299-0201
Patterson Vegetable Company
Patterson, CA....209-892-2611
Prima® Wawona
Fresno, CA....559-787-8780
Sunfood
El Cajon, CA....888-729-3663
Sunsweet Growers Inc.
Yuba City, CA....800-417-2253
Terri Lynn Inc
Elgin, IL....800-323-0775
Trinity Fruit Sale Co
Fresno, CA....559-433-3777
Tufts Ranch
Winters, CA....530-795-4144
Unique Ingredients LLC
Gold Canyon, AZ....480-983-2498
Viva Tierra
Mt Vernon, WA....360-855-0566
Z&S Distributing
Fresno, CA....800-467-0788

Canned

Emerling International Foods
Buffalo, NY....716-833-7381

Dried

American Importing Co.
Minneapolis, MN....855-273-0466
Bedemco Inc
White Plains, NY....914-683-1119
California Fruit
San Diego, CA....877-378-4811
Central California Raisin Packing Co, Inc.
Del Rey, CA....559-888-2195
Green Earth Orchards
Salt Lake City, UT....801-888-7161
Kalustyan
New York, NY....800-352-3451
King Arthur Flour
Norwich, VT....800-827-6836
Made In Nature
Boulder, CO....800-906-7426
Mariani Packing Co.
Vacaville, CA....707-452-2800
Natural Foods Inc
Toledo, OH....419-537-1711
Setton International Foods
Commack, NY....800-227-4397
Sunridge Farms
Royal Oaks, CA....831-786-7000
Sunsweet Growers Inc.
Yuba City, CA....800-417-2253
Timber Crest Farms
Healdsburg, CA....888-766-4233
Weaver Nut Co. Inc.
Ephrata, PA....800-473-2688

Frozen

Emerling International Foods
Buffalo, NY....716-833-7381

Kernals

Emerling International Foods
Buffalo, NY....716-833-7381

Artichoke

Fayter Farms Produce
Bradley, CA....831-385-8515
Ocean Mist Farms
Castroville, CA....831-633-2144
Orleans Packing Co
Hyde Park, MA....617-361-6611
SupHerb Farms
Turlock, CA....800-787-4372
Vegetable Juices Inc
Chicago, IL....888-776-9752

Canned

Agrocan
Ville St Laurent, QC....877-247-6226
Emerling International Foods
Buffalo, NY....716-833-7381
Ron Son Foods Inc
Swedesboro, NJ....856-241-7333

Frozen

Emerling International Foods
Buffalo, NY....716-833-7381
SupHerb Farms
Turlock, CA....800-787-4372
Vegetable Juices Inc
Chicago, IL....888-776-9752

Hearts

Castella Imports Inc
Brentwood, NY....631-231-5500
Colonna Brothers Inc
North Bergen, NJ....201-864-1115
SupHerb Farms
Turlock, CA....800-787-4372

Arugula

80 Acres Farms
Hamilton, OH....888-574-1569
AeroFarms
Newark, NJ....973-242-2495
Bowery Farming Inc.
New York, NY
BrightFarms
Irvington, NY....866-857-8745
Earthbound Farm
San Jn Bautista, CA....800-690-3200
Plenty
San Francisco, CA....650-735-3737

Asparagus

Arbre Farms Inc
Walkerville, MI....231-873-3337
Boskovich Farms Inc
Oxnard, CA....805-487-2299
Brock Seed Company
Finley, TN....731-286-2430
Burnette Foods
Elk Rapids, MI....231-264-8116
Cal Harvest Marketing Inc
Hanford, CA....559-582-4494
Coloma Frozen Foods Inc
Coloma, MI....800-642-2723
Delta Packing
Lodi, CA....209-334-1023
Di Mare Fresh Inc
Fort Worth, TX....817-385-3000
Earthbound Farm
San Jn Bautista, CA....800-690-3200
Foster Family Farm
South Windsor, CT....860-648-9366
George W Saulpaugh & Son
Germantown, NY....518-537-6500
Giumarra Companies
Los Angeles, CA....213-627-2900
Heartland Strawberry Farm
Waterloo, IA....888-747-7423
Lakeside Foods Inc.
Manitowoc, WI....800-466-3834
Metzger Specialty Brands
New York, NY....212-957-0055
Michigan Freeze Pack
Hart, MI....231-873-2175
Miss Scarlett's Flowers
Juneau, AK....800-345-6734
New Era Canning Company
New Era, MI....231-861-2151
North Bay Produce Inc
Traverse City, MI....231-946-1941
Ocean Mist Farms
Castroville, CA....831-633-2144
Pictsweet Co
Bells, TN....731-663-7600
Sedlock Farm
Lynn Center, IL....309-521-8284
Shafer Lake Fruit Inc
Hartford, MI....269-621-3194
Smeltzer Orchard Co
Frankfort, MI....231-882-4421
Snowcrest Packer
Abbotsford, BC....800-265-3686
Symms Fruit Ranch Inc
Caldwell, ID....208-459-4821
T.S. Smith & Sons
Bridgeville, DE....302-337-8271
Weil's Food Processing
Wheatley, ON....519-825-4572

Canned

Carriere Foods Inc
Saint-Denis-Sur-Richelie, QC....450-787-3411
Emerling International Foods
Buffalo, NY....716-833-7381
Fruit Belt Canning Inc
Lawrence, MI....269-674-3939
Unique Ingredients LLC
Gold Canyon, AZ....480-983-2498

Frozen

Emerling International Foods
Buffalo, NY....716-833-7381
Fruit Belt Canning Inc
Lawrence, MI....269-674-3939

Paris Foods Corporation
Trappe, MD....410-200-9595
Unique Ingredients LLC
Gold Canyon, AZ....480-983-2498

Avocado

Brooks Tropicals Inc
Homestead, FL....800-327-4833
Calavo Growers
Santa Paula, CA....805-525-1245
Castellini Group
Newport, KY....800-233-8560
Del Monte Fresh Produce Inc.
Coral Gables, FL....800-950-3683
Diversified Avocado Products
Mission Viejo, CA....800-879-2555
Earthbound Farm
San Jn Bautista, CA....800-690-3200
Emerling International Foods
Buffalo, NY....716-833-7381
Giumarra Companies
Los Angeles, CA....213-627-2900
J. R. Simplot Co.
Boise, ID....208-336-2110
McDaniel Fruit
Fallbrook, CA....760-728-8438
Prime Produce
Orange, CA....714-771-0718
Reed Lang Farms
Rio Hondo, TX....956-748-2354
Simpatica
Camarillo, CA....310-286-2236
West Pak Avocado Inc
Murrieta, CA....800-266-4414

Bamboo Shoots

Dong Kee Company
Chicago, IL....312-225-6340
Emerling International Foods
Buffalo, NY....716-833-7381
Lee's Food Products
Toronto, ON....416-465-2407
SupHerb Farms
Turlock, CA....800-787-4372

Banana

A. Gagliano Co Inc
Milwaukee, WI....800-272-1516
Chiquita Brands LLC.
Fort Lauderdale, FL....954-924-5700
Del Monte Fresh Produce Inc.
Coral Gables, FL....800-950-3683
Emerling International Foods
Buffalo, NY....716-833-7381
Organics Unlimited
San Diego, CA....619-710-0658
Paris Foods Corporation
Trappe, MD....410-200-9595
Santanna Banana Company
Harrisburg, PA....717-238-8321
Surface Banana Company
Parkersburg, WV....304-485-2400
Unique Ingredients LLC
Gold Canyon, AZ....480-983-2498

Banana Products

Banana Distributing Company
San Antonio, TX....210-227-8285
Confoco USA, Inc.
Elizabeth, NJ....908-659-0566
KOZY Shack Enterprises Inc
St Paul, MN....855-716-1555
Spreda Group
Louisville, KY....502-426-9411

Dried

Barnana
Santa Monica, CA....858-480-1543
Bedemco Inc
White Plains, NY....914-683-1119
Fine Dried Foods Intl
Santa Cruz, CA....831-426-1413
Made In Nature
Boulder, CO....800-906-7426
Mariani Packing Co.
Vacaville, CA....707-452-2800
Setton International Foods
Commack, NY....800-227-4397
Sunridge Farms
Royal Oaks, CA....831-786-7000

Plantain

MIC Foods
Miami, FL....800-788-9335
Organics Unlimited
San Diego, CA....619-710-0658
Tantos Foods International
Markham, ON....905-943-9993

Beans

A. Lassonde Inc.
Rougemont, QC....866-552-7643
Abbott & Cobb Inc
Feasterville, PA....800-345-7333
Agricore United
St Louis Park, MN....877-509-5865
Amigos Canning Company
San Antonio, TX....210-798-5360
B & G Foods Inc.
Parsippany, NJ....973-401-6500
Beckman & Gast Co
St Henry, OH....419-678-4195
Buckhead Gourmet
Atlanta, GA....800-673-6338
Burnette Foods
Elk Rapids, MI....231-264-8116
Burnham & Morrill Co
Portland, ME....800-813-2165
Buxton Foods
Buxton, ND....800-726-8057
Cajun Boy's Louisiana Products
Church Point, LA....800-880-9575
California Fruit and Tomato Kitchens
Modesto, CA....209-574-9407
California Garden Products
San Juan Capistrano, CA....949-215-0000
Camellia Beans
Harahan, LA....504-733-8480
Campbell Soup Co.
Camden, NJ....800-257-8443
Capco Enterprises
East Hanover, NJ....800-252-1011
Castella Imports Inc
Brentwood, NY....631-231-5500
Chef Merito Inc
Van Nuys, CA....800-637-4861
Cooperative Elevator Co
Pigeon, MI....800-968-0601
Country Cupboard
Lewisburg, PA....570-523-3211
Crookston Bean
Crookston, MN....218-281-2567
Eckroat Seed Company
Oklahoma City, OK....800-331-7333
Eden Foods Inc
Clinton, MI....888-424-3336
Everspring Farms
Seaforth, ON....519-527-0990
Faribault Foods, Inc.
Fairbault, MN....507-331-1400
Foster Family Farm
South Windsor, CT....860-648-9366
Furmano's Foods
Northumberland, PA....800-952-1111
Goya Foods Inc.
Jersey City, NJ....201-348-4900
Grandma Browns Beans Inc
Mexico, NY....315-963-7221
Green Valley Foods
Salem, OR....844-588-3535
Hanover Foods Corp
Hanover, PA....717-632-6000
HealthBest
San Marcos, CA....760-752-5230
Heartline Foods
Westport, CT....203-222-0381
Hoopeston Foods Inc
Burnsville, MN....952-854-0903
Hormel Foods Corp.
Austin, MN....507-437-5611
Houston Calco, Inc
Houston, TX....713-236-8668
HP Schmid
San Francisco, CA....415-765-5925
In Harvest Inc
Bemidji, MN....800-346-7032
Inland Empire Foods
Riverside, CA....888-452-3267
Inter-American Products
Cincinnati, OH....800-645-2233
International Home Foods
Parsippany, NJ....973-359-9920

Kalustyan
New York, NY....800-352-3451
Knight Seed Company
Burnsville, MN....800-328-2999
Krinos Foods
Bronx, NY....718-729-9000
L & S Packing Co
Farmingdale, NY....800-286-6487
Lakeside Foods Inc.
Plainview, MN....507-534-3141
Les Aliments Ramico Foods
St. Leonard, QC....514-329-1844
Louis Dreyfus Corporation
Rotterdam,
Meridian Foods New Inc
Eaton, IN....765-396-3344
Mills Brothers Intl
Seattle, WA....206-575-3000
Miramar Fruit Trading Company
Doral, FL....305-883-4774
Miyako Oriental Foods Inc
Baldwin Park, CA....877-788-6476
Morgan Foods Inc
Austin, IN....888-430-1780
Nation Wide Canning Ltd.
Cottam, ON....519-839-4831
National Frozen Foods Corp
Seattle, WA....206-322-8900
Natural Foods Inc
Toledo, OH....419-537-1711
New Era Canning Company
New Era, MI....231-861-2151
New Harvest Foods
Washington, DC....920-822-2578
NORPAC Foods Inc
Salem, OR
North Bay Trading Co
Brule, WI....800-348-0164
Northern Feed & Bean Company
Lucerne, CO....800-316-2326
Osowski Farms
Minto, ND....701-248-3341
Pacific Collier Fresh Company
Immokalee, FL....800-226-7274
Paisano Food Products
Elk Grove Village, IL....800-672-4726
Pictsweet Co
Bells, TN....731-663-7600
Pleasant Grove Farms
Pleasant Grove, CA....916-655-3391
Producers Cooperative
Bryan, TX....979-778-6000
Produits Ronald
St. Damase, QC....800-465-0118
Purity Foods Inc
Hudson, MI....800-997-7358
Quetzal Internet Cafe
San Francisco, CA....888-673-8181
R&J Farms
West Salem, OH....419-846-3179
Randall Food Products
Cincinnati, OH....513-793-6525
Raymond-Hadley Corporation
Spencer, NY....800-252-5220
Red River Commodities Inc
Fargo, ND....800-437-5539
Rice Company
Fair Oaks, CA....916-784-7745
Riceland Foods Inc.
Stuttgart, AR....855-742-3929
Roberts Seed
Axtell, NE....308-743-2565
Sambets Cajun Deli
Austin, TX....800-472-6238
Seabrook Brothers & Sons
Seabrook, NJ....856-455-8080
Seapoint Farms
Huntington Beach, CA....714-374-9831
Smith Frozen Foods Inc
Weston, OR....541-566-3515
Snowcrest Packer
Abbotsford, BC....800-265-3686
Sole Grano LLC
Fair Lawn, NJ....201-797-7100
SOPAKCO Foods
Mullins, SC....800-276-9678
Spokane Seed Co
Spokane Valley, WA....800-359-8478
Sprague Foods
Belleville, ON....613-966-1200
Sugai Kona Coffee
Holualoa, HI....808-322-7717

Talley Farms
Arroyo Grande, CA 805-489-5400

Tipiak Inc
Stamford, CT 203-961-9117

Torn & Glasser
Los Angeles, CA 800-282-6887

Torrefazione Barzula & Import
Mississauga, ON 866-358-5488

Trinidad Benham Corporation
Denver, CO 303-220-1400

Twin City Foods Inc.
Stanwood, WA 206-515-2400

United Intertrade Corporation
Houston, TX 800-969-2233

Vegetarian Traveler
Woodbury, MN

Veronica Foods Inc
Oakland, CA 800-370-5554

Vincent Formusa Company
Des Plaines, IL 847-813-6040

Weaver Nut Co. Inc.
Ephrata, PA 800-473-2688

Webster Farms
Cambridge, NS 800-507-8844

WG Thompson & Sons
Blenheim, ON 800-265-5225

Wicklund Farms
Springfield, OR 541-747-5998

Wildcat Produce
McGrew, NE 308-783-2438

Z&S Distributing
Fresno, CA 800-467-0788

Zarda Bar-B-Q & Catering Company
Blue Springs, MO 800-776-7427

Adzuki

Bob's Red Mill Natural Foods
Milwaukie, OR 800-349-2173

Emerling International Foods
Buffalo, NY 716-833-7381

New Organics
Kenwood, CA 734-677-5570

Organic Planet
San Francisco, CA 415-765-5590

Baked

A. Lassonde Inc.
Rougemont, QC 866-552-7643

Burnham & Morrill Co
Portland, ME 800-813-2165

California Garden Products
San Juan Capistrano, CA 949-215-0000

Capco Enterprises
East Hanover, NJ 800-252-1011

Captain Ken's Foods Inc
St Paul, MN 800-510-3811

Grandma Browns Beans Inc
Mexico, NY 315-963-7221

Hanover Foods Corp
Hanover, PA 717-632-6000

Produits Ronald
St. Damase, QC 800-465-0118

TyRy Inc
Rocklin, CA 800-322-6325

Wornick Company
Cincinnati, OH 800-860-4555

Zarda Bar-B-Q & Catering Company
Blue Springs, MO 800-776-7427

Beans: Snap Blue Lake

Arbre Farms Inc
Walkerville, MI 231-873-3337

Black

Agricore United
St Louis Park, MN 877-509-5865

Buckhead Gourmet
Atlanta, GA 800-673-6338

Country Cupboard
Lewisburg, PA 570-523-3211

Miyako Oriental Foods Inc
Baldwin Park, CA 877-788-6476

Teasdale Quality Foods Inc
Atwater, CA 209-358-5616

Blackeye (Cowpeas)

Hanover Foods Corp
Hanover, PA 717-632-6000

Trinidad Benham Corporation
Denver, CO 303-220-1400

Blue Lake

Canned

Emerling International Foods
Buffalo, NY 716-833-7381

New Era Canning Company
New Era, MI 231-861-2151

NORPAC Foods Inc
Salem, OR

Frozen

Emerling International Foods
Buffalo, NY 716-833-7381

NORPAC Foods Inc
Salem, OR

Pictsweet Co
Bells, TN 731-663-7600

Seabrook Brothers & Sons
Seabrook, NJ 856-455-8080

Twin City Foods Inc.
Stanwood, WA 206-515-2400

Broad

Park 100 Foods Inc
Tipton, IN 800-854-6504

Butter

Canned

Emerling International Foods
Buffalo, NY 716-833-7381

Frozen

Emerling International Foods
Buffalo, NY 716-833-7381

Canned

Bush Brothers & Co
. 800-590-3797

California Garden Products
San Juan Capistrano, CA 949-215-0000

Carriere Foods Inc
Saint-Denis-Sur-Richelie, QC 450-787-3411

Pastene Co LTD
Canton, MA 781-298-3397

Seneca Foods Corp
Marion, NY 315-926-8100

Teasdale Quality Foods Inc
Atwater, CA 209-358-5616

Cannellini

Bob's Red Mill Natural Foods
Milwaukie, OR 800-349-2173

Emerling International Foods
Buffalo, NY 716-833-7381

New Organics
Kenwood, CA 734-677-5570

Organic Planet
San Francisco, CA 415-765-5590

Chick

Agrocan
Ville St Laurent, QC 877-247-6226

Emerling International Foods
Buffalo, NY 716-833-7381

New Organics
Kenwood, CA 734-677-5570

Organic Planet
San Francisco, CA 415-765-5590

Saffron Road
Stamford, CT 877-425-2587

The Amazing Chickpea
St. Louis Park, MN 612-548-1099

Timeless Seeds
Ulm, MT 406-866-3340

Chili

Emerling International Foods
Buffalo, NY 716-833-7381

Faribault Foods, Inc.
Fairbault, MN 507-331-1400

Hanover Foods Corp
Hanover, PA 717-632-6000

Milnot Company
Litchfield, IL 800-877-6455

Organic Planet
San Francisco, CA 415-765-5590

SOPAKCO Foods
Mullins, SC 800-276-9678

Dried

Bland

Kelley Bean Co Inc
Scottsbluff, NE 308-635-6438

Dry

Agfinity Inc
Eaton, CO 800-433-4688

Basic American Foods
Walnut Creek, CA 925-472-4000

Berberian Nut Company
Chico, CA 530-981-4900

Burnette Foods
Elk Rapids, MI 231-264-8116

C & F Foods Inc
City Of Industry, CA 626-723-1000

Camellia Beans
Harahan, LA 504-733-8480

Central Bean Co
Quincy, WA 509-787-1544

Commodities Marketing Inc
Clarksburg, NJ 732-516-0700

Cooperative Elevator Co
Pigeon, MI 800-968-0601

Crookston Bean
Crookston, MN 218-281-2567

Eckhart Seed Company
Salinas, CA 831-758-0925

Eckroat Seed Company
Oklahoma City, OK 800-331-7333

Emerling International Foods
Buffalo, NY 716-833-7381

Farmers Cooperative Grain Co
Kinde, MI 989-874-4200

Freeland Bean & Grain Inc
Freeland, MI 800-447-9131

H.K. Canning
Ventura, CA 805-652-1392

High Country Elevators Inc
Dove Creek, CO 970-677-2251

Hoopeston Foods Inc
Burnsville, MN 952-854-0903

HP Schmid
San Francisco, CA 415-765-5925

Jack's Bean Co LLC
Holyoke, CO 970-854-3702

Kalustyan
New York, NY 800-352-3451

Knight Seed Company
Burnsville, MN 800-328-2999

Luxor California Exports Corp.
San Diego, CA 619-465-7777

Meridian Foods New Inc
Eaton, IN 765-396-3344

Mills Brothers Intl
Seattle, WA 206-575-3000

Morrison Farms
Clearwater, NE 402-887-5335

Nature's Legacy Inc.
Hudson, MI 517-448-2050

New Organics
Kenwood, CA 734-677-5570

Nk Hurst Co Inc
Indianapolis, IN 800-426-2336

Northern Feed & Bean Company
Lucerne, CO 800-316-2326

Northwest Pea & Bean Co
Spokane Valley, WA 509-534-3821

Oakland Bean Cleaning & Storage
Knights Landing, CA 530-735-6203

Organic Planet
San Francisco, CA 415-765-5590

Osowski Farms
Minto, ND 701-248-3341

Paisano Food Products
Elk Grove Village, IL 800-672-4726

Producers Cooperative
Bryan, TX 979-778-6000

R&J Farms
West Salem, OH 419-846-3179

Randall Food Products
Cincinnati, OH 513-793-6525

Red River Commodities Inc
Fargo, ND 800-437-5539

Rhodes Bean & Supply Co-Op
Tracy, CA 209-835-1284

Roberts Seed
Axtell, NE........................308-743-2565
Russell E. Womack, Inc.
Lubbock, TX.....................877-787-3559
S & E Organic Farms Inc
Bakersfield, CA 661-325-2644
Seed Enterprises Inc
West Point, NE 888-440-7333
Smith Frozen Foods Inc
Weston, OR.......................541-566-3515
Sprague Foods
Belleville, ON.....................613-966-1200
Terra Ingredients LLC
Minneapolis, MN 855-497-3308
Trinidad Benham Company
Bridgeport, NE 308-262-1361
Trinidad Benham Corporation
Denver, CO.......................303-220-1400
Vege-Cool
Newman, CA.....................209-862-2360
Webster Farms
Cambridge, NS 800-507-8844
Westbrae Natural Foods
Melville, NY.......................800-434-4246
WG Thompson & Sons
Blenheim, ON......................800-265-5225

Canned

Carriere Foods Inc
Saint-Denis-Sur-Richelie, QC 450-787-3411
Emerling International Foods
Buffalo, NY.......................716-833-7381

Edible

Agfinity Inc
Eaton, CO.........................800-433-4688
Russell E. Womack, Inc.
Lubbock, TX.......................877-787-3559

Fava

Bob's Red Mill Natural Foods
Milwaukie, OR....................800-349-2173
Emerling International Foods
Buffalo, NY.......................716-833-7381
Kalustyan
New York, NY 800-352-3451
Organic Planet
San Francisco, CA 415-765-5590
Tarazi Specialty Foods
Chino, CA.........................909-628-3601

Frozen

Agfinity Inc
Eaton, CO.........................800-433-4688
Amigos Canning Company
San Antonio, TX...................210-798-5360
Buxton Foods
Buxton, ND.......................800-726-8057
Campbell Soup Co.
Camden, NJ.......................800-257-8443
Captain Ken's Foods Inc
St Paul, MN.......................800-510-3811
Diversified Foods & Seasonings
Covington, LA 800-914-2382
Emerling International Foods
Buffalo, NY.......................716-833-7381
Hanover Foods Corp
Hanover, PA 717-632-6000
Lakeside Foods Inc.
Plainview, MN 507-534-3141
Lakeside Foods Inc.
Manitowoc, WI....................800-466-3834
Meridian Foods New Inc
Eaton, IN.........................765-396-3344
National Frozen Foods Corp
Seattle, WA 206-322-8900
NORPAC Foods Inc
Salem, OR
Pictsweet Co
Bells, TN..........................731-663-7600
Seabrook Brothers & Sons
Seabrook, NJ......................856-455-8080
Smith Frozen Foods Inc
Weston, OR.......................541-566-3515
Snowcrest Packer
Abbotsford, BC....................800-265-3686
Twin City Foods Inc.
Stanwood, WA 206-515-2400

Garbanzo

Bob's Red Mill Natural Foods
Milwaukie, OR 800-349-2173
Buckhead Gourmet
Atlanta, GA.......................800-673-6338
California Fruit and Tomato Kitchens
Modesto, CA......................209-574-9407
Capco Enterprises
East Hanover, NJ..................800-252-1011
Emerling International Foods
Buffalo, NY.......................716-833-7381
In Harvest Inc
Bemidji, MN.......................800-346-7032
Kalustyan
New York, NY 800-352-3451
New Organics
Kenwood, CA.....................734-677-5570
Northwest Pea & Bean Co
Spokane Valley, WA 509-534-3821
Organic Planet
San Francisco, CA 415-765-5590
Sprague Foods
Belleville, ON.....................613-966-1200
Teasdale Quality Foods Inc
Atwater, CA 209-358-5616
Vana Life Foods
Seattle, WA.......................347-446-6504

Great Northern

Agricore United
St Louis Park, MN 877-509-5865
Bob's Red Mill Natural Foods
Milwaukie, OR....................800-349-2173
Emerling International Foods
Buffalo, NY.......................716-833-7381
Hanover Foods Corp
Hanover, PA 717-632-6000
Jack's Bean Co LLC
Holyoke, CO......................970-854-3702
New Organics
Kenwood, CA.....................734-677-5570
Organic Planet
San Francisco, CA 415-765-5590
Randall Food Products
Cincinnati, OH 513-793-6525

Greek

Canned

Agrocan
Ville St Laurent, QC...............877-247-6226

Green

Beckman & Gast Co
St Henry, OH......................419-678-4195
Burnette Foods
Elk Rapids, MI 231-264-8116
Faribault Foods, Inc.
Fairbault, MN 507-331-1400
Hanover Foods Corp
Hanover, PA 717-632-6000
Miss Scarlett's Flowers
Juneau, AK 800-345-6734
National Frozen Foods Corp
Seattle, WA.......................206-322-8900
New Era Canning Company
New Era, MI......................231-861-2151
New Harvest Foods
Washington, DC 920-822-2578
NORPAC Foods Inc
Salem, OR
Patterson Frozen Foods
Patterson, CA 209-892-2611
Pictsweet Co
Bells, TN..........................731-663-7600
Seabrook Brothers & Sons
Seabrook, NJ......................856-455-8080
Seneca Foods Corp
Princeville, IL.....................309-385-4301
Twin City Foods Inc.
Stanwood, WA 206-515-2400
Veronica Foods Inc
Oakland, CA......................800-370-5554
Wicklund Farms
Springfield, OR....................541-747-5998
Wildcat Produce
McGrew, NE......................308-783-2438

Canned

Beckman & Gast Co
St Henry, OH......................419-678-4195
Burnette Foods
Elk Rapids, MI 231-264-8116
Carriere Foods Inc
Saint-Denis-Sur-Richelie, QC 450-787-3411
Commodities Marketing Inc
Clarksburg, NJ 732-516-0700
Emerling International Foods
Buffalo, NY.......................716-833-7381
Faribault Foods, Inc.
Fairbault, MN 507-331-1400
New Era Canning Company
New Era, MI......................231-861-2151
New Harvest Foods
Washington, DC 920-822-2578
NORPAC Foods Inc
Salem, OR
Seneca Foods Corp
Princeville, IL.....................309-385-4301
Truitt Bros Inc
Salem, OR........................800-547-8712

Frozen

Lisa's Organics
Carnelian Bay, CA 877-584-5711
National Frozen Foods Corp
Seattle, WA.......................206-322-8900
NORPAC Foods Inc
Salem, OR
Paris Foods Corporation
Trappe, MD.......................410-200-9595
Pictsweet Co
Bells, TN..........................731-663-7600
Seabrook Brothers & Sons
Seabrook, NJ......................856-455-8080
Twin City Foods Inc.
Stanwood, WA 206-515-2400

Green Mung

New Organics
Kenwood, CA.....................734-677-5570
Organic Planet
San Francisco, CA 415-765-5590

Italian

National Frozen Foods Corp
Seattle, WA.......................206-322-8900
Pictsweet Co
Bells, TN..........................731-663-7600

Kidney

Agfinity Inc
Eaton, CO 800-433-4688
Bob's Red Mill Natural Foods
Milwaukie, OR....................800-349-2173
Burnette Foods
Elk Rapids, MI 231-264-8116
California Garden Products
San Juan Capistrano, CA 949-215-0000
Cordon Bleu International
Anjou, QC........................800-363-1182
Hanover Foods Corp
Hanover, PA 717-632-6000
International Home Foods
Parsippany, NJ.....................973-359-9920
Jack's Bean Co LLC
Holyoke, CO......................970-854-3702
Nation Wide Canning Ltd.
Cottam, ON.......................519-839-4831
New Era Canning Company
New Era, MI......................231-861-2151
Oakland Bean Cleaning & Storage
Knights Landing, CA 530-735-6203
Pleasant Grove Farms
Pleasant Grove, CA 916-655-3391
Red River Commodities Inc
Fargo, ND........................800-437-5539
Sprague Foods
Belleville, ON.....................613-966-1200
Teasdale Quality Foods Inc
Atwater, CA 209-358-5616
WG Thompson & Sons
Blenheim, ON.....................800-265-5225

Canned

Burnette Foods
Elk Rapids, MI 231-264-8116

Cordon Bleu International
Anjou, QC........800-363-1182
Emerling International Foods
Buffalo, NY........716-833-7381
International Home Foods
Parsippany, NJ........973-359-9920
Nation Wide Canning Ltd.
Cottam, ON........519-839-4831
New Era Canning Company
New Era, MI........231-861-2151
Red River Commodities Inc
Fargo, ND........800-437-5539
Vegetable Juices Inc
Chicago, IL........888-776-9752

Dark Red

Agrocan
Ville St Laurent, QC........877-247-6226
Cordon Bleu International
Anjou, QC........800-363-1182
Red River Commodities Inc
Fargo, ND........800-437-5539
Sprague Foods
Belleville, ON........613-966-1200

Frozen

Emerling International Foods
Buffalo, NY........716-833-7381
Vegetable Juices Inc
Chicago, IL........888-776-9752

Light Red

Jack's Bean Co LLC
Holyoke, CO........970-854-3702
Red River Commodities Inc
Fargo, ND........800-437-5539

Lentil

Agricore United
St Louis Park, MN........877-509-5865
Bob's Red Mill Natural Foods
Milwaukie, OR........800-349-2173
C & F Foods Inc
City Of Industry, CA........626-723-1000
Camellia Beans
Harahan, LA........504-733-8480
Emerling International Foods
Buffalo, NY........716-833-7381
Farmer Direct Organic
Regina, SK........306-563-7815
Garden Valley Corp
Sutherlin, OR........541-459-9565
HP Schmid
San Francisco, CA........415-765-5925
In Harvest Inc
Bemidji, MN........800-346-7032
Inland Empire Foods
Riverside, CA........888-452-3267
Kalustyan
New York, NY........800-352-3451
Mezza
Lake Forest, IL........888-206-6054
Mills Brothers Intl
Seattle, WA........206-575-3000
New Organics
Kenwood, CA........734-677-5570
Northwest Pea & Bean Co
Spokane Valley, WA........509-534-3821
Primo Foods
Toronto, ON........800-377-6945
Shah Trading Company
Scarborough, ON........416-292-6927
Spokane Seed Co
Spokane Valley, WA........800-359-8478
Timeless Seeds
Ulm, MT........406-866-3340
United Pulse Trading Inc
Bismarck, ND........701-751-1623
Wallace Grain & Pea Company
Pullman, WA........509-878-1561

Canned

Organic Planet
San Francisco, CA........415-765-5590

Lima

Bob's Red Mill Natural Foods
Milwaukie, OR........800-349-2173
California Fruit and Tomato Kitchens
Modesto, CA........209-574-9407
Country Cupboard
Lewisburg, PA........570-523-3211
Hanover Foods Corp
Hanover, PA........717-632-6000
In Harvest Inc
Bemidji, MN........800-346-7032
Lakeside Foods Inc.
Plainview, MN........507-534-3141
National Frozen Foods Corp
Seattle, WA........206-322-8900
Patterson Frozen Foods
Patterson, CA........209-892-2611
Pictsweet Co
Bells, TN........731-663-7600
Seabrook Brothers & Sons
Seabrook, NJ........856-455-8080
Smith Frozen Foods Inc
Weston, OR........541-566-3515
Trinidad Benham Corporation
Denver, CO........303-220-1400
Vege-Cool
Newman, CA........209-862-2360

Canned

Emerling International Foods
Buffalo, NY........716-833-7381
Hanover Foods Corp
Hanover, PA........717-632-6000
Lakeside Foods Inc.
Plainview, MN........507-534-3141

Frozen

Hanover Foods Corp
Hanover, PA........717-632-6000
National Frozen Foods Corp
Seattle, WA........206-322-8900
Paris Foods Corporation
Trappe, MD........410-200-9595
Pictsweet Co
Bells, TN........731-663-7600
Seabrook Brothers & Sons
Seabrook, NJ........856-455-8080
Smith Frozen Foods Inc
Weston, OR........541-566-3515

Lupini

Castella Imports Inc
Brentwood, NY........631-231-5500
Emerling International Foods
Buffalo, NY........716-833-7381
L & S Packing Co
Farmingdale, NY........800-286-6487

Mung

Green

Bob's Red Mill Natural Foods
Milwaukie, OR........800-349-2173
Commodities Marketing Inc
Clarksburg, NJ........732-516-0700
Eckroat Seed Company
Oklahoma City, OK........800-331-7333
Emerling International Foods
Buffalo, NY........716-833-7381
Jonathan's Sprouts
Rochester, MA........508-763-2577
Kalustyan
New York, NY........800-352-3451

Navy

Bob's Red Mill Natural Foods
Milwaukie, OR........800-349-2173
Central Bean Co
Quincy, WA........509-787-1544
Jack's Bean Co LLC
Holyoke, CO........970-854-3702
New Era Canning Company
New Era, MI........231-861-2151
Sprague Foods
Belleville, ON........613-966-1200

Canned

Emerling International Foods
Buffalo, NY........716-833-7381
New Era Canning Company
New Era, MI........231-861-2151

Pink

Central Bean Co
Quincy, WA........509-787-1544
Oakland Bean Cleaning & Storage
Knights Landing, CA........530-735-6203

Pinto

Agfinity Inc
Eaton, CO........800-433-4688
Agricore United
St Louis Park, MN........877-509-5865
Buxton Foods
Buxton, ND........800-726-8057
Central Bean Co
Quincy, WA........509-787-1544
Crookston Bean
Crookston, MN........218-281-2567
Emerling International Foods
Buffalo, NY........716-833-7381
Hanover Foods Corp
Hanover, PA........717-632-6000
International Home Foods
Parsippany, NJ........973-359-9920
Jack's Bean Co LLC
Holyoke, CO........970-854-3702
New Organics
Kenwood, CA........734-677-5570
Northern Feed & Bean Company
Lucerne, CO........800-316-2326
Organic Planet
San Francisco, CA........415-765-5590
Producers Cooperative
Bryan, TX........979-778-6000
Randall Food Products
Cincinnati, OH........513-793-6525
Russell E. Womack, Inc.
Lubbock, TX........877-787-3559
Teasdale Quality Foods Inc
Atwater, CA........209-358-5616
Trinidad Benham Corporation
Denver, CO........303-220-1400
Vegetable Juices Inc
Chicago, IL........888-776-9752

Refried

Amigos Canning Company
San Antonio, TX........210-798-5360
Hormel Foods Corp.
Austin, MN........507-437-5611
Teasdale Quality Foods Inc
Atwater, CA........209-358-5616

Canned

Amigos Canning Company
San Antonio, TX........210-798-5360
Morgan Foods Inc
Austin, IN........888-430-1780

Shoots

Houston Calco, Inc
Houston, TX........713-236-8668

Small Red

Central Bean Co
Quincy, WA........509-787-1544

Snap Green

Arbre Farms Inc
Walkerville, MI........231-873-3337
Boskovich Farms Inc
Oxnard, CA........805-487-2299

Snap Wax

Arbre Farms Inc
Walkerville, MI........231-873-3337

Wax

Hanover Foods Corp
Hanover, PA........717-632-6000
National Frozen Foods Corp
Seattle, WA........206-322-8900
New Era Canning Company
New Era, MI........231-861-2151
NORPAC Foods Inc
Salem, OR
Pictsweet Co
Bells, TN........731-663-7600

Seabrook Brothers & Sons
Seabrook, NJ 856-455-8080
Twin City Foods Inc.
Stanwood, WA 206-515-2400

Canned

Arbre Farms Inc
Walkerville, MI 231-873-3337
Carriere Foods Inc
Saint-Denis-Sur-Richelie, QC 450-787-3411
Emerling International Foods
Buffalo, NY 716-833-7381
New Era Canning Company
New Era, MI 231-861-2151
NORPAC Foods Inc
Salem, OR

Frozen

Arbre Farms Inc
Walkerville, MI 231-873-3337
Emerling International Foods
Buffalo, NY 716-833-7381
National Frozen Foods Corp
Seattle, WA 206-322-8900
NORPAC Foods Inc
Salem, OR
Pictsweet Co
Bells, TN 731-663-7600
Seabrook Brothers & Sons
Seabrook, NJ 856-455-8080
Twin City Foods Inc.
Stanwood, WA 206-515-2400

Beets

Boskovich Farms Inc
Oxnard, CA 805-487-2299
Dehydrates Inc
Hewlett, NY 800-983-4443
Earthbound Farm
San Jn Bautista, CA 800-690-3200
Gouw Quality Onions
Taber, AB 403-223-1440
Local Roots Farms
Burt, NY 716-946-3198
Love Beets
Bala Cynwyd, PA 856-692-1740
Old Country Packers
Duryea, PA 570-655-9608
Osowski Farms
Minto, ND 701-248-3341
Plenty
San Francisco, CA 650-735-3737
Sargent and Greenleaf
Nicholasville, KY 800-826-7652
Schiff Food Products Co Inc
Totowa, NJ 973-237-1990
Vegetable Juices Inc
Chicago, IL 888-776-9752

Canned

Emerling International Foods
Buffalo, NY 716-833-7381

Frozen

Emerling International Foods
Buffalo, NY 716-833-7381
Vegetable Juices Inc
Chicago, IL 888-776-9752

Sugar

Agri-Dairy Products
Purchase, NY 914-697-9580
Michigan Sugar Company
Bay City, MI 989-686-0161
Nyssa-Nampa Beet Growers
Nyssa, OR 541-372-2904
Osowski Farms
Minto, ND 701-248-3341
Western Sugar Cooperative
Denver, CO 800-523-7497

Berries

Abbotsford Growers Ltd.
Abbotsford, BC 604-864-0022
Allen's Blueberry Freezer Inc
Ellsworth, ME 207-667-5561
Atlantic Blueberry
Hammonton, NJ 609-561-8600
Behm Blueberry Farms
Grand Haven, MI 616-846-1650
Bluechip Group
Salt Lake City, UT 800-878-0099
Carolina Blueberry Co-Op Assn
Garland, NC 910-588-4220
Cherry Central Cooperative, Inc.
Traverse City, MI 231-946-1860
Coastal Classics
Duxbury, MA 508-746-6058
Country Fresh Inc
Spring, TX 281-453-3300
Crop Pharms, LLC
Staatsburg, NY 845-266-8999
Custom Produce Sales
Parlier, CA 559-254-5800
Decas Cranberry Sales Inc
Carver, MA 800-649-9811
Del Mar Food Products Corp
Watsonville, CA 831-722-3516
E.W. Bowker Company
Pemberton, NJ 609-894-9508
Earth Circle Organics
Auburn, CA 877-922-3663
Firestone Pacific Foods Co
Vancouver, WA 360-695-9484
From Oregon
Springfield, OR 541-747-4222
Giumarra Companies
Los Angeles, CA 213-627-2900
Graysmarsh Berry Farm
Sequim, WA 800-683-4367
Grow-Pac
Cornelius, OR 503-357-9691
J H Verbridge & Son Inc
Williamson, NY 315-589-2366
Jersey Fruit Co-Op
Glassboro, NJ 856-863-9100
K.B. Hall Ranch
Ojai, CA 805-525-5875
KERR Concentrates Inc
Salem, OR 800-910-5377
Krupka's Blueberries
Fennville, MI 269-857-4278
Leelanau Fruit Co
Peshawbestown, MI 231-271-3514
Macrie Brothers
Hammonton, NJ 609-561-6822
Meduri Farms
Dallas, OR 877-388-8800
Midwest Blueberry Farms
Holland, MI 616-399-2133
Norm's Farms
Purdy, MO 417-522-1375
North American Blueberry Council
Folsom, CA 800-824-6395
Oregon Raspberry & Blackberry Commission
Corvallis, OR 541-758-4043
Organic Nectars LLC
Malden On Hudson, NY 845-246-0506
Oxford Frozen Foods
Oxford, NS 902-447-2100
Pamlico Packing Company
Grantsboro, NC 800-682-1113
Peterson Farms Inc
Shelby, MI 231-861-0119
Plaidberry Company
Vista, CA 760-727-5403
R M Lawton Cranberries Inc
Middleboro, MA 508-947-7465
Ragold Confections
Wilton Manors, FL 954-566-9092
Reiter Affiliated Companies
Oxnard, CA 805-483-1000
Scenic Fruit Co
Gresham, OR 877-927-3434
Setton International Foods
Commack, NY 800-227-4397
Smeltzer Orchard Co
Frankfort, MI 231-882-4421
Snowcrest Packer
Abbotsford, BC 800-265-3686
Sunfood
El Cajon, CA 888-729-3663
Terri Lynn Inc
Elgin, IL 800-323-0775
Timber Crest Farms
Healdsburg, CA 888-766-4233
Tom Ringhausen Orchards
Hardin, IL 800-258-6645
Topaz Farm
Portland, OR 503-708-0008
Tru-Blu Cooperative Associates
New Lisbon, NJ 609-894-8717
True Blue Farms
Grand Junction, MI 877-654-2400
Valley View Blueberries
Vancouver, WA 360-892-2839
Vilore Foods Co Inc
Laredo, TX 956-722-7190
Well-Pict Inc
Watsonville, CA 831-722-3871
Wetherby Cranberry Company
Warrens, WI 608-378-4813
Wilhelm Foods
Newberg, OR 503-538-2929
Wish Farms
Plant City, FL 813-752-5111

Canned & Frozen

Abbotsford Growers Ltd.
Abbotsford, BC 604-864-0022
Allen's Blueberry Freezer Inc
Ellsworth, ME 207-667-5561
Atlantic Blueberry
Hammonton, NJ 609-561-8600
Carolina Blueberry Co-Op Assn
Garland, NC 910-588-4220
Cherry Central Cooperative, Inc.
Traverse City, MI 231-946-1860
E.W. Bowker Company
Pemberton, NJ 609-894-9508
G M Allen & Son Inc
Orland, ME 207-469-7060
Grow-Pac
Cornelius, OR 503-357-9691
J H Verbridge & Son Inc
Williamson, NY 315-589-2366
KERR Concentrates Inc
Salem, OR 800-910-5377
Leelanau Fruit Co
Peshawbestown, MI 231-271-3514
Oxford Frozen Foods
Oxford, NS 902-447-2100
Plaidberry Company
Vista, CA 760-727-5403
Scenic Fruit Co
Gresham, OR 877-927-3434
Snowcrest Packer
Abbotsford, BC 800-265-3686
Tru-Blu Cooperative Associates
New Lisbon, NJ 609-894-8717
True Blue Farms
Grand Junction, MI 877-654-2400
Unique Ingredients LLC
Gold Canyon, AZ 480-983-2498
Wawona Frozen Foods Inc
Clovis, CA 559-299-2901

Blackberry

Coloma Frozen Foods Inc
Coloma, MI 800-642-2723
Driscoll Strawberry Assoc Inc
Watsonville, CA 831-424-0506
Grow-Pac
Cornelius, OR 503-357-9691
KERR Concentrates Inc
Salem, OR 800-910-5377
North Bay Produce Inc
Traverse City, MI 231-946-1941
Oregon Fruit Products Co
Salem, OR 800-394-9333
Rainsweet Inc
Salem, OR 800-363-4293
Reiter Affiliated Companies
Oxnard, CA 805-483-1000
Sand Hill Berries
Mt Pleasant, PA 724-547-4760
Symons Frozen Foods
Centralia, WA 360-736-1321
Tom Ringhausen Orchards
Hardin, IL 800-258-6645
Unique Ingredients LLC
Gold Canyon, AZ 480-983-2498
Venture Vineyards
Lodi, NY 888-635-6277
Wish Farms
Plant City, FL 813-752-5111

Frozen

Coloma Frozen Foods Inc
Coloma, MI 800-642-2723

Emerling International Foods
Buffalo, NY....716-833-7381
Grow-Pac
Cornelius, OR....503-357-9691
KERR Concentrates Inc
Salem, OR....800-910-5377
Merrill's Blueberry Farms
Ellsworth, ME....800-711-6551
Oregon Fruit Products Co
Salem, OR....800-394-9333
Overlake Foods
Olympia, WA....800-683-1078
Paris Foods Corporation
Trappe, MD....410-200-9595
Rainsweet Inc
Salem, OR....800-363-4293
Symons Frozen Foods
Centralia, WA....360-736-1321
Townsend Farms Inc
Fairview, OR....503-666-1780
Unique Ingredients LLC
Gold Canyon, AZ....480-983-2498

Blueberry

Agvest
Cleveland, OH....216-464-3737
Allen's Blueberry Freezer Inc
Ellsworth, ME....207-667-5561
Blueberry Store
Grand Junction, MI....877-654-2400
Christy Wild Blueberry Farms
Amherst, NS....902-667-3013
Coloma Frozen Foods Inc
Coloma, MI....800-642-2723
Custom Produce Sales
Parlier, CA....559-254-5800
Diamond Blueberry Inc
Hammonton, NJ....609-561-3661
Driscoll Strawberry Assoc Inc
Watsonville, CA....831-424-0506
E.W. Bowker Company
Pemberton, NJ....609-894-9508
Earthbound Farm
San Jn Bautista, CA....800-690-3200
Enfield Farms Inc
Lynden, WA....360-354-2919
Fruit d'Or
Villeroy, QC....819-385-1126
G M Allen & Son Inc
Orland, ME....207-469-7060
Hawkins Farm
Bristol, WI....262-857-2616
Hialeah Products Co
Hollywood, FL....800-923-3379
Honee Bear Canning
Lawton, MI....800-626-2327
Indian Bay Frozen Foods
Centreville, NL....709-678-2844
Just Tomatoes
Westley, CA....800-537-1985
Krupka's Blueberries
Fennville, MI....269-857-4278
Maberry & Maberry Berry Associates
Lynden, WA....360-354-7708
Macrie Brothers
Hammonton, NJ....609-561-6822
Maine Wild Blueberry Company
Cherryfield, ME....800-243-4005
Meduri Farms
Dallas, OR....877-388-8800
Merrill's Blueberry Farms
Ellsworth, ME....800-711-6551
Midwest Blueberry Farms
Holland, MI....616-399-2133
New England Cranberry
Lynn, MA....800-410-2892
Niagara Foods
Middleport, NY....716-735-7722
North American Blueberry Council
Folsom, CA....800-824-6395
North Bay Produce Inc
Traverse City, MI....231-946-1941
Oregon Fruit Products Co
Salem, OR....800-394-9333
Pacific Coast Fruit Co
Portland, OR....503-234-6411
Pandol Brothers Inc
Delano, CA....661-725-3755
Peterson Farms Inc
Shelby, MI....231-861-0119
Producer Marketing Overlake
Olympia, WA....360-352-9096
Rainsweet Inc
Salem, OR....800-363-4293
Reiter Affiliated Companies
Oxnard, CA....805-483-1000
Royal Ridge Fruits
Royal City, WA....509-346-1520
Smeltzer Orchard Co
Frankfort, MI....231-882-4421
Snowcrest Packer
Abbotsford, BC....800-265-3686
Symons Frozen Foods
Centralia, WA....360-736-1321
Terri Lynn Inc
Elgin, IL....800-323-0775
Timber Crest Farms
Healdsburg, CA....888-766-4233
Townsend Farms Inc
Fairview, OR....503-666-1780
Unique Ingredients LLC
Gold Canyon, AZ....480-983-2498
Valley View Blueberries
Vancouver, WA....360-892-2839
Venture Vineyards
Lodi, NY....888-635-6277
Wild Blueberries
Old Town, ME....207-570-3535
Wish Farms
Plant City, FL....813-752-5111

Canned

Honee Bear Canning
Lawton, MI....800-626-2327
Maine Wild Blueberry Company
Cherryfield, ME....800-243-4005
Merrill's Blueberry Farms
Ellsworth, ME....800-711-6551
Oregon Fruit Products Co
Salem, OR....800-394-9333

Dried

Atwater Foods
Lyndonville Orleans, NY....585-765-2639
Bedemco Inc
White Plains, NY....914-683-1119
Golden Valley Natural
Shelley, ID....888-270-7147
Hodgson Mill Inc
Effingham, IL....800-347-0198
Setton International Foods
Commack, NY....800-227-4397

Frozen

Agvest
Cleveland, OH....216-464-3737
Allen's Blueberry Freezer Inc
Ellsworth, ME....207-667-5561
Bleuet Nordic
Dolbeau-Mistassini, QC....418-239-1001
Blueberry Store
Grand Junction, MI....877-654-2400
Christy Wild Blueberry Farms
Amherst, NS....902-667-3013
Diamond Blueberry Inc
Hammonton, NJ....609-561-3661
E.W. Bowker Company
Pemberton, NJ....609-894-9508
Earthbound Farm
San Jn Bautista, CA....800-690-3200
Emerling International Foods
Buffalo, NY....716-833-7381
Enfield Farms Inc
Lynden, WA....360-354-2919
Fruit d'Or
Villeroy, QC....819-385-1126
G M Allen & Son Inc
Orland, ME....207-469-7060
Maberry & Maberry Berry Associates
Lynden, WA....360-354-7708
Maine Wild Blueberry Company
Cherryfield, ME....800-243-4005
Oregon Fruit Products Co
Salem, OR....800-394-9333
Overlake Foods
Olympia, WA....800-683-1078
Pacific Coast Fruit Co
Portland, OR....503-234-6411
Paris Foods Corporation
Trappe, MD....410-200-9595
Rainsweet Inc
Salem, OR....800-363-4293
Snowcrest Packer
Abbotsford, BC....800-265-3686
Townsend Farms Inc
Fairview, OR....503-666-1780
Unique Ingredients LLC
Gold Canyon, AZ....480-983-2498

High Bush

Victor Packing
Madera, CA....559-673-5908

Boysenberry

KERR Concentrates Inc
Salem, OR....800-910-5377
Oregon Fruit Products Co
Salem, OR....800-394-9333
Rainsweet Inc
Salem, OR....800-363-4293

Canned

Oregon Fruit Products Co
Salem, OR....800-394-9333

Frozen

Emerling International Foods
Buffalo, NY....716-833-7381
KERR Concentrates Inc
Salem, OR....800-910-5377
Oregon Fruit Products Co
Salem, OR....800-394-9333
Rainsweet Inc
Salem, OR....800-363-4293
Townsend Farms Inc
Fairview, OR....503-666-1780

Canned

Emerling International Foods
Buffalo, NY....716-833-7381
Maine Wild Blueberry Company
Cherryfield, ME....800-243-4005
Plaidberry Company
Vista, CA....760-727-5403

Cranberry

Agvest
Cleveland, OH....216-464-3737
Coastal Classics
Duxbury, MA....508-746-6058
Decas Cranberry Sales Inc
Carver, MA....800-649-9811
E.W. Bowker Company
Pemberton, NJ....609-894-9508
Fruit d'Or
Villeroy, QC....819-385-1126
Hialeah Products Co
Hollywood, FL....800-923-3379
Joseph J. White
Browns Mills, NJ....609-893-2332
New England Cranberry
Lynn, MA....800-410-2892
Niagara Foods
Middleport, NY....716-735-7722
Pacific Coast Fruit Co
Portland, OR....503-234-6411
R M Lawton Cranberries Inc
Middleboro, MA....508-947-7465
Setton International Foods
Commack, NY....800-227-4397
Smeltzer Orchard Co
Frankfort, MI....231-882-4421
Snowcrest Packer
Abbotsford, BC....800-265-3686
Terri Lynn Inc
Elgin, IL....800-323-0775
Timber Crest Farms
Healdsburg, CA....888-766-4233
Unique Ingredients LLC
Gold Canyon, AZ....480-983-2498
Wetherby Cranberry Company
Warrens, WI....608-378-4813

Dried

American Importing Co.
Minneapolis, MN....855-273-0466
Atwater Foods
Lyndonville Orleans, NY....585-765-2639
Bedemco Inc
White Plains, NY....914-683-1119

Fruit d'Or	Villeroy, QC	819-385-1126
King Arthur Flour	Norwich, VT	800-827-6836
Mariani Packing Co.	Vacaville, CA	707-452-2800
Patience Fruit & Co.	Villeroy, QC	
Simply Incredible Foods	Port Edwards, WI	715-697-6232
Sunridge Farms	Royal Oaks, CA	831-786-7000

Frozen

Agvest	Cleveland, OH	216-464-3737
E.W. Bowker Company	Pemberton, NJ	609-894-9508
Fruit d'Or	Villeroy, QC	819-385-1126
Niagara Foods	Middleport, NY	716-735-7722
Pacific Coast Fruit Co	Portland, OR	503-234-6411
Simply Incredible Foods	Port Edwards, WI	715-697-6232
Snowcrest Packer	Abbotsford, BC	800-265-3686

Products

Emerling International Foods	Buffalo, NY	716-833-7381
Simply Incredible Foods	Port Edwards, WI	715-697-6232
Unique Ingredients LLC	Gold Canyon, AZ	480-983-2498

Whole

Patience Fruit & Co.	Villeroy, QC	
Simply Incredible Foods	Port Edwards, WI	715-697-6232

Currants

Crop Pharms, LLC	Staatsburg, NY	845-266-8999
Emerling International Foods	Buffalo, NY	716-833-7381
Milne Fruit Products Inc	Prosser, WA	509-786-2611
Pacific Coast Fruit Co	Portland, OR	503-234-6411
Setton International Foods	Commack, NY	800-227-4397

Red

Pacific Coast Fruit Co	Portland, OR	503-234-6411

Frozen

Abbotsford Growers Ltd.	Abbotsford, BC	604-864-0022
Agvest	Cleveland, OH	216-464-3737
Christy Wild Blueberry Farms	Amherst, NS	902-667-3013
Coloma Frozen Foods Inc	Coloma, MI	800-642-2723
Diamond Blueberry Inc	Hammonton, NJ	609-561-3661
E.W. Bowker Company	Pemberton, NJ	609-894-9508
Earthbound Farm	San Jn Bautista, CA	800-690-3200
Emerling International Foods	Buffalo, NY	716-833-7381
Enfield Farms Inc	Lynden, WA	360-354-2919
G M Allen & Son Inc	Orland, ME	207-469-7060
Grow-Pac	Cornelius, OR	503-357-9691
J H Verbridge & Son Inc	Williamson, NY	315-589-2366
Maberry & Maberry Berry Associates	Lynden, WA	360-354-7708
Maine Wild Blueberry Company	Cherryfield, ME	800-243-4005
Niagara Foods	Middleport, NY	716-735-7722
Ocean Spray International	Lakeville-Middleboro, MA	800-662-3263
Oregon Fruit Products Co	Salem, OR	800-394-9333
Overlake Foods	Olympia, WA	800-683-1078
Pacific Coast Fruit Co	Portland, OR	503-234-6411
Prairie Berries Inc.	Keeler, SK	306-788-2018
Rainsweet Inc	Salem, OR	800-363-4293
Snowcrest Packer	Abbotsford, BC	800-265-3686
Sunrise Growers	Placentia, CA	714-630-6292
Symons Frozen Foods	Centralia, WA	360-736-1321
Webster Farms	Cambridge, NS	800-507-8844

Goose

Oregon Fruit Products Co	Salem, OR	800-394-9333

Juniper

Schiff Food Products Co Inc	Totowa, NJ	973-237-1990

Lingonberries

Indian Bay Frozen Foods	Centreville, NL	709-678-2844

Mulberries

Kalustyan	New York, NY	800-352-3451

Raspberries

Bridenbaugh Orchards	Martinsburg, PA	814-793-2364
Coloma Frozen Foods Inc	Coloma, MI	800-642-2723
Decker Farms Inc	Hillsboro, OR	503-628-1532
Driscoll Strawberry Assoc Inc	Watsonville, CA	831-424-0506
Enfield Farms Inc	Lynden, WA	360-354-2919
Graysmarsh Berry Farm	Sequim, WA	800-683-4367
Heartland Strawberry Farm	Waterloo, IA	888-747-7423
Just Tomatoes	Westley, CA	800-537-1985
KERR Concentrates Inc	Salem, OR	800-910-5377
Mike & Jean's Berry Farm	Mt Vernon, WA	360-424-7220
Oregon Fruit Products Co	Salem, OR	800-394-9333
Pacific Coast Fruit Co	Portland, OR	503-234-6411
Rainsweet Inc	Salem, OR	800-363-4293
Reiter Affiliated Companies	Oxnard, CA	805-483-1000
Royal Ridge Fruits	Royal City, WA	509-346-1520
Sand Hill Berries	Mt Pleasant, PA	724-547-4760
Snowcrest Packer	Abbotsford, BC	800-265-3686
Strebin Farms	Troutdale, OR	503-665-8328
Symons Frozen Foods	Centralia, WA	360-736-1321
Terri Lynn Inc	Elgin, IL	800-323-0775
Townsend Farms Inc	Fairview, OR	503-666-1780
Unique Ingredients LLC	Gold Canyon, AZ	480-983-2498
Venture Vineyards	Lodi, NY	888-635-6277
Wish Farms	Plant City, FL	813-752-5111

Frozen

Abbotsford Growers Ltd.	Abbotsford, BC	604-864-0022
Coloma Frozen Foods Inc	Coloma, MI	800-642-2723
Earthbound Farm	San Jn Bautista, CA	800-690-3200
Emerling International Foods	Buffalo, NY	716-833-7381
Enfield Farms Inc	Lynden, WA	360-354-2919
KERR Concentrates Inc	Salem, OR	800-910-5377
Oregon Fruit Products Co	Salem, OR	800-394-9333
Overlake Foods	Olympia, WA	800-683-1078
Pacific Coast Fruit Co	Portland, OR	503-234-6411
Rainsweet Inc	Salem, OR	800-363-4293
Snowcrest Packer	Abbotsford, BC	800-265-3686
Strebin Farms	Troutdale, OR	503-665-8328
Symons Frozen Foods	Centralia, WA	360-736-1321
Townsend Farms Inc	Fairview, OR	503-666-1780
Unique Ingredients LLC	Gold Canyon, AZ	480-983-2498

Strawberry

Bluechip Group	Salt Lake City, UT	800-878-0099
Boskovich Farms Inc	Oxnard, CA	805-487-2299
Bridenbaugh Orchards	Martinsburg, PA	814-793-2364
Clofine Dairy Products Inc	Linwood, NJ	609-653-1000
Coloma Frozen Foods Inc	Coloma, MI	800-642-2723
Decker Farms Inc	Hillsboro, OR	503-628-1532
Del Mar Food Products Corp	Watsonville, CA	831-722-3516
Driscoll Strawberry Assoc Inc	Watsonville, CA	831-424-0506
Etchandy Farms	Anaheim, CA	
Grow-Pac	Cornelius, OR	503-357-9691
Hialeah Products Co	Hollywood, FL	800-923-3379
J H Verbridge & Son Inc	Williamson, NY	315-589-2366
KERR Concentrates Inc	Salem, OR	800-910-5377
Mike & Jean's Berry Farm	Mt Vernon, WA	360-424-7220
Niagara Foods	Middleport, NY	716-735-7722
Oregon Fruit Products Co	Salem, OR	800-394-9333
Pacific Coast Fruit Co	Portland, OR	503-234-6411
Paradise Inc	Plant City, FL	813-752-1155
Producer Marketing Overlake	Olympia, WA	360-352-9096
Rainsweet Inc	Salem, OR	800-363-4293
Reiter Affiliated Companies	Oxnard, CA	805-483-1000
Smeltzer Orchard Co	Frankfort, MI	231-882-4421
Snowcrest Packer	Abbotsford, BC	800-265-3686
Sunrise Growers	Placentia, CA	714-630-6292
T.S. Smith & Sons	Bridgeville, DE	302-337-8271
Terri Lynn Inc	Elgin, IL	800-323-0775
Townsend Farms Inc	Fairview, OR	503-666-1780
Unique Ingredients LLC	Gold Canyon, AZ	480-983-2498
Valley View Blueberries	Vancouver, WA	360-892-2839
Webster Farms	Cambridge, NS	800-507-8844
Well-Pict Inc	Watsonville, CA	831-722-3871

Wish Farms
Plant City, FL 813-752-5111

Canned

Emerling International Foods
Buffalo, NY.................... 716-833-7381
Oregon Fruit Products Co
Salem, OR.................... 800-394-9333
Overlake Foods
Olympia, WA 800-683-1078
Unique Ingredients LLC
Gold Canyon, AZ 480-983-2498

Dried

Atwater Foods
Lyndonville Orleans, NY 585-765-2639
Bedemco Inc
White Plains, NY 914-683-1119

Frozen

Coloma Frozen Foods Inc
Coloma, MI.................... 800-642-2723
Earthbound Farm
San Jn Bautista, CA 800-690-3200
Emerling International Foods
Buffalo, NY.................... 716-833-7381
Fruit Belt Canning Inc
Lawrence, MI 269-674-3939
Grow-Pac
Cornelius, OR.................... 503-357-9691
J H Verbridge & Son Inc
Williamson, NY 315-589-2366
KERR Concentrates Inc
Salem, OR.................... 800-910-5377
Niagara Foods
Middleport, NY.................... 716-735-7722
Overlake Foods
Olympia, WA 800-683-1078
Pacific Coast Fruit Co
Portland, OR 503-234-6411
Rainsweet Inc
Salem, OR.................... 800-363-4293
Snowcrest Packer
Abbotsford, BC.................... 800-265-3686
Sunrise Growers
Placentia, CA 714-630-6292
Townsend Farms Inc
Fairview, OR.................... 503-666-1780
Webster Farms
Cambridge, NS 800-507-8844

Brandied Fruits

Au Printemps Gourmet
Saint-Jerome, QC 800-438-6676
Dundee Brandied Fruit Co
Dundee, OR.................... 503-537-2500
Hurd Orchards
Holley, NY 585-638-8838
Jubilee Gourmet Creations
Manchester, NH 603-625-0654
Silver Palate Kitchens
Cresskill, NJ 201-568-0110

Broccoli

Boskovich Farms Inc
Oxnard, CA.................... 805-487-2299
Cal Harvest Marketing Inc
Hanford, CA 559-582-4494
D'Arrigo Brothers Company of California
Salinas, CA.................... 831-455-4500
Dehydrates Inc
Hewlett, NY 800-983-4443
Earthbound Farm
San Jn Bautista, CA 800-690-3200
Great American Appetizers
Nampa, ID.................... 800-282-4834
Hanover Foods Corp
Hanover, PA 717-632-6000
Kuhlmann's Market Gardens & Greenhouses
Edmonton, AB 780-475-7500
Mann Packing Co
Salinas, CA.................... 800-285-1002
Michigan Freeze Pack
Hart, MI.................... 231-873-2175
Patterson Frozen Foods
Patterson, CA 209-892-2611
Patterson Vegetable Company
Patterson, CA 209-892-2611
Pictsweet Co
Bells, TN.................... 731-663-7600
Snowcrest Packer
Abbotsford, BC.................... 800-265-3686
Talley Farms
Arroyo Grande, CA.................... 805-489-5400
Tanimura Antle Inc
Salinas, CA 800-772-4542
Teixeira Farms, Inc.
Santa Maria, CA 805-928-3801
Titan Farms
Ridge Spring, SC 803-685-5381
Vegetable Juices Inc
Chicago, IL 888-776-9752
Western Pacific Produce
Santa Barbara, CA 800-963-4451

Chopped

80 Acres Farms
Hamilton, OH 888-574-1569
Pictsweet Co
Bells, TN.................... 731-663-7600

Frozen

Emerling International Foods
Buffalo, NY.................... 716-833-7381
Great American Appetizers
Nampa, ID.................... 800-282-4834
Lisa's Organics
Carnelian Bay, CA 877-584-5711
Paris Foods Corporation
Trappe, MD.................... 410-200-9595
Pictsweet Co
Bells, TN.................... 731-663-7600
Snowcrest Packer
Abbotsford, BC.................... 800-265-3686
Sun Harvest Foods Inc
San Diego, CA 619-661-0909
Sure-Fresh Produce Inc
Santa Maria, CA 888-423-5379
Unique Ingredients LLC
Gold Canyon, AZ 480-983-2498
Vegetable Juices Inc
Chicago, IL 888-776-9752

Brussel Sprouts

Boskovich Farms Inc
Oxnard, CA.................... 805-487-2299
Miss Scarlett's Flowers
Juneau, AK 800-345-6734
Patterson Frozen Foods
Patterson, CA 209-892-2611
Pictsweet Co
Bells, TN.................... 731-663-7600
Snowcrest Packer
Abbotsford, BC.................... 800-265-3686
Star Fine Foods
Fresno, CA 559-498-2900

Frozen

Emerling International Foods
Buffalo, NY.................... 716-833-7381
Paris Foods Corporation
Trappe, MD.................... 410-200-9595
Pictsweet Co
Bells, TN.................... 731-663-7600
Snowcrest Packer
Abbotsford, BC.................... 800-265-3686

Cabbage

Boskovich Farms Inc
Oxnard, CA.................... 805-487-2299
Carando Gourmet Frozen Foods
Agawam, MA 888-227-2636
Club Chef LLC
Covington, KY 859-578-3100
Dehydrates Inc
Hewlett, NY 800-983-4443
Eckert Cold Storage
Manteca, CA.................... 209-823-3181
Exeter Produce
Exeter, ON.................... 519-235-0141
F & S Produce Co Inc
Vineland, NJ 800-886-3316
HH Dobbins Inc
Lyndonville, NY.................... 877-362-2467
Kuhlmann's Market Gardens & Greenhouses
Edmonton, AB 780-475-7500
Pacific Collier Fresh Company
Immokalee, FL 800-226-7274
R.C. McEntire & Company
Columbia, SC 803-799-3388
Russo Farms
Vineland, NJ 856-692-5942
Sales USA
Salado, TX 800-766-7344
Sure-Fresh Produce Inc
Santa Maria, CA 888-423-5379
Teixeira Farms, Inc.
Santa Maria, CA 805-928-3801
Vegetable Juices Inc
Chicago, IL 888-776-9752
Vessey & Co Inc
Holtville, CA.................... 760-356-0130

Bok Choy

AeroFarms
Newark, NJ 973-242-2495
Boskovich Farms Inc
Oxnard, CA.................... 805-487-2299
Eckert Cold Storage
Manteca, CA.................... 209-823-3181
Sure-Fresh Produce Inc
Santa Maria, CA 888-423-5379
Talley Farms
Arroyo Grande, CA.................... 805-489-5400
Vessey & Co Inc
Holtville, CA.................... 760-356-0130

Canned

Emerling International Foods
Buffalo, NY.................... 716-833-7381
Sure-Fresh Produce Inc
Santa Maria, CA 888-423-5379

Chinese

Pioneer Growers
Belle Glade, FL.................... 229-243-9306

Frozen

Carando Gourmet Frozen Foods
Agawam, MA 888-227-2636
Eckert Cold Storage
Manteca, CA.................... 209-823-3181
Emerling International Foods
Buffalo, NY.................... 716-833-7381
Ripon Pickle Co Inc
Ripon, WI 920-748-7110
Sure-Fresh Produce Inc
Santa Maria, CA 888-423-5379
Vegetable Juices Inc
Chicago, IL 888-776-9752

Green

Seneca Foods Corp
Princeville, IL.................... 309-385-4301
Vessey & Co Inc
Holtville, CA.................... 760-356-0130

Processed

Mama O's Premium Kimchi
Brooklyn, NY 917-326-1557

Red

F & S Produce Co Inc
Vineland, NJ 800-886-3316
Vessey & Co Inc
Holtville, CA.................... 760-356-0130

Cactus

D'Arrigo Brothers Company of California
Salinas, CA.................... 831-455-4500
True Nopal Cactus Water
Scottsdale, AZ.................... 480-636-8044

Candied Fruits

Crystallized, Glace

American Key Food Products Inc
Closter, NJ.................... 877-263-7539
California Custom Fruits
Baldwin Park, CA.................... 877-558-0056
Emerling International Foods
Buffalo, NY.................... 716-833-7381
Gray & Company
Hart, MI.................... 800-551-6009
Hialeah Products Co
Hollywood, FL 800-923-3379
King Arthur Flour
Norwich, VT.................... 800-827-6836

Limpert Bros Inc
Vineland, NJ 800-691-1353
Olde Tyme Food Corporation
East Longmeadow, MA 800-356-6533
Paradise Inc
Plant City, FL 813-752-1155
Reinhart Foods
Toronto, ON 416-645-4910
Scala-Wisell International Inc.
Floral Park, NY 516-437-8600
Setton International Foods
Commack, NY 800-227-4397
Unique Ingredients LLC
Gold Canyon, AZ 480-983-2498
Weaver Nut Co. Inc.
Ephrata, PA 800-473-2688

Canned Fruits

Agrocan
Ville St Laurent, QC 877-247-6226
B.M. Lawrence & Company
San Francisco, CA 415-981-2926
BGS Jourdan & Sons
Darlington, MD 410-457-4904
Bob Gordon & Associates
Oak Park, IL 708-524-9611
Burnette Foods
Elk Rapids, MI 231-264-8116
Coco Lopez Inc
Miramar, FL 800-341-2242
Curtice Burns Foods
Shortsville, NY 585-289-4414
Del Monte Foods Inc.
Walnut Creek, CA
Derco Foods Intl
Fresno, CA 559-435-2664
Emerling International Foods
Buffalo, NY 716-833-7381
Florida Citrus
Bartow, FL 863-537-3999
Hurd Orchards
Holley, NY 585-638-8838
International Home Foods
Parsippany, NJ 973-359-9920
Knouse Foods Co-Op Inc.
Peach Glen, PA 717-677-8181
L & S Packing Co
Farmingdale, NY 800-286-6487
Lancaster Packing Company
Myerstown, PA 717-397-9727
Maine Wild Blueberry Company
Cherryfield, ME 800-243-4005
Majestic Foods
Huntington, NY 631-424-9444
Manzana Products Co.
Sebastopol, CA 707-823-5313
Maui Gold Pineapple Company
Pukalani, HI 808-877-3805
Neil Jones Food Company
Vancouver, WA 800-291-3862
New Era Canning Company
New Era, MI 231-861-2151
Ntc Marketing
Williamsville, NY 800-333-1637
Oregon Cherry Growers Inc
Salem, OR
Oregon Fruit Products Co
Salem, OR 800-394-9333
Pacific Coast Producers
Lodi, CA 877-618-4776
Patterson Frozen Foods
Patterson, CA 209-892-2611
Plaidberry Company
Vista, CA 760-727-5403
Snokist Growers
Yakima, WA 800-377-2857
Triple D Orchards Inc
Empire, MI 231-326-5174
Truitt Bros Inc
Salem, OR 800-547-8712

Canned Vegetables

A. Lassonde Inc.
Rougemont, QC 866-552-7643
Appleton Produce Company
Weiser, ID 208-414-3352
B.M. Lawrence & Company
San Francisco, CA 415-981-2926
BGS Jourdan & Sons
Darlington, MD 410-457-4904
Bob Gordon & Associates
Oak Park, IL 708-524-9611
Border Foods
New Hope, MN 763-559-7338
Burnette Foods
Elk Rapids, MI 231-264-8116
Capitol Foods
Memphis, TN 662-781-9021
Carriere Foods Inc
Saint-Denis-Sur-Richelie, QC 450-787-3411
Coco Lopez Inc
Miramar, FL 800-341-2242
Cordon Bleu International
Anjou, QC 800-363-1182
Curtice Burns Foods
Shortsville, NY 585-289-4414
Deep Foods Inc
Union, NJ 908-810-7500
Del Monte Foods Inc.
Walnut Creek, CA
Dong Kee Company
Chicago, IL 312-225-6340
Ebro Foods
Chicago, IL 773-696-0150
Emerling International Foods
Buffalo, NY 716-833-7381
Escalon Premier Brand
Escalon, CA 209-838-7341
Fiesta Canning Co
Phoenix, AZ 602-212-2424
Ful-Flav-R Foods
Alamo, CA 925-838-0300
Gl Mezzetta Inc
American Canyon, CA 800-941-7044
Green Valley Foods
Salem, OR 844-588-3535
GWB Foods Corporation
Brooklyn, NY 877-977-7610
Hanover Foods Corp
Hanover, PA 717-632-6000
Hermann Pickle Co
Garrettsville, OH 800-245-2696
International Home Foods
Parsippany, NJ 973-359-9920
John N Wright Jr Inc
Federalsburg, MD 410-754-9044
Juanita's Foods
Wilmington, CA 800-303-2965
L & S Packing Co
Farmingdale, NY 800-286-6487
Lakeside Foods Inc.
Plainview, MN 507-534-3141
Lakeside Foods Inc.
Manitowoc, WI 800-466-3834
Lakeside Packing Company
Harrow, ON 519-738-2314
Lodi Canning Co
Lodi, WI 608-592-4236
Majestic Foods
Huntington, NY 631-424-9444
Mccall Farms
Effingham, SC 800-277-2012
Meridian Foods New Inc
Eaton, IN 765-396-3344
Miami Purveyors Inc
Miami, FL 800-966-6328
Milroy Canning Company
Milroy, IN 765-629-2221
Monterey Mushrooms Inc
Watsonville, CA 800-333-6874
Monticello Canning Company
Crossville, TN
Musco Family Olive Co
Tracy, CA 800-523-9828
Nation Wide Canning Ltd.
Cottam, ON 519-839-4831
Neil Jones Food Company
Vancouver, WA 800-291-3862
New Era Canning Company
New Era, MI 231-861-2151
New Harvest Foods
Washington, DC 920-822-2578
Nickabood's Inc
Los Angeles, CA 213-746-1541
NORPAC Foods Inc
Salem, OR
Northwest Packing Co
Vancouver, WA 800-543-4356
Pacific Coast Producers
Lodi, CA 877-618-4776
Paradise Products Corporation
Boca Raton, FL 800-826-1235
Pastene Co LTD
Canton, MA 781-298-3397
Patterson Frozen Foods
Patterson, CA 209-892-2611
Produits Ronald
St. Damase, QC 800-465-0118
Pure Food Ingredients
Verona, WI 800-355-9601
Ralph Sechler & Son Inc
St Joe, IN 800-332-5461
Red Gold Inc.
Elwood, IN 866-729-7187
Red River Commodities Inc
Fargo, ND 800-437-5539
Ron Son Foods Inc
Swedesboro, NJ 856-241-7333
San Antonio Farms
Platteville, WI 800-236-1119
Seneca Foods Corp
Marion, NY 315-926-8100
Simplot Food Group
Boise, ID 800-572-7783
Sun Harvest Foods Inc
San Diego, CA 619-661-0909
Sun-Brite Canning
Kingsville, ON 519-326-9033
Thomas Canning/Maidstone
Maidstone, ON 519-737-1531
Tolteca Foodservice
Norcross, GA 800-541-6835
Truitt Bros Inc
Salem, OR 800-547-8712
Unilever Food Solutions
Englewood Cliffs, NJ
United Canning Corporation
North Lima, OH 216-549-9807
Weil's Food Processing
Wheatley, ON 519-825-4572
Wornick Company
Cincinnati, OH 800-860-4555

Carrot

Boskovich Farms Inc
Oxnard, CA 805-487-2299
De Bruyn Produce Company
Ponpano Beach, FL 800-733-9177
Dehydrates Inc
Hewlett, NY 800-983-4443
Del Monte Fresh Produce Inc.
Coral Gables, FL 800-950-3683
Earthbound Farm
San Jn Bautista, CA 800-690-3200
Exeter Produce
Exeter, ON 519-235-0141
F & S Produce Co Inc
Vineland, NJ 800-886-3316
Fresh Express, Inc.
Salinas, CA 800-242-5472
Grimmway Farms
Bakersfield, CA 800-301-3101
Hanover Foods Corp
Hanover, PA 717-632-6000
JES Foods
Cleveland, OH 216-883-8987
Just Tomatoes
Westley, CA 800-537-1985
KERN Ridge Growers LLC
Arvin, CA 661-854-3141
Kuhlmann's Market Gardens & Greenhouses
Edmonton, AB 780-475-7500
Local Roots Farms
Burt, NY 716-946-3198
Miss Scarlett's Flowers
Juneau, AK 800-345-6734
National Frozen Foods Corp
Seattle, WA 206-322-8900
New Harvest Foods
Washington, DC 920-822-2578
Patterson Frozen Foods
Patterson, CA 209-892-2611
Pictsweet Co
Bells, TN 731-663-7600
Pioneer Growers
Belle Glade, FL 229-243-9306
R.C. McEntire & Company
Columbia, SC 803-799-3388
Ripon Pickle Co Inc
Ripon, WI 920-748-7110
Rousseau Farming Co
Phoenix, AZ 623-936-7100
Smith Frozen Foods Inc
Weston, OR 541-566-3515

Strathroy Foods
Strathroy, ON 519-245-4600
Twin City Foods Inc.
Stanwood, WA 206-515-2400
Vegetable Juices Inc
Chicago, IL 888-776-9752

Baby

Sales USA
Salado, TX 800-766-7344

Canned

Arbre Farms Inc
Walkerville, MI 231-873-3337
Emerling International Foods
Buffalo, NY 716-833-7381
Hanover Foods Corp
Hanover, PA 717-632-6000
New Harvest Foods
Washington, DC 920-822-2578

Dehydrated

Advanced Spice & Trading
Carrollton, TX 800-872-7811
Tova Industries LLC
Louisville, KY 888-532-8682

Frozen

Arbre Farms Inc
Walkerville, MI 231-873-3337
Emerling International Foods
Buffalo, NY 716-833-7381
Hanover Foods Corp
Hanover, PA 717-632-6000
National Frozen Foods Corp
Seattle, WA 206-322-8900
Paris Foods Corporation
Trappe, MD 410-200-9595
Pictsweet Co
Bells, TN 731-663-7600
Smith Frozen Foods Inc
Weston, OR 541-566-3515
Strathroy Foods
Strathroy, ON 519-245-4600
Twin City Foods Inc.
Stanwood, WA 206-515-2400
Vegetable Juices Inc
Chicago, IL 888-776-9752

Organic

Seneca Foods Corp
Princeville, IL 309-385-4301

Peeled

Chiquita Brands LLC.
Fort Lauderdale, FL 954-924-5700
Rousseau Farming Co
Phoenix, AZ 623-936-7100

with Greens

Boskovich Farms Inc
Oxnard, CA 805-487-2299

Cauliflower

Al Pete Meats
Muncie, IN 765-288-8817
Crown Packing Company
Salinas, CA 831-424-2067
Earthbound Farm
San Jn Bautista, CA 800-690-3200
EDCO Food Products Inc
Hobart, WI 800-255-3768
Exeter Produce
Exeter, ON 519-235-0141
F & S Produce Co Inc
Vineland, NJ 800-886-3316
Great American Appetizers
Nampa, ID 800-282-4834
Lake Erie Frozen Foods Co
Ashland, OH 800-766-8501
Long Island Cauliflower Assn
Riverhead, NY 631-727-2212
Mike & Jean's Berry Farm
Mt Vernon, WA 360-424-7220
Paradise Products Corporation
Boca Raton, FL 800-826-1235
Patterson Frozen Foods
Patterson, CA 209-892-2611
Pictsweet Co
Bells, TN 731-663-7600
Ripon Pickle Co Inc
Ripon, WI 920-748-7110
Sargent and Greenleaf
Nicholasville, KY 800-826-7652
Snowcrest Packer
Abbotsford, BC 800-265-3686
Tanimura Antle Inc
Salinas, CA 800-772-4542
Vegetable Juices Inc
Chicago, IL 888-776-9752

Canned

Emerling International Foods
Buffalo, NY 716-833-7381
Paradise Products Corporation
Boca Raton, FL 800-826-1235
Seneca Foods Corp
Marion, NY 315-926-8100

Frozen

Al Pete Meats
Muncie, IN 765-288-8817
Emerling International Foods
Buffalo, NY 716-833-7381
Great American Appetizers
Nampa, ID 800-282-4834
Paris Foods Corporation
Trappe, MD 410-200-9595
Pictsweet Co
Bells, TN 731-663-7600
Snowcrest Packer
Abbotsford, BC 800-265-3686

Celery

Boskovich Farms Inc
Oxnard, CA 805-487-2299
Crown Packing Company
Salinas, CA 831-424-2067
Dehydrates Inc
Hewlett, NY 800-983-4443
Earthbound Farm
San Jn Bautista, CA 800-690-3200
F & S Produce Co Inc
Vineland, NJ 800-886-3316
JES Foods
Cleveland, OH 216-883-8987
Leach Farms Inc
Berlin, WI 920-361-1880
Michigan Celery Cooperative
Hudsonville, MI 616-669-1250
Michigan Freeze Pack
Hart, MI 231-873-2175
Nature Quality
San Martin, CA 408-683-2182
Pioneer Growers
Belle Glade, FL 229-243-9306
R.C. McEntire & Company
Columbia, SC 803-799-3388
State Garden Inc.
Chelsea, MA
Sure-Fresh Produce Inc
Santa Maria, CA 888-423-5379
Tanimura Antle Inc
Salinas, CA 800-772-4542
Teixeira Farms, Inc.
Santa Maria, CA 805-928-3801
Tri-Counties Packing Company
Salinas, CA 831-422-7841

Canned

Emerling International Foods
Buffalo, NY 716-833-7381
Sure-Fresh Produce Inc
Santa Maria, CA 888-423-5379

Dehydrated

Advanced Spice & Trading
Carrollton, TX 800-872-7811
Emerling International Foods
Buffalo, NY 716-833-7381
Tova Industries LLC
Louisville, KY 888-532-8682
Unique Ingredients LLC
Gold Canyon, AZ 480-983-2498

Frozen

Emerling International Foods
Buffalo, NY 716-833-7381
Nature Quality
San Martin, CA 408-683-2182
Paris Foods Corporation
Trappe, MD 410-200-9595
Sure-Fresh Produce Inc
Santa Maria, CA 888-423-5379
Vegetable Juices Inc
Chicago, IL 888-776-9752

Sticks

R.C. McEntire & Company
Columbia, SC 803-799-3388

Cherries

Agvest
Cleveland, OH 216-464-3737
Bob Gordon & Associates
Oak Park, IL 708-524-9611
Bridenbaugh Orchards
Martinsburg, PA 814-793-2364
Brothers International Food Corporation
Rochester, NY 585-343-3007
Burnette Foods
Elk Rapids, MI 231-264-8116
Cahoon Farms
Wolcott, NY 315-594-9610
Cal Harvest Marketing Inc
Hanford, CA 559-582-4494
California Fruit Processors
Stockton, CA 209-931-1760
Castella Imports Inc
Brentwood, NY 631-231-5500
Chelan Fresh Marketing
Chelan, WA 509-682-2591
Cherry Central Cooperative, Inc.
Traverse City, MI 231-946-1860
Cherry Hill Orchards
Lancaster, PA 717-872-9311
Cherry Hut
Traverse City, MI 888-882-4431
Cherry Lane Frozen Fruits
Vineland Station, ON 877-243-7796
Chief Wenatchee
Wenatchee, WA 509-662-5197
Christopher Ranch LLC
Gilroy, CA 408-847-1100
Chukar Cherries
Prosser, WA 800-624-9544
Coloma Frozen Foods Inc
Coloma, MI 800-642-2723
Delta Packing
Lodi, CA 209-334-1023
Diamond Fruit Growers
Hood River, OR 541-354-5300
Earthbound Farm
San Jn Bautista, CA 800-690-3200
Fruit Acres Farm Market and U-Pick
Coloma, MI 269-208-3591
Giumarra Companies
Los Angeles, CA 213-627-2900
Gl Mezzetta Inc
American Canyon, CA 800-941-7044
Gray & Company
Hart, MI 800-551-6009
Harner Farms
State College, PA 814-237-7919
Honee Bear Canning
Lawton, MI 800-626-2327
J H Verbridge & Son Inc
Williamson, NY 315-589-2366
Just Tomatoes
Westley, CA 800-537-1985
Kalustyan
New York, NY 800-352-3451
L & S Packing Co
Farmingdale, NY 800-286-6487
Leroux Creek
Hotchkiss, CO 877-970-5670
Mason County Fruit Packers Cooperative
Hart, MI 231-873-7504
Meduri Farms
Dallas, OR 877-388-8800
Miss Scarlett's Flowers
Juneau, AK 800-345-6734
Natural Foods Inc
Toledo, OH 419-537-1711
Niagara Foods
Middleport, NY 716-735-7722

North Bay Produce Inc
Traverse City, MI 231-946-1941
Oneonta Starr Ranch Growers
Wenatchee, WA 509-663-2191
Oregon Cherry Growers Inc
Salem, OR
Oregon Fruit Products Co
Salem, OR 800-394-9333
Pandol Brothers Inc
Delano, CA 661-725-3755
Paradise Inc
Plant City, FL 813-752-1155
Paradise Products Corporation
Boca Raton, FL 800-826-1235
Peterson Farms Inc
Shelby, MI 231-861-0119
Price Co
Yakima, WA 509-966-4110
Purity Products
Plainview, NY 800-256-6102
Reinhart Foods
Toronto, ON 416-645-4910
Smeltzer Orchard Co
Frankfort, MI 231-882-4421
Snowcrest Packer
Abbotsford, BC 800-265-3686
Stadelman Fruit LLC
Zillah, WA 509-829-5145
Symms Fruit Ranch Inc
Caldwell, ID 208-459-4821
Terri Lynn Inc
Elgin, IL 800-323-0775
Timber Crest Farms
Healdsburg, CA 888-766-4233
Trinity Fruit Sale Co
Fresno, CA 559-433-3777
Triple D Orchards Inc
Empire, MI 231-326-5174
Unique Ingredients LLC
Gold Canyon, AZ 480-983-2498
Yakima Fresh
Yakima, WA 509-248-5770

Canned

Arbre Farms Inc
Walkerville, MI 231-873-3337
Bob Gordon & Associates
Oak Park, IL 708-524-9611
Burnette Foods
Elk Rapids, MI 231-264-8116
Emerling International Foods
Buffalo, NY 716-833-7381
Honee Bear Canning
Lawton, MI 800-626-2327
L & S Packing Co
Farmingdale, NY 800-286-6487
Oregon Cherry Growers Inc
Salem, OR
Oregon Fruit Products Co
Salem, OR 800-394-9333
Paradise Products Corporation
Boca Raton, FL 800-826-1235
Triple D Orchards Inc
Empire, MI 231-326-5174
Truitt Bros Inc
Salem, OR 800-547-8712
Unique Ingredients LLC
Gold Canyon, AZ 480-983-2498

Dried

American Importing Co.
Minneapolis, MN 855-273-0466
Atwater Foods
Lyndonville Orleans, NY 585-765-2639
Bedemco Inc
White Plains, NY 914-683-1119
King Arthur Flour
Norwich, VT 800-827-6836
Setton International Foods
Commack, NY 800-227-4397
South Bend Chocolate Co
South Bend, IN 800-301-4961

Frozen

Agvest
Cleveland, OH 216-464-3737
Arbre Farms Inc
Walkerville, MI 231-873-3337
Cahoon Farms
Wolcott, NY 315-594-9610
Cherry Lane Frozen Fruits
Vineland Station, ON 877-243-7796
Coloma Frozen Foods Inc
Coloma, MI 800-642-2723
Emerling International Foods
Buffalo, NY 716-833-7381
Fruithill Inc
Yamhill, OR 503-662-3926
Great Lakes Packing Co
Kewadin, MI 231-264-5561
Honee Bear Canning
Lawton, MI 800-626-2327
J H Verbridge & Son Inc
Williamson, NY 315-589-2366
Leelanau Fruit Co
Peshawbestown, MI 231-271-3514
Mason County Fruit Packers Cooperative
Hart, MI 231-873-7504
Muir Copper Canyon Farms
Salt Lake City, UT 800-564-0949
Niagara Foods
Middleport, NY 716-735-7722
Norfood Cherry Growers
Simcoe, ON 519-426-5784
Oregon Cherry Growers Inc
Salem, OR
Oregon Fruit Products Co
Salem, OR 800-394-9333
Smeltzer Orchard Co
Frankfort, MI 231-882-4421
Snowcrest Packer
Abbotsford, BC 800-265-3686
Townsend Farms Inc
Fairview, OR 503-666-1780
Triple D Orchards Inc
Empire, MI 231-326-5174
Unique Ingredients LLC
Gold Canyon, AZ 480-983-2498

Maraschino

Bells Foods International
Gervais, OR 503-390-1425
Bob Gordon & Associates
Oak Park, IL 708-524-9611
Eden Processing
Poplar Grove, IL 815-765-2000
Emerling International Foods
Buffalo, NY 716-833-7381
Gl Mezzetta Inc
American Canyon, CA 800-941-7044
Gray & Company
Hart, MI 800-551-6009
Johnson Foods, Inc. - Cannery Plant
Sunnyside, WA 509-837-4188
L & S Packing Co
Farmingdale, NY 800-286-6487
Metzger Specialty Brands
New York, NY 212-957-0055
Oregon Cherry Growers Inc
Salem, OR
Pacific Choice Brands
Fresno, CA 559-476-3581
Paradise Products Corporation
Boca Raton, FL 800-826-1235
Purity Products
Plainview, NY 800-256-6102
Reinhart Foods
Toronto, ON 416-645-4910
Seneca Foods Corp
Marion, NY 315-926-8100
Unique Ingredients LLC
Gold Canyon, AZ 480-983-2498

Sweet

Peterson Farms Inc
Shelby, MI 231-861-0119
Royal Ridge Fruits
Royal City, WA 509-346-1520

Tart

Cherry Hill Orchards
Lancaster, PA 717-872-9311
Fruit Belt Canning Inc
Lawrence, MI 269-674-3939
Royal Ridge Fruits
Royal City, WA 509-346-1520
South Bend Chocolate Co
South Bend, IN 800-301-4961

Chicory

Whole Herb Co
Sonoma, CA 707-935-1077

Chives

SupHerb Farms
Turlock, CA 800-787-4372
Vegetable Juices Inc
Chicago, IL 888-776-9752

Citrus Fruits

Armistead Citrus Company
Mesa, AZ 480-830-2491
Brooks Tropicals Inc
Homestead, FL 800-327-4833
Brothers International Food Corporation
Rochester, NY 585-343-3007
Conoley Citrus Packers Inc
Winter Garden, FL 407-656-3300
Corona College Heights
Riverside, CA 951-351-7880
Crown Processing Company
Cerritos, CA 562-865-0293
Del Monte Fresh Produce Inc.
Coral Gables, FL 800-950-3683
Di Mare Fresh Inc
Fort Worth, TX 817-385-3000
DNE World Fruit Sales
Fort Pierce, FL 800-327-6676
Dundee Citrus Growers Assn
Dundee, FL 800-447-1574
Dundee Groves
Dundee, FL 800-294-2266
Evans Properties
Vero Beach, FL 772-234-2410
Fillmore Piru Citrus
Piru, CA 805-521-1781
Golden River Fruit Company
Vero Beach, FL 772-562-8610
Haines City Citrus Growers
Haines City, FL 800-327-6676
Heller Brothers Packing Corp
Winter Garden, FL 855-543-5537
Hunt Brothers Cooperative
Lake Wales, FL 863-676-1411
Magnolia Citrus Assn
Porterville, CA 559-784-4455
Mixon Fruit Farms Inc
Bradenton, FL 800-608-2525
North Bay Produce Inc
Traverse City, MI 231-946-1941
Oneonta Starr Ranch Growers
Wenatchee, WA 509-663-2191
Orange Cove-Sanger Citrus
Orange Cove, CA 559-626-4453
P R Farms Inc
Clovis, CA 559-299-0201
Reed Lang Farms
Rio Hondo, TX 956-748-2354
Shields Date Garden
Indio, CA 800-414-2555
Sun Groves Inc
Safety Harbor, FL 800-672-6438
Sun Pacific
Pasadena, CA 213-612-9957
Tony Vitrano Company
Jessup, MD 800-481-3784
Visalia Citrus Packing Group
Woodlake, CA 559-564-3351
Wileman Brothers & Elliott Inc
Cutler, CA 559-528-4772
Wonderful Citrus
Mission, TX 956-205-7300
Yokohl Packing Co
Lindsay, CA 559-562-1327

Peels

Con Yeager Spice Co
Zelienople, PA 800-222-2460
Crown Processing Company
Cerritos, CA 562-865-0293
Paradise Inc
Plant City, FL 813-752-1155
Vita-Pakt Citrus Products Co
Covina, CA 888-684-8272

Citrus Peel Products

Eden Processing
Poplar Grove, IL 815-765-2000

Fmali Herb
Santa Cruz, CA 831-423-7913
Vita-Pakt Citrus Products Co
Covina, CA 888-684-8272

Coconut & Coconut Products

Alpha Health
Burnaby, BC 888-826-9625
American Key Food Products Inc
Closter, NJ 877-263-7539
Baker's Coconut
East Hanover, NJ 855-535-5648
Blue Marble Brands
Providence, RI 888-534-0246
Coconut Beach
Bonita, CA
Commodities Marketing Inc
Clarksburg, NJ 732-516-0700
Eden Processing
Poplar Grove, IL 815-765-2000
Emerling International Foods
Buffalo, NY 716-833-7381
Hawaii Candy Inc
Honolulu, HI 800-303-2507
Hearty Naturals
West McLean, VA 513-443-2789
Hialeah Products Co
Hollywood, FL 800-923-3379
L & M Bakery
Riverside, NJ 888-887-1335
Marx Brothers Inc
Birmingham, AL 800-633-6376
Maverick Brands, LLC
Palo Alto, CA 424-571-7230
Mehaffies Pies
Dayton, OH 800-289-7437
Miramar Fruit Trading Company
Doral, FL 305-883-4774
Munkijo
Irvine, CA 949-861-2798
Olde Tyme Mercantile
Arroyo Grande, CA 805-489-7991
Organics Unlimited
San Diego, CA 619-710-0658
Premier Organics
Oakland, CA 866-237-8688
Red V Foods
Buford, GA 770-729-8983
Reinhart Foods
Toronto, ON 416-645-4910
Rv Industries
Buford, GA 770-729-8983
Sally Lane's Candy Farm
Paris, TN 731-642-5801
Spicy Sense
Kearny, NJ 718-790-0070
White-Stokes Company
Chicago, IL 800-978-6537
Wildly Organic
Silver Bay, MN 800-945-3801

Desiccated & Shredded

Commodities Marketing Inc
Clarksburg, NJ 732-516-0700
Emerling International Foods
Buffalo, NY 716-833-7381
International Coconut Corp
Elizabeth, NJ 908-289-1555
King Arthur Flour
Norwich, VT 800-827-6836
Loghouse Foods
Minneapolis, MN 763-546-8395
Organic Planet
San Francisco, CA 415-765-5590
Rv Industries
Buford, GA 770-729-8983
Service Packing Company
Vancouver, BC 604-681-0264
Setton International Foods
Commack, NY 800-227-4397

Dried

Bedemco Inc
White Plains, NY 914-683-1119
Hialeah Products Co
Hollywood, FL 800-923-3379
King Arthur Flour
Norwich, VT 800-827-6836
To Your Health Sprouted Flour Co., Inc.
Floyd, VA 540-283-9589

Frozen

Emerling International Foods
Buffalo, NY 716-833-7381

Processed

Hialeah Products Co
Hollywood, FL 800-923-3379

Collard Greens

Earthbound Farm
San Jn Bautista, CA 800-690-3200
Emerling International Foods
Buffalo, NY 716-833-7381
Oxford Frozen Foods
Oxford, NS 902-447-2100
Pictsweet Co
Bells, TN 731-663-7600
Seabrook Brothers & Sons
Seabrook, NJ 856-455-8080

Canned & Frozen

Paris Foods Corporation
Trappe, MD 410-200-9595
Pictsweet Co
Bells, TN 731-663-7600
Seabrook Brothers & Sons
Seabrook, NJ 856-455-8080
Walter P Rawl & Sons Inc
Pelion, SC 803-894-1900

Corn

A. Lassonde Inc.
Rougemont, QC 866-552-7643
Abbott & Cobb Inc
Feasterville, PA 800-345-7333
Christopher Ranch LLC
Gilroy, CA 408-847-1100
Coutts Specialty Foods Inc
Boxborough, MA 800-919-2952
Dehydrates Inc
Hewlett, NY 800-983-4443
Didion Milling Inc
Johnson Creek, WI 920-348-6816
DuPont Pioneer
Johnston, IA 515-535-5954
F & S Produce Co Inc
Vineland, NJ 800-886-3316
Fruit Acres Farm Market and U-Pick
Coloma, MI 269-208-3591
Furmano's Foods
Northumberland, PA 800-952-1111
John Copes Food Products
Hanover, PA 800-888-4646
Just Tomatoes
Westley, CA 800-537-1985
Lakeside Foods Inc.
Plainview, MN 507-534-3141
Miss Scarlett's Flowers
Juneau, AK 800-345-6734
National Frozen Foods Corp
Seattle, WA 206-322-8900
Natural Way Mills Inc
Middle River, MN 218-222-3677
New Harvest Foods
Washington, DC 920-822-2578
NSG Transport Inc
Gothenburg, NE 308-537-7191
Paradise Products Corporation
Boca Raton, FL 800-826-1235
Pioneer Growers
Belle Glade, FL 229-243-9306
Pop Art Snacks
Salt Lake City, UT 801-983-7470
Produits Ronald
St. Damase, QC 800-465-0118
Roberts Seed
Axtell, NE 308-743-2565
Smith Frozen Foods Inc
Weston, OR 541-566-3515
Sno-Pac Foods Inc
Caledonia, MN 800-533-2215
Snowcrest Packer
Abbotsford, BC 800-265-3686
Sonne
Wahpeton, ND 800-727-6663
Subco Foods Inc
Sheboygan, WI 800-473-0757
Symons Frozen Foods
Centralia, WA 360-736-1321
Twin City Foods Inc.
Stanwood, WA 206-515-2400
Unique Ingredients LLC
Gold Canyon, AZ 480-983-2498
Vegetable Juices Inc
Chicago, IL 888-776-9752
Veronica Foods Inc
Oakland, CA 800-370-5554
Z&S Distributing
Fresno, CA 800-467-0788

Canned

A. Lassonde Inc.
Rougemont, QC 866-552-7643
Carriere Foods Inc
Saint-Denis-Sur-Richelie, QC 450-787-3411
Emerling International Foods
Buffalo, NY 716-833-7381
Lakeside Foods Inc.
Plainview, MN 507-534-3141
Lakeside Foods Inc.
Manitowoc, WI 800-466-3834
Lodi Canning Co
Lodi, WI 608-592-4236
New Harvest Foods
Washington, DC 920-822-2578
Paradise Products Corporation
Boca Raton, FL 800-826-1235
Produits Ronald
St. Damase, QC 800-465-0118
SEW Friel
Queenstown, MD 410-827-8841

Canned & Frozen

Seneca Foods Corp
Princeville, IL 309-385-4301

Corn-on-the-Cob

A. Lassonde Inc.
Rougemont, QC 866-552-7643
AgriNorthwest
Kennewick, WA 509-734-1195
Emerling International Foods
Buffalo, NY 716-833-7381
National Frozen Foods Corp
Seattle, WA 206-322-8900
Pictsweet Co
Bells, TN 731-663-7600
Produits Ronald
St. Damase, QC 800-465-0118
Smith Frozen Foods Inc
Weston, OR 541-566-3515
Twin City Foods Inc.
Stanwood, WA 206-515-2400

Frozen

Bennett's Apples & Cider
Ancaster, ON 905-648-6878
National Frozen Foods Corp
Seattle, WA 206-322-8900
Pictsweet Co
Bells, TN 731-663-7600
Smith Frozen Foods Inc
Weston, OR 541-566-3515
Twin City Foods Inc.
Stanwood, WA 206-515-2400
Vessey & Co Inc
Holtville, CA 760-356-0130

Frozen

Lakeside Foods Inc.
Plainview, MN 507-534-3141
Lakeside Foods Inc.
Manitowoc, WI 800-466-3834
Lisa's Organics
Carnelian Bay, CA 877-584-5711
Lodi Canning Co
Lodi, WI 608-592-4236
Ocean Mist Farms
Castroville, CA 831-633-2144
Paris Foods Corporation
Trappe, MD 410-200-9595
Smith Frozen Foods Inc
Weston, OR 541-566-3515
Snowcrest Packer
Abbotsford, BC 800-265-3686
Symons Frozen Foods
Centralia, WA 360-736-1321
Zuccaro Produce
Columbia Heights, MN 612-333-1122

Stored

Acme Steak & Seafood
Youngstown, OH. 800-686-2263
Seneca Foods Corp
Marion, NY. 315-926-8100

Sweet

Christopher Ranch LLC
Gilroy, CA. 408-847-1100
New Harvest Foods
Washington, DC 920-822-2578
T.S. Smith & Sons
Bridgeville, DE. 302-337-8271

Cranberries

Rainsweet Inc
Salem, OR. 800-363-4293

Crushed

Baldwin Richardson Foods
Oakbrook Terrace, IL 866-644-2732
Clofine Dairy Products Inc
Linwood, NJ 609-653-1000
Emerling International Foods
Buffalo, NY. 716-833-7381

Crysanthemums

Heritage Farms Dairy
Murfreesboro, TN. 615-895-2790

Cucumber

Abbott & Cobb Inc
Feasterville, PA. 800-345-7333
Ben B. Schwartz & Sons
Detroit, MI 313-841-8300
Carson City Pickle Company
Carson City, MI. 989-584-3148
Cates Addis Company
Parkton, NC 800-423-1883
Earthbound Farm
San Jn Bautista, CA 800-690-3200
F & S Produce Co Inc
Vineland, NJ 800-886-3316
Giumarra Companies
Los Angeles, CA. 213-627-2900
Nash Produce
Nashville, NC 800-334-3032
Pacific Collier Fresh Company
Immokalee, FL 800-226-7274
Rene Produce Dist
Rio Rico, AZ. 520-281-0806
Russo Farms
Vineland, NJ 856-692-5942
United Pickles
Bronx, NY. 718-933-6060
United With Earth
Berkeley, CA. 510-210-4359
Vegetable Juices Inc
Chicago, IL 888-776-9752
Wholesum Family Farms
Nogales, AZ 520-281-9233
Wildcat Produce
McGrew, NE. 308-783-2438
Z&S Distributing
Fresno, CA 800-467-0788

for Pickling

Bissett Produce Company
Spring Hope, NC. 800-849-5073
Rick's Picks
Brooklyn, NY 212-358-0428

Dates

Alya Foods
North Brunswick, NJ 917-495-0815
American Importing Co.
Minneapolis, MN 855-273-0466
Amport Foods
St. Paul, MN 800-236-1119
Bard Valley Medjool Date Growers
Yuma, AZ 928-726-0901
Bautista Family Organic Date
Mecca, CA 760-396-2337
Date Lady Inc.
Springfield, MO 417-414-2282
Desert Valley Date
Coachella, CA. 760-398-0999
Double Date Packing
Coachella, CA. 760-398-8900
Emerling International Foods
Buffalo, NY. 716-833-7381
Hadley's Date Gardens
Thermal, CA 760-399-5191
Kalustyan
New York, NY 800-352-3451
Lee Andersons
Coachella, CA. 760-398-3441
Marin Food Specialties
Byron, CA. 925-634-6126
New Organics
Kenwood, CA 734-677-5570
Noour Inc.
Huntington Beach, CA 800-621-1378
Nut Factory
Spokane Valley, WA 888-239-5288
Peter Rabbit Farms
Coachella, CA. 760-398-0136
Reinhart Foods
Toronto, ON 416-645-4910
Royal Medjool Date Gardens
Bard, CA 760-572-0524
Sahara Date Company
Vienna, VA 703-745-7463
Service Packing Company
Vancouver, BC 604-681-0264
Setton International Foods
Commack, NY 800-227-4397
Shields Date Garden
Indio, CA. 800-414-2555
Sunfood
El Cajon, CA. 888-729-3663
Sweet Pillar
Newport Beach, CA 310-913-7261
Terri Lynn Inc
Elgin, IL 800-323-0775
Timber Crest Farms
Healdsburg, CA 888-766-4233
To Your Health Sprouted Flour Co., Inc.
Floyd, VA 540-283-9589
United With Earth
Berkeley, CA. 510-210-4359

Dehydrated

Abbotsford Growers Ltd.
Abbotsford, BC. 604-864-0022
Advanced Spice & Trading
Carrollton, TX. 800-872-7811
Agvest
Cleveland, OH 216-464-3737
Amport Foods
St. Paul, MN 800-236-1119
Associated Fruit Company
Phoenix, OR 541-535-1787
Atlantic Blueberry
Hammonton, NJ 609-561-8600
Bay Cities Produce Co Inc
San Leandro, CA. 510-346-4943
California Fruit and Tomato Kitchens
Modesto, CA. 209-574-9407
Caltex Foods
Canoga Park, CA 800-522-5839
Carolina Blueberry Co-Op Assn
Garland, NC 910-588-4220
Century Blends LLC
Hunt Valley, MD. 410-771-6606
Chazy Orchards
Chazy, NY. 518-846-7171
Cherry Central Cooperative, Inc.
Traverse City, MI 231-946-1860
Cherry Hill Orchards
Lancaster, PA. 717-872-9311
Chooljian Bros Packing Co
Sanger, CA 559-875-5501
Chukar Cherries
Prosser, WA. 800-624-9544
Congdon Orchards Inc.
Yakima, WA 509-966-4440
Cooperative Elevator Co
Pigeon, MI 800-968-0601
Crane & Crane Inc
Brewster, WA 509-689-3447
Del Rey Packing
Del Rey, CA. 559-888-2031
Fig Garden Packing Inc
Fresno, CA 559-271-9000
Fine Dried Foods Intl
Santa Cruz, CA. 831-426-1413
Hialeah Products Co
Hollywood, FL 800-923-3379
Larsen Farms
Hamer, ID 208-374-5592
Made In Nature
Boulder, CO 800-906-7426
Mayfield Farms and Nursery
Athens, TN 423-746-9859
Mercer Processing
Modesto, CA. 209-529-0150
Oxford Frozen Foods
Oxford, NS 902-447-2100
Paisano Food Products
Elk Grove Village, IL 800-672-4726
Powder Pure
The Dalles, OR 541-298-4800
Red River Foods Inc
Richmond, VA. 804-320-1800
Reinhart Foods
Toronto, ON 416-645-4910
RFi Ingredients
Blauvelt, NY. 800-962-7663
Serv-Agen Corporation
Cherry Hill, NJ 856-663-6966
Shields Date Garden
Indio, CA. 800-414-2555
Smeltzer Orchard Co
Frankfort, MI 231-882-4421
Solana Gold Organics
Sebastopol, CA 800-459-1121
Terri Lynn Inc
Elgin, IL 800-323-0775
Timber Crest Farms
Healdsburg, CA 888-766-4233
Tova Industries LLC
Louisville, KY 888-532-8682
Tru-Blu Cooperative Associates
New Lisbon, NJ 609-894-8717
True Blue Farms
Grand Junction, MI. 877-654-2400
Ursula's Island Farms Company
Seattle, WA 206-762-3113
Valley View Packing Co
Yuba City, CA. 530-673-7356
Washington Potato Company
Pasco, WA. 800-897-2726
Wenda America Inc
Naperville, IL 844-999-3632
White Oaks Frozen Foods
Merced, CA. 209-725-9492
Zuccaro Produce
Columbia Heights, MN. 612-333-1122

Freeze Dried

Advanced Spice & Trading
Carrollton, TX. 800-872-7811
Oregon Freeze Dry, Inc.
Albany, OR 541-926-6001
RFi Ingredients
Blauvelt, NY. 800-962-7663
Setton International Foods
Commack, NY 800-227-4397
SupHerb Farms
Turlock, CA 800-787-4372
Unique Ingredients LLC
Gold Canyon, AZ 480-983-2498
Van Drunen Farms
Momence, IL. 815-472-3100

Dipping Fruit

Confectioners'

Baldwin Richardson Foods
Oakbrook Terrace, IL 866-644-2732
Bella Viva Orchards
Hughson, CA 800-552-8218
Terri Lynn Inc
Elgin, IL 800-323-0775

Dried & Dehydrated Fruits

Dehydrated Fruit

Agvest
Cleveland, OH 216-464-3737
American Nut & Chocolate Co
Boston, MA. 800-797-6887
Amport Foods
St. Paul, MN 800-236-1119
Bautista Family Organic Date
Mecca, CA 760-396-2337
Casados Farms
Ohkay Owingeh, NM 505-852-2433

Century Blends LLC
Hunt Valley, MD . . . 410-771-6606
Chaucer Foods, Inc. USA
Forest Grove, OR
Cherry Central Cooperative, Inc.
Traverse City, MI . . . 231-946-1860
Chukar Cherries
Prosser, WA . . . 800-624-9544
Clic International Inc
Laval, QC . . . 450-669-2663
Desert Valley Date
Coachella, CA . . . 760-398-0999
Fig Garden Packing Inc
Fresno, CA . . . 559-271-9000
Fine Dried Foods Intl
Santa Cruz, CA . . . 831-426-1413
Freeman Industries
Tuckahoe, NY . . . 800-666-6454
Fruition Northwest LLC
North Plains, OR . . . 503-880-5193
Golden Town Apple Products
Rougemont, QC . . . 866-552-7643
Gulf Pecan Company
Mobile, AL . . . 251-661-2931
Hialeah Products Co
Hollywood, FL . . . 800-923-3379
Hurd Orchards
Holley, NY . . . 585-638-8838
Kamish Food Products
Chicago, IL . . . 773-725-6959
Kozlowski Farms
Forestville, CA . . . 800-473-2767
Leroux Creek
Hotchkiss, CO . . . 877-970-5670
Made In Nature
Boulder, CO . . . 800-906-7426
Maine Wild Blueberry Company
Cherryfield, ME . . . 800-243-4005
Mariani Packing Co.
Vacaville, CA . . . 707-452-2800
Marshall Ingredients
Wolcott, NY . . . 800-796-9353
Mercer Processing
Modesto, CA . . . 209-529-0150
Niagara Foods
Middleport, NY . . . 716-735-7722
Organic Planet
San Francisco, CA . . . 415-765-5590
Ramos Orchards
Winters, CA . . . 530-795-4748
Red River Foods Inc
Richmond, VA . . . 804-320-1800
S&P Marketing, Inc.
Maple Grove, MN . . . 763-559-0436
Sensible Foods LLC
Santa Rosa, CA . . . 888-222-0170
Shields Date Garden
Indio, CA . . . 800-414-2555
Silva International
Momence, IL . . . 815-472-3535
Specialty Ingredients
Buffalo Grove, IL . . . 847-419-9595
Spice King Corporation
Beverly Hills, CA . . . 310-836-7770
Spreda Group
Louisville, KY . . . 502-426-9411
Sunridge Farms
Royal Oaks, CA . . . 831-786-7000
Timber Crest Farms
Healdsburg, CA . . . 888-766-4233
Torn & Glasser
Los Angeles, CA . . . 800-282-6887
Torn Ranch
Novato, CA . . . 707-796-7800
Ursula's Island Farms Company
Seattle, WA . . . 206-762-3113
Valley View Packing Co
Yuba City, CA . . . 530-673-7356
Van Drunen Farms
Momence, IL . . . 815-472-3100
World Nutrition, Inc.
Scottsdale, AZ . . . 800-548-2710
Yogavive
Tiburon, CA . . . 415-366-6226

Desiccated Fruit

Fig Garden Packing Inc
Fresno, CA . . . 559-271-9000
Hialeah Products Co
Hollywood, FL . . . 800-923-3379
Kozlowski Farms
Forestville, CA . . . 800-473-2767
Leroux Creek
Hotchkiss, CO . . . 877-970-5670
Maine Wild Blueberry Company
Cherryfield, ME . . . 800-243-4005
Ramos Orchards
Winters, CA . . . 530-795-4748
San Joaquin Figs Inc
Fresno, CA . . . 559-224-4963
Spreda Group
Louisville, KY . . . 502-426-9411

Dried Fruit

Agrexco USA
Jamaica, NY . . . 718-481-8700
Amalgamated Produce
Bridgeport, CT . . . 800-358-3808
American Food Ingredients Inc
Oceanside, CA . . . 760-967-6287
American Importing Co.
Minneapolis, MN . . . 855-273-0466
American Key Food Products Inc
Closter, NJ . . . 877-263-7539
American Nuts Inc.
Sylmar, CA . . . 818-364-8855
American Spoon Foods Inc
Petoskey, MI . . . 888-735-6700
Amphora International
Lake Forest, CA . . . 888-380-4808
Amport Foods
St. Paul, MN . . . 800-236-1119
Ann's House of Nuts, Inc.
Columbia, MD . . . 410-309-6887
Atwater Foods
Lyndonville Orleans, NY . . . 585-765-2639
Aurora Products
Orange, CT . . . 800-398-1048
Azar Nut Co
El Paso, TX . . . 800-351-8178
Bazzini Holdings LLC
Allentown, PA . . . 610-366-1606
Bella Viva Orchards
Hughson, CA . . . 800-552-8218
Blueberry Store
Grand Junction, MI . . . 877-654-2400
Boghosian Raisin Packing Co
Fowler, CA . . . 559-834-5348
Buchanan Hollow Nut Co
Le Grand, CA . . . 800-532-1500
Cal Ranch
Concord, CA . . . 925-429-2900
California Fruit
San Diego, CA . . . 877-378-4811
California Fruit & Nut
Gustine, CA . . . 888-747-8224
California Packing Company
Olivehurst, CA . . . 530-740-1040
Casados Farms
Ohkay Owingeh, NM . . . 505-852-2433
Christy Wild Blueberry Farms
Amherst, NS . . . 902-667-3013
Chukar Cherries
Prosser, WA . . . 800-624-9544
Cibo Vita
Totowa, NJ . . . 862-238-8020
Colorado Nut Co
Denver, CO . . . 800-876-1625
Creative Snacks Co LLC
Greensboro, NC . . . 336-668-4151
Dan-D Foods Ltd
Richmond, BC . . . 800-633-4788
Dardimans California
Panorama City, CA . . . 818-849-5770
Derco Foods Intl
Fresno, CA . . . 559-435-2664
Desert Valley Date
Coachella, CA . . . 760-398-0999
Diamond Foods
Santa Cruz, CA . . . 831-457-3200
Fannie May Fine Chocolate
Oakdale, MN . . . 800-999-3629
Fine Dried Foods Intl
Santa Cruz, CA . . . 831-426-1413
Frontier Co-op
Norway, IA . . . 844-550-6200
Fruit d'Or
Villeroy, QC . . . 819-385-1126
Ganong Bros Ltd
St. Stephen, NB . . . 888-270-8222
GNS Foods
Arlington, TX . . . 817-795-4671
Gold Pure Food Products Co. Inc.
Hempstead, NY . . . 800-422-4681
Golden Town Apple Products
Rougemont, QC . . . 866-552-7643
Hadley's Date Gardens
Thermal, CA . . . 760-399-5191
HealthBest
San Marcos, CA . . . 760-752-5230
Healthco Canada Enterprises
Victoria, BC . . . 877-468-2875
Heartland Ingredients LLC
Troy, MO . . . 800-557-2621
Hialeah Products Co
Hollywood, FL . . . 800-923-3379
Hickory Harvest Foods
Akron, OH . . . 800-448-6887
HP Schmid
San Francisco, CA . . . 415-765-5925
International Harvest Inc
Mt Vernon, NY . . . 800-277-4268
JF Braun & Sons Inc.
Elizabeth, NJ . . . 800-997-7177
Just Tomatoes
Westley, CA . . . 800-537-1985
Kalustyan
New York, NY . . . 800-352-3451
Kamish Food Products
Chicago, IL . . . 773-725-6959
Kendall Frozen Fruits, Inc.
Beverly Hills, CA . . . 310-288-9920
King Nut Co
Solon, OH . . . 800-860-5464
Kiwi Kiss
Boca Raton, FL
Kozlowski Farms
Forestville, CA . . . 800-473-2767
Krispy Kernels
Quebec, QC . . . 877-791-9986
Leroux Creek
Hotchkiss, CO . . . 877-970-5670
Made In Nature
Boulder, CO . . . 800-906-7426
Maine Wild Blueberry Company
Cherryfield, ME . . . 800-243-4005
Majestic Foods
Huntington, NY . . . 631-424-9444
Mariani Packing Co.
Vacaville, CA . . . 707-452-2800
Marx Brothers Inc
Birmingham, AL . . . 800-633-6376
Mavuno Harvest
Philadelphia, PA
Meduri Farms
Dallas, OR . . . 877-388-8800
Mezza
Lake Forest, IL . . . 888-206-6054
Midwest Nut Co
Minneapolis, MN . . . 800-328-5502
Mountain High Organics
New Milford, CT . . . 860-210-7805
Natural Food Source
Bethlehem, PA . . . 610-997-0500
Natural Foods Inc
Toledo, OH . . . 419-537-1711
Natural Sins
New York, NY
Nature's Bandits
Riverside, CT . . . 203-571-2040
Navitas Naturals
Novato, CA . . . 888-645-4282
New Century Snacks
City of Commerce, CA . . . 800-688-6887
New Organics
Kenwood, CA . . . 734-677-5570
Newtown Foods USA Inc
Newtown, PA . . . 215-579-2120
Niagara Foods
Middleport, NY . . . 716-735-7722
Nimeks Organics
Bethlehem, PA . . . 610-997-0500
Nothing But The Fruit
Concord, MA . . . 978-341-1221
Nspired Natural Foods
Boulder, CO . . . 800-434-4246
Nut Factory
Spokane Valley, WA . . . 888-239-5288
Organically Grown Co
Eugene, OR . . . 800-937-9677
Osage Pecan Co
Butler, MO . . . 800-748-8305
Pacific Fruit Processors
Suite 600, CA . . . 952-820-2518
Pacific Gold Marketing
Arlington, TX . . . 817-795-4671

Paradise Fruits NA
Norwood, MA....781-769-4900
Patsy's Candy
Colorado Springs, CO....866-372-8797
Primex International Trading
Los Angeles, CA....310-410-7100
Ramos Orchards
Winters, CA....530-795-4748
Raymond-Hadley Corporation
Spencer, NY....800-252-5220
Red River Foods Inc
Richmond, VA....804-320-1800
Regal Health Food
Chicago, IL....773-252-1044
Reinhart Foods
Toronto, ON....416-645-4910
Royal Ridge Fruits
Royal City, WA....509-346-1520
Service Packing Company
Vancouver, BC....604-681-0264
Setton Farms
Terra Bella, CA....559-535-6050
Setton International Foods
Commack, NY....800-227-4397
Shields Date Garden
Indio, CA....800-414-2555
Shoei Foods USA Inc
Olivehurst, CA....530-237-1295
Shoreline Fruit
Traverse City, MI....800-836-3972
Sigona's
San Carlos, CA....650-368-6992
Smeltzer Orchard Co
Frankfort, MI....231-882-4421
Snackerz
Commerce, CA....888-576-2253
Society Hill Snacks
Philadelphia, PA....800-595-0050
Solana Gold Organics
Sebastopol, CA....800-459-1121
Sole Grano LLC
Fair Lawn, NJ....201-797-7100
Specialty Commodities Inc
Fargo, ND....701-282-8222
Spreda Group
Louisville, KY....502-426-9411
Star Snacks
Jersey City, NJ....888-782-7688
Stretch Island Fruit
Solana Beach, CA....800-700-9687
Sun Empire Foods
Kerman, CA....800-252-4786
Sun-Maid Growers of California
Kingsburg, CA....559-896-8000
Sunridge Farms
Royal Oaks, CA....831-786-7000
Sunridge Farms Inc
Salinas, CA....831-755-1530
Sunsweet Growers Inc.
Yuba City, CA....800-417-2253
Swerseys Chocolate
Brooklyn, NY....718-497-8800
Terri Lynn Inc
Elgin, IL....800-323-0775
Timber Crest Farms
Healdsburg, CA....888-766-4233
Todd's
Vernon, CA....800-938-6337
Torn & Glasser
Los Angeles, CA....800-282-6887
Traina Foods Inc
Patterson, CA....209-892-5472
Trophy Nut Co
Tipp City, OH....800-219-9004
Tropical Foods
Charlotte, NC....800-438-4470
Tropical Foods
Lithia Springs, GA....800-544-3762
Tropical Nut Fruit & Bulk Cndy
Lithia Springs, GA....800-544-3762
Twenty First Century Snacks
Ronkonkoma, NY....800-975-2883
TyRy Inc
Rocklin, CA....800-322-6325
Unique Ingredients LLC
Gold Canyon, AZ....480-983-2498
Ursula's Island Farms Company
Seattle, WA....206-762-3113
Vacaville Fruit Co
Vacaville, CA....707-447-1085
Valley View Blueberries
Vancouver, WA....360-892-2839
Valley View Packing Co
Yuba City, CA....530-673-7356
Van Drunen Farms
Momence, IL....815-472-3100
Waymouth Farms Inc
Minneapolis, MN....800-527-0094
Weaver Nut Co. Inc.
Ephrata, PA....800-473-2688
Z Foods Inc.
Madera, CA....888-400-1015

Fig

Fig Garden Packing Inc
Fresno, CA....559-271-9000
Kalustyan
New York, NY....800-352-3451
Natural Foods Inc
Toledo, OH....419-537-1711
Nut Factory
Spokane Valley, WA....888-239-5288
San Joaquin Figs Inc
Fresno, CA....559-224-4963
Timber Crest Farms
Healdsburg, CA....888-766-4233
Unique Ingredients LLC
Gold Canyon, AZ....480-983-2498

Freeze Dried

BCFoods
Santa Rosa, CA....707-547-1776
Brothers All Natural
Rochester, NY....877-842-7477
Chaucer Consumer Solutions
Calabasas, CA
Crispy Green Inc.
Fairfield, NJ....973-679-4515
Homegrown Organic Farms
Porterville, CA....559-306-1750
Mercer Foods
Modesto, CA....209-529-0150
Oregon Freeze Dry, Inc.
Albany, OR....541-926-6001
Paradise Fruits NA
Norwood, MA....781-769-4900
Wolf Canyon Foods
Carmel, CA....831-626-1323

Dried & Dehydrated Vegetables

AgroCepia
Miami, FL....305-704-3488
Bautista Family Organic Date
Mecca, CA....760-396-2337
Emerling International Foods
Buffalo, NY....716-833-7381
Frontier Co-op
Norway, IA....844-550-6200
Healthco Canada Enterprises
Victoria, BC....877-468-2875
Hialeah Products Co
Hollywood, FL....800-923-3379
High Quality Organics
Reno, NV....775-971-8550
International Harvest Inc
Mt Vernon, NY....800-277-4268
Jain Americas Inc
Columbus, OH....888-473-7539
Just Tomatoes
Westley, CA....800-537-1985
Made In Nature
Boulder, CO....800-906-7426
Maine Coast Sea Vegetables
Franklin, ME....207-565-2907
Mills Brothers Intl
Seattle, WA....206-575-3000
Nimeks Organics
Bethlehem, PA....610-997-0500
RFi Ingredients
Blauvelt, NY....800-962-7663
Sensible Foods LLC
Santa Rosa, CA....888-222-0170
Specialty Ingredients
Buffalo Grove, IL....847-419-9595
Sun Ray International
Davis, CA....530-297-1688
Sunco & Frenchie
Clifton, NJ....973-478-1011
SupHerb Farms
Turlock, CA....800-787-4372
Traina Foods Inc
Patterson, CA....209-892-5472
Van Eeghen International Inc
St Laurent, QC....514-332-6455

Beet Powder

RFi Ingredients
Blauvelt, NY....800-962-7663
Seneca Foods Corp
Marion, NY....315-926-8100

Bell Peppers

Green

RFi Ingredients
Blauvelt, NY....800-962-7663

Red

RFi Ingredients
Blauvelt, NY....800-962-7663

Broccoli

Chopped

RFi Ingredients
Blauvelt, NY....800-962-7663

Cabbage Flakes

RFi Ingredients
Blauvelt, NY....800-962-7663

Celery Flakes

RFi Ingredients
Blauvelt, NY....800-962-7663

Dehydrated Vegetables

AgroCepia
Miami, FL....305-704-3488
American Food Ingredients Inc
Oceanside, CA....760-967-6287
Caltex Foods
Canoga Park, CA....800-522-5839
Dehydrates Inc
Hewlett, NY....800-983-4443
Freeman Industries
Tuckahoe, NY....800-666-6454
Garden Valley Corp
Sutherlin, OR....541-459-9565
Inland Empire Foods
Riverside, CA....888-452-3267
Larsen Farms
Hamer, ID....208-374-5592
Mercer Processing
Modesto, CA....209-529-0150
New Season Foods Inc
Forest Grove, OR....503-357-7124
Oregon Potato Co
Boardman, OR....800-336-6311
Paisano Food Products
Elk Grove Village, IL....800-672-4726
Sarant International Cmmdts
Stony Brook, NY....631-675-2875
Schiff Food Products Co Inc
Totowa, NJ....973-237-1990
Serv-Agen Corporation
Cherry Hill, NJ....856-663-6966
Silva International
Momence, IL....815-472-3535
South Mill
Kennett Square, PA....610-444-4800
Spice King Corporation
Beverly Hills, CA....310-836-7770
Two Guys Spice Company
Jacksonville, FL....800-874-5656
Unified Food Ingredients
San Marcos, CA....760-744-7225
Vauxhall Foods
Vauxhall, AB....403-654-2771
Washington Potato Company
Pasco, WA....800-897-2726
World Spice
Roselle, NJ....800-234-1060

Dried Chives

SupHerb Farms
Turlock, CA....800-787-4372

Eggplant

Setton International Foods
Commack, NY....800-227-4397

Freeze Dried

American Food Ingredients Inc
Oceanside, CA 760-967-6287
BCFoods
Santa Rosa, CA 707-547-1776
Hanover Foods Corp
Hanover, PA 717-632-6000
Ocean Mist Farms
Castroville, CA 831-633-2144
Oregon Freeze Dry, Inc.
Albany, OR 541-926-6001
RFi Ingredients
Blauvelt, NY 800-962-7663
SupHerb Farms
Turlock, CA 800-787-4372
Wolf Canyon Foods
Carmel, CA 831-626-1323
Zuccaro Produce
Columbia Heights, MN 612-333-1122

Leeks - Chopped

RFi Ingredients
Blauvelt, NY 800-962-7663

Mushrooms

North American Reishi/Nammex
Gibsons, BC 604-886-7799
South Mill
Kennett Square, PA 610-444-4800

Mushroom Powder

Mushroom Harvest
Athens, OH 740-448-7376

Onion

Dehydrated

Advanced Spice & Trading
Carrollton, TX 800-872-7811
American Key Food Products Inc
Closter, NJ 877-263-7539
Emerling International Foods
Buffalo, NY 716-833-7381
Jain Americas Inc
Columbus, OH 888-473-7539
Schiff Food Products Co Inc
Totowa, NJ 973-237-1990
Swagger Foods Corp
Vernon Hills, IL 847-913-1200

Granulated

Acme Steak & Seafood
Youngstown, OH 800-686-2263
Basic American Foods
Walnut Creek, CA 925-472-4000
Bottom Line Foods
Pembroke Pines, FL 954-843-0562
Bryant Preserving Company
Alma, AR 800-634-2413
Burnham & Morrill Co
Portland, ME 800-813-2165
H.K. Canning
Ventura, CA 805-652-1392
Hye Cuisine
Del Rey, CA 559-834-3000
Les Aliments Livabec Foods
Sherrington, QC 450-454-7971
Nor-Cliff Farms
Port Colborne, ON 905-835-0808
Oxford Frozen Foods
Oxford, NS 902-447-2100
Pacific Valley Foods Inc
Bellevue, WA 425-643-1805
Seneca Foods Corp
Princeville, IL 309-385-4301
Seneca Foods Corp
Marion, NY 315-926-8100
Supreme Dairy Farms Co
Warwick, RI 401-739-8180

for Dehydration

Ful-Flav-R Foods
Alamo, CA 925-838-0300

Peas - Air-dried

Bryant Preserving Company
Alma, AR 800-634-2413
Oxford Frozen Foods
Oxford, NS 902-447-2100

Shallots - Freeze Dried

Oxford Frozen Foods
Oxford, NS 902-447-2100
RFi Ingredients
Blauvelt, NY 800-962-7663
SupHerb Farms
Turlock, CA 800-787-4372

Soup Blend

Sentry Seasonings
Elmhurst, IL 630-530-5370

Spinach Powder

RFi Ingredients
Blauvelt, NY 800-962-7663

Tomatoes

Halves

Bryant Preserving Company
Alma, AR 800-634-2413
Oxford Frozen Foods
Oxford, NS 902-447-2100
Zuccaro Produce
Columbia Heights, MN 612-333-1122

Tomato Powder

Bryant Preserving Company
Alma, AR 800-634-2413

Eggplant

Buona Vita Inc
Bridgeton, NJ 856-453-7972
Castella Imports Inc
Brentwood, NY 631-231-5500
Dolce Nonna
Whitestone, NY 718-767-3501
Dominex
St Augustine, FL 904-810-2132
Giumarra Companies
Los Angeles, CA 213-627-2900
L & S Packing Co
Farmingdale, NY 800-286-6487
Michigan Freeze Pack
Hart, MI 231-873-2175
Miss Scarlett's Flowers
Juneau, AK 800-345-6734
Ocean Mist Farms
Castroville, CA 831-633-2144
Peter Rabbit Farms
Coachella, CA 760-398-0136
Rene Produce Dist
Rio Rico, AZ 520-281-0806
Russo Farms
Vineland, NJ 856-692-5942
Turri's Italian Foods
Roseville, MI 586-773-6010
Vegetable Juices Inc
Chicago, IL 888-776-9752
Wholesum Family Farms
Nogales, AZ 520-281-9233
Z&S Distributing
Fresno, CA 800-467-0788

Figs

Fig Garden Packing Inc
Fresno, CA 559-271-9000
Figamajigs
San Mateo, CA 650-227-3830
Hadley's Date Gardens
Thermal, CA 760-399-5191
Kalustyan
New York, NY 800-352-3451
Made In Nature
Boulder, CO 800-906-7426
Natural Foods Inc
Toledo, OH 419-537-1711
New Organics
Kenwood, CA 734-677-5570
North Bay Produce Inc
Traverse City, MI 231-946-1941
Prima® Wawona
Fresno, CA 559-787-8780
Service Packing Company
Vancouver, BC 604-681-0264
Setton International Foods
Commack, NY 800-227-4397
Sunfood
El Cajon, CA 888-729-3663
Terri Lynn Inc
Elgin, IL 800-323-0775
Timber Crest Farms
Healdsburg, CA 888-766-4233
To Your Health Sprouted Flour Co., Inc.
Floyd, VA 540-283-9589
United With Earth
Berkeley, CA 510-210-4359
Valley Fig Growers
Fresno, CA 559-237-3893

Frozen

FDI Inc
Berkeley, IL 708-544-1880

Fire Roasted Vegetables

SupHerb Farms
Turlock, CA 800-787-4372

Flowers - Edible

Fmali Herb
Santa Cruz, CA 831-423-7913
Wild Hibiscus Flower Company
Richford, VT 800-499-8490

Fresh Fruit

Bay Cities Produce Co Inc
San Leandro, CA 510-346-4943
Belleharvest Sales Inc
Belding, MI 800-452-7753
Cherry Hill Orchards
Lancaster, PA 717-872-9311
Diamond Blueberry Inc
Hammonton, NJ 609-561-3661
Dole Food Company, Inc.
Thousand Oaks, CA 800-356-3111
Family Tree Farms
Reedley, CA 866-352-8671
Florida Citrus
Bartow, FL 863-537-3999
Glacier Foods
Houston, TX 832-375-6300
Golden Town Apple Products
Rougemont, QC 866-552-7643
Homegrown Organic Farms
Porterville, CA 559-306-1750
Limehouse Produce Co
North Charleston, SC 843-556-3400
Maui Gold Pineapple Company
Pukalani, HI 808-877-3805
Muir Copper Canyon Farms
Salt Lake City, UT 800-564-0949
Silver Creek Farms
Twin Falls, ID 208-736-0829
Snokist Growers
Yakima, WA 800-377-2857
Sun Rich Fresh Foods USA Inc
Corona, CA 800-735-3801
Townsend Farms Inc
Fairview, OR 503-666-1780
Washington Fruit & Produce Company
Yakima, WA 509-457-6177

Fresh Vegetables

Bay Cities Produce Co Inc
San Leandro, CA 510-346-4943
Boskovich Farms Inc
Oxnard, CA 805-487-2299
Dole Food Company, Inc.
Thousand Oaks, CA 800-356-3111
Glacier Foods
Houston, TX 832-375-6300
Hanover Foods Corp
Hanover, PA 717-632-6000
International Specialty Supply
Cookeville, TN 931-526-1106
Lennox Farm
Shelburne, ON 519-925-6444
Limehouse Produce Co
North Charleston, SC 843-556-3400
Monterey Mushrooms Inc
Watsonville, CA 800-333-6874
Muir Copper Canyon Farms
Salt Lake City, UT 800-564-0949
Musco Family Olive Co
Tracy, CA 800-523-9828

R.C. McEntire & Company
Columbia, SC 803-799-3388
Silver Creek Farms
Twin Falls, ID 208-736-0829
Western Pacific Produce
Santa Barbara, CA 800-963-4451

Prepared

DNO Inc
Columbus, OH 614-231-3601
Dole Food Company, Inc.
Thousand Oaks, CA 800-356-3111
Risvold's Inc.
Gardena, CA 323-770-2674

Frozen Fruit

Abbotsford Growers Ltd.
Abbotsford, BC 604-864-0022
Agvest
Cleveland, OH 216-464-3737
Bay Cities Produce Co Inc
San Leandro, CA 510-346-4943
BCFoods
Santa Rosa, CA 707-547-1776
Beta Pure Foods
Santa Cruz, CA 831-685-6565
Blue Marble Brands
Providence, RI 888-534-0246
Bonduelle North America
Quebec, ON 450-787-3411
Cahoon Farms
Wolcott, NY 315-594-9610
Carriere Foods Inc
Saint-Denis-Sur-Richelie, QC 450-787-3411
Cherry Lane Frozen Fruits
Vineland Station, ON 877-243-7796
Christy Wild Blueberry Farms
Amherst, NS 902-667-3013
Clofine Dairy Products Inc
Linwood, NJ 609-653-1000
Coloma Frozen Foods Inc
Coloma, MI 800-642-2723
Decker Farms Inc
Hillsboro, OR 503-628-1532
Diamond Blueberry Inc
Hammonton, NJ 609-561-3661
E.W. Bowker Company
Pemberton, NJ 609-894-9508
Eckert Cold Storage
Manteca, CA 209-823-3181
Emerling International Foods
Buffalo, NY 716-833-7381
Enfield Farms Inc
Lynden, WA 360-354-2919
Ever Fresh Fruit Co
Boring, OR 800-239-8026
Froozer
Denver, CO 720-446-0145
Frozfruit Corporation
Gardena, CA 310-217-1034
Fru-V
Stouffville, ON
Fruit Belt Canning Inc
Lawrence, MI 269-674-3939
Glacier Foods
Houston, TX 832-375-6300
Golden Town Apple Products
Rougemont, QC 866-552-7643
Grow-Pac
Cornelius, OR 503-357-9691
Hartog Rahal Foods
Norwood, NJ 201-750-0500
Inn Foods Inc
Watsonville, CA 800-708-7836
Interfrost
East Rochester, NY 585-381-0320
J H Verbridge & Son Inc
Williamson, NY 315-589-2366
Kendall Frozen Fruits, Inc.
Beverly Hills, CA 310-288-9920
KERR Concentrates Inc
Salem, OR 800-910-5377
Maine Wild Blueberry Company
Cherryfield, ME 800-243-4005
Majestic Foods
Huntington, NY 631-424-9444
Mason County Fruit Packers Cooperative
Hart, MI 231-873-7504
Midwest Frozen Foods, Inc.
Hanover Park, IL 866-784-0123
Milne Fruit Products Inc
Prosser, WA 509-786-2611
National Frozen Foods Corp
Seattle, WA 206-322-8900
Natural Food Source
Bethlehem, PA 610-997-0500
Nature's Touch
Saint-Laurent, QC
Niagara Foods
Middleport, NY 716-735-7722
Ocean Spray International
Lakeville-Middleboro, MA 800-662-3263
Oregon Cherry Growers Inc
Salem, OR
Oregon Fruit Products Co
Salem, OR 800-394-9333
Overlake Foods
Olympia, WA 800-683-1078
Pacific Coast Fruit Co
Portland, OR 503-234-6411
Paris Foods Corporation
Trappe, MD 410-200-9595
Patterson Frozen Foods
Patterson, CA 209-892-2611
Rainsweet Inc
Salem, OR 800-363-4293
Small Planet Foods
Minneapolis, MN 800-624-4123
Smeltzer Orchard Co
Frankfort, MI 231-882-4421
Snowcrest Packer
Abbotsford, BC 800-265-3686
Sparboe Foods Corp
New Hampton, IA 641-394-3040
Stahlbush Island Farms Inc
Corvallis, OR 541-757-1497
Sunrise Growers
Placentia, CA 714-630-6292
Superior Foods
Watsonville, CA 831-728-3691
Symons Frozen Foods
Centralia, WA 360-736-1321
Tatangelo's Wholesale Fruit & Vegetables
Woodbridge, ON 877-328-8503
Townsend Farms Inc
Fairview, OR 503-666-1780
Triple D Orchards Inc
Empire, MI 231-326-5174
Unique Ingredients LLC
Gold Canyon, AZ 480-983-2498
VIP Sales Company
Hayward, CA 866-536-8008
Webster Farms
Cambridge, NS 800-507-8844
Willamette Valley Pie Co
Salem, OR 503-362-8857

Berries

Cherry Central Cooperative, Inc.
Traverse City, MI 231-946-1860
Froozer
Denver, CO 720-446-0145
Royal Ridge Fruits
Royal City, WA 509-346-1520
Small Planet Foods
Minneapolis, MN 800-624-4123
Stahlbush Island Farms Inc
Corvallis, OR 541-757-1497

Frozen Vegetables

Al Pete Meats
Muncie, IN 765-288-8817
Appleton Produce Company
Weiser, ID 208-414-3352
BCFoods
Santa Rosa, CA 707-547-1776
Beta Pure Foods
Santa Cruz, CA 831-685-6565
Bonduelle North America
Quebec, ON 450-787-3411
Boskovich Farms Inc
Oxnard, CA 805-487-2299
Bright Harvest Sweet Potato Co
Clarksville, AR 800-793-7440
Carando Gourmet Frozen Foods
Agawam, MA 888-227-2636
Carriere Foods Inc
Saint-Denis-Sur-Richelie, QC 450-787-3411
Coloma Frozen Foods Inc
Coloma, MI 800-642-2723
Dairy King Milk Farms/Foodservice
Whitter, CA 800-900-6455
Deep Foods Inc
Union, NJ 908-810-7500
Dickinson Frozen Foods
Eagle, ID 800-886-4326
Eckert Cold Storage
Manteca, CA 209-823-3181
Fresh Frozen Foods
Jefferson, GA 800-277-9851
Froozer
Denver, CO 720-446-0145
Fru-V
Stouffville, ON
Fruit Belt Canning Inc
Lawrence, MI 269-674-3939
GC Farms
Morgan Hill, CA 408-778-0562
Glacier Foods
Houston, TX 832-375-6300
Great American Appetizers
Nampa, ID 800-282-4834
Hanover Foods Corp
Hanover, PA 717-632-6000
Hermann Pickle Co
Garrettsville, OH 800-245-2696
Inn Foods Inc
Watsonville, CA 800-708-7836
Interfrost
East Rochester, NY 585-381-0320
International Specialty Supply
Cookeville, TN 931-526-1106
J G Townsend Jr & Co
Georgetown, DE 302-856-2525
John Copes Food Products
Hanover, PA 800-888-4646
Juanita's Foods
Wilmington, CA 800-303-2965
Lakeside Foods Inc.
Plainview, MN 507-534-3141
Lakeside Foods Inc.
Manitowoc, WI 800-466-3834
Lennox Farm
Shelburne, ON 519-925-6444
Lodi Canning Co
Lodi, WI 608-592-4236
Meridian Foods New Inc
Eaton, IN 765-396-3344
Miami Purveyors Inc
Miami, FL 800-966-6328
Midwest Frozen Foods, Inc.
Hanover Park, IL 866-784-0123
Milroy Canning Company
Milroy, IN 765-629-2221
Monticello Canning Company
Crossville, TN
National Frozen Foods Corp
Seattle, WA 206-322-8900
Natural Food Source
Bethlehem, PA 610-997-0500
Nature Quality
San Martin, CA 408-683-2182
Niagara Foods
Middleport, NY 716-735-7722
NORPAC Foods Inc
Salem, OR
Oregon Potato Co
Boardman, OR 800-336-6311
Paris Foods Corporation
Trappe, MD 410-200-9595
Patterson Frozen Foods
Patterson, CA 209-892-2611
Pictsweet Co
Bells, TN 731-663-7600
Rainsweet Inc
Salem, OR 800-363-4293
Red Gold Inc.
Elwood, IN 866-729-7187
RFS Limited
Roswell, GA 770-993-0030
San Antonio Farms
Platteville, WI 800-236-1119
Seabrook Brothers & Sons
Seabrook, NJ 856-455-8080
Seenergy Foods
Woodbridge, ON 800-609-7674
Simplot Food Group
Boise, ID 800-572-7783
Small Planet Foods
Minneapolis, MN 800-624-4123
Smeltzer Orchard Co
Frankfort, MI 231-882-4421

Smith Frozen Foods Inc
Weston, OR....541-566-3515
Snowcrest Packer
Abbotsford, BC....800-265-3686
Stahlbush Island Farms Inc
Corvallis, OR....541-757-1497
Strathroy Foods
Strathroy, ON....519-245-4600
Superior Foods
Watsonville, CA....831-728-3691
SupHerb Farms
Turlock, CA....800-787-4372
Symons Frozen Foods
Centralia, WA....360-736-1321
Tatangelo's Wholesale Fruit & Vegetables
Woodbridge, ON....877-328-8503
Trans Pecos Foods
San Antonio, TX....210-228-0896
Twin City Foods Inc.
Stanwood, WA....206-515-2400
Unique Ingredients LLC
Gold Canyon, AZ....480-983-2498
VIP Sales Company
Hayward, CA....866-536-8008
Washington Potato Company
Pasco, WA....800-897-2726
Washington Rhubarb Grower Assn
Sumner, WA....800-435-9911
Webster Farms
Cambridge, NS....800-507-8844
Westin Foods
Omaha, NE....800-228-6098
Wornick Company
Cincinnati, OH....800-860-4555

Fruit

A. Gagliano Co Inc
Milwaukee, WI....800-272-1516
Adobe Creek Packing Co Inc
Kelseyville, CA....707-279-4204
Agvest
Cleveland, OH....216-464-3737
American Yeast
Memphis, TN....866-920-9885
Amport Foods
St. Paul, MN....800-236-1119
Anastasia Confections Inc
Orlando, FL....800-329-7100
Andros Foods North America
Mount Jackson, VA....844-426-3767
Applewood Orchards Inc
Deerfield, MI....800-447-3854
Arcor USA
Coral Gables, FL....800-572-7267
Ariel Natural Foods
Bellevue, WA....425-637-3345
Atlanta Bread Co.
Smyrna, GA....800-398-3728
BCFoods
Santa Rosa, CA....707-547-1776
Ben B. Schwartz & Sons
Detroit, MI....313-841-8300
Bilgore's Groves
Clearwater, FL....727-442-2171
Bissinger's Handcrafted Chocolatier
St. Louis, MO....314-615-2400
Bob Gordon & Associates
Oak Park, IL....708-524-9611
Bridenbaugh Orchards
Martinsburg, PA....814-793-2364
Burnette Foods
Elk Rapids, MI....231-264-8116
Cahoon Farms
Wolcott, NY....315-594-9610
Casados Farms
Ohkay Owingeh, NM....505-852-2433
Cascadian Farm Inc
Sedro Woolley, WA....360-855-0542
Castellini Group
Newport, KY....800-233-8560
Cherry Lane Frozen Fruits
Vineland Station, ON....877-243-7796
Christy Wild Blueberry Farms
Amherst, NS....902-667-3013
Chudleigh's
Milton, ON....800-387-4028
Chukar Cherries
Prosser, WA....800-624-9544
Cinnabar Specialty Foods Inc
Prescott, AZ....866-293-6433
Citrosuco North America Inc
Lake Wales, FL....800-356-4592
Classic Commissary
Binghamton, NY....800-929-3486
Clements Foods Co
Oklahoma City, OK....800-654-8355
Concannon Vineyard
Livermore, CA....800-258-9866
Concord Foods, LLC
Brockton, MA....508-580-1700
Country Fresh Inc
Spring, TX....281-453-3300
Decas Cranberry Sales Inc
Carver, MA....800-649-9811
Del Mar Food Products Corp
Watsonville, CA....831-722-3516
Del Monte Fresh Produce Inc.
Coral Gables, FL....800-950-3683
Delta Packing
Lodi, CA....209-334-1023
Desert Valley Date
Coachella, CA....760-398-0999
Diamond Blueberry Inc
Hammonton, NJ....609-561-3661
Diamond Fruit Growers
Hood River, OR....541-354-5300
DMH Ingredients Inc
Libertyville, IL....847-362-9977
DNO Inc
Columbus, OH....614-231-3601
E Waldo Ward & Son Marmalades
Sierra Madre, CA....800-355-9273
E.D. Smith Foods Ltd
Hamilton, ON....905-573-1207
E.W. Bowker Company
Pemberton, NJ....609-894-9508
Earth Circle Organics
Auburn, CA....877-922-3663
East Coast Fresh Cuts Inc
Laurel, MD
Eckert Cold Storage
Manteca, CA....209-823-3181
El Brands
Ozark, AL....334-445-2828
Enfield Farms Inc
Lynden, WA....360-354-2919
Ever Fresh Fruit Co
Boring, OR....800-239-8026
Family Tree Farms
Reedley, CA....866-352-8671
Fannie May Fine Chocolate
Oakdale, MN....800-999-3629
Fernando C Pujals & Bros
Guaynabo, PR....787-792-3080
Fillmore Piru Citrus
Piru, CA....805-521-1781
Fine Dried Foods Intl
Santa Cruz, CA....831-426-1413
Firestone Pacific Foods Co
Vancouver, WA....360-695-9484
Flippin-Seaman Inc
Tyro, VA....434-277-5828
Frieda's Inc
Los Alamitos, CA....714-826-6100
Frozfruit Corporation
Gardena, CA....310-217-1034
Fruit Fillings Inc
Fresno, CA....800-995-4514
Ganong Bros Ltd
St. Stephen, NB....888-270-8222
Gene Belk Briners
Bloomington, CA....909-877-1819
Gl Mezzetta Inc
American Canyon, CA....800-941-7044
Glacier Foods
Houston, TX....832-375-6300
Graceland Fruit Inc
Frankfort, MI....800-352-7181
Gray & Company
Hart, MI....800-551-6009
Graysmarsh Berry Farm
Sequim, WA....800-683-4367
Grouse Hunt Farm Inc
Tamaqua, PA....570-467-2850
Grow-Pac
Cornelius, OR....503-357-9691
Gurley's Foods
Willmar, MN....800-426-7845
Hallcrest Vineyards
Felton, CA....831-335-4441
Harris Farms Inc
Coalinga, CA....800-311-6211
Harry & David
Medford, OR....877-322-1200
Hartog Rahal Foods
Norwood, NJ....201-750-0500
Heller Brothers Packing Corp
Winter Garden, FL....855-543-5537
Henggeler Packing Company
Fruitland, ID....208-452-4212
HH Dobbins Inc
Lyndonville, NY....877-362-2467
Hialeah Products Co
Hollywood, FL....800-923-3379
Hickory Farms
Maumee, OH....800-753-8558
Indian Bay Frozen Foods
Centreville, NL....709-678-2844
Indian Hollow Farms
Richland Center, WI....800-236-3944
International Home Foods
Parsippany, NJ....973-359-9920
J C Watson Co
Parma, ID....208-722-5141
J H Verbridge & Son Inc
Williamson, NY....315-589-2366
J. R. Simplot Co.
Boise, ID....208-336-2110
Jersey Fruit Co-Op
Glassboro, NJ....856-863-9100
JES Foods
Cleveland, OH....216-883-8987
JF Braun & Sons Inc.
Elizabeth, NJ....800-997-7177
Johnson Foods, Inc.
Sunnyside, WA....509-837-4214
Joseph J. White
Browns Mills, NJ....609-893-2332
K.B. Hall Ranch
Ojai, CA....805-525-5875
Kalustyan
New York, NY....800-352-3451
Kiona Vineyards Winery
Benton City, WA....509-588-6716
Knight's Appleden Fruit LTD
Colborne, ON....905-349-2521
Knouse Foods Co-Op Inc.
Peach Glen, PA....717-677-8181
Kozlowski Farms
Forestville, CA....800-473-2767
Krupka's Blueberries
Fennville, MI....269-857-4278
L & S Packing Co
Farmingdale, NY....800-286-6487
La Vigne Enterprises
Fallbrook, CA....760-723-9997
Lee Andersons
Coachella, CA....760-398-3441
Leroux Creek
Hotchkiss, CO....877-970-5670
Liberty Orchards Co Inc
Cashmere, WA....800-231-3242
Macrie Brothers
Hammonton, NJ....609-561-6822
Made In Nature
Boulder, CO....800-906-7426
Maine Wild Blueberry Company
Cherryfield, ME....800-243-4005
Majestic Foods
Huntington, NY....631-424-9444
Mange
Somerville, MA....917-880-2104
Mariani Packing Co.
Vacaville, CA....707-452-2800
Mason County Fruit Packers Cooperative
Hart, MI....231-873-7504
Maui Gold Pineapple Company
Pukalani, HI....808-877-3805
Mayer's Cider Mill
Webster, NY....800-543-0043
Mayfield Farms and Nursery
Athens, TN....423-746-9859
Mccartney Produce Co
Paris, TN....731-642-2362
Mercer Processing
Modesto, CA....209-529-0150
Midwest Blueberry Farms
Holland, MI....616-399-2133
Mira International Foods
East Brunswick, NJ....800-818-6472
Miramar Fruit Trading Company
Doral, FL....305-883-4774
Moonlight Co
Reedley, CA....559-638-7799
Naraghi Group
Escalon, CA....209-579-5253

Nassau Candy Distributors
Hicksville, NY 516-433-7100
National Flavors
Kalamazoo, MI 800-525-2431
Natural Fruit Corp
Hialeah, FL 305-887-7525
Nekta
Auckland, ... 649-250-2789
New Century Snacks
City of Commerce, CA 800-688-6887
New Era Canning Company
New Era, MI 231-861-2151
New York Apple Sales Inc
Glenmont, NY 888-477-6770
North American Blueberry Council
Folsom, CA 800-824-6395
Northern Orcharad Co Inc
Peru, NY 518-643-2367
Nutri Fruit
Gresham, OR 503-663-2680
Oneonta Starr Ranch Growers
Wenatchee, WA 509-663-2191
Orange Bang Inc
Sylmar, CA 818-833-1000
Orange Cove-Sanger Citrus
Orange Cove, CA 559-626-4453
Oregon Cherry Growers Inc
Salem, OR
Oregon Fruit Products Co
Salem, OR 800-394-9333
Organically Grown Co
Eugene, OR 800-937-9677
Ouhlala Gourmet
Coral Gables, FL 305-774-7332
Pacific Coast Fruit Co
Portland, OR 503-234-6411
Pacific Trellis
Reedley, CA 559-638-5100
Pacific Westcoast Foods
Beaverton, OR 800-874-9333
Palmer Candy Co
Sioux City, IA 800-831-0828
Paradise Products Corporation
Boca Raton, FL 800-826-1235
Pavero Cold Storage
Highland, NY 800-435-2994
Peaceful Fruits
. 330-356-8515
Plaidberry Company
Vista, CA 760-727-5403
Purity Products
Plainview, NY 800-256-6102
R M Lawton Cranberries Inc
Middleboro, MA 508-947-7465
Rainsweet Inc
Salem, OR 800-363-4293
Ramos Orchards
Winters, CA 530-795-4748
Reed Lang Farms
Rio Hondo, TX 956-748-2354
Regal Health Food
Chicago, IL 773-252-1044
Reinhart Foods
Toronto, ON 416-645-4910
Reter Fruit
Medford, OR 541-772-9560
Rice Fruit Co
Gardners, PA 800-627-3359
Russo Farms
Vineland, NJ 856-692-5942
S A Carlson Inc
Yakima, WA 509-965-8333
S Zitner Co
Philadelphia, PA 215-229-9828
Sand Hill Berries
Mt Pleasant, PA 724-547-4760
Santanna Banana Company
Harrisburg, PA 717-238-8321
SAPNA Foods
Atlanta, GA 404-589-0977
Satiety Winery & Cafe
Davis, CA 530-757-2699
Scotian Gold
Coldbrook, NS 888-726-8426
Shafer Lake Fruit Inc
Hartford, MI 269-621-3194
Shields Date Garden
Indio, CA 800-414-2555
Signature Fruit
Bloomingdale, IL 630-980-2481
Silver Palate Kitchens
Cresskill, NJ 201-568-0110
Smeltzer Orchard Co
Frankfort, MI 231-882-4421
Snackerz
Commerce, CA 888-576-2253
Snowcrest Packer
Abbotsford, BC 800-265-3686
Solana Gold Organics
Sebastopol, CA 800-459-1121
SOPAKCO Foods
Mullins, SC 800-276-9678
Southern Okie
Edmond, OK 405-657-7765
Sparboe Foods Corp
New Hampton, IA 641-394-3040
Specialty Food Association
New York, NY 646-878-0301
Spreda Group
Louisville, KY 502-426-9411
Spring Ledge Farm Stand
New London, NH 603-526-6253
Sun Groves Inc
Safety Harbor, FL 800-672-6438
Sundia Corp
Oakland, CA 415-762-0600
Sunrise Growers
Placentia, CA 714-630-6292
Sunsweet Growers Inc.
Yuba City, CA 800-417-2253
Surface Banana Company
Parkersburg, WV 304-485-2400
Sweet Candy Company
Salt Lake City, UT 855-772-7720
T.S. Smith & Sons
Bridgeville, DE 302-337-8271
Tastee Apple
Newcomerstown, OH 800-262-7753
Taylor Farms
Salinas, CA 831-754-0471
Taylor Farms Pacific
Tracy, CA 209-830-1086
Tejon Ranch Co
Lebec, CA 661-248-3000
Tom Ringhausen Orchards
Hardin, IL 800-258-6645
Tony Vitrano Company
Jessup, MD 800-481-3784
Trailblazer Foods
Portland, OR 800-777-7179
Trefethen Family Vineyards
Napa, CA 707-255-7700
Tri-Boro Fruit Co
Fresno, CA 559-486-4141
Triple D Orchards Inc
Empire, MI 231-326-5174
Trophy Nut Co
Tipp City, OH 800-219-9004
Truitt Bros Inc
Salem, OR 800-547-8712
Tuscarora Organic Growers Cooperative
Hustontown, PA 814-448-2173
United Marketing Exchange
Delta, CO 970-874-3332
Ursula's Island Farms Company
Seattle, WA 206-762-3113
Valley Fig Growers
Fresno, CA 559-237-3893
Valley View Blueberries
Vancouver, WA 360-892-2839
Valley View Packing Co
Yuba City, CA 530-673-7356
Varet Street Market
Brooklyn, NY 718-302-0560
Vilore Foods Co Inc
Laredo, TX 956-722-7190
Visalia Produce Sales
Kingsburg, CA 559-897-6652
Warner Candy
El Paso, TX 847-928-7200
Washington Fruit & Produce Company
Yakima, WA 509-457-6177
Webster Farms
Cambridge, NS 800-507-8844
Well-Pict Inc
Watsonville, CA 831-722-3871
Wetherby Cranberry Company
Warrens, WI 608-378-4813
Wiards Orchards Inc
Ypsilanti, MI 734-390-9211
World Nutrition, Inc.
Scottsdale, AZ 800-548-2710
Yakima Fresh
Yakima, WA 509-248-5770
Yokohl Packing Co
Lindsay, CA 559-562-1327

Aseptic Packaged

Cherry Moon Farms
San Diego, CA 800-580-2913

Cocktail

Emerling International Foods
Buffalo, NY 716-833-7381

Jarred or Cupped

Emerling International Foods
Buffalo, NY 716-833-7381
Keep Moving Inc.
New York, NY
Kurtz Orchards Farms
Niagra-on-the-Lake, ON 905-468-2937

Salad

Risvold's Inc.
Gardena, CA 323-770-2674

Galangal

Nickabood's Inc
Los Angeles, CA 213-746-1541

Garlic

Black Garlic
Hayward, CA 888-811-9065
California Garlic Co
San Diego, CA 951-506-8883
Colonna Brothers Inc
North Bergen, NJ 201-864-1115
Country Cupboard
Lewisburg, PA 570-523-3211
Earthbound Farm
San Jn Bautista, CA 800-690-3200
Emerling International Foods
Buffalo, NY 716-833-7381
Garlic Co
Bakersfield, CA 661-393-4212
Miss Scarlett's Flowers
Juneau, AK 800-345-6734
Obis One
Blacksburg, VA 609-202-9766
Stinking Rose, The
San Francisco, CA 800-995-7674
Sunny Dell Foods Inc
Oxford, PA 610-932-5164
SupHerb Farms
Turlock, CA 800-787-4372
Vegetable Juices Inc
Chicago, IL 888-776-9752

Dehydrated

Bedemco Inc
White Plains, NY 914-683-1119

Granulated

American Key Food Products Inc
Closter, NJ 877-263-7539
Emerling International Foods
Buffalo, NY 716-833-7381
Vegetable Juices Inc
Chicago, IL 888-776-9752

Ginger

Christopher Ranch LLC
Gilroy, CA 408-847-1100
Christopher's Herb Shop
Springville, UT 888-372-4372
Con Yeager Spice Co
Zelienople, PA 800-222-2460
Emerling International Foods
Buffalo, NY 716-833-7381
Ful-Flav-R Foods
Alamo, CA 925-838-0300
Ginger People, The
Marina, CA 800-551-5284
International Glace
Spokane, WA 800-884-5041
Morris J Golombeck Inc
Brooklyn, NY 718-284-3505
Paradise Inc
Plant City, FL 813-752-1155
Schiff Food Products Co Inc
Totowa, NJ 973-237-1990

SupHerb Farms
Turlock, CA 800-787-4372
Texas Coffee Co
Beaumont, TX. . . . 800-259-3400
Triple Leaf Tea Inc
S San Francisco, CA 800-552-7448
Ungerer & Co
Lincoln Park, NJ 973-706-7381
Vegetable Juices Inc
Chicago, IL 888-776-9752

Crystallized

Emerling International Foods
Buffalo, NY. . . . 716-833-7381
King Arthur Flour
Norwich, VT. . . . 800-827-6836
Organic Planet
San Francisco, CA 415-765-5590
Setton International Foods
Commack, NY 800-227-4397
Verdant Kitchen
Norcross, GA 912-349-2958

Pickled

Paradise Inc
Plant City, FL 813-752-1155

Glace

Dixie Dew Prods Co
Erlanger, KY. . . . 800-867-8548
Fruit Fillings Inc
Fresno, CA 800-995-4514
International Glace
Spokane, WA. . . . 800-884-5041

Grape

Ballantine Produce Company
Reedley, CA 559-875-2583
Brothers International Food Corporation
Rochester, NY. . . . 585 343 3007
Cal Harvest Marketing Inc
Hanford, CA 559-582-4494
Concannon Vineyard
Livermore, CA 800-258-9866
Custom Produce Sales
Parlier, CA 559-254-5800
Delta Packing
Lodi, CA 209-334-1023
Fowler Packing Co
Fresno, CA 559-834-5911
George W Saulpaugh & Son
Germantown, NY 518-537-6500
Giumarra Companies
Los Angeles, CA. . . . 213-627-2900
Hallcrest Vineyards
Felton, CA. . . . 831-335-4441
Hillcrest Orchard
Lake Placid, FL. . . . 865-397-5273
Jasmine Vineyards, Inc.
Delano, CA 661-792-2141
Moonlight Co
Reedley, CA 559-638-7799
Naraghi Group
Escalon, CA 209-579-5253
Oneonta Starr Ranch Growers
Wenatchee, WA. . . . 509-663-2191
Pacific Trellis
Reedley, CA 559-638-5100
Pandol Brothers Inc
Delano, CA 661-725-3755
Prima® Wawona
Fresno, CA 559-787-8780
Royal Vista Marketing Inc
Visalia, CA 559-636-9198
Satiety Winery & Cafe
Davis, CA 530-757-2699
Spiech Farms Fruit & Floral
Paw Paw, MI 269-657-1980
Spring Ledge Farm Stand
New London, NH 603-526-6253
Tejon Ranch Co
Lebec, CA 661-248-3000
Trefethen Family Vineyards
Napa, CA. . . . 707-255-7700
Venture Vineyards
Lodi, NY 888-635-6277
Z&S Distributing
Fresno, CA 800-467-0788

Leaves

Castella Imports Inc
Brentwood, NY. . . . 631-231-5500
Corfu Foods Inc
Bensenville, IL 630-595-2510
Grecian Delight Foods Inc
Elk Grove Village, IL 800-621-4387
Hye Cuisine
Del Rey, CA 559-834-3000
Pacific Choice Brands
Fresno, CA 559-476-3581
Setton International Foods
Commack, NY 800-227-4397
Yergat Packing Co
Fresno, CA 559-276-9180

Table

Anton Caratan & Son
Bakersfield, CA 661-725-2575
Corrin Produce Sales
Dinuba, CA. . . . 559-596-0517
Lucich Santos Farms
Patterson, CA 209-892-6500
Peter Rabbit Farms
Coachella, CA. . . . 760-398-0136
Richard Bagdasarian Inc
Mecca, CA 760-396-2168
Satiety Winery & Cafe
Davis, CA 530-757-2699
Sun Pacific
Pasadena, CA 213-612-9957
Vincent B Zaninovich & Sons
Richgrove, CA 661-725-2497
Z&S Distributing
Fresno, CA 800-467-0788

Wine

Delta Packing
Lodi, CA. . . . 209-334-1023
Galleano Winery
Mira Loma, CA. . . . 951-685-5376
Kiona Vineyards Winery
Benton City, WA. . . . 509-588-6716
Satiety Winery & Cafe
Davis, CA 530-757-2699
Symms Fruit Ranch Inc
Caldwell, ID 208-459-4821
Talbott Farms
Palisade, CO 970-464-5656
Tejon Ranch Co
Lebec, CA. . . . 661-248-3000
The Wine RayZyn Company
Napa, CA. . . . 707-251-1600
Trefethen Family Vineyards
Napa, CA. . . . 707-255-7700

Grapefruit

Agrexco USA
Jamaica, NY 718-481-8700
Bautista Family Organic Date
Mecca, CA 760-396-2337
Corona College Heights
Riverside, CA 951-351-7880
DNE World Fruit Sales
Fort Pierce, FL 800-327-6676
Dundee Groves
Dundee, FL. . . . 800-294-2266
Gene's Citrus Ranch
Palmetto, FL. . . . 888-723-2006
Golden River Fruit Company
Vero Beach, FL. . . . 772-562-8610
Haines City Citrus Growers
Haines City, FL. . . . 800-327-6676
Hale Indian River Groves
Vero Beach, FL. . . . 800-562-4502
Heller Brothers Packing Corp
Winter Garden, FL 855-543-5537
Hunt Brothers Cooperative
Lake Wales, FL. . . . 863-676-1411
Lane Southern Orchards
Fort Valley, GA. . . . 800-277-3224
Leroy Smith Inc
Vero Beach, FL. . . . 772-569-2059
Reed Lang Farms
Rio Hondo, TX. . . . 956-748-2354
Seald Sweet
Vero Beach, FL. . . . 559-636-4400
Wonderful Citrus
Mission, TX 956-205-7300

Pink

DNE World Fruit Sales
Fort Pierce, FL 800-327-6676

White

DNE World Fruit Sales
Fort Pierce, FL 800-327-6676

Guava

Brooks Tropicals Inc
Homestead, FL 800-327-4833
Unique Ingredients LLC
Gold Canyon, AZ 480-983-2498

Canned & Frozen

Emerling International Foods
Buffalo, NY. . . . 716-833-7381
Unique Ingredients LLC
Gold Canyon, AZ 480-983-2498

Kale

AeroFarms
Newark, NJ 973-242-2495
Alive and Radiant
Needham, MA. . . . 800-385-1417
Bowery Farming Inc.
New York, NY
BrightFarms
Irvington, NY 866-857-8745
Earthbound Farm
San Jn Bautista, CA 800-690-3200
Emerling International Foods
Buffalo, NY. . . . 716-833-7381
Plenty
San Francisco, CA 650-735-3737
Rhythm Superfoods
Austin, TX. . . . 512-441-5667
Seabrook Brothers & Sons
Seabrook, NJ. . . . 856-455-8080

Fresh

80 Acres Farms
Hamilton, OH 888-574-1569
Boskovich Farms Inc
Oxnard, CA. . . . 805-487-2299

Frozen

Paris Foods Corporation
Trappe, MD. . . . 410-200-9595
Vegetable Juices Inc
Chicago, IL 888-776-9752

Kelp Products

Acadian Seaplants
Dartmouth, NS 800-575-9100
Atlantic Laboratories Inc
Waldoboro, ME. . . . 888-662-5357
Gum Technology Corporation
Tucson, AZ 800-369-4867
Maine Coast Sea Vegetables
Franklin, ME. . . . 207-565-2907
Silver Fern Chemical Inc
Seattle, WA 866-282-3384

Kiwi

Giumarra Companies
Los Angeles, CA. . . . 213-627-2900
Nekta
Auckland, ... 649-250-2789
Oneonta Starr Ranch Growers
Wenatchee, WA. . . . 509-663-2191
Royal Vista Marketing Inc
Visalia, CA 559-636-9198
Setton International Foods
Commack, NY 800-227-4397
Sun Pacific
Pasadena, CA 213-612-9957
Unique Ingredients LLC
Gold Canyon, AZ 480-983-2498
Viva Tierra
Mt Vernon, WA. . . . 360-855-0566

Gold

Brandt Farms Inc
Reedley, CA 559-638-6961

Kohlrabi

Seneca Foods Corp
Princeville, IL . . . 309-385-4301

Kumquat

Paradise Products Corporation
Boca Raton, FL . . . 800-826-1235
Setton International Foods
Commack, NY . . . 800-227-4397
West Pak Avocado Inc
Murrieta, CA . . . 800-266-4414

Leek

Calif Watercress Inc
Fillmore, CA . . . 805-524-4808
SupHerb Farms
Turlock, CA . . . 800-787-4372
Sure-Fresh Produce Inc
Santa Maria, CA . . . 888-423-5379
VCPB Transportation
Secaucus, NJ . . . 201-770-0070
Vegetable Juices Inc
Chicago, IL . . . 888-776-9752

Lemon

Corona College Heights
Riverside, CA . . . 951-351-7880
Di Mare Fresh Inc
Fort Worth, TX . . . 817-385-3000
DNE World Fruit Sales
Fort Pierce, FL . . . 800-327-6676
Oneonta Starr Ranch Growers
Wenatchee, WA . . . 509-663-2191
Paradise Inc
Plant City, FL . . . 813-752-1155
Seald Sweet
Vero Beach, FL . . . 559-636-4400
Wonderful Citrus
Mission, TX . . . 956-205-7300
Z&S Distributing
Fresno, CA . . . 800-467-0788

Peels

Fmali Herb
Santa Cruz, CA . . . 831-423-7913

Lettuce

Ben B. Schwartz & Sons
Detroit, MI . . . 313-841-8300
Boskovich Farms Inc
Oxnard, CA . . . 805-487-2299
BrightFarms
Irvington, NY . . . 866-857-8745
Cal Harvest Marketing Inc
Hanford, CA . . . 559-582-4494
Club Chef LLC
Covington, KY . . . 859-578-3100
Crop One
Oakland, CA
Crown Packing Company
Salinas, CA . . . 831-424-2067
Del Monte Fresh Produce Inc.
Coral Gables, FL . . . 800-950-3683
Earthbound Farm
San Jn Bautista, CA . . . 800-690-3200
F & S Produce Co Inc
Vineland, NJ . . . 800-886-3316
Fresh Express, Inc.
Salinas, CA . . . 800-242-5472
Hari Om Farms
Eagleville, TN . . . 615-368-7778
Live Gourmet
Carpinteria, CA
R.C. McEntire & Company
Columbia, SC . . . 803-799-3388
Ready Pac Foods Inc
Irwindale, CA . . . 800-800-4088
Sales USA
Salado, TX . . . 800-766-7344
State Garden Inc.
Chelsea, MA
Talley Farms
Arroyo Grande, CA . . . 805-489-5400
Tanimura Antle Inc
Salinas, CA . . . 800-772-4542
Teixeira Farms, Inc.
Santa Maria, CA . . . 805-928-3801
Vegetable Juices Inc
Chicago, IL . . . 888-776-9752

Butterhead

Boston

Tanimura Antle Inc
Salinas, CA . . . 800-772-4542

Looseleaf

Green

80 Acres Farms
Hamilton, OH . . . 888-574-1569
Bowery Farming Inc.
New York, NY
BrightFarms
Irvington, NY . . . 866-857-8745
Tanimura Antle Inc
Salinas, CA . . . 800-772-4542

Red

80 Acres Farms
Hamilton, OH . . . 888-574-1569
Bowery Farming Inc.
New York, NY
Tanimura Antle Inc
Salinas, CA . . . 800-772-4542

Romaine

80 Acres Farms
Hamilton, OH . . . 888-574-1569
Bowery Farming Inc.
New York, NY
Royce C. Bone Farms
Nashville, NC . . . 252-443-3773
Talley Farms
Arroyo Grande, CA . . . 805-489-5400
Tanimura Antle Inc
Salinas, CA . . . 800-772-4542

Lime

Agri-Dairy Products
Purchase, NY . . . 914-697-9580
Brooks Tropicals Inc
Homestead, FL . . . 800-327-4833
DNE World Fruit Sales
Fort Pierce, FL . . . 800-327-6676
Hunt Brothers Cooperative
Lake Wales, FL . . . 863-676-1411
Key West Key Lime Pie Co
Big Pine Key, FL . . . 877-882-7437
Shanley Farms
Morro Bay, CA . . . 805-323-6525
Wonderful Citrus
Mission, TX . . . 956-205-7300

Loganberries

KERR Concentrates Inc
Salem, OR . . . 800-910-5377

Mango

Brooks Tropicals Inc
Homestead, FL . . . 800-327-4833
Clofine Dairy Products Inc
Linwood, NJ . . . 609-653-1000
Commodities Marketing Inc
Clarksburg, NJ . . . 732-516-0700
Couture Farms
Kettleman City, CA . . . 559-386-9865
Earthbound Farm
San Jn Bautista, CA . . . 800-690-3200
Eckert Cold Storage
Manteca, CA . . . 209-823-3181
Just Tomatoes
Westley, CA . . . 800-537-1985
Natural Foods Inc
Toledo, OH . . . 419-537-1711
North Bay Produce Inc
Traverse City, MI . . . 231-946-1941
Organic Planet
San Francisco, CA . . . 415-765-5590
Setton International Foods
Commack, NY . . . 800-227-4397
Simply Panache
Hampton, VA . . . 800-313-5613
Townsend Farms Inc
Fairview, OR . . . 503-666-1780
Unique Ingredients LLC
Gold Canyon, AZ . . . 480-983-2498

Dried

American Importing Co.
Minneapolis, MN . . . 855-273-0466
Bedemco Inc
White Plains, NY . . . 914-683-1119
Fine Dried Foods Intl
Santa Cruz, CA . . . 831-426-1413
Made In Nature
Boulder, CO . . . 800-906-7426
Mariani Packing Co.
Vacaville, CA . . . 707-452-2800
Sunfood
El Cajon, CA . . . 888-729-3663
Sunridge Farms
Royal Oaks, CA . . . 831-786-7000

Melon

Del Monte Fresh Produce Inc.
Coral Gables, FL . . . 800-950-3683
Emerling International Foods
Buffalo, NY . . . 716-833-7381
Giumarra Companies
Los Angeles, CA . . . 213-627-2900

Balls

Frozen

Emerling International Foods
Buffalo, NY . . . 716-833-7381

Cantaloupe

Couture Farms
Kettleman City, CA . . . 559-386-9865
Earthbound Farm
San Jn Bautista, CA . . . 800-690-3200
F & S Produce Co Inc
Vineland, NJ . . . 800-886-3316
Hialeah Products Co
Hollywood, FL . . . 800-923-3379
Vessey & Co Inc
Holtville, CA . . . 760-356-0130
Zuccaro Produce
Columbia Heights, MN . . . 612-333-1122

Dried

Setton International Foods
Commack, NY . . . 800-227-4397

Honeydew

Couture Farms
Kettleman City, CA . . . 559-386-9865
Turlock Fruit Co
Turlock, CA . . . 209-634-7207
Zuccaro Produce
Columbia Heights, MN . . . 612-333-1122

Watermelon

Bryant Preserving Company
Alma, AR . . . 800-634-2413
F & S Produce Co Inc
Vineland, NJ . . . 800-886-3316
Zuccaro Produce
Columbia Heights, MN . . . 612-333-1122

Seedless

Bissett Produce Company
Spring Hope, NC . . . 800-849-5073

Miso

Great Eastern Sun Trading Co
Asheville, NC . . . 800-334-5809
Miyako Oriental Foods Inc
Baldwin Park, CA . . . 877-788-6476
Organic Gourmet
Sherman Oaks, CA . . . 800-400-7772

Mushrooms

Al Pete Meats
Muncie, IN . . . 765-288-8817
Alimentaire Whyte's Inc
Laval, QC . . . 866-420-9520
Basciani Foods Inc
Avondale, PA . . . 610-268-3610
Bob Gordon & Associates
Oak Park, IL . . . 708-524-9611
Buonitalia
New York, NY . . . 212-633-9090

Colonna Brothers Inc
North Bergen, NJ ... 201-864-1115
Country Fresh Mushroom Co
Toughkenamon, PA ... 610-268-3033
Crazy Jerrys Inc Kahuna-Sauces
Woodstock, GA ... 800-347-2823
Cutone Specialty Foods
Chelsea, MA ... 617-889-1122
Dong Kee Company
Chicago, IL ... 312-225-6340
Emerling International Foods
Buffalo, NY ... 716-833-7381
Flavor House, Inc.
Adelanto, CA ... 760-246-9131
Fungus Among Us
Snohomish, WA ... 360-568-3403
Giorgio Foods
Temple, PA ... 800-220-2139
Giovanni's Appetizing Food Co
Richmond, MI ... 586-727-9355
Gourmet's Finest
Avondale, PA ... 610-268-6910
Great American Appetizers
Nampa, ID ... 800-282-4834
Great Lakes Foods
Menominee, MI ... 800-800-7492
H.K. Canning
Ventura, CA ... 805-652-1392
Hanover Foods Corp
Hanover, PA ... 717-632-6000
Health Concerns
Oakland, CA ... 800-233-9355
Kitchen Pride Mushrooms Farm
Gonzales, TX ... 830-540-4528
L & S Packing Co
Farmingdale, NY ... 800-286-6487
L F Lambert Spawn Co
Coatesville, PA ... 610-384-5031
L K Bowman
Nottingham, PA ... 800-853-1919
Lake Erie Frozen Foods Co
Ashland, OH ... 800-766-8501
Lee's Food Products
Toronto, ON ... 416-465-2407
Les Aliments Livabec Foods
Sherrington, QC ... 450-454-7971
Matador Processors
Blanchard, OK ... 800-847-0797
Miss Scarlett's Flowers
Juneau, AK ... 800-345-6734
Money's Mushrooms
Vancouver, BC ... 800-669-7992
Monterey Mushrooms Inc
Watsonville, CA ... 800-333-6874
Mushroom Co
Cambridge, MD ... 410-221-8971
Nation Wide Canning Ltd.
Cottam, ON ... 519-839-4831
North American Reishi/Nammex
Gibsons, BC ... 604-886-7799
Ntc Marketing
Williamsville, NY ... 800-333-1637
Om Mushrooms
Carlsbad, CA ... 866-740-6874
Ostrom Mushrooms
Olympia, WA ... 360-491-1410
Paradise Products Corporation
Boca Raton, FL ... 800-826-1235
Phillips Gourmet Inc
Kennett Square, PA ... 610-925-0520
Prairie Mushrooms
Ardrossan, AB ... 780-467-3555
Rainsweet Inc
Salem, OR ... 800-363-4293
Ron Son Foods Inc
Swedesboro, NJ ... 856-241-7333
S.D. Mushrooms
Avondale, PA ... 610-268-8082
Sabatino Truffles USA
West Haven, CT ... 888-444-9971
Setton International Foods
Commack, NY ... 800-227-4397
South Mill
Kennett Square, PA ... 610-444-4800
Star Fine Foods
Fresno, CA ... 559-498-2900
Sunny Dell Foods Inc
Oxford, PA ... 610-932-5164
Superior Mushroom Farms
Ardrossan, AB ... 866-687-2242
SupHerb Farms
Turlock, CA ... 800-787-4372
Tiger Mushroom Farm
Nanton, AB ... 403-646-2578
Unique Foods
Raleigh, NC ... 919-779-5600
United Canning Corporation
North Lima, OH ... 216-549-9807
VCPB Transportation
Secaucus, NJ ... 201-770-0070
Vegetable Juices Inc
Chicago, IL ... 888-776-9752

Beech

Country Fresh Mushroom Co
Toughkenamon, PA ... 610-268-3033
Monterey Mushrooms Inc
Watsonville, CA ... 800-333-6874
Phillips Gourmet Inc
Kennett Square, PA ... 610-925-0520

Canned

Agrocan
Ville St Laurent, QC ... 877-247-6226
Bob Gordon & Associates
Oak Park, IL ... 708-524-9611
Dong Kee Company
Chicago, IL ... 312-225-6340
Giorgio Foods
Temple, PA ... 800-220-2139
Great Lakes Foods
Menominee, MI ... 800-800-7492
Lee's Food Products
Toronto, ON ... 416-465-2407
Money's Mushrooms
Vancouver, BC ... 800-669-7992
Monterey Mushrooms Inc
Watsonville, CA ... 800-333-6874
Mushroom Co
Cambridge, MD ... 410-221-8971
Nation Wide Canning Ltd.
Cottam, ON ... 519-839-4831
Ntc Marketing
Williamsville, NY ... 800-333-1637
Paradise Products Corporation
Boca Raton, FL ... 800-826-1235
Ron Son Foods Inc
Swedesboro, NJ ... 856-241-7333
Shafer-Haggart
Vancouver, BC ... 604-669-5512
Sunny Dell Foods Inc
Oxford, PA ... 610-932-5164
Unique Foods
Raleigh, NC ... 919-779-5600
United Canning Corporation
North Lima, OH ... 216-549-9807

Chanterelle

Country Fresh Mushroom Co
Toughkenamon, PA ... 610-268-3033
Emerling International Foods
Buffalo, NY ... 716-833-7381

Criminis

Country Fresh Mushroom Co
Toughkenamon, PA ... 610-268-3033
Giorgio Foods
Temple, PA ... 800-220-2139
Ostrom Mushrooms
Olympia, WA ... 360-491-1410
Phillips Gourmet Inc
Kennett Square, PA ... 610-925-0520

Dehydrated

Emerling International Foods
Buffalo, NY ... 716-833-7381
Nikken Foods
St Louis, MO ... 314-881-5818
South Mill
Kennett Square, PA ... 610-444-4800
Unique Ingredients LLC
Gold Canyon, AZ ... 480-983-2498

Enokis

Country Fresh Mushroom Co
Toughkenamon, PA ... 610-268-3033
Giorgio Foods
Temple, PA ... 800-220-2139
Ostrom Mushrooms
Olympia, WA ... 360-491-1410
Phillips Gourmet Inc
Kennett Square, PA ... 610-925-0520

Fresh

Country Fresh Mushroom Co
Toughkenamon, PA ... 610-268-3033
Giorgio Foods
Temple, PA ... 800-220-2139

Frozen

Al Pete Meats
Muncie, IN ... 765-288-8817
Giorgio Foods
Temple, PA ... 800-220-2139
Great American Appetizers
Nampa, ID ... 800-282-4834
Hanover Foods Corp
Hanover, PA ... 717-632-6000
Lake Erie Frozen Foods Co
Ashland, OH ... 800-766-8501
Matador Processors
Blanchard, OK ... 800-847-0797
Monterey Mushrooms Inc
Watsonville, CA ... 800-333-6874
Mushroom Co
Cambridge, MD ... 410-221-8971
Paris Foods Corporation
Trappe, MD ... 410-200-9595
Rainsweet Inc
Salem, OR ... 800-363-4293

Lobster

Country Fresh Mushroom Co
Toughkenamon, PA ... 610-268-3033

Maitakes

Country Fresh Mushroom Co
Toughkenamon, PA ... 610-268-3033
Hardscrabble Enterprises
Franklin, WV ... 304-358-2921
Phillips Gourmet Inc
Kennett Square, PA ... 610-925-0520

Morel

Country Fresh Mushroom Co
Toughkenamon, PA ... 610-268-3033
Emerling International Foods
Buffalo, NY ... 716-833-7381

Oyster

Concord Farms
Union City, CA ... 510-429-8855
Country Fresh Mushroom Co
Toughkenamon, PA ... 610-268-3033
Emerling International Foods
Buffalo, NY ... 716-833-7381
Giorgio Foods
Temple, PA ... 800-220-2139
Ostrom Mushrooms
Olympia, WA ... 360-491-1410
Phillips Gourmet Inc
Kennett Square, PA ... 610-925-0520

Porcini

Country Fresh Mushroom Co
Toughkenamon, PA ... 610-268-3033
Emerling International Foods
Buffalo, NY ... 716-833-7381

Portobello

Country Fresh Mushroom Co
Toughkenamon, PA ... 610-268-3033
Giorgio Foods
Temple, PA ... 800-220-2139
Ostrom Mushrooms
Olympia, WA ... 360-491-1410
Phillips Gourmet Inc
Kennett Square, PA ... 610-925-0520

Shiitake

Baycliff Co Inc
Garwood, NJ ... 866-772-7569
Concord Farms
Union City, CA ... 510-429-8855
Country Fresh Mushroom Co
Toughkenamon, PA ... 610-268-3033
Emerling International Foods
Buffalo, NY ... 716-833-7381

Hardscrabble Enterprises
Franklin, WV 304-358-2921
Monterey Mushrooms Inc
Watsonville, CA 800-333-6874
Ostrom Mushrooms
Olympia, WA 360-491-1410
Phillips Gourmet Inc
Kennett Square, PA................610-925-0520
SupHerb Farms
Turlock, CA 800-787-4372

Truffles

Buonitalia
New York, NY 212-633-9090
Garland Truffles, Inc.
Hillsborough, NC 919-732-3041

White

Country Fresh Mushroom Co
Toughkenamon, PA................610-268-3033
Giorgio Foods
Temple, PA 800-220-2139
Monterey Mushrooms Inc
Watsonville, CA 800-333-6874
Ostrom Mushrooms
Olympia, WA 360-491-1410
Phillips Gourmet Inc
Kennett Square, PA................610-925-0520

Wild

Country Fresh Mushroom Co
Toughkenamon, PA................610-268-3033
Grapevine Trading Company
Santa Rosa, CA...................800-469-6478

Wood Ear

Country Fresh Mushroom Co
Toughkenamon, PA................610-268-3033

Mustard

Arbor Hill Grapery & Winery
Naples, NY 800-554-7553
Ashman Manufacturing & Distributing Company
Virginia Beach, VA................800-641-9924
Bauer's Mustard
Flushing, NY.....................718-821-3570
Baumer Foods Inc
Metairie, LA 504-482-5761
Beaverton Foods Inc
Hillsboro, OR 800-223-8076
Boetje Foods Inc
Rock Island, IL 877-726-3853
Booneway Farms
Berea, KY 859-986-2636
Boston Spice & Tea Company
Boston, VA 800-966-4372
Brad's Taste of New York
Floral Park, NY...................516-354-9004
Bread & Chocolate Inc
Wells River, VT 800-524-6715
Buonitalia
New York, NY 212-633-9090
Casa Visco
Schenectady, NY..................888-607-2823
Casually Gourmet
New Haven, VT 800-639-7604
Cedarvale Food Products
Toronto, ON 416-656-3330
Cherchies
Malvern, PA 800-644-1980
Ciro Foods
Pittsburgh, PA....................412-771-9018
Clements Foods Co
Oklahoma City, OK 800-654-8355
Coastal Classics
Duxbury, MA 508-746-6058
Delicae Gourmet
Tarpon Springs, FL................800-942-2502
Dorina So-Good Inc
Union, IL........................815-923-2144
East Shore Specialty Foods
Hartland, WI.....................800-236-1069
Erba Food Products
Brooklyn, NY 718-272-7700
Fischer & Wieser Spec Foods
Fredericksburg, TX................877-861-0260
Ford's Gourmet Foods
Raleigh, NC 800-446-0947
Fox Hollow
Crestwood, KY 502-241-8621
G.E. Barbour
Sussex, NB 506-432-2300
Garden Complements Inc
Kansas City, MO..................800-966-1091
Garlic Festival Foods
Hollister, CA.....................888-427-5423
Gold Pure Food Products Co. Inc.
Hempstead, NY...................800-422-4681
Golden State Foods Corp
Irvine, CA 949-247-8000
Grapevine Trading Company
Santa Rosa, CA...................800-469-6478
Grouse Hunt Farm Inc
Tamaqua, PA 570-467-2850
GS Dunn & Company
Hamilton, ON 905-522-0833
Heinz Portion Control
Jacksonville, FL 904-695-1300
Hot Licks
Spring Valley, CA.................888-766-6468
International Home Foods
Parsippany, NJ....................973-359-9920
J.N. Bech
Elk Rapids, MI 800-232-4583
KARI-Out Co
White Plains, NY 800-433-8799
Kathy's Gourmet Specialties
Mendocino, CA...................707-937-1383
Kelchner's Horseradish
Allentown, PA....................800-424-1952
Knese Enterprise
Bellerose, NY 516-354-9004
Koloa Rum Corp
Kalaheo, HI......................808-332-9333
Kozlowski Farms
Forestville, CA 800-473-2767
Lounsbury Foods
Toronto, ON 416-656-6330
Mad Will's Food Company
Auburn, CA......................888-275-9455
Mccutcheon Apple Products
Frederick, MD....................800-888-7537
Mizkan Americas Inc
Kansas City, MO..................800-323-4358
Morehouse Foods Inc
City Of Industry, CA...............888-297-9800
Mother's Mountain Pantry
Falmouth, ME....................800-440-9891
Mountainbrook of Vermont
Jeffersonville, VT.................802-644-1988
Mucky Duck Mustard Company
Ferndale, MI 248-544-4610
Mutchler's Dakota Gold Mustard
Spearfish, SD 605-642-8166
New Canaan Farms
Dripping Springs, TX..............800-727-5267
Northeast Kingdom Mustard Company
Derby, VT 866-478-7388
Old Cavendish Products
Cavendish, VT 800-536-7899
Olde Tyme Mercantile
Arroyo Grande, CA................805-489-7991
Olds Products Co
Pleasant Prairie, WI 262-947-3500
Paris Foods Corporation
Trappe, MD......................410-200-9595
Pemberton's Foods Inc
Gray, ME........................800-255-8401
Pictsweet Co
Bells, TN........................731-663-7600
Piknik Products Company
Montgomery, AL..................334-240-2218
Pilgrim Foods
Great Neck, NY 516-466-0522
Plochman Inc
Manteno, IL 800-843-4566
Purity Products
Plainview, NY....................800-256-6102
Quality Foods
Qualicum Beach, BC 877-833-7890
Rapazzini Winery
Gilroy, CA.......................800-842-6262
Red Pelican Food Products
Detroit, MI 313-881-4095
Restaurant Lulu Gourmet Products
San Francisco, CA 888-693-5800
REX Pure Foods
New Orleans, LA 800-344-8314
Riba Foods
Houston, TX 800-327-7422
Rising Sun Farms
Phoenix, OR 800-888-0795
Robert Rothschild Farm
Cincinnati, OH 800-222-9966
Schlotterbeck & Foss Company
Portland, ME.....................800-777-4666
Scott-Bathgate
Winnipeg, MB....................800-216-2990
Select Food Products
Toronto, ON 800-699-8016
Silver Palate Kitchens
Cresskill, NJ 201-568-0110
Stello Foods Inc
Punxsutawney, PA................800-849-4599
TexaFrance
Round Rock, TX..................800-776-8937
Tropical Foods
Charlotte, NC 800-438-4470
UFL Foods
Mississauga, ON..................905-670-7776
Ultra Seal
New Paltz, NY 845-255-2490
Uncle Fred's Fine Foods
Rockport, TX 361-729-8320
Westport Rivers Vineyard
Westport, MA 800-993-9695
Wild Thymes Farm Inc
Greenville, NY 845-266-8387
William Poll Inc
New York, NY 800-993-7655
Wing Nien Food
Hayward, CA 510-487-8877
Wing's Food Products
Toronto, ON 416-259-2662
Wisconsin Spice Inc
Berlin, WI.......................920-361-3555
Woeber Mustard Mfg Co
Springfield, OH...................800-548-2929
Wood Brothers Inc
West Columbia, SC................803-796-5146

Cress

Koppert Cress USA
Cutchogue, NY 631-734-8500

Greens

Canned & Frozen

Barhyte Specialty Foods Inc
Pendleton, OR....................800-227-4983
Bauer's Mustard
Flushing, NY.....................718-821-3570
Heintz & Weber Co
Buffalo, NY......................716-852-7171
Mendocino Mustard
Fort Bragg, CA 800-964-2270
Montana Specialty Mills LLC
Great Falls, MT...................800-332-2024
Mrs. Dog's Products
Grand Rapids, MI 800-267-7364
Seabrook Brothers & Sons
Seabrook, NJ.....................856-455-8080
Terrapin Ridge
Clearwater, FL 800-999-4052
Wisconsin Wilderness Food Products
Lake Bluff, IL 800-359-3039

Osaka Purple

Alfred L. Wolff, Inc.
Park Ridge, IL....................847-759-8888

Nectar

Mira International Foods
East Brunswick, NJ................800-818-6472
WCC Honey Marketing
City Of Industry, CA...............626-855-3086

Canned

Healthmate Products
Highland Park, IL 847-579-1051

Nectarines

Ballantine Produce Company
Reedley, CA 559-875-2583
Brandt Farms Inc
Reedley, CA 559-638-6961
California Fruit
San Diego, CA 877-378-4811
Cherry Hill Orchards
Lancaster, PA.....................717-872-9311

Copper Hills Fruit Sales
Fresno, CA 559-432-5400
Corrin Produce Sales
Dinuba, CA 559-596-0517
Custom Produce Sales
Parlier, CA 559-254-5800
Earthbound Farm
San Jn Bautista, CA 800-690-3200
Fowler Packing Co
Fresno, CA 559-834-5911
HMC Farms
Kingsburg, CA 559-897-1025
Mountain View Fruit Sales
Reedley, CA 559-637-9933
Oneonta Starr Ranch Growers
Wenatchee, WA 509-663-2191
P R Farms Inc
Clovis, CA 559-299-0201
Pandol Brothers Inc
Delano, CA 661-725-3755
Prima® Wawona
Fresno, CA 559-787-8780
Stadelman Fruit LLC
Zillah, WA 509-829-5145
Sun Valley Packing
Reedley, CA 559-591-1515
Symms Fruit Ranch Inc
Caldwell, ID 208-459-4821
T.S. Smith & Sons
Bridgeville, DE 302-337-8271
Tom Ringhausen Orchards
Hardin, IL 800-258-6645
Trinity Fruit Sale Co
Fresno, CA 559-433-3777
Unique Ingredients LLC
Gold Canyon, AZ 480-983-2498
Z&S Distributing
Fresno, CA 800-467-0788

Okra

Boskovich Farms Inc
Oxnard, CA 805-487-2299
Miss Scarlett's Flowers
Juneau, AK 800-345-6734
Pictsweet Co
Bells, TN 731-663-7600
Talk O'Texas Brands Inc
San Angelo, TX 800-749-6572
Trappey's Fine Foods Inc
New Iberia, LA 337-365-8281

Canned

Emerling International Foods
Buffalo, NY 716-833-7381

Frozen

Emerling International Foods
Buffalo, NY 716-833-7381
Paris Foods Corporation
Trappe, MD 410-200-9595
Pictsweet Co
Bells, TN 731-663-7600

Olives

Aceitunas Losada
Carmona, Sevilla,
Adams Olive Ranch
Lindsay, CA 888-216-5483
Agrocan
Ville St Laurent, QC 877-247-6226
Alimentaire Whyte's Inc
Laval, QC 866-420-9520
Alive & Well Olives
Ponte Vedra Beach, FL
Bahama Specialty Foods
Durham, NC 919-471-4051
Bari Olive Oil Co
Dinuba, CA 877-638-3626
Bell-Carter Foods Inc
Walnut Creek, CA 800-252-3557
Blue Marble Brands
Providence, RI 888-534-0246
Bob Gordon & Associates
Oak Park, IL 708-524-9611
C.C. Graber Company
Ontario, CA 800-996-5483
California Olive Growers
Fresno, CA 888-965-4837
Caltex Foods
Canoga Park, CA 800-522-5839
Castella Imports Inc
Brentwood, NY 631-231-5500
Corfu Foods Inc
Bensenville, IL 630-595-2510
Cormier Rice Milling Co Inc
De Witt, AR 870-946-3561
Cosmo Food Products
West Haven, CT 800-942-6766
Country Cupboard
Lewisburg, PA 570-523-3211
Crazy Jerrys Inc Kahuna-Sauces
Woodstock, GA 800-347-2823
DeLallo Italian Foods
Jeannette, PA 800-433-9100
E Waldo Ward & Son Marmalades
Sierra Madre, CA 800-355-9273
Emerling International Foods
Buffalo, NY 716-833-7381
Fantis Foods Inc
Carlstadt, NJ 201-933-6200
FoodMatch Inc
New York, NY 800-350-3411
Gl Mezzetta Inc
American Canyon, CA 800-941-7044
Grainaissance
Emeryville, CA 800-472-4697
Jeff's Garden
American Canyon, CA 707-266-7444
Kaiser Pickles
Cincinnati, OH 888-291-0608
Krinos Foods
Bronx, NY 718-729-9000
L & S Packing Co
Farmingdale, NY 800-286-6487
Lakeside Packing Company
Harrow, ON 519-738-2314
Leonard Mountain Inc
Bixby, OK 800-822-7700
M & CP FARMS
Orland, CA 530-865-9810
Mancuso Cheese Co
Joliet, IL 815-722-2475
Manhattan Food Brands, LLC
Metuchen, NJ 732-906-2168
Mario Camancho Foods
Plant City, FL 800-293-9783
Musco Family Olive Co
Tracy, CA 800-523-9828
Nature Quality
San Martin, CA 408-683-2182
Ntc Marketing
Williamsville, NY 800-333-1637
Oil & Olives Company
Miami, FL 305-670-0979
Olde Tyme Mercantile
Arroyo Grande, CA 805-489-7991
Orleans Packing Co
Hyde Park, MA 617-361-6611
Pacific Choice Brands
Fresno, CA 559-476-3581
Paradise Products Corporation
Boca Raton, FL 800-826-1235
Pastene Co LTD
Canton, MA 781-298-3397
Picklesmith Inc
Taft, TX 800-499-3401
Price Co
Yakima, WA 509-966-4110
Proacec USA
Santa Monica, CA 310-996-7770
Pure Food Ingredients
Verona, WI 800-355-9601
Ron Son Foods Inc
Swedesboro, NJ 856-241-7333
San Marzano Imports
Howell, NJ 732-364-1724
Sandt's Honey Co
Easton, PA 800-935-3960
Santa Barbara Olive Company
Santa Barbara, CA 800-624-4896
Sargent and Greenleaf
Nicholasville, KY 800-826-7652
Sieco USA Corporation
Houston, TX 713-464-1726
Silverleaf International Corp
Rosharon, TX 800-442-7542
Spruce Foods
San Clemente, CA 800-326-3612
Stinking Rose, The
San Francisco, CA 800-995-7674
Sunfood
El Cajon, CA 888-729-3663
Sutter Buttes Olive Oil
Sutter, CA 530-763-7921
Tee Pee Olives, Inc.
Rye, NY 800-431-1529
Trattore Farms
Geyserville, CA 707-431-7200
Vegetable Juices Inc
Chicago, IL 888-776-9752
Veronica Foods Inc
Oakland, CA 800-370-5554
Vincent Formusa Company
Des Plaines, IL 847-813-6040
West Coast Products
Orland, CA 800-382-3072
Woodlake Ranch
Woodlake, CA 559-564-2161

Black

Agrocan
Ville St Laurent, QC 877-247-6226
Bell-Carter Foods Inc
Walnut Creek, CA 800-252-3557
Bob Gordon & Associates
Oak Park, IL 708-524-9611
Musco Family Olive Co
Tracy, CA 800-523-9828

Whole

Adams Olive Ranch
Lindsay, CA 888-216-5483

Greek

Adams Olive Ranch
Lindsay, CA 888-216-5483
Castella Imports Inc
Brentwood, NY 631-231-5500
Taziki's Cafe
Birmingham, AL

Green

Agrocan
Ville St Laurent, QC 877-247-6226
Bob Gordon & Associates
Oak Park, IL 708-524-9611
Musco Family Olive Co
Tracy, CA 800-523-9828
Ron Son Foods Inc
Swedesboro, NJ 856-241-7333
Woodlake Ranch
Woodlake, CA 559-564-2161

with Pimiento

Bell-Carter Foods Inc
Walnut Creek, CA 800-252-3557
Musco Family Olive Co
Tracy, CA 800-523-9828

Italian

Adams Olive Ranch
Lindsay, CA 888-216-5483
Bono USA
Fairfield, NJ 862-485-8729
Castella Imports Inc
Brentwood, NY 631-231-5500

Onion

Agri-Pack
Pasco, WA 509-545-6181
Alsum Farms & Produce
Cambria, WI 800-236-5127
Appleton Produce Company
Weiser, ID 208-414-3352
Baker Produce
Kennewick, WA 800-624-7553
Boardman Foods Inc
Boardman, OR 541-481-3000
Bob Gordon & Associates
Oak Park, IL 708-524-9611
Boskovich Farms Inc
Oxnard, CA 805-487-2299
Cascade Specialties, Inc.
Boardman, OR 541-481-2522
Castella Imports Inc
Brentwood, NY 631-231-5500
Christopher Ranch LLC
Gilroy, CA 408-847-1100
Club Chef LLC
Covington, KY 859-578-3100

Coulter Giufre & Co Inc
Chittenango, NY . . . 315-687-6510
De Bruyn Produce Company
Ponpano Beach, FL . . . 800-733-9177
Del Monte Fresh Produce Inc.
Coral Gables, FL . . . 800-950-3683
Delta Packing
Lodi, CA . . . 209-334-1023
Dickinson Frozen Foods
Eagle, ID . . . 800-886-4326
Earthbound Farm
San Jn Bautista, CA . . . 800-690-3200
Exeter Produce
Exeter, ON . . . 519-235-0141
F & S Produce Co Inc
Vineland, NJ . . . 800-886-3316
Fiesta Farms
Toronto, ON . . . 416-537-1235
Fresh Express, Inc.
Salinas, CA . . . 800-242-5472
Ful-Flav-R Foods
Alamo, CA . . . 925-838-0300
Gill's Onions LLC
Oxnard, CA . . . 800-348-2255
Gl Mezzetta Inc
American Canyon, CA . . . 800-941-7044
Gouw Quality Onions
Taber, AB . . . 403-223-1440
Haliburton International Inc
Ontario, CA . . . 877-980-4295
Harris Farms Inc
Coalinga, CA . . . 800-311-6211
Isadore A. Rapasadi & Son
Canastota, NY . . . 800-828-7277
J C Watson Co
Parma, ID . . . 208-722-5141
JES Foods
Cleveland, OH . . . 216-883-8987
L & S Packing Co
Farmingdale, NY . . . 800-286-6487
Magic Valley Growers
Wendell, ID . . . 208-536-6693
Miss Scarlett's Flowers
Juneau, AK . . . 800-345-6734
Muir Copper Canyon Farms
Salt Lake City, UT . . . 800-564-0949
Murakami Farms
Ontario, OR . . . 800-421-8814
National Frozen Foods Corp
Seattle, WA . . . 206-322-8900
Nature Quality
San Martin, CA . . . 408-683-2182
Oneonta Starr Ranch Growers
Wenatchee, WA . . . 509-663-2191
Ontario Produce Company
Ontario, OR . . . 541-889-6485
Paradise Products Corporation
Boca Raton, FL . . . 800-826-1235
Peri & Sons Farms
Yerington, NV . . . 775-463-4444
POG
Grand Bend, ON . . . 519-238-5704
R.C. McEntire & Company
Columbia, SC . . . 803-799-3388
Rainsweet Inc
Salem, OR . . . 800-363-4293
Sargent and Greenleaf
Nicholasville, KY . . . 800-826-7652
Schiff Food Products Co Inc
Totowa, NJ . . . 973-237-1990
Seald Sweet
Vero Beach, FL . . . 559-636-4400
Superior Nutrition Corporation
Wilmington, DE . . . 302-655-5762
SupHerb Farms
Turlock, CA . . . 800-787-4372
Swagger Foods Corp
Vernon Hills, IL . . . 847-913-1200
Symms Fruit Ranch Inc
Caldwell, ID . . . 208-459-4821
Tanimura Antle Inc
Salinas, CA . . . 800-772-4542
United Marketing Exchange
Delta, CO . . . 970-874-3332
Vegetable Juices Inc
Chicago, IL . . . 888-776-9752
Vessey & Co Inc
Holtville, CA . . . 760-356-0130
Viva Tierra
Mt Vernon, WA . . . 360-855-0566
Wildcat Produce
McGrew, NE . . . 308-783-2438
Z&S Distributing
Fresno, CA . . . 800-467-0788

Canned

Appleton Produce Company
Weiser, ID . . . 208-414-3352
Bob Gordon & Associates
Oak Park, IL . . . 708-524-9611
Ful-Flav-R Foods
Alamo, CA . . . 925-838-0300
Gl Mezzetta Inc
American Canyon, CA . . . 800-941-7044
L & S Packing Co
Farmingdale, NY . . . 800-286-6487
Paradise Products Corporation
Boca Raton, FL . . . 800-826-1235
Reckitt Benckiser LLC
Parsippany, NJ . . . 973-404-2600

Cocktail

Castella Imports Inc
Brentwood, NY . . . 631-231-5500

Crushed

Schiff Food Products Co Inc
Totowa, NJ . . . 973-237-1990

Frozen

Appleton Produce Company
Weiser, ID . . . 208-414-3352
Dickinson Frozen Foods
Eagle, ID . . . 800-886-4326
National Frozen Foods Corp
Seattle, WA . . . 206-322-8900
Nature Quality
San Martin, CA . . . 408-683-2182
Paris Foods Corporation
Trappe, MD . . . 410-200-9595
POG
Grand Bend, ON . . . 519-238-5704
Rainsweet Inc
Salem, OR . . . 800-363-4293
SupHerb Farms
Turlock, CA . . . 800-787-4372
Vegetable Juices Inc
Chicago, IL . . . 888-776-9752

Green

Di Mare Fresh Inc
Fort Worth, TX . . . 817-385-3000
Russo Farms
Vineland, NJ . . . 856-692-5942
SupHerb Farms
Turlock, CA . . . 800-787-4372
Tanimura Antle Inc
Salinas, CA . . . 800-772-4542
Walter P Rawl & Sons Inc
Pelion, SC . . . 803-894-1900

Minced

Swagger Foods Corp
Vernon Hills, IL . . . 847-913-1200

Pearl & Cocktail Onions

Kingston Fresh
Idaho Falls, ID . . . 208-522-2365
L & S Packing Co
Farmingdale, NY . . . 800-286-6487
Magic Valley Growers
Wendell, ID . . . 208-536-6693
National Frozen Foods Corp
Seattle, WA . . . 206-322-8900
POG
Grand Bend, ON . . . 519-238-5704
Weiser River Packing
Weiser, ID . . . 208-549-0200

Red

Baker Produce
Kennewick, WA . . . 800-624-7553
Pawelski Farm
Goshen, NY . . . 845-772-2600
Peri & Sons Farms
Yerington, NV . . . 775-463-4444
SupHerb Farms
Turlock, CA . . . 800-787-4372
Vessey & Co Inc
Holtville, CA . . . 760-356-0130

Spanish

SupHerb Farms
Turlock, CA . . . 800-787-4372

Orange

A. Gagliano Co Inc
Milwaukee, WI . . . 800-272-1516
Agrexco USA
Jamaica, NY . . . 718-481-8700
Bissinger's Handcrafted Chocolatier
St. Louis, MO . . . 314-615-2400
Cal Harvest Marketing Inc
Hanford, CA . . . 559-582-4494
Corona College Heights
Riverside, CA . . . 951-351-7880
Di Mare Fresh Inc
Fort Worth, TX . . . 817-385-3000
DNE World Fruit Sales
Fort Pierce, FL . . . 800-327-6676
Dundee Groves
Dundee, FL . . . 800-294-2266
Fillmore Piru Citrus
Piru, CA . . . 805-521-1781
Gene's Citrus Ranch
Palmetto, FL . . . 888-723-2006
Haines City Citrus Growers
Haines City, FL . . . 800-327-6676
Hale Indian River Groves
Vero Beach, FL . . . 800-562-4502
Heller Brothers Packing Corp
Winter Garden, FL . . . 855-543-5537
Hunt Brothers Cooperative
Lake Wales, FL . . . 863-676-1411
Lane Southern Orchards
Fort Valley, GA . . . 800-277-3224
Leroy Smith Inc
Vero Beach, FL . . . 772-569-2059
Magnolia Citrus Assn
Porterville, CA . . . 559-784-4455
Oneonta Starr Ranch Growers
Wenatchee, WA . . . 509-663-2191
Orange Cove-Sanger Citrus
Orange Cove, CA . . . 559-626-4453
P R Farms Inc
Clovis, CA . . . 559-299-0201
Paradise Inc
Plant City, FL . . . 813-752-1155
Reed Lang Farms
Rio Hondo, TX . . . 956-748-2354
Seald Sweet
Vero Beach, FL . . . 559-636-4400
Tony Vitrano Company
Jessup, MD . . . 800-481-3784
Unique Ingredients LLC
Gold Canyon, AZ . . . 480-983-2498
Wonderful Citrus
Mission, TX . . . 956-205-7300
Yokohl Packing Co
Lindsay, CA . . . 559-562-1327
Z&S Distributing
Fresno, CA . . . 800-467-0788

Blood

Z&S Distributing
Fresno, CA . . . 800-467-0788

Mandarin

Agrocan
Ville St Laurent, QC . . . 877-247-6226
Au Printemps Gourmet
Saint-Jerome, QC . . . 800-438-6676
DNE World Fruit Sales
Fort Pierce, FL . . . 800-327-6676
Ntc Marketing
Williamsville, NY . . . 800-333-1637

Canned

Ntc Marketing
Williamsville, NY . . . 800-333-1637

Naval

DNE World Fruit Sales
Fort Pierce, FL . . . 800-327-6676
Johnston Farms
Bakersfield, CA . . . 661-366-3201
KERN Ridge Growers LLC
Arvin, CA . . . 661-854-3141
Magnolia Citrus Assn
Porterville, CA . . . 559-784-4455

Z&S Distributing
Fresno, CA 800-467-0788

Peels

Fmali Herb
Santa Cruz, CA 831-423-7913

Pieces

Citrico
Northbrook, IL 800-445-2171

Sections

Canned

Emerling International Foods
Buffalo, NY. 716-833-7381

Valencia

Magnolia Citrus Assn
Porterville, CA 559-784-4455
Z&S Distributing
Fresno, CA 800-467-0788

Oriental Vegetables

Canned

Lee's Food Products
Toronto, ON 416-465-2407
Nikken Foods
St Louis, MO. 314-881-5818

Papaya

Brooks Tropicals Inc
Homestead, FL 800-327-4833
Calavo Growers
Santa Paula, CA 805-525-1245
Natural Foods Inc
Toledo, OH 419-537-1711
Organic Planet
San Francisco, CA 415-765-5590
Setton International Foods
Commack, NY 800-227-4397
Timber Crest Farms
Healdsburg, CA 888-766-4233
Unique Ingredients LLC
Gold Canyon, AZ 480-983-2498

Dried

American Importing Co.
Minneapolis, MN 855-273-0466
Bedemco Inc
White Plains, NY 914-683-1119
Fine Dried Foods Intl
Santa Cruz, CA 831-426-1413
Sunridge Farms
Royal Oaks, CA 831-786-7000

Peach

Ballantine Produce Company
Reedley, CA 559-875-2583
Ben B. Schwartz & Sons
Detroit, MI 313-841-8300
Brandt Farms Inc
Reedley, CA 559-638-6961
Bridenbaugh Orchards
Martinsburg, PA 814-793-2364
California Fruit
San Diego, CA 877-378-4811
Capitol Foods
Memphis, TN 662-781-9021
Central California Raisin Packing Co, Inc.
Del Rey, CA 559-888-2195
Cherry Hill Orchards
Lancaster, PA. 717-872-9311
Cherry Lane Frozen Fruits
Vineland Station, ON 877-243-7796
Clofine Dairy Products Inc
Linwood, NJ 609-653-1000
Copper Hills Fruit Sales
Fresno, CA 559-432-5400
Corrin Produce Sales
Dinuba, CA. 559-596-0517
Custom Produce Sales
Parlier, CA 559-254-5800
Del Mar Food Products Corp
Watsonville, CA 831-722-3516
Fruit Acres Farm Market and U-Pick
Coloma, MI. 269-208-3591
Hialeah Products Co
Hollywood, FL 800-923-3379
HMC Farms
Kingsburg, CA 559-897-1025
Kings Canyon
Reedley, CA 559-638-3571
Lane Southern Orchards
Fort Valley, GA. 800-277-3224
Livingston Farmers Assn
Livingston, CA 209-394-7941
Mason County Fruit Packers Cooperative
Hart, MI. 231-873-7504
Miss Scarlett's Flowers
Juneau, AK 800-345-6734
Naraghi Group
Escalon, CA 209-579-5253
Natural Foods Inc
Toledo, OH 419-537-1711
North Bay Produce Inc
Traverse City, MI 231-946-1941
Nut Factory
Spokane Valley, WA 888-239-5288
Oneonta Starr Ranch Growers
Wenatchee, WA. 509-663-2191
Organic Planet
San Francisco, CA 415-765-5590
Overlake Foods
Olympia, WA 800-683-1078
P R Farms Inc
Clovis, CA 559-299-0201
Pandol Brothers Inc
Delano, CA 661-725-3755
Patterson Vegetable Company
Patterson, CA 209-892-2611
Peterson Farms Inc
Shelby, MI. 231-861-0119
Prima® Wawona
Fresno, CA 559-787-8780
Rice Fruit Co
Gardners, PA. 800-627-3359
Shafer Lake Fruit Inc
Hartford, MI 269-621-3194
Shawnee Canning Co
Cross Junction, VA 800-713-1414
Sun Valley Packing
Reedley, CA 559-591-1515
Sunsweet Growers Inc.
Yuba City, CA. 800-417-2253
Symms Fruit Ranch Inc
Caldwell, ID 208-459-4821
T.S. Smith & Sons
Bridgeville, DE. 302-337-8271
Talbott Farms
Palisade, CO 970-464-5656
Taylor Orchards
Reynolds, GA 478-847-5963
Terri Lynn Inc
Elgin, IL 800-323-0775
Timber Crest Farms
Healdsburg, CA 888-766-4233
Titan Farms
Ridge Spring, SC 803-685-5381
Tom Ringhausen Orchards
Hardin, IL 800-258-6645
Trinity Fruit Sale Co
Fresno, CA 559-433-3777
Unique Ingredients LLC
Gold Canyon, AZ 480-983-2498
Viva Tierra
Mt Vernon, WA. 360-855-0566
Wawona Frozen Foods Inc
Clovis, CA 559-299-2901
Z&S Distributing
Fresno, CA 800-467-0788

Canned

Agrocan
Ville St Laurent, QC. 877-247-6226
Emerling International Foods
Buffalo, NY. 716-833-7381
George Noroian
Oakland, CA. 510-591-7044
Overlake Foods
Olympia, WA 800-683-1078
Shafer-Haggart
Vancouver, BC 604-669-5512
Shawnee Canning Co
Cross Junction, VA 800-713-1414

Dried

Bedemco Inc
White Plains, NY 914-683-1119

Frozen

Cherry Lane Frozen Fruits
Vineland Station, ON 877-243-7796
Emerling International Foods
Buffalo, NY. 716-833-7381
George Noroian
Oakland, CA 510-591-7044
Overlake Foods
Olympia, WA 800-683-1078

Klingstone

Canned - Sliced & Diced

Mountain View Fruit Sales
Reedley, CA 559-637-9933

Sliced

Producer Marketing Overlake
Olympia, WA 360-352-9096

Pear

A. Gagliano Co Inc
Milwaukee, WI 800-272-1516
Adobe Creek Packing Co Inc
Kelseyville, CA. 707-279-4204
Ben B. Schwartz & Sons
Detroit, MI 313-841-8300
Brothers International Food Corporation
Rochester, NY. 585-343-3007
California Fruit
San Diego, CA 877-378-4811
Chelan Fresh Marketing
Chelan, WA. 509-682-2591
Chief Wenatchee
Wenatchee, WA. 509-662-5197
D'Arrigo Brothers Company of California
Salinas, CA 831-455-4500
Delta Packing
Lodi, CA 209-334-1023
Diamond Fruit Growers
Hood River, OR 541-354-5300
Earthbound Farm
San Jn Bautista, CA 800-690-3200
George W Saulpaugh & Son
Germantown, NY 518-537-6500
Giumarra Companies
Los Angeles, CA. 213-627-2900
HH Dobbins Inc
Lyndonville, NY 877-362-2467
Hialeah Products Co
Hollywood, FL 800-923-3379
Matson Fruit Co
Selah, WA 509-697-7100
Miss Scarlett's Flowers
Juneau, AK 800-345-6734
Mt. Konocti Growers
Kelseyville, CA. 707-279-4213
New York Apple Sales Inc
Glenmont, NY. 888-477-6770
Nuchief Sales Inc
Wenatchee, WA. 888-269-4638
Oneonta Starr Ranch Growers
Wenatchee, WA. 509-663-2191
Pavero Cold Storage
Highland, NY 800-435-2994
Reter Fruit
Medford, OR. 541-772-9560
Rice Fruit Co
Gardners, PA. 800-627-3359
Scotian Gold
Coldbrook, NS 888-726-8426
Stadelman Fruit LLC
Zillah, WA. 509-829-5145
Stanley Orchards Sales, Inc.
Modena, NY 845-883-7351
Symms Fruit Ranch Inc
Caldwell, ID 208-459-4821
Terri Lynn Inc
Elgin, IL 800-323-0775
Timber Crest Farms
Healdsburg, CA 888-766-4233
Trinity Fruit Sale Co
Fresno, CA 559-433-3777
Truitt Bros Inc
Salem, OR. 800-547-8712

Unique Ingredients LLC
Gold Canyon, AZ 480-983-2498
Viva Tierra
Mt Vernon, WA 360-855-0566
Yakima Fresh
Yakima, WA 509-248-5770

Asian

Ballantine Produce Company
Reedley, CA 559-875-2583
Fowler Packing Co
Fresno, CA 559-834-5911
Giumarra Companies
Los Angeles, CA 213-627-2900
Naumes, Inc.
Medford, OR 541-772-6268
Price Co
Yakima, WA 509-966-4110

Bartlett

Adobe Creek Packing Co Inc
Kelseyville, CA 707-279-4204

Bosc

Adobe Creek Packing Co Inc
Kelseyville, CA 707-279-4204

Canned

Agrocan
Ville St Laurent, QC 877-247-6226
Arbre Farms Inc
Walkerville, MI 231-873-3337
Emerling International Foods
Buffalo, NY 716-833-7381
Seneca Foods Corp
Marion, NY 315-926-8100

D'Anjou/Bosc

Associated Fruit Company
Phoenix, OR 541-535-1787

Dried

Bedemco Inc
White Plains, NY 914-683-1119

Frozen

Arbre Farms Inc
Walkerville, MI 231-873-3337
Emerling International Foods
Buffalo, NY 716-833-7381

Red

Adobe Creek Packing Co Inc
Kelseyville, CA 707-279-4204

Peas

Boskovich Farms Inc
Oxnard, CA 805-487-2299
Camellia Beans
Harahan, LA 504-733-8480
Caribbean Food Delights Inc
Tappan, NY 845-398-3000
Castella Imports Inc
Brentwood, NY 631-231-5500
Garden Valley Corp
Sutherlin, OR 541-459-9565
Hanover Foods Corp
Hanover, PA 717-632-6000
Inland Empire Foods
Riverside, CA 888-452-3267
International Home Foods
Parsippany, NJ 973-359-9920
Knight Seed Company
Burnsville, MN 800-328-2999
Lakeside Foods Inc.
Plainview, MN 507-534-3141
Mezza
Lake Forest, IL 888-206-6054
Mills Brothers Intl
Seattle, WA 206-575-3000
Miramar Fruit Trading Company
Doral, FL 305-883-4774
National Frozen Foods Corp
Seattle, WA 206-322-8900
New Harvest Foods
Washington, DC 920-822-2578
Norben Co
Willoughby, OH 888-466-7236
Northwest Pea & Bean Co
Spokane Valley, WA 509-534-3821
Pictsweet Co
Bells, TN 731-663-7600
Royal Caribbean Bakery
Mt Vernon, NY 888-818-0971
Smith Frozen Foods Inc
Weston, OR 541-566-3515
Snowcrest Packer
Abbotsford, BC 800-265-3686
Spokane Seed Co
Spokane Valley, WA 800-359-8478
Strathroy Foods
Strathroy, ON 519-245-4600
Symons Frozen Foods
Centralia, WA 360-736-1321
Talley Farms
Arroyo Grande, CA 805-489-5400
Twin City Foods Inc.
Stanwood, WA 206-515-2400
Vege-Cool
Newman, CA 209-862-2360
Veronica Foods Inc
Oakland, CA 800-370-5554
Wallace Grain & Pea Company
Pullman, WA 509-878-1561
Z&S Distributing
Fresno, CA 800-467-0788

Black-eyed

Pictsweet Co
Bells, TN 731-663-7600

Canned

Emerling International Foods
Buffalo, NY 716-833-7381

Frozen

Emerling International Foods
Buffalo, NY 716-833-7381
Pictsweet Co
Bells, TN 731-663-7600

Canned

Blue Runner Foods Inc
Gonzales, LA 225-647-3016
Carriere Foods Inc
Saint-Denis-Sur-Richelie, QC 450-787-3411
Emerling International Foods
Buffalo, NY 716-833-7381
Hanover Foods Corp
Hanover, PA 717-632-6000
International Home Foods
Parsippany, NJ 973-359-9920
Lakeside Foods Inc.
Plainview, MN 507-534-3141
Lakeside Foods Inc.
Manitowoc, WI 800-466-3834
Lodi Canning Co
Lodi, WI 608-592-4236
New Harvest Foods
Washington, DC 920-822-2578

Dry

Camellia Beans
Harahan, LA 504-733-8480
Just Tomatoes
Westley, CA 800-537-1985
Mills Brothers Intl
Seattle, WA 206-575-3000
Spokane Seed Co
Spokane Valley, WA 800-359-8478

Frozen

Cavendish Farms
Dieppe, NB 506-858-7710
Emerling International Foods
Buffalo, NY 716-833-7381
Hanover Foods Corp
Hanover, PA 717-632-6000
Lakeside Foods Inc.
Plainview, MN 507-534-3141
Lakeside Foods Inc.
Manitowoc, WI 800-466-3834
Lisa's Organics
Carnelian Bay, CA 877-584-5711
Lodi Canning Co
Lodi, WI 608-592-4236
National Frozen Foods Corp
Seattle, WA 206-322-8900
Paris Foods Corporation
Trappe, MD 410-200-9595
Pictsweet Co
Bells, TN 731-663-7600
Smith Frozen Foods Inc
Weston, OR 541-566-3515
Snowcrest Packer
Abbotsford, BC 800-265-3686
Strathroy Foods
Strathroy, ON 519-245-4600
Symons Frozen Foods
Centralia, WA 360-736-1321
Twin City Foods Inc.
Stanwood, WA 206-515-2400

Green

Knight Seed Company
Burnsville, MN 800-328-2999
Northwest Pea & Bean Co
Spokane Valley, WA 509-534-3821
Pictsweet Co
Bells, TN 731-663-7600
Sno-Pac Foods Inc
Caledonia, MN 800-533-2215

Green & Yellow Split - Dried

Country Cupboard
Lewisburg, PA 570-523-3211
Emerling International Foods
Buffalo, NY 716-833-7381
New Organics
Kenwood, CA 734-677-5570
Organic Planet
San Francisco, CA 415-765-5590
Spokane Seed Co
Spokane Valley, WA 800-359-8478
Unique Ingredients LLC
Gold Canyon, AZ 480-983-2498
Vege-Cool
Newman, CA 209-862-2360

Snap

Miss Scarlett's Flowers
Juneau, AK 800-345-6734
National Frozen Foods Corp
Seattle, WA 206-322-8900
Pictsweet Co
Bells, TN 731-663-7600

Snow

North Bay Produce Inc
Traverse City, MI 231-946-1941

Southern

Trinidad Benham Corporation
Denver, CO 303-220-1400

Yellow Split

Knight Seed Company
Burnsville, MN 800-328-2999
Northwest Pea & Bean Co
Spokane Valley, WA 509-534-3821
Timeless Seeds
Ulm, MT 406-866-3340
United Pulse Trading Inc
Bismarck, ND 701-751-1623

Peppers

Abbott & Cobb Inc
Feasterville, PA 800-345-7333
AgroCepia
Miami, FL 305-704-3488
B & G Foods Inc.
Parsippany, NJ 973-401-6500
Baumer Foods Inc
Metairie, LA 504-482-5761
Bifulco Four Seasons
Pittsgrove, NJ 856-692-0778
Big B Barbecue
Evansville, IN 812-425-5235
Blue Marble Brands
Providence, RI 888-534-0246
Bob Gordon & Associates
Oak Park, IL 708-524-9611
Border Foods
New Hope, MN 763-559-7338
Boskovich Farms Inc
Oxnard, CA 805-487-2299

Carando Gourmet Frozen Foods
Agawam, MA 888-227-2636
Cherchies
Malvern, PA 800-644-1980
Christopher Ranch LLC
Gilroy, CA. 408-847-1100
Chugwater Chili
Chugwater, WY 800-972-4454
Comanche Tortilla Factory
Fort Stockton, TX. 432-336-3245
Del Mar Food Products Corp
Watsonville, CA 831-722-3516
Delta Packing
Lodi, CA. 209-334-1023
Dickinson Frozen Foods
Eagle, ID. 800-886-4326
Dolce Nonna
Whitestone, NY 718-767-3501
Eckert Cold Storage
Manteca, CA. 209-823-3181
EDCO Food Products Inc
Hobart, WI 800-255-3768
Emerling International Foods
Buffalo, NY. 716-833-7381
F & S Produce Co Inc
Vineland, NJ 800-886-3316
Fiesta Canning Co
Phoenix, AZ 602-212-2424
Food City Pickle Company
Battle Creek, MI 269-781-9135
Fountain Valley Foods
Colorado Springs, CO. 719-573-6012
Frog Ranch Foods
Glouster, OH. 800-742-2488
Ful-Flav-R Foods
Alamo, CA 925-838-0300
Garon Foods
Herrin, IL 618-942-4810
George Chiala Farms Inc
Morgan Hill, CA. 408-778-0562
Giuliano's Specialty Foods
Garden Grove, CA 714-895-9661
Giumarra Companies
Los Angeles, CA. 213-627-2900
Gl Mezzetta Inc
American Canyon, CA 800-941-7044
GNS Spices
Walnut, CA 909-594-9505
Great American Appetizers
Nampa, ID. 800-282-4834
GWB Foods Corporation
Brooklyn, NY 877-977-7610
Haliburton International Inc
Ontario, CA. 877-980-4295
Harris Farms Inc
Coalinga, CA. 800-311-6211
Hermann Pickle Co
Garrettsville, OH. 800-245-2696
JES Foods
Cleveland, OH 216-883-8987
Johnston Farms
Bakersfield, CA 661-366-3201
Kaiser Pickles
Cincinnati, OH 888-291-0608
Kaplan & Zubrin
Camden, NJ. 856-964-1083
Krinos Foods
Bronx, NY. 718-729-9000
Kruger Foods
Stockton, CA. 209-941-8518
L & S Packing Co
Farmingdale, NY 800-286-6487
Lakeside Packing Company
Harrow, ON. 519-738-2314
Landry's Pepper Co
St Martinville, LA. 337-394-6097
Mama Lil's Peppers
Portland, OR 503-206-6746
Matador Processors
Blanchard, OK 800-847-0797
Michigan Freeze Pack
Hart, MI. 231-873-2175
Miguel's Stowe Away
Stowe, VT. 800-448-6517
Monticello Canning Company
Crossville, TN
Mt Olive Pickle Co
Mt Olive, NC 800-672-5041
Nature Quality
San Martin, CA. 408-683-2182
Norpaco Inc
Middletown, CT 800-252-0222

Pacific Choice Brands
Fresno, CA 559-476-3581
Pastene Co LTD
Canton, MA 781-298-3397
Pastorelli Food Products
Chicago, IL 800-767-2829
Pepper Creek Farms
Lawton, OK. 800-526-8132
Peter Rabbit Farms
Coachella, CA. 760-398-0136
Pure Food Ingredients
Verona, WI 800-355-9601
Ralph Sechler & Son Inc
St Joe, IN. 800-332-5461
Rene Produce Dist
Rio Rico, AZ. 520-281-0806
Ripon Pickle Co Inc
Ripon, WI 920-748-7110
Ron Son Foods Inc
Swedesboro, NJ 856-241-7333
Sargent and Greenleaf
Nicholasville, KY. 800-826-7652
Schiff Food Products Co Inc
Totowa, NJ 973-237-1990
Sedlock Farm
Lynn Center, IL. 309-521-8284
Snowcrest Packer
Abbotsford, BC. 800-265-3686
South Mill
Kennett Square, PA. 610-444-4800
Strub Pickles
Brantford, ON. 519-751-1717
SupHerb Farms
Turlock, CA 800-787-4372
Topor's Pickle & Food Svc Inc
Detroit, MI 313-237-0288
Tropical Foods
Charlotte, NC 800-438-4470
Vega Food Industries Inc
Cranston, RI 800-973-7737
Vegetable Juices Inc
Chicago, IL. 888-776-9752
Vincent Formusa Company
Des Plaines, IL 847-813-6040
Violet Packing Holdings LLC
Williamstown, NJ. 856-629-7428
Wholesum Family Farms
Nogales, AZ 520-281-9233
Z&S Distributing
Fresno, CA 800-467-0788

Banana

Food City Pickle Company
Battle Creek, MI 269-781-9135
Gl Mezzetta Inc
American Canyon, CA 800-941-7044
Kaplan & Zubrin
Camden, NJ. 856-964-1083
Topor's Pickle & Food Svc Inc
Detroit, MI 313-237-0288
Trappey's Fine Foods Inc
New Iberia, LA. 337-365-8281

Bell

Christopher Ranch LLC
Gilroy, CA. 408-847-1100
Dehydrates Inc
Hewlett, NY 800-983-4443
Dickinson Frozen Foods
Eagle, ID. 800-886-4326
Earthbound Farm
San Jn Bautista, CA 800-690-3200
Eckert Cold Storage
Manteca, CA. 209-823-3181
F & S Produce Co Inc
Vineland, NJ. 800-886-3316
Ful-Flav-R Foods
Alamo, CA 925-838-0300
Gel Spice Co LLC
Bayonne, NJ 800-922-0230
George Chiala Farms Inc
Morgan Hill, CA. 408-778-0562
Grasso Foods Inc
Swedesboro, NJ 856-467-2222
KERN Ridge Growers LLC
Arvin, CA 661-854-3141
Moody Dunbar Inc
Johnson City, TN 423-952-0100
Nature Quality
San Martin, CA. 408-683-2182

Oxford Frozen Foods
Oxford, NS 902-447-2100
Rene Produce Dist
Rio Rico, AZ. 520-281-0806
Ripon Pickle Co Inc
Ripon, WI. 920-748-7110
Schiff Food Products Co Inc
Totowa, NJ 973-237-1990
SupHerb Farms
Turlock, CA 800-787-4372
Sure-Fresh Produce Inc
Santa Maria, CA 888-423-5379
Talley Farms
Arroyo Grande, CA. 805-489-5400
Titan Farms
Ridge Spring, SC 803-685-5381
Tropical Foods
Charlotte, NC 800-438-4470
Vegetable Juices Inc
Chicago, IL. 888-776-9752
Z&S Distributing
Fresno, CA 800-467-0788

Canned

Bob Gordon & Associates
Oak Park, IL 708-524-9611
Colonna Brothers Inc
North Bergen, NJ 201-864-1115
Emerling International Foods
Buffalo, NY. 716-833-7381
Ful-Flav-R Foods
Alamo, CA 925-838-0300
L & S Packing Co
Farmingdale, NY 800-286-6487
Mancini Packing Co
Zolfo Springs, FL 800-741-1778
Moody Dunbar Inc
Johnson City, TN 423-952-0100
Ron Son Foods Inc
Swedesboro, NJ 856-241-7333
Violet Packing Holdings LLC
Williamstown, NJ 856-629-7428

Capsicums

Advanced Spice & Trading
Carrollton, TX. 800-872-7811
Emerling International Foods
Buffalo, NY. 716-833-7381
Vegetable Juices Inc
Chicago, IL 888-776-9752

Frozen

SupHerb Farms
Turlock, CA 800-787-4372

Cayenne

Trappey's Fine Foods Inc
New Iberia, LA. 337-365-8281

Cherry

B & G Foods Inc.
Parsippany, NJ. 973-401-6500
F & S Produce Co Inc
Vineland, NJ 800-886-3316
Kaplan & Zubrin
Camden, NJ. 856-964-1083
L & S Packing Co
Farmingdale, NY 800-286-6487
Norpaco Inc
Middletown, CT 800-252-0222
Trappey's Fine Foods Inc
New Iberia, LA. 337-365-8281

Chile

American Key Food Products Inc
Closter, NJ. 877-263-7539
Border Foods
New Hope, MN. 763-559-7338
Chili Dude
Dallas, TX. 214-354-9906
Chugwater Chili
Chugwater, WY 800-972-4454
Dave's Gourmet
San Rafael, CA 800-758-0372
Emerling International Foods
Buffalo, NY. 716-833-7381
Fiesta Canning Co
Phoenix, AZ 602-212-2424
Ful-Flav-R Foods
Alamo, CA 925-838-0300

George Chiala Farms Inc
Morgan Hill, CA 408-778-0562
Gl Mezzetta Inc
American Canyon, CA 800-941-7044
KERN Ridge Growers LLC
Arvin, CA 661-854-3141
Magic Seasoning Blends
New Orleans, LA 800-457-2857
Mancini Packing Co
Zolfo Springs, FL 800-741-1778
New Mexico Green Chile Company
Artesia, NM 505-503-0996
Pepperland Farms
Ponchatoula, LA 985-956-6703
Pure Food Ingredients
Verona, WI 800-355-9601
SupHerb Farms
Turlock, CA 800-787-4372
Tropical Commodities
Miami, FL 305-471-8120
Vega Food Industries Inc
Cranston, RI 800-973-7737
Vegetable Juices Inc
Chicago, IL 888-776-9752
Walker Foods
Los Angeles, CA 800-966-5199
Z&S Distributing
Fresno, CA 800-467-0788

Dried Pods

American Key Food Products Inc
Closter, NJ 877-263-7539
Emerling International Foods
Buffalo, NY 716-833-7381
Gel Spice Co LLC
Bayonne, NJ 800-922-0230
Magic Seasoning Blends
New Orleans, LA 800-457-2857

Chipotle

Emerling International Foods
Buffalo, NY 716-833-7381
Magic Seasoning Blends
New Orleans, LA 800-457-2857
Ripon Pickle Co Inc
Ripon, WI 920-748-7110
Vegetable Juices Inc
Chicago, IL 888-776-9752

Frozen

Carando Gourmet Frozen Foods
Agawam, MA 888-227-2636
Dickinson Frozen Foods
Eagle, ID 800-886-4326
Eckert Cold Storage
Manteca, CA 209-823-3181
Emerling International Foods
Buffalo, NY 716-833-7381
Grasso Foods Inc
Swedesboro, NJ 856-467-2222
Great American Appetizers
Nampa, ID 800-282-4834
Hermann Pickle Co
Garrettsville, OH 800-245-2696
Matador Processors
Blanchard, OK 800-847-0797
Monticello Canning Company
Crossville, TN
Paris Foods Corporation
Trappe, MD 410-200-9595
Rainsweet Inc
Salem, OR 800-363-4293
San Antonio Farms
Platteville, WI 800-236-1119
Snowcrest Packer
Abbotsford, BC 800-265-3686
SupHerb Farms
Turlock, CA 800-787-4372
Vegetable Juices Inc
Chicago, IL 888-776-9752

Habanero

Brooks Tropicals Inc
Homestead, FL 800-327-4833
Garon Foods
Herrin, IL 618-942-4810
George Chiala Farms Inc
Morgan Hill, CA 408-778-0562

Jalapeno

Advanced Spice & Trading
Carrollton, TX 800-872-7811
AgroCepia
Miami, FL 305-704-3488
Arbre Farms Inc
Walkerville, MI 231-873-3337
Dehydrates Inc
Hewlett, NY 800-983-4443
Eckert Cold Storage
Manteca, CA 209-823-3181
EDCO Food Products Inc
Hobart, WI 800-255-3768
Emerling International Foods
Buffalo, NY 716-833-7381
F & S Produce Co Inc
Vineland, NJ 800-886-3316
Fountain Valley Foods
Colorado Springs, CO 719-573-6012
Ful-Flav-R Foods
Alamo, CA 925-838-0300
Garon Foods
Herrin, IL 618-942-4810
George Chiala Farms Inc
Morgan Hill, CA 408-778-0562
Gl Mezzetta Inc
American Canyon, CA 800-941-7044
Great American Appetizers
Nampa, ID 800-282-4834
L & S Packing Co
Farmingdale, NY 800-286-6487
Leon's Texas Cuisine
Mckinney, TX 972-529-5050
Limited Edition
Midland, TX 432-686-2008
Matador Processors
Blanchard, OK 800-847-0797
Miguel's Stowe Away
Stowe, VT 800-448-6517
Nature Quality
San Martin, CA 408-683-2182
Pepper Creek Farms
Lawton, OK 800-526-8132
Pure Food Ingredients
Verona, WI 800-355-9601
San Antonio Farms
Platteville, WI 800-236-1119
Strub Pickles
Brantford, ON 519-751-1717
SupHerb Farms
Turlock, CA 800-787-4372
Trappey's Fine Foods Inc
New Iberia, LA 337-365-8281
Vegetable Juices Inc
Chicago, IL 888-776-9752
Walker Foods
Los Angeles, CA 800-966-5199

Jalapeno & Chiles

Grasso Foods Inc
Swedesboro, NJ 856-467-2222
La Victoria Foods
Austin, MN 800-725-7212
Matador Processors
Blanchard, OK 800-847-0797
Nature Quality
San Martin, CA 408-683-2182
Pure Food Ingredients
Verona, WI 800-355-9601
SupHerb Farms
Turlock, CA 800-787-4372

Non-Bell

Grasso Foods Inc
Swedesboro, NJ 856-467-2222

Pepperoncini

Agrocan
Ville St Laurent, QC 877-247-6226
Baumer Foods Inc
Metairie, LA 504-482-5761
Big B Barbecue
Evansville, IN 812-425-5235
Bob Gordon & Associates
Oak Park, IL 708-524-9611
Castella Imports Inc
Brentwood, NY 631-231-5500
Emerling International Foods
Buffalo, NY 716-833-7381
Food City Pickle Company
Battle Creek, MI 269-781-9135
Gl Mezzetta Inc
American Canyon, CA 800-941-7044
L & S Packing Co
Farmingdale, NY 800-286-6487
Ron Son Foods Inc
Swedesboro, NJ 856-241-7333
Vegetable Juices Inc
Chicago, IL 888-776-9752

Roasted

Agrocan
Ville St Laurent, QC 877-247-6226
Bedemco Inc
White Plains, NY 914-683-1119
Castella Imports Inc
Brentwood, NY 631-231-5500
Ful-Flav-R Foods
Alamo, CA 925-838-0300
Mancini Packing Co
Zolfo Springs, FL 800-741-1778
Moody Dunbar Inc
Johnson City, TN 423-952-0100
Ron Son Foods Inc
Swedesboro, NJ 856-241-7333
Sunny Dell Foods Inc
Oxford, PA 610-932-5164
SupHerb Farms
Turlock, CA 800-787-4372

Serrano

EDCO Food Products Inc
Hobart, WI 800-255-3768
Emerling International Foods
Buffalo, NY 716-833-7381
F & S Produce Co Inc
Vineland, NJ 800-886-3316
San Antonio Farms
Platteville, WI 800-236-1119
SupHerb Farms
Turlock, CA 800-787-4372

Sweet

Carando Gourmet Frozen Foods
Agawam, MA 888-227-2636
Coutts Specialty Foods Inc
Boxborough, MA 800-919-2952
Kaplan & Zubrin
Camden, NJ 856-964-1083
Mancini Packing Co
Zolfo Springs, FL 800-741-1778
Ripon Pickle Co Inc
Ripon, WI 920-748-7110

Persimmons

Ballantine Produce Company
Reedley, CA 559-875-2583
Copper Hills Fruit Sales
Fresno, CA 559-432-5400
Emerling International Foods
Buffalo, NY 716-833-7381
HMC Farms
Kingsburg, CA 559-897-1025
Just Tomatoes
Westley, CA 800-537-1985
Naumes, Inc.
Medford, OR 541-772-6268
Pandol Brothers Inc
Delano, CA 661-725-3755
Tufts Ranch
Winters, CA 530-795-4144
West Pak Avocado Inc
Murrieta, CA 800-266-4414

Pimientos

Emerling International Foods
Buffalo, NY 716-833-7381
Monticello Canning Company
Crossville, TN
Moody Dunbar Inc
Johnson City, TN 423-952-0100
Paradise Products Corporation
Boca Raton, FL 800-826-1235
Strub Pickles
Brantford, ON 519-751-1717

Pineapple

Chiquita Brands LLC.
Fort Lauderdale, FL ... 954-924-5700
Del Monte Fresh Produce Inc.
Coral Gables, FL ... 800-950-3683
F & S Produce Co Inc
Vineland, NJ ... 800-886-3316
Hialeah Products Co
Hollywood, FL ... 800-923-3379
J H Verbridge & Son Inc
Williamson, NY ... 315-589-2366
Maui Gold Pineapple Company
Pukalani, HI ... 808-877-3805
Ntc Marketing
Williamsville, NY ... 800-333-1637
Nut Factory
Spokane Valley, WA ... 888-239-5288
Organic Planet
San Francisco, CA ... 415-765-5590
Pacific Coast Fruit Co
Portland, OR ... 503-234-6411
Paradise Inc
Plant City, FL ... 813-752-1155
Setton International Foods
Commack, NY ... 800-227-4397
Sunfood
El Cajon, CA ... 888-729-3663
Terri Lynn Inc
Elgin, IL ... 800-323-0775
Timber Crest Farms
Healdsburg, CA ... 888-766-4233
Transpacific Foods Inc
Irvine, CA ... 949-975-9900
Unique Ingredients LLC
Gold Canyon, AZ ... 480-983-2498

Canned

Agrocan
Ville St Laurent, QC ... 877-247-6226
Emerling International Foods
Buffalo, NY ... 716-833-7381
Maui Gold Pineapple Company
Pukalani, HI ... 808-877-3805
Ntc Marketing
Williamsville, NY ... 800-333-1637
Transpacific Foods Inc
Irvine, CA ... 949-975-9900

Chunks

Transpacific Foods Inc
Irvine, CA ... 949-975-9900

Crushed

Transpacific Foods Inc
Irvine, CA ... 949-975-9900

Dried

American Importing Co.
Minneapolis, MN ... 855-273-0466
Bedemco Inc
White Plains, NY ... 914-683-1119
Fine Dried Foods Intl
Santa Cruz, CA ... 831-426-1413
Golden Valley Natural
Shelley, ID ... 888-270-7147
King Arthur Flour
Norwich, VT ... 800-827-6836
Made In Nature
Boulder, CO ... 800-906-7426
Mariani Packing Co.
Vacaville, CA ... 707-452-2800
Sunridge Farms
Royal Oaks, CA ... 831-786-7000

Frozen

Emerling International Foods
Buffalo, NY ... 716-833-7381
J H Verbridge & Son Inc
Williamson, NY ... 315-589-2366
Pacific Coast Fruit Co
Portland, OR ... 503-234-6411
Townsend Farms Inc
Fairview, OR ... 503-666-1780

Plums

Ballantine Produce Company
Reedley, CA ... 559-875-2583
Brandt Farms Inc
Reedley, CA ... 559-638-6961
Burnette Foods
Elk Rapids, MI ... 231-264-8116
Copper Hills Fruit Sales
Fresno, CA ... 559-432-5400
Corrin Produce Sales
Dinuba, CA ... 559-596-0517
Custom Produce Sales
Parlier, CA ... 559-254-5800
Fowler Packing Co
Fresno, CA ... 559-834-5911
Henggeler Packing Company
Fruitland, ID ... 208-452-4212
J C Watson Co
Parma, ID ... 208-722-5141
Mountain View Fruit Sales
Reedley, CA ... 559-637-9933
North Bay Produce Inc
Traverse City, MI ... 231-946-1941
Oneonta Starr Ranch Growers
Wenatchee, WA ... 509-663-2191
Oregon Fruit Products Co
Salem, OR ... 800-394-9333
Organic Planet
San Francisco, CA ... 415-765-5590
P R Farms Inc
Clovis, CA ... 559-299-0201
Pandol Brothers Inc
Delano, CA ... 661-725-3755
Peterson Farms Inc
Shelby, MI ... 231-861-0119
Prima® Wawona
Fresno, CA ... 559-787-8780
Shafer Lake Fruit Inc
Hartford, MI ... 269-621-3194
Stadelman Fruit LLC
Zillah, WA ... 509-829-5145
Sun Valley Packing
Reedley, CA ... 559-591-1515
Symms Fruit Ranch Inc
Caldwell, ID ... 208-459-4821
Terri Lynn Inc
Elgin, IL ... 800-323-0775
Timber Crest Farms
Healdsburg, CA ... 888-766-4233
Trinity Fruit Sale Co
Fresno, CA ... 559-433-3777
Unique Ingredients LLC
Gold Canyon, AZ ... 480-983-2498
Viva Tierra
Mt Vernon, WA ... 360-855-0566
Z&S Distributing
Fresno, CA ... 800-467-0788

Canned

Burnette Foods
Elk Rapids, MI ... 231-264-8116
Emerling International Foods
Buffalo, NY ... 716-833-7381
Honee Bear Canning
Lawton, MI ... 800-626-2327
Oregon Fruit Products Co
Salem, OR ... 800-394-9333
Truitt Bros Inc
Salem, OR ... 800-547-8712

Dried

American Importing Co.
Minneapolis, MN ... 855-273-0466
Bedemco Inc
White Plains, NY ... 914-683-1119
Made In Nature
Boulder, CO ... 800-906-7426
Mariani Packing Co.
Vacaville, CA ... 707-452-2800
Setton International Foods
Commack, NY ... 800-227-4397

Frozen

Coloma Frozen Foods Inc
Coloma, MI ... 800-642-2723
Emerling International Foods
Buffalo, NY ... 716-833-7381
Fruithill Inc
Yamhill, OR ... 503-662-3926
Oregon Fruit Products Co
Salem, OR ... 800-394-9333

Pomegranate

Ballantine Produce Company
Reedley, CA ... 559-875-2583
Copper Hills Fruit Sales
Fresno, CA ... 559-432-5400
Emerling International Foods
Buffalo, NY ... 716-833-7381
Fowler Packing Co
Fresno, CA ... 559-834-5911
HMC Farms
Kingsburg, CA ... 559-897-1025
Naumes, Inc.
Medford, OR ... 541-772-6268
North Bay Produce Inc
Traverse City, MI ... 231-946-1941
POM Wonderful LLC
Los Angeles, CA ... 866-976-6999

Potatoes

Au Gratin

Captain Ken's Foods Inc
St Paul, MN ... 800-510-3811
Idahoan Foods LLC
Idaho Falls, ID ... 800-746-7999

Frozen

Captain Ken's Foods Inc
St Paul, MN ... 800-510-3811

Baked & Stuffed

Sun Glo Of Idaho
Sugar City, ID ... 208-356-7346

Frozen

Penobscot Mccrum LLC
Belfast, ME ... 800-435-4456
Sun Glo Of Idaho
Sugar City, ID ... 208-356-7346

Canned

Burnette Foods
Elk Rapids, MI ... 231-264-8116
Emerling International Foods
Buffalo, NY ... 716-833-7381
Nation Wide Canning Ltd.
Cottam, ON ... 519-839-4831
New Harvest Foods
Washington, DC ... 920-822-2578
Nickabood's Inc
Los Angeles, CA ... 213-746-1541
Ore-Ida Foods
Pittsburgh, PA ... 800-255-5750
Weil's Food Processing
Wheatley, ON ... 519-825-4572

Dehydrated

Idahoan Foods LLC
Idaho Falls, ID ... 800-746-7999
Specialty Ingredients
Buffalo Grove, IL ... 847-419-9595

Frozen

Agri-Dairy Products
Purchase, NY ... 914-697-9580
Emerling International Foods
Buffalo, NY ... 716-833-7381
Oregon Potato Co
Boardman, OR ... 800-336-6311
Unique Ingredients LLC
Gold Canyon, AZ ... 480-983-2498

Fresh

AgriNorthwest
Kennewick, WA ... 509-734-1195
Beamon Brothers
Goldsboro, NC ... 919-734-4931
Circle Valley Produce LLC
Idaho Falls, ID ... 208-524-2628
Earthbound Farm
San Jn Bautista, CA ... 800-690-3200
Hanover Potato Products Inc
Hanover, PA ... 717-632-0700
Oneonta Starr Ranch Growers
Wenatchee, WA ... 509-663-2191
Oregon Potato Co
Boardman, OR ... 800-336-6311
Oregon Potato Co
Pasco, WA ... 800-987-2726
Pacific Collier Fresh Company
Immokalee, FL ... 800-226-7274

R.D. Offutt Farms
Park Rapids, MN. 218-732-1461
Seald Sweet
Vero Beach, FL 559-636-4400
Symms Fruit Ranch Inc
Caldwell, ID 208-459-4821

Russet

Baker Produce
Kennewick, WA 800-624-7553
Bottom Line Foods
Pembroke Pines, FL 954-843-0562
Les Aliments Livabec Foods
Sherrington, QC 450-454-7971
McCain Produce Inc.
Florenceville-Bristol, NB 506-392-3036

White

McCain Produce Inc.
Florenceville-Bristol, NB 506-392-3036

Frozen

Cavendish Farms
Dieppe, NB 506-858-7710
Emerling International Foods
Buffalo, NY. 716-833-7381
Endico Potatoes Inc
Mt Vernon, NY 914-664-1151
McCain Foods USA Inc.
Oakbrook Terace, IL. 800-938-7799
Michael Foods, Inc.
Minnetonka, MN. 952-258-4000
Mr Dell Foods
Kearney, MO. 816-628-4644
Nickabood's Inc
Los Angeles, CA. 213-746-1541
Ore-Ida Foods
Pittsburgh, PA. 800-255-5750
Oregon Potato Co
Boardman, OR 800-336-6311
Paris Foods Corporation
Trappe, MD. 410-200-9595
Small Planet Foods
Minneapolis, MN 800-624-4123
Sun Glo Of Idaho
Sugar City, ID. 208-356-7346
Twin City Foods Inc.
Stanwood, WA 206-515-2400
Washington Potato Company
Pasco, WA. 800-897-2726

Rounds

Penobscot Mccrum LLC
Belfast, ME. 800-435-4456

Wedges

Ore-Ida Foods
Pittsburgh, PA. 800-255-5750
Penobscot Mccrum LLC
Belfast, ME. 800-435-4456

Instant

Gilster-Mary Lee Corp
Chester, IL. 618-826-2361
Idahoan Foods LLC
Idaho Falls, ID 800-746-7999

Oven Type

Frozen

Sun Glo Of Idaho
Sugar City, ID. 208-356-7346

Potatoes

Aaland Potato Company
Hoople, ND. 701-894-6144
Alsum Farms & Produce
Cambria, WI 800-236-5127
Baker Produce
Kennewick, WA 800-624-7553
Ben B. Schwartz & Sons
Detroit, MI 313-841-8300
Burnette Foods
Elk Rapids, MI 231-264-8116
Byrnes Packing Shed
Hastings, FL 904-692-1643
Canon Potato Company
Center, CO 719-754-3445
Crystal Potato Seed Co
Crystal, ND 701-657-2143
Dr. Oetker Canada Ltd.
Mississauga, ON 800-387-6939
Edmonton Potato Growers
Edmonton, AB 780-447-1860
Grower Shipper Potato Company
Monte Vista, CO 719-852-3569
Hanover Potato Products Inc
Hanover, PA 717-632-0700
Idaho Supreme Potatoes Inc
Firth, ID. 208-346-4100
Idahoan Foods LLC
Idaho Falls, ID 800-746-7999
Isadore A. Rapasadi & Son
Canastota, NY. 800-828-7277
J C Watson Co
Parma, ID 208-722-5141
J. R. Simplot Co.
Boise, ID 208-336-2110
Johnston Farms
Bakersfield, CA 661-366-3201
Kingston Fresh
Idaho Falls, ID 208-522-2365
Kiska Farms
Burbank, WA. 509-547-7746
Larsen Farms
Hamer, ID 208-374-5592
Lehr Brothers
Edison, CA 661-366-3244
Livingston Farmers Assn
Livingston, CA 209-394-7941
Lone Wolf Farms
Minto, ND. 701-248-3482
Maple Leaf Foods International
North York, ON. 800-268-3708
Martens Fresh
Port Byron, NY. 315-776-8821
McCain Foods USA Inc.
Oakbrook Terace, IL 800-938-7799
McCain Produce Inc.
Florenceville-Bristol, NB 506-392-3036
Michael Foods, Inc.
Minnetonka, MN. 952-258-4000
Mr Dell Foods
Kearney, MO. 816-628-4644
Muir Copper Canyon Farms
Salt Lake City, UT 800-564-0949
Nation Wide Canning Ltd.
Cottam, ON. 519-839-4831
National Harvest
Kansas City, MO. 816-842-9600
New Harvest Foods
Washington, DC 920-822-2578
Nonpareil Farms
Blackfoot, ID 800-522-2223
Nu-Way Potato Products
North York, ON. 416-241-9151
O C Schulz & Sons
Crystal, ND 701-657-2152
Oregon Potato Co
Boardman, OR 800-336-6311
Penobscot Mccrum LLC
Belfast, ME. 800-435-4456
Sun Glo Of Idaho
Sugar City, ID 208-356-7346
Twin City Foods Inc.
Stanwood, WA 206-515-2400
Vauxhall Foods
Vauxhall, AB. 403-654-2771
Vessey & Co Inc
Holtville, CA. 760-356-0130
Washington Potato Company
Pasco, WA. 800-897-2726
Weil's Food Processing
Wheatley, ON 519-825-4572
Wildcat Produce
McGrew, NE. 308-783-2438

Red

Baker Produce
Kennewick, WA 800-624-7553
Kiska Farms
Burbank, WA. 509-547-7746
McCain Produce Inc.
Florenceville-Bristol, NB 506-392-3036
Vessey & Co Inc
Holtville, CA. 760-356-0130

Powdered Vegetables

Emerling International Foods
Buffalo, NY. 716-833-7381
Green Foods Corp.
Oxnard, CA. 800-777-4430
Green Source Organics
Boynton Beach, FL. 561-740-8595
LYNQ
Montreal, QC
Marshall Ingredients
Wolcott, NY 800-796-9353
Niagara Foods
Middleport, NY. 716-735-7722
Spreda Group
Louisville, KY. 502-426-9411
Vegetable Juices Inc
Chicago, IL 888-776-9752
Weinberg Foods
Kirkland, WA 800-866-3447

Produce

Aaland Potato Company
Hoople, ND. 701-894-6144
Adobe Creek Packing Co Inc
Kelseyville, CA. 707-279-4204
AgriNorthwest
Kennewick, WA 509-734-1195
Alsum Farms & Produce
Cambria, WI 800-236-5127
Annapolis Produce & Restaurant
Annapolis, MD 410-266-5211
Anton Caratan & Son
Bakersfield, CA 661-725-2575
Apple Acres
La Fayette, NY 603-893-8596
Appleton Produce Company
Weiser, ID 208-414-3352
Applewood Orchards Inc
Deerfield, MI 800-447-3854
Argee Corp
Santee, CA 800-449-3030
Associated Fruit Company
Phoenix, OR 541-535-1787
Atlantic Blueberry
Hammonton, NJ 609-561-8600
Babe Farms Inc
Santa Maria, CA 800-648-6772
Baker Produce
Kennewick, WA 800-624-7553
Ballantine Produce Company
Reedley, CA 559-875-2583
Banana Distributing Company
San Antonio, TX. 210-227-8285
Bay Cities Produce Co Inc
San Leandro, CA. 510-346-4943
Ben B. Schwartz & Sons
Detroit, MI 313-841-8300
Ben-Bud Growers Inc.
Boca Raton, FL. 561-347-3120
Bifulco Four Seasons
Pittsgrove, NJ 856-692-0778
Bodek Kosher Produce Inc
Brooklyn, NY 718-377-4163
Boggiatto Produce Inc
Salinas, CA. 831-424-8952
Boskovich Farms Inc
Oxnard, CA. 805-487-2299
Brandt Farms Inc
Reedley, CA 559-638-6961
Bridenbaugh Orchards
Martinsburg, PA 814-793-2364
Brooks Tropicals Inc
Homestead, FL 800-327-4833
Byrnes Packing Shed
Hastings, FL 904-692-1643
Cal Harvest Marketing Inc
Hanford, CA 559-582-4494
Calco of Calgary
Calgary, AB. 403-295-3578
Calif Watercress Inc
Fillmore, CA. 805-524-4808
Capital Produce II Inc
Jessup, MD 443-755-1733
Caro Foods
Houma, LA 800-395-2276
Carolina Blueberry Co-Op Assn
Garland, NC 910-588-4220
Carson City Pickle Company
Carson City, MI. 989-584-3148
Castellini Group
Newport, KY. 800-233-8560

Cates Addis Company
Parkton, NC 800-423-1883
Chazy Orchards
Chazy, NY....................... 518-846-7171
Chief Wenatchee
Wenatchee, WA.................... 509-662-5197
Chris' Farm Stand
Peabody, MA...................... 978-994-4315
Christopher Ranch LLC
Gilroy, CA....................... 408-847-1100
Circle Valley Produce LLC
Idaho Falls, ID 208-524-2628
Concannon Vineyard
Livermore, CA 800-258-9866
Congdon Orchards Inc.
Yakima, WA 509-966-4440
Corona College Heights
Riverside, CA 951-351-7880
Corrin Produce Sales
Dinuba, CA....................... 559-596-0517
Coulter Giufre & Co Inc
Chittenango, NY.................. 315-687-6510
Country Fresh Mushroom Co
Toughkenamon, PA................. 610-268-3033
Couture Farms
Kettleman City, CA................ 559-386-9865
Crane & Crane Inc
Brewster, WA 509-689-3447
Crown Packing Company
Salinas, CA 831-424-2067
Crystal Potato Seed Co
Crystal, ND....................... 701-657-2143
D'Arrigo Brothers Company of California
Salinas, CA....................... 831-455-4500
Delta Packing
Lodi, CA 209-334-1023
Di Mare Fresh Inc
Fort Worth, TX 817-385-3000
Diamond Blueberry Inc
Hammonton, NJ 609-561-3661
Diamond Fruit Growers
Hood River, OR 541-354-5300
Dimond Tager Company Products
Tampa, FL 813-238-3111
DNE World Fruit Sales
Fort Pierce, FL 800-327-6676
DNO Inc
Columbus, OH 614-231-3601
Dundee Citrus Growers Assn
Dundee, FL........................ 800-447-1574
E.W. Bowker Company
Pemberton, NJ..................... 609-894-9508
Exeter Produce
Exeter, ON........................ 519-235-0141
F & S Produce Co Inc
Vineland, NJ 800-886-3316
Farm Pak Products Inc
Spring Hope, NC................... 800-367-2799
Federation-Southern Cprtvs
Atlanta, GA....................... 404-765-0991
Ferris Organic Farms
Eaton Rapids, MI 800-628-8736
Fiesta Farms
Toronto, ON 416-537-1235
Fig Garden Packing Inc
Fresno, CA 559-271-9000
Fillmore Piru Citrus
Piru, CA 805-521-1781
Finer Foods Inc
Chicago, IL....................... 773-579-3870
Flippin-Seaman Inc
Tyro, VA 434-277-5828
Florida Citrus
Bartow, FL 863-537-3999
Fresh Express, Inc.
Salinas, CA 800-242-5472
Fruit Ranch Inc
Milwaukee, WI..................... 800-433-3289
Ful-Flav-R Foods
Alamo, CA 925-838-0300
G Cefalu & Brother Inc
Jessup, MD 410-799-2910
Garber Farms
Iota, LA.......................... 800-824-2284
Gentile Brothers Company
Cincinnati, OH 800-877-7954
George Chiala Farms Inc
Morgan Hill, CA................... 408-778-0562
George W Saulpaugh & Son
Germantown, NY 518-537-6500
Glacier Foods
Houston, TX 832-375-6300
Godwin Produce Co
Dunn, NC 910-892-4171
Golden River Fruit Company
Vero Beach, FL.................... 772-562-8610
Golden Town Apple Products
Rougemont, QC 866-552-7643
Great Eastern Sun Trading Co
Asheville, NC 800-334-5809
Grimmway Farms
Bakersfield, CA 800-301-3101
Grower Shipper Potato Company
Monte Vista, CO................... 719-852-3569
Haines City Citrus Growers
Haines City, FL.................... 800-327-6676
Half Moon Fruit & Produce Company
Yolo, CA 530-662-1727
Harlin Fruit Co
Monett, MO 417-235-7370
Harner Farms
State College, PA 814-237-7919
Harris Farms Inc
Coalinga, CA...................... 800-311-6211
Heller Brothers Packing Corp
Winter Garden, FL 855-543-5537
Henggeler Packing Company
Fruitland, ID 208-452-4212
Herold's Salads
Cleveland, OH 800-427-2523
HH Dobbins Inc
Lyndonville, NY.................... 877-362-2467
Horton Fruit Co Inc
Louisville, KY 800-626-2245
Hunt Brothers Cooperative
Lake Wales, FL..................... 863-676-1411
Indian Bay Frozen Foods
Centreville, NL.................... 709-678-2844
Indian Hollow Farms
Richland Center, WI................ 800-236-3944
International Specialty Supply
Cookeville, TN 931-526-1106
Isadore A. Rapasadi & Son
Canastota, NY..................... 800-828-7277
J C Watson Co
Parma, ID 208-722-5141
J J Produce
Loxahatchee, FL................... 561-791-1796
Jack Brown Produce
Sparta, MI........................ 800-348-0834
Jasmine Vineyards, Inc.
Delano, CA 661-792-2141
JES Foods
Cleveland, OH 216-883-8987
Jonathan's Sprouts
Rochester, MA 508-763-2577
Joseph J. White
Browns Mills, NJ 609-893-2332
Kaiser Pickles
Cincinnati, OH 888-291-0608
Kingston Fresh
Idaho Falls, ID 208-522-2365
Kitchen Pride Mushrooms Farm
Gonzales, TX 830-540-4528
Knight Seed Company
Burnsville, MN.................... 800-328-2999
Knight's Appleden Fruit LTD
Colborne, ON 905-349-2521
L F Lambert Spawn Co
Coatesville, PA.................... 610-384-5031
Lagorio Enterprises
Manteca, CA...................... 209-982-5691
Lane Southern Orchards
Fort Valley, GA.................... 800-277-3224
Lehr Brothers
Edison, CA 661-366-3244
Lennox Farm
Shelburne, ON 519-925-6444
Livingston Farmers Assn
Livingston, CA 209-394-7941
Lone Wolf Farms
Minto, ND........................ 701-248-3482
Long Island Cauliflower Assn
Riverhead, NY 631-727-2212
Lou Pizzo Produce
Parkland, FL...................... 954-941-8830
Lucich Santos Farms
Patterson, CA 209-892-6500
M & S Tomato Repacking Co Inc
Springfield, MA 413-737-1308
Magnolia Citrus Assn
Porterville, CA 559-784-4455
Mancuso Cheese Co
Joliet, IL 815-722-2475
Mann Packing Co
Salinas, CA....................... 800-285-1002
Manzana Products Co.
Sebastopol, CA.................... 707-823-5313
Maple Leaf Foods International
North York, ON.................... 800-268-3708
Marley Orchards Corporation
Yakima, WA 509-248-5231
Martens Fresh
Port Byron, NY.................... 315-776-8821
Matson Fruit Co
Selah, WA........................ 509-697-7100
Maui Gold Pineapple Company
Pukalani, HI 808-877-3805
McDaniel Fruit
Fallbrook, CA..................... 760-728-8438
Mcfarling Foods Inc
Indianapolis, IN 317-635-2633
Merrill's Blueberry Farms
Ellsworth, ME..................... 800-711-6551
Michigan Celery Cooperative
Hudsonville, MI 616-669-1250
Mike & Jean's Berry Farm
Mt Vernon, WA.................... 360-424-7220
Mister Spear
Stockton, CA...................... 800-677-7327
Mixon Fruit Farms Inc
Bradenton, FL..................... 800-608-2525
Montreal Chop Suey Company
Montreal, QC 514-522-3134
Naraghi Group
Escalon, CA 209-579-5253
National Raisin Co.
Fowler, CA 559-834-5981
New York Apple Sales Inc
Glenmont, NY..................... 888-477-6770
Nonpareil Farms
Blackfoot, ID 800-522-2223
Nor-Cliff Farms
Port Colborne, ON 905-835-0808
North Bay Produce Inc
Traverse City, MI 231-946-1941
Northern Feed & Bean Company
Lucerne, CO 800-316-2326
Northwest Pea & Bean Co
Spokane Valley, WA 509-534-3821
NSG Transport Inc
Gothenburg, NE 308-537-7191
Nuchief Sales Inc
Wenatchee, WA.................... 888-269-4638
Nunes Co Inc
Salinas, CA 831-751-7500
Nut Factory
Spokane Valley, WA............... 888-239-5288
O C Schulz & Sons
Crystal, ND....................... 701-657-2152
Ocean Mist Farms
Castroville, CA.................... 831-633-2144
Ocean Spray International
Lakeville-Middleboro, MA 800-662-3263
Ontario Produce Company
Ontario, OR....................... 541-889-6485
Orange Cove-Sanger Citrus
Orange Cove, CA 559-626-4453
Oregon Potato Co
Boardman, OR 800-336-6311
Oxford Frozen Foods
Oxford, NS 902-447-2100
P R Farms Inc
Clovis, CA 559-299-0201
Pandol Brothers Inc
Delano, CA....................... 661-725-3755
Pavero Cold Storage
Highland, NY 800-435-2994
Peter Rabbit Farms
Coachella, CA..................... 760-398-0136
Pioneer Growers
Belle Glade, FL.................... 229-243-9306
Pleasant Grove Farms
Pleasant Grove, CA 916-655-3391
Post Familie Vineyards
Altus, AR 800-275-8423
Pots de Creme
Lexington, KY 859-299-2254
Prairie Mushrooms
Ardrossan, AB 780-467-3555
Price Co
Yakima, WA 509-966-4110
Prime Produce
Orange, CA....................... 714-771-0718
Produce Buyers Company
Detroit, MI 313-843-0132

Producers Cooperative
Bryan, TX........................979-778-6000
Quillin Produce Co
Huntsville, AL....................256-883-7374
R & S Mexican Food
Glendale, AZ......................602-272-2727
R.C. McEntire & Company
Columbia, SC......................803-799-3388
Red Hat Cooperative
Redcliff, AB......................403-548-6208
Reed Lang Farms
Rio Hondo, TX.....................956-748-2354
Reinhart Foods
Toronto, ON.......................416-645-4910
Rene Produce Dist
Rio Rico, AZ......................520-281-0806
Reter Fruit
Medford, OR.......................541-772-9560
Rice Fruit Co
Gardners, PA......................800-627-3359
Russo Farms
Vineland, NJ......................856-692-5942
S & E Organic Farms Inc
Bakersfield, CA...................661-325-2644
S & L Produce Inc
Walnut Hill, IL...................618-532-8344
Sales USA
Salado, TX........................800-766-7344
Santanna Banana Company
Harrisburg, PA....................717-238-8321
Schmidt Bros Inc
Swanton, OH.......................800-200-7318
Scotian Gold
Coldbrook, NS.....................888-726-8426
Seald Sweet
Vero Beach, FL....................559-636-4400
Sedlock Farm
Lynn Center, IL...................309-521-8284
Segall Nathan Co Inc
Montgomery, AL....................334-279-3174
Shields Date Garden
Indio, CA.........................800-414-2555
Snokist Growers
Yakima, WA........................800-377-2857
Solana Gold Organics
Sebastopol, CA....................800-459-1121
South Mill
Kennett Square, PA................610-444-4800
Spring Ledge Farm Stand
New London, NH....................603-526-6253
Stadelman Fruit LLC
Zillah, WA........................509-829-5145
Star Route Farms
Bolinas, CA.......................415-868-1658
Strube Celery & Vegetable Co
Chicago, IL.......................773-446-4000
Sun Pacific
Pasadena, CA......................213-612-9957
Superior Mushroom Farms
Ardrossan, AB.....................866-687-2242
Sure-Fresh Produce Inc
Santa Maria, CA...................888-423-5379
Surface Banana Company
Parkersburg, WV...................304-485-2400
Talley Farms
Arroyo Grande, CA.................805-489-5400
Tanimura Antle Inc
Salinas, CA.......................800-772-4542
Taylor Farms
Salinas, CA.......................831-754-0471
Taylor Farms Pacific
Tracy, CA.........................209-830-1086
Taylor Orchards
Reynolds, GA......................478-847-5963
Teixeira Farms, Inc.
Santa Maria, CA...................805-928-3801
Tejon Ranch Co
Lebec, CA.........................661-248-3000
Tiger Mushroom Farm
Nanton, AB........................403-646-2578
Tony Vitrano Company
Jessup, MD........................800-481-3784
Topaz Farm
Portland, OR......................503-708-0008
Trefethen Family Vineyards
Napa, CA..........................707-255-7700
Tru-Blu Cooperative Associates
New Lisbon, NJ....................609-894-8717
True Blue Farms
Grand Junction, MI................877-654-2400
Tufts Ranch
Winters, CA.......................530-795-4144

Turlock Fruit Co
Turlock, CA.......................209-634-7207
Ultimate Foods
Linden, NJ........................908-486-0800
United Apple Sales
New Paltz, NY.....................585-765-2460
United Marketing Exchange
Delta, CO.........................970-874-3332
United Pickles
Bronx, NY.........................718-933-6060
Van de Kamps
Peoria, IL........................800-798-3318
Vaughn Rue Produce
Wilson, NC........................800-388-8138
Venture Vineyards
Lodi, NY..........................888-635-6277
Veronica Foods Inc
Oakland, CA.......................800-370-5554
Vidalia Sweets Brand
Lyons, GA.........................912-565-8881
Vincent B Zaninovich & Sons
Richgrove, CA.....................661-725-2497
Walter P Rawl & Sons Inc
Pelion, SC........................803-894-1900
Washington Fruit & Produce Company
Yakima, WA........................509-457-6177
Waugh Foods Inc
East Peoria, IL...................309-427-8000
Weiser River Packing
Weiser, ID........................208-549-0200
West Pak Avocado Inc
Murrieta, CA......................800-266-4414
Wetherby Cranberry Company
Warrens, WI.......................608-378-4813
Whitney & Sons Seafood
Hudson, FL........................727-869-3728
Wileman Brothers & Elliott Inc
Cutler, CA........................559-528-4772
Worldwide Specialties In
Los Angeles, CA...................800-437-2702
Yakima Fresh
Yakima, WA........................509-248-5770
Yokohl Packing Co
Lindsay, CA.......................559-562-1327
Zentis Sweet Ovations
Philadelphia, PA..................800-223-7073
Zuccaro Produce
Columbia Heights, MN..............612-333-1122

Prunes

Central California Raisin Packing Co, Inc.
Del Rey, CA.......................559-888-2195
George W Saulpaugh & Son
Germantown, NY....................518-537-6500
Henggeler Packing Company
Fruitland, ID.....................208-452-4212
HH Dobbins Inc
Lyndonville, NY...................877-362-2467
Hialeah Products Co
Hollywood, FL.....................800-923-3379
Kalustyan
New York, NY......................800-352-3451
Organic Planet
San Francisco, CA.................415-765-5590
Ramos Orchards
Winters, CA.......................530-795-4748
Service Packing Company
Vancouver, BC.....................604-681-0264
Sowden Brothers Farm
Live Oak, CA......................530-695-3750
Stadelman Fruit LLC
Zillah, WA........................509-829-5145
Sunsweet Growers Inc.
Yuba City, CA.....................800-417-2253
Sutter Foods LLC
Yuba City, CA.....................530-682-7776
Terri Lynn Inc
Elgin, IL.........................800-323-0775
Timber Crest Farms
Healdsburg, CA....................888-766-4233
Tufts Ranch
Winters, CA.......................530-795-4144
Unique Ingredients LLC
Gold Canyon, AZ...................480-983-2498
Valley View Packing Co
Yuba City, CA.....................530-673-7356
Wilbur Packing Company
Yuba City, CA.....................530-671-4911

Canned

Emerling International Foods
Buffalo, NY.......................716-833-7381
Valley View Packing Co
Yuba City, CA.....................530-673-7356

Dried

Bedemco Inc
White Plains, NY..................914-683-1119
Setton International Foods
Commack, NY.......................800-227-4397

Frozen

Emerling International Foods
Buffalo, NY.......................716-833-7381
Honee Bear Canning
Lawton, MI........................800-626-2327

Pulps & Purees

Amafruits
Mokena, IL........................877-818-1262
Buddy Fruits
Rye, NY...........................914-514-2098
Homemade Harvey
Los Angeles, CA...................310-472-4410
Nimeks Organics
Bethlehem, PA.....................610-997-0500
Pastorelli Food Products
Chicago, IL.......................800-767-2829
Perfect Puree of Napa Valley
Napa, CA..........................707-261-5100
Rainsweet Inc
Salem, OR.........................800-363-4293
Rv Industries
Buford, GA........................770-729-8983
Sunrise Growers
Placentia, CA.....................714-630-6292
SupHerb Farms
Turlock, CA.......................800-787-4372
Tulkoff's Food Products Inc
Baltimore, MD.....................800-638-7343

Fruit & Vegetable

California Custom Fruits
Baldwin Park, CA..................877-558-0056
Emerling International Foods
Buffalo, NY.......................716-833-7381
Golden Town Apple Products
Rougemont, QC.....................866-552-7643
Greenwood Associates
Niles, IL.........................847-579-5500
Hirzel Canning Co & Farms
Luckey, OH........................419-419-7525
Louis Dreyfus Company Citrus Inc
Winter Garden, FL.................407-656-1000
Pastorelli Food Products
Chicago, IL.......................800-767-2829
Peace River Citrus Products
Vero Beach, FL....................772-492-4050
Prima Foods International
Silver Springs, FL.................800-774-8751
Red Gold Inc.
Elwood, IN........................866-729-7187
S & E Organic Farms Inc
Bakersfield, CA...................661-325-2644
Seneca Foods Corp
Marion, NY........................315-926-8100
True Blue Farms
Grand Junction, MI................877-654-2400
Vegetable Juices Inc
Chicago, IL.......................888-776-9752
Vita-Pakt Citrus Products Co
Covina, CA........................888-684-8272

Pulp

Dried Beet

Emerling International Foods
Buffalo, NY.......................716-833-7381

Fruit

3V Company
Brooklyn, NY......................718-858-7333
Avo-King Internatl
Orange, CA........................800-286-5464
Calavo Growers
Santa Paula, CA...................805-525-1245
Miramar Fruit Trading Company
Doral, FL.........................305-883-4774

Sunny Avocado
Jamul, CA 800-999-2862
Tantos Foods International
Markham, ON 905-943-9993

Vegetable

Pastorelli Food Products
Chicago, IL 800-767-2829

Puree

Fruit

Beta Pure Foods
Santa Cruz, CA 831-685-6565
Calavo Growers
Santa Paula, CA 805-525-1245
Fruithill Inc
Yamhill, OR 503-662-3926
Gerber Products Co
Arlington, VA 800-284-9488
Golden Town Apple Products
Rougemont, QC 866-552-7643
Granny's Best Strawberry Products
Victoria, ON 519-426-0705
Greenwood Associates
Niles, IL 847-579-5500
Hartog Rahal Foods
Norwood, NJ 201-750-0500
Johnson Foods, Inc.
Sunnyside, WA 509-837-4214
Milne Fruit Products Inc
Prosser, WA 509-786-2611
Munk Pack
Greenwich, CT
National Frozen Foods Corp
Seattle, WA 206-322-8900
Pacific Coast Fruit Co
Portland, OR 503-234-6411
Rainsweet Inc
Salem, OR 800-363-4293
RFi Ingredients
Blauvelt, NY 800-962-7663
Rv Industries
Buford, GA 770-729-8983
Seneca Foods Corp
Princeville, IL 309-385-4301
Summerland Sweets
Summerland, BC 800-577-1277
Sunrise Growers
Placentia, CA 714-630-6292

Fruit & Vegetable

Ful-Flav-R Foods
Alamo, CA 925-838-0300
National Frozen Foods Corp
Seattle, WA 206-322-8900
Pastorelli Food Products
Chicago, IL 800-767-2829

Orange

KMC Citrus Enterprises Inc
Weirsdale, FL 863-298-8270

Tomato

Emerling International Foods
Buffalo, NY 716-833-7381
Hirzel Canning Co & Farms
Luckey, OH 419-419-7525
Pastorelli Food Products
Chicago, IL 800-767-2829

Vegetable

Beta Pure Foods
Santa Cruz, CA 831-685-6565
National Frozen Foods Corp
Seattle, WA 206-322-8900
Otsuka America Foods Inc
San Francisco, CA 415-986-5300
Pastorelli Food Products
Chicago, IL 800-767-2829

Tomato

Canned

Nation Wide Canning Ltd.
Cottam, ON 519-839-4831
Pastorelli Food Products
Chicago, IL 800-767-2829

Red Gold Inc.
Elwood, IN 866-729-7187
Seneca Foods Corp
Marion, NY 315-926-8100
Tip Top Canning Co
Tipp City, OH 800-352-2635
Vegetable Juices Inc
Chicago, IL 888-776-9752
Violet Packing Holdings LLC
Williamstown, NJ 856-629-7428

Pumpkin

Abbott & Cobb Inc
Feasterville, PA 800-345-7333
Bay Baby Produce
Burlington, WA 360-755-2299
Bennett's Apples & Cider
Ancaster, ON 905-648-6878
Heartland Strawberry Farm
Waterloo, IA 888-747-7423
Organic Planet
San Francisco, CA 415-765-5590
Schmidt Bros Inc
Swanton, OH 800-200-7318
Tom Ringhausen Orchards
Hardin, IL 800-258-6645
Topaz Farm
Portland, OR 503-708-0008
Unique Ingredients LLC
Gold Canyon, AZ 480-983-2498
Wildcat Produce
McGrew, NE 308-783-2438

Canned

Agrocan
Ville St Laurent, QC 877-247-6226
Emerling International Foods
Buffalo, NY 716-833-7381
Harvest-Pac Products
Chatham, ON 519-436-0446
Lakeside Foods Inc.
Manitowoc, WI 800-466-3834

Frozen

Emerling International Foods
Buffalo, NY 716-833-7381
Lakeside Foods Inc.
Manitowoc, WI 800-466-3834

Radish

Boskovich Farms Inc
Oxnard, CA 805-487-2299
F & S Produce Co Inc
Vineland, NJ 800-886-3316
Gouw Quality Onions
Taber, AB 403-223-1440
Pioneer Growers
Belle Glade, FL 229-243-9306
Vegetable Juices Inc
Chicago, IL 888-776-9752

Raisins

Amazing Fruit Products
Fort Payne, AL 256-273-5363
American Key Food Products Inc
Closter, NJ 877-263-7539
Bedemco Inc
White Plains, NY 914-683-1119
Boghosian Raisin Packing Co
Fowler, CA 559-834-5348
Central California Raisin Packing Co, Inc.
Del Rey, CA 559-888-2195
Chooljian Bros Packing Co
Sanger, CA 559-875-5501
Del Rey Packing
Del Rey, CA 559-888-2031
Dipasa USA Inc
Brownsville, TX 956-831-4072
Emerling International Foods
Buffalo, NY 716-833-7381
Fig Garden Packing Inc
Fresno, CA 559-271-9000
Foley's Chocolates & Candies
Richmond, BC 888-236-5397
Green Earth Orchards
Salt Lake City, UT 801-888-7161
Jason & Son Specialty Foods
Rancho Cordova, CA 800-810-9093
Jewel Date Co
Thermal, CA 760-399-4474
Just Tomatoes
Westley, CA 800-537-1985
Kalustyan
New York, NY 800-352-3451
Lion Raisins Inc
Selma, CA 559-834-6677
Made In Nature
Boulder, CO 800-906-7426
Mariani Packing Co.
Vacaville, CA 707-452-2800
National Raisin Co.
Fowler, CA 559-834-5981
New Organics
Kenwood, CA 734-677-5570
Nut Factory
Spokane Valley, WA 888-239-5288
Organic Planet
San Francisco, CA 415-765-5590
Reinhart Foods
Toronto, ON 416-645-4910
Setton International Foods
Commack, NY 800-227-4397
Sun Valley Raisins Inc
Fresno, CA 559-233-8070
Sun-Maid Growers of California
Kingsburg, CA 559-896-8000
Sunfood
El Cajon, CA 888-729-3663
Sunridge Farms
Royal Oaks, CA 831-786-7000
Terri Lynn Inc
Elgin, IL 800-323-0775
Timber Crest Farms
Healdsburg, CA 888-766-4233
Unique Ingredients LLC
Gold Canyon, AZ 480-983-2498
Victor Packing
Madera, CA 559-673-5908
Waymouth Farms Inc
Minneapolis, MN 800-527-0094

Chocolate Coated

Sun-Maid Growers of California
Kingsburg, CA 559-896-8000

Dried

Boghosian Raisin Packing Co
Fowler, CA 559-834-5348
Fig Garden Packing Inc
Fresno, CA 559-271-9000
Jason & Son Specialty Foods
Rancho Cordova, CA 800-810-9093
Kalustyan
New York, NY 800-352-3451
National Raisin Co.
Fowler, CA 559-834-5981
Nut Factory
Spokane Valley, WA 888-239-5288

Yogurt Coated

Foley's Chocolates & Candies
Richmond, BC 888-236-5397
GKI Foods
Brighton, MI 248-486-0055
Mariani Packing Co.
Vacaville, CA 707-452-2800
Setton International Foods
Commack, NY 800-227-4397
Sun-Maid Growers of California
Kingsburg, CA 559-896-8000
Terri Lynn Inc
Elgin, IL 800-323-0775

Rhubarb

Bryant Preserving Company
Alma, AR 800-634-2413
Cajun Brands
New Iberia, LA 504-408-2252
Coloma Frozen Foods Inc
Coloma, MI 800-642-2723
Lennox Farm
Shelburne, ON 519-925-6444
Snowcrest Packer
Abbotsford, BC 800-265-3686
Washington Rhubarb Grower Assn
Sumner, WA 800-435-9911
Webster Farms
Cambridge, NS 800-507-8844

Canned

Emerling International Foods
Buffalo, NY....716-833-7381

Frozen

Coloma Frozen Foods Inc
Coloma, MI....800-642-2723
Emerling International Foods
Buffalo, NY....716-833-7381
Lennox Farm
Shelburne, ON....519-925-6444
Snowcrest Packer
Abbotsford, BC....800-265-3686
Washington Rhubarb Grower Assn
Sumner, WA....800-435-9911
Webster Farms
Cambridge, NS....800-507-8844

Roasted Vegetables

SupHerb Farms
Turlock, CA....800-787-4372

Roots & Tubers

American Botanicals
Eolia, MO....800-684-6070
Emerling International Foods
Buffalo, NY....716-833-7381
Penn Herb Co
Philadelphia, PA....800-523-9971

Rutabaga

Arbre Farms Inc
Walkerville, MI....231-873-3337
Exeter Produce
Exeter, ON....519-235-0141

Canned

Arbre Farms Inc
Walkerville, MI....231-873-3337
Emerling International Foods
Buffalo, NY....716-833-7381

Frozen

Arbre Farms Inc
Walkerville, MI....231-873-3337
Emerling International Foods
Buffalo, NY....716-833-7381
Paris Foods Corporation
Trappe, MD....410-200-9595

Salad Greens

AeroFarms
Newark, NJ....973-242-2495
Atlanta Bread Co.
Smyrna, GA....800-398-3728
Boskovich Farms Inc
Oxnard, CA....805-487-2299
Earthbound Farm
San Jn Bautista, CA....800-690-3200
Risvold's Inc.
Gardena, CA....323-770-2674
Taylor Farms Pacific
Tracy, CA....209-830-1086

Mustard Tips

AeroFarms
Newark, NJ....973-242-2495

Sauces

Apple

Andros Foods North America
Mount Jackson, VA....844-426-3767
Blue Jay Orchards
Bethel, CT....203-748-0119
Cold Hollow Cider Mill
Waterbury Center, VT....800-327-7537
Commodities Marketing Inc
Clarksburg, NJ....732-516-0700
Coutts Specialty Foods Inc
Boxborough, MA....800-919-2952
Del Mar Food Products Corp
Watsonville, CA....831-722-3516
Emerling International Foods
Buffalo, NY....716-833-7381
Graves Mountain Lodge Inc.
Syria, VA....540-923-4231
Knouse Foods Co-Op Inc.
Peach Glen, PA....717-677-8181
Leahy Orchards
Franklin Centre, QC....800-667-7380
Leroux Creek
Hotchkiss, CO....877-970-5670
Love Creek Orchards
Medina, TX....800-449-0882
Mott's LLP
Plano, TX....800-426-4891
Nana Mae's Organics
Sebastopol, CA....707-829-7359
New Era Canning Company
New Era, MI....231-861-2151
Solana Gold Organics
Sebastopol, CA....800-459-1121
Tree Top Inc
Selah, WA....509-697-7251
Unique Ingredients LLC
Gold Canyon, AZ....480-983-2498
White House Foods
Winchester, VA....540-662-3401

Canned

Leahy Orchards
Franklin Centre, QC....800-667-7380
New Era Canning Company
New Era, MI....231-861-2151

with Other Fruit or Spices

Leahy Orchards
Franklin Centre, QC....800-667-7380

Cranberry

Coastal Classics
Duxbury, MA....508-746-6058
Delectable Gourmet LLC
Deer Park, NY....800-696-1350
Fireside Kitchen
Halifax, NS....902-454-7387
Johnston's Home Style Products
Charlottetown, PE....902-629-1300
Ocean Spray International
Lakeville-Middleboro, MA....800-662-3263
Skjodt-Barrett Foods
Brampton, ON....877-600-1200
Steel's Gourmet Foods, Ltd.
Bridgeport, PA....800-678-3357

Jellied

Ocean Spray International
Lakeville-Middleboro, MA....800-662-3263

Scallions

Emerling International Foods
Buffalo, NY....716-833-7381
Ferris Organic Farms
Eaton Rapids, MI....800-628-8736
S & E Organic Farms Inc
Bakersfield, CA....661-325-2644
SupHerb Farms
Turlock, CA....800-787-4372
Tanimura Antle Inc
Salinas, CA....800-772-4542

Seaweeds & Sea Vegetables

Acadian Seaplants
Dartmouth, NS....800-575-9100
Gimme Health Foods
San Rafael, CA
Great Eastern Sun Trading Co
Asheville, NC....800-334-5809
Maine Coast Sea Vegetables
Franklin, ME....207-565-2907
Maine Seaweed Company
Steuben, ME....207-546-2875
Ocean's Halo
Burlingame, CA....650-642-5907
Sea Veggies
Commerce, CA....323-728-4762

Shallot

California Garlic Co
San Diego, CA....951-506-8883
Christopher Ranch LLC
Gilroy, CA....408-847-1100
Haliburton International Inc
Ontario, CA....877-980-4295
SupHerb Farms
Turlock, CA....800-787-4372
Vegetable Juices Inc
Chicago, IL....888-776-9752

Soy

Agri-Dairy Products
Purchase, NY....914-697-9580
Ajinomoto Heartland Inc
Chicago, IL....773-380-7000
Avatar Corp
University Park, IL....800-255-3181
Basic Food Flavors
North Las Vegas, NV....702-643-0043
Bluechip Group
Salt Lake City, UT....800-878-0099
California Natural Products
Lathrop, CA....209-858-2525
Cedar Lake Foods
Cedar Lake, MI....800-246-5039
Clofine Dairy Products Inc
Linwood, NJ....609-653-1000
Cricklewood Soyfoods
Mertztown, PA....610-682-4109
Ener-G Foods
Seattle, WA....800-331-5222
Flavor House, Inc.
Adelanto, CA....760-246-9131
Genisoy
Downsview, OH....866-972-6879
Glennys
Brooklyn, NY....888-864-1243
Healthy Food Ingredients
Fargo, ND....844-275-3443
Hialeah Products Co
Hollywood, FL....800-923-3379
House Foods America Corp
Garden Grove, CA....877-333-7077
International Service Group
Alpharetta, GA....770-518-0988
Island Spring Inc
Vashon, WA....206-463-9848
Lee's Food Products
Toronto, ON....416-465-2407
Lightlife
Turners Falls, MA....800-769-3279
Lisanatti Foods
Oregon City, OR....866-864-3922
Mandarin Soy Sauce Inc
Middletown, NY....845-343-1505
Mei Shun Tofu Products Company
Chicago, IL....312-842-7000
MicroSoy Corporation
Jefferson, IA....515-386-2100
Miyako Oriental Foods Inc
Baldwin Park, CA....877-788-6476
Modesto WholeSoy
Ceres, CA....209-523-5119
N D Labs
Lynbrook, NY....888-263-5227
Nature Soy Inc
Philadelphia, PA....215-765-3289
Northern Soy Inc
Rochester, NY....585-235-8970
Pokonobe Industries
Santa Monica, CA....310-392-1259
Pulmuone Foods USA Inc.
Fullerton, CA....800-588-7782
Red River Commodities Inc
Fargo, ND....800-437-5539
San-Ei Gen FFI
New York, NY....212-315-7850
Schillinger Genetics Inc
West Des Moines, IA....866-769-7200
Solnuts
Hudson, IA....800-648-3503
Soyfoods of America
Washington, DC....202-659-3520
SoyLife Division
Edina, MN....952-920-7700
Specialty Ingredients
Buffalo Grove, IL....847-419-9595
Spectrum Foods Inc
Springfield, IL....217-528-5301
Sunrich LLC
Hope, MN....800-297-5997
Turtle Island Foods
Hood River, OR....800-508-8100
Vitasoy USA
Woburn, MA....800-848-2769

Fresh

Smoke & Fire Natural Food
Great Barrington, MA. 413-528-8008
Vitasoy USA
Woburn, MA. 800-848-2769

Protein

Texturized

Seneca Foods Corp
Princeville, IL 309-385-4301
Spectrum Foods Inc
Springfield, IL. 217-528-5301

Soy Bean

Aak USA Inc
Newark, NJ. 973-344-1300
AG Processing Inc
Omaha, NE 800-247-1345
American Culinary Garden
Springfield, MO 888-831-2433
DuPont Nutrition & Biosciences
New Century, KS 913-764-8100
DuPont Pioneer
Johnston, IA 515-535-5954
Durey-Libby Edible Nuts
Carlstadt, NJ 800-332-6887
Fizzle Flat Farm, L.L.C.
Yale, IL 618-793-2060
IMAC
Oklahoma City, OK 888-878-7827
Ingredient Innovations
Kansas City, MO. 816-587-1426
Knight Seed Company
Burnsville, MN. 800-328-2999
Lone Pine Enterprise Inc
Carlisle, AR 870-552-3217
Louis Dreyfus Corporation
Rotterdam,
Myron's Fine Foods, Inc.
Millers Falls, MA 800-730-2820
Producers Rice Mill Inc.
Stuttgart, AR. 870-673-4444
R&J Farms
West Salem, OH 419-846-3179
Red River Commodities Inc
Fargo, ND 800-437-5539
Roberts Seed
Axtell, NE. 308-743-2565
Schillinger Genetics Inc
West Des Moines, IA 866-769-7200
Seed Enterprises Inc
West Point, NE 888-440-7333
Shepherd Farms Inc
Hillsboro, IL 800-383-2676
Sno-Pac Foods Inc
Caledonia, MN 800-533-2215
Sonne
Wahpeton, ND. 800-727-6663
T.S. Smith & Sons
Bridgeville, DE. 302-337-8271
Tofu Shop Specialty Foods Inc
Arcata, CA 707-822-7401

Roasted Whole

Greenwave Foods
Berkeley, CA. 510-898-1973

Soy Milk

Agri-Dairy Products
Purchase, NY 914-697-9580
Chunco Foods Inc
Kansas City, MO. 816-283-0716
Clofine Dairy Products Inc
Linwood, NJ 609-653-1000
Commodities Marketing Inc
Clarksburg, NJ 732-516-0700
Devansoy Farms
Carroll, IA. 800-747-8605
Eden Foods Inc
Clinton, MI 888-424-3336
Ener-G Foods
Seattle, WA 800-331-5222
FarmSoy Company
Summertown, TN 931-964-2411
Mighty Soy Inc
Los Angeles, CA. 323-266-6969
Nutrisoya Foods
Saint-Hyacinthe, QC. 877-769-2645
San Diego Soy Dairy
El Cajon, CA. 619-447-8638
Soyfoods of America
Washington, DC 202-659-3520
Sunrise Markets
Vancouver, BC 800-661-2326
Tofu Shop Specialty Foods Inc
Arcata, CA 707-822-7401
Twin Oaks Community
Louisa, VA 540-894-5141
Vance's Foods
San Francisco, CA 415-621-1171
WhiteWave Foods
Denver, CO 800-488-9283

Soy Protein

DuPont Nutrition & Biosciences
New Century, KS 913-764-8100
Farbest-Tallman Foods Corp
Montvale, NJ. 201-573-4900
N D Labs
Lynbrook, NY 888-263-5227
SoyTex
West Orange, NJ 888-769-8391

Concentrate

DuPont Nutrition & Biosciences
New Century, KS 913-764-8100
Spectrum Foods Inc
Springfield, IL. 217-528-5301

Grits

Spectrum Foods Inc
Springfield, IL. 217-528-5301

Spinach

Avon Heights Mushrooms
Avondale, PA 610-268-2092
Boskovich Farms Inc
Oxnard, CA. 805-487-2299
Earthbound Farm
San Jn Bautista, CA 800-690-3200
F & S Produce Co Inc
Vineland, NJ 800-886-3316
Patterson Frozen Foods
Patterson, CA 209-892-2611
Patterson Vegetable Company
Patterson, CA 209-892-2611
Pictsweet Co
Bells, TN. 731-663-7600
Seabrook Brothers & Sons
Seabrook, NJ. 856-455-8080
Snowcrest Packer
Abbotsford, BC. 800-265-3686
State Garden Inc.
Chelsea, MA
Unique Ingredients LLC
Gold Canyon, AZ 480-983-2498
Vegetable Juices Inc
Chicago, IL 888-776-9752

Canned

Emerling International Foods
Buffalo, NY. 716-833-7381

Frozen

Emerling International Foods
Buffalo, NY. 716-833-7381
Paris Foods Corporation
Trappe, MD. 410-200-9595
Vegetable Juices Inc
Chicago, IL 888-776-9752

Sponge Gourd

Acme Steak & Seafood
Youngstown, OH. 800-686-2263
Bifulco Four Seasons
Pittsgrove, NJ 856-692-0778
Cajun Brands
New Iberia, LA 504-408-2252

Sprouts

Amigos Canning Company
San Antonio, TX. 210-798-5360
Boskovich Farms Inc
Oxnard, CA. 805-487-2299
Calco of Calgary
Calgary, AB. 403-295-3578
Chunco Foods Inc
Kansas City, MO. 816-283-0716
Houston Calco, Inc
Houston, TX 713-236-8668
International Specialty Supply
Cookeville, TN 931-526-1106
Jonathan's Sprouts
Rochester, MA 508-763-2577
Montreal Chop Suey Company
Montreal, QC 514-522-3134
Mung Dynasty
Pittsburgh, PA 412-381-1350
Snowcrest Packer
Abbotsford, BC. 800-265-3686

Alfalfa

Chunco Foods Inc
Kansas City, MO. 816-283-0716
International Specialty Supply
Cookeville, TN 931-526-1106
Jonathan's Sprouts
Rochester, MA 508-763-2577
Marjon Specialty Foods Inc
Plant City, FL 813-752-3482

Bean

Emerling International Foods
Buffalo, NY. 716-833-7381
International Specialty Supply
Cookeville, TN 931-526-1106
Marjon Specialty Foods Inc
Plant City, FL 813-752-3482

Mung Bean

Chunco Foods Inc
Kansas City, MO. 816-283-0716
NOW Foods
Bloomingdale, IL 888-669-3663

Squash

Abbott & Cobb Inc
Feasterville, PA. 800-345-7333
Bay Baby Produce
Burlington, WA. 360-755-2299
Boskovich Farms Inc
Oxnard, CA. 805-487-2299
Earthbound Farm
San Jn Bautista, CA 800-690-3200
F & S Produce Co Inc
Vineland, NJ 800-886-3316
Giumarra Companies
Los Angeles, CA. 213-627-2900
Haliburton International Inc
Ontario, CA. 877-980-4295
Michigan Freeze Pack
Hart, MI. 231-873-2175
National Frozen Foods Corp
Seattle, WA 206-322-8900
Organically Grown Co
Eugene, OR. 800-937-9677
Pacific Collier Fresh Company
Immokalee, FL 800-226-7274
Pictsweet Co
Bells, TN. 731-663-7600
Rene Produce Dist
Rio Rico, AZ. 520-281-0806
Snowcrest Packer
Abbotsford, BC. 800-265-3686
Tom Ringhausen Orchards
Hardin, IL 800-258-6645
Vegetable Juices Inc
Chicago, IL 888-776-9752
Walter P Rawl & Sons Inc
Pelion, SC. 803-894-1900
Wholesum Family Farms
Nogales, AZ 520-281-9233

Acorn

Bay Baby Produce
Burlington, WA. 360-755-2299

Canned

Emerling International Foods
Buffalo, NY. 716-833-7381
Sure-Fresh Produce Inc
Santa Maria, CA 888-423-5379

Frozen

Emerling International Foods
Buffalo, NY....716-833-7381
Paris Foods Corporation
Trappe, MD....410-200-9595
Sure-Fresh Produce Inc
Santa Maria, CA....888-423-5379
Vegetable Juices Inc
Chicago, IL....888-776-9752

Golden Scallopino

Zuccaro Produce
Columbia Heights, MN....612-333-1122

Star Fruit

Brooks Tropicals Inc
Homestead, FL....800-327-4833

Succotash

Emerling International Foods
Buffalo, NY....716-833-7381
Pictsweet Co
Bells, TN....731-663-7600
Symons Frozen Foods
Centralia, WA....360-736-1321
Twin City Foods Inc.
Stanwood, WA....206-515-2400

Canned

Emerling International Foods
Buffalo, NY....716-833-7381
Patterson Frozen Foods
Patterson, CA....209-892-2611

Frozen

Emerling International Foods
Buffalo, NY....716-833-7381
Paris Foods Corporation
Trappe, MD....410-200-9595
Patterson Frozen Foods
Patterson, CA....209-892-2611
Pictsweet Co
Bells, TN....731-663-7600
Symons Frozen Foods
Centralia, WA....360-736-1321

Sun Dried Fruit

Chooljian Bros Packing Co
Sanger, CA....559-875-5501
Del Rey Packing
Del Rey, CA....559-888-2031

Sweet Potatoes

B & B Produce
Cana, VA....800-633-4902
Best Ever Bakery
Massapequa, NY....516-795-5590
Bissett Produce Company
Spring Hope, NC....800-849-5073
Bright Harvest Sweet Potato Co
Clarksville, AR....800-793-7440
Burch Farms
Hilton, NY....800-466-9668
Carolina Pride Products
Enfield, NC....252-445-3154
Earthbound Farm
San Jn Bautista, CA....800-690-3200
Godwin Produce Co
Dunn, NC....910-892-4171
Johnson Brothers Produce Company
Whitakers, NC....252-437-2111
Joseph D Teachey Jr Produce Co
Wallace, NC....910-285-4502
Livingston Farmers Assn
Livingston, CA....209-394-7941
Moody Dunbar Inc
Johnson City, TN....423-952-0100
Nash Produce
Nashville, NC....800-334-3032
Royce C. Bone Farms
Nashville, NC....252-443-3773
Scott Farms Inc
Lucama, NC....877-284-4030
Spring Acres Sales Company
Spring Hope, NC....800-849-5436
Tull Hill Farms Inc
Kinston, NC....252-523-8052
Wayne E Bailey Produce Co Inc
Chadbourn, NC....800-845-6149

Frozen

Bright Harvest Sweet Potato Co
Clarksville, AR....800-793-7440
Emerling International Foods
Buffalo, NY....716-833-7381

Mashed

Bright Harvest Sweet Potato Co
Clarksville, AR....800-793-7440

Frozen

Bright Harvest Sweet Potato Co
Clarksville, AR....800-793-7440

Swiss Chard

Earthbound Farm
San Jn Bautista, CA....800-690-3200

Tamarind

Cinnabar Specialty Foods Inc
Prescott, AZ....866-293-6433

Tangelos

Heller Brothers Packing Corp
Winter Garden, FL....855-543-5537

Tangerines

DNE World Fruit Sales
Fort Pierce, FL....800-327-6676
Haines City Citrus Growers
Haines City, FL....800-327-6676
Hale Indian River Groves
Vero Beach, FL....800-562-4502
Heller Brothers Packing Corp
Winter Garden, FL....855-543-5537
Hunt Brothers Cooperative
Lake Wales, FL....863-676-1411
Seald Sweet
Vero Beach, FL....559-636-4400

Taro

Sweety Novelty
Monterey Park, CA....626-282-4482

Tartufo

Gelato Fresco
Toronto, ON....416-785-5415
Vigneri Chocolate Inc.
Rochester, NY....877-844-6374

Textured Vegetable Protein

Advanced Spice & Trading
Carrollton, TX....800-872-7811
Clofine Dairy Products Inc
Linwood, NJ....609-653-1000
DuPont Nutrition & Biosciences
New Century, KS....913-764-8100
First Spice Mixing Co
Long Island City, NY....800-221-1105
New Organics
Kenwood, CA....734-677-5570
Westin Foods
Omaha, NE....800-228-6098

Tomatillos

Emerling International Foods
Buffalo, NY....716-833-7381
George Chiala Farms Inc
Morgan Hill, CA....408-778-0562
Haliburton International Inc
Ontario, CA....877-980-4295

Tomato

AgroCepia
Miami, FL....305-704-3488
Agrusa
Leonia, NJ....201-592-5950
Ballantine Produce Company
Reedley, CA....559-875-2583
BGS Jourdan & Sons
Darlington, MD....410-457-4904
Castellini Group
Newport, KY....800-233-8560
Char-Wil Canning Company
Trappe, MD....410-476-3167
Del Monte Fresh Produce Inc.
Coral Gables, FL....800-950-3683
Di Mare Fresh Inc
Fort Worth, TX....817-385-3000
Earthbound Farm
San Jn Bautista, CA....800-690-3200
Eden Foods Inc
Clinton, MI....888-424-3336
Escalon Premier Brand
Escalon, CA....209-838-7341
F & S Produce Co Inc
Vineland, NJ....800-886-3316
Fresh Express, Inc.
Salinas, CA....800-242-5472
George Chiala Farms Inc
Morgan Hill, CA....408-778-0562
Giumarra Companies
Los Angeles, CA....213-627-2900
Haliburton International Inc
Ontario, CA....877-980-4295
Harris Farms Inc
Coalinga, CA....800-311-6211
Henry Broch & Co
Gurnee, IL....847-816-6225
Hermann Pickle Co
Garrettsville, OH....800-245-2696
John N Wright Jr Inc
Federalsburg, MD....410-754-9044
Kaplan & Zubrin
Camden, NJ....856-964-1083
Lagorio Enterprises
Manteca, CA....209-982-5691
Local Roots Farms
Burt, NY....716-946-3198
M & S Tomato Repacking Co Inc
Springfield, MA....413-737-1308
Mangia Inc.
Mission Viejo, CA....866-462-6442
Miramar Pickles & Food Products
Fort Lauderdale, FL....954-463-0222
Nation Wide Canning Ltd.
Cottam, ON....519-839-4831
Neil Jones Food Company
Vancouver, WA....800-291-3862
Northwest Packing Co
Vancouver, WA....800-543-4356
Pacific Collier Fresh Company
Immokalee, FL....800-226-7274
Pastorelli Food Products
Chicago, IL....800-767-2829
Patterson Vegetable Company
Patterson, CA....209-892-2611
Pure Food Ingredients
Verona, WI....800-355-9601
Rene Produce Dist
Rio Rico, AZ....520-281-0806
Royce C. Bone Farms
Nashville, NC....252-443-3773
Sofo Foods
Toledo, OH....800-447-4211
Spreda Group
Louisville, KY....502-426-9411
Stanislaus Food Prod
Modesto, CA....800-327-7201
Sun Pacific
Pasadena, CA....213-612-9957
Sun-Brite Canning
Kingsville, ON....519-326-9033
Surface Banana Company
Parkersburg, WV....304-485-2400
Talley Farms
Arroyo Grande, CA....805-489-5400
Thomas Canning/Maidstone
Maidstone, ON....519-737-1531
Timber Crest Farms
Healdsburg, CA....888-766-4233
Tip Top Canning Co
Tipp City, OH....800-352-2635
Topor's Pickle & Food Svc Inc
Detroit, MI....313-237-0288
Unilever Food Solutions
Englewood Cliffs, NJ
Vegetable Juices Inc
Chicago, IL....888-776-9752
Veronica Foods Inc
Oakland, CA....800-370-5554
Vincent Formusa Company
Des Plaines, IL....847-813-6040
Violet Packing Holdings LLC
Williamstown, NJ....856-629-7428

Waterfield Farms
Amherst, MA 413-549-3558
Weil's Food Processing
Wheatley, ON 519-825-4572
Wholesum Family Farms
Nogales, AZ 520-281-9233
Z&S Distributing
Fresno, CA 800-467-0788

Canned

Agrocan
Ville St Laurent, QC 877-247-6226
Agusa
Lemoore, CA....................559-924-4785
B & G Foods Inc.
Parsippany, NJ....................973-401-6500
Char-Wil Canning Company
Trappe, MD....................410-476-3167
Dei Fratelli
Toledo, OH 800-837-1631
Eden Foods Inc
Clinton, MI 888-424-3336
Escalon Premier Brand
Escalon, CA 209-838-7341
Hirzel Canning Co.
Ottawa, OH....................800-837-1631
John N Wright Jr Inc
Federalsburg, MD....................410-754-9044
Milroy Canning Company
Milroy, IN 765-629-2221
Morningstar Foods
Los Banos, CA 209-826-8000
Nation Wide Canning Ltd.
Cottam, ON....................519-839-4831
Natural Value
Sacramento, CA 916-836-3561
Neil Jones Food Company
Vancouver, WA....................800-291-3862
Northwest Packing Co
Vancouver, WA....................800-543-4356
Pastene Co LTD
Canton, MA 781-298-3397
Pastorelli Food Products
Chicago, IL....................800-767-2829
Pure Food Ingredients
Verona, WI 800-355-9601
Red Gold Inc.
Elwood, IN 866-729-7187
Rio Valley Canning Co
Donna, TX....................956-464-7843
Shafer-Haggart
Vancouver, BC 604-669-5512
Small Planet Foods
Minneapolis, MN 800-624-4123
Stanislaus Food Prod
Modesto, CA....................800-327-7201
Sun-Brite Canning
Kingsville, ON 519-326-9033
Thomas Canning/Maidstone
Maidstone, ON 519-737-1531
Tip Top Canning Co
Tipp City, OH 800-352-2635
Violet Packing Holdings LLC
Williamstown, NJ....................856-629-7428
Weil's Food Processing
Wheatley, ON 519-825-4572

Crushed

Agrocan
Ville St Laurent, QC...............877-247-6226
Colonna Brothers Inc
North Bergen, NJ 201-864-1115
Furmano's Foods
Northumberland, PA 800-952-1111
Hirzel Canning Co & Farms
Luckey, OH....................419-419-7525
Small Planet Foods
Minneapolis, MN 800-624-4123
Violet Packing Holdings LLC
Williamstown, NJ 856-629-7428

Cherry

80 Acres Farms
Hamilton, OH 888-574-1569
Exeter Produce
Exeter, ON....................519-235-0141
Talley Farms
Arroyo Grande, CA...............805-489-5400

Cocktail

Miss Scarlett's Flowers
Juneau, AK 800-345-6734
Seneca Foods Corp
Princeville, IL 309-385-4301

Diced

Furmano's Foods
Northumberland, PA 800-952-1111
Hirzel Canning Co & Farms
Luckey, OH....................419-419-7525
Ingomar Packing Co
Los Banos, CA 209-826-9494
Small Planet Foods
Minneapolis, MN 800-624-4123
Tip Top Canning Co
Tipp City, OH 800-352-2635

Dried

Agusa
Lemoore, CA....................559-924-4785
Emerling International Foods
Buffalo, NY....................716-833-7381
Fine Dried Foods Intl
Santa Cruz, CA 831-426-1413
Grapevine Trading Company
Santa Rosa, CA....................800-469-6478
Just Tomatoes
Westley, CA....................800-537-1985
Rising Sun Farms
Phoenix, OR 800-888-0795
Setton International Foods
Commack, NY 800-227-4397
Terri Lynn Inc
Elgin, IL 800-323-0775
Timber Crest Farms
Healdsburg, CA 888-766-4233
Unique Ingredients LLC
Gold Canyon, AZ 480-983-2498
Valley Sun Products Inc
Newman, CA....................800-426-5444

Fresh

F & S Produce Co Inc
Vineland, NJ 800-886-3316
Fresh Express, Inc.
Salinas, CA 800-242-5472
G Cefalu & Brother Inc
Jessup, MD 410-799-2910
Harris Farms Inc
Coalinga, CA....................800-311-6211
Lagorio Enterprises
Manteca, CA....................209-982-5691
Mixon Fruit Farms Inc
Bradenton, FL....................800-608-2525
Rene Produce Dist
Rio Rico, AZ....................520-281-0806
Talley Farms
Arroyo Grande, CA...............805-489-5400

Frozen

Milroy Canning Company
Milroy, IN 765-629-2221
Ocean Mist Farms
Castroville, CA....................831-633-2144
Red Gold Inc.
Elwood, IN 866-729-7187
SupHerb Farms
Turlock, CA 800-787-4372
Vegetable Juices Inc
Chicago, IL 888-776-9752

Marinated

American Importing Co.
Minneapolis, MN 855-273-0466

Plum

Kaplan & Zubrin
Camden, NJ....................856-964-1083

Processed

Agusa
Lemoore, CA....................559-924-4785
Escalon Premier Brand
Escalon, CA 209-838-7341
Pastorelli Food Products
Chicago, IL 800-767-2829
Weil's Food Processing
Wheatley, ON 519-825-4572

Products

Agusa
Lemoore, CA....................559-924-4785
American Chalkis Intl. Food Corp.
Walnut, CA 562-232-4105
Emerling International Foods
Buffalo, NY....................716-833-7381
Escalon Premier Brand
Escalon, CA 209-838-7341
F & S Produce Co Inc
Vineland, NJ 800-886-3316
Fresh Express, Inc.
Salinas, CA....................800-242-5472
George Chiala Farms Inc
Morgan Hill, CA....................408-778-0562
Henry Broch & Co
Gurnee, IL....................847-816-6225
Hermann Pickle Co
Garrettsville, OH....................800-245-2696
International Home Foods
Parsippany, NJ....................973-359-9920
Lagorio Enterprises
Manteca, CA....................209-982-5691
Lake Packing Co Inc
Lottsburg, VA 800-324-2759
Los Gatos Tomato Products
Huron, CA....................559-945-2700
Milroy Canning Company
Milroy, IN 765-629-2221
Morningstar Foods
Los Banos, CA 209-826-8000
Nation Wide Canning Ltd.
Cottam, ON....................519-839-4831
Northwest Packing Co
Vancouver, WA 800-543-4356
Paradise Tomato Kitchens
Louisville, KY 502-637-1700
Pasta Factory
Melrose Park, IL....................800-615-6951
Pastorelli Food Products
Chicago, IL 800-767-2829
Progresso Quality Foods
Vineland, NJ 856-691-1565
Pure Food Ingredients
Verona, WI 800-355-9601
Red Gold Inc.
Elwood, IN 866-729-7187
Small Planet Foods
Minneapolis, MN 800-624-4123
Spreda Group
Louisville, KY....................502-426-9411
Talley Farms
Arroyo Grande, CA....................805-489-5400
Thomas Canning/Maidstone
Maidstone, ON 519-737-1531
Timber Crest Farms
Healdsburg, CA 888-766-4233
Tip Top Canning Co
Tipp City, OH 800-352-2635
Unilever Food Solutions
Englewood Cliffs, NJ
Unique Ingredients LLC
Gold Canyon, AZ 480-983-2498
VCPB Transportation
Secaucus, NJ....................201-770-0070
Vegetable Juices Inc
Chicago, IL 888-776-9752
Veronica Foods Inc
Oakland, CA 800-370-5554
Walker Foods
Los Angeles, CA....................800-966-5199
Weil's Food Processing
Wheatley, ON 519-825-4572
Welch Foods Inc.
Concord, MA 800-340-6870

Roma (Egg)

Lagorio Enterprises
Manteca, CA....................209-982-5691

Stewed

Furmano's Foods
Northumberland, PA 800-952-1111
Nation Wide Canning Ltd.
Cottam, ON....................519-839-4831
Northwest Packing Co
Vancouver, WA....................800-543-4356

Tip Top Canning Co
Tipp City, OH 800-352-2635

Sun-Dried

Agrocan
Ville St Laurent, QC 877-247-6226
American Importing Co.
Minneapolis, MN 855-273-0466
Bedemco Inc
White Plains, NY 914-683-1119
Bella Sun Luci
Chico, CA 530-899-2661
Castella Imports Inc
Brentwood, NY 631-231-5500
Martin Farms
Brockport, NY 877-838-7369
Mezza
Lake Forest, IL 888-206-6054
Pacific Choice Brands
Fresno, CA 559-476-3581
Veronica Foods Inc
Oakland, CA 800-370-5554

Yellow Cherry

Beckman & Gast Co
St Henry, OH 419-678-4195
California Fruit and Tomato Kitchens
Modesto, CA 209-574-9407
Supreme Dairy Farms Co
Warwick, RI 401-739-8180

for Processing

Agusa
Lemoore, CA 559-924-4785

Tropical & Exotic Fruit

Ntc Marketing
Williamsville, NY 800-333-1637
Sambazon
San Clemente, CA 877-726-2296
Varet Street Market
Brooklyn, NY 718-302-0560

Turnip

Boskovich Farms Inc
Oxnard, CA 805-487-2299
Pictsweet Co
Bells, TN 731-663-7600
Snowcrest Packer
Abbotsford, BC 800-265-3686
Tom Ringhausen Orchards
Hardin, IL 800-258-6645
Walter P Rawl & Sons Inc
Pelion, SC 803-894-1900

Canned

Emerling International Foods
Buffalo, NY 716-833-7381

Frozen

Emerling International Foods
Buffalo, NY 716-833-7381
Paris Foods Corporation
Trappe, MD 410-200-9595

Vegetables

A. Lassonde Inc.
Rougemont, QC 866-552-7643
Aaland Potato Company
Hoople, ND 701-894-6144
Acme Steak & Seafood
Youngstown, OH 800-686-2263
Affiliated Rice Milling
Alvin, TX 281-331-6176
Agro Foods, Inc.
Miami, FL 786-552-9006
Al Pete Meats
Muncie, IN 765-288-8817
ALDI
Cincinnati, OH 513-421-1671
Alimentaire Whyte's Inc
Laval, QC 866-420-9520
Associated Potato Growers
Grand Forks, ND 800-437-4685
B & G Foods Inc.
Parsippany, NJ 973-401-6500
B.M. Lawrence & Company
San Francisco, CA 415-981-2926
Baker Produce
Kennewick, WA 800-624-7553
Baumer Foods Inc
Metairie, LA 504-482-5761
Bay Cities Produce Co Inc
San Leandro, CA 510-346-4943
BCFoods
Santa Rosa, CA 707-547-1776
Bean Buddies
New Hyde Park, NY 516-775-3706
Ben B. Schwartz & Sons
Detroit, MI 313-841-8300
Big B Barbecue
Evansville, IN 812-425-5235
Birdseye Food
Mountain Lakes, NJ 585-383-1850
Bob Gordon & Associates
Oak Park, IL 708-524-9611
Border Foods
New Hope, MN 763-559-7338
Bornt & Sons Inc
Holtville, CA 760-356-1066
Bottom Line Foods
Pembroke Pines, FL 954-843-0562
Bright Harvest Sweet Potato Co
Clarksville, AR 800-793-7440
Bryant Preserving Company
Alma, AR 800-634-2413
Bubbles of San Francisco
Stockton, CA 209-951-6071
Burnette Foods
Elk Rapids, MI 231-264-8116
Burnham & Morrill Co
Portland, ME 800-813-2165
Byrnes Packing Shed
Hastings, FL 904-692-1643
C.C. Graber Company
Ontario, CA 800-996-5483
Cajun Brands
New Iberia, LA 504-408-2252
California Fruit and Tomato Kitchens
Modesto, CA 209-574-9407
Caltex Foods
Canoga Park, CA 800-522-5839
Carando Gourmet Frozen Foods
Agawam, MA 888-227-2636
Caribbean Food Delights Inc
Tappan, NY 845-398-3000
Cascadian Farm Inc
Sedro Woolley, WA 360-855-0542
Castellini Group
Newport, KY 800-233-8560
Cates Addis Company
Parkton, NC 800-423-1883
Cebro Frozen Food
Newman, CA 209-862-0150
Christopher Ranch LLC
Gilroy, CA 408-847-1100
Chugwater Chili
Chugwater, WY 800-972-4454
Club Chef LLC
Covington, KY 859-578-3100
Coloma Frozen Foods Inc
Coloma, MI 800-642-2723
Coulter Giufre & Co Inc
Chittenango, NY 315-687-6510
Country Fresh Inc
Spring, TX 281-453-3300
Coutts Specialty Foods Inc
Boxborough, MA 800-919-2952
Crystal Potato Seed Co
Crystal, ND 701-657-2143
D'Arrigo Brothers Company of California
Salinas, CA 831-455-4500
Dairy King Milk Farms/Foodservice
Whitter, CA 800-900-6455
Dairy Management Inc
Rosemont, IL 800-853-2479
Deep Foods Inc
Union, NJ 908-810-7500
Del Mar Food Products Corp
Watsonville, CA 831-722-3516
Del Monte Fresh Produce Inc.
Coral Gables, FL 800-950-3683
Delicious Valley Frozen Foods
McAllen, TX 956-631-7177
Delta Packing
Lodi, CA 209-334-1023
Dickinson Frozen Foods
Eagle, ID 800-886-4326
DMH Ingredients Inc
Libertyville, IL 847-362-9977
DNO Inc
Columbus, OH 614-231-3601
Dong Kee Company
Chicago, IL 312-225-6340
East Coast Fresh Cuts Inc
Laurel, MD
Eckert Cold Storage
Manteca, CA 209-823-3181
Eden Foods Inc
Clinton, MI 888-424-3336
Erba Food Products
Brooklyn, NY 718-272-7700
Escalon Premier Brand
Escalon, CA 209-838-7341
F & S Produce Co Inc
Vineland, NJ 800-886-3316
Faribault Foods, Inc.
Fairbault, MN 507-331-1400
Federation-Southern Cprtvs
Atlanta, GA 404-765-0991
Fiesta Canning Co
Phoenix, AZ 602-212-2424
Florida Citrus
Bartow, FL 863-537-3999
Fort Boise Produce Company
Nyssa, OR 541-372-5174
Foster Family Farm
South Windsor, CT 860-648-9366
Fountain Valley Foods
Colorado Springs, CO 719-573-6012
Fresh Frozen Foods
Jefferson, GA 800-277-9851
Frieda's Inc
Los Alamitos, CA 714-826-6100
Ful-Flav-R Foods
Alamo, CA 925-838-0300
Garber Farms
Iota, LA 800-824-2284
Garden Valley Corp
Sutherlin, OR 541-459-9565
Garon Foods
Herrin, IL 618-942-4810
GC Farms
Morgan Hill, CA 408-778-0562
Gene Belk Briners
Bloomington, CA 909-877-1819
George Chiala Farms Inc
Morgan Hill, CA 408-778-0562
Gl Mezzetta Inc
American Canyon, CA 800-941-7044
Glacier Foods
Houston, TX 832-375-6300
GLK Foods, LLC
Shortsville, NY 855-572-8800
Glory Foods
Columbus, OH 800-414-5679
Godwin Produce Co
Dunn, NC 910-892-4171
Gotliebs Guacamole
Sharon, CT 860-365-0842
Great American Appetizers
Nampa, ID 800-282-4834
GS Dunn & Company
Hamilton, ON 905-522-0833
GWB Foods Corporation
Brooklyn, NY 877-977-7610
H.K. Canning
Ventura, CA 805-652-1392
Haliburton International Inc
Ontario, CA 877-980-4295
Hard-E Foods
St Louis, MO 314-533-2211
Harner Farms
State College, PA 814-237-7919
Harris Farms Inc
Coalinga, CA 800-311-6211
Harvest-Pac Products
Chatham, ON 519-436-0446
Heirloom Organic Gardens
Hollister, CA 831-637-8497
Henderson's Gardens
Berwyn, AB 780-338-2128
Henry Broch & Co
Gurnee, IL 847-816-6225
Herold's Salads
Cleveland, OH 800-427-2523
HH Dobbins Inc
Lyndonville, NY 877-362-2467
HMC Farms
Kingsburg, CA 559-897-1025
Houston Calco, Inc
Houston, TX 713-236-8668

Inland Empire Foods
Riverside, CA . . . 888-452-3267
International Home Foods
Parsippany, NJ. . . . 973-359-9920
International Specialty Supply
Cookeville, TN . . . 931-526-1106
J C Watson Co
Parma, ID . . . 208-722-5141
J. R. Simplot Co.
Boise, ID . . . 208-336-2110
JES Foods
Cleveland, OH . . . 216-883-8987
John N Wright Jr Inc
Federalsburg, MD. . . . 410-754-9044
Jyoti Cuisine India
Berwyn, PA . . . 610-296-4620
Kaplan & Zubrin
Camden, NJ. . . . 856-964-1083
Kings Processing
Middleton, NS. . . . 902-825-2188
Knight Seed Company
Burnsville, MN . . . 800-328-2999
L & S Packing Co
Farmingdale, NY . . . 800-286-6487
L H Hayward & Co
New Orleans, LA . . . 504-733-8480
Lagorio Enterprises
Manteca, CA . . . 209-982-5691
Lakeside Foods Inc.
Plainview, MN . . . 507-534-3141
Lakeside Packing Company
Harrow, ON. . . . 519-738-2314
Lennox Farm
Shelburne, ON . . . 519-925-6444
Les Trois Petits Cochons
Brooklyn, NY . . . 800-537-7283
Limited Edition
Midland, TX . . . 432-686-2008
Livingston Farmers Assn
Livingston, CA . . . 209-394-7941
Lodi Canning Co
Lodi, WI . . . 608-592-4236
Lone Wolf Farms
Minto, ND. . . . 701-248-3482
Long Island Cauliflower Assn
Riverhead, NY . . . 631-727-2212
Made In Nature
Boulder, CO . . . 800-906-7426
Mancini Packing Co
Zolfo Springs, FL . . . 800-741-1778
Maple Leaf Foods International
North York, ON. . . . 800-268-3708
Martens Fresh
Port Byron, NY. . . . 315-776-8821
Martha's Garden
Toronto, ON . . . 866-773-2887
Matador Processors
Blanchard, OK . . . 800-847-0797
Mccartney Produce Co
Paris, TN. . . . 731-642-2362
Mercer Processing
Modesto, CA. . . . 209-529-0150
Meridian Foods New Inc
Eaton, IN. . . . 765-396-3344
Miami Purveyors Inc
Miami, FL. . . . 800-966-6328
Michael Foods, Inc.
Minnetonka, MN. . . . 952-258-4000
Michigan Celery Cooperative
Hudsonville, MI . . . 616-669-1250
Miguel's Stowe Away
Stowe, VT . . . 800-448-6517
Millie's Pierogi
Chicopee Falls, MA . . . 800-743-7641
Mills Brothers Intl
Seattle, WA . . . 206-575-3000
Milos
New York, NY . . . 212-245-7400
Minnesota Dehydrated Veg Inc
Fosston, MN . . . 218-435-1997
Miramar Fruit Trading Company
Doral, FL. . . . 305-883-4774
Mister Spear
Stockton, CA. . . . 800-677-7327
Mixon Fruit Farms Inc
Bradenton, FL. . . . 800-608-2525
Mother Teresa's
Clute, TX. . . . 888-265-7429
Mrs Mazzula Food Products Inc
Edison, NJ. . . . 732-248-0555
Mt Olive Pickle Co
Mt Olive, NC . . . 800-672-5041

Nation Wide Canning Ltd.
Cottam, ON. . . . 519-839-4831
National Frozen Foods Corp
Seattle, WA . . . 206-322-8900
Natural Choice Distribution
Oakland, CA . . . 510-653-8212
Nature Quality
San Martin, CA. . . . 408-683-2182
New Era Canning Company
New Era, MI . . . 231-861-2151
New Harvest Foods
Washington, DC . . . 920-822-2578
Nicola International
Los Angeles, CA. . . . 818-545-1515
Nonpareil Farms
Blackfoot, ID . . . 800-522-2223
NORPAC Foods Inc
Salem, OR
Northwest Packing Co
Vancouver, WA. . . . 800-543-4356
Nunes Co Inc
Salinas, CA. . . . 831-751-7500
O C Schulz & Sons
Crystal, ND. . . . 701-657-2152
Ocean Mist Farms
Castroville, CA. . . . 831-633-2144
Ohio Mushroom Company
Lima, OH . . . 419-221-1721
Olive Growers Council
Visalia, CA . . . 559-734-1710
Ontario Produce Company
Ontario, OR. . . . 541-889-6485
Oregon Potato Co
Boardman, OR . . . 800-336-6311
Organically Grown Co
Eugene, OR. . . . 800-937-9677
Osowski Farms
Minto, ND. . . . 701-248-3341
Pacific Choice Brands
Fresno, CA . . . 559-476-3581
Pacific Collier Fresh Company
Immokalee, FL . . . 800-226-7274
Pacific Valley Foods Inc
Bellevue, WA . . . 425-643-1805
Paradise Products Corporation
Boca Raton, FL. . . . 800-826-1235
Paris Foods Corporation
Trappe, MD. . . . 410-200-9595
Pastorelli Food Products
Chicago, IL . . . 800-767-2829
Pictsweet Co
Bells, TN. . . . 731-663-7600
Pride Enterprises Glades
Belle Glade, FL. . . . 561-996-1091
Proacec USA
Santa Monica, CA. . . . 310-996-7770
Produits Ronald
St. Damase, QC. . . . 800-465-0118
Pure Food Ingredients
Verona, WI . . . 800-355-9601
Queensway Foods Company
Burlingame, CA . . . 650-871-7770
R & S Mexican Food
Glendale, AZ. . . . 602-272-2727
R.C. McEntire & Company
Columbia, SC . . . 803-799-3388
Rainsweet Inc
Salem, OR. . . . 800-363-4293
Ralph Sechler & Son Inc
St Joe, IN. . . . 800-332-5461
Raymond-Hadley Corporation
Spencer, NY . . . 800-252-5220
Ready Pac Foods Inc
Irwindale, CA . . . 800-800-4088
Red River Commodities Inc
Fargo, ND . . . 800-437-5539
Rene Produce Dist
Rio Rico, AZ. . . . 520-281-0806
Ripon Pickle Co Inc
Ripon, WI . . . 920-748-7110
Ron Son Foods Inc
Swedesboro, NJ . . . 856-241-7333
Salad Depot
Moonachie, NJ . . . 201-507-1980
Santa Barbara Olive Company
Santa Barbara, CA . . . 800-624-4896
Sargent and Greenleaf
Nicholasville, KY. . . . 800-826-7652
Schiff Food Products Co Inc
Totowa, NJ . . . 973-237-1990
Schmidt Bros Inc
Swanton, OH. . . . 800-200-7318

Seabrook Brothers & Sons
Seabrook, NJ. . . . 856-455-8080
Sedlock Farm
Lynn Center, IL. . . . 309-521-8284
Seneca Foods Corp
Princeville, IL. . . . 309-385-4301
Seneca Foods Corp
Marion, NY. . . . 315-926-8100
Serv-Agen Corporation
Cherry Hill, NJ . . . 856-663-6966
Seville Olive Company
Los Angeles, CA. . . . 323-261-2218
Shafer Lake Fruit Inc
Hartford, MI . . . 269-621-3194
Silva Farms
Gonzales, CA . . . 831-675-2428
Small Planet Foods
Minneapolis, MN . . . 800-624-4123
Smeltzer Orchard Co
Frankfort, MI . . . 231-882-4421
Smith Frozen Foods Inc
Weston, OR. . . . 541-566-3515
Snowcrest Packer
Abbotsford, BC. . . . 800-265-3686
Sonne
Wahpeton, ND. . . . 800-727-6663
SOPAKCO Foods
Mullins, SC. . . . 800-276-9678
South Mill
Kennett Square, PA. . . . 610-444-4800
Specialty Food Association
New York, NY . . . 646-878-0301
Spokane Seed Co
Spokane Valley, WA . . . 800-359-8478
Spreda Group
Louisville, KY. . . . 502-426-9411
Strathroy Foods
Strathroy, ON . . . 519-245-4600
Strub Pickles
Brantford, ON. . . . 519-751-1717
Sun Glo Of Idaho
Sugar City, ID . . . 208-356-7346
Sun-Brite Canning
Kingsville, ON . . . 519-326-9033
Sunnyside Vegetable Packing
Millville, NJ . . . 856-451-5077
Superior Bean & Spice Company
Brush Prairie, WA. . . . 360-694-0819
SupHerb Farms
Turlock, CA . . . 800-787-4372
Surface Banana Company
Parkersburg, WV. . . . 304-485-2400
T.S. Smith & Sons
Bridgeville, DE. . . . 302-337-8271
Talk O'Texas Brands Inc
San Angelo, TX . . . 800-749-6572
Taylor Farms
Salinas, CA. . . . 831-754-0471
Taylor Farms Pacific
Tracy, CA . . . 209-830-1086
Teixeira Farms, Inc.
Santa Maria, CA. . . . 805-928-3801
Thomas Canning/Maidstone
Maidstone, ON . . . 519-737-1531
Timber Crest Farms
Healdsburg, CA . . . 888-766-4233
Tom Ringhausen Orchards
Hardin, IL . . . 800-258-6645
Topor's Pickle & Food Svc Inc
Detroit, MI . . . 313-237-0288
Trans Pecos Foods
San Antonio, TX. . . . 210-228-0896
Tropic Fish Hawaii LLC
Honolulu, HI. . . . 808-591-2936
Tropical Foods
Charlotte, NC . . . 800-438-4470
Tuscarora Organic Growers Cooperative
Hustontown, PA . . . 814-448-2173
Twin City Foods Inc.
Stanwood, WA . . . 206-515-2400
Unilever Food Solutions
Englewood Cliffs, NJ
United Marketing Exchange
Delta, CO . . . 970-874-3332
Vegetable Juices Inc
Chicago, IL. . . . 888-776-9752
Veronica Foods Inc
Oakland, CA. . . . 800-370-5554
Violet Packing Holdings LLC
Williamstown, NJ. . . . 856-629-7428
Visalia Produce Sales
Kingsburg, CA . . . 559-897-6652

Wagshal's Imports
Washington, DC 202-363-5698
Wallace Grain & Pea Company
Pullman, WA 509-878-1561
Washington Potato Company
Pasco, WA 800-897-2726
Washington Rhubarb Grower Assn
Sumner, WA 800-435-9911
Webster Farms
Cambridge, NS 800-507-8844
Weil's Food Processing
Wheatley, ON 519-825-4572
Westin Foods
Omaha, NE 800-228-6098
Wildcat Produce
McGrew, NE 308-783-2438
Zuccaro Produce
Columbia Heights, MN 612-333-1122

IQF (Individual Quick Frozen)

Eckert Cold Storage
Manteca, CA 209-823-3181
Rainsweet Inc
Salem, OR 800-363-4293
SupHerb Farms
Turlock, CA 800-787-4372
Washington Rhubarb Grower Assn
Sumner, WA 800-435-9911

Vegetables Mixed

Agrocan
Ville St Laurent, QC 877-247-6226
Birdseye Food
Mountain Lakes, NJ 585-383-1850
Deep Foods Inc
Union, NJ 908-810-7500
Di Mare Fresh Inc
Fort Worth, TX 817-385-3000
Just Tomatoes
Westley, CA 800-537-1985
New Harvest Foods
Washington, DC 920-822-2578
Patterson Frozen Foods
Patterson, CA 209-892-2611
Risvold's Inc.
Gardena, CA 323-770-2674
Strathroy Foods
Strathroy, ON 519-245-4600

Broccoli, Peas & Carrots

Faribault Foods, Inc.
Fairbault, MN 507-331-1400

California Blend

Paris Foods Corporation
Trappe, MD 410-200-9595

Canned

Bryant Preserving Company
Alma, AR 800-634-2413
Carriere Foods Inc
Saint-Denis-Sur-Richelie, QC 450-787-3411
Cates Addis Company
Parkton, NC 800-423-1883
Deep Foods Inc
Union, NJ 908-810-7500
Emerling International Foods
Buffalo, NY 716-833-7381
Faribault Foods, Inc.
Fairbault, MN 507-331-1400
Moody Dunbar Inc
Johnson City, TN 423-952-0100
New Harvest Foods
Washington, DC 920-822-2578

Frozen

Birdseye Food
Mountain Lakes, NJ 585-383-1850
Deep Foods Inc
Union, NJ 908-810-7500
Paris Foods Corporation
Trappe, MD 410-200-9595
Strathroy Foods
Strathroy, ON 519-245-4600
Symons Frozen Foods
Centralia, WA 360-736-1321

Peas & Carrots

Cates Addis Company
Parkton, NC 800-423-1883
Strathroy Foods
Strathroy, ON 519-245-4600
Symons Frozen Foods
Centralia, WA 360-736-1321
Twin City Foods Inc.
Stanwood, WA 206-515-2400

Frozen

Cates Addis Company
Parkton, NC 800-423-1883
Strathroy Foods
Strathroy, ON 519-245-4600
Symons Frozen Foods
Centralia, WA 360-736-1321
Twin City Foods Inc.
Stanwood, WA 206-515-2400

Water Chestnuts

Dong Kee Company
Chicago, IL 312-225-6340
Emerling International Foods
Buffalo, NY 716-833-7381
Lee's Food Products
Toronto, ON 416-465-2407
SupHerb Farms
Turlock, CA 800-787-4372

Watercress

AeroFarms
Newark, NJ 973-242-2495
Calif Watercress Inc
Fillmore, CA 805-524-4808

Yams

AgriNorthwest
Kennewick, WA 509-734-1195
Arbre Farms Inc
Walkerville, MI 231-873-3337
Bright Harvest Sweet Potato Co
Clarksville, AR 800-793-7440
F & S Produce Co Inc
Vineland, NJ 800-886-3316
Garber Farms
Iota, LA 800-824-2284
Godwin Produce Co
Dunn, NC 910-892-4171
Ocean Mist Farms
Castroville, CA 831-633-2144
Seneca Foods Corp
Marion, NY 315-926-8100
Vaughn Rue Produce
Wilson, NC 800-388-8138
Zuccaro Produce
Columbia Heights, MN 612-333-1122

Frozen

Bright Harvest Sweet Potato Co
Clarksville, AR 800-793-7440

Zucchini

Arbre Farms Inc
Walkerville, MI 231-873-3337
Bifulco Four Seasons
Pittsgrove, NJ 856-692-0778
Earthbound Farm
San Jn Bautista, CA 800-690-3200
Emerling International Foods
Buffalo, NY 716-833-7381
F & S Produce Co Inc
Vineland, NJ 800-886-3316
Great American Appetizers
Nampa, ID 800-282-4834
Haliburton International Inc
Ontario, CA 877-980-4295
Miss Scarlett's Flowers
Juneau, AK 800-345-6734
Paris Foods Corporation
Trappe, MD 410-200-9595
Pictsweet Co
Bells, TN 731-663-7600
Sure-Fresh Produce Inc
Santa Maria, CA 888-423-5379
Talley Farms
Arroyo Grande, CA 805-489-5400
Vegetable Juices Inc
Chicago, IL 888-776-9752

General Grocery

General

731 North Beach LLC
La Habra, CA 562-697-8888
99 Ranch Market
Hacienda Heights, CA 626-839-2899
A Gift Basket by Carmela
Longmeadow, MA 413-746-1400
A.T. Gift Company
Harpers Ferry, WV 304-876-6680
Aliments Fontaine Sant, Inc
Ville Saint-Laurent, QC 888-627-2683
Allied Food Products
Brooklyn, NY 718-230-4227
AmeriQual Foods
Evansville, IN 812-867-1444
Arctic Glacier
Winnipeg, MB 888-573-9237
Ashley Food Co Inc
Sudbury, MA 800-617-2823
Baldwin Richardson Foods
Oakbrook Terrace, IL 866-644-2732
Binding Brauerei USA
Norwalk, CT 203-229-0111
Boyajian LLC
Canton, MA 800-965-0665
Brazilian Home Collection
Passaic, NJ 973-365-5800
Brookshire Grocery Company
Tyler, TX 888-937-3776
Capalbo's Fruit Baskets
Clifton, NJ 800-252-6262
Chicken Of The Sea
El Segundo, CA 844-267-8862
Chong Mei Trading
East Point, GA 404-768-3838
Choyce Produce
Honolulu, HI 808 839 1502
Christmas Point Wild Rice Co
Baxter, MN 218-828-0603
Classic Foods
San Francisco, CA 800-574-8122
Colony Foods
Lawrence, MA 978-682-9677
Cosgrove Distributors Inc
Spring Valley, IL 800-347-3071
Creative Food Ingredients
Perry, NY 585-237-2213
Culinary Farms Inc
Woodland, CA 888-383-2767
DeLallo Foods
Mount Pleasant, PA 877-355-2556
Dogswell LLC
Los Angeles, CA 888-559-8833
Eat It Corporation
Brooklyn, NY 718 768-7950
Ellsworth Foods
Tifton, GA 229-386-8448
Fabrique Delices
Hayward, CA 510-441-9500
Farallon Fisheries Co
S San Francisco, CA 650-583-3474
Fast Fixing Foods
Boaz, AL 800-317-4232
Festive Foods
Virginia Beach, VA 757-490-9186
Figueroa Brothers
Irving, TX 800-886-6354
Formost Friedman Company
Merrick, NY 516-378-4919
Fountain Shakes/MS Foods
Minnetonka, MN 952-988-6940
French & Brawn Marketplace
Camden, ME 207-236-3361
Galland's Institutional Food
Bakersfield, CA 661-631-5505
Giulia Speciality Food
Lodi, NJ 973-478-3111
Gold Mine Natural Food Company
Poway, CA 800-475-3663
Great River Organic Milling
Arcadia, WI 608-687-9580
Gulf Marine & Industrial Supplies Inc
Houston, TX 800-886-6252
H & W Foods
Kapolei, HI 808-682-8300
H-E-B Grocery Co. LP
San Antonio, TX 800-432-3113
Haile Resources
Dallas, TX 800-357-1471
Hain Celestial Group Inc
Lake Success, NY 800-434-4246
Hanmi Inc
Chicago, IL 773-271-0730
Hatch Chile Company
Albuquerque, NM 912-267-9909
Healthy Food Ingredients
Fargo, ND 844-275-3443
Hickey Foods
Sun Valley, ID 800-215-0646
Holly's Oatmeal Inc
Torrington, CT 860-618-0090
Ingles Markets
Black Mountain, NC 828-669-2941
Inland Products
Carthage, MO 417-358-4048
International Delicacies Inc
San Pablo, CA 844-974-1030
Ira Higdon Grocery Company
Cairo, GA 229-377-1272
Island Treasures Gourmet
Manassas, VA 703-801-4671
Itella Foods
San Pedro, CA 310-732-5875
Johnston County Hams
Smithfield, NC 800-543-4267
Julian's Recipe
Brooklyn, NY 888-640-8880
Kaladi Brothers
Anchorage, AK 907-644-7400
Karlin Foods
Northfield, IL 847-441-8330
Kaurina's, LLC
Dallas, TX 972-888-9990
Kusha Inc.
Cypress, CA 800-550-7423
La Superior Food Products
Shawnee Mission, KS 913-432-4933
Lahaha Tea Co
Arcadia, CA 626-215-6960
Lance Private Brands
Charlotte, NC 888-722-1163
Lemke Wholesale
Rogers, AR 479-751-4671
Lopez Foods
Oklahoma City, OK 405-603-7500
Lotus Manufacturing Company
San Antonio, TX 210-223-1421
M & M Label Co
Malden, MA 800-637-6628
M&L Ventures
Tucson, AZ 520-884-8232
Maher Marketing Services
Irving, TX 972-751-7700
Marukan Vinegar USA Inc.
Paramount, CA 562-630-6060
Mathews Packing
Marysville, CA 530-743-9000
Mcfarling Foods Inc
Indianapolis, IN 317-635-2633
Meijer Inc
Grand Rapids, MI 616-453-6711
Milton A. Klein Company
New York, NY 800-221-0248
Minh Food Corporation
Pasadena, TX 800-344-7655
Miss Jenny's Pickles
Kernersville, NC 336-978-0041
Mission Valley Foods
Fremont, CA 408-254-9387
Mj Kellner Co
Springfield, IL 217-483-1700
MKE Enterprises LTD
New York, NY 212-447-0051
Moledina Commodities
Flower Mound, TX 817-490-1101
Monte Cristo Trading
Scarsdale, NY 914-725-8025
National Food Co LTD
Honolulu, HI 808-839-1118
National Importers
Richmond, BC 888-894-6464
O'Brines Pickling
Spokane, WA 509-534-7255
Olde Estate
Boca Raton, FL 561-400-7444
Particle Control
Albertville, MN 763-497-3075
Penn Dutch Meat & Seafood Market
Hollywood, FL 954-921-7144
Pon Food Corp
Ponchatoula, LA 985-386-6941
Publix Super Market
Lakeland, FL 800-242-1227
Pure Inventions LLC
Little Silver, NJ 732-842-5777
Quality Food Products Inc
Chicago, IL 312-666-4559
Ramsen Inc
Lakeville, MN 952-431-0400
Richards Natural Foods
Eagle, MI 517-627-7965
Schnuck Markets, Inc.
St. Louis, MO 800-264-4400
Select Origins
Mansfield, OH 419-924-5447
Severance Foods Inc
Hartford, CT 860-724-7063
Solo Worldwide Enterprises
Falls Church, VA 703-845-7072
Sprouts Farmers Market Inc.
Phoenix, AZ
Stassen North America
Louisville, CO 303-563-1016
Sun Garden Sprouts
Cookeville, TN 931-400-2710
Sun World Intl LLC
Palm Desert, CA 760-398-9450
Sun-Rise
Alexandria, MN 320-846-5720
Sunny Delight Beverage Company
Cincinnati, OH
Tase-Rite Co
Wakefield, RI 401-783-7300
The Procter & Gamble Company
Cincinnati, OH 800-692-0132
Thermice Company
Old Greenwich, CT 203-637-4500
Topco Associates LLC
Elk Grove Village, IL 847-676-3030
Trade Marcs Group
Brooklyn, NY 718-387-9696
Tradeshare Corporation
Brooklyn, NY 718-237-2295
Transnational Foods
Miami, FL 305-415-9970
Ultimate Foods
Linden, NJ 908-486-0800
Valley Sun Products Inc
Newman, CA 800-426-5444
VIP Food Svc
Kahului, HI 808-877-5055
Wallace Edwards & Sons
Surry, VA 800-200-4267
WEIS Markets Inc.
Sunbury, PA 866-999-9347
Winn-Dixie Stores
Jacksonville, FL 800-967-9105
Wonder Natural Foods Corp
Water Mill, NY 631-726-4433
Yamamotoyama of America
Pomona, CA 909-594-7356
Zuccaro Produce
Columbia Heights, MN 612-333-1122

Ingredients, Flavors & Additives

Freeze Dried Ingredients

Freeze-Dry Ingredients
Elmhurst, IL 630-530-1880
Oregon Freeze Dry, Inc.
Albany, OR 541-926-6001
SupHerb Farms
Turlock, CA 800-787-4372
Y Not Foods
Cape Coral, FL 608-222-2860

General

A Hill of Beans Coffee Roasters
Omaha, NE 402-333-6048
Accurate Ingredients Inc
Farmingdale, NY 516-496-2500
AEP Colloids
Hadley, NY 800-848-0658
Ajinomoto Frozen Foods USA, Inc.
Ontario, CA 866-536-8008
Aloecorp, Inc.
Seattle, WA 800-458-2563
AMCO Proteins
Burlington, NJ 609-387-3130
AME Nutrition
Dublin, OH 614-766-3638
American Ingredients Co
Lenexa, KS 800-669-4092
American Specialty Foods
Lancaster, PA 800-335-6663
Ames Company, Inc
New Ringgold, PA 610-750-1032
AMF Pharma
Ontario, CA 888-666-1016
Analyticon Discovery LLC
Rockville, MD 240-406-1256
Asiamerica Ingredients
Westwood, NJ 201-497-5531
AuNutra Industries Inc
Chino, CA 909-628-2600
Axiom Foods, Inc.
Los Angeles, CA 800-711-3587
Bakto Flavors
North Brunswick, NJ 732-354-4492
Batory Foods
Des Plaines, IL 847-299-1999
Beverage Flavors Intl
Chicago, IL 773-248-3860
Biothera
St Paul, MN 651-675-0300
Blanver USA
Boca Raton, FL 561-416-5513
Blue Marble Biomaterials
Missoula, MT 800-738-0849
Bonnie & Don Flavours Inc.
Mississauga, ON 905-625-1813
Budenheim USA, Inc.
Columbus, OH 614-345-2400
Caldic USA Inc
Elgin, IL 847-468-0001
Caremoli USA
Ames, IA 515-233-1255
Carolina Innovative Food Ingredients, Inc.
Nashville, NC 252-462-1551
Catherych
Warren, NJ 732-566-6625
Centerchem, Inc.
Norwalk, CT 203-822-9800
Chaucer Foods, Inc. USA
Forest Grove, OR
CJ America
Los Angeles, CA 213-427-5566
Clara Foods
San Francisco, CA
Clariant
Charlottte, NC 704-331-7000
Corbion
S San Francisco, CA
Corbion
Blair, NE 402-426-0377
Corbion
Tucker, GA 470-545-7100
Corbion
Dolton, IL 708-849-8590
Corbion
Mississauga, ON 800-324-8802
Corbion
Totowa, NJ 800-526-5261
Corbion
Lenexa, KS 800-669-4092
Corbion
Grandview, MO 816-763-8377
Creative Flavors & Specialties LLP
Linden, NJ 908-862-4678
D F Ingredients Inc
Washington, MO 888-583-0802
D2 Ingredients, LP.
De Pere, WI 920-425-8870
Darling Ingredients Inc.
Irving, TX 800-800-4841
Deko International Company
Earth City, MO 314-298-0910
Denomega Pure Health
Brighton, CO 479-181-2845
Dohler-Milne Aseptics LLC
Prosser, WA 509-786-2240
Draco Natural Products Inc
San Jose, CA 408-287-7871
Dulcette Technologies
Lindenhurst, NY 631-752-8700
DuPont Tate & Lyle BioProducts Company, LLC.
Loudon, TN 866-404-7933
DyStar Hilton Davis/DyStar Foam Control
Cuyahoga Falls, OH 330-916-6726
Edlong Corporation
Elk Grove Village, IL 847-631-6700
Embria Health Sciences
Ankeny, IA 877-362-7421
EMD Performance Materials
Philadelphia, PA 888-367-3275
Emerald Hilton Davis LLC
Cincinnati, OH 513-841-0057
Emerald Performance Materials
Cuyahoga Falls, OH 330-916-6700
Epogee
Indianapolis, IN
Escalade Limited
Huntington, NY 631-659-3373
Ethical Naturals
San Anselmo, CA 866-459-4454
Expro Manufacturing
Vernon, CA 323-415-8544
Fallwood Corp
White Plains, NY 914-304-4065
Fenchem Inc
Chino, CA 909-597-1113
Fiberstar
River Falls, WI 715-425-7550
First Choice Ingredients
Germantown, WI 262-251-4322
FlavorHealth
North Brunswick, NJ 732-875-4799
Flavors and Color
Walnut, CA 909-598-4441
Fontana Flavors Inc
Janesville, WI 608-754-9668
Fontana Flavors Inc
Janesville, WI 608-754-9668
Foreign Domestic Chemicals
Oakland, NJ 201-651-9700
Freeze-Dry Foods Inc
Albion, NY 585-589-6399
FrieslandCampina Ingredients North America, Inc.
Paramus, NJ 551-497-7300
Fuji Health Science/Inc
Burlington, NJ 609-386-3030
GAF Seelig Inc
Flushing, NY 718-899-5000
Garuda International
Exeter, CA 559-594-4380
Gelnex Gelatins
Chicago, IL 312-577-4275
Glanbia Nutritionals
Twin Falls, ID 208-733-7555
GLG Life Tech Corporation
Richmond, BC 855-454-7587
Global Preservatives
Lake Charles, LA 866-491-0816
Golden 100
Deland, FL 386-734-0113
Graham Chemical Corporation
Barrington, IL 847-304-4400
Great Earth Chemical
Portland, OR 503-620-7130
GTC Nutrition
Westchester, IL 800-443-2746
Hangzhou Sanhe USA Inc.
Walnut, CA 909-869-6016
Hard Eight Nutrition LLC
Henderson, NV 702-425-7638
Hawkins Inc
Roseville, MN 800-328-5460
Heartland Flax
Valley City, ND 866-599-3529
Helm New York Chemical Corp
Piscataway, NJ 732-981-0528
High Quality Organics
Reno, NV 775-971-8550
Hilmar Ingredients
Hilmar, CA 888-300-4465
Horner International
Raleigh, NC 919-787-3112
I P Callison & Sons
Lacey, WA 360-412-3340
ICL Performance Products
St. Louis, MO 800-244-6169
IFC Solutions
Linden, NJ 800-875-9393
Imperial Sensus
Sugar Land, TX 281-490-9522
Ingredia Inc
Wapakoneta, OH 419-738-4060
Ingredient Specialties
Exeter, CA 559-594-4380
Innophos Holdings Inc.
Cranbury, NJ 609-495-2495
Innova Flavors
Lombard, IL 630-928-4800
Interfood Ingredients
Miami, FL 786-953-8320
J & K Ingrediants
Paterson, NJ 973-340-8700
J Rettenmaier USA LP
Schoolcraft, MI 877-895-4099
Javo Beverage Co., Inc.
Vista, CA 760-330-1141
Jel Sert
West Chicago, IL 800-323-2592
Jost Chemical
St Louis, MO 314-428-4300
Kenko International
Los Angeles, CA 323-721-8300
Latitude, LTD
Huntington, NY 631-659-3374
Lekithos
Palm Beach Gardens, FL
Lionel Hitchen Essitional Oils
Sarasota, FL 941-379-1400
Lipid Nutrition
Channahan, IL 815-730-5208
Log 5 Corporation
Phoenix, MD 410-329-9580
Log House Foods
Plymouth, MN 763-546-8395
Magrabar Chemical Corp
Morton Grove, IL 847-965-7550
MAK Wood Inc
Grafton, WI 262-387-1200
Marroquin Organic Intl.
Santa Cruz, CA 831-423-3442
Marukan Vinegar USA Inc.
Paramount, CA 562-630-6060
MGP Ingredients Inc
Atchison, KS 800-255-0302
Moore Organics
Hamilton, OH 513-881-7144
Muntons Ingredients
Bellevue, WA 425-372-3082
Nantong Acetic Acid Chemical Co., Ltd.
Hilliard, OH 614-947-0249
Nature's Products Inc
Sunrise, FL 800-752-7873
New Hope Natural Media
Boulder, CO 303-939-8440
Newport Ingredients
Los Angeles, CA 323-284-5959
North Taste Flavourings
Anse-Bleue, NB 506-732-0010

Nutraceutical International
Park City, UT 800-669-8877
Nutralliance
Yorba Linda, CA 844-410-1400
NutriFusion
Naples, FL 239-300-9702
Old Cavendish Products
Cavendish, VT 800-536-7899
Peter Cremer North America
Cincinnati, OH 877-901-7262
Phamous Phloyd's Barbecue
Denver, CO 800-497-3281
Piveg, Inc.
San Diego, CA 858-688-3070
Procell Polymers
Baton Rouge, LA 225-978-8069
Reheis Co
Berkeley Heights, NJ 908-464-1500
San Joaquin Vly Concentrates
Fresno, CA 800-557-0220
Shanghai Freemen
Edison, NJ 732-981-1288
SoluBlend Technologies LLC
Frankfort, IL 815-534-5778
Specialty Minerals Inc
Bethlehem, PA 800-801-1031
Sunshine International Foods
Methuen, MA 978-837-3209
Suzhou-Chem Inc
Wellesley, MA 781-433-8618
Svzusa Inc
Othello, WA 509-488-6563
Vanilla Corp Of America LLC
Hatfield, PA 215-996-1978
Ventura Foods LLC
Brea, CA 800-421-6257
Vida Blend
Amsterdam, NY 518-620-6216
Wiberg Corporation
Oakville, ON 905-825-9900
Wildly Organic
Silver Bay, MN 800-945-3801
Z-Trim Holdings, Inc
Mundelein, IL 847-549-6002

Acids

Amerol Chemical Corporation
Farmingdale, NY 631-694-4700
Bartek Ingredients, Inc.
Stoney Creek, ON 800-263-4165
BASF Corp.
Florham Park, NJ 800-526-1072
Cargill Inc.
Minneapolis, MN 800-227-4455
J M Swank Co
North Liberty, IA 800-593-6375
Jarchem Industries
Newark, NJ 973-578-4560
Jungbunzlauer Inc
Newton, MA 617-969-0900
Particle Dynamics
Saint Louis, MO 800-452-4682
Pfanstiehl Inc
Waukegan, IL 847-623-0370
PMP Fermentation Products
Peoria, IL 800-558-1031
Profood International
Naperville, IL 888-288-0081
Protein Research
Livermore, CA 800-948-1991
Roquette America Inc.
Geneva, IL 630-463-9430
Shanghai Freemen
Edison, NJ 732-981-1288
Silver Fern Chemical Inc
Seattle, WA 866-282-3384
Symrise Inc.
Teterboro, NJ 201-288-3200
Trumark
Linden, NJ 800-752-7877
Wilke International Inc
Lenexa, KS 800-779-5545

Adipic

Shanghai Freemen
Edison, NJ 732-981-1288
Silver Fern Chemical Inc
Seattle, WA 866-282-3384
Universal Preservachem Inc
Somerset, NJ 732-568-1266

Aminoacetic

ADH Health Products Inc
Congers, NY 845-268-0027
Ajinomoto Heartland Inc
Chicago, IL 773-380-7000
AMT Labs Inc
North Salt Lake, UT 801-294-3126
Anabol Naturals
Santa Cruz, CA 800-426-2265
Asiamerica Ingredients
Westwood, NJ 201-497-5531
Belmont Chemicals
Clifton, NJ 800-722-5070
Catherych
Warren, NJ 732-566-6625
DMH Ingredients Inc
Libertyville, IL 847-362-9977
Eckhart Corporation
Novato, CA 800-200-4201
Jo Mar Laboratories
Campbell, CA 800-538-4545
Kyowa Hakko
New York, NY 800-596-9252
NOW Foods
Bloomingdale, IL 888-669-3663
Nu Naturals Inc
Eugene, OR 800-753-4372
Stauber Performance Ingrdients
Fullerton, CA 888-441-4233
Universal Preservachem Inc
Somerset, NJ 732-568-1266

Benzoic

Emerald Kalama Chemical, LLC
Kalama, WA 800-223-0035
Luyties Pharmacal Company
Saint Louis, MO 800-325-8080
Universal Preservachem Inc
Somerset, NJ 732-568-1266

Boric/Boracic

Universal Preservachem Inc
Somerset, NJ 732-568-1266

Gluconic (Gluconolactone)

Glucona America
Janesville, WI 608-752-0449
Jungbunzlauer Inc
Newton, MA 617-969-0900
PMP Fermentation Products
Peoria, IL 800-558-1031
Roquette America Inc.
Geneva, IL 630-463-9430
Universal Preservachem Inc
Somerset, NJ 732-568-1266

Glutamic

Shanghai Freemen
Edison, NJ 732-981-1288
Universal Preservachem Inc
Somerset, NJ 732-568-1266

Succinic

BioAmber
Plymouth, MN 763-253-4480
Shanghai Freemen
Edison, NJ 732-981-1288

Tannic

Silvateam USA
Ontario, CA 909-635-2870

Acidulants

Asiamerica Ingredients
Westwood, NJ 201-497-5531
Marukan Vinegar USA Inc.
Paramount, CA 562-630-6060
Newport Ingredients
Los Angeles, CA 323-284-5959
Tate & Lyle PLC
Hoffman Estates, IL 847-396-7500
Wenda America Inc
Naperville, IL 844-999-3632

Acetic

Asiamerica Ingredients
Westwood, NJ 201-497-5531
Jarchem Industries
Newark, NJ 973-578-4560
Universal Preservachem Inc
Somerset, NJ 732-568-1266

Citric

American Key Food Products Inc
Closter, NJ 877-263-7539
Asiamerica Ingredients
Westwood, NJ 201-497-5531
Cargill Inc.
Minneapolis, MN 800-227-4455
Embassy Flavours Ltd.
Brampton, ON 800-334-3371
FBC Industries
Schaumburg, IL 888-322-4637
Hosemen & Roche Vitamins & Fine Chemicals
Nutley, NJ 800-526-6367
International Chemical Corp
Melbourne, FL 800-914-2436
Jungbunzlauer Inc
Newton, MA 617-969-0900
Luyties Pharmacal Company
Saint Louis, MO 800-325-8080
Nichem Co
Newark, NJ 973-399-9810
Shekou Chemicals
Waltham, MA 781-893-6878
Universal Preservachem Inc
Somerset, NJ 732-568-1266

Fumaric

Asiamerica Ingredients
Westwood, NJ 201-497-5531
Bartek Ingredients, Inc.
Stoney Creek, ON 800-263-4165
Jungbunzlauer Inc
Newton, MA 617-969-0900
Silver Fern Chemical Inc
Seattle, WA 866-282-3384
Universal Preservachem Inc
Somerset, NJ 732-568-1266

Lactic

Asiamerica Ingredients
Westwood, NJ 201-497-5531
Fleurchem Inc
Middletown, NY 845-341-2100
Jungbunzlauer Inc
Newton, MA 617-969-0900
Pfanstiehl Inc
Waukegan, IL 847-623-0370
Trumark
Linden, NJ 800-752-7877
Universal Preservachem Inc
Somerset, NJ 732-568-1266
Varied Industries Corp
Mason City, IA 800-654-5617
Wilke International Inc
Lenexa, KS 800-779-5545

Malic

Asiamerica Ingredients
Westwood, NJ 201-497-5531
Bartek Ingredients, Inc.
Stoney Creek, ON 800-263-4165
Jungbunzlauer Inc
Newton, MA 617-969-0900
Universal Preservachem Inc
Somerset, NJ 732-568-1266

Phosphoric

Asiamerica Ingredients
Westwood, NJ 201-497-5531
ICL Performance Products
St. Louis, MO 800-244-6169
Universal Preservachem Inc
Somerset, NJ 732-568-1266

Sorbic

Asiamerica Ingredients
Westwood, NJ 201-497-5531
International Chemical Corp
Melbourne, FL 800-914-2436
Jungbunzlauer Inc
Newton, MA 617-969-0900
Silver Fern Chemical Inc
Seattle, WA 866-282-3384

Universal Preservachem Inc
Somerset, NJ 732-568-1266

Tartaric

American Tartaric Products
Larchmont, NY 914-834-1881
Asiamerica Ingredients
Westwood, NJ 201-497-5531
Bartek Ingredients, Inc.
Stoney Creek, ON 800-263-4165
Frontier Co-op
Norway, IA 844-550-6200
H. Interdonati
Cold Spring Harbour, NY 800-367-6617
International Chemical Corp
Melbourne, FL 800-914-2436
Jungbunzlauer Inc
Newton, MA 617-969-0900
Universal Preservachem Inc
Somerset, NJ 732-568-1266

Additives

Foreign Domestic Chemicals
Oakland, NJ 201-651-9700
Great Earth Chemical
Portland, OR 503-620-7130
ICL Performance Products
St. Louis, MO 800-244-6169
Jost Chemical
St Louis, MO 314-428-4300
Latitude, LTD
Huntington, NY 631-659-3374
Magrabar Chemical Corp
Morton Grove, IL 847-965-7550

Anticaking

Allied Blending & Ingredients
Keokuk, IA 800-758-4080
Asiamerica Ingredients
Westwood, NJ 201-497-5531
Atlantic Chemicals Trading
Glendale, CA 818-246-0077

Enrichment & Nutrient

Single & Blended

Asiamerica Ingredients
Westwood, NJ 201-497-5531

Enzymes

D F Ingredients Inc
Washington, MO 888-583-0802
Deerland Probiotics & Enzymes
Forsyth, MO 800-825-8545
DSM
Heerlen,

Free Flow

Amerol Chemical Corporation
Farmingdale, NY 631-694-4700
Asiamerica Ingredients
Westwood, NJ 201-497-5531
Crompton Corporation
Greenwich, CT 800-295-2392
Garuda International
Exeter, CA 559-594-4380
Prolume
Lakeside, AZ 928-367-1200

Nutrient

Provitas LLC
Plano, TX 972-767-8867
Shanghai Freemen
Edison, NJ 732-981-1288

Adjuncts

Torkelson Cheese Co
Lena, IL 815-369-4265

Brewing

Acadian Seaplants
Dartmouth, NS 800-575-9100
Boyd's Coffee Co
Portland, OR 800-735-2878
Shanghai Freemen
Edison, NJ 732-981-1288
Thymly Products Inc
Colora, MD 877-710-2340

Agents

Asiamerica Ingredients
Westwood, NJ 201-497-5531
Crest Foods Inc
Ashton, IL 877-273-7893
IFC Solutions
Linden, NJ 800-875-9393
International Foodcraft Corp
Linden, NJ 800-875-9393
MAFCO Worldwide
Camden, NJ 856-986-4050
Magrabar Chemical Corp
Morton Grove, IL 847-965-7550

Buffering

Thymly Products Inc
Colora, MD 877-710-2340

Clarifying

American Laboratories
Omaha, NE 402-339-2494

Release, Grease

Edible

International Foodcraft Corp
Linden, NJ 800-875-9393

Thickening

PLT Health Solutions Inc
Morristown, NJ 973-984-0900
Sno Shack Inc
Rexburg, ID 888-766-7425

Arrowroot

Advanced Spice & Trading
Carrollton, TX 800-872-7811
Frontier Co-op
Norway, IA 844-550-6200
Schiff Food Products Co Inc
Totowa, NJ 973-237-1990

Whipping

Kolatin Real Kosher Gelatin
Lakewood, NJ 732-364-8700

Alkalis

Caustic

Sodium & Potassium Hydroxides

Xena International
Polo, IL 815-946-2626

Ammonium Carbonate

King Arthur Flour
Norwich, VT 800-827-6836
Luyties Pharmacal Company
Saint Louis, MO 800-325-8080
Universal Preservachem Inc
Somerset, NJ 732-568-1266

Analogs

Meat

Caribbean Food Delights Inc
Tappan, NY 845-398-3000
Cedar Lake Foods
Cedar Lake, MI 800-246-5039
Ivy Foods
Phoenix, AZ 877-223-5459
Oogolow Enterprises
Chico, CA 800-816-6873
Vitasoy USA
Woburn, MA 800-848-2769
Westin Foods
Omaha, NE 800-228-6098
Winmix/Natural Care Products
Englewood, FL 941-475-7432

Antioxidants

Amerol Chemical Corporation
Farmingdale, NY 631-694-4700
Asiamerica Ingredients
Westwood, NJ 201-497-5531
Avatar Corp
University Park, IL 800-255-3181
Body Breakthrough Inc
Deer Park, NY 800-924-3343
Dulcette Technologies
Lindenhurst, NY 631-752-8700
Escalade Limited
Huntington, NY 631-659-3373
Ethical Naturals
San Anselmo, CA 866-459-4454
Fuji Health Science/Inc
Burlington, NJ 609-386-3030
Herbal Products & Development
Aptos, CA 831-688-8706
International Vitamin Corporation
Freehold, NJ 800-666-8482
J M Swank Co
North Liberty, IA 800-593-6375
Kenko International
Los Angeles, CA 323-721-8300
Latitude, LTD
Huntington, NY 631-659-3374
Newport Ingredients
Los Angeles, CA 323-284-5959
NOW Foods
Bloomingdale, IL 888-669-3663
Nutraceutical International
Park City, UT 800-669-8877
PLT Health Solutions Inc
Morristown, NJ 973-984-0900
Premier Organics
Oakland, CA 866-237-8688
QBI
South Plainfield, NJ 908-668-0088
RFi Ingredients
Blauvelt, NY 800-962-7663
RPM Total Vitality
Yorba Linda, CA 800-234-3092
Shanghai Freemen
Edison, NJ 732-981-1288
Uas Laboratories
Eden Prairie, MN 800-422-3371
Wenda America Inc
Naperville, IL 844-999-3632

Ascorbic Acid

Asiamerica Ingredients
Westwood, NJ 201-497-5531
China Pharmaceutical Enterprises
Baton Rouge, LA 800-345-1658
International Chemical Corp
Melbourne, FL 800-914-2436
King Arthur Flour
Norwich, VT 800-827-6836
Shekou Chemicals
Waltham, MA 781-893-6878
Universal Preservachem Inc
Somerset, NJ 732-568-1266

Aroma Chemicals

Asiamerica Ingredients
Westwood, NJ 201-497-5531
Astral Extracts
Syosset, NY 516-496-2505
Firmenich Inc.
Plainsboro, NJ 800-257-9591
Powder Pure
The Dalles, OR 541-298-4800
Terra Flavors & Fragrances
New York, NY 212-244-1181

Aroma Chemicals & Materials

Chemicals

Asiamerica Ingredients
Westwood, NJ 201-497-5531
Native Scents
Taos, NM 800-645-3471

Methyl Salicylate

Asiamerica Ingredients
Westwood, NJ 201-497-5531

Fragrances

AFF International
Marietta, GA 800-241-7764
AM Todd Co
Kalamazoo, MI 269-343-2603
Aroma Vera
Los Angeles, CA 800-669-9514

Aromachem
Brooklyn, NY 718-497-4664
Asiamerica Ingredients
Westwood, NJ 201-497-5531
Avoca
Merry Hill, NC 252-482-2133
Avri Co Inc
Richmond, CA 800-883-9574
Centflor Manufacturing Co
New York, NY 212-246-8307
Classic Flavors & Fragrances
New York, NY 212-777-0004
DreamTime, Inc
Santa Cruz, CA 877-464-6702
Elan Vanilla Co
Newark, NJ 973-344-8014
Essential Products of America
Tampa, FL 800-822-9698
Firmenich Inc.
Plainsboro, NJ 800-257-9591
Flavor & Fragrance Specialties
Mahwah, NJ 800-998-4337
Flavormatic Industries
Wappingers Falls, NY 845-297-9100
Fleurchem Inc
Middletown, NY 845-341-2100
Flower Essence Svc
Nevada City, CA 800-548-0075
Green Spot Packaging
Claremont, CA 800-456-3210
International Flavors & Fragrances Inc.
New York, NY 212-765-5500
Jogue Inc
Northville, MI 800-531-3888
Newport Flavours & Fragrances
Orange, CA 714-744-3700
PMC Specialties Group Inc
Cincinnati, OH 800-543-2466
SKW Nature Products
Langhorne, PA 215-702-1000
Symrise Inc.
Teterboro, NJ 201-288-3200
T Hasegawa USA Inc
Cerritos, CA 714-522-1900
Technology Flavors & Fragrances
Amityville, NY 631-789-8228
Treatt USA Inc
Lakeland, FL 863-668-9500
Ungerer & Co
Lincoln Park, NJ 973-706-7381

Bases

Al-Rite Fruits & Syrups Co
Miami, FL 305-652-2540
Ariake USA Inc
Harrisonburg, VA 540-432-6550
BakeMark Canada
Laval, QC 800-361-4998
BakeMark Ingredients Canada
Richmond, BC 800-665-9441
Bartush Schnitzius Foods Co
Lewisville, TX 972-219-1270
Blount Fine Foods
Fall River, MA 774-888-1300
California Dairies Inc.
Visalia, CA 559-625-2200
Chef Hans' Gourmet Foods
Monroe, LA 800-890-4267
Citrosuco North America Inc
Lake Wales, FL 800-356-4592
Classic Tea
Libertyville, IL 630-680-9934
Clofine Dairy Products Inc
Linwood, NJ 609-653-1000
Concord Foods, LLC
Brockton, MA 508-580-1700
Consolidated Mills Inc
Houston, TX 713-896-4196
Crest Foods Inc
Ashton, IL 877-273-7893
CTL Foods
Colfax, WI 800-962-5227
Custom Culinary Inc.
Schaumberg, IL 800-621-8827
Dorothy Dawson Food Products
Jackson, MI 517-788-9830
Eatem Foods Co
Vineland, NJ 800-683-2836
Erba Food Products
Brooklyn, NY 718-272-7700
Finlays
Lincoln, RI 800-288-6272
Flavor House, Inc.
Adelanto, CA 760-246-9131
Folklore Foods
Selby, SD 605-649-1144
Fuji Foods Corp
Browns Summit, NC 336-375-3111
Global Food Industries
Townville, SC 800-225-4152
GS-AFI
South Plainfield, NJ 800-345-4342
Gum Technology Corporation
Tucson, AZ 800-369-4867
Hormel Foods Corp.
Austin, MN 507-437-5611
Illes Seasonings & Flavors
Carrollton, TX 800-683-4553
Integrative Flavors
Michigan City, IN 800-837-7687
JMH International
Park City, UT 888-741-4564
Johnson's Food Products
Dorchester, MA 617-265-3400
Manildra Milling Corporation
Fairway, KS 800-323-8435
Meat-O-Mat Corp
Brooklyn, NY 718-965-7250
Merci Spring Water
Maryland Heights, MO 314-872-9323
MicroSoy Corporation
Jefferson, IA 515-386-2100
Midas Foods Intl
Oak Park, MI 877-728-2379
Olympia Oyster Co
Shelton, WA 877-427-3193
Pacific Harvest Products
Bellevue, WA 425-401-7990
Particle Dynamics
Saint Louis, MO 800-452-4682
Produits Ronald
St. Damase, QC 800-465-0118
Roos Foods
Kenton, DE 800-343-3642
Serv-Agen Corporation
Cherry Hill, NJ 856-663-6966
Skjodt-Barrett Foods
Brampton, ON 877-600-1200
Spice Hunter Inc
Richmond, VA 800-444-3061
Spicetec Flavors & Seasonings
Omaha, NE 800-921-7502
Stevens Tropical Plantation
West Palm Beach, FL 561-683-4701
Sweet Sue Kitchens
Athens, AL 256-216-0500
Swiss Food Products
Chicago, IL 312-829-0100
Texas Spice Co
Round Rock, TX 800-880-8007
Tone Products Inc
Melrose Park, IL 800-536-8663
United Citrus
Norwood, MA 800-229-7300
V & E Kohnstamm Inc
Brooklyn, NY 800-847-4500
Vita-Pakt Citrus Products Co
Covina, CA 888-684-8272
Welch Foods Inc.
Concord, MA 800-340-6870
Western Syrup Company
Santa Fe Springs, CA 562-921-4485
White Coffee Corporation
Long Island City, NY 800-221-0140

Beef

Castella Imports Inc
Brentwood, NY 631-231-5500
Golden Specialty Foods Inc
Norwalk, CA 562-802-2537

Broth Cubes

Gel Spice Co LLC
Bayonne, NJ 800-922-0230

Beverage

Allen Flavors Inc
Edison, NJ 908-561-5995
Astral Extracts
Syosset, NY 516-496-2505
Baldwin Richardson Foods
Oakbrook Terrace, IL 866-644-2732
Bartush Schnitzius Foods Co
Lewisville, TX 972-219-1270
California Custom Fruits
Baldwin Park, CA 877-558-0056
Carmi Flavor & Fragrance Company
Commerce, CA 800-421-9647
Century Foods Intl LLC
Sparta, WI 800-269-1901
Classic Tea
Libertyville, IL 630-680-9934
Consolidated Mills Inc
Houston, TX 713-896-4196
CTL Foods
Colfax, WI 800-962-5227
Delano Growers Grape Products
Delano, CA 661-725-3255
Essential Flavors & Fragrances
Corona, CA 888-333-9935
Finlays
Lincoln, RI 800-288-6272
Folklore Foods
Selby, SD 605-649-1144
Franco's Cocktail Mixes
Pompano Beach, FL 800-782-4508
Fruitcrown Products Corp
Farmingdale, NY 800-441-3210
Global Food Industries
Townville, SC 800-225-4152
I Rice & Co Inc
Philadelphia, PA 800-232-6022
Milne Fruit Products Inc
Prosser, WA 509-786-2611
Nedlog Company
Wheeling, IL 800-323-6201
New Organics
Kenwood, CA 734-677-5570
Plaidberry Company
Vista, CA 760-727-5403
Quality Naturally Foods
City Of Industry, CA 888-498-6986
Rio Syrup Co
St Louis, MO 800-325-7666
Roos Foods
Kenton, DE 800-343-3642
Schlotterbeck & Foss Company
Portland, ME 800-777-4666
Singer Extract Laboratory
Livonia, MI 313-345-5880
Skjodt-Barrett Foods
Brampton, ON 877-600-1200
Stevens Tropical Plantation
West Palm Beach, FL 561-683-4701
Tampico Beverages Inc
Chicago, IL 877-826-7426
Thirs-Tea Corp
Boca Raton, FL 561-948-5600
Tova Industries LLC
Louisville, KY 888-532-8682
Vance's Foods
San Francisco, CA 415-621-1171
Vegetable Juices Inc
Chicago, IL 888-776-9752
Wechsler Coffee Corporation
Teterboro, NJ 800-800-2633
Welch Foods Inc.
Concord, MA 800-340-6870
Western Syrup Company
Santa Fe Springs, CA 562-921-4485
Wild Aseptics, LLC
Erlanger, KY 877-787-7221
Winmix/Natural Care Products
Englewood, FL 941-475-7432

Bouillon

Gel Spice Co LLC
Bayonne, NJ 800-922-0230
Hormel Foods Corp.
Austin, MN 507-437-5611
Massel USA
Carol Stream, IL 704-573-2299
Organic Gourmet
Sherman Oaks, CA 800-400-7772

Beef

Hormel Foods Corp.
Austin, MN 507-437-5611
Supreme Dairy Farms Co
Warwick, RI 401-739-8180

Candy

Kolatin Real Kosher Gelatin
Lakewood, NJ 732-364-8700

Chicken

Castella Imports Inc
Brentwood, NY 631-231-5500
Golden Specialty Foods Inc
Norwalk, CA 562-802-2537
Swiss Food Products
Chicago, IL 312-829-0100

Chocolate

Forbes Chocolate BP
Broadview Hts, OH 440-838-4400
US Chocolate Corp
Brooklyn, NY 718-788-8555

Dairy

Johnson's Food Products
Dorchester, MA 617-265-3400
WILD Flavors (Canada)
Mississauga, ON 800-263-5286

Non-Dairy & Imitation

Al-Rite Fruits & Syrups Co
Miami, FL 305-652-2540
BakeMark Ingredients Canada
Richmond, BC 800-665-9441
California Custom Fruits
Baldwin Park, CA 877-558-0056
Century Foods Intl LLC
Sparta, WI 800-269-1901
Clofine Dairy Products Inc
Linwood, NJ 609-653-1000
Forbes Chocolate BP
Broadview Hts, OH 440-838-4400
Freeman Industries
Tuckahoe, NY 800-666-6454
Galloway Co
Neenah, WI 800-722-8903
Global Food Industries
Townville, SC 800-225-4152
I Rice & Co Inc
Philadelphia, PA 800-232-6022
Johnson's Food Products
Dorchester, MA 617-265-3400
Land O'Lakes Inc
Arden Hills, MN 800-328-9680
Limpert Bros Inc
Vineland, NJ 800-691-1353
New Organics
Kenwood, CA 734-677-5570
Nog Incorporated
Dunkirk, NY 800-332-2664
Plaidberry Company
Vista, CA 760-727-5403
Quality Naturally Foods
City Of Industry, CA 888-498-6986
Tova Industries LLC
Louisville, KY 888-532-8682
Welsh Farms
Wallington, NJ 800-221-0663
Westin Foods
Omaha, NE 800-228-6098

Flavor

Creative Flavors & Specialties LLP
Linden, NJ 908-862-4678
Essentia Protein Solutions
Ankeny, IA 515-289-5100
Forbes Chocolate BP
Broadview Hts, OH 440-838-4400
GS-AFI
South Plainfield, NJ 800-345-4342
JMH International
Park City, UT 888-741-4564
Pecan Deluxe Candy Co
Dallas, TX 800-733-3589

Food

Abimco USA, Inc.
Mendham, NJ 973-543-7393
Clofine Dairy Products Inc
Linwood, NJ 609-653-1000
GS-AFI
South Plainfield, NJ 800-345-4342
I Rice & Co Inc
Philadelphia, PA 800-232-6022
Summit Hill Flavors
Somerset, NJ 732-805-0335
Tova Industries LLC
Louisville, KY 888-532-8682
Vita-Pakt Citrus Products Co
Covina, CA 888-684-8272
Wild Aseptics, LLC
Erlanger, KY 877-787-7221

Fruit

Agrana Fruit US Inc
Cleveland, OH 800-477-3788
California Custom Fruits
Baldwin Park, CA 877-558-0056
Fee Brothers
Rochester, NY 800-961-3337
Tova Industries LLC
Louisville, KY 888-532-8682
Wild Aseptics, LLC
Erlanger, KY 877-787-7221

Gravy

Bernard Food Industries Inc
Evanston, IL 800-323-3663
Con Yeager Spice Co
Zelienople, PA 800-222-2460
Cordon Bleu International
Anjou, QC 800-363-1182
Custom Culinary Inc.
Schaumberg, IL 800-621-8827
Dorothy Dawson Food Products
Jackson, MI 517-788-9830
Eatem Foods Co
Vineland, NJ 800-683-2836
Felbro Food Products
Los Angeles, CA 323-936-5266
Fuji Foods Corp
Browns Summit, NC 336-375-3111
Gel Spice Co LLC
Bayonne, NJ 800-922-0230
Griffith Foods Inc.
Alsip, IL 708-371-0900
Hormel Foods Corp.
Austin, MN 507-437-5611
Integrative Flavors
Michigan City, IN 800-837-7687
Karlsburger Foods Inc
Monticello, MN 800-383-6549
Lasco Foods Inc
St Louis, MO 314-832-1906
Lawry's Foods
Hunt Valley, MD 800-952-9797
Magic Seasoning Blends
New Orleans, LA 800-457-2857
Meat-O-Mat Corp
Brooklyn, NY 718-965-7250
More Than Gourmet
Akron, OH 800-860-9385
Pacific Foods
Kent, WA 800-347-9444
Produits Ronald
St. Damase, QC 800-465-0118
Serv-Agen Corporation
Cherry Hill, NJ 856-663-6966
Shenandoah Mills
Lebanon, TN 615-444-0841
Sweet Sue Kitchens
Athens, AL 256-216-0500
Swiss Food Products
Chicago, IL 312-829-0100
Tova Industries LLC
Louisville, KY 888-532-8682
Vogue Cuisine Foods
Sunnyvale, CA 888-236-4144
World Flavors Inc
Warminster, PA 215-672-4400

Juice

Citrosuco North America Inc
Lake Wales, FL 800-356-4592
Delano Growers Grape Products
Delano, CA 661-725-3255
Merci Spring Water
Maryland Heights, MO 314-872-9323
Welch's Global Ingredients Group
Concord, MA 978-371-3692

Sauce

Eatem Foods Co
Vineland, NJ 800-683-2836
Illes Seasonings & Flavors
Carrollton, TX 800-683-4553
JMH International
Park City, UT 888-741-4564
Produits Ronald
St. Damase, QC 800-465-0118
Summit Hill Flavors
Somerset, NJ 732-805-0335
UFL Foods
Mississauga, ON 905-670-7776

Seafood

Blount Fine Foods
Fall River, MA 774-888-1300
Swiss Food Products
Chicago, IL 312-829-0100

Soup

Bernard Food Industries Inc
Evanston, IL 800-323-3663
Blount Fine Foods
Fall River, MA 774-888-1300
Bluechip Group
Salt Lake City, UT 800-878-0099
Chef Hans' Gourmet Foods
Monroe, LA 800-890-4267
Con Yeager Spice Co
Zelienople, PA 800-222-2460
Custom Culinary Inc.
Schaumberg, IL 800-621-8827
Dean Distributors, Inc.
Burlingame, CA 800-792-0816
Dismat Corporation
Toledo, OH 419-531-8963
Dorothy Dawson Food Products
Jackson, MI 517-788-9830
Erba Food Products
Brooklyn, NY 718-272-7700
Five Star Food Base Company
St Paul, MN 800-505-7827
Flavor House, Inc.
Adelanto, CA 760-246-9131
Fuji Foods Corp
Browns Summit, NC 336-375-3111
Gel Spice Co LLC
Bayonne, NJ 800-922-0230
Griffith Foods Inc.
Alsip, IL 708-371-0900
Hormel Foods Corp.
Austin, MN 507-437-5611
Integrative Flavors
Michigan City, IN 800-837-7687
JMH International
Park City, UT 888-741-4564
Kent Precision Foods Group Inc
Muscatine, IA 800-442-5242
Lake City Foods
Mississauga, ON 905-625-8244
Lasco Foods Inc
St Louis, MO 314-832-1906
LonoLife
Oceanside, CA 855-843-8566
Magic Seasoning Blends
New Orleans, LA 800-457-2857
Meat-O-Mat Corp
Brooklyn, NY 718-965-7250
Mermaid Spice Corporation
Fort Myers, FL 239-693-1986
Olympia Oyster Co
Shelton, WA 877-427-3193
Oskri Corporation
Lake Mills, WI 920-648-8300
Pacific Foods
Kent, WA 800-347-9444
Produits Alimentaire
Laval, QC 800-361-9326
Produits Ronald
St. Damase, QC 800-465-0118
R C Fine Foods Inc
Hillsborough, NJ 800-526-3953
R L Schreiber Inc
Ft Lauderdale, FL 800-624-8777
Senba USA
Hayward, CA 888-922-5852
Serv-Agen Corporation
Cherry Hill, NJ 856-663-6966
Spice Hunter Inc
Richmond, VA 800-444-3061
St. Ours & Company
East Weymouth, MA 781-331-8520

Summit Hill Flavors
Somerset, NJ 732-805-0335
Superior Quality Foods
Ontario, CA. 800-300-4210
Sweet Sue Kitchens
Athens, AL 256-216-0500
Swiss Food Products
Chicago, IL 312-829-0100
Tone Products Inc
Melrose Park, IL. 800-536-8663
Tova Industries LLC
Louisville, KY 888-532-8682
UBF Food Solutions
Lisle, IL. 630-955-5394
UFL Foods
Mississauga, ON. 905-670-7776
Unilever US
Englewood Cliffs, NJ 800-298-5018
Vogue Cuisine Foods
Sunnyvale, CA 888-236-4144
White Coffee Corporation
Long Island City, NY 800-221-0140
World Flavors Inc
Warminster, PA 215-672-4400
Young Winfield
Hamilton, ON 905-893-2536

Seafood

Blount Fine Foods
Fall River, MA 774-888-1300

Vegetable

California Custom Fruits
Baldwin Park, CA. 877-558-0056
Wild Aseptics, LLC
Erlanger, KY. 877-787-7221

Yogurt

Gum Technology Corporation
Tucson, AZ 800-369-4867
Johanna Foods Inc.
Flemington, NJ 800-727-6700
Maple Island
Saint Paul, MN 800-369-1022
Plaidberry Company
Vista, CA. 760-727-5403

Benzoate of Soda

Xena International
Polo, IL 815-946-2626

Binders

Cereal

Sentry Seasonings
Elmhurst, IL 630-530-5370

Sausage

Roland Machinery
Springfield, IL. 800-325-1183
Sentry Seasonings
Elmhurst, IL 630-530-5370
World Flavors Inc
Warminster, PA 215-672-4400

for Meat Products

Sentry Seasonings
Elmhurst, IL 630-530-5370

Bioflavinoids

Asiamerica Ingredients
Westwood, NJ. 201-497-5531
H. Interdonati
Cold Spring Harbour, NY. 800-367-6617
PLT Health Solutions Inc
Morristown, NJ. 973-984-0900
QBI
South Plainfield, NJ 908-668-0088
Test Laboratories Inc
Reseda, CA 818-881-4251

Biopolymers

CP Kelco
Atlanta, GA. 800-535-2687

Bits

Baking

Erba Food Products
Brooklyn, NY 718-272-7700

Ham

Imitation

Gel Spice Co LLC
Bayonne, NJ 800-922-0230

Blends

Cheese

Classic Tea
Libertyville, IL 630-680-9934
Leprino Foods Co.
Denver, CO 800-537-7466
Sentry Seasonings
Elmhurst, IL 630-530-5370

Custom

Maple Island
Saint Paul, MN 800-369-1022
Old Dominion Spice Company
Ashland, VA 804-550-2780
Sentry Seasonings
Elmhurst, IL 630-530-5370
World Flavors Inc
Warminster, PA 215-672-4400

Enrichment

Sentry Seasonings
Elmhurst, IL 630-530-5370

Herbs

All Purpose

Sentry Seasonings
Elmhurst, IL 630-530-5370
Shaanxi Jiahe Phytochem Co., Ltd.
Parsippany, NJ. 973-439-6869
SupHerb Farms
Turlock, CA 800-787-4372

Herbs & Spices

Asiamerica Ingredients
Westwood, NJ. 201-497-5531
Cajohn's Fiery Foods Co
Westerville, OH. 888-703-3473
Colorado Spice Co
Boulder, CO 800-677-7423
Georgia Spice Company
Atlanta, GA. 800-453-9997
Jodie's Kitchen
Pinellas Park, FL. 800-728-3704
La Flor Spices
Hauppaugue, NY 631-885-9601
Marion-Kay Spice Co
Brownstown, IN 800-627-7423
Marnap Industries
Buffalo, NY. 716-897-1220
Pendery's
Dallas, TX. 800-533-1870
Sentry Seasonings
Elmhurst, IL 630-530-5370
St John's Botanicals
Bowie, MD 301-262-5302
SupHerb Farms
Turlock, CA 800-787-4372
Wisconsin Spice Inc
Berlin, WI. 920-361-3555

Pepper

Sentry Seasonings
Elmhurst, IL 630-530-5370

Caffeine

Asiamerica Ingredients
Westwood, NJ. 201-497-5531
Jungbunzlauer Inc
Newton, MA. 617-969-0900
Natra US
Chula Vista, CA 800-262-6216

Casein & Caseinates

Agri-Dairy Products
Purchase, NY 914-697-9580
AME Nutrition
Dublin, OH 614-766-3638
American Pasien Co
Burlington, NJ. 609-387-3130
Blossom Farm Products
Ridgewood, NJ 800-729-1818
Crest Foods Inc
Ashton, IL 877-273-7893
Erie Foods Intl Inc
Erie, IL 309-659-2233
Kantner Group
Wapakoneta, OH 877-738-3448

Casein

Austrade
Palm Beach Gdns, FL. 561-209-2447
Century Foods Intl LLC
Sparta, WI. 800-269-1901
Clofine Dairy Products Inc
Linwood, NJ 609-653-1000
International Casein Corporation
Great Neck, NY 516-466-4363
Oxford Frozen Foods
Oxford, NS 902-447-2100
Pacific Cheese Co
Hayward, CA 510-784-8800
Prestige Proteins
Boca Raton, FL. 561-997-8770
Prestige Technology
Boca Raton, FL. 888-697-4141
Silver Creek Specialty Meats
Oshkosh, WI 800-729-2849

Cellulose Gel

Aromi d'Italia
Baltimore, MD 877-435-2869
Asiamerica Ingredients
Westwood, NJ 201-497-5531
J Rettenmaier USA LP
Schoolcraft, MI. 877-895-4099
PLT Health Solutions Inc
Morristown, NJ 973-984-0900

Chemicals

Natural

Asiamerica Ingredients
Westwood, NJ 201-497-5531
BASF Corp.
Florham Park, NJ 800-526-1072
Chempacific Corp
Baltimore, MD 410-633-5771
Crompton Corporation
Greenwich, CT 800-295-2392
Flavorchem Corp
Downers Grove, IL. 800-435-2867
Graham Chemical Corporation
Barrington, IL 847-304-4400
Symrise Inc.
Teterboro, NJ. 201-288-3200
Van Waters & Roger
Summit, IL 708-728-6830
Vanco Trading Inc
Darien, CT. 203-656-2800

Chlorophyll

Asiamerica Ingredients
Westwood, NJ 201-497-5531
Christopher's Herb Shop
Springville, UT 888-372-4372
De Souza's
Banning, CA 800-373-5171
H. Interdonati
Cold Spring Harbour, NY. 800-367-6617
Verday
New York, NY
World Organics Corporation
Huntington Beach, CA 714-893-0017

Chocolate Products

Byrnes & Kiefer Company
Callery, PA 724-538-5200
Forbes Chocolate BP
Broadview Hts, OH. 440-838-4400
Golden 100
Deland, FL 386-734-0113

Log House Foods
Plymouth, MN....................763-546-8395

Coagulants

Dairy

Forbes Chocolate BP
Broadview Hts, OH................440-838-4400

Coatings

Compound

BASF Corp.
Florham Park, NJ.................800-526-1072

Edible

Golden 100
Deland, FL......................386-734-0113
Mantrose-Haeuser Co Inc
Westport, CT....................800-344-4229

Cocoa Butter

Aak USA Inc
Newark, NJ......................973-344-1300
Barry Callebaut USA
Chicago, IL.....................866-443-0460
Natra US
Chula Vista, CA..................800-262-6216

Colors

Americolor Corp
Placentia, CA....................800-556-0233
Color Garden
Anaheim, CA.....................714-572-0444
ColorKitchen
Bend, OR........................510-227-6174
ColorMaker, Inc.
Anaheim, CA.....................714-572-0444
D D Williamson & Co Inc
Louisville, KY...................502-895-2438
DDW: The Color House
Louisville, KY...................502-895-2438
Emerald Performance Materials
Cuyahoga Falls, OH...............330-916-6700
Erba Food Products
Brooklyn, NY....................718-272-7700
Flavorchem Corp
Downers Grove, IL................800-435-2867
GNT USA
Tarrytown, NY...................914-524-0600
Golden 100
Deland, FL......................386-734-0113
IFC Solutions
Linden, NJ......................800-875-9393
International Foodcraft Corp
Linden, NJ......................800-875-9393
Lubrizol Corp
Wickliffe, OH....................440-943-4200
Newport Ingredients
Los Angeles, CA..................323-284-5959
Particle Dynamics
Saint Louis, MO..................800-452-4682
Prova
Danvers, MA.....................877-776-8287
Roha USA LTD
St Louis, MO.....................888-533-7642
San Joaquin Vly Concentrates
Fresno, CA......................800-557-0220
Sensient Technologies Corp
Milwaukee, WI...................414-271-6755
Shank's Extracts Inc
Lancaster, PA....................800-346-3135
Weber Flavors
Wheeling, IL.....................800-558-9078

Annatto

Schiff Food Products Co Inc
Totowa, NJ......................973-237-1990
SJH Enterprises
Middleton, WI....................888-745-3845

Burnt Sugar

D D Williamson & Co Inc
Louisville, KY...................502-895-2438
Four Percent Company
Highland Park, MI.................313-345-5880
Produits Alimentaire
St Lambert De Lauzon, QC.........800-463-1787
RFi Ingredients
Blauvelt, NY.....................800-962-7663
Seydel Co
Pendergrass, GA..................706-693-2266

Caramel

Carmi Flavor & Fragrance Company
Commerce, CA....................800-421-9647
Gel Spice Co LLC
Bayonne, NJ.....................800-922-0230

Butter & Cheese

Agri-Dairy Products
Purchase, NY....................914-697-9580
Carmi Flavor & Fragrance Company
Commerce, CA....................800-421-9647
Prime Ingredients Inc
Saddle Brook, NJ.................888-791-6655
SJH Enterprises
Middleton, WI....................888-745-3845

Caramel

D D Williamson & Co Inc
Louisville, KY...................502-895-2438
Sethness Caramel Color
Skokie, IL.......................847-329-2080

Cider & Vinegar

Asiamerica Ingredients
Westwood, NJ....................201-497-5531
Prime Ingredients Inc
Saddle Brook, NJ.................888-791-6655

Dyes

Certified

Castella Imports Inc
Brentwood, NY...................631-231-5500

Grape Skin Extract Color

Asiamerica Ingredients
Westwood, NJ....................201-497-5531

Natural

Asiamerica Ingredients
Westwood, NJ....................201-497-5531
D D Williamson & Co Inc
Louisville, KY...................502-895-2438
LaMonde Wild Flavors
Mississauga, CA..................800-263-5286
PLT Health Solutions Inc
Morristown, NJ...................973-984-0900

Annatto

SJH Enterprises
Middleton, WI....................888-745-3845

Anthocyanins Grape Skin

Asiamerica Ingredients
Westwood, NJ....................201-497-5531
RFi Ingredients
Blauvelt, NY.....................800-962-7663

Betaine Beet

RFi Ingredients
Blauvelt, NY.....................800-962-7663

Carmine

Asiamerica Ingredients
Westwood, NJ....................201-497-5531
RFi Ingredients
Blauvelt, NY.....................800-962-7663

Carotenoids

Asiamerica Ingredients
Westwood, NJ....................201-497-5531
RFi Ingredients
Blauvelt, NY.....................800-962-7663

Others

Asiamerica Ingredients
Westwood, NJ....................201-497-5531

Turmeric

Asiamerica Ingredients
Westwood, NJ....................201-497-5531
RFi Ingredients
Blauvelt, NY.....................800-962-7663

Compounds

Cooking

Coast Packing Co
Vernon, CA......................323-277-7700
Prime Ingredients Inc
Saddle Brook, NJ.................888-791-6655

Tenderizing

Chicago Pastry
Bloomingdale, IL.................630-529-6391
Custom Culinary Inc.
Schaumberg, IL...................800-621-8827
Tova Industries LLC
Louisville, KY...................888-532-8682
World Flavors Inc
Warminster, PA...................215-672-4400

Concentrates

Fruit

3V Company
Brooklyn, NY....................718-858-7333
Apple & Eve LLC
Port Washington, NY..............800-969-8018
Beta Pure Foods
Santa Cruz, CA...................831-685-6565
Citrosuco North America Inc
Lake Wales, FL...................800-356-4592
Coloma Frozen Foods Inc
Coloma, MI......................800-642-2723
Greenwood Associates
Niles, IL........................847-579-5500
KERR Concentrates Inc
Salem, OR.......................800-910-5377
Minute Maid Company
Atlanta, GA......................800-520-2653
Monin Inc.
Clearwater, FL...................855-352-8671
Paragon Fruits
Maple Grove, MN.................763-559-0436
Stiebs
Madera, CA......................559-661-0031
Svzusa Inc
Othello, WA......................509-488-6563

Fruit Puree

Greenwood Associates
Niles, IL........................847-579-5500
Milne Fruit Products Inc
Prosser, WA.....................509-786-2611
RFi Ingredients
Blauvelt, NY.....................800-962-7663

Vegetable

Beta Pure Foods
Santa Cruz, CA...................831-685-6565
Greenwood Associates
Niles, IL........................847-579-5500

Whey Protein Concentrates & Isolates

Calpro Ingredients
Corona, CA......................909-493-4890
Hilmar Ingredients
Hilmar, CA......................888-300-4465
Ingredia Inc
Wapakoneta, OH..................419-738-4060
Kantner Group
Wapakoneta, OH..................877-738-3448
Main Street Ingredients
La Crosse, WI....................800-359-2345
Milky Whey Inc
Missoula, MT.....................800-379-6455

Confectionery

Bakers' & Confectioners' Supplies

Abel & Schafer Inc
Ronkonkoma, NY..................800-443-1260
Al-Rite Fruits & Syrups Co
Miami, FL.......................305-652-2540
American Almond Products Co
Brooklyn, NY....................800-825-6663
American Key Food Products Inc
Closter, NJ......................877-263-7539

AnaCon Foods Company
Atchison, KS . . . 800-328-0291
Ann's House of Nuts, Inc.
Columbia, MD . . . 410-309-6887
Arcor USA
Coral Gables, FL . . . 800-572-7267
Astor Chocolate Corp
Lakewood, NJ . . . 732-901-1001
Baker Boy Bake Shop Inc
Dickinson, ND . . . 800-437-2008
Bama Foods LTD
Tulsa, OK . . . 800-756-2262
Bartlett Milling Co.
Statesville, NC . . . 800-438-6016
Best Maid Cookie Co
River Falls, WI . . . 888-444-0322
Bette's Oceanview Diner
Berkeley, CA . . . 510-644-3230
Blend Pak Inc
Bloomfield, KY . . . 502-252-8000
Blommer Chocolate Co
Chicago, IL . . . 800-621-1606
Blue Pacific Flavors & Fragrances
City of Industry, CA . . . 626-934-0099
Blue Planet Foods
Collegedale, TN . . . 877-396-3145
Bob's Red Mill Natural Foods
Milwaukie, OR . . . 800-349-2173
Brass Ladle Products
Concordville, PA . . . 800-955-2353
Brown & Haley
Fife, WA . . . 800-426-8400
Byrd Mill Co
Ashland, VA . . . 888-897-3336
Byrnes & Kiefer Company
Callery, PA . . . 724-538-5200
California Independent Almond Growers
Merced, CA . . . 209-667-4855
Cangel
Toronto, ON . . . 800-267-4795
Carol Lee Donuts
Salina, KS . . . 785-827-2402
Century Foods Intl LLC
Sparta, WI . . . 800-269-1901
Cereal Food Processors Inc
Mcpherson, KS . . . 800-835-2067
Charles H Baldwin & Sons
West Stockbridge, MA . . . 413-232-7785
Chase Brothers Dairy
Oxnard, CA . . . 800-438-6455
CHS Inc.
Inver Grove Hts., MN . . . 800-328-6539
Commodities Marketing Inc
Clarksburg, NJ . . . 732-516-0700
Cream Of The West
Harlowton, MT . . . 800-477-2383
Dakota Specialty Milling, Inc.
Fargo, ND . . . 844-633-2746
De Iorio's Foods Inc
Utica, NY . . . 800-649-7612
Dessert Innovations Inc
Atlanta, GA . . . 800-359-7351
Devansoy Farms
Carroll, IA . . . 800-747-8605
Dorothy Dawson Food Products
Jackson, MI . . . 517-788-9830
Eden Foods Inc
Clinton, MI . . . 888-424-3336
Eden Processing
Poplar Grove, IL . . . 815-765-2000
EFCO Products Inc
Poughkeepsie, NY . . . 800-284-3326
Fizzle Flat Farm, L.L.C.
Yale, IL . . . 618-793-2060
Food Concentrate Corporation
Oklahoma City, OK . . . 405-840-5633
Frankford Candy & Chocolate Co
Philadelphia, PA . . . 800-523-9090
Franklin Foods
Enosburg Falls, VT . . . 800-933-6114
Galloway Co
Neenah, WI . . . 800-722-8903
Ghirardelli Chocolate Co
San Leandro, CA . . . 800-877-9338
Golden Fluff Popcorn Co
Lakewood, NJ . . . 732-367-5448
Gorant Chocolatier
Youngstown, OH . . . 330-726-8821
Greenfield Mills
North Howe, IN . . . 260-367-2394
Guittard Chocolate Co
Burlingame, CA . . . 800-468-2462
Gurley's Foods
Willmar, MN . . . 800-426-7845
Gust John Foods & Products
Batavia, IL . . . 800-756-5886
H B Taylor Co
Chicago, IL . . . 773-254-4805
Hamersmith, Inc.
Miami, FL . . . 305-685-7451
Harlan Bakeries
Avon, IN . . . 800-435-2738
Healthy Food Ingredients
Fargo, ND . . . 844-275-3443
Heartland Food Products
Westwood, KS . . . 866-571-0222
Heidi's Gourmet Desserts
Tucker, GA . . . 800-241-4166
Holton Food Products
La Grange, IL . . . 708-352-5599
Homestead Mills
Cook, MN . . . 800-652-5233
Honeyville Grain Inc
Brigham City, UT . . . 435-494-4200
I Rice & Co Inc
Philadelphia, PA . . . 800-232-6022
J M Swank Co
North Liberty, IA . . . 800-593-6375
J.R. Short Canadian Mills
Toronto, ON . . . 416-421-3463
Kalsec
Kalamazoo, MI . . . 800-323-9320
Kargher Corp
Hatfield, PA . . . 800-355-1247
Kencraft, Inc.
Alpine, UT . . . 800-377-4368
Kimmie Candy Company
Reno, NV . . . 888-532-1325
King Milling Co Inc
Lowell, MI . . . 616-897-9264
Knappen Milling Co
Augusta, MI . . . 800-562-7736
Knouse Foods Co-Op Inc.
Peach Glen, PA . . . 717-677-8181
L & S Packing Co
Farmingdale, NY . . . 800-286-6487
Lacey Milling Company
Hanford, CA . . . 559-584-6634
Lake States Yeast
Rhinelander, WI . . . 715-369-4949
Lawrence Foods Inc
Elk Grove Village, IL . . . 847-437-2400
Leon's Bakery
North Haven, CT . . . 800-223-6844
Little Crow Foods
Warsaw, IN . . . 800-288-2769
Loghouse Foods
Minneapolis, MN . . . 763-546-8395
Louisiana Gourmet Enterprises
Houma, LA . . . 800-328-5586
Lucas Meyer
Decatur, IL . . . 800-769-3660
Lyoferm & Vivolac Cultures
Indianapolis, IN . . . 317-356-8460
Main Street Ingredients
La Crosse, WI . . . 800-359-2345
Malt Diastase Co
Saddle Brook, NJ . . . 800-526-0180
Marx Brothers Inc
Birmingham, AL . . . 800-633-6376
Merlino Italian Baking Company
Kent, WA . . . 800-800-9490
Mills Brothers Intl
Seattle, WA . . . 206-575-3000
Minn-Dak Yeast Co Inc
Wahpeton, ND . . . 701-642-3300
Moorhead & Company
Rocklin, CA . . . 800-322-6325
Morris J Golombeck Inc
Brooklyn, NY . . . 718-284-3505
Northwestern Foods
Arden Hills, MN . . . 800-236-4937
Orlinda Milling Company
Orlinda, TN . . . 615-654-3633
Pacific Westcoast Foods
Beaverton, OR . . . 800-874-9333
Palmer Candy Co
Sioux City, IA . . . 800-831-0828
Pasta Factory
Melrose Park, IL . . . 800-615-6951
Pelican Bay Ltd.
Dunedin, FL . . . 800-826-8982
Pied-Mont/Dora
Anne Des Plaines, QC . . . 800-363-8003
Plaidberry Company
Vista, CA . . . 760-727-5403
Quali Tech Inc
Chaska, MN . . . 800-328-5870
Quality Naturally Foods
City Of Industry, CA . . . 888-498-6986
R&J Farms
West Salem, OH . . . 419-846-3179
Reinhart Foods
Toronto, ON . . . 416-645-4910
Rene Rey Chocolates Ltd
North Vancouver, BC . . . 888-985-0949
Rhodes International Inc
Salt Lake City, UT . . . 800-876-7333
Richmond Baking Co
Richmond, IN . . . 765-962-8535
Roland Machinery
Springfield, IL . . . 800-325-1183
Rv Industries
Buford, GA . . . 770-729-8983
Schlotterbeck & Foss Company
Portland, ME . . . 800-777-4666
Scott's Auburn Mills
Russellville, KY . . . 270-726-2080
Serv-Agen Corporation
Cherry Hill, NJ . . . 856-663-6966
Service Packing Company
Vancouver, BC . . . 604-681-0264
Shawnee Milling Co
Shawnee, OK . . . 405-273-7000
Signature Brands LLC
Ocala, FL . . . 800-456-9573
Skjodt-Barrett Foods
Brampton, ON . . . 877-600-1200
SOUPerior Bean & Spice Company
Vancouver, WA . . . 800-878-7687
Southeastern Mills Inc
Rome, GA . . . 800-334-4468
Star of the West Milling Co.
Frankenmuth, MI . . . 989-652-9971
Strossner's Bakery & Cafe
Greenville, SC . . . 864-233-2990
Sucesores de Pedro Cortes
Hato Rey, PR . . . 787-754-7040
Swatt Baking Co
Olean, NY . . . 800-370-6656
Tara Foods
Atlanta, GA . . . 404-559-0605
Taste Maker Foods
Memphis, TN . . . 800-467-1407
The Lollipop Tree, Inc
Auburn, NY . . . 800-842-6691
TNT Crust
Green Bay, WI . . . 920-431-7240
Tova Industries LLC
Louisville, KY . . . 888-532-8682
Uhlmann Co
Kansas City, MO . . . 866-866-8627
Valley View Blueberries
Vancouver, WA . . . 360-892-2839
VIP Foods
Flushing, NY . . . 718-821-5330
Watson Inc
West Haven, CT . . . 800-388-3481
Weaver Nut Co. Inc.
Ephrata, PA . . . 800-473-2688
West Pac
Idaho Falls, ID . . . 800-973-7407
Whitaker & Assoc Architects
Atlanta, GA . . . 404-266-1265
White-Stokes Company
Chicago, IL . . . 800-978-6537
Willmark Sales Company
Brooklyn, NY . . . 718-388-7141
Yohay Baking Co
Lindenhurst, NY . . . 631-225-0300
Young Winfield
Hamilton, ON . . . 905-893-2536

Cultures & Yeasts

Bacteria

Sour Dough

Cultures for Health
Morrisville, NC

Yogurt

Cultures for Health
Morrisville, NC

Bacterial Cultures & Starter Media

Cultures for Health
Morrisville, NC
Kantner Group
Wapakoneta, OH....877-738-3448

Cultures

Alfer Laboratories
Chatsworth, CA....818-709-0737
Alternative Health & Herbs
Albany, OR....800-345-4152
Berkshire Dairy
Wyomissing, PA....877-696-6455
Crystal Creamery
Modesto, CA....866-225-4821
Cultures for Health
Morrisville, NC
Dairy Connection Inc
Madison, WI....608-242-9030
GEM Cultures
Lakewood, WA....253-588-2922
IMAC
Oklahoma City, OK....888-878-7827
Ingredient Innovations
Kansas City, MO....816-587-1426
Lallemand
Montreal, QC....514-522-2133
Lallemand American Yeast
Addison, IL....630-932-1290
Lyoferm & Vivolac Cultures
Indianapolis, IN....317-356-8460
Old Home Foods Inc
New Brighton, MN....651-312-8900
Quality Ingredients
Burnsville, MN....952-898-4002
Sunshine Dairy Foods Inc
Portland, OR....503-234-7526
Test Laboratories Inc
Reseda, CA....818-881-4251
Vivolac Cultures Corporation
Indianapolis, IN....317-356-8460

Yeast

Bakon Yeast
Scottsdale, AZ....480-595-9370
Bluechip Group
Salt Lake City, UT....800-878-0099
California Blending Co
El Monte, CA....626-448-1918
Cardi Foods
Fuquay Varina, NC....919-557-3866
DSM
Heerlen,
Fleischmann's Yeast
Chesterfield, MO....800-777-4959
Hodgson Mill Inc
Effingham, IL....800-347-0198
Kyowa Hakko
New York, NY....800-596-9252
Lake States Yeast
Rhinelander, WI....715-369-4949
Lallemand American Yeast
Addison, IL....630-932-1290
Lesaffre Yeast Corporation
Milwaukee, WI....800-770-2714
Luxor California Exports Corp.
San Diego, CA....619-465-7777
Minn-Dak Yeast Co Inc
Wahpeton, ND....701-642-3300
Natural Foods Inc
Toledo, OH....419-537-1711
Organic Gourmet
Sherman Oaks, CA....800-400-7772
Pascobel Inc
Longueuil, QC....450-677-2443
Red Star Yeast
Milwaukee, WI....800-445-4746
Vinquiry Wine Analysis
Windsor, CA....707-838-6312
Wausau Paper Corp.
Mosinee, WI....866-722-8675

Autolysates

Lake States Yeast
Rhinelander, WI....715-369-4949

Bakers'

Lallemand/American Yeast
Long Island City, NY....773-267-2223
Minn-Dak Yeast Co Inc
Wahpeton, ND....701-642-3300

Brewers'

Energen Products Inc
Norwalk, CA....800-423-8837
NPC Dehydrators
Payette, ID....208-642-4471
Watson Inc
West Haven, CT....800-388-3481

Extracts

Organic Gourmet
Sherman Oaks, CA....800-400-7772

Fresh

Lallemand American Yeast
Addison, IL....630-932-1290

Primary Dried

Lallemand American Yeast
Addison, IL....630-932-1290

Torula Dried

Lake States Yeast
Rhinelander, WI....715-369-4949

Whey

Hilmar Ingredients
Hilmar, CA....888-300-4465

Wine

Lallemand/American Yeast
Petaluma, CA....800-423-6625

Yogurt

Lyo-San
Lachute, QC....800-363-3697

Curing Preparations

Meat

First Spice Mixing Co
Long Island City, NY....800-221-1105

Decorative Items

Petra International
Mississauga, ON....800-261-7226
Pfeil & Holding Inc
Woodside, NY....800-247-7955
Scala-Wisell International Inc.
Floral Park, NY....516-437-8600
Sugar Flowers Plus
Glendale, CA....800-972-2935

Digestive Aids

Arise & Shine Herbal Products
Medford, OR....800-688-2444
Bio-K + International Inc.
Laval, QC....800-593-2465
Bionutritional Research Group
Irvine, CA....714-427-6990
Deerland Probiotics & Enzymes
Kennesaw, GA....800-697-8179
Deerland Probiotics & Enzymes
Forsyth, MO....800-825-8545
Enzymatic Therapy Inc
Green Bay, WI....800-783-2286
Enzyme Formulations Inc
Madison, WI....800-614-4400
Russo Farms
Vineland, NJ....856-692-5942

Emulsifiers

Aromatech USA
Orlando, FL....407-277-5727
Asiamerica Ingredients
Westwood, NJ....201-497-5531
Avatar Corp
University Park, IL....800-255-3181
Bunge Canada
Oakville, ON....905-825-7900
Enterprise Foods
Atlanta, GA....404-351-2251
Kerry, Inc
Beloit, WI....608-363-1200
Lambent Technologies
Skokie, IL....800-432-7187
Mitsubishi Intl. Corp.
New York, NY....800-442-6266
Montello Inc
Tulsa, OK....800-331-4628
Mother Murphy's
Greensboro, NC....800-849-1277
Newport Ingredients
Los Angeles, CA....323-284-5959
PLT Health Solutions Inc
Morristown, NJ....973-984-0900
Profood International
Naperville, IL....888-288-0081
Ribus Inc.
St. Louis, MO....314-727-4287
Taiyo International Inc.
Minneapolis, MN....763-398-3003
Tate & Lyle PLC
Hoffman Estates, IL....847-396-7500
Wenda America Inc
Naperville, IL....844-999-3632

Lecithin

Acatris USA
Edina, MN....952-920-7700
AG Processing Inc
Omaha, NE....800-247-1345
American Lecithin Company
Oxford, CT....800-364-4416
Asiamerica Ingredients
Westwood, NJ....201-497-5531
Avatar Corp
University Park, IL....800-255-3181
Blue Chip Baker
Salt Lake City, UT....800-878-0099
Bluechip Group
Salt Lake City, UT....800-878-0099
CanAmera Foods
Edmonton, AL....780-447-6960
DuPont Nutrition & Biosciences
New Century, KS....913-764-8100
Homefree LLC
Windham, NH....800-552-7172
International Foodcraft Corp
Linden, NJ....800-875-9393
King Arthur Flour
Norwich, VT....800-827-6836
Lucas Meyer
Decatur, IL....800-769-3660
Mid Atlantic Vegetable Shortening Company
Kearny, NJ....800-966-1645
Natural Foods Inc
Toledo, OH....419-537-1711
Westin Foods
Omaha, NE....800-228-6098

Enhancers

Apple Flavor & Fragrance USA
Edison, NJ....732-393-0600
Bluechip Group
Salt Lake City, UT....800-878-0099
Cinnabar Specialty Foods Inc
Prescott, AZ....866-293-6433
First Spice Mixing Co
Long Island City, NY....800-221-1105
King Arthur Flour
Norwich, VT....800-827-6836
Lora Brody Products Inc
Waltham, MA....781-899-3910
Newport Ingredients
Los Angeles, CA....323-284-5959
Seattle Seasonings
Port Orchard, WA....360-871-1511

Enzymes

Ajinomoto Heartland Inc
Chicago, IL....773-380-7000
Amano Enzyme USA Company, Ltd
Elgin, IL....800-446-7652
American Laboratories
Omaha, NE....402-339-2494
American Yeast
Memphis, TN....866-920-9885
Asiamerica Ingredients
Westwood, NJ....201-497-5531
Bio-Nutritional Products
Northvale, NJ....201-784-8200
Catherych
Warren, NJ....732-566-6625

Enzyme Development Corporation
New York, NY 212-736-1580
Enzyme Innovation
Chino, CA 909-203-4620
George A Jeffreys & Company
Salem, VA 540-389-8220
Malabar Formulas
Nuevo, CA 909-866-3678
Mitsubishi Intl. Corp.
New York, NY 800-442-6266
Novozymes North America Inc
Franklinton, NC 800-879-6686
Profood International
Naperville, IL 888-288-0081
SKW Nature Products
Dubuque, IA 563-588-6244
Test Laboratories Inc
Reseda, CA 818-881-4251
Universal Formulas
Kalamazoo, MI 800-342-6960

Extenders

Arboris LLC
Savannah, GA 912-238-7537
MAFCO Worldwide
Camden, NJ 856-986-4050
Thymly Products Inc
Colora, MD 877-710-2340

Chicken

Valley Grain Products
Fresno, CA 559-675-3400

Coffee

I Rice & Co Inc
Philadelphia, PA 800-232-6022

Meat

Flavor House, Inc.
Adelanto, CA 760-246-9131
Gum Technology Corporation
Tucson, AZ 800-369-4867
Tova Industries LLC
Louisville, KY 888-532-8682
World Flavors Inc
Warminster, PA 215-672-4400

Extracts

Active Organics
Lewisville, TX 800-541-1478
Advanced Food Systems
Somerset, NJ 800-787-3067
Al-Rite Fruits & Syrups Co
Miami, FL 305-652-2540
AM Todd Co
Kalamazoo, MI 269-343-2603
American Instants Inc
Flanders, NJ 973-584-8811
American Laboratories
Omaha, NE 402-339-2494
American Mercantile Corp
Memphis, TN 901-454-1900
Apotheca Inc
Woodbine, IA 800-736-3130
Asiamerica Ingredients
Westwood, NJ 201-497-5531
Bakto Flavors
North Brunswick, NJ 732-354-4492
Bartek Ingredients, Inc.
Stoney Creek, ON 800-263-4165
Bear Stewart Corp
Chicago, IL 800-697-2327
Berghausen E Cheml Co
Cincinnati, OH 800-648-5887
Beta Pure Foods
Santa Cruz, CA 831-685-6565
Bickford Flavors
Euclid, OH 800-283-8322
Blessed Herbs
Oakham, MA 800-489-4372
Blue California Co
Rancho Sta Marg, CA 949-459-2729
Blue Mountain Enterprise Inc
Kinston, NC 800-522-1544
Briess Malt & Ingredients Co.
Chilton, WI 800-657-0806
Brucia Plant Extracts
Shingle Springs, CA 530-676-2774
Byrnes & Kiefer Company
Callery, PA 724-538-5200
Cafe Du Monde Coffee Stand
New Orleans, LA 800-772-2927
Cajun Brands
New Iberia, LA 504-408-2252
California Custom Foods
Fullerton, CA 714-870-0490
Capri Sun
Granite City, IL
Cargill Inc.
Minneapolis, MN 800-227-4455
Castella Imports Inc
Brentwood, NY 631-231-5500
Cellucon Inc
Strathmore, CA 559-568-0190
Century Blends LLC
Hunt Valley, MD 410-771-6606
Chas Boggini Co.
Coventry, CT 860-742-2652
Christopher's Herb Shop
Springville, UT 888-372-4372
Classic Flavors & Fragrances
New York, NY 212-777-0004
Clements Foods Co
Oklahoma City, OK 800-654-8355
Concord Foods, LLC
Brockton, MA 508-580-1700
Consolidated Mills Inc
Houston, TX 713-896-4196
Crestmont Enterprises
Camden, NJ 856-966-0700
Dean Distributors, Inc.
Burlingame, CA 800-792-0816
Draco Natural Products Inc
San Jose, CA 408-287-7871
Edgar A Weber & Co
Wheeling, IL 800-558-9078
Erba Food Products
Brooklyn, NY 718-272-7700
Ethical Naturals
San Anselmo, CA 866-459-4454
Everfresh Food Corporation
Minneapolis, MN 612-331-6393
Fenchem Inc
Chino, CA 909-597-1113
Finlays
Lincoln, RI 800-288-6272
Flavor House, Inc.
Adelanto, CA 760-246 9131
Flavor Sciences Inc
Lenoir, NC 800-535-2867
Flavorchem Corp
Downers Grove, IL 800-435-2867
Florida Food Products Inc
Eustis, FL 800-874-2331
Fona International
Geneva, IL 630-578-8600
Foodscience Corp
Essex Junction, VT 800-874-9444
Genarom International
Cranbury, NJ 609-409-6200
Green Foods Corp.
Oxnard, CA 800-777-4430
H B Taylor Co
Chicago, IL 773-254-4805
Herbs Etc
Santa Fe, NM 888-694-3727
High Quality Organics
Reno, NV 775-971-8550
Horner International
Raleigh, NC 919-787-3112
Inter-American Products
Cincinnati, OH 800-645-2233
J M Swank Co
North Liberty, IA 800-593-6375
Jiaherb
Pine Brook, NJ 888-542-4372
Kalsec
Kalamazoo, MI 800-323-9320
Kefiplant
Drummondville, QC 819-477-2345
Kerry Foodservice
Mansfield, OH 800-533-2722
Kerry, Inc
Beloit, WI 608-363-1200
Lochhead Mfg. Co.
Fenton, MO 800-776-2088
MAFCO Worldwide
Camden, NJ 856-986-4050
Malt Diastase Co
Garfield, NJ 800-772-0416
Metarom Corporation
Newport, VT 888-882-5555
Mother Murphy's
Greensboro, NC 800-849-1277
Muntons Ingredients
Bellevue, WA 425-372-3082
Natra US
Chula Vista, CA 800-262-6216
Naturex Inc
South Hackensack, NJ 201-440-5000
Newtown Foods USA Inc
Newtown, PA 215-579-2120
Nutricepts
Burnsville, MN 800-949-9060
Oregon Flavor Rack
Parker Flavors Inc
Baltimore, MD 800-336-9113
Particle Control
Albertville, MN 763-497-3075
Particle Dynamics
Saint Louis, MO 800-452-4682
Perlarom Technology
Columbia, MD 410-997-5114
Phyto-Technologies
Woodbine, IA 877-809-3404
Phytotherapy Research Laboratory
Lobelville, TN 800-274-3727
PLT Health Solutions Inc
Morristown, NJ 973-984-0900
PMC Specialties Group Inc
Cincinnati, OH 800-543-2466
Prova
Danvers, MA 877-776-8287
R C Fine Foods Inc
Hillsborough, NJ 800-526-3953
RFi Ingredients
Blauvelt, NY 800-962-7663
Royal Foods & Flavor
Elk Grove Vlg, IL 847-595-9166
San-Ei Gen FFI
New York, NY 212-315-7850
SAPNA Foods
Atlanta, GA 404-589-0977
Senba USA
Hayward, CA 888-922-5852
Shank's Extracts Inc
Lancaster, PA 800-346-3135
Simpson Spring Co
South Easton, MA 508-238-4472
Singer Extract Laboratory
Livonia, MI 313-345-5880
Sivetz Coffee
Corvallis, OR 541-753-9713
SJH Enterprises
Middleton, WI 888-745-3845
Sno Shack Inc
Rexburg, ID 888-766-7425
Spicely
Fremont, CA 510-440-1044
Star Kay White Inc
Congers, NY 800-874-8518
Sterling Extract Co Inc
Franklin Park, IL 847-451-9728
Stiebs
Madera, CA 559-661-0031
Target Flavors Inc
Brookfield, CT 800-538-3350
Technology Flavors & Fragrances
Amityville, NY 631-789-8228
Texas Coffee Co
Beaumont, TX 800-259-3400
Texas Spice Co
Round Rock, TX 800-880-8007
Triple K Manufacturing Company, Inc.
Shenandoah, IA 712-246-4376
United Canadian Malt
Peterborough, ON 800-461-6400
V & E Kohnstamm Inc
Brooklyn, NY 800-847-4500
Virginia Dare Extract Co
Brooklyn, NY 718-788-1776
Weber Flavors
Wheeling, IL 800-558-9078
Young Winfield
Hamilton, ON 905-893-2536

Beef

Blue Mountain Enterprise Inc
Kinston, NC 800-522-1544
Flavor House, Inc.
Adelanto, CA 760-246-9131
Gold Coast Ingredients
Commerce, CA 800-352-8673

Prime Ingredients Inc
Saddle Brook, NJ 888-791-6655
RFi Ingredients
Blauvelt, NY 800-962-7663
Savoury Systems Inc
Branchburg, NJ 888-534-6621
Superior Quality Foods
Ontario, CA 800-300-4210
Tastepoint
Philadelphia, PA 800-363-5286
Vital Proteins LLC
Elk Grove Village, IL 224-544-9110

Beverages

Muntons Ingredients
Bellevue, WA 425-372-3082

Botanical

Abkit Camocare Nature Works
New York, NY 800-226-6227
Active Organics
Lewisville, TX 800-541-1478
American Biosciences
Blauvelt, NY 888-884-7770
Apex Marketing Group
Las Vegas, NV 888-990-2739
Apotheca Inc
Woodbine, IA 800-736-3130
Asiamerica Ingredients
Westwood, NJ 201-497-5531
Avoca
Merry Hill, NC 252-482-2133
Blue California Co
Rancho Sta Marg, CA 949-459-2729
Botanical Products
Springville, CA 559-539-3432
Brucia Plant Extracts
Shingle Springs, CA 530-676-2774
Christopher's Herb Shop
Springville, UT 888-372-4372
Danisco-Cultor
Ardsley, NY 914-674-6300
Dolisos America
Henderson, NV 800-365-4767
Eclectic Institute
Sandy, OR 503-668-4120
Emerling International Foods
Buffalo, NY 716-833-7381
Energique
Woodbine, IA 800-869-8078
Excellentia Intl.
Fairfield, NJ 737-749-9840
Frutarom Meer Corporation
Hertzeliya Pituach,
GCI Nutrients
Foster City, CA 866-580-6549
Graminex
Saginaw, MI 877-472-6469
Health from the Sun
Maynard, MA 800-447-2229
Herb Pharm
Williams, OR 800-348-4372
Herbalist & Alchemist Inc
Washington, NJ 908-689-9020
Horner International
Raleigh, NC 919-787-3112
Nature's Apothecary
Bloomingdale, IL 888-669-3663
Nature's Products Inc
Sunrise, FL 800-752-7873
Naturex Inc
South Hackensack, NJ 201-440-5000
Parker Flavors Inc
Baltimore, MD 800-336-9113
Pharmachem Laboratories
Kearny, NJ 800-526-0609
PLT Health Solutions Inc
Morristown, NJ 973-984-0900
Plus Pharma
Vista, CA 760-597-0200
RFi Ingredients
Blauvelt, NY 800-962-7663
Sabinsa Corp
East Windsor, NJ 732-777-1111
Synthite USA Inc.
Oak Park, IL 708-446-1716
Terra Botanica Products
Dahlonega, GA 770-718-9340
Terra Flavors & Fragrances
New York, NY 212-244-1181
Test Laboratories Inc
Reseda, CA 818-881-4251
Universal Preservachem Inc
Somerset, NJ 732-568-1266
Verdure Sciences
Noblesville, IN 888-656-4364
Whole Herb Co
Sonoma, CA 707-935-1077

Chicken

Blue Mountain Enterprise Inc
Kinston, NC 800-522-1544
Flavor House, Inc.
Adelanto, CA 760-246-9131
Prime Ingredients Inc
Saddle Brook, NJ 888-791-6655

Coffee

Amelia Bay
Suwanee, GA 770-772-6360
American Instants Inc
Flanders, NJ 973-584-8811
California Custom Fruits
Baldwin Park, CA 877-558-0056
Coffee Enterprises
Burlington, VT 800-375-3398
Finlays
Lincoln, RI 800-288-6272
Kerry Foodservice
Mansfield, OH 800-533-2722
Prime Ingredients Inc
Saddle Brook, NJ 888-791-6655
S & D Coffee Inc
Concord, NC 800-933-2210
Synergy Flavors Inc
Wauconda, IL 847-487-1011
Synthite USA Inc.
Oak Park, IL 708-446-1716
Teawolf LLC
Pine Brook, NJ 973-575-4600
Virginia Dare Extract Co
Brooklyn, NY 718-788-1776

Crab

ADM Wild Flavors & Specialty
Erlanger, KY 859-342-3600
American Instants Inc
Flanders, NJ 973-584-8811
Barlean's Fisheries
Ferndale, WA 360-384-0325
Blue Mountain Enterprise Inc
Kinston, NC 800-522-1544
Boyajian LLC
Canton, MA 800-965-0665
Cajun Brands
New Iberia, LA 504-408-2252
Delmonaco Winery & Vineyards
Baxter, TN 931-858-1177
Embassy Flavours Ltd.
Brampton, ON 800-334-3371
Empire Spice Mills
Winnipeg, NB 204-786-1594
FBC Industries
Schaumburg, IL 888-322-4637
Felbro Food Products
Los Angeles, CA 323-936-5266
Flavor Sciences Inc
Lenoir, NC 800-535-2867
Flavor Systems Intl.
Cincinnati, OH 800-498-2783
Flavormatic Industries
Wappingers Falls, NY 845-297-9100
Fleurchem Inc
Middletown, NY 845-341-2100
Four Percent Company
Highland Park, MI 313-345-5880
Glucona America
Janesville, WI 608-752-0449
Gold Coast Ingredients
Commerce, CA 800-352-8673
GSB & Assoc
Kennesaw, GA 877-472-2776
Ingredient Innovations
Kansas City, MO 816-587-1426
John I. Haas
Washington, DC
Joseph Adams Corp
Valley City, OH 330-225-9135
Lochhead Mfg. Co.
Fenton, MO 800-776-2088
Magic Ice Products
Cincinnati, OH 800-776-7923
Ottens Flavors
Philadelphia, PA 800-523-0767
Prime Ingredients Inc
Saddle Brook, NJ 888-791-6655
SKW Nature Products
Langhorne, PA 215-702-1000
Stirling Foods
Renton, WA 800-332-1714
Takasago International Corp
Rockleigh, NJ 201-767-9001
Test Laboratories Inc
Reseda, CA 818-881-4251
The Stephan Company
Tampa, FL 954-971-0600
Torre Products Co Inc
New York, NY 212-925-8989
Triple K Manufacturing Company, Inc.
Shenandoah, IA 712-246-4376

Flavoring

Amoretti
Oxnard, CA 800-266-7388
Dohler-Milne Aseptics LLC
Prosser, WA 509-786-2240
I Rice & Co Inc
Philadelphia, PA 800-232-6022
Paradigm Foodworks Inc
Lake Oswego, OR 800-234-0250

Fruit

Agrana Fruit US Inc
Cleveland, OH 800-477-3788
Byrnes & Kiefer Company
Callery, PA 724-538-5200
Dohler-Milne Aseptics LLC
Prosser, WA 509-786-2240
Horner International
Raleigh, NC 919-787-3112
Parker Flavors Inc
Baltimore, MD 800-336-9113
Synergy Flavors Inc
Wauconda, IL 847-487-1011
Test Laboratories Inc
Reseda, CA 818-881-4251

Root Beer

California Custom Fruits
Baldwin Park, CA 877-558-0056
Four Percent Company
Highland Park, MI 313-345-5880
Gold Coast Ingredients
Commerce, CA 800-352-8673
Prime Ingredients Inc
Saddle Brook, NJ 888-791-6655
Rio Syrup Co
St Louis, MO 800-325-7666

Seafood

Ocean Cliff Corp
New Bedford, MA 508-990-7900

Tea

California Custom Fruits
Baldwin Park, CA 877-558-0056
Ethical Naturals
San Anselmo, CA 866-459-4454
Jogue Inc
Northville, MI 800-531-3888
Kerry Foodservice
Mansfield, OH 800-533-2722
PLT Health Solutions Inc
Morristown, NJ 973-984-0900
RFi Ingredients
Blauvelt, NY 800-962-7663
S & D Coffee Inc
Concord, NC 800-933-2210
Synergy Flavors Inc
Wauconda, IL 847-487-1011
Synthite USA Inc.
Oak Park, IL 708-446-1716
Teawolf LLC
Pine Brook, NJ 973-575-4600
Virginia Dare Extract Co
Brooklyn, NY 718-788-1776

Vanilla

Astral Extracts
Syosset, NY....516-496-2505
Bakto Flavors
North Brunswick, NJ....732-354-4492
Bickford Flavors
Euclid, OH....800-283-8322
California Custom Fruits
Baldwin Park, CA....877-558-0056
Carmi Flavor & Fragrance Company
Commerce, CA....800-421-9647
Castella Imports Inc
Brentwood, NY....631-231-5500
Clements Foods Co
Oklahoma City, OK....800-654-8355
Consolidated Mills Inc
Houston, TX....713-896-4196
Elan Vanilla Co
Newark, NJ....973-344-8014
Embassy Flavours Ltd.
Brampton, ON....800-334-3371
Emerling International Foods
Buffalo, NY....716-833-7381
Everfresh Food Corporation
Minneapolis, MN....612-331-6393
Flavorchem Corp
Downers Grove, IL....800-435-2867
Flavorganics
Newark, NJ....866-972-6879
Four Percent Company
Highland Park, MI....313-345-5880
Frontier Co-op
Norway, IA....844-550-6200
Gel Spice Co LLC
Bayonne, NJ....800-922-0230
Gold Coast Ingredients
Commerce, CA....800-352-8673
Grapevine Trading Company
Santa Rosa, CA....800-469-6478
H B Taylor Co
Chicago, IL....773-254-4805
Homefree LLC
Windham, NH....800-552-7172
Horner International
Raleigh, NC....919-787-3112
I Rice & Co Inc
Philadelphia, PA....800-232-6022
Jogue Inc
Northville, MI....800-531-3888
Lafaza Foods
Oakland, CA....510-282-1138
Lochhead Mfg. Co.
Fenton, MO....800-776-2088
Nielsen-Massey Vanillas Inc
Waukegan, IL....800-525-7873
Parker Flavors Inc
Baltimore, MD....800-336-9113
Prime Ingredients Inc
Saddle Brook, NJ....888-791-6655
Rio Syrup Co
St Louis, MO....800-325-7666
Rodelle Inc
Fort Collins, CO....800-898-5457
Shank's Extracts Inc
Lancaster, PA....800-346-3135
Singing Dog Vanilla
Eugene, OR....888-343-0002
Sterling Extract Co Inc
Franklin Park, IL....847-451-9728
Synergy Flavors Inc
Wauconda, IL....847-487-1011
Tastepoint
Philadelphia, PA....800-363-5286
Teawolf LLC
Pine Brook, NJ....973-575-4600
Triple K Manufacturing Company, Inc.
Shenandoah, IA....712-246-4376
V & E Kohnstamm Inc
Brooklyn, NY....800-847-4500
Van Tone Creative
Terrell, TX....800-856-0802
Virginia Dare Extract Co
Brooklyn, NY....718-788-1776
Weber Flavors
Wheeling, IL....800-558-9078

Vegetable

Basic American Foods
Walnut Creek, CA....925-472-4000
Cajun Brands
New Iberia, LA....504-408-2252
Gold Coast Ingredients
Commerce, CA....800-352-8673
Kalsec
Kalamazoo, MI....800-323-9320
Prime Ingredients Inc
Saddle Brook, NJ....888-791-6655
Silvateam USA
Ontario, CA....909-635-2870
Ted Shear Assoc Inc
Larchmont, NY....914-833-0017
Varied Industries Corp
Mason City, IA....800-654-5617
Vegetable Juices Inc
Chicago, IL....888-776-9752

Yeast

Royal Foods & Flavor
Elk Grove Vlg, IL....847-595-9166
Savoury Systems Inc
Branchburg, NJ....888-534-6621

Fatty Acids

Essential

Childlife
Culver City, CA....800-993-0332
RFi Ingredients
Blauvelt, NY....800-962-7663

Fillers

Meal

Agri-Dairy Products
Purchase, NY....914-697-9580

Flakes

Banana

Agvest
Cleveland, OH....216-464-3737
Emerling International Foods
Buffalo, NY....716-833-7381
Gerber Products Co
Arlington, VA....800-284-9488
Spreda Group
Louisville, KY....502-426-9411
Unique Ingredients LLC
Gold Canyon, AZ....480-983-2498

Oats

Bob's Red Mill Natural Foods
Milwaukie, OR....800-349-2173
LaCrosse Milling Company
Cochrane, WI....800-441-5411

Potato

AgraWest Foods
Prince Edward Island, NS....877-687-1400
Bob's Red Mill Natural Foods
Milwaukie, OR....800-349-2173
Emerling International Foods
Buffalo, NY....716-833-7381
Idaho Pacific Holdings Inc
Rigby, ID....800-238-5503
Idaho Supreme Potatoes Inc
Firth, ID....208-346-4100
New Organics
Kenwood, CA....734-677-5570
Oregon Potato Co
Boardman, OR....800-336-6311
Tova Industries LLC
Louisville, KY....888-532-8682
Unique Ingredients LLC
Gold Canyon, AZ....480-983-2498
VCPB Transportation
Secaucus, NJ....201-770-0070

Soy

MicroSoy Corporation
Jefferson, IA....515-386-2100
New Organics
Kenwood, CA....734-677-5570

Flavor Enhancers

Asiamerica Ingredients
Westwood, NJ....201-497-5531
Batory Foods
Des Plaines, IL....847-299-1999
International Flavors & Fragrances Inc.
New York, NY....212-765-5500
Lifem Spice Ingredients
Palm Beach, FL....561-844-6334
MAFCO Worldwide
Camden, NJ....856-986-4050
Mixerz All Natural Cocktail Mixers
Beverly, MA....978-922-6497
Nutra Food Ingredients, LLC
Kentwood, MI....616-656-9928
QST Ingredients
Rancho Cucamonga, CA....909-989-4343
Savoury Systems Inc
Branchburg, NJ....888-534-6621
Summit Hill Flavors
Somerset, NJ....732-805-0335

Gluconates

Asiamerica Ingredients
Westwood, NJ....201-497-5531
Lifewise Ingredients
Brookfield, IL....262-788-9141

Flavors

Advanced Food Systems
Somerset, NJ....800-787-3067
AFF International
Marietta, GA....800-241-7764
Ajinomoto Heartland Inc
Chicago, IL....773-380-7000
Al-Rite Fruits & Syrups Co
Miami, FL....305-652-2540
Allen Flavors Inc
Edison, NJ....908-561-5995
AM Todd Co
Kalamazoo, MI....269-343-2603
American Fruits & Flavors
Pacoima, CA....818-899-9574
American Instants Inc
Flanders, NJ....973-584-8811
American Laboratories
Omaha, NE....402-339-2494
Aromor Flavors & Fragrances
Englewood Cliffs, NJ....866-425-1600
Arylessence Inc
Marietta, GA....800-553-2440
Asiamerica Ingredients
Westwood, NJ....201-497-5531
Austin Special Foods Company
Austin, TX....512-372-8665
Avri Co Inc
Richmond, CA....800-883-9574
AVRON Resources Inc
Richmond, CA....800-883-9574
Baker's Coconut
East Hanover, NJ....855-535-5648
Bakto Flavors
North Brunswick, NJ....732-354-4492
Bartek Ingredients, Inc.
Stoney Creek, ON....800-263-4165
Bear Stewart Corp
Chicago, IL....800-697-2327
Bedoukian Research Inc
Danbury, CT....800-424-9300
Beta Pure Foods
Santa Cruz, CA....831-685-6565
Blendex Co
Louisville, KY....800-626-6325
Blue Pacific Flavors & Fragrances
City of Industry, CA....626-934-0099
Cajun Brands
New Iberia, LA....504-408-2252
California Custom Foods
Fullerton, CA....714-870-0490
Capri Sun
Granite City, IL
Capriccio
Chatsworth, CA....818-718-7620
Cargill Inc.
Minneapolis, MN....800-227-4455
Century Blends LLC
Hunt Valley, MD....410-771-6606
Chr Hansen Inc
Milwaukee, WI....414-607-5700
Citrop Inc
Tampa, FL....813-249-5955
Citrus and Allied Essences
New Hyde Park, NY....516-354-1200
Classic Flavors & Fragrances
New York, NY....212-777-0004

Clements Foods Co
Oklahoma City, OK 800-654-8355
Comax Flavors
Melville, NY 800-992-0629
Commercial Creamery Co
Spokane, WA 509-747-4131
Consolidated Mills Inc
Houston, TX 713-896-4196
Cosco International
Chicago, IL 800-621-4549
Creative Flavors Inc
Chagrin Falls, OH 800-848-9043
Crestmont Enterprises
Camden, NJ 856-966-0700
Danisco-Cultor
Ardsley, NY 914-674-6300
Dean Distributors, Inc.
Burlingame, CA 800-792-0816
Dohler-Milne Aseptics LLC
Prosser, WA 509-786-2240
Ecom Manufacturing Corporation
Markham, ON 905-477-2441
Edlong Corporation
Elk Grove Village, IL 847-631-6700
Emerald Performance Materials
Cuyahoga Falls, OH 330-916-6700
Essential Flavors & Fragrances
Corona, CA 888-333-9935
Everfresh Food Corporation
Minneapolis, MN 612-331-6393
Excellentia Intl.
Fairfield, NJ 737-749-9840
Fee Brothers
Rochester, NY 800-961-3337
Finlays
Lincoln, RI 800-288-6272
First Choice Ingredients
Germantown, WI 262-251-4322
Flavor Dynamics Two
South Plainfield, NJ 888-271-8424
Flavor House, Inc.
Adelanto, CA 760-246-9131
Flavor Producers
West Hills, CA 818-835-1850
Flavor Systems Intl.
Cincinnati, OH 800-498-2783
Flavorchem Corp
Downers Grove, IL 800-435-2867
Florida Food Products Inc
Eustis, FL 800-874-2331
Fona International
Geneva, IL 630-578-8600
Fontana Flavors Inc
Janesville, WI 608-754-9668
Food Ingredient Solutions
Teterboro, NJ 917-449-9558
French's Flavor Ingredients
Springfield, MO 800-841-1256
Fuchs North America
Hampstead, MD 800-365-3229
Genarom International
Cranbury, NJ 609-409-6200
Givaudan Fragrances Corp
East Hanover, NJ 973-386-9800
Golden 100
Deland, FL 386-734-0113
Great Northern Maple Products
Saint Honor, De Shenley, QC 418-485-7777
Green Spot Packaging
Claremont, CA 800-456-3210
Griffith Foods Inc.
Alsip, IL 708-371-0900
Grow Co
Ridgefield, NJ 201-941-8777
Gum Technology Corporation
Tucson, AZ 800-369-4867
H B Taylor Co
Chicago, IL 773-254-4805
Horner International
Raleigh, NC 919-787-3112
I Rice & Co Inc
Philadelphia, PA 800-232-6022
Illes Seasonings & Flavors
Carrollton, TX 800-683-4553
Innova Flavors
Lombard, IL 630-928-4800
International Bakers Services, Inc.
South Bend, IN 574-287-7111
International Flavors & Fragrances Inc.
New York, NY 212-765-5500
J M Swank Co
North Liberty, IA 800-593-6375

Jean Niel Inc
Odessa, FL 727-834-8855
Johnson's Food Products
Dorchester, MA 617-265-3400
Kalsec
Kalamazoo, MI 800-323-9320
Kerry Foodservice
Mansfield, OH 800-533-2722
Kerry, Inc
Beloit, WI 608-363-1200
Latitude, LTD
Huntington, NY 631-659-3374
Liberty Natural Products Inc
Oregon City, OR 800-289-8427
Lionel Hitchen Essitional Oils
Sarasota, FL 941-379-1400
Lochhead Mfg. Co.
Fenton, MO 800-776-2088
MAFCO Worldwide
Camden, NJ 856-986-4050
Mane Inc.
Lebanon, OH 513-248-9876
Marukome USA Inc.
Irvine, CA 949-863-0110
Metarom Corporation
Newport, VT 888-882-5555
Mother Murphy's
Greensboro, NC 800-849-1277
Natural Flavors
Newark, NJ 973-589-1230
Nature's Products Inc
Sunrise, FL 800-752-7873
Naturex Inc
South Hackensack, NJ 201-440-5000
Northeastern Products Company
S Plainfield, NJ 908-561-1660
Northwestern Extract
Germantown, WI 800-466-3034
Nutricepts
Burnsville, MN 800-949-9060
Ocean Cliff Corp
New Bedford, MA 508-990-7900
Oregon Flavor Rack
OSF Flavors Inc
Windsor, CT 800-466-6015
Parker Flavors Inc
Baltimore, MD 800-336-9113
Parrish's Cake Decorating
Gardena, CA 800-736-8443
Particle Control
Albertville, MN 763-497-3075
Particle Dynamics
Saint Louis, MO 800-452-4682
Perlarom Technology
Columbia, MD 410-997-5114
PMC Specialties Group Inc
Cincinnati, OH 800-543-2466
Progressive Flavors
Madison, WI 800-827-0555
Richard E. Colgin Company
Dallas, TX 888-226-5446
Rio Syrup Co
St Louis, MO 800-325-7666
Rosebrand Corp
Brooklyn, NY 800-854-5356
Royal Foods & Flavor
Elk Grove Vlg, IL 847-595-9166
San-Ei Gen FFI
New York, NY 212-315-7850
Savoury Systems Inc
Branchburg, NJ 888-534-6621
Senomyx Inc
San Diego, CA 858-646-8300
Sensient Flavors and Fragrances
Hoffman Estates, IL 847-755-5300
Sensient Technologies Corp
Milwaukee, WI 414-271-6755
Serv-Agen Corporation
Cherry Hill, NJ 856-663-6966
Shank's Extracts Inc
Lancaster, PA 800-346-3135
Silesia Flavors
Hoffman Estates, IL 847-645-0270
Singer Extract Laboratory
Livonia, MI 313-345-5880
SJH Enterprises
Middleton, WI 888-745-3845
SKW Nature Products
Dubuque, IA 563-588-6244
Sno Shack Inc
Rexburg, ID 888-766-7425

Southern Flavoring Co
Bedford, VA 800-765-8565
Spicetec Flavors & Seasonings
Omaha, NE 800-921-7502
Star Kay White Inc
Congers, NY 800-874-8518
Stauber Performance Ingrdients
Fullerton, CA 888-441-4233
Sterling Extract Co Inc
Franklin Park, IL 847-451-9728
Symrise Inc.
Teterboro, NJ 201-288-3200
Synergy Flavors Inc
Wauconda, IL 847-487-1011
T Hasegawa USA Inc
Cerritos, CA 714-522-1900
Taiyo International Inc.
Minneapolis, MN 763-398-3003
Target Flavors Inc
Brookfield, CT 800-538-3350
Tate & Lyle PLC
Hoffman Estates, IL 847-396-7500
Technology Flavors & Fragrances
Amityville, NY 631-789-8228
Terra Flavors & Fragrances
New York, NY 212-244-1181
Test Laboratories Inc
Reseda, CA 818-881-4251
Texas Spice Co
Round Rock, TX 800-880-8007
Triple K Manufacturing Company, Inc.
Shenandoah, IA 712-246-4376
Ungerer & Co
Lincoln Park, NJ 973-706-7381
US Chocolate Corp
Brooklyn, NY 718-788-8555
US Ingredients
Naperville, IL 630-820-1711
V & E Kohnstamm Inc
Brooklyn, NY 800-847-4500
Valley Grain Products
Fresno, CA 559-675-3400
Vanlab Corporation
Rochester, NY 585-232-6647
Virginia Dare Extract Co
Brooklyn, NY 718-788-1776
Webbpak Inc
Trussville, AL 800-655-3500
Weber Flavors
Wheeling, IL 800-558-9078
Western Syrup Company
Santa Fe Springs, CA 562-921-4485
WILD Flavors (Canada)
Mississauga, ON 800-263-5286
World Flavors Inc
Warminster, PA 215-672-4400

Almond

Castella Imports Inc
Brentwood, NY 631-231-5500
Flavorganics
Newark, NJ 866-972-6879
Gold Coast Ingredients
Commerce, CA 800-352-8673
Nielsen-Massey Vanillas Inc
Waukegan, IL 800-525-7873

Amaretto

Allen Flavors Inc
Edison, NJ 908-561-5995
Flavorganics
Newark, NJ 866-972-6879
Gold Coast Ingredients
Commerce, CA 800-352-8673

Anise (See also Spices/Anise Seed)

Castella Imports Inc
Brentwood, NY 631-231-5500
Gold Coast Ingredients
Commerce, CA 800-352-8673

Apple

Allen Flavors Inc
Edison, NJ 908-561-5995
Gold Coast Ingredients
Commerce, CA 800-352-8673

Apricot

Gold Coast Ingredients
Commerce, CA 800-352-8673

Artificial

Citrus and Allied Essences
New Hyde Park, NY 516-354-1200
Clarendon Flavor Engineering
Louisville, KY 502-634-9215

Banana

Allen Flavors Inc
Edison, NJ 908-561-5995
Castella Imports Inc
Brentwood, NY 631-231-5500
Flavorganics
Newark, NJ 866-972-6879
Gold Coast Ingredients
Commerce, CA 800-352-8673

Beer

Gold Coast Ingredients
Commerce, CA 800-352-8673

Berry

Gold Coast Ingredients
Commerce, CA 800-352-8673

Beverage

Allen Flavors Inc
Edison, NJ 908-561-5995
Clarendon Flavor Engineering
Louisville, KY 502-634-9215
Flavor & Fragrance Specialties
Mahwah, NJ 800-998-4337
Flavors from Florida
Bartow, FL 800-888-0409
Synergy Flavors Inc
Wauconda, IL 847-487-1011

Blackberry

Allen Flavors Inc
Edison, NJ 908-561-5995
Gold Coast Ingredients
Commerce, CA 800-352-8673

Blueberry

Allen Flavors Inc
Edison, NJ 908-561-5995
Gold Coast Ingredients
Commerce, CA 800-352-8673

Brown Sugar

Gold Coast Ingredients
Commerce, CA 800-352-8673

Butter

DairyChem Inc.
Fishers, IN 317-849-8400
Edlong Corporation
Elk Grove Village, IL 847-631-6700
First Choice Ingredients
Germantown, WI 262-251-4322
Gold Coast Ingredients
Commerce, CA 800-352-8673

Pecan

Edlong Corporation
Elk Grove Village, IL 847-631-6700
Gold Coast Ingredients
Commerce, CA 800-352-8673

Vanilla

Edlong Corporation
Elk Grove Village, IL 847-631-6700
Gold Coast Ingredients
Commerce, CA 800-352-8673

Buttermilk

DairyChem Inc.
Fishers, IN 317-849-8400
Edlong Corporation
Elk Grove Village, IL 847-631-6700
Gold Coast Ingredients
Commerce, CA 800-352-8673

Butterscotch

Edlong Corporation
Elk Grove Village, IL 847-631-6700
Gold Coast Ingredients
Commerce, CA 800-352-8673

Cajeta

Edlong Corporation
Elk Grove Village, IL 847-631-6700

Caramel

Edlong Corporation
Elk Grove Village, IL 847-631-6700
Gold Coast Ingredients
Commerce, CA 800-352-8673
Mont Blanc Gourmet
Denver, CO 800-877-3811

Cheese

Dean Distributors, Inc.
Burlingame, CA 800-792-0816
Edlong Corporation
Elk Grove Village, IL 847-631-6700
Flavor Dynamics Two
South Plainfield, NJ 888-271-8424
Gold Coast Ingredients
Commerce, CA 800-352-8673
H B Taylor Co
Chicago, IL 773-254-4805
Ingretec
Lebanon, PA 717-273-0711
Thiel Cheese & Ingredients
Hilbert, WI 920-989-1440

Cheesecake

Edlong Corporation
Elk Grove Village, IL 847-631-6700
Gold Coast Ingredients
Commerce, CA 800-352-8673

Cherry

Allen Flavors Inc
Edison, NJ 908-561-5995
AM Todd Co
Kalamazoo, MI 269-343-2603

Chocolate

Allen Flavors Inc
Edison, NJ 908-561-5995
Gold Coast Ingredients
Commerce, CA 800-352-8673
H B Taylor Co
Chicago, IL 773-254-4805
Mont Blanc Gourmet
Denver, CO 800-877-3811
US Chocolate Corp
Brooklyn, NY 718-788-8555

Cinnamon

Gold Coast Ingredients
Commerce, CA 800-352-8673

Citrus

Allen Flavors Inc
Edison, NJ 908-561-5995
Asiamerica Ingredients
Westwood, NJ 201-497-5531
Citrus and Allied Essences
New Hyde Park, NY 516-354-1200
Flavorganics
Newark, NJ 866-972-6879
Gold Coast Ingredients
Commerce, CA 800-352-8673
H B Taylor Co
Chicago, IL 773-254-4805

Cocoa

Batory Foods
Des Plaines, IL 847-299-1999
Flavor Dynamics Two
South Plainfield, NJ 888-271-8424
Gold Coast Ingredients
Commerce, CA 800-352-8673
Horner International
Raleigh, NC 919-787-3112
Prova
Danvers, MA 877-776-8287

Coconut

Castella Imports Inc
Brentwood, NY 631-231-5500
Gold Coast Ingredients
Commerce, CA 800-352-8673

Coffee

A Hill of Beans Coffee Roasters
Omaha, NE 402-333-6048
Acqua Blox LLC
Santa Fe Springs, CA 562-693-9599
American Instants Inc
Flanders, NJ 973-584-8811
Beck Flavors
Loveland, OH 314-878-7522
Coffee Grounds
Falcon Heights, MN 651-644-9959
Finlays
Lincoln, RI 800-288-6272
Flavor & Fragrance Specialties
Mahwah, NJ 800-998-4337
Flavor Dynamics Two
South Plainfield, NJ 888-271-8424
Gold Coast Ingredients
Commerce, CA 800-352-8673
Prova
Danvers, MA 877-776-8287
U Roast Em Inc
Hayward, WI 715-634-6255

Cultured

DairyChem Inc.
Fishers, IN 317-849-8400
Edlong Corporation
Elk Grove Village, IL 847-631-6700

Dairy

Beck Flavors
Loveland, OH 314-878-7522
Blossom Farm Products
Ridgewood, NJ 800-729-1818
Dairy Farmers Of America
Kansas City, KS 888-332-6455
DairyChem Inc.
Fishers, IN 317-849-8400
Edlong Corporation
Elk Grove Village, IL 847-631-6700
First Choice Ingredients
Germantown, WI 262-251-4322
Gold Coast Ingredients
Commerce, CA 800-352-8673
H B Taylor Co
Chicago, IL 773-254-4805
Hilmar Ingredients
Hilmar, CA 888-300-4465
Ingretec
Lebanon, PA 717-273-0711
Nature's Products Inc
Sunrise, FL 800-752-7873
Saputo Inc.
Montreal, QC 800-672-8866

Egg

Gold Coast Ingredients
Commerce, CA 800-352-8673

Extract

Asiamerica Ingredients
Westwood, NJ 201-497-5531
Bell Flavors & Fragrances
Northbrook, IL 847-291-8300
Bickford Flavors
Euclid, OH 800-283-8322
California Custom Fruits
Baldwin Park, CA 877-558-0056
Carmi Flavor & Fragrance Company
Commerce, CA 800-421-9647
Charles H Baldwin & Sons
West Stockbridge, MA 413-232-7785
Citrus and Allied Essences
New Hyde Park, NY 516-354-1200
Crest Foods Inc
Ashton, IL 877-273-7893
Crestmont Enterprises
Camden, NJ 856-966-0700
Edlong Corporation
Elk Grove Village, IL 847-631-6700
Essentia Protein Solutions
Ankeny, IA 515-289-5100
Fona International
Geneva, IL 630-578-8600
Freeman Industries
Tuckahoe, NY 800-666-6454

Frutarom Meer Corporation
Hertzeliya Pituach,
Fuji Foods Corp
Browns Summit, NC 336-375-3111
GLCC Co
Paw Paw, MI 269-657-3167
H R Nicholson Co
Baltimore, MD 800-638-3514
Hosemen & Roche Vitamins & Fine Chemicals
Nutley, NJ 800-526-6367
Jogue Inc
Northville, MI 800-531-3888
Kloss Manufacturing Co Inc
Allentown, PA 800-445-7100
Marnap Industries
Buffalo, NY 716-897-1220
Master Mix
Placentia, CA 714-524-1698
National Flavors
Kalamazoo, MI 800-525-2431
Newport Flavours & Fragrances
Orange, CA 714-744-3700
Nielsen-Massey Vanillas Inc
Waukegan, IL 800-525-7873
Pecan Deluxe Candy Co
Dallas, TX 800-733-3589
Red Arrow Products Co LLC
Manitowoc, WI 920-769-1100
Robertet Flavors
Piscataway, NJ 732-981-8300
Senomyx Inc
San Diego, CA 858-646-8300
Simpson Spring Co
South Easton, MA 508-238-4472
Sno Wizard Inc
New Orleans, LA 800-366-9766
Southern Flavoring Co
Bedford, VA 800-765-8565
Southern Snow
Belle Chasse, LA 504-393-8967
Tara Foods
Atlanta, GA 404-559-0605
Tastepoint
Philadelphia, PA 800-363-5286
Van Tone Creative
Terrell, TX 800-856-0802
Vegetable Juices Inc
Chicago, IL 888-776-9752

Fat

Choco Finesse, LLC
Indianapolis, IN 317-476-6034
Edlong Corporation
Elk Grove Village, IL 847-631-6700
Gold Coast Ingredients
Commerce, CA 800-352-8673

Fish

Fontana Flavors Inc
Janesville, WI 608-754-9668
Gold Coast Ingredients
Commerce, CA 800-352-8673
North Taste Flavourings
Anse-Bleue, NB 506-732-0010

Flavors

Dressing

Edlong Corporation
Elk Grove Village, IL 847-631-6700

Enhancers

Edlong Corporation
Elk Grove Village, IL 847-631-6700
Essentia Protein Solutions
Ankeny, IA 515-289-5100
Flavor & Fragrance Specialties
Mahwah, NJ 800-998-4337
H&A Health Products, Inc
Richmond Hill, ON 514-979-3589
Serious Foodie
Bradenton, FL 844-736-6343
W.T.I.
Jefferson, GA 800-827-1727

Fruit

Agrana Fruit US Inc
Cleveland, OH 800-477-3788
Dohler-Milne Aseptics LLC
Prosser, WA 509-786-2240
Gold Coast Ingredients
Commerce, CA 800-352-8673
H B Taylor Co
Chicago, IL 773-254-4805
Silesia Flavors
Hoffman Estates, IL 847-645-0270

Grain

GKI Foods
Brighton, MI 248-486-0055

Half & Half

Edlong Corporation
Elk Grove Village, IL 847-631-6700

Hazelnut

Allen Flavors Inc
Edison, NJ 908-561-5995
Flavorganics
Newark, NJ 866-972-6879
Gold Coast Ingredients
Commerce, CA 800-352-8673

Heat Stable

Edlong Corporation
Elk Grove Village, IL 847-631-6700

Hickory Smoke Oil

Gold Coast Ingredients
Commerce, CA 800-352-8673
Talk O'Texas Brands Inc
San Angelo, TX 800-749-6572

Irish Creme

Edlong Corporation
Elk Grove Village, IL 847-631-6700
Gold Coast Ingredients
Commerce, CA 800-352-8673

Lemon

Allen Flavors Inc
Edison, NJ 908-561-5995
Castella Imports Inc
Brentwood, NY 631-231-5500
Charles H Baldwin & Sons
West Stockbridge, MA 413-232-7785
Citromax Flavors Inc
Carlstadt, NJ 201-933-8405
Frontier Co-op
Norway, IA 844-550-6200
Gold Coast Ingredients
Commerce, CA 800-352-8673
Nielsen-Massey Vanillas Inc
Waukegan, IL 800-525-7873
Serv-Agen Corporation
Cherry Hill, NJ 856-663-6966
Test Laboratories Inc
Reseda, CA 818-881-4251
Ungerer & Co
Lincoln Park, NJ 973-706-7381

Licorice

AM Todd Co
Kalamazoo, MI 269-343-2603
Asiamerica Ingredients
Westwood, NJ 201-497-5531
Gold Coast Ingredients
Commerce, CA 800-352-8673
Horner International
Raleigh, NC 919-787-3112

Lime

Allen Flavors Inc
Edison, NJ 908-561-5995
Gold Coast Ingredients
Commerce, CA 800-352-8673
Ungerer & Co
Lincoln Park, NJ 973-706-7381

Liqueur

Edgar A Weber & Co
Wheeling, IL 800-558-9078

Macadamia

Allen Flavors Inc
Edison, NJ 908-561-5995
Buonitalia
New York, NY 212-633-9090
Gold Coast Ingredients
Commerce, CA 800-352-8673

Maple

Allen Flavors Inc
Edison, NJ 908-561-5995
Castella Imports Inc
Brentwood, NY 631-231-5500
Gold Coast Ingredients
Commerce, CA 800-352-8673

Butter

Edlong Corporation
Elk Grove Village, IL 847-631-6700

Masking

Edlong Corporation
Elk Grove Village, IL 847-631-6700
Gold Coast Ingredients
Commerce, CA 800-352-8673
Silesia Flavors
Hoffman Estates, IL 847-645-0270
Virginia Dare Extract Co
Brooklyn, NY 718-788-1776
Watson Inc
West Haven, CT 800-388-3481

Meat

First Choice Ingredients
Germantown, WI 262-251-4322
Flavor & Fragrance Specialties
Mahwah, NJ 800-998-4337
Flavor House, Inc.
Adelanto, CA 760-246-9131
Fontana Flavors Inc
Janesville, WI 608-754-9668
Genarom International
Cranbury, NJ 609-409-6200
Innova Flavors
Lombard, IL 630-928-4800

Microwave

Edlong Corporation
Elk Grove Village, IL 847-631-6700

Milk

DairyChem Inc.
Fishers, IN 317-849-8400
Edlong Corporation
Elk Grove Village, IL 847-631-6700
Fonterra Co-operative Group Limited
Chicago, IL 888-869-6455
Gold Coast Ingredients
Commerce, CA 800-352-8673
Ingredia Inc
Wapakoneta, OH 419-738-4060

Butter

Edlong Corporation
Elk Grove Village, IL 847-631-6700
Fonterra Co-operative Group Limited
Chicago, IL 888-869-6455

Nut

Gold Coast Ingredients
Commerce, CA 800-352-8673
H B Taylor Co
Chicago, IL 773-254-4805

Orange

Allen Flavors Inc
Edison, NJ 908-561-5995
Castella Imports Inc
Brentwood, NY 631-231-5500
Charles H Baldwin & Sons
West Stockbridge, MA 413-232-7785
Frontier Co-op
Norway, IA 844-550-6200
Gold Coast Ingredients
Commerce, CA 800-352-8673
Nielsen-Massey Vanillas Inc
Waukegan, IL 800-525-7873
Ungerer & Co
Lincoln Park, NJ 973-706-7381

Passion Fruit

Allen Flavors Inc
Edison, NJ....908-561-5995
Gold Coast Ingredients
Commerce, CA....800-352-8673

Peach

Allen Flavors Inc
Edison, NJ....908-561-5995
Gold Coast Ingredients
Commerce, CA....800-352-8673

Peanut

Gold Coast Ingredients
Commerce, CA....800-352-8673

Pear

Allen Flavors Inc
Edison, NJ....908-561-5995
Gold Coast Ingredients
Commerce, CA....800-352-8673

Peppermint

Castella Imports Inc
Brentwood, NY....631-231-5500
Frontier Co-op
Norway, IA....844-550-6200
Gold Coast Ingredients
Commerce, CA....800-352-8673
Ungerer & Co
Lincoln Park, NJ....973-706-7381

Pickle

Gold Coast Ingredients
Commerce, CA....800-352-8673

Pineapple

Allen Flavors Inc
Edison, NJ....908-561-5995
Castella Imports Inc
Brentwood, NY....631-231-5500
Gold Coast Ingredients
Commerce, CA....800-352-8673

Pistachio

Gold Coast Ingredients
Commerce, CA....800-352-8673

Potato

Gold Coast Ingredients
Commerce, CA....800-352-8673

Poultry

Flavor House, Inc.
Adelanto, CA....760-246-9131

Raspberry

Allen Flavors Inc
Edison, NJ....908-561-5995
Gold Coast Ingredients
Commerce, CA....800-352-8673

Root Beer

Allen Flavors Inc
Edison, NJ....908-561-5995
Gold Coast Ingredients
Commerce, CA....800-352-8673

Rum

Butter Toffee

Edlong Corporation
Elk Grove Village, IL....847-631-6700

Seafood

Flavor House, Inc.
Adelanto, CA....760-246-9131

Smoke

Dean Distributors, Inc.
Burlingame, CA....800-792-0816
Gold Coast Ingredients
Commerce, CA....800-352-8673
Red Arrow Products Co LLC
Manitowoc, WI....920-769-1100

Sour

Senomyx Inc
San Diego, CA....858-646-8300

Cream

DairyChem Inc.
Fishers, IN....317-849-8400
Edlong Corporation
Elk Grove Village, IL....847-631-6700
Gold Coast Ingredients
Commerce, CA....800-352-8673

Sour Dough

Gold Coast Ingredients
Commerce, CA....800-352-8673

Spearmint

Gold Coast Ingredients
Commerce, CA....800-352-8673
I P Callison & Sons
Lacey, WA....360-412-3340
Ungerer & Co
Lincoln Park, NJ....973-706-7381

Strawberry

Allen Flavors Inc
Edison, NJ....908-561-5995
Castella Imports Inc
Brentwood, NY....631-231-5500
Gold Coast Ingredients
Commerce, CA....800-352-8673

Sweet Cream

Gold Coast Ingredients
Commerce, CA....800-352-8673

Tea

Acqua Blox LLC
Santa Fe Springs, CA....562-693-9599
Allen Flavors Inc
Edison, NJ....908-561-5995
Beck Flavors
Loveland, OH....314-878-7522
Flavor & Fragrance Specialties
Mahwah, NJ....800-998-4337
Flavor Dynamics Two
South Plainfield, NJ....888-271-8424
Gold Coast Ingredients
Commerce, CA....800-352-8673

Vanilla

Agri-Dairy Products
Purchase, NY....914-697-9580
Allen Flavors Inc
Edison, NJ....908-561-5995
Bakto Flavors
North Brunswick, NJ....732-354-4492
Carmi Flavor & Fragrance Company
Commerce, CA....800-421-9647
Charles H Baldwin & Sons
West Stockbridge, MA....413-232-7785
Clements Foods Co
Oklahoma City, OK....800-654-8355
Everfresh Food Corporation
Minneapolis, MN....612-331-6393
Gold Coast Ingredients
Commerce, CA....800-352-8673
Helm New York Chemical Corp
Piscataway, NJ....732-981-0528
Jogue Inc
Northville, MI....800-531-3888
Lafaza Foods
Oakland, CA....510-282-1138
Lemur International
Richmond, CA....510-620-9708
New Organics
Kenwood, CA....734-677-5570
Prova
Danvers, MA....877-776-8287
Serv-Agen Corporation
Cherry Hill, NJ....856-663-6966
Singing Dog Vanilla
Eugene, OR....888-343-0002
Sno Wizard Inc
New Orleans, LA....800-366-9766
Sterling Extract Co Inc
Franklin Park, IL....847-451-9728
Triple K Manufacturing Company, Inc.
Shenandoah, IA....712-246-4376
Webbpak Inc
Trussville, AL....800-655-3500

Vanillin

Agri-Dairy Products
Purchase, NY....914-697-9580
AM Todd Co
Kalamazoo, MI....269-343-2603
Asiamerica Ingredients
Westwood, NJ....201-497-5531
Astral Extracts
Syosset, NY....516-496-2505
California Custom Fruits
Baldwin Park, CA....877-558-0056
Gold Coast Ingredients
Commerce, CA....800-352-8673
International Chemical Corp
Melbourne, FL....800-914-2436
Nichem Co
Newark, NJ....973-399-9810
Universal Preservachem Inc
Somerset, NJ....732-568-1266
Zink & Triest Company
Montgomeryville, PA....800-537-5070

Variegates

Triple K Manufacturing Company, Inc.
Shenandoah, IA....712-246-4376

Vegetable

Gold Coast Ingredients
Commerce, CA....800-352-8673
Kalsec
Kalamazoo, MI....800-323-9320
Summit Hill Flavors
Somerset, NJ....732-805-0335

Watermelon

Gold Coast Ingredients
Commerce, CA....800-352-8673

Wine

Edgar A Weber & Co
Wheeling, IL....800-558-9078
Gold Coast Ingredients
Commerce, CA....800-352-8673

Wintergreen

Gold Coast Ingredients
Commerce, CA....800-352-8673

Yogurt

DairyChem Inc.
Fishers, IN....317-849-8400
Edlong Corporation
Elk Grove Village, IL....847-631-6700
Gold Coast Ingredients
Commerce, CA....800-352-8673
Gum Technology Corporation
Tucson, AZ....800-369-4867
Johanna Foods Inc.
Flemington, NJ....800-727-6700
Plaidberry Company
Vista, CA....760-727-5403

Glandulars

Ultra Enterprises
Whittier, CA....800-543-0627

Grain-Based

Beaumont Rice Mills
Beaumont, TX....409-832-2521

Gums

AM Todd Co
Kalamazoo, MI....269-343-2603
Asiamerica Ingredients
Westwood, NJ....201-497-5531
Au'some Candies
Monmouth Junction, NJ....877-287-6649
Batory Foods
Des Plaines, IL....847-299-1999
Beehive Botanicals
Hayward, WI....800-233-4483

Cap Candy
Napa, CA. 707-251-9321
DMH Ingredients Inc
Libertyville, IL 847-362-9977
El Brands
Ozark, AL 334-445-2828
Food Ingredient Solutions
Teterboro, NJ. 917-449-9558
Fun Factory
Milwaukee, WI 877-894-6767
Gum Technology Corporation
Tucson, AZ 800-369-4867
Gurley's Foods
Willmar, MN 800-426-7845
H&A Health Products, Inc
Richmond Hill, ON. 514-979-3589
Jungbunzlauer Inc
Newton, MA 617-969-0900
Kolatin Real Kosher Gelatin
Lakewood, NJ 732-364-8700
Lotte USA Inc
Battle Creek, MI 269-963-6664
Magic Gumball Intl
Chatsworth, CA 800-576-2020
Main Street Ingredients
La Crosse, WI 800-359-2345
Montello Inc
Tulsa, OK 800-331-4628
Oak Leaf Confections
. . . . 877-261-7887
PLT Health Solutions Inc
Morristown, NJ. 973-984-0900
Polypro International Inc
Edina, MN. 800-765-9776
Profood International
Naperville, IL 888-288-0081
Richardson Brands Co
Canajoharie, NY 518-673-3553
Sahagian & Associates
Oak Park, IL 800-327-9273
Scripture Candy
Birmingham, AL. 888-317-7333
Snackerz
Commerce, CA 888-576-2253
SP Enterprises, Inc.
Las Vegas, NV 800-746-4774
SWELL Philadelphia Chewing Gum Corporation
Havertown, PA 610-449-1700
Thymly Products Inc
Colora, MD. 877-710-2340
TIC Gums
Belcamp, MD 800-899-3953
Triple-C
Hamilton, ON 800-263-9105
Whetstone Chocolates
St Augustine, FL. 877-261-7887
World Confections Inc
South Orange, NJ 718-768-8100

Acacia Gum

Alfred L. Wolff, Inc.
Park Ridge, IL. 847-759-8888
Gum Technology Corporation
Tucson, AZ 800-369-4867
Gumix International Inc
Fort Lee, NJ 800-248-6492
Main Street Ingredients
La Crosse, WI 800-359-2345
Nexira
Somerville, NJ 800-872-1850
PLT Health Solutions Inc
Morristown, NJ. 973-984-0900

Agar-Agar

AM Todd Co
Kalamazoo, MI 269-343-2603
Gum Technology Corporation
Tucson, AZ 800-369-4867
PLT Health Solutions Inc
Morristown, NJ. 973-984-0900
Universal Preservachem Inc
Somerset, NJ. 732-568-1266

Algin & Alginates

PLT Health Solutions Inc
Morristown, NJ. 973-984-0900

Arabic

PLT Health Solutions Inc
Morristown, NJ. 973-984-0900

Carboxymethylcellulose

PLT Health Solutions Inc
Morristown, NJ. 973-984-0900

Carrageenan

CP Kelco
Atlanta, GA. 800-535-2687
GPI USA LLC.
Mokena, IL 800-929-4248
PLT Health Solutions Inc
Morristown, NJ. 973-984-0900

Gellan

CP Kelco
Atlanta, GA. 800-535-2687
PLT Health Solutions Inc
Morristown, NJ. 973-984-0900

Ghatti

PLT Health Solutions Inc
Morristown, NJ. 973-984-0900

Guar Gum

Agri-Dairy Products
Purchase, NY 914-697-9580
Asiamerica Ingredients
Westwood, NJ 201-497-5531
Commodities Marketing Inc
Clarksburg, NJ 732-516-0700
Gum Technology Corporation
Tucson, AZ 800-369-4867
H Fox & Co Inc
Brooklyn, NY 718-385-4600
PLT Health Solutions Inc
Morristown, NJ. 973-984-0900
Polypro International Inc
Edina, MN. 800-765-9776
Universal Preservachem Inc
Somerset, NJ. 732-568-1266

Hydroxypropyl Methylcellulose

Asiamerica Ingredients
Westwood, NJ 201-497-5531

Karaya Gum

Gum Technology Corporation
Tucson, AZ 800-369-4867
Universal Preservachem Inc
Somerset, NJ. 732-568-1266

Locust Bean Gum

CP Kelco
Atlanta, GA. 800-535-2687
Gum Technology Corporation
Tucson, AZ 800-369-4867
PLT Health Solutions Inc
Morristown, NJ. 973-984-0900

Methylcellulose

PLT Health Solutions Inc
Morristown, NJ. 973-984-0900

Natural

PLT Health Solutions Inc
Morristown, NJ. 973-984-0900

Pectin

Asiamerica Ingredients
Westwood, NJ 201-497-5531
CP Kelco
Atlanta, GA. 800-535-2687
Silvateam USA
Ontario, CA. 909-635-2870

Tara

PLT Health Solutions Inc
Morristown, NJ. 973-984-0900
Silvateam USA
Ontario, CA. 909-635-2870

Tragacanth

Gum Technology Corporation
Tucson, AZ 800-369-4867
Universal Preservachem Inc
Somerset, NJ. 732-568-1266

Vegetable Gum

Functional Foods
Englishtown, NJ 800-442-9524
Gum Technology Corporation
Tucson, AZ 800-369-4867
Gumix International Inc
Fort Lee, NJ 800-248-6492

Xanthan Gum

AM Todd Co
Kalamazoo, MI 269-343-2603
Asiamerica Ingredients
Westwood, NJ 201-497-5531
CP Kelco
Atlanta, GA. 800-535-2687
Deosen USA
Piscataway, NJ 908-292-1165
Gum Technology Corporation
Tucson, AZ 800-369-4867
Hodgson Mill Inc
Effingham, IL 800-347-0198
Homefree LLC
Windham, NH. 800-552-7172

Humectants

Nutricepts
Burnsville, MN 800-949-9060

Hydrocolloids

PLT Health Solutions Inc
Morristown, NJ. 973-984-0900
Silvateam USA
Ontario, CA. 909-635-2870
TIC Gums
Belcamp, MD 800-899-3953

Hydrolyzed Products

Milk Proteins

First Spice Mixing Co
Long Island City, NY 800-221-1105
Kantner Group
Wapakoneta, OH. 877-738-3448
Milk Specialties Global
Eden Prairie, MN 952-942-7310

Vegetable Proteins

Flavor House, Inc.
Adelanto, CA 760-246-9131
Savoury Systems Inc
Branchburg, NJ. 888-534-6621
Valley Meats
Coal Valley, IL 309-517-6639

Inclusions

Paradise Fruits NA
Norwood, MA. 781-769-4900

Ingredients

Avafina Organics
Coquitlam, BC 604-292-0022
Blue California Co
Rancho Sta Marg, CA. 949-459-2729
Carolina Ingredients Inc
Rock Hill, SC 803-323-6550
Century Foods Intl LLC
Sparta, WI. 800-269-1901
Diana Naturals
Saddle Brook, NJ 845-729-0942
DSM Food Specialties
Parsippany, NJ
Espro Manufacturing
Vernon, CA 323-415-8544
Excellentia Intl.
Fairfield, NJ 737-749-9840
Fallwood Corp
White Plains, NY 914-304-4065
Ful-Flav-R Foods
Alamo, CA 925-838-0300
Global Organics
Cambridge, MA 781-648-8844
Hayashibara International Inc.
New York, NY 212-703-1340
Heartland Ingredients LLC
Troy, MO. 800-557-2621
Helm New York Chemical Corp
Piscataway, NJ 732-981-0528

International Food Products
Fenton, MO 800-227-8427
Marukan Vinegar USA Inc.
Paramount, CA 562-630-6060
Newtown Foods USA Inc
Newtown, PA 215-579-2120
PGP International
Woodland, CA 800-233-0110
PLT Health Solutions Inc
Morristown, NJ 973-984-0900
Quali Tech Inc
Chaska, MN 800-328-5870
SAPNA Foods
Atlanta, GA 404-589-0977
Sentry Seasonings
Elmhurst, IL 630-530-5370
Sun Ray International
Davis, CA 530-297-1688
Universal Impex Corporation
Toronto, ON 416-743-7778
Van Hees Gmbh
Cary, NC 919-654-6862

Bakery

American Pasien Co
Burlington, NJ 609-387-3130
Amoretti
Oxnard, CA 800-266-7388
Caremoli USA
Ames, IA 515-233-1255
Chaucer Foods, Inc. USA
Forest Grove, OR
International Food Products
Fenton, MO 800-227-8427
New Horizon Foods
Union City, CA 510-489-8600
P&H Milling Group
Cambridge, ON 519-650-6400
White Stokes International
Chicago, IL 800-978-6537

Dairy

Century Foods Intl LLC
Sparta, WI 800-269-1901
Interfood Ingredients
Miami, FL 786-953-8320
Kantner Group
Wapakoneta, OH 877-738-3448
Trega Foods
Weyauwega, WI 920-867-2137

Food

AmTech Ingredients
Hudson, WI 715-381-5746
Anchor Ingredients
Fargo, ND 701-499-1480
Capriccio
Chatsworth, CA 818-718-7620
Catherych
Warren, NJ 732-566-6625
Century Foods Intl LLC
Sparta, WI 800-269-1901
Interfood Ingredients
Miami, FL 786-953-8320
International Food Products
Fenton, MO 800-227-8427
Land O'Frost Inc.
Lansing, IL 800-323-3308
Mantrose-Haeuser Co Inc
Westport, CT 800-344-4229
PLT Health Solutions Inc
Morristown, NJ 973-984-0900
Summit Hill Flavors
Somerset, NJ 732-805-0335
White Stokes International
Chicago, IL 800-978-6537

Leaveners

Baking Soda

Agri-Dairy Products
Purchase, NY 914-697-9580
Bunny Bread
Evansville, IN
Church & Dwight Co., Inc.
Ewing, NJ 800-833-9532
Clabber Girl Corporation
Terre Haute, IN 812-232-9446
Frontier Co-op
Norway, IA 844-550-6200

GloryBee
Eugene, OR 800-456-7923
Natrium Products Inc
Cortland, NY 800-962-4203

Maltodextrin

Agri-Dairy Products
Purchase, NY 914-697-9580
California Natural Products
Lathrop, CA 209-858-2525
Clofine Dairy Products Inc
Linwood, NJ 609-653-1000
Grain Processing Corp
Muscatine, IA 800-448-4472
Ingredion Inc.
Westchester, IL 800-713-0208
Malt Diastase Co
Saddle Brook, NJ 800-526-0180
New Organics
Kenwood, CA 734-677-5570
Roquette America Inc.
Geneva, IL 630-463-9430

Milk Calcium

Ingredia Inc
Wapakoneta, OH 419-738-4060
Kantner Group
Wapakoneta, OH 877-738-3448

Pastes

Almond

Emerling International Foods
Buffalo, NY 716-833-7381

Fig

Emerling International Foods
Buffalo, NY 716-833-7381
Fig Garden Packing Inc
Fresno, CA 559-271-9000
Unique Ingredients LLC
Gold Canyon, AZ 480-983-2498

Fruit

Cinnabar Specialty Foods Inc
Prescott, AZ 866-293-6433
Citadelle Maple Syrup Producers' Cooperative
Plessisville, QC 819-362-3241
Emerling International Foods
Buffalo, NY 716-833-7381
Fig Garden Packing Inc
Fresno, CA 559-271-9000
Kapaa Poi Factory
Kapaa, HI 808-822-5426
Lion Raisins Inc
Selma, CA 559-834-6677
Unique Ingredients LLC
Gold Canyon, AZ 480-983-2498
Vacaville Fruit Co
Vacaville, CA 707-447-1085

Tomato

Emerling International Foods
Buffalo, NY 716-833-7381
Ingomar Packing Co
Los Banos, CA 209-826-9494
International Home Foods
Parsippany, NJ 973-359-9920
Northwest Packing Co
Vancouver, WA 800-543-4356
Pastene Co LTD
Canton, MA 781-298-3397
Spreda Group
Louisville, KY 502-426-9411
Stanislaus Food Prod
Modesto, CA 800-327-7201
Unilever Food Solutions
Englewood Cliffs, NJ

Canned & Frozen

International Home Foods
Parsippany, NJ 973-359-9920
Unilever Food Solutions
Englewood Cliffs, NJ

Pectins

Apple

Asiamerica Ingredients
Westwood, NJ 201-497-5531
Century Blends LLC
Hunt Valley, MD 410-771-6606
Gum Technology Corporation
Tucson, AZ 800-369-4867
Spreda Group
Louisville, KY 502-426-9411
Universal Preservachem Inc
Somerset, NJ 732-568-1266

Citrus

Asiamerica Ingredients
Westwood, NJ 201-497-5531
Century Blends LLC
Hunt Valley, MD 410-771-6606
Citrico
Northbrook, IL 800-445-2171
Gum Technology Corporation
Tucson, AZ 800-369-4867
Universal Preservachem Inc
Somerset, NJ 732-568-1266

Fruit

Century Blends LLC
Hunt Valley, MD 410-771-6606
Kent Precision Foods Group Inc
Muscatine, IA 800-442-5242
Spreda Group
Louisville, KY 502-426-9411

Phosphates

Asiamerica Ingredients
Westwood, NJ 201-497-5531
BK Giulini Corporation
Ladenburg,
Escalade Limited
Huntington, NY 631-659-3373
Fiberstar
River Falls, WI 715-425-7550
First Spice Mixing Co
Long Island City, NY 800-221-1105
Hawkins Inc
Roseville, MN 800-328-5460
ICL Performance Products
St. Louis, MO 800-244-6169
Innophos Holdings Inc.
Cranbury, NJ 609-495-2495
International Food Products
Fenton, MO 800-227-8427
Prayon Inc.
Augusta, GA 206-213-5572
Wiberg Corporation
Oakville, ON 905-825-9900

Ammonium Phosphates

Luyties Pharmacal Company
Saint Louis, MO 800-325-8080
Universal Preservachem Inc
Somerset, NJ 732-568-1266

Calcium Phosphate

Asiamerica Ingredients
Westwood, NJ 201-497-5531
Luyties Pharmacal Company
Saint Louis, MO 800-325-8080
Natural Enrichment Industries
Herrin, IL 618-942-2112

Potassium Bicarbonate

Innophos Holdings Inc.
Cranbury, NJ 609-495-2495

Sodium Phosphate

Agri-Dairy Products
Purchase, NY 914-697-9580
Asiamerica Ingredients
Westwood, NJ 201-497-5531
Luyties Pharmacal Company
Saint Louis, MO 800-325-8080
Universal Preservachem Inc
Somerset, NJ 732-568-1266

Potassium Bitartrate (Cream of Tartar)

Advanced Spice & Trading
Carrollton, TX. 800-872-7811
American Tartaric Products
Larchmont, NY. 914-834-1881
Jungbunzlauer Inc
Newton, MA 617-969-0900

Potassium Bromate

Morre-Tec Ind Inc
Union, NJ 908-686-0307

Potassium Citrate

Agri-Dairy Products
Purchase, NY 914-697-9580
Asiamerica Ingredients
Westwood, NJ 201-497-5531
Cargill Inc.
Minneapolis, MN 800-227-4455
Jungbunzlauer Inc
Newton, MA 617-969-0900
Shekou Chemicals
Waltham, MA 781-893-6878
Universal Preservachem Inc
Somerset, NJ. 732-568-1266

Potassium Lactate

Hawkins Inc
Roseville, MN. 800-328-5460
Trumark
Linden, NJ. 800-752-7877

Potassium Sorbate

Agri-Dairy Products
Purchase, NY 914-697-9580
Asiamerica Ingredients
Westwood, NJ 201-497-5531
Jungbunzlauer Inc
Newton, MA 617-969-0900
Shekou Chemicals
Waltham, MA 781-893-6878
Silver Fern Chemical Inc
Seattle, WA. 866-282-3384
Universal Preservachem Inc
Somerset, NJ. 732-568-1266

Powders

Expro Manufacturing
Vernon, CA 323-415-8544
First Choice Ingredients
Germantown, WI. 262-251-4322
Hayashibara International Inc.
New York, NY 212-703-1340
Marroquin Organic Intl.
Santa Cruz, CA. 831-423-3442

Adobo

American Key Food Products Inc
Closter, NJ. 877-263-7539
Gel Spice Co LLC
Bayonne, NJ 800-922-0230
Magic Seasoning Blends
New Orleans, LA 800-457-2857

Arrowroot

GloryBee
Eugene, OR. 800-456-7923

Baking

Agri-Dairy Products
Purchase, NY 914-697-9580
American Tartaric Products
Larchmont, NY. 914-834-1881
Erba Food Products
Brooklyn, NY 718-272-7700
Frontier Co-op
Norway, IA 844-550-6200
King Arthur Flour
Norwich, VT. 800-827-6836
Lallemand American Yeast
Addison, IL. 630-932-1290
Lynch Foods
North York, ON. 416-449-5464
Roland Machinery
Springfield, IL. 800-325-1183
Tasty Mix Quality Foods
Brooklyn, NY 718-855-7680
Young Winfield
Hamilton, ON 905-893-2536

Beverage

Aromatech USA
Orlando, FL. 407-277-5727
Baldwin Richardson Foods
Oakbrook Terrace, IL 866-644-2732
Best Foods
Englewood Cliffs, NJ 201-894-4000
Cappuccine
Corona, CA 800-511-3127
First Choice Ingredients
Germantown, WI. 262-251-4322
Instant Products of America
Columbus, IN 812-372-9100
J. Crow Company
New Ipswich, NH 800-878-1965
Lynch Foods
North York, ON. 416-449-5464
Mele-Koi Farms
Newport Beach, CA 949-660-9000
Natural Formulas
Hayward, CA 510-372-1800
Northwestern Foods
Arden Hills, MN. 800-236-4937
Wechsler Coffee Corporation
Teterboro, NJ. 800-800-2633

Broth

Ancient Nutrition
North Palm Beach, FL 888-823-4468
Essentia Protein Solutions
Ankeny, IA 515-289-5100
International Dehydrated Foods
Springfield, MO 800-641-6509

Buttermilk

Diehl Food Ingredients
Defiance, OH 800-251-3033
Kantner Group
Wapakoneta, OH. 877-738-3448

Carob

Earth Circle Organics
Auburn, CA. 877-922-3663
NOW Foods
Bloomingdale, IL 888-669-3663
Universal Preservachem Inc
Somerset, NJ. 732-568-1266

Carob & Cocoa

Dairy House
Fenton, MO. 636-343-5444
Earth Circle Organics
Auburn, CA. 877-922-3663
GloryBee
Eugene, OR. 800-456-7923
Jedwards International Inc
Braintree, MA 781-848-1473
Kana Organics
Westlake Village, CA 213-603-0448

Celery

Advanced Spice & Trading
Carrollton, TX. 800-872-7811
American Key Food Products Inc
Closter, NJ. 877-263-7539
Con Yeager Spice Co
Zelienople, PA. 800-222-2460
Emerling International Foods
Buffalo, NY. 716-833-7381
Gel Spice Co LLC
Bayonne, NJ 800-922-0230
Unique Ingredients LLC
Gold Canyon, AZ 480-983-2498

Cheese

Anderson Custom Processing
New Ulm, MN. 877-588-4950
Commercial Creamery Co
Spokane, WA. 509-747-4131
DMH Ingredients Inc
Libertyville, IL 847-362-9977
First Choice Ingredients
Germantown, WI. 262-251-4322
Kantner Group
Wapakoneta, OH. 877-738-3448
Kerry, Inc
Beloit, WI 608-363-1200
King Arthur Flour
Norwich, VT. 800-827-6836

American

Kantner Group
Wapakoneta, OH. 877-738-3448

Bakers

Kantner Group
Wapakoneta, OH. 877-738-3448

Cheddar

Commercial Creamery Co
Spokane, WA. 509-747-4131
Kantner Group
Wapakoneta, OH. 877-738-3448

Cream

Kantner Group
Wapakoneta, OH. 877-738-3448

Chicken Stock

Summit Hill Flavors
Somerset, NJ. 732-805-0335

Chili

Advanced Spice & Trading
Carrollton, TX. 800-872-7811
American Key Food Products Inc
Closter, NJ. 877-263-7539
Bruce Foods Corporation
Lafayette, LA 800-299-9082
Bueno Foods
Albuquerque, NM. 800-888-7336
Commercial Creamery Co
Spokane, WA. 509-747-4131
Dave's Gourmet
San Rafael, CA 800-758-0372
Fernandez Chili Co
Alamosa, CO. 719-589-6043
Gel Spice Co LLC
Bayonne, NJ 800-922-0230
Monterrey Products
San Antonio, TX. 210-435-2872
Morris J Golombeck Inc
Brooklyn, NY 718-284-3505
Santa Cruz Chili & Spice
Tumacacori, AZ 520-398-2591
Swagger Foods Corp
Vernon Hills, IL 847-913-1200
Texas Coffee Co
Beaumont, TX. 800-259-3400
Whole Herb Co
Sonoma, CA 707-935-1077

Cocoa

Batory Foods
Des Plaines, IL 847-299-1999
Forbes Chocolate BP
Broadview Hts, OH. 440-838-4400
Frontier Co-op
Norway, IA 844-550-6200
Gilster-Mary Lee Corp
Chester, IL. 618-826-2361
Mont Blanc Gourmet
Denver, CO 800-877-3811
Natra US
Chula Vista, CA 800-262-6216
Northwestern Foods
Arden Hills, MN. 800-236-4937
NOW Foods
Bloomingdale, IL 888-669-3663
Sucesores de Pedro Cortes
Hato Rey, PR. 787-754-7040
Vivoo
Verona,
Wildly Organic
Silver Bay, MN 800-945-3801

Curry

American Key Food Products Inc
Closter, NJ. 877-263-7539
Commissariat Imports
Los Angeles, CA. 310-475-5628

Gel Spice Co LLC
Bayonne, NJ 800-922-0230

Hot

Commissariat Imports
Los Angeles, CA..................310-475-5628

Echinacea Purpurea

Asiamerica Ingredients
Westwood, NJ....................201-497-5531
RFi Ingredients
Blauvelt, NY....................800-962-7663

Egg

Batory Foods
Des Plaines, IL..................847-299-1999

Feverfew

Asiamerica Ingredients
Westwood, NJ....................201-497-5531
RFi Ingredients
Blauvelt, NY....................800-962-7663

Fruit

Agvest
Cleveland, OH..................216-464-3737
Blue California Co
Rancho Sta Marg, CA..............949-459-2729
Carmi Flavor & Fragrance Company
Commerce, CA....................800-421-9647
Emerling International Foods
Buffalo, NY......................716-833-7381
Jiaherb
Pine Brook, NJ..................888-542-4372
Mayfield Farms and Nursery
Athens, TN......................423-746-9859
Niagara Foods
Middleport, NY..................716-735-7722
Paragon Fruits
Maple Grove, MN..................763-559-0436
Powder Pure
The Dalles, OR..................541-298-4800
Prime Ingredients Inc
Saddle Brook, NJ................888-791-6655
QBI
South Plainfield, NJ............908-668-0088
RFi Ingredients
Blauvelt, NY....................800-962-7663
Spreda Group
Louisville, KY..................502-426-9411
Unique Ingredients LLC
Gold Canyon, AZ..................480-983-2498
United Citrus
Norwood, MA....................800-229-7300
Valley Fig Growers
Fresno, CA......................559-237-3893

Garlic (See also Spices/Garlic Powder)

Advanced Spice & Trading
Carrollton, TX..................800-872-7811
Alfred L. Wolff, Inc.
Park Ridge, IL..................847-759-8888
American Key Food Products Inc
Closter, NJ......................877-263-7539
Asiamerica Ingredients
Westwood, NJ....................201-497-5531
Emerling International Foods
Buffalo, NY......................716-833-7381
Gel Spice Co LLC
Bayonne, NJ....................800-922-0230
Great Garlic Foods
Bradley Beach, NJ................732-775-3311
Italian Rose Garlic Products
Riviera Beach, FL................800-338-8899
RFi Ingredients
Blauvelt, NY....................800-962-7663
Texas Coffee Co
Beaumont, TX....................800-259-3400
Vegetable Juices Inc
Chicago, IL......................888-776-9752

Gingko

Asiamerica Ingredients
Westwood, NJ....................201-497-5531
RFi Ingredients
Blauvelt, NY....................800-962-7663

Ginseng

Asiamerica Ingredients
Westwood, NJ....................201-497-5531
RFi Ingredients
Blauvelt, NY....................800-962-7663

Gotu Kola

Asiamerica Ingredients
Westwood, NJ....................201-497-5531
RFi Ingredients
Blauvelt, NY....................800-962-7663

Ice Cream

Agri-Dairy Products
Purchase, NY....................914-697-9580
America's Classic Foods
Cambria, CA......................805-927-0745
Clofine Dairy Products Inc
Linwood, NJ......................609-653-1000
Quality Naturally Foods
City Of Industry, CA............888-498-6986

Jelly

Lake City Foods
Mississauga, ON..................905-625-8244

Meat

American Key Food Products Inc
Closter, NJ......................877-263-7539
Flavor House, Inc.
Adelanto, CA....................760-246-9131
QST Ingredients
Rancho Cucamonga, CA............909-989-4343
Summit Hill Flavors
Somerset, NJ....................732-805-0335

Mesquite Smoke

Earth Circle Organics
Auburn, CA......................877-922-3663

Milk

Abunda Life
Asbury Park, NJ..................732-775-9338
Agri-Dairy Products
Purchase, NY....................914-697-9580
All American Foods Inc
Mankato, MN......................800-833-2661
Berkshire Dairy
Wyomissing, PA..................877-696-6455
Blossom Farm Products
Ridgewood, NJ....................800-729-1818
California Dairies Inc.
Visalia, CA......................559-625-2200
Century Foods Intl LLC
Sparta, WI......................800-269-1901
Challenge Dairy Products, Inc.
Dublin, CA......................800-733-2479
Clofine Dairy Products Inc
Linwood, NJ......................609-653-1000
Commercial Creamery Co
Spokane, WA......................509-747-4131
Con Yeager Spice Co
Zelienople, PA..................800-222-2460
Country Fresh Farms
Salt Lake City, UT..............800-878-0099
CTL Foods
Colfax, WI......................800-962-5227
Devansoy Farms
Carroll, IA......................800-747-8605
F C C
Mcminnville, OR..................503-472-2157
First District Association
Litchfield, MN..................320-693-3236
First Spice Mixing Co
Long Island City, NY............800-221-1105
Fonterra Co-operative Group Limited
Chicago, IL......................888-869-6455
Graf Creamery Co
Bonduel, WI......................715-758-2137
Humboldt Creamery
Modesto, CA......................888-316-6064
IMAC
Oklahoma City, OK................888-878-7827
Kantner Group
Wapakoneta, OH..................877-738-3448
Kelly Flour Company
Addison, IL......................630-678-5300
Lake Country Foods Inc
Oconomowoc, WI..................262-567-5521
Land O'Lakes Inc
Arden Hills, MN..................800-328-9680
Main Street Ingredients
La Crosse, WI....................800-359-2345
Maple Island
Saint Paul, MN..................800-369-1022
Meyenberg Goat Milk
Turlock, CA......................800-891-4628
Plainview Milk Products
Plainview, MN....................800-356-5606
Protient
St Paul, MN......................800-328-9680
Ramsen Inc
Lakeville, MN....................952-431-0400
Rv Industries
Buford, GA......................770-729-8983
Saint Albans Cooperative Creamery
Saint Albans, VT................802-524-6581
Thymly Products Inc
Colora, MD......................877-710-2340
United Dairymen of Arizona
Tempe, AZ........................480-966-7211
Vance's Foods
San Francisco, CA................415-621-1171
Weinberg Foods
Kirkland, WA....................800-866-3447
Welsh Farms
Wallington, NJ..................800-221-0663
Westin Foods
Omaha, NE........................800-228-6098

Molasses

Rogers Sugar Inc.
Montreal, QC....................514-527-8686
Smolich Bros. Home Made Sausage
Crest Hill, IL..................815-727-2144

Mustard

Kathy's Gourmet Specialties
Mendocino, CA....................707-937-1383

Onion (See also Spices/Onion Powder)

Advanced Spice & Trading
Carrollton, TX..................800-872-7811
American Key Food Products Inc
Closter, NJ......................877-263-7539
Con Yeager Spice Co
Zelienople, PA..................800-222-2460
Emerling International Foods
Buffalo, NY......................716-833-7381
Erba Food Products
Brooklyn, NY....................718-272-7700
Gel Spice Co LLC
Bayonne, NJ....................800-922-0230
Texas Coffee Co
Beaumont, TX....................800-259-3400
Vegetable Juices Inc
Chicago, IL......................888-776-9752

Pau D'Arco Bark

Asiamerica Ingredients
Westwood, NJ....................201-497-5531
RFi Ingredients
Blauvelt, NY....................800-962-7663

Peanut Butter

Crazy Richard's
Dublin, OH......................614-889-4824

Prepared for Further Processing

Akay USA LLC
Sayreville, NJ..................732-254-7177

Protein

Clif Bar & Co
Emeryville, CA..................802-254-3227
Fonterra Co-operative Group Limited
Chicago, IL......................888-869-6455
Kiss My Keto
Los Angeles, CA..................310-765-1553
Lekithos
Palm Beach Gardens, FL
LonoLife
Oceanside, CA....................855-843-8566
Onnit Labs
Austin, TX......................855-666-4899
Terra Origin, Inc.
Hauppauge, NY....................631-300-2306

Universal Nutrition
New Brunswick, NJ 800-872-0101
Wisconsin Specialty Protein
Madison, WI
Zego Foods
San Francisco, CA 415-706-8094

Saw Palmetto Berry

Asiamerica Ingredients
Westwood, NJ 201-497-5531
RFi Ingredients
Blauvelt, NY 800-962-7663

Seafood

American Key Food Products Inc
Closter, NJ. 877-263-7539
Flavor House, Inc.
Adelanto, CA 760-246-9131

Seasoning

Advanced Food Services
Lenexa, KS 913-888-8088
American Key Food Products Inc
Closter, NJ. 877-263-7539
Gel Spice Co LLC
Bayonne, NJ 800-922-0230
Magic Seasoning Blends
New Orleans, LA 800-457-2857
Summit Hill Flavors
Somerset, NJ. 732-805-0335
Vegetable Juices Inc
Chicago, IL 888-776-9752

Soy Milk

Cedar Lake Foods
Cedar Lake, MI. 800-246-5039

St. John's Wort

RFi Ingredients
Blauvelt, NY. 800-962-7663

Tofu

Aloha Tofu Factory Inc
Honolulu, HI. 808-845-2669
Clofine Dairy Products Inc
Linwood, NJ 609-653-1000
Dixie USA
Tomball, TX 800-233-3668

Tomato

Henry Broch & Co
Gurnee, IL. 847-816-6225

Valerian Root

Asiamerica Ingredients
Westwood, NJ. 201-497-5531
RFi Ingredients
Blauvelt, NY. 800-962-7663

Vanilla

Agri-Dairy Products
Purchase, NY 914-697-9580
Carmi Flavor & Fragrance Company
Commerce, CA. 800-421-9647
Emerling International Foods
Buffalo, NY. 716-833-7381
H B Taylor Co
Chicago, IL 773-254-4805
Helm New York Chemical Corp
Piscataway, NJ 732-981-0528
Prime Ingredients Inc
Saddle Brook, NJ 888-791-6655
Sterling Extract Co Inc
Franklin Park, IL. 847-451-9728
Sunfood
El Cajon, CA. 888-729-3663
Whole Herb Co
Sonoma, CA 707-935-1077

Yogurt

Commercial Creamery Co
Spokane, WA. 509-747-4131
Kantner Group
Wapakoneta, OH. 877-738-3448
Maple Island
Saint Paul, MN 800-369-1022
Master Mix
Placentia, CA 714-524-1698

Quality Ingredients
Burnsville, MN 952-898-4002

Preservatives

Atlantic Chemicals Trading
Glendale, CA 818-246-0077
Emerald Performance Materials
Cuyahoga Falls, OH 330-916-6700
Escalade Limited
Huntington, NY 631-659-3373
Grace & I
Los Angeles, CA. 800-584-1736
Great Earth Chemical
Portland, OR 503-620-7130
Kenko International
Los Angeles, CA. 323-721-8300
Profood International
Naperville, IL 888-288-0081
Simply Panache
Hampton, VA 800-313-5613

Food

Brenntag North America
Reading, PA 610-926-6100
Cargill Inc.
Minneapolis, MN 800-227-4455
Emerald Kalama Chemical, LLC
Kalama, WA 800-223-0035
FBC Industries
Schaumburg, IL. 888-322-4637
Hosemen & Roche Vitamins & Fine Chemicals
Nutley, NJ 800-526-6367
Hurd Orchards
Holley, NY 585-638-8838
Jarchem Industries
Newark, NJ 973-578-4560
Jungbunzlauer Inc
Newton, MA 617-969-0900
Kent Precision Foods Group Inc
Muscatine, IA 800-442-5242
Macco Organiques
Valleyfield, QC 450-371-1066
Nutricepts
Burnsville, MN 800-949-9060
Parish Chemical Company
Orem, UT 801-226-2018
PMC Specialties Group Inc
Cincinnati, OH 800-543-2466
Shekou Chemicals
Waltham, MA 781-893-6878
Silver Fern Chemical Inc
Seattle, WA. 866-282-3384
Tasty Mix Quality Foods
Brooklyn, NY 718-855-7680
Universal Preservachem Inc
Somerset, NJ. 732-568-1266
Wisconsin Wilderness Food Products
Lake Bluff, IL 800-359-3039

Proteins

AME Nutrition
Dublin, OH 614-766-3638
American Pasien Co
Burlington, NJ. 609-387-3130
BioExx Specialty Proteins
Toronto, ON 416-588-4442
Clara Foods
San Francisco, CA
Clofine Dairy Products Inc
Linwood, NJ 609-653-1000
Essentia Protein Solutions
Ankeny, IA 515-289-5100
Fonterra Co-operative Group Limited
Chicago, IL. 888-869-6455
Ingredia Inc
Wapakoneta, OH. 419-738-4060
International Food Products
Fenton, MO. 800-227-8427
Kantner Group
Wapakoneta, OH. 877-738-3448
Milk Specialties Global
Eden Prairie, MN 952-942-7310

Releases

Food

Barlean's Fisheries
Ferndale, WA 360-384-0325
Capri Bagel & Pizza Corporation
Brooklyn, NY 718-497-4431

Cloud Nine
Claremont, CA 909-624-3147
Corn Popper
Tulsa, OK 918-250-9317
Desert King International
San Diego, CA 800-982-2235
EcoNatural Solutions
Boulder, CO 303-357-5682
Ferris Organic Farms
Eaton Rapids, MI 800-628-8736
Flavorganics
Newark, NJ 866-972-6879
Ingredient Innovations
Kansas City, MO. 816-587-1426
Jewel Date Co
Thermal, CA 760-399-4474
Leech Lake Wild Rice
Cass Lake, MN 218-335-8200
Lone Pine Enterprise Inc
Carlisle, AR 870-552-3217
Lowell Farms
El Campo, TX. 888-484-9213
Marantha Natural Foods
San Francisco, CA 866-972-6879
Martha Olson's Great Foo
Sutter Creek, CA. 800-973-3966
Montana Specialty Mills LLC
Great Falls, MT. 800-332-2024
Nicola Valley Apiaries
Merritt, BC 250-378-5208
S & E Organic Farms Inc
Bakersfield, CA 661-325-2644
Southern Brown Rice
Weiner, AR 800-421-7423
Stengel Seed & Grain Co
Milbank, SD 605-432-6030
Sunnyland Mills
Fresno, CA 800-501-8017
Top Hat Co Inc
Wilmette, IL 847-256-6565
US Mills
Bala Cynwyd, PA 800-422-1125

Replacers

Savoury Systems Inc
Branchburg, NJ. 888-534-6621

Egg

Clara Foods
San Francisco, CA

Fat

Edlong Corporation
Elk Grove Village, IL 847-631-6700
Epogee
Indianapolis, IN

Raisin Juice

Dry

Cajun Brands
New Iberia, LA. 504-408-2252

Sodium

Asiamerica Ingredients
Westwood, NJ. 201-497-5531
Erie Foods Intl Inc
Erie, IL 309-659-2233
Gum Technology Corporation
Tucson, AZ 800-369-4867
International Food Products
Fenton, MO. 800-227-8427
Jungbunzlauer Inc
Newton, MA 617-969-0900
Nu-Tek Food Science
Minnetouka, MN. 952-683-7580
Nutricepts
Burnsville, MN 800-949-9060
PMP Fermentation Products
Peoria, IL. 800-558-1031
Trumark
Linden, NJ. 800-752-7877

Sodium Alginates

Asiamerica Ingredients
Westwood, NJ. 201-497-5531
Gum Technology Corporation
Tucson, AZ 800-369-4867

PLT Health Solutions Inc
Morristown, NJ....................973-984-0900
TIC Gums
Belcamp, MD....................800-899-3953

Sodium Benzoate

Agri-Dairy Products
Purchase, NY....................914-697-9580
Asiamerica Ingredients
Westwood, NJ....................201-497-5531
Cargill Inc.
Minneapolis, MN....................800-227-4455
Emerald Kalama Chemical, LLC
Kalama, WA....................800-223-0035
Jarchem Industries
Newark, NJ....................973-578-4560
Jungbunzlauer Inc
Newton, MA....................617-969-0900
Luyties Pharmacal Company
Saint Louis, MO....................800-325-8080
Shekou Chemicals
Waltham, MA....................781-893-6878
Silver Fern Chemical Inc
Seattle, WA....................866-282-3384
Universal Preservachem Inc
Somerset, NJ....................732-568-1266

Sodium Citrate

Asiamerica Ingredients
Westwood, NJ....................201-497-5531
Cargill Inc.
Minneapolis, MN....................800-227-4455
International Chemical Corp
Melbourne, FL....................800-914-2436
Jungbunzlauer Inc
Newton, MA....................617-969-0900
Shekou Chemicals
Waltham, MA....................781-893-6878
Universal Preservachem Inc
Somerset, NJ....................732-568-1266

Sodium Lactate

Hawkins Inc
Roseville, MN....................800-328-5460

Spirulina

Alternative Health & Herbs
Albany, OR....................800-345-4152
Asiamerica Ingredients
Westwood, NJ....................201-497-5531
Christopher's Herb Shop
Springville, UT....................888-372-4372
Cyanotech Corp
Kailua Kona, HI....................800-395-1353
Earth Circle Organics
Auburn, CA....................877-922-3663

Stabilizers

King Arthur Flour
Norwich, VT....................800-827-6836
Marukan Vinegar USA Inc.
Paramount, CA....................562-630-6060
PLT Health Solutions Inc
Morristown, NJ....................973-984-0900
Silvateam USA
Ontario, CA....................909-635-2870
Taiyo International Inc.
Minneapolis, MN....................763-398-3003
Tate & Lyle PLC
Hoffman Estates, IL....................847-396-7500
TIC Gums
Belcamp, MD....................800-899-3953
Watson Inc
West Haven, CT....................800-388-3481
Wenda America Inc
Naperville, IL....................844-999-3632

Lecithinated

Agri-Dairy Products
Purchase, NY....................914-697-9580
Arnhem Group
Cranford, NJ....................800-851-1052
New Organics
Kenwood, CA....................734-677-5570
Universal Preservachem Inc
Somerset, NJ....................732-568-1266

Yogurt

Johanna Foods Inc.
Flemington, NJ....................800-727-6700
Maple Island
Saint Paul, MN....................800-369-1022

Starches

Anderson Custom Processing
New Ulm, MN....................877-588-4950
Cargill Inc.
Minneapolis, MN....................800-227-4455
Evergreen Sweeteners, Inc
Hollywood, FL....................954-381-7776
Marroquin Organic Intl.
Santa Cruz, CA....................831-423-3442
Marsan Foods
Toronto, ON....................416-755-9262
National Starch Food Innovation
Bridgewater, NJ....................800-743-6343
Norben Co
Willoughby, OH....................888-466-7236
Raymond-Hadley Corporation
Spencer, NY....................800-252-5220
Roquette America Inc.
Geneva, IL....................630-463-9430
Seydel Co
Pendergrass, GA....................706-693-2266
St. Lawrence Starch
Mississauga, ON....................905-271-8396
Tate & Lyle PLC
Hoffman Estates, IL....................847-396-7500
Westin Foods
Omaha, NE....................800-228-6098

Arrowroot

American Key Food Products Inc
Closter, NJ....................877-263-7539

Corn

American Key Food Products Inc
Closter, NJ....................877-263-7539
Evergreen Sweeteners, Inc
Hollywood, FL....................954-381-7776
GloryBee
Eugene, OR....................800-456-7923
Grain Processing Corp
Muscatine, IA....................800-448-4472
Hodgson Mill Inc
Effingham, IL....................800-347-0198
Ingredion Inc.
Westchester, IL....................800-713-0208
International Food Products
Fenton, MO....................800-227-8427
Meelunie America
Farmington Hills, MI....................248-473-2100
Mills Brothers Intl
Seattle, WA....................206-575-3000
Nacan Products
Brampton, ON....................905-454-4466
New Organics
Kenwood, CA....................734-677-5570
Westin Foods
Omaha, NE....................800-228-6098

Dextrin

Seydel Co
Pendergrass, GA....................706-693-2266

Potato

Homefree LLC
Windham, NH....................800-552-7172
International Food Products
Fenton, MO....................800-227-8427
King Arthur Flour
Norwich, VT....................800-827-6836
VCPB Transportation
Secaucus, NJ....................201-770-0070

Rice

American Key Food Products Inc
Closter, NJ....................877-263-7539
Avebe America Inc.
Cranbury, NJ....................609-865-8981
International Food Products
Fenton, MO....................800-227-8427

Tapioca

Homefree LLC
Windham, NH....................800-552-7172
King Arthur Flour
Norwich, VT....................800-827-6836

Wheat

Caremoli USA
Ames, IA....................515-233-1255
International Food Products
Fenton, MO....................800-227-8427

Surfactants & Solubilizers

Stepan Co.
Northfield, IL....................847-446-7500

Solubilizers

PLT Health Solutions Inc
Morristown, NJ....................973-984-0900

Sweeteners

Agri-Dairy Products
Purchase, NY....................914-697-9580
Atlantic Chemicals Trading
Glendale, CA....................818-246-0077
Catherych
Warren, NJ....................732-566-6625
Dulcette Technologies
Lindenhurst, NY....................631-752-8700
Escalade Limited
Huntington, NY....................631-659-3373
Evergreen Sweeteners, Inc
Hollywood, FL....................954-381-7776
GLG Life Tech Corporation
Vancouver, BC....................604-669-2602
GLG Life Tech Corporation
Richmond, BC....................855-454-7587
H&A Health Products, Inc
Richmond Hill, ON....................514-979-3589
Helm New York Chemical Corp
Piscataway, NJ....................732-981-0528
Ingredient Specialties
Exeter, CA....................559-594-4380
International Food Products
Fenton, MO....................800-227-8427
J M Swank Co
North Liberty, IA....................800-593-6375
Kenko International
Los Angeles, CA....................323-721-8300
Log House Foods
Plymouth, MN....................763-546-8395
Louisiana Sugar Cane Cooperative
St Martinville, LA....................337-394-3785
Marroquin Organic Intl.
Santa Cruz, CA....................831-423-3442
Natur Sweeteners, Inc.
Los Angeles, CA....................310-445-0020
NOW Foods
Bloomingdale, IL....................888-669-3663
Rare Hawaiian Honey Company
Kamuela, HI....................888-663-6639
Rio Naturals
El Dorado Hills, CA....................916-719-4514
Stauber Performance Ingrdients
Fullerton, CA....................888-441-4233
Sweet'N Low
Brooklyn, NY
Sweetleaf Co
Gilbert, AZ....................480-921-2160
Techno Food Ingredients Co., Ltd
San Gabriel, CA....................626-288-8478
Wenda America Inc
Naperville, IL....................844-999-3632
Wildly Organic
Silver Bay, MN....................800-945-3801

Dextrose

Agri-Dairy Products
Purchase, NY....................914-697-9580
Cargill Inc.
Minneapolis, MN....................800-227-4455
Evergreen Sweeteners, Inc
Hollywood, FL....................954-381-7776
Ingredion Inc.
Westchester, IL....................800-713-0208
Malt Diastase Co
Saddle Brook, NJ....................800-526-0180
Roquette America Inc.
Geneva, IL....................630-463-9430

Westin Foods
Omaha, NE 800-228-6098

Lactose

Agri-Dairy Products
Purchase, NY 914-697-9580
Asiamerica Ingredients
Westwood, NJ 201-497-5531
Blossom Farm Products
Ridgewood, NJ 800-729-1818
Century Foods Intl LLC
Sparta, WI 800-269-1901
Clofine Dairy Products Inc
Linwood, NJ 609-653-1000
First District Association
Litchfield, MN 320-693-3236
Grande Custom Ingredients Group
Fond du Lac, WI 800-772-3210
Hilmar Ingredients
Hilmar, CA 888-300-4465
Leprino Foods Co.
Denver, CO 800-537-7466
Main Street Ingredients
La Crosse, WI 800-359-2345
Universal Preservachem Inc
Somerset, NJ 732-568-1266

Sorbitol

Agri-Dairy Products
Purchase, NY 914-697-9580
Asiamerica Ingredients
Westwood, NJ 201-497-5531
Roquette America Inc.
Geneva, IL 630-463-9430
Universal Preservachem Inc
Somerset, NJ 732-568-1266

Tenderizers

3V Company
Brooklyn, NY 718-858-7333
AM Todd Co
Kalamazoo, MI 269-343-2603
Dean Distributors, Inc.
Burlingame, CA 800-792-0816
Phamous Phloyd's Barbecue
Denver, CO 800-497-3281
Sentry Seasonings
Elmhurst, IL 630-530-5370
W.T.I.
Jefferson, GA 800-827-1727

Meat

3V Company
Brooklyn, NY 718-858-7333
Alltech Inc
Nicholasville, KY 859-885-9613
AM Todd Co
Kalamazoo, MI 269-343-2603
American Key Food Products Inc
Closter, NJ 877-263-7539
Custom Culinary Inc.
Schaumberg, IL 800-621-8827
Enzyme Development Corporation
New York, NY 212-736-1580
Oregon Flavor Rack
Sentry Seasonings
Elmhurst, IL 630-530-5370
Texas Coffee Co
Beaumont, TX 800-259-3400
World Flavors Inc
Warminster, PA 215-672-4400

Thickeners

Gelnex Gelatins
Chicago, IL 312-577-4275

Gelatin

Asiamerica Ingredients
Westwood, NJ 201-497-5531
Cangel
Toronto, ON 800-267-4795
Con Yeager Spice Co
Zelienople, PA 800-222-2460
Erba Food Products
Brooklyn, NY 718-272-7700
First Food Co
Dallas, TX 800-527-1866
Gelita North America
Sergeant Bluff, IA 800-223-9244
Gelnex Gelatins
Chicago, IL 312-577-4275
Golden Fluff Popcorn Co
Lakewood, NJ 732-367-5448
Inter-American Products
Cincinnati, OH 800-645-2233
Marquez Brothers International
Hanford, CA 800-858-1119
Milligan & Higgins
Johnstown, NY 518-762-4638
Nature's Products Inc
Sunrise, FL 800-752-7873
Nitta Gelatin NA
Morrisville, NC 800-278-7680
PB Leiner USA
Plainview, NY 516-822-4040
Protica Inc
Whitehall, PA 800-776-8422
Qualicaps Inc
Whitsett, NC 800-227-7853
Rousselot Inc
Mukwonago, WI 888-455-3556
SKW Nature Products
Langhorne, PA 215-702-1000
Spring Glen Fresh Foods
Ephrata, PA 800-641-2853
Tessenderlo Kerley Inc
Phoenix, AZ 800-669-0559
Tova Industries LLC
Louisville, KY 888-532-8682
Vital Proteins LLC
Elk Grove Village, IL 224-544-9110
Vyse Gelatin Co
Schiller Park, IL 800-533-2152
White Coffee Corporation
Long Island City, NY 800-221-0140

Toppings

Al-Rite Fruits & Syrups Co
Miami, FL 305-652-2540
Bake N Joy Foods
North Andover, MA 800-666-4937
Baldwin Richardson Foods
Oakbrook Terrace, IL 866-644-2732
Consolidated Mills Inc
Houston, TX 713-896-4196
Dark Tickle Company
St Lunaire-Griquet, NL 709-623-2354
Golden State Foods Corp
Irvine, CA 949-247-8000
Gumpert's Canada
Mississauga, ON 800-387-9324
Instant Products of America
Columbus, IN 812-372-9100
Kerry Foodservice
Mansfield, OH 800-533-2722
Paulaur Corp
Cranbury, NJ 609-395-8844
Phillips Syrup Corp
Cleveland, OH 800-350-8443
Presto Avoset Group
Claremont, CA 909-399-0062
Scala-Wisell International Inc.
Floral Park, NY 516-437-8600
Shine Companies
Spring, TX 281-353-8392

Cakes & Donuts

Signature Brands LLC
Ocala, FL 800-456-9573

Confectionery

Paulaur Corp
Cranbury, NJ 609-395-8844
Ribble Production
Warminster, PA 215-674-1706

Crunch

American Almond Products Co
Brooklyn, NY 800-825-6663
Paulaur Corp
Cranbury, NJ 609-395-8844

Dessert

3V Company
Brooklyn, NY 718-858-7333
Al-Rite Fruits & Syrups Co
Miami, FL 305-652-2540
American Almond Products Co
Brooklyn, NY 800-825-6663
American Classic Ice Cream Company
Bay Shore, NY 800-736-4100
Aunt Aggie De's Pralines
Sinton, TX 800-333-9354
Baldwin Richardson Foods
Oakbrook Terrace, IL 866-644-2732
Brighams
Arlington, MA 800-242-2423
Calhoun Bend Mill
Libuse, LA 800-519-6455
California Balsamic Inc
Ukiah, CA 888-644-5127
California Custom Foods
Fullerton, CA 714-870-0490
California Custom Fruits
Baldwin Park, CA 877-558-0056
Carole's Cheesecake Company
Toronto, ON 416-256-0000
Chocolaterie Bernard Callebaut
Calgary, AB 800-661-8367
Conagra Brands Inc
Chicago, IL 877-266-2472
Conagra Foodservice
Chicago, IL 877-266-2472
Consolidated Mills Inc
Houston, TX 713-896-4196
Country Fresh Food & Confections, Inc.
Oliver Springs, TN 800-545-8782
Creme Unlimited
Matteson, IL 800-227-3637
Durkee-Mower
Lynn, MA 781-593-8007
Felbro Food Products
Los Angeles, CA 323-936-5266
Gold Coast Ingredients
Commerce, CA 800-352-8673
Golden West Fruit Company
Commerce, CA 323-726-9419
H Fox & Co Inc
Brooklyn, NY 718-385-4600
Hanan Products Co
Hicksville, NY 516-938-1000
Homemade By Dorothy Boise
Boise, ID 800-657-7449
I Rice & Co Inc
Philadelphia, PA 800-232-6022
Instant Products of America
Columbus, IN 812-372-9100
Instantwhip Foods Inc
Columbus, OH 800-544-9447
J.M. Smucker Co.
Orrville, OH 888-550-9555
JER Creative Food Concepts, Inc.
Commerce, CA 800-350-2462
Jogue Inc
Northville, MI 800-531-3888
Johnson's Food Products
Dorchester, MA 617-265-3400
Kraus & Co
Irvine, CA 800-662-5871
Lyons Magnus
Fresno, CA 800-344-7130
Masterson Co Inc
Milwaukee, WI 414-647-1132
Michigan Desserts
Oak Park, MI 800-328-8632
Newport Flavours & Fragrances
Orange, CA 714-744-3700
Oak State Products Inc
Wenona, IL 815-853-4348
Oregon Hill Farms
St Helens, OR 800-243-4541
Parker Products
Fort Worth, TX 817-336-7441
Paulaur Corp
Cranbury, NJ 609-395-8844
Pearson's Berry Farm
Bowden, AB 403-224-3011
Pecan Deluxe Candy Co
Dallas, TX 800-733-3589
Phillips Syrup Corp
Cleveland, OH 800-350-8443
Rich Products Corp
Buffalo, NY 800-828-2021
Rosebrand Corp
Brooklyn, NY 800-854-5356
Rowena
Norfolk, VA 800-627-8699
Sea Breeze Fruit Flavors
Towaco, NJ 800-732-2733
Somebody's Mother's Chocolate
Houston, TX 713-627-3055

Sonoma Syrup Co. Inc.
Sonoma, CA 707-996-4070
Spruce Mountain Blueberries
West Rockport, ME................ 207-236-3538
Steel's Gourmet Foods, Ltd.
Bridgeport, PA 800-678-3357
Swatt Baking Co
Olean, NY......................... 800-370-6656
The Great San Saba River Pecan Company
San Saba, TX 800-621-8121
Tiller Foods Company
Dayton, OH......................... 937-435-4601
Tom & Sally's Handmade Chocolates
Brattleboro, VT.................... 800-827-0800
Tone Products Inc
Melrose Park, IL................... 800-536-8663
Top Hat Co Inc
Wilmette, IL 847-256-6565
Tropical Foods
Lithia Springs, GA 800-544-3762
Valley Grain Products
Fresno, CA 559-675-3400
Wax Orchards
Seattle, WA........................ 800-634-6132
Western Syrup Company
Santa Fe Springs, CA 562-921-4485
White-Stokes Company
Chicago, IL 800-978-6537
Williamsburg Chocolatier
Williamsburg, VA 757-253-1474

Fruit

E.D. Smith Foods Ltd
Hamilton, ON 905-573-1207

Meringue

Zuccaro Produce
Columbia Heights, MN............. 612-333-1122

Sprinkles

Erba Food Products
Brooklyn, NY 718-272-7700
King Arthur Flour
Norwich, VT 800-827-6836
Weaver Nut Co. Inc.
Ephrata, PA........................ 800-473-2688

Whipped

Bunge Canada
Oakville, ON....................... 905-825-7900
CanAmera Foods
Edmonton, AL....................... 780-447-6960
Fieldbrook Foods Corp.
Dunkirk, NY 800-333-0805
Johnson's Food Products
Dorchester, MA.................... 617-265-3400
Now & Zen
Louisville, CO..................... 800-779-6383
Rich Products Corp
Buffalo, NY........................ 800-828-2021
Schneider's Dairy Inc
Pittsburgh, PA..................... 412-881-3525
Tiller Foods Company
Dayton, OH......................... 937-435-4601

Dairy

Brighams
Arlington, MA 800-242-2423
Elgin Dairy Foods
Chicago, IL 800-786-9900
Instantwhip Foods Inc
Columbus, OH 800-544-9447
Johnson's Food Products
Dorchester, MA.................... 617-265-3400

Non-Dairy

Elgin Dairy Foods
Chicago, IL 800-786-9900
Instantwhip Foods Inc
Columbus, OH 800-544-9447
Johnson's Food Products
Dorchester, MA.................... 617-265-3400

Vitamins & Supplements

Aloecorp, Inc.
Seattle, WA........................ 800-458-2563
Embria Health Sciences
Ankeny, IA 877-362-7421
Fallwood Corp
White Plains, NY 914-304-4065
Fenchem Inc
Chino, CA.......................... 909-597-1113
Great Earth Chemical
Portland, OR....................... 503-620-7130
Latitude, LTD
Huntington, NY 631-659-3374

A

Asiamerica Ingredients
Westwood, NJ....................... 201-497-5531
Banner Pharmacaps
High Point, NC..................... 800-526-6993
Dong Us I
Irvine, CA......................... 888-580-0088
Ganeden, Inc
Mayfield Hts, OH 440-229-5200
New Hope Natural Media
Boulder, CO 303-939-8440
Synergy Plus
Freehold, NJ 732-308-3000

B1 - Thiamine

Prinova
Carol Stream, IL................... 630-868-0300

B12

Prinova
Carol Stream, IL................... 630-868-0300

B2 - Riboflavin

Prinova
Carol Stream, IL................... 630-868-0300

B5

Prinova
Carol Stream, IL................... 630-868-0300

B6 - Pyridoxine

Prinova
Carol Stream, IL................... 630-868-0300

Beta Carotene

Asiamerica Ingredients
Westwood, NJ....................... 201-497-5531

Biotin

Asiamerica Ingredients
Westwood, NJ....................... 201-497-5531

C

Asiamerica Ingredients
Westwood, NJ....................... 201-497-5531
Childlife
Culver City, CA 800-993-0332
Marlyn Nutraceuticals
Phoenix, AZ 800-899-4499
Prinova
Carol Stream, IL................... 630-868-0300

Ascorbic Acid

World Ginseng Ctr Inc
San Francisco, CA 800-747-8808

Calcium

Allied Custom Gypsum Company
Norman, OK......................... 800-624-5963
American Micronutrients
Independence, MO 816-252-1060
Asiamerica Ingredients
Westwood, NJ....................... 201-497-5531
Specialty Minerals Inc
Bethlehem, PA 800-801-1031

E - Tocopherol

Asiamerica Ingredients
Westwood, NJ....................... 201-497-5531
World Ginseng Ctr Inc
San Francisco, CA 800-747-8808

Inositol

Asiamerica Ingredients
Westwood, NJ....................... 201-497-5531
Tabco Enterprises
Pomona, CA 909-623-4565

Medical Nutritionals

Alternative Health & Herbs
Albany, OR......................... 800-345-4152
Apotheca Inc
Woodbine, IA 800-736-3130
Asiamerica Ingredients
Westwood, NJ....................... 201-497-5531
Atrium Biotech
Quebec, QC......................... 418-652-1116
Brenntag North America
Reading, PA 610-926-6100
Champion Nutrition Inc
Sunrise, FL 800-225-4831
Chattem Chemicals Inc
Chattanooga, TN.................... 423-822-5000
Eatem Foods Co
Vineland, NJ 800-683-2836
Green Turtle Bay Vitamin Company
Summit, NJ......................... 800-887-8535
Penta Manufacturing Company
Livingston, NJ..................... 973-740-2300
Tova Industries LLC
Louisville, KY 888-532-8682
Westar Nutrition Corporation
Costa Mesa, CA 800-645-1868

Mineral Blends

Asiamerica Ingredients
Westwood, NJ....................... 201-497-5531
Coral LLC
Carson City, NV 800-882-9577
M-CAP Technologies
Wilmington, DE 302-695-5329
World Nutrition, Inc.
Scottsdale, AZ..................... 800-548-2710

Minerals

Acta Health Products
Sunnyvale, CA 408-732-6830
ADH Health Products Inc
Congers, NY........................ 845-268-0027
Alacer Corp
Carlisle, PA....................... 888-425-2362
Alta Health Products
Idaho City, ID 800-423-4155
Ameri-Kal Inc
Wichita Falls, TX 940-322-5400
Anabol Naturals
Santa Cruz, CA..................... 800-426-2265
Asiamerica Ingredients
Westwood, NJ....................... 201-497-5531
Beverly International
Cold Spring, KY.................... 800-781-3475
Bio-Tech Pharmacal Inc
Fayetteville, AR 800-345-1199
Brenntag North America
Reading, PA 610-926-6100
Champion Nutrition Inc
Sunrise, FL........................ 800-225-4831
Childlife
Culver City, CA 800-993-0332
Coral LLC
Carson City, NV 800-882-9577
Designed Nutritional Products
Orem, UT 801-224-4518
DSM Fortitech Premixes
Schenectady, NY
Eidon
Poway, CA.......................... 800-700-1169
Grow Co
Ridgefield, NJ..................... 201-941-8777
Healthy N Fit International
Croton On Hudson, NY 800-338-5200
Herbal Products & Development
Aptos, CA.......................... 831-688-8706
J R Carlson Laboratories Inc
Arlington Heights, IL 888-234-5656
Jamieson Laboratories
Windsor, ON........................ 800-265-5088
Jungbunzlauer Inc
Newton, MA......................... 617-969-0900
Marlyn Nutraceuticals
Phoenix, AZ 800-899-4499
Michael's Naturopathic Prgms
San Antonio, TX.................... 800-845-2730
Milwhite Inc
Brownsville, TX 800-442-0082
Naturalife Laboratories
Torrance, CA....................... 800-231-3670
Nature Most Laboratories
Middletown, CT 800-234-2112

Nature's Bounty Co.
Ronkonkoma, NY 877-774-3361
Nature's Sunshine Products Company
Lehi, UT 800-223-8225
NOW Foods
Bloomingdale, IL 888-669-3663
Nutricepts
Burnsville, MN 800-949-9060
Nutritech Corporation
Santa Barbara, CA 800-235-5727
Nutrition 21 Inc
Purchase, NY 914-701-4500
Particle Dynamics
Saint Louis, MO 800-452-4682
Performance Labs
Calabasas, CA 800-848-2537
PLT Health Solutions Inc
Morristown, NJ 973-984-0900
PMP Fermentation Products
Peoria, IL 800-558-1031
Pro Pac Labs
Ogden, UT 888-277-6722
Protein Research
Livermore, CA 800-948-1991
Randal Optimal Nutrients
Santa Rosa, CA 800-221-1697
San Francisco Salt
Hayward, CA 800-480-4540
Seppic Inc
Fairfield, NJ 877-737-7421
Universal Formulas
Kalamazoo, MI 800-342-6960
US Foods & Pharmaceuticals Inc
Madison, WI 800-362-8294
USA Laboratories Inc
Burns, TN 800-489-4872

Niacin

Asiamerica Ingredients
Westwood, NJ 201-497-5531
Nu Naturals Inc
Eugene, OR 800-753-4372

Nutraceuticals

Amcan Industries
Elmsford, NY 914-347-4838
AquaTec Development
Sugar Land, TX 281-491-0808
Asiamerica Ingredients
Westwood, NJ 201-497-5531
BASF Corp.
Florham Park, NJ 800-526-1072
Bio-Foods
Pine Brook, NJ 973-808-5856
Bio-Tech Pharmacal Inc
Fayetteville, AR 800-345-1199
BioTech Corporation
Glastonbury, CT 800-886-9052
Brenntag North America
Reading, PA 610-926-6100
Century Foods Intl LLC
Sparta, WI 800-269-1901
Cyanotech Corp
Kailua Kona, HI 800-395-1353
Dulcette Technologies
Lindenhurst, NY 631-752-8700
Embria Health Sciences
Ankeny, IA 877-362-7421
Fallwood Corp
White Plains, NY 914-304-4065
Farbest-Tallman Foods Corp
Montvale, NJ 201-573-4900
GloryBee
Eugene, OR 800-456-7923
Jarrow Industries Inc
Santa Fe Springs, CA 562-906-1919
Lallemand Inc
Montreal, QC 800-452-4364
Natra US
Chula Vista, CA 800-262-6216
Naturex Inc
South Hackensack, NJ 201-440-5000
Nutraceutics Corp
St Louis, MO 877-664-6684
Nutranique Labs
Santa Rosa, CA 707-545-9017
PLT Health Solutions Inc
Morristown, NJ 973-984-0900
QBI
South Plainfield, NJ 908-668-0088
Soluble Products Company
Lakewood, NJ 732-364-8855
SoyLife Division
Edina, MN 952-920-7700
Trans-Packers Svc Corp
Brooklyn, NY 877-787-8837
Unique Ingredients LLC
Gold Canyon, AZ 480-983-2498
Vitakem Neutraceutical Inc
Smithtown, NY 855-837-0430
Vitarich Laboratories
Naples, FL 800-817-9999
Vivolac Cultures Corporation
Indianapolis, IN 317-356-8460
Westar Nutrition Corporation
Costa Mesa, CA 800-645-1868

Nutritional Supplements

ADH Health Products Inc
Congers, NY 845-268-0027
Alfer Laboratories
Chatsworth, CA 818-709-0737
Ameri-Kal Inc
Wichita Falls, TX 940-322-5400
American Health
Ronkonkoma, NY 800-445-7137
Anabol Naturals
Santa Cruz, CA 800-426-2265
Arizona Natural Products
Phoenix, AZ 800-255-2823
Arizona Nutritional Supplements
Chandler, AZ 888-742-7675
Asiamerica Ingredients
Westwood, NJ 201-497-5531
Atrium Biotech
Quebec, QC 418-652-1116
Belmont Chemicals
Clifton, NJ 800-722-5070
Bio-Foods
Pine Brook, NJ 973-808-5856
BioSynergy
Boise, ID 800-554-7145
Brickerlabs.Com
Chandler, AZ 800-274-2537
Bristol-Myers Squibb Co.
New York, NY 800-332-2056
Century Foods Intl LLC
Sparta, WI 800-269-1901
Champion Nutrition Inc
Sunrise, FL 800-225-4831
Cognis
Cincinnati, OH 800-526-1072
Cyanotech Corp
Kailua Kona, HI 800-395-1353
Dean Distributors, Inc.
Burlingame, CA 800-792-0816
Dr. Christopher's Herbal Supplements
Spanish Fork, UT 800-453-1406
Embria Health Sciences
Ankeny, IA 877-362-7421
Esteem Products
Bellevue, WA 800-255-7631
Fallwood Corp
White Plains, NY 914-304-4065
Food Sciences Corp
Mt Laurel, NJ 800-346-4422
Foodscience Corp
Essex Junction, VT 800-874-9444
Genisoy
San Francisco, CA 866-972-6879
Herbal Products & Development
Aptos, CA 831-688-8706
I-Health Inc
Cromwell, CT 800-990-3476
Klaire Laboratories
Reno, NV 888-488-2488
Lewis Laboratories International Ltd.
Southport, CT 800-243-6020
Lifestar Millennium
Sedona, AZ 877-422-4739
Lifestyle Health Guide
Cheyenne, WY 800-822-3712
Matrix Health Products
Santee, CA 888-736-5609
Mega Pro Intl
St George, UT 800-541-9469
Metagenics, Inc.
Aliso Viejo, CA 800-692-9400
Mushroom Wisdom, Inc
East Rutherford, NJ 800-747-7418
N D Labs
Lynbrook, NY 888-263-5227
Natural Balance
Englewood, CO 800-624-4260
Naturalife Laboratories
Torrance, CA 800-231-3670
Naturally Scientific
Leonia, NJ 888-428-0700
Nature's Best Inc
Hauppauge, NY 800-345-2378
Nature's Nutrition
Marysville, OH 800-242-1115
New Horizon Foods
Union City, CA 510-489-8600
Nurture
Devon, PA 888-395-3300
Nutrition Center Inc
Douglas, WY 800-443-3333
Nutrition Supply Corp
Liberty, TX 888-541-3997
Nutritional Labs Intl
Missoula, MT 406-273-5493
Nutritional Specialties
Orange, CA 800-333-6168
O'Donnell Formulas Inc
San Marcos, CA 800-736-1991
Orange Peel Enterprises
Vero Beach, FL 800-643-1210
P-Bee Products
Oak Harbor, WA 800-322-5572
Pacific Nutritional
Vancouver, WA 360-896-2297
Pacific Standard Distributors
Sandy, OR 760-479-1460
Performance Labs
Calabasas, CA 800-848-2537
Phoenician Herbals
Scottsdale, AZ 800-966-8144
Phyto-Technologies
Woodbine, IA 877-809-3404
Pioneer Nutritional Formula
Shelburne Falls, MA 800-458-8483
Premier Protein
Emeryville, CA 888-836-8977
Pro-Source Performance Prods
Manasquan, NJ 732-528-3260
Protein Research
Livermore, CA 800-948-1991
Randal Optimal Nutrients
Santa Rosa, CA 800-221-1697
Royal Products
Scottsdale, AZ 480-948-2509
Schiff Nutrition International
Parsippany, NJ 800-526-6251
Shaklee Corp
Pleasanton, CA 800-742-5533
Soft Cell Technology
Commerce, CA 800-360-7484
Solgar Vitamin & Herbal
Leonia, NJ 877-765-4274
St John's Botanicals
Bowie, MD 301-262-5302
Stimo-O-Stam, Ltd.
Covington, LA 800-562-7514
Tabco Enterprises
Pomona, CA 909-623-4565
Twinlab Corporation
Boca Raton, FL 800-645-5626
Uas Laboratories
Eden Prairie, MN 800-422-3371
USA Laboratories Inc
Burns, TN 800-489-4872
Vita-Pure Inc
Roselle, NJ 908-245-1212
Vitatech Nutritional Sciences
Tustin, CA 714-832-9700
Wakunaga Of America Co LTD
Mission Viejo, CA 800-421-2998
WCC Honey Marketing
City Of Industry, CA 626-855-3086
Wellesse
Ferndale, WA 800-232-4005
Wilke International Inc
Lenexa, KS 800-779-5545
World Ginseng Ctr Inc
San Francisco, CA 800-747-8808
Zone Perfect Nutrition Company
Columbus, OH 800-390-6690

Pantothenic Acid

Asiamerica Ingredients
Westwood, NJ 201-497-5531

Protein Supplements

Alkinco
New York, NY....800-424-7118
Asiamerica Ingredients
Westwood, NJ....201-497-5531
Belmont Chemicals
Clifton, NJ....800-722-5070
Bio-Foods
Pine Brook, NJ....973-808-5856
Croda Inc
Edison, NJ....732-417-0800
Designer Protein
Carlsbad, CA....800-337-4463
Energenetics International
Keokuk, IA....319-535-0760
Hilmar Ingredients
Hilmar, CA....888-300-4465
Mariner Neptune Fish & Seafood Company
Winnipeg, NB....800-668-8862
World Ginseng Ctr Inc
San Francisco, CA....800-747-8808

Supplements

Acta Health Products
Sunnyvale, CA....408-732-6830
ADH Health Products Inc
Congers, NY....845-268-0027
Agger Fish Corp
Brooklyn, NY....718-855-1717
Alfer Laboratories
Chatsworth, CA....818-709-0737
Alkinco
New York, NY....800-424-7118
Aloe Farms Inc
Harlingen, TX....800-262-6771
AMT Labs Inc
North Salt Lake, UT....801-294-3126
Anabol Naturals
Santa Cruz, CA....800-426-2265
Archon Vitamin Corp
Edison, NJ....800-848-0089
Arizona Natural Products
Phoenix, AZ....800-255-2823
Asiamerica Ingredients
Westwood, NJ....201-497-5531
Atrium Biotech
Quebec, QC....418-652-1116
Beehive Botanicals
Hayward, WI....800-233-4483
Belmont Chemicals
Clifton, NJ....800-722-5070
Bestco Inc
Mooresville, NC....704-664-4300
Brassica Protection Products
Baltimore, MD....866-747-0001
CactuLife, LLC
Corona Del Mar, CA....800-500-1713
Century Foods Intl LLC
Sparta, WI....800-269-1901
Champion Nutrition Inc
Sunrise, FL....800-225-4831
Christopher's Herb Shop
Springville, UT....888-372-4372
Clear Products Inc.
San Diego, CA....888-257-2532
Dean Distributors, Inc.
Burlingame, CA....800-792-0816
Deerland Probiotics & Enzymes
Kennesaw, GA....800-697-8179
Doctor's Best Inc
San Clemente, CA....800-333-6977
Eckhart Corporation
Novato, CA....800-200-4201
En Garde Health Products, Inc.
Van Nuys, CA....800-955-4633
GCI Nutrients
Foster City, CA....866-580-6549
Global Health Laboratories
Amityville, NY....631-777-2134
Good For You America
Concordia, MO....866-329-5969
Herbal Products & Development
Aptos, CA....831-688-8706
Heritage Books & Gifts
Virginia Beach, VA....800-862-2923
Hillestad Pharmaceuticals
Woodruff, WI....800-535-7742
International Vitamin Corporation
Freehold, NJ....800-666-8482
J R Carlson Laboratories Inc
Arlington Heights, IL....888-234-5656
Jo Mar Laboratories
Campbell, CA....800-538-4545
Kiss My Keto
Los Angeles, CA....310-765-1553
Lang Pharma Nutrition Inc
Middletown, RI....401-848-7700
LonoLife
Oceanside, CA....855-843-8566
Maju Superfoods
San Diego, CA....619-736-0622
Mantrose-Haeuser Co Inc
Westport, CT....800-344-4229
MegaFood
Manchester, NH....800-848-2542
Natural Balance
Englewood, CO....800-624-4260
Nature's Bounty Co.
Ronkonkoma, NY....877-774-3361
Nature's Herbs
Merritt, BC....800-437-2257
Nature's Plus
Melville, NY....800-645-9500
Nature's Provision Company
Olivebridge, NY....845-657-6020
Nature's Way
Green Bay, WI....800-962-8873
Navitas Naturals
Novato, CA....888-645-4282
New Chapter
Brattleboro, VT....800-543-7279
Nutraceutical International
Park City, UT....800-669-8877
Nutricepts
Burnsville, MN....800-949-9060
Nutritional Counselors of America
Spencer, TN....931-946-3600
Nutriwest
Douglas, WY....800-443-3333
O'Donnell Formulas Inc
San Marcos, CA....800-736-1991
Old Fashioned Natural Products
Santa Ana, CA....800-552-9045
Onnit Labs
Austin, TX....855-666-4899
Pharmavite LLC
Northridge, CA....800-276-2878
Pro Form Labs
Orinda, CA....707-752-9010
Protein Research
Livermore, CA....800-948-1991
Randal Optimal Nutrients
Santa Rosa, CA....800-221-1697
Rejuvila
Boulder, CO....877-480-4402
Source Naturals
Scotts Valley, CA....800-815-2333
Tova Industries LLC
Louisville, KY....888-532-8682
TruBrain
Santa Monica, CA....650-241-8372
Twinlab Corporation
Boca Raton, FL....800-645-5626
Universal Nutrition
New Brunswick, NJ....800-872-0101
Vit-Best Nutrition
Tustin, CA....714-832-9700
Vita-Pure Inc
Roselle, NJ....908-245-1212
Vitakem Neutraceutical Inc
Smithtown, NY....855-837-0430
Vital Choice
Bellingham, WA....800-608-4825
Vitamer Laboratories
Irvine, CA....800-432-8355
Vitaminerals
Glendale, CA....800-432-1856
Wakunaga Of America Co LTD
Mission Viejo, CA....800-421-2998
Wilke International Inc
Lenexa, KS....800-779-5545
World Organics Corporation
Huntington Beach, CA....714-893-0017

Minerals

AMT Labs Inc
North Salt Lake, UT....801-294-3126
Asiamerica Ingredients
Westwood, NJ....201-497-5531
Bestco Inc
Mooresville, NC....704-664-4300
BetterBody Foods & Nutrition LLC
Lindon, UT....866-404-6582
Jamieson Laboratories
Windsor, ON....800-265-5088
Matrix Health Products
Santee, CA....888-736-5609
Nutraceutical International
Park City, UT....800-669-8877
Nutricepts
Burnsville, MN....800-949-9060
Protein Research
Livermore, CA....800-948-1991
Randal Optimal Nutrients
Santa Rosa, CA....800-221-1697
Watson Inc
West Haven, CT....800-388-3481

Vitamins

AHD International, LLC
Atlanta, GA....404-233-4022
Asiamerica Ingredients
Westwood, NJ....201-497-5531
Foodscience Corp
Essex Junction, VT....800-874-9444
Freeda Vitamins Inc
Long Island City, NY....800-777-3737
Garcoa Laboratories Inc
Calabasas, CA....800-831-4247
Healthy N Fit International
Croton On Hudson, NY....800-338-5200
International Vitamin Corporation
Freehold, NJ....800-666-8482
Jamieson Laboratories
Windsor, ON....800-265-5088
MegaFood
Manchester, NH....800-848-2542
Nature's Way
Green Bay, WI....800-962-8873
Nhs Labs Inc
Star, ID....888-546-8694
Nutribiotic
Lakeport, CA....800-225-4345
Nutrilabs
San Francisco, CA....877-468-8745
Nutrisciences Labs
Farmingdale, NY....855-492-7388
Optimum Nutrition
Aurora, IL....800-763-3444
Protein Research
Livermore, CA....800-948-1991
Randal Optimal Nutrients
Santa Rosa, CA....800-221-1697
Sandco International
Northport, AL....800-382-2075
Scandinavian Formulas Inc
Sellersville, PA....800-288-2844
Solgar Vitamin & Herbal
Leonia, NJ....877-765-4274
Twinlab Corporation
Boca Raton, FL....800-645-5626
Vitatech Nutritional Sciences
Tustin, CA....714-832-9700
Watson Inc
West Haven, CT....800-388-3481
Wilke International Inc
Lenexa, KS....800-779-5545

Vitamins

21st Century Products, Inc.
Fort Worth, TX....817-284-8299
A.Vogel USA
Ghent, NY....800-641-7555
Abunda Life
Asbury Park, NJ....732-775-9338
Acta Health Products
Sunnyvale, CA....408-732-6830
Action Labs
Anaheim, CA....800-400-5696
ADH Health Products Inc
Congers, NY....845-268-0027
Agumm
Coral Springs, FL....954-344-0607
AHD International, LLC
Atlanta, GA....404-233-4022
Alacer Corp
Carlisle, PA....888-425-2362
Alfer Laboratories
Chatsworth, CA....818-709-0737
Alternative Health & Herbs
Albany, OR....800-345-4152
Ameri-Kal Inc
Wichita Falls, TX....940-322-5400

American Biosciences
Blauvelt, NY 888-884-7770
Anabol Naturals
Santa Cruz, CA 800-426-2265
Animal Pak
New Brunswick, NJ 800-872-0101
Anmar Nutrition
Bridgeport, CT 203-336-8330
Apotheca Inc
Woodbine, IA 800-736-3130
Apple Valley Market
Berrien Springs, MI 800-237-7436
Archon Vitamin Corp
Edison, NJ 800-848-0089
Argee Corp
Santee, CA 800-449-3030
Asiamerica Ingredients
Westwood, NJ 201-497-5531
At Last Naturals Inc
Valhalla, NY 800-527-8123
Atkins Nutritionals Inc.
Denver, CO 800-628-5467
Banner Pharmacaps
High Point, NC 800-526-6993
BASF Corp.
Florham Park, NJ 800-526-1072
Belmont Chemicals
Clifton, NJ 800-722-5070
Beverly International
Cold Spring, KY 800-781-3475
Bio-Tech Pharmacal Inc
Fayetteville, AR 800-345-1199
Botanical Products
Springville, CA 559-539-3432
Brenntag North America
Reading, PA 610-926-6100
Capsule Works
Ronkonkoma, NY 877-435-2277
Carob Tree
Arcadia, CA 626-445-0215
Champion Nutrition Inc
Sunrise, FL 800-225-4831
Childlife
Culver City, CA 800-993-0332
China Pharmaceutical Enterprises
Baton Rouge, LA 800-345-1658
Country Life
Hauppauge, NY 800-645-5768
CVC4Health
Vernon, CA 800-421-6175
Cyanotech Corp
Kailua Kona, HI 800-395-1353
De Souza's
Banning, CA 800-373-5171
Deerland Probiotics & Enzymes
Kennesaw, GA 800-697-8179
DMH Ingredients Inc
Libertyville, IL 847-362-9977
DSM Fortitech Premixes
Schenectady, NY
Dynapro International
Kaysville, UT 800-877-1413
Earth Science
Corona, CA 951-371-7565
Eckhart Corporation
Novato, CA 800-200-4201
Eclectic Institute
Sandy, OR 503-668-4120
Edom Labs Inc
Deer Park, NY 800-723-3366
Energen Products Inc
Norwalk, CA 800-423-8837
Enzymatic Therapy Inc
Green Bay, WI 800-783-2286
ERBL
Vista, CA 800-275-3725
Esteem Products
Bellevue, WA 800-255-7631
Europa Sports Products
Charlotte, NC 800-447-4795
Farbest-Tallman Foods Corp
Montvale, NJ 201-573-4900
Figuerola Laboratories
Santa Ynez, CA 800-219-1147
Fortress Systems LLC
Omaha, NE 888-331-6601
Freeda Vitamins Inc
Long Island City, NY 800-777-3737
Freeman Industries
Tuckahoe, NY 800-666-6454
Functional Products LLC
Atlantic Beach, FL 904-249-8074

Futurebiotics LLC
Hauppauge, NY 800-645-1721
G M P Laboratories Of Amer Inc
Anaheim, CA 714-630-2467
Garcoa Laboratories Inc
Calabasas, CA 800-831-4247
GCI Nutrients
Foster City, CA 866-580-6549
Goen Technologies Inc
Wilkes Barre, PA 800-467-3041
Graminex
Saginaw, MI 877-472-6469
Green Foods Corp.
Oxnard, CA 800-777-4430
Green Turtle Bay Vitamin Company
Summit, NJ 800-887-8535
Grow Co
Ridgefield, NJ 201-941-8777
H. Reisman Corporation
Orange, NJ 973-882-1670
Health Products Corp
Yonkers, NY 914-423-2900
Healthy N Fit International
Croton On Hudson, NY 800-338-5200
Helmuth Country Bakery Inc
Hutchinson, KS 800-567-6360
Herbal Products & Development
Aptos, CA 831-688-8706
Heritage Books & Gifts
Virginia Beach, VA 800-862-2923
Heterochemical Corp
Valley Stream, NY 516-561-8225
Highland Laboratories
Mount Angel, OR 888-717-4917
Hillestad Pharmaceuticals
Woodruff, WI 800-535-7742
Hosemen & Roche Vitamins & Fine Chemicals
Nutley, NJ 800-526-6367
I-Health Inc
Cromwell, CT 800-990-3476
Indiana Botanic Gardens Inc
Hobart, IN 877-909-1502
International Vitamin Corporation
Freehold, NJ 800-666-8482
J R Carlson Laboratories Inc
Arlington Heights, IL 888-234-5656
Jamieson Laboratories
Windsor, ON 800-265-5088
Jarrow Industries Inc
Santa Fe Springs, CA 562-906-1919
Kemin Industries Inc
Des Moines, IA 800-777-8307
Lang Pharma Nutrition Inc
Middletown, RI 401-848-7700
Leiner Health Products
Carson, CA 310-835-8400
Liberty Natural Products Inc
Oregon City, OR 800-289-8427
Luyties Pharmacal Company
Saint Louis, MO 800-325-8080
Madys Company
San Francisco, CA 415-822-2227
Marlyn Nutraceuticals
Phoenix, AZ 800-899-4499
Mega Pro Intl
St George, UT 800-541-9469
MegaFood
Manchester, NH 800-848-2542
Metabolic Nutrition
Tamarac, FL 800-626-1022
Metagenics, Inc.
Aliso Viejo, CA 800-692-9400
Michael's Naturopathic Prgms
San Antonio, TX 800-845-2730
Mission Pharmacal Company
San Antonio, TX 210-696-8400
Motherland International Inc
Rancho Cucamonga, CA 800-590-5407
Natural Food Supplements Inc
Canoga Park, CA 818-341-3375
Naturalife Laboratories
Torrance, CA 800-231-3670
Nature Most Laboratories
Middletown, CT 800-234-2112
Nature's Bounty Co.
Ronkonkoma, NY 877-774-3361
Nature's Sunshine Products Company
Lehi, UT 800-223-8225
New Chapter
Brattleboro, VT 800-543-7279
Northridge Laboratories
Chatsworth, CA 818-882-5622

NOW Foods
Bloomingdale, IL 888-669-3663
Noyes, P J
Lancaster, NH 800-522-2469
Nu Naturals Inc
Eugene, OR 800-753-4372
Nutraceutical International
Corpus Christi, TX 800-338-4788
Nutraceutical International
Park City, UT 800-669-8877
Nutraceutics Corp
St Louis, MO 877-664-6684
Nutri-Cell
Naples, FL 866-953-2355
Nutribiotic
Lakeport, CA 800-225-4345
Nutrilabs
San Francisco, CA 877-468-8745
Nutritech Corporation
Santa Barbara, CA 800-235-5727
Nutritional Counselors of America
Spencer, TN 931-946-3600
Nutritional Research Associates
South Whitley, IN 800-456-4931
Nutro Laboratories
South Plainfield, NJ 800-446-8876
O'Donnell Formulas Inc
San Marcos, CA 800-736-1991
Oc Lugo Co Inc
New City, NY 845-480-5121
Old Fashioned Natural Products
Santa Ana, CA 800-552-9045
Optimal Nutrients
Foster City, CA 707-528-1800
Ortho-Molecular Products Inc
Stevens Point, WI 800-332-2351
Pacific Nutritional
Vancouver, WA 360-896-2297
Parish Chemical Company
Orem, UT 801-226-2018
Particle Dynamics
Saint Louis, MO 800-452-4682
Pharmachem Laboratories
Kearny, NJ 800-526-0609
Phoenix Laboratories
Farmingdale, NY 800-236-6583
Pro Pac Labs
Ogden, UT 888-277-6722
Proper-Chem
Dix Hills, NY 631-420-8000
Protein Research
Livermore, CA 800-948-1991
Pure Source LLC
Doral, FL 800-324-6273
Randal Optimal Nutrients
Santa Rosa, CA 800-221-1697
SADKHIN Complex
Brooklyn, NY 800-723-5446
Sandco International
Northport, AL 800-382-2075
Scandinavian Formulas Inc
Sellersville, PA 800-288-2844
Select Supplements Inc
Carlsbad, CA 760-431-7509
Solgar Vitamin & Herbal
Leonia, NJ 877-765-4274
Source Naturals
Scotts Valley, CA 800-815-2333
Sportabs International
Los Angeles, CA 888-814-7767
Super Nutrition Life Extension
Fort Lauderdale, FL 800-678-8989
Tabco Enterprises
Pomona, CA 909-623-4565
Terra Botanica Products
Dahlonega, GA 770-718-9340
Texas Coffee Co
Beaumont, TX 800-259-3400
Thor Inc
Ogden, UT 888-846-7462
Twinlab Corporation
Boca Raton, FL 800-645-5626
Unique Vitality Products
Agoura Hills, CA 818-889-7739
USA Laboratories Inc
Burns, TN 800-489-4872
Vita-Pure Inc
Roselle, NJ 908-245-1212
Vitamer Laboratories
Irvine, CA 800-432-8355
Vitaminerals
Glendale, CA 800-432-1856

Vitamins
Chicago, IL 312-861-0700
Vitarich Laboratories
Naples, FL 800-817-9999
Wakunaga Of America Co LTD
Mission Viejo, CA 800-421-2998
Westar Nutrition Corporation
Costa Mesa, CA 800-645-1868
Whole Life Nutritional Supplements
North Hollywood, CA 800-748-5841
Wilke International Inc
Lenexa, KS 800-779-5545
World Ginseng Ctr Inc
San Francisco, CA 800-747-8808
World Nutrition, Inc.
Scottsdale, AZ 800-548-2710
World Organics Corporation
Huntington Beach, CA 714-893-0017
Wright Enrichment Inc
Crowley, LA 800-201-3096
Wysong Corp
Midland, MI 800-748-0188

Waxes

Lanaetex Products Incorporated
Elizabeth, NJ 908-351-9700

Paraffin

International Food Products
Fenton, MO 800-227-8427
Stevenson-Cooper Inc
Philadelphia, PA 215-223-2600

Rice

International Food Products
Fenton, MO 800-227-8427

Jams, Jellies & Spreads

Jams

A Taste of the Kingdom
Kingdom City, MO ... 888-592-5080
Alaska Herb & Tea Co
Anchorage, AK ... 800-654-2764
Algood Food Co
Louisville, KY ... 502-637-3631
Amberland Foods
Harvey, ND ... 800-950-4558
Andros Foods North America
Mount Jackson, VA ... 844-426-3767
Au Printemps Gourmet
Saint-Jerome, QC ... 800-438-6676
B & R Classics LLC
Huntington, NY ... 631-427-5675
BakeMark Ingredients Canada
Richmond, BC ... 800-665-9441
Bear Meadow Farm
Ashfield, MA ... 413-628-3970
Bear Stewart Corp
Chicago, IL ... 800-697-2327
Bella Vista Farm
Lawton, OK ... 866-237-8526
Benbow's Coffee Roasters
Bar Harbor, ME ... 207-288-2552
Blake Hill Preserves
Grafton, VT ... 802-289-1636
Blue Marble Brands
Providence, RI ... 888-534-0246
Bonnie's Jams
Cambridge, MA ... 617-714-5380
Brad's Organic
Haverstraw, NY ... 845-429-9080
Bread & Chocolate Inc
Wells River, VT ... 800-524-6715
BRINS
Brooklyn, NY
Buckhead Gourmet
Atlanta, GA ... 800-673-6338
Buonitalia
New York, NY ... 212-633-9090
Calamondin Cafe
Fort Myers, FL ... 239-288-5535
California Custom Fruits
Baldwin Park, CA ... 877-558-0056
Carol Hall's Hot Pepper Jelly
Fort Bragg, CA ... 866-737-7379
Carr Valley Cheese Company
La Valle, WI ... 800-462-7258
Chelsea Flower Market
New York, NY ... 888-727-7887
Choice of Vermont
Destin, FL ... 800-444-6261
Clements Foods Co
Oklahoma City, OK ... 800-654-8355
Coco Lopez Inc
Miramar, FL ... 800-341-2242
Colorado Mountain Jams & Jellies
Palisade, CO ... 970-464-0745
Cornabys
Spanish Fork, UT ... 801-830-4530
Cotswold Cottage Foods
Arvada, CO ... 800-208-1977
Crop Pharms, LLC
Staatsburg, NY ... 845-266-8999
Daregal
Princeton, NJ ... 609-375-2312
Dark Tickle Company
St Lunaire-Griquet, NL ... 709-623-2354
Deborah's Kitchen Inc.
Littleton, MA ... 617-216-9908
Delicae Gourmet
Tarpon Springs, FL ... 800-942-2502
Diane's Sweet Heat
McKinleyville, CA
Doral International
Bayside, NY ... 718-224-7413
Doves and Figs LLC
Arlington, MA ... 781-646-2272
E.D. Smith Foods Ltd
Hamilton, ON ... 905-573-1207
Eat This
Erwinna, PA ... 215-391-5807
EFCO Products Inc
Poughkeepsie, NY ... 800-284-3326
Eleanor's Best LLC
Garrison, NY ... 646-296-6870
Erba Food Products
Brooklyn, NY ... 718-272-7700
Family Food Company
Paramount, CA ... 310-715-2698
Fruit Fillings Inc
Fresno, CA ... 800-995-4514
Fruit of the Land Products
Thornhill, ON ... 877-311-5267
GEM Berry Products
Orofino, ID ... 888-231-1699
Heinz Portion Control
Jacksonville, FL ... 904-695-1300
Herb Bee's Products
Colchester, VT ... 802-864-7387
House of Webster
Rogers, AR ... 800-369-4641
Jim's Cheese Pantry
Waterloo, WI ... 800-345-3571
Just Jan's Inc.
Calabasas, CA ... 818-282-6236
Kozlowski Farms
Forestville, CA ... 800-473-2767
Lowcountry Produce
Raleigh, NC ... 800-935-2792
Mad River Farm Kitchen
Arcata, CA ... 707-822-0248
Manassero Farms
Irvine, CA ... 949-554-5103
Mardale Specialty Foods
Waukegan, IL ... 845-299-0285
Middlefield Cheese House
Middlefield, OH ... 800-327-9477
Mixon Fruit Farms Inc
Bradenton, FL ... 800-608-2525
National Grape Co-Op
Westfield, NY ... 800-340-6870
Nature's Hollow
Charleston, UT
New Canaan Farms
Dripping Springs, TX ... 800-727-5267
Oasis Food Co
Hillside, NJ ... 800-275-0477
Old Country Cheese
Cashton, WI ... 888-320-9469
Pacific Westcoast Foods
Beaverton, OR ... 800-874-9333
Peanut Butter & Co.
New York, NY ... 866-456-8372
Pemberton's Foods Inc
Gray, ME ... 800-255-8401
Potlicker Kitchen
Stowe, VT ... 802-760-6111
Reid Foods
Gurnee, IL ... 888-295-8478
Rowena
Norfolk, VA ... 800-627-8699
Sapore della Vita
Sarasota, FL ... 941-914-4256
Sargent's Bear Necessities
North Troy, VT ... 802-988-2903
Scott Hams
Greenville, KY ... 800-318-1353
Shawnee Canning Co
Cross Junction, VA ... 800-713-1414
Side Hill Farm
Brattleboro, VT ... 802-254-2018
Sidehill Farm
Brattleboro, VT ... 802-254-2018
Something Special Deli-Foods
Sherwood Park, AB ... 800-461-5892
Spruce Mountain Blueberries
West Rockport, ME ... 207-236-3538
Stanchfield Farms
Milo, ME ... 207-732-5173
Steel's Gourmet Foods, Ltd.
Bridgeport, PA ... 800-678-3357
Stonewall Kitchen
York, ME ... 800-826-1752
Summer In Vermont Jams
Hinesburg, VT ... 802-453-3793
Sunfresh Foods
Seattle, WA ... 800-669-9625
Sutter Buttes Olive Oil
Sutter, CA ... 530-763-7921
T.J. Blackburn Syrup Works
Jefferson, TX ... 800-657-5073
T.W. Garner Food Company
Winston Salem, NC ... 800-476-7383
TBJ Gourmet
West Chester, PA ... 856-222-2000
The Jam Stand
Brooklyn, NY ... 718-218-5194
Universal Impex Corporation
Toronto, ON ... 416-743-7778
Valley View Blueberries
Vancouver, WA ... 360-892-2839
Vermont Harvest Spec Food LLC
Stowe, VT ... 800-338-5354
Vista D'Oro Farms
Langley, BC ... 855-514-3539
Welch Foods Inc.
Concord, MA ... 800-340-6870
Willamette Valley Pie Co
Salem, OR ... 503-362-8857

Apricot

Allied Old English Inc
Port Reading, NJ ... 732-602-8955
Erba Food Products
Brooklyn, NY ... 718-272-7700

Grape

Allied Old English Inc
Port Reading, NJ ... 732-602-8955
T.W. Garner Food Company
Winston Salem, NC ... 800-476-7383

Strawberry

Allied Old English Inc
Port Reading, NJ ... 732-602-8955
Bear Stewart Corp
Chicago, IL ... 800-697-2327
Erba Food Products
Brooklyn, NY ... 718-272-7700
Knott's Berry Farms
Orrville, OH ... 866-828-5502
New Canaan Farms
Dripping Springs, TX ... 800-727-5267
T.W. Garner Food Company
Winston Salem, NC ... 800-476-7383

Jellies

Alaska Herb & Tea Co
Anchorage, AK ... 800-654-2764
Aloha From Oregon
Eugene, OR ... 800-241-0300
B & B Pecan Processors
Turkey, NC ... 866-328-7322
Bear Meadow Farm
Ashfield, MA ... 413-628-3970
Beetroot Delights
Foothill, ON ... 888-842-3387
Carr Valley Cheese Company
La Valle, WI ... 800-462-7258
Coco Lopez Inc
Miramar, FL ... 800-341-2242
Colorado Mountain Jams & Jellies
Palisade, CO ... 970-464-0745
Deborah's Kitchen Inc.
Littleton, MA ... 617-216-9908
Dundee Groves
Dundee, FL ... 800-294-2266
Just Jan's Inc.
Calabasas, CA ... 818-282-6236
Kettle Master
Hillsville, VA ... 276-728-7571
Low Country Produce
Lobeco, SC ... 800-935-2792
Lowcountry Produce
Raleigh, NC ... 800-935-2792
McIlhenny Company
Avery Island, LA ... 800-634-9599
Northeast Kingdom Mustard Company
Derby, VT ... 866-478-7388
Palmetto Canning
Palmetto, FL ... 941-722-1100
Pennacook Peppers
Virginia Beach, VA ... 757-663-8798

Potlicker Kitchen
Stowe, VT 802-760-6111

Shenk's Foods
Lancaster, PA 717-393-4240

Something Special Deli-Foods
Sherwood Park, AB 800-461-5892

Beets

Beetroot Delights
Foothill, ON 888-842-3387

Royal

Algood Food Co
Louisville, KY 502-637-3631

Bear Stewart Corp
Chicago, IL 800-697-2327

C C Pollen
Phoenix, AZ 800-875-0096

Campagna Distinct Flavor
Lebanon, OR 800-959-4372

Dawes Hill Honey Company
Nunda, NY 888-800-8075

Delicae Gourmet
Tarpon Springs, FL 800-942-2502

Fiesta Gourmet of Tejas
Canyon Lake, TX 800-585-8250

Herb Bee's Products
Colchester, VT 802-864-7387

Royal Resources
New Orleans, LA 800-888-9932

Sargent's Bear Necessities
North Troy, VT 802-988-2903

Stanchfield Farms
Milo, ME 207-732-5173

Summer In Vermont Jams
Hinesburg, VT 802-453-3793

Vermont Harvest Spec Food LLC
Stowe, VT 800-338-5354

WCC Honey Marketing
City Of Industry, CA 626-855-3086

Z Specialty Food, LLC
Woodland, CA 800-678-1226

Marmalades & Preserves

A Perfect Pear
Napa, CA 800-553-5753

A Southern Season
Hillsborough, NC 800-253-3663

Alaska Jacks
Anchorage, AK 888-660-2257

Algood Food Co
Louisville, KY 502-637-3631

Allied Old English Inc
Port Reading, NJ 732-602-8955

Amberland Foods
Harvey, ND 800-950-4558

Amcan Industries
Elmsford, NY 914-347-4838

American Spoon Foods Inc
Petoskey, MI 888-735-6700

Ana's Salsa
Austin, TX 888-849-7054

Arbor Hill Grapery & Winery
Naples, NY 800-554-7553

Arizona Cowboy
Phoenix, AZ 800-529-8627

Arome Fleurs & Fruits
Saint-Jean-Baptiste Day, QC 877-349-3282

Au Printemps Gourmet
Saint-Jerome, QC 800-438-6676

Bainbridge Festive Foods
Farmington, TN 800-545-9205

Bartons Fine Foods
Denniston, KY 888-810-3750

Baumer Foods Inc
Metairie, LA 504-482-5761

Bear Meadow Farm
Ashfield, MA 413-628-3970

Bear Stewart Corp
Chicago, IL 800-697-2327

Blackberry Patch
Thomasville, GA 800-853-5598

Blake Hill Preserves
Grafton, VT 802-289-1636

Blue Marble Brands
Providence, RI 888-534-0246

Blueberry Store
Grand Junction, MI 877-654-2400

Bono USA
Fairfield, NJ 862-485-8729

Booneway Farms
Berea, KY 859-986-2636

BRINS
Brooklyn, NY

C W Resources Inc
New Britain, CT 860-229-7700

California Custom Fruits
Baldwin Park, CA 877-558-0056

Castella Imports Inc
Brentwood, NY 631-231-5500

Casually Gourmet
New Haven, VT 800-639-7604

Catamount Specialties of Vermont
Plainfield, VT 800-639-2406

Cherchies
Malvern, PA 800-644-1980

Cheri's Desert Harvest
Tucson, AZ 800-743-1141

Cherith Valley Gardens
Fort Worth, TX 800-610-9813

Cherry Hut
Traverse City, MI 888-882-4431

Chris' Farm Stand
Peabody, MA 978-994-4315

Chugwater Chili
Chugwater, WY 800-972-4454

Chukar Cherries
Prosser, WA 800-624-9544

Cincinnati Preserving Co
Cincinnati, OH 800-222-9966

Clements Foods Co
Oklahoma City, OK 800-654-8355

Coco Lopez Inc
Miramar, FL 800-341-2242

Cold Hollow Cider Mill
Waterbury Center, VT 800-327-7537

Country Cupboard
Lewisburg, PA 570-523-3211

Coutts Specialty Foods Inc
Boxborough, MA 800-919-2952

Dillman Farm Inc
Bloomington, IN 800-359-1362

Dundee Groves
Dundee, FL 800-294-2266

E Waldo Ward & Son Marmalades
Sierra Madre, CA 800-355-9273

Eat This
Erwinna, PA 215-391-5807

EFCO Products Inc
Poughkeepsie, NY 800-284-3326

Eleanor's Best LLC
Garrison, NY 646-296-6870

Erba Food Products
Brooklyn, NY 718-272-7700

Esper Products DeLuxe
Kissimmee, FL 800-268-0892

Eva Gates Homemade Preserves
Bigfork, MT 800-682-4283

Eweberry Farms
Brownsville, OR 541-466-3470

Fiesta Gourmet of Tejas
Canyon Lake, TX 800-585-8250

Fireside Kitchen
Halifax, NS 902-454-7387

Fischer & Wieser Spec Foods
Fredericksburg, TX 877-861-0260

Food For Thought Inc
Honor, MI 231-326-5444

Forge Mountain Foods
Hendersonville, NC 800-823-6743

Freed, Teller & Freed
South San Francisco, CA 800-370-7371

From Oregon
Springfield, OR 541-747-4222

Frostproof Sunkist Groves
Frostproof, FL 863-635-4873

Gem Berry Products
Sandpoint, ID 800-231-1699

Graves Mountain Lodge Inc.
Syria, VA 540-923-4231

Graysmarsh Berry Farm
Sequim, WA 800-683-4367

Great Northern Maple Products
Saint Honor, De Shenley, QC 418-485-7777

Greaves Jams & Marmalades
Niagara-on-the-Lake, ON 800-515-9939

Green Grown Products Inc
Marina Del Ray, CA 310-828-1686

Grouse Hunt Farm Inc
Tamaqua, PA 570-467-2850

H Cantin
Beauport, QC 800-463-5268

Heinz Portion Control
Jacksonville, FL 904-695-1300

Hillcrest Orchard
Lake Placid, FL 865-397-5273

Hollman Foods
Des Moines, IA 888-926-2879

Homemade By Dorothy Boise
Boise, ID 800-657-7449

Honey Bear Fruit Basket
Denver, CO 888-330-2327

Huckleberry Patch
Hungry Horse, MT 800-527-7340

Hurd Orchards
Holley, NY 585-638-8838

Indian Bay Frozen Foods
Centreville, NL 709-678-2844

Inter-American Products
Cincinnati, OH 800-645-2233

J.M. Smucker Co.
Orrville, OH 888-550-9555

Jim's Cheese Pantry
Waterloo, WI 800-345-3571

JMS Specialty Foods
Ripon, WI 800-535-5437

Kamish Food Products
Chicago, IL 773-725-6959

Kent Precision Foods Group Inc
Muscatine, IA 800-442-5242

Kerr Jellies
Dana, NC 877-685-8381

Knott's Berry Farms
Orrville, OH 866-828-5502

Knouse Foods Co-Op Inc.
Peach Glen, PA 717-677-8181

Koloa Rum Corp
Kalaheo, HI 808-332-9333

Kozlowski Farms
Forestville, CA 800-473-2767

La Caboose Specialties
Sunset, LA 337-662-5401

Lancaster Packing Company
Myerstown, PA 717-397-9727

Lawrence Foods Inc
Elk Grove Village, IL 847-437-2400

Lehi Mills
Lehi, UT 877-311-3566

Leona's Restaurante
Chimayo, NM 888-561-5569

Lillie's Q
Chicago, IL 773-772-5500

Love Creek Orchards
Medina, TX 800-449-0882

Lowcountry Produce
Raleigh, NC 800-935-2792

Lynch Foods
North York, ON 416-449-5464

Lyons Magnus
Fresno, CA 800-344-7130

Mad River Farm Kitchen
Arcata, CA 707-822-0248

Meier's Wine Cellars Inc
Cincinnati, OH 800-346-2941

Minnestalgia Foods LLC
Mcgregor, MN 800-328-6731

Mixon Fruit Farms Inc
Bradenton, FL 800-608-2525

Mountainbrook of Vermont
Jeffersonville, VT 802-644-1988

Mrs Auld's Gourmet Foods Inc
Reno, NV 800-322-8537

New Canaan Farms
Dripping Springs, TX 800-727-5267

New England Cranberry
Lynn, MA 800-410-2892

Oregon Hill Farms
St Helens, OR 800-243-4541

Pacific Westcoast Foods
Beaverton, OR 800-874-9333

Palmetto Canning
Palmetto, FL 941-722-1100

Pearson's Berry Farm
Bowden, AB 403-224-3011

Pepper Creek Farms
Lawton, OK 800-526-8132

Pied-Mont/Dora
Anne Des Plaines, QC 800-363-8003

Plaidberry Company
Vista, CA 760-727-5403

Poiret International
Tamarac, FL 800-237-9151

Post Familie Vineyards
Altus, AR 800-275-8423

Purity Factories
St. John's, NL 800-563-3411
Purity Products
Plainview, NY 800-256-6102
Quality Naturally Foods
City Of Industry, CA 888-498-6986
Rapazzini Winery
Gilroy, CA 800-842-6262
Restaurant Lulu Gourmet Products
San Francisco, CA 888-693-5800
Robert Rothschild Farm
Cincinnati, OH 800-222-9966
Rocky Top Farms
Ellsworth, MI 800-862-9303
Rose City Pepperheads
Tigard, OR 503-443-3873
Roseland Manufacturing
Roseland, NJ 973-228-2500
Rowena
Norfolk, VA 800-627-8699
Sambets Cajun Deli
Austin, TX 800-472-6238
Sand Hill Berries
Mt Pleasant, PA 724-547-4760
SBK Preserves
Bronx, NY 800-773-7378
Sedlock Farm
Lynn Center, IL 309-521-8284
Seven Keys Co Of Florida
Pompano Beach, FL 954-946-5010
Shawnee Canning Co
Cross Junction, VA 800-713-1414
Shenk's Foods
Lancaster, PA 717-393-4240
Shooting Star Farms
Bartlesville, OK 888-850-8540
Silver Palate Kitchens
Cresskill, NJ 201-568-0110
Skjodt-Barrett Foods
Brampton, ON 877-600-1200
Stickney & Poor Company
Peterborough, NH 603-924-2259
Sugarman of Vermont
Hardwick, VT 800-932-7700
Summerland Sweets
Summerland, BC 800-577-1277
T.J. Blackburn Syrup Works
Jefferson, TX 800-657-5073
T.W. Garner Food Company
Winston Salem, NC 800-476-7383
Tait Farm Foods
Centre Hall, PA 800-787-2716
Tex-Mex Gourmet
Brenham, TX 888-345-8467
The Great San Saba River Pecan Company
San Saba, TX 800-621-8121
The Lollipop Tree, Inc
Auburn, NY 800-842-6691
Trailblazer Foods
Portland, OR 800-777-7179
Trappist Preserves
Cleveland, OH 800-472-0425
Tropical Preserving Co Inc
Los Angeles, CA 213-748-5108
Uncle Fred's Fine Foods
Rockport, TX 361-729-8320
Valley View Blueberries
Vancouver, WA 360-892-2839
Vista D'Oro Farms
Langley, BC 855-514-3539
Wagner Gourmet Foods
Lenexa, KS 913-469-5411
Wax Orchards
Seattle, WA 800-634-6132
WCC Honey Marketing
City Of Industry, CA 626-855-3086
Welch Foods Inc
Concord, MA 800-340-6870
Welch Foods Inc.
Concord, MA 800-340-6870
Westport Rivers Vineyard
Westport, MA 800-993-9695
Wild Thyme Cottage Products
Pointe Claire, QC 514-695-3602
Z Specialty Food, LLC
Woodland, CA 800-678-1226

Spreads

A Southern Season
Hillsborough, NC 800-253-3663
Aak USA Inc
Newark, NJ 973-344-1300
Alaska Smokehouse
Woodinville, WA 800-422-0852
Alexian Pâtés
Neptune, NJ 800-927-9473
Algood Food Co
Louisville, KY 502-637-3631
Allfresh Food Products
Evanston, IL 847-869-3100
Allied Old English Inc
Port Reading, NJ 732-602-8955
Amcan Industries
Elmsford, NY 914-347-4838
American Almond Products Co
Brooklyn, NY 800-825-6663
American Spoon Foods Inc
Petoskey, MI 888-735-6700
Arbor Hill Grapery & Winery
Naples, NY 800-554-7553
B & G Foods Inc.
Parsippany, NJ 973-401-6500
Bainbridge Festive Foods
Farmington, TN 800-545-9205
BakeMark Ingredients Canada
Richmond, BC 800-665-9441
Bauer's Mustard
Flushing, NY 718-821-3570
Baumer Foods Inc
Metairie, LA 504-482-5761
Bear Meadow Farm
Ashfield, MA 413-628-3970
Beekman 1802
Sharon Springs, NY 888-801-1802
Bel Brands USA
Chicago, IL 312-462-1500
Betty Lou's
McMinnville, OR 800-242-5205
Black Bear Fruits
New Lisbon, WI 608-547-6133
Blake Hill Preserves
Grafton, VT 802-289-1636
Blue Jay Orchards
Bethel, CT 203-748-0119
Boulder Brands, Inc.
Paramus, NJ 201-421-3970
BP Gourmet
Hauppauge, NY 631-234-8200
Bread Dip Company
Maple Valley, WA 425-358-7386
Butterball Farms
Grand Rapids, MI 888-828-8837
Butternut Mountain Farm
Morrisville, VT 800-828-2376
Carolina Food Company
Tulsa, OK 918-519-9338
Castella Imports Inc
Brentwood, NY 631-231-5500
Chelsea Flower Market
New York, NY 888-727-7887
Cheri's Desert Harvest
Tucson, AZ 800-743-1141
Cherry Hut
Traverse City, MI 888-882-4431
Chocolaterie Bernard Callebaut
Calgary, AB 800-661-8367
Chris' Farm Stand
Peabody, MA 978-994-4315
Chugwater Chili
Chugwater, WY 800-972-4454
Cinnabar Specialty Foods Inc
Prescott, AZ 866-293-6433
Citadelle Maple Syrup Producers' Cooperative
Plessisville, QC 819-362-3241
Clements Foods Co
Oklahoma City, OK 800-654-8355
Cleveland Kraut
Cleveland, OH 216-264-6895
Cold Hollow Cider Mill
Waterbury Center, VT 800-327-7537
Consumer Guild Foods Inc
Toledo, OH 419-726-3406
Cook's Pantry
Ventura, CA 805-947-4622
Cowboy Caviar
Berkeley, CA 877-509-1796
Crofter's Food
Parry Sound, ON 705-746-6301
Cugino's Gourmet Foods
Crystal Lake, IL 888-592-8446
Dawes Hill Honey Company
Nunda, NY 888-800-8075
Dutch Gold Honey Inc
Lancaster, PA 800-338-0587
E Waldo Ward & Son Marmalades
Sierra Madre, CA 800-355-9273
Earth Balance
Boulder, CO 866-234-6429
East Wind Inc
Tecumseh, MO 417-679-4682
Erba Food Products
Brooklyn, NY 718-272-7700
Esper Products DeLuxe
Kissimmee, FL 800-268-0892
Eva Gates Homemade Preserves
Bigfork, MT 800-682-4283
Fireside Kitchen
Halifax, NS 902-454-7387
Flaum Appetizing
Brooklyn, NY 718-821-1970
Follow Your Heart
Chatsworth, CA 818-725-2820
Forge Mountain Foods
Hendersonville, NC 800-823-6743
Fox Hollow
Crestwood, KY 502-241-8621
From Oregon
Springfield, OR 541-747-4222
Gardners Candies Inc
Tyrone, PA 800-242-2639
GEM Berry Products
Orofino, ID 888-231-1699
Gem Berry Products
Sandpoint, ID 800-231-1699
GFA Brands Inc
Paramus, NJ 201-568-9300
Giovanni's Appetizing Food Co
Richmond, MI 586-727-9355
Graham Cheese Corporation
Elnora, IN 800-472-9178
Graves Mountain Lodge Inc.
Syria, VA 540-923-4231
Graysmarsh Berry Farm
Sequim, WA 800-683-4367
Great Garlic Foods
Bradley Beach, NJ 732-775-3311
Greaves Jams & Marmalades
Niagara-on-the-Lake, ON 800-515-9939
Groeb Farms
Onsted, MI 800-530-9969
Grouse Hunt Farm Inc
Tamaqua, PA 570-467-2850
H & B Packing Co
Waco, TX 254-752-2506
Harold Food Company
Charlotte, NC 704-588-8061
Heinz Portion Control
Jacksonville, FL 904-695-1300
Herb Bee's Products
Colchester, VT 802-864-7387
Hillcrest Orchard
Lake Placid, FL 865-397-5273
Hillside Lane Farm
Randolph, VT 802-728-0070
Hollman Foods
Des Moines, IA 888-926-2879
Homemade By Dorothy Boise
Boise, ID 800-657-7449
Honey Bear Fruit Basket
Denver, CO 888-330-2327
Honey Butter Products Co
Manheim, PA 717-665-9323
Hope Foods
Boulder, CO 303-248-7019
Huckleberry Patch
Hungry Horse, MT 800-527-7340
Indian Bay Frozen Foods
Centreville, NL 709-678-2844
J.M. Smucker Co.
Orrville, OH 888-550-9555
JMS Specialty Foods
Ripon, WI 800-535-5437
Just Jan's Inc.
Calabasas, CA 818-282-6236
Kapow Now!
North Vancouver, BC 604-726-6391
Kent Precision Foods Group Inc
Muscatine, IA 800-442-5242
Kerr Jellies
Dana, NC 877-685-8381
Kevala
Dallas, TX 877-379-1179
Kind Snacks
New York, NY 855-884-5463
Knott's Berry Farms
Orrville, OH 866-828-5502

Knotts Fine Foods
Paris, TN . . . 731-642-1961
Knouse Foods Co-Op Inc.
Peach Glen, PA . . . 717-677-8181
Koloa Rum Corp
Kalaheo, HI . . . 808-332-9333
Kozlowski Farms
Forestville, CA . . . 800-473-2767
Krema Nut Co
Columbus, OH . . . 800-222-4132
Kween Foods
San Diego, CA . . . 401-343-0805
La Caboose Specialties
Sunset, LA . . . 337-662-5401
Lancaster Packing Company
Myerstown, PA . . . 717-397-9727
Land O'Lakes Inc
Arden Hills, MN . . . 800-328-9680
Landis Peanut Butter
Souderton, PA . . . 215-723-9366
Lasco Foods Inc
St Louis, MO . . . 314-832-1906
Lawry's Foods
Hunt Valley, MD . . . 800-952-9797
Leavitt Corp., The
Everett, MA . . . 617-389-2600
Leroux Creek
Hotchkiss, CO . . . 877-970-5670
Lost Trail Root Beer
Louisburg, KS . . . 800-748-7765
Love Creek Orchards
Medina, TX . . . 800-449-0882
Lynch Foods
North York, ON . . . 416-449-5464
Mad River Farm Kitchen
Arcata, CA . . . 707-822-0248
Madison Foods
Saint Paul, MN . . . 651-265-8212
Manassero Farms
Irvine, CA . . . 949-554-5103
Marantha Natural Foods
San Francisco, CA . . . 866-972-6879
Marin Food Specialties
Byron, CA . . . 925-634-6126
Mccutcheon Apple Products
Frederick, MD . . . 800-888-7537
Meier's Wine Cellars Inc
Cincinnati, OH . . . 800-346-2941
Minnestalgia Foods LLC
Mcgregor, MN . . . 800-328-6731
Miss Scarlett's Flowers
Juneau, AK . . . 800-345-6734
Mixon Fruit Farms Inc
Bradenton, FL . . . 800-608-2525
Montana Mountain Smoked Fish
Montana City, MT . . . 800-649-2959
Mountainbrook of Vermont
Jeffersonville, VT . . . 802-644-1988
Mrs Annie's Peanut Patch
Floresville, TX . . . 830-393-7845
National Grape Co-Op
Westfield, NY . . . 800-340-6870
New Canaan Farms
Dripping Springs, TX . . . 800-727-5267
Nikki's Coconut Butter
Hudson, WI
Nutiva
Richmond, CA . . . 800-993-4367
Once Again Nut Butter
Nunda, NY . . . 888-800-8075
Oregon Hill Farms
St Helens, OR . . . 800-243-4541
Organic Gourmet
Sherman Oaks, CA . . . 800-400-7772
Original Herkimer Cheese
Ilion, NY . . . 315-895-7428
Pacific Beach Peanut Butter
La Mesa, CA . . . 630-329-0792
Palmetto Canning
Palmetto, FL . . . 941-722-1100
Parkers Farm
Coon Rapids, MN . . . 800-869-6685
Peaceworks
New York, NY . . . 212-897-3985
Penotti USA
Westport, CT . . . 877-720-0896
Pied-Mont/Dora
Anne Des Plaines, QC . . . 800-363-8003
Pine River Pre-Pack Inc
Newton, WI . . . 920-726-4216
Plochman Inc
Manteno, IL . . . 800-843-4566
Private Harvest
El Dorado Hills, CA . . . 916-933-7080
Producers Peanut Company
Suffolk, VA . . . 800-847-5491
Protient
St Paul, MN . . . 800-328-9680
Purity Factories
St. John's, NL . . . 800-563-3411
Purity Farms
La Farge, WI . . . 877-211-4819
Purity Products
Plainview, NY . . . 800-256-6102
Quong Hop & Company
S San Francisco, CA . . . 650-553-9900
Rachael's Smoked Fish
Springfield, MA . . . 800-327-3412
Rapazzini Winery
Gilroy, CA . . . 800-842-6262
Rapunzel Pure Organics
Bloomfield, NJ . . . 800-225-1449
Regal Food Service
Houston, TX . . . 281-477-3683
Restaurant Lulu Gourmet Products
San Francisco, CA . . . 888-693-5800
Rocky Top Farms
Ellsworth, MI . . . 800-862-9303
Roseland Manufacturing
Roseland, NJ . . . 973-228-2500
Rowena
Norfolk, VA . . . 800-627-8699
Sabra Blue & White Food Products
Dallas, TX . . . 888-957-2272
Salmolux Inc
Federal Way, WA . . . 253-874-6570
Sassafras Enterprises Inc
Chicago, IL . . . 800-537-4941
SBK Preserves
Bronx, NY . . . 800-773-7378
Schlotterbeck & Foss Company
Portland, ME . . . 800-777-4666
Scott-Bathgate
Winnipeg, MB . . . 800-216-2990
Sedlock Farm
Lynn Center, IL . . . 309-521-8284
Shawnee Canning Co
Cross Junction, VA . . . 800-713-1414
Shenk's Foods
Lancaster, PA . . . 717-393-4240
Silver Palate Kitchens
Cresskill, NJ . . . 201-568-0110
Skjodt-Barrett Foods
Brampton, ON . . . 877-600-1200
Small Planet Foods
Minneapolis, MN . . . 800-624-4123
Something Special Deli-Foods
Sherwood Park, AB . . . 800-461-5892
Sommer Maid Creamery Inc
Pipersville, PA . . . 215-345-6160
Southern Gold Honey Co
Vidor, TX . . . 808-899-2494
Southern Peanut Co Inc
Dublin, NC . . . 800-330-3141
St Laurent Brothers
Bay City, MI . . . 800-289-7688
Stello Foods Inc
Punxsutawney, PA . . . 800-849-4599
Sugarman of Vermont
Hardwick, VT . . . 800-932-7700
Summerland Sweets
Summerland, BC . . . 800-577-1277
Suzanne's Specialties
New Brunswick, NJ . . . 800-762-2135
Sweetstacks LLC
San Diego, CA . . . 619-997-1097
T.W. Garner Food Company
Winston Salem, NC . . . 800-476-7383
Tait Farm Foods
Centre Hall, PA . . . 800-787-2716
Tara Foods
Atlanta, GA . . . 404-559-0605
Tarazi Specialty Foods
Chino, CA . . . 909-628-3601
Terrapin Ridge
Clearwater, FL . . . 800-999-4052
The Great San Saba River Pecan Company
San Saba, TX . . . 800-621-8121
The Lollipop Tree, Inc
Auburn, NY . . . 800-842-6691
Thistledew Farm
Proctor, WV . . . 800-854-6639
Timber Crest Farms
Healdsburg, CA . . . 888-766-4233
Trappist Preserves
Cleveland, OH . . . 800-472-0425
Treasure Foods
West Valley, UT . . . 801-974-0911
Tribe Mediterranean
Taunton, MA . . . 800-848-6687
Tropical Foods
Charlotte, NC . . . 800-438-4470
Tropical Preserving Co Inc
Los Angeles, CA . . . 213-748-5108
Valley View Blueberries
Vancouver, WA . . . 360-892-2839
Ventura Foods LLC
Brea, CA . . . 800-421-6257
Virginia & Spanish Peanut Co
Providence, RI . . . 800-673-3562
Wagner Gourmet Foods
Lenexa, KS . . . 913-469-5411
WCC Honey Marketing
City Of Industry, CA . . . 626-855-3086
Welch Foods Inc
Concord, MA . . . 800-340-6870
Welch Foods Inc.
Concord, MA . . . 800-340-6870
Westbrae Natural Foods
Melville, NY . . . 800-434-4246
Wild Thymes Farm Inc
Greenville, NY . . . 845-266-8387
WillowOak Farms
Amherst, VA . . . 888-963-2767
Wisconsin Milk Mktng Board Inc
Madison, WI . . . 800-589-5127
Wisconsin Wilderness Food Products
Lake Bluff, IL . . . 800-359-3039
World Art Foods
Temple, TX . . . 254-774-8322
Z Specialty Food, LLC
Woodland, CA . . . 800-678-1226
Zesty Z: The Za'atar Company
Brooklyn, NY . . . 917-740-5241

Apple Butter

A.W. Jantzi & Sons
Wellesley, ON . . . 519-656-2400
Bear Meadow Farm
Ashfield, MA . . . 413-628-3970
Betty Lou's
McMinnville, OR . . . 800-242-5205
Blue Jay Orchards
Bethel, CT . . . 203-748-0119
Centennial Farms
Augusta, MO . . . 636-228-4338
Clements Foods Co
Oklahoma City, OK . . . 800-654-8355
Cold Hollow Cider Mill
Waterbury Center, VT . . . 800-327-7537
Coutts Specialty Foods Inc
Boxborough, MA . . . 800-919-2952
Father's Country Hams
Bremen, KY . . . 270-525-3554
Graves Mountain Lodge Inc.
Syria, VA . . . 540-923-4231
Hillcrest Orchard
Lake Placid, FL . . . 865-397-5273
Kime's Cider Mill
Bendersville, PA . . . 717-677-7539
Knouse Foods Co-Op Inc.
Peach Glen, PA . . . 717-677-8181
Lost Trail Root Beer
Louisburg, KS . . . 800-748-7765
Love Creek Orchards
Medina, TX . . . 800-449-0882
Mccutcheon Apple Products
Frederick, MD . . . 800-888-7537
Shawnee Canning Co
Cross Junction, VA . . . 800-713-1414
Shenk's Foods
Lancaster, PA . . . 717-393-4240
Timber Crest Farms
Healdsburg, CA . . . 888-766-4233
Tropical Preserving Co Inc
Los Angeles, CA . . . 213-748-5108

Fruit Butter

American Almond Products Co
Brooklyn, NY . . . 800-825-6663
Applecreek Speciality Foods
Lexington, KY . . . 800-747-8871
Betty Lou's
McMinnville, OR . . . 800-242-5205

Clements Foods Co
Oklahoma City, OK 800-654-8355
Cold Hollow Cider Mill
Waterbury Center, VT. 800-327-7537
Dillman Farm Inc
Bloomington, IN. 800-359-1362
Hollman Foods
Des Moines, IA. 888-926-2879
JMS Specialty Foods
Ripon, WI 800-535-5437
Knouse Foods Co-Op Inc.
Peach Glen, PA 717-677-8181
Kozlowski Farms
Forestville, CA 800-473-2767
Lancaster Packing Company
Myerstown, PA 717-397-9727
Leroux Creek
Hotchkiss, CO. 877-970-5670
Lost Trail Root Beer
Louisburg, KS. 800-748-7765
Mccutcheon Apple Products
Frederick, MD. 800-888-7537
Oregon Hill Farms
St Helens, OR 800-243-4541
Scott Hams
Greenville, KY 800-318-1353
Shenk's Foods
Lancaster, PA 717-393-4240
Timber Crest Farms
Healdsburg, CA 888-766-4233
Tropical Preserving Co Inc
Los Angeles, CA. 213-748-5108
World of Chia
The Woodlands, TX 800-251-6973

Meats & Meat Products

Canned

ADJR Inc
Paulding, OH 419-399-3182
Aunt Kitty's Foods Inc
Vineland, NJ 856-691-2100
B & G Foods Inc.
Parsippany, NJ 973-401-6500
Calihan Pork Processors Inc
Peoria, IL 309-674-9175
Campbell Soup Co.
Camden, NJ 800-257-8443
Cordon Bleu International
Anjou, QC 800-363-1182
Dorina So-Good Inc
Union, IL 815-923-2144
Gary's Frozen Foods
Lubbock, TX 806-745-1933
Grabill Country Meats
Grabill, IN 866-333-6328
Hormel Foods Corp.
Austin, MN 507-437-5611
Hsin Tung Yang Foods Inc
S San Francisco, CA 650-589-6789
J & B Sausage Co Inc
Waelder, TX 830-788-7511
Kelly Foods
Jackson, TN 731-424-2255
Mertz Sausage Co
San Antonio, TX 210-433-3263
Opa's Smoked Meats
Fredericksburg, TX 800-543-6750
Triple U Enterprises
Fort Pierre, SD 605-567-3624

Cooked

Burke Corp
Nevada, IA 800-654-1152
Golden West Food Group
Vernon, CA 888-807-3663
Omaha Steaks Inc
.... 800-960-8400
Specialty Foods Group Inc
Owensboro, KY 800-238-0020

Dried

Alderfer Inc
Harleysville, PA 800-341-1121
Arctic Beverages
Winnipeg, MB 866-503-1270
Asiago PDO & Speck Alto Adige PGI
New York, NY 646-624-2885
Breslow Deli Products
Philadelphia, PA 215-739-4200
Chomps
Naples, FL
Chops Snacks
Lebanon, GA 888-571-4442
Citterio USA
Freeland, PA 800-435-8888
Country Archer Jerky Co.
San Bernardino, CA 909-370-0155
Duke's
Henningsen Foods Inc
Omaha, NE 800-228-2769
Hoopeston Foods Inc
Burnsville, MN 952-854-0903
Hsin Tung Yang Foods Inc
S San Francisco, CA 650-589-6789
Oregon Freeze Dry, Inc.
Albany, OR 541-926-6001
Perky Jerky
Greenwood Vlg, CO 888-343-6113
Prime Smoked Meats Inc
Oakland, CA 510-832-7167
Ralph's Packing Co
Perkins, OK 800-522-3979
Riverview Foods
Warsaw, KY 859-567-5211
Serv-Rite Meat Co Inc
Los Angeles, CA 323-227-1911
Shelton's Poultry Inc
Pomona, CA 800-541-1833
Silver Star Meats Inc
Mc Kees Rocks, PA 800-548-1321
SlantShack Jerky
Brooklyn, NY 201-632-1035
Tillamook Country Smoker
Bay City, OR
True Jerky
San Francisco, CA 858-336-2005
Wolf Canyon Foods
Carmel, CA 831-626-1323

Frozen

Acme Steak & Seafood
Youngstown, OH 800-686-2263
Al Pete Meats
Muncie, IN 765-288-8817
American Foods Group LLC
Green Bay, WI 800-345-0293
AquaCuisine
Portland, OR 208-323-2782
Armbrust Meats
Medford, WI 715-748-3102
Atlantic Meat Company
Savannah, GA 912-964-8511
Atlantic Veal & Lamb Inc
Brooklyn, NY 800-222-8325
B & D Foods
Boise, ID 208-344-1183
Blakely Freezer Locker
Blakeley, GA 229-723-3622
Bouma Meats
Provost, AB 780-753-2092
Branding Iron
Sauget, IL 800-851-4684
Broadleaf Venison USA Inc
Vernon, CA 800-336-3844
Brook Locker Plant
Brook, IN 219-275-2611
Brookside Foods
Cleveland, OH 216-991-7600
Burke Corp
Nevada, IA 800-654-1152
Bush Brothers Provision Co
West Palm Beach, FL 800-327-1345
Butterfield Foods
Noblesville, IN 317-776-4775
Calihan Pork Processors Inc
Peoria, IL 309-674-9175
Carando Gourmet Frozen Foods
Agawam, MA 888-227-2636
Cardinal Meat Specialists
Brampton, ON 800-363-1439
Caribbean Food Delights Inc
Tappan, NY 845-398-3000
Carriage House Foods
Ames, IA 515-232-2273
Centennial Food Corporation
Calgary, AB 403-214-0044
Chef's Requested Foods
Oklahoma City, OK 405-239-2610
Cher-Make Sausage Co
Manitowoc, WI 800-242-7679
Cheraw Packing Plant
Cheraw, SC 843-537-7426
Clifty Farm Country Meats
Paris, TN 800-486-4267
Curly's Foods Inc
Edina, MN 612-920-3400
Devault Foods
Devault, PA 800-426-2874
Dold Foods
Wichita, KS 316-838-9101
Duis Meat Processing
Concordia, KS 800-281-4295
Duma Meats Inc
Mogadore, OH 330-628-3438
El Rey Cooked Meats
St Louis, MO 314-521-3113
Florida Veal Processors
Wimauma, FL 813-634-5545
Garden Protein International
Richmond, BC 877-305-6777
Gaucho Foods
Fayetteville, IL 877-677-2282
Golden West Food Group
Vernon, CA 888-807-3663
Grecian Delight Foods Inc
Elk Grove Village, IL 800-621-4387
Hall Brothers Meats
Olmsted Twp, OH 440-235-3262
Hamms Custom Meats
Mckinney, TX 972-542-3359
Hanover Foods Corp
Hanover, PA 717-632-6000
Hatfield Quality Meats
Hatfield, PA 800-743-1191
Heringer Meats Inc
Covington, KY 859-291-2000
Homestead Meats
Delta, CO 970-874-1145
Hormel Foods Corp.
Austin, MN 507-437-5611
International Food Packers Corporation
Miami, FL 305-740-5847
John Garner Meats
Van Buren, AR 800-543-5473
K & K Gourmet Meats Inc
Leetsdale, PA 724-266-8400
Kelley Foods
Elba, AL 334-897-5761
Kenosha Beef International LTD
Kenosha, WI
King Kold Meats
Englewood, OH 800-836-2797
Kutztown Bologna Company
Leola, PA 800-723-8824
Ladoga Frozen Food & Retail
Ladoga, IN 765-942-2225
Leo G. Fraboni Sausage Company
Hibbing, MN 218-263-5074
M Buono Beef Co
Philadelphia, PA 215-463-3600
Macfarlane Pheasants
Janesville, WI 800-345-8348
Mada'n Kosher Foods
Dania, FL 954-925-0077
Maid-Rite Steak Company
Dunmore, PA 800-233-4259
Maple Leaf Foods International
North York, ON 800-268-3708
Morrison Lamothe
Toronto, ON 877-677-6533
Omaha Steaks Inc
.... 800-960-8400
On-Cor Frozen Foods Redi-Serve
Aurora, IL 920-563-6391
P.A. Braunger Institutional Foods
Sioux City, IA 712-258-4515
Pacific Valley Foods Inc
Bellevue, WA 425-643-1805
Phoenix Agro-Industrial Corporation
Westbury, NY 516-334-1194
Pierceton Foods Inc
Pierceton, IN 574-594-2344
Prime Smoked Meats Inc
Oakland, CA 510-832-7167
R Four Meats
Chatfield, MN 507-867-4180
Rich Products Corp
Vineland, NJ 800-818-9261
Rymer Foods
Chicago, IL 800-247-9637
Shelley's
Jersey City, NJ 201-433-2900
Smith Packing Regional Meat
Utica, NY 315-732-5125
Smoked Turkey Inc
Marshville, NC 704-624-6628
Steak-Umm Company
Shillington, PA 860-928-5900
Sudlersville Frozen Food Locker
Sudlersville, MD 410-438-3106
Thompson Packers
Slidell, LA 800-989-6328
Travis Meats Inc
Powell, TN 800-247-7606
Triple U Enterprises
Fort Pierre, SD 605-567-3624
Tucker Packing Co
Orrville, OH 330-683-3311
United Meat Company
San Francisco, CA 415-864-2118
United Supermarkets
Lubbock, TX 806-745-9667

Valley Meat Company
Modesto, CA....800-222-6328
Valley Meats
Coal Valley, IL....309-517-6639
W & G Marketing Company
Ames, IA....515-233-4774
Zartic Inc
Rome, GA....800-241-0516

Ingredients

Burke Corp
Nevada, IA....800-654-1152
GPI USA LLC.
Mokena, IL....800-929-4248

Minced

Groff's Meats
Elizabethtown, PA....717-367-1246
Reinhart Foods
Toronto, ON....416-645-4910

Packers

1000 Islands River Rat Cheese
Clayton, NY....800-752-1341
A.C. Kissling Company
Philadelphia, PA....800-445-1943
A.L. Duck Jr Inc
Zuni, VA....757-562-2387
Abattoir Aliments Asta Inc.
St Alexandre De Kamouras, QC....800-463-1355
Ajinomoto Foods North America, Inc.
Ontario, CA....909-477-4700
AJM Meat Packing
San Juan, PR....787-787-4050
Al Safa Halal
New York City, NY....800-268-8147
Alaska Sausage & Seafood
Anchorage, AK....800-798-3636
Alewel's Country Meats
Warrensburg, MO....800-353-8553
Alexian Pâtés
Neptune, NJ....800-927-9473
Alle Processing Corp
Flushing, NY....718-894-2000
Amcan Industries
Elmsford, NY....914-347-4838
Atlantic Meat Company
Savannah, GA....912-964-8511
Atlantic Veal & Lamb Inc
Brooklyn, NY....800-222-8325
Atlantis Pak USA Inc
Coral Gables, FL....305-403-2603
B & D Foods
Boise, ID....208-344-1183
B & R Quality Meats Inc
Waterloo, IA....319-232-6328
Bakalars Sausage Co
La Crosse, WI....608-784-0384
Ball Park Franks
Peoria, IL....888-317-5867
Baretta Provision
East Berlin, CT....860-828-0802
Barone Foods
Tucson, AZ....520-623-8571
BCFoods
Santa Rosa, CA....707-547-1776
Bellville Meat Market
Bellville, TX....800-571-6328
Bierig Brothers Inc
Vineland, NJ....856-691-9765
Big B Barbecue
Evansville, IN....812-425-5235
Binkert's Meat Products
Baltimore, MD....410-687-5959
Birchwood Foods Inc
Kenosha, WI....800-541-1685
Blakely Freezer Locker
Blakeley, GA....229-723-3622
Blue Ribbon Meats
Cleveland, OH....800-262-0395
Bluebonnet Meat Company
Trenton, TX....903-989-2293
Boesl Packing Co
Baltimore, MD....800-675-1471
Bowser Meat Processing
Meriden, KS....785-484-2454
Braham Food Locker Service
Braham, MN....320-396-2636
Branding Iron
Sauget, IL....800-851-4684
Branding Iron Meats
Sauk Rapids, MN....800-851-4684
Breslow Deli Products
Philadelphia, PA....215-739-4200
Broadaway Ham Co
Jonesboro, AR....870-932-6688
Broadleaf Venison USA Inc
Vernon, CA....800-336-3844
Brook Locker Plant
Brook, IN....219-275-2611
Brook Meadow Meats
Hagerstown, MD....301-739-3107
Brown Packing Company
South Holland, IL....800-832-8325
Brucepac
Woodburn, OR....800-899-3629
Brush Locker
Fort Morgan, CO....970-842-2660
Bryant's Meat Inc.
Taylorsville, MS....800-844-0507
Buckhead Beef
Atlanta, GA....800-888-5578
Burgers' Smokehouse
California, MO....800-345-5185
Burnett & Son
Monrovia, CA....877-632-5467
Burton Meat Processing
Burton, TX....979-289-4022
Busseto Foods
Fresno, CA....800-628-2633
C & C Packing Co
Stamps, AR....866-365-3759
C Roy & Sons Processing
Yale, MI....810-387-3957
C&S Wholesale Meat Company
Atlanta, GA....404-627-3547
Callaway Packing Inc
Delta, CO....970-874-9743
Calumet Diversified Meats Company
Pleasant Prairie, WI....800-752-7427
Cambridge Packing Company
Boston, MA....800-722-6726
Carando Gourmet Frozen Foods
Agawam, MA....888-227-2636
Cardinal Meat Specialists
Brampton, ON....800-363-1439
Caribbean Food Delights Inc
Tappan, NY....845-398-3000
Carl Venezia Fresh Meats
Plymouth Meeting, PA....610-239-6750
Carlton Farms
Carlton, OR....800-932-0946
Carolina Packers Inc
Smithfield, NC....800-682-7675
Catelli Brothers Inc
Collingswood, NJ....856-869-9293
Caughman's Meat Plant
Lexington, SC....803-356-0076
Cavens Meats
Conover, OH....937-368-3841
Caviness Beef Packers LTD
Hereford, TX....806-357-2333
Caviness Beef Packers LTD
Amarillo, TX....806-372-5781
Centennial Food Corporation
Calgary, AB....403-214-0044
Center Locker Svc
Center, MO....800-884-0737
Central Meat & Provision
San Diego, CA....619-239-1391
Central Meat Market
Providence, RI....401-751-6935
Charlie's Country Sausage
Minot, ND....701-838-6302
Chef's Requested Foods
Oklahoma City, OK....405-239-2610
Chicago 58 Food Products
Woodbridge, ON....416-603-4244
Chino Meat Provision Corporation
Chino, CA....909-627-1997
Chisesi Brothers Meat Packing
New Orleans, LA....800-966-3550
Cibao Meat Products Inc
Bronx, NY....718-993-5072
Cifelli & Sons Inc
South River, NJ....732-238-0090
Clay Center Locker Plant
Clay Center, KS....800-466-5543
Clifty Farm Country Meats
Paris, TN....800-486-4267
Cloud's Meat Processing
Carthage, MO....417-358-5855
Clyde's Italian & German Sausage
Denver, CO....303-433-8744
Conagra Brands Inc
Chicago, IL....877-266-2472
Conagra Foodservice
Chicago, IL....877-266-2472
Conecuh Sausage Co
Evergreen, AL....800-726-0507
Corfu Foods Inc
Bensenville, IL....630-595-2510
Country Butcher Shop
Carlisle, PA....800-272-9223
Country Smoked Meats
Bowling Green, OH....800-321-4766
Crater Meat Co Inc
Medford, OR....541-772-6966
Crofton & Sons Inc
Tampa, FL....800-878-7675
Crystal Lake Farms
Decatur, AR....800-382-4425
Cudlin's Meat Market
Newfield, NY....607-564-3443
Culver Duck Farms Inc
Middlebury, IN....800-825-9225
Curly's Foods Inc
Edina, MN....612-920-3400
Custom-Pak Meats
Knoxville, TN....615-687-0871
Dale T Smith & Sons Inc
Draper, UT....801-571-3611
David Mosner Meat Products
Bronx, NY....866-928-6428
Dean Sausage Co Inc
Attalla, AL....800-228-0704
Debragga & Spitler
Jersey City, NJ
Dennison Meat Locker
Dennison, MN....507-645-8734
Diggs Packing Company
Columbia, MO....573-449-2995
Dinner Bell Meat Product
Lynchburg, VA....434-847-7766
Dold Foods
Wichita, KS....316-838-9101
Dolores Canning Co Inc
Los Angeles, CA....323-263-9155
Duis Meat Processing
Concordia, KS....800-281-4295
Dunham's Meats
Urbana, WA....509-924-9821
Dutterer's Home Food Service
Baltimore, MD....410-298-3663
Dyna Tabs LLC
Brooklyn, NY....718-376-6084
E&H Packing Company
Detroit, MI....313-567-8286
E.W. Knauss & Son
Quakertown, PA....800-648-4220
East Dayton Meat & Poultry
Dayton, OH....937-253-6185
Edelman Meats Inc
Antigo, WI....715-623-7686
Ehresman Packaging Co
Garden City, KS....620-276-3791
El Paso Meat Co
El Paso, TX....915-838-8600
El Rey Cooked Meats
St Louis, MO....314-521-3113
Elba Custom Meats
Elba, AL....334-897-2007
Ellsworth Locker
Ellsworth, MN....507-967-2544
ELP Inc
Elizabeth, CO....303-688-2240
Enslin & Son Packing Company
Hattiesburg, MS....800-898-4687
F&Y Enterprises
Wauconda, IL....847-526-0620
Fairbury Food Products
Fairbury, NE....402-729-3379
Far West Meats
Highland, CA....909-864-1990
Farm Boy Food Svc
Evansville, IN....800-852-3976
Farmers Produce
Ashby, MN....218-747-2749
Farmington Foods Inc
Forest Park, IL....800-609-3276
Finchville Farms Country Ham
Finchville, KY....800-678-1521
Fineberg Packing Company
Memphis, TN....901-458-2622

Fiorucci Foods USA Inc
S Chesterfield, VA 800-524-7775
Fischer Meats
Issaquah, WA 425-392-3131
Flanders
Waycross, GA 912-283-5191
Florida Veal Processors
Wimauma, FL 813-634-5545
Foell Packing Company
Naperville, IL 919-776-0592
Fortenberry Mini-Storage
Kodak, TN. 865-933-2568
Frank Wardynski & Sons Inc
Buffalo, NY. 716-854-6083
Freirich Foods
Salisbury, NC 800-221-1315
Fresh Mark Inc.
Massillon, OH. 330-832-7491
Frick's Quality Meats
Washington, MO 800-241-2209
Froehlich Alex Packing Co
Johnstown, PA. 814-535-7694
Fulton Provision Co
Portland, OR 800-333-6328
Gaiser's European Style
Union, NJ 908-686-3421
Gem Meat Packing Co
Garden City, ID. 208-375-9424
Gibbon Packing
Gibbon, NE. 308-468-5771
Glazier Packing Co
Malone, NY. 518-483-4990
Glen's Packing Co
Hallettsville, TX 800-368-2333
Glier's Meats Inc
Covington, KY 800-446-3882
Global Food Industries
Townville, SC. 800-225-4152
Gouvea's & Purity Foods Inc
Honolulu, HI 808-847-3717
Grabill Country Meats
Grabill, IN. 866-333-6328
Grandpa Ittel's Meats Inc
Howard Lake, MN 320-543-2285
Grant Park Packing
Chicago, IL 312-421-4096
Greater Omaha Packing Co Inc.
Omaha, NE 800-747-5400
Grecian Delight Foods Inc
Elk Grove Village, IL 800-621-4387
Grote & Weigel Inc
Bloomfield, CT. 860-242-8528
Gulf Packing Company
San Benito, TX. 956-399-2631
Gunnoe Farms Sausage & Salad
Charleston, WV 304-343-7686
H&K Packers Company
Winnipeg, NB 204-233-2354
Hansen Packing Co
Jerseyville, IL 618-498-3714
Harvest Direct
Norwell, MA 800-733-2106
Hastings Meat Supply
Hastings, NE. 402-463-9857
Hatfield Quality Meats
Hatfield, PA. 800-743-1191
Henningsen Foods Inc
Omaha, NE 800-228-2769
Herman Falter Packing Co
Columbus, OH 800-325-6328
Herring Brothers Meats
Guilford, ME. 207-876-2631
Hightower's Packing
Minden, LA. 318-377-5459
Hilltop Meat Co
Andalusia, AL. 800-781-0053
Hofmann Sausage Co Inc
Mattydale, NY. 800-724-8410
Holly Hill Locker Company
Holly Hill, SC. 803-496-3611
Holton Meat Processing
Holton, KS 785-364-2331
Home Delivery Food Service
Jefferson, GA 706-367-9551
Homestead Meats
Delta, CO 970-874-1145
Hoopeston Foods Inc
Burnsville, MN 952-854-0903
Hoople Country Kitchen Inc
Rockport, IN 877-466-7537
Hormel Foods Corp.
Austin, MN 507-437-5611

Hot Springs Packing Co Inc
Hot Springs, AR 800-535-0449
Hsin Tung Yang Foods Inc
S San Francisco, CA. 650-589-6789
Hughes Springs Frozen Food Center
Hughes Springs, TX 903-639-2941
Hughson Meat Company
San Marcos, TX 877-462-6328
Humphrey's Market
Springfield, IL. 800-747-6328
Indian Valley Meats
Indian, AK. 907-653-7511
International Food Packers Corporation
Miami, FL. 305-740-5847
International Meat Co
Chicago, IL 773-622-1400
Isernio Sausage Company
Seattle, WA 888-495-8674
Ito Cariani Sausage Company
Hayward, CA 510-887-0882
J F O'Neill & Packing Co
Omaha, NE 402-733-1200
J W Treuth & Sons
Catonsville, MD 410-747-6281
Jackson Brothers Food Locker
Post, TX 806-495-3245
Jackson Meat
Hutchinson, KS. 620-259-6066
Jacob & Sons Wholesale Meats
Martins Ferry, OH. 740-633-3091
Jacobsmuhlen's Meats
Cornelius, OR 503-359-0479
JD Sweid Foods
Langley, BC 800-665-4355
Jemm Wholesale Meat Company
Chicago, IL 773-523-8161
Jensen Meat Company
San Diego, CA 619-754-6400
John Garner Meats
Van Buren, AR 800-543-5473
John Volpi & Co
St Louis, MO. 800-288-3439
Johnson's Wholesale Meats
Opelousas, LA 337-948-4444
Johnson, Nash & Sons Farms
Warsaw, NC. 910-289-6842
Johnsonville Sausage LLC
Watertown, WI 888-556-2728
Jones Dairy Farm
Fort Atkinson, WI. 800-563-6637
Jordahl Meats
Manchester, MN 507-826-3418
Joseph Kirschner & Company
Augusta, ME. 207-623-3544
Keeter's Meat Company
Tulia, TX. 800-456-5019
Kelley Foods
Elba, AL 334-897-5761
Kelly Packing Company
Torrington, WY. 307-532-2210
Kenosha Beef International LTD
Kenosha, WI
Kent Quality Foods Inc
Grand Rapids, MI 800-748-0141
Kershenstine Beef Jerky
Eupora, MS 662-258-2049
Ketters Meat Market & Locker Plant
Frazee, MN. 218-334-2351
Kingsbury Country Market
La Porte, IN. 219-393-3016
Kiolbassa Provision Co
San Antonio, TX. 800-456-5465
Koegel Meats Inc
Flint, MI 810-238-3685
Konetzko's Meat Market
Browerville, MN. 320-594-2915
Kowalski Sausage Co
Hamtramck, MI. 800-482-2400
Kruse & Son
Monrovia, CA. 626-358-4536
Kruse Meat Products
Alexander, AR 501-316-2100
Kutztown Bologna Company
Leola, PA. 800-723-8824
L & L Packing Co
Chicago, IL 800-628-6328
L & M Lockers
Belt, MT 406-277-3522
Lad's Smokehouse Catering
Needville, TX 979-793-6210
Ladoga Frozen Food & Retail
Ladoga, IN 765-942-2225

Lakeside Foods Inc.
Plainview, MN 507-534-3141
Lampost Meats
Grimes, IA. 515-288-6111
Land O'Frost Inc
Searcy, AR 800-643-5654
Lee's Sausage Co
Orangeburg, SC 803-534-5517
Lengerich Meats Inc
Zanesville, IN 260-638-4123
Leo G. Fraboni Sausage Company
Hibbing, MN. 218-263-5074
Lindner Bison
Northern, CA 530-254-6337
Lombardi Brothers Meat Packers
Denver, CO 303-458-7441
Lord's Sausage & Country Ham
Dexter, GA 800-342-6002
Lynden Meat Co
Lynden, WA 360-354-2449
M Buono Beef Co
Philadelphia, PA 215-463-3600
Mac's Meats Inc
Las Cruces, NM 575-524-2751
Macfarlane Pheasants
Janesville, WI 800-345-8348
MacGregors Meat & Seafood
Toronto, ON 888-383-3663
Maid-Rite Steak Company
Dunmore, PA. 800-233-4259
Manger Packing Corp
Baltimore, MD 800-227-9262
Maple Leaf Foods International
North York, ON. 800-268-3708
Maple Leaf Meats
Motreal, QC 800-268-3708
Marcel et Henri Charcuterie Francaise
South San Francisco, CA 800-227-6436
Marks Meat
Holmen, WI. 608-526-6058
Mclemores Abattoir Inc
Vidalia, GA. 912-537-4476
Meat Center
Edna, TX. 361-782-3776
Meating Place
Buffalo, NY. 716-885-3623
Medeiros Farms
Kalaheo, HI. 808-332-8211
Merkley & Sons Packing Co Inc
Jasper, IN 812-482-7020
Michael's Finer Meats/Seafoods
Columbus, OH 800-282-0518
Miller Brothers Packing Company
Sylvester, GA 229-776-2014
Moonlite Bar-B-Q Inn
Owensboro, KY 800-322-8989
Morreale John R Inc
Chicago, IL 312-421-3664
Morrison Lamothe
Toronto, ON 877-677-6533
Morrison Meat Packers
Miami, FL. 800-330-4267
Mountain States Rosen
Bronx, NY. 800-872-5262
Moyer Packing Co.
Elroy, PA. 800-967-8325
Mucke's Meat Products
Hartford, CT 800-726-5598
Napoleon Locker
Napoleon, IN. 812-852-4333
National Foods
Indianapolis, IN 800-683-6565
Natural Food Holdings
Sioux Center, IA 800-735-7765
New City Packing Company
Aurora, IL. 630-851-8800
New Generation Foods
Burnaby, BC 604-515-7438
Nicky USA Inc
Portland, OR 800-469-4162
Niemuth's Steak & Chop Shop
Waupaca, WI. 715-258-2666
Oklahoma City Meat Co Inc
Oklahoma City, OK 405-235-3308
Olson Locker
Fairmont, MN 507-238-2563
Omaha Meat Processors
Omaha, NE 402-554-1965
On-Cor Frozen Foods Redi-Serve
Aurora, IL. 920-563-6391
Original Chili Bowl
Ontario, CA. 800-548-6363

Oscar's Wholesale Meats
Ogden, UT........................801-621-5655
Ossian Smoked Meats
Ossian, IN........................800-535-8862
Our Best Foods
Tewksbury, MA....................978-858-0077
Palmer Meat Packing Co
Tremonton, UT....................435-257-5329
Paradise Locker Inc.
Trimble, MO......................816-370-6328
Pasqualichio Brothers Inc
Scranton, PA.....................800-232-6233
Peco Foods Inc.
Tuscaloosa, AL...................205-345-4711
Pekarna Meat Market
Jordan, MN.......................952-492-6101
Pender Packing Co Inc
Rocky Point, NC..................910-675-3311
Petschl's Quality Meats
Tukwila, WA......................206-575-4400
Phoenix Agro-Industrial Corporation
Westbury, NY.....................516-334-1194
Pie Piper Products
Wheeling, IL.....................800-621-8183
Pierceton Foods Inc
Pierceton, IN....................574-594-2344
Piller Sausages & Delicatessens
Waterloo, ON.....................800-265-2628
Piller's Fine Foods
Waterloo, ON.....................800-265-2627
Pinter's Packing Plant
Dorchester, WI...................715-654-5444
Plymouth Beef Co.
Bronx, NY........................718-589-8600
Prairie Cajun Wholesale
Eunice, LA.......................337-546-6195
Premium Meat Co
Brigham City, UT.................435-723-5944
Prime Smoked Meats Inc
Oakland, CA......................510-832-7167
Pruden Packing Company
Suffolk, VA......................757-539-8773
Puueo Poi Shop
Hilo, HI.........................808-935-8435
Quality Food Company
Providence, RI...................877-233-3462
Quality Meats & Seafood
West Fargo, ND...................800-342-4250
Quality Sausage Company
Dallas, TX.......................214-634-3400
R Four Meats
Chatfield, MN....................507-867-4180
R M Felts' Packing Co
Ivor, VA.........................757-859-6131
R.E. Meyer Company
Lincoln, NE......................888-990-2333
Rabbit Barn
Turlock, CA......................209-632-1123
Raber Packing Co
Peoria, IL.......................800-331-0543
Ralph's Packing Co
Perkins, OK......................800-522-3979
Randolph Packing Co
Asheboro, NC.....................336-672-1470
Ray's Sausage Co
Cleveland, OH....................216-921-8782
Real Kosher Sausage Company
Newark, NJ.......................973-690-5394
Red Smith Foods Inc
Davie, FL........................954-581-1996
Register Meat Co
Cottondale, FL...................850-352-4269
Rich Products Corp
Vineland, NJ.....................800-818-9261
Rinehart Meat Processing
Branson, MO......................417-869-2041
Riverton Packing
Riverton, WY.....................307-856-3838
Robbins Packing Company
Statesboro, GA...................912-764-7503
Robinson Distributing Co
London, KY.......................800-230-5131
Rocky Mountain Packing Company
Havre, MT........................406-265-3401
Roman Packing Company
Norfolk, NE......................800-373-5990
Roman Sausage Company
Santa Clara, CA..................800-497-7462
Roode Packing Company
Fairbury, NE.....................402-729-2253
Rose Packing Co Inc
South Barrington, IL.............800-323-7363
Royal Center Locker Plant
Royal Center, IN.................574-643-3275
Royal Home Bakery
Newmarket, ON....................905-715-7044
Royal Palate Foods
Inglewood, CA....................310-330-7701
Rudolph's Market & Sausage
Dallas, TX.......................214-741-1874
Rymer Foods
Chicago, IL......................800-247-9637
S.W. Meat & Provision Company
Phoenix, AZ......................602-275-2000
Sadler's Smokehouse
Henderson, TX....................903-657-5581
Sahlen's
Buffalo, NY......................800-466-8165
Sambol Meat Company
Overland Park, KS................913-334-8404
San Angelo Packing
San Angelo, TX...................325-949-9401
San Antonio Packing Co
San Antonio, TX..................210-224-5441
Sanders Meat Packing Inc
Custer, MI.......................800-968-5035
Sardinha's Sausage
Somerset, MA.....................800-678-0178
Saval Foods Corp
Elkridge, MD.....................800-527-2825
Savoie's Sausage and Food Products
Opelousas, LA....................337-942-7241
Schaefers Market
Sauk Centre, MN..................320-352-6490
Schleswig Specialty Meats
Schleswig, IA....................712-676-3324
Schumacher Wholesale Meats
Golden Valley, MN................800-432-7020
Seaboard Foods
Shawnee Mission, KS..............800-262-7907
Serv-Rite Meat Co Inc
Los Angeles, CA..................323-227-1911
Shaker Valley Foods
Cleveland, OH....................216-961-8600
Shamrock Slaughter Plant
Shamrock, TX.....................806-256-3241
Shelley's
Jersey City, NJ..................201-433-2900
Shelton's Poultry Inc
Pomona, CA.......................800-541-1833
Siena Foods
Toronto, ON......................800-465-0422
Silver Creek Specialty Meats
Oshkosh, WI......................800-729-2849
Silver Star Meats Inc
Mc Kees Rocks, PA................800-548-1321
Skylark Meats
Omaha, NE........................800-759-5275
Smith Meat Packing
Detroit, MI......................313-833-1590
Smith Packing Regional Meat
Utica, NY........................315-732-5125
Smith Provision Co Inc
Erie, PA.........................800-334-9151
SOPAKCO Foods
Mullins, SC......................800-276-9678
Souris Valley Processors
Melita, MB.......................204-522-8210
Southern Packing Corp
Chesapeake, VA...................757-421-2131
Spencer Packing Company
Washington, NC...................252-946-4161
Spring Hill Meat Market
Spring Hill, KS..................913-592-3501
Springville Meat & Cold Storage
Springville, UT..................801-489-6391
Stampede Meat, Inc.
Bridgeview, IL...................800-353-0933
Standard Meat Co LP
Dallas, TX.......................866-859-6313
Statewide Meats & Poultry
New Haven, CT....................203-777-6669
Steak-Umm Company
Shillington, PA..................860-928-5900
Stewarts Market
Yelm, WA.........................360-458-2091
Stock Yards Packing Company
Melrose Park, IL.................877-785-9273
Stone Meat Processor
Ogden, UT........................801-782-9825
Stonie's Sausage Shop
Perryville, MO...................888-546-2540
Strasburg Provision
Strasburg, OH....................800-207-6009
Streit Carl & Son Co
Neptune, NJ......................732-775-0803
Stripling's General Store
Moultrie, GA.....................229-985-4226
Sudlersville Frozen Food Locker
Sudlersville, MD.................410-438-3106
Sunergia Soyfoods
Charlottesville, VA..............800-693-5134
Sunnydale Meats Inc
Gaffney, SC......................864-489-6091
Superior Meat Co
Vernal, UT.......................435-789-3274
Suzanna's Kitchen
Peachtree Cor, GA................770-476-9900
Swiss-American Sausage Company
Lathrop, CA......................209-858-5555
T O Williams Inc
Portsmouth, VA...................757-397-0771
T.L. Herring & Company
Wilson, NC.......................252-291-1141
Taylor Provisions Company
Trenton, NJ......................609-392-1113
Temptee Specialty Foods
Denver, CO.......................800-842-1233
Tennessee Valley Packing Co
Columbia, TN.....................931-388-2623
Theriault's Abattoir Inc
Hamlin, ME.......................207-868-3344
Thomas Brothers Country Ham
Asheboro, NC.....................336-672-0337
Thomas Packing Company
Columbus, GA.....................800-729-0976
Thompson Packers
Slidell, LA......................800-989-6328
Thumann Inc.
Carlstadt, NJ....................201-935-3636
Tiger Meat & Provisions
Miami, FL........................305-324-0083
Tillamook Meat Inc
Tillamook, OR....................503-842-4802
Travis Meats Inc
Powell, TN.......................800-247-7606
Triple U Enterprises
Fort Pierre, SD..................605-567-3624
Troy Pork Store
Troy, NY.........................518-272-8291
Tyler Packing Co
Tyler, TX........................903-593-9592
Une-Viandi
St. Jean Sur Richelieu, NB.......800-363-1955
United Meat Company
San Francisco, CA................415-864-2118
United Provision Meat Company
Columbus, OH.....................614-252-1126
V.W. Joyner & Company
Smithfield, VA...................757-357-2161
Valley Meat Company
Modesto, CA......................800-222-6328
Victor Ostrowski & Son
Baltimore, MD....................410-327-8935
Vienna Meat Products
Scarborough, ON..................800-588-1931
Vollwerth & Baroni Companies
Hancock, MI......................800-562-7620
W & G Marketing Company
Ames, IA.........................515-233-4774
WACO Beef & Pork Processors
Waco, TX.........................254-772-4669
Wall Meat Processing
Wall, SD.........................605-279-2348
Wampler's Farm Sausage Company
Lenoir City, TN..................800-728-7243
Wasatch Meats Inc
Salt Lake City, UT...............800-631-8294
Wayco Ham Co
Goldsboro, NC....................800-962-2614
Western Buffalo Company
Rapid City, SD...................800-247-3263
Westport Locker LLC
Westport, IN.....................877-265-0551
Whitaker & Assoc Architects
Atlanta, GA......................404-266-1265
White Packing Company
Fredericksburg, VA...............540-373-9883
Wichita Packing Co Inc
Chicago, IL......................312-763-3965
Willcox Meat Packing House
Willcox, AZ......................520-384-2015
Willie's Smoke House LLC
Harrisville, PA..................800-742-4184
Windcrest Meat Packers
Port Perry, ON...................800-750-2542

Woodbine
Norfolk, VA ... 757-461-2731

World Casing Corp
Maspeth, NY ... 800-221-4887

Y & T Packing Co
Springfield, IL ... 217-522-3345

Yoakum Packing Co
Yoakum, TX ... 800-999-6997

Zartic Inc
Rome, GA ... 800-241-0516

Zerna Packing
Labadie, MO ... 636-742-4190

Zummo Meat Co
Beaumont, TX ... 409-842-1810

Zweigle's Inc
Rochester, NY ... 585-546-1740

Patties

Acme Steak & Seafood
Youngstown, OH ... 800-686-2263

Branding Iron
Sauget, IL ... 800-851-4684

Brucepac
Woodburn, OR ... 800-899-3629

Burger Maker Inc
Carlstadt, NJ ... 201-939-0444

Caribbean Food Delights Inc
Tappan, NY ... 845-398-3000

Chicago Meat Authority Inc
Chicago, IL ... 800-383-3811

Corfu Foods Inc
Bensenville, IL ... 630-595-2510

CTI Foods
Wilder, ID ... 208-482-7844

Fair Oaks Farms LLC
Pleasant Prairie, WI ... 800-528-8615

Gouvea's & Purity Foods Inc
Honolulu, HI ... 808-847-3717

Karn Meats
Columbus, OH ... 800-221-9585

Kenosha Beef International LTD
Kenosha, WI

Kutztown Bologna Company
Leola, PA ... 800-723-8824

Laurent's Meat Market
Marrero, LA ... 504-341-1771

Meating Place
Buffalo, NY ... 716-885-3623

Mishler Packing Co
Lagrange, IN ... 800-860-4156

On-Cor Frozen Foods Redi-Serve
Aurora, IL ... 920-563-6391

Pulmuone Foods USA Inc.
Fullerton, CA ... 800-588-7782

Roman Sausage Company
Santa Clara, CA ... 800-497-7462

S.W. Meat & Provision Company
Phoenix, AZ ... 602-275-2000

Springville Meat & Cold Storage
Springville, UT ... 801-489-6391

Travis Meats Inc
Powell, TN ... 800-247-7606

Valley Meat Company
Modesto, CA ... 800-222-6328

Wisconsin Packaging Corp
Fort Atkinson, WI ... 920-563-9363

Zartic Inc
Rome, GA ... 800-241-0516

Frozen

Birchwood Foods Inc
Kenosha, WI ... 800-541-1685

Branding Iron
Sauget, IL ... 800-851-4684

Burke Corp
Nevada, IA ... 800-654-1152

Cardinal Meat Specialists
Brampton, ON ... 800-363-1439

Caribbean Food Delights Inc
Tappan, NY ... 845-398-3000

Chicago Meat Authority Inc
Chicago, IL ... 800-383-3811

Corfu Foods Inc
Bensenville, IL ... 630-595-2510

Edmond's Chile Co
St Louis, MO ... 314-772-1499

Flanders
Waycross, GA ... 912-283-5191

Jemm Wholesale Meat Company
Chicago, IL ... 773-523-8161

John Garner Meats
Van Buren, AR ... 800-543-5473

Kenosha Beef International LTD
Kenosha, WI

King Kold Meats
Englewood, OH ... 800-836-2797

Kutztown Bologna Company
Leola, PA ... 800-723-8824

Leo G. Fraboni Sausage Company
Hibbing, MN ... 218-263-5074

Maid-Rite Steak Company
Dunmore, PA ... 800-233-4259

Mellos North End Mfr
Fall River, MA ... 800-673-2320

On-Cor Frozen Foods Redi-Serve
Aurora, IL ... 920-563-6391

Plymouth Beef Co.
Bronx, NY ... 718-589-8600

Thompson Packers
Slidell, LA ... 800-989-6328

Valley Meat Company
Modesto, CA ... 800-222-6328

Wisconsin Packaging Corp
Fort Atkinson, WI ... 920-563-9363

Zartic Inc
Rome, GA ... 800-241-0516

Portion Cuts

A To Z Portion Control Meats
Bluffton, OH ... 800-338-6328

Atlantic Veal & Lamb Inc
Brooklyn, NY ... 800-222-8325

B & D Foods
Boise, ID ... 208-344-1183

Beef Products Inc.
North Sioux City, SD ... 605-217-8000

Boar's Head
Sarasota, FL ... 800-352-6277

Bouma Meats
Provost, AB ... 780-753-2092

Broadleaf Venison USA Inc
Vernon, CA ... 800-336-3844

Brucepac
Woodburn, OR ... 800-899-3629

Bush Brothers Provision Co
West Palm Beach, FL ... 800-327-1345

C&S Wholesale Meat Company
Atlanta, GA ... 404-627-3547

Cambridge Packing Company
Boston, MA ... 800-722-6726

Canal Fulton Provision
Canal Fulton, OH ... 800-321-3502

Caribbean Food Delights Inc
Tappan, NY ... 845-398-3000

Carolina Pride Foods
Greenwood, SC ... 864-229-5611

Chicago Meat Authority Inc
Chicago, IL ... 800-383-3811

Clifty Farm Country Meats
Paris, TN ... 800-486-4267

Cloverdale Foods
Mandan, ND ... 800-669-9511

Corfu Foods Inc
Bensenville, IL ... 630-595-2510

Crescent Duck Farm
Aquebogue LI, NY ... 631-722-8000

Dairy Fresh Foods Inc
Taylor, MI ... 313-299-0735

Devault Foods
Devault, PA ... 800-426-2874

Frank Brunckhorst Company
Sarasota, FL ... 804-722-4100

King Kold Meats
Englewood, OH ... 800-836-2797

L & L Packing Co
Chicago, IL ... 800-628-6328

Land O'Frost Inc
Searcy, AR ... 800-643-5654

Marshallville Packing Co
Marshallville, OH ... 330-855-2871

National Foods
Indianapolis, IN ... 800-683-6565

Ohio Association Of Meat
Frazeysburg, OH ... 740-828-9900

Pacific Poultry Company
Honolulu, HI ... 808-841-2828

Paulsen Foods
Atlanta, GA ... 404-873-1804

Quality Meats & Seafood
West Fargo, ND ... 800-342-4250

Robinson Distributing Co
London, KY ... 800-230-5131

S.W. Meat & Provision Company
Phoenix, AZ ... 602-275-2000

SOPAKCO Foods
Mullins, SC ... 800-276-9678

Standard Meat Co LP
Dallas, TX ... 866-859-6313

Streit Carl & Son Co
Neptune, NJ ... 732-775-0803

The Bruss Company
Chicago, IL ... 773-282-2900

Triple U Enterprises
Fort Pierre, SD ... 605-567-3624

United Meat Company
San Francisco, CA ... 415-864-2118

WACO Beef & Pork Processors
Waco, TX ... 254-772-4669

Wisconsin Packaging Corp
Fort Atkinson, WI ... 920-563-9363

Prepared

Ajinomoto Foods North America, Inc.
Ontario, CA ... 909-477-4700

American Foods Group LLC
Green Bay, WI ... 800-345-0293

Burke Corp
Nevada, IA ... 800-654-1152

Charlito's Cocina
Brooklyn, NY ... 718-482-7890

Fair Oaks Farms LLC
Pleasant Prairie, WI ... 800-528-8615

Gutheinz Meats Inc
Scranton, PA ... 570-344-1191

Henry J's Meat Specialties
Chicago, IL ... 800-242-1314

Meat & Supply Co
New York, NY ... 646-864-0967

Piller's Fine Foods
Waterloo, ON ... 800-265-2627

Roger Wood Foods Inc
Savannah, GA ... 800-849-9272

Sofo Foods
Toledo, OH ... 800-447-4211

Specialty Foods Group Inc
Owensboro, KY ... 800-238-0020

Wisconsin Cheeseman
Madison, WI ... 800-693-0834

Proteins

Abbot's Butcher
Costa Mesa, CA ... 949-726-2156

Burke Corp
Nevada, IA ... 800-654-1152

Fork & Goode
Brooklyn, NY

Spice Of Life Co
Sherman Oaks, CA ... 818-909-0052

General

Aala Meat Market Inc
Honolulu, HI ... 808-832-6650

Ajinomoto Foods North America, Inc.
Ontario, CA ... 909-477-4700

Alef Sausage Inc
Mundelein, IL ... 847-968-2533

Annapolis Produce & Restaurant
Annapolis, MD ... 410-266-5211

Arnold's Meat Food Products
Brooklyn, NY ... 800-633-7023

Asiago PDO & Speck Alto Adige PGI
New York, NY ... 646-624-2885

Aufschnitt Meats
Owings Mills, MD ... 410-356-7745

B & R Quality Meats Inc
Waterloo, IA ... 319-232-6328

Ballard Custom Meats
Manchester, ME ... 207-622-9764

Belleville Brothers Packing
North Baltimore, OH ... 419-257-3529

Bernard & Sons
Bakersfield, CA ... 661-327-4431

Blalock Seafood & Specialty
Orange Beach, AL ... 251-974-5811

Boar's Head
Sarasota, FL ... 800-352-6277

Boyle Meat Company
Kansas City, MO ... 800-821-3626

Bradley Technologies Canada Inc.
Delta, BC ... 866-508-7514

Broadbent B & B Food Products
Kuttawa, KY ... 800-841-2202

Brookshire Grocery Company
Tyler, TX........................888-937-3776
Brown Foods
Dallas, GA........................770-445-4358
Burke Corp
Nevada, IA........................800-654-1152
C & J Tender Meat Co
Anchorage, AK........................907-562-2838
Casper Foodservice Company
Chicago, IL........................312-226-2265
Charlito's Cocina
Brooklyn, NY........................718-482-7890
Chicago Premier Meats
Chicago, IL........................800-385-0661
Chipper Snax
Salt Lake City, UT........................801-977-0742
Chong Mei Trading
East Point, GA........................404-768-3838
Cimpl Meats
Yankton, SD........................605-665-1665
Coleman Natural
Kings Mountain, NC........................800-442-8666
Consumers Packing Co
Melrose Park, IL........................800-356-9876
Creminelli Fine Meats
Salt Lake City, UT........................801-428-1820
CTI Foods
Wilder, ID........................208-482-7844
Devro Inc
Swansea, SC........................803-796-9730
DiMario Foods
Oak Brook, IL........................630-581-5250
Double B Distributors
Lexington, KY........................859-255-8822
Dr. Pete's/J.C. Specialty Foods
Savannah, GA........................912-233-3035
E-Fish-Ent Fish Company
Sooke, BC........................250-642-4007
Ellsworth Foods
Tifton, GA........................229-386-8448
Fa Lu Cioli
Union, NJ........................908-258-8651
Fork & Goode
Brooklyn, NY
Frank Brunckhorst Company
Sarasota, FL........................804-722-4100
Galvinell Meat Co Inc
Conowingo, MD........................410-378-3032
Garden Protein International
Richmond, BC........................877-305-6777
Glenoaks Food Inc
Sun Valley, CA........................818-768-9091
Golden Valley Natural
Shelley, ID........................888-270-7147
Golden West Food Group
Vernon, CA........................888-807-3663
Gopicnic Inc
Chicago, IL........................773-328-2490
Grayson Naturla Farms
Independence, VA........................276-773-3712
Gulf Marine & Industrial Supplies Inc
Houston, TX........................800-886-6252
H-E-B Grocery Co. LP
San Antonio, TX........................800-432-3113
Harbison Wholesale Meats
Cullman, AL........................256-739-5105
Heinkel's Packing Co
Decatur, IL........................800-594-2738
Henry J's Meat Specialties
Chicago, IL........................800-242-1314
Higa Food Service
Honolulu, HI........................808-531-3591
Highland Family Farms
Mapleton, MN........................507-524-3797
Ingles Markets
Black Mountain, NC........................828-669-2941
International Farmers Market
Chamblee, GA........................770-455-1777
Ira Higdon Grocery Company
Cairo, GA........................229-377-1272
J M Swank Co
North Liberty, IA........................800-593-6375
Jacob & Sons Wholesale Meats
Martins Ferry, OH........................740-633-3091
Jordan's Meats & Deli
Lakeland, MN........................651-337-2224
JUST Inc
San Francisco, CA........................844-423-6637
Kern Meat Distributing
Brooksville, KY........................606-756-2255
Lamex Foods Inc.
Bloomington, MN........................952-844-0585
Layman Distributing
Salem, VA........................800-237-1319
Les Trois Petits Cochons
Brooklyn, NY........................800-537-7283
Link Snacks Inc.
Minong, WI........................715-466-2234
Lubbers Family Farm
Grand Rapids, MI........................616-453-4257
Manda Fine Meats Inc
Baton Rouge, LA........................800-343-2642
Marathon Enterprises Inc
Englewood, NJ........................800-722-7388
Mcfarling Foods Inc
Indianapolis, IN........................317-635-2633
Mcredmond Brothers
Nashville, TN........................800-251-5930
Me At Corral
Gainesville, GA........................770-536-9188
Meat & Fish Fellas
Glendale, AZ........................623-931-6190
Meijer Inc
Grand Rapids, MI........................616-453-6711
Memphis Meats
Berkeley, CA
Miami Beef Co
Miami Lakes, FL........................305-621-3252
My Favorite Jerky
Boulder, CO........................303-444-2846
National Meat & Provision Company
Reserve, LA........................985-479-4200
New Grass Bison
Shawnee, KS........................866-422-5888
New Horizon Farms
Pipestone, MN........................800-906-7447
Newport Meat Co North
Irvine, CA........................949-474-4040
Northern Meats
Anchorage, AK........................907-561-1729
Northwest Meat Company
Chicago, IL........................312-733-1418
Oberto Brands
Kent, WA........................877-453-7591
Oberweis Dairy Inc
North Aurora, IL........................866-623-7934
Ohio Association Of Meat
Frazeysburg, OH........................740-828-9900
Olympic Provisions Northwest
Portland, OR........................503-894-8136
Omaha Steaks Inc
........................800-960-8400
Oscar's Wholesale Meats
Ogden, UT........................801-621-5655
Park 100 Foods Inc
Tipton, IN........................800-854-6504
Piggie Park Enterprises
West Columbia, SC........................800-628-7423
Piller's Fine Foods
Waterloo, ON........................800-265-2627
Pilot Meat & Sea Food Company
Galena, IL........................319-556-0760
Pioneer Snacks
Farmington Hills, MI........................248-862-1990
Pluester Quality Meat Co
Hardin, IL........................618-396-2224
Pocino Foods
City Of Industry, CA........................800-345-0150
Pon Food Corp
Ponchatoula, LA........................985-386-6941
Porkie Company of Wisconsin
Cudahy, WI........................800-333-2588
Prime Cut Meat & Seafood Company
Phoenix, AZ........................800-277-1054
Primera Meat Service
Harlingen, TX........................956-423-3721
Primo Foods
Oceanside, CA........................760-439-8711
Protos Inc
Greensburg, PA........................724-836-1802
Publix Super Market
Lakeland, FL........................800-242-1227
Quality Snack Foods Inc
Alsip, IL........................708-377-7120
Quirch Foods
Coral Gables, FL........................800-458-5252
RM Heagy Foods
Lancaster, PA........................717-569-1032
Rocky Mountain Natural Meats
Henderson, CO........................800-327-2706
Rougie Foie Gras
Marieville, QC........................450-460-2107
Safeway Inc.
Pleasanton, CA........................877-723-3929
Schenk Packing Co Inc
Mt Vernon, WA........................360-336-2128
Schisa Brothers
Syracuse, NY........................315-463-0213
Seafood Dimensions Intl
Yorba Linda, CA........................714-692-6464
Service Foods
Norcross, GA........................800-872-3484
Shuff's Meat Market
Thurmont, MD........................301-271-2231
Smoke House
Sagle, ID........................208-263-6312
Smoked Turkey Inc
Marshville, NC........................704-624-6628
Snak King Corp
City Of Industry, CA........................626-336-7711
Sofina Foods Inc
Markham, ON........................855-763-4621
Sommers Organic
Wheeling, IL........................877-377-9797
Specialty Food Association
New York, NY........................646-878-0301
Speco Inc
Schiller Park, IL........................800-541-5415
SRA Foods
Birmingham, AL........................205-323-7447
Strassburger Steaks
Carlstadt, NJ........................201-842-8890
Surlean Foods
San Antonio, TX........................800-999-4370
Sweetwood Cattle Co
Steamboat Spgs, CO........................970-879-7456
Teddy's Tasty Meats
Anchorage, AK........................907-562-2320
Thanasi Foods LLC
Boulder, CO........................866-558-7379
The New Primal
Johns Island, SC........................866-723-1386
The Shed Saucery
Ocean Springs, MS........................228-875-9590
Think Jerky
Chicago, IL........................312-380-0039
Thumann Inc.
Carlstadt, NJ........................201-935-3636
Todd's
Vernon, CA........................800-938-6337
Trail's Best Snacks
Memphis, TN........................800-852-1863
Trenton Processing Ctr
Trenton, IL........................800-871-7675
Troyer Foods Inc
Goshen, IN........................800-876-9377
Turkey Creeks Snacks Inc
Thomaston, GA........................800-329-8875
Tuscan Eat/Perdinci
Sarasota, FL........................941-565-7382
UTZ Quality Foods Inc.
Hanover, PA........................800-367-7629
Vanee Foods Co
Berkeley, IL........................708-449-7300
Vantage Foods
Calgary, AB........................403-215-2820
Vermont Smoke and Cure
Hinesburg, VT........................802-482-4666
Vestergaard Farms
Ann Arbor, MI........................734-929-2875
Vity Meat & Provisions Company
Phoenix, AZ........................602-269-7768
Volpi Foods
St Louis, MO........................800-288-3439
Wegmans Food Markets Inc.
Rochester, NY........................800-934-6267
White Oak Pastures
Bluffton, GA........................229-641-2081
Winn-Dixie Stores
Jacksonville, FL........................800-967-9105
YB Meats of Wichita
Wichita, KS........................316-942-1213
Zabiha Halal Meat Processors
Addison, IL........................630-620-5000
Zoe's Meats
Santa Rosa, CA........................707-545-9637
Zuccaro Produce
Columbia Heights, MN........................612-333-1122

Beef & Beef Products

A To Z Portion Control Meats
Bluffton, OH........................800-338-6328
A&H Products, Inc
Hillsdale, NJ........................908-206-8886
A.C. Kissling Company
Philadelphia, PA........................800-445-1943

Abbott's Meat Inc
Flint, MI 800-678-1907
Abbyland Foods Inc
Abbotsford, WI.................... 800-732-5483
Acme Steak & Seafood
Youngstown, OH.................... 800-686-2263
Adolf's Meats & Sausage Kitchen
Hartford, CT...................... 860-522-1588
Advance Pierre Foods
Cincinnati, OH.................... 800-969-2747
AFI-FlashGril'd Steak
Salt Lake City, UT................ 800-382-2862
AJ's Lena Maid Meats Inc
Lena, IL.......................... 815-369-4522
Al Safa Halal
New York City, NY................. 800-268-8147
Albert's Meats
Claysville, PA.................... 800-522-9970
Alderfer Inc
Harleysville, PA.................. 800-341-1121
Alpine Butcher
Lowell, MA........................ 978-256-7771
Alpine Cheese Company
Winesburg, OH..................... 330-359-6291
Alpine Meats
Stockton, CA...................... 800-399-6328
American Foods Group LLC
Green Bay, WI..................... 800-345-0293
Amity Packing Co Inc
Chicago, IL....................... 800-837-0270
Andrews Dried Beef Company
Quakertown, PA.................... 610-759-5180
Anmar Foods
Chicago, IL....................... 312-421-6500
Arena & Sons
Redwood City, CA.................. 650-366-1750
Arizona Sunland Foods
Tucson, AZ........................ 520-624-7068
Armbrust Meats
Medford, WI....................... 715-748-3102
Arrowhead Beef
Chipley, FL....................... 850-270-8804
Atlantic Meat Company
Savannah, GA...................... 912-964-8511
Aunt Kitty's Foods Inc
Vineland, NJ...................... 856-691-2100
Aurora Packing Co Inc
North Aurora, IL.................. 630-897-0551
Ayoba-Yo
Oakton, VA........................ 202-796-8554
B & R Quality Meats Inc
Waterloo, IA...................... 319-232-6328
B.W.J.W. Inc.
Fort Worth, TX.................... 817-831-0051
Bakalars Sausage Co
La Crosse, WI..................... 608-784-0384
Ball Park Franks
Peoria, IL........................ 888-317-5867
Baretta Provision
East Berlin, CT................... 860-828-0802
Barney Pork House
Decatur, AL....................... 256-353-8688
Beef Products Inc.
North Sioux City, SD.............. 605-217-8000
Bellville Meat Market
Bellville, TX..................... 800-571-6328
Berks Packing Company, Inc.
Reading, PA....................... 800-882-3757
Berry Processing
Walla Walla, IL................... 509-529-2161
Best Chicago Meat
Chicago, IL
Best Provision Co Inc
Union, NJ......................... 800-631-4466
Big B Barbecue
Evansville, IN.................... 812-425-5235
Birchwood Foods Inc
Kenosha, WI....................... 800-541-1685
Blakely Freezer Locker
Blakeley, GA...................... 229-723-3622
Bluebonnet Meat Company
Trenton, TX....................... 903-989-2293
Boone's Butcher Shop
Bardstown, KY..................... 888-253-3384
Borders Sporting Goods
Ashland, KY....................... 606-928-6326
Boulder Sausage Co
Louisville, CO.................... 866-529-0595
Bouma Meats
Provost, AB....................... 780-753-2092
Bouvry Exports Calgary
Calgary, AB....................... 403-253-0717

Boyd's Sausage Co
Washington, IA.................... 319-653-5715
Bradley 3 Ranch
Memphis, TX....................... 806-888-1062
Braham Food Locker Service
Braham, MN........................ 320-396-2636
Branding Iron
Sauget, IL........................ 800-851-4684
Breslow Deli Products
Philadelphia, PA.................. 215-739-4200
Brook Locker Plant
Brook, IN......................... 219-275-2611
Brook Meadow Meats
Hagerstown, MD.................... 301-739-3107
Brookfield Farm
Amherst, MA....................... 413-253-7991
Brown Foods
Dallas, GA........................ 770-445-4358
Brown Packing Company
South Holland, IL................. 800-832-8325
Brown Thompson & Sons
Fancy Farm, KY.................... 270-623-6321
Burgers' Smokehouse
California, MO.................... 800-345-5185
Burke Corp
Nevada, IA........................ 800-654-1152
Burnett & Son
Monrovia, CA...................... 877-632-5467
Burton Meat Processing
Burton, TX........................ 979-289-4022
Bush Brothers Provision Co
West Palm Beach, FL............... 800-327-1345
C & J Tender Meat Co
Anchorage, AK..................... 907-562-2838
C&S Wholesale Meat Company
Atlanta, GA....................... 404-627-3547
Caddo Packing Co
Marshall, TX...................... 903-935-2211
Callaway Packing Inc
Delta, CO......................... 970-874-9743
Campbell Soup Co.
Camden, NJ........................ 800-257-8443
Campbell's Quality Cuts
Sidney, OH........................ 937-492-2194
Camrose Packers
Camrose, AB....................... 780-672-4887
Canal Fulton Provision
Canal Fulton, OH.................. 800-321-3502
Candelari's Specialty Sausage
Houston, TX....................... 800-953-5343
Capital Packers Inc
Edmonton, AB...................... 800-272-8868
Capolla Food Inc
North York, ON.................... 416-633-0389
Carando Gourmet Frozen Foods
Agawam, MA........................ 888-227-2636
Cargill Protein
Wichita, KS
Caribbean Food Delights Inc
Tappan, NY........................ 845-398-3000
Caribbean Products
Baltimore, MD..................... 410-235-7700
Carl Rittberger Sr Inc
Zanesville, OH.................... 740-452-2767
Caro Foods
Houma, LA......................... 800-395-2276
Castle Rock Meats
Denver, CO........................ 303-292-0855
Cattaneo Brothers Inc
San Luis Obispo, CA............... 800-243-8537
Centennial Food Corporation
Calgary, AB....................... 403-214-0044
Center Locker Svc
Center, MO........................ 800-884-0737
Central Meat & Provision
San Diego, CA..................... 619-239-1391
Century Agricultural Products LLC
Greenback, TN..................... 865-980-8522
Chandler Foods Inc
Greensboro, NC.................... 800-537-6219
Charlito's Cocina
Brooklyn, NY...................... 718-482-7890
Chef's Requested Foods
Oklahoma City, OK................. 405-239-2610
Cher-Make Sausage Co
Manitowoc, WI..................... 800-242-7679
Cheraw Packing Plant
Cheraw, SC........................ 843-537-7426
Chicago 58 Food Products
Woodbridge, ON.................... 416-603-4244
Chicago Meat Authority Inc
Chicago, IL....................... 800-383-3811

Chicago Steaks
Chicago, IL....................... 773-847-5400
Chip Steak & Provision Co
Mankato, MN....................... 507-388-6277
Cimpl Meats
Yankton, SD....................... 605-665-1665
Circle V Meats
Spanish Fork, UT.................. 801-798-3081
Clay Center Locker Plant
Clay Center, KS................... 800-466-5543
Clovervale Farms
Amherst, OH....................... 800-433-0146
Columbia Packing Co Inc
Dallas, TX........................ 214-946-8171
Conagra Brands Inc
Chicago, IL....................... 877-266-2472
Conagra Foodservice
Chicago, IL....................... 877-266-2472
Continental Grain Company
New York, NY...................... 212-207-5100
Continental Sausage
Denver, CO........................ 866-794-7727
Corfu Foods Inc
Bensenville, IL................... 630-595-2510
Couch's Country Style Sausages
Cleveland, OH..................... 216-823-2332
Country Butcher Shop
Carlisle, PA...................... 800-272-9223
Country Village Meats Inc
Sublette, IL...................... 800-700-4545
Crescent Foods
Chicago, IL....................... 800-939-6268
Creuzebergers Meats
Duncansville, PA.................. 814-695-3061
Critchfield Meats Inc
Lexington, KY..................... 800-866-2901
Crofton & Sons Inc
Tampa, FL......................... 800-878-7675
CTI Foods
Wilder, ID........................ 208-482-7844
Curley's Custom Meats
Jackson Center, OH................ 937-596-6518
Curly's Foods Inc
Edina, MN......................... 612-920-3400
Curtis Packing Co
Greensboro, NC.................... 336-275-7684
Cyclone Enterprises Inc
Houston, TX....................... 281-872-0087
Dale T Smith & Sons Inc
Draper, UT........................ 801-571-3611
Day-Lee Foods, Inc.
Santa Fe Springs, CA.............. 800-329-5331
Dearborn Sausage Co Inc
Dearborn, MI...................... 866-900-4426
Debragga & Spitler
Jersey City, NJ
Decker Food Company
Garland, TX....................... 972-278-6192
Deen Meat & Cooked Foods
Fort Worth, TX.................... 800-333-3953
Devault Foods
Devault, PA....................... 800-426-2874
Dewig Brothers Packing Company
Haubstadt, IN..................... 812-768-6208
Diazteca Inc
Rio Rico, AZ...................... 520-761-4621
Diestel Family Turkey Ranch
.... 209-532-4950
Diggs Packing Company
Columbia, MO...................... 573-449-2995
Dino's Sausage & Meat Co Inc
Utica, NY......................... 315-732-2661
Dole & Bailey Inc
Woburn, MA........................ 781-935-1234
Dom's Sausage Co Inc
Malden, MA........................ 781-324-6390
Donald E Hunter Meats
Hillsboro, OH..................... 937-466-2311
Dorina So-Good Inc
Union, IL......................... 815-923-2144
Drier's Meats
Three Oaks, MI.................... 269-756-3101
Dryden Provision Co Inc
Louisville, KY.................... 502-583-1777
Dugdale Beef Company
Indianapolis, IN.................. 317-520-9981
Duma Meats Inc
Mogadore, OH...................... 330-628-3438
Dutch Packing Co., Inc.
Doral, FL......................... 800-723-9249
Dutterer's Home Food Service
Baltimore, MD..................... 410-298-3663

Dynamic Foods
Lubbock, TX 806-723-5600
E&H Packing Company
Detroit, MI 313-567-8286
E.W. Knauss & Son
Quakertown, PA 800-648-4220
East Dayton Meat & Poultry
Dayton, OH 937-253-6185
Ed Miniat Inc
South Holland, IL 708-589-2400
Edelman Meats Inc
Antigo, WI 715-623-7686
Eickman's Processing Co
Seward, IL 815-247-8451
Eiserman Meats
Slave Lake, AB 780-849-5507
El Paso Meat Co
El Paso, TX 915-838-8600
Ellsworth Locker
Ellsworth, MN 507-967-2544
ELP Inc
Elizabeth, CO 303-688-2240
Enjoy Foods International
Fontana, CA 909-823-2228
Eureka Locker Inc
Eureka, IL 309-467-2731
Eurocaribe Packing Company
Vega Baja, PR 787-793-6900
Ezzo Sausage Company
Columbus, OH 800-558-8841
Fabbri Sausage Mfg Co
Chicago, IL 312-829-6363
Fair Oaks Farms LLC
Pleasant Prairie, WI 800-528-8615
Far West Meats
Highland, CA 909-864-1990
Farm Boy Food Svc
Evansville, IN 800-852-3976
FDI Inc
Berkeley, IL 708-544-1880
Feed The Party
Louisville, KY
First Original Texas Chili Company
Fort Worth, TX 800-507-0009
Flanders
Waycross, GA 912-283-5191
Four Star Beef
Omaha, NE
Fred Usinger Inc
Milwaukee, WI 800-558-9998
Freirich Foods
Salisbury, NC 800-221-1315
Fremont Beef Co
Fremont, NE 800-331-4788
Fulton Provision Co
Portland, OR 800-333-6328
Gary's Frozen Foods
Lubbock, TX 806-745-1933
Gaucho Foods
Fayetteville, IL 877-677-2282
Gelsinger Food Products
Montrose, CA 818-248-7811
Gem Meat Packing Co
Garden City, ID 208-375-9424
Georgetown Farm
Free Union, VA 888-328-5326
Godshall's Quality Meats
Telford, PA 888-463-7425
Golden West Food Group
Vernon, CA 888-807-3663
GoodMark Foods
Edina, MN 952-835-6900
Grandpa Ittel's Meats Inc
Howard Lake, MN 320-543-2285
Grant Park Packing
Chicago, IL 312-421-4096
Grass Run Farms
Greeley, CO 800-727-2333
Great Plains Beef LLC
Lincoln, NE 402-479-2115
Greater Omaha Packing Co Inc.
Omaha, NE 800-747-5400
Grimm's Fine Food
Richmond, BC 866-663-4746
Grimm's Locker Service
Sherwood, OH 419-899-2655
Groff's Meats
Elizabethtown, PA 717-367-1246
Gwinn's Foods
St Louis, MO 314-521-8792
H&K Packers Company
Winnipeg, NB 204-233-2354
Hall Brothers Meats
Olmsted Twp, OH 440-235-3262
Ham I Am
Dallas, TX 800-742-6426
Hamilos Bros Inspected Meat
Madison, IL 618-876-3710
Hamms Custom Meats
Mckinney, TX 972-542-3359
Happy Acres Packing Company
Petal, MS 601-584-8301
Harper's Country Hams
Clinton, KY 888-427-7377
Harris Ranch Beef Co
Selma, CA 800-742-1955
Hausman Foods LLC
Corpus Christi, TX 361-883-5521
Heinke Family Farm
Paradise, CA 530-877-5264
Heinkel's Packing Co
Decatur, IL 800-594-2738
Henry J's Meat Specialties
Chicago, IL 800-242-1314
Heringer Meats Inc
Covington, KY 859-291-2000
Hickory Baked Ham Co
Castle Rock, CO 303-688-2633
Hickory Farms
Maumee, OH 800-753-8558
High Valley Farm
Castle Rock, CO 303-634-2944
Hillbilly Smokehouse
Rogers, AR 479-636-1927
Hoff's United Food
Brownsville, WI 800-852-9658
Holly Hill Locker Company
Holly Hill, SC 803-496-3611
Holton Meat Processing
Holton, KS 785-364-2331
Home Market Food Inc
Norwood, MA 800-367-8325
Honeybaked Ham
Cincinnati, OH 513-583-8792
Horlacher Meats
Logan, UT 435-752-1287
Hormel Foods Corp.
Austin, MN 507-437-5611
Houser Meats
Rushville, IL 217-322-4994
Hsin Tung Yang Foods Inc
S San Francisco, CA 650-589-6789
Humeniuk's Meat Cutting
Ranfurly, AB 780-658-2381
Huse's Country Meats
Malone, TX 254-533-2205
Independent Meat Co
Twin Falls, ID 800-284-4626
International Food Packers Corporation
Miami, FL 305-740-5847
International Meat Co
Chicago, IL 773-622-1400
Isernio Sausage Company
Seattle, WA 888-495-8674
Ito Cariani Sausage Company
Hayward, CA 510-887-0882
J F O'Neill & Packing Co
Omaha, NE 402-733-1200
J W Treuth & Sons
Catonsville, MD 410-747-6281
J.M. Schneider
Saint Anselme, QC 418-885-4474
Jackson Brothers Food Locker
Post, TX 806-495-3245
Jacob's Meats Inc
Defiance, OH 419-782-7831
Jacobsmuhlen's Meats
Cornelius, OR 503-359-0479
Jakes Brothers Country Meats
Joelton, TN 615-876-2911
Janowski's Hamburgers Inc
Rockville Centre, NY 516-764-9591
JBS USA LLC
Greeley, CO 970-506-8000
Jemm Wholesale Meat Company
Chicago, IL 773-523-8161
Jensen Meat Company
San Diego, CA 619-754-6400
John Garner Meats
Van Buren, AR 800-543-5473
Jones Packing Co
Harvard, IL 815-943-4488
Jordahl Meats
Manchester, MN 507-826-3418
Joyce Farms
Winston Salem, NC 800-755-6923
K & K Gourmet Meats Inc
Leetsdale, PA 724-266-8400
Karl Ehmer
Flushing, NY 800-487-5275
Kelble Brothers Inc
Berlin Heights, OH 800-247-2333
Kelly Corned Beef Co
Chicago, IL 800-624-5617
Kelly Packing Company
Torrington, WY 307-532-2210
Kelly-Eisenberg Gourmet Deli Products
Chicago, IL 800-624-5617
Kenosha Beef International LTD
Kenosha, WI
Kershenstine Beef Jerky
Eupora, MS 662-258-2049
Ketters Meat Market & Locker Plant
Frazee, MN 218-334-2351
King Kold Meats
Englewood, OH 800-836-2797
King's Command Foods Inc
Green Bay, WA 800-345-0293
Kingsbury Country Market
La Porte, IN 219-393-3016
Kiolbassa Provision Co
San Antonio, TX 800-456-5465
Klement Sausage Co Inc
Milwaukee, WI 800-553-6368
Kulana Foods LTD
Hilo, HI 808-959-9144
Kutztown Bologna Company
Leola, PA 800-723-8824
L & L Packing Co
Chicago, IL 800-628-6328
L & M Lockers
Belt, MT 406-277-3522
L & M Slaughterhouse
Georgetown, IL 217-662-6841
L. A. Smoking & Curing Company
Los Angeles, CA 213-624-2369
Ladoga Frozen Food & Retail
Ladoga, IN 765-942-2225
Lampost Meats
Grimes, IA 515-288-6111
Land O'Frost Inc
Searcy, AR 800-643-5654
Land O'Frost Inc.
Lansing, IL 800-323-3308
Lay Packing Company
Knoxville, TN 865-522-1147
Lehmann Farms
Lakeville, MN 800-446-5276
Lengerich Meats Inc
Zanesville, IN 260-638-4123
Leo G. Fraboni Sausage Company
Hibbing, MN 218-263-5074
Link Snacks Inc.
Minong, WI 715-466-2234
Lisbon Sausage Co Inc
New Bedford, MA 508-994-0453
Lombardi Brothers Meat Packers
Denver, CO 303-458-7441
Long Food Industries
Fripp Island, SC 843-838-3205
Longview Meat & Merchandise Ltd
Longview, AB 866-355-3759
Mac's Meats Inc
Las Cruces, NM 575-524-2751
MacGregors Meat & Seafood
Toronto, ON 888-383-3663
Mada'n Kosher Foods
Dania, FL 954-925-0077
Magnolia Meats
Knoxville, TN 865-546-7702
Maid-Rite Steak Company
Dunmore, PA 800-233-4259
Manger Packing Corp
Baltimore, MD 800-227-9262
Manley Meats Inc
Decatur, IN 260-592-7313
Marie F
Markham, ON 800-365-4464
Marks Meat
Holmen, WI 608-526-6058
Marshallville Packing Co
Marshallville, OH 330-855-2871
Marubeni America Corp.
New York, NY 212-450-0100
Matthiesen's Deer & Custom
De Witt, IA 563-659-8409

Mclemores Abattoir Inc
Vidalia, GA 912-537-4476
Meadowbrook Meat Company
Rocky Mount, NC 252-985-7200
Meatco Sales Ltd.
Mirror, AB 403-788-2292
Meating Place
Buffalo, NY 716-885-3623
Meatland Packers
Medicine Hat, AB 403-528-4321
Medeiros Farms
Kalaheo, HI 808-332-8211
Memphis Meats
Berkeley, CA
Merkley & Sons Packing Co Inc
Jasper, IN 812-482-7020
Merrill Meat Co
Encampment, WY 307-327-5345
Mesquite Organic Beef LLC
Aurora, CO 888-480-2333
Metafoods LLC
Brookhaven, GA 404-843-2400
Metropolitan Sausage Manufacturing Company
Flossmoor, IL 708-331-3232
Michael's Finer Meats/Seafoods
Columbus, OH 800-282-0518
Miko Meat
Hilo, HI 808-935-0841
Miller Brothers Packing Company
Sylvester, GA 229-776-2014
Miller's Country Hams
Dresden, TN 800-622-0606
Miller's Meat Market
Red Bud, IL 618-282-3334
Mims Meat Company
Houston, TX 713-453-0151
Mirasco
Atlanta, GA 770-956-1945
Montana Ranch Brand
Billings, MT 406-294-2333
Morreale John R Inc
Chicago, IL 312-421-3664
Mortimer's Fine Foods
Burlington, ON 905-336-0000
Moweaqua Packing Plant
Moweaqua, IL 217-768-4714
Munsee Meats
Muncie, IN 800-662-8001
Napoleon Locker
Napoleon, IN 812-852-4333
National Foods
Indianapolis, IN 800-683-6565
National Steak & Poultry
Owasso, OK 918-274-8787
Natures Sungrown Foods Inc
San Rafael, CA 415-491-4944
Nebraska Beef Council
Kearney, NE 800-421-5326
Nema Food Distribution
Fairfield, NJ 973-256-4415
Nesbitt Processing
Aledo, IL 309-582-5183
New Braunfels Smokehouse
New Braunfels, TX 800-537-6932
Nick's Sticks
Marshfield, WI 715-257-0636
Nodine's Smokehouse Inc
Torrington, CT 800-222-2059
Nolechek Meats Inc
Thorp, WI 800-454-5580
Northern Packing Company
Brier Hill, NY 315-375-8801
Northwest Meat Company
Chicago, IL 312-733-1418
Nossack Fine Meats
Red Deer, AB 403-346-5006
Nueske's Applewood Smoked Meat
Wittenberg, WI 800-720-1153
Oklahoma City Meat Co Inc
Oklahoma City, OK 405-235-3308
Old Country Meat & Sausage Company
San Diego, CA 619-297-4301
Old Kentucky Hams
Cynthiana, KY 859-234-5015
Old Neighborhood
Lynn, MA 781-595-1557
Olson Locker
Fairmont, MN 507-238-2563
Omaha Meat Processors
Omaha, NE 402-554-1965
Omaha Steaks Inc
. 800-960-8400

On-Cor Frozen Foods Redi-Serve
Aurora, IL 920-563-6391
Onoway Custom Packers
Onoway, AB 780-967-2727
Ossian Smoked Meats
Ossian, IN 800-535-8862
P G Molinari & Sons
San Francisco, CA 415-822-5555
Palmer Meat Packing Co
Tremonton, UT 435-257-5329
Palmyra Bologna Co Inc
Palmyra, PA 800-282-6336
Panorama Meats
Fresno, CA 707-765-6756
Paradise Locker Inc.
Trimble, MO 816-370-6328
Pasqualichio Brothers Inc
Scranton, PA 800-232-6233
Pat's Meat Discounter
Mills, WY 307-237-7549
Patrick Cudahy LLC
Cudahy, WI 800-486-6900
Paul Schafer Meat Products
Baltimore, MD 410-528-1250
Payne Packing Co
Artesia, NM 575-746-2779
Pekarna Meat Market
Jordan, MN 952-492-6101
Pekarski Sausage
South Deerfield, MA 413-665-4537
Petschl's Quality Meats
Tukwila, WA 206-575-4400
Pierceton Foods Inc
Pierceton, IN 574-594-2344
Piller's Fine Foods
Waterloo, ON 800-265-2627
Pinter's Packing Plant
Dorchester, WI 715-654-5444
Piper Meat Processing
Andover, OH 440-293-7170
Plymouth Beef Co.
Bronx, NY 718-589-8600
Poche's Smokehouse
Breaux Bridge, LA 800-376-2437
Polarica USA, Inc.
Pacheco, CA 800-426-3872
Pork Shop of Vermont
Charlotte, VT 800-458-3441
Premium Meat Co
Brigham City, UT 435-723-5944
Prime Pak Foods Inc
Gainesville, GA 770-536-8708
Provost Packers
Provost, AB 780-753-2415
Quaker Maid Meats
Reading, PA 610-376-1500
Quality Food Company
Providence, RI 877-233-3462
Quality Sausage Company
Dallas, TX 214-634-3400
Quirch Foods
Coral Gables, FL 800-458-5252
R Four Meats
Chatfield, MN 507-867-4180
R I Provision Co
Johnston, RI 401-831-0815
R.E. Meyer Company
Lincoln, NE 888-990-2333
Ranch Oak Farm
Fort Worth, TX 800-888-0327
Randall Foods Inc
Vernon, CA 800-372-6581
Ray's Sausage Co
Cleveland, OH 216-921-8782
Real Sausage Co
Chicago, IL 312-842-5330
Red Deer Lake Meat Processing
Calgary, AB 403-256-4925
Red Hot Chicago
Chicago, IL 800-249-5226
Red Steer Meats
Phoenix, AZ 602-272-6677
Redondo's LLC
Waipahu, HI 808-671-5444
Rinehart Meat Processing
Branson, MO 417-869-2041
Robbins Packing Company
Statesboro, GA 912-764-7503
Robertson's Country Meat Hams
Finchville, KY 800-678-1521
Rocky Mountain Meats
Rocky Mountain House, AB 403-845-3434

Rocky Mountain Packing Company
Havre, MT 406-265-3401
Rolet Food Products Company
Brooklyn, NY 718-497-0476
Roman Packing Company
Norfolk, NE 800-373-5990
Romanian Kosher Sausage Co
Chicago, IL 773-761-4141
Roode Packing Company
Fairbury, NE 402-729-2253
Rosen's Diversified Inc.
Fairmont, MN 507-238-6001
Royal Center Locker Plant
Royal Center, IN 574-643-3275
Royal Palate Foods
Inglewood, CA 310-330-7701
Rubashkin
Brooklyn, NY 718-436-5511
Rude Custom Butchering
Mt Morris, IL 815-946-3795
Ruef's Meat Market
New Glarus, WI 608-527-2554
Rymer Foods
Chicago, IL 800-247-9637
S.W. Meat & Provision Company
Phoenix, AZ 602-275-2000
Sadler's Smokehouse
Henderson, TX 903-657-5581
Salwa Foods
Lawrenceville, GA 770-263-8207
Sam KANE Beef Processors Inc
Corpus Christi, TX 800-242-4142
Sampco
Chicago, IL 800-767-1689
San Angelo Packing
San Angelo, TX 325-949-9401
Sanders Meat Packing Inc
Custer, MI 800-968-5035
Sangudo Custom Meat Packers
Sangudo, AB 888-785-3353
Santa's Smokehouse
Fairbanks, AK 800-478-3885
Saval Foods Corp
Elkridge, MD 800-527-2825
Sculli Brothers
Yeadon, PA 215-336-1223
Shamrock Foods Co
Phoenix, AZ 800-289-3663
Shelley's
Jersey City, NJ 201-433-2900
Shirer Brothers Meats
Adamsville, OH 740-796-3214
Shreve Meats Processing
Shreve, OH 330-567-2142
Shrums Sausage & Meats
Stettler, AB 403-742-1427
Silver Lake Sausage Shop
Providence, RI 401-944-4081
Sky Haven Farm
Cincinnati, OH 513-681-2303
Skylark Meats
Omaha, NE 800-759-5275
Slathars Smokehouse
Lake City, MN 507-753-2080
Slim Jim
Chicago, IL 877-266-2472
Smith Packing Regional Meat
Utica, NY 315-732-5125
Smith Provision Co Inc
Erie, PA 800-334-9151
Smokey Denmark Sausage Co
Austin, TX 512-385-0718
Sofina Foods Inc
Markham, ON 855-763-4621
Sommers Organic
Wheeling, IL 877-377-9797
Souris Valley Processors
Melita, MB 204-522-8210
Southern Packing Corp
Chesapeake, VA 757-421-2131
Specialty Foods Group Inc
Owensboro, KY 800-238-0020
Spring Grove Foods
Miamisburg, OH 937-866-4311
Springville Meat & Cold Storage
Springville, UT 801-489-6391
Square-H Brands Inc
Vernon, CA 323-267-4600
SRA Foods
Birmingham, AL 205-323-7447
Stallings Head Cheese Co
Houston, TX 713-523-1751

Standard Meat Co LP
Dallas, TX 866-859-6313
Steak-Umm Company
Shillington, PA 860-928-5900
Stehlin & Sons Company
Cincinnati, OH 800-352-7396
Stock Yards Packing Company
Melrose Park, IL 877-785-9273
Stone Meat Processor
Ogden, UT 801-782-9825
Straub's
Clayton, MO 888-725-2121
Strauss Brands International
Franklin, WI 414-421-5250
Streit Carl & Son Co
Neptune, NJ 732-775-0803
Stripling's General Store
Moultrie, GA 229-985-4226
Sudlersville Frozen Food Locker
Sudlersville, MD 410-438-3106
Sugardale Foods Inc
.... 800-860-6333
Sun-Rise
Alexandria, MN 320-846-5720
SunFed Ranch
Woodland, CA 530-723-5373
Sunnydale Meats Inc
Gaffney, SC 864-489-6091
Suzanna's Kitchen
Peachtree Cor, GA 770-476-9900
Sweetwood Cattle Co
Steamboat Spgs, CO 970-879-7456
Tank's Meats Inc
Elmore, OH 419-862-3312
Taylor Meat Co
Taylor, TX 512-352-6357
Taylor's Sausage Co
St Louis, MO 314-652-3476
Tayse Meats
Cleveland, OH 216-664-1799
Temptee Specialty Foods
Denver, CO 800-842-1233
Terra's
Perham, MN 218-346-4100
Terrell Meats
Delta, UT 435-864-2600
Texas Reds Steak House
Red River, NM 575-754-2922
The Bruss Company
Chicago, IL 773-282-2900
Thompson Packers
Slidell, LA 800-989-6328
Thomson Meats
Melfort, SK 306-752-2802
Three Jerks Jerky
Pacific Palisades, CA 424-703-5375
Tillamook Meat Inc
Tillamook, OR 503-842-4802
Tolteca Foodservice
Norcross, GA 800-541-6835
Travis Meats Inc
Powell, TN 800-247-7606
Tri State Beef Co
Cincinnati, OH 513-579-1722
Troy Pork Store
Troy, NY 518-272-8291
Troyer Foods Inc
Goshen, IN 800-876-9377
Tucker Packing Co
Orrville, OH 330-683-3311
Turk Brothers Custom Meats Inc
Ashland, OH 800-789-1051
Tyler Packing Co
Tyler, TX 903-593-9592
Tyson Foods Inc.
Springdale, AR 479-290-4000
Tyson Foods Inc.
Springdale, AR 800-233-6332
Uncle Charley's Sausage
Vandergrift, PA 724-845-3302
Une-Viandi
St. Jean Sur Richelieu, NB 800-363-1955
United Meat Company
San Francisco, CA 415-864-2118
United Provision Meat Company
Columbus, OH 614-252-1126
Universal Beef Products
Houston, TX 713-224-6043
US Wellness Meats
Canton, MO 877-383-0051
Uvalde Meat Processing
Uvalde, TX 830-278-6247
Valley Meat Company
Modesto, CA 800-222-6328
Valley Meats
Coal Valley, IL 309-517-6639
Verde Farms, LLC
Woburn, MA 617-221-8922
Vestergaard Farms
Ann Arbor, MI 734-929-2875
Victoria Fancy Sausage
Edmonton, AB 780-471-2283
Vienna Beef LTD
Chicago, IL 800-366-3647
Vienna Meat Products
Scarborough, ON 800-588-1931
Vital Choice
Bellingham, WA 800-608-4825
Voget Meats Inc
Hubbard, OR 503-981-6271
W & G Marketing Company
Ames, IA 515-233-4774
W.A. Beans & Sons
Bangor, ME 800-649-1958
W.R. Delozier Sausage Company
Seymour, TN 865-577-5907
WACO Beef & Pork Processors
Waco, TX 254-772-4669
Waken Meat Co
Atlanta, GA 404-627-3537
Walker Meats
Carrollton, GA 800-741-3601
Wall Meat Processing
Wall, SD 605-279-2348
Waltham Beef Company
Boston, MA 617-269-2250
Warren & Son Meat Processing
Whipple, OH 740-585-2421
Wasatch Meats Inc
Salt Lake City, UT 800-631-8294
Webster City Custom Meats Inc
Webster City, IA 515-832-1130
Weiss Brothers Smoke House
Johnstown, PA 814-539-4085
West Liberty Foods LLC
West Liberty, IA 888-511-4500
Westbrook Trading Company
Calgary, AB 800-563-5785
Western Buffalo Company
Rapid City, SD 800-247-3263
Western Meat Co
Tumwater, WA 866-357-6601
Westport Locker LLC
Westport, IN 877-265-0551
White Oak Pastures
Bluffton, GA 229-641-2081
White's Meat Processing
Fort Gibson, OK 918-478-2347
Willcox Meat Packing House
Willcox, AZ 520-384-2015
Windcrest Meat Packers
Port Perry, ON 800-750-2542
Winona Packing Company
Winona, MS 662-283-4317
Winter Sausage Manufacturing Company
Eastpointe, MI 800-321-2987
Wisconsin Packaging Corp
Fort Atkinson, WI 920-563-9363
Wohrles Foods
Pittsfield, MA 800-628-6114
Woodbine
Norfolk, VA 757-461-2731
Woods Smoked Meats Inc
Bowling Green, MO 800-458-8426
Yoakum Packing Co
Yoakum, TX 800-999-6997
Zartic Inc
Rome, GA 800-241-0516

Barbecued

Art's Tamales
Metamora, IL 309-367-2850
Bear Creek Smokehouse Inc
Marshall, TX 800-950-2327
Burke Corp
Nevada, IA 800-654-1152
Curly's Foods Inc
Edina, MN 612-920-3400
Dorina So-Good Inc
Union, IL 815-923-2144
Gary's Frozen Foods
Lubbock, TX 806-745-1933
Gaucho Foods
Fayetteville, IL 877-677-2282
King Kold Meats
Englewood, OH 800-836-2797
Moonlite Bar-B-Q Inn
Owensboro, KY 800-322-8989
Sadler's Smokehouse
Henderson, TX 903-657-5581
The Shed Saucery
Ocean Springs, MS 228-875-9590
Travis Meats Inc
Powell, TN 800-247-7606
W & G Marketing Company
Ames, IA 515-233-4774

Frozen

Art's Tamales
Metamora, IL 309-367-2850
Burke Corp
Nevada, IA 800-654-1152
El Rey Cooked Meats
St Louis, MO 314-521-3113
Gary's Frozen Foods
Lubbock, TX 806-745-1933
Gaucho Foods
Fayetteville, IL 877-677-2282
Hormel Foods Corp.
Austin, MN 507-437-5611
King Kold Meats
Englewood, OH 800-836-2797

Brisket

Bear Creek Smokehouse Inc
Marshall, TX 800-950-2327
Henry J's Meat Specialties
Chicago, IL 800-242-1314
Nueces Canyon Range
Brenham, TX 800-925-5058
Saval Foods Corp
Elkridge, MD 800-527-2825

Canned with Natural Juices

Aunt Kitty's Foods Inc
Vineland, NJ 856-691-2100
International Food Packers Corporation
Miami, FL 305-740-5847

Chipped

Alderfer Inc
Harleysville, PA 800-341-1121

Dinners

Campbell Soup Co.
Camden, NJ 800-257-8443
Henry J's Meat Specialties
Chicago, IL 800-242-1314

Filet Mignon

Amana Meat Shop & Smoke House
Amana, IA 800-373-6328
American Foods Group LLC
Green Bay, WI 800-345-0293
Chef's Requested Foods
Oklahoma City, OK 405-239-2610
Chicago Steaks
Chicago, IL 773-847-5400
Miami Beef Co
Miami Lakes, FL 305-621-3252

Fresh

Amity Packing Co Inc
Chicago, IL 800-837-0270
Brook Locker Plant
Brook, IN 219-275-2611
Brookfield Farm
Amherst, MA 413-253-7991
Buckhead Beef
Atlanta, GA 800-888-5578
Cattleman Meat & Produce
Taylor, MI 734-287-8260
Certified Piedmontese Beef
Lincoln, NE 800-414-3487
Farm Boy Food Svc
Evansville, IN 800-852-3976
Farmstead At Long Meadow Ranch
St Helena, CA 877-627-2645
Great Plains Beef LLC
Lincoln, NE 402-479-2115
Heinkel's Packing Co
Decatur, IL 800-594-2738

International Meat Co
Chicago, IL 773-622-1400
Lengerich Meats Inc
Zanesville, IN 260-638-4123
Munsee Meats
Muncie, IN 800-662-8001
National Beef Packing Co LLC
Kansas City, MO. 800-449-2333
Plymouth Beef Co.
Bronx, NY. 718-589-8600
R Four Meats
Chatfield, MN 507-867-4180
Schneider Foods
Etobicoke, ON 416-252-5790
Shelley's
Jersey City, NJ 201-433-2900
Smith Packing Regional Meat
Utica, NY 315-732-5125
Temptee Specialty Foods
Denver, CO 800-842-1233
Teton Waters Ranch LLC
Denver, CO 720-340-4590
Thumann Inc.
Carlstadt, NJ 201-935-3636
Tomer Kosher Foods
Skokie, IL 847-779-4870
Troy Pork Store
Troy, NY 518-272-8291
W.A. Beans & Sons
Bangor, ME. 800-649-1958
WACO Beef & Pork Processors
Waco, TX 254-772-4669

Frozen

Amity Packing Co Inc
Chicago, IL 800-837-0270
Armbrust Meats
Medford, WI 715-748-3102
Art's Tamales
Metamora, IL 309-367-2850
Atlantic Meat Company
Savannah, GA 912-964-8511
Birchwood Foods Inc
Kenosha, WI 800-541-1685
Birdie Pak Products
Chicago, IL 773-247-5293
Blakely Freezer Locker
Blakeley, GA. 229-723-3622
Bob's Custom Cuts
Bonnyville, AB 780-826-2627
Branding Iron
Sauget, IL 800-851-4684
Brook Locker Plant
Brook, IN 219-275-2611
Brookfield Farm
Amherst, MA 413-253-7991
Brookview Farms
Manakin-Sabot, VA 804-784-3131
Buckhead Beef
Atlanta, GA. 800-888-5578
Burke Corp
Nevada, IA 800-654-1152
Bush Brothers Provision Co
West Palm Beach, FL 800-327-1345
Carando Gourmet Frozen Foods
Agawam, MA 888-227-2636
Caribbean Food Delights Inc
Tappan, NY. 845-398-3000
Caribbean Products
Baltimore, MD 410-235-7700
Carl Buddig & Co.
Homewood, IL 888-633-5684
Cattleman Meat & Produce
Taylor, MI 734-287-8260
Chip Steak & Provision Co
Mankato, MN 507-388-6277
City Foods Inc
Chicago, IL. 773-523-1566
Curly's Foods Inc
Edina, MN. 612-920-3400
Devault Foods
Devault, PA. 800-426-2874
Duma Meats Inc
Mogadore, OH 330-628-3438
Dynamic Foods
Lubbock, TX. 806-723-5600
Edmond's Chile Co
St Louis, MO. 314-772-1499
El Rey Cooked Meats
St Louis, MO. 314-521-3113
Fox Deluxe Inc
Chicago, IL 312-421-3737
Gary's Frozen Foods
Lubbock, TX. 806-745-1933
Gaucho Foods
Fayetteville, IL 877-677-2282
Hall Brothers Meats
Olmsted Twp, OH 440-235-3262
Hamms Custom Meats
Mckinney, TX. 972-542-3359
Hausman Foods LLC
Corpus Christi, TX 361-883-5521
Heringer Meats Inc
Covington, KY 859-291-2000
Hormel Foods Corp.
Austin, MN 507-437-5611
International Food Packers Corporation
Miami, FL. 305-740-5847
Jemm Wholesale Meat Company
Chicago, IL 773-523-8161
JTM Food Group
Harrison, OH. 800-626-2308
K & K Gourmet Meats Inc
Leetsdale, PA 724-266-8400
King Kold Meats
Englewood, OH 800-836-2797
Kutztown Bologna Company
Leola, PA. 800-723-8824
Ladoga Frozen Food & Retail
Ladoga, IN 765-942-2225
Lengerich Meats Inc
Zanesville, IN 260-638-4123
Leo G. Fraboni Sausage Company
Hibbing, MN. 218-263-5074
M Buono Beef Co
Philadelphia, PA 215-463-3600
Maid-Rite Steak Company
Dunmore, PA. 800-233-4259
Meat-O-Mat Corp
Brooklyn, NY 718-965-7250
Northern Packing Company
Brier Hill, NY 315-375-8801
On-Cor Frozen Foods Redi-Serve
Aurora, IL. 920-563-6391
Phoenix Agro Industrial Corporation
Westbury, NY 516-334-1194
Pierceton Foods Inc
Pierceton, IN. 574-594-2344
Plymouth Beef Co.
Bronx, NY. 718-589-8600
R Four Meats
Chatfield, MN. 507-867-4180
Sam KANE Beef Processors Inc
Corpus Christi, TX 800-242-4142
Schneider Foods
Etobicoke, ON 416-252-5790
Shelley's
Jersey City, NJ 201-433-2900
Smith Packing Regional Meat
Utica, NY 315-732-5125
Steak-Umm Company
Shillington, PA 860-928-5900
Sudlersville Frozen Food Locker
Sudlersville, MD. 410-438-3106
Thompson Packers
Slidell, LA. 800-989-6328
Travis Meats Inc
Powell, TN 800-247-7606
Tucker Packing Co
Orrville, OH 330-683-3311
United Meat Company
San Francisco, CA 415-864-2118
Zartic Inc
Rome, GA. 800-241-0516

Ground

Acme Steak & Seafood
Youngstown, OH. 800-686-2263
American Foods Group LLC
Green Bay, WI. 800-345-0293
Atlantic Meat Company
Savannah, GA 912-964-8511
Caribbean Food Delights Inc
Tappan, NY. 845-398-3000
Centennial Food Corporation
Calgary, AB. 403-214-0044
Chicago Steaks
Chicago, IL 773-847-5400
Chip Steak & Provision Co
Mankato, MN 507-388-6277
Devault Foods
Devault, PA. 800-426-2874
Fulton Provision Co
Portland, OR 800-333-6328
Grass Run Farms
Greeley, CO. 800-727-2333
Jensen Meat Company
San Diego, CA 619-754-6400
John Garner Meats
Van Buren, AR 800-543-5473
Karn Meats
Columbus, OH 800-221-9585
Kenosha Beef International LTD
Kenosha, WI
Miami Beef Co
Miami Lakes, FL. 305-621-3252
Nurture Ranch
Frisco, TX. 866-467-2624
Palmer Meat Packing Co
Tremonton, UT 435-257-5329
Quality Food Company
Providence, RI 877-233-3462
Rinehart Meat Processing
Branson, MO. 417-869-2041
S.W. Meat & Provision Company
Phoenix, AZ 602-275-2000
Sommers Organic
Wheeling, IL. 877-377-9797
Springville Meat & Cold Storage
Springville, UT 801-489-6391
Stanley Provision Company
Manchester, CT. 888-688-6347
Stone Meat Processor
Ogden, UT. 801-782-9825
Thompson Packers
Slidell, LA. 800-989-6328
Valley Meat Company
Modesto, CA. 800-222-6328
Valley Meats
Coal Valley, IL 309-517-6639

Coarse Frozen

Devault Foods
Devault, PA. 800-426-2874

Frozen

Acme Steak & Seafood
Youngstown, OH. 800-686-2263
Caribbean Food Delights Inc
Tappan, NY. 845-398-3000
Chip Steak & Provision Co
Mankato, MN 507-388-6277
Kenosha Beef International LTD
Kenosha, WI
Thompson Packers
Slidell, LA. 800-989-6328

Hamburger

Acme Steak & Seafood
Youngstown, OH. 800-686-2263
Alpine Butcher
Lowell, MA. 978-256-7771
American Foods Group LLC
Green Bay, WI. 800-345-0293
Atlantic Meat Company
Savannah, GA 912-964-8511
Bakalars Sausage Co
La Crosse, WI 608-784-0384
Birchwood Foods Inc
Kenosha, WI 800-541-1685
Brucepac
Woodburn, OR 800-899-3629
Burger Maker Inc
Carlstadt, NJ 201-939-0444
Burke Corp
Nevada, IA 800-654-1152
Chicago Meat Authority Inc
Chicago, IL 800-383-3811
Chicopee Provision Co Inc
Chicopee, MA. 800-924-6328
Crocetti's Oakdale Packing Co
East Bridgewater, MA 508-587-0035
Devault Foods
Devault, PA. 800-426-2874
Edmond's Chile Co
St Louis, MO. 314-772-1499
Gouvea's & Purity Foods Inc
Honolulu, HI. 808-847-3717
Hormel Foods Corp.
Austin, MN 507-437-5611
Marathon Enterprises Inc
Englewood, NJ 800-722-7388
Miami Beef Co
Miami Lakes, FL. 305-621-3252

Ossian Smoked Meats
Ossian, IN........................800-535-8862
Pierceton Foods Inc
Pierceton, IN......................574-594-2344
Rinehart Meat Processing
Branson, MO.....................417-869-2041
Rymer Foods
Chicago, IL.......................800-247-9637
Saad Wholesale Meats
Detroit, MI.......................313-831-8126
Thompson Packers
Slidell, LA........................800-989-6328
Travis Meats Inc
Powell, TN........................800-247-7606
Valley Meat Company
Modesto, CA......................800-222-6328

Cooked Frozen

Burke Corp
Nevada, IA........................800-654-1152
Maid-Rite Steak Company
Dunmore, PA.....................800-233-4259

Uncooked Frozen

Al Safa Halal
New York City, NY...............800-268-8147
Caribbean Food Delights Inc
Tappan, NY........................845-398-3000
Maid-Rite Steak Company
Dunmore, PA......................800-233-4259
Pierceton Foods Inc
Pierceton, IN......................574-594-2344

Italian

Burke Corp
Nevada, IA........................800-654-1152
Henry J's Meat Specialties
Chicago, IL........................800-242-1314

Liver

American Foods Group LLC
Green Bay, WI....................800-345-0293
Caughman's Meat Plant
Lexington, SC.....................803-356-0076
Dynamic Foods
Lubbock, TX.......................806-723-5600
Fremont Beef Co
Fremont, NE.......................800-331-4788
Giovanni's Appetizing Food Co
Richmond, MI.....................586-727-9355
Lee's Sausage Co
Orangeburg, SC..................803-534-5517
Skylark Meats
Omaha, NE........................800-759-5275

London Broil

Burnett & Son
Monrovia, CA.....................877-632-5467

NY Strip Steak

Amana Meat Shop & Smoke House
Amana, IA.........................800-373-6328
Certified Piedmontese Beef
Lincoln, NE........................800-414-3487
Chef's Requested Foods
Oklahoma City, OK..............405-239-2610
Sommers Organic
Wheeling, IL.......................877-377-9797

Patties

Alpine Butcher
Lowell, MA.........................978-256-7771
Brucepac
Woodburn, OR....................800-899-3629
Burke Corp
Nevada, IA........................800-654-1152
Field Roast
Seattle, WA.......................800-311-9497
Fulton Provision Co
Portland, OR......................800-333-6328
Grass Run Farms
Greeley, CO........................800-727-2333
International Meat Co
Chicago, IL........................773-622-1400
Jensen Meat Company
San Diego, CA....................619-754-6400
Miami Beef Co
Miami Lakes, FL..................305-621-3252
On-Cor Frozen Foods
Sommers Organic
Wheeling, IL.......................877-377-9797

Frozen

Branding Iron
Sauget, IL..........................800-851-4684
Caribbean Food Delights Inc
Tappan, NY........................845-398-3000
Centennial Food Corporation
Calgary, AB........................403-214-0044
Corfu Foods Inc
Bensenville, IL....................630-595-2510
John Garner Meats
Van Buren, AR....................800-543-5473
Kenosha Beef International LTD
Kenosha, WI
King Kold Meats
Englewood, OH...................800-836-2797
Kutztown Bologna Company
Leola, PA...........................800-723-8824
Maid-Rite Steak Company
Dunmore, PA......................800-233-4259
Meat-O-Mat Corp
Brooklyn, NY......................718-965-7250
SunFed Ranch
Woodland, CA.....................530-723-5373
Travis Meats Inc
Powell, TN.........................800-247-7606
Valley Meat Company
Modesto, CA......................800-222-6328
Wisconsin Packaging Corp
Fort Atkinson, WI................920-563-9363

Jamaçaín

Royal Home Bakery
Newmarket, ON...................905-715-7044

Porterhouse

Arrowhead Beef
Chipley, FL........................850-270-8804
Certified Piedmontese Beef
Lincoln, NE........................800-414-3487
Chef's Requested Foods
Oklahoma City, OK..............405-239-2610
Chicago Steaks
Chicago, IL........................773-847-5400

Pot Roast

Fontanini Italian Meats
McCook, IL........................800-331-6328
Freirich Foods
Salisbury, NC.....................800-221-1315

Processed

Al Safa Halal
New York City, NY...............800-268-8147
Alderfer Inc
Harleysville, PA..................800-341-1121
Alewel's Country Meats
Warrensburg, MO................800-353-8553
Alpine Meats
Stockton, CA......................800-399-6328
American Foods Group LLC
Green Bay, WI....................800-345-0293
Aunt Kitty's Foods Inc
Vineland, NJ.......................856-691-2100
Best Chicago Meat
Chicago, IL
Best Provision Co Inc
Union, NJ..........................800-631-4466
Big B Barbecue
Evansville, IN.....................812-425-5235
Buckhead Beef
Atlanta, GA........................800-888-5578
Bush Brothers Provision Co
West Palm Beach, FL...........800-327-1345
Caddo Packing Co
Marshall, TX.......................903-935-2211
Campbell Soup Co.
Camden, NJ........................800-257-8443
Carando Gourmet Frozen Foods
Agawam, MA......................888-227-2636
Caribbean Food Delights Inc
Tappan, NY........................845-398-3000
Cattaneo Brothers Inc
San Luis Obispo, CA............800-243-8537
Central Meat & Provision
San Diego, CA....................619-239-1391
Chandler Foods Inc
Greensboro, NC...................800-537-6219
Cher-Make Sausage Co
Manitowoc, WI...................800-242-7679
Cheraw Packing Plant
Cheraw, SC........................843-537-7426
Chip Steak & Provision Co
Mankato, MN.....................507-388-6277
Columbia Packing Co Inc
Dallas, TX..........................214-946-8171
Corfu Foods Inc
Bensenville, IL....................630-595-2510
Dutterer's Home Food Service
Baltimore, MD....................410-298-3663
E.W. Knauss & Son
Quakertown, PA..................800-648-4220
F&Y Enterprises
Wauconda, IL.....................847-526-0620
Hamms Custom Meats
Mckinney, TX.....................972-542-3359
Horlacher Meats
Logan, UT..........................435-752-1287
Hsin Tung Yang Foods Inc
S San Francisco, CA............650-589-6789
Jensen Meat Company
San Diego, CA....................619-754-6400
John Garner Meats
Van Buren, AR....................800-543-5473
Kershenstine Beef Jerky
Eupora, MS........................662-258-2049
King's Command Foods Inc
Green Bay, WA....................800-345-0293
Kutztown Bologna Company
Leola, PA...........................800-723-8824
Land O'Frost Inc
Searcy, AR.........................800-643-5654
Link Snacks Inc.
Minong, WI........................715-466-2234
Longview Meat & Merchandise Ltd
Longview, AB......................866-355-3759
Lower Foods, Inc.
Richmond, UT.....................800-295-7898
Moyer Packing Co.
Elroy, PA...........................800-967-8325
National Beef Packing Co LLC
Kansas City, MO..................800-449-2333
Nebraska Beef Council
Kearney, NE.......................800-421-5326
People's Sausage Co
Los Angeles, CA..................213-627-8633
Pierceton Foods Inc
Pierceton, IN......................574-594-2344
Plumrose USA
Chicago, IL........................800-526-4909
Plymouth Beef Co.
Bronx, NY..........................718-589-8600
Rinehart Meat Processing
Branson, MO......................417-869-2041
Saval Foods Corp
Elkridge, MD......................800-527-2825
Smith Provision Co Inc
Erie, PA.............................800-334-9151
Sunset Farm Foods Inc
Valdosta, GA......................800-882-1121
Temptee Specialty Foods
Denver, CO........................800-842-1233
Terrell Meats
Delta, UT...........................435-864-2600
The Bruss Company
Chicago, IL........................773-282-2900
Thompson Packers
Slidell, LA.........................800-989-6328
Tri State Beef Co
Cincinnati, OH....................513-579-1722
Tyson Foods Inc.
Springdale, AR...................800-233-6332
Valley Meat Company
Modesto, CA......................800-222-6328
Weaver Nut Co. Inc.
Ephrata, PA........................800-473-2688
Wisconsin Packaging Corp
Fort Atkinson, WI................920-563-9363
Woods Smoked Meats Inc
Bowling Green, MO..............800-458-8426

Products

Alderfer Inc
Harleysville, PA..................800-341-1121
Alewel's Country Meats
Warrensburg, MO................800-353-8553
Bakalars Sausage Co
La Crosse, WI.....................608-784-0384
Best Chicago Meat
Chicago, IL

Big B Barbecue
Evansville, IN 812-425-5235
Birchwood Foods Inc
Kenosha, WI 800-541-1685
Branding Iron
Sauget, IL 800-851-4684
Buona Vita Inc
Bridgeton, NJ 856-453-7972
Bush Brothers Provision Co
West Palm Beach, FL 800-327-1345
Caddo Packing Co
Marshall, TX 903-935-2211
Campbell Soup Co.
Camden, NJ 800-257-8443
Caribbean Food Delights Inc
Tappan, NY 845-398-3000
Carl Buddig & Co.
Homewood, IL 888-633-5684
Chicago Meat Authority Inc
Chicago, IL 800-383-3811
Columbia Packing Co Inc
Dallas, TX 214-946-8171
Daily Nutrition
Tucson, AZ 888-612-5037
Dino's Sausage & Meat Co Inc
Utica, NY 315-732-2661
Dutterer's Home Food Service
Baltimore, MD 410-298-3663
E.W. Knauss & Son
Quakertown, PA 800-648-4220
Edmond's Chile Co
St Louis, MO 314-772-1499
El Rey Cooked Meats
St Louis, MO 314-521-3113
Elmwood Locker Svc
Elmwood, IL 309-742-8929
F&Y Enterprises
Wauconda, IL 847-526-0620
Grandpa Ittel's Meats Inc
Howard Lake, MN 320-543-2285
Groff's Meats
Elizabethtown, PA 717-367-1246
Harris Ranch Beef Co
Selma, CA 800-742-1955
Hazle Park Quality Meats
West Hazleton, PA 800-238-4331
Holly Hill Locker Company
Holly Hill, SC 803-496-3611
Hormel Foods Corp.
Austin, MN 507-437-5611
Ito Cariani Sausage Company
Hayward, CA 510-887-0882
John Garner Meats
Van Buren, AR 800-543-5473
K & K Gourmet Meats Inc
Leetsdale, PA 724-266-8400
Karn Meats
Columbus, OH 800-221-9585
Kelly Corned Beef Co
Chicago, IL 800-624-5617
Kenosha Beef International LTD
Kenosha, WI
Kershenstine Beef Jerky
Eupora, MS 662-258-2049
Kutztown Bologna Company
Leola, PA 800-723-8824
Leo G. Fraboni Sausage Company
Hibbing, MN 218-263-5074
Lower Foods, Inc.
Richmond, UT 800-295-7898
Maid-Rite Steak Company
Dunmore, PA 800-233-4259
Meating Place
Buffalo, NY 716-885-3623
National Foods
Indianapolis, IN 800-683-6565
On-Cor Frozen Foods Redi-Serve
Aurora, IL 920-563-6391
Opa's Smoked Meats
Fredericksburg, TX 800-543-6750
Peer Foods Group Inc
Chicago, IL 800-365-5644
People's Sausage Co
Los Angeles, CA 213-627-8633
Pinter's Packing Plant
Dorchester, WI 715-654-5444
Plumrose USA
Chicago, IL 800-526-4909
Plymouth Beef Co.
Bronx, NY 718-589-8600
Rinehart Meat Processing
Branson, MO 417-869-2041
Rymer Foods
Chicago, IL 800-247-9637
S.W. Meat & Provision Company
Phoenix, AZ 602-275-2000
Sadler's Smokehouse
Henderson, TX 903-657-5581
Sanders Meat Packing Inc
Custer, MI 800-968-5035
Saval Foods Corp
Elkridge, MD 800-527-2825
Sheinman Provision Co
Philadelphia, PA 215-473-7065
Steak-Umm Company
Shillington, PA 860-928-5900
Stripling's General Store
Moultrie, GA 229-985-4226
Temptee Specialty Foods
Denver, CO 800-842-1233
Terrell Meats
Delta, UT 435-864-2600
The Bruss Company
Chicago, IL 773-282-2900
Une-Viandi
St. Jean Sur Richelieu, NB 800-363-1955
Vienna Meat Products
Scarborough, ON 800-588-1931
Weaver Nut Co. Inc.
Ephrata, PA 800-473-2688
Wisconsin Packaging Corp
Fort Atkinson, WI 920-563-9363
Woods Smoked Meats Inc
Bowling Green, MO 800-458-8426

Raw

Caribbean Food Delights Inc
Tappan, NY 845-398-3000
Maid-Rite Steak Company
Dunmore, PA 800-233-4259

Rib Eye Roast

Certified Piedmontese Beef
Lincoln, NE 800-414-3487

Rib Eye Steak

Amana Meat Shop & Smoke House
Amana, IA 800-373-6328
Arrowhead Beef
Chipley, FL 850-270-8804
Chef's Requested Foods
Oklahoma City, OK 405-239-2610
Chicago Steaks
Chicago, IL 773-847-5400
Father's Country Hams
Bremen, KY 270-525-3554
Sommers Organic
Wheeling, IL 877-377-9797
Woods Smoked Meats Inc
Bowling Green, MO 800-458-8426

Rib Steak

Chicago Steaks
Chicago, IL 773-847-5400

Roast Beef

Alderfer Inc
Harleysville, PA 800-341-1121
Alpine Butcher
Lowell, MA 978-256-7771
Applegate Farms
Bridgewater, NJ 866-587-5858
Arrowhead Beef
Chipley, FL 850-270-8804
Berks Packing Company, Inc.
Reading, PA 800-882-3757
Burnett & Son
Monrovia, CA 877-632-5467
Carando Gourmet Frozen Foods
Agawam, MA 888-227-2636
Chip Steak & Provision Co
Mankato, MN 507-388-6277
Curly's Foods Inc
Edina, MN 612-920-3400
Dom's Sausage Co Inc
Malden, MA 781-324-6390
Dorina So-Good Inc
Union, IL 815-923-2144
Dutterer's Home Food Service
Baltimore, MD 410-298-3663
El Rey Cooked Meats
St Louis, MO 314-521-3113
Hormel Foods Corp.
Austin, MN 507-437-5611
Ito Cariani Sausage Company
Hayward, CA 510-887-0882
Lower Foods, Inc.
Richmond, UT 800-295-7898
Miami Beef Co
Miami Lakes, FL 305-621-3252
Saval Foods Corp
Elkridge, MD 800-527-2825
Sheinman Provision Co
Philadelphia, PA 215-473-7065
Vienna Meat Products
Scarborough, ON 800-588-1931

Rolls - Frozen

Columbia Packing Co Inc
Dallas, TX 214-946-8171
Travis Meats Inc
Powell, TN 800-247-7606

Sirloin Cubes

Chicago Steaks
Chicago, IL 773-847-5400

Sliced

E.W. Knauss & Son
Quakertown, PA 800-648-4220
Henry J's Meat Specialties
Chicago, IL 800-242-1314
Plymouth Beef Co.
Bronx, NY 718-589-8600

Dried

Alderfer Inc
Harleysville, PA 800-341-1121
E.W. Knauss & Son
Quakertown, PA 800-648-4220
Palmyra Bologna Co Inc
Palmyra, PA 800-282-6336

Frozen

Burke Corp
Nevada, IA 800-654-1152
Philadelphia Cheese Steak
Philadelphia, PA 800-342-9771

Special Trim

Buckhead Beef
Atlanta, GA 800-888-5578

Steak

Alaskan Gourmet Seafoods
Anchorage, AK 800-288-3740
Alpine Butcher
Lowell, MA 978-256-7771
American Foods Group LLC
Green Bay, WI 800-345-0293
Arrowhead Beef
Chipley, FL 850-270-8804
Bakalars Sausage Co
La Crosse, WI 608-784-0384
Bear Creek Smokehouse Inc
Marshall, TX 800-950-2327
Burnett & Son
Monrovia, CA 877-632-5467
Campbell Soup Co.
Camden, NJ 800-257-8443
Dom's Sausage Co Inc
Malden, MA 781-324-6390
Grass Run Farms
Greeley, CO 800-727-2333
Jemm Wholesale Meat Company
Chicago, IL 773-523-8161
Joe Fazio's Famous Italian
Charleston, WV 304-344-3071
Karn Meats
Columbus, OH 800-221-9585
Kutztown Bologna Company
Leola, PA 800-723-8824
Mattingly Foods Of Louisville
Louisville, KY 502-253-2000
Omaha Steaks Inc
.... 800-960-8400
Pine Point Seafood
Scarborough, ME 207-883-4701
Pinter's Packing Plant
Dorchester, WI 715-654-5444

Rymer Foods
Chicago, IL 800-247-9637
Sommers Organic
Wheeling, IL 877-377-9797
Steak-Umm Company
Shillington, PA 860-928-5900
Strassburger Steaks
Carlstadt, NJ 201-842-8890
Woods Smoked Meats Inc
Bowling Green, MO 800-458-8426

Stew

Burnett & Son
Monrovia, CA 877-632-5467
Campbell Soup Co.
Camden, NJ 800-257-8443
Johnston's Home Style Products
Charlottetown, PE 902-629-1300
Miami Beef Co
Miami Lakes, FL 305-621-3252
Plymouth Beef Co.
Bronx, NY 718-589-8600

Frozen

Edmond's Chile Co
St Louis, MO 314-772-1499

Tongue

Fremont Beef Co
Fremont, NE 800-331-4788
Saval Foods Corp
Elkridge, MD 800-527-2825

Veal

A To Z Portion Control Meats
Bluffton, OH 800-338-6328
A.C. Kissling Company
Philadelphia, PA 800-445-1943
Adolf's Meats & Sausage Kitchen
Hartford, CT 860-522-1588
Alpine Butcher
Lowell, MA 978-256-7771
Arena & Sons
Redwood City, CA 650-366-1750
Atlantic Veal & Lamb Inc
Brooklyn, NY 800-222-8325
B & R Quality Meats Inc
Waterloo, IA 319-232-6328
Baretta Provision
East Berlin, CT 860-828-0802
Borders Sporting Goods
Ashland, KY 606-928-6326
Branding Iron
Sauget, IL 800-851-4684
Brook Locker Plant
Brook, IN 219-275-2611
Buckhead Beef
Atlanta, GA 800-888-5578
Bush Brothers Provision Co
West Palm Beach, FL 800-327-1345
Buzz Food Svc
Charleston, WV 304-925-4781
Capital Packers Inc
Edmonton, AB 800-272-8868
Catelli Brothers Inc
Collingswood, NJ 856-869-9293
Central Meat & Provision
San Diego, CA 619-239-1391
Country Village Meats Inc
Sublette, IL 800-700-4545
Cusack Meats
Oklahoma City, OK 800-241-6328
David Mosner Meat Products
Bronx, NY 866-928-6428
Debragga & Spitler
Jersey City, NJ
Dom's Sausage Co Inc
Malden, MA 781-324-6390
Feed The Party
Louisville, KY
Florida Veal Processors
Wimauma, FL 813-634-5545
Fulton Provision Co
Portland, OR 800-333-6328
Heringer Meats Inc
Covington, KY 859-291-2000
International Meat Co
Chicago, IL 773-622-1400
Jordahl Meats
Manchester, MN 507-826-3418
King Kold Meats
Englewood, OH 800-836-2797
King's Command Foods Inc
Green Bay, WA 800-345-0293
L & L Packing Co
Chicago, IL 800-628-6328
L & M Slaughterhouse
Georgetown, IL 217-662-6841
Lay Packing Company
Knoxville, TN 865-522-1147
Lombardi Brothers Meat Packers
Denver, CO 303-458-7441
Maid-Rite Steak Company
Dunmore, PA 800-233-4259
Malcolm Meats Co
Northwood, OH 800-822-6328
Marcho Farms Inc
Harleysville, PA 215-721-7131
Meat-O-Mat Corp
Brooklyn, NY 718-965-7250
Miami Beef Co
Miami Lakes, FL 305-621-3252
Michael's Finer Meats/Seafoods
Columbus, OH 800-282-0518
Mountain States Rosen
Bronx, NY 800-872-5262
Northwest Meat Company
Chicago, IL 312-733-1418
On-Cor Frozen Foods Redi-Serve
Aurora, IL 920-563-6391
Pasqualichio Brothers Inc
Scranton, PA 800-232-6233
Petschl's Quality Meats
Tukwila, WA 206-575-4400
Quaker Maid Meats
Reading, PA 610-376-1500
Rendulic Meat Packing Corp
Mckeesport, PA 412-678-9541
Sculli Brothers
Yeadon, PA 215-336-1223
Shelley's
Jersey City, NJ 201-433-2900
Smith Packing Regional Meat
Utica, NY 315-732-5125
Southern Packing Corp
Chesapeake, VA 757-421-2131
Standard Meat Co LP
Dallas, TX 866-859-6313
Stock Yards Packing Company
Melrose Park, IL 877-785-9273
Strassburger Steaks
Carlstadt, NJ 201-842-8890
Streit Carl & Son Co
Neptune, NJ 732-775-0803
Superior Farms
Sacramento, CA 800-228-5262
Suzanna's Kitchen
Peachtree Cor, GA 770-476-9900
The Bruss Company
Chicago, IL 773-282-2900
Thompson Packers
Slidell, LA 800-989-6328
Travis Meats Inc
Powell, TN 800-247-7606
Tyler Packing Co
Tyler, TX 903-593-9592
Une-Viandi
St. Jean Sur Richelieu, NB 800-363-1955
United Meat Company
San Francisco, CA 415-864-2118
United Provision Meat Company
Columbus, OH 614-252-1126
Valley Meats
Coal Valley, IL 309-517-6639
Wasatch Meats Inc
Salt Lake City, UT 800-631-8294
Windcrest Meat Packers
Port Perry, ON 800-750-2542

Breaded Frozen

Branding Iron
Sauget, IL 800-851-4684
King's Command Foods Inc
Green Bay, WA 800-345-0293
Meat-O-Mat Corp
Brooklyn, NY 718-965-7250
On-Cor Frozen Foods Redi-Serve
Aurora, IL 920-563-6391
Valley Meats
Coal Valley, IL 309-517-6639

Burgers

Meat-O-Mat Corp
Brooklyn, NY 718-965-7250

Cutlet

On-Cor Frozen Foods Redi-Serve
Aurora, IL 920-563-6391

Fresh

Florida Veal Processors
Wimauma, FL 813-634-5545
Provimi Foods
Seymour, WI 800-833-8325
Shelley's
Jersey City, NJ 201-433-2900
Smith Packing Regional Meat
Utica, NY 315-732-5125

Frozen

Atlantic Veal & Lamb Inc
Brooklyn, NY 800-222-8325
Branding Iron
Sauget, IL 800-851-4684
Brook Locker Plant
Brook, IN 219-275-2611
Buckhead Beef
Atlanta, GA 800-888-5578
Bush Brothers Provision Co
West Palm Beach, FL 800-327-1345
Florida Veal Processors
Wimauma, FL 813-634-5545
Heringer Meats Inc
Covington, KY 859-291-2000
King Kold Meats
Englewood, OH 800-836-2797
Maid-Rite Steak Company
Dunmore, PA 800-233-4259
Meat-O-Mat Corp
Brooklyn, NY 718-965-7250
On-Cor Frozen Foods Redi-Serve
Aurora, IL 920-563-6391
Provimi Foods
Seymour, WI 800-833-8325
Shelley's
Jersey City, NJ 201-433-2900
Smith Packing Regional Meat
Utica, NY 315-732-5125
Thompson Packers
Slidell, LA 800-989-6328
Travis Meats Inc
Powell, TN 800-247-7606
United Meat Company
San Francisco, CA 415-864-2118

Ground

M Buono Beef Co
Philadelphia, PA 215-463-3600

Loin Chop

Chicago Steaks
Chicago, IL 773-847-5400

Rib Chop

Chicago Steaks
Chicago, IL 773-847-5400

Frankfurters

Al Pete Meats
Muncie, IN 765-288-8817
Albert's Meats
Claysville, PA 800-522-9970
Anmar Foods
Chicago, IL 312-421-6500
Applegate Farms
Bridgewater, NJ 866-587-5858
AquaCuisine
Portland, OR 208-323-2782
Ball Park Franks
Peoria, IL 888-317-5867
Best Provision Co Inc
Union, NJ 800-631-4466
Big City Reds
Omaha, NE 800-759-5275
Boesl Packing Co
Baltimore, MD 800-675-1471
C.W. Brown Foods, Inc.
Mountt Royal, NJ 856-423-3700
Carolina Packers Inc
Smithfield, NC 800-682-7675

Chicago 58 Food Products
Woodbridge, ON 416-603-4244
Chicopee Provision Co Inc
Chicopee, MA 800-924-6328
Chisesi Brothers Meat Packing
New Orleans, LA 800-966-3550
Cloverdale Foods
Mandan, ND 800-669-9511
Country Village Meats Inc
Sublette, IL 800-700-4545
Curtis Packing Co
Greensboro, NC 336-275-7684
Dennison Meat Locker
Dennison, MN 507-645-8734
Dietz & Watson Inc.
Philadelphia, PA 215-831-9000
Double B Foods Inc
Arlington, TX 800-679-0349
Dutterer's Home Food Service
Baltimore, MD 410-298-3663
Fair Oaks Farms LLC
Pleasant Prairie, WI 800-528-8615
Far West Meats
Highland, CA 909-864-1990
Fare Foods Corp
Du Quoin, IL 618-542-2155
Field Roast
Seattle, WA 800-311-9497
Gary's Frozen Foods
Lubbock, TX 806-745-1933
Glazier Packing Co
Malone, NY 518-483-4990
Gouvea's & Purity Foods Inc
Honolulu, HI 808-847-3717
Grote & Weigel Inc
Bloomfield, CT 860-242-8528
Hatfield Quality Meats
Hatfield, PA 800-743-1191
Hazle Park Quality Meats
West Hazleton, PA 800-238-4331
Health is Wealth Foods
Moonachie, NJ 201-933-7474
Hormel Foods Corp.
Austin, MN 507-437-5611
Hummel Brothers Inc
New Haven, CT 800-828-8978
Kayem Foods
Chelsea, MA 800-426-6100
Kelly Corned Beef Co
Chicago, IL 800-624-5617
Kent Quality Foods Inc
Grand Rapids, MI 800-748-0141
Kilgus Meats
Toledo, OH 419-472-9721
Koegel Meats Inc
Flint, MI 810-238-3685
Little Rhody Brand Frankfurts
Johnston, RI 401-831-0815
Marathon Enterprises Inc
Englewood, NJ 800-722-7388
Martin Rosols
New Britain, CT 860-223-2707
Matthiesen's Deer & Custom
De Witt, IA 563-659-8409
Milling Sausage Inc
Milwaukee, WI 414-645-2677
National Foods
Indianapolis, IN 800-683-6565
Omaha Steaks Inc
. . . . 800-960-8400
P & L Poultry
Spokane, WA 509-892-1242
Pie Piper Products
Wheeling, IL 800-621-8183
Principe Foods USA
Long Beach, CA 310-680-5500
Quong Hop & Company
S San Francisco, CA 650-553-9900
R.L. Zeigler Company
Selma, AL 800-392-6328
Roger Wood Foods Inc
Savannah, GA 800-849-9272
Saag's Products LLC
San Leandro, CA 855-287-6562
Sahlen's
Buffalo, NY 800-466-8165
Saugy Inc.
Cranston, RI 866-467-2849
Schaefers Market
Sauk Centre, MN 320-352-6490
Schneider Foods
Kitchener, ON 519-741-5000

Sechrist Brothers
Dallastown, PA 717-244-2975
Shelton's Poultry Inc
Pomona, CA 800-541-1833
Smith Packing Regional Meat
Utica, NY 315-732-5125
Smith Provision Co Inc
Erie, PA 800-334-9151
Smithfield Foods Inc.
Smithfield, VA 757-365-3000
Stawnichy Holdings
Mundare, AB 888-764-7646
Stevens Sausage Co
Smithfield, NC 800-338-0561
Sunnydale Meats Inc
Gaffney, SC 864-489-6091
Tecumseh Poultry, LLC
Waverly, NE 402-786-1000
Tennessee Valley Packing Co
Columbia, TN 931-388-2623
Teton Waters Ranch LLC
Denver, CO 720-340-4590
Thomas Packing Company
Columbus, GA 800-729-0976
Thumann Inc.
Carlstadt, NJ 201-935-3636
Troy Foods Inc
Troy, IL 618-667-6332
Tyson Foods Inc.
Springdale, AR 800-233-6332
Vienna Beef LTD
Chicago, IL 800-366-3647
Zweigle's Inc
Rochester, NY 585-546-1740

Beef

American Foods Group LLC
Green Bay, WI 800-345-0293
Berks Packing Company, Inc.
Reading, PA 800-882-3757
Big City Reds
Omaha, NE 800-759-5275
Grote & Weigel Inc
Bloomfield, CT 860-242-8528
Health is Wealth Foods
Moonachie, NJ 201-933-7474
Heinkel's Packing Co
Decatur, IL 800-594-2738
Hormel Foods Corp.
Austin, MN 507-437-5611
Kelly Corned Beef Co
Chicago, IL 800-624-5617
Milling Sausage Inc
Milwaukee, WI 414-645-2677
National Foods
Indianapolis, IN 800-683-6565
Pie Piper Products
Wheeling, IL 800-621-8183
Red Hot Chicago
Chicago, IL 800-249-5226
Teton Waters Ranch LLC
Denver, CO 720-340-4590
True Story Foods
San Francisco, CA 888-277-1171

Kosher

American Foods Group LLC
Green Bay, WI 800-345-0293

Chicken

Applegate Farms
Bridgewater, NJ 866-587-5858
P & L Poultry
Spokane, WA 509-892-1242
True Story Foods
San Francisco, CA 888-277-1171

Corn Dogs

Al Pete Meats
Muncie, IN 765-288-8817
Fare Foods Corp
Du Quoin, IL 618-542-2155
Foster Farms Inc.
Livingston, CA 800-255-7227
Hormel Foods Corp.
Austin, MN 507-437-5611
Suzanna's Kitchen
Peachtree Cor, GA 770-476-9900
Tyson Foods Inc.
Springdale, AR 479-290-4000

Hot Dogs

Grass Run Farms
Greeley, CO 800-727-2333
Harvin Choice Meats
Sumter, SC 800-849-6328
Heinkel's Packing Co
Decatur, IL 800-594-2738
Saad Wholesale Meats
Detroit, MI 313-831-8126
Specialty Foods Group Inc
Owensboro, KY 800-238-0020
SunFed Ranch
Woodland, CA 530-723-5373
Vermont Smoke and Cure
Hinesburg, VT 802-482-4666

Mini

Grote & Weigel Inc
Bloomfield, CT 860-242-8528
Hormel Foods Corp.
Austin, MN 507-437-5611

Pork

C.W. Brown Foods, Inc.
Mountt Royal, NJ 856-423-3700
Heinkel's Packing Co
Decatur, IL 800-594-2738

Soy

Lightlife
Turners Falls, MA 800-769-3279
Quong Hop & Company
S San Francisco, CA 650-553-9900

Turkey

Applegate Farms
Bridgewater, NJ 866-587-5858
P & L Poultry
Spokane, WA 509-892-1242
Sardinha's Sausage
Somerset, MA 800-678-0178

Game

Alewel's Country Meats
Warrensburg, MO 800-353-8553
Alpine Butcher
Lowell, MA 978-256-7771
Bayou Land Seafood
Breaux Bridge, LA 337-667-6118
Bob's Custom Cuts
Bonnyville, AB 780-826-2627
Boyd's Sausage Co
Washington, IA 319-653-5715
Broadleaf Venison USA Inc
Vernon, CA 800-336-3844
Brome Lake Ducks Ltd
Knowlton, QC 888-956-1977
Bryant Preserving Company
Alma, AR 800-634-2413
Burgers' Smokehouse
California, MO 800-345-5185
Camrose Packers
Camrose, AB 780-672-4887
Carolina Blueberry Co-Op Assn
Garland, NC 910-588-4220
Charlito's Cocina
Brooklyn, NY 718-482-7890
Clay Center Locker Plant
Clay Center, KS 800-466-5543
Debragga & Spitler
Jersey City, NJ
Eickman's Processing Co
Seward, IL 815-247-8451
Eiserman Meats
Slave Lake, AB 780-849-5507
Ellsworth Locker
Ellsworth, MN 507-967-2544
Farmers Meat Market
Viking, AB 780-336-3241
Fossil Farms
Boonton, NJ 973-917-3155
Georgetown Farm
Free Union, VA 888-328-5326
Goodheart Brand Specialty Food
San Antonio, TX 888-466-3992
Grandview Farms
Thornbury, ON 519-599-6368
Hickory Baked Ham Co
Castle Rock, CO 303-688-2633

Humeniuk's Meat Cutting
Ranfurly, AB 780-658-2381
Indian Valley Meats
Indian, AK 907-653-7511
Jewel Date Co
Thermal, CA 760-399-4474
Joyce Farms
Winston Salem, NC. 800-755-6923
Ketters Meat Market & Locker Plant
Frazee, MN 218-334-2351
Macfarlane Pheasants
Janesville, WI 800-345-8348
Mahantongo Game Farm
Dalmatia, PA 800-982-9913
Matthiesen's Deer & Custom
De Witt, IA 563-659-8409
McLane's Meats
Wetaskiwin, AB 780-352-4321
Meat-O-Mat Corp
Brooklyn, NY 718-965-7250
Meatco Sales Ltd.
Mirror, AB 403-788-2292
Michael's Finer Meats/Seafoods
Columbus, OH 800-282-0518
Miller's Meat Market
Red Bud, IL 618-282-3334
Musicon Deer Farm
Goshen, NY 845-294-6378
Nicky USA Inc
Portland, OR 800-469-4162
Onoway Custom Packers
Onoway, AB 780-967-2727
Oxford Frozen Foods
Oxford, NS 902-447-2100
Palmetto Pigeon Plant
Sumter, SC 803-775-1204
Payne Packing Co
Artesia, NM 575-746-2779
Pekarna Meat Market
Jordan, MN 952-492-6101
Pinter's Packing Plant
Dorchester, WI 715-654-5444
Prairie Cajun Wholesale
Eunice, LA 337-546-6195
R Four Meats
Chatfield, MN 507-867-4180
Rabbit Barn
Turlock, CA 209-632-1123
Rocky Mountain Meats
Rocky Mountain House, AB 403-845-3434
Specialty Meats & Gourmet
Hudson, WI 800-310-2360
Springville Meat & Cold Storage
Springville, UT 801-489-6391
Squab Producers of California
Modesto, CA 209-537-4744
Stonie's Sausage Shop
Perryville, MO 888-546-2540
Tofield Packers Ltd
Tofield, AB 780-662-4842
United Meat Company
San Francisco, CA 415-864-2118
Uvalde Meat Processing
Uvalde, TX 830-278-6247
Victoria Fancy Sausage
Edmonton, AB 780-471-2283
Wall Meat Processing
Wall, SD 605-279-2348
Western Buffalo Company
Rapid City, SD 800-247-3263
White Oak Pastures
Bluffton, GA 229-641-2081

Alligator

Acadian Ostrich Ranch
Clinton, LA 800-350-0167
Alpine Butcher
Lowell, MA 978-256-7771
Bayou Land Seafood
Breaux Bridge, LA 337-667-6118
Nicky USA Inc
Portland, OR 800-469-4162
Prairie Cajun Wholesale
Eunice, LA 337-546-6195

Boar

Alpine Butcher
Lowell, MA 978-256-7771
Broadleaf Venison USA Inc
Vernon, CA 800-336-3844
Grandview Farms
Thornbury, ON 519-599-6368
Nicky USA Inc
Portland, OR 800-469-4162

Buffalo

Alewel's Country Meats
Warrensburg, MO 800-353-8553
Alpine Butcher
Lowell, MA 978-256-7771
Broadleaf Venison USA Inc
Vernon, CA 800-336-3844
Clay Center Locker Plant
Clay Center, KS 800-466-5543
Golden Valley Natural
Shelley, ID 888-270-7147
Miller's Meat Market
Red Bud, IL 618-282-3334
Nicky USA Inc
Portland, OR 800-469-4162
Pinter's Packing Plant
Dorchester, WI 715-654-5444
Rocky Mountain Natural Meats
Henderson, CO 800-327-2706
Springville Meat & Cold Storage
Springville, UT 801-489-6391
Superior Farms
Sacramento, CA 800-228-5262
Triple U Enterprises
Fort Pierre, SD 605-567-3624
Vital Choice
Bellingham, WA 800-608-4825
Wall Meat Processing
Wall, SD 605-279-2348
Western Buffalo Company
Rapid City, SD 800-247-3263
YB Meats of Wichita
Wichita, KS 316-942-1213

Caribou

Grandview Farms
Thornbury, ON 519-599-6368

Emu

Dino-Meat Company
White House, TN 877-557-6493
Grandview Farms
Thornbury, ON 519-599-6368
YB Meats of Wichita
Wichita, KS 316-942-1213

Farm-Raised

Clay Center Locker Plant
Clay Center, KS 800-466-5543
Sunnyside Farms LLC
Washington, VA 540-675-3669
Triple U Enterprises
Fort Pierre, SD 605-567-3624
Wall Meat Processing
Wall, SD 605-279-2348
Western Buffalo Company
Rapid City, SD 800-247-3263

Meat & Poultry

Becker Foods
Westminster, CA 714-891-9474
Bon Secour Fisheries Inc
Bon Secour, AL 251-949-7411
Broadleaf Venison USA Inc
Vernon, CA 800-336-3844
Clay Center Locker Plant
Clay Center, KS 800-466-5543
Crescent Duck Farm
Aquebogue LI, NY 631-722-8000
Czimer's Game & Seafoods
Homer Glen, IL 888-294-6377
Eickman's Processing Co
Seward, IL 815-247-8451
Ellsworth Locker
Ellsworth, MN 507-967-2544
Fox Deluxe Inc
Chicago, IL 312-421-3737
Grandview Farms
Thornbury, ON 519-599-6368
Grimaud Farms-California Inc
Stockton, CA 800-466-9955
Hickory Baked Ham Co
Castle Rock, CO 303-688-2633
Indian Valley Meats
Indian, AK 907-653-7511
Ketters Meat Market & Locker Plant
Frazee, MN 218-334-2351
Lindner Bison
Northern, CA 530-254-6337
Macfarlane Pheasants
Janesville, WI 800-345-8348
Metzer Farms
Gonzales, CA 800-424-7755
Miller Brothers Packing Company
Sylvester, GA 229-776-2014
Musicon Deer Farm
Goshen, NY 845-294-6378
Palmetto Pigeon Plant
Sumter, SC 803-775-1204
Pekarna Meat Market
Jordan, MN 952-492-6101
Pinter's Packing Plant
Dorchester, WI 715-654-5444
R Four Meats
Chatfield, MN 507-867-4180
Schiltz Foods Inc
Sisseton, SD 877-872-4458
Springville Meat & Cold Storage
Springville, UT 801-489-6391
Squab Producers of California
Modesto, CA 209-537-4744
Stonie's Sausage Shop
Perryville, MO 888-546-2540
Triple U Enterprises
Fort Pierre, SD 605-567-3624
United Meat Company
San Francisco, CA 415-864-2118
Uvalde Meat Processing
Uvalde, TX 830-278-6247
Wall Meat Processing
Wall, SD 605-279-2348
Wapsie Produce
Decorah, IA 563-382-4271
Western Buffalo Company
Rapid City, SD 800-247-3263

Muskox

Grandview Farms
Thornbury, ON 519-599-6368

Ostrich

Acadian Ostrich Ranch
Clinton, LA 800-350-0167
Broadleaf Venison USA Inc
Vernon, CA 800-336-3844
Clay Center Locker Plant
Clay Center, KS 800-466-5543
Grandview Farms
Thornbury, ON 519-599-6368
Kingsbury Country Market
La Porte, IN 219-393-3016
Meat-O-Mat Corp
Brooklyn, NY 718-965-7250
Nicky USA Inc
Portland, OR 800-469-4162
Pokanoket Ostrich Farm
South Dartmouth, MA 508-992-6188
Prime Ostrich International
Morinville, AB 800-340-2311
Protos Inc
Greensburg, PA 724-836-1802
YB Meats of Wichita
Wichita, KS 316-942-1213

Pheasant

Alpine Butcher
Lowell, MA 978-256-7771
Burgers' Smokehouse
California, MO 800-345-5185
Hickory Baked Ham Co
Castle Rock, CO 303-688-2633
Macfarlane Pheasants
Janesville, WI 800-345-8348
Mahantongo Game Farm
Dalmatia, PA 800-982-9913
Nicky USA Inc
Portland, OR 800-469-4162
Squab Producers of California
Modesto, CA 209-537-4744

Quail (See also Eggs: Quail)

Alpine Butcher
Lowell, MA 978-256-7771
Burgers' Smokehouse
California, MO 800-345-5185

Manchester Farms
Columbia, SC 800-845-0421
Nicky USA Inc
Portland, OR 800-469-4162
Nueces Canyon Range
Brenham, TX. 800-925-5058
Squab Producers of California
Modesto, CA. 209-537-4744
Urgasa
Coral Gables, FL. 786-543-6693

Rabbit

Nicky USA Inc
Portland, OR 800-469-4162
Rabbit Barn
Turlock, CA. 209-632-1123

Fryer

Mahantongo Game Farm
Dalmatia, PA 800-982-9913
Squab Producers of California
Modesto, CA. 209-537-4744
Tarazi Specialty Foods
Chino, CA 909-628-3601

Squab

Palmetto Pigeon Plant
Sumter, SC 803-775-1204
Squab Producers of California
Modesto, CA. 209-537-4744

Venison

AJ's Lena Maid Meats Inc
Lena, IL. 815-369-4522
Alewel's Country Meats
Warrensburg, MO 800-353-8553
Alpine Butcher
Lowell, MA. 978-256-7771
Bellville Meat Market
Bellville, TX 800-571-6328
Blakely Freezer Locker
Blakeley, GA. 229-723-3622
Boyd's Sausage Co
Washington, IA 319-653-5715
Broadleaf Venison USA Inc
Vernon, CA 800-336-3844
Brookview Farms
Manakin-Sabot, VA 804-784-3131
Ellsworth Locker
Ellsworth, MN 507-967-2544
Grandview Farms
Thornbury, ON 519-599-6368
Heinkel's Packing Co
Decatur, IL 800-594-2738
Houser Meats
Rushville, IL 217-322-4994
Indian Valley Meats
Indian, AK. 907-653-7511
Jackson Brothers Food Locker
Post, TX 806-495-3245
Ketters Meat Market & Locker Plant
Frazee, MN 218-334-2351
MacGregors Meat & Seafood
Toronto, ON 888-383-3663
Matthiesen's Deer & Custom
De Witt, IA 563-659-8409
Musicon Deer Farm
Goshen, NY. 845-294-6378
Nesbitt Processing
Aledo, IL. 309-582-5183
Nicky USA Inc
Portland, OR 800-469-4162
R Four Meats
Chatfield, MN 507-867-4180
Smokey Denmark Sausage Co
Austin, TX. 512-385-0718
Specialty Meats & Gourmet
Hudson, WI. 800-310-2360
Stonie's Sausage Shop
Perryville, MO 888-546-2540
Superior Farms
Sacramento, CA 800-228-5262
United Meat Company
San Francisco, CA 415-864-2118
Uvalde Meat Processing
Uvalde, TX 830-278-6247
YB Meats of Wichita
Wichita, KS. 316-942-1213

Canned

Indian Valley Meats
Indian, AK. 907-653-7511

Frozen

Broadleaf Venison USA Inc
Vernon, CA 800-336-3844
Brookview Farms
Manakin-Sabot, VA 804-784-3131
Indian Valley Meats
Indian, AK. 907-653-7511
R Four Meats
Chatfield, MN. 507-867-4180
United Meat Company
San Francisco, CA 415-864-2118

Wild

Clay Center Locker Plant
Clay Center, KS 800-466-5543
Eickman's Processing Co
Seward, IL. 815-247-8451
Triple U Enterprises
Fort Pierre, SD 605-567-3624
Wall Meat Processing
Wall, SD 605-279-2348
Western Buffalo Company
Rapid City, SD 800-247-3263

Goat

Braham Food Locker Service
Braham, MN 320-396-2636
Caribbean Food Delights Inc
Tappan, NY. 845-398-3000
ELP Inc
Elizabeth, CO 303-688-2240
Halsted Packing House
Chicago, IL 312-421-5147
Jones Packing Co
Harvard, IL 815-943-4488
Madani Halal
Ozone Park, NY 718-323-9732
Nesbitt Processing
Aledo, IL. 309-582-5183
Red Deer Lake Meat Processing
Calgary, AB. 403-256-4925
White Oak Pastures
Bluffton, GA. 229-641-2081
Windcrest Meat Packers
Port Perry, ON. 800-750-2542

Horse

Bouvry Exports Calgary
Calgary, AB. 403-253-0717
Phoenix Agro-Industrial Corporation
Westbury, NY 516-334-1194

Lamb

A.C. Kissling Company
Philadelphia, PA 800-445-1943
Acme Steak & Seafood
Youngstown, OH. 800-686-2263
AJ's Lena Maid Meats Inc
Lena, IL. 815-369-4522
Alpine Butcher
Lowell, MA. 978-256-7771
Alpine Meats
Stockton, CA. 800-399-6328
B & R Quality Meats Inc
Waterloo, IA 319-232-6328
Blakely Freezer Locker
Blakeley, GA. 229-723-3622
Borders Sporting Goods
Ashland, KY 606-928-6326
Brookview Farms
Manakin-Sabot, VA 804-784-3131
Bush Brothers Provision Co
West Palm Beach, FL 800-327-1345
Callaway Packing Inc
Delta, CO 970-874-9743
Campbell's Quality Cuts
Sidney, OH 937-492-2194
Canal Fulton Provision
Canal Fulton, OH 800-321-3502
Catelli Brothers Inc
Collingswood, NJ 856-869-9293
Center Locker Svc
Center, MO 800-884-0737
Chicago Steaks
Chicago, IL 773-847-5400
Clay Center Locker Plant
Clay Center, KS 800-466-5543
Country Butcher Shop
Carlisle, PA 800-272-9223
Country Village Meats Inc
Sublette, IL 800-700-4545
Cusack Meats
Oklahoma City, OK 800-241-6328
Dale T Smith & Sons Inc
Draper, UT 801-571-3611
David Mosner Meat Products
Bronx, NY. 866-928-6428
Debragga & Spitler
Jersey City, NJ
Dino's Sausage & Meat Co Inc
Utica, NY 315-732-2661
Dole & Bailey Inc
Woburn, MA 781-935-1234
Dom's Sausage Co Inc
Malden, MA 781-324-6390
Duma Meats Inc
Mogadore, OH 330-628-3438
Eickman's Processing Co
Seward, IL. 815-247-8451
Eiserman Meats
Slave Lake, AB 780-849-5507
ELP Inc
Elizabeth, CO 303-688-2240
Eureka Locker Inc
Eureka, IL 309-467-2731
Feed The Party
Louisville, KY
Fulton Provision Co
Portland, OR 800-333-6328
Halsted Packing House
Chicago, IL 312-421-5147
Heringer Meats Inc
Covington, KY 859-291-2000
Houser Meats
Rushville, IL 217-322-4994
International Meat Co
Chicago, IL 773 622 1400
Isernio Sausage Company
Seattle, WA 888-495-8674
JBS USA LLC
Greeley, CO. 970-506-8000
Jones Packing Co
Harvard, IL 815-943-4488
Jordahl Meats
Manchester, MN 507-826-3418
Kelble Brothers Inc
Berlin Heights, OH 800-247-2333
Kelly Packing Company
Torrington, WY. 307-532-2210
L & L Packing Co
Chicago, IL 800-628-6328
L & M Slaughterhouse
Georgetown, IL. 217-662-6841
Lay Packing Company
Knoxville, TN 865-522-1147
Lombardi Brothers Meat Packers
Denver, CO 303-458-7441
Madani Halal
Ozone Park, NY 718-323-9732
Maid-Rite Steak Company
Dunmore, PA. 800-233-4259
Malcolm Meats Co
Northwood, OH 800-822-6328
Manger Packing Corp
Baltimore, MD 800-227-9262
Marks Meat
Holmen, WI. 608-526-6058
Matthiesen's Deer & Custom
De Witt, IA 563-659-8409
Meatland Packers
Medicine Hat, AB 403-528-4321
Miami Beef Co
Miami Lakes, FL. 305-621-3252
Miller Brothers Packing Company
Sylvester, GA 229-776-2014
Mountain States Rosen
Bronx, NY. 800-872-5262
Nesbitt Processing
Aledo, IL. 309-582-5183
Northwest Meat Company
Chicago, IL 312-733-1418
Oklahoma City Meat Co Inc
Oklahoma City, OK 405-235-3308
Omaha Steaks Inc
. 800-960-8400
Onoway Custom Packers
Onoway, AB 780-967-2727

Pasqualichio Brothers Inc
Scranton, PA....................800-232-6233
Petschl's Quality Meats
Tukwila, WA....................206-575-4400
Premium Meat Co
Brigham City, UT....................435-723-5944
R Four Meats
Chatfield, MN....................507-867-4180
Ralph's Packing Co
Perkins, OK....................800-522-3979
Red Deer Lake Meat Processing
Calgary, AB....................403-256-4925
Rendulic Meat Packing Corp
Mckeesport, PA....................412-678-9541
Rocky Mountain Meats
Rocky Mountain House, AB....................403-845-3434
Royal Center Locker Plant
Royal Center, IN....................574-643-3275
Shelley's
Jersey City, NJ....................201-433-2900
Smith Packing Regional Meat
Utica, NY....................315-732-5125
Springville Meat & Cold Storage
Springville, UT....................801-489-6391
SRA Foods
Birmingham, AL....................205-323-7447
Standard Meat Co LP
Dallas, TX....................866-859-6313
Stock Yards Packing Company
Melrose Park, IL....................877-785-9273
Strassburger Steaks
Carlstadt, NJ....................201-842-8890
Strauss Brands International
Franklin, WI....................414-421-5250
Streit Carl & Son Co
Neptune, NJ....................732-775-0803
Superior Farms
Sacramento, CA....................800-228-5262
Terrell Meats
Delta, UT....................435-864-2600
Thompson Packers
Slidell, LA....................800-989-6328
Tillamook Meat Inc
Tillamook, OR....................503-842-4802
Tucker Packing Co
Orrville, OH....................330-683-3311
Turk Brothers Custom Meats Inc
Ashland, OH....................800-789-1051
Une-Viandi
St. Jean Sur Richelieu, NB....................800-363-1955
United Meat Company
San Francisco, CA....................415-864-2118
United Provision Meat Company
Columbus, OH....................614-252-1126
Uvalde Meat Processing
Uvalde, TX....................830-278-6247
Vestergaard Farms
Ann Arbor, MI....................734-929-2875
Victoria Fancy Sausage
Edmonton, AB....................780-471-2283
Wall Meat Processing
Wall, SD....................605-279-2348
Warren & Son Meat Processing
Whipple, OH....................740-585-2421
Wasatch Meats Inc
Salt Lake City, UT....................800-631-8294
Westport Locker LLC
Westport, IN....................877-265-0551
White's Meat Processing
Fort Gibson, OK....................918-478-2347
Willcox Meat Packing House
Willcox, AZ....................520-384-2015
Windcrest Meat Packers
Port Perry, ON....................800-750-2542
YB Meats of Wichita
Wichita, KS....................316-942-1213

Fresh

Atlantic Veal & Lamb Inc
Brooklyn, NY....................800-222-8325
R Four Meats
Chatfield, MN....................507-867-4180
Shelley's
Jersey City, NJ....................201-433-2900
Smith Packing Regional Meat
Utica, NY....................315-732-5125

Frozen

Atlantic Veal & Lamb Inc
Brooklyn, NY....................800-222-8325
Maid-Rite Steak Company
Dunmore, PA....................800-233-4259
Phoenix Agro-Industrial Corporation
Westbury, NY....................516-334-1194
R Four Meats
Chatfield, MN....................507-867-4180
Shelley's
Jersey City, NJ....................201-433-2900
Smith Packing Regional Meat
Utica, NY....................315-732-5125
Thompson Packers
Slidell, LA....................800-989-6328
United Meat Company
San Francisco, CA....................415-864-2118

Leg of

Alpine Butcher
Lowell, MA....................978-256-7771
Chicago Steaks
Chicago, IL....................773-847-5400

Loin Chop

Alpine Butcher
Lowell, MA....................978-256-7771
Chicago Steaks
Chicago, IL....................773-847-5400

Loin Roast

Alpine Butcher
Lowell, MA....................978-256-7771

Rib Chop

Chicago Steaks
Chicago, IL....................773-847-5400

Meat Meal

Mcredmond Brothers
Nashville, TN....................800-251-5930

Mutton

Center Locker Svc
Center, MO....................800-884-0737

Packaged

Burke Corp
Nevada, IA....................800-654-1152
Fair Oaks Farms LLC
Pleasant Prairie, WI....................800-528-8615

Pates & Fois Gras

Foie Gras

Hudson Valley Foie Gras
Ferndale, NY....................845-292-2500

Pates

Alexian Pâtés
Neptune, NJ....................800-927-9473
Caughman's Meat Plant
Lexington, SC....................803-356-0076
Cordon Bleu International
Anjou, QC....................800-363-1182
Ducktrap River Of Maine
Belfast, ME....................800-434-8727
Giovanni's Appetizing Food Co
Richmond, MI....................586-727-9355
Hickory Baked Ham Co
Castle Rock, CO....................303-688-2633
International Trading Company
Houston, TX....................713-224-5901
Les Trois Petits Cochons
Brooklyn, NY....................800-537-7283
Marcel et Henri Charcuterie Francaise
South San Francisco, CA....................800-227-6436
Michel's Magnifique
New York, NY....................212-431-1070
Olympic Provisions Northwest
Portland, OR....................503-894-8136
Organic Gourmet
Sherman Oaks, CA....................800-400-7772
Phoenicia Patisserie
Arlington, TX....................817-261-2898
Piller's Fine Foods
Waterloo, ON....................800-265-2627
Salmolux Inc
Federal Way, WA....................253-874-6570
Sunset Farm Foods Inc
Valdosta, GA....................800-882-1121
Taste of Gourmet
Indianola, MS....................800-833-7731

Pork & Pork Products

A To Z Portion Control Meats
Bluffton, OH....................800-338-6328
Abattoir Aliments Asta Inc.
St Alexandre De Kamouras, QC....................800-463-1355
Acornseekers Inc
Flatonia, TX....................786-338-8160
Alaska Sausage & Seafood
Anchorage, AK....................800-798-3636
Albert's Meats
Claysville, PA....................800-522-9970
Alderfer Inc
Harleysville, PA....................800-341-1121
Alpine Butcher
Lowell, MA....................978-256-7771
Amana Meat Shop & Smoke House
Amana, IA....................800-373-6328
Arizona Sunland Foods
Tucson, AZ....................520-624-7068
Armbrust Meats
Medford, WI....................715-748-3102
Atlantic Pork & Provisions
Jamaica, NY....................800-245-3536
B & D Foods
Boise, ID....................208-344-1183
B & R Quality Meats Inc
Waterloo, IA....................319-232-6328
Bear Creek Smokehouse Inc
Marshall, TX....................800-950-2327
Best Chicago Meat
Chicago, IL
Big B Barbecue
Evansville, IN....................812-425-5235
Bluebonnet Meat Company
Trenton, TX....................903-989-2293
Bodin Foods
New Iberia, LA....................337-367-1344
Boone's Butcher Shop
Bardstown, KY....................888-253-3384
Brucepac
Woodburn, OR....................800-899-3629
Burgers' Smokehouse
California, MO....................800-345-5185
Burke Corp
Nevada, IA....................800-654-1152
Burnett & Son
Monrovia, CA....................877-632-5467
Bush Brothers Provision Co
West Palm Beach, FL....................800-327-1345
Buzz Food Svc
Charleston, WV....................304-925-4781
C Roy & Sons Processing
Yale, MI....................810-387-3957
Caddo Packing Co
Marshall, TX....................903-935-2211
Calihan Pork Processors Inc
Peoria, IL....................309-674-9175
Calumet Diversified Meats Company
Pleasant Prairie, WI....................800-752-7427
Cargill Protein
Wichita, KS
Caribbean Products
Baltimore, MD....................410-235-7700
Carmelita Provisions Company
Monterey Park, CA....................323-262-6751
Carolina Pride Foods
Greenwood, SC....................864-229-5611
Caughman's Meat Plant
Lexington, SC....................803-356-0076
Central Meat & Provision
San Diego, CA....................619-239-1391
Chandler Foods Inc
Greensboro, NC....................800-537-6219
Chef's Requested Foods
Oklahoma City, OK....................405-239-2610
Cheraw Packing Plant
Cheraw, SC....................843-537-7426
Chicago Steaks
Chicago, IL....................773-847-5400
Chip Steak & Provision Co
Mankato, MN....................507-388-6277
Chisesi Brothers Meat Packing
New Orleans, LA....................800-966-3550
Cimpl Meats
Yankton, SD....................605-665-1665
Circle B Ranch
Seymour, MO....................417-683-0271
Circle V Meats
Spanish Fork, UT....................801-798-3081

Clem Becker Meats
Two Rivers, WI....................920-793-1391
Clougherty Packing LLC
Los Angeles, CA..................800-846-7635
Cloverdale Foods
Mandan, ND.......................800-669-9511
Coleman Natural
Kings Mountain, NC...............800-442-8666
Columbia Packing Co Inc
Dallas, TX........................214-946-8171
Continental Grain Company
New York, NY.....................212-207-5100
Cordon Bleu International
Anjou, QC.........................800-363-1182
Country Butcher Shop
Carlisle, PA......................800-272-9223
Country Smoked Meats
Bowling Green, OH................800-321-4766
Country Village Meats Inc
Sublette, IL......................800-700-4545
Crawford Sausage Co Inc
Chicago, IL.......................773-277-3095
Crofton & Sons Inc
Tampa, FL.........................800-878-7675
Curtis Packing Co
Greensboro, NC...................336-275-7684
Cusack Meats
Oklahoma City, OK...............800-241-6328
Dailys Premium Meats
Salt Lake City, UT...............800-328-7695
Debragga & Spitler
Jersey City, NJ
Diestel Family Turkey Ranch
..................................209-532-4950
Dietz & Watson Inc.
Philadelphia, PA.................215-831-9000
Dohar Meats Inc
Cleveland, OH....................216-241-4197
Dolores Canning Co Inc
Los Angeles, CA..................323-263-9155
Dom's Sausage Co Inc
Malden, MA.......................781-324-6390
Dreymiller & KRAY Inc
Hampshire, IL.....................847-683-2271
Duma Meats Inc
Mogadore, OH.....................330-628-3438
East Dayton Meat & Poultry
Dayton, OH........................937-253-6185
Edelmann Provision Company
Harrison, OH......................513-881-5800
Edmond's Chile Co
St Louis, MO......................314-772-1499
Fabbri Sausage Mfg Co
Chicago, IL.......................312-829-6363
Fair Oaks Farms LLC
Pleasant Prairie, WI.............800-528-8615
Fanestil Packing Company
Emporia, KS.......................800-658-1652
Feed The Party
Louisville, KY
Fletcher's Fine Foods
Auburn, WA.......................253-735-0800
Fork & Goode
Brooklyn, NY
Fortenberry Mini-Storage
Kodak, TN.........................865-933-2568
Freirich Foods
Salisbury, NC.....................800-221-1315
Frick's Quality Meats
Washington, MO...................800-241-2209
Fulton Provision Co
Portland, OR......................800-333-6328
Golden West Food Group
Vernon, CA........................888-807-3663
Gouvea's & Purity Foods Inc
Honolulu, HI......................808-847-3717
Grant Park Packing
Chicago, IL.......................312-421-4096
Groff's Meats
Elizabethtown, PA................717-367-1246
Gulf Marine & Industrial Supplies Inc
Houston, TX.......................800-886-6252
Hamms Custom Meats
Mckinney, TX.....................972-542-3359
Harvin Choice Meats
Sumter, SC........................800-849-6328
Hatfield Quality Meats
Hatfield, PA.......................800-743-1191
Hazle Park Quality Meats
West Hazleton, PA................800-238-4331
Hickory Baked Ham Co
Castle Rock, CO..................303-688-2633
Higa Food Service
Honolulu, HI......................808-531-3591
Hillbilly Smokehouse
Rogers, AR.......................479-636-1927
Holly Hill Locker Company
Holly Hill, SC.....................803-496-3611
Hoople Country Kitchen Inc
Rockport, IN......................877-466-7537
Hormel Foods Corp.
Austin, MN.......................507-437-5611
Humphrey's Market
Springfield, IL....................800-747-6328
JBS USA LLC
Greeley, CO......................970-506-8000
John Hofmeister & Son Inc
Chicago, IL.......................800-923-4267
Johnsonville Sausage LLC
Watertown, WI....................888-556-2728
Jones Dairy Farm
Fort Atkinson, WI................800-563-6637
JTM Food Group
Harrison, OH......................800-626-2308
Karn Meats
Columbus, OH....................800-221-9585
Kelley Foods
Elba, AL..........................334-897-5761
Kilgus Meats
Toledo, OH........................419-472-9721
Kowalski Sausage Co
Hamtramck, MI....................800-482-2400
Kubla Khan Food Company
Portland, OR......................503-234-7494
Kutztown Bologna Company
Leola, PA.........................800-723-8824
L & L Packing Co
Chicago, IL.......................800-628-6328
Land O'Frost Inc
Searcy, AR.......................800-643-5654
Lay Packing Company
Knoxville, TN.....................865-522-1147
Lee's Sausage Co
Orangeburg, SC..................803-534-5517
Leidy's
Harleysville, PA..................800-222-2319
Leo G. Fraboni Sausage Company
Hibbing, MN......................218-263-5074
Leona Meat Plant
Troy, PA..........................570-297-3574
Les Trois Petits Cochons
Brooklyn, NY.....................800-537-7283
Levesque
Montreal, QC.....................877-539-1702
Locustdale Meat Packing
Locustdale, PA...................570-875-1270
Lord's Sausage & Country Ham
Dexter, GA........................800-342-6002
Lubbers Family Farm
Grand Rapids, MI.................616-453-4257
Malcolm Meats Co
Northwood, OH....................800-822-6328
Maple Leaf Foods
Winnipeg, NB.....................800-564-6253
Marshallville Packing Co
Marshallville, OH.................330-855-2871
Marubeni America Corp.
New York, NY.....................212-450-0100
Meating Place
Buffalo, NY.......................716-885-3623
Mellos North End Mfr
Fall River, MA....................800-673-2320
Metafoods LLC
Brookhaven, GA..................404-843-2400
Miami Beef Co
Miami Lakes, FL..................305-621-3252
Mirasco
Atlanta, GA.......................770-956-1945
Mitchell Foods
Barbourville, KY.................888-202-9745
Montana Ranch Brand
Billings, MT.......................406-294-2333
Morreale John R Inc
Chicago, IL.......................312-421-3664
Morrison Meat Packers
Miami, FL.........................800-330-4267
Morse's Sauerkraut
Waldoboro, ME...................866-832-5569
National Steak & Poultry
Owasso, OK.......................918-274-8787
New Braunfels Smokehouse
New Braunfels, TX................800-537-6932
New Horizon Farms
Pipestone, MN....................800-906-7447
Niemuth's Steak & Chop Shop
Waupaca, WI......................715-258-2666
Northwest Meat Company
Chicago, IL.......................312-733-1418
Oklahoma City Meat Co Inc
Oklahoma City, OK...............405-235-3308
Olymel
Saint-Hyacinthe, QC..............450-771-0400
Omaha Steaks Inc
..................................800-960-8400
Ossian Smoked Meats
Ossian, IN........................800-535-8862
Parma Sausage Products
Pittsburgh, PA....................877-294-4207
Pasqualichio Brothers Inc
Scranton, PA.....................800-232-6233
Payne Packing Co
Artesia, NM.......................575-746-2779
Pederson's Natural Farms
Hamilton, TX
Peer Foods Group Inc
Chicago, IL.......................800-365-5644
Perdue Farms Inc.
Salisbury, MD....................800-473-7383
Pierceton Foods Inc
Pierceton, IN......................574-594-2344
Pioneer Packing Co
Bowling Green, OH...............419-352-5283
Plumrose USA
Chicago, IL.......................800-526-4909
Quality Snack Foods Inc
Alsip, IL..........................708-377-7120
Quirch Foods
Coral Gables, FL.................800-458-5252
R M Felts' Packing Co
Ivor, VA..........................757-859-6131
R.L. Zeigler Company
Selma, AL.........................800-392-6328
Randall Foods Inc
Vernon, CA........................800-372-6581
Ray's Sausage Co
Cleveland, OH....................216-921-8782
Red Smith Foods Inc
Davie, FL.........................954-581-1996
Register Meat Co
Cottondale, FL....................850-352-4269
Rendulic Meat Packing Corp
Mckeesport, PA...................412-678-9541
Rinehart Meat Processing
Branson, MO......................417-869-2041
Robertson's Country Meat Hams
Finchville, KY....................800-678-1521
Rose Packing Co Inc
South Barrington, IL..............800-323-7363
Sadler's Smokehouse
Henderson, TX....................903-657-5581
Sanders Meat Packing Inc
Custer, MI........................800-968-5035
Saval Foods Corp
Elkridge, MD.....................800-527-2825
Savoie's Sausage and Food Products
Opelousas, LA....................337-942-7241
Schaller & Weber Inc
Astoria, NY.......................800-847-4115
Sculli Brothers
Yeadon, PA.......................215-336-1223
Seaboard Foods
Shawnee Mission, KS.............800-262-7907
Sechrist Brothers
Dallastown, PA...................717-244-2975
Sheinman Provision Co
Philadelphia, PA.................215-473-7065
Smolich Bros. Home Made Sausage
Crest Hill, IL......................815-727-2144
Sofina Foods Inc
Markham, ON......................855-763-4621
Sommers Organic
Wheeling, IL......................877-377-9797
SRA Foods
Birmingham, AL...................205-323-7447
Stevens Sausage Co
Smithfield, NC....................800-338-0561
Stevison Ham Co
Portland, TN......................800-844-4267
Stonie's Sausage Shop
Perryville, MO....................888-546-2540
Strassburger Steaks
Carlstadt, NJ......................201-842-8890
Stripling's General Store
Moultrie, GA......................229-985-4226
Sugar Creek
Washington Ct Hs, OH............800-848-8205

Suncrest Farms
Princeton, KY 973-595-0214
Sunnydale Meats Inc
Gaffney, SC 864-489-6091
Taylor Meat Co
Taylor, TX 512-352-6357
Teton Waters Ranch LLC
Denver, CO 720-340-4590
The Bruss Company
Chicago, IL 773-282-2900
Thomas Packing Company
Columbus, GA 800-729-0976
Tolteca Foodservice
Norcross, GA 800-541-6835
Triumph Foods, LLC
St. Joseph, MO 800-262-7907
Troy Foods Inc
Troy, IL 618-667-6332
Tyson Foods Inc.
Springdale, AR 479-290-4000
Tyson Foods Inc.
Springdale, AR 800-233-6332
V.W. Joyner & Company
Smithfield, VA 757-357-2161
Valley Meats
Coal Valley, IL 309-517-6639
Vestergaard Farms
Ann Arbor, MI 734-929-2875
Vital Choice
Bellingham, WA 800-608-4825
Vollwerth & Baroni Companies
Hancock, MI 800-562-7620
W.A. Beans & Sons
Bangor, ME 800-649-1958
WACO Beef & Pork Processors
Waco, TX 254-772-4669
Waken Meat Co
Atlanta, GA 404-627-3537
Wayco Ham Co
Goldsboro, NC 800-962-2614
White Oak Pastures
Bluffton, GA 229-641-2081
Wichita Packing Co Inc
Chicago, IL 312-763-3965
Williams Pork
Chadbourn, NC 910-654-0204
Willie's Smoke House LLC
Harrisville, PA 800-742-4184
YB Meats of Wichita
Wichita, KS 316-942-1213

Barbecued

Big B Barbecue
Evansville, IN 812-425-5235
Chandler Foods Inc
Greensboro, NC 800-537-6219
Dorina So-Good Inc
Union, IL 815-923-2144
Moonlite Bar-B-Q Inn
Owensboro, KY 800-322-8989
Piggie Park Enterprises
West Columbia, SC 800-628-7423
Sadler's Smokehouse
Henderson, TX 903-657-5581
Stevison Ham Co
Portland, TN 800-844-4267
W & G Marketing Company
Ames, IA 515-233-4774
Woods Smoked Meats Inc
Bowling Green, MO 800-458-8426

Frozen

Burke Corp
Nevada, IA 800-654-1152
Clifty Farm Country Meats
Paris, TN 800-486-4267

Boneless Picnic

Roger Wood Foods Inc
Savannah, GA 800-849-9272

Breaded

King's Command Foods Inc
Green Bay, WA 800-345-0293
Valley Meats
Coal Valley, IL 309-517-6639

Fresh

Abattoir A. Trahan Company
Yamachiche, QC 819-296-3791
Aliments Jolibec, Inc
St Jacques De Montcalm, QC 450-861-6082
Amity Packing Co Inc
Chicago, IL 800-837-0270
Botsford Fisheries
Cap Pele, NB 506-577-4327
Brook Locker Plant
Brook, IN 219-275-2611
Buckhead Beef
Atlanta, GA 800-888-5578
Camrose Packers
Camrose, AB 780-672-4887
Charcuterie LaTour Eiffel
Blainville, QC 800-361-0001
Farm Boy Food Svc
Evansville, IN 800-852-3976
Independent Meat Co
Twin Falls, ID 800-284-4626
J & M Wholesale Meat Inc
Modesto, CA 855-522-1248
J W Treuth & Sons
Catonsville, MD 410-747-6281
Les Salaisons Brochu
St. Henri De Levis, QC 418-882-2282
Les Viandes or Fil
Laval, QC 450-687-5664
Maple Leaf Pork
Montreal, QC 800-268-3708
Ontario Pork
Guelph, ON 877-668-7675
Pure Foods Meat
Toronto, ON 416-236-1163
R Four Meats
Chatfield, MN 507-867-4180
Schwab Meat Co
Oklahoma City, OK 800-888-8668
Shelley's
Jersey City, NJ 201-433-2900
Smith Packing Regional Meat
Utica, NY 315-732-5125
Sommers Organic
Wheeling, IL 877-377-9797
Sunterra Meats
Trochu, AB 403-442-4202
Thomson Meats
Melfort, SK 306-752-2802
Troy Pork Store
Troy, NY 518-272-8291
True Story Foods
San Francisco, CA 888-277-1171

Frozen

Abattoir A. Trahan Company
Yamachiche, QC 819-296-3791
Aliments Jolibec, Inc
St Jacques De Montcalm, QC 450-861-6082
Amity Packing Co Inc
Chicago, IL 800-837-0270
B & D Foods
Boise, ID 208-344-1183
Blakely Freezer Locker
Blakeley, GA 229-723-3622
Bob's Custom Cuts
Bonnyville, AB 780-826-2627
Botsford Fisheries
Cap Pele, NB 506-577-4327
Branding Iron
Sauget, IL 800-851-4684
Brook Locker Plant
Brook, IN 219-275-2611
Brookfield Farm
Amherst, MA 413-253-7991
Buckhead Beef
Atlanta, GA 800-888-5578
Burke Corp
Nevada, IA 800-654-1152
Charcuterie LaTour Eiffel
Blainville, QC 800-361-0001
Clifty Farm Country Meats
Paris, TN 800-486-4267
Curly's Foods Inc
Edina, MN 612-920-3400
Edmond's Chile Co
St Louis, MO 314-772-1499
El Rey Cooked Meats
St Louis, MO 314-521-3113
Hatfield Quality Meats
Hatfield, PA 800-743-1191
J & M Wholesale Meat Inc
Modesto, CA 855-522-1248
Kutztown Bologna Company
Leola, PA 800-723-8824
Ladoga Frozen Food & Retail
Ladoga, IN 765-942-2225
Lengerich Meats Inc
Zanesville, IN 260-638-4123
Les Salaisons Brochu
St. Henri De Levis, QC 418-882-2282
Les Viandes du Breton
Riviere-Du-Lup, QC 418-863-6711
Les Viandes or Fil
Laval, QC 450-687-5664
M Buono Beef Co
Philadelphia, PA 215-463-3600
Maid-Rite Steak Company
Dunmore, PA 800-233-4259
Maple Leaf Pork
Montreal, QC 800-268-3708
Phoenix Agro-Industrial Corporation
Westbury, NY 516-334-1194
Pierceton Foods Inc
Pierceton, IN 574-594-2344
Pure Foods Meat
Toronto, ON 416-236-1163
R Four Meats
Chatfield, MN 507-867-4180
Schwab Meat Co
Oklahoma City, OK 800-888-8668
Shelley's
Jersey City, NJ 201-433-2900
Smith Packing Regional Meat
Utica, NY 315-732-5125
Sommers Organic
Wheeling, IL 877-377-9797
Springhill Farms
Neepawa, NB 204-476-3393
Steak-Umm Company
Shillington, PA 860-928-5900
Sudlersville Frozen Food Locker
Sudlersville, MD 410-438-3106
Thompson Packers
Slidell, LA 800-989-6328
Thomson Meats
Melfort, SK 306-752-2802
Travis Meats Inc
Powell, TN 800-247-7606

Loin Baby Back Ribs

Wichita Packing Co Inc
Chicago, IL 312-763-3965

Loin Chop

Amana Meat Shop & Smoke House
Amana, IA 800-373-6328
Calumet Diversified Meats Company
Pleasant Prairie, WI 800-752-7427
Chicago Steaks
Chicago, IL 773-847-5400

Loins

Bear Creek Smokehouse Inc
Marshall, TX 800-950-2327
Black's Barbecue
Lockhart, TX 888-632-8225
Calihan Pork Processors Inc
Peoria, IL 309-674-9175
Calumet Diversified Meats Company
Pleasant Prairie, WI 800-752-7427
Chicago Steaks
Chicago, IL 773-847-5400
Country Smoked Meats
Bowling Green, OH 800-321-4766
Father's Country Hams
Bremen, KY 270-525-3554
Pasqualichio Brothers Inc
Scranton, PA 800-232-6233
Saval Foods Corp
Elkridge, MD 800-527-2825

Pigs' Feet

Canned

Peer Foods Group Inc
Chicago, IL 800-365-5644
Red Smith Foods Inc
Davie, FL 954-581-1996

Prepared

Frozen

Advance Pierre Foods
Cincinnati, OH 800-969-2747

Branding Iron
Sauget, IL . . . 800-851-4684
Brookview Farms
Manakin-Sabot, VA . . . 804-784-3131
Buckhead Beef
Atlanta, GA . . . 800-888-5578
Burke Corp
Nevada, IA . . . 800-654-1152
Chicago Meat Authority Inc
Chicago, IL . . . 800-383-3811
Hall Brothers Meats
Olmsted Twp, OH . . . 440-235-3262
Hamms Custom Meats
Mckinney, TX . . . 972-542-3359
King Kold Meats
Englewood, OH . . . 800-836-2797
Land O'Frost Inc
Searcy, AR . . . 800-643-5654
Pierceton Foods Inc
Pierceton, IN . . . 574-594-2344
Puueo Poi Shop
Hilo, HI . . . 808-935-8435
Roger Wood Foods Inc
Savannah, GA . . . 800-849-9272
Tucker Packing Co
Orrville, OH . . . 330-683-3311

Raw

Duma Meats Inc
Mogadore, OH . . . 330-628-3438
Ralph's Packing Co
Perkins, OK . . . 800-522-3979

Rib Center Cut

Bear Creek Smokehouse Inc
Marshall, TX . . . 800-950-2327
Chicago Steaks
Chicago, IL . . . 773-847-5400
Farm Boy Food Svc
Evansville, IN . . . 800-852-3976
Stevison Ham Co
Portland, TN . . . 800-844-4267

Sausage

Alaska Sausage & Seafood
Anchorage, AK . . . 800-798-3636
Albert's Meats
Claysville, PA . . . 800-522-9970
Alef Sausage Inc
Mundelein, IL . . . 847-968-2533
Arnold's Meat Food Products
Brooklyn, NY . . . 800-633-7023
Battistoni Italian Spec Meats
Buffalo, NY . . . 800-248-2705
Bear Creek Smokehouse Inc
Marshall, TX . . . 800-950-2327
Bellville Meat Market
Bellville, TX . . . 800-571-6328
Big Fork Brands
Chicago, IL . . . 321-206-9444
Bilinski Sausage Mfg Co
Cohoes, NY . . . 877-873-9102
Broadbent B & B Food Products
Kuttawa, KY . . . 800-841-2202
Brooklyn Cured LLC
New York, NY . . . 907-282-2221
Brucepac
Woodburn, OR . . . 800-899-3629
Burke Corp
Nevada, IA . . . 800-654-1152
C.W. Brown Foods, Inc.
Mountt Royal, NJ . . . 856-423-3700
Carr Valley Cheese Company
La Valle, WI . . . 800-462-7258
Caughman's Meat Plant
Lexington, SC . . . 803-356-0076
Chisesi Brothers Meat Packing
New Orleans, LA . . . 800-966-3550
Cimpl Meats
Yankton, SD . . . 605-665-1665
Clougherty Packing LLC
Los Angeles, CA . . . 800-846-7635
Crofton & Sons Inc
Tampa, FL . . . 800-878-7675
Den's Hot Dogs
Brooklyn, NY . . . 718-355-9636
Devro Inc
Swansea, SC . . . 803-796-9730
Dom's Sausage Co Inc
Malden, MA . . . 781-324-6390
East Dayton Meat & Poultry
Dayton, OH . . . 937-253-6185
Ebro Foods
Chicago, IL . . . 773-696-0150
Edelmann Provision Company
Harrison, OH . . . 513-881-5800
F B Purnell Sausage Co Inc
Simpsonville, KY . . . 800-626-1512
Field Roast
Seattle, WA . . . 800-311-9497
Fortenberry Mini-Storage
Kodak, TN . . . 865-933-2568
Fred Usinger Inc
Milwaukee, WI . . . 800-558-9998
Gouvea's & Purity Foods Inc
Honolulu, HI . . . 808-847-3717
Hoople Country Kitchen Inc
Rockport, IN . . . 877-466-7537
Humphrey's Market
Springfield, IL . . . 800-747-6328
International Meat Co
Chicago, IL . . . 773-622-1400
Johnsonville Sausage LLC
Watertown, WI . . . 888-556-2728
Korte Meat Processors Inc
Highland, IL . . . 618-654-3813
Kowalski Sausage Co
Hamtramck, MI . . . 800-482-2400
Kramarczuk's Sausage Co
Minneapolis, MN . . . 612-379-3018
Kubisch Sausage Mfg Co
Shelby Twp, MI . . . 800-852-5019
Laxson Co
San Antonio, TX . . . 210-226-8397
Lee's Sausage Co
Orangeburg, SC . . . 803-534-5517
Leidy's
Harleysville, PA . . . 800-222-2319
Leo G. Fraboni Sausage Company
Hibbing, MN . . . 218-263-5074
Les Trois Petits Cochons
Brooklyn, NY . . . 800-537-7283
Lord's Sausage & Country Ham
Dexter, GA . . . 800-342-6002
Magic Seasoning Blends
New Orleans, LA . . . 800-457-2857
Manns Sausage Company
Blacksburg, VA . . . 540-605-0867
Meating Place
Buffalo, NY . . . 716-885-3623
Miami Beef Co
Miami Lakes, FL . . . 305-621-3252
Morrison Meat Packers
Miami, FL . . . 800-330-4267
Morse's Sauerkraut
Waldoboro, ME . . . 866-832-5569
New Braunfels Smokehouse
New Braunfels, TX . . . 800-537-6932
Niemuth's Steak & Chop Shop
Waupaca, WI . . . 715-258-2666
Nodine's Smokehouse Inc
Torrington, CT . . . 800-222-2059
Old Wisconsin Sausage Inc
Sheboygan, WI . . . 877-451-7988
Olympic Provisions Northwest
Portland, OR . . . 503-894-8136
R M Felts' Packing Co
Ivor, VA . . . 757-859-6131
Ray's Sausage Co
Cleveland, OH . . . 216-921-8782
Red Smith Foods Inc
Davie, FL . . . 954-581-1996
Register Meat Co
Cottondale, FL . . . 850-352-4269
Rinehart Meat Processing
Branson, MO . . . 417-869-2041
Roger Wood Foods Inc
Savannah, GA . . . 800-849-9272
Rose Packing Co Inc
South Barrington, IL . . . 800-323-7363
Sausage Kitchen
Lisbon Falls, ME . . . 888-453-5503
Savoie's Sausage and Food Products
Opelousas, LA . . . 337-942-7241
Smith Provision Co Inc
Erie, PA . . . 800-334-9151
Specialty Foods Group Inc
Owensboro, KY . . . 800-238-0020
Stonie's Sausage Shop
Perryville, MO . . . 888-546-2540
Stripling's General Store
Moultrie, GA . . . 229-985-4226
Sunnydale Meats Inc
Gaffney, SC . . . 864-489-6091
Sunset Farm Foods Inc
Valdosta, GA . . . 800-882-1121
Teton Waters Ranch LLC
Denver, CO . . . 720-340-4590
Thomas Packing Company
Columbus, GA . . . 800-729-0976
Vermont Smoke and Cure
Hinesburg, VT . . . 802-482-4666
Vollwerth & Baroni Companies
Hancock, MI . . . 800-562-7620
WACO Beef & Pork Processors
Waco, TX . . . 254-772-4669
Williams Pork
Chadbourn, NC . . . 910-654-0204
YB Meats of Wichita
Wichita, KS . . . 316-942-1213
Zweigle's Inc
Rochester, NY . . . 585-546-1740

Ardouille

Burke Corp
Nevada, IA . . . 800-654-1152
Magic Seasoning Blends
New Orleans, LA . . . 800-457-2857
Sunset Farm Foods Inc
Valdosta, GA . . . 800-882-1121

Scrapple

Arnold's Meat Food Products
Brooklyn, NY . . . 800-633-7023
Kirby Holloway Provision Co
Harrington, DE . . . 800-995-4729

Spareribs

Calihan Pork Processors Inc
Peoria, IL . . . 309-674-9175
RJ Balson and Sons Inc
Asheville, NC . . . 321-281-9473

Tenderloin Roast

Amana Meat Shop & Smoke House
Amana, IA . . . 800-373-6328
Bear Creek Smokehouse Inc
Marshall, TX . . . 800-950-2327
New Braunfels Smokehouse
New Braunfels, TX . . . 800-537-6932
Opa's Smoked Meats
Fredericksburg, TX . . . 800-543-6750

Poultry

50th State Poultry Processors
Pearl City, HI . . . 808-845-5902
Adolf's Meats & Sausage Kitchen
Hartford, CT . . . 860-522-1588
AJM Meat Packing
San Juan, PR . . . 787-787-4050
Al Safa Halal
New York City, NY . . . 800-268-8147
Alderfer Inc
Harleysville, PA . . . 800-341-1121
All-States Quality Foods
Charles City, IA . . . 800-247-4195
Allen Harim Foods LLC
Seaford, DE . . . 877-397-9191
Alpine Butcher
Lowell, MA . . . 978-256-7771
American Egg Products Inc
Blackshear, GA . . . 912-449-5700
Amick Farms LLC
Batesburg, SC . . . 800-926-4257
Anmar Foods
Chicago, IL . . . 312-421-6500
Applegate Farms
Bridgewater, NJ . . . 866-587-5858
Arizona Sunland Foods
Tucson, AZ . . . 520-624-7068
Armbrust Meats
Medford, WI . . . 715-748-3102
B & B Poultry Co
Norma, NJ . . . 800-535-7646
B & D Foods
Boise, ID . . . 208-344-1183
Barber Foods
Kings Mountain, NC . . . 877-447-3279
Bear Creek Smokehouse Inc
Marshall, TX . . . 800-950-2327
Becker Foods
Westminster, CA . . . 714-891-9474

Bell & Evans
Fredericksburg, PA 717-865-6626
Bird-In-Hand Farms Inc
Lancaster, PA 717-291-9904
Birdie Pak Products
Chicago, IL 773-247-5293
Black's Barbecue
Lockhart, TX 888-632-8225
Blakely Freezer Locker
Blakeley, GA 229-723-3622
Blue Ridge Poultry
Athens, GA 706-546-6767
Boar's Head
Sarasota, FL 800-352-6277
Bon Ton Products
Wheeling, IL 847-520-8300
Bowman & Landes Turkeys
New Carlisle, OH 877-466-9466
Brakebush Brothers
Westfield, WI 800-933-2121
Brook Locker Plant
Brook, IN 219-275-2611
Brown Foods
Dallas, GA 770-445-4358
Bryant's Meat Inc.
Taylorsville, MS 800-844-0507
Burgers' Smokehouse
California, MO 800-345-5185
Burke Corp
Nevada, IA 800-654-1152
Bush Brothers Provision Co
West Palm Beach, FL 800-327-1345
Butterball LLC
Garner, NC 919-255-7900
Butterfield Foods
Noblesville, IN 317-776-4775
Campbell Soup Co.
Camden, NJ 800-257-8443
Canal Fulton Provision
Canal Fulton, OH 800-321-3502
Caribbean Food Delights Inc
Tappan, NY 845-398-3000
Case Farms Ohio Division
Winesburg, OH 330-359-7141
Chandler Foods Inc
Greensboro, NC 800-537-6219
Charles Poultry Company
Lancaster, PA 717-872-7621
Chef Hans' Gourmet Foods
Monroe, LA 800-890-4267
Chef's Requested Foods
Oklahoma City, OK 405-239-2610
Chester's International , LLC
Mountain Brook, AL 800-288-1555
Chestertown Natural Foods
Chestertown, MD 410-778-1677
Chick-Fil-A Inc.
Atlanta, GA 866-232-2040
Chisesi Brothers Meat Packing
New Orleans, LA 800-966-3550
Choctaw Maid Farms
Jackson, MS 601-683-4000
Clifty Farm Country Meats
Paris, TN 800-486-4267
Conagra Brands Inc
Chicago, IL 877-266-2472
Conagra Foodservice
Chicago, IL 877-266-2472
Continental Grain Company
New York, NY 212-207-5100
Cordon Bleu International
Anjou, QC 800-363-1182
Corfu Foods Inc
Bensenville, IL 630-595-2510
Couch's Country Style Sausages
Cleveland, OH 216-823-2332
Country Smoked Meats
Bowling Green, OH 800-321-4766
Crescent Duck Farm
Aquebogue LI, NY 631-722-8000
Crescent Foods
Chicago, IL 800-939-6268
Crystal Lake Farms
Decatur, AR 800-382-4425
Culver Duck Farms Inc
Middlebury, IN 800-825-9225
Cusack Meats
Oklahoma City, OK 800-241-6328
Debel Food Products
Elizabeth, NJ 800-421-3447
Debragga & Spitler
Jersey City, NJ

Delphos Poultry Products
Delphos, OH 419-692-5816
Dietz & Watson Inc.
Philadelphia, PA 215-831-9000
Dole & Bailey Inc
Woburn, MA 781-935-1234
Double B Foods Inc
Arlington, TX 800-679-0349
Draper Valley Farms
Mt Vernon, WA 800-562-2012
Dutterer's Home Food Service
Baltimore, MD 410-298-3663
E.C. Phillips & Son
Ketchikan, AK 907-247-7975
East Dayton Meat & Poultry
Dayton, OH 937-253-6185
East Poultry Co
Austin, TX 512-476-5367
Eberly Poultry, Inc.
Stevens, PA 717-336-6440
Edelman Meats Inc
Antigo, WI 715-623-7686
El Jay Poultry Corporation
Voorhees, NJ 856-435-0900
Empire Kosher Foods
Mifflintown, PA 800-367-4734
Exceldor Cooperative
Levis, QC 418-830-5600
Fair Oaks Farms LLC
Pleasant Prairie, WI 800-528-8615
Farbest Foods Inc
Jasper, IN 812-683-4200
Farmers Produce
Ashby, MN 218-747-2749
Feed The Party
Louisville, KY
Fieldale Farms
Baldwin, GA 800-241-5400
Fried Provisions Company
Evans City, PA 724-538-3160
Gentry's Poultry
Ward, SC 800-926-2161
George's Inc
Springdale, AR 800-800-2449
Gerber's Poultry Inc
Kidron, OH 800-362-7381
Giovanni's Appetizing Food Co
Richmond, MI 586-727-9355
Golden Platter Foods
Newark, NJ 973-344-8770
Golden West Food Group
Vernon, CA 888-807-3663
Grabill Country Meats
Grabill, IN 866-333-6328
Grant Park Packing
Chicago, IL 312-421-4096
Gress Enterprises
Scranton, PA 570-561-0150
Grimaud Farms-California Inc
Stockton, CA 800-466-9955
Hall Brothers Meats
Olmsted Twp, OH 440-235-3262
Hamilos Bros Inspected Meat
Madison, IL 618-876-3710
Health is Wealth Foods
Moonachie, NJ 201-933-7474
Heinkel's Packing Co
Decatur, IL 800-594-2738
Hickory Baked Ham Co
Castle Rock, CO 303-688-2633
Hillbilly Smokehouse
Rogers, AR 479-636-1927
Hollman Foods
Des Moines, IA 888-926-2879
Hormel Foods Corp.
Austin, MN 507-437-5611
House of Raeford Farms Inc.
Rose Hill, NC 910-289-3191
Indian Valley Meats
Indian, AK 907-653-7511
International Home Foods
Parsippany, NJ 973-359-9920
International Meat Co
Chicago, IL 773-622-1400
J & G Poultry & Seafood
Gainesville, GA 770-536-5540
J.R. Poultry
Fults, IL 618-458-7194
Jacob's Meats Inc
Defiance, OH 419-782-7831
Janes Family Foods
Mississauga, ON 800-565-2637

JD Sweid Foods
Langley, BC 800-665-4355
Jennie-O Turkey Store
Willmar, MN 320-235-6080
Joe Jurgielwicz & Sons
Hamburg, PA 800-543-8257
John Garner Meats
Van Buren, AR 800-543-5473
Johnson, Nash & Sons Farms
Warsaw, NC 910-289-6842
Joyce Farms
Winston Salem, NC 800-755-6923
K & K Gourmet Meats Inc
Leetsdale, PA 724-266-8400
Kelly Gourmet Foods Inc
San Francisco, CA 415-648-9200
King Cole Ducks Limited
Newmarket, ON 800-363-3825
King's Command Foods Inc
Green Bay, WA 800-345-0293
L. Craelius & Company
Chicago, IL 312-666-7100
Lake Charles Poultry
Lake Charles, LA 337-433-6818
Land O'Frost Inc
Searcy, AR 800-643-5654
Land O'Frost Inc.
Lansing, IL 800-323-3308
Lendy's Cafe Raw Bar
Virginia Beach, VA 757-491-3511
Lilydale Foods
Markham, ON 800-661-5341
Locustdale Meat Packing
Locustdale, PA 570-875-1270
Long Food Industries
Fripp Island, SC 843-838-3205
LSK Smoked Turkey Products
Bronx, NY 718-792-1300
Macfarlane Pheasants
Janesville, WI 800-345-8348
MacGregors Meat & Seafood
Toronto, ON 888-383-3663
Mada'n Kosher Foods
Dania, FL 954-925-0077
Madani Halal
Ozone Park, NY 718-323-9732
Mahantongo Game Farm
Dalmatia, PA 800-982-9913
Maid-Rite Steak Company
Dunmore, PA 800-233-4259
Malcolm Meats Co
Northwood, OH 800-822-6328
Manchester Farms
Columbia, SC 800-845-0421
Manger Packing Corp
Baltimore, MD 800-227-9262
Manley Meats Inc
Decatur, IN 260-592-7313
Maple Leaf Farms
St Leesburg, IN 800-348-2812
Mar-Jac Poultry Inc.
Gainesville, GA 770-531-5000
Marshall Durbin Companies
Birmingham, AL 800-768-2456
Marshallville Packing Co
Marshallville, OH 330-855-2871
McFarland Foods
Riverton, UT 800-441-9596
Meat-O-Mat Corp
Brooklyn, NY 718-965-7250
Metafoods LLC
Brookhaven, GA 404-843-2400
Miami Beef Co
Miami Lakes, FL 305-621-3252
Miller Brothers Packing Company
Sylvester, GA 229-776-2014
Mirasco
Atlanta, GA 770-956-1945
Moretti's Poultry
Columbus, OH 614-486-2333
Moroni Feed Company
Moroni, UT 435-436-8202
Mountain Valley Poultry
Brandon, FL 813-689-2616
Mountaire Corporation
Millsboro, DE 877-887-1490
Murray's Chickens
South Fallsburg, NY 800-588-5051
Nema Food Distribution
Fairfield, NJ 973-256-4415
New Braunfels Smokehouse
New Braunfels, TX 800-537-6932

New Wave Cuisine
Mount Holly, NJ . . . 800-486-0276
Nodine's Smokehouse Inc
Torrington, CT . . . 800-222-2059
Norfolk Hatchery
Norfolk, NE. . . . 800-345-2449
Northwest Meat Company
Chicago, IL . . . 312-733-1418
Ok Industries
Fort Smith, AR . . . 800-635-9441
Olson Locker
Fairmont, MN . . . 507-238-2563
Omaha Steaks Inc
. . . 800-960-8400
On-Cor Frozen Foods Redi-Serve
Aurora, IL . . . 920-563-6391
P & L Poultry
Spokane, WA. . . . 509-892-1242
Pacific Poultry Company
Honolulu, HI . . . 808-841-2828
Paisano Food Products
Elk Grove Village, IL . . . 800-672-4726
Palmetto Pigeon Plant
Sumter, SC . . . 803-775-1204
Pasqualichio Brothers Inc
Scranton, PA . . . 800-232-6233
Peco Foods Inc.
Tuscaloosa, AL . . . 205-345-4711
Pennfield Farms
Mt Joy, PA. . . . 800-732-0009
Petaluma Poultry
Petaluma, CA . . . 800-556-6789
Petschl's Quality Meats
Tukwila, WA. . . . 206-575-4400
Piller's Fine Foods
Waterloo, ON . . . 800-265-2627
Pinty's Premium Foods
Burlington, ON. . . . 800-263-7223
Pintys Delicious Foods
Burlington, ON. . . . 800-263-9710
Prime Pak Foods Inc
Gainesville, GA . . . 770-536-8708
Puueo Poi Shop
Hilo, HI. . . . 808-935-8435
Quirch Foods
Coral Gables, FL. . . . 800-458-5252
Randall Foods Inc
Vernon, CA . . . 800-372-6581
Ray's Sausage Co
Cleveland, OH . . . 216-921-8782
Registry Steak & Seafood
Bridgeview, IL . . . 708-458-3100
Rod Golden Hatchery Inc
Cullman, AL. . . . 256-734-0941
Roman Sausage Company
Santa Clara, CA . . . 800-497-7462
Rose Acre Farms
Wolcott, IN . . . 765-258-4015
Rose Hill Distributors
Branford, CT. . . . 203-488-7231
Rus Dun Farms Inc
Collierville, TN. . . . 901-853-0931
Rymer Foods
Chicago, IL . . . 800-247-9637
Sadler's Smokehouse
Henderson, TX . . . 903-657-5581
Schaefers Market
Sauk Centre, MN . . . 320-352-6490
Schaller & Weber Inc
Astoria, NY. . . . 800-847-4115
Schiltz Foods Inc
Sisseton, SD . . . 877-872-4458
Schneider Foods
Kitchener, ON. . . . 519-741-5000
Schneider Foods
Saint Marys, ON. . . . 800-567-1890
Selwoods Farm Hunting Preserve
Alpine, AL . . . 800-522-0403
Serenade Foods
Milford, IN . . . 574-658-4121
Shelley's
Jersey City, NJ . . . 201-433-2900
Shelton's Poultry Inc
Pomona, CA . . . 800-541-1833
Simmons Foods Inc
Siloam Springs, AR . . . 888-831-7007
SJH Enterprises
Middleton, WI. . . . 888-745-3845
Smith Packing Regional Meat
Utica, NY . . . 315-732-5125
Smoked Turkey Inc
Marshville, NC . . . 704-624-6628
Sofina Foods Inc
Markham, ON. . . . 855-763-4621
Sommers Organic
Wheeling, IL. . . . 877-377-9797
SOPAKCO Foods
Mullins, SC. . . . 800-276-9678
Springville Meat & Cold Storage
Springville, UT . . . 801-489-6391
Squab Producers of California
Modesto, CA. . . . 209-537-4744
Standard Meat Co LP
Dallas, TX. . . . 866-859-6313
Starkel Poultry
Puyallup, WA . . . 253-845-2876
Steak-Umm Company
Shillington, PA . . . 860-928-5900
Streit Carl & Son Co
Neptune, NJ . . . 732-775-0803
Sunday House Foods
Fredericksburg, TX. . . . 830-997-2136
Sunnydale Meats Inc
Gaffney, SC. . . . 864-489-6091
Sure-Good Food Distributors
Syracuse, NY . . . 315-422-1196
Suzanna's Kitchen
Peachtree Cor, GA . . . 770-476-9900
Sweet Sue Kitchens
Athens, AL . . . 256-216-0500
Taylor's Poultry Place
Lexington, SC. . . . 803-356-3431
Thomas Packing Company
Columbus, GA . . . 800-729-0976
Tillamook Meat Inc
Tillamook, OR . . . 503-842-4802
Tip Top Poultry Inc
Marietta, GA. . . . 800-241-5230
Tolteca Foodservice
Norcross, GA . . . 800-541-6835
Troyer Foods Inc
Goshen, IN . . . 800-876-9377
Turkey Store
Faribault, MN. . . . 507-334-5555
Tyson Foods Inc.
Springdale, AR . . . 479-290-4000
United Provision Meat Company
Columbus, OH . . . 614-252-1126
Universal Poultry Company
Athens, GA . . . 706-546-6767
Vestergaard Farms
Ann Arbor, MI . . . 734-929-2875
Vienna Meat Products
Scarborough, ON . . . 800-588-1931
Vitale Poultry Company
Columbus, OH . . . 614-267-1874
W & G Marketing Company
Ames, IA. . . . 515-233-4774
WACO Beef & Pork Processors
Waco, TX . . . 254-772-4669
Walden Foods
Winchester, VA . . . 800-648-7688
Walker Meats
Carrollton, GA . . . 800-741-3601
Waltkoch Limited
Tucker, GA . . . 404-378-3666
Wapsie Produce
Decorah, IA. . . . 563-382-4271
Wasatch Meats Inc
Salt Lake City, UT . . . 800-631-8294
Wayco Ham Co
Goldsboro, NC . . . 800-962-2614
Wayne Farms LLC.
Oakwood, GA. . . . 800-392-0844
Whitaker & Assoc Architects
Atlanta, GA. . . . 404-266-1265
White Fence Farm
Romeoville, IL . . . 630-739-1720
White Oak Pastures
Bluffton, GA. . . . 229-641-2081
Willie's Smoke House LLC
Harrisville, PA. . . . 800-742-4184
Willow Tree Poultry Farm Inc
Attleboro, MA. . . . 508-222-3621
Woods Smoked Meats Inc
Bowling Green, MO . . . 800-458-8426
World Flavors Inc
Warminster, PA . . . 215-672-4400
Wornick Company
Cincinnati, OH . . . 800-860-4555
Yoakum Packing Co
Yoakum, TX . . . 800-999-6997
Zabiha Halal Meat Processors
Addison, IL. . . . 630-620-5000
Zacky Farms
Fresno, CA . . . 800-888-0235
Zartic Inc
Rome, GA. . . . 800-241-0516

Chicken

50th State Poultry Processors
Pearl City, HI . . . 808-845-5902
Al Safa Halal
New York City, NY. . . . 800-268-8147
All-States Quality Foods
Charles City, IA . . . 800-247-4195
Alpine Butcher
Lowell, MA. . . . 978-256-7771
Amylu Foods
Chicago, IL
B & D Foods
Boise, ID . . . 208-344-1183
Bear Creek Smokehouse Inc
Marshall, TX. . . . 800-950-2327
Black's Barbecue
Lockhart, TX. . . . 888-632-8225
Blakely Freezer Locker
Blakeley, GA. . . . 229-723-3622
Brakebush Brothers
Westfield, WI . . . 800-933-2121
Brook Locker Plant
Brook, IN . . . 219-275-2611
Brucepac
Woodburn, OR . . . 800-899-3629
Bryant's Meat Inc.
Taylorsville, MS . . . 800-844-0507
Burgers' Smokehouse
California, MO . . . 800-345-5185
Burke Corp
Nevada, IA . . . 800-654-1152
Buzz Food Svc
Charleston, WV . . . 304-925-4781
Caribbean Food Delights Inc
Tappan, NY. . . . 845-398-3000
Caribbean Products
Baltimore, MD . . . 410-235-7700
Case Farms
Troutman, NC. . . . 704-528-4501
CBP Resources
Gastonia, NC. . . . 704-868-4573
Cericola Farms
Bradford, ON . . . 905-939-2962
Charles Poultry Company
Lancaster, PA . . . 717-872-7621
Chef Hans' Gourmet Foods
Monroe, LA. . . . 800-890-4267
Chester's International , LLC
Mountain Brook, AL . . . 800-288-1555
Chick-Fil-A Inc.
Atlanta, GA. . . . 866-232-2040
Chisesi Brothers Meat Packing
New Orleans, LA . . . 800-966-3550
Choctaw Maid Farms
Jackson, MS . . . 601-683-4000
Coleman Natural
Kings Mountain, NC. . . . 800-442-8666
Cordon Bleu International
Anjou, QC. . . . 800-363-1182
Corfu Foods Inc
Bensenville, IL . . . 630-595-2510
Crystal Lake Farms
Decatur, AR . . . 800-382-4425
Culver Duck Farms Inc
Middlebury, IN . . . 800-825-9225
Delphos Poultry Products
Delphos, OH. . . . 419-692-5816
Dom's Sausage Co Inc
Malden, MA . . . 781-324-6390
Double B Foods Inc
Arlington, TX . . . 800-679-0349
East Poultry Co
Austin, TX. . . . 512-476-5367
Eberly Poultry, Inc.
Stevens, PA . . . 717-336-6440
Exceldor Cooperative
Levis, QC . . . 418-830-5600
Fair Oaks Farms LLC
Pleasant Prairie, WI . . . 800-528-8615
Farmers Produce
Ashby, MN . . . 218-747-2749
Fieldale Farms
Baldwin, GA. . . . 800-241-5400
Foster Farms Inc.
Livingston, CA . . . 800-255-7227
Golden West Food Group
Vernon, CA . . . 888-807-3663

Gress Enterprises
Scranton, PA ... 570-561-0150
Health is Wealth Foods
Moonachie, NJ ... 201-933-7474
Home Delivery Food Service
Jefferson, GA ... 706-367-9551
Horizon Poultry
Toronto, ON ... 519-364-3200
Hormel Foods Corp.
Austin, MN ... 507-437-5611
Hunter Food Inc
Anaheim, CA ... 714-666-1888
International Home Foods
Parsippany, NJ. ... 973-359-9920
Janes Family Foods
Mississauga, ON ... 800-565-2637
Javed & Sons
Houston, TX ... 713-835-6850
JBS USA LLC
Greeley, CO. ... 970-506-8000
JD Sweid Foods
Langley, BC ... 800-665-4355
Joyce Farms
Winston Salem, NC. ... 800-755-6923
K & K Gourmet Meats Inc
Leetsdale, PA ... 724-266-8400
Karn Meats
Columbus, OH ... 800-221-9585
Kelly Gourmet Foods Inc
San Francisco, CA ... 415-648-9200
King Food Service
Rock Island, IL ... 309-787-4488
King's Command Foods Inc
Green Bay, WA ... 800-345-0293
Koch Foods Inc
Park Ridge, IL. ... 800-837-2778
La Nova Wings
Buffalo, NY. ... 800-652-6682
Land O'Frost Inc
Searcy, AR ... 800-643-5654
Land O'Frost Inc.
Lansing, IL ... 800-323-3308
Locustdale Meat Packing
Locustdale, PA ... 570-875-1270
Magnolia Meats
Knoxville, TN. ... 865-546-7702
Manger Packing Corp
Baltimore, MD ... 800-227-9262
Maple Leaf Farms
St Leesburg, IN. ... 800-348-2812
Mar-Jac Poultry Inc.
Gainesville, GA ... 770-531-5000
Meat-O-Mat Corp
Brooklyn, NY ... 718-965-7250
Memphis Meats
Berkeley, CA
Mexi-Frost Specialties Company
Brooklyn, NY ... 718-625-3324
Michael's Finer Meats/Seafoods
Columbus, OH ... 800-282-0518
Mitchell Foods
Barbourville, KY ... 888-202-9745
Moretti's Poultry
Columbus, OH ... 614-486-2333
Murray's Chickens
South Fallsburg, NY. ... 800-588-5051
Norfolk Hatchery
Norfolk, NE. ... 800-345-2449
North Country Smokehouse
Claremont, NH ... 800-258-4304
Ok Industries
Fort Smith, AR ... 800-635-9441
Oklahoma City Meat Co Inc
Oklahoma City, OK ... 405-235-3308
Olymel
Saint-Hyacinthe, QC. ... 450-771-0400
On-Cor Frozen Foods Redi-Serve
Aurora, IL ... 920-563-6391
P & L Poultry
Spokane, WA. ... 509-892-1242
Paisano Food Products
Elk Grove Village, IL ... 800-672-4726
Palmetto Pigeon Plant
Sumter, SC ... 803-775-1204
Perdue Farms Inc.
Salisbury, MD ... 800-473-7383
Petaluma Poultry
Petaluma, CA ... 800-556-6789
Petschl's Quality Meats
Tukwila, WA. ... 206-575-4400
Pinty's Premium Foods
Burlington, ON ... 800-263-7223
Prime Pak Foods Inc
Gainesville, GA ... 770-536-8708
Pueo Poi Shop
Hilo, HI ... 808-935-8435
Randall Foods Inc
Vernon, CA ... 800-372-6581
Roman Sausage Company
Santa Clara, CA ... 800-497-7462
Roy Dick Company
Griffin, GA ... 770-227-3916
Royal Harvest Foods Inc
Springfield, MA ... 413-737-8392
Royal Palate Foods
Inglewood, CA ... 310-330-7701
Rymer Foods
Chicago, IL ... 800-247-9637
Salwa Foods
Lawrenceville, GA ... 770-263-8207
Shamrock Foods Co
Phoenix, AZ ... 800-289-3663
Simmons Foods Inc
Siloam Springs, AR ... 888-831-7007
SJH Enterprises
Middleton, WI. ... 888-745-3845
Smith Packing Regional Meat
Utica, NY ... 315-732-5125
Sommers Organic
Wheeling, IL. ... 877-377-9797
SOPAKCO Foods
Mullins, SC. ... 800-276-9678
SRA Foods
Birmingham, AL. ... 205-323-7447
Steak-Umm Company
Shillington, PA ... 860-928-5900
Sunnydale Meats Inc
Gaffney, SC. ... 864-489-6091
Suzanna's Kitchen
Peachtree Cor, GA ... 770-476-9900
Sweet Sue Kitchens
Athens, AL ... 256-216-0500
Tecumseh Poultry, LLC
Waverly, NE ... 402-786-1000
Thomson Meats
Melfort, SK ... 306-752-2802
Tony Downs Foods
Mankato, MN ... 866-731-4561
True Story Foods
San Francisco, CA ... 888-277-1171
Vital Choice
Bellingham, WA ... 800-608-4825
WACO Beef & Pork Processors
Waco, TX ... 254-772-4669
Waken Meat Co
Atlanta, GA. ... 404-627-3537
Wasatch Meats Inc
Salt Lake City, UT ... 800-631-8294
Wayne Farms LLC.
Oakwood, GA. ... 800-392-0844
West Liberty Foods LLC
West Liberty, IA ... 888-511-4500
Wornick Company
Cincinnati, OH ... 800-860-4555
Zartic Inc
Rome, GA. ... 800-241-0516

Barbecued

Black's Barbecue
Lockhart, TX. ... 888-632-8225
The Shed Saucery
Ocean Springs, MS. ... 228-875-9590
Woods Smoked Meats Inc
Bowling Green, MO ... 800-458-8426

Barbecued Frozen

Burke Corp
Nevada, IA ... 800-654-1152

Breaded

Americhicken
Cape Girardeau, MO. ... 573-651-6485
Barber Foods
Kings Mountain, NC. ... 877-447-3279
Blendco Inc
Hattiesburg, MS ... 888-253-6326
Delphos Poultry Products
Delphos, OH ... 419-692-5816
House-Autry Mills Inc
Four Oaks, NC ... 800-849-0802
Janes Family Foods
Mississauga, ON ... 800-565-2637
Meat-O-Mat Corp
Brooklyn, NY ... 718-965-7250

Broilers

Holmes Foods
Nixon, TX ... 830-582-1551
Koala Moa
Honolulu, HI ... 808-523-6701

Bulk - Leg Quarters - Legs - Thighs

Pennfield Farms
Mt Joy, PA ... 800-732-0009

Canned Boned

Criders Poultry
Stillmore, GA ... 800-342-3851
International Home Foods
Parsippany, NJ. ... 973-359-9920

Cooked - Breaded - Frozen

Advance Pierre Foods
Cincinnati, OH ... 800-969-2747
Bear Creek Smokehouse Inc
Marshall, TX. ... 800-950-2327

Cut-Up Frozen

Wayne Farms LLC.
Oakwood, GA. ... 800-392-0844

Cut-Up IQF (Individually Quick Frozen)

Bell & Evans
Fredericksburg, PA ... 717-865-6626

Diced & Cooked

Brucepac
Woodburn, OR ... 800-899-3629

Diced Frozen

Burke Corp
Nevada, IA ... 800-654-1152

Fajita Strips

Burke Corp
Nevada, IA ... 800-654-1152
Chef's Requested Foods
Oklahoma City, OK ... 405-239-2610

Fillets

Delphos Poultry Products
Delphos, OH ... 419-692-5816
Eberly Poultry, Inc.
Stevens, PA ... 717-336-6440

Fresh

Becker Foods
Westminster, CA. ... 714-891-9474
Bell & Evans
Fredericksburg, PA ... 717-865-6626
Brook Locker Plant
Brook, IN ... 219-275-2611
Choctaw Maid Farms
Jackson, MS ... 601-683-4000
Exceldor Cooperative
Levis, QC ... 418-830-5600
Fieldale Farms
Baldwin, GA. ... 800-241-5400
Holmes Foods
Nixon, TX ... 830-582-1551
Just Bare
Greeley, CO. ... 877-328-2838
Koch Foods Inc
Park Ridge, IL. ... 800-837-2778
Petaluma Poultry
Petaluma, CA ... 800-556-6789
Pilgrim's Pride Corp.
Greeley, CO. ... 970-506-8000
Sanderson Farms
Laurel, MS ... 800-844-4030
Smith Packing Regional Meat
Utica, NY ... 315-732-5125
Sommers Organic
Wheeling, IL. ... 877-377-9797
Wayne Farms LLC.
Oakwood, GA. ... 800-392-0844

Frozen

Americhicken
Cape Girardeau, MO ... 573-651-6485

B & D Foods
Boise, ID ... 208-344-1183

Blakely Freezer Locker
Blakeley, GA ... 229-723-3622

Brakebush Brothers
Westfield, WI ... 800-933-2121

Brook Locker Plant
Brook, IN ... 219-275-2611

Burke Corp
Nevada, IA ... 800-654-1152

Caribbean Food Delights Inc
Tappan, NY ... 845-398-3000

Caribbean Products
Baltimore, MD ... 410-235-7700

Choctaw Maid Farms
Jackson, MS ... 601-683-4000

Draper Valley Farms
Mt Vernon, WA ... 800-562-2012

Exceldor Cooperative
Levis, QC ... 418-830-5600

Fieldale Farms
Baldwin, GA ... 800-241-5400

Foster Farms Inc.
Livingston, CA ... 800-255-7227

Gress Enterprises
Scranton, PA ... 570-561-0150

Health is Wealth Foods
Moonachie, NJ ... 201-933-7474

Janes Family Foods
Mississauga, ON ... 800-565-2637

K & K Gourmet Meats Inc
Leetsdale, PA ... 724-266-8400

Koch Foods Inc
Park Ridge, IL ... 800-837-2778

Manchester Farms
Columbia, SC ... 800-845-0421

Maple Leaf Farms
St Leesburg, IN ... 800-348-2812

Mar-Jac Poultry Inc.
Gainesville, GA ... 770-531-5000

Mexi-Frost Specialties Company
Brooklyn, NY ... 718-625-3324

On-Cor Frozen Foods Redi-Serve
Aurora, IL ... 920-563-6391

Paisano Food Products
Elk Grove Village, IL ... 800-672-4726

Palmetto Pigeon Plant
Sumter, SC ... 803-775-1204

Phoenix Agro-Industrial Corporation
Westbury, NY ... 516-334-1194

Pilgrim's Pride Corp.
Greeley, CO ... 970-506-8000

Rymer Foods
Chicago, IL ... 800-247-9637

Sanderson Farms
Laurel, MS ... 800-844-4030

Simmons Foods Inc
Siloam Springs, AR ... 888-831-7007

SJH Enterprises
Middleton, WI ... 888-745-3845

Smith Packing Regional Meat
Utica, NY ... 315-732-5125

Sommers Organic
Wheeling, IL ... 877-377-9797

Steak-Umm Company
Shillington, PA ... 860-928-5900

Tecumseh Poultry, LLC
Waverly, NE ... 402-786-1000

Tony Downs Foods
Mankato, MN ... 866-731-4561

Wayne Farms LLC.
Oakwood, GA ... 800-392-0844

Zartic Inc
Rome, GA ... 800-241-0516

Liver

Holmes Foods
Nixon, TX ... 830-582-1551

Nuggets

Bell & Evans
Fredericksburg, PA ... 717-865-6626

Crafty Counter
Austin, TX ... 512-643-2412

Health is Wealth Foods
Moonachie, NJ ... 201-933-7474

JD Sweid Foods
Langley, BC ... 800-665-4355

On-Cor Frozen Foods Redi-Serve
Aurora, IL ... 920-563-6391

Pinty's Premium Foods
Burlington, ON ... 800-263-7223

Saad Wholesale Meats
Detroit, MI ... 313-831-8126

Patties

Caribbean Food Delights Inc
Tappan, NY ... 845-398-3000

Royal Caribbean Bakery
Mt Vernon, NY ... 888-818-0971

Saad Wholesale Meats
Detroit, MI ... 313-831-8126

Sommers Organic
Wheeling, IL ... 877-377-9797

Patties Breaded

Americhicken
Cape Girardeau, MO ... 573-651-6485

Meat-O-Mat Corp
Brooklyn, NY ... 718-965-7250

Prepared

Caribbean Food Delights Inc
Tappan, NY ... 845-398-3000

Delphos Poultry Products
Delphos, OH ... 419-692-5816

Foster Farms Inc.
Livingston, CA ... 800-255-7227

Pasqualichio Brothers Inc
Scranton, PA ... 800-232-6233

Sommers Organic
Wheeling, IL ... 877-377-9797

Prepared Frozen

Americhicken
Cape Girardeau, MO ... 573-651-6485

Burke Corp
Nevada, IA ... 800-654-1152

Caribbean Food Delights Inc
Tappan, NY ... 845-398-3000

Chang Food Company
Garden Grove, CA ... 714-265-9990

Chef Hans' Gourmet Foods
Monroe, LA ... 800-890-4267

Hormel Foods Corp.
Austin, MN ... 507-437-5611

Meat-O-Mat Corp
Brooklyn, NY ... 718-965-7250

Morrison Lamothe
Toronto, ON ... 877-677-6533

Paisano Food Products
Elk Grove Village, IL ... 800-672-4726

SJH Enterprises
Middleton, WI ... 888-745-3845

Raw

Caribbean Food Delights Inc
Tappan, NY ... 845-398-3000

Eberly Poultry, Inc.
Stevens, PA ... 717-336-6440

J W Treuth & Sons
Catonsville, MD ... 410-747-6281

Kelly Gourmet Foods Inc
San Francisco, CA ... 415-648-9200

Tenders

Americhicken
Cape Girardeau, MO ... 573-651-6485

Cornish Game Hens

Eberly Poultry, Inc.
Stevens, PA ... 717-336-6440

Norfolk Hatchery
Norfolk, NE ... 800-345-2449

Woods Smoked Meats Inc
Bowling Green, MO ... 800-458-8426

Duck

Bear Creek Smokehouse Inc
Marshall, TX ... 800-950-2327

Crescent Duck Farm
Aquebogue LI, NY ... 631-722-8000

Culver Duck Farms Inc
Middlebury, IN ... 800-825-9225

Hudson Valley Foie Gras
Ferndale, NY ... 845-292-2500

Memphis Meats
Berkeley, CA

North Country Smokehouse
Claremont, NH ... 800-258-4304

Goose

Schiltz Foods Inc
Sisseton, SD ... 877-872-4458

Wenk Foods Inc
Madison, SD ... 605-256-4569

Guineas

Eberly Poultry, Inc.
Stevens, PA ... 717-336-6440

Turkey

Alderfer Inc
Harleysville, PA ... 800-341-1121

Alpine Butcher
Lowell, MA ... 978-256-7771

Amana Meat Shop & Smoke House
Amana, IA ... 800-373-6328

Applegate Farms
Bridgewater, NJ ... 866-587-5858

Bear Creek Smokehouse Inc
Marshall, TX ... 800-950-2327

Becker Foods
Westminster, CA ... 714-891-9474

Bowman & Landes Turkeys
New Carlisle, OH ... 877-466-9466

Brucepac
Woodburn, OR ... 800-899-3629

Burgers' Smokehouse
California, MO ... 800-345-5185

Burke Corp
Nevada, IA ... 800-654-1152

Campbell Soup Co.
Camden, NJ ... 800-257-8443

Cargill Protein
Wichita, KS

Carl Buddig & Co.
Homewood, IL ... 888-633-5684

Cericola Farms
Bradford, ON ... 905-939-2962

Charles Poultry Company
Lancaster, PA ... 717-872-7621

Chef's Requested Foods
Oklahoma City, OK ... 405-239-2610

Clifty Farm Country Meats
Paris, TN ... 800-486-4267

Couch's Country Style Sausages
Cleveland, OH ... 216-823-2332

Country Smoked Meats
Bowling Green, OH ... 800-321-4766

Diestel Family Turkey Ranch
... 209-532-4950

Dietz & Watson Inc.
Philadelphia, PA ... 215-831-9000

Eberly Poultry, Inc.
Stevens, PA ... 717-336-6440

Far West Meats
Highland, CA ... 909-864-1990

Farbest Foods Inc
Jasper, IN ... 812-683-4200

Foster Farms Inc.
Livingston, CA ... 800-255-7227

Godshall's Quality Meats
Telford, PA ... 888-463-7425

Grabill Country Meats
Grabill, IN ... 866-333-6328

Heinkel's Packing Co
Decatur, IL ... 800-594-2738

Hickory Baked Ham Co
Castle Rock, CO ... 303-688-2633

Hillbilly Smokehouse
Rogers, AR ... 479-636-1927

Hollman Foods
Des Moines, IA ... 888-926-2879

Hormel Foods Corp.
Austin, MN ... 507-437-5611

Jaindl Farms
Orefield, PA ... 800-475-6654

Jennie-O Turkey Store
Willmar, MN ... 320-235-6080

Land O'Frost Inc
Searcy, AR ... 800-643-5654

Lindner Bison
Northern, CA ... 530-254-6337

Locustdale Meat Packing
Locustdale, PA ... 570-875-1270

Mada'n Kosher Foods
Dania, FL 954-925-0077
Meat-O-Mat Corp
Brooklyn, NY 718-965-7250
Moretti's Poultry
Columbus, OH 614-486-2333
Moroni Feed Company
Moroni, UT....435-436-8202
New Braunfels Smokehouse
New Braunfels, TX....800-537-6932
Norbest, LLC
Moroni, UT....800-453-5327
Norfolk Hatchery
Norfolk, NE....800-345-2449
Olymel
Saint-Hyacinthe, QC....450-771-0400
P & L Poultry
Spokane, WA....509-892-1242
Pasqualichio Brothers Inc
Scranton, PA 800-232-6233
Perdue Farms Inc.
Salisbury, MD....800-473-7383
Piggie Park Enterprises
West Columbia, SC....800-628-7423
Plainville Farms
New Oxford, PA 800-724-0206
Quaker Maid Meats
Reading, PA 610-376-1500
Ray's Sausage Co
Cleveland, OH 216-921-8782
Roman Sausage Company
Santa Clara, CA 800-497-7462
Sahlen's
Buffalo, NY....800-466-8165
Selwoods Farm Hunting Preserve
Alpine, AL 800-522-0403
Smith Packing Regional Meat
Utica, NY 315-732-5125
Smoked Turkey Inc
Marshville, NC 704-624-6628
Sommers Organic
Wheeling, IL....877-377-9797
Specialty Foods Group Inc
Owensboro, KY 800-238-0020
Standard Meat Co LP
Dallas, TX....866-859-6313
Sunnydale Meats Inc
Gaffney, SC....864-489-6091
Suzanna's Kitchen
Peachtree Cor, GA 770-476-9900
Sweet Sue Kitchens
Athens, AL 256-216-0500
Talisman Foods
Salt Lake City, UT 801-487-6409
Thomas Packing Company
Columbus, GA 800-729-0976
Turkey Store
Faribault, MN....507-334-5555
Vienna Meat Products
Scarborough, ON 800-588-1931
W & G Marketing Company
Ames, IA....515-233-4774
Wayco Ham Co
Goldsboro, NC 800-962-2614
West Liberty Foods LLC
West Liberty, IA 888-511-4500
Woods Smoked Meats Inc
Bowling Green, MO 800-458-8426
Zacky Farms
Fresno, CA 800-888-0235

Breast

Alderfer Inc
Harleysville, PA 800-341-1121
Amana Meat Shop & Smoke House
Amana, IA....800-373-6328
Berks Packing Company, Inc.
Reading, PA 800-882-3757
Dietz & Watson Inc.
Philadelphia, PA 215-831-9000
Grote & Weigel Inc
Bloomfield, CT....860-242-8528
Hickory Baked Ham Co
Castle Rock, CO 303-688-2633
Rose Packing Co Inc
South Barrington, IL....800-323-7363
Smith Packing Regional Meat
Utica, NY 315-732-5125
Woods Smoked Meats Inc
Bowling Green, MO 800-458-8426

Canned

Bowman & Landes Turkeys
New Carlisle, OH 877-466-9466
Grabill Country Meats
Grabill, IN....866-333-6328
Sweet Sue Kitchens
Athens, AL 256-216-0500

Fresh

Becker Foods
Westminster, CA....714-891-9474
Blue Ridge Poultry
Athens, GA....706-546-6767
Cooper Farms Cooked Meats
Van Wert, OH 419-238-4056
Moroni Feed Company
Moroni, UT....435-436-8202
Smith Packing Regional Meat
Utica, NY 315-732-5125
Turkey Store
Faribault, MN....507-334-5555

Frozen

Burke Corp
Nevada, IA 800-654-1152

Ground

Eberly Poultry, Inc.
Stevens, PA....717-336-6440
Sommers Organic
Wheeling, IL....877-377-9797

Leg

Karn Meats
Columbus, OH 800-221-9585

Patties

Brucepac
Woodburn, OR 800-899-3629
Sommers Organic
Wheeling, IL....877-377-9797

Raw

Carl Buddig & Co.
Homewood, IL 888-633-5684

Sausage

C.W. Brown Foods, Inc.
Mountt Royal, NJ 856-423-3700
Golden Platter Foods
Newark, NJ....973-344-8770
Roger Wood Foods Inc
Savannah, GA....800-849-9272

Whole Frozen

Hickory Baked Ham Co
Castle Rock, CO 303-688-2633

Smoked, Cured & Deli Meats

814 Americas Inc
Elizabeth, NJ....908-354-2674
Andalusia Distributing Co Inc
Andalusia, AL....334-222-3671
Applegate Farms
Bridgewater, NJ 866-587-5858
Aries Prepared Beef
Burbank, CA....800-424-2333
Best Chicago Meat
Chicago, IL
Blue Grass Quality Meat
Covington, KY 859-331-7100
Boone's Butcher Shop
Bardstown, KY 888-253-3384
Boyd's Sausage Co
Washington, IA....319-653-5715
Braham Food Locker Service
Braham, MN....320-396-2636
Buffalo Bills Premium Snacks
Lebanon, PA 717-273-7499
Burke Corp
Nevada, IA 800-654-1152
Caddo Packing Co
Marshall, TX....903-935-2211
Campbell Soup Co.
Camden, NJ....800-257-8443
Chef's Cut: Real Jerky
Naples, FL....586-615-0329
Chicopee Provision Co Inc
Chicopee, MA....800-924-6328
Chip Steak & Provision Co
Mankato, MN 507-388-6277
Circle V Meats
Spanish Fork, UT 801-798-3081
Cloverdale Foods
Mandan, ND 800-669-9511
Columbia Packing Co Inc
Dallas, TX....214-946-8171
Crawford Sausage Co Inc
Chicago, IL 773-277-3095
Curtis Packing Co
Greensboro, NC 336-275-7684
Cusack Meats
Oklahoma City, OK 800-241-6328
Daniele Inc
Pascoag, RI....800-451-2535
Di Bruno Bros
Philadelphia, PA 215-922-2876
Field Roast
Seattle, WA 800-311-9497
Foster Farms Inc.
Livingston, CA 800-255-7227
Freirich Foods
Salisbury, NC 800-221-1315
Freybe Gourmet Foods Ltd
Langley, BC 800-879-3739
Frick's Quality Meats
Washington, MO....800-241-2209
Fusion Jerky
South San Francisco, CA 650-589-8899
Gary's Frozen Foods
Lubbock, TX....806-745-1933
H & B Packing Co
Waco, TX 254-752-2506
Harrington's of Vermont
Richmond, VT
Heringer Meats Inc
Covington, KY 859-291-2000
Hummel Brothers Inc
New Haven, CT 800-828-8978
Independent Meat Co
Twin Falls, ID....800-284-4626
J & B Sausage Co Inc
Waelder, TX 830-788-7511
Kayem Foods
Chelsea, MA....800-426-6100
Koegel Meats Inc
Flint, MI 810-238-3685
Korte Meat Processors Inc
Highland, IL 618-654-3813
LA Quercia LLC
Norwalk, IA 515-981-1625
Lay Packing Company
Knoxville, TN....865-522-1147
Liguria Foods Inc
Humboldt, IA 515-332-4121
Little Rhody Brand Frankfurts
Johnston, RI 401-831-0815
Lord's Sausage & Country Ham
Dexter, GA 800-342-6002
Mada'n Kosher Foods
Dania, FL 954-925-0077
Matthiesen's Deer & Custom
De Witt, IA 563-659-8409
Mckenzie Country Classic's
Burlington, VT 800-426-6100
Mertz Sausage Co
San Antonio, TX....210-433-3263
Milano's Of New York City
New York, NY 800-643-6328
Miller's Meat Market
Red Bud, IL....618-282-3334
Neese Country Sausage Inc
Greensboro, NC 800-632-1010
Nema Food Distribution
Fairfield, NJ 973-256-4415
New Packing Company
Chicago, IL....312-666-1314
OLLI Salumeria Americana
Oceanside, CA 877-655-4937
Olympia Provisions
Portland, OR....503-894-8275
Olympic Provisions Northwest
Portland, OR....503-894-8136
Opa's Smoked Meats
Fredericksburg, TX....800-543-6750
Patrick Cudahy LLC
Cudahy, WI....800-486-6900
Paulsen Foods
Atlanta, GA....404-873-1804

Pederson's Natural Farms
Hamilton, TX
Peer Foods Group Inc
Chicago, IL 800-365-5644
Piller's Fine Foods
Waterloo, ON 800-265-2627
Plumrose USA
Chicago, IL 800-526-4909
Pocino Foods
City Of Industry, CA. . . . 800-345-0150
Principe Foods USA
Long Beach, CA 310-680-5500
Quirch Foods
Coral Gables, FL. . . . 800-458-5252
R M Felts' Packing Co
Ivor, VA. . . . 757-859-6131
Shaker Valley Foods
Cleveland, OH 216-961-8600
SnackMasters, LLC
Hilmar, CA 800-597-9770
Stevens Sausage Co
Smithfield, NC 800-338-0561
Stonie's Sausage Shop
Perryville, MO 888-546-2540
SunFed Ranch
Woodland, CA. . . . 530-723-5373
Terrell Meats
Delta, UT. . . . 435-864-2600
Thomas Packing Company
Columbus, GA 800-729-0976
Thumann Inc.
Carlstadt, NJ 201-935-3636
Troy Foods Inc
Troy, IL 618-667-6332
True Story Foods
San Francisco, CA 888-277-1171
Tyson Foods Inc.
Springdale, AR 479-290-4000
Tyson Foods Inc.
Springdale, AR 800-233-6332
Vermilion Packers Ltd
Vermilion, AB. . . . 780-853-4622
Vermont Smoke and Cure
Hinesburg, VT. . . . 802-482-4666
Vienna Beef LTD
Vernon, CA 800-733-6063
Wagshal's Imports
Washington, DC 202-363-5698
Webster City Custom Meats Inc
Webster City, IA 515-832-1130
Weyauwega Star Dairy
Weyauwega, WI 888-813-9720
Yoakum Packing Co
Yoakum, TX 800-999-6997

Bacon

Alderfer Inc
Harleysville, PA 800-341-1121
Aliments Prince SEC
Anjou, QC. . . . 800-361-3898
Amana Meat Shop & Smoke House
Amana, IA. . . . 800-373-6328
Applegate Farms
Bridgewater, NJ 866-587-5858
Arnold's Meat Food Products
Brooklyn, NY 800-633-7023
Bacon America
Drummondville, QC. . . . 819-475-3030
Bear Creek Smokehouse Inc
Marshall, TX. . . . 800-950-2327
Blakely Freezer Locker
Blakeley, GA. . . . 229-723-3622
Broadbent B & B Food Products
Kuttawa, KY. . . . 800-841-2202
Burke Corp
Nevada, IA 800-654-1152
Chef's Requested Foods
Oklahoma City, OK 405-239-2610
Chisesi Brothers Meat Packing
New Orleans, LA 800-966-3550
Circle B Ranch
Seymour, MO 417-683-0271
Cloverdale Foods
Mandan, ND 800-669-9511
Di Bruno Bros
Philadelphia, PA 215-922-2876
Father's Country Hams
Bremen, KY 270-525-3554
Ferris, Stahl-Meyer
Fort Lee, NJ 201-242-5500
Hickory Baked Ham Co
Castle Rock, CO 303-688-2633
Leidy's
Harleysville, PA 800-222-2319
Manda Fine Meats Inc
Baton Rouge, LA 800-343-2642
Maple Leaf Consumer Foods
Fair Oaks, CA. . . . 800-999-7603
Naked Bacon
Ste. Genevieve, MO
Niemuth's Steak & Chop Shop
Waupaca, WI. . . . 715-258-2666
North Country Smokehouse
Claremont, NH 800-258-4304
Olympic Provisions Northwest
Portland, OR 503-894-8136
Outstanding Foods
Venice, CA
Patrick Cudahy LLC
Cudahy, WI 800-486-6900
Pederson's Natural Farms
Hamilton, TX
Piller's Fine Foods
Waterloo, ON 800-265-2627
R.L. Zeigler Company
Selma, AL. . . . 800-392-6328
Rinehart Meat Processing
Branson, MO. . . . 417-869-2041
Rose Packing Co Inc
South Barrington, IL. . . . 800-323-7363
Saad Wholesale Meats
Detroit, MI 313-831-8126
Scott Hams
Greenville, KY 800-318-1353
Seaboard Foods
Shawnee Mission, KS. . . . 800-262-7907
Sugar Creek
Washington Ct Hs, OH. . . . 800-848-8205
Sunnydale Meats Inc
Gaffney, SC. . . . 864-489-6091
Sunset Farm Foods Inc
Valdosta, GA. . . . 800-882-1121
Thomas Packing Company
Columbus, GA 800-729-0976
V.W. Joyner & Company
Smithfield, VA 757-357-2161
Vermont Smoke and Cure
Hinesburg, VT. . . . 802-482-4666
Woods Smoked Meats Inc
Bowling Green, MO 800-458-8426

Bits Imitation

American Key Food Products Inc
Closter, NJ. . . . 877-263-7539
Con Yeager Spice Co
Zelienople, PA. . . . 800-222-2460
Fairbury Food Products
Fairbury, NE 402-729-3379
Schiff Food Products Co Inc
Totowa, NJ 973-237-1990
Tova Industries LLC
Louisville, KY 888-532-8682
Westin Foods
Omaha, NE 800-228-6098

Bits Real

Burke Corp
Nevada, IA 800-654-1152
Con Yeager Spice Co
Zelienople, PA. . . . 800-222-2460
Sugar Creek
Washington Ct Hs, OH 800-848-8205
Tova Industries LLC
Louisville, KY 888-532-8682

Canadian Style

Al & John's Glen Rock Ham
West Caldwell, NJ. . . . 800-969-4990
Burgers' Smokehouse
California, MO 800-345-5185
Burke Corp
Nevada, IA 800-654-1152
Calihan Pork Processors Inc
Peoria, IL. . . . 309-674-9175
Country Smoked Meats
Bowling Green, OH 800-321-4766
Hickory Baked Ham Co
Castle Rock, CO 303-688-2633
Hormel Foods Corp.
Austin, MN. . . . 507-437-5611
Peer Foods Group Inc
Chicago, IL 800-365-5644
Pioneer Packing Co
Bowling Green, OH 419-352-5283
Rose Packing Co Inc
South Barrington, IL. . . . 800-323-7363

Slices

Carolina Pride Foods
Greenwood, SC. . . . 864-229-5611
Country Smoked Meats
Bowling Green, OH 800-321-4766
Jimmy Dean Foods
Springdale, AR 800-925-3326
Sugar Creek
Washington Ct Hs, OH 800-848-8205
Webster City Custom Meats Inc
Webster City, IA 515-832-1130

Slices Thick

Jimmy Dean Foods
Springdale, AR 800-925-3326
Westbrae Natural Foods
Melville, NY 800-434-4246

Beef Jerky

Alderfer Inc
Harleysville, PA 800-341-1121
Alewel's Country Meats
Warrensburg, MO 800-353-8553
Amana Meat Shop & Smoke House
Amana, IA. . . . 800-373-6328
Baier's Sausage & Meats
Red Deer, AB 403-346-1535
Better Made Snack Foods
Detroit, MI 800-332-2394
Big Chief Meat Snacks Inc
Calgary, AB. . . . 403-264-2641
Boyd's Sausage Co
Washington, IA. . . . 319-653-5715
Brooklyn Biltong
Brooklyn, NY 407-538-8876
Buffalo Bills Premium Snacks
Lebanon, PA 717-273-7499
Cattaneo Brothers Inc
San Luis Obispo, CA 800-243-8537
Chickasaw Trading Company
Denver City, TX 800-848-3515
Chudabeef Jerky Co.
Long Beach, CA
Debbie D's Jerky & Sausage
Tillamook, OR 503-842-2622
E.W. Knauss & Son
Quakertown, PA 800-648-4220
Eastside Deli Supply
Lansing, MI. . . . 800-349-6694
Eiserman Meats
Slave Lake, AB. . . . 780-849-5507
Enjoy Foods International
Fontana, CA 909-823-2228
F&Y Enterprises
Wauconda, IL 847-526-0620
Golden Valley Natural
Shelley, ID. . . . 888-270-7147
Grandpa Ittel's Meats Inc
Howard Lake, MN 320-543-2285
Hi Country Snack Foods
Lincoln, MT 406-362-4050
Hsin Tung Yang Foods Inc
S San Francisco, CA. . . . 650-589-6789
J & B Sausage Co Inc
Waelder, TX 830-788-7511
Kershenstine Beef Jerky
Eupora, MS. . . . 662-258-2049
King B Meat Snacks
Minong, WI. . . . 800-346-6896
Link Snacks Inc.
Minong, WI. . . . 715-466-2234
Longview Meat & Merchandise Ltd
Longview, AB. . . . 866-355-3759
Middlefield Cheese House
Middlefield, OH 800-327-9477
New Braunfels Smokehouse
New Braunfels, TX. . . . 800-537-6932
Norpaco Inc
Middletown, CT 800-252-0222
Palmer Meat Packing Co
Tremonton, UT 435-257-5329
Patagonia Provisions
Sausalito, CA 888-221-8208
People's Sausage Co
Los Angeles, CA. . . . 213-627-8633

Rinehart Meat Processing
Branson, MO. 417-869-2041
Terrell Meats
Delta, UT. 435-864-2600
Tommy's Jerky Outlet
Mentor, OH. 866-448-6942
Trail's Best Snacks
Memphis, TN 800-852-1863
W.A. Beans & Sons
Bangor, ME. 800-649-1958
Weaver Nut Co. Inc.
Ephrata, PA 800-473-2688
Western Beef Jerky
Edmonton, AB 780-469-4817
Wild Bill's Foods
Martinsville, VA 800-848-3236
Willie's Smoke House LLC
Harrisville, PA. 800-742-4184
Woods Smoked Meats Inc
Bowling Green, MO 800-458-8426

Frozen

KRAVE Jerky
Sonoma, CA 707-935-1035

Bologna

Alderfer Inc
Harleysville, PA 800-341-1121
Atlantic Pork & Provisions
Jamaica, NY 800-245-3536
Boesl Packing Co
Baltimore, MD 800-675-1471
Boyd's Sausage Co
Washington, IA. 319-653-5715
C Roy & Sons Processing
Yale, MI. 810-387-3957
Carolina Packers Inc
Smithfield, NC 800-682-7675
Carolina Pride Foods
Greenwood, SC. 864-229-5611
Chisesi Brothers Meat Packing
New Orleans, LA 800-966-3550
Curtis Packing Co
Greensboro, NC 336-275-7684
Far West Meats
Highland, CA 909-864-1990
Frank Wardynski & Sons Inc
Buffalo, NY. 716-854-6083
Gouvea's & Purity Foods Inc
Honolulu, HI. 808-847-3717
Groff's Meats
Elizabethtown, PA. 717-367-1246
Grote & Weigel Inc
Bloomfield, CT. 860-242-8528
Hazle Park Quality Meats
West Hazleton, PA 800-238-4331
Ito Cariani Sausage Company
Hayward, CA 510-887-0882
Kilgus Meats
Toledo, OH 419-472-9721
Kitt's Meat Processing
Dedham, IA. 712-683-5622
Locustdale Meat Packing
Locustdale, PA 570-875-1270
Palmyra Bologna Co Inc
Palmyra, PA. 800-282-6336
Rendulic Meat Packing Corp
Mckeesport, PA. 412-678-9541
Saad Wholesale Meats
Detroit, MI 313-831-8126
Schaefers Market
Sauk Centre, MN 320-352-6490
Sechrist Brothers
Dallastown, PA 717-244-2975
Sheinman Provision Co
Philadelphia, PA 215-473-7065
Silver Star Meats Inc
Mc Kees Rocks, PA 800-548-1321
Spring Grove Foods
Miamisburg, OH. 937-866-4311
Stawnichy Holdings
Mundare, AB 888-764-7646
Sunset Farm Foods Inc
Valdosta, GA. 800-882-1121
Tennessee Valley Packing Co
Columbia, TN. 931-388-2623
Thumann Inc.
Carlstadt, NJ 201-935-3636
Troy Foods Inc
Troy, IL 618-667-6332
Zweigle's Inc
Rochester, NY. 585-546-1740

Bratwurst

Country Smoked Meats
Bowling Green, OH 800-321-4766
Elmwood Locker Svc
Elmwood, IL. 309-742-8929
Far West Meats
Highland, CA 909-864-1990
Fontanini Italian Meats
McCook, IL. 800-331-6328
Kilgus Meats
Toledo, OH 419-472-9721
Koegel Meats Inc
Flint, MI 810-238-3685
S.W. Meat & Provision Company
Phoenix, AZ 602-275-2000
Saugy Inc.
Cranston, RI 866-467-2849
Silver Star Meats Inc
Mc Kees Rocks, PA 800-548-1321
Smolich Bros. Home Made Sausage
Crest Hill, IL. 815-727-2144
Sunset Farm Foods Inc
Valdosta, GA. 800-882-1121
WACO Beef & Pork Processors
Waco, TX 254-772-4669
Woods Smoked Meats Inc
Bowling Green, MO 800-458-8426

Corned Beef

Alderfer Inc
Harleysville, PA 800-341-1121
Art's Tamales
Metamora, IL 309-367-2850
Best Provision Co Inc
Union, NJ 800-631-4466
Burnett & Son
Monrovia, CA. 877-632-5467
Carando Gourmet Frozen Foods
Agawam, MA 888-227-2636
Chicopee Provision Co Inc
Chicopee, MA. 800-924-6328
Curly's Foods Inc
Edina, MN. 612-920-3400
Dutterer's Home Food Service
Baltimore, MD 410-298-3663
Hormel Foods Corp.
Austin, MN 507-437-5611
International Food Packers Corporation
Miami, FL. 305-740-5847
Kelly Corned Beef Co
Chicago, IL 800-624-5617
Kelly Foods
Jackson, TN 731-424-2255
Lower Foods, Inc.
Richmond, UT. 800-295-7898
Nossack Fine Meats
Red Deer, AB 403-346-5006
Peer Foods Group Inc
Chicago, IL 800-365-5644
Plumrose USA
Chicago, IL 800-526-4909
Saval Foods Corp
Elkridge, MD 800-527-2825
Sheinman Provision Co
Philadelphia, PA 215-473-7065
Stawnichy Holdings
Mundare, AB 888-764-7646
Thompson Packers
Slidell, LA. 800-989-6328
Vienna Meat Products
Scarborough, ON 800-588-1931

Deli Foods

ASK Foods Inc
Palmyra, PA. 800-879-4275
Bagels By Bell
Brooklyn, NY 718-272-2780
Billingsgate Fish Company
Calgary, AB. 403-571-7700
Bloomfield Bakers
Los Alamitos, CA 800-594-4111
Bottom Line Foods
Pembroke Pines, FL 954-843-0562
Bouma Meats
Provost, AB. 780-753-2092
Boyd's Sausage Co
Washington, IA. 319-653-5715
Carl Buddig & Co.
Homewood, IL 888-633-5684
Carolina Packers Inc
Smithfield, NC 800-682-7675
Chicago 58 Food Products
Woodbridge, ON. 416-603-4244
Cibao Meat Products Inc
Bronx, NY. 718-993-5072
Corfu Foods Inc
Bensenville, IL 630-595-2510
Cumberland Gap Provision Company
Middlesboro, KY 855-411-7675
Curtis Packing Co
Greensboro, NC 336-275-7684
Czimer's Game & Seafoods
Homer Glen, IL. 888-294-6377
Dairy Fresh Foods Inc
Taylor, MI 313-299-0735
Eastside Deli Supply
Lansing, MI. 800-349-6694
Frank Brunckhorst Company
Sarasota, FL 804-722-4100
Fratelli Beretta USA
Mount Olive, NJ 201-438-0723
Global Food Industries
Townville, SC 800-225-4152
Heinkel's Packing Co
Decatur, IL 800-594-2738
HFI Foods
Redmond, WA. 425-883-1320
Home Style Foods Inc
Hamtramck, MI. 313-874-3250
Hormel Foods Corp.
Austin, MN 507-437-5611
Hummel Brothers Inc
New Haven, CT 800-828-8978
Kay Foods Co
Detroit, MI 313-393-1100
Kelly Corned Beef Co
Chicago, IL. 800-624-5617
Kelly Foods
Jackson, TN 731-424-2255
Kitt's Meat Processing
Dedham, IA. 712-683-5622
Klein's Kosher Pickles
Phoenix, AZ 800-437-4255
Liguria Foods Inc
Humboldt, IA 515-332-4121
Lower Foods, Inc.
Richmond, UT. 800-295-7898
Manda Fine Meats Inc
Baton Rouge, LA 800-343-2642
Marshallville Packing Co
Marshallville, OH 330-855-2871
Meadows Country Products
Hollidaysburg, PA. 888-499-1001
Norbest, LLC
Moroni, UT 800-453-5327
Palmyra Bologna Co Inc
Palmyra, PA. 800-282-6336
Pederson's Natural Farms
Hamilton, TX
Plumrose USA
Chicago, IL 800-526-4909
Rachael's Smoked Fish
Springfield, MA 800-327-3412
Real Kosher Sausage Company
Newark, NJ 973-690-5394
Schneider Foods
Kitchener, ON. 519-741-5000
Siena Foods
Toronto, ON 800-465-0422
Silver Star Meats Inc
Mc Kees Rocks, PA 800-548-1321
Smith Provision Co Inc
Erie, PA 800-334-9151
Smithfield Foods Inc.
Smithfield, VA 757-365-3000
Spring Glen Fresh Foods
Ephrata, PA 800-641-2853
Spring Grove Foods
Miamisburg, OH. 937-866-4311
Stevens Sausage Co
Smithfield, NC 800-338-0561
Temptee Specialty Foods
Denver, CO 800-842-1233
Tyson Foods Inc.
Springdale, AR 800-233-6332
Vegi-Deli
San Rafael, CA 888-473-3667

Deli Meats

Alderfer Inc
Harleysville, PA 800-341-1121

Alpine Butcher
Lowell, MA 978-256-7771

Atlantic Pork & Provisions
Jamaica, NY 800-245-3536

Berks Packing Company, Inc.
Reading, PA 800-882-3757

Binkert's Meat Products
Baltimore, MD 410-687-5959

Boar's Head
Sarasota, FL 800-352-6277

Boesl Packing Co
Baltimore, MD 800-675-1471

Broadaway Ham Co
Jonesboro, AR 870-932-6688

Burke Corp
Nevada, IA 800-654-1152

C Roy & Sons Processing
Yale, MI 810-387-3957

Carl Buddig & Co.
Homewood, IL 888-633-5684

Carolina Packers Inc
Smithfield, NC 800-682-7675

Carolina Pride Foods
Greenwood, SC 864-229-5611

Charlie's Country Sausage
Minot, ND 701-838-6302

Charlie's Pride
Vernon, CA 877-866-0992

Citterio USA
Freeland, PA 800-435-8888

Country Smoked Meats
Bowling Green, OH 800-321-4766

Curtis Packing Co
Greensboro, NC 336-275-7684

Dietz & Watson Inc.
Philadelphia, PA 215-831-9000

Dohar Meats Inc
Cleveland, OH 216-241-4197

Dutterer's Home Food Service
Baltimore, MD 410-298-3663

Far West Meats
Highland, CA 909-864-1990

Frank Brunckhorst Company
Sarasota, FL 804-722-4100

Frank Wardynski & Sons Inc
Buffalo, NY 716-854-6083

Fried Provisions Company
Evans City, PA 724-538-3160

Gaiser's European Style
Union, NJ 908-686-3421

Gouvea's & Purity Foods Inc
Honolulu, HI 808-847-3717

Groff's Meats
Elizabethtown, PA 717-367-1246

Hans Kissle Co
Haverhill, MA 978-556-4500

Hazle Park Quality Meats
West Hazleton, PA 800-238-4331

Heinkel's Packing Co
Decatur, IL 800-594-2738

Hummel Brothers Inc
New Haven, CT 800-828-8978

Kelly Corned Beef Co
Chicago, IL 800-624-5617

Kelly Foods
Jackson, TN 731-424-2255

Kilgus Meats
Toledo, OH 419-472-9721

Kitt's Meat Processing
Dedham, IA 712-683-5622

Land O'Frost Inc
Searcy, AR 800-643-5654

Lengerich Meats Inc
Zanesville, IN 260-638-4123

Leona Meat Plant
Troy, PA 570-297-3574

Liguria Foods Inc
Humboldt, IA 515-332-4121

Locustdale Meat Packing
Locustdale, PA 570-875-1270

Lower Foods, Inc.
Richmond, UT 800-295-7898

Manda Fine Meats Inc
Baton Rouge, LA 800-343-2642

Marathon Enterprises Inc
Englewood, NJ 800-722-7388

Marshallville Packing Co
Marshallville, OH 330-855-2871

Martin Rosols
New Britain, CT 860-223-2707

Parma Sausage Products
Pittsburgh, PA 877-294-4207

Plumrose USA
Chicago, IL 800-526-4909

Queen City Sausage & Provision
Cincinnati, OH 877-544-5588

R.L. Zeigler Company
Selma, AL 800-392-6328

Rendulic Meat Packing Corp
Mckeesport, PA 412-678-9541

Robinson Distributing Co
London, KY 800-230-5131

Roman Packing Company
Norfolk, NE 800-373-5990

Saag's Products LLC
San Leandro, CA 855-287-6562

Saval Foods Corp
Elkridge, MD 800-527-2825

Schaefers Market
Sauk Centre, MN 320-352-6490

Schaller & Weber Inc
Astoria, NY 800-847-4115

Sculli Brothers
Yeadon, PA 215-336-1223

Sechrist Brothers
Dallastown, PA 717-244-2975

Sheinman Provision Co
Philadelphia, PA 215-473-7065

Smith Packing Regional Meat
Utica, NY 315-732-5125

Smith Provision Co Inc
Erie, PA 800-334-9151

Specialities Importers & Distributers
Millington, NJ 800-899-6689

Spring Grove Foods
Miamisburg, OH 937-866-4311

Standard Meat Co LP
Dallas, TX 866-859-6313

Stawnichy Holdings
Mundare, AB 888-764-7646

Stevens Sausage Co
Smithfield, NC 800-338-0561

Stonie's Sausage Shop
Perryville, MO 888-546-2540

Temptee Specialty Foods
Denver, CO 800-842-1233

Tennessee Valley Packing Co
Columbia, TN 931-388-2623

Troy Foods Inc
Troy, IL 618-667-6332

Tyson Foods Inc.
Springdale, AR 800-233-6332

United Provision Meat Company
Columbus, OH 614-252-1126

V.W. Joyner & Company
Smithfield, VA 757-357-2161

Vienna Beef LTD
Chicago, IL 800-366-3647

Vienna Meat Products
Scarborough, ON 800-588-1931

Warren & Son Meat Processing
Whipple, OH 740-585-2421

Ham

Albert's Meats
Claysville, PA 800-522-9970

Aliments Prince SEC
Anjou, QC 800-361-3898

Ashland Sausage Co
Carol Stream, IL 630-690-2600

Badger Gourmet Ham
Milwaukee, WI 414-645-1756

Broadbent B & B Food Products
Kuttawa, KY 800-841-2202

Calihan Pork Processors Inc
Peoria, IL 309-674-9175

Chicago Steaks
Chicago, IL 773-847-5400

Chisesi Brothers Meat Packing
New Orleans, LA 800-966-3550

Cloverdale Foods
Mandan, ND 800-669-9511

Father's Country Hams
Bremen, KY 270-525-3554

Frick's Quality Meats
Washington, MO 800-241-2209

Grote & Weigel Inc
Bloomfield, CT 860-242-8528

Hickory Baked Ham Co
Castle Rock, CO 303-688-2633

Holly Hill Locker Company
Holly Hill, SC 803-496-3611

Humphrey's Market
Springfield, IL 800-747-6328

Leidy's
Harleysville, PA 800-222-2319

Maple Leaf Consumer Foods
Fair Oaks, CA 800-999-7603

Milling Sausage Inc
Milwaukee, WI 414-645-2677

Niemuth's Steak & Chop Shop
Waupaca, WI 715-258-2666

Patrick Cudahy LLC
Cudahy, WI 800-486-6900

Pederson's Natural Farms
Hamilton, TX

Piller's Fine Foods
Waterloo, ON 800-265-2627

Redondo Iglesias USA
Bayonne, NJ 201-455-5266

Rinehart Meat Processing
Branson, MO 417-869-2041

Rose Packing Co Inc
South Barrington, IL 800-323-7363

Scott Hams
Greenville, KY 800-318-1353

Silver Star Meats Inc
Mc Kees Rocks, PA 800-548-1321

Smoked Turkey Inc
Marshville, NC 704-624-6628

Specialty Foods Group Inc
Owensboro, KY 800-238-0020

Stonie's Sausage Shop
Perryville, MO 888-546-2540

Thomas Packing Company
Columbus, GA 800-729-0976

Thumann Inc.
Carlstadt, NJ 201-935-3636

V.W. Joyner & Company
Smithfield, VA 757-357-2161

Vermont Smoke and Cure
Hinesburg, VT 802-482-4666

Wayco Ham Co
Goldsboro, NC 800-962-2614

Canned

Clifty Farm Country Meats
Paris, TN 800-486-4267

Dold Foods
Wichita, KS 316-838-9101

Hickory Baked Ham Co
Castle Rock, CO 303-688-2633

Horlacher Meats
Logan, UT 435-752-1287

International Trading Company
Houston, TX 713-224-5901

S. Wallace Edward & Sons
Surry, VA 800-222-4267

Wayco Ham Co
Goldsboro, NC 800-962-2614

Cooked - Water-added Chilled

Ferris, Stahl-Meyer
Fort Lee, NJ 201-242-5500

Madrange
Millington, NJ 800-899-6689

Fresh

Amana Meat Shop & Smoke House
Amana, IA 800-373-6328

Smith Provision Co Inc
Erie, PA 800-334-9151

Smithfield Foods Inc.
Smithfield, VA 757-365-3000

Frozen

Burke Corp
Nevada, IA 800-654-1152

Smoked

Alderfer Inc
Harleysville, PA 800-341-1121

Badger Gourmet Ham
Milwaukee, WI 414-645-1756

Bear Creek Smokehouse Inc
Marshall, TX 800-950-2327

Blakely Freezer Locker
Blakeley, GA 229-723-3622

Carolina Packers Inc
Smithfield, NC 800-682-7675

Cumberland Gap Provision Company
Middlesboro, KY 855-411-7675
Finchville Farms Country Ham
Finchville, KY 800-678-1521
Fresh Mark Inc.
Massillon, OH.......... 330-832-7491
Frick's Quality Meats
Washington, MO.......... 800-241-2209
Gaiser's European Style
Union, NJ 908-686-3421
Groff's Meats
Elizabethtown, PA.......... 717-367-1246
Hillbilly Smokehouse
Rogers, AR 479-636-1927
Humphrey's Market
Springfield, IL.......... 800-747-6328
J & B Sausage Co Inc
Waelder, TX 830-788-7511
John Hofmeister & Son Inc
Chicago, IL.......... 800-923-4267
Manger Packing Corp
Baltimore, MD 800-227-9262
North Country Smokehouse
Claremont, NH 800-258-4304
Nueske's Applewood Smoked Meat
Wittenberg, WI 800-720-1153
Parma Sausage Products
Pittsburgh, PA.......... 877-294-4207
Peer Foods Group Inc
Chicago, IL.......... 800-365-5644
Quality Meats & Seafood
West Fargo, ND.......... 800-342-4250
R M Felts' Packing Co
Ivor, VA.......... 757-859-6131
Rinehart Meat Processing
Branson, MO.......... 417-869-2041
Rose Packing Co Inc
South Barrington, IL.......... 800-323-7363
S. Wallace Edward & Sons
Surry, VA.......... 800-222-4267
Sahlen's
Buffalo, NY.......... 800-466-8165
Sechrist Brothers
Dallastown, PA 717-244-2975
Selwoods Farm Hunting Preserve
Alpine, AL 800-522-0403
Serv-Rite Meat Co Inc
Los Angeles, CA.......... 323-227-1911
Smith Provision Co Inc
Erie, PA.......... 800-334-9151
Swiss-American Sausage Company
Lathrop, CA 209-858-5555
Thomas Packing Company
Columbus, GA 800-729-0976
Troy Foods Inc
Troy, IL.......... 618-667-6332
Tyson Foods Inc.
Springdale, AR 800-233-6332
V.W. Joyner & Company
Smithfield, VA 757-357-2161
Webster City Custom Meats Inc
Webster City, IA 515-832-1130
Willie's Smoke House LLC
Harrisville, PA.......... 800-742-4184

Steak

Grote & Weigel Inc
Bloomfield, CT.......... 860-242-8528

Head Cheese

Ashland Sausage Co
Carol Stream, IL.......... 630-690-2600
Chicopee Provision Co Inc
Chicopee, MA.......... 800-924-6328
Savoie's Sausage and Food Products
Opelousas, LA 337-942-7241
Sweet Traders
Huntington Beach, CA 714-903-6800

Knockwurst

Boesl Packing Co
Baltimore, MD 800-675-1471
Chicopee Provision Co Inc
Chicopee, MA.......... 800-924-6328
Country Smoked Meats
Bowling Green, OH 800-321-4766
Far West Meats
Highland, CA 909-864-1990
Ferris, Stahl-Meyer
Fort Lee, NJ 201-242-5500
Gouvea's & Purity Foods Inc
Honolulu, HI.......... 808-847-3717
Matthiesen's Deer & Custom
De Witt, IA 563-659-8409
Sunset Farm Foods Inc
Valdosta, GA.......... 800-882-1121

Liverwurst

Atlantic Pork & Provisions
Jamaica, NY 800-245-3536
Chicopee Provision Co Inc
Chicopee, MA.......... 800-924-6328
Gaiser's European Style
Union, NJ 908-686-3421
Grote & Weigel Inc
Bloomfield, CT.......... 860-242-8528
Silver Star Meats Inc
Mc Kees Rocks, PA 800-548-1321
Sunset Farm Foods Inc
Valdosta, GA.......... 800-882-1121

Luncheon Meat

Alderfer Inc
Harleysville, PA 800-341-1121
Atlantic Pork & Provisions
Jamaica, NY 800-245-3536
Berks Packing Company, Inc.
Reading, PA 800-882-3757
Binkert's Meat Products
Baltimore, MD 410-687-5959
Birchwood Foods Inc
Kenosha, WI.......... 800-541-1685
Boar's Head
Sarasota, FL 800-352-6277
Boesl Packing Co
Baltimore, MD 800-675-1471
Boyd's Sausage Co
Washington, IA.......... 319-653-5715
Broadaway Ham Co
Jonesboro, AR.......... 870-932-6688
C Roy & Sons Processing
Yale, MI.......... 810-387-3957
Carl Buddig & Co.
Homewood, IL 888-633-5684
Carolina Packers Inc
Smithfield, NC 800-682-7675
Carolina Pride Foods
Greenwood, SC.......... 864-229-5611
Charlie's Country Sausage
Minot, ND.......... 701-838-6302
Chicopee Provision Co Inc
Chicopee, MA.......... 800-924-6328
Chisesi Brothers Meat Packing
New Orleans, LA 800-966-3550
Cibao Meat Products Inc
Bronx, NY.......... 718-993-5072
Citterio USA
Freeland, PA 800-435-8888
Country Smoked Meats
Bowling Green, OH 800-321-4766
Curtis Packing Co
Greensboro, NC 336-275-7684
Dietz & Watson Inc.
Philadelphia, PA 215-831-9000
Dutterer's Home Food Service
Baltimore, MD 410-298-3663
Far West Meats
Highland, CA 909-864-1990
Ferris, Stahl-Meyer
Fort Lee, NJ 201-242-5500
Frank Brunckhorst Company
Sarasota, FL 804-722-4100
Frank Wardynski & Sons Inc
Buffalo, NY.......... 716-854-6083
Fried Provisions Company
Evans City, PA 724-538-3160
Gouvea's & Purity Foods Inc
Honolulu, HI.......... 808-847-3717
Groff's Meats
Elizabethtown, PA.......... 717-367-1246
Hazle Park Quality Meats
West Hazleton, PA 800-238-4331
Hofmann Sausage Co Inc
Mattydale, NY.......... 800-724-8410
Hormel Foods Corp.
Austin, MN 507-437-5611
Hummel Brothers Inc
New Haven, CT 800-828-8978
Ito Cariani Sausage Company
Hayward, CA 510-887-0882
John Volpi & Co
St Louis, MO.......... 800-288-3439
Kelly Corned Beef Co
Chicago, IL 800-624-5617
Kilgus Meats
Toledo, OH 419-472-9721
Kitt's Meat Processing
Dedham, IA.......... 712-683-5622
Land O'Frost Inc
Searcy, AR 800-643-5654
Land O'Frost Inc.
Lansing, IL 800-323-3308
Lengerich Meats Inc
Zanesville, IN 260-638-4123
Leona Meat Plant
Troy, PA.......... 570-297-3574
Liguria Foods Inc
Humboldt, IA 515-332-4121
Locustdale Meat Packing
Locustdale, PA 570-875-1270
Lower Foods, Inc.
Richmond, UT.......... 800-295-7898
Manda Fine Meats Inc
Baton Rouge, LA 800-343-2642
Marshallville Packing Co
Marshallville, OH.......... 330-855-2871
Martin Rosols
New Britain, CT 860-223-2707
Norbest, LLC
Moroni, UT.......... 800-453-5327
Palmyra Bologna Co Inc
Palmyra, PA.......... 800-282-6336
Parma Sausage Products
Pittsburgh, PA.......... 877-294-4207
Patrick Cudahy LLC
Cudahy, WI.......... 800-486-6900
Plumrose USA
Chicago, IL.......... 800-526-4909
R.L. Zeigler Company
Selma, AL.......... 800-392-6328
Rendulic Meat Packing Corp
Mckeesport, PA.......... 412-678-9541
Robinson Distributing Co
London, KY 800-230-5131
Roman Packing Company
Norfolk, NE.......... 800-373-5990
Saad Wholesale Meats
Detroit, MI 313-831-8126
Saag's Products LLC
San Leandro, CA.......... 855-287-6562
Saval Foods Corp
Elkridge, MD 800-527-2825
Schaefers Market
Sauk Centre, MN 320-352-6490
Schaller & Weber Inc
Astoria, NY.......... 800-847-4115
Sculli Brothers
Yeadon, PA 215-336-1223
Sechrist Brothers
Dallastown, PA 717-244-2975
Sheinman Provision Co
Philadelphia, PA 215-473-7065
Siena Foods
Toronto, ON 800-465-0422
Smith Packing Regional Meat
Utica, NY 315-732-5125
Smith Provision Co Inc
Erie, PA.......... 800-334-9151
Spring Grove Foods
Miamisburg, OH.......... 937-866-4311
Standard Meat Co LP
Dallas, TX.......... 866-859-6313
Stevens Sausage Co
Smithfield, NC 800-338-0561
Stonie's Sausage Shop
Perryville, MO 888-546-2540
Sunset Farm Foods Inc
Valdosta, GA.......... 800-882-1121
Tennessee Valley Packing Co
Columbia, TN.......... 931-388-2623
Thumann Inc.
Carlstadt, NJ 201-935-3636
Troy Foods Inc
Troy, IL 618-667-6332
United Provision Meat Company
Columbus, OH 614-252-1126
V.W. Joyner & Company
Smithfield, VA 757-357-2161
Vienna Meat Products
Scarborough, ON 800-588-1931
Warren & Son Meat Processing
Whipple, OH.......... 740-585-2421

Canned

Alpine Butcher
Lowell, MA 978-256-7771
Tyson Foods Inc.
Springdale, AR 800-233-6332

Olive Loaf

Bryant Preserving Company
Alma, AR 800-634-2413
Cajun Brands
New Iberia, LA 504-408-2252

Pastrami

Alderfer Inc
Harleysville, PA 800-341-1121
Best Provision Co Inc
Union, NJ 800-631-4466
Bottom Line Foods
Pembroke Pines, FL 954-843-0562
Carando Gourmet Frozen Foods
Agawam, MA 888-227-2636
Carl Buddig & Co.
Homewood, IL 888-633-5684
Chicago 58 Food Products
Woodbridge, ON 416-603-4244
Curly's Foods Inc
Edina, MN 612-920-3400
Dutterer's Home Food Service
Baltimore, MD 410-298-3663
Ferris, Stahl-Meyer
Fort Lee, NJ 201-242-5500
Kelly Corned Beef Co
Chicago, IL 800-624-5617
Lower Foods, Inc.
Richmond, UT 800-295-7898
Marathon Enterprises Inc
Englewood, NJ 800-722-7388
Nossack Fine Meats
Red Deer, AB 403-346-5006
Saval Foods Corp
Elkridge, MD 800-527-2825
Vienna Meat Products
Scarborough, ON 800-588-1931
Volpi Foods
St Louis, MO 800-288-3439

Pepperoni

Battistoni Italian Spec Meats
Buffalo, NY 800-248-2705
Big Chief Meat Snacks Inc
Calgary, AB 403-264-2641
Burke Corp
Nevada, IA 800-654-1152
Busseto Foods
Fresno, CA 800-628-2633
Cattaneo Brothers Inc
San Luis Obispo, CA 800-243-8537
Country Smoked Meats
Bowling Green, OH 800-321-4766
Fiorucci Foods USA Inc
S Chesterfield, VA 800-524-7775
Hormel Foods Corp.
Austin, MN 507-437-5611
Ito Cariani Sausage Company
Hayward, CA 510-887-0882
Liguria Foods Inc
Humboldt, IA 515-332-4121
Quality Sausage Company
Dallas, TX 214-634-3400
Sangudo Custom Meat Packers
Sangudo, AB 888-785-3353
Spring Grove Foods
Miamisburg, OH 937-866-4311
Stawnichy Holdings
Mundare, AB 888-764-7646
Swiss-American Sausage Company
Lathrop, CA 209-858-5555
Viau Foods
Laval, QC 800-663-5492
Volpi Foods
St Louis, MO 800-288-3439

Prosciutto

Fiorucci Foods USA Inc
S Chesterfield, VA 800-524-7775
Hormel Foods Corp.
Austin, MN 507-437-5611
Olympic Provisions Northwest
Portland, OR 503-894-8136
Parma Sausage Products
Pittsburgh, PA 877-294-4207
Santa Maria Foods
Branpton, ON 905-790-1991
Siena Foods
Toronto, ON 800-465-0422
Volpi Foods
St Louis, MO 800-288-3439

Salami

Alef Sausage Inc
Mundelein, IL 847-968-2533
Applegate Farms
Bridgewater, NJ 866-587-5858
Baier's Sausage & Meats
Red Deer, AB 403-346-1535
Battistoni Italian Spec Meats
Buffalo, NY 800-248-2705
Boesl Packing Co
Baltimore, MD 800-675-1471
Burke Corp
Nevada, IA 800-654-1152
Busseto Foods
Fresno, CA 800-628-2633
Charlie's Country Sausage
Minot, ND 701-838-6302
Chicago 58 Food Products
Woodbridge, ON 416-603-4244
Chicopee Provision Co Inc
Chicopee, MA 800-924-6328
Chisesi Brothers Meat Packing
New Orleans, LA 800-966-3550
Cibao Meat Products Inc
Bronx, NY 718-993-5072
Far West Meats
Highland, CA 909-864-1990
Fiorucci Foods USA Inc
S Chesterfield, VA 800-524-7775
Hormel Foods Corp.
Austin, MN 507-437-5611
Ito Cariani Sausage Company
Hayward, CA 510-887-0882
John Volpi & Co
St Louis, MO 800-288-3439
Liguria Foods Inc
Humboldt, IA 515-332-4121
Marathon Enterprises Inc
Englewood, NJ 800-722-7388
OLLI Salumeria Americana
Oceanside, CA 877-655-4937
Parma Sausage Products
Pittsburgh, PA 877-294-4207
Patrick Cudahy LLC
Cudahy, WI 800-486-6900
Plumrose USA
Chicago, IL 800-526-4909
Santa Maria Foods
Branpton, ON 905-790-1991
Schaller & Weber Inc
Astoria, NY 800-847-4115
Sculli Brothers
Yeadon, PA 215-336-1223
Siena Foods
Toronto, ON 800-465-0422
Spring Grove Foods
Miamisburg, OH 937-866-4311
Stawnichy Holdings
Mundare, AB 888-764-7646
Swiss-American Sausage Company
Lathrop, CA 209-858-5555
Volpi Foods
St Louis, MO 800-288-3439

Sausages

A.L. Duck Jr Inc
Zuni, VA 757-562-2387
Abbyland Foods Inc
Abbotsford, WI 800-732-5483
Adolf's Meats & Sausage Kitchen
Hartford, CT 860-522-1588
Aidells Sausage Co
San Lorenzo, CA 800-546-5795
Alaska Sausage & Seafood
Anchorage, AK 800-798-3636
Alewel's Country Meats
Warrensburg, MO 800-353-8553
Aliments Prince SEC
Anjou, QC 800-361-3898
Alpine Meats
Stockton, CA 800-399-6328
Applegate Farms
Bridgewater, NJ 866-587-5858
AquaCuisine
Portland, OR 208-323-2782
Aries Prepared Beef
Burbank, CA 800-424-2333
Armbrust Meats
Medford, WI 715-748-3102
Arnold's Meat Food Products
Brooklyn, NY 800-633-7023
Ashland Sausage Co
Carol Stream, IL 630-690-2600
Baier's Sausage & Meats
Red Deer, AB 403-346-1535
Baja Foods LLC
Chicago, IL 773-376-9030
Bakalars Sausage Co
La Crosse, WI 608-784-0384
Berks Packing Company, Inc.
Reading, PA 800-882-3757
Big City Reds
Omaha, NE 800-759-5275
Bilinski Sausage Mfg Co
Cohoes, NY 877-873-9102
Binkert's Meat Products
Baltimore, MD 410-687-5959
Black's Barbecue
Lockhart, TX 888-632-8225
Blue Grass Quality Meat
Covington, KY 859-331-7100
Bob Evans Farms Inc.
800-939-2338
Boesl Packing Co
Baltimore, MD 800-675-1471
Bouma Meats
Provost, AB 780-753-2092
Bowser Meat Processing
Meriden, KS 785-484-2454
Boyd's Sausage Co
Washington, IA 319-653-5715
Braham Food Locker Service
Braham, MN 320 396 2636
Bridgford Foods Corp
Anaheim, CA 800-527-2105
Broadleaf Venison USA Inc
Vernon, CA 800-336-3844
Brook Meadow Meats
Hagerstown, MD 301-739-3107
Bryant's Meat Inc.
Taylorsville, MS 800-844-0507
Burgers' Smokehouse
California, MO 800-345-5185
Burke Corp
Nevada, IA 800-654-1152
Burton Meat Processing
Burton, TX 979-289-4022
Camellia General Provision Co
Buffalo, NY 716-893-5352
Caribbean Food Delights Inc
Tappan, NY 845-398-3000
Carl Buddig & Co.
Homewood, IL 888-633-5684
Carolina Packers Inc
Smithfield, NC 800-682-7675
Casa di Carfagna
Columbus, OH 614-846-6340
Casual Gourmet Foods
Clearwater, FL 727-298-8307
Cattaneo Brothers Inc
San Luis Obispo, CA 800-243-8537
Caughman's Meat Plant
Lexington, SC 803-356-0076
Center Locker Svc
Center, MO 800-884-0737
Central Meat Market
Providence, RI 401-751-6935
Charlie's Country Sausage
Minot, ND 701-838-6302
Cher-Make Sausage Co
Manitowoc, WI 800-242-7679
Chicopee Provision Co Inc
Chicopee, MA 800-924-6328
Chisesi Brothers Meat Packing
New Orleans, LA 800-966-3550
Cibao Meat Products Inc
Bronx, NY 718-993-5072
Cifelli & Sons Inc
South River, NJ 732-238-0090
Cimpl Meats
Yankton, SD 605-665-1665
Cloverdale Foods
Mandan, ND 800-669-9511

Clyde's Italian & German Sausage
Denver, CO 303-433-8744
Conecuh Sausage Co
Evergreen, AL 800-726-0507
Couch's Country Style Sausages
Cleveland, OH 216-823-2332
Country Smoked Meats
Bowling Green, OH 800-321-4766
Crawford Sausage Co Inc
Chicago, IL 773-277-3095
Crocetti's Oakdale Packing Co
East Bridgewater, MA 508-587-0035
Crofton & Sons Inc
Tampa, FL 800-878-7675
Culver Duck Farms Inc
Middlebury, IN 800-825-9225
Cumberland Gap Provision Company
Middlesboro, KY 855-411-7675
Dean Sausage Co Inc
Attalla, AL 800-228-0704
Debbie D's Jerky & Sausage
Tillamook, OR 503-842-2622
Dennison Meat Locker
Dennison, MN 507-645-8734
Diggs Packing Company
Columbia, MO 573-449-2995
DiGregorio Food Products
St Louis, MO 314-776-1062
Dinner Bell Meat Product
Lynchburg, VA 434-847-7766
Dino's Sausage & Meat Co Inc
Utica, NY 315-732-2661
Dohar Meats Inc
Cleveland, OH 216-241-4197
Dreymiller & KRAY Inc
Hampshire, IL 847-683-2271
Duis Meat Processing
Concordia, KS 800-281-4295
Dutch Packing Co., Inc.
Doral, FL 800-723-9249
E.W. Knauss & Son
Quakertown, PA 800-648-4220
Ellsworth Locker
Ellsworth, MN 507-967-2544
Elmwood Locker Svc
Elmwood, IL 309-742-8929
Elore Enterprises Inc
Miami Gardens, FL 305-477-1650
Enslin & Son Packing Company
Hattiesburg, MS 800-898-4687
European Egg Noodle Manufacturing
Edmonton, AB 780-453-6767
Evergood Fine Foods
San Francisco, CA 800-253-6733
F&Y Enterprises
Wauconda, IL 847-526-0620
Fabbri Sausage Mfg Co
Chicago, IL 312-829-6363
Fanestil Packing Company
Emporia, KS 800-658-1652
Far West Meats
Highland, CA 909-864-1990
Ferris, Stahl-Meyer
Fort Lee, NJ 201-242-5500
Foell Packing Company
Naperville, IL 919-776-0592
Fontanini Italian Meats
McCook, IL 800-331-6328
Fortenberry Mini-Storage
Kodak, TN 865-933-2568
Frank Wardynski & Sons Inc
Buffalo, NY 716-854-6083
Fresh Mark Inc.
Massillon, OH 330-832-7491
Frick's Quality Meats
Washington, MO 800-241-2209
Fried Provisions Company
Evans City, PA 724-538-3160
Gaiser's European Style
Union, NJ 908-686-3421
Gaspar's Linguica Co Inc
North Dartmouth, MA 800-542-2038
Gem Meat Packing Co
Garden City, ID 208-375-9424
Glazier Packing Co
Malone, NY 518-483-4990
Glier's Meats Inc
Covington, KY 800-446-3882
Gouvea's & Purity Foods Inc
Honolulu, HI 808-847-3717
Grandpa Ittel's Meats Inc
Howard Lake, MN 320-543-2285

Grant Park Packing
Chicago, IL 312-421-4096
Grimm's Fine Food
Richmond, BC 866-663-4746
Grote & Weigel Inc
Bloomfield, CT 860-242-8528
Gunnoe Farms Sausage & Salad
Charleston, WV 304-343-7686
H & B Packing Co
Waco, TX 254-752-2506
Hatfield Quality Meats
Hatfield, PA 800-743-1191
Hazle Park Quality Meats
West Hazleton, PA 800-238-4331
Heinkel's Packing Co
Decatur, IL 800-594-2738
Hillbilly Smokehouse
Rogers, AR 479-636-1927
Hofmann Sausage Co Inc
Mattydale, NY 800-724-8410
Homestead Meats
Delta, CO 970-874-1145
Hoople Country Kitchen Inc
Rockport, IN 877-466-7537
Hormel Foods Corp.
Austin, MN 507-437-5611
Hot Springs Packing Co Inc
Hot Springs, AR 800-535-0449
Hummel Brothers Inc
New Haven, CT 800-828-8978
Humphrey's Market
Springfield, IL 800-747-6328
Huse's Country Meats
Malone, TX 254-533-2205
Independent Meat Co
Twin Falls, ID 800-284-4626
Indian Valley Meats
Indian, AK 907-653-7511
Isernio Sausage Company
Seattle, WA 888-495-8674
Ito Cariani Sausage Company
Hayward, CA 510-887-0882
J & B Sausage Co Inc
Waelder, TX 830-788-7511
Jody Maroni's Sausage Kingdom
Burbank, CA 818-760-2004
Johnsonville Sausage LLC
Watertown, WI 888-556-2728
Jones Dairy Farm
Fort Atkinson, WI 800-563-6637
Kayem Foods
Chelsea, MA 800-426-6100
Kelley Foods
Elba, AL 334-897-5761
Kent Quality Foods Inc
Grand Rapids, MI 800-748-0141
Kilgus Meats
Toledo, OH 419-472-9721
Kiolbassa Provision Co
San Antonio, TX 800-456-5465
Kirby Holloway Provision Co
Harrington, DE 800-995-4729
Klement Sausage Co Inc
Milwaukee, WI 800-553-6368
Koegel Meats Inc
Flint, MI 810-238-3685
Konetzko's Meat Market
Browerville, MN 320-594-2915
Kowalski Sausage Co
Hamtramck, MI 800-482-2400
Lad's Smokehouse Catering
Needville, TX 979-793-6210
Larry's Sausage Corporation
Fayetteville, NC 910-483-5148
Laurent's Meat Market
Marrero, LA 504-341-1771
Le Pique-Nique
New York, NY 800-699-9822
Lee's Sausage Co
Orangeburg, SC 803-534-5517
Leona Meat Plant
Troy, PA 570-297-3574
Lewis Sausage Corporation
Burgaw, NC 910-259-2642
Liguria Foods Inc
Humboldt, IA 515-332-4121
Link Snacks Inc.
Minong, WI 715-466-2234
Little Rhody Brand Frankfurts
Johnston, RI 401-831-0815
Locustdale Meat Packing
Locustdale, PA 570-875-1270

Lord's Sausage & Country Ham
Dexter, GA 800-342-6002
Louie's Finer Meats
Cumberland, WI 800-270-4297
Lucy's Foods
Latrobe, PA 724-539-1430
Mac's Farms Sausage Co Inc
Newton Grove, NC 910-594-0095
Manda Fine Meats Inc
Baton Rouge, LA 800-343-2642
Marathon Enterprises Inc
Englewood, NJ 800-722-7388
Marcel et Henri Charcuterie Francaise
South San Francisco, CA 800-227-6436
Marshallville Packing Co
Marshallville, OH 330-855-2871
Mckenzie Country Classic's
Burlington, VT 800-426-6100
McLane's Meats
Wetaskiwin, AB 780-352-4321
Meating Place
Buffalo, NY 716-885-3623
Mellos North End Mfr
Fall River, MA 800-673-2320
Mertz Sausage Co
San Antonio, TX 210-433-3263
Michael's Provision Co
Fall River, MA 508-672-0982
Michel's Magnifique
New York, NY 212-431-1070
Milan Provision Co
Corona, NY 718-899-7678
Miller Brothers Packing Company
Sylvester, GA 229-776-2014
Miller's Meat Market
Red Bud, IL 618-282-3334
Milling Sausage Inc
Milwaukee, WI 414-645-2677
Momence Packing Company
Sheboygan Falls, WI 888-556-2728
Neese Country Sausage Inc
Greensboro, NC 800-632-1010
Neto's Market & Grill
Santa Clara, CA 888-482-6386
New Packing Company
Chicago, IL 312-666-1314
Niemuth's Steak & Chop Shop
Waupaca, WI 715-258-2666
Norpaco Inc
Middletown, CT 800-252-0222
North Country Smokehouse
Claremont, NH 800-258-4304
Nossack Fine Meats
Red Deer, AB 403-346-5006
Nueske's Applewood Smoked Meat
Wittenberg, WI 800-720-1153
Odom's Tennessee Pride Sausage Company
Madison, TN 615-868-1360
Omaha Steaks Inc
. . . . 800-960-8400
Opa's Smoked Meats
Fredericksburg, TX 800-543-6750
Ossian Smoked Meats
Ossian, IN 800-535-8862
Parma Sausage Products
Pittsburgh, PA 877-294-4207
Patrick Cudahy LLC
Cudahy, WI 800-486-6900
Peer Foods Group Inc
Chicago, IL 800-365-5644
Pekarna Meat Market
Jordan, MN 952-492-6101
Piller Sausages & Delicatessens
Waterloo, ON 800-265-2628
Pinter's Packing Plant
Dorchester, WI 715-654-5444
Pioneer Packing Co
Bowling Green, OH 419-352-5283
Pokanoket Ostrich Farm
South Dartmouth, MA 508-992-6188
Polka Home Style Sausage
Chicago, IL 773-221-0395
Quality Meats & Seafood
West Fargo, ND 800-342-4250
Queen City Sausage & Provision
Cincinnati, OH 877-544-5588
R & D Sausage Co
Cleveland, OH 216-692-1832
Ray's Sausage Co
Cleveland, OH 216-921-8782
Real Kosher Sausage Company
Newark, NJ 973-690-5394

Red Smith Foods Inc
Davie, FL 954-581-1996
Register Meat Co
Cottondale, FL 850-352-4269
Rich Products Corp
Vineland, NJ 800-818-9261
Rinehart Meat Processing
Branson, MO. 417-869-2041
Robbins Packing Company
Statesboro, GA 912-764-7503
Robinson Distributing Co
London, KY 800-230-5131
Roma Packing Company
East Providence, RI 401-228-7170
Roman Packing Company
Norfolk, NE. 800-373-5990
Roman Sausage Company
Santa Clara, CA 800-497-7462
Roode Packing Company
Fairbury, NE 402-729-2253
Rudolph's Market & Sausage
Dallas, TX. 214-741-1874
S. Wallace Edward & Sons
Surry, VA. 800-222-4267
S.W. Meat & Provision Company
Phoenix, AZ 602-275-2000
Saag's Products LLC
San Leandro, CA. 855-287-6562
Sahlen's
Buffalo, NY. 800-466-8165
Sangudo Custom Meat Packers
Sangudo, AB. 888-785-3353
Sardinha's Sausage
Somerset, MA. 800-678-0178
Sausages by Amy
Chicago, IL 312-829-2250
Savoie's Sausage and Food Products
Opelousas, LA 337-942-7241
Schaefers Market
Sauk Centre, MN 320-352-6490
Schaller & Weber Inc
Astoria, NY. 800-847-4115
Scott Hams
Greenville, KY 800-318-1353
Sculli Brothers
Yeadon, PA 215-336-1223
Sechrist Brothers
Dallastown, PA 717-244-2975
Selecto Sausage Co
Houston, TX 713-926-1626
Serv-Rite Meat Co Inc
Los Angeles, CA. 323-227-1911
Sheinman Provision Co
Philadelphia, PA 215-473-7065
Siena Foods
Toronto, ON 800-465-0422
Silver Creek Specialty Meats
Oshkosh, WI. 800-729-2849
Silver Star Meats Inc
Mc Kees Rocks, PA 800-548-1321
Smith Packing Regional Meat
Utica, NY 315-732-5125
Smith Provision Co Inc
Erie, PA. 800-334-9151
Smokey Denmark Sausage Co
Austin, TX. 512-385-0718
Smolich Bros. Home Made Sausage
Crest Hill, IL. 815-727-2144
Spring Grove Foods
Miamisburg, OH. 937-866-4311
Stanley Provision Company
Manchester, CT. 888-688-6347
Stawnichy Holdings
Mundare, AB 888-764-7646
Stevens Sausage Co
Smithfield, NC 800-338-0561
Stewarts Market
Yelm, WA 360-458-2091
Stonie's Sausage Shop
Perryville, MO 888-546-2540
Strasburg Provision
Strasburg, OH 800-207-6009
Streit Carl & Son Co
Neptune, NJ 732-775-0803
Stripling's General Store
Moultrie, GA. 229-985-4226
Sunergia Soyfoods
Charlottesville, VA 800-693-5134
Sunnydale Meats Inc
Gaffney, SC. 864-489-6091
Swiss-American Sausage Company
Lathrop, CA 209-858-5555

T.L. Herring & Company
Wilson, NC 252-291-1141
Tennessee Valley Packing Co
Columbia, TN. 931-388-2623
Texas Sausage Co
Austin, TX. 512-472-6707
Thomas Packing Company
Columbus, GA 800-729-0976
Tofield Packers Ltd
Tofield, AB 780-662-4842
Troy Foods Inc
Troy, IL 618-667-6332
Uvalde Meat Processing
Uvalde, TX 830-278-6247
Vermilion Packers Ltd
Vermilion, AB. 780-853-4622
Viau Foods
Laval, QC 800-663-5492
Victor Ostrowski & Son
Baltimore, MD 410-327-8935
Vienna Beef LTD
Chicago, IL 800-366-3647
Vienna Meat Products
Scarborough, ON 800-588-1931
Vollwerth & Baroni Companies
Hancock, MI. 800-562-7620
Volpi Foods
St Louis, MO. 800-288-3439
W.A. Beans & Sons
Bangor, ME. 800-649-1958
WACO Beef & Pork Processors
Waco, TX 254-772-4669
Wampler's Farm Sausage Company
Lenoir City, TN. 800-728-7243
Warren & Son Meat Processing
Whipple, OH. 740-585-2421
Willie's Smoke House LLC
Harrisville, PA. 800-742-4184
Wolfson Casing Corp
Mt Vernon, NY 800-221-8042
Woods Smoked Meats Inc
Bowling Green, MO 800-458-8426
Zummo Meat Co
Beaumont, TX. 409-842-1810
Zweigle's Inc
Rochester, NY. 585-546-1740

Andouille

Applegate Farms
Bridgewater, NJ 866-587-5858
Burke Corp
Nevada, IA 800-654-1152
Grote & Weigel Inc
Bloomfield, CT. 860-242-8528
Laurent's Meat Market
Marrero, LA 504-341-1771
Parma Sausage Products
Pittsburgh, PA. 877-294-4207
Savoie's Sausage and Food Products
Opelousas, LA 337-942-7241
Thomas Packing Company
Columbus, GA 800-729-0976

Blood

Bavarian Meat Products
Seattle, WA 206-448-3540
Chicopee Provision Co Inc
Chicopee, MA. 800-924-6328
Gouvea's & Purity Foods Inc
Honolulu, HI. 808-847-3717

Bockwurst

Chicopee Provision Co Inc
Chicopee, MA. 800-924-6328
Country Smoked Meats
Bowling Green, OH 800-321-4766
Koegel Meats Inc
Flint, MI 810-238-3685

Boudin

Comeaux's
Lafayette, LA 888-264-5460
Marcel et Henri Charcuterie Francaise
South San Francisco, CA 800-227-6436
Savoie's Sausage and Food Products
Opelousas, LA 337-942-7241
Stallings Head Cheese Co
Houston, TX 713-523-1751
Sunset Farm Foods Inc
Valdosta, GA. 800-882-1121

Woods Smoked Meats Inc
Bowling Green, MO 800-458-8426
Zummo Meat Co
Beaumont, TX. 409-842-1810

Bratwurst

Chicopee Provision Co Inc
Chicopee, MA. 800-924-6328
Country Smoked Meats
Bowling Green, OH 800-321-4766
Elmwood Locker Svc
Elmwood, IL. 309-742-8929
F B Purnell Sausage Co Inc
Simpsonville, KY 800-626-1512
Far West Meats
Highland, CA 909-864-1990
Grote & Weigel Inc
Bloomfield, CT. 860-242-8528
Kayem Foods
Chelsea, MA. 800-426-6100
Kilgus Meats
Toledo, OH 419-472-9721
Koegel Meats Inc
Flint, MI 810-238-3685
New Braunfels Smokehouse
New Braunfels, TX. 800-537-6932
S.W. Meat & Provision Company
Phoenix, AZ 602-275-2000
Smolich Bros. Home Made Sausage
Crest Hill, IL. 815-727-2144
WACO Beef & Pork Processors
Waco, TX 254-772-4669

Cajun

Fontanini Italian Meats
McCook, IL. 800-331-6328

Casings: Sausage, Pork, Beef

Austrade
Palm Beach Gdns, FL. 561-209-2447
Con Yeager Spice Co
Zelienople, PA. 800-222-2460
Dewied International Inc
San Antonio, TX. 800-992-5600
International Casings Group
Chicago, IL. 800-825-5151
Koegel Meats Inc
Flint, MI 810-238-3685
Marie F
Markham, ON. 800-365-4464
Nitta Casings Inc
Bridgewater, NJ 800-526-3970
Oversea Casing Co
Seattle, WA 206-682-6845
Syracuse Casing Co
Syracuse, NY 315-475-0309
World Casing Corp
Maspeth, NY. 800-221-4887

Chicken

Bell & Evans
Fredericksburg, PA 717-865-6626
Kayem Foods
Chelsea, MA 800-426-6100
Lucy's Foods
Latrobe, PA. 724-539-1430
W.A. Beans & Sons
Bangor, ME. 800-649-1958

Chorizo

Arnold's Meat Food Products
Brooklyn, NY 800-633-7023
Burke Corp
Nevada, IA 800-654-1152
Cacique
Monrovia, CA. 800-521-6987
Carmelita Provisions Company
Monterey Park, CA. 323-262-6751
Country Smoked Meats
Bowling Green, OH 800-321-4766
F B Purnell Sausage Co Inc
Simpsonville, KY 800-626-1512
Lucy's Foods
Latrobe, PA. 724-539-1430
Parma Sausage Products
Pittsburgh, PA. 877-294-4207
Sunset Farm Foods Inc
Valdosta, GA. 800-882-1121
WACO Beef & Pork Processors
Waco, TX 254-772-4669

Chourico

Gaspar's Linguica Co Inc
North Dartmouth, MA 800-542-2038
Manuel's Odessa Tortilla
Odessa, TX 800-753-2445
Mertz Sausage Co
San Antonio, TX.............210-433-3263
Sardinha's Sausage
Somerset, MA.............800-678-0178

Hot

Boesl Packing Co
Baltimore, MD 800-675-1471
Chicopee Provision Co Inc
Chicopee, MA.............800-924-6328
E.W. Knauss & Son
Quakertown, PA 800-648-4220
H & B Packing Co
Waco, TX 254-752-2506
Hormel Foods Corp.
Austin, MN 507-437-5611
Ray's Sausage Co
Cleveland, OH 216-921-8782
Sheinman Provision Co
Philadelphia, PA 215-473-7065
Siena Foods
Toronto, ON 800-465-0422

Hot Italian

Eagle Rock Food Co
Albuquerque, NM.............505-323-1183
F B Purnell Sausage Co Inc
Simpsonville, KY 800-626-1512
Grote & Weigel Inc
Bloomfield, CT.............860-242-8528
Siena Foods
Toronto, ON 800-465-0422

Kielbasa

Berks Packing Company, Inc.
Reading, PA 800-882-3757
Boesl Packing Co
Baltimore, MD 800-675-1471
Chicopee Provision Co Inc
Chicopee, MA.............800-924-6328
Country Smoked Meats
Bowling Green, OH 800-321-4766
Far West Meats
Highland, CA 909-864-1990
Frank Wardynski & Sons Inc
Buffalo, NY.............716-854-6083
Gaspar's Linguica Co Inc
North Dartmouth, MA 800-542-2038
Grote & Weigel Inc
Bloomfield, CT.............860-242-8528
Hot Springs Packing Co Inc
Hot Springs, AR 800-535-0449
Leo G. Fraboni Sausage Company
Hibbing, MN.............218-263-5074
Locustdale Meat Packing
Locustdale, PA 570-875-1270
Marathon Enterprises Inc
Englewood, NJ 800-722-7388
Martin Rosols
New Britain, CT 860-223-2707
Norpaco Inc
Middletown, CT.............800-252-0222
Parma Sausage Products
Pittsburgh, PA.............877-294-4207
Roma Packing Company
East Providence, RI 401-228-7170
Sardinha's Sausage
Somerset, MA.............800-678-0178
Silver Star Meats Inc
Mc Kees Rocks, PA 800-548-1321
Smith Packing Regional Meat
Utica, NY 315-732-5125
Stanley Provision Company
Manchester, CT.............888-688-6347
Victor Ostrowski & Son
Baltimore, MD 410-327-8935

Knockwurst

Boesl Packing Co
Baltimore, MD 800-675-1471
Country Smoked Meats
Bowling Green, OH 800-321-4766
Far West Meats
Highland, CA 909-864-1990
Gouvea's & Purity Foods Inc
Honolulu, HI.............808-847-3717
Grote & Weigel Inc
Bloomfield, CT.............860-242-8528

Legonica (Thin Italian)

Gaspar's Linguica Co Inc
North Dartmouth, MA 800-542-2038

Linguica

Burke Corp
Nevada, IA 800-654-1152
Swiss-American Sausage Company
Lathrop, CA 209-858-5555

Link

Bakalars Sausage Co
La Crosse, WI.............608-784-0384
Bellville Meat Market
Bellville, TX.............800-571-6328
Burke Corp
Nevada, IA 800-654-1152
Country Smoked Meats
Bowling Green, OH 800-321-4766
F B Purnell Sausage Co Inc
Simpsonville, KY.............800-626-1512
Father's Country Hams
Bremen, KY 270-525-3554
Fontanini Italian Meats
McCook, IL.............800-331-6328
H & B Packing Co
Waco, TX 254-752-2506
Hormel Foods Corp.
Austin, MN.............507-437-5611
Jimmy Dean Foods
Springdale, AR 800-925-3326
Mellos North End Mfr
Fall River, MA 800-673-2320
Opa's Smoked Meats
Fredericksburg, TX.............800-543-6750
Ray's Sausage Co
Cleveland, OH 216-921-8782

Mortadella

Fiorucci Foods USA Inc
S Chesterfield, VA 800-524-7775
John Volpi & Co
St Louis, MO.............800-288-3439
Parma Sausage Products
Pittsburgh, PA.............877-294-4207
Siena Foods
Toronto, ON 800-465-0422

Patti

F B Purnell Sausage Co Inc
Simpsonville, KY.............800-626-1512
Father's Country Hams
Bremen, KY 270-525-3554
Fontanini Italian Meats
McCook, IL.............800-331-6328
Hormel Foods Corp.
Austin, MN 507-437-5611
Jimmy Dean Foods
Springdale, AR.............800-925-3326
Mellos North End Mfr
Fall River, MA 800-673-2320
Ray's Sausage Co
Cleveland, OH 216-921-8782
Roman Sausage Company
Santa Clara, CA 800-497-7462

Polish

Crawford Sausage Co Inc
Chicago, IL 773-277-3095
Fontanini Italian Meats
McCook, IL.............800-331-6328

Pork

Crawford Sausage Co Inc
Chicago, IL.............773-277-3095
Grote & Weigel Inc
Bloomfield, CT.............860-242-8528
Lucy's Foods
Latrobe, PA.............724-539-1430

Salmon

Aquatec Seafoods Ltd.
Comox, BC.............250-339-6412

Sicilian Style (with Cheese)

Volpi Foods
St Louis, MO.............800-288-3439

Sweet

Chicopee Provision Co Inc
Chicopee, MA.............800-924-6328

Sweet Italian

Grote & Weigel Inc
Bloomfield, CT.............860-242-8528

Turkey

Couch's Country Style Sausages
Cleveland, OH 216-823-2332
Eagle Rock Food Co
Albuquerque, NM.............505-323-1183
Gaspar's Linguica Co Inc
North Dartmouth, MA 800-542-2038
Lucy's Foods
Latrobe, PA.............724-539-1430

Venison

Broadleaf Venison USA Inc
Vernon, CA.............800-336-3844

Smoked Meat

Alewel's Country Meats
Warrensburg, MO 800-353-8553
Alpine Meats
Stockton, CA.............800-399-6328
Applegate Farms
Bridgewater, NJ 866-587-5858
Bellville Meat Market
Bellville, TX.............800-571-6328
Berks Packing Company, Inc.
Reading, PA 800-882-3757
Boesl Packing Co
Baltimore, MD 800-675-1471
Braham Food Locker Service
Braham, MN.............320-396-2636
Brook Meadow Meats
Hagerstown, MD.............301-739-3107
Burgers' Smokehouse
California, MO 800-345-5185
Carolina Pride Foods
Greenwood, SC.............864-229-5611
Chicago 58 Food Products
Woodbridge, ON.............416-603-4244
Cloud's Meat Processing
Carthage, MO 417-358-5855
Country Smoked Meats
Bowling Green, OH 800-321-4766
Crofton & Sons Inc
Tampa, FL.............800-878-7675
Duis Meat Processing
Concordia, KS.............800-281-4295
E.W. Knauss & Son
Quakertown, PA 800-648-4220
F&Y Enterprises
Wauconda, IL 847-526-0620
Fairbury Food Products
Fairbury, NE 402-729-3379
Far West Meats
Highland, CA 909-864-1990
Fiorucci Foods USA Inc
S Chesterfield, VA 800-524-7775
Fresh Mark Inc.
Massillon, OH.............330-832-7491
Frick's Quality Meats
Washington, MO.............800-241-2209
Gaiser's European Style
Union, NJ 908-686-3421
Grandpa Ittel's Meats Inc
Howard Lake, MN 320-543-2285
Hickory Baked Ham Co
Castle Rock, CO 303-688-2633
Hollman Foods
Des Moines, IA.............888-926-2879
Homestead Meats
Delta, CO 970-874-1145
Hormel Foods Corp.
Austin, MN 507-437-5611
Humphrey's Market
Springfield, IL.............800-747-6328
John Hofmeister & Son Inc
Chicago, IL.............800-923-4267
John Volpi & Co
St Louis, MO.............800-288-3439

Koegel Meats Inc
Flint, MI 810-238-3685
Konetzko's Meat Market
Browerville, MN 320-594-2915
Laurent's Meat Market
Marrero, LA 504-341-1771
Leo G. Fraboni Sausage Company
Hibbing, MN 218-263-5074
Lord's Sausage & Country Ham
Dexter, GA 800-342-6002
Manger Packing Corp
Baltimore, MD 800-227-9262
Mckenzie Country Classic's
Burlington, VT 800-426-6100
Nodine's Smokehouse Inc
Torrington, CT 800-222-2059
Nueces Canyon Range
Brenham, TX 800-925-5058
Original Chili Bowl
Ontario, CA 800-548-6363
People's Sausage Co
Los Angeles, CA 213-627-8633
Pioneer Packing Co
Bowling Green, OH 419-352-5283
Quality Meats & Seafood
West Fargo, ND 800-342-4250
R M Felts' Packing Co
Ivor, VA 757-859-6131
Rinehart Meat Processing
Branson, MO 417-869-2041
Robbins Packing Company
Statesboro, GA 912-764-7503
Rose Packing Co Inc
South Barrington, IL 800-323-7363
Saag's Products LLC
San Leandro, CA 855-287-6562
Sahlen's
Buffalo, NY 800-466-8165
Sardinha's Sausage
Somerset, MA 800-678-0178
Savoie's Sausage and Food Products
Opelousas, LA 337-942-7241
Schaller & Weber Inc
Astoria, NY 800-847-4115
Sechrist Brothers
Dallastown, PA 717-244-2975
Smith Meat Packing
Detroit, MI 313-833-1590
Stonie's Sausage Shop
Perryville, MO 888-546-2540
Stripling's General Store
Moultrie, GA 229-985-4226
Swiss-American Sausage Company
Lathrop, CA 209-858-5555
Thomas Packing Company
Columbus, GA 800-729-0976
Triple U Enterprises
Fort Pierre, SD 605-567-3624

Troy Pork Store
Troy, NY 518-272-8291
V.W. Joyner & Company
Smithfield, VA 757-357-2161
Warren & Son Meat Processing
Whipple, OH 740-585-2421
Wayco Ham Co
Goldsboro, NC 800-962-2614
Willie's Smoke House LLC
Harrisville, PA 800-742-4184
Woods Smoked Meats Inc
Bowling Green, MO 800-458-8426
Yoakum Packing Co
Yoakum, TX 800-999-6997
Zerna Packing
Labadie, MO 636-742-4190

Poultry & Game

Selwoods Farm Hunting Preserve
Alpine, AL 800-522-0403

Tasso

Comeaux's
Lafayette, LA 888-264-5460
Savoie's Sausage and Food Products
Opelousas, LA 337-942-7241

Turkey

Deli Breast - Fresh

Norbest, LLC
Moroni, UT 800-453-5327

Deli Breast - Frozen

Norbest, LLC
Moroni, UT 800-453-5327

Deli Breast - Honey

Albert's Meats
Claysville, PA 800-522-9970

Deli Breast - Smoked

Applegate Farms
Bridgewater, NJ 866-587-5858

Smoked

Applegate Farms
Bridgewater, NJ 866-587-5858
Burgers' Smokehouse
California, MO 800-345-5185
Chickasaw Trading Company
Denver City, TX 800-848-3515
Crofton & Sons Inc
Tampa, FL 800-878-7675

Hollman Foods
Des Moines, IA 888-926-2879
North Country Smokehouse
Claremont, NH 800-258-4304
Ranch Oak Farm
Fort Worth, TX 800-888-0327
Selwoods Farm Hunting Preserve
Alpine, AL 800-522-0403
Thomas Packing Company
Columbus, GA 800-729-0976
Wayco Ham Co
Goldsboro, NC 800-962-2614

Steaks

B & D Foods
Boise, ID 208-344-1183
Bakalars Sausage Co
La Crosse, WI 608-784-0384
Burnett & Son
Monrovia, CA 877-632-5467
Cambridge Packing Company
Boston, MA 800-722-6726
Centennial Food Corporation
Calgary, AB 403-214-0044
Devault Foods
Devault, PA 800-426-2874
Dynamic Foods
Lubbock, TX 806-723-5600
Feed The Party
Louisville, KY
Kutztown Bologna Company
Leola, PA 800-723-8824
Ossian Smoked Meats
Ossian, IN 800-535-8862
Pierceton Foods Inc
Pierceton, IN 574-594-2344
Pinter's Packing Plant
Dorchester, WI 715-654-5444
Rymer Foods
Chicago, IL 800-247-9637
S.W. Meat & Provision Company
Phoenix, AZ 602-275-2000
Stampede Meat, Inc.
Bridgeview, IL 800-353-0933
Steak-Umm Company
Shillington, PA 860-928-5900
Valley Meats
Coal Valley, IL 309-517-6639

Tripe

Bradshaw's Food Products
Dighton, MA 508-669-6088

Nuts & Nut Butters

Nut Butters

88 Acres
Allston, MA 617-208-8651
Abby's Better Nut Butter
American Almond Products Co
Brooklyn, NY 800-825-6663
Amoretti
Oxnard, CA.........................800-266-7388
Andalucia Nuts
Houston, TX 713-977-9090
Betsy's Best
....888-483-2019
Big Spoon Roasters
Durham, NC 919-309-9100
Cache Creek Foods LLC
Woodland, CA......................530-662-1764
Crazy Go Nuts
Fower, CA
Crazy Richard's
Dublin, OH 614-889-4824
Earth Balance
Boulder, CO 866-234-6429
East Wind Inc
Tecumseh, MO 417-679-4682
Eliot's Adult Nut Butters
....503-847-9457
Everland Foods
Burnaby, BC
Everland Parks
Burnaby, BC
Farmtrue
North Stonington, CT...............860-495-2231
Feridies
Courtland, VA.......................800-544-0896
Food Mill
Oakland, CA........................510-482-3848
Fresh Hemp Foods
Winnipeg, NB 800-665-4367
Georgia Grinders
Chamblee, GA
Gopal's Healthfoods
Sidney, TX 866-646-7257
Healing Home Foods
Pound Ridge, NY 914-764-1303
Jonny Almond Nut Co
Flint, MI 810-767-6887
Julie's Real
Dallas, TX...........................877-659-4375
Justin's Nut Butter
Boulder, CO 844-448-0302
Kalot Superfood
Denver, CO.........................561-757-6541
Laurel Foods
Hillsboro, OR 503-692-3663
Legendary Foods
Pasadena, CA 888-698-1708
Love You Foods
Flagstaff, AZ.......................844-693-2662
Maisie Jane's California Sunshine
Chico, CA...........................530-899-7909
Marin Food Specialties
Byron, CA...........................925-634-6126
Naturally Nutty
Traverse City, MI 888-224-9988
Nikki's Coconut Butter
Hudson, WI
Nuttzo
San Diego, CA 888-325-0553
Once Again Nut Butter
Nunda, NY 888-800-8075
Pacific Grain & Foods
Fresno, CA 559-276-2580
Perfect Snacks
Sorrento Valley, CA 866-628-8548
Premier Organics
Oakland, CA........................866-237-8688
Probar
Salt Lake City, UT 800-921-2294
Purely Pecans
Valdosta, GA.......................800-627-6630
Reginald's Homemade LLC
Manakin Sabot, VA.................804-972-4040
Saratoga Peanut Butter Company
Saratoga Springs, NY..............888-967-3268
Solo Foods
Countryside, IL.....................800-328-7656
Soynut Butter Co
Glenview, IL 847-635-9960
SunButter
Fargo, ND 877-873-4501
SuperFat
Beaverton, OR
Tierra Farm
Valatie, NY 519-392-8300
To Your Health Sprouted Flour Co., Inc.
Floyd, VA 540-283-9589
Tribe 9 Foods
Madison, WI........................608-257-7216
Winn-Dixie Stores
Jacksonville, FL 800-967-9105
Z Specialty Food, LLC
Woodland, CA......................800-678-1226

Almond

Argania Butter
Rancho Palos Verdes, CA
Barney Butter
Fresno, CA 559-442-1752
Big Spoon Roasters
Durham, NC 919-309-9100
Buff Bake
Santa Ana, CA 949-274-9464
COnut Butter
New Orleans, LA
Crazy Richard's
Dublin, OH 614-889-4824
Everland Foods
Burnaby, BC
Georgia Grinders
Chamblee, GA
GloryBee
Eugene, OR.........................800-456-7923
Julie's Real
Dallas, TX...........................877-659-4375
Justin's Nut Butter
Boulder, CO 844-448-0302
Marin Food Specialties
Byron, CA...........................925-634-6126
Naturalmond Almond Butter
Chamblee, GA......................866-327-9301
No Cow
Denver, CO
Noosh Brands
Simi Valley, CA....................805-522-5744
Nuts 'N More
Providence, RI 844-413-2344
Once Again Nut Butter
Nunda, NY 888-800-8075
Premier Organics
Oakland, CA 866-237-8688
To Your Health Sprouted Flour Co., Inc.
Floyd, VA 540-283-9589

Hazelnut

Fine & Raw Chocolate
Brooklyn, NY 718-366-3633
Nuts 'N More
Providence, RI 844-413-2344

Peanut Butter

Algood Food Co
Louisville, KY 502-637-3631
American Almond Products Co
Brooklyn, NY 800-825-6663
Azar Nut Co
El Paso, TX.........................800-351-8178
Bell Plantation
Tifton, GA..........................229-387-7238
Bella Vista Farm
Lawton, OK.........................866-237-8526
Big Spoon Roasters
Durham, NC 919-309-9100
Bnutty
Merrillville, IN 844-426-8889
Buff Bake
Santa Ana, CA 949-274-9464
CB's Nuts
Kingston, WA 360-297-1213
Clements Foods Co
Oklahoma City, OK 800-654-8355
COnut Butter
New Orleans, LA
Crazy Richard's
Dublin, OH 614-889-4824
E.F. Lane & Son
Oakland, CA 510-569-8980
East Wind Inc
Tecumseh, MO 417-679-4682
Eliot's Adult Nut Butters
....503-847-9457
G.E. Barbour
Sussex, NB 506-432-2300
Gardners Candies Inc
Tyrone, PA.........................800-242-2639
Georgia Grinders
Chamblee, GA
Good Spread
Boulder, CO
HomePlate Peanut Butter
Austin, TX..........................512-580-9980
J.M. Smucker Co.
Orrville, OH 888-550-9555
JER Creative Food Concepts, Inc.
Commerce, CA 800-350-2462
JMS Specialty Foods
Ripon, WI 800-535-5437
Justin's Nut Butter
Boulder, CO 844-448-0302
Krema Nut Co
Columbus, OH 800-222-4132
Landis Peanut Butter
Souderton, PA.....................215-723-9366
Leavitt Corp., The
Everett, MA.........................617-389-2600
Lynch Foods
North York, ON....................416-449-5464
Marantha Natural Foods
San Francisco, CA 866-972-6879
Mrs Annie's Peanut Patch
Floresville, TX 830-393-7845
Nuts 'N More
Providence, RI 844-413-2344
Once Again Nut Butter
Nunda, NY 888-800-8075
Pacific Beach Peanut Butter
La Mesa, CA.......................630-329-0792
Peanut Butter & Co.
New York, NY 866-456-8372
Producers Peanut Company
Suffolk, VA 800-847-5491
Reginald's Homemade LLC
Manakin Sabot, VA.................804-972-4040
Scott-Bathgate
Winnipeg, MB......................800-216-2990
Sessions Co Inc
Enterprise, AL.....................334-393-0200
Simple Foods
Tonawanda, NY 800-234-8850
Southern Peanut Co Inc
Dublin, NC 800-330-3141
St Laurent Brothers
Bay City, MI 800-289-7688
Sunland Inc/Peanut Better
Portales, NM.......................575-356-6638
Sweet Harvest Foods
Rosemount, MN 507-263-8599
Tara Foods
Atlanta, GA.........................404-559-0605
Virginia & Spanish Peanut Co
Providence, RI 800-673-3562

Crunchy

Everland Foods
Burnaby, BC
International Food Products
Fenton, MO.........................800-227-8427

Smooth

International Food Products
Fenton, MO.........................800-227-8427

Nut Pastes

American Almond Products Co
Brooklyn, NY 800-825-6663

Amoretti
Oxnard, CA ... 800-266-7388
Georgia Nut Co
Skokie, IL ... 877-674-2993
Solo Foods
Countryside, IL ... 800-328-7656

Almond

Bear Stewart Corp
Chicago, IL ... 800-697-2327
Georgia Nut Co
Skokie, IL ... 877-674-2993
Putney Pasta
Brattleboro, VT ... 800-253-3683

Nuts

A La Carte
Chicago, IL ... 800-722-2370
Adams & Brooks Inc
Los Angeles, CA ... 213-749-3226
Adkin & Son Associated Food Products
South Haven, MI ... 269-637-7450
Albanese Confectionery Group
Merrillville, IN ... 800-536-0581
All Wrapped Up
Plantation, FL ... 800-891-2194
Alldrin Brothers
Ballico, CA ... 209-667-1600
American Almond Products Co
Brooklyn, NY ... 800-825-6663
American Key Food Products Inc
Closter, NJ ... 877-263-7539
American Nut & Chocolate Co
Boston, MA ... 800-797-6887
American Yeast
Memphis, TN ... 866-920-9885
Ames International Inc
Fife, WA ... 888-469-2637
AnaCon Foods Company
Atchison, KS ... 800-328-0291
Andalucia Nuts
Houston, TX ... 713-977-9090
Ann's House of Nuts, Inc.
Columbia, MD ... 410-309-6887
Archer Daniels Midland Company
Chicago, IL ... 312-634-8100
Arizona Cowboy
Phoenix, AZ ... 800-529-8627
Arizona Pistachio Company
Tucson, AZ ... 800-333-8575
Arway Confections Inc
Chicago, IL ... 800-695-0612
Aunt Aggie De's Pralines
Sinton, TX ... 800-333-9354
Aurora Products
Orange, CT ... 800-398-1048
Azar Nut Co
El Paso, TX ... 800-351-8178
Baldwin-Minkler Farms
Orland, CA ... 530-865-8080
Balsu
Bay Harbour Islands, FL ... 305-993-5045
Barcelona Nut Co
Baltimore, MD ... 800-296-6887
Bavarian Nut Co
Buffalo, NY ... 716-810-6887
Bazzini Holdings LLC
Allentown, PA ... 610-366-1606
Bedemco Inc
White Plains, NY ... 914-683-1119
Beer Nuts Co Store-Plant
Bloomington, IL ... 309-827-8580
Ben Heggy's Candy Co
Canton, OH ... 330-455-7703
Berberian Nut Company
Chico, CA ... 530-981-4900
Berson Peanuts
Opp, AL ... 334-493-0655
Beta Pure Foods
Santa Cruz, CA ... 831-685-6565
Birdsong Corp.
Suffolk, VA ... 757-539-3456
Bissinger's Handcrafted Chocolatier
St. Louis, MO ... 314-615-2400
Blue Diamond Growers
Sacramento, CA ... 800-987-2329
Brooks Peanut Co
Samson, AL ... 334-898-7194
Buchanan Hollow Nut Co
Le Grand, CA ... 800-532-1500
Buddy Squirrel LLC
St Francis, WI ... 800-972-2658
Byrd's Pecans
Butler, MO ... 866-679-5583
C J Dannemiller Co
Norton, OH ... 800-624-8671
Cache Creek Foods LLC
Woodland, CA ... 530-662-1764
Cajun Creole Products Inc
New Iberia, LA ... 800-946-8688
Cal-Grown Nut Company
Hughson, CA ... 209-883-4081
California Almond Packers
Modesto, CA ... 209-549-8262
California Fruit & Nut
Gustine, CA ... 888-747-8224
California Independent Almond Growers
Merced, CA ... 209-667-4855
California Walnut Co
Los Molinos, CA ... 530-527-2616
California Wholesale Nut
Chico, CA ... 530-895-0512
Camilla Pecan Company
Camilla, GA ... 800-526-8770
Capay Canyon Ranch
Esparto, CA ... 530-662-2372
Capco Enterprises
East Hanover, NJ ... 800-252-1011
Carolina Cracker
Garner, NC ... 919-779-6899
Cheese Straws & More
Monroe, LA ... 800-997-1921
Chico Nut Company
Chico, CA ... 530-891-1493
CHS Inc.
Inver Grove Hts., MN ... 800-328-6539
Clic International Inc
Laval, QC ... 450-669-2663
Colorado Nut Co
Denver, CO ... 800-876-1625
Commodities Marketing Inc
Clarksburg, NJ ... 732-516-0700
Crain Ranch
Los Molinos, CA ... 530-527-1077
D Steengrafe Co Inc
Pleasant Valley, NY ... 845-635-4067
Dakota Gourmet
Wahpeton, ND ... 800-727-6663
Del Rio Nut Company
Livingston, CA ... 209-394-7945
Derco Foods Intl
Fresno, CA ... 559-435-2664
Desert Pepper Trading Co
El Paso, TX ... 888-472-5727
Diamond of California
San Francisco, CA ... 415-912-3180
Durey-Libby Edible Nuts
Carlstadt, NJ ... 800-332-6887
E.F. Lane & Son
Oakland, CA ... 510-569-8980
Edison Grainery
Benicia, CA ... 510-382-0202
El Brands
Ozark, AL ... 334-445-2828
Elegant Edibles
Houston, TX ... 800-227-3226
Everland Foods
Burnaby, BC
Everland Parks
Burnaby, BC
Fastachi
Watertown, MA ... 800-466-3022
Flanigan Farms
Culver City, CA ... 800-525-0228
Foley's Chocolates & Candies
Richmond, BC ... 888-236-5397
Ford's Gourmet Foods
Raleigh, NC ... 800-446-0947
Frazier Nut Farms Inc
Waterford, CA ... 209-522-1406
Fresh Roasted Almond Company
Warren, MI ... 877-478-6887
Fun Factory
Milwaukee, WI ... 877-894-6767
G Scaccianoce & Co
Bronx, NY ... 718-991-4462
GAF Seelig Inc
Flushing, NY ... 718-899-5000
Georgia Nut Co
Skokie, IL ... 877-674-2993
Germack Pistachio Co
Detroit, MI ... 800-872-4006
Glennys
Brooklyn, NY ... 888-864-1243
GNS Foods
Arlington, TX ... 817-795-4671
Golden Kernel Pecan Co
Cameron, SC ... 803-823-2311
Goodart Candy Inc
Lubbock, TX ... 806-747-2600
Gourmet Nut
Brooklyn, NY ... 347-413-5180
Govadinas Fitness Foods
San Diego, CA ... 800-900-0108
Grace & I
Los Angeles, CA ... 800-584-1736
Great Northern Maple Products
Saint Honor, De Shenley, QC ... 418-485-7777
Guerra Nut Shelling Co Inc
Hollister, CA ... 831-637-4471
Gulf Pecan Company
Mobile, AL ... 251-661-2931
Gurley's Foods
Willmar, MN ... 800-426-7845
H&S Edible Products Corporation
Mount Vernon, NY ... 800-253-3364
Hammons Products Co
Stockton, MO ... 888-429-6887
Hampton Farms
Severn, NC ... 800-313-2748
Hancock Peanut Company
Courtland, VA ... 757-653-9351
Harris Farms Inc
Coalinga, CA ... 800-311-6211
Haven's Candies
Westbrook, ME ... 800-639-6309
Hawaiian King Candies
Honolulu, HI ... 800-570-1902
Hazelnut Growers Of Oregon
Cornelius, OR ... 800-273-4676
HempNut
Henderson, NV ... 707-576-7050
Hialeah Products Co
Hollywood, FL ... 800-923-3379
Hickory Farms
Maumee, OH ... 800-753-8558
Hickory Harvest Foods
Akron, OH ... 800-448-6887
HP Schmid
San Francisco, CA ... 415-765-5925
Hubbard Peanut Co Inc
Sedley, VA ... 800-889-7688
Idaho Candy Co
Boise, ID ... 800-898-6986
International Harvest Inc
Mt Vernon, NY ... 800-277-4268
International Service Group
Alpharetta, GA ... 770-518-0988
Island Snacks
Buena Park, CA ... 714-994-1228
Jardine Ranch
Paso Robles, CA ... 866-833-5050
Jason & Son Specialty Foods
Rancho Cordova, CA ... 800-810-9093
Jerry's Nut House
Denver, CO ... 303-861-2262
Jewel Date Co
Thermal, CA ... 760-399-4474
JF Braun & Sons Inc.
Elizabeth, NJ ... 800-997-7177
Jimbo's Jumbos Inc
Edenton, NC ... 800-334-4771
John B. Sanfilippo & Son
Elgin, IL ... 847-289-1800
Kalustyan
New York, NY ... 800-352-3451
King Nut Co
Solon, OH ... 800-860-5464
Koeze Company
Grand Rapids, MI ... 800-555-9688
Krema Nut Co
Columbus, OH ... 800-222-4132
Krispy Kernels
Quebec, QC ... 877-791-9986
L & S Packing Co
Farmingdale, NY ... 800-286-6487
LA Wholesale Produce Market
Los Angeles, CA ... 888-454-6887
Laurel Foods
Hillsboro, OR ... 503-692-3663
Leavitt Corp., The
Everett, MA ... 617-389-2600
Lee Seed Co
Inwood, IA ... 800-736-6530

Legendary Foods
Pasadena, CA 888-698-1708
Livingston Farmers Assn
Livingston, CA 209-394-7941
Lodi Nut Company
Lodi, CA 800-234-6887
Lou-Retta's Custom Chocolates
Buffalo, NY 716-833-7111
Lowery's Home Made Candies
Muncie, IN 800-541-3340
Mac Farms Of Hawaii Inc
Captain Cook, HI 808-328-2435
Majestic Foods
Huntington, NY 631-424-9444
Marantha Natural Foods
San Francisco, CA 866-972-6879
Mariani Nut Co
Winters, CA 530-795-1546
Mavuno Harvest
Philadelphia, PA
McCleskey Mills
Smithville, GA 229-846-2003
Merritt Pecan Co
Weston, GA 800-762-9152
Mezza
Lake Forest, IL 888-206-6054
Midwest Nut Co
Minneapolis, MN 800-328-5502
Mister Snacks Inc
Amherst, NY 800-333-6393
Monte Vista Farming Co
Denair, CA 209-874-1866
Moonlight Mixes LLC
Little Rock, AR 501-374-2244
Mound City Shelled Nut Inc
St Louis, MO 888-338-6887
Mount Franklin Foods
El Paso, TX 800-351-8178
Mrs. Dog's Products
Grand Rapids, MI 800-267-7364
Mrs. May's Naturals
Carson, CA 877-677-6297
Naraghi Group
Escalon, CA 209-579-5253
Natural Foods Inc
Toledo, OH 419-537-1711
Nature's Candy
Fredericksburg, TX 800-729-0085
Nature's Select Inc
Grand Rapids, MI 888-715-4321
Navarro Pecan Co
Corsicana, TX 800-333-9507
Naylor Candies Inc
Mt Wolf, PA 717-266-2706
New Century Snacks
City of Commerce, CA 800-688-6887
New Nissi Corp.
Paterson, NJ 973-278-4400
New Organics
Kenwood, CA 734-677-5570
Nichols Farms
Hanford, CA 559-584-6811
Nimeks Organics
Bethlehem, PA 610-997-0500
Northwest Chocolate Factory
Salem, OR 503-362-1340
Northwest Hazelnut Company
Hubbard, OR 503-982-8030
Nspired Natural Foods
Boulder, CO 800-434-4246
Nutorious LLC
Green Bay, WI 920-288-0483
Nuts + Nuts
Brooklyn, NY 347-513-9670
Nutty Bavarian
Sanford, FL 800-382-4788
Olam Spices
Fresno, CA 559-447-1390
Old Dominion Peanut Corp
Norfolk, VA 800-368-6887
Once Again Nut Butter
Nunda, NY 888-800-8075
Orangeburg Pecan Co
Orangeburg, SC 803-534-4277
Organic Planet
San Francisco, CA 415-765-5590
Original Herkimer Cheese
Ilion, NY 315-895-7428
Osage Pecan Co
Butler, MO 800-748-8305
Pacific Gold Marketing
Arlington, TX 817-795-4671
Panoche Creek Packing
Fresno, CA 559-449-1721
Papes Pecan House
Seguin, TX 888-688-7273
Patagonia Provisions
Sausalito, CA 888-221-8208
Patsy's Candy
Colorado Springs, CO 866-372-8797
Peanut Patch Gift Shop
Courtland, VA 800-544-0896
Peanut Roaster
Henderson, NC 800-445-1404
Pear's Coffee
Bellevue, NE 800-828-7688
Pease's Candy
Springfield, IL 217-523-3721
Pecan Deluxe Candy Co
Dallas, TX 800-733-3589
Picard Peanuts
Waterdown, ON 888-244-7688
Pippin Snack Pecans
Albany, GA 800-554-6887
Pleasant Grove Farms
Pleasant Grove, CA 916-655-3391
Porkie Company of Wisconsin
Cudahy, WI 800-333-2588
Priester's Pecans
Fort Deposit, AL 866-477-4736
Prince of Peace
Hayward, CA 800-732-2328
Producers Peanut Company
Suffolk, VA 800-847-5491
Quality Nut Co
Modesto, CA 209-526-3590
Ramos Orchards
Winters, CA 530-795-4748
Red River Foods Inc
Richmond, VA 804-320-1800
Reed Lang Farms
Rio Hondo, TX 956-748-2354
Regal Health Food
Chicago, IL 773-252-1044
Restaurant Data
Irvington, NY 800-346-9390
Richard Green Company
Indianapolis, IN 317-972-0941
Roberts Ferry Nut Co
Waterford, CA 209-874-3247
Ross-Smith Pecan Company
Thomasville, GA 800-841-5503
Rpac LLC
Los Banos, CA 209-826-0272
Sambets Cajun Deli
Austin, TX 800-472-6238
Santa Clara Nut Co
San Jose, CA 408-298-2425
Sante Specialty Foods
Santa Clara, CA 408-451-9585
Scala-Wisell International Inc.
Floral Park, NY 516-437-8600
Schermer Pecan Co
Glennville, GA 800-841-3403
Service Packing Company
Vancouver, BC 604-681-0264
Setton Farms
Terra Bella, CA 559-535-6050
Setton International Foods
Commack, NY 800-227-4397
Severn Peanut Co
Severn, NC 252-585-1744
Shields Date Garden
Indio, CA 800-414-2555
Shoei Foods USA Inc
Olivehurst, CA 530-237-1295
Sivetz Coffee
Corvallis, OR 541-753-9713
Snackerz
Commerce, CA 888-576-2253
Society Hill Snacks
Philadelphia, PA 800-595-0050
Sole Grano LLC
Fair Lawn, NJ 201-797-7100
Solnuts
Hudson, IA 800-648-3503
South Bend Chocolate Co
South Bend, IN 800-301-4961
South Georgia Pecan Co
Valdosta, GA 800-627-6630
South Valley Farms
Wasco, CA 661-391-9000
Southern Peanut Co Inc
Dublin, NC 800-330-3141
Southern Season
Chapel Hill, NC 877-929-7133
Southern Style Nuts
Denison, TX 903-463-3161
Specialty Commodities Inc
Fargo, ND 701-282-8222
Sprucewood Handmade Cookie Company
Warkworth, ON 877-632-1300
Squirrel Brand Company
McKinney, TX 800-624-8242
St Laurent Brothers
Bay City, MI 800-289-7688
Stahmann Farms
La Mesa, NM 575-526-2453
Star Snacks
Jersey City, NJ 888-782-7688
Stone Mountain Pecan Co
Monroe, GA 800-633-6887
Sugai Kona Coffee
Holualoa, HI 808-322-7717
Sun Empire Foods
Kerman, CA 800-252-4786
Sun-Maid Growers of California
Kingsburg, CA 559-896-8000
Sunny South Pecan Company
Statesboro, GA 800-764-3687
Sunnyland Farms
Albany, GA 800-999-2488
Sunray Food Products Corporation
Bronx, NY 718-548-2255
Sunridge Farms
Royal Oaks, CA 831-786-7000
Sunridge Farms Inc
Salinas, CA 831-755-1530
Sunshine Nut Company
Lewes, DE 210-732-9460
SunWest Foods, Inc.
Davis, CA 530-758-8550
Superior Nut & Candy
Chicago, IL 800-843-2238
Superior Nut Company
Cambridge, MA 800-251-6060
Superior Pecans
Eufaula, AL 800-628-2350
Swerseys Chocolate
Brooklyn, NY 718-497-8800
T M Duche Nut Co
Orland, CA 530-865-5511
Tejon Ranch Co
Lebec, CA 661-248-3000
Terri Lynn Inc
Elgin, IL 800-323-0775
Thanasi Foods LLC
Boulder, CO 866-558-7379
The Kroger Co.
Murray, KY 800-632-6900
The Peanut Butter Shop of Williamsburg
Toano, VA 800-831-1828
Thunderbird Real Food Bar
Austin, TX 512-383-8334
Timber Crest Farms
Healdsburg, CA 888-766-4233
To Your Health Sprouted Flour Co., Inc.
Floyd, VA 540-283-9589
Todd's
Vernon, CA 800-938-6337
Torn & Glasser
Los Angeles, CA 800-282-6887
Torn Ranch
Novato, CA 707-796-7800
Tracy Luckey Pecans
Harlem, GA 800-476-4796
Treehouse Farms
Elgin, AZ 559-757-5020
Trophy Nut Co
Tipp City, OH 800-219-9004
Tropical Foods
Charlotte, NC 800-438-4470
Tropical Foods
Lithia Springs, GA 800-544-3762
Tropical Nut & Fruit Co
Orlando, FL 800-749-8869
Tucker Pecan Co
Montgomery, AL 800-239-6540
Twenty First Century Snacks
Ronkonkoma, NY 800-975-2883
UTZ Quality Foods Inc.
Hanover, PA 800-367-7629
Vending Nut Co
Fort Worth, TX 800-429-9260
Virginia & Spanish Peanut Co
Providence, RI 800-673-3562

Virginia Diner Inc
Wakefield, VA....................888-823-4637
Warner Candy
El Paso, TX....................847-928-7200
Warrell Corp
Camp Hill, PA....................800-233-7082
Waymouth Farms Inc
Minneapolis, MN....................800-527-0094
Weaver Nut Co. Inc.
Ephrata, PA....................800-473-2688
Westnut
Cornelius, OR....................800-382-5339
Whaley Pecan Co Inc
Troy, AL....................800-824-6827
Whitley Peanut Factory Inc
Hayes, VA....................800-470-2244
Willamette Valley Walnuts
McMinnville, OR....................503-472-3215
Willmar Cookie & Nut Company
Willmar, MN....................800-426-7845
Wisconsin Cheeseman
Madison, WI....................800-693-0834
Wolfies Roasted Nut Co
Findlay, OH....................419-423-1355
Wonderful Pistachios & Almonds
Lost Hills, CA....................661-797-6500
Young Pecan
Las Cruces, NM....................575-524-4321
Young Pecan, Inc.
Florence, SC....................800-729-6003
Zenobia Co
Bronx, NY....................866-936-6242
Zuccaro Produce
Columbia Heights, MN....................612-333-1122

Almonds

AgStandard Smoked Almonds
Los Angeles, CA
Alldrin Brothers
Ballico, CA....................209-667-1600
Almond Brothers
Pheonix, AZ....................602-955-0909
American Almond Products Co
Brooklyn, NY....................800-825-6663
American Key Food Products Inc
Closter, NJ....................877-263-7539
Baldwin-Minkler Farms
Orland, CA....................530-865-8080
Barcelona Nut Co
Baltimore, MD....................800-296-6887
Bavarian Nut Co
Buffalo, NY....................716-810-6887
Bedemco Inc
White Plains, NY....................914-683-1119
Bobalu Nuts
CA....................805-223-0919
Buchanan Hollow Nut Co
Le Grand, CA....................800-532-1500
Cache Creek Foods LLC
Woodland, CA....................530-662-1764
Cal-Grown Nut Company
Hughson, CA....................209-883-4081
California Almond Packers
Modesto, CA....................209-549-8262
California Independent Almond Growers
Merced, CA....................209-667-4855
Capay Canyon Ranch
Esparto, CA....................530-662-2372
Capco Enterprises
East Hanover, NJ....................800-252-1011
Charles H Baldwin & Sons
West Stockbridge, MA....................413-232-7785
Chico Nut Company
Chico, CA....................530-891-1493
Chocolate Moon
Asheville, NC....................800-723-1236
Commodities Marketing Inc
Clarksburg, NJ....................732-516-0700
Creative Snacks Co LLC
Greensboro, NC....................336-668-4151
Del Rio Nut Company
Livingston, CA....................209-394-7945
Durey-Libby Edible Nuts
Carlstadt, NJ....................800-332-6887
Equal Exchange Inc
West Bridgewater, MA....................774-776-7400
Erba Food Products
Brooklyn, NY....................718-272-7700
Fastachi
Watertown, MA....................800-466-3022
Foley's Chocolates & Candies
Richmond, BC....................888-236-5397
Frazier Nut Farms Inc
Waterford, CA....................209-522-1406
Fresh Roasted Almond Company
Warren, MI....................877-478-6887
G Scaccianoce & Co
Bronx, NY....................718-991-4462
Gourmet Nut
Brooklyn, NY....................347-413-5180
Harris Farms Inc
Coalinga, CA....................800-311-6211
Healing Home Foods
Pound Ridge, NY....................914-764-1303
Hialeah Products Co
Hollywood, FL....................800-923-3379
Hughson Nut Inc
Hughson, CA....................209-883-0403
Jardine Ranch
Paso Robles, CA....................866-833-5050
Jasmine Vineyards, Inc.
Delano, CA....................661-792-2141
Jerry's Nut House
Denver, CO....................303-861-2262
John B. Sanfilippo & Son
Elgin, IL....................847-289-1800
Krema Nut Co
Columbus, OH....................800-222-4132
Legendary Foods
Pasadena, CA....................888-698-1708
Livingston Farmers Assn
Livingston, CA....................209-394-7941
Lodi Nut Company
Lodi, CA....................800-234-6887
Lou-Retta's Custom Chocolates
Buffalo, NY....................716-833-7111
Maisie Jane's California Sunshine
Chico, CA....................530-899-7909
Mariani Nut Co
Winters, CA....................530-795-1546
Monte Vista Farming Co
Denair, CA....................209-874-1866
Naraghi Group
Escalon, CA....................209-579-5253
Navitas Naturals
Novato, CA....................888-645-4282
Nichols Farms
Hanford, CA....................559-584-6811
NOW Foods
Bloomingdale, IL....................888-669-3663
Nunes Farms Marketing
Gustine, CA....................209-862-3033
Nut Factory
Spokane Valley, WA....................888-239-5288
Nuts About You
Los Angeles, CA
Nutty Bavarian
Sanford, FL....................800-382-4788
Olomomo Nut Company
Boulder, CO....................877-923-6888
Omega Nutrition
Bellingham, WA....................800-661-3529
Once Again Nut Butter
Nunda, NY....................888-800-8075
Organic Planet
San Francisco, CA....................415-765-5590
Osage Pecan Co
Butler, MO....................800-748-8305
P R Farms Inc
Clovis, CA....................559-299-0201
Pacific Gold Marketing
Arlington, TX....................817-795-4671
Panoche Creek Packing
Fresno, CA....................559-449-1721
Patterson Vegetable Company
Patterson, CA....................209-892-2611
Pearl Crop
Stockton, CA....................209-808-7575
Pleasant Grove Farms
Pleasant Grove, CA....................916-655-3391
Primex International Trading
Los Angeles, CA....................310-410-7100
Q's Nuts
Somerville, MA....................617-764-3741
Ramos Orchards
Winters, CA....................530-795-4748
Red River Foods Inc
Richmond, VA....................804-320-1800
Roberts Ferry Nut Co
Waterford, CA....................209-874-3247
Rotteveel Orchards
Dixon, CA....................707-678-1495
Rpac LLC
Los Banos, CA....................209-826-0272
Select Harvest USA
Turlock, CA....................209-668-2471
Service Packing Company
Vancouver, BC....................604-681-0264
Setton International Foods
Commack, NY....................800-227-4397
Simple Foods
Tonawanda, NY....................800-234-8850
South Valley Farms
Wasco, CA....................661-391-9000
Southern Style Nuts
Denison, TX....................903-463-3161
Sunridge Farms
Royal Oaks, CA....................831-786-7000
SunWest Foods, Inc.
Davis, CA....................530-758-8550
T M Duche Nut Co
Orland, CA....................530-865-5511
Tejon Ranch Co
Lebec, CA....................661-248-3000
Terri Lynn Inc
Elgin, IL....................800-323-0775
The Mapled Nut Co.
Morrisville, VT....................800-726-4661
Timber Crest Farms
Healdsburg, CA....................888-766-4233
To Your Health Sprouted Flour Co., Inc.
Floyd, VA....................540-283-9589
Treehouse Farms
Elgin, AZ....................559-757-5020
Unique Ingredients LLC
Gold Canyon, AZ....................480-983-2498
Weaver Nut Co. Inc.
Ephrata, PA....................800-473-2688
Whitley Peanut Factory Inc
Hayes, VA....................800-470-2244
Wild Things Snacks
Seattle, WA....................720-231-9196
Wolfies Roasted Nut Co
Findlay, OH....................419-423-1355
Wonderful Pistachios & Almonds
Lost Hills, CA....................661-797-6500

Salted

Cache Creek Foods LLC
Woodland, CA....................530-662-1764
Hialeah Products Co
Hollywood, FL....................800-923-3379
NOW Foods
Bloomingdale, IL....................888-669-3663
Setton International Foods
Commack, NY....................800-227-4397
Terri Lynn Inc
Elgin, IL....................800-323-0775

Brazil

American Almond Products Co
Brooklyn, NY....................800-825-6663
Bedemco Inc
White Plains, NY....................914-683-1119
Cache Creek Foods LLC
Woodland, CA....................530-662-1764
Durey-Libby Edible Nuts
Carlstadt, NJ....................800-332-6887
Hialeah Products Co
Hollywood, FL....................800-923-3379
LA Wholesale Produce Market
Los Angeles, CA....................888-454-6887
NOW Foods
Bloomingdale, IL....................888-669-3663
Setton International Foods
Commack, NY....................800-227-4397
Terri Lynn Inc
Elgin, IL....................800-323-0775
Weaver Nut Co. Inc.
Ephrata, PA....................800-473-2688

Cashews

American Almond Products Co
Brooklyn, NY....................800-825-6663
American Key Food Products Inc
Closter, NJ....................877-263-7539
Bavarian Nut Co
Buffalo, NY....................716-810-6887
Bedemco Inc
White Plains, NY....................914-683-1119
Cache Creek Foods LLC
Woodland, CA....................530-662-1764
California Fruit & Nut
Gustine, CA....................888-747-8224

Commodities Marketing Inc
Clarksburg, NJ 732-516-0700
Dan-D Foods Ltd
Richmond, BC 800-633-4788
Durey-Libby Edible Nuts
Carlstadt, NJ 800-332-6887
Earth Circle Organics
Auburn, CA. 877-922-3663
Equal Exchange Inc
West Bridgewater, MA 774-776-7400
Fastachi
Watertown, MA. 800-466-3022
Fresh Roasted Almond Company
Warren, MI 877-478-6887
Germack Pistachio Co
Detroit, MI 800-872-4006
Gourmet Nut
Brooklyn, NY 347-413-5180
Healing Home Foods
Pound Ridge, NY 914-764-1303
Hialeah Products Co
Hollywood, FL 800-923-3379
Jerry's Nut House
Denver, CO 303-861-2262
John B. Sanfilippo & Son
Elgin, IL 847-289-1800
Karma Nuts
Dublin, CA 925-961-5491
Koeze Company
Grand Rapids, MI 800-555-9688
Krema Nut Co
Columbus, OH 800-222-4132
LA Wholesale Produce Market
Los Angeles, CA. 888-454-6887
Landies Candies Co
Buffalo, NY. 800-955-2634
Lou-Retta's Custom Chocolates
Buffalo, NY. 716-833-7111
Marantha Natural Foods
San Francisco, CA 866-972-6879
Maxwell's Gourmet Food
Raleigh, NC 800-952-6887
Navitas Naturals
Novato, CA. 888-645-4282
Naylor Candies Inc
Mt Wolf, PA 717-266-2706
New Organics
Kenwood, CA 734-677-5570
NOW Foods
Bloomingdale, IL 888-669-3663
Nut Factory
Spokane Valley, WA 888-239-5288
Nuts & Stems
Rosharon, TX 281-464-6887
Nutty Bavarian
Sanford, FL. 800-382-4788
Olomomo Nut Company
Boulder, CO 877-923-6888
Once Again Nut Butter
Nunda, NY 888-800-8075
Organic Planet
San Francisco, CA 415-765-5590
Osage Pecan Co
Butler, MO 800-748-8305
Pacific Gold Marketing
Arlington, TX. 817-795-4671
Q's Nuts
Somerville, MA 617-764-3741
Restaurant Data
Irvington, NY 800-346-9390
Setton International Foods
Commack, NY 800-227-4397
Southern Style Nuts
Denison, TX 903-463-3161
Sunfood
El Cajon, CA. 888-729-3663
Sunray Food Products Corporation
Bronx, NY. 718-548-2255
Sunridge Farms
Royal Oaks, CA 831-786-7000
Terri Lynn Inc
Elgin, IL 800-323-0775
The Mapled Nut Co.
Morrisville, VT. 800-726-4661
To Your Health Sprouted Flour Co., Inc.
Floyd, VA 540-283-9589
Tropical Foods
Lithia Springs, GA 800-544-3762
Weaver Nut Co. Inc.
Ephrata, PA 800-473-2688
Wolfies Roasted Nut Co
Findlay, OH. 419-423-1355

Chestnuts

Adkin & Son Associated Food Products
South Haven, MI. 269-637-7450

Coated

Golden Kernel Pecan Co
Cameron, SC. 803-823-2311
Wolfies Roasted Nut Co
Findlay, OH. 419-423-1355

Chocolate

Bazzini Holdings LLC
Allentown, PA. 610-366-1606
Bissinger's Handcrafted Chocolatier
St. Louis, MO 314-615-2400
Jerry's Nut House
Denver, CO 303-861-2262
Lowery's Home Made Candies
Muncie, IN 800-541-3340
Osage Pecan Co
Butler, MO 800-748-8305
Ripple Brand Collective
Congers, NY 845-353-1251
Schermer Pecan Co
Glennville, GA 800-841-3403
Weaver Nut Co. Inc.
Ephrata, PA 800-473-2688

Yogurt

GKI Foods
Brighton, MI 248-486-0055
Jerry's Nut House
Denver, CO 303-861-2262
Setton International Foods
Commack, NY 800-227-4397
Terri Lynn Inc
Elgin, IL 800-323-0775

Filberts

American Almond Products Co
Brooklyn, NY 800-825-6663
Cache Creek Foods LLC
Woodland, CA. 530-662-1764
Commodities Marketing Inc
Clarksburg, NJ 732-516-0700
Durey-Libby Edible Nuts
Carlstadt, NJ 800-332-6887
Erba Food Products
Brooklyn, NY 718-272-7700
Germack Pistachio Co
Detroit, MI 800-872-4006
Hialeah Products Co
Hollywood, FL 800-923-3379
Jerry's Nut House
Denver, CO 303-861-2262
Krema Nut Co
Columbus, OH 800-222-4132
Nut Factory
Spokane Valley, WA 888-239-5288
Organic Planet
San Francisco, CA 415-765-5590
Setton International Foods
Commack, NY 800-227-4397
Terri Lynn Inc
Elgin, IL 800-323-0775
Weaver Nut Co. Inc.
Ephrata, PA 800-473-2688

Glazed & Coated

Arway Confections Inc
Chicago, IL 800-695-0612
Bazzini Holdings LLC
Allentown, PA. 610-366-1606
Betty Lou's
McMinnville, OR 800-242-5205
Bissinger's Handcrafted Chocolatier
St. Louis, MO 314-615-2400
Cache Creek Foods LLC
Woodland, CA. 530-662-1764
Cheese Straws & More
Monroe, LA. 800-997-1921
Chocolate Moon
Asheville, NC 800-723-1236
Crown Candy Corp
Macon, GA 800-241-3529
Dillon Candy Co
Boston, GA 800-382-8338
Farr Candy Company
Idaho Falls, ID 208-522-8215
Foley's Chocolates & Candies
Richmond, BC 888-236-5397
G Scaccianoce & Co
Bronx, NY. 718-991-4462
GKI Foods
Brighton, MI 248-486-0055
Golden Kernel Pecan Co
Cameron, SC 803-823-2311
Goodart Candy Inc
Lubbock, TX. 806-747-2600
Haven's Candies
Westbrook, ME 800-639-6309
Jason & Son Specialty Foods
Rancho Cordova, CA 800-810-9093
Jerry's Nut House
Denver, CO 303-861-2262
Kay Foods Co
Detroit, MI 313-393-1100
King Nut Co
Solon, OH 800-860-5464
Knudsen Candy
Hayward, CA 800-736-6887
Layman Distributing
Salem, VA 800-237-1319
Lowery's Home Made Candies
Muncie, IN 800-541-3340
Mac Farms Of Hawaii Inc
Captain Cook, HI 808-328-2435
Marich Confectionery
Hollister, CA. 800-624-7055
Matangos Candies
Harrisburg, PA 717-234-0882
Midwest Nut Co
Minneapolis, MN 800-328-5502
Moore's Candies
Baltimore, MD 410-836-8840
Mrs Annie's Peanut Patch
Floresville, TX 830-393-7845
Muth's Candy Store
Louisville, KY 502-582-2639
Nature's Candy
Fredericksburg, TX. 800-729-0085
Naylor Candies Inc
Mt Wolf, PA 717-266-2706
Northwest Chocolate Factory
Salem, OR. 503-362-1340
Nuts About You
Los Angeles, CA
Nutty Bavarian
Sanford, FL. 800-382-4788
Old Dominion Peanut Corp
Norfolk, VA. 800-368-6887
Pippin Snack Pecans
Albany, GA. 800-554-6887
Popcorn Connection
North Hollywood, CA 800-852-2676
Priester's Pecans
Fort Deposit, AL. 866-477-4736
Prince of Peace
Hayward, CA 800-732-2328
Setton International Foods
Commack, NY 800-227-4397
Southern Style Nuts
Denison, TX 903-463-3161
St Laurent Brothers
Bay City, MI. 800-289-7688
Superior Nut & Candy
Chicago, IL 800-843-2238
Terri Lynn Inc
Elgin, IL 800-323-0775
Tom & Sally's Handmade Chocolates
Brattleboro, VT. 800-827-0800
Tonex
Wallington, NJ 973-773-5135
Tropical Nut Fruit & Bulk Cndy
Lithia Springs, GA 800-544-3762
Warrell Corp
Camp Hill, PA. 844-234-3217
Waymouth Farms Inc
Minneapolis, MN 800-527-0094
Weaver Nut Co. Inc.
Ephrata, PA 800-473-2688
Webb's Candy
Davenport, FL. 800-289-9322
Whitley Peanut Factory Inc
Hayes, VA. 800-470-2244
Wolfies Roasted Nut Co
Findlay, OH. 419-423-1355

Hazelnuts

Balsu
Bay Harbour Islands, FL. 305-993-5045

Bedemco Inc
White Plains, NY 914-683-1119
Cache Creek Foods LLC
Woodland, CA. 530-662-1764
Commodities Marketing Inc
Clarksburg, NJ 732-516-0700
Fancy's Candy's
Rougemont, NC 888-403-2629
Fastachi
Watertown, MA. 800-466-3022
Hazelnut Growers Of Oregon
Cornelius, OR 800-273-4676
Hazy Grove Nuts
Portland, OR 800-574-6887
Hialeah Products Co
Hollywood, FL 800-923-3379
Jerry's Nut House
Denver, CO 303-861-2262
Krema Nut Co
Columbus, OH 800-222-4132
LA Wholesale Produce Market
Los Angeles, CA. 888-454-6887
Northwest Chocolate Factory
Salem, OR. 503-362-1340
Northwest Hazelnut Company
Hubbard, OR. 503-982-8030
Omega Nutrition
Bellingham, WA 800-661-3529
Organic Planet
San Francisco, CA 415-765-5590
Setton International Foods
Commack, NY 800-227-4397
Terri Lynn Inc
Elgin, IL 800-323-0775
Westnut
Cornelius, OR 800-382-5339

Macadamia

American Key Food Products Inc
Closter, NJ. 877-263-7539
Bedemco Inc
White Plains, NY 914-683-1119
Cache Creek Foods LLC
Woodland, CA. 530-662-1764
Durey-Libby Edible Nuts
Carlstadt, NJ 800-332-6887
Hawaiian Host Inc
Honolulu, HI. 888-414-4678
Hawaiian Sun Products
Honolulu, HI. 808-845-3211
Hialeah Products Co
Hollywood, FL 800-923-3379
Island Princess
Honolulu, HI. 866-872-8601
Jerry's Nut House
Denver, CO. 303-861-2262
Koeze Company
Grand Rapids, MI. 800-555-9688
Legendary Foods
Pasadena, CA 888-698-1708
Lodi Nut Company
Lodi, CA 800-234-6887
Mac Farms Of Hawaii Inc
Captain Cook, HI 808-328-2435
Menehune Mac
Honolulu, HI. 808-841-3344
NOW Foods
Bloomingdale, IL 888-669-3663
Organic Planet
San Francisco, CA 415-765-5590
Prince of Peace
Hayward, CA 800-732-2328
Royal Hawaiian Orchards LP
Dana Point, CA. 949-661-6304
Setton International Foods
Commack, NY 800-227-4397
Sugai Kona Coffee
Holualoa, HI 808-322-7717
Terri Lynn Inc
Elgin, IL 800-323-0775

Mixed Nuts

Bavarian Nut Co
Buffalo, NY. 716-810-6887
Bazzini Holdings LLC
Allentown, PA. 610-366-1606
Cibo Vita
Totowa, NJ 862-238-8020
Crazy Jerrys Inc Kahuna-Sauces
Woodstock, GA. 800-347-2823
Gopal's Healthfoods
Sidney, TX 866-646-7257
Gourmet Nut
Brooklyn, NY 347-413-5180
Jerry's Nut House
Denver, CO 303-861-2262
Moonlight Mixes LLC
Little Rock, AR. 501-374-2244
Nichols Farms
Hanford, CA 559-584-6811
Osage Pecan Co
Butler, MO 800-748-8305
Sunridge Farms
Royal Oaks, CA 831-786-7000
Swerseys Chocolate
Brooklyn, NY 718-497-8800
The Mapled Nut Co.
Morrisville, VT. 800-726-4661
Wisconsin Cheeseman
Madison, WI 800-693-0834

Nut Meats

American Almond Products Co
Brooklyn, NY 800-825-6663
Baldwin-Minkler Farms
Orland, CA 530-865-8080
Cache Creek Foods LLC
Woodland, CA. 530-662-1764
Durey-Libby Edible Nuts
Carlstadt, NJ 800-332-6887
Hammons Products Co
Stockton, MO 888-429-6887
Jerry's Nut House
Denver, CO. 303-861-2262
King Nut Co
Solon, OH 800-860-5464
Mid Valley Nut Co
Hughson, CA 209-883-4491
Mother Earth Enterprises
New York, NY 866-436-7688
Service Packing Company
Vancouver, BC 604-681-0264
Setton International Foods
Commack, NY 800-227-4397
Superior Nut & Candy
Chicago, IL 800-843-2238
Superior Pecans
Eufaula, AL. 800-628-2350
Terri Lynn Inc
Elgin, IL 800-323-0775
Waymouth Farms Inc
Minneapolis, MN 800-527-0094
Whaley Pecan Co Inc
Troy, AL 800-824-6827
Willamette Valley Walnuts
McMinnville, OR 503-472-3215
Young Pecan, Inc.
Florence, SC 800-729-6003

Nut Products

Georgia Nut Co
Skokie, IL 877-674-2993
NutRaw Foods
Delano, CA
Nuts 'N More
Providence, RI 844-413-2344
Royal Hawaiian Orchards LP
Dana Point, CA. 949-661-6304
Two Moms In The Raw
Longmont, CO 720-221-8555
Wisconsin Cheeseman
Madison, WI 800-693-0834

Peanuts

Barcelona Nut Co
Baltimore, MD 800-296-6887
Bavarian Nut Co
Buffalo, NY. 716-810-6887
Belmont Peanuts-Southampton
Capron, VA 434-658-4613
Berson Peanuts
Opp, AL 334-493-0655
E.F. Lane & Son
Oakland, CA 510-569-8980
Feridies
Courtland, VA. 866-732-6883
Hampton Farms
Severn, NC 800-313-2748
Hardy Farms
Hawkinsville, GA. 888-368-6887
Jerry's Nut House
Denver, CO 303-861-2262
Kameda USA Inc.
Torrance, CA. 310-944-9639
Koeze Company
Grand Rapids, MI 800-555-9688
Krema Nut Co
Columbus, OH 800-222-4132
New Organics
Kenwood, CA 734-677-5570
Osage Pecan Co
Butler, MO 800-748-8305
Peanut Corporation of America
Lynchburg, VA 434-384-7098
Peanut Processors Inc
Dublin, NC 800-330-3141
Peanut Shop
Toano, VA. 800-637-3268
Q's Nuts
Somerville, MA 617-764-3741
Queensway Foods Company
Burlingame, CA 650-871-7770
Royal Oak Peanuts
Drewryville, VA 800-608-4590
Setton International Foods
Commack, NY 800-227-4397
Southern Peanut Co Inc
Dublin, NC 800-330-3141
Sunfood
El Cajon, CA. 888-729-3663
Terri Lynn Inc
Elgin, IL 800-323-0775
Virginia Diner Inc
Wakefield, VA. 888-823-4637
Wolfies Roasted Nut Co
Findlay, OH. 419-423-1355

Granulated

American Almond Products Co
Brooklyn, NY 800-825-6663
American Key Food Products Inc
Closter, NJ. 877-263-7539
Cajun Creole Products Inc
New Iberia, LA 800-946-8688
Hialeah Products Co
Hollywood, FL 800-923-3379
Producers Peanut Company
Suffolk, VA. 800-847-5491
Terri Lynn Inc
Elgin, IL 800-323-0775

Raw

American Almond Products Co
Brooklyn, NY 800-825-6663
Birdsong Corp.
Suffolk, VA. 757-539-3456
Cajun Creole Products Inc
New Iberia, LA 800-946-8688
Hialeah Products Co
Hollywood, FL 800-923-3379
Krema Nut Co
Columbus, OH 800-222-4132
LA Wholesale Produce Market
Los Angeles, CA. 888-454-6887
St Laurent Brothers
Bay City, MI 800-289-7688

Raw & Shelled

American Key Food Products Inc
Closter, NJ. 877-263-7539
Cajun Creole Products Inc
New Iberia, LA 800-946-8688
Feridies
Courtland, VA. 866-732-6883
Hialeah Products Co
Hollywood, FL 800-923-3379
King Nut Co
Solon, OH 800-860-5464
McCleskey Mills
Smithville, GA 229-846-2003
New Organics
Kenwood, CA 734-677-5570
Royal Oak Peanuts
Drewryville, VA 800-608-4590
Setton International Foods
Commack, NY 800-227-4397
Southern Peanut Co Inc
Dublin, NC 800-330-3141
Terri Lynn Inc
Elgin, IL 800-323-0775

Roasted

American Almond Products Co
Brooklyn, NY 800-825-6663
C J Dannemiller Co
Norton, OH 800-624-8671
Cajun Creole Products Inc
New Iberia, LA 800-946-8688
E.F. Lane & Son
Oakland, CA 510-569-8980
King Nut Co
Solon, OH 800-860-5464
Naylor Candies Inc
Mt Wolf, PA 717-266-2706
Queensway Foods Company
Burlingame, CA 650-871-7770
Southern Peanut Co Inc
Dublin, NC 800-330-3141
St Laurent Brothers
Bay City, MI 800-289-7688

Salted

Cajun Creole Products Inc
New Iberia, LA 800-946-8688
Durey-Libby Edible Nuts
Carlstadt, NJ 800-332-6887
Feridies
Courtland, VA 866-732-6883
Hialeah Products Co
Hollywood, FL 800-923-3379
Koeze Company
Grand Rapids, MI 800-555-9688
LA Wholesale Produce Market
Los Angeles, CA 888-454-6887
New Organics
Kenwood, CA 734-677-5570
Setton International Foods
Commack, NY 800-227-4397
Southern Peanut Co Inc
Dublin, NC 800-330-3141
St Laurent Brothers
Bay City, MI 800-289-7688
Terri Lynn Inc
Elgin, IL 800-323-0775
Virginia & Spanish Peanut Co
Providence, RI 800-673-3562
Virginia Diner Inc
Wakefield, VA 888-823-4637

Pecan

American Key Food Products Inc
Closter, NJ 877-263-7539
Aunt Aggie De's Pralines
Sinton, TX 800-333-9354
Bavarian Nut Co
Buffalo, NY 716-810-6887
Bedemco Inc
White Plains, NY 914-683-1119
Cache Creek Foods LLC
Woodland, CA 530-662-1764
Carolina Cracker
Garner, NC 919-779-6899
Carolyn's Gourmet
Concord, MA 800-656-2940
Cheese Straws & More
Monroe, LA 800-997-1921
Claxton Bakery Inc
Claxton, GA 800-841-4211
Country Estate Pecans
Goldwaite, TX 800-473-2267
Durey-Libby Edible Nuts
Carlstadt, NJ 800-332-6887
Elegant Edibles
Houston, TX 800-227-3226
Fancy's Candy's
Rougemont, NC 888-403-2629
Fresh Roasted Almond Company
Warren, MI 877-478-6887
George's Candy Shop Inc
Mobile, AL 800-633-1306
Golden Harvest Pecans
Cairo, GA 800-597-0968
Golden Kernel Pecan Co
Cameron, SC 803-823-2311
Green Valley Pecan Company
Sahuarita, AZ 520-791-2880
Gulf Pecan Company
Mobile, AL 251-661-2931
Healing Home Foods
Pound Ridge, NY 914-764-1303
Hialeah Products Co
Hollywood, FL 800-923-3379
Indianola Pecan House Inc
Indianola, MS 800-541-6252
Jewel Date Co
Thermal, CA 760-399-4474
John B. Sanfilippo & Son
Elgin, IL 847-289-1800
Koeze Company
Grand Rapids, MI 800-555-9688
Krema Nut Co
Columbus, OH 800-222-4132
Landies Candies Co
Buffalo, NY 800-955-2634
Lane Southern Orchards
Fort Valley, GA 800-277-3224
Lou-Retta's Custom Chocolates
Buffalo, NY 716-833-7111
Maxwell's Gourmet Food
Raleigh, NC 800-952-6887
Merritt Pecan Co
Weston, GA 800-762-9152
Mingo River Pecan Company
Florence, SC 800-440-6442
Mountain States Pecan
Roswell, NM 575-623-2216
Navarro Pecan Co
Corsicana, TX 800-333-9507
New Organics
Kenwood, CA 734-677-5570
NOW Foods
Bloomingdale, IL 888-669-3663
Nutty Bavarian
Sanford, FL 800-382-4788
Orangeburg Pecan Co
Orangeburg, SC 803-534-4277
Osage Pecan Co
Butler, MO 800-748-8305
Papes Pecan House
Seguin, TX 888-688-7273
Pippin Snack Pecans
Albany, GA 800-554-6887
Priester's Pecans
Fort Deposit, AL 866-477-4736
Q's Nuts
Somerville, MA 617-764-3741
Reed Lang Farms
Rio Hondo, TX 956-748-2354
Ross-Smith Pecan Company
Thomasville, GA 800-841-5503
Schermer Pecan Co
Glennville, GA 800-841-3403
Setton International Foods
Commack, NY 800-227-4397
South Georgia Pecan Co
Valdosta, GA 800-627-6630
Southern Style Nuts
Denison, TX 903-463-3161
Stahmann Farms
La Mesa, NM 575-526-2453
Stone Mountain Pecan Co
Monroe, GA 800-633-6887
Sunny South Pecan Company
Statesboro, GA 800-764-3687
Sunnyland Farms
Albany, GA 800-999-2488
Sunridge Farms
Royal Oaks, CA 831-786-7000
SunWest Foods, Inc.
Davis, CA 530-758-8550
Superior Pecans
Eufaula, AL 800-628-2350
Terri Lynn Inc
Elgin, IL 800-323-0775
The Mapled Nut Co.
Morrisville, VT 800-726-4661
Tracy Luckey Pecans
Harlem, GA 800-476-4796
Tucker Pecan Co
Montgomery, AL 800-239-6540
Weaver Nut Co. Inc.
Ephrata, PA 800-473-2688
Whaley Pecan Co Inc
Troy, AL 800-824-6827
Whitley Peanut Factory Inc
Hayes, VA 800-470-2244
Wolfies Roasted Nut Co
Findlay, OH 419-423-1355
Young Pecan
Las Cruces, NM 575-524-4321
Young Pecan, Inc.
Florence, SC 800-729-6003

Salted

Golden Kernel Pecan Co
Cameron, SC 803-823-2311
Schermer Pecan Co
Glennville, GA 800-841-3403
Stahmann Farms
La Mesa, NM 575-526-2453

Pignolias

Bedemco Inc
White Plains, NY 914-683-1119
Castella Imports Inc
Brentwood, NY 631-231-5500
L & S Packing Co
Farmingdale, NY 800-286-6487

Pine

American Importing Co.
Minneapolis, MN 855-273-0466
American Key Food Products Inc
Closter, NJ 877-263-7539
Durey-Libby Edible Nuts
Carlstadt, NJ 800-332-6887
Grapevine Trading Company
Santa Rosa, CA 800-469-6478
Hialeah Products Co
Hollywood, FL 800-923-3379
NOW Foods
Bloomingdale, IL 888-669-3663
Setton International Foods
Commack, NY 800-227-4397
Sunridge Farms
Royal Oaks, CA 831-786-7000
Terri Lynn Inc
Elgin, IL 800-323-0775

Pistachio

Arizona Pistachio Company
Tucson, AZ 800-333-8575
Barcelona Nut Co
Baltimore, MD 800-296-6887
Bavarian Nut Co
Buffalo, NY 716-810-6887
Bedemco Inc
White Plains, NY 914-683-1119
Buchanan Hollow Nut Co
Le Grand, CA 800-532-1500
Cache Creek Foods LLC
Woodland, CA 530-662-1764
California Fruit & Nut
Gustine, CA 888-747-8224
Capco Enterprises
East Hanover, NJ 800-252-1011
Commodities Marketing Inc
Clarksburg, NJ 732-516-0700
Durey-Libby Edible Nuts
Carlstadt, NJ 800-332-6887
Fastachi
Watertown, MA 800-466-3022
Germack Pistachio Co
Detroit, MI 800-872-4006
Healing Home Foods
Pound Ridge, NY 914-764-1303
Hialeah Products Co
Hollywood, FL 800-923-3379
Jardine Ranch
Paso Robles, CA 866-833-5050
Kalustyan
New York, NY 800-352-3451
Keenan Farms
Kettleman City, CA 559-945-1400
Koeze Company
Grand Rapids, MI 800-555-9688
Krema Nut Co
Columbus, OH 800-222-4132
LA Wholesale Produce Market
Los Angeles, CA 888-454-6887
Leona's Restaurante
Chimayo, NM 888-561-5569
Maisie Jane's California Sunshine
Chico, CA 530-899-7909
Mrs. Dog's Products
Grand Rapids, MI 800-267-7364
Naraghi Group
Escalon, CA 209-579-5253
Nichols Farms
Hanford, CA 559-584-6811
NOW Foods
Bloomingdale, IL 888-669-3663

Nunes Farms Marketing
Gustine, CA 209-862-3033
NutRaw Foods
Delano, CA
Nuts & Stems
Rosharon, TX 281-464-6887
Omega Nutrition
Bellingham, WA 800-661-3529
Organic Planet
San Francisco, CA 415-765-5590
Pacific Gold Marketing
Arlington, TX 817-795-4671
Primex International Trading
Los Angeles, CA 310-410-7100
Santa Barbara Pistachio Co
Maricopa, CA 800-896-1044
Setton Farms
Terra Bella, CA 559-535-6050
Setton International Foods
Commack, NY 800-227-4397
Setton Pistachio
Terra Bella, CA 559-535-6050
South Valley Farms
Wasco, CA 661-391-9000
Sunfood
El Cajon, CA 888-729-3663
Sunray Food Products Corporation
Bronx, NY 718-548-2255
Sunridge Farms
Royal Oaks, CA 831-786-7000
SunWest Foods, Inc.
Davis, CA 530-758-8550
Tejon Ranch Co
Lebec, CA 661-248-3000
Terri Lynn Inc
Elgin, IL 800-323-0775
Timber Crest Farms
Healdsburg, CA 888-766-4233
Weaver Nut Co. Inc.
Ephrata, PA 800-473-2688
Wonderful Pistachios & Almonds
Lost Hills, CA 661-797-6500

Pralines (See also Confectionery)

Aunt Aggie De's Pralines
Sinton, TX 800-333-9354
B & B Pecan Processors
Turkey, NC 866-328-7322
Blueberry Store
Grand Junction, MI 877-654-2400
Creole Delicacies Gourmet Shop
New Orleans, LA 504-525-9508
Landies Candies Co
Buffalo, NY 800-955-2634
Pecan Deluxe Candy Co
Dallas, TX 800-733-3589

Roasted

Adkin & Son Associated Food Products
South Haven, MI 269-637-7450
American Almond Products Co
Brooklyn, NY 800-825-6663
Baker Candy Company
Snohomish, WA 425-422-6331
C J Dannemiller Co
Norton, OH 800-624-8671
Dakota Gourmet
Wahpeton, ND 800-727-6663
GrandyOats
Hiram, ME 207-935-7415
Osage Pecan Co
Butler, MO 800-748-8305
Pacific Grain & Foods
Fresno, CA 559-276-2580
Q's Nuts
Somerville, MA 617-764-3741
Solnuts
Hudson, IA 800-648-3503
Superior Nut & Candy
Chicago, IL 800-843-2238
Tropical Foods
Charlotte, NC 800-438-4470
Tropical Nut & Fruit Co
Orlando, FL 800-749-8869
Willmar Cookie & Nut Company
Willmar, MN 800-426-7845

Shelled

Alldrin Brothers
Ballico, CA 209-667-1600
Country Estate Pecans
Goldwaite, TX 800-473-2267
Crain Walnut Shelling, Inc.
Los Molinos, CA 530-529-1585
Frazier Nut Farms Inc
Waterford, CA 209-522-1406
Jerry's Nut House
Denver, CO 303-861-2262
Pippin Snack Pecans
Albany, GA 800-554-6887
Ross-Smith Pecan Company
Thomasville, GA 800-841-5503
Santa Clara Nut Co
San Jose, CA 408-298-2425
Tracy Luckey Pecans
Harlem, GA 800-476-4796
Whaley Pecan Co Inc
Troy, AL 800-824-6827

Soy

Almost Nuts
Denmark, WI 920-915-0152
American Importing Co.
Minneapolis, MN 855-273-0466
Amport Foods
St. Paul, MN 800-236-1119
Don't Go Nuts
Salida, CO 855-666-8826
Hialeah Products Co
Hollywood, FL 800-923-3379
Just Tomatoes
Westley, CA 800-537-1985
Lee Seed Co
Inwood, IA 800-736-6530
Nature's Select Inc
Grand Rapids, MI 888-715-4321
New Organics
Kenwood, CA 734-677-5570
Solnuts
Hudson, IA 800-648-3503
Sunridge Farms
Royal Oaks, CA 831-786-7000

Walnuts

American Almond Products Co
Brooklyn, NY 800-825-6663
Bavarian Nut Co
Buffalo, NY 716-810-6887
Bedemco Inc
White Plains, NY 914-683-1119
Berberian Nut Company
Chico, CA 530-981-4900
Byrd's Pecans
Butler, MO 866-679-5583
California Walnut Co
Los Molinos, CA 530-527-2616
Crain Ranch
Los Molinos, CA 530-527-1077
Crain Walnut Shelling, Inc.
Los Molinos, CA 530-529-1585
Durey-Libby Edible Nuts
Carlstadt, NJ 800-332-6887
Erba Food Products
Brooklyn, NY 718-272-7700
Frazier Nut Farms Inc
Waterford, CA 209-522-1406
Fresh Roasted Almond Company
Warren, MI 877-478-6887
Guerra Nut Shelling Co Inc
Hollister, CA 831-637-4471
Hammons Products Co
Stockton, MO 888-429-6887
Healing Home Foods
Pound Ridge, NY 914-764-1303
Hialeah Products Co
Hollywood, FL 800-923-3379
Jerry's Nut House
Denver, CO 303-861-2262
John B. Sanfilippo & Son
Elgin, IL 847-289-1800
Lodi Nut Company
Lodi, CA 800-234-6887
Mariani Nut Co
Winters, CA 530-795-1546
Mid Valley Nut Co
Hughson, CA 209-883-4491
Naraghi Group
Escalon, CA 209-579-5253
New Organics
Kenwood, CA 734-677-5570
NOW Foods
Bloomingdale, IL 888-669-3663
Nut Factory
Spokane Valley, WA 888-239-5288
Osage Pecan Co
Butler, MO 800-748-8305
Pearl Crop
Stockton, CA 209-808-7575
Primex International Trading
Los Angeles, CA 310-410-7100
Quality Nut Co
Modesto, CA 209-526-3590
Ramos Orchards
Winters, CA 530-795-4748
Santa Clara Nut Co
San Jose, CA 408-298-2425
Service Packing Company
Vancouver, BC 604-681-0264
Sunridge Farms
Royal Oaks, CA 831-786-7000
SunWest Foods, Inc.
Davis, CA 530-758-8550
Tejon Ranch Co
Lebec, CA 661-248-3000
The Mapled Nut Co.
Morrisville, VT 800-726-4661
Weaver Nut Co. Inc.
Ephrata, PA 800-473-2688
Wilbur Packing Company
Yuba City, CA 530-671-4911
Willamette Valley Walnuts
McMinnville, OR 503-472-3215

Black

American Key Food Products Inc
Closter, NJ 877-263-7539
Cache Creek Foods LLC
Woodland, CA 530-662-1764
Frazier Nut Farms Inc
Waterford, CA 209-522-1406
Guerra Nut Shelling Co Inc
Hollister, CA 831-637-4471
Hammons Black Walnuts
Stockton, MO 888-429-6887
Hammons Products Co
Stockton, MO 888-429-6887
Hialeah Products Co
Hollywood, FL 800-923-3379
John B. Sanfilippo & Son
Elgin, IL 847-289-1800
Lodi Nut Company
Lodi, CA 800-234-6887
New Organics
Kenwood, CA 734-677-5570
Organic Planet
San Francisco, CA 415-765-5590
Setton International Foods
Commack, NY 800-227-4397
Terri Lynn Inc
Elgin, IL 800-323-0775
Unique Ingredients LLC
Gold Canyon, AZ 480-983-2498

Oils, Shortening & Fats

General

Akicorp
N Miami Beach, FL 786-426-5750
American Hawaiian Soy Company
Honolulu, HI..................... 800-841-8435
Austrian Trade Commission
New York, NY 212-421-5250
Capa Di Roma Inc
East Hartford, CT 860-282-0298
Central Soyfoods
Lawrence, KS 785-312-8698
CHS Inc.
Inver Grove Hts., MN.............. 800-328-6539
Denomega Pure Health
Brighton, CO..................... 479-181-2845
DuPont Pioneer
Johnston, IA 515-535-3200
First Food International
Linden, NJ....................... 908-862-5558
Fruit of the Land Products
Thornhill, ON 877-311-5267
Frutech International Corp
Pasadena, CA 626-844-0200
G. Banis Company
Wilmington, DE 617-516-9092
Gourmet Mondiale
Ste-Catherine, QC................. 450-638-6380
Heartland Flax
Valley City, ND.................. 866-599-3529
I Heart Olive Oil
Ft Lauderdale, FL 954-607-1539
International Food Products
Fenton, MO..................... 800-227-8427
Maywood International Sales
Sante Fe, NM 805-500-5500
NAR
Nashua, NH..................... 603-888-5420
Nealanders Food Ingredients
Mississauga, ON.................. 800-263-1939
Oasis Food Co
Hillside, NJ 800-275-0477
Oilseeds International LTD
San Francisco, CA 415-956-7251
Pacific Soybean & Grain
San Mateo, CA 650-525-0500
Patrick Cudahy LLC
Cudahy, WI...................... 800-486-6900
Pondini Imports
Somerset, NJ.................... 732-545-1255
Rallis Whole Foods
Windsor, ON..................... 519-796-9712
SIGCO Sun Products
Breckenridge, MN 800-654-4145
Spectrum Foods Inc
Springfield, IL................... 217-528-5301
Sutter Buttes Olive Oil
Sutter, CA 530-763-7921
Wegmans Food Markets Inc.
Rochester, NY.................... 800-934-6267
Western Pacific Oils, Inc.
Los Angeles, CA.................. 213-232-5117

Fats & Lard

Beef

Fatworks
Niwot, CO

Chicken

All-States Quality Foods
Charles City, IA 800-247-4195

Dried

Agri-Dairy Products
Purchase, NY 914-697-9580

Frozen

Clofine Dairy Products Inc
Linwood, NJ..................... 609-653-1000

Liquid

Agri-Dairy Products
Purchase, NY 914-697-9580
Clofine Dairy Products Inc
Linwood, NJ 609-653-1000

Powdered

Clofine Dairy Products Inc
Linwood, NJ 609-653-1000

Hydrogenated

AG Processing Inc
Omaha, NE 800-247-1345
Agri-Dairy Products
Purchase, NY 914-697-9580
Baker Commodities Inc
Vernon, CA 800-427-0696
Blossom Farm Products
Ridgewood, NJ 800-729-1818
Bunge Loders Croklaan
Channahon, IL 800-621-4710
National Starch Food Innovation
Bridgewater, NJ 800-743-6343
Theriault's Abattoir Inc
Hamlin, ME...................... 207-868-3344
Werling & Sons Slaughterhouse
Burkettsville, OH 937-338-3281

Lard

CanAmera Foods
Edmonton, AL.................... 780-447-6960
Fatworks
Niwot, CO
OLLI Salumeria Americana
Oceanside, CA 877-655-4937

Margarine

Allfresh Food Products
Evanston, IL 847-869-3100
Bunge Canada
Oakville, ON..................... 905-825-7900
Butterball Farms
Grand Rapids, MI 888-828-8837
CanAmera Foods
Edmonton, AL.................... 780-447-6960
CHS Inc.
Inver Grove Hts., MN.............. 800-328-6539
GFA Brands Inc
Paramus, NJ 201-568-9300
Hamersmith, Inc.
Miami, FL....................... 305-685-7451
JE Bergeron & Sons
Bromptonville, QC 800-567-2798
Keller's Creamery
Kansas City, MO.................. 800-535-5371
Land O'Lakes Inc
Arden Hills, MN.................. 800-328-9680
Madison Foods
Saint Paul, MN 651-265-8212
Oasis Food Co
Hillside, NJ 800-275-0477
Parmalat Canada
Toronto, ON 800-563-1515
Protient
St Paul, MN...................... 800-328-9680
Richardson International
Winnipeg, MB.................... 866-217-6211
Schneider's Dairy Inc
Pittsburgh, PA................... 412-881-3525
Sommer Maid Creamery Inc
Pipersville, PA................... 215-345-6160
Ventura Foods LLC
Brea, CA 800-421-6257
Western Pacific Oils, Inc.
Los Angeles, CA.................. 213-232-5117

Oils

AAK
Louisville, KY 800-622-3055
Abitec Corp
Columbus, OH 800-555-1255
ACH Food Co Inc
Oakbrook Terrace, IL 630-586-3740
Agrusa
Leonia, NJ...................... 201-592-5950
Akicorp
N Miami Beach, FL 786-426-5750
Alexander International (USA)
Brightwaters, NY 866-965-0143
AM Todd Co
Kalamazoo, MI 269-343-2603
AME Nutrition
Dublin, OH 614-766-3638
American Hawaiian Soy Company
Honolulu, HI..................... 800-841-8435
American Mercantile Corp
Memphis, TN 901-454-1900
American Yeast
Memphis, TN 866-920-9885
Archer Daniels Midland Company
Decatur, IL 217-424-5200
Archer Daniels Midland Company
Chicago, IL 312-634-8100
Arista Industries Inc
Wilton, CT 800-255-6457
Aroma Vera
Los Angeles, CA.................. 800-669-9514
Aroma-Life
Encino, CA 818-905-7761
Arro Corp
Hodgkins, IL..................... 877-929-2776
Astral Extracts
Syosset, NY...................... 516-496-2505
Au Printemps Gourmet
Saint-Jerome, QC 800-438-6676
Avatar Corp
University Park, IL 800-255-3181
Beta Pure Foods
Santa Cruz, CA................... 831-685-6565
Bioriginal Food and Science Corp
Saskatoon, SK.................... 306-975-1166
Bittersweet Herb Farm
Shelburne Falls, MA............... 800-456-1599
Brand Aromatics Inc
Lakewood, NJ.................... 800-363-2080
Bridgewell Resources LLC
Clackamas, OR 800-481-3557
Buonitalia
New York, NY 212-633-9090
C W Resources Inc
New Britain, CT 860-229-7700
C.F. Sauer Co.
Richmond, VA.................... 888-723-0052
California Balsamic Inc
Ukiah, CA....................... 888-644-5127
California Olive Oil Council
Berkeley, CA..................... 888-718-9830
CanAmera Foods
Edmonton, AL.................... 780-447-6960
Catania Oils
Ayer, MA........................ 978-772-7900
Centflor Manufacturing Co
New York, NY 212-246-8307
CHS Inc.
Inver Grove Hts., MN.............. 800-328-6539
Classic Flavors & Fragrances
New York, NY 212-777-0004
Clic International Inc
Laval, QC 450-669-2663
Coast Packing Co
Vernon, CA...................... 323-277-7700
Coldani Olive Ranch LLC
Lodi, CA 209-334-0527
Colonna Brothers Inc
North Bergen, NJ 201-864-1115
Columbus Vegetable Oils
Des Plaines, IL 847-257-8920
Consumer Guild Foods Inc
Toledo, OH 419-726-3406
Critelli Olive Oil
Fairfield, CA..................... 800-865-4836
Delicae Gourmet
Tarpon Springs, FL................ 800-942-2502
Denomega Pure Health
Brighton, CO..................... 479-181-2845
Dow AgroSciences Canada
Calgary, AB...................... 403-735-8800
DuPont Nutrition & Biosciences
New Century, KS 913-764-8100
Erba Food Products
Brooklyn, NY 718-272-7700
Everland Foods
Burnaby, BC

Everland Parks
Burnaby, BC
Flavorchem Corp
Downers Grove, IL 800-435-2867
Follmer Development, Inc
Newbury Park, CA 805-498-4531
Fratelli Mantova
Naperville, IL 630-904-0002
Freed, Teller & Freed
South San Francisco, CA 800-370-7371
Frutech International Corp
Pasadena, CA 626-844-0200
GFA Brands Inc
Paramus, NJ 201-568-9300
Golden Eagle Olive Products
Porterville, CA 559-784-3468
Good Food Inc
Honey Brook, PA 800-327-4406
Grapevine Trading Company
Santa Rosa, CA 800-469-6478
Hamersmith, Inc.
Miami, FL 305-685-7451
Hartsville Oil Mill
Darlington, SC 843-393-1501
Herbal Products & Development
Aptos, CA 831-688-8706
Hybco USA
Los Angeles, CA 323-269-3111
II Sisters
Moss Beach, CA 800-282-7058
Ingredion Inc.
Westchester, IL 800-713-0208
International Food Products
Fenton, MO 800-227-8427
International Home Foods
Parsippany, NJ 973-359-9920
J.M. Smucker Co.
Orrville, OH 888-550-9555
Kalsec
Kalamazoo, MI 800-323-9320
Kalustyan
New York, NY 800-352-3451
Kevala
Dallas, TX 877-379-1179
La Tourangelle
Berkeley, CA 866-688-6457
Lebermuth Company
South Bend, IN 800-648-1123
Lesley Elizabeth Inc
Lapeer, MI 800-684-3300
Liberty Natural Products Inc
Oregon City, OR 800-289-8427
Liberty Vegetable Oil Co
Santa Fe Springs, CA 562-921-3567
Loriva Culinary Oils
San Francisco, CA 866-972-6879
Love You Foods
Flagstaff, AZ 844-693-2662
Lowcountry Produce
Raleigh, NC 800-935-2792
Lucini Italia Company
San Francisco, CA 888-558-2464
Marathon Packing Corp
San Leandro, CA 510-895-2000
Marnap Industries
Buffalo, NY 716-897-1220
Maywood International Sales
Sante Fe, NM 805-500-5500
Mc Glaughlin Oil Co
Columbus, OH 614-231-2518
Medallion International Inc
Pompton Plains, NJ 973-616-3401
Monini North America
Shelton, CT 203-513-2685
Mosby Winery
Buellton, CA 800-706-6729
Mott's LLP
Plano, TX 800-426-4891
Mountain High Organics
New Milford, CT 860-210-7805
Mountainbrook of Vermont
Jeffersonville, VT 802-644-1988
Napa Valley Kitchens
Napa, CA 707-254-3700
National Flavors
Kalamazoo, MI 800-525-2431
Natural Value
Sacramento, CA 916-836-3561
Nature Most Laboratories
Middletown, CT 800-234-2112
Nealanders Food Ingredients
Mississauga, ON 800-263-1939

Newport Flavours & Fragrances
Orange, CA 714-744-3700
Nexcel Natural Ingredients
Springfield, IL 217-391-0091
North American Enterprises
Tucson, AZ 800-817-8666
Nutiva
Richmond, CA 800-993-4367
O Olive Oil
Petaluma, CA 888-827-7148
Odell's
Reno, NV 800-635-0436
Omega Protein
Reedville, VA 804-453-6262
Organic Gemini
Brooklyn, NY 347-662-2900
Pacifica Culinaria
Vista, CA 800-622-8880
Paradise Products Corporation
Boca Raton, FL 800-826-1235
Pastene Co LTD
Canton, MA 781-298-3397
Pastorelli Food Products
Chicago, IL 800-767-2829
Patsy's Italian Restaurant
New York, NY 212-247-3491
Pompeian Inc
Baltimore, MD 800-766-7342
Prairie Thyme LTD
Santa Fe, NM 800-869-0009
Proacec USA
Santa Monica, CA 310-996-7770
Pure Indian
Princeton Jct., NJ 877-588-4433
Purity Products
Plainview, NY 800-256-6102
Rising Sun Farms
Phoenix, OR 800-888-0795
Ron Son Foods Inc
Swedesboro, NJ 856-241-7333
Rosa Food Products
Philadelphia, PA 215-467-2214
S S Steiner Inc
New York, NY 212-838-8901
Salute Sante! Food & Wine
Napa, CA 707-251-3900
Santa Barbara Pistachio Co
Maricopa, CA 800-896-1044
Santini Foods
San Lorenzo, CA 800-835-6888
Sieco USA Corporation
Houston, TX 713-464-1726
Silver Palate Kitchens
Cresskill, NJ 201-568-0110
Source Food Technology
Durham, NC 866-277-3849
Sovena USA Inc
Rome, NY 315-797-7070
Sparboe Foods Corp
New Hampton, IA 641-394-3040
Sparrow Lane
Ceres, CA 866-515-2477
Stauber Performance Ingrdients
Fullerton, CA 888-441-4233
Sun Grove Foods Inc
Passaic, NJ 973-574-1110
Sutter Buttes Olive Oil
Sutter, CA 530-763-7921
Tait Farm Foods
Centre Hall, PA 800-787-2716
Tee Pee Olives, Inc.
Rye, NY 800-431-1529
The Coromega Company
Carlsbad, CA 877-275-3725
The Dow Chemical Company
Midland, MI 800-331-6451
Tropical Foods
Charlotte, NC 800-438-4470
Veronica Foods Inc
Oakland, CA 800-370-5554
Vitamins
Chicago, IL 312-861-0700
Viterra, Inc
Regina, SK 866-647-4090
Wine Country Kitchens
Napa, CA 866-767-9463
Wing Nien Food
Hayward, CA 510-487-8877

Almond

AG Processing Inc
Omaha, NE 800-247-1345

Aroma-Life
Encino, CA 818-905-7761
Astral Extracts
Syosset, NY 516-496-2505
Embassy Flavours Ltd.
Brampton, ON 800-334-3371
Emerling International Foods
Buffalo, NY 716-833-7381
Flora Inc
Lynden, WA 800-446-2110
Gold Coast Ingredients
Commerce, CA 800-352-8673
K L Keller Imports
Oakland, CA 510-839-7890
Pokonobe Industries
Santa Monica, CA 310-392-1259
Tri-State Ingredients
Mason, OH 800-622-1050
Universal Preservachem Inc
Somerset, NJ 732-568-1266

Anise or Aniseed

Astral Extracts
Syosset, NY 516-496-2505
Embassy Flavours Ltd.
Brampton, ON 800-334-3371
Emerling International Foods
Buffalo, NY 716-833-7381
Medallion International Inc
Pompton Plains, NJ 973-616-3401
Tri-State Ingredients
Mason, OH 800-622-1050

Avocado

Arista Industries Inc
Wilton, CT 800-255-6457
Chosen Foods, Inc.
San Diego, CA 877-674-2244
Everland Foods
Burnaby, BC
Primal Kitchen
Oxnard, CA 888-774-6259
Primal Nutrition
Malibu, CA 888-774-6259

Bean

Avatar Corp
University Park, IL 800-255-3181
Tri-State Ingredients
Mason, OH 800-622-1050

Black Pepper

Medallion International Inc
Pompton Plains, NJ 973-616-3401
Tri-State Ingredients
Mason, OH 800-622-1050

Borage

Omega Nutrition
Bellingham, WA 800-661-3529

Canola

ACH Food Co Inc
Oakbrook Terrace, IL 630-586-3740
AG Processing Inc
Omaha, NE 800-247-1345
American Vegetable Oils
Commerce, CA 800-728-8089
Avatar Corp
University Park, IL 800-255-3181
Bunge Canada
Oakville, ON 905-825-7900
California Olive Oil Council
Berkeley, CA 888-718-9830
DuPont Pioneer
Johnston, IA 515-535-5954
Emerling International Foods
Buffalo, NY 716-833-7381
Flora Inc
Lynden, WA 800-446-2110
Gama Products
Miami, FL 786-235-1515
Good Food Inc
Honey Brook, PA 800-327-4406
Intermountain Canola Cargill
Minneapolis, MN 800-822-6652
International Foodcraft Corp
Linden, NJ 800-875-9393

Loriva Culinary Oils
San Francisco, CA 866-972-6879
Maywood International Sales
Sante Fe, NM 805-500-5500
Montana Specialty Mills LLC
Great Falls, MT.................. 800-332-2024
Nealanders Food Ingredients
Mississauga, ON.................. 800-263-1939
New Organics
Kenwood, CA...................... 734-677-5570
Nexcel Natural Ingredients
Springfield, IL.................. 217-391-0091
Odell's
Reno, NV 800-635-0436
Omega Nutrition
Bellingham, WA 800-661-3529
Pokonobe Industries
Santa Monica, CA................. 310-392-1259
Riceland Foods Inc.
Stuttgart, AR.................... 855-742-3929
Richardson International
Winnipeg, MB..................... 866-217-6211
Tri-State Ingredients
Mason, OH 800-622-1050
Universal Preservachem Inc
Somerset, NJ..................... 732-568-1266

Caraway

Emerling International Foods
Buffalo, NY...................... 716-833-7381
Medallion International Inc
Pompton Plains, NJ............... 973-616-3401
Tri-State Ingredients
Mason, OH 800-622-1050

Cardamom

Medallion International Inc
Pompton Plains, NJ............... 973-616-3401
Tri-State Ingredients
Mason, OH 800-622-1050

Cassia

Embassy Flavours Ltd.
Brampton, ON..................... 800-334-3371
Tri-State Ingredients
Mason, OH 800-622-1050

Castor

Arista Industries Inc
Wilton, CT 800-255-6457
Avatar Corp
University Park, IL.............. 800-255-3181
Heritage Books & Gifts
Virginia Beach, VA............... 800-862-2923
Leatex Chemical Co
Philadelphia, PA 215-739-2000
Salem Oil & Grease Company
Salem, MA 978-745-0585
Tri-State Ingredients
Mason, OH 800-622-1050

Celery

Tri-State Ingredients
Mason, OH 800-622-1050

Cinnamon - Leaf & Bark

Medallion International Inc
Pompton Plains, NJ............... 973-616-3401
Tri-State Ingredients
Mason, OH 800-622-1050

Citrus

Astral Extracts
Syosset, NY...................... 516-496-2505
Boyajian LLC
Canton, MA 800-965-0665
California Olive Oil Council
Berkeley, CA..................... 888-718-9830
Diana's Specialty Foods
Pingree Grove, IL 847-683-1200
Embassy Flavours Ltd.
Brampton, ON..................... 800-334-3371
Emerling International Foods
Buffalo, NY...................... 716-833-7381
Frutech International Corp
Pasadena, CA 626-844-0200
Gold Coast Ingredients
Commerce, CA..................... 800-352-8673
Louis Dreyfus Company Citrus Inc
Winter Garden, FL 407-656-1000
Medallion International Inc
Pompton Plains, NJ............... 973-616-3401
Peace River Citrus Products
Vero Beach, FL................... 772-492-4050
Prime Ingredients Inc
Saddle Brook, NJ 888-791-6655
Robertet Flavors
Piscataway, NJ 732-981-8300
Tri-State Ingredients
Mason, OH 800-622-1050
Ungerer & Co
Lincoln Park, NJ................. 973-706-7381

Clove

Tri-State Ingredients
Mason, OH 800-622-1050

Coconut

Aak USA Inc
Newark, NJ....................... 973-344-1300
AG Processing Inc
Omaha, NE 800-247-1345
Avatar Corp
University Park, IL 800-255-3181
Blue Marble Brands
Providence, RI 888-534-0246
Clofine Dairy Products Inc
Linwood, NJ 609-653-1000
Emerling International Foods
Buffalo, NY...................... 716-833-7381
Everland Foods
Burnaby, BC
First Food International
Linden, NJ....................... 908-862-5558
GloryBee
Eugene, OR....................... 800-456-7923
Gold Coast Ingredients
Commerce, CA..................... 800-352-8673
Good Food Inc
Honey Brook, PA 800-327-4406
Kelapo
Tampa, FL........................ 800-230-5952
Maywood International Sales
Sante Fe, NM 805-500-5500
Odell's
Reno, NV 800-635-0436
Pokonobe Industries
Santa Monica, CA................. 310-392-1259
Pure Life Organic Foods
Las Vegas, NV 708-990-5817
RE Botanicals
Boulder, CO 303-214-2118
Sunfood
El Cajon, CA..................... 888-729-3663
Tri-State Ingredients
Mason, OH 800-622-1050
Tropical Link Canada Ltd.
Burnaby, BC...................... 778-379-3510
Universal Impex Corporation
Toronto, ON 416-743-7778
Western Pacific Oils, Inc.
Los Angeles, CA.................. 213-232-5117

Cod Liver

Jamieson Laboratories
Windsor, ON...................... 800-265-5088

Cooking

ACH Food Co Inc
Oakbrook Terrace, IL 630-586-3740
Agrusa
Leonia, NJ....................... 201-592-5950
Allfresh Food Products
Evanston, IL 847-869-3100
Arista Industries Inc
Wilton, CT 800-255-6457
Arro Corp
Hodgkins, IL..................... 877-929-2776
Avatar Corp
University Park, IL.............. 800-255-3181
Butter Buds Food Ingredients
Racine, WI....................... 800-426-1119
C&T Refinery
Minneapolis, MN 800-227-4455
California Oils Corp
Richmond, CA 800-225-6457
California Olive Oil Council
Berkeley, CA..................... 888-718-9830
Capital City Processors
Winchester, VA................... 800-473-2731
Coast Packing Co
Vernon, CA 323-277-7700
Colonna Brothers Inc
North Bergen, NJ 201-864-1115
Diana's Specialty Foods
Pingree Grove, IL................ 847-683-1200
Dipasa USA Inc
Brownsville, TX.................. 956-831-4072
Embassy Flavours Ltd.
Brampton, ON..................... 800-334-3371
Emerling International Foods
Buffalo, NY...................... 716-833-7381
Flora Inc
Lynden, WA....................... 800-446-2110
Follmer Development, Inc
Newbury Park, CA 805-498-4531
Gateway Food Products Co
Dupo, IL 877-220-1963
Good Food Inc
Honey Brook, PA 800-327-4406
Intermountain Canola Cargill
Minneapolis, MN 800-822-6652
Liberty Vegetable Oil Co
Santa Fe Springs, CA 562-921-3567
Loriva Culinary Oils
San Francisco, CA 866-972-6879
Louis Dreyfus Company Citrus Inc
Winter Garden, FL 407-656-1000
Marathon Packing Corp
San Leandro, CA.................. 510-895-2000
Marina Foods
Medley, FL....................... 786-888-0129
Morris J Golombeck Inc
Brooklyn, NY 718-284-3505
Mother Earth Enterprises
New York, NY 866-436-7688
Mott's LLP
Plano, TX 800-426-4891
Natural Oils International
Simi Valley, CA.................. 805-433-0160
Nick Sciabica & Sons
Modesto, CA...................... 800-551-9612
North American Enterprises
Tucson, AZ 800-817-8666
PAR-Way Tryson Co
St Clair, MO 636-629-4545
Pastorelli Food Products
Chicago, IL 800-767-2829
Pokonobe Industries
Santa Monica, CA................. 310-392-1259
Producers Cooperative Oil Mill
Oklahoma City, OK 405-232-7555
Progresso Quality Foods
Vineland, NJ 856-691-1565
Purity Products
Plainview, NY.................... 800-256-6102
Ron Son Foods Inc
Swedesboro, NJ 856-241-7333
Sovena USA Inc
Rome, NY......................... 315-797-7070
Spectrum Foods Inc
Springfield, IL.................. 217-528-5301
Thyme Garden Herb Co
Alsea, OR 800-482-4372
Tri-State Ingredients
Mason, OH 800-622-1050

Spray

ACH Food Co Inc
Oakbrook Terrace, IL 630-586-3740
Butter Buds Food Ingredients
Racine, WI....................... 800-426-1119
Follmer Development, Inc
Newbury Park, CA 805-498-4531
International Home Foods
Parsippany, NJ................... 973-359-9920
PAR-Way Tryson Co
St Clair, MO 636-629-4545

Coriander Seed

Tri-State Ingredients
Mason, OH 800-622-1050

Corn

ACH Food Co Inc
Oakbrook Terrace, IL 630-586-3740
AG Processing Inc
Omaha, NE 800-247-1345

Arro Corp
Hodgkins, IL 877-929-2776
Avatar Corp
University Park, IL 800-255-3181
Erba Food Products
Brooklyn, NY 718-272-7700
Gama Products
Miami, FL 786-235-1515
Good Food Inc
Honey Brook, PA 800-327-4406
Ingredion Inc.
Westchester, IL 800-713-0208
Maywood International Sales
Sante Fe, NM 805-500-5500
Nealanders Food Ingredients
Mississauga, ON 800-263-1939
Olde Tyme Food Corporation
East Longmeadow, MA 800-356-6533
Pacific Soybean & Grain
San Mateo, CA 650-525-0500
Pastorelli Food Products
Chicago, IL 800-767-2829
Pokonobe Industries
Santa Monica, CA 310-392-1259
Purity Products
Plainview, NY 800-256-6102
Riceland Foods Inc.
Stuttgart, AR 855-742-3929
Sovena USA Inc
Rome, NY 315-797-7070
Tri-State Ingredients
Mason, OH 800-622-1050
Universal Preservachem Inc
Somerset, NJ 732-568-1266

Cottonseed

AAK
Louisville, KY 800-622-3055
Aak USA Inc
Newark, NJ 973-344-1300
Abitec Corp
Columbus, OH 800 555 1255
AG Processing Inc
Omaha, NE 800-247-1345
Emerling International Foods
Buffalo, NY 716-833-7381
Good Food Inc
Honey Brook, PA 800-327-4406
Hartsville Oil Mill
Darlington, SC 843-393-1501
Maywood International Sales
Sante Fe, NM 805-500-5500
Nealanders Food Ingredients
Mississauga, ON 800-263-1939
Producers Cooperative Oil Mill
Oklahoma City, OK 405-232-7555
PYCO Industries Inc
Lubbock, TX 806-747-3434
Riceland Foods Inc.
Stuttgart, AR 855-742-3929
Southern Cotton Oil Co
Memphis, TN 901-452-3151
Stevenson-Cooper Inc
Philadelphia, PA 215-223-2600
Tri-State Ingredients
Mason, OH 800-622-1050

Dillweed

Tri-State Ingredients
Mason, OH 800-622-1050

Edible

Aak USA Inc
Newark, NJ 973-344-1300
Abitec Corp
Columbus, OH 800-555-1255
ACH Food Co Inc
Oakbrook Terrace, IL 630-586-3740
AG Processing Inc
Omaha, NE 800-247-1345
Agri-Dairy Products
Purchase, NY 914-697-9580
Agrusa
Leonia, NJ 201-592-5950
Allfresh Food Products
Evanston, IL 847-869-3100
Arista Industries Inc
Wilton, CT 800-255-6457
Arro Corp
Hodgkins, IL 877-929-2776
Avatar Corp
University Park, IL 800-255-3181
Barlean's Fisheries
Ferndale, WA 360-384-0325
Boyajian LLC
Canton, MA 800-965-0665
Bunge Loders Croklaan
Channahon, IL 800-621-4710
Butter Buds Food Ingredients
Racine, WI 800-426-1119
C P Vegetable Oil
Fort Lauderdale, FL 800-398-7154
California Oils Corp
Richmond, CA 800-225-6457
California Olive Oil Council
Berkeley, CA 888-718-9830
Capital City Processors
Winchester, VA 800-473-2731
Capitol Foods
Memphis, TN 662-781-9021
Colavita USA
Edison, NJ 888-265-2848
Colonna Brothers Inc
North Bergen, NJ 201-864-1115
Con Agra Snack Foods
Hamburg, IA 800-831-5818
Consumer Guild Foods Inc
Toledo, OH 419-726-3406
Dipasa USA Inc
Brownsville, TX 956-831-4072
Embassy Flavours Ltd.
Brampton, ON 800-334-3371
Emerling International Foods
Buffalo, NY 716-833-7381
Energen Products Inc
Norwalk, CA 800-423-8837
Erba Food Products
Brooklyn, NY 718-272-7700
Flora Inc
Lynden, WA 800-446-2110
Gama Products
Miami, FL 786-235-1515
Gateway Food Products Co
Dupo, IL 877-220-1963
Good Food Inc
Honey Brook, PA 800-327-4406
Grassland Dairy Products Inc
Greenwood, WI 800-428-8837
Herbal Products & Development
Aptos, CA 831-688-8706
Intermountain Canola Cargill
Minneapolis, MN 800-822-6652
John I. Haas
Washington, DC
Liberty Vegetable Oil Co
Santa Fe Springs, CA 562-921-3567
Loriva Culinary Oils
San Francisco, CA 866-972-6879
Louis Dreyfus Company Citrus Inc
Winter Garden, FL 407-656-1000
Marina Foods
Medley, FL 786-888-0129
Medallion International Inc
Pompton Plains, NJ 973-616-3401
Morris J Golombeck Inc
Brooklyn, NY 718-284-3505
Mother Earth Enterprises
New York, NY 866-436-7688
Natural Oils International
Simi Valley, CA 805-433-0160
New Organics
Kenwood, CA 734-677-5570
Nick Sciabica & Sons
Modesto, CA 800-551-9612
North American Enterprises
Tucson, AZ 800-817-8666
Oils Of Aloha
Waialua, HI 800-367-6010
Ottens Flavors
Philadelphia, PA 800-523-0767
Paradise Products Corporation
Boca Raton, FL 800-826-1235
Pastorelli Food Products
Chicago, IL 800-767-2829
Perdue Farms Inc.
Salisbury, MD 800-473-7383
Pokonobe Industries
Santa Monica, CA 310-392-1259
Pompeian Inc
Baltimore, MD 800-766-7342
Progresso Quality Foods
Vineland, NJ 856-691-1565
Purity Products
Plainview, NY 800-256-6102
Ron Son Foods Inc
Swedesboro, NJ 856-241-7333
Sessions Co Inc
Enterprise, AL 334-393-0200
Silver Palate Kitchens
Cresskill, NJ 201-568-0110
Sovena USA Inc
Rome, NY 315-797-7070
Stuart Hale Co
Chicago, IL 773-638-1800
Thyme Garden Herb Co
Alsea, OR 800-482-4372
Tri-State Ingredients
Mason, OH 800-622-1050
Tropical Foods
Charlotte, NC 800-438-4470
Universal Preservachem Inc
Somerset, NJ 732-568-1266
Veronica Foods Inc
Oakland, CA 800-370-5554

Essential

Allylix Inc
San Diego, CA 858-909-0595
AM Todd Co
Kalamazoo, MI 269-343-2603
American Mercantile Corp
Memphis, TN 901-454-1900
Aroma Vera
Los Angeles, CA 800-669-9514
Aroma-Life
Encino, CA 818-905-7761
Aromachem
Brooklyn, NY 718-497-4664
Avri Co Inc
Richmond, CA 800-883-9574
Bioriginal Food and Science Corp
Saskatoon, SK 306-975-1166
Blue California Co
Rancho Sta Marg, CA 949-459-2729
Centflor Manufacturing Co
New York, NY 212-246-8307
Classic Flavors & Fragrances
New York, NY 212-777-0004
Colin Ingram
Comptche, CA 707-937-1824
Embassy Flavours Ltd.
Brampton, ON 800-334-3371
Emerling International Foods
Buffalo, NY 716-833-7381
Essential Products of America
Tampa, FL 800-822-9698
Excellentia Intl.
Fairfield, NJ 737-749-9840
Flavor Sciences Inc
Lenoir, NC 800-535-2867
Flavorchem Corp
Downers Grove, IL 800-435-2867
Flavormatic Industries
Wappingers Falls, NY 845-297-9100
Global Botanical
Barrie, ON 705-733-2117
Green Turtle Bay Vitamin Company
Summit, NJ 800-887-8535
Greenwood Associates
Niles, IL 847-579-5500
GuruNanda
Buena Park, CA 866-421-0309
H B Taylor Co
Chicago, IL 773-254-4805
Healing Solutions
Phoenix, AZ 800-819-4098
Heritage Books & Gifts
Virginia Beach, VA 800-862-2923
Joseph Adams Corp
Valley City, OH 330-225-9135
Kalsec
Kalamazoo, MI 800-323-9320
Lebermuth Company
Mishawaka, IN 800-648-1123
Leeward Resources
Baltimore, MD 410-837-9003
Lemur International
Richmond, CA 510-620-9708
Loriva Culinary Oils
San Francisco, CA 866-972-6879
Maple Ridge Farms
Mosinee, WI 715-693-4346
Marnap Industries
Buffalo, NY 716-897-1220

Medallion International Inc
Pompton Plains, NJ................973-616-3401
Mother Earth Enterprises
New York, NY 866-436-7688
Native Scents
Taos, NM........................800-645-3471
Nature's Fusions
Provo, UT 801-872-9500
NOW Foods
Bloomingdale, IL 888-669-3663
Prova
Danvers, MA......................877-776-8287
Robertet Flavors
Piscataway, NJ 732-981-8300
Starwest Botanicals Inc
Sacramento, CA 800-800-4372
Synthite USA Inc.
Oak Park, IL 708-446-1716
Terra Flavors & Fragrances
New York, NY....................212-244-1181
Torre Products Co Inc
New York, NY 212-925-8989
Treatt USA Inc
Lakeland, FL......................863-668-9500
Tri-State Ingredients
Mason, OH 800-622-1050
Ungerer & Co
Lincoln Park, NJ 973-706-7381
Whole Herb Co
Sonoma, CA 707-935-1077

Natural

Jedwards International Inc
Braintree, MA.....................781-848-1473

Fish

Aker BioMarine Antarctic US, LLC.
Metuchen, NJ 732-917-4000
Daybrook Fisheries
New Orleans, LA 504-561-6163
Eckhart Corporation
Novato, CA.......................800-200-4201
J R Carlson Laboratories Inc
Arlington Heights, IL 888-234-5656
Jamieson Laboratories
Windsor, ON......................800-265-5088
Omega Pure
Irvine, CA........................562-429-3335
Scandinavian Laboratories
Belvidere, PA 866-623-2650
Tabco Enterprises
Pomona, CA 909-623-4565

Fruit

Arista Industries Inc
Wilton, CT 800-255-6457
Kurtz Orchards Farms
Niagra-on-the-Lake, ON............905-468-2937

Garlic

Astral Extracts
Syosset, NY.......................516-496-2505
California Olive Oil Council
Berkeley, CA......................888-718-9830
Diana's Specialty Foods
Pingree Grove, IL..................847-683-1200
Emerling International Foods
Buffalo, NY.......................716-833-7381
Halladay's Harvest Barn
Bellows Falls, VT..................802-463-3471
Lebermuth Company
Mishawaka, IN 800-648-1123
Loriva Culinary Oils
San Francisco, CA 866-972-6879
Prime Ingredients Inc
Saddle Brook, NJ 888-791-6655
Thyme Garden Herb Co
Alsea, OR 800-482-4372
Tri-State Ingredients
Mason, OH.......................800-622-1050
Vegetable Juices Inc
Chicago, IL.......................888-776-9752

Ginger

Astral Extracts
Syosset, NY.......................516-496-2505
Tri-State Ingredients
Mason, OH 800-622-1050
Ungerer & Co
Lincoln Park, NJ 973-706-7381

Grapefruit

Astral Extracts
Syosset, NY.......................516-496-2505
Emerling International Foods
Buffalo, NY.......................716-833-7381
Gold Coast Ingredients
Commerce, CA....................800-352-8673
Tri-State Ingredients
Mason, OH 800-622-1050

Grapeseed

AG Processing Inc
Omaha, NE 800-247-1345
Ameri-Kal Inc
Wichita Falls, TX 940-322-5400
Arista Industries Inc
Wilton, CT 800-255-6457
Cuisine Perel
Richmond, CA 800-887-3735
Diana's Specialty Foods
Pingree Grove, IL.................847-683-1200
Emerling International Foods
Buffalo, NY.......................716-833-7381
Food & Vine Inc.
Napa, CA.........................707-251-3900
GloryBee
Eugene, OR.......................800-456-7923
Lifestar Millennium
Sedona, AZ.......................877-422-4739
Pokonobe Industries
Santa Monica, CA.................310-392-1259
Queensway Foods Company
Burlingame, CA...................650-871-7770
Salute Sante! Food & Wine
Napa, CA.........................707-251-3900
Tabco Enterprises
Pomona, CA 909-623-4565
Tri-State Ingredients
Mason, OH 800-622-1050

Hazelnut

K L Keller Imports
Oakland, CA 510-839-7890
Loriva Culinary Oils
San Francisco, CA 866-972-6879
Tri-State Ingredients
Mason, OH 800-622-1050

Hemp Nut

Ananda Hemp
Cynthiana, KY
Foods Alive
Angola, IN........................260-488-4497
Herbal Products & Development
Aptos, CA 831-688-8706
Mother Earth Enterprises
New York, NY 866-436-7688
Tri-State Ingredients
Mason, OH 800-622-1050

Lemon

AG Processing Inc
Omaha, NE 800-247-1345
Astral Extracts
Syosset, NY.......................516-496-2505
Boyajian LLC
Canton, MA 800-965-0665
Citromax Flavors Inc
Carlstadt, NJ 201-933-8405
Diana's Specialty Foods
Pingree Grove, IL 847-683-1200
Embassy Flavours Ltd.
Brampton, ON.....................800-334-3371
Emerling International Foods
Buffalo, NY.......................716-833-7381
Gold Coast Ingredients
Commerce, CA....................800-352-8673
Prime Ingredients Inc
Saddle Brook, NJ 888-791-6655
Tri-State Ingredients
Mason, OH 800-622-1050
Ungerer & Co
Lincoln Park, NJ 973-706-7381

Lemon Grass

Emerling International Foods
Buffalo, NY.......................716-833-7381
Tri-State Ingredients
Mason, OH 800-622-1050

Lime

Astral Extracts
Syosset, NY.......................516-496-2505
Boyajian LLC
Canton, MA 800-965-0665
Emerling International Foods
Buffalo, NY.......................716-833-7381
Gold Coast Ingredients
Commerce, CA....................800-352-8673
Tri-State Ingredients
Mason, OH 800-622-1050
Ungerer & Co
Lincoln Park, NJ 973-706-7381

Mustard

Emerling International Foods
Buffalo, NY.......................716-833-7381
Montana Specialty Mills LLC
Great Falls, MT....................800-332-2024
Tri-State Ingredients
Mason, OH 800-622-1050

Nutmeg

Emerling International Foods
Buffalo, NY.......................716-833-7381
Tri-State Ingredients
Mason, OH 800-622-1050
Whole Herb Co
Sonoma, CA 707-935-1077

Olive

Acesur North America
Purchase, NY 914-925-0450
ACH Food Co Inc
Oakbrook Terrace, IL 630-586-3740
Advanced Bio Development
Piermont, NY 845-365-3838
AG Processing Inc
Omaha, NE 800-247-1345
Agrocan
Ville St Laurent, QC 877-247-6226
Agrusa
Leonia, NJ........................201-592-5950
Alba Foods, Inc
Stone Mountain, GA...............888-725-4605
Amira Nature Foods Ltd.
Irvine, CA........................949-852-4468
Amphora International
Lake Forest, CA 888-380-4808
Aralia Olive Oils
Cambridge, MA 877-585-9510
Arista Industries Inc
Wilton, CT 800-255-6457
Ariston Specialties
Bloomfield, CT....................860-224-7184
Arnabal International, Inc.
Tustin, CA........................714-665-9477
Athena Oil Inc
Astoria, NY.......................718-956-8893
Avatar Corp
University Park, IL 800-255-3181
B R Cohn Winery & Olive Oil Co
Glen Ellen, CA 800-330-4064
Bari Olive Oil Co
Dinuba, CA.......................877-638-3626
Bella Cucina
Atlanta, GA.......................866-350-9040
Bella Vista Farm
Lawton, OK.......................866-237-8526
Bozzano Olive Ranch
Stockton, CA......................209-451-3665
Bragg Live Food Products Inc
Goleta, CA 800-446-1990
California Coast Naturals
Santa Barbara, CA 805-685-2076
California Olive Growers
Fresno, CA 888-965-4837
California Olive Oil Council
Berkeley, CA......................888-718-9830
Calio Groves
Piedmont, CA 800-865-4836
Calivirgin Olive Oils
Lodi, CA..........................209-210-3142
Castella Imports Inc
Brentwood, NY....................631-231-5500
Chacewater Winery and Olive Mill
Kelseyville, CA....................707-279-2995
Chaparral Gardens
Atascadero, CA....................805-703-0829

Cibaria International	Riverside, CA	951-823-8490
Colavita USA	Edison, NJ	888-265-2848
Coldani Olive Ranch LLC	Lodi, CA	209-334-0527
Colonna Brothers Inc	North Bergen, NJ	201-864-1115
Corning Olive Oil Company	Corning, CA	530-824-5447
Creagri Inc	Hayward, CA	510-732-6478
Critelli Olive Oil	Fairfield, CA	800-865-4836
Diana's Specialty Foods	Pingree Grove, IL	847-683-1200
Emerling International Foods	Buffalo, NY	716-833-7381
Enzo Olive Oil Co.	Madera, CA	559-299-7278
Erba Food Products	Brooklyn, NY	718-272-7700
Extravagonzo Gourmet Foods	Boise, ID	208-639-2926
Fantis Foods Inc	Carlstadt, NJ	201-933-6200
Farmstead At Long Meadow Ranch	St Helena, CA	877-627-2645
Filippo Berio Brand	Lyndhurst, NJ	201-525-2900
Gaea North America LLC	Hollywood, FL	954-923-7723
GB Ratto International Grocery	Oakland, CA	800-325-3483
Golden Eagle Olive Products	Porterville, CA	559-784-3468
Good Food Inc	Honey Brook, PA	800-327-4406
Grapevine Trading Company	Santa Rosa, CA	800-469-6478
Holy Smoke LLC	Johns Island, SC	843-343-5581
Krinos Foods	Bronx, NY	718-729-9000
La Piccolina	Decatur, GA	800-626-1624
Laird & Company	Scobeyville, NJ	877-438-5247
Loriva Culinary Oils	San Francisco, CA	866-972-6879
Lucero Olive Oil Mfr	Corning, CA	530-824-2190
Lucero Olive Oil Mfr	Corning, CA	877-330-2190
Lucini Italia Company	San Francisco, CA	888-558-2464
M&H Erickson Ranch	Orland, CA	530-865-9587
Manassero Farms	Irvine, CA	949-554-5103
Mancini Packing Co	Zolfo Springs, FL	800-741-1778
Mancuso Cheese Co	Joliet, IL	815-722-2475
Marconi Italian Specialty Foods	Chicago, IL	312-421-0485
Marina Foods	Medley, FL	786-888-0129
Mario Camancho Foods	Plant City, FL	800-293-9783
McEvoy Ranch	Petaluma, CA	866-617-6779
Mosti Mondiale/Gourmet Mondiale	Ste-Catherine, QC	450-638-6380
Mountainbrook of Vermont	Jeffersonville, VT	802-644-1988
Nick Sciabica & Sons	Modesto, CA	800-551-9612
North American Enterprises	Tucson, AZ	800-817-8666
Oliva Verde USA	Raleigh, NC	919-846-9020
Olive Oil Factor	Waterbury, CT	475-235-2666
Olive Oil Source	Santa Ynez, CA	805-688-1014
Olivina. LLC	Livermore, CA	925-455-8710
Organic Olive Juice	New York, NY	
Organic Planet	San Francisco, CA	415-765-5590
P R Farms Inc	Clovis, CA	559-299-0201
Pacific Sun Olive Oil	Gerber, CA	530-385-1475
Paradise Products Corporation	Boca Raton, FL	800-826-1235
Pasolivo Willow Creek Olive Ranch	Paso Robles, CA	805-227-0186
Pastorelli Food Products	Chicago, IL	800-767-2829
Pokonobe Industries	Santa Monica, CA	310-392-1259
Pompeian Inc	Baltimore, MD	800-766-7342
Proacec USA	Santa Monica, CA	310-996-7770
Purity Products	Plainview, NY	800-256-6102
Queensway Foods Company	Burlingame, CA	650-871-7770
Ron Son Foods Inc	Swedesboro, NJ	856-241-7333
Silverleaf International Corp	Rosharon, TX	800-442-7542
Southern Season	Chapel Hill, NC	877-929-7133
Sovena USA Inc	Rome, NY	315-797-7070
Sun Olive Oil Company	Jacksonville, FL	904-645-6630
Sutter Buttes Olive Oil	Sutter, CA	530-763-7921
Sweet Corn Products Co	Bloomfield, NE	877-628-6115
Tee Pee Olives, Inc.	Rye, NY	800-431-1529
Terry Foods	Stoke-on-Trent,	
Thyme Garden Herb Co	Alsea, OR	800-482-4372
Trattore Farms	Geyserville, CA	707-431-7200
Tri-State Ingredients	Mason, OH	800-622-1050
Valley Grain Products	Fresno, CA	559-675-3400
Veronica Foods Inc	Oakland, CA	800-370-5554
Villa Barone	Middletown, CA	707-987-8823
Vincent Formusa Company	Des Plaines, IL	847-813-6040
William Hill Estate Winery	Napa, CA	707-265-3024

Extra Virgin

Adams Olive Ranch	Lindsay, CA	888-216-5483
Agrocan	Ville St Laurent, QC	877-247-6226
Agrusa	Leonia, NJ	201-592-5950
Arnabal International, Inc.	Tustin, CA	714-665-9477
Bari Olive Oil Co	Dinuba, CA	877-638-3626
Bellucci	Fresno, CA	
Bono USA	Fairfield, NJ	862-485-8729
Bozzano Olive Ranch	Stockton, CA	209-451-3665
California Olive Ranch	Chico, CA	530-592-3700
Calio Groves	Piedmont, CA	800-865-4836
Castella Imports Inc	Brentwood, NY	631-231-5500
Chacewater Winery and Olive Mill	Kelseyville, CA	707-279-2995
CHO America	Baytown, TX	281-712-1549
Colonna Brothers Inc	North Bergen, NJ	201-864-1115
Corning Olive Oil Company	Corning, CA	530-824-5447
Critelli Olive Oil	Fairfield, CA	800-865-4836
Di Alfredo Foods	Garnet Valley, PA	610-558-2802
Farmstead At Long Meadow Ranch	St Helena, CA	877-627-2645
Filippo Berio Brand	Lyndhurst, NJ	201-525-2900
Gemsa Oils	La Mirada, CA	714-521-1736
GloryBee	Eugene, OR	800-456-7923
Golden Eagle Olive Products	Porterville, CA	559-784-3468
Green Gorilla	Malibu, CA	323-452-5919
K L Keller Imports	Oakland, CA	510-839-7890
Kana Organics	Westlake Village, CA	213-603-0448
Lucero Olive Oil Mfr	Corning, CA	530-824-2190
Lucini Italia Company	San Francisco, CA	888-558-2464
Natural Earth Products	Brooklyn, NY	718-552-2727
O Olive Oil	Petaluma, CA	888-827-7148
Olive Oil Source	Santa Ynez, CA	805-688-1014
Oliveo LLC	Rosenberg, TX	888-924-6687
Olivina. LLC	Livermore, CA	925-455-8710
Pacific Sun Olive Oil	Gerber, CA	530-385-1475
Paesana Products	East Farmingdale, NY	631-845-1717
Paradise Products Corporation	Boca Raton, FL	800-826-1235
Pastorelli Food Products	Chicago, IL	800-767-2829
Pepper Mill Imports	Seaside, CA	800-928-1744
Proacec USA	Santa Monica, CA	310-996-7770
Queensway Foods Company	Burlingame, CA	650-871-7770
Ron Son Foods Inc	Swedesboro, NJ	856-241-7333
Sabatino Truffles USA	West Haven, CT	888-444-9971
Sieco USA Corporation	Houston, TX	713-464-1726
Specialty Food Association	New York, NY	646-878-0301
Spruce Foods	San Clemente, CA	800-326-3612
Stinking Rose, The	San Francisco, CA	800-995-7674
Sun Grove Foods Inc	Passaic, NJ	973-574-1110
Sunfood	El Cajon, CA	888-729-3663
Sutter Buttes Olive Oil	Sutter, CA	530-763-7921
Terry Foods	Stoke-on-Trent,	
Trattore Farms	Geyserville, CA	707-431-7200
Veronica Foods Inc	Oakland, CA	800-370-5554
Villa Barone	Middletown, CA	707-987-8823

Pomace

Agrocan	Ville St Laurent, QC	877-247-6226
Olive Oil Source	Santa Ynez, CA	805-688-1014
Pacific Sun Olive Oil	Gerber, CA	530-385-1475
Villa Barone	Middletown, CA	707-987-8823

Onion

Astral Extracts	Syosset, NY	516-496-2505
Tri-State Ingredients	Mason, OH	800-622-1050
Vegetable Juices Inc	Chicago, IL	888-776-9752
Whole Herb Co	Sonoma, CA	707-935-1077

Orange

Astral Extracts
Syosset, NY....516-496-2505
Boyajian LLC
Canton, MA....800-965-0665
Diana's Specialty Foods
Pingree Grove, IL....847-683-1200
Embassy Flavours Ltd.
Brampton, ON....800-334-3371
Emerling International Foods
Buffalo, NY....716-833-7381
Gold Coast Ingredients
Commerce, CA....800-352-8673
Tri-State Ingredients
Mason, OH....800-622-1050
Ungerer & Co
Lincoln Park, NJ....973-706-7381
V & E Kohnstamm Inc
Brooklyn, NY....800-847-4500
Whole Herb Co
Sonoma, CA....707-935-1077

Palm

Aak USA Inc
Newark, NJ....973-344-1300
AG Processing Inc
Omaha, NE....800-247-1345
American Palm Oil
Washington, DC....202-333-0661
Daabon Organic USA, Inc.
Miami, FL....305-358-7667
Emerling International Foods
Buffalo, NY....716-833-7381
Maywood International Sales
Sante Fe, NM....805-500-5500
Natural Habitats USA
Boulder, CO....888-958-1967
Nealanders Food Ingredients
Mississauga, ON....800-263-1939
Pokonobe Industries
Santa Monica, CA....310-392-1259
Stevenson-Cooper Inc
Philadelphia, PA....215-223-2600
Tri-State Ingredients
Mason, OH....800-622-1050
Western Pacific Oils, Inc.
Los Angeles, CA....213-232-5117

Peanut

AG Processing Inc
Omaha, NE....800-247-1345
Arro Corp
Hodgkins, IL....877-929-2776
Avatar Corp
University Park, IL....800-255-3181
California Olive Oil Council
Berkeley, CA....888-718-9830
First Food International
Linden, NJ....908-862-5558
Good Food Inc
Honey Brook, PA....800-327-4406
K L Keller Imports
Oakland, CA....510-839-7890
Loriva Culinary Oils
San Francisco, CA....866-972-6879
Maywood International Sales
Sante Fe, NM....805-500-5500
Nealanders Food Ingredients
Mississauga, ON....800-263-1939
Pastorelli Food Products
Chicago, IL....800-767-2829
Pokonobe Industries
Santa Monica, CA....310-392-1259
Purity Products
Plainview, NY....800-256-6102
Riceland Foods Inc.
Stuttgart, AR....855-742-3929
Sessions Co Inc
Enterprise, AL....334-393-0200
Sovena USA Inc
Rome, NY....315-797-7070
Tri-State Ingredients
Mason, OH....800-622-1050

Pecan

Schermer Pecan Co
Glennville, GA....800-841-3403

Pepper

Tri-State Ingredients
Mason, OH....800-622-1050
Whole Herb Co
Sonoma, CA....707-935-1077

Peppermint

Emerling International Foods
Buffalo, NY....716-833-7381
Gold Coast Ingredients
Commerce, CA....800-352-8673
Lebermuth Company
Mishawaka, IN....800-648-1123
Medallion International Inc
Pompton Plains, NJ....973-616-3401
Tri-State Ingredients
Mason, OH....800-622-1050
Ungerer & Co
Lincoln Park, NJ....973-706-7381

Pimiento

Tri-State Ingredients
Mason, OH....800-622-1050

Popping Corn

Acatris USA
Edina, MN....952-920-7700
Avatar Corp
University Park, IL....800-255-3181
Con Agra Snack Foods
Hamburg, IA....800-831-5818
Delicious Popcorn
Waupaca, WI....715-258-7683
Great Western Co LLC
Hollywood, AL....256-259-3578
Tri-State Ingredients
Mason, OH....800-622-1050

Poppy Seed

Herbal Products & Development
Aptos, CA....831-688-8706
Tri-State Ingredients
Mason, OH....800-622-1050
Whole Herb Co
Sonoma, CA....707-935-1077

Pumpkin Seed

Arista Industries Inc
Wilton, CT....800-255-6457

Rice Bran

Arista Industries Inc
Wilton, CT....800-255-6457
Oilseeds International LTD
San Francisco, CA....415-956-7251
RiceBran Technologies
Scottsdale, AZ....602-522-3000
Riceland Foods Inc.
Stuttgart, AR....855-742-3929

Safflower

AG Processing Inc
Omaha, NE....800-247-1345
Arista Industries Inc
Wilton, CT....800-255-6457
California Oils Corp
Richmond, CA....800-225-6457
Flora Inc
Lynden, WA....800-446-2110
Loriva Culinary Oils
San Francisco, CA....866-972-6879
New Organics
Kenwood, CA....734-677-5570
Pokonobe Industries
Santa Monica, CA....310-392-1259
Tri-State Ingredients
Mason, OH....800-622-1050

Sage

Astral Extracts
Syosset, NY....516-496-2505
Emerling International Foods
Buffalo, NY....716-833-7381
Tri-State Ingredients
Mason, OH....800-622-1050
Whole Herb Co
Sonoma, CA....707-935-1077

Salad

Arista Industries Inc
Wilton, CT....800-255-6457
Arro Corp
Hodgkins, IL....877-929-2776
Avatar Corp
University Park, IL....800-255-3181
Consumer Guild Foods Inc
Toledo, OH....419-726-3406
Emerling International Foods
Buffalo, NY....716-833-7381
Sovena USA Inc
Rome, NY....315-797-7070
Spectrum Foods Inc
Springfield, IL....217-528-5301
Tri-State Ingredients
Mason, OH....800-622-1050
Ventura Foods LLC
Brea, CA....800-421-6257

Sassafras

Astral Extracts
Syosset, NY....516-496-2505
Tri-State Ingredients
Mason, OH....800-622-1050
Whole Herb Co
Sonoma, CA....707-935-1077

Sesame

AG Processing Inc
Omaha, NE....800-247-1345
Arista Industries Inc
Wilton, CT....800-255-6457
Avatar Corp
University Park, IL....800-255-3181
California Olive Oil Council
Berkeley, CA....888-718-9830
Dipasa USA Inc
Brownsville, TX....956-831-4072
Emerling International Foods
Buffalo, NY....716-833-7381
Everland Foods
Burnaby, BC
Flora Inc
Lynden, WA....800-446-2110
Loriva Culinary Oils
San Francisco, CA....866-972-6879
Organic Planet
San Francisco, CA....415-765-5590
Pokonobe Industries
Santa Monica, CA....310-392-1259
Tri-State Ingredients
Mason, OH....800-622-1050
Universal Preservachem Inc
Somerset, NJ....732-568-1266

Soybean

AAK
Louisville, KY....800-622-3055
Aak USA Inc
Newark, NJ....973-344-1300
Abitec Corp
Columbus, OH....800-555-1255
AG Processing Inc
Omaha, NE....800-247-1345
Agri-Dairy Products
Purchase, NY....914-697-9580
American Hawaiian Soy Company
Honolulu, HI....800-841-8435
Arro Corp
Hodgkins, IL....877-929-2776
Avatar Corp
University Park, IL....800-255-3181
California Olive Oil Council
Berkeley, CA....888-718-9830
Central Soyfoods
Lawrence, KS....785-312-8698
CHS Inc.
Inver Grove Hts., MN....800-328-6539
Clofine Dairy Products Inc
Linwood, NJ....609-653-1000
Dixie USA
Tomball, TX....800-233-3668
DuPont Pioneer
Johnston, IA....515-535-3200
Emerling International Foods
Buffalo, NY....716-833-7381
First Food International
Linden, NJ....908-862-5558

Gama Products
Miami, FL....786-235-1515
International Foodcraft Corp
Linden, NJ....800-875-9393
Maywood International Sales
Sante Fe, NM....805-500-5500
Nealanders Food Ingredients
Mississauga, ON....800-263-1939
New Organics
Kenwood, CA....734-677-5570
Nexcel Natural Ingredients
Springfield, IL....217-391-0091
Organic Planet
San Francisco, CA....415-765-5590
Owensboro Grain Co
Owensboro, KY....800-874-0305
Pacific Soybean & Grain
San Mateo, CA....650-525-0500
Pastorelli Food Products
Chicago, IL....800-767-2829
Pokonobe Industries
Santa Monica, CA....310-392-1259
Purity Products
Plainview, NY....800-256-6102
Riceland Foods Inc.
Stuttgart, AR....855-742-3929
Sovena USA Inc
Rome, NY....315-797-7070
Tri-State Ingredients
Mason, OH....800-622-1050
Universal Preservachem Inc
Somerset, NJ....732-568-1266

Sunflower

Aak USA Inc
Newark, NJ....973-344-1300
ACH Food Co Inc
Oakbrook Terrace, IL....630-586-3740
AG Processing Inc
Omaha, NE....800-247-1345
Emerling International Foods
Buffalo, NY....716-833-7381
Everland Foods
Burnaby, BC
First Food International
Linden, NJ....908-862-5558
Flora Inc
Lynden, WA....800-446-2110
GloryBee
Eugene, OR....800-456-7923
Loriva Culinary Oils
San Francisco, CA....866-972-6879
Maywood International Sales
Sante Fe, NM....805-500-5500
New Organics
Kenwood, CA....734-677-5570
Nexcel Natural Ingredients
Springfield, IL....217-391-0091
Odell's
Reno, NV....800-635-0436
Pacific Soybean & Grain
San Mateo, CA....650-525-0500
Pokonobe Industries
Santa Monica, CA....310-392-1259
SIGCO Sun Products
Breckenridge, MN....800-654-4145
Tri-State Ingredients
Mason, OH....800-622-1050

Tangerine

Astral Extracts
Syosset, NY....516-496-2505
Emerling International Foods
Buffalo, NY....716-833-7381
Gold Coast Ingredients
Commerce, CA....800-352-8673
Tri-State Ingredients
Mason, OH....800-622-1050

Thyme

Astral Extracts
Syosset, NY....516-496-2505
Emerling International Foods
Buffalo, NY....716-833-7381
Tri-State Ingredients
Mason, OH....800-622-1050
Whole Herb Co
Sonoma, CA....707-935-1077

Truffle

Alba Foods, Inc
Stone Mountain, GA....888-725-4605

Vegetable

Aak USA Inc
Newark, NJ....973-344-1300
Abitec Corp
Columbus, OH....800-555-1255
ACH Food Co Inc
Oakbrook Terrace, IL....630-586-3740
Adams Vegetable Oils Inc
Arbuckle, CA....530-668-2005
AG Processing Inc
Omaha, NE....800-247-1345
Allfresh Food Products
Evanston, IL....847-869-3100
Arista Industries Inc
Wilton, CT....800-255-6457
Arro Corp
Hodgkins, IL....877-929-2776
Athena Oil Inc
Astoria, NY....718-956-8893
Avatar Corp
University Park, IL....800-255-3181
Blue California Co
Rancho Sta Marg, CA....949-459-2729
Bunge Canada
Oakville, ON....905-825-7900
C P Vegetable Oil
Fort Lauderdale, FL....800-398-7154
C&T Refinery
Minneapolis, MN....800-227-4455
California Oils Corp
Richmond, CA....800-225-6457
CHS Inc.
Inver Grove Hts., MN....800-328-6539
Cibaria International
Riverside, CA....951-823-8490
DuPont Nutrition & Biosciences
New Century, KS....913-764-8100
Emerling International Foods
Buffalo, NY....716-833-7381
Follmer Development, Inc
Newbury Park, CA....805-498-4531
Fuji Vegetable Oil Inc
White Plains, NY....914-761-7900
Gateway Food Products Co
Dupo, IL....877-220-1963
Good Food Inc
Honey Brook, PA....800-327-4406
Hybco USA
Los Angeles, CA....323-269-3111
International Food Products
Fenton, MO....800-227-8427
Liberty Vegetable Oil Co
Santa Fe Springs, CA....562-921-3567
Loriva Culinary Oils
San Francisco, CA....866-972-6879
Montana Specialty Mills LLC
Great Falls, MT....800-332-2024
Natural Oils International
Simi Valley, CA....805-433-0160
Oasis Food Co
Hillside, NJ....800-275-0477
Ottens Flavors
Philadelphia, PA....800-523-0767
Pokonobe Industries
Santa Monica, CA....310-392-1259
Purity Products
Plainview, NY....800-256-6102
Spruce Foods
San Clemente, CA....800-326-3612
Starwest Botanicals Inc
Sacramento, CA....800-800-4372
Tri-State Ingredients
Mason, OH....800-622-1050
Universal Preservachem Inc
Somerset, NJ....732-568-1266

Vitamin

Arista Industries Inc
Wilton, CT....800-255-6457
Green Turtle Bay Vitamin Company
Summit, NJ....800-887-8535
Jedwards International Inc
Braintree, MA....781-848-1473
Noyes, P J
Lancaster, NH....800-522-2469
Tri-State Ingredients
Mason, OH....800-622-1050

Universal Preservachem Inc
Somerset, NJ....732-568-1266

Walnut

K L Keller Imports
Oakland, CA....510-839-7890
Loriva Culinary Oils
San Francisco, CA....866-972-6879

Wheat Germ

Arista Industries Inc
Wilton, CT....800-255-6457
Avatar Corp
University Park, IL....800-255-3181
Energen Products Inc
Norwalk, CA....800-423-8837
Pokonobe Industries
Santa Monica, CA....310-392-1259
Tri-State Ingredients
Mason, OH....800-622-1050
Universal Preservachem Inc
Somerset, NJ....732-568-1266
Viobin USA
Monticello, IL....888-473-9645
Vitamins
Chicago, IL....312-861-0700

Pan Coatings & Sprays

Richardson International
Winnipeg, MB....866-217-6211

Shortening

AAK
Louisville, KY....800-622-3055
ACH Food Co Inc
Oakbrook Terrace, IL....630-586-3740
Allfresh Food Products
Evanston, IL....847-869-3100
Brand Aromatics Inc
Lakewood, NJ....800-363-2080
C.F. Sauer Co.
Richmond, VA....888-723-0052
CanAmera Foods
Edmonton, AL....780-447-6960
Clofine Dairy Products Inc
Linwood, NJ....609-653-1000
Coast Packing Co
Vernon, CA....323-277-7700
DuPont Nutrition & Biosciences
New Century, KS....913-764-8100
Hamersmith, Inc.
Miami, FL....305-685-7451
International Food Products
Fenton, MO....800-227-8427
J.M. Smucker Co.
Orrville, OH....888-550-9555
JE Bergeron & Sons
Bromptonville, QC....800-567-2798
Marina Foods
Medley, FL....786-888-0129
Mid Atlantic Vegetable Shortening Company
Kearny, NJ....800-966-1645
Pastorelli Food Products
Chicago, IL....800-767-2829
Richardson International
Winnipeg, MB....866-217-6211
Source Food Technology
Durham, NC....866-277-3849
Spectrum Foods Inc
Springfield, IL....217-528-5301
Ventura Foods LLC
Brea, CA....800-421-6257
Western Pacific Oils, Inc.
Los Angeles, CA....213-232-5117

Fluid

DuPont Nutrition & Biosciences
New Century, KS....913-764-8100
Pastorelli Food Products
Chicago, IL....800-767-2829

Vegetable

Bunge Canada
Oakville, ON....905-825-7900
DuPont Nutrition & Biosciences
New Century, KS....913-764-8100
Gateway Food Products Co
Dupo, IL....877-220-1963

JE Bergeron & Sons
Bromptonville, QC 800-567-2798
Pastorelli Food Products
Chicago, IL 800-767-2829

Liquid

DuPont Nutrition & Biosciences
New Century, KS 913-764-8100

Pastorelli Food Products
Chicago, IL 800-767-2829

Organic Foods *See also* Organic Foods Major

General

Abunda Life
Asbury Park, NJ 732-775-9338
Adrienne's Gourmet Foods
Santa Barbara, CA 800-937-7010
Allegro Coffee Co
Thornton, CO 800-666-4869
Alliston Creamery
Alliston, ON 705-435-6751
Alta Dena Certified Dairy LLC
City Of Industry, CA. 800-535-1369
Alvarado Street Bakery
Petaluma, CA 707-789-6700
American Natural & Organic
Fremont, CA 510-440-1044
Amy's Kitchen Inc
Santa Rosa, CA. 707-781-6600
Andre-Boudin Bakeries
San Francisco, CA 415-882-1849
Ankeny Lake Wild Rice
Salem, OR. 800-555-5380
Annie's Naturals
Berkeley, CA. 800-434-1234
Applegate Farms
Bridgewater, NJ 866-587-5858
Argee Corp
Santee, CA 800-449-3030
Arico Natural Foods
Beaverton, OR 503-259-0871
Atwater Foods
Lyndonville Orleans, NY 585-765-2639
Avalon Organic Coffees
Albuquerque, NM 800-662-2575
Avenue Gourmet
Owings Mills, MD 410-902-5701
Barrows Tea Company
New Bedford, MA 800-832-5024
Beehive Botanicals
Hayward, WI. 800-233-4483
Bel Brands USA
Chicago, IL 312-462-1500
Belgravia Imports
Portsmouth, RI 800-848-1127
Bella Vista Farm
Lawton, OK. 866-237-8526
Berardi's Fresh Roast
Cleveland, OH 800-876-9109
Beta Pure Foods
Santa Cruz, CA. 831-685-6565
Beth's Fine Desserts
Mill Valley, CA. 415-383-3991
Blessed Herbs
Oakham, MA. 800-489-4372
Blue Marble Brands
Providence, RI 888-534-0246
Boehringer Ingelheim Corp
Ridgefield, CT 800-243-0127
Brad's Organic
Haverstraw, NY. 845-429-9080
Brass Ladle Products
Concordville, PA. 800-955-2353
Brewster Dairy Inc
Brewster, OH 800-874-8874
Briess Malt & Ingredients Co.
Chilton, WI. 800-657-0806
Buchanan Hollow Nut Co
Le Grand, CA 800-532-1500
Bunker Hill Cheese Co Inc
Millersburg, OH 800-253-6636
Buns & Roses Organic Wholegrain Bakery
Edmonton, AB 780-438-0098
Buywell Coffee
Colorado Springs, CO. 877-294-6246
Cache Creek Foods LLC
Woodland, CA. 530-662-1764
Cafe Altura
Santa Paula, CA 800-526-8328
Cafe Society Coffee Company
Dallas, TX. 800-717-6000
California Custom Fruits
Baldwin Park, CA. 877-558-0056
California Independent Almond Growers
Merced, CA. 209-667-4855
California Olive Oil Council
Berkeley, CA. 888-718-9830
Cascadian Farm Inc
Sedro Woolley, WA. 360-855-0542
Cedarlane Foods
Carson, CA 800-826-3322
Century Foods Intl LLC
Sparta, WI 800-269-1901
Champlain Valley Milling Corp
Westport, NY. 518-962-4711
Chelten House Products
Swedesboro, NJ
Cherith Valley Gardens
Fort Worth, TX 800-610-9813
Chino Valley Ranchers
Colton, CA 800-354-4503
Chris' Farm Stand
Peabody, MA. 978-994-4315
Christopher Ranch LLC
Gilroy, CA. 408-847-1100
CHS Sunprairie
Minot, ND. 800-556-6807
Chunco Foods Inc
Kansas City, MO. 816-283-0716
Citrus Service
Winter Garden, FL 407-656-4999
Clear Mountain Coffee Company
Silver Spring, MD. 301-587-2233
Coleman Natural
Kings Mountain, NC. 800-442-8666
Country Choice Organic
Eden Prairie, MN 952-829-8824
CROPP Cooperative
La Farge, WI. 888-444-6455
Cuizina Food Company
Woodinville, WA. 425-486-7000
Cyanotech Corp
Kailua Kona, HI 800-395-1353
Daymar Select Fine Coffees
El Cajon, CA. 800-466-7590
Dorothy Dawson Food Products
Jackson, MI. 517-788-9830
Earth Island
Chatsworth, CA 888-394-3949
East Wind Inc
Tecumseh, MO 417-679-4682
Eatem Foods Co
Vineland, NJ 800-683-2836
Eberly Poultry, Inc.
Stevens, PA 717-336-6440
Eden Foods Inc
Clinton, MI 888-424-3336
Eden Organic Pasta Company
Clinton, MI 888-424-3336
Eggology
Canoga Park, CA 818-610-2222
Emerling International Foods
Buffalo, NY. 716-833-7381
Equal Exchange Inc
West Bridgewater, MA 774-776-7400
Ethical Naturals
San Anselmo, CA. 866-459-4454
Extracts and Ingredients Ltd
Union, NJ 908-688-9009
Fairhaven Cooperative Flour Mill
Bellingham, WA 360-757-9947
FarmGro Organic Foods
Regina, SK 306-751-2449
Fine Dried Foods Intl
Santa Cruz, CA. 831-426-1413
Fireside Kitchen
Halifax, NS 902-454-7387
Florence Macaroni Manufacturing
Chicago, IL 800-647-2782
Florida Crystals Corporation
West Palm Beach, FL 844-344-9497
Florida Food Products Inc
Eustis, FL 800-874-2331
French Meadow Bakery & Cafe
Minneapolis, MN 612-870-7855
Fresh Tofu Inc
Allentown, PA. 610-433-4711
Frontier Co-op
Norway, IA 844-550-6200
Fungus Among Us
Snohomish, WA 360-568-3403
Gelato Fresco
Toronto, ON 416-785-5415
George Chiala Farms Inc
Morgan Hill, CA 408-778-0562
Ginseng Up Corp
Worcester, MA 800-446-7364
GKI Foods
Brighton, MI 248-486-0055
Golden Harvest Pecans
Cairo, GA 800-597-0968
Golden Town Apple Products
Rougemont, QC 866-552-7643
Good Groceries
Brooklyn, NY 347-853-7462
Good Stuff Cacao
Metamora, MI. 248-690-5114
Grandpa Po's Nutra Nuts
Commerce, CA. 323-260-7457
Great Eastern Sun Trading Co
Asheville, NC 800-334-5809
Great River Organic Milling
Arcadia, WI. 608-687-9580
Green & Black's Organic Chocolate
Plano, TX 877-299-1254
Grounds for Change
Poulsbo, WA 800-796-6820
Guayaki
Sebastopol, CA. 888-482-9254
Hain Celestial Group Inc
Boulder, CO 800-434-4246
Hallcrest Vineyards
Felton, CA. 831-335-4441
Harbar LLC
Canton, MA 800-881-7040
Hawkhaven Greenhouse International
Wautoma, WI 800-745-4295
Health Valley Company
Irwindale, CA 800-334-3204
Healthy Food Ingredients
Fargo, ND 844-275-3443
HempNut
Henderson, NV 707-576-7050
Herbal Magic
Toronto, ON 877-237-7225
Heritage Short Bread
Hilton Head Isle, SC. 843-422-3458
Hialeah Products Co
Hollywood, FL 800-923-3379
Highland Sugarworks
Websterville, VT. 800-452-4012
Homestead Mills
Cook, MN 800-652-5233
Horizon Organic Dairy
Broomfield, CO 888-494-3020
Horner International
Raleigh, NC. 919-787-3112
Hoyt's Honey Farm
Baytown, TX. 281-576-5383
HP Schmid
San Francisco, CA 415-765-5925
IMAG Organics
Dallas, TX. 855-301-0400
Indigo Coffee Roasters
Florence, MA 800-447-5450
Ineeka Inc
Chicago, IL 312-733-8327
Integrative Flavors
Michigan City, IN 800-837-7687
International Foods
Bloomfield, NJ 800-225-1449
Island Spring Inc
Vashon, WA. 206-463-9848
Johnson Foods, Inc.
Sunnyside, WA 509-837-4214
Jonathan's Sprouts
Rochester, MA 508-763-2577
Kashi Company
Solana Beach, CA. 877-747-2467
KD Canners Inc
Mississauga, ON. 905-602-1825
Kopali Organics
Miami, FL. 305-751-7341
Kozlowski Farms
Forestville, CA 800-473-2767
Lakeview Bakery
Calgary, AB. 403-246-6127
Larabar
Denver, CO 800-543-2147

Late July Snacks
Norwalk, CT 888-857-6225
Lifeway
Morton Grove, IL 877-281-3874
Lily of the Desert
Denton, TX 800-229-5459
Lowell Farms
El Campo, TX 888-484-9213
Lundberg Family Farms
Richvale, CA 530-538-3500
Made In Nature
Boulder, CO 800-906-7426
Magnum Coffee Roastery
Nunica, MI 888-937-5282
Mandarin Soy Sauce Inc
Middletown, NY 845-343-1505
Marroquin Organic Intl.
Santa Cruz, CA 831-423-3442
Mcfadden Farm
Potter Valley, CA 800-544-8230
Mediterranean Snack Food Co
Boonton, NJ 973-402-2644
Mellace Family Brands
Carlsbad, CA 866-255-6887
Merlino Italian Baking Company
Kent, WA 800-800-9490
Mills Brothers Intl
Seattle, WA 206-575-3000
Minnestalgia Foods LLC
Mcgregor, MN 800-328-6731
Miyako Oriental Foods Inc
Baldwin Park, CA 877-788-6476
Mom's Gourmet, LLC
Chagrin Falls, OH 440-564-9702
Moore Organics
Hamilton, OH 513-881-7144
Mountain High Organics
New Milford, CT 860-210-7805
Mr Espresso
Oakland, CA 510-287-5200
Mrs. Leeper's Pasta
Excelsior Springs, MO 800-848-5266
Mrs. Miller's Homemade Noodles
Fredericksburg, OH 800-227-4487
Mushroom Co
Cambridge, MD 410-221-8971
Mustard Seed
Central, SC 877-621-2591
Najla's Specialty Foods Inc
Louisville, KY 877-962-5527
Native American Natural Foods
Kyle, SD 800-416-7212
Natural Food Mill
Corona, CA 800-797-5090
Natural Way Mills Inc
Middle River, MN 218-222-3677
Nature's Candy
Fredericksburg, TX 800-729-0085
Nature's Legacy Inc.
Hudson, MI 517-448-2050
Nature's Nutrition
Marysville, OH 800-242-1115
Naturel
Rancho Cucamonga, CA 877-242-8344
Natures Sungrown Foods Inc
San Rafael, CA 415-491-4944
New England Natural Bakers
Greenfield, MA 800-910-2884
New Organics
Kenwood, CA 734-677-5570
North Bay Trading Co
Brule, WI 800-348-0164
North Country Natural Spring Water
Port Kent, NY 518-834-9400
NOW Foods
Bloomingdale, IL 888-669-3663
Nu-World Amaranth Inc
Naperville, IL 630-369-6851
Nutra Nuts
Commerce, CA 323-260-7457
Nutrex Hawaii Inc
Kailua Kona, HI 800-453-1187
O Olive Oil
Petaluma, CA 888-827-7148
OMG! Superfoods
Rancho Dominguez, CA 855-664-3663
Once Again Nut Butter
Nunda, NY 888-800-8075
Organic Germinal
Los Angeles, CA 310-846-5901
Organic Girl Produce
Salinas, CA 831-758-7800
Organic Gourmet
Sherman Oaks, CA 800-400-7772
Organic Liaison, LLC
Coral Springs, FL 954-755-4405
Organic Planet
San Francisco, CA 415-765-5590
Organic Wine Co Inc
San Francisco, CA 888-326-9463
Oskri Corporation
Lake Mills, WI 920-648-8300
Pacari Organic Chocolate
Boca Raton, FL
Palmieri Food Products
New Haven, CT 800-845-5447
Panos Brands
Rochelle Park, NJ 201-843-8900
Pappy's Sassafras Tea
Columbus Grove, OH 877-659-5110
Parthenon Food Products
Ann Arbor, MI 734-994-1012
Pasta Prima
Benicia, CA 530-671-7200
Peace Mountain Natural Beverages
Springfield, MA 413-567-4942
Peace Village Organic Foods
Berkeley, CA 510-524-4420
Pearl Valley Cheese Inc
Fresno, OH 740-545-6002
Personal Edge Nutrition
Ballwin, MO 514-636-4512
Pleasant Grove Farms
Pleasant Grove, CA 916-655-3391
Prairie Mills Products LLC
Rochester, IN 574-223-3177
Price Co
Yakima, WA 509-966-4110
Progenix Corporation
Wausau, WI 800-233-3356
Purity Farms
La Farge, WI 877-211-4819
Quality Naturally Foods
City Of Industry, CA 888-498-6986
R&J Farms
West Salem, OH 419-846-3179
R.J. Corr Naturals
Posen, IL 708-389-4200
RAJB Hog Foods Inc
Jersey City, NJ 201-395-9400
Rapunzel Pure Organics
Bloomfield, NJ 800-225-1449
Ravioli Store
Long Island City, NY 877-727-8269
Red River Commodities Inc
Fargo, ND 800-437-5539
Regenie's Crunchy Pi
Haverhill, MA 877-734-3643
RFi Ingredients
Blauvelt, NY 800-962-7663
Roberts Seed
Axtell, NE 308-743-2565
Rocky Mountain Honey Company
Salt Lake City, UT 801-355-2054
Run-A-Ton Group Inc
Chester, NJ 800-247-6580
Rustic Crust Inc
Pittsfield, NH 603-435-5119
Seitenbacher America LLC
Odessa, FL 727-376-3000
Shariann's Organics
Boulder, CO 800-434-4246
Sierra Madre Coffee
Denver, CO 303-446-0050
Silver Creek Specialty Meats
Oshkosh, WI 800-729-2849
SJH Enterprises
Middleton, WI 888-745-3845
Sno-Pac Foods Inc
Caledonia, MN 800-533-2215
Solana Gold Organics
Sebastopol, CA 800-459-1121
Solnuts
Hudson, IA 800-648-3503
Sophia's Sauce Works
Carson City, NV 800-718-7769
Spicely
Fremont, CA 510-440-1044
Springfield Creamery Inc
Eugene, OR 541-689-2911
Straus Family Creamery
Petaluma, CA 800-572-7783
Sunergia Soyfoods
Charlottesville, VA 800-693-5134
Sunnyside Organics Seedlings
Washington, VA 510-221-5050
Sunridge Farms
Royal Oaks, CA 831-786-7000
Sunridge Farms Inc
Salinas, CA 831-755-1530
Sunshine Farm & Garden
Renick, WV 304-497-2208
Sure-Fresh Produce Inc
Santa Maria, CA 888-423-5379
Sustainable Sourcing
Great Barrington, MA 413-528-5141
Suzanne's Specialties
New Brunswick, NJ 800-762-2135
Synergy
Moab, UT 800-804-3211
Tastybaby
Malibu, CA 866-588-8278
Tea-n-Crumpets
San Rafael, CA 415-457-2495
Teeny Tiny Spice Company of Vermont LLC
Shelburne, VT 802-598-6800
Templar Food Products
New Providence, NJ 800-883-6752
Thomas Canning/Maidstone
Maidstone, ON 519-737-1531
Thoughtful Food
Lafayette, CA 510-910-2581
Three Trees Almondmilk
San Mateo, CA 855-863-8733
Tomanetti Food Products Inc
Oakmont, PA 800-875-3040
Tova Industries LLC
Louisville, KY 888-532-8682
Travel Chocolate
New York, NY 718-841-7030
Treehouse Farms
Elgin, AZ 559-757-5020
Triple Springs Spring Water Co
Meriden, CT 203-235-8374
Tripper Inc
Oxnard, CA 805-988-8851
True Organic Product Inc
Helm, CA 800-487-0379
Tuscarora Organic Growers Cooperative
Hustontown, PA 814-448-2173
Twin Marquis
Brooklyn, NY 800-367-6868
Unique Ingredients LLC
Gold Canyon, AZ 480-983-2498
Vegetable Juices Inc
Chicago, IL 888-776-9752
Ventre Packing Company
Syracuse, NY 315-463-2384
Vienna Bakery
Barrington, RI 401-245-2355
Vogue Cuisine Foods
Sunnyvale, CA 888-236-4144
WCC Honey Marketing
City Of Industry, CA 626-855-3086
Westbrae Natural Foods
Melville, NY 800-434-4246
Wholesome!
Sugar Land, TX 800-680-1896
Wild Aseptics, LLC
Erlanger, KY 877-787-7221
Wild Rice Exchange
Woodland, CA 800-223-7423
Wine Country Chef LLC
Hidden Valley Lake, CA 707-322-0406
Wing Nien Food
Hayward, CA 510-487-8877
Wizards Cauldron, LTD
Yanceyville, NC 336-694-5665
Wood Sugarbush
Spring Valley, WI 715-772-4656
Woodstock Farms Manufacturing
Edison, NJ 800-526-4349
World Casing Corp
Maspeth, NY 800-221-4887
Xochitl
Dallas, TX 866-595-8917
Y Z Enterprises Inc
Maumee, OH 800-736-8779
Your Bar Factory
LaSalle, QC 888-366-0258
Zhena's Gypsy Tea
Commerce, CA 800-448-0803

Baby Foods

Ella's Kitchen
New Castle, DE 800-685-7799

Gerber Products Co
Arlington, VA 800-284-9488
Hain Celestial Group Inc
Lake Success, NY 800-434-4246
Happy Family
New York, NY 855-644-2779
Little Duck Organics
New York, NY 877-458-1321
Oh Baby Foods, Inc.
Fayetteville, AR 800-788-1451
Plum Organics
Emeryville, CA 877-914-7586
Square One Organics
River Forest, IL 866-771-7138
Stonyfield Organic
Londonderry, NH 800-776-2697

Baked Goods

Alvarado Street Bakery
Petaluma, CA 707-789-6700
Blue Marble Brands
Providence, RI 888-534-0246
Bread Alone Bakery
Lake Katrine, NY 800-769-3328
Country Choice Organic
Eden Prairie, MN 952-829-8824
Fillo Factory, The
Northvale, NJ 800-653-4556
Foods Alive
Angola, IN 260-488-4497
French Meadow Bakery & Cafe
Minneapolis, MN 612-870-7855
Fullbloom Baking Co
Newark, CA 800-201-9909
Good Groceries
Brooklyn, NY 347-853-7462
Homefree LLC
Windham, NH 800-552-7172
Inked Organics
Petaluma, CA
Kashi Company
Solana Beach, CA 877-747-2467
Kerri Kreations
Santa Cruz, CA 831-429-5129
Mary's Gone Crackers
Gridley, CA 888-258-1250
Natural Food Mill
Corona, CA 800-797-5090
Nature's Path Foods
Blaine, WA 888-808-9505
Rudi's Organic Bakery
Boulder, CO 877-293-0876
Rustic Crust Inc
Pittsfield, NH 603-435-5119
Tram Bar LLC
Victor, ID 208-354-4790

Beverages

24 Mantra Organic
Fremont, CA
Allegro Coffee Co
Thornton, CO 800-666-4869
ALO Drinks
San Francisco, CA
Bhakti
Boulder, CO 303-484-8770
Blue Marble Brands
Providence, RI 888-534-0246
Cafe Kreyol
Manassas, VA
Caffe Ibis Gallery Deli
Logan, UT 888-740-4777
California Juice Co.
Santa Barbara, CA 805-738-8723
Celebrity Tea, LLC
Tampa, FL 813-600-3317
Cell-Nique
Norwalk, CT 888-417-9343
Chartreuse Organic Tea
Trenton, MI 866-315-7832
Choice Organic Teas
Seattle, WA 866-972-6879
Citromax Flavors Inc
Carlstadt, NJ 201-933-8405
Dark Dog
Miami Beach, FL
Davidson's Organics
Reno, NV 800-882-5888
Evolution Fresh
Seattle, WA 800-794-9986
Faribault Foods, Inc.
Fairbault, MN 507-331-1400
Florida Food Products Inc
Eustis, FL 800-874-2331
Foods Alive
Angola, IN 260-488-4497
Frey Vineyards
Redwood Valley, CA 800-760-3739
Great Eastern Sun Trading Co
Asheville, NC 800-334-5809
Hain Celestial Group Inc
Lake Success, NY 800-434-4246
Happy Family
New York, NY 855-644-2779
Honest Tea Inc
Atlanta, GA 800-520-2653
J.M. Smucker Co.
Orrville, OH 888-550-9555
Kombucha Wonder Drink
Portland, OR 877-224-7331
Lakewood Juice Co.
Miami, FL 866-324-5900
Mamma Chia
Carlsbad, CA 855-588-2442
New Barn Organics
Rohnert Park, CA 888-635-7102
Organic Girl Produce
Salinas, CA 831-758-7800
Perricone Juices
Beaumont, CA 951-769-7171
Pyure Brands
Naples, FL 305-509-5096
Rooibee Red Tea
Louisville, KY 502-749-0800
Sambazon
San Clemente, CA 877-726-2296
Small Planet Foods
Minneapolis, MN 800-624-4123
Stash Tea Co
Portland, OR 800-547-1514
Stonyfield Organic
Londonderry, NH 800-776-2697
Suntood
El Cajon, CA 888-729-3663
Tazo Tea
Kent, WA 855-829-6832
Templar Food Products
New Providence, NJ 800-883-6752
The Healthy Beverage Company
Doylestown, PA 800-295-1388
Third Street Inc
Louisville, CO 800-636-3790

Candy & Confectionery

Cocoa Parlor
Laguna Niguel, CA 949-877-9549
DAGOBA Organic Chocolate
Ashland, OR 866-972-6879
Dina's Organic Chocolate
Mt Kisco, NY 888-625-2008
Earth Source Organics
Vista, CA 760-734-1867
Good Stuff Cacao
Metamora, MI 248-690-5114
Justin's Nut Butter
Boulder, CO 844-448-0302
Nelly's Organics
Chatsworth, CA 310-756-0738
NuGo Nutrition
Oakmont, PA 888-421-2032
Organic Nectars LLC
Malden On Hudson, NY 845-246-0506
Pascha Chocolate
Toronto, Ontario, ... 855-472-7242
Sjaak's Organic Chocolates
Petaluma, CA 707-775-2434
Sunridge Farms
Royal Oaks, CA 831-786-7000
Theo Chocolate
Seattle, WA 206-632-5100
Zazubean
Vancouver, BC 604-801-5488

Cereals, Grains, Rice & Flour

Back to the Roots
Oakland, CA 510-922-9758
Bob's Red Mill Natural Foods
Milwaukie, OR 800-349-2173
Boulder Granola
Boulder, CO 303-443-1136
Foods Alive
Angola, IN 260-488-4497
Great River Organic Milling
Arcadia, WI 608-687-9580
Hain Celestial Group Inc
Lake Success, NY 800-434-4246
Happy Family
New York, NY 855-644-2779
Heartland Mills Shipping
Marienthal, KS 800-232-8533
Hodgson Mill Inc
Effingham, IL 800-347-0198
Homefree LLC
Windham, NH 800-552-7172
IMAG Organics
Dallas, TX 855-301-0400
Kashi Company
Solana Beach, CA 877-747-2467
King Arthur Flour
Norwich, VT 800-827-6836
Lundberg Family Farms
Richvale, CA 530-538-3500
Natural Food Mill
Corona, CA 800-797-5090
Nature's Legacy Inc.
Hudson, MI 517-448-2050
Nature's Path Foods
Blaine, WA 888-808-9505
New England Natural Bakers
Greenfield, MA 800-910-2884
NOW Foods
Bloomingdale, IL 888-669-3663
Pacific Grain & Foods
Fresno, CA 559-276-2580
Santa Barbara Pistachio Co
Maricopa, CA 800-896-1044
Small Batch Organics
Manchester Center, VT 802-367-1054
Small Planet Foods
Minneapolis, MN 800-624-4123
Smirk's
Fort Morgan, CO 970-762-0202
Spectrum Foods Inc
Springfield, IL 217-528-5301
Teeccino
Carpinteria, CA 800-498-3434
The Real Co
Wilmington, DE 347-433-8945
Timeless Seeds
Ulm, MT 406-866-3340
TresOmega
New Milford, CT 860-210-7805

Cheese & Cheese Products

Blue Marble Brands
Providence, RI 888-534-0246
Horizon Organic Dairy
Broomfield, CO 888-494-3020
Pennsylvania Macaroni Company
Pittsburgh, PA 800-223-5928

Dairy Products

Ahara Ghee
Portland, OR 503-997-5050
Alden's Organic
Camas, WA
Ancient Organics
Berkeley, CA 510-280-5043
Aurora Organic Dairy
Boulder, CO 303-284-3313
Boulder Homemade Inc
Boulder, CO 800-691-5002
Cloud Top
Pasadena, CA 888-263-1778
Horizon Organic Dairy
Broomfield, CO 888-494-3020
Oregon Ice Cream Co.
Vancouver, WA 360-713-6800
Springfield Creamery Inc
Eugene, OR 541-689-2911
Stonyfield Organic
Londonderry, NH 800-776-2697
WhiteWave Foods
Denver, CO 800-488-9283
Windy City Organics
Northbrook, IL 800-925-0577

Doughs, Mixes & Fillings

Bob's Red Mill Natural Foods
Milwaukie, OR 800-349-2173

French Meadow Bakery & Cafe
Minneapolis, MN 612-870-7855
Hodgson Mill Inc
Effingham, IL 800-347-0198
Homefree LLC
Windham, NH 800-552-7172
Nature's Path Foods
Blaine, WA 888-808-9505

Eggs & Egg Products

Horizon Organic Dairy
Broomfield, CO 888-494-3020
Pete and Gerry's Organic Eggs
Monroe, NH 800-210-6657

Ethnic Foods

Bob's Red Mill Natural Foods
Milwaukie, OR 800-349-2173
French Meadow Bakery & Cafe
Minneapolis, MN 612-870-7855
Great Eastern Sun Trading Co
Asheville, NC 800-334-5809
Harbar LLC
Canton, MA 800-881-7040
San-J International Inc
Henrico, VA 800-446-5500
SLT Group
Dayton, NJ 732-837-3096
The Food Collective
Irvine, CA 866-328-8638

Fruits & Vegetables

Atlantic Laboratories Inc
Waldoboro, ME 888-662-5357
Bay Baby Produce
Burlington, WA 360-755-2299
Bedemco Inc
White Plains, NY 914-683-1119
Blue Marble Brands
Providence, RI 888-534-0246
Bob's Red Mill Natural Foods
Milwaukie, OR 800-349-2173
Dole Food Company, Inc.
Thousand Oaks, CA 800-356-3111
Driscoll Strawberry Assoc Inc
Watsonville, CA 831-424-0506
Earthbound Farm
San Jn Bautista, CA 800-690-3200
Faribault Foods, Inc.
Fairbault, MN 507-331-1400
Farm Fresh to You
Anaheim, CA 800-796-6009
Fine Dried Foods Intl
Santa Cruz, CA 831-426-1413
Golden Valley Natural
Shelley, ID 888-270-7147
Great Eastern Sun Trading Co
Asheville, NC 800-334-5809
Happy Family
New York, NY 855-644-2779
Hodgson Mill Inc
Effingham, IL 800-347-0198
Lisa's Organics
Carnelian Bay, CA 877-584-5711
Made In Nature
Boulder, CO 800-906-7426
Maine Coast Sea Vegetables
Franklin, ME 207-565-2907
Mushroom Co
Cambridge, MD 410-221-8971
Mushroom Harvest
Athens, OH 740-448-7376
Nature's Legacy Inc.
Hudson, MI 517-448-2050
Organic Girl Produce
Salinas, CA 831-758-7800
Organics Unlimited
San Diego, CA 619-710-0658
Ready Pac Foods Inc
Irwindale, CA 800-800-4088
Sambazon
San Clemente, CA 877-726-2296
Season Harvest Foods
Los Altos, CA 650-968-2273
Small Planet Foods
Minneapolis, MN 800-624-4123
Spectrum Foods Inc
Springfield, IL 217-528-5301
Sunfood
El Cajon, CA 888-729-3663
Sunridge Farms
Royal Oaks, CA 831-786-7000
Sutter Foods LLC
Yuba City, CA 530-682-7776
Tradin Organics USA
Scotts Valley, CA 831-685-6565
Viva Tierra
Mt Vernon, WA 360-855-0566
WhiteWave Foods
Denver, CO 800-488-9283
Wholesum Family Farms
Nogales, AZ 520-281-9233

General Grocery

Blue Marble Brands
Providence, RI 888-534-0246
Faribault Foods, Inc.
Fairbault, MN 507-331-1400
Happy Family
New York, NY 855-644-2779
Lisa's Organics
Carnelian Bay, CA 877-584-5711
Small Planet Foods
Minneapolis, MN 800-624-4123

Hemp

Colorado Hemp Honey
Parker, CO 833-233-2256
Curaleaf
Wakefield, MA 833-760-4367
Earth Circle Organics
Auburn, CA 877-922-3663
Ella's Flats
Naples, FL
Hemp Fusion
Roswell, GA 877-669-4367
Hemp Oil Canada
Ste. Agathe, MB 800-289-4367
Hemp Production Services
Saskatoon, SK 844-436-7477
Humming Hemp
Richland, WA 503-559-6476
Isodiol
Escondido, CA 855-979-6751
Lumen
Oakland, CA
Manitoba Harvest Hemp
Minneapolis, MN 800-665-4367
Minnesota Hemp Farms
Hastings, MN 877-205-4367
Nature's Love
Snyder, CO 970-571-7959
Phivida Organics
San Diego, CA 844-744-6646
RE Botanicals
Boulder, CO 303-214-2118
San Luis Valley Hemp Co.
Del Norte, CO 719-299-5000

Ingredients, Flavors & Additives

Aromatech USA
Orlando, FL 407-277-5727
Briess Malt & Ingredients Co.
Chilton, WI 800-657-0806
California Natural Products
Lathrop, CA 209-858-2525
Citromax Flavors Inc
Carlstadt, NJ 201-933-8405
Flavorganics
Newark, NJ 866-972-6879
Frontier Co-op
Norway, IA 844-550-6200
Futurebiotics LLC
Hauppauge, NY 800-645-1721
GloryBee
Eugene, OR 800-456-7923
Gold Coast Ingredients
Commerce, CA 800-352-8673
Homefree LLC
Windham, NH 800-552-7172
International Foodcraft Corp
Linden, NJ 800-875-9393
Lang Pharma Nutrition Inc
Middletown, RI 401-848-7700
Moore Organics
Hamilton, OH 513-881-7144
New Chapter
Brattleboro, VT 800-543-7279
NOW Foods
Bloomingdale, IL 888-669-3663
Organic Partners Intl.
Portland, OR 503-445-1065
Premier Organics
Oakland, CA 866-237-8688
Primal Essence
Oxnard, CA 877-774-6253
Rejuvila
Boulder, CO 877-480-4402
RFi Ingredients
Blauvelt, NY 800-962-7663
Sunfood
El Cajon, CA 888-729-3663

Jams, Jellies & Spreads

Cook's Pantry
Ventura, CA 805-947-4622
Food For Thought Inc
Honor, MI 231-326-5444
Good Spread
Boulder, CO
Small Planet Foods
Minneapolis, MN 800-624-4123

Meats & Meat Products

Bilinski Sausage Mfg Co
Cohoes, NY 877-873-9102
Coleman Natural
Kings Mountain, NC 800-442-8666
Eberly Poultry, Inc.
Stevens, PA 717-336-6440
Golden Valley Natural
Shelley, ID 888-270-7147
Mesquite Organic Beef LLC
Aurora, CO 888-480-2333
Osso Good, LLC
San Rafael, CA
Panorama Meats
Fresno, CA 707-765-6756
Petaluma Poultry
Petaluma, CA 800-556-6789
Sommers Organic
Wheeling, IL 877-377-9797

Nuts & Nut Butters

Bedemco Inc
White Plains, NY 914-683-1119
Blue Marble Brands
Providence, RI 888-534-0246
Divine Organics
CA 209-532-4950
J.M. Smucker Co.
Orrville, OH 888-550-9555
Justin's Nut Butter
Boulder, CO 844-448-0302
NOW Foods
Bloomingdale, IL 888-669-3663
Nuttzo
San Diego, CA 888-325-0553
Once Again Nut Butter
Nunda, NY 888-800-8075
Pacific Grain & Foods
Fresno, CA 559-276-2580
Premier Organics
Oakland, CA 866-237-8688
Santa Barbara Pistachio Co
Maricopa, CA 800-896-1044
Sunco & Frenchie
Clifton, NJ 973-478-1011
Sunfood
El Cajon, CA 888-729-3663
Sunridge Farms
Royal Oaks, CA 831-786-7000
Windy City Organics
Northbrook, IL 800-925-0577

Oils, Shortening & Fats

Blue Marble Brands
Providence, RI 888-534-0246
CHO America
Baytown, TX 281-712-1549
Cibaria International
Riverside, CA 951-823-8490
Citromax Flavors Inc
Carlstadt, NJ 201-933-8405
Critelli Olive Oil
Fairfield, CA 800-865-4836
GloryBee
Eugene, OR 800-456-7923
International Foodcraft Corp
Linden, NJ 800-875-9393

Santa Barbara Pistachio Co
Maricopa, CA 800-896-1044
Solazyme Inc
S San Francisco, CA 650-589-5883
Spectrum Foods Inc
Springfield, IL 217-528-5301
Sunfood
El Cajon, CA 888-729-3663
TresOmega
New Milford, CT 860-210-7805
Vital Choice
Bellingham, WA 800-608-4825

Pasta & Noodles

Blue Marble Brands
Providence, RI 888-534-0246
Caesar's Pasta
Blackwood, NJ 888-432-2372
Good Citizens
Simi Valley, CA
Great Eastern Sun Trading Co
Asheville, NC 800-334-5809
Hain Celestial Group Inc
Lake Success, NY 800-434-4246
Hodgson Mill Inc
Effingham, IL 800-347-0198
Lundberg Family Farms
Richvale, CA 530-538-3500
Natural Food Mill
Corona, CA 800-797-5090
Nature's Legacy Inc.
Hudson, MI 517-448-2050

Prepared Foods

24 Mantra Organic
Fremont, CA
Blue Marble Brands
Providence, RI 888-534-0246
Boulder Organic Foods
Niwot, CO 303-530-0470
Caesar's Pasta
Blackwood, NJ 888-432-2372
Faribault Foods, Inc.
Fairbault, MN 507-331-1400
Fig Food Co.
New York, NY 855-344-3663
Fillo Factory, The
Northvale, NJ 800-653-4556
Great Eastern Sun Trading Co
Asheville, NC 800-334-5809
Hain Celestial Group Inc
Lake Success, NY 800-434-4246
Happy Family
New York, NY 855-644-2779
Kashi Company
Solana Beach, CA 877-747-2467
Lightlife
Turners Falls, MA 800-769-3279
Lisa's Organics
Carnelian Bay, CA 877-584-5711
Made In Nature
Boulder, CO 800-906-7426
Sommers Organic
Wheeling, IL 877-377-9797
The Food Collective
Irvine, CA 866-328-8638
Vital Choice
Bellingham, WA 800-608-4825

Relishes & Pickled Products

Food For Thought Inc
Honor, MI 231-326-5444
Great Eastern Sun Trading Co
Asheville, NC 800-334-5809
Small Planet Foods
Minneapolis, MN 800-624-4123

Sauces, Dips & Dressings

Banzos
Denver, CO 303-447-2133
Chelten House Products
Swedesboro, NJ
Drew's Organics
Chester, VT 800-228-2980
Earth Island
Chatsworth, CA 888-394-3949
Flamous Brands
Duarte, CA 626-799-7909
Follow Your Heart
Chatsworth, CA 818-725-2820
Frontier Co-op
Norway, IA 844-550-6200
Klein Foods, Inc
Marshall, MN 800-657-0174
Organic Girl Produce
Salinas, CA 831-758-7800
Salad Girl Inc
Mahtomedi, MN 651-653-9155
San-J International Inc
Henrico, VA 800-446-5500
Small Planet Foods
Minneapolis, MN 800-624-4123

Snack Foods

ALOHA
New York, NY
Bearded Brothers
Austin, TX
Bhu Foods
San Diego, CA 619-855-3258
Blue Marble Brands
Providence, RI 888-534-0246
Charlton Natural Foods, Inc.
Huntington Beach, CA 888-611-7753
Dharma Bars
Earthbound Farm
San Jn Bautista, CA 800-690-3200
Flamous Brands
Duarte, CA 626-799-7909
Fullbloom Baking Co
Newark, CA 800-201-9909
Happy Family
New York, NY 855-644-2779
Late July Snacks
Norwalk, CT 888-857-6225
Lundberg Family Farms
Richvale, CA 530-538-3500
Maine Coast Sea Vegetables
Franklin, ME 207-565-2907
Mary's Gone Crackers
Gridley, CA 888-258-1250
Mountain Organic Foods
Moraga, CA 925-377-0119
Nature's Legacy Inc.
Hudson, MI 517-448-2050
Nature's Path Foods
Blaine, WA 888-808-9505
New England Natural Bakers
Greenfield, MA 800-910-2884
NOW Foods
Bloomingdale, IL 888-669-3663
NuGo Nutrition
Oakmont, PA 888-421-2032
Organic Germinal
Los Angeles, CA 310-846-5901
Plum Organics
Emeryville, CA 877-914-7586
Raw Bite
Hudson, MA 844-729-2483
Rhythm Superfoods
Austin, TX 512-441-5667
Rudi's Organic Bakery
Boulder, CO 877-293-0876
Sunridge Farms
Royal Oaks, CA 831-786-7000
Vegan Rob's
Sea Cliff, NY 516-671-4411
Vege USA
Monrovia, CA 888-772-8343
Watusee Foods
Washington, DC 202-281-8245
Way Better Snacks
Minneapolis, MN 612-314-2060
Yogavive
Tiburon, CA 415-366-6226

Specialty Processed Foods

Cell-Nique
Norwalk, CT 888-417-9343
Earth Island
Chatsworth, CA 888-394-3949
Happy Family
New York, NY 855-644-2779
Heritage Health Food
Collegedale, TN 888-237-0807
Homefree LLC
Windham, NH 800-552-7172
Lightlife
Turners Falls, MA 800-769-3279
Lundberg Family Farms
Richvale, CA 530-538-3500
Natural Food Mill
Corona, CA 800-797-5090
NuGo Nutrition
Oakmont, PA 888-421-2032
Osso Good, LLC
San Rafael, CA
Prosperity Organic Foods
Boise, ID 888-557-5741
Sunshine Burger & Spec Food Co
Fort Atkinson, WI 920-568-1100
The Food Collective
Irvine, CA 866-328-8638
Wisconsin Specialty Protein
Madison, WI

Spices, Seasonings & Seeds

24 Mantra Organic
Fremont, CA
American Natural & Organic
Fremont, CA 510-440-1044
Blue Marble Brands
Providence, RI 888-534-0246
Bob's Red Mill Natural Foods
Milwaukie, OR 800-349-2173
Davidson's Organics
Reno, NV 800-882-5888
Foods Alive
Angola, IN 260-488-4497
Frontier Co-op
Norway, IA 844-550-6200
GoAvo
Montville, NJ 973-534-9951
Great Eastern Sun Trading Co
Asheville, NC 800-334-5809
Hodgson Mill Inc
Effingham, IL 800-347-0198
Homefree LLC
Windham, NH 800-552-7172
Maine Coast Sea Vegetables
Franklin, ME 207-565-2907
Mountain Rose Herbs
Pleasant Hill, OR 800-879-3337
Nature's Legacy Inc.
Hudson, MI 517-448-2050
NOW Foods
Bloomingdale, IL 888-669-3663
Pacific Grain & Foods
Fresno, CA 559-276-2580
Primal Essence
Oxnard, CA 877-774-6253
Red Monkey Foods
Springfield, MO 417-319-7300
Smith & Truslow
Denver, CO 303-339-6967
Spicely
Fremont, CA 510-440-1044
Sunfood
El Cajon, CA 888-729-3663
Sunridge Farms
Royal Oaks, CA 831-786-7000
Sustainable Sourcing
Great Barrington, MA 413-528-5141
The Real Co
Wilmington, DE 347-433-8945
Vital Choice
Bellingham, WA 800-608-4825

Sugars, Syrups & Sweeteners

Bascom Family Farms Inc
Brattleboro, VT 888-266-6271
Bee Seasonal
Gilbert, AZ
Blue Marble Brands
Providence, RI 888-534-0246
Divine Organics
CA 209-532-4950
Finding Home Farms
Middletown, NY 845-355-4335
Flavorganics
Newark, NJ 866-972-6879
Florida Crystals Corporation
West Palm Beach, FL 844-344-9497
Food For Thought Inc
Honor, MI 231-326-5444
GloryBee
Eugene, OR 800-456-7923
Lundberg Family Farms
Richvale, CA 530-538-3500
Madhava Natural Sweeteners
Boulder, CO 800-530-2900

Maple Valley Cooperative
Cashton, WI 608-654-7319
NOW Foods
Bloomingdale, IL 888-669-3663
Once Again Nut Butter
Nunda, NY 888-800-8075
Organic Nectars LLC
Malden On Hudson, NY. 845-246-0506
Pyure Brands
Naples, FL. 305-509-5096
Runamok Maple
Fairfax, VT 802-849-7943
SBS Americas
Valley Cottage, NY. 844-727-0827
Skedaddle Maple
Florenceville-Bristol, NB
Sugar Bob's Smoked Maple Syrup
Londonderry, VT. 802-297-7665
Sunfood
El Cajon, CA. 888-729-3663
Suzanne's Specialties
New Brunswick, NJ 800-762-2135
Sweet Harvest Foods
Rosemount, MN 507-263-8599
The Real Co
Wilmington, DE 347-433-8945
UBC Food Distributors
Dearborn, MI. 877-846-8117
Xooz Gear
Frisco, TX 214-206-1222

Pasta & Noodles

General

A Zerega's Sons Inc
Fair Lawn, NJ 201-797-1400
Agrusa
Leonia, NJ 201-592-5950
Al Dente Pasta Co
Whitmore Lake, MI 800-536-7278
Alaska Pasta Co
Anchorage, AK 907-276-2632
Alaska Smokehouse
Woodinville, WA 800-422-0852
American Italian Pasta Company
Excelsior Springs, MO 877-328-7278
Armanino Foods of Distinction
Hayward, CA 800-255-8588
Arrowhead Mills
Boulder, CO 800-434-4246
Atlanta Bread Co.
Smyrna, GA 800-398-3728
Belletieri Company
Allentown, PA 610-433-4334
Bernie's Foods
Brooklyn, NY 718-417-6677
Better Than Foods USA
Brookfield, WI 855-691-5900
Bgreen Food
San Diego, CA 619-825-9330
Biagio's Banquets
Chicago, IL 800-392-2837
Blue Evolution
San Mateo, CA 605-741-4074
Blue Marble Brands
Providence, RI 888-534-0246
Boudreaux's Foods
New Orleans, LA 504-733-8440
Bruno Specialty Foods
West Sayville, NY 631-589-1700
Buona Vita Inc
Bridgeton, NJ 856-453-7972
Buonitalia
New York, NY 212-633-9090
Caesar's Pasta
Blackwood, NJ 888-432-2372
Cando Pasta
Cando, ND 701-968-4401
Canton Noodle Corporation
New York, NY 212-226-3276
Cappello's
Denver, CO 844-353-2863
Carando Gourmet Frozen Foods
Agawam, MA 888-227-2636
Carla's Pasta
South Windsor, CT 860-436-4042
Castella Imports Inc
Brentwood, NY 631-231-5500
Cedarlane Foods
Carson, CA 800-826-3322
Chicago Avenue Pizza
Chicago, IL 800-244-8935
Chickapea
Collingwood, ON 888-868-9968
Clic International Inc
Laval, QC 450-669-2663
Codinos Food Inc
Scotia, NY 800-246-8908
Colavita USA
Edison, NJ 888-265-2848
Colony Brands Inc
Monroe, WI 800-544-9036
Corsetti's Pasta Products
Woodbury, NJ 800-989-1188
Costas Pasta
Kennesaw, GA 770-514-8814
Cottage Street Pasta
Barre, VT 802-476-4024
Country Foods
Polson, MT 406-883-4384
Cuizina Food Company
Woodinville, WA 425-486-7000
Dairy Maid Ravioli Mfg Co
Brooklyn, NY 866-777-3661
Di Fiore Pasta Co
Hartford, CT 860-296-1077
Drakes Fresh Pasta Co
High Point, NC 800-737-2782
E.D. Smith Foods Ltd
Hamilton, ON 905-573-1207
Eden Foods Inc
Clinton, MI 888-424-3336
Eden Organic Pasta Company
Clinton, MI 888-424-3336
El Peto Products
Cambridge, ON 800-387-4064
Elena's
Auburn Hills, MI 800-723-5362
Ener-G Foods
Seattle, WA 800-331-5222
Ethnic Gourmet Foods
Boulder, CO 800-434-4246
European Egg Noodle Manufacturing
Edmonton, AB 780-453-6767
Explore Cuisine
Red Bank, NJ
FDI Inc
Berkeley, IL 708-544-1880
Fiori Bruna Pasta Products
Miami Lakes, FL 305-705-2534
Florence Macaroni Manufacturing
Chicago, IL 800-647-2782
Florence Pasta & Cheese
Marshall, MN 800-533-5290
Florentyna's Fresh Pasta Factory
Los angles, CA 800-747-2782
Food City USA
Arvada, CO 303-321-4447
Fratelli Mantova
Naperville, IL 630-904-0002
Fresh Market Pasta Company
Portland, ME 207-773-7146
Fresh Pasta Delights
Plano, TX 972-422-5907
Fun Foods
East Rutherford, NJ 800-507-2782
Gaston Dupre
Excelsior Springs, MO 817-629-6275
Genki USA
Torrance, CA
Gilster-Mary Lee Corp
Chester, IL 618-826-2361
Gluten Free Foods Mfg.
Chino, CA 909-823-8230
Good Old Dad Food Products
Sault Ste. Marie, ON 800-267-7426
Gourmet's Fresh Pasta
Pasadena, CA 626-798-0841
Great Eastern Sun Trading Co
Asheville, NC 800-334-5809
Greenfield Noodle & Spec Co
Detroit, MI 313-873-2212
Heartline Foods
Westport, CT 203-222-0381
HFI Foods
Redmond, WA 425-883-1320
Hodgson Mill Inc
Effingham, IL 800-347-0198
Hong Tou Noodle Company
Los Angeles, CA 323-256-3843
Hung's Noodle House
Calgary, AB 403-250-1663
International Harvest Inc
Mt Vernon, NY 800-277-4268
International Home Foods
Parsippany, NJ 973-359-9920
International Noodle Co
Madison Heights, MI 248-583-2479
Italia Foods
Schaumburg, IL 800-747-1109
Italian Gourmet Foods Canada
Calgary, AB 403-283-5350
Itarca
Los Angeles, CA 800-747-2782
J B & Son LTD
Yonkers, NY 914-963-5192
Joseph's Gourmet Pasta
Haverhill, MA 800-863-8998
JSL Foods
Los Angeles, CA 800-745-3236
Juno Chef's
Goshen, NY 845-294-5400
Kay Foods Co
Detroit, MI 313-393-1100
Kemach Food Products
Brooklyn, NY 718-272-5655
Kozlowski Farms
Forestville, CA 800-473-2767
La Moderna
Toluca, MX
LA Pasta Inc
Silver Spring, MD 301-588-1111
La Piccolina
Decatur, GA 800-626-1624
La Romagnola
Orlando, FL 800-843-8359
La Spiga D'Oro Fresh Pasta Co
Pacifica, CA 800-847-2782
Ladson Homemade Pasta Company
Charleston, SC 843-588-5088
Landolfi's Food Products
Trenton, NJ 609-392-1830
Lotsa Pasta
San Diego, CA 858-581-6777
Louisa Food Products Inc
St Louis, MO 314-868-3000
Mama Del's Macacroni
East Haven, CT 203-469-6255
Mama Rosie's Ravioli
Charlestown, MA 888-246-4300
Mamma Lina Ravioli Company
San Diego, CA 858-535-0620
Marconi Italian Specialty Foods
Chicago, IL 312-421-0485
Marsan Foods
Toronto, ON 416-755-9262
Maruchan Inc
Irvine, CA 949-789-2300
MI-AL. Corp
Glen Cove, NY 516-759-0652
Michael Angelo's Inc
Austin, TX 877-482-5426
Midwest Food
Chicago, IL 773-927-8870
Modern Macaroni Co LTD
Honolulu, HI 808-845-6841
Montreal Chop Suey Company
Montreal, QC 514-522-3134
Morii Foods, Inc.
Tualatin, OR 503-691-7007
Morrison Lamothe
Toronto, ON 877-677-6533
Mountain High Organics
New Milford, CT 860-210-7805
Mrs. Leeper's Pasta
Excelsior Springs, MO 800-848-5266
Mucci Food Products LTD
Canton, MI 734-453-4555
MXO Global
Mount Royal, QC
Nantucket Pasta Company, Inc.
Nantucket, MA 508-494-5209
Napoli Pasta Manufacturers
Miami, FL 305-666-1942
Natural Value
Sacramento, CA 916-836-3561
Nature's Legacy Inc.
Hudson, MI 517-448-2050
Nissin Foods USA Co Inc
Gardena, CA 310-327-8478
North American Enterprises
Tucson, AZ 800-817-8666
Northern Farmhouse Pasta LLC
Roscoe, NY 607-290-4064
NuPasta
Markham, ON 855-910-8800
O'Sole Mio
Boisbriand, QC 844-696-8933
Oakland Noodle Co
Oakland, IL 217-346-2322
OB Macaroni Company
. 844-837-6259
Ocean's Halo
Burlingame, CA 650-642-5907
Okahara Saimin Factory LTD
Honolulu, HI 808-949-0588
P & S Ravioli Co
Philadelphia, PA 215-339-9929
Pappardelle's Inc
Denver, CO 800-607-2782

Pasta Del Mondo
Carmel, NY....800-392-8887
Pasta Factory
Melrose Park, IL....800-615-6951
Pasta International
Mississauga, ON....905-890-5550
Pasta Mami
Smyrna, GA....770-438-6022
Pasta Mill
Edmonton, AB....780-454-8665
Pasta Montana
Great Falls, MT....406-761-1516
Pasta Prima
Benicia, CA....530-671-7200
Pasta Quistini
Toronto, ON....416-742-3222
Pasta Shoppe
Nashville, TN....800-247-0188
Pasta Sonoma
Rohnert Park, CA....707-584-0800
Pastorelli Food Products
Chicago, IL....800-767-2829
Peace Village Organic Foods
Berkeley, CA....510-524-4420
Pede Brothers Italian Food
Schenectady, NY....518-356-3042
Peking Noodle Co Inc
Los Angeles, CA....323-223-0897
Pennsylvania Macaroni Company
Pittsburgh, PA....800-223-5928
Philadelphia Macaroni Co
Philadelphia, PA....215-923-3141
Pierino Frozen Foods
Lincoln Park, MI....313-928-0950
Pondini Imports
Somerset, NJ....732-545-1255
Porinos Gourmet Food
Central Falls, RI....800-826-3938
Publix Super Market
Lakeland, FL....800-242-1227
Pure Sales
Costa Mesa, CA....714-540-5455
Queen Ann Ravioli & Macaroni
Brooklyn, NY....718-256-1061
Quinoa Corporation
Gardena, CA....310-217-8125
Ranieri Fine Foods
Brooklyn, NY....718-599-9520
Ravioli Store
Long Island City, NY....877-727-8269
Rice Innovations
Fontana, CA....909-823-8230
Riviera Ravioli Company
Bronx, NY....718-823-0260
Rocca's Italian Foods Inc
New Castle, PA....724-654-3344
Ron Son Foods Inc
Swedesboro, NJ....856-241-7333
Ronzoni
Largo, FL....800-730-5957
Rosa Food Products
Philadelphia, PA....215-467-2214
Roses Ravioli
Oglesby, IL....815-883-8011
Rossi Pasta LTD
Marietta, OH....800-227-6774
S T Specialty Foods Inc
Brooklyn Park, MN....763-493-9600
Sabatino Truffles USA
West Haven, CT....888-444-9971
Salt Lake Macaroni & Noodle Company
Salt Lake City, UT....801-969-9855
Sam Mills USA
Boynton Beach, FL....561-572-0510
Savoia Foods
Chicago Heights, IL....800-867-2782
Sedlock Farm
Lynn Center, IL....309-521-8284
Sempio Foods
Cerritos, CA....562-207-9540
Serro Foods LLC
Catskill, NY....518-943-9255
Severino Pasta Mfg Co Inc
Westmont, NJ....856-854-3716
Seviroli Foods
Garden City, NY....516-222-6220
Sfoglia Fine Pastas & Gourmet
Freeland, WA....360-331-4080
Shanghai Co
Portland, OR....503-235-2525
Silver Palate Kitchens
Cresskill, NJ....201-568-0110
Silver State Foods Inc
Denver, CO....800-423-3351
SOPAKCO Foods
Mullins, SC....800-276-9678
SOUPerior Bean & Spice Company
Vancouver, WA....800-878-7687
Spring Glen Fresh Foods
Ephrata, PA....800-641-2853
Spruce Foods
San Clemente, CA....800-326-3612
Star Ravioli Mfg Co
Moonachie, NJ....201-933-6427
Stellar Pasta Company
Great Barrington, MA....413-528-2150
Sun Noodle
Honolulu, HI....808-841-5808
Taif Inc
Folcroft, PA....610-522-0122
Tasty Mix Quality Foods
Brooklyn, NY....718-855-7680
TexaFrance
Round Rock, TX....800-776-8937
Tomasso Corporation
Baie D'Urfe, QC....514-325-3000
Trio's Original Italian Pasta Co.
Chelsea, MA....800-999-9603
Tropical Foods
Charlotte, NC....800-438-4470
Turri's Italian Foods
Roseville, MI....586-773-6010
Twin Marquis
Brooklyn, NY....800-367-6868
Union
Irvine, CA....800-854-7292
United Noodle Manufacturing Company
Salt Lake City, UT....801-485-0951
US Durum Products LTD
Lancaster, PA....866-268-7268
Varco Brothers
Chicago, IL....312-642-4740
Vitasoy USA
Woburn, MA....800-848-2769
Wan Hua Foods
Seattle, WA....206-622-8417
Wegmans Food Markets Inc.
Rochester, NY....800-934-6267
Willow Foods
Beaverton, OR....800-338-3609
Wine Country Pasta
Sonoma, CA....707-935-1366
Wing's Food Products
Toronto, ON....416-259-2662
Winn-Dixie Stores
Jacksonville, FL....800-967-9105
Wisconsin Whey International
Juda, WI....608-233-5101
Wonton Food
Brooklyn, NY....800-776-8889
Wornick Company
Cincinnati, OH....800-860-4555
Young's Noodle Factory Inc
Honolulu, HI....808-533-6478
Zeroodle
Richmond Hill, ON....905-889-9880

Agnolotti

Agrusa
Leonia, NJ....201-592-5950
Caesar's Pasta
Blackwood, NJ....888-432-2372
Pasta Factory
Melrose Park, IL....800-615-6951
Putney Pasta
Brattleboro, VT....800-253-3683
Queen Ann Ravioli & Macaroni
Brooklyn, NY....718-256-1061
Supreme Dairy Farms Co
Warwick, RI....401-739-8180
Wisconsin Whey International
Juda, WI....608-233-5101

Angel Hair

Al Dente Pasta Co
Whitmore Lake, MI....800-536-7278
Backyard Safari Co
Covington, GA....770-385-3273
Barilla USA
Northbrook, IL....800-922-7455
Bgreen Food
San Diego, CA....619-825-9330
Caesar's Pasta
Blackwood, NJ....888-432-2372
Cipriani's Spaghetti & Sauce Company
Chicago Heights, IL....708-755-6212
Costa Macaroni Manufacturing
Los Angeles, CA....800-433-7785
Food City USA
Arvada, CO....303-321-4447
Hodgson Mill Inc
Effingham, IL....800-347-0198
La Romagnola
Orlando, FL....800-843-8359
Lucy's Foods
Latrobe, PA....724-539-1430
Mrs. Leeper's Pasta
Excelsior Springs, MO....800-848-5266
NuPasta
Markham, ON....855-910-8800
Pasta Factory
Melrose Park, IL....800-615-6951
Pasta Valente
Charlottesville, VA....888-575-7670
Putney Pasta
Brattleboro, VT....800-253-3683

Bows

Hodgson Mill Inc
Effingham, IL....800-347-0198

Canned

Canton Noodle Corporation
New York, NY....212-226-3276
Faribault Foods, Inc.
Fairbault, MN....507-331-1400
International Home Foods
Parsippany, NJ....973-359-9920
Midwest Food
Chicago, IL....773-927-8870
Natural Value
Sacramento, CA....916-836-3561
Seneca Foods Corp
Marion, NY....315-926-8100
Shanghai Co
Portland, OR....503-235-2525

Cannelloni

Louisa Food Products Inc
St Louis, MO....314-868-3000
Marsan Foods
Toronto, ON....416-755-9262
Pasta Factory
Melrose Park, IL....800-615-6951
Pasta International
Mississauga, ON....905-890-5550
Riviera Ravioli Company
Bronx, NY....718-823-0260
Star Ravioli Mfg Co
Moonachie, NJ....201-933-6427
Tomasso Corporation
Baie D'Urfe, QC....514-325-3000
Turri's Italian Foods
Roseville, MI....586-773-6010

Cavatappi

Costa Macaroni Manufacturing
Los Angeles, CA....800-433-7785

Cavatelli

Alfredo Aiello Italian Food
Quincy, MA....617-770-6360
Caesar's Pasta
Blackwood, NJ....888-432-2372
Fiori Bruna Pasta Products
Miami Lakes, FL....305-705-2534
J B & Son LTD
Yonkers, NY....914-963-5192
Landolfi's Food Products
Trenton, NJ....609-392-1830
Pasta Del Mondo
Carmel, NY....800-392-8887
Pasta Factory
Melrose Park, IL....800-615-6951
Queen Ann Ravioli & Macaroni
Brooklyn, NY....718-256-1061
Riviera Ravioli Company
Bronx, NY....718-823-0260
Star Ravioli Mfg Co
Moonachie, NJ....201-933-6427

Wisconsin Whey International
Juda, WI 608-233-5101

Elbow Macaroni

A Zerega's Sons Inc
Fair Lawn, NJ 201-797-1400
Cando Pasta
Cando, ND 701-968-4401
Costa Macaroni Manufacturing
Los Angeles, CA. 800-433-7785
Cuizina Food Company
Woodinville, WA. 425-486-7000
Good Citizens
Simi Valley, CA
Hodgson Mill Inc
Effingham, IL 800-347-0198
Lundberg Family Farms
Richvale, CA. 530-538-3500
Philadelphia Macaroni Co
Philadelphia, PA 215-923-3141
Superior Pasta Co
Philadelphia, PA 215-627-3306

Farfalle

Costa Macaroni Manufacturing
Los Angeles, CA. 800-433-7785
Italia Foods
Schaumburg, IL. 800-747-1109

Fettuccine

Barilla USA
Northbrook, IL 800-922-7455
Hodgson Mill Inc
Effingham, IL 800-347-0198
Lucy's Foods
Latrobe, PA. 724-539-1430
NuPasta
Markham, ON. 855-910-8800
Pasta Valente
Charlottesville, VA 888-575-7670

Gnocchi

Agrusa
Leonia, NJ. 201-592-5950
Capone Foods
Somerville, MA 617-629-2296
Dixie USA
Tomball, TX 800-233-3668
Italian Foods Corporation
Raleigh, NC 888-516-7262
Lucy's Foods
Latrobe, PA. 724-539-1430
Queen Ann Ravioli & Macaroni
Brooklyn, NY 718-256-1061

Frozen

Lucy's Foods
Latrobe, PA. 724-539-1430
Queen Ann Ravioli & Macaroni
Brooklyn, NY 718-256-1061
Turri's Italian Foods
Roseville, MI 586-773-6010

Lasagna

Capone Foods
Somerville, MA 617-629-2296
Carla's Pasta
South Windsor, CT 860-436-4042
Hodgson Mill Inc
Effingham, IL 800-347-0198
Philadelphia Macaroni Co
Philadelphia, PA 215-923-3141

Frozen

Alfredo Aiello Italian Food
Quincy, MA. 617-770-6360
Bruno Specialty Foods
West Sayville, NY. 631-589-1700
Caesar's Pasta
Blackwood, NJ 888-432-2372
Cedarlane Foods
Carson, CA 800-826-3322
Codinos Food Inc
Scotia, NY. 800-246-8908
Italia Foods
Schaumburg, IL. 800-747-1109
Landolfi's Food Products
Trenton, NJ 609-392-1830
Mamma Lina Ravioli Company
San Diego, CA 858-535-0620
Marsan Foods
Toronto, ON 416-755-9262
Molinaro's Fine Italian Foods Ltd.
Mississauga, ON. 905-281-0352
Pasta Factory
Melrose Park, IL. 800-615-6951
Pasta International
Mississauga, ON. 905-890-5550
Riviera Ravioli Company
Bronx, NY. 718-823-0260
Seviroli Foods
Garden City, NY 516-222-6220
Tomasso Corporation
Baie D'Urfe, QC. 514-325-3000
Wisconsin Whey International
Juda, WI 608-233-5101

Noodles

A Zerega's Sons Inc
Fair Lawn, NJ. 201-797-1400
Costa Macaroni Manufacturing
Los Angeles, CA. 800-433-7785

Canned

Canton Noodle Corporation
New York, NY 212-226-3276
Shanghai Co
Portland, OR 503-235-2525
United Noodle Manufacturing Company
Salt Lake City, UT 801-485-0951

Chow Mein

Everfresh Food Corporation
Minneapolis, MN 612-331-6393
Nanka Seimen Company
Vernon, CA. 323-585-9967
Passport Food Group
Ontario, CA. 310-463-0954
Valdez Food Inc
Philadelphia, PA 215-634-6106
Wan Hua Foods
Seattle, WA 206-622-8417
Willow Foods
Beaverton, OR 800-338-3609
Wonton Food
Brooklyn, NY 800-776-8889

Egg

A Zerega's Sons Inc
Fair Lawn, NJ. 201-797-1400
Costa Macaroni Manufacturing
Los Angeles, CA. 800-433-7785
Eden Organic Pasta Company
Clinton, MI 888-424-3336
Hodgson Mill Inc
Effingham, IL 800-347-0198
Manischewitz Co
Newark, NJ 201-553-1100
Nanka Seimen Company
Vernon, CA. 323-585-9967
Silver State Foods Inc
Denver, CO 800-423-3351

Mung Bean

Explore Cuisine
Red Bank, NJ

Oriental

Allied Old English Inc
Port Reading, NJ. 732-602-8955
Annie Chun's
Los Angeles, CA. 415-479-8272
Union
Irvine, CA 800-854-7292
Vitasoy USA
Woburn, MA. 800-848-2769
Wonton Food
Brooklyn, NY 800-776-8889

Ramen

Bgreen Food
San Diego, CA 619-825-9330
Blue Marble Brands
Providence, RI 888-534-0246
Maruchan Inc
Irvine, CA. 949-789-2300
Pressery
Denver, CO
Sun Noodle New Jersey
Carlstadt, NJ 201-530-1100
Union
Irvine, CA. 800-854-7292

Soba

Miracle Noodle
Los Angeles, CA. 800-948-4205
Sun Noodle New Jersey
Carlstadt, NJ 201-530-1100

Pasta

Alba Foods, Inc
Stone Mountain, GA. 888-725-4605
Banza
Barilla USA
Northbrook, IL 800-922-7455
Caesar's Pasta
Blackwood, NJ 888-432-2372
Conte's Pasta Co.
Vineland, NJ 800-211-6607
Costa Macaroni Manufacturing
Los Angeles, CA. 800-433-7785
Cuizina Food Company
Woodinville, WA. 425-486-7000
Cybele's Free To Eat
Los Angeles, CA. 877-895-3729
Edison Grainery
Benicia, CA. 510-382-0202
Fantis Foods Inc
Carlstadt, NJ 201-933-6200
Faribault Foods, Inc.
Fairbault, MN 507-331-1400
Fiore Di Pasta
Fresno, CA 559-457-0431
Gabriella's Kitchen
Mississauga, ON. 844-754-6690
Gia Russa
Boardman, OH 800-527-8772
Intermountain Specialty Food Group
Salt Lake City, UT 801-977-9077
Jovial Foods
North Stonington, CT. 877-642-0644
Kana Organics
Westlake Village, CA 213-603-0448
Kashi Company
Solana Beach, CA. 877-747-2467
Krinos Foods
Bronx, NY. 718-729-9000
LA Pasta Inc
Silver Spring, MD. 301-588-1111
La Romagnola
Orlando, FL. 800-843-8359
Lucy's Foods
Latrobe, PA. 724-539-1430
Mezza
Lake Forest, IL 888-206-6054
MI-AL. Corp
Glen Cove, NY 516-759-0652
Park 100 Foods Inc
Tipton, IN 800-854-6504
Pasta Prima
Benicia, CA. 530-671-7200
Queen Ann Ravioli & Macaroni
Brooklyn, NY 718-256-1061
Ragozzino Foods Inc
Meriden, CT 800-348-1240
Reid Foods
Gurnee, IL. 888-295-8478
Ronzoni
Largo, FL 800-730-5957
RP's Pasta Company
Madison, WI. 608-257-7216
Serro Foods LLC
Catskill, NY 518-943-9255
Sfoglini Pasta Shop
Brooklyn, NY 917-338-5955
Simply Shari's Gluten Free
Thousand Oaks, CA 805-241-5676
Sophia Foods
Brooklyn, NY 718-272-1110
Superior Pasta Co
Philadelphia, PA 215-627-3306
Surgital America
Miramar, FL 954-538-6891
Tribe 9 Foods
Madison, WI. 608-257-7216
Turri's Italian Foods
Roseville, MI 586-773-6010

Vincent Formusa Company
Des Plaines, IL 847-813-6040
Wisconsin Whey International
Juda, WI 608-233-5101

Frozen

Fiore Di Pasta
Fresno, CA 559-457-0431
Homestead Ravioli Company
South San Francisco, CA 650-615-0750
LA Pasta Inc
Silver Spring, MD 301-588-1111

Penne

A Zerega's Sons Inc
Fair Lawn, NJ 201-797-1400
Cando Pasta
Cando, ND 701-968-4401
Costa Macaroni Manufacturing
Los Angeles, CA 800-433-7785
Cuizina Food Company
Woodinville, WA 425-486-7000
Turri's Italian Foods
Roseville, MI 586-773-6010

Ravioli

Agrusa
Leonia, NJ 201-592-5950
Alfonso Gourmet Pasta
Pompano Beach, FL 800-370-7278
Alfredo Aiello Italian Food
Quincy, MA 617-770-6360
Antoni Ravioli Co
North Massapequa, NY 800-783-0350
Armanino Foods of Distinction
Hayward, CA 800-255-8588
Aunt Kitty's Foods Inc
Vineland, NJ 856-691-2100
Bella Ravioli
Medford, MA 781-396-0875
Borgattis Ravioli
Bronx, NY 718-367-3799
Bruno Specialty Foods
West Sayville, NY 631-589-1700
Caesar's Pasta
Blackwood, NJ 888-432-2372
Campbell Soup Co.
Camden, NJ 800-257-8443
Capone Foods
Somerville, MA 617-629-2296
Chinese Spaghetti Factory
Boston, MA 617-445-7714
Codinos Food Inc
Scotia, NY 800-246-8908
Cottage Street Pasta
Barre, VT 802-476-4024
Cuizina Food Company
Woodinville, WA 425-486-7000
Dairy Maid Ravioli Mfg Co
Brooklyn, NY 866-777-3661
Fiori Bruna Pasta Products
Miami Lakes, FL 305-705-2534
International Home Foods
Parsippany, NJ 973-359-9920
Italia Foods
Schaumburg, IL 800-747-1109
J B & Son LTD
Yonkers, NY 914-963-5192
La Romagnola
Orlando, FL 800-843-8359
Landolfi's Food Products
Trenton, NJ 609-392-1830
Louisa Food Products Inc
St Louis, MO 314-868-3000
Lucy's Foods
Latrobe, PA 724-539-1430
Mamma Lina Ravioli Company
San Diego, CA 858-535-0620
Maria & Son
St Louis, MO 866-481-9009
MI-AL. Corp
Glen Cove, NY 516-759-0652
New York Ravioli
New Hyde Park, NY 888-588-7287
Nuovo Pasta Productions LTD
Stratford, CT 800-803-0033
Pasta Del Mondo
Carmel, NY 800-392-8887
Pasta Factory
Melrose Park, IL 800-615-6951
Pasta International
Mississauga, ON 905-890-5550
Pasta Mill
Edmonton, AB 780-454-8665
Pasta Prima
Benicia, CA 530-671-7200
Queen Ann Ravioli & Macaroni
Brooklyn, NY 718-256-1061
Roses Ravioli
Oglesby, IL 815-883-8011
Seviroli Foods
Garden City, NY 516-222-6220
Star Ravioli Mfg Co
Moonachie, NJ 201-933-6427
Tomasso Corporation
Baie D'Urfe, QC 514-325-3000
Wisconsin Whey International
Juda, WI 608-233-5101

Canned

Alfredo Aiello Italian Food
Quincy, MA 617-770-6360
Campbell Soup Co.
Camden, NJ 800-257-8443
Cuizina Food Company
Woodinville, WA 425-486-7000
International Home Foods
Parsippany, NJ 973-359-9920

Cheese

Alfredo Aiello Italian Food
Quincy, MA 617-770-6360
Aunt Kitty's Foods Inc
Vineland, NJ 856-691-2100
Fiori Bruna Pasta Products
Miami Lakes, FL 305-705-2534
La Romagnola
Orlando, FL 800-843-8359
Louisa Food Products Inc
St Louis, MO 314-868-3000
Queen Ann Ravioli & Macaroni
Brooklyn, NY 718-256-1061

Frozen

Alfredo Aiello Italian Food
Quincy, MA 617-770-6360
Bruno Specialty Foods
West Sayville, NY 631-589-1700
Caesar's Pasta
Blackwood, NJ 888-432-2372
Carla's Pasta
South Windsor, CT 860-436-4042
Codinos Food Inc
Scotia, NY 800-246-8908
Cuizina Food Company
Woodinville, WA 425-486-7000
Fiori Bruna Pasta Products
Miami Lakes, FL 305-705-2534
Homestead Ravioli Company
South San Francisco, CA 650-615-0750
Italia Foods
Schaumburg, IL 800-747-1109
J B & Son LTD
Yonkers, NY 914-963-5192
Kiki's Gluten-Free
Park Ridge, IL
Landolfi's Food Products
Trenton, NJ 609-392-1830
Louisa Food Products Inc
St Louis, MO 314-868-3000
MI-AL. Corp
Glen Cove, NY 516-759-0652
Pasta Del Mondo
Carmel, NY 800-392-8887
Pasta Factory
Melrose Park, IL 800-615-6951
Pasta International
Mississauga, ON 905-890-5550
Pasta Prima
Benicia, CA 530-671-7200
Seviroli Foods
Garden City, NY 516-222-6220
Star Ravioli Mfg Co
Moonachie, NJ 201-933-6427
Tomasso Corporation
Baie D'Urfe, QC 514-325-3000
Turri's Italian Foods
Roseville, MI 586-773-6010
Wisconsin Whey International
Juda, WI 608-233-5101

Meat

La Romagnola
Orlando, FL 800-843-8359
Queen Ann Ravioli & Macaroni
Brooklyn, NY 718-256-1061

Seafood

La Romagnola
Orlando, FL 800-843-8359
Queen Ann Ravioli & Macaroni
Brooklyn, NY 718-256-1061

Vegetable

La Romagnola
Orlando, FL 800-843-8359
Queen Ann Ravioli & Macaroni
Brooklyn, NY 718-256-1061

Rigatoni

Al Dente Pasta Co
Whitmore Lake, MI 800-536-7278
Codinos Food Inc
Scotia, NY 800-246-8908
Landolfi's Food Products
Trenton, NJ 609-392-1830
Lucy's Foods
Latrobe, PA 724-539-1430
Pasta Factory
Melrose Park, IL 800-615-6951

Rotelle

Cuizina Food Company
Woodinville, WA 425-486-7000

Rotini

A Zerega's Sons Inc
Fair Lawn, NJ 201-797-1400
Al Dente Pasta Co
Whitmore Lake, MI 800-536-7278
Cando Pasta
Cando, ND 701-968-4401
Hodgson Mill Inc
Effingham, IL 800-347-0198
Lundberg Family Farms
Richvale, CA 530-538-3500
Turri's Italian Foods
Roseville, MI 586-773-6010

Semolina

Florence Macaroni Manufacturing
Chicago, IL 800-647-2782

Shells

A Zerega's Sons Inc
Fair Lawn, NJ 201-797-1400
Barilla USA
Northbrook, IL 800-922-7455
Cando Pasta
Cando, ND 701-968-4401
Costa Macaroni Manufacturing
Los Angeles, CA 800-433-7785
Hodgson Mill Inc
Effingham, IL 800-347-0198

Spaghetti

Barilla USA
Northbrook, IL 800-922-7455
Caesar's Pasta
Blackwood, NJ 888-432-2372
Campbell Soup Co.
Camden, NJ 800-257-8443
Costa Macaroni Manufacturing
Los Angeles, CA 800-433-7785
Country Cupboard
Lewisburg, PA 570-523-3211
Hodgson Mill Inc
Effingham, IL 800-347-0198
International Home Foods
Parsippany, NJ 973-359-9920
Iwamoto Natto Factory
Paia, HI 808-579-9935
La Romagnola
Orlando, FL 800-843-8359
Ladson Homemade Pasta Company
Charleston, SC 843-588-5088
Landolfi's Food Products
Trenton, NJ 609-392-1830

Lucy's Foods
Latrobe, PA 724-539-1430
Lundberg Family Farms
Richvale, CA 530-538-3500
NuPasta
Markham, ON 855-910-8800
Pasta Factory
Melrose Park, IL 800-615-6951
Pasta International
Mississauga, ON 905-890-5550
Philadelphia Macaroni Co
Philadelphia, PA 215-923-3141
Superior Pasta Co
Philadelphia, PA 215-627-3306
Varco Brothers
Chicago, IL 312-642-4740
Wisconsin Whey International
Juda, WI 608-233-5101

Canned

International Home Foods
Parsippany, NJ 973-359-9920
Seneca Foods Corp
Marion, NY 315-926-8100

Frozen

Caesar's Pasta
Blackwood, NJ 888-432-2372
Landolfi's Food Products
Trenton, NJ 609-392-1830
Pasta International
Mississauga, ON 905-890-5550

Spelt

A Zerega's Sons Inc
Fair Lawn, NJ 201-797-1400
Costa Macaroni Manufacturing
Los Angeles, CA 800-433-7785
Nature's Legacy Inc.
Hudson, MI 517-448-2050

Spinach

Cipriani's Spaghetti & Sauce Company
Chicago Heights, IL 708-755-6212
La Romagnola
Orlando, FL 800-843-8359
Marsan Foods
Toronto, ON 416-755-9262
Wonton Food
Brooklyn, NY 800-776-8889

Stuffed Shells

Armanino Foods of Distinction
Hayward, CA 800-255-8588
Lucy's Foods
Latrobe, PA 724-539-1430
Queen Ann Ravioli & Macaroni
Brooklyn, NY 718-256-1061
Turri's Italian Foods
Roseville, MI 586-773-6010

Tagliatelle

Costa Macaroni Manufacturing
Los Angeles, CA 800-433-7785

Tortellini

Agrusa
Leonia, NJ 201-592-5950
Alfredo Aiello Italian Food
Quincy, MA 617-770-6360
Armanino Foods of Distinction
Hayward, CA 800-255-8588
Bruno Specialty Foods
West Sayville, NY 631-589-1700
Costa Macaroni Manufacturing
Los Angeles, CA 800-433-7785
Cuizina Food Company
Woodinville, WA 425-486-7000
Dairy Maid Ravioli Mfg Co
Brooklyn, NY 866-777-3661
Fiori Bruna Pasta Products
Miami Lakes, FL 305-705-2534
Italia Foods
Schaumburg, IL 800-747-1109
Landolfi's Food Products
Trenton, NJ 609-392-1830
Lucy's Foods
Latrobe, PA 724-539-1430
MI-AL. Corp
Glen Cove, NY 516-759-0652
New York Ravioli
New Hyde Park, NY 888-588-7287
Pasta Del Mondo
Carmel, NY 800-392-8887
Pasta Factory
Melrose Park, IL 800-615-6951
Pasta International
Mississauga, ON 905-890-5550
Pasta Mill
Edmonton, AB 780-454-8665
Putney Pasta
Brattleboro, VT 800-253-3683
Queen Ann Ravioli & Macaroni
Brooklyn, NY 718-256-1061
Riviera Ravioli Company
Bronx, NY 718-823-0260
Roses Ravioli
Oglesby, IL 815-883-8011
Turri's Italian Foods
Roseville, MI 586-773-6010

Vermicelli

Cipriani's Spaghetti & Sauce Company
Chicago Heights, IL 708-755-6212
Costa Macaroni Manufacturing
Los Angeles, CA 800-433-7785
Iwamoto Natto Factory
Paia, HI 808-579-9935
Superior Pasta Co
Philadelphia, PA 215-627-3306

Prepared Foods

Battered

BlueWater Seafoods
Gloucester, MA....888-560-2539
Strong Roots
Brooklyn, NY....929-466-1639

Refrigerated

Alderfer Inc
Harleysville, PA....800-341-1121
Alpine Butcher
Lowell, MA....978-256-7771
AquaCuisine
Portland, OR....208-323-2782
Atlantic Pork & Provisions
Jamaica, NY....800-245-3536
Avon Heights Mushrooms
Avondale, PA....610-268-2092
Binkert's Meat Products
Baltimore, MD....410-687-5959
Boesl Packing Co
Baltimore, MD....800-675-1471
Boudreaux's Foods
New Orleans, LA....504-733-8440
Brookside Foods
Cleveland, OH....216-991-7600
C Roy & Sons Processing
Yale, MI....810-387-3957
Charlie's Country Sausage
Minot, ND....701-838-6302
Chicago 58 Food Products
Woodbridge, ON....416-603-4244
Chisesi Brothers Meat Packing
New Orleans, LA....800-966-3550
Citterio USA
Freeland, PA....800-435-8888
Corfu Foods Inc
Bensenville, IL....630-595-2510
Country Maid Inc
Milwaukee, WI....800-628-4354
Dairy Fresh Foods Inc
Taylor, MI....313-299-0735
Dawn's Foods
Portage, WI....800-993-2967
Dietz & Watson Inc.
Philadelphia, PA....215-831-9000
Dohar Meats Inc
Cleveland, OH....216-241-4197
F & S Produce Co Inc
Vineland, NJ....800-886-3316
Frank Wardynski & Sons Inc
Buffalo, NY....716-854-6083
Fried Provisions Company
Evans City, PA....724-538-3160
Gouvea's & Purity Foods Inc
Honolulu, HI....808-847-3717
Green Garden Food Products
Sandpoint, ID....800-669-3169
Groff's Meats
Elizabethtown, PA....717-367-1246
Hazle Park Quality Meats
West Hazleton, PA....800-238-4331
Helen's Pure Foods
Cheltenham, PA....215-379-6433
Herold's Salads
Cleveland, OH....800-427-2523
HFI Foods
Redmond, WA....425-883-1320
Hoople Country Kitchen Inc
Rockport, IN....877-466-7537
House of Thaller Inc
Knoxville, TN....800-462-3365
Ito Cariani Sausage Company
Hayward, CA....510-887-0882
John Volpi & Co
St Louis, MO....800-288-3439
Kelly Corned Beef Co
Chicago, IL....800-624-5617
Kilgus Meats
Toledo, OH....419-472-9721
Knotts Fine Foods
Paris, TN....731-642-1961
Lakeside Foods Inc.
Manitowoc, WI....800-466-3834
Land O'Frost Inc
Searcy, AR....800-643-5654
Lengerich Meats Inc
Zanesville, IN....260-638-4123
Leona Meat Plant
Troy, PA....570-297-3574
Locustdale Meat Packing
Locustdale, PA....570-875-1270
Marshallville Packing Co
Marshallville, OH....330-855-2871
Martin Rosols
New Britain, CT....860-223-2707
Meadows Country Products
Hollidaysburg, PA....888-499-1001
Mrs Grissom's Salads Inc
Nashville, TN....800-255-0571
Parma Sausage Products
Pittsburgh, PA....877-294-4207
Queen City Sausage & Provision
Cincinnati, OH....877-544-5588
R.C. McEntire & Company
Columbia, SC....803-799-3388
Rachael's Smoked Fish
Springfield, MA....800-327-3412
Real Kosher Sausage Company
Newark, NJ....973-690-5394
Rendulic Meat Packing Corp
Mckeesport, PA....412-678-9541
Roman Packing Company
Norfolk, NE....800-373-5990
Saag's Products LLC
San Leandro, CA....855-287-6562
Sandridge Food Corp
Medina, OH....800-627-2523
Saval Foods Corp
Elkridge, MD....800-527-2825
Schaefers Market
Sauk Centre, MN....320-352-6490
Schaller & Weber Inc
Astoria, NY....800-847-4115
Sculli Brothers
Yeadon, PA....215-336-1223
Sechrist Brothers
Dallastown, PA....717-244-2975
Sheinman Provision Co
Philadelphia, PA....215-473-7065
Smith Packing Regional Meat
Utica, NY....315-732-5125
Spring Glen Fresh Foods
Ephrata, PA....800-641-2853
Spring Grove Foods
Miamisburg, OH....937-866-4311
Standard Meat Co LP
Dallas, TX....866-859-6313
Stawnichy Holdings
Mundare, AB....888-764-7646
Stonie's Sausage Shop
Perryville, MO....888-546-2540
Suter Co Inc
Sycamore, IL....800-435-6942
Tennessee Valley Packing Co
Columbia, TN....931-388-2623
Teti Bakery
Etobicoke, ON....800-465-0123
Troy Foods Inc
Troy, IL....618-667-6332
United Provision Meat Company
Columbus, OH....614-252-1126
Upstate Niagara Co-Op Inc.
Buffalo, NY....716-892-3156
Vienna Meat Products
Scarborough, ON....800-588-1931
Warren & Son Meat Processing
Whipple, OH....740-585-2421
Wornick Company
Cincinnati, OH....800-860-4555

General

A Gift Basket by Carmela
Longmeadow, MA....413-746-1400
Acme Steak & Seafood
Youngstown, OH....800-686-2263
Advance Pierre Foods
Cincinnati, OH....800-969-2747
Agrusa
Leonia, NJ....201-592-5950
Ajinomoto Foods North America, Inc.
Ontario, CA....909-477-4700
Al Pete Meats
Muncie, IN....765-288-8817
Alderfer Inc
Harleysville, PA....800-341-1121
Alfonso Gourmet Pasta
Pompano Beach, FL....800-370-7278
Alfonso Gourmet Pasta
Pompano Beach, FL....800-370-7278
Alfonso Gourmet Pasta
Pompano Beach, FL....800-370-7278
Alfredo Aiello Italian Food
Quincy, MA....617-770-6360
Alpine Butcher
Lowell, MA....978-256-7771
Armanino Foods of Distinction
Hayward, CA....800-255-8588
Atlantic Pork & Provisions
Jamaica, NY....800-245-3536
Avalon Gourmet
Phoenix, AZ....602-253-0343
Avon Heights Mushrooms
Avondale, PA....610-268-2092
Bake Crafters Food Company
McDonald, TN....423-396-3392
Barber Foods
Kings Mountain, NC....877-447-3279
Bay Cities Produce Co Inc
San Leandro, CA....510-346-4943
Beaver Street Fisheries
Jacksonville, FL....800-874-6426
Bellisio Foods
Minneapolis, MN
Bernardi Italian Foods Company
Bloomsburg, PA....570-389-5500
Biagio's Banquets
Chicago, IL....800-392-2837
Biagio's Banquets
Chicago, IL....800-392-2837
Big B Barbecue
Evansville, IN....812-425-5235
Binkert's Meat Products
Baltimore, MD....410-687-5959
Blue Marble Brands
Providence, RI....888-534-0246
BlueWater Seafoods
Gloucester, MA....888-560-2539
Boesl Packing Co
Baltimore, MD....800-675-1471
Bouma Meats
Provost, AB....780-753-2092
Boyd's Sausage Co
Washington, IA....319-653-5715
Brookside Foods
Cleveland, OH....216-991-7600
Bruno Specialty Foods
West Sayville, NY....631-589-1700
Buxton Foods
Buxton, ND....800-726-8057
C Roy & Sons Processing
Yale, MI....810-387-3957
Cajun Brands
New Iberia, LA....504-408-2252
Calendar Islands Maine Lobster LLC
Portland, ME....207-541-9140
Camino Real Foods Inc
Vernon, CA....800-421-6201
Campbell Soup Co.
Camden, NJ....800-257-8443
Campbell Soup Co.
Camden, NJ....800-257-8443
Canada Bread Co, Ltd
Etobicoke, ON....800-465-5515
Caribbean Food Delights Inc
Tappan, NY....845-398-3000
Carl Buddig & Co.
Homewood, IL....888-633-5684
Carolina Packers Inc
Smithfield, NC....800-682-7675
Carrington Foods Co Inc
Saraland, AL....251-675-9700
Cedar Lake Foods
Cedar Lake, MI....800-246-5039
Cedarlane Foods
Carson, CA....800-826-3322
Chang Food Company
Garden Grove, CA....714-265-9990

Channel Fish Processing
Gloucester, MA....................800-457-0054
Charlie's Country Sausage
Minot, ND....................701-838-6302
Chateau Food Products Inc
Cicero, IL....................708-863-4207
Chef America
Chatsworth, CA....................818-718-8111
Chef Hans' Gourmet Foods
Monroe, LA....................800-890-4267
Chicago 58 Food Products
Woodbridge, ON....................416-603-4244
Chicago Meat Authority Inc
Chicago, IL....................800-383-3811
Chincoteague Seafood Co Inc
Parsonsburg, MD....................443-260-4800
Chisesi Brothers Meat Packing
New Orleans, LA....................800-966-3550
Citterio USA
Freeland, PA....................800-435-8888
Colony Brands Inc
Monroe, WI....................800-544-9036
Conagra Brands Inc
Chicago, IL....................877-266-2472
Conagra Foodservice
Chicago, IL....................877-266-2472
Continental Mills Inc
Tukwila, WA....................206-816-7000
Corfu Foods Inc
Bensenville, IL....................630-595-2510
County Gourmet Foods, LLC
Sewickley, PA....................412-741-8902
Cuisine Solutions Inc
Sterling, VA....................888-285-4679
Cumberland Gap Provision Company
Middlesboro, KY....................855-411-7675
Curtis Packing Co
Greensboro, NC....................336-275-7684
Dairy Fresh Foods Inc
Taylor, MI....................313-299-0735
Deep Foods Inc
Union, NJ....................908-810-7500
Devault Foods
Devault, PA....................800-426-2874
Dietz & Watson Inc.
Philadelphia, PA....................215-831-9000
Ding Hau Food Co, Ltd
Richmond, BC....................604-273-1188
Dippy Foods
Cypress, CA....................800-819-8551
Doerle Food Svc LLC
Broussard, LA....................800-256-1631
Dohar Meats Inc
Cleveland, OH....................216-241-4197
Earth Island
Chatsworth, CA....................888-394-3949
Earth Island
Chatsworth, CA....................888-394-3949
Emerling International Foods
Buffalo, NY....................716-833-7381
Enjoy Foods International
Fontana, CA....................909-823-2228
Euro Source Gourmet
Cedar Grove, NJ....................973-857-6000
F & S Produce Co Inc
Vineland, NJ....................800-886-3316
F & S Produce Co Inc
Vineland, NJ....................800-886-3316
Fine Choice Foods
Richmond, BC....................866-760-0888
Fishpeople
Portland, OR....................503-342-2424
Flavor Right Foods Group
St Phoenix, AZ....................888-464-3734
Frank Wardynski & Sons Inc
Buffalo, NY....................716-854-6083
Fried Provisions Company
Evans City, PA....................724-538-3160
Garden Protein International
Richmond, BC....................877-305-6777
GeeFree
Marina del Ray, CA....................310-862-8686
Glendora Quiche Company
San Dimas, CA....................909-394-1777
Golden Gulf Coast Packing Co
Biloxi, MS....................228-374-6121
Gonard Foods
Calgary, AB....................403-277-0991
Gopicnic Inc
Chicago, IL....................773-328-2490
Gouvea's & Purity Foods Inc
Honolulu, HI....................808-847-3717

Grecian Delight Foods Inc
Elk Grove Village, IL....................800-621-4387
Groff's Meats
Elizabethtown, PA....................717-367-1246
Gutheinz Meats Inc
Scranton, PA....................570-344-1191
H-E-B Grocery Co. LP
San Antonio, TX....................800-432-3113
Harold Food Company
Charlotte, NC....................704-588-8061
Hartselle Frozen Foods
Hartselle, AL....................256-773-7261
Harvest Time Foods
Ayden, NC....................252-746-6675
Hazle Park Quality Meats
West Hazleton, PA....................800-238-4331
Heinkel's Packing Co
Decatur, IL....................800-594-2738
Helen's Pure Foods
Cheltenham, PA....................215-379-6433
Herold's Salads
Cleveland, OH....................800-427-2523
HFI Foods
Redmond, WA....................425-883-1320
HFI Foods
Redmond, WA....................425-883-1320
Hip Chick Farms
....................707-861-9010
Holland American International Specialties
Bellflower, CA....................562-925-6914
Homestead Fine Foods
S San Francisco, CA....................650-615-0750
Homestead Fine Foods
S San Francisco, CA....................650-615-0750
Hoople Country Kitchen Inc
Rockport, IN....................877-466-7537
House of Thaller Inc
Knoxville, TN....................800-462-3365
HSR Associates Inc
Tarzana, CA....................818-757-7152
Hummel Brothers Inc
New Haven, CT....................800-828-8978
Ian's Natural Food
Framingham, MA....................508-283-1174
Independent Packers Corporation
Seattle, WA....................206-285-6000
Independent Packers Corporation
Seattle, WA....................206-285-6000
Ise America Inc
Galena, MD....................410-755-6300
Ise America Inc
Galena, MD....................410-755-6300
Ito Cariani Sausage Company
Hayward, CA....................510-887-0882
John Volpi & Co
St Louis, MO....................800-288-3439
Karine & Jeff
Los Angeles, CA
Kay Foods Co
Detroit, MI....................313-393-1100
Kelly Corned Beef Co
Chicago, IL....................800-624-5617
Kelly Foods
Jackson, TN....................731-424-2255
Kerala Curry
Pittsboro, NC....................919-545-9401
Kilgus Meats
Toledo, OH....................419-472-9721
King Kold Meats
Englewood, OH....................800-836-2797
Kitt's Meat Processing
Dedham, IA....................712-683-5622
Knotts Fine Foods
Paris, TN....................731-642-1961
Kubla Khan Food Company
Portland, OR....................503-234-7494
Lafitte Frozen Foods Corp
Lafitte, LA....................504-689-2041
Lakeside Foods Inc.
Manitowoc, WI....................800-466-3834
Land O'Frost Inc
Searcy, AR....................800-643-5654
Landolfi's Food Products
Trenton, NJ....................609-392-1830
Lengerich Meats Inc
Zanesville, IN....................260-638-4123
Leona Meat Plant
Troy, PA....................570-297-3574
Liguria Foods Inc
Humboldt, IA....................515-332-4121
Lisa Shively's Kitchen Helpers, LLC
Eden, NC....................336-623-7511

Locustdale Meat Packing
Locustdale, PA....................570-875-1270
Louisiana Packing Company
Westwego, LA....................800-666-1293
Love Quiches Desserts
Freeport, NY....................516-623-8800
Lower Foods, Inc.
Richmond, UT....................800-295-7898
Macabee Foods
West Nyack, NY....................845-623-1300
Made Rite Foods
Burlington, NC....................336-229-5728
Mah Chena Company
Chicago, IL....................312-226-5100
Manda Fine Meats Inc
Baton Rouge, LA....................800-343-2642
Maria & Son
St Louis, MO....................866-481-9009
Marsan Foods
Toronto, ON....................416-755-9262
Marshallville Packing Co
Marshallville, OH....................330-855-2871
Martin Rosols
New Britain, CT....................860-223-2707
Martin Rosols
New Britain, CT....................860-223-2707
Martin Seafood Company
Jessup, MD....................410-799-5822
Mcfarling Foods Inc
Indianapolis, IN....................317-635-2633
Mcgraths Seafood
Streator, IL....................815-672-2654
Meadows Country Products
Hollidaysburg, PA....................888-499-1001
Menemsha Fish Market
Chilmark, MA....................508-645-2282
Metafoods LLC
Brookhaven, GA....................404-843-2400
Mexi-Frost Specialties Company
Brooklyn, NY....................718-625-3324
Michael Foods, Inc.
Minnetonka, MN....................952-258-4000
Molinaro's Fine Italian Foods Ltd.
Mississauga, ON....................905-281-0352
Molinaro's Fine Italian Foods Ltd.
Mississauga, ON....................905-281-0352
Mrs Grissom's Salads Inc
Nashville, TN....................800-255-0571
Naleway Foods
Winnipeg, MB....................800-665-7448
Naleway Foods
Winnipeg, MB....................800-665-7448
Nestle USA
Mt Sterling, KY....................859-499-1100
Nestle USA Inc
Glendale, CA....................800-225-2270
Night Hawk Frozen Foods Inc
Buda, TX....................800-580-4166
Old Fashioned Kitchen Inc
Lakewood, NJ....................732-364-4100
On-Cor Frozen Foods
On-Cor Frozen Foods Redi-Serve
Aurora, IL....................920-563-6391
P.A. Braunger Institutional Foods
Sioux City, IA....................712-258-4515
Parma Sausage Products
Pittsburgh, PA....................877-294-4207
Pasta Factory
Melrose Park, IL....................800-615-6951
Paulsen Foods
Atlanta, GA....................404-873-1804
Pictsweet Co
Bells, TN....................731-663-7600
Plumrose USA
Chicago, IL....................800-526-4909
Pon Food Corp
Ponchatoula, LA....................985-386-6941
Preferred Meal Systems Inc
Moosic, PA....................570-457-8311
Prolimer Foods
Candiac, QC....................877-535-4631
Queen International Foods
Monterey Park, CA....................800-423-4414
R.C. McEntire & Company
Columbia, SC....................803-799-3388
R.L. Zeigler Company
Selma, AL....................800-392-6328
Rachael's Smoked Fish
Springfield, MA....................800-327-3412
Ramona's Mexican Foods
Gardena, CA....................310-323-1950

Rancho Sierra
Salinas, CA 800-398-2929
Real Kosher Sausage Company
Newark, NJ 973-690-5394
Regal Food Service
Houston, TX 281-477-3683
Rendulic Meat Packing Corp
Mckeesport, PA 412-678-9541
Request Foods Inc
Holland, MI 800-786-0900
Rich Products Corp
Vineland, NJ 800-818-9261
Roman Packing Company
Norfolk, NE 800-373-5990
Ruiz Food Products Inc.
Dinuba, CA 800-477-6474
Saag's Products LLC
San Leandro, CA 855-287-6562
Sales Associates Of Alaska
Fairbanks, AK 800-478-2371
Sanderson Farms
Laurel, MS 800-844-4030
Sandridge Food Corp
Medina, OH 800-627-2523
Saval Foods Corp
Elkridge, MD 800-527-2825
Schaefers Market
Sauk Centre, MN 320-352-6490
Schaller & Weber Inc
Astoria, NY 800-847-4115
Sculli Brothers
Yeadon, PA 215-336-1223
Sechrist Brothers
Dallastown, PA 717-244-2975
Seneca Foods Corp
Marion, NY 315-926-8100
Seviroli Foods
Garden City, NY 516-222-6220
Shamrock Foods Co
Phoenix, AZ 800-289-3663
Sheinman Provision Co
Philadelphia, PA 215-473-7065
Sims Wholesale
Batesville, AR 870-793-1109
Smith Packing Regional Meat
Utica, NY 315-732-5125
SONOCO
Houma, LA 800-458-7012
Souperb LLC
Emeryville, CA 415-685-8508
Spring Glen Fresh Foods
Ephrata, PA 800-641-2853
Spring Grove Foods
Miamisburg, OH 937-866-4311
Standard Meat Co LP
Dallas, TX 866-859-6313
Star Ravioli Mfg Co
Moonachie, NJ 201-933-6427
Starbucks
Seattle, WA 800-782-7282
Stawnichy Holdings
Mundare, AB 888-764-7646
Steak-Umm Company
Shillington, PA 860-928-5900
Stevens Sausage Co
Smithfield, NC 800-338-0561
Stonie's Sausage Shop
Perryville, MO 888-546-2540
Strong Roots
Brooklyn, NY 929-466-1639
Sunburst Foods
Goldsboro, NC 919-778-2151
Sunset Specialty Foods
Lake Arrowhead, CA 909-337-7643
Symphony Foods
Berkeley, CA 510-845-8275
Tampa Maid Foods Inc
Lakeland, FL 800-237-7637
Tasty Mix Quality Foods
Brooklyn, NY 718-855-7680
Tennessee Valley Packing Co
Columbia, TN 931-388-2623
Teti Bakery
Etobicoke, ON 800-465-0123
Thermo Pac LLC
Stone Mountain, GA 770-934-3200
Tomanetti Food Products Inc
Oakmont, PA 800-875-3040
Tomasso Corporation
Baie D'Urfe, QC 514-325-3000
Troy Foods Inc
Troy, IL 618-667-6332
Tyson Foods Inc.
Springdale, AR 800-233-6332
United Provision Meat Company
Columbus, OH 614-252-1126
Upstate Niagara Co-Op Inc.
Buffalo, NY 716-892-3156
Vanee Foods Co
Berkeley, IL 708-449-7300
Vienna Meat Products
Scarborough, ON 800-588-1931
Viking Seafoods Inc
Malden, MA 800-225-3020
W.A. Beans & Sons
Bangor, ME 800-649-1958
Warren & Son Meat Processing
Whipple, OH 740-585-2421
Wawona Frozen Foods Inc
Clovis, CA 559-299-2901
Wegmans Food Markets Inc.
Rochester, NY 800-934-6267
Winn-Dixie Stores
Jacksonville, FL 800-967-9105
Wornick Company
Cincinnati, OH 800-860-4555
Wornick Company
Cincinnati, OH 800-860-4555
Wornick Company
Cincinnati, OH 800-860-4555
Zartic Inc
Rome, GA 800-241-0516
Zuccaro Produce
Columbia Heights, MN 612-333-1122

Appetizers

Ajinomoto Foods North America, Inc.
Ontario, CA 909-477-4700
Anchor Appetizer Group
Appleton, WI 920-997-2200
Appetizers And, Inc.
Wilmington, WA 800-224-7630
B & D Foods
Boise, ID 208-344-1183
Belle River Enterprises
Belle River, PE 902-962-2248
Better Baked Foods Inc
North East, PA 814-725-8778
Biagio's Banquets
Chicago, IL 800-392-2837
Bylada Foods
Moonachie, NJ 201-933-7474
Caribbean Food Delights Inc
Tappan, NY 845-398-3000
Cateraid Inc
Howell, MI 800-508-8217
Cathay Foods Corporation
Boston, MA 617-427-1507
Chang Food Company
Garden Grove, CA 714-265-9990
Chateau Food Products Inc
Cicero, IL 708-863-4207
Chinese Spaghetti Factory
Boston, MA 617-445-7714
Conagra Brands Inc
Chicago, IL 877-266-2472
Conagra Foodservice
Chicago, IL 877-266-2472
Cordon Bleu International
Anjou, QC 800-363-1182
Culinaire
Denver, CO 877-502-9100
Dominex
St Augustine, FL 904-810-2132
Dufour Pastry Kitchens Inc
Bronx, NY 800-439-1282
Egg Roll Fantasy
Auburn, CA 530-887-9197
Fillo Factory, The
Northvale, NJ 800-653-4556
Fine Choice Foods
Richmond, BC 866-760-0888
Frozen Specialties Inc
Perrysburg, OH 419-867-2005
Fry Foods Inc
Tiffin, OH 800-626-2294
Glendora Quiche Company
San Dimas, CA 909-394-1777
Great American Appetizers
Nampa, ID 800-282-4834
Harvest Food Products Co Inc
Hayward, CA 510-675-0383
Health is Wealth Foods
Moonachie, NJ 201-933-7474
L & S Packing Co
Farmingdale, NY 800-286-6487
La Tang Cuisine Manufacturing
Houston, TX 713-780-4876
Lamb Weston Holdings Inc.
Eagle, ID 800-766-7783
Lee's Sausage Co
Orangeburg, SC 803-534-5517
Lemon & Vine
Napa, CA 707-926-6073
Lucky Foods
Tualatin, OR 503-612-1300
Mama Amy's Quality Foods
Mississauga, ON 905-456-0056
Matador Processors
Blanchard, OK 800-847-0797
McCain Foods USA Inc.
Oakbrook Terace, IL 800-938-7799
Mt. Olympus Specialty Foods
Buffalo, NY 716-874-0771
Nancy's Specialty Foods
Newark, CA 510-494-1100
Paulsen Foods
Atlanta, GA 404-873-1804
Perfect Bite Co
Glendale, CA 818-507-1527
Pie Piper Products
Wheeling, IL 800-621-8183
Piller's Fine Foods
Waterloo, ON 800-265-2627
Plenus Group Inc
Lowell, MA 978-970-3832
Produits Belle Baie
Caraquet, NB 506-727-4414
Sable & Rosenfeld Foods
Toronto, ON 416-929-4214
Sabra Blue & White Food Products
Dallas, TX 888-957-2272
Shonna's Gourmet Goodies
West Bridgewater, MA 888-312-7868
Sinbad Sweets
Madera, CA 866-746-2232
Sofo Foods
Toledo, OH 800-447-4211
Steak-Umm Company
Shillington, PA 860-928-5900
Tampa Maid Foods Inc
Lakeland, FL 800-237-7637
The Perfect Pita
Springfield, VA 703-644-0004
Thyme & Truffles Hors d'Oeuvres
Dollard-Des-Ormeaux, QC 877-785-9759
Tipiak Inc
Stamford, CT 203-961-9117
Valdez Food Inc
Philadelphia, PA 215-634-6106
Van-Lang Food Products
Countryside, IL 708-588-0800
William Poll Inc
New York, NY 800-993-7655
Willow Foods
Beaverton, OR 800-338-3609
Wonton Food
Brooklyn, NY 800-776-8889

Fresh, Canned & Frozen

Belle River Enterprises
Belle River, PE 902-962-2248
Biagio's Banquets
Chicago, IL 800-392-2837
Caribbean Food Delights Inc
Tappan, NY 845-398-3000
Cateraid Inc
Howell, MI 800-508-8217
Cathay Foods Corporation
Boston, MA 617-427-1507
Caughman's Meat Plant
Lexington, SC 803-356-0076
Cedar Key Aquaculture Farms
Riverview, FL 888-252-6735
Chang Food Company
Garden Grove, CA 714-265-9990
Chateau Food Products Inc
Cicero, IL 708-863-4207
Chinese Spaghetti Factory
Boston, MA 617-445-7714
Cordon Bleu International
Anjou, QC 800-363-1182
Dufour Pastry Kitchens Inc
Bronx, NY 800-439-1282
Fine Choice Foods
Richmond, BC 866-760-0888

Frozen Specialties Inc
Perrysburg, OH....419-867-2005
Glendora Quiche Company
San Dimas, CA....909-394-1777
Good Wives
Wilmington, MA....800-521-8160
Gourmet Foods Inc
Compton, CA....310-632-3300
Great American Appetizers
Nampa, ID....800-282-4834
La Tang Cuisine Manufacturing
Houston, TX....713-780-4876
Lancaster Colony Corporation
Westerville, OH....614-224-7141
Lee's Sausage Co
Orangeburg, SC....803-534-5517
Matador Processors
Blanchard, OK....800-847-0797
Nancy's Specialty Foods
Newark, CA....510-494-1100
Pie Piper Products
Wheeling, IL....800-621-8183
Piller's Fine Foods
Waterloo, ON....800-265-2627
Produits Belle Baie
Caraquet, NB....506-727-4414
Royal Palate Foods
Inglewood, CA....310-330-7701
Shonna's Gourmet Goodies
West Bridgewater, MA....888-312-7868
Silverleaf International Corp
Rosharon, TX....800-442-7542
Steak-Umm Company
Shillington, PA....860-928-5900
Tampa Maid Foods Inc
Lakeland, FL....800-237-7637
Thyme & Truffles Hors d'Oeuvres
Dollard-Des-Ormeaux, QC....877-785-9759
Tipiak Inc
Stamford, CT....203-961-9117
Van-Lang Food Products
Countryside, IL....708-588-0800
VLR Food Corporation
Vaughan, ON....800-387-7437

Frozen

Ajinomoto Foods North America, Inc.
Ontario, CA....909-477-4700
Appetizers And, Inc.
Wilmington, WA....800-224-7630
B & D Foods
Boise, ID....208-344-1183
Bylada Foods
Moonachie, NJ....201-933-7474
Caribbean Food Delights Inc
Tappan, NY....845-398-3000
Cathay Foods Corporation
Boston, MA....617-427-1507
Chang Food Company
Garden Grove, CA....714-265-9990
Chateau Food Products Inc
Cicero, IL....708-863-4207
Coastal Seafoods
Ridgefield, CT....203-431-0453
Cordon Bleu International
Anjou, QC....800-363-1182
Dufour Pastry Kitchens Inc
Bronx, NY....800-439-1282
Giorgio Foods
Temple, PA....800-220-2139
Good Wives
Wilmington, MA....800-521-8160
Great American Appetizers
Nampa, ID....800-282-4834
Health is Wealth Foods
Moonachie, NJ....201-933-7474
Matador Processors
Blanchard, OK....800-847-0797
McCain Foods Ltd.
Toronto, ON....416-955-1700
McCain Foods USA Inc.
Oakbrook Terace, IL....800-938-7799
Neilly's Foods
York, PA....717-668-3722
Paulsen Foods
Atlanta, GA....404-873-1804
Stacey's Famous Foods
Hayden, ID....800-782-2395
Steak-Umm Company
Shillington, PA....860-928-5900
Strong Roots
Brooklyn, NY....929-466-1639
Tampa Maid Foods Inc
Lakeland, FL....800-237-7637
Thyme & Truffles Hors d'Oeuvres
Dollard-Des-Ormeaux, QC....877-785-9759
Tipiak Inc
Stamford, CT....203-961-9117
William Poll Inc
New York, NY....800-993-7655

Refrigerated

Cyclone Enterprises Inc
Houston, TX....281-872-0087

Baked Beans (see also Pork & Beans)

Canned

Agfinity Inc
Eaton, CO....800-433-4688
Amigos Canning Company
San Antonio, TX....210-798-5360
Blue Runner Foods Inc
Gonzales, LA....225-647-3016
Burnette Foods
Elk Rapids, MI....231-264-8116
Burnham & Morrill Co
Portland, ME....800-813-2165
California Fruit and Tomato Kitchens
Modesto, CA....209-574-9407
Campbell Soup Co.
Camden, NJ....800-257-8443
Carriere Foods Inc
Saint-Denis-Sur-Richelie, QC....450-787-3411
Cordon Bleu International
Anjou, QC....800-363-1182
Eden Foods Inc
Clinton, MI....888-424-3336
Grandma Browns Beans Inc
Mexico, NY....315-963-7221
H.K. Canning
Ventura, CA....805-652-1392
Hanover Foods Corp
Hanover, PA....717-632-6000
Hoopeston Foods Inc
Burnsville, MN....952-854-0903
International Home Foods
Parsippany, NJ....973-359-9920
L & S Packing Co
Farmingdale, NY....800-286-6487
Lakeside Foods Inc.
Plainview, MN....507-534-3141
Lakeside Foods Inc.
Manitowoc, WI....800-466-3834
Mccall Farms
Effingham, SC....800-277-2012
Meridian Foods New Inc
Eaton, IN....765-396-3344
Miyako Oriental Foods Inc
Baldwin Park, CA....877-788-6476
Morgan Foods Inc
Austin, IN....888-430-1780
Nation Wide Canning Ltd.
Cottam, ON....519-839-4831
Natural Value
Sacramento, CA....916-836-3561
New Era Canning Company
New Era, MI....231-861-2151
New Harvest Foods
Washington, DC....920-822-2578
NORPAC Foods Inc
Salem, OR
Red River Commodities Inc
Fargo, ND....800-437-5539
Rio Valley Canning Co
Donna, TX....956-464-7843
Seneca Foods Corp
Princeville, IL....309-385-4301
Truitt Bros Inc
Salem, OR....800-547-8712
TyRy Inc
Rocklin, CA....800-322-6325
United Intertrade Corporation
Houston, TX....800-969-2233
Wornick Company
Cincinnati, OH....800-860-4555

Breaded Vegetables

Al Pete Meats
Muncie, IN....765-288-8817
Great American Appetizers
Nampa, ID....800-282-4834
Lake Erie Frozen Foods Co
Ashland, OH....800-766-8501
Pictsweet Co
Bells, TN....731-663-7600
Trans Pecos Foods
San Antonio, TX....210-228-0896
Westin Foods
Omaha, NE....800-228-6098

Breakfast Foods: Instant

Bake Crafters Food Company
McDonald, TN....423-396-3392
Bede Inc
Haledon, NJ....866-239-6565
Brekki
Carlsbad, CA....760-487-8895
California Cereal Products
Oakland, CA....510-452-4500
Campbell Soup Co.
Camden, NJ....800-257-8443
Continental Mills Inc
Tukwila, WA....206-816-7000
Country Smoked Meats
Bowling Green, OH....800-321-4766
Cream Of The West
Harlowton, MT....800-477-2383
Five Star Home Foods, Inc.
King of Prussia, PA....800-246-5405
GeeFree
Marina del Ray, CA....310-862-8686
GFA Brands Inc
Paramus, NJ....201-568-9300
Hodgson Mill Inc
Effingham, IL....800-347-0198
Homestead Mills
Cook, MN....800-652-5233
Ian's Natural Food
Framingham, MA....508-283-1174
International Home Foods
Parsippany, NJ....973-359-9920
Jimmy Dean Foods
Springdale, AR....800-925-3326
Kellogg Co.
Battle Creek, MI....800-962-1413
Little Crow Foods
Warsaw, IN....800-288-2769
Maxwell House & Post
Rye Brook, NY....914-335-2500
Nature's Legacy Inc.
Hudson, MI....517-448-2050
Quaker Oats Company
Peterborough, ON....800-267-6287
Real Food Marketing
Kansas City, MO....816-221-4100
San Francisco Spice Co.
Woodland, CA....866-972-6879
Sturm Foods Inc
Manawa, WI....800-347-8876
Tova Industries LLC
Louisville, KY....888-532-8682
US Mills
Bala Cynwyd, PA....800-422-1125

Broth

Canned, Frozen, Powdered

Blount Fine Foods
Fall River, MA....774-888-1300
Bookbinder Specialties LLC
Media, PA....215-322-1305
Clofine Dairy Products Inc
Linwood, NJ....609-653-1000
Cordon Bleu International
Anjou, QC....800-363-1182
Fuji Foods Corp
Browns Summit, NC....336-375-3111
Hormel Foods Corp.
Austin, MN....507-437-5611
International Dehydrated Foods
Springfield, MO....800-641-6509
Organic Gourmet
Sherman Oaks, CA....800-400-7772
Osso Good, LLC
San Rafael, CA
Sentry Seasonings
Elmhurst, IL....630-530-5370
SOUPerior Bean & Spice Company
Vancouver, WA....800-878-7687
St. Ours & Company
East Weymouth, MA....781-331-8520

Sweet Sue Kitchens
Athens, AL 256-216-0500
Tova Industries LLC
Louisville, KY 888-532-8682

Chicken

All-States Quality Foods
Charles City, IA 800-247-4195
Bonafide Provisions
San Diego, CA
Clofine Dairy Products Inc
Linwood, NJ 609-653-1000
Hain Celestial Group Inc
Lake Success, NY 800-434-4246
Imagine Foods
Boulder, CO 800-434-4246
Kettle & Fire
Austin, TX 415-857-0024
Sentry Seasonings
Elmhurst, IL 630-530-5370
Sweet Sue Kitchens
Athens, AL 256-216-0500
The Art of Broth, LLC
CA 818-715-9320
Vanee Foods Co
Berkeley, IL 708-449-7300

Chili

Aunt Kitty's Foods Inc
Vineland, NJ 856-691-2100
Baja Foods LLC
Chicago, IL 773-376-9030
Big B Barbecue
Evansville, IN 812-425-5235
Bruce Foods Corporation
Lafayette, LA 800-299-9082
Burnett & Son
Monrovia, CA 877-632-5467
Buxton Foods
Buxton, ND 800-726-8057
Campbell Soup Co.
Camden, NJ 800-257-8443
Carolina Packers Inc
Smithfield, NC 800-682-7675
Chandler Foods Inc
Greensboro, NC 800-537-6219
Cherchies
Malvern, PA 800-644-1980
Detroit Chili Co
Southfield, MI 248-440-5933
Edmond's Chile Co
St Louis, MO 314-772-1499
El Rey Cooked Meats
St Louis, MO 314-521-3113
Faribault Foods, Inc.
Fairbault, MN 507-331-1400
Fillo Factory, The
Northvale, NJ 800-653-4556
Harold Food Company
Charlotte, NC 704-588-8061
Health Valley Company
Irwindale, CA 800-334-3204
Hoopeston Foods Inc
Burnsville, MN 952-854-0903
International Home Foods
Parsippany, NJ 973-359-9920
Kelly Foods
Jackson, TN 731-424-2255
Kettle & Fire
Austin, TX 415-857-0024
Las Cruces Brand Products
El Paso, TX 915-779-5709
Lee's Sausage Co
Orangeburg, SC 803-534-5517
Leonard Mountain Inc
Bixby, OK 800-822-7700
Mi Ranchito Foods
Phoenix, AZ 602-272-3949
Milnot Company
Litchfield, IL 800-877-6455
Moonlite Bar-B-Q Inn
Owensboro, KY 800-322-8989
Mr Jay's Tamales & Chili
Lynwood, CA 310-537-3932
North of the Border
Tesuque, NM 800-860-0681
Original Chili Bowl
Ontario, CA 800-548-6363
Patagonia Provisions
Sausalito, CA 888-221-8208
Pokanoket Ostrich Farm
South Dartmouth, MA 508-992-6188
Supreme Frozen Products
Chicago, IL 773-622-3777
T.L. Herring & Company
Wilson, NC 252-291-1141
Taylor's Mexican Chili Co Inc
Carlinville, IL 800-382-4454
Terra Sol Chile Company
Austin, TX 512-836-3525
Texas Tamale Co
Houston, TX 713-795-5500
TODDS Enterprises Inc
Irvine, CA 800-568-6337
Torn & Glasser
Los Angeles, CA 800-282-6887
Vienna Beef LTD
Chicago, IL 800-366-3647
Vietti Foods Co Inc
Nashville, TN 615-244-7864
Wisconsin Packaging Corp
Fort Atkinson, WI 920-563-9363
Yankee Specialty Foods
Boston, MA 800-688-9904

Canned

Milnot Company
Litchfield, IL 800-877-6455
Pure Food Ingredients
Verona, WI 800-355-9601
Vanee Foods Co
Berkeley, IL 708-449-7300

Canned & Frozen

Aunt Kitty's Foods Inc
Vineland, NJ 856-691-2100
Baja Foods LLC
Chicago, IL 773-376-9030
Big B Barbecue
Evansville, IN 812-425-5235
Campbell Company of Canada
Toronto, ON 800-410-7687
Caughman's Meat Plant
Lexington, SC 803-356-0076
Chandler Foods Inc
Greensboro, NC 800-537-6219
Edmond's Chile Co
St Louis, MO 314-772-1499
First Original Texas Chili Company
Fort Worth, TX 800-507-0009
Kelly Foods
Jackson, TN 731-424-2255
Marsan Foods
Toronto, ON 416-755-9262
Mi Ranchito Foods
Phoenix, AZ 602-272-3949
Milnot Company
Litchfield, IL 800-877-6455
North of the Border
Tesuque, NM 800-860-0681
SOPAKCO Foods
Mullins, SC 800-276-9678
TODDS Enterprises Inc
Irvine, CA 800-568-6337
Westbrae Natural Foods
Melville, NY 800-434-4246
Worthmore Food Products Co
Cincinnati, OH 866-837-7687

Frozen

Bueno Foods
Albuquerque, NM 800-888-7336
Texas Chili Co
Fort Worth, TX 800-507-0009

with Cheese

Las Cruces Brand Products
El Paso, TX 915-779-5709

Chowder

Bay Shore Chowders & Bisques
Fall River, MA 888-675-6892
Blount Fine Foods
Fall River, MA 774-888-1300
Campbell Company of Canada
Toronto, ON 800-410-7687
Campbell Soup Co.
Camden, NJ 800-257-8443
Cherchies
Malvern, PA 800-644-1980
Denzer's Food Products
Baltimore, MD 410-889-1500
Fish Hopper
Monterey, CA 831-372-3406
LA Monica Fine Foods
Millville, NJ
Mid-Atlantic Foods Inc
Easton, MD 800-922-4688
Ronzoni
Largo, FL 800-730-5957
Triton Seafood Co
Medley, FL 305-888-0051
Valdez Food Inc
Philadelphia, PA 215-634-6106
Yankee Specialty Foods
Boston, MA 800-688-9904

Clam & Fish

Bay Shore Chowders & Bisques
Fall River, MA 888-675-6892
Blount Fine Foods
Fall River, MA 774-888-1300
Campbell Company of Canada
Toronto, ON 800-410-7687
Campbell Soup Co.
Camden, NJ 800-257-8443
Chincoteague Seafood Co Inc
Parsonsburg, MD 443-260-4800
Fish Hopper
Monterey, CA 831-372-3406
Kettle Cuisine
Lynn, MA 877-302-7687
LA Monica Fine Foods
Millville, NJ
Mid-Atlantic Foods Inc
Easton, MD 800-922-4688
Sea Watch Intl
Easton, MD 410-822-7500

Chutney

A Perfect Pear
Napa, CA 800-553-5753
Blue Jay Orchards
Bethel, CT 203-748-0119
Blueberry Store
Grand Junction, MI 877-654-2400
Chelsea Flower Market
New York, NY 888-727-7887
Chicama Vineyards
West Tisbury, MA 888-244-2262
Cinnabar Specialty Foods Inc
Prescott, AZ 866-293-6433
Coastal Classics
Duxbury, MA 508-746-6058
Commissariat Imports
Los Angeles, CA 310-475-5628
Creative Foodworks Inc
San Antonio, TX 210-212-4761
Cuizina Food Company
Woodinville, WA 425-486-7000
Curry King Corporation
Waldwick, NJ 800-287-7987
Delicae Gourmet
Tarpon Springs, FL 800-942-2502
Graves Mountain Lodge Inc.
Syria, VA 540-923-4231
Great American Foods Commissary
Hughes Springs, TX 903-639-1482
J.M. Smucker Co.
Orrville, OH 888-550-9555
Jay Shah Foods
Mississauga, ON 905-696-0172
Koloa Rum Corp
Kalaheo, HI 808-332-9333
Kozlowski Farms
Forestville, CA 800-473-2767
Outback Kitchens LLC
Huntington, VT 802-434-5262
Silver Palate Kitchens
Cresskill, NJ 201-568-0110
Solo Foods
Countryside, IL 800-328-7656
Spruce Mountain Blueberries
West Rockport, ME 207-236-3538
Steel's Gourmet Foods, Ltd.
Bridgeport, PA 800-678-3357
Tait Farm Foods
Centre Hall, PA 800-787-2716
Vermont Harvest Spec Food LLC
Stowe, VT 800-338-5354

Wild Thymes Farm Inc
Greenville, NY 845-266-8387
Wisconsin Wilderness Food Products
Lake Bluff, IL 800-359-3039

Convenience Food

American Wholesale Grocery
Mobile, AL 251-433-2528
Andalusia Distributing Co Inc
Andalusia, AL 334-222-3671
Anmar Foods
Chicago, IL 312-421-6500
Biagio's Banquets
Chicago, IL 800-392-2837
Big B Barbecue
Evansville, IN 812-425-5235
Camino Real Foods Inc
Vernon, CA 800-421-6201
Crum Creek Mils
Springfield, PA 888-607-3500
Delicious Frookie
Des Plaines, IL 847-699-3200
Dorothy Dawson Food Products
Jackson, MI 517-788-9830
Fantastic World Foods
Providence, RI
Forkless Gourmet Inc
Chicago, IL 312-474-5746
Grecian Delight Foods Inc
Elk Grove Village, IL 800-621-4387
Kelly Foods
Jackson, TN 731-424-2255
Kraft Heinz Canada
North York, ON 416-441-5000
Lundberg Family Farms
Richvale, CA 530-538-3500
McCain Foods Ltd.
Toronto, ON 416-955-1700
Michael Foods, Inc.
Minnetonka, MN 952-258-4000
Minsley, Inc.
Ontario, CA 909 458 1100
Movie Breads Food
Chateauguay, QC 450-692-7606
Naleway Foods
Winnipeg, MB 800-665-7448
Nancy's Specialty Foods
Newark, CA 510-494-1100
Natural Quick Foods
Seattle, WA 206-365-5757
Sunburst Foods
Goldsboro, NC 919-778-2151
Super Mom's LLC
St Paul Park, MN 800-944-7276
Suzanna's Kitchen
Peachtree Cor, GA 770-476-9900
Troverco
St. Louis, MO 800-468-3354

Frozen

Advance Pierre Foods
Cincinnati, OH 800-969-2747
Agrusa
Leonia, NJ 201-592-5950
Ajinomoto Foods North America, Inc.
Ontario, CA 909-477-4700
Al Pete Meats
Muncie, IN 765-288-8817
Applegate Farms
Bridgewater, NJ 866-587-5858
Barber Foods
Kings Mountain, NC 877-447-3279
Bernardi Italian Foods Company
Bloomsburg, PA 570-389-5500
Biagio's Banquets
Chicago, IL 800-392-2837
Buxton Foods
Buxton, ND 800-726-8057
Bylada Foods
Moonachie, NJ 201-933-7474
Camino Real Foods Inc
Vernon, CA 800-421-6201
Campbell Soup Co.
Camden, NJ 800-257-8443
Canada Bread Co, Ltd
Etobicoke, ON 800-465-5515
Catch Up Logistics
Pittsburgh, PA 412-441-9512
Cedar Lake Foods
Cedar Lake, MI 800-246-5039
Cedarlane Foods
Carson, CA 800-826-3322
Endico Potatoes Inc
Mt Vernon, NY 914-664-1151
English Bay Batter Us Inc
Columbus, OH 800-253-6844
Fine Choice Foods
Richmond, BC 866-760-0888
Forte Stromboli Company
Philadelphia, PA 215-463-6336
Giorgio Foods
Temple, PA 800-220-2139
Gonard Foods
Calgary, AB 403-277-0991
Harvest Time Foods
Ayden, NC 252-746-6675
High Liner Foods Inc.
Lunenburg, NS 902-634-8811
Hormel Foods Corp.
Austin, MN 507-437-5611
Juno Chef's
Goshen, NY 845-294-5400
Landolfi's Food Products
Trenton, NJ 609-392-1830
Love Quiches Desserts
Freeport, NY 516-623-8800
Macabee Foods
West Nyack, NY 845-623-1300
Made Rite Foods
Burlington, NC 336-229-5728
Maple Leaf Farms
St Leesburg, IN 800-348-2812
Marsan Foods
Toronto, ON 416-755-9262
Martin Seafood Company
Jessup, MD 410-799-5822
Michael Foods, Inc.
Minnetonka, MN 952-258-4000
Milnot Company
Litchfield, IL 800-877-6455
Miracapo Pizza
Elk Grove Village, IL 847-631-3500
Morningstar Farms
Zanesville, OH 800-535-5644
Morrison Lamothe
Toronto, ON 877-677-6533
Naleway Foods
Winnipeg, MB 800-665-7448
Nestle USA Inc
Glendale, CA 800-225-2270
Nickabood's Inc
Los Angeles, CA 213-746-1541
Night Hawk Frozen Foods Inc
Buda, TX 800-580-4166
Old Fashioned Kitchen Inc
Lakewood, NJ 732-364-4100
On-Cor Frozen Foods Redi-Serve
Aurora, IL 920-563-6391
Ore-Ida Foods
Pittsburgh, PA 800-255-5750
Pasta Factory
Melrose Park, IL 800-615-6951
Queen International Foods
Monterey Park, CA 800-423-4414
Ragozzino Foods Inc
Meriden, CT 800-348-1240
Ramona's Mexican Foods
Gardena, CA 310-323-1950
Request Foods Inc
Holland, MI 800-786-0900
Ruiz Food Products Inc.
Dinuba, CA 800-477-6474
Saffron Road
Stamford, CT 877-425-2587
Steak-Umm Company
Shillington, PA 860-928-5900
Sunset Specialty Foods
Lake Arrowhead, CA 909-337-7643
The Food Collective
Irvine, CA 866-328-8638
Thyme & Truffles Hors d'Oeuvres
Dollard-Des-Ormeaux, QC 877-785-9759
Tomasso Corporation
Baie D'Urfe, QC 514-325-3000
Turri's Italian Foods
Roseville, MI 586-773-6010
United Supermarkets
Lubbock, TX 806-745-9667
Wawona Frozen Foods Inc
Clovis, CA 559-299-2901
Zartic Inc
Rome, GA 800-241-0516

Crepes

Crepini
Pleasantville, NY 914-533-6645
Echo Lake Foods, Inc.
Burlington, WI 262-763-9551
Old Fashioned Kitchen Inc
Lakewood, NJ 732-364-4100
Table De France
Ontario, CA 909-923-5205

Croquettes

Hanover Foods Corp
Hanover, PA 717-632-6000

French Fries

Endico Potatoes Inc
Mt Vernon, NY 914-664-1151
Hanover Potato Products Inc
Hanover, PA 717-632-0700
Healthy Life Brands LLC
Wellesley, MA 508-401-7040
Lamb Weston Holdings Inc.
Eagle, ID 800-766-7783
McCain Foods Ltd.
Toronto, ON 416-955-1700
McCain Foods USA Inc.
Oakbrook Terace, IL 800-938-7799
Ore-Ida Foods
Pittsburgh, PA 800-255-5750
Qualifresh Michel St. Arneault
St. Hubert, QC 800-565-0550
Strong Roots
Brooklyn, NY 929-466-1639
Twin City Foods Inc.
Stanwood, WA 206-515-2400
VCPB Transportation
Secaucus, NJ 201-770-0070
Yum Yum Potato Chips
Warwick, QC 800-567-5792

Baked

McCain Foods Ltd.
Toronto, ON 416-955-1700

Canned

Emerling International Foods
Buffalo, NY 716-833-7381

Crinkle Cut

Lamb Weston Holdings Inc.
Eagle, ID 800-766-7783
McCain Foods Ltd.
Toronto, ON 416-955-1700

Frozen

Emerling International Foods
Buffalo, NY 716-833-7381
Endico Potatoes Inc
Mt Vernon, NY 914-664-1151
McCain Foods Ltd.
Toronto, ON 416-955-1700
Ore-Ida Foods
Pittsburgh, PA 800-255-5750
Qualifresh Michel St. Arneault
St. Hubert, QC 800-565-0550
Twin City Foods Inc.
Stanwood, WA 206-515-2400

Shoestring

Emerling International Foods
Buffalo, NY 716-833-7381
Ore-Ida Foods
Pittsburgh, PA 800-255-5750

Sweet

Lamb Weston Holdings Inc.
Eagle, ID 800-766-7783
McCain Foods Ltd.
Toronto, ON 416-955-1700

Tater Tots

McCain Foods Ltd.
Toronto, ON 416-955-1700

Wedges

Lamb Weston Holdings Inc.
Eagle, ID 800-766-7783

McCain Foods Ltd.
Toronto, ON 416-955-1700

French Toast

Continental Mills Inc
Tukwila, WA....................206-816-7000

Frozen

Continental Mills Inc
Tukwila, WA....................206-816-7000

Fresh

Cece's Veggie Co.
Austin, TX....................512-200-3337
DNO Inc
Columbus, OH 614-231-3601
G A Food Svc Inc
St Petersburg, FL....................800-852-2211
Garden Protein International
Richmond, BC 877-305-6777

Frozen

Ajinomoto Foods North America, Inc.
Ontario, CA....................909-477-4700
Best Chicago Meat
Chicago, IL
Better Baked Foods Inc
North East, PA....................814-725-8778
Blue Marble Brands
Providence, RI 888-534-0246
Burke Corp
Nevada, IA 800-654-1152
Caulipower
Encino, CA 844-422-8544
Charles Rockel & Son
Cincinnati, OH 513-631-3009
Conagra Brands Inc
Chicago, IL....................877-266-2472
Conagra Foodservice
Chicago, IL....................877-266-2472
Discovery Foods
Hayward, CA 510-780-9238
Emerling International Foods
Buffalo, NY....................716-833-7381
Freeze-Dry Foods Inc
Albion, NY 585-589-6399
Garden Protein International
Richmond, BC 877-305-6777
Giorgio Foods
Temple, PA 800-220-2139
Grainful
Ithaca, NY
Hook Line and Savor
Gloucester, MA....................833-457-2867
Ian's Natural Food
Framingham, MA 508-283-1174
Kraft Heinz Co.
Chicago, IL....................800-543-5335
Lisa's Organics
Carnelian Bay, CA 877-584-5711
Luvo Inc.
Blaine, WA 844-880-5886
Mamie's Pies
San Francisco, CA 415-870-0390
McCain Foods Ltd.
Toronto, ON 416-955-1700
On-Cor Frozen Foods
Oscar's Wholesale Meats
Ogden, UT....................801-621-5655
Paulsen Foods
Atlanta, GA....................404-873-1804
Popkoff's
City of Industry, CA....................844-767-5633
Red's All Natural
North Sioux City, SD 605-956-7337
Saffron Road
Stamford, CT....................877-425-2587
Schwan's Company
Marshall, MN 800-533-5290
Strong Roots
Brooklyn, NY 929-466-1639
The Food Collective
Irvine, CA....................866-328-8638
TMI Trading Co
Brooklyn, NY 718-821-5052

Giardiniera

Castella Imports Inc
Brentwood, NY....................631-231-5500

Colonna Brothers Inc
North Bergen, NJ 201-864-1115
Fontanini Italian Meats
McCook, IL....................800-331-6328
L & S Packing Co
Farmingdale, NY 800-286-6487
Orleans Packing Co
Hyde Park, MA....................617-361-6611

Hash

Canned & Frozen

Caughman's Meat Plant
Lexington, SC....................803-356-0076
Hormel Foods Corp.
Austin, MN 507-437-5611
Kelly Foods
Jackson, TN 731-424-2255
Lee's Sausage Co
Orangeburg, SC 803-534-5517
Ninety Six Canning Company
Ninety Six, SC 864-543-2700
SOPAKCO Foods
Mullins, SC....................800-276-9678

Hush Puppies

Atkinson Milling Co.
Selma, NC....................800-948-5707
Delta Pride Catfish
Indianola, MS 800-228-3474
Fry Krisp Food Products
Jackson, MI....................877-854-5440
Great American Foods Commissary
Hughes Springs, TX 903-639-1482
Lakeside Mills
Rutherfordton, NC 828-286-4866
Lone Star Consolidated Foods Inc.
Dallas, TX....................800-658-5637
Savannah Food Co
Savannah, TN 800-795-2550
Shenandoah Mills
Lebanon, TN....................615-444-0841
Triton Seafood Co
Medley, FL 305-888-0051

Frozen & Mixes

Tova Industries LLC
Louisville, KY 888-532-8682
Triton Seafood Co
Medley, FL 305-888-0051
Weisenberger Mills
Midway, KY 800-643-8678

Individual Packets

Foodservice

Baldwin Richardson Foods
Oakbrook Terrace, IL 866-644-2732
Heinz Portion Control
Jacksonville, FL 904-695-1300
Magic Seasoning Blends
New Orleans, LA 800-457-2857

Individual Quick Frozen Food

Applegate Farms
Bridgewater, NJ 866-587-5858
Appleton Produce Company
Weiser, ID 208-414-3352
Bandon Bay Fisheries
Bandon, OR 541-347-4454
Beef Products Inc.
North Sioux City, SD 605-217-8000
Boardman Foods Inc
Boardman, OR 541-481-3000
Burke Corp
Nevada, IA 800-654-1152
Cherryfield Foods
Cherryfield, ME 207-546-7573
Christy Wild Blueberry Farms
Amherst, NS 902-667-3013
Cuizina Food Company
Woodinville, WA....................425-486-7000
Eckert Cold Storage
Manteca, CA....................209-823-3181
Emerling International Foods
Buffalo, NY....................716-833-7381
Fish King
Glendale, CA 818-244-2161

Gay's Wild Maine Blueberries
Old Town, ME 207-570-3535
High Liner Foods Inc.
Lunenburg, NS 902-634-8811
Hillmans Shrimp & Oyster
Port Lavaca, TX 800-582-4416
Kashi Company
Solana Beach, CA....................877-747-2467
LA Monica Fine Foods
Millville, NJ
Leach Farms Inc
Berlin, WI 920-361-1880
Lef Bleuges Marinor
St-Felicien, QC 418-679-4577
Louisiana Packing Company
Westwego, LA....................800-666-1293
Merrill's Blueberry Farms
Ellsworth, ME....................800-711-6551
Mr Dell Foods
Kearney, MO....................816-628-4644
Nature Quality
San Martin, CA....................408-683-2182
On-Cor Frozen Foods
Ore-Cal Corp
Los Angeles, CA....................800-827-7474
Rainsweet Inc
Salem, OR....................800-363-4293
Sea Snack Foods Inc
Los Angeles, CA....................213-622-2204
Sun Glo Of Idaho
Sugar City, ID 208-356-7346
Sun Harvest Foods Inc
San Diego, CA 619-661-0909
Sure-Fresh Produce Inc
Santa Maria, CA 888-423-5379
The Food Collective
Irvine, CA....................866-328-8638
Unique Ingredients LLC
Gold Canyon, AZ 480-983-2498
Washington Rhubarb Grower Assn
Sumner, WA 800-435-9911

Knishes

Gabila's Knishes
Copiague, NY 631-789-2220
Oceanside Knish Factory
Oceanside, NY 516-766-4445

Meat Balls

Armanino Foods of Distinction
Hayward, CA 800-255-8588
Buona Vita Inc
Bridgeton, NJ 856-453-7972
Carando Gourmet Frozen Foods
Agawam, MA 888-227-2636
Cordon Bleu International
Anjou, QC....................800-363-1182
DelGrosso Foods
Tipton, PA....................800-521-5880
Devault Foods
Devault, PA....................800-426-2874
Fontanini Italian Meats
McCook, IL....................800-331-6328
King's Command Foods Inc
Green Bay, WA....................800-345-0293
Maid-Rite Steak Company
Dunmore, PA....................800-233-4259
Marcho Farms Inc
Harleysville, PA 215-721-7131
On-Cor Frozen Foods Redi-Serve
Aurora, IL 920-563-6391
Quality Sausage Company
Dallas, TX....................214-634-3400
Rich Products Corp
Vineland, NJ 800-818-9261

Canned

Acme Steak & Seafood
Youngstown, OH....................800-686-2263
Campbell Soup Co.
Camden, NJ....................800-257-8443
Cordon Bleu International
Anjou, QC....................800-363-1182

Frozen

Burke Corp
Nevada, IA 800-654-1152
Carando Gourmet Frozen Foods
Agawam, MA 888-227-2636

Devault Foods
Devault, PA........ 800-426-2874
Maid-Rite Steak Company
Dunmore, PA........ 800-233-4259
Mom's Food Company
Osterville, MA........ 800-969-6667
On-Cor Frozen Foods
On-Cor Frozen Foods Redi-Serve
Aurora, IL........ 920-563-6391
Quaker Maid Meats
Reading, PA........ 610-376-1500
Rich Products Corp
Vineland, NJ........ 800-818-9261
Turri's Italian Foods
Roseville, MI........ 586-773-6010
West Liberty Foods LLC
West Liberty, IA........ 888-511-4500

Swedish

Burke Corp
Nevada, IA........ 800-654-1152
Rose Packing Co Inc
South Barrington, IL........ 800-323-7363

Meat Loaf

Buona Vita Inc
Bridgeton, NJ........ 856-453-7972
Burnett & Son
Monrovia, CA........ 877-632-5467
Corfu Foods Inc
Bensenville, IL........ 630-595-2510
Fontanini Italian Meats
McCook, IL........ 800-331-6328
King's Command Foods Inc
Green Bay, WA........ 800-345-0293
Marcho Farms Inc
Harleysville, PA........ 215-721-7131
Mitchell Foods
Barbourville, KY........ 888-202-9745
On-Cor Frozen Foods
Rymer Foods
Chicago, IL........ 800-247-9637
Sandridge Food Corp
Medina, OH........ 800-627-2523
Sunset Farm Foods Inc
Valdosta, GA........ 800-882-1121

Onion Rings

Agri-Pack
Pasco, WA........ 509-545-6181
Great American Appetizers
Nampa, ID........ 800-282-4834
Matador Processors
Blanchard, OK........ 800-847-0797
Oxford Frozen Foods
Oxford, NS........ 902-447-2100
Westin Foods
Omaha, NE........ 800-228-6098
Yum Yum Potato Chips
Warwick, QC........ 800-567-5792

Frozen

Emerling International Foods
Buffalo, NY........ 716-833-7381
Fry Foods Inc
Tiffin, OH........ 800-626-2294
Great American Appetizers
Nampa, ID........ 800-282-4834
Lamb Weston Holdings Inc.
Eagle, ID........ 800-766-7783
Matador Processors
Blanchard, OK........ 800-847-0797
Oxford Frozen Foods
Oxford, NS........ 902-447-2100
Westin Foods
Omaha, NE........ 800-228-6098

Pancakes

Continental Mills Inc
Tukwila, WA........ 206-816-7000
Cook-In-The-Kitchen
Hampden, ME........ 207-848-4900
Old Fashioned Kitchen Inc
Lakewood, NJ........ 732-364-4100
Pamela's Products
Ukiah, CA........ 707-462-6605
Red Rose Trading Company
Lancaster, PA........ 717-293-7833
Ungars Food
Elmwood Park, NJ........ 201-773-6846

Frozen

Bake Crafters Food Company
McDonald, TN........ 423-396-3392
Continental Mills Inc
Tukwila, WA........ 206-816-7000
Old Fashioned Kitchen Inc
Lakewood, NJ........ 732-364-4100
Thomas Brothers Country Ham
Asheboro, NC........ 336-672-0337

Refrigerated

Echo Lake Foods, Inc.
Burlington, WI........ 262-763-9551

with Fruit

Continental Mills Inc
Tukwila, WA........ 206-816-7000

Pierogies

Ateeco Inc
Shenandoah, PA........ 800-743-7649
Aunt Kathy's Homestyle Products
Waldheim, SK........ 306-945-2181
Babci's Specialty Foods
Chicopee, MA........ 413-598-8158
Brom Food Group
St. Laurent, QC........ 514-744-5152
Giorgio Foods
Temple, PA........ 800-220-2139
Heritage Foods USA
New York, NY........ 718-389-0985
Millie's Pierogi
Chicopee Falls, MA........ 800-743-7641
Mrs. Ts Pierogies
Shenandoah, PA........ 800-743-7649
Naleway Foods
Winnipeg, MB........ 800-665-7448
Old Fashioned Kitchen Inc
Lakewood, NJ........ 732-364-4100
Popkoff's
City of Industry, CA........ 844-767-5633
Schwan's Company
Marshall, MN........ 800-533-5290

Pizza & Pizza Products

Al Safa Halal
New York City, NY........ 800-268-8147
Andre-Boudin Bakeries
San Francisco, CA........ 415-882-1849
Avanti Foods Co
Walnut, IL........ 800-243-3739
Baja Foods LLC
Chicago, IL........ 773-376-9030
BBU Bakeries
Horsham, PA........ 800-984-0989
Biagio's Banquets
Chicago, IL........ 800-392-2837
Blue Planet Foods
Collegedale, TN........ 877-396-3145
Burke Corp
Nevada, IA........ 800-654-1152
Bylada Foods
Moonachie, NJ........ 201-933-7474
California Blending Co
El Monte, CA........ 626-448-1918
Calise & Sons Bakery Inc
Lincoln, RI........ 800-225-4737
Canada Bread Co, Ltd
Etobicoke, ON........ 800-465-5515
Cappello's
Denver, CO........ 844-353-2863
Capri Bagel & Pizza Corporation
Brooklyn, NY........ 718-497-4431
Catch Up Logistics
Pittsburgh, PA........ 412-441-9512
Chelsea Milling Co.
Chelsea, MI........ 800-727-2460
Crestar Crusts
Washington Court House, OH........ 740-335-4813
Delgrosso Foods Inc.
Tipton, PA........ 800-521-5880
Dorothy Dawson Food Products
Jackson, MI........ 517-788-9830
Farm Boy Food Svc
Evansville, IN........ 800-852-3976
Fresh Mark Inc.
Massillon, OH........ 330-832-7491
Frozen Specialties Inc
Perrysburg, OH........ 419-867-2005
GeeFree
Marina del Ray, CA........ 310-862-8686
General Mills
Minneapolis, MN........ 800-248-7310
Gold Standard Baking Inc
Chicago, IL........ 800-648-7904
Home Run Inn Frozen Foods
Woodridge, IL........ 800-636-9696
Indian Foods Company, Inc.
Osseo, MN........ 866-331-7684
Kamish Food Products
Chicago, IL........ 773-725-6959
Kiki's Gluten-Free
Park Ridge, IL
Kosto Food Products Co
Wauconda, IL........ 847-487-2600
KT's Kitchens
Carson, CA........ 310-764-0850
L & S Packing Co
Farmingdale, NY........ 800-286-6487
Lamonaca Bakery
Windber, PA........ 814-467-4909
Leprino Foods Co.
Denver, CO........ 800-537-7466
Livermore Falls Baking Company
Livermore Falls, ME........ 207-897-3442
Longo's Bakery Inc
Hazleton, PA........ 570-454-5825
Magic Seasoning Blends
New Orleans, LA........ 800-457-2857
Mama Amy's Quality Foods
Mississauga, ON........ 905-456-0056
McCain Foods Ltd.
Toronto, ON........ 416-955-1700
Miracapo Pizza
Elk Grove Village, IL........ 847-631-3500
Molinaro's Fine Italian Foods Ltd.
Mississauga, ON........ 905-281-0352
Nardone Brothers
Hanover Twp, PA........ 800-822-5320
Nation Pizza & Foods
Schaumburg, IL........ 847-397-3320
Nation Wide Canning Ltd.
Cottam, ON........ 519-839-4831
Nestle USA Inc
Glendale, CA........ 800-225-2270
Northwestern Foods
Arden Hills, MN........ 800-236-4937
O'Neal's Fresh Frozen Pizza Crust
Springfield, OH........ 937-323-0050
Palmieri Food Products
New Haven, CT........ 800-845-5447
Pecoraro Dairy Products
Brooklyn, NY........ 718-388-2379
Pennsylvania Macaroni Company
Pittsburgh, PA........ 800-223-5928
Perky's Pizza
Oldsmar, FL........ 800-473-7597
Piqua Pizza Supply Co Inc
Piqua, OH........ 800-521-4442
Quality Sausage Company
Dallas, TX........ 214-634-3400
Rosina Food Holdings Inc
Buffalo, NY........ 888-767-4621
Schwan's Company
Marshall, MN........ 800-533-5290
Sunset Farm Foods Inc
Valdosta, GA........ 800-882-1121
Supreme Dairy Farms Co
Warwick, RI........ 401-739-8180
Swiss-American Sausage Company
Lathrop, CA........ 209-858-5555
Teeny Foods Inc
Portland, OR........ 503-252-3006
Teti Bakery
Etobicoke, ON........ 800-465-0123
Tip Top Canning Co
Tipp City, OH........ 800-352-2635
TNT Crust
Green Bay, WI........ 920-431-7240
Tomanetti Food Products
Oakmont, PA........ 800-875-3040
Tomanetti Food Products Inc
Oakmont, PA........ 800-875-3040
Tomaro's Bakery
Clarksburg, WV........ 304-622-0691
Triple K Manufacturing Company, Inc.
Shenandoah, IA........ 712-246-4376
Tyson Foods Inc.
Springdale, AR........ 479-290-4000
Valdez Food Inc
Philadelphia, PA........ 215-634-6106

Violet Packing Holdings LLC
Williamstown, NJ . . . 856-629-7428
Wanda's Nature Farm
Lincoln, NE . . . 800-735-6828
Weisenberger Mills
Midway, KY . . . 800-643-8678
Worthmore Food Products Co
Cincinnati, OH . . . 866-837-7687

Pizza

Amy's Kitchen Inc
Santa Rosa, CA . . . 707-781-6600
Andre-Boudin Bakeries
San Francisco, CA . . . 415-882-1849
Art's Tamales
Metamora, IL . . . 309-367-2850
Atlanta Bread Co.
Smyrna, GA . . . 800-398-3728
Aunt Kathy's Homestyle Products
Waldheim, SK . . . 306-945-2181
Berkshire Mountain Bakery
Housatonic, MA . . . 866-274-6124
Biagio's Banquets
Chicago, IL . . . 800-392-2837
BJ's Restaurants Inc.
Huntington Beach, CA . . . 714-500-2400
Bylada Foods
Moonachie, NJ . . . 201-933-7474
Cafe Moak
Rockford, MI . . . 616-866-7625
Catch Up Logistics
Pittsburgh, PA . . . 412-441-9512
Cedarlane Foods
Carson, CA . . . 800-826-3322
Chelsea Milling Co.
Chelsea, MI . . . 800-727-2460
Colors Gourmet Pizza
Vista, CA . . . 760-597-1400
Dorothy Dawson Food Products
Jackson, MI . . . 517-788-9830
European Egg Noodle Manufacturing
Edmonton, AB . . . 780-453-6767
Frozen Specialties Inc
Perrysburg, OH . . . 419-867-2005
Joe Corbis' Wholesale Pizza
Darnestown, MD . . . 888-526-7247
Kashi Company
Solana Beach, CA . . . 877-747-2467
Lucia's Pizza Co
St Louis, MO . . . 314-843-2553
Macabee Foods
West Nyack, NY . . . 845-623-1300
McCain Foods Ltd.
Toronto, ON . . . 416-955-1700
Molinaro's Fine Italian Foods Ltd.
Mississauga, ON . . . 905-281-0352
Mozzicato De Pasquale Bakery
Hartford, CT . . . 860-296-0426
Nardone Brothers
Hanover Twp, PA . . . 800-822-5320
Nestle USA Inc
Glendale, CA . . . 800-225-2270
New York Pizza
Daytona Beach, FL . . . 386-257-2050
Newman's Own
Westport, CT . . . 203-222-0136
Sunset Specialty Foods
Lake Arrowhead, CA . . . 909-337-7643
Superbrand Dairies
Montgomery, AL . . . 334-277-6010
Teeny Foods Inc
Portland, OR . . . 503-252-3006
Teti Bakery
Etobicoke, ON . . . 800-465-0123
The Perfect Pita
Springfield, VA . . . 703-644-0004
Troverco
St. Louis, MO . . . 800-468-3354

Cheese

Avanti Foods Co
Walnut, IL . . . 800-243-3739
Farm Boy Food Svc
Evansville, IN . . . 800-852-3976
Leprino Foods Co.
Denver, CO . . . 800-537-7466
Oh Yes! Foods
Los Angeles, CA . . . 855-696-4937
Pecoraro Dairy Products
Brooklyn, NY . . . 718-388-2379
Sun-Re Cheese Co
Sunbury, PA . . . 570-286-1511
Tomanetti Food Products Inc
Oakmont, PA . . . 800-875-3040

Crust

Berkshire Mountain Bakery
Housatonic, MA . . . 866-274-6124
Cali'flour Foods
Chico, CA . . . 866-422-3568
Calise & Sons Bakery Inc
Lincoln, RI . . . 800-225-4737
Chelsea Milling Co.
Chelsea, MI . . . 800-727-2460
Colors Gourmet Pizza
Vista, CA . . . 760-597-1400
Dorothy Dawson Food Products
Jackson, MI . . . 517-788-9830
Flamin' Red's Woodfired
Pawlet, VT . . . 802-325-3641
Giorgio Foods
Temple, PA . . . 800-220-2139
Livermore Falls Baking Company
Livermore Falls, ME . . . 207-897-3442
Lone Star Bakery
Round Rock, TX . . . 512-255-7268
Mama Mary's
Fairforest, SC . . . 800-813-7574
Mikey's
. . . 480-696-2483
Molinaro's Fine Italian Foods Ltd.
Mississauga, ON . . . 905-281-0352
Nation Pizza & Foods
Schaumburg, IL . . . 847-397-3320
Northwestern Foods
Arden Hills, MN . . . 800-236-4937
Pacific Ocean Produce
Santa Cruz, CA . . . 831-423-2654
Piqua Pizza Supply Co Inc
Piqua, OH . . . 800-521-4442
Rustic Crust Inc
Pittsfield, NH . . . 603-435-5119
Teeny Foods Inc
Portland, OR . . . 503-252-3006
Teti Bakery
Etobicoke, ON . . . 800-465-0123
TNT Crust
Green Bay, WI . . . 920-431-7240
Tomanetti Food Products Inc
Oakmont, PA . . . 800-875-3040
Tomaro's Bakery
Clarksburg, WV . . . 304-622-0691
Wrawp
Pomona, CA . . . 855-972-9748

Frozen

Badger Best Pizzas
De Pere, WI . . . 920-336-6464
Better Baked Foods Inc
North East, PA . . . 814-725-8778
Biagio's Banquets
Chicago, IL . . . 800-392-2837
Bylada Foods
Moonachie, NJ . . . 201-933-7474
Calise & Sons Bakery Inc
Lincoln, RI . . . 800-225-4737
Catch Up Logistics
Pittsburgh, PA . . . 412-441-9512
Caulipower
Encino, CA . . . 844-422-8544
Cedarlane Foods
Carson, CA . . . 800-826-3322
Chelsea Milling Co.
Chelsea, MI . . . 800-727-2460
Chicago Avenue Pizza
Chicago, IL . . . 800-244-8935
Giorgio Foods
Temple, PA . . . 800-220-2139
Kashi Company
Solana Beach, CA . . . 877-747-2467
Lucia's Pizza Co
St Louis, MO . . . 314-843-2553
Macabee Foods
West Nyack, NY . . . 845-623-1300
Made In Nature
Boulder, CO . . . 800-906-7426
Molinaro's Fine Italian Foods Ltd.
Mississauga, ON . . . 905-281-0352
Nation Pizza & Foods
Schaumburg, IL . . . 847-397-3320
Nestle USA Inc
Glendale, CA . . . 800-225-2270
Palermo's Pizza
Milwaukee, WI . . . 414-643-0919
Randy's Frozen Meats
Faribault, MN . . . 507-334-7177
Spinato's Fine Foods
Tempe, AZ . . . 480-275-4319
Sunset Specialty Foods
Lake Arrowhead, CA . . . 909-337-7643
Superbrand Dairies
Montgomery, AL . . . 334-277-6010
Tony's Pizza
Marshall, MN . . . 888-465-8324

Pizza Bagels

Giorgio Foods
Temple, PA . . . 800-220-2139

Pizza Toppings

Avanti Foods Co
Walnut, IL . . . 800-243-3739
Baja Foods LLC
Chicago, IL . . . 773-376-9030
Buona Vita Inc
Bridgeton, NJ . . . 856-453-7972
Burke Corp
Nevada, IA . . . 800-654-1152
Farm Boy Food Svc
Evansville, IN . . . 800-852-3976
Fontanini Italian Meats
McCook, IL . . . 800-331-6328
Fresh Mark Inc.
Massillon, OH . . . 330-832-7491
Mama Mary's
Fairforest, SC . . . 800-813-7574
Patrick Cudahy LLC
Cudahy, WI . . . 800-486-6900
Pocino Foods
City Of Industry, CA . . . 800-345-0150
Quality Sausage Company
Dallas, TX . . . 214-634-3400
Swiss-American Sausage Company
Lathrop, CA . . . 209-858-5555

Shells

Bowness Bakery
Calgary, AB . . . 403-250-9760
Lamonaca Bakery
Windber, PA . . . 814-467-4909
Livermore Falls Baking Company
Livermore Falls, ME . . . 207-897-3442
Longo's Bakery Inc
Hazleton, PA . . . 570-454-5825

Frozen

Rosina Food Holdings Inc
Buffalo, NY . . . 888-767-4621

Pork & Beans (see also Baked Beans)

International Home Foods
Parsippany, NJ . . . 973-359-9920
Morgan Foods Inc
Austin, IN . . . 888-430-1780

Canned

Grandma Browns Beans Inc
Mexico, NY . . . 315-963-7221
International Home Foods
Parsippany, NJ . . . 973-359-9920

Porkskins

Fried

Cajun

Quality Snack Foods Inc
Alsip, IL . . . 708-377-7120

Portion Contol & Packaged Foods

A To Z Portion Control Meats
Bluffton, OH . . . 800-338-6328
Acme Steak & Seafood
Youngstown, OH . . . 800-686-2263
Advance Pierre Foods
Cincinnati, OH . . . 800-969-2747
Al Pete Meats
Muncie, IN . . . 765-288-8817

ASC Seafood Inc
Largo, FL 800-876-3474

Baldwin Richardson Foods
Oakbrook Terrace, IL 866-644-2732

Bouma Meats
Provost, AB 780-753-2092

Branding Iron
Sauget, IL 800-851-4684

Broadleaf Venison USA Inc
Vernon, CA 800-336-3844

Bruno Specialty Foods
West Sayville, NY 631-589-1700

Bush Brothers Provision Co
West Palm Beach, FL 800-327-1345

C&S Wholesale Meat Company
Atlanta, GA 404-627-3547

Cal-Tex Citrus Juice LP
Houston, TX 800-231-0133

Cambridge Packing Company
Boston, MA 800-722-6726

Canal Fulton Provision
Canal Fulton, OH 800-321-3502

Cardinal Meat Specialists
Brampton, ON 800-363-1439

Cloverdale Foods
Mandan, ND 800-669-9511

Cloverland Dairy
Saint Clairsville, OH 740-699-0509

Colony Brands Inc
Monroe, WI 800-544-9036

Cuizina Food Company
Woodinville, WA 425-486-7000

Devault Foods
Devault, PA 800-426-2874

Dynamic Foods
Lubbock, TX 806-723-5600

Elwood International Inc
Copiague, NY 631-842-6600

Fancy Farms Popcorn
Bernie, MO 800-833-8154

Good Old Days Foods
Little Rock, AR 501-565-1257

Gouvea's & Purity Foods Inc
Honolulu, HI 808-847-3717

Heinz Portion Control
Jacksonville, FL 904-695-1300

Italia Foods
Schaumburg, IL 800-747-1109

Jemm Wholesale Meat Company
Chicago, IL 773-523-8161

John Garner Meats
Van Buren, AR 800-543-5473

Kenosha Beef International LTD
Kenosha, WI

King Kold Meats
Englewood, OH 800-836-2797

King's Command Foods Inc
Green Bay, WA 800-345-0293

Knouse Foods Co-Op Inc.
Peach Glen, PA 717-677-8181

Kutiks Honey Farm
Norwich, NY 607-336-4105

Kutztown Bologna Company
Leola, PA 800-723-8824

L & L Packing Co
Chicago, IL 800-628-6328

Land O'Frost Inc
Searcy, AR 800-643-5654

Leahy Orchards
Franklin Centre, QC 800-667-7380

Love Quiches Desserts
Freeport, NY 516-623-8800

Lynch Foods
North York, ON 416-449-5464

M Buono Beef Co
Philadelphia, PA 215-463-3600

Maid-Rite Steak Company
Dunmore, PA 800-233-4259

Marcho Farms Inc
Harleysville, PA 215-721-7131

Mardale Specialty Foods
Waukegan, IL 845-299-0285

Maxim's Import Corporation
Miami, FL 800-331-6652

Meat-O-Mat Corp
Brooklyn, NY 718-965-7250

National Foods
Indianapolis, IN 800-683-6565

New Generation Foods
Burnaby, BC 604-515-7438

Ocean Beauty Seafoods Inc
Seattle, WA 800-365-8950

Okuhara Foods Inc
Honolulu, HI 808-848-0581

Omaha Steaks Inc
800-960-8400

On-Cor Frozen Foods Redi-Serve
Aurora, IL 920-563-6391

Ossian Smoked Meats
Ossian, IN 800-535-8862

Pacific Poultry Company
Honolulu, HI 808-841-2828

Peggy Lawton Kitchens
East Walpole, MA 800-843-7325

Pierceton Foods Inc
Pierceton, IN 574-594-2344

Plymouth Beef Co.
Bronx, NY 718-589-8600

Pokanoket Ostrich Farm
South Dartmouth, MA 508-992-6188

Preferred Meal Systems Inc
Moosic, PA 570-457-8311

Premier Meat Co
Vernon, CA 800-555-5539

Prime Ostrich International
Morinville, AB 800-340-2311

Quality Croutons
Chicago, IL 800-334-2796

Quality Meats & Seafood
West Fargo, ND 800-342-4250

Quality Naturally Foods
City Of Industry, CA 888-498-6986

Schneider's Dairy Inc
Pittsburgh, PA 412-881-3525

Serv-Rite Meat Co Inc
Los Angeles, CA 323-227-1911

Skylark Meats
Omaha, NE 800-759-5275

Smith Packing Regional Meat
Utica, NY 315-732-5125

Spilke's Baking Company
Moosic, PA 570-457-2400

Stampede Meat, Inc.
Bridgeview, IL 800-353-0933

Stickney & Poor Company
Peterborough, NH 603-924-2259

Streit Carl & Son Co
Neptune, NJ 732-775-0803

Taku Smokehouse
Juneau, AK 800-582-5122

Temptee Specialty Foods
Denver, CO 800-842-1233

The Bruss Company
Chicago, IL 773-282-2900

Tiller Foods Company
Dayton, OH 937-435-4601

Travis Meats Inc
Powell, TN 800-247-7606

Triple U Enterprises
Fort Pierre, SD 605-567-3624

TyRy Inc
Rocklin, CA 800-322-6325

Tyson Foods Inc.
Springdale, AR 479-290-4000

Ultra Seal
New Paltz, NY 845-255-2490

United Meat Company
San Francisco, CA 415-864-2118

United Provision Meat Company
Columbus, OH 614-252-1126

Valley Meat Company
Modesto, CA 800-222-6328

WACO Beef & Pork Processors
Waco, TX 254-772-4669

Wawona Frozen Foods Inc
Clovis, CA 559-299-2901

Wing Nien Food
Hayward, CA 510-487-8877

Wing's Food Products
Toronto, ON 416-259-2662

Pot Pies

Cedarlane Foods
Carson, CA 800-826-3322

Morrison Lamothe
Toronto, ON 877-677-6533

Real Food Marketing
Kansas City, MO 816-221-4100

Stacey's Famous Foods
Hayden, ID 800-782-2395

Twin Hens
Princeton, NJ 908-925-9040

Pot Stickers

Ajinomoto Foods North America, Inc.
Ontario, CA 909-477-4700

Chang Food Company
Garden Grove, CA 714-265-9990

Harvest Food Products Co Inc
Hayward, CA 510-675-0383

Health is Wealth Foods
Moonachie, NJ 201-933-7474

Kubla Khan Food Company
Portland, OR 503-234-7494

Peking Noodle Co Inc
Los Angeles, CA 323-223-0897

Shine Foods Inc
Torrance, CA 310-533-6010

Wan Hua Foods
Seattle, WA 206-622-8417

Potato Products

Alexia Foods
Long Island City, NY 718-937-0100

Bob Evans Farms Inc.
800-939-2338

Idahoan Foods LLC
Idaho Falls, ID 800-746-7999

Maple Leaf Foods International
North York, ON 800-268-3708

McCain Foods Ltd.
Toronto, ON 416-955-1700

McCain Produce Inc.
Florenceville-Bristol, NB 506-392-3036

Pacific Valley Foods Inc
Bellevue, WA 425-643-1805

Rices Potato Chips
Biloxi, MS 228-396-5775

Seneca Foods Corp
Marion, NY 315-926-8100

Hash Browned Potatoes

Emerling International Foods
Buffalo, NY 716-833-7381

Idahoan Foods LLC
Idaho Falls, ID 800-746-7999

McCain Foods Ltd.
Toronto, ON 416-955-1700

Michael Foods, Inc.
Minnetonka, MN 952-258-4000

Mr Dell Foods
Kearney, MO 816-628-4644

Sun Glo Of Idaho
Sugar City, ID 208-356-7346

Prepared Meals

A Dozen Cousins
Berkeley, CA

Amigos Canning Company
San Antonio, TX 210-798-5360

Aunt Kitty's Foods Inc
Vineland, NJ 856-691-2100

Bakkavor USA
Charlotte, NC 800-842-3025

Barber Foods
Kings Mountain, NC 877-447-3279

Big Mountain Foods
Vancouver, BC

BlueWater Seafoods
Gloucester, MA 888-560-2539

Chandler Foods Inc
Greensboro, NC 800-537-6219

Cheating Gourmet
Auburn, ME 800-239-9731

Chef Hans' Gourmet Foods
Monroe, LA 800-890-4267

Feel Good Foods
Brooklyn, NY 800-638-8949

Gardein
Marina del Ray, CA 310-862-8686

Garden Protein International
Richmond, BC 877-305-6777

Good Food Made Simple
Wellesley, MA 800-535-3447

Grandcestors
Golden, CO

Halal Fine Foods
Toronto, ON 416-679-8000

Hans Kissle Co
Haverhill, MA 978-556-4500

Henry J's Meat Specialties
Chicago, IL 800-242-1314

J B & Son LTD
Yonkers, NY . . . 914-963-5192
J&M Food Products Co
Deerfield, IL . . . 847-948-1290
Jackfruit Company, The
Boulder, CO . . . 877-433-4024
JTM Food Group
Harrison, OH. . . . 800-626-2308
Kashi Company
Solana Beach, CA. . . . 877-747-2467
Melba's Old School Po Boys
New Orleans, LA . . . 504-267-7765
Modern Table
Walnut Creek, CA
Molinaro's Fine Italian Foods Ltd.
Mississauga, ON. . . . 905-281-0352
O'Sole Mio
Boisbriand, QC. . . . 844-696-8933
Pacific Foods of Oregon
Tualatin, OR . . . 503-692-9666
Patty Palace Foods
Toronto, ON . . . 416-297-0510
Rosina Food Holdings Inc
Buffalo, NY. . . . 888-767-4621
Schwan's Company
Marshall, MN . . . 800-533-5290
Seneca Foods Corp
Marion, NY. . . . 315-926-8100
Snapdragon Foods
Oakland, CA . . . 877-881-7627
Soylent
Los Angeles, CA
Stonewall Kitchen
York, ME. . . . 800-826-1752
Suji's Korean Cuisine
Seattle, WA . . . 206-985-6640
The Food Collective
Irvine, CA . . . 866-328-8638
TreeHouse Foods, Inc.
Oak Brook, IL. . . . 708-483-1300
Tyson Foods Inc.
Springdale, AR . . . 479-290-4000

Beef Dinner

Big B Barbecue
Evansville, IN . . . 812-425-5235
Henry J's Meat Specialties
Chicago, IL . . . 800-242-1314
Kelly Foods
Jackson, TN . . . 731-424-2255
Melba's Old School Po Boys
New Orleans, LA . . . 504-267-7765
Night Hawk Frozen Foods Inc
Buda, TX. . . . 800-580-4166

Breakfast

Good Food Made Simple
Wellesley, MA. . . . 800-535-3447
Ise America Inc
Galena, MD. . . . 410-755-6300
Jimmy Dean Foods
Springdale, AR . . . 800-925-3326
Michael Foods, Inc.
Minnetonka, MN. . . . 952-258-4000

Burritos

Chimichangas

Burrito Kitchens
Longmont, CO . . . 720-652-9000
Camino Real Foods Inc
Vernon, CA . . . 800-421-6201
Good Food Made Simple
Wellesley, MA. . . . 800-535-3447
Queen International Foods
Monterey Park, CA. . . . 800-423-4414
Red's All Natural
North Sioux City, SD . . . 605-956-7337
Troverco
St. Louis, MO . . . 800-468-3354

Canned

Kelly Foods
Jackson, TN . . . 731-424-2255

Casseroles

Dynamic Foods
Lubbock, TX. . . . 806-723-5600
Good Old Days Foods
Little Rock, AR. . . . 501-565-1257
Marsan Foods
Toronto, ON . . . 416-755-9262
Savannah Food Co
Savannah, TN . . . 800-795-2550

Convenience

Chef Hans' Gourmet Foods
Monroe, LA. . . . 800-890-4267
Crafty Counter
Austin, TX. . . . 512-643-2412
Homegrown Naturals
Napa, CA. . . . 800-288-1089
Patty Palace Foods
Toronto, ON . . . 416-297-0510
Soylent
Los Angeles, CA

Corn Fritters

Triton Seafood Co
Medley, FL . . . 305-888-0051

Crab

Stuffed

Boja's Foods Inc
Bayou La Batre, AL . . . 251-824-4186

Eggplant Parmigiana

Bruno Specialty Foods
West Sayville, NY. . . . 631-589-1700
Pasta Factory
Melrose Park, IL. . . . 800-615-6951

Eggs

Dixie Egg Co
Jacksonville, FL . . . 800-394-3447
Good Food Made Simple
Wellesley, MA. . . . 800-535-3447
Great Valley Mills
Barto, PA. . . . 800-688-6455
Ise America Inc
Galena, MD. . . . 410-755-6300
Michael Foods, Inc.
Minnetonka, MN. . . . 952-258-4000

Entrees

Ajinomoto Frozen Foods USA, Inc.
Ontario, CA. . . . 866-536-8008
Bellisio Foods
Minneapolis, MN
Bernardi Italian Foods Company
Bloomsburg, PA . . . 570-389-5500
Blue Runner Foods Inc
Gonzales, LA . . . 225-647-3016
Boudreaux's Foods
New Orleans, LA . . . 504-733-8440
Burnett & Son
Monrovia, CA. . . . 877-632-5467
Carando Gourmet Frozen Foods
Agawam, MA . . . 888-227-2636
Culinary Revolution
La Jolla, CA . . . 858-454-4390
Deep Foods Inc
Union, NJ . . . 908-810-7500
Ethnic Gourmet Foods
Boulder, CO . . . 800-434-4246
Five Star Home Foods, Inc.
King of Prussia, PA. . . . 800-246-5405
Good Food Made Simple
Wellesley, MA. . . . 800-535-3447
Heinz Quality Chef Foods Inc
Cedar Rapids, IA. . . . 800-356-8307
HFI Foods
Redmond, WA. . . . 425-883-1320
JTM Food Group
Harrison, OH. . . . 800-626-2308
Kent Precision Foods Group Inc
Muscatine, IA . . . 800-442-5242
King Kold Meats
Englewood, OH . . . 800-836-2797
Marsan Foods
Toronto, ON . . . 416-755-9262
Melba's Old School Po Boys
New Orleans, LA . . . 504-267-7765
Natural Quick Foods
Seattle, WA . . . 206-365-5757
Paulsen Foods
Atlanta, GA. . . . 404-873-1804
Plenus Group Inc
Lowell, MA. . . . 978-970-3832
Ragozzino Foods Inc
Meriden, CT . . . 800-348-1240
Ruggiero Seafood
Newark, NJ . . . 866-225-2627
Spring Glen Fresh Foods
Ephrata, PA . . . 800-641-2853
Steak-Umm Company
Shillington, PA . . . 860-928-5900
Stefano Foods
Charlotte, NC . . . 800-340-4019
Sugar Foods Corp
Sun Valley, CA . . . 818-768-7900
Tamarind Tree
Neshanic Station, NJ. . . . 800-432-8733
Taste Traditions Inc
Omaha, NE . . . 800-228-2170
Thyme & Truffles Hors d'Oeuvres
Dollard-Des-Ormeaux, QC. . . . 877-785-9759
Wild Zora Foods
Loveland, CO . . . 970-541-9672

Frozen

Alfredo Aiello Italian Food
Quincy, MA. . . . 617-770-6360
Amy's Kitchen Inc
Santa Rosa, CA. . . . 707-781-6600
Beetnik Foods, LLC
Austin, TX. . . . 512-548-8228
Bellisio Foods
Minneapolis, MN
Bernardi Italian Foods Company
Bloomsburg, PA . . . 570-389-5500
Carando Gourmet Frozen Foods
Agawam, MA . . . 888-227-2636
CK Living LLC
River Edge, NJ . . . 201-261-2078
Deep Foods Inc
Union, NJ . . . 908-810-7500
Dynamic Foods
Lubbock, TX. . . . 806-723-5600
Fairfield Farm Kitchens
Brockton, MA . . . 508-584-9300
Grainful
Ithaca, NY
HFI Foods
Redmond, WA. . . . 425-883-1320
Kashi Company
Solana Beach, CA. . . . 877-747-2467
Kelly Gourmet Foods Inc
San Francisco, CA . . . 415-648-9200
Kent Precision Foods Group Inc
Muscatine, IA . . . 800-442-5242
King Kold Meats
Englewood, OH . . . 800-836-2797
Lenchner Bakery
Concord, ON. . . . 905-738-8811
Marsan Foods
Toronto, ON . . . 416-755-9262
Michael Angelo's Inc
Austin, TX. . . . 877-482-5426
Milmar Food Group
Goshen, NY. . . . 845-294-5400
Night Hawk Frozen Foods Inc
Buda, TX. . . . 800-580-4166
Oven Poppers
Manchester, NH . . . 603-644-3773
Paulsen Foods
Atlanta, GA. . . . 404-873-1804
Royal Palate Foods
Inglewood, CA . . . 310-330-7701
Ruggiero Seafood
Newark, NJ . . . 866-225-2627
Steak-Umm Company
Shillington, PA . . . 860-928-5900
The Food Collective
Irvine, CA. . . . 866-328-8638
Thyme & Truffles Hors d'Oeuvres
Dollard-Des-Ormeaux, QC. . . . 877-785-9759

Microwavable

Conagra Brands Inc
Chicago, IL . . . 877-266-2472
Conagra Foodservice
Chicago, IL . . . 877-266-2472
Vana Life Foods
Seattle, WA . . . 347-446-6504

Shelf Stable

Cordon Bleu International
Anjou, QC 800-363-1182
Dorina So-Good Inc
Union, IL. . . . 815-923-2144
Good For You America
Concordia, MO 866-329-5969
Hanover Foods Corp
Hanover, PA 717-632-6000
Health Valley Company
Irwindale, CA 800-334-3204
Hormel Foods Corp.
Austin, MN 507-437-5611
Joelle's Choice Specialty Foods LLC
Fairfield, IA 800-880-2779
Lundberg Family Farms
Richvale, CA. . . . 530-538-3500
Mr Jay's Tamales & Chili
Lynwood, CA 310-537-3932
My Own Meals Inc
Deerfield, IL 847-948-1118
Sabra Dipping Company,LL
Oceanside, CA 800-748-5523
SOPAKCO Foods
Mullins, SC. . . . 800-276-9678
Spring Glen Fresh Foods
Ephrata, PA 800-641-2853
Sugar Foods Corp
Sun Valley, CA 818-768-7900
Truitt Bros Inc
Salem, OR. . . . 800-547-8712
Vigo Importing Co
Tampa, FL. . . . 800-282-4130

Etoufee

Chef Hans' Gourmet Foods
Monroe, LA. . . . 800-890-4267

Fish

Carrington Foods Co Inc
Saraland, AL 251-675-9700
Cuizina Food Company
Woodinville, WA. . . . 425-486-7000
Fishpeople
Portland, OR 503-342-2424
Janes Family Foods
Mississauga, ON. . . . 800-565-2637
Love The Wild
Boulder, CO 844-424-9875
Melba's Old School Po Boys
New Orleans, LA 504-267-7765
Menemsha Fish Market
Chilmark, MA. . . . 508-645-2282
Quinault Pride
Taholah, WA 360-276-4431
Stacey's Famous Foods
Hayden, ID 800-782-2395

Stuffed

Anchor Frozen Foods
Westbury, NY 800-566-3474
Beaver Street Fisheries
Jacksonville, FL 800-874-6426
King & Prince Seafood Corp
Brunswick, GA 800-841-0205
Sweet Water Seafood
Carlstadt, NJ 201-939-6622
Tampa Maid Foods Inc
Lakeland, FL. . . . 800-237-7637

Fish & Chips

Viking Seafoods Inc
Malden, MA 800-225-3020

Fish Patties

Pacific Salmon Company
Edmonds, WA. . . . 425-774-1315
Viking Seafoods Inc
Malden, MA 800-225-3020

Fish Sticks

Channel Fish Processing
Gloucester, MA. . . . 800-457-0054
Ungars Food
Elmwood Park, NJ 201-773-6846
Viking Seafoods Inc
Malden, MA 800-225-3020

Frozen

Al Safa Halal
New York City, NY. . . . 800-268-8147
BlueWater Seafoods
Gloucester, MA. . . . 888-560-2539
Tichon Sea Food Corp
New Bedford, MA 508-999-5607
Viking Seafoods Inc
Malden, MA 800-225-3020

Fried Rice

Willow Foods
Beaverton, OR 800-338-3609

Frozen

Bake Crafters Food Company
McDonald, TN 423-396-3392
Biagio's Banquets
Chicago, IL. . . . 800-392-2837
Birdseye Food
Mountain Lakes, NJ 585-383-1850
Cuizina Food Company
Woodinville, WA. . . . 425-486-7000
G A Food Svc Inc
St Petersburg, FL. . . . 800-852-2211
Grandcestors
Golden, CO
Heinkel's Packing Co
Decatur, IL 800-594-2738
High Liner Foods Inc.
Lunenburg, NS 902-634-8811
Kidfresh
New York, NY 212-686-4303
McCain Foods Ltd.
Toronto, ON 416-955-1700
Monsoon Kitchens
Shrewsbury, MA 508-842-0070
Neilly's Foods
York, PA 717-668-3722
Path of Life
Warrenville, IL 844-248-9997
Philadelphia Cheese Steak
Philadelphia, PA 800-342-9771
Quorn Foods
Chicago, IL
The Food Collective
Irvine, CA. . . . 866-328-8638

Gyros

Corfu Foods Inc
Bensenville, IL 630-595-2510
Corfu Foods Inc
Bensenville, IL 800-874-9767
Kronos
Glendale Heights, IL. . . . 800-621-0099

Lasagna

Alfredo Aiello Italian Food
Quincy, MA. . . . 617-770-6360
Homestead Fine Foods
S San Francisco, CA. . . . 650-615-0750

Macaroni

Campbell Soup Co.
Camden, NJ. . . . 800-257-8443
Gilster-Mary Lee Corp
Chester, IL. . . . 618-826-2361
Molinaro's Fine Italian Foods Ltd.
Mississauga, ON. . . . 905-281-0352

Mozzarella Sticks

Giorgio Foods
Temple, PA 800-220-2139
Matador Processors
Blanchard, OK 800-847-0797

Pasta & Noodle Dishes

Agrusa
Leonia, NJ. . . . 201-592-5950
Alfredo Aiello Italian Food
Quincy, MA. . . . 617-770-6360
Antoni Ravioli Co
North Massapequa, NY 800-783-0350
Barilla USA
Northbrook, IL 800-922-7455
Bernardi Italian Foods Company
Bloomsburg, PA 570-389-5500
Bruno Specialty Foods
West Sayville, NY. . . . 631-589-1700
Carando Gourmet Frozen Foods
Agawam, MA 888-227-2636
Cuizina Food Company
Woodinville, WA. . . . 425-486-7000
Dabruzzi's Italian Foods
Hudson, WI. . . . 715-386-3653
Food City USA
Arvada, CO. . . . 303-321-4447
Landolfi's Food Products
Trenton, NJ 609-392-1830
On-Cor Frozen Foods
Plentiful Pantry
Salt Lake City, UT 801-977-9077
Ragozzino Foods Inc
Meriden, CT 800-348-1240
Rich Products Corp
Vineland, NJ 800-818-9261
S T Specialty Foods Inc
Brooklyn Park, MN. . . . 763-493-9600
Sandridge Food Corp
Medina, OH. . . . 800-627-2523
Seviroli Foods
Garden City, NY. . . . 516-222-6220
Sidari's Italian Foods
Cleveland, OH 216-431-3344
Star Ravioli Mfg Co
Moonachie, NJ 201-933-6427
The Food Collective
Irvine, CA 866-328-8638

Rice

Amalgamated Produce
Bridgeport, CT 800-358-3808
Chef Soraya
Boulder, CO 800-677-7423
Minsley, Inc.
Ontario, CA. . . . 909-458-1100
Penguin Natural Food Inc
Vernon, CA 323-727-7980
Tony Chachere's Creole Foods
Opelousas, LA 800-551-9066

Salad

Classic Commissary
Binghamton, NY. . . . 800-929-3486
Club Chef LLC
Covington, KY 859-578-3100
F & S Produce Co Inc
Vineland, NJ 800-886-3316
Hans Kissle Co
Haverhill, MA. . . . 978-556-4500
Lakeside Foods Inc.
Manitowoc, WI. . . . 800-466-3834
Paisley Farms Inc
Willoughby, OH 800-474-5688
R.C. McEntire & Company
Columbia, SC 803-799-3388
Ready Pac Foods Inc
Irwindale, CA 800-800-4088
Sandridge Food Corp
Medina, OH. . . . 800-627-2523
Suter Co Inc
Sycamore, IL. . . . 800-435-6942
Troverco
St. Louis, MO 800-468-3354

Sandwiches

B-S Foods Company
Oklahoma City, OK 405-949-9797
Bake Crafters Food Company
McDonald, TN 423-396-3392
Better Baked Foods Inc
North East, PA. . . . 814-725-8778
Black's Barbecue
Lockhart, TX. . . . 888-632-8225
Bridgford Foods Corp
Anaheim, CA 800-527-2105
Camino Real Foods Inc
Vernon, CA 800-421-6201
Chef's Pride Gifts LLC
Taylor, MI 800-878-1800
Chicken Salad Chick
Auburn, AL. . . . 334-275-4578
Classic Delight Inc
St Marys, OH 800-274-9828
Corfu Foods Inc
Bensenville, IL 630-595-2510
Country Smoked Meats
Bowling Green, OH 800-321-4766

E A Sween Co
Eden Prairie, MN 800-328-8184
Eastside Deli Supply
Lansing, MI. 800-349-6694
Food Factory
Honolulu, HI. 808-593-2633
Helen's Pure Foods
Cheltenham, PA 215-379-6433
Hormel Foods Corp.
Austin, MN 507-437-5611
JTM Food Group
Harrison, OH. 800-626-2308
Knotts Fine Foods
Paris, TN. 731-642-1961
Lilydale Foods
Markham, ON. 800-661-5341
Made-Rite Sandwich Co
Ooltewah, TN 800-343-1327
Maui Bagel
Kahului, HI. 808-270-7561
Meat & Supply Co
New York, NY 646-864-0967
Piemonte Bakery Co
Rockford, IL 815-962-4833
Royal Touch Foods
Etobicoke, ON 416-213-1077
Safeway Inc.
Pleasanton, CA 877-723-3929
Southern Belle Sandwich Company
Baton Rouge, LA 800-344-4670
Steak-Umm Company
Shillington, PA 860-928-5900
Sunburst Foods
Goldsboro, NC 919-778-2151
Troverco
St. Louis, MO 800-468-3354
UBF Food Solutions
Lisle, IL. 630-955-5394
Zartic Inc
Rome, GA 800-241-0516

Pocket

Applegate Farms
Bridgewater, NJ 866-587-5858
Nestle USA Inc
Glendale, CA 800-225-2270
Patty Palace Foods
Toronto, ON 416-297-0510

Scampi

Shrimp Frozen

Cheating Gourmet
Auburn, ME 800-239-9731

Seafood

AquaCuisine
Portland, OR. 208-323-2782
Carnival Brands Mfg
New Orleans, LA 800-925-2774
Carrington Foods Co Inc
Saraland, AL. 251-675-9700
Channel Fish Processing
Gloucester, MA. 800-457-0054
Chincoteague Seafood Co Inc
Parsonsburg, MD 443-260-4800
Cuizina Food Company
Woodinville, WA. 425-486-7000
Fish King
Glendale, CA 818-244-2161
Gulf City Marine Supply
Bayou La Batre, AL 251-824-2516
King & Prince Seafood Corp
Brunswick, GA. 800-841-0205
Melba's Old School Po Boys
New Orleans, LA 504-267-7765
Menemsha Fish Market
Chilmark, MA. 508-645-2282
Neptune Fisheries
Newport News, VA. 800-545-7474
Oven Poppers
Manchester, NH 603-644-3773
Ruggiero Seafood
Newark, NJ. 866-225-2627
Sea Pearl Seafood
Bayou La Batre, AL 800-872-8804
Tex-Mex Cold Storage
Brownsville, TX. 956-831-9433
Triton Seafood Co
Medley, FL 305-888-0051

Weyand's Fishery
Wyandotte, MI 800-521-9815

Spaghetti

Canned

Campbell Soup Co.
Camden, NJ. 800-257-8443
Hormel Foods Corp.
Austin, MN 507-437-5611
Seneca Foods Corp
Marion, NY. 315-926-8100

with Meatballs

Burnett & Son
Monrovia, CA. 877-632-5467
JTM Food Group
Harrison, OH. 800-626-2308

Stuffed Cabbage

Morrison Lamothe
Toronto, ON 877-677-6533

Stuffed Peppers

L & S Packing Co
Farmingdale, NY 800-286-6487
Matador Processors
Blanchard, OK 800-847-0797
Norpaco Inc
Middletown, CT 800-252-0222
Vega Food Industries Inc
Cranston, RI 800-973-7737

Stuffed Shells

Antoni Ravioli Co
North Massapequa, NY 800-783-0350
Bruno Specialty Foods
West Sayville, NY. 631-589-1700
Caesar's Pasta
Blackwood, NJ 888-432-2372
Codinos Food Inc
Scotia, NY. 800-246-8908
J B & Son LTD
Yonkers, NY 914-963-5192
Landolfi's Food Products
Trenton, NJ 609-392-1830
Pasta Del Mondo
Carmel, NY. 800-392-8887
Pasta Factory
Melrose Park, IL. 800-615-6951
Seviroli Foods
Garden City, NY. 516-222-6220
Star Ravioli Mfg Co
Moonachie, NJ 201-933-6427
Wisconsin Whey International
Juda, WI 608-233-5101

Tamales

Tucson Tamale Company
Tucson, AZ. 520-398-6282

Turkey Dinner

Morrison Lamothe
Toronto, ON 877-677-6533

Vegetarian

Atlantic Natural Foods
Nashville, NC 888-491-0524
Dixie USA
Tomball, TX 800-233-3668
F & S Produce Co Inc
Vineland, NJ 800-886-3316
Garden Protein International
Richmond, BC 877-305-6777
Health Valley Company
Irwindale, CA 800-334-3204
Kashi Company
Solana Beach, CA. 877-747-2467
Les Palais Des Thes
New York, NY 917-515-2887
Mortimer's Fine Foods
Burlington, ON. 905-336-0000
Tamarind Tree
Neshanic Station, NJ. 800-432-8733
The Food Collective
Irvine, CA 866-328-8638

Prepared Salads

Avon Heights Mushrooms
Avondale, PA 610-268-2092
Baba Foods
San Diego, CA 619-426-6946
Bay Cities Produce Co Inc
San Leandro, CA. 510-346-4943
Black's Barbecue
Lockhart, TX. 888-632-8225
Brookside Foods
Cleveland, OH 216-991-7600
Cedar's Mediterranean Foods
Ward Hill, MA 978-372-8010
Chef's Pride Gifts LLC
Taylor, MI 800-878-1800
Chiquita Brands LLC.
Fort Lauderdale, FL 954-924-5700
Conifer Foods
Medina, WA 800-588-9160
Dole Food Company, Inc.
Thousand Oaks, CA 800-356-3111
FiveStar Gourmet Foods
Ontario, CA. 909-390-0032
Giovanni's Appetizing Food Co
Richmond, MI. 586-727-9355
Hanover Foods Corp
Hanover, PA 717-632-6000
Harold Food Company
Charlotte, NC 704-588-8061
Helen's Pure Foods
Cheltenham, PA 215-379-6433
Herold's Salads
Cleveland, OH 800-427-2523
HFI Foods
Redmond, WA. 425-883-1320
Home Style Foods Inc
Hamtramck, MI. 313-874-3250
Hoople Country Kitchen Inc
Rockport, IN 877-466-7537
House of Thaller Inc
Knoxville, TN. 800-462-3365
Kay Foods Co
Detroit, MI 313-393-1100
Kings Processing
Middleton, NS. 902-825-2188
L & S Packing Co
Farmingdale, NY 800-286-6487
Meadows Country Products
Hollidaysburg, PA. 888-499-1001
Melba's Old School Po Boys
New Orleans, LA 504-267-7765
Mrs Grissom's Salads Inc
Nashville, TN 800-255-0571
Mrs Stratton's Salads Inc
Birmingham, AL. 205-940-9640
Sally Sherman
Mt Vernon, NY. 718-822-1100
Sandridge Food Corp
Medina, OH. 800-627-2523
Sidari's Italian Foods
Cleveland, OH 216-431-3344
Soupergirl
Washington, DC 202-609-7177
Spring Glen Fresh Foods
Ephrata, PA. 800-641-2853
Summer Fresh
Woodbridge, ON. 877-472-5237
Vega Food Industries Inc
Cranston, RI 800-973-7737
Zuccaro Produce
Columbia Heights, MN. 612-333-1122

Antipasto

Giovanni's Appetizing Food Co
Richmond, MI. 586-727-9355
L & S Packing Co
Farmingdale, NY 800-286-6487
Pastene Co LTD
Canton, MA 781-298-3397

Chicken

Chicken Salad Chick
Auburn, AL. 334-275-4578
Mrs Stratton's Salads Inc
Birmingham, AL. 205-940-9640
Old Dutch Mustard Company
Great Neck, NY 516-466-0522

Cole Slaw

Avon Heights Mushrooms
Avondale, PA 610-268-2092
Black's Barbecue
Lockhart, TX 888-632-8225
Dawn's Foods
Portage, WI 800-993-2967
Flaum Appetizing
Brooklyn, NY 718-821-1970
Kay Foods Co
Detroit, MI 313-393-1100
Mrs Stratton's Salads Inc
Birmingham, AL 205-940-9640
Spring Glen Fresh Foods
Ephrata, PA 800-641-2853

Egg

Dawn's Foods
Portage, WI 800-993-2967

Iceberg Lettuce Based

Bay Cities Produce Co Inc
San Leandro, CA 510-346-4943
Zuccaro Produce
Columbia Heights, MN 612-333-1122

Macaroni

Black's Barbecue
Lockhart, TX 888-632-8225
Hanover Foods Corp
Hanover, PA 717-632-6000
Spring Glen Fresh Foods
Ephrata, PA 800-641-2853

Pasta

Dawn's Foods
Portage, WI 800-993-2967
Herold's Salads
Cleveland, OH 800-427-2523
HFI Foods
Redmond, WA 425-883-1320
Home Style Foods Inc
Hamtramck, MI 313-874-3250
Kay Foods Co
Detroit, MI 313-393-1100
Sandridge Food Corp
Medina, OH 800-627-2523
Spring Glen Fresh Foods
Ephrata, PA 800-641-2853

Potato

Black's Barbecue
Lockhart, TX 888-632-8225
Dawn's Foods
Portage, WI 800-993-2967
Hanover Foods Corp
Hanover, PA 717-632-6000
Herold's Salads
Cleveland, OH 800-427-2523
Kay Foods Co
Detroit, MI 313-393-1100
Mrs Stratton's Salads Inc
Birmingham, AL 205-940-9640
Sandridge Food Corp
Medina, OH 800-627-2523
Spring Glen Fresh Foods
Ephrata, PA 800-641-2853

Salmon

Rachael's Smoked Fish
Springfield, MA 800-327-3412

Seafood

Rachael's Smoked Fish
Springfield, MA 800-327-3412

Tuna

Flaum Appetizing
Brooklyn, NY 718-821-1970
Mrs Stratton's Salads Inc
Birmingham, AL 205-940-9640

Quiche

Classic Cookings, LLC
Jamaica, NY 718-439-0200
Glendora Quiche Company
San Dimas, CA 909-394-1777
Hans Kissle Co
Haverhill, MA 978-556-4500
Love Quiches Desserts
Freeport, NY 516-623-8800
Nancy's Specialty Foods
Newark, CA 510-494-1100
Pie Piper Products
Wheeling, IL 800-621-8183
Quelle Quiche
Brentwood, MO 314-961-6554
Stacey's Famous Foods
Hayden, ID 800-782-2395
Wholesome Bakery
San Francisco, CA 415-343-5414

Soups & Stews

4C Foods Corp
Brooklyn, NY 718-272-4242
Alaska Smokehouse
Woodinville, WA 800-422-0852
All American Foods Inc
Mankato, MN 800-833-2661
Alvalle
Denver, CO
Andersen's Pea Soup
Buellton, CA 805-688-5581
Annie Chun's
Los Angeles, CA 415-479-8272
Atlanta Bread Co.
Smyrna, GA 800-398-3728
Aunt Kitty's Foods Inc
Vineland, NJ 856-691-2100
B&H Foods
Charlotte, NC 704-332-4106
Back to Nature Foods
.... 855-346-2225
Bakkavor USA
Charlotte, NC 800-842-3025
Bay Shore Chowders & Bisques
Fall River, MA 888-675-6892
Baycliff Co Inc
Garwood, NJ 866-772-7569
Bear Creek Country Kitchens
Heber City, UT 800-516-7286
Bellisio Foods
Minneapolis, MN
Blount Fine Foods
Fall River, MA 774-888-1300
Blue Crab Bay
Melfa, VA 800-221-2722
Boston Chowda
Haverhill, MA 800-992-0054
Bou Brands
New York, NY 858-401-3356
Boudreaux's Foods
New Orleans, LA 504-733-8440
Boulder Organic Foods
Niwot, CO 303-530-0470
Cajun Fry Co Inc
Pierre Part, LA 888-272-2586
California Natural Products
Lathrop, CA 209-858-2525
California Wild Rice Growers
Fall River Mills, CA 800-626-4366
Caltex Foods
Canoga Park, CA 800-522-5839
Cambridge Food
Monterey, CA 800-433-2584
Campbell Company of Canada
Toronto, ON 800-410-7687
Campbell Soup Co.
Camden, NJ 800-257-8443
Catania Hospitality Group
Hyannis, MA 888-774-5511
Chef Hans' Gourmet Foods
Monroe, LA 800-890-4267
Cherchies
Malvern, PA 800-644-1980
Chimayo To Go / Cibolo Junction
Albuquerque, NM 800-683-9628
Chincoteague Seafood Co Inc
Parsonsburg, MD 443-260-4800
Christie's
Stroughton, MA 781-341-3341
Clarmil Manufacturing Corp
Hayward, CA 888-252-7645
Classic Cookings, LLC
Jamaica, NY 718-439-0200
Comfort Foods
Albuquerque, NM 800-460-5803
Conifer Specialties Inc
Woodinville, WA 800-588-9160
Cooke Tavern LTD
Spring Mills, PA 866-422-7687
Country Cupboard
Lewisburg, PA 570-523-3211
Crush Foods Service
Westlake Village, CA 818-699-6381
Cugino's Gourmet Foods
Crystal Lake, IL 888-592-8446
Custom Culinary Inc.
Schaumberg, IL 800-621-8827
Daily Soup
New York, NY 888-393-7687
Denzer's Food Products
Baltimore, MD 410-889-1500
Diversified Foods & Seasonings
Covington, LA 800-914-2382
Dorothy Dawson Food Products
Jackson, MI 517-788-9830
Dr. McDougall's Right Foods
Woodland, CA 866-972-6879
Eatem Foods Co
Vineland, NJ 800-683-2836
Edmond's Chile Co
St Louis, MO 314-772-1499
El Peto Products
Cambridge, ON 800-387-4064
Ellie's Country Delights
Wainscott, NY 631-478-5200
Erba Food Products
Brooklyn, NY 718-272-7700
Fair Scones
Medina, WA 800-588-9160
Fantastic World Foods
Providence, RI
Fawen
Brooklyn, NY 888-737-7052
Fig Food Co.
New York, NY 855-344-3663
Fish Hopper
Monterey, CA 831-372-3406
Flavor House, Inc.
Adelanto, CA 760-246-9131
FOND Bone Broth
San Antonio, TX
George F Brocke & Sons
Moscow, ID 208-289-4231
GoBio!
Action, ON 519-853-2958
Grace Foods International
Astoria, NY 718-433-4789
Grandma Browns Beans Inc
Mexico, NY 315-963-7221
Grandma Pat's Products
Albin, WY 307-631-0801
Great Eastern Sun Trading Co
Asheville, NC 800-334-5809
Griffith Foods Inc.
Alsip, IL 708-371-0900
H.K. Canning
Ventura, CA 805-652-1392
Hain Celestial Group Inc
Lake Success, NY 800-434-4246
Halal Fine Foods
Toronto, ON 416-679-8000
Hale and Hearty Soups
New York, NY 212-255-2433
Hanover Foods Corp
Hanover, PA 717-632-6000
Hans Kissle Co
Haverhill, MA 978-556-4500
Health Valley Company
Irwindale, CA 800-334-3204
Heartline Foods
Westport, CT 203-222-0381
Heinz Quality Chef Foods Inc
Cedar Rapids, IA 800-356-8307
Hirzel Canning Co & Farms
Luckey, OH 419-419-7525
Hoopeston Foods Inc
Burnsville, MN 952-854-0903
Hormel Foods Corp.
Austin, MN 507-437-5611
Idaho Pacific Holdings Inc
Rigby, ID 800-238-5503
Imagine Foods
Boulder, CO 800-434-4246
Integrative Flavors
Michigan City, IN 800-837-7687
Jager Foods
Sauk Centre, MN 800-358-7251
JMAC Trading, Inc.
Torrance, CA 877-566-4569

Juanita's Foods
Wilmington, CA 800-303-2965
Just Delicious Gourmet Foods
Seal Beach, CA 800-871-6085
Jyoti Cuisine India
Berwyn, PA 610-296-4620
Karine & Jeff
Los Angeles, CA
Karlsburger Foods Inc
Monticello, MN 800-383-6549
Kay Foods Co
Detroit, MI 313-393-1100
KD Canners Inc
Mississauga, ON 905-602-1825
Kent Precision Foods Group Inc
Muscatine, IA 800-442-5242
Kettle Cuisine
Lynn, MA 877-302-7687
Le Grand
Blainville, QC 450-623-3000
Leonard Mountain Inc
Bixby, OK 800-822-7700
Les Aliments Ramico Foods
St. Leonard, QC 514-329-1844
Loffredo Produce
Rock Island, IL 800-383-3367
LonoLife
Oceanside, CA 855-843-8566
Manischewitz Co
Newark, NJ 201-553-1100
Marsan Foods
Toronto, ON 416-755-9262
McCormick & Company
Hunt Valley, MD 410-527-6189
Meat-O-Mat Corp
Brooklyn, NY 718-965-7250
Mercer Processing
Modesto, CA 209-529-0150
Mid-Atlantic Foods Inc
Easton, MD 800-922-4688
Moonlite Bar-B-Q Inn
Owensboro, KY 800-322-8989
Morgan Foods Inc
Austin, IN 888-430-1780
Near East Food Products
Leominster, MA 800-822-7423
Nissin Foods USA Co Inc
Gardena, CA 310-327-8478
Nona Lim
Oakland, CA 415-513-5328
North Aire Market, Inc.
Shakopee, MN 800-662-3781
North of the Border
Tesuque, NM 800-860-0681
Numo Broth
San Jose, CA
Organic Gourmet
Sherman Oaks, CA 800-400-7772
Overhill Farms Inc
Vernon, CA 800-859-6406
Pacific Foods of Oregon
Tualatin, OR 503-692-9666
Park 100 Foods Inc
Tipton, IN 800-854-6504
Patagonia Provisions
Sausalito, CA 888-221-8208
Perez Food Products
Kansas City, MO 816-931-8761
Pioneer Foods Industries
Stuttgart, AR 870-673-4444
Plentiful Pantry
Salt Lake City, UT 801-977-9077
Plenus Group Inc
Lowell, MA 978-970-3832
Pressery
Denver, CO
Progresso Quality Foods
Vineland, NJ 856-691-1565
Ragozzino Foods Inc
Meriden, CT 800-348-1240
Rapunzel Pure Organics
Bloomfield, NJ 800-225-1449
Ronzoni
Largo, FL 800-730-5957
Royal Palate Foods
Inglewood, CA 310-330-7701
San Francisco Spice Co.
Woodland, CA 866-972-6879
Sandridge Food Corp
Medina, OH 800-627-2523
Sea Watch Intl
Easton, MD 410-822-7500
Shelton's Poultry Inc
Pomona, CA 800-541-1833
Skinny Souping
Chicago, IL
Souperb LLC
Emeryville, CA 415-685-8508
Soupergirl
Washington, DC 202-609-7177
SOUPerior Bean & Spice Company
Vancouver, WA 800-878-7687
Spice Hunter Inc
Richmond, VA 800-444-3061
Sprague Foods
Belleville, ON 613-966-1200
Spring Glen Fresh Foods
Ephrata, PA 800-641-2853
St. Ours & Company
East Weymouth, MA 781-331-8520
Sudbury Soups and Salads
Sudbury, MA 888-783-7687
Sun Opta Inc.
Mississauga, ON 952-820-2518
Sweet Earth Foods
Moss Landing, CA 800-737-3311
Sweet Sue Kitchens
Athens, AL 256-216-0500
Swiss Food Products
Chicago, IL 312-829-0100
Tabatchinick Fine Foods
Somerset, NJ 732-247-6668
Tex-Mex Gourmet
Brenham, TX 888-345-8467
The Sprout House
Lake Katrine, NY 800-777-6887
Timber Peaks Gourmet
Parker, CO 800-982-7687
Tio Gazpacho
New York, NY 917-946-1160
Turtle Island Foods
Hood River, OR 800-508-8100
Twin Marquis
Brooklyn, NY 800-367-6868
Unilever Canada
Toronto, ON 416-415-3000
Unilever Food Solutions
Englewood Cliffs, NJ
Vienna Beef LTD
Chicago, IL 800-366-3647
Vietti Foods Co Inc
Nashville, TN 615-244-7864
Vince's Seafoods
Gretna, LA 504-368-1544
VIP Foods
Flushing, NY 718-821-5330
Westbrae Natural Foods
Melville, NY 800-434-4246
White Coffee Corporation
Long Island City, NY 800-221-0140
Wild Zora Foods
Loveland, CO 970-541-9672
William Poll Inc
New York, NY 800-993-7655
Wong Wing
Florenceville-Bristol, NB 866-622-2461
Worthmore Food Products Co
Cincinnati, OH 866-837-7687
Yankee Specialty Foods
Boston, MA 800-688-9904

Beef Soup

Country Cupboard
Lewisburg, PA 570-523-3211
Erba Food Products
Brooklyn, NY 718-272-7700
Integrative Flavors
Michigan City, IN 800-837-7687

Beef Stew

Aunt Kitty's Foods Inc
Vineland, NJ 856-691-2100
Caltex Foods
Canoga Park, CA 800-522-5839
Campbell Company of Canada
Toronto, ON 800-410-7687
Chimayo To Go / Cibolo Junction
Albuquerque, NM 800-683-9628
Hoopeston Foods Inc
Burnsville, MN 952-854-0903
Kelly Foods
Jackson, TN 731-424-2255
Marsan Foods
Toronto, ON 416-755-9262
Midwest Food
Chicago, IL 773-927-8870
Spring Glen Fresh Foods
Ephrata, PA 800-641-2853
Sweet Sue Kitchens
Athens, AL 256-216-0500

Borscht

Gold Pure Food Products Co. Inc.
Hempstead, NY 800-422-4681

Canned Soup

Amy's Kitchen Inc
Santa Rosa, CA 707-781-6600
Bookbinder Specialties LLC
Media, PA 215-322-1305
Caltex Foods
Canoga Park, CA 800-522-5839
Carriere Foods Inc
Saint-Denis-Sur-Richelie, QC 450-787-3411
Chef Hans' Gourmet Foods
Monroe, LA 800-890-4267
Chincoteague Seafood Co Inc
Parsonsburg, MD 443-260-4800
Colonna Brothers Inc
North Bergen, NJ 201-864-1115
Dynamic Foods
Lubbock, TX 806-723-5600
Faribault Foods, Inc.
Fairbault, MN 507-331-1400
Hoopeston Foods Inc
Burnsville, MN 952-854-0903
Mid-Atlantic Foods Inc
Easton, MD 800-922-4688
Overhill Farms Inc
Vernon, CA 800-859-6406
Progresso Quality Foods
Vineland, NJ 856-691-1565
Sea Watch Intl
Easton, MD 410-822-7500
Shelton's Poultry Inc
Pomona, CA 800-541-1833
Sweet Sue Kitchens
Athens, AL 256-216-0500
Unilever US
Englewood Cliffs, NJ 800-298-5018
Vanee Foods Co
Berkeley, IL 708-449-7300
Worthmore Food Products Co
Cincinnati, OH 866-837-7687

Canned Stew

Aunt Kitty's Foods Inc
Vineland, NJ 856-691-2100
Caltex Foods
Canoga Park, CA 800-522-5839
Campbell Company of Canada
Toronto, ON 800-410-7687
Campbell Soup Co.
Camden, NJ 800-257-8443
Cordon Bleu International
Anjou, QC 800-363-1182
Faribault Foods, Inc.
Fairbault, MN 507-331-1400
Hoopeston Foods Inc
Burnsville, MN 952-854-0903
Kelly Foods
Jackson, TN 731-424-2255
Midwest Food
Chicago, IL 773-927-8870
Sweet Sue Kitchens
Athens, AL 256-216-0500

Chicken & Noodles

Aunt Kathy's Homestyle Products
Waldheim, SK 306-945-2181
Country Cupboard
Lewisburg, PA 570-523-3211
Hain Celestial Group Inc
Lake Success, NY 800-434-4246
Imagine Foods
Boulder, CO 800-434-4246
Shelton's Poultry Inc
Pomona, CA 800-541-1833
Swagger Foods Corp
Vernon Hills, IL 847-913-1200

Chicken & Rice

Hain Celestial Group Inc
Lake Success, NY.................800-434-4246
Hale and Hearty Soups
New York, NY....................212-255-2433

Chowder

Fish Hopper
Monterey, CA....................831-372-3406
Fishpeople
Portland, OR....................503-342-2424
LA Monica Fine Foods
Millville, NJ
Mid-Atlantic Foods Inc
Easton, MD......................800-922-4688
Plenus Group Inc
Lowell, MA......................978-970-3832
Ronzoni
Largo, FL.......................800-730-5957
Sea Watch Intl
Easton, MD......................410-822-7500
Vanee Foods Co
Berkeley, IL....................708-449-7300
Yankee Specialty Foods
Boston, MA......................800-688-9904

Corn

Hain Celestial Group Inc
Lake Success, NY.................800-434-4246

Manhattan

LA Monica Fine Foods
Millville, NJ

New England

Campbell Company of Canada
Toronto, ON.....................800-410-7687
Custom Culinary Inc.
Schaumberg, IL..................800-621-8827
Hormel Foods Corp.
Austin, MN......................507-437-5611
LA Monica Fine Foods
Millville, NJ
Vanee Foods Co
Berkeley, IL....................708-449-7300

Cream of Broccoli

Imagine Foods
Boulder, CO.....................800-434-4246

Cream of Mushroom

Aunt Kitty's Foods Inc
Vineland, NJ....................856-691-2100
Imagine Foods
Boulder, CO.....................800-434-4246
Vanee Foods Co
Berkeley, IL....................708-449-7300

Dehydrated Soup

Chef Merito Inc
Van Nuys, CA....................800-637-4861
Conifer Foods
Medina, WA......................800-588-9160
Dorothy Dawson Food Products
Jackson, MI.....................517-788-9830
Flavor House, Inc.
Adelanto, CA....................760-246-9131
Frontier Soups
Waukegan, IL....................800-300-7867
Integrative Flavors
Michigan City, IN...............800-837-7687
Maruchan Inc
Irvine, CA......................949-789-2300
Mayacamas Fine Foods
Sonoma, CA......................800-826-9621
Northwestern Foods
Arden Hills, MN.................800-236-4937
Sentry Seasonings
Elmhurst, IL....................630-530-5370
Serv-Agen Corporation
Cherry Hill, NJ.................856-663-6966
SOUPerior Bean & Spice Company
Vancouver, WA...................800-878-7687
Tropical Nut Fruit & Bulk Cndy
Lithia Springs, GA..............800-544-3762
VIP Foods
Flushing, NY....................718-821-5330
Vogue Cuisine Foods
Sunnyvale, CA...................888-236-4144

Fresh Stew

Midwest Food
Chicago, IL.....................773-927-8870

Frozen Soup

Bellisio Foods
Minneapolis, MN
Chincoteague Seafood Co Inc
Parsonsburg, MD.................443-260-4800
Crystal Noodle
Torrance, CA....................310-781-9734
Dorothy Dawson Food Products
Jackson, MI.....................517-788-9830
Edmond's Chile Co
St Louis, MO....................314-772-1499
Fairfield Farm Kitchens
Brockton, MA....................508-584-9300
Marsan Foods
Toronto, ON.....................416-755-9262
Progresso Quality Foods
Vineland, NJ....................856-691-1565
Shelton's Poultry Inc
Pomona, CA......................800-541-1833
Taste Traditions Inc
Omaha, NE.......................800-228-2170
William Poll Inc
New York, NY....................800-993-7655

Frozen Stew

Campbell Soup Co.
Camden, NJ......................800-257-8443
Edmond's Chile Co
St Louis, MO....................314-772-1499
Marsan Foods
Toronto, ON.....................416-755-9262
Midwest Food
Chicago, IL.....................773-927-8870

Gumbo

Cajun Crawfish Distributors
Branch, LA......................888-254-8626
Cajun Fry Co Inc
Pierre Part, LA.................888-272-2586
Chef Hans' Gourmet Foods
Monroe, LA......................800-890-4267
Cuizina Food Company
Woodinville, WA.................425-486-7000
Kajun Kettle Foods
New Orleans, LA.................800-331-9612
Louisiana Gourmet Enterprises
Houma, LA.......................800-328-5586
Vince's Seafoods
Gretna, LA......................504-368-1544
Yankee Specialty Foods
Boston, MA......................800-688-9904

Lentil Soup

Boulder Organic Foods
Niwot, CO.......................303-530-0470
Colonna Brothers Inc
North Bergen, NJ................201-864-1115
Country Cupboard
Lewisburg, PA...................570-523-3211
Hain Celestial Group Inc
Lake Success, NY................800-434-4246

Miso

Great Eastern Sun Trading Co
Asheville, NC...................800-334-5809
Kettle & Fire
Austin, TX......................415-857-0024
Ocean's Halo
Burlingame, CA..................650-642-5907
San-J International Inc
Henrico, VA.....................800-446-5500

Potato Leek Soup

Boulder Organic Foods
Niwot, CO.......................303-530-0470

Wonton Soup

Maruchan Inc
Irvine, CA......................949-789-2300

Stuffing

Meat

Texas Crumb & Food Products
Farmers Branch, TX..............800-522-7862
World Flavors Inc
Warminster, PA..................215-672-4400

Relishes & Pickled Products

Pickled Products

A-1 Eastern-Homemade Pickle Co
Los Angeles, CA . . . 323-223-1141
Baensch Food Products Co
Milwaukee, WI . . . 414-562-4643
Big B Barbecue
Evansville, IN . . . 812-425-5235
Bob Gordon & Associates
Oak Park, IL . . . 708-524-9611
Bryant Preserving Company
Alma, AR . . . 800-634-2413
Cajun Brands
New Iberia, LA . . . 504-408-2252
Campbell Soup Co.
Camden, NJ . . . 800-257-8443
Carson City Pickle Company
Carson City, MI . . . 989-584-3148
Commissariat Imports
Los Angeles, CA . . . 310-475-5628
Cordon Bleu International
Anjou, QC . . . 800-363-1182
Corsair Pepper Sauce
Gulfport, MS . . . 228-452-0311
Dolores Canning Co Inc
Los Angeles, CA . . . 323-263-9155
F & S Produce Co Inc
Vineland, NJ . . . 800-886-3316
Feature Foods
Brampton, ON . . . 905-452-7741
Flamm Pickle & Packing
Eau Claire, MI . . . 800-742-5531
Food City Pickle Company
Battle Creek, MI . . . 269-781-9135
Food For Thought Inc
Honor, MI . . . 231-326-5444
Foster Family Farm
South Windsor, CT . . . 860-648-9366
Freestone Pickle Co
Bangor, MI . . . 877-874-2553
Gene Belk Briners
Bloomington, CA . . . 909-877-1819
Giovanni's Appetizing Food Co
Richmond, MI . . . 586-727-9355
Gl Mezzetta Inc
American Canyon, CA . . . 800-941-7044
Granny Blossom Specialty Foods
Wells, VT . . . 802-645-0507
Grillo's Pickles
Needham Heights, MA
Hell On The Red Inc
Telephone, TX . . . 903-664-2573
Hermann Pickle Co
Garrettsville, OH . . . 800-245-2696
JNB Foods, LLC
Albany, NY . . . 607-267-5874
L & S Packing Co
Farmingdale, NY . . . 800-286-6487
Lakeside Packing Company
Harrow, ON . . . 519-738-2314
Lancaster Packing Company
Myerstown, PA . . . 717-397-9727
Mama O's Premium Kimchi
Brooklyn, NY . . . 917-326-1557
McClure's Pickles LLC
Detroit, MI . . . 248-837-9323
Mccutcheon Apple Products
Frederick, MD . . . 800-888-7537
Money's Mushrooms
Vancouver, BC . . . 800-669-7992
Paisley Farms Inc
Willoughby, OH . . . 800-474-5688
Paradise Products Corporation
Boca Raton, FL . . . 800-826-1235
Peer Foods Group Inc
Chicago, IL . . . 800-365-5644
Pepperland Farms
Ponchatoula, LA . . . 985-956-6703
Pernicious Pickling
Costa Mesa, CA . . . 714-794-9845
Pickled Pink
Norcross, GA . . . 770-998-1500
Porinos Gourmet Food
Central Falls, RI . . . 800-826-3938
Rachael's Smoked Fish
Springfield, MA . . . 800-327-3412
Red Smith Foods Inc
Davie, FL . . . 954-581-1996
Renfro Foods
Fort Worth, TX . . . 800-332-2456
Safie Specialty Foods
Chesterfield, MI . . . 586-598-8282
Sargent and Greenleaf
Nicholasville, KY . . . 800-826-7652
Seneca Foods Corp
Marion, NY . . . 315-926-8100
Stanchfield Farms
Milo, ME . . . 207-732-5173
Stonewall Kitchen
York, ME . . . 800-826-1752
Talk O'Texas Brands Inc
San Angelo, TX . . . 800-749-6572
Troy Pork Store
Troy, NY . . . 518-272-8291
Tucker Cellars
Sunnyside, WA . . . 509-837-8701
United Pickles
Bronx, NY . . . 718-933-6060
Yergat Packing Co
Fresno, CA . . . 559-276-9180

Cauliflower

Gene Belk Briners
Bloomington, CA . . . 909-877-1819
Paisley Farms Inc
Willoughby, OH . . . 800-474-5688
Sargent and Greenleaf
Nicholasville, KY . . . 800-826-7652

Eggs

Cordon Bleu International
Anjou, QC . . . 800-363-1182
Feature Foods
Brampton, ON . . . 905-452-7741
Red Smith Foods Inc
Davie, FL . . . 954-581-1996

Meats

Troy Pork Store
Troy, NY . . . 518-272-8291

Onions

Screamin' Onionz
Poughkeepsie, NY

Peppers

Apecka Peppered Pickles
Rockwall, TX . . . 972-771-7628
F & S Produce Co Inc
Vineland, NJ . . . 800-886-3316
Gene Belk Briners
Bloomington, CA . . . 909-877-1819
Gl Mezzetta Inc
American Canyon, CA . . . 800-941-7044
Paisley Farms Inc
Willoughby, OH . . . 800-474-5688
Porinos Gourmet Food
Central Falls, RI . . . 800-826-3938
Sargent and Greenleaf
Nicholasville, KY . . . 800-826-7652

Pickles

A-1 Eastern-Homemade Pickle Co
Los Angeles, CA . . . 323-223-1141
Alimentaire Whyte's Inc
Laval, QC . . . 866-420-9520
Allen's Pickle Works
Glen Cove, NY . . . 516-676-0640
B & G Foods Inc.
Parsippany, NJ . . . 973-401-6500
Bainbridge Festive Foods
Farmington, TN . . . 800-545-9205
Batampte Pickle Prods Inc
Brooklyn, NY . . . 718-251-2100
Bay Valley Foods
El Paso, TX . . . 800-236-1119
Bessinger Pickle Co
Au Gres, MI . . . 989-876-8008
Best Maid Products, Inc.
Fort Worth, TX . . . 800-447-3581
Blazzin Pickle Company
McAllen, TX . . . 956-630-0733
Brooklyn Brine Co LLC
Brooklyn, NY . . . 347-223-4345
Bubbies Fine Foods
Stockton, CA . . . 805-947-4622
Caltex Foods
Canoga Park, CA . . . 800-522-5839
Campbell Soup Co.
Camden, NJ . . . 800-257-8443
Carson City Pickle Company
Carson City, MI . . . 989-584-3148
Clic International Inc
Laval, QC . . . 450-669-2663
Commissariat Imports
Los Angeles, CA . . . 310-475-5628
Conscious Choice Foods
Lewisville, TX . . . 877-898-6158
Cook's Pantry
Ventura, CA . . . 805-947-4622
Country Cupboard
Lewisburg, PA . . . 570-523-3211
Erba Food Products
Brooklyn, NY . . . 718-272-7700
Flaum Appetizing
Brooklyn, NY . . . 718-821-1970
Forge Mountain Foods
Hendersonville, NC . . . 800-823-6743
Gene Belk Briners
Bloomington, CA . . . 909-877-1819
GFA Brands Inc
Paramus, NJ . . . 201-568-9300
Gielow Pickles Inc
Lexington, MI . . . 810-359-7680
GWB Foods Corporation
Brooklyn, NY . . . 877-977-7610
Hausbeck Pickle Co
Saginaw, MI . . . 866-754-4721
Hermann Pickle Co
Garrettsville, OH . . . 800-245-2696
House of Herbs LLC
Passaic, NJ . . . 973-779-2422
House of Spices
Flushing, NY . . . 718-507-4600
Howard Foods Inc
Danvers, MA . . . 978-774-6207
Hurd Orchards
Holley, NY . . . 585-638-8838
Island Spring Inc
Vashon, WA . . . 206-463-9848
J G Van Holten & Son Inc
Waterloo, WI . . . 800-256-0619
Kaiser Pickles
Cincinnati, OH . . . 888-291-0608
Kaplan & Zubrin
Camden, NJ . . . 856-964-1083
Klein's Kosher Pickles
Phoenix, AZ . . . 800-437-4255
Kruger Foods
Stockton, CA . . . 209-941-8518
L & S Packing Co
Farmingdale, NY . . . 800-286-6487
Lakeside Packing Company
Harrow, ON . . . 519-738-2314
Lancaster Packing Company
Myerstown, PA . . . 717-397-9727
Limited Edition
Midland, TX . . . 432-686-2008
Lowcountry Produce
Raleigh, NC . . . 800-935-2792
Miramar Pickles & Food Products
Fort Lauderdale, FL . . . 954-463-0222
Miss Ginny's Orginal Vermont Pickle Works
Northfield, VT . . . 802-485-3057
Mister Pickle's Inc
Auburn, CA . . . 530-885-1000
Mixon Fruit Farms Inc
Bradenton, FL . . . 800-608-2525
Mt Olive Pickle Co
Mt Olive, NC . . . 800-672-5041
Olde Tyme Mercantile
Arroyo Grande, CA . . . 805-489-7991
Olympic Provisions Northwest
Portland, OR . . . 503-894-8136

Original Tony Packo's
Toledo, OH 866-472-2567
Paisley Farms Inc
Willoughby, OH 800-474-5688
Paradise Products Corporation
Boca Raton, FL. 800-826-1235
Patriot Pickel Inc
Wayne, NJ. 973-709-9487
Pemberton's Foods Inc
Gray, ME. 800-255-8401
Picklesmith Inc
Taft, TX. 800-499-3401
Porter's Pick-A-Dilly
Stowe, VT 802-253-6338
Purity Products
Plainview, NY. 800-256-6102
Ralph Sechler & Son Inc
St Joe, IN. 800-332-5461
Regal Crown Foods Inc
Worcester, MA 508-752-2679
Ripon Pickle Co Inc
Ripon, WI 920-748-7110
Sambets Cajun Deli
Austin, TX. 800-472-6238
Sargent and Greenleaf
Nicholasville, KY 800-826-7652
Sargent's Bear Necessities
North Troy, VT 802-988-2903
Shawnee Canning Co
Cross Junction, VA. 800-713-1414
Stan-Mark Food Products Inc
Chicago, IL 800-651-0994
Strub Pickles
Brantford, ON 519-751-1717
SuckerPunch Gourmet
Bridgeview, IL 708-784-3000
Sunshine Fresh
North Las Vegas, NV 800-832-8081
Sutter Buttes Olive Oil
Sutter, CA 530-763-7921
Topor's Pickle & Food Svc Inc
Detroit, MI 313-237-0288
United Pickles
Bronx, NY. 718-933-6060
Vaughn Rue Produce
Wilson, NC 800-388-8138
William Harrison Winery LLC
St Helena, CA 800-913-9463

Dill

Allen's Pickle Works
Glen Cove, NY 516-676-0640
Batampte Pickle Prods Inc
Brooklyn, NY 718-251-2100
Bessinger Pickle Co
Au Gres, MI 989-876-8008
Best Maid Products, Inc.
Fort Worth, TX 800-447-3581
Bubbies Fine Foods
Stockton, CA. 805-947-4622
Conscious Choice Foods
Lewisville, TX 877-898-6158
Flamm Pickle & Packing
Eau Claire, MI. 800-742-5531
Food City Pickle Company
Battle Creek, MI 269-781-9135
Hausbeck Pickle Co
Saginaw, MI 866-754-4721
Hermann Pickle Co
Garrettsville, OH. 800-245-2696
Kaplan & Zubrin
Camden, NJ. 856-964-1083
Sechler's Fine Pickles
Saint Joe, IN 800-332-5461
Strub Pickles
Brantford, ON. 519-751-1717
United Pickles
Bronx, NY. 718-933-6060

Gherkins

Conscious Choice Foods
Lewisville, TX 877-898-6158
Paradise Products Corporation
Boca Raton, FL. 800-826-1235
Sargent and Greenleaf
Nicholasville, KY 800-826-7652
Sechler's Fine Pickles
Saint Joe, IN 800-332-5461

Kosher

Best Maid Products, Inc.
Fort Worth, TX 800-447-3581
Bubbies Fine Foods
Stockton, CA. 805-947-4622
Kaplan & Zubrin
Camden, NJ. 856-964-1083

Sweet

Best Maid Products, Inc.
Fort Worth, TX 800-447-3581
Flamm Pickle & Packing
Eau Claire, MI. 800-742-5531
Food City Pickle Company
Battle Creek, MI 269-781-9135
Hausbeck Pickle Co
Saginaw, MI 866-754-4721
Kaplan & Zubrin
Camden, NJ. 856-964-1083
Sechler's Fine Pickles
Saint Joe, IN 800-332-5461
United Pickles
Bronx, NY. 718-933-6060

Vegetables

Apecka Peppered Pickles
Rockwall, TX 972-771-7628
Batampte Pickle Prods Inc
Brooklyn, NY 718-251-2100
Bob Gordon & Associates
Oak Park, IL 708-524-9611
Carson City Pickle Company
Carson City, MI. 989-584-3148
Columbia Valley Farms Inc.
Pasco, WA. 855-261-6395
EDCO Food Products Inc
Hobart, WI 800-255-3768
F & S Produce Co Inc
Vineland, NJ 800-886-3316
Foster Family Farm
South Windsor, CT 860-648-9366
Gene Belk Briners
Bloomington, CA 909-877-1819
Gl Mezzetta Inc
American Canyon, CA 800-941-7044
Hell On The Red Inc
Telephone, TX. 903-664-2573
Hermann Pickle Co
Garrettsville, OH. 800-245-2696
Johnson Foods, Inc. - Cannery Plant
Sunnyside, WA 509-837-4188
L & S Packing Co
Farmingdale, NY 800-286-6487
Lancaster Packing Company
Myerstown, PA 717-397-9727
Leonard Mountain Inc
Bixby, OK. 800-822-7700
Miramar Pickles & Food Products
Fort Lauderdale, FL 954-463-0222
Money's Mushrooms
Vancouver, BC 800-669-7992
Olympic Provisions Northwest
Portland, OR 503-894-8136
Paisley Farms Inc
Willoughby, OH 800-474-5688
Paradise Products Corporation
Boca Raton, FL. 800-826-1235
Pepperland Farms
Ponchatoula, LA 985-956-6703
Pickled Planet
Ashland, OR 541-201-2689
Talk O'Texas Brands Inc
San Angelo, TX 800-749-6572
Tucker Cellars
Sunnyside, WA 509-837-8701
Yergat Packing Co
Fresno, CA 559-276-9180

Relishes

Alimentaire Whyte's Inc
Laval, QC 866-420-9520
Aloha From Oregon
Eugene, OR. 800-241-0300
Alto Rey Food Corp
Studio City, CA. 323-969-0178
American Culinary Garden
Springfield, MO 888-831-2433
American Fine Food Corporation
Doral, FL. 305-392-5000
Amigos Canning Company
San Antonio, TX. 210-798-5360
Arizona Pepper Products
Mesa, AZ. 800-359-3912
Au Printemps Gourmet
Saint-Jerome, QC 800-438-6676
Baldwin Richardson Foods
Oakbrook Terrace, IL 866-644-2732
Barhyte Specialty Foods Inc
Pendleton, OR. 800-227-4983
Bauer's Mustard
Flushing, NY. 718-821-3570
Bay Valley Foods
El Paso, TX. 800-236-1119
BBQ Bunch
Kansas City, MO. 816-941-4534
Best Provision Co Inc
Union, NJ 800-631-4466
Big B Barbecue
Evansville, IN 812-425-5235
Blue Jay Orchards
Bethel, CT. 203-748-0119
Boetje Foods Inc
Rock Island, IL 877-726-3853
Bogland
Pembroke, MA 781-829-9549
Bryant Preserving Company
Alma, AR 800-634-2413
C & E Canners Inc
Hammonton, NJ 609-561-1078
C.F. Sauer Co.
Richmond, VA. 888-723-0052
Cajun Brands
New Iberia, LA 504-408-2252
Campbell Soup Co.
Camden, NJ. 800-257-8443
Carolina Treet
Wilmington, NC 800-616-6344
Catskill Mountain Specialties
Saugerties, NY 800-311-3473
Chandler Foods Inc
Greensboro, NC 800-537-6219
Cherith Valley Gardens
Fort Worth, TX 800-610-9813
Christie's
Stroughton, MA 781-341-3341
Cinnabar Specialty Foods Inc
Prescott, AZ 866-293-6433
Clements Foods Co
Oklahoma City, OK 800-654-8355
Commissariat Imports
Los Angeles, CA. 310-475-5628
Conroy Foods
Pittsburgh, PA. 412-781-0977
Consumer Guild Foods Inc
Toledo, OH 419-726-3406
Corfu Foods Inc
Bensenville, IL 630-595-2510
Cosmopolitan Foods
Glen Ridge, NJ 973-680-4560
Country Cupboard
Lewisburg, PA. 570-523-3211
Curry King Corporation
Waldwick, NJ 800-287-7987
Cyclone Enterprises Inc
Houston, TX 281-872-0087
Daisy Brand
Dallas, TX. 877-292-9830
Davis Food Company
Plantation, FL 954-791-5868
Delallo's Italian Store
Jeannette, PA. 724-523-5000
Delgrosso Foods Inc.
Tipton, PA 800-521-5880
Dhidow Enterprises
Oxford, PA 610-932-7868
Dickson's Pure Honey
San Angelo, TX 915-655-9233
E Waldo Ward & Son Marmalades
Sierra Madre, CA 800-355-9273
Elwood International Inc
Copiague, NY 631-842-6600
Firth Maple Products
Spartansburg, PA. 814-654-2435
Flamm Pickle & Packing
Eau Claire, MI. 800-742-5531
Flavormatic Industries
Wappingers Falls, NY. 845-297-9100
Flavors of the Heartland
Rocheport, MO 800-269-3210
Fliinko
South Dartmouth, MA 800-266-9609

Food City Pickle Company
Battle Creek, MI 269-781-9135
Forge Mountain Foods
Hendersonville, NC 800-823-6743
Fountain Valley Foods
Colorado Springs, CO. 719-573-6012
Fox Hollow
Crestwood, KY 502-241-8621
Garden Row Foods
St Charles, IL 800-505-9999
Garden Row Foods
Franklin Park, IL. 800-555-9798
Gil's Gourmet Gallery
Seaside, CA. 800-438-7480
Golding Farms Foods
Winston Salem, NC. 336-766-6161
Graves Mountain Lodge Inc.
Syria, VA. 540-923-4231
Green Garden Food Products
Sandpoint, ID 800-669-3169
Grouse Hunt Farm Inc
Tamaqua, PA. 570-467-2850
Half Moon Bay Trading Co
Atlantic Beach, FL 888-447-2823
Halifax Group
Washington, DC 202-530-8300
Hanson Thompson Honey Farms
Redfield, SD 605-472-0474
Hausbeck Pickle Co
Saginaw, MI 866-754-4721
Heintz & Weber Co
Buffalo, NY. 716-852-7171
Heluva Good Cheese
Lynnfield, MA 800-644-5473
Hendon & David
Millbrook, NY 845-677-9696
Herlocher Foods
State College, PA 800-437-5625
Howard Foods Inc
Danvers, MA. 978-774-6207
Hudson Valley Homestead
Craryville, NY. 518-851-7336
Hume Specialties
Chester, VT. 802-875-3117
Imus Ranch Foods
Darien, CT. 888-284-4687
J G Van Holten & Son Inc
Waterloo, WI. 800-256-0619
J.N. Bech
Elk Rapids, MI 800-232-4583
Jardine Foods
Buda, TX. 800-544-1880
Jay Shah Foods
Mississauga, ON. 905-696-0172
Joe Hutson Foods
Jacksonville, FL 904-731-9065
Kaiser Pickles
Cincinnati, OH 888-291-0608
Khatsa & Company
Bellevue, WA 888-234-6781
Klein's Kosher Pickles
Phoenix, AZ 800-437-4255
Kozlowski Farms
Forestville, CA 800-473-2767
Kruger Foods
Stockton, CA. 209-941-8518
LA Vencedora Products Inc
Los Angeles, CA. 800-327-2572
Lakeside Packing Company
Harrow, ON. 519-738-2314
Lancaster Packing Company
Myerstown, PA 717-397-9727
Landry's Pepper Co
St Martinville, LA. 337-394-6097
Laredo Tortilleria & Mexican
Fort Wayne, IN 800-252-7336
Lounsbury Foods
Toronto, ON 416-656-6330
M.A. Hatt & Sons
Lunenburg, NS 902-634-8407
Mardale Specialty Foods
Waukegan, IL 845-299-0285
Mccutcheon Apple Products
Frederick, MD. 800-888-7537
Mendocino Mustard
Fort Bragg, CA 800-964-2270
Mo Hotta Mo Betta
Savannah, GA. 912-748-2766
Monticello Canning Company
Crossville, TN
Mrs. Dog's Products
Grand Rapids, MI 800-267-7364

Mt Olive Pickle Co
Mt Olive, NC 800-672-5041
Nature Quality
San Martin, CA. 408-683-2182
Nestelle's, Inc.
Salem, OR. 503-393-7056
New Canaan Farms
Dripping Springs, TX 800-727-5267
Newly Weds Foods Inc
Modesto, CA. 800-487-7423
NPC Dehydrators
Eden, NC. 336-635-5190
NutraSweet Company
Chicago, IL 800-323-5321
O'Garvey Sauces
New Braunfels, TX 830-620-6127
Oasis Food Co
Hillside, NJ 800-275-0477
Ocean Spray International
Lakeville-Middleboro, MA 800-662-3263
Ojai Cook
Los Angeles, CA. 886-571-1551
Old Dutch Mustard Company
Great Neck, NY 516-466-0522
Olds Products Co
Pleasant Prairie, WI 262-947-3500
Original Tony Packo's
Toledo, OH 866-472-2567
Orleans Packing Co
Hyde Park, MA. 617-361-6611
Paisley Farms Inc
Willoughby, OH 800-474-5688
Palmieri Food Products
New Haven, CT 800-845-5447
Peaceworks
New York, NY 212-897-3985
Pepper Creek Farms
Lawton, OK. 800-526-8132
Peter's Mustards
Sharon, CT 860-364-0842
Plochman Inc
Manteno, IL 800-843-4566
Precise Food Ingredients
Carrollton, TX. 972-323-4951
Quaker Sugar Company
Brooklyn, NY 718-387-6500
Ragsdale-Overton Food Traditions
Smithfield, NC 888-424-8863
Raye's Mustard
Eastport, ME. 800-853-1903
Red Pelican Food Products
Detroit, MI 313-881-4095
RENFRO Foods Inc
Fort Worth, TX 817-336-3849
Ripon Pickle Co Inc
Ripon, WI 920-748-7110
Robert & James Brands
Birmingham, MI. 248-646-0578
Rubys Apiaries
Milnor, ND 701-427-5200
Salad Oils Intl Corp
Chicago, IL. 773-261-0500
San Antonio Farms
Platteville, WI 800-236-1119
Seminole Foods
Springfield, OH. 800-881-1177
Seneca Foods Corp
Marion, NY. 315-926-8100
Shenk's Foods
Lancaster, PA 717-393-4240
Silver Spring Foods
Eau Clair, MI. 800-826-7322
Smiling Fox Pepper Company
North Aurora, IL. 972-754-2820
Snowizard Extracts
New Orleans, LA 800-366-9766
Sperry Apiaries
Kindred, ND 701-428-3000
St Mary Sugar Co-Op
Jeanerette, LA. 337-276-6761
Stan-Mark Food Products Inc
Chicago, IL. 800-651-0994
Stickney & Poor Company
Peterborough, NH. 603-924-2259
Strub Pickles
Brantford, ON. 519-751-1717
Sun Valley Mustard
Hailey, ID 800-628-7124
Sunshine Fresh
North Las Vegas, NV 800-832-8081
Tapatio Hot Sauce
Vernon, CA. 323-587-8933

Target Flavors Inc
Brookfield, CT 800-538-3350
Terrapin Ridge
Clearwater, FL 800-999-4052
Thistledew Farm
Proctor, WV 800-854-6639
Tipp Distributors Inc
El Paso, TX. 888-668-2639
Ultimate Gourmet
Hillsborough, NJ. 908-359-4050
United Pickles
Bronx, NY. 718-933-6060
Vidalia Sweets Brand
Lyons, GA. 912-565-8881
Wild Thyme Cottage Products
Pointe Claire, QC 514-695-3602
Wing's Food Products
Toronto, ON 416-259-2662
Wing-Time
Lynn, MA 781-592-1069
Wisconsin Wilderness Food Products
Lake Bluff, IL. 800-359-3039
Ye Olde Pepper Co
Salem, MA 866-526-2376

Beets

Beetroot Delights
Foothill, ON 888-842-3387
Bubbies Fine Foods
Stockton, CA. 805-947-4622
Paisley Farms Inc
Willoughby, OH 800-474-5688

Relishes & Condiments

Baldwin Richardson Foods
Oakbrook Terrace, IL 866-644-2732
Best Maid Products, Inc.
Fort Worth, TX 800-447-3581
Bubbies Fine Foods
Stockton, CA. 805-947-4622
Grandma Hoerner's Inc
Alma, KS. 785-765-2300
HerbNZest LLC
Princeton, NJ. 917-582-1191
Howard Foods Inc
Danvers, MA. 978-774-6207
J.M. Smucker Co.
Orrville, OH 888-550-9555
JaynRoss Creations LLC
Whitmore Lake, MI 734-657-5852
JNB Foods, LLC
Albany, NY. 607-267-5874
Lowcountry Produce
Raleigh, NC 800-935-2792
Marathon Enterprises Inc
Englewood, NJ 800-722-7388
Paisley Farms Inc
Willoughby, OH 800-474-5688
Reva Foods
Saint Petersburg, FL. 727-692-1292
Shawnee Canning Co
Cross Junction, VA 800-713-1414
Small Planet Foods
Minneapolis, MN 800-624-4123
Virginia Chutney Company
Washington, VA 540-675-1984

Sauerkraut

A.C. Kissling Company
Philadelphia, PA 800-445-1943
Alimentaire Whyte's Inc
Laval, QC 866-420-9520
Batampte Pickle Prods Inc
Brooklyn, NY 718-251-2100
Bubbies Fine Foods
Stockton, CA. 805-947-4622
Cook's Pantry
Ventura, CA. 805-947-4622
Dietz & Watson Inc.
Philadelphia, PA 215-831-9000
Emerling International Foods
Buffalo, NY. 716-833-7381
Farmhouse Culture
Watsonville, CA 831-466-0499
Fermenting Fairy
Santa Monica, CA
Flaum Appetizing
Brooklyn, NY 718-821-1970
Fremont Authentic Brands
Fremont, OH. 419-334-8995

GLK Foods, LLC
Shortsville, NY 855-572-8800
Hirzel Canning Co & Farms
Luckey, OH 419-419-7525
Kaiser Pickles
Cincinnati, OH 888-291-0608
Kaplan & Zubrin
Camden, NJ 856-964-1083
Kruger Foods
Stockton, CA 209-941-8518
Lakeside Packing Company
Harrow, ON 519-738-2314
Marathon Enterprises Inc
Englewood, NJ 800-722-7388
Miramar Pickles & Food Products
Fort Lauderdale, FL 954-463-0222
New Harvest Foods
Washington, DC 920-822-2578
Pickled Planet
Ashland, OR 541-201-2689
Red Pelican Food Products
Detroit, MI 313-881-4095
Ripon Pickle Co Inc
Ripon, WI 920-748-7110
Strub Pickles
Brantford, ON 519-751-1717
United Pickles
Bronx, NY 718-933-6060
Victor Preserving Company
Ontario, NY 315-524-2711

Juice

Fremont Authentic Brands
Fremont, OH 419-334-8995
Hirzel Canning Co & Farms
Luckey, OH 419-419-7525
Kaiser Pickles
Cincinnati, OH 888-291-0608
Leo G. Fraboni Sausage Company
Hibbing, MN 218-263-5074
M.A. Hatt & Sons
Lunenburg, NS 902-634-8407
Smithfield Foods Inc.
Smithfield, VA 757-365-3000

Sauces, Dips & Dressings

Condiments

3 Gyros Inc
Tecumseh, ON. 519-737-0389
505 Southwestern
Meridian, ID
A Taste of the Kingdom
Kingdom City, MO 888-592-5080
A&B American Style, LLC
New York, NY 917-720-7009
Ajinomoto Foods North America, Inc.
Ontario, CA. 909-477-4700
Alimentaire Whyte's Inc
Laval, QC 866-420-9520
Allied Old English Inc
Port Reading, NJ 732-602-8955
Aloha Shoyu Co LTD
Pearl City, HI 808-456-5929
American Spoon Foods Inc
Petoskey, MI 888-735-6700
Amphora International
Lake Forest, CA 888-380-4808
Appledore Cove LLC
North Berwick, ME. 207-676-4088
Ashman Manufacturing & Distributing Company
Virginia Beach, VA 800-641-9924
Au Printemps Gourmet
Saint-Jerome, QC 800-438-6676
August Kitchen
Armonk, NY 914-219-5249
Bartush Schnitzius Foods Co
Lewisville, TX 972-219-1270
Baumer Foods Inc
Metairie, LA 504-482-5761
Bear Meadow Farm
Ashfield, MA 413-628-3970
Beetroot Delights
Foothill, ON 888-842-3387
Bel Brands USA
Chicago, IL 312-462-1500
Bessinger Pickle Co
Au Gres, MI 989-876-8008
Bettah Buttah, LLC
Kansas City, KS 800-568-8468
Betty Lou's
McMinnville, OR 800-242-5205
Big B Barbecue
Evansville, IN 812-425-5235
Bob Gordon & Associates
Oak Park, IL 708-524-9611
Bobby D'S
Minnetonka, MN. 952-278-7810
Boetje Foods Inc
Rock Island, IL 877-726-3853
Bone Doctors' BBQ, LLC
Charlottesville, VA 434-296-7766
Border Foods
New Hope, MN. 763-559-7338
Brad's Taste of New York
Floral Park, NY 516-354-9004
Bradley Technologies Canada Inc.
Delta, BC. 866-508-7514
Brooklyn Delhi
Brooklyn, NY
Brothers Sauces
Fort Worth, TX 817-821-3374
Bryant Preserving Company
Alma, AR 800-634-2413
C & E Canners Inc
Hammonton, NJ 609-561-1078
Cajohn's Fiery Foods Co
Westerville, OH. 888-703-3473
Cajun Brands
New Iberia, LA 504-408-2252
Caltex Foods
Canoga Park, CA 800-522-5839
Canyon Specialty Foods
Dallas, TX. 214-352-1771
Capa Di Roma Inc
East Hartford, CT 860-282-0298
Carol Hall's Hot Pepper Jelly
Fort Bragg, CA 866-737-7379
Carolina Treet
Wilmington, NC 800-616-6344
Casa Visco
Schenectady, NY. 888-607-2823
Cedarvale Food Products
Toronto, ON 416-656-3330
Chandler Foods Inc
Greensboro, NC 800-537-6219
Chef Silvio's of Wooster Street
Guilford, CT 203-453-1064
Chef Tim Foods, LLC
Etters, PA 717-802-0350
Chicago 58 Food Products
Woodbridge, ON. 416-603-4244
Christie's
Stroughton, MA 781-341-3341
Christopher Ranch LLC
Gilroy, CA. 408-847-1100
Cinnabar Specialty Foods Inc
Prescott, AZ 866-293-6433
Clements Foods Co
Oklahoma City, OK 800-654-8355
Clic International Inc
Laval, QC 450-669-2663
CMS Fine Foods
Healdsburg, CA 707-473-9561
Cold Hollow Cider Mill
Waterbury Center, VT. 800-327-7537
Commissariat Imports
Los Angeles, CA. 310-475-5628
Cook's Pantry
Ventura, CA. 805-947-4622
Cordoba Foods LLC
Hialeah, FL 786-202-2988
Corfu Foods Inc
Bensenville, IL 630-595-2510
Creative Foodworks Inc
San Antonio, TX. 210-212-4761
Creole Fermentation Indu
Abbeville, LA. 337-898-9377
Cuizina Food Company
Woodinville, WA. 425-486-7000
Del Monte Foods Inc.
Walnut Creek, CA
Desert Pepper Trading Co
El Paso, TX. 888-472-5727
Diamond Crystal Brands Inc
Savannah, GA. 800-654-5115
Doral International
Bayside, NY 718-224-7413
Dorina So-Good Inc
Union, IL. 815-923-2144
Dragunara LLC
Palos Verdes Estate, CA 310-618-8818
Earth Island
Chatsworth, CA 888-394-3949
Ed Roller Inc
Rochester, NY. 585-458-8020
Edward & Sons Trading Co
Carpinteria, CA. 805-684-8500
El Toro Food Products
Watsonville, CA 831-728-9266
Elwood International Inc
Copiague, NY 631-842-6600
Enrico's/Ventre Packing
Syracuse, NY 888-472-8237
Erba Food Products
Brooklyn, NY 718-272-7700
Famous Chili Inc
Fort Smith, AR 479-782-0096
Fernandez Chili Co
Alamosa, CO. 719-589-6043
Filfil Foods LLC
Brooklyn, NY 917-971-3493
Fireside Kitchen
Halifax, NS 902-454-7387
Follow Your Heart
Chatsworth, CA 818-725-2820
Ford's Gourmet Foods
Raleigh, NC 800-446-0947
Fountain Valley Foods
Colorado Springs, CO. 719-573-6012
Fratelli Mantova
Naperville, IL 630-904-0002
Fremont Authentic Brands
Fremont, OH. 419-334-8995
G.E. Barbour
Sussex, NB 506-432-2300
Garden Complements Inc
Kansas City, MO. 800-966-1091
Gedney Foods Co
Sun Valley, CA 888-244-0653
GFA Brands Inc
Paramus, NJ 201-568-9300
Gibbons Bee Farm
Ballwin, MO 877-736-8607
Gingras Vinegar
Rougemont, QC 866-469-4954
Girard's Food Service Dressings
City of Industry, CA 888-327-8442
GoAvo
Montville, NJ 973-534-9951
Golden Specialty Foods Inc
Norwalk, CA. 562-802-2537
Good Food For Good
Markham, ON. 647-449-4922
Goya Foods Inc.
Jersey City, NJ 201-348-4900
Graysmarsh Berry Farm
Sequim, WA 800-683-4367
Greaves Jams & Marmalades
Niagara-on-the-Lake, ON. 800-515-9939
Green Garden Food Products
Sandpoint, ID 800-669-3169
GWB Foods Corporation
Brooklyn, NY 877-977-7610
H-E-B Grocery Co. LP
San Antonio, TX. 800-432-3113
Happy Goat
Boston, MA. 617-549-2776
Harpo's
Honolulu, HI. 808-735-6456
Heinz Portion Control
Jacksonville, FL 904-695-1300
Hell On The Red Inc
Telephone, TX. 903-664-2573
Homegrown Naturals
Napa, CA. 800-288-1089
Hoople Country Kitchen Inc
Rockport, IN 877-466-7537
Hormel Foods Corp.
Austin, MN 507-437-5611
House of Spices
Flushing, NY. 718-507-4600
Howjax
Pembroke Pines, FL 954-441-2491
HSR Associates Inc
Tarzana, CA 818-757-7152
Hyde & Hyde Inc
Corona, CA. 951-279-5239
I Heart Olive Oil
Ft Lauderdale, FL. 954-607-1539
International Food Products
Fenton, MO. 800-227-8427
International Home Foods
Parsippany, NJ. 973-359-9920
J.N. Bech
Elk Rapids, MI 800-232-4583
Jasmine & Bread
South Royalton, VT 802-763-7115
Jayone Foods Inc
Paramount, CA 562-633-7400
JMS Specialty Foods
Ripon, WI 800-535-5437
Joe Bertman Foods
Cleveland, OH 216-431-4460
John Volpi & Co
St Louis, MO. 800-288-3439
Junuis Food Products
Palatine, IL 847-359-4300
Kamish Food Products
Chicago, IL. 773-725-6959
KARI-Out Co
White Plains, NY 800-433-8799
Kathy's Gourmet Specialties
Mendocino, CA. 707-937-1383
KC Innovations Inc
Kansas City, KS 816-506-9023
Ken's Foods Inc
Marlborough, MA. 508-229-1100
Knese Enterprise
Bellerose, NY 516-354-9004
Koloa Rum Corp
Kalaheo, HI. 808-332-9333
Kozlowski Farms
Forestville, CA 800-473-2767

Kraft Heinz Canada
North York, ON. 416-441-5000
Kraft Heinz Co.
Chicago, IL 800-543-5335
Krinos Foods
Bronx, NY. 718-729-9000
Kruger Foods
Stockton, CA. 209-941-8518
L & S Packing Co
Farmingdale, NY 800-286-6487
La Ferme Martinette
Coaticook, QC 888-881-4561
La Morena
Huamantla, ... 222-211-0515
Lakeside Packing Company
Harrow, ON. 519-738-2314
Landry's Pepper Co
St Martinville, LA. 337-394-6097
Lasco Foods Inc
St Louis, MO. 314-832-1906
Le Caramel
La Mesa, CA. 619-562-0713
Lea & Perrins
Glenview, IL
Lefty Spices
Waldorf, MD. 301-399-3145
Letterman Enterprises Inc.
State College, PA 814-574-4339
Li'l Guy Foods
Kansas City, MO. 800-886-8226
Lounsbury Foods
Toronto, ON 416-656-6330
Mad Will's Food Company
Auburn, CA. 888-275-9455
Marathon Enterprises Inc
Englewood, NJ 800-722-7388
Mardale Specialty Foods
Waukegan, IL 845-299-0285
Marsa Specialty Products
Vernon, CA 800-628-0500
Marukan Vinegar USA Inc.
Paramount, CA 562-630-6060
McIlhenny Company
Avery Island, LA. 800-634-9599
Miguel's Stowe Away
Stowe, VT. 800-448-6517
Mizkan Americas Inc
Kansas City, MO. 800-323-4358
Modern Packaging
Duluth, GA 770-622-1500
Montana Mex
Bozeman, MT
Morgan Foods Inc
Austin, IN 888-430-1780
Morse's Sauerkraut
Waldoboro, ME. 866-832-5569
Mother Raw
Toronto, ON 855-464-0117
Mother Shucker's Original Cocktail Sauce
Columbia, SC 803-261-3802
Mrs Clark's Foods
Ankeny, IA 800-736-5674
Mullins Food Products
Broadview, IL 708-344-3224
Nature Quality
San Martin, CA. 408-683-2182
New Canaan Farms
Dripping Springs, TX 800-727-5267
Northwest Packing Co
Vancouver, WA 800-543-4356
Oasis Food Co
Hillside, NJ 800-275-0477
Oberweis Dairy Inc
North Aurora, IL. 866-623-7934
Ojai Cook LLC
Ojai, CA 888-657-1155
Olde Tyme Mercantile
Arroyo Grande, CA. 805-489-7991
Olympia International
Belvidere, IL. 815-547-5972
Pacific Choice Brands
Fresno, CA 559-476-3581
Palmieri Food Products
New Haven, CT 800-845-5447
Paradise Products Corporation
Boca Raton, FL. 800-826-1235
Passage Foods LLC
Collinsville, CT. 800-860-1045
Pastene Co LTD
Canton, MA 781-298-3397
Phamous Phloyd's Barbecue
Denver, CO 800-497-3281
Piknik Products Company
Montgomery, AL. 334-240-2218
Pilgrim Foods
Great Neck, NY 516-466-0522
Pineland Farms
New Gloucester, ME. 207-688-4539
Pondini Imports
Somerset, NJ. 732-545-1255
Porinos Gourmet Food
Central Falls, RI 800-826-3938
Prairie Thyme LTD
Santa Fe, NM 800-869-0009
Primal Kitchen
Oxnard, CA. 888-774-6259
Primal Nutrition
Malibu, CA 888-774-6259
Productos Del Plata
Miami, FL. 786-357-8261
Purity Farms
La Farge, WI 877-211-4819
Purity Products
Plainview, NY. 800-256-6102
Ralph Sechler & Son Inc
St Joe, IN. 800-332-5461
Rapazzini Winery
Gilroy, CA. 800-842-6262
Raye's Mustard
Eastport, ME. 800-853-1903
Ready Foods Inc
Denver, CO 800-748-1218
Reckitt Benckiser LLC
Parsippany, NJ. 973-404-2600
Red Duck Foods
Portland, OR 530-219-0150
Renfro Foods
Fort Worth, TX 800-332-2456
Restaurant Lulu Gourmet Products
San Francisco, CA 888-693-5800
REX Pure Foods
New Orleans, LA 800-344-8314
Rowena
Norfolk, VA. 800-627-8699
Royal Food Products
Indianapolis, IN 317-782-2660
Sabra Dipping Company,LL
Oceanside, CA 800-748-5523
Sambets Cajun Deli
Austin, TX. 800-472-6238
Santa Barbara Olive Company
Santa Barbara, CA 800-624-4896
Sargent and Greenleaf
Nicholasville, KY. 800-826-7652
Savoie's Sausage and Food Products
Opelousas, LA 337-942-7241
Schlotterbeck & Foss Company
Portland, ME. 800-777-4666
Scott-Bathgate
Winnipeg, MB. 800-216-2990
Sea Salt Superstore
Everett, WA. 425-249-2331
Seneca Foods Corp
Marion, NY. 315-926-8100
Shenk's Foods
Lancaster, PA 717-393-4240
Silver Palate Kitchens
Cresskill, NJ 201-568-0110
Silver Spring Foods
Eau Clair, MI. 800-826-7322
Sir Kensington's
New York, NY 646-450-5735
Sisler's Ice & Ice Cream
Ohio, IL. 888-891-3856
Skillet Street Food
Seattle, WA 425-998-9817
Skjodt-Barrett Foods
Brampton, ON. 877-600-1200
Sky Valley Foods
Danville, VA
Spanish Gardens Food Manufacturing
Kansas City, KS 913-831-4242
Sprague Foods
Belleville, ON. 613-966-1200
Steel's Gourmet Foods, Ltd.
Bridgeport, PA 800-678-3357
Stickney & Poor Company
Peterborough, NH. 603-924-2259
Stonewall Kitchen
York, ME. 800-826-1752
Strub Pickles
Brantford, ON 519-751-1717
T. Marzetti Company
Westerville, OH. 800-999-1835
Tamarind Tree
Neshanic Station, NJ. 800-432-8733
Target Flavors Inc
Brookfield, CT 800-538-3350
Taste Teasers
Dallas, TX. 800-526-1840
Terrell's Potato Chip Co
Syracuse, NY 315-437-2786
Tessemae's All Natural
Essex, MD. 855-698-3773
Texas Heat
San Antonio, TX. 800-656-5916
The Lollipop Tree, Inc
Auburn, NY. 800-842-6691
The Truffleist
Astoria, NY. 917-325-3374
Thompson's Fine Foods
Shoreview, MN. 800-807-0025
Thor-Shackel Horseradish Company
Eau Claire, WI 800-826-7322
Trappist Preserves
Cleveland, OH 800-472-0425
TreeHouse Foods, Inc.
Oak Brook, IL. 708-483-1300
Tropical Foods
Charlotte, NC 800-438-4470
Tulkoff's Food Products Inc
Baltimore, MD 800-638-7343
Twang Partners LTD
San Antonio, TX. 800-950-8095
Two Chefs on a Roll
Carson, CA 800-842-3025
Ultra Seal
New Paltz, NY 845-255-2490
Unilever Food Solutions
Englewood Cliffs, NJ
Ventura Foods LLC
Brea, CA 800-421-6257
Victoria Fine Foods
Brooklyn, NY 718-927-3000
Vienna Beef LTD
Chicago, IL 800-366-3647
Wagner Gourmet Foods
Lenexa, KS 913-469-5411
Walker Foods
Los Angeles, CA. 800-966-5199
Wei-Chuan USA Inc
Bell Gardens, CA 562-372-2020
Welch Foods Inc
Concord, MA 800-340-6870
Welch Foods Inc.
Concord, MA 800-340-6870
Westbrae Natural Foods
Melville, NY. 800-434-4246
Westin Foods
Omaha, NE 800-228-6098
Westport Rivers Vineyard
Westport, MA 800-993-9695
Wild Thymes Farm Inc
Greenville, NY 845-266-8387
Wing Nien Food
Hayward, CA 510-487-8877
Wings Foods of Alberta Ltd
Edmonton, AB 780-433-6406
Winn-Dixie Stores
Jacksonville, FL 800-967-9105
Wisconsin Spice Inc
Berlin, WI 920-361-3555
Woeber Mustard Mfg Co
Springfield, OH. 800-548-2929
Wood Brothers Inc
West Columbia, SC. 803-796-5146
Woodlake Ranch
Woodlake, CA. 559-564-2161
Woody's Bar-B-Q Sauce Company
Waldenburg, AR 888-747-9229
World Harbors
Auburn, ME 800-355-6221
York Mountain Winery
Templeton, CA 805-237-7575

Dips

A&B American Style, LLC
New York, NY 917-720-7009
Abraham's Natural Foods
Long Branch, NJ. 800-327-9903
Amigos Canning Company
San Antonio, TX. 210-798-5360
Anderson Erickson Dairy
Des Moines, IA. 515-265-2521
Anderson Erickson Dairy
Kansas City, KS 913-621-4801

Appledore Cove LLC
North Berwick, ME. 207-676-4088
Arbor Hill Grapery & Winery
Naples, NY 800-554-7553
Ashman Manufacturing & Distributing Company
Virginia Beach, VA. 800-641-9924
ASK Foods Inc
Palmyra, PA. 800-879-4275
Au Printemps Gourmet
Saint-Jerome, QC 800-438-6676
Baba Foods
San Diego, CA 619-426-6946
Banzos
Denver, CO 303-447-2133
Baptista's Bakery
Franklin, WI 414-409-2000
Baruvi Fresh LLC
New York, NY 646-346-1074
Bel Brands USA
Chicago, IL 312-462-1500
Bison Foods
Buffalo, NY. 716-892-3156
Bitchin' Sauce
Carlsbad, CA
Blue Moose of Boulder
Lafayette, CO 303-926-0664
Bread Dip Company
Maple Valley, WA. 425-358-7386
Byrne Dairy, Inc.
Syracuse, NY 800-899-1535
Cass-Clay Creamery
Fargo, ND 701-293-6455
Cedar's Mediterranean Foods
Ward Hill, MA 978-372-8010
Chelten House Products
Swedesboro, NJ
Country Cupboard
Lewisburg, PA. 570-523-3211
Crazy Jerrys Inc Kahuna-Sauces
Woodstock, GA. 800-347-2823
Creamland Dairies Inc
Albuquerque, NM. 505-247-0721
Creative Foodworks Inc
San Antonio, TX. 210-212-4761
Custom Ingredients Inc
New Braunfels, TX. 800-457-8935
Delighted By
Dixie Dew Prods Co
Erlanger, KY. 800-867-8548
Do Anything Foods
New York, NY
Dorina So-Good Inc
Union, IL. 815-923-2144
El Toro Food Products
Watsonville, CA 831-728-9266
Elki Coporation
Everett, WA. 425-261-1002
Flamous Brands
Duarte, CA 626-799-7909
Foods Alive
Angola, IN. 260-488-4497
Fountain Valley Foods
Colorado Springs, CO. 719-573-6012
Franklin Foods
Enosburg Falls, VT. 800-933-6114
Fresh Nature Foods
Spokane, WA. 509-368-7260
Frontier Co-op
Norway, IA 844-550-6200
Garden Complements Inc
Kansas City, MO. 800-966-1091
Golden Specialty Foods Inc
Norwalk, CA. 562-802-2537
Goldwater's Food's Of Arizona
Fredericksburg, TX. 866-779-7241
Gourmet du Village
Morin-Heights, QC. 800-668-2314
Guiltless Gourmet
Newark, NJ 201-553-1100
Haig's Delicacies
Hayward, CA 510-782-6285
Halladay's Harvest Barn
Bellows Falls, VT. 802-463-3471
Havana's Limited
Titusville, FL. 321-267-0513
Havoc Maker Products
Guilford, CT 800-681-3909
Heidi's Salsa
Los Angeles, CA. 310-821-0211
Helen's Pure Foods
Cheltenham, PA 215-379-6433
Heluva Good Cheese
Lynnfield, MA 800-644-5473
Herb Patch of Vermont
Bellows Falls, VT. 800-282-4372
Herlocher Foods
State College, PA 800-437-5625
Hirzel Canning Co & Farms
Luckey, OH. 419-419-7525
Hope Foods
Boulder, CO 303-248-7019
Hummustir
New York, NY
Intercorp Excelle Foods
North York, ON. 888-473-6337
Kentucky Beer Cheese
Nicholasville, KY 859-887-1645
Knese Enterprise
Bellerose, NY 516-354-9004
Lakeview Farms
Delphos, OH 800-755-9925
Lancaster Colony Corporation
Westerville, OH. 614-224-7141
Lantana Hummus
Austin, TX. 844-907-7626
Leigh Olivers
Tyler, TX. 903-245-9183
Litehouse Foods
Sandpoint, ID 800-669-3169
Lost Trail Root Beer
Louisburg, KS. 800-748-7765
Low Country Produce
Lobeco, SC 800-935-2792
Lowcountry Produce
Raleigh, NC 800-935-2792
Manassero Farms
Irvine, CA 949-554-5103
Mayfield Dairy Farms LLC
Athens, TN 800-362-9546
Michelle's RawFoodz
Chicago, IL 312-442-0406
Mixon Fruit Farms Inc
Bradenton, FL. 800-608-2525
Mother Raw
Toronto, ON 855-464-0117
New Canaan Farms
Dripping Springs, TX 800-727-5267
One Culture Foods
Duarte, CA 646-650-2989
Oregon Harvest
Portland, OR 503-249-0092
Original Herkimer Cheese
Ilion, NY. 315-895-7428
Outta the Park Eats
Cary, NC 919-462-0012
Pied-Mont/Dora
Anne Des Plaines, QC 800-363-8003
Prairie Farms Dairy Inc.
Edwardsville, IL 618-659-5700
Productos Del Plata
Miami, FL. 786-357-8261
Quality Foods
Qualicum Beach, BC 877-833-7890
Renfro Foods
Fort Worth, TX 800-332-2456
RENFRO Foods Inc
Fort Worth, TX 817-336-3849
Road's End Organics
Carpinteria, CA. 877-247-3373
S A L T Sisters
Goshen, IN 574-971-8368
Sabra Blue & White Food Products
Dallas, TX. 888-957-2272
Sabra-Go Mediterranean
Dallas, TX. 888-957-2272
Salvy Sousa Dealer Locator
Arkansas City, KS. 620-442-2700
Sambets Cajun Deli
Austin, TX. 800-472-6238
Schneider-Valley Farms Inc
Williamsport, PA. 570-326-2021
Sea Gold Seafood Products Inc
New Bedford, MA 508-993-3060
Sentry Seasonings
Elmhurst, IL 630-530-5370
Sheila's Select Gourmet Recipe
Heber City, UT 800-516-7286
Shine Companies
Spring, TX. 281-353-8392
Shooting Star Farms
Bartlesville, OK 888-850-8540
Smith Dairy
Orrville, OH 800-776-7076
Sterzing Food Co
Burlington, IA. 800-754-8467
Taste Weavers
Urbana, OH. 888-810-8365
Texas Heat
San Antonio, TX. 800-656-5916
The Honest Stand
Denver, CO
Thompson's Fine Foods
Shoreview, MN. 800-807-0025
Toom Dips
Saint Paul, MN 651-447-8666
Tova Industries LLC
Louisville, KY 888-532-8682
Tribe Mediterranean
Taunton, MA. 800-848-6687
Tropical Link Canada Ltd.
Burnaby, BC 778-379-3510
Two Chefs on a Roll
Carson, CA 800-842-3025
United Dairy Inc.
Martins Ferry, OH. 800-252-1542
US Chocolate Corp
Brooklyn, NY 718-788-8555
Vegy Vida
Cincinnati, OH 513-659-0781
Ventre Packing Company
Syracuse, NY 315-463-2384
Victoria Fine Foods
Brooklyn, NY 718-927-3000
White Camel Foods Group
Carlstadt, NJ 201-848-1215
Wild West Spices
Cody, WY 888-587-8887
William Poll Inc
New York, NY 800-993-7655

Bean

Collaborative Advantage Marketing
Detroit, MI 248-723-0793
Garden Complements Inc
Kansas City, MO. 800-966-1091
Hormel Foods Corp.
Austin, MN 507-437-5611
La Esquina Food Products
New York, NY 646-710-3183
Sentry Seasonings
Elmhurst, IL 630-530-5370
Ventre Packing Company
Syracuse, NY 315-463-2384

Cheese

Better Made Snack Foods
Detroit, MI 800-332-2394
Hell On The Red Inc
Telephone, TX. 903-664-2573
Hormel Foods Corp.
Austin, MN 507-437-5611
JTM Food Group
Harrison, OH. 800-626-2308
Kentucky Beer Cheese
Nicholasville, KY 859-887-1645
Leaf Cuisine
Santa Monica, CA
Litehouse Foods
Sandpoint, ID 800-669-3169
Sentry Seasonings
Elmhurst, IL 630-530-5370
Texas Heat
San Antonio, TX. 800-656-5916
Ventre Packing Company
Syracuse, NY 315-463-2384

Chili

Food Processor of New Mexico
Albuquerque, NM. 877-634-3772
Golden Specialty Foods Inc
Norwalk, CA. 562-802-2537
Sentry Seasonings
Elmhurst, IL 630-530-5370

Chip

Amigos Canning Company
San Antonio, TX. 210-798-5360
Dorina So-Good Inc
Union, IL. 815-923-2144
Sentry Seasonings
Elmhurst, IL 630-530-5370

Guacamole

Frontera Foods
Chicago, IL 800-509-4441
Sentry Seasonings
Elmhurst, IL 630-530-5370

Salsa

A&B American Style, LLC
New York, NY 917-720-7009
Alicita-Salsa
Great Falls, VA 703-340-5323
Allied Old English Inc
Port Reading, NJ. . . . 732-602-8955
Arizona Beverage Company
Cincinnati, OH 800-832-3775
Bachman Company
Wyamissing, PA 800-523-8253
Bel Brands USA
Chicago, IL 312-462-1500
Bettah Buttah, LLC
Kansas City, KS 800-568-8468
Bingo Salsa, LLC
Poulsbo, WA 360-779-6746
Border Foods
New Hope, MN. . . . 763-559-7338
C & G Salsa
Fishers, IN. . . . 317-569-9099
Canyon Specialty Foods
Dallas, TX. . . . 214-352-1771
Casa Visco
Schenectady, NY. . . . 888-607-2823
Choice of Vermont
Destin, FL 800-444-6261
Colorado Salsa Company
Littleton, CO. . . . 303-932-2617
Desert Pepper Trading Co
El Paso, TX. . . . 888-472-5727
Food For Thought Inc
Honor, MI 231-326-5444
Fountain Valley Foods
Colorado Springs, CO. . . . 719-573-6012
Franklin Foods
Enosburg Falls, VT. . . . 800-933-6114
Frontera Foods
Chicago, IL 800-509-4441
Golden Specialty Foods Inc
Norwalk, CA. . . . 562-802-2537
Granny Blossom Specialty Foods
Wells, VT 802-645-0507
Green Mountain Gringo
Winston-Salem, NC 888-875-3111
Heidi's Salsa
Los Angeles, CA. . . . 310-821-0211
Herlocher Foods
State College, PA 800-437-5625
JNB Foods, LLC
Albany, NY. . . . 607-267-5874
Kind Snacks
New York, NY 855-884-5463
Li'l Guy Foods
Kansas City, MO. . . . 800-886-8226
Maggie's Salsa
Charleston, WV 304-550-5460
Mesa Salsa
Santa Barbara, CA 805-448-3836
Mission Foods Corp.
Irving, TX. . . . 214-583-5113
My Brother Bobby's Salsa
Poughkeepsie, NY 845-462-6227
New Canaan Farms
Dripping Springs, TX 800-727-5267
North of the Border
Tesuque, NM. . . . 800-860-0681
Old Home Foods Inc
New Brighton, MN 651-312-8900
Oregon Harvest
Portland, OR. . . . 503-249-0092
Pacific Choice Brands
Fresno, CA 559-476-3581
Pita Pal
Houston, TX 713-777-7482
Quality Foods
Qualicum Beach, BC 877-833-7890
Ready Foods Inc
Denver, CO. . . . 800-748-1218
Royal Resources
New Orleans, LA 800-888-9932
Sentry Seasonings
Elmhurst, IL 630-530-5370
Shooting Star Farms
Bartlesville, OK 888-850-8540
Small Planet Foods
Minneapolis, MN 800-624-4123
Stinking Rose, The
San Francisco, CA 800-995-7674
T.W. Garner Food Company
Winston Salem, NC. . . . 800-476-7383
Terrell's Potato Chip Co
Syracuse, NY 315-437-2786
Ventre Packing Company
Syracuse, NY 315-463-2384

Glazes

A Taste of the Kingdom
Kingdom City, MO. . . . 888-592-5080
Abel & Schafer Inc
Ronkonkoma, NY. . . . 800-443-1260
Ashman Manufacturing & Distributing Company
Virginia Beach, VA. . . . 800-641-9924
BakeMark Ingredients Canada
Richmond, BC 800-665-9441
De Nigris
Totowa, NJ 973-837-6791
Genarom International
Cranbury, NJ. . . . 609-409-6200
Gracious Gourmet
Bridgewater, CT 860-350-1213
Howard Foods Inc
Danvers, MA. . . . 978-774-6207
International Food Products
Fenton, MO. . . . 800-227-8427
Newly Weds Foods Inc
Chicago, IL. . . . 800-621-7521
Newport Flavours & Fragrances
Orange, CA. . . . 714-744-3700
Puratos Canada
Mississauga, ON. . . . 905-362-3668
Sentry Seasonings
Elmhurst, IL 630-530-5370
Valley View Blueberries
Vancouver, WA. . . . 360-892-2839

Gravy

Atlantic Seasonings
Kinston, NC 800-433-5261
Aunt Kitty's Foods Inc
Vineland, NJ 856-691-2100
Campbell Soup Co.
Camden, NJ. . . . 800-257-8443
Cordon Bleu International
Anjou, QC. . . . 800-363-1182
Custom Culinary Inc.
Schaumberg, IL. . . . 800-621-8827
Diversified Foods & Seasonings
Covington, LA 800-914-2382
Edmond's Chile Co
St Louis, MO. . . . 314-772-1499
Griffith Foods Inc.
Alsip, IL 708-371-0900
Imagine Foods
Boulder, CO 800-434-4246
Mayacamas Fine Foods
Sonoma, CA 800-826-9621
Mcclancy Seasonings Co
Fort Mill, SC. . . . 800-843-1968
R L Schreiber Inc
Ft Lauderdale, FL. . . . 800-624-8777
Sambets Cajun Deli
Austin, TX. . . . 800-472-6238
Schlotterbeck & Foss Company
Portland, ME. . . . 800-777-4666
Select Food Products
Toronto, ON 800-699-8016
Sentry Seasonings
Elmhurst, IL 630-530-5370
Taste Maker Foods
Memphis, TN 800-467-1407
United Supermarkets
Lubbock, TX. . . . 806-745-9667
Vanee Foods Co
Berkeley, IL. . . . 708-449-7300

Prepared

Aunt Kitty's Foods Inc
Vineland, NJ 856-691-2100
Campbell Soup Co.
Camden, NJ. . . . 800-257-8443
Cordon Bleu International
Anjou, QC. . . . 800-363-1182
Custom Culinary Inc.
Schaumberg, IL. . . . 800-621-8827
Lawry's Foods
Hunt Valley, MD. . . . 800-952-9797
Mayacamas Fine Foods
Sonoma, CA 800-826-9621
Sentry Seasonings
Elmhurst, IL 630-530-5370
United Supermarkets
Lubbock, TX. . . . 806-745-9667

Ketchup

A&B American Style, LLC
New York, NY 917-720-7009
Alimentaire Whyte's Inc
Laval, QC 866-420-9520
Baldwin Richardson Foods
Oakbrook Terrace, IL 866-644-2732
C & E Canners Inc
Hammonton, NJ 609-561-1078
De Nigris
Totowa, NJ 973-837-6791
E.D. Smith Foods Ltd
Hamilton, ON 905-573-1207
Erba Food Products
Brooklyn, NY 718-272-7700
Fine Foods Of America Inc
Leawood, KS. . . . 913-451-2525
Golden State Foods Corp
Irvine, CA 949-247-8000
Good Food For Good
Markham, ON 647-449-4922
Heinz Portion Control
Jacksonville, FL 904-695-1300
KARI-Out Co
White Plains, NY 800-433-8799
Mountain Fire Foods
Huntington, VT. . . . 802-434-2685
Mucky Duck Mustard Company
Ferndale, MI 248-544-4610
Nature's Hollow
Charleston, UT
New Business Corp
Gary, IN. . . . 219-885-1476
Northwest Packing Co
Vancouver, WA. . . . 800-543-4356
Portlandia Foods
Portland, OR 833-739-3663
Red Duck Foods
Portland, OR 530-219-0150
Salvy Sousa Dealer Locator
Arkansas City, KS. . . . 620-442-2700
Sir Kensington's
New York, NY 646-450-5735
Small Planet Foods
Minneapolis, MN 800-624-4123
Stickney & Poor Company
Peterborough, NH. . . . 603-924-2259
Ultra Seal
New Paltz, NY 845-255-2490
Victoria Amory & Co LLC
Greenwich, CT 203-220-6454
Westport Rivers Vineyard
Westport, MA 800-993-9695
Wing's Food Products
Toronto, ON 416-259-2662
World Art Foods
Temple, TX. . . . 254-774-8322

Marinades

A Perfect Pear
Napa, CA. . . . 800-553-5753
A. Lassonde Inc.
Rougemont, QC 866-552-7643
Allegro Fine Foods Inc
Paris, TN 731-642-6113
Angelo Pietro Honolulu
Honolulu, HI. . . . 808-941-0555
Annie's Naturals
Berkeley, CA. . . . 800-434-1234
Applecreek Speciality Foods
Lexington, KY 800-747-8871
Appledore Cove LLC
North Berwick, ME. . . . 207-676-4088
Ashman Manufacturing & Distributing Company
Virginia Beach, VA. . . . 800-641-9924
B & G Foods Inc.
Parsippany, NJ. . . . 973-401-6500
Bavaria Corp International
Apopka, FL. . . . 407-880-0322
Bea & B Foods
San Diego, CA 858-490-6205

Blendex Co
Louisville, KY 800-626-6325
Blue Smoke Salsa
Ansted, WV. 888-725-7298
Bunker Foods Corp.
New York, NY 646-738-4020
Cajohn's Fiery Foods Co
Westerville, OH. 888-703-3473
Cajun Original Foods Inc
New Iberia, LA. 337-367-1344
Chaparral Gardens
Atascadero, CA. 805-703-0829
CHS Inc.
Inver Grove Hts., MN. 800-328-6539
Cinnabar Specialty Foods Inc
Prescott, AZ 866-293-6433
CMS Fine Foods
Healdsburg, CA 707-473-9561
Colonna Brothers Inc
North Bergen, NJ 201-864-1115
Con Yeager Spice Co
Zelienople, PA. 800-222-2460
Creative Foodworks Inc
San Antonio, TX. 210-212-4761
Cugino's Gourmet Foods
Crystal Lake, IL 888-592-8446
Cuizina Food Company
Woodinville, WA. 425-486-7000
Dixie Trail Farms
Wilmington, NC 800-665-3968
Dorothy Dawson Food Products
Jackson, MI. 517-788-9830
Dr Pete's
Savannah, GA. 888-599-0047
Dr. Pete's
Savannah, GA. 912-233-3035
Ford's Gourmet Foods
Raleigh, NC 800-446-0947
Fox Hollow
Crestwood, KY 502-241-8621
Funnibonz LLC
Princeton Jct, NJ. 877-300-2669
Garden Complements Inc
Kansas City, MO. 800-966-1091
Genarom International
Cranbury, NJ. 609-409-6200
Girard's Food Service Dressings
City of Industry, CA 888-327-8442
Halmoni's Divine Marinade
Demarest, NJ. 917-913-8961
Havana's Limited
Titusville, FL. 321-267-0513
Intercorp Excelle Foods
North York, ON. 888-473-6337
J.T. Pappy's Sauce
Los Angeles, CA. 323-969-9605
Jake's Grillin
Hopewell Jct, NY 845-226-4656
Judicial Flavors
Auburn, CA. 530-885-1298
Kaari Foods
Brooklyn, NY
Kinder's BBQ
Walnut Creek, CA. 925-939-7242
L & S Packing Co
Farmingdale, NY 800-286-6487
Lawry's Foods
Hunt Valley, MD. 800-952-9797
Louisiana Fish Fry Products
Baton Rouge, LA 800-356-2905
Love'n Herbs
Waterbury, CT. 203-756-4932
Mad Will's Food Company
Auburn, CA. 888-275-9455
Magic Seasoning Blends
New Orleans, LA 800-457-2857
Manassero Farms
Irvine, CA 949-554-5103
Maple Grove Farms Of Vermont
St Johnsbury, VT. 802-748-5141
Marin Food Specialties
Byron, CA. 925-634-6126
McIlhenny Company
Avery Island, LA. 800-634-9599
Mod Squad Martha
Johns Island, SC 615-476-3696
Molli
Dallas, TX
Montebello Kitchens
Gordonsville, VA 800-743-7687
Mountain Fire Foods
Huntington, VT. 802-434-2685
Mt. Olympus Specialty Foods
Buffalo, NY. 716-874-0771
Napa Valley Kitchens
Napa, CA. 707-254-3700
Nature's Kitchen
Roswell, GA 678-845-6897
Newly Weds Foods Inc
Chicago, IL 800-621-7521
Newman's Own
Westport, CT. 203-222-0136
North Coast Processing
Carlsbad, CA. 760-931-6809
One Culture Foods
Duarte, CA 646-650-2989
Parthenon Food Products
Ann Arbor, MI 734-994-1012
Phamous Phloyd's Barbecue
Denver, CO. 800-497-3281
Porinos Gourmet Food
Central Falls, RI 800-826-3938
Primal Kitchen
Oxnard, CA. 888-774-6259
Primal Nutrition
Malibu, CA 888-774-6259
Produits Ronald
St. Damase, QC. 800-465-0118
Quality Foods
Qualicum Beach, BC 877-833-7890
Red Creek Marinade Company
Amarillo, TX. 800-687-9114
Restaurant Lulu Gourmet Products
San Francisco, CA 888-693-5800
River Town Foods Corp
St Louis, MO. 800-844-3210
Rosmarino Foods/R.Z. Humbert Company
Odessa, FL 888-926-9053
Salvy Sousa Dealer Locator
Arkansas City, KS. 620-442-2700
Sambets Cajun Deli
Austin, TX. 800-472-6238
Santa Barbara Salsa/California Creative
Oceanside, CA 800-748-5523
Sentry Seasonings
Elmhurst, IL 630-530-5370
Serro Foods LLC
Catskill, NY 518-943-9255
Soy Vay Enterprises
Felton, CA. 800-444-6369
Surlean Foods
San Antonio, TX. 800-999-4370
Swagger Foods Corp
Vernon Hills, IL 847-913-1200
Sweet Peas Floral Design
Stockton, CA. 209-472-9284
Sweetwater Spice Company
Austin, TX. 800-531-6079
Tessemae's All Natural
Essex, MD. 855-698-3773
Tillie's Gourmet
Doylestown, PA 215-272-8326
Tone Products Inc
Melrose Park, IL. 800-536-8663
Tova Industries LLC
Louisville, KY 888-532-8682
Trailblazer Foods
Portland, OR. 800-777-7179
Ultimate Gourmet
Hillsborough, NJ. 908-359-4050
Vita Food Products Inc
Chicago, IL 800-989-8482
Wickers Food Products Inc
Hornersville, MO 800-847-0032
Wild Thymes Farm Inc
Greenville, NY 845-266-8387
Wine Country Chef LLC
Hidden Valley Lake, CA. 707-322-0406

Beef

Lawry's Foods
Hunt Valley, MD. 800-952-9797
Sentry Seasonings
Elmhurst, IL 630-530-5370

Chicken

Delphos Poultry Products
Delphos, OH 419-692-5816
Sentry Seasonings
Elmhurst, IL 630-530-5370
Sunchef Farms
Vernon, CA 323-588-5800

Fajita

Magic Seasoning Blends
New Orleans, LA 800-457-2857
San Antonio Farms
Platteville, WI 800-236-1119
Sentry Seasonings
Elmhurst, IL 630-530-5370
Tova Industries LLC
Louisville, KY 888-532-8682

Lamb

Sentry Seasonings
Elmhurst, IL 630-530-5370

Meat

A. Lassonde Inc.
Rougemont, QC 866-552-7643
Allegro Fine Foods Inc
Paris, TN. 731-642-6113
American Culinary Garden
Springfield, MO 888-831-2433
Booneway Farms
Berea, KY. 859-986-2636
Bunker Foods Corp.
New York, NY 646-738-4020
Cajun Original Foods Inc
New Iberia, LA. 337-367-1344
Centennial Food Corporation
Calgary, AB. 403-214-0044
Cinnabar Specialty Foods Inc
Prescott, AZ 866-293-6433
Con Yeager Spice Co
Zelienople, PA. 800-222-2460
D & D Foods Inc
West Des Moines, IA 800-772-4098
Favorite Foods
Burnaby, BC 604-420-5100
Genarom International
Cranbury, NJ. 609-409-6200
L & S Packing Co
Farmingdale, NY 800-286-6487
Lawry's Foods
Hunt Valley, MD. 800-952-9797
Magic Seasoning Blends
New Orleans, LA 800-457-2857
Mrs. Dog's Products
Grand Rapids, MI 800-267-7364
Newly Weds Foods Inc
Chicago, IL. 800-621-7521
Parthenon Food Products
Ann Arbor, MI 734-994-1012
Passetti's Pride
Hayward, CA 800-521-4659
Produits Ronald
St. Damase, QC. 800-465-0118
Red Creek Marinade Company
Amarillo, TX. 800-687-9114
Rob Salamida Co Inc
Johnson City, NY 800-545-5072
San Antonio Farms
Platteville, WI 800-236-1119
Sentry Seasonings
Elmhurst, IL 630-530-5370
Sparrow Lane
Ceres, CA 866-515-2477
Stanchfield Farms
Milo, ME. 207-732-5173
Sweet Peas Floral Design
Stockton, CA. 209-472-9284
Tova Industries LLC
Louisville, KY 888-532-8682

Mayonaise

C.F. Sauer Co.
Richmond, VA. 888-723-0052
Clements Foods Co
Oklahoma City, OK 800-654-8355
Consumer Guild Foods Inc
Toledo, OH 419-726-3406
Conway Import Co Inc
Franklin Park, IL. 800-323-8801
Cuisine Perel
Richmond, CA 800-887-3735
Empire Mayonnaise Company, LLC.
Brooklyn, NY 718-636-2069
Erba Food Products
Brooklyn, NY 718-272-7700
GFA Brands Inc
Paramus, NJ 201-568-9300

Girard's Food Service Dressings
City of Industry, CA 888-327-8442
GoAvo
Montville, NJ 973-534-9951
Green Garden Food Products
Sandpoint, ID 800-669-3169
Heinz Portion Control
Jacksonville, FL 904-695-1300
IFM
New York, NY 212-229-1633
Intercorp Excelle Foods
North York, ON. 888-473-6337
JUST Inc
San Francisco, CA 844-423-6637
Kruger Foods
Stockton, CA. 209-941-8518
Litehouse Foods
Sandpoint, ID 800-669-3169
Mardale Specialty Foods
Waukegan, IL 845-299-0285
Oasis Food Co
Hillside, NJ. 800-275-0477
Olde Tyme Mercantile
Arroyo Grande, CA. 805-489-7991
Piknik Products Company
Montgomery, AL. 334-240-2218
Primal Nutrition
Malibu, CA 888-774-6259
Purity Products
Plainview, NY. 800-256-6102
Rapazzini Winery
Gilroy, CA. 800-842-6262
Restaurant Lulu Gourmet Products
San Francisco, CA 888-693-5800
Royal Food Products
Indianapolis, IN 317-782-2660
San Gennaro Foods Inc
Kent, WA. 800-462-1916
Stickney & Poor Company
Peterborough, NH 603-924-2259
Stonewall Kitchen
York, ME. 800-826-1752
Unilever US
Englewood Cliffs, NJ 800-298-5018
Ventura Foods LLC
Brea, CA 800-421-6257
Victoria Amory & Co LLC
Greenwich, CT 203-220-6454
Wood Brothers Inc
West Columbia, SC. 803-796-5146

Mustard

G.S. Dunn Limited
Hamilton, ON 905-522-0833

Brown

G.S. Dunn Limited
Hamilton, ON 905-522-0833
GoldRush Mustard
Dallas, TX. 214-335-8345
International Food Products
Fenton, MO. 800-227-8427
Mizkan Americas Inc
Mount Prospect, IL 800-323-4358
Monastary Mustard
Angel, OR. 503-949-6321
Raye's Old Fashioned Gourmet Mustard
Eastport, ME. 800-853-1903
Reckitt Benckiser LLC
Parsippany, NJ. 973-404-2600
Stickney & Poor Company
Peterborough, NH 603-924-2259
Stonewall Kitchen
York, ME. 800-826-1752

Oriental

G.S. Dunn Limited
Hamilton, ON 905-522-0833
GS Dunn & Company
Hamilton, ON 905-522-0833
HerbNZest LLC
Princeton, NJ. 917-582-1191

Yellow

CMS Fine Foods
Healdsburg, CA 707-473-9561
Country Cupboard
Lewisburg, PA. 570-523-3211
Finding Home Farms
Middletown, NY. 845-355-4335
Flaherty Inc
Skokie, IL 847-966-1005
G.S. Dunn Limited
Hamilton, ON 905-522-0833
GS Dunn & Company
Hamilton, ON 905-522-0833
Honey Acres
Neosho, WI 920-474-4411
International Food Products
Fenton, MO. 800-227-8427
Marathon Enterprises Inc
Englewood, NJ 800-722-7388
Miller's Mustard LLC
Gibsonia, PA 412-894-7172
Portlandia Foods
Portland, OR 833-739-3663
Raye's Mustard
Eastport, ME 800-853-1903
Reckitt Benckiser LLC
Parsippany, NJ. 973-404-2600
Silver Spring Foods
Eau Clair, MI. 800-826-7322
Stickney & Poor Company
Peterborough, NH 603-924-2259
Stonewall Kitchen
York, ME. 800-826-1752
Victoria Amory & Co LLC
Greenwich, CT 203-220-6454

Salad Dressings

A Perfect Pear
Napa, CA. 800-553-5753
Allied Old English Inc
Port Reading, NJ. 732-602-8955
American Spoon Foods Inc
Petoskey, MI 888-735-6700
Angelo Pietro Honolulu
Honolulu, HI 808-941-0555
Annie's Naturals
Berkeley, CA. 800-434-1234
Arbor Hill Grapery & Winery
Naples, NY 800-554-7553
Arcobasso Foods Inc
Hazlewood, MO 800-284-0620
Argee Corp
Santee, CA 800-449-3030
Argo Century, Inc.
Jacksonville, FL 800-446-7108
Arizona Sunland Foods
Tucson, AZ 520-624-7068
Ashman Manufacturing & Distributing Company
Virginia Beach, VA. 800-641-9924
Atlantic Seasonings
Kinston, NC 800-433-5261
B & G Foods Inc.
Parsippany, NJ. 973-401-6500
Bahama Specialty Foods
Durham, NC 919-471-4051
Baldwin Richardson Foods
Oakbrook Terrace, IL 866-644-2732
Bartush Schnitzius Foods Co
Lewisville, TX 972-219-1270
Baycliff Co Inc
Garwood, NJ. 866-772-7569
Bear Meadow Farm
Ashfield, MA 413-628-3970
Best Foods
Englewood Cliffs, NJ 201-894-4000
Best Maid Products, Inc.
Fort Worth, TX 800-447-3581
Betty Lou's
McMinnville, OR 800-242-5205
Boudreaux's Foods
New Orleans, LA 504-733-8440
BP Gourmet
Hauppauge, NY 631-234-8200
Buckhead Gourmet
Atlanta, GA. 800-673-6338
C W Resources Inc
New Britain, CT 860-229-7700
C.F. Sauer Co.
Richmond, VA. 888-723-0052
California Custom Foods
Fullerton, CA 714-870-0490
Carole's Cheesecake Company
Toronto, ON 416-256-0000
Chelten House Products
Swedesboro, NJ
Chicama Vineyards
West Tisbury, MA. 888-244-2262
Choice Food Distributors LLC
Nashville, TN 615-350-6070
Christie's
Stroughton, MA 781-341-3341
CHS Inc.
Inver Grove Hts., MN. 800-328-6539
Clements Foods Co
Oklahoma City, OK 800-654-8355
CMS Fine Foods
Healdsburg, CA 707-473-9561
Consumer Guild Foods Inc
Toledo, OH 419-726-3406
Conway Import Co Inc
Franklin Park, IL. 800-323-8801
Corsair Pepper Sauce
Gulfport, MS. 228-452-0311
Country Fresh Food & Confections, Inc.
Oliver Springs, TN 800-545-8782
Creative Foodworks Inc
San Antonio, TX. 210-212-4761
Cuisine Perel
Richmond, CA 800-887-3735
D & D Foods Inc
West Des Moines, IA 800-772-4098
Delicae Gourmet
Tarpon Springs, FL. 800-942-2502
Diane's Signature Products
Edmond, OK. 405-509-3311
Dorina So-Good Inc
Union, IL. 815-923-2144
Drusilla Seafood
Baton Rouge, LA 800-364-8844
Dynamic Foods
Lubbock, TX. 806-723-5600
Earth & Vine Provisions Inc
Lincoln, CA 888-723-8463
Earth Balance
Boulder, CO 866-234-6429
Earth Island
Chatsworth, CA 888-394-3949
Farmdale Creamery Inc
San Bernardino, CA 800-346-7306
Food Source Company
Mississauga, ON 905-625-8404
Foods Alive
Angola, IN. 260-488-4497
Gedney Foods Co
Sun Valley, CA 888-244-0653
GFA Brands Inc
Paramus, NJ 201-568-9300
Girard's Food Service Dressings
City of Industry, CA 888-327-8442
Gold Pure Food Products Co. Inc.
Hempstead, NY. 800-422-4681
Golden Specialty Foods Inc
Norwalk, CA. 562-802-2537
Golden State Foods Corp
Irvine, CA 949-247-8000
Green Garden Food Products
Sandpoint, ID 800-669-3169
Greenjoy
Okatie, SC
Griffith Foods Inc.
Alsip, IL 708-371-0900
Grouse Hunt Farm Inc
Tamaqua, PA 570-467-2850
Hagerty Foods
Orange, CA. 714-628-1230
Hanley's Foods Inc.
Baton Rouge, LA 225-366-0992
Harpo's
Honolulu, HI. 808-735-6456
Hartville Kitchen
Hartville, OH 330-877-9353
Haven's Kitchen Sauces
New York, NY 212-929-7900
Hell On The Red Inc
Telephone, TX. 903-664-2573
House of Herbs LLC
Passaic, NJ 973-779-2422
IFM
New York, NY 212-229-1633
Intercorp Excelle Foods
North York, ON. 888-473-6337
Jed's Maple Products
Derby, VT 802-766-2700
JUST Inc
San Francisco, CA 844-423-6637
Kaari Foods
Brooklyn, NY
Kauai Organic Farms
Kilauea, HI 808-651-8843
Ken's Foods Inc
Marlborough, MA. 508-229-1100

Kerry Foodservice
Mansfield, OH 800-533-2722
Kosto Food Products Co
Wauconda, IL 847-487-2600
Kozlowski Farms
Forestville, CA 800-473-2767
Kraft Heinz Canada
North York, ON. 416-441-5000
KT's Kitchens
Carson, CA 310-764-0850
L & S Packing Co
Farmingdale, NY 800-286-6487
Lasco Foods Inc
St Louis, MO. 314-832-1906
Litehouse Foods
Sandpoint, ID 800-669-3169
Live A Little Gourmet Foods
Oakland, CA 888-744-2300
Love'n Herbs
Waterbury, CT. 203-756-4932
Lynch Foods
North York, ON. 416-449-5464
Mad Will's Food Company
Auburn, CA. 888-275-9455
Maple Grove Farms Of Vermont
St Johnsbury, VT. 802-748-5141
Mardale Specialty Foods
Waukegan, IL 845-299-0285
Marie's Quality Foods
Brea, CA 800-339-1051
Marina Foods
Medley, FL 786-888-0129
Marjon Specialty Foods Inc
Plant City, FL 813-752-3482
Marukan Vinegar USA Inc.
Paramount, CA 562-630-6060
Marzetti
Columbus, OH 614-846-2232
Mayacamas Fine Foods
Sonoma, CA 800-826-9621
Mccutcheon Apple Products
Frederick, MD. 800-888-7537
Mermaid Spice Corporation
Fort Myers, FL 239-693-1986
Michelle's RawFoodz
Chicago, IL 312-442-0406
Milani
Muscatine, IA 800-442-5242
Milos Whole World Gourmet
Athens, OH 866-589-6456
Mixon Fruit Farms Inc
Bradenton, FL. 800-608-2525
Mod Squad Martha
Johns Island, SC 615-476-3696
Mother Raw
Toronto, ON 855-464-0117
Mother Teresa's
Clute, TX. 888-265-7429
Mucky Duck Mustard Company
Ferndale, MI 248-544-4610
Mullens Dressing
Palestine, IL 618-586-2727
Mullins Food Products
Broadview, IL 708-344-3224
Napa Valley Kitchens
Napa, CA. 707-254-3700
Nonna Pia's Gourmet Sauces
Whistler, BC 888-372-1534
North American Enterprises
Tucson, AZ 800-817-8666
North Coast Farms
Santa Cruz, CA. 831-426-3733
North Coast Processing
Carlsbad, CA. 760-931-6809
O'Brian Brothers Food
Cincinnati, OH 513-791-9909
Oasis Food Co
Hillside, NJ 800-275-0477
Ocean Spray International
Lakeville-Middleboro, MA 800-662-3263
Olde Tyme Mercantile
Arroyo Grande, CA. 805-489-7991
Ott Food Products Co
Carthage, MO 800-866-2585
Pacific Harvest Products
Bellevue, WA 425-401-7990
Pacific Westcoast Foods
Beaverton, OR 800-874-9333
Parthenon Food Products
Ann Arbor, MI 734-994-1012
Piknik Products Company
Montgomery, AL. 334-240-2218

Porinos Gourmet Food
Central Falls, RI 800-826-3938
Primal Kitchen
Oxnard, CA. 888-774-6259
Primal Nutrition
Malibu, CA 888-774-6259
Purity Products
Plainview, NY. 800-256-6102
Quality Foods
Qualicum Beach, BC 877-833-7890
Quong Hop & Company
S San Francisco, CA. 650-553-9900
Risvold's Inc.
Gardena, CA 323-770-2674
River Town Foods Corp
St Louis, MO. 800-844-3210
Rosmarino Foods/R.Z. Humbert Company
Odessa, FL 888-926-9053
Royal Food Products
Indianapolis, IN 317-782-2660
Royal Resources
New Orleans, LA 800-888-9932
Salad Girl Inc
Mahtomedi, MN 651-653-9155
San Diego Soy Dairy
El Cajon, CA. 619-447-8638
San Gennaro Foods Inc
Kent, WA. 800-462-1916
San-J International Inc
Henrico, VA 800-446-5500
Saratoga Salad Dressing
Canton, MA 781-821-1010
Schlotterbeck & Foss Company
Portland, ME. 800-777-4666
Select Food Products
Toronto, ON 800-699-8016
Sentry Seasonings
Elmhurst, IL 630-530-5370
Shawnee Canning Co
Cross Junction, VA. 800-713-1414
Silver Palate Kitchens
Cresskill, NJ 201-568-0110
Sky Valley Foods
Danville, VA
Southern Art Company, LLC
Atlanta, GA. 800-257-6606
Sprague Foods
Belleville, ON. 613-966-1200
Stickney & Poor Company
Peterborough, NH. 603-924-2259
Swagger Foods Corp
Vernon Hills, IL 847-913-1200
Sweet Earth Foods
Moss Landing, CA 800-737-3311
T'Lish Dressings and Marinades
Opelika, AL. 205-503-8603
T. Marzetti Company
Westerville, OH. 800-999-1835
Tasty Toppings Inc
Columbus, NE. 800-228-4148
Tessemae's All Natural
Essex, MD. 855-698-3773
Tex-Mex Gourmet
Brenham, TX. 888-345-8467
TexaFrance
Round Rock, TX. 800-776-8937
The Lollipop Tree, Inc
Auburn, NY. 800-842-6691
Thistledew Farm
Proctor, WV 800-854-6639
Tillie's Gourmet
Doylestown, PA 215-272-8326
Trader Vic's Food Products
Emeryville, CA 877-762-4824
Triple H Food Processors Inc
Riverside, CA 951-352-5700
Tulocay Cemetery
Napa, CA. 888-627-2859
Unilever US
Englewood Cliffs, NJ. 800-298-5018
Valley Grain Products
Fresno, CA 559-675-3400
Ventura Foods LLC
Brea, CA. 800-421-6257
Vincent Formusa Company
Des Plaines, IL 847-813-6040
Virginia Honey Company
Inwood, WV 304-267-8500
Vita Food Products Inc
Chicago, IL 800-989-8482
Vitasoy USA
Woburn, MA. 800-848-2769

Walden Farms
Linden, NJ. 800-229-1706
Westin Foods
Omaha, NE 800-228-6098
White Oak Farm and Table
Westport, CT. 203-716-1577
Wild Thymes Farm Inc
Greenville, NY 845-266-8387
WillowOak Farms
Amherst, VA 888-963-2767
Wine Country Kitchens
Napa, CA. 866-767-9463
Wizards Cauldron, LTD
Yanceyville, NC 336-694-5665
Wood Brothers Inc
West Columbia, SC. 803-796-5146
World Flavors Inc
Warminster, PA 215-672-4400
Yo Mama's Foods
Gainesville, FL
York Mountain Winery
Templeton, CA 805-237-7575

Balsamic Vinegar

Adams Olive Ranch
Lindsay, CA 888-216-5483
Buckhead Gourmet
Atlanta, GA. 800-673-6338
Colonna Brothers Inc
North Bergen, NJ 201-864-1115
Conway Import Co Inc
Franklin Park, IL. 800-323-8801
De Nigris
Totowa, NJ 973-837-6791
Manassero Farms
Irvine, CA 949-554-5103
Milani
Muscatine, IA 800-442-5242
Newman's Own
Westport, CT. 203-222-0136

Blue Cheese

Conway Import Co Inc
Franklin Park, IL. 800-323-8801
Litehouse Foods
Sandpoint, ID 800-669-3169
Wood Brothers Inc
West Columbia, SC. 803-796-5146

Ceasar

Conway Import Co Inc
Franklin Park, IL. 800-323-8801
HV Food Products Co
Oakland, CA 877-853-7262
Litehouse Foods
Sandpoint, ID 800-669-3169
Newman's Own
Westport, CT. 203-222-0136

Creamy Dijon

Conway Import Co Inc
Franklin Park, IL. 800-323-8801
Mullens Dressing
Palestine, IL 618-586-2727
Stinking Rose, The
San Francisco, CA 800-995-7674

French

Litehouse Foods
Sandpoint, ID 800-669-3169
Milani
Muscatine, IA 800-442-5242
O'Brian Brothers Food
Cincinnati, OH 513-791-9909
Ott Food Products Co
Carthage, MO 800-866-2585
Wood Brothers Inc
West Columbia, SC. 803-796-5146

Gourmet

Betty Lou's
McMinnville, OR 800-242-5205
Olde Tyme Mercantile
Arroyo Grande, CA. 805-489-7991
Salad Girl Inc
Mahtomedi, MN 651-653-9155

Italian Style

Conway Import Co Inc
Franklin Park, IL 800-323-8801
Hartville Kitchen
Hartville, OH 330-877-9353
HV Food Products Co
Oakland, CA 877-853-7262
Litehouse Foods
Sandpoint, ID 800-669-3169
Mullens Dressing
Palestine, IL 618-586-2727
Newman's Own
Westport, CT 203-222-0136
O'Brian Brothers Food
Cincinnati, OH 513-791-9909
Olde Tyme Mercantile
Arroyo Grande, CA 805-489-7991
Ott Food Products Co
Carthage, MO 800-866-2585
Wood Brothers Inc
West Columbia, SC 803-796-5146

Mixes

CHS Inc.
Inver Grove Hts., MN 800-328-6539
Frontier Co-op
Norway, IA 844-550-6200
Gourmet du Village
Morin-Heights, QC 800-668-2314
House of Thaller Inc
Knoxville, TN 800-462-3365
Kokopelli's Kitchen
Phoenix, AZ 888-943-9802
R C Fine Foods Inc
Hillsborough, NJ 800-526-3953

Oil & Vinegar

Marukan Vinegar USA Inc.
Paramount, CA 562-630-6060

Ranch

Ott Food Products Co
Carthage, MO 800-866-2585

Non-Fat

Betty Lou's
McMinnville, OR 800-242-5205
Marukan Vinegar USA Inc.
Paramount, CA 562-630-6060
Walden Farms
Linden, NJ 800-229-1706

Oil & Vinegar

Au Printemps Gourmet
Saint-Jerome, QC 800-438-6676
Conway Import Co Inc
Franklin Park, IL 800-323-8801
Gourm, Mist
Sunny Isles Beach, FL 866-502-8472
Litehouse Foods
Sandpoint, ID 800-669-3169
Marukan Vinegar USA Inc.
Paramount, CA 562-630-6060
Newman's Own
Westport, CT 203-222-0136

Ranch

Conway Import Co Inc
Franklin Park, IL 800-323-8801
Hartville Kitchen
Hartville, OH 330-877-9353
HV Food Products Co
Oakland, CA 877-853-7262
Litehouse Foods
Sandpoint, ID 800-669-3169
Newman's Own
Westport, CT 203-222-0136
O'Brian Brothers Food
Cincinnati, OH 513-791-9909

Raspberry Vinegrette

Litehouse Foods
Sandpoint, ID 800-669-3169
Rising Sun Farms
Phoenix, OR 800-888-0795

Thousand Island

Conway Import Co Inc
Franklin Park, IL 800-323-8801
Wood Brothers Inc
West Columbia, SC 803-796-5146

Salsa

505 Southwestern
Meridian, ID
Alimentaire Whyte's Inc
Laval, QC 866-420-9520
Allied Old English Inc
Port Reading, NJ 732-602-8955
American Spoon Foods Inc
Petoskey, MI 888-735-6700
Amigos Canning Company
San Antonio, TX 210-798-5360
Ana's Salsa
Austin, TX 888-849-7054
Appledore Cove LLC
North Berwick, ME 207-676-4088
Arizona Cowboy
Phoenix, AZ 800-529-8627
Ashman Manufacturing & Distributing Company
Virginia Beach, VA 800-641-9924
B & G Foods Inc.
Parsippany, NJ 973-401-6500
Bartush Schnitzius Foods Co
Lewisville, TX 972-219-1270
BBQ Bunch
Kansas City, MO 816-941-4534
Beaverton Foods Inc
Hillsboro, OR 800-223-8076
Bel Brands USA
Chicago, IL 312-462-1500
Better Made Snack Foods
Detroit, MI 800-332-2394
Bien Padre Foods Inc
Eureka, CA 707-442-4585
Big B Barbecue
Evansville, IN 812-425-5235
Blueberry Store
Grand Junction, MI 877-654-2400
Border Foods
New Hope, MN 763-559-7338
C W Resources Inc
New Britain, CT 860-229-7700
Cajohn's Fiery Foods Co
Westerville, OH 888-703-3473
California-Antilles Trading
San Diego, CA 800-330-6450
Casa Visco
Schenectady, NY 888-607-2823
Catamount Specialties of Vermont
Plainfield, VT 800-639-2406
Cedar's Mediterranean Foods
Ward Hill, MA 978-372-8010
Cervantes Food Products Inc
Albuquerque, NM 877-982-4453
Charlie Beigg's Sauce Company
Windham, ME 888-502-8595
Chelten House Products
Swedesboro, NJ
Chimayo To Go / Cibolo Junction
Albuquerque, NM 800-683-9628
Choice of Vermont
Destin, FL 800-444-6261
Cinnabar Specialty Foods Inc
Prescott, AZ 866-293-6433
Circle R Ranch
Flower Mound, TX 800-247-3077
Ciro Foods
Pittsburgh, PA 412-771-9018
Colorado Salsa Company
Littleton, CO 303-932-2617
Country Cupboard
Lewisburg, PA 570-523-3211
Cowgirl Chocolates
Moscow, ID 888-882-4098
Creative Foodworks Inc
San Antonio, TX 210-212-4761
Cuizina Food Company
Woodinville, WA 425-486-7000
Custom Food Solutions LLC
Louisville, KY 800-767-2993
Dave's Gourmet
San Rafael, CA 800-758-0372
Dei Fratelli
Toledo, OH 800-837-1631
DelGrosso Foods
Tipton, PA 800-521-5880
Delgrosso Foods Inc.
Tipton, PA 800-521-5880
Desert Pepper Trading Co
El Paso, TX 888-472-5727
Dockside Market
Key Largo, FL 800-813-2253
Dorina So-Good Inc
Union, IL 815-923-2144
E.D. Smith Foods Ltd
Hamilton, ON 905-573-1207
Edward Johnson's Salsa
Flemington, NJ
El Toro Food Products
Watsonville, CA 831-728-9266
Famous Chili Inc
Fort Smith, AR 479-782-0096
Fiesta Gourmet of Tejas
Canyon Lake, TX 800-585-8250
Fischer & Wieser Spec Foods
Fredericksburg, TX 877-861-0260
Food Processor of New Mexico
Albuquerque, NM 877-634-3772
Ford's Gourmet Foods
Raleigh, NC 800-446-0947
Forge Mountain Foods
Hendersonville, NC 800-823-6743
Fountain Valley Foods
Colorado Springs, CO 719-573-6012
Fremont Authentic Brands
Fremont, OH 419-334-8995
Frog Ranch Foods
Glouster, OH 800-742-2488
Galena Canning Co
Galena, IL 815-777-9495
Garden Complements Inc
Kansas City, MO 800-966-1091
Garden Fresh Gourmet
Ferndale, MI 866-725-7239
Gedney Foods Co
Sun Valley, CA 888-244-0653
Gingro Corp
Manchester Center, VT 802-362-0836
Giovanni Food Co Inc
Syracuse, NY 315-457-2373
Gold Pure Food Products Co. Inc.
Hempstead, NY 800-422-4681
Golden Specialty Foods Inc
Norwalk, CA 562-802-2537
Green Mountain Gringo
Winston-Salem, NC 888-875-3111
Gringo Jack's
Manchester Ctr, VT 802-362-0836
Guiltless Gourmet
Newark, NJ 201-553-1100
Gumpert's Canada
Mississauga, ON 800-387-9324
Hagerty Foods
Orange, CA 714-628-1230
Havana's Limited
Titusville, FL 321-267-0513
Heidi's Salsa
Los Angeles, CA 310-821-0211
Hirzel Canning Co & Farms
Luckey, OH 419-419-7525
Hol, Mol,
Long Beach, CA 877-310-8453
Hormel Foods Corp.
Austin, MN 507-437-5611
Hot Licks
Spring Valley, CA 888-766-6468
Hot Mama's Foods
Springfield, MA 413-737-6572
Hot Wachula's
Lakeland, FL 877-883-8700
Hume Specialties
Chester, VT 802-875-3117
Imus Ranch Foods
Darien, CT 888-284-4687
Indel Food Products Inc
El Paso, TX 800-472-0159
JC's Midnite Salsa
Tucson, AZ 800-817-2572
Jillipepper
Albuquerque, NM 505-609-8409
JNB Foods, LLC
Albany, NY 607-267-5874
Joe Hutson Foods
Jacksonville, FL 904-731-9065
Kettle Master
Hillsville, VA 276-728-7571
Kind Snacks
New York, NY 855-884-5463

Kozlowski Farms
Forestville, CA 800-473-2767
LA Canasta Mexican Foods
Phoenix, AZ 855-269-7721
La Esquina Food Products
New York, NY 646-710-3183
LA Vencedora Products Inc
Los Angeles, CA 800-327-2572
La Victoria Foods
Austin, MN 800-725-7212
Laredo Tortilleria & Mexican
Fort Wayne, IN 800-252-7336
Las Cruces Brand Products
El Paso, TX 915-779-5709
Leigh Olivers
Tyler, TX 903-245-9183
Leona's Restaurante
Chimayo, NM 888-561-5569
Li'l Guy Foods
Kansas City, MO 800-886-8226
Litehouse Foods
Sandpoint, ID 800-669-3169
Los Chileros
Albuquerque, NM 505-768-1100
Lowcountry Produce
Raleigh, NC 800-935-2792
Mad Will's Food Company
Auburn, CA 888-275-9455
Miguel's Stowe Away
Stowe, VT 800-448-6517
Mixon Fruit Farms Inc
Bradenton, FL 800-608-2525
My Brother's Salsa
Bentonville, AR 479-271-9404
Naked Infusions LLC
Calabasas, CA 818-239-9058
Native Kjalii Foods
San Francisco, CA 415-522-5580
O'Garvey Sauces
New Braunfels, TX 830-620-6127
Ocean Spray International
Lakeville-Middleboro, MA 800-662-3263
Paisley Farms Inc
Willoughby, OH 800-474-5688
Palmieri Food Products
New Haven, CT 800-845-5447
Paradise Products Corporation
Boca Raton, FL 800-826-1235
Patricia Quintana
Los Angeles, CA
Pepper Creek Farms
Lawton, OK 800-526-8132
Plocky's Fine Snacks
Hinsdale, IL 630-323-8888
Quality Foods
Qualicum Beach, BC 877-833-7890
Rapazzini Winery
Gilroy, CA 800-842-6262
Ready Foods Inc
Denver, CO 800-748-1218
Red Gold Inc.
Elwood, IN 866-729-7187
Renfro Foods
Fort Worth, TX 800-332-2456
Reva Foods
Saint Petersburg, FL 727-692-1292
Riba Foods
Houston, TX 800-327-7422
Royal Resources
New Orleans, LA 800-888-9932
Ruffner's
Wayne, PA 610-687-9800
Sabor Mexicano
Berkeley, CA
Sabra Dipping Company,LL
Oceanside, CA 800-748-5523
Sabra-Go Mediterranean
Dallas, TX 888-957-2272
Salsa God
New York, NY 646-359-0573
Sambets Cajun Deli
Austin, TX 800-472-6238
San Antonio Farms
Platteville, WI 800-236-1119
Santa Barbara Olive Company
Santa Barbara, CA 800-624-4896
Santa Barbara Salsa/California Creative
Oceanside, CA 800-748-5523
Sechler's Fine Pickles
Saint Joe, IN 800-332-5461
Select Food Products
Toronto, ON 800-699-8016

Shawnee Canning Co
Cross Junction, VA 800-713-1414
Sky Valley Foods
Danville, VA
Slawsa
Cramerton, NC
Smiling Fox Pepper Company
North Aurora, IL 972-754-2820
Southern Bar-B-Que
Jennings, LA 866-612-2586
Southwest Spirit
Socorro, NM 800-838-0773
Soylent Brand
Irving, TX 972-255-4747
Spruce Foods
San Clemente, CA 800-326-3612
Steel's Gourmet Foods, Ltd.
Bridgeport, PA 800-678-3357
Stello Foods Inc
Punxsutawney, PA 800-849-4599
Steve Mendez
Woodland, CA 530-662-0512
Stinking Rose, The
San Francisco, CA 800-995-7674
SuckerPunch Gourmet
Bridgeview, IL 708-784-3000
Sun Harvest Foods Inc
San Diego, CA 619-661-0909
Sunny Dell Foods Inc
Oxford, PA 610-932-5164
T.W. Garner Food Company
Winston Salem, NC 800-476-7383
Taste Weavers
Urbana, OH 888-810-8365
Tenayo
New York, NY 917-677-7607
Terrell's Potato Chip Co
Syracuse, NY 315-437-2786
Texas Heat
San Antonio, TX 800-656-5916
Texas Tamale Co
Houston, TX 713-795-5500
The Brooklyn Salsa Co LLC
Ridgewood, NY 347-470-5493
The Vine
Manhasset, NY 516-365-8463
Timber Peaks Gourmet
Parker, CO 800-982-7687
Todd's Salsa
Bangor, ME 844-328-7257
Ultimate Salsa
Charlotte, NC 888-827-2572
Uncle Fred's Fine Foods
Rockport, TX 361-729-8320
Vegetable Juices Inc
Chicago, IL 888-776-9752
Vita Food Products Inc
Chicago, IL 800-989-8482
Walker Foods
Los Angeles, CA 800-966-5199
Wing Nien Food
Hayward, CA 510-487-8877
Ximena's Latin Flavors
Spicewood, TX 817-821-3246
Xochitl
Dallas, TX 866-595-8917
Zuni Foods
San Antonio, TX 800-906-3876

Canned

Kozlowski Farms
Forestville, CA 800-473-2767
Palmieri Food Products
New Haven, CT 800-845-5447
T.W. Garner Food Company
Winston Salem, NC 800-476-7383

Chunky

Newman's Own
Westport, CT 203-222-0136
T.W. Garner Food Company
Winston Salem, NC 800-476-7383

Mild

Garden Fresh Gourmet
Ferndale, MI 866-725-7239
Hot Wachula's
Lakeland, FL 877-883-8700
JC's Midnite Salsa
Tucson, AZ 800-817-2572

Sabra Dipping Company,LL
Oceanside, CA 800-748-5523
T.W. Garner Food Company
Winston Salem, NC 800-476-7383
Ultimate Salsa
Charlotte, NC 888-827-2572

Picante

Bartush Schnitzius Foods Co
Lewisville, TX 972-219-1270
Garden Fresh Gourmet
Ferndale, MI 866-725-7239
Hormel Foods Corp.
Austin, MN 507-437-5611
Hot Wachula's
Lakeland, FL 877-883-8700
JC's Midnite Salsa
Tucson, AZ 800-817-2572
T.W. Garner Food Company
Winston Salem, NC 800-476-7383
Texas Heat
San Antonio, TX 800-656-5916
Ultimate Salsa
Charlotte, NC 888-827-2572

with Cheese

Amigos Canning Company
San Antonio, TX 210-798-5360
Delgrosso Foods Inc.
Tipton, PA 800-521-5880

Sauces

505 Southwestern
Meridian, ID
A Southern Season
Hillsborough, NC 800-253-3663
Ajinomoto Foods North America, Inc.
Ontario, CA 909-477-4700
Ajinomoto Heartland Inc
Chicago, IL 773-380-7000
Al Dente Pasta Co
Whitmore Lake, MI 800-536-7278
Alimentaire Whyte's Inc
Laval, QC 866-420-9520
Allegro Fine Foods Inc
Paris, TN 731-642-6113
Allied Old English Inc
Port Reading, NJ 732-602-8955
American Culinary Garden
Springfield, MO 888-831-2433
American Spoon Foods Inc
Petoskey, MI 888-735-6700
Amigos Canning Company
San Antonio, TX 210-798-5360
Amy's Kitchen Inc
Santa Rosa, CA 707-781-6600
Angelo Pietro Honolulu
Honolulu, HI 808-941-0555
Ankle Deep Foods
Norfolk, NE 402-371-6707
Annie Chun's
Los Angeles, CA 415-479-8272
Annie's Naturals
Berkeley, CA 800-434-1234
Apecka Peppered Pickles
Rockwall, TX 972-771-7628
Archie Moore's
Milford, CT 203-876-5088
Argo Century, Inc.
Jacksonville, FL 800-446-7108
Arizona Sunland Foods
Tucson, AZ 520-624-7068
Arlen S Gould & Assoc
Arlington Hts, IL 847-577-2122
Armanino Foods of Distinction
Hayward, CA 800-255-8588
Ashman Manufacturing & Distributing Company
Virginia Beach, VA 800-641-9924
ASK Foods Inc
Palmyra, PA 800-879-4275
Atlanta Burning Bush
Newnan, GA 800-665-5611
Atlantic Seasonings
Kinston, NC 800-433-5261
Au Printemps Gourmet
Saint-Jerome, QC 800-438-6676
Aunt Aggie De's Pralines
Sinton, TX 800-333-9354
Aunt Jenny's Sauces/Melba Foods
Brooklyn, NY 718-383-3192

Austin Slow Burn
Austin, TX........................877-513-3192
B & B Pecan Processors
Turkey, NC........................866-328-7322
B & G Foods Inc.
Parsippany, NJ........................973-401-6500
Bainbridge Festive Foods
Farmington, TN........................800-545-9205
Bakkavor USA
Charlotte, NC........................800-842-3025
Baldwin Richardson Foods
Oakbrook Terrace, IL........................866-644-2732
Barefoot Contessa Pantry
York, ME........................800-826-1752
Barhyte Specialty Foods Inc
Pendleton, OR........................800-227-4983
Bartush Schnitzius Foods Co
Lewisville, TX........................972-219-1270
Basic Food Flavors
North Las Vegas, NV........................702-643-0043
Baumer Foods Inc
Metairie, LA........................504-482-5761
Bay Valley Foods
El Paso, TX........................800-236-1119
Baycliff Co Inc
Garwood, NJ........................866-772-7569
BBQ Bunch
Kansas City, MO........................816-941-4534
BBQ Shack
Paola, KS........................913-294-5908
BBQ'n Fools Catering, LLC
Greenfield, IN........................800-671-8652
Beaverton Foods Inc
Hillsboro, OR........................800-223-8076
Beetnik Foods, LLC
Austin, TX........................512-548-8228
Bel Brands USA
Chicago, IL........................312-462-1500
Bellisio Foods
Minneapolis, MN
Berner Food & Beverage LLC
Dakota, IL........................800-819-8199
Bettah Buttah, LLC
Kansas City, KS........................800-568-8468
Bien Padre Foods Inc
Eureka, CA........................707-442-4585
Big B Barbecue
Evansville, IN........................812-425-5235
Big Poppa Smokers
Coachella, CA........................877-828-0727
Bittersweet Herb Farm
Shelburne Falls, MA........................800-456-1599
Blackberry Patch
Thomasville, GA........................800-853-5598
Blair's Sauces & Snacks
Highlands, NJ........................800-982-5247
Blue Jay Orchards
Bethel, CT........................203-748-0119
Blue Smoke Salsa
Ansted, WV........................888-725-7298
Bodin Foods
New Iberia, LA........................337-367-1344
Bongiovi Brand Pasta Sauces
Valley Village, CA........................434-296-7766
Border Foods
New Hope, MN........................763-559-7338
Bove's of Vermont
Burlington, VT........................802-862-6651
Brateka Enterprises
Ocala, FL........................877-549-3227
Brooklyn Delhi
Brooklyn, NY
Brother Bru Bru's
Venice, CA........................310-396-9033
Bruno Specialty Foods
West Sayville, NY........................631-589-1700
Buckhead Gourmet
Atlanta, GA........................800-673-6338
Buffalo Wild Wings
Minneapolis, MN........................763-546-1891
Bunker Foods Corp.
New York, NY........................646-738-4020
C & E Canners Inc
Hammonton, NJ........................609-561-1078
C.F. Sauer Co.
Richmond, VA........................888-723-0052
Cafe Chilku
Colchester, VT........................802-878-4645
Cafe Tequila
San Francisco, CA........................415-264-0106
Cajohn's Fiery Foods Co
Westerville, OH........................888-703-3473

Cajun Brands
New Iberia, LA........................504-408-2252
California Balsamic Inc
Ukiah, CA........................888-644-5127
California Custom Foods
Fullerton, CA........................714-870-0490
Campagna Distinct Flavor
Lebanon, OR........................800-959-4372
Campbell Soup Co.
Camden, NJ........................800-257-8443
Canada Bread Co, Ltd
Etobicoke, ON........................800-465-5515
Canyon Specialty Foods
Dallas, TX........................214-352-1771
Capone Foods
Somerville, MA........................617-629-2296
Captain Bob's Jet Fuel
Fort Wayne, IN........................877-486-6468
Carando Gourmet Frozen Foods
Agawam, MA........................888-227-2636
Carmela's Gourmet
Monterey, CA........................831-373-6291
Carol's Country Cuisine
Glen Ellen, CA........................707-996-1124
Carole's Cheesecake Company
Toronto, ON........................416-256-0000
Carolina Treet
Wilmington, NC........................800-616-6344
Carriere Foods Inc
Saint-Denis-Sur-Richelie, QC........................450-787-3411
Cary Randall's Sauces & Dressings
Highlands, NJ........................732-872-6353
Casa di Carfagna
Columbus, OH........................614-846-6340
Casa Di Lisio Products Inc
Mt Kisco, NY........................800-247-4199
Casa Visco
Schenectady, NY........................888-607-2823
Catamount Specialties of Vermont
Plainfield, VT........................800-639-2406
Catskill Mountain Specialties
Saugerties, NY........................800-311-3473
Cattle Boyz Foods
Okotoks, Alberta,, CA........................888-662-9366
Cedarvale Food Products
Toronto, ON........................416-656-3330
Cervantes Food Products Inc
Albuquerque, NM........................877-982-4453
Charlie Palmer Group
New York, NY........................866-458-7224
Chef Merito Inc
Van Nuys, CA........................800-637-4861
Chef Philippe LLC
Arlington, TX........................817-461-9049
Chef Shells Catering & Roadside Cafe
Downtown Port Huron, MI........................810-966-8371
Chef-A-Roni Fancy Foods
East Greenwich, RI........................401-884-8798
Chelten House Products
Swedesboro, NJ
Cherchies
Malvern, PA........................800-644-1980
Cherry Hut
Traverse City, MI........................888-882-4431
Chincoteague Seafood Co Inc
Parsonsburg, MD........................443-260-4800
Choclatique
Los Angeles, CA........................310-479-3849
Chocolaterie Bernard Callebaut
Calgary, AB........................800-661-8367
Christie's
Stroughton, MA........................781-341-3341
Christopher Ranch LLC
Gilroy, CA........................408-847-1100
Chukar Cherries
Prosser, WA........................800-624-9544
Cinnabar Specialty Foods Inc
Prescott, AZ........................866-293-6433
Cipriani's Spaghetti & Sauce Company
Chicago Heights, IL........................708-755-6212
Circle B Ranch
Seymour, MO........................417-683-0271
Ciro Foods
Pittsburgh, PA........................412-771-9018
City Saucery
Staten Island, NY........................718-753-4006
Clarmil Manufacturing Corp
Hayward, CA........................888-252-7645
Classy Delites
Austin, TX........................800-440-2648
Clements Foods Co
Oklahoma City, OK........................800-654-8355

Clofine Dairy Products Inc
Linwood, NJ........................609-653-1000
CMS Fine Foods
Healdsburg, CA........................707-473-9561
Coach Sposato's Bar-B-Que
Lincoln, AR........................800-264-7535
Cold Hollow Cider Mill
Waterbury Center, VT........................800-327-7537
Colgin Co
Dallas, TX........................888-226-5446
Colonna Brothers Inc
North Bergen, NJ........................201-864-1115
Colorado Salsa Company
Littleton, CO........................303-932-2617
Conifer Foods
Medina, WA........................800-588-9160
Continental Seasoning
Teaneck, NJ........................800-631-1564
Cook's Pantry
Ventura, CA........................805-947-4622
Cookies Food Products
Wall Lake, IA........................800-331-4995
Cordon Bleu International
Anjou, QC........................800-363-1182
Corfu Foods Inc
Bensenville, IL........................630-595-2510
Corine's Cuisine
Sparks, MD
Corsair Pepper Sauce
Gulfport, MS........................228-452-0311
Costa Deano's Gourmet Foods
Canton, OH........................800-337-2823
Country Bob's Inc
Centralia, IL........................800-373-2140
Country Fresh Food & Confections, Inc.
Oliver Springs, TN........................800-545-8782
Country Village Meats Inc
Sublette, IL........................800-700-4545
Cowboy Food & Drink
Chagrin Falls, OH........................800-759-5489
Crave Natural Foods
Los Angeles, CA........................877-425-2599
Crazy Jerrys Inc Kahuna-Sauces
Woodstock, GA........................800-347-2823
Creative Foodworks Inc
San Antonio, TX........................210-212-4761
Crustacean Foods
Los Angeles, CA........................866-263-2625
Cucina Antica Foods Corp
Mt Kisco, NY........................877-728-2462
Cugino's Gourmet Foods
Crystal Lake, IL........................888-592-8446
Cuizina Food Company
Woodinville, WA........................425-486-7000
Curry King Corporation
Waldwick, NJ........................800-287-7987
Custom Culinary Inc.
Schaumberg, IL........................800-621-8827
Custom Food Solutions LLC
Louisville, KY........................800-767-2993
Custom Ingredients Inc
New Braunfels, TX........................800-457-8935
Cyclone Enterprises Inc
Houston, TX........................281-872-0087
D & D Foods Inc
West Des Moines, IA........................800-772-4098
D'Oni Enterprises
San Juan Capistrano, CA........................800-809-8298
Dabruzzi's Italian Foods
Hudson, WI........................715-386-3653
Daregal
Princeton, NJ........................609-375-2312
Dean Distributors, Inc.
Burlingame, CA........................800-792-0816
Del Mar Food Products Corp
Watsonville, CA........................831-722-3516
Delgrosso Foods Inc.
Tipton, PA........................800-521-5880
Dell'Amore Enterprises
Colchester, VT........................800-962-6673
Desert Pepper Trading Co
El Paso, TX........................888-472-5727
Dhidow Enterprises
Oxford, PA........................610-932-7868
DiGregorio Food Products
St Louis, MO........................314-776-1062
Dillard's Bar-B-Q Sauce
Durham, NC........................919-286-1080
Dipasa USA Inc
Brownsville, TX........................956-831-4072
Diversified Foods & Seasonings
Covington, LA........................800-914-2382

Divine Foods
Elizabethtown, NC 910-862-2576
Dixie Trail Farms
Wilmington, NC 800-665-3968
Do Anything Foods
New York, NY
Dorina So-Good Inc
Union, IL........815-923-2144
Dorothy Dawson Food Products
Jackson, MI........517-788-9830
Dr Pete's
Savannah, GA........888-599-0047
Drew's Organics
Chester, VT........800-228-2980
E Waldo Ward & Son Marmalades
Sierra Madre, CA 800-355-9273
E.D. Smith Foods Ltd
Hamilton, ON 905-573-1207
Earth & Vine Provisions Inc
Lincoln, CA 888-723-8463
East Wind Inc
Tecumseh, MO 417-679-4682
Eastern Food Industries Inc
East Greenwich, RI........401-884-8798
Eatem Foods Co
Vineland, NJ 800-683-2836
Eden Foods Inc
Clinton, MI 888-424-3336
Edmond's Chile Co
St Louis, MO........314-772-1499
El Charro Mexican Food Ind
Roswell, NM........575-622-8590
El Rancho Tortilla
San Antonio, TX........210-922-8411
El Rey Cooked Meats
St Louis, MO........314-521-3113
El Toro Food Products
Watsonville, CA 831-728-9266
EMD Sales Inc
Baltimore, MD 410-385-3023
Escalon Premier Brand
Escalon, CA 209-838-7341
Essen Nutrition Corp
Romeoville, IL 800-582-6064
Ethnic Gourmet Foods
Boulder, CO 800-434-4246
Excalibur Seasoning
Pekin, IL 800-444-2169
Famous Chili Inc
Fort Smith, AR 479-782-0096
Father's Country Hams
Bremen, KY 270-525-3554
Favorite Foods
Burnaby, BC 604-420-5100
Felbro Food Products
Los Angeles, CA........323-936-5266
Fernandez Chili Co
Alamosa, CO........719-589-6043
Festive Foods
Virginia Beach, VA........757-490-9186
Fiesta Canning Co
Phoenix, AZ 602-212-2424
Figaro Company
Mesquite, TX 972-288-3587
Fireside Kitchen
Halifax, NS........902-454-7387
Fischer & Wieser Spec Foods
Fredericksburg, TX........877-861-0260
Flavor House, Inc.
Adelanto, CA 760-246-9131
Follow Your Heart
Chatsworth, CA 818-725-2820
Food Concentrate Corporation
Oklahoma City, OK 405-840-5633
Food Masters
Griffin, GA 888-715-4394
Food Source Company
Mississauga, ON........905-625-8404
Fool Proof Gourmet Products
Grapevine, TX 817-329-1839
Ford's Gourmet Foods
Raleigh, NC 800-446-0947
Formosa Enterprises Inc
San Jose, CA........408-297-3300
Fountain Valley Foods
Colorado Springs, CO........719-573-6012
Fox Hollow
Crestwood, KY........502-241-8621
Fremont Authentic Brands
Fremont, OH........419-334-8995
Fresh Pasta Delights
Plano, TX 972-422-5907
Frontera Foods
Chicago, IL........800-509-4441
Frontier Co-op
Norway, IA 844-550-6200
Fusion Gourmet
Gardena, CA........310-532-8938
Fuzzy's Wholesale Bar-B-Q
Madison, NC........336-548-2283
Galassi Foods
Coralville, IA 319-339-7409
Galena Canning Co
Galena, IL 815-777-9495
Garden Complements Inc
Kansas City, MO........800-966-1091
Garden Row Foods
Franklin Park, IL........800-555-9798
Garlic Festival Foods
Hollister, CA........888-427-5423
Gator Hammock Corp
Felda, FL........800-664-2867
Gayle's Sweet N' Sassy Foods
Beverly Hills, CA 310-246-1792
Gedney Foods Co
Sun Valley, CA 888-244-0653
Gehl Foods, Inc.
Germantown, WI........800-521-2873
Genarom International
Cranbury, NJ........609-409-6200
Gia Russa
Boardman, OH 800-527-8772
Gingro Corp
Manchester Center, VT........802-362-0836
Giovanni Food Co Inc
Syracuse, NY 315-457-2373
Girard's Food Service Dressings
City of Industry, CA 888-327-8442
GMB Specialty Foods
San Juan Capistrano, CA 800-809-8298
GoBio!
Action, ON 519-853-2958
Gold Dollar Products
Memphis, TN 800-971-8964
Gold Pure Food Products Co. Inc.
Hempstead, NY........800-422-4681
Golden Specialty Foods Inc
Norwalk, CA........562-802-2537
Golden State Foods Corp
Irvine, CA........949-247-8000
Golden West Specialty Foods
Brisbane, CA........800-584-4481
Goldwater's Food's Of Arizona
Fredericksburg, TX........866-779-7241
Good Food For Good
Markham, ON........647-449-4922
Gourmet Conveniences Ltd
Litchfield, CT 866-793-3801
Gourmet's Secret
North Highlands, CA 916-334-6161
Grain Processing Corp
Muscatine, IA 800-448-4472
Gravymaster, Inc.
Canajoharie, NY........800-839-8938
Great American Barbecue Company
White Plains, NY 914-686-2277
Green Garden Food Products
Sandpoint, ID 800-669-3169
Griffith Foods Inc.
Alsip, IL 708-371-0900
Gringo Jack's
Manchester Ctr, VT 802-362-0836
Grouse Hunt Farm Inc
Tamaqua, PA........570-467-2850
Guido's International Foods
Pasadena, CA 877-994-8436
Gumpert's Canada
Mississauga, ON........800-387-9324
Gunther's Gourmet
Richmond, VA........804-240-1796
Habby Habanero's Food Products
Jacksonville, FL 904-333-9758
Hagerty Foods
Orange, CA........714-628-1230
Haig's Delicacies
Hayward, CA 510-782-6285
Halal Fine Foods
Toronto, ON 416-679-8000
Halifax Group
Washington, DC 202-530-8300
Hampton Chutney Company
Amagansett, NY........631-267-3131
Hanan Products Co
Hicksville, NY 516-938-1000
Hanover Foods Corp
Hanover, PA 717-632-6000
Harry's Cafe
Mount Holly, VT........802-259-2996
Hartville Kitchen
Hartville, OH 330-877-9353
Hartville Locker Service
Hartville, OH 330-877-9547
Harvest-Pac Products
Chatham, ON 519-436-0446
Havana's Limited
Titusville, FL........321-267-0513
Havoc Maker Products
Guilford, CT 800-681-3909
Heartbreaking Dawns Artisan Foods
Glendale, AZ........646-957-3484
Heartline Foods
Westport, CT........203-222-0381
Heffy's BBQ Co.
Kansas City, MO........816-200-2271
Heidi's Salsa
Los Angeles, CA........310-821-0211
Heintz & Weber Co
Buffalo, NY........716-852-7171
Heinz Portion Control
Jacksonville, FL 904-695-1300
Heinz Quality Chef Foods Inc
Cedar Rapids, IA........800-356-8307
Heluva Good Cheese
Lynnfield, MA 800-644-5473
Heritage Family Specialty Foods Inc
Grand Prairie, TX 800-648-2837
Hillside Lane Farm
Randolph, VT 802-728-0070
Hirzel Canning Co & Farms
Luckey, OH 419-419-7525
Hollman Foods
Des Moines, IA........888-926-2879
Homestead Fine Foods
S San Francisco, CA........650-615-0750
Honey Bear Fruit Basket
Denver, CO........888-330-2327
Honeydrop Beverages
Houston, TX
HongryHawg of Louisiana
Prairieville, LA 888-772-4294
Hoopeston Foods Inc
Burnsville, MN 952-854-0903
Hopkins Inn Of Lake Waramaug
Warren, CT 860-868-7295
Hormel Foods Corp.
Austin, MN 507-437-5611
Horseshoe Brand
Milan, NY........845-240-2390
House of Herbs LLC
Passaic, NJ 973-779-2422
Howjax
Pembroke Pines, FL 954-441-2491
Hume Specialties
Chester, VT........802-875-3117
HV Food Products Co
Oakland, CA........877-853-7262
Illes Seasonings & Flavors
Carrollton, TX........800-683-4553
Imus Ranch Foods
Darien, CT........888-284-4687
Integrative Flavors
Michigan City, IN........800-837-7687
Intercorp Excelle Foods
North York, ON........888-473-6337
International Home Foods
Parsippany, NJ........973-359-9920
Island Spice
Doral, FL........786-473-3465
Italia Foods
Schaumburg, IL........800-747-1109
Iya Foods LLC
North Aurora, IL........630-854-7107
J.A.M.B. Low Carb Distributor
Pompano Beach, FL 800-708-6738
J.N. Bech
Elk Rapids, MI 800-232-4583
J.T. Pappy's Sauce
Los Angeles, CA........323-969-9605
Jack Miller's Food Products
Ville Platte, LA........800-646-1541
Jake's Grillin
Hopewell Jct, NY 845-226-4656
Jesben
Pittsburgh, PA
Jets Le Frois Corp
Brockport, NY 585-637-5003

Jillipepper
Albuquerque, NM 505-609-8409
Jimtown Store
Healdsburg, CA 707-433-1212
JMS Specialty Foods
Ripon, WI 800-535-5437
Joe Hutson Foods
Jacksonville, FL 904-731-9065
Johnny Harris Famous Barbecue Sauce
Savannah, GA 888-547-2823
Juanita's Foods
Wilmington, CA 800-303-2965
Kaari Foods
Brooklyn, NY
Kagome USA Inc
Los Banos, CA 209-826-8850
Kajun Kettle Foods
New Orleans, LA 800-331-9612
KARI-Out Co
White Plains, NY 800-433-8799
Kathy's Gourmet Specialties
Mendocino, CA 707-937-1383
Kelchner's Horseradish
Allentown, PA 800-424-1952
Kemach Food Products
Brooklyn, NY 718-272-5655
Ken's Foods Inc
Marlborough, MA 508-229-1100
Kent Precision Foods Group Inc
Muscatine, IA 800-442-5242
Kentucky Bourbon
Louisville, KY 866-472-7797
Kerala Curry
Pittsboro, NC 919-545-9401
Kettle Master
Hillsville, VA 276-728-7571
Kill Sauce
Pasadena, CA
Kilwons Foods
Santa Cruz, CA 831-426-9670
Kind Snacks
New York, NY 855-884-5463
Kinder's BBQ
Walnut Creek, CA 925-939-7242
King Cupboard
Red Lodge, MT 800-962-6555
Knouse Foods Co-Op Inc.
Peach Glen, PA 717-677-8181
Koloa Rum Corp
Kalaheo, HI 808-332-9333
Kozlowski Farms
Forestville, CA 800-473-2767
Kraft Heinz Co.
Chicago, IL 800-543-5335
Kraus & Co
Irvine, CA 800-662-5871
L & S Packing Co
Farmingdale, NY 800-286-6487
L & S Packing Co
Farmingdale, NY 877-879-6453
La Piccolina
Decatur, GA 800-626-1624
LA Vencedora Products Inc
Los Angeles, CA 800-327-2572
Lancaster Fine Foods
Lancaster, PA 717-397-9578
Laredo Tortilleria & Mexican
Fort Wayne, IN 800-252-7336
Las Cruces Brand Products
El Paso, TX 915-779-5709
Lasco Foods Inc
St Louis, MO 314-832-1906
Lassonde Pappas & Company, Inc.
Carneys Point, NJ 800-257-7019
Le Frois Foods Corporation
Brockport, NY 585-637-5003
Le Grand
Blainville, QC 450-623-3000
Lea & Perrins
Glenview, IL
Leams
Hutchinson, KS 316-662-4287
Lee Kum Kee USA Inc
City Of Industry, CA 800-654-5082
Lee's Sausage Co
Orangeburg, SC 803-534-5517
Lemmes Company
Coventry, RI 401-821-2575
Lendy's Cafe Raw Bar
Virginia Beach, VA 757-491-3511
Leroux Creek
Hotchkiss, CO 877-970-5670

Les Aliments Livabec Foods
Sherrington, QC 450-454-7971
Li'l Guy Foods
Kansas City, MO 800-886-8226
LiDestri Food & Drink
Fairport, NY 585-377-7700
Lillie's Q
Chicago, IL 773-772-5500
Longmeadow Building Dept
Longmeadow, MA 413-565-4153
Louis Maull Co
St Louis, MO 314-241-8410
Louisa Food Products Inc
St Louis, MO 314-868-3000
Louisiana Fish Fry Products
Baton Rouge, LA 800-356-2905
Louisiana Gourmet Enterprises
Houma, LA 800-328-5586
Lounsbury Foods
Toronto, ON 416-656-6330
Lowcountry Produce
Raleigh, NC 800-935-2792
Lucky Foods
Tualatin, OR 503-612-1300
LWC Brands Inc.
Dallas, TX 800-552-8006
Lynch Foods
North York, ON 416-449-5464
Lyons Magnus
Fresno, CA 800-344-7130
Mad Chef Enterprise
Mentor, OH 800-951-2433
Mad Will's Food Company
Auburn, CA 888-275-9455
Madison Foods
Saint Paul, MN 651-265-8212
Magic Seasoning Blends
New Orleans, LA 800-457-2857
Mandarin Soy Sauce Inc
Middletown, NY 845-343-1505
Mansmith's Barbeque
San Jn Bautista, CA 800-626-7648
Maple Grove Farms Of Vermont
St Johnsbury, VT 802-748-5141
Marina Foods
Medley, FL 786-888-0129
Marsan Foods
Toronto, ON 416-755-9262
Martha Olson's Great Foo
Sutter Creek, CA 800-973-3966
Matouk International USA Inc
Sunrise, FL 954-742-2204
Mayacamas Fine Foods
Sonoma, CA 800-826-9621
Mcclancy Seasonings Co
Fort Mill, SC 800-843-1968
McCormick & Company
Hunt Valley, MD 410-527-6189
Mccutcheon Apple Products
Frederick, MD 800-888-7537
Meditalia
New York, NY 212-616-3006
Mid-Atlantic Foods Inc
Easton, MD 800-922-4688
Midas Foods Intl
Oak Park, MI 877-728-2379
Miguel's Stowe Away
Stowe, VT 800-448-6517
Millflow Spice Corp.
Hauppauge, NY 866-227-8355
Minnestalgia Foods LLC
Mcgregor, MN 800-328-6731
Mix-A-Lota Stuff LLC
Fort Pierce, FL 727-365-7328
Miyako Oriental Foods Inc
Baldwin Park, CA 877-788-6476
Mizkan Americas Inc
Kansas City, MO 800-323-4358
Mo Hotta Mo Betta
Savannah, GA 912-748-2766
Mod Squad Martha
Johns Island, SC 615-476-3696
Molinaro's Fine Italian Foods Ltd.
Mississauga, ON 905-281-0352
Molli
Dallas, TX
Monin Inc.
Clearwater, FL 855-352-8671
Montebello Kitchens
Gordonsville, VA 800-743-7687
Monterrey Products
San Antonio, TX 210-435-2872

Monterrey Products
San Antonio, TX 800-872-1652
Moonlite Bar-B-Q Inn
Owensboro, KY 800-322-8989
More Than Gourmet
Akron, OH 800-860-9385
Morgan Foods Inc
Austin, IN 888-430-1780
Morningstar Foods
Los Banos, CA 209-826-8000
Mother Teresa's
Clute, TX 888-265-7429
Mott's
Plano, TX 800-426-4891
Mott's LLP
Plano, TX 800-426-4891
Mrs. Dog's Products
Grand Rapids, MI 800-267-7364
Mullens Dressing
Palestine, IL 618-586-2727
Mullins Food Products
Broadview, IL 708-344-3224
Myron's Fine Foods, Inc.
Millers Falls, MA 800-730-2820
Nana Mae's Organics
Sebastopol, CA 707-829-7359
Nation Wide Canning Ltd.
Cottam, ON 519-839-4831
Native Kjalii Foods
San Francisco, CA 415-522-5580
New Business Corp
Gary, IN 219-885-1476
New Canaan Farms
Dripping Springs, TX 800-727-5267
New Era Canning Company
New Era, MI 231-861-2151
Nog Incorporated
Dunkirk, NY 800-332-2664
Nonna Pia's Gourmet Sauces
Whistler, BC 888-372-1534
North American Enterprises
Tucson, AZ 800-817-8666
North Coast Processing
Carlsbad, CA 760-931-6809
Northwest Packing Co
Vancouver, WA 800-543-4356
Nuovo Pasta Productions LTD
Stratford, CT 800-803-0033
O'Brian Brothers Food
Cincinnati, OH 513-791-9909
O'Garvey Sauces
New Braunfels, TX 830-620-6127
O'Sole Mio
Boisbriand, QC 844-696-8933
Ocean Spray International
Lakeville-Middleboro, MA 800-662-3263
Ocean's Halo
Burlingame, CA 650-642-5907
Ojai Cook
Los Angeles, CA 886-571-1551
Old World Spices Inc
Overland Park, KS 800-241-0070
On The Verandah
Highlands, NC 828-526-2338
One Culture Foods
Duarte, CA 646-650-2989
Otafuku Foods
Santa Fe Springs, CA 562-404-4700
Ott Food Products Co
Carthage, MO 800-866-2585
Overhill Farms Inc
Vernon, CA 800-859-6406
Pacific Choice Brands
Fresno, CA 559-476-3581
Pacific Foods of Oregon
Tualatin, OR 503-692-9666
Pacific Harvest Products
Bellevue, WA 425-401-7990
Pacific Poultry Company
Honolulu, HI 808-841-2828
Palmieri Food Products
New Haven, CT 800-845-5447
Papa Leone Food Enterprises
Beverly Hills, CA 310-552-1660
Paradise Products Corporation
Boca Raton, FL 800-826-1235
Park 100 Foods Inc
Tipton, IN 800-854-6504
Parthenon Food Products
Ann Arbor, MI 734-994-1012
Passetti's Pride
Hayward, CA 800-521-4659

Pasta Factory
Melrose Park, IL 800-615-6951
Pastor Chuck Orchards
Portland, ME 207-773-1314
Pastorelli Food Products
Chicago, IL 800-767-2829
Peaceworks
New York, NY 212-897-3985
Pearson's Homestyle
Bowden, AB 877-224-3339
Pecan Deluxe Candy Co
Dallas, TX 800-733-3589
Pemberton's Foods Inc
Gray, ME 800-255-8401
Pepper Creek Farms
Lawton, OK 800-526-8132
Peppers
Lewes, DE 800-998-3473
Perky's Pizza
Oldsmar, FL 800-473-7597
Pett Spice Products Inc
Atlanta, GA 404-691-5235
Pierino Frozen Foods
Lincoln Park, MI 313-928-0950
Piggie Park Enterprises
West Columbia, SC 800-628-7423
Pino's Pasta Veloce
Staten Island, NY 718-273-6660
Plenus Group Inc
Lowell, MA 978-970-3832
Poison Pepper Company
Floral City, FL 888-539-5540
Pomodoro Fresca Foods
Millburn, NJ 973-467-6609
Ponti USA
New York, NY
Porinos Gourmet Food
Central Falls, RI 800-826-3938
Porky's Gourmet Foods
Gallatin, TN 800-767-5911
Prairie Thyme LTD
Santa Fe, NM 800-869-0009
Private Harvest
El Dorado Hills, CA 916-933-7080
Private Label Foods
Rochester, NY 585-254-9205
Produits Ronald
St. Damase, QC 800-465-0118
Progresso Quality Foods
Vineland, NJ 856-691-1565
PS Seasoning & Spices
Iron Ridge, WI 920-387-2204
Purity Products
Plainview, NY 800-256-6102
Quality Foods
Qualicum Beach, BC 877-833-7890
R L Schreiber Inc
Ft Lauderdale, FL 800-624-8777
R&R Homestead Kitchen
Saumico, WI 888-779-8245
Ragozzino Foods Inc
Meriden, CT 800-348-1240
Ragsdale-Overton Food Traditions
Smithfield, NC 888-424-8863
Rancho's
Memphis, TN 901-276-8820
Randazzo's Honest To Goodness Sauces
Glen Rock, NJ 201-543-1195
Rao's Specialty Foods Inc
New York, NY 212-269-0151
Ray's Sausage Co
Cleveland, OH 216-921-8782
Raye's Mustard
Eastport, ME 800-853-1903
Raye's Old Fashioned Gourmet Mustard
Eastport, ME 800-853-1903
Reckitt Benckiser LLC
Parsippany, NJ 973-404-2600
Red Lion Spicy Foods Company
Red Lion, PA 717-309-8303
Reily Foods Company
New Orleans, LA 800-535-1961
Renfro Foods
Fort Worth, TX 800-332-2456
RENFRO Foods Inc
Fort Worth, TX 817-336-3849
Restaurant Lulu Gourmet Products
San Francisco, CA 888-693-5800
Reva Foods
Saint Petersburg, FL 727-692-1292
REX Pure Foods
New Orleans, LA 800-344-8314
Reynolds Sugar Bush
Aniwa, WI 715-449-2057
Riba Foods
Houston, TX 800-327-7422
Richelieu Foods Inc
Braintree, MA 781-786-6800
Rio Valley Canning Co
Donna, TX 956-464-7843
River Town Foods Corp
St Louis, MO 800-844-3210
Robert Rothschild Farm
Cincinnati, OH 800-222-9966
Robinson's No 1 Ribs
Oak Park, IL 800-836-6750
Ronzoni
Largo, FL 800-730-5957
Rosa Mexicano
New York, NY 212-757-5447
Roses Ravioli
Oglesby, IL 815-883-8011
Rosmarino Foods/R.Z. Humbert Company
Odessa, FL 888-926-9053
Rossi Pasta LTD
Marietta, OH 800-227-6774
Routin America
Delray Beach, FL
Rowena
Norfolk, VA 800-627-8699
Royal Baltic LTD
Brooklyn, NY 718-385-8300
Royal Food Products
Indianapolis, IN 317-782-2660
Rufus Teague
Shawnee, KS 913-706-3814
Ruskin Redneck Trading Company
Ruskin, FL 813-645-7710
S.D. Mushrooms
Avondale, PA 610-268-8082
Sabatino Truffles USA
West Haven, CT 888-444-9971
Sable & Rosenfeld Foods
Toronto, ON 416-929-4214
Sabra Dipping Company,LL
Oceanside, CA 800-748-5523
Sadler's Smokehouse
Henderson, TX 903-657-5581
Saffron Road
Stamford, CT 877-425-2587
Salvy Sousa Dealer Locator
Arkansas City, KS 620-442-2700
Sambets Cajun Deli
Austin, TX 800-472-6238
Santa Barbara Olive Company
Santa Barbara, CA 800-624-4896
Santa Barbara Salsa/California Creative
Oceanside, CA 800-748-5523
Santa Cruz Chili & Spice
Tumacacori, AZ 520-398-2591
Saratoga Salad Dressing
Canton, MA 781-821-1010
Sau-Sea Foods
Tarrytown, NY 914-631-1717
Sauces N' Love
Lynn, MA 781-595-7771
Savoie's Sausage and Food Products
Opelousas, LA 337-942-7241
Schiavone's Casa Mia
Middletown, OH 513-422-8650
Schlotterbeck & Foss Company
Portland, ME 800-777-4666
Scott's Sauce Co Inc
Goldsboro, NC 800-734-7282
Select Food Products
Toronto, ON 800-699-8016
Seminole Foods
Springfield, OH 800-881-1177
Senba USA
Hayward, CA 888-922-5852
Seneca Foods Corp
Marion, NY 315-926-8100
Sentry Seasonings
Elmhurst, IL 630-530-5370
Serious Foodie
Bradenton, FL 844-736-6343
Serro Foods LLC
Catskill, NY 518-943-9255
Shirley J Ventures, LLC
Lindon, UT 801-225-5073
Sidari's Italian Foods
Cleveland, OH 216-431-3344
Sieco USA Corporation
Houston, TX 713-464-1726
Silver Palate Kitchens
Cresskill, NJ 201-568-0110
Silver Spring Foods
Eau Clair, MI 800-826-7322
Silver State Foods Inc
Denver, CO 800-423-3351
Simply Delicious
Cedar Grove, NC 919-732-5294
Skjodt-Barrett Foods
Brampton, ON 877-600-1200
Slather Brand Foods LLC
Charleston, SC 843-513-1750
Solana Gold Organics
Sebastopol, CA 800-459-1121
Solo Foods
Countryside, IL 800-328-7656
SOPAKCO Foods
Mullins, SC 800-276-9678
Sopakco Foods
Mullins, SC 843-464-7851
Sopako Foods
Mullins, SC 843-464-7851
Sophia Foods
Brooklyn, NY 718-272-1110
Sophia's Sauce Works
Carson City, NV 800-718-7769
South Ceasar Dressing Company
Novato, CA 415-897-0605
Southern Art Company, LLC
Atlanta, GA 800-257-6606
Southern Delight Gourmet Foods
Bowling Green, KY 866-782-9943
Southern Okie
Edmond, OK 405-657-7765
Southwest Specialty Food
Goodyear, AZ 800-536-3131
Soy Vay Enterprises
Felton, CA 800-444-6369
Spanish Gardens Food Manufacturing
Kansas City, KS 913-831-4242
Stanislaus Food Prod
Modesto, CA 800-327-7201
Starport Foods
San Francisco, CA 866-206-9343
Stello Foods Inc
Punxsutawney, PA 800-849-4599
Stickney & Poor Company
Peterborough, NH 603-924-2259
Stonewall Kitchen
York, ME 800-826-1752
Stubb's Legendary BBQ
Austin, TX 800-227-2283
Sun Harvest Foods Inc
San Diego, CA 619-661-0909
Sunny Dell Foods Inc
Oxford, PA 610-932-5164
Super Smokers Bar-B-Que
Eureka, MO 636-938-9742
Surlean Foods
San Antonio, TX 800-999-4370
Sutter Buttes Olive Oil
Sutter, CA 530-763-7921
Swatt Baking Co
Olean, NY 800-370-6656
Sweet & Saucy Inc
Centennial, CO 303-807-5132
Sweet Baby Ray's
Chicago, IL 877-729-2229
Sweet Peas Floral Design
Stockton, CA 209-472-9284
Sweetwater Spice Company
Austin, TX 800-531-6079
Swiss Food Products
Chicago, IL 312-829-0100
T. Marzetti Company
Westerville, OH 800-999-1835
T.W. Garner Food Company
Winston Salem, NC 800-476-7383
Tait Farm Foods
Centre Hall, PA 800-787-2716
Tantos Foods International
Markham, ON 905-943-9993
Tapatio Hot Sauce
Vernon, CA 323-587-8933
Taste Weavers
Urbana, OH 888-810-8365
Tasty Tomato
San Antonio, TX 210-822-2443
Teasdale Quality Foods Inc
Atwater, CA 209-358-5616
Terlato Kitchen
Bannockburn, IL 855-805-7221

Tex-Mex Gourmet
Brenham, TX. . . . 888-345-8467
Texas Heat
San Antonio, TX. . . . 800-656-5916
Texas Tamale Co
Houston, TX. . . . 713-795-5500
The Saucey Sauce CompanyInc.
Brooklyn, NY 646-648-0159
Thistledew Farm
Proctor, WV 800-854-6639
Thomas Gourmet Foods
Greensboro, NC 800-867-2823
Thompson's Fine Foods
Shoreview, MN. . . . 800-807-0025
Thor-Shackel Horseradish Company
Eau Claire, WI 800-826-7322
Thornton Foods Company
Eden Prairie, MN 952-944-1735
Timber Crest Farms
Healdsburg, CA 888-766-4233
Tip Top Canning Co
Tipp City, OH 800-352-2635
TMI Trading Co
Brooklyn, NY 718-821-5052
Todd's
Des Moines, IA. . . . 800-247-5363
Tomasso Corporation
Baie D'Urfe, QC. . . . 514-325-3000
Tone Products Inc
Melrose Park, IL. . . . 800-536-8663
Top Hat Co Inc
Wilmette, IL 847-256-6565
Trader Vic's Food Products
Emeryville, CA. . . . 877-762-4824
Trappey's Fine Foods Inc
New Iberia, LA. . . . 337-365-8281
Trio's Original Italian Pasta Co.
Chelsea, MA. . . . 800-999-9603
Triple H Food Processors Inc
Riverside, CA 951-352-5700
Triple K Manufacturing Company, Inc.
Shenandoah, IA. . . . 712-246-4376
Tulkoff's Food Products Inc
Baltimore, MD 800-638-7343
Twin Marquis
Brooklyn, NY 800-367-6868
Two Chefs on a Roll
Carson, CA 800-842-3025
UBF Food Solutions
Lisle, IL. . . . 630-955-5394
Ultimate Gourmet
Hillsborough, NJ. . . . 908-359-4050
United Foods USA
Hayward, CA 510-264-5850
Valley Grain Products
Fresno, CA 559-675-3400
Vegetable Juices Inc
Chicago, IL 888-776-9752
Ventre Packing Company
Syracuse, NY 315-463-2384
Vermont Signature Sauces
Saxtons River, VT. . . . 802-869-5000
Vidalia Brands Inc
Reidsville, GA 800-752-0206
Vidalia Sweets Brand
Lyons, GA. . . . 912-565-8881
Viki's Montana Classics
Bigfork, MT 800-248-1222
Vincent's Food Corporation
Carle Place, NY 516-481-3544
Violet Packing Holdings LLC
Williamstown, NJ 856-629-7428
Vivienne Dressings
St Louis, MO. . . . 800-827-0778
Wagner Gourmet Foods
Lenexa, KS 913-469-5411
Wagshal's Imports
Washington, DC 202-363-5698
Walden Farms
Linden, NJ. . . . 800-229-1706
Walker Foods
Los Angeles, CA. . . . 800-966-5199
Webbpak Inc
Trussville, AL 800-655-3500
Wei-Chuan USA Inc
Bell Gardens, CA 562-372-2020
Well Dressed Food Company
Tupper Lake, NY 518-359-5280
West Pac
Idaho Falls, ID 800-973-7407
Westbrae Natural Foods
Melville, NY. . . . 800-434-4246

Westin Foods
Omaha, NE 800-228-6098
Whole in the Wall
Binghamton, NY. . . . 607-722-5138
Wickers Food Products Inc
Hornersville, MO 800-847-0032
Widow's Mite Vinegar Company
Washington, DC 877-678-5854
WILD Flavors (Canada)
Mississauga, ON. . . . 800-263-5286
Wild Thymes Farm Inc
Greenville, NY 845-266-8387
William Poll Inc
New York, NY 800-993-7655
Williamsburg Chocolatier
Williamsburg, VA 757-253-1474
WillowOak Farms
Amherst, VA 888-963-2767
Wing It Inc
Falmouth, MA. . . . 508-540-9860
Wing Nien Food
Hayward, CA 510-487-8877
Wing-Time
Lynn, MA 781-592-1069
Wizards Cauldron, LTD
Yanceyville, NC 336-694-5665
Woeber Mustard Mfg Co
Springfield, OH. . . . 800-548-2929
Wood Brothers Inc
West Columbia, SC. . . . 803-796-5146
World Art Foods
Temple, TX 254-774-8322
World Famous Buffalo Wing Sauce
Buffalo, NY. . . . 716-912-9068
World Flavors Inc
Warminster, PA 215-672-4400
World Harbors
Auburn, ME 800-355-6221
World Herbs Gourmet
Old Saybrook, CT. . . . 860-388-3781
Worthmore Food Products Co
Cincinnati, OH 866-837-7687
Yai's Thai
Denver, CO
Yamasa Corp USA
Salem, OR. . . . 503-363-8550
Ying's Kitchen
Lake Villa, IL 847-403-7078
Yo Mama's Foods
Gainesville, FL
Yoshida Food Products Co
Portland, OR 800-653-1114
Zarda Bar-B-Q & Catering Company
Blue Springs, MO. . . . 800-776-7427

Alfredo

Al Dente Pasta Co
Whitmore Lake, MI 800-536-7278
Amanida USA Corp
Coral Gables, FL
Barilla USA
Northbrook, IL 800-922-7455
Casa Di Lisio Products Inc
Mt Kisco, NY 800-247-4199
Classy Delites
Austin, TX. . . . 800-440-2648
Cuizina Food Company
Woodinville, WA. . . . 425-486-7000
Genarom International
Cranbury, NJ. . . . 609-409-6200
LiDestri Food & Drink
Fairport, NY 585-377-7700
Marsan Foods
Toronto, ON 416-755-9262
Newman's Own
Westport, CT. . . . 203-222-0136
Pasta Factory
Melrose Park, IL. . . . 800-615-6951
Sargento Foods Inc
Plymouth, WI 800-243-3737
Tomasso Corporation
Baie D'Urfe, QC. . . . 514-325-3000
Victoria Fine Foods
Brooklyn, NY 718-927-3000

Barbecue

A Southern Season
Hillsborough, NC 800-253-3663
A. Lassonde Inc.
Rougemont, QC 866-552-7643

Allied Old English Inc
Port Reading, NJ. . . . 732-602-8955
Annie's Naturals
Berkeley, CA. . . . 800-434-1234
Arbor Hill Grapery & Winery
Naples, NY 800-554-7553
Ashman Manufacturing & Distributing Company
Virginia Beach, VA. . . . 800-641-9924
Baker's Ribs No 2
Dallas, TX. . . . 214-748-5433
Baldwin Richardson Foods
Oakbrook Terrace, IL 866-644-2732
Bartush Schnitzius Foods Co
Lewisville, TX 972-219-1270
Baumer Foods Inc
Metairie, LA 504-482-5761
BBQ Bunch
Kansas City, MO. . . . 816-941-4534
BBQ'n Fools Catering, LLC
Greenfield, IN 800-671-8652
BBS Bodacious BBQ Company
Coral Springs, FL 800-537-5928
Bettah Buttah, LLC
Kansas City, KS 800-568-8468
Big B Barbecue
Evansville, IN 812-425-5235
Blair's Sauces & Snacks
Highlands, NJ 800-982-5247
Blueberry Store
Grand Junction, MI. . . . 877-654-2400
Bone Suckin' Sauce
Raleigh, NC 919-833-7647
Buffalo Wild Wings
Minneapolis, MN 763-546-1891
Bunker Foods Corp.
New York, NY 646-738-4020
Cafe Chilku
Colchester, VT 802-878-4645
Cafe Tequila
San Francisco, CA 415-264-0106
Cajohn's Fiery Foods Co
Westerville, OH. . . . 888-703-3473
California-Antilles Trading
San Diego, CA 800-330-6450
Captain Bob's Jet Fuel
Fort Wayne, IN 877-486-6468
Carolina Treet
Wilmington, NC 800-616-6344
Casa Visco
Schenectady, NY. . . . 888-607-2823
Casually Gourmet
New Haven, VT 800-639-7604
Catamount Specialties of Vermont
Plainfield, VT 800-639-2406
Catskill Mountain Specialties
Saugerties, NY 800-311-3473
Charlie Beigg's Sauce Company
Windham, ME. . . . 888-502-8595
CHS Inc.
Inver Grove Hts., MN. . . . 800-328-6539
Cinnabar Specialty Foods Inc
Prescott, AZ 866-293-6433
Clements Foods Co
Oklahoma City, OK 800-654-8355
Coach Sposato's Bar-B-Que
Lincoln, AR 800-264-7535
Colgin Co
Dallas, TX. . . . 888-226-5446
Conway Import Co Inc
Franklin Park, IL. . . . 800-323-8801
Cookies Food Products
Wall Lake, IA 800-331-4995
Cookshack
Ponca City, OK 800-423-0698
Country Bob's Inc
Centralia, IL 800-373-2140
Country Cupboard
Lewisburg, PA. . . . 570-523-3211
Crazy Mary's
New York, NY 212-889-8124
Creative Foodworks Inc
San Antonio, TX. . . . 210-212-4761
Cugino's Gourmet Foods
Crystal Lake, IL 888-592-8446
Cuisine Perel
Richmond, CA 800-887-3735
Cuizina Food Company
Woodinville, WA. . . . 425-486-7000
Culver Duck Farms Inc
Middlebury, IN 800-825-9225
D & D Foods Inc
West Des Moines, IA 800-772-4098

Desert Pepper Trading Co
El Paso, TX....................888-472-5727
Dillard's Bar-B-Q Sauce
Durham, NC....................919-286-1080
Dorina So-Good Inc
Union, IL....................815-923-2144
Douglas Cross Enterprises
Seattle, WA....................206-448-1193
Dynamic Foods
Lubbock, TX....................806-723-5600
E.D. Smith Foods Ltd
Hamilton, ON....................905-573-1207
El Rey Cooked Meats
St Louis, MO....................314-521-3113
Favorite Foods
Burnaby, BC....................604-420-5100
Felbro Food Products
Los Angeles, CA....................323-936-5266
Fiesta Gourmet of Tejas
Canyon Lake, TX....................800-585-8250
Figaro Company
Mesquite, TX....................972-288-3587
Food Concentrate Corporation
Oklahoma City, OK....................405-840-5633
Food Ingredient Solutions
Teterboro, NJ....................917-449-9558
Food Processor of New Mexico
Albuquerque, NM....................877-634-3772
Fremont Authentic Brands
Fremont, OH....................419-334-8995
Funnibonz LLC
Princeton Jct, NJ....................877-300-2669
Garden Complements Inc
Kansas City, MO....................800-966-1091
Gayle's Sweet N' Sassy Foods
Beverly Hills, CA....................310-246-1792
Gedney Foods Co
Sun Valley, CA....................888-244-0653
Golden Specialty Foods Inc
Norwalk, CA....................562-802-2537
Golding Farms Foods
Winston Salem, NC....................336-766-6161
Good Food For Good
Markham, ON....................647-449-4922
Gumpert's Canada
Mississauga, ON....................800-387-9324
Hak's
Los Angeles, CA....................424-235-0516
Havana's Limited
Titusville, FL....................321-267-0513
Head Country
Ponca City, OK....................888-762-1227
Heinz Portion Control
Jacksonville, FL....................904-695-1300
Hollman Foods
Des Moines, IA....................888-926-2879
Hormel Foods Corp.
Austin, MN....................507-437-5611
Horseshoe Brand
Milan, NY....................845-240-2390
Hot Licks
Spring Valley, CA....................888-766-6468
Hot Wachula's
Lakeland, FL....................877-883-8700
J.N. Bech
Elk Rapids, MI....................800-232-4583
JMS Specialty Foods
Ripon, WI....................800-535-5437
Johnny Harris Famous Barbecue Sauce
Savannah, GA....................888-547-2823
Judicial Flavors
Auburn, CA....................530-885-1298
Kinder's BBQ
Walnut Creek, CA....................925-939-7242
King's Hawaiian Holding Co Inc.
Torrance, CA....................877-695-4227
Kozlowski Farms
Forestville, CA....................800-473-2767
L & S Packing Co
Farmingdale, NY....................800-286-6487
Lea & Perrins
Glenview, IL
Lee's Sausage Co
Orangeburg, SC....................803-534-5517
Lendy's Cafe Raw Bar
Virginia Beach, VA....................757-491-3511
Litehouse Foods
Sandpoint, ID....................800-669-3169
Lounsbury Foods
Toronto, ON....................416-656-6330
Mad Will's Food Company
Auburn, CA....................888-275-9455
Mansmith's Barbeque
San Jn Bautista, CA....................800-626-7648
Mccutcheon Apple Products
Frederick, MD....................800-888-7537
Millflow Spice Corp.
Hauppauge, NY....................866-227-8355
Mucky Duck Mustard Company
Ferndale, MI....................248-544-4610
Nature's Hollow
Charleston, UT
New Business Corp
Gary, IN....................219-885-1476
North of the Border
Tesuque, NM....................800-860-0681
O'Brian Brothers Food
Cincinnati, OH....................513-791-9909
Ott Food Products Co
Carthage, MO....................800-866-2585
Pacific Choice Brands
Fresno, CA....................559-476-3581
Pacific Poultry Company
Honolulu, HI....................808-841-2828
Palmetto Canning
Palmetto, FL....................941-722-1100
Palmieri Food Products
New Haven, CT....................800-845-5447
Paradise Products Corporation
Boca Raton, FL....................800-826-1235
Passetti's Pride
Hayward, CA....................800-521-4659
Piggie Park Enterprises
West Columbia, SC....................800-628-7423
Porinos Gourmet Food
Central Falls, RI....................800-826-3938
Produits Ronald
St. Damase, QC....................800-465-0118
Reckitt Benckiser LLC
Parsippany, NJ....................973-404-2600
Rib Rack
Birmingham, MI
River Town Foods Corp
St Louis, MO....................800-844-3210
Rob Salamida Co Inc
Johnson City, NY....................800-545-5072
Robbie's Natural Products
Vancouver, WA....................360-433-2325
Robinson's No 1 Ribs
Oak Park, IL....................800-836-6750
Rosmarino Foods/R.Z. Humbert Company
Odessa, FL....................888-926-9053
Sadler's Smokehouse
Henderson, TX....................903-657-5581
Sambets Cajun Deli
Austin, TX....................800-472-6238
San Gennaro Foods Inc
Kent, WA....................800-462-1916
Savoie's Sausage and Food Products
Opelousas, LA....................337-942-7241
Schlotterbeck & Foss Company
Portland, ME....................800-777-4666
Scott's Sauce Co Inc
Goldsboro, NC....................800-734-7282
Sky Valley Foods
Danville, VA
Southern Bar-B-Que
Jennings, LA....................866-612-2586
Southern Delight Gourmet Foods
Bowling Green, KY....................866-782-9943
Stanchfield Farms
Milo, ME....................207-732-5173
Steel's Gourmet Foods, Ltd.
Bridgeport, PA....................800-678-3357
Stinking Rose, The
San Francisco, CA....................800-995-7674
Stuart & CO
Brooklyn, NY....................347-292-7456
Subco Foods Inc
Sheboygan, WI....................800-473-0757
Sweet Baby Ray's
Chicago, IL....................877-729-2229
Sweet Peas Floral Design
Stockton, CA....................209-472-9284
T. Marzetti Company
Westerville, OH....................800-999-1835
T.W. Garner Food Company
Winston Salem, NC....................800-476-7383
Taste Weavers
Urbana, OH....................888-810-8365
The Shed Saucery
Ocean Springs, MS....................228-875-9590
Thompson's Fine Foods
Shoreview, MN....................800-807-0025
Todd's
Des Moines, IA....................800-247-5363
Triple H Food Processors Inc
Riverside, CA....................951-352-5700
Tulkoff's Food Products Inc
Baltimore, MD....................800-638-7343
Ubons Sauce LLC
Yazoo City, MS....................662-716-7100
Valley Grain Products
Fresno, CA....................559-675-3400
Ventre Packing Company
Syracuse, NY....................315-463-2384
Vermont Made Richard's Sauces
St Albans, VT....................802-524-3196
Vidalia Sweets Brand
Lyons, GA....................912-565-8881
We Rub You
Brooklyn, NY....................718-387-9797
Webbpak Inc
Trussville, AL....................800-655-3500
Wei-Chuan USA Inc
Bell Gardens, CA....................562-372-2020
West Pac
Idaho Falls, ID....................800-973-7407
Westin Foods
Omaha, NE....................800-228-6098
Wine Country Chef LLC
Hidden Valley Lake, CA....................707-322-0406
Wing Nien Food
Hayward, CA....................510-487-8877
Wing-Time
Lynn, MA....................781-592-1069
Wizards Cauldron, LTD
Yanceyville, NC....................336-694-5665
Wood Brothers Inc
West Columbia, SC....................803-796-5146
World Famous Buffalo Wing Sauce
Buffalo, NY....................716-912-9068
World Flavors Inc
Warminster, PA....................215-672-4400
Zarda Bar-B-Q & Catering Company
Blue Springs, MO....................800-776-7427

Black Bean

Favorite Foods
Burnaby, BC....................604-420-5100
Lee Kum Kee USA Inc
City Of Industry, CA....................800-654-5082

Cheese

Berner Food & Beverage LLC
Dakota, IL....................800-819-8199
Clofine Dairy Products Inc
Linwood, NJ....................609-653-1000
Cuizina Food Company
Woodinville, WA....................425-486-7000
Fountain Valley Foods
Colorado Springs, CO....................719-573-6012
Galassi Foods
Coralville, IA....................319-339-7409
Genarom International
Cranbury, NJ....................609-409-6200
Kent Precision Foods Group Inc
Muscatine, IA....................800-442-5242
Knouse Foods Co-Op Inc.
Peach Glen, PA....................717-677-8181
Marsan Foods
Toronto, ON....................416-755-9262
Sargento Foods Inc
Plymouth, WI....................800-243-3737
Thornton Foods Company
Eden Prairie, MN....................952-944-1735

Nacho

Bel Brands USA
Chicago, IL....................312-462-1500
Knouse Foods Co-Op Inc.
Peach Glen, PA....................717-677-8181
Olde Tyme Food Corporation
East Longmeadow, MA....................800-356-6533
Vanee Foods Co
Berkeley, IL....................708-449-7300

Chili

Baldwin Richardson Foods
Oakbrook Terrace, IL....................866-644-2732
Big B Barbecue
Evansville, IN....................812-425-5235
Cervantes Food Products Inc
Albuquerque, NM....................877-982-4453

Commodities Marketing Inc
Clarksburg, NJ 732-516-0700
El Charro Mexican Food Ind
Roswell, NM.....................575-622-8590
Fernandez Chili Co
Alamosa, CO.....................719-589-6043
Fiesta Canning Co
Phoenix, AZ 602-212-2424
First Original Texas Chili Company
Fort Worth, TX 800-507-0009
Hurd Orchards
Holley, NY 585-638-8838
Ingleby Farms
Dublin, PA.......................877-728-7277
Las Cruces Brand Products
El Paso, TX......................915-779-5709
Le Grand
Blainville, QC....................450-623-3000
Lee Kum Kee USA Inc
City Of Industry, CA...............800-654-5082
Miguel's Stowe Away
Stowe, VT........................800-448-6517
Mrs Auld's Gourmet Foods Inc
Reno, NV 800-322-8537
North of the Border
Tesuque, NM.....................800-860-0681
Red Gold Inc.
Elwood, IN 866-729-7187
Santa Cruz Chili & Spice
Tumacacori, AZ 520-398-2591
Sky Valley Foods
Danville, VA
Stokes Canning Company
Aurora, CO 800-978-6537
T.W. Garner Food Company
Winston Salem, NC................800-476-7383

Clam

Casa Di Lisio Products Inc
Mt Kisco, NY 800-247-4199
Chincoteague Seafood Co Inc
Parsonsburg, MD 443-260-4800
Colonna Brothers Inc
North Bergen, NJ 201-864-1115
Cuizina Food Company
Woodinville, WA..................425-486-7000
Mid-Atlantic Foods Inc
Easton, MD......................800-922-4688
Pasta Factory
Melrose Park, IL..................800-615-6951
Victoria Fine Foods
Brooklyn, NY 718-927-3000

Cocktail

Baldwin Richardson Foods
Oakbrook Terrace, IL 866-644-2732
Cedarvale Food Products
Toronto, ON 416-656-3330
Clements Foods Co
Oklahoma City, OK 800-654-8355
Cuizina Food Company
Woodinville, WA..................425-486-7000
E Waldo Ward & Son Marmalades
Sierra Madre, CA 800-355-9273
Ed Roller Inc
Rochester, NY....................585-458-8020
Golding Farms Foods
Winston Salem, NC................336-766-6161
Joe Hutson Foods
Jacksonville, FL 904-731-9065
Kelchner's Horseradish
Allentown, PA....................800-424-1952
Lounsbury Foods
Toronto, ON 416-656-6330
Palmieri Food Products
New Haven, CT 800-845-5447
Paradise Products Corporation
Boca Raton, FL...................800-826-1235
Sau-Sea Foods
Tarrytown, NY 914-631-1717
T.W. Garner Food Company
Winston Salem, NC................800-476-7383
Thor-Shackel Horseradish Company
Eau Claire, WI 800-826-7322
Tulkoff's Food Products Inc
Baltimore, MD 800-638-7343
Vegetable Juices Inc
Chicago, IL 888-776-9752

Curry

Baldwin Richardson Foods
Oakbrook Terrace, IL 866-644-2732
Curry King Corporation
Waldwick, NJ 800-287-7987
HerbNZest LLC
Princeton, NJ.....................917-582-1191

Dessert

Amoretti
Oxnard, CA......................800-266-7388
Applecreek Speciality Foods
Lexington, KY 800-747-8871
Graeter's Mfg. Co.
Cincinnati, OH 800-721-3323
Sutter Buttes Olive Oil
Sutter, CA 530-763-7921

Duck

Allied Old English Inc
Port Reading, NJ..................732-602-8955
KARI-Out Co
White Plains, NY 800-433-8799
L & S Packing Co
Farmingdale, NY 800-286-6487

Fish

24Vegan
Arcadia, CA
Stacey's Famous Foods
Hayden, ID 800-782-2395

Fra Diavolo

Cuizina Food Company
Woodinville, WA..................425-486-7000
L & S Packing Co
Farmingdale, NY 800-286-6487
Palmieri Food Products
New Haven, CT 800-845-5447
Papa Leone Food Enterprises
Beverly Hills, CA 310-552-1660
Victoria Fine Foods
Brooklyn, NY 718-927-3000

Frozen

Bellisio Foods
Minneapolis, MN
Carando Gourmet Frozen Foods
Agawam, MA 888-227-2636
Casa Di Lisio Products Inc
Mt Kisco, NY 800-247-4199
Cuizina Food Company
Woodinville, WA..................425-486-7000
Dynamic Foods
Lubbock, TX.....................806-723-5600
Louisa Food Products Inc
St Louis, MO.....................314-868-3000
Marsan Foods
Toronto, ON 416-755-9262
Overhill Farms Inc
Vernon, CA 800-859-6406
Pierino Frozen Foods
Lincoln Park, MI..................313-928-0950
Tomasso Corporation
Baie D'Urfe, QC..................514-325-3000
Trio's Original Italian Pasta Co.
Chelsea, MA 800-999-9603
Two Chefs on a Roll
Carson, CA 800-842-3025
Vegetable Juices Inc
Chicago, IL 888-776-9752

Fudge

Paradigm Foodworks Inc
Lake Oswego, OR.................800-234-0250

Garlic

Baldwin Richardson Foods
Oakbrook Terrace, IL 866-644-2732
Bunker Foods Corp.
New York, NY 646-738-4020
Captain Bob's Jet Fuel
Fort Wayne, IN 877-486-6468
CHS Inc.
Inver Grove Hts., MN..............800-328-6539
Cuizina Food Company
Woodinville, WA..................425-486-7000

L & S Packing Co
Farmingdale, NY 800-286-6487
Lee Kum Kee USA Inc
City Of Industry, CA...............800-654-5082
Marsan Foods
Toronto, ON 416-755-9262
Pasta Factory
Melrose Park, IL..................800-615-6951
Robbie's Natural Products
Vancouver, WA 360-433-2325
Soy Vay Enterprises
Felton, CA.......................800-444-6369
Vegetable Juices Inc
Chicago, IL 888-776-9752

Ginger

Baldwin Richardson Foods
Oakbrook Terrace, IL 866-644-2732
Bunker Foods Corp.
New York, NY 646-738-4020
Cuizina Food Company
Woodinville, WA..................425-486-7000
Vegetable Juices Inc
Chicago, IL 888-776-9752

Gourmet

Beaverton Foods Inc
Hillsboro, OR 800-223-8076
Hot Mama's Foods
Springfield, MA 413-737-6572
Kagome USA Inc
Los Banos, CA 209-826-8850
Vita Food Products Inc
Chicago, IL 800-989-8482
Wildly Delicious
Toronto, ON 888-545-9995

Habanero

Baldwin Richardson Foods
Oakbrook Terrace, IL 866-644-2732
Captain Bob's Jet Fuel
Fort Wayne, IN 877-486-6468
Catskill Mountain Specialties
Saugerties, NY 800-311-3473
Chili Dude
Dallas, TX.......................214-354-9906
Havana's Limited
Titusville, FL.....................321-267-0513
Horseshoe Brand
Milan, NY.......................845-240-2390
Kill Sauce
Pasadena, CA
Lendy's Cafe Raw Bar
Virginia Beach, VA................757-491-3511
Mo Hotta Mo Betta
Savannah, GA 912-748-2766
Mrs. Dog's Products
Grand Rapids, MI 800-267-7364
New Canaan Farms
Dripping Springs, TX 800-727-5267
Porky's Gourmet Foods
Gallatin, TN 800-767-5911
Tex-Mex Gourmet
Brenham, TX.....................888-345-8467
Vegetable Juices Inc
Chicago, IL 888-776-9752
Wing-Time
Lynn, MA 781-592-1069

Hoisin

Baldwin Richardson Foods
Oakbrook Terrace, IL 866-644-2732
Cuizina Food Company
Woodinville, WA..................425-486-7000
Hormel Foods Corp.
Austin, MN......................507-437-5611
Lee Kum Kee USA Inc
City Of Industry, CA...............800-654-5082
Miyako Oriental Foods Inc
Baldwin Park, CA.................877-788-6476
Soy Vay Enterprises
Felton, CA.......................800-444-6369
Wei-Chuan USA Inc
Bell Gardens, CA 562-372-2020

Hollandaise

Century Blends LLC
Hunt Valley, MD..................410-771-6606
Cuizina Food Company
Woodinville, WA..................425-486-7000

Teasdale Quality Foods Inc
Atwater, CA 209-358-5616

Horseradish

Bartush Schnitzius Foods Co
Lewisville, TX 972-219-1270
Beaverton Foods Inc
Hillsboro, OR 800-223-8076
Cedarvale Food Products
Toronto, ON 416-656-3330
Ed Roller Inc
Rochester, NY 585-458-8020
Grouse Hunt Farm Inc
Tamaqua, PA 570-467-2850
Hoople Country Kitchen Inc
Rockport, IN 877-466-7537
Kelchner's Horseradish
Allentown, PA 800-424-1952
Lounsbury Foods
Toronto, ON 416-656-6330
Mother's Mountain Pantry
Falmouth, ME 800-440-9891
Sau-Sea Foods
Tarrytown, NY 914-631-1717
Seminole Foods
Springfield, OH 800-881-1177
Silver Spring Foods
Eau Clair, MI 800-826-7322
Southwest Specialty Food
Goodyear, AZ 800-536-3131
Strub Pickles
Brantford, ON 519-751-1717
Thor-Shackel Horseradish Company
Eau Claire, WI 800-826-7322
Tulkoff's Food Products Inc
Baltimore, MD 800-638-7343
Westin Foods
Omaha, NE 800-228-6098
Woeber Mustard Mfg Co
Springfield, OH 800-548-2929

Hot

Archie Moore's
Milford, CT 203-876-5088
Arizona Cowboy
Phoenix, AZ 800-529-8627
Ashman Manufacturing & Distributing Company
Virginia Beach, VA 800-641-9924
B & G Foods Inc.
Parsippany, NJ 973-401-6500
Baldwin Richardson Foods
Oakbrook Terrace, IL 866-644-2732
Baumer Foods Inc
Metairie, LA 504-482-5761
BBQ'n Fools Catering, LLC
Greenfield, IN 800-671-8652
Blair's Sauces & Snacks
Highlands, NJ 800-982-5247
Boston Spice & Tea Company
Boston, VA 800-966-4372
Brother Bru Bru's
Venice, CA 310-396-9033
Bruce Foods Corporation
Lafayette, LA 800-299-9082
Buds Kitchen
New Castle, PA 724-654-9216
Buffalo Wild Wings
Minneapolis, MN 763-546-1891
Cafe Tequila
San Francisco, CA 415-264-0106
Cajohn's Fiery Foods Co
Westerville, OH 888-703-3473
Cajun Brands
New Iberia, LA 504-408-2252
California-Antilles Trading
San Diego, CA 800-330-6450
Cannon's Sweets Hots
Las Cruces, NM 800-214-6639
Canyon Specialty Foods
Dallas, TX 214-352-1771
Captain Bob's Jet Fuel
Fort Wayne, IN 877-486-6468
Carriere Foods Inc
Saint-Denis-Sur-Richelie, QC 450-787-3411
Colorado Salsa Company
Littleton, CO 303-932-2617
Country Bob's Inc
Centralia, IL 800-373-2140
Cyclone Enterprises Inc
Houston, TX 281-872-0087
Dave's Gourmet
San Rafael, CA 800-758-0372
Dhidow Enterprises
Oxford, PA 610-932-7868
Dockside Market
Key Largo, FL 800-813-2253
E. H. Gourmet
Virginia Beach, VA 757-431-1996
Favorite Foods
Burnaby, BC 604-420-5100
Festive Foods
Virginia Beach, VA 757-490-9186
Fire Fruits International
Orlando, FL 407-480-6580
Ford's Gourmet Foods
Raleigh, NC 800-446-0947
Forge Mountain Foods
Hendersonville, NC 800-823-6743
Garden Complements Inc
Kansas City, MO 800-966-1091
Garden Row Foods
Franklin Park, IL 800-555-9798
Havana's Limited
Titusville, FL 321-267-0513
Heartbreaking Dawns Artisan Foods
Glendale, AZ 646-957-3484
Heintz & Weber Co
Buffalo, NY 716-852-7171
Hormel Foods Corp.
Austin, MN 507-437-5611
Horseshoe Brand
Milan, NY 845-240-2390
Hot Licks
Spring Valley, CA 888-766-6468
Hot Wachula's
Lakeland, FL 877-883-8700
Ingleby Farms
Dublin, PA 877-728-7277
Joe Hutson Foods
Jacksonville, FL 904-731-9065
Juanita's Foods
Wilmington, CA 800-303-2965
Judicial Flavors
Auburn, CA 530-885-1298
K-Mama Sauce
Minneapolis, MN 612-460-5156
KARI-Out Co
White Plains, NY 800-433-8799
L & S Packing Co
Farmingdale, NY 800-286-6487
LA Canasta Mexican Foods
Phoenix, AZ 855-269-7721
Las Cruces Brand Products
El Paso, TX 915-779-5709
Lendy's Cafe Raw Bar
Virginia Beach, VA 757-491-3511
Leonard Mountain Inc
Bixby, OK 800-822-7700
Lounsbury Foods
Toronto, ON 416-656-6330
Mad Will's Food Company
Auburn, CA 888-275-9455
Magic Seasoning Blends
New Orleans, LA 800-457-2857
MAK Enterprises
Palmdale, CA 661-272-1867
Maple Grove Farms Of Vermont
St Johnsbury, VT 802-748-5141
Millflow Spice Corp.
Hauppauge, NY 866-227-8355
Mizkan Americas Inc
Kansas City, MO 800-323-4358
Mo Hotta Mo Betta
Savannah, GA 912-748-2766
Mrs. Dog's Products
Grand Rapids, MI 800-267-7364
Native Kjalii Foods
San Francisco, CA 415-522-5580
Natural Value
Sacramento, CA 916-836-3561
North of the Border
Tesuque, NM 800-860-0681
O'Garvey Sauces
New Braunfels, TX 830-620-6127
Original Juan
Kansas City, KS 800-568-8468
Paradise Products Corporation
Boca Raton, FL 800-826-1235
Pepper Creek Farms
Lawton, OK 800-526-8132
Pepper Island Beach
Lawrence, PA 724-746-2401
Peppered Palette
Bellingham, WA 866-829-9151
Peppers
Lewes, DE 800-998-3473
Picaflor
Boulder, CO 720-442-3816
Porky's Gourmet Foods
Gallatin, TN 800-767-5911
Quality Foods
Qualicum Beach, BC 877-833-7890
Ray's Sausage Co
Cleveland, OH 216-921-8782
Reckitt Benckiser LLC
Parsippany, NJ 973-404-2600
Red Hot Foods
Santa Paula, CA 805-258-3650
Robinson's No 1 Ribs
Oak Park, IL 800-836-6750
Royal Resources
New Orleans, LA 800-888-9932
Sabra Dipping Company,LL
Oceanside, CA 800-748-5523
Sam's Leon Mexican Food
Omaha, NE 402-733-3809
Sambets Cajun Deli
Austin, TX 800-472-6238
San Antonio Farms
Platteville, WI 800-236-1119
Simmons Hot Gourmet Products Corp.
Lethbridge, AB 403-327-9087
Sinai Gourmet
Montreal, QC 844-887-4624
Southwest Specialty Food
Goodyear, AZ 800-536-3131
Spice House International Specialties
Hicksville, NY 516-942-7248
Sweet Baby Ray's
Chicago, IL 877-729-2229
T.W. Garner Food Company
Winston Salem, NC 800-476-7383
Tantos Foods International
Markham, ON 905-943-9993
Tapatio Hot Sauce
Vernon, CA 323-587-8933
Texas Tamale Co
Houston, TX 713-795-5500
Thistledew Farm
Proctor, WV 800-854-6639
Thompson's Fine Foods
Shoreview, MN 800-807-0025
Tomorrow Enterprise
New Iberia, LA 337-783-2666
Trappey's Fine Foods Inc
New Iberia, LA 337-365-8281
Tucson Tamale Company
Tucson, AZ 520-398-6282
Uncle Dougie's
Chicago, IL
Vegetable Juices Inc
Chicago, IL 888-776-9752
Whitfield Foods Inc
Montgomery, AL 800-633-8790
Wing It Inc
Falmouth, MA 508-540-9860
Wing-Time
Lynn, MA 781-592-1069
Wizards Cauldron, LTD
Yanceyville, NC 336-694-5665
World Famous Buffalo Wing Sauce
Buffalo, NY 716-912-9068

Jerk

Baldwin Richardson Foods
Oakbrook Terrace, IL 866-644-2732
Buffalo Wild Wings
Minneapolis, MN 763-546-1891
Catskill Mountain Specialties
Saugerties, NY 800-311-3473
Cinnabar Specialty Foods Inc
Prescott, AZ 866-293-6433
Cuizina Food Company
Woodinville, WA 425-486-7000
Doctor Dread's Jerk
Glen Echo, MD 301-908-9450
Mix-A-Lota Stuff LLC
Fort Pierce, FL 727-365-7328
Nature's Kitchen
Roswell, GA 678-845-6897

Lemon

Baldwin Richardson Foods
Oakbrook Terrace, IL 866-644-2732
Genarom International
Cranbury, NJ 609-409-6200
Wei-Chuan USA Inc
Bell Gardens, CA 562-372-2020

Marinara

Baldwin Richardson Foods
Oakbrook Terrace, IL 866-644-2732
Campbell Soup Co.
Camden, NJ 800-257-8443
Casa Di Lisio Products Inc
Mt Kisco, NY 800-247-4199
CHS Inc.
Inver Grove Hts., MN 800-328-6539
Colonna Brothers Inc
North Bergen, NJ 201-864-1115
Cowboy Caviar
Berkeley, CA 877-509-1796
Cuizina Food Company
Woodinville, WA 425-486-7000
Dell'Amore Enterprises
Colchester, VT 800-962-6673
Hot Wachula's
Lakeland, FL 877-883-8700
Kozlowski Farms
Forestville, CA 800-473-2767
L & S Packing Co
Farmingdale, NY 800-286-6487
LiDestri Food & Drink
Fairport, NY 585-377-7700
Mad Will's Food Company
Auburn, CA 888-275-9455
Mamma Lombardi's All Natural Sauces
Holbrook, NY 631-471-6609
Marsan Foods
Toronto, ON 416-755-9262
Molinaro's Fine Italian Foods Ltd.
Mississauga, ON 905-281-0352
Nello's Sauce
Raleigh, NC 919-428-4338
Newman's Own
Westport, CT 203-222-0136
Palmieri Food Products
New Haven, CT 800-845-5447
Pasta Factory
Melrose Park, IL 800-615-6951
Pasta Valente
Charlottesville, VA 888-575-7670
Pastorelli Food Products
Chicago, IL 800-767-2829
Red Gold Inc.
Elwood, IN 866-729-7187
Sargento Foods Inc
Plymouth, WI 800-243-3737
Stanislaus Food Prod
Modesto, CA 800-327-7201
Vanee Foods Co
Berkeley, IL 708-449-7300
Ventre Packing Company
Syracuse, NY 315-463-2384
Victoria Fine Foods
Brooklyn, NY 718-927-3000
Violet Packing Holdings LLC
Williamstown, NJ 856-629-7428
Webbpak Inc
Trussville, AL 800-655-3500

Meat

J.M. Smucker Co.
Orrville, OH 888-550-9555
Victoria Fine Foods
Brooklyn, NY 718-927-3000
Woods Smoked Meats Inc
Bowling Green, MO 800-458-8426

Mediterranean

Baldwin Richardson Foods
Oakbrook Terrace, IL 866-644-2732
Cookies Food Products
Wall Lake, IA 800-331-4995
Cuizina Food Company
Woodinville, WA 425-486-7000
L & S Packing Co
Farmingdale, NY 800-286-6487
Papa Leone Food Enterprises
Beverly Hills, CA 310-552-1660
Parthenon Food Products
Ann Arbor, MI 734-994-1012

Mexican Food

Art's Mexican Products
Kansas City, KS 913-371-2163
B & G Foods Inc.
Parsippany, NJ 973-401-6500
Big B Barbecue
Evansville, IN 812-425-5235
Border Foods
New Hope, MN 763-559-7338
Casa Visco
Schenectady, NY 888-607-2823
Fernandez Chili Co
Alamosa, CO 719-589-6043
Garden Complements Inc
Kansas City, MO 800-966-1091
Golden Specialty Foods Inc
Norwalk, CA 562-802-2537
Golding Farms Foods
Winston Salem, NC 336-766-6161
Heluva Good Cheese
Lynnfield, MA 800-644-5473
New Canaan Farms
Dripping Springs, TX 800-727-5267
Palmieri Food Products
New Haven, CT 800-845-5447
Pepper Creek Farms
Lawton, OK 800-526-8132
Subco Foods Inc
Sheboygan, WI 800-473-0757
Walker Foods
Los Angeles, CA 800-966-5199

Mint

Baldwin Richardson Foods
Oakbrook Terrace, IL 866-644-2732
Cedarvale Food Products
Toronto, ON 416-656-3330
Lounsbury Foods
Toronto, ON 416-656-6330
Top Hat Co Inc
Wilmette, IL 847-256-6565

Mixes

Century Blends LLC
Hunt Valley, MD 410-771-6606
CHS Inc.
Inver Grove Hts., MN 800-328-6539
Clorox Company
Oakland, CA 510-271-7000
Lawry's Foods
Hunt Valley, MD 800-952-9797
Produits Alimentaire
Laval, QC 800-361-9326
R C Fine Foods Inc
Hillsborough, NJ 800-526-3953
Serv-Agen Corporation
Cherry Hill, NJ 856-663-6966
Superior Quality Foods
Ontario, CA 800-300-4210
UFL Foods
Mississauga, ON 905-670-7776

Mole

Juanita's Foods
Wilmington, CA 800-303-2965

Mushroom

Cipriani's Spaghetti & Sauce Company
Chicago Heights, IL 708-755-6212
Cuizina Food Company
Woodinville, WA 425-486-7000
Galassi Foods
Coralville, IA 319-339-7409
The Truffleist
Astoria, NY 917-325-3374
Vanee Foods Co
Berkeley, IL 708-449-7300
Vegetable Juices Inc
Chicago, IL 888-776-9752
Worthmore Food Products Co
Cincinnati, OH 866-837-7687

Orange

Bunker Foods Corp.
New York, NY 646-738-4020
Papa Leone Food Enterprises
Beverly Hills, CA 310-552-1660
San-J International Inc
Henrico, VA 800-446-5500

Organic

Fiore Di Pasta
Fresno, CA 559-457-0431
Imagine Foods
Boulder, CO 800-434-4246
Lassonde Pappas & Company, Inc.
Carneys Point, NJ 800-257-7019
Vegy Vida
Cincinnati, OH 513-659-0781

Oyster

Favorite Foods
Burnaby, BC 604-420-5100
Lee Kum Kee USA Inc
City Of Industry, CA 800-654-5082
Wei-Chuan USA Inc
Bell Gardens, CA 562-372-2020

Pasta

Amanida USA Corp
Coral Gables, FL
Barilla USA
Northbrook, IL 800-922-7455
Colavita USA
Edison, NJ 888-265-2848
Coupla Guys Foods
Chicago, IL 312-829-2332
Dei Fratelli
Toledo, OH 800-837-1631
Del Monte Foods Inc.
Walnut Creek, CA
Fiore Di Pasta
Fresno, CA 559-457-0431
Milos Whole World Gourmet
Athens, OH 866-589-6456
Mondiv/Division of Lassonde Inc
Boisbriand, QC 450-979-0717
Newman's Own
Westport, CT 203-222-0136
Nona Vegan Foods
Toronto, ON 416-836-9387
Pacific Choice Brands
Fresno, CA 559-476-3581
Paesana Products
East Farmingdale, NY 631-845-1717
Pastene Co LTD
Canton, MA 781-298-3397
Patsy's Brands
New York, NY 212-247-3491
Serro Foods LLC
Catskill, NY 518-943-9255
Summer Garden Food Manufacturing
Boardman, OH 330-965-8455
The Sunshine Tomato Company
New Cumberland, PA 717-909-0844
Victoria Fine Foods
Brooklyn, NY 718-927-3000
White Oak Farm and Table
Westport, CT 203-716-1577

Peanut

Rowena
Norfolk, VA 800-627-8699

Pepper

Brother Bru Bru's
Venice, CA 310-396-9033
Colibri Pepper Company
Elmer, LA 316-730-6528
Genarom International
Cranbury, NJ 609-409-6200
Judicial Flavors
Auburn, CA 530-885-1298
Landry's Pepper Co
St Martinville, LA 337-394-6097
Pepper Source Inc
Metairie, LA 504-885-3223
Pepper Source LTD
Rogers, AR 479-246-1030
Pepper Source, Rogers
Van Buren, AR 479-474-5178
Porky's Gourmet Foods
Gallatin, TN 800-767-5911
Small Axe Peppers
Long Island City, NY

T.W. Garner Food Company
Winston Salem, NC. 800-476-7383

Hot

Brother Bru Bru's
Venice, CA 310-396-9033
Horseshoe Brand
Milan, NY. 845-240-2390
Kill Sauce
Pasadena, CA
Mother's Mountain Pantry
Falmouth, ME. 800-440-9891
Porky's Gourmet Foods
Gallatin, TN 800-767-5911

Pesto

Al Dente Pasta Co
Whitmore Lake, MI 800-536-7278
Armanino Foods of Distinction
Hayward, CA 800-255-8588
Barilla USA
Northbrook, IL 800-922-7455
Bella Cucina
Atlanta, GA. 866-350-9040
Casa Di Lisio Products Inc
Mt Kisco, NY 800-247-4199
Christopher Ranch LLC
Gilroy, CA. 408-847-1100
Cuizina Food Company
Woodinville, WA. 425-486-7000
Delectable Gourmet LLC
Deer Park, NY. 800-696-1350
Golden Specialty Foods Inc
Norwalk, CA. 562-802-2537
Gracious Gourmet
Bridgewater, CT 860-350-1213
Great Garlic Foods
Bradley Beach, NJ 732-775-3311
HerbNZest LLC
Princeton, NJ. 917-582-1191
Kind Snacks
New York, NY 855-884-5463
La Maison Le Grand
St-Joseph-du-Lac, QC. 450-623-3000
Le Grand
Blainville, QC 450-623-3000
Les Aliments Livabec Foods
Sherrington, QC 450-454-7971
Millflow Spice Corp.
Hauppauge, NY 866-227-8355
Mondiv/Division of Lassonde Inc
Boisbriand, QC 450-979-0717
North American Enterprises
Tucson, AZ 800-817-8666
Pasta Factory
Melrose Park, IL 800-615-6951
Peaceworks
New York, NY 212-897-3985
Pestos with Panache
Brooklyn, NY 917-656-3082
Randazzo's Honest To Goodness Sauces
Glen Rock, NJ. 201-543-1195
Red Gold Inc.
Elwood, IN 866-729-7187
Rising Sun Farms
Phoenix, OR 800-888-0795
TexaFrance
Round Rock, TX. 800-776-8937
Tulkoff's Food Products Inc
Baltimore, MD 800-638-7343
Victoria Fine Foods
Brooklyn, NY 718-927-3000
Waterfield Farms
Amherst, MA 413-549-3558

Pizza

Alimentaire Whyte's Inc
Laval, QC 866-420-9520
Baldwin Richardson Foods
Oakbrook Terrace, IL 866-644-2732
Big B Barbecue
Evansville, IN 812-425-5235
Canada Bread Co, Ltd
Etobicoke, ON 800-465-5515
Cuizina Food Company
Woodinville, WA. 425-486-7000
DelGrosso Foods
Tipton, PA 800-521-5880
Delgrosso Foods Inc.
Tipton, PA. 800-521-5880
Dorothy Dawson Food Products
Jackson, MI. 517-788-9830
Furmano's Foods
Northumberland, PA 800-952-1111
Giovanni Food Co Inc
Syracuse, NY 315-457-2373
Hirzel Canning Co & Farms
Luckey, OH. 419-419-7525
Leonardo's of Vermont, LLC
South Burlington, VT 902-863-8404
Mama Mary's
Fairforest, SC 800-813-7574
Nation Wide Canning Ltd.
Cottam, ON. 519-839-4831
Palmieri Food Products
New Haven, CT 800-845-5447
Paradise Tomato Kitchens
Louisville, KY 502-637-1700
Pastorelli Food Products
Chicago, IL 800-767-2829
Perky's Pizza
Oldsmar, FL 800-473-7597
Rustic Crust Inc
Pittsfield, NH 603-435-5119
Sargento Foods Inc
Plymouth, WI 800-243-3737
Sassafras Enterprises Inc
Chicago, IL 800-537-4941
Sky Valley Foods
Danville, VA
Spinato's Fine Foods
Tempe, AZ 480-275-4319
Stanislaus Food Prod
Modesto, CA. 800-327-7201
Tip Top Canning Co
Tipp City, OH 800-352-2635
Triple K Manufacturing Company, Inc.
Shenandoah, IA. 712-246-4376
Violet Packing Holdings LLC
Williamstown, NJ 856-629-7428
Worthmore Food Products Co
Cincinnati, OH 866-837-7687

Plum

Baldwin Richardson Foods
Oakbrook Terrace, IL 866-644-2732
Cuizina Food Company
Woodinville, WA. 425-486-7000
Favorite Foods
Burnaby, BC 604-420-5100
Lee Kum Kee USA Inc
City Of Industry, CA. 800-654-5082
Wei-Chuan USA Inc
Bell Gardens, CA 562-372-2020
Wing's Food Products
Toronto, ON 416-259-2662

Primavera

Cuizina Food Company
Woodinville, WA. 425-486-7000
L & S Packing Co
Farmingdale, NY 800-286-6487

Puttanesca

Baldwin Richardson Foods
Oakbrook Terrace, IL 866-644-2732
Casa Di Lisio Products Inc
Mt Kisco, NY 800-247-4199
Cuizina Food Company
Woodinville, WA. 425-486-7000
L & S Packing Co
Farmingdale, NY 800-286-6487
Papa Leone Food Enterprises
Beverly Hills, CA 310-552-1660

Seafood

Beaverton Foods Inc
Hillsboro, OR 800-223-8076
Blue Crab Bay
Melfa, VA 800-221-2722
Chincoteague Seafood Co Inc
Parsonsburg, MD 443-260-4800
Clements Foods Co
Oklahoma City, OK 800-654-8355
Cuizina Food Company
Woodinville, WA. 425-486-7000
E Waldo Ward & Son Marmalades
Sierra Madre, CA 800-355-9273
Heinz Portion Control
Jacksonville, FL 904-695-1300
J.M. Smucker Co.
Orrville, OH 888-550-9555
Lounsbury Foods
Toronto, ON 416-656-6330
Mid-Atlantic Foods Inc
Easton, MD 800-922-4688
Myron's Fine Foods, Inc.
Millers Falls, MA 800-730-2820
New Business Corp
Gary, IN. 219-885-1476
New Canaan Farms
Dripping Springs, TX 800-727-5267
Palmieri Food Products
New Haven, CT 800-845-5447
Paradise Products Corporation
Boca Raton, FL. 800-826-1235
Rosmarino Foods/R.Z. Humbert Company
Odessa, FL 888-926-9053
Silver Spring Foods
Eau Clair, MI. 800-826-7322
T.W. Garner Food Company
Winston Salem, NC. 800-476-7383
Woeber Mustard Mfg Co
Springfield, OH. 800-548-2929

Soy

Ajinomoto Heartland Inc
Chicago, IL 773-380-7000
Alimentaire Whyte's Inc
Laval, QC 866-420-9520
American Culinary Garden
Springfield, MO 888-831-2433
Baldwin Richardson Foods
Oakbrook Terrace, IL 866-644-2732
Bartush Schnitzius Foods Co
Lewisville, TX 972-219-1270
Basic Food Flavors
North Las Vegas, NV 702-643-0043
Baumer Foods Inc
Metairie, LA 504-482-5761
Baycliff Co Inc
Garwood, NJ. 866-772-7569
Castella Imports Inc
Brentwood, NY. 631-231-5500
Clements Foods Co
Oklahoma City, OK 800-654-8355
Commodities Marketing Inc
Clarksburg, NJ 732-516-0700
Dixie USA
Tomball, TX 800-233-3668
Edward & Sons Trading Co
Carpinteria, CA. 805-684-8500
Favorite Foods
Burnaby, BC 604-420-5100
Felbro Food Products
Los Angeles, CA. 323-936-5266
Flavor House, Inc.
Adelanto, CA 760-246-9131
Hormel Foods Corp.
Austin, MN 507-437-5611
Inter-American Products
Cincinnati, OH 800-645-2233
KARI-Out Co
White Plains, NY 800-433-8799
Lee Kum Kee USA Inc
City Of Industry, CA. 800-654-5082
Lee's Food Products
Toronto, ON 416-465-2407
Mandarin Soy Sauce Inc
Middletown, NY. 845-343-1505
McIlhenny Company
Avery Island, LA. 800-634-9599
Millflow Spice Corp.
Hauppauge, NY 866-227-8355
Myron's Fine Foods, Inc.
Millers Falls, MA 800-730-2820
Nikken Foods
St Louis, MO. 314-881-5818
San-J International Inc
Henrico, VA 800-446-5500
Sempio Foods
Cerritos, CA 562-207-9540
Serv-Agen Corporation
Cherry Hill, NJ 856-663-6966
Sobaya
Cowansville, QC. 800-319-8808
Tomasso Corporation
Baie D'Urfe, QC. 514-325-3000
Wei-Chuan USA Inc
Bell Gardens, CA 562-372-2020
Wing Nien Food
Hayward, CA 510-487-8877

Wing's Food Products
Toronto, ON 416-259-2662
Wizards Cauldron, LTD
Yanceyville, NC 336-694-5665
Yamasa Corp USA
Salem, OR 503-363-8550

Spaghetti

Alimentaire Whyte's Inc
Laval, QC 866-420-9520
Baldwin Richardson Foods
Oakbrook Terrace, IL 866-644-2732
Campbell Soup Co.
Camden, NJ 800-257-8443
Casa Visco
Schenectady, NY 888-607-2823
Chef-A-Roni Fancy Foods
East Greenwich, RI 401-884-8798
Cipriani's Spaghetti & Sauce Company
Chicago Heights, IL 708-755-6212
Cuizina Food Company
Woodinville, WA 425-486-7000
DelGrosso Foods
Tipton, PA 800-521-5880
Delgrosso Foods Inc.
Tipton, PA 800-521-5880
Eden Foods Inc
Clinton, MI 888-424-3336
Furmano's Foods
Northumberland, PA 800-952-1111
Giovanni Food Co Inc
Syracuse, NY 315-457-2373
Gumpert's Canada
Mississauga, ON 800-387-9324
Hagerty Foods
Orange, CA 714-628-1230
Hanover Foods Corp
Hanover, PA 717-632-6000
Hirzel Canning Co & Farms
Luckey, OH 419-419-7525
L & S Packing Co
Farmingdale, NY 800-286-6487
Marsan Foods
Toronto, ON 416-755-9262
Molinaro's Fine Italian Foods Ltd.
Mississauga, ON 905-281-0352
Mom's Food Company
Osterville, MA 800-969-6667
Nation Wide Canning Ltd.
Cottam, ON 519-839-4831
Nicola Pizza
Rehoboth Beach, DE 302-226-2654
Palmieri Food Products
New Haven, CT 800-845-5447
Peaceworks
New York, NY 212-897-3985
Pino's Pasta Veloce
Staten Island, NY 718-273-6660
Porinos Gourmet Food
Central Falls, RI 800-826-3938
Progresso Quality Foods
Vineland, NJ 856-691-1565
Ragozzino Foods Inc
Meriden, CT 800-348-1240
Red Gold Inc.
Elwood, IN 866-729-7187
Seneca Foods Corp
Marion, NY 315-926-8100
Silver State Foods Inc
Denver, CO 800-423-3351
Todd's
Des Moines, IA 800-247-5363
Triple H Food Processors Inc
Riverside, CA 951-352-5700
Violet Packing Holdings LLC
Williamstown, NJ 856-629-7428
Westin Foods
Omaha, NE 800-228-6098
Worthmore Food Products Co
Cincinnati, OH 866-837-7687

Meat

Campbell Soup Co.
Camden, NJ 800-257-8443
Chef-A-Roni Fancy Foods
East Greenwich, RI 401-884-8798
Cipriani's Spaghetti & Sauce Company
Chicago Heights, IL 708-755-6212
DelGrosso Foods
Tipton, PA 800-521-5880
Gaucho Foods
Fayetteville, IL 877-677-2282
Vanee Foods Co
Berkeley, IL 708-449-7300

Meatless

Campbell Soup Co.
Camden, NJ 800-257-8443
Chef-A-Roni Fancy Foods
East Greenwich, RI 401-884-8798
DelGrosso Foods
Tipton, PA 800-521-5880
Molinaro's Fine Italian Foods Ltd.
Mississauga, ON 905-281-0352

Steak

Ashman Manufacturing & Distributing Company
Virginia Beach, VA 800-641-9924
Baumer Foods Inc
Metairie, LA 504-482-5761
Creative Foodworks Inc
San Antonio, TX 210-212-4761
Golding Farms Foods
Winston Salem, NC 336-766-6161
Joe Hutson Foods
Jacksonville, FL 904-731-9065
Kozlowski Farms
Forestville, CA 800-473-2767
L & S Packing Co
Farmingdale, NY 800-286-6487
Lea & Perrins
Glenview, IL
Magic Seasoning Blends
New Orleans, LA 800-457-2857
Myron's Fine Foods, Inc.
Millers Falls, MA 800-730-2820
Newman's Own
Westport, CT 203-222-0136
Paradise Products Corporation
Boca Raton, FL 800-826-1235
Quality Foods
Qualicum Beach, BC 877-833-7890
Webbpak Inc
Trussville, AL 800-655-3500
Wine Country Chef LLC
Hidden Valley Lake, CA 707-322-0406
Wizards Cauldron, LTD
Yanceyville, NC 336-694-5665

Stir-Fry

Baldwin Richardson Foods
Oakbrook Terrace, IL 866-644-2732
Cuizina Food Company
Woodinville, WA 425-486-7000
Flavor House, Inc.
Adelanto, CA 760-246-9131
Hormel Foods Corp.
Austin, MN 507-437-5611
L & S Packing Co
Farmingdale, NY 800-286-6487
Marjon Specialty Foods Inc
Plant City, FL 813-752-3482
Myron's Fine Foods, Inc.
Millers Falls, MA 800-730-2820
Wei-Chuan USA Inc
Bell Gardens, CA 562-372-2020
Wing Nien Food
Hayward, CA 510-487-8877
Wizards Cauldron, LTD
Yanceyville, NC 336-694-5665

Sweet & Sour

Baldwin Richardson Foods
Oakbrook Terrace, IL 866-644-2732
Big B Barbecue
Evansville, IN 812-425-5235
Cuizina Food Company
Woodinville, WA 425-486-7000
Garden Complements Inc
Kansas City, MO 800-966-1091
Gumpert's Canada
Mississauga, ON 800-387-9324
KARI-Out Co
White Plains, NY 800-433-8799
L & S Packing Co
Farmingdale, NY 800-286-6487
Lee Kum Kee USA Inc
City Of Industry, CA 800-654-5082
Robbie's Natural Products
Vancouver, WA 360-433-2325
Vanee Foods Co
Berkeley, IL 708-449-7300
Wei-Chuan USA Inc
Bell Gardens, CA 562-372-2020
Wing Nien Food
Hayward, CA 510-487-8877

Szechuan

Baldwin Richardson Foods
Oakbrook Terrace, IL 866-644-2732
Favorite Foods
Burnaby, BC 604-420-5100
Myron's Fine Foods, Inc.
Millers Falls, MA 800-730-2820
San-J International Inc
Henrico, VA 800-446-5500

Taco

Amigos Canning Company
San Antonio, TX 210-798-5360
Baldwin Richardson Foods
Oakbrook Terrace, IL 866-644-2732
Bartush Schnitzius Foods Co
Lewisville, TX 972-219-1270
Bien Padre Foods Inc
Eureka, CA 707-442-4585
Big B Barbecue
Evansville, IN 812-425-5235
Cookies Food Products
Wall Lake, IA 800-331-4995
El Rancho Tortilla
San Antonio, TX 210-922-8411
Famous Chili Inc
Fort Smith, AR 479-782-0096
Fernandez Chili Co
Alamosa, CO 719-589-6043
Golden Specialty Foods Inc
Norwalk, CA 562-802-2537
Golding Farms Foods
Winston Salem, NC 336-766-6161
Hagerty Foods
Orange, CA 714-628-1230
Heluva Good Cheese
Lynnfield, MA 800-644-5473
Hirzel Canning Co & Farms
Luckey, OH 419-419-7525
Hormel Foods Corp.
Austin, MN 507-437-5611
Hume Specialties
Chester, VT 802-875-3117
Imus Ranch Foods
Darien, CT 888-284-4687
Judicial Flavors
Auburn, CA 530-885-1298
LA Vencedora Products Inc
Los Angeles, CA 800-327-2572
La Victoria Foods
Austin, MN 800-725-7212
Laredo Tortilleria & Mexican
Fort Wayne, IN 800-252-7336
Li'l Guy Foods
Kansas City, MO 800-886-8226
New Canaan Farms
Dripping Springs, TX 800-727-5267
Palmieri Food Products
New Haven, CT 800-845-5447
Pepper Creek Farms
Lawton, OK 800-526-8132
Red Duck Foods
Portland, OR 530-219-0150
Red Gold Inc.
Elwood, IN 866-729-7187
Spanish Gardens Food Manufacturing
Kansas City, KS 913-831-4242

Tahini

Dipasa USA Inc
Brownsville, TX 956-831-4072
East Wind Inc
Tecumseh, MO 417-679-4682
Once Again Nut Butter
Nunda, NY 888-800-8075
Premier Organics
Oakland, CA 866-237-8688

Tartar

Baldwin Richardson Foods
Oakbrook Terrace, IL 866-644-2732
Cedarvale Food Products
Toronto, ON 416-656-3330

Cuizina Food Company
Woodinville, WA. 425-486-7000
Golding Farms Foods
Winston Salem, NC. 336-766-6161
Heinz Portion Control
Jacksonville, FL 904-695-1300
Kelchner's Horseradish
Allentown, PA. 800-424-1952
Lounsbury Foods
Toronto, ON 416-656-6330
Sau-Sea Foods
Tarrytown, NY 914-631-1717
Schlotterbeck & Foss Company
Portland, ME. 800-777-4666
Silver Spring Foods
Eau Clair, MI. 800-826-7322
Westin Foods
Omaha, NE 800-228-6098
Wood Brothers Inc
West Columbia, SC. 803-796-5146

Teriyaki

Argo Century, Inc.
Jacksonville, FL 800-446-7108
Baldwin Richardson Foods
Oakbrook Terrace, IL 866-644-2732
Baycliff Co Inc
Garwood, NJ. 866-772-7569
BBQ'n Fools Catering, LLC
Greenfield, IN. 800-671-8652
Buffalo Wild Wings
Minneapolis, MN 763-546-1891
California Custom Foods
Fullerton, CA 714-870-0490
Conway Import Co Inc
Franklin Park, IL. 800-323-8801
Cuizina Food Company
Woodinville, WA. 425-486-7000
Dynamic Foods
Lubbock, TX. 806-723-5600
Favorite Foods
Burnaby, BC 604-420-5100
Golden Specialty Foods Inc
Norwalk, CA. 562-802-2537
Hormel Foods Corp.
Austin, MN 507-437-5611
L & S Packing Co
Farmingdale, NY 800-286-6487
Miyako Oriental Foods Inc
Baldwin Park, CA. 877-788-6476
Myron's Fine Foods, Inc.
Millers Falls, MA 800-730-2820
Passetti's Pride
Hayward, CA 800-521-4659
Red Duck Foods
Portland, OR 530-219-0150
Sagawa's Savory Sauces
Tualatin, OR 503-692-4334
San-J International Inc
Henrico, VA 800-446-5500
Sky Valley Foods
Danville, VA
T. Marzetti Company
Westerville, OH. 800-999-1835
Triple H Food Processors Inc
Riverside, CA 951-352-5700
Valley Grain Products
Fresno, CA 559-675-3400
World Flavors Inc
Warminster, PA. 215-672-4400
Yamasa Corp USA
Salem, OR. 503-363-8550

Tomato

Barilla USA
Northbrook, IL 800-922-7455
City Saucery
Staten Island, NY 718-753-4006
Furmano's Foods
Northumberland, PA 800-952-1111
Galassi Foods
Coralville, IA 319-339-7409
Mamma Lombardi's All Natural Sauces
Holbrook, NY. 631-471-6609
Rosa Food Products
Philadelphia, PA 215-467-2214
Small Planet Foods
Minneapolis, MN 800-624-4123
The Jersey Tomato Company
Hillsdale, NJ

Canned

Bartush Schnitzius Foods Co
Lewisville, TX 972-219-1270
Bruno Specialty Foods
West Sayville, NY. 631-589-1700
Cajun Brands
New Iberia, LA. 504-408-2252
Casa Di Lisio Products Inc
Mt Kisco, NY 800-247-4199
Casa Visco
Schenectady, NY. 888-607-2823
City Saucery
Staten Island, NY 718-753-4006
Colonna Brothers Inc
North Bergen, NJ 201-864-1115
Costa Deano's Gourmet Foods
Canton, OH. 800-337-2823
Cucina Antica Foods Corp
Mt Kisco, NY 877-728-2462
Cuizina Food Company
Woodinville, WA. 425-486-7000
Escalon Premier Brand
Escalon, CA 209-838-7341
Gumpert's Canada
Mississauga, ON. 800-387-9324
Hanover Foods Corp
Hanover, PA 717-632-6000
Hirzel Canning Co & Farms
Luckey, OH. 419-419-7525
International Home Foods
Parsippany, NJ. 973-359-9920
Kozlowski Farms
Forestville, CA 800-473-2767
L & S Packing Co
Farmingdale, NY 800-286-6487
Molinaro's Fine Italian Foods Ltd.
Mississauga, ON. 905-281-0352
Nation Wide Canning Ltd.
Cottam, ON. 519-839-4831
Northwest Packing Co
Vancouver, WA 800-543-4356
Palmieri Food Products
New Haven, CT 800-845-5447
Papa Leone Food Enterprises
Beverly Hills, CA 310-552-1660
Pasta Factory
Melrose Park, IL. 800-615-6951
Pastorelli Food Products
Chicago, IL 800-767-2829
Progresso Quality Foods
Vineland, NJ 856-691-1565
Seneca Foods Corp
Marion, NY. 315-926-8100
Small Planet Foods
Minneapolis, MN 800-624-4123
Tip Top Canning Co
Tipp City, OH 800-352-2635
Tomasso Corporation
Baie D'Urfe, QC. 514-325-3000
Walker Foods
Los Angeles, CA. 800-966-5199

Diced

Small Planet Foods
Minneapolis, MN 800-624-4123

Frozen

Cajun Brands
New Iberia, LA. 504-408-2252
Casa Di Lisio Products Inc
Mt Kisco, NY 800-247-4199
Cuizina Food Company
Woodinville, WA. 425-486-7000
Hanover Foods Corp
Hanover, PA 717-632-6000
Marsan Foods
Toronto, ON 416-755-9262
Molinaro's Fine Italian Foods Ltd.
Mississauga, ON. 905-281-0352
Progresso Quality Foods
Vineland, NJ 856-691-1565
Seneca Foods Corp
Marion, NY. 315-926-8100

with Spices

Palmieri Food Products
New Haven, CT 800-845-5447
Patsy's Italian Restaurant
New York, NY 212-247-3491

Small Planet Foods
Minneapolis, MN 800-624-4123

Worcestershire

A. Lassonde Inc.
Rougemont, QC 866-552-7643
Annie's Naturals
Berkeley, CA. 800-434-1234
Baldwin Richardson Foods
Oakbrook Terrace, IL 866-644-2732
Baumer Foods Inc
Metairie, LA 504-482-5761
Big B Barbecue
Evansville, IN 812-425-5235
Cajun Brands
New Iberia, LA. 504-408-2252
Clements Foods Co
Oklahoma City, OK 800-654-8355
Colgin Co
Dallas, TX. 888-226-5446
Felbro Food Products
Los Angeles, CA. 323-936-5266
Gold Coast Ingredients
Commerce, CA. 800-352-8673
Illes Seasonings & Flavors
Carrollton, TX. 800-683-4553
Inter-American Products
Cincinnati, OH 800-645-2233
Lea & Perrins
Glenview, IL
McIlhenny Company
Avery Island, LA. 800-634-9599
Millflow Spice Corp.
Hauppauge, NY 866-227-8355
New Business Corp
Gary, IN. 219-885-1476
Portlandia Foods
Portland, OR 833-739-3663
Reckitt Benckiser LLC
Parsippany, NJ. 973-404-2600
Robbie's Natural Products
Vancouver, WA 360-433-2325
Serv-Agen Corporation
Cherry Hill, NJ 856-663-6966
T.W. Garner Food Company
Winston Salem, NC. 800-476-7383
Vegetable Juices Inc
Chicago, IL 888-776-9752

Vinegar

A Perfect Pear
Napa, CA. 800-553-5753
Agrusa
Leonia, NJ. 201-592-5950
American Culinary Garden
Springfield, MO 888-831-2433
Arbor Hill Grapery & Winery
Naples, NY 800-554-7553
Arnabal International, Inc.
Tustin, CA. 714-665-9477
Au Printemps Gourmet
Saint-Jerome, QC 800-438-6676
B R Cohn Winery & Olive Oil Co
Glen Ellen, CA 800-330-4064
Baycliff Co Inc
Garwood, NJ. 866-772-7569
Belton Foods Inc
Dayton, OH. 800-443-2266
Big B Barbecue
Evansville, IN 812-425-5235
Bittersweet Herb Farm
Shelburne Falls, MA. 800-456-1599
Blueberry Store
Grand Junction, MI. 877-654-2400
Boston Spice & Tea Company
Boston, VA 800-966-4372
Boyajian LLC
Canton, MA 800-965-0665
Buonitalia
New York, NY 212-633-9090
C W Resources Inc
New Britain, CT 860-229-7700
California Balsamic Inc
Ukiah, CA. 888-644-5127
California Olive Oil Council
Berkeley, CA. 888-718-9830
Castella Imports Inc
Brentwood, NY. 631-231-5500
Chicama Vineyards
West Tisbury, MA. 888-244-2262

Clements Foods Co
Oklahoma City, OK 800-654-8355
Colonna Brothers Inc
North Bergen, NJ 201-864-1115
Consumers Vinegar & Spice Co
Chicago, IL 773-376-4100
Creole Fermentation Indu
Abbeville, LA 337-898-9377
Dark Tickle Company
St Lunaire-Griquet, NL. 709-623-2354
De Nigris
Totowa, NJ 973-837-6791
Delicae Gourmet
Tarpon Springs, FL 800-942-2502
Eden Foods Inc
Clinton, MI 888-424-3336
Emerling International Foods
Buffalo, NY. 716-833-7381
Fleischmann's Vinegar Co Inc
Cerritos, CA 800-443-1067
Fleischmann's Yeast
Chesterfield, MO 800-777-4959
Four Chimneys Farm Winery Trust
Himrod, NY 607-243-7502
Fredericksburg Herb Farm
Fredericksburg, TX. 800-259-4372
Gedney Foods Co
Sun Valley, CA 888-244-0653
Gold Pure Food Products Co. Inc.
Hempstead, NY. 800-422-4681
Grapevine Trading Company
Santa Rosa, CA. 800-469-6478
Halladay's Harvest Barn
Bellows Falls, VT 802-463-3471
Herb Bee's Products
Colchester, VT 802-864-7387
Hinzerling Winery
Prosser, WA. 800-727-6702
Hudson Valley Fruit Juice
Highland, NY 845-691-8061
Hurd Orchards
Holley, NY 585-638-8838
II Sisters
Moss Beach, CA 800-282-7058
K L Keller Imports
Oakland, CA 510-839-7890
KARI-Out Co
White Plains, NY 800-433-8799
Kedem
Bayonne, NJ 718-369-4600
Ken's Foods Inc
Marlborough, MA 508-229-1100
Knouse Foods Co-Op Inc.
Peach Glen, PA 717-677-8181
Kozlowski Farms
Forestville, CA 800-473-2767
Lesley Elizabeth Inc
Lapeer, MI. 800-684-3300
Lounsbury Foods
Toronto, ON 416-656-6330
Mandarin Soy Sauce Inc
Middletown, NY 845-343-1505
Mange
Somerville, MA 917-880-2104
Marina Foods
Medley, FL 786-888-0129
Marukan Vinegar USA Inc.
Paramount, CA 562-630-6060
Mizkan Americas Inc
Kansas City, MO. 800-323-4358
Modena Fine Foods Inc
Clifton, NJ. 973-470-8499
Morehouse Foods Inc
City Of Industry, CA. 888-297-9800
Myron's Fine Foods, Inc.
Millers Falls, MA 800-730-2820
Nakano Foods
Mt Prospect, IL 800-323-4358
National Fruit Product Co Inc
Winchester, VA 540-723-9614
National Vinegar Co
St Louis, MO. 314-962-4111
Nonna Pia's Gourmet Sauces
Whistler, BC 888-372-1534
North American Enterprises
Tucson, AZ 800-817-8666
O Olive Oil
Petaluma, CA 888-827-7148
Oasis Food Co
Hillside, NJ 800-275-0477
Old Dutch Mustard Company
Great Neck, NY 516-466-0522
Olds Products Co
Pleasant Prairie, WI 262-947-3500
Pastorelli Food Products
Chicago, IL 800-767-2829
Patsy's Italian Restaurant
New York, NY 212-247-3491
Pilgrim Foods
Great Neck, NY 516-466-0522
Pompeian Inc
Baltimore, MD 800-766-7342
Ponti USA
New York, NY
Prairie Thyme LTD
Santa Fe, NM 800-869-0009
Proacec USA
Santa Monica, CA. 310-996-7770
Purity Products
Plainview, NY. 800-256-6102
Red Pelican Food Products
Detroit, MI 313-881-4095
Reinhart Foods
Toronto, ON 416-645-4910
Restaurant Lulu Gourmet Products
San Francisco, CA 888-693-5800
REX Pure Foods
New Orleans, LA 800-344-8314
Roanoke Apple Products
Salem, VA 540-375-3782
Robert Rothschild Farm
Cincinnati, OH 800-222-9966
Rosa Food Products
Philadelphia, PA 215-467-2214
Santa Barbara Olive Company
Santa Barbara, CA 800-624-4896
Sargent and Greenleaf
Nicholasville, KY 800-826-7652
Satiety Winery & Cafe
Davis, CA 530-757-2699
Sedlock Farm
Lynn Center, IL. 309-521-8284
Sempio Foods
Cerritos, CA 562-207-9540
Sherrill Orchards
Arvin, CA 661-858-2035
Sieco USA Corporation
Houston, TX 713-464-1726
Silver Palate Kitchens
Cresskill, NJ 201-568-0110
Slide Ridge LLC
Mendon, UT 435-752-4956
Solana Gold Organics
Sebastopol, CA 800-459-1121
Southern Season
Chapel Hill, NC 877-929-7133
Sparrow Lane
Ceres, CA 866-515-2477
Spruce Mountain Blueberries
West Rockport, ME. 207-236-3538
Stickney & Poor Company
Peterborough, NH. 603-924-2259
Thistledew Farm
Proctor, WV 800-854-6639
Thyme Garden Herb Co
Alsea, OR 800-482-4372
Todhunter Foods
Lake Alfred, FL. 863-956-1116
Tropical Foods
Charlotte, NC 800-438-4470
Vincent Formusa Company
Des Plaines, IL 847-813-6040
Walker Foods
Los Angeles, CA. 800-966-5199
Webbpak Inc
Trussville, AL 800-655-3500
White House Foods
Winchester, VA 540-662-3401
Widow's Mite Vinegar Company
Washington, DC 877-678-5854
Wild Thymes Farm Inc
Greenville, NY 845-266-8387
Wing's Food Products
Toronto, ON 416-259-2662
Woeber Mustard Mfg Co
Springfield, OH. 800-548-2929

Apple Cider

Bragg Live Food Products Inc
Goleta, CA 800-446-1990
Comvita USA
Santa Barbara, CA 855-449-2201
De Nigris
Totowa, NJ 973-837-6791
Eden Foods Inc
Clinton, MI 888-424-3336
Emerling International Foods
Buffalo, NY. 716-833-7381
Ethan's
Boulder, CO 720-432-8384
GloryBee
Eugene, OR. 800-456-7923
Kevala
Dallas, TX. 877-379-1179
Knouse Foods Co-Op Inc.
Peach Glen, PA 717-677-8181
Mizkan Americas Inc
Kansas City, MO. 800-323-4358
Nana Mae's Organics
Sebastopol, CA 707-829-7359
National Vinegar Co
St Louis, MO. 314-962-4111
Pastorelli Food Products
Chicago, IL 800-767-2829
Ponti USA
New York, NY
Reinhart Foods
Toronto, ON 416-645-4910
Roanoke Apple Products
Salem, VA 540-375-3782
Sieco USA Corporation
Houston, TX 713-464-1726
Solana Gold Organics
Sebastopol, CA 800-459-1121
Vermont Village
Barre, VT
Walker Foods
Los Angeles, CA. 800-966-5199
Webbpak Inc
Trussville, AL 800-655-3500
White House Foods
Winchester, VA 540-662-3401
Widow's Mite Vinegar Company
Washington, DC 877-678-5854

Balsamic

Acetifico Marcello Denigris
Westwood, NJ 973-837-6791
Agrusa
Leonia, NJ. 201-592-5950
California Olive Oil Council
Berkeley, CA. 888-718-9830
Chaparral Gardens
Atascadero, CA. 805-703-0829
Coldani Olive Ranch LLC
Lodi, CA 209-334-0527
Consumers Vinegar & Spice Co
Chicago, IL 773-376-4100
Emerling International Foods
Buffalo, NY. 716-833-7381
Enzo Olive Oil Co.
Madera, CA. 559-299-7278
Modena Fine Foods Inc
Clifton, NJ. 973-470-8499
Mosby Winery
Buellton, CA. 800-706-6729
Mosti Mondiale/Gourmet Mondiale
Ste-Catherine, QC. 450-638-6380
North American Enterprises
Tucson, AZ 800-817-8666
Olive Oil Factor
Waterbury, CT. 475-235-2666
Organic Planet
San Francisco, CA 415-765-5590
Pastorelli Food Products
Chicago, IL 800-767-2829
Ponti USA
New York, NY
Proacec USA
Santa Monica, CA. 310-996-7770
Putney House Trading LLC
New London, NH 603-526-2336
Reinhart Foods
Toronto, ON 416-645-4910
Restaurant Lulu Gourmet Products
San Francisco, CA 888-693-5800
S A L T Sisters
Goshen, IN 574-971-8368
Sieco USA Corporation
Houston, TX 713-464-1726
Sutter Buttes Olive Oil
Sutter, CA 530-763-7921
Valley Grain Products
Fresno, CA 559-675-3400
Wild Thymes Farm Inc
Greenville, NY 845-266-8387

Liquid

Clements Foods Co
Oklahoma City, OK 800-654-8355
Colonna Brothers Inc
North Bergen, NJ 201-864-1115

Malt

Consumers Vinegar & Spice Co
Chicago, IL 773-376-4100
Eden Foods Inc
Clinton, MI 888-424-3336
Reinhart Foods
Toronto, ON 416-645-4910

Raspberry

Reinhart Foods
Toronto, ON 416-645-4910
Thistledew Farm
Proctor, WV 800-854-6639

Sherry

National Vinegar Co
St Louis, MO........................ 314-962-4111

White Distilled

Big B Barbecue
Evansville, IN 812-425-5235
Consumers Vinegar & Spice Co
Chicago, IL 773-376-4100
Creole Fermentation Indu
Abbeville, LA 337-898-9377
Emerling International Foods
Buffalo, NY......................... 716-833-7381
Knouse Foods Co-Op Inc.
Peach Glen, PA 717-677-8181
Mizkan Americas Inc
Kansas City, MO.................... 800-323-4358
National Vinegar Co
St Louis, MO........................ 314-962-4111
Pastorelli Food Products
Chicago, IL 800-767-2829
Reinhart Foods
Toronto, ON 416-645-4910
Roanoke Apple Products
Salem, VA 540-375-3782
Walker Foods
Los Angeles, CA.................... 800-966-5199
Webbpak Inc
Trussville, AL 800-655-3500
White House Foods
Winchester, VA 540-662-3401

Wine

B & G Foods Inc.
Parsippany, NJ..................... 973-401-6500
California Balsamic Inc
Ukiah, CA 888-644-5127
Consumers Vinegar & Spice Co
Chicago, IL 773-376-4100
De Nigris
Totowa, NJ 973-837-6791
Eden Foods Inc
Clinton, MI 888-424-3336
Knouse Foods Co-Op Inc.
Peach Glen, PA 717-677-8181
Modena Fine Foods Inc
Clifton, NJ......................... 973-470-8499
Nakano Foods
Mt Prospect, IL..................... 800-323-4358
National Vinegar Co
St Louis, MO........................ 314-962-4111
Pastorelli Food Products
Chicago, IL 800-767-2829
Pompeian Inc
Baltimore, MD 800-766-7342
Ponti USA
New York, NY
Reinhart Foods
Toronto, ON 416-645-4910
Roanoke Apple Products
Salem, VA 540-375-3782
Satiety Winery & Cafe
Davis, CA 530-757-2699
Sieco USA Corporation
Houston, TX 713-464-1726
Wine Country Kitchens
Napa, CA........................... 866-767-9463

Snack Foods

General

34-Degrees
Denver, CO 303-861-4818
3PM Bites
New York, NY
88 Acres
Allston, MA 617-208-8651
Ajinomoto Frozen Foods USA, Inc.
Ontario, CA........ 866-536-8008
America's Classic Foods
Cambria, CA........ 805-927-0745
American Importing Co.
Minneapolis, MN 855-273-0466
Amplify Snack Brands
Austin, TX........ 512-600-9893
Arico Natural Foods
Beaverton, OR 503-259-0871
B.O.S.S. Food Co.
.... 800-344-8584
Bake City
Atlanta, GA........ 855-336-4777
Balance Bar Company
Bohemia, NY 800-346-2194
Barbara's Bakery
Lakeville, MN........ 800-343-0590
Barkthins Snacking Chocolate
Congers, NY 845-770-5802
Barrel O' Fun Snack Foods
Perham, MN 800-346-4910
Bazaar Inc
River Grove, IL........ 800-736-1888
Beanitos
Austin, TX........ 512-609-8017
Bearded Brothers
Austin, TX
Bearitos
Boulder, CO 310-886-8200
Because Cookie Dough
Betsy's Cheese Straws
Millbrook, AZ........ 877-902-3141
Biena Foods
Allston, MA 617-202-5210
Big Spoon Roasters
Durham, NC 919-309-9100
Big Steer
Houston, TX 800-421-4951
Blue Crab Bay
Melfa, VA 800-221-2722
Bountiful Larder LLC
Crested Butte, CO........ 800-676-5057
Brothers All Natural
Rochester, NY........ 877-842-7477
Buffalo Bills Premium Snacks
Lebanon, PA 717-273-7499
Calif Snack Foods
South El Monte, CA 626-454-4099
CarbRite Diet
New Brunswick, NJ 800-872-0101
Caveman Foods
Lafayette, CA 925-979-9515
Chasquis Natural Foods
St. Catharines, ON
Chic Naturals
Lahaina, HI........ 808-463-7878
Conn's Potato Chips
Zanesville, OH 740-452-4615
Cornfields Inc
Waukegan, IL 847-263-7000
Countertop Productions
Alexandria, VA
Crazy Richard's
Dublin, OH 614-889-4824
Creative Snacks Co LLC
Greensboro, NC 336-668-4151
Crunch-A-Mame
Mulberry, AR
Crunchsters
.... 303-545-9000
Crunchy Rollers
Dallas, TX
Del Monte Foods Inc.
Walnut Creek, CA
Dieffenbach's Potato Chips
Womelsdorf, PA 610-589-2385
Divvies
South Salem, NY 914-533-2804
DNX Foods
Tucson, AZ 888-612-5037
Don Bugito
San Francisco, CA
Double B Distributors
Lexington, KY 859-255-8822
Eagle Family Foods
Richfield, OH 888-656-3245
East Kentucky Foods
Winchester, KY........ 859-744-2218
Eat Your Coffee
Boston, MA
EatKeenwa, Inc.
Jersey City, NJ 855-453-3692
Elemental Superfood
Torrance, CA
Ello Raw
Empact Bars
Boulder, CO 877-836-7228
Enjoy Life Foods
Chicago, IL........ 888-503-6569
Farmwise LLC
Wellesley, MA........ 508-401-7040
Flamous Brands
Duarte, CA 626-799-7909
From the Ground Up
Fairfield, NJ
General Mills
Minneapolis, MN 800-248-7310
GKI Foods
Brighton, MI........ 248-486-0055
Gluck Brands
Sugar Land, TX........ 281-903-7082
Golden Flake Snack Foods
Birmingham, AL........ 800-367-7629
Golden Island Jerky Co.
Rancho Cucamonga, CA 844-362-3222
Goldilocks USA
Hayward, CA 510-476-0700
Good Lovin' Foods
.... 877-760-6833
Good! Snacks
Walnut, CA........ 415-762-0600
GoodBites Snacks
Venice, CA
Goodness Knows
Gopal's Healthfoods
Sidney, TX 866-646-7257
Gourmet Basics
Brooklyn, NY 718-509-9366
Gourmet Kitchen, Inc.
Neptune, NJ 800-492-3663
Govadinas Fitness Foods
San Diego, CA 800-900-0108
Grandma Emily
Montreal, QC 877-943-3661
Growing Roots Foods
Englewood Cliffs, NJ
H-E-B Grocery Co. LP
San Antonio, TX........ 800-432-3113
Hale and Hearty Soups
New York, NY 212-255-2433
Happy Family
New York, NY 855-644-2779
Happy Herberts Food Co Inc
Jersey City, NJ 800-764-2779
Hearthside Food Solutions
Downers Grove, IL........ 630-967-3600
Hippeas
Plainview, NY
Hippie Snacks
Burnaby, BC........ 877-769-6887
Humbly Hemp
Los Angeles, CA........ 424-259-3521
Humming Hemp
Richland, WA 503-559-6476
Hungry Sultan
Lake Forest, CA 949-215-0000
Husman Snack Food Company
Peoria, IL........ 859-282-7490
I'm Different Snacks
Los Angeles, CA
Ideal Snacks Corp
Liberty, NY........ 845-292-7000
Jonny Almond Nut Co
Flint, MI 810-767-6887
Kateri Foods
Hopkins, MN 800-330-8351
KAYS Processing LLC
Clara City, MN 320-847-3220
Kellogg Co.
Battle Creek, MI........ 800-962-1413
Kind Snacks
New York, NY 855-884-5463
King Henry's Inc
Valencia, CA........ 661-295-5566
Kraft Heinz Co.
Chicago, IL........ 800-543-5335
Krema Nut Co
Columbus, OH 800-222-4132
Late July Snacks
Norwalk, CT........ 888-857-6225
Laurel Hill Foods
Attleboro, MA........ 877-759-8141
Leaf Jerky
Battle Creek, MI........ 800-962-1413
Lesserevil Brand Snack Co
Danbury, CT 203-529-3555
Levant Mediterranean Snack Foods LLC
Haverhill, MA........ 978-241-9986
Lillie's Q
Chicago, IL........ 773-772-5500
LivBar
Salem, OR........ 971-239-1209
Lost Trail Root Beer
Louisburg, KS........ 800-748-7765
Love Good Fats
Toronto, ON
Love You Foods
Flagstaff, AZ........ 844-693-2662
Lundberg Family Farms
Richvale, CA........ 530-538-3500
LWC Brands Inc.
Dallas, TX........ 800-552-8006
Maine Coast Sea Vegetables
Franklin, ME........ 207-565-2907
Manischewitz Co
Newark, NJ 201-553-1100
Maplegrove Foods
Ontario, CA........ 909-545-6075
McIlhenny Company
Avery Island, LA........ 800-634-9599
Mediterranean Snack Food Co
Boonton, NJ 973-402-2644
MetaBall
Chester, NJ 800-247-6580
Mezza
Lake Forest, IL 888-206-6054
Mister Bee Potato Chips Co
Parkersburg, WV........ 304-428-6133
Modern Pod Co.
Providence, RI
Mondelez International
East Hanover, NJ 855-535-5648
Mountain Organic Foods
Moraga, CA........ 925-377-0119
Nebraska Bean
Clearwater, NE 800-253-6502
New Nissi Corp.
Paterson, NJ 973-278-4400
Nomi Snacks
Minneapolis, MN
Nora Snacks
Santa Fe Springs, CA 562-404-9888
NOW Foods
Bloomingdale, IL 888-669-3663
Nu-World Amaranth Inc
Naperville, IL 630-369-6851
Nush Foods
Salt Lake City, UT 801-953-1370
Nutty Goodness
Charleston, SC
OHi Food
Costa Mesa, CA 808-281-7815
ONE Brands
Charlotte, NC 888-231-2684
Organic Amazon
Key Biscayne, FL
Organic Gemini
Brooklyn, NY........ 347-662-2900
Organic RealBar
Diamond Bar, CA........ 888-622-8828

Orto Foods
Congers, NY 516-725-5422
Pacific Gold Snacks
Kent, WA. 253-854-7056
Paleo Ranch
Lakeway, TX
Papa Dean's Popcorn
San Antonio, TX. 877-855-7272
Patagonia Provisions
Sausalito, CA 888-221-8208
Peaceful Fruits
. 330-356-8515
Peeled Snacks
Cumberland, RI. 401-437-4386
Perfect Snacks
Sorrento Valley, CA 866-628-8548
Phyter Foods
West Chicago, IL 630-206-3701
Pippin Snack Pecans
Albany, GA 800-554-6887
Power Crunch
Irvine, CA
Prana
Ville St Laurent, QC 844-447-7262
Probar
Salt Lake City, UT 800-921-2294
Ramsey Popcorn Co Inc
Ramsey, IN 800-624-2060
Raw Rev
Hawthorne, NY. 914-326-4095
Real Coconut Co. Inc., The
CA
Rhythm Superfoods
Austin, TX. 512-441-5667
Ripple Brand Collective
Congers, NY 845-353-1251
Rise Bar
Irvine, CA 800-440-6476
Royal Hawaiian Orchards LP
Dana Point, CA. 949-661-6304
Rudolph Foods Co
Lima, OH. 419-648-3611
Safely Delicious
Overland Park, KS 913-963-5140
Sargento Foods Inc
Plymouth, WI 800-243-3737
Schwan's Company
Marshall, MN 800-533-5290
Seapoint Farms
Huntington Beach, CA 714-374-9831
Sensible Foods LLC
Santa Rosa, CA. 888-222-0170
Setton International Foods
Commack, NY 800-227-4397
Sheffa Foods
New York, NY 800-494-1956
Simply 7 Snacks
Houston, TX 877-682-2359
Small Planet Foods
Minneapolis, MN 800-624-4123
Snack Works/Metrovox Snacks
Orange, CA 800-783-9870
Snikiddy, LLC
Boulder, CO 303-444-4405
Snyder's-Lance Inc.
Charlotte, NC 800-438-1880
Sophia Foods
Brooklyn, NY 718-272-1110
Squire Boone Village
New Albany, IN 888-934-1804
Sugar Foods Corp
New York, NY
Sun Opta Inc.
Mississauga, ON. 952-820-2518
Sun-Maid Growers of California
Kingsburg, CA 559-896-8000
Sun-Rype Products
Kelowna, BC. 888-786-7973
Sunridge Farms Inc
Salinas, CA 831-755-1530
SuperEats
New York, NY 802-760-7075
Superseedz
North Haven, CT. 203-407-0546
Sweetwood Cattle Co
Steamboat Spgs, CO. 970-879-7456
Terrell's Potato Chip Co
Syracuse, NY 315-437-2786
Terri Lynn Inc
Elgin, IL 800-323-0775
Thanasi Foods LLC
Boulder, CO 866-558-7379
Thatcher's Gourmet Specialties
San Francisco, CA 800-926-2676
The Humphrey Co
Lockport, NY 716-597-1974
The Konery
Brooklyn, NY 917-750-4147
The Matzo Project
Brooklyn, NY 929-276-2896
The Naked Edge, LLC
Boulder, CO 888-297-9426
The Safe + Fair Food Company
Chicago, IL
TMI Trading Co
Brooklyn, NY 718-821-5052
Touche Bakery
London, ON 518-455-0044
TreeHouse Foods, Inc.
Oak Brook, IL. 708-483-1300
Tri-Sum Potato Chip Company
Leominster, MA 978-697-2447
Tropical Valley Foods
Plattsburgh, NY 877-756-6831
Watusee Foods
Washington, DC 202-281-8245
Wegmans Food Markets Inc.
Rochester, NY. 800-934-6267
WholeMe
Minneapolis, MN 612-247-9728
Wicked Crisps
Greensboro, NC
Wicked Mix
Little Rock, AR. 501-374-2244
Wild Zora Foods
Loveland, CO 970-541-9672
Wilde Brands
Boulder, CO 720-328-0843
Windy City Organics
Northbrook, IL 800-925-0577
Winn-Dixie Stores
Jacksonville, FL 800-967-9105
Wise Foods Inc
Berwick, PA 888-438-9473
Wyandot Inc
Marion, OH. 800-992-6368
Yogavive
Tiburon, CA 415-366-6226
Your Bar Factory
LaSalle, QC. 888-366-0258

Cheese Curls

Cheeze Kurls
Grand Rapids, MI 616-784-6095
Elmers Fine Foods Inc
New Orleans, LA 888-570-0764
Golden Flake Snack Foods
Birmingham, AL. 800-367-7629
Happy's Potato Chip Co
Minneapolis, MN 612-781-3121
Hartley's Potato Chip Co
Lewistown, PA 717-248-0526
Tri-Sum Potato Chip Company
Leominster, MA 978-697-2447
Wyandot Inc
Marion, OH. 800-992-6368

Cheese Twists

Aileen Quirk & Sons Inc
Kansas City, MO. 816-471-4580
American Blanching Company
Fitzgerald, GA 229-423-4098
American Nut & Chocolate Co
Boston, MA. 800-797-6887
American Skin LLC
Burgaw, NC. 800-248-7463
Amsnack
Stockton, CA. 209-982-5545
Archie Moore's
Milford, CT. 203-876-5088
Arizona Pistachio Company
Tucson, AZ 800-333-8575
Austinuts
Austin, TX. 877-329-6887
B. Lloyd's Pecans
Barwick, GA. 800-322-6887
Bachman Company
Wyamissing, PA 800-523-8253
Ballreich's Potato Chips
Tiffin, OH 800-323-2447
Barrel O' Fun Snack Foods
Perham, MN 800-346-4910
Berberian Nut Company
Chico, CA 530-981-4900
Bickel's Snack Foods Inc
York, PA 800-233-1933
Black Jewell Popcorn
Columbus, IN 800-948-2302
Boyd's Sausage Co
Washington, IA 319-653-5715
Brandmeyer Popcorn Co
Ankeny, IA 800-568-8276
Bremner Biscuit Company
Denver, CO 866-972-6879
Brennan Snacks Manufacturing
Bogalusa, LA 800-290-7486
Browns' Ice Cream Company
Minneapolis, MN 612-378-1075
C.J. Distributing
Surf City, NC 800-990-2366
Cafe Fanny
Berkeley, CA. 800-441-5413
Calbee America Inc
Fairfield, CA 707-427-2500
California Fruit & Nut
Gustine, CA 888-747-8224
Capri Bagel & Pizza Corporation
Brooklyn, NY 718-497-4431
Carolina Fine Snacks
Greensboro, NC 336-605-0773
Cattaneo Brothers Inc
San Luis Obispo, CA 800-243-8537
Central Snacks
Carthage, MS 601-267-3112
Chappaqua Crunch
Marblehead, MA. 781-631-8118
Cheese Straws & More
Monroe, LA. 800-997-1921
Chelsea Milling Co.
Chelsea, MI. 800-727-2460
City Farm/Rocky Peanut Company
Detroit, MI 800-437-6825
Cloud Nine
Claremont, CA 909-624-3147
Colorado Popcorn Co
Sterling, CO 866-491-2676
Columbia Empire Farms Inc
Sherwood, OR. 503-538-2156
Community Orchards
Fort Dodge, IA 888-573-8212
Con Agra Snack Foods
Hamburg, IA. 800-831-5818
Corbin Foods-Edibowls
Santa Ana, CA 800-695-5655
Corn Popper
Tulsa, OK 918-250-9317
Dellaco Classic Confections
Burlington, WI 866-537-2656
Dieffenbach's Potato Chips
Womelsdorf, PA 610-589-2385
Door County Potato Chips
Milwaukee, WI 414-964-1428
Durey-Libby Edible Nuts
Carlstadt, NJ 800-332-6887
Durham Ellis Pecan Co
Comanche, TX 800-732-2629
Eddy's Bakery
Boise, ID 208-377-8100
El Grano De Oro
Pacifica, CA 650-355-8417
Elegant Edibles
Houston, TX 800-227-3226
Exquisita Tortillas Inc
Edinburg, TX 956-383-6712
Fairchester Snacks Corp
White Plains, NY 914-761-2824
Fairmont Snacks Group
Independence, OH 216-642-3336
Fastachi
Watertown, MA. 800-466-3022
Fisher's Popcorn
Ocean City, MD 888-395-0335
Foley's Chocolates & Candies
Richmond, BC 888-236-5397
Fontazzi/Metrovox Snacks
Orange, CA 800-428-0522
Food Products Corporation
Phoenix, AZ 602-273-7139
Fortella Fortune Cookies
Chicago, IL. 312-567-9000
Fresh Roasted Almond Company
Warren, MI 877-478-6887
Fun City Popcorn
Las Vegas, NV 800-423-1710

Furukawa Potato Chip Factory
Captain Cook, HI 808-323-3785
Garrett Popcorn Shops
Chicago, IL 888-476-7267
Germack Pistachio Co
Detroit, MI 800-872-4006
GH Bent Company
Milton, MA 617-322-9287
Gilda Industries Inc
Hialeah, FL 305-887-8286
Glacial Ridge Foods
Starbuck, MN 320-239-2215
Golden Peanut and Tree Nuts
Alpharetta, GA 770-752-8160
Govatos Chocolates
Wilmington, DE 888-799-5252
Great Western Co LLC
Hollywood, AL 256-259-3578
Guy's Food
Overland Park, KS 800-821-2405
Haby's Alsatian Bakery
Castroville, TX 830-538-2118
Hammond's Candies
Denver, CO 888-226-3999
Happy Herberts Food Co Inc
Jersey City, NJ 800-764-2779
Harvest Manor Farms
Princeton, KY 877-984-6639
Hazelnut Growers Of Oregon
Cornelius, OR 800-273-4676
Hillson Nut Co
Cleveland, OH 800-333-2818
Hume Specialties
Chester, VT 802-875-3117
Humphrey Co
Cleveland, OH 800-486-3739
Imus Ranch Foods
Darien, CT 888-284-4687
J.W. Haywood & Sons Dairy
Louisville, KY 502-774-2311
Jay Shah Foods
Mississauga, ON 905-696-0172
Jenny's Old Fashioned
North Ridgeville, OH 800-452-3235
Jerrell Packaging
Birmingham, AL 205-426-8930
JMS Specialty Foods
Ripon, WI 800-535-5437
Joel Harvey Distributing
Brooklyn, NY 718-629-2690
John W Macy's Cheesesticks Inc
Elmwood Park, NJ 800-643-0573
Judy's Cream Caramels
Sherwood, OR 503-625-7161
Kendrick Gourmet Products
Columbus, GA 800-356-1858
Kevton Gourmet Tea
Streetman, TX 888-538-8668
Kids Kookie Company
San Clemente, CA 800-350-7577
LA Vencedora Products Inc
Los Angeles, CA 800-327-2572
Laredo Tortilleria & Mexican
Fort Wayne, IN 800-252-7336
Larosa Bakery Inc
Shrewsbury, NJ 800-527-6722
Las Cruces Brand Products
El Paso, TX 915-779-5709
Lima Grain Cereal Seeds LLC
Fort Collins, CO 970-498-2200
Longleaf Plantation
Purvis, MS 800-421-7370
Longview Meat & Merchandise Ltd
Longview, AB 866-355-3759
Los Angeles Nut House Brands
Los Angeles, CA 213-481-0134
Louise's
Shelbyville, KY 502-633-9700
Ludwick's Frozen Donuts
Grand Rapids, MI 800-366-8816
Madhouse Munchies
South Burlington, VT 888-323-4687
Mama Amy's Quality Foods
Mississauga, ON 905-456-0056
Manuel's Odessa Tortilla
Odessa, TX 800-753-2445
Marantha Natural Foods
San Francisco, CA 866-972-6879
Maxin Marketing Corporation
Aliso Viejo, CA 949-362-1177
Mexican Accent
New Berlin, WI 262-784-4422
Mission Foods Corp.
Irving, TX 972-232-5200
Mitchum Potato Chips
Charlotte, NC 704-372-6744
Molinaro's Fine Italian Foods Ltd.
Mississauga, ON 905-281-0352
Mrs. Dog's Products
Grand Rapids, MI 800-267-7364
Natchez Pecan Shelling Company
Taylorsville, MS 601-785-4333
National Foods
Bronx, NY 800-683-6565
Nips Potato Chips
Honolulu, HI 808-593-8549
Noble Popcorn
Sac City, IA 800-537-9554
Northwoods Candy Emporium
Branson, MO 417-332-1010
Nustef Foods
Mississauga, ON 877-306-7562
Nutty Bavarian
Sanford, FL 800-382-4788
Oasis Mediterranean Cuisine
Toledo, OH 419-269-1516
Old Dutch Foods LTD
Roseville, MN
Old Sacramento Popcorn Company
Sacramento, CA 916-446-1980
Packaged Products Division
Largo, FL 888-833-2247
Paddack Enterprises
Escalon, CA 209-838-1536
Papes Pecan House
Seguin, TX 888-688-7273
Pepe's Mexican Restaurant
Anaheim, CA 714-952-9410
Perfections by Allan
Owings Mills, MD 800-581-8670
Picard Peanuts
Waterdown, ON 888-244-7688
Pickle Cottage
Bucklin, KS 316-826-3502
Pizza Products
Farmington Hills, MI 800-600-7482
Plantation Pecan & Gift Company
Waterproof, LA 800-477-3226
Plehn's Bakery Inc
Louisville, KY 502-896-4438
Pond Brothers Peanut Company
Suffolk, VA 757-539-2356
Poore Brothers
Phoenix, AZ 623-932-6200
Popcorn Popper
Monon, IN 800-270-2705
Popcorner
Swansea, IL 618-277-2676
Poppin Popcorn
Naples, FL 941-262-1691
Premiere Packing Company
Greenacres, WA 888-239-5288
REED'S Inc
Los Angeles, CA 800-997-3337
Reiter Dairy
Newport, KY 800-544-6455
Rices Potato Chips
Biloxi, MS 228-396-5775
Ricos Candy Snack & Bakery
Hialeah, FL 305-885-7392
Ripensa A/S
Lehigh Acres, FL 941-561-5882
Rolet Food Products Company
Brooklyn, NY 718-497-0476
Route 11 Potato Chips
Mount Jackson, VA 800-294-7783
Rural Route 1 Popcorn Co
Livingston, WI 800-828-8115
Rygmyr Foods
South Saint Paul, MN 800-545-3903
Sanarak Paper & Popcorn Supplies
Buffalo, NY 716-874-5662
Savory Foods
Grand Rapids, MI 800-878-2583
Sesaco Corp
Austin, TX 800-737-2260
Severance Foods Inc
Hartford, CT 860-724-7063
Shallowford Farms Popcorn, Inc.
Yadkinville, NC 800-892-9539
Shearer's Foods Inc
Massillon, OH 330-767-4030
Snack Factory
Princeton, NJ 888-683-5400
Snappy Popcorn
Breda, IA 800-742-0228
Snelgrove Ice Cream Company
Salt Lake City, UT 800-569-0005
Snikiddy, LLC
Boulder, CO 303-444-4405
Sommer's Food Products
Salisbury, MO 660-388-5511
Southern Popcorn Company
Memphis, TN 901-362-5238
Southern Roasted Nuts
Fitzgerald, GA 912-423-5616
Spilke's Baking Company
Moosic, PA 570-457-2400
St. Amour Inc/French Cookies
Costa Mesa, CA 714-754-1900
Story's Popcorn Company
Charleston, MO 573-649-2727
Sunnyside Farms
Neligh, NE 402-791-2210
Tabard Farm Potato Chips
Middletown, VA 540-869-0104
Texas Tito's
Austin, TX . . . . . 877-99 -OTEX
The Great Western Tortilla Co.
Denver, CO 303-298-0705
Thyme Garden Herb Co
Alsea, OR 800-482-4372
Tim's Cascade Snacks
Auburn, WA 800-533-8467
Tom Sturgis Pretzels Inc
Reading, PA 800-817-3834
Trinidad Benham Corporation
Denver, CO 303-220-1400
Trotter Soft Pretzels
Hatfield, PA 215-855-2197
Tuscan Bakery
Portland, OR 800-887-2261
Twin Valley Developmental Services
Greenleaf, KS 800-748-7416
Uncle Ralph's Cookies
Frederick, MD 800-422-0626
Uncle Ray's Potato Chips
Detroit, MI 800-800-3286
Van-Lang Food Products
Countryside, IL 708-588-0800
Vande Walle's Candies Inc
Appleton, WI 800-738-1020
Vic's Corn Popper
Omaha, NE 402-932-0426
Wachusset Potato Chip Co Inc
Fitchburg, MA 800-551-5539
Warden Peanut Company
Portales, NM 575-356-6691
Weaver Popcorn Co Inc
Van Buren, IN
Wynnewood Pecan Company
Wynnewood, OK 800-892-4985
Yick Lung Company
Honolulu, HI 808-841-3611
Young Pecan
Las Cruces, NM 575-524-4321

Chips

Bagel Chips

Basic Grain Products
Coldwater, OH 866-411-6677
Greater Knead, The
Bensalem, PA 267-522-8523
Harlan Bakeries
Avon, IN 800-435-2738
Hometown Bagel Inc
Alsip, IL 708-385-0002
Old London Foods
Yadkinville, NC
Soloman Baking Company
Denver, CO 303-371-2777
Weaver Nut Co. Inc.
Ephrata, PA 800-473-2688

Baked

Abuelita Mexican Foods
Manassas Park, VA 703-369-0232
Azteca Foods Inc
Chicago, IL 708-563-6600
C J Vitner Co
Chicago, IL 773-523-7900
Dang Foods
Berkeley, CA 510-338-3345

Fuller Foods
Portland, OR 503-308-3814
Golden Fluff Popcorn Co
Lakewood, NJ 732-367-5448
Harlan Bakeries
Avon, IN 800-435-2738
Imus Ranch Foods
Darien, CT. 888-284-4687
LA Canasta Mexican Foods
Phoenix, AZ 855-269-7721
LA Mexicana Tortilleria
Chicago, IL 773-247-5443
Laredo Tortilleria & Mexican
Fort Wayne, IN 800-252-7336
Li'l Guy Foods
Kansas City, MO. 800-886-8226
Luna's Tortillas
Dallas, TX. 214-747-2661
Mexican Accent
New Berlin, WI. 262-784-4422
Natural Intentions, Inc.
Folsom, CA
Olde Tyme Food Corporation
East Longmeadow, MA 800-356-6533
Ozuna Food Products Corporation
Sunnyvale, CA 408-400-0495
Pepe's Mexican Restaurant
Anaheim, CA 714-952-9410
Puebla Foods Inc
Passaic, NJ 973-473-0201
R&J Farms
West Salem, OH 419-846-3179
Rudy's Tortillas
Carrollton, TX. 800-878-2401
Severance Foods Inc
Hartford, CT 860-724-7063
Shallowford Farms Popcorn, Inc.
Yadkinville, NC 800-892-9539
Spanish Gardens Food Manufacturing
Kansas City, KS 913-831-4242
TH Foods, Inc.
Loves Park, IL. 815-636-9500
The Safe + Fair Food Company
Chicago, IL
Tom's Snacks Company
Charlotte, NC 800-995-2623
Vintage Italia
Windermere, FL 407-217-5910
Westbrae Natural Foods
Melville, NY. 800-434-4246

Banana

American Importing Co.
Minneapolis, MN 855-273-0466
Bubba's Fine Foods
Loveland, CO

Cassava

Arico Natural Foods
Beaverton, OR 503-259-0871
Tantos Foods International
Markham, ON. 905-943-9993
Wai Lana Snacks
Sacramento, CA 888-924-5262

Chocolate

Sheryl's Chocolate Creations
Hicksville, NY 888-882-2462
The Good Bean
Berkeley, CA. 561-243-7773

Corn

Abuelita Mexican Foods
Manassas Park, VA. 703-369-0232
Art's Mexican Products
Kansas City, KS 913-371-2163
Barrel O' Fun Snack Foods
Perham, MN 800-346-4910
C J Vitner Co
Chicago, IL. 773-523-7900
Delicious Popcorn
Waupaca, WI. 715-258-7683
Frito-Lay Inc.
Plano, TX 800-352-4477
G.E.F. Gourmet Foods Inc
Mountain Lake, MN. 800-692-6762
Golden Flake Snack Foods
Birmingham, AL. 800-367-7629
Inka Crops
Citrus Heights, CA 916-723-1450
LA Mexicana Tortilleria
Chicago, IL. 773-247-5443
Old Dutch Foods LTD
Roseville, MN
Pippin Snack Pecans
Albany, GA. 800-554-6887
Tom's Snacks Company
Charlotte, NC 800-995-2623
Xochitl
Dallas, TX. 866-595-8917

Fried

Abuelita Mexican Foods
Manassas Park, VA. 703-369-0232
Archie Moore's
Milford, CT. 203-876-5088
Bickel's Potato Chip Company
York, PA 800-233-1933
C J Vitner Co
Chicago, IL 773-523-7900
Calbee America Inc
Fairfield, CA. 707-427-2500
Delicious Popcorn
Waupaca, WI. 715-258-7683
El Milagro
Chicago, IL. 773-579-6120
Elmers Fine Foods Inc
New Orleans, LA 888-570-0764
Evans Food Group LTD
Chicago, IL. 866-254-7400
Happy's Potato Chip Co
Minneapolis, MN 612-781-3121
Hartley's Potato Chip Co
Lewistown, PA 717-248-0526
Jones Potato Chip Co
Mansfield, OH 800-466-9424
Kitchen Cooked Inc
Farmington, IL 800-752-1535
LA Mexicana Tortilleria
Chicago, IL. 773-247-5443
LA Vencedora Products Inc
Los Angeles, CA. 800-327-2572
Laredo Tortilleria & Mexican
Fort Wayne, IN 800-252-7336
Manhattan Food Brands, LLC
Metuchen, NJ 732-906-2168
Maui Potato Chip Factory
Kahului, HI 808-877-3652
Mexican Accent
New Berlin, WI. 262-784-4422
Middleswarth Potato Chips
Kingston, PA. 570-288-2447
Miguel's Stowe Away
Stowe, VT. 800-448-6517
Mrs Fisher's Potato Chips
Rockford, IL 815-964-9114
Olde Tyme Food Corporation
East Longmeadow, MA 800-356-6533
Ozuna Food Products Corporation
Sunnyvale, CA 408-400-0495
Pepe's Mexican Restaurant
Anaheim, CA 714-952-9410
Puebla Foods Inc
Passaic, NJ 973-473-0201
Revonah Pretzel LLC
Hanover, PA 717-630-2883
Route 11 Potato Chips
Mount Jackson, VA. 800-294-7783
Severance Foods Inc
Hartford, CT 860-724-7063
Shearer's Foods Inc
Massillon, OH. 330-767-4030
Spanish Gardens Food Manufacturing
Kansas City, KS 913-831-4242
Sun Pac Foods
Brampton, ON. 905-792-2700
Terrell's Potato Chip Co
Syracuse, NY 315-437-2786
Tim's Cascade Snacks
Auburn, WA 800-533-8467
Tom's Foods
Charlotte, NC 877-309-6361
Tom's Snacks Company
Charlotte, NC 800-995-2623
Westbrae Natural Foods
Melville, NY. 800-434-4246
Yum Yum Potato Chips
Warwick, QC. 800-567-5792

Nacho

Arizona Beverage Company
Cincinnati, OH 800-832-3775
Luna's Tortillas
Dallas, TX. 214-747-2661
Old Dutch Foods LTD
Roseville, MN
Olde Tyme Food Corporation
East Longmeadow, MA 800-356-6533
Ozuna Food Products Corporation
Sunnyvale, CA 408-400-0495

Peanut Butter

Perfect Life Nutrition
West Orange, NJ 973-980-2298

Pita

Argo Fine Foods
Saint James, NY 631-703-0443
Baba Foods
San Diego, CA 619-426-6946
Basic Grain Products
Coldwater, OH 866-411-6677
Bearitos
Boulder, CO 310-886-8200
Cedar's Mediterranean Foods
Ward Hill, MA 978-372-8010
Regco
Haverhill, MA. 978-521-4370
Regenie's Crunchy Pi
Haverhill, MA. 877-734-3643
Sensible Portions
Boulder, CO 800-913-6637
Soloman Baking Company
Denver, CO. 303-371-2777

Plantain

ARA Food Corp
Miami, FL. 800-533-8831
Inka Crops
Citrus Heights, CA 916-723-1450
Lam's Food Inc
Queens Village, NY 718-217-0476

Potato

All American Snacks
Midland, TX 800-840-2455
Arctic Beverages
Winnipeg, MB. 866-503-1270
Bachman Company
Wyamissing, PA 800-523-8253
Backer's Potato Chip Company
Fulton, MO 573-642-2833
Barrel O' Fun Snack Foods
Perham, MN 800-346-4910
Better Made Snack Foods
Detroit, MI 800-332-2394
Bickel's Potato Chip Company
York, PA 800-233-1933
Bickel's Snack Foods Inc
York, PA 800-233-1933
Bountiful Larder LLC
Crested Butte, CO. 800-676-5057
Brad's Taste of New York
Floral Park, NY. 516-354-9004
Coney Island Classics
Valley Stream, NY 516-823-3001
Conn's Potato Chips
Zanesville, OH 740-452-4615
Covered Bridge Potato Chip Company
Waterville, NB 506-375-2447
Deep River Snacks
Deep River, CT. 860-434-7347
Delicious Popcorn
Waupaca, WI. 715-258-7683
Dieffenbach's Potato Chips
Womelsdorf, PA 610-589-2385
Doctor Dread's Jerk
Glen Echo, MD. 301-908-9450
Eli's Bread Inc
New York, NY 866-354-3547
Elmers Fine Foods Inc
New Orleans, LA 888-570-0764
Frito-Lay Inc.
Plano, TX 800-352-4477
Golden Flake Snack Foods
Birmingham, AL. 800-367-7629
Gringo Jack's
Manchester Ctr, VT 802-362-0836

Grippo Foods
Cincinnati, OH 800-626-1824
Hanover Foods Corp
Hanover, PA 717-632-6000
Happy's Potato Chip Co
Minneapolis, MN 612-781-3121
Hartley's Potato Chip Co
Lewistown, PA 717-248-0526
Herr Foods Inc.
Nottingham, PA.................... 800-523-5030
Husman Snack Food Company
Peoria, IL.................... 859-282-7490
Inka Crops
Citrus Heights, CA 916-723-1450
Jackson's Honest
Crested Butte, CO
Joe Tea and Joe Chips
Upper Montclair, NJ.................... 973-744-7502
Jones Potato Chip Co
Mansfield, OH 800-466-9424
Kay's Naturals, Inc.
Clara City, MN 866-873-5499
Kettle Brand
Charlotte, NC 800-438-1880
Kitchen Cooked Inc
Farmington, IL 800-752-1535
Knese Enterprise
Bellerose, NY 516-354-9004
Luke's Organic
Santa Cruz, CA
Martin's Potato Chips
Thomasville, PA 800-272-4477
Maui Potato Chip Factory
Kahului, HI.................... 808-877-3652
Mediterranean Snack Food Co
Boonton, NJ 973-402-2644
Middleswarth Potato Chips
Kingston, PA.................... 570-288-2447
Mikesell's Potato Chip Company
Dayton, OH.................... 937-228-9400
Mister Bee Potato Chips Co
Parkersburg, WV.................... 304-428-6133
Mrs Fisher's Potato Chips
Rockford, IL 815-964-9114
Naturally Homegrown
Surrey, BC.................... 604-465-7751
Old Dutch Foods LTD
Roseville, MN
Ole Salty's Potato Chips
Loves Park, IL.................... 815-637-2447
One Potato Two Potato
Womelsdorf, PA 610-589-6500
Osem USA Inc
Englewood Cliffs, NJ 800-200-6736
PepsiCo.
Purchase, NY 914-253-2000
Pippin Snack Pecans
Albany, GA.................... 800-554-6887
Pop Gourmet LLC
Tukwila, WA.................... 206-397-3896
Popchips
San Francisco, CA 866-217-9327
Revonah Pretzel LLC
Hanover, PA.................... 717-630-2883
Rick's Chips
San Anselmo, CA 415-420-8151
Rock-N-Roll Gourmet
Marina Del Ray, CA 800-518-3891
Snak King Corp
City Of Industry, CA.................... 626-336-7711
Snyder's-Lance Inc.
Charlotte, NC 800-438-1880
Sterzing Food Co
Burlington, IA.................... 800-754-8467
Stuart & CO
Brooklyn, NY 347-292-7456
Terrell's Potato Chip Co
Syracuse, NY 315-437-2786
That's How We Roll, LLC
Fairfield, NJ 973-602-3011
The Good Crisp Company
Tim's Cascade Snacks
Auburn, WA 800-533-8467
Tom's Foods
Charlotte, NC 877-309-6361
Tom's Snacks Company
Charlotte, NC 800-995-2623
Tri-Sum Potato Chip Company
Leominster, MA 978-697-2447
UTZ Quality Foods Inc.
Hanover, PA 800-367-7629
Wachusset Potato Chip Co Inc
Fitchburg, MA 800-551-5539
Westbrae Natural Foods
Melville, NY.................... 800-434-4246
Wysong Corp
Midland, MI 800-748-0188
Yum Yum Potato Chips
Warwick, QC.................... 800-567-5792

Alternative

AvoLov
Bend, OR.................... 541-419-4078
Bare Snacks
.... 800-940-0019
Beanfields
.... 855-328-2326
Daily Crave, The
Folsom, CA
Ka-POP!
Erie, CO
Kiwa
Ontario, CA
Mediterranean Snack Food Co
Boonton, NJ 973-402-2644
Naturally Homegrown
Surrey, BC.................... 604-465-7751
Pop Gourmet LLC
Tukwila, WA.................... 206-397-3896
ProFormance Foods
Brooklyn, NY 703-869-3413
Snikiddy, LLC
Boulder, CO 303-444-4405
The Good Crisp Company

Baked

Bickel's Snack Foods Inc
York, PA 800-233-1933
That's How We Roll, LLC
Fairfield, NJ 973-602-3011
Wyandot Inc
Marion, OH.................... 800-992-6368

Barbecue

Backer's Potato Chip Company
Fulton, MO 573-642-2833
Barrel O' Fun Snack Foods
Perham, MN 800-346-4910
Martin's Potato Chips
Thomasville, PA 800-272-4477
Mister Bee Potato Chips Co
Parkersburg, WV.................... 304-428-6133
Tim's Cascade Snacks
Auburn, WA 800-533-8467
Wachusset Potato Chip Co Inc
Fitchburg, MA 800-551-5539

Gourmet

Boulder Canyon Natural Foods
Boulder, CO 303-546-9939

No Salt

Wachusset Potato Chip Co Inc
Fitchburg, MA 800-551-5539

Ridges

Arctic Beverages
Winnipeg, MB.................... 866-503-1270
Backer's Potato Chip Company
Fulton, MO 573-642-2833
Barrel O' Fun Snack Foods
Perham, MN 800-346-4910
Wachusset Potato Chip Co Inc
Fitchburg, MA 800-551-5539

Salt & Vinegar

Small Planet Foods
Minneapolis, MN 800-624-4123
Tim's Cascade Snacks
Auburn, WA 800-533-8467
Wachusset Potato Chip Co Inc
Fitchburg, MA 800-551-5539

Salted

Barrel O' Fun Snack Foods
Perham, MN 800-346-4910
International Trading Company
Houston, TX 713-224-5901
Mediterranean Snack Food Co
Boonton, NJ 973-402-2644

Sour Cream & Onion

Backer's Potato Chip Company
Fulton, MO 573-642-2833
Barrel O' Fun Snack Foods
Perham, MN 800-346-4910
Martin's Potato Chips
Thomasville, PA 800-272-4477
Mister Bee Potato Chips Co
Parkersburg, WV.................... 304-428-6133
Tim's Cascade Snacks
Auburn, WA 800-533-8467
Wachusset Potato Chip Co Inc
Fitchburg, MA 800-551-5539

Sweet Potatoes

ARA Food Corp
Miami, FL 800-533-8831
Rhythm Superfoods
Austin, TX.................... 512-441-5667
Small Planet Foods
Minneapolis, MN 800-624-4123
The Good Bean
Berkeley, CA.................... 561-243-7773

Taco

Li'l Guy Foods
Kansas City, MO.................... 800-886-8226

Tortilla

Abuelita Mexican Foods
Manassas Park, VA 703-369-0232
Arizona Cowboy
Phoenix, AZ 800-529-8627
Art's Mexican Products
Kansas City, KS 913-371-2163
Azteca Foods Inc
Chicago, IL 708-563-6600
Bachman Company
Wyamissing, PA 800-523-8253
Bake Crafters Food Company
McDonald, TN 423-396-3392
Barrel O' Fun Snack Foods
Perham, MN 800-346-4910
Bearitos
Boulder, CO 310-886-8200
Better Made Snack Foods
Detroit, MI 800-332-2394
Bickel's Snack Foods Inc
York, PA 800-233-1933
Bountiful Larder LLC
Crested Butte, CO.................... 800-676-5057
C J Vitner Co
Chicago, IL 773-523-7900
Copak Solutions
Conover, NC 828-261-0255
Deep River Snacks
Deep River, CT.................... 860-434-7347
El Matador Foods
Baytown, TX.................... 800-470-2447
El Milagro
Chicago, IL 773-579-6120
Food Should Taste Good
Denver, CO 877-588-3784
Frog Ranch Foods
Glouster, OH 800-742-2488
Golden Flake Snack Foods
Birmingham, AL.................... 800-367-7629
Golden Fluff Popcorn Co
Lakewood, NJ 732-367-5448
Herr Foods Inc.
Nottingham, PA.................... 800-523-5030
Husman Snack Food Company
Peoria, IL.................... 859-282-7490
LA Canasta Mexican Foods
Phoenix, AZ 855-269-7721
LA Mexicana Tortilleria
Chicago, IL 773-247-5443
LA Tapatia Tortilleria Inc
Fresno, CA 559-441-1030
Los Amigo Tortilla Mfg Co
Atlanta, GA.................... 800-969-8226
Luke's Organic
Santa Cruz, CA
Miguel's Stowe Away
Stowe, VT 800-448-6517
Mikesell's Potato Chip Company
Dayton, OH.................... 937-228-9400
Mission Foodservice
Oldsmar, FL 800-443-7994

Ozuna Food Products Corporation
Sunnyvale, CA 408-400-0495
Pan De Oro Tortilla Chip Co
Hartford, CT 860-724-7063
PepsiCo.
Purchase, NY 914-253-2000
Plocky's Fine Snacks
Hinsdale, IL 630-323-8888
Puebla Foods Inc
Passaic, NJ 973-473-0201
R.W. Garcia
Scotts Valley, CA 408-287-4616
Rudy's Tortillas
Carrollton, TX. 800-878-2401
RW Garcia
San Jose, CA. 408-287-4616
Small Planet Foods
Minneapolis, MN 800-624-4123
Snak King Corp
City Of Industry, CA. 626-336-7711
Snyder's-Lance Inc.
Charlotte, NC 800-438-1880
Spanish Gardens Food Manufacturing
Kansas City, KS 913-831-4242
Sun Pac Foods
Brampton, ON. 905-792-2700
T.W. Garner Food Company
Winston Salem, NC. 800-476-7383
Tom's Snacks Company
Charlotte, NC 800-995-2623
UTZ Quality Foods Inc.
Hanover, PA 800-367-7629
Way Better Snacks
Minneapolis, MN 612-314-2060
Westbrae Natural Foods
Melville, NY. 800-434-4246
Wyandot Inc
Marion, OH. 800-992-6368

Corn Nuts

California Nuggets Inc
Ripon, CA. 209-599-7131
Dakota Gourmet
Wahpeton, ND. 800-727-6663
Hialeah Products Co
Hollywood, FL 800-923-3379
Setton International Foods
Commack, NY 800-227-4397
Waymouth Farms Inc
Minneapolis, MN 800-527-0094

Popcorn

479 Degrees
San Francisco, CA 815-552-6039
A La Carte
Chicago, IL 800-722-2370
American Pop Corn Co
Sioux City, IA. 712-239-1232
Angelic Gourmet Inc
Naples, NY 800-294-0947
Angie's Artisan Treats LLC
North Mankato, MN. 888-982-4984
Bachman Company
Wyamissing, PA 800-523-8253
Better Made Snack Foods
Detroit, MI 800-332-2394
Black Jewell Popcorn
Columbus, IN 800-948-2302
Black Shield
Albuquerque, NM. 800-653-9357
Brandmeyer Popcorn Co
Ankeny, IA 800-568-8276
Brimhall Foods
Bartlett, TN. 800-628-6559
Buddy Squirrel LLC
St Francis, WI 800-972-2658
C & F Foods Inc
City Of Industry, CA. 626-723-1000
C J Dannemiller Co
Norton, OH 800-624-8671
C J Vitner Co
Chicago, IL 773-523-7900
Calif Snack Foods
South El Monte, CA 626-454-4099
Cape Cod Potato Chips
Hyannis, MA. 800-438-1880
Carmadhy's Foods
Waterloo, ON 519-746-0551
Cheeze Kurls
Grand Rapids, MI 616-784-6095
Chester Inc Information
Valparaiso, IN 800-778-1131
Cloud Nine
Claremont, CA 909-624-3147
Clutter Farms
Gambier, OH. 740-427-3515
Colorado Popcorn Co
Sterling, CO 866-491-2676
Con Agra Snack Foods
Hamburg, IA. 800-831-5818
Coney Island Classics
Valley Stream, NY 516-823-3001
Corn Popper
Tulsa, OK 918-250-9317
Crickle Company
Thomasville, GA. 800-237-8689
De Met's Candy Co
Stamford, CT. 800-872-7622
Deep River Snacks
Deep River, CT. 860-434-7347
Delicious Popcorn
Waupaca, WI. 715-258-7683
Double Good
Burr Ridge, IL. 630-568-5544
Eagle Family Foods
Richfield, OH 888-656-3245
Elmers Fine Foods Inc
New Orleans, LA 888-570-0764
Fancy Farms Popcorn
Bernie, MO 800-833-8154
Fernando C Pujals & Bros
Guaynabo, PR. 787-792-3080
Fizzle Flat Farm, L.L.C.
Yale, IL 618-793-2060
Frankford Candy & Chocolate Co
Philadelphia, PA 800-523-9090
Fresh Ideas
Las Vegas, NV 702-701-4272
Frito-Lay Inc.
Plano, TX 800-352-4477
Front Range Snacks Inc
Centennial, CO 303-744-8850
Fun City Popcorn
Las Vegas, NV 800-423-1710
Funkychunky Inc.
Edina, MN. 888-473-8659
Gaslamp Co Popcorn
Riverside, CA 877-237-8276
Gilster-Mary Lee Corp
Chester, IL. 618-826-2361
Gluck Brands
Sugar Land, TX. 281-903-7082
Golden Flake Snack Foods
Birmingham, AL. 800-367-7629
Golden Fluff Popcorn Co
Lakewood, NJ 732-367-5448
Grandpa Po's Nutra Nuts
Commerce, CA 323-260-7457
Great American Popcorn Works of Pennsylvania
Telford, PA 855-542-2676
Great Western Co LLC
Hollywood, AL. 256-259-3578
Hain Celestial Group Inc
Lake Success, NY. 800-434-4246
Halfpops Inc
Scottsdale, AZ. 480-494-5117
Happy Herberts Food Co Inc
Jersey City, NJ 800-764-2779
Happy's Potato Chip Co
Minneapolis, MN 612-781-3121
Herr Foods Inc.
Nottingham, PA. 800-523-5030
International Home Foods
Parsippany, NJ. 973-359-9920
International Service Group
Alpharetta, GA 770-518-0988
Jerry's Nut House
Denver, CO. 303-861-2262
Jess Jones Vineyard
Dixon, CA. 707-678-3839
Jody's Gourmet Popcorn
Virginia Beach, VA. 757-422-8646
Kernel Fabyan's Gourmet Popcorn
St Charles, IL 847-483-1377
Kernel Seasons LLC
Elk Grove Vlg, IL. 866-328-7672
Kloss Manufacturing Co Inc
Allentown, PA. 800-445-7100
Koeze Company
Grand Rapids, MI 800-555-9688
Kornfections
Chantilly, VA. 800-469-8886
Krispy Kernels
Quebec, QC. 877-791-9986
Lima Grain Cereal Seeds LLC
Fort Collins, CO 970-498-2200
Martin's Potato Chips
Thomasville, PA 800-272-4477
Metzger Popcorn Co
Delphos, OH 800-819-6072
Michele's Chocolate Truffles
Clackamas, OR 800-656-7112
Midwest Nut Co
Minneapolis, MN 800-328-5502
Mikesell's Potato Chip Company
Dayton, OH. 937-228-9400
Mills Brothers Intl
Seattle, WA 206-575-3000
Morrison Farms
Clearwater, NE 402-887-5335
Nebraska Bean
Clearwater, NE 800-253-6502
Newman's Own
Westport, CT. 203-222-0136
Noble Popcorn
Sac City, IA. 800-537-9554
Nutra Nuts
Commerce, CA 323-260-7457
Old Dutch Foods LTD
Roseville, MN
Old Sacramento Popcorn Company
Sacramento, CA 916-446-1980
Olson Livestock & Seed
Haigler, NE 308-297-3283
Oogie's Snack LLC
Denver, CO 303-455-2107
Organic Planet
San Francisco, CA 415-765-5590
Papa Dean's Popcorn
San Antonio, TX. 877-855-7272
Patsy's Candy
Colorado Springs, CO. 866-372-8797
Pleasant Grove Farms
Pleasant Grove, CA 916-655-3391
Pop Art Snacks
Salt Lake City, UT 801-983-7470
Pop Gourmet LLC
Tukwila, WA. 206-397-3896
Popcorn Connection
North Hollywood, CA 800-852-2676
Popcorn Popper
Monon, IN. 800-270-2705
Popcorn World
Sedalia, MO 800-443-8226
Popcorner
Swansea, IL. 618-277-2676
Popcornopolis LLC
Vernon, CA 800-767-2489
Poppers Supply Company
Allentown, PA. 800-457-9810
Popsalot
Beverly Hills, CA 213-761-0156
Preferred Popcorn
Chapman, NE. 308-986-2526
Preston Farms Popcorn
Louisville, KY 866-767-7464
Primrose Candy Co
Chicago, IL. 800-268-9522
Quinn Snacks
Boulder, CO 303-927-6655
R&J Farms
West Salem, OH 419-846-3179
Ramsey Popcorn Co Inc
Ramsey, IN 800-624-2060
Reist Popcorn Co
Mt Joy, PA. 717-653-8078
Richard Green Company
Indianapolis, IN 317-972-0941
Rivard Popcorn Products
Lancaster, PA 717-898-7131
Roberts Ferry Nut Co
Waterford, CA. 209-874-3247
Rock-N-Roll Gourmet
Marina Del Ray, CA 800-518-3891
Rygmyr Foods
South Saint Paul, MN. 800-545-3903
Sahagian & Associates
Oak Park, IL 800-327-9273
Sexy Pop LLC
Sea Cliff, NY 877-476-2755
Shallowford Farms Popcorn, Inc.
Yadkinville, NC 800-892-9539
Shepherd Farms Inc
Hillsboro, IL 800-383-2676

Sheryl's Chocolate Creations
Hicksville, NY 888-882-2462
Snack Works/Metrovox Snacks
Orange, CA 800-783-9870
Snak King Corp
City Of Industry, CA 626-336-7711
Snappy Popcorn
Breda, IA 800-742-0228
Snikiddy, LLC
Boulder, CO 303-444-4405
Snyder's-Lance Inc.
Charlotte, NC 800-438-1880
Stock Popcorn Ind Inc
Lake View, IA 712-657-2811
Sugar Plum
Kingston, PA 800-447-8427
Teelee Popcorn
Shannon, IL 800-578-2363
The Hampton Popcorn Company
Bethpage, NY 888-947-6726
The Little Kernel
Manalapan, NJ 732-607-3880
Tiny But Mighty Popcorn
Shellsburg, IA 800-330-4692
Todd's
Vernon, CA 800-938-6337
Treier Popcorn Farms
Bloomdale, OH 419-454-2811
Tri-Sum Potato Chip Company
Leominster, MA 978-697-2447
Trinidad Benham Corporation
Denver, CO 303-220-1400
UTZ Quality Foods Inc.
Hanover, PA 800-367-7629
Vande Walle's Candies Inc
Appleton, WI 800-738-1020
Vegan Rob's
Sea Cliff, NY 516-671-4411
Velvet Creme Popcorn Co
Westwood, KS 888-553-6708
Vogel Popcorn
Lakeville, MN 952-469-7482
Wabash Valley Farms
Monon, IN 877-888-7077
Wachusset Potato Chip Co Inc
Fitchburg, MA 800-551-5539
Weaver Popcorn Co Inc
Van Buren, IN
Westbrae Natural Foods
Melville, NY 800-434-4246
Wildly Organic
Silver Bay, MN 800-945-3801
Yaya's
Corona Del Mar, CA 949-675-7708

Coated

Black Shield
Albuquerque, NM 800-653-9357
Calif Snack Foods
South El Monte, CA 626-454-4099
Double Good
Burr Ridge, IL 630-568-5544
Golden Fluff Popcorn Co
Lakewood, NJ 732-367-5448
Jody's Gourmet Popcorn
Virginia Beach, VA 757-422-8646
Kernel Seasons LLC
Elk Grove Vlg, IL 866-328-7672
Lou-Retta's Custom Chocolates
Buffalo, NY 716-833-7111
The Safe + Fair Food Company
Chicago, IL

Flavored

479 Degrees
San Francisco, CA 815-552-6039
Black Shield
Albuquerque, NM 800-653-9357
Calif Snack Foods
South El Monte, CA 626-454-4099
Dale & Thomas Popcorn
Englewood, NJ 800-767-4444
DGZ Chocolate
Houston, TX 877-949-9444
Double Good
Burr Ridge, IL 630-568-5544
Eda's Sugar Free
Philadelphia, PA 215-324-3412
G.H. Cretors
Richfield, OH
Golden Fluff Popcorn Co
Lakewood, NJ 732-367-5448
Halfpops Inc
Scottsdale, AZ 480-494-5117
Happy's Potato Chip Co
Minneapolis, MN 612-781-3121
Jody's Gourmet Popcorn
Virginia Beach, VA 757-422-8646
Kernel Seasons LLC
Elk Grove Vlg, IL 866-328-7672
Live Love Pop
Addison, TX 214-697-6370
Maddy & Maize
Saint Paul, MN 612-405-9155
Maria's Premium
Middlefield Cheese House
Middlefield, OH 800-327-9477
Midwest Nut Co
Minneapolis, MN 800-328-5502
Mini Pops Inc
Stoughton, MA 781-436-5864
Noble Popcorn
Sac City, IA 800-537-9554
Nouveau Foods
Mountain View, CA
Oogie's Snack LLC
Denver, CO 303-455-2107
Pipsnacks
New York, NY 973-723-4246
Pop Gourmet LLC
Tukwila, WA 206-397-3896
Pop Zero
Salt Lake City, UT 801-456-5757
Popcorn World
Sedalia, MO 800-443-8226
Popcornopolis LLC
Vernon, CA 800-767-2489
Poppy Hand-Crafted Popcorn
Asheville, NC 828-552-3149
POPTime
Clifton, NJ 862-225-9549
Quality Snacks
New York, NY
Quinn Snacks
Boulder, CO 303-927-6655
Rivard Popcorn Products
Lancaster, PA 717-898-7131
Tastebuds Popcorn
Belmont, NC 704-461-8755
The Little Kernel
Manalapan, NJ 732-607-3880
Tim's Cascade Snacks
Auburn, WA 800-533-8467
Tri-Sum Potato Chip Company
Leominster, MA 978-697-2447
Velvet Creme Popcorn Co
Westwood, KS 888-553-6708
Victoria's Catered Traditions
Manteca, CA 877-272-5208
Wabash Valley Farms
Monon, IN 877-888-7077
Yaya's
Corona Del Mar, CA 949-675-7708

Pork Rinds

ARA Food Corp
Miami, FL 800-533-8831
Bacon's Heir
. . . . 706-688-9534
Better Made Snack Foods
Detroit, MI 800-332-2394
Evans Food Group LTD
Chicago, IL 866-254-7400
Golden Flake Snack Foods
Birmingham, AL 800-367-7629
Mac's Snacks
Arlington, TX 817-640-5626
Manda Fine Meats Inc
Baton Rouge, LA 800-343-2642
Rudolph Foods Co
Lima, OH 419-648-3611
Sau-Sea Foods
Tarrytown, NY 914-631-1717
Tom's Snacks Company
Charlotte, NC 800-995-2623

Bacon

Evans Food Group LTD
Chicago, IL 866-254-7400
Rudolph Foods Co
Lima, OH 419-648-3611

Potato Sticks

Golden Fluff Popcorn Co
Lakewood, NJ 732-367-5448
Wachusset Potato Chip Co Inc
Fitchburg, MA 800-551-5539

Pretzels

All American Snacks
Midland, TX 800-840-2455
All Wrapped Up
Plantation, FL 800-891-2194
Amoroso's Baking Co
Bellmawr, NJ 215-471-4740
Angelic Gourmet Inc
Naples, NY 800-294-0947
Bachman Company
Wyamissing, PA 800-523-8253
Bake Crafters Food Company
McDonald, TN 423-396-3392
Barrel O' Fun Snack Foods
Perham, MN 800-346-4910
Benzel's Pretzel Bakery
Altoona, PA 800-344-4438
Better Made Snack Foods
Detroit, MI 800-332-2394
Bickel's Snack Foods Inc
York, PA 800-233-1933
Bissinger's Handcrafted Chocolatier
St. Louis, MO 314-615-2400
Brad's Taste of New York
Floral Park, NY 516-354-9004
Brimhall Foods
Bartlett, TN 800-628-6559
Buckeye Pretzel Company
Williamsport, PA 800-257-6029
Buddy Squirrel LLC
St Francis, WI 800-972-2658
Candy Cottage Company
Huntingdon Valley, PA 215-953-8288
Cape Cod Potato Chips
Hyannis, MA 800-438-1880
Clara Foods
Clara City, MN 888-844-8518
Dave's Gourmet
San Rafael, CA 800-758-0372
Dieffenbach's Potato Chips
Womelsdorf, PA 610-589-2385
Dream Confectioners LTD
Teaneck, NJ 201-836-9000
Fatty Sundays
Brooklyn, NY 646-762-2555
Frito-Lay Inc.
Plano, TX 800-352-4477
From the Ground Up
Fairfield, NJ
GKI Foods
Brighton, MI 248-486-0055
Gratify Gluten Free
Englewood Cliffs, NJ 800-200-6736
GWB Foods Corporation
Brooklyn, NY 877-977-7610
Happy Herberts Food Co Inc
Jersey City, NJ 800-764-2779
Hartley's Potato Chip Co
Lewistown, PA 717-248-0526
Herr Foods Inc.
Nottingham, PA 800-523-5030
Hialeah Products Co
Hollywood, FL 800-923-3379
J & J Snack Foods Corp
Pennsauken, NJ 800-486-9533
Julius Sturgis Pretzel Bakery
Lititz, PA 717-626-4354
Kay's Naturals, Inc.
Clara City, MN 866-873-5499
Key III Candies
Fort Wayne, IN 800-752-2382
Keystone Pretzel Bakery
Lititz, PA 888-572-4500
Kim & Scott's Gourmet Pretzels
Chicago, IL 800-578-9478
Knese Enterprise
Bellerose, NY 516-354-9004
Krispy Kernels
Quebec, QC 877-791-9986
Martin's Potato Chips
Thomasville, PA 800-272-4477
Mary's Gone Crackers
Gridley, CA 888-258-1250
Mikesell's Potato Chip Company
Dayton, OH 937-228-9400

Mister Snacks Inc
Amherst, NY 800-333-6393
Nature's Legacy Inc.
Hudson, MI 517-448-2050
Old Dutch Foods LTD
Roseville, MN
Palmer Candy Co
Sioux City, IA 800-831-0828
PepsiCo.
Purchase, NY 914-253-2000
Porkie Company of Wisconsin
Cudahy, WI 800-333-2588
Port City Pretzels
Portsmouth, NH 603-502-7946
Pretzel Perfection
Vancouver, WA 360-635-3886
Pretzel Pete
Montgomeryville, PA 877-857-1727
Pretzels Inc
Bluffton, IN 800-456-4838
Quinn Snacks
Boulder, CO 303-927-6655
R&J Farms
West Salem, OH 419-846-3179
S B Global Foods Inc
Lansdale, PA 877-857-1727
Savor Street
Reading, PA 800-523-8253
Sheryl's Chocolate Creations
Hicksville, NY 888-882-2462
Snack Works/Metrovox Snacks
Orange, CA 800-783-9870
Snak King Corp
City Of Industry, CA 626-336-7711
Snyder's of Hanover
Charlotte, NC 800-233-7125
Sole Grano LLC
Fair Lawn, NJ 201-797-7100
Sporting Colors LLC
St. Louis, MO 888-394-2292
Sweet City Supply
Virginia Beach, VA 888-793-3824
Tell City Pretzel Company
Tell City, IN 812-548-4499
Todd's
Vernon, CA 800-938-6337
Triple-C
Hamilton, ON 800-263-9105
Tru Chocolate
Medford, MA 855-878-2462
Unique Pretzel Bakery, Inc.
Reading, PA 610-929-3172
UTZ Quality Foods Inc.
Hanover, PA 800-367-7629
Vermont Pretzel & Cookie Co.
Bellows Falls, VT 888-671-4774
Weaver Nut Co. Inc.
Ephrata, PA 800-473-2688
Wege Pretzel Company
Hanover, PA 800-888-4646
Westbrae Natural Foods
Melville, NY 800-434-4246

Flavored

Creative Snacks Co LLC
Greensboro, NC 336-668-4151
Dream Pretzels
New York, NY 877-966-8434
Grippo Foods
Cincinnati, OH 800-626-1824
Kim & Scott's Gourmet Pretzels
Chicago, IL 800-578-9478
Unique Pretzel Bakery, Inc.
Reading, PA 610-929-3172

Nubs

Kim & Scott's Gourmet Pretzels
Chicago, IL 800-578-9478
Pretzel Pete
Montgomeryville, PA 877-857-1727

Soft

Bakers Best Snack Food Corp.
Pennsauken, NJ 215-822-3511
Hammond Pretzel Bakery Inc
Lancaster, PA 717-392-7532
Kim & Scott's Gourmet Pretzels
Chicago, IL 800-578-9478
New York Pretzel
Brooklyn, NY 718-366-9800
Rudi's Organic Bakery
Boulder, CO 877-293-0876
Vermont Pretzel & Cookie Co.
Bellows Falls, VT 888-671-4774

Sticks or Rods

Barrel O' Fun Snack Foods
Perham, MN 800-346-4910
Confectionately Yours LTD
Buffalo Grove, IL 800-875-6978
Handy Pax
Randolph, MA 781-963-8300
Kim & Scott's Gourmet Pretzels
Chicago, IL 800-578-9478
Quinn Snacks
Boulder, CO 303-927-6655
Sheryl's Chocolate Creations
Hicksville, NY 888-882-2462

Twists

Jerry's Nut House
Denver, CO 303-861-2262
Kim & Scott's Gourmet Pretzels
Chicago, IL 800-578-9478
Pretzel Pete
Montgomeryville, PA 877-857-1727
Sheryl's Chocolate Creations
Hicksville, NY 888-882-2462

Rice Cakes

Basic Grain Products
Coldwater, OH 866-411-6677
Blue Marble Brands
Providence, RI 888-534-0246
Element Snacks
New York, NY 212-966-7696
GWB Foods Corporation
Brooklyn, NY 877-977-7610
Happy Family
New York, NY 855-644-2779
Hawaii Candy Inc
Honolulu, HI 800-303-2507
Lundberg Family Farms
Richvale, CA 530-538-3500
Ohta Wafer Factory
Honolulu, HI 808-949-2775
Westbrae Natural Foods
Melville, NY 800-434-4246

Snack Pellets

Preformed

Fashion Snackz
Pomona, CA 909-598-0880
Rudolph Foods Co
Lima, OH 419-648-3611
Urban Foods LLC
Sacramento, CA 916-372-3663

Trail Mix

American Importing Co.
Minneapolis, MN 855-273-0466
Bavarian Nut Co
Buffalo, NY 716-810-6887
Bhuja Snacks
Kennesaw, GA
Big Steer
Houston, TX 800-421-4951
Bite Fuel
Oregon City, OR
Bubba's Fine Foods
Loveland, CO
C J Vitner Co
Chicago, IL 773-523-7900
Cibo Vita
Totowa, NJ 862-238-8020
Creative Snacks Co LLC
Greensboro, NC 336-668-4151
Desert Pepper Trading Co
El Paso, TX 888-472-5727
East Kentucky Foods
Winchester, KY 859-744-2218
Essential Living Foods
Torrance, CA 310-319-1555
Grandma Emily
Montreal, QC 877-943-3661
GrandyOats
Hiram, ME 207-935-7415
Greenjoy
Okatie, SC
Healing Home Foods
Pound Ridge, NY 914-764-1303
Hickory Harvest Foods
Akron, OH 800-448-6887
Inn Maid Food
Lenox, MA 413-637-2732
Jerry's Nut House
Denver, CO 303-861-2262
Kohler Original Recipe Chocolates
Kohler, WI 920-208-4930
Lehi Valley Trading Company
Mesa, AZ 480-684-1402
Marin Food Specialties
Byron, CA 925-634-6126
Midwest Nut Co
Minneapolis, MN 800-328-5502
Mister Snacks Inc
Amherst, NY 800-333-6393
Nature Kist Snacks
Commerce, CA 323-278-9578
Navitas Naturals
Novato, CA 888-645-4282
New England Natural Bakers
Greenfield, MA 800-910-2884
Nspired Natural Foods
Boulder, CO 800-434-4246
Nut Factory
Spokane Valley, WA 888-239-5288
Old Dutch Foods LTD
Roseville, MN
Patience Fruit & Co.
Villeroy, QC
Prana
Ville St Laurent, QC 844-447-7262
Setton Farms
Terra Bella, CA 559-535-6050
Setton International Foods
Commack, NY 800-227-4397
Sole Grano LLC
Fair Lawn, NJ 201-797-7100
Sonne
Wahpeton, ND 800-727-6663
Sun-Rype Products
Kelowna, BC 888-786-7973
Sunridge Farms
Royal Oaks, CA 831-786-7000
Sunridge Farms Inc
Salinas, CA 831-755-1530
Superior Nut & Candy
Chicago, IL 800-843-2238
Terri Lynn Inc
Elgin, IL 800-323-0775
Thoughtful Food
Lafayette, CA 510-910-2581
Tierra Farm
Valatie, NY 519-392-8300
Timber Peaks Gourmet
Parker, CO 800-982-7687
Tropical Foods
Charlotte, NC 800-438-4470
Valley View Blueberries
Vancouver, WA 360-892-2839
Waymouth Farms Inc
Minneapolis, MN 800-527-0094
Weaver Nut Co. Inc.
Ephrata, PA 800-473-2688
Wysong Corp
Midland, MI 800-748-0188

Specialty & Organic Foods

General

Arico Natural Foods
Beaverton, OR . . . 503-259-0871
Fallwood Corp
White Plains, NY . . . 914-304-4065

Aquaculture

Bayou Land Seafood
Breaux Bridge, LA . . . 337-667-6118
Bourbon Barrel Foods
Louisville, KY . . . 502-333-6103
Chef Silvio's of Wooster Street
Guilford, CT . . . 203-453-1064
GS Gelato & Desserts Inc
Fort Walton Bch, FL . . . 888-435-2767
Idaho Trout Company
Buhl, ID . . . 866-878-7688
Marion's Smart Delights
Arlington, VA . . . 703-593-3450
Nora Snacks
Santa Fe Springs, CA . . . 562-404-9888
Ocean's Balance
Cape Elizabeth, ME
Silver Streak Bass Co
El Campo, TX . . . 979-543-6343
Southern Pride Catfish Company
Seattle, WA . . . 800-343-8046
T. Marzetti Company
Westerville, OH . . . 800-999-1835
Treats Island Fisheries
Scaly Mountain, NC . . . 207-733-4580

CBD

Curaleaf
Wakefield, MA . . . 833-760-4367
GoodBites Snacks
Venice, CA
Green Gorilla
Malibu, CA . . . 323-452-5919
Green Roads CBD
Deerfield Beach, FL . . . 833-462-8922
Irwin Naturals
Los Angeles, CA . . . 888-223-1548
Medterra CBD
Irvine, CA . . . 800-971-1288
Nature's Fusions
Provo, UT . . . 801-872-9500
NuLeaf Naturals
Denver, CO . . . 720-372-4842
Plus CBD Oil
San Diego, CA . . . 855-758-7223
PureForm CBD
Los Angeles, CA
Sagely Naturals
Santa Monica, CA . . . 424-262-6614

Dietary Products

Alfred L. Wolff, Inc.
Park Ridge, IL . . . 847-759-8888
Avenue Gourmet
Owings Mills, MD . . . 410-902-5701
Cave Shake
Los Angeles, CA
Cell-Nique
Norwalk, CT . . . 888-417-9343
Clara Foods
San Francisco, CA
Grandcestors
Golden, CO
Health Warrior
Richmond, VA . . . 804-381-5305
Kalifornia Keto
Villa Park, CA
Personal Edge Nutrition
Ballwin, MO . . . 514-636-4512
Prosperity Organic Foods
Boise, ID . . . 888-557-5741
Steve's PaleoGoods
Pennsauken, NJ . . . 856-356-2258
Synergy
Moab, UT . . . 800-804-3211

Diet & Weight Loss Aids

Alkinco
New York, NY . . . 800-424-7118
Almased USA
St. Petersburg, FL . . . 727-867-4444
Body Breakthrough Inc
Deer Park, NY . . . 800-924-3343
CarbRite Diet
New Brunswick, NJ . . . 800-872-0101
Eckhart Corporation
Novato, CA . . . 800-200-4201
Himalayan Heritage
Fredonia, WI . . . 888-414-9500
Inbalance Health
Wayland, MI . . . 269-792-1977
LonoLife
Oceanside, CA . . . 855-843-8566
Natural Balance
Englewood, CO . . . 800-624-4260
Nature's Plus
Melville, NY . . . 800-645-9500
Nellson Candies Inc
Irwindale, CA . . . 626-334-4508
Nestle USA Inc
Glendale, CA . . . 800-225-2270
Nutraceutical International
Park City, UT . . . 800-669-8877
Organic Liaison, LLC
Coral Springs, FL . . . 954-755-4405
Pro Form Labs
Orinda, CA . . . 707-752-9010
Russo Farms
Vineland, NJ . . . 856-692-5942
Soluble Products Company
Lakewood, NJ . . . 732-364-8855
The Sola Company
Houston, TX . . . 800-277-1486
Tova Industries LLC
Louisville, KY . . . 888-532-8682
USA Laboratories Inc
Burns, TN . . . 800-489-4872
VitaThinQ Inc.
Davie, FL
Zevia
Culver City, CA . . . 855-469-3842

Dietary Supplements

Acta Health Products
Sunnyvale, CA . . . 408-732-6830
Alacer Corp
Carlisle, PA . . . 888-425-2362
Archon Vitamin Corp
Edison, NJ . . . 800-848-0089
Balanced Health Products
New York, NY . . . 212-794-9878
BetaStatin Nutritional Rsearch
Greenwich, CT . . . 800-660-9570
Century Foods Intl LLC
Sparta, WI . . . 800-269-1901
CHiKPRO
. . . 417-708-0988
Edom Labs Inc
Deer Park, NY . . . 800-723-3366
Green Roads CBD
Deerfield Beach, FL . . . 833-462-8922
Hero Nutritionals
Santa Ana, CA . . . 800-500-4376
Immu Dyne Inc
Florence, KY . . . 888-246-6839
Life Extension Foundation
Fort Lauderdale, FL . . . 888-895-4771
Maat Nutritionals
Los Angeles, CA . . . 888-818-6228
Montana Naturals
Park City, UT . . . 800-650-9597
Naturalife Laboratories
Torrance, CA . . . 800-231-3670
Nature's Herbs
Merritt, BC . . . 800-437-2257
Nellson Nutraceutical LLC
Anaheim, CA . . . 844-635-5766
North West Pharmanaturals Inc
Brea, CA . . . 714-529-0980
NOW Foods
Bloomingdale, IL . . . 888-669-3663
Power Crunch
Irvine, CA
QBI
South Plainfield, NJ . . . 908-668-0088
Rainbow Light Nutritional Systems
Santa Cruz, CA . . . 800-635-1233
SimplyFUEL, LLC
Leawood, KS . . . 913-269-1889
Source Naturals
Scotts Valley, CA . . . 800-815-2333
Trace Minerals Research
West Haven, UT . . . 800-624-7145
Valentine Enterprises Inc
Lawrenceville, GA . . . 770-995-0661
Vita-Pure Inc
Roselle, NJ . . . 908-245-1212
Vitamer Laboratories
Irvine, CA . . . 800-432-8355
Wilke International Inc
Lenexa, KS . . . 800-779-5545

Health Products

Abunda Life
Asbury Park, NJ . . . 732-775-9338
Acta Health Products
Sunnyvale, CA . . . 408-732-6830
Action Labs
Anaheim, CA . . . 800-400-5696
ADH Health Products Inc
Congers, NY . . . 845-268-0027
Agger Fish Corp
Brooklyn, NY . . . 718-855-1717
Alacer Corp
Carlisle, PA . . . 888-425-2362
Alfer Laboratories
Chatsworth, CA . . . 818-709-0737
Alkinco
New York, NY . . . 800-424-7118
Alli & Rose
Lincolnton, NC . . . 828-446-8420
Aloe Farms Inc
Harlingen, TX . . . 800-262-6771
Aloe Laboratories
Harlingen, TX . . . 800-258-5380
Alternative Health & Herbs
Albany, OR . . . 800-345-4152
Amcan Industries
Elmsford, NY . . . 914-347-4838
American Almond Products Co
Brooklyn, NY . . . 800-825-6663
American Spoon Foods Inc
Petoskey, MI . . . 888-735-6700
Anabol Naturals
Santa Cruz, CA . . . 800-426-2265
Annie's Naturals
Berkeley, CA . . . 800-434-1234
Apotheca Inc
Woodbine, IA . . . 800-736-3130
Archon Vitamin Corp
Edison, NJ . . . 800-848-0089
Arizona Natural Products
Phoenix, AZ . . . 800-255-2823
Arro Corp
Hodgkins, IL . . . 877-929-2776
Aspire
Chicago, OH
Atkins Nutritionals Inc.
Denver, CO . . . 800-628-5467
Atrium Biotech
Quebec, QC . . . 418-652-1116
Bake N Joy Foods
North Andover, MA . . . 800-666-4937
BBS Bodacious BBQ Company
Coral Springs, FL . . . 800-537-5928
Bede Inc
Haledon, NJ . . . 866-239-6565
Beehive Botanicals
Hayward, WI . . . 800-233-4483
Bel Brands USA
Chicago, IL . . . 312-462-1500
Betty Lou's
McMinnville, OR . . . 800-242-5205
Bevco Sales International Inc.
Surrey, BC . . . 800-663-0090
Beverly International
Cold Spring, KY . . . 800-781-3475

Bio-Foods
Pine Brook, NJ . . . 973-808-5856
Black Ranch Organic Grains
Etna, CA . . . 916-467-3387
Blessed Herbs
Oakham, MA. . . . 800-489-4372
Blue Chip Baker
Salt Lake City, UT . . . 800-878-0099
Blue Planet Foods
Collegedale, TN . . . 877-396-3145
Botanical Products
Springville, CA. . . . 559-539-3432
Brucia Plant Extracts
Shingle Springs, CA . . . 530-676-2774
Buckhead Gourmet
Atlanta, GA. . . . 800-673-6338
Bunker Hill Cheese Co Inc
Millersburg, OH . . . 800-253-6636
Butter Buds Food Ingredients
Racine, WI. . . . 800-426-1119
CactuLife, LLC
Corona Del Mar, CA. . . . 800-500-1713
California Fruit
San Diego, CA . . . 877-378-4811
California Natural Products
Lathrop, CA . . . 209-858-2525
California Olive Oil Council
Berkeley, CA. . . . 888-718-9830
Caltex Foods
Canoga Park, CA . . . 800-522-5839
Carole's Cheesecake Company
Toronto, ON . . . 416-256-0000
Cascade Fresh
Seattle, WA . . . 800-511-0057
Caveman Foods
Lafayette, CA . . . 925-979-9515
Cedar Crest Specialties
Cedarburg, WI. . . . 800-877-8341
Cedar Lake Foods
Cedar Lake, MI. . . . 800-246-5039
Cedarlane Foods
Carson, CA. . . . 800-826-3322
Champlain Valley Milling Corp
Westport, NY. . . . 518-962-4711
Chase Brothers Dairy
Oxnard, CA. . . . 800-438-6455
China Mist Brands
Scottsdale, AZ. . . . 800-242-8807
Christopher Ranch LLC
Gilroy, CA. . . . 408-847-1100
Christopher's Herb Shop
Springville, UT . . . 888-372-4372
Clif Bar & Co
Emeryville, CA. . . . 802-254-3227
Coca-Cola Beverages Northeast
Bedford, NH . . . 844-619-3388
Cookie Tree Bakeries
Salt Lake City, UT . . . 801-268-2253
Countertop Productions
Alexandria, VA
Cyanotech Corp
Kailua Kona, HI . . . 800-395-1353
Dairy Maid Dairy LLC
Frederick, MD. . . . 301-663-5114
Dean Distributors, Inc.
Burlingame, CA . . . 800-792-0816
Deerland Probiotics & Enzymes
Kennesaw, GA . . . 800-697-8179
Devansoy Farms
Carroll, IA. . . . 800-747-8605
Diamond Crystal Brands Inc
Savannah, GA. . . . 800-654-5115
Dolphin Natural Chocolates
Cambria, CA. . . . 800-236-5744
Dorothy Dawson Food Products
Jackson, MI. . . . 517-788-9830
Dr. In The Kitchen
Minneapolis, MN . . . 952-746-3007
DSM Fortitech Premixes
Schenectady, NY
Dulce de Leche Delcampo Products
Miami, FL. . . . 877-472-9408
Earth Island
Chatsworth, CA . . . 888-394-3949
Eda's Sugar Free
Philadelphia, PA . . . 215-324-3412
Edner Corporation
Hayward, CA . . . 510-441-8504
Elwood International Inc
Copiague, NY . . . 631-842-6600
Emkay Trading Corporation
Elmsford, NY . . . 914-592-9000

Ener-G Foods
Seattle, WA . . . 800-331-5222
Energen Products Inc
Norwalk, CA. . . . 800-423-8837
Essential Nutrients Inc
Emery, UT. . . . 435-286-2460
Evo Hemp
Boulder, CO
Evolve
Walnut Creek, CA. . . . 888-298-6629
Faber Foods and Aeronautics
Evergreen, CO. . . . 800-237-3255
Falcone's Cookie Land LTD
Brooklyn, NY . . . 718-236-4200
Fat Snax
Brooklyn, NY . . . 347-496-5834
Fieldbrook Foods Corp.
Dunkirk, NY . . . 800-333-0805
First District Association
Litchfield, MN . . . 320-693-3236
FitPro USA
Fairfield, CA. . . . 877-645-5776
FODY Food Co.
Westmount, QC. . . . 818-835-1850
Food First
Walhalla, ND. . . . 800-241-0799
Freeda Vitamins Inc
Long Island City, NY . . . 800-777-3737
Frontier Co-op
Norway, IA . . . 844-550-6200
Garuda International
Exeter, CA. . . . 559-594-4380
Germack Pistachio Co
Detroit, MI . . . 800-872-4006
Gertrude & Bronner's Magic Alpsnack
Vista, CA. . . . 877-786-3649
Gifford's Ice Cream
Skowhegan, ME . . . 800-950-2604
Ginger Shots
Huntington Beach, CA . . . 888-413-1487
Ginseng Up Corp
Worcester, MA . . . 800-446-7364
Global Health Laboratories
Amityville, NY . . . 631-777-2134
Glover's Ice Cream Inc
Frankfort, IN. . . . 800-686-5163
Goldthread
Santa Monica, CA. . . . 413-325-8987
GoMacro
Viola, WI. . . . 800-788-9540
GoodBelly Probiotics
Boulder, CO . . . 303-443-3631
Govadinas Fitness Foods
San Diego, CA . . . 800-900-0108
Great Circles
Bellows Falls, VT. . . . 877-877-2120
Green Foods Corp.
Oxnard, CA. . . . 800-777-4430
Green Options
San Rafael, CA . . . 888-473-3667
Grow Co
Ridgefield, NJ. . . . 201-941-8777
Gust John Foods & Products
Batavia, IL. . . . 800-756-5886
GWB Foods Corporation
Brooklyn, NY . . . 877-977-7610
H Fox & Co Inc
Brooklyn, NY . . . 718-385-4600
H. Reisman Corporation
Orange, NJ . . . 973-882-1670
H2rOse, LLC
Los Angeles, CA
Harvest Valley Bakery Inc
La Salle, IL. . . . 815-224-9030
Haydenergy Health
Valley Stream, NY . . . 800-255-1660
Health Valley Company
Irwindale, CA . . . 800-334-3204
Healthy Grain Foods LLC
Northbrook, IL . . . 847-272-5576
Healthy Skoop
Boulder, CO . . . 720-545-1753
Healthy Times Baby Food
San Diego, CA . . . 858-513-1550
Heart to Heart Foods
Hyde Park, UT . . . 435-753-9602
Heavenly Hemp Foods
Nederland, CO . . . 888-328-4367
Hello Water
. . . 888-474-3556
Hemp Fusion
Roswell, GA . . . 877-669-4367

Hemp2o
San Leandro, CA. . . . 510-382-1231
Herbal Products & Development
Aptos, CA . . . 831-688-8706
Herbs America
Murphy, OR . . . 541-846-6222
Heritage Books & Gifts
Virginia Beach, VA. . . . 800-862-2923
Heritage Farms Dairy
Murfreesboro, TN. . . . 615-895-2790
Heterochemical Corp
Valley Stream, NY . . . 516-561-8225
HFI Foods
Redmond, WA. . . . 425-883-1320
Hillestad Pharmaceuticals
Woodruff, WI . . . 800-535-7742
Hillside Candy Co
Hillside, NJ. . . . 800-524-1304
Hinckley Springs Bottled Water
. . . 800-201-6218
Holistic Products Corporation
Englewood, NJ . . . 800-221-0308
Homestead Mills
Cook, MN. . . . 800-652-5233
Hormel Foods Corp.
Austin, MN. . . . 507-437-5611
Host Defense Mushrooms
. . . 800-780-9126
House Foods America Corp
Garden Grove, CA . . . 877-333-7077
Howard Foods Inc
Danvers, MA. . . . 978-774-6207
Hsu's Ginseng Enterprises Inc
Wausau, WI. . . . 800-826-1577
Humbly Hemp
Los Angeles, CA. . . . 424-259-3521
Humco Holding Group Inc
Texarkana, TX. . . . 903-831-7808
I-Health Inc
Cromwell, CT. . . . 800-990-3476
ICONIC Protein
San Clemente, CA
Imlak'esh Organics
Goleta, CA . . . 805-689-2269
Integrative Flavors
Michigan City, IN. . . . 800-837-7687
Inter Health Nutraceuticals
Benicia, CA. . . . 800-783-4636
Interbake Foods
Richmond, VA. . . . 800-221-1002
International Casings Group
Chicago, IL . . . 800-825-5151
International Vitamin Corporation
Freehold, NJ . . . 800-666-8482
Island Spring Inc
Vashon, WA. . . . 206-463-9848
J R Carlson Laboratories Inc
Arlington Heights, IL . . . 888-234-5656
J.N. Bech
Elk Rapids, MI . . . 800-232-4583
Jamieson Laboratories
Windsor, ON. . . . 800-265-5088
Jason & Son Specialty Foods
Rancho Cordova, CA. . . . 800-810-9093
Jason Pharmaceuticals
Owings Mills, MD . . . 800-638-7867
Jaxon's Ice Cream Parlor
Dania Beach, FL. . . . 954-923-4445
JiMMY! Bars
Chicago, IL . . . 888-676-7971
JMS Specialty Foods
Ripon, WI . . . 800-535-5437
Jonathan's Sprouts
Rochester, MA . . . 508-763-2577
Julian Bakery
Oceanside, CA . . . 760-721-5200
Kapaa Poi Factory
Kapaa, HI . . . 808-822-5426
Kemach Food Products
Brooklyn, NY . . . 718-272-5655
Keto Foods
Neptune, NJ . . . 732-922-0009
KiiTO, Inc.
Los Angeles, CA
Klinke Brothers Ice Cream Co
Memphis, TN . . . 901-322-6640
Knouse Foods Co-Op Inc.
Peach Glen, PA . . . 717-677-8181
Koia
Los Angeles, CA
Kolb-Lena Bresse Bleu Inc
Lena, IL. . . . 815-369-4577

Kor Shots
Malibu, CA
Korea Ginseng Corp.
Cerritos, CA
Kozlowski Farms
Forestville, CA 800-473-2767
Kura Nutrition
Manchester, NH 603-217-2665
Le Bleu Corp
Advance, NC. 800-854-4471
Life Extension Foundation
Fort Lauderdale, FL 888-895-4771
Lifeway
Morton Grove, IL 877-281-3874
Lifewise Ingredients
Brookfield, IL 262-788-9141
Living Farms
Tracy, MN. 507-629-3517
Longreen Corp.
San Gabriel, CA 626-287-4700
Lucas Meyer
Decatur, IL 800-769-3660
Lukas Confections
York, PA 717-843-0921
Magnetic Springs
Columbus, OH 800-572-2990
Main Street Gourmet
Cuyahoga Falls, OH 800-678-6246
Maju Superfoods
San Diego, CA 619-736-0622
Manhattan Food Brands, LLC
Metuchen, NJ 732-906-2168
Maple Grove Farms Of Vermont
St Johnsbury, VT. 802-748-5141
Marsa Specialty Products
Vernon, CA 800-628-0500
Marsan Foods
Toronto, ON 416-755-9262
Masala Chai Company
Santa Cruz, CA 831-475-8881
Master Mix
Placentia, CA 714-524-1698
Mayway Corp
Oakland, CA 800-262-9929
Mccutcheon Apple Products
Frederick, MD. 800-888-7537
Meadow Brook Dairy Co
Erie, PA 800-352-4010
MegaFood
Manchester, NH 800-848-2542
Mei Shun Tofu Products Company
Chicago, IL 312-842-7000
Merlino Italian Baking Company
Kent, WA. 800-800-9490
Michigan Dairy LLC
Livonia, MI 734-367-5390
Michigan Desserts
Oak Park, MI. 800-328-8632
MicroSoy Corporation
Jefferson, IA 515-386-2100
Midwest Nut Co
Minneapolis, MN 800-328-5502
Mills Brothers Intl
Seattle, WA 206-575-3000
Monarch Beverage Company
Atlanta, GA. 800-241-3732
Morinaga Nutritional Foods, Inc.
Torrance, CA. 310-787-0200
Morningland Dairy Cheese Company
Mountain View, MO 417-855-0588
Mountain High Yogurt
Minneapolis, MN 866-964-4878
Mrs. Leeper's Pasta
Excelsior Springs, MO 800-848-5266
Mrs. Malibu Foods
Malibu, CA 800-677-6254
Mt Sterling Co-Op Creamery
Highland, WI 866-289-4628
Murray Cider Co Inc
Roanoke, VA. 540-977-9000
Mustard Seed
Central, SC 877-621-2591
Natural Balance
Englewood, CO. 800-624-4260
Natural Company
Baltimore, MD 410-628-1262
Natural Food Supplements Inc
Canoga Park, CA 818-341-3375
Natural Food World
Culver City, CA 310-836-7770
Nature Zen USA
Essex Junction, VT
Nature's Bounty Co.
Ronkonkoma, NY. 877-774-3361
Nature's Herbs
Merritt, BC 800-437-2257
Nature's Legacy Inc.
Hudson, MI. 517-448-2050
Nature's Plus
Melville, NY 800-645-9500
Naturex Inc
South Hackensack, NJ 201-440-5000
Nellson Candies Inc
Irwindale, CA 626-334-4508
Nestle USA Inc
Glendale, CA 800-225-2270
New Chapter
Brattleboro, VT. 800-543-7279
New England Country Bakers
Watertown, CT 800-225-3779
NewGem Products
Fife, WA 253-896-3089
Nomolas Corp
Woodmere, NY. 516-569-3093
Nootra Life
Norimoor Lic
Flushing, NY. 718-423-6667
North Country Natural Spring Water
Port Kent, NY. 518-834-9400
North Peace Apiaries
Fort St. John, BC. 250-785-4808
Now & Zen
Louisville, CO. 800-779-6383
NOW Foods
Bloomingdale, IL 888-669-3663
Noyes, P J
Lancaster, NH 800-522-2469
NuGo Nutrition
Oakmont, PA. 888-421-2032
Nush Foods
Salt Lake City, UT 801-953-1370
Nut Factory
Spokane Valley, WA 888-239-5288
Nutraceutical International
Park City, UT 800-669-8877
Nutrilabs
San Francisco, CA 877-468-8745
Nutrisport Pharmacal
Franklin, NJ 833-403-2861
Nutriwest
Douglas, WY. 800-443-3333
O'Boyle's Ice Cream Company
Bristol, PA. 215-788-3882
O'Donnell Formulas Inc
San Marcos, CA 800-736-1991
Ola Loa
San Francisco, CA 800-800-9550
Old Fashioned Natural Products
Santa Ana, CA 800-552-9045
Olde Tyme Mercantile
Arroyo Grande, CA. 805-489-7991
OMG! Superfoods
Rancho Dominguez, CA. 855-664-3663
Once Again Nut Butter
Nunda, NY 888-800-8075
Onnit Labs
Austin, TX. 855-666-4899
Oorganik
Houston, TX 281-240-7992
Optimum Nutrition
Aurora, IL. 800-763-3444
Organic Gourmet
Sherman Oaks, CA 800-400-7772
Osso Good, LLC
San Rafael, CA
Ota Tofu
Portland, OR 503-232-8947
OWYN
Fairfield, NJ 833-533-7061
Pappy's Sassafras Tea
Columbus Grove, OH 877-659-5110
Particle Dynamics
Saint Louis, MO 800-452-4682
Pecan Deluxe Candy Co
Dallas, TX. 800-733-3589
Pecoraro Dairy Products
Brooklyn, NY 718-388-2379
Peggy Lawton Kitchens
East Walpole, MA. 800-843-7325
Penta Manufacturing Company
Livingston, NJ. 973-740-2300
Perfect Foods Inc
Goshen, NY. 800-933-3288
Perry's Ice Cream Co Inc
Akron, NY. 800-873-7797
Phillips Syrup Corp
Cleveland, OH 800-350-8443
Pied-Mont/Dora
Anne Des Plaines, QC 800-363-8003
Pines International
Lawrence, KS 800-697-4637
Plainview Milk Products
Plainview, MN 800-356-5606
Pleasant View Dairy
Highland, IN 219-838-0155
Pleasoning Gourmet Seasonings
La Crosse, WI. 800-279-1614
Power of 3
Tenants Harbor, ME 888-211-7911
Premium Water
Kansas City, MO. 800-332-3332
Pro Form Labs
Orinda, CA 707-752-9010
Pro Portion Food
Sayville, NY 631-567-4494
Progenix Corporation
Wausau, WI. 800-233-3356
Proper-Chem
Dix Hills, NY 631-420-8000
Protein Research
Livermore, CA 800-948-1991
Protient
Woodland, CA. 651-638-2600
Purity Dairies LLC
Nashville, TN 615-244-1900
Quality Naturally Foods
City Of Industry, CA. 888-498-6986
Quong Hop & Company
S San Francisco, CA. 650-553-9900
R.J. Corr Naturals
Posen, IL. 708-389-4200
Ramos Orchards
Winters, CA 530-795-4748
Ramsen Inc
Lakeville, MN. 952-431-0400
Randal Optimal Nutrients
Santa Rosa, CA. 800-221-1697
RawFusion
Oxnard, CA. 888-852-3350
Regal Health Food
Chicago, IL 773-252-1044
Rinehart Meat Processing
Branson, MO. 417-869-2041
Rio Syrup Co
St Louis, MO. 800-325-7666
Roquette America Inc.
Geneva, IL. 630-463-9430
Royal Products
Scottsdale, AZ. 480-948-2509
Russo Farms
Vineland, NJ 856-692-5942
Sahadi Fine Foods Inc
Brooklyn, NY 800-724-2341
Sally Lane's Candy Farm
Paris, TN. 731-642-5801
Saratoga Spring Water Co
Saratoga Springs, NY 888-426-8642
Schneider's Dairy Inc
Pittsburgh, PA. 412-881-3525
Sells Best
Mishawaka, IN 800-837-8368
Setton International Foods
Commack, NY 800-227-4397
Shenk's Foods
Lancaster, PA 717-393-4240
Siren Snacks
San Francisco, CA
Sisler's Ice & Ice Cream
Ohio, IL. 888-891-3856
Sneaky Chef Foods, The
Boca Raton, FL. 561-757-6541
So Delicious Dairy Free
Springfield, OR. 866-388-7853
Solana Gold Organics
Sebastopol, CA 800-459-1121
Solnuts
Hudson, IA 800-648-3503
Source Naturals
Scotts Valley, CA 800-815-2333
Sovena USA Inc
Rome, NY. 315-797-7070
Staff Of Life Natural Foods
Santa Cruz, CA 831-423-8632
Star of the West Milling Co.
Frankenmuth, MI 989-652-9971

Subco Foods Inc
Sheboygan, WI 800-473-0757
Sunergia Soyfoods
Charlottesville, VA 800-693-5134
Sunfood
El Cajon, CA. 888-729-3663
Sunray Food Products Corporation
Bronx, NY. 718-548-2255
Sunsweet Growers Inc.
Yuba City, CA. 800-417-2253
Super Stores Industries
Turlock, CA 209-668-2100
Swagger Foods Corp
Vernon Hills, IL 847-913-1200
Swiss Premium Dairy Inc
Lebanon, PA 800-222-2129
Synergy
Moab, UT 800-804-3211
Terra Origin, Inc.
Hauppauge, NY 631-300-2306
The Coromega Company
Carlsbad, CA. 877-275-3725
The Valpo Velvet Shoppe
Valparaiso, IN 219-464-4141
Tigo+
FL 786-207-4772
Timber Crest Farms
Healdsburg, CA 888-766-4233
Toft Dairy Inc
Sandusky, OH 800-521-4606
Tomanetti Food Products Inc
Oakmont, PA. 800-875-3040
Tova Industries LLC
Louisville, KY 888-532-8682
Tropical Foods
Charlotte, NC 800-438-4470
Tropical Foods
Lithia Springs, GA 800-544-3762
Truth Bar LLC
Waltham, MA 888-886-8959
TruVibe Organics
Santa Monica, CA
Tu Me Beverage Company
CA. 818-237-5105
Tulkoff's Food Products Inc
Baltimore, MD 800-638-7343
Turveda
CA
Twinlab Corporation
Boca Raton, FL. 800-645-5626
TyRy Inc
Rocklin, CA 800-322-6325
Ultima Health Products Inc.
Cortland, OH. 888-663-8584
Unique Ingredients LLC
Gold Canyon, AZ 480-983-2498
Urban Moonshine
Burlington, VT 802-428-4707
Utzy, Inc.
Lake Geneva, WI 877-307-6142
Valley View Blueberries
Vancouver, WA. 360-892-2839
Vance's Foods
San Francisco, CA 415-621-1171
Varni Brothers/7-Up Bottling
Modesto, CA. 209-521-1777
Vaxa International
Tampa, FL. 877-622-8292
Ventre Packing Company
Syracuse, NY 315-463-2384
Venus Wafers Inc
Hingham, MA. 800-545-4538
Verday
New York, NY
VIP Foods
Flushing, NY. 718-821-5330
Vit-Best Nutrition
Tustin, CA. 714-832-9700
Vital Proteins LLC
Elk Grove Village, IL 224-544-9110
Vitality Works
Albuquerque, NM. 505-268-9950
Vitamer Laboratories
Irvine, CA 800-432-8355
Vitamins
Chicago, IL. 312-861-0700
Vitasoy USA
Woburn, MA. 800-848-2769
Vitatech Nutritional Sciences
Tustin, CA. 714-832-9700
Vive Organic
Venice, CA 877-774-9291

Vogue Cuisine Foods
Sunnyvale, CA 888-236-4144
Wah Yet Group
Hayward, CA 800-229-3392
Walden Farms
Linden, NJ. 800-229-1706
Wax Orchards
Seattle, WA 800-634-6132
Wellington Foods
Corona, CA 951-547-7000
Westin Foods
Omaha, NE 800-228-6098
White Rock Products Corp
Flushing, NY. 800-969-7625
Whitey's Ice Cream Inc
Moline, IL. 888-594-4839
Whole Herb Co
Sonoma, CA 707-935-1077
Wilke International Inc
Lenexa, KS 800-779-5545
Wilson's Fantastic Candy
Memphis, TN 901-767-1900
Wing Nien Food
Hayward, CA 510-487-8877
Winmix/Natural Care Products
Englewood, FL 941-475-7432
Wisconsin Specialty Protein
Madison, WI
World Flavors Inc
Warminster, PA. 215-672-4400
World Ginseng Ctr Inc
San Francisco, CA 800-747-8808
World Organics Corporation
Huntington Beach, CA 714-893-0017
Y Z Enterprises Inc
Maumee, OH. 800-736-8779
Yoshida Food Products Co
Portland, OR 800-653-1114

Low-Calorie Desserts

Eden Creamery
Los Angeles, CA
Wink Frozen Desserts
Stamford, CT. 516-323-5283

Sugar-Free Foods

American Instants Inc
Flanders, NJ 973-584-8811
Aunt Gussie Cookies & Crackers
Garfield, NJ. 800-422-6654
Bissinger's Handcrafted Chocolatier
St Louis, MO. 800-325-8881
California Custom Fruits
Baldwin Park, CA. 877-558-0056
Clemmy's
Randcho Mirage, CA 877-253-6698
Dresden Stollen Co USA
Albertson, NY. 516-746-5802
Eda's Sugar Free
Philadelphia, PA 215-324-3412
GKI Foods
Brighton, MI 248-486-0055
Gust John Foods & Products
Batavia, IL. 800-756-5886
Howard Foods Inc
Danvers, MA. 978-774-6207
Inn Maid Food
Lenox, MA 413-637-2732
International Brownie
East Weymouth, MA. 800-230-1588
Kinnikinnick Foods
Edmonton, AB 877-503-4466
Kiss My Keto
Los Angeles, CA. 310-765-1553
Main Street Gourmet
Cuyahoga Falls, OH 800-678-6246
Maple Grove Farms Of Vermont
St Johnsbury, VT. 802-748-5141
MATI Energy
Durham, NC 866-924-8005
Mccutcheon Apple Products
Frederick, MD. 800-888-7537
Michigan Desserts
Oak Park, MI. 800-328-8632
Mrs. Leeper's Pasta
Excelsior Springs, MO 800-848-5266
NuGo Nutrition
Oakmont, PA. 888-421-2032
Nui Foods
Anaheim, CA

Olde Tyme Mercantile
Arroyo Grande, CA. 805-489-7991
Perry's Ice Cream Co Inc
Akron, NY. 800-873-7797
Sally Lane's Candy Farm
Paris, TN 731-642-5801
Sells Best
Mishawaka, IN 800-837-8368
Setton International Foods
Commack, NY 800-227-4397
Shenk's Foods
Lancaster, PA 717-393-4240
Silver Tray Cookies
Fort Lauderdale, FL 305-883-0800
The Sola Company
Houston, TX 800-277-1486
Tova Industries LLC
Louisville, KY 888-532-8682
Unique Beverage Company
Everett, WA. 425-267-0959

Gluten-Free

3 Gyros Inc
Tecumseh, ON. 519-737-0389
Alicita-Salsa
Great Falls, VA 703-340-5323
American Natural & Organic
Fremont, CA 510-440-1044
American Specialty Foods
Lancaster, PA 800-335-6663
Amrita Snacks
Hartsdale, NY 888-728-7779
Andean Naturals LLC
Foster City, CA 650-303-1780
Antoni Ravioli Co
North Massapequa, NY 800-783-0350
Ariel Natural Foods
Bellevue, WA 425-637-3345
Aunt Aggie De's Pralines
Sinton, TX. 800-333-9354
Aunt Gussie Cookies & Crackers
Garfield, NJ. 800-422-6654
Avena Foods Ltd.
Regina, SK 306-757-3663
Beanitos
Austin, TX. 512-609-8017
Beetnik Foods, LLC
Austin, TX. 512-548-8228
Boulder Granola
Boulder, CO 303-443-1136
Brothers Sauces
Fort Worth, TX 817-821-3374
Buns & Roses Organic Wholegrain Bakery
Edmonton, AB 780-438-0098
Chef Tim Foods, LLC
Etters, PA 717-802-0350
Cherrybrook Kitchen
Burlington, MA. 866-458-8225
Clemmy's
Randcho Mirage, CA 877-253-6698
Cup 4 Cup LLC
Napa, CA. 707-754-4263
D I Mfg LLC
Omaha, NE 402-330-5650
Delicious Without Gluten
Dollard Des Ormeaux, QC 514-542-3943
Dharma Bars
Dowd & Rogers
San Clemente, CA. 800-232-8619
Dream Foods Intl
Santa Monica, CA. 310-315-5739
Earth Source Organics
Vista, CA. 760-734-1867
Eat Real Snacks USA
Marietta, GA. 404-432-0842
Emmy's Organics
Ithaca, NY. 855-463-6697
Ener-G Foods
Seattle, WA. 800-331-5222
Enjoy Life Foods
Chicago, IL 888-503-6569
FAGE USA Dairy Ind Inc
Johnstown, NY 866-962-5912
Falafel Republic
Needham Heights, MA 781-878-6027
Feridies
Courtland, VA. 800-544-0896
Figamajigs
San Mateo, CA 650-227-3830
Firebird Artisan Mills
Harvey, ND. 701-324-4330

Foods Alive
Angola, IN. 260-488-4497
French Meadow Bakery & Cafe
Minneapolis, MN 612-870-7855
Garden Spot Distributors
New Holland, PA 800-829-5100
Glutino
Laval, QC 800-363-3438
Go Max Go Foods
Gold Mine Natural Food Company
Poway, CA 800-475-3663
Gopicnic Inc
Chicago, IL. 773-328-2490
Gracious Gourmet
Bridgewater, CT 860-350-1213
Grain-Free JK Gourmet, Inc.
Toronto, ON 800-608-0465
Greater Knead, The
Bensalem, PA 267-522-8523
GS Gelato & Desserts Inc
Fort Walton Bch, FL. 888-435-2767
Healing Home Foods
Pound Ridge, NY 914-764-1303
Hearthy Foods
Los Angeles, CA. 213-372-5093
Hodgson Mill Inc
Effingham, IL 800-347-0198
Honey Mama's
Portland, OR. 888-506-2627
Integrative Flavors
Michigan City, IN. 800-837-7687
Jayone Foods Inc
Paramount, CA 562-633-7400
Jilz Gluten Free
Ventura, CA. 805-585-5297
Jovial Foods
North Stonington, CT 877-642-0644
Julian Bakery
Oceanside, CA 760-721-5200
Kateri Foods
Hopkins, MN 800-330-8351
Kay's Naturals, Inc.
Clara City, MN 866-873-5499
Kayco
Bayonne, NJ 718-369-4600
Kedem
Bayonne, NJ 718-369-4600
Kerala Curry
Pittsboro, NC 919-545-9401
Kerri Kreations
Santa Cruz, CA. 831-429-5129
Kind Snacks
New York, NY 855-884-5463
King Arthur Flour
Norwich, VT. 800-827-6836
Kinnikinnick Foods
Edmonton, AB 877-503-4466
Koegel Meats Inc
Flint, MI 810-238-3685
Lifeway
Morton Grove, IL 877-281-3874
Lisa Shively's Kitchen Helpers, LLC
Eden, NC. 336-623-7511
Litehouse Foods
Sandpoint, ID 800-669-3169
Little Duck Organics
New York, NY 877-458-1321
LivBar
Salem, OR. 971-239-1209
Luna & Larry's Coconut Bliss
Eugene, OR. 541-345-0020
Maple Grove Farms Of Vermont
St Johnsbury, VT. 802-748-5141
MariGold Foods
Willis, TX 936-344-0444
Marion's Smart Delights
Arlington, VA 703-593-3450
Marjie's Plantain Foods, Inc.
New York, NY 908-627-5627
Mary's Gone Crackers
Gridley, CA. 888-258-1250
Mediterranean Snack Food Co
Boonton, NJ 973-402-2644
Mercer's Dairy
Boonville, NY. 866-637-2377
Mikey's
. . . . 480-696-2483
Mini Pops Inc
Stoughton, MA 781-436-5864
Minsa Corp
Lubbock, TX. 800-852-8291
Modern Day Masala, LLC
Marietta, GA 866-611-3757
Mom's Gourmet, LLC
Chagrin Falls, OH. 440-564-9702
Moo Chocolate/Organic Children's Chocolate LLC
Cos Cob, CT 203-561-8864
Mrs. Leeper's Pasta
Excelsior Springs, MO 800-848-5266
Mrs. May's Naturals
Carson, CA 877-677-6297
Native American Natural Foods
Kyle, SD 800-416-7212
Nature's Hilights
Chico, CA. 800-313-6454
Now & Zen
Louisville, CO. 800-779-6383
NOW Foods
Bloomingdale, IL 888-669-3663
Nu-World Amaranth Inc
Naperville, IL 630-369-6851
Omega Nutrition
Bellingham, WA 800-661-3529
Oregon Bark
Portland, OR
Outta the Park Eats
Cary, NC 919-462-0012
Pamela's Products
Ukiah, CA. 707-462-6605
Pineland Farms
New Gloucester, ME. 207-688-4539
Plocky's Fine Snacks
Hinsdale, IL 630-323-8888
Pocino Foods
City Of Industry, CA. 800-345-0150
Preferred Brands Inc
Stamford, CT. 800-827-8900
Purely Elizabeth
Boulder, CO 720-242-7525
Real Coconut Co. Inc., The
CA
Red Rose Trading Company
Lancaster, PA 717-293-7833
Rhythm Superfoods
Austin, TX. 512-441-5667
Rice Innovations
Fontana, CA 909-823-8230
Rigoni Di Asiago
Miami, FL. 305-470-7583
Root Cellar Preserves
Wellesley, MA. 781-864-7440
San-J International Inc
Henrico, VA 800-446-5500
Sensible Foods LLC
Santa Rosa, CA. 888-222-0170
Soozy's Grain-Free
New York, NY
Soynut Butter Co
Glenview, IL. 847-635-9960
Sprecher Brewing Co
Milwaukee, WI. 888-650-2739
Suzanne's Specialties
New Brunswick, NJ 800-762-2135
Swapples
Washington, DC
Tamarind Tree
Neshanic Station, NJ. 800-432-8733
The Amazing Chickpea
St. Louis Park, MN. 612-548-1099
The Art of Broth, LLC
CA. 818-715-9320
The Good Crisp Company
The Piping Gourmets
. . . . 786-233-8660
The Power of Fruit
Lebanon, NJ 908-450-9806
The Safe + Fair Food Company
Chicago, IL
The Soulfull Project
Camden, NJ
The Toasted Oat Bakehouse
Columbus, OH
Thinkthin, LLC
Los Angeles, CA. 866-988-4465
This Bar Saves Lives, LLC
Culver City, CA 310-730-5060
Thoughtful Food
Lafayette, CA 510-910-2581
Thunderbird Real Food Bar
Austin, TX. 512-383-8334
Tierra Farm
Valatie, NY 519-392-8300
Tribe 9 Foods
Madison, WI. 608-257-7216
Trumps Food Interest
Vancouver, BC 604-732-8473
Twin Hens
Princeton, NJ. 908-925-9040
Ultimate Biscotti
Eugene, OR. 541-344-8220
UnReal Brands
Boston, MA
Urban Foods LLC
Sacramento, CA 916-372-3663
Van's International Foods
Torrance, CA. 310-320-8611
West Thomas Partners, LLC
Grand Rapids, MI 616-755-8432
Wholesome Bakery
San Francisco, CA 415-343-5414
Wrawp
Pomona, CA 855-972-9748
Yai's Thai
Denver, CO
Yogavive
Tiburon, CA 415-366-6226

Gourmet & Specialty Foods

Gourmet & Specialty Foods

4th & Heart
CA. 213-880-2559
Aketta
Al Safa Halal
New York City, NY. 800-268-8147
Alexian Pâtés
Neptune, NJ 800-927-9473
Alfonso Gourmet Pasta
Pompano Beach, FL 800-370-7278
Amaranth Resources
Albert Lea, MN. 800-842-6689
American Lecithin Company
Oxford, CT 800-364-4416
Ames International Inc
Fife, WA 888-469-2637
Ancora Coffee Roasters
Madison, WI 800-260-0217
Andre-Boudin Bakeries
San Francisco, CA 415-882-1849
Annie's Homegrown
Berkeley, CA. 800-288-1089
Applecreek Speciality Foods
Lexington, KY 800-747-8871
Arbor Hill Grapery & Winery
Naples, NY 800-554-7553
Arbuckle Coffee Roasters
Tucson, AZ 800-533-8278
Art CoCo Chocolate Company
Geneva, IL. 877-232-9901
Ashland Plantation Gourmet
Bunkie, LA 318-346-6600
Ashman Manufacturing & Distributing Company
Virginia Beach, VA. 800-641-9924
Avary Farms
Odessa, TX 432-332-4139
Babe Farms Inc
Santa Maria, CA 800-648-6772
Barhyte Specialty Foods Inc
Pendleton, OR. 800-227-4983
Barrie House Gourmet Coffee
Elmsford, NY 800-876-2233
Basketfull
New York, NY 800-645-4438
Bay Shore Chowders & Bisques
Fall River, MA 888-675-6892
Bella Cucina
Atlanta, GA. 866-350-9040
Berardi's Fresh Roast
Cleveland, OH 800-876-9109
Biagio's Banquets
Chicago, IL. 800-392-2837
Big Steer
Houston, TX 800-421-4951
Biscotti & Co.
White Plains, NY 914-682-2165
Blue Crab Bay
Melfa, VA 800-221-2722
Boetje Foods Inc
Rock Island, IL. 877-726-3853
Boston's Best Coffee Roasters
South Easton, MA. 800-898-8393
Boyd's Coffee Co
Portland, OR. 800-735-2878

Brad's Taste of New York
Floral Park, NY....516-354-9004
Brandmeyer Popcorn Co
Ankeny, IA....800-568-8276
Brass Ladle Products
Concordville, PA....800-955-2353
Brateka Enterprises
Ocala, FL....877-549-3227
Brazos Legends
Houston, TX....800-882-6253
Breaktime Snacks
Paramount, CA....800-677-1968
Bremner Biscuit Company
Denver, CO....866-972-6879
British American Tea & Coffee
Durham, NC....919-471-1357
Brutocao Cellars
Hopland, CA....800-433-3689
BTS Company/Hail Caesar Dressings
Nashville, TN....800-617-8899
Bubbles Baking Co
Van Nuys, CA....800-777-4970
Buckmaster Coffee Co
Hillsboro, OR....800-962-9148
Buona Vita Inc
Bridgeton, NJ....856-453-7972
Busseto Foods
Fresno, CA....800-628-2633
Buxton Foods
Buxton, ND....800-726-8057
Buzzn Bee Farms
West Palm Beach, FL....561-881-1551
Byrd Cookie
Savannah, GA....800-291-2973
C W Resources Inc
New Britain, CT....860-229-7700
C.C. Graber Company
Ontario, CA....800-996-5483
Cafe Sark's Gourmet Coffee
Yorba Linda, CA....626-579-6000
Caffe D'Oro
Chino, CA....800-200-5005
California Balsamic Inc
Ukiah, CA....888-644-5127
California Oils Corp
Richmond, CA....800-225-6457
Calistoga Food Company
New York, NY....212-879-4940
Caltex Foods
Canoga Park, CA....800-522-5839
Cape Cod Specialty Foods
Sagamore, MA....508-888-7099
Cappuccine
Corona, CA....800-511-3127
Carando Gourmet Frozen Foods
Agawam, MA....888-227-2636
Carl Buddig & Co.
Homewood, IL....888-633-5684
Carolyn's Gourmet
Concord, MA....800-656-2940
Cateraid Inc
Howell, MI....800-508-8217
Cedarlane Foods
Carson, CA....800-826-3322
Champignon North America Inc
Englewood Cliffs, NJ....201-871-7211
Chatz Roasting Co
Ceres, CA....209-541-1100
Chef Hans' Gourmet Foods
Monroe, LA....800-890-4267
Chef Zachary's Gourmet Blended Spices
Detroit, MI....313-226-0000
Chef's Pride Gifts LLC
Taylor, MI....800-878-1800
Cherchies
Malvern, PA....800-644-1980
Cheryl's Cookies
Westerville, OH....800-443-8124
Chewys Rugulach
San Diego, CA....800-241-3456
Chex Finer Foods Inc
Mansfield, MA....800-227-8114
Chocolate Street of Hartville
Hartville, OH....888-853-5904
Chocolates by Mark
Houston, TX....832-736-2626
Choice of Vermont
Destin, FL....800-444-6261
Christie's
Stroughton, MA....781-341-3341
Christopher Ranch LLC
Gilroy, CA....408-847-1100
Citterio USA
Freeland, PA....800-435-8888
Clara Foods
San Francisco, CA
Clem's Seafood & Specialties
Buckner, KY....502-222-7571
Clement's Pastry Shops Inc
Hyattsville, MD....301-277-6300
Cloud Nine
Claremont, CA....909-624-3147
Coffee Masters
Spring Grove, IL....800-334-6485
Cold Fusion Foods
West Hollywood, CA....310-287-3244
Colony Brands Inc
Monroe, WI....800-544-9036
Colorado Popcorn Co
Sterling, CO....866-491-2676
Colors Gourmet Pizza
Vista, CA....760-597-1400
Coltsfoot/Golden Eagle Herb
Grants Pass, OR....800-736-8749
Conifer Foods
Medina, WA....800-588-9160
Cook's Gourmet Foods
Riverside, CA....951-352-5700
Cookie Tree Bakeries
Salt Lake City, UT....801-268-2253
Cordon Bleu International
Anjou, QC....800-363-1182
Corfu Foods Inc
Bensenville, IL....630-595-2510
Corn Popper
Tulsa, OK....918-250-9317
Cosentino Winery
Napa, CA....800-764-1220
Costa Deano's Gourmet Foods
Canton, OH....800-337-2823
CostaDeano's Enterprises
Canton, OH....330-453-1555
Cottonwood Canyon Vineyard
Santa Maria, CA....805-937-8463
Cowboy Caviar
Berkeley, CA....877-509-1796
Creative Cotton
Northbrook, IL....847-291-4128
Creole Delicacies Gourmet Shop
New Orleans, LA....504-525-9508
Crown Pacific Fine Foods
Kent, WA....425-251-8750
Crustacean Foods
Los Angeles, CA....866-263-2625
CTC Manufacturing
Calgary, AB....800-668-7677
Cucina & Amore
San Pablo, CA....510-964-4838
Cugino's Gourmet Foods
Crystal Lake, IL....888-592-8446
Culinary Masters Corporation
Alpharetta, GA....800-261-5261
Cyclone Enterprises Inc
Houston, TX....281-872-0087
Dave's Gourmet
San Rafael, CA....800-758-0372
Davis Bakery & Delicatessen
Cleveland, OH....216-292-3060
Dean Distributors, Inc.
Burlingame, CA....800-792-0816
Deep Foods Inc
Union, NJ....908-810-7500
Delftree Corp
North Adams, MA....800-243-3742
DeMedici Imports
Elizabeth, NJ....908-372-0965
Deneen Foods
Santa Fe, NM....800-866-4695
Desserts by David Glass
South Windsor, CT....860-462-7520
Diana's Specialty Foods
Pingree Grove, IL....847-683-1200
Dinkel's Bakery Inc
Chicago, IL....800-822-8817
Dobake
Oakland, CA....800-834-3134
Dole & Bailey Inc
Woburn, MA....781-935-1234
Dolores Canning Co Inc
Los Angeles, CA....323-263-9155
Don Alfonso Foods
Austin, TX....800-456-6100
Dorina So-Good Inc
Union, IL....815-923-2144
Dowd & Rogers
San Clemente, CA....800-232-8619
Dr. Tima Natural Products
Los Angeles, CA....310-472-2181
Dufour Pastry Kitchens Inc
Bronx, NY....800-439-1282
Dumbee Gourmet Foods
Albany, GA....800-569-1657
E Waldo Ward & Son Marmalades
Sierra Madre, CA....800-355-9273
Eagle Coffee Co Inc
Baltimore, MD....410-685-5893
East Indies Coffee & Tea Co
Lebanon, PA....800-220-2326
East Shore Specialty Foods
Hartland, WI....800-236-1069
Egg Roll Fantasy
Auburn, CA....530-887-9197
Eilenberger Bakeries
Palestine, TX....800-831-2544
Endangered Species Chocolate
Indianapolis, IN....800-293-0160
Enjoy Life Foods
Chicago, IL....888-503-6569
Eweberry Farms
Brownsville, OR....541-466-3470
Exo Inc.
Brooklyn, NY....818-744-4140
Fairwinds Gourmet Coffee
Lincoln, CA....800-829-1300
Fantasy Chocolates
Boynton Beach, FL....800-804-4962
Fantis Foods Inc
Carlstadt, NJ....201-933-6200
Fillo Factory, The
Northvale, NJ....800-653-4556
Finlays
Lincoln, RI....800-288-6272
Fiorucci Foods USA Inc
S Chesterfield, VA....800-524-7775
First District Association
Litchfield, MN....320-693-3236
Fliinko
South Dartmouth, MA....800-266-9609
Food For Thought Inc
Honor, MI....231-326-5444
Fox Hollow
Crestwood, KY....502-241-8621
Fox Meadow Farm
Chester Springs, PA....610-827-9731
Fox's Fine Foods
Laguna Beach, CA....888-522-3697
France Delices
Montreal, QC....800-663-1365
Fratello Coffee Roasters
Calgary, AB....800-465-7227
Frontera Foods
Chicago, IL....800-509-4441
Fruit Ranch Inc
Milwaukee, WI....800-433-3289
Fun Foods
East Rutherford, NJ....800-507-2782
Future Bakery & Cafe
Toronto, ON....416-231-1491
Gadsden Coffee/Caffe
Arivaca, AZ....888-514-5282
Geneva Food Products
Sanford, FL....800-240-2326
Gift Basket Supply World
Jacksonville, FL....800-786-4438
Gillies Coffee
Brooklyn, NY....800-344-5526
Giovanni's Appetizing Food Co
Richmond, MI....586-727-9355
GKI Foods
Brighton, MI....248-486-0055
Glacial Ridge Foods
Starbuck, MN....320-239-2215
Golden Malted
South Bend, IN....888-596-4040
Golden Moon Tea
Bristow, VA....877-327-5473
Golden West Specialty Foods
Brisbane, CA....800-584-4481
Goldstar Brands LLC
Tucker, GA....888-296-7191
Good Fortunes & Edible Art
Canoga Park, CA....800-644-9474
Good Health Natural Foods
Greensboro, NC....336-285-0735
Gourmet Market
Knoxville, TN....865-330-0123

Gourmet Products
Thomaston, CT....860-283-5147
Goya Foods Inc.
Jersey City, NJ....201-348-4900
Grace Tea Co
Acton, MA....978-635-9500
Granowska's
Toronto, ON....416-533-7755
Great American Popcorn Works of Pennsylvania
Telford, PA....855-542-2676
Green Mountain Gringo
Winston-Salem, NC....888-875-3111
Greenwell Farms Inc
Kealakekua, HI....888-592-5662
Grey Owl Foods
Grand Rapids, MN....800-527-0172
Grounds For Thought
Bowling Green, OH....419-354-3266
GWB Foods Corporation
Brooklyn, NY....877-977-7610
Habby Habanero's Food Products
Jacksonville, FL....904-333-9758
Hale and Hearty Soups
New York, NY....212-255-2433
Hancock Gourmet Lobster Co
Topsham, ME....207-725-1855
Happy & Healthy Products Inc
Boca Raton, FL....561-367-0739
Harbar LLC
Canton, MA....800-881-7040
Harrington's of Vermont
Richmond, VT
Harrison Napa Valley
Saint Helena, CA....707-963-8762
Hawthorne Valley Farm
Ghent, NY....518-672-7500
Hearthstone Whole Grain Bakery
Bozeman, MT....800-757-7919
Hendricks Apiaries
Englewood, CO....303-789-3209
Heritage Fancy Foods Marketing
Erlanger, KY....859-282-3782
Hialeah Products Co
Hollywood, FL....800-923-3379
Hickory Baked Ham Co
Castle Rock, CO....303-688-2633
Hickory Farms
Maumee, OH....800-753-8558
High Liner Foods Inc.
Lunenburg, NS....902-634-8811
Hollman Foods
Des Moines, IA....888-926-2879
Homestead Baking Co
Rumford, RI....800-556-7216
Honey Acres
Neosho, WI....920-474-4411
House of Coffee Beans
Houston, TX....800-422-1799
Humphrey's Market
Springfield, IL....800-747-6328
Hungry Sultan
Lake Forest, CA....949-215-0000
Hunt Country Foods Inc
Marshall, VA....540-364-2622
Hye Cuisine
Del Rey, CA....559-834-3000
Hye Quality Bakery
Fresno, CA....877-445-1778
Impromtu Gourmet
Owings Mills, MD....877-632-5766
Improved Nature
Gardner, NC
Indian Foods Company, Inc.
Osseo, MN....866-331-7684
Indigo Coffee Roasters
Florence, MA....800-447-5450
Intermountain Canola Cargill
Minneapolis, MN....800-822-6652
International Brownie
East Weymouth, MA....800-230-1588
International Trading Company
Houston, TX....713-224-5901
Ivy Foods
Phoenix, AZ....877-223-5459
J.A.M.B. Low Carb Distributor
Pompano Beach, FL....800-708-6738
J.B. Peel Coffee Roasters
Red Hook, NY....800-231-7372
J.N. Bech
Elk Rapids, MI....800-232-4583
James Frasinetti & Sons
Sacramento, CA....916-383-2444

Jason & Son Specialty Foods
Rancho Cordova, CA....800-810-9093
Jay Shah Foods
Mississauga, ON....905-696-0172
Jeremiah's Pick Coffee Co
San Francisco, CA....877-537-3642
Jim's Cheese Pantry
Waterloo, WI....800-345-3571
Jodyana Corporation
Miami, FL....888-563-5282
Joy's Specialty Foods
Mancos, CO....800-831-5697
Joyva Corp
Brooklyn, NY....718-497-0170
Just Desserts
Fairfield, CA....415-780-6860
Kay Foods Co
Detroit, MI....313-393-1100
KD Canners Inc
Mississauga, ON....905-602-1825
Kelly Gourmet Foods Inc
San Francisco, CA....415-648-9200
Kennedy Gourmet
Glendale Heights, IL....800-729-8116
Kerry Foodservice
Mansfield, OH....800-533-2722
Kevton Gourmet Tea
Streetman, TX....888-538-8668
Keystone Coffee Co
San Jose, CA....408-998-2221
Kids Kookie Company
San Clemente, CA....800-350-7577
Knese Enterprise
Bellerose, NY....516-354-9004
Knudsen Candy
Hayward, CA....800-736-6887
Koegel Meats Inc
Flint, MI....810-238-3685
Kokopelli's Kitchen
Phoenix, AZ....888-943-9802
Kolb-Lena Bresse Bleu Inc
Lena, IL....815-369-4577
Kornfections
Chantilly, VA....800-469-8886
Krinos Foods
Bronx, NY....718-729-9000
L & S Packing Co
Farmingdale, NY....800-286-6487
L'Esprit De Campagne
Berryville, VA....800-692-8008
L.A. Libations
El Segundo, CA
La Cookie
Houston, TX....713-784-2722
La Vigne Enterprises
Fallbrook, CA....760-723-9997
Larosa Bakery Inc
Shrewsbury, NJ....800-527-6722
Laska Stuff
Rochester, MI....248-652-8473
Leech Lake Wild Rice
Deer River, MN....877-246-0620
Lesley Elizabeth Inc
Lapeer, MI....800-684-3300
Lindsay Farms
Pike Road, AL....800-243-4608
Live A Little Gourmet Foods
Oakland, CA....888-744-2300
Lodi Nut Company
Lodi, CA....800-234-6887
Lotus Brands
Twin Lakes, WI....800-824-6396
Louisiana Fish Fry Products
Baton Rouge, LA....800-356-2905
Louisiana Gourmet Enterprises
Houma, LA....800-328-5586
Love Creek Orchards
Medina, TX....800-449-0882
Lovebiotics LLC
Los Osos, CA
M&L Gourmet Ice Cream
Baltimore, MD....410-276-4880
M. Marion & Company
Santa Rosa, CA....707-836-0551
Mad Chef Enterprise
Mentor, OH....800-951-2433
Mad Will's Food Company
Auburn, CA....888-275-9455
Madhava Natural Sweeteners
Boulder, CO....800-530-2900
Madrona Specialty Foods LLC
Seattle, WA....425-656-2997

Magic Ice Products
Cincinnati, OH....800-776-7923
Magnum Coffee Roastery
Nunica, MI....888-937-5282
Main Street Gourmet
Cuyahoga Falls, OH....800-678-6246
Mama Rose's Gourmet Foods
Phoenix, AZ....855-809-2848
Mama Vida's Inc
Randallstown, MD....877-521-0742
Mancini Packing Co
Zolfo Springs, FL....800-741-1778
Manitok Food & Gifts
Callaway, MN....800-726-1863
Maple Leaf Foods International
North York, ON....800-268-3708
Marantha Natural Foods
San Francisco, CA....866-972-6879
Marcel et Henri Charcuterie Francaise
South San Francisco, CA....800-227-6436
Mardi Gras
Verona, NJ....973-857-3777
Marich Confectionery
Hollister, CA....800-624-7055
Marin Food Specialties
Byron, CA....925-634-6126
Market Square Food Co.
Park City, IL....800-232-2299
Marukai Market
Gardena, CA....310-660-6300
MarySue.com
Baltimore, MD....800-662-2639
Meat-O-Mat Corp
Brooklyn, NY....718-965-7250
Mendocino Mustard
Fort Bragg, CA....800-964-2270
Merlino Italian Baking Company
Kent, WA....800-800-9490
Mills Brothers Intl
Seattle, WA....206-575-3000
Minnestalgia Foods LLC
Mcgregor, MN....800-328-6731
Miracapo Pizza
Elk Grove Village, IL....847-631-3500
Modern Gourmet Foods
Irvine, CA....949-250-3129
Morningland Dairy Cheese Company
Mountain View, MO....417-855-0588
Mother Earth Enterprises
New York, NY....866-436-7688
Mrs Auld's Gourmet Foods Inc
Reno, NV....800-322-8537
Mrs. Leeper's Pasta
Excelsior Springs, MO....800-848-5266
MSRF, Inc.
Chicago, IL....773-227-1115
Mt. Olympus Specialty Foods
Westminster, MD....410-848-7080
Mt. Olympus Specialty Foods
Buffalo, NY....716-874-0771
Murvest
Fort Lauderdale, FL....954-772-6440
Mustard Seed
Central, SC....877-621-2591
Nancy's Specialty Foods
Newark, CA....510-494-1100
National Foods
Kansas City, MO....620-624-1851
National Importers
Richmond, BC....888-894-6464
Natural Exotic Tropicals
Pompano Beach, FL....800-756-5267
Natural Intentions, Inc.
Folsom, CA
Natural Quick Foods
Seattle, WA....206-365-5757
Nature's Finest Products
Dallas, TX....800-237-5205
Nell Baking Company
Kenedy, TX....800-215-9190
Neshaminy Valley Natural Foods
Warminster, PA....215-443-5545
Nest Eggs
Chicago, IL....773-525-4952
New Canaan Farms
Dripping Springs, TX....800-727-5267
Newmarket Foods
Petaluma, CA....707-778-3400
Niche Import Co
Cedar Knolls, NJ....800-548-6882
Nina's Gourmet Dip
Mc Lean, VA....703-356-1667

North American Enterprises
Tucson, AZ 800-817-8666
Northern Flair Foods
Mound, MN 888-530-4453
Northwoods Candy Emporium
Branson, MO. 417-332-1010
Nostalgic Specialty Foods
Boca Raton, FL 561-391-8600
Nueske's Applewood Smoked Meat
Wittenberg, WI 800-720-1153
Nutty Bavarian
Sanford, FL 800-382-4788
OH Chocolate
Seattle, WA 206-329-8777
Olde Tyme Mercantile
Arroyo Grande, CA. 805-489-7991
Oregon Hill Farms
St Helens, OR 800-243-4541
Oregon Pride
The Dalles, OR 888-697-4767
Organic Gourmet
Sherman Oaks, CA 800-400-7772
Organic Nectars LLC
Malden On Hudson, NY. 845-246-0506
Orleans Packing Co
Hyde Park, MA 617-361-6611
P & M Staiger Vineyard
Boulder Creek, CA 831-338-0172
Pacific Westcoast Foods
Beaverton, OR 800-874-9333
Palmetto Pigeon Plant
Sumter, SC 803-775-1204
Palmieri Food Products
New Haven, CT 800-845-5447
Panola Pepper Co
Lake Providence, LA 800-256-3013
Papa Dean's Popcorn
San Antonio, TX. 877-855-7272
Paradise Products Corporation
Boca Raton, FL 800-826-1235
Parma Sausage Products
Pittsburgh, PA 877-294-4207
Parny Gourmet
Miami, FL 305-798-5177
Pastry Chef
Pawtucket, RI 800-639-8606
Pati-Petite Cookies Inc
Bridgeville, PA 800-253-5805
Paulaur Corp
Cranbury, NJ. 609-395-8844
Paulsen Foods
Atlanta, GA. 404-873-1804
Peanut Patch Gift Shop
Courtland, VA 800-544-0896
Pearl Coffee Co
Akron, OH. 800-822-5282
Peerless Coffee & Tea
Oakland, CA 800-310-5662
Pelican Bay Ltd.
Dunedin, FL 800-826-8982
Phipps Desserts
North York, ON. 416-391-5800
Picard Peanuts
Waterdown, ON 888-244-7688
Pickwick Catfish Farm
Counce, TN. 731-689-3805
PJ's Coffee & Tea
Covington, LA 800-527-1055
Plaidberry Company
Vista, CA. 760-727-5403
Plaza de Espana Gourmet
Sunny Isles Beach, FL 305-971-3468
Pontiac Coffee Break
Waterford, MI 248-332-6333
POP Fishing & Marine
Honolulu, HI. 808-537-2905
Popcorn Connection
North Hollywood, CA 800-852-2676
Popcorner
Swansea, IL. 618-277-2676
Porinos Gourmet Food
Central Falls, RI 800-826-3938
Prairie Thyme LTD
Santa Fe, NM 800-869-0009
Premium Brands
Bardstown, KY 502-348-0081
Prince of Peace
Hayward, CA 800-732-2328
Private Harvest
El Dorado Hills, CA 916-933-7080
Pulmuone Foods USA Inc.
Fullerton, CA 800-588-7782
Pure Planet
Rancho Dominguez, CA. 800-695-2017
Purely American
Norfolk, VA. 800-359-7873
Purity Farms
La Farge, WI 877-211-4819
R C Fine Foods Inc
Hillsborough, NJ. 800-526-3953
R L Schreiber Inc
Ft Lauderdale, FL 800-624-8777
Rabbit Barn
Turlock, CA. 209-632-1123
Rainbow Valley Frozen Yogurt
White Lake, MI. 800-979-8669
Rainforest Company
Maryland Heights, MO. 314-344-1000
Rao's Specialty Foods Inc
New York, NY 212-269-0151
Raymond-Hadley Corporation
Spencer, NY 800-252-5220
Reading Coffee Roasters
Birdsboro, PA 800-331-6713
Real Coconut Co. Inc., The
CA
Restaurant Lulu Gourmet Products
San Francisco, CA 888-693-5800
Rich Products Corp
Buffalo, NY. 800-828-2021
Righetti Specialties Inc
Santa Maria, CA 800-268-1041
Rio Trading Company
Baltimore, MD 443-384-2500
Robert Rothschild Farm
Cincinnati, OH 800-222-9966
Ron Son Foods Inc
Swedesboro, NJ 856-241-7333
Rosmarino Foods/R.Z. Humbert Company
Odessa, FL 888-926-9053
Rossi Pasta LTD
Marietta, OH. 800-227-6774
Rowena
Norfolk, VA. 800-627-8699
Royal Baltic LTD
Brooklyn, NY 718-385-8300
Royal Palm Popcorn Company
Edison, NJ. 800-526-8865
Rubschlager Baking Corp
. 800-661-7246
Rudolph's Specialty Bakery
Toronto, ON 800-268-1589
Russ & Daughters
New York, NY 800-787-7229
Russian Chef
New York, NY 212-249-1550
Saguaro Food Products
Tucson, AZ 800-732-2447
Sambets Cajun Deli
Austin, TX. 800-472-6238
San Francisco Popcorn Works
San Francisco, CA 800-777-2676
San Gennaro Foods Inc
Kent, WA. 800-462-1916
Sandridge Food Corp
Medina, OH. 800-627-2523
Santa Barbara Olive Company
Santa Barbara, CA 800-624-4896
Santa Barbara Salsa
Oceanside, CA 800-748-5523
Santa Fe Seasons
Belen, NM. 800-866-4695
Sardinha's Sausage
Somerset, MA. 800-678-0178
Sassafras Enterprises Inc
Chicago, IL 800-537-4941
Savannah Cinnamon & Cookie Company
Bradenton, FL. 800-288-0854
Schwan's Food Service Inc.
Marshall, MN 877-302-7426
Scooty's Wholesome Foods
Boulder, CO 303-440-4025
Selma's Cookies
Apopka, FL. 800-992-6654
Senor Felix's Gourmet Mexican
Baldwin Park, CA. 626-960-2800
Serranos Salsa
Austin, TX. 512-328-9200
Sfoglia Fine Pastas & Gourmet
Freeland, WA 360-331-4080
Shady Grove Orchards
Onalaska, WA 360-985-7033
Sheila's Select Gourmet Recipe
Heber City, UT 800-516-7286
Shine Foods Inc
Torrance, CA. 310-533-6010
Signature Foods
Pendergrass, DR 706-693-0098
Silver Palate Kitchens
Cresskill, NJ 201-568-0110
Simply Divine
New York, NY 212-541-7300
Simpson & Vail
Brookfield, CT 800-282-8327
Sonoma Gourmet
Sonoma, CA 707-939-3700
Southern Gold Honey Co
Vidor, TX 808-899-2494
Southern Heritage Coffee Company
Indianapolis, IN 800-486-1198
Southern Season
Chapel Hill, NC 877-929-7133
Southern Style Nuts
Denison, TX 903-463-3161
Specialty Coffee Roasters
Delray Beach, FL 800-253-9363
Specialty Foods South LLC
Charleston, SC 800-538-0003
Spice Galleon
Belgium, WI. 877-668-4800
Spring Creek Natural Foods
Spencer, WV. 518-436-7603
Sprout House
Ramona, CA 800-777-6887
Star Ravioli Mfg Co
Moonachie, NJ 201-933-6427
Steel's Gourmet Foods, Ltd.
Bridgeport, PA 800-678-3357
Stirling Foods
Renton, WA. 800-332-1714
Summerfield Farm Products
Orange, VA 800-898-3276
Sun West Foods
Davis, CA 530-758-8550
Sunfood
El Cajon, CA. 888-729-3663
Sunset Specialty Foods
Lake Arrowhead, CA 909-337-7643
Sweet Shop USA
Mt Pleasant, TX 888-957-9338
Sweety Novelty
Monterey Park, CA. 626-282-4482
Swiss American Inc
St Louis, MO. 800-325-8150
Swiss Chalet Fine Foods
Doral, FL. 800-347-9477
T.W. Garner Food Company
Winston Salem, NC. 800-476-7383
Table De France
Ontario, CA. 909-923-5205
Taft Street Winery
Sebastopol, CA 707-823-2049
Tait Farm Foods
Centre Hall, PA. 800-787-2716
Tarazi Specialty Foods
Chino, CA. 909-628-3601
Teeccino
Carpinteria, CA. 800-498-3434
Thackrey & Co
Bolinas, CA. 415-868-9543
The Honest Stand
Denver, CO
The Real Co
Wilmington, DE 347-433-8945
The Water Kefir People
Bend, OR
Thistledew Farm
Proctor, WV 800-854-6639
Tipiak Inc
Stamford, CT. 203-961-9117
Tokunaga Farms
Selma, CA. 559-896-0949
Tom & Sally's Handmade Chocolates
Brattleboro, VT. 800-827-0800
Tomanetti Food Products Inc
Oakmont, PA. 800-875-3040
Too Good Gourmet
San Lorenzo, CA. 877-850-4663
Topolos at Russian River Vine
Forestville, CA 707-887-3344
Torn Ranch
Novato, CA. 707-796-7800
Torrefazione Italia
Seattle, WA. 800-827-2333
Tova Industries LLC
Louisville, KY 888-532-8682

Treat Ice Cream Co
San Jose, CA....408-292-9321
Trinity Spice
Midland, TX....800-460-1149
Tropical Foods
Charlotte, NC....800-438-4470
Tropical Foods
Lithia Springs, GA....800-544-3762
Tropical Nut & Fruit Co
Orlando, FL....800-749-8869
Two Chefs on a Roll
Carson, CA....800-842-3025
Uncle Ralph's Cookies
Frederick, MD....800-422-0626
Unibroue/Unibrew
Chambly, QC....450-658-7658
Unique Foods
Raleigh, NC....919-779-5600
Upton's Naturals
Chicago, IL
Valley View Blueberries
Vancouver, WA....360-892-2839
Van-Lang Food Products
Countryside, IL....708-588-0800
Vega Food Industries Inc
Cranston, RI....800-973-7737
VegGuide.org
Chicago, IL....773-363-3939
Venus Wafers Inc
Hingham, MA....800-545-4538
Vermont Food Experience
Shelburne, VT....802-985-8101
Vermont Natural Co
Jacksonville, VT....802-368-2231
Vermont Village
Barre, VT
Vigneri Chocolate Inc.
Rochester, NY....877-844-6374
Vine Village Day
Napa, CA....707-255-4116
Viola's Gourmet Goodies
Los Angeles, CA....323-731-5277
Vital Proteins LLC
Elk Grove Village, IL....224-544-9110
Volcano Island Honey Company
Honokaa, HI....888-663-6639
W.S. Wells & Sons
Wilton, ME....207-645-3393
Wagner Gourmet Foods
Lenexa, KS....913-469-5411
Walden Foods
Winchester, VA....800-648-7688
Warren & Son Meat Processing
Whipple, OH....740-585-2421
Weaver Nut Co. Inc.
Ephrata, PA....800-473-2688
Wechsler Coffee Corporation
Teterboro, NJ....800-800-2633
Wege of Hanover
Hanover, PA....800-888-4646
Wenner Bakery
Bayport, NY....800-869-6262
Westbrae Natural Foods
Melville, NY....800-434-4246
Wild Rice Exchange
Woodland, CA....800-223-7423
Will-Pak Foods
Ontario, CA....800-874-0883
Woeber Mustard Mfg Co
Springfield, OH....800-548-2929
Worldwide Specialties In
Los Angeles, CA....800-437-2702
Yankee Specialty Foods
Boston, MA....800-688-9904
Yayin Corporation
Valley Village, CA....707-829-5686
Yorktown Baking Company
Yorktown Heights, NY....800-235-3961
Your Bar Factory
LaSalle, QC....888-366-0258
Yvonne's Gourmet Sensations
Marlton, NJ....856-985-7677
Z Specialty Food, LLC
Woodland, CA....800-678-1226
Zitos Specialty Foods
Port Charlotte, FL....941-625-0806

Health & Dietary

Energy Bars

Abbott Laboratories
Abbott Park, IL....847-938-3887
Amrita Snacks
Hartsdale, NY....888-728-7779
Barn Stream Natural Foods
Alstead, NH....603-756-4395
Better Than Coffee
Torrance, CA
Bonk Breaker
Santa Monica, CA....310-315-4129
CarbRite Diet
New Brunswick, NJ....800-872-0101
Clif Bar & Co
Emeryville, CA....802-254-3227
Dharma Bars
DNX Foods
Tucson, AZ....888-612-5037
Epic Provisions
Austin, TX....512-944-8502
Foodie Fuel
Boulder, CO
Gertrude & Bronner's Magic Alpsnack
Vista, CA....877-786-3649
GU Energy Labs
Berkeley, CA....800-400-1995
GURU Organic Energy
San Francisco, CA
Immordl
San Clemente, CA....844-466-6735
Joj, Bar
Encinitas, CA....877-643-3575
Kalifornia Keto
Villa Park, CA
Kiss My Keto
Los Angeles, CA....310-765-1553
KiZE Concepts
Oklahoma City, OK
LivBar
Salem, OR....971-239-1209
MariGold Foods
Willis, TX....936-344-0444
MATI Energy
Durham, NC....866-924-8005
MetaBall
Chester, NJ....800-247-6580
MODe Sports Nutrition
Costa Mesa, CA....949-274-9948
Navitas Naturals
Novato, CA....888-645-4282
Nutraplex
Altamonte Springs, FL
Nutri-Nation
Port Coquitlam, BC....604-552-5549
ONE Brands
Charlotte, NC....888-231-2684
Onnit Labs
Austin, TX....855-666-4899
Optimum Nutrition
Aurora, IL....800-763-3444
Phat Fudge
Marina del Rey, CA
Probar
Salt Lake City, UT....800-921-2294
Quantum Energy Squares
Santa Monica, CA
Rise Bar
Irvine, CA....800-440-6476
Skratch Labs
Boulder, CO....800-735-8904
This Bar Saves Lives, LLC
Culver City, CA....310-730-5060
Thunderbird Real Food Bar
Austin, TX....512-383-8334
Tram Bar LLC
Victor, ID....208-354-4790
TruBrain
Santa Monica, CA....650-241-8372
West Thomas Partners, LLC
Grand Rapids, MI....616-755-8432
YoFiit
Vaughan, ON....647-997-7846

Organic Foods

Abunda Life
Asbury Park, NJ....732-775-9338
Adrienne's Gourmet Foods
Santa Barbara, CA....800-937-7010
Alliston Creamery
Alliston, ON....705-435-6751
Alta Dena Certified Dairy LLC
City Of Industry, CA....800-535-1369
American Natural & Organic
Fremont, CA....510-440-1044
Amy's Kitchen Inc
Santa Rosa, CA....707-781-6600
Andre-Boudin Bakeries
San Francisco, CA....415-882-1849
Ankeny Lake Wild Rice
Salem, OR....800-555-5380
Annie's Naturals
Berkeley, CA....800-434-1234
Applegate Farms
Bridgewater, NJ....866-587-5858
Atlantic Laboratories Inc
Waldoboro, ME....888-662-5357
Aurora Organic Dairy
Boulder, CO....303-284-3313
Avalon Organic Coffees
Albuquerque, NM....800-662-2575
Barrows Tea Company
New Bedford, MA....800-832-5024
Bedemco Inc
White Plains, NY....914-683-1119
Bedrock Farm Certified Organic Medicinal Herbs
Wakefield, RI....888-874-7393
Beech-Nut Nutrition Corp
Amsterdam, NY....518-595-6600
Beetnik Foods, LLC
Austin, TX....512-548-8228
Bel Brands USA
Chicago, IL....312-462-1500
Belgravia Imports
Portsmouth, RI....800-848-1127
Bella Vista Farm
Lawton, OK....866-237-8526
Berardi's Fresh Roast
Cleveland, OH....800-876-9109
Beta Pure Foods
Santa Cruz, CA....831-685-6565
Beth's Fine Desserts
Mill Valley, CA....415-383-3991
Blessed Herbs
Oakham, MA....800-489-4372
Blue Marble Brands
Providence, RI....888-534-0246
Boehringer Ingelheim Corp
Ridgefield, CT....800-243-0127
Boulder Granola
Boulder, CO....303-443-1136
Brad's Organic
Haverstraw, NY....845-429-9080
Brass Ladle Products
Concordville, PA....800-955-2353
Brewster Dairy Inc
Brewster, OH....800-874-8874
Buchanan Hollow Nut Co
Le Grand, CA....800-532-1500
Buchi Kombucha
Marshall, NC....828-394-2360
Bunker Hill Cheese Co Inc
Millersburg, OH....800-253-6636
Buns & Roses Organic Wholegrain Bakery
Edmonton, AB....780-438-0098
Butter Buds Food Ingredients
Racine, WI....800-426-1119
Buywell Coffee
Colorado Springs, CO....877-294-6246
Cafe Altura
Santa Paula, CA....800-526-8328
Cafe Society Coffee Company
Dallas, TX....800-717-6000
Caffe Ibis Gallery Deli
Logan, UT....888-740-4777
California Custom Fruits
Baldwin Park, CA....877-558-0056
California Independent Almond Growers
Merced, CA....209-667-4855
California Olive Oil Council
Berkeley, CA....888-718-9830
Carob Tree
Arcadia, CA....626-445-0215
Cascadian Farm Inc
Sedro Woolley, WA....360-855-0542
Cedarlane Foods
Carson, CA....800-826-3322
Celebrity Tea, LLC
Tampa, FL....813-600-3317
Cell-Nique
Norwalk, CT....888-417-9343
Century Foods Intl LLC
Sparta, WI....800-269-1901
Champlain Valley Milling Corp
Westport, NY....518-962-4711
Chartreuse Organic Tea
Trenton, MI....866-315-7832

Chelten House Products
Swedesboro, NJ
Cherith Valley Gardens
Fort Worth, TX 800-610-9813
Chino Valley Ranchers
Colton, CA 800-354-4503
Chris' Farm Stand
Peabody, MA. 978-994-4315
Christopher Ranch LLC
Gilroy, CA. 408-847-1100
CHS Sunprairie
Minot, ND. 800-556-6807
Chunco Foods Inc
Kansas City, MO. 816-283-0716
Citromax Flavors Inc
Carlstadt, NJ 201-933-8405
Citrus Service
Winter Garden, FL 407-656-4999
Clear Mountain Coffee Company
Silver Spring, MD. 301-587-2233
Cloud Top
Pasadena, CA 888-263-1778
Coleman Natural
Kings Mountain, NC. 800-442-8666
Country Choice Organic
Eden Prairie, MN 952-829-8824
CROPP Cooperative
La Farge, WI. 888-444-6455
Cuizina Food Company
Woodinville, WA. 425-486-7000
Cyanotech Corp
Kailua Kona, HI 800-395-1353
DAGOBA Organic Chocolate
Ashland, OR 866-972-6879
Daymar Select Fine Coffees
El Cajon, CA. 800-466-7590
Dharma Bars
Dorothy Dawson Food Products
Jackson, MI. 517-788-9830
East Wind Inc
Tecumseh, MO 417-679-4682
Eatem Foods Co
Vineland, NJ 800-683-2836
Eberly Poultry, Inc.
Stevens, PA 717-336-6440
Eden Foods Inc
Clinton, MI 888-424-3336
Eden Organic Pasta Company
Clinton, MI 888-424-3336
Eggology
Canoga Park, CA 818-610-2222
Extracts and Ingredients Ltd
Union, NJ 908-688-9009
Fairhaven Cooperative Flour Mill
Bellingham, WA 360-757-9947
FarmGro Organic Foods
Regina, SK 306-751-2449
Fig Food Co.
New York, NY 855-344-3663
Fine Dried Foods Intl
Santa Cruz, CA. 831-426-1413
Firebird Artisan Mills
Harvey, ND 701-324-4330
Fireside Kitchen
Halifax, NS 902-454-7387
Flamous Brands
Duarte, CA 626-799-7909
Florence Macaroni Manufacturing
Chicago, IL 800-647-2782
Florida Crystals Corporation
West Palm Beach, FL 844-344-9497
Florida Food Products Inc
Eustis, FL 800-874-2331
Foods Alive
Angola, IN. 260-488-4497
French Meadow Bakery & Cafe
Minneapolis, MN 612-870-7855
Fresh Tofu Inc
Allentown, PA. 610-433-4711
Frey Vineyards
Redwood Valley, CA. 800-760-3739
Frontera Foods
Chicago, IL 800-509-4441
Fruit d'Or
Villeroy, QC 819-385-1126
Fullbloom Baking Co
Newark, CA 800-201-9909
Fungus Among Us
Snohomish, WA 360-568-3403
Gelato Fresco
Toronto, ON 416-785-5415

George Chiala Farms Inc
Morgan Hill, CA. 408-778-0562
Gerber Products Co
Arlington, VA 800-284-9488
Ginseng Up Corp
Worcester, MA 800-446-7364
Golden Harvest Pecans
Cairo, GA 800-597-0968
Good Groceries
Brooklyn, NY 347-853-7462
Good Stuff Cacao
Metamora, MI 248-690-5114
Grandpa Po's Nutra Nuts
Commerce, CA. 323-260-7457
Great Eastern Sun Trading Co
Asheville, NC 800-334-5809
Great River Organic Milling
Arcadia, WI. 608-687-9580
Green & Black's Organic Chocolate
Plano, TX 877-299-1254
Guayaki
Sebastopol, CA. 888-482-9254
Hain Celestial Group Inc
Boulder, CO 800-434-4246
Hallcrest Vineyards
Felton, CA. 831-335-4441
Happy Family
New York, NY 855-644-2779
Harbar LLC
Canton, MA 800-881-7040
Hawkhaven Greenhouse International
Wautoma, WI 800-745-4295
Healing Home Foods
Pound Ridge, NY. 914-764-1303
Health Valley Company
Irwindale, CA 800-334-3204
Healthy Food Ingredients
Fargo, ND 844-275-3443
Healthy Times Baby Food
San Diego, CA 858-513-1550
HempNut
Henderson, NV. 707-576-7050
Herbal Magic
Toronto, ON 877-237-7225
Heritage Short Bread
Hilton Head Isle, SC. 843-422-3458
Highland Sugarworks
Websterville, VT. 800-452-4012
Hodgson Mill Inc
Effingham, IL 800-347-0198
Hodo
Oakland, CA 510-464-2977
Homefree LLC
Windham, NH. 800-552-7172
Homestead Mills
Cook, MN. 800-652-5233
HP Schmid
San Francisco, CA 415-765-5925
Indigo Coffee Roasters
Florence, MA 800-447-5450
Ineeka Inc
Chicago, IL 312-733-8327
Internatural Foods
Bloomfield, NJ 800-225-1449
Island Spring Inc
Vashon, WA. 206-463-9848
Johnson Foods, Inc.
Sunnyside, WA 509-837-4214
Kay's Naturals, Inc.
Clara City, MN 866-873-5499
KD Canners Inc
Mississauga, ON. 905-602-1825
Kombucha Wonder Drink
Portland, OR. 877-224-7331
Kopali Organics
Miami, FL. 305-751-7341
Kozlowski Farms
Forestville, CA 800-473-2767
Lakeview Bakery
Calgary, AB. 403-246-6127
Lakewood Juice Co.
Miami, FL. 866-324-5900
Late July Snacks
Norwalk, CT. 888-857-6225
Lifeway
Morton Grove, IL 877-281-3874
Little Duck Organics
New York, NY 877-458-1321
LivBar
Salem, OR. 971-239-1209
Lowell Farms
El Campo, TX. 888-484-9213

Luna & Larry's Coconut Bliss
Eugene, OR. 541-345-0020
Lundberg Family Farms
Richvale, CA. 530-538-3500
Made In Nature
Boulder, CO 800-906-7426
Magnum Coffee Roastery
Nunica, MI 888-937-5282
Maine Coast Sea Vegetables
Franklin, ME. 207-565-2907
Makana Beverages Inc.
Oxnard, CA
Mamma Chia
Carlsbad, CA. 855-588-2442
Mandarin Soy Sauce Inc
Middletown, NY. 845-343-1505
MariGold Foods
Willis, TX 936-344-0444
Mary's Gone Crackers
Gridley, CA. 888-258-1250
Mcfadden Farm
Potter Valley, CA 800-544-8230
Mediterranean Snack Food Co
Boonton, NJ 973-402-2644
Mellace Family Brands
Carlsbad, CA. 866-255-6887
Merlino Italian Baking Company
Kent, WA. 800-800-9490
Mills Brothers Intl
Seattle, WA. 206-575-3000
Minnestalgia Foods LLC
Mcgregor, MN 800-328-6731
Miyako Oriental Foods Inc
Baldwin Park, CA. 877-788-6476
Mom's Gourmet, LLC
Chagrin Falls, OH. 440-564-9702
Mountain Organic Foods
Moraga, CA. 925-377-0119
Mr Espresso
Oakland, CA 510-287-5200
Mrs. Leeper's Pasta
Excelsior Springs, MO 800-848-5266
Mrs. Miller's Homemade Noodles
Fredericksburg, OH 800-227-4487
Mushroom Co
Cambridge, MD 410-221-8971
Mushroom Harvest
Athens, OH 740-448-7376
Mustard Seed
Central, SC 877-621-2591
Najla's Specialty Foods Inc
Louisville, KY 877-962-5527
Native American Natural Foods
Kyle, SD 800-416-7212
Natural Food Mill
Corona, CA. 800-797-5090
Natural Way Mills Inc
Middle River, MN. 218-222-3677
Nature's Candy
Fredericksburg, TX. 800-729-0085
Nature's Legacy Inc.
Hudson, MI. 517-448-2050
Nature's Nutrition
Marysville, OH 800-242-1115
Naturel
Rancho Cucamonga, CA 877-242-8344
Natures Sungrown Foods Inc
San Rafael, CA. 415-491-4944
New England Natural Bakers
Greenfield, MA. 800-910-2884
North Bay Trading Co
Brule, WI. 800-348-0164
North Country Natural Spring Water
Port Kent, NY. 518-834-9400
NOW Foods
Bloomingdale, IL 888-669-3663
NuGo Nutrition
Oakmont, PA. 888-421-2032
Nutra Nuts
Commerce, CA. 323-260-7457
Nutrex Hawaii Inc
Kailua Kona, HI 800-453-1187
O Olive Oil
Petaluma, CA 888-827-7148
Once Again Nut Butter
Nunda, NY 888-800-8075
Organic Gourmet
Sherman Oaks, CA. 800-400-7772
Organic Nectars LLC
Malden On Hudson, NY. 845-246-0506
Organic Wine Co Inc
San Francisco, CA 888-326-9463

Oskri Corporation
Lake Mills, WI 920-648-8300
Pacari Organic Chocolate
Boca Raton, FL
Palmieri Food Products
New Haven, CT 800-845-5447
Panos Brands
Rochelle Park, NJ 201-843-8900
Pappy's Sassafras Tea
Columbus Grove, OH 877-659-5110
Parthenon Food Products
Ann Arbor, MI 734-994-1012
Pasta Prima
Benicia, CA.................... 530-671-7200
Peace Mountain Natural Beverages
Springfield, MA 413-567-4942
Peace Village Organic Foods
Berkeley, CA.................... 510-524-4420
Peaceful Fruits
.... 330-356-8515
Pearl Valley Cheese Inc
Fresno, OH 740-545-6002
Perricone Juices
Beaumont, CA.................... 951-769-7171
Personal Edge Nutrition
Ballwin, MO.................... 514-636-4512
Phillips Gourmet Inc
Kennett Square, PA.................... 610-925-0520
Pleasant Grove Farms
Pleasant Grove, CA 916-655-3391
Prairie Mills Products LLC
Rochester, IN 574-223-3177
Probar
Salt Lake City, UT 800-921-2294
Progenix Corporation
Wausau, WI.................... 800-233-3356
Purity Farms
La Farge, WI.................... 877-211-4819
R&J Farms
West Salem, OH 419-846-3179
R.J. Corr Naturals
Posen, IL.................... 708-389-4200
RAJB Hog Foods Inc
Jersey City, NJ 201-395-9400
Rapunzel Pure Organics
Bloomfield, NJ 800-225-1449
Ravioli Store
Long Island City, NY 877-727-8269
Red River Commodities Inc
Fargo, ND.................... 800-437-5539
Regenie's Crunchy Pi
Haverhill, MA.................... 877-734-3643
Rhythm Superfoods
Austin, TX.................... 512-441-5667
Rocky Mountain Honey Company
Salt Lake City, UT 801-355-2054
Rooibee Red Tea
Louisville, KY 502-749-0800
Run-A-Ton Group Inc
Chester, NJ 800-247-6580
Rustic Crust Inc
Pittsfield, NH 603-435-5119
Santa Barbara Pistachio Co
Maricopa, CA 800-896-1044
Shariann's Organics
Boulder, CO 800-434-4246
Sierra Madre Coffee
Denver, CO.................... 303-446-0050
Silver Creek Specialty Meats
Oshkosh, WI.................... 800-729-2849
Simply Gum
New York, NY
SJH Enterprises
Middleton, WI.................... 888-745-3845
Small Planet Foods
Minneapolis, MN 800-624-4123
Solana Gold Organics
Sebastopol, CA 800-459-1121
Solnuts
Hudson, IA 800-648-3503
Sophia's Sauce Works
Carson City, NV 800-718-7769
Springfield Creamery Inc
Eugene, OR.................... 541-689-2911
Sprouts Farmers Market Inc.
Phoenix, AZ
Straus Family Creamery
Petaluma, CA 800-572-7783
Sunergia Soyfoods
Charlottesville, VA 800-693-5134
Sunfood
El Cajon, CA.................... 888-729-3663

Sunridge Farms
Royal Oaks, CA 831-786-7000
Sunridge Farms Inc
Salinas, CA.................... 831-755-1530
Sunshine Burger & Spec Food Co
Fort Atkinson, WI.................... 920-568-1100
SunWest Foods, Inc.
Davis, CA 530-758-8550
Sustainable Sourcing
Great Barrington, MA.................... 413-528-5141
Suzanne's Specialties
New Brunswick, NJ 800-762-2135
Tastybaby
Malibu, CA.................... 866-588-8278
Tea-n-Crumpets
San Rafael, CA 415-457-2495
Teeny Tiny Spice Company of Vermont LLC
Shelburne, VT.................... 802-598-6800
Templar Food Products
New Providence, NJ.................... 800-883-6752
The Coromega Company
Carlsbad, CA.................... 877-275-3725
The Naked Edge, LLC
Boulder, CO 888-297-9426
The Tea Spot, Inc.
Boulder, CO 303-444-8324
Thomas Canning/Maidstone
Maidstone, ON 519-737-1531
Tierra Farm
Valatie, NY 519-392-8300
Tomanetti Food Products Inc
Oakmont, PA.................... 800-875-3040
Tova Industries LLC
Louisville, KY 888-532-8682
Travel Chocolate
New York, NY 718-841-7030
Treehouse Farms
Elgin, AZ.................... 559-757-5020
Triple Springs Spring Water Co
Meriden, CT 203-235-8374
Tripper Inc
Oxnard, CA.................... 805-988-8851
Tropical Açaí LLC
Pompano Beach, FL 855-550-2224
True Organic Product Inc
Helm, CA 800-487-0379
TruVibe Organics
Santa Monica, CA
Twin Marquis
Brooklyn, NY 800-367-6868
Uncle Matt's Organic
Clermont, FL.................... 833-729-8625
Unique Beverage Company
Everett, WA.................... 425-267-0959
Vegetable Juices Inc
Chicago, IL 888-776-9752
Ventre Packing Company
Syracuse, NY 315-463-2384
Verde Farms, LLC
Woburn, MA.................... 617-221-8922
Vermont Village
Barre, VT
Vienna Bakery
Barrington, RI.................... 401-245-2355
Vive Organic
Venice, CA 877-774-9291
Vivoo
Verona,
Vixen Kitchen
Santa Cruz, CA.................... 707-223-5627
Vogue Cuisine Foods
Sunnyvale, CA 888-236-4144
WCC Honey Marketing
City Of Industry, CA.................... 626-855-3086
Westbrae Natural Foods
Melville, NY.................... 800-434-4246
Wild Rice Exchange
Woodland, CA.................... 800-223-7423
Wing Nien Food
Hayward, CA 510-487-8877
Wizards Cauldron, LTD
Yanceyville, NC 336-694-5665
World Casing Corp
Maspeth, NY.................... 800-221-4887
Xochitl
Dallas, TX.................... 866-595-8917
Y Z Enterprises Inc
Maumee, OH.................... 800-736-8779
Yogavive
Tiburon, CA 415-366-6226
Your Bar Factory
LaSalle, QC.................... 888-366-0258

Zhena's Gypsy Tea
Commerce, CA 800-448-0803

Certified

Briess Malt & Ingredients Co.
Chilton, WI 800-657-0806
Caffe Ibis Gallery Deli
Logan, UT.................... 888-740-4777
California Custom Fruits
Baldwin Park, CA.................... 877-558-0056
Clofine Dairy Products Inc
Linwood, NJ 609-653-1000
Crosby Molasses Company
Saint John, NB 800-561-2206
Emerling International Foods
Buffalo, NY.................... 716-833-7381
Frontier Co-op
Norway, IA 844-550-6200
Gold Mine Natural Food Company
Poway, CA 800-475-3663
Hoyt's Honey Farm
Baytown, TX.................... 281-576-5383
Jonathan's Sprouts
Rochester, MA 508-763-2577
Kozlowski Farms
Forestville, CA 800-473-2767
Lily of the Desert
Denton, TX 800-229-5459
Marukan Vinegar USA Inc.
Paramount, CA 562-630-6060
New Organics
Kenwood, CA.................... 734-677-5570
Nu-World Amaranth Inc
Naperville, IL 630-369-6851
Once Again Nut Butter
Nunda, NY 888-800-8075
Organic Gourmet
Sherman Oaks, CA 800-400-7772
Organic Planet
San Francisco, CA 415-765-5590
Osso Good, LLC
San Rafael, CA
Raye's Mustard
Eastport, ME.................... 800-853-1903
Red Monkey Foods
Springfield, MO 417-319-7300
RFi Ingredients
Blauvelt, NY.................... 800-962-7663
Roberts Seed
Axtell, NE.................... 308-743-2565
Sure-Fresh Produce Inc
Santa Maria, CA 888-423-5379
The Food Collective
Irvine, CA.................... 866-328-8638
The Honest Stand
Denver, CO
The Lancaster Food Company
Lancaster, PA
True Story Foods
San Francisco, CA 888-277-1171
Tuscarora Organic Growers Cooperative
Hustontown, PA 814-448-2173
Wild Aseptics, LLC
Erlanger, KY.................... 877-787-7221
Wisconsin Specialty Protein
Madison, WI
Wood Sugarbush
Spring Valley, WI 715-772-4656

Beef

Sunnyside Organics Seedlings
Washington, VA 510-221-5050
Tribali Foods
San Marino, CA 310-592-5420

Fruit

Kozlowski Farms
Forestville, CA 800-473-2767

Poultry

Tribali Foods
San Marino, CA 310-592-5420

Produce

Argee Corp
Santee, CA 800-449-3030
Price Co
Yakima, WA 509-966-4110
Tierra Farm
Valatie, NY 519-392-8300

Fruits

Atwater Foods
Lyndonville Orleans, NY 585-765-2639
California Custom Fruits
Baldwin Park, CA................ 877-558-0056
Crunchies Natural Food Company
Westlake Village, CA 888-997-1866
Emerling International Foods
Buffalo, NY.................... 716-833-7381
Fine Dried Foods Intl
Santa Cruz, CA.................. 831-426-1413
Global Organics
Cambridge, MA 781-648-8844
Golden Town Apple Products
Rougemont, QC 866-552-7643
Hallcrest Vineyards
Felton, CA..................... 831-335-4441
Hialeah Products Co
Hollywood, FL 800-923-3379
Made In Nature
Boulder, CO 800-906-7426
Organic Planet
San Francisco, CA 415-765-5590
Price Co
Yakima, WA 509-966-4110
Setton International Foods
Commack, NY 800-227-4397
Solana Gold Organics
Sebastopol, CA 800-459-1121
Sunfood
El Cajon, CA.................... 888-729-3663
Sunshine Farm & Garden
Renick, WV..................... 304-497-2208
Tropical Açaí LLC
Pompano Beach, FL 855-550-2224
Unique Ingredients LLC
Gold Canyon, AZ 480-983-2498

Ingredients

Global Organics
Cambridge, MA 781-648-8844
Marroquin Organic Intl.
Santa Cruz, CA.................. 831-423-3442
Wildly Organic
Silver Bay, MN 800-945-3801

Natural

Amrita Snacks
Hartsdale, NY................... 888-728-7779
Arico Natural Foods
Beaverton, OR 503-259-0871
Avenue Gourmet
Owings Mills, MD 410-902-5701
Cache Creek Foods LLC
Woodland, CA................... 530-662-1764
California Custom Fruits
Baldwin Park, CA................ 877-558-0056
Earthrise Nutritionals
Irvine, CA...................... 800-949-7473
Ethical Naturals
San Anselmo, CA................ 866-459-4454
GKI Foods
Brighton, MI.................... 248-486-0055
Global Organics
Cambridge, MA 781-648-8844
Healthy Times Baby Food
San Diego, CA 858-513-1550
Horner International
Raleigh, NC..................... 919-787-3112
Hudson River Foods
Castleton, NY 888-417-9343
Internatural Foods
Bloomfield, NJ 800-225-1449
Larabar
Denver, CO..................... 800-543-2147
New Organics
Kenwood, CA................... 734-677-5570
Organic Planet
San Francisco, CA 415-765-5590
Pasta Prima
Benicia, CA..................... 530-671-7200
Pyure Brands
Naples, FL...................... 305-509-5096
Quality Naturally Foods
City Of Industry, CA.............. 888-498-6986
Seitenbacher America LLC
Odessa, FL 727-376-3000
Sure-Fresh Produce Inc
Santa Maria, CA................. 888-423-5379
Unique Ingredients LLC
Gold Canyon, AZ 480-983-2498
Vegetable Juices Inc
Chicago, IL 888-776-9752
Wine Country Chef LLC
Hidden Valley Lake, CA........... 707-322-0406
Your Bar Factory
LaSalle, QC..................... 888-366-0258

Antioxidants

Ax Water
Fargo, ND

Vegetables

CROPP Cooperative
La Farge, WI.................... 888-444-6455
Emerling International Foods
Buffalo, NY..................... 716-833-7381
Global Organics
Cambridge, MA 781-648-8844
Healthy Times Baby Food
San Diego, CA 858-513-1550
Made In Nature
Boulder, CO 800-906-7426
Pleasant Grove Farms
Pleasant Grove, CA 916-655-3391
R&J Farms
West Salem, OH 419-846-3179
Sno-Pac Foods Inc
Caledonia, MN 800-533-2215
The Naked Edge, LLC
Boulder, CO 888-297-9426
Vegetable Juices Inc
Chicago, IL 888-776-9752

Sun-Dried Foods

Tropical Link Canada Ltd.
Burnaby, BC 778-379-3510

Survival Foods

Good For You America
Concordia, MO 866-329-5969
Hialeah Products Co
Hollywood, FL 800-923-3379
J&M Food Products Co
Deerfield, IL 847-948-1290
SOPAKCO Packaging
Mullins, SC..................... 843-464-7851
TyRy Inc
Rocklin, CA 800-322-6325

Vegetarian Products

Abbot's Butcher
Costa Mesa, CA 949-726-2156
Adventist Book & Food
Trenton, NJ 800-765-6955
Big Mountain Foods
Vancouver, BC
Bixby & Co., LLC
Rockland, ME.................... 207-691-1778
Boulder Organic Foods
Niwot, CO...................... 303-530-0470
Butler Foods LLC
Grand Ronde, OR 503-437-9133
Caribbean Food Delights Inc
Tappan, NY..................... 845-398-3000
CHS Inc.
Inver Grove Hts., MN............. 800-328-6539
Cricklewood Soyfoods
Mertztown, PA 610-682-4109
Dixie USA
Tomball, TX 800-233-3668
Earth Island
Chatsworth, CA 888-394-3949
EatPastry LLC
San Diego, CA 858-755-7456
Emmy's Organics
Ithaca, NY...................... 855-463-6697
Flamous Brands
Duarte, CA 626-799-7909
Fora Foods
Brooklyn, NY
Forager Project
San Francisco, CA
Franklin Farms
Parsippany, NJ
Go Max Go Foods
Gold Mine Natural Food Company
Poway, CA 800-475-3663
Good PLANeT Foods
Bellevue, WA 425-449-8134
Gopal's Healthfoods
Sidney, TX 866-646-7257
Hilary's Eat Well
Lawrence, KS 785-856-3399
Hudson River Foods
Castleton, NY 888-417-9343
JUST Inc
San Francisco, CA 844-423-6637
Jyoti Cuisine India
Berwyn, PA..................... 610-296-4620
Levant Mediterranean Snack Foods LLC
Haverhill, MA................... 978-241-9986
Lightlife
Turners Falls, MA................ 800-769-3279
Marjon Specialty Foods Inc
Plant City, FL 813-752-3482
Modern Table
Walnut Creek, CA
Morningstar Farms
Zanesville, OH 800-535-5644
N D Labs
Lynbrook, NY................... 888-263-5227
Natural Food Mill
Corona, CA..................... 800-797-5090
Nature's Path Foods
Blaine, WA 888-808-9505
Neat Foods
Lancaster, PA 866-637-6328
New Barn Organics
Rohnert Park, CA 888-635-7102
No Evil Foods
Asheville, NC 828-367-1536
Nona Vegan Foods
Toronto, ON 416-836-9387
Nuts For Cheese
London, ON 519-601-5070
Oogolow Enterprises
Chico, CA...................... 800-816-6873
Pita Pal
Houston, TX 713-777-7482
Probar
Salt Lake City, UT 800-921-2294
Quorn Foods
Chicago, IL
Small Planet Foods
Minneapolis, MN 800-624-4123
Spice Of Life Co
Sherman Oaks, CA 818-909-0052
Sweet Earth Foods
Moss Landing, CA 800-737-3311
The Art of Broth, LLC
CA............................ 818-715-9320
The Piping Gourmets
.... 786-233-8660
The Soulfull Project
Camden, NJ
Turtle Island Foods
Hood River, OR 800-508-8100
Twin Oaks Community
Louisa, VA 540-894-5141
Unique Ingredients LLC
Gold Canyon, AZ................. 480-983-2498
Upton's Naturals
Chicago, IL
Vana Life Foods
Seattle, WA..................... 347-446-6504
Vegetable Juices Inc
Chicago, IL..................... 888-776-9752
Veggie Land
Parsippany, NJ................... 888-808-5540
Vegi-Deli
San Rafael, CA 888-473-3667
Violife
Thessaloniki,
Vitasoy USA
Woburn, MA.................... 800-848-2769
Vtopian Artisan Cheeses
Portland, OR
Wholesome Bakery
San Francisco, CA 415-343-5414
Wine Country Chef LLC
Hidden Valley Lake, CA........... 707-322-0406
Yai's Thai
Denver, CO
Your Bar Factory
LaSalle, QC..................... 888-366-0258

Burgers

Beyond Meat
El Segundo, CA 866-756-4112
Big Mountain Foods
Vancouver, BC

Boca Foods Company
Madison, WI 608-285-3311
Dixie USA
Tomball, TX 800-233-3668
Five Star Foodies
Cincinnati, OH
Goodseed Burgers
. . . . 512-698-7907
Impossible Foods
Redwood City, CA 855-877-6365
Neat Foods
Lancaster, PA 866-637-6328
Quaker Maid Meats
Reading, PA 610-376-1500
Quorn Foods
Chicago, IL

Sunshine Burger & Spec Food Co
Fort Atkinson, WI. 920-568-1100
Ungars Food
Elmwood Park, NJ 201-773-6846
Vitasoy USA
Woburn, MA. 800-848-2769

Patties

Big Mountain Foods
Vancouver, BC
Caribbean Food Delights Inc
Tappan, NY. 845-398-3000
Hilary's Eat Well
Lawrence, KS 785-856-3399
JD Sweid Foods
Langley, BC 800-665-4355

Neat Foods
Lancaster, PA 866-637-6328
Neese Country Sausage Inc
Greensboro, NC 800-632-1010
Pulmuone Foods USA Inc.
Fullerton, CA 800-588-7782
Quorn Foods
Chicago, IL
Vitasoy USA
Woburn, MA. 800-848-2769

Breaded

Neat Foods
Lancaster, PA 866-637-6328

Specialty Processed Foods

Barbecue Products (See also Specific Foods)

A Southern Season
Hillsborough, NC . . . 800-253-3663
A. Lassonde Inc.
Rougemont, QC . . . 866-552-7643
Allied Old English Inc
Port Reading, NJ . . . 732-602-8955
Arbor Hill Grapery & Winery
Naples, NY . . . 800-554-7553
Art's Tamales
Metamora, IL . . . 309-367-2850
Aunt Kitty's Foods Inc
Vineland, NJ . . . 856-691-2100
Baker's Ribs No 2
Dallas, TX . . . 214-748-5433
Bartush Schnitzius Foods Co
Lewisville, TX . . . 972-219-1270
Baumer Foods Inc
Metairie, LA . . . 504-482-5761
BBQ Bunch
Kansas City, MO . . . 816-941-4534
Big B Barbecue
Evansville, IN . . . 812-425-5235
Black's Barbecue
Lockhart, TX . . . 888-632-8225
Broadaway Ham Co
Jonesboro, AR . . . 870-932-6688
Bunker Foods Corp.
New York, NY . . . 646-738-4020
Cafe Tequila
San Francisco, CA . . . 415-264-0106
California Custom Foods
Fullerton, CA . . . 714-870-0490
California-Antilles Trading
San Diego, CA . . . 800-330-6450
Calumet Diversified Meats Company
Pleasant Prairie, WI . . . 800-752-7427
Captain Bob's Jet Fuel
Fort Wayne, IN . . . 877-486-6468
Carolina Treet
Wilmington, NC . . . 800-616-6344
Casa Visco
Schenectady, NY . . . 888-607-2823
Catskill Mountain Specialties
Saugerties, NY . . . 800-311-3473
Caughman's Meat Plant
Lexington, SC . . . 803-356-0076
Chandler Foods Inc
Greensboro, NC . . . 800-537-6219
Cinnabar Specialty Foods Inc
Prescott, AZ . . . 866-293-6433
Clements Foods Co
Oklahoma City, OK . . . 800-654-8355
Clifty Farm Country Meats
Paris, TN . . . 800-486-4267
Coach Sposato's Bar-B-Que
Lincoln, AR . . . 800-264-7535
Colgin Co
Dallas, TX . . . 888-226-5446
Cookies Food Products
Wall Lake, IA . . . 800-331-4995
Corky's Ribs & BBQ
Pigeon Forge, TN . . . 865-453-7427
Creative Foodworks Inc
San Antonio, TX . . . 210-212-4761
Curly's Foods Inc
Edina, MN . . . 612-920-3400
D & D Foods Inc
West Des Moines, IA . . . 800-772-4098
Dillard's Bar-B-Q Sauce
Durham, NC . . . 919-286-1080
Dorina So-Good Inc
Union, IL . . . 815-923-2144
Dorothy Dawson Food Products
Jackson, MI . . . 517-788-9830
El Rey Cooked Meats
St Louis, MO . . . 314-521-3113
Favorite Foods
Burnaby, BC . . . 604-420-5100
Felbro Food Products
Los Angeles, CA . . . 323-936-5266
Figaro Company
Mesquite, TX . . . 972-288-3587
Food Concentrate Corporation
Oklahoma City, OK . . . 405-840-5633
Fremont Authentic Brands
Fremont, OH . . . 419-334-8995
Fry Krisp Food Products
Jackson, MI . . . 877-854-5440
Garden Complements Inc
Kansas City, MO . . . 800-966-1091
Gary's Frozen Foods
Lubbock, TX . . . 806-745-1933
Gaucho Foods
Fayetteville, IL . . . 877-677-2282
Gayle's Sweet N' Sassy Foods
Beverly Hills, CA . . . 310-246-1792
Gedney Foods Co
Sun Valley, CA . . . 888-244-0653
Golden Specialty Foods Inc
Norwalk, CA . . . 562-802-2537
Golding Farms Foods
Winston Salem, NC . . . 336-766-6161
Gumpert's Canada
Mississauga, ON . . . 800-387-9324
Harold Food Company
Charlotte, NC . . . 704-588-8061
Head Country
Ponca City, OK . . . 888-762-1227
Heinz Portion Control
Jacksonville, FL . . . 904-695-1300
Hollman Foods
Des Moines, IA . . . 888-926-2879
Hormel Foods Corp.
Austin, MN . . . 507-437-5611
J & B Sausage Co Inc
Waelder, TX . . . 830-788-7511
J.N. Bech
Elk Rapids, MI . . . 800-232-4583
JD Sweid Foods
Langley, BC . . . 800-665-4355
JMS Specialty Foods
Ripon, WI . . . 800-535-5437
Johnny Harris Famous Barbecue Sauce
Savannah, GA . . . 888-547-2823
King Kold Meats
Englewood, OH . . . 800-836-2797
Kozlowski Farms
Forestville, CA . . . 800-473-2767
Kubla Khan Food Company
Portland, OR . . . 503-234-7494
L & S Packing Co
Farmingdale, NY . . . 800-286-6487
Lea & Perrins
Glenview, IL
Lee's Sausage Co
Orangeburg, SC . . . 803-534-5517
Lendy's Cafe Raw Bar
Virginia Beach, VA . . . 757-491-3511
Lounsbury Foods
Toronto, ON . . . 416-656-6330
Mad Will's Food Company
Auburn, CA . . . 888-275-9455
Magic Seasoning Blends
New Orleans, LA . . . 800-457-2857
Mansmith's Barbeque
San Jn Bautista, CA . . . 800-626-7648
Mccutcheon Apple Products
Frederick, MD . . . 800-888-7537
Mitchell Foods
Barbourville, KY . . . 888-202-9745
Moonlite Bar-B-Q Inn
Owensboro, KY . . . 800-322-8989
Mullens Dressing
Palestine, IL . . . 618-586-2727
New Business Corp
Gary, IN . . . 219-885-1476
Ninety Six Canning Company
Ninety Six, SC . . . 864-543-2700
O'Brian Brothers Food
Cincinnati, OH . . . 513-791-9909
Original Chili Bowl
Ontario, CA . . . 800-548-6363
Ott Food Products Co
Carthage, MO . . . 800-866-2585
Pacific Poultry Company
Honolulu, HI . . . 808-841-2828
Palmieri Food Products
New Haven, CT . . . 800-845-5447
Paradise Products Corporation
Boca Raton, FL . . . 800-826-1235
Piggie Park Enterprises
West Columbia, SC . . . 800-628-7423
Porinos Gourmet Food
Central Falls, RI . . . 800-826-3938
Produits Ronald
St. Damase, QC . . . 800-465-0118
River Town Foods Corp
St Louis, MO . . . 800-844-3210
Riverview Foods
Warsaw, KY . . . 859-567-5211
Robinson's No 1 Ribs
Oak Park, IL . . . 800-836-6750
Roos Foods
Kenton, DE . . . 800-343-3642
Rosmarino Foods/R.Z. Humbert Company
Odessa, FL . . . 888-926-9053
Sadler's Smokehouse
Henderson, TX . . . 903-657-5581
Savoie's Sausage and Food Products
Opelousas, LA . . . 337-942-7241
Schiff Food Products Co Inc
Totowa, NJ . . . 973-237-1990
Schlotterbeck & Foss Company
Portland, ME . . . 800-777-4666
Scott's Sauce Co Inc
Goldsboro, NC . . . 800-734-7282
Steel's Gourmet Foods, Ltd.
Bridgeport, PA . . . 800-678-3357
Suzanna's Kitchen
Peachtree Cor, GA . . . 770-476-9900
Sweet Baby Ray's
Chicago, IL . . . 877-729-2229
Sweet Peas Floral Design
Stockton, CA . . . 209-472-9284
T. Marzetti Company
Westerville, OH . . . 800-999-1835
T.W. Garner Food Company
Winston Salem, NC . . . 800-476-7383
Thompson's Fine Foods
Shoreview, MN . . . 800-807-0025
Todd's
Des Moines, IA . . . 800-247-5363
Travis Meats Inc
Powell, TN . . . 800-247-7606
Triple H Food Processors Inc
Riverside, CA . . . 951-352-5700
Triple K Manufacturing Company, Inc.
Shenandoah, IA . . . 712-246-4376
Triple U Enterprises
Fort Pierre, SD . . . 605-567-3624
Valley Grain Products
Fresno, CA . . . 559-675-3400
Vidalia Sweets Brand
Lyons, GA . . . 912-565-8881
W & G Marketing Company
Ames, IA . . . 515-233-4774
Webbpak Inc
Trussville, AL . . . 800-655-3500
Wei-Chuan USA Inc
Bell Gardens, CA . . . 562-372-2020
West Pac
Idaho Falls, ID . . . 800-973-7407
Westin Foods
Omaha, NE . . . 800-228-6098
Wing Nien Food
Hayward, CA . . . 510-487-8877
Wood Brothers Inc
West Columbia, SC . . . 803-796-5146
Woods Smoked Meats Inc
Bowling Green, MO . . . 800-458-8426
World Famous Buffalo Wing Sauce
Buffalo, NY . . . 716-912-9068
Zarda Bar-B-Q & Catering Company
Blue Springs, MO . . . 800-776-7427

Dehydrated Food (See also Specific Foods)

Agvest
Cleveland, OH . . . 216-464-3737
Alkinco
New York, NY . . . 800-424-7118
American Dehydrated Foods, Inc.
Springfield, MO . . . 800-456-3447
American Nut & Chocolate Co
Boston, MA . . . 800-797-6887

Amport Foods
St. Paul, MN 800-236-1119
Anderson Custom Processing
New Ulm, MN. 877-588-4950
Atrium Biotech
Quebec, QC. 418-652-1116
Basic American Foods
Walnut Creek, CA. 925-472-4000
Blossom Farm Products
Ridgewood, NJ. 800-729-1818
Boghosian Raisin Packing Co
Fowler, CA 559-834-5348
California Fruit
San Diego, CA 877-378-4811
Caltex Foods
Canoga Park, CA 800-522-5839
Casados Farms
Ohkay Owingeh, NM 505-852-2433
Century Blends LLC
Hunt Valley, MD. 410-771-6606
Challenge Dairy Products, Inc.
Dublin, CA 800-733-2479
Chef Merito Inc
Van Nuys, CA. 800-637-4861
Chooljian Bros Packing Co
Sanger, CA 559-875-5501
Chukar Cherries
Prosser, WA. 800-624-9544
Clofine Dairy Products Inc
Linwood, NJ 609-653-1000
Commercial Creamery Co
Spokane, WA. 509-747-4131
Consumers Vinegar & Spice Co
Chicago, IL 773-376-4100
Country Cupboard
Lewisburg, PA. 570-523-3211
Dairy King Milk Farms/Foodservice
Whitter, CA. 800-900-6455
Dairy-Mix Inc
St Petersburg, FL 800-955-6101
Del Rey Packing
Del Rey, CA 559-888-2031
Desert Valley Date
Coachella, CA. 760-398-0999
Devansoy Farms
Carroll, IA. 800-747-8605
Dismat Corporation
Toledo, OH 419-531-8963
Emerling International Foods
Buffalo, NY. 716-833-7381
Fig Garden Packing Inc
Fresno, CA 559-271-9000
Fine Dried Foods Intl
Santa Cruz, CA. 831-426-1413
First District Association
Litchfield, MN 320-693-3236
Freeman Industries
Tuckahoe, NY. 800-666-6454
Fuji Foods Corp
Browns Summit, NC. 336-375-3111
Garden Valley Corp
Sutherlin, OR 541-459-9565
Global Food Industries
Townville, SC. 800-225-4152
Golden Town Apple Products
Rougemont, QC 866-552-7643
Good For You America
Concordia, MO 866-329-5969
Graf Creamery Co
Bonduel, WI 715-758-2137
Grandpa Ittel's Meats Inc
Howard Lake, MN 320-543-2285
Henningsen Foods Inc
Omaha, NE 800-228-2769
Hialeah Products Co
Hollywood, FL 800-923-3379
Honeyville Grain Inc
Brigham City, UT 435-494-4200
Humco Holding Group Inc
Texarkana, TX. 903-831-7808
Idaho Pacific Holdings Inc
Rigby, ID. 800-238-5503
Idaho Supreme Potatoes Inc
Firth, ID. 208-346-4100
Kamish Food Products
Chicago, IL 773-725-6959
Kozlowski Farms
Forestville, CA 800-473-2767
Land O'Lakes Inc
Arden Hills, MN. 800-328-9680
Larsen Farms
Hamer, ID 208-374-5592
Leroux Creek
Hotchkiss, CO. 877-970-5670
Made In Nature
Boulder, CO 800-906-7426
Main Street Ingredients
La Crosse, WI. 800-359-2345
Maine Wild Blueberry Company
Cherryfield, ME 800-243-4005
Maruchan Inc
Irvine, CA. 949-789-2300
Master Mix
Placentia, CA 714-524-1698
Mayacamas Fine Foods
Sonoma, CA 800-826-9621
Mercer Processing
Modesto, CA. 209-529-0150
Morris J Golombeck Inc
Brooklyn, NY 718-284-3505
Niagara Foods
Middleport, NY. 716-735-7722
North Bay Trading Co
Brule, WI. 800-348-0164
Northern Feed & Bean Company
Lucerne, CO 800-316-2326
Oakland Bean Cleaning & Storage
Knights Landing, CA 530-735-6203
Ontario Foods
Guelph, ON. 888-466-2372
Oregon Potato Co
Boardman, OR 800-336-6311
Paisano Food Products
Elk Grove Village, IL 800-672-4726
Pines International
Lawrence, KS 800-697-4637
Plainview Milk Products
Plainview, MN 800-356-5606
Pro Form Labs
Orinda, CA 707-752-9010
Producers Cooperative
Bryan, TX. 979-778-6000
Produits Alimentaire
Laval, QC 800-361-9326
Protient
St Paul, MN. 800-328-9680
Quality Ingredients
Burnsville, MN. 952-898-4002
Ramos Orchards
Winters, CA 530-795-4748
Ramsen Inc
Lakeville, MN. 952-431-0400
Reinhart Foods
Toronto, ON 416-645-4910
Rinehart Meat Processing
Branson, MO. 417-869-2041
Russell E. Womack, Inc.
Lubbock, TX. 877-787-3559
Schiff Food Products Co Inc
Totowa, NJ 973-237-1990
Serv-Agen Corporation
Cherry Hill, NJ 856-663-6966
Shields Date Garden
Indio, CA. 800-414-2555
SlantShack Jerky
Brooklyn, NY 201-632-1035
Smeltzer Orchard Co
Frankfort, MI 231-882-4421
Smuggler's Kitchen
Dundee, FL. 800-604-6793
Solana Gold Organics
Sebastopol, CA. 800-459-1121
SOUPerior Bean & Spice Company
Vancouver, WA. 800-878-7687
South Mill
Kennett Square, PA. 610-444-4800
Spice Hunter Inc
Richmond, VA. 800-444-3061
Spreda Group
Louisville, KY. 502-426-9411
St. Ours & Company
East Weymouth, MA. 781-331-8520
Sugar Foods Corp
Sun Valley, CA 818-768-7900
ThreeWorks Snacks
259 Niagara St., ON
Tova Industries LLC
Louisville, KY 888-532-8682
Triple U Enterprises
Fort Pierre, SD 605-567-3624
Tropical Foods
Charlotte, NC 800-438-4470
Tropical Foods
Lithia Springs, GA 800-544-3762
Tropical Nut Fruit & Bulk Cndy
Lithia Springs, GA 800-544-3762
Unique Ingredients LLC
Gold Canyon, AZ 480-983-2498
United Dairymen of Arizona
Tempe, AZ. 480-966-7211
Ursula's Island Farms Company
Seattle, WA 206-762-3113
Valley View Packing Co
Yuba City, CA. 530-673-7356
Verhoff Alfalfa Mill Inc
Ottawa, OH 800-834-8563
VIP Foods
Flushing, NY. 718-821-5330
Vogue Cuisine Foods
Sunnyvale, CA 888-236-4144
W.A. Beans & Sons
Bangor, ME. 800-649-1958
Washington Potato Company
Pasco, WA. 800-897-2726
Welsh Farms
Wallington, NJ 800-221-0663
Westin Foods
Omaha, NE 800-228-6098

Fermented Products (See also Specific Foods)

Lovebiotics LLC
Los Osos, CA
Makana Beverages Inc.
Oxnard, CA
Roland Machinery
Springfield, IL. 800-325-1183
The Water Kefir People
Bend, OR

Freeze Dried Food (See also Specific Foods)

BCFoods
Santa Rosa, CA. 707-547-1776
Emerling International Foods
Buffalo, NY. 716-833-7381
Good For You America
Concordia, MO 866-329-5969
Hanover Foods Corp
Hanover, PA 717-632-6000
Tierra Farm
Valatie, NY 519-392-8300
Tru Fru, LLC
Salt Lake City, UT 888-437-2497
Unique Ingredients LLC
Gold Canyon, AZ 480-983-2498
Van Drunen Farms
Momence, IL. 815-472-3100
Vivolac Cultures Corporation
Indianapolis, IN 317-356-8460

Frozen Foods (See also Specific Foods)

Abbotsford Growers Ltd.
Abbotsford, BC. 604-864-0022
Acme Steak & Seafood
Youngstown, OH. 800-686-2263
Agfinity Inc
Eaton, CO 800-433-4688
Aglamesis Bros Ice Cream
Cincinnati, OH 513-531-5196
Agripac
Denver, CO 503-981-0111
Agropur
Granby, QC. 800-363-5686
Agvest
Cleveland, OH 216-464-3737
Ajinomoto Foods North America, Inc.
Ontario, CA. 909-477-4700
Al Gelato Bornay
Franklin Park, IL. 847-455-5355
Al Pete Meats
Muncie, IN 765-288-8817
Al-Rite Fruits & Syrups Co
Miami, FL. 305-652-2540
Aladdin Bakers
Brooklyn, NY 718-499-1818
Alaskan Gourmet Seafoods
Anchorage, AK. 800-288-3740
Alati-Caserta Desserts
Montr,al, QC. 877-377-5680
Alexia Foods
Long Island City, NY 718-937-0100

Alfredo Aiello Italian Food
Quincy, MA....617-770-6360
Aliotti Wholesale Fish Company
Monterey, CA....408-722-4597
All Round Foods Bakery Prod
Westbury, NY....800-428-8802
Allen Harim Foods LLC
Seaford, DE....877-397-9191
Allen's Blueberry Freezer Inc
Ellsworth, ME....207-667-5561
Alpenrose Dairy
Portland, OR....503-244-1133
Alyeska Seafoods
Unalaska, AK....907-581-1211
Amano Fish Cake Factory
Hilo, HI....808-935-5555
American Classic Ice Cream Company
Bay Shore, NY....800-736-4100
American Seafoods
Seattle, WA....206-448-0300
Andrew & Williamson Sales Co
San Diego, CA....619-661-6000
Angy's Food Products Inc
Westfield, MA....413-572-1010
Annie's Frozen Yogurt
Minneapolis, MN....800-969-9648
Appleton Produce Company
Weiser, ID....208-414-3352
AquaCuisine
Portland, OR....208-323-2782
Arista Industries Inc
Wilton, CT....800-255-6457
Armbrust Meats
Medford, WI....715-748-3102
Arrowac Fisheries
Seattle, WA....206-282-5655
Art's Tamales
Metamora, IL....309-367-2850
Artuso Pastry
Bronx, NY....718-367-2515
ASC Seafood Inc
Largo, FL....800-876-3474
Athens Foods Inc
Brookpark, OH....843-916-2000
Atkinson Milling Co.
Selma, NC....800-948-5707
Atlantic Blueberry
Hammonton, NJ....609-561-8600
Atlantic Meat Company
Savannah, GA....912-964-8511
Atlantic Veal & Lamb Inc
Brooklyn, NY....800-222-8325
Aurora Frozen Foods Division
Saint Louis, MO....314-801-2800
Austin Special Foods Company
Austin, TX....512-372-8665
Avanti Foods Co
Walnut, IL....800-243-3739
Avo-King Internatl
Orange, CA....800-286-5464
Awrey Bakeries
Livonia, MI....800-950-2253
B & D Foods
Boise, ID....208-344-1183
B G Smith & Sons Oyster Co
Sharps, VA....877-483-8279
Badger Best Pizzas
De Pere, WI....920-336-6464
Baja Foods LLC
Chicago, IL....773-376-9030
Baker Boy Bake Shop Inc
Dickinson, ND....800-437-2008
Baker Boys
Calgary, AB....877-246-6036
Baker's Point Fisheries
Oyster Pond Jeddore, NS....902-845-2347
Balboa Dessert Co Inc
Santa Ana, CA....800-974-9699
Bama Foods LTD
Tulsa, OK....800-756-2262
Bama Frozen Dough
Tulsa, OK....800-756-2262
Bandon Bay Fisheries
Bandon, OR....541-347-4454
Barber Foods
Kings Mountain, NC....877-447-3279
Barnes Ice Cream Company
Manchester, ME....207-622-0827
Bavarian Specialty Foods, LLC
Los Angeles, CA....626-856-3188
Bay Oceans Sea Foods
Garibaldi, OR....503-322-3316

Bayou Land Seafood
Breaux Bridge, LA....337-667-6118
BCFoods
Santa Rosa, CA....707-547-1776
Beaver Street Fisheries
Jacksonville, FL....800-874-6426
Beck's Waffles of Oklahoma
Shawnee, OK....800-646-6254
Becker Foods
Westminster, CA....714-891-9474
Behm Blueberry Farms
Grand Haven, MI....616-846-1650
Bellisio Foods
Minneapolis, MN
Bernardi Italian Foods Company
Bloomsburg, PA....570-389-5500
Bernie's Foods
Brooklyn, NY....718-417-6677
Best Maid Cookie Co
River Falls, WI....888-444-0322
Beta Pure Foods
Santa Cruz, CA....831-685-6565
Biagio's Banquets
Chicago, IL....800-392-2837
Biloxi Freezing Processing Inc.
Biloxi, MS....228-436-0017
Birch Street Seafoods
Digby, NS....902-245-6551
Birchwood Foods Inc
Kenosha, WI....800-541-1685
Birdie Pak Products
Chicago, IL....773-247-5293
Birdsall Ice Cream Company
Mason City, IA....641-423-5365
Blakely Freezer Locker
Blakeley, GA....229-723-3622
Bland Farms INC
Glennville, GA....800-752-0206
Blend Pak Inc
Bloomfield, KY....502-252-8000
Blount Fine Foods
Fall River, MA....774-888-1300
Blue Ridge Poultry
Athens, GA....706-546-6767
BlueWater Seafoods
Gloucester, MA....888-560-2539
Bob's Custom Cuts
Bonnyville, AB....780-826-2627
Boboli Intl. Inc.
Stockton, CA....209-473-3507
Bodin Foods
New Iberia, LA....337-367-1344
Bon Secour Fisheries Inc
Bon Secour, AL....251-949-7411
Bonnie Doon LLC
Elkhart, IN....574-264-3390
Boston Chowda
Haverhill, MA....800-992-0054
Brakebush Brothers
Westfield, WI....800-933-2121
Branding Iron
Sauget, IL....800-851-4684
Bridgford Foods Corp
Anaheim, CA....800-527-2105
Brighams
Arlington, MA....800-242-2423
Bright Harvest Sweet Potato Co
Clarksville, AR....800-793-7440
Broadleaf Venison USA Inc
Vernon, CA....800-336-3844
Brom Food Group
St. Laurent, QC....514-744-5152
Brook Locker Plant
Brook, IN....219-275-2611
Brooklyn Bagel Company
Staten Island, NY....800-349-3055
Brookside Foods
Cleveland, OH....216-991-7600
Brookview Farms
Manakin-Sabot, VA....804-784-3131
Brown Produce Company
Farina, IL....618-245-3301
Brown's Ice Cream Co
Minneapolis, MN....612-378-1075
Browns' Ice Cream Company
Minneapolis, MN....612-378-1075
Bruno Specialty Foods
West Sayville, NY....631-589-1700
Bubbies Homemade Ice Cream
Aiea, HI....808-487-7218
Buck's Spumoni Company
Milford, CT....888-222-8257

Bueno Foods
Albuquerque, NM....800-888-7336
Burke Corp
Nevada, IA....800-654-1152
Bush Brothers Provision Co
West Palm Beach, FL....800-327-1345
Butterfield Foods
Noblesville, IN....317-776-4775
Buxton Foods
Buxton, ND....800-726-8057
Bylada Foods
Moonachie, NJ....201-933-7474
C F Gollott & Son Seafood
Diberville, MS....228-392-2747
Caesar's Pasta
Blackwood, NJ....888-432-2372
Cahoon Farms
Wolcott, NY....315-594-9610
Callis Seafood
Lancaster, VA....804-462-7634
Camino Real Foods Inc
Vernon, CA....800-421-6201
Campbell Soup Co.
Camden, NJ....800-257-8443
Captain Ken's Foods Inc
St Paul, MN....800-510-3811
Carando Gourmet Frozen Foods
Agawam, MA....888-227-2636
Caribbean Food Delights Inc
Tappan, NY....845-398-3000
Caribbean Products
Baltimore, MD....410-235-7700
Carla's Pasta
South Windsor, CT....860-436-4042
Carolina Blueberry Co-Op Assn
Garland, NC....910-588-4220
Carolina Foods Inc
Charlotte, NC....800-234-0441
Carousel Cakes
Nanuet, NY....800-659-2253
Carriere Foods Inc
Saint-Denis-Sur-Richelie, QC....450-787-3411
Carrington Foods Co Inc
Saraland, AL....251-675-9700
Casa di Carfagna
Columbus, OH....614-846-6340
Casa Di Lisio Products Inc
Mt Kisco, NY....800-247-4199
Catch Up Logistics
Pittsburgh, PA....412-441-9512
Cateraid Inc
Howell, MI....800-508-8217
Cathay Foods Corporation
Boston, MA....617-427-1507
CBC Foods
Little River, KS....800-276-4770
Cedar Crest Specialties
Cedarburg, WI....800-877-8341
Cedar Key Aquaculture Farms
Riverview, FL....888-252-6735
Cedar Lake Foods
Cedar Lake, MI....800-246-5039
Cedarlane Foods
Carson, CA....800-826-3322
Centreside Dairy
Renfrew, ON....800-889-9974
Challenge Dairy Products, Inc.
Dublin, CA....800-733-2479
Chandler Foods Inc
Greensboro, NC....800-537-6219
Chang Food Company
Garden Grove, CA....714-265-9990
Channel Fish Processing
Gloucester, MA....800-457-0054
Chases Lobster Pound
Port Howe, NS....902-243-2408
Chateau Food Products Inc
Cicero, IL....708-863-4207
Chef America
Chatsworth, CA....818-718-8111
Chef Hans' Gourmet Foods
Monroe, LA....800-890-4267
Chef's Pride Gifts LLC
Taylor, MI....800-878-1800
Cher-Make Sausage Co
Manitowoc, WI....800-242-7679
Cherbogue Fisheries
Yarmouth, NS....902-742-9157
Cherry Hill Orchards
Lancaster, PA....717-872-9311
Cherry Lane Frozen Fruits
Vineland Station, ON....877-243-7796

Chester W. Howeth & Brother
Crisfield, MD 410-968-1398
Chewys Rugulach
San Diego, CA 800-241-3456
Chicago Meat Authority Inc
Chicago, IL 800-383-3811
Chill & Moore
Fort Worth, TX 800-676-3055
Chincoteague Seafood Co Inc
Parsonsburg, MD 443-260-4800
Chocolate Shoppe Ice Cream Co
Madison, WI 800-466-8043
Chocolaterie Bernard Callebaut
Calgary, AB 800-661-8367
Choctaw Maid Farms
Jackson, MS 601-683-4000
CHR Foods
Watsonville, CA 831-728-0157
Christie Cookie
Nashville, TN 800-458-2447
Christy Wild Blueberry Farms
Amherst, NS 902-667-3013
Ciao Bella Gelato Company
Irvington, NJ 800-435-2863
Cinderella Cheese Cake Co
Riverside, NJ 800-521-1171
Citrico
Northbrook, IL 800-445-2171
Citrosuco North America Inc
Lake Wales, FL 800-356-4592
Citrus Service
Winter Garden, FL 407-656-4999
Classic Delight Inc
St Marys, OH 800-274-9828
Clear Springs Foods Inc.
Buhl, ID 800-635-8211
Clearwater Fine Foods
Bedford, NS 902-443-0550
Clifty Farm Country Meats
Paris, TN 800-486-4267
Clyde's Delicious Donuts
Addison, IL 630-628-6555
Coastal Seafoods
Ridgefield, CT 203-431-0453
Codinos Food Inc
Scotia, NY 800-246-8908
Cohen's Bakery
Ellenville, NY 845-647-2200
Cole's Quality Foods
Grand Rapids, MI 616-975-0081
Coloma Frozen Foods Inc
Coloma, MI 800-642-2723
Con Agra Foods Inc
Troy, OH 937-335-2115
Conoley Citrus Packers Inc
Winter Garden, FL 407-656-3300
Consolidated Mills Inc
Houston, TX 713-896-4196
Continental Mills Inc
Tukwila, WA 206-816-7000
Cookie Tree Bakeries
Salt Lake City, UT 801-268-2253
Corky's Ribs & BBQ
Pigeon Forge, TN 865-453-7427
Cozy Harbor Seafood Inc
Portland, ME 800-225-2586
Creighton Brothers
Warsaw, IN 574-267-3101
Creme Curls
Hudsonville, MI 800-466-1219
Creme D'Lite
Irving, TX 972-255-7255
Crescent Duck Farm
Aquebogue LI, NY 631-722-8000
Crest International Corporation
San Diego, CA 800-548-1232
Crestar Crusts
Washington Court House, OH 740-335-4813
Crevettes Du Nord
Gaspe, QC 418-368-1414
Crown Valley Food Service
Beaumont, CA 951-769-8786
Crystal Creamery
Modesto, CA 866-225-4821
Cuisine Solutions Inc
Sterling, VA 888-285-4679
Cuizina Food Company
Woodinville, WA 425-486-7000
Culinary Institute Lenotre
Houston, TX 888-536-6873
Culver Duck Farms Inc
Middlebury, IN 800-825-9225
Curly's Foods Inc
Edina, MN 612-920-3400
Cutie Pie Corp
Salt Lake City, UT 800-453-4575
Cyclone Enterprises Inc
Houston, TX 281-872-0087
Dairy Fresh Foods Inc
Taylor, MI 313-299-0735
Dairy King Milk Farms/Foodservice
Whitter, CA 800-900-6455
Dakota Brands Intl
Jamestown, ND 800-844-5073
Dannon Yo Cream
Portland, OR 800-962-7326
De Iorio's Foods Inc
Utica, NY 800-649-7612
Deconna Ice Cream
Reddick, FL 800-824-8254
Deep Creek Custom Packing
Ninilchik, AK 800-764-0078
Deep Foods Inc
Union, NJ 908-810-7500
Del's Lemonade & Refreshments
Cranston, RI 401-463-6190
Del's Seaway Shrimp & Oyster Company
Biloxi, MS 228-432-2604
Delta Pride Catfish
Indianola, MS 800-228-3474
Desserts Of Distinction
Tigard, OR 503-654-8370
Detroit Chili Co
Southfield, MI 248-440-5933
Devault Foods
Devault, PA 800-426-2874
Devine Foods
Elwyn, PA 888-338-4631
Diamond Blueberry Inc
Hammonton, NJ 609-561-3661
Dickinson Frozen Foods
Eagle, ID 800-886-4326
Dillman Farm Inc
Bloomington, IN 800-359-1362
Dimitria Delights Baking Co
North Grafton, MA 800-763-1113
Diversified Avocado Products
Mission Viejo, CA 800-879-2555
Dol Cice' Gelato Company
Yardley, PA 215-499-5661
Dold Foods
Wichita, KS 316-838-9101
Dorothy Dawson Food Products
Jackson, MI 517-788-9830
Dr Praeger's Sensible Foods
Elmwood Park, NJ 877-772-3437
Draper Valley Farms
Mt Vernon, WA 800-562-2012
Dufour Pastry Kitchens Inc
Bronx, NY 800-439-1282
Duma Meats Inc
Mogadore, OH 330-628-3438
Dutch Ann Foods Company
Natchez, MS 601-445-5566
Dwayne Keith Brooks Company
Orangevale, CA 916-988-1030
Dynamic Foods
Lubbock, TX 806-723-5600
E. Gagnon & Fils
St Therese-De-Gaspe, QC 418-385-3011
E.W. Bowker Company
Pemberton, NJ 609-894-9508
Eastern Fish Company
Teaneck, NJ 800-526-9066
Eberhard Creamery
Redmond, OR 541-548-5181
Eckert Cold Storage
Manteca, CA 209-823-3181
Edmond's Chile Co
St Louis, MO 314-772-1499
Edner Corporation
Hayward, CA 510-441-8504
Edwards Baking Company
Marshall, MN 866-739-2328
El Paso Meat Co
El Paso, TX 915-838-8600
El Rey Cooked Meats
St Louis, MO 314-521-3113
Elena's Food Specialties
S San Francisco, CA 800-376-5368
Eli's Cheesecake
Chicago, IL 800-354-2253
Endico Potatoes Inc
Mt Vernon, NY 914-664-1151
Enfield Farms Inc
Lynden, WA 360-354-2919
English Bay Batter Us Inc
Columbus, OH 800-253-6844
Enterprises Pates et Croutes
Boucherville, QC 800-265-7790
Ever Fresh Fruit Co
Boring, OR 800-239-8026
Exceldor Cooperative
Levis, QC 418-830-5600
Fairmont Foods Of Minnesota
Fairmont, MN 507-238-9001
Fairview Dairy Inc
Latrobe, PA 724-537-7111
Fantasia
Sedalia, MO 660-827-1172
Farr Candy Company
Idaho Falls, ID 208-522-8215
Fendall Ice Cream Company
Salt Lake City, UT 801-355-3583
Ferroclad Fishery
Batchawana Bay, ON 705-882-2295
Field's Pies
Pauls Valley, OK 800-286-7501
Fieldale Farms
Baldwin, GA 800-241-5400
Fieldbrook Foods Corp.
Dunkirk, NY 800-333-0805
Fiera Foods
Toronto, ON 800-675-6356
Fine Choice Foods
Richmond, BC 866-760-0888
Fiori Bruna Pasta Products
Miami Lakes, FL 305-705-2534
First Original Texas Chili Company
Fort Worth, TX 800-507-0009
Fish King
Glendale, CA 818-244-2161
Fish Market Inc
Louisville, KY 502-587-7474
Flavors from Florida
Bartow, FL 800-888-0409
Fleischer's Bagels
Macedon, NY 315-986-9999
Florentyna's Fresh Pasta Factory
Los angeles, CA 800-747-2782
Florida Veal Processors
Wimauma, FL 813-634-5545
Florida's Natural Growers
Lake Wales, FL 888-657-6600
Food City USA
Arvada, CO 303-321-4447
Forte Stromboli Company
Philadelphia, PA 215-463-6336
Fran's Healthy Helpings
Burlingame, CA 650-652-5772
France Delices
Montreal, QC 800-663-1365
French Gourmet Inc
Sparks, NV 775-525-2525
Fresh Frozen Foods
Jefferson, GA 800-277-9851
Fresh Juice Delivery
Beverly Hills, CA 310-271-7373
Frio Foods
San Antonio, TX 210-278-4525
Frozen Specialties Inc
Perrysburg, OH 419-867-2005
Frozfruit Corporation
Gardena, CA 310-217-1034
Fruit Belt Canning Inc
Lawrence, MI 269-674-3939
Fruithill Inc
Yamhill, OR 503-662-3926
Fry Foods Inc
Tiffin, OH 800-626-2294
G M Allen & Son Inc
Orland, ME 207-469-7060
Gabila's Knishes
Copiague, NY 631-789-2220
Gad Cheese Retail Store
Medford, WI 715-748-4273
Galliker Dairy Co
Johnstown, PA 800-477-6455
Galloway Co
Neenah, WI 800-722-8903
Garber Ice Cream Co Inc
Winchester, VA 800-662-5422
Gardner Pie Co
Akron, OH 330-245-2030
Gary's Frozen Foods
Lubbock, TX 806-745-1933

Gaucho Foods
Fayetteville, IL 877-677-2282
Gelato Fresco
Toronto, ON 416-785-5415
George Chiala Farms Inc
Morgan Hill, CA 408-778-0562
George Robberecht Seafood
Montross, VA 804-472-3556
Gerard & Dominique Seafoods
Harbor, OR 800-858-0449
Gesco ENR
Gaspe, QC 418-368-1414
Gifford's Ice Cream
Skowhegan, ME 800-950-2604
Giorgio Foods
Temple, PA 800-220-2139
Glacier Foods
Houston, TX 832-375-6300
Glendora Quiche Company
San Dimas, CA 909-394-1777
Glover's Ice Cream Inc
Frankfort, IN 800-686-5163
Gold Standard Baking Inc
Chicago, IL 800-648-7904
Golden Gulf Coast Packing Co
Biloxi, MS 228-374-6121
Golden Platter Foods
Newark, NJ 973-344-8770
Golden Town Apple Products
Rougemont, QC 866-552-7643
Gonard Foods
Calgary, AB 403-277-0991
Gonnella Baking Company
Schamburg, IL 800-322-8829
Good Harbor Fillet Company
New Bedford, MA 800-343-8046
Good Old Days Foods
Little Rock, AR 501-565-1257
Good Wives
Wilmington, MA 800-521-8160
Gorton's Inc.
Gloucester, MA 800-222-6846
Gourmet Croissant
Brooklyn, NY 718-499-4911
Goya Foods Inc.
Jersey City, NJ 201-348-4900
Great American Appetizers
Nampa, ID 800-282-4834
Great Northern Baking Company
Minneapolis, MN 612-331-1043
Great Northern Products Inc
Cranston, RI 401-490-4590
Great Valley Mills
Barto, PA 800-688-6455
Grecian Delight Foods Inc
Elk Grove Village, IL 800-621-4387
Gregory's Foods, Inc.
St Paul, MN 800-231-4734
Gress Enterprises
Scranton, PA 570-561-0150
Grimaud Farms-California Inc
Stockton, CA 800-466-9955
Grossingers Home Bakery
New York, NY 800-479-6996
Grow-Pac
Cornelius, OR 503-357-9691
Gulf Pride Enterprises
Biloxi, MS 888-689-0560
Guttenplan's Frozen Dough
Middletown, NJ 888-422-4357
GWB Foods Corporation
Brooklyn, NY 877-977-7610
H&H Fisheries Limited
Eastern Passage, NS 866-773-4400
Haines Packing Company
Haines, AK 907-766-2883
Hall Brothers Meats
Olmsted Twp, OH 440-235-3262
Hallmark Fisheries
Charleston, OR 541-888-3253
Hamms Custom Meats
Mckinney, TX 972-542-3359
Handy International Inc
Salisbury, MD 800-426-3977
Hanover Foods Corp
Hanover, PA 717-632-6000
Harker's Distribution
Le Mars, IA 800-798-7700
Harlan Bakeries
Avon, IN 800-435-2738
Harold Food Company
Charlotte, NC 704-588-8061
Harrisburg Dairies Inc
Harrisburg, PA 800-692-7429
Hartog Rahal Foods
Norwood, NJ 201-750-0500
Harvest Time Foods
Ayden, NC 252-746-6675
Hatfield Quality Meats
Hatfield, PA 800-743-1191
Health is Wealth Foods
Moonachie, NJ 201-933-7474
Heidi's Gourmet Desserts
Tucker, GA 800-241-4166
Heinz Quality Chef Foods Inc
Cedar Rapids, IA 800-356-8307
Herb's Seafood
Westampton, NJ 800-486-0276
Heringer Meats Inc
Covington, KY 859-291-2000
Hermann Pickle Co
Garrettsville, OH 800-245-2696
Hershey Creamery Co
Harrisburg, PA 888-240-1905
HFI Foods
Redmond, WA 425-883-1320
Higgins Seafood
Lafitte, LA 504-689-3577
Hillard Bloom Packing Co Inc
Port Norris, NJ 856-785-0120
Hillmans Shrimp & Oyster
Port Lavaca, TX 800-582-4416
Holton Food Products
La Grange, IL 708-352-5599
Home Delivery Food Service
Jefferson, GA 706-367-9551
Home Market Foods Inc.
Norwood, MA 781-948-1500
Home Run Inn Frozen Foods
Woodridge, IL 800-636-9696
Homer's Ice Cream
Wilmette, IL 847-251-0477
Homestead Meats
Delta, CO 970-874-1145
Hormel Foods Corp.
Austin, MN 507-437-5611
Horst Seafood
Juneau, AK 877-518-4300
Houdini Inc
Fullerton, CA 714-525-0325
House of Flavors Inc
Ludington, MI 800-930-7740
House of Spices
Flushing, NY 718-507-4600
Hudsonville Ice Cream
Holland, MI 616-546-4005
Humboldt Creamery
Modesto, CA 888-316-6064
Hunter Farms - High Point Division
High Point, NC 800-446-8035
Ice Cream Bowl
Zanesville, OH 740-452-5267
Ice Cream Club Inc
Boynton Beach, FL 800-535-7711
Ice Cream Specialties Inc
St Louis, MO 800-662-7550
Ideal Dairy Farms
Hudson Falls, NY 518-747-5059
Il Gelato
Astoria, NY 800-899-9299
Incredible Cheesecake
San Diego, CA 619-563-9722
Independent Packers Corporation
Seattle, WA 206-285-6000
Indian Ridge Shrimp Co
Chauvin, LA 800-594-0920
Indian Valley Meats
Indian, AK 907-653-7511
Inn Foods Inc
Watsonville, CA 800-708-7836
Inovata Foods
Tillsonburg, ON 800-265-5731
Inshore Fisheries
Middle West Pubnico, NS 902-762-2522
International Food Packers Corporation
Miami, FL 305-740-5847
International Specialty Supply
Cookeville, TN 931-526-1106
Island Marine Products
Clarks Harbour, NS 902-745-2222
Island Oasis Frozen Cocktail
Beloit, WI 800-777-4752
Island Scallops
Qualicum Beach, BC 250-757-9811
It's It Ice Cream Co
Burlingame, CA 800-345-1928
Italia Foods
Schaumburg, IL 800-747-1109
Itarca
Los Angeles, CA 800-747-2782
J & J Wall Bakery Co
Sacramento, CA 916-381-1410
J B & Son LTD
Yonkers, NY 914-963-5192
J H Verbridge & Son Inc
Williamson, NY 315-589-2366
J. Matassini & Sons Fish Company
Tampa, FL 813-229-0829
J.W. Haywood & Sons Dairy
Louisville, KY 502-774-2311
Jack & Jill Ice Cream
Moorestown, NJ 856-813-2300
James Skinner Company
Omaha, NE 800-358-7428
Janes Family Foods
Mississauga, ON 800-565-2637
Jaxon's Ice Cream Parlor
Dania Beach, FL 954-923-4445
Jazz Fine Foods
Montreal, QC 514-255-0110
JBS Packing Inc
Port Arthur, TX 409-982-3216
Jecky's Best
Santa Clarita, CA 888-532-5972
Jel Sert
West Chicago, IL 800-323-2592
Jemm Wholesale Meat Company
Chicago, IL 773-523-8161
Jessie's Ilwaco Fish Company
San Francisco, CA 360-642-3773
Joe Jurgielwicz & Sons
Hamburg, PA 800-543-8257
John Garner Meats
Van Buren, AR 800-543-5473
Johnson's Real Ice Cream
Columbus, OH 614-231-0014
Josh & John's Ice Cream
Colorado Springs, CO 800-530-2855
Jubilee Foods
Bayou La Batre, AL 251-824-2110
Juno Chef's
Goshen, NY 845-294-5400
Junuis Food Products
Palatine, IL 847-359-4300
K & K Gourmet Meats Inc
Leetsdale, PA 724-266-8400
Kan-Pak
Arkansas City, KS 800-378-1265
Karn Meats
Columbus, OH 800-221-9585
Katrina's Tartufo
Port Jeffrsn Sta, NY 800-480-8836
Kelley Foods
Elba, AL 334-897-5761
Kenosha Beef International LTD
Kenosha, WI
Kent Foods Inc
Gonzales, TX 830-672-7993
Kent Precision Foods Group Inc
Muscatine, IA 800-442-5242
Key Largo Fisheries
Key Largo, FL 800-432-4358
Keyser Brothers
Lottsburg, VA 804-529-6837
King Cole Ducks Limited
Newmarket, ON 800-363-3825
King Kold Meats
Englewood, OH 800-836-2797
Kitchens Seafood
Plant City, FL 800-327-0132
Klinke Brothers Ice Cream Co
Memphis, TN 901-322-6640
Kodiak Salmon Packers
Larsen Bay, AK 907-847-2250
Kona Cold Lobsters
Kailua Kona, HI 808-329-4332
Konto's Foods
Patterson, NJ 973-278-2800
KT's Kitchens
Carson, CA 310-764-0850
Kubla Khan Food Company
Portland, OR 503-234-7494
Kutztown Bologna Company
Leola, PA 800-723-8824
Kyger Bakery Products
Lafayette, IN 765-447-1252

L&C Fisheries
Kensington, PE....902-886-2770
La Cookie
Burbank, CA....818-495-5732
LA Monica Fine Foods
Millville, NJ
La Nova Wings
Buffalo, NY....800-652-6682
Ladoga Frozen Food & Retail
Ladoga, IN....765-942-2225
Lady Gale Seafood
Baldwin, LA....337-923-2060
Lafitte Frozen Foods Corp
Lafitte, LA....504-689-2041
Lake Packing Co Inc
Lottsburg, VA....800-324-2759
Lakeside Foods Inc.
Plainview, MN....507-534-3141
Land O'Lakes Inc
Arden Hills, MN....800-328-9680
Landolfi's Food Products
Trenton, NJ....609-392-1830
Leader Candies
Brooklyn, NY....718-366-6900
Leelanau Fruit Co
Peshawbestown, MI....231-271-3514
Leidenheimer Baking Co
New Orleans, LA....800-259-9099
Lenchner Bakery
Concord, ON....905-738-8811
Lengerich Meats Inc
Zanesville, IN....260-638-4123
Lennox Farm
Shelburne, ON....519-925-6444
Leon's Bakery
North Haven, CT....800-223-6844
Leonetti's Frozen Food
Philadelphia, PA....866-551-7168
Les Boulangers Associes Inc
Seatac, WA....800-522-1185
Lombardi's Seafood
Winter Park, FL....800-879-8411
Lone Star Bakery
Round Rock, TX....512-255-7268
Lougheed Fisheries
Owen Sound, ON....519-376-1586
Louis Dreyfus Company Citrus Inc
Winter Garden, FL....407-656-1000
Louisa Food Products Inc
St Louis, MO....314-868-3000
Louisiana Packing Company
Westwego, LA....800-666-1293
Love Quiches Desserts
Freeport, NY....516-623-8800
Lucia's Pizza Co
St Louis, MO....314-843-2553
Ludwick's Frozen Donuts
Grand Rapids, MI....800-366-8816
Ludwig Fish & Produce Company
La Porte, IN....800-362-2608
Luxury Crab
St John's, NL....709-739-6668
M Buono Beef Co
Philadelphia, PA....215-463-3600
M&L Gourmet Ice Cream
Baltimore, MD....410-276-4880
M.A. Johnson Frozen Foods
Marion, IN....317-664-8023
Macabee Foods
West Nyack, NY....845-623-1300
Macfarlane Pheasants
Janesville, WI....800-345-8348
Mack's Bill Ice Cream
Dover, PA....717-292-1931
Mackie International, Inc.
Riverside, CA....800-733-9762
Mada'n Kosher Foods
Dania, FL....954-925-0077
Maid-Rite Steak Company
Dunmore, PA....800-233-4259
Main Street Gourmet
Cuyahoga Falls, OH....800-678-6246
Maine Wild Blueberry Company
Cherryfield, ME....800-243-4005
Majestic Foods
Huntington, NY....631-424-9444
Mama Rosie's Ravioli
Charlestown, MA....888-246-4300
Mamma Lina Ravioli Company
San Diego, CA....858-535-0620
Manchester Farms
Columbia, SC....800-845-0421
Mancuso Cheese Co
Joliet, IL....815-722-2475
Mannhardt Inc
Sheboygan Falls, WI....800-423-2327
Maola Milk & Ice Cream Co.
....844-287-1970
Maple Donuts Inc
Lake City, PA....877-774-3668
Maple Leaf Farms
St Leesburg, IN....800-348-2812
Maple Leaf Foods International
North York, ON....800-268-3708
Maplehurst Bakeries LLC
Brownsburg, IN....800-428-3200
Mar-Jac Poultry Inc.
Gainesville, GA....770-531-5000
Mar-Key Foods
Vidalia, GA....912-537-4204
Mardi Gras
Verona, NJ....973-857-3777
Mario's Gelati
Vancouver, BC....604-879-9411
Marsan Foods
Toronto, ON....416-755-9262
Martin Brothers Seafood Co
Westwego, LA....504-341-2251
Martin Seafood Company
Jessup, MD....410-799-5822
Marzetti Foodservice
Westerville, OH....800-247-4194
Mason County Fruit Packers Cooperative
Hart, MI....231-873-7504
Matador Processors
Blanchard, OK....800-847-0797
Maxim's Import Corporation
Miami, FL....800-331-6652
Mayfield Farms and Nursery
Athens, TN....423-746-9859
McCain Foods Ltd.
Toronto, ON....416-955-1700
McCain Foods USA Inc.
Oakbrook Terace, IL....800-938-7799
McConnell's Fine Ice Cream
Santa Barbara, CA....805-963-8813
Meat-O-Mat Corp
Brooklyn, NY....718-965-7250
Mehaffies Pies
Dayton, OH....800-289-7437
Mel-O-Cream Donuts Intl
Springfield, IL....800-500-5414
Meleddy Cherry Plant
Sturgeon Bay, WI....920-743-2858
Menemsha Fish Market
Chilmark, MA....508-645-2282
Merrill's Blueberry Farms
Ellsworth, ME....800-711-6551
Mexi-Frost Specialties Company
Brooklyn, NY....718-625-3324
Mi Ranchito Foods
Phoenix, AZ....602-272-3949
Mia Products
Scranton, PA....570-207-5328
Michael Foods, Inc.
Minnetonka, MN....952-258-4000
Michael's Cookies
Clear Lake, IA....800-822-5384
Michele's Family Bakery
York, PA....717-741-2027
Michelle Chocolatiers
Colorado Springs, CO....888-447-3654
Michigan Dairy LLC
Livonia, MI....734-367-5390
Mid-Atlantic Foods Inc
Easton, MD....800-922-4688
Mikawaya LLC
Vernon, CA....323-587-5504
Mike & Jean's Berry Farm
Mt Vernon, WA....360-424-7220
Mill Cove Lobster Pound
Trevett, ME....207-633-3340
Milmar Food Group
Goshen, NY....845-294-5400
Milne Fruit Products Inc
Prosser, WA....509-786-2611
Minh Food
Pasadena, TX....713-475-1970
Minh Food Corporation
Pasadena, TX....800-344-7655
Minor Fisheries
Port Colborne, ON....905-834-9232
Minterbrook Oyster Co
Gig Harbor, WA....253-857-5251
Minute Maid Company
Atlanta, GA....800-520-2653
Miracapo Pizza
Elk Grove Village, IL....847-631-3500
Mister Cookie Face
Dunkirk, NY....800-333-0305
Mobile Processing
Mobile, AL....251-438-6944
Model Dairy LLC
Reno, NV....800-433-2030
Modern Pod Co.
Providence, RI
Molinaro's Fine Italian Foods Ltd.
Mississauga, ON....905-281-0352
Momence Packing Company
Sheboygan Falls, WI....888-556-2728
Mooresville Ice Cream Co
Mooresville, NC....800-304-7172
Morey's Seafood Intl LLC
Motley, MN....800-808-3474
Morgan Foods Inc
Austin, IN....888-430-1780
Moroni Feed Company
Moroni, UT....435-436-8202
Morrison Lamothe
Toronto, ON....877-677-6533
Morrison Meat Pies
West Valley, UT....801-977-0181
Morrison Milling Co
Denton, TX....800-531-7912
Mortimer's Fine Foods
Burlington, ON....905-336-0000
Mozzicato De Pasquale Bakery
Hartford, CT....860-296-0426
Mushroom Co
Cambridge, MD....410-221-8971
Mutual Fish Co
Seattle, WA....206-322-4368
Myers Frozen Food Provisions
St Paul, IN....765-525-6304
Naleway Foods
Winnipeg, MB....800-665-7448
Nan Sea Enterprises of Wisconsin
Waukesha, WI....262-542-8841
Nancy's Specialty Foods
Newark, CA....510-494-1100
National Fish & Oyster
Olympia, WA....360-491-5550
National Frozen Foods Corp
Seattle, WA....206-322-8900
Natural Feast Corporation
Dover, MA....508-785-3322
Natural Fruit Corp
Hialeah, FL....305-887-7525
Nature Quality
San Martin, CA....408-683-2182
Nelson Crab Inc
Tokeland, WA....800-262-0069
Nelson Ice Cream
Stillwater, MN....651-430-1103
Neptune Fisheries
Newport News, VA....800-545-7474
Nestle USA
Mt Sterling, KY....859-499-1100
Nestle USA Inc
Glendale, CA....800-225-2270
New England Muffin Co Inc
Fall River, MA....508-675-2833
New York Frozen Foods Inc
Bedford, OH....216-292-5655
Newfound Resources
St Josephs, NL....709-579-7676
Niagara Foods
Middleport, NY....716-735-7722
Nickabood's Inc
Los Angeles, CA....213-746-1541
Night Hawk Frozen Foods Inc
Buda, TX....800-580-4166
Nor-Cliff Farms
Port Colborne, ON....905-835-0808
Norbest, LLC
Moroni, UT....800-453-5327
Nordic Group Inc
Boston, MA....800-486-4002
Norfood Cherry Growers
Simcoe, ON....519-426-5784
NORPAC Foods Inc
Salem, OR
North Pacific Seafoods Inc
Seattle, WA....206-726-9900
Northern Products Corporation
Seattle, WA....888-599-6290

Northern Wind Inc
New Bedford, MA 888-525-2525
Notre Dame Seafoods Inc.
Comfort Cove, NL 709-244-5511
O'Boyle's Ice Cream Company
Bristol, PA. 215-788-3882
O'Hara Corp
Rockland, ME. 207-594-4444
Ocean Beauty Seafoods Inc
Seattle, WA 800-365-8950
Ocean Food Co. Ltd.
Toronto, ON 416-285-6487
Ocean Spray International
Lakeville-Middleboro, MA 800-662-3263
Ocean Springs Seafood
Ocean Springs, MS 228-875-0104
Okuhara Foods Inc
Honolulu, HI. 808-848-0581
Old Fashioned Kitchen Inc
Lakewood, NJ. 732-364-4100
Omaha Steaks Inc
. . . . 800-960-8400
On-Cor Frozen Foods
On-Cor Frozen Foods Redi-Serve
Aurora, IL. 920-563-6391
Orange Bakery
Irvine, CA 949-863-1377
Ore-Ida Foods
Pittsburgh, PA. 800-255-5750
Oregon Fruit Products Co
Salem, OR. 800-394-9333
Oregon Potato Co
Boardman, OR 800-336-6311
Otis Spunkmeyer
Brockport, NY 855-427-9982
Out of a Flower
Lancaster, TX 800-743-4696
Oven Poppers
Manchester, NH 603-644-3773
Overhill Farms Inc
Vernon, CA 800-859-6406
Overlake Foods
Olympia, WA 800-683-1078
Oxford Frozen Foods
Oxford, NS 902-447-2100
P. Janes & Sons
Hant's Harbor, NL. 709-586-2252
Pacific American Fish Co Inc
Vernon, CA 800-625-2525
Pacific Coast Fruit Co
Portland, OR 503-234-6411
Pacific Ocean Produce
Santa Cruz, CA 831-423-2654
Pacific Salmon Company
Edmonds, WA. 425-774-1315
Pacific Seafoods International
Port Hardy, BC 250-949-8781
Pacific Valley Foods Inc
Bellevue, WA 425-643-1805
Paisano Food Products
Elk Grove Village, IL 800-672-4726
Palmetto Pigeon Plant
Sumter, SC 803-775-1204
Pamlico Packing Company
Grantsboro, NC. 800-682-1113
Paradise Island Foods
Nanaimo, BC. 800-889-3370
Pasta Del Mondo
Carmel, NY. 800-392-8887
Pasta Factory
Melrose Park, IL. 800-615-6951
Pasta International
Mississauga, ON. 905-890-5550
Pastry Chef
Pawtucket, RI 800-639-8606
Patterson Frozen Foods
Patterson, CA 209-892-2611
Paul Piazza & Son Inc
New Orleans, LA 800-969-6011
Pede Brothers Italian Food
Schenectady, NY. 518-356-3042
PEI Mussel King
Morrell, PE 800-673-2767
Pellman Foods Inc
New Holland, PA 717-354-8070
Penguin Frozen Foods Inc
Northbrook, IL 800-323-1485
Penobscot Mccrum LLC
Belfast, ME. 800-435-4456
Pepe's Inc
Chicago, IL 312-733-2500
Pepe's Mexican Restaurant
Anaheim, CA 714-952-9410
Perfect Addition
Newport Beach, CA 949-640-0220
Perfect Foods Inc
Goshen, NY. 800-933-3288
Perry's Ice Cream Co Inc
Akron, NY. 800-873-7797
Peter Pan Seafoods Inc.
Bellevue, WA 206-728-6000
Petersen Ice Cream Company
Oak Park, IL 708-386-6130
Phillips Foods
Baltimore, MD 888-234-2722
Phoenix Agro-Industrial Corporation
Westbury, NY 516-334-1194
Phranil Foods
Spokane, WA. 509-534-7770
Pictsweet Co
Bells, TN. 731-663-7600
Pierceton Foods Inc
Pierceton, IN. 574-594-2344
Pierino Frozen Foods
Lincoln Park, MI. 313-928-0950
Pinocchio Italian Ice Cream Company
Edmonton, AB 780-455-1905
Piqua Pizza Supply Co Inc
Piqua, OH 800-521-4442
Platte Valley Creamery
Scottsbluff, NE 308-632-4225
Plehn's Bakery Inc
Louisville, KY 502-896-4438
Plymouth Beef Co.
Bronx, NY. 718-589-8600
POG
Grand Bend, ON 519-238-5704
Portland Shellfish Company
Portland, ME. 207-799-9290
Positively 3rd St Bakery
Duluth, MN. 218-724-8619
Prairie Cajun Wholesale
Eunice, LA 337-546-6195
Prairie Farms Dairy Inc.
Edwardsville, IL 618-659-5700
Preferred Meal Systems Inc
Moosic, PA 570-457-8311
Price's Creameries
El Paso, TX. 915-565-2711
Pride Dairies
Bottineau, ND. 701-228-2216
Prime Smoked Meats Inc
Oakland, CA 510-832-7167
Puritan/ATZ Ice Cream
Kendallville, IN 260-347-2700
Purity Dairies LLC
Nashville, TN 615-244-1900
Purity Ice Cream Co
Ithaca, NY. 607-272-1545
QualiGourmet
Boisbriand, QC 514-287-3530
Quality Food Products Inc
Chicago, IL 312-666-4559
Quality Seafood
Apalachicola, FL. 850-653-9696
Queen International Foods
Monterey Park, CA. 800-423-4414
Quelle Quiche
Brentwood, MO 314-961-6554
R Four Meats
Chatfield, MN. 507-867-4180
Ragozzino Foods Inc
Meriden, CT 800-348-1240
Rainsweet Inc
Salem, OR. 800-363-4293
Ralph's Famous Italian Ices
Babylon, NY. 631-893-5646
Ramona's Mexican Foods
Gardena, CA. 310-323-1950
Ranaldi Bros. Frozen Food Products
Warwick, RI 401-737-5130
Ready Foods Inc
Denver, CO 800-748-1218
Red Baron
Marshall, MN 800-769-7980
Reinhold Ice Cream Company
Pittsburgh, PA 412-321-7600
Reiter Dairy
Newport, KY. 800-544-6455
Reiter Dairy LLC
Springfield, OH. 937-323-5777
Request Foods Inc
Holland, MI. 800-786-0900
Resource Trading Company
Portland, ME. 207-772-2299
Restaurant Systems International
Staten Island, NY 718-494-8888
Rhodes International Inc
Salt Lake City, UT 800-876-7333
Rich Products Corp
Vineland, NJ 800-818-9261
Rich Products Corp
Buffalo, NY. 800-828-2021
Rich's Ice Cream Co Inc
West Palm Beach, FL 561-833-7585
Riviera Ravioli Company
Bronx, NY. 718-823-0260
Rosati Italian Water Ice
Clifton Heights, PA. 855-476-7284
Rose Frozen Shrimp
Los Angeles, CA. 213-626-8251
Roselani Tropics Ice Cream
Wailuku, HI. 808-244-7951
Rowena
Norfolk, VA. 800-627-8699
Royal Harvest Foods Inc
Springfield, MA 413-737-8392
Royal Madera Vineyards
Madera, CA. 559-486-6666
Royal Seafood Inc
Brooklyn, NY 718-769-1517
Rubschlager Baking Corp
. . . . 800-661-7246
Ruggiero Seafood
Newark, NJ 866-225-2627
Ruiz Food Products Inc.
Dinuba, CA 800-477-6474
Rymer Foods
Chicago, IL 800-247-9637
S & E Organic Farms Inc
Bakersfield, CA 661-325-2644
S.D. Mushrooms
Avondale, PA 610-268-8082
Sahadi Fine Foods Inc
Brooklyn, NY. 800-724-2341
Santa Monica Seafood Co.
Rancho Dominguez, CA. 800-969-8862
Saveur Food Group
New york, NY 212-595-5425
Savino's Italian Ices
Deerfield Beach, FL 954-426-4119
Saxby Foods
Edmonton, AB 780-440-4179
Scenic Fruit Co
Gresham, OR. 877-927-3434
Schaefers Market
Sauk Centre, MN 320-352-6490
Schneider Foods
Saint Marys, ON 800-567-1890
Schneider's Dairy Inc
Pittsburgh, PA. 412-881-3525
Schneider-Valley Farms Inc
Williamsport, PA. 570-326-2021
Sea Pearl Seafood
Bayou La Batre, AL 800-872-8804
Sea Safari
Belhaven, NC 800-688-6174
Sea Snack Foods Inc
Los Angeles, CA. 213-622-2204
Sea Watch Intl
Easton, MD. 410-822-7500
Seaberghs Frozen Foods
White Plains, NY 914-948-6377
Seabrook Brothers & Sons
Seabrook, NJ. 856-455-8080
Seafood Producers Co-Op
Bellingham, WA 360-733-0120
Seatech Corporation
Lynnwood, WA. 425-487-3231
Sesinco Foods
New York, NY 212-243-1306
Seviroli Foods
Garden City, NY. 516-222-6220
Seviroli Foods Inc
Garden City, NY. 516-222-6220
Seymour & Sons Seafoods Inc
Diberville, MS 228-392-4020
Shaw's Southern Belle Frozen, Inc.
Jacksonville, FL 888-742-9772
Shawmut Fishing Company
Anchorage, AK. 709-334-2559
Shelley's
Jersey City, NJ 201-433-2900
Shonna's Gourmet Goodies
West Bridgewater, MA 888-312-7868

Sidari's Italian Foods
Cleveland, OH 216-431-3344
Sill Farm Market
Lawrence, MI 269-674-3755
Silver Lining Seafood
Seattle, WA....................800-426-5490
Silver State Foods Inc
Denver, CO....................800-423-3351
Simmons Foods Inc
Siloam Springs, AR 888-831-7007
Sisler's Ice & Ice Cream
Ohio, IL....................888-891-3856
Smeltzer Orchard Co
Frankfort, MI 231-882-4421
Smith Dairy
Orrville, OH 800-776-7076
Smith Frozen Foods Inc
Weston, OR....................541-566-3515
Smith Packing Regional Meat
Utica, NY 315-732-5125
Smoked Turkey Inc
Marshville, NC 704-624-6628
Snelgrove Ice Cream Company
Salt Lake City, UT 800-569-0005
Sno-Co Berry Pak
Marysville, WA....................360-659-3555
Snowbear Frozen Custard
W Lafayette, IN....................765-746-2930
Snowcrest Packer
Abbotsford, BC....................800-265-3686
So Delicious Dairy Free
Springfield, OR....................866-388-7853
Southern Ice Cream Specialties
Marietta, GA....................770-428-0452
Sparboe Foods Corp
New Hampton, IA....................641-394-3040
Specialty Meats & Gourmet
Hudson, WI....................800-310-2360
Spruce Lane Investments
Stratford, PE 902-892-2600
Squab Producers of California
Modesto, CA....................209-537-4744
St. Ours & Company
East Weymouth, MA....................781-331-8520
Star Ravioli Mfg Co
Moonachie, NJ 201-933-6427
Starkel Poultry
Puyallup, WA 253-845-2876
Steak-Umm Company
Shillington, PA 860-928-5900
Sterling Caviar LLC
Elverta, CA....................800-525-0333
Stewart's Shops Corp
Ballston Spa, NY 518-581-1200
Stone Crabs Inc
Miami Beach, FL 800-260-2722
Stone's Home Made Candy Shop
Oswego, NY....................888-223-3928
Strathroy Foods
Strathroy, ON 519-245-4600
Strebin Farms
Troutdale, OR....................503-665-8328
Sudlersville Frozen Food Locker
Sudlersville, MD....................410-438-3106
SugarCreek
Cincinnati, OH 800-445-2715
Sun Glo Of Idaho
Sugar City, ID....................208-356-7346
Sunny Avocado
Jamul, CA....................800-999-2862
Sunrise Growers
Placentia, CA 714-630-6292
Sunset Specialty Foods
Lake Arrowhead, CA 909-337-7643
Sunshine Dairy Foods Inc
Portland, OR....................503-234-7526
Sunshine Food Sales
Miami, FL....................305-696-2885
Super Snooty Sea Food Corporation
Boston, MA....................617-426-6390
Super Stores Industries
Turlock, CA 209-668-2100
Superbrand Dairies
Montgomery, AL....................334-277-6010
Supreme Frozen Products
Chicago, IL 773-622-3777
Sutherland's Foodservice
Forest Park, GA 404-366-8550
Suzanna's Kitchen
Peachtree Cor, GA 770-476-9900
Sweet Fortunes of America
Woodstock, NY....................845-679-7327
Sweet Water Seafood
Carlstadt, NJ 201-939-6622
Sweety Novelty
Monterey Park, CA....................626-282-4482
Switzer's Inc
Belleville, IL....................618-234-2225
Symons Frozen Foods
Centralia, WA 360-736-1321
Table De France
Ontario, CA....................909-923-5205
Taif Inc
Folcroft, PA....................610-522-0122
Taku Smokehouse
Juneau, AK 800-582-5122
Tampa Maid Foods Inc
Lakeland, FL....................800-237-7637
Tantos Foods International
Markham, ON....................905-943-9993
Tasty Mix Quality Foods
Brooklyn, NY 718-855-7680
Tasty Selections
Concord, ON....................905-760-2353
Taylor Shellfish Farms
Shelton, WA 360-426-6178
Tebay Dairy Company
Parkersburg, WV....................304-863-3705
Tex-Mex Cold Storage
Brownsville, TX 956-831-9433
The Pillsbury Company
Chelsea, MA....................800-370-7834
The Valpo Velvet Shoppe
Valparaiso, IN 219-464-4141
Thompson Packers
Slidell, LA....................800-989-6328
Thyme & Truffles Hors d'Oeuvres
Dollard-Des-Ormeaux, QC....................877-785-9759
Tichon Sea Food Corp
New Bedford, MA 508-999-5607
Tillamook County Creamery Association
Tillamook, OR 503-842-4481
Tipiak Inc
Stamford, CT....................203-961-9117
TNT Crust
Green Bay, WI....................920-431-7240
Toft Dairy Inc
Sandusky, OH....................800-521-4606
Tolteca Foodservice
Norcross, GA 800-541-6835
Tomanetti Food Products Inc
Oakmont, PA....................800-875-3040
Tomasso Corporation
Baie D'Urfe, QC....................514-325-3000
Tony's Ice Cream Co
Gastonia, NC....................704-867-7085
Totino's
Minneapolis, MN 800-248-7310
Trade Winds Pizza
Green Bay, WI....................920-336-7810
Trans Pecos Foods
San Antonio, TX....................210-228-0896
Travis Meats Inc
Powell, TN 800-247-7606
Trident Seafoods Corp
Wrangell, AK 907-874-3346
Trio's Original Italian Pasta Co.
Chelsea, MA....................800-999-9603
Triple D Orchards Inc
Empire, MI 231-326-5174
Triple U Enterprises
Fort Pierre, SD 605-567-3624
Triton Seafood Co
Medley, FL 305-888-0051
Tropical Illusions
Trenton, MO 660-359-5422
Tropical Treets
North York, ON....................888-424-8229
Tropicana Products Inc.
Chicago, IL....................800-237-7799
Tru-Blu Cooperative Associates
New Lisbon, NJ 609-894-8717
True Blue Farms
Grand Junction, MI....................877-654-2400
Turano Baking
Berwyn, IL 708-788-9220
Turk Brothers Custom Meats Inc
Ashland, OH....................800-789-1051
Turkey Store
Faribault, MN....................507-334-5555
Turri's Italian Foods
Roseville, MI 586-773-6010
Two Chefs on a Roll
Carson, CA 800-842-3025
Umpqua Dairy
Roseburg, OR....................888-672-6455
Uncle Ralph's Cookies
Frederick, MD....................800-422-0626
Unique Ingredients LLC
Gold Canyon, AZ 480-983-2498
United Meat Company
San Francisco, CA 415-864-2118
United Supermarkets
Lubbock, TX....................806-745-9667
Valley Meat Company
Modesto, CA....................800-222-6328
Valley Meats
Coal Valley, IL 309-517-6639
Van Oriental Food Inc
Dallas, TX....................214-630-0111
Van-Lang Food Products
Countryside, IL....................708-588-0800
VegGuide.org
Chicago, IL....................773-363-3939
Velda Farms
Orlando, FL....................800-795-4649
Velvet Ice Cream Co Inc
Utica, OH 800-589-5000
Viking Seafoods Inc
Malden, MA 800-225-3020
Vince's Seafoods
Gretna, LA 504-368-1544
Vincent Piazza Jr & Sons
Harahan, LA....................800-259-5016
Virginia Trout Co
Monterey, VA 540-468-2280
Vitamilk Dairy
Bellingham, WA 206-529-4128
Vivolac Cultures Corporation
Indianapolis, IN 317-356-8460
W & G Marketing Company
Ames, IA....................515-233-4774
W.L. Petrey Wholesale Inc.
Luverne, AL 334-230-5674
Waltkoch Limited
Tucker, GA 404-378-3666
Wanchese Fish Co Inc
Suffolk, VA....................757-673-4500
Wapsie Produce
Decorah, IA....................563-382-4271
Warwick Ice Cream
Warwick, RI 401-821-8403
Washington Potato Company
Pasco, WA....................800-897-2726
Washington Rhubarb Grower Assn
Sumner, WA 800-435-9911
Waugh Foods Inc
East Peoria, IL....................309-427-8000
Wawona Frozen Foods Inc
Clovis, CA 559-299-2901
Wayfield Foods
Atlanta, GA....................404-559-3200
Wayne Dairy Products Inc
Richmond, IN 765-935-7521
Webster Farms
Cambridge, NS 800-507-8844
Welch Foods Inc
Concord, MA 800-340-6870
Welch Foods Inc.
Concord, MA 800-340-6870
Weldon Ice Cream Co
Millersport, OH....................740-467-2400
Welsh Farms
Wallington, NJ 800-221-0663
Welsh Farms
Clifton, NJ....................973-772-2388
Wenk Foods Inc
Madison, SD 605-256-4569
Wenner Bakery
Bayport, NY 800-869-6262
Westco-BakeMark
Pico Rivera, CA 562-949-1054
Westin Foods
Omaha, NE 800-228-6098
Weyand's Fishery
Wyandotte, MI 800-521-9815
White Cap Fish Market
Islip, NY 631-277-6577
White Toque
Secaucus, NJ....................800-237-6936
Whitey's Ice Cream Inc
Moline, IL....................888-594-4839
Wick's Pies Inc
Winchester, IN 800-642-5880
Wild Rice Exchange
Woodland, CA....................800-223-7423

Williams Institutional Foods
Douglas, GA 912-384-5270
Winmix/Natural Care Products
Englewood, FL 941-475-7432
Wolferman's
Medford, OR 800-798-6241
Wolfgang Puck Food Company
Santa Monica, CA 310-432-1350
Wornick Company
Cincinnati, OH 800-860-4555
Wright's Ice Cream Co
Cayuga, IN 800-686-9561
Ya-Hoo Baking Co
Sherman, TX 888-869-2466
Yamasa Fish Cake Co
Los Angeles, CA 213-626-2211
Yorktown Baking Company
Yorktown Heights, NY 800-235-3961
Zartic Inc
Rome, GA 800-241-0516
Ziegenfelder Ice Cream Co
Wheeling, WV 800-322-3642

Spices, Seasonings & Seeds

General

Deko International Company
Earth City, MO 314-298-0910

Herbs

ACH Food Co Inc
Oakbrook Terrace, IL 630-586-3740
Agrexco USA
Jamaica, NY 718-481-8700
AM Todd Co
Kalamazoo, MI 269-343-2603
American Botanicals
Eolia, MO 800-684-6070
American Mercantile Corp
Memphis, TN 901-454-1900
Ana's Salsa
Austin, TX 888-849-7054
Ashland Sausage Co
Carol Stream, IL 630-690-2600
August Kitchen
Armonk, NY 914-219-5249
Backyard Safari Co
Covington, GA 770-385-3273
Badia Spices Inc.
Doral, FL 877-629-8000
BDS Natural
Long Beach, CA 310-747-0444
Belmont Chemicals
Clifton, NJ 800-722-5070
Beta Pure Foods
Santa Cruz, CA 831-685-6565
Better Living Products
Princeton, TX 972-736-6691
Bijol & Spices Inc
Miami, FL 888-245-6570
Bolner's Fiesta Spices
San Antonio, TX
Castella Imports Inc
Brentwood, NY 631-231-5500
Chef Tim Foods, LLC
Etters, PA 717-802-0350
Choice Food Distributors LLC
Nashville, TN 615-350-6070
Christopher's Herb Shop
Springville, UT 888-372-4372
Cinnabar Specialty Foods Inc
Prescott, AZ 866-293-6433
Colorado Spice Co
Boulder, CO 800-677-7423
Crush Foods Service
Westlake Village, CA 818-699-6381
Crystal Star Herbal Nutrition
Salinas, CA 831-422-7500
Cyclone Enterprises Inc
Houston, TX 281-872-0087
Daregal
Princeton, NJ 609-375-2312
Dion Herbs & Spices
St-Jerome, QC 877-569-8001
Dizzy Pig BBQ Co
Manassas, VA 571-379-4884
Dragunara LLC
Palos Verdes Estate, CA 310-618-8818
Dried Ingredients, LLC.
Miami, FL 786-999-8499
Dynapro International
Kaysville, UT 800-877-1413
Eckhart Corporation
Novato, CA 800-200-4201
Fantis Foods Inc
Carlstadt, NJ 201-933-6200
Freed, Teller & Freed
South San Francisco, CA 800-370-7371
Georgia Spice Company
Atlanta, GA 800-453-9997
Golden State Herbs
Thermal, CA 800-730-3575
Great Spice Company
Reno, NV 800-730-3575
Guayaki
Sebastopol, CA 888-482-9254
Hari Om Farms
Eagleville, TN 615-368-7778
Health Concerns
Oakland, CA 800-233-9355
Health Products Corp
Yonkers, NY 914-423-2900
HealthBest
San Marcos, CA 760-752-5230
Heffy's BBQ Co.
Kansas City, MO 816-200-2271
Herb Patch of Vermont
Bellows Falls, VT 800-282-4372
Herbal Science LLC
Bonita Springs, FL 239-597-8822
Herbs Etc
Santa Fe, NM 888-694-3727
High Quality Organics
Reno, NV 775-971-8550
International Spice
Lakewood, NJ 609-838-1717
Jodie's Kitchen
Pinellas Park, FL 800-728-3704
Kalustyan
New York, NY 800-352-3451
Kevala
Dallas, TX 877-379-1179
La Flor Spices
Hauppauge, NY 631-885-9601
Lebermuth Company
South Bend, IN 800-648-1123
Leeward Resources
Baltimore, MD 410-837-9003
Lefty Spices
Waldorf, MD 301-399-3145
Maine Coast Sea Vegetables
Franklin, ME 207-565-2907
McCormick & Company
Hunt Valley, MD 410-527-6189
Mermaid Spice Corporation
Fort Myers, FL 239-693-1986
Mezza
Lake Forest, IL 888-206-6054
Modern Day Masala, LLC
Marietta, GA 866-611-3757
Mom's Gourmet, LLC
Chagrin Falls, OH 440-564-9702
Morris J Golombeck Inc
Brooklyn, NY 718-284-3505
Mother Shucker's Original Cocktail Sauce
Columbia, SC 803-261-3802
Mountain Rose Herbs
Pleasant Hill, OR 800-879-3337
Nature's Sunshine Products Company
Lehi, UT 800-223-8225
Oak Hill Farm
Glen Ellen, CA 800-878-7808
Pacific Spice Co
Commerce, CA 323-890-0895
Pereg Gourmet Spices
Flushing, NY 718-261-6767
Phamous Phloyd's Barbecue
Denver, CO 800-497-3281
Pots de Creme
Lexington, KY 859-299-2254
Primal Essence
Oxnard, CA 877-774-6253
Prince of Peace
Hayward, CA 800-732-2328
Pure Ground Ingredients
Minden, NV 775-297-4047
QBI
South Plainfield, NJ 908-668-0088
Realsalt
Heber City, UT 800-367-7258
Red Monkey Foods
Springfield, MO 417-319-7300
Republic of Tea
Novato, CA 800-298-4832
Rodelle Inc
Fort Collins, CO 800-898-5457
S A L T Sisters
Goshen, IN 574-971-8368
Sampac Enterprises
S San Francisco, CA 650-876-0808
SAPNA Foods
Atlanta, GA 404-589-0977
See Smell Taste
San Francisco, CA 415-986-4216
Sentry Seasonings
Elmhurst, IL 630-530-5370
Shashi Foods
Toronto, ON 866-748-7441
Silva International
Momence, IL 815-472-3535
Smith & Truslow
Denver, CO 303-339-6967
Specialty Food America Inc
Hopkinsville, KY 888-881-1633
Spice House International Specialties
Hicksville, NY 516-942-7248
Spicely
Fremont, CA 510-440-1044
Sunshine Farm & Garden
Renick, WV 304-497-2208
Sup Herb Farms
Turlock, CA 800-787-4372
Superior Foods
Watsonville, CA 831-728-3691
SupHerb Farms
Turlock, CA 800-787-4372
Test Laboratories Inc
Reseda, CA 818-881-4251
Tolteca Foodservice
Norcross, GA 800-541-6835
Universal Formulas
Kalamazoo, MI 800-342-6960
Van Drunen Farms
Momence, IL 815-472-3100
Van Eeghen International Inc
St Laurent, QC 514-332-6455
Wagner Gourmet Foods
Lenexa, KS 913-469-5411
Whole Herb Co
Sonoma, CA 707-935-1077
Wisdom Natural Brands-Uani
Gilbert, AZ 800-899-9908
World Spice
Roselle, NJ 800-234-1060
Yellow Emperor Inc
Eugene, OR 877-485-6664
Young Winfield
Hamilton, ON 905-893-2536
Zuccaro Produce
Columbia Heights, MN 612-333-1122

Herbal Supplements

Abunda Life
Asbury Park, NJ 732-775-9338
Acta Health Products
Sunnyvale, CA 408-732-6830
ADH Health Products Inc
Congers, NY 845-268-0027
Advanced Spice & Trading
Carrollton, TX 800-872-7811
Agumm
Coral Springs, FL 954-344-0607
Alfred L. Wolff, Inc.
Park Ridge, IL 847-759-8888
Alta Health Products
Idaho City, ID 800-423-4155
Alternative Health & Herbs
Albany, OR 800-345-4152
AM Todd Co
Kalamazoo, MI 269-343-2603
Amazing Herbs Nutraceuticals
Buford, GA 800-241-9138
Ameri-Kal Inc
Wichita Falls, TX 940-322-5400
American Biosciences
Blauvelt, NY 888-884-7770
Arise & Shine Herbal Products
Medford, OR 800-688-2444
Asiamerica Ingredients
Westwood, NJ 201-497-5531
Auroma International Inc
Silver Lake, WI 262-889-8569
Bedrock Farm Certified Organic Medicinal Herbs
Wakefield, RI 888-874-7393
Bionutritional Research Group
Irvine, CA 714-427-6990
Blessed Herbs
Oakham, MA 800-489-4372
Bodyonics Limited
Farmingdale, NY 516-822-1230
Botanical Products
Springville, CA 559-539-3432

Brucia Plant Extracts
Shingle Springs, CA . . . 530-676-2774
Christopher's Herb Shop
Springville, UT . . . 888-372-4372
CHS Sunprairie
Minot, ND . . . 800-556-6807
Cinnabar Specialty Foods Inc
Prescott, AZ . . . 866-293-6433
Country Life
Hauppauge, NY . . . 800-645-5768
Cyanotech Corp
Kailua Kona, HI . . . 800-395-1353
Dr. Christopher's Herbal Supplements
Spanish Fork, UT . . . 800-453-1406
Eclectic Institute
Sandy, OR . . . 503-668-4120
Emerling International Foods
Buffalo, NY . . . 716-833-7381
Empire Spice Mills
Winnipeg, NB . . . 204-786-1594
En Garde Health Products, Inc.
Van Nuys, CA . . . 800-955-4633
Essential Flavors & Fragrances
Corona, CA . . . 888-333-9935
Essiac Canada International
Ottawa, ON . . . 888-900-2299
Fmali Herb
Santa Cruz, CA . . . 831-423-7913
Freeman Industries
Tuckahoe, NY . . . 800-666-6454
Functional Products LLC
Atlantic Beach, FL . . . 904-249-8074
Fungi Perfecti
Olympia, WA . . . 800-780-9126
Gaia Herbs Inc
Brevard, NC . . . 888-917-8269
GCI Nutrients
Foster City, CA . . . 866-580-6549
Ginco International
Simi Valley, CA . . . 800-284-2598
Global Botanical
Barrie, ON . . . 705-733-2117
Global Health Laboratories
Amityville, NY . . . 631-777-2134
Graminex
Saginaw, MI . . . 877-472-6469
Green Gold Group LLC
Marathon, WI . . . 888-533-7288
Green Grown Products Inc
Marina Del Ray, CA . . . 310-828-1686
Green Turtle Bay Vitamin Company
Summit, NJ . . . 800-887-8535
H. Reisman Corporation
Orange, NJ . . . 973-882-1670
Health & Nutrition Systems International
Boynton Beach, FL . . . 561-433-0733
Health & Wholeness Store
Fairfield, IA . . . 800-255-8332
Health Plus
Chino, CA . . . 800-822-6225
Health Products Corp
Yonkers, NY . . . 914-423-2900
Heart Foods Company
Minneapolis, MN . . . 800-229-3663
Herbal Magic
Toronto, ON . . . 877-237-7225
Herbal Products & Development
Aptos, CA . . . 831-688-8706
Herbalist & Alchemist Inc
Washington, NJ . . . 908-689-9020
HerbaSway Laboratories
Wallingford, CT . . . 800-672-7322
HerbCo International
Duvall, WA . . . 888-643-7226
Himalayan Heritage
Fredonia, WI . . . 888-414-9500
Honso USA
Chandler, AZ . . . 888-461-5808
Humco Holding Group Inc
Texarkana, TX . . . 903-831-7808
ILHWA American Corporation
Belleville, NJ . . . 800-446-7364
Indena USA Inc
Seattle, WA . . . 206-340-0863
Indiana Botanic Gardens Inc
Hobart, IN . . . 877-909-1502
International Vitamin Corporation
Freehold, NJ . . . 800-666-8482
Jaguar Yerba Company
Ashland, OR . . . 800-839-0775
Jarrow Industries Inc
Santa Fe Springs, CA . . . 562-906-1919

JR Laboratories
Honesdale, PA . . . 570-253-5826
Kalustyan
New York, NY . . . 800-352-3451
Kingchem
Allendale, NJ . . . 800-211-4330
LA Lifestyle Nutritional Products
Santa Ana, CA . . . 800-387-4786
LifeTime
Orange, CA . . . 800-333-6168
Mayway Corp
Oakland, CA . . . 800-262-9929
Mcfadden Farm
Potter Valley, CA . . . 800-544-8230
Meridian Trading Co.
Boulder, CO . . . 303-442-8683
Michael's Naturopathic Prgms
San Antonio, TX . . . 800-845-2730
Mincing Overseas Spice Company
Dayton, NJ . . . 732-355-9944
Motherland International Inc
Rancho Cucamonga, CA . . . 800-590-5407
Naturalife Laboratories
Torrance, CA . . . 800-231-3670
Nature Most Laboratories
Middletown, CT . . . 800-234-2112
Nature's Bounty Co.
Ronkonkoma, NY . . . 877-774-3361
Nature's Herbs
Merritt, BC . . . 800-437-2257
North West Pharmanaturals Inc
Brea, CA . . . 714-529-0980
Northridge Laboratories
Chatsworth, CA . . . 818-882-5622
Pendery's
Dallas, TX . . . 800-533-1870
Phyto-Technologies
Woodbine, IA . . . 877-809-3404
Prince of Peace
Hayward, CA . . . 800-732-2328
Pro Form Labs
Orinda, CA . . . 707-752-9010
Pro Pac Labs
Ogden, UT . . . 888-277-6722
Progenix Corporation
Wausau, WI . . . 800-233-3356
Rainbow Light Nutritional Systems
Santa Cruz, CA . . . 800-635-1233
Restaurant Lulu Gourmet Products
San Francisco, CA . . . 888-693-5800
SADKHIN Complex
Brooklyn, NY . . . 800-723-5446
Sandbar Trading Corp
Louisville, CO . . . 303-499-7480
Schiff Food Products Co Inc
Totowa, NJ . . . 973-237-1990
Shaker Museum
New Gloucester, ME . . . 888-624-6345
Soft Cell Technology
Commerce, CA . . . 800-360-7484
Starwest Botanicals Inc
Sacramento, CA . . . 800-800-4372
Sundial Herb Garden
Higganum, CT . . . 860-345-4290
Swagger Foods Corp
Vernon Hills, IL . . . 847-913-1200
Test Laboratories Inc
Reseda, CA . . . 818-881-4251
Tova Industries LLC
Louisville, KY . . . 888-532-8682
Turtle Island Herbs
Boulder, CO . . . 800-684-4060
Tusitala
Grand Bay, AL . . . 251-865-4353
Twin Oaks Community
Louisa, VA . . . 540-894-5141
Uptime Energy, Inc.
Canoga Park, CA
Urban Moonshine
Burlington, VT . . . 802-428-4707
Utzy, Inc.
Lake Geneva, WI . . . 877-307-6142
Verdure Sciences
Noblesville, IN . . . 888-656-4364
Virgin Raw Foods LLC
Los Angeles, CA . . . 800-830-7047
Vit-Best Nutrition
Tustin, CA . . . 714-832-9700
Vitality Works
Albuquerque, NM . . . 505-268-9950
Vitamer Laboratories
Irvine, CA . . . 800-432-8355

Vitarich Laboratories
Naples, FL . . . 800-817-9999
Whole Herb Co
Sonoma, CA . . . 707-935-1077
World Ginseng Ctr Inc
San Francisco, CA . . . 800-747-8808
World Organics Corporation
Huntington Beach, CA . . . 714-893-0017
Yerba Prima
Ashland, OR . . . 800-488-4339

for Beef

Sentry Seasonings
Elmhurst, IL . . . 630-530-5370

for Pork

Sentry Seasonings
Elmhurst, IL . . . 630-530-5370

for Poultry

Sentry Seasonings
Elmhurst, IL . . . 630-530-5370

for Seafood

Hsu's Ginseng Enterprises Inc
Wausau, WI . . . 800-826-1577
Sentry Seasonings
Elmhurst, IL . . . 630-530-5370

Salt

Adluh Flour
Columbia, SC . . . 800-692-3584
Agri-Dairy Products
Purchase, NY . . . 914-697-9580
Ajinomoto Heartland Inc
Chicago, IL . . . 773-380-7000
Amphora International
Lake Forest, CA . . . 888-380-4808
Bespoke Provisions
Boulder, CO . . . 646-963-1245
Bluechip Group
Salt Lake City, UT . . . 800-878-0099
Cabo Rojo Enterprises
Boqueron, PR . . . 787-254-0015
Chef Salt
Center Valley, PA . . . 215-782-1730
Con Yeager Spice Co
Zelienople, PA . . . 800-222-2460
Dr. Paul Lohmann Inc.
Islandia, NY . . . 631-851-8810
Earth Circle Organics
Auburn, CA . . . 877-922-3663
Foods Alive
Angola, IN . . . 260-488-4497
Franco's Cocktail Mixes
Pompano Beach, FL . . . 800-782-4508
Frontier Co-op
Norway, IA . . . 844-550-6200
Gustus Vitae Condiments LLC
Pasadena, CA . . . 424-229-2367
Heinz Portion Control
Jacksonville, FL . . . 904-695-1300
HimalaSalt
Sheffield, MA . . . 413-528-5141
Himalayan Chef
Sheffield, MA . . . 413-528-5141
ICL Performance Products
St. Louis, MO . . . 800-244-6169
Java-Gourmet/Keuka Lake Coffee Roaster
Penn Yan, NY . . . 888-478-2739
Jungbunzlauer Inc
Newton, MA . . . 617-969-0900
K+S Windsor Salt Ltd.
Pointe Claire, QC . . . 514-630-0900
Lawry's Foods
Hunt Valley, MD . . . 800-952-9797
Morton Salt Inc.
Chicago, IL . . . 800-725-8847
Nutricepts
Burnsville, MN . . . 800-949-9060
Peg's Salt
Greenwood, VA . . . 434-249-2495
Rapunzel Pure Organics
Bloomfield, NJ . . . 800-225-1449
S A L T Sisters
Goshen, IN . . . 574-971-8368
Salty Wahine Gourmet Hawaiian Sea Salt
Hanapepe, HI . . . 808-378-4089
Seattle Seasonings
Port Orchard, WA . . . 360-871-1511

Smith & Truslow
Denver, CO 303-339-6967
Stickney & Poor Company
Peterborough, NH 603-924-2259
Sunfood
El Cajon, CA 888-729-3663
Sustainable Sourcing
Great Barrington, MA 413-528-5141
Sutter Buttes Olive Oil
Sutter, CA 530-763-7921
Swagger Foods Corp
Vernon Hills, IL 847-913-1200
The Chili Lab
Brooklyn, NY
Twang Partners LTD
San Antonio, TX 800-950-8095
United Salt Corp
Houston, TX 800-554-8658
WBM International
Flemington, NJ 866-802-9366

Active

Dr. Paul Lohmann Inc.
Islandia, NY 631-851-8810
Particle Dynamics
Saint Louis, MO 800-452-4682

Celery

American Key Food Products Inc
Closter, NJ 877-263-7539
Gel Spice Co LLC
Bayonne, NJ 800-922-0230

Garlic

American Key Food Products Inc
Closter, NJ 877-263-7539
Bolner's Fiesta Spices
San Antonio, TX
Gel Spice Co LLC
Bayonne, NJ 800-922-0230

MSG & Salt Mixture

ACH Food Co Inc
Oakbrook Terrace, IL 630-586-3740
American Food Ingredients Inc
Oceanside, CA 760-967-6287
Compass Minerals
Overland Park, KS 913-344-9200
De Souza's
Banning, CA 800-373-5171
Dr. Paul Lohmann Inc.
Islandia, NY 631-851-8810

Onion

American Key Food Products Inc
Closter, NJ 877-263-7539
Gel Spice Co LLC
Bayonne, NJ 800-922-0230

Rock

Frontier Co-op
Norway, IA 844-550-6200
Morton Salt Inc.
Chicago, IL 800-725-8847

Sea

Blue Crab Bay
Melfa, VA 800-221-2722
Blue Marble Brands
Providence, RI 888-534-0246
Celtic Sea Salt
Arden, NC 800-867-7258
Evolution Salt Co.
Austin, TX 877-868-7979
Jacobsen's Salt Co.
Portland, OR 503-719-4973
Redmond Minerals Inc
Heber City, UT 866-312-7258
Riega
Kansas City, MO 816-744-8260
Sea Salt Superstore
Lynnwood, WA 866-999-7258
Selina Naturally
Arden, NC 800-867-7258
Smith & Truslow
Denver, CO 303-339-6967
Spice Lab
Pompano Beach, FL 954-275-4478

Sutter Buttes Olive Oil
Sutter, CA 530-763-7921

Substitutes

Ajinomoto Heartland Inc
Chicago, IL 773-380-7000
Mermaid Spice Corporation
Fort Myers, FL 239-693-1986
Morre-Tec Ind Inc
Union, NJ 908-686-0307
Spice Hunter Inc
Richmond, VA 800-444-3061

Tablets

Dr. Paul Lohmann Inc.
Islandia, NY 631-851-8810

Enriched

Dr. Paul Lohmann Inc.
Islandia, NY 631-851-8810

Seasonings

A.C. Legg
Calera, AL 800-422-5344
Adluh Flour
Columbia, SC 800-692-3584
Advanced Food Systems
Somerset, NJ 800-787-3067
All American Seasonings
Denver, CO 303-623-2320
All Seasonings Ingredients Inc
Oneida, NY 800-255-7748
Alpine Touch Spices
Choteau, MT 877-755-2525
AM Todd Co
Kalamazoo, MI 269-343-2603
American Food Ingredients Inc
Oceanside, CA 760-967-6287
American Key Food Products Inc
Closter, NJ 877-263-7539
Andy's Seasoning
St Louis, MO 800-305-3004
Arizona Natural Products
Phoenix, AZ 800-255-2823
Atlantic Seasonings
Kinston, NC 800-433-5261
Au Printemps Gourmet
Saint-Jerome, QC 800-438-6676
Autin's Cajun Cookery
Covington, LA 800-877-7290
Backyard Safari Co
Covington, GA 770-385-3273
Badia Spices Inc.
Doral, FL 877-629-8000
Baker's Ribs No 2
Dallas, TX 214-748-5433
Bakon Yeast
Scottsdale, AZ 480-595-9370
Barataria Spice Company
Barataria, LA 800-793-7650
BBQ'n Fools Catering, LLC
Greenfield, IN 800-671-8652
Bell Flavors & Fragrances
Northbrook, IL 847-291-8300
Benson's Gourmet Seasonings
Azusa, CA 800-325-5619
Bettah Buttah, LLC
Kansas City, KS 800-568-8468
Big Poppa Smokers
Coachella, CA 877-828-0727
Bittersweet Herb Farm
Shelburne Falls, MA 800-456-1599
BKW Seasonings
Knoxville, TN 865-851-8657
Blend Pak Inc
Bloomfield, KY 502-252-8000
Blendex Co
Louisville, KY 800-626-6325
Blue Crab Bay
Melfa, VA 800-221-2722
Bolner's Fiesta Spices
San Antonio, TX
Boston Spice & Tea Company
Boston, VA 800-966-4372
C&P Additives
Boca Raton, FL 877-857-2623
C.F. Sauer Co.
Richmond, VA 888-723-0052
Cabo Rojo Enterprises
Boqueron, PR 787-254-0015

Cajun Boy's Louisiana Products
Church Point, LA 800-880-9575
Cajun Brands
New Iberia, LA 504-408-2252
Cajun Original Foods Inc
New Iberia, LA 337-367-1344
California Blending Co
El Monte, CA 626-448-1918
Caribbean Food Delights Inc
Tappan, NY 845-398-3000
Catamount Specialties of Vermont
Plainfield, VT 800-639-2406
Cedar Hill Seasonings
Edmond, OK 800-342-1986
Char Crust
Chicago, IL 800-311-9884
Chef Hans' Gourmet Foods
Monroe, LA 800-890-4267
Chef Merito Inc
Van Nuys, CA 800-637-4861
Chef Paul Prudhomme's Magic Seasonings Blends
New Orleans, LA 800-457-2857
Chef Shells Catering & Roadside Cafe
Downtown Port Huron, MI 810-966-8371
Cherchies
Malvern, PA 800-644-1980
Chester's International , LLC
Mountain Brook, AL 800-288-1555
Chimayo To Go / Cibolo Junction
Albuquerque, NM 800-683-9628
Chr Hansen Inc
Milwaukee, WI 414-607-5700
Christie's
Stroughton, MA 781-341-3341
Christopher Ranch LLC
Gilroy, CA 408-847-1100
Chugwater Chili
Chugwater, WY 800-972-4454
Colonna Brothers Inc
North Bergen, NJ 201-864-1115
Colorado Spice Co
Boulder, CO 800-677-7423
Commercial Creamery Co
Spokane, WA 509-747-4131
Common Folk Farm
Naples, ME 207-787-2764
Con Yeager Spice Co
Zelienople, PA 800-222-2460
Consumers Vinegar & Spice Co
Chicago, IL 773-376-4100
Continental Seasoning
Teaneck, NJ 800-631-1564
Creative Seasonings
Wakefield, MA 617-246-1461
Crest Foods Inc
Ashton, IL 877-273-7893
Custom Culinary Inc.
Schaumberg, IL 800-621-8827
Davis & Davis Gourmet Foods
Allison Park, PA 412-487-7770
Dean Distributors, Inc.
Burlingame, CA 800-792-0816
Deko International Company
Earth City, MO 314-298-0910
Demitri's Bloody Mary Seasonings
Seattle, WA 800-627-9649
Dismat Corporation
Toledo, OH 419-531-8963
Dona Yiya Foods
San Sebastian, PR 787-896-4007
Dorothy Dawson Food Products
Jackson, MI 517-788-9830
Elite Spice Inc
Jessup, MD 800-232-3531
Enrico's/Ventre Packing
Syracuse, NY 888-472-8237
Erba Food Products
Brooklyn, NY 718-272-7700
Everglades Foods
Sebring, FL 800-689-2221
Everson Spice Co
Signal Hill, CA 800-421-3753
Excalibur Seasoning
Pekin, IL 800-444-2169
Fernandez Chili Co
Alamosa, CO 719-589-6043
First Spice Mixing Co
Long Island City, NY 800-221-1105
Five Star Food Base Company
St Paul, MN 800-505-7827
Flavor Dynamics Two
South Plainfield, NJ 888-271-8424

Flavorbank Company
Tucson, AZ 800-835-7603
Fmali Herb
Santa Cruz, CA 831-423-7913
Food Concentrate Corporation
Oklahoma City, OK 405-840-5633
Food Ingredient Solutions
Teterboro, NJ. 917-449-9558
Foran Spice Inc
Oak Creek, WI 800-558-6030
Fox Meadow Farm of Vermont
Rutland, VT 888-754-4204
Fresh Ideas
Las Vegas, NV 702-701-4272
Fuchs North America
Hampstead, MD 800-365-3229
Garden of the Gods Gourmet
Colorado Springs, CO. 877-229-1548
Georgia Spice Company
Atlanta, GA. 800-453-9997
Golden Specialty Foods Inc
Norwalk, CA. 562-802-2537
Good Rub
Morrisville, NC. 919-371-0329
Gravymaster, Inc.
Canajoharie, NY 800-839-8938
Green Mountain Gringo
Winston-Salem, NC 888-875-3111
Grouse Hunt Farm Inc
Tamaqua, PA 570-467-2850
Guapo Spices Company
Los Angeles, CA. 213-322-8900
Guido's International Foods
Pasadena, CA 877-994-8436
Gustus Vitae Condiments LLC
Pasadena, CA 424-229-2367
Halladay's Harvest Barn
Bellows Falls, VT. 802-463-3471
Harris Farms Inc
Coalinga, CA. 800-311-6211
Head Country
Ponca City, OK 888-762-1227
Health & Wholeness Store
Fairfield, IA 800-255-8332
Heartline Foods
Westport, CT. 203-222-0381
Heidi's Salsa
Los Angeles, CA. 310-821-0211
Herb Society Of America
Willoughby, OH 440-256-0514
Himalayan Chef
Sheffield, MA 413-528-5141
Hollman Foods
Des Moines, IA. 888-926-2879
Homegrown Naturals
Napa, CA. 800-288-1089
Illes Seasonings & Flavors
Carrollton, TX. 800-683-4553
Ingredients Corp Of America
Memphis, TN 888-242-2669
Integrative Flavors
Michigan City, IN. 800-837-7687
International Spice
Lakewood, NJ. 609-838-1717
Jagulana Herbal Products
Badger, CA 888-465-3686
JM All Purpose Seasoning
Lincoln, NE. 402-421-8326
K+S Windsor Salt Ltd.
Pointe Claire, QC 514-630-0900
Kent Precision Foods Group Inc
Muscatine, IA 800-442-5242
La Flor Spices
Hauppaugue, NY 631-885-9601
Lawry's Foods
Hunt Valley, MD. 800-952-9797
Life Spice & Ingredients LLC
Chicago, IL. 312-274-9992
Louisiana Gourmet Enterprises
Houma, LA 800-328-5586
Lucile's
Boulder, CO 800-727-3653
Luhr Jensen & Sons Inc
Hood River, OR 541-386-3811
Mad Chef Enterprise
Mentor, OH. 800-951-2433
Magic Seasoning Blends
New Orleans, LA 800-457-2857
Mane Inc.
Lebanon, OH. 513-248-9876
Mansmith's Barbeque
San Jn Bautista, CA 800-626-7648

Marin Food Specialties
Byron, CA. 925-634-6126
Marion-Kay Spice Co
Brownstown, IN 800-627-7423
Marnap Industries
Buffalo, NY. 716-897-1220
Massel USA
Carol Stream, IL 704-573-2299
Mayacamas Fine Foods
Sonoma, CA 800-826-9621
Mcclancy Seasonings Co
Fort Mill, SC. 800-843-1968
McCormick & Company
Hunt Valley, MD. 410-527-6189
Meat-O-Mat Corp
Brooklyn, NY 718-965-7250
Mermaid Spice Corporation
Fort Myers, FL 239-693-1986
Metarom Corporation
Newport, VT. 888-882-5555
Mild Bill's Spices
Ennis, TX 972-875-2975
Misty's Restaurant & Lounge
Lincoln, NE. 402-466-7222
Modern Products Inc
Mequon, WI 800-877-8935
Morris J Golombeck Inc
Brooklyn, NY 718-284-3505
Morton Salt Inc.
Chicago, IL 800-725-8847
Mrs. McGarrigle's Fine Foods
Merrickville, ON. 877-768-7827
Newly Weds Foods Inc
Chicago, IL 800-621-7521
Nonna Pia's Gourmet Sauces
Whistler, BC 888-372-1534
North Coast Farms
Santa Cruz, CA. 831-426-3733
North Coast Processing
Carlsbad, CA. 760-931-6809
Nu Products Co Inc
South Hackensack, NJ 800-836-7692
Old World Spices Inc
Overland Park, KS 800-241-0070
One Source
Concord, MA 800-554-5501
Oregon Flavor Rack
Oregon Spice Co Inc
Portland, OR. 800-565-1599
Organic Gourmet
Sherman Oaks, CA 800-400-7772
Pacific Foods
Kent, WA. 800-347-9444
Paleo Powder Seasoning
. 979-540-9137
Pappy Meat Company
Fresno, CA 559-291-0218
PAR-Way Tryson Co
St Clair, MO 636-629-4545
Pearson's Homestyle
Bowden, AB 877-224-3339
Pelican Bay Ltd.
Dunedin, FL 800-826-8982
Pemberton's Foods Inc
Gray, ME. 800-255-8401
Pleasoning Gourmet Seasonings
La Crosse, WI 800-279-1614
Precise Food Ingredients
Carrollton, TX. 972-323-4951
Produits Alimentaire
Laval, QC 800-361-9326
PS Seasoning & Spices
Iron Ridge, WI 920-387-2204
R C Fine Foods Inc
Hillsborough, NJ. 800-526-3953
Rector Foods
Brampton, ON. 888-314-7834
Red Lion Spicy Foods Company
Red Lion, PA. 717-309-8303
Restaurant Lulu Gourmet Products
San Francisco, CA 888-693-5800
Reva Foods
Saint Petersburg, FL 727-692-1292
REX Pure Foods
New Orleans, LA 800-344-8314
Rezolex LLC
Radium Springs, NM 575-527-1730
Riega
Kansas City, MO. 816-744-8260
Robinson's No 1 Ribs
Oak Park, IL 800-836-6750

Royal Foods & Flavor
Elk Grove Vlg, IL. 847-595-9166
S&B International Corporation
Torrance, CA. 310-257-0177
Salmolux Inc
Federal Way, WA 253-874-6570
Saratoga Food Specialties
Bolingbrook, IL 800-451-0407
Schiff Food Products Co Inc
Totowa, NJ 973-237-1990
Seattle Seasonings
Port Orchard, WA 360-871-1511
Secret Garden
Park Rapids, MN. 800-950-4409
Sentry Seasonings
Elmhurst, IL 630-530-5370
Shine Companies
Spring, TX. 281-353-8392
Shirley J Ventures, LLC
Lindon, UT 801-225-5073
Silver Palate Kitchens
Cresskill, NJ 201-568-0110
Soteria
Fairburn, GA. 404-768-5161
SOUPerior Bean & Spice Company
Vancouver, WA 800-878-7687
Southern Culture Foods
Peachtree Corners, GA
Southern Delight Gourmet Foods
Bowling Green, KY 866-782-9943
Spice Galleon
Belgium, WI 877-668-4800
Spice Hunter Inc
Richmond, VA. 800-444-3061
Spice King Corporation
Beverly Hills, CA 310-836-7770
Spicely
Fremont, CA 510-440-1044
Spicetec Flavors & Seasonings
Omaha, NE 800-921-7502
Spike Seasoning Magic
Mequon, WI 262-242-2400
St Charles Trading Inc
Batavia, IL. 630-377-0608
Superior Quality Foods
Ontario, CA. 800-300-4210
Swagger Foods Corp
Vernon Hills, IL 847-913-1200
T Hasegawa USA Inc
Cerritos, CA 714-522-1900
Tampico Spice Co
Los Angeles, CA. 323-235-3154
Taste Maker Foods
Memphis, TN 800-467-1407
Texas Coffee Co
Beaumont, TX. 800-259-3400
Texas Crumb & Food Products
Farmers Branch, TX 800-522-7862
Texas Traditions Gourmet
Georgetown, TX 800-547-7062
Todd's
Des Moines, IA. 800-247-5363
Tommy Tang's Thai Seasonings
Los Angeles, CA. 818-442-0219
Tony Chachere's Creole Foods
Opelousas, LA 800-551-9066
Trader Vic's Food Products
Emeryville, CA 877-762-4824
Tropical Foods
Charlotte, NC 800-438-4470
Tropical Link Canada Ltd.
Burnaby, BC 778-379-3510
UFL Foods
Mississauga, ON. 905-670-7776
Unilever Food Solutions
Englewood Cliffs, NJ
United Foods USA
Hayward, CA 510-264-5850
US Ingredients
Naperville, IL 630-820-1711
Vanns Spices LTD
Gwynn Oak, MD. 800-583-1693
Victoria Gourmet Inc
Woburn, MA. 800-403-8981
Wagner Gourmet Foods
Lenexa, KS 913-469-5411
West Pac
Idaho Falls, ID 800-973-7407
Whole Herb Co
Sonoma, CA 707-935-1077
WILD Flavors (Canada)
Mississauga, ON. 800-263-5286

Wildly Delicious
Toronto, ON 888-545-9995
William E. Martin & Sons Company
Roslyn, NY 516-605-2444
Wixon Inc.
St. Francis, WI 800-841-5304
Woody's Bar-B-Q Sauce Company
Waldenburg, AR 888-747-9229
World Flavors Inc
Warminster, PA 215-672-4400
World Harbors
Auburn, ME 800-355-6221
Young Winfield
Hamilton, ON 905-893-2536

Baking

Hodgson Mill Inc
Effingham, IL 800-347-0198
Sentry Seasonings
Elmhurst, IL 630-530-5370
World Spice
Roselle, NJ 800-234-1060

Barbecue

Applecreek Speciality Foods
Lexington, KY 800-747-8871
Bolner's Fiesta Spices
San Antonio, TX
Captain Foods, Inc.
Edgewater, FL 800-749-5047
Frontier Co-op
Norway, IA 844-550-6200
Mansmith's Barbeque
San Jn Bautista, CA 800-626-7648
Red Monkey Foods
Springfield, MO 417-319-7300
Rufus Teague
Shawnee, KS 913-706-3814
Sentry Seasonings
Elmhurst, IL 630-530-5370

Blackening

Sentry Seasonings
Elmhurst, IL 630-530-5370

Cajun Style

A Cajun Life®, LLC
Damascus, OR
Bolner's Fiesta Spices
San Antonio, TX
Cajun Creole Products Inc
New Iberia, LA 800-946-8688
Frontier Co-op
Norway, IA 844-550-6200
Louisiana Fish Fry Products
Baton Rouge, LA 800-356-2905
Red Monkey Foods
Springfield, MO 417-319-7300
Reggie Balls Cajun Foods
Lake Charles, LA 337-436-0291
Sentry Seasonings
Elmhurst, IL 630-530-5370
Slap Ya Mama Cajun Seasoning
Ville Platte, LA 800-485-5217

Cheese

Sentry Seasonings
Elmhurst, IL 630-530-5370

Chinese Style

Sentry Seasonings
Elmhurst, IL 630-530-5370
Smith & Truslow
Denver, CO 303-339-6967

Curd

Sentry Seasonings
Elmhurst, IL 630-530-5370

Dairy Products

Sentry Seasonings
Elmhurst, IL 630-530-5370

Fajita

Bolner's Fiesta Spices
San Antonio, TX
Sentry Seasonings
Elmhurst, IL 630-530-5370

Fried Rice

Sentry Seasonings
Elmhurst, IL 630-530-5370

Greek Style

Sentry Seasonings
Elmhurst, IL 630-530-5370
Smith & Truslow
Denver, CO 303-339-6967

Italian Herbs

Sentry Seasonings
Elmhurst, IL 630-530-5370
Smith & Truslow
Denver, CO 303-339-6967

Italian Style

Schiff Food Products Co Inc
Totowa, NJ 973-237-1990
Sentry Seasonings
Elmhurst, IL 630-530-5370

Lemon & Basil

Sentry Seasonings
Elmhurst, IL 630-530-5370

Lemon & Dill

Sentry Seasonings
Elmhurst, IL 630-530-5370

Lemon Pepper

Red Monkey Foods
Springfield, MO 417-319-7300
Sentry Seasonings
Elmhurst, IL 630-530-5370

Meat Products

A.C. Legg
Calera, AL 800-422-5344
All American Seasonings
Denver, CO 303-623-2320
Charissa
Cutchogue, NY 631-734-8878
JM All Purpose Seasoning
Lincoln, NE 402-421-8326
Nueces Canyon Range
Brenham, TX 800-925-5058
Ralph's Packing Co
Perkins, OK 800-522-3979
Rector Foods
Brampton, ON 888-314-7834
Robinson's No 1 Ribs
Oak Park, IL 800-836-6750
Sentry Seasonings
Elmhurst, IL 630-530-5370
Wixon Inc.
St. Francis, WI 800-841-5304
World Flavors Inc
Warminster, PA 215-672-4400

Mexican Style

Bea & B Foods
San Diego, CA 858-490-6205
Bolner's Fiesta Spices
San Antonio, TX
Golden Specialty Foods Inc
Norwalk, CA 562-802-2537
Red Monkey Foods
Springfield, MO 417-319-7300
Schiff Food Products Co Inc
Totowa, NJ 973-237-1990
Sentry Seasonings
Elmhurst, IL 630-530-5370

Pizza

California Blending Co
El Monte, CA 626-448-1918
Dorothy Dawson Food Products
Jackson, MI 517-788-9830
Sentry Seasonings
Elmhurst, IL 630-530-5370

Rib Rub

Bolner's Fiesta Spices
San Antonio, TX
Reva Foods
Saint Petersburg, FL 727-692-1292

Rufus Teague
Shawnee, KS 913-706-3814
Sentry Seasonings
Elmhurst, IL 630-530-5370
Swagger Foods Corp
Vernon Hills, IL 847-913-1200
Uncle Dougie's
Chicago, IL

Sausage

Sentry Seasonings
Elmhurst, IL 630-530-5370

Andouille

Sentry Seasonings
Elmhurst, IL 630-530-5370

Hot Italian

Sentry Seasonings
Elmhurst, IL 630-530-5370

Kielbasa

Sentry Seasonings
Elmhurst, IL 630-530-5370

Sweet Italian

Sentry Seasonings
Elmhurst, IL 630-530-5370

Snack

Butter

Sentry Seasonings
Elmhurst, IL 630-530-5370

Cajun Spice

Sentry Seasonings
Elmhurst, IL 630 530-5370

Cheddar

Sentry Seasonings
Elmhurst, IL 630-530-5370

Cinnamon Toast

Bolner's Fiesta Spices
San Antonio, TX
Sentry Seasonings
Elmhurst, IL 630-530-5370

Mesquite BBQ

Middleswarth Potato Chips
Kingston, PA 570-288-2447
Mrs Fisher's Potato Chips
Rockford, IL 815-964-9114
Sentry Seasonings
Elmhurst, IL 630-530-5370

Nacho Cheese

Sentry Seasonings
Elmhurst, IL 630-530-5370

Ranch

Sentry Seasonings
Elmhurst, IL 630-530-5370

Sour Cream & Onion

Middleswarth Potato Chips
Kingston, PA 570-288-2447
Mrs Fisher's Potato Chips
Rockford, IL 815-964-9114
Sentry Seasonings
Elmhurst, IL 630-530-5370

Southwest

Sentry Seasonings
Elmhurst, IL 630-530-5370

Tomato Pesto

Sentry Seasonings
Elmhurst, IL 630-530-5370

for Corned Beef

Sentry Seasonings
Elmhurst, IL 630-530-5370

for Tacos

Badia Spices Inc.
Doral, FL 877-629-8000
Bolner's Fiesta Spices
San Antonio, TX
Riega
Kansas City, MO 816-744-8260
Sentry Seasonings
Elmhurst, IL 630-530-5370

Seeds

American Mercantile Corp
Memphis, TN 901-454-1900
Ann's House of Nuts, Inc.
Columbia, MD 410-309-6887
Brock Seed Company
Finley, TN 731-286-2430
Buddy Squirrel LLC
St Francis, WI 800-972-2658
CHS Sunflower
Grandin, ND 701-484-5313
Cibo Vita
Totowa, NJ 862-238-8020
Con Yeager Spice Co
Zelienople, PA 800-222-2460
Corteva Agriscience
Wilmington, DE 302-485-3000
Dipasa USA Inc
Brownsville, TX 956-831-4072
DuPont Pioneer
Johnston, IA 515-535-5954
Eden Foods Inc
Clinton, MI 888-424-3336
Edison Grainery
Benicia, CA 510-382-0202
El Brands
Ozark, AL 334-445-2828
Everspring Farms
Seaforth, ON 519-527-0990
Farmer Direct Organic
Regina, SK 306-563-7815
Fernando C Pujals & Bros
Guaynabo, PR 787-792-3080
Foods Alive
Angola, IN 260-488-4497
Fresh Hemp Foods
Winnipeg, NB 800-665-4367
Frito-Lay Inc.
Plano, TX 800-352-4477
Giusto's Specialty Foods Inc
S San Francisco, CA 650-873-6566
Go Raw
San Jose, CA 408-272-4722
GoldFoods
Miami, FL 305-924-4825
Gourmet Nut
Brooklyn, NY 347-413-5180
Govadinas Fitness Foods
San Diego, CA 800-900-0108
Gurley's Foods
Willmar, MN 800-426-7845
H B Taylor Co
Chicago, IL 773-254-4805
HempNut
Henderson, NV 707-576-7050
Hialeah Products Co
Hollywood, FL 800-923-3379
High Mowing Organic Seeds
Wolcott, VT 866-735-4454
HP Schmid
San Francisco, CA 415-765-5925
International Harvest Inc
Mt Vernon, NY 800-277-4268
Kalustyan
New York, NY 800-352-3451
King Arthur Flour
Norwich, VT 800-827-6836
Krispy Kernels
Quebec, QC 877-791-9986
Mezza
Lake Forest, IL 888-206-6054
Midwest Nut Co
Minneapolis, MN 800-328-5502
Mincing Overseas Spice Company
Dayton, NJ 732-355-9944
Minn-Dak Growers LTD
Grand Forks, ND 701-746-7453
Monsanto Co
West Fargo, ND 800-437-4120
Natural Foods Inc
Toledo, OH 419-537-1711
Nature's Candy
Fredericksburg, TX 800-729-0085
Nature's Select Inc
Grand Rapids, MI 888-715-4321
New Century Snacks
City of Commerce, CA 800-688-6887
New Nissi Corp.
Paterson, NJ 973-278-4400
Nu-World Amaranth Inc
Naperville, IL 630-369-6851
Nutiva
Richmond, CA 800-993-4367
One Degree Organic Foods
Abbotsford, BC 855-834-2642
Osage Pecan Co
Butler, MO 800-748-8305
Patsy's Candy
Colorado Springs, CO 866-372-8797
Plantation Products Inc
Norton, MA 508-285-5800
R&J Farms
West Salem, OH 419-846-3179
Red River Commodities Inc
Fargo, ND 800-437-5539
Schiff Food Products Co Inc
Totowa, NJ 973-237-1990
Scott-Bathgate
Winnipeg, MB 800-216-2990
Seeds of Change
Rancho Dominguez, CA 888-762-7333
Smirk's
Fort Morgan, CO 970-762-0202
Snackerz
Commerce, CA 888-576-2253
Sole Grano LLC
Fair Lawn, NJ 201-797-7100
Sonne
Wahpeton, ND 800-727-6663
Specialty Commodities Inc
Fargo, ND 701-282-8222
Spitz USA
Loveland, CO 970-613-9319
Sunray Food Products Corporation
Bronx, NY 718-548-2255
Sunridge Farms
Royal Oaks, CA 831-786-7000
Sunshine Farm & Garden
Renick, WV 304-497-2208
Tantos Foods International
Markham, ON 905-943-9993
Tasty Seeds Ltd
Winkler, NB 888-632-6906
Texas Coffee Co
Beaumont, TX 800-259-3400
Thanasi Foods LLC
Boulder, CO 866-558-7379
To Your Health Sprouted Flour Co., Inc.
Floyd, VA 540-283-9589
Todd's
Vernon, CA 800-938-6337
Torn & Glasser
Los Angeles, CA 800-282-6887
Trophy Nut Co
Tipp City, OH 800-219-9004
Tropical Foods
Charlotte, NC 800-438-4470
Tropical Foods
Lithia Springs, GA 800-544-3762
Tropical Nut & Fruit Co
Orlando, FL 800-749-8869
TruVibe Organics
Santa Monica, CA
Urban Foods LLC
Sacramento, CA 916-372-3663
Weaver Nut Co. Inc.
Ephrata, PA 800-473-2688
Westin Foods
Omaha, NE 800-228-6098
Whole Herb Co
Sonoma, CA 707-935-1077
Willmar Cookie & Nut Company
Willmar, MN 800-426-7845
Zenobia Co
Bronx, NY 866-936-6242

Alfalfa

Corteva Agriscience
Wilmington, DE 302-485-3000
DuPont Pioneer
Johnston, IA 515-535-5954
NOW Foods
Bloomingdale, IL 888-669-3663

Anise or Aniseed

Chesapeake Spice Company
Belcamp, MD 410-272-6100
Commodities Marketing Inc
Clarksburg, NJ 732-516-0700
Morris J Golombeck Inc
Brooklyn, NY 718-284-3505
Smith & Truslow
Denver, CO 303-339-6967

Annatto

Gel Spice Co LLC
Bayonne, NJ 800-922-0230
Morris J Golombeck Inc
Brooklyn, NY 718-284-3505
Organic Planet
San Francisco, CA 415-765-5590
Schiff Food Products Co Inc
Totowa, NJ 973-237-1990

Caraway

Bedemco Inc
White Plains, NY 914-683-1119
Bob's Red Mill Natural Foods
Milwaukie, OR 800-349-2173
Chesapeake Spice Company
Belcamp, MD 410-272-6100
Frontier Co-op
Norway, IA 844-550-6200
Organic Planet
San Francisco, CA 415-765-5590
Smith & Truslow
Denver, CO 303-339-6967

Cardamom

Advanced Spice & Trading
Carrollton, TX 800-872-7811
American Key Food Products Inc
Closter, NJ 877-263-7539
Con Yeager Spice Co
Zelienople, PA 800-222-2460
Consumers Vinegar & Spice Co
Chicago, IL 773-376-4100
Frontier Co-op
Norway, IA 844-550-6200
Organic Planet
San Francisco, CA 415-765-5590
Schiff Food Products Co Inc
Totowa, NJ 973-237-1990
Smith & Truslow
Denver, CO 303-339-6967

Celery

Advanced Spice & Trading
Carrollton, TX 800-872-7811
American Key Food Products Inc
Closter, NJ 877-263-7539
Con Yeager Spice Co
Zelienople, PA 800-222-2460
Schiff Food Products Co Inc
Totowa, NJ 973-237-1990
Smith & Truslow
Denver, CO 303-339-6967
Unique Ingredients LLC
Gold Canyon, AZ 480-983-2498
Whole Herb Co
Sonoma, CA 707-935-1077

Ground

Chesapeake Spice Company
Belcamp, MD 410-272-6100

Coriander

Smith & Truslow
Denver, CO 303-339-6967

Whole

Smith & Truslow
Denver, CO 303-339-6967

Cumin

Con Yeager Spice Co
Zelienople, PA 800-222-2460
Consumers Vinegar & Spice Co
Chicago, IL 773-376-4100
Smith & Truslow
Denver, CO 303-339-6967

Ground

Bolner's Fiesta Spices
San Antonio, TX
Smith & Truslow
Denver, CO 303-339-6967

Dill

Advanced Spice & Trading
Carrollton, TX. 800-872-7811
Con Yeager Spice Co
Zelienople, PA. 800-222-2460
Organic Planet
San Francisco, CA 415-765-5590
Schiff Food Products Co Inc
Totowa, NJ 973-237-1990
Smith & Truslow
Denver, CO 303-339-6967
Vegetable Juices Inc
Chicago, IL 888-776-9752

Fennel

Acatris USA
Edina, MN. 952-920-7700
Advanced Spice & Trading
Carrollton, TX. 800-872-7811
American Key Food Products Inc
Closter, NJ. 877-263-7539
Commodities Marketing Inc
Clarksburg, NJ 732-516-0700
Con Yeager Spice Co
Zelienople, PA. 800-222-2460
Organic Planet
San Francisco, CA 415-765-5590
Schiff Food Products Co Inc
Totowa, NJ 973-237-1990
Smith & Truslow
Denver, CO 303-339-6967

Ground

Smith & Truslow
Denver, CO 303-339-6967

Fenugreek

Acatris USA
Edina, MN. 952-920-7700
Smith & Truslow
Denver, CO 303-339-6967

Flax

Bedemco Inc
White Plains, NY 914-683-1119
Bob's Red Mill Natural Foods
Milwaukie, OR 800-349-2173
Dixie USA
Tomball, TX 800-233-3668
Foods Alive
Angola, IN. 260-488-4497
Gel Spice Co LLC
Bayonne, NJ 800-922-0230
Gourmet Nut
Brooklyn, NY 347-413-5180
Hialeah Products Co
Hollywood, FL 800-923-3379
King Arthur Flour
Norwich, VT 800-827-6836
Minn-Dak Growers LTD
Grand Forks, ND. 701-746-7453
Montana Specialty Mills LLC
Great Falls, MT. 800-332-2024
Natural Way Mills Inc
Middle River, MN. 218-222-3677
New Organics
Kenwood, CA 734-677-5570
Organic Planet
San Francisco, CA 415-765-5590
Pizzey's Milling & Baking Company
Twin Falls, ID 208-733-7555
Premium Gold Flax Products & Processing
Denhoff, ND 866-570-1234
Red River Commodities Inc
Fargo, ND 800-437-5539

Mustard

American Key Food Products Inc
Closter, NJ. 877-263-7539
Commodities Marketing Inc
Clarksburg, NJ 732-516-0700
Con Yeager Spice Co
Zelienople, PA. 800-222-2460
New Organics
Kenwood, CA 734-677-5570
Phamous Phloyd's Barbecue
Denver, CO 800-497-3281

Ground Yellow

Smith & Truslow
Denver, CO 303-339-6967

Whole Brown

Smith & Truslow
Denver, CO 303-339-6967

Whole Yellow

Smith & Truslow
Denver, CO 303-339-6967

Peanut

Adkin & Son Associated Food Products
South Haven, MI. 269-637-7450

Poppy

Advanced Spice & Trading
Carrollton, TX. 800-872-7811
American Key Food Products Inc
Closter, NJ. 877-263-7539
Bedemco Inc
White Plains, NY 914-683-1119
Bob's Red Mill Natural Foods
Milwaukie, OR 800-349-2173
Con Yeager Spice Co
Zelienople, PA. 800-222-2460
Frontier Co-op
Norway, IA 844-550-6200
HP Schmid
San Francisco, CA 415-765-5925
New Organics
Kenwood, CA 734-677-5570
Organic Planet
San Francisco, CA 415-765-5590
Patisserie Wawel
Montreal, QC 614-524-3348
Red Monkey Foods
Springfield, MO 417-319-7300
Schiff Food Products Co Inc
Totowa, NJ 973-237-1990
Smith & Truslow
Denver, CO 303-339-6967
Texas Coffee Co
Beaumont, TX. 800-259-3400

Pumpkin

Advanced Spice & Trading
Carrollton, TX. 800-872-7811
American Key Food Products Inc
Closter, NJ. 877-263-7539
Bedemco Inc
White Plains, NY 914-683-1119
Bob's Red Mill Natural Foods
Milwaukie, OR 800-349-2173
Cache Creek Foods LLC
Woodland, CA. 530-662-1764
Durey-Libby Edible Nuts
Carlstadt, NJ 800-332-6887
Emerling International Foods
Buffalo, NY. 716-833-7381
Hialeah Products Co
Hollywood, FL 800-923-3379
Kathie's Kitchen
North Haven, CT. 203-407-0546
Midwest Nut Co
Minneapolis, MN 800-328-5502
New Organics
Kenwood, CA 734-677-5570
NOW Foods
Bloomingdale, IL 888-669-3663
Organic Planet
San Francisco, CA 415-765-5590
Sunfood
El Cajon, CA. 888-729-3663
Sunray Food Products Corporation
Bronx, NY. 718-548-2255
Sunridge Farms
Royal Oaks, CA 831-786-7000
Superseedz
North Haven, CT. 203-407-0546

Rape

American Key Food Products Inc
Closter, NJ. 877-263-7539
New Organics
Kenwood, CA 734-677-5570

Rice

Bob's Red Mill Natural Foods
Milwaukie, OR 800-349-2173

Sesame

American Key Food Products Inc
Closter, NJ. 877-263-7539
Bedemco Inc
White Plains, NY 914-683-1119
Chesapeake Spice Company
Belcamp, MD 410-272-6100
New Organics
Kenwood, CA 734-677-5570
NOW Foods
Bloomingdale, IL 888-669-3663
Organic Planet
San Francisco, CA 415-765-5590
Red Monkey Foods
Springfield, MO 417-319-7300
Setton International Foods
Commack, NY 800-227-4397
Spice & Spice
Rolling Hills Estates, CA 866-729-7742

Black

Foods Alive
Angola, IN. 260-488-4497

White

Bob's Red Mill Natural Foods
Milwaukie, OR 800-349-2173
Spice & Spice
Rolling Hills Estates, CA 866-729-7742

Spice

Advanced Spice & Trading
Carrollton, TX. 800-872-7811
American Key Food Products Inc
Closter, NJ. 877-263-7539
Fantis Foods Inc
Carlstadt, NJ 201-933-6200
Stan-Mark Food Products Inc
Chicago, IL 800-651-0994

Sunflower

Advanced Sunflower
Huron, SD. 605-554-1301
American Importing Co.
Minneapolis, MN 855-273-0466
American Key Food Products Inc
Closter, NJ. 877-263-7539
Bedemco Inc
White Plains, NY 914-683-1119
Cache Creek Foods LLC
Woodland, CA. 530-662-1764
CHS Sunflower
Grandin, ND 701-484-5313
Commodities Marketing Inc
Clarksburg, NJ 732-516-0700
Corteva Agriscience
Wilmington, DE 302-485-3000
DuPont Pioneer
Johnston, IA 515-535-5954
Durey-Libby Edible Nuts
Carlstadt, NJ 800-332-6887
Eden Foods Inc
Clinton, MI 888-424-3336
Fastachi
Watertown, MA. 800-466-3022
Heartland Mills Shipping
Marienthal, KS 800-232-8533
Hialeah Products Co
Hollywood, FL 800-923-3379
HP Schmid
San Francisco, CA 415-765-5925
Inn Maid Food
Lenox, MA 413-637-2732
Marantha Natural Foods
San Francisco, CA 866-972-6879
Midwest Nut Co
Minneapolis, MN 800-328-5502
Minn-Dak Growers LTD
Grand Forks, ND. 701-746-7453

New Organics
Kenwood, CA 734-677-5570
NOW Foods
Bloomingdale, IL 888-669-3663
Organic Planet
San Francisco, CA 415-765-5590
R&J Farms
West Salem, OH 419-846-3179
Red River Commodities Inc
Fargo, ND 800-437-5539
Scott-Bathgate
Winnipeg, MB. 800-216-2990
Setton International Foods
Commack, NY 800-227-4397
Sonne
Wahpeton, ND. 800-727-6663
Sunray Food Products Corporation
Bronx, NY. 718-548-2255
Sunridge Farms
Royal Oaks, CA 831-786-7000
Westin Foods
Omaha, NE 800-228-6098

Vegetable

Abbott & Cobb Inc
Feasterville, PA. 800-345-7333
Corteva Agriscience
Wilmington, DE 302-485-3000
Harris Moran Seed Co
Modesto, CA. 209-579-7333
Plantation Products Inc
Norton, MA. 508-285-5800
Seeds of Change
Rancho Dominguez, CA. 888-762-7333
Seminis Vegetable Seeds Inc
Oxnard, CA. 805-485-7317

Spices

A.C. Legg
Calera, AL. 800-422-5344
Abunda Life
Asbury Park, NJ 732-775-9338
Adventure Foods
Whittier, NC 828-497-4113
All American Seasonings
Denver, CO 303-623-2320
AM Todd Co
Kalamazoo, MI. 269-343-2603
American Food Ingredients Inc
Oceanside, CA 760-967-6287
American Key Food Products Inc
Closter, NJ. 877-263-7539
American Mercantile Corp
Memphis, TN 901-454-1900
American Natural & Organic
Fremont, CA. 510-440-1044
Arizona Natural Products
Phoenix, AZ 800-255-2823
Au Printemps Gourmet
Saint-Jerome, QC 800-438-6676
Badia Spices Inc.
Doral, FL. 877-629-8000
Barataria Spice Company
Barataria, LA. 800-793-7650
Bell Flavors & Fragrances
Northbrook, IL 847-291-8300
Bi Nutraceuticals
Long Beach, CA. 310-669-2100
Big B Barbecue
Evansville, IN. 812-425-5235
Bijol & Spices Inc
Miami, FL. 888-245-6570
Boston Spice & Tea Company
Boston, VA 800-966-4372
Boyd's Coffee Co
Portland, OR. 800-735-2878
Bueno Foods
Albuquerque, NM. 800-888-7336
C.F. Sauer Co.
Richmond, VA. 888-723-0052
California Blending Co
El Monte, CA 626-448-1918
Castella Imports Inc
Brentwood, NY. 631-231-5500
Century Blends LLC
Hunt Valley, MD. 410-771-6606
Chef Hans' Gourmet Foods
Monroe, LA. 800-890-4267
Chef Merito Inc
Van Nuys, CA. 800-637-4861
Chef Paul Prudhomme's Magic Seasonings Blends
New Orleans, LA 800-457-2857
Chef Zachary's Gourmet Blended Spices
Detroit, MI 313-226-0000
Chesapeake Spice Company
Belcamp, MD 410-272-6100
Chic Naturals
Lahaina, HI 808-463-7878
Chimayo To Go / Cibolo Junction
Albuquerque, NM. 800-683-9628
Choice Food Distributors LLC
Nashville, TN 615-350-6070
Christopher Ranch LLC
Gilroy, CA. 408-847-1100
Christopher's Herb Shop
Springville, UT 888-372-4372
Chugwater Chili
Chugwater, WY 800-972-4454
Colonna Brothers Inc
North Bergen, NJ 201-864-1115
Colorado Spice Co
Boulder, CO 800-677-7423
Commodities Marketing Inc
Clarksburg, NJ 732-516-0700
Con Yeager Spice Co
Zelienople, PA. 800-222-2460
Consolidated Mills Inc
Houston, TX 713-896-4196
Consumers Vinegar & Spice Co
Chicago, IL 773-376-4100
Continental Seasoning
Teaneck, NJ. 800-631-1564
Creole Delicacies Gourmet Shop
New Orleans, LA 504-525-9508
Cyclone Enterprises Inc
Houston, TX 281-872-0087
D Steengrafe Co Inc
Pleasant Valley, NY 845-635-4067
Davidson's Organics
Reno, NV 800-882-5888
Delicae Gourmet
Tarpon Springs, FL. 800-942-2502
Desert Pepper Trading Co
El Paso, TX. 888-472-5727
Dona Yiya Foods
San Sebastian, PR. 787-896-4007
Drusilla Seafood
Baton Rouge, LA 800-364-8844
Ecom Manufacturing Corporation
Markham, ON. 905-477-2441
Elite Spice Inc
Jessup, MD 800-232-3531
Emerling International Foods
Buffalo, NY. 716-833-7381
Empire Spice Mills
Winnipeg, NB 204-786-1594
Enrico's/Ventre Packing
Syracuse, NY 888-472-8237
Erba Food Products
Brooklyn, NY 718-272-7700
Excalibur Seasoning
Pekin, IL. 800-444-2169
Excellentia Intl.
Fairfield, NJ 737-749-9840
Farmtrue
North Stonington, CT 860-495-2231
Feature Foods
Brampton, ON. 905-452-7741
Fernandez Chili Co
Alamosa, CO. 719-589-6043
Flavorbank Company
Tucson, AZ 800-835-7603
Fmali Herb
Santa Cruz, CA 831-423-7913
Food Ingredient Solutions
Teterboro, NJ. 917-449-9558
Fool Proof Gourmet Products
Grapevine, TX 817-329-1839
Foran Spice Inc
Oak Creek, WI 800-558-6030
Fox Meadow Farm of Vermont
Rutland, VT 888-754-4204
Freed, Teller & Freed
South San Francisco, CA 800-370-7371
Frontier Co-op
Norway, IA 844-550-6200
Ful-Flav-R Foods
Alamo, CA 925-838-0300
GB Ratto International Grocery
Oakland, CA 800-325-3483
George Chiala Farms Inc
Morgan Hill, CA. 408-778-0562
Georgia Spice Company
Atlanta, GA. 800-453-9997
Giusto's Specialty Foods Inc
S San Francisco, CA. 650-873-6566
Global Botanical
Barrie, ON. 705-733-2117
Gourmantra Foods
Markham, ON 416-225-6711
Great Lakes Tea & Spice
Glen Arbor, MI 877-645-9363
Great Spice Company
Reno, NV 800-730-3575
Green Mountain Gringo
Winston-Salem, NC 888-875-3111
Griffith Foods Inc.
Alsip, IL 708-371-0900
GS Dunn & Company
Hamilton, ON 905-522-0833
Guapo Spices Company
Los Angeles, CA. 213-322-8900
Gustus Vitae Condiments LLC
Pasadena, CA 424-229-2367
Hamersmith, Inc.
Miami, FL. 305-685-7451
Harbor Spice
Forest Hill, MD. 410-893-9500
Harris Farms Inc
Coalinga, CA. 800-311-6211
HealthBest
San Marcos, CA 760-752-5230
Henry Broch & Co
Gurnee, IL. 847-816-6225
Herb Society Of America
Willoughby, OH 440-256-0514
Hollman Foods
Des Moines, IA. 888-926-2879
Homegrown Naturals
Napa, CA. 800-288-1089
Ingretec
Lebanon, PA 717-273-0711
Instant Products of America
Columbus, IN 812-372-9100
International Spice
Lakewood, NJ. 609-838-1717
Italian Rose Garlic Products
Riviera Beach, FL. 800-338-8899
Iya Foods LLC
North Aurora, IL. 630-854-7107
Jagulana Herbal Products
Badger, CA 888-465-3686
Jiaherb
Pine Brook, NJ 888-542-4372
Just Cook Foods
San Francisco, CA 415-269-2705
K+S Windsor Salt Ltd.
Pointe Claire, QC 514-630-0900
Kalsec
Kalamazoo, MI. 800-323-9320
Kalustyan
New York, NY 800-352-3451
Kent Precision Foods Group Inc
Muscatine, IA 800-442-5242
Kevala
Dallas, TX. 877-379-1179
La Flor Spices
Hauppauge, NY 631-885-9601
La Flor Spices Company
Hauppauge, NY 631-851-9601
Lakeside Mills
Rutherfordton, NC 828-286-4866
Lawry's Foods
Hunt Valley, MD. 800-952-9797
Lebermuth Company
Mishawaka, IN 800-648-1123
Leeward Resources
Baltimore, MD 410-837-9003
Li'l Guy Foods
Kansas City, MO. 800-886-8226
Lillie's Q
Chicago, IL 773-772-5500
Lost Trail Root Beer
Louisburg, KS. 800-748-7765
Lowcountry Produce
Raleigh, NC 800-935-2792
Magic Seasoning Blends
New Orleans, LA 800-457-2857
Mansmith's Barbeque
San Jn Bautista, CA 800-626-7648
Maple Grove Farms Of Vermont
St Johnsbury, VT. 802-748-5141
Marin Food Specialties
Byron, CA. 925-634-6126

Marion-Kay Spice Co
Brownstown, IN 800-627-7423

Marnap Industries
Buffalo, NY 716-897-1220

Mcclancy Seasonings Co
Fort Mill, SC 800-843-1968

McCormick & Company
Hunt Valley, MD 410-527-6189

Mermaid Spice Corporation
Fort Myers, FL 239-693-1986

Mezza
Lake Forest, IL 888-206-6054

Mild Bill's Spices
Ennis, TX 972-875-2975

Milton A. Klein Company
New York, NY 800-221-0248

Mincing Overseas Spice Company
Dayton, NJ 732-355-9944

Modern Products Inc
Mequon, WI 800-877-8935

Monterrey Products
San Antonio, TX 210-435-2872

Morris J Golombeck Inc
Brooklyn, NY 718-284-3505

Morton & Bassett Spices
Rohnert Park, CA 415-883-8530

Morton Salt Inc.
Chicago, IL 800-725-8847

Mountain High Organics
New Milford, CT 860-210-7805

Mountain Rose Herbs
Pleasant Hill, OR 800-879-3337

Natural Foods Inc
Toledo, OH 419-537-1711

Nature Quality
San Martin, CA 408-683-2182

Northwestern Coffee Mills
Mason, WI 800-243-5283

Oak Grove Smoke House Inc
Prairieville, LA 225-673-6857

Ocean Cliff Corp
New Bedford, MA 508-990-7900

Olam Spices
Fresno, CA 559-447-1390

Old Mansion Inc
Petersburg, VA 800-476-1877

Old World Spices Inc
Overland Park, KS 800-241-0070

One Source
Concord, MA 800-554-5501

Oregon Flavor Rack

Oregon Spice Co Inc
Portland, OR 800-565-1599

Organic Planet
San Francisco, CA 415-765-5590

Ottens Flavors
Philadelphia, PA 800-523-0767

Paca Foods Inc
Tampa, FL 800-388-7419

Pacific Grain & Foods
Fresno, CA 559-276-2580

Pacific Spice Co
Commerce, CA 323-890-0895

Palmieri Food Products
New Haven, CT 800-845-5447

Pappy Meat Company
Fresno, CA 559-291-0218

Papy's Foods Inc
Mchenry, IL 815-385-3313

Particle Dynamics
Saint Louis, MO 800-452-4682

Pearson's Homestyle
Bowden, AB 877-224-3339

Pecos Valley Spice Company
Corrales, NM 505-243-2622

Pelican Bay Ltd.
Dunedin, FL 800-826-8982

Pemberton's Foods Inc
Gray, ME 800-255-8401

Pendery's
Dallas, TX 800-533-1870

Pereg Gourmet Spices
Flushing, NY 718-261-6767

Pett Spice Products Inc
Atlanta, GA 404-691-5235

Precise Food Ingredients
Carrollton, TX 972-323-4951

Precision Blends
Baldwin Park, CA 800-836-9979

Proacec USA
Santa Monica, CA 310-996-7770

PS Seasoning & Spices
Iron Ridge, WI 920-387-2204

Pure Indian
Princeton Jct., NJ 877-588-4433

R & S Mexican Food
Glendale, AZ 602-272-2727

R C Fine Foods Inc
Hillsborough, NJ 800-526-3953

R L Schreiber Inc
Ft Lauderdale, FL 800-624-8777

Rapazzini Winery
Gilroy, CA 800-842-6262

Raymond-Hadley Corporation
Spencer, NY 800-252-5220

Red Lion Spicy Foods Company
Red Lion, PA 717-309-8303

REX Pure Foods
New Orleans, LA 800-344-8314

Rufus Teague
Shawnee, KS 913-706-3814

Sambets Cajun Deli
Austin, TX 800-472-6238

Sandbar Trading Corp
Louisville, CO 303-499-7480

Santa Cruz Chili & Spice
Tumacacori, AZ 520-398-2591

Saratoga Food Specialties
Bolingbrook, IL 800-451-0407

Schiff Food Products Co Inc
Totowa, NJ 973-237-1990

Sea Salt Superstore
Lynnwood, WA 866-999-7258

Season Harvest Foods
Los Altos, CA 650-968-2273

See Smell Taste
San Francisco, CA 415-986-4216

Selecto Sausage Co
Houston, TX 713-926-1626

Sentry Seasonings
Elmhurst, IL 630-530-5370

Serv-Agen Corporation
Cherry Hill, NJ 856-663-6966

Shank's Extracts Inc
Lancaster, PA 800-346-3135

SJH Enterprises
Middleton, WI 888-745-3845

SOUPerior Bean & Spice Company
Vancouver, WA 800-878-7687

South Texas Spice Co LTD
San Antonio, TX 210-436-2280

Spanish Gardens Food Manufacturing
Kansas City, KS 913-831-4242

Specialty Commodities Inc
Fargo, ND 701-282-8222

Specialty Food America Inc
Hopkinsville, KY 888-881-1633

Spice & Spice
Rolling Hills Estates, CA 866-729-7742

Spice Chain
Avenel, NJ 732-499-9070

Spice Hunter Inc
Richmond, VA 800-444-3061

Spice O' Life
Seattle, WA 206-789-4195

Spiceland
Chicago, IL 800-352-8671

Spicely
Fremont, CA 510-440-1044

St Charles Trading Inc
Batavia, IL 630-377-0608

St John's Botanicals
Bowie, MD 301-262-5302

Stan-Mark Food Products Inc
Chicago, IL 800-651-0994

Starwest Botanicals Inc
Sacramento, CA 800-800-4372

Stickney & Poor Company
Peterborough, NH 603-924-2259

Sundial Herb Garden
Higganum, CT 860-345-4290

SupHerb Farms
Turlock, CA 800-787-4372

Sutter Buttes Olive Oil
Sutter, CA 530-763-7921

Swagger Foods Corp
Vernon Hills, IL 847-913-1200

Tampico Spice Co
Los Angeles, CA 323-235-3154

Taste Maker Foods
Memphis, TN 800-467-1407

Teeny Tiny Spice Company of Vermont LLC
Shelburne, VT 802-598-6800

Terra Flavors & Fragrances
New York, NY 212-244-1181

Texas Coffee Co
Beaumont, TX 800-259-3400

Texas Traditions Gourmet
Georgetown, TX 800-547-7062

To Market To Market
Loveland, CO 970-278-1000

Tommy Tang's Thai Seasonings
Los Angeles, CA 818-442-0219

Trader Vic's Food Products
Emeryville, CA 877-762-4824

Trinity Spice
Midland, TX 800-460-1149

Triple H Food Processors Inc
Riverside, CA 951-352-5700

Tripper Inc
Oxnard, CA 805-988-8851

Tropical Foods
Charlotte, NC 800-438-4470

Tropical Nut & Fruit Co
Orlando, FL 800-749-8869

Two Guys Spice Company
Jacksonville, FL 800-874-5656

Uncle Fred's Fine Foods
Rockport, TX 361-729-8320

Urban Accents
Chicago, IL 877-872-7742

Us Spice Mill Inc
Chicago, IL 773-378-6800

Van Eeghen International Inc
St Laurent, QC 514-332-6455

Van Roy Coffee Co
Cleveland, OH 877-826-7669

Vanns Spices LTD
Gwynn Oak, MD 800-583-1693

Vegetable Juices Inc
Chicago, IL 888-776-9752

Vincent Formusa Company
Des Plaines, IL 847-813-6040

Wabash Heritage Mfg LLC
Vincennes, IN 812-886-0147

Wagner Gourmet Foods
Lenexa, KS 913-469-5411

Weaver Nut Co. Inc.
Ephrata, PA 800-473-2688

West Pac
Idaho Falls, ID 800-973-7407

Wheeling Coffee & Spice Co
Wheeling, WV 800-500-0141

Whole Herb Co
Sonoma, CA 707-935-1077

Wild West Spices
Cody, WY 888-587-8887

William Bounds
Torrance, CA 800-473-0504

William E. Martin & Sons Company
Roslyn, NY 516-605-2444

Wine Country Chef LLC
Hidden Valley Lake, CA 707-322-0406

Wisconsin Spice Inc
Berlin, WI 920-361-3555

Wixon Inc.
St. Francis, WI 800-841-5304

World Flavors Inc
Warminster, PA 215-672-4400

World Harbors
Auburn, ME 800-355-6221

World of Spices
Stirling, NJ 908-647-1218

World Spice
Roselle, NJ 800-234-1060

Young Winfield
Hamilton, ON 905-893-2536

Adobo

Frontier Co-op
Norway, IA 844-550-6200

Allspice

Chesapeake Spice Company
Belcamp, MD 410-272-6100

Commodities Marketing Inc
Clarksburg, NJ 732-516-0700

Ecom Manufacturing Corporation
Markham, ON 905-477-2441

Emerling International Foods
Buffalo, NY 716-833-7381

Erba Food Products
Brooklyn, NY 718-272-7700

Frontier Co-op
Norway, IA 844-550-6200
Gel Spice Co LLC
Bayonne, NJ 800-922-0230
Morris J Golombeck Inc
Brooklyn, NY 718-284-3505
Old Mansion Inc
Petersburg, VA 800-476-1877
Organic Planet
San Francisco, CA 415-765-5590
Red Monkey Foods
Springfield, MO 417-319-7300
Schiff Food Products Co Inc
Totowa, NJ 973-237-1990
Smith & Truslow
Denver, CO 303-339-6967
Texas Coffee Co
Beaumont, TX 800-259-3400
Tova Industries LLC
Louisville, KY 888-532-8682
Whole Herb Co
Sonoma, CA 707-935-1077

Ground

Con Yeager Spice Co
Zelienople, PA 800-222-2460
Consumers Vinegar & Spice Co
Chicago, IL 773-376-4100
Schiff Food Products Co Inc
Totowa, NJ 973-237-1990
Smith & Truslow
Denver, CO 303-339-6967
Wabash Heritage Mfg LLC
Vincennes, IN 812-886-0147
Whole Herb Co
Sonoma, CA 707-935-1077

Whole

Con Yeager Spice Co
Zelienople, PA 800-222-2460
Whole Herb Co
Sonoma, CA 707-935-1077

Anise - Star

Ground

Chesapeake Spice Company
Belcamp, MD 410-272-6100
Frontier Co-op
Norway, IA 844-550-6200
Smith & Truslow
Denver, CO 303-339-6967

Whole

Smith & Truslow
Denver, CO 303-339-6967

Apple Pie Spices

Frontier Co-op
Norway, IA 844-550-6200
Smith & Truslow
Denver, CO 303-339-6967

Basil

Advanced Spice & Trading
Carrollton, TX 800-872-7811
American Key Food Products Inc
Closter, NJ 877-263-7539
Chesapeake Spice Company
Belcamp, MD 410-272-6100
Con Yeager Spice Co
Zelienople, PA 800-222-2460
Emerling International Foods
Buffalo, NY 716-833-7381
Gel Spice Co LLC
Bayonne, NJ 800-922-0230
Golden State Herbs
Thermal, CA 800-730-3575
Lebermuth Company
Mishawaka, IN 800-648-1123
Morris J Golombeck Inc
Brooklyn, NY 718-284-3505
Red Monkey Foods
Springfield, MO 417-319-7300
Schiff Food Products Co Inc
Totowa, NJ 973-237-1990
Smith & Truslow
Denver, CO 303-339-6967
Specialty Food America Inc
Hopkinsville, KY 888-881-1633
Spice Chain
Avenel, NJ 732-499-9070
SupHerb Farms
Turlock, CA 800-787-4372
Tova Industries LLC
Louisville, KY 888-532-8682
Vegetable Juices Inc
Chicago, IL 888-776-9752
Waterfield Farms
Amherst, MA 413-549-3558
Whole Herb Co
Sonoma, CA 707-935-1077

Basil Leaf

Frontier Co-op
Norway, IA 844-550-6200
Morris J Golombeck Inc
Brooklyn, NY 718-284-3505
Old Mansion Inc
Petersburg, VA 800-476-1877
Schiff Food Products Co Inc
Totowa, NJ 973-237-1990

Bay Leaves

Advanced Spice & Trading
Carrollton, TX 800-872-7811
American Key Food Products Inc
Closter, NJ 877-263-7539
Bolner's Fiesta Spices
San Antonio, TX
Chesapeake Spice Company
Belcamp, MD 410-272-6100
Con Yeager Spice Co
Zelienople, PA 800-222-2460
Consumers Vinegar & Spice Co
Chicago, IL 773-376-4100
Frontier Co-op
Norway, IA 844-550-6200
Gel Spice Co LLC
Bayonne, NJ 800-922-0230
Pendery's
Dallas, TX 800-533-1870
Red Monkey Foods
Springfield, MO 417-319-7300
Smith & Truslow
Denver, CO 303-339-6967
Spice Chain
Avenel, NJ 732-499-9070
Tova Industries LLC
Louisville, KY 888-532-8682
Vegetable Juices Inc
Chicago, IL 888-776-9752
Wabash Heritage Mfg LLC
Vincennes, IN 812-886-0147
Whole Herb Co
Sonoma, CA 707-935-1077

Ground

Emerling International Foods
Buffalo, NY 716-833-7381

Black Pepper - Ground

Chesapeake Spice Company
Belcamp, MD 410-272-6100
Spice & Spice
Rolling Hills Estates, CA 866-729-7742
Swagger Foods Corp
Vernon Hills, IL 847-913-1200

Capers

Alimentaire Whyte's Inc
Laval, QC 866-420-9520
Blue Marble Brands
Providence, RI 888-534-0246
Castella Imports Inc
Brentwood, NY 631-231-5500
Emerling International Foods
Buffalo, NY 716-833-7381
Gl Mezzetta Inc
American Canyon, CA 800-941-7044
J.M. Smucker Co.
Orrville, OH 888-550-9555
L & S Packing Co
Farmingdale, NY 800-286-6487
Orleans Packing Co
Hyde Park, MA 617-361-6611
Paradise Products Corporation
Boca Raton, FL 800-826-1235
Proacec USA
Santa Monica, CA 310-996-7770
Ron Son Foods Inc
Swedesboro, NJ 856-241-7333
Vegetable Juices Inc
Chicago, IL 888-776-9752

Cardamom

Fiesta Gourmet of Tejas
Canyon Lake, TX 800-585-8250
Flavouressence Products
Mississauga, ON 866-209-7778
Min Tong Herbs
Oakland, CA 800-562-5777
Old Mansion Inc
Petersburg, VA 800-476-1877
Sill Farm Market
Lawrence, MI 269-674-3755
Sunja's Oriental Foods
Waterbury, VT 802-244-7644

Ground

Chesapeake Spice Company
Belcamp, MD 410-272-6100
Smith & Truslow
Denver, CO 303-339-6967
Wabash Heritage Mfg LLC
Vincennes, IN 812-886-0147

Whole

Smith & Truslow
Denver, CO 303-339-6967

Carob Powder

American Key Food Products Inc
Closter, NJ 877-263-7539
Gel Spice Co LLC
Bayonne, NJ 800-922-0230

Cassia (Cinnamon)

American Key Food Products Inc
Closter, NJ 877-263-7539
Commodities Marketing Inc
Clarksburg, NJ 732-516-0700
Smith & Truslow
Denver, CO 303-339-6967

Cayenne

Chesapeake Spice Company
Belcamp, MD 410-272-6100
Frontier Co-op
Norway, IA 844-550-6200
Marion-Kay Spice Co
Brownstown, IN 800-627-7423
Vegetable Juices Inc
Chicago, IL 888-776-9752

Cayenne Pepper

American Key Food Products Inc
Closter, NJ 877-263-7539
Christopher's Herb Shop
Springville, UT 888-372-4372
Morris J Golombeck Inc
Brooklyn, NY 718-284-3505
Pepper Creek Farms
Lawton, OK 800-526-8132
Red Monkey Foods
Springfield, MO 417-319-7300
Tova Industries LLC
Louisville, KY 888-532-8682
Wabash Heritage Mfg LLC
Vincennes, IN 812-886-0147

Ground

Smith & Truslow
Denver, CO 303-339-6967

Whole

Texas Coffee Co
Beaumont, TX 800-259-3400

Celery Flakes

Frontier Co-op
Norway, IA 844-550-6200
Swagger Foods Corp
Vernon Hills, IL 847-913-1200

Celery Salt

Frontier Co-op
Norway, IA 844-550-6200
Old Mansion Inc
Petersburg, VA 800-476-1877
Red Monkey Foods
Springfield, MO 417-319-7300

Chervil

American Key Food Products Inc
Closter, NJ. 877-263-7539
Frontier Co-op
Norway, IA 844-550-6200
Muirhead Canning Co
The Dalles, OR 541-298-1660
SupHerb Farms
Turlock, CA 800-787-4372

Chile Pepper

Chesapeake Spice Company
Belcamp, MD 410-272-6100
Chugwater Chili
Chugwater, WY 800-972-4454
Frontier Co-op
Norway, IA 844-550-6200
Pendery's
Dallas, TX. 800-533-1870

Chili Crush

Spice & Spice
Rolling Hills Estates, CA 866-729-7742

Chili Pods

Whole & Dried

Spice & Spice
Rolling Hills Estates, CA 866-729-7742

Chili Powder

Frontier Co-op
Norway, IA 844-550-6200
Leona's Restaurante
Chimayo, NM 888-561-5569
Mezza
Lake Forest, IL 888-206-6054
Red Monkey Foods
Springfield, MO 417-319-7300
Smith & Truslow
Denver, CO 303-339-6967
Spice & Spice
Rolling Hills Estates, CA 866-729-7742
The Chili Lab
Brooklyn, NY

Chinese

Red Monkey Foods
Springfield, MO 417-319-7300
Smith & Truslow
Denver, CO 303-339-6967

Chipotle Chile Peppers

Dried

Frontier Co-op
Norway, IA 844-550-6200

Chives

Advanced Spice & Trading
Carrollton, TX. 800-872-7811
American Key Food Products Inc
Closter, NJ. 877-263-7539
Chesapeake Spice Company
Belcamp, MD 410-272-6100
Frontier Co-op
Norway, IA 844-550-6200
Gel Spice Co LLC
Bayonne, NJ 800-922-0230
Red Monkey Foods
Springfield, MO 417-319-7300
Schiff Food Products Co Inc
Totowa, NJ 973-237-1990
Smith & Truslow
Denver, CO 303-339-6967
SupHerb Farms
Turlock, CA 800-787-4372

Cinnamon

Advanced Spice & Trading
Carrollton, TX. 800-872-7811
American Key Food Products Inc
Closter, NJ. 877-263-7539
Chesapeake Spice Company
Belcamp, MD 410-272-6100
Con Yeager Spice Co
Zelienople, PA. 800-222-2460
Emerling International Foods
Buffalo, NY. 716-833-7381
Erba Food Products
Brooklyn, NY 718-272-7700
Frontier Co-op
Norway, IA 844-550-6200
Lebermuth Company
Mishawaka, IN 800-648-1123
Morris J Golombeck Inc
Brooklyn, NY 718-284-3505
Organic Planet
San Francisco, CA 415-765-5590
Pendery's
Dallas, TX. 800-533-1870
Red Monkey Foods
Springfield, MO 417-319-7300
Schiff Food Products Co Inc
Totowa, NJ 973-237-1990
Spice & Spice
Rolling Hills Estates, CA 866-729-7742
Swagger Foods Corp
Vernon Hills, IL 847-913-1200
Texas Coffee Co
Beaumont, TX. 800-259-3400
Tova Industries LLC
Louisville, KY 888-532-8682
Tripper Inc
Oxnard, CA. 805-988-8851

Cassia

Advanced Spice & Trading
Carrollton, TX. 800-872-7811
Morris J Golombeck Inc
Brooklyn, NY 718-284-3505
Schiff Food Products Co Inc
Totowa, NJ 973-237-1990
Tova Industries LLC
Louisville, KY 888-532-8682

Ground

Con Yeager Spice Co
Zelienople, PA. 800-222-2460
Homefree LLC
Windham, NH 800-552-7172
Jedwards International Inc
Braintree, MA 781-848-1473
Smith & Truslow
Denver, CO 303-339-6967
Wabash Heritage Mfg LLC
Vincennes, IN 812-886-0147

Whole

Red Monkey Foods
Springfield, MO 417-319-7300
Smith & Truslow
Denver, CO 303-339-6967
Spice & Spice
Rolling Hills Estates, CA 866-729-7742

Citron

Emerling International Foods
Buffalo, NY. 716-833-7381
Seald Sweet
Vero Beach, FL 559-636-4400

Cloves

Chesapeake Spice Company
Belcamp, MD 410-272-6100
Con Yeager Spice Co
Zelienople, PA. 800-222-2460
Emerling International Foods
Buffalo, NY. 716-833-7381
Frontier Co-op
Norway, IA 844-550-6200
Old Mansion Inc
Petersburg, VA 800-476-1877
Red Monkey Foods
Springfield, MO 417-319-7300
Schiff Food Products Co Inc
Totowa, NJ 973-237-1990
Smith & Truslow
Denver, CO 303-339-6967
Tova Industries LLC
Louisville, KY 888-532-8682

Ground

Con Yeager Spice Co
Zelienople, PA. 800-222-2460
Schiff Food Products Co Inc
Totowa, NJ 973-237-1990
Smith & Truslow
Denver, CO 303-339-6967
Texas Coffee Co
Beaumont, TX. 800-259-3400
Wabash Heritage Mfg LLC
Vincennes, IN 812-886-0147

Coriander (Cilantro)

Advanced Spice & Trading
Carrollton, TX. 800-872-7811
Chesapeake Spice Company
Belcamp, MD 410-272-6100
Con Yeager Spice Co
Zelienople, PA. 800-222-2460
Frontier Co-op
Norway, IA 844-550-6200
Gel Spice Co LLC
Bayonne, NJ 800-922-0230
Morris J Golombeck Inc
Brooklyn, NY 718-284-3505
Red Monkey Foods
Springfield, MO 417-319-7300
Schiff Food Products Co Inc
Totowa, NJ 973-237-1990
Smith & Truslow
Denver, CO 303-339-6967
Spice & Spice
Rolling Hills Estates, CA 866-729-7742
Tova Industries LLC
Louisville, KY 888-532-8682

Cumin

Advanced Spice & Trading
Carrollton, TX. 800-872-7811
American Key Food Products Inc
Closter, NJ. 877-263-7539
Chesapeake Spice Company
Belcamp, MD 410-272-6100
Commodities Marketing Inc
Clarksburg, NJ 732-516-0700
Con Yeager Spice Co
Zelienople, PA. 800-222-2460
Emerling International Foods
Buffalo, NY. 716-833-7381
Famarco Limited
Virginia Beach, VA. 757-460-3573
Frontier Co-op
Norway, IA 844-550-6200
Gel Spice Co LLC
Bayonne, NJ 800-922-0230
Red Monkey Foods
Springfield, MO 417-319-7300
Smith & Truslow
Denver, CO 303-339-6967
Spice & Spice
Rolling Hills Estates, CA 866-729-7742
Tova Industries LLC
Louisville, KY 888-532-8682
Wabash Heritage Mfg LLC
Vincennes, IN 812-886-0147

Curry Powder

Frontier Co-op
Norway, IA 844-550-6200
Red Monkey Foods
Springfield, MO 417-319-7300
Smith & Truslow
Denver, CO 303-339-6967
Texas Coffee Co
Beaumont, TX. 800-259-3400

Dill

Chesapeake Spice Company
Belcamp, MD 410-272-6100
Con Yeager Spice Co
Zelienople, PA. 800-222-2460
Frontier Co-op
Norway, IA 844-550-6200
Gel Spice Co LLC
Bayonne, NJ 800-922-0230

SupHerb Farms
Turlock, CA 800-787-4372
Tova Industries LLC
Louisville, KY 888-532-8682

Dill Weed

Con Yeager Spice Co
Zelienople, PA. 800-222-2460
Golden State Herbs
Thermal, CA 800-730-3575
Red Monkey Foods
Springfield, MO 417-319-7300
Smith & Truslow
Denver, CO 303-339-6967
SupHerb Farms
Turlock, CA 800-787-4372

Dried

Island Spice
Doral, FL 786-473-3465
Van Drunen Farms
Momence, IL 815-472-3100

Extracts

Norac Technologies
Edmonton, AB 780-414-9595
Synthite USA Inc.
Oak Park, IL 708-446-1716

Fennel

Chesapeake Spice Company
Belcamp, MD 410-272-6100
Frontier Co-op
Norway, IA 844-550-6200
Old Mansion Inc
Petersburg, VA 800-476-1877
Red Monkey Foods
Springfield, MO 417-319-7300
Smith & Truslow
Denver, CO 303-339-6967
SupHerb Farms
Turlock, CA 800-787-4372
Wabash Heritage Mfg LLC
Vincennes, IN 812-886-0147

Fenugreek

Advanced Spice & Trading
Carrollton, TX 800-872-7811
Chesapeake Spice Company
Belcamp, MD 410-272-6100
Gel Spice Co LLC
Bayonne, NJ 800-922-0230

Garam Masala

Frontier Co-op
Norway, IA 844-550-6200

Garlic

Arizona Natural Products
Phoenix, AZ 800-255-2823
Badia Spices Inc.
Doral, FL 877-629-8000
Beaverton Foods Inc
Hillsboro, OR 800-223-8076
Bio-Nutritional Products
Northvale, NJ 201-784-8200
Bolner's Fiesta Spices
San Antonio, TX
California Garlic Co
San Diego, CA 951-506-8883
Christopher Ranch LLC
Gilroy, CA 408-847-1100
Christopher's Herb Shop
Springville, UT 888-372-4372
Con Yeager Spice Co
Zelienople, PA. 800-222-2460
Derlea Foods
Pickering, ON 888-430-7777
Ecom Manufacturing Corporation
Markham, ON 905-477-2441
Freeda Vitamins Inc
Long Island City, NY 800-777-3737
Frontier Co-op
Norway, IA 844-550-6200
Ful-Flav-R Foods
Alamo, CA 925-838-0300
Garlic Co
Bakersfield, CA 661-393-4212
Garlic Valley Farms Inc
Glendale, CA 800-424-7990
George Chiala Farms Inc
Morgan Hill, CA 408-778-0562
Haliburton International Inc
Ontario, CA 877-980-4295
Hamersmith, Inc.
Miami, FL 305-685-7451
Harris Farms Inc
Coalinga, CA 800-311-6211
Kimball Enterprise International
Hacienda Heights, CA 213-276-8898
L & S Packing Co
Farmingdale, NY 800-286-6487
Lawry's Foods
Hunt Valley, MD 800-952-9797
Lebermuth Company
Mishawaka, IN 800-648-1123
Marin Food Specialties
Byron, CA 925-634-6126
Morris J Golombeck Inc
Brooklyn, NY 718-284-3505
Nature Quality
San Martin, CA 408-683-2182
Nu Naturals Inc
Eugene, OR 800-753-4372
Old Mansion Inc
Petersburg, VA 800-476-1877
Pacific Choice Brands
Fresno, CA 559-476-3581
Pendery's
Dallas, TX 800-533-1870
Rapazzini Winery
Gilroy, CA 800-842-6262
Schiff Food Products Co Inc
Totowa, NJ 973-237-1990
Specialty Food America Inc
Hopkinsville, KY 888-881-1633
Spice Chain
Avenel, NJ 732-499-9070
Spice World Inc
Orlando, FL
SupHerb Farms
Turlock, CA 800-787-4372
Swagger Foods Corp
Vernon Hills, IL 847-913-1200
Texas Coffee Co
Beaumont, TX 800-259-3400
Three Springs Farm
Oaks, OK 918-868-5450
Tova Industries LLC
Louisville, KY 888-532-8682
Trout Lake Farm
Trout Lake, WA 800-655-6988
Tulkoff's Food Products Inc
Baltimore, MD 800-638-7343
Vessey & Co Inc
Holtville, CA 760-356-0130

Chopped

California Garlic Co
San Diego, CA 951-506-8883
Ful-Flav-R Foods
Alamo, CA 925-838-0300
L & S Packing Co
Farmingdale, NY 800-286-6487
Spice World Inc
Orlando, FL
Tulkoff's Food Products Inc
Baltimore, MD 800-638-7343

Granulated

Advanced Spice & Trading
Carrollton, TX 800-872-7811
Gel Spice Co LLC
Bayonne, NJ 800-922-0230
Smith & Truslow
Denver, CO 303-339-6967
Spice & Spice
Rolling Hills Estates, CA 866-729-7742
Tova Industries LLC
Louisville, KY 888-532-8682
Wabash Heritage Mfg LLC
Vincennes, IN 812-886-0147

Minced

Con Yeager Spice Co
Zelienople, PA. 800-222-2460
Red Monkey Foods
Springfield, MO 417-319-7300
Smith & Truslow
Denver, CO 303-339-6967
Spice World Inc
Orlando, FL
Wabash Heritage Mfg LLC
Vincennes, IN 812-886-0147

Powdered

Con Yeager Spice Co
Zelienople, PA. 800-222-2460
Erba Food Products
Brooklyn, NY 718-272-7700
Red Monkey Foods
Springfield, MO 417-319-7300
Smith & Truslow
Denver, CO 303-339-6967
Texas Coffee Co
Beaumont, TX 800-259-3400
Whole Herb Co
Sonoma, CA 707-935-1077

Garlic Salt

Red Monkey Foods
Springfield, MO 417-319-7300
Smith & Truslow
Denver, CO 303-339-6967
Texas Coffee Co
Beaumont, TX 800-259-3400

Ginger

Advanced Spice & Trading
Carrollton, TX 800-872-7811
American Key Food Products Inc
Closter, NJ 877-263-7539
California Garlic Co
San Diego, CA 951-506-8883
Chesapeake Spice Company
Belcamp, MD 410-272-6100
Christopher Ranch LLC
Gilroy, CA 408-847-1100
Christopher's Herb Shop
Springville, UT 888-372-4372
Con Yeager Spice Co
Zelienople, PA. 800-222-2460
D Steengrafe Co Inc
Pleasant Valley, NY 845-635-4067
Erba Food Products
Brooklyn, NY 718-272-7700
Frontier Co-op
Norway, IA 844-550-6200
Gel Spice Co LLC
Bayonne, NJ 800-922-0230
Hialeah Products Co
Hollywood, FL 800-923-3379
Morris J Golombeck Inc
Brooklyn, NY 718-284-3505
Old Mansion Inc
Petersburg, VA 800-476-1877
Pendery's
Dallas, TX 800-533-1870
Red Monkey Foods
Springfield, MO 417-319-7300
Royal Foods Inc
Marina, CA 800-551-5284
Specialty Food America Inc
Hopkinsville, KY 888-881-1633
Spice World Inc
Orlando, FL
SupHerb Farms
Turlock, CA 800-787-4372
Texas Coffee Co
Beaumont, TX 800-259-3400
Tova Industries LLC
Louisville, KY 888-532-8682
Wabash Heritage Mfg LLC
Vincennes, IN 812-886-0147

Crystallized

Frontier Co-op
Norway, IA 844-550-6200
Hialeah Products Co
Hollywood, FL 800-923-3379

Ground

Con Yeager Spice Co
Zelienople, PA. 800-222-2460
Smith & Truslow
Denver, CO 303-339-6967

Pieces

Ful-Flav-R Foods
Alamo, CA 925-838-0300
Spice World Inc
Orlando, FL

Ginseng

Alternative Health & Herbs
Albany, OR 800-345-4152
Atkins Ginseng Farms
Waterford, ON........................ 800-265-0239
Fmali Herb
Santa Cruz, CA........................ 831-423-7913
Ginco International
Simi Valley, CA........................ 800-284-2598
Heise Wausau Farms
Wausau, WI........................ 800-764-1010
ILHWA American Corporation
Belleville, NJ 800-446-7364
Madys Company
San Francisco, CA 415-822-2227
Master Mix
Placentia, CA 714-524-1698
Penn Herb Co
Philadelphia, PA 800-523-9971
Prince of Peace
Hayward, CA 800-732-2328
Progenix Corporation
Wausau, WI........................ 800-233-3356
St John's Botanicals
Bowie, MD 301-262-5302
Sun Chlorella USA
Torrance, CA........................ 800-829-2828
Triple Leaf Tea Inc
S San Francisco, CA........................ 800-552-7448
Yellow Emperor Inc
Eugene, OR........................ 877-485-6664

Gumbo File (Powdered Sassafras)

Frontier Co-op
Norway, IA 844-550-6200

Herbes de Provence

Frontier Co-op
Norway, IA 844-550-6200
King Arthur Flour
Norwich, VT 800-827-6836
Red Monkey Foods
Springfield, MO 417-319-7300
Smith & Truslow
Denver, CO 303-339-6967
SupHerb Farms
Turlock, CA 800-787-4372

Horseradish

Buedel Food Products
Bridgeview, IL 708-496-3500
Feature Foods
Brampton, ON........................ 905-452-7741
Frontier Co-op
Norway, IA 844-550-6200
Gold Pure Food Products Co. Inc.
Hempstead, NY........................ 800-422-4681
Heintz & Weber Co
Buffalo, NY........................ 716-852-7171
Junuis Food Products
Palatine, IL 847-359-4300
Palmieri Food Products
New Haven, CT 800-845-5447
Red Pelican Food Products
Detroit, MI 313-881-4095
Strub Pickles
Brantford, ON........................ 519-751-1717
Thor-Shackel Horseradish Company
Eau Claire, WI 800-826-7322
United Pickles
Bronx, NY........................ 718-933-6060

Jerk Chicken

Bolner's Fiesta Spices
San Antonio, TX
Frontier Co-op
Norway, IA 844-550-6200

Juniper Berries

Frontier Co-op
Norway, IA 844-550-6200

Lavender

Smith & Truslow
Denver, CO 303-339-6967

Lavender Flowers

Wabash Heritage Mfg LLC
Vincennes, IN 812-886-0147

Lemon Grass

SupHerb Farms
Turlock, CA 800-787-4372

Lemon Peel

Frontier Co-op
Norway, IA 844-550-6200
Smith & Truslow
Denver, CO 303-339-6967

Liquid

Emerling International Foods
Buffalo, NY........................ 716-833-7381
Jogue Inc
Northville, MI........................ 800-531-3888
Sentry Seasonings
Elmhurst, IL 630-530-5370
Spice World Inc
Orlando, FL
Vegetable Juices Inc
Chicago, IL........................ 888-776-9752
World Flavors Inc
Warminster, PA........................ 215-672-4400

Mace (See also Nutmeg)

Advanced Spice & Trading
Carrollton, TX........................ 800-872-7811
American Key Food Products Inc
Closter, NJ........................ 877-263-7539
Chesapeake Spice Company
Belcamp, MD 410-272-6100
Con Yeager Spice Co
Zelienople, PA........................ 800-222-2460
Emerling International Foods
Buffalo, NY........................ 716-833-7381
Frontier Co-op
Norway, IA 844-550-6200
Gel Spice Co LLC
Bayonne, NJ 800-922-0230
Old Mansion Inc
Petersburg, VA 800-476-1877
Specialty Food America Inc
Hopkinsville, KY 888-881-1633
Tova Industries LLC
Louisville, KY 888-532-8682

Ground

Con Yeager Spice Co
Zelienople, PA........................ 800-222-2460

Marjoram

American Key Food Products Inc
Closter, NJ........................ 877-263-7539
Con Yeager Spice Co
Zelienople, PA........................ 800-222-2460
Emerling International Foods
Buffalo, NY........................ 716-833-7381
Frontier Co-op
Norway, IA 844-550-6200
Gel Spice Co LLC
Bayonne, NJ 800-922-0230
Golden State Herbs
Thermal, CA 800-730-3575
Old Mansion Inc
Petersburg, VA 800-476-1877
Red Monkey Foods
Springfield, MO 417-319-7300
Smith & Truslow
Denver, CO 303-339-6967
SupHerb Farms
Turlock, CA 800-787-4372
Tova Industries LLC
Louisville, KY 888-532-8682
Wabash Heritage Mfg LLC
Vincennes, IN 812-886-0147

Mint

Whole Herb Co
Sonoma, CA 707-935-1077

Mint Leaves

Advanced Spice & Trading
Carrollton, TX........................ 800-872-7811
Charles H Baldwin & Sons
West Stockbridge, MA 413-232-7785
Emerling International Foods
Buffalo, NY........................ 716-833-7381

Spearmint

Gel Spice Co LLC
Bayonne, NJ 800-922-0230
SupHerb Farms
Turlock, CA 800-787-4372

Mulling

Aspen Mulling Company Inc.
San Francisco, CA 866-972-6879

Mustard

Dry - Prepared

American Key Food Products Inc
Closter, NJ........................ 877-263-7539
Au Printemps Gourmet
Saint-Jerome, QC 800-438-6676
Baldwin Richardson Foods
Oakbrook Terrace, IL 866-644-2732
Catamount Specialties of Vermont
Plainfield, VT 800-639-2406
Frontier Co-op
Norway, IA 844-550-6200
GS Dunn & Company
Hamilton, ON 905-522-0833
Herlocher Foods
State College, PA 800-437-5625
J.N. Bech
Elk Rapids, MI 800-232-4583
Kozlowski Farms
Forestville, CA 800-473-2767
Minn-Dak Growers LTD
Grand Forks, ND........................ 701-746-7453
New Canaan Farms
Dripping Springs, TX 800-727-5267
Old Mansion Inc
Petersburg, VA 800-476-1877
Pepper Creek Farms
Lawton, OK........................ 800-526-8132

Prepared

Walker Foods
Los Angeles, CA........................ 800-966-5199

Mustard Powder

Red Monkey Foods
Springfield, MO 417-319-7300
Wabash Heritage Mfg LLC
Vincennes, IN 812-886-0147

Mustards

Chesapeake Spice Company
Belcamp, MD 410-272-6100
Con Yeager Spice Co
Zelienople, PA........................ 800-222-2460

Natural Flavorings

Spice King Corporation
Beverly Hills, CA........................ 310-836-7770

Nutmeg (See also Mace)

Advanced Spice & Trading
Carrollton, TX........................ 800-872-7811
American Key Food Products Inc
Closter, NJ........................ 877-263-7539
Commodities Marketing Inc
Clarksburg, NJ 732-516-0700
Con Yeager Spice Co
Zelienople, PA........................ 800-222-2460
Emerling International Foods
Buffalo, NY........................ 716-833-7381
Frontier Co-op
Norway, IA 844-550-6200
Gel Spice Co LLC
Bayonne, NJ 800-922-0230
Red Monkey Foods
Springfield, MO 417-319-7300
Schiff Food Products Co Inc
Totowa, NJ 973-237-1990

Smith & Truslow
Denver, CO 303-339-6967
Spice & Spice
Rolling Hills Estates, CA 866-729-7742
Texas Coffee Co
Beaumont, TX. 800-259-3400
Tripper Inc
Oxnard, CA. 805-988-8851

Ground

Con Yeager Spice Co
Zelienople, PA. 800-222-2460

Whole

Con Yeager Spice Co
Zelienople, PA. 800-222-2460

Onion

ACH Food Co Inc
Oakbrook Terrace, IL 630-586-3740
Con Yeager Spice Co
Zelienople, PA. 800-222-2460
Frontier Co-op
Norway, IA 844-550-6200
Ful-Flav-R Foods
Alamo, CA 925-838-0300
Gel Spice Co LLC
Bayonne, NJ 800-922-0230
Marin Food Specialties
Byron, CA. 925-634-6126
Old Mansion Inc
Petersburg, VA 800-476-1877
Red Monkey Foods
Springfield, MO 417-319-7300
Texas Coffee Co
Beaumont, TX. 800-259-3400

Chopped

Con Yeager Spice Co
Zelienople, PA. 800-222-2460
Ful-Flav-R Foods
Alamo, CA 925-838-0300

Granulated

Con Yeager Spice Co
Zelienople, PA. 800-222-2460
Smith & Truslow
Denver, CO. 303-339-6967
Wabash Heritage Mfg LLC
Vincennes, IN 812-886-0147

Minced

Con Yeager Spice Co
Zelienople, PA. 800-222-2460
Erba Food Products
Brooklyn, NY 718-272-7700
Red Monkey Foods
Springfield, MO 417-319-7300
Smith & Truslow
Denver, CO. 303-339-6967

Onion Salt

Red Monkey Foods
Springfield, MO 417-319-7300

Oregano

Advanced Spice & Trading
Carrollton, TX. 800-872-7811
Bolner's Fiesta Spices
San Antonio, TX
Castella Imports Inc
Brentwood, NY. 631-231-5500
Chesapeake Spice Company
Belcamp, MD 410-272-6100
Con Yeager Spice Co
Zelienople, PA. 800-222-2460
Emerling International Foods
Buffalo, NY. 716-833-7381
Frontier Co-op
Norway, IA 844-550-6200
Morris J Golombeck Inc
Brooklyn, NY 718-284-3505
Old Mansion Inc
Petersburg, VA 800-476-1877
Red Monkey Foods
Springfield, MO 417-319-7300
Schiff Food Products Co Inc
Totowa, NJ 973-237-1990
Smith & Truslow
Denver, CO 303-339-6967
Specialty Food America Inc
Hopkinsville, KY 888-881-1633
Spice Chain
Avenel, NJ. 732-499-9070
SupHerb Farms
Turlock, CA 800-787-4372
Texas Coffee Co
Beaumont, TX. 800-259-3400
Trout Lake Farm
Trout Lake, WA. 800-655-6988
Vegetable Juices Inc
Chicago, IL 888-776-9752
Whole Herb Co
Sonoma, CA 707-935-1077

Greek

Agrocan
Ville St Laurent, QC 877-247-6226
Golden State Herbs
Thermal, CA 800-730-3575

Mexican

Wabash Heritage Mfg LLC
Vincennes, IN 812-886-0147

Paprika

Advanced Spice & Trading
Carrollton, TX. 800-872-7811
American Key Food Products Inc
Closter, NJ. 877-263-7539
Chesapeake Spice Company
Belcamp, MD 410-272-6100
Con Yeager Spice Co
Zelienople, PA. 800-222-2460
Emerling International Foods
Buffalo, NY. 716-833-7381
Erba Food Products
Brooklyn, NY 718-272-7700
Frontier Co-op
Norway, IA 844-550-6200
Gel Spice Co LLC
Bayonne, NJ 800-922-0230
Heartline Foods
Westport, CT. 203-222-0381
Morris J Golombeck Inc
Brooklyn, NY 718-284-3505
Old Mansion Inc
Petersburg, VA 800-476-1877
Pendery's
Dallas, TX. 800-533-1870
Red Monkey Foods
Springfield, MO 417-319-7300
Schiff Food Products Co Inc
Totowa, NJ 973-237-1990
SJH Enterprises
Middleton, WI. 888-745-3845
Smith & Truslow
Denver, CO. 303-339-6967
Spice & Spice
Rolling Hills Estates, CA 866-729-7742
Spice Chain
Avenel, NJ. 732-499-9070
Swagger Foods Corp
Vernon Hills, IL 847-913-1200
Wabash Heritage Mfg LLC
Vincennes, IN 812-886-0147

Parsley

Bifulco Four Seasons
Pittsgrove, NJ 856-692-0778
Chesapeake Spice Company
Belcamp, MD 410-272-6100
Frontier Co-op
Norway, IA 844-550-6200
Golden State Herbs
Thermal, CA 800-730-3575
Red Monkey Foods
Springfield, MO 417-319-7300
Smith & Truslow
Denver, CO. 303-339-6967
Specialty Food America Inc
Hopkinsville, KY 888-881-1633
SupHerb Farms
Turlock, CA 800-787-4372

Dehydrated

Alfred L. Wolff, Inc.
Park Ridge, IL. 847-759-8888
American Key Food Products Inc
Closter, NJ. 877-263-7539
Emerling International Foods
Buffalo, NY. 716-833-7381
Gel Spice Co LLC
Bayonne, NJ 800-922-0230
Unique Ingredients LLC
Gold Canyon, AZ 480-983-2498

Pepper

Advanced Spice & Trading
Carrollton, TX. 800-872-7811
American Key Food Products Inc
Closter, NJ. 877-263-7539
Casablanca Foods LLC
New York, NY. 212-317-1111
Con Yeager Spice Co
Zelienople, PA. 800-222-2460
Eatem Foods Co
Vineland, NJ 800-683-2836
Lawry's Foods
Hunt Valley, MD 800-952-9797
Morris J Golombeck Inc
Brooklyn, NY 718-284-3505
Old Mansion Inc
Petersburg, VA 800-476-1877
Pepper Mill Imports
Seaside, CA. 800-928-1744
Red Monkey Foods
Springfield, MO 417-319-7300
Schiff Food Products Co Inc
Totowa, NJ 973-237-1990
Smith & Truslow
Denver, CO 303-339-6967
Spice & Spice
Rolling Hills Estates, CA 866-729-7742
Swagger Foods Corp
Vernon Hills, IL 847-913-1200
Texas Coffee Co
Beaumont, TX. 800-259-3400
Tripper Inc
Oxnard, CA. 805-988-8851
Walker Foods
Los Angeles, CA. 800-966-5199
Wine Country Chef LLC
Hidden Valley Lake, CA. 707-322-0406

Black - White - Red

ACH Food Co Inc
Oakbrook Terrace, IL 630-586-3740
Frontier Co-op
Norway, IA 844-550-6200
Marion-Kay Spice Co
Brownstown, IN 800-627-7423
Spice & Spice
Rolling Hills Estates, CA 866-729-7742

White Ground

Chesapeake Spice Company
Belcamp, MD 410-272-6100
Smith & Truslow
Denver, CO 303-339-6967

White Whole

Frontier Co-op
Norway, IA 844-550-6200
Smith & Truslow
Denver, CO 303-339-6967

Pepper Mash

Emerling International Foods
Buffalo, NY. 716-833-7381
Vegetable Juices Inc
Chicago, IL 888-776-9752

Peppercorns

Amphora International
Lake Forest, CA 888-380-4808
Frontier Co-op
Norway, IA 844-550-6200
Smith & Truslow
Denver, CO. 303-339-6967
Wabash Heritage Mfg LLC
Vincennes, IN 812-886-0147

Whole

Smith & Truslow
Denver, CO 303-339-6967

Peppermint

Smith & Truslow
Denver, CO 303-339-6967
Trout Lake Farm
Trout Lake, WA 800-655-6988

Pickling Spices

Frontier Co-op
Norway, IA 844-550-6200
Texas Coffee Co
Beaumont, TX 800-259-3400

Red Pepper

Crushed

Marion-Kay Spice Co
Brownstown, IN 800-627-7423
Swagger Foods Corp
Vernon Hills, IL 847-913-1200

Flaked

Smith & Truslow
Denver, CO 303-339-6967

Rosemary

Advanced Spice & Trading
Carrollton, TX 800-872-7811
American Key Food Products Inc
Closter, NJ 877-263-7539
Chesapeake Spice Company
Belcamp, MD 410-272-6100
Con Yeager Spice Co
Zelienople, PA 800-222-2460
Emerling International Foods
Buffalo, NY 716-833-7381
Frontier Co-op
Norway, IA 844-550-6200
Gel Spice Co LLC
Bayonne, NJ 800-922-0230
Morris J Golombeck Inc
Brooklyn, NY 718-284-3505
Old Mansion Inc
Petersburg, VA 800-476-1877
Red Monkey Foods
Springfield, MO 417-319-7300
RFi Ingredients
Blauvelt, NY 800-962-7663
Schiff Food Products Co Inc
Totowa, NJ 973-237-1990
Smith & Truslow
Denver, CO 303-339-6967
SupHerb Farms
Turlock, CA 800-787-4372
Universal Preservachem Inc
Somerset, NJ 732-568-1266
Wabash Heritage Mfg LLC
Vincennes, IN 812-886-0147

Cut

RFi Ingredients
Blauvelt, NY 800-962-7663

Ground

Con Yeager Spice Co
Zelienople, PA 800-222-2460
RFi Ingredients
Blauvelt, NY 800-962-7663
Schiff Food Products Co Inc
Totowa, NJ 973-237-1990

Saffron

Advanced Spice & Trading
Carrollton, TX 800-872-7811
American Key Food Products Inc
Closter, NJ 877-263-7539
Chesapeake Spice Company
Belcamp, MD 410-272-6100
Emerling International Foods
Buffalo, NY 716-833-7381
Gel Spice Co LLC
Bayonne, NJ 800-922-0230
Rumi Spice
Chicago, IL 213-447-6112
Schiff Food Products Co Inc
Totowa, NJ 973-237-1990
Shank's Extracts Inc
Lancaster, PA 800-346-3135
Smith & Truslow
Denver, CO 303-339-6967
Whole Herb Co
Sonoma, CA 707-935-1077

Sage

Castella Imports Inc
Brentwood, NY 631-231-5500
Chesapeake Spice Company
Belcamp, MD 410-272-6100
Con Yeager Spice Co
Zelienople, PA 800-222-2460
Consumers Vinegar & Spice Co
Chicago, IL 773-376-4100
Frontier Co-op
Norway, IA 844-550-6200
Old Mansion Inc
Petersburg, VA 800-476-1877
Red Monkey Foods
Springfield, MO 417-319-7300
Smith & Truslow
Denver, CO 303-339-6967
SupHerb Farms
Turlock, CA 800-787-4372

Leaves

Advanced Spice & Trading
Carrollton, TX 800-872-7811
Con Yeager Spice Co
Zelienople, PA 800-222-2460
Emerling International Foods
Buffalo, NY 716-833-7381
Gel Spice Co LLC
Bayonne, NJ 800-922-0230
SupHerb Farms
Turlock, CA 800-787-4372

Rubbed

Con Yeager Spice Co
Zelienople, PA 800-222-2460

Savory

All American Foods Inc
Mankato, MN 800-833-2661
American Key Food Products Inc
Closter, NJ 877-263-7539
Flavor House, Inc.
Adelanto, CA 760-246-9131
Golden State Herbs
Thermal, CA 800-730-3575
Silver Palate Kitchens
Cresskill, NJ 201-568-0110
Smith & Truslow
Denver, CO 303-339-6967
Swagger Foods Corp
Vernon Hills, IL 847-913-1200
Tastepoint
Philadelphia, PA 800-363-5286

Shallots

Spice World Inc
Orlando, FL
SupHerb Farms
Turlock, CA 800-787-4372

Sorrel

SupHerb Farms
Turlock, CA 800-787-4372

Spearmint

Golden State Herbs
Thermal, CA 800-730-3575
SupHerb Farms
Turlock, CA 800-787-4372
Trout Lake Farm
Trout Lake, WA 800-655-6988

Star Anise

Chesapeake Spice Company
Belcamp, MD 410-272-6100
Frontier Co-op
Norway, IA 844-550-6200
Smith & Truslow
Denver, CO 303-339-6967

Tandoori

Frontier Co-op
Norway, IA 844-550-6200

Tarragon

Advanced Spice & Trading
Carrollton, TX 800-872-7811
Chesapeake Spice Company
Belcamp, MD 410-272-6100
Con Yeager Spice Co
Zelienople, PA 800-222-2460
Frontier Co-op
Norway, IA 844-550-6200
Old Mansion Inc
Petersburg, VA 800-476-1877
Red Monkey Foods
Springfield, MO 417-319-7300
Schiff Food Products Co Inc
Totowa, NJ 973-237-1990
Smith & Truslow
Denver, CO 303-339-6967
Specialty Food America Inc
Hopkinsville, KY 888-881-1633
SupHerb Farms
Turlock, CA 800-787-4372
Wabash Heritage Mfg LLC
Vincennes, IN 812-886-0147

Tartar

Cream

King Arthur Flour
Norwich, VT 800-827-6836
Universal Preservachem Inc
Somerset, NJ 732-568-1266

Teas

Castella Imports Inc
Brentwood, NY 631-231-5500
O'Neill Coffee Co
West Middlesex, PA 724-528-2244

Thyme

Advanced Spice & Trading
Carrollton, TX 800-872-7811
American Key Food Products Inc
Closter, NJ 877-263-7539
Chesapeake Spice Company
Belcamp, MD 410-272-6100
Con Yeager Spice Co
Zelienople, PA 800-222-2460
Emerling International Foods
Buffalo, NY 716-833-7381
Frontier Co-op
Norway, IA 844-550-6200
Golden State Herbs
Thermal, CA 800-730-3575
Morris J Golombeck Inc
Brooklyn, NY 718-284-3505
Old Mansion Inc
Petersburg, VA 800-476-1877
Red Monkey Foods
Springfield, MO 417-319-7300
Schiff Food Products Co Inc
Totowa, NJ 973-237-1990
Smith & Truslow
Denver, CO 303-339-6967
Specialty Food America Inc
Hopkinsville, KY 888-881-1633
SupHerb Farms
Turlock, CA 800-787-4372

Ground

Schiff Food Products Co Inc
Totowa, NJ 973-237-1990
Wabash Heritage Mfg LLC
Vincennes, IN 812-886-0147

Turmeric

Agri-Dairy Products
Purchase, NY 914-697-9580
American Key Food Products Inc
Closter, NJ 877-263-7539
Con Yeager Spice Co
Zelienople, PA 800-222-2460
Emerling International Foods
Buffalo, NY 716-833-7381
Frontier Co-op
Norway, IA 844-550-6200
Red Monkey Foods
Springfield, MO 417-319-7300
Schiff Food Products Co Inc
Totowa, NJ 973-237-1990

SJH Enterprises
Middleton, WI 888-745-3845
Tu Me Beverage Company
CA 818-237-5105
Tumericalive Healing Enterprise
New York, NY 347-559-6760
Turveda
CA

Ground

Natural Earth Products
Brooklyn, NY 718-552-2727
Schiff Food Products Co Inc
Totowa, NJ 973-237-1990
Smith & Truslow
Denver, CO 303-339-6967
Wabash Heritage Mfg LLC
Vincennes, IN 812-886-0147

Vanilla

Agri-Dairy Products
Purchase, NY 914-697-9580
Nielsen-Massey Vanillas Inc
Waukegan, IL 800-525-7873
Texas Coffee Co
Beaumont, TX 800-259-3400
Tripper Inc
Oxnard, CA 805-988-8851
Wabash Heritage Mfg LLC
Vincennes, IN 812-886-0147

Vanilla Beans

Emerling International Foods
Buffalo, NY 716-833-7381
Jedwards International Inc
Braintree, MA 781-848-1473
Red Monkey Foods
Springfield, MO 417-319-7300
Smith & Truslow
Denver, CO 303-339-6967
Zink & Triest Company
Montgomeryville, PA 800-537-5070

Wasabi

Great Eastern Sun Trading Co
Asheville, NC 800-334-5809

White Pepper

Ground

Smith & Truslow
Denver, CO 303-339-6967
Spice & Spice
Rolling Hills Estates, CA 866-729-7742

Sugars, Syrups & Sweeteners

General

Bear Stewart Corp
Chicago, IL ... 800-697-2327
Century Blends LLC
Hunt Valley, MD ... 410-771-6606
Colorado Sweet Gold
Lakewood, CO ... 303-384-1101
Crop Pharms, LLC
Staatsburg, NY ... 845-266-8999
Crosby Molasses Company
Saint John, NB ... 800-561-2206
Deborah's Kitchen Inc.
Littleton, MA ... 617-216-9908
Deer Creek Honey Farms LTD
London, OH ... 740-852-0899
E.F. Lane & Son
Oakland, CA ... 510-569-8980
EFCO Products Inc
Poughkeepsie, NY ... 800-284-3326
Evergreen Sweeteners, Inc
Hollywood, FL ... 954-381-7776
Hoyt's Honey Farm
Baytown, TX ... 281-576-5383
In The Raw
Brooklyn, NY ... 800-611-7434
Indiana Sugars
Lemont, IL ... 630-986-9150
JK Sucralose
Edison, NJ ... 732-512-0889
Kerry Foodservice
Mansfield, OH ... 800-533-2722
Kevala
Dallas, TX ... 877-379-1179
Maple Products
Sherbrooke, QC ... 819-569-5161
Monin Inc.
Clearwater, FL ... 855-352-8671
NOW Foods
Bloomingdale, IL ... 888-669-3663
Particle Control
Albertville, MN ... 763-497-3075
Paulaur Corp
Cranbury, NJ ... 609-395-8844
PureCircle USA
Chicago, IL ... 630-361-0374
Sugarright
Fairless Hills, PA ... 215-486-2105
Swerve Sweetener
New Orleans, LA ... 888-979-3783
Tate & Lyle PLC
Hoffman Estates, IL ... 847-396-7500
TresOmega
New Milford, CT ... 860-210-7805
Tropical Link Canada Ltd.
Burnaby, BC ... 778-379-3510
Western New York Syrup Corporation
Lakeville, NY ... 585-346-2311
Whitfield Foods Inc
Montgomery, AL ... 800-633-8790

Artificial

Heartland Sweeteners
Carmel, IN ... 317-566-9750
Merisant
Chicago, IL ... 312-840-6000
Niutang Chemical, Inc.
Chino, CA ... 909-631-2895
Silver Fern Chemical Inc
Seattle, WA ... 866-282-3384
Sweet'N Low
Brooklyn, NY
Techno USA
San Gabriel, CA ... 626-288-8478
Universal Preservachem Inc
Somerset, NJ ... 732-568-1266
US Sugar Company
Clewiston, FL ... 863-983-8121

Fructose

Agri-Dairy Products
Purchase, NY ... 914-697-9580
Cargill Inc.
Minneapolis, MN ... 800-227-4455
Evergreen Sweeteners, Inc
Hollywood, FL ... 954-381-7776
H. Interdonati
Cold Spring Harbour, NY ... 800-367-6617
Hunter Farms - High Point Division
High Point, NC ... 800-446-8035
Malt Diastase Co
Saddle Brook, NJ ... 800-526-0180
Oxford Frozen Foods
Oxford, NS ... 902-447-2100
Scenic Fruit Co
Gresham, OR ... 877-927-3434
Sensus America Inc
Lawrence Twp, NJ ... 646-452-6140
St. Lawrence Starch
Mississauga, ON ... 905-271-8396
True Blue Farms
Grand Junction, MI ... 877-654-2400

Crystalline

Farbest-Tallman Foods Corp
Montvale, NJ ... 201-573-4900

Honey

Adee Honey Farm
Bruce, SD ... 605-627-5621
Alaska Herb & Tea Co
Anchorage, AK ... 800-654-2764
Apiterra
Garland, TX ... 972-485-1005
Babe's Honey Farm
Victoria, BC ... 250-658-8319
Barkman Honey
Hillsboro, KS ... 800-364-6623
Bee Harmony Honey
Hillsboro, KS
Bee Raw Honey
Brooklyn, NY ... 888-660-0090
Bella Vista Farm
Lawton, OK ... 866-237-8526
Bloom Honey
... 877-555-9300
Burleson Honey
Waxahachie, TX ... 972-937-2809
Castella Imports Inc
Brentwood, NY ... 631-231-5500
Cloister Honey LLC
Charlotte, NC ... 704-517-6190
Clover Blossom Honey
La Fontaine, IN ... 765-981-4443
Colorado Hemp Honey
Parker, CO ... 833-233-2256
Comvita USA
Santa Barbara, CA ... 855-449-2201
Country Cupboard
Lewisburg, PA ... 570-523-3211
Dundee Groves
Dundee, FL ... 800-294-2266
Dutch Gold Honey Inc
Lancaster, PA ... 800-338-0587
Ed's Honey Co
Dickinson, ND ... 701-225-9223
Eleanor's Best LLC
Garrison, NY ... 646-296-6870
Emerling International Foods
Buffalo, NY ... 716-833-7381
Fischer Honey Company
North Little Rock, AR ... 501-758-1123
Fisher Honey Co
Lewistown, PA ... 717-242-4373
GloryBee
Eugene, OR ... 800-456-7923
Gold Sweet Company
Lake Wales, FL ... 863-676-0963
Govadinas Fitness Foods
San Diego, CA ... 800-900-0108
Hanna's Honey
Salem, OR ... 503-393-2945
Honey Acres
Neosho, WI ... 920-474-4411
Honey Bee Company
Alpharetta, GA ... 800-572-8838
Honey Blossom
The Colony, TX ... 469-582-7508
Honey Stinger
Steamboat Sprints, CO ... 866-464-6639
Hoyt's Honey Farm
Baytown, TX ... 281-576-5383
Island of the Moon Apiaries
Esparto, CA ... 530-787-3993
John Paton Inc
Doylestown, PA ... 215-348-7050
Kevala
Dallas, TX ... 877-379-1179
Klein Foods, Inc
Marshall, MN ... 800-657-0174
Leighton's Honey Inc
Haines City, FL ... 863-422-1773
Life Force Specialty Foods
Moscow, ID ... 877-657-9471
Madhava Natural Sweeteners
Boulder, CO ... 800-530-2900
Malt Diastase Co
Saddle Brook, NJ ... 800-526-0180
Meluka Honey
Santa Clarita, CA
Merrimack Valley Apiaries
Billerica, MA ... 978-667-2337
Mike's Hot Honey
Brooklyn, NY ... 347-450-4722
Mixon Fruit Farms Inc
Bradenton, FL ... 800-608-2525
Monin Inc.
Clearwater, FL ... 855-352-8671
Nature's Hollow
Charleston, UT
Once Again Nut Butter
Nunda, NY ... 888-800-8075
Orchard Pond
Tallahassee, FL ... 850-894-0154
Queen of America
Belleview, FL ... 352-245-3600
R D Laney Family Honey Co
North Liberty, IN ... 574-656-8701
Round Rock Honey Co, LLC
Round Rock, TX ... 512-828-5416
Savannah Bee Co.
Savannah, GA ... 800-955-5080
Scott Hams
Greenville, KY ... 800-318-1353
Shawnee Canning Co
Cross Junction, VA ... 800-713-1414
Sioux Honey Assn.
Sioux City, IA ... 712-258-0638
Slide Ridge LLC
Mendon, UT ... 435-752-4956
Strawberry Hill Grand Delights
Everett, MA ... 617-319-3557
Sutter Buttes Olive Oil
Sutter, CA ... 530-763-7921
Sutton Honey Farms
Lancaster, KY ... 859-792-4277
Suzanne's Specialties
New Brunswick, NJ ... 800-762-2135
Sweet Harvest Foods
Rosemount, MN ... 507-263-8599
Sweetener Supply Corp
Brookfield, IL ... 888-784-2799
Tropical Blossom Honey Co
Edgewater, FL ... 386-428-9027
Vintage Bee Inc.
Durham, NC ... 919-699-6788
Virgin Raw Foods LLC
Los Angeles, CA ... 800-830-7047
Virginia Honey Company
Inwood, WV ... 304-267-8500
Vita Food Products Inc
Chicago, IL ... 800-989-8482

Bee Pollen & Propolis

Alfred L. Wolff, Inc.
Park Ridge, IL ... 847-759-8888
Babe's Honey Farm
Victoria, BC ... 250-658-8319
C C Pollen
Phoenix, AZ ... 800-875-0096
Green Grown Products Inc
Marina Del Ray, CA ... 310-828-1686
Hsu's Ginseng Enterprises Inc
Wausau, WI ... 800-826-1577
Island of the Moon Apiaries
Esparto, CA ... 530-787-3993

Lenny's Bee Productions
Bearsville, NY 845-679-4514
Natural Foods Inc
Toledo, OH 419-537-1711
Nature Cure Northwest
Poulsbo, WA 800-957-8048
Nicola Valley Apiaries
Merritt, BC 250-378-5208
North Peace Apiaries
Fort St. John, BC 250-785-4808
Paradis Honey
Girouxville, AB 780-323-4283
Penauta Products
Stouffville, ON 905-640-1564
QBI
South Plainfield, NJ 908-668-0088
Rocky Mountain Honey Company
Salt Lake City, UT 801-355-2054
Southern Gold Honey Co
Vidor, TX 808-899-2494
Thistledew Farm
Proctor, WV 800-854-6639
Z Specialty Food, LLC
Woodland, CA 800-678-1226

Bees Wax

Adee Honey Farm
Bruce, SD 605-627-5621
Babe's Honey Farm
Victoria, BC 250-658-8319
D Steengrafe Co Inc
Pleasant Valley, NY 845-635-4067
Paradis Honey
Girouxville, AB 780-323-4283
Pure Food Ingredients
Verona, WI 800-355-9601
Rocky Mountain Honey Company
Salt Lake City, UT 801-355-2054
Silverbow Honey Company
Moses Lake, WA 866-444-6639
Southern Gold Honey Co
Vidor, TX 808-899-2494
Thistledew Farm
Proctor, WV 800-854-6639
Wixson Honey Inc
Dundee, NY 800-363-8209
Z Specialty Food, LLC
Woodland, CA 800-678-1226

Butter

Dundee Groves
Dundee, FL 800-294-2266
Honey Acres
Neosho, WI 920-474-4411
Honey Butter Products Co
Manheim, PA 717-665-9323
Kevala
Dallas, TX 877-379-1179
Kurtz Orchards Farms
Niagra-on-the-Lake, ON 905-468-2937
Limited Edition
Midland, TX 432-686-2008
Treasure Foods
West Valley, UT 801-974-0911

Granules

Natural

Groeb Farms
Onsted, MI 800-530-9969

Liquid

Champlain Valley Apiaries
Middlebury, VT 800-841-7334
Deer Creek Honey Farms LTD
London, OH 740-852-0899
Dutch Gold Honey Inc
Lancaster, PA 800-338-0587
E.F. Lane & Son
Oakland, CA 510-569-8980
Fischer Honey Company
North Little Rock, AR 501-758-1123
GloryBee
Eugene, OR 800-456-7923
Groeb Farms
Onsted, MI 800-530-9969
Honey Acres
Neosho, WI 920-474-4411
Hoyt's Honey Farm
Baytown, TX 281-576-5383
In The Raw
Brooklyn, NY 800-611-7434
Jacobsen's Salt Co.
Portland, OR 503-719-4973
Leighton's Honey Inc
Haines City, FL 863-422-1773
Leona's Restaurante
Chimayo, NM 888-561-5569
Nature Nate's
McKinney, TX 469-452-4429
Western New York Syrup Corporation
Lakeville, NY 585-346-2311

Molasses

Alma Plantation
Lakeland, LA 225-627-6632
Amalgamated Sugar Company
Boise, ID 208-383-6500
B & G Foods Inc.
Parsippany, NJ 973-401-6500
Baldwin Richardson Foods
Oakbrook Terrace, IL 866-644-2732
C & H Sugar Co Inc
Crockett, CA 800-773-1803
C S Steen Syrup Mill Inc
Abbeville, LA 800-725-1654
Cora Texas Mfg Co Inc
White Castle, LA 225-545-3679
Crosby Molasses Company
Saint John, NB 800-561-2206
Deer Creek Honey Farms LTD
London, OH 740-852-0899
Emerling International Foods
Buffalo, NY 716-833-7381
GloryBee
Eugene, OR 800-456-7923
Golding Farms Foods
Winston Salem, NC 336-766-6161
Lafourche Sugar LLC
Thibodaux, LA 985-447-3210
Louisiana Sugar Cane Co-Op Inc
St Martinville, LA 337-394-3785
Malt Diastase Co
Saddle Brook, NJ 800-526-0180
Malt Diastase Co
Garfield, NJ 800-772-0416
Michigan Desserts
Oak Park, MI 800-328-8632
Mott's LLP
Plano, TX 800-426-4891
New Organics
Kenwood, CA 734-677-5570
Osceola Farms Sugar Warehouse
Pahokee, FL 561-924-7156
Pacific Westcoast Foods
Beaverton, OR 800-874-9333
Pure Foods
Sultan, WA 360-793-2241
Pure Life Organic Foods
Las Vegas, NV 708-990-5817
Pure Sweet Honey Farms Inc
Verona, WI 800-355-9601
Raceland Raw Sugar Corporation
Raceland, LA 985-537-3533
Rio Grande Valley Sugar Growers
Santa Rosa, TX 956-636-1411
Rogers Sugar Inc.
Montreal, QC 514-527-8686
Savoie Industries
Belle Rose, LA 225-473-9293
Scott Hams
Greenville, KY 800-318-1353
Southern Minnesota Beet Sugar Cooperative
Renville, MN 320-329-8305
St. James Sugar Cooperative
Saint James, LA 225-265-4056
Sugar Cane Growers Co-Op of Florida
Belle Glade, FL 561-996-5556
Suzanne's Specialties
New Brunswick, NJ 800-762-2135
Sweetener Supply Corp
Brookfield, IL 888-784-2799
T.J. Blackburn Syrup Works
Jefferson, TX 800-657-5073
Tova Industries LLC
Louisville, KY 888-532-8682
WCC Honey Marketing
City Of Industry, CA 626-855-3086
Westway Trading Corporation
New Orleans, LA 701-282-5010
Whitfield Foods Inc
Montgomery, AL 800-633-8790
Wholesome!
Sugar Land, TX 800-680-1896

Natural Sweeteners

Abunda Life
Asbury Park, NJ 732-775-9338
Adee Honey Farm
Bruce, SD 605-627-5621
Alfred L. Wolff, Inc.
Park Ridge, IL 847-759-8888
Alma Plantation
Lakeland, LA 225-627-6632
Amalgamated Sugar Company
Boise, ID 208-383-6500
Artesian Honey Producers
Artesian, SD 605-527-2423
Babe's Honey Farm
Victoria, BC 250-658-8319
Barkman Honey
Hillsboro, KS 800-364-6623
BioVittoria USA
Libertyville, IL 847-226-3467
Briess Malt & Ingredients Co.
Chilton, WI 800-657-0806
C S Steen Syrup Mill Inc
Abbeville, LA 800-725-1654
California Natural Products
Lathrop, CA 209-858-2525
Cargill Inc.
Minneapolis, MN 800-227-4455
Champlain Valley Apiaries
Middlebury, VT 800-841-7334
Cleveland Syrup Corporation
Cleveland, OH 216-883-1845
Clover Blossom Honey
La Fontaine, IN 765-981-4443
Cora Texas Mfg Co Inc
White Castle, LA 225-545-3679
Crockett Honey
Tempe, AZ 800-291-3969
Crop Pharms, LLC
Staatsburg, NY 845-266-8999
Dawes Hill Honey Company
Nunda, NY 888-800-8075
Deer Creek Honey Farms LTD
London, OH 740-852-0899
Dixie USA
Tomball, TX 800-233-3668
Domino Specialty Ingredients
West Palm Beach, FL
Doyon
.... 800-265-2600
Dutch Gold Honey Inc
Lancaster, PA 800-338-0587
E.F. Lane & Son
Oakland, CA 510-569-8980
Eden Foods Inc
Clinton, MI 888-424-3336
Evergreen Sweeteners, Inc
Hollywood, FL 954-381-7776
Farbest-Tallman Foods Corp
Montvale, NJ 201-573-4900
Fischer Honey Company
North Little Rock, AR 501-758-1123
Florida Crystals Corporation
West Palm Beach, FL 844-344-9497
Garuda International
Exeter, CA 559-594-4380
Gateway Food Products Co
Dupo, IL 877-220-1963
Golding Farms Foods
Winston Salem, NC 336-766-6161
Grain Processing Corp
Muscatine, IA 800-448-4472
Great Eastern Sun Trading Co
Asheville, NC 800-334-5809
Greenwood Associates
Niles, IL 847-579-5500
Groeb Farms
Onsted, MI 800-530-9969
H. Interdonati
Cold Spring Harbour, NY 800-367-6617
Hanna's Honey
Salem, OR 503-393-2945
Healthy Food Ingredients
Fargo, ND 844-275-3443
Heinz Portion Control
Jacksonville, FL 904-695-1300
Hendricks Apiaries
Englewood, CO 303-789-3209
Honey World
Parker, SD 605-297-4188

Hoyt's Honey Farm
Baytown, TX....................281-576-5383
Indiana Sugars
Lemont, IL....................630-986-9150
Ingredion Inc.
Westchester, IL....................800-713-0208
Jiaherb
Pine Brook, NJ....................888-542-4372
Jogue Inc
Northville, MI....................800-531-3888
Kerry Foodservice
Mansfield, OH....................800-533-2722
Kutiks Honey Farm
Norwich, NY....................607-336-4105
Lafourche Sugar LLC
Thibodaux, LA....................985-447-3210
Leighton's Honey Inc
Haines City, FL....................863-422-1773
Leprino Foods Co.
Denver, CO....................800-537-7466
Les Industries Bernard et Fils
Saint Victor, QC....................418-588-3590
Louisiana Sugar Cane Co-Op Inc
St Martinville, LA....................337-394-3785
M.A. Patout & Son LTD
Jeanerette, LA....................337-276-4592
Madhava Natural Sweeteners
Boulder, CO....................800-530-2900
Malt Diastase Co
Saddle Brook, NJ....................800-526-0180
Maple Products
Sherbrooke, QC....................819-569-5161
Michele Foods
South Holland, IL....................708-331-7453
Minn-Dak Farmers Co-Op
Wahpeton, ND....................701-642-8411
Minnestalgia Foods LLC
Mcgregor, MN....................800-328-6731
New Organics
Kenwood, CA....................734-677-5570
Nickabood's Inc
Los Angeles, CA....................213-746-1541
Nicola Valley Apiaries
Merritt, BC....................250-378-5208
North Peace Apiaries
Fort St. John, BC....................250-785-4808
NOW Foods
Bloomingdale, IL....................888-669-3663
Once Again Nut Butter
Nunda, NY....................888-800-8075
Organic Nectars LLC
Malden On Hudson, NY....................845-246-0506
Organic Planet
San Francisco, CA....................415-765-5590
Osceola Farms Sugar Warehouse
Pahokee, FL....................561-924-7156
Ouachita Lumber Co
West Monroe, LA....................318-396-1960
Particle Control
Albertville, MN....................763-497-3075
Paulaur Corp
Cranbury, NJ....................609-395-8844
Pied-Mont/Dora
Anne Des Plaines, QC....................800-363-8003
Pure Food Ingredients
Verona, WI....................800-355-9601
Pure Foods
Sultan, WA....................360-793-2241
Pure Sweet Honey Farms Inc
Verona, WI....................800-355-9601
Pyure Brands
Naples, FL....................305-509-5096
R Weaver Apiaries
Navasota, TX....................936-825-2333
Raceland Raw Sugar Corporation
Raceland, LA....................985-537-3533
Rio Grande Valley Sugar Growers
Santa Rosa, TX....................956-636-1411
Rocky Mountain Honey Company
Salt Lake City, UT....................801-355-2054
Roquette America Inc.
Geneva, IL....................630-463-9430
Sandt's Honey Co
Easton, PA....................800-935-3960
Savoie Industries
Belle Rose, LA....................225-473-9293
Shady Maple Farm
Mississauga, ON....................905-206-1455
Silverbow Honey Company
Moses Lake, WA....................866-444-6639
Sno Shack Inc
Rexburg, ID....................888-766-7425
Southern Minnesota Beet Sugar Cooperative
Renville, MN....................320-329-8305
St. James Sugar Cooperative
Saint James, LA....................225-265-4056
Steviva Ingredients
Portland, OR....................800-851-6314
Stickney & Poor Company
Peterborough, NH....................603-924-2259
Sugar Cane Growers Co-Op of Florida
Belle Glade, FL....................561-996-5556
Sunfood
El Cajon, CA....................888-729-3663
Suzanne's Specialties
New Brunswick, NJ....................800-762-2135
Thistledew Farm
Proctor, WV....................800-854-6639
Unique Ingredients LLC
Gold Canyon, AZ....................480-983-2498
United Canadian Malt
Peterborough, ON....................800-461-6400
Universal Preservachem Inc
Somerset, NJ....................732-568-1266
Valentine Chemicals
Lockport, LA....................985-532-2541
Valley View Blueberries
Vancouver, WA....................360-892-2839
VIP Foods
Flushing, NY....................718-821-5330
WCC Honey Marketing
City Of Industry, CA....................626-855-3086
Western New York Syrup Corporation
Lakeville, NY....................585-346-2311
Westway Trading Corporation
New Orleans, LA....................701-282-5010
Whitfield Foods Inc
Montgomery, AL....................800-633-8790
Wholesome!
Sugar Land, TX....................800-680-1896
Wixson Honey Inc
Dundee, NY....................800-363-8209
Woodworth Honey & Bee Co
Halliday, ND....................701-938-4647
Z Specialty Food, LLC
Woodland, CA....................800-678-1226

Sucrose

Evergreen Sweeteners, Inc
Hollywood, FL....................954-381-7776
NOW Foods
Bloomingdale, IL....................888-669-3663
Rogers Sugar Inc.
Montreal, QC....................514-527-8686
Universal Preservachem Inc
Somerset, NJ....................732-568-1266

Sugar

Adirondack Maple Farms
Fonda, NY....................518-853-4022
Agri-Dairy Products
Purchase, NY....................914-697-9580
Alma Plantation
Lakeland, LA....................225-627-6632
Amalgamated Sugar Company
Boise, ID....................208-383-6500
American Crystal Sugar Co.
Moorhead, MN....................218-236-4400
Bateman Products
Rigby, ID....................208-745-9033
Beneo Inc
Morris Plains, NJ....................973-539-6644
Bonumose LLC
Charlottesville, VA
C & H Sugar Co Inc
Crockett, CA....................800-773-1803
Cleveland Syrup Corporation
Cleveland, OH....................216-883-1845
Cora Texas Mfg Co Inc
White Castle, LA....................225-545-3679
Domino Specialty Ingredients
West Palm Beach, FL
ECOM Agroindustrial Corporation Ltd
Pully,
Erba Food Products
Brooklyn, NY....................718-272-7700
Evergreen Sweeteners, Inc
Hollywood, FL....................954-381-7776
Florida Crystals Corporation
West Palm Beach, FL....................844-344-9497
Franco's Cocktail Mixes
Pompano Beach, FL....................800-782-4508
Global Organics
Cambridge, MA....................781-648-8844
Greenwell Farms Inc
Kealakekua, HI....................888-592-5662
Heinz Portion Control
Jacksonville, FL....................904-695-1300
Honey Ridge Farms
Brush Prairie, WA....................360-256-0086
Imperial Sugar Company
Sugar Land, TX....................800-727-8427
Indiana Sugars
Lemont, IL....................630-986-9150
Jakeman's Maple Products
Beachville, ON....................800-382-9795
Kerry Foodservice
Mansfield, OH....................800-533-2722
Lafourche Sugar LLC
Thibodaux, LA....................985-447-3210
Lantic Sugar
Montreal, QC....................514-527-8686
Louisiana Sugar Cane Co-Op Inc
St Martinville, LA....................337-394-3785
M.A. Patout & Son LTD
Jeanerette, LA....................337-276-4592
Madhava Natural Sweeteners
Boulder, CO....................800-530-2900
Maple Products
Sherbrooke, QC....................819-569-5161
Mapleland Farm
Salem, NY....................518-854-7669
Marubeni America Corp.
New York, NY....................212-450-0100
Michigan Sugar Company
Bay City, MI....................989-686-0161
Minn-Dak Farmers Co-Op
Wahpeton, ND....................701-642-8411
Olam Spices
Fresno, CA....................559-447-1390
Organic Planet
San Francisco, CA....................415-765-5590
Osceola Farms Sugar Warehouse
Pahokee, FL....................561-924-7156
Particle Control
Albertville, MN....................763-497-3075
Paulaur Corp
Cranbury, NJ....................609-395-8844
Penta Manufacturing Company
Livingston, NJ....................973-740-2300
Quaker Sugar Company
Brooklyn, NY....................718-387-6500
Raceland Raw Sugar Corporation
Raceland, LA....................985-537-3533
Rapunzel Pure Organics
Bloomfield, NJ....................800-225-1449
Rice Company
Fair Oaks, CA....................916-784-7745
Rio Grande Valley Sugar Growers
Santa Rosa, TX....................956-636-1411
Rogers Sugar Inc.
Taber, AB....................403-223-3535
Rogers Sugar Inc.
Montreal, QC....................514-527-8686
Rogers Sugar Inc.
Vancouver, BC....................604-253-1131
S A L T Sisters
Goshen, IN....................574-971-8368
Savoie Industries
Belle Rose, LA....................225-473-9293
Shady Maple Farm
Mississauga, ON....................905-206-1455
Southern Minnesota Beet Sugar Cooperative
Renville, MN....................320-329-8305
St. James Sugar Cooperative
Saint James, LA....................225-265-4056
Sugar Foods Corp
Sun Valley, CA....................818-768-7900
Sugarright
Fairless Hills, PA....................215-486-2105
Sweeteners Plus Inc
Lakeville, NY....................585-346-3193
US Sugar Company
Clewiston, FL....................863-983-8121
Valentine Chemicals
Lockport, LA....................985-532-2541
Western Sugar Cooperative
Denver, CO....................800-523-7497
Westin Foods
Omaha, NE....................800-228-6098
William Bounds
Torrance, CA....................800-473-0504

Brown

Agri-Dairy Products
Purchase, NY 914-697-9580
C & H Sugar Co Inc
Crockett, CA....................800-773-1803
Evergreen Sweeteners, Inc
Hollywood, FL....................954-381-7776
Florida Crystals Corporation
West Palm Beach, FL....................844-344-9497
Sweetener Supply Corp
Brookfield, IL....................888-784-2799
US Sugar Company
Clewiston, FL....................863-983-8121
Westin Foods
Omaha, NE....................800-228-6098

Cane

Agri-Dairy Products
Purchase, NY....................914-697-9580
C & H Sugar Co Inc
Crockett, CA....................800-773-1803
Evergreen Sweeteners, Inc
Hollywood, FL....................954-381-7776
Global Organics
Cambridge, MA....................781-648-8844
Homefree LLC
Windham, NH....................800-552-7172
Just Panela
Boulder, CO....................720-600-0522
M.A. Patout & Son LTD
Jeanerette, LA....................337-276-4592
New Organics
Kenwood, CA....................734-677-5570
Organic Planet
San Francisco, CA....................415-765 5590
Rio Grande Valley Sugar Growers
Santa Rosa, TX....................956-636-1411
Sweetener Supply Corp
Brookfield, IL....................888-784-2799
Wholesome!
Sugar Land, TX....................800-680-1896

Granulated

Amalgamated Sugar Company
Boise, ID....................208-383-6500
Diazteca Inc
Rio Rico, AZ....................520-761-4621
Evergreen Sweeteners, Inc
Hollywood, FL....................954-381-7776
Michigan Sugar Company
Bay City, MI....................989-686-0161
Paulaur Corp
Cranbury, NJ....................609-395-8844
Rogers Sugar Inc.
Montreal, QC....................514-527-8686
Sweetener Supply Corp
Brookfield, IL....................888-784-2799
US Sugar Company
Clewiston, FL....................863-983-8121
Westin Foods
Omaha, NE....................800-228-6098

Icing

BakeMark USA
Schaumburg, IL....................847-519-3135
Domino Specialty Ingredients
West Palm Beach, FL
Lantic Sugar
Montreal, QC....................514-527-8686
Signature Brands LLC
Ocala, FL....................800-456-9573

Invert

Agri-Dairy Products
Purchase, NY....................914-697-9580
Evergreen Sweeteners, Inc
Hollywood, FL....................954-381-7776
Florida Crystals Corporation
West Palm Beach, FL....................844-344-9497
Malt Diastase Co
Saddle Brook, NJ....................800-526-0180
Paulaur Corp
Cranbury, NJ....................609-395-8844

Liquid

Amalgamated Sugar Company
Boise, ID....................208-383-6500
Evergreen Sweeteners, Inc
Hollywood, FL....................954-381-7776
Flavouressence Products
Mississauga, ON....................866-209-7778
Lantic Sugar
Montreal, QC....................514-527-8686
Paulaur Corp
Cranbury, NJ....................609-395-8844
Wholesome!
Sugar Land, TX....................800-680-1896

Liquid & Granulated

Agri-Dairy Products
Purchase, NY....................914-697-9580
Amalgamated Sugar Company
Boise, ID....................208-383-6500
C & H Sugar Co Inc
Crockett, CA....................800-773-1803
Evergreen Sweeteners, Inc
Hollywood, FL....................954-381-7776
Lantic Sugar
Montreal, QC....................514-527-8686

Maple

Brown Family Farm
Brattleboro, VT....................866-254-8718
Butternut Mountain Farm
Morrisville, VT....................800-828-2376
Citadelle Maple Syrup Producers' Cooperative
Plessisville, QC....................819-362-3241
Emerling International Foods
Buffalo, NY....................716-833-7381
Finding Home Farms
Middletown, NY....................845-355-4335
Food For Thought Inc
Honor, MI....................231-326-5444
GloryBee
Eugene, OR....................800-456-7923
J.M. Smucker Co.
Orrville, OH....................888-550-9555
Maple Hollow
Merrill, WI....................715-536-7251
Maple Products
Sherbrooke, QC....................819-569-5161
Maple Valley Cooperative
Cashton, WI....................608-654-7319
Richards Maple Products
Chardon, OH....................800-352-4052
Shady Maple Farm
Mississauga, ON....................905-206-1455
Vermont Country Naturals
Charlotte, VT....................800-528-7021
Whitfield Foods Inc
Montgomery, AL....................800-633-8790

Butter

Butternut Mountain Farm
Morrisville, VT....................800-828-2376
Choice of Vermont
Destin, FL....................800-444-6261
Whitfield Foods Inc
Montgomery, AL....................800-633-8790

Organic

Florida Crystals Corporation
West Palm Beach, FL....................844-344-9497
In The Raw
Brooklyn, NY....................800-611-7434
NOW Foods
Bloomingdale, IL....................888-669-3663
Sunfood
El Cajon, CA....................888-729-3663
Wholesome!
Sugar Land, TX....................800-680-1896

Powdered

Agri-Dairy Products
Purchase, NY....................914-697-9580
C & H Sugar Co Inc
Crockett, CA....................800-773-1803
Cleveland Syrup Corporation
Cleveland, OH....................216-883-1845
Evergreen Sweeteners, Inc
Hollywood, FL....................954-381-7776
Flavouressence Products
Mississauga, ON....................866-209-7778
Michigan Sugar Company
Bay City, MI....................989-686-0161
US Sugar Company
Clewiston, FL....................863-983-8121
Vermont Country Naturals
Charlotte, VT....................800-528-7021
Westin Foods
Omaha, NE....................800-228-6098

Turbinado

In The Raw
Brooklyn, NY....................800-611-7434

Sugar Substitutes

Abunda Life
Asbury Park, NJ....................732-775-9338
Agri-Dairy Products
Purchase, NY....................914-697-9580
Amcan Industries
Elmsford, NY....................914-347-4838
Fasweet Co
Jonesboro, AR....................888-223-6693
Franco's Cocktail Mixes
Pompano Beach, FL....................800-782-4508
GLG Life Tech Corporation
Richmond, BC....................855-454-7587
GloryBee
Eugene, OR....................800-456-7923
Great Eastern Sun Trading Co
Asheville, NC....................800-334-5809
H. Interdonati
Cold Spring Harbour, NY....................800-367-6617
Health Garden USA
Spring Valley, NY....................845-877-7090
Jungbunzlauer Inc
Newton, MA....................617-969-0900
M. Licht & Son
Knoxville, TN....................865-523-5593
Madhava Natural Sweeteners
Boulder, CO....................800-530-2900
Malt Diastase Co
Saddle Brook, NJ....................800-526-0180
McNeil Nutritionals
Fort Washington, PA....................215-273-7000
McNeil Specialty Products Company
New Brunswick, NJ....................732-524-3799
Minnestalgia Foods LLC
Mcgregor, MN....................800-328-6731
Nickabood's Inc
Los Angeles, CA....................213-746-1541
North Peace Apiaries
Fort St. John, BC....................250-785-4808
NOW Foods
Bloomingdale, IL....................888-669-3663
NuNaturals
Eugene, OR....................800-753-4372
Once Again Nut Butter
Nunda, NY....................888-800-8075
Paulaur Corp
Cranbury, NJ....................609-395-8844
PMC Specialties Group Inc
Cincinnati, OH....................800-543-2466
Rocky Mountain Honey Company
Salt Lake City, UT....................801-355-2054
Roquette America Inc.
Geneva, IL....................630-463-9430
St. Lawrence Starch
Mississauga, ON....................905-271-8396
Steviva Ingredients
Portland, OR....................800-851-6314
Stickney & Poor Company
Peterborough, NH....................603-924-2259
Sugar Foods Corp
Sun Valley, CA....................818-768-7900
Suzanne's Specialties
New Brunswick, NJ....................800-762-2135
Sweet'N Low
Brooklyn, NY
Sweetleaf Co
Gilbert, AZ....................800-899-9908
Universal Preservachem Inc
Somerset, NJ....................732-568-1266
VIP Foods
Flushing, NY....................718-821-5330
WCC Honey Marketing
City Of Industry, CA....................626-855-3086
Westin Foods
Omaha, NE....................800-228-6098
Wholesome!
Sugar Land, TX....................800-680-1896

Aspartame

Ajinomoto Heartland Inc
Chicago, IL....................773-380-7000
McNeil Nutritionals
Fort Washington, PA....................215-273-7000

Saccharin

Jungbunzlauer Inc
Newton, MA 617-969-0900
PMC Specialties Group Inc
Cincinnati, OH 800-543-2466
Roquette America Inc.
Geneva, IL 630-463-9430
Sweet'N Low
Brooklyn, NY

Sugar Alternatives

GLG Life Tech Corporation
Richmond, BC 855-454-7587
McNeil Nutritionals
Fort Washington, PA 215-273-7000
Stevita Naturals
Arlington, TX 800-577-8409

Syrups

A.C. Calderoni
Brisbane, CA 866-468-1897
A.W. Jantzi & Sons
Wellesley, ON 519-656-2400
Abunda Life
Asbury Park, NJ 732-775-9338
Advanced Ingredients, Inc.
Minneapolis, MN 888-238-4647
Al-Rite Fruits & Syrups Co
Miami, FL 305-652-2540
Alaska Herb & Tea Co
Anchorage, AK 800-654-2764
Alimentaire Whyte's Inc
Laval, QC 866-420-9520
Amalgamated Sugar Company
Boise, ID 208-383-6500
Baldwin Richardson Foods
Oakbrook Terrace, IL 866-644-2732
Bay Valley Foods
El Paso, TX 800-236-1119
Belton Foods Inc
Dayton, OH 800-443-2266
Ben's Sugar Shack
Temple, NH 603-924-3177
Blueberry Store
Grand Junction, MI 877-654-2400
Bosco Products Inc
Towaco, NJ 800-438-2672
Boyd's Coffee Co
Portland, OR 800-735-2878
Briess Malt & Ingredients Co.
Chilton, WI 800-657-0806
C S Steen Syrup Mill Inc
Abbeville, LA 800-725-1654
California Custom Foods
Fullerton, CA 714-870-0490
California Natural Products
Lathrop, CA 209-858-2525
Cameron Birch Syrup & Confections
Wasilla, AK 800-962-4724
Carborator Rental Svc
Philadelphia, PA 800-220-3556
Cargill Inc.
Minneapolis, MN 800-227-4455
Carolina Beverage Corp
Salisbury, NC 704-633-4550
Carolina Treet
Wilmington, NC 800-616-6344
Castella Imports Inc
Brentwood, NY 631-231-5500
Cheri's Desert Harvest
Tucson, AZ 800-743-1141
Citadelle Maple Syrup Producers' Cooperative
Plessisville, QC 819-362-3241
Classic Tea
Libertyville, IL 630-680-9934
Clear Mountain Coffee Company
Silver Spring, MD 301-587-2233
Clements Foods Co
Oklahoma City, OK 800-654-8355
Cleveland Syrup Corporation
Cleveland, OH 216-883-1845
Cold Hollow Cider Mill
Waterbury Center, VT 800-327-7537
Con Yeager Spice Co
Zelienople, PA 800-222-2460
Consolidated Mills Inc
Houston, TX 713-896-4196
Cora Italian Specialties
Countryside, IL 800-696-2672
Cora Texas Mfg Co Inc
White Castle, LA 225-545-3679
Crosby Molasses Company
Saint John, NB 800-561-2206
Davinci Gourmet LTD
Seattle, WA 800-640-6779
Daymar Select Fine Coffees
El Cajon, CA 800-466-7590
Dean Distributors, Inc.
Burlingame, CA 800-792-0816
Deer Creek Honey Farms LTD
London, OH 740-852-0899
Domino Specialty Ingredients
West Palm Beach, FL
E.D. Smith Foods Ltd
Hamilton, ON 905-573-1207
Emerling International Foods
Buffalo, NY 716-833-7381
Entner-Stuart Premium Syrups
Albany, OR 800-926-6886
Eva Gates Homemade Preserves
Bigfork, MT 800-682-4283
Evergreen Sweeteners, Inc
Hollywood, FL 954-381-7776
Eweberry Farms
Brownsville, OR 541-466-3470
Felbro Food Products
Los Angeles, CA 323-936-5266
Ferrara Bakery & Cafe
New York, NY 212-226-6150
Finlays
Lincoln, RI 800-288-6272
Flavorganics
Newark, NJ 866-972-6879
Flavors from Florida
Bartow, FL 800-888-0409
Flavors of Hawaii Inc
Honolulu, HI 808-597-1727
Flavouressence Products
Mississauga, ON 866-209-7778
Florida Citrus
Bartow, FL 863-537-3999
Folklore Foods
Selby, SD 605-649-1144
Forge Mountain Foods
Hendersonville, NC 800-823-6743
Foxtail Foods
Fairfield, OH 800-487-2253
Gateway Food Products Co
Dupo, IL 877-220-1963
Gedney Foods Co
Sun Valley, CA 888-244-0653
GEM Berry Products
Orofino, ID 888-231-1699
Gem Berry Products
Sandpoint, ID 800-231-1699
Golden Eagle Syrup
Fayette, AL 205-932-5294
Golden State Foods Corp
Irvine, CA 949-247-8000
Great Valley Mills
Barto, PA 800-688-6455
Great Western Co LLC
Hollywood, AL 256-259-3578
Great Western Juice Co
Maple Heights, OH 800-321-9180
Groeb Farms
Onsted, MI 800-530-9969
Gust John Foods & Products
Batavia, IL 800-756-5886
H & H Products Co
Orlando, FL 800-678-8448
H Fox & Co Inc
Brooklyn, NY 718-385-4600
Heinz Portion Control
Jacksonville, FL 904-695-1300
Highland Sugarworks
Websterville, VT 800-452-4012
Homemade By Dorothy Boise
Boise, ID 800-657-7449
Honey Run Winery
Chico, CA 530-345-6405
Howard Foods Inc
Danvers, MA 978-774-6207
Huckleberry Patch
Hungry Horse, MT 800-527-7340
I Rice & Co Inc
Philadelphia, PA 800-232-6022
Ingredion Inc.
Westchester, IL 800-713-0208
Instant Products of America
Columbus, IN 812-372-9100
International Food Products
Fenton, MO 800-227-8427
J.M. Smucker Co.
Orrville, OH 888-550-9555
Jakeman's Maple Products
Beachville, ON 800-382-9795
JER Creative Food Concepts, Inc.
Commerce, CA 800-350-2462
JMS Specialty Foods
Ripon, WI 800-535-5437
Jogue Inc
Northville, MI 800-531-3888
Josef Aaron Syrup Company
Redmond, WA 425-820-7221
Jus-Made
Dallas, TX 800-969-3746
Just Date Syrup
San Mateo, CA
Kemach Food Products
Brooklyn, NY 718-272-5655
Kerry Foodservice
Mansfield, OH 800-533-2722
Kloss Manufacturing Co Inc
Allentown, PA 800-445-7100
Koloa Rum Corp
Kalaheo, HI 808-332-9333
Kozlowski Farms
Forestville, CA 800-473-2767
Kurtz Orchards Farms
Niagra-on-the-Lake, ON 905-468-2937
Lafourche Sugar LLC
Thibodaux, LA 985-447-3210
Lancaster Packing Company
Myerstown, PA 717-397-9727
Les Industries Bernard et Fils
Saint Victor, QC 418-588-3590
Limpert Bros Inc
Vineland, NJ 800-691-1353
Lost Trail Root Beer
Louisburg, KS 800-748-7765
Louisiana Sugar Cane Co-Op Inc
St Martinville, LA 337-394-3785
Lowery's Premium Roast Gourmet Coffee
Snohomish, WA 800-767-1783
Lundberg Family Farms
Richvale, CA 530-538-3500
Lynch Foods
North York, ON 416-449-5464
Lyons Magnus
Fresno, CA 800-344-7130
Magic Ice Products
Cincinnati, OH 800-776-7923
Malt Diastase Co
Garfield, NJ 800-772-0416
Maple Grove Farms Of Vermont
St Johnsbury, VT 802-748-5141
Maple Products
Sherbrooke, QC 819-569-5161
Mapleland Farm
Salem, NY 518-854-7669
Mardale Specialty Foods
Waukegan, IL 845-299-0285
Marsa Specialty Products
Vernon, CA 800-628-0500
Masterson Co Inc
Milwaukee, WI 414-647-1132
Melchers Flavors of America
Indianapolis, IN 800-235-2867
Michele Foods
South Holland, IL 708-331-7453
Michigan Sugar Company
Bay City, MI 989-686-0161
Minnestalgia Foods LLC
Mcgregor, MN 800-328-6731
Monin Inc.
Clearwater, FL 855-352-8671
Morris Kitchen
Brooklyn, NY 347-457-6994
National Flavors
Kalamazoo, MI 800-525-2431
National Fruit Flavor Co Inc
New Orleans, LA 800-966-1123
Naturel
Rancho Cucamonga, CA 877-242-8344
New Organics
Kenwood, CA 734-677-5570
Newport Flavours & Fragrances
Orange, CA 714-744-3700
Nog Incorporated
Dunkirk, NY 800-332-2664
Northwestern Extract
Germantown, WI 800-466-3034
Orange Bang Inc
Sylmar, CA 818-833-1000

Oregon Hill Farms
St Helens, OR 800-243-4541
Organic Nectars LLC
Malden On Hudson, NY. 845-246-0506
Osceola Farms Sugar Warehouse
Pahokee, FL 561-924-7156
Pacific Westcoast Foods
Beaverton, OR 800-874-9333
Paradigm Foodworks Inc
Lake Oswego, OR. 800-234-0250
Paulaur Corp
Cranbury, NJ 609-395-8844
Phillips Syrup Corp
Cleveland, OH 800-350-8443
Pied-Mont/Dora
Anne Des Plaines, QC 800-363-8003
Poppers Supply Company
Allentown, PA. 800-457-9810
Pride of Dixie Syrup Company
Bono, AR 800-530-7654
Prima Foods International
Silver Springs, FL. 800-774-8751
Pure Foods
Sultan, WA 360-793-2241
Purity Factories
St. John's, NL 800-563-3411
R Torre & Co
S San Francisco, CA 800-775-1925
Raceland Raw Sugar Corporation
Raceland, LA 985-537-3533
Richards Maple Products
Chardon, OH. 800-352-4052
Rio Syrup Co
St Louis, MO. 800-325-7666
Rocky Ridge Maple
Middlebury Center, PA 607-742-9566
Roquette America Inc.
Geneva, IL. 630-463-9430
Routin America
Delray Beach, FL
Santini Foods
San Lorenzo, CA. 800-835-6888
Savoie Industries
Belle Rose, LA 225-473-9293
SBK Preserves
Bronx, NY. 800-773-7378
Sea Breeze Fruit Flavors
Towaco, NJ 800-732-2733
Shady Maple Farm
Mississauga, ON. 905-206-1455
Shank's Extracts Inc
Lancaster, PA 800-346-3135
Shawnee Canning Co
Cross Junction, VA. 800-713-1414
Singer Extract Laboratory
Livonia, MI. 313-345-5880
Skjodt-Barrett Foods
Brampton, ON. 877-600-1200
Somerset Syrup & Concessions
Edison, NJ. 800-526-8865
Sonoma Syrup Co. Inc.
Sonoma, CA 707-996-4070
St. James Sugar Cooperative
Saint James, LA 225-265-4056
Star Kay White Inc
Congers, NY 800-874-8518
Stasero International
Kent, WA. 888-929-2378
Steel's Gourmet Foods, Ltd.
Bridgeport, PA 800-678-3357
Stevens Tropical Plantation
West Palm Beach, FL 561-683-4701
Stirling Foods
Renton, WA. 800-332-1714
Sugar Cane Growers Co-Op of Florida
Belle Glade, FL. 561-996-5556
Sugarman of Vermont
Hardwick, VT 800-932-7700
Sugarright
Fairless Hills, PA 215-486-2105
Suzanne's Specialties
New Brunswick, NJ 800-762-2135
Sweet Additions
Palm Beach Gardens, NY. 561-472-0178
Sweetstacks LLC
San Diego, CA 619-997-1097
T. Marzetti Company
Westerville, OH. 800-999-1835
T.J. Blackburn Syrup Works
Jefferson, TX. 800-657-5073
Texas Coffee Traders Inc
Austin, TX. 800-343-4875
Toms Moms Foods, LLC
Centreville, VA 614-716-9436
Tone Products Inc
Melrose Park, IL 800-536-8663
Tonewood Maple
Waitsfield, VT. 802-496-5512
Torani
San Francisco, CA 855-972-0508
Tova Industries LLC
Louisville, KY 888-532-8682
Trader Vic's Food Products
Emeryville, CA. 877-762-4824
Trailblazer Foods
Portland, OR 800-777-7179
Triple H Food Processors Inc
Riverside, CA 951-352-5700
Turtle Island Herbs
Boulder, CO 800-684-4060
United Canadian Malt
Peterborough, ON. 800-461-6400
Valley Grain Products
Fresno, CA 559-675-3400
Valley View Blueberries
Vancouver, WA 360-892-2839
Van Tone Creative
Terrell, TX. 800-856-0802
Ventura Foods LLC
Brea, CA 800-421-6257
Vita Food Products Inc
Chicago, IL 800-989-8482
Wagner Excello Food Products
Broadview, IL 708-338-4488
WCC Honey Marketing
City Of Industry, CA. 626-855-3086
Webbpak Inc
Trussville, AL 800-655-3500
Western Syrup Company
Santa Fe Springs, CA 562-921-4485
Westin Foods
Omaha, NE 800-228-6098
Westway Trading Corporation
New Orleans, LA 701-282-5010
White-Stokes Company
Chicago, IL 800-978-6537
Whitfield Foods Inc
Montgomery, AL. 800-633-8790
Willamette Valley Pie Co
Salem, OR. 503-362-8857
Wing Nien Food
Hayward, CA 510-487-8877

Bar

Davinci Gourmet LTD
Seattle, WA 800-640-6779

Beverages

ARCO Coffee
Superior, WI 800-283-2726
Davinci Gourmet LTD
Seattle, WA 800-640-6779
EFCO Products Inc
Poughkeepsie, NY 800-284-3326
Flavouressence Products
Mississauga, ON. 866-209-7778
Folklore Foods
Selby, SD. 605-649-1144
Great Western Juice Co
Maple Heights, OH. 800-321-9180
Refresco Beverages US Inc.
Tampa, FL. 888-260-3776
Rio Syrup Co
St Louis, MO. 800-325-7666
Skjodt-Barrett Foods
Brampton, ON. 877-600-1200
Van Tone Creative
Terrell, TX. 800-856-0802

Cane

Agri-Dairy Products
Purchase, NY 914-697-9580
Evergreen Sweeteners, Inc
Hollywood, FL 954-381-7776
Flavorganics
Newark, NJ 866-972-6879
Malt Diastase Co
Saddle Brook, NJ 800-526-0180
New Organics
Kenwood, CA 734-677-5570
Osceola Farms Sugar Warehouse
Pahokee, FL 561-924-7156
Ouachita Lumber Co
West Monroe, LA 318-396-1960
Webbpak Inc
Trussville, AL 800-655-3500

Corn

Archer Daniels Midland Company
Decatur, IL 217-424-5200
Archer Daniels Midland Company
Chicago, IL 312-634-8100
Crosby Molasses Company
Saint John, NB 800-561-2206
Evergreen Sweeteners, Inc
Hollywood, FL 954-381-7776
Malt Diastase Co
Saddle Brook, NJ 800-526-0180
Whitfield Foods Inc
Montgomery, AL. 800-633-8790

Blends

Evergreen Sweeteners, Inc
Hollywood, FL 954-381-7776

Dextrose

Archer Daniels Midland Company
Decatur, IL 217-424-5200
Archer Daniels Midland Company
Chicago, IL 312-634-8100
Evergreen Sweeteners, Inc
Hollywood, FL 954-381-7776

Glucose - Etc.

Archer Daniels Midland Company
Decatur, IL 217-424-5200
Archer Daniels Midland Company
Chicago, IL 312-634-8100
Baldwin Richardson Foods
Oakbrook Terrace, IL 866-644-2732
Cargill Inc.
Minneapolis, MN 800-227-4455
Con Yeager Spice Co
Zelienople, PA. 800-222-2460
Evergreen Sweeteners, Inc
Hollywood, FL 954-381-7776
Gateway Food Products Co
Dupo, IL 877-220-1963
Ingredion Inc.
Westchester, IL 800-713-0208
Malt Diastase Co
Saddle Brook, NJ 800-526-0180
New Organics
Kenwood, CA 734-677-5570
Paulaur Corp
Cranbury, NJ 609-395-8844
Roquette America Inc.
Geneva, IL. 630-463-9430
WCC Honey Marketing
City Of Industry, CA. 626-855-3086
Westin Foods
Omaha, NE 800-228-6098

High Fructose

Evergreen Sweeteners, Inc
Hollywood, FL 954-381-7776
Ingredion Inc.
Westchester, IL 800-713-0208
Sweetener Supply Corp
Brookfield, IL 888-784-2799

Fruit

3V Company
Brooklyn, NY 718-858-7333
Al-Rite Fruits & Syrups Co
Miami, FL. 305-652-2540
Baldwin Richardson Foods
Oakbrook Terrace, IL 866-644-2732
Bernard & Sons Maple Products
St-Victor, QC. 418-588-6109
Blackberry Patch
Thomasville, GA. 800-853-5598
California Custom Fruits
Baldwin Park, CA. 877-558-0056
Cold Hollow Cider Mill
Waterbury Center, VT. 800-327-7537
Davinci Gourmet LTD
Seattle, WA 800-640-6779
Eva Gates Homemade Preserves
Bigfork, MT 800-682-4283
GEM Berry Products
Orofino, ID 888-231-1699

Great Valley Mills
Barto, PA........................800-688-6455
H & H Products Co
Orlando, FL......................800-678-8448
H Fox & Co Inc
Brooklyn, NY.....................718-385-4600
I Rice & Co Inc
Philadelphia, PA.................800-232-6022
Inn Maid Food
Lenox, MA........................413-637-2732
J.M. Smucker Co.
Orrville, OH.....................888-550-9555
Jogue Inc
Northville, MI...................800-531-3888
Koloa Rum Corp
Kalaheo, HI......................808-332-9333
Maple Grove Farms Of Vermont
St Johnsbury, VT.................802-748-5141
Minnestalgia Foods LLC
Mcgregor, MN.....................800-328-6731
Orange Bang Inc
Sylmar, CA.......................818-833-1000
Pacific Westcoast Foods
Beaverton, OR....................800-874-9333
Phillips Syrup Corp
Cleveland, OH....................800-350-8443
Purity Factories
St. John's, NL...................800-563-3411
Sea Breeze Fruit Flavors
Towaco, NJ.......................800-732-2733
Summerland Sweets
Summerland, BC...................800-577-1277
Valley View Blueberries
Vancouver, WA....................360-892-2839
Van Tone Creative
Terrell, TX......................800-856-0802
Vermont Specialty Food Association
Randolph, VT.....................802-728-0070
Western Syrup Company
Santa Fe Springs, CA.............562-921-4485

Malt Extract

Briess Malt & Ingredients Co.
Chilton, WI......................800-657-0806
Grounds For Thought
Bowling Green, OH................419-354-3266
Lake Country Foods Inc
Oconomowoc, WI...................262-567-5521
Malt Diastase Co
Saddle Brook, NJ.................800-526-0180
Premier Malt Products Inc
Warren, MI.......................800-521-1057
Roquette America Inc.
Geneva, IL.......................630-463-9430
United Canadian Malt
Peterborough, ON.................800-461-6400

Maple

A Perfect Pear
Napa, CA.........................800-553-5753
Adirondack Maple Farms
Fonda, NY........................518-853-4022
Arnold Farm Sugarhouse
Jackman, ME......................207-668-4110
B & G Foods Inc.
Parsippany, NJ...................973-401-6500
Baldwin Richardson Foods
Oakbrook Terrace, IL.............866-644-2732
Bascom Family Farms Inc
Brattleboro, VT..................888-266-6271
Bernard & Sons Maple Products
St-Victor, QC.....................418-588-6109
Brown Family Farm
Brattleboro, VT..................866-254-8718
Butternut Mountain Farm
Morrisville, VT..................800-828-2376
Citadelle Maple Syrup Producers' Cooperative
Plessisville, QC.................819-362-3241
Coombs Family Farm
Brattleboro, VT..................888-266-6271
Couture's Maple Shop/B & B
Westfield, VT....................800-845-2733
D & D Sugarwoods Farm
Glover, VT.......................800-245-3718
Dole Pond Maple Products
Jackman, ME......................418-653-5322
Eleanor's Best LLC
Garrison, NY.....................646-296-6870
Emerling International Foods
Buffalo, NY......................716-833-7381
Green River Chocolates
Hinesburg, VT....................802-482-6727
Hidden Springs Maple
Putney, VT.......................802-387-5200
Highland Sugarworks
Websterville, VT.................800-452-4012
Hillside Lane Farm
Randolph, VT.....................802-728-0070
Howard Foods Inc
Danvers, MA......................978-774-6207
Jed's Maple Products
Derby, VT........................802-766-2700
JMS Specialty Foods
Ripon, WI........................800-535-5437
King Arthur Flour
Norwich, VT......................800-827-6836
L.B. Maple Treat
Granby, QC.......................888-775-1111
Les Industries Bernard et Fils
Saint Victor, QC.................418-588-3590
Maple Acres Inc
Kewadin, MI......................231-264-9265
Maple Grove Farms Of Vermont
St Johnsbury, VT.................802-748-5141
Maple Hollow
Merrill, WI......................715-536-7251
Maple Products
Sherbrooke, QC...................819-569-5161
Maple Valley Cooperative
Cashton, WI......................608-654-7319
Mc Lure's Honey & Maple Prod
Littleton, NH....................603-444-6246
Middlefield Cheese House
Middlefield, OH..................800-327-9477
Minnestalgia Foods LLC
Mcgregor, MN.....................800-328-6731
Mount Mansfield Maple Products
Winooski, VT.....................802-497-1671
Nature's Hollow
Charleston, UT
NOW Foods
Bloomingdale, IL.................888-669-3663
Phillips Syrup Corp
Cleveland, OH....................800-350-8443
Pride of Dixie Syrup Company
Bono, AR.........................800-530-7654
Richards Maple Products
Chardon, OH......................800-352-4052
Sea Breeze Fruit Flavors
Towaco, NJ.......................800-732-2733
Shady Maple Farm
Mississauga, ON..................905-206-1455
Subco Foods Inc
Sheboygan, WI....................800-473-0757
Sugarman of Vermont
Hardwick, VT.....................800-932-7700
Swisser Sweet Maple
Castorland, NY...................315-346-1034
The Maple Guild
Island Pond, VT..................802-723-6753
Tonewood Maple
Waitsfield, VT...................802-496-5512
Turkey Hill Sugarbush
Waterloo, QC.....................450-539-4822
Vermont Specialty Food Association
Randolph, VT.....................802-728-0070
Wagner Excello Food Products
Broadview, IL....................708-338-4488
Webbpak Inc
Trussville, AL...................800-655-3500

Pancake

Bernard & Sons Maple Products
St-Victor, QC.....................418-588-6109
California Custom Foods
Fullerton, CA....................714-870-0490
Finding Home Farms
Middletown, NY...................845-355-4335
Golden Eagle Syrup
Fayette, AL......................205-932-5294
Gust John Foods & Products
Batavia, IL......................800-756-5886
Marina Foods
Medley, FL.......................786-888-0129
Pride of Dixie Syrup Company
Bono, AR.........................800-530-7654
Sea Breeze Fruit Flavors
Towaco, NJ.......................800-732-2733
T. Marzetti Company
Westerville, OH..................800-999-1835
Tone Products Inc
Melrose Park, IL.................800-536-8663
Vermont Country Naturals
Charlotte, VT....................800-528-7021
Whitfield Foods Inc
Montgomery, AL...................800-633-8790

Toppings

Sundae

California Custom Fruits
Baldwin Park, CA.................877-558-0056
I Rice & Co Inc
Philadelphia, PA.................800-232-6022
Tahana Confections LLC
Portsmouth, NH...................603-498-6246

Waffle

Golden Eagle Syrup
Fayette, AL......................205-932-5294
Pride of Dixie Syrup Company
Bono, AR.........................800-530-7654
T. Marzetti Company
Westerville, OH..................800-999-1835

1 **1-2-3 Gluten Free**
125 Orange Tree Dr.
Chagrin Falls, OH 44022
216-378-9233
info@123glutenfree.com
www.123glutenfree.com
Gluten free baking mixes.
Owner: Kimberlee Ullner
kim@123glutenfree.com
Square Footage: 80000
Brands:
1-2-3 Gluten Free

2 **10 Strawberry Street**
3837 Monaco Pkwy
Denver, CO 80207
800-428-9397
www.tenstrawberrystreet.com
Serveware, dinnerwear, glassware and flatware
VP, Sales & Marketing: Ruby Hershberger
Year Founded: 1983

3 **1000 Islands River Rat Cheese**
242 James St
Clayton, NY 13624-1010
315-686-2480
Fax: 315-686-4701 800-752-1341
support@riverratcheese.net
www.riverratcheese.net
Distributor: NYS Cheese, Adirondack Sausage
President: Mary Scudera
1000islandsriverratcheese@gmail.com
Estimated Sales: $2,500,000
Number Employees: 10-19
Type of Packaging: Consumer, Food Service, Private Label, Bulk
Brands:
Adirondack Cheese
Gold Cup
River Rat Cheese

4 **1642**
2025 rue Parthenais
Suite 318
Montreal, QC H2K 3T2
Canada
800-774-4907
info@1642.ca www.1642.ca
Soft drinks

5 **18 Rabbits Inc.**
995 Market Street
2nd Floor
San Francisco, CA 94103
415-922-6006
blackjack@18rabbits.com
www.18rabbits.com
Organic, non-GMO and kosher granola bars
Founder and CEO: Alison Vercruysse
COO: Kent Spalding
Brands:
18 RABBITS

6 **21st Century Products, Inc.**
2692 Gravel Dr
Bldg 5
Fort Worth, TX 76118-6976
817-284-8299
Fax: 817-284-4844
Processor and exporter of vitamins; also, mineral and weight loss drinks
President: Greg Harris
Vice President: Dixon Ray
National Sales Director: Richard Fabose
Estimated Sales: $100,000
Number Employees: 2
Type of Packaging: Consumer, Food Service, Private Label, Bulk

7 **21st Century Snack Foods**
921 S 2nd St
Ronkonkoma, NY 11779
631-588-8000
www.21snackshop.com
Chocolate, nuts, seeds, trail mixes, dried fruit, candy, gummies, marzipan and gifts.
President: Royce Keller
Estimated Sales: $2.5-5 Million
Number Employees: 20-49
Type of Packaging: Bulk

8 **24 Mantra Organic**
Fremont, CA 94538
www.24mantra.com
Organic processed foods and drinks

9 **24Vegan**
Arcadia, CA 91077-1743
www.24vegan.com
Fish sauce

10 **3 Gyros Inc**
5270 Brendan Lane
Tecumseh, ON N0R 1L0
Canada
519-737-0389
Fax: 888-678-8584 info@3gyros.com
Gluten-free, sugar-free, other condiments, salad dressing, other sauces, seasonings and cooking enhancers.
President/Founder: Thanos Zikantas
National Account Manager: Tim Fittler
Customer Service: Angelo Zikantas
Product Development: Jason Verbeen

11 **3 Springs Water Co**
1800 Pine Run Rd
Laurel Run, PA 18706-9419
570-823-7019
Fax: 570-822-6177 800-332-7873
info@3springs.com www.3springs.com
Processor and bottler of low-mineral and sodium-free spring water
President: Jim Tosh
info@3springs.com
Estimated Sales: $3-5 Million
Number Employees: 20-49
Square Footage: 80000
Type of Packaging: Consumer, Food Service, Private Label
Brands:
3 Springs

12 **3 Water**
Huntington, NY 11743
877-371-8704
info@drink3water.com www.drink3water.com
Caffeinated water
Parent Co: EuroVita Corp.
Type of Packaging: Consumer

13 **34-Degrees**
2825 Larimer St
Denver, CO 80216
303-861-4818
Fax: 303-484-4664 info@34-degrees.com
www.34-degrees.com
Wafer crackers made with all natural ingredients. Natural, sesame, cracked pepper, rosemary, and whole grain varieties.
Founder/President: Craig Lierberman
EVP: Jennifer Margoles
Marketing Manager: Jen Swift
VP of Operations: Wes Brasher
Number Employees: 5-9
Type of Packaging: Consumer
Brands:
34 Degrees

14 **350 Cheese Straws**
1003 Lennoxville Rd.
Beaufort, NC 28516
252-838-9080
www.350cheesestraw.com
Cheese straws.
Founder and President: Ashley Sellars
Square Footage: 330230

15 **360 Nutrition**
1689 Beverly Blvd
Los Angeles, CA 90026
213-805-3015
inquiry@360nutritionusa.com
360nutritionusa.com
Drink blends
Number of Brands: 5
Number of Products: 20
Type of Packaging: Consumer
Brands:
360 NUTRITION
BLENDS WITH BENEFITS
GO MATCHA
PRO-SHAKE
SLIM SHAKE

16 **3PM Bites**
New York, NY
3pmbites.com
Superfood snacks
Founder: Tisha Agarwal
Year Founded: 2016
Number Employees: 1-10
Number of Brands: 1
Number of Products: 3
Type of Packaging: Consumer
Brands:
3PM BITES

17 **3V Company**
110 Bridge Street
Brooklyn, NY 11201
718-858-7333
Fax: 718-858-7371 3v.co
Fruit-based beverage products.
CEO: Eren Spring
Contact: Hershy Gombo
hgombo@3v.co
Number of Brands: 3
Type of Packaging: Consumer, Food Service, Private Label, Bulk
Brands:
3V Classic™
3V Fresh™
Smartfruit™

18 **4505 Meats LLC**
1246 Howard St
San Francisco, CA 94103
415-255-3094
Pork rinds
General Manager: Adam Bailey
Culinary Operations Manager: Cole Mayfield

19 **479 Degrees**
3450 Sacramento Street
San Francisco, CA 94118
815-552-6039
customer_service@479degrees.com
www.479degrees.com
Flavored popcorn.
Founder: Jean Arnold
Contact: Virginia Bryant
virginia@479degrees.com
Brands:
479 Degrees

20 **4C Foods Corp**
580 Fountain Ave
Brooklyn, NY 11208-6002
718-272-4242
Fax: 718-272-2899 inthekitchen@4c.com
www.4c.com
Iced tea, soft drink mix; imported cheese; bread crumbs and soup mix.
Founder and President: John Celauro
sally@4c.com
SVP Operations: Wayne Celauro
Number Employees: 100-249
Square Footage: 420000
Type of Packaging: Food Service, Private Label
Brands:
4C Foods
4C Beverages

21 **4Pure**
207-831-1030
www.drink4pure.com
Lemonade
Founder & CEO: Will Boyle
Number of Brands: 1
Number of Products: 3
Type of Packaging: Consumer
Brands:
4PURE

22 **4th & Heart**
213-880-2559
wecare@4thandheart.com
fourthandheart.com
Modern food staples
Co-Founder: Raquel Gunsagar
Co-Founder: Lillian Wunsch
Number of Brands: 1
Number of Products: 12
Type of Packaging: Consumer
Brands:
4TH & HEART

23 **505 Southwestern**
Meridian, ID 83642
www.flagshipfoodgroup.com
Salsas, cooking sauces and condiments

24 **50th State Poultry Processors**
98-715 Kuahao Place
Pearl City, HI 96782
808-845-5902
Fax: 808-847-7040 derronuezu@yahoo.com
www.50thstatepoultry.biz

Poultry
President: Darryl Uezu
VP: Linda Uezu
Estimated Sales: $10-20 Million
Number Employees: 20-49
Type of Packaging: Consumer, Food Service

25 **51 Fifty Enterprises**
436 Second St
Livingston, CA 95334
855-513-4389
info@51fiftyenergydrink.com
www.51fiftyenergydrink.com

Energy drinks
Number of Brands: 1
Number of Products: 11
Type of Packaging: Consumer
Brands:
51FIFTY

26 **731 North Beach LLC**
731 N. Beach Blvd
La Habra, CA 90631-3657
562-697-8888
Fax: 562-697-8288

Groceries
Owner: Han K Ng
Estimated Sales: $2.5-5 000,000
Number Employees: 5-9

27 **80 Acres Farms**
345 High St.
7th Fl.
Hamilton, OH 45011
888-574-1569
www.80acresfarms.com

Herbs, leafy greens, and select vegetables.
Co-Founder & President: Tisha Livingston
Co-Founder & CEO: Mike Zelkind
Year Founded: 2015
Type of Packaging: Private Label

28 **814 Americas Inc**
814 2nd Ave
Elizabeth, NJ 07202-3804
908-354-2674
Fax: 908-354-7170 www.814americas.com
Sausage
Founder: Severino Abuin
CFO: Michael Patratuolla
Manager: Michael Patracuolla
Estimated Sales: $5-10 Million
Number Employees: 20-49
Brands:
El Mino
Riojano

29 **88 Acres**
P.O. Box 79
Allston, MA 02121
617-208-8651
hello@88acres.com
88acres.com

Seed bars, seed granola, and seed butters
Co-Founder: Rob Dalton
Co-Founder: Nicole Ledoux
Marketing Manager: Dayna Scandone
Director of Sales: J.D. Collins
Other Locations:
Bakery
Dorchester MA

30 **8th Wonder**
Denver, CO 80209
303-868-6296
reed@8thwondertea.com
www.8thwondertea.com

Superfood RTD teas
Founder: Parker Rush

31 **99 Ranch Market**
1625 S Azusa Ave
Hacienda Heights, CA 91745-3832
626-839-2899
Fax: 626-839-2127 www.99ranch.com
Asian American groceries
Founder/CEO: Roger Chen

Year Founded: 1984
Estimated Sales: $500,000
Number Employees: 50-99
Other Locations:
Manufacturing Facility-Sugarland
Sugarland TX

32 **A B Munroe Dairy Inc**
151 N Brow St
East Providence, RI 02914-4415
401-438-4450
Fax: 401-438-0035 info@cowtruck.com
Fluid milk
President: Robert Armstrong
Director, Sales: Bob Munroe
Site Manager: Steve Viall
sviall@monroedairy.com
Plant Manager: John Sherman
Estimated Sales: $7-20 Million
Number Employees: 50-99
Brands:
Munroe Dairy

33 **A Cajun Life®, LLC**
Damascus, OR 97089
info@acajunlife.com
www.acajunlife.com

Cajun seasonings
Founder: Chris Fontenot

34 **A Couple of Squares, Inc**
501-B Nightingale Avenue
London, ON N5W 4C4
Canada
519-672-6979
Fax: 519-672-4487 866-672-6979
info@acoupleofsquares.com
www.acoupleofsquares.com

Cookie manufacturer and wholesaler.
Director of Marketing: Bernadette Erb
Sales Marketing: Carol Dobbin
Square Footage: 9000

35 **A Dozen Cousins**
Berkeley, CA 94710
support@adozencousins.com
adozencousins.com

Ready-to-heat beans
Founder & CEO: Ibraheem Basir

36 **A Gift Basket by Carmela**
64 Magnolia Cir
Longmeadow, MA 01106
413-746-1400
Fax: 413-746-1441
Customized gift baskets; importer of plum tomatoes, olive oil, balsamic vinegar, coffee, cookies, cakes, artichokes and gourmet foods from Italy
President: Carmela Denille
Estimated Sales: Less than $500,000
Number Employees: 1-4
Square Footage: 32800
Brands:
Gift Baskets By Carmela

37 **A Hill of Beans Coffee Roasters**
14512 West Center Rd
Omaha, NE 68144
402-333-6048
Fax: 402-333-7113 www.ahillofbeans.com
Roasted coffee beans.
Owner: Leo Hill
Estimated Sales: $5-10 000,000 appx.
Number Employees: 2-10

38 **A J's Edible Arts**
313 S 4th Ave
Pasco, WA 99301-5510
USA
509-547-3440
Fax: 509-380-0142 www.ajsediblearts.com
Mustard, sauces, giftboxes
Presiden: Alice Jones
alice@ajsediblearts.com
Co-Owner: Juli Massingale
Number Employees: 1-4

39 **A La Carte**
5610 W Bloomingdale Ave
Chicago, IL 60639-4110
773-237-3000
Fax: 773-237-3075 800-722-2370
service@alacarteline.com
Custom promotional products including hard candy and popcorn in decorative tins, jars, boxes, etc.

President: Michael Shulkin
CEO: Adam Robins
Sales Director: James Janowski
Purchasing: Marly Robins
Estimated Sales: $10-20 Million
Number Employees: 50-99
Parent Co: David Scott Industries
Type of Packaging: Food Service, Private Label, Bulk

40 **A Perfect Pear**
1283 Monticello Rd
Napa, CA 94558
707-251-8532
Fax: 707-257-6830 800-553-5753
All natural pear products to include vinegars, preserves, jellies, chutneys, marinades, salad dressings and maple syrup

41 **A Plus Label**
3215 W Warner Ave
Santa Ana, CA 92704
714-229-9811
apluslabel.com

Tag and label manufacturer

42 **A Southern Season**
505 Eno St
Hillsborough, NC 27278-2357
919-929-7133
Fax: 800-646-1118 800-253-3663
www.southernseason.com
Cheesestraws, BBQ sauces, lemon drops, cookies, jams and jellies
Owner: Michael Barefoot
Marketing Director: Deborah Miller
Manager: Tom Baker
tom@southernseason.com
Number Employees: 10-19
Brands:
Carolina Cupboard

43 **A Taste of the Kingdom**
3773 County Road 210
Kingdom City, MO 65262-2018
573-592-7373
Fax: 573-642-8680 888-592-5080
Natural, kosher condiments and glazes
Owner: Julie Price
Estimated Sales: $3-5 Million
Number Employees: 5-9

44 **A Tavola Together**
6262 Crooked Stick Cir
Stockton, CA 95219-1857
USA
209-608-5455
Fax: 209-475-0954
Focaccia, pizza dough, baking mixes, gluten free, recipes
Owner: Rima Barkett
Owner: Claudia Pruett
Estimated Sales: 500,000.00
Number Employees: 4

45 **A To Z Portion Control Meats**
201 N Main St
Bluffton, OH 45817-1297
419-358-2926
Fax: 419-358-8876 800-338-6328
www.atozmeats.com
Beef and pork products.
President: Lee A Kagy
leek@atozmeats.com
Year Founded: 1945
Estimated Sales: G
Number Employees: 20-49
Type of Packaging: Consumer, Food Service, Private Label, Bulk

46 **A Zerega's Sons Inc**
20-01 Broadway
P.O. Box 241
Fair Lawn, NJ 07410
201-797-1400
Fax: 201-797-0148 sales@zerega.com
www.zerega.com

Dry pasta.
Director: John Vermylen
jvermylen@zerega.com
Treasurer: Nicholas Pugliese
Vice President: Mark Vermylen
Marketing Project Manager: Judi Pollack
Production Manager: Joseph Anzalone

Year Founded: 1848
Estimated Sales: $48.1 Million
Number Employees: 100-249
Square Footage: 125000
Type of Packaging: Consumer, Food Service, Private Label, Bulk
Other Locations:
Zerega's Pasta Plant
Lee's Summit MO
Zerega's Pasta Plant
Fair Lawn NJ
Brands:
Antoine's
Columbia

47 **A la Cart**
Advanced meal delivery systems
President, Unified Brands: Dave Herring
Parent Co: Unified Brands

48 **A to Z Wineworks**
30835 N Hwy 99 W
Newburg, OR 97132
800-739-4455
info@AtoZwineworks.com
www.AtoZwineworks.com
Wine
Founder, CEO: Bill Hatcher
Founder, Chief Marketing & Sales Officer: Deb Hatcher
Founder, Consulting Winemaker: Cheryl Francis
Founder, Director of Winemaking: Sam Tannahill
Year Founded: 2002
Number Employees: 20-49
Brands:
Rex Hill

49 **A&A Marine & Drydock Company**
10417 Front Line
PO Box 547
Blenheim, ON N0P 1A0
Canada
519-676-2030
Fax: 519-676-4343 www.aamarine.ca
Frozen perch and pickerel.
President: George Anderson
Vice President: Sherry Anderson
Estimated Sales: $3.5 Million
Number Employees: 25
Type of Packaging: Consumer, Food Service

50 **A&B American Style, LLC**
PO Box 949
New York, NY 10013-0861
917-720-7009
www.abamerican.com
Sauces, seasonings, condiments: mayo, ketchup, salsa, dips.
Co-Founder: Arial Fliman
Co-Founder: Brian Ballan
brianballan@abamerican.com
Number Employees: 2

51 **A&C Quinlin Fisheries**
1220 Highway 330
Centreville, NS B0W 2G0
Canada
902-745-2742
Fax: 902-745-1788
Salted fish and seafood.
President: Aaron Quinlin
Estimated Sales: $5-10 Million
Number Employees: 20
Type of Packaging: Consumer, Food Service
Brands:
A&C
Chelsea

52 **A&H Products, Inc**
739 Ramsey Avenue
Hillsdale, NJ 07205
908-206-8886
Fax: 908-206-8632 sl@aandh.us
www.abeles-heymann.com
Producer of salami, pastrami, corned beef, brisket, hot dogs, beef fry, smoked turkey, and knockwurst.
President: Seth Leavitt
Estimated Sales: $5-10 Million
Number Employees: 5-9

53 **A-1 Eastern-Homemade Pickle Co**
1832 Johnston St
Los Angeles, CA 90031-3499
323-223-1141
Fax: 323-227-8951 info@a1pickle.com
www.a1pickle.com
Kosher pickles and assorted pickle products
President: Martin Morhar
Vice President: Murray Berger
Estimated Sales: $3.6 Million
Number Employees: 20-49
Type of Packaging: Food Service
Brands:
A-1 Pickle

54 **A-Treat Bottling Co**
2001 Union Blvd
Allentown, PA 18109-1631
610-434-6139
Fax: 610-434-5511 800-220-1531
www.a-treat.com
Soft drinks
President: Joseph Garvey
j.garvey@a-treat.com
VP: Curt Thomas
Estimated Sales: $9 Million
Number Employees: 50-99
Brands:
A-Treat
Big Blue
Green Spot
Treat-Up

55 **A. Gagliano Co Inc**
300 N Jefferson St # 1
PO Box 511382
Milwaukee, WI 53202-5920
414-272-1515
Fax: 414-272-7215 800-272-1516
info@agagliano.com
Fresh fruits and vegetables
Owner: Anthony Gagliano
tony@agagliano.com
Owner: Nick Gagliano
Owner: Mike Gagliano
Warehouse Manager: Rick Alsum
Estimated Sales: $20 Million
Number Employees: 50-99
Number of Brands: 1
Number of Products: 500
Square Footage: 200000
Type of Packaging: Consumer, Food Service, Private Label, Bulk
Brands:
A. Gagliano

56 **A. Lassonde Inc.**
755 Rue Principale
Rougemont, QC J0L 1M0
Canada
866-552-7643
www.lassonde.com
Fruit juices and drinks.
President/CEO: Jean Gattuso
Chairman/CEO: Pierre-Paul Lassonde
Vice President/CFO: Guy Blanchette
Year Founded: 1918
Estimated Sales: 1.5 Billion
Number Employees: 2,100
Number of Brands: 32
Parent Co: Lassonde Industries, Inc.
Type of Packaging: Food Service
Brands:
Allen's
Rougemont
Fairlee
Orange Maison
Everfresh
Fruite
Graves
Oasis
Sunlike
Del Monte
Tropical Grove
Fruit Drop
Ruby Kist
Bombay
Apple & Eve
Northland
Old Orchard
Madeleine
Canadian Club
Antico
Canton
The Shrink
Pomme De Coeur
Aroma Mi Amore
Bortilly
Arte Nova
Au Quotidien
Vivre Une Double Vie
Dublin's Pub
Vivre Dans La Nuit
Facies
The Red Plane

57 **A. Nonini Winery**
2640 N Dickenson Ave
Fresno, CA 93723-9644
559-275-1936
Fax: 209-241-7119 noniniwinery@gmail.com
Wine
President & Wine Maker: James Jordan
noniniwinery@gmail.com
Estimated Sales: $1-2.5 Million
Number Employees: 1-4
Type of Packaging: Private Label
Brands:
A Nonini

58 **A. Rafanelli Winery**
4685 W Dry Creek Rd
Healdsburg, CA 95448-8124
707-433-1385
Fax: 707-433-3836 www.arafanelliwinery.com
Wines which include; Zinfandel, Cabernet Sauvignon and Merlot
Owner: Stacy Rafanelli
stacy@arafanelliwinery.com
Estimated Sales: $500,000-$1 Million
Number Employees: 1-4
Number of Brands: 1
Number of Products: 1
Type of Packaging: Private Label
Brands:
A. Rafanelli

59 **A. Smith Bowman Distillery**
1 Bowman Dr
Fredericksburg, VA 22408
540-373-4555
Fax: 540-371-2236 www.asmithbowman.com
Bourbon, scotch, rum, tequila, whiskey, gin and vodka
President/CEO: John Adams Jr
CFO/COO: Kent Broussard
VP Production and Distiller: Joseph Dangler
Estimated Sales: $20-50 Million
Number Employees: 20-49
Number of Brands: 2
Number of Products: 9
Brands:
Bowman's
Virginia Gentleman

60 **A.C. Calderoni**
99 N. Hill Dr
Brisbane, CA 94005-1201
415-468-2282
Fax: 415-468-5967 866-468-1897
calderoni@value.net www.accalderoni.com
Juices, juice concentrates, and cocktail mixes
President: Bob Baciocco
Purchasing: Scott Hawley
Estimated Sales: $2.5-5 Million
Number Employees: 1-4
Brands:
A.C. Calderoni

61 **A.C. Inc.**
125 Black Duck Cove Rd
Beals, ME 04611
207-497-2261
Fax: 207-497-2731
Seafood wholesaler
President, CEO & Co-Owner: Albert Carver
Vice President & Co-Owner: Patrick Robinson

62 **A.C. Kissling Company**
161 E Allen St
Philadelphia, PA 19125-4194
215-423-4700
Fax: 215-425-0525 800-445-1943
Sauerkraut
President: R W Kissling Jr
Contact: R Kissling
kaultejk@yahoo.com

Estimated Sales: $2 Million
Number Employees: 10-19
Type of Packaging: Consumer
Brands:
Kissling

63 **A.C. LaRocco Pizza**
12412 E. Desmet Ave
Suite D
Spokane Valley, WA 99216-5082
509-924-9113
Fax: 509-922-3085
Vegetarian pizzas
President/CEO: Clarence Scott
Marketing Director: Karen Leffler
k.leffler@aclarocco.com
Estimated Sales: $2 Million
Number Employees: 1-4
Brands:
A.C. Larocco Vegetarian Pizza

64 **A.C. Legg**
6330 Highway 31
PO Box 709
Calera, AL 35040-5131
205-324-3451
Fax: 205-324-5971 800-422-5344
sales@aclegg.com www.aclegg.com
Processor of custom-blended seasonings for meat, poultry, seafood and snack foods.
President/CEO: James Purvis
jpurvis@aclegg.com
EVP: Charles Purvis
EVP: Sandra Purvis
Year Founded: 1923
Estimated Sales: $20-50 Million
Number Employees: 100-249
Number of Brands: 1
Square Footage: 131000
Type of Packaging: Food Service, Private Label, Bulk
Brands:
Legg's Old Plantation

65 **A.L. Duck Jr Inc**
26231 River Run Trail
Zuni, VA 23898-3215
757-562-2387
Smoked sausage
President: Brenda Redd
Estimated Sales: $1-2.5 Million
Number Employees: 5-9
Type of Packaging: Consumer, Food Service

66 **A.T. Gift Company**
RR 3
Box 802
Harpers Ferry, WV 25425-9310
304-876-6680
Fax: 304-876-2757
Wine related products
President: Angela Gift
Sales Manager: Frank Gift
Estimated Sales: Less than $500,000
Number Employees: 2

67 **A.Vogel USA**
6 Grandinetti Drive
Ghent, NY 12075
518-828-9111
Fax: 888-798-7555 800-641-7555
info@BioforceUSA.com www.bioforceusa.com
Natural products, vitamins, etc.
President: Paul Ross
Sales Manager: Rich Manziello
Operations Manager: Roberts Sheets
Estimated Sales: $300,000-500,000
Number Employees: 1-4
Parent Co: Bioforce USA
Brands:
A. Vogel

68 **A.W. Jantzi & Sons**
3800 Nafziger Rd
PO Box 27
Wellesley, ON N0B 2T0
Canada
519-656-2400
Fax: 519-656-3370 info@wellappleproducts.com
www.wellappleproducts.com
Apple cider and apple butter
President: Steve Jantzi
Vice President: Kevin Jantzi
Number Employees: 15
Square Footage: 40000
Type of Packaging: Consumer, Bulk
Brands:
Wellesley

69 **A2 Milk Company**
P.O. Box 20651
Boulder, CO 80308
844-422-6455
hello@a2milk.com
www.a2milk.com
Milk
Chief Executive USA: Blake Waltrip
Parent Co: Hain Celestial Group

70 **AAK**
2520 7th Street Rd
Louisville, KY 40208-1029
502-636-1321
Fax: 502-636-3904 800-622-3055
www.aak.com
Shortenings including flaked, creamy liquid and votated; also, soybean and cottonseed oils; as well as identity preserved oils for GMO-free market.
President/CEO: Timothy Helson
Regional Sales Manager: Jason Glaser
Operations Manager: Sam Marrillia
Estimated Sales: $11.6 Million
Number Employees: 100-249
Square Footage: 200000
Parent Co: AAK USA Inc.
Type of Packaging: Food Service, Bulk
Brands:
Golden Brands
Golden Foods

71 **AB InBev**
One Busch Pl.
St. Louis, MO 63118
314-577-7427
www.ab-inbev.com
Beer, malt liquor, ales, lagers, and non-alcoholic brews.
Zone President, North America: Michel Dukeris
CEO: Carlos Brito
Chief Financial/Solutions Officer: Felipe Dutra
Chief Marketing Officer: Pedro Earp
Chief Sales Officer: Ricardo Tadeu
Year Founded: 2008
Estimated Sales: $56.6 Billion
Number Employees: 182,915
Number of Brands: 500+
Type of Packaging: Consumer, Food Service, Bulk
Other Locations:
Brewery
Baldwinsville NY
Brewery
Cartersville GA
Brewery
Columbus OH
Brewery
Fairfield CA
Brewery
Fort Collins CO
Brewery
Houston TX
Brewery
Jacksonville FL
Brewery
Los Angeles CA
Brewery
Merrimack NH
Brewery
St. Louis MO
Brewery
Williamsburg VA
Brewery
Newark NJ
Brands:
Budweiser
Corona
Stella Artois
Beck's
Leffe
Hoegaarden
Aguila
Brahma
Canvas
Cass
Eagle Lager
Hero
Jupiler
Modelo
Patagonia
Victoria
Wals Brut

72 **ABC Tea House**
14520 Arrow Hwy
Baldwin Park, CA 91706-1732
626-813-1333
Fax: 626-813-1338 888-220-3988
Tea and teabags
Owner: West Huang
west_huang@solteras.com
Estimated Sales: $5-10 Million
Number Employees: 20-49
Parent Co: Cathay International
Brands:
Abc Tea (A Better Choice)

73 **ACH Food Co Inc**
One Parkview Plz
5th Floor
Oakbrook Terrace, IL 60181
630-586-3740
Fax: 630-954-6661 www.achfood.com
ACH's spice and seasonings brands, oils and shortenings, canola, vegetable, olive, and mixed blends.
Vice President & General Manager: Robert Soth
Chief Executive Officer: Imad Bazzi
EVP & Chief Financial Officer: Steve Zaruba
Vice President, Human Resources: Sarah Blankenship
sblankenship@achfood.com
Year Founded: 1868
Estimated Sales: $20-50 Million
Number Employees: 1000-4999
Square Footage: 768000
Type of Packaging: Consumer, Food Service, Private Label
Brands:
Argo Corn Starch
Decacake
French's Dry Spice Mixes
Spice Islands
Durkee
French's
Patak's
Wber Seasonings

74 **ACP, Inc.**
225 49th Avenue Dr SW
Cedar Rapids, IA 52404
319-368-8120
Fax: 319-368-8198 800-233-2366
acpsolutions.com
Commercial ovens
President/Owner: Tim Garbett
Parent Co: Ali Group

75 **ADH Health Products Inc**
215 N Route 303
Congers, NY 10920-1726
845-268-0027
Fax: 845-268-2988 info@adhhealth.com
www.adhhealth.com
All-natural vitamins, minerals, botanicals and high-quality health supplements.
President: Balu Advani
Chairman/CEO: Balram Advani
CFO: Navin Advani
VP/Vice Chairman/Human Resource Director: Maya Advani
COO: Ashwin Advani
VP Production: Arun Deshpande
Estimated Sales: $12.6 Million
Number Employees: 50-99
Square Footage: 100000
Type of Packaging: Private Label
Brands:
Centra-Vit
Daily Multiple S/C
One Daily Essential With Iron
Prenatal Formula
Stress Formula With Zinc
Thera-M Multiple

76 **ADJR Inc**
7909 Broughton Pike
Paulding, OH 45879
419-399-3182
Fax: 419-399-3189
Canned meat

President: Rex Bowersock
Treasurer: Angela Bowersock
Vice President: Dean Bowesock
Manager: Dawn Trentman
Estimated Sales: $2.6 Million
Number Employees: 20
Square Footage: 44100
Type of Packaging: Consumer, Food Service, Private Label

77 **ADM Wild Flavors & Specialty**
1261 Pacific Ave
Erlanger, KY 41018-1260
859-342-3600
Fax: 859-342-3610 info@wildflavors.com
www.wildflavors.com
Processor and exporter of flavors, colors and other ingredients for food and beverage
President: Kody Gibson
kcgibson@sbts.edu
Marketing Manager: Oliver Hodapp
Estimated Sales: $5-10 Million
Number Employees: 1000-4999
Parent Co: Archer Daniels Midland Company
Type of Packaging: Food Service, Private Label

78 **AEP Colloids**
6299 Route 9N
Hadley, NY 12835
518-696-9900
Fax: 518-696-9997 800-848-0658
www.aepcolloids.com
Supplier and manufacturer of gums including agar agar, guar, karaya, locust bean, tragacanth, carrageenan and psyllium husk.
Quality Manager: Drew Tomis
Contact: Adam Strouse
a.strouse@aepcolloids.com
Year Founded: 1966
Number Employees: 5-9
Square Footage: 40000
Parent Co: Sarcom Inc
Type of Packaging: Bulk

79 **AFF International**
1265 Kennestone Circle
Marietta, GA 30066-6037
770-427-8177
Fax: 770-427-0964 800-241-7764
Processor and exporter of aromatic flavors and fragrances
President/Owner: Richard Neill
Estimated Sales: $10-20 Million
Number Employees: 20-49
Type of Packaging: Bulk

80 **AFI-FlashGril'd Steak**
780 Layton Ave
Salt Lake City, UT 84104-1727
801-972-0055
Fax: 801-972-2050 800-382-2862
afisteak@aol.com
Frozen sandwich steaks
Manager: Goran Cvetkovic
CFO: Eugene Hill
VP, Marketing: Noel Working
Estimated Sales: $5-10 Million
Number Employees: 20-49
Brands:
Flashgril'd

81 **AG Processing Inc**
12700 W Dodge Rd
Omaha, NE 68154-2154
402-496-7809
Fax: 402-492-7721 800-247-1345
info@agp.com www.agp.com
Emulsifiers, lecithin, vegetable fats, soybean flours, soy proteins and oils including vegetable, almond, amaranth, avocado, canola, coconut, corn, cottonseed, grape seed, lemon, olive, palm, peanut, and safflower.
Chairman: Brad Davis
CEO: J Keith Spackler
CFO/Group VP: Scott Simmelink
Senior VP: Mark Craigmile
mcraigmile@agp.com
VP: Matt Caswell
SVP, HR: Duke Vair
SVP, Operations: Mark Craigmile
Estimated Sales: Over $1 Billion
Number Employees: 1000-4999
Parent Co: AGP
Other Locations:
AG Processing Plant
Eagle Grove IA
AG Processing Plant
Emmetsburg IA
AG Processing Plant
Manning IA
AG Processing Plant
Mason City IA
AG Processing Plant
Sergeant Bluff IA
AG Processing Plant
Sheldon IA
AG Processing Plant
Dawson MN
AG Processing Plant
St. Joseph MO
AG Processing Plant
Hastings NE
Brands:
Aep
Agp Grain Ltd
Agp Grain Marketing
Aminoplus
Masterfeeds
Soygold

82 **AGRO Merchants Grp NA**
1150 Sanctuary Pkwy
Suite 125
Alpharetta, GA 30009
888-599-5512
info@agromerchants.com agromerchants.com
Fresh and frozen food handling solutions
President, North America: Dave Moore
CEO: Carlos Rodriguez
CFO: Arjan Kaaks
Year Founded: 2013

83 **AGT Foods USA**
1611 E Century Ave
Suite 102
Bismarck, ND 58503-0780
701-751-1623
Fax: 701-751-1626 info@agtfoods.com
www.agtfoods.com
Supplier of food ingredients. Specialize in red split lentils, football red lentils, whole lentils, chickpeas/garbonzo beans, peas and yellow split peas.
President/CEO: Murad Al-Katib
Parent Co: AGT Food & Ingredients
Type of Packaging: Consumer, Food Service, Private Label, Bulk
Other Locations:
Williston Facility
Williston ND
Minot Factory
Minot ND

84 **AHD International, LLC**
3340 Peachtree Rd NE
Suite 1685
Atlanta, GA 30326-1143
404-233-4022
Fax: 404-233-4041 info@ahdintl.com
www.ahdintl.com
Contract manufacturer of vitamins and nutritional products; Importer and exporter of nutritional raw materials and oils
President: John Alkire
Estimated Sales: $10-20 Million
Number Employees: 10-19
Type of Packaging: Bulk

85 **AJ's Lena Maid Meats Inc**
500 W Main St
Lena, IL 61048-9726
815-369-4522
Fax: 815-369-2075
Beef, pork, lamb and venison
Owner: Marcia Pax
Secretary/Treasurer: Suzanne McGiveron
Estimated Sales: $500000
Number Employees: 10-19
Type of Packaging: Bulk
Brands:
Lena Maid

86 **AJM Meat Packing**
PO Box 13922
Park Court
San Juan, PR 00926-3922
787-787-4050
Fax: 787-787-2445
Manufactures approved USDA, FDA, and AMS meat and poultry for the industry which processes products for the school lunch program
VP of Operations: Sabah Yassin

87 **ALDI**
220 E 4th St
Cincinnati, OH 45202-4102
513-421-1671
Fax: 513-421-1671 www.aldi.us
Manager: Amy Denny
Marketing Director: Bill Still
Estimated Sales: Under $500,000
Number Employees: 20-49

88 **ALO Drink**
377 Swift Ave
South San Francisco, CA 94080
650-616-7777
Fax: 650-616-4808 info@alodrink.com
www.alodrink.com
Non-carbonated beverage: juice, cider
Executive VP: Henry Chen
Sales&Marketing: Jordan Ferchill
Contact: Brian Choi
brianchoi@alodrink.com
Parent Co: SPI West Port, Inc.

89 **ALO Drinks**
377 Swift Ave
San Francisco, CA 94080
info@alodrink.com
alodrink.com
Aloe vera drinks
Brands:
alo

90 **ALOHA**
New York, NY 10005
aloha.com
Organic protein drinks, bars and powders

91 **AM Todd Co**
1717 Douglas Ave
Kalamazoo, MI 49007
269-343-2603
Fax: 269-343-3399 www.wildflavors.com
Processor and exporter of natural flavor extracts including alfalfa, black walnut hulls, wild cherry bark, dandelion, spice, oleoresins, xanthan gum, agar agar, fruit aromas (essences), essential oils, ethyl vanillin, papain, coffeeechinacea and ginseng
Director, Business Development: Matt Redd
Estimated Sales: $50-100 Million
Number Employees: 50-99
Square Footage: 95000
Parent Co: Wild Flavours
Type of Packaging: Bulk

92 **AMCO Proteins**
109 Elbow Lane
Burlington, NJ 08016-4123
609-387-3130
Fax: 609-387-7204 info@amcoproteins.com
www.amcoproteins.com
Manufacturer of functional protein ingredients.
CEO: Adam Cabot
Vice President: Nancy Kraus
Product Development Manager: Jeffrey Brous
Other Locations:
Quality Distribution Inc.
Salt Lake City UT

93 **AME Nutrition**
545 Metro Place S
Suite 100
Dublin, OH 43017
614-766-3638
sales@amenutrition.com
www.amenutrition.com
Plant- and dairy-based ingredients manufacturer
Director of Sales & Marketing: Bill Brickson

94 **AMF Pharma**
1931 S Lynx Place
Ontario, CA 91761
909-930-9599
Fax: 909-930-9499 888-666-1016
info@amfpharma.com amfpharma.com
Dietary supplements
Number of Brands: 1
Type of Packaging: Private Label

95 **AMT Labs Inc**
680 N 700 W
North Salt Lake, UT 84054-2733
801-294-3126
Fax: 801-299-0220 customercare@amtlabs.net

Processor and exporter of food supplements including mineral supplements, amino acid chelates, ascorbates, citrates, etc.
President: Bing Fang
President: Layne Hadley
Chairman: Dr Sen-Maw Fang PhD
VP/Research & Development: Dr. Oliver Fang MD
VP Manufacturing: Todd Rasmussen
Estimated Sales: $8.2 Million
Number Employees: 50-99
Square Footage: 400000
Type of Packaging: Private Label, Bulk

96 **AOI Matcha**
16651 Gothard St
Unit M
Huntington Beach, CA 92647
714-841-2716
877-264-0877
info@aoimatcha.com www.aoimatcha.com
Green tea
Type of Packaging: Bulk

97 **AOI Tea Company**
16651 Gothard Street
Unit M
Huntington Beach, CA 92647
714-841-2716
877-264-0877
consumer@AOItea.com www.aoitea.com
Matcha green tea
Madam President: Ayano Honda
Contact: Andrew Ge
age@aoimatcha.com

98 **APC Inc**
2425 SE Oak Tree Ct
Ankeny, IA 50021-7199
515-289-7600
Fax: 515-289-4360 800-369-2672
www.functionalproteins.com
Manufacturer of dairy replacer for bakery, confectionery and beverage applications.
CEO: Ryan Black
rblack@proliant.com
Number Employees: 50-99
Parent Co: Lauridsen Group
Other Locations:
U.S. Office
Ankeny IA
Mexico Office
El Marqu,s, Quer,taro
Production
Melrose MN
Brands:
VersiLac®

99 **APS BioGroup**
2235 South Central Ave
Phoenix, AZ 85004
602-353-8800
info@apsbiogroup.com
www.apsbiogroup.com
Producer of colostrum, and private label vitamins.
CEO: Bob Davies
Parent Co: Pantheryx, Inc.
Type of Packaging: Consumer, Private Label

100 **ARA Food Corp**
8001 NW 60th St
Miami, FL 33166-3412
305-468-6659
Fax: 305-592-6035 800-533-8831
info@arafood.com www.tropicalchips.net
Plantain, taro and cassava tropical chips
Vice President: Alberto Abrante
salesdep@arafood.com
Estimated Sales: $10-20 Million
Number Employees: 50-99
Number of Brands: 9
Type of Packaging: Private Label
Brands:
Bananitas
Donita
Rico's
ARA Real
Top Banana
Yu-qui-tas
Mariquitas Classic
Natura
Tropical Chips

101 **ARCO Coffee**
2206 Winter St
Superior, WI 54880-1400
715-392-4771
Fax: 715-392-4776 800-283-2726
Pete@arcocoffee.com www.arcocoffee.com
Coffee and coffee syrups
Owner: John Andresen
President: B Fleming
Contact: Chris Devaney
chris@arcocoffee.com
Director Manufacturing: Vern Suby
Estimated Sales: Less than $500,000
Number Employees: 1-4
Type of Packaging: Consumer, Food Service
Brands:
Arco

102 **ASC Seafood Inc**
6340 118th Ave
Largo, FL 33773-3728
727-541-6896
Fax: 727-545-0582 800-876-3474
fred@ascseafood.com www.ascseafood.com
Quality seafood products
Owner: Steve Annas
steve@ascseafood.com
VP Sales/Marketing: Fred Kunder
Estimated Sales: $4 Million
Number Employees: 5-9
Brands:
Gulf-Maid

103 **ASK Foods Inc**
77 N Hetrick Ave
Palmyra, PA 17078-1529
717-838-6356
Fax: 717-838-7458 800-879-4275
tasmith@askfoods.com www.askfoods.com
Desserts, dips, deli salads, sauces, soups, entrees and natural juices.
CEO: Wendy Dimatteo
wdimatteo@askfoods.com
CFO: Rich Rutowski
Director Sales & Marketing: Terry Smith
Estimated Sales: $10-20 Million
Number Employees: 100-249
Square Footage: 400
Type of Packaging: Consumer, Food Service, Private Label, Bulk
Brands:
Ask Foods
Homestyle

104 **ASV Wines**
1998 Road 152
Delano, CA 93215-9437
661-792-3159
Fax: 661-792-3995 sales@asvwines.com
www.asvwines.com
Wines
CEO: Marko Zaninovich
markozaninovich@asvwines.com
Vice President: William Nakata
Plant Manager: John Sleeman
Estimated Sales: $3.2 Million
Number Employees: 20-49
Type of Packaging: Food Service, Private Label, Bulk
Other Locations:
San Martin Winery
San Martin CA
Brands:
Canyon Oaks
Crow Canyon
Muirwood
Steel Creek

105 **AVRON Resources Inc**
1080 Essex Ave
Richmond, CA 94801-2113
510-233-0633
Fax: 510-233-0636 800-883-9574
avron@avron.com
Flavors
President: Carl Arvold
Estimated Sales: $5-10 Million
Number Employees: 5-9
Type of Packaging: Private Label

106 **Aak USA Inc**
131 Marsh St
Newark, NJ 07114
973-344-1300
betterwithaak@aak.com
www.aak.com
Processor and importer of cocoa butter substitutes and oils including coconut, cottonseed, palm, soybean, sunflower, vegetable, etc.; exporter of lauric oil products
President, USA & North Latin America: Octavio Diaz de Leon
VP, Operations: Frank Miller
Estimated Sales: $50-100 Million
Number Employees: 50-99
Parent Co: AAK AB
Type of Packaging: Bulk
Other Locations:
AAK USA Inc-Port Newark Plant
Port Newark NJ
AAK USA K1/K2-Lousiville Plant
Louisville KY
AAK Foodservice, USA
Hillside NJ
AAK USA Richmond Corp.
Richmond CA

107 **Aala Meat Market Inc**
751 Waiakamilo Rd
Honolulu, HI 96817-4312
808-832-6650
Fax: 808-832-6659
Meats
President: Sandra Moribe
gmoribe5@hawaiiantel.net
Estimated Sales: $1-3 Million
Number Employees: 10-19

108 **Aaland Potato Company**
PO Box 304
101 Railroad Avenue
Hoople, ND 58243
701-894-6144
Fax: 701-894-6423
Potatoes
Manager: Jim Bailey
Estimated Sales: $2.5-5 Million
Number Employees: 10-19
Type of Packaging: Consumer
Brands:
Aaland

109 **Abattoir A. Trahan Company**
860 Chemin Des Acadiens
Yamachiche, QC G0X 3L0
Canada
819-296-3791
Fax: 819-296-3364
Fresh and frozen pork
President: Rene Trahan
Marketing Director: Dennis Trahan
Number Employees: 50-99
Type of Packaging: Consumer, Food Service, Private Label, Bulk

110 **Abattoir Aliments AstaInc.**
511 Av De La Gare
St Alexandre De Kamouras, QC G0L 2G0
Canada
418-495-2728
Fax: 418-495-2879 800-463-1355
www.alimentsasta.com
Pork. Slaughtering services available
CEO: Jacques Poitras
Financial Services Director: Carol Levesque
Supervisor, IT Services And Procurement: Jean Francois Thoral
Quality Services Director: Chanel Fournier
Sales Director: Andre Poitras
Human Resources Director: Edith Laplante
VP, Operations: Stephanie Poitras
Number Employees: 405
Type of Packaging: Bulk

111 **Abbot's Butcher**
350 Clinton St.
Costa Mesa, CA 92626
949-726-2156
hello@theabbotsbutcher.com
www.abbotsbutcher.com
Plant-based meats including imitation ground beef, chicken, and chorizo
Founder, CEO: Kerry Song

112 **Abbotsford Growers Ltd.**
31825 Marshall Road
Abbotsford, BC V2T 5Z8
Canada
604-864-0022
Fax: 604-864-0020 info@abbotsfordgrowers.com
www.abbotsfordgrowers.com
Raspberry & blueberry packer; frozen purees; and pasteurized and aseptic purees.
General Manager: Colin Hutchinson
Quality Assurance Supervisor: Dan Sigfusson
Sales/Plant/Production: Stephen Evans
Estimated Sales: $10-24 Million
Number Employees: 250
Square Footage: 100000
Type of Packaging: Bulk
Brands:
Abbotsford Growers Co-Op

113 **Abbott & Cobb Inc**
4151 E Street Rd
Feasterville, PA 19053-4995
215-245-6666
Fax: 215-245-9043 800-345-7333
acseed@abbottcobb.com www.abbottcobb.com
Breeder, producer and marketer of vegetable seeds, specifically corn, peppers, pumpkins, beans, squash and cucumbers.
Owner: Art Abbott
aandcseeds@aol.com
VP of Sales & Product Management: Luther McLaugglin
Vice President of Public Relations: Harriett Ryan
Senior Vice President of Operations: Bob Rumer
Estimated Sales: $38.7 Million
Number Employees: 20-49
Type of Packaging: Private Label, Bulk
Other Locations:
Nogales AZ
West Palm Beach FL
Caldwell ID
Los Mochis, Mexico

114 **Abbott Laboratories**
100 Abbott Park Rd
Abbott Park, IL 60064-3500
847-938-3887
Fax: 847-937-9555 www.abbottvascular.com
Offers a variety of pediatric and adult nutritional products, pharmaceuticals and enteral feeding products. Processor of evaporated and condensed milk.
Chairman/CEO: Miles White
CFO: Thomas Freyman
Senior VP: Gary McCullough
Contact: Roberto Abalos
roberto.abalos@abbott.com
Number Employees: 1-4
Parent Co: Abbott Laboratories
Type of Packaging: Consumer

115 **Abbott's Candy Shop**
48 E Walnut St
Hagerstown, IN 47346-1542
765-489-4442
Fax: 765-489-5501 877-801-1200
abbottscandy@abbottscandy.com
www.abbottscandy.com
Gourmet chocolates and caramels
President: Suanna Goodnight
Vice President: Gordon Goodnight
Manager: Becky Diercks
abbottscandy@abbottscandy.com
Estimated Sales: $780,000
Number Employees: 20-49
Square Footage: 28
Type of Packaging: Private Label
Brands:
Abbott's Candy

116 **Abbott's Meat Inc**
3623 Blackington Ave
Flint, MI 48532-3874
810-232-7128
Fax: 810-232-7960 800-678-1907
www.abbottsmeat.com
Beef and beef products
President: Rebecca Shepler
rshepler@abbottsmeat.com
Estimated Sales: $5-10 Million
Number Employees: 10-19
Brands:
Abbotts Meat

117 **Abby's Better Nut Butter**
abbysbetter.com
Nut butters
Founder: Abby Kircher
Number of Brands: 1
Number of Products: 5
Type of Packaging: Consumer
Brands:
ABBY'S BETTER NUT BUTTER

118 **Abbyland Foods Inc**
502 E Linden St
P.O. Box 69
Abbotsford, WI 54405
715-223-6386
Fax: 715-223-6388 800-732-5483
abbyland@abbyland.com www.abbyland.com
Meat, sausage and boneless beef.
Chief Insurance & Financial Officer: Paul Hess
Director of Specialty Meats: Brian O'Connor
Specialty Meats Sales: Patty Patterson
Office Manager: Jane Langman
715-223-6386 Ext. 7216
Sausage Production: Sean Wagner
Year Founded: 1977
Estimated Sales: $127 Million
Number Employees: 1,000
Square Footage: 122000
Type of Packaging: Food Service, Private Label, Bulk
Brands:
Abbuland
London Classic Broil
Tailgate

119 **Abdallah Candies & Gifts**
3501 County Road 42 W
Burnsville, MN 55306-3805
952-890-0859
Fax: 952-890-3664 service@abdallahcandies.com
www.abdallahcandies.com
Chocolate, caramels and candy mixes.
President: Steve Hegedus
stevenh@abdallahcandies.com
Number Employees: 100-249
Number of Brands: 5
Square Footage: 55000

120 **Abe's Vegan Muffins**
845-735-5100
www.abesmuffins.com
Muffins and cakes
Number of Brands: 1
Number of Products: 30
Type of Packaging: Consumer
Brands:
ABE'S

121 **Abel & Schafer Inc**
20 Alexander Ct
Ronkonkoma, NY 11779-6573
631-737-2220
Fax: 631-737-2335 800-443-1260
info@kompletusa.com us.komplet.com
Mixes including bread, cake, muffin, dough conditioners, glazes and fillings
Vice President: Joanne Oakes
roy.donna@cdphp.com
VP: Frank Triedman
R&D Manager: Diego Grassi
Head of Quality Control: Bert Wiegand
Sales Manager: Joseph Piotte
Director of Operations: Carl Wittig
Production Manager: Christopher Weber
Estimated Sales: $20-25 Million
Number Employees: 50-99
Parent Co: Abel & Schafer Group
Type of Packaging: Private Label

122 **Abimar Foods Inc**
5425 N 1st St
Abilene, TX 79603-6424
325-691-5425
Fax: 325-691-5471
salesinquiry@abimarfoods.com
Bakery products including cookies and crackers.
Chief Executive Officer: Patricia Canal
pcanal@abimarfoods.com
Director, Business Development: Rafael Henao
Director, Operations: Brandon Heiser
Plant Manager: Luis Felipe Velasquez Lopez
Director, Procurement: Mauricio Perez
Estimated Sales: $29 Million
Number Employees: 100-249
Number of Brands: 4
Parent Co: Grupo Empresarial Nutresa
Type of Packaging: Consumer
Brands:
Festy
Lil Dutch Maid
Nucita
Tru Blu

123 **Abimco USA, Inc.**
43 Hampshire Dr
Mendham, NJ 07945
973-543-7393
Fax: 973-543-2948
Fruit juice concentrates; importer and exporter of dried and frozen fruits and vegetables; Importer of juice concentrates, honey and tomato paste; exporter of fresh mushrooms
President: Paulette Krelman
General Manager: Arthur Kupperman
Number Employees: 1-4
Type of Packaging: Bulk

124 **Abingdon Vineyard & Winery**
20530 Alvarado Rd
Abingdon, VA 24211
276-623-1255
Fax: 276-623-0125 info@abingdonwinery.com
www.abingdonwinery.com
Wines
Owner: Bob Carlson
Co-Owner: Janet Lee Nordin
Vineyard Manager: Kevin Sutherland
Estimated Sales: $.5-1 million
Number Employees: 1-4

125 **Abita Brewing Co**
166 Barbee Rd
Covington, LA 70433-8651
985-893-3143
Fax: 985-898-3546 800-737-2311
friends@abita.com www.abita.com
Lager, ale and caffeine-free root beer.
President: Jim Andrews
jimandrews.mail@abitalumber.com
Year Founded: 1986
Estimated Sales: $20-50 Million
Number Employees: 20-49
Square Footage: 14000
Type of Packaging: Consumer, Private Label
Brands:
Abita
Golden
Purple Haze
Turbodog

126 **(HQ)Abitec Corp**
501 W 1st Ave
Columbus, OH 43215
614-429-6464
800-555-1255
info@abiteccorp.com www.abiteccorp.com
Producer of specialty chemicals including vegetable oils and powders.
CEO: Jeff Walton
CFO: Brad Orders
Head, R&D: Jim Williams
VP, Operations: John Bielas
Estimated Sales: $50-100 Million
Number Employees: 50-200
Number of Brands: 9
Parent Co: ABF Ingredients
Other Locations:
Abitec Corporation
Janesville WI
Abitec Corporation
Paris IL
Brands:
Acconon®
Accoquat®
Capmul®
Caprol®
Captex®
Hydro-Kote®
Nutri Sperse®
Pureco®
Sterotex®

127 **Abkit Camocare Nature Works**
61 Broadway
Room 1310
New York, NY 10006-2722
212-292-1550
Fax: 212-292-1542 800-226-6227
www.abkit.com
Natural products, vitamins, etc

President: Claus Ghringer
Director International Sales: Alison Carley
Estimated Sales: $3-5 Million
Number Employees: 10-19
Brands:
Catuama
Kwai
Nature Works

128 **Abraham's Natural Foods**
9 Long Branch Ave
PO Box 89
Long Branch, NJ 07740-7121
732-229-5799
Fax: 732-571-0890 800-327-9903
abrahamshummos@gmail.com
www.abrahamsnatural.com
Natural gourmet dips, salads and cookies, and kosher and Middle Eastern foods
President: Louis Fellman
taboule@yahoo.com
Estimated Sales: $1 Million
Number Employees: 5-9
Brands:
Baba Ghannouj
Hummos

129 **Absopure Water Company**
8835 General Drive
Plymouth, MI 48170
800-422-7678
www.absopure.com
Bottled water
President: William Young
Contact: Art Amelotte
amelotte@absopure.com
Estimated Sales: $22.9 Million
Number Employees: 100-249
Number of Brands: 1
Type of Packaging: Consumer, Private Label, Bulk
Brands:
Absopure

130 **Abuelita Mexican Foods**
9209 Enterprise Ct
Manassas Park, VA 20111-4809
703-369-0232
Fax: 703-369-0875 office@abuelita.com
www.abuelita.com
Corn tortillas and corn tortilla chips.
President: Eugene Suarez
General Manager: Peggy Suarez
Sales Director: Steve Dill
Estimated Sales: $4.7 Million
Number Employees: 1-4
Number of Brands: 3
Number of Products: 45
Square Footage: 106000
Brands:
Abuelita
Casa De Carmen
Nana's Cocina

131 **Abunda Life**
208 3rd Ave
Asbury Park, NJ 07712-6097
732-775-9338
Fax: 732-502-0899
Natural health products including vitamins, goat milk powder, fiber supplements, herbal spices, herbal teas, rice bran syrups and sweeteners including: banana, grape, pineapple and orange.
Founder: Dr Robert Sorge
Estimated Sales: $300,000-500,000
Number Employees: 10-19
Square Footage: 16800
Type of Packaging: Consumer, Private Label
Brands:
24 Super Amino Acids
Abunda Body
Blood Building Broth
Blood Building Powder
Brain Invigoration Powder
Cholesterol Solve
Cram For Students
Dieters Tea
Energy Powder
Essaic Formula
Fruit Fiber
Live Plant Juice
Liver Detox Formula
Parasite Annihilation Powder
Royal Pollen Complex
Super Bowl Cleanse
Super C Active
Super Detox
Super Green
Super Salad Oil
Super Tonic

132 **Acacia Vineyard**
2750 Las Amigas Rd
Napa, CA 94559
707-226-9991
Fax: 707-226-1685 877-226-1700
acacia.info@acaciavineyard.com
www.acaciavineyard.com
Wines
Owner: Matthew Glynn
Contact: Dawn Angelosante
dangelosante@acaciawinery.com
Estimated Sales: $10-20 Million
Number Employees: 20-49
Parent Co: Chalone Wine Group
Brands:
Acacia

133 **Acadian Fine Foods**
228 Saint Charles Ave # 1323
New Orleans, LA 70130-2646
504-581-2355
Fax: 504-525-9841
Frozen stuffed chicken, seafood pies, canned blue crabmeat, frozen crabs, crawfish
President: Charles Williams
VP: Russell Raelston
Estimated Sales: $.5-1 million
Number Employees: 5-9

134 **Acadian Ostrich Ranch**
9010 Highway 961
Clinton, LA 70722
225-683-9988
Fax: 225-683-9988 800-350-0167
Ostrich and alligator meats
President: Marco Dermody

135 **Acadian Seaplants**
30 Brown Avenue
Dartmouth, NS B3B 1X8
Canada
902-468-2840
Fax: 902-468-3474 800-575-9100
info@acadian.ca www.acadianseaplants.com
Seaweed based products for food, biochemical, agricultural, and agrichemical markets.
Director of Sales: Robert Sperdakes
Account Manager: Linda Linquist
Year Founded: 1981
Estimated Sales: $20 Million
Number Employees: 300
Type of Packaging: Private Label, Bulk
Brands:
Drewclar
Hana-Nori
Nutramer

136 **Açai Roots**
5920 Friars Rd
Suite 206
San Diego, CA 92108
Fax: 619-330-2465 866-401-2224
info@açairoots.com www.açairoots.com
Açaí products
Number of Brands: 1
Number of Products: 10
Type of Packaging: Consumer
Brands:
ACAI ROOTS

137 **Acatris USA**
3300 Edinborough Way
Suite 712
Edina, MN 55435-5963
952-920-7700
Fax: 952-920-7704 www.acatris.com
Blended dough conditioners, antioxidant solutions, release agents and lubricants; wholesaler/distributor of soy flour, vitamin/mineral blends and oils including soybean and canola
President: Laurent Leduc
Manager: Joni Johnson
Sales Manager: Cherie Jones
Estimated Sales: $5-10 Million
Number Employees: 20-49
Number of Brands: 15
Square Footage: 64000
Parent Co: Royal Schouten Group
Type of Packaging: Bulk
Brands:
Alube
Dadex
Daedol
Daejel
Daelube
Daminaide
Daminco
Daminet
Extol
Fenulife
Lesoy
Linumlife
Myvacet
Myverol
Soylife

138 **AccuTemp**
8415 N Clinton Park Dr
Fort Wayne, IN 46825
800-210-5907
www.accutemp.net
Commercial kitchen equipment, including steamers and griddles
President & CEO: Scott Swogger
EVP, Sales & Marketing: John Pennington
COO: Dave Ogram
Year Founded: 1993

139 **Accurate Ingredients Inc**
125 Schmitt Blvd
Farmingdale, NY 11735-1403
516-496-2500
Fax: 516-496-2516 info@acing.net
Ingredients
President: Dan Saber
Vice President of Sales: Vince Pasquale
Sales, Vice President of Operations: Rich Hamerschlag
Estimated Sales: $15.6 Million
Number Employees: 20-49
Type of Packaging: Consumer, Food Service, Bulk
Other Locations:
Accurate Ingredients
Santa Ana CA

140 **Accurex**
PO Box 410
Schofield, WI 54476
Fax: 715-241-6191 800-333-1400
www.accurex.com
Kitchen ventilation systems
President/Owner: Damon Childers

141 **Ace Bakery**
1 Hafis Rd
North York, ON M6M 2V6
Canada
416-241-8433
Fax: 905-565-7098 800-443-7929
bread@acebakery.com www.acebakery.com
Fresh and frozen baguettes, loaves, buns, and bagels; chips, toasts, croutons and granola.
President: Lee Andrews
Year Founded: 1993
Number Employees: 500-999
Parent Co: George Weston Ltd.

142 **Ace Development**
31194 State Highway 51
Bruneau, ID 83604-5076
208-845-2487
Fax: 208-845-2274 copakarobert@hotmail.com
Aquaculture fisheries.
President: Robert Williams
Year Founded: 1984
Estimated Sales: $800,000
Number Employees: 1-4

143 **Ace Farm USA Inc**
1343 Lafayette Ave
Bronx, NY 10474-4806
718-991-3816
Fax: 718-679-9125 info@acefarmusa.com
Non-alcoholic beverages, soft drinks.
Marketing: Jean Park
Manager: Jina Park
jina@acefarmusa.com
Number Employees: 20-49

144 **Aceitunas Losada**
Ctra. A-398 km 21.3
Carmona, Sevilla, 41410
Spain
export@aceitunaslosada.com
aceitunaslosada.com
Olives

145 **Acesur North America**
2700 Westchester Ave
Suite 105
Purchase, NY 10577-2554
914-925-0450
Fax: 914-925-0458 info@acesur.com
www.acesur.com
Olive oil and other specialty Spanish products
USA Director: Antonio Rubiales

146 **Acetifico Marcello Denigris**
P.O. Box 53
Westwood, NJ 07675-0053
973-837-6791
Fax: 973-837-6794 denigris1889.com
Vinegars
Type of Packaging: Consumer, Food Service, Private Label

147 **Acharice Specialties**
PO Box 690
Greenville, MS 38702-0690
800-432-4901
Fax: 901-381-3287
Rice and grain products
President/CEO: Jack Stratol
Research & Development: Bill Land
Sales/Marketing: Nelson Wurth
Operations/Production: Mike Well
Plant Manager: Pat Roy
Number Employees: 500-999
Type of Packaging: Private Label

148 **Achatz Handmade Pie Co**
30301 Commerce Blvd
Chesterfield, MI 48051-1243
586-749-2882
www.achatzpies.com
Handmade pies
Manager: Wendy Achatz
vparis@slpr.net
Estimated Sales: Less Than $500,000
Number Employees: 1-4

149 **Ackerman Winery**
4406 220th Trl
Amana, IA 52203-8035
319-622-3379
Fax: 319-622-6513 info@ackermanwinery.com
www.ackermanwinery.com
Wine
President: Les Ackerman
Manager: Cassie Bott
cassie@firesidewinery.com
Estimated Sales: $1-2.5 Million
Number Employees: 1-4
Type of Packaging: Bulk

150 **Acme Bread Co**
1601 San Pablo Ave
Berkeley, CA 94702-1317
510-524-1327
www.acmebread.com
Bread
Founder: Steven Sullivan
Contact: Hannah Jukovsky
hannah@acmebread.com
Estimated Sales: Less Than $500,000
Number Employees: 5-9

151 **Acme Smoked Fish Corporation**
30-56 Gem Street
Brooklyn, NY 11222
718-383-8585
Fax: 718-383-9115 www.acmesmokedfish.com
Processor and importer of smoked fish and herring.
President: Eric Caslow
CFO: Eduardo Carlajasa
EVP: Robert Caslow
Director of Sales: Buzz Billik
VP of Operations: Davis Caslow
Year Founded: 1901
Estimated Sales: $20-50 Million
Number Employees: 100-249
Brands:
Acme
Blue Hill Bay

152 **Acme Steak & Seafood**
31 Bissell Ave
Youngstown, OH 44505-2707
330-270-8000
Fax: 330-270-8006 800-686-2263
support@acmesteak.com www.acmesteak.com
Fresh produce, seafood, sausage, hamburgers and portion controlled meat.
Owner/President: Michael Mike
mike@acmesteak.com
Year Founded: 1947
Estimated Sales: $2.40 Million
Number Employees: 10-19
Square Footage: 68000
Type of Packaging: Consumer, Food Service, Private Label

153 **Acornseekers Inc**
5294 FM1115
Flatonia, TX 78941
786-338-8160
www.acornseekers.com
Spanish-style pork
Co-Founder & CEO: Sergio Marsal
Co-Founder & Chief Operations Officer: Manuel Murga

154 **Acqua Blox LLC**
12000 East Slauson Ave
Suite 3
Santa Fe Springs, CA 90670
562-693-9599
Fax: 562-945-3133 info@aquablox.com
www.aquablox.com
Purified and bacteria free water products specifically designed for emergency preparedness, first responders, and disaster victims
Manager: Mike Harris
Estimated Sales: Below $5 Million
Number Employees: 1-4
Type of Packaging: Consumer, Bulk
Brands:
Aqua Blox®

155 **Across Foods, LLC**
608 Coach Drive
New Hope, PA 18938
215-693-6274
Fax: 267-895-6311 info@acrossfoods.com
www.acrossfoods.com
Kosher, organic/natiral, cookies, full-line candy, gummies/jellies/pates de fruits, licorice, health, fitness and energy bars, dried fruit.
President: Michael Sas
mjmas@acrossfoods.com

156 **Acta Health Products**
380 N Pastoria Avenue
Sunnyvale, CA 94085-4108
408-732-6830
Fax: 408-732-0208 www.actaproducts.com
Processor and exporter of vitamins, minerals, herbal extracts and other dietary supplements; importer of raw materials
President: David Chang
david.chang@actaproducts.com
VP: K Y Chang
Director Quality Control: Michael Chang
Director Marketing/Sales: Cal Bewicke
Director Purchasing: Leo Liu
Estimated Sales: $3 Million
Number Employees: 30
Square Footage: 124000
Type of Packaging: Private Label, Bulk

157 **Action Labs**
PO Box 1090
2915 East Rickerway
Anaheim, CA 92806
714-630-5941
Fax: 714-630-8221 800-400-5696
actionvit@aol.com www.actionlab.com
Specialty diet and energy supplements for men and women.
President: James R Bailey
Marketing: Mandy Ray
Sales: John Russo
Brands:
Ginseng 4x

158 **Active Organics**
1097 Yates St
Lewisville, TX 75057-4829
972-221-7500
Fax: 972-221-3324 800-541-1478
info@activeorganics.com
www.activeorganics.com
Botanical extracts
Vice President: Linda Defratus
ldefratus@organics.com
CFO: Glen Guthmann
VP: Bill Hynes
Human Resources Executive: Angi Rene
VP Operations: Bill Heinz
Estimated Sales: $9.9 Million
Number Employees: 100-249
Square Footage: 484000

159 **Acushnet Fish Corporation**
46 Middle Street
Fairhaven, MA 02719-3086
508-997-7482
Fax: 508-999-6697
Fish
President: Ralph Parsons

160 **Adair Vineyards**
52 Allhusen Rd
New Paltz, NY 12561-4217
845-255-1377
adairwines@aol.com
www.adairwine.com
Wines
Owner: Mark Stopkie
Estimated Sales: Less Than $500,000
Number Employees: 1-4
Type of Packaging: Private Label

161 **Adam Matthews Inc**
2104 Plantside Dr
Jeffersontown, KY 40299-1924
502-499-1244
Fax: 502-499-8331
Bakery products including cheesecakes,and Festival Pie.
President: Vicky Meeks
vmeeks@promediagroup.com
Office Operations: Christie Schneider
Bakery Operations: Matt Mead
National Sales Representative: Mary Anne Burch
VP Operations: Cathy Fleig
Estimated Sales: $1-2.5 Million
Number Employees: 20-49
Square Footage: 80000
Brands:
Adam Matthews

162 **Adam Puchta Winery**
1947 Frene Creek Rd
Hermann, MO 65041-4103
573-486-5596
Fax: 573-486-2361 info@adampuchtawine.com
www.adampuchtawine.com
Wines
President: Timothy Puchta
tjp_apwinery@centurytel.net
Estimated Sales: $1-2.5 Million
Number Employees: 10-19
Type of Packaging: Private Label

163 **Adams & Brooks Inc**
1915 S Hoover St
Los Angeles, CA 90007-1322
213-749-3226
Fax: 213-746-7614 info@adams-brooks.com
Bagged candy including: chocolate cups, candy bars, lollypops, novelty, nut, caramel and taffy. Also vending, fund raising and theatre packaging.
President: John Brooks
Cmo: Steve Misinger
steve.misingerbrooks@adams-brooks.com
VP of Marketing & Product Development: Cindy Brooks
Estimated Sales: $10-20 Million
Number Employees: 100-249
Type of Packaging: Consumer, Private Label, Bulk
Brands:
Adams & Brooks
Coffee Rio
Comic Animal
Cup-O-Gold
Fairtime
P-Nuttles
P-Nuttles Butter Toffee Peanuts

Psycho Pops
Psycho Psours
Unicorn Pops

164 **Adams County Winery**
251 Peach Tree Rd
Orrtanna, PA 17353-9753
717-334-4631
Fax: 717-334-4026 877-601-7936
vintner@adamscountywinery.com
www.adamscountywinery.com

Wines
Owner: Katherine Bigler
vintner@adamscountywinery.com
Estimated Sales: $1-2.5 Million
Number Employees: 10-19

165 **Adams Fisheries Ltd**
617 Bear Point Rd
Shag Harbour, NS B0T 1W0
Canada
902-723-2435
Fax: 902-723-2325
Salted cod, pollack and haddock and live lobster
President: Donald Adams
Estimated Sales: $3.2 Million
Number Employees: 8
Square Footage: 34000

166 **Adams Foods & Milling**
146 Industrial Dr
Box 143a
Dothan, AL 36303
334-983-4233
Fax: 334-983-5596
Cakes including pound, sheet and decorated
President: Ted Adams
Manager: Larry Nowkaiski
Manager: Joy Pettis
Estimated Sales: $5-10 Million
Number Employees: 5-9
Parent Co: Adams Milling Company
Type of Packaging: Consumer, Food Service, Private Label, Bulk
Brands:
Adams
Avery
Baker's Best
Home Style
Mother's

167 **Adams Olive Ranch**
1200 S Aster Ave
Lindsay, CA 93247
559-562-2882
Fax: 559-562-2272 888-216-5483
www.adamsoliveranch.com
Olives
Owner: Denis Bonfilio
Estimated Sales: Less than $500,000
Number Employees: 10-19
Square Footage: 24000
Type of Packaging: Consumer, Private Label
Brands:
Adam's Ranch
Raw Earth Organics
Smith Home Cured

168 **Adams USA Inc.**
610 S. Jefferson Avenue
Cookeville, TN 10017
212-733-2323
Fax: 800-946-4102 800-251-6857
www.adamsusa.com
Health products
CEO: Ian Read
Contact: Dani Boger
dani.boger@adamsusa.com

169 **Adams Vegetable Oils Inc**
P.O. Box 956
Arbuckle, CA 95912
530-668-2005
Fax: 530-476-2315 info@adamsgrp.com
www.adamsvegetableoils.com
Vegetable oils, grain and seeds.
Sales Manager: David Hoffsten
Estimated Sales: $100+ Million
Number Employees: 50-99
Square Footage: 5889
Type of Packaging: Bulk

170 **AddGarlic!**
617 Broadway
Unit 1576
Sonoma, CA 95476
707-996-2999
www.addgarlic.com

Pureed Garlic
President: Andy Davis
andy@addgarlic.com
Brands:
Aglio Di Mirabella(c)

171 **Adee Honey Farm**
517 Jay St.
Bruce, SD 57220
605-627-5621
Fax: 605-627-5622 www.adeehoneyfarms.com
Processor of honey and beeswax. Pollination services also available
Owner: Richard Adee
Owner: Kelvin Adee
Owner: Bret Adee
Contact: Kirk Adee
kirkadee@adeehoneyfarms.com
Year Founded: 1957
Estimated Sales: $20-50 Million
Number Employees: 50-99
Type of Packaging: Bulk
Other Locations:
Bakersfield CA
Cedar Rapids NE
Roscoe SD
Woodville MS

172 **Adelaida Cellars Inc**
5805 Adelaida Rd
Paso Robles, CA 93446-9783
805-239-8980
Fax: 805-239-4671 800-676-1232
wines@adelaida.com www.adelaida.com
Wines
Owner: Elizabeth Vansteenwyk
wines@adelaida.com
General Manager: Jessica Kollhoff
Director of Retail Sales and Marketing: Sunni Mullinax
National Sales: Paul Sowerby
Hospitality Manager: Pati Coelho
Production: Lalo Escalante
Estimated Sales: $1-2.5 Million
Number Employees: 10-19

173 **Adelsheim Vineyard**
16800 NE Calkins Ln
Newberg, OR 97132-6572
503-538-3652
Fax: 503-538-2248 info@adelsheim.com
www.chehalemmountains.org
Pinot noir wines and cool-climae white wines from Pinot gris; Chardonnay; Pinot blanc and Auxerrois.
President: David Adelsheim
info@adelsheim.com
Owner: Virginia Adelsheim
Marketing & Communications Manager: Catherine Douglas
Manager of Sales Operations: Kim Bellingar
Controller: Kathi Neal
Vineyard Manager: Chad Vargas
Winemaker: Dave Paige
Estimated Sales: $7 Million
Number Employees: 20-49
Square Footage: 160000
Brands:
Adelsheim Vineyard

174 **Adirondack Beverages Inc**
701 Corporation Park
Scotia, NY 12302-1065
518-370-3622
Fax: 518-370-3762 800-316-6096
contact@adkbev.com
www.adirondackbeverages.com
Carbonated and noncarbonated beverages including cola, ginger ale, tonic, fruit drink, seltzer and sparkling and still water
President: Douglas Martin
CFO: Ray Demers
rdemers@adkbev.com
Estimated Sales: $500,000-1 Million
Number Employees: 100-249
Square Footage: 3000000
Parent Co: Polar Corporation
Type of Packaging: Consumer, Food Service, Private Label
Brands:
Adironack
Clear 'n' Natural
Waist Watcher

175 **Adirondack Maple Farms**
490 Persse Rd
Fonda, NY 12068-5716
518-853-4022
Fax: 518-853-3791 bruceroblee@yahoo.com
www.adirondackmaplefarms.com
Pure maple syrup, sugar and candy.
Owner: Bruce Roblee
broblee@adirondackmaplefarms.com
General Manager: Bruce Roblee
Estimated Sales: Less Than $500,000
Number Employees: 1-4
Type of Packaging: Private Label
Brands:
Adirondack Maple Farms

176 **Adkin & Son Associated Food Products**
6645 107th Ave
South Haven, MI 49090-9366
269-637-7450
Fax: 269-637-2636
Edible fresh chestnut
President: Roy Adkin
National Accounts: L Adkin
Research & Development: Shelly Newton
Marketing Director: K Johnson
Production/Quality Control: Harold Bennett
Estimated Sales: $15 Million
Number Employees: 5-9
Square Footage: 44000
Type of Packaging: Food Service, Bulk
Brands:
Adkin's
Adkin's Royal Blue

177 **Adler Fels Winery**
980 Airway Ct
Unit B
Santa Rosa, CA 95403-2000
707-539-3123
Fax: 707-569-8301 info@adlerfels.com
Wines
Owner: David Coleman
Estimated Sales: $20 Million
Number Employees: 5-9
Parent Co: Adams Wine Group

178 **Adluh Flour**
804 Gervais St
PO Box 1437
Columbia, SC 29201-3126
803-779-2460
Fax: 803-252-0014 800-692-3584
info@adluh.com www.adluh.com
Flour and corn meal
President: William Allen
info@adluh.com
Year Founded: 1900
Estimated Sales: $5 Million
Number Employees: 10-19
Type of Packaging: Food Service
Brands:
Adluh
Carolina Gem
Eatmor
Gold Bond

179 **Admiral Beverage Corp**
821 Pulliam Ave
Worland, WY 82401-2325
307-347-4201
Fax: 307-347-3571
meumann@admiralbeverage.com
www.admiralbeverage.com
Soft drinks
President: Forrest K Clay
fclay@admiralbeverage.com
Chief Financial Officer: Keith Hartnett
EVP, General Counsel: Bob Callan
Director of Human Resources: AJ Jenness
VP Operations: Kelly Clay
Estimated Sales: $20-50 Million
Number Employees: 100-249
Parent Co: Pepsi Company
Type of Packaging: Consumer, Food Service

180 **Adobe Creek Packing Co Inc**
4825 Loasa Dr
Kelseyville, CA 95451
707-279-4204
Fax: 707-279-0366 shirleyacp@sbcglobal.net
Bartlett pears
President/Grower: Kenneth Barr
Controller: Shirley Campbell
Shipping Manager: Floyd Saderlund
Office Manager: Margot Hoyt
Estimated Sales: $2.7 Million
Number Employees: 250-499
Type of Packaging: Consumer, Food Service, Bulk
Brands:
Blazing Star

181 **Adobe Springs**
PO Box 1417
Patterson, CA 95363-1417
408-897-3023
Fax: 408-897-3028 www.mgwater.com
Bulk magnesium rich mineral water
President: Gary Dutey
Vice President: Paul Mason
paulmason@mgwater.com
Brands:
Hi0spring
Noah's Spring Water
Seven-Up

182 **(HQ)Adolf's Meats & Sausage Kitchen**
35 New Britain Ave
Hartford, CT 06106-3306
860-522-1588
Meats
President: Joseph Gorski
joegorski@live.com
Estimated Sales: Less Than $500,000
Number Employees: 1-4
Type of Packaging: Consumer, Food Service, Bulk
Other Locations:
Adolf's Meat & Sausage
Norwalk CT

183 **Adrienne's Gourmet Foods**
849 Ward Dr
Santa Barbara, CA 93111
805-964-6848
Fax: 805-964-8698 800-937-7010
Organic and kosher cookies, crackers and high protein pastas.
President: John O'Donnell
Vice President: Adrienne O'Donnell
Contact: Sarah Guiginano
sarah@adriennes.com
Estimated Sales: $5-10 Million
Number Employees: 20-49
Type of Packaging: Consumer, Food Service, Private Label, Bulk
Brands:
Appeteasers
California Crisps
Courtney's
Courtney's Organic Water Crackers
Darcia's Organic Crostini
Lavosh Hawaii
Papadina Pasta
Papadini Hi-Protein

184 **Advance Pierre Foods**
9987 Carver Rd.
Suite 500
Cincinnati, OH 45242
800-969-2747
www.advancepierre.com
Packaged sandwiches, fully cooked chicken and beef products, Philly-style steak, breaded beef, pork and poultry, and bakery products.
President/CEO: John Simons
CFO: Michael Sims
Year Founded: 1946
Estimated Sales: $600 Million
Number Employees: 4,000+
Number of Brands: 10
Parent Co: Tyson Foods
Type of Packaging: Consumer, Food Service, Private Label
Other Locations:
Advance Food Company
Caryville TN
Advance Food Company
Scanton PA
Advance Food Company-Sales
Oklahoma City OK
Brands:
Barber Foods®
Better Bakery™
BIG AZ®
Fast Fixin'®
Hot 'n' Ready®
PB Jamwich®
Landshire®
Pierre™
Steak-EZE®
The Pub®

185 **Advanced Aquaculture Systems**
4509 Hickory Creek Ln
Brandon, FL 33511-8013
813-653-2823
Fax: 813-684-7773 800-994-7599
info@advancedaquaculture.com
www.advancedaquaculture.com
Hybrid striped bass
President: Gary Miller
Vice President: Barbara Miller
Estimated Sales: $65,000
Number Employees: 5-9

186 **Advanced Bio Development**
768 Piermont Ave
Piermont, NY 10968
845-365-3838
info@x2performance.com
www.x2performance.com
Natural energy products
CEO: Dr. Ralph Ferrante

187 **(HQ)Advanced Food Products LLC**
402 S Custer Ave
New Holland, PA 17557
800-732-5373
info@afpllc.com www.afpllc.com
Dairy based products such as puddings, dips, sauces, spreads, nutritional beverages and soups.
President & CEO: Miro Hosek
miroslav.hosek@afpllc.com
CFO: Kris Smith
R&D Manager: Deb Holzhueter
Director, Quality Assurance: Matthew Brown
Director, National Sales & Marketing: Joe Hillen
SVP, Operations: Gregg Kenitz
Year Founded: 1940
Estimated Sales: $100+ Million
Number Employees: 100-249
Type of Packaging: Private Label
Other Locations:
Manufacturing Facility
Clear Lake WI
Manufacturing Facility
Visalia CA
Brands:
Andersen's(c) Soup
Caf, Classics(c)
Campo Lindo(c)
Encircle(c)
Muy Fresco(c)
Real Fresh(c)

188 **Advanced Food Services**
9807 Lackman Rd
Lenexa, KS 66219-1209
913-888-8088
Fax: 913-888-8075 info@advancedfood.com
www.advancedfood.com
Seasonings and bakery mixes
President: Raju Shah
rshah@advancedfood.com
Number Employees: 10-19

189 **Advanced Food Systems**
21 Roosevelt Ave
Somerset, NJ 08873-5030
732-873-6776
Fax: 732-873-4177 800-787-3067
info@afsnj.com www.afsnj.com
Customized ingredient systems for meat and poultry products, frozen foods, sauces and marinades, and more.
President: Yongkeun Joh
arun.abraham@acegroup.com
CFO: Pamela Cooper
EVP: Warren Love
Sales Executive: Chris Kelly
Operations Director: Bob Lijana
Purchasing Director: Mike Walker
Estimated Sales: $6.5 Million
Number Employees: 50-99
Square Footage: 107200

190 **Advanced Ingredients, Inc.**
401 N 3rd St
Suite 400
Minneapolis, MN 55401
Fax: 763-201-5820 888-238-4647
info@advancedingredients.com
www.advancedingredients.com
Specialty ingredients
President: Fred Greenland
Estimated Sales: $1-3 Million
Number Employees: 5-9
Brands:
Bakesmart®
Energysmart®
Energysource®
Fruitrim®
Fruitsavr®
Fruitsource®
Moisturlok®
Plus and Moisturlok®

191 **Advanced Spice & Trading**
1808 Monetary Ln Ste 100
Carrollton, TX 75006
972-242-8580
Fax: 972-242-6920 800-872-7811
sales@advancedspice.com
www.advancedspice.com
Spices and ingredients
President: Douglas Hank
CEO: Greg Hank
greg@advancedspice.com
Estimated Sales: $2.3 Million
Number Employees: 15
Square Footage: 268800
Type of Packaging: Consumer, Food Service, Private Label, Bulk
Brands:
Santaka Chili Pods
Supper Topper

192 **Advanced Sunflower**
PO Box 902
740 2nd St SW
Huron, SD 57350
605-554-1301
advancedsunflower.com
Sunflower seeds
CEO: Danny Dale
Number of Brands: 1
Type of Packaging: Consumer, Bulk
Brands:
ADVANCED

193 **Adventist Book & Food**
2160 Us Highway 1
Trenton, NJ 08648-4447
609-392-8010
Fax: 609-392-4477 800-765-6955
www.adventistbookcenter.com
Vegetarian meat substitutes
CFO: Herb Shiroma
Owner: New Jersey
Estimated Sales: $.5-1 million
Number Employees: 1-4

194 **Adventure Foods**
481 Banjo Lane
Whittier, NC 28789-7999
828-497-4113
Fax: 828-497-7529
CustomerService@adventurefoods.com
www.adventurefoods.com
Freeze-dried; dehydrated; shelf stable foods and instant food; food storage programs; health food markets; baking mixes, bulk spices and ingredients; specialty foods and special packing for vegetarian, diabetics, gluten intolerance andother food or health restrictions.
President: Jean Spangenberg
jean@adventurefoods.com
CEO: Sam Spangenberg
Number Employees: 5-9
Parent Co: Jean's Garden Greats
Type of Packaging: Consumer, Food Service, Private Label, Bulk
Brands:
Adventure Foods
Bake Packers
Gsi

Heartline
Lumen
Open Country
Well Seasoned Traveler

195 **AeroFarms**
212 Rome St
Newark, NJ 07105
973-242-2495
info@aerofarms.com
www.aerofarms.com
Baby greens, microgreens, herbs; Aeroponic technology
Chief Executive Officer: David Rosenberg
Chief Financial Officer: Guy Blanchard
Chief Operating Officer: Roger Post
Chief Science Officer: Ed Harwood
Chief Technology Officer: Roger Buelow
Chief Marketing Officer: Marc Oshima
General Counsel: Ariel Lager
Year Founded: 2004
Number Employees: 50-99
Type of Packaging: Food Service
Brands:
Dream Greens

196 **Affiliated Rice Milling**
715 N. 2nd St.
Alvin, TX 77511-3674
281-331-6176
Fax: 281-585-0336
Rice and rice flour.
Manager: Johnny Dunham
VP, Operations: Johnny Dunham
Estimated Sales: $20-50 Million
Number Employees: 1-10
Square Footage: 130000
Parent Co: Rice Belt Warehouse
Brands:
Eminence

197 **Afia Foods**
P.O. Box 170651
Austin, TX 78717
512-698-8448
sales@afiafoods.com
www.afiafoods.com
Greek, Mediterranean, and Middle Eastern foods
President: Farrah Moussallati Sibai

198 **Afieneur**
172 Montague St
Brooklyn, NY 11201
617-480-1340
www.afineur.com
Coffee
CEO & Co-Founder: Camille Delebecque, PhD
CTO & Co-Founder: Sophie Deterre, PhD

199 **Afineur**
172 Montague St
Brooklyn, NY 11201
617-480-1340
Coffee
Ceo & Co-Founder: Camille Delebecque PhD
Cto & Co-Founder: Sophie Deterre PhD

200 **Afton Mountain Vineyards Inc**
234 Vineyard Ln
Afton, VA 22920-3702
540-456-8667
Fax: 540-456-8002
finewines@aftonmountainvineyards.com
www.aftonmountainvineyards.com
Wines
President: Tom Corpora
Estimated Sales: $1-2.5 Million
Number Employees: 20-49
Type of Packaging: Private Label

201 **AgSource Milk Analysis Laboratory**
106 North Cecil Street
Bonduel, WI 54107
715-758-2178
Fax: 715-758-2620 bonduel@agsource.com
Farmer-owned and client focused, we are dedicated to providing comprehensive laboratory analysis.
Co-Owner: Don Niles
Co-Owner: John Pagel
VP: Joel Amdall
Vice President Laboratory: Steve Peterson
Personnel Manager: Bruce Cornish
General Manager: C Smith
Estimated Sales: $1-3 Million
Number Employees: 20-49
Brands:
Ag Co-Op

202 **AgStandard Smoked Almonds**
Los Angeles, CA
getagstandard.com
Smoked almonds
Number of Brands: 1
Type of Packaging: Consumer

203 **Agave Dream**
PO Box 1382
La Canada, CA 91012
USA
818-425-7378
Fax: 800-719-0950 310-619-1575
www.agavedream.com
Frozen desserts, ice cream, sorbet
Owner and Co-Founder: Jean Zwarg
Co-Founder: Stacey Ralphs
Estimated Sales: 150,000
Number Employees: 2
Brands:
Agave Dream

204 **Agfinity Inc**
260 Factory Rd
Eaton, CO 80615-3481
970-454-4000
Fax: 970-454-2144 800-433-4688
www.agfinityinc.com
Agricultural services, agronomy, fertilizer, fuel/propane, car maintenance, and hardware equipment.
President: Stuart Agfinity
sagfinity@agfinityinc.com
CEO: Jason Brancel
CFO: Rob Lyons
Year Founded: 1905
Estimated Sales: $10-20 Million
Number Employees: 201-500
Type of Packaging: Consumer
Brands:
Red Bird

205 **Agger Fish Corp**
63 Flushing Ave # 313
Brooklyn, NY 11205-1081
718-855-1717
Fax: 718-855-4545 marcagger@gmail.com
www.aggerfish.com
Monkfish, fluke, monkfish liver and shark fins, bones and cartilage for food supplements and ingredients.
President: Marc Agger
marcagger@gmail.com
Estimated Sales: $500,000-$1 Million
Number Employees: 500-999
Square Footage: 12000
Type of Packaging: Bulk

206 **Aglamesis Bros Ice Cream**
3046 Madison Rd
Cincinnati, OH 45209-1797
513-531-5196
Fax: 513-531-5403 www.aglamesis.com
Ice cream and confectionery products
President: James Aglamesis
sales@aglamesis.com
Estimated Sales: $2.5-5 Million
Number Employees: 20-49
Type of Packaging: Consumer, Food Service

207 **AgraWest Foods**
PO Box 760
Souris
Prince Edward Island, NS C0A 2B0
Canada
902-687-1400
Fax: 902-687-1401 877-687-1400
agrawest@agrawest.com www.agrawest.com
Dehydrated potato granules
President/CEO: Wally Browning
VP Finance: Baden Burt
VP/GM: John Schodde
Quality Assurance Manager: Kendra Deagle
Sales Manager: Mary Croucher
Production Manager: Jamie Trainor
Parent Co: Idaho Pacific Corporation
Type of Packaging: Food Service, Bulk
Brands:
Chef Master

208 **Agrana Fruit US Inc**
6850 Southpointe Pkwy
Cleveland, OH 44141-3260
440-546-1199
Fax: 440-546-0038 800-477-3788
www.agrana.us
Sugar; starch; and processed fruits.
President/CEO: Johann Marihart
Board Member: Fritz Gattermeyer
Estimated Sales: $10-20 Million
Number Employees: 50-99
Parent Co: SIAS MPA
Type of Packaging: Food Service, Private Label, Bulk

209 **Agrexco USA**
15012 132nd Ave
Jamaica, NY 11434
718-481-8700
Fax: 718-481-8710 amoso@agrexco.com
www.agrexco.com
Fruits including dried dates, grapefruits and oranges, vegetables, herbs, and flowers.
President: Yoram Shalev
CFO/VP, Quality Control: Jack Aschkeigi
Produce Sales Manager: Joseph Benjuya
Contact: Abelardo Zeron
abelardoz@agrexco.com
Estimated Sales: $20-50 Million
Number Employees: 20-49
Brands:
Alesia
Carmel

210 **Agri-Dairy Products**
3020 Westchester Ave
Purchase, NY 10577
914-697-9580
Fax: 914-697-9586
customerservice@agridairy.com
www.agridairy.com
Dairy and food ingredients including whey and lactose, milkfat, milk powders, casein, milk proteins, cheese and butter.
President: Steven Bronfield
CEO: Frank Reeves III
CFO: Mary Ellen Storino
Year Founded: 1985
Estimated Sales: $52 Million
Number Employees: 10
Number of Products: 50+
Square Footage: 1600
Type of Packaging: Bulk

211 **Agri-Mark Inc**
958 Riverdale St
West Springfield, MA 01089-4621
978-552-5500
Fax: 978-552-5587 information@agrimark.net
www.agrimark.net
whey and Dairy products including butter and non-fat, skim and condensed milk; exporter of butter powder.
President/CEO: Richard Stammer
SVP: Robert Wellington
VP/Marketing: John Burke
Communications Director: Douglas DiMento
Plant Manager: Gary Carlow
Year Founded: 1919
Estimated Sales: $20-50 Million
Number Employees: 50-99
Type of Packaging: Private Label, Bulk
Other Locations:
Agri-Mark Manufacturing Plant
West Springfield MA
Agri-Mark Manufacturing Plant
Middlebury VT
Agri-Mark Manufacturing Plant
Cabot VT
Agri-Mark Manufacturing Plant
Chateaugay NY
Brands:
Cabot
McCadam

212 **Agri-Pack**
28 Pasco Kahlotus Road
Pasco, WA 99301
509-545-6181
Fax: 509-545-5748 steve@agri-pack.com
Onions including whole, rings, diced and strips
Manager: Tim Sessions
Account Executive: Jon Josephson
Director Sales/Marketing: Steve Shepard
Plant Manager: Todd Daniko

Estimated Sales: $2.5-5 Million
Number Employees: 20-49
Square Footage: 600000
Parent Co: Agri Pack
Type of Packaging: Food Service, Bulk

213 **(HQ)AgriNorthwest**
6716 W Rio Grande
Kennewick, WA 99336
509-734-1195
contactus@agrinw.com
www.agrinorthwest.com
Grower & supplier of corn, wheat and potatoes.
President: Todd Jones
General Manager: Tom Mackay
Farm Unit Manager: Mike Monger
Year Founded: 1968
Estimated Sales: $31.6 Million
Number Employees: 150
Type of Packaging: Food Service, Bulk
Other Locations:
Plymouth WA
Prescott WA

214 **Agricor Inc**
1626 S Joaquin Dr
Marion, IN 46953-9633
765-662-0606
Fax: 765-662-7189 www.grainmillers.com
Whole grain ingredients
President: Steve Wickes
IT: Bill Cramer
bill.cramer@grainmillers.com
Year Founded: 1983
Number Employees: 20-49
Type of Packaging: Bulk
Brands:
Grain Millers

215 **(HQ)Agricore United**
1600 Utica Avenue South
Suite 350
St Louis Park, MN 55416
952-460-7450
Fax: 952-460-7404 877-509-5865
Wheat; barley; oats; 3-grain and instant cereals; pancake mix; organic flour and herb food bars and beans.
President/CEO: Mayo Schmidt
CFO: Rex McLennan
COO-Grain: Fran Malecha
Parent Co: Agricore United Int'l.
Type of Packaging: Consumer, Food Service, Bulk
Other Locations:
Manitoba
Saskatchewan
Alberta
British Columbia

216 **Agripac**
PO Box 5110
Denver, CO 80217-5110
503-981-0111
Fax: 503-982-3550 consultas@agripac.com.ar
Frozen red raspberries, strawberries, marionberries, rhubarb, snap beans, broccoli, cauliflower, corn, whole onions, peas and carrots, squash, mixed vegetables, prepared vegetables
Director: Pablo Adreani
Senior VP: Patrick Monaghan
Senior VP, Operations: Russ Grubb
Brands:
Agripac

217 **Agro Farma Inc.**
669 County Road 25
New Berlin, NY 13411
607-847-6181
Fax: 607-847-8847 877-847-6181
contact@chobani.com www.chobani.com
Greek yogurt
President/CEO: Hamdi Ulukaya
COO: Mikael Pederson
Controller: Besnik Fetoski
Communications Director: Nicki Briggs
VP/Sales: Kyle O'Brien
Contact: Amanda Adams
a.adams@agro-farma.com
Estimated Sales: $35.0 Million
Number Employees: 12000
Other Locations:
Manufacturing Facility
Twin Falls ID
Brands:
Chobani

218 **Agro Foods, Inc.**
3531 SW 13th St
Miami, FL 33145
786-552-9006
Fax: 305-361-7639 www.agrofoods.com
Spanish olives
Manager: Isa Knight
Estimated Sales: $1-2.5 Million
Number Employees: 5-9
Square Footage: 526000
Parent Co: Agro Aceitunera SA
Type of Packaging: Consumer, Food Service, Private Label, Bulk
Brands:
Candelita
Exporsevilla
Lola

219 **AgroCepia**
9703 Dixie Highway
Suite 3
Miami, FL 33156
305-704-3488
Fax: 305-666-6930 www.agrocepia.cl
Low moisture colored apple flakes and nuggets, evaporated apple dices, grinds, rings and wedges, low moisture powders, dehydrated tomato, green bell pepper, red bell pepper and jalapeno pepper dices and granules
Sales Director: Mike Zobel
Contact: George Bartels
gbartels@acusallc.com
Estimated Sales: $3-5 Million
Number Employees: 1-4

220 **(HQ)Agrocan**
176 Benjamin Hudon
Ville St Laurent, QC H4N 1H8
Canada
514-272-2512
Fax: 514-270-6370 877-247-6226
info@agrocanfoods.com www.agrocanfoods.com
Manufacturer and exporter of fruit, olives, oil, vegetables and miscellaneous products
President: John Karellis
Number Employees: 3
Type of Packaging: Private Label
Other Locations:
Agrocan
Aeginion, N. Pierias
Brands:
Sunmed

221 **Agropur**
2701 Freedom Rd
Appleton, WI 54913-9315
920-687-2489
Fax: 608-441-3031 kevin.thomson@agropur.com
www.agropur.com
Cheese and cheese products.
Director of Sales: Kevin Thomson
Contact: David Hitner
david.hitner@agropur.com
Number Employees: 50-99
Parent Co: Agropur

222 **(HQ)Agropur**
510 Rue Principale
Granby, QC J2G 7G2
Canada
450-375-1991
Fax: 450-375-7160 800-363-5686
jarollan@agropur.com www.agropur.com
Dairy products
Chairman: Jacques Cartier
CEO: Claude Menard
Secretary: Andre Gauthier
Director, Dairy Ingredient Sales: Kevin Thomson
Number Employees: 650
Parent Co: Agropur MSI, LLC
Type of Packaging: Consumer, Food Service
Other Locations:
Agropur Coop. Agro-Alimentair
Markham ON

223 **Agrusa**
PO Box 267
117 Fort Lee Road
Leonia, NJ 07605-7244
201-592-5950
Fax: 201-585-7244 agrusa@agrusainc.com
www.agritalia.com
Italian foods, including: pasta, olive oil, balsamic vinegar, tomatoes, risotto, rice and frozen pizza.
President: Jill Bush
Number Employees: 5
Square Footage: 8000
Type of Packaging: Consumer, Food Service, Private Label, Bulk
Brands:
Bella Italia
Celio
Don Peppe
Private Label

224 **Agumm**
10636 NW 49th Street
Coral Springs, FL 33076-2702
954-344-0607
Fax: 305-341-6667
Baked products, batters, breading, confectionery, dry mixes
President: Matthew Rutter

225 **Agusa**
1055 S 19th Ave
Lemoore, CA 93245-9747
559-924-4785
Fax: 559-924-0933 jeff.babb@agusa.biz
www.agusa.biz
Tomato based products
President: Pedro Souchard
COO: Inigo Martinez
CFO: Javier Souchard
VP: Craig Shimomura
Sales Manager: Jeff Babb
jeff.babb@agusa.biz
General Manager: Joel Lira
Estimated Sales: $5.9 Million
Number Employees: 20-49
Square Footage: 56000
Type of Packaging: Food Service, Private Label, Bulk

226 **Agvest**
7589 First Pl Ste 2
Cleveland, OH 44146
216-464-3737
Fax: 440-735-1680 www.agvest.com
Frozen apples, elderberries, bilberries; sugar infused blueberries, cranberries and cherries; and fruit flakes and powders.
President/CEO: Barry Schneider
CFO: Steve Hamilton
Contact: Bob Newman
bob@agvest.com
Estimated Sales: $1-2.5 Million
Number Employees: 5-9
Type of Packaging: Food Service
Brands:
North Eastern
Quality

227 **Ah Dor Kosher Fish Corporation**
25 Maple Terrace
Monsey, NY 10952-3707
845-425-2060
Fish
President: Joseph Neuman
Estimated Sales: Less than $500,000
Number Employees: 1-4
Type of Packaging: Private Label

228 **Ahara Ghee**
1630 SE 3rd Ave
Portland, OR 97214
503-997-5050
ahararasaghee@gmail.com
www.iloveghee.com
Organic ghee (clarified butter)
Founder/CEO: Andrea Shuman
Co-Founder/COO: Martin Lemke
Year Founded: 2011

229 **Ahlgren Vineyard**
Bonded Winery 7464
Boulder Creek, CA 95006
831-338-6071
Fax: 831-338-9111 800-338-6071
www.ahlgrenvineyard.com
Wines
Co-Owner: Valerie Ahlgren
Co-Owner/CEO/Winemaker: Dexter Ahlgren
Estimated Sales: $1-2.5 Million
Number Employees: 1-4
Type of Packaging: Food Service, Private Label
Brands:
Ahlgren Vineyard
Tre Vini Rossi

230 **Ahmad Tea**
P.O.Box 876
Deer Park, TX 77536
281-478-0957
Fax: 281-479-0521 800-637-7704
info@ahmadteausa.com www.ahmadtea.com
Tea and tea gift producer
Marketing: Karim Afshar
Contact: Ali Afshar
ali@ahmadtea.com

231 **Ai Vy Springrolls, Llc**
515 East 72nd St
Suite 4j
New York, NY 10021
897-394-3657
info@aivyspringrolls.com
www.aivyspringrolls.com
Spring rolls
Square Footage: 80000

232 **Aidells Sausage Co**
2411 Baumann Ave
San Lorenzo, CA 94580-1801
510-614-5450
Fax: 510-614-2287 800-546-5795
info@aidells.com www.aidells.com
Sausage and other deli products.
Founder: Chef Bruce Aidells
CEO: Bob Mc Henry
Manager: Rosa Anders
randers@aidells.com
Number Employees: 20-49
Type of Packaging: Consumer, Food Service, Bulk
Brands:
Aidell's

233 **Aileen Quirk & Sons Inc**
235 W 12th Ave
Kansas City, MO 64116-4178
816-471-4580
Fax: 816-842-8063 info@aileenquirkandsons.com
www.aileenquirkandsons.com
Dried edible beans for wholesalers and grocery stores.
Owner: Kelly Quirk
quirksons@aol.com
CEO: Larry Quirk
Traffic Manager: Leslie Quirk
Office Manager: Frances Kuhn
Estimated Sales: $3 Million
Number Employees: 10-19
Type of Packaging: Food Service, Private Label, Bulk
Brands:
PDQ Puncher

234 **Aimonetto and Sons**
720 N 10th St
Renton, WA 98057
206-767-2777
Fax: 206-762-6792 866-823-2777
Milk, juice, cottage cheese, sour cream and yogurt; wholesaler/distributor of dairy products
Owner: Jim Aimonetto
Estimated Sales: $10-20 Million
Number Employees: 10-19
Type of Packaging: Consumer, Food Service

235 **Airlie Winery**
15305 Dunn Forest Rd
Monmouth, OR 97361-9570
503-838-6013
Fax: 503-838-6279 airlie@airliewinery.com
www.airliewinery.com
Wines
Owner: Mary Olson
airlie@airliewinery.com
Marketing/Sales VP: Barry Glassman
Marketing and Sales Director: Sue Shay
Winemaker: Elizabeth Ogg
Estimated Sales: $500,000-$1 Million
Number Employees: 1-4
Type of Packaging: Private Label
Brands:
Airlie

236 **Aiya America Inc**
2807 Oregon Ct
Unit D-5
Torrance, CA 90503-2635
310-212-1395
Fax: 310-212-1386 info@aiya-america.com
www.aiya-america.com
Wholesaler and distributor of matcha green tea and premium leaf teas used in many types of food and beverage applications.
Sales Assistant/Customer Service: Daniel Coniglio
daniel@aiya-america.com

237 **(HQ)Ajinomoto Foods North America, Inc.**
4200 Concours St.
Suite 100
Ontario, CA 91764
909-477-4700
Fax: 919-477-4600 www.ajinomotofoods.com
Specializes in frozen ethnic dishes, such as Italian, Mexican and Asian including lasagna, meat balls, ravioli, spaghetti sauce, potstickers, spring rolls, and burritos.
President/CEO: Takaaki Nishii
President, North America: Bernard Kreilmann
Year Founded: 1909
Estimated Sales: $670 Million
Number Employees: 2,500+
Number of Brands: 14
Parent Co: Ajinomoto Co., Inc.
Type of Packaging: Consumer, Food Service
Other Locations:
Amino Acid Technologies
Raleigh NC
Wellness & Sports Nutrition
Raleigh NC
Food Ingredients
Itasca IL
Ajinomoto Windsor, Inc.
Ontario, Canada
Ajinomoto Heartland, Inc.
Chicago IL
Ajinomoto Althea, Inc.
San Diego CA
Ajinomoto De Mexico
Col. Juarez, Mexico
Brands:
Ajinomoto®
Posada®
Bernardi®
Amoy®
Fred's®
Whitey's®
Chili Bowl®
Golden Tiger®
Tai Pei®
Ling Ling®
Jose Ole®
VIP®

238 **Ajinomoto Frozen Foods USA, Inc.**
4200 Concours Street
Suite 100
Ontario, CA 91764
866-536-8008
www.ajifrozenusa.com
Asian ingredients and prepared foods.
Parent Co: Ajinomoto Co., Inc.
Type of Packaging: Consumer, Food Service, Private Label
Other Locations:
Los Angeles CA
Portland OR
Honolulu HI
Brands:
Tai Pei®
Ling Ling®
Jose Ole®
Ajinomoto®
VIP®
Posada®
Bernardi®
Amoy®
Fred's®
Whitey's®
Chili Bowl®
Golden Tiger®

239 **Ajinomoto Heartland Inc**
8430 W Bryn Mawr Ave
Suite 650
Chicago, IL 60631-3421
773-380-7000
Fax: 773-380-7006 www.lysine.com
Feed-grade amino acids
President: Daniel Bercovici
Number Employees: 10-19
Parent Co: Ajinomoto Co., Inc.
Type of Packaging: Bulk
Brands:
L-Lysine
L-Threonine
AjiLys®
L-Tryptophan
AjiPro®-L
L-Valine

240 **Ajiri Tea Company**
PO Box 162
Upper Black Eddy, PA 18972
610-982-5075
Fax: 610-982-9346 ajirifoundation@gmail.com
www.ajiritea.com
Tea and coffee.
Owner: Sara Holby

241 **Ak Mak Bakeries**
89 Academy Ave
Sanger, CA 93657-2104
559-875-5511
Fax: 559-875-2472 www.akmakbakeries.com
Armenian flat bread and cracker bread.
President: Manoog Soojian
manoog@akmakbakeries.com
Controller: Tanya Hodge
Year Founded: 1893
Estimated Sales: $20-50 Million
Number Employees: 20-49
Number of Brands: 2
Type of Packaging: Consumer
Brands:
Ak Mak
Country Style

242 **Akay USA LLC**
500 Hartle St
Suite E
Sayreville, NJ 08872-2770
732-254-7177
akayusallc@gmail.com
www.akay-group.com
Paprika and other spices.
Senior Vice President of Sales USA: Rajive Joseph
Manager: Balu Maliakel
balu.maliakel@akay-group.com
Number Employees: 1-4
Parent Co: Akay Group

243 **Aker BioMarine Antarctic US, LLC.**
312 Amboy Ave
Metuchen, NJ 08840
732-917-4000
www.superbakrill.com
Krill oil
Brands:
Superba

244 **Aketta**
www.aketta.com
Cricket protein powder
CEO: Mohammed Ashour
COO: Gabriel Mott
Number of Brands: 1
Number of Products: 5
Type of Packaging: Consumer
Brands:
AKETTA

245 **Akicorp**
20145 NE 21st CT
N Miami Beach, FL 33179
786-426-5750
ysaac@akinin.com
Oilseeds
Manager: Ysaac Akinin
yakinin@akinin.com

246 **Al & John's Glen Rock Ham**
147 Clinton Rd.
West Caldwell, NJ 07006
973-521-7928
Fax: 973-521-7929 800-969-4990
www.glenrockhams.com
Canadian bacon and fresh ham including cooked, ready-to-eat, fat-free, semi-boneless, smoked boneless, honey, Virginia maple, apple cinnamon, Black Forest.
President/CEO: Alex Oldja
VP: Jennifer Oldja
Director Quality Assurance: Daniel Oldja
Plant Manager: Alex Oldja, Jr.

Estimated Sales: $20-50 Million
Number Employees: 100-249
Brands:
Kohler Deli Meats
Freda Deli Meats

247 **Al Dente Pasta Co**
9815 Main St
Whitmore Lake, MI 48189-9438
734-449-8522
800-536-7278
info@aldentepasta.com www.aldentepasta.com
Specialty flavored pasta and sauces.
President/Founder: Monique Deschaine
VP: Dennis Deschaine
Contact: Nanette Carson
nanette@aldentepasta.com
Estimated Sales: $5-10 Million
Number Employees: 50-99
Brands:
Al Dente
Al Dente Pasta Selecta
Al Dente Sure Success
Monique's Pasta Sauces

248 **Al Gelato Bornay**
9133 Belden Ave
Franklin Park, IL 60131-3505
847-455-5355
Fax: 847-455-7553 algelatochicago@gmail.com
www.algelatochicago.com
Ice cream, sorbet, spumoni, natural fruit sorbets, and frozen desserts.
President: Paula DiNardo
pdinardo@laibensebornay.com
Estimated Sales: Less Than $500,000
Number Employees: 5-9
Square Footage: 20000
Type of Packaging: Food Service, Private Label, Bulk
Brands:
Al Gelato

249 **(HQ)Al Pete Meats**
2100 E Willard St
Muncie, IN 47302-3737
765-288-8817
Fax: 765-281-2759 www.petespride.net
Frozen portion control foods; including corn dogs, breaded meat and cheese, raw and cooked breaded mushrooms and cauliflower; Exporter of frozen portion controlled breaded meat products.
President: Arlin Mann
CEO: John Hartmeyer
Purchasing Manager: Paul Whitechair
Estimated Sales: $10-20 Million
Number Employees: 20-49
Square Footage: 450000
Type of Packaging: Consumer, Food Service, Private Label
Other Locations:
Manufacturing Facility
Muncie IN
Manufacturing Facility
Fairbury IL
Brands:
Al Pete
Pete's Pride

250 **Al Richard's Chocolates**
851 Broadway
Bayonne, NJ 07002
201-436-0915
Fax: 201-436-0485 888-777-6964
www.alrichardschocolates.com
Chocolates
Estimated Sales: $300,000-500,000
Number Employees: 1-4

251 **Al Safa Halal**
100 Church St
8th Floor
New York City, NY 10007
800-268-8147
connect@alsafafoods.com www.alsafahalal.com
Processor and exporter of halal processed foods including pizza, beef burgers, chicken nuggets, fish sticks.
President: David Muller
VP: Steve Hahn
Number Employees: 10-19
Number of Brands: 40
Parent Co: Engro Foods Canada Ltd.
Type of Packaging: Consumer, Food Service
Other Locations:
Al Safa Halal
Cambridge, Ontario
Brands:
Al Safa Halal

252 **Al's Beverage Company**
1-3 Revay Rd
East Windsor, CT 06088
860-627-7003
Fax: 860-627-8067 888-257-7632
mfeldman@alsbeverage.com
www.alsbeverage.com
Fountain soft drinks
Owner: Marjorie Feldman
Sr. VP Sales: John Martin
VP: William Melcher
Marketing Consultant: Todd Lemieux
Sales Director: Art Gallegos
Contact: Leslie Gengenbach
lgengenbach@alsbeverage.com
Operations Manager: Michael McCarthy
Estimated Sales: $3-5 Million
Number Employees: 50-99
Type of Packaging: Private Label
Brands:
Al's
Barrel Head
Canada Dry
Rc
Stewarts
Sunkist

253 **Al-Rite Fruits & SyrupsCo**
18524 NE 2nd Ave
Miami, FL 33179-4427
305-652-2540
Fax: 305-652-4478 www.al-rite.com
Processor and exporter of kosher products including isotonic iced tea, fountain and slush beverage, ice cream and nondairy bases. Also fudge and chocolate syrups, toppings, frozen cocktail/bar mixes and extracts and flavors forbeverages and desserts
Manager: Alfredo Faubel
Vice President: Cliff Spring
cspring@al-rite.com
Estimated Sales: $5-10 Million
Number Employees: 10-19
Type of Packaging: Consumer, Food Service, Private Label, Bulk
Brands:
Al-Rite
Iso-Sport
Tropical

254 **Alabama Gulf Seafood**
9280 Seafood House Rd
Bayou La Batre, AL 36509
251-824-4396
Fax: 251-824-7579 eatalabamaseafood.com
Seafood
President: Richard Gazzier
Vice President: Donna Gazzier
Estimated Sales: $5-10 Million
Number Employees: 10-19

255 **Alacer Corp**
Carlisle, PA 17013
888-425-2362
www.emergenc.com
Dietary supplements, mineral ascorbates, vitamins and distilled water.
President: Ron Fugate
Vice President: Bruce Sweyd
Year Founded: 1978
Estimated Sales: $20-50 Million
Number Employees: 50-99
Square Footage: 57000
Type of Packaging: Consumer
Brands:
Emer'gen-C
Miracle

256 **Aladdin Bakers**
240 25th St
Brooklyn, NY 11232-1338
718-499-1818
Fax: 718-788-5174 kasindorf@aladdinbakers.com
www.aladdinbakers.com
Sandwich wraps and gourmet flour tortillas; pita; panini and specialty breads; bagels; bread sticks; toast; croutons; and flatbreads.
President: Joseph Ayoub
ayoub@aladdinbakers.com
CFO/GM: Donald Guzzi
Quality Control Director: Javier Vasquez
VP Sales/Marketing: Paul Kasindorf
Human Resources Director: Barbara Adams
COO/Plant Manager: Arkadi Karachun
Production Manager: Ed Curran
Year Founded: 1972
Estimated Sales: $20-50 Million
Number Employees: 100-249
Square Footage: 9774
Type of Packaging: Consumer, Food Service, Private Label, Bulk
Brands:
Aladdin

257 **Alakef Coffee Roasters Inc**
1330 E Superior St
Suite 1
Duluth, MN 55805-3855
218-724-6849
Fax: 218-724-7727 800-438-9228
info@alakef.com www.alakef.com
Roasted coffee
Co-Owner: Nessim Bohbot
coffee@alakef.com
VP: Deborah Bohbot
Estimated Sales: $1.7 Million
Number Employees: 10-19
Type of Packaging: Private Label

258 **Alamance Foods**
840 Plantation Dr
Burlington, NC 27215
info@alamancefoods.com
www.alamancefoods.com
Freeze popsicles; whip cream and classic creamer, water.
President: Bill Scott
Regional Sales Manager: Jerry Schumate
Estimated Sales: $10-100 Million
Number Employees: 100-249
Brands:
Classic Cream
Fun Pops
Fun Whip
Happy Drinks
Triton Water

259 **(HQ)Alamo Tamale Corporation**
3713 Jensen Dr
Houston, TX 77026
713-228-6446
Fax: 713-228-7513 800-252-0586
www.alamotamale.com
Tamales
President: Louis Webster
VP: Shirleen Webster
Estimated Sales: $10-20 Million
Number Employees: 50-99
Square Footage: 75000
Type of Packaging: Consumer, Food Service, Private Label
Brands:
Alamo

260 **Alaska Aquafarms**
P.O. Box 7
Moose Pass, AK 99631-0007
907-288-3667
Fax: 907-288-3667 jjh@seward.net
Shellfish
Owner: James Hetrick
President/CEO: Willard Fehr
Estimated Sales: $300,000-500,000
Number Employees: 1-4

261 **Alaska Bounty Seafoods & Smokery**
110 Jarvis Street
Sitka, AK 99835-9806
907-747-3730
Smoked salmon
Partner: Carol Petraborg
Partner: Gerold Brager
Estimated Sales: $1-2.5 Million
Number Employees: 5-9
Type of Packaging: Consumer, Food Service, Bulk

262 **Alaska General Seafoods**
6425 NE 175th St
Kenmore, WA 98028-4808
425-485-7755
Fax: 425-485-5172 info@akgen.com
www.akgen.com
Socially responsible seafood including fresh, frozen, canned, and roe
Vice President: Gordon Lindquist
g.lindquist@alaskageneralseafoods.com
Controller: Brad Wilkins
Estimated Sales: $20-50 Million
Number Employees: 10-19
Parent Co: Jim Pattison Group
Other Locations:
Kenmore Warehouse
Kenmore WA
Naknek Plant
Naknek AK
Ketchikan Plant
Ketchikan AK
Egegik Office
Egegik AK
Ferndale Shop
Ferndale WA
Brands:
Gold Seal

263 **Alaska Herb & Tea Co**
6710 Weimer Dr
Anchorage, AK 99502-2054
907-245-3499
Fax: 907-245-3499 800-654-2764
herbtea@alaska.net www.alaskaherbtea.com
Tea, honey, syrups, jams and jellies, cocoa, vinegars
President: Charles Walsh
herbtea@alaska.net
VP: Sandra Fongemie
Operations Manager: Ann Stewart
Production Manager: Maria Salizar
Estimated Sales: Less than $500,000
Number Employees: 1-4
Type of Packaging: Private Label
Brands:
Alaska Wild Teas
Alaskan Boreal Bouquet
Alaskan Fireweed
Alaskan Gold
Cocoalaska

264 **Alaska Jacks**
6251 Tuttle Pl
Suite 101
Anchorage, AK 99507-2099
907-248-9999
Fax: 907-243-2044 888-660-2257
Smoked salmon, chocolate, taffy, jams and jellies, salmon, gold crunch, chikoot chews, klondike krisp, sourdough starters, and earthquake bars.
President: Starr Horton
Sales Manager: Dave Berry
Estimated Sales: $5-10 Million
Number Employees: 20-49
Brands:
Alaska Jack's
Alaska Tea Traders

265 **Alaska Ocean Trading**
4101 Westland Cir
Anchorage, AK 99517-1430
907-243-4399
Fax: 907-243-4399
Fish and seafood
CFO: Roger Park
Estimated Sales: Under $500,000
Number Employees: 1-4

266 **Alaska Pacific Seafoods**
627 Shelikof St
Kodiak, AK 99615
907-486-3234
Seafood
Estimated Sales: $50-100 Million
Number Employees: 100-249
Parent Co: North Pacific Seafoods
Brands:
North Pacific Seafood

267 **Alaska Pasta Co**
511 W 41st Ave
Suite A
Anchorage, AK 99503-6643
907-276-2632
Fax: 907-276-2632
Pasta
Owner: Hope Nelson
rvnelson@dci.net
Estimated Sales: $1-2.5 Million
Number Employees: 1-4

268 **Alaska Sausage & Seafood**
2914 Arctic Blvd
Anchorage, AK 99503-3811
907-562-3636
Fax: 907-562-7343 800-798-3636
aks@ak.net www.alaskasausage.com
Sausage, processed meats and smoked fish; exporter of smoked salmon
President: Herbert Eckmann
Secretary/Treasurer: Eva Eckmann
Quality Control Manager: Martin Eckmann
IT: Amanda Ingram
aks@ak.net
Estimated Sales: $10-20 Million
Number Employees: 20-49
Square Footage: 30000
Type of Packaging: Consumer, Food Service, Private Label, Bulk
Brands:
Alaskan

269 **Alaska Seafood Co**
5731 Concrete Way
Juneau, AK 99801-9543
907-780-4808
Fax: 907-780-5140 800-451-1400
info@alaskaseafoodcompany.com
www.alaskaseafoodcompany.com
Fish.
President: Richard Hand
Year Founded: 1987
Estimated Sales: $800,000
Number Employees: 10-19

270 **Alaska Smokehouse**
21616 87th Ave SE
Woodinville, WA 98072-8017
360-668-9404
Fax: 360-668-1005 800-422-0852
service@alaskasmokehouse.com
www.alaskasmokehouse.com
Smoked salmon, spreads, jerky, cookies, fruit purees and coffee.
President/CEO: Jack Praino
customerservice@alaskasmokehouse.com
SVP: Tiffany Andriesen
Estimated Sales: $1.5 Million
Number Employees: 20-49
Square Footage: 60000
Type of Packaging: Consumer, Private Label
Brands:
Alaska Smokehouse
Sleepless In Seattle Coffee
The Famous Pacific Dessert Company

271 **Alaska Brewing Company**
5429 Shaune Drive
Juneau, AK 99801-9540
907-780-5866
Fax: 907-780-4514 www.alaskanbeer.com
Beer, amber, pale and stouts.
Co-Founder/President: Geoffrey Larson
Co-Founder: Marcy Larson
CEO: Linda Thomas
Contact: Cindy Burchfield
lostinalaska@gci.net
Plant Manager: Curtis Holmes
Estimated Sales: $20-50 Million
Number Employees: 56
Number of Brands: 10
Type of Packaging: Private Label
Brands:
Alaskan Amber
Alaskan Freeride APA
Alaskan Hopothermia
Alaskan Icy Bay IPA
Alaskan Imperial Red
Alaskan Kicker Session IPA
Alaskan Stout
Alaskan Summer Ale
Alaskan White
AlaskaN Winter Ale

272 **Alaskan Gourmet Seafoods**
1020 International Airport Road
Anchorage, AK 99518
Fax: 907-563-2592 800-288-3740
www.akgourmet.com
Frozen and canned smoked halibut and salmon.
President: Paul Schilling
Estimated Sales: $5-10 Million
Number Employees: 18
Square Footage: 40000
Brands:
Alaskan Gourmet

273 **Alaskan Leader Fisheries**
8874 Bender Rd
Suite 201
Lynden, WA 98264-8550
360-318-1280
Fax: 866-649-2675 www.alaskanleader.com
Owner: Rob Wurm
rob@alaskanleaderfisheries.com
Partner: Kevin O'Leary
Partner: Richard Thummel
Estimated Sales: $.5-1 million
Number Employees: 1-4
Brands:
Alaskan Leader Fisheries

274 **Alaskan Smoked Salmon &Seafood**
8430 Laviento Dr
Anchorage, AK 99515-1914
907-349-8234
Fax: 907-344-7666
Smoked salmon
President: Christopher Rosauer
aksam@alaska.net
Estimated Sales: $200,000
Number Employees: 1-4
Type of Packaging: Consumer, Food Service

275 **Alati-Caserta Desserts**
277 Rue Dante
Montr,al, QC H2S 1K3
Canada
514-271-3013
Fax: 514-277-5860 877-377-5680
info@alaticaserta.com www.alaticaserta.com
Desserts including almond cakes, cannoli ricotta and chocolate mousse.
President: Vittorio Caldarone
Co-Owner: Marco Caldarone
Estimated Sales: $243,000
Number Employees: 6
Type of Packaging: Food Service
Brands:
Alati-Casserta

276 **Alba Foods, Inc**
1355 Rock Mountain Blvd
Stone Mountain, GA 30083
888-725-4605
info@albafoods.us www.albafoods.us
Tart shells and baking ingredients

277 **Alba Vineyard & Winery**
269 Route 627
Village of Finesville
Milford, NJ 08848-1771
908-995-7800
Fax: 908-995-7155 wine@albavineyard.com
www.albavineyard.com
Wines
President/Owner: Thomas Sharko
Partner: Rudy Marchesi
Estimated Sales: $2.5-5 Million
Number Employees: 5-9
Type of Packaging: Private Label, Bulk
Brands:
Alba

278 **Albanese Confectionery Group**
5441 E Lincoln Hwy
Merrillville, IN 46410-5947
219-942-1877
Fax: 219-769-6897 800-536-0581
retail@albaneseconfectionery.com
www.albanesecandy.com
Chocolate covered nuts, candies, and gummies.
President: Scott Albanese
ciaoalbanese@albaneseconfectionary.com
Vice President: Richard Albanese
Purchasing: Alan Levinson
Estimated Sales: $5-10 Million
Number Employees: 5-9
Other Locations:
Hobart Manufacturing Facility
Hobart IN

279 **Albert's Meats**
2992 Green Valley Rd
Claysville, PA 15323
800-522-9970
freshflavor@albertsmeats.com albertsmeats.com
Smoked hams, luncheon meats, sausages and kielbasa.
Owner: George Weiss
Sales Manager: Brian Weiss
Number Employees: 50-99
Parent Co: Green Valley Packing
Type of Packaging: Consumer

280 **Alberta Cheese Company**
8420 26th Street SE
Calgary, AB T2C 1C7
Canada
403-279-4353
Fax: 403-279-4795 info@albertacheese.com
www.albertacheese.com
Cheese: mozzarella, ricotta, cheddar, feta, provolone and monterey jack
President: Frank Talarico
Sales Manager/GM: Michael Talarico
Estimated Sales: $5-10 Million
Number Employees: 20
Type of Packaging: Consumer, Food Service
Brands:
Franco's
Sorento

281 **Alca Trading Co.**
5301 Blue Lagoon Dr
Suite 570
Miami, FL 33126
305-265-8331
www.alcatradingcorp.com
Banana juices and mango purees.
Contact: Andrea Cordova
andrea@alcatradingcorp.com

282 **Alcove Chocolate**
1929 Hillhurst Ave.
Los Angeles, CA 90027
USA
323-284-2229
Fax: 323-644-0111 www.alcovecafe.com
Chocolate Bars
Founder: Tom Trellis

283 **Alden's Organic**
Camas, WA 98607
www.aldensicecream.com
Organic ice cream
Brands:
Alden's Organic

284 **Alder Springs Smoked Salmon**
PO Box 97
61 River Road
Sequim, WA 98382-0097
360-683-2829
Fax: 360-683-5359
Smoked salmon, salmon jerky, oysters, cod and trout
Owner: Robert Bearden
Estimated Sales: Less than $500,000
Number Employees: 1-4
Type of Packaging: Private Label
Brands:
Alder Springs

285 **Alderfer Inc**
382 Main St
PO Box 2
Harleysville, PA 19438-2310
215-256-8818
Fax: 215-256-6120 800-341-1121
www.alderfermeats.com
Pork, beef and turkey products
President/CEO: Jim Van Stone
jvanstone@alderfermeats.com
CFO: Sandy Sloyer
Marketing Manager: Samantha Alderfer
Sales Executive: Chet Dudzinski
Human Resources Manager: Janise Stauffer
Plant Manager: Brent Shoemaker
Purchasing Manager: Ray Ganser
Estimated Sales: $12 Million
Number Employees: 50-99
Number of Brands: 1
Number of Products: 300
Square Footage: 60000
Type of Packaging: Consumer, Food Service, Private Label, Bulk
Brands:
Alderfer
Leidy's

286 **AleSmith Brewing Company**
9368 Cabot Dr
San Diego, CA 92126
858-549-9888
Fax: 858-549-1052 peter@alesmith.com
www.alesmith.com
Ale including seasonal
Owner: Peter Zien
Contact: Peter Cronin
pcronin@alesmith.com
Estimated Sales: $3-5 Million
Number Employees: 1-4
Square Footage: 12800
Type of Packaging: Food Service, Bulk

287 **Alef Sausage Inc**
1026 Campus Dr
Mundelein, IL 60060-3831
847-968-2533
Fax: 847-968-3095 www.alefsausage.com
Saugage
President: Alec Mikhaylov
alec@alefsausage.com
Estimated Sales: Less Than $500,000
Number Employees: 5-9

288 **Aleias Gluten Free Foods**
4 Pin Oak Dr
Branford, CT 06405-6506
203-488-5556
connect@aleias.com
www.aleias.com
Gluten-free cookies, bread crumbs, panko, croutons, breads and stuffing mixes.
Contact: Jim Snow
jims@aleias.com
Estimated Sales: Less Than $500,000
Number Employees: 1-4

289 **Alessi Bakery**
2909 W Cypress St
Tampa, FL 33609-1630
813-879-4544
Fax: 813-872-9103
Tortes, pastry desserts, cakes, cookies
President: Philip Alessi
pjr@alessibakeries.com
CFO: Debrah Herman
Estimated Sales: $5-10 Million
Number Employees: 50-99
Square Footage: 60000
Type of Packaging: Consumer, Food Service
Brands:
Alessi Bakery

290 **Alewel's Country Meats**
911 N Simpson Dr
Junction 13 & 50
Warrensburg, MO 64093-9277
660-747-8261
Fax: 660-747-1857 800-353-8553
ralewel@alewels.com www.country-meats.com
Dry, shelf stable, game and summer sausage, and game jerky including deer and buffalo.
Owner: Randy Alewel
alewels@sprintmail.com
Estimated Sales: $2.5-5 Million
Number Employees: 5-9
Square Footage: 20000
Type of Packaging: Consumer, Food Service, Private Label, Bulk
Brands:
Alewel's Country Meats
Grandpa A'S

291 **Alexander Gourmet Beverages**
670 Hardwick Rd
Bolton, ON L7C 5R5
Canada
905-361-2577
Fax: 905-282-0601 800-265-5081
info@alexanderstea.com www.alexanderstea.com
Teas
President: Dave Elliott
Estimated Sales: $3.5 Million
Number Employees: 60+
Number of Brands: 6
Square Footage: 60000
Type of Packaging: Consumer, Food Service, Private Label, Bulk
Brands:
Alexander's Gourmet Tea
Cocoa Creations
Herbal Teazers

292 **Alexander International(USA)**
132 Concourse East
Brightwaters, NY 11718
805-218-6628
866-965-0143
service@alexander-usa.com
Drink mixes, herbs and spices, olive and other oils.
Owner: F.Matthias Alexander

293 **Alexandra & Nicolay Chocolate Company**
507 Delaware Avenue
PO Box 14
Portaland, PA 18351
570-897-6223
Fax: 570-897-5954 anchocolatiers@aol.com
www.alexandraandnicolay.com
Chocolates in milk, white and dark
Founder: Alexandra Mazhirov
Founder: Nicolay Mazhirov
Estimated Sales: $300,000-500,000
Number Employees: 5-9

294 **Alexia Foods**
5102 21st Street
Suite 3B
Long Island City, NY 11101
718-937-0100
Fax: 718-937-0110 info@alexiafoods.com
www.alexiafoods.com
Frozen potato products including artisan breads, oven blends, onion rings, organic products, mashed potatoes, oven fries and oven reds, julienne fries, and appetizers.
President/CEO: Alex Dzieduszycki
Senior Marketing Manager: Michael Smith
Director of Sales: Jack Acree
Contact: Christine Dubois
christine.dubois@alexiafoods.com
Estimated Sales: G
Parent Co: ConAgra Foods
Type of Packaging: Food Service

295 **Alexian Pâtés**
1200 7th Ave
Neptune, NJ 07753-5176
732-775-3220
Fax: 732-775-3223 800-927-9473
informationrequest@alexianpate.com
www.alexianpate.com
Specialty meats and sausages. All natural preservative free pâtés and mousses; pork, poultry, vegetarian and vegan pâtés
President: Laurie Cummins
Sales Manager: Paul Klempert
Contact: Alexian Terrines
alexian@alexianpate.com
Accountant: John Stevens
Estimated Sales: $10-20 Million
Number Employees: 10-19

296 **Alexis Bailly Vineyard**
18200 Kirby Ave S
Hastings, MN 55033-9340
651-437-1413
info@abvwines.com
www.abvwines.com
Wines
Founder: David Bailly
Owner/CEO: Nan Bailly
Estimated Sales: $500,000-$1 Million
Number Employees: 1-4
Type of Packaging: Consumer, Private Label
Brands:
Alexis Bailly

297 **Alfer Laboratories**
9566 Vassar Ave
Chatsworth, CA 91311-4141
818-709-0737
Fax: 818-709-5360
Nutritional supplements and vitamins including liquid cal-mag, acidophilus cultures and aloe vera gels/juices
President: Ines Gutierrez
alferlabs@aol.com
Purchasing Manager: Ines Gutierrez
Estimated Sales: $2.5-5 Million
Number Employees: 5-9

Type of Packaging: Private Label

298 **Alfonso Gourmet Pasta**
2211 NW 30th Pl
Pompano Beach, FL 33069-1026
954-960-1010
Fax: 954-974-2773 800-370-7278
customerservice@alfonsogourmetpasta.com
Ravioli and prepared foods including fresh, frozen and processed.
President: Joseph Delfavero
jdelfavero@ppg.com
Estimated Sales: $2.5 Million
Number Employees: 5-9
Square Footage: 48000
Type of Packaging: Food Service
Brands:
Alfonso Gourmet Pasta

299 **Alfred & Sam's Italian Bakery**
17 Fairview Ave
Lancaster, PA 17603-5594
717-392-6311
Fax: 717-392-6311
Rolls, breads, cannolis and cookies.
President: Tim Mineo
Owner: Sam Borsellino
Estimated Sales: $500,000-$1 Million
Number Employees: 10-19
Type of Packaging: Consumer
Brands:
Alfred & Sam's

300 **Alfred L. Wolff, Inc.**
1440 Renaissance Drive
Park Ridge, IL 60068
847-759-8888
Fax: 312-265-9888 www.alwolff.com
Importer of dehydrated vegetables, herbs, honey and other bee products including royal jelly, bee pollen and propolis; also, gum arabic, acidulating agents and nutritional fiber
General Manager: Magnus von Buddenbrock
Estimated Sales: $5 Million
Number Employees: 3
Parent Co: Alfred L. Wolff GmbH
Type of Packaging: Bulk
Brands:
Big Onion
Finest Honey Organic
Finest Honey Selection
Qslic
Quick Acid
Quick Chew
Quick Coat
Quick Fibre
Quick Glanz
Quick Gum
Quick Lac
Quick Oil
Quick Shine
Shellac

301 **Alfred Louie Inc**
4501 Shepard St
Bakersfield, CA 93313-2310
661-831-2520
Fax: 661-833-9197
Fruits and vegetables, pasta, and Chinese canned goods and vegetables.
President: Susan Louie
Manager: Gordon Louie
peakdragon@yahoo.com
Estimated Sales: $5,115,628
Number Employees: 10-19

302 **Alfred Nickles Bakery Inc**
26 N Main St
Navarre, OH 44662
330-879-5635
customerservice@nicklesbakery.com
www.nicklesbakery.com
Baked goods
President & CEO: David Gardner
SVP, Finance: Mark Sponseller
Plant Manager: John Nixon
Year Founded: 1909
Estimated Sales: $153 Million
Number Employees: 50-99

303 **Alfredo Aiello Italian Food**
8 Franklin St
Quincy, MA 02169-4944
617-770-6360
Fax: 617-773-3342 info@aapasta.com
www.aapasta.com
Fresh lasagna, ravioli, cavatelli, tortellini, fettuccini
Owner: Alfredo Aiello
alfredo@aapasta.com
Operations Manager: Lino Aiello
Purchasing Manager: John Lucca
Estimated Sales: $5-10 Million
Number Employees: 1-4
Type of Packaging: Consumer, Food Service, Private Label, Bulk
Brands:
Alfredo

304 **Algonquin Tea**
RR#5, 106 Augsburg Road
Eganville, ON K0J 1T0
Canada
613-628-6157
800-292-6671
spirit@algonquintea.com algonquintea.com
Herbal tea
Co-Owner & Office Manager: Kim Elkington
Co-Owner: Steven Martyn
Estimated Sales: $1 Million
Number Employees: 10
Brands:
The Algonquin Tea Co

305 **Algood Food Co**
7401 Trade Port Dr
Louisville, KY 40258-1896
502-637-3631
Fax: 502-637-1502 bmcdonald@algoodfood.com
www.algoodfood.com
Processor and exporter of peanut butter, jams, jellies and preserves
President: Nicolas Melhuish
CEO: Cecil Barnett
VP & CFO: Kathleen Powell
Vice President: Gillian Barnett
Sales Manager: Ashley Keeney
Operations Executive: Dan Schmidt
Production Manager: Danny Ludwig
Number Employees: 100-249
Square Footage: 400000
Brands:
Algood Blue Label
Algood Jelly
Algood Marmalade
Algood Old Fashioned
Algood Preserves
Algood Red Label
Cap 'n Kid

306 **Alicita-Salsa**
737 Walker Road
Suite 2, Po Box 1064
Great Falls, VA 22066
703-340-5323
Fax: 703-406-1276
Dairy-free, gluten-free, sugar-free, vegetarian, salsa/dips, other sauces, seasonings and cooking enhancers, other snacks, other vegetables/fruit.
Marketing: Suzanne Fields

307 **Alimentaire Whyte's Inc**
1540 Rue Des Patriotes
Laval, QC H7L 2N6
Canada
866-420-9520
customer.service@whytes.ca www.whytes.ca
Sauces, cherries, olives, condiments, relish, cooking oils, and table syrup
Year Founded: 1892
Estimated Sales: $32.35 Million
Number Employees: 325
Square Footage: 250000

308 **Alimentos Finisterre**
1109 Little Harbor Drive
Deerfield Beach, FL 33441
954-570-5886
Fax: 954-719-2445
Kosher, full-line cold non-carbonated beverages, RTD-ready to drink (coffee, tea, concentrates, powders), full-line condiments, marinades, full-line spreads & syrup, olives, private label.
Marketing: Tony Grivnovics

309 **Aliments Fontaine Sant, Inc**
450 Rue Deslauriers
Ville Saint-Laurent, QC H4N 1V8
Canada
514-956-7730
Fax: 514-956-7734 888-627-2683
info@fontainesante.com www.fontainesante.com
Health foods.
Marketing: Sami Damnati

310 **Aliments Jolibec, Inc**
149 Montee Allard
St Jacques De Montcalm, QC J0K 2R0
Canada
450-861-6082
Fresh and frozen pork
President: Roger Ethier
Number Employees: 43
Type of Packaging: Bulk

311 **Aliments Prince SEC**
11053 Louis H Lafontaine
Anjou, QC H1J 2Z4
Canada
514-383-0556
Fax: 514-383-4332 800-361-3898
Bacon, ham and sausages
President: Marcel Heroux
GM: Alain Heroux
Director Sales: Sylvain Blais
Number Employees: 800
Type of Packaging: Consumer, Food Service, Private Label

312 **Aliments Trigone**
93 Ch De L'Aqueduc Rr 1
St-Francois-De-La-Rivier, QC G0R 3A0
Canada
418-259-7414
Fax: 418-259-2417 877-259-7491
bio@alimentstrigone.com
www.alimentstrigone.com
Buckwheat and shelled hempseeds.
President: Jacques Cote
Estimated Sales: $1.3 Million
Number Employees: 9
Brands:
Trigone

313 **Aliotti Wholesale Fish Company**
2 Wharf II
PO Box 3325
Monterey, CA 93940
408-722-4597
Fax: 408-722-3456
Processor and exporter of frozen squid
President/Purchasing Manager: Joe Aliotii
Estimated Sales: $2.7 Million
Number Employees: 8
Type of Packaging: Food Service
Brands:
Prima Quality

314 **Alive & Well Olives**
Ponte Vedra Beach, FL 32004
www.aliveandwellolives.com
Olives
Founding Partner: Greg Leonard
Founding Partner: Martin Roth
Founding Partner: Bruce Kern
Brands:
Alive & Well

315 **Alive and Radiant**
PO Box 920096
Needham, MA 02492
800-385-1417
Fax: 617-229-6244
Kale chips
CEO: Blessing Horowytz
Director of Marketing: Melanie Kingsley
Square Footage: 80000
Brands:
Alive & Radiant

316 **Alkinco**
PO Box 278
New York, NY 10116-0278
212-719-3070
Fax: 212-764-7804 800-424-7118
info@Alkincohair.com www.alkincohair.com
Beverage mixes including sugared, chocolate and weight control; also, protein supplements

President: Julius Klugman
VP: Stewart Hoffman
Estimated Sales: $5-10 Million
Number Employees: 20-49
Square Footage: 200000
Type of Packaging: Consumer, Private Label
Brands:
Alkinco

317 All American Foods Inc
121 Mohr Dr
Mankato, MN 56001-3000
507-387-6480
Fax: 507-387-6111 800-833-2661
info@aafoods.com www.aafoods.com
Dairy and non-dairy ingredients, including cheese powders and cheese flavorings, dried cultural ingredients, high-fat powders, dried flavoring ingredients, egg replacement powders, and replacers and substitutes for non-fat dry milkpowder, dry buttermilk powder and dry whole milk powder
President: Connie Stokman
Chief Executive Officer: Jeff Thom
Year Founded: 1987
Estimated Sales: $20 Million
Number Employees: 50-99
Number of Brands: 1
Number of Products: 150
Square Footage: 80000
Parent Co: All American Foods
Type of Packaging: Private Label, Bulk
Brands:
PRO MIX

318 All American Seasonings
10600 E 54th Ave
Suite B
Denver, CO 80239-2132
303-623-2320
Fax: 303-623-1920
www.allamericanseasonings.com
Baking mixes for bread, cakes, other pasteries; assorted seasoned snacks including: chips, popcorn, nuts, & pretzels; sauces; variety of hot and cold beverages, energy drinks, and mixers.
Chairman: Andy Rodriguez
Director Of Quality Assurance: Mary Davis
Marketing Director: Joseph Gallagher
Year Founded: 1968
Estimated Sales: $12 Million
Number Employees: 20-49
Square Footage: 70000
Type of Packaging: Consumer, Food Service, Private Label, Bulk
Brands:
All American

319 All American Snacks
P.O.Box 3
Midland, TX 79702
432-687-6666
Fax: 915-699-2305 800-840-2455
www.allamericansnacks.com
White chocolate; cereals; pretzels; and pecan halves.
Owner/Public Relations: Lexie Kauffman
Co-Owner/Manager: Sheri Brockett
Sales Director: Kimberlea Bryand
Estimated Sales: $5-10 Million
Number Employees: 20-49
Brands:
All American Afternoon Delight
All American Precious Stones
All American White Trash

320 All Goode Organics
PO Box 61256
Santa Barbara, CA 93160
805-683-3370
Fax: 805-683-7669
Organic foods, herbal teas

321 All Juice Food & Beverage
740 SE Dalbey Drive
Ankeny, IA 50021
515-299-6457
Fax: 515-964-0697 800-736-5674
info@mrsclarks.com www.mrsclarks.com
Beverages, apple juice
President: Ron Kahrer
Plant Manager: John Weber
Number Employees: 20-49

322 All Round Foods Bakery Prod
437 Railroad Ave
Westbury, NY 11590-4314
516-338-1888
Fax: 516-338-5151 800-428-8802
www.allroundfoods.com
Processor and exporter of frozen doughnuts including plain, glazed, sugar, cinnamon, jelly, etc.
Owner: Glen Wolther
glen@allroundfoods.com
VP, Sales (Central): John Brahm
Executive VP: Robert Glasser
VP, Sales/Marketing (South): Greg Hanson
Purchasing: Steven Finkelstein
Estimated Sales: $3-5 Million
Number Employees: 10-19
Square Footage: 336000
Type of Packaging: Food Service
Brands:
All Round Foods

323 All Seasonings Ingredients Inc
1043 Freedom Dr
Oneida, NY 13421-7108
315-361-1066
Fax: 315-361-1048 800-255-7748
bfarnach@allseasonings.com
www.allseasonings.com
Custom blended spices and seasonings
President: Cheryl Ano
cano@allseasonings.com
Controller: Steven Tornabene
VP: Brendan Farnach
Manager/Director: Darby Smith
Estimated Sales: Less than $500,000
Number Employees: 1-4
Square Footage: 199504
Type of Packaging: Consumer, Food Service, Private Label, Bulk

324 All Wrapped Up
801 W Tropical Way
Plantation, FL 33317
954-648-3051
Fax: 954-587-2144 800-891-2194
pam@allwrappedup-gifts.com
www.allwrappedup-gifts.com
Candies, cookies, chocolates, nuts, and pretzels, professionally wrapped.
President/CEO: Pam Schwimmer
pam@allwrappedup-gifts.com
VP: Donna Merill
Estimated Sales: Less than $500,000
Number Employees: 5-9
Type of Packaging: Consumer, Private Label

325 All-States Quality Foods
901 N Main Street
Charles City, IA 50616-2109
641-228-5023
Fax: 641-228-2624 800-247-4195
Chicken products including broth, rendered fat, diced cooked meat and turkey and chicken quesadillas.
President: Elliot Jones
Marketing Director: Steve Tenney
Operations Manager: Dan Anderegg
dan@allstates.com
Estimated Sales: $17 Million
Number Employees: 150
Number of Products: 10
Type of Packaging: Consumer, Food Service, Private Label, Bulk

326 Allan Bros. Inc.
31 Allan Rd.
Naches, WA 98937
509-653-2625
info@allanbrosfruit.com
www.allanbrosfruit.com
Apples, apple juice, and cherries.
CEO: Miles Kohl
Year Founded: 1951
Number Employees: 200-500
Type of Packaging: Private Label

327 Allann Brothers Coffee Roasters
1852 Fescue St SE
Albany, OR 97322-7075
541-812-8013
Fax: 541-812-8010 800-926-6886
sales@allannbroscoffee.com
Coffee and teas
Owner: Allan Stuart
Sales Director: Michael Harris
info@allannbroscoffee.com
Estimated Sales: Less than $500,000
Number Employees: 10-19
Type of Packaging: Consumer, Food Service, Private Label, Bulk

328 Alldrin Brothers
P.O.Box 10
Ballico, CA 95303-0010
209-667-1600
Fax: 209-667-0463 www.almondcafe.com
Processor and exporter of almonds.
President: Gary Alldrin
Purchasing Manager: Gary Alldrin
Estimated Sales: $1-2.5 Million
Number Employees: 50-99
Type of Packaging: Bulk
Brands:
Alldrin

329 Alle Processing Corp
5620 59th St
Flushing, NY 11378-2314
718-894-2000
Fax: 718-326-4642 www.alleprocessing.com
Kosher fresh and frozen meat products, entrees and deli meats.
President: Mendel Weinstock
IT: Shlomo Halberstam
halbycpa@alleprocessing.com
Estimated Sales: $10-20 Million
Number Employees: 50-99
Number of Brands: 4
Square Footage: 150000
Parent Co: Alle Processing
Type of Packaging: Consumer, Food Service, Private Label, Bulk
Brands:
Meal Mart
Mou Cuisine
New York Kosher Deli
Amazing Meals

330 Alleghany's Fish Farm
2755 Route 281
Saint Philemon, QC G0R 4A0
Canada
418-469-2823
Fax: 418-469-2872
Live trout eggs
GM: Yves Boulanger
Estimated Sales: $1-5 Million
Number Employees: 22
Type of Packaging: Consumer, Food Service
Brands:
Alleghanys

331 Allegria Italian Bakers
233 E Weddell Dr # I
Sunnyvale, CA 94089-1659
408-734-4300
Fax: 408-734-2444 800-467-8648
Baked goods
President: G Giurlani
italbisco@yahoo.com
CFO: Claire Baxter
Marketing Director: R Giurlani
Plant Manager: G Portida
Year Founded: 1984
Estimated Sales: $5-10 Million
Number Employees: 5-9
Type of Packaging: Consumer, Food Service, Private Label, Bulk

332 Allegro Coffee Co
12799 Claude Ct
Suite B
Thornton, CO 80241-3828
303-444-4844
Fax: 303-920-5468 800-666-4869
www.allegrocoffee.com
Roasted specialty coffees; importer of green coffee beans.
President/General Manager: Jeff Teter
jeff_teter@allegro-coffee.com
CFO: Clarence Peterson
VP: David Kubena
Marketing Director: Tara Cross
Sales Director: Glenda Chamberlain
Human Resources Director: Mimi Fins
Plant Operations Manager: Alejandro Rodolfo
Marketing/Purchasing Manager: Susan Drexel

Estimated Sales: $10 Million
Number Employees: 50-99
Square Footage: 50000
Parent Co: Whole Foods Market
Brands:
Allegro Coffee
Allegro Tea
Organic Coffee

333 Allegro Fine Foods Inc
1595 Highway 218 Byp
PO Box 1262
Paris, TN 38242-6632
731-642-6113
Fax: 731-642-6116 info@allegromarinade.com
www.allegromarinade.com
Meat and vegetable marinades
President: John Fuqua
john@allegromarinade.com
VP: Thomas Harrison
Quality Assurance Manager: Marti Jones
Marketing Manager: Tim Phifer
VP Operations: Stan Nelms
Purchasing: Melanie Mathis
Estimated Sales: $3 Million
Number Employees: 50-99
Square Footage: 80000
Type of Packaging: Consumer, Food Service, Private Label, Bulk
Brands:
Allegro

334 Allegro Winery & Vineyards
3475 Sechrist Rd
Brogue, PA 17309-9415
717-927-9148
Fax: 717-927-1521 info@allegrowines.com
www.cadenzavineyards.com
Wines
Owner: Kris Miller
kris@allegrowines.com
Owner: Carl Helrich
Estimated Sales: $500,000-$1 Million
Number Employees: 1-4
Square Footage: 16000
Brands:
Allegro

335 (HQ)Allen Flavors Inc
23 Progress St
Edison, NJ 08820-1102
908-561-5995
Fax: 908-561-4164 info@allenflavors.com
www.allenflavors.com
Beverage formulation, flavor and ingredient supply company.
President: Joseph Allen
joeyallen@allenflavors.com
VP: Michel Allen
Chemist: Donald Mull
Vice President of Sales & Marketing: Joe Moran
Assistant Vice President: Dana Allen
Estimated Sales: $38.7 Million
Number Employees: 50-99
Square Footage: 300000
Type of Packaging: Bulk
Other Locations:
Wet Blending & Distribution Center
South Plainfield NJ

336 (HQ)Allen Harim Foods LLC
126 N Shipley St
Seaford, DE 19973-3100
302-629-9136
Fax: 302-629-5081 877-397-9191
info@allenharimllc.com www.allenharimllc.com
Poultry products including frozen parts and whole birds; exporter of frozen poultry items
CEO: Steve Evans
Chairman: Warren Allen
CFO: Brian Hildreth
Director of Planning, IT and QA: Allen Harim
Director of Sales and Marketing: Dr.Key Lee
VP Human Resources: Tracy Morris
VP Live Operations: Gary Gladys
Production Coordinator: Karlyn Lemon
Purchasing Director: Gary Lacher
Number Employees: 1000-4999
Type of Packaging: Consumer, Food Service, Private Label, Bulk
Other Locations:
Allen Family Foods
Delmar DE
Allen Family Foods
Hurlock MD
Allen Family Foods
Linkwood MD
Brands:
Allens

337 Allen's Blueberry Freezer Inc
PO Box 536
Ellsworth, ME 04605
207-667-5561
Fax: 207-667-8315 allensblueberries@gmail.com
Frozen wild blueberries.
President/CEO: Roy Allen
allen@acadia.net
Estimated Sales: $10-20 Million
Number Employees: 10-19
Type of Packaging: Consumer, Food Service
Brands:
Allen's

338 Allen's Pickle Works
36 Garvies Point Rd
Glen Cove, NY 11542-2821
516-676-0640
Fax: 516-759-5780 bgpickl@aol.com
www.newyorkdelipickle.com
Cold packed sour dill and half sour pickles including whole, spears and chips.
President: Ronald Horman
Estimated Sales: $2.5-5 Million
Number Employees: 10-19
Square Footage: 72000
Type of Packaging: Private Label
Brands:
Allens
Alma
Butterfield
Clear Sailing

339 Alley Kat Brewing Co, Ltd
9929-60th Avenue
Edmonton, AB T6E 0C7
Canada
780-436-8922
Fax: 780-430-7363 thekats@alleykatbeer.com
www.alleykatbeer.com
Beer, ale, lager and stout
Co-Owner: Neil Herbst
Co-Owner: Lavonne Herbst
Sales Director: Christopher Ducharme
Estimated Sales: $500,000
Number Employees: 8
Square Footage: 15000
Type of Packaging: Consumer, Food Service
Brands:
Alley Kat Amber
Aprikat
Charlie Flint's Original Lager
Ein Prosit!
Full Moon Pale Ale
Olde Deuteronomy
Razzykat
Smoked Porter
St. Paddy's
Weihnachtskatze

340 Allfresh Food Products
2156 Green Bay Rd
Evanston, IL 60201-3046
847-869-3100
Fax: 847-869-3103 www.allfreshfoodproducts.com
Butter blends, margarine, shortening and vegetable oil
President: Gulshan Wadhwa
allfreshfood@aol.com
VP: Anil Wadhwa
Purchasing Manager: Gulshan Wadhwa
Estimated Sales: $5-10 Million
Number Employees: 5-9
Parent Co: Food Corporation of America
Type of Packaging: Consumer, Food Service
Brands:
All Fresh
Big Boy
Buckson
Farmer Brothers
Top Notch

341 Alli & Rose
1422 E Main St
PMB #210
Lincolnton, NC 28092
828-446-8420
Fax: 828-333-5591 customerservice@alli-rose.com
www.alli-rose.com
Chocolate, snacks: pretzels, munchi bites, wafer sticks, veggie straws
Parent Co: C.A.L. Marketing

342 Allied Blending & Ingredients
121 Royal Rd
Keokuk, IA 52632-2028
319-524-1235
Fax: 319-524-9889 800-758-4080
cs@alliedblending.com www.alliedblending.com
Cheese and tortilla products; also baked goods and ingredients.
President: Randy Schmelzel
rschmelzel@alliedblending.com
CFO: Charles Cross
VP Technical Services: John Fannon
Director, Sales & Marketing: Tara Perry
Operations: Matt Stelzer
Plant Manager: Jeff Brunenn
Purchasing: Stephanie Slattery
Number Employees: 50-99
Square Footage: 1200
Brands:
Free Flow®
SureFlo™
SecureFlo™
Flow Lite®
Cheese-Mor™
BatchPak™
No-Stick™

343 (HQ)Allied Custom Gypsum Company
1550 Double Drive
Norman, OK 73069-8288
Fax: 405-366-9515 800-624-5963
customerservice@alliedcustomgypsum.com
www.alliedcustomgypsum.com
Food
Manager & CFO: Tracy Shirley
Executive VP: Dan Northcutt
VP Operations: Kris Kinder
Estimated Sales: $1-5 Million
Number Employees: 10-19
Number of Products: 1
Square Footage: 200000
Parent Co: Harrison Gypsum
Type of Packaging: Food Service
Brands:
Acg
Acg Broadcast Gypsum
Terra Alba
Valu-Fil

344 Allied Food Products
251-253 Saint Marks Ave
Brooklyn, NY 11238
718-230-4227
Fax: 718-230-4229 info@alliedfoodproducts.com
www.alliedfoodproducts.com
Kosher soup and gravy bases, gourmet sauces and dressings, dessert mixes and seasoning blends
General Manager: Ernest Stern
Estimated Sales: $1-2,500,000
Number Employees: 5-9
Brands:
E&S

345 Allied Old English Inc
100 Markley St
Port Reading, NJ 07064-1897
732-602-8955
Fax: 732-636-2538 info@alliedoldenglish.com
www.alliedoldenglish.com
Processor and exporter of Oriental prepared foods including noodles and sauces; also, pancake syrup, molasses, salad dressings, jams, jellies, preserves, salsa and barbecue sauce
President: Brian Dean
COO: Sean Colon
scolon@alliedoldenglish.com
Director of Purchasing: Beverley Gould
Estimated Sales: $8 Million
Number Employees: 50-99
Square Footage: 2000
Type of Packaging: Consumer, Food Service, Private Label, Bulk
Brands:
Ah-So
China Pride
Dai Dairy
Mee Tu
Plantation
Polynesian

Rio Grande
Saucy Susan

346 **Allied Wine Corporation**
70 Berme Rd
Ellenville, NY 12428
845-796-4160
Fax: 845-796-4161 800-796-4100
l.goldman@alliedwine.com www.alliedwine.com
Kosher wines and spirits
Manager: David Fieldman
VP: Herman Schwartz
Estimated Sales: $500,000-$1 Million
Number Employees: 1-4
Type of Packaging: Food Service, Private Label
Brands:
Armon

347 **Alliston Creamery**
26 Dominion Street
Alliston, ON L9R 1L5
Canada
705-435-6751
Fax: 705-435-6797 info@allistoncreamery.com
Butter
President: David Kennedy
Number Employees: 9
Square Footage: 60000
Type of Packaging: Consumer, Food Service, Private Label, Bulk
Brands:
Golden Dawn

348 **Alltech Inc**
3031 Catnip Hill Rd
Nicholasville, KY 40356-9765
859-885-9613
Fax: 859-887-3223 info@alltech.com
www.alltech.com
Meat tenderizers, gelating agents, flavor bases and sequestrants
President & CEO: Mark Lyons
COO: Alric Blake
CFO, North America Feed Division: Nathan Hohman
EVP: E Michael Castle II
Chief Marketing Officer: Orla McAleer
VP Business Development: Marc Larousse
VP Operations: Dan Haney
Estimated Sales: $20-50 Million
Number Employees: 500-999

349 **Alluserv**
4900 W Electric Ave
West Milwaukee, WI 53219
414-902-6400
Fax: 414-902-6446 800-558-8565
info@elakeside.com alluserv.com
Equipment for healthcare food service meal assembly and delivery
President/Owner: Joe Carlson
Principal: Larry Moon
General Manager: Tony Yenzer

350 **Allylix Inc**
7220 Trade St
Suite 209
San Diego, CA 92121
858-909-0595
Fax: 858-909-0695 info@allylix.com
www.allylix.com
Terpene products and derivatives; food ingredients.
President & CEO: Carolyn Fritz
VP Business Development: Seth Goldblum
VP Research & Development: Richard Burlingame
sgoldblum@allylix.com
VP Sales & Marketing: Leandro Nonino
Contact: Seth Goldblum
sgoldblum@allylix.com
Estimated Sales: $280,000
Number Employees: 5-9

351 **Alma Plantation**
4612 Alma Plantation Rd
Lakeland, LA 70752
225-627-6632
www.amscl.org
Blackstrap molasses; beet sugar; pure cane sugar; and raw sugars.
CEO: David Stewart
Year Founded: 1859
Estimated Sales: Less than $500,000
Number Employees: 5-9
Type of Packaging: Bulk

352 **Almark Foods**
2118 Centennial Dr
Gainesville, GA 30504
770-536-4520
Fax: 770-536-4793 800-849-3447
almarkfoods@msn.com www.almarkeggs.com
Egg products
President: Don Stoner
CEO: Mark Papp
Contact: David Cathey
d.cathey@almarkeggs.com
Operations Manager: Paul Heard
Estimated Sales: $5-10 Million
Number Employees: 90
Square Footage: 60000
Type of Packaging: Food Service
Brands:
Almark

353 **Almarla Vineyards & Winery**
Highway 510
Shubuta, MS 39360
601-687-5548
Wines
President: Timothy Dunbar
Brands:
Almarla Black Lightning
Almarla Soul Train
Sautene
Thunder McCloud

354 **Almased USA**
2861 34th Street South
St. Petersburg, FL 33711
727-867-4444
Fax: 727-866-1438 www.almased.com
Meal replacement powder
Number of Brands: 1
Number of Products: 1
Type of Packaging: Consumer
Brands:
ALMASED

355 **Almond Brothers**
4102 Air Lane
Pheonix, AZ 85034
602-955-0909
info@almondbrothers.com
almondbrothers.com
Almonds
Owner: Steve Godber

356 **Almost Nuts**
PO Box 19
Denmark, WI 54208-0019
920-915-0152
sales@soyalmostnuts.com
www.soyalmostnuts.com
Dry roasted soybeans covered in dark chocolate.
Owner: Darren Kornowske
darren@soyalmostnuts.com
Estimated Sales: $80,000
Number Employees: 2
Square Footage: 3890

357 **Aloe Commodities International**
2161 Hutton Dr.
Suite 126
Carrollton, TX 75006-8333
972-241-4251
Fax: 972-241-4376 800-701-2563
Aloe vera products, cosmetics and dietary supplement drinks
President/Director: Mark McKnight
CEO: Scott McKnight
CFO: Richard Ellis
VP Sales/Marketing: Jennifer Larson
COO/General Manager: Fred Lauterbach
Estimated Sales: $20-50 Million
Number Employees: 20-49
Number of Brands: 20
Number of Products: 100
Square Footage: 64000
Type of Packaging: Consumer, Private Label
Brands:
Avera Sport
Carbmate
El Toro Loco
Katahna
Naturally Aloe

358 **Aloe Farms Inc**
3102 Wilson Rd
Harlingen, TX 78552-5011
956-425-1289
Fax: 956-425-3390 800-262-6771
info@aloeverafarms.com www.aloeverafarms.com
Aloe vera juice, gel and capsules.
President: Mark Berry
VP: Elvia Berry
Estimated Sales: Less Than $500,000
Number Employees: 1-4
Square Footage: 4224
Type of Packaging: Consumer, Private Label, Bulk
Brands:
Aloe Farms

359 **Aloe Laboratories**
5821 E Harrison Ave
Harlingen, TX 78550-1811
956-428-8416
Fax: 956-428-8482 800-258-5380
lrodriguez@aloelabs.com www.aloelabs.com
Organic and conventional aloe vera gel, juice, concentrates and powder.
President: Luis Rodriguez
lrodriguez@aolelabs.com
CEO: Hide Aragaki
Operations and Logistics: Mike Hernandez
Estimated Sales: $3-5 Million
Number Employees: 50-99
Square Footage: 160000
Parent Co: Aloe Farms, Inc.
Brands:
Aloe Burst
Aloe Labs

360 **Aloe'Ha Drink Products**
1908 Augusta Drive
Apt 2
Houston, TX 77057-3717
713-978-6359
Fax: 713-978-6858 www.aloeha.com
Carbonated fruit drinks including rasberry, kiwi-strawberry, peach, lemon-lime, etc.
Operations Manager: Doyle Gaskamp
Number Employees: 5
Type of Packaging: Consumer, Food Service
Brands:
Aloe'ha

361 **Aloecorp, Inc.**
3005 1st Ave
Seattle, WA 98121
360-486-7415
800-458-2563
www.aloecorp.com
Aloe vera and other aloe ingredients.
CEO: KS Yoon
Vice President, Chief Scientific Officer: Ken Jones
Quality Unit & Scientific Reg. Affairs: Ramiro Gallegos
Sales Representative: Julia Foo
Customer Service Manager: Norma Garza
Director of Operations: Juan Saldana
Number Employees: 5-9
Other Locations:
Hainan Aloecorp Co. Ltd
Shanghai, China

362 **Aloha Distillers**
5 Sand Island Access Rd
Unit 118
Honolulu, HI 96819-2222
808-841-5787
Fax: 808-847-2903 alohadistillersinc@yahoo.com
Processor and exporter of liqueurs including coffee, chocolate-coconut and chi-chi
President/Purchasing Manager: Dave Fazendin
alohadistillersinc@yahoo.com
Marketing: Ann Fazendin
Estimated Sales: $1-2.5 Million
Number Employees: 1-4
Number of Brands: 1
Number of Products: 1
Type of Packaging: Consumer
Brands:
Coffee
Gold
Kona
Liqueur

363 **Aloha From Oregon**
1471 Railroad Blvd
Unit 6
Eugene, OR 97402-4187
541-343-5519
Fax: 541-343-5499 800-241-0300
www.alohafromoregon.com
Pepper jellies, chutneys, and other specialty items.
President: Judy Dodson
jd@alohafromoregon.com
Estimated Sales: $5-10 Million
Number Employees: 5-9
Type of Packaging: Consumer, Food Service, Private Label

364 **Aloha Poi Factory Inc**
800 Lower Main St
Wailuku, HI 96793-1417
808-244-3536
Fax: 808-244-1914
Poi
President: Lester Nakama
Estimated Sales: $2.5-5 Million
Number Employees: 10-19
Type of Packaging: Consumer, Food Service

365 **Aloha Shoyu Co LTD**
96-1205 Waihona St
Pearl City, HI 96782-1969
808-456-5929
Fax: 808-456-5093 gotshoyu@alohashoyu.com
www.alohashoyu.com
Sauces
President: Brian Tanigawa
btanigawa@alohashoyu.com
Number Employees: 20-49

366 **Aloha Tofu Factory Inc**
961 Akepo Ln
Honolulu, HI 96817-4503
808-845-2669
Fax: 808-848-4607 www.aloha-tofu.com
Tofu
President: Sharren Sakamaki
VP/Office Manager: Jane Uyehara
Estimated Sales: $2.3 Million
Number Employees: 20-49
Square Footage: 44000

367 **Alois J Binder Bakery**
940 Frenchmen St
New Orleans, LA 70116-1683
504-947-1111
Fax: 504-947-1122 www.binderbakery.com
Bread and other bakery products
Owner: Alois Binder Jr
Treasurer: Joseph Binder
Estimated Sales: $4 Million
Number Employees: 20-49
Type of Packaging: Consumer, Food Service, Private Label, Bulk

368 **Alouette Cheese USA**
400 S Custer Ave
New Holland, PA 17557
800-322-2743
customer.service@alouettecheese.com
www.alouettecheese.com
French cheese
President & CEO: Dominique Huth
Director, Research & Development: Steve Schalow
Year Founded: 1974
Estimated Sales: $100 Million
Number Employees: 200-500
Brands:
alouette(c)

369 **Alpen Cellars**
2000 E Fork Rd
Trinity Center, CA 96091
530-266-9513
Fax: 530-266-3363 winemaker@alpencellars.com
www.alpencellars.com
Wine
Owner: Mark Groves
winemaker@alpencellars.com
Winemaker: Keith Grooves
Estimated Sales: Less than $500,000
Number Employees: 10-19
Brands:
Alpen Cellars

370 **Alpen Sierra Coffee Company**
2222 Park Place
Suite 1A
Minden, NV 89423
775-783-7263
Fax: 775-783-7293 800-531-1405
coffeentea@alpensierra.com www.alpensierra.com
Coffee and tea
President: Christian Waskiewicz
coffeentea@alpensierra.com
Marketing: Megan Waskiewicz
Estimated Sales: $1-2.5 Million
Number Employees: 5-9
Brands:
Alpen Sierra

371 **Alpendough**
Cookies and cookie dough
President/Owner: Andrew McKean
Number of Brands: 1
Number of Products: 6
Type of Packaging: Consumer
Brands:
ALPENDOUGH

372 **Alpenglow Beverage Company**
3056 Dismel Hollow Road
Linden, VA 22642
540-635-2118
Fax: 304-229-4377
Kosher, organic/natural, juice/cider, non-alcoholic beverages, RTD-ready to drink (coffee, tea, concentrates, powders).
President: Ben Lacy, III
Marketing: Terry Hess

373 **Alpenrose Dairy**
6149 SW Shattuck Rd
P.O.Box 25030
Portland, OR 97221-1044
503-244-1133
Fax: 503-452-2139 TomBaker@alpenrose.com
www.alpenrose.com
Ice cream; milk; farm eggs; yogurt; orange juice; and butter.
President: Carl Cadanau III
Cmo: Tom Baker
tombaker@alpenrose.com
Operations: Tom Nieradka
Purchasing: Rocky Amick
Estimated Sales: $1.6 Million
Number Employees: 100-249
Type of Packaging: Consumer, Food Service
Brands:
Alpenrose

374 **(HQ)Alpha Baking Company**
1910 Lincoln Way West
South Bend, IN 46628
773-261-6000
spowell@alphabaking.com
www.alphabaking.com
Fresh and frozen bread, buns, and bagels sold through wholesale or retail
CEO: Lawrence Marcucci
Vice President of Division: Gary Narcisi
VP of Sales & Marketing: Tim Gill
Estimated Sales: $7 Million
Number Employees: 1000
Square Footage: 600000
Type of Packaging: Consumer, Food Service
Brands:
S. Rosen's
Natural Ovens Bakery

375 **Alpha Health**
104-3686 Bonneville Place
Burnaby, BC V3N 4T6
Canada
888-826-9625
info@assurednatural.com www.alphahealth.ca
Coconut oil, coconut sugar, coconut flour, MCT oil, red palm oil
Number Employees: 10-19
Parent Co: Assured Natural

376 **Alpina**
5011 AG Park Dr West
Batavia, NY 14020
855-886-1914
alpinaus.com
Smoothies and other dairy products

377 **(HQ)Alpine Butcher**
963 Chelmsford St
Lowell, MA 01851-5131
978-256-7771
Processor of beef, pork, lamb, chicken, seafood and game meat.
President: Peter Doyle
Treasurer: Dennis Doyle
Owner: Greg Doyle
Owner: Thomas Doyle
Year Founded: 1913
Estimated Sales: $20-50 Million
Number Employees: 10-19
Number of Brands: 1
Square Footage: 3000
Type of Packaging: Consumer, Food Service, Private Label, Bulk
Brands:
Doyle's

378 **Alpine Cheese Company**
US Highway 62 E
Winesburg, OH 44690
330-359-6291
Fax: 330-359-0035
Dairy products, natural cheeses and deli
President: Robert Ramseyer
Manager: Joe Nisley
Plant Manager: Brian Barbey
Purchasing Manager: Donald Fudge
Estimated Sales: $35 Million
Number Employees: 45
Type of Packaging: Private Label

379 **Alpine Coffee Roasters**
894 US Highway 2
Suite J
Leavenworth, WA 98826-1340
509-548-3313
Fax: 509-548-4251 800-246-2761
Coffee
Co-Owner: Dale Harrison
Co-Owner: Veronica Harrison
java@alpinecoffeeroasters.com
Roastmaster: Bill Harrison
Estimated Sales: $2.5-5 Million
Number Employees: 1-4
Brands:
Alpine Coffee

380 **Alpine Meats**
7850 Lower Sacramento Rd
Stockton, CA 95210-3912
209-477-2691
Fax: 209-477-1994 800-399-6328
info@alpinemeats.com www.alpinemeats.com
Frankfurters, sausages and hams.
President: Jerry Singer
Quality Control: James Sturgeon
Controller: Cecil McKie
Production: Dennis Saragoza
Purchasing: Robby Jaynes
Estimated Sales: $8 Million
Number Employees: 50-99
Square Footage: 196000
Type of Packaging: Consumer, Food Service, Private Label, Bulk
Brands:
Alpine

381 **Alpine Pure USA**
421 Currant Road
Falls River, MA 02720
617-548-8301
Fax: 888-311-6541 888-332-3392
www.alpinepure.net
Teas

382 **Alpine Start Foods**
1911 11th St
Suite 207
Boulder, CO 80302
info@alpinestartfoods.com
alpinestartfoods.com
Instant coffee
Number of Brands: 1
Number of Products: 1
Type of Packaging: Consumer
Brands:
ALPINE START

383 **Alpine Touch Spices**
101 3rd St
714 Main Avenue North
Choteau, MT 59422
406-466-2063
Fax: 406-466-2076 877-755-2525
montanaalpinetouch@gmail.com
www.alpinetouch.com
Seasonings
Owner: Mark Southard
Co-Owner: Vicki Southard
Estimated Sales: $500,000-$1 Million
Number Employees: 1-4

384 **Alpine Valley Water**
16900 Lathrop Ave
Harvey, IL 60426
708-333-3910
Fax: 708-333-3921 sales@AlpineValleyWater.com
www.alpinevalleywater.com
Distilled and bottled water
Owner: Tim Rausch
Estimated Sales: Less than $500,000
Number Employees: 1-4
Square Footage: 40000
Type of Packaging: Food Service
Brands:
Alpine Valley

385 **Alpine Vineyards**
25904 Green Peak Rd
Monroe, OR 97456-9773
541-424-5851
Fax: 541-424-5891 www.actionnet.net
Wines
Owner: Dan Jepsen
alpinevineyards@actionnet.net
Estimated Sales: $1-2.5 Million
Number Employees: 5-9

386 **Alsum Farms & Produce**
N9083 County Road E
Cambria, WI 53923-9668
920-348-5127
Fax: 920-348-5174 800-236-5127
www.alsum.com
Potatoes and onions; fresh fruits and vegetables.
President & CEO: Larry Alsum
CEO: Randy Fischer
randy.fischer@alsum.com
National Sales & Marketing Manager: Heidi Alsum-Randall
Year Founded: 1972
Number Employees: 100-249
Number of Brands: 4
Number of Products: 300
Type of Packaging: Consumer, Food Service, Private Label, Bulk
Brands:
Alsum Farms & Produce
Alsum Organics
Rainbow Organics
Family Favorite

387 **Alta Dena Certified Dairy LLC**
17851 E Railroad
City Of Industry, CA 91748
626-923-3182
800-535-1369
www.altadenadairy.com
Dairy products.
Logistics: Carl Reynolds
Year Founded: 1945
Estimated Sales: $48.1 Million
Number Employees: 500-999
Square Footage: 100000
Parent Co: Dean Foods
Brands:
Alta Dena Classic
Caribbean Chill
Crazy Cow
Dairy Mart
Decadent Temptations
Le Younghurt
Old Tyme

388 **Alta Dena Heartland Farms**
17851 Railroad St
City Of Industry, CA 91748-1118
626-923-3000
Fax: 626-923-3038 800-395-7004
deanfoods@casupport.com
www.heartlandfarms.com
Dairy products
Manager: Mary Armstrong
mary.armstrong@heartlandfarms.com
Number Employees: 250-499
Square Footage: 500000
Parent Co: Dean Foods
Type of Packaging: Consumer, Private Label
Other Locations:
Heartland Farms Distribution
Anaheim CA
Heartland Farms Distribution
San Diego CA
Heartland Farms Distribution
El Centro CA
Heartland Farms Distribution
Ventura CA
Heartland Farms Distribution
Santa Barbara CA
Heartland Farms Distribution
Desert Hot Springs CA
Brands:
Knudsen®
Foremost®
Arnold Palmer
Trumoo Chocolate Milk
Swiss Premium

389 **Alta Health Products**
300 Main St
Idaho City, ID 83631
208-392-4170
Fax: 208-392-4185 800-423-4155
info@altahealthproducts.com
www.altahealthproducts.com
Herbal supplements, teas and minerals
President: Judy Haswell
Founder: Richard Barmakian
Vice President: Deborah Saw Kims
Product Promotion: Kelli Fischer
Estimated Sales: Less than $500,000
Number Employees: 1-4
Brands:
Alta

390 **Alta Vineyard Cellar**
PO Box 980
3081 Lake County Hwy
Calistoga, CA 94515-0980
707-942-6708
Fax: 707-942-5065
Wines
President: Benjamin Falk
Estimated Sales: $500,000-$1 Million
Number Employees: 1-4
Brands:
Alta

391 **Altamura Winery**
1700 Wooden Valley Rd
Napa, CA 94558-9617
707-253-2000
Fax: 707-255-3937 altamurawinery@aol.com
www.altamura.com
Wines
President: Frank C Altamura
Estimated Sales: $3-5 Million
Number Employees: 5-9
Number of Brands: 1
Number of Products: 2

392 **Alter Eco**
2339 3rd St
Suite 70
San Francisco, CA 94107-3100
415-701-1214
Fax: 415-701-1213 sales@alterecofoods.com
www.alterecofoods.com
Fair trade and organic quinoa, rice, sugar, cacao
Co-founder/Co-CEO: Edouard Rollet
Co-founder/Co-CEO: Mathieu Senard
President: Kate Tierney
Quality Assurance: Anissa Bouziane
Director, Marketing: Antoine Ambert
Director, Operations: Jeanne Cloutier
Number Employees: 1-4

393 **Alternative Health & Herbs**
425 Jackson St SE
Albany, OR 97321
541-791-8400
Fax: 541-791-8401 800-345-4152
healthinfo@healthherbs.com
www.healthherbs.com
Liquid herbal formulations; herbal teas and vitamins.
Owner: Bishop Truman Berst
Estimated Sales: Less than $500,000
Number Employees: 1-4
Square Footage: 12000
Type of Packaging: Consumer, Private Label, Bulk
Brands:
American Health & Herbs Ministry
American Naturals
Truman's

394 **Alto Rey Food Corp**
11468 Dona Teresa Dr
Studio City, CA 91604-4271
323-969-0178
Fax: 323-969-0197
Condiments, dips, salsas, dressings
President: David Ufberg
davidu@altorey.com
Estimated Sales: $1-2.5 Million
Number Employees: 1-4
Brands:
Alto Rey

395 **Alto Vineyards & Winery**
8515 Highway 127
Alto Pass, IL 62905-2033
618-893-4898
Fax: 618-893-4935 www.altovineyards.net
Wines
President / General Manager: Paul Renzaglia
altovin@midwest.net
Estimated Sales: $5-10 Million
Number Employees: 5-9
Type of Packaging: Bulk
Other Locations:
Alto Vineyards
Champaign IL

396 **Alvalle**
Denver, CO 80212
www.alvalle.us
Gazpacho
Brands:
ALOHA

397 **Alvarado Street Bakery**
2225 S McDowell Blvd.
Petaluma, CA 94954-5661
707-789-6700
Fax: 707-283-0350
info@alvaradostreetbakery.com
www.alvaradostreetbakery.com
Organic goods including sprouted wheat bread, kosher bagels, tortillas and whole grain and oil-free granola; exporter of frozen organic wheat bread and kosher bagels.
CEO: Bryan Long
Sales Director: Jim Canterbury
Purchasing: Jamie Mitchell
Year Founded: 1979
Estimated Sales: $23 Million
Number Employees: 100-249
Number of Brands: 2
Number of Products: 27
Square Footage: 75000
Type of Packaging: Consumer, Private Label
Brands:
Alvarado Street Bakery

398 **Alvita**
8600 Transit Dr
Suite B1
Amherst, NY 14051
833-258-4821
www.alvita.com
Herbal teas and supplement.
Year Founded: 1922
Estimated Sales: $100+ Million
Number Employees: 250-499
Parent Co: Twinlab
Brands:
Alvita Tea
Remeteas Detoxitea
Remeteas Masculinitea
Remeteas Pms Rescue
Remeteas Visibilitea

399 **Alya Foods**
2227 US Hwy 1 #279
North Brunswick, NJ 08902
917-495-0815
info@alyafoods.com
www.alyafoods.com
Dates

400 **Alyeska Seafoods**
551 W Broadway
P.O. Box 530
Unalaska, AK 99685
907-581-1211
Fresh and frozen seafoods
Sales Coordinator: Theresa Koonce
Estimated Sales: $50-100 Million
Number Employees: 20-49
Parent Co: Maruha Nichiro Corporation

401 **AmByth Estate**
510 Sequoia Ln
Templeton, CA 93465
805-319-6967
gelert@ambythestate.com
www.ambythestate.com
Organic vineyard
Co-Owner: Mary Hart
Co-Owner: Gelert Hart
Estimated Sales: Less than $500,000
Number Employees: 1-4

402 **AmTech Ingredients**
573 County Route A
Suite 102
Hudson, WI 54016
715-381-5746
www.amtechingredients.com
Producer/distributor of specialty food ingredients, primarily in powder form.
Contact: Andrew Brudevold
abrudevold@amtechingredients.com
Estimated Sales: $330,000
Number Employees: 3
Square Footage: 6734

403 **Amador Foothill Winery**
12500 Steiner Rd
Plymouth, CA 95669-9510
209-245-6307
Fax: 209-245-3280 800-778-9463
info@amadorfoothill.com
Wines
Owner/President: Ben Zeitman
Owner/Winemaker: Katie Quinn
katie@amadorfoothill.com
Estimated Sales: Less Than $500,000
Number Employees: 1-4
Type of Packaging: Private Label
Brands:
Amador Foothill

404 **Amafruits**
8940 W 192nd St
Suite C
Mokena, IL 60448
877-818-1262
custserv@amafruits.com www.amafruits.com
Fruit purees & sorbets
Number of Brands: 1
Number of Products: 11
Type of Packaging: Consumer
Brands:
AMAFRUITS

405 **Amalfitano's Italian Bakery**
29 E Commons Blvd
Suite 700
New Castle, DE 19720-1740
302-324-9005
Fax: 302-324-9008
Bakery products
Owner: Ralph Jacobs
Estimated Sales: $2.5-5 Million
Number Employees: 20-49

406 **Amalgamated Produce**
P.O. Box 5159
1318 Kossuth Street
Bridgeport, CT 06610
203-366-6919
Fax: 203-339-3773 800-358-3808
www.inbusiness.com
Bean soup mixes, dried fruits, stuffings, sprout products and wild rice dishes.
CEO/President: Richard Blackwell
Chief Executive Officer: Richard Westin
Vice President: Adriana Alvarez
Estimated Sales: $10-50 Million
Number Employees: 20-49
Square Footage: 24000
Brands:
Specialty Farms

407 **Amalgamated Sugar Company**
1951 S. Saturn Way
Suite 100
Boise, ID 83709
208-383-6500
Fax: 208-383-6688 www.amalgamatedsugar.com
Beet sugar.
President/CEO: John McCreedy
Chairman: Duane Grant
VP of Finance: Craig Hanks
Executive VP/Chief Buisness Dev. Officer: Joe Huff
Vice President, Operations: Kent Quinney
Year Founded: 1897
Estimated Sales: $907 Million
Number Employees: 1,600+
Square Footage: 20000
Parent Co: Snake River Sugar Company
Type of Packaging: Consumer, Food Service, Private Label, Bulk
Brands:
White Satin®

408 **Amalthea Cellars Farm Winery**
209 Vineyard Rd
Atco, NJ 08004-2369
856-768-8585
AmaltheaCellars@gmail.com
www.amaltheacellars.com
Wines
Owner: Louis Caracciolo
Manager: Virginia Caracciolo
Estimated Sales: $1-2.5 Million
Number Employees: 5-9

409 **Amana Meat Shop & SmokeHouse**
4513 F St
Amana, IA 52203-8027
319-622-7586
Fax: 319-622-6245 800-373-6328
info@amanameatshop.com
Hickory-smoked meats including sausage, ham, bacon, pork tenderloin and bratwurst.
Manager: Greg Hergert
Director: Mike Shoup
Estimated Sales: Less than $500,000
Number Employees: 10-19
Parent Co: Amana Society Corporation
Type of Packaging: Consumer, Food Service
Brands:
Amana Meats

410 **Amanda Hills Spring Water**
9756 National Road SW
PO Box 301
Etna, OH 43018
740-927-3422
Fax: 740-927-1856 800-375-0885
info@amandahills.com www.amandahills.com
Spring water
Owner: David Betts
Contact: Michael Betts
michael@amandahills.com
Estimated Sales: $300,000-500,000
Number Employees: 1-4
Number of Brands: 1
Square Footage: 40000
Type of Packaging: Private Label
Brands:
Amanda Hills

411 **Amanida USA Corp**
2655 Lejeune Rd
Suite 810
Coral Gables, FL 33134
amanida.com/en/
Gourmet Italian and Spanish products
Parent Co: Amanida

412 **Amano Artisan Chocolate**
496 S 1325 W
Orem, UT 84058-5877
801-655-1996
amano@amanochocolate.com
www.amanochocolate.com
Chocolates
Owner: Art Pollard
Pastry Chef: Rebecca Millican
Number Employees: 20-49
Type of Packaging: Private Label
Brands:
Amano Ocumare
Amano Jenbrana

413 **Amano Enzyme USA Company, Ltd**
1415 Madeline Ln
Elgin, IL 60124
847-649-0101
Fax: 847-649-0205 800-446-7652
sales@amanoenzymeusa.com
Non-animal and non-GMO enzymes for the dietary supplement, nutraceutical, food, diagnostic and pharmaceutical industries.
President: Motoyuki Amano
VP Science/Technology: James Jolly
Contact: Kumiko Paik
kpaik@amanoenzymeusa.com
Estimated Sales: $15 Million
Number Employees: 440
Square Footage: 50000
Parent Co: Amano Enzyme

414 **Amano Fish Cake Factory**
30 Holomua St
Hilo, HI 96720-5102
808-935-5555
Fax: 808-961-2154
Frozen and canned fish cakes
Owner: Hiroshi Mathubara
Estimated Sales: $1-2.5 Million
Number Employees: 5-9
Type of Packaging: Consumer
Brands:
Amano

415 **Amara Organic Baby Food**
584 Page St
San Francisco, CA 94117
267-981-6411
hello@amaraorganicfoods.com
amaraorganicfoods.com
Baby food
Number of Brands: 1
Type of Packaging: Consumer
Brands:
AMARA

416 **Amaranth Resources**
139 E William Street
Suite 325
Albert Lea, MN 56007-2535
507-373-0356
Fax: 507-373-4753 800-842-6689
Grains, cereals, spices, seasonings, condiments, allergy free products
CEO: Edward Hubbard
Vice President: R Merrell
Estimated Sales: $2.5-5 Million
Brands:
Ambake
Amban
Amburst
Amgrain
Best of Health

417 **Amavi Cellars**
3796 Peppers Bridge Rd
Walla Walla, WA 99362-7007
509-525-3541
Fax: 509-522-5011 info@amavicellars.com
www.amavicellars.com
Wines
Winemaker/Partner: Jean Francois Pellet
Partner: Eric McKibben
Partner: Travis Goff
Partner: Shane McKibben
Managing Partner: Ray Goff
Tasting Room Manager: Patty Lynch
Number Employees: 5-9

418 **Amazing Candy Craft Company**
18408 Jamaica Avenue
Hollis, NY 11423-2431
718-264-3031
Fax: 718-264-8437 800-429-9368
Candy
President: Frank Salacuse
VP: Catherine Salacuse
VP Marketing/Sales: Brad Demsky
Brands:
Candy Activity
Make Your Own Gummies

419 **Amazing Fruit Products**
501 Airport Rd
Fort Payne, AL 35968
256-273-5363
info@afp-us.com
amazingfruitproducts.com
Flavor-infused raisins
Number of Brands: 1
Number of Products: 7
Type of Packaging: Consumer
Brands:
AMAZIN' RAISIN

420 **Amazing Herbs Nutraceuticals**
2709 Faith Industrial Dr
Ste 500
Buford, GA 30518-3564
770-982-4780
Fax: 770-982-0273 800-241-9138
info@amazingherbs.com www.amazingherbs.com
Supplements and natural products
Owner: Tony Goreja
Brands:
Amazing Herbs
Theramune Nutritionals

421 **Amazon Trading, Ltd.**
257 Siri Dhamma Mawatha
Colombo, 10
Sri Lanka
www.amazontea.biz
Loose leaf teas and tea bags.
Owner: Gamini Jayaweera
CEO: Suranga Herath
Square Footage: 80000
Brands:
Tea of Life
SUN LEAF

422 **Amberg Wine Cellars**
2412 Seneca Castle Orleans Road
Clifton Springs, NY 14432
315-462-3455
Fax: 315-462-6512 www.ambergwine.com
Wines
Owner: Ute Amberg
President: Herman Amberg
CFO: Eric Amberg
Marketing Manager: Debbie Amberg
Estimated Sales: $500,000-$1 Million
Number Employees: 1-4
Type of Packaging: Private Label
Brands:
Amberg Wine Cellars

423 **Amberland Foods**
1350 Frontage Road
Harvey, ND 58341
701-324-4804
Fax: 701-324-4805 800-950-4558
amberlandfoods@gondtc.com
Dehydrated soup mixes, scone and dip mixes, jams, jellies, seasonings, syrups and toppings
Owner/Manager: Susan K Schwarz
Operations Manager: Elreen Olson
Estimated Sales: $1-2.5 Million
Number Employees: 10-19
Number of Brands: 1
Number of Products: 50
Square Footage: 16000
Type of Packaging: Consumer, Private Label
Brands:
Dakota Seasonings

424 **Ambootia Tea Estate**
PO Box 11696
400 N McClurg Ct, Suite 1103
Chicago, IL 60611-0696
312-661-1550
Fax: 312-661-1523 www.teareport.com
Tea
President: Shashank Goel
Estimated Sales: Less than $500,000
Number Employees: 5-9
Brands:
Ambootia

425 **Ambrosi Cheese USA**
57-01 49th Place
Maspeth, NY 11378
USA
sales@ambrosifoodusa.com
Cheese
Owner: Ottorino Ambrosi
Sales & Marketing: Giacomo Veraldi

426 **Ambrosial Granola**
Po Box 090712
Brooklyn, NY 11209
718-491-1335
Fax: 718-425-9932
Granola cereals
President: Hariclia Makoulis

427 **Amcan Beverages Inc**
1201 Commerce Blvd
American Canyon, CA 94503-9611
707-557-0500
Fax: 707-557-0100 800-972-5962
www.pokka.com.sg
Fruit juices, canned iced coffee, iced tea and yogurt flavored drinks
President: Don Soetaert
CFO: George Lewis
Vice President: Joe Inazuka
Manager: Dave Baldwin
dabaldwin@na.ko.com
Estimated Sales: $18 Million
Number Employees: 100-249
Square Footage: 500000
Parent Co: Pokka Corporation
Type of Packaging: Private Label
Brands:
Fruit Ole
Hawaiian Sun
Premium Tea
The Coffee

428 **Amcan Industries**
570 Taxter Road
Elmsford, NY 10523-2356
914-347-4838
Fax: 914-347-4960
Meat, jam, jelly, preserves, health food, nutriceuticals, confectionery, fish, seafood, dairy, beverage and juices, bakery and cereal, natural and artificial sweeteners
President: Bowes Dempsey
VP: Benjamin Dempsey
Contact: Guylaine Boucher
guylaine@dempseycorporation.com
Estimated Sales: $5-10 Million
Number Employees: 7

429 **Amelia Bay**
3851 Lakefield Dr
Suite 120
Suwanee, GA 30024-1242
770-772-6360
Fax: 770-772-4766 www.ameliabay.com
Liquid concentrates for coffees, teas, cappucinos, chais.
President: John Crandall
john@ameliabay.com
Sales Manager: Ralph Lane
Estimated Sales: $5-10 Million
Number Employees: 5-9
Type of Packaging: Food Service

430 **Amella**
214 Main Street
Suite 376
El Segundo, CA 90245
USA
Fax: 310-388-3105 800-205-0080
Carmel candy
Owner: Elena Kiamileva
Contact: Emir Kiamilev
ekiamilev@amellacaramels.com

431 **Ameri Candy**
3618 Saint Germaine Ct
Louisville, KY 40207-3722
502-583-1776
Fax: 502-583-1776 omar@americandybar.com
www.americandybar.com
Chocolates
Owner: Omar Patum
omar@americandybar.com
Estimated Sales: Less than $500,000
Number Employees: 1-4
Type of Packaging: Consumer, Private Label, Bulk
Brands:
Americandy
Asher
Jim Candy
Rooster Run

432 **Ameri-Kal Inc**
5405 Centime Drive
Suite 400
Wichita Falls, TX 76305-5271
940-322-5400
Nutritional supplements, vitamins, minerals, herbal formulations, sports nutrition products, herb flavored grapeseed oil, capsules, tablets, bulk powder, liquids, soft gel, etc.
Director: Djoko Soejoto
CEO: Tom Soejoto
Director/Of Marketing: Ron Soejoto
Contact: Keith Mccray
keith@ameri-kal.com
Number Employees: 18
Square Footage: 142000
Type of Packaging: Private Label, Bulk

433 **Ameri-Suisse Group**
157 Helen Street
South Plainfield, NJ 07080
908-222-1001
Fax: 732-222-1929
Novelty candies
Owner: Lew Demeter

434 **AmeriGift**
P.O. Box 5767
2300 Celcius Avenue
Oxnard, CA 93030
805-988-0350
Fax: 805-988-4668 800-421-9039
Candy gift items
Owner: Lionel Meff
Estimated Sales: $2.5-5 Million
Number Employees: 50-99
Brands:
Amerigift Sweet Tooth Originals
Ghirardelli

435 **AmeriQual Foods**
18200 Highway 41 North
Evansville, IN 47725
812-867-1444
Fax: 812-867-0278 www.ameriqual.com
Supplier of pre-made food items and manufacturer of heat-sealed microwavable bowls, trays and flexible pouches
CEO: Steve Chancellor
CFO: Sandra Rasche
Finance: Dave Barnes
Contact: Casey Elliott
casey.elliott@thementornetwork.com
Number Employees: 650
Other Locations:
AmeriQual Packaging
Evansville IN

436 **America's Catch**
PO Box 584
Itta Bena, MS 38941
662-254-7207
Fax: 662-254-9776 800-242-0041
solons@catfish.com www.catfish.com
Fresh and frozen farm-raised catfish
President: Solon Scott
VP Sales: John Nelms
Plant Manager: Bill Martin
Estimated Sales: $20-50 Million
Number Employees: 250-499
Type of Packaging: Consumer, Food Service, Private Label, Bulk
Brands:
America's Catch

437 **America's Classic Foods**
1298 Warren Rd
Cambria, CA 93428-4642
805-927-0745
Fax: 805-927-2280 webmail@amcf.com
www.amcf.com
Powdered ice cream mix, ice cream freezers, processor and exporter of mixes including ice cream, baking, doughnut, etc.
President: Monty Rice
mgr@amcf.com
Estimated Sales: $1 Million
Number Employees: 1-4
Square Footage: 120000
Type of Packaging: Food Service, Private Label, Bulk
Brands:
America's Classic Foods
American Creamery

Empower
Mommy's Choice
Smooth & Creamy

438 American Almond Products Co
103 Walworth St
Brooklyn, NY 11205-2807
718-875-8310
Fax: 718-935-1505 800-825-6663
info@americanalmond.com
Processed nuts, natural nut butters & pastes, specialty pastes, marzipan, lekvar, poppy butter, piping gelee, crunch toppings and coconut macaroon mix.
President: Kevin Burn
kbyrne@americanalmond.com
Customer Service: Priscilla Morales
Estimated Sales: $5-10 Million
Number Employees: 20-49
Square Footage: 160000
Type of Packaging: Consumer, Food Service, Private Label, Bulk
Brands:
America Almond
American Almond

439 American Beverage Marketers
New Albany, IN 47151
812-944-3585
abm@abmcocktails.com
abmcocktails.com
Liquid cocktail mixes
Brands:
Agalima
Master of Mixes
Finest Call
Re...l Cocktail

440 American Biosciences
560 Bradley Parkway
Blauvelt, NY 10913
845-727-0800
888-884-7770
info@americanbiosciences.com
www.americanbiosciences.com
Herbs and supplements.
President: David Wales
Vice President: Rick Jahnke
Estimated Sales: $5-10 Million
Number Employees: 5-9
Type of Packaging: Consumer

441 American Blanching Company
155 Rip Wiley Rd
PO Box 1028
Fitzgerald, GA 31750
229-423-4098
Fax: 229-423-3842 info@AmericanBlanching.com
www.americanblanching.com
Blanched peanuts
President/CEO: Jack Warden
Contact: Michael Davis
mdavis@americanblanching.com

442 American Botanicals
24750 Highway Ff
Eolia, MO 63344
573-485-2300
Fax: 573-485-3801 800-684-6070
info@americanbotanicals.com
www.americanbotanicals.com
American herbs.
President: Allen Lockard
ambotncls@aol.com
Quality Control: Denise Kunzweiler
Operations: Chris Zumwalt
Milling Production: Ron Kunzweiler
Purchasing Agent: Tom Duncan
Purchasing Agent: Gennie Martinez
Estimated Sales: $12 Million
Number Employees: 20-49
Number of Products: 200
Square Footage: 35000
Type of Packaging: Bulk

443 American Bottling & Beverage
1756 Industrial Rd
Walterboro, SC 29488-9368
843-538-7937
Fax: 801-975-7185 www.abbperformance.com
Sport beverages
Owner: Olivia Hall
Manager: Ken Farley
kfarley@glanbia.com
Number Employees: 20-49

444 American Canadian Fisheries
6069 Hannegan Rd
Bellingham, WA 98226
360-398-1117
Fax: 360-398-8801 800-344-7942
Fish and gift boxes
President: Andy Vitaljic
Estimated Sales: $500,000-$1 Million
Number Employees: 1-4
Brands:
Hannegan Seafoods

445 American Chalkis Intl. Food Corp.
20120 Paseo Del Prado Ste A
Walnut, CA 91789
562-232-4105
Fax: 562-232-4106 info@chalkistomato.us
Tomato products & tomato paste, apricot puree, pomegranate, apple & grape concentrates.

446 American Cheesemen
PO Box 261
2522 South Shore Dr
Clear Lake, IA 50428-0261
641-357-7176
Fax: 641-357-7177
Cheese
President: Paul Austin
Estimated Sales: $5-10 Million
Number Employees: 1-4
Brands:
American Cheesemen
Choppin N Block
E-Z Keep

447 American Classic Ice Cream Company
1565 5th Industrial Ct
Bay Shore, NY 11706
631-666-1000
Fax: 631-666-2934 800-736-4100
www.americanclassicicecream.com
Ice cream and novelties including sandwiches, cups, pies, etc.; also, toppings
Owner: Edgar Williams
Owner/VP: Gregory Kronrad
Contact: Greg Kronrad
gregkronrad@yahoo.com
General Manager: Theresa Bellizzi
Estimated Sales: Under $500,000
Number Employees: 5-9
Type of Packaging: Consumer, Food Service

448 American Copak Corporation
9175 Eton Ave
Chatsworth, CA 91311-5806
818-576-1000
Fax: 818-882-1637 www.americancopak.com
Bakers' and confectioners' supplies, beverages, candy, cereals, snack foods, condiments, dairy products, spreads, kosher foods, mixes, pasta, sauces, soups, sugar, syrups, etc.
President: Steven Brooker
Business Development: Wanda Walk
Estimated Sales: $5-10 Million
Number Employees: 50-99
Square Footage: 400000

449 American Crystal Sugar Co.
101 N. 3rd St.
Moorhead, MN 56560
218-236-4400
feedback@crystalsugar.com
www.crystalsugar.com
Sugarbeet cooperative.
President/CEO: Thomas Astrup
Year Founded: 1899
Estimated Sales: Over $1 Billion
Number Employees: 1000-4999
Type of Packaging: Consumer, Private Label, Bulk
Other Locations:
Crookston MN
Drayton ND
East Grand Forks MN
Hillsboro ND
Corporate Headquarters
Moorhead MN
Sidney MT

450 American Culinary Garden
3508 E Division St
Springfield, MO 65802-2499
417-799-1410
Fax: 417-831-9933 888-831-2433
Balsamic vinegar and soy sauce and also dessert glazes and burgundy soy marinade.
Manager/Sales Director: Gary Anderson
Vice President: Judy Sipe
Order Desk: Lisa Clifford
Estimated Sales: $2.5-5 Million
Number Employees: 1
Type of Packaging: Consumer, Food Service
Brands:
American Culinary Gardens
Teatro

451 American Dehydrated Foods, Inc.
3801 E Sunshine St
PO Box 4087
Springfield, MO 65809-2800
417-881-7755
Fax: 417-881-4963 800-456-3447
info@adf.com www.adf.com
Dehydrated foods.
Chairman: Thomas Slaight
CEO: Kurt Hellweg
President: Mike Gerke
Contact: Dan Beeman
dbeeman@adfinc.com
Plant Manager: Mike Scabarozi
Estimated Sales: $20-50 Million
Number Employees: 20-49
Number of Brands: 1
Brands:
ADF

452 American Egg Products Inc
375 Pierce Industrial Blvd
Blackshear, GA 31516-2358
912-449-5700
Fax: 912-449-2438 www.calmainefoods.com
Egg products
President: James D Hull
CEO: Ken Looper
CFO: Richard Looper
Office Manager: Michelle Kersey
Estimated Sales: $7 Million
Number Employees: 50-99
Parent Co: Cal-Maine Foods, Inc.

453 American Fine Food Corporation
3600 NW 114th Ave
Doral, FL 33178-1842
305-392-5000
Fax: 305-392-5400
Groceries
President: Sam Amoudi
Marketing/Export Manager: Fadi Ladki
Estimated Sales: $5-10 Million
Number Employees: 5-9

454 American Flatbread
Pittsfield, NH 03263
603-435-5119
info@americanflatbreadproducts.com
americanflatbreadproducts.com
Flatbreads
President: George Schenk
flatbread@americanflatbread.com
VP: Camilla Behn
Marketing Director: Jennifer Moffroid
Manager: Paul Krcmar
Purchasing: Amy Troiano
Estimated Sales: $13.9 Million
Number Employees: 20-49

455 American Food Ingredients Inc
4021 Avenida DE LA Plata
Suite 501
Oceanside, CA 92056-5849
760-967-6287
Fax: 760-967-1952 amerfood@aol.com
www.americanfoodingredients.com
Dehydrated fruits and vegetables, mushrooms, truffles, non GMO ingredients, salt and salt mixtures, seasonings, spices and herbs
President/CEO: Karen Koppenhaver
amerfood@aol.com
Estimated Sales: $5-10 Million
Number Employees: 20-49
Brands:
American Food

456 American Food Products Inc
983 Riverside Dr
Methuen, MA 01844
978-682-1855
www.candybreak.com
Candy
Year Founded: 1950
Estimated Sales: $50-100 Million
Number Employees: 50-99
Type of Packaging: Private Label, Bulk

457 American Foods Group LLC
500 S. Washington St.
Green Bay, WI 54301-4219
800-345-0293
info@AmericanFoodsGroup.com
www.americanfoodsgroup.com
Beef products.
President/COO: Steven Van Lannen
Chairman/CEO: Tom Rosen
CFO: David Jagodzinske
Executive Vice President: Jeff Jones
Year Founded: 2005
Estimated Sales: $225.5 Million
Number Employees: 4,500
Square Footage: 60000
Parent Co: Rosen's Diversified, Inc.
Type of Packaging: Consumer, Food Service
Other Locations:
Mitchell SD
Sharonville OH
Brands:
Halal Meats
America's Heartland Organic Beef
Server's Choice
Meyer Natural Angus Beef
Sheboygan Sausage Company
Skylark
Big City Reds
Great American Hamburgers
Rock River Cattle

458 American Fruits & Flavors
10725 Sutter Ave
Pacoima, CA 91331
818-899-9574
SalesTeam@americanfruit.com
www.americanfruits-flavors.com
Custom flavors, fruit juice blends, natural sweeteners, juice concentrates and liquid powder blends. Specializing in fruit, vegetable, sweet and savory flavors, flavor bases, fruit concentrates, coconut products, smoothies, andtropical blends.
President: Bill Haddad
CEO: Rodney Sacks
Corporate Controller: Michael Model
Senior Research & Development Chemist: Martin Goldberg
Quality Control Chemist: Linda Valenzuela
VP of Marketing: Richard Linn
Director of Human Resources: Regina Rodriguez
Year Founded: 2016
Estimated Sales: $168 Million
Number Employees: 100-249
Square Footage: 20000
Parent Co: Monster Beverage Corporation

459 American Halal Company
1177 Summer St
3rd Floor
Stamford, CT 06905
203-961-1954
877-425-2587
info@saffronroadfood.com saffronroadfood.com
Gourmet foods
Chief Executive Officer: Adnan Durrani

460 American Hawaiian Soy Company
274 Kalihi Street
Honolulu, HI 96819
808-841-8435
800-841-8435
Soybean
President: John Morita

461 American Health
2100 Smithtown Avenue
Ronkonkoma, NY 11779
631-244-2021
Fax: 631-244-1777 800-445-7137
www.americanhealthus.com
Vitamins, minerals, food supplements
President/CEO: Dorie Greenblatt
doriegreenblatt@americanhealthus.com
Vice President: Robert Silverman
Estimated Sales: $3-5 Million
Number Employees: 5-9
Type of Packaging: Consumer

462 American Importing Co.
550 Kasota Ave SE
Minneapolis, MN 55414
855-273-0466
www.amportfoods.com
Snack foods including trail mixes, dried fruits and sunflower seeds.
President: Jeff Vogel
Contact: Kim Ewanika
kim@amportfoods.com
Parent Co: Flagstone Foods
Type of Packaging: Consumer, Private Label, Bulk
Brands:
Amport Foods
Dessert Jewell
Salad Expressions

463 American Ingredients Co
7905 Quivira Rd
Lenexa, KS 66215-2732
913-888-4540
Fax: 913-888-4970 800-669-4092
info@caravaningredients.com
Food ingredients including fortification, emulsifiers, functional blends, bakery mixes and bases, frozen dough, and fillings, icings and glazes
President: Les Stanbery
Chairman: Jaap Vink
VP CFO: Joel Krichiver
Product Manager: Dave Pfefer
Marketing Director: Kerrie Medlicott
VP Sales: Jim Eastan
VP Human Resources: Pam Parker
Engineering Director: Bill Becicka
Director of Operations: Gordon Nolan
Plant Manager: Ian Trod
Number Employees: 350
Type of Packaging: Food Service, Bulk
Other Locations:
North Kansas City MO
Mississauga ON
Brands:
Invisible Goodness
Nutrivan
Trancendim
Pristine
Bake-Soft
Alphadim
Bfp
Pationic

464 American Instants Inc
117 Bartley Flanders Rd
Flanders, NJ 07836
973-584-8811
sales@americaninstants.com
www.americaninstants.com
Instant coffees and teas, cappuccino, granita, chai, fresh brew tea, hot chocolate, drink mixes and liquid coffee extract
President: Martin Wagner
CEO: Christopher Roche
rshipe@americaninstants.com
Director, R&D: Kristin Truglio
Estimated Sales: $30 Million
Number Employees: 50-99
Square Footage: 72000
Type of Packaging: Food Service, Private Label
Brands:
Cappuccino Supreme
Deep Rich
Hot Chocolate Supreme

465 (HQ)American Italian Pasta Company
1000 Italian Way
Excelsior Springs, MO 64024
877-328-7278
www.makesameal.com
Dry pasta
President, TreeHouse Foods: Dennis Riordan
CEO, TreeHouse Foods: Sam Reed
Parent Co: TreeHouse Private Brands, Inc.
Type of Packaging: Consumer, Food Service, Private Label, Bulk
Other Locations:
Columbia SC
Kenosha WI
Brands:
Ronco
Anthony's
Luxury
Mueller's
Pennsylvania Dutch
Golden Grain
Heartland

466 American Key Food Products Inc
1 Reuten Dr
Closter, NJ 07624-2115
201-767-8022
Fax: 201-767-9124 877-263-7539
contactus@akfponline.com www.akfponline.com
Bulk quantity starches, spices and ingredients.
Manager: Luis Mansueto
VP: Ivan Sarda
Sales: Mel Festejo
Manager: Foss Carter
cfoss@akfponline.com
Operations: Edwin Pacia
Purchasing: Connie Ponce de Leon
Number Employees: 1-4
Type of Packaging: Bulk
Brands:
Emsland
King Lion

467 American Laboratories
4410 South 102nd Street
Omaha, NE 68127
402-339-2494
Fax: 402-339-0801
sales@americanlaboratories.com
www.americanlaboratories.com
Pancreatin and pepsin enzymes
President: Kenny Soejoto
Chairman/CEO: Jeff Jackson
Senior Vice President: Rod Schake
Vice President of Administration: Janet Giwoyna
Vice President of Quality Assurance: Thomas Langdon
Vice President of Sales: Bret Wyant
Contact: Dan Aase
d.aase@americanlaboratories.com
Vice President of Production: Mark Schufeldt
Purchasing Manager: Tom Hall
Number Employees: 50-99
Number of Products: 960
Type of Packaging: Bulk

468 American Lecithin Company
115 Hurley Road
Unit 2B
Oxford, CT 06478
203-262-7100
Fax: 203-262-7101 800-364-4416
www.americanlecithin.com
Lecithin products and specialty phospholipids; importer of lecithin
President: Randall Zigmont
Contact: Dianne Bukowski
customerService@americanLecithin.Com
Year Founded: 1928
Estimated Sales: $.5-1 million
Number Employees: 6
Square Footage: 28000
Parent Co: The Lipod Group
Type of Packaging: Consumer, Bulk
Brands:
Alcolec

469 (HQ)American Licorice
1914 Happiness Way
La Porte, IL 46350
219-324-1400
Fax: 219-324-1490 866-442-2783
insidesales@americ.com
www.americanlicorice.com
Licorice twists, pieces, and ropes in various flavors. Also sour hard candies and drinking straws.
President & CEO: John Kretchmer
Director of Business Strategy: Aaron Johnson
Director of Innovation: Tim Walsh
Quality Assurance Manager: Ed Silva
Corporate Logistic Manager: Ernie Dacanay
Corporate Supply Chain Manager: Dennie Carff
Year Founded: 1914
Estimated Sales: $39.9 Million
Number Employees: 201-500
Square Footage: 126521

Type of Packaging: Consumer, Food Service, Private Label, Bulk
Other Locations:
Consumer Service
La Porte IN
Brands:
Natural Vines
Black Licorice Vines
Licorice Ropes
Red Ropes
Red Vines
Snaps
Sour Punch
Sugar Free Vines
Super Ropes
Twisty Punch
Sip-N-Chew
Extinguisher

470 **American Mercantile Corp**
1270 Warford St
Memphis, TN 38108-3421
901-454-1900
Fax: 901-454-0207 amc@memphi.net
www.americanmercantile.com
Spices, seeds, herbs, botanicals, extracts, essential oils and related natural products
President: Damond Arney
amc@memphi.net
Estimated Sales: Less Than $500,000
Number Employees: 1-4

471 **American Micronutrients**
PO Box 7129
3120 Weatherford Road
Independence, MO 64055
816-254-6000
Fax: 816-254-6004 816-252-1060
Chelated calcium
President: Mike Davison
Brands:
American Micronutrients

472 **American Mint**
1107 Braodway
New York, NY 10010-2731
212-929-1410
Fax: 212-929-1864 800-401-6468
Natural mints
Owner: Sam Hamirani
Estimated Sales: Less than $500,000
Number Employees: 1-4
Type of Packaging: Private Label, Bulk

473 **American Natural & Organic**
4180 Business Center Dr
Fremont, CA 94538-6354
510-440-1044
info@organicspices.com
www.organicspices.com
Natural and organic spices
CEO & President: John Chansari
Contact: Clara Bonner
clara@organicspices.com
Estimated Sales: $1.2 Million
Number Employees: 5-9
Type of Packaging: Bulk
Brands:
SPICELY

474 **American Nut & Chocolate Co**
121 Newmarket Sq
Boston, MA 02118-2603
617-427-1510
Fax: 617-427-1805 800-797-6887
info@amnut.com www.amnut.com
Roasted nuts, chocolates, dried fruits and candies.
President: Robert Novack
Year Founded: 1927
Estimated Sales: $500,000
Number Employees: 1-4
Square Footage: 64000
Type of Packaging: Food Service, Bulk
Brands:
Harvard

475 **American Nuts Inc.**
12950 San Fernando Rd
Sylmar, CA 91342
USA
818-364-8855
contact@americannuts.com
www.americannuts.com
Nuts and dried fruits
CEO/Founder: Gary Eshgian
Number Employees: 20-49

476 **American Palm Oil**
1010 Wisconsin Avenue NW
Suite 307
Washington, DC 20007
202-333-0661
Fax: 202-333-0331 info@americanpalmoil.com
Palm oils
Executive Director: Mohd Salleh Kassim
Contact: Manny Amaya
manuel.amaya@unitedpharmallc.com
Number Employees: 15

477 **American Pasien Co**
109 Elbow Ln
Burlington, NJ 08016-4123
609-387-3130
Fax: 609-387-7204 info@109elbow.com
www.amcocustomdrying.biz
Functional protein ingredients and protein polymers for edible applications
CEO: Jamil Ahmed
jamilahmed@americancasein.com
CEO: Dennis Bobker
CFO: Jack Pipala
Account Manager: Jane Macey
Sales Manager: Cliff Lang
Human Resources Manager/IT Manager: Ellen Iuliucci
Facilities Manager: Chris Lockard
Estimated Sales: $5.8 Million
Number Employees: 20-49
Square Footage: 120000
Type of Packaging: Bulk

478 **American Pop Corn Co**
1 Fun Pl
P.O. Box 178
Sioux City, IA 51102
712-239-1232
Fax: 712-239-1268 henry@jollytime-export.com
www.jollytime.com
Various flavours of microwavable and pre-popped popcorn.
President: Jeff Naslund
naslund@americanpopdigital.com
Chairman: Carlton Smith
VP, Production: Greg Hoffman
Year Founded: 1914
Estimated Sales: $30.60 Million
Number Employees: 185
Type of Packaging: Consumer, Bulk
Brands:
Jolly Time

479 **American Quality Foods**
353 Banner Farm Rd
Mills River, NC 28759-8707
828-890-8344
www.americanqualityfoods.com
Gluten free and diet dessert mixes
Manager: Debbie Allison
debbie@americanqualityfoods.com
Number Employees: 20-49
Square Footage: 17000

480 **American Seafoods**
Market Place Tower
2025 First Ave, Suite 900
Seattle, WA 98121
206-448-0300
www.americanseafoods.com
Seafood, including Alaska pollock, Pacific Hake, Yellowfin sole, and Pacific cod.
Chief Executive Officer: Mikel Durham
President: Inge Andreassen
Chief Financial Officer: Kevin McMenimen
EVP, Product & Business Development: Scott McNair
scott.mcnair@americanseafoods.com
Estimated Sales: $430 Million
Number Employees: 1000+
Type of Packaging: Bulk
Other Locations:
Seattle WA
Dutch Harbor AK
New Bedford MA
Greensboro AL

481 **American Skin LLC**
140 Industrial Dr
Burgaw, NC 28425
910-259-2232
Fax: 910-259-2535 800-248-7463
Sales@americanskin.net www.pork-rinds.com
Pork rings and pork rinds
Manager: Wes Blake
wes@americanskin.net
Estimated Sales: $300,000-500,000
Number Employees: 20-49

482 **American Soy Products Inc**
1474 Woodland Dr
Saline, MI 48176-1282
734-429-2310
Fax: 734-429-2112 www.americansoy.com
Aseptic packer of juices, teas and soy products
President: Ron Roller
Estimated Sales: $2.5-5 Million
Number Employees: 50-99
Square Footage: 260000
Type of Packaging: Consumer, Private Label

483 **American Specialty Confections**
888 County Road D W Ste 100
Saint Paul, MN 55112
651-251-7000
Fax: 651-251-7070 800-776-2085
Candy
President: Jeff Haynes
Marketing Director: Chris Dusk
Sales Manager: Mike Gardener
Number Employees: 100

484 **American Specialty Foods**
2316 Norman Road
Lancaster, PA 17601
717-397-9578
Fax: 717-397-0951 800-335-6663
www.asfbrands.com
Gluten-free, baking mixes and ingredients, tea, condiments, spices, dessert toppings.
Marketing: Doug Harris
Contact: Michael Fry
mike.fry@asfbrands.com

485 **(HQ)American Spoon Foods Inc**
1668 Clarion Ave
PO Box 566
Petoskey, MI 49770-9263
231-347-9030
Fax: 231-347-2512 888-735-6700
hello@spoon.com www.spoon.com
Jams, jellies, salsas and condiments.
President: Chris Chickering
chris@spoon.com
VP: Larry Forgione
Human Resources Manager: Dorothy Felton
Plant Manager: Paul Ramey
Purchasing Director: John Kafer
Estimated Sales: $10-20 Million
Number Employees: 50-99
Square Footage: 24000
Type of Packaging: Consumer, Food Service
Other Locations:
Petosky MI
Charlevoix MI
Traverse City MI
Harbor Springs MI
Saugatuck MI
Northville MI
Ann Arbor MI
Brands:
American Chef Larry Forgione's
American Fruit Butters
American Fruit Toppings
American Salad Dazzlers
American Spoon Foods
American Spoon Fruits
Salad Dazzlers
Spoon Fruit
Spoon Toppers

486 **American Tartaric Products**
1865 Palmer Ave
Larchmont, NY 10538
914-834-1881
Fax: 914-834-4611 atp@americantartaric.com
www.americantartaric.com
Tartaric acid, cream of tartar and baking powder
President: Emilio Zanin
Vice President: Luca Zanin
Estimated Sales: $5-10 Million
Number Employees: 27

Other Locations:
American Tartaric Products
Windsor CA

487 **American Tuna**
4364 Bonita Rd
Unit 331
Bonita, CA 91902
866-817-0497
americantuna.com
Canned tuna
Number of Brands: 1
Number of Products: 9
Type of Packaging: Consumer
Brands:
AMERICAN TUNA

488 **American Vegetable Oils**
7244 Condor St
Commerce, CA 90040
800-728-8089
americanvegoil.com
Vegetable oil
Number of Brands: 1
Number of Products: 14
Type of Packaging: Consumer, Bulk
Brands:
AVO

489 **American Vintage Wine Biscuits**
4003 27th St
Long Island City, NY 11101-3814
718-361-1003
Fax: 718-361-0204 info@americanvintage.com
www.americanvintage.com
Crackers and snacks made with wine
Owner: Mary Lynn Mondich
Estimated Sales: Less than $500,000
Number Employees: 1-4
Type of Packaging: Consumer

490 **American Wholesale Grocery**
131 New Jersey Street
Mobile, AL 36603-2111
251-433-2528
Fax: 251-432-7982
Groceries
President: Harold Owens
Secretary/Treasurer: James Statter
Vice President: John Carpenter

491 **American Yeast**
251 Stiles Dr
Memphis, TN 38127-3500
901-358-4788
Fax: 901-795-6948 866-920-9885
asbe@asbe.org www.lallemand.com
Baking enzymes and baking ingredients
Manager: Bud Spooner
First Vice Chairwoman: Theresa S Cogswell
VP: Christine Merenova
Second Vice-Chairman: Eddie Perrou
Manager: Darrell Philips
Estimated Sales: $5-10 Million
Number Employees: 10-19
Brands:
Essential
Fermaid

492 **Americana Vineyards & Winery**
4367 E Covert Rd
Interlaken, NY 14847-9720
607-387-6801
Fax: 607-387-3852 888-600-8067
gotwine@americanavineyards.com
www.americanavineyards.com
Wines
Owner: Joe Gober
wineinny@aol.com
Estimated Sales: $840,000
Number Employees: 10-19
Brands:
Americana

493 **Americhicken**
1330 Copper Dr
Cape Girardeau, MO 63701-1730
573-651-6485
Fax: 573-651-4669 www.americhicken.com
Frozen chicken and entrees
President: Taylor Bass
taylor@americhicken.com
Number Employees: 5-9

494 **Americolor Corp**
341 S Melrose St
Suite C
Placentia, CA 92870-5974
714-996-1820
Fax: 714-996-7422 800-556-0233
info@americolorcorp.com
www.americolorcorp.com
Food colors for the bakery industry
President: Monika Molina
monika@americolorcorp.com
CFO: Fay Molina
Estimated Sales: $500,000-$1 Million
Number Employees: 1-4
Brands:
Ameri Color

495 **Ameripure Processing Co**
803 Willow St
Franklin, LA 70538-6030
337-413-8000
Fax: 337-413-8003 800-328-6729
pfahey@ameripure.com www.ameripure.com
Oysters
President: John Jestvich
john@ameripure.com
Estimated Sales: $5 Million
Number Employees: 50-99
Type of Packaging: Consumer, Food Service, Private Label
Brands:
Ameripure

496 **Amerol Chemical Corporation**
71 Carolyn Blvd
Farmingdale, NY 11735
631-694-4700
Fax: 631-694-9177
Synthetic and natural antioxidants and mixed tocopherols.
President: C J Monteleone
CEO: D Sartorio
CFO: A Diaz
R&D: Y Liang
Marketing: S Jean Charles
Operations: F Monteleone
Production: D Ghiglieri
Purchasing Director: D Raleigh
Estimated Sales: $300,000-500,000
Number Employees: 1-4
Square Footage: 46000
Type of Packaging: Private Label, Bulk

497 **Ames Company, Inc**
PO Box 46
45 Pine Hill Road
New Ringgold, PA 17960
610-750-1032
Fax: 413-604-0541 info@theingredientstore.com
www.theingredientstore.com
Vegetarian meat analogs and dry mixes
Owner: Joseph Ames, Sr.
Number Employees: 5-9

498 **Ames International Inc**
4401 Industry Dr E
Bldg. A
Fife, WA 98424-1832
253-946-4779
Fax: 253-926-4127 888-469-2637
questions@emilyschocolates.com
www.emilyschocolates.com
Nut products, gourmet chocolates and cookies
President: George Paulose
gpaulose@amesinternational.com
VP: Susan Paulose
Marketing: Amy Paulose
Estimated Sales: $5-10 Million
Number Employees: 50-99
Square Footage: 220000
Type of Packaging: Private Label, Bulk
Brands:
Amy's
Ecosnax
Emily's
Orchard Hills
Santa Cruz
Seven Seas

499 **Amest Food**
Stony Point, NY 10980
718-360-0886
info@amest.com
www.amest.com
Estonian chocolate, marzipan and dark rye bread

500 **Amick Farms LLC**
2079 Batesburg Hwy.
Batesburg, SC 29006
803-532-1400
Fax: 803-532-1491 800-926-4257
www.amickfarms.com
Chicken products.
Chief Executive Officer: Ben Harrison
bharrison@amickfarms.com
Vice President, Sales & Marketing: Steve Kernen
Year Founded: 1941
Estimated Sales: $100-499 Million
Number Employees: 1000-4999
Number of Brands: 2
Square Footage: 10992
Parent Co: OSI Industries, LLC
Type of Packaging: Consumer, Food Service, Private Label, Bulk
Other Locations:
Hurlock MD
Brands:
Amick Farms Poultry
Sunrise Farm Fresh

501 **Amigos Canning Company**
4669 Highway 90 W
San Antonio, TX 78237
210-798-5360
www.amigosfoods.com
Mexican foods, including refried beans, dips, sauces, peppers, and taco shells.
Manager: Clint McNew
Controller: Ivan Kerr
ikerr@amigosfoods.com
Sales Contact: Heather McNew
Plant Manager: Carlos Menchaca
Year Founded: 1925
Estimated Sales: $11.5 Million
Number Employees: 90
Square Footage: 39000
Parent Co: Durrset Amigos
Type of Packaging: Consumer, Private Label
Brands:
Amigos

502 **Amira Nature Foods Ltd.**
1 Park Plz Ste 600
Irvine, CA 92614-5987
USA
949-852-4468
Fax: 949-271-3615 amira.net
Grain, cereal, pasta, olive oils, baked goods, dairy products
CEO/Chairman: Karan Chanana
Vice President: Alireza Yazdi

503 **Amity Packing Co Inc**
4220 S Kildare Ave
Chicago, IL 60632-3930
773-475-9398
Fax: 312-942-0413 800-837-0270
byanz@amitypacking.com www.amitypacking.com
Fresh and frozen pork and beef products.
President: Richard T Samuel
Vice President: Matt Buol
VP Sales/Marketing: Tom Laplant
Contact: Ray Green
rgreen@amitypacking.com
Operations Manager: Jim Stamm
Estimated Sales: $110,000
Number Employees: 10-19
Square Footage: 11224

504 **Amity Vineyards**
18150 SE Amity Vineyards Rd
Amity, OR 97101-2304
503-835-2362
Fax: 503-835-6451 888-264-8966
amity@amityvineyards.com
www.coelhowinery.com
Wines
President: Myron Redford
myronamity@amityvineyards.com
Sales/Manager: Peter Higbee
Estimated Sales: $830,000
Number Employees: 10-19
Square Footage: 60

505 **Amizetta Vineyards**
1099 Greenfield Rd
St Helena, CA 94574-9625
707-963-1460
Fax: 707-963-1460 cab@amizetta.com
www.amizetta.com
Wines
Owner: Wendy Edelstein
wendy.n.edelstein@nasa.gov
Co-Owner: Amisetta Clark
President: Perry McFadden Clark
Operations/Winemaker: Robert Egelhoff
Estimated Sales: $1-2.5 Million
Number Employees: 1-4

506 **Ammerland America**
134 South Dixie Hwy
Suite 110
Hallandale Beach, FL 33009
954-350-0325
yunger@molkerei-ammerland.de
www.molkerei-ammerland.de
Dairy Products
President/CEO: Israel Yunger
Parent Co: Molkerei Ammerland eG

507 **Amoretti**
451 Lombard St
Oxnard, CA 93030-5143
805-983-2903
Fax: 818-718-0204 800-266-7388
www.amoretti.com
Nut flour, paste and butter
Founder, CEO: Jack Barsoumian
info@amoretti.com
Marketing President: Maral Barsoumian
Manufacturing President: Ara Barsoumian
Year Founded: 1989
Estimated Sales: $20+ Million
Number Employees: 20-49
Type of Packaging: Food Service, Bulk
Brands:
Amoretti
Baristella
Capriccio

508 **Amoroso's Baking Co**
151 Benigno Blvd
Bellmawr, NJ 08031
215-471-4740
info@amorosobaking.com
amorosobaking.com
Rolls, breads, bagels, Jewish bread and pretzels.
President: Lenny Amoroso
lmamoroso@amorosobaking.com
Vice President: Jesse Amoroso
CFO: Preston Thomas
Year Founded: 1904
Estimated Sales: $27.7 Million
Number Employees: 400
Square Footage: 80000
Type of Packaging: Consumer, Food Service, Private Label
Brands:
Merion Park Rye Bread
Richmond Rye Bread
Amoroso's Hearth Baked

509 **Amphora International**
20622 Canada Rd
Lake Forest, CA 92630
949-609-0600
888-380-4808
amphorafoods.com
Olive oil, organic dried fruit, condiments and spices
Number of Brands: 1
Number of Products: 19
Type of Packaging: Consumer
Brands:
AMPHORA

510 **Amplify Snack Brands**
500 W 5th St
Suite 1350
Austin, TX 78701
512-600-9893
Fax: 512-640-8757 info@amplifysnacks.com
amplifysnackbrands.com
Healthy snacks

511 **Amport Foods**
380 St. Peter St.
Suite 1000
St. Paul, MN 55102
612-331-7000
Fax: 612-331-1122 800-236-1119
customers@amportfoods.com
www.amportfoods.com
Dates, dried fruits whole and pressed, soy nuts, and sunflower seeds
President: Andrew Stillman
Vice President: Jeff Vogel
Contact: Aaron Anderson
aaron@amportfoods.com
Production Manager: Mike McIvor
Estimated Sales: $20-50 Million
Number Employees: 20-49
Type of Packaging: Bulk

512 **Amrhein's Wine Cellars**
9243 Patterson Dr
Bent Mountain, VA 24059-2215
540-929-4632
Fax: 540-929-4632 info@amrheins.com
www.amrheinshop.us
Wines
Owner: Russel Amrhein
vinapple@att.net
Estimated Sales: Less Than $500,000
Number Employees: 1-4

513 **Amrita Health Foods**
37 Harvard Dr.
Hartsdale, NY 10530
888-728-7779
800-523-8644
www.amritahealthfoods.com
Energy bars
Founder and CEO: Arshad Bahl
Square Footage: 80000

514 **Amrita Snacks**
Hartsdale, NY 10530
888-728-7779
www.amritahealthfoods.com
Plant-based, vegan, all-natural protein bars, protein snack bites and energy bars in various flavors
Founder/CEO: Arshad Bahl
Number of Brands: 1
Number of Products: 21
Type of Packaging: Consumer, Private Label
Brands:
Amrita

515 **Amsnack**
7770 Longe Street
Stockton, CA 95206-3925
209-982-5545
Fax: 209-982-4955
Rice crackers, cookies crackers and chips
President: Satoshi Yamada
Shipping Coordinator: Karen Valterza
Estimated Sales: $5-9.9 Million
Number Employees: 20-49

516 **Amstell Holding**
209 Theodore Rice Boulevard
New Bedford, MA 02745-1213
508-995-6100
Fax: 508-995-2912
Shelf-stable nonrefrigerated milk, nutritional supplements, juices, teas, and drink beverages.
Director Operations: Cindy Aldrich

517 **Amsterdam Brewing Company**
21 Bathurst Street
Toronto, ON M5V 2N6
Canada
416-504-1040
Fax: 416-504-1043 416-504-6882
info@amsterdambeer.com
www.amsterdambeer.com
Beer, lager and ale including stout
President: Jeff Carefoote
Number Employees: 12
Type of Packaging: Consumer, Food Service

518 **Amwell Valley Vineyard**
80 Old York Road
Ringoes, NJ 08551
908-788-5852
Fax: 908-788-1030
Wines
Owner: Jeff Fischer
President: Dr Michael Fisher
Operations Manager: Scott Gares
Estimated Sales: $1-2.5 Million
Number Employees: 1-4
Number of Brands: 1
Number of Products: 20
Type of Packaging: Consumer
Brands:
Amwell Valley Vineyard

519 **Amy & Brian Naturals**
6905 Aragon Circle
Buena Park, CA 90620
info@amyandbriannaturals.com
www.amyandbriannaturals.com
Coconut water
Number of Brands: 1
Number of Products: 5
Type of Packaging: Consumer
Brands:
AMY & BRIAN

520 **Amy Food Inc**
3324 S Richey St
Houston, TX 77017-6259
713-910-5860
Fax: 713-910-4812 www.amyfood.com
Egg rolls, potstickers, empanadas and party platters, natural and organic foods.
Owner: Phyllis Hsu
amyfood@aol.com
Number Employees: 50-99
Square Footage: 40000
Type of Packaging: Consumer, Food Service, Private Label
Brands:
Jamy's Three Dragon

521 **Amy's Candy Bar**
4704 N Damen Ave
Chicago, IL 60625-1512
773-942-6386
amyscandybar@gmail.com
www.amyscandybar.com
Candy and confections
Estimated Sales: Less Than $500,000
Number Employees: 1-4

522 **Amy's Kitchen Inc**
2330 Northpoint Pkwy
Santa Rosa, CA 95407
707-781-6600
www.amys.com
Frozen organic meals and entrees; also canned soups and bottled pasta sauces.
Co-Owner: Andy Berliner
Co-Owner: Rachel Berliner
EVP: Jack Chipman
Director, Contract Manufacturing: Norma Mery
Estimated Sales: $92.3 Million
Number of Brands: 1
Number of Products: 146
Square Footage: 100000
Type of Packaging: Consumer, Food Service
Brands:
Amys Kitchen

523 **Amylu Foods**
1143 West Lake St
Chicago, IL 60607
www.amylufoods.com
Craft meats
CEO: Amylu Kurzawski
Brands:
Amylu
Leon's Sausage
Slotkowski

524 **Ana's Salsa**
17503 La Cantera Pkwy
Suite 104-473
Austin, TX 78257
512-837-2203
Fax: 512-837-0003 888-849-7054
info@anasfoods.com www.anasfoods.com
Salsas, herbs and jams.
President: Anna Olvera-Ullrich
COO/SVP: Jim Ullrich
Estimated Sales: $500,000
Number Employees: 1-4
Number of Brands: 3
Number of Products: 8
Type of Packaging: Consumer, Food Service, Bulk

Brands:
Ana's

525 **AnaCon Foods Company**
1145 Main St
PO Box 651
Atchison, KS 66002
913-367-2885
Fax: 913-367-1794 800-328-0291
anacon@journey.com
Processor and exporter of simulated nut and fruit particulates and analogs
Executive Director: Tom Miller
VP Sales/Marketing: Jane Hallas
Director Operations: Marvin Mikkelson
Estimated Sales: $2.5-5 Million
Number Employees: 20-49
Brands:
Bits'n'pops
Bowlby's Bits
Mix-Ups
Nuts'n'pops
Wheat Nuts

526 **Anabol Naturals**
1550 Mansfield St
Santa Cruz, CA 95062-1720
831-479-1403
Fax: 831-479-1406 800-426-2265
www.anabolnaturals.com
Sports nutrition supplements
President: Roger Prince
anabol@cruzio.com
Estimated Sales: $500,000-$1 Million
Number Employees: 5-9
Square Footage: 20000
Brands:
Anabol Naturals

527 **Analyticon Discovery LLC**
9700 Great Seneca Hwy
Rockville, MD 20850-3307
240-406-1256
Fax: 240-453-6208 info@ac-discovery.com
www.ac-discovery.com
Natural active ingredients and products.
CEO/Co-Founder: Lutz Muller-Kuhrt
CFO/Co-Founder: Jochen Gatter
VP Research & Development: Karsten Siems
North American/UK Sales Representative: Andrea Christes
Contact: Betsy Manikowski
b.manikowski@ac-discovery.com
VP Operations & Research: Martina Jaensch
Estimated Sales: $4.64 Million
Number Employees: 1-4

528 **Ananda Hemp**
PO Box 648
Cynthiana, KY 41031
hello@anandahemp.com
www.anandahemp.com
Hemp extract
Number of Brands: 1
Number of Products: 5
Type of Packaging: Consumer
Brands:
ANANDA HEMP

529 **Anastasia Confections Inc**
1815 Cypress Lake Dr
Orlando, FL 32837-8457
407-816-9944
Fax: 407-816-9901 800-329-7100
customerservice@anastasiaconfections.com
www.anastasiaconfections.com
Specialty candy
President: Mike Constantine
customerservice@anastasiaconfections.com
Estimated Sales: $2 Million
Number Employees: 20-49

530 **Anchor Appetizer Group**
PO Box 2518
Appleton, WI 54912
920-997-2200
Fax: 920-734-2828
Appetizers
President: Mark Follett
Vice President: Scott Follet
Estimated Sales: $6 Million
Parent Co: McCain Foods USA/H.J. Heinz Company
Type of Packaging: Consumer, Food Service
Brands:
Brew City
Cheese Senasations
Golden Crisp
Golden Crisp
Moore's
Mozzaluna
Mozzamia
Olivenos
Poppers
Primasamo Cubes
Provago Wheels
Queso Triangulos
Wrappetizers

531 **Anchor Brewing Company**
1705 Mariposa St
San Francisco, CA 94107
415-863-8350
Fax: 415-552-7094 info@anchorbrewing.com
www.anchorbrewing.com
Beer and ale
Marketing, Communications & Events: Teagan Thompson
VP Sales: Martin Geraghty
VP Logistics: Alfredo Mialma
Year Founded: 1896
Estimated Sales: $20-50 Million
Number Employees: 50-99
Parent Co: Sapporo Holdings
Type of Packaging: Consumer, Private Label
Brands:
Anchor Steam
Liberty Ale
Anchor Porter
Summer Beer
Olf Foghorn
Anchor Small
Christmas Ale

532 **Anchor Frozen Foods**
32 Urban Ave
PO Box 887
Westbury, NY 11590
516-333-6344
Fax: 516-997-1823 800-566-3474
info@anchorfrozenfoods.com
Seafood including stuffed sole, conch, shrimp, lobster tails, octopus, calamari and king crab legs.
President: Roy Tuccillo
Contact: Stephanie Rusellan
stephanie@anchorfrozenfoods.com
Estimated Sales: $500,000- 1 Million
Number Employees: 5-9
Type of Packaging: Consumer, Food Service, Bulk

533 **Anchor Ingredients**
5181 38th Street South
Suite B
Fargo, ND 58104
701-499-1480
Fax: 701-499-1481 info@anchoringredients.com
anchoringredients.com
Food ingredients
Co-Founder, Managing Director: Al Yablonski
Co-Founder, Managing Director: Seth Novak
Number of Brands: 1
Type of Packaging: Bulk

534 **Ancient Harvest**
PO Box 4240
Boulder, CO 80306
310-217-8125
ancientharvest.com
Organic grains
Number of Brands: 1
Number of Products: 10
Brands:
ANCIENT HARVEST
POW! PASTA

535 **Ancient Nutrition**
1201 US Highway One
Suite 350
North Palm Beach, FL 33408
888-823-4468
info@ancientnutrition.com ancientnutrition.com
Protein supplement
Co-Founder: Jordan Rubin
Number of Brands: 1
Number of Products: 8
Brands:
ANCIENT NUTRITION

536 **Ancient Organics**
726 Allston Way
Berkeley, CA 94710
510-280-5043
morgyne@ancientorganics.com
www.ancientorganics.com
Organic ghee (clarified butter)
Founder: Peter Malakoff
Owner: Matteo Girard Maxon
CFO: Abinashi Khalsa
VP Sales & Marketing: Greg Glass
National Sales Manager: Tim Transon

537 **Ancient Peaks Winery**
22720 El Camino Real
Santa Margarita, CA 93453-8668
805-365-7045
Fax: 805-365-7046 info@apwinery.com
www.ancientpeaks.com
Wines
Type of Packaging: Private Label

538 **Anco Foods**
11421 NW 107 St
Miami, FL 33178
305-651-8489
866-343-1108
www.ancofinecheese.com
Cheese
CEO: Arno Leoni
Estimated Sales: $207 Million
Parent Co: Schratter Foods Inc
Type of Packaging: Bulk

539 **Ancora Coffee Roasters**
3701 Orin Road
Madison, WI 53704
608-255-2900
Fax: 608-255-2901 800-260-0217
service@ancoracoffee.com www.ancoracoffee.com
Coffees, whole bean and ground; loose leaf teas
President/CEO: George Krug
Quality Control/Production: Rob Jeffrics
Marketing: Christy Gibbs
cgibbs@ancoracoffee.com
Estimated Sales: $1-5 Million
Number Employees: 10-19
Square Footage: 60000
Type of Packaging: Consumer, Food Service, Bulk

540 **Andalucia Nuts**
3505 Bering Dr
Houston, TX 77057
713-977-9090
www.andalucianuts.com
Nuts and nut butters
Type of Packaging: Bulk

541 **Andalusia Distributing Co Inc**
117 Allen Ave
Andalusia, AL 36420-2501
334-222-3671
www.adc1.com
Deli products
President: Ricky Jones
Vice President: Billy Jones
CFO: Chris Jones
General Manager: Ronnie Taylor
Year Founded: 1956
Estimated Sales: $50-100 Million
Number Employees: 50-99
Brands:
Sara Lee
Bellarico's
Altria
RJReynolds
Hershey's
MARS
Mondelez International
Wrigley
KRAFT
General Mills
Jack Link's
Nestle

542 **Andean Naturals LLC**
393 Catamaran St
Foster City, CA 94404-2907
650-303-1780
Fax: 707-202-2838 info@andeannaturals.com
www.andeannaturals.com
Quinoa

Owner: Sergio Nunez De Arco
sergio_nunez@andeannaturals.com
Finance & Operations Manager: Marcos Guevara
Estimated Sales: $100 Thousand
Number Employees: 1-4
Type of Packaging: Bulk

543 **Andersen's Pea Soup**
376 Avenue of the Flags
Buellton, CA 93427
805-688-5581
Fax: 805-686-5670 info@peasoupandersens.net
www.peasoupandersens.net
Canned split pea soup
Manager: Tony Picard
Purchasing Director: Brinda Wolf
Estimated Sales: $2.5-5 Million
Number Employees: 50-99

544 **Anderson Custom Processing**
PO Box 279
New Ulm, MN 56073
507-233-2800
Fax: 507-233-2806 877-588-4950
acpi@newulmtel.net
www.andersonprocessing.com
Spray-dried food products including whey, starches, cheese and cream powders
President: Brian Anderson
brian.anderson@andersonprocessing.com
Founder/CEO: Glen Anderson
Production Manager: Jerome Braun
Estimated Sales: $3-5 Million
Number Employees: 1-4
Type of Packaging: Bulk
Other Locations:
Sleepy Eye MN
Little Falls WI
Belleville WI

545 **Anderson Dairy Inc**
801 Searles Ave
Las Vegas, NV 89101
702-642-7507
Fax: 702-642-3480 comments@andersondairy.com
www.andersondairy.com
Milk and dairy products including milk, cottage cheese, sour cream, cream, buttermilk, half & half, butter, eggs, ice cream and eggnog
President: Dave Coon
Year Founded: 1907
Estimated Sales: $76 Million
Number Employees: 100-249
Number of Brands: 1
Square Footage: 130000
Type of Packaging: Consumer, Bulk
Brands:
Anderson Dairy

546 **Anderson Erickson Dairy**
2420 E University Ave
Des Moines, IA 50317
515-265-2521
www.aedairy.com
Milks, orange juice, lemonade, yogurt, cottage cheese, dips, sour cream, eggnog, buttermilk and creams, and ice cream mix.
President: Miriam Erickson Brown
Chief Financial Officer: Warren Erickson
Director of Marketing: Kim Peter
Year Founded: 1930
Estimated Sales: $44.40 Million
Number Employees: 250-499
Square Footage: 190000
Type of Packaging: Food Service
Other Locations:
Kansas City KS

547 **Anderson Erickson Dairy**
5431 Speaker Rd
Kansas City, KS 66106
913-621-4801
www.aedairy.com
Milks, orange juice, lemonade, yogurt, cottage cheese, dips, sour cream, eggnog, buttermilk and creams, and ice cream mix.
President: Miriam Erickson Brown
Year Founded: 1930
Estimated Sales: $20-50 Million
Number Employees: 250-499
Type of Packaging: Food Service

548 **Anderson Seafood**
4780 E Bryson St
Anaheim, CA 92807-1901
714-777-7100
Fax: 714-777-7116
contactus@andersonseafoods.com
www.shopandersonseafoods.com
Fresh and frozen seafood
President: Dennis Anderson
CFO: Alberto Andrade
Vice President: Todd Anderson
VP, Procurement, Sales & Operations: Carl Oliphant
Year Founded: 1979
Number Employees: 20-49
Type of Packaging: Consumer, Food Service

549 **Anderson Valley Brewing Co**
17700 Highway 253
Boonville, CA 95415
707-895-2337
Fax: 707-895-2353 800-207-2237
info@avbc.com www.avbc.com
Seasonal beer, ale, porter, stout, lager and pilsner
President: Trey White
trewhite@avbc.com
VP Sales: David Gatlin
Estimated Sales: $7 Million
Number Employees: 20-49
Square Footage: 80000
Type of Packaging: Consumer
Brands:
Barney Flats Oatmeal Stout
Beik's Esb
Boont Amber
High Rollers Wheat
Hop Ottin' Ipa
Poleeko Gold
Winter Solstice

550 **Anderson's Conn Valley Vineyards**
680 Rossi Rd
St Helena, CA 94574-9646
707-963-8600
Fax: 707-963-7818 800-946-3497
info@connvalleyvineyards.com
www.connvalleyvineyards.com
Wines
President: Todd Anderson
todd@connvalleyvineyards.com
Operations: Mac Sawyer
Estimated Sales: $2.5-5 Million
Number Employees: 5-9

551 **Andre Prost Inc**
680 Middlesex Tpke
Old Saybrook, CT 06475-1303
860-388-0838
Fax: 860-388-0830 800-243-0897
www.andreprost.com
Candy, confectionery, seasonings and spices.
Owner: Lori Montano
Vice President: Peter Cumings
VP Finance: Charles Landrey
lorimontano@andreprost.com
Estimated Sales: $2 Million
Number Employees: 10-19
Brands:
A Taste of China
A Taste of India
A Taste of Thai
Ginger Snaps
Honees
Notta Pasta
Odense
Zotz

552 **Andre's Confiserie Suisse**
5018 Main St
Kansas City, MO 64112-2755
816-561-3440
Fax: 816-561-2922 800-892-1234
customer_service@andreschocolates.com
www.andreschocolates.com
Swiss style chocolate candies
President: Marcel Bollier
customerservice@andreschocolates.com
CEO: Rene Bollier
CFO: Connie Bollier
Estimated Sales: $2.5-5 Million
Number Employees: 50-99
Type of Packaging: Consumer
Other Locations:
Andre's Confiserie Suisse
Overland Park KS
Andre's Confiserie Suisse
Denver CO

553 **Andre-Boudin Bakeries**
221 Main St Ste 1230
San Francisco, CA 94105
415-882-1849
Fax: 415-913-1818 boudin@boudinbakery.com
www.boudinbakery.com
Sourdough bread, specialty breads, and sweet goods
Owner: Sharon Duvall
VP Sales/Marketing: Terry Wight
Contact: Kayla Alexis
kalexis@boudinbakery.com
Plant Manager: Rick Rodrick
Estimated Sales: $300,000-500,000
Number Employees: 1,000-4,999
Type of Packaging: Private Label, Bulk
Brands:
Boudin

554 **Andrew & Williamson Sales Co**
9940 Marconi Dr
San Diego, CA 92154-7270
619-661-6000
Fax: 619-661-6007
accounting@andrew-williamson.com
www.bajaclassic.com
Frozen strawberries
President: Fred Williamson
fredwilliamson@andrew-williamson.com
Estimated Sales: $2.5-5 Million
Number Employees: 20-49
Brands:
A&W

555 **Andrew Peller Limited**
697 S. Service Rd.
Grimsby, ON L3M 4E8
Canada
905-643-4131
Fax: 905-643-4944 info@andrewpeller.com
www.andrewpeller.com
Wines.
President: Randy Powell
Chairman/CEO: John Peller
Executive VP, IT/CFO: Steve Attridge
Executive VP, Marketing: Shawn MacLeod
Executive VP, National Sales: Erin Rooney
Executive VP, Human Resources: Sara Presutto
Executive VP, Operations: Brendan Wall
Year Founded: 1927
Estimated Sales: $363.8 Million
Number Employees: 1,198
Number of Brands: 10
Square Footage: 89782
Type of Packaging: Consumer, Food Service, Bulk
Brands:
Peller Estates
Sandhill
Wayne Gretzky Estates
Trius Winery
Red Rooster
Calona Vineyards
Thirty Bench
Roundpetal
Vineco
Winexpert

556 **Andrews Brewing Co**
565 Aquone Rd
Andrews, NC 28901-7004
828-321-2006
www.andrewsbrewing.com
Beer
Owner: Andrew Hazen
Estimated Sales: $500,000-$1 Million
Number Employees: 1-4
Brands:
Brown Ale
English Pale Ale
St. Nicks Poter
Summer Golden Ale

557 **Andrews Caramel Apples**
5001 W Belmont Ave
Chicago, IL 60642
773-286-2224
Fax: 773-286-2258 800-305-3004
Info@AndysSeasoning.com
Caramel apples
President: Daniel De Marco
Treasurer: Sylvia Schuman
Purchasing: Rick Walker

Estimated Sales: $2.5-5 Million
Number Employees: 10-19
Type of Packaging: Consumer
Brands:
Andrews
Ms. Kays

558 **Andrews Dried Beef Company**
625 E Broad Street
Quakertown, PA 18951-1713
610-759-5180
Fax: 610-759-1529

Dried beef
President: E William Knauss
Estimated Sales: $10-24.9 Million
Number Employees: 50-99
Parent Co: E.W. Knauss & Sons

559 **Andros Foods North America**
10119 Old Valley Pike
Mount Jackson, VA 22842
540-217-4100
844-426-3767
sales@androsna.com www.androsna.com
Fruit based food and beverages, confectionary, preserves, frozen desserts
CEO/COO: Terry Stoehr
Estimated Sales: $52.3 Million
Number Employees: 500-999
Parent Co: Andros Group

560 **Andy's Seasoning**
2829 Chouteau Ave
St Louis, MO 63103-3016
314-664-2149
Fax: 314-664-2149 800-305-3004
www.andysseasoning.com
Seasoning salt and breadings for fish and chicken.
President/CEO: Larry Lee
Manager: Michael Lee
michael@andysseasoning.com
Year Founded: 1981
Estimated Sales: $20-50 Million
Number Employees: 20-49
Number of Brands: 9
Number of Products: 12
Square Footage: 27000
Type of Packaging: Consumer, Food Service, Private Label, Bulk
Brands:
Andy's Cajun Fish Breading
Andy's Golden Fish Batter
Andy's Hot 'N' Spicy Breading
Andy's Mild Chicken Breading
Andy's Red Fish Breading
Andy's Seasoned Salt
Andy's Shrimp Tempura Batter
Andy's Vegetable Breading
Andy's Yellow Fish Breading

561 **Anette's Chocolate & Ice Cream**
1321 1st St
Napa, CA 94559-2927
707-252-4228
Fax: 707-252-8074 mary@anettes.com
Truffles, creams, brittles, chews, chocolate sauces, caramel sauces, traditional and unique seasonal specialties.
President: Helen Krasovic
helen.krasovic@lajollasportsclub.com
VP: Brent Madsen
Marketing: Mary Stornetta
Number Employees: 10-19

562 **Angel's Bakeries**
29 Norman Avenue
Brooklyn, NY 11222
718-389-1400
Fax: 718-389-3928 joe@angelsbakery.com
www.angelsbakery.com
Cookies, muffin tops, muffins, florentines, cakes and cake slices.
President: Joseph Angel
Vice President: Adi Angel
Marketing Director: Bill McNamee
Production Manager: Eloy Rojas
Estimated Sales: $4.1 Million
Number Employees: 45

563 **Angelic Bakehouse**
3275 East Layton Ave
Cudahy, WI 53110
www.angelicbakehouse.com
Crusts, wraps, bread, buns, rolls, baguettes and bread crisps
Co-Founder: Jenny Marino
Co-Founder: James Marino
Year Founded: 2009
Number of Brands: 1
Number of Products: 20
Brands:
ANGELIC BAKEHOUSE
FLATZZA
SPROUTED

564 **Angelic Gourmet Inc**
P.O.Box 127
8629 State Route 21 South
Naples, NY 14512
800-294-0947
Fax: 800-947-5371
Chocolate dipped pretzels and chocolate drizzled popcorn.
President: Donna Scott
Estimated Sales: $1.8 Million
Number Employees: 20

565 **Angelo & Franco U.S.A.**
3441 Jack Northrop Ave.
Building 14
Hawthorne, CA 90250
USA
310-263-0506
www.angeloandfranco.com
A variety of cheeses.
Co-Owner: Angelo Tartaglia
Co-Owner: Franco Russo
Brands:
angelo & franco

566 **Angelo Pietro Honolulu**
1108 12th Ave # C
Honolulu, HI 96816-3767
USA
808-941-0555
Fax: 808-440-0385 www.angelopietro.com
Sauces, seasonings, cooking enhancers, marinades, salad dressing
President: Kunihiko Murata
Manager: Tomohiko Shiomi
Number Employees: 20-49

567 **Angie's Artisan Treats LLC**
1918 Lookout Dr
North Mankato, MN 56003-1705
507-387-3886
888-982-4984
www.boomchickapop.com
Kettle corn.
Co-Owner: Dan Bastian
Co-Owner: Angie Bastian
Manager: Joe Atkinson
jatkinson@angiespopcorn.com
Number Employees: 100-249
Square Footage: 80000
Brands:
BOOMCHICKAPOP

568 **Anglo American Trading**
P.O.Box 97
Harvey, LA 70059-0097
504-341-5631
Fax: 504-341-5635
Manager: Dennis Skrmetta
CEO: Eric Skrmetta

569 **Angry Orchard Cider Company, LLC**
2241 Albany Post Rd.
Walden, NY 12586
888-845-3311
www.angryorchard.com
Apple, pear and ros, hard ciders
Head Producer: Ryan Burk
Number of Brands: 1
Number of Products: 6
Type of Packaging: Consumer, Private Label
Brands:
Angry Orchard

570 **Angy's Food Products Inc**
77 Servistar Industrial Way
Westfield, MA 01085-5601
413-572-1010
Fax: 413-572-4785 www.angyslandolfi.com
Frozen tortellini, gnocchi, cavatelli, stuffed shells, manicotti and ravioli
Owner: Edward Debartolo
edd@angyslandolfi.com
CFO: Liz Campanini
VP: Steve Campanini
Number Employees: 20-49
Square Footage: 92000
Type of Packaging: Consumer, Food Service, Private Label, Bulk
Brands:
Angy's
Big Y
Finast
Introvigne's
Shaw's

571 **Anheuser-Busch**
One Busch Place
St. Louis, MO 63118
800-342-5283
www.anheuser-busch.com
Beers
President & CEO, North America: Michel Doukeris
VP, Finance & Solutions: Nelson Jamel
VP, People: Agostino De Gasperis
VP, Procurement & Sustainability: Ingrid De Ryck
VP, Business & Wholesaler Development: Bob Tallett
VP, Marketing: Marcel Marcondes
VP, Sales: Brendan Whitworth
VP, Legal & Corporate Affairs: Cesar Vargas
Year Founded: 1852
Estimated Sales: $15.5 Billion
Number Employees: 19,000+
Number of Brands: 100+
Type of Packaging: Consumer, Food Service, Private Label
Brands:
Budweiser
Bud Light
Michelob Ultra
Stella Artois
Patagonia Cerveza
Estrella Jalisco
Busch
Natural Light
Landshark Lager
Presedente
Hoegaarden
Shock Top
10 Barrel Brewing Co.
Breckenridge Brewery
Blue Point Brewing Company
Devils Backbone Brewing Company
Elysian Brewing
Golden Road Brewing
Four Peaks Brewing Co.
Goose Isalnd
Karbach Brewing Company
Platform Beer Co.
Wicked Weed Brewing
Veza Sur Brewing Co.
Virture Cider
Maha Organic Hard Cider
LQD
Ritas
Bon & Viv Spiked Seltzer
Babe
Cutwater Spirits
Hi Ball Energy
Kombrewcha

572 **Animal Pak**
3 Terminal Rd
New Brunswick, NJ 08901-3615
732-545-3130
Fax: 732-509-0458 800-872-0101
info@animalpak.com www.animalpak.com
Vitamins, supplements, and powdered proteins
President: Clyde Rockoff
VP Marketing: Michael Rockoff
VP Sales: Tim Tantum
VP Operations: Bob Glucken
Plant Manager: Dave Mitchell
Estimated Sales: $35.1 Million
Number Employees: 100-249
Square Footage: 100000
Parent Co: Universal Nutrition
Brands:
Animal Pak
Forza
Hardfast
Natural Sterols
Yohimbe Bar

573 **Anita's Mexican Foods Corporation**
1390 West 4th Street
San Bernardino, CA 92408
909-884-8706
Mexican foods including tortilla chips and taco and tostada shells, plus organic snacks, chips and popcorn
President: Jose Gomez
Contact: Mark Schneeberger
mark.schneeberger@anitasmexicanfood.com
Plant Manager: Frank Coser
Estimated Sales: $20-50 Million
Number Employees: 100-249
Square Footage: 30000
Parent Co: La Reina
Type of Packaging: Consumer, Food Service, Private Label, Bulk
Brands:
Anita's
Go-Mex
La Reina
Old Pueblo Ranch

574 **Anita's Yogurt**
Brooklyn, NY 11211
anitas.com
Coconut yogurt
Founder: Anita Shepherd

575 **Ankeny Lake Wild Rice**
9594 Sidney Rd S
PO Box 3667
Salem, OR 97306-9448
503-363-3241
Fax: 503-371-9080 800-555-5380
ankenylakes_st.maries@yahoo.com
www.wildriceonline.com
Certified organic wild rice and nonorganic and wild rice blends
Owner: Larry Payne
paynels@netzero.com
Co-Owner: Sharon Jenkins-Payne
Estimated Sales: $500,000
Number Employees: 1-4
Square Footage: 12000
Type of Packaging: Consumer, Food Service, Private Label, Bulk
Brands:
Canadian Jumbo Lake
Idaho Lake Wild Rice
Oregon
Wild & Ricey

576 **Ankle Deep Foods**
912 W Omaha Avenue
Norfolk, NE 68701-5842
402-371-6707
wings@buffalomaid.com
www.buffalomaid.com
Hot suaces and marinades
Brands:
Buffalo Maid

577 **Anmar Foods**
2150 W Carroll Ave
Chicago, IL 60612-1604
312-421-6500
Fax: 312-421-4765 www.anmarfoods.com
Beef, burgers, chicken, turkey, pork, and lamb
Owner: Bob Martinelli
President: Michael Casper
Estimated Sales: $20-50 Million
Number Employees: 20-49

578 **Anmar Nutrition**
P.O.Box 2343
540 Barnum Avenue
Bridgeport, CT 06608-0343
203-336-8330
Fax: 203-336-5508 www.anmarinternational.com
Vitamins, nutritional products, excipients, non-prescription pharmaceutical products, herbs, and amino acids.
President: John Blanco
VP: Hongbing Deng
Sales Director: Allan Pollard
Production Manager: John Blanco
Estimated Sales: $10-20 Million
Number Employees: 10-19
Number of Products: 100+
Square Footage: 15000
Type of Packaging: Bulk

579 **Ann Hemyng Candy Inc**
118 N Main St
Trumbauersville, PA 18970
215-536-7004
Fax: 215-536-6848 800-779-7004
ahcchocolate@verizon.net
www.chocolateshop.com
Molded chocolate including lollypops, novelties in chocolates, custom corporate logos
President/Owner: Louise Spindler
Estimated Sales: $.5-1 million
Number Employees: 5-9

580 **Ann's House of Nuts, Inc.**
9212 Berger Road
Suite 300
Columbia, MD 21046
410-309-6887
Fax: 410-312-9144
Nuts, dried fruits and mixes
President: Edward Zinke
Estimated Sales: $2.5-5 Million
Number Employees: 50-99
Square Footage: 800000
Type of Packaging: Consumer, Food Service, Private Label

581 **Anna's Oatcakes**
988 Route 100
Weston, VT 05161-5414
802-824-3535
Oatcakes and other baked goods

582 **Annabella**
Longmont, CO 80504
www.annabella.com
Water buffalo milk yogurt

583 **Annabelle Candy Co Inc**
27211 Industrial Blvd
Hayward, CA 94545-3392
510-783-2900
Fax: 510-785-7675 info@annabellecandy.com
www.annabellecandy.info
Processor of confectionery products including chocolate truffles, candy bars, nougats and taffy
CEO: Susan G Karl
susan@annabelle-candy.com
Year Founded: 1950
Estimated Sales: $15 Million
Number Employees: 50-99
Square Footage: 60000
Type of Packaging: Consumer, Bulk
Brands:
ABBA-ZABBA(c)
BIG HUNK(c)
LOOK!(c)
Rocky Road(c)
U-NO(c)

584 **Annabelle Lee**
70 Rear Mills Road
Kennebunkport, ME 04046
207-967-4611
Fax: 207-832-7795
Seafood
President: Frank Minio
Number Employees: 30

585 **Annapolis Produce & Restaurant**
15 Lee St
Annapolis, MD 21401-3980
410-266-5211
Fax: 410-266-0568
Groceries, fish, meats and dairy products.
President: Charles Bassford
Chief Financial Officer: Bobby Goldbeck
Vice President: Elaine Bassford
Estimated Sales: $10-19.9 Million
Number Employees: 5-9

586 **Annapolis Winery**
26055 Soda Springs Rd
Annapolis, CA 95412-9728
707-886-5460
Fax: 707-886-5460 annapoliswinery@gmail.com
www.annapoliswinery.com
Wines
President: Basil Scalabrini
Co- Owner: Barbara Scalabrini
Estimated Sales: $2.5-5 Million
Number Employees: 5-9

587 **Annette Island Packing Company**
PO Box 8
Metlakatla, AK 99926
907-886-4441
Fax: 907-886-4471 info@metlakatla.com
www.metlakatla.com
Salmon and cured seafood
Manager: Freeman McGilton

588 **Annette's Donuts Ltd.**
1965 Lawrence Ave W
Toronto, ON M9N 1H5
Canada
416-656-3444
Fax: 416-656-5400 888-839-7857
Bread, pastries and other bakery products
President: Nicolas Yannopoulos
Board Member: Ariadni Yannopoulos
Estimated Sales: $5.9 Million
Number Employees: 85
Square Footage: 124000
Type of Packaging: Consumer, Food Service, Bulk

589 **Annie Chun's**
PO Box 911170
Los Angeles, CA 90091
415-479-8272
Fax: 415-479-8274 info@anniechun.com
www.anniechun.com
Soup bowls, noodle bowls, noodle express, rice express and organic noodles and sauce kits.
Owner: Annie Chun
President: Mike Keeland
CFO: Han Kim
Estimated Sales: Less than $500,000
Number Employees: 5-9

590 **Annie's Frozen Yogurt**
5200 W 74th St # A
Minneapolis, MN 55439-2223
952-835-2110
Fax: 952-835-2378 800-969-9648
www.anniesyogurt.com
Frozen yogurt
President: Lawrence Cerf
ldcerf@aol.com
Estimated Sales: $500,000-$1 Million
Number Employees: 10-19

591 **Annie's Homegrown**
1610 5th St
Berkeley, CA 94710-1715
510-558-7500
800-288-1089
bernie@annies.com www.annies.com
Vegan and organic foods
President: Mark Mortimer
CEO: John Foraker
CFO: Zahir Ibrahim
Chief Innovation Officer: Bob Kaake
VP Marketing: Sarah Bird
Strategic Planning: ED Aaron
IT: Kristin Gibson-Lynn
kgibsonlynn@annies.com
Estimated Sales: Less Than $500,000
Number Employees: 5-9
Type of Packaging: Private Label
Brands:
Annie's Macaroni & Cheese
Tamarind Tree
Annie's Organic Foods

592 **Annie's Naturals**
1610 5th St
Berkeley, CA 94710-1715
510-558-7500
Fax: 802-456-8865 800-434-1234
www.annies.com
Dressings and vinaigrettes, BBQ sauces, marinades and Worcestershire sauce.
Owner/Production Development: Annie Christopher
Owner/Sales/Marketing: Peter Backman
Number Employees: 10-19
Type of Packaging: Consumer, Food Service, Private Label
Brands:
Annie's Naturals
Annie's Naturals Magic Sauces
Annie's Naturals Salad Dressings

593 **Antelope Valley Winery**
42041 20th St W
Lancaster, CA 93534-6912
661-722-0145
Fax: 661-722-6035 800-282-8332
wines@avwinery.com www.avwinery.com
Wines
Owner: Cyndee Donato
Winemaker: Cecil McLester
Estimated Sales: $2.5-5 Million
Number Employees: 5-9
Type of Packaging: Private Label
Brands:
Antelope Valley

594 **Anthony & Sons Italian Bakery**
1275 Bloomfield Ave
Fairfield, NJ 07004-2708
973-575-5865
Fax: 973-244-1298 anthonyandsons@aol.com
Bread
Owner: Anthony Pio Costa
Plant Manager: Robert Tobia
Estimated Sales: Less than $500,000
Number Employees: 5-9

595 **Anthony Road Wine Co**
1020 Anthony Rd
Penn Yan, NY 14527-9632
315-536-2182
Fax: 315-536-5851 800-559-2182
info@anthonyroadwine.com
www.anthonyroadwine.com
Wines
Estimated Sales: $2.5-5 Million
Number Employees: 10-19

596 **Anthony Thomas Candy Co**
1777 Arlingate Ln
Columbus, OH 43228-4114
614-272-1870
877-226-3921
www.anthony-thomas.com
Gourmet-style chocolate including truffles, real butter creams, cordial cherries, creams, peanut butter cups, pecans and English Toffee.
President: Joe Zanetos
EVP Administration/Finance: Greg Zanetos
Marketing/Sales Manager: Clara Davis
EVP Production: Tim Zanetos
Plant Manager: Paul Reeder
Estimated Sales: Less Than $500,000
Number Employees: 1-4
Square Footage: 456000
Type of Packaging: Consumer
Brands:
Anthony-Thomas Chocolates

597 **Anton Caratan & Son**
PO Box 2797
1625 Road 160
Bakersfield, CA 93303-2797
661-725-2575
Fax: 661-725-5829
Table grapes
President: Anton Caratan
Sales Manager: George Ann Caratan
Estimated Sales: $10-20 Million
Number Employees: 250-499
Type of Packaging: Consumer
Brands:
Good Times
Prosperity

598 **Antoni Ravioli Co**
879 N Broadway
North Massapequa, NY 11758-2353
516-799-0350
Fax: 516-799-0357 800-783-0350
www.antoniravioli.com
Ravioli, stuffed shells and manicotti, tortellini, cavatelli and gnocchi, fresh pasta, also gluten free products.
President: Gene Saucci
philrino@msn.com
Estimated Sales: $1.5 Million
Number Employees: 10-19
Square Footage: 12000
Type of Packaging: Food Service, Private Label, Bulk
Brands:
Antoni Ravioli

599 **Antonio Mozzarella Factory**
71 Springfield Ave
Springfield, NJ 07081-1303
973-379-0033
Fax: 973-379-0099 antoniomozz@verizon.net
www.antoniomozzarella.com
Fresh mozarella
President: Tom Pagpugliese
thomas@antoniomozzarella.com
Estimated Sales: $7.1 Million
Number Employees: 1-4

600 **Apac Chemical Corporation**
150 N Santa Anita Ave
Suite 850
Arcadia, CA 91006
626-203-0066
Fax: 626-203-0067 866-849-2722
sales@apacchemical.com www.apacchemical.com
Potassium sorbate and sorbic acid
President: Sun Chang
Vice President: Tom Kusaka
Account Executive: Sergio Scarcella
Account Executive: Dave Plowman
Estimated Sales: $4 Million
Number Employees: 7

601 **Apani Southwest**
5401 N 1st St
Abilene, TX 79603-6424
325-690-1550
Fax: 325-690-1412 drinkapak@sbcglobal.net
www.apanisw.com
Premium drinking water
Owner: Glenda Pickens
Estimated Sales: $2 Million
Number Employees: 10-19
Type of Packaging: Private Label

602 **Apecka Peppered Pickles**
371 Stevens Road
Rockwall, TX 75032-6754
972-771-7628
Fax: 973-772-2655
Peppered pickles, pickled okra and garlic, green chile sauce
President: Sharon Eisenbraun
Estimated Sales: Less than $500,000
Number Employees: 1-4

603 **Apex Marketing Group**
7835 S Rainbow Blvd
Suite 17-300
Las Vegas, NV 89139
866-610-6165
Fax: 805-499-4204 888-990-2739
apexmktg@earthlink.net www.hairnomore.com
Personal care products
President/CEO: Mel Landyn
Vice President: Carole Landyn
Marketing Director: Mark Landyn
Operations Manager: Armen Grigorian
Product Manager: Mel Landyn
Estimated Sales: $5 Million
Number Employees: 25
Number of Brands: 2
Number of Products: 6
Square Footage: 32000
Type of Packaging: Consumer, Private Label, Bulk
Other Locations:
Apex Marketing Group
Newbury Park CA

604 **Aphrodite Divine Confections**
2677 Forest Lane
Garland, TX 75042
972-485-1005
Fax: 972-485-8866 baker@aphroditedesserts.com
www.aphroditedesserts.com
Frozen cookie dough and desserts
Founder: Dean d'Ambrosia

605 **Apiterra**
2677 Forest Lane
Garland, TX 75042
972-485-1005
Fax: 972-485-8866 baker@aphroditedesserts.com
www.aphroditedesserts.com
Flavor-infused honey
Co-Founder & CEO: Dzmitry Hryharovich
Co-Founder & CTO: Aleh Svirchou
Co-Founder: Daria Zarubina
Brands:
APITERRA

606 **Apotheca Inc**
201 Apple Boulevard
Woodbine, IA 51579
712-647-3133
Fax: 888-898-0401 800-736-3130
info@apothecacompany.com
www.apothecacompany.com
Homeopathics, botanical extracts, capsules, tablets and sports nutritionals
President: Kathryn Simon
Contact: Mike Evans
mike@apothecacompany.com
Estimated Sales: $10-20 Million
Number Employees: 100
Square Footage: 140000

607 **Appetizers And, Inc.**
330 Ballardvalle Street
Wilmington, WA 01887
773-227-0400
Fax: 773-227-0448 800-224-7630
Frozen hors d'oeuvres
President/CEO/Co-Owner: George King
EVP/Co-Owner: Patricia Domanik
CFO: Scott Forester
SVP Operations/COO: Kristine Holtz
VP Manufacturing: John Trellicoso
Number Employees: 250-499
Type of Packaging: Consumer, Food Service

608 **Apple & Eve LLC**
2 Seaview Blvd # 100
3rd Floor
Port Washington, NY 11050-4634
516-621-1122
Fax: 516-621-2164 800-969-8018
info@appleandeve.com www.appleandeve.com
Natural juices and juice blends; importer of fruit concentrates
Founder/CEO: Gordon Crane
gordon@appleandeve.com
CFO: Paul Devilacqua
VP: Joan Segal
VP Innovation & Development: Ken Gootkind
Director of Marketing/Advertising: Jeff Damiano
VP Sales/Marketing: Cary Crane
Operations Executive: Tyron Charles
Plant Manager: John Donlon
Purchasing Manager: Mary Ellen Brothers
Estimated Sales: $15.1 Million
Number Employees: 50-99
Number of Products: 100+
Square Footage: 42000
Type of Packaging: Consumer
Brands:
Apple & Eve
Made In the Shade
Sesame Street
Tribal

609 **Apple Acres**
4633 Cherry Valley Turnpike
La Fayette, NY 13084
603-893-8596
Fax: 315-677-5143 sam@appleacres.com
www.appleacres.com
Apples
CEO: Walter Blackler
Co-Owner: Bob Rigdon
Estimated Sales: $10 Million
Number Employees: 20-49
Square Footage: 128000
Type of Packaging: Consumer

610 **Apple Flavor & Fragrance USA**
55 Carter Dr
Edison, NJ 08817-2066
732-393-0600
Fax: 732-393-1933 www.cnaff.com
Flavor ingredients and enhancers.
President: Maggie Wu
maggieapff@cnaffusa.com
Number Employees: 5-9

611 **Apple Valley Market**
9067 US Highway 31 # A
Berrien Springs, MI 49103-1806
269-471-3282
Fax: 269-471-6035 800-237-7436
avnf@avnf.com www.avnf.com
Vitamins and vegetarian groceries
Manager: George Schmidt
george@avnf.com
CEO: Frank Williams

Estimated Sales: $5-10 Million
Number Employees: 100-249
Square Footage: 200000

612 **Applecreek Speciality Foods**
PO Box 910089
Lexington, KY 40591
859-881-8010
Fax: 877-869-9184 800-747-8871
bhall@mis.net
Preserves, fruit butters, marinade, salsa, relish, caramel and chocolate fidge dessert sauces, dressings, BBQ seasonings and homemade candies.
Owner: Buddy Hall
Operations Manager: Lynn Abshear
Estimated Sales: $1-3 Million
Number Employees: 1-4
Brands:
Applecreek Orchards

613 **Appledore Cove LLC**
19 Buffum Rd Unit 6
North Berwick, ME 03906
207-676-4088
Fax: 207-636-8100
Salsas, condiments & dips, sauces & marinades, preserves & dessert sauces
President: Jeff Garstka

614 **Applegate Farms**
Rt 202 South
Suite 300
Bridgewater, NJ 08807-5530
908-725-2768
Fax: 908-725-3383 866-587-5858
Organic meat including beef, chicken, turkey and pork. Also cheese, sausage and hotdogs.
Owner: Seven McDonald
Co-Founder: Chris Ely
Number Employees: 50-99
Square Footage: 28000
Type of Packaging: Consumer, Food Service, Private Label, Bulk
Brands:
Applegate Farms
Great Organic Hotdog
Joy Stick

615 **Appleton Produce Company**
1408 Weiser River Road
PO Box 110
Weiser, ID 83672
208-414-3352
Fax: 208-414-1862 onions@appletonproduce.com
Onions
President: C. Robert Woods
President/Owner: Steve Woods
Marketing/Sales Manager: Steve Walker
Purchasing Manager: Dave Price
Estimated Sales: $12 Million
Number Employees: 50
Type of Packaging: Consumer, Food Service, Private Label, Bulk
Brands:
Apco
Appleton
Gold Nugget

616 **Applewood Orchards Inc**
2998 Rodesiler Hwy
Deerfield, MI 49238-9789
517-447-3002
Fax: 517-447-3006 800-447-3854
jim@applewoodapples.com
www.applewoodapples.com
Apples
Owner: James Swindeman
james@applewoodapples.com
Vice President: Steve Swindeman
VP: Scott Swindeman
Estimated Sales: $5-10 Million
Number Employees: 20-49
Type of Packaging: Consumer

617 **Applewood Seed & Garden Group**
5380 Vivian Street
Arvada, CO 80002-1959
303-431-7333
Fax: 303-467-7886 800-232-0666
sales@applewoodseed.com
www.applewoodseed.com
Wildflower and garden seed producers
President: Gene Milstein
General Manager: Norm Poppe
Contact: Kendall Holdrem
kholdren@applewoodseed.com
Estimated Sales: $5-10 Million
Parent Co: Applewood Seed & Garden Group

618 **Applewood Winery**
82 Four Corners Rd.
Warwick, NY 10990
845-988-9292
info@applewoodwinery.com
www.applewoodwinery.com
Merlot, Cabernet, Riesling, Chardonnay, Red wine blends, fruit-flavoured wine, hard cider
Owner: Jonathan Hull
Year Founded: 1993
Number of Brands: 2
Number of Products: 21
Type of Packaging: Consumer, Private Label
Brands:
Applewood Winery
Naked Flock

619 **April Hill Inc**
190 28th St SE
Grand Rapids, MI 49548
616-245-0595
Fax: 616-245-2368 www.aprilhill.com
Breads, rolls
Plant Manager: William MacKenzie
Estimated Sales: $2.5-5 Million
Number Employees: 10-19

620 **Aqua Clara Bottling & Distribution**
1315 Cleveland Street
Clearwater, FL 33755-5102
727-446-2999
Fax: 727-446-3999
Oxygen-enriched premium drinking water
Chairman: E Douglas Cifers
President & CEO: Jack Plunkett
Number Employees: 5-9
Brands:
Aqua Clara

621 **Aqua Vie Beverage Corporation**
PO Box 6759
333 South Main Street
Ketchum, ID 83340-6759
208-622-7792
Fax: 208-622-8829 800-744-7500
www.aquavie.com
Natural falvored water without carbonation, low-calorie and exotic flavors
President: Thomas Gillespie
Estimated Sales: $1-2.5 Million
Number Employees: 20-49
Type of Packaging: Bulk
Brands:
Avalanche

622 **AquaCuisine**
11560 SW 67th Avenue
Suite 200W
Portland, OR 97223
208-323-2782
Fax: 208-323-4730 mgoforth@aquacuisine.com
www.aquacuisine.com
Seafood products as well as fresh and frozen burgers, franks and refrigerated seafood entrees.
President: Mark Goforth
Estimated Sales: $5 Million
Number Employees: 1-4
Number of Products: 7
Square Footage: 20000
Type of Packaging: Consumer
Brands:
Aquacuisine

623 **AquaTec Development**
1543 Locke Ln
Sugar Land, TX 77478
281-491-0808
Fax: 281-242-7771
Bulk production of algae and nutraceutical extracts and concentrates. Algae food supplements and food fortificial bulk only
President: Howard Stern
hstern@aquatec.com
Number Employees: 1-4
Type of Packaging: Bulk

624 **Aquatec Seafoods Ltd.**
820 Shamrock Place
Comox, BC V9M 3P6
Canada
250-339-6412
Fax: 250-339-4951
Fresh and frozen salmon and oysters
President: Malena Tutte
Estimated Sales: $2.7 Million
Number Employees: 20
Square Footage: 28000
Type of Packaging: Consumer, Food Service, Private Label, Bulk

625 **Aquatech**
6221 Petersburg St
Anchorage, AK 99507-2006
907-563-1387
Fax: 907-563-1852 877-938-2722
www.crabfactory.com
Live, fresh and frozen Alaskan king crab.
Partner: Miki Ballard
Partner: Lamar Ballard
aquatech@ak.net
General Manager: Sarah Ballard
Estimated Sales: $3-5 Million
Number Employees: 5-9

626 **Aralia Olive Oils**
1105 Massachusetts Avenue
Suite 2E
Cambridge, MA 02138
617-354-8556
Fax: 617-249-1855 877-585-9510
www.araliaoliveoils.com
Olive Oils
President: Emmanuel Daskalakis
Number Employees: 2

627 **Arbor Crest Wine Cellars**
4705 N Fruit Hill Rd
Spokane, WA 99217-9562
509-927-9463
Fax: 509-927-0574 www.arborcrest.com
Wine
Head Winemaker: Kristina Mielke-van L"ben Sels
Estimated Sales: $1.25 Million
Number Employees: 20-49
Type of Packaging: Private Label
Brands:
Arbor Crest

628 **Arbor Hill Grapery & Winery**
6461 State Route 64
Naples, NY 14512-9726
585-374-2870
Fax: 585-374-9198 800-554-7553
www.thegrapery.com
Wines, grape- and fruit-based products, fruit preservatives, wine jellies, dressings, vinegars, barbeque sauces, mustard, spreadable sauces and dips, pretzel dips, wine sauces and tea concentrates.
President: John Brahm
john@thegrapery.com
VP: Katharine Brahm
Public Relations: Sherry Brahm-Orlando
Estimated Sales: Less than $5 Million
Number Employees: 5-9
Type of Packaging: Consumer, Private Label
Brands:
Arbor Hill Wine
Brahm's Wine Country
Mrs. Brahms

629 **Arbor Mist Winery**
116 Buffalo St
Canandaigua, NY 14424
866-396-7394
www.arbormist.com
Fruit-flavored wines

630 **Arbor Springs Water Co**
950 Orchard St
Ferndale, MI 48220-1439
248-543-7151
Fax: 248-543-0488 sales@arborspringswater.com
Bottled spring and purified water.
Owner: John Niel
j.niel@arborspringswater.com
Estimated Sales: $5-10 Million
Number Employees: 10-19
Other Locations:
Arbor Springs Water Company
Ann Arbor MI

631 **Arboris LLC**
1101 W Lathrop Ave
PO Box 2008
Savannah, GA 31415-1021
912-238-7537
Fax: 912-238-7454 info@arboris-us.com
www.arboris-us.com
Sterols used in yogurt, milks, juices and breads.
Vice President/General Manager: Peter Acton
Contact: Elliot Abemayor
elliot.abemayor@arboris-us.com
Purchasing: Jeanne Anderson
Number Employees: 10-19

632 **Arbre Farms Inc**
6362 N 192nd Ave
Walkerville, MI 49459-8601
231-873-3337
Fax: 231-873-5699 www.arbrefarms.com
Provides food service and frozen food manufacturing industries with the finest quality frozen fruits and vegetables.
President: C O Johnson
cjohnson@arbrefarms.com
Quality Control: Robert Anderson
Marketing: Tripper Showell
Sales: Jean Hovey
Plant Manager: Vince Miskosky
Number Employees: 250-499
Type of Packaging: Food Service, Bulk
Other Locations:
Willow Cold Storage
Walkerville MI

633 **Arbuckle Coffee Roasters**
3550 E Corporate Dr
Tucson, AZ 85706-1821
520-790-5282
Fax: 520-748-7910 800-533-8278
www.arbucklecoffee.com
Coffee and tea.
President: Denney Willis
VP: Josh Willis
Estimated Sales: $500,000-$1 Million
Number Employees: 10-19
Brands:
Arbuckle

634 **Arcadia Biosciences**
202 Cousteau Pl.
Ste. 105
Davis, CA 95618
530-756-7077
Fax: 530-756-7027 info@arcadiabio.com
arcadiabio.com
Non-GMO specialty wheat ingredients.
President & CEO: Matthew Plavan
Chief Commercial Officer: Sarah Reiter
CFO: Pam Haley
CTO: Randall Shultz
Year Founded: 2002
Number of Brands: 1
Type of Packaging: Food Service
Brands:
GoodWheat™

635 **Arcadia Dairy Farms Inc**
1869 Brevard Rd
34 Arcadia Farms Road
Arden, NC 28704
828-684-3556
Fax: 828-684-7988 info@arcadiafarms.com
www.arcadiadairyfarms.com
Juices including orange, apple, strawberry and grape; also, water
President: James Ward
arcdfinc@aol.com
Vice President: Carolyn Arthur
Estimated Sales: $1 Million
Number Employees: 20-49
Type of Packaging: Consumer
Brands:
Arcadia
Sunrise

636 **Arcadian Estate Winery**
4184 State Route 14
Rock Stream, NY 14878
607-535-2068
Fax: 607-535-4692 800-298-1346
info@arcadianwine.com www.arcadianwine.com
Wines.
Owner: John Dalonzo
Number Employees: 10-19
Type of Packaging: Consumer

637 **Archer Daniels Midland Company**
4666 Faries Parkway
Decatur, IL 62526
217-424-5200
www.adm.com
Food and feed ingredients, industrial chemicals and biofuels.
Type of Packaging: Food Service, Bulk

638 **(HQ)Archer Daniels Midland Company**
77 West Wacker Dr.
Suite 4600
Chicago, IL 60601
312-634-8100
www.adm.com
Food and feed ingredients, industrial chemicals and biofuels.
Chairman/CEO: Juan Luciano
Executive VP/CFO: Ray Young
Senior VP/General Counsel: D. Cameron Findlay
Year Founded: 1902
Estimated Sales: $64.3 Billion
Number Employees: 32,000

639 **Archibald Frozen Desserts**
990 Progress Blvd
New Albany, IN 47150-2259
812-941-8267
Fax: 812-941-5374
Soft serve ice cream and frozen yogurt
CEO: Ed Meyer
Executive VP: Greg Gilbert
greg.gilbert@archibaldfrozendesserts.com
Sales & Marketing Coordinator: Lindsay Usher
National Sales Manager: Alex Mohler
Warehouse/Service Manager: Tim Coy
Estimated Sales: Less Than $500,000
Number Employees: 1-4

640 **Archie Moore's**
15 Factory Ln
Milford, CT 06460-3306
203-876-5088
Fax: 203-876-0525
Manufacturer and exporter of buffalo wing sauce and flavored potato chips
President: Todd Ressler
tressler@archiemoores.com
Estimated Sales: $.5-1 million
Number Employees: 20-49
Square Footage: 10000
Parent Co: Archie Moore's Bar & Restaurant
Type of Packaging: Consumer, Food Service, Private Label, Bulk
Brands:
Archie Moore's

641 **Archon Vitamin Corp**
3775 Park Ave
Suite 1
Edison, NJ 08820-2566
973-371-1700
Fax: 973-371-1277 800-848-0089
purchasing@archonvitamin.com
www.archonvitamin.com
Vitamins, minerals, herbs, and other nutritionals.
President: Tom Pugsley
tpugsley@archonvitamin.com
VP Products Division: Paul Stevens
Quality Assurance Manager: Susan Jackson
Sales Manager: Rick McNall
Operations Executive: Jose Camaano
Purchasing Director: Tracy Daniiel
Estimated Sales: $5-10 Million
Number Employees: 50-99
Number of Brands: 1
Square Footage: 200000
Type of Packaging: Consumer, Private Label, Bulk
Brands:
Bionutrient

642 **Arcobasso Foods Inc**
8850 Pershall Road
Hazlewood, MO 63042
314-381-8083
Fax: 314-381-4522 800-284-0620
pat@arcobasso.com www.arcobasso.com
Salad dressings, sauces and marinades.
President: Pat Newsham
Contact: Phyllis Alberici
phyllis@arcobasso.com
Type of Packaging: Food Service

643 **Arcor USA**
550 Biltmore Way-PH11A
Coral Gables, FL 33134
305-592-1080
Fax: 305-592-1081 800-572-7267
info@arcor.com www.arcor.com.ar
Candies
President: Luis Alejandro Pagani
National Sales Manager: Michael Figueras
Product Manager: Damian Cordova
Estimated Sales: $10-20 Million
Number Employees: 20-49
Type of Packaging: Private Label
Brands:
Arcor Premium Hard Filled Candies
Arcor Value Line Hard Candies
Rocklets
Whisper Chocolate Bon Bons

644 **(HQ)Arctic Beverages**
107 Mountainview Road
Unit 2
Winnipeg, MB R3C 2E6
Can
204-633-8686
866-503-1270
winnipeg@arcticbev.com www.arcticbev.com
Soft drinks, juices, snack foods, bread, frozen food, chocolate.
Year Founded: 1991
Estimated Sales: $6 Million
Number Employees: 44
Number of Products: 68
Square Footage: 68000
Parent Co: Tribal Councils Investment Group of Manitoba Ltd.
Other Locations:
Arctic Beverages Ltd.
The Pas MB
Arctic Beverages Ltd.
Thompson MB
Arctic Beverages Ltd.
Winnipeg MB

645 **Arctic Glacier**
625 Henry Avenue
Winnipeg, MB R3A 0V1
Canada
204-772-2473
Fax: 204-783-9857 888-573-9237
info@arcticglacierinc.com
www.arcticglacierinc.com
Ice
President/CEO: Keith McMahon
EVP Operations: Mike Wohlgemuth
Chief Financial Officer: Douglas Bailey
VP Accounting/Financial Reporting: Rosemary Brisson
VP Sales/Marketing: Michael Busch
Estimated Sales: $10-20 Million
Number Employees: 20-49
Parent Co: Arctic Glacier
Other Locations:
Happy Ice Manufacturing Plant
Buffalo NY
Happy Ice Manufacturing Plant
Utica NY
Happy Ice Manufacturing Plant
Corning NY
Happy Ice Manufacturing Plant
Albany NY

646 **Arctic Ice Cream Co**
22 Arctic Pkwy
Ewing, NJ 08638-3093
609-393-4264
Fax: 609-392-3663 800-858-8966
arcticicecream@hotmail.com
www.arcticicecreamco.com
Ice cream
President: Thomas Green
CEO: John Connors
Vice President: Christine Green
Estimated Sales: $1 Million
Number Employees: 10-19

647 **Arctic Zero**
4241 Jutland Drive
Suite 305
San Diego, CA 92117
888-272-1715
www.arcticzero.com
Low glycemic, lactose free, gluten free and GMO free frozen desserts

Founder: Greg Holtman
Contact: Megan Abordo
megan@myarcticzero.com

648 **Ardent Mills Corp**
1875 Lawrence St
Suite 200
Denver, CO 80202-1847
510-999-2877
800-851-9618
www.ardentmills.com
Flours, mixes, blends, and specialty products.
CEO: Dan Dye
Chief Financial Officer: John Barton
Director of Marketing: Don Trouba
Vice President, Sales: Dean Grossmann
Contact: Andy Alan
andy.allen@ardentmills.com
Senior Director Operations: Troy Anderson
Number Employees: 10-19
Type of Packaging: Food Service, Bulk
Brands:
American Beauty
Buccaneer
Denrado
Full Power
Hummer
Kyrol
Magnifico Special
Minnesota Girl
Pikes Peak
Producer
Ramsey Medium Rye
Urban Special
and many more

649 **Ardith Mae Farmstead Goat Cheese**
1094 State Route 9J
Stuyvesant , NY 12173
917-744-4314
www.ardithmae.com
Goat cheese

650 **Ardmore Cheese Company**
26366 Main Street
Ardmore, TN 38449
931-427-2191
Fax: 931-427-4116
Cheddar cheese
Manager: Abby Woods
VP: Joe Madeo
Plant Manager: Brad Jackson
Estimated Sales: $500-1 Million appx.
Number Employees: 1-4
Square Footage: 40000
Type of Packaging: Consumer, Private Label
Brands:
Ardmore
Avalon

651 **Ardy Fisher**
201-244-3436
877-699-5066
info@ardyfisher.com brislingsardines.com
Sardines
Number of Brands: 1
Number of Products: 5
Brands:
BRISLING SARDINES

652 **Arel Group Wine & Spirits Inc**
2870 Pharr Court South NW
Suite 2009
Atlanta, GA 30305-2174
404-869-4387
Fax: 404-506-9242 info@arelgroupws.com
www.tenutapolvaro.com
Wines and spirits
President & Co-Founder: Elviana Candoni
Co-Founder: Armando De Zan
admin@candoniwines.com
Estimated Sales: $1.3 Million
Number Employees: 10-19
Number of Brands: 2
Brands:
Candoni de Zan
Tenuta Polvaro

653 **Arena & Sons**
746 Maple St
Redwood City, CA 94063-2025
650-366-1750
Fax: 650-366-4679
Veal and beef
Owner: Jim Arena
President: Joanne Arena
Estimated Sales: $2.5-5 Million
Number Employees: 5-9
Type of Packaging: Bulk

654 **Argania Butter**
Rancho Palos Verdes, CA 90275
info@arganiabutter.com
arganiabutter.com
Almond butter
Founder: Nadia Gara

655 **Argee Corp**
9550 Pathway St
Santee, CA 92071-4169
619-449-5050
Fax: 619-449-8392 800-449-3030
argeecorp@sbcglobal.net www.argeecorp.com
President: Robert Goldman
rgoldman@argeecorp.com
VP Sales/Marketing: Ruth Goldman
Estimated Sales: $10-20 Million
Number Employees: 50-99

656 **Argo Century, Inc.**
840 Edgewood Ave
Suite 202
Jacksonville, FL 32205
704-525-6180
Fax: 704-525-6280 800-446-7108
info@tontonsauce.com www.tontonsauce.com
Ginger dressing, teriyaki sauce and vinaigrettes.
President: Yoshi Shioda
Estimated Sales: $1-3 Million
Number Employees: 1-4
Type of Packaging: Consumer

657 **Argo Fine Foods**
PO Box 2077
Saint James, NY 11780
631-703-0443
Tzatziki (yogurt sauce), pita snacks
President/Owner: Christel DeBlasio-Pavlidis

658 **Argo Tea**
16 W Randolph St
Chicago, IL 60601
612-553-1550
info@argotea.com
www.argotea.com
Tea

659 **Argyle Winery**
691 Highway 99 W
PO Box 280
Dundee, OR 97115-0280
503-538-8520
Fax: 503-538-2055 888-427-4953
customerservice@argylewinery.com
www.argylewinery.com
Wines.
Director, Sales & Marketing: Chris Cullina
Head, Vineyard Operations: Allen Holstein
Year Founded: 1987
Estimated Sales: $20-50 Million
Number Employees: 50-99
Number of Brands: 3
Parent Co: Distinguished Vineyards & Wine Partners
Type of Packaging: Private Label
Brands:
Argyle Brut
Nuthouse
Spirithouse

660 **Ariake USA Inc**
1711 N Liberty St
Harrisonburg, VA 22802-4518
540-432-6550
Fax: 540-432-6549 www.ariakeusa.com
Meat stocks, broths, bases, and seasonings.
Technical Manager: Kyle Wellsford
kylewellsford@va.ariake.com
Manager: Joseph Brisby
Purchasing Specialist: Aaron Robinson
Estimated Sales: $18 Million
Number Employees: 50-99
Square Footage: 58000
Parent Co: Ariake Japan Co., Ltd.

661 **Arico Natural Foods**
3720 Sw 141st Ave
Suite 210
Beaverton, OR 97005
503-259-0871
www.crisproot.com
Casava root chips
President/CEO: Angela Ichwan
CFO/VP: Hermanto Hidajat
Vice President of Sales and Marketing: Duke Field
Estimated Sales: $500,000-1 Million
Number Employees: 5-9

662 **Ariel Natural Foods**
13400 N 20th St
Suite 32
Bellevue, WA 98005
425-637-3345
Fax: 425-637-8655 www.arielfoods.com
Sugar-free, dairy-free and gluten-free premium dried snacks.

663 **Ariel Vineyards**
860 Napa Valley Corporate Way
Suite C
Napa, CA 94558-6281
707-258-8050
Fax: 707-258-8052 800-456-9472
info@arielvineyards.com www.arielvineyards.com
Nonalcoholic wine
Manager: Craig Rosser
info@jlohr.com
VP Operations: Jeff Meier
Estimated Sales: $5-10 Million
Number Employees: 1-4
Square Footage: 256000
Parent Co: J. Lohr Vineyards & Wines
Brands:
Ariel
Ariel Blanc
Ariel Brut Cuve
Ariel Cabernet
Ariel Chardonnay
Ariel Merlot
Ariel Rouge
Ariel White Zinfandel

664 **Aries Prepared Beef**
17 W Magnolia Blvd
Burbank, CA 91502-1719
818-526-4855
Fax: 818-845-3041 800-424-2333
aileen@ariesbeef.com www.ariesbeef.com
Meats and sausage including; roast beef, pastrami, corned beef, hot dogs, sausages, and pickled and fresh meats
Owner: Ragip Unal
Director of Quality Control: Rob Unal
VP Sales: Fred Weiss
ragipunal@gmail.com
Director of Production: Luis Rolon
General Manager: Ken McLaughlin
Estimated Sales: $19 Million
Number Employees: 50-99
Type of Packaging: Consumer, Food Service

665 **Arise & Shine Herbal Products**
P.O.Box 400
Medford, OR 97501
541-282-0891
Fax: 541-773-8866 800-688-2444
www.ariseandshine.com
Digestive aids and herbal supplements.
Founder: Dr. Richard Anderson
CEO: Avona L'Carttier
Contact: Denise Shannon
dshannon@ariseandshine.com
Brands:
Chomper
Flora Grow
Herbal Nutrition
Super Antioxidant Blend
Ultimate Food Complex

666 **Arista Industries Inc**
557 Danbury Rd
Wilton, CT 06897-2218
203-761-1009
Fax: 203-761-4980 800-255-6457
info@aristaindustries.com
www.aristaindustries.com
Oils, frozen shrimp, lobster tails and octopus. Importer of octopus, shrimp, squid, lobster tails, oils and surimi products.

President: Alan Weitzer
CEO: Charles Hillyer
Chairman: Stephen Weitzer
steve@aristaindustries.com
Estimated Sales: $2.5-5 Million
Number Employees: 20-49
Type of Packaging: Consumer, Food Service
Brands:
Arista
Pacific Treasures
Sea Devils

667 **Ariston Specialties**
PO Box 306
Bloomfield, CT 06002
860-224-7184
Fax: 860-726-1263
aristonspecialties@hotmail.com
Olive Oils
Owner: Thomas Doukas
tom.doukas@aristonspecialties.com

668 **Ariza Cheese Co**
7602 Jackson St
Paramount, CA 90723-4912
562-630-4144
Fax: 562-630-4174 800-762-4736
Mexican cheese
President: Fatima Ariza
Estimated Sales: $5.5 Million
Number Employees: 20-49
Type of Packaging: Consumer, Food Service

669 **Arizmendi Bakery**
1331 9th Ave
San Francisco, CA 94122-2308
415-566-3117
info@arizmendibakery.com
www.arizmendibakery.com
Pastries, artisan breads, gourmet pizza
Owner: Isaac Hee
isaachee@yahoo.com
Number Employees: 10-19

670 **Arizona Beverage Company**
644 Linn Street
Suite 318
Cincinnati, OH 45203
Fax: 516-326-4988 800-832-3775
info@drinkarizona.com www.drinkarizona.com
Teas, juices and iced coffees.
President: John Ferolito
Chairman: Don Vultagglio
CFO/CEO: Rick Adonailo
VP National Sales: Paul O'Donnell
Contact: Taiwo Adekoya
tadekoya@drinkarizona.com
Year Founded: 1992
Estimated Sales: $5-10 Million
Number Employees: 500-999
Brands:
Arizona
Ferolito, Vultaggio & Sons
Rx Extreme Energy Shot

671 **Arizona Cowboy**
3010 N 24th St
Phoenix, AZ 85016-7816
602-278-1427
Fax: 602-484-9482 800-529-8627
www.ameliocenterprises.com
Salsa, jellies, hot sauces, tortilla chips, honey, candy and nuts.
Owner/President: Amelio Casciato
Estimated Sales: $500,000-1 Million
Number Employees: 5-9
Square Footage: 6600
Type of Packaging: Consumer, Food Service, Private Label

672 **Arizona Natural Products**
12815 N Cave Creek Rd
Phoenix, AZ 85022-5834
602-997-6098
Fax: 602-288-8331 800-255-2823
info@arizonanatural.com www.arizonanatural.com
Herbal and vitamin supplements.
President/CEO: Michael Hanna
Contact: Ranna Hanna
rhanna@arizonanatural.com
Estimated Sales: Less Than $500,000
Number Employees: 5-9
Square Footage: 40000

Brands:
Allirich

673 **Arizona Nutritional Supplements**
210 S Beck Ave
Chandler, AZ 85226-3311
480-753-3510
Fax: 480-966-9640 888-742-7675
www.aznutritional.com
Nutritional and dietary supplements
Owner: Jonathan Pinkus
jonpinkus@aznutritional.com
Co-Owner: Aaron Blunck
Estimated Sales: $10-20 Million
Number Employees: 100-249
Square Footage: 50000

674 **Arizona Pepper Products**
710 E Broadway Rd
Mesa, AZ 85204-2081
480-833-1908
Fax: 480-833-0309 800-359-3912
info@azgunslinger.com www.azgunslinger.com
Hot sauces, olives, spices and pistachios
President: Bill Marko
Year Founded: 1987
Estimated Sales: $2.5-5 Million
Number Employees: 10-19

675 **Arizona Pistachio Company**
3865 N Businesss Ctr Drive
Suite 115
Tucson, AZ 85705
520-746-0880
Fax: 520-741-9797 800-333-8575
salesapc@azpistachio.com
Pistachios
President: Henry Mollner
Year Founded: 1969
Estimated Sales: $2.5-5 Million
Number Employees: 5-9
Type of Packaging: Consumer, Food Service, Bulk

676 **Arizona Sunland Foods**
3752 S Broadmont Drive
Tucson, AZ 85713
520-624-7068
www.azsunlandfoods.com
Breaded proteins, sauces and dressings
President: Arnie Jacobsen
arnie@azsunlandfoods.com
Director of Sales & Marketing: Josh Jacobsen
Director of Product Dev. & Operations: Joel Jacobsen
Year Founded: 1983
Type of Packaging: Food Service, Private Label
Brands:
Sunland

677 **Arizona Vineyards**
1830 E Patagonia Hwy
Nogales, AZ 85621
520-287-7972
Fax: 520-287-7597
Wines
Owner/President: Arthur Ocheltree
Owner/CEO: Tino Ocheltree
Estimated Sales: Less than $150,000
Number Employees: 1-4
Brands:
Arizona Vineyards

678 **Arla Foods Inc**
675 Rivermede Road
Concord, ON L4K 2G9
Canada
905-669-9393
Fax: 905-669-5614 www.arlafoods.com
Cheese
President: Andrew Simpson
Estimated Sales: $19 Million
Number Employees: 120
Square Footage: 200000
Type of Packaging: Consumer, Food Service, Private Label, Bulk
Brands:
Tre Stelle

679 **Arlen S Gould & Assoc**
2821 N Vista Rd
Arlington Hts, IL 60004-2108
847-577-2122
Fax: 708-577-4244
Sauces, dips and dressings

Owner: Arlen Gould
Number Employees: 1-4
Brands:
Dolefam

680 **Armanino Foods of Distinction**
30588 San Antonio St
Hayward, CA 94544-7102
510-441-9300
Fax: 510-441-0101 800-255-8588
customerservice@armanino.biz
Exporter of Italian foods including sauces, pasta, meatballs and bread. Importer of Italian cheeses.
CEO: Edmond Pera
Estimated Sales: F
Number Employees: 20-49
Square Footage: 24000
Type of Packaging: Consumer, Food Service
Brands:
Armanino

681 **Armbrust Meats**
224 S Main St
Medford, WI 54451
715-748-3102
Fax: 715-748-6399
Fresh and frozen sausage, beef, pork and poultry
President: Thomas Armbrust
Estimated Sales: $500,000-$1 Million
Square Footage: 132000
Type of Packaging: Consumer, Bulk

682 **Armenia Coffee Corporation**
2975 Westchester Avenue
Purchase, NY 10577
914-694-6100
Fax: 914-694-5622 j.apuzzo@armeniacoffee.com
armeniacoffee.net
Coffee
President: Joe Apuzzo
Owner: John Randall
CFO: Alan Macek
VP: Robert Tapia
Estimated Sales: $1.4 Million
Number Employees: 9

683 **Armeno Coffee Roasters LTD**
75 Otis St
Northborough, MA 01532-2412
508-393-2821
Fax: 508-393-2818 beans@armeno.com
www.armeno.com
Coffee roaster
Owner: Chuck Koffman
beans@armeno.com
Co-Owner: John Parks
Estimated Sales: Under $1 Million
Number Employees: 1-4
Square Footage: 20000
Type of Packaging: Consumer, Private Label
Brands:
Armeno

684 **Armistead Citrus Company**
1057 N Greenfield Rd
Mesa, AZ 85205
480-830-2491
Citrus products
Owner: Ken Armistead
Estimated Sales: Under $500,000
Number Employees: 1-4
Brands:
Armistead Citrus Products

685 **Arnabal International, Inc.**
13459 Savanna
Tustin, CA 92782
714-665-9477
Fax: 714-665-9477 armen@arnabal.com
www.arnabal.com
Oils and vinegars
Owner: Nairy Balian
Co-Owner: Jeff Stratton
Estimated Sales: $.5-1 million
Number Employees: 1-4

686 **Arnel's Originals, Inc**
381 Sonoma Ct
Ventura, CA 93004-1169
USA
805-322-6900
www.arnelsoriginals.com
Baking mixes

President: Arnel McAtee
Contact: Gabriela Eisenberg
eisenbergg@svusd.org
Estimated Sales: 52,000
Number Employees: 1

687 **Arnhem Group**
25 Commerce Drive
Suite 130
Cranford, NJ 07016-3605
908-709-4045
Fax: 908-709-9221 800-851-1052
info@arnhemgroup.com www.arnhemgroup.com
Binders and extenders, fat replacers, flavor enhancers, milk products and stabilizers.
President, Chairman, CEO: Michael Bonner
Account Manager: Karyn Rosenberg
National Accounts Manager: Sandra Lyna
Contact: Milagros Fernandez
mfernandez@arnhemgroup.com
Estimated Sales: $1-2.5 Million
Number Employees: 1-4

688 **Arnold Farm Sugarhouse**
P.O. Box 63
Jackman, ME 04945
207-668-4110
www.arnoldfarm.com
Maple syrup

689 **Arnold Foods Company**
PO Box 976
Horsham, PA 19044
203-531-2043
Fax: 203-531-2170 800-984-0989
www.gwbakeries.com
Baked goods
Vice President: Rod Cuha
Manager: Vinnie Greco
Number Employees: 1-4
Brands:
Beck's
Beck's Dark
Beck's For Oktoberfest
Haake Beck Non-Alcoholic

690 **Arnold's Meat Food Products**
274 Heyward Street
Brooklyn, NY 11209
718-963-1400
Fax: 718-963-2303 800-633-7023
www.arnolds-sausage.com
Smoked sausage, scrapple, chorizos, kielbasa and bacon.
President: Sheldon Dosik
michelle_shao@colpal.com
VP: Jason Judd
Year Founded: 1967
Estimated Sales: $3.6 Million
Number Employees: 25
Square Footage: 33940
Type of Packaging: Consumer, Food Service, Private Label, Bulk
Brands:
Arnold's Meats
Caroline's Sausage
El Cerdito

691 **Arns Winery**
601 Mund Rd
St Helena, CA 94574-9738
707-963-3429
Fax: 707-963-5780 info@arnswinery.com
www.arnswinery.com
Wines
Owner: John Arns
Co-Owner: Sandi Belcher
sandi@arnswinery.com
Marketing: Sandi Belcher
Sales: Kathi Belcher-Tyler
Purchasing: John Arns
Estimated Sales: $100,000
Number Employees: 1-4
Number of Brands: 1
Number of Products: 1
Square Footage: 4800
Type of Packaging: Consumer
Brands:
Arns

692 **Aroma Coffee Company**
7650 Industrial Dr
Forest Park, IL 60130
708-488-8340
Fax: 708-488-8366
Roasted whole bean coffee
President: Gust Papanicholas
Estimated Sales: $5-10 Million
Number Employees: 6
Type of Packaging: Consumer, Food Service, Private Label, Bulk
Brands:
Aroma Cuisiner's Choice
Aroma Southern Maison
Aroma Turkish
Cuisiniers Choice

693 **Aroma Coffee Roasters Inc**
1601 Madison St
Hoboken, NJ 07030-2313
201-792-1730
Fax: 201-659-1883 www.aromacoffee.com
Coffee wholesaler
Manager: Ruth Santuccio
Estimated Sales: $1-2.5 Million
Number Employees: 20-49

694 **Aroma Ridge**
1831 W Oak Pkwy
Suite C
Marietta, GA 30062-2246
770-421-9600
Fax: 770-421-9116 800-528-2123
contact@aromaridge.com www.aromaridge.com
Coffee
Owner: Nawal Shadeed
Number Employees: 5-9

695 **Aroma Vera**
5310 Beethoven St
Los Angeles, CA 90066-7015
310-204-3392
Fax: 310-306-5873 800-669-9514
cservice@aromavera.com
Processor, importer and exporter of essential oils
President: Marcel Lavabre
CEO: Klee Irwin
Estimated Sales: $59,000
Number Employees: 1
Square Footage: 200000
Brands:
Aroma Vera

696 **Aroma-Life**
16161 Ventura Boulevard
Encino, CA 91436-2522
818-905-7761
Fax: 818-905-0292 mzwan@aol.com
Almond and macadamia oils
President: Moshe Zwang
CEO: Diana Zwang
Estimated Sales: $300,000-500,000
Number Employees: 1-4
Number of Brands: 18
Number of Products: 16
Square Footage: 110000
Type of Packaging: Private Label, Bulk
Brands:
Aroma-Life

697 **Aromachem**
599 Johnson Ave
Brooklyn, NY 11237
718-497-4664
Fax: 718-821-2193
Flavors, essential oils and fragrances
President: M Edwards
CEO: Leona Levine
Estimated Sales: $3 Million
Number Employees: 30
Square Footage: 100000
Type of Packaging: Bulk

698 **Aromatech USA**
5770 Hoffner Avenue
Suite 103
Orlando, FL 32822
407-277-5727
Fax: 407-277-5725 americas@aromatech.fr
www.aromatech.fr/en/f.usa.htm
Flavorings for beverages, candies, baking, snacks and pastries.

699 **Arome Fleurs & Fruits**
6600, chemin des Sept
Saint-Jean-Baptiste Day, QC J0L 2B0
Canada
450-281-0911
Fax: 450-281-0917 877-349-3282
Floral products incorporated into spreads, jellies and syrups.

700 **Aromi d'Italia**
5 N Calhoun St
Baltimore, MD 21223-1814
443-703-4001
Fax: 443-703-2194 877-435-2869
ashworth@ashworth.com
Gelato
Owner: Boris Ghazarian
Contact: Hannah Follis
hfollis@aromibeauty.com
Estimated Sales: $200,000
Number Employees: 5-9
Brands:
Aromi D'Italia

701 **Aromor Flavors & Fragrances**
560 Sylvan Ave # 2030
Englewood Cliffs, NJ 07632-3165
201-503-1662
Fax: 201-503-1663 866-425-1600
Flavors and fragrances
Manager: Carol Feldman
cfeldman@aromor-usa.com
General Manager: Gary Romans
Number Employees: 1-4

702 **Arro Corp**
7440 Santa Fe Dr # A
Hodgkins, IL 60525-5076
708-639-9063
Fax: 708-352-5293 877-929-2776
Sales@arro.com www.arro.com
Corn, peanut, salad, soybean and vegetable oils.
Owner: Pat Gaughn
arrosales@aol.com
Sales Exec: Timothy Mcnicholas
Estimated Sales: $500,000-1 Million
Number Employees: 50-99
Type of Packaging: Food Service, Private Label, Bulk
Other Locations:
Chicago IL
Hodgkins IL

703 **Arrowac Fisheries**
Fisherman's Commerce Building
4039 21st Ave W, Suite 200
Seattle, WA 98199-1252
206-282-5655
Fax: 206-282-9329 info@arrowac-merco.com
www.arrowac-merco.com
Fresh and frozen seafood.
President: Frank Mercker
Vice President: Waltraut Yanagisawa
Estimated Sales: $25 Million
Number of Brands: 3
Number of Products: 15
Square Footage: 2000
Type of Packaging: Consumer, Food Service, Private Label, Bulk
Brands:
Arrow
Merco
Ocean Dawn

704 **Arrowhead Beef**
982 Hutchins Ln.
Chipley, FL 32428
850-270-8804
info@arrowheadbeef.com
arrowheadbeef.com
Grass-fed and Waygu beef.
Co-Owner: George Fisher
Co-Owner: Tony DeBlauw
Year Founded: 2010
Type of Packaging: Private Label

705 **Arrowhead Mills**
4600 Sleepytime Dr.
Boulder, CO 80301
866-595-8917
Fax: 806-364-8242 800-434-4246
www.arrowheadmills.com
Pasta

President/CEO: Irwin Simon
Operations: Gary Schultz
Purchasing: Dale Hollingswoth
Number Employees: 50-99
Parent Co: Hain Food Group

706 **Arrowood Winery**
14347 Hwy 12
PO Box 1240
Glen Ellen, CA 95442-9445
707-935-2600
Fax: 707-938-5947 800-938-5170
www.arrowoodvineyards.com
Wines.
Founder: Richard Arrowood
Founder: Alis Arrowood
Winemaker: Kristina Werner
Manager: Lisa Evich
lisa.evich@arrowoodwinery.com
Estimated Sales: $10-20 Million
Number Employees: 20-49
Number of Brands: 2
Type of Packaging: Private Label
Brands:
Arrowood
Grand Archer

707 **Art CoCo Chocolate Company**
2248 Gary Lane
Geneva, IL 60134
630-232-2500
Fax: 630-232-2528 877-232-9901
info@artcoco.com www.artcoco.com
Chocolates
President: Kenneth Wolf
VP: Gail Zucker
National Retail Sales Director: Michelle Bonnick
Production Manager: Charles Martinez
Estimated Sales: $5-9.9 Million
Number Employees: 5-9
Parent Co: Silvestri Sweets, Inc.
Type of Packaging: Private Label
Brands:
Art Coco
Art Fidos Cookies
Art Topo

708 **Art's Mexican Products**
615 Kansas Ave
Kansas City, KS 66105-1311
913-371-2163
Fax: 913-371-2052
www.artsmexicanfoodproducts.com
Mexican food specialties including corn chips, tortilla chips and sauces.
Owner: Angela Gutierrez
Owner: Rachael Gutierrez
Manager: Rachael Kelly
Estimated Sales: $10-20 Million
Number Employees: 10-19
Number of Brands: 1
Brands:
Art's Mexican Products

709 **Art's Tamales**
574-576 Hickory Point Rd
Metamora, IL 61548
309-367-2850
Beef tamales and BBQ
President: David Chinuge
CEO: Zack Fosdyck
Public Relations: Robin Fosdyck
Production Manager: Bill Sanders
Estimated Sales: $300,000-500,000
Number Employees: 5
Square Footage: 20000
Type of Packaging: Consumer, Food Service, Private Label
Brands:
Art's Tamales
Party Time

710 **Arteasans Beverages LLC**
801 New 167th St
Suite 312
North Miami Beach, FL 33162-3729
305-363-5410
www.arteasan.com
Cold tea

711 **Artek USA**
3915 Freshwind Circle
Westlake Village, CA 91361
818-874-0885
Fax: 818-874-0802 866-278-3501
sales@artekusa.com www.artekusa.com
President: Larry Jones
Estimated Sales: $.5-1 million
Number Employees: 5

712 **Artesa Vineyards & Winery**
1345 Henry Rd
Napa, CA 94559-9705
707-224-1668
Fax: 707-224-1672 Info@artesawinery.com
www.artesawinery.com
Wines
President: Mark Beringer
djohnson@nspit.nashville.ihs.gov
CFO: Tim O'Leary
Winemaker: Ana Diogo-Draper
VP Production: Dave Dobson
Estimated Sales: $20-50 Million
Number Employees: 50-99
Type of Packaging: Private Label

713 **Artesian Honey Producers**
PO Box 6
100 West 1st Ave
Artesian, SD 57314
605-527-2423
Honey, candy, and confectionary
Owner: John Zen
Estimated Sales: $1-2.5 Million
Number Employees: 5-9
Type of Packaging: Bulk

714 **Artisan Confections**
100 Crystal A Dr
Hershey, PA 17033-9524
717-534-4200
Fax: 415-626-7991 866 237 0152
Chocolate truffles and chocolate novelties
President: Charles Huggins
CEO: Joseph Scmidt
CFO: Jeff Smith
VP Marketing: Ellen Meuse
Production Manager: Richard Chaeniot
Estimated Sales: $5-10 Million
Number Employees: 50-99
Brands:
Chocolate Slicks

715 **Artisan Kettle**
833-605-6929
info@artisankettle.com artisankettle.com
Chocolate chips and bars
Number of Brands: 1
Number of Products: 2
Brands:
ARTISAN KETTLE

716 **Artist Coffee**
51 Harvey Road
Unit D
Londonderry, NH 03053-7414
603-434-9385
Fax: 603-216-8029 866-440-4511
Producer of gourmet coffee, tea and candy for promotional trade. Specializing in Custom Labeling with very special products.
President: Tom Rushton
Marketing Director: Dan Sewell
Estimated Sales: $3-5 Million
Number Employees: 1-4
Type of Packaging: Consumer, Private Label
Other Locations:
Lambent Technologies
Gurnee IL
Brands:
Cirashine
Erucical
Hodag
Lamchem
Lumisolve
Lumisorb
Lumulse
Oleocal
Polycal

717 **Arturo's Spinella's Bakery**
750 North Main Street
Waterbury, CT 06705
203-754-3056
Cookies
President: Fred Napolitano
Estimated Sales: $1-2.5 Million appx.
Number Employees: 5-9

718 **Artuso Pastry**
670 E 187th St
Bronx, NY 10458
718-367-2515
Fax: 718-367-2553 sales@artusopastry.com
artusopastry.com
Italian pastry ingredients, fresh and frozen
CEO: Anthony Artuso
Sales Exec: Natalie Corridori
Estimated Sales: $3 Million
Number Employees: 20-49
Brands:
Artuso

719 **Arway Confections Inc**
3425 N Kimball Ave
Chicago, IL 60618-5505
773-267-5770
Fax: 773-267-0610 800-695-0612
craigleva@arwayconfections.com
www.arwayconfections.com
Candy including brittles, butter toffee, panned and enrobed products, sponge candy and glazed nuts
President: James Resnick
jamesresnick@arwayconfections.com
President/Marketing Manager: Craig Leva
General Manager/Purchasing: Rick Johnson
Estimated Sales: $5-10 Million
Number Employees: 20-49
Square Footage: 320000
Type of Packaging: Bulk

720 **Arylessence Inc**
1091 Lake Dr
Marietta, GA 30066-1073
770-924-3775
Fax: 770-928-5671 800-553-2440
gcoffG@arylessence.com www.arylessence.com
Fragrance and flavors
President & CEO: Steve Tanner
ctanner@arylessence.com
Executive Vice President: Cynthia Reichard
Estimated Sales: $23 Million
Number Employees: 50-99
Type of Packaging: Private Label

721 **Aryzta**
6080 Center Dr
Suite 900
Los Angeles, CA 90045
855-427-9982
www.aryztaamericas.com
Baked and unbaked desserts and breakfast pastries.
Chairman: Gary McGann
CEO: Kevin Toland
Year Founded: 1897
Estimated Sales: $300 Million
Number Employees: 10,000+
Type of Packaging: Consumer, Food Service, Private Label
Other Locations:
Gourmet Baker
Burnaby BC
Gourmet Baker
Winnipeg MT
Brands:
Fantasia
Gourmet Baker

722 **Asael Farr & Sons Co**
2575 S 300 W
Salt Lake City, UT 84115-2908
801-484-8724
Fax: 801-484-8768 877-553-2777
info@farrsicecream.com www.farrsicecream.com
Ice creams, yogurts, sorbets, ice cream and yogurt mixes, specialty foods, etc
President: Dexter Farr
CEO: Michael Farr
Contact: Blair Boelter
blair.boelter@farrsicecream.com
Estimated Sales: $.5-1 million
Number Employees: 5-9
Brands:
Farr
Russell's

723 **Asarasi**
23 Turner Rd #61
Danbury, CT 06810
info@asarasiwater.com
asarasi.com
Bottled water extracted from maple trees
CEO: Adam Lazar

724 **Aseltine Cider Company**
533 Lamoreaux Dr NW
Comstock Park, MI 49321
616-784-6615
Fax: 616-784-7676
Bottled apple products, manufacturing food preparations
Owner: John Klamt
Secretary: Ronald Klamt
General Manager: John Klamt
Estimated Sales: $2.5-5 Million
Number Employees: 10-19

725 **Asher's Chocolates**
1555 Gehman Road
Kulpsville, PA 19443
215-721-3276
Fax: 215-721-3265 855-827-4377
customers@ashers.com www.ashers.com
Chocolate and confections, including chocolate-covered pretzels potato chips, and graham crackers. The company also produces boxed assortments (including truffles, chews, nuts, cordials, and creams) and gift baskets, fudgepecan-caramel patties, almond bark, and sugar-free and low-carb assortments.
President/CEO: David Asher
CFO: Charles Clark
VP Sales/Marketing: Jeff Asher
Contact: Lisa Wylie
lwylie@ashers.com
VP Operations: Steve Marcanello
Estimated Sales: A
Number Employees: 120

726 **Ashland Milling**
PO Box 1775
14471 Washington Highway
Ashland, VA 23005
804-798-8329
Fax: 804-798-9357 888-897-3336
sales@byrdmill.com www.byrdmill.com
Flour, cornmeal and mixes
President: Todd Attkisson
General Manager: Lynwood Atkinson
attkisson@byrdmill.com
Estimated Sales: $10-20 Million
Number Employees: 20-49
Brands:
Blue Barn
Diamond
Eukanuba
Hyland
Kalmbach
Purina

727 **Ashland Plantation Gourmet**
133 Highway 1177
Bunkie, LA 71322-9773
318-346-6600
Fax: 318-346-4666
Food Producers
President: Kim White
Estimated Sales: Less than $500,000
Number Employees: 1-4

728 **Ashland Sausage Co**
280 S Westgate Dr
Carol Stream, IL 60188-2243
630-690-2600
Fax: 630-690-2612 contact@ashlandsausage.com
www.ashlandsausage.com
Sausage
President: Stanley Podgorski
ashlandsausage@yahoo.com
Purchasing: Stanley Podgorski
Estimated Sales: $1-2.5 Million
Number Employees: 10-19
Type of Packaging: Consumer, Food Service
Brands:
Ashland

729 **Ashland Vineyards & Winery**
2775 E Main St
Ashland, OR 97520-9781
541-488-0088
Fax: 541-488-5857 www.winenet.com
Wines
Owner: Phil Kodak
wines@winenet.com
Owner/CEO: Kathleen Kodak
Estimated Sales: Less Than $500,000
Number Employees: 1-4
Brands:
Ashland

730 **Ashley Food Co Inc**
443 North Rd
Sudbury, MA 01776-1017
978-579-8988
Fax: 978-579-8989 800-617-2823
maddog@ashleyfood.com www.ashleyfoodco.com
Sauces
President: David Ashley
maddog@ashleyfood.com
Estimated Sales: $1-2.5 Million
Number Employees: 1-4
Brands:
Joe Perry's
Mad Cat
Mad Dog Hot Sauce
Weir's

731 **Ashman Manufacturing & Distributing Company**
P.O.Box 1068
1120 Jensen Drive
Virginia Beach, VA 23451-0068
757-428-6734
Fax: 757-437-0398 800-641-9924
admin@ashmanco.com www.ashmanco.com
A wide variety of gourmet sauces, salsas, hot sauces, dry blends, marinades, dessert sauces and drink mixes
President, Co-Founder: Tim Ashman
Co-Founder: Katharine Ashman
Sales Manager: Joel Lutchin
Estimated Sales: $5-10 million
Number Employees: 10-19
Type of Packaging: Consumer, Private Label

732 **Asiago PDO & Speck AltoAdige PGI**
26 West 23rd Street
6th Floor
New York, NY 10010
646-624-2885
Fax: 646-624-2893
Cheese, cured meats i.e. prosciutto/bacon.
Marketing: Flavio Innocenzi

733 **Asiamerica Ingredients**
245 Old Hood Rd #3
Westwood, NJ 07675-3174
201-497-5993
Fax: 201-497-5994 201-497-5531
info@asiamericaingredients.com
www.asiamericaingredients.com
Processor, importer, exporter and distributor of bulk vitamins, amino acids, nutraceuticals, aromatic chemicals, food additives, herbs, mineral nutrients and pharmaceuticals.
President/Owner: Mark Zhang
CFO: Lillian Yang
Quality Control: Michelle Naomi
Sales: Cari Pandero
Contact: Elizabeth Gysbers
egysbers@asiamericaingredients.com
Purchasing: Michelle N. Riley
Estimated Sales: $5-10 Million
Number Employees: 10
Type of Packaging: Bulk

734 **Asian Foods Inc**
1300 L'Orient St
St Paul, MN 55117
651-558-2400
www.asianfoods.com
Ethnic food products
CEO: Kevin Hourican
Vice President, Sales: Jim Hamel
Estimated Sales: $100+ Million
Number Employees: 100-249
Number of Brands: 3
Square Footage: 68000
Parent Co: SYSCO
Type of Packaging: Food Service, Private Label
Other Locations:
Kansas City MO
Hampshire IL
Brands:
Ji Hao
Shang Pin

735 **Askinosie Chocolate**
514 E Commercial St
Springfield, MO 65803-2946
417-862-9900
Fax: 417-862-9904 lawren@askinosie.com
www.askinosie.com
Chocolate/cocoa products
Owner: Shawn Askinosie
mshawn@askinosie.com
Operations Manager: Jill Tilman
Number Employees: 10-19

736 **Aspen Mulling Company Inc.**
C/O World Pantry Company
1192 Illinois Street
San Francisco, CA 94107
800-622-7736
Fax: 970-925-5408 866-972-6879
aspenspices@worldpantry.com
www.aspenspices.com
Manufacturer and exporter of mulling spices
Manager: Leo Varade
Marketing: David Kallen
Estimated Sales: Under $5 Million
Number Employees: 5-9
Type of Packaging: Consumer, Food Service

737 **Aspire**
500 N Michigan Ave.
Suite 600
Chicago, OH 60611
customerservice@aspiredrinks.com
aspiredrinks.com
Energy drinks with zero sugar and zero calories.
CEO: Chris Wadlington
Co-Founder & Intl. Sales Director: Neil Blewitt
Co-Founder & COO: Darren Linnell
Year Founded: 2010
Number Employees: 11-50
Type of Packaging: Private Label

738 **Assets Grille & Southwest Brewing Company**
6910 Montgomery Boulevard NE
Albuquerque, NM 87109-1406
505-889-6400
Fax: 505-889-0264
Brewer of beer, ale and stout
Owner: Mark Devesti
Estimated Sales: $2.5-5 Million
Number Employees: 50-99
Parent Co: Assets Brewing Company
Type of Packaging: Consumer, Food Service, Bulk

739 **Associated Fruit Company**
3721 Colver Rd
Phoenix, OR 97535-9705
541-535-1787
Fax: 541-535-6936
Manufacturer and exporter of fresh fruit including plums and pears
President: David Lowry
Purchasing: Scott Martinez
delrae.erickson@exchangebank.com
Estimated Sales: $1-2.5 Million
Number Employees: 6
Type of Packaging: Bulk

740 **Associated Milk Producers Inc.**
315 N. Broadway St.
PO Box 455
New Ulm, MN 56073
507-354-8295
800-533-3580
www.ampi.com
Cheese, butter and powdered milk products.
Co-President/Co-CEO: Donn DeVelder
Co-President/Co-CEO: Sheryl Meshke
Chairman: Steve Schlangen
schlangens@ampi.com
Estimated Sales: $1.7 Billion
Number Employees: 1000-4999
Type of Packaging: Consumer, Food Service, Private Label

741 **(HQ)Associated Potato Growers**
2001 N 6th St
Grand Forks, ND 58203-1584
701-775-4614
Fax: 701-746-5767 800-437-4685
www.apgspud.com
Potatoes and potato products
CEO: Bryan Miller
Director Sales: Greg Holtman
Estimated Sales: $26 Million
Number Employees: 100-249
Other Locations:
Associated Potato Growers
Grafton ND
Associated Potato Growers
Drayton ND
Brands:
Apg
Dole
Holsom
Natives Pride
Nodark
Potato Mity Red

742 **Asti Holdings Ltd**
320 Stewardson Way
Unit 2-3
New Westminster, BC V3M 6C3
Canada
604-523-6866
Fax: 604-523-6880 info@goldenbonbon.com
www.goldenbonbon.com
Nougat candy and caramels
President: Ricardo Mazzucco
Estimated Sales: $1.7 Million
Number Employees: 100-500

743 **Astor Chocolate Corp**
651 New Hampshire Ave
Lakewood, NJ 08701-5452
732-901-1001
Fax: 732-901-1003 info@astorchocolate.com
www.astorchocolate.com
Manufacturer, importer and exporter of chocolate including fund raising, foiled novelties, bars, truffles, mints, shells and boxed.
President: Teri Aboud
teri.aboud@gmail.com
President: David Grunhut
CFO: Nat Vernaci
Sales Director: Howard Cubberly
Human Resource Executive: Arie Lax
Purchasing Manager: Karen Garrison
Estimated Sales: $25,000
Number Employees: 50-99
Square Footage: 66162
Type of Packaging: Consumer, Food Service, Private Label, Bulk
Brands:
After Dark
Le Belge Chocolatier
Party Favors By Astor
Pastry Essentials
Square One

744 **Astral Extracts**
50 Eileen Way
Unit 6
Syosset, NY 11791-5313
516-496-2505
Fax: 516-496-4248 info@astralextracts.com
www.astralextracts.com
Processor, wholesaler, distributor, importer and exporter of fruit juice concentrates, essential oils and citrus products
President: Cynthia Astrack
info@astralextracts.com
General Manager: Joan Pace
Estimated Sales: $5-10 Million
Number Employees: 5-9
Square Footage: 30000
Type of Packaging: Food Service, Private Label, Bulk

745 **Astro Dairy Products**
405 The West Mall
10th Floor
Toronto, ON M9C 5S1
Canada
416-622-2811
Fax: 416-622-4180 www.astro.ca
Dairy products including yogurt, cottage cheese, sour cream and cream cheese
President: James Biltekoff
Number Employees: 200
Parent Co: Parmalat Canada
Type of Packaging: Consumer, Food Service, Private Label, Bulk
Brands:
Astro
Biobest

746 **At Last Naturals Inc**
401 Columbus Ave # 2
Valhalla, NY 10595-1375
914-747-3599
Fax: 914-747-3791 800-527-8123
www.alast.com
Manufacturer and exporter of laxative tea and natural herbal health products.
Vice President: Fred Rosen
fred@alast.com
Estimated Sales: $1-3 Million
Number Employees: 1-4
Square Footage: 148000
Type of Packaging: Consumer
Brands:
Dhea
Innerclean
Sul-Ray
Valerian

747 **Ateeco Inc**
600 E Centre St
PO Box 606
Shenandoah, PA 17976-1825
570-462-2745
Fax: 570-462-3299 800-743-7649
consumercontact@pierogies.com
www.pierogies.com
Frozen pierogies.
President: Thomas Twardzik
tcoyle@pierogies.com
Director, Public Relations: Wayne Holben
Director, Operations: Ray Stasulli
Estimated Sales: $20-50 Million
Number Employees: 100-249
Number of Brands: 1
Square Footage: 350
Type of Packaging: Private Label
Brands:
Mrs. T's Pierogies

748 **Athena Oil Inc**
3082 36th St
Astoria, NY 11103-4705
718-956-8893
Fax: 718-956-5813 info@athenaoil.com
www.athenaoil.com
Wholes sale oils vegetable and olive
President/Owner: Moschos Scoullis
mscoullis@gmail.com
Estimated Sales: $1.2 Million
Number Employees: 10-19

749 **Athens Baking Company**
4589 W Jacquelyn Ave
Fresno, CA 93722-6442
559-485-3024
Fax: 559-485-0671 800-775-2867
sales@athensbaking.com www.athensbaking.com
Baked beans, rolls, and buns
Owner: Dave Smart
Estimated Sales: $5-10 Million
Type of Packaging: Consumer, Food Service, Private Label
Brands:
Athens

750 **Athens Foods Inc**
13600 Snow Rd
Brookpark, OH 44142-2546
216-676-8500
Fax: 216-676-0609 843-916-2000
www.athensfoods.com
Fillo dough, fillo shells and other fillo products.
CEO: Scott Sumser
CFO: Bob Tansing
R&D Manager: Jean Myers
VP of Sales/Marketing: Bill Buckingham
VP of Operations: Jeff Swint
Estimated Sales: $29.5 Million
Number Employees: 100-249
Number of Brands: 2
Number of Products: 200
Square Footage: 120000
Type of Packaging: Consumer, Food Service, Private Label, Bulk
Brands:
Apollo®
Athens®

751 **Athletic Brewing Co.**
350 Long Beach Rd
Stratford, CT 06615
203-273-0422
info@athleticbrewing.com
www.athleticbrewing.com
Non-alcoholic craft beer
Founder: Bill Shufelt
Year Founded: 2017

752 **Atka Pride Seafoods Inc**
302 Gold St
Suite 202
Juneau, AK 99801-1127
907-586-0161
Fax: 907-586-0165 888-927-4232
info@apicda.com www.apicda.com
Supplier of seafood
Chief Executive Officer: Larry Cotter
Chief Financial Officer: Robert Smith
Chief Operating Officer: John Sevier
Number Employees: 1-4
Parent Co: Aleutian Pribilof Island Community Development Association

753 **Atkins Elegant Desserts**
11852 Allisonville Rd
Fishers, IN 46038-2312
317-570-1850
Fax: 317-773-3766 800-887-8808
Frozen cheesecakes, pies, cakes and pastries.
Manager: Debbie Llewellyn
CEO: Tom Atkins Jr
CFO: Tom Atkins
R&D: Darrell Bell
Quality Control: John Parent
Canadian National Manager: Wayne Barefoot
VP Sales & Marketing: Bob Barry
National Accounts Manager: Lisa Atkins Miller
Operations: Bill Beglin
Production: Jeff Fascko
Plant Manager: Terry Graves
Purchasing: Denise Miller
Estimated Sales: $12-13 Million
Number Employees: 50-99
Square Footage: 70000
Type of Packaging: Consumer, Food Service, Private Label
Brands:
Atkins

754 **Atkins Ginseng Farms**
RR 1
PO Box 1125
Waterford, ON N0E 1Y0
Canada
519-443-7236
Fax: 519-443-4565 800-265-0239
Manufacturer, importer and exporter of ginseng products including capsules, also grower of american ginseng
Owner/President: Micheal Atkins
Estimated Sales: $20-50 Million
Number Employees: 5-9
Square Footage: 6000
Type of Packaging: Consumer, Private Label, Bulk
Brands:
Atkins
Gin Ultimate
Golden Dreams
Golden Grower
Northern Serenitea
Northern Spirit

755 **Atkins Nutritionals Inc.**
1050 17th St
Suite 1000
Denver, CO 80265-2078
303-633-2840
800-628-5467
www.atkins.com
Atkins diet food, candy and nutritional bars.
President & CEO: Joseph Scalzo
Estimated Sales: $5-10 Million
Number Employees: 1-4
Type of Packaging: Consumer, Food Service

756 **Atkinson Candy Co**
1608 W Frank Ave
Lufkin, TX 75904-3109
936-639-2333
Fax: 936-639-2337 contact@atkinsoncandy.com
Manufacturer of candies.
President: Eric Atkinson
eatkinson@atkinsoncandy.com
COO: Doug Hanks
Estimated Sales: $21.8 Million
Number Employees: 100-249
Square Footage: 100000
Type of Packaging: Consumer, Food Service
Brands:
Mint Twists
Peanut Butter Bars
Chick-O-Stick
Long Boys
Gemstone Gourmet Candies
Sophie Mae
Slo Poke
Black Cow

757 **Atkinson Milling Co.**
95 Atkinson Mill Rd.
Intersection Hwy. 42 & 39
Selma, NC 27576
919-965-3547
Fax: 919-202-0523 800-948-5707
information@atkinsonmilling.com
www.atkinsonmilling.com
Flour and other grain mill products including corn meal, hushpuppy mixes, breaders, biscuit mixes, cornbread sticks, and chicken dumplings.
President: Glen Wheeler
Year Founded: 1757
Estimated Sales: $8.3 Million
Number Employees: 50-99
Type of Packaging: Consumer, Food Service, Private Label, Bulk
Brands:
Atkinson's
Boddie
Cattail
Ellis Davis

758 **Atlanta Bread Co.**
1200 Wilson Way SE
Suite 100
Smyrna, GA 30082-7212
770-432-0933
Fax: 770-444-1991 800-398-3728
www.atlantabread.com
Bread, pastries, bagels, rolls,muffins,sandwiches,salads and desserts. Also featuring expanded coffee selection
President & CEO: Jerry Couvaras
COO: Basil Couvaras
Estimated Sales: $1-2.5 Million
Number Employees: 100-249
Type of Packaging: Consumer, Food Service
Brands:
Atlanta Bread

759 **Atlanta Burning Bush**
3781 Happy Valley Cir
Newnan, GA 30263
770-253-4443
Fax: 770-253-9941 800-665-5611
Hot sauces, BBQ sauce. Supplier of food related products
Owner: Marilyn Witt
Estimated Sales: $500,000-$1,000,000
Number Employees: 1-4
Type of Packaging: Consumer, Bulk
Brands:
Atlanta Burning

760 **Atlanta Coffee & Tea Co**
770-981-6774
Fax: 770-981-6697 800-426-4781
sales@atlantacoffeeandtea.com
shop.atlantacoffeeandtea.com/contact-us
Processor and importer of coffee and tea; coffee roaster and tea packer, private label packaging available
VP: Harris Carver
Estimated Sales: Less Than $500,000
Number Employees: 1-4
Number of Products: 16
Type of Packaging: Food Service, Private Label

761 **Atlanta Coffee Roasters**
2205 Lavista Rd NE
Atlanta, GA 30329-3917
404-636-1038
Fax: 404-255-1189 800-252-8211
info@atlantacoffeeroasters.com
www.atlantacoffeeroasters.com
Coffee
Owner: William Letbetter
bill@atlantacoffeeroasters.com
CFO: Stephen Burress
Estimated Sales: $910,000
Number Employees: 5-9
Brands:
Brazil Celebes
Celebes
Columbian
Costa Rica
Jamaica Bluemountain
Laminita

762 **Atlanta Fish Market**
265 Pharr Rd NE
Atlanta, GA 30305-2243
404-262-3165
Fax: 404-240-6665 www.buckheadrestaurants.com
Seafood
Manager: Jason Zaleski
bcompton@buckheadrestaurants.com
Site Manager: Brandon Compton
bcompton@buckheadrestaurants.com
Estimated Sales: $5-10 Million
Number Employees: 100-249

763 **Atlantic Aqua Farms**
918 Brush Wharf Rd
Orwell Cove, PE C0A 2E0
Canada
902-651-2563
Fax: 902-651-2513 terry@canadiancove.pe.ca
www.canadiancove.com
Manufacturer and exporter of fresh mussels, oysters and clams-hardshell
GM: Brian Fortune
Number Employees: 50
Type of Packaging: Consumer, Food Service, Private Label, Bulk

764 **Atlantic Blueberry**
7201 Weymouth Rd # A
Hammonton, NJ 08037-3414
609-561-8600
Fax: 609-561-5033 staff@atlanticblueberry.com
www.atlanticblueberry.com
Processor and exporter of fresh and frozen blueberries
President/CEO: Arthur Galletta
Harvest Crew Supervisor: Paul Galletta
Food Safety, Security, and Defense, QC: John Galletta
Sales: Art Galletta
General Inquiries, Press Inquiries: Denny Doyle
Operations: Robert Galletta
Year Founded: 1935
Estimated Sales: $5-10 Million
Number Employees: 10-19
Number of Brands: 1
Number of Products: 1
Square Footage: 320000
Type of Packaging: Private Label
Brands:
Atlantic Blueberry

765 **(HQ)Atlantic Capes Fisheries**
985 Ocean Dr
Cape May, NJ 08204-1855
609-884-3000
Fax: 609-884-3261 info@atlanticapes.com
www.atlanticapes.com
Fresh and frozen scallops, fish, clams, mackerel, squid and monkfish; importer of scallops; exporter of fresh and frozen scallops, squid, butterfish and mackerel
President: Daniel Cohen
dcohen@atlanticcapesfisheries.com
VP, Sales/Marketing: Jeff Bolton
VP, Operations: David Shaw
Estimated Sales: $15 Million
Number Employees: 20-49
Square Footage: 40000
Other Locations:
ACF Production Facility
Point Pleasant Beach NJ
ACF Sales/Marketing Office
New Bedford MA
Brands:
Atlantic Capes
Cape May Salt

766 **Atlantic Chemicals Trading**
116 N Maryland Ave # 210
Glendale, CA 91206-4270
818-246-0077
Fax: 617-292-0073 usa@act.de
www.act.de
Manufacturer and distributor of flavors such as peppermint & menthol, sweeteners, acidifiers and preservatives. Food additives and preservatives
General Manager: Jaklin Minasian
Number Employees: 5-9

767 **Atlantic Fish Specialties**
17 Walker Drive
Charlottetown, PE C1A 8S5
Canada
902-894-7005
Fax: 902-566-3546 macneill@cookeaqua.com
www.cookeaqua.com
Manufacturer and exporter of smoked salmon, mackerel and trout
President: Glenn Cooke
General Manager: Doug Galen
Number Employees: 40
Type of Packaging: Consumer, Food Service, Private Label, Bulk

768 **Atlantic Foods**
2560 US Highway 22
Scotch Plains, NJ 07076
908-889-8182
Fax: 909-322-9993
Seafood
President: Derek Ivey
Estimated Sales: $50-100 Million
Number Employees: 100-200
Type of Packaging: Consumer, Food Service, Private Label, Bulk

769 **Atlantic Laboratories Inc**
41 Cross St
Waldoboro, ME 04572-5634
207-832-5376
Fax: 207-832-6905 888-662-5357
nak@noamkelp.com www.noamkelp.com
Harvests and processes kelp.
President: Robert Morse, Jr.
Contact: Edward Ernste
eernste@noamkelp.com
Number Employees: 5-9
Type of Packaging: Consumer, Bulk

770 **Atlantic Meat Company**
2600 Louisville Rd
Savannah, GA 31415
912-964-8511
Fax: 912-964-6831
Fresh and frozen ground beef, including hamburger patties
President/CEO: Lee Javetz
Purchasing Agent: Marc Javetz
Estimated Sales: $20-50 Million
Number Employees: 50
Square Footage: 30000
Type of Packaging: Consumer, Food Service, Private Label, Bulk
Brands:
Atlantic Meat
Circle a Brands Beef Patties
Circlea Beef Patties

771 **Atlantic Mussel Growers Corporation**
PO Box 70
Pointe Pleasant Road
Murray Harbour, PE C0A 1R0
Canada
902-962-3089
Fax: 902-962-3741 800-838-3106
Manufacturer and exporter of fresh mussels
Executive Manager: John Sullivan
Business Manager: Rollie McInnis
Operations Manager: Marjorie Henderson
Number Employees: 25
Type of Packaging: Consumer, Private Label, Bulk

772 **Atlantic Natural Foods**
110 Industry Ct
Nashville, NC 27856
888-491-0524
www.atlanticnaturalfoods.com
Vegetarian foods and beverages
Number of Brands: 3
Square Footage: 53000
Brands:
LOMA LINDA
KAFFREE ROMA
NEAT

773 **Atlantic Pork & Provisions**
14707 94th Ave
Jamaica, NY 11435-4513
718-272-9550
Fax: 718-272-9630 800-245-3536
Fresh hams; also, bologna and liverwurst loaves
President/Ceo: Jack Antinori
Number Employees: 50
Type of Packaging: Consumer
Brands:
Atlantic
Eidelweiss
Laurel Hill
Lifeline

774 **Atlantic Salmon of Maine**
57 Little River Dr
Belfast, ME 4915
207-338-9028
Fax: 207-338-6288 800-508-7861
www.cookeaqua.com
Fresh salmon
GM: David Peterson
CFO: John Thibodeau
Sales Manager: Mary Warner
Contact: Peter Christensen
pchristensen@majesticsalmon.com
Receptionist: Becky Darres
Number Employees: 200
Type of Packaging: Food Service
Other Locations:
Atlantic Salmon of Maine
Swan Island ME

775 **Atlantic Sea Pride**
16 Fish Pier
Boston, MA 02210-2054
617-269-7700
Fax: 617-269-7766
Processor and wholesaler/distributor of fresh fish and fillets; serving the food service market
President: Anthony Correnti
VP: Frank Mazza
Estimated Sales: $4.30 Million
Number Employees: 20
Type of Packaging: Consumer, Food Service, Bulk

776 **Atlantic Seacove Inc**
20 Newmarket Sq
Boston, MA 02118-2601
617-442-6206
Fax: 617-482-7733
Wholesale dealers in fresh and frozen fish
President/CEO: John Wojitasinski
Owner: Andrew Bunten
Treasurer: Mitchell Wojitasinski
Estimated Sales: $3.3 Million
Number Employees: 10-19

777 **Atlantic Seafood Direct**
12 A Portland Fish Pier
PO Box 682
Portland, ME 04104
800-774-6025
Seafood fresh and frozen
President: Jerry Knecht
VP/General Manager: Mike Norton

778 **Atlantic Seasonings**
417 E Vernon Ave
Kinston, NC 28501-4456
252-522-1515
Fax: 252-522-2485 800-433-5261
Salad dressing and drink mixes, gravies, seasoning and flour blends and sauces; custom blending available
President: Jay Neuhoff
VP Marketing: Ken Neuhoff
Estimated Sales: $2.5-5 Million
Number Employees: 10-19
Square Footage: 72000
Type of Packaging: Food Service, Private Label, Bulk
Brands:
Atlantic Seasonings

779 **Atlantic Veal & Lamb Inc**
275 Morgan Ave
Brooklyn, NY 11211
800-222-8325
info@atlanticveal.com www.atlanticveal.com
Processor and exporter of individually vacuumed frozen veal including portion controlled, hand sliced, leg cutlets, roasts and cubed.
Chief Executive Officer: Phillip Peerless
ppeerless@atlanticveal.com
Chairman: Marty Weiner
CFO: Joe Saccardi
VP: Martin Weiner
Lamb Sales Director: Dan Salmon
National Sales Director: John Ricci
Customer Service Manager: Mario Vigorito
Chief Operating Officer: Shawn Peerless
Estimated Sales: $20-50 Million
Number Employees: 100-249
Type of Packaging: Consumer, Food Service
Brands:
Farm Fed Veal
Plume De Veau
The Epicurean

780 **Atlantis Pak USA Inc**
75 Valencia Ave # 701
Coral Gables, FL 33134-6132
305-403-2603
Fax: 786-249-0454
customerservice@atlantis-pak.com
www.atlantis-pak.com
Meat Packing, manufacturer of acid free packing paper, and recycled paper for meat.
Principle: Vladimir Zhamgotsev
zhamgotsev@atlantis-pak.com
Number Employees: 1-4
Parent Co: Atlantis Pak

781 **Atlas Peak Vineyards**
3700 Sada Canyon Road
Napa, CA 94558
866-522-9463
Fax: 707-226-2306 707-252-7971
wineclub@atlaspeak.com www.vineyards.com
Red and white wines
Owner: Marchese Piero-Antinori
CFO: Chris Stenzel
Contact: Carlos Ladeland
carlos.ladeland@atlaspeakvineyards.com
VP Operations: Darren Procsal
VP Production: Tony Fernandez
Estimated Sales: $5-10 Million
Number Employees: 20-49
Type of Packaging: Consumer, Food Service
Brands:
Atlas Peak
Consenso

782 **Atoka Cranberries, Inc.**
3025 Route 218
Manseau, Quebec, QC G0X 1VO
Canada
819-356-2001
Fax: 819-356-2111 infoatoka@atoka.qc.ca
Grower and processor of fresh and dried cranberries, and cranberry juice concentrate for industrial applications. Founded in 1984.
President: Mark Bieler

783 **(HQ)Atrium Biotech**
1405 Boul
Quebec, QC G1P 4P5
Canada
418-652-1116
Fax: 866-628-6661
Processor, importer and exporter of shark cartilage, nutritional supplements and powders. Developers and marketing of value added ingrediants
President: Richard Bordeleau
CEO: Luc Dupont
Vice President/CFO: Jocelyn Harvey
Development: Serge Yelle
Sales: Johan Aerts
Purchasing: Rene Augstburger
Estimated Sales: $1.5 Million
Number Employees: 20
Number of Brands: 3
Number of Products: 20
Square Footage: 400000
Brands:
2-Mix
Biomega
Cartcelt
Cartilade
Dermanex
Genista
Natcelt
Pepogest
Phyto-Est
Prostacare
Prostavite

784 **Attala Development Corporation**
101 North Natchez Street
Kosciusko, MS 39090
662-289-2981
Fax: 662-289-3288 info@kadcorp.org
www.kosciusko.ms/development
Corn flour meal and blended wheat flour
President/CEO: Steve Zea
VP Economic Development: Greg Cooper
VP Community Development: Tonya Threet
Purchasing: Joe Cain
Estimated Sales: $345
Number Employees: 4
Type of Packaging: Consumer, Private Label
Brands:
Magnolia

785 **Atwater Block Brewing Company**
237 Joseph Campau St
Detroit, MI 48207
313-877-9205
Fax: 313-877-9241 atwater@atwaterbeer.com
www.atwaterbeer.com
German-style lager, ale and beer; importer of malt and hops
President: Mark Rieth
Contact: Chelsea Iadipaolo
chelsea@atwaterbeer.com
Estimated Sales: $.5-1 million
Number Employees: 10-19
Square Footage: 80000
Type of Packaging: Consumer, Food Service, Private Label
Brands:
Atwater
Stoney

786 **Atwater Foods**
10182 Roosevelt Hwy
Route 18
Lyndonville Orleans, NY 14098-9785
585-765-2639
Fax: 585-765-9443 www.shorelinefruit.com
Manufacturer, exporter and wholesaler of many kinds of dried fruit, including apples, cherries, cranberries, blueberries and strawberries. Star-K Kosher. Our customer service support is responsive to timelines and responsible forkeeping everything on track
Manager: Randy Atwater
Quality Control: Chris Fraser
Sales/Marketing: Jim Palmer
Contact: Fred Freeman
fred@atwaterfoods.com
Plant Manager: Steve Mohr
Purchasing Manager: Pat Glidden
Estimated Sales: 15-20 Million
Number Employees: 50-99
Number of Products: 50+
Square Footage: 180000
Type of Packaging: Private Label, Bulk
Brands:
Atwater
Atwater Dried Fruits
Shoreline Fruit

787 **Atwood Cheese Company**
Rural Route 1
7412 Highway 235
Atwood, ON N0G 1B0
Canada
519-356-2271
Fax: 519-356-2170
Largest manufacturer of cheeses including mozzarella, feta, fontina, emmental and parmesan
Manager: Samuel Cadeddo
Number Employees: 19
Square Footage: 120000
Type of Packaging: Bulk

Brands:
Tre Stelle

788 **Au Bon Climat Winery**
PO Box 113
Los Olivos, CA 93441
805-937-9801
Fax: 805-937-2539 info@auboncimat.com
www.auboncimat.com
Wines
Owner: Robert Lindquist
Contact: Michael Main
michael@auboncimat.com
Winemaker: Jim Clendenen
Estimated Sales: $.5-1 million
Number Employees: 1-4
Type of Packaging: Private Label

789 **Au Printemps Gourmet**
101-765 Nobel Street
Saint-Jerome, QC J7Z 7A3
Canada
450-438-6676
Fax: 450-438-0080 800-438-6676
services@beaulieuinstant.com
www.beaulieuinstantane.com/en/home-apgourmet
Vinegars, jams, jelly seasonings and gift sets, gourmet foods.
Owner: Chantal Desjardins
Finance Director: Tim Dick
Vice President, Sales/Marketing: Marilyn O'Connell
Operations: Dolores Wilson
Year Founded: 1978
Estimated Sales: $5-9 Million
Number Employees: 20
Number of Brands: 1
Brands:
Au Printemps Gourmet

790 **(HQ)Au'some Candies**
2031 Route 130
Suite E, Bldg A
Monmouth Junction, NJ 08852-3014
732-951-8818
Fax: 732-951-8828 877-287-6649
Candy
President: Carlos Yeung
CEO: David Tsu
Sales Manager: Marcos Perales
VP Operations: Rose Downey
Year Founded: 1998
Estimated Sales: $5-10 Million
Number Employees: 10-19
Other Locations:
Au'some Candies
Mission Viejo CA
Au'some Candies
Coppell TX
Au'Some Candies
Mississauga, Ontario
Au'Some Candies Europe S.L.
Sitges, Spain
Au'Some Candy Asia
Kowloon, Hong Kong
Brands:
Candy Yo-Yo
Gummi Alien Invaders
Pop Magic
Super Sucker

791 **AuNutra Industries Inc**
5625 Daniels Street
Chino, CA 91710
909-628-2600
Fax: 909-628-8110 info@aunutra.com
www.aunutra.com
Manufacturer and supplier of botanicals and nutritional ingredients
VP Sales/Marketing: Ken Guest
Regional Sales Manager: Tara Trainor
Contact: Jing Ang
jang@aunutra.com

792 **Auburn Dairy Products Inc**
702 W Main St
Auburn, WA 98001-5299
253-833-3400
Fax: 253-833-3751 800-950-9264
info@yamiyogurt.com www.instantwhip.com
Sour cream, half and half and yogurt including plain, orange, cherry, strawberry, blueberry and lemon. Lactose free and 100 percent dairy.
Manager: Jerry Dinsmore
Executive Director: Martin Lavine
Purchasing & Plant Manager: Marv Query
Estimated Sales: $10-20 Million
Number Employees: 20-49
Parent Co: Instantwhip Foods
Type of Packaging: Consumer, Food Service
Brands:
Yami(c) Yogurt
Zoi Greek Yogurt

793 **Aufschnitt Meats**
7 Gwynns Mill
Owings Mills, MD 21117
410-356-7745
www.aufschnittmeats.com
Meat products

794 **August Foods LTD**
4820 Avenue Q
Lubbock, TX 79412-2210
806-744-1918
Fax: 806-744-4934
Fried pies
Owner: Brian Seely
Estimated Sales: $750
Number Employees: 10-19
Square Footage: 14400
Brands:
August's Fried

795 **August Kitchen**
PO Box 54
Armonk, NY 10504-0054
914-219-5249
info@augustkitchen.com
Marinades, other sauces, seasonings and cooking enhancers.
Contact: Zina Ovchinnikoff-Santos
zina@augustkitchen.com
Number Employees: 1-4
Brands:
J-Burger Seasoning

796 **August Schell Brewing Co**
1860 Schells Rd
New Ulm, MN 56073
507-354-5528
Fax: 507-359-9119 800-770-5020
schells@schellsbrewery.com schellsbrewery.com
Manufacturer of beer, ale and lager.
Year Founded: 1828
Estimated Sales: $21 Million
Number Employees: 50-99
Type of Packaging: Consumer, Private Label
Brands:
Grain Belt
Schell's

797 **Augusta Winery**
5601 High St
Augusta, MO 63332-1703
636-228-4301
Fax: 636-228-4683 888-667-9463
info@augustawinery.com
www.augustawinery.com
Manufacturer of handcrafted wines
President: Tony Kooyumjian
augustawinery@aol.com
Year Founded: 1988
Estimated Sales: $2.5-5 Million
Number Employees: 5-9
Type of Packaging: Bulk

798 **Augustin's Waffles**
51 Glen Ridge Drive
Long Valley, NJ 07853
908-684-0830
Fax: 908-684-4878
Presweetened belgian waffles, with pearl sugars, dough, cooked waffles, sales of equipment and waffle tools.
President: Al Poe
Vice President: Henry Picquet

799 **Aunt Aggie De's Pralines**
311 W Sinton St
Sinton, TX 78387-2556
361-364-2711
Fax: 361-692-2971 800-333-9354
sales@auntaggiede.com www.auntaggiede.com
Processor of original, all natural chocolate, chewy, and coconut pralines.
Founder & CEO: Eleanor Harren
aggiede@aol.com
General Counsel & Marketing: Amy Harren de Villarreal
Chief Operating Officer: Michael Pocrass
Year Founded: 1987
Estimated Sales: $5-10 Million
Number Employees: 20-49
Square Footage: 2200
Brands:
Aunt Aggie De's Pralines

800 **Aunt Fannie's Bakery**
1039 Grant Street SE
Atlanta, GA 30315-2014
404-622-8146
Baked goods
Manager: Earl Stallworth
Estimated Sales: $20-50 Million
Number Employees: 100-249
Parent Co: Flowers Industries

801 **Aunt Gussie Cookies & Crackers**
141 Lanza Ave
Bldg 8
Garfield, NJ 07026-3538
973-340-4480
Fax: 973-340-3501 800-422-6654
info@auntgussies.com www.auntgussies.com
Processor of cookies and crackers including sugar-free and gluten-free
President: David Caine
Contact: Joyce Parker
joyce@auntgussies.com
Year Founded: 1980
Estimated Sales: $2.5-5 Million
Number Employees: 5-9
Number of Brands: 1
Number of Products: 45
Square Footage: 60000
Type of Packaging: Consumer, Private Label, Bulk
Brands:
Aunt Gussie's Cookies & Crackers

802 **Aunt Heddy's Bakery**
234 N 9th Street
Brooklyn, NY 11211-2012
718-782-0582
Food wholsaler and maufacturer of breads and babka
Owner: Rich Zablocki
Estimated Sales: $63 Thousand
Number Employees: 2

803 **Aunt Jenny's Sauces/Melba Foods**
186 Huron St
Brooklyn, NY 11222-1706
718-383-3192
Fax: 718-383-3191 www.melbafoods.com
Sauces, melba foods, groceries
President: Marie Cuoco
Year Founded: 1962
Estimated Sales: $2.5-5 Million
Number Employees: 10-20
Type of Packaging: Private Label

804 **Aunt Kathy's Homestyle Products**
PO Box 279
Waldheim, SK S0K 4R0
Canada
306-945-2181
Fax: 306-945-2043
Manufacturer and distributor of cabbage rolls, filled perogies, pizza, Mennonite farmer sausage and smokies, chicken strips, dry ribs, pies, and crumbles.
Owner: Deah Scott
Owner: Derek Scott
Production Manager: Willie Curtis
Year Founded: 1986
Estimated Sales: A
Number Employees: 5-9
Type of Packaging: Consumer, Bulk

805 **Aunt Kitty's Foods Inc**
270 N Mill Road
Vineland, NJ 08360
856-691-2100
Fax: 856-696-1295 www.auntkittys.com
Manufacturer, retail private label, and packaging of chili, stew, beef hash, hot dog chili, gravy, condensed soups, broth, beef cubes, and pasta.
Vice President: Craig Adams
Plant Manager: J Keith Griffis

Year Founded: 1924
Estimated Sales: $1-3 Million
Number Employees: 100-249
Number of Brands: 6
Square Footage: 480000
Parent Co: Hanover Foods Corp
Type of Packaging: Consumer, Food Service, Private Label
Brands:
Aunt Kitty's
Austex Products
Bryan Products
Bunker Hill
Castleberry Products
Venice Maid Products

806 **Aunt Lizzie's Inc**
1531 Overton Park Ave
Memphis, TN 38112-5138
901-274-2966
Fax: 901-274-2902 800-993-7788
www.auntlizzie.com
Gourmet southern cheese straws and other products
President: Ginna Kelley
Founder: Elizabeth Harwell
Year Founded: 1983
Estimated Sales: Under $500,000
Number Employees: 5-9
Type of Packaging: Private Label
Brands:
Aunt Lizzie's
Lemon Shortbread
Libby's Pecan Cookies
Sharp Cheddar Cheese
Sun-Dried Tomato Str
Wind & Willow Key Lime Cheeseball

807 **(HQ)Aunt Millie's Bakeries**
350 Pearl St
Fort Wayne, IN 46802-1508
260-424-8245
Fax: 260-424-5047 855-755-2253
customerservice@auntmillies.com
www.auntmillies.com
Breads, buns, English muffins, rolls, as well as bread and muffin mixes
President: John Popp
VP Finance: Jay Miller
Estimated Sales: $10-15 Million
Number Employees: 1000-4999
Type of Packaging: Consumer, Food Service
Other Locations:
Perfection Bakeries Plant
Michigan
Perfection Bakeries Plant
Illinois
Perfection Bakeries Plant
Ohio
Perfection Bakeries Plant
Kentucky
Brands:
Aunt Millie's
Sumbeam

808 **Aunt Sally's Praline Shops**
750 Saint Charles Ave
New Orleans, LA 70130-3714
504-522-2126
Fax: 504-944-5925 800-642-7257
service@auntsallys.com www.auntsallys.com
New Orleans style creamy praline candies in four flavors, and other specialty food items.
Manager: Bethany Gex
CEO: Frank Simoncioni
Sales: Becky Hebert
Sales: Cherie Cunningham
Director Of Operations: Karl Schmidt
Estimated Sales: $5 Million+
Number Employees: 20-49
Square Footage: 20000
Type of Packaging: Consumer, Food Service, Private Label, Bulk
Brands:
Aunt Sally's Creamy Pralines
Aunt Sally's Gourmet

809 **Auroma International Inc**
1100 E Lotus Dr
Silver Lake, WI 53170-1668
262-889-8569
Fax: 262-889-2461 auroma@lotuspress.com
www.auromaintl.com
Dietary supplements, herbs and herbal formulas.
CEO: Santosh Krinsky
Number Employees: 50-99

810 **Aurora Alaska Premium Smoked Salmon & Seafood**
PO Box 211376
Anchorage, AK 99521-1376
907-338-2229
Fax: 907-338-2228 800-653-3474
Seafood products
Owner: Bill Dornberger
Owner: Gloria Dornberger

811 **Aurora Frozen Foods Division**
2067 Westport Center Drive
Saint Louis, MO 63146-2800
314-801-2800
Fax: 314-801-2550
Frozen sea food, pizza and breakfast products, including waffles, french toast
Chairman: Ian Wilson
COO: Eric D Brenk
CFO: William R McManaman
Number Employees: 1017
Brands:
Aunt Jemima
Celeste
Duncan Hines
Lender's
Log Cabin
Mrs Butterworth's
Mrs Paul's
Van De Kamp's

812 **Aurora Organic Dairy**
1919 14th St
Suite 300
Boulder, CO 80302-5321
303-284-3313
Fax: 720-564-0409 info@auroraorganic.com
www.auroraorganic.com
Producer of private-brand organic milk and butter for U.S. retailers.
President and CEO: Marcus Peperzak
President. Scott McGinty
CFO: Cammie Muller
Vice President: Clark Driftmier
Director of Quality: Peggy Colfelt
Marketing Manager: Sonia Tuatelli
Contact: Kristin Anderson
kristin.anderson@auroraorganic.com
Senior VP Farm Operations: Juan Velez
Plant Manager: John Beutler
Estimated Sales: 23.9 Million
Number Employees: 5-9
Square Footage: 2835
Type of Packaging: Private Label, Bulk

813 **Aurora Packing Co Inc**
125 S Grant St
North Aurora, IL 60542-1603
630-897-0551
Fax: 630-897-0647 www.aurorabeef.com
Processor and exporter of beef. Meat packing plant founded in 1939.
CFO: Don Tanis
dtanis@aurorapacking.com
VP: Marvin Doty
Estimated Sales: $41 Million
Number Employees: 100-249
Number of Brands: 1
Type of Packaging: Consumer, Food Service, Private Label
Brands:
Aurora Angus Beef

814 **Aurora Products**
205 Edison Road
Orange, CT 06477
203-375-9956
Fax: 203-375-9734 800-398-1048
ANatural@auroraproduct.com
www.auroraproduct.com
Trail mixes, nuts, dried fruits and candy
Owner/President: Stephanie Blackwell
VP Operations: Scott Magner
Year Founded: 1998
Estimated Sales: $30-40 Million
Number Employees: 100+

815 **Aussie Crunch**
1877 Air Lane Drive
Suite 4
Nashville, TN 37210-3814
615-983-8280
Fax: 615-261-9055 800-401-6534
Makers of gourmet popcorn, and popcorn supplies
President: Andy Moore
Year Founded: 2004
Number Employees: 7

816 **Austin Chase Coffee**
4001 21st Ave W
Seattle, WA 98199-1201
206-282-7045
Fax: 206-282-5218 888-502-2333
Coffee
President: Phil Sancken
jane@caffeappassionato.com
Sales Exec: Jane Galloway
Year Founded: 1989
Estimated Sales: $5-10 Million
Number Employees: 20-49
Type of Packaging: Private Label
Brands:
Nescafe
Green Mountain
Peets

817 **Austin Slow Burn**
PO Box 150042
Austin, TX 78715-0042
512-282-7140
Fax: 512-282-7140 877-513-3192
www.austinslowburn.com
Gourmet fiery foods. Marinades, jams, jellies, hot pepper sauce, red sauce, green sauce and special variety sauces.
President: Jill Lewis
jilllewis@austin.rr.com
VP: Kevin Lewis
Estimated Sales: $300,000-500,000
Number Employees: 1-4

818 **Austin Special Foods Company**
10000 Inshore Drive
Austin, TX 78730
512-372-8665
Fax: 512-652-2699
Wholesaler of all natural and kosher dairy biscotti, cookies and frozen cookie dough. Many biscotti flavors
Owner: Laura Logan
CEO: Gene Austin
Year Founded: 1994
Estimated Sales: $10-20 Million
Number Employees: 3
Brands:
Dog Bakery Products
M&M Cookies
Granny Cookies

819 **Austinuts**
2900 W Anderson Ln # 19b
Austin, TX 78757-1364
512-323-6887
Fax: 512-323-6889 877-329-6887
info@austinuts.com www.austinuts.com
Dry Roasted Gourmet Nuts and Seeds, Dried Fruits, Chocolates, Candy, Trail Mixes, Gourmet Food, Go Texan Products, Gift Baskets & Corporate Gifts.
Founder: Doron Ilai
Estimated Sales: $650,000
Number Employees: 5-9
Square Footage: 8
Type of Packaging: Private Label
Brands:
Austinuts

820 **Austrade**
3309 Northlake Blvd # 201
Suite 201
Palm Beach Gdns, FL 33403-1705
561-209-2447
Fax: 561-585-7164 info@austradeinc.com
The leader in importing fine chemicals and food products.
President: Gary Bartl
VP: Stephen Barti
Marketing: Joseph Schantl
Sales: Sandra Barti
Year Founded: 1997
Estimated Sales: Less than $500,000
Number Employees: 1-4

821 **Austrian Trade Commission**
120 W 45th St # 900
7th Avenue
New York, NY 10036-4062
212-421-5250
Fax: 212-751-4675
newyork@advantageaustria.org
Specialty foods. Non-alcoholic beverages, water, beer, salad dressing, full-line vinegar, full-line chcoolate, cheese, agency/trade organization.
Contact: Christian Kesberg
Contact: Maichaela Lausegger
Manager: Salomeh Saidi
tehran@advantageaustria.org
Number Employees: 5-9

822 **Authentic Marotti Biscotti**
749 Red Wing Dr
Lewisville, TX 75067
972-221-7295
Fax: 972-436-4547
Wholesome bakers of gourmet biscotti, brownies and bar cookies.
Owner: Joann Marotti
VP: Glenn Mancini
Estimated Sales: $2.5-5 Million
Number Employees: 1-4
Type of Packaging: Consumer, Private Label, Bulk
Brands:
Marotti Biscotti

823 **Autin's Cajun Cookery**
804 W 8th Ave
Covington, LA 70433-2306
985-871-1199
Fax: 985-871-7290 800-877-7290
autinskjun@aol.com www.autinscajuncookery.com
Manufacturer of Cajun dinner mixes and seasonings including jambalaya, etouffee, dirty rice, chili, gumbo, etc
President: Gibson Autin
autinskjun@aol.com
Year Founded: 1910
Estimated Sales: $500,000-$1 Million
Number Employees: 1-4
Type of Packaging: Consumer, Food Service, Private Label, Bulk
Brands:
Autin's

824 **Automatic Rolls Of New Jersey**
1 Gourmet Ln
Edison, NJ 08837
877-222-2867
www.nefoods.com
Soft hamburger rolls; serving McDonalds chains
Plant Manager: Charlies Colli
Estimated Sales: $50-100 Million
Number Employees: 100-249
Parent Co: Northeast Foods
Type of Packaging: Food Service

825 **Autumn Hill Vineyards/Blue Ridge Wine**
301 River Drive
Stanardsville, VA 22973
434-985-6100
autumnhillwine@gmail.com
www.autumnhillwine.com
Wine
Owner: Avra Schwab
Owner: Ed Schwab
Estimated Sales: $1-3 Million
Number Employees: 1-4

826 **Autumn Wind Vineyard**
15225 NE North Valley Rd
Newberg, OR 97132
503-538-6931
Fax: 503-538-6931
Manufacturer of fine wines
Owner: Patricia Green
Co-Owner: Jim Anderson
Estimated Sales: $500,000-$1 Million
Number Employees: 1-4
Square Footage: 12
Type of Packaging: Private Label
Brands:
Patricia Green Cellars

827 **Avafina Organics**
100-1580 Brigantine Dr
Coquitlam, BC V3K 7C1
Canada
604-292-0022
Fax: 604-292-0024 hello@avafina.com
www.avafina.com
Organic ingredients

828 **Avalon Gourmet**
1051 E Broadway Rd
Phoenix, AZ 85040-2301
602-253-0343
Fax: 480-253-0432
Manufacturer of gourmet foods
President: Richard Du Pree
richdupree@fsiaz.com
Owner: Alan Parker
VP: Dolores DuPree
Year Founded: 1994
Estimated Sales: $5-10 Million
Number Employees: 5-9

829 **Avalon International Breads**
422 W Willis St
Detroit, MI 48201-1702
313-832-0008
Fax: 313-832-0018 www.avalonbreads.net
Organic breads and baked goods
CEO: Vanessa Blanchard
vanessablanchard@avalonbreads.net
Number Employees: 50-99

830 **Avalon Organic Coffees**
8308 Corona Loop NE
Albuquerque, NM 87113-1665
505-856-5582
Fax: 505-856-5588 800-662-2575
e-mail@avalonorganic.com
Organic coffee
Contact: Tanya Archuleta

831 **Avanti Foods Co**
109 Depot Street
Walnut, IL 61376
815-379-2155
800-243-3739
www.avantifoods.com
Frozen pizzas and walnut cheeses
Year Founded: 1964
Estimated Sales: $6 Million
Number Employees: 20-49
Number of Brands: 3
Type of Packaging: Consumer, Food Service, Private Label, Bulk
Brands:
Gino's
Swiss Party

832 **Avary Farms**
2513 North Jackson
Odessa, TX 79761
432-332-4139
Fax: 915-332-4130
Owner: Bob Avary
Sales/Marketing Manager: Angela Avery
Estimated Sales: $300,000-500,000
Number Employees: 1-4

833 **Avatar Corp**
500 Central Ave
University Park, IL 60484-3147
708-534-5511
Fax: 708-534-0123 800-255-3181
inquiries@avatarcorp.com www.avatarcorp.com
Manufacture, refine and supply raw materials and ingrdients for the food, drug and personal care industries.
Owner: Kari Boykin
k.boykin@avatarholdings.com
President: Michael Shamie
VP Marketing: David Darwin
Chief Operating Officer: Phil Ternes
Plant Manager: Kent Taylor
Purchasing: Kristina Gutyan
Year Founded: 1982
Estimated Sales: $9 Million
Number Employees: 10-19
Square Footage: 80000
Type of Packaging: Private Label, Bulk
Brands:
Arol
Arox
Avox
Avagel
Avapol
Avatar
Avatech
Brown 'n' Serve
Citation
Dpo
Lsc
Protrolley
Paneze
Pankote
Pinnacle
Probio
Prochill
Procon
Prokote
Prophos
Prosyn
Protech
Snow White
Soft White
Trokote
Wintrex

834 **Avebe America Inc.**
101 Interchange Plaza
Suite 101
Cranbury, NJ 08512
609-865-8981
www.avebe.com
Starch specialties for texture, protein enrichment, stability and appearance.
Estimated Sales: $20-50 Million
Number Employees: 20-49
Parent Co: AVEBE Group

835 **Aveka Inc**
2045 Wooddale Dr
St Paul, MN 55125-2904
651-730-1729
Fax: 651-730-1826 888-317-3700
aveka@aveka.com www.aveka.com
Contract manufacturer and research and development company that focuses on particle technology including spray drying, particle coating or microcapsule technologies.
Owner: John Anderson
aveka@avekamfg.com
CEO/Owvnder: William Hendrickson
Environmental Manager: Shain Kroenecke
Process Engineer: Matthew Timmers
Number Employees: 50-99
Other Locations:
Aveka Manufacturing
Fredericksberg IA
Cresco Food Technologies
Cresco IA
Aveka Nutra Processing
Waukon IA
Aveka CCE Technologies
Cottage Grove MN

836 **Avena Foods Ltd.**
316 1st Ave. E
Regina, SK S4N 5H2
Canada
306-757-3663
Fax: 306-757-1218 drichardson@avenafoods.com
www.avenafoods.com
Processor and supplier of gluten-free/wheat free oat products for private label/ingredients market. Allergen free plant with GFCO and OU Kosher Certification. Products include rolled oats, quick flakes, flour, steel cuts oats andbran.
Director: Kevin Meadows
Director: Maryellen Carlson
Quality Control: Nicole Gudmundsson
Sales: Dale Richardson
Operations: Rod Lechner
Plant Manager: Nathalie Paquin
Purchasing: Carryl Litzenberger
Estimated Sales: $746.93 Thousand
Number Employees: 26
Type of Packaging: Private Label, Bulk

837 **Avenue Gourmet**
11445 Cronridge Drive
Suite Q
Owings Mills, MD 21117
410-902-5701
Fax: 410-902-0600 www.avenuegourmet.com
Manufacturer of specialty and natural foods distribution

President: Patricia Lobel
patricia.lobel@avenuegourmet.com
Sales Manager: Sandra Hoffman
Year Founded: 1998
Number Employees: 10-19

838 **Avery Brewing Company**
5763 Arapahoe Ave. Unit E
Boulder, CO 80303
303-440-4324
Fax: 303-786-8790 877-844-5679
info@averybrewing.com www.averybrewing.com
Producer of various beers
President: Adam Avery
CEO/CFO: Larry Avery
Vice President: Thomas Boogaard
Quality Control Manager: Matt Thrall
Contact: Bernardo Alatorre
bernardo@averybrewing.com
Operations Manager: Steve Breezley
Chief Technology Officer: Shaun Nanavati
Year Founded: 1993
Estimated Sales: $5-10 Million
Number Employees: 9
Brands:
14'er Esb
Avery
Ellie's Brown
Hog Heaven
Out of Bounds
Redpoint
Salvation
The Reverend
White Rascal

839 **Avery Dennison Corporation**
207 N Goode Avenue
Suite 500
Glendale, CA 91203-1301
626-304-2000
www.averydennison.com
Manufacturer and exporter of pressure sensitive labels.
Chairman/President/CEO: Mitch Butier
SVP/Chief Financial Officer: Greg Lovins
SVP/Chief Human Resources Officer: Anne Hill
SVP/General Counsel/Secretary: Susan Miller
VP/General Manager, Retail Branding: Deon Stander
VP/Global Operations/Supply Chain: Kamran Kian
Year Founded: 1935
Estimated Sales: $7.5 Billion
Number Employees: 30,000
Other Locations:
Avery Research Center (AEM)
Irwindale CA
Business Media
Buffalo NY
Corporate
Framingham MA
Corporate Int'l Manufacturing
Covina CA
Corporate Office at Brea
Brea CA
Corporate Office at Framingham
Framingham MA
Corporate Shared EHS at Milford
Milford MA
Engineered Films Division
Greenfield IN
Engineered Films Division
Painesville OH

840 **Avitae**
PO Box 93686
Cleveland, OH 44101
888-228-4823
goavitae.com
Caffeinated water
Number of Brands: 3
Number of Products: 15
Brands:
AVITAE
SPARKLING AVITAE
AVITAE XR

841 **Avo-King Internatl**
2050 W Chapman Ave
Suite 210
Orange, CA 92868-2649
714-937-1551
Fax: 714-937-1974 800-286-5464
info@avo-king.com www.avo-king.com
Processor and importer of frozen guacamole and avocado pulp
Owner: Guido Doddoli
Controller: Francisco Philibert
commets@avo-king.com
Vice President: Pablo Doddoli
Estimated Sales: $2.5 Million
Number Employees: 1-4
Parent Co: Doddoli Hermanos Group
Brands:
Avo-King

842 **AvoLov**
20724 Carmen Loop
Suite 120
Bend, OR 97702
541-419-4078
www.avocadochips.com
Avocado chips
Number of Brands: 1
Number of Products: 3
Brands:
AVOLOV

843 **Avoca**
PO Box 129
841 Avoca Road
Merry Hill, NC 27957
252-482-2133
Fax: 252-482-8622 www.avocainc.com
Manufacturer and exporter of flavors and fragrances
President: David Peele
Director/ Business Development: Richard Maier
COO: Danny White
Research & Development: Richard Teague
Marketing Director: Shannon Sloan
Plant Manager: Danny White
Number Employees: 50-99

844 **Avon Heights Mushrooms**
50 Old Baltimore Pike
Avondale, PA 19311
610-268-2092
Fax: 610 268-8706
Manufacturer of coleslaw and salad mixes; also, packer of spinach, broker of vegetables
Owner: Philip Pusey Jr
Year Founded: 1972
Estimated Sales: $2 Millio
Number Employees: 20
Square Footage: 32000

845 **Avri Co Inc**
1080 Essex Ave
Richmond, CA 94801-2113
510-233-0633
Fax: 510-233-0636 800-883-9574
avrico@avrico.com
Flavoring supplies, flavors, fragrances, essential oils
President: Carl Arvold
av@avrico.com
Estimated Sales: Less than $1 Million
Number Employees: 5-9
Brands:
Avri Companies

846 **Award Baking Intl**
206 State Ave S
New Germany, MN 55367-9521
952-353-2533
Fax: 952-353-8066 800-333-3523
awardbaking@oblaten.com www.oblaten.com
Biscottis and all natural specialty baked goods.
Owner: Tim Kraft
tkraft@oblaten.com
Co-Owner: Ken Barron
Marketing: Rhonda Kossack
Year Founded: 1948
Estimated Sales: $1-2.5 Million
Number Employees: 20-49
Square Footage: 40000
Parent Co: Kenny B's Cookie
Brands:
Auer
Award Auer/Blaschke
Award Crunchy Dunkers
Biscotti Di Roma
Carlsbad Oblaten

847 **Awrey Bakeries**
12301 Farmington Rd
Livonia, MI 48150
734-522-1100
Fax: 734-522-1585 800-950-2253
personnel@awrey.com
Frozen baked goods including cakes, bagels, muffins, doughnuts, danish, croissants, biscuits, rolls, english muffins, and marquise desserts.
VP, Contract Sales: Diane Lynch
Contact: Betty Awrey
b.j.awrey@netscape.com
Plant Manager and Director of Operations: Kurt Eddy
Estimated Sales: $34.6 Million
Number Employees: 380
Number of Brands: 4
Number of Products: 200
Square Footage: 60000
Type of Packaging: Consumer, Food Service, Private Label
Brands:
Awrey's Maestro
Grande
Marquise
Atkins Elegant Desserts

848 **Ax Water**
Fargo, ND 58104
info@drinkaxwater.com
drinkaxwater.com
Antioxidant water
CEO and Co-Founder: Blake Johnson
President and Co-Founder: Wade Gronwold
Year Founded: 2017

849 **Axelsson & Johnson Fish Company**
PO Box 180
933 Ocean Drive
Cape May, NJ 08204-0180
609-884-8426
Fax: 609-898-0221 ajfish@bellatlantic.net
www.jerseyseafood.nj.gov
Exporter and importer of fresh seafood
Manager: Andrew Axelsson
Estimated Sales: $5-10 Million
Number Employees: 10-19
Brands:
A&J Brand

850 **Axiom Foods, Inc.**
12100 Wilshire Blvd
Suite 800
Los Angeles, CA 90025
310-264-2606
800-711-3587
info@axiomfoods.com www.axiomfoods.com
Organic WGBR protein concentrates and isolates, sugars, sugar solids, honey, milks, flours and starches. (brown rice products)
President & CEO: David Janow
Sales Director: Jason Lee
Estimated Sales: $.5-1 Million

851 **Axium Foods**
239 Oak Grove Ave
PO Box 187
South Beloit, IL 61080-1936
815-389-3053
800-523-8644
www.axiumfoods.com
Corn-based snack foods
President: Jerry Stokely
jstokely@axiumfoods.com
Number Employees: 100-249
Type of Packaging: Consumer, Food Service, Private Label

852 **Ayara Products**
6245 W. 87th St.
Los Angeles, CA 90045
310-410-8848
www.ayaraproducts.com
Ethnic sauces.
Founder: Vanda Asapahu
vanda@ayarathaicuisine.com
Square Footage: 80000

853 **Ayoba-Yo**
P.O. Box 3666
Oakton, VA 22124
202-796-8554
www.ayoba-yo.com
Dried meat snacks

854 **Azar Nut Co**
1800 Northwestern Dr
El Paso, TX 79912-1125
915-877-4079
Fax: 915-877-1198 800-351-8178
www.mountfranklinfoods.com
Peanuts, almonds, pecans, walnuts, pine and mixed nuts, dried fruit, candy and snack mixes
CEO: Richard Condie
condie@azarnutco.com
New Business Development Manager: Jay Roehner
VP, Sales & Marketing: Barbara Powell
Operations Manager: James Jamison
Warehouse Manager: Art Romero
Number Employees: 100-249
Other Locations:
Sunlight Plant
Juarez, Mexico

855 **Azteca Foods Inc**
5005 S Nagle Ave
Chicago, IL 60638-1318
708-563-6600
Fax: 708-563-0331 info@aztecafoods.com
www.baja-tortillas.com
Mexican food products including salad shells, tortilla chips and tortillas
President: Renee Togher
renee.togher@aztecafoods.com
Chairman: Arthur Velasquez
Vice President, Finance: Joseh Klomes
Vice President Operations: Julio Martinez
Estimated Sales: $34 Million
Number Employees: 100-249
Number of Brands: 3
Square Footage: 120000
Type of Packaging: Consumer, Food Service
Brands:
Azteca®
Buena Vida®
Ultragrain® Tortillas

856 **Azteca Milling**
5601 Executive Dr.
Suite 650
Irving, TX 75038-6118
972-232-5300
Fax: 972-232-5370 800-364-0040
info@aztecamilling.com www.aztecamilling.com
Corn tortilla flours; snack flours; retail flours, and speciality flours.
President: Ignacio Hernandez
Vice President: Don Schleppegrell
Corporate Sales Manager: Rick Norton
Snack Manager Sales: Alan Davis
Contact: Hernan Guevara
hernan_guevara@aztecamilling.com
Estimated Sales: $40 Million
Number Employees: 100-249
Parent Co: Gruma Corporation
Type of Packaging: Bulk
Brands:
Masa Mixta ®
Maseca ®
Selecta ®

857 **(HQ)Azuma Foods Intl Inc USA**
20201 Mack St
Hayward, CA 94545-1224
510-782-1112
Fax: 510-782-1188 www.azumafoods.com
Processor, exporter and importer of frozen seafood, caviar and ready-made sushi
President/CEO: Takahiro Tamura
Chairman: Toshinobu Azuma
Estimated Sales: $5-10 Million
Number Employees: 50-99
Other Locations:
New York Branch
East Rutherford NJ
Hawaii Sales Office
Honolulu HI
West Coast American Division Sales
Novato CA
East Coast American Division Sales
Boston MA
Brands:
Ichiban Delight®
My-Dol®
Sea Salad
Takohachi
Taste of Island Legends
Tobikko®

858 **B & B Food DistributorsInc**
724 S 13th St
Terre Haute, IN 47807-4997
812-238-1438
Fax: 812-232-0670 800-264-1438
www.bandbfoods.net
Manufacturer of general merchandise and foodservice equipment
President: Scott Isles
scott@bandbfoods.net
Year Founded: 1952
Estimated Sales: $10-20 Million
Number Employees: 50-99

859 **B & B Pecan Processors**
106 Thomson Ave
Turkey, NC 28393-9132
910-533-2229
Fax: 919-553-4610 866-328-7322
bandbpecans@intrstar.net
www.elizabethspecans.com
Pecan praline, brittle, chocolate covered pecans, butter-roasted pecans and BBQ sauce
Owner: Alan Bundy
bandbpecans@intrstar.net
Estimated Sales: $.5-1 million
Number Employees: 5-9
Brands:
Elizabeth's

860 **B & B Poultry Co**
110 Almond Rd
Norma, NJ 08347
856-692-8893
Fax: 856-455-7681 800-535-7646
information@bandbpoultry.com
www.bandbpoultry.com
Refrigerated chickens, whole and parts
President: Josh Fisher
CEO: Mark Fisher
Treasurer: Dorothy Fisher
Vice President: Mark Fisher
Contact: Benjamin Fisher
Year Founded: 1945
Estimated Sales: $25 Million
Number Employees: 100-249

861 **B & B Produce**
12902 Fancy Gap Hwy.
Cana, VA 24317
276-755-4441
Fax: 919-894-2127 800-633-4902
www.bandbproducecana.com
Fruits, vegetables, plants, hanging baskets, candy, jams, jelly, honey, molasses
Founder & Owner: Burlie Bowman
Owner: Eddie Bowman
Owner: Gary Bowman
Estimated Sales: $20-50 Million
Number Employees: 20-49
Brands:
Sun Beauty

862 **B & C Riverside**
2155 Highway 18
Vacherie, LA 70090-5405
225-265-8356
Fax: 225-265-9960 www.bncrestaurant.com
Vacuum packed, fresh and frozen alligator and seafood
Owner: Tommy Breaux
Estimated Sales: Under $1 Million
Number Employees: 5-9
Type of Packaging: Consumer, Food Service

863 **B & D Foods**
3494 S Tk Ave
Boise, ID 83705-5278
208-344-1183
Fax: 208-344-6825 sales@banddfoods.net
www.banddfoods.com
Processor of frozen finger steaks, pork and chicken strips and battered mozzarella cheese sticks
Contact: Tim Anderson
Contact: Don Emlet
Contact: John Tolman
Contact: Carma Christensen
cchristensen@banddfoods.net
Year Founded: 1972
Estimated Sales: $10-20 Million
Number Employees: 10-19
Square Footage: 24000
Type of Packaging: Food Service, Private Label

864 **B & G Foods Inc.**
4 Gatehall Dr.
Parsippany, NJ 07054
973-401-6500
Fax: 973-630-6522 customercare@mybrands.com
www.bgfoods.com
Frozen and shelf-stable products including hot cereals, jams, jellies, fruit spreads, canned meats, beans and vegetables, taco shells, vinegars and cooking wines, sweeteners, seasonings, pickles, peppers, salsas and various saucessyrups and condiments.
Chairman: Stephen Sherrill
President/CEO/Director: Kenneth Romanzi
EVP, Finance/Chief Financial Officer: Bruce Wacha
EVP/Chief Compliance Officer: Scott Lerner
EVP, Human Resources: Eric Hart
Executive VP/Chief Customer Officer: Ellen Schum
Chief Supply Chain Officer: Erich Fritz
Year Founded: 1889
Estimated Sales: $1.7 Billion
Number Employees: 2,500+
Number of Brands: 50+
Square Footage: 200000
Type of Packaging: Consumer, Food Service
Brands:
Back to Nature
Bear Creek®
Cream of Wheat®
Green Giant™
B&M®
Mrs Dash®
Ortega
Victoria®
Ac'cent®
Ac'cent Sa-son®
B&G®
Baker's Joys®
Brer Rabbit®
Buena Vida™
Canoleo®
Carey's®
Crock Pot®
Dec A Cake®
Devonsheer®
Don Pepino®
Durkee®
Emeril's®
Grandma's Molasses®
Henri's®
Joan of Arc®
Las Palmas®
Le Sueur®
MacDonald's™
Mama Mary's™
Maple Grove Farms of Vermont®
McCann's®
Molly McButter
New York Flatbreads™
New York Style™
Old London®
Polaner®
Regina®
Scalfani®
Skinnygirl™
SnackWell's®d
Spice Islands®
Spring Tree®
Static Guard®
Sugar Twin®
Tone's®
Trappey's®
True North®
Underwood®
Vermont Maid®
Weber®
Wright's®

865 **B & J Seafood**
1101 US Highway 70 E
New Bern, NC 28560-6617
252-637-0483
Fax: 252-633-0775
Wholesaler of fish and seafood. Canned, frozen and refrigerated blue crabmeat, frozen and refrigerated flounder fillets.
President: Brent Fulcher
bjseafood@earthlink.net
Year Founded: 2006
Estimated Sales: $14 Million
Number Employees: 100-249
Type of Packaging: Private Label
Brands:
Upper Bay

866 **B & R Classics LLC**
56 Old Field Rd
Huntington, NY 11743
631-427-5675
Fax: 631-421-7471 ctr@brclassics.com
www.brclassics.com
Gluten-free, cakes/pastries, cookies, chocolate bars, chocolate truffles, gummies/jellies/pates de fruits, chips, gift packs.
Marketing: Chris Riley
Contact: Chris Johnson
chris@johnsco-investments.com

867 **B & R Quality Meats Inc**
200 Park Rd
Waterloo, IA 50703
319-232-6328
Fax: 319-232-8623
customerservice@b-rqualitymeats.com
www.b-rqualitymeats.com
Processor and wholesaler/distributor of meat including beef, pork, veal and poultry; serving the foodservice market
Estimated Sales: $5-10 Million
Number Employees: 10-19
Square Footage: 24000
Type of Packaging: Consumer, Food Service, Bulk

868 **B G Smith & Sons Oyster Co**
787 Oakley Ln
Sharps, VA 22548
804-394-2721
Fax: 804-394-2741 877-483-8279
Manufacturer and exporter of fresh and frozen oysters; processor and packager of ice
President/CEO: B Smith
Estimated Sales: $2.5-5 Million
Number Employees: 10-19
Number of Brands: 3
Number of Products: 1
Square Footage: 400000
Type of Packaging: Consumer, Food Service, Private Label
Brands:
Chesapeake Bay Ice
Chesapeake Pride
Ocean Spray
Perch Creek

869 **B R Cohn Winery & Olive Oil Co**
15000 Hwy 12
Glen Ellen, CA 95442-9454
707-938-4064
Fax: 707-938-4585 800-330-4064
info@brcohn.com www.brcohnwinery.com
Wine, olive oils, vinegars
President: Daniel Cohn
Owner: Bruce Cohn
Accounts Manager: Kelly Johnson
Marketing and Design Manager: Trevor Swallow
National Sales Manager: Lezette Yearby
Public Relations: Micheal Coats
Winemaker: Tom Montgomery
Purchasing: Bruce Cohn
Estimated Sales: $2.5-5 Million
Number Employees: 20-49
Type of Packaging: Private Label
Brands:
Balsamic and Herb Dipping Oil
Balsamic Vinegar of Modena
Cabernet Vinegar
Carneros Chardonnay
Champagne Vinegar
Chardonnay Vinegar
Mendocino Cty. Sauvignon Blanc
Olive Hill Cabernet Sauvignon
Olive Hill Cabernet Sauvignon
Olive Hill Pinot Noir
Organic Extra Virgin Olive Oil
Raspberry Champagne Vinegar
Reserve Carneros Chardonnay
Silver Label Cabernet Sauvigno
Sonoma Extra Virgin Olive Oil
Sonoma Valley Merlot
Sonoma Valley Zinfandel

870 **B S & B Safety Systems LLC**
7455 E 46th St
Tulsa, OK 74145-6301
918-622-5950
Fax: 918-492-1559 800-272-3475
sales@bsbsystems.com www.bsbsystems.com
Manufactures overpressure protection safety products, pressure relief, both positive and vacuum with pressure relieving products including rupture disks.
VP: Dave Garrison
Number Employees: 5-9

871 **B&A Bakery**
1820 Ellesmere Road
Toronto, ON M1H 2V5
Canada
416-289-9600
Fax: 416-289-2445 800-263-2878
freshness@breadsource.com
www.breadsource.com
Processor of homestyle sandwich bread and rolls including hamburger, submarine, hot dog, dinner and kaiser
Proprietor: Arif Sunderji
Year Founded: 1985
Estimated Sales: $1.4 Million
Number Employees: 40
Square Footage: 48000
Type of Packaging: Food Service

872 **B&D Food Corporation**
575 Madison Ave
Suite 1006
New York, NY 10022-8511
212-937-8456
Fax: 212-412-9034
Roasted, ground coffee; chocolate beverages and cappaccinos; and spray dried agglomerated soluble coffee and powdered tea.
Chief Executive Officer/Board Directors: Yaron Arbell
Chief Financial Officer/Board Directors: Yossi Haras
Number Employees: 1-4
Type of Packaging: Food Service

873 **B&H Foods**
P.O.Box 668568
Charlotte, NC 28266-8568
704-332-4106
Fax: 704-332-5980
Shellfish Shippers
President: Stan Bracey
Plant Manager: Dennis Frost
Estimated Sales: $20-50 Million
Number Employees: 50-99
Parent Co: B&H Foods

874 **B&K Coffee**
PO Box 1238
Oneonta, NY 13820-5238
607-432-1499
Fax: 607-432-1592 800-432-1499
www.bkcoffee.com
Manufacturer of coffee and tea.
Owner: Paul Karabinis
Owner: Gene Bettiol
Year Founded: 1991
Estimated Sales: $10-24.9 Million
Number Employees: 20-49
Number of Brands: 1
Type of Packaging: Private Label
Brands:
B&K Coffee

875 **B&M Enterprises**
4818 S 76th St
Suite 130
Greenfield, WI 53220
414-399-7402
Fax: 414-461-2009 www.bmenterprisez.com
Manufacturer of dairy products
Owner: Marson Berry
Account Manager: Billy Anderson
Year Founded: 1982
Estimated Sales: Under $500,000
Number Employees: 1-4

876 **B&M Fisheries**
15 Pingree Farm Road
Georgetown, MA 01833
978-352-6663
Fax: 978-352-7565
Manufacturer of seafood
Manager: Matt Lofton
Manager: Brad Zimmerman
Contact: Allan Robicheau
allan@houmardacadie.com

877 **B-S Foods Company**
1000 Cornell Pkwy
Suite 600
Oklahoma City, OK 73108-1800
405-949-9797
Fax: 405-949-9802
Pre-packaged luncheon meats and sandwiches
Owner: Sandra Henager
Sales Manager: Dave Heinecke
Estimated Sales: $2.5-5 Million
Number Employees: 5-9
Parent Co: B-S Foods Company
Type of Packaging: Consumer

878 **B-Tea Beverage, LLC**
One International Blvd
Suite 720
Mahwah, NJ 07495
201-512-8400
Fax: 201-791-5800 btkombucha.com
Organic kombucha, organic tea
Operations Manager: Katie Scully
Year Founded: 2016
Number Employees: 1-10

879 **B. Lloyd's Pecans**
PO Box 354
1073 Clifford Street
Barwick, GA 31720
404-759-2441
800-322-6887
Supplier of Pecans and pecan confections
Owner: Heeth Varnedoe
Estimated Sales: $500-1 Million appx.
Number Employees: 30-99
Type of Packaging: Food Service

880 **B. Nutty**
655 12th St Apt 305
Oakland, CA 94607-3667
USA
510-374-4658
nutty@nuttyness.com
Chocolate bars, candy, gift packs
CEO: Kristian Salvesen
Chief Marketing: Anis Salvesen
Number Employees: 2

881 **B.B. Bean, Coffee**
583 County Line Rd
Monument, CO 80132
719-481-1170
bbcoffee@aol.com
Coffee
CEO: Elizabeth Kawczynski
Marketing Director: Elizabeth Kawczynski
Roastmaster: Bob Polito
Brands:
Bean Coffee

882 **B.C. Fisheries**
P.O.Box 334
Hanckock Point Road
Hancock, ME 04640-0334
207-422-8205
Fax: 207-422-8206
Seafood
Manager: Pete Daley

883 **B.M. Lawrence & Company**
601 Montgomery St
Suite 1115
San Francisco, CA 94111-2614
415-981-2926
Fax: 415-981-2926 info@bmlawrence.com
Wholesaler/Processor and distributor of soft drinks, nonalcoholic beer, canned fruits, vegetables, juices and fish
President: B Lawrence
Purchasing Agent: Hugh Ditzler
info@bmlawrence.com
Estimated Sales: $5-10 Million
Number Employees: 5-9
Square Footage: 8000
Brands:
California Farms
Grapefruit
Lemon-Lime
Us Cola
Us Select

884 **B.O.S.S. Food Co.**
800-344-8584
info@bossfoodco.com bossfoodco.com

Superfood snack bars
Number of Brands: 1
Number of Products: 5

885 **B.W.J.W. Inc.**
3517 Conway St
Fort Worth, TX 76111
817-831-0051
Fax: 817-834-6766
Meat
President: John Wehba
Contact: Bill Louis
b.louis@barwmeat.com
Estimated Sales: $10 Million
Number Employees: 65

886 **BASF Corp.**
100 Park Ave.
Florham Park, NJ 07932
973-245-6000
800-526-1072
www.basf.com
Vitamins and feed additives for human and livestock nutrition and fungicides, insecticides and herbicides for crop protection.
Chairman/CEO, BASF North America: Wayne Smith
Executive VP/CFO, BASF Corporation: Tobias Dratt
Senior VP/General Counsel: Stefan John
Year Founded: 1865
Estimated Sales: $63.8 Billion
Number Employees: 117,628
Parent Co: BASF SE
Other Locations:
Geismar LA
Shreveport LA
Livonia MI
Wyandotte MI
Sparks GA
Aberdeen MI
Palmyra MO
Belvidere NJ
Jamesburg NJ
Washington NJ
Enka NC
Morganton NC
Wilmington NC

887 **BBQ Bunch**
13100 Woodland Avenue
Kansas City, MO 64146-1801
816-941-4534
Fax: 816-941-0263 lewieb@aol.com
BBQ and mustard sauce; wholesaler/distrinutor of BBQ products; marketing consultant to the BBQ industry.
Owner: Lewis Bunch
Estimated Sales: $500,000-$1 Million
Number Employees: 1-4
Type of Packaging: Food Service, Private Label, Bulk
Brands:
Jazzy Barbecue Sauce

888 **BBQ Shack**
1613 E Peoria St
Paola, KS 66071-1893
913-294-5908
pitmaster@thebbqshack.com
Barbacue meats
Owner: Rick Schoenberger
Director Marketing/Sales: Debbie McCrackin
Estimated Sales: Less Than $500,000
Number Employees: 5-9
Brands:
Bbq Shack

889 **BBQ'n Fools Catering, LLC**
20 W. South Street
Greenfield, IN 46140
317-448-5873
Fax: 800-671-8652 800-671-8652
www.bbqnfools.com
BBQ sauces and seasonings.
Owner: Tom Brohamer
Co-Owner: Kurt Weidmann
Contact: Grant Ford
grant@bbqnfools.com
Estimated Sales: $40,000
Number Employees: 3
Brands:
Bbq'n Fools
Papa Dan's World Famous Jerky

890 **BBS Bodacious BBQ Company**
8411 Forest Hills Dr
Suite 103
Coral Springs, FL 33065
954-752-0909
Fax: 954-345-3482 800-537-5928
bbsbbq@aol.com www.800jerky2u.com
Natural and fat-free barbecue sauces, spicy jellies and steak, turkey jerky
President/CEO: Susan Sheldon
Estimated Sales: $500,000-$1 Million
Number Employees: 10-19
Brands:
Aunt Jayne's
Bbs Bodacious
Sammye's Sumptuous

891 **BBS Lobster Co**
141 Smalls Point Rd
Machiasport, ME 04655-3231
207-255-8888
Fax: 207-255-3987 info@lobstertrap.com
www.lobstertrap.com
Wholesaler of lobsters
Owner: Susan West
General Manager: Blair West
CFO: Greg Menzel
Assistant General Manager: Rosie Barrett
Domestic/International Sales: David Madden
Lobster Purchasing/Operations: Tom Platt
Estimated Sales: $1,600,000
Number Employees: 5-9
Parent Co: Lobster Trap Wholesale Seafood Dealers

892 **BBU Bakeries**
255 Business Ctr Drive
PO Box 976
Horsham, PA 19044
213-672-8010
Fax: 610-320-9286 800-984-0989
Manufacturer of cakes, pies, muffins, doughnuts, breads, pizza dough and bagels
President: Gary Prince
Plant Manager: Ron Schulthies
Year Founded: 1983
Estimated Sales: $300,000-500,000
Number Employees: 10000-25000
Type of Packaging: Consumer
Brands:
Mrs Bairds
Orowheat
Entemanns
Thomas
Arnorld
Boboli
Freihoffer

893 **BCFoods**
1330 N Dutton Ave
Suite 100
Santa Rosa, CA 95401
707-547-1776
Fax: 707-545-5270 www.bcfoods.com
Industrial ingredients, dehydrated and freeze dried vegetables, freeze dried fruit, dairy and meat products.
President North America: Adam Lee
Director of Sales & Marketing: Mike Bray
Global Operations Manager: Daniel Mabee
Estimated Sales: $20-50 Million
Number Employees: 20-49

894 **BCGA Concept Corporation**
39 Canal Street
New York, NY 10002
212-488-0661
Fax: 212-488-0700 info@freshgingerale.com
Soft Drinks, Non Alcoholic.
Founder/CEO: Bruce Cost
Marketing: Jenny Chen

895 **BDS Natural**
2779 E El Presidio St
Long Beach, CA 90810-1118
310-747-0444
Fax: 310-518-2577 info@bdsnatural.com
www.bdsnatural.com
Manufacturer and distributor of spices and seasoning blends, botanical powders, and herbal teas.
Co-Founder: Steve Brennis
Co-Founder: David Soloman
General Manager: Donna Cook
R&D Manager/Technical Foods Sales: Daniel Alexander
Technnical Director: Pauline Lu
Customer Service Manager: Marlene Sellers
Human Resources Manager: Alexis Torres
Director of Operations: Kevin Witt
Operations Manager: John Kapski
Purchasing: Brandy Guedea
Number Employees: 5-9
Other Locations:
Operations
Carson, CA

896 **BGS Jourdan & Sons**
1415 Stafford Rd
Darlington, MD 21034-1801
410-457-4904
Canned whole tomatoes and various other fruits and vegetables.
Owner: Scott Reezes
Estimated Sales: Less than $120,000
Number Employees: 1-4
Type of Packaging: Consumer, Private Label
Brands:
Point Pleasant

897 **BJ's Restaurants Inc.**
7755 Center Ave
Suite 300
Huntington Beach, CA 92647-3084
714-500-2400
Fax: 714-848-8287 dianne@bjsbrewhouse.com
www.bjsrestaurants.com
Beer, ale and lager; also, pizza
President/CEO: Gerald Deitchle
Cfo/Evp: Gregory Levin
Executive VP: Lon F Ledwith
lon@bjsbrewhouse.com
Estimated Sales: 513,000
Number Employees: 10000+
Parent Co: BJ's Restaurants Inc
Brands:
Bj Beer

898 **BK Giulini Corporation**
Dr.-Albert-Reimann-Str. 2
Ladenburg, 68526
Germany
Phosphate-based food ingredients for further processed meat, poultry, dairy and seafood.
Chief Scientific Officer: Wolfgang Schneider
Estimated Sales: $24 Million
Number Employees: 15
Square Footage: 4129
Parent Co: ICL
Brands:
Bekaplus®
Brifisol®
Johr®
Turrisin®

899 **BK Specialty Foods**
200 Eagle Court
Swedesboro, NJ 08085-1799
856-294-600
Fax: 856-241-8942 800-354-9445
bkfoods.com
Gourmet foods including dairy, baked goods, desserts, beans & rice, fruit and ethnic foods.
CFO: Scott Carey
Vice President of Sales and Marketing: Karen Kratchman-Gold
Number Employees: 51-200

900 **BKW Seasonings**
3110 Henson Rd
Suite 7
Knoxville, TN 37921-5392
865-851-8657
Fax: 865-966-6963 matt@bkwseasonings.com
www.bkwseasonings.com
Various types of seasonings
Owner: Matt Boeler
Contact: Karen Webb
kwebb@bkwseasonings.com
Year Founded: 2007
Number Employees: 5-9

901 BN Soda
PO Box 11
Brookline, MA 02446
617-782-7888
Fax: 240-536-3079
Soda made of natural flavors and cane sugar, also caffeine-free
Founder: Tom Bleier
tombleier@aol.com

902 BOLD Organics
2090 7th Avenue
Suite 201A
New York, NY 10027
consumerinfo@bold-organics.com
Organic foods
President/CEO: Aaron Greenwald
CFO/COO: Justin Kniepman
National Sales Manager: Sasha Sherman

903 BP Gourmet
135 Ricefield Ln
Hauppauge, NY 11788-2046
631-234-8200
Fax: 631-234-8200
Fat-free and organic cookies, sugar free cookies, fruit spreads and salad dressing. Also produces bread sticks and croutons
President: Florence Boris
Estimated Sales: $2.5-5 Million
Number Employees: 20-49
Brands:
Bp Gourmet
Freida's Kitchen
Monte Carlo Bake Shop
Sweet Nothings

904 BRAMI Snacks
154 Grand St
New York, NY 10013-3141
917-291-1945
info@bramisnacks.com
www.bramisnacks.com
Beans and wholegrain snacks
CEO: Dillon Dandurand
Brands:
BRAMI Beans

905 BRINS
Brooklyn, NY
orders@staggjam.com
www.brinsjam.com
Jams and marmalades
Founder: Candice Ross
Year Founded: 2015

906 BTS Company/Hail CaesarDressings
PO Box 218015
5157 Traceway Drive
Nashville, TN 37221-8015
615-646-3125
Fax: 615-226-6867 800-617-8899
Gourmet dressings, pasta sauces, marinades. Available in Original, Low-Fat and Fat Free, Wide variety of flavors & sizes.
Owner: Bunny Sundock
Estimated Sales: $1-3 Million
Number Employees: 1-4

907 Baba Foods
San Diego, CA
619-426-6946
Fax: 619-810-0755 inforequest@babafoods.com
www.babafoods.com
Hummus, pita chips, dips and salads
Number of Brands: 1
Number of Products: 33
Brands:
BABA FOODS

908 Babci's Specialty Foods
193 Fairview Avenue
Chicopee, MA 01013
413-598-8158
Pierogies, kapusta, chrust
President: Eugene Kirejczyk
Year Founded: 1986
Type of Packaging: Food Service, Private Label

909 Babcock Winery & Vineyards
5175 E Highway 246
Lompoc, CA 93436-9613
805-736-1455
Fax: 805-736-3886 info@babcockwinery.com
www.babcockwinery.com
Red and white wines
Owner: Bryan Babcock
info@babcockwinery.com
Year Founded: 1984
Estimated Sales: $5-10 Million
Number Employees: 20-49
Type of Packaging: Private Label

910 Babe Farms Inc
1485 N Blosser Rd
Santa Maria, CA 93458-2043
805-925-4144
Fax: 805-922-3950 800-648-6772
customerservice@babefarms.com
www.babefarms.com
Specialty and baby produce items, including peeled carrots and root vegetables
Founder: Will Souza
CEO: Judy Lundberg
judy@babefarms.com
Finance Manager: Carrie Jordan
Operations: Jeff Lundberg
Year Founded: 1986
Estimated Sales: $7 Million
Number Employees: 100-249
Type of Packaging: Food Service, Private Label
Brands:
Babe Farms

911 Babe's Honey Farm
4150 Blenkinsop Road
Victoria, BC V8X 2C4
Canada
250-658-8319
Fax: 250-658-8149 www.babes-honey-farm.com
Fireweed and wild flower honey, beeswax
Owner: Brandon Schwartz
Year Founded: 1945
Estimated Sales: $585,000
Number Employees: 60
Square Footage: 48000
Type of Packaging: Food Service
Brands:
Babe's

912 Baby's Coffee
U.S. 1 Mile Marker 15
Key West, FL 33040
337-442-6359
Fax: 305-744-9843 800-523-2326
info@babyscoffee.com www.babyscoffee.com
Coffee
Manager: Mary Browman
Co-Owner: Olga Teplitsky
Marketing Manager: Alfonse Manosalvas
Estimated Sales: Less than $500,000
Number Employees: 1-4
Type of Packaging: Private Label
Brands:
Baby's Breakfast Roast
Baby's Private Buzz
Baby's Wrelker's Roa
Hemingway's Hair Of
Killer Joe
Old Town Roast
Sexpresso

913 Bacardi Canada, Inc.
3250 Bloor St. W
East Tower, Suite 1050
Toronto, ON M8X 2X9
Canada
905-451-6100
Fax: 905-451-6753 www.bacardi.com
Rum, vodka, scotch, gin, vermouth, carbonated low proof beverages, liqueurs
General Manager: Blair MacNeil
Estimated Sales: 250-499
Number Employees: 100
Parent Co: Bacardi Limited
Type of Packaging: Consumer, Food Service
Brands:
Barcardi
Grey Goose
Martini & Rossi
Russian Prince
Bombay

914 Bacardi USA Inc
2701 S Le Jeune Rd
Suite 400
Coral Gables, FL 33134-5809
305-573-8511
Fax: 305-573-0756 800-222-2734
hrbmusa@bacardi.com
www.bacardilimited.com/us/en
Tropical drink flavored coolers, rum, vodka, prepared mixed drinks
President: Pete Carr
CEO: Mahesh Madhavan
Estimated Sales: $650 Million
Number Employees: 250-499
Parent Co: Bacardi International
Type of Packaging: Consumer, Food Service
Brands:
Anejo
B&B/Benedictine
Bacardi Breezers
Bacardi Limon
Bacardi Rum
Bacardi Spice
Bombay
Castillo Rums
Dewar's Scotch
Hatuey Beers
Martini & Rossi Asti
Martini & Rossi Vermouth
Pommeroy

915 Bacci Chocolate Design
17 Columbia St # 4
Swampscott, MA 01907-1788
781-595-1511
Fax: 781-595-1544 888-725-2877
sales@baccichocolatedesign.com
Chocolate bars, other chocolate, toffee.
Owner: Carlo Bacci
carlobacci@hotmail.com
Sr VP Marketing/Sales: Erin Calvo-Bacci
Estimated Sales: Less Than $500,000
Number Employees: 1-4

916 Bachman Company
801 Hill Avenue
Wyamissing, PA 19610
610-320-7800
Fax: 610-320-7897 800-523-8253
www.bachmanco.com
Pretzels, jax, tortilla chips, popcorn, potato chips, party mix and onion rings.
President: Scott Carpenter
CEO: Joanne Millisock
Director: Marcia Welch
Sales: Andy Kapusta
Director of Human Resources: Deanna Williams
VP Manufacturing/Operations: Mark Miller
VP Manufacturing: Daniel Meyers
Purchasing Director: Lisa George
Estimated Sales: $10-20 Million
Number Employees: 350
Square Footage: 40000
Type of Packaging: Consumer, Food Service
Brands:
Bachman
Kidzels
Treat
Valley Maid

917 Back Bay Trading
11800 Wills Rd
Suite 120
Alpharetta, GA 30024
770-772-6360
Fax: 770-772-4766 800-650-8327
info@ameliabay.com www.ameliabay.com
Liquid tea and Coffee Bag-N-box
President/CEO: John Crandall
CFO: Sherry Harder
Vice President: Jason Crandall
Sales Director: Marshall Cartmill
Public Relations: Jackie Hewitt
Operations Manager: Dudley Blizzard
Estimated Sales: $5-10 Million
Number Employees: 5-9
Type of Packaging: Private Label
Brands:
Amelia Bay
Private Label

918 **Back to Basics**
PO Box 2780
West Bend, WI 53095-0278
801-523-6500
800-688-1989
www.backtobasicsproducts.com
Confections, candy, equipment
Estimated Sales: $5-10 Million
Number Employees: 50-99
Brands:
Back To Basics
Hawaiice
Nutri Source
Peel Away

919 **Back to Nature Foods**
855-346-2225
www.backtonaturefoods.com
Cereal, cookies, crackers, granola, nuts, trail mix, soup and juice
Brands:
BACK TO NATURE

920 **Back to the Roots**
424 2nd St
Oakland, CA 94607
510-922-9758
www.backtotheroots.com
Organic cereal and windowsill gardens
Co-Founder: Nikhil Arora
Co-Founder: Alejandro Velez
Year Founded: 2009

921 **Backer's Potato Chip Company**
1 West Industrial Road
PO Box 128
Fulton, MO 65251
573-642-2833
Fax: 573-642-7617 john@backerchips.com
www.backerchips.com
Potato chips
President: Vicki McDaniel
Contact: Eric Milius
eric@backerchips.com
Estimated Sales: $10-20 Million
Number Employees: 50-99
Number of Brands: 1
Type of Packaging: Consumer, Private Label
Brands:
Backer's

922 **Backyard Safari Co**
303 Campbell Rd
Covington, GA 30014-6110
770-385-3273
Fax: 888-821-2241
support@backyardsafarico.com
www.backyardsafarico.com
Spices, herbs, and pastas
Owner: Sherri Hutchison
Contact: Clyde Hutchison
clyde_hutchison@att.net
Estimated Sales: Less Than $500,000
Number Employees: 1-4
Square Footage: 80000
Brands:
Clyde's Soon to be Famous
GROW Gardens

923 **Bacon America**
255 Rue Rocheleau
Drummondville, QC J2C 7G2
Canada
819-475-3030
Fax: 819-475-4164
Bacon
President: Marcel Heroux
Estimated Sales: $5-10 Million
Number Employees: 500-999
Parent Co: J.M. Schneider
Type of Packaging: Consumer, Food Service, Private Label

924 **Bacon's Heir**
706-688-9534
info@baconsheir.com
baconsheir.com
Pork rinds and pork panko
Number of Brands: 2
Number of Products: 10
Brands:
PORK PANKO
PORK CLOUDS

925 **Bad Frog Brewery Co**
1093 A1a Beach Blvd
Suite 346
St Augustine, FL 32080-6733
904-687-5939
Fax: 734-629-1777 888-223-3764
badfrog@badfrog.com www.badfrog.com
Beer
President: Jim Wauldron
Contact: William Ostrander
williamostrander@badfrog.com
Estimated Sales: $2.5-5 Million
Number Employees: 10-19
Type of Packaging: Private Label
Brands:
Bad Frog Amber Lager
Bad Frog Bad Light
Bad Frog Micro Malt

926 **Bad Seed Cider Company, LLC**
43 Baileys Gap Rd.
Highland, NY 12528
845-236-0956
info@badseedhardcider.com
www.badseedhardcider.com
Hard dry ciders
Co-Owner/Partner: Albert Wilklow
Co-Owner/Partner: Devin Britton
Co-Owner/Partner: Bram Kincheloe
Year Founded: 2011
Number of Brands: 1
Number of Products: 4
Type of Packaging: Consumer, Private Label
Brands:
Bad Seed

927 **Badger Best Pizzas**
1548 Deckner Avenue
De Pere, WI 54185
920-336-6464
Frozen pizza
President: Herm Fredericks
Plant Manager: Peggy Seefeldt
Estimated Sales: $2.5-5 Million
Number Employees: 5-9

928 **Badger Gourmet Ham**
3521 W Lincoln Avenue
Milwaukee, WI 53215-2394
414-645-1756
Fax: 414-645-5189 www.badgergourmetham.com
Ham
President: Mark Schwellinger
Estimated Sales: $10-20 Million
Number Employees: 20-49
Number of Brands: 1
Type of Packaging: Consumer
Brands:
Badger

929 **Badger Island Shell-Fish & Lobster**
2 Badgers Is W
Kittery, ME 03904-1601
207-703-0431
Fax: 207-703-0432 joe@herbertbrothers.com
www.herbertbrothers.com
Seafood, shellfish, lobster
Owner: Joe Herbert
Co-Owner: Dave Herbert
Estimated Sales: $.5-1 million
Number Employees: 1-4
Parent Co: Herbert Brothers Entertainment Inc

930 **Badia Spices Inc.**
PO Box 226497
Doral, FL 33322-4697
305-629-8000
877-629-8000
info@badiaspices.com www.badiaspices.com
Herbs, spices and seasonings including garlic, buboric, jalapeno, lindo and taco flavoring.
President: Joseph Badia
info@badia-spices.com
Year Founded: 1967
Estimated Sales: $100 Million
Number Employees: 100-249
Number of Brands: 1
Square Footage: 100000
Type of Packaging: Consumer, Food Service, Private Label, Bulk
Brands:
Badia Spices
Badia Canned Vegetables
Badia Hot Sauces
Badia Nuts & Seeds
Badia Seasoning Blends
Badia Teas

931 **Baensch Food Products Co**
1025 E Locust St
Milwaukee, WI 53212
414-562-4643
Fax: 414-562-5525 www.mabaensch.com
Pickled & creamed herring
Owner/President: Kim Wall
kim@mabaensch.com
GM: David Jackson
Year Founded: 1932
Number Employees: 10-19
Square Footage: 120000
Parent Co: Wild Foods
Type of Packaging: Consumer, Food Service, Private Label, Bulk
Brands:
Ma Baensch
Ma Baensch Herring

932 **Bagai Tea Company**
PO Box 1046
San Marcos, CA 92079-1046
760-591-3084
Fax: 760-510-1904
Tea
President: Arun Bagai
CFO: Sanjay Bagai
VP: Vik Bagai
Production Manager: Maria Bagai
Purchasing Manager: Arun Bagai
Estimated Sales: $1-5 Million
Number Employees: 5-9
Type of Packaging: Private Label
Brands:
Chaya
Emerald Green
Golden Amber

933 **Bagel Factory**
2320 S Robertson Blvd # 202
Boulevard
Los Angeles, CA 90034-2053
310-836-9865
www.bagelfactoryinc.com
Bagels
Owner: Sanford Brody
sanford@thebagelfactory.com
CEO/President: Jay Epstein
Estimated Sales: Less Than $500,000
Number Employees: 1-4
Square Footage: 10000

934 **Bagel Guys**
102 Willoughby Street
Brooklyn, NY 11201-5318
718-222-4361
Fax: 718-222-4362 bagelguyscorp@AOL.com
Bagels
President: Jeffrey Gargiulo
Estimated Sales: $120,000
Number Employees: 3

935 **Bagel Lites**
240 51st Ave
Apt. 1F
Long Island City, NY 11101
844-678-5544
sales@bagellites.com
www.bagellites.com
Bite-size bagels
Owner: Raquel Salas
Estimated Sales: $100,000
Number Employees: 1-4
Type of Packaging: Private Label

936 **Bagels By Bell**
10013 Foster Avenue
Brooklyn, NY 11236
718-272-2780
Fax: 718-272-2789 info@bialy.com
www.bialy.com
Bagels and bialy
President: Warren Bell
Estimated Sales: $1 Million
Number Employees: 10-19
Type of Packaging: Private Label
Brands:
Bell Bialy

Bell Mini Bagel
Bagel By Bell

937 **Bagelworks**
1229 1st Ave # 2
New York, NY 10065-6314
212-744-6444
Fax: 718-358-3076 www.bagelworks-nyc.com
Muffins and bagels including oat bran, sesame, poppy, cinnamon raisin, sundried tomato, chocolate, sourdough, spinach, herb, wholewheat, cheese, broccoli, rye, peanut butter, etc. including fat free
Owner: Mona Hinnawi
munayah@aol.com
CEO: Aliyeh Hinnawi
CFO: Joseph Hinnawi
VP: Ramsey Hinnawi
Estimated Sales: Less Than $500,000
Number Employees: 5-9
Square Footage: 3400
Other Locations:
Bagelworks
New York NY

938 **Bagley's**
9782 Rt. 414
Hector, NY 14841
607-582-6421
Fax: 607-582-6421
www.Brittany@BagleysPRV.com
Wines
President: Dave Bagley
Estimated Sales: Less than $200,000
Number Employees: 1-4
Type of Packaging: Private Label
Brands:
Poplar Ridge Vineyards

939 **Bahama Specialty Foods**
614 Shepherd Street
Durham, NC 27701-3133
919-471-4051
Fax: 919-479-4916
Pepper sauces and salad dressings
President: Robert Maehr
CEO: Jeffrey Ensminger
Estimated Sales: $250,000-500,000
Number Employees: 1-4
Number of Brands: 2
Number of Products: 5
Square Footage: 26000
Type of Packaging: Consumer

940 **Baier's Sausage & Meats**
6022 67a Street
Red Deer, AB T4P 3E8
Canada
403-346-1535
Fax: 403-346-1773
Ham, sausage, beef jerky, bacon and salami
CEO: Keith Baires
Marketing: Keith Baires
Estimated Sales: $5-10 Million
Type of Packaging: Consumer, Food Service, Bulk
Brands:
Baier's

941 **Bailey's Basin Seafood**
1683 Front Street
Morgan City, LA 70380-3034
985-384-4926
Fax: 985-384-4926
Fish and seafood
President: Nolton Bailey
Estimated Sales: $2.6 Million
Number Employees: 30
Type of Packaging: Consumer, Food Service

942 **Baileyana Winery**
4915 Orcutt Rd
San Luis Obispo, CA 93401-8335
805-544-9080
Fax: 805-781-3635 www.baileyana.com
Wine
Manager: Michael Blaney
michael@paragonvineyard.com
CFO: John R Nevin
Estimated Sales: Below $5 Million
Number Employees: 20-49
Brands:
Ecclestone
Vintage Port

943 **Baily Tea USA Inc**
2275 research blvd
Suite 720
Rockville, MD 20850
301-704-1739
sales@bailytea.com
www.bailytea.com
Tea
CEO: Sudath Munasinghe
s.munasinghe@bailytea.com

944 **Baily Vineyard & Winery**
33440 LA Serena Way
Temecula, CA 92591-5104
951-676-9463
Fax: 951-676-1276 contact@bailywinery.com
www.bailywinery.com
Wine
Owner: Phil Baily
phil@bailywinery.com
Owner: Carol Baily
Year Founded: 1986
Estimated Sales: $2,800,000
Number Employees: 5-9
Brands:
Baily

945 **Bainbridge Festive Foods**
2630 Nashville Highway
Farmington, TN 37091
931-359-8000
Fax: 662-363-9895 800-545-9205
www.bainbridgefestivefoods.com
Jellies, pickles, preserves, spice tea mix, and parsley mustard sauce
President: Anthony Altavilla
Owner: Kathleen Pegram
Year Founded: 1981
Estimated Sales: $150,000
Number Employees: 1-4
Number of Products: 12
Square Footage: 14000
Type of Packaging: Private Label

946 **Baird Dairy LLC**
110 N Randolph Ave
Clarksville, IN 47129-2761
812-283-3345
Fax: 812-283-8701
Ice cream
Owner: Randall Baird
Estimated Sales: Less Than $500,000
Number Employees: 1-4
Type of Packaging: Consumer

947 **Baja Foods LLC**
636 W Root St
Chicago, IL 60609-2630
773-376-9030
Fax: 773-376-9245 lisa@bajafoodsllc.com
Frozen tamales, quesadillas, chimichangas, burritos, enchiladas, taco meat and chili
Owner: Art Velasquez
donraezler@aol.com
Sales/Marketing: Jeff Rothschild
General Manager: Timothy Poisson
Purchasing Manager: Cheryl Canning
Year Founded: 2001
Estimated Sales: $10-20 Million
Number Employees: 20-49
Square Footage: 30000
Type of Packaging: Consumer, Food Service, Private Label, Bulk
Brands:
Amigo
Cafe Amigo
La Marca
Tango

948 **Bakalars Sausage Co**
2760 Hemstock St
La Crosse, WI 54603-2345
608-784-0384
Fax: 608-784-8361 info@bakalarssausage.com
www.bakalarssausage.com
Sausage, beef, fish, pork, hamburger meat, steak, etc
President: Mike Bakalars
bakalars@centurytel.net
Purchasing Manager: Mike Bakalars
Estimated Sales: $15 Million
Number Employees: 20-49
Type of Packaging: Consumer, Food Service, Private Label, Bulk
Brands:
Bakalars

949 **Bake City**
1235 Hightower Trail
Suite 300
Atlanta, GA 30350
855-336-4777
info@bakecityusa.com www.bakecityusa.com
Vegan, organic baked snacks

950 **Bake Crafters Food Company**
10673 S Lee Highway
McDonald, TN 37353
423-396-3392
Fax: 423-396-9604 support@bakecrafters.com
bakecrafters.com
Baked goods manufacturer specializing in school foodservice nationwide.
General Manager: Michael Byrd
Contact: Lonny Byrd
lonny@bakecrafters.com
Type of Packaging: Consumer, Food Service, Private Label, Bulk
Brands:
Bake Crafters

951 **Bake N Joy Foods**
351 Willow St
North Andover, MA 01845-5973
978-521-5946
Fax: 978-683-1713 800-666-4937
productinfo@bakenjoy.com www.bakenjoy.com
Low-fat, fat-free and frozen batters, bakery mixes, fillings, toppings, icings and ready-to-bake items
President/CEO: Robert Ogan
rogan@bakenjoy.com
CFO: Alice Shephard
VP Sales: Mark Ake
VP Marketing/Business Development: George Fregone
Marketing Manager: Tara Oleary O Donovan
Estimated Sales: $20-50 Million
Number Employees: 100-249
Type of Packaging: Food Service, Bulk
Other Locations:
Bake'n Joy Foods
Chuluota FL
Brands:
Freshbakes
Strawberry Colada Frozen Batter
Triple Berry Blast Frozen Batter

952 **Bake Rite Rolls Inc**
2945 Samuel Dr
Bensalem, PA 19020
215-638-2400
800-949-5623
www.nefoods.com
Soft sandwich rolls, english muffins, hamburger and hot dog rolls.
Plant Manager: Jackie Eddis
Estimated Sales: $20-50 Million
Number Employees: 100-249
Parent Co: Northeast Foods
Type of Packaging: Private Label

953 **BakeMark Canada**
2345 Francis-Hughes Avenue
Laval, QC H7S 1N5
Canada
450-667-8888
Fax: 450-667-3342 800-361-4998
www.bakemarkcanada.com
Processor and exporter of bakers' and confectioners' supplies including fondants, cocoa chips and pieces, apricot and strawberry glazes, rainbow and chocolate sprinkles and fruit pie fillings
President: Larry Sullivan
Contact: Stephanie Corrente
Year Founded: 1915
Number Employees: 10-19
Square Footage: 280000
Parent Co: CSM Bakery Supplies North America
Type of Packaging: Food Service, Private Label
Brands:
Golden
Lafave

954 **BakeMark Ingredients Canada**
2480 Viking Way
Richmond, BC V6V 1N2
Canada
604-303-1700
Fax: 604-270-8002 800-665-9441
www.yourbakemark.com
Baked goods, breads, baking mixes, cookies, pie filling, icing, frozen fruit
President: Larry Sullivan
Vice President: Michael Armstrong
Marketing: David Lopez
Sales Manager: Jeff Bligh
General Manager: Rick Barnes
Manufacturing: Ellen Tsang
Estimated Sales: $23 Million
Number Employees: 160
Number of Brands: 12
Number of Products: 2000
Type of Packaging: Private Label, Bulk
Brands:
Bakemark
Bib Ulmer Spatz
Brill
Caravan
Degoede
Diamalt
Dreidoppel
Marquerite
Meistermarken

955 **BakeMark USA**
1933 N Meacham Road
Suite 530
Schaumburg, IL 60173-4342
847-519-3135
Fax: 847-925-2101 www.bakemarkusa.com
Bakery products
President/CEO: Robert Wallace
CFO: Herman Brons
VP: Tom Gumkowski
Branch Manager: Karen Werner
Estimated Sales: $4 Million
Type of Packaging: Private Label
Other Locations:
Phoenix AZ
Burlington NJ
Pico Rivera CA
North Las Vegas NV
Rancho Cordova CA
Reno NV
Union City CA
Buffalo NY
Denver CO
Saratoga Springs NY
Altanta GA
Fairfield OH
Carol Stream IL
Brands:
Bakeqwik
Bakesense
Flour Brands
Produits Marguerite
Trigal Dorado
Westco

956 **(HQ)BakeMark USA**
7351 Crider Ave
Pico Rivera, CA 90660-3705
562-949-1054
Fax: 562-948-5506 866-232-8575
information@bakemark.com
www.yourbakemark.com
Baking mixes, fillings, icings, glazes, and bakery supplies
President & CEO: Gary Schmidt
CFO: Refugio Reynoso
VP Sales & Marketing: Rick Bennett
Estimated Sales: $20-50 Million
Number Employees: 20-49

957 **Baked & Wired**
1052 Thomas Jefferson St NW
Washington, DC 20007-3813
703-663-8727
info@bakedandwired.com
www.bakedandwired.com
Baked goods, espresso and bread
Owner: Tony Velazquez
email@bakedandwired.com
Number Employees: 5-9

958 **Bakeology**
Torrance, CA
bakeology.co
Cookies, snack bites and bars
Co-Founder: Dawn Martel
Co-Founder: Sasha Crescentini
Number of Brands: 1
Number of Products: 5
Brands:
BAKEOLOGY

959 **Baker Boy Bake Shop Inc**
170 Gta Dr
Dickinson, ND 58601-7200
701-225-4444
Fax: 701-225-7981 800-437-2008
Processor of frozen dough products; wholesaler/distributor of bakery supplies including flour, sugar, etc.; serving the foodservice market.
CEO: Guy Moos
guym@bakerboy.com
Year Founded: 1955
Number Employees: 250-499
Square Footage: 135000
Type of Packaging: Consumer, Food Service, Private Label
Brands:
Baker Boy

960 **Baker Boys**
2140 Pegasus Road NE
Calgary, AB T2E 8G8
Canada
403-255-4556
Fax: 403-259-5124 877-246-6036
info@bakerboys.net www.bakerboys.net
Processor of cinnamon rolls including thaw and serve, pre-proofed and frozen
President: Barry Walton
Year Founded: 1987
Number Employees: 20-49
Type of Packaging: Consumer, Food Service
Brands:
Baker Boys Baked Goods

961 **Baker Candy Company**
12345 139th St Se
Snohomish, WA 98290
425-422-6331
Fax: 206-361-7009 www.bakerscandies.com
Manufacturer of roasted nuts, chocolates and hard candy
Owner: Randy Spoo
VP: Ronald Prevele
Treasurer: Ronald Prevele
VP: Lee Prevele
Year Founded: 2009
Estimated Sales: $5-10 Million
Number Employees: 2
Square Footage: 60000
Type of Packaging: Consumer, Bulk
Brands:
Pop Candy
Mars
Pez
Skull
Dylan's

962 **Baker Cheese Factory Inc**
N5279 County Road G
St Cloud, WI 53079-1644
920-477-7871
Fax: 920-477-2404 info@bakercheese.com
www.bakercheese.com
Manufacturer of various cheese specializing in string cheese.
President: Brian Baker
CFO: Kevin Baker
Cheese Operations Manager: Jeff LeBleu
Year Founded: 1916
Estimated Sales: $25-50 Million
Number Employees: 100-249
Type of Packaging: Consumer, Private Label
Brands:
Baker

963 **Baker Commodities Inc**
4020 Bandini Blvd
Vernon, CA 90058-4274
323-268-2883
Fax: 323-268-5166 800-427-0696
info@bakercommodities.com
Protein meal and feeding fats. Rendering company that recycles fats and oils.
Owner: James M Andreoli
jan@bakercommodities.com
CFO: Jim Reynolds
Executive VP: Dennis Luckey
VP Operations: Bill Sikes
Estimated Sales: $10-20 Million
Number Employees: 500-999
Type of Packaging: Bulk
Other Locations:
Seattle WA
Spokane WA
Kerman CA
Phoenix AZ
Rochester NY
North Billerica MA

964 **Baker Maid Products, Inc.**
2419 Java Street
New Orleans, LA 70119
504-827-5500
Fax: 504-827-5400 800-664-7882
info@bakermaid.com www.bakermaid.com
Brandied fruit cake and cookies
President & CEO: Darryl Sorrensen
Marketing Director: Adrian Smith
Operations Director: Colin Manikin
Plant Manager: Greg Marigny
Year Founded: 1953
Estimated Sales: $1-2.5 Million
Number Employees: 20-49

965 **Baker Produce**
212 W Railroad Avenue
PO Box 6757
Kennewick, WA 99336
509-586-6174
Fax: 509-582-3694 800-624-7553
pquinn@bakerproduce.com
www.bakerproduce.com
Apples, onions, potatoes
Sales Manager: Pam Quinn
Sales Representative: Savannah Dean
Shipping Clerk: Kiley Dean
Number Employees: 250-499
Type of Packaging: Consumer, Food Service, Bulk
Brands:
Baker Supreme
Bakers Beauties
Golden Beauties
Goose Hill
Western Beauty

966 **Baker's Candies Factory Store**
831 S Baker St
PO Box 88
Greenwood, NE 68366-1000
402-789-2700
Fax: 402-789-2013 800-804-7330
info@bakerscandies.com www.bakerscandies.com
Fine chocolates, including our chocolate meltaways in seven flavors
Owner: Todd Baker
todd@bakerscandies.com
VP: Patty Baker
Estimated Sales: $3-5 Million
Number Employees: 5-9
Type of Packaging: Consumer

967 **Baker's Coconut**
100 Deforest Ave
East Hanover, NJ 07936
901-381-6636
Fax: 901-381-6524 855-535-5648
www.mondelezinternational.com
Coconut concentrate
Contact: Mary Taylor
Number Employees: 100-249
Parent Co: Kraft Foods
Type of Packaging: Bulk

968 **Baker's Dozen & Cafe**
225 E State St
Herkimer, NY 13350
315-866-6770
Baked goods including bread, rolls and doughnuts
Owner: Tom Watkins
Manager: Tony Durso
Estimated Sales: Less Than $500,000
Number Employees: 10-19

969 **Baker's Point Fisheries**
33 Bakers Point Rd East
Oyster Pond Jeddore, NS B0J 1W0
Canada
902-845-2347
Fax: 902-845-2770 janette@bakerspoint.ca
Fresh and frozen haddock, cod, pollack, hake and cusk
Co-Owner: Janette Faulkner
Co-Owner: Wyman Baker
Number Employees: 50-99
Type of Packaging: Bulk

970 **Baker's Ribs No 2**
3033 Main St
Dallas, TX 75226-1506
214-748-5433
Fax: 214-748-8544 www.bakersribs.com
BBQ sauces and seasonings
General Manager: Robert Austin
Owners: Joe and Suzanne Duncan
Estimated Sales: Less Than $500,000
Number Employees: 1-4
Type of Packaging: Consumer, Food Service
Brands:
Baker's Rib Inc

971 **Bakerhaus Veit Limited**
70 Whitmore Road
Woodbridge, ON L4L 7Z4
Canada
905-850-9229
Fax: 905-850-9292 800-387-8860
info@backerhausveit.com
www.backerhausveit.com
Artisan breads
President/CEO: Sabine C Veit
Sales/Marketing/Development: Doug Fleck
Brands:
Bakerhaus Veit

972 **Bakers Best Snack Food Corp.**
6000 Central Highway
Pennsauken, NJ 08109
215-822-3511
Fax: 215-997-2049
Soft pretzels
Manager: Wayne Childs
President: Jerry Driver
Sales Exec: John Lewandoski
Marketing Manager: Michael Karaban
G.M.: Wayne Childs
Year Founded: 1989
Number Employees: 50-99
Parent Co: J&J Snack Foods Company
Type of Packaging: Consumer
Brands:
Rold Gold
Mustard Pretzels
Peanut Butter Pretzels
Unique Pretzels

973 **Bakers Breakfast Cookie**
427 Ohio St.
Bellingham, WA 98225
360-714-9585
Fax: 360-715-8011 877-889-1090
www.bbcookies.com
All natural cookies
Owner: Erin Baker
Contact: G Bryan
bryang@bbcookies.com
Estimated Sales: $5-10 Million
Number Employees: 20-49
Square Footage: 8000

974 **Bakers of Paris**
99 Park Ln
Brisbane, CA 94005-1309
415-468-9100
Fax: 415-468-4320
customer-service@bakersofparis.com
www.bakersofparis.com
French bread and French pastries
Owner: Lionel Robbe-Jeadu
lionel@bakersofparis.com
VP: Gilles Wicker
Sales Executive: Caroline Hughes
Estimated Sales: $5-10 Million
Number Employees: 20-49

975 **Bakery Barn Inc**
111 Terence Dr
Pittsburgh, PA 15236-4133
412-655-1113
Fax: 412-655-8566 888-322-BARN
sales@bakery-barn.com
High-protein cookies
President/Owner: Sean Perich
frontoffice@bakery-barn.com
Number Employees: 100-249
Type of Packaging: Private Label

976 **Bakery Essentials Inc**
2007 Inverness Dr
Vernon Hills, IL 60061-4530
847-573-0844
Fax: 847-573-0945
Flour, wheat and grain
Owner: Michael Kaufman
Estimated Sales: $500,000-$1 Million
Number Employees: 1-4

977 **Bakery on Main**
127 Park Ave
Suite 100
East Hartford, CT 6108
860-895-6622
Fax: 860-895-6624 info@bakeryonmain.com
bakeryonmain.com
Gluten free baked goods
President/Founder: Michael Smulders
Quality Assurance Manager: Jennifer Salisbury
Senior Marketing Associate: Curtis Dalbon
VP, Sales: Paul Connolly
Operations Manager: Melissa Carducci-Brooks
Production Manager: Frank Guiliano

978 **BakeryCorp**
15625 NW 15th Ave
Miami, FL 33169-5601
305-623-3838
Fax: 305-626-9189 info@bakerycorp.com
www.bakerycorp.com
Breads, cakes and pastries
Vice President: Juan Carlos Lacal
Operations General Manager: Luis Lacal
Estimated Sales: $10-20 Million
Number Employees: 20-49
Number of Brands: 1
Type of Packaging: Food Service, Bulk
Brands:
BakeryCorp

979 **Baking Leidenheimer**
1501 Simon Bolivar Ave
New Orleans, LA 70113-2329
504-525-1596
Fax: 504-525-1596 800-259-9099
info@leidenheimer.com www.leidenheimer.com
Breads
President: Sandy Whann
Estimated Sales: $10-20,000,000
Number Employees: 10-19

980 **Bakkavor USA**
2700 Westinghouse Blvd
Charlotte, NC 28273
800-842-3025
sales@bakkavor.us www.bakkavor.com
Fresh soups, breads, sauces, hummus, burritos, dips, and ready meals
President & CEO: Ben Waldron
CFO: Mary Barnett
Quality Assurance Manager: Julie Morrison
Director of Marketing: Therese Griffin
VP Strategic Business Development: Stephen Young
Number Employees: 500-999
Parent Co: Bakkavor Group

981 **Bakon Yeast**
33415 N 64th Place
Scottsdale, AZ 85266-7363
480-595-9370
Fax: 480-595-9371 bakonyeast@aol.com
bakonyeast.samsbiz.com
Vegetable derived bacon flavored seasonings and hickory smoked torula yeast
President: Phyll Ray
VP: Larry Ray
Plant Manager: Rebecca Schaefer
Year Founded: 1933
Estimated Sales: $600,000
Number Employees: 2-4
Square Footage: 40000
Parent Co: Bakon Yeast
Type of Packaging: Consumer, Food Service, Bulk
Brands:
Bakon Seasonings
Bakon Yeast

982 **Bakto Flavors**
59 Dudley Rd.
North Brunswick, NJ
732-354-4492
Fax: 732-626-5677 info@baktoflavors.com
www.baktoflavors.com
Vanilla products, flavors, spices & herbs, and vinegars
Founder: Daphna Havkin-Frenkel
Square Footage: 80000
Brands:
Visionary Vinegars

983 **Balagna Winery Company**
223 Rio Bravo Dr
Los Alamos, NM 87544
505-672-3678
Fax: 505-672-1482
Wines
Proprietor: John Balagna
Estimated Sales: $.5-1 million
Number Employees: 1-4
Brands:
Balagna Winery

984 **Balance Bar Company**
110 Orville Drive
Bohemia, NY 11716
800-346-2194
info@balance.com www.balance.com
Meal replacement dieting aids, energy bars
President/CEO: Peter Wilson
Chief Executive Officer: Jeff Nagel
Vice President, Finance: Kristina Eriksen
Chief Operating Officer: Michele ABO
Estimated Sales: $8 Million
Number Employees: 29
Parent Co: The Carlyle Group, L P
Type of Packaging: Private Label
Brands:
Balance

985 **Balanced Health Products**
215 E 68th St Ste 33a
New York, NY 10065
212-794-9878
Fax: 212-794-5108
Dietetic candy and food health supplements
President: Nikki Haskell
Estimated Sales: $790,000
Number Employees: 1-4
Square Footage: 4000
Brands:
Nikki Bars
Star Blend
Star Caps
Star Sucker Sour
Star Suckers

986 **Balboa Dessert Co Inc**
1760 E Wilshire Ave
Santa Ana, CA 92705-4615
714-972-4972
Fax: 714-972-0605 800-974-9699
customerservice@balboadessert.com
Processor and exporter of desserts including frozen cakes, cheesecakes and tortes, gourmet baked goods, wholesale and retail
Owner: Anna Ochoa
aochoa@balboadessert.com
Owner: Brett Pollack
Vice President: Dan Hamilton
Year Founded: 1987
Estimated Sales: $4 Million
Number Employees: 5-9
Square Footage: 72000
Type of Packaging: Food Service

987 **Baldinger Baking Co**
1256 Phalen Blvd
St Paul, MN 55106-2156
651-224-5761
Fax: 651-224-9047 www.baldingerbakery.com
Breads, breadsticks, buns, rolls, bagels and more.

Partner: Bob Baldinger
President: Steve Baldinger
Contact: Dawn Almen
dawnalmen@gmail.com
Year Founded: 1888
Estimated Sales: $22 Million
Number Employees: 50-99
Square Footage: 145000
Type of Packaging: Consumer, Food Service, Private Label
Brands:
Baldinger

988 **Baldwin Richardson Foods**
#2390, One Tower Lane
Oakbrook Terrace, IL 60181
866-644-2732
www.brfoods.com
Liquid ingredient manufacturer specializing in signature sauces, dessert toppings, beverage and pancake syrups, specialty fruit fillings and condiments. The company also offers processing options such as hot-fill, cold-fillhomogenization, and emulsion.
President & CEO: Eric Johnson
Chief Financial Officer: Evelyn White
Sr. Director of Sales: Cara Hughes
Year Founded: 1916
Estimated Sales: $5-10,000,000
Number Employees: 200-500
Square Footage: 900000
Type of Packaging: Consumer, Food Service, Private Label, Bulk
Other Locations:
Macedon Manufacturing Facility
Macedon NY
Williamson Manufacturing
East Williamson NY
Brands:
Mrs. Richardson Toppings
Nance's Mustards

989 **Baldwin Vineyards**
176 Hardenburgh Rd
Pine Bush, NY 12566-5720
845-744-2226
Fax: 845-744-6321 Info@BaldwinVineyards.com
www.baldwinvineyards.com
Wines
Owner: Pat Baldwin
bv2@frontiernet.net
Owner/President: Jack Baldwin
VP: John Baldwin
Estimated Sales: $500,000-$1 Million
Number Employees: 1-4
Brands:
Baldwin

990 **Baldwin-Minkler Farms**
320 E South St
Orland, CA 95963-9111
530-865-8080
Fax: 530-865-8085 djsoetaert@aol.com
Almonds
Owner: Bill Minkler
Estimated Sales: $20-50 Million
Number Employees: 50-99
Type of Packaging: Bulk

991 **Balic Winery**
6623 Harding Hwy
Mays Landing, NJ 08330-1022
609-625-2166
Fax: 609-625-1904 www.balicwinery.com
Wine
Owner: Bojan Boskodich
b.boskodich@balicwinery.com
Year Founded: 1933
Estimated Sales: Less than $200,000
Number Employees: 1-4

992 **Ball Park Franks**
PO Box 3901
Peoria, IL 61612
888-317-5867
www.ballparkbrand.com
Hot dogs, packaged meat products, kosher meats, jerky, beef and chicken patties.
President/CEO: Donnie Smith
Number of Brands: 1
Parent Co: Tyson Foods
Brands:
Ball Park

993 **Ballantine Produce Company**
P.O.Box 756
10550 S Button Willeen Ave
Reedley, CA 93654-4400
559-875-2583
Fax: 559-637-2159
Manufacturer and processor of over 200 varieties of plums, peaches, nectarines, pluots, white flesh, apricots, grapes, Asian pears, quince, pomegranates, persimmons and apples.
President: Virgil Rasmussen
Partner: Herbert Kaprielian
CFO: Richard Graham
Manufacturing Executive: Ron Fraughenheim
Year Founded: 1919
Estimated Sales: $10-20 Million
Number Employees: 1-4
Type of Packaging: Consumer, Food Service
Other Locations:
Reedley Sales Office
Reedley CA
Brands:
Ballantine

994 **Ballard Custom Meats**
55 Myrtle St
Manchester, ME 04351-3251
207-622-9764
Fax: 207-621-0242
Meats and seafood
President: Kenneth Ballard
Year Founded: 1969
Estimated Sales: $2,000,000
Number Employees: 10-19

995 **Ballas Egg Products Corp**
40 N 2nd St
Zanesville, OH 43701-3446
740-453-0386
Fax: 740-453-0491 www.ballasegg.com
Frozen, dried and liquid egg products.
President: Craig Ballas
Estimated Sales: $10 Million
Number Employees: 50-99
Type of Packaging: Consumer, Bulk
Brands:
Ballas

996 **Ballreich's Potato Chips**
186 Ohio Ave
Tiffin, OH 44883-1746
419-447-1814
Fax: 419-447-5635 800-323-2447
chips@ballreich.com www.ballreich.com
Snacks including potato chips; flavors include BBQ, sour cream and onion, southwestern BBQ, salt and vinegar, no salt added, and marcelled
Owner: Brian Reis
brian@ballreich.com
VP: Linda Reis
Year Founded: 1920
Estimated Sales: $4 Million
Number Employees: 20-49
Number of Brands: 1
Number of Products: 52
Square Footage: 200000
Type of Packaging: Private Label

997 **Balsu**
1160 Kane Concourse
Suite 100A
Bay Harbour Islands, FL 33154
305-993-5045
Fax: 305-993-5047 balsu@balsusa.com
www.balsusa.com
Hazelnuts
President/CHR: H. Zapsu
Director/Sales And Marketing: Sezen Donmezer
Sales Director: Karim Azzaoui
kazzaoui@aol.com
Year Founded: 1980
Estimated Sales: A
Number Employees: 1-4
Type of Packaging: Bulk

998 **Balticshop.Com LLC**
2842 Main Street
Suite 333
Glastonbury, CT 06033-1036
Fax: 201-300-0146 800-506-2312
margita@balticshop.com www.balticshop.com
Bread, candy & cookies.

999 **Baltimore Brewing Company**
104 Albemarle St
Baltimore, MD 21202
410-837-5000
Fax: 410-837-5024 theo@degroens.com
www.degroens.com
Beers
President: Theo De Groen
groen@degroens.com
Secretary: Irntraud De Groen
Estimated Sales: Under $500,000
Number Employees: 1-4
Brands:
De Groen's

1000 **Baltimore Coffee & Tea Co Inc**
9 W Aylesbury Rd # T
Lutherville, MD 21093-4121
410-561-1080
Fax: 410-561-4816 800-823-1408
orders@baltcoffee.com www.baltcoffee.com
Coffee and tea
Owner: Paul Jakubowski
pjakubowski@easternshoretea.com
VP: Norman Loverde
Estimated Sales: $2.5-5 Million
Number Employees: 50-99
Type of Packaging: Private Label
Brands:
Easten Shore Tea
Peets
Costa Rica
Lavazza Coffee

1001 **Bama Fish Atlanta**
3113 Main Street
East Point, GA 30344-4802
404-765-9896
Fax: 404-765-9874
Fresh and frozen fish

1002 **Bama Foods LTD**
5377 E 66th St N
Tulsa, OK 74117-1813
918-592-0778
Fax: 918-732-2902 800-756-2262
www.bama.com
Frozen baked goods including cookies, pies and biscuits; dough, pastry and crumb crust pie shells
CEO: Matt Alley
alley@bama.com
Chief Executive Officer: Paula A. Marshall
Chief Financial Officer-US Operations: Rocky Moore
Executive Vice President: William L. Chew
Vice President of Research and Developme: Joe McDilda
QC Manager: Maurice Lawry
Director Brand Sales: Gary Wilson
Vice President of Operations: Kevin C. Wilson
Number Employees: 100-249
Type of Packaging: Consumer, Food Service

1003 **Bama Frozen Dough**
2745 East 11th Street
PO Box 4829
Tulsa, OK 74104
918-732-2600
Fax: 918-592-7499 800-756-2262
dwilson@bama.com www.bama.com
Frozen pizza, yeast, pastry sheet dough
CEO: Paula Marshall
Chief Financial Officer: Rocky Moore
VP R&D/Quality Assurance: Mike Martin
VP Sales/Marketing: Alvaro Gomez
Contact: Adam Ailey
aailey@bama.com
VP Operations: Kevin Wilson
Estimated Sales: $20-50 Million
Number Employees: 100-249
Parent Co: Bama Companies
Other Locations:
Bama Companies
Tulsa OK
Bama Foods Ltd.
Tulsa OK
Beijing Bama Food Processing Co.
Daxing County, Beijing

1004 **Banana Distributing Company**
1500 S Zarzamora Street
Unit 405
San Antonio, TX 78207
210-227-8285
Fax: 210-227-8285 www.banana-distributing.com

Bananas, plantains, hass avocados, oranges, apples, sugar cane
Owner/Manager: Jim Scarsdale
Year Founded: 2007
Estimated Sales: $5-10 Million
Number Employees: 10-19
Parent Co: Barshop Enterprises
Type of Packaging: Consumer, Food Service, Bulk

1005 **Bandon Bay Fisheries**
PO Box 485
250 1st Street SW
Bandon, OR 97411-0485
541-347-4454
Fax: 541-347-4313
Seafood, shrimp meat and crab meat
Manager: Graydon Stinnett
Number Employees: 50-99
Square Footage: 40000
Parent Co: S&S Seafood
Type of Packaging: Private Label

1006 **Banfi Vintners**
1111 Cedar Swamp Rd
Old Brookville, NY 11545-2109
516-626-9200
Fax: 516-626-9218 800-645-6511
banfiwines@gmail.com www.banfiwines.com
Wine
Principal: James Mariani
President & CEO: Cristina Mariani-May
Marketing Director: Gary Clayton
VP Public Relations: Lars Leicht
Estimated Sales: $34 Million
Number Employees: 50-99
Brands:
Almaviva
Bell' Agio
Borgogno
Cecchi
Concha Y Toro
Cono Sur
Costello Banfi
Entree
Florio
Old Brookville
Placido
Riunite
Sartori
Sincerity
Stone Haven
Stone Haven
Stone's
Sunrise
Vigne Regali
Walnut Crest
Wisdom & Warter

1007 **Bang & Soderlund Inc**
9240 Bonita Beach Rd SE # 1118
Bonita Springs, FL 34135-4250
239-498-0600
Fax: 239-498-0606 soderlund@aol.com
Dairy products
Manager: Michael Cunningham
Estimated Sales: $2.5-5,000,000
Number Employees: 1-4
Type of Packaging: Private Label

1008 **Banner Candy Manufacturing Company**
700 Liberty Avenue
Brooklyn, NY 11208-2115
718-647-4747
Candy and confectionary
President: Peter Stone
Partner: Laura Stone
Contact: Rose Grunther
bannercandy700@yahoo.com
Estimated Sales: $10-20 Million
Number Employees: 29-49
Type of Packaging: Bulk

1009 **Banner Pharmacaps**
4100 Mendenhall Oaks Pkwy
Suite 301
High Point, NC 27265
336-812-7003
Fax: 336-812-7030 800-526-6993
www.patheon.com
Vitamins
President/CEO: Roger Gordon
CFO: Damien Reynolds
Global VP/R&D/Operations: Aqeel Fatmi
kevin.cogdell@wellsfargo.com
Contact: Kevin Cogdell
kevin.cogdell@wellsfargo.com
Global VP/Commercial Operations: Timothy Doran
Parent Co: Sobel-Holland
Other Locations:
Banner Pharmacaps
Chatsworth CA
Banner Pharmacaps
Alberta, Canada
Gelcaps Exportadora De Mexico
Naucalpan, Edo. de Mexico
Banner Pharmacaps Europe BV
Tilburg, The Netherlands
Banner Pharmacaps India Pvt. Ltd.
Bangalore, India
Brands:
Sofgels®
Entericare®
Solvatrol™
Soflet® Gelcaps
Liquisoft™
Chewels®
Versatrol™
Ecocaps®

1010 **Banquet Schusters Bakery**
115 E Abriendo Ave
Pueblo, CO 81004-4201
719-544-1062
Baked goods
President: Janet Monack
Year Founded: 1946
Estimated Sales: Less Than $500,000
Number Employees: 10-19
Type of Packaging: Consumer

1011 **Bantam Bagels**
283 Bleecker St
New York, NY 10014
646-852-6320
contact@bantambagels.com
www.bantambagels.com
Gourmet bagels
Co-Owner: Nick Oleksak
Co-Owner: Elyse Olesak
Year Founded: 2015
Estimated Sales: $500,000
Number Employees: 1-4
Type of Packaging: Consumer, Food Service
Brands:
MarieBelle(c)

1012 **Banza**
info@eatbanza.com
www.eatbanza.com
Chickpea pasta
Number of Brands: 1
Type of Packaging: Consumer
Brands:
BANZA

1013 **Banzos**
5500 East Pacific Place
Denver, CO 80222
303-447-2133
info@eatbanzos.com
Garbonzo bean dips and snacks
Parent Co: Wild Thyme Naturals
Type of Packaging: Consumer

1014 **Baptista's Bakery**
4625 W Oakwood Park Dr
Franklin, WI 53132-8872
414-409-2000
Fax: 414-423-4375 info@baptistas.com
www.baptistas.com
Snack products
President: Thomas Howe
thowe@baptistas.com
Research & Development: Kelli Lara
Product Development & Culinary Science: Mike Huber
Business Development & Customer Service: Ed Creamean
Materials/Distribution Manager: Neil Stockman
Plant Technical Manager: Brent Butterfield
Supply Chain Process Specialist: John Susko
Number Employees: 100-249
Square Footage: 135000
Parent Co: Snyder's-Lance Inc.
Type of Packaging: Food Service, Private Label

1015 **Bar Harbor Brewing Company**
8 Mount Desert Street
Bar Harbor, ME 04609
207-288-4592
www.barharborbrewing.com
Brewering company
President: Andre Lozano
Operations: Tod Foster
Year Founded: 1990
Estimated Sales: $1-2.5 Million
Number Employees: 1-4
Brands:
Bar Harbor Ginger Ale
Bar Harbor Peach Ale
Cadillac Mountain Stout
Harbor Lighthouse Ale
Thunder Hole Ale
True Blue

1016 **Bar Harbor Foods**
1112 Cutler Rd
Whiting, ME 04691-3436
207-259-3341
Fax: 207-259-3343 info@barharborfoods.com
www.barharborfoods.com
Seafood
Contact: Mike Sansing
msansing@barharborfoods.com

1017 **Bar-S Foods Co**
5090 N 40th St # 300
Phoenix, AZ 85018-2185
602-264-7272
Fax: 602-285-5252 800-699-4115
www.bar-s.com
Meat products
CEO: Delilah Aguilar
delilah.aguilar@bar-sfoods.com
Number Employees: 50-99

1018 **Baraboo Candy Co LLC**
E10891 Coop Ln
Baraboo, WI 53913
608-356-7425
Fax: 608-356-1815 800-967-1690
sales@baraboocandy.com www.baraboocandy.com
Chocolate candy sugar free, dark, milk and white chocolate
President: Michael Ford
CEO: Walter Smith
Chief Executive: Dennis Roney
Year Founded: 1981
Estimated Sales: $1 Million
Number Employees: 5-9
Type of Packaging: Private Label, Bulk
Brands:
Chewy Gooey Pretzel Sticks
Cow Lick
Cow Pie
Green Bay Puddles
Lick-A-Pig
Moo Chew
Upper Fingers
Wally Walleye

1019 **Barataria Spice Company**
PO Box 239
Barataria, LA 70036
504-689-7650
800-793-7650
www.seasoningspice.com
Spices
Co-Owner/President: Mike Hymel
Co-Owner/CEO: Cynthia Hymel
Estimated Sales: Less than $500,000
Number Employees: 2
Type of Packaging: Consumer, Food Service
Brands:
Captain Mike's

1020 **Barbara's Bakery**
20802 Kensington Blvd
Lakeville, MN 55044
800-343-0590
www.barbaras.com
Organic and natural cereals, crackers, cookies, bars, puffs and chips.
President: Barabara Jaffe
Research & Development Manager: Deborah Flindall
Vice President, Marketing: Kent Spalding
Year Founded: 1971
Estimated Sales: $20-50 Million

Number Employees: 175
Square Footage: 102500
Type of Packaging: Consumer, Private Label
Other Locations:
Barbara's Bakery
Sacramento CA
Brands:
Barbara's Bakery
Nature's Choice
Weetabix

1021 **Barber Dairies**
36 Barber Ct
Birmingham, AL 35209-6435
205-942-2351
Fax: 205-943-0296 www.barbersdairy.com
Dairy products, fruit juices and teas.
Controller: Martin Walden
General Manager/VP: P Flagg
Chief Marketing Officer: Johnny Collins
Sales: Terri Smith
Human Resource Executive: Sharon Williams
Manager: Lew Mccravy
Plant Manager: Valerie Meyers
Estimated Sales: $5-10 Million
Number Employees: 250-499
Parent Co: Dean Foods
Type of Packaging: Consumer, Food Service, Private Label, Bulk

1022 **Barber Foods**
PO Box 219
Kings Mountain, NC 28086
877-447-3279
www.barberfoods.com
Frozen chicken: stuffed breasts
Year Founded: 1955
Estimated Sales: $3-5 Million
Square Footage: 600000
Parent Co: Advance Pierre Foods
Type of Packaging: Consumer, Food Service
Other Locations:
Barber Foods Production Plant
Portland ME
Brands:
Barber Foods

1023 **Barber's Farm Distillery LLC**
3609 NY-30
Middleburgh, NY 12122
www.1857spirits.com
Gluten-free, farm-to-bottle vodka
President/General Manager: Dorcas Roehrs
Head Distiller: Elias Barber
Marketing/Sales Director: Larry Friedberg
Number of Brands: 1
Number of Products: 1
Type of Packaging: Consumer, Private Label
Brands:
1857 Spirits

1024 **Barbero Bakery, Inc.**
61 Conrad St
Trenton, NJ 08611
609-394-5122
Fax: 609-394-5567 www.barberobakery.com
Specialty cakes, pastries, italian cookies, deserts, deli breads and rolls
President: Robert McVicker
Contact: Lou Commiso
lcommiso@barberobakery.com
Year Founded: 1925
Estimated Sales: $2.5-5 Million
Number Employees: 20-49

1025 **Barboursville Vineyards**
17655 Winery Rd
P.O. Box 136
Barboursville, VA 22923-8321
540-832-3824
Fax: 540-832-7572 bvvy@barboursvillewine.com
Wines
Manager: Luca Paschina
CMO: Carter Nicholas
nicholas.carter@barboursvillewine.com
Number Employees: 20-49

1026 **Barca Wine Cellars**
PO Box 1150
Roseville, CA 95678
916-786-0770
Fax: 916-740-2220
barcaintlwines@barcawines.net
barcawines.net
Wines
General Manager/CEO: Gino Barca
Year Founded: 1881
Estimated Sales: $3-5 Million
Number Employees: 5-9
Brands:
Barbousville Vineyards

1027 **Barcelona Nut Co**
502 S Mount St
Baltimore, MD 21223-3495
410-233-5252
Fax: 410-233-6555 800-296-6887
sales@barcelonanut.com www.barcelonanut.com
Trail mixes, snack mixes, popcorn and cotton candy
President: Tony Tsonis
ttsonis@barcelonanut.com
EVP: Mike Adams
Estimated Sales: $20-50 Million
Number Employees: 100-249
Number of Brands: 5
Square Footage: 55000
Type of Packaging: Consumer, Food Service, Private Label, Bulk
Brands:
Barcelona
Candyman Lane
Healthnut
Snacknut
Stonehedge

1028 **Bard Valley Medjool Date Growers**
2575 E 23rd Lane
Yuma, AZ 85365
928-726-0901
Fax: 928-726-9413 edwardo@datepac.com
www.datepac.com
Medjool dates
President: Edward O'Malley
President of Sales Operations: Dave Nelson
Production Manager: Camen Wilson
General Manager: Glen Vandervoort
Year Founded: 2004
Number Employees: 50-99

1029 **Bare Snacks**
800-940-0019
baresnacks.com
Fruit and vegetable chips
Number of Brands: 1
Type of Packaging: Consumer
Brands:
BARE

1030 **Barefoot Contessa Pantry**
2 Stonewall Lane
York, ME 03909
207-351-2712
Fax: 207-351-2715 800-826-1752
kbouchie@stonewallkitchen.com
www.stonewallkitchen.com
French citrus, dessert baking mixes, breakfast baking mixes, dessert toppings, sauces and marinades, pancakes and syrups, preserves and lemon curd, coffee and hot chocolate
Co-Founder/President/CEO: Jonathan King
Co-Founder/VP: James Stott
Year Founded: 1991

1031 **Barely Bread**
www.barelybread.com
Grain-free bread and bagels
Founder: Amanda Orso
Chief Marketing Officer: Elyssa Sanders
Number of Brands: 1
Type of Packaging: Consumer
Brands:
BARELY BREAD

1032 **Baretta Provision**
172 Commerce St
East Berlin, CT 06023-1105
860-828-0802
Fax: 860-828-8699 www.barettaprovision.com
Meats including beef, pork and veal
Owner: William Baretta
President: Daniel Baretta
Contact: Lori Wright
lori.wright@barettaprovision.com
Year Founded: 1967
Estimated Sales: $3-5 Million
Number Employees: 10-19
Type of Packaging: Food Service
Brands:
Lenora

1033 **Bargetto Winery**
3535 N Main St
Soquel, CA 95073-2530
831-475-2258
Fax: 831-475-2664 800-422-7438
customerservice@bargetto.com www.bargetto.com
Wines
President: Martin Bargetto
Operations: Michael Sones
Year Founded: 1918
Estimated Sales: $5-9.9 Million
Number Employees: 20-49
Type of Packaging: Private Label
Brands:
Bargetto
Chaucers
Lavita

1034 **Barhyte Specialty Foods Inc**
912 Airport Rd
Pendleton, OR 97801-4589
541-276-0259
Fax: 503-691-8918 800-227-4983
chris@mustardpeople.com www.barhyte.com
Mustards
Owner: Brad Hill
Secretary/Treasurer: Irene Barhyte
Director Sales Marketing: Chris Barhyte
chris@barhyte.com
Public Relation President: Kelly M. Mooney
Year Founded: 1982
Estimated Sales: $2.5-5,000,000
Number Employees: 5-9
Brands:
Aviator Ale Micro Brew Mustards
Food and Wine
Food and Wine Mustards
Haus Barhyte Mustard
Williamette Valley Mustard

1035 **Bari & Gail**
761 Main Street
Walpole, MA 02081
508-668-2634
Fax: 508-850-9555 800-828-9318
Chocolates
President: Joseph Sesnovich
Owner: Barrie Steinberg
Vice President: Lisa Gail Sesnovich
Year Founded: 1932
Estimated Sales: $500,000
Number Employees: 1-4
Type of Packaging: Bulk

1036 **Bari Olive Oil Co**
40063 Road 56
Dinuba, CA 93618-9708
559-595-9260
877-638-3626
orders@barioliveoil.com www.barioliveoil.com
Olive oils
President: Robert Sawatzky
Contact: Breann Borges
borgesbreann@barioliveoil.com
Number Employees: 1-4

1037 **Barilla USA**
885 Sunset Ridge Road
Northbrook, IL 60062
847-405-7500
Fax: 847-405-7505 800-922-7455
www.barilla.com
Pastas and pasta sauces.
President: Jean-Pierre Comte
VP Marketing: Melissa Tendick
Contact: Carroll Alba
alba.carroll@barilla.com
Logistics Customer Manager: Pasquale DeChiara
Number Employees: 100-249
Number of Brands: 3
Type of Packaging: Food Service
Brands:
Barilla Pasta
Barilla Pronto™
Barilla ProteinPLUS™

1038 **Barkeater Chocolates**
3235 State Route 28
PO Box 286
North Creek, NY 12853
518-251-4438
www.barkeaterchocolates.com
Chocolates
Co-Founder: Jim Morris
Co-Founder: Deb Morris
Contact: Louisa Giaquinto
lgiaquinto@allstatecorporateservices.com
Square Footage: 80000
Brands:
Barkeater Chocolates

1039 **Barker System Bakery**
209 S Oak St
Mt Carmel, PA 17851-2147
570-339-3380
Baked goods
President: Cathy Saukatis
Owner: Paul Saukatis
Estimated Sales: Less than $500,000
Number Employees: 1-4

1040 **Barkman Honey**
120 Santa Fe St
Hillsboro, KS 67063-9688
620-947-3173
Fax: 620-947-3640 800-364-6623
www.barkmanhoney.com
Honey
CEO: Dwight Stoller
dstoller@ghfllc.com
Director of Operations: Tom Harmon
Year Founded: 1920
Number Employees: 50-99
Type of Packaging: Consumer, Food Service
Other Locations:
Latty OH
Brands:
Naked Wild Honey
Busy Bee
Pure Harmony Dakota Clover
Pure 'N Simple
Thrifty Bee

1041 **Barkthins Snacking Chocolate**
225 N Route 303 Ste 101
Congers, NY 10920-3001
USA
845-770-5802
Fax: 845-353-5276 www.barkTHINS.com
Chocolate
Executive Vice President: Tom Riggio
Chief Marketing Officer: Deborah Holt
Contact: Dominic Alvarado
dalvarack@barkthins.com

1042 **Barlean's Fisheries**
3660 Slater Rd
Ferndale, WA 98248-9518
360-384-0325
Fax: 360-384-1746 bfmain@barleansfishery.com
www.barleansfishery.com
Organic flaxseed oil, fish oil
Owner/President: Cindy Smith
Vice President: Ronan Smith
Marketing Director: Andreas Koch
Manager: Yehya Ahmed
yahmed@barleans.com
Year Founded: 1972
Number Employees: 10-19

1043 **Barn Stream Natural Foods**
PO Box 896
52 McClean Road
Alstead, NH 03602-3326
603-756-4395
Health foods
Owner: Nicholas Raynor
Year Founded: 1992
Estimated Sales: $1 Million
Number Employees: 2

1044 **Barnana**
1746 Berkeley St
Unit B
Santa Monica, CA 90404
858-480-1543
info@barnana.com
barnana.com
Dried banana snacks
Co-Founder/CEO: Caue Suplicy
CMO: Nik Ingersoll
COO: Matt Clifford
Year Founded: 2012
Type of Packaging: Private Label

1045 **Barnes & Watson Fine Teas**
270 S Hanford St # 211
Seattle, WA 98134-1941
206-625-9435
Fax: 206-625-0345 800-447-8832
tea@barnesandwatson.com www.bwt.com
Tea
Owner: Ken Rudee
Estimated Sales: $1-2,500,000
Number Employees: 1-4
Number of Products: 50+
Type of Packaging: Consumer, Food Service, Bulk
Brands:
Barnes
Watson Fine Teas

1046 **Barnes Ice Cream Company**
475 Pond Rd
Manchester, ME 04351-3612
207-622-0827
Ice cream and frozen desserts
Owner: Richard Barnes
Owner: Carl Barnes
Estimated Sales: $500,000-$1 Million
Number Employees: 1-4
Type of Packaging: Consumer

1047 **Barney Butter**
2925 S Elm Ave
Suite 101
Fresno, CA 93706-5465
USA
559-442-1752
info@barneybutter.com
www.barneybutter.com
Almond based butters
Chief Financial Officer: Dawn Kelley
Estimated Sales: Less Than $500,000
Number Employees: 1-4

1048 **Barney Pork House**
New Mourten Road
Decatur, AL 35601-1471
256-353-8688
Sausage
Partner: Billy C Burney II
Estimated Sales: $.5-1 million
Number Employees: 49

1049 **Barnie's Coffee and Tea**
1030 N Orange Ave
Suite 220
Orlando, FL 32801
800-284-1416
customerservice@barniescoffee.com
www.barniescoffee.com
Coffee and tea
CFO: Tricia Relvini
VP, Sales & Marketing: Scott Uguccioni
Estimated Sales: $94 Million
Number Employees: 50-99

1050 **Baron Vineyards**
PO Box 624
1516 Fairway Drive
Paso Robles, CA 93446
805-239-3313
Fax: 805-239-2789
Wines
Owner: Tom Baron
Co-Owner: Sharon Baron
Number Employees: 20-49
Brands:
Baron

1051 **Barone Foods**
345 S Kino Pkwy
Tucson, AZ 85719
520-623-8571
Fax: 520-622-1599
Cooked and processed meats including sausage
Chief Operating Officer: Tim Barone
Estimated Sales: $5-10 Million
Number Employees: 10-19
Parent Co: City Meat
Type of Packaging: Consumer, Food Service, Private Label, Bulk

1052 **Barrel O' Fun Snack Foods**
400 Lakeside Dr
PO Box 230
Perham, MN 56573-2202
330-346-7000
Fax: 218-346-7003 800-346-4910
www.barrelofunsnacks.com
Snacks
President/CEO: Ken Nelson
VP: Charlie Nelson
VP Sales & Marketing: Randy Johnson
Contact: Terry Enerson
tenerson@klnfamilybrands.com
General Manager: Kevin Keil
Estimated Sales: $20-50 Million
Number Employees: 5-9
Number of Brands: 1
Parent Co: Shearer's Foods
Type of Packaging: Private Label
Brands:
Barrel O'Fun

1053 **Barrie House Gourmet Coffee**
4 Warehouse Lane
Elmsford, NY 10523
914-233-1561
800-876-2233
www.barriehouse.com
Coffees, teas, accessories and equipment
President: Paul Goldstein
CEO: Craig M James
CFO/COO: George Ercolino
Quality/R&D Director: Zurab Jacobi
VP Sales & Customer Service: Kathleen Collins
Contact: Edward Goldstein
egoldstein@barriehouse.com
Year Founded: 1934
Estimated Sales: $20-50 Million
Number Employees: 20-49
Number of Products: 200
Type of Packaging: Food Service, Private Label, Bulk
Brands:
Barrie House
Cafe Bodega
Cafe Excellence
Donut Shop

1054 **Barrington Coffee Roasting**
165 Quarry Hill Rd
Lee, MA 01238-9623
413-243-3008
Fax: 413-528-0614 800-528-0998
coffee@barringtoncoffee.com
www.barringtoncoffee.com
Coffee
Owner: Barth Anderson
barth@barringtoncoffee.com
Owner: Gregg Charbonneau
General Manager: Christina Stanton
Production Director: Karli Cassavant
Year Founded: 1993
Estimated Sales: $2.5-5 Million
Number Employees: 5-9
Type of Packaging: Private Label
Brands:
Barrington Estate
Barrington Gold
Dark Roast
Limited Edition
Organic/Fair Trade
Single Origin

1055 **Barrows Tea Company**
PO Box 40278
New Bedford, MA 02744-0003
774-488-8684
Fax: 508-990-2760 800-832-5024
www.barrowstea.com
Teas
President: Sam Barrows
Estimated Sales: $1-2.5 Million
Number Employees: 1-4
Number of Brands: 1
Number of Products: 15
Type of Packaging: Consumer, Food Service
Brands:
Barrows

1056 **Barry Callebaut USA**
600 West Chicago Ave
Suite 860
Chicago, IL 60654
312-496-7300
866-443-0460
www.barry-callebaut.com
Chocolate and cocoa
Chief Executive Officer: Antoine de Saint-Affrique
Chief Financial Officer: Victor Balli
President, Americas: David Johnson
Contact: Mark Adriaenssens
mark.adriaenssens@barry-callebaut.com
Number Employees: 10,000
Number of Brands: 14
Brands:
Barry Callebaut
Bensdorp
Cacao Barry
Callebaut®
Caprimo
Carma®
Chocolate Masters™
Chocovic
IBC
Le Royal
Mona Lisa
Sicao
Van Houten Drinks
Van Houten Professional
VanLeer
La Morella Nuts

1057 **Barry Group**
415 Griffin Dr
Corner Brook, NL A2H 3E9
Canada
709-785-7387
bgi@barrygroupinc.com
www.barrygroupinc.com
Frozen fish and seafood; grenadier fillets; fish oil.
Founder & CEO: Bill Barry
VP, Sales: Kevin Baldwin
Year Founded: 1854
Estimated Sales: $283.03 Million
Number Employees: 3,000
Parent Co: Westfish International
Type of Packaging: Consumer, Food Service, Private Label, Bulk
Brands:
Ocean Leader
Seafreez
Pacific
Icelandic

1058 **Barsotti Family Juice Co.**
2239 Hidden Valley Lane
Camino, CA 95709-9722
530-622-4629
Fax: 530-642-9703 info@barsottijuice.com
www.barsottijuice.com
Fruit and vegetable juices
Co-Founder: Gael Barsotti
Co-Founder: Joan Barsotti
Number of Brands: 1
Number of Products: 11
Type of Packaging: Consumer

1059 **Bartek Ingredients, Inc.**
421 Seaman Street
Stoney Creek, ON L8E 3J4
Canada
905-662-1127
Fax: 905-662-8849 800-263-4165
sales@bartek.ca www.bartek.ca
Acidulants
Chief Executive Officer: Raffaele Brancato
Vice President: David Tapajna
Vice President: Jason Perry
Year Founded: 1978
Estimated Sales: $40 Million
Number Employees: 80
Square Footage: 40000

1060 **Bartlett Dairy & Food Service**
90-04 161 St
Suite 609
Jamaica, NY 11435
718-658-2299
www.bartlettny.com
Dairy and general grocery products
President: Thomas Malave, Jr.
Senior Logistics Analyst: Gary Kwan
gkwan@bartlettny.com
Year Founded: 1990
Estimated Sales: $123.3 Million
Number Employees: 171
Number of Brands: 1
Brands:
Bartlett Dairy

1061 **Bartlett Milling Co.**
701 S Center St
Box 831
Statesville, NC 28677
704-872-9581
Fax: 704-873-8956 800-438-6016
www.bartlettmillingfeed.com
Grain merchandising, flour and feed milling
Vice President: Trey Sebus
Year Founded: 1907
Estimated Sales: $50-100 Million
Number Employees: 100-249
Parent Co: Bartlett & Company
Type of Packaging: Consumer, Food Service, Private Label, Bulk
Brands:
Diamond Cake
Fine Spun
Palace Pastry
White Rock
Wigwam

1062 **Bartolini Ice Cream**
967 E 167th St
Bronx, NY 10459-1951
718-589-5151
Fax: 718-893-3171
Ice cream, ices, cheese, eggs, and dairy products
Owner: Michael Bartolini
Year Founded: 1971
Estimated Sales: $3 Million
Number Employees: 10-19

1063 **Bartons Fine Foods**
Highway 460
Denniston, KY 40316
606-768-3750
Fax: 606-768-3737 888-810-3750
Jellies, jams, mustards, barbecue sauces, molasses and relishes
President: Bryan Allphin
Operations Director: Phil Madrio
Estimated Sales: $2.5-5 Million
Number Employees: 5-9
Square Footage: 24000
Type of Packaging: Consumer, Food Service, Private Label

1064 **Bartush Schnitzius Foods Co**
425 E Jones St
1137 North Kealy
Lewisville, TX 75057-2613
972-219-1270
Fax: 972-436-5719 sales@bartushfoods.com
www.bartushfoods.com
Bar mixes, salad dressing and sauces including horseradish, salsa, barbecue, taco, picante and tomato
President/CEO: John Rubi
jrubi@bartushfoods.com
Sales Executive: Joe Bartush
Year Founded: 1968
Estimated Sales: $12 Million
Number Employees: 50-99
Number of Products: 200+
Square Footage: 100000
Type of Packaging: Consumer, Food Service, Private Label
Brands:
Bar-Snitz
Fairway
Melcer
Schnitzius
Texas

1065 **Baruvi Fresh LLC**
535 Fifth Ave
27th Flr
New York, NY 10017
646-346-1074
info@baruvi.com
www.hummustir.com
Hummus
CEO/Co-Founder: Rakesh Barmecha
COO/Co-Founder: Alon Kruvi
Vice President of Sales: Brian Stuckleman
Operations Manager: Johnny Makkar
Year Founded: 2015
Number Employees: 1-10
Type of Packaging: Food Service, Private Label

1066 **Basciani Foods Inc**
944 Penn Green Rd.
Avondale, PA 19311-9749
610-268-3610
Fax: 610-268-2186 john@bascianifoods.com
www.bascianifoods.com
Mushrooms including crimini, portabella, oyster, shiitake, white, and other exotic mushrooms; Blackberries
President: Mario Basciani Sr
COO: Michael Basciani Sr
Food Safety & Sanitation Specialist: Fred Recchiuti
Head of Sales/Logistics: John Basciani Sr
Head of Sales/Logistics: Richard Basciani Jr
Estimated Sales: $20-50 Million
Number Employees: 100-249

1067 **Bascom Family Farms Inc**
74 Cotton Mill Hl # A106
Brattleboro, VT 05301-8603
802-254-5529
Fax: 802-257-8111 888-266-6271
sales@bascomfamilyfarms.com
www.maplesource.com
Pure maple syrup and sugar; organic and kosher varieties available
President: Bruce Bascom
Director of Sales and Marketing: Arnold Coombs
Estimated Sales: $.5-1 million
Number Employees: 10-19
Number of Brands: 3
Type of Packaging: Consumer, Food Service, Private Label, Bulk
Brands:
Coombs Family Farms

1068 **Base Culture**
5160 140th Ave N
Clearwater, FL 33760
baseculture.com
Paleo baked goods
Founder & CEO: Jordan Windschauer
Number of Brands: 1
Type of Packaging: Consumer

1069 **Basic American Foods**
2185 N California Blvd
Suite 215
Walnut Creek, CA 94596-3566
925-472-4000
Fax: 925-472-4360 www.baf.com
Mashed potatoes, hashbrowns & cut potatoes, potato casseroles, and beans & chili
President & CEO: Loren Kimura
lkimura@baf.com
CFO: John Argent
Brand Manager: Hans Kohte
Development Manager: Gary Eversoll
Production Supervisor: Leon Mortensen
Marketing Manager: Jane Foreman
Director, Ingredient Sales: Daniela Boyd
Senior Manager Media Relations: Pat Burke
VP Supply Chain Operations: Mark Klompien
Project Manager: Jerome Bullock
Purchasing: Chris Gentry
Number Employees: 100-249
Square Footage: 13814
Type of Packaging: Consumer, Food Service, Private Label, Bulk
Brands:
Hungry Jack
Nana's Own
Basic American Foods
Nature's Own Potato Pearls
Potato Pearls Excel
Potato Pearls
Golden Grill
Redi-Shred
Quick-Start Home Style Chili
Santiago Beans
Classic Casserole
Redi-Shred Potato Cheese Bake

1070 **Basic Food Flavors**
3950 E Craig Rd
North Las Vegas, NV 89030-7504
702-643-0043
Fax: 702-643-6149 info@basicfoodflavors.com
www.basicfoodflavors.com

Industrial ingredients, including hydrolyzed vegetable proteins, processed flavors, soy sauce and soy bases
President & CFO: Cathy Staley
cstaley@staleyinc.com
Vice President: Bill Robertson
Lab Manager; R&D: Randy Pierce
Quality Assurance Manager: Geetika Duggal
Customer Service: Cathy Hooper
Director of Sales & Marketing: Dave Wood
Operations Director: Phil Price
Estimated Sales: $10 Million
Number Employees: 50-99
Square Footage: 60000
Type of Packaging: Food Service, Bulk

1071 **Basic Grain Products**
300-310 East Vine Street
Coldwater, OH 45828-1399
614-408-3091
Fax: 419-678-4647 866-411-6677
info@tastemorr.com www.tastemorr.com
Whole grain rice cakes, multigrain crisps, pita chips, and potato crisps.
President: Carol Knapke
Estimated Sales: $20-50 Million
Number Employees: 100-249
Number of Brands: 1
Type of Packaging: Consumer, Private Label
Brands:
Tastemorr Snacks

1072 **Basignani Winery**
15722 Falls Rd
Sparks Glencoe, MD 21152-9582
410-472-0703
Fax: 410-472-2536
Wines
Owner: Lynne Basignani
lynne@basignani.com
Year Founded: 1986
Estimated Sales: Less Than $500,000
Number Employees: 1-4

1073 **Basin Crawfish Processors**
P.O.Box 25
522 Parkway Drive
Breaux Bridge, LA 70517-4306
337-332-6655
Fax: 337-332-5917 www.bbcrawfest.com
Crawfish, frozen fish and seafood
President: Brayon Blanchard
Estimated Sales: $300,000-500,000
Number Employees: 1-4

1074 **Basketfull**
276 5th Ave Rm 201
New York, NY 10001
212-686-2175
Fax: 212-255-9019 800-645-4438
Gourmet food and fruit and gift baskets
President: Nancy Forest
Estimated Sales: Less than $500,000
Number Employees: 5-9

1075 **Baskin-Robbins LLC**
130 Royall St
Canton, MA 02021
800-859-5339
www.baskinrobbins.com
Ice cream, specialty frozen desserts, bases for dairy beverages, nondairy flavors
President: David Hoffmann
CEO: Nigel Travis
Chief Information & Strategy Officer: Jack Clare
COO: Scott Murphy
Year Founded: 1945
Estimated Sales: Over $1 Billion
Number Employees: 1,000-4,999
Number of Brands: 2
Parent Co: Dunkin' Brands, Inc.
Type of Packaging: Consumer, Food Service
Brands:
Baskin Robbins
Dunkin' Donuts

1076 **Basque French Bakery**
2625 Inyo St
Fresno, CA 93721-2787
559-268-7088
Fax: 559-268-0510 www.pyreneesbakery.com
Baked goods, breads and rolls
President/Owner: Al Lewis
al.lewis@pyreneesbakery.com
Vice President: Rita Ingmire
Production Manager: Ed Kwiecien
Year Founded: 1994
Estimated Sales: $2.5-5 Million
Number Employees: 20-49

1077 **Bass Lake Cheese Factory**
598 Valley View Trl
Somerset, WI 54025-6800
715-247-5586
Fax: 715-549-6617 800-368-2437
blcheese@blcheese.com www.blcheese.com
Cheese
Owner: Scott Erickson
Co-Owner: Julie Erickson
Year Founded: 1918
Estimated Sales: 500,000
Number Employees: 5-9
Type of Packaging: Consumer
Brands:
Master's Mark

1078 **(HQ)Bassett's**
1211 Chestnut St
Suite 410
Philadelphia, PA 19107-4114
215-864-2771
Fax: 215-864-2766 888-999-6314
www.bassettsicecream.com
Ice cream, yogurt, sorbet
President: Michael Strange
CEO: Ann Bassett
Estimated Sales: $5-10 Million
Number Employees: 5-9
Other Locations:
Bassetts Ice Cream
Philadelphia PA
Brands:
Bassett's

1079 **Batampte Pickle Prods Inc**
77 Brooklyn Terminal Market
Brooklyn, NY 11236-1511
718-251-2100
Fax: 718-531-9212
Pickles and pickled products.
President/CEO: Barry Silberstein
Vice President: Scott Silberstein
Estimated Sales: $20-50 Million
Number Employees: 50-99
Number of Brands: 1
Type of Packaging: Consumer
Brands:
Ba-Tampte

1080 **Batavia Wine Cellars**
235 N Bloomfield Road
Canandaigua, NY 14424-1059
585-396-7600
Fax: 585-396-7833
Wines
President: Ned Cooper
Ceo/Vice President: Tim Richenberg
Contact: Marty Bognanno
marty.bognanno@cwine.com
Number Employees: 100-249
Parent Co: Canandaigua Wine Company
Type of Packaging: Consumer, Food Service, Private Label, Bulk
Brands:
Capri
Henri Merchant
Vinter's Choice

1081 **Batdorf & Bronson**
200 Market St NE
Olympia, WA 98501-6965
360-753-7531
Fax: 360-754-5283 800-955-5282
coffee@batdorf.com www.batdorfcoffee.com
Coffee
President: Larry Challain
larryc@batdorf.com
CFO: Dave Wasson
Vice President: Scott Merle
Quality Control: Michael Elvin
Public Relations: Lois Maffeo
Operations Manager: Heather Ringwood
Production Manager: Brian Meyers
Plant Manager: Shelia Smith
Estimated Sales: $5-10 Million
Number Employees: 20-49
Type of Packaging: Consumer, Food Service, Private Label, Bulk

1082 **Bateman Products**
251 W Main Street
Rigby, ID 83442-1351
208-745-9033
Fax: 208-357-5317 www.mrsbateman.com
Fat products, sugar and egg replacements
Owner: Mrs Bateman
Estimated Sales: $.5-1 million
Number Employees: 5-9

1083 **Batory Foods**
1700 E Higgins Rd
Suite 300
Des Plaines, IL 60018-3800
847-299-1999
Fax: 847-299-2750 info@batoryfoods.com
www.batoryfoods.com
Distributor of cocoa products, dairy products, cereals, candies and corn syrup solids, commodity syrups, condiments, sauces, egg powders, dough conditioners, emulsifiers and fibers.
President: Ron Friedman
CFO: Alan Kessler
Number Employees: 50-99

1084 **Battistoni Italian SpecMeats**
81 Dingens St
Buffalo, NY 14206-2307
716-826-2700
Fax: 716-826-0603 800-248-2705
Italian meat products including salami, pepperoni, capacollo and chorizo.
President: Eric Naber
Manager: Anne Ashley
aashley@battistonibrand.com
Year Founded: 1931
Estimated Sales: $10-24.9 Million
Number Employees: 20-49
Number of Brands: 1
Parent Co: Providential Foods Corporation
Type of Packaging: Private Label
Brands:
Battistoni

1085 **Bauducco Foods Inc.**
1705 NW 133 Ave
Suite 101
Miami, FL 33182
305-477-9270
Fax: 305-477-4703 sales@bauduccofoods.com
www.bauducco.com
Panettone, wafers, cookies, crackers and bars
President/General Manager: Stefano Mozzi
Manager: Fred Rodrigues
Contact: Alfredo Rivera
alfredor@bauduccofoods.com
Year Founded: 2004
Estimated Sales: $5 Million
Number Employees: 1-4
Brands:
Bauducco

1086 **Bauer's Mustard**
5340 Metropolitan Ave
Flushing, NY 11385-1218
718-821-3570
Fax: 718-366-3055 bart@abauersmustard.com
www.abauersmustard.com
Mustard
Owner: Bart Druery
bart@abauersmustard.com
Number Employees: 1-4
Type of Packaging: Consumer, Food Service
Brands:
A. Bauer's

1087 **Baumer Foods Inc**
2424 Edenborn Ave
Suite 510
Metairie, LA 70001
504-482-5761
www.baumerfoods.com
Sauces, including hot sauce, steak sauce, worcestershire, oriental and wing sauce.
Regional Sales Manager: Kevin Eber
Vice President, Exports: Marwan Kabbani
Year Founded: 1923
Estimated Sales: $39.9 Million
Number Employees: 100-249
Number of Brands: 1

Number of Products: 11
Square Footage: 120000
Type of Packaging: Consumer, Food Service, Private Label
Brands:
Chef's Recipe
Figaro
Ditka
Crystal

1088 **Bautista Family OrganicDate**
93800 Hammond Rd
Mecca, CA 92254-6706
760-396-2337
www.7hotdates.com
Dehydrated fruits and vegetables
Owner: Enrique Bautista
Year Founded: 1975
Estimated Sales: Less Than $500,000
Number Employees: 1-4

1089 **Bavaria Corp International**
515 Cooper Commerce Dr
Suite 100
Apopka, FL 32703-6222
407-880-0322
Fax: 407-880-1932 bavaria@bavariacorp.com
www.bavariacorp.com
Specialty blends, marinades, and dips
Owner: Dennis Koo
Sales Director, North America: Steven Fore
bavaria@fdn.com
Estimated Sales: $5-$10 Million
Number Employees: 5-9
Type of Packaging: Food Service, Bulk
Brands:
Bafos

1090 **Bavarian Meat Products**
2934 Western Ave
Seattle, WA 98121-1021
206-448-3540
Fax: 206-956-0526
Sausage
Owner: Lila Ridgeway
lila@bavarianmeats.com
Co-Owner: Robert Hofstatter
Vice President: Lynn Stewart
Estimated Sales: $2.5-5 Million
Number Employees: 10-19
Type of Packaging: Consumer, Food Service

1091 **Bavarian Nut Co**
822 Elmwood Ave
Buffalo, NY 14222-1408
716-810-6887
sales@bavariannut.com
www.bavariannut.com
Nuts, including almonds, pecans, cashews, pistachios, salted peanuts, walnuts and trail mixes
Owner: Dan Desrosiers
Year Founded: 1994
Estimated Sales: $20-50 Million
Number Employees: 50-99

1092 **Bavarian Specialty Foods, LLC**
22417 S Vermont St
Los Angeles, CA 90502-2449
626-856-3188
Bakery products
Number Employees: 100-249
Type of Packaging: Food Service, Private Label, Bulk

1093 **Baxters Vineyards & Winery**
2010 Parley St
Nauvoo, IL 62354-1355
217-453-2528
Fax: 217-453-6600 800-854-1396
www.nauvoowinery.com
Wines
Co-owner: Kelly Logan
Co-owner: Brenda Logan
baxters@nauvoo.net
Year Founded: 1857
Estimated Sales: $500,000-$1 Million
Number Employees: 5-9
Brands:
Baxters Old Nauvoo

1094 **Bay Baby Produce**
424 Greenleaf Ave
Burlington, WA 98233-1800
360-755-2299
Fax: 360-755-8010 info@baybabyproduce.com
www.baybabyproduce.com
Organic pie pumpkins, spaghetti squash, butternut squash, acorn squash, carnival squash, delicata squash, kabocha squash, and red kuri squash
Founder/President: Michele Youngquist
Sales: Tyann Schlimmer

1095 **Bay Cities Produce Co Inc**
2109 Williams St
San Leandro, CA 94577
510-346-4943
Fax: 510-352-4704 www.baycitiesproduce.com
Frozen and prepared fruits and vegetables.
President: Steve Del Masso
Vice President: Vince Del Masso
Secretary/Treasurer/VP: Diana Del Masso
diana@baycitiesproduce.com
Office Manager/Accounts Payable: JoLynn Eala
Quality Control: Luis Vaca
General Manager: Jason Shipps
Sales Manager: Tony D'Amato
Frozen Foods Supervisor: Jeff Christensen
Senior Buyer: Mike Short
Year Founded: 1947
Estimated Sales: $20-50 Million
Number Employees: 20-49
Square Footage: 55000
Type of Packaging: Food Service

1096 **Bay Haven Lobster Pound**
280 Chases Pond Rd
York, ME 3909
207-363-5265
Fax: 907-486-6417
Lobster, fish, and seafood
Owner: Randy Small
President: Tim Small
Year Founded: 1998
Estimated Sales: $1-3 Million
Number Employees: 5-9

1097 **Bay Hawk Ales**
2000 Main St
Irvine, CA 92614-7202
949-442-7565
Fax: 949-442-7566 info@bayhawkales.com
Beers
Manager: Carl Zappa
President: David Voorhies
Sales: Robert Fischer
General Manager: Karl Zappa
Year Founded: 1994
Estimated Sales: $2.5-5 Million
Number Employees: 5
Type of Packaging: Consumer, Food Service, Private Label
Brands:
Amber Ale
Bayhawk Ipa
Bayhawk Stout
Beach Blonde
California Pale Ale (Cpa)
Chocolate Porter
Hefe Weizen
Honey Blonde
O.C. Lager

1098 **Bay Hundred Seafood Inc**
23713 Saint Michaels Rd
St Michaels, MD 21663-2431
410-745-9329
Fax: 410-745-9176
www.chesapeakelandingrestaurant.com
Oysters and crabs
President: Joseph Spurry
Estimated Sales: $10-20 Million
Number Employees: 10-19
Type of Packaging: Consumer
Brands:
Miles River

1099 **Bay Oceans Sea Foods**
PO Box 348
Garibaldi, OR 97118-0348
503-322-3316
Fax: 503-322-0049 www.localocean.net
Products include gourmet albacore tuna, chinook salmon, dungeness crab and shrimp, as well as canned tuna and salmon.

Owner: Jeff Princehouse
Estimated Sales: $10-20 Million
Number Employees: 20-49
Type of Packaging: Consumer, Food Service

1100 **Bay Pac Beverages**
1150 Civic Drive
Suite 300
Walnut Creek, CA 94596-8221
925-279-0800
Fax: 925-279-0804 baypac@pacbell.net
Sports beverages
President: Jackson Bays
Manager of Export Sales: Alan Wirsig
Estimated Sales: $2.5-5 Million
Number Employees: 5-9
Type of Packaging: Bulk

1101 **Bay Shore Chowders & Bisques**
360 Currant Road
Fall River, MA 02720
888-675-6892
info@bayshorechowders.com
www.bayshorechowders.com
Gourmet lobster bisque, New England and Manhattan clam chowders, New England fish chowder, lobster, mussels, shrimp and roasted corn chowder, crab bisque
Estimated Sales: $780,000
Number Employees: 4
Type of Packaging: Consumer, Food Service, Bulk
Brands:
Bay Shore

1102 **Bay State Milling Co.**
100 Congress St.
Quincy, MA 02169
800-553-5687
infobsm@bsm.com www.baystatemilling.com
Flour and grain products.
President/CEO: Peter Levangie
Head of Business Development: Brian Rothwell
CFO: Peter Banat
Senior Director Marketing & Product Dev.: Colleen Zammar
VP, Sales & Customer Development: Douglas Dewitt
Vice President of Operations: Kevin Kavanaugh
Year Founded: 1899
Estimated Sales: $61.2 Million
Type of Packaging: Consumer, Food Service, Private Label, Bulk
Other Locations:
Tolleson AZ
Platteville CO
Minneapolis MN
Winona MN
Indiantown FL
Mooresville NC
Clifton NJ
Wichita KS

1103 **Bay Valley Foods**
1390 Pullman Dr.
El Paso, TX 79936
800-236-1119
www.bayvalleyfoods.com
Pickles, powder, syrups & sauces, aseptic, liquid creamer, refrigerated dressing & egg substitutes, soup, broth & gravy, infant foods, salsa, salad dressings, marinades & barbecue sauces, fruit spreads & sauces, salad dressingsmarinades and mayonnaise.
President/CEO: Steve Oakland
CFO: Matthew Foulston
Executive VP/General Counsel: Thomas O'Neill
Year Founded: 1862
Estimated Sales: $116.3 Million
Number Employees: 1,000
Square Footage: 50000
Parent Co: TreeHouse Foods, Inc.
Type of Packaging: Consumer, Food Service, Private Label, Bulk
Brands:
Hoffman House®
Bennetts®
Mocha Mix®
Borden®
Cremora®
Flavor Charm
Bay Valley™
E.D. Smith
Second Nature®
Steinfeld's®
Nalley®
Farman's®

Heifetz®
Roddenbery's®
Northwoods®

1104 **Bay View Farm**
PO Box 680
Honaunau, HI 96726
808-328-9658
Fax: 808-328-8693 800-662-5880
www.bayviewfarmcoffees.com
Coffee
President: Andrew Roy
VP: Roslyn Roy
Estimated Sales: $5-10 Million
Number Employees: 10-19

1105 **Baycliff Co Inc**
608 South Ave.
Garwood, NJ 07027
212-772-6078
Fax: 212-472-8980 866-772-7569
www.sushichef.com
Rice vinegar, soy sauce, soy salad dressing, teriyaki sauce, rice, rice cracker mix, green tea, and soups
President: Helen Tandler
ht@sushichef.com
VP: Alan Johnson
Estimated Sales: $20-50 Million
Number Employees: 20-49
Type of Packaging: Consumer, Food Service
Brands:
Sushi Chef

1106 **Baycliff Company**
242 E 72nd St
New York, NY 10021
212-772-6078
Fax: 212-472-8980 www.sushichef.com
Japanese food and ingredients; vinegar; sauces; vegetables; spices.
President: Helen Tandler
Year Founded: 1982
Brands:
The Sushi Chef

1107 **Bayley's Lobster Pound**
9 Avenue Six
Pine Point
Scarborough, ME 04074-8838
207-883-4571
Fax: 207-510-7317 800-932-6456
bayleys@bayleys.com www.bayleys.com
Fresh and frozen shrimp, clams and lobster
Owner: William Bayley
bill@bayleys.com
Year Founded: 1915
Number Employees: 5-9

1108 **Bayou Crab**
10380 Foots Rd
Grand Bay, AL 36541-6491
251-824-2076
Fax: 251-824-1484
Cajum foods
Owner: Dan Viravong
Estimated Sales: $3-5 Million
Number Employees: 10-19

1109 **Bayou Food Distributors**
949 Industry Rd
Kenner, LA 70062-6848
504-469-1745
Fax: 504-469-1852 800-516-8283
bayoufoods@hughes.com
Fillet fish, crabs, shrimp; frozen foods, such as beef, pork, poultry and seafood
CEO: Arthur Mitchell
bayoufoods@hughes.net
Estimated Sales: $5-10 Million
Number Employees: 5-9
Square Footage: 54400
Type of Packaging: Food Service

1110 **Bayou Land Seafood**
1108 Vincent Berard Rd
Breaux Bridge, LA 70517
337-667-6118
Fax: 337-667-6059 bayoulandseafood@aol.com
Seafood, including fresh and frozen crawfish, fish, crabs and shrimp; also, alligator and turtle
Owner: Adam Johnson
bayoulandseafood@aol.com
VP: Sharon Difatta
Plant Manager: Jeff Guidry
Year Founded: 2000
Estimated Sales: $2 Million
Number Employees: 50-99
Number of Products: 100
Square Footage: 38400
Type of Packaging: Consumer, Food Service, Bulk
Brands:
Bayou Land Seafood

1111 **Bays English Muffin Corporation**
PO Box 1455
1026 Jackson Blvd
Chicago, IL 60607-2914
312-346-5757
Fax: 316-226-3435 800-367-2297
www.bays.com
Breads, rolls, buns
President: James Bay
Year Founded: 1933
Estimated Sales: $1-2.5 Million
Number Employees: 35

1112 **Baywood Cellars**
5573 W Woodbridge Rd
Lodi, CA 95242
209-334-0445
Fax: 209-334-0132 800-214-0445
Wines
Founder: Joe Cotta Jr
President: John Cotta
Co-Owner: James Cotta
Estimated Sales: Under $500,000
Number Employees: 1-4
Brands:
Baywood Cellars

1113 **Bazaar Inc**
1900 5th Ave
River Grove, IL 60171-1931
708-583-1800
Fax: 708-583-9782 800-736-1888
www.thebazaarinc.com
Candy, snacks and spices
President: Rob Nardick
rnardick@thebazaarinc.com
Finance Executive: Tony Ligenza
VP: Arlene Nardick
Sales Executive: Arnie Fishbain
VP Purchasing: Gene Wisniewski
Year Founded: 1960
Estimated Sales: $15 Million
Number Employees: 100-249
Square Footage: 590000

1114 **Bazzini Holdings LLC**
1035 Mill Rd
Allentown, PA 18106-3101
610-366-1606
Fax: 610-366-1606 www.bazzininuts.com
Nuts, mixes, bars and pistachios
Owner/President: Rocco Damato
COO: Richard Toltzis
VP of Marketing: Carrie Madigan
Manager: Jen Bowman
jbowman@cherrydalefarms.com
Number Employees: 1-4
Square Footage: 200000
Other Locations:
Allentown PA
Brands:
Bazzini
Candy Club
House of Bazzini
Natures Club
Nut Club

1115 **Be-Bop Biscotti**
601 NE 1st St
Bend, OR 97701
Fax: 541-389-6185 888-545-7487
info@be-bop.net www.be-bop.net
Biscotti
President/Owner: Robert Golden
Contact: Glenna Gibson
ggibson@be-bop.net
Number Employees: 99

1116 **Bea & B Foods**
PO Box 178837
San Diego, CA 92117
858-490-6205
pilarcitas@aol.com
www.pilarcitas.com
Mexican seasonings and marinades
President: Bea Knapp
Estimated Sales: $3-5 Million
Number Employees: 1-4
Brands:
Pilarcitas

1117 **Beachaven Vineyards & Winery**
1100 Dunlop Ln
Clarksville, TN 37040-9319
931-645-8867
Fax: 931-645-3522
thefolks@beachavenwinery.com
www.westgateinnclarksville.com
Wines
President/Owner: Louisa Cooke
bbwinery@aol.com
VP: Edward Cooke
Estimated Sales: $2.5-5 Million
Number Employees: 10-19

1118 **Beacon Drive Inn**
255 John B White Sr Blvd
Spartanburg, SC 29306-6047
864-585-9387
Fax: 864-585-2888
Iced tea
General Manager: Kenny Church
CEO: Steve McManus
CEO: Sam Maw
Year Founded: 1946
Estimated Sales: $3-5 Million
Number Employees: 50-99
Square Footage: 20000
Type of Packaging: Food Service, Private Label
Brands:
Beacon Drive-In Iced Tea

1119 **Beal's Lobster Pier**
186 Clark Point Rd
SW Harbor, ME 04679
207-244-3202
Fax: 207-244-9479 800-244-7178
orders@bealslobster.com www.bealslobster.com
Lobster
President/Owner: Sam Beal
Year Founded: 1930
Estimated Sales: $1-3 Million
Number Employees: 10-19

1120 **Beam Suntory**
222 W. Merchandise Mart Plaza
Suite 1600
Chicago, IL 60654
312-964-6999
www.beamsuntory.com
Alcohol, including cognac, bourbon and bourbon mixes, whisky, rum, and tequila.
President/CEO: Albert Baladi
President, Brands: Jessica Spence
Senior VP/CFO: Marc Andre Tousignant
Senior VP/General Counsel: Todd Bloomquist
Senior VP/Chief Human Resources Officer: Paula Erickson
EVP/Chief Supply Chain Officer: David Hunter
Year Founded: 2014
Estimated Sales: $3.1 Billion
Number Employees: 4,800
Number of Brands: 50+
Square Footage: 50000
Parent Co: Suntory Holdings
Type of Packaging: Consumer, Food Service
Other Locations:
Jim Beam Brands Co.
Geyserville CA
Brands:
Baker's®
Basil Hayden's®
Booker's®
Bourbon deLuxe®
Jim Beam®
Knob Creek®
Maker's Mark®
Old Crow®
Old Grand-Dad®
Red Stag
Ardmore®
Auchentoshan
Bowmore
Glen Garioch
Laphroaig®
McClelland's
Teacher's®
Sumiwataru Umeshu
Suntory Umeshu
Yamazaki Aged Umeshu
Dai Juhyo

Kuromaru
Muginoka
Nanko
Super Juhyo
Wanko
Suntory Whisky
2 GINGERS®
Connemara®
Kilbeggan®
Tyrconnell®
Alberta Premium®
Canadian Club®
Tangle Ridge®
Old Overholt®
DYC Whisky
100 ANOS®
El Tesoro de Don Felipe®
Hornitos®
Sauza®
Tres Generaciones®
Calico Jack®
Cruzan®
Ronrico®
AO Vodka
EFFEN®
Kamchatka®
Pinnacle®
VOX®
Courvoisier®
Salignac®
After Shock®
DeKuyper®
Hermes
Japone
JDK & Sons™
Kamora®
Lejay Lagoute
Leroux®
Midori Melon
Sourz®
Square
The Blue
Gilbey's®
Larios®
Sipsmith®
SkinnygirL®
Larios®
Sipsmith®
SkinnygirL®
-196 C
Kaori Horoyoi
Kokushibori

1121 Beamon Brothers

3392 Us Highway 117 N
Goldsboro, NC 27530-8175
919-734-4931
Fax: 919-736-1849
Potatoes, sweet potatoes
President: Robert Rackley
Estimated Sales: Under $500,000
Number Employees: 3
Brands:
Mount Herman
Stoney Hill

1122 Bean Buddies

1804 Plaza Avenue
New Hyde Park, NY 11040-4937
516-775-3706
Fax: 516-775-3706
Chocolate, coffee candy, candy and confectionary retail
President: Nina Cole
Estimated Sales: $2.5-5 Million
Number Employees: 5-9

1123 Bean Forge

93753 Coos Sumner Lane
PO Box 1073
Coos Bay, OR 97420-1614
541-267-5191
Fax: 888-354-0491 888-292-1632
sales@thebeanforge.com www.thebeanforge.com
Coffees
Manager: Adam Hinkle
Owner: David Herold
Estimated Sales: $500,000-$1 Million
Number Employees: 5-9
Brands:
Bean Forge
Guido & Sals Old Chicago
Kenya Aa
Lighthouse
Menehune Magic
Tanzanian Peaberry
Whiskey Run

1124 Beanfields

855-328-2326
info@beanfields.com www.beanfields.com
Bean chips
CEO: Mark Rampolla
Number of Brands: 1
Number of Products: 7
Type of Packaging: Consumer
Brands:
BEANFIELDS

1125 Beanitos

3601 South Congress
Suite B-500
Austin, TX 78704
512-609-8017
Fax: 512-609-8094 www.beanitos.com
Vegetarian chips and snacks
Marketing: Dave Forman
Contact: Mike Larocca
mike@beanitos.com
Type of Packaging: Private Label

1126 Bear Creek Country Kitchens

325 W 600 S
Heber City, UT 84032-2230
516-333-9326
Fax: 435-654-5449 800-516-7286
www.bearcreekcountrykitchens.com
Soup and pasta mixes
Owner: Donald White
President/CEO: Kevin Ruda
CFO: Al Van Leeuwen
Director R&D: Brian Brinkerhoff
VP Sales/Marketing: Stephen White
VP Operations: Kevin Kowalski
Purchasing Manager: Mark Hartman
Estimated Sales: $40 Million
Number Employees: 100-249
Square Footage: 180000
Parent Co: American Capital Strategies
Type of Packaging: Consumer, Food Service
Brands:
Bear Creek Country Kitchens
Sheila's Select Gourmet Recipes

1127 Bear Creek Smokehouse Inc

10857 State Highway 154
Marshall, TX 75670-8105
903-935-5217
Fax: 903-935-2871 800-950-2327
info@bearcreeksmokehouse.com
www.bearcreeksmokehouse.com
Smoked chicken, turkey and turkey products, smoked and cured ham, salted pork, soup mixes, smoked bacon, sausages, pork ribs and desserts.
President: Charles Shoults
VP: Robbie Shoults
Secretary/Treasurer: Brenda Shoults
Year Founded: 1943
Estimated Sales: $10-20 Million
Number Employees: 20-49
Square Footage: 60000
Type of Packaging: Consumer
Brands:
Bear Creek Brand

1128 Bear Creek Winery

4210 Holland Loop Road
PO Box 609
Cave Junction, OR 97523
541-592-3977
Fax: 541-592-2127 877-273-4843
bvw@bridgeviewwine.com
www.bridgeviewwine.com
Wines
CEO: Rene Eichmann
Marketing: Lorie Eichmann
Year Founded: 1997
Estimated Sales: Less than $500,000
Number Employees: 1-4
Brands:
Dijon Clone
Rogue Valley

1129 Bear Meadow Farm

926 Watson-Spruce Corner Rd
Ashfield, MA 01330
413-628-3970
Apples, jellies, preserves, jams, salad dressings
Owner: Matt Shearer
Year Founded: 2002
Estimated Sales: $1-2.5 Million
Number Employees: 1-4
Square Footage: 12000
Type of Packaging: Consumer, Food Service, Private Label
Brands:
Bear Meadow Farm
Rt 66 Foods

1130 Bear Naked, Inc.

PO Box 649
Solana Beach, CA 92075
866-374-4442
www.bearnaked.com
Granola, energy bars, snack bars and trail mix.
Parent Co: Kellogg Company

1131 Bear Stewart Corp

1025 N Damen Avenue
Chicago, IL 60622
773-276-0400
Fax: 773-276-3512 800-697-2327
info@bearstewart.com www.bearstewart.com
Fillings, jams, jellies, and premade mixes for bakers and confectioners.
VP of Sales: Michael Hoffman
COO: Jason Brooks
Year Founded: 1966
Estimated Sales: $5-10 Million
Number Employees: 1-4
Square Footage: 200000
Type of Packaging: Food Service, Bulk

1132 Bearded Brothers

Austin, TX 78736
www.beardedbros.com
Vegan, organic snack bars
Co-Founder: Caleb Simpson
Co-Founder: Chris Simpson

1133 Bearitos

4600 Sleepytime Drive
Boulder, CO 80301
310-886-8200
Fax: 310-886-8219 www.bearitos.com
Puffed snacks and tortilla chips.
President/CEO: Irwin Simon
Estimated Sales: $10-20 Million
Number Employees: 20-49
Brands:
Bearitos

1134 Beatrice Bakery Co

201 S 5th St
Beatrice, NE 68310-4408
402-223-2358
Fax: 402-223-4465 800-228-4030
www.beatricebakery.com
Dessert cakes, fruit cakes, and liqueur-filled cakes
President: Greg Leech
greg@beatricebakery.com
Quality Control/Production Manager: Robin Dickinson
Sales Manager: Connie Warnsing
Public Relations: Brooklyn Soft
Estimated Sales: $5-10 Million
Number Employees: 20-49
Number of Brands: 10
Number of Products: 125
Square Footage: 200000
Type of Packaging: Private Label
Brands:
Grandma's Bake Shoppe
Grandma's Fruit Cake
Innkeeper's Own
Ye Olde English

1135 Beaucanon Estate Wines

1006 Monticello Rd
Napa, CA 94558-2032
707-254-1460
Fax: 707-254-1462 800-660-3520
www.beaucanonestate.com
Wines
President: Louis De Coninck
louis@beaucanonestate.com
Estimated Sales: $2.5-5,000,000
Number Employees: 10-19

1136 **Beaujolais Panforte**
3200 Dutton Ave
Suite 320
Santa Rosa, CA 95407-5735
707-357-1566
Fax: 707-937-3656 800-776-1778
www.beaujolaisgranola.com
Granola products
CEO: David LaMonica
Partner: Andrea Sarnataro
Type of Packaging: Private Label
Brands:
McConnell's(c)

1137 **Beaulieu Vineyard**
1960 St. Helena Hwy
Rutherford, CA 94573
707-257-5749
cs_bv@bvwines.com
www.bvwines.com
Wines
Marketing Manager: Graham Jones
Estimated Sales: $25-49 Million
Number Employees: 80
Parent Co: Diageo Chateau & Estate Wines Co.
Type of Packaging: Bulk

1138 **Beaumont Rice Mills**
1800 Pecos Street
Beaumont, TX 77701
409-832-2521
lbroussard@gtbizclass.com
www.bmtricemills.com
Rice
President: Louis Broussard
lbroussard@gtbizclass.com
Vice President: Ben Broussard
Secretary: Sheryl Graham
Assistant Secretary/Treasurer: Brenda Cook
Estimated Sales: $17.5 Million
Number Employees: 50-99
Type of Packaging: Consumer

1139 **Beaver Street Brewery**
11 S Beaver St # 1
Flagstaff, AZ 86001-5500
928-779-0079
Fax: 928-779-0029 info@beaverstreetbrewery.com
www.beaverstreetbrewery.com
Beers
President/Owner: Evan Hanseth
we2k@aol.com
VP: Winnie Hanseth
Estimated Sales: $248 Million
Number Employees: 100-249
Type of Packaging: Consumer, Food Service
Brands:
Bramble Berry Brew
Hefe Weizen
India Pale Ale
Marzen Lager
Pilsener
R&R Oatmeal Stout
Rail Head Red Ale
Vienna Lager

1140 **Beaver Street Fisheries**
1741 W. Beaver St.
Jacksonville, FL 32209
800-252-5661
800-874-6426
www.beaverstreetfisheries.com
Lobster tail, clams, oysters, shrimp, crab, mussels, swai fillets, tilapia fillets, breaded fish, imitation crab, smoked salmon, frog legs, crawfish, conch, squid & calamari and octopus & scallops. Also manufactures beef, porkpoultryand lamb.
President: Alfred Frisch
CFO: Jeff Edwards
Executive Vice President: Mark Frisch
Director, Marketing: Bluzette Carline
Year Founded: 1950
Estimated Sales: $442.8 Million
Number Employees: 250-499
Number of Brands: 5
Square Footage: 300000
Type of Packaging: Consumer, Food Service, Private Label, Bulk
Brands:
Sea Best®
Tropic Seafood®
Island Queen®
Island Prince®
HF's Outstanding

1141 **Beaverton Foods Inc**
7100 NE Century Boulevard
Hillsboro, OR 97124
503-646-8138
800-223-8076
www.beavertonfoods.com
Horseradish, mustard, garlic and sauces.
Founder: Rose Biggi
CEO: Domonic Biggi
Business/Customer Service Manager: Roger Klingsporn
Estimated Sales: $10-20 Million
Number Employees: 50-99
Number of Brands: 6
Number of Products: 150
Square Footage: 65000
Type of Packaging: Consumer, Food Service, Private Label, Bulk
Brands:
Beaver
Charlie's Salsa
Inglehoffer
Napa Valley
Pacific Farms
Tulelake

1142 **Because Cookie Dough**
hello@becausecookiedough.com
www.becausecookiedough.com
Cookie dough
Founder: Alexis Chan
Number of Brands: 1
Type of Packaging: Consumer
Brands:
BECAUSE COOKIE DOUGH

1143 **Beck Flavors**
1301 Mattec Drive
Loveland, OH 45140
314-878-7522
Fax: 513-889-1268 beckflavors.net
Bakery, beverage, coffee, tea, and dairy flavors
General Manager: Joe Willoughby
Contact: Darienne Bils
dbils@beckflavors.net
Type of Packaging: Bulk
Other Locations:
Ardsley NY
Bakersfield CA
Lakeland FL
New Century KS
Brands:
Beck Cafe
Beck Flavors

1144 **Beck's Ice Cream**
3610 Lewisberry Rd
York, PA 17404-8382
717-764-4585
Fax: 717-846-5121
Ice cream
Owner: Jerry Beck
CEO: Lynne Beck
CFO: Kerry Beck
Year Founded: 1979
Estimated Sales: $250,000
Number Employees: 1-4
Brands:
Becks Ice Cream

1145 **Beck's Waffles of Oklahoma**
101 S Kickapoo Ave
Shawnee, OK 74801-7686
405-878-0615
Fax: 405-878-8546 800-646-6254
wafflman@swbell.net
Frozen Belgian waffles
President: Betty Beck
Sales: Doyle Beck
Year Founded: 1998
Estimated Sales: $1-3 Million
Number Employees: 10
Square Footage: 80000
Type of Packaging: Consumer, Food Service

1146 **Becker Foods**
15136 Goldenwest Cir
Westminster, CA 92683-5235
714-891-9474
www.beckerfoods.com
Custom processor and packager of; fresh and frozen poultry, beef, pork, lamb, veal, cheese products, and more
President: Stan Becker
stan@beckerfoods.com
Vice President: Dian Vendel
Number Employees: 5-9
Type of Packaging: Food Service, Private Label

1147 **Beckman & Gast Co**
282 W Kremer-Hoying Road
PO Box 307
St Henry, OH 45883
419-678-4195
Fax: 419-678-3005 www.beckmangast.com
Canned goods including tomato juice, tomatoes, and cut green beans.
President: William Gast
william.gast@beckmangast.com
Secretary/Treasurer: Paul Moorman
Customer Service Manager: Terri Gast
Operations Manager: Paul Moorman
VP of Manufacturing: Karl Gast
Estimated Sales: $5-9.9 Million
Number Employees: 10-19
Type of Packaging: Consumer, Private Label
Brands:
Beckman's

1148 **Beckmann's Old World Bakery**
104 Bronson St # 6
Santa Cruz, CA 95062-3487
831-423-9242
Fax: 831-426-3548
customerhelp@beckmannsbakery.com
www.beckmannsbakery.com
Breads and other baked goods.
President: Peter Beckmann
pbeckmann@beckmannsbakery.com
CEO: Beth Holland
Estimated Sales: $24.2 Million
Number Employees: 100-249
Number of Brands: 1
Square Footage: 17000
Brands:
Beckmann's

1149 **Beckmen Vineyards**
2670 Ontiveros Rd
Los Olivos, CA 93441
805-688-8664
Fax: 805-688-9983 info@beckmenvineyards.com
www.beckmenvineyards.com
Wines
President: Tom Beckmen
info@beckmenvineyards.com
Operations Manager: Steve Beckmen
Estimated Sales: $500-1 Million appx.
Number Employees: 5-9

1150 **Becky's Blissful Bakery**
PO Box 252
Pewaukee, WI 53072
262-327-4111
www.beckysblissfulbakery.com
Manufacturer of desserts made from all natural ingredients. Specializes in caramel.
Owner: Rebecca Scarberry
Square Footage: 80000

1151 **Bede Inc**
PO Box 8263
Haledon, NJ 07538-0263
973-956-2900
Fax: 973-956-0600 866-239-6565
bedeinc@aol.com
Processor and exporter of instant hot cereals including peanut porridge, banana, plantain, etc.; also, peanut-based health beverage mixes
President: Jasseth Cummings
CFO: Gloria Johnson
Buyer: Sam Cummings
Quality Control: King H
Estimated Sales: $2.5-5,000,000
Number Employees: 1-4
Brands:
Cream of Peanut
Crema De Many
Malted Peanut
Quick Peanut Porridge
Vigorteen

1152 **Bedell Northfork LLC**
36225 Main Rd
RT 25
Cutchogue, NY 11935-1346
631-734-7537
Fax: 631-734-5788 wine@bedellcellars.com
www.bedellcellars.com
Wines
Owner: Michael Lynne
CEO: Trent Preszler
Senior Vice President, Events: Amy Finno
EVP- Sales & Marketing: Jonathan Lynne
Contact: Suzanne Baird
sue@bedellcellars.com
COO: Trent Preszler
Plant Manager: Dave Thompson
Estimated Sales: $1-2.5 Million
Number Employees: 5-9
Other Locations:
Corey Creek Vineyards(Tasting Room)
Southold NY
Brands:
Bedell Cellars
Corey Creek

1153 **Bedemco Inc**
3 Barker Ave Ste 325
White Plains, NY 10601
914-683-1119
Fax: 914-683-1482 info@bedemco.com
www.bedemco.com
Organic dried fruit, dried vegetables, nuts and seeds.
President: Elazar Demeshulam
Vice President: Roy Demeshulam
Quality Control Manager: Natalie Levy
Marketing Director: Emily Cantor
Sales: Murray Feinblatt
Contact: Roni Detoledo
roni@bedemco.com
Production Manager: Robert Haas
Estimated Sales: $3-5 Million
Number Employees: 1-4
Type of Packaging: Food Service, Private Label, Bulk
Brands:
HUDSON VALLEY FARMS

1154 **Bedoukian Research Inc**
21 Finance Dr
Danbury, CT 06810-4133
203-830-4000
Fax: 203-830-4010 800-424-9300
customerservice@bedoukian.com
www.bedoukian.com
Flavors and aromas.
President: Robert Bedoukian
robert@bedoukian.com
Regulatory and Technical Services: Joseph Bania
Year Founded: 1972
Estimated Sales: $10-24 Million
Number Employees: 50-99

1155 **Bedre Fine Chocolate**
37 N Colbert Rd
Davis, OK 73030-9338
580-369-4200
800-367-5390
bedre.chocolates@chickasaw.net
www.bedrechocolates.com
Chocolate
Contact: Brenda Cloud
brenda.cloud@chickasaw.net
Number Employees: 10-19
Type of Packaging: Consumer, Private Label

1156 **Bedrock Farm Certified Organic Medicinal Herbs**
106 Woodland Trail
Wakefield, RI 55105
401-789-9943
Fax: 651-227-1387 888-874-7393
Organic medicinal herbs. Founded in 1992.
President: Angie Geary

1157 **Bee Harmony Honey**
Hillsboro, KS 67063
www.beesponsible.com
Raw honey

1158 **Bee International**
2311 Boswell Rd
Suite 1
Chula Vista, CA 91914-3512
619-710-1800
Fax: 619-710-1822 800-421-6465
info@beeinc.com www.beeinc.com
Manufacturer and importer of Easter, Valentine, Halloween, Christmas and novelty candy items
Owner/CEO: Louis Block
louisblock@beeinc.com
Quality Assurance Manager: Martin Quezada
VP Operations: Charles Block
Estimated Sales: $18 Million
Number Employees: 20-49
Square Footage: 165000
Type of Packaging: Consumer
Brands:
Chicle Chips
Micro Bmx Bike
Micro Scooter

1159 **Bee Raw Honey**
Brooklyn, NY 11231
888-660-0090
www.beeraw.com
Honey
Founder: Zeke Freeman
Square Footage: 80000
Brands:
Bee Raw

1160 **Bee Seasonal**
Gilbert, AZ 85234
beeseasonal.com
Organic raw honey
Founder: Thomas H□bbe

1161 **Beech-Nut Nutrition Corp**
1 Nutritious Pl
Amsterdam, NY 12010-8105
518-595-6600
Fax: 518-595-6601 www.beechnut.com
Organic baby foods
CEO: Jeff Boutelle
Chief Financial Officer: Alain Souligny
Vice President of Human Resources: Erin Clemens
Controlled: Marc Ruf
Estimated Sales: $10-20 Million
Number Employees: 20-49
Number of Brands: 2
Parent Co: Hero Group
Type of Packaging: Consumer
Brands:
Beech-Nut
Beech-Nut Organic

1162 **Beecher's Handmade Cheese**
1600 Pike Place
Seattle, WA 98101
206-956-1964
sales@beecherscheese.com
www.beechershandmadecheese.com
Cheese
Owner: Kurt Beecher Dammeier
Year Founded: 2003
Number Employees: 20-40

1163 **(HQ)Beef Products Inc.**
891 Two Rivers Dr
North Sioux City, SD 57049-5391
605-217-8000
Fax: 605-217-8001 www.beefproducts.com
Lean beef processed from fresh beef trimmings
President/Owner: Richard Jochum
CEO: Eldon Roth
Director: Regina Roth
Contact: David Berghult
dberghult@beefproducts.com
Facilities: Brian Goeden
Purchasing: Dave Rose
Number Employees: 1400
Square Footage: 144000
Type of Packaging: Consumer, Food Service
Other Locations:
BPI Plant
South Sioux City NE
BPI Plant
Amarillo TX
BPI Plant
Garden City KS
BPI Plant
Waterloo IA
BPI Plant
Finney County KS
Brands:
Bpi®

1164 **Beehive Botanicals**
16297 W Nursery Rd
Hayward, WI 54843-7138
715-634-4274
Fax: 715-634-3523 800-233-4483
www.beehivebotanicals.com
Processor and exporter of health supplements derived from honey, propolis, pollen and royal jelly; also, sugar-free propolis chewing gum.
President/CEO: Linda Graham
linda.graham@beehivebotanicals.com
Quality Control Manager: Denise Gregory
Purchasing Manager: Lisa Johnson
Year Founded: 1972
Estimated Sales: $6.5 Million
Number Employees: 20-49
Square Footage: 24000
Brands:
Beehive Botanicals
Honey Silk
Royal Jelly
Bee Pollen

1165 **Beehive Cheese**
2440 East 6600 South
Suite 8
Uintah, UT 84405
801-476-0900
Fax: 801-476-3308 www.beehivecheese.com
Cheese
Owner: Tim Welsh
Owner: Pat Ford
Estimated Sales: B
Number Employees: 10-19

1166 **Beekman 1802**
187 Main St
Sharon Springs, NY 13459
888-801-1802
shop.beekman1802.com
Organic jams, honey, concentrates, coffee beans, and cookbooks.
Co-Founder: Josh Kilmer-Purcell
Co-Founder: Brent Ridge
Year Founded: 2008

1167 **Beer Bakers Inc.**
5515 Edmondson Pike
Suite 121
Nashville, TN 37211
615-775-3329
soberdough.com
Baked goods made with beer.
Co-Owner: Jordan Mychal
Co-Owner: Veronic Mychal
Type of Packaging: Consumer, Private Label
Brands:
Soberdough

1168 **Beer Nuts Co Store-Plant**
103 N Robinson St
Bloomington, IL 61701-5424
309-827-8580
Fax: 309-827-0914 info@beernuts.com
Nuts
President: James Shirk
ashirk@beernuts.com
Marketing Manager: Cindy Shirk
Public Relations: Tom Foster
Media Relations: Georgia Dawson
Year Founded: 1937
Estimated Sales: G
Number Employees: 50-99
Square Footage: 100000
Type of Packaging: Food Service
Brands:
Beer Nuts(c)

1169 **Beetnik Foods, LLC**
2600 E. Cesar Chavez
Austin, TX 78702
512-548-8228
customersupport@beetnikfoods.com
www.beetnikfoods.com
Organic sauces and frozen, ready-to-eat meals.
Founder: David Perkins
Contact: Rustin Dodd
rdodd@beetnikfoods.com
Square Footage: 330230
Brands:
beetnik

1170 **Beetroot Delights**
72 Sprucesside Crescent
Foothill, ON L0S 1E1
Canada
888-842-3387
Fax: 905-892-1080
Manufacturer and exporter of beetroot condiments including cherry beet pepper and ginger beet jelly, spiced beet ketchup and beet relish. Founded in 1985.
President: Grace Lallemand
Number Employees: 3
Square Footage: 3200
Type of Packaging: Consumer, Food Service
Brands:
Beetroot Delights

1171 **Behm Blueberry Farms**
14904 Canary Drive
Grand Haven, MI 49417
616-846-1650
http://www.behmblueberryfarms.com/
Fresh blueberries. Founded in 1953.
President: Howard Behm
VP: Sharon Behm
Estimated Sales: $3-5 Million
Number Employees: 5
Brands:
Blueberry King

1172 **Bel Brands USA**
30 S. Wacker Dr.
Suite 3000
Chicago, IL 60606-7413
312-462-1500
Fax: 847-879-1999 www.belbrandsusa.com
Nacho sauce, salsa and cheeses.
CEO: Bill Graham
Vice President, Human Resources: Kerri Gollias
Vice President, Marketing: Shannon Maher
Year Founded: 1865
Estimated Sales: $103 Million
Number Employees: 250-499
Number of Brands: 7
Square Footage: 130000
Type of Packaging: Consumer, Food Service, Bulk
Other Locations:
Bel Brands USA
Little Chute WI
Bel Brands USA
Leitchfield KY
Bel Brands USA
Brookings SD
Brands:
Boursin
Kaukauna
Laughing Cow
Merkts
Mini Babybel
Owl's Nest
Price*s

1173 **Bel Cheese USA**
602 W Main St
Leitchfield, KY 42754-1347
270-259-4071
Fax: 270-259-4560
Manufacturer of spreadable cheese and individual serving-sized cheese wheels.
Plant Manager: Francine Moudry
fmoudry@belbrandsusa.com
Estimated Sales: $20-50 Million
Number Employees: 250-499
Number of Brands: 2
Square Footage: 57500
Parent Co: Bel Brands USA
Type of Packaging: Consumer, Food Service, Bulk
Brands:
Laughing Cow
Mini Babybel

1174 **BelGioioso Cheese Inc.**
4200 Main St
Green Bay, WI 54311
920-863-2123
Fax: 920-863-8791 info@belgioioso.com
www.belgioioso.com
Italian cheeses including provolone, parmesan, romano, asiago, fontina, kasseri, mascarpone, gorgonzola, fresh mozzarella, pepato, peperoncino, parveggiano.
Sales Manager: Mimmo Bruno
Quality Assurance Manager: Helen Schmude
Vice President of Marketing: Francis Wall
Vice President Foodservice Sales: Bob Ekstrom
Human Resources Manager: Barb Altschwager
Year Founded: 1979
Estimated Sales: $31.5 Million
Number Employees: 100-249
Square Footage: 30000
Type of Packaging: Consumer, Food Service, Bulk
Brands:
Belgioioso
American Grana
Auribella
Unwrap & Roll
Italico
Peperoncino
Ricotta Con Latte

1175 **Belcolade**
Industriezone Zuid III-B-9320
Pennsauken, NJ 08110
856-661-9123
Fax: 856-665-0005 www.belcolade.com
Couverture chocolate, wholesaler of chocolate and cocoa.
Principak: Taygun Basaran
Estimated Sales: $5-10 Million
Number Employees: 5-9
Parent Co: Belcolade NV/SA
Brands:
Belcolade
Belcolade
Carat

1176 **Belgian Boys**
140 Carolyn Blvd
Farmingdale, NY 11735
info@belgianboys.com
belgianboys.com
Peanute butter; chips; cookies; pancake and waffle mixes
Co-Founder: Gregory Galel
Number Employees: 11-50

1177 **Belgravia Imports**
275 Highpoint Ave
Portsmouth, RI 02871
401-683-3323
Fax: 401-683-2717 800-848-1127
belgravia@belgraviaimports.com
www.belgraviaimports.com
Organic and natural gourmet foods.
President: Ronald Dick
Contact: Vinny Constanza
vin-warehouse@belgraviaimports.com
Year Founded: 1937
Estimated Sales: $1-2.5 Million
Number Employees: 5-9

1178 **Bell & Evans**
154 W Main St
Fredericksburg, PA 17026
717-865-6626
info@bellandevans.com
www.bellandevans.com
Processor and exporter of fresh chicken, chicken nuggets, sausages, burgers, and diced IQF chicken breast
President: Scott Sechler
CFO: Dan Chirico
Year Founded: 1894
Estimated Sales: Over $1 Billion
Number Employees: 500-999
Number of Brands: 2
Square Footage: 180000
Brands:
Bell & Evans the Excellent Chicken
Farmers Pride Natural

1179 **Bell Flavors & Fragrances**
500 Academy Dr
Northbrook, IL 60062-2497
847-291-8300
Fax: 847-291-1217 info@bellff.com
www.bellff.com
Manufacturer and exporter of natural and artificial flavoring extracts for food and beverages; also, spice compounds.
President: Jim Heinz
jheinz@bellff.com
Director of Marketing: Kelli Heinz
Year Founded: 1912
Estimated Sales: $39 Million
Number Employees: 50-99
Square Footage: 100000
Type of Packaging: Consumer, Food Service
Brands:
Yuccafoam

1180 **Bell Foods International**
3213 Waconda Rd.
Gervais, OR 97026
503-390-1425
Fax: 503-390-9526 info@bellfoodsintl.com
www.bellfoodsintl.com
Maraschino cherry manufacturers
Contact: Monica Guzman
monicag@bellfoodsintl.com
Type of Packaging: Consumer, Private Label

1181 **Bell Marketing Inc**
10135 S Roberts Rd # 208
Palos Hills, IL 60465-1500
708-598-8873
Fax: 708-598-8968 800-426-6113
www.bellmarketing.com
Fruit ingredients, juice concentrates, purees, dried fruit-essences-botanicals
Owner: Mary Bell
Sales Director: Karen McNichols
mbell@bellmktg.com
Operations Manager: Jim Kusmierek
Estimated Sales: $5 Million
Number Employees: 1-4
Type of Packaging: Bulk

1182 **Bell Mountain Vineyards**
463 Bell Mountain Rd
Willow City, TX 78675-8501
830-685-3297
Fax: 830-685-3657
evelyn@bellmountainwine.com
www.bellmountainwine.com
Wines.
Owner: Robert P Oberhelman
bellmountainwine@ctesc.net
VP: Ames Morrison
Year Founded: 1968
Estimated Sales: $2.5-5 Million
Number Employees: 5-9

1183 **Bell Plantation**
P.O. Box 943
Tifton, GA 31793
229-387-7238
customerservice@bellplantation.com
bellplantation.com
Organic peanute butter, peanute cooking oil, chocolate and spreads.
Owner: Jill St John
Year Founded: 2007

1184 **Bell's Brewery Inc**
355 E Kalamazoo Ave
Kalamazoo, MI 49053
269-382-2338
Fax: 269-382-3820 www.bellsbeer.com
Ale and stout
President: Larry Bell
VP: Angie Bell
Estimated Sales: $5-10 Million
Number Employees: 50-99
Type of Packaging: Consumer, Food Service

1185 **Bell-Carter Foods Inc**
590 Ygnacio Valley Rd.
Suite 300
Walnut Creek, CA 94596
925-284-5933
Fax: 925-284-1289 800-252-3557
contactus@bellcarter.com www.bellcarter.com
Black ripe, spanish, sicilian, kalamata, and other specialty olive products
CEO: Tim Carter
CFO: Paul Adcock
EVP: Doug Reifsteck
Quality Assurance & R/D: Julie Tinsley
VP Strategy & Marketing: Colleen Sparda
VP Sales: Tom Rickard
Director of Operations: Ron Kerr
Estimated Sales: $20-50 Million
Number Employees: 20-49
Type of Packaging: Consumer, Food Service, Private Label, Bulk
Brands:
Lindsay Olives

1186 Bella Chi-Cha Products
216-B Fern Street
Santa Cruz, CA 95060
831-423-1851
Fax: 831-423-0212 ccrusso@pacbell.net
www.bellachicha.com
Pesto and layered tortas
President/Owner: Chi-Cha Russo

1187 Bella Coola Fisheries
3133 188 St
Surrey, BC V3S 9V5
Canada
604-541-0339
Fax: 604-541-0370
Processor and exporter of fresh and frozen herring roe and salmon
General Manager: Frank Taylor
Number Employees: 10-19
Type of Packaging: Consumer, Food Service, Private Label, Bulk

1188 Bella Cucina
1870 Murphy Ave SW
Atlanta, GA 30310-4837
404-755-0404
Fax: 678-539-8401 866-350-9040
customerservice@bellacucina.com
www.bellacucina.com
Olive oils and pestos
Owner: Louise Fili
customerservice@bellacucina.com
Manager: Reginald Weeks
Estimated Sales: $2.5-5 Million
Number Employees: 5-9
Type of Packaging: Private Label

1189 Bella Ravioli
369 Main St
Medford, MA 02155-6149
781-396-0875
Fax: 781-396-0876
Pasta. Founded in 1981.
Owner: Robert DE Pasquale
Co-Owner: Robert De Pasquale
Estimated Sales: Less Than $500,000
Number Employees: 1-4
Brands:
Bella Ravioli

1190 Bella Sun Luci
1220 Fortress St
Chico, CA 95973-9029
530-899-2661
Fax: 530-899-7746 mooneyfarm@aol.com
www.bellasunluci.com
Sun dried tomatoes, pesto, risotto, olive oil, BBQ marinade and tomato sauces.
Owner: Maryellen Mooney
Partner/Production: Stephen Mooney
Quality Assurance Manager: Jett Uribe
Sales/Marketing: Lisa Mooney
Business Management: Tammy Goss
Estimated Sales: $30 Million
Number Employees: 20-49
Square Footage: 100000
Type of Packaging: Consumer, Food Service, Private Label, Bulk
Brands:
Bella Sun Luci
Summer's Choice

1191 Bella Vista Farm
1002 SW Ard St
Lawton, OK 73505-9660
580-536-1300
Fax: 580-536-4886 866-237-8526
craig@peppercreekfarms.com
www.peppercreekfarms.com
Organic jams, honey, peanut butter, popcorn, all nautral pasta sauces, organic pasta and organic olive oil.
Owner: Craig Weissman
Year Founded: 1984
Estimated Sales: Less than $500,000
Number Employees: 5-9
Brands:
Bella Vista

1192 Bella Viva Orchards
7030 Hughson Ave
Hughson, CA 95326-8014
209-883-9015
Fax: 209-883-0215 800-552-8218
CustomerCare@BellaViva.com
Kosher dried fruit and chocolate fruits packaged for gifts.
Owner: Victor Martino
Year Founded: 1994
Estimated Sales: Less Than $500,000
Number Employees: 1-4

1193 Bella-Napoli Italian Bakery
721 River St
Troy, NY 12180-1233
518-274-8277
Fax: 518-274-2625 888-800-0103
www.bellanapolibakery.com
Italian specialties
President: Dominic Mainella
Sales Executive: Victoria Signore
Estimated Sales: $2.5-5 Million
Number Employees: 50-99
Other Locations:
Bella Napoli Italian Bakery
Latham NY

1194 Belle Plaine Cheese Factory
N3473 Wisconsin Ave
Shawano, WI 54166
715-526-2789
866-245-5924
Retailer of cheese including colby, cheddar, monterey jack, rainbow and pepper jack. Founded in 1972.
President: Donald Brandl
Estimated Sales: Less Than $500,000
Number Employees: 1-4
Type of Packaging: Consumer

1195 Belle River Enterprises
12 Waterview Lane
Belle River, PE C0A 1B0
Canada
902-962-2248
Fax: 902-962-4276
Processor and exporter of rock crab combo and minced crab, cocktail claws and salad meat and lobsters. Founded in 1982.
General Manager: Howard Hancock
Vice President: Dean Hancock
Estimated Sales: $1-5 Million
Number Employees: 75
Square Footage: 32000
Brands:
Belle River

1196 Belleharvest Sales Inc
11900 Fisk Road
Belding, MI 48809-9413
800-452-7753
sales@belleharvest.com www.belleharvest.com
Manufacturer, wholesaler/distributor, exporter, and packer of fresh apples.
President/CEO: Mike Rothwell
bellehar@iserv.net
Controller: Tony Kramer
Director of Marketing: Chris Sandwick
Director of Field Operations: Tony Blattner
Plant Manager: Brad Pitsch
Number Employees: 50-99
Parent Co: Belding Fruit Storage
Type of Packaging: Private Label, Bulk
Brands:
Evercrisp®
Smitten®
SweeTango® Apples
Topaz

1197 Bellerose Vineyard
435 W Dry Creek Rd
Healdsburg, CA 95448
707-433-1637
Fax: 707-433-7024
Wines (Winery)
Founder/Owner: Charles Richard
Estimated Sales: $500,000 appx.
Number Employees: 5-9
Brands:
Bellerose

1198 (HQ)Belletieri Company
1207 W Chew St
Allentown, PA 18102-3751
610-433-4334
Italian specialty foods, condiments and sauces. Founded in 1994.
President: Loui Belletieri
Treasurer: Peter Belletieri
Estimated Sales: Under $500,000
Number Employees: 4-6

1199 Belleville Brothers Packing
2545 Insley Rd
North Baltimore, OH 45872
419-257-3529
Fax: 419-257-3529 www.bellevillebrothers.com
Meat products. Founded in 1999.
President: James Belleville
Owner: Ivan Bellevue
Estimated Sales: $500,000
Number Employees: 1-4
Type of Packaging: Consumer, Bulk

1200 (HQ)Bellisio Foods
1201 Harman Pl
Ste 302
Minneapolis, MN 55403
info@bellisiofoods.com
www.bellisiofoods.com
Frozen entrees, sauces and soups.
CEO: Tom Smith
SVP & CFO: Doug Kooren
SVP & Chief People Officer: Margot McManus
SVP, Marketing & Sales: John Plaso
Year Founded: 1912
Estimated Sales: $140.9 Million
Number Employees: 1000+
Square Footage: 40280
Parent Co: Charoen Pokphand Foods
Type of Packaging: Consumer, Food Service
Brands:
Authentico®
Budget Gourmet®
Michelina's Grande
Michelina's Lean Gourmet®
Michelina's Pizza Snack Rolls
Michelina's Signature®
Zap'ems®

1201 Bellocq
104 West St
Brooklyn, NY 11222
347-463-9231
inquiries@bellocq.com
www.bellocq.com
Manufacturer of a variety of teas and tea sets.
Co-Founder: Michael Shannon
Co-Founder: Heidi Stewart
Co-Founder: Scott Stewart
Square Footage: 80000
Brands:
Bellocq

1202 Bells Foods International
3213 Waconda Rd NE
Gervais, OR 97026
503-390-1425
Fax: 503-390-9526 info@bellfoodsintl.com
www.bellfoodsintl.com
A food processor, manufacturer specialized in co-packing
President: Craig Bell
CFO: Paul Leipzig
Marketing Director: Cody Bell
VP Sales: Doug Zibell
Plant Manager: Monica Guzman
Estimated Sales: $65,000
Number Employees: 20-49
Parent Co: Bell Farms
Type of Packaging: Consumer, Food Service, Private Label, Bulk
Brands:
Eola

1203 Bellucci
2904 S Angus Avenue
Fresno, CA 93727
info@belluccipremium.com
belluccipremium.com
Organic extra virgin olive oil

1204 **Bellville Meat Market**
36 S Front St
Bellville, TX 77418-2406
979-865-5782
Fax: 979-865-0550 800-571-6328
www.bellvillemeatmarket.com
Regular and flavored beef and pork smoked sausage links including garlic, jalapeno, cayenne pepper, etc.; also, fresh pork links, dry, all beef summer and pan sausages and venison products available
Owner: Jerrod Poffenberger
jerrod@bellvillemeatmarket.com
Office Manager: Sara Barnet
Plant Manager: Jerrod Daniel Poffenberger
Plant Operator: Marcus J. Poffenberger
Estimated Sales: $2.5-5 Million
Number Employees: 10-19
Square Footage: 6000
Type of Packaging: Consumer, Food Service, Private Label, Bulk
Brands:
Poffenberger's Bellville

1205 **Bellwether Farms**
PO Box 299
Valley Ford, CA 94972
707-478-8067
Fax: 707-763-2443 info@bellwethercheese.com
Fresh and aged cheese
Owner: Cynthia Callahan
Founder: Cindy Callahan
Vice President: Liam Callahan
liam@bellwetherfarms.com
Sales/Marketing: Lenny Rice Moonsammy
Estimated Sales: Under $500,000
Number Employees: 5-9
Type of Packaging: Private Label
Brands:
Bellwether

1206 **Belly Treats, Inc.**
210-200 Wellington St W
Toronto, ON M5V 3C7
Canada
416-418-3285
Fax: 905-479-4135 www.bellytreats.com
Candies and nuts
Owner/Sales & Marketing: George Tsioros
Estimated Sales: $1 Million
Number of Products: 500+
Type of Packaging: Bulk

1207 **Belmar Spring Water**
410 Grove Street
Glen Rock, NJ 07452
201-444-1010
Fax: 201-444-2801 www.belmarspringwater.com
Processor and bottler of spring water.
Estimated Sales: $1-2.5 Million
Number Employees: 10-19
Type of Packaging: Consumer, Private Label

1208 **Belmont Brewing Co**
25 39th Pl # 25
Long Beach, CA 90803-2806
562-433-3891
Fax: 562-434-0604 www.belmontbrewing.com
Beer and micro brews. Founded in 1990.
Owner: David Hansen
davidhansen@belmontbrewing.com
General Manager: Ben Patterson
VP: Tom Avila
Estimated Sales: $2.5-5 Million
Number Employees: 50-99
Brands:
Bitburger
Black & Tan
Franziskaner Hefe-Weisse
Growler
Long Beach Crude
Marathon
Penny Fogger
Shandy
Strawberry Blonde
Top Sail Amber
Woodchuck Pear Cider

1209 **Belmont Chemicals**
50 Mount Prospect Ave
Clifton, NJ 07013-1900
973-777-2225
Fax: 973-777-6384 800-722-5070
Processor and exporter of vitamins, nutritional and protein supplements, herbs and amino acids
Owner/President: Paul Egyes
Sales Manager: Paul Egyes
Public Relations: Mary Apuzzo
Estimated Sales: $4.5 Million
Number Employees: 4
Number of Products: 50
Square Footage: 4000
Type of Packaging: Bulk

1210 **Belmont Peanuts-Southampton**
23195 Popes Station Rd
Capron, VA 23829-2501
434-658-4613
info@belmontpeanuts.com
www.belmontpeanuts.com
Peanut and peanut products. Founded in 1993.
President/Owner: Patsy Marks
pastymarks@belmontpeanuts.com
VP: Robert Marks
Number Employees: 1-4

1211 **Belton Foods Inc**
2701 Thunderhawk Ct
Dayton, OH 45414-3445
937-890-7768
Fax: 937-890-7780 800-443-2266
dsipos@beltonfoods.com www.beltonfoods.com
Beverages, concentrates, pancake and table syrups, vinegars, drink mixes, enhancing syrups and slush base. Founded in 1971.
President: David Sipos
dsipos@beltonfoods.com
Vice President: Cynthia Gillespie
Sales Executive: Ted Doron
Sales Director: Don Fox
Production Manager: Joe Reece
Manager: Tony Dudon
Estimated Sales: $3.4 Million
Number Employees: 20-49
Number of Brands: 20
Number of Products: 120
Square Footage: 96
Type of Packaging: Consumer, Food Service, Private Label, Bulk

1212 **(HQ)Ben & Jerry's Homemade Inc**
30 Community Dr # 1
South Burlington, VT 05403-6828
802-846-1500
Fax: 802-846-1555 866-258-6877
info@benjerry.com www.benjerry.com
Processor of ice cream, frozen yogurt, sorbet and smoothies
President/CEO: Perry Odak
CEO: Jostein Solheim
CFO: Michael Graning
Marketing Director: David Stever
Public Relations Manager: Sean Greenwood
Senior Director Operations: Bruce Bowman
Plant Manager: Janette Cole
Purchasing: Daniel Scheidt
Year Founded: 1978
Number Employees: 500-999
Square Footage: 276000
Type of Packaging: Consumer
Other Locations:
Ben & Jerry's
Waterbury VT
Brands:
Ben & Jerry's
Ben & Jerry's Frozen Smoothies
Ben & Jerry's Ice Cream

1213 **Ben B. Schwartz & Sons**
7201 W. Fort Street
Suite #27
Detroit, MI 48209
313-841-8300
Fax: 313-841-1253 www.benbdetroit.com
Grower of fruits and vegetables including apples, peaches, pears, cucumbers, lettuce and potatoes. Founded in 1906.
Owner/President/CEO: Chris Billmeyer
Contact: Zeena Toma
ztoma@wescommtech.com
COO: Nathan Stone
Estimated Sales: $10-20 Million
Number Employees: 20-49
Type of Packaging: Consumer

1214 **Ben Heggy's Candy Co**
743 Cleveland Ave NW
Canton, OH 44702-1884
330-455-7703
Fax: 330-455-9865 info@heggys.com
www.heggys.com
Old fashioned candies and handcrafted chocolates.
President/Owner: Richard Wollenberg
info@heggys.com
Estimated Sales: $10-20 Million
Number Employees: 20-49
Type of Packaging: Private Label

1215 **Ben's Sugar Shack**
83 Webster Hwy
Temple, NH 03084-4124
603-924-3177
benssugarshack@gmail.com
www.bensmaplesyrup.com
Manufacturer of syrup.
Owner: Ben Fisk

1216 **Ben-Bud Growers Inc.**
9210 Glades Rd
Boca Raton, FL 33434
561-347-3120
Fax: 561-347-3101 www.ben-bud.com
Processor and importer of vegetables.
President: Ben Litowich
Quality Control Manager: Robert Graham
Sales Manager: Andrew Wilson
Year Founded: 1910
Estimated Sales: $20-50 Million
Number Employees: 10-19
Type of Packaging: Consumer, Bulk

1217 **Benbow's Coffee Roasters**
8 Access Alley
Bar Harbor, ME 04609
207-288-2552
Fax: 207-288-8227 www.benbows.com
Coffee roasters and jams
President/Owner: Ron Greenberg
CEO: Jaren Greenberg
Estimated Sales: Less than $500,000
Number Employees: 1-4
Type of Packaging: Private Label
Brands:
Benbow's

1218 **Beneficial Blends**
6304 Benjamin Road
Suite 507
Tampa, FL 33634-5128
Fax: 813-902-7261 800-230-5952
erin@beneficialblends.com www.kelapo.com
Other baking mixes and ingredients, other condiments, other oils, other spreads & syrup.
Marketing: Erin Meagher
erin@beneficialblends.com

1219 **Beneo Inc**
201 Littleton Rd # 100
1st Floor
Morris Plains, NJ 07950-2939
973-539-6644
Fax: 973-867-2141 contact@beneo.com
www.beneo.com
Manufacturer of ingredients derived from chicory roots, beer sugar, rice and wheat.
President: Jon Peters
Executive VP: Joe O'Neill
joe.oneill@beneo.com
Estimated Sales: $170,000
Number Employees: 10-19
Parent Co: Beneo GmbH
Brands:
Isomalt

1220 **Benmarl Wine Co**
156 Highland Ave
Marlboro, NY 12542-6304
845-236-4265
Fax: 845-236-7271 benmarlwinery@gmail.com
www.benmarl.com
Wines including white, blended red, rose and Chardonnay. Founded in 1971.
Owner: Victor Spaccerelli
President: Mark Miller
General Manager: Matthew Spaccarelli
Estimated Sales: $2.5-5 Million
Number Employees: 5-9
Type of Packaging: Consumer, Food Service

Brands:
Marlboro Village

1221 **Bennett's Apples & Cider**
944 Garner Road East
Ancaster, ON L9G 3K9
Canada
905-648-6878
Fax: 905-648-3647 www.bennettsapples.com
Sweet and mulled apple and apple cranberry cider, apples, pumpkins and sweet corn; contract packaging available. Founded in 1978.
CEO/President: Todd Bennett
Vice President: Richard Bennett
Estimated Sales: $3 Million
Number Employees: 27
Square Footage: 40000
Type of Packaging: Consumer, Food Service, Private Label, Bulk
Brands:
Bennett's

1222 **Benson's Gourmet Seasonings**
P.O.Box 638
Azusa, CA 91702-0638
626-969-4443
Fax: 626-969-2912 800-325-5619
bensons4u@aol.com www.bensonsseasonings.com
Kosher, salt-free and sugar-free seasoning blends including herb/pepper, natural salty flavor, Southwestern, Jamaican, lemon and garlic/herb, big game, game bird and chili. Founded in 1989.
President: Debbie Benson
Estimated Sales: Less than $500,000
Number Employees: 1-4
Square Footage: 4000
Type of Packaging: Consumer, Food Service, Bulk

1223 **Benton's Seafood Ctr**
711 Central Ave S
Tifton, GA 31794-5212
229-382-4976
Fax: 229-382-0779
Seafood. Founded in 1987.
Owner: Tim Benton
Estimated Sales: $1-3 Million
Number Employees: 1-4

1224 **Benzel's Pretzel Bakery**
5200 6th Ave
Altoona, PA 16602-1435
814-942-5062
Fax: 814-942-4133 800-344-4438
pretzels@benzels.com www.benzels.com
Pretzels. Founded in 1911.
President: Ann Benzel
pretzels@benzels.com
Owner: William Benzel
Sales Director: Shaun Benzel
Production Manager: Erkin McCaulley
Estimated Sales: $10-20 Million
Number Employees: 98
Number of Products: 36
Square Footage: 180000
Type of Packaging: Consumer, Food Service, Private Label, Bulk
Brands:
Benzel's Brand
Pennysticks Brand

1225 **Benziger Family Winery**
1883 London Ranch Rd
Glen Ellen, CA 95442-9728
707-935-3000
Fax: 707-935-3016 888-490-2739
greatwine@benziger.com www.benziger.com
Fine wines
President: Tim Wallace
erinnbz@benziger.com
VP Winegrowing: Mark Burningham
Marketing: Jennifer Seekon
Sales: Erinn Benziger
General Manager: Mike Benziger
Estimated Sales: $20-50 Million
Number Employees: 5-9

1226 **Bequet Confections**
8235 Huffine Ln
Bozeman, MT 59718-5986
406-586-2191
Fax: 406-586-7003 877-423-7838
sales@bequetconfections.com
www.bequetconfections.com
Caramels and flavored caramels. Founded in 2001.
President: Joe Sharber
Owner: Robin Bequet
robin@bequetconfections.com
Number Employees: 20-49

1227 **Berardi's Fresh Roast**
12029 Abbey Rd
Cleveland, OH 44133-2637
440-582-4303
Fax: 440-582-4359 800-876-9109
sales@berardiscoffee.com
www.berardiscoffee.com
Specialty coffees, estates, organic, signature blends, espresso and espresso pods. Green, black, organic and herbal teas. Founded in 1987.
Owner: Sean Leneghan
sleneghan@berardiscoffee.com
CEO: Patrick Leneghan
Estimated Sales: $2.5-5 Million
Number Employees: 20-49
Type of Packaging: Private Label

1228 **Berberian Nut Company**
6100 Wilson Landing Rd.
Chico, CA 95973-8902
530-981-4900
Fax: 209-465-6008 www.berberiannut.com
Chandler, Howard, Tulare, and Hartley walnuts
Principal: Pete Turner
Quality Assurance Supervisor: Yesica Salcido
Marketing Manager: Ken Wagner
General Manager: Terry Turner
Plant Manager: Ren Fairbanks
Estimated Sales: $20-50 Million
Number Employees: 50-99
Type of Packaging: Consumer, Food Service, Private Label, Bulk

1229 **Bergen Marzipan & Chocolate**
205 S Washington Ave
Bergenfield, NJ 07621-2918
201-385-8343
Fax: 201-385-0042 bergenmarzipan@optonline.net
www.bergenmarzipan.net
Confections, marzipan and chocolate. Founded in 1987.
Owner: Eddie Sarpon
bergenmarzipan@yahoo.com
Principal: Gunter Schott
Estimated Sales: Under $500,000
Number Employees: 5-9

1230 **Berghausen E Cheml Co**
4524 Este Ave
Cincinnati, OH 45232-1763
513-541-5631
Fax: 530-683-4011 800-648-5887
www.berghausen.com
Processor and finisher of quillaja and yucca extracts (powder and liquid forms) and food colors. Founded in 1863.
President: Beth Baker
bbaker@berghausen.com
Quality Control Manager: Tom Davlin
Estimated Sales: $1-5 Million
Number Employees: 10-19

1231 **Berghoff Brewery**
1730 W Superior St # 3w
Chicago, IL 60622-5639
608-358-4992
Fax: 608-325-3198 www.berghoffbeer.com
Beer and malt liquor in kegs, bottles and cans
President/Plant Manager: Gary Olson
CEO: Harry Cumberbatch
Director of Brewing/Quality Control: Kris Kalav
Production Manager: Dick Tschanz
Estimated Sales: $10 Million
Number Employees: 20-49
Brands:
Berghoff Family
Blumer's Root Beer
Braumeister
Braumeister Light
Huber
Huber Bock
Wisi Club

1232 **Bering Sea Fisheries**
4413 83rd Avenue SE
Snohomish, WA 98290-5204
425-334-1498
Processor and exporter of frozen salmon. Founded in 1961.
President: H William Bodey
Vice President: Russell Bodey
Estimated Sales: $780,000
Number Employees: 10
Type of Packaging: Private Label

1233 **Berke-Blake Fancy Foods, Inc.**
150 National Pl # 140
Longwood, FL 32750-6431
407-831-7288
Fax: 407-831-7065 888-386-2253
www.anniepiesbakery.com
Cakes including cheesecakes, and pies. Founded in 1991.
CEO: Anne Resnick
Sales Executive: Marnie Blake Zahn
General Manager: Mark Hanft
Production Manager: Daniele Sansone
Estimated Sales: $5-10 Million
Number Employees: 5-9
Number of Brands: 1
Number of Products: 100
Square Footage: 36000
Type of Packaging: Food Service
Brands:
Annie Pie's

1234 **Berkeley Farms**
25500 Clawiter Rd
Hayward, CA 94545
510-265-8600
Fax: 510-265-8748 800-395-7004
sharon_cornelius@deanfoods.com
www.berkeleyfarms.com
Dairy products
Manager: Nick Kelble
Quality Control: Besty Raasch
VP Sales/Marketing: Mike Lasky
General Sales Manager: Dan Atkins
Distribution Manager: Richard Hunter
General Manager: Derek Allbee
Plant Manager: Randy Vick
Number Employees: 500-999
Parent Co: Dean Foods Company

1235 **Berks Packing Company, Inc.**
307-323 Bingaman St
PO Box 5919
Reading, PA 19610-5919
610-376-7291
Fax: 610-378-1210 800-882-3757
hr@berksfoods.com www.berksfoods.com
Beef frankfurters, smoked sausage and kielbasa, roast beef, turkey breast, regular and reduced-sodium ham, deli meats, etc
President: Mike Boylan
CEO: Charles Boylan
Purchasing Director: David Boylan
Brands:
Berks

1236 **Berkshire Bark Inc**
18 Elm Ct
Sheffield, MA 1257
413-229-8120
info@berkshirebark.com
www.berkshirebark.com
Manufacturer of top quality Belgian chocolate.
President: Jerome Bertuglia
Number Employees: 1-4
Brands:
berkshire bark

1237 **Berkshire Brewing Co Inc**
12 Railroad St
South Deerfield, MA 01373-1034
413-665-6600
Fax: 413-665-7837 877-222-7468
www.berkshire-brewing.com
Ale and seasonal beer. Founded in 1992.
Owner: Dan Bisson
dbisson@berkshirebrewingcompany.com
CEO: Christopher Lalli
Director: Julia Dvorko
Estimated Sales: $1.2 Million
Number Employees: 20-49
Type of Packaging: Consumer, Food Service
Brands:
Berkshire Ale
Cabin Fever Ale
Coffeehouse Porter
Drayman's Porter
Gold Spike Ale
Hefeweizen

Holidale Barley Wine
Imperial Stout
Lost Sailor India Pale Ale
Mailbock Lager
Oktoberfest Lager
Raspberry Barley Wine
River Ale
Shabadoo Black and Tan Ale
Steel Rail Extra Pale Ale

1238 **Berkshire Dairy**
1258 Penn Ave
Wyomissing, PA 19610-2147
610-378-9999
Fax: 610-378-4975 877-696-6455
info@berkshiredairy.com www.berkshiredairy.com
Manufacturer, importer and exporter of analog extenders, dehydrated dairy products, powders, cheese, creamers, lactose, milk and whey, whole milk powder, Anhydreos milkfat butter, nonfat dry milk, permeate
President & CEO: Dale Mills
dmills@berkshiredairy.com
Sales Director: Steve Cinesi
Estimated Sales: $2.7 Million
Number Employees: 10-19
Parent Co: Dairy Farmers of America, Inc.
Type of Packaging: Private Label, Bulk
Brands:
Berk-Cap

1239 **Berkshire Mountain Bakery**
367 Park St
Housatonic, MA 1236
413-274-3412
Fax: 413-274-6124 866-274-6124
info@berkshiremountainbakery.com
www.berkshiremountainbakery.com
Baked goods such as; sourdough bread, ciabatta bread, bread w/chocolate, oat pecan cookies, pizza crusts and pizza's
President: Richard Bourdon
bourdon592@yahoo.com
Number Employees: 10-19

1240 **Berlin Natural Bakery**
5126 County Rd 120
Berlin, OH 44610
330-893-2734
Fax: 330-893-2157 800-686-5334
www.berlinnaturalbakery.com
Bakery products made with spelt. Founded in 1997.
President: Joy Schrock
cindy@berlinnaturalbakery.com
Managing Executive: Karl Widder
Estimated Sales: $1.3 Million
Number Employees: 20-49
Type of Packaging: Private Label

1241 **Bernadette Baking Company**
85 Commercial St
Medford, MA 02155
781-393-8700
Fax: 781-393-0414
Crunchy biscotti dipped in brews, coffees, teas, or wines. Founded in 1998.
President: Bernadette De Vergilio
Vice President: Marie Cooke
Plant Manager: Mario Ruiz
Estimated Sales: Under $500,000
Number Employees: 5-9
Type of Packaging: Private Label
Brands:
Bernadette's Biscotti
Bernadette's Biscotti Soave
Bernadette's Cookies

1242 **Bernard & Sons**
4011 Jewett Ave
Bakersfield, CA 93301
661-327-4431
Fax: 661-327-7461 www.bernardandsons.com
Meat Products. Founded in 1965.
Owner: Dennis Bernard
General Manager: Hal Ulmer
Estimated Sales: $11,100,000
Number Employees: 20-49

1243 **Bernard & Sons Maple Products**
104, rue Industrielle du Bois,
St-Victor, QC GOM 2B0
Canada
418-588-6109
Fax: 418-588-6836 info@bernards.ca
www.bernards.ca
Pure maple and fruit syrups

1244 **Bernard Food IndustriesInc**
P.O. Box 1497
Evanston, IL 60204
Fax: 847-869-5315 800-323-3663
www.bernardfoods.com
Dessert toppings, soup bases, drinks and baking ingredients.
President & CEO: Steve Bernard
VP, Sales & Operations: Lou Haan
Year Founded: 1947
Estimated Sales: $20-50 Million
Number Employees: 50-99
Square Footage: 60000
Type of Packaging: Consumer, Food Service, Private Label, Bulk
Brands:
Bernard
Beta-Care
Calorie Control
Hola
Kwik-Dish
Lite-95
Longhorn Grill
Sans Sucre
Tex-Pro
Thixx

1245 **Bernardi Italian Foods Company**
595 W 11th St
Bloomsburg, PA 17815
570-389-5500
Fax: 570-784-0293 www.bernardifoodservice.com
Frozen and prepared Italian dinners and cheese foods
Plant Manager: Howard Teufel
Q/A Manager: Julie Simcox
Purchasing: Sharon Lawrence
Year Founded: 1969
Estimated Sales: $20-50 Million
Number Employees: 100-249
Square Footage: 70000
Parent Co: Ajinomoto Foods
Type of Packaging: Consumer, Food Service, Private Label, Bulk

1246 **Bernardo Winery**
13330 Paseo Del Verano Norte
San Diego, CA 92128-1899
858-487-1866
Fax: 858-673-5376 jim@bernardowinery.com
www.bernardowinery.com
Wine and brandy. Founded in 1932.
President: Ross Rizzo
ross@bernardowinery.com
Marketing & Advertising Manager: Samantha Pewitt
General Manager: Selena Roberts
Estimated Sales: $500,000-$1 Million
Number Employees: 20-49
Type of Packaging: Private Label
Brands:
Bernardo

1247 **Bernardus Winery Tasting Rm**
5 W Carmel Valley Rd
21810 Parrot Ranch Road
Carmel Valley, CA 93924
831-298-8021
Fax: 831-659-1676 800-223-2533
www.bernardus.com
Wines
Owner: Ben Pon
bpon@bernardus.com
Operations Manager: Dean DeKorth
Plant Manager: Matthew Shea
Estimated Sales: $5-10 Million
Number Employees: 5-9
Type of Packaging: Private Label
Brands:
Bernardus

1248 **Bernatello's Foods**
5625 W 78th St
Suite B
Edina, MN 55439-3153
952-831-6622
800-878-5001
www.bernatellos.com
Frozen pizza manufacturer in the Midwest.
Number Employees: 100-249
Brands:
Brew Pub
Bellatoria
Orv's
Roma
Pizza Corner

1249 **Berner Food & Beverage LLC**
2034 E Factory Rd
Dakota, IL 61018
800-819-8199
berner.sales@bernerfoods.com
bernerfoodandbeverage.com
Shelf stable RTD coffee beverages, dips, and aerosol cheese.
CEO: Kurt Seagrist
CFO: Scott Edgcomb
VP, Manufacturing: Alan Davis
Chief Commercial Officer: Kirby Harris
Year Founded: 1943
Estimated Sales: $250 Million
Number Employees: 600-800
Square Footage: 200000
Type of Packaging: Consumer, Private Label, Bulk
Other Locations:
Berner Cheese Corp.
Rock City IL

1250 **Bernheim Distilling Company**
1416 S 3rd Street
Louisville, KY 40208-2117
502-638-1387
Fax: 502-585-9110 800-303-0053
Bookings@bernheimmansion.com
www.bernheimmansion.com
Spirits, wheat whiskey and bourbon
Owner: Bernard Bernheim
Estimated Sales: $300,000-500,000
Number Employees: 5-9

1251 **Bernie's Foods**
158 Cook Street
Brooklyn, NY 11206
718-417-6677
Fax: 201-445-2003 www.ratners.com
Canner and food processors of frozen kosher foods.
President: Abraham Ostreicher
Number Employees: 20-49
Number of Brands: 3
Number of Products: 50
Square Footage: 40000
Type of Packaging: Consumer, Food Service, Private Label
Brands:
Frankel's Homestyle
Tovli

1252 **Berres Brothers Coffee**
202 Air Park Dr
PO Box 578
Watertown, WI 53094-7411
920-261-6158
Fax: 920-261-9390 800-233-5443
info@bbcoffee.com www.berresbrothers.com
Coffee
Owner: Pete Berres
info@bbcoffee.com
Number Employees: 50-99

1253 **Berri Pro**
3159 Donald Douglas Loop S
Santa Monica, CA 90405
berripro.com
Fitness beverage
Founder: Jerome Tse
Number of Brands: 1
Type of Packaging: Consumer
Brands:
BERRI PRO

1254 **Berry Processing**
150 Avery Street
Walla Walla, IL 99362
509-529-2161
Fax: 509-527-1331
Beef and pork. Founded in 1955.

Owner: Kathreen Berry
Co-Owner: Lowell Berry
Estimated Sales: $500,000-$1 Million
Number Employees: 1-4
Type of Packaging: Consumer, Food Service, Private Label, Bulk

1255 Berryessa Gap Tasting Room
15 Main St
Winters, CA 95694-1722
530-795-3201
Fax: 916-795-1119 orrin@berryessagap.com
www.berryessagap.com
Processors of fine wines
CFO & Owner: Dan Martinez
Owner, Marketing & Sales Director: Corinne Martinez
Owner & Winemaker: Mike Anderson
Owner & Vineyard Operations Manager: Santiago Moreno
Hospitality & Marketing Manager: Megan Foley
Sales Manager: Clint Crow
clintcrow@berryessagap.com
Estimated Sales: $220,000
Number Employees: 1-4

1256 Berson Peanuts
113 Highway 52 E
Opp, AL 36467-3767
334-493-0655
Fax: 334-493-7767
Peanuts
Division Manager: Dennis Finch
Contact: John Reed
john@alafarm.com
Estimated Sales: Less Than $500,000
Number Employees: 5-9
Type of Packaging: Bulk

1257 Bertie County Peanuts
217 U.S. 13 North
Windsor, NC 27983
252-794-2138
Fax: 252-794-9267 800-457-0005
jon@pnuts.net www.pnuts.net
Sugar-free, other chocolate, other candy, health, fitness and energy bars, nuts, gift packs, private label.
Marketing: Jon Powell

1258 Besco Grain Ltd
PO Box 166
30 Railway Avenue
Brunkild, MB R0G 0E0
Canada
204-736-3570
Fax: 204-736-3575 www.bescograin.ca
Grains
President: Renee Caners
Quality Control: Carol Schulz
International Sales: Anthony Krijger
Sales Manager: Fred Nicholson
Office Manager: Sheri Hiebert
Plant Manager: Jamie Stelmachowich

1259 Bespoke Provisions
PO Box 225
Boulder, CO 80306
646-963-1245
hello@bespoke-provisions.com
www.bespoke-provisions.com
Manufacturer of crackers, salt, and candles.
Founder: Rachelle Miller
Square Footage: 80000

1260 Bess Eaton
127 High St
Westerly, RI 02891-1821
401-596-5533
www.besseaton.com
Coffee and baked goods
Management: David Liguori
Estimated Sales: Less Than $500,000
Number Employees: 5-9

1261 Bessinger Pickle Co
537 N Court Street
Au Gres, MI 48703-9204
989-876-8008
Dill pickles, pickled fruits and vegetables.
Year Founded: 1974
Estimated Sales: $1 Million
Number Employees: 50-99
Square Footage: 104000
Type of Packaging: Consumer

1262 Best Chicago Meat
4649 W Armitage Ave
Chicago, IL 60639
www.bestchicagomeat.com
Meat products including frozen hamburger patties, sausages, spare ribs, chitterlings, bacon, ham, breakfast links, chicken nuggets, rib tips and kosher hot dogs
CFO: Paul Dwyer
Regional Sales Manager: Edward Allaway
Estimated Sales: $20-50 Million
Number Employees: 20-49
Number of Brands: 4
Square Footage: 20000
Parent Co: Beavers Holdings
Type of Packaging: Consumer, Food Service
Brands:
David's Kosher
Glenmark
JEMMBURGER
Moo & Oink

1263 Best Chocolate In Town
880 Massachusetts Avenue
Indianapolis, IN 46204
317-636-2800
Fax: 317-636-2822 888-294-2378
info@bestchocolateintown.com
www.bestchocolateintown.com
Hand-made chocolates
Owner: Elizabeth Garber
Estimated Sales: $100,000
Number Employees: 5-9

1264 Best Cooking Pulses, Inc.
110 10th St NE
Portage la Prairie, MB R1N 1B5
Canada
204-857-4451
margaret@bestcookingpulses.com
www.bestcookingpulses.com
Peas, chickpea, lentil and bean flours and pea fiber. Certified Kosher, Halal, Conventional or Certified-Organic, free of all major allergens, and gluten free.
President: Trudy Heal
Director, Sales & Marketing: Jennifer Evancio
General Manager: Mike Gallais
Estimated Sales: $11.25 Million
Number Employees: 23
Type of Packaging: Bulk

1265 Best Ever Bakery
17 Broadway
Massapequa, NY 11758-5003
516-795-5590
Fax: 516-804-1144 besteverbakery@gmail.com
www.besteverbakeshop.com
Sweet potato and pecan pie, cakes, cookies, and dessert designs.
Owner: Ashley D Elia
President: Vincent D Elia
Estimated Sales: A
Number Employees: 5-9
Type of Packaging: Consumer

1266 Best Express Foods Inc
1458 E Grand River Rd
Williamston, MI 48895-9336
517-655-2288
Fax: 517-655-8568
Frozen pizza and pizza related items
Contact: Dave Spencer
dspencer@bestexpressfoods.com
Number Employees: 20-49
Type of Packaging: Consumer

1267 Best Foods
700 Sylvan Ave
Englewood Cliffs, NJ 07632
201-894-4000
Fax: 201-894-2186 www.bestfoods.com
Best Foods manufactures the best-selling mayonnaise in the United States. East of the Rockies, Best Foods is known as Hellman's.
President, Unilever Foods: Amanda Sourry
Contact: Cordell Price
cordell.price@unilever.com
Number Employees: 44,000
Number of Products: 13
Parent Co: Unilever
Type of Packaging: Consumer, Food Service
Brands:
Best Foods
Hellmann's

1268 Best Harvest Bakeries
530 S 65th St
Kansas City, KS 66111-2324
913-287-6300
Fax: 913-287-5408 800-811-5715
info@bestharvest.com www.bestharvest.com
Buns and rolls and breads. Founded in 1999.
President/COO: Ed Honesty
Chairman/CEO: Robert Beavers
VP: Brandon Beavers
Quality Assurance Supervisor: Jason McConico
Manufacturing Executive: Brad Wolf
Purchasing: Rich Lingo
Estimated Sales: $3.4 Million
Number Employees: 20-49
Square Footage: 128000
Type of Packaging: Consumer, Food Service

1269 Best Maid Cookie Co
1147 Benson St
River Falls, WI 54022-1594
715-426-2090
Fax: 715-426-1950 888-444-0322
customerservice@bestmaid.com
www.bestmaid.com
Pre-formed frozen cookie dough and baked cookies; also specialty products available. Founded in 1943.
Owner: Byron Grickson
Vice President: Ron Thielen
Human Resource Manager: Deb Dartsch
Number Employees: 100-249
Square Footage: 80000
Type of Packaging: Food Service, Private Label

1270 Best Maid Products, Inc.
1401 S Riverside Drive
PO Box 1809
Fort Worth, TX 76101-1809
817-335-5494
Fax: 817-534-7117 800-447-3581
www.bestmaidproducts.com
Pickles, sauces, dressings and condiments.
President: Brian Dalton
Technical Director: Mike Wuller
Marketing Director: Roger Fort
Contact: Diaz Alfonso
diaza@aldeasa.com
Estimated Sales: $44.1 Million
Number Employees: 250
Number of Brands: 1
Square Footage: 200000
Type of Packaging: Consumer
Brands:
Best Maid

1271 Best Provision Co Inc
2401 Morris Ave.
Union, NJ 07083
973-242-5000
Fax: 973-648-0041 800-631-4466
info@bestprovision.com www.bestprovision.com
Corned beef, roast beef, frankfurters, pastrami and bacon
President: Floyd Jason
fjayson@bestprovision.com
Co-Owner: Kevin Karp
Co-Owner: Richard Dolinko
Human Resource Director: Clara Mendez
Year Founded: 1938
Estimated Sales: $35 Million
Number Employees: 100-249
Square Footage: 65000
Type of Packaging: Consumer, Food Service

1272 Bestco Inc
288 Mazeppa Rd
Mooresville, NC 28115-7928
704-664-4300
Fax: 704-664-7493 www.bestco.com
Nutritional supplements, cough drops, lozenges and antacids.
President: Tim Condron
CEO: Richard Zulman
rzulman@bestco.com
CFO: Scott Wattenberg
EVP: Mark Knight
EVP: Steve Berkowitz
EVP: Jonathan Zulman

Estimated Sales: $1-9.99 Million
Number Employees: 250-499
Parent Co: Tamanda Holdings USA Inc.
Type of Packaging: Private Label

1273 Beta Pure Foods
2100 Deleware Avenue
Santa Cruz, CA 95060
831-685-6565
Fax: 831-685-6569 www.betapure.com
Organic frozen fruits and vegetables, concentrates and purees, sweeteners. Founded in 1994.
President: Loren Morr
Number Employees: 5-9
Parent Co: SunOpta
Type of Packaging: Food Service, Private Label, Bulk

1274 BetaStatin Nutritional Rsearch
299 Riversville Rd
Greenwich, CT 06831
203-869-7778
Fax: 203-869-7778 800-660-9570
www.betastatin.com
Nutritional and weight loss supplements.
Managing Director: Dr Stephen L Newman

1275 Beth's Fine Desserts
34 Miller Aveue
Mill Valley, CA 94941
415-383-3991
Fax: 707-792-0399
Bite-sized cookies and savory cheese wafers, gourmet gift items, gingerbreads. Produces and markets desserts.
President: Beth Setrakian
Brands:
Beth's
Beth's Baking Basics
Heavenly Little Cookies

1276 Bethel Heights Vineyard
6060 Bethel Heights Rd NW
Salem, OR 97304-9733
503-399-9588
Fax: 503-581-0943 info@bethelheights.com
www.bethelheights.com
Wines
President: Pat Dudley
pat@bethelheights.com
Winemaker: Terry Casteel
Vice President: Ted Casteel
Marketing Director: Pat Dudley
Estimated Sales: $2 Million
Number Employees: 20-49
Type of Packaging: Private Label

1277 Betsy's Best
888-483-2019
info@betsysbest.com betsysbest.com
Nut and seed butters
Founder: Betsy Opyt
Number of Brands: 1
Number of Products: 4
Type of Packaging: Consumer
Brands:
BETSY'S BEST

1278 Betsy's Cheese Straws
3761 Grandview Road
Millbrook, AZ 36054-3203
334-285-1354
Fax: 800-625-9700 877-902-3141
info@belmontpeanuts.com
Cheese straws. Founded in 1998.
President/Owner: Betsy Parker
Contact: Elizabeth Campbell
elizabethc@betsyscheesestraws.com
Number Employees: 6

1279 Bettah Buttah, LLC
111 Southwest Blvd
Kansas City, KS 66103
913-432-5228
Fax: 913-432-5880 800-568-8468
www.bettahbuttah.com
Specialty foods, snacks, hot sauces, condiments, seasonings, salsas, barbeque sauces. Flavored butters. Founded in 1996.
President: Joe Polo
Branch Manager: Jana Kirke
Contact: Kit Maxfield
Contact: Bryan Richards
Estimated Sales: Less than $500,000
Number Employees: 20-49
Brands:
Cajun Bayou
Calido Chile Traders
Fiesta
Jose Goldstein
Original Juan
Panisgood
Texas Longhorn
Wild and Mild

1280 Bette's Oceanview Diner
1807 4th St
Berkeley, CA 94710-1910
510-644-3230
Fax: 510-644-3209 bettesdiner@worldpantry.com
www.bettesdiner.com
Manufacturer and exporter of pancake mixes including buttermilk, oatmeal and buckwheat; also, scone mixes including raisin, cranberry and lemon currant
Owner: Bette Kroening
Number Employees: 20-49
Type of Packaging: Consumer, Food Service
Brands:
Bette's Oceanview Diner

1281 Better Bagel Bakery
4854 S Tamiami Trl
Sarasota, FL 34231-4352
941-924-0393
Fax: 941-924-0358
Baked goods such as; breads, rolls, bagels, etc
Owner: Jun Park
Estimated Sales: Less than $100,000
Number Employees: 1-4

1282 Better Baked Foods Inc
56 Smedley St
North East, PA 16428-1632
814-725-8778
Fax: 814-725-5021 www.betterbaked.com
French bread pizza, panini sandwiches, appetizers, garlic breads, breakfast items, and desserts.
President/COO: Joseph Pacinelli
CEO: Chris Miller
Director of Manufacturing Operations: Jerry Pacinelli
IT Manager: Brad Harrison
davide@betterbaked.com
Plant Manager: Scott Carpenter
Estimated Sales: $20-50 Million
Number Employees: 100-249
Number of Brands: 3
Square Footage: 200000
Type of Packaging: Food Service, Private Label
Brands:
Daybreak Classics
Papa Presto
Two Sicily's

1283 Better Beverages Inc
10624 Midway Ave
Cerritos, CA 90703-1581
562-924-8321
Fax: 562-924-6204 800-344-5219
customercare@betbev.com www.betbev.com
Soft drinks, juices, energy drinks, coffee, punch syrups, bar mixes, beverage dispensers, and glass washer and sanitizer.
Owner: Harold Harris
haroldh@betbev.com
CEO: G Harris
Estimated Sales: $20-50 Million
Number Employees: 20-49
Type of Packaging: Consumer, Food Service
Brands:
Rc Cola

1284 Better Bites Bakery
Austin, TX 78737
rachel@betterbitesbakery.com
www.betterbitesbakery.com
Bites, cupcakes and brownies
Founder & CEO: Leah Lopez

1285 Better Living Products
208 Harvard Drive
Princeton, TX 75407
972-736-6691
Fax: 903-298-0014 zetawize@yahoo.com
www.betterlivingusa.com
Processor, importer of kava kava powder, aloe vera juice and herbs. Founded in 1996.
Founder: Don Ansley
COO: Ed Carter
Estimated Sales: Less than $500,000
Number Employees: 1-4
Parent Co: Zeta Wize LLC Company
Brands:
Kava Kava
Noni Nonu

1286 Better Made Snack Foods
10148 Gratiot Ave
Detroit, MI 48213
313-925-4774
Fax: 313-925-6028 800-332-2394
info@bettermadesnackfoods.com
www.bettermadesnackfoods.com
Potato chips, popcorn, crunchy chips, pretzels, pork rinds, tortilla chips, beef jerky, chocolate covered potato chips and pretzels, salsas and cheese dips.
President: David Jones
Year Founded: 1930
Estimated Sales: $62 Million
Number Employees: 100-249
Type of Packaging: Consumer, Food Service
Brands:
Better Made

1287 Better Than Coffee
Torrance, CA 90503
contact@betterthancoffee.com
www.betterthancoffee.com
High energy bars
Founder & Managing Partner: Valerie Milovic

1288 Better Than Foods USA
17000 W Capitol Dr
Brookfield, WI 53005
855-691-5900
www.betterthanfoodsusa.com
Organic noodles, pasta and rice
Number of Brands: 1
Number of Products: 3
Type of Packaging: Consumer
Brands:
BETTER THAN

1289 BetterBody Foods & Nutrition LLC
1762 W 20 S Ste 500
Lindon, UT 84042-1762
Fax: 801-456-2601 866-404-6582
info@xagave.com www.xagave.com
Supplements
President/Owner: Stephen Richards
Contact: Joshua Faber
jfaber@betterbodyfoods.com

1290 Betty Jane Homemade Candy
3049 Asbury Rd
Dubuque, IA 52001-8459
563-582-4668
Fax: 563-582-2150 800-642-1254
www.bettyjanecandies.com
Candy
President/CEO: Drew Siegert
bjcgremlin@aol.com
Vice President: George Hagge
Sales Exec: Linnae Heinz
Plant Mgr./Head of Production: John Heinz
Estimated Sales: $2 Million
Number Employees: 20-49
Type of Packaging: Consumer
Brands:
Gremlins

1291 Betty Lou's
750 SE Booth Bend Rd
PO Box 537
McMinnville, OR 97128
503-434-5205
Fax: 503-472-8643 800-242-5205
www.bettylousinc.com
Processor and exporter of oil and, low-fat oven baked apple butter, low-fat and wheat-free fruit bars and fat-free cookies, snack foods and candies, protein bars. Founded in 1978.
Owner: Betty Carrier
VP Sales: John Sizemore
Estimated Sales: $2.5-5 Million
Number Employees: 20-49
Square Footage: 36000
Type of Packaging: Consumer, Private Label
Brands:
Betty Lou's

1292 **Bevco Sales International Inc.**
9354-194th Street
Surrey, BC V4N 4E9
Canada
604-888-1455
Fax: 604-888-2887 800-663-0090
info@bevco.net www.bevco.net
Processor and co-packer of fruit juices, citrus drinks and bottled water
President/Board Member: Brian Fortier
Board Member: Donna Fortier
Estimated Sales: $5-10 Million
Number Employees: 10-19
Type of Packaging: Consumer, Private Label
Brands:
Juicetyme Delites
O-Jay
Watertyme
Wild Springs

1293 **Beverage America**
545 E 32nd St
Holland, MI 49423-5495
616-396-1281
Fax: 616-396-8121
Bottled water, fruit beverages, Snapple, and Dr. Pepper
Plant Manufacturing: Dale Stein
Estimated Sales: $5-10 Million
Number Employees: 5-9

1294 **Beverage Capital Corporation**
2209 Sulphur Spring Rd
Baltimore, MD 21227-2933
410-242-7404
Fax: 410-247-2977
bevcapsales@beveragecapital.com
Bottled and canned soft and juice drinks and juice; also, seltzer water; contract packaging available
Chairman: Harold Honickman
Controller: John Schmitj
Treasurer: Walter Wilkinson
Vice President: Rick Smith
Contact: Florence Stewart
fstewart@capitol-beverage.com
Purchasing Agent: Kim Quinn
Estimated Sales: $28 Million
Number Employees: 350
Square Footage: 365000
Type of Packaging: Consumer, Private Label
Other Locations:
Whitehead Court Manufacturing
Baltimore MD
30th Street Manufacturing
Baltimore MD
Brands:
Bevnet
Cadbury Schweppes
Canada Dry
Energy Brand
Mistic
Snapple

1295 **Beverage Flavors Intl**
3150 N Campbell Ave
Chicago, IL 60618-7921
773-248-3860
Fax: 773-248-3862 info@beverageflavorsintl.com
www.beverageflavorsinternational.com
Beverage flavor emulsions and concentrates to bottlers. Flavor selection includes citrus punch, tropical fruit punch, pineapple-banana, mango peach, apple, strawberry-kiwi, aloha punch and pineapple-guava.
Manager: Daniel Manoogian
Contact: Gregg Goga
ggoga@beverageflavorsintl.com
Office Manager: Barbara Martinez
Estimated Sales: Less Than $500,000
Number Employees: 1-4
Type of Packaging: Bulk

1296 **Beverage House Inc**
400 High Point Rd SE # 100
Cartersville, GA 30120-6610
770-387-0451
Fax: 770-387-1809 888-367-8327
www.beveragehouse.com
Coffee, tea and beverage concentrates. Founded in 1984.
Manager: Jimmy Garren
CEO: Jim Gollhoffer
Marketing Manager: Robbin McCool
Manager: Monte Ammons
monte@beveragehouse.com
Number Employees: 20-49
Type of Packaging: Private Label
Brands:
New Southern Tradition Teas
Reedy Brew Teas

1297 **Beverly International**
1768 Industrial Rd
Cold Spring, KY 41076-8610
859-781-3474
Fax: 859-781-7590 800-781-3475
www.beverlyinternational.net
Manufacturer and exporter of multiple vitamin and mineral packs; also, protein powders. Founded in 1967.
Owner: Roger Riedinger
Owner: Sandy Riedinger
sandyr@beverlyinternational.net
Estimated Sales: Less Than $500,000
Number Employees: 5-9
Type of Packaging: Consumer, Food Service, Private Label
Brands:
Beverly International

1298 **Bevsource**
219 Little Canada Road East
St. Paul, MN 55117
651-797-0113
Fax: 651-482-1337 866-956-4608
sales@bevsource.com www.bevsource.com
Ingredients and packaging for the beverage industry, specifically sweeteners, vitamin blends, juice concentrates, and alcohol.

1299 **Beyond Meat**
1325 E El Segundo Blvd
El Segundo, CA 90245
866-756-4112
beyondmeat.com
Plant-based burgers and sausages
CEO: Ethan Brown
Number of Brands: 1
Number of Products: 11
Type of Packaging: Consumer
Brands:
BEYOND MEAT

1300 **Bgreen Food**
6977 Navajo Rd
Suite 116
San Diego, CA 92119
619-825-9330
hello@bgreenfood.com
www.bgreenfood.com
Organic rice and noodles

1301 **Bhakti**
939 Pearl St
Suite 200
Boulder, CO 80302-5067
303-484-8770
www.drinkbhakti.com
Chai made with fresh pressed organic ginger and fiery spices.
Founder & CEO: Brook Eddy
brook@bhaktichai.com
Quality Assurance Supervisor: Matthew Sessa
Marketing & Events Manager: Allison Salvati
Food Service Sales Manager: Austin Doll
Director Of Plant Operations: Beau Hagberry
Head Brewer: Jared Mandeville
Shipping Manager: Kyle Hameister
Number Employees: 1-4
Type of Packaging: Consumer, Food Service

1302 **Bhu Foods**
San Diego, CA 92110
619-855-3258
www.bhufoods.com
Vegan protein bars
Contact: Laura Katleman
Number of Brands: 1
Number of Products: 12
Type of Packaging: Consumer
Brands:
BHU FIT

1303 **Bhuja Snacks**
Kennesaw, GA 30152
majans.com
Snack mixes
Parent Co: Majans

1304 **Bi Nutraceuticals**
2550 El Presidio St
Long Beach, CA 90810-1193
310-669-2100
Fax: 310-637-3644 contact@botanicals.com
www.binutraceuticals.com
Manufacturer and distributor of water soluable extracts, pre-mixes, herb powders and teas.
President: George Pontiakos
Director of Fulfillment Services: Corey Leon
CFO: Christoph Kirchner
VP Technical Services: Emilio Gutierrez
VP Global Quality & Compliance: Rupa Das
Director of Marketing: Randy Kreienbrink
Sales Manager-Pacific Territory: Nicole Robertson
Contact: Patrisha Abergas
patrishaabergas@tmmc.com
Director, Extract Operations: Dr. William Meer

1305 **Biagio's Banquets**
4242 N Central Ave
Chicago, IL 60634-1810
773-736-9009
Fax: 773-587-3011 800-392-2837
rperrye@aol.com www.suparossa.com
Processor and exporter of pasta, breaded appetizers and pizza including deep dish, thin crust, pan and self-rising. Founded in 1977.
President: Samuel Cirrincione
Sales Director: Michelle Rubino
Contact: Peter Lesniak
peter@suparossa.com
General Manager: Tom Cirrincione
Estimated Sales: $10-20 Million
Number Employees: 50-99
Square Footage: 60000
Brands:
Suparossa

1306 **Bianchi Winery**
3380 Branch Rd
Paso Robles, CA 93446-8314
805-226-9922
Fax: 805-226-8230 info@bianchiwine.com
www.bianchiwine.com
Manufacturer and exporter of red and white wines. Founded in 2001.
Owner: Glenn A Bianchi
gl@bianchiwine.com
Principal: Al Smart
CFO: Mike Gardnier
Vice President: Albert Paul
Operations: Edward Ortease
Manager/Winemaster: Tom Lane
Estimated Sales: $5 Million
Number Employees: 5-9
Number of Brands: 3
Number of Products: 20
Type of Packaging: Consumer, Food Service, Bulk
Brands:
Bianchi Vineyards
Chateau Cellars
Domaine Noel
Vista Verde

1307 **Bias Vineyards & Winery**
3166 Highway B
Berger, MO 63014-1418
573-834-5475
Fax: 573-834-2046 800-905-2427
info@biaswinery.com www.biaswinery.com
Wines
President: Carol Grass
biaswinery@fenit.com
VP: Kirk Grass
Purchasing Director: Carol Grass
Estimated Sales: Less Than $500,000
Number Employees: 1-4
Type of Packaging: Private Label

1308 **Biazzo Dairy Products Inc**
1145 Edgewater Ave
Ridgefield, NJ 07657-2102
201-941-6800
Fax: 201-941-4151 info@biazzo.com
www.biazzo.com
Fresh, chunk and shredded mozzarella, ricotta and string cheese.
President: Sergio Espinoza
sergio.espinoza@schreiberfoods.com
Vice President: John Iapichino, Jr.
Food Safety & Quality Assurance Manager: Sanya Bici
Director of Sales: Steven Cilento

Estimated Sales: $20-50 Million
Number Employees: 50-99
Square Footage: 58000
Type of Packaging: Consumer, Food Service, Private Label, Bulk
Brands:
Biazzo Brand

1309 Bickel's Potato Chip Company
51 N Main St
PO Box 2427
York, PA 17405
717-665-2002
Fax: 717-665-5449 800-233-1933
www.bickelssnacks.com
Warehouse location for Bickel's potato chips. Founded in 1954.
President: John Wareheine
Controller: Gary Knisely
Director Sales: Ed Dobkel
Plant Manager: Jay Epstein
Purchasing Director: Nellie Redding
Estimated Sales: $10-24.9 Million
Number Employees: 5-9
Type of Packaging: Consumer
Brands:
Bickel's

1310 Bickel's Snack Foods Inc
1120 Zinns Quarry Rd
P.O. Box 2427
York, PA 17404-3533
717-843-0738
Fax: 717-843-5192 800-233-1933
www.bickelssnacks.com
Snack food products including barrels, tortilla chips, corn chips, wedge pretzels, kettle cooked chips, cheese products, and potato chips.
General Manager: Dale Warfel
Year Founded: 1954
Estimated Sales: $20-50 Million
Number Employees: 1000-4999
Parent Co: Hanover Foods Corporation
Type of Packaging: Private Label
Brands:
Bickle Snacks
Bon Ton
Cabana
Golden Gourmet
Wege

1311 Bickford Daniel LobsterCompany
Lanes Is
Vinalhaven, ME 04863
207-863-4688
Fax: 207-863-4525
Lobster
Estimated Sales: $1-3 Million
Number Employees: 5-9

1312 Bickford Flavors
19007 Saint Clair Ave
Euclid, OH 44117-1001
216-531-6006
Fax: 216-531-2006 800-283-8322
orders@bickfordflavors.com
www.bickfordflavors.com
Extracts including vanilla and assorted flavoring and syrups.
President: Barbara Sofer
orders@bickfordflavors.com
Vice President: Scott Sofer
Operations: Heather Noel
Estimated Sales: $2.5-5 Million
Number Employees: 5-9
Number of Brands: 1
Number of Products: 150
Square Footage: 60000
Type of Packaging: Private Label
Brands:
Bickford

1313 Bidwell Candies
1610 Broadway Ave
Mattoon, IL 61938-5751
217-234-3858
Fax: 217-234-3856
Manufactures chocolates and candies
Owner: Greg Kuhl
Co-Owner: Lori Kuhl
Plant Manager: Judy Brown
Estimated Sales: Less than $500,000
Number Employees: 5-9

1314 Bidwell Vineyard
18910 Middle Rd
Vineyard 48
Cutchogue, NY 11935-1069
631-734-5200
Fax: 631-734-6763
Fine wines. Founded in 1982.
Owner: Rose Pipia
General Manager: Joseph Pipia
Purchasing Director: James Bidwell
Estimated Sales: $1-2.5 Million appx.
Number Employees: 1-4
Brands:
Carbernet Sauvignon
Chardonnay
Country Gardens Blush Banquet
Merlot
Sauvignon Blanc
White Riesling

1315 Bien Cuit
120 Smith St.
Brooklyn, NY 11201
718-852-0200
info@biencuit.com
www.biencuit.com
Various types of bread.
Chef & Owner: Zachary Golper
Owner: Kate Wheatcroft
Head Baker: Sarah Wilkens
Director, Sales & Marketing: Shelby Jones
Director, Operations: Zachary Greenspon
Type of Packaging: Consumer

1316 Bien Padre Foods Inc
1459 Railroad St
Eureka, CA 95501-2147
707-442-4585
Fax: 707-269-2140 www.bienpadre.com
Manufacturer and exporter of tortilla chips, corn and flour tortillas and salsas. Founded in 1974.
President/Owner: Benito Lim
stevebpf@gmail.com
Sales Exec: Steve Frenz
Estimated Sales: $1-2.5 Million
Number Employees: 20-49
Square Footage: 56000
Type of Packaging: Consumer, Food Service, Private Label, Bulk

1317 Biena Foods
119 Braintree St
Suite 409
Allston, MA 02134-1642
617-202-5210
hello@bienafoods.com
Manufacturer of flavoured chickpea snacks.
Founder and CEO: Poorvi Patodia
poorvi@bienafoods.com
Number Employees: 1-4
Square Footage: 80000
Brands:
Biena Chickpea Snacks

1318 Bieri's Jackson Cheese
3271 Hwy. P
Jackson, WI 53037
262-677-3227
Fax: 262-677-3480 800-321-6077
annette@bierischeese.com www.bierischeese.com
Retailers of the finest Wisconsin cheeses
Owner: Annette Du Bois
Co-Owner/CEO: Wayne Dubois
Estimated Sales: $300,000-500,000
Number Employees: 5-9
Type of Packaging: Bulk

1319 Bierig Brothers Inc
3539 Reilly Ct
Vineland, NJ 08360-1500
856-691-9765
Fax: 856-692-7869 www.bierigbrothers.com
Veal and lamb products.
Vice President: David Bierig
biebros@aol.com
Operations Manager: Danny Bierig
General Manager: Alan Bierig
Vice President: David Bierig
biebros@aol.com
Estimated Sales: $25 Million
Number Employees: 20-49

1320 Biery Cheese Co
6544 Paris Ave
Louisville, OH 44641-9544
330-875-3381
Fax: 330-875-5896 www.bierycheese.com
Family-owned award-winning cheese manufacturer.
President: Jeff Fairless
CEO: Ben Biery
Number Employees: 100-249
Type of Packaging: Consumer, Food Service, Private Label, Bulk
Brands:
Biery

1321 Bifulco Four Seasons
590 Almond Rd
Pittsgrove, NJ 08318-4070
856-692-0778
Fax: 856-691-1529 www.bifulcos.com/
Parsley, peppers, tomatoes, zucchini, and melons. Founded in 1971.
President/Owner: Bert Bifullo
Contact: Umberto Bifulco
umbertobifulco@bifulcos.com
Secretary/Sales: Kathleen Bifulco
Estimated Sales: $2.5-5 Million
Number Employees: 10-19
Type of Packaging: Consumer, Bulk
Brands:
Tall-Boy

1322 Big Al's Seafood
7701 Quacker Neck Rd
PO Box 293
Bozman, MD 21612
410-745-2637
Fax: 410-745-9046
Wholesaler/distributor of crabs, clams, fish and oysters. Founded in 1979.
President: Alan Poore
Estimated Sales: Less than $500,000
Number Employees: 5
Square Footage: 24000
Type of Packaging: Consumer

1323 Big Apple Bagels
500 Lake Cook Rd # 475
Suite 475
Deerfield, IL 60015-5240
847-948-7520
800-251-6101
www.bigapplebagels.com
Bagels and baked goods
Contact: Richard Chou
richard@bodypoint.com
Number Employees: 10-19

1324 Big B Barbecue
2727 N Kentucky Ave
Evansville, IN 47711-6203
812-425-5235
Fax: 812-428-8432 www.bigbbarbecue.com
Sauces, pepperoncinis, chili, pork barbecue, sloppy joes, vinegar, salsa and pickled products. Founded in 1962.
President & CEO: Richard Bonenberger
Estimated Sales: Less Than $500,000
Number Employees: 10-19
Type of Packaging: Consumer, Food Service, Private Label, Bulk
Brands:
Big B
Frontier Gold

1325 Big Boss Baking Co
629 Mcway Dr
High Point, NC 27263-2059
336-861-1212
www.bigbossbaking.com
Manufacturer of granola and granola bites.
President and Owner: Lavinia Hensley
lavinia@bigbossbaking.com
Estimated Sales: Less Than $500,000
Number Employees: 5-9
Square Footage: 80000

1326 Big Bucks Brewery & Steakhouse
550 S Wisconsin Street
Gaylord, MI 49735
989-731-0401
Fax: 989-731-2788 info@bigbuck.com
Beer, ale, lager and stout. Founded in 1994.

Manager: Tracy Dalman
Contact: Anthony Dombrowski
anthonydombrowski@mathworks.com
Estimated Sales: $2.5-5 Million
Number Employees: 376
Type of Packaging: Consumer, Food Service

1327 **Big Chief Meat Snacks Inc**
3900 52 Ave NE
Calgary, AB T3J 3X4
Canada
403-264-2641
Fax: 403-262-9053 biteme@bigchief.ca
www.bigchiefbeefjerky.com
Snack meats including pepperoni and teriyaki sticks, beef jerky and kippered beef. Founded in 1971.
Founder: William Klein
Contact: Mary Bendzik
Estimated Sales: C
Number Employees: 20
Type of Packaging: Consumer
Brands:
Big Chief
Old Dutch

1328 **Big City Reds**
4430 S 110th Street
Omaha, NE 68137-1217
847-714-1640
Fax: 847-714-1647 800-759-5275
www.americanfoodsgroup.com
All beef hotdogs, frankfurters and sausage including Polish and cocktail. FOunded in 1996.
President: Michael Sternberg
VP Marketing: Rebecca Sternberg
National Sales Manager: Robin Warren
Estimated Sales: $500,000
Number Employees: 5-10
Type of Packaging: Consumer, Food Service, Private Label
Brands:
Big City Reds

1329 **Big Dipper Dough Co.**
2819 Cass Rd E4
Traverse City, MI 49684
231-883-6035
bigdipperdough.com
Cookie dough
Co-Owner/Co-Founder: Dan Fuller
Co-Owner/Co-Founder: Austin Groesser
Type of Packaging: Consumer
Brands:
BIG DIPPER

1330 **Big Easy Foods**
3935 Ryan St
Lake Charles, LA 70605-2817
337-477-5499
Fax: 985-563-4202 855-477-9296
info@bigeasyfoods.com www.bigeasyfoods.com
Turduckens, stuffed chickens, shrimp, sausage, boudin, jalapeno poppers, cornbread casserole
Managing Partner: Larry Avery
lavery@bigeasyfoods.com
Managing Partner: Mark Abraham
COO: Scott Arrant
Estimated Sales: $20-50 Million
Number Employees: 50-99

1331 **Big Fatty's Flaming Foods**
639 County Road 240
Valley View, TX 76272-5912
940-726-3741
Fax: 940-726-6257 888-248-6332
Spicy foods; biscotti, spice rubs and cornbread. Founded in 1996.
President/Owner: Gail Patterson
gforcewind@aol.com
VP: Ricky Patterson
Estimated Sales: Less Than $500,000
Number Employees: 1-4

1332 **Big Fork Brands**
4241 N Ravenswood Ave
Chicago, IL 60613
321-206-9444
contact@bigforkbrands.com
bigforkbrands.com
Bacon and sausage
Co-Founder/Chef: Lance Avery
Co-Founder: Ann Avery
Year Founded: 2011

1333 **Big Island Candies Inc**
585 Hinano St
Hilo, HI 96720-4428
808-946-9213
Fax: 808-961-6941 800-935-5510
contactus@bigislandcandies.com
www.bigislandcandies.com
Manufacturer of shortbread cookies, chocolates and baked goods.
President/CEO: Allan Ikawa
allan@bigislandcandies.com
Chief Financial Officer: Bonnie Honda
Estimated Sales: $7 Million
Number Employees: 50-99
Number of Brands: 1
Type of Packaging: Consumer
Brands:
Big Island Candies

1334 **Big Island Seafood, LLC**
1201 University Drive NE
Atlanta, GA 30306-2504
404-366-8943
Fax: 404-366-9129
Tuna, swordfish, snapper, grouper, sea bass, mahi-mahi, tilapia, seafood

1335 **Big J Milling Co**
733 W Forest St
Brigham City, UT 84302-2052
435-723-3459
Fax: 435-723-3450 www.brigham.net
Grain and flour. Founded in 1909.
President: Brent Baugh
bgbaugh@brigham.net
Owner: Mike Chadwick
Owner: Ken Sutton
Vice President: Ray Reese
Sales Executive: Scott Reese
Estimated Sales: $2.6 Million
Number Employees: 10-19
Type of Packaging: Consumer, Food Service, Private Label

1336 **Big Mountain Foods**
Vancouver, BC V5X 3E8
Canada
bigmountainfoods.com
Vegan prepared meals
Year Founded: 1987

1337 **Big Picture Farm LLC**
1600 Peaked Mountain Road
PO Box 344
Townshend, VT 05353
802-221-0547
bigpicturefarm@gmail.com
www.bigpicturefarm.com
Candy, caramels, and cheese.
Founder: Iouisa Conrad
Co-Founder: Luke Farrell
Square Footage: 80000

1338 **Big Poppa Smokers**
53973 Polk St.
Coachella, CA 92236
877-828-0727
customerservice@bigpoppasmokers.com
www.bigpoppasmokers.com
Manufacturer of grills & smokers, rubs, meat sauces and cutlery.
President and CEO: Sterling Ball
Square Footage: 80000

1339 **Big Red Bottling**
6500 River Place Boulevard
Building 1, Suite 450
Austin, TX 78730
254-772-7791
Fax: 254-772-2441 www.bigred.com
Carbonated soft drinks
Chairman & CEO: Gary Smith
Year Founded: 1937
Estimated Sales: $20-50 Million
Number Employees: 20-49
Parent Co: Dr Pepper Snapple Group
Brands:
Diet Big Red ®
Big Blue ®
Big Red Vanilla Float ®
Big Peach ®
Big Pineapple ®
Nugrape ®
Nesbitts ®

1340 **Big Rock Brewery**
5555 76th Avenue SE
Calgary, AB T2C 4L8
Canada
403-720-3239
Fax: 403-236-7523 800-242-3107
beer@bigrockbeer.com www.bigrockbeer.com
Beer, ale, stout and lager
President & CEO: Wayne Arsenault
Chief Financial Officer: Don Sewell
Head Brewmaster: Paul Gautreau
Director of Marketing: Susanne Fox
VP Sales: Paul Howden
Business Development Manager: Dennis Carr
Estimated Sales: G
Number Employees: 100-249
Type of Packaging: Consumer, Food Service

1341 **Big Russ Beer Cheese**
237 South Main St.
Beaver Dam, KY 42320
270-485-6544
www.bigrussbeercheese.com
Manufacturer of beer cheese.
Square Footage: 80000

1342 **Big Shoulders Coffee**
1105 W Chicago Ave
Chicago, IL 60642
312-846-1883
information@bigshoulderscoffee.com
www.bigshoulderscoffee.com
Coffee
Founder: Tim Coonan
General Manager: Abigail Helmus
VP Operations: Gregg Piazzi
Director of Sales: Dave Marsalek
Year Founded: 2012
Number Employees: 20-49

1343 **(HQ)Big Sky Brands**
3289 Lenworth Dr
Unit A
Mississauga, ON L4X 2H1
Canada
416-599-5415
www.bigskybrands.com
Candy, mints and soda.
Co-Founder: Ron Cheng
Co-Founder: Steve Yacht
Type of Packaging: Private Label
Other Locations:
Big Sky Brands
Chicago IL
Big Sky Brands
Buffalo NY
Big Sky Brands
Los Angeles CA
Brands:
Co2 Hard Candy
Diablo Ignited Sours
Drive Activated
Green-T Energy Mints
Jones Soda Carbonated Candy
Jones Soda Carbonated Sours
Jones Soda Energy Boosters
Jones Sours
Love Mints
Make Out Mints
Playboy Mints
Warp Energy Mints
Warp Micro Hyper Charged Mints
Sunkist Citrus

1344 **Big Sky Brewing Co**
5417 Trumpeter Way
P.O.Box 17170
Missoula, MT 59808-8680
406-549-2777
Fax: 406-549-1919 800-559-2774
info@bigskybrew.com www.bigskybrew.com
Ale and stout. Founded in 1995.
President: Neal Leathers
neal@bigskybrew.com
Sales Executive: Bjorn Nabozney
VP Production: Kris Nabozney
Estimated Sales: $3 Million
Number Employees: 20-49
Square Footage: 96000
Type of Packaging: Consumer, Food Service, Bulk
Brands:
Big Sky Ipa
Moose Drool Brown Ale
Powder Hound Winter Ale
Scape Goat Pale Ale

Summer Honey Seasonal Ale
Trout Slayer Ale

1345 **Big Spoon Roasters**
4517 Hillsborough Rd
#101-B
Durham, NC 27705
919-309-9100
info@bigspoonroasters.com
www.bigspoonroasters.com
Nut butters and nut butter snack bars
Founder: Mark Overbay
Marketing & Communications Manager: Mackenzie Props
Regional Sales Representative: Andrew Anderson
Director of Operations: Michael Silver
Year Founded: 2011
Number Employees: 10-19

1346 **Big Steer**
9101 Lipan Rd # 108
Houston, TX 77063-5559
713-782-2444
Fax: 713-785-0730 800-421-4951
bigsteer@live.com www.bigsteer.biz
Manufacturer microwave fudge and gourmet snack mixes. Founded in 1989.
President: Grant Nichols
Estimated Sales: $1-5 Million
Number Employees: 5-9
Type of Packaging: Private Label

1347 **Big Train Inc**
25392 Commercentre Dr
Lake Forest, CA 92630
949-340-8800
Fax: 949-707-1000 800-244-8724
www.bigtrain.com
Ice blended coffees, flavored syrups, and specialty beverage mixes. Founded in 1991.
CEO: Mike Dunn
CFO: Kevin Smith
VP, Supply Chain: Steve Schartg
International Sales: Rachel Pena
Customer Service Supervisor: Shannon Haskill
Estimated Sales: $10-12 Million
Number Employees: 1-4
Square Footage: 72000
Type of Packaging: Bulk

1348 **Big Tree Farms**
2305 Ashland St
Suite C506
Ashland, OR 97520
541-488-5605
info@bigtreefarms.com
bigtreefarms.com
Coconut products including oil and sugar.
Co-Founder: Ben Ripple
Number Employees: 11-50
Brands:
Los Cantores

1349 **Big Watt Coffee**
Minneapolis, MN 55408
info@bigwattcoffee.com
bigwattcoffee.com
Cold press coffee
Co-Founder: Lee Carter
Co-Founder: Jason Westplate
Co-Founder: Caleb Garn

1350 **Bigelow Tea**
201 Black Rock Tpke
Fairfield, CT 06825
888-244-3569
info@bigelowtea.com www.bigelowtea.com
Tea bags and tea including organic, loose, hot and iced
President: David Bigelow
Executive Vice President: Donald Janezic
Assistant Marketing Manager: Cindy Manning
Warehouse Coordinator: Steve Koch
Year Founded: 1945
Estimated Sales: $94 Million
Number Employees: 250-499
Number of Brands: 1
Brands:
Bigelow

1351 **Bijol & Spices Inc**
2154 NW 22nd Ct
Miami, FL 33142-7346
305-634-9030
Fax: 305-634-7454 888-245-6570
info@bijol.com www.bijol.com
Contract packager and exporter of spices and herbs. Founded in 1991.
President: Ida Borges
Vice President: Diego Borges
Estimated Sales: $2.5-5 Million
Number Employees: 5-9
Type of Packaging: Consumer

1352 **Bilgore's Groves**
807 Court Street
Clearwater, FL 34616-1525
727-442-2171
Fax: 727-446-3998
Fruits
Manager: Evelyn Tumber
Estimated Sales: $500-1 Million appx.
Number Employees: 1-4

1353 **Bilinski Sausage Mfg Co**
41 Lark St
Cohoes, NY 12047-4618
518-237-0171
Fax: 518-237-0205 877-873-9102
info@bilinski.com www.bilinski.com
Many flavors of all natural and organic chicken sausages. 100% all natural, antibiotic-free, and fully cooked.
Owner: Steve Schonwetter
info@bilinski.com
Number Employees: 20-49
Type of Packaging: Consumer

1354 **Bill's Seafood**
9016 Belair Rd
Baltimore, MD 21236-2120
410-256-9520
Fax: 410-256-3491
www.billsseafoodandcatering.net
Seafood
Owner: Bill Paulshock
bscrabs@aol.com
Estimated Sales: $5-10 Million
Number Employees: 20-49

1355 **(HQ)Billingsgate Fish Company**
1941 Uxbridge Drive NW
Calgary, AB T2N 2V2
Canada
403-571-7700
Fax: 403-571-7717 www.billingsgate.com
Processor and packager of fish, meat and deli products; wholesaler/distributor of meats and seafood; serving the food service market. Founded in 1966.
President/Board Member: Bryan Fallwell
Sales Representative: Brenda Shreindorfer
Operations Manager: Mark Puffer
Estimated Sales: $2.8 Million
Number Employees: 20
Square Footage: 140000
Type of Packaging: Consumer, Food Service
Other Locations:
Billingsgate Fish Company
Edmonton, Alberta
Billingsgate Fish Company
St. Albert, Alberta
Brands:
Billingsgate
King of Fish
Plough Boy

1356 **Billy's Seafood Inc**
16780 River Rd
Bon Secour, AL 36511-3428
251-949-6288
Fax: 251-949-6505 888-424-5597
billys@gulftel.com www.billys-seafood.com
Seafood
Owner: Billy Parks
billys@gulftel.com
Estimated Sales: $2,000,000
Number Employees: 1-4

1357 **Biloxi Freezing Processing Inc.**
PO Box 730
Biloxi, MS 39533
228-436-0017
Fax: 228-436-0019 biloxifreezing.com
Frozen shrimp
President: Mark Mavar
Number Employees: 20-49
Type of Packaging: Consumer, Food Service, Private Label
Brands:
Captain Joey
M&M
Suarez

1358 **Biltmore Estate Wine Company**
1 Lodge St
Asheville, NC 28803
800-411-3812
www.biltmore.com
Wines
President & CEO: Bill Cecil
SVP & CFO: Steve Watson
Director of Marketing: Heather Jordan
hjordan@biltmore.com
Estimated Sales: $138.8 Million
Number Employees: 1,800
Number of Brands: 2
Brands:
Biltmore
Antler Hill

1359 **Bimbo Bakeries USA Inc.**
255 Business Center Dr.
PO Box 976
Horsham, PA 19044
Fax: 610-320-9286 800-984-0989
www.bimbobakeriesusa.com
Bread and sweet baked goods.
President: Fred Penny
Year Founded: 1998
Estimated Sales: Over $1 Billion
Number Employees: 20,000
Number of Brands: 20
Parent Co: Grupo Bimbo
Brands:
Thomas'®
Sara Lee®
Nature's Harvest®
Arnold®
Brownberry®
Oroweat®
Entenmann's®
Ball Park®
Marinela®
Bimbo®
Maier's®
eureka!®
Beefsteak®
Boboli®
Mrs Baird's®
Freihofer's®
Heiner's
Grandma Sycamore's®
Tia Rosa®
Stroehmann®
Beefsteak(c)
D'Italiano(c)

1360 **Bindi North America**
630 Belleville Tpke
Kearny, NJ 07032-4407
973-812-8118
Fax: 973-812-5020 info@bindiusa.com
www.bindiusa.com
Manufacturer of cakes, gelato, croissants, dessert sauces and other delicacies.
President: Attilio Bindi
Vice President: Stefano Del Verme
sdelverme@bindiusa.com
Number Employees: 100-249
Square Footage: 80000
Brands:
bindi

1361 **Binding Brauerei USA**
194 Main St # 1
Norwalk, CT 06851-3502
203-229-0111
Fax: 203-229-0105 www.bindingusa-beers.com
Beer and ale.
President: Hans Schliebs
CEO: Dilip Mehta
VP Sales: Dave Deuser
Estimated Sales: $5-10 Million
Number Employees: 10-19
Parent Co: Radeberger Gruppe GmbH
Brands:
Clausthaler
Dab
Krusovice

Radeberger
Tucher

1362 **Bingo Salsa, LLC**
2001 Nw Swanlund Street
Poulsbo, WA 98370-9528
360-779-6746
Fax: 360-930-8377 bingosalsa67@yahoo.com
www.bingosalsas.com
Makers of canned fruits and specialties. Founded in 2004.
Principal: Lisa Hudson
mamabread@yahoo.com

1363 **Binkert's Meat Products**
8805 Philadelphia Rd
Baltimore, MD 21237-4310
410-687-5959
Fax: 410-687-5023 binkertsmeat@comcast.net
www.binkerts.com
Manufacturer and distributor of German style lunch meats and sausages. FOunded in 1964.
President: Sonya Weber
Managing Partner: Luthar Weber
Estimated Sales: $300,000-500,000
Number Employees: 5
Square Footage: 11200

1364 **Binns Vineyards & Winery**
525 Roadrunner Lane
Las Cruces, NM 8800550348
575-526-6738
Fax: 575-522-1112
Wines
Owner: Eddie Binns
Vice President: Glenn Binns
Estimated Sales: $1-4.9 Million
Number Employees: 5-9
Type of Packaging: Private Label

1365 **Bio-Botanica Inc**
75 Commerce Dr
Hauppauge, NY 11788-3943
631-231-5522
Fax: 631-231-7332 800-645-5720
www.bio-botanica.com
Botanical extracts and flavors
Owner/CEO: Frank D'Amelio
President: Josephine Perricone
CFO: William O'Reilly
VP R&D: Dr. Youssef Mirhom
Quality Control: William Wilson
Marketing Director: Dorie Greenblatt
VP Sales: Mark Sysler
Estimated Sales: $5-10 Million
Number Employees: 100-249
Number of Products: 300
Square Footage: 560000
Type of Packaging: Food Service, Private Label, Bulk

1366 **Bio-Foods**
104 Bloomfield Avenue
Pine Brook, NJ 07058
973-808-5856
Fax: 973-396-2999 bobkoetzner@aol.com
www.biofoodsltd.com
Manufacturer and exporter of nutrients and spices.
President: Bharat Patel
Vice President: Robert Koetzner
Number Employees: 5-9
Square Footage: 36000
Type of Packaging: Bulk
Brands:
Bio-Foods

1367 **Bio-Hydration Research Lab**
2091 Rutherford Road
Carlsbad, CA 92008
760-438-6686
Fax: 760-268-0808 800-531-5088
sales@pentawater.com www.pentawater.com
Bio-Hydration; a molecular restructured water that hydrates faster and provides enhanced performance and healthy living. Founded in 1999.
CEO: Bill Holloway
Chief Financial Officer: Ernest Ho
CEO: Dennis O'Bryan
Public Relations Manager: Jeffrey Pizzino
Estimated Sales: $5-10 Million
Number Employees: 50-99
Number of Brands: 1
Number of Products: 2
Square Footage: 220000
Type of Packaging: Consumer
Brands:
Penta

1368 **Bio-K + International Inc.**
Parc Scientifique
495 boul. Armand-Frappier
Laval, QC H7V 4B3
Canada
450-978-2465
Fax: 450-978-9729 800-593-2465
info@biokplus.com www.biokplus.com
President: Pavel Hamet
Marketing Director: Michael Sirdemt
CFO: Michael Rheault
Year Founded: 1996
Brands:
Bio K

1369 **Bio-Nutritional Products**
119 Rockland Ave
Northvale, NJ 07647-2144
201-784-8200
Fax: 201-784-8201
President: Stephen Difolco
Brands:
Eugalan
Lacto

1370 **Bio-Tech Pharmacal Inc**
3481 N Hwy 112
Fayetteville, AR 72704-7437
479-443-9148
Fax: 479-443-5643 800-345-1199
customerservice@bio-tech-pharm.com
www.biotechpharmacal.com
Hypo-allergenic nutraceuticals, vitamins, minerals, herbals, anti-oxidants, amino acids, etc. Founded in 1984.
Chairman: Dale Benedict
service@bio-tech-pharm.com
Director, Sales/Marketing: Lora Daniel
Facility Manager: Mark Leason
Number Employees: 10-19
Number of Brands: 1
Type of Packaging: Consumer, Private Label, Bulk
Brands:
Bio-Tech Pharmacal

1371 **BioAmber**
3850 Annapolis Ln N
Suite 180
Plymouth, MN 55447
763-253-4480
kristine.weigal@bio-amber.com
Succinic acid, BDO, plasticizers, polymers and C6 chemicals
President & CEO: Jean-Francois HUC
CTO: Jim Millis
CFO: Andrew Ashworth
Executive VP: Mike Hartmann
Chief Commercial Officer: Babette Pettersen
Contact: Marie Beaumont
marie.beaumont@bio-amber.com
Chief Operations Officer: Fabrice Orecchioni
Estimated Sales: $560 Thousand
Number Employees: 74

1372 **BioExx Specialty Proteins**
33 Fraser Ave
Suite G11
Toronto, ON M6K 3J9
Canada
416-588-4442
Fax: 416-588-1999 www.bioexx.com
Oil and high-value proteins from Canola.
CEO & Director: Chris Schnarr
CFO: Greg Furyk
EVP: Samah Garringer
VP Operations: Clinton Smith

1373 **BioSynergy**
PO Box 16833
Boise, ID 83706-6414
208-342-6660
Fax: 208-342-0880 800-554-7145
email@biosynergy.com www.biosynergy.com
Health related products and nutritional supplements. FOunded in 1994.
President/Owner: Ted Kremer
tdoty@cves.org
CEO: Hidemi Ogino
Marketing Director: Hidemi Kremer
Estimated Sales: $200,000
Number Employees: 1-4
Brands:
Nojo

1374 **(HQ)BioTech Corporation**
107 Oakwood Dr Ste E
Glastonbury, CT 06033
860-633-8111
Fax: 860-682-6863 800-886-9052
info@dermasilkbrands.com
Nutraceuticals and nutritional supplements. Founded in 1994.
President: Gregory Kelly
Contact: Lisa Livingston
llivingston@biotechcorp.com
Estimated Sales: $5-10 Million
Number Employees: 10-19

1375 **BioVittoria USA**
357 N Milwaukee Rd
Libertyville, IL 60048
847-226-3467
Processor and supplier of monk fruit, a natural calorie-free sweetener that is a new alternative to sugar and artificial sweeteners.
President: Lan Fusheng
CEO: David Thorrold
CFO: Danny Wai Yen
VP: Garth Smith
VP Sales & Marketing: Paul Paslaski
Estimated Sales: $500 Thousand
Type of Packaging: Food Service, Private Label, Bulk

1376 **Bioenergy Life Science**
13840 Johnson St NE
Andover, MN 55304-6922
763-757-0032
Fax: 763-757-0588 877-474-2673
info@bioenergyls.com www.theribosecompany.biz
Our focus is on the bulk ribose sale business for food and beverage and dietary supplements. Supplement
President: Tom VonderBrink
Chairman/Chief Executive Officer: Leo Zhang
Regional Director: Marianne McDonagh
EVP/Chief Technology Officer: Alex Xue
Technical Sales Manager: Michael Crabtree
Executive Director, Supply Chain Mgmt.: Adia Edwards
Director of Marketing: Penny Portner
Office Administrator: Greta Kaster
Director, Business Administration: Michelle Wald
Research Scientist: Pat Starks
Warehouse Manager: Nick Jacobson
Shipping & Receiving Manager: Lori Huntley
Number Employees: 10-19

1377 **Bionutritional ResearchGroup**
15375 Barranca Pkwy
Suite C104
Irvine, CA 92618-2206
714-427-6990
Fax: 714-427-6998
Nutritional products, protein powder and bars, supplements. Founded in 1991.
Owner: Kevin Lawrence
President/CEO: Kevin Stensby
Sales Executive: Ken Braunstein
VP Operations: Tom Williams
Estimated Sales: $15 Million
Number Employees: 5-9
Brands:
Alpha Glutamine
Cell Charge®
Power Crunch®
Proto Whey®

1378 **Bioriginal Food and Science Corp**
102 Melville Street
Saskatoon, SK S7J 0R1
Canada
306-975-1166
Fax: 306-242-3829 business@bioriginal.com
www.bioriginal.com
Essential fatty acids, omega 3, omega 6, and omega 9.
President/CEO: Joe Vidal
EVP Global Marketing/Sales: Johan Kamphuis
VP Operations: Cameron Kupper

1379 **Biospringer**
7475 West Main St
Milwaukee, WI 53214
414-615-4100
Fax: 414-615-4005 866-424-1158
customer.service@biospringer-na.com
www.biospringer-na.com
Natural yeast
Marketing Manager: Marilyn Stieve
Contact: Chris Kaltenbach
chris.kaltenbach@lsaf.com

1380 **Biotec A Z Laboratories**
20809 N 19th Avenue
Suite 1
Phoenix, AZ 85027-3519
800-218-6979
Fax: 623-576-2285
Supplements and vitamins.
President: Tyler Rosales

1381 **Biothera**
3388 Mike Collins Dr # A
Suite A
St Paul, MN 55121-2409
651-675-0300
Fax: 651-657-0400 info@biothera.com
www.biothera.com
Food-grade immune-enhancing ingredients for the nutritional supplement, functional food, cosmetic and animal feed nutrition markets.
Founder/Chairman: Daniel Conners
Chief Executive Officer: Richard G Mueller
rmueller@biotherapharma.com
Chief Financial Officer: William Gacki
Senior Vice President: James Horstmann
SVP, Research & Development: Donald Cox, Ph.D.
SVP, Marketing & Communications: David Walsh
SVP, Business Development: Steve Smith
COO, Research & Technology: Steven Karel
Estimated Sales: $3-5 Million
Number Employees: 50-99
Type of Packaging: Bulk

1382 **Birch Benders**
3316 Tejon St
Unit 107
Denver, CO 80211
855-572-6225
Fax: 303-502-1112 info@birchbenders.com
birchbenders.com
Toaster waffles and pancake and waffle mixes
Co-Founder: Matt Lacasse
Co-Founder: Lizzi Ackerman

1383 **Birch Street Seafoods**
31 Birch St
Digby, NS B0V 1A0
Canada
902-245-6551
Fax: 902-245-6554
Processor and exporter of fresh and frozen salted groundfish
Vice President: William Cottreau
Contact: Janice Oliver
Plant Manager: Alan Frankland
Estimated Sales: $500,000-1 Million
Number Employees: 25
Type of Packaging: Consumer, Food Service, Private Label, Bulk

1384 **Birchwood Foods Inc**
3111 152nd Ave
PO Box 639
Kenosha, WI 53144-7630
262-859-2272
Fax: 262-859-2078 800-541-1685
bwinfo@bwfoods.com www.bwfoods.com
Manufactuer and exporter of cryogenically frozen and vacuum-packed fresh ground beef in bulk and patties; importer of boneless beef
President, CEO & Director: Dennis Vignieri
CEO: Cindy Anderson
canderson@bwfoods.com
CFO & Director: Jerry King
VP HR & Safety: Phyllis Murray
Quality Assurance Supervisor: Cathy Miller
VP Sales & Marketing: Wayne Wehking
EVP Operations & Procurement: John Ruffolo
Product Manager: Doug Ladd
Manager of Purchasing: Alex Savaglio
Estimated Sales: $2.76 Million
Number Employees: 500-999
Square Footage: 240000
Type of Packaging: Consumer, Food Service, Private Label, Bulk
Other Locations:
Frankfort Manufacturing Facility
Frankfort IN
Columbus Manufacturing Facility
Columbus OH
Atlanta Manufacturing Facility
Atlanta GA

1385 **(HQ)Bird-In-Hand Farms Inc**
1708 Columbia Ave # 1
Lancaster, PA 17603-4550
717-291-9904
Fax: 717-291-1990 www.bihfarms.com
Poultry. Founded in 1949.
Owner: Frederick Bloom
VP Sales: Ted Bloom
fred.bloom@bihfarms.com
Estimated Sales: $5-10 Million
Number Employees: 5-9
Type of Packaging: Private Label
Other Locations:
Bird-In-Hand Farms
Chapin SC
Bird-In-Hand Farms
Jackson MI
Bird-In-Hand Farms
Huntington IN
Bird-In-Hand Farms
Nacogdoches TX
Bird-In-Hand Farms
Monett MO
Bird-In-Hand Farms
Topsail Beach NC
Bird-In-Hand Farms
Russellville AR
Bird-In-Hand Farms
Southern Pines NC
Brands:
Bird-In-Hand
Truly Dutch

1386 **Birdie Pak Products**
3925 W 31st St
Chicago, IL 60623-4934
773-247-5293
Fax: 773-247-4280 www.birdiepak.com
Processor and distributor of frozen beef, poultry and fish
President: Thomas Krueger
VP: Kevin Krueger
Estimated Sales: $2.5-5 Million
Number Employees: 10-19
Type of Packaging: Consumer, Food Service, Private Label
Brands:
Birdie Pak

1387 **Birdsall Ice Cream Company**
518 N Federal Ave
Mason City, IA 50401-3216
641-423-5365
Ice cream. Founded in 1968.
Owner: Vaughn Escher
Owner: Dave Escher
Estimated Sales: $1 Million
Number Employees: 22
Type of Packaging: Consumer, Food Service

1388 **Birdseye Dairy-Morning Glory**
2325 Memorial Dr
Green Bay, WI 54303-6399
920-494-5388
Fax: 920-494-4388 www.birdseyejuice.com
Apple and orange juice; wholesaler/distributor of dairy products including milk, ice cream, butter and sour cream; serving the food service market. Founded in 1925.
President: Steven Williams
steve.williamss@birdseye.com
Estimated Sales: $10-20 Million
Number Employees: 10-19
Type of Packaging: Consumer, Food Service, Private Label, Bulk
Brands:
Birdseye
Morning Glory

1389 **Birdseye Food**
1 Old Bloomfield Rd.
Mountain Lakes, NJ 07046
585-383-1850
Fax: 585-385-1281 www.birdseye.com
Frozen vegetables, frozen complete bagged meals, canned pie fillings, chili and bottled salad dressings.
President/CEO, Conagra Brands: Sean Connolly
Year Founded: 1923
Estimated Sales: $399 Million
Number Employees: 100-249
Square Footage: 15333
Parent Co: Conagra Brands, Inc.
Type of Packaging: Consumer, Food Service, Bulk
Other Locations:
Fennville MI
Waseca MN
Fulton NY
Berlin PA
Algona WA
Tacoma WA
Darien WI
Green Bay WI
Brands:
Birds Eye®

1390 **Birdsong Corp.**
612 Madison Ave.
PO Box 1400
Suffolk, VA 23434-1400
757-539-3456
Fax: 757-539-7360 www.birdsongpeanuts.com
Raw peanuts.
President: Jeff Johnson
CEO: George Birdsong
gbirdsong@birdsong-peanuts.com
CFO: Stephen Huber
Year Founded: 1914
Estimated Sales: $50.50 Million
Number Employees: 500-999
Square Footage: 10000
Type of Packaging: Food Service
Other Locations:
Birdsong Corp.
Gorman TX

1391 **Birkett Mills**
PO Box 440
Penn Yan, NY 14527
315-536-3311
Fax: 315-536-6740 contact@thebirkettmills.com
www.thebirkettmills.com
Flour
President & COO: Jeff Gifford
CEO: Wayne Wagner
Sales Executive: Cliff Orr
Contact: Don Habberfield
dhabberfield@thebirkettmills.com
Estimated Sales: $1-2.5 Million
Number Employees: 40
Type of Packaging: Consumer, Private Label, Bulk
Brands:
Bessie
Pocono
Puritan
Wolffs

1392 **Birkholm's Solvang Bakery**
460 Alisal Rd
Solvang, CA 93463-2726
805-688-8188
Fax: 805-686-4407 800-377-4253
www.birkholmsbakery.com
Processor and exporter of bread, cake and Danish tarts
President: Susan Halme
susan@solvangbakery.com
General manager: Melissa Redell
Estimated Sales: Less Than $500,000
Number Employees: 5-9
Type of Packaging: Consumer, Food Service

1393 **Birnn Chocolates of Vermont**
102 Kimball Ave
Suite 4
South Burlington, VT 05403
Fax: 802-860-1256 800-338-3141
www.birnn.com
Premium wholesale truffles
President: H Birnn
bh@birnn.com
Co-Owner: Bill Birnn
VP: Bill Birnn
Estimated Sales: $2 Million
Number Employees: 20-49
Type of Packaging: Private Label

1394 **(HQ)Biscomerica Corporation**
565 West Slover Avenue
PO Box 1070
Rialto, CA 92377-1070
909-877-5997
Fax: 909-877-3593 info@biscomerica.com
www.biscomerica.com
Manufacturer of cookies, chocolates and candies.
President/CEO: Nadi Soltan
Contact: Dina Fangary
dfangar@biscomerica.com
Year Founded: 1980
Estimated Sales: $30 Million
Number Employees: 250-499
Number of Brands: 4
Square Footage: 250000
Type of Packaging: Consumer, Food Service, Private Label, Bulk
Brands:
Checkers Cookies
Granny's Oven
Knott's Berry Farms
Sun Maid

1395 **(HQ)Biscoti Di Suzy**
1070 40th St
Oakland, CA 94608-3617
510-923-0446
Fax: 510-923-0344 800-211-5903
info@crunchyfoods.com www.crunchyfoods.com
Cookies, other baked goods.
Owner/CEO: Karen Jackson
Marketing: Will Tassi
Estimated Sales: $5-9.9 Million
Number Employees: 10-19
Type of Packaging: Consumer, Food Service, Private Label, Bulk
Brands:
Biscotti Di Suzy™

1396 **Biscottea**
23216 SE 135th Ct
Issaquah, WA 98027
425-313-1993
Fax: 425-427-0709 info@biscottea.net
www.biscottea.net
Organic, all natural flavored shortbread
President/Owner: Laurance Milner
Number Employees: 2

1397 **Biscotti & Co.**
145-157 St John Street
White Plains, NY EC1V 4PW
914-682-2165
Fax: 914-328-4276
Bulk and wrapped shelf stable biscotti and gourmet cookies
President: Gary Spirer
Marketing Director: Jerry O'Donnell
Sales Director: Debbie Rittberg
General Manager: Jerry O'Donnell
Number Employees: 10-19
Square Footage: 36000
Type of Packaging: Consumer, Bulk
Brands:
Alex & Dani's Biscotti
Karen's Fabulous Biscotti

1398 **Biscotti Goddess**
3910 Amberleigh Blvd
Richmond, VA 23236
804-745-9490
www.biscotti-goddess.com
Manufacturer of biscotti. Founded in 2007.
Owner: Jan Defalco
Number Employees: 1-4

1399 **Bishop Brothers**
113 W 5th Ave
Bristow, OK 74010-2824
918-367-2270
Fax: 918-367-2270 800-859-8304
info@bishoptaboli.com www.bishoptaboli.com
Wholesaler/distributor of bulgur wheat including tabbouleh; custom packaging services available. Founded in 1962.
Owner: Eddie Bishop
ebishop07@aol.com
Estimated Sales: $2.5-5 Million
Number Employees: 1-4
Type of Packaging: Consumer, Food Service, Bulk

1400 **Bishop Farms Winery**
500 S Meriden Rd
Cheshire, CT 06410-2968
203-272-8243
Fax: 203-272-7344
Manufacturer of wines
President: John Romanik
Owner: Mary Romanik
Marketing Director: Mary Romanik
Contact: Kevin Clark
crystal6156@yahoo.com
Estimated Sales: $500,000-$1 Million
Number Employees: 1-4

1401 **Bison Brewing Company**
PO Box 4821
Berkeley, CA 94704-4821
510-697-1537
Fax: 510-217-4332 info@bisonbrew.com
www.bisonbrew.com
Organic Beer. Founded in 1989.
Owner: Dan DelGarande
Sales Representative: Rich Schwanbeck
Estimated Sales: $5-10 Million
Number Employees: 10-19
Brands:
Barley Wine Ale
Belgian Ale
Chocolate Stout
Farmhouse Saison
Gingerbread Ale
Honey Basil Ale
India Pale Ale
Red Ale
Winter Warmer

1402 **Bison Foods**
25 Anderson Rd
Buffalo, NY 14225
716-892-3156
www.bisonfoods.com
Dips and sour cream.
Chief Executive Officer: Larry Webster
Chief Operating Officer: Joe Duscher
Year Founded: 1931
Parent Co: Upstate Niagara Cooperative Inc.
Type of Packaging: Consumer

1403 **Bissett Produce Company**
P.O.Box 279
1436 North NC Hwy 581
Spring Hope, NC 27882-0279
252-478-4158
Fax: 252-478-7798 800-849-5073
Bissettproducecompanyinc@msn.com
Grower, packer and exporter of sweet potatoes, pickling cucumbers and banana and specialty peppers and seedless watermelons. Founded in 2001.
Manager: Don Sparks
Finance Executive: Dan Bissett
Vice President: Lee Bissett
Sales Director: Don Sparks
Contact: Dan Bissett
bissettproducecompanyinc@msn.com
Estimated Sales: $2.5-5 Million
Number Employees: 20
Square Footage: 240000
Type of Packaging: Consumer, Food Service, Private Label, Bulk
Brands:
Bissett's
Rue's Choice

1404 **(HQ)Bissinger's Handcrafted Chocolatier**
3983 Gratiot Street
St Louis, MO 63110
314-534-2401
Fax: 314-534-2419 800-325-8881
sales@bissingers.com www.bissingers.com
Boxed chocolates, sugar free chocolate and classic gourmet candies. Founded in 1995.
President: Ken Kellerhals
Contact: Charles Anton
canton@bissingers.com
Number Employees: 40

1405 **Bissinger's HandcraftedChocolatier**
1600 North Broadway
St. Louis, MO 63102
314-615-2400
www.bissingers.com
Fine chocolates and caramels.
CEO: Tim Fogerty
Estimated Sales: $6000000
Number Employees: 5-9
Type of Packaging: Consumer, Bulk

1406 **Bitchin' Sauce**
Carlsbad, CA 92010
www.bitchinsauce.com
Almond dip
Number of Brands: 1
Number of Products: 6
Type of Packaging: Consumer
Brands:
BITCHIN' SAUCE

1407 **Bite Fuel**
Oregon City, OR 97045
info@bitefuel.com
www.bitefuel.com
Cookies and trail mix
CEO: Eric Shen
Production Manager: Isabel Ayala
Number of Brands: 1
Number of Products: 8
Type of Packaging: Consumer
Brands:
BITE FUEL

1408 **Bite Size Bakery**
504 Frontage Rd NE
Rio Rancho, NM 87124
505-994-3093
www.bitesizebakery.com
Manufacturer of bite-sized cookies in a variety of flavours, including bizcochitos, pinon nut chocolate chip, lemon verde pistachio. ginger snap, and raisin oatmeal.
Owner: Lucia Deichmann
Parent Co: KDK Enterprises
Brands:
Bite-Size Bakery

1409 **Bitsy's Brainfood**
1 Little West 12th Street
New York, NY 10014
212-461-1572
www.bitsysbrainfood.com
Cookies and crackers
Co-Founder: Maggie Patton
Co-Founder: Alex Voris
Number of Brands: 1
Number of Products: 8
Type of Packaging: Consumer
Brands:
SMART CRACKERS
SMART COOKIES

1410 **Bitter Love**
Portland, ME 04101
www.bitterlove.com
Sparkling drinking bitters

1411 **Bittermilk LLC**
P.O. Box 13371
Charleston, SC 29422
843-641-0455
drink@bittermilk.com
bittermilk.com
Alcoholic cocktail mixers with natural ingredients
Co-Founder: Joe Raya
Co-Founder: MariElena Raya
Brands:
Michel de France(c)

1412 **Bittersweet Herb Farm**
635 Mohawk Trl
Shelburne Falls, MA 01370-9775
413-625-6523
Fax: 413-625-0166 800-456-1599
dave@bittersweetherbfarm.com
www.bittersweetherbfarm.com
Wasabi ginger sauce, lemon garlic sauce, strawberry jam and all natural seasonings. Also flavored oils and balsamic vinegars. Founded in 1983.
Owner: Dave Lemon
dave@bittersweetherbfarm.com
Estimated Sales: $1-2.5 Million
Number Employees: 10-19

1413 **Bittersweet Pastries**
385 Chestnut St
Norwood, NJ 07648-2001
201-768-7005
Fax: 973-882-6998 800-217-2938

Desserts including tarts, layer cakes, and flourless chocolate truffle cakes. Also sold frozen and dessert bars. Founded in 1984.
President: Bob Trier
Vice President: Louis Florencia
info@bittersweetpastries.com
Estimated Sales: $1-5 Million
Number Employees: 20-49
Square Footage: 18000
Parent Co: Fairfield Gourmet Foods Corporation
Type of Packaging: Food Service

1414 **Bixby & Co., LLC**
One Sea Street Place
Rockland, ME 04841
207-691-1778
info@bixbyco.com
www.bixbyco.com
Manufacturer of vegan chocolates.
Founder: Kate McAleer
kate@bixbyco.com
Brands:
Bixby Bar

1415 **Black Bear Farm Winery**
248 County Road 1
Chenango Forks, NY 13746-2208
607-656-9863
mamabear@blackbearwinery.com
www.blackbearwinery.com
Wines
President: Mark Stacey
Co-Owner: Sandy Stacey
Chief of Cider Production: Joe Stacey
Number Employees: 1-4

1416 **Black Bear Fruits**
N7832 County Rd M
New Lisbon, WI 53950
608-547-6133
www.blackbearfruits.com
Fruits and vegetables. Founded in 2010.
Contact: Ron Krizan
greenrugger@yahoo.com

1417 **Black Forest Organic**
Oakbrook Terrace Tower
1 Tower Lane, Suite 2700
Oakbrook Terrace, IL 60181
800-323-1768
www.ferrarausa.com
Non-chocolate confection
CEO: Todd Siwak
CFO: Tom Polke
Chief Operating Officer: Michael Murray
Year Founded: 1908
Number of Brands: 1
Number of Products: 16
Parent Co: Ferrara Candy Company
Type of Packaging: Consumer
Brands:
BLACK FOREST ORGANIC
TROLLI
NOW AND LATER
BRACH'S
BOB'S
RED HOTS
LEMONHEAD
SATHERS
JUJYFRUITS
BOSTON BAKED BEANS
ATOMIC FIREBALL
JAW BUSTERS
CHUCKLES
RAIN BLO
SUPER BUBBLE
FRUIT STRIPE

1418 **Black Garlic**
2499 American Ave
Hayward, CA 94545-1809
510-264-0227
888-811-9065
info@blackgarlic.com www.blackgarlic.com
Garlic. Founded in 2008.
CEO: Scott Kim
Contact: Sohee Lee
slee@myblackgarlic.com
Number Employees: 5-9

1419 **Black Hound New York**
226 India Street
Brooklyn, NY 11222
212-97 -505
Fax: 718-782-0621 800-344-4417
customerservice@blackhoundny.com
www.blackhoundny.com
Hard, soft and chocolate candies, cakes and delectibles. Founded in 2003.
President: Debbie Miller
Estimated Sales: $500,000-$1 Million
Number Employees: 10-19

1420 **Black Jewell Popcorn**
417 Washington St
Columbus, IN 47201
618-948-2303
Fax: 618-948-2505 800-948-2302
www.blackjewell.com
Black and red popcorn
President: Carole Klein
Owner: Charles Klein
Estimated Sales: $2.5-5 Million
Number Employees: 10-19
Type of Packaging: Private Label
Brands:
Black Jewell®
Crimson Jewell®

1421 **Black Market Gelato**
13158 Saticoy St
North Hollywood, CA 91605
818-983-6040
blackmarketgelato.com
Gelato and sorbet
Owner: Spin Mllynarik
Estimated Sales: Less than $500,000
Number Employees: 1-4
Type of Packaging: Consumer, Private Label

1422 **Black Mesa Winery**
1502 Highway 68
Velarde, NM 87582
505-852-2820
Fax: 505-852-2820 800-852-6372
jer@blackmesawinery.com
www.blackmesawinery.com
Wine
Co-Owner: Jerry Burd
Co-Owner: Lynda Burd
Event Coordinator: Karen Fielding
Estimated Sales: $500,000-$1 Million
Number Employees: 1-4
Type of Packaging: Private Label
Brands:
Black Mesa
Coyote Wine

1423 **Black Prince Distillery Inc**
691 Clifton Ave
PO Box 1999
Clifton, NJ 07011-4203
973-365-2050
Fax: 973-365-0746 rickn@blackprincedist.com
www.blackprincedistillery.com
Liquor, liqueurs and cordials
President: Robert Guttag
VP, Operations: Rick Noone
rnoone@blackprincedistillery.com
Estimated Sales: $3.2 Million
Number Employees: 20-49
Square Footage: 120000
Brands:
Black Prince
Devils Spring
Dorado
Llord's
Tj Toad

1424 **Black Ranch Organic Grains**
5800 Eastside Road
Etna, CA 96027-9753
916-467-3387
Seven grain cereals including wheat and barley
Owner: Dave Black
Co-Owner: Dawn Black
Estimated Sales: Under $500,000
Number Employees: 1-4
Type of Packaging: Consumer, Food Service
Brands:
Black Ranch Gourmet Grains

1425 **Black River Caviar**
0075 Sunset Dr
Breckenridge, CO 80424-7218
970-547-1542
Fax: 970-547-9707 888-315-0575
graham@blackrivercaviar.com
www.blackrivercaviar.com
Caviar
President: Graham Gaspard
Estimated Sales: $500 Thousand
Number Employees: 5
Type of Packaging: Consumer, Food Service

1426 **Black Sheep Vintners**
221 Main Street
PO Box 1851
Murphys, CA 95247
209-728-2157
Fax: 209-728-2157 info@blacksheepwinery.com
www.blacksheepwinery.com
Fine wines. Founded in 1983.
Owner: Steve Millier
CEO: David Olson
Marketing Director: Janis Olson
Estimated Sales: Less than $500,000
Number Employees: 1-4
Type of Packaging: Private Label

1427 **Black Shield**
5620 Venice Avenue NE
Albuquerque, NM 87113-2306
562- Ve-ice
Fax: 505-884-5643 800-653-9357
Specialty gourmet popcorn
President: Marc Moore
Estimated Sales: Less than $500,000
Number Employees: 1-4

1428 **Black's Barbecue**
215 N Main St
Lockhart, TX 78644-2121
512-398-2712
Fax: 512-398-6000 888-632-8225
info@blacksbbq.com www.blacksbbq.com
Barbequed sausage; wholesaler/distributor of meats including brisket, ribs, chicken, pork and loin. Established in 2009.
Manager: Steve Cloud
CEO: Terry Black
Owner: Norma Black
Co-Owner: Edgar Black
Manager: Barrett Black
barrett@blacksbbq.com
Estimated Sales: $300,000-500,000
Number Employees: 5-9
Type of Packaging: Bulk

1429 **Blackbear Coffee Company**
318 N Main St
Hendersonville, NC 28792-0407
828-692-6333
Fax: 828-692-6333
www.mountainshops.com/bear.html
Coffee
Manager: Bo Rodriquez
Estimated Sales: Less than $500,000
Number Employees: 5-9

1430 **Blackberry Patch**
PO Box 1639
Thomasville, GA 31799
229-558-9996
Fax: 229-558-9998 800-853-5598
fruittreats@blackberrypatch.com
www.blackberrypatch.com
Natural fruit syrups, jams, jellies, chocolate sauces and pancake mixes. Founded in 1999.
President: Randy Harvey
Owner: Harry Jones
Contact: Sabrina Cannon
sabrinac@blackberrypatch.com
Estimated Sales: $870,000
Number Employees: 11
Number of Brands: 2
Number of Products: 48
Type of Packaging: Consumer, Private Label

1431 **Blair's Sauces & Snacks**
188 Bay Ave
PO Box 363
Highlands, NJ 07732-1624
732-872-0755
Fax: 732-872-2035 800-982-5247
www.extremefood.com

Manufacturer of hot sauces, BBQ rubs and snacks.
Owner: Blair Lazar
Number of Brands: 1
Type of Packaging: Consumer
Brands:
Blair's

1432 **Blake Hill Preserves**
PO Box 118
Grafton, VT 05146-0118
802-289-1636
vicky@blakehillpreserves.com
www.blakehillpreserves.com
Manufacturer of chutneys, conserves, preserves and marmaldes made from organic ingredients.
Co-Founder: Vicky Allard
vicky@blakehillpreserves.com
Co-Founder: Joe Hanglin
Number Employees: 1-4
Square Footage: 80000

1433 **Blake's All Natural Foods**
178 Silk Farm Rd
Concord, NH 03301-8411
603-225-3532
Fax: 603-225-3390 info@blakesallnatural.com
www.blakesallnatural.com
Frozen natural, organic and family-sized meals
CEO: Sean M Connolly
sean@blakesallnature.com
Number Employees: 20-49

1434 **Blakely Freezer Locker**
12850 Magnolia Street
Blakeley, GA 31758-7055
229-723-3622
Fax: 229-723-9156
Frozen beef, pork and chicken, also hardwood smoked sausages and hams.
Owner: Douglas Huey Johnson
Owner: Deeann Benton Johnson
Estimated Sales: $2.5-5 Million
Number Employees: 5-9
Type of Packaging: Consumer
Other Locations:
Blakely GA

1435 **Blalock Seafood & Specialty**
24822 Canal Rd
Orange Beach, AL 36561-3894
251-974-5811
Fax: 251-974-5812
Manufacturer and wholesaler of seafood. Founded in 1992.
Owner: Pete Blalock
pblalock419@gmail.com
Estimated Sales: $4,000,000
Number Employees: 5-9
Type of Packaging: Consumer

1436 **Bland Farms INC**
1126 Raymond D Bland Rd
Glennville, GA 30427-7020
912-654-3048
Fax: 912-654-1330 800-752-0206
info@blandfarms.com www.blandfarms.com
Frozen foods and sweet onions. Founded in 2000.
Owner: Delbert Bland
delbert@blandfarms.com
Manager: Elbert Bland
Number Employees: 100-249

1437 **Blansh International**
2340 West Monte Vista Avenue
Turlock, CA 95380
209-250-1237
Fax: 408-279-8444
Ethnic foods. Founded in 1991.
President: Atoor Eliasnia
Estimated Sales: $250,000
Number Employees: 2

1438 **Blanton's**
229 West Main Street
Suite 202
Frankfort, KY 40601
502-223-9874
Fax: 423-337-3487 www.blantonsbourbon.com
Hard stick candy, molded and regular chocolate; also, seasonal products available. Founded in 1967.
Owner: Harld Blanton
Vice President: Betty Blanton
Estimated Sales: $500,000
Number Employees: 5-9
Type of Packaging: Consumer
Brands:
Blanton's

1439 **Blanver USA**
1515 S Federal Hwy
Suite 204
Boca Raton, FL 33432-7404
561-416-5513
Fax: 561-416-5563 tesau@blanver.com
www.blanver.com.br
Purified cellulose excipients, gums and gels used to increase fiber content, improve texture, stabilize and thicken food products.
President: Sergio Frangioni
Founder: Valdemir Passos
Contact: Scott Geary
scott.geary@blanver.com
Operations Manager: Rehanna Birbal
Estimated Sales: $1.3 Million
Parent Co: Blanver
Type of Packaging: Bulk

1440 **Blaser's USA, Inc.**
1858 US Highway 63
Comstock, WI 54826
715-822-2437
Fax: 715-822-8459 866-570-2439
Cheeses. Founded in 1947.
CEO: Paul Bauer
National VP Sales/Marketing: Jim Grande
Operations Manager: John Freyholtz
Plant Superintendent: Joe Hines
Estimated Sales: $500,000-$1 Million
Number Employees: 50-99
Parent Co: The Ellsworth Cooperative Creamery
Type of Packaging: Private Label
Brands:
Blaser's

1441 **Blau Oyster Co Inc**
11321 Blue Heron Rd
Bow, WA 98232-9326
360-766-6171
Fax: 360-766-6115 www.blauoyster.com
Processor and exporter of oysters. Founded in 1933.
President: Paul E Blau
blauoysterco@gmail.com
Marketing Manager: Pete Nordlund
Director of Operations: Paul Blau
Estimated Sales: $2.5-5 Million
Number Employees: 10-19
Type of Packaging: Consumer, Food Service, Private Label, Bulk

1442 **Blazzin Pickle Company**
6105 N 32nd Street
McAllen, TX 78505-5006
956-630-0733
Pickles including chips and spears
President: Craig Johnson
VP: Kathy Johnson
Number Employees: 1-4
Square Footage: 8000
Type of Packaging: Consumer, Food Service
Brands:
Blazzin

1443 **Blend Pak Inc**
10039 High Grove Rd
PO Box 458
Bloomfield, KY 40008-7178
502-252-8000
Fax: 502-252-8001 salesinfo@blendpak.com
www.blendpak.com
Manufactures batter, breaders, marinades, seasoning blends, specialty mixes, and custom blended dry formulas. Founded in 1990.
CEO/Human Resources Director: Dan Sutherland
dan@blendpak.com
EVP: Sue Sutherland
R&D: Linda Mikels
Quality Control: Rob Elkin
Operations: Dave Montgomery
Plant Manager: Matt Elder
Estimated Sales: $10 Million
Number Employees: 20-49
Square Footage: 44000
Type of Packaging: Food Service, Private Label, Bulk
Brands:
Blend Pak
Bloomfield Farms
Pier Fresh

1444 **Blendco Inc**
8 J M Tatum Industrial Dr
Hattiesburg, MS 39401-8341
601-544-9800
Fax: 601-544-5634 888-253-6326
csr@blendcoinc.com www.blendcoinc.com
Dry food manufacturer. Provide custom blending and packaging, as well as private labeling and contract packaging services.
President: Charles McCaffrey
Chief Financial Officer: Ken Hrdlica
Estimated Sales: $8 Million
Number Employees: 20-49
Number of Brands: 2
Type of Packaging: Food Service, Private Label, Bulk
Brands:
Ezy Time
Chicken-To-Go

1445 **Blendex Co**
11208 Electron Dr
Louisville, KY 40299-3875
502-267-1003
Fax: 502-267-1024 800-626-6325
www.blendex.com
Dry ingredients blending company specializing in batters, breadings, seasonings, seasonings and marinades. 12 distribution warehouses located across the US.
President: Jacquelyn Bailey
CEO: Ronald Pottinger
rpottinger@blendex.com
Director: Olin Cook
Executive Vice President: Tony Jessee
Vice President Research/Development: Jordan Stivers
Vice President of Sales: Ron Carr
Estimated Sales: $28.5 Million
Number Employees: 50-99
Type of Packaging: Food Service, Private Label, Bulk

1446 **Blendtopia**
Nashville, TN 37217
www.blendtopiafoods.com
Superfood smoothie kits
Founder: Tiffany Taylor

1447 **Blenheim Bottling Company**
P0 Box 452
Hamer, SC 29547
843-774-0322
Fax: 843-774-4018 800-270-9344
info@blenheimgingerale.com
www.blenheimgingerale.com
Jamaican ginger ale manufacturer. Founded in 1993.
President: Patty Schafer
CEO: Mackie Hayes
Manager: Ryan Schafer
Sales Director: Sheila McDowell
Estimated Sales: $2.5-5 Million
Number Employees: 5-9
Brands:
Blenheim

1448 **Blessed Herbs**
109 Barre Plains Rd
Oakham, MA 01068
508-882-3839
Fax: 508-882-3755 800-489-4372
info@blessedherbs.com www.blessedherbs.com
Manufacturer, importer and exporter of organic and wildcrafted dried herbs, extracts, formulas and tablets; also, echinacea angustifolia root; exporter and importer of dried herbs and colon cleansers.
Co-Founder: Michael Volchok
Co-Founder: Martha Volchok
CEO: Scott Leonard
Marketing Director: Shalom Volchok
Contact: Alicia Rocco
alicia@blessedherbs.com
Estimated Sales: $500,000-$1 Million
Number Employees: 14
Square Footage: 24000
Type of Packaging: Consumer, Bulk

1449 **Bletsoe's Cheese Inc**
8281 3rd Ln
Marathon, WI 54448-9522
715-443-2526
Fax: 715-443-6407 bletsoecheese@frontier.com

This company was founded in 1983 and is a producer of cheeses. Bletsoe's products include up to 27 types of cheese. Varieties include cheese curds, 22 lb. cheddar daises, 40 pound cheddar, pepper jack and colby.
President: David Bletsoe
Marketing Director: Bonnie Bletsoe
Estimated Sales: $5-10 Million
Number Employees: 10-19
Type of Packaging: Consumer
Brands:
Bletsoe's Cheese

1450 **Bleuet Nordic**
103 rue Boulianne
Dolbeau-Mistassini, QC G8L 6B1
Canada
418-239-1001
Fax: 418-239-0565 info@bleuetnordic.com
bleuetnordic.com
Frozen wild blueberries
Sales: Tim Dohan

1451 **Bliss Brothers Dairy, Inc.**
PO Box 2288
711 Park Street
Attleboro, MA 02703
508-222-2884
Fax: 508-226-6320 800-622-8789
www.blissdairy.com
Manufacturers of ice cream, frozen yogurt, sherbert, sorbet, and ice cream mixes
President: Dave Bliss
Chief Financial Officer: Kent Bliss
Contact: Thomas Bliss
tbliss@bristolfarms.com
Estimated Sales: $1-2.5 Million
Number Employees: 50-99

1452 **Bliss Gourmet Foods**
St. Paul, MN
blissgourmetfoods.com
Granola and muesli
Founder and Chef: Lesley Powers
Year Founded: 1908
Number of Brands: 1
Number of Products: 16
Type of Packaging: Consumer

1453 **Blissfully Better**
Chester, NJ 07930
www.blissfullybetter.com
Toffee sweetened with coconut nectar
CEO: Bonnie Boroian
Number of Brands: 1
Number of Products: 4
Type of Packaging: Consumer
Brands:
BLISSFULLY BETTER

1454 **Blk Enterprises**
214 W 39th Street
Room 202
New York, NY 10018-8323
212-764-3331
Fax: 212-764-3338 c.laurita@blkbeverages.com
Beverages. Founded in 2011
Contact: Chris Laurita
Number Employees: 1

1455 **(HQ)Blommer Chocolate Co**
600 W Kinzie St
Chicago, IL 60654-5585
312-226-7700
Fax: 312-226-4141 800-621-1606
www.blommer.com
Processor and exporter of chocolate ingredients for the bakery, dairy and confectionery industries including milk and dark chocolate, confectioner and pastel coatings, cookie drops, chocolate liquor, cocoa butter, cocoa powder, icecream ingredients, etc. Founded in 1939.
President: Peter Blommer
Founder, Chairman & CEO: Henry Blommer
CFO: Jack S Larsen
jack@blommer.com
Vice President: Rich Blommer
Manager of Quality Assurance: Radka Kacena
Marketing & Purchasing Manager: Leanna Hicks
Sales Support: Chief Marketing Officer Kidd
VP of Operations: Rich Blommer
Plant Mnaager: Joe Chwala
Purchasing Manager: Faye Garcia
Estimated Sales: $38.4 Million
Number Employees: 1-4
Square Footage: 340000
Type of Packaging: Bulk
Other Locations:
Union City CA
East Greenville PA
Campbellford ON

1456 **Blommer Chocolate Co**
1101 Blommer Dr
East Greenville, PA 18041-2140
215-679-4472
Fax: 215-679-4196 800-825-8181
klhicks@uc.blommer.com www.blommer.com
Chocolate
President: Peter Blommer
pblommer@uc.blommer.com
Estimated Sales: Less than $500,000
Number Employees: 100-249
Type of Packaging: Bulk
Other Locations:
Chicago IL
Union City CA

1457 **Bloom Honey**
805-379-0040
877-555-9300
www.bloomhoney.com
Raw honey
President/Owner: David Jefferson
Number of Brands: 1
Number of Products: 8
Type of Packaging: Consumer
Brands:
BLOOM

1458 **Bloomfield Bakers**
10711 Bloomfield St
Los Alamitos, CA 90720-2503
562-594-4411
Fax: 562-742-0408 800-594-4111
Cookies, cereals, crackers, bars and mixes. Founded in 1981.
President: Sam Calderon
Owner/CEO: William Ross
Research & Development Manager: Christina Lates
Quality Control Manager: Steve Huber
National Sales Manager: Russ Case
Contact: Raiza Bastidas
braiza@phonewareinc.com
COO: Gary Marx
Plant/Production Manager: Ricardo Gonzalez
Estimated Sales: $5-10 Million
Number Employees: 850
Square Footage: 300000
Type of Packaging: Private Label

1459 **Bloomfield Farms**
575 Spencer Mattingly Ln
Bardstown, KY 40004-9103
502-348-0012
Fax: 502-348-7711 www.thebloomfieldfarms.com
Gluten free mixes including brownies, pancakes, pizza dough and cake mixes
Manager: Davis Chesser
davisc@blendpak.com
Number Employees: 10-19

1460 **Bloomington Brewing Co**
1795 E 10th St
Bloomington, IN 47408-3975
812-323-2112
Fax: 812-333-3200 www.bloomingtonbrew.com
Ale and stout
Owner: Jessica May
jessica@bloomington.com
General Manager: Micheal Fox
Business Manager: Mark Cady
Marketing Director: Sera Shikh
Number Employees: 1-4
Parent Co: One World Enterprises
Type of Packaging: Consumer, Food Service, Bulk
Brands:
Bloomington Brewing
Quarrymen Pale

1461 **Bloomsberry LLC**
92 Jackson St
Salem, MA 01970-3068
978-745-9100
Fax: 978-745-9150 800-745-5154
sales@bloomsberry.com www.praimgroup.com
Chocolates. Founded in 2005.
Owner: Vanessa Kettelwell
vanessa@bloomsberry.com
VP: Kerry Francis
Estimated Sales: Less Than $500,000
Number Employees: 1-4

1462 **Blossom Farm Products**
545 State Rt 17
Suite 2003
Ridgewood, NJ 07450
201-493-2626
Fax: 201-493-2666 800-729-1818
Processor, importer and exporter of dairy products including milk powders, dry blends, whey, caseinates, lactose, butter fats, etc.
President: Paul Podell
Manager: Kathy Oviedo
VP: Marcia Podell
Operations Manager: Kathy Oviedo
Number Employees: 5-9
Type of Packaging: Consumer, Food Service, Bulk

1463 **Blossom Water, LLC**
PO Box 393
Westwood, MA 02090
855-325-5777
info@drinkblossomwater.com
www.drinkblossomwater.com
Flavoured water.
Founder & President: Steve Fortuna
Director of Sales: Mike Penta
Square Footage: 80000
Brands:
blossom water

1464 **Blount Fine Foods**
630 Currant Rd
Fall River, MA 02720
774-888-1300
www.blountfinefoods.com
Frozen seafood products including chopped clams, lobster bisque, clam chowder, variety of meats, hearty soups and an array of dips.
President: Todd Blount
Chief Innovation Officer: William Bigelow
bsewall@blountseafood.com
VP, Sales & Marketing: Bob Sewall
Director, Purchasing: Ed Sheehan
Estimated Sales: $46.60 Million
Number Employees: 50-99
Square Footage: 65000
Type of Packaging: Consumer, Food Service, Private Label, Bulk
Brands:
Blount
Gourmet Stuffed Clams
Point Judith
Sams Clams
White Cap

1465 **Blue Bell Creameries LP**
1101 S Blue Bell Rd
Brenham, TX 77833-4413
979-836-7977
Fax: 979-830-7398 800-327-8135
www.bluebell.com
Ice milk mix, ices, ice cream and frozen yogurt. FOunded in 1907.
CEO: Paul W Kruse
paul.kruse@bluebell.com
President/CEO: Paul Kruse
Chief Managing Officer: Melvin Zeigenbein
Number Employees: 1000-4999
Type of Packaging: Consumer, Food Service
Other Locations:
Sylacauga AL
Broken Arrow OK
Brenham TX
Brands:
Blue Bell Ice Cream
Blue Bell Dairy

1466 **(HQ)Blue California Co**
30111 Tomas
Rancho Sta Marg, CA 92688-2125
949-459-2729
Fax: 949-635-1986 info@bluecal-ingredients.com
www.bluecal-ingredients.com
Developer and manufacturer of food ingredients.
President: Steven Chen
steven.chen@gmail.com
Executive Vice President: Cecilia McCollum
Quality Control Manager: Carl Lai
Estimated Sales: $10-20 Million
Number Employees: 10-19

Other Locations:
Rockaway NJ

1467 **Blue Chip Baker**
1911 S 3850 W
Salt Lake City, UT 84104-4914
801-269-0997
Fax: 801-269-9666 800-878-0099
info@bluechipgroup.net www.augasonfarms.com
Lecithins, health foods, wild Mexican yam cream, colloidal silver
President: Mark Augason
CEO: Gary Bringhurst
HR Vice President: Jeff Augason
VP of Information Technology: Fabio Demelo
Estimated Sales: $500,000-$1 Million
Number Employees: 100-249
Square Footage: 40
Type of Packaging: Consumer, Food Service, Private Label, Bulk
Brands:
Trophic

1468 **Blue Chip Cookies**
5991 Meijer Dr
Suite 24
Milford, OH 45150-1531
513-697-6610
Fax: 513-297-9494 800-888-9866
www.bluechipcookiesdirect.com
Manufacturer and wholesaler of fresh baked cookies
President/Chief Cookie Officer: Donna Drury
Estimated Sales: Less Than $500,000
Number Employees: 1-4

1469 **Blue Circle Foods**
4600 Argyle Terrace NW
Washington, DC 20011
202-232-5282
www.bluecirclefoods.com
Fresh and frozen fish
Year Founded: 2005

1470 **Blue Crab Bay**
29368 Atlantic Dr.
Melfa, VA 23410
757-787-3602
Fax: 757-787-3430 800-221-2722
sales@bluecrabbay.com www.bluecrabbay.com
Wholesaler & retailer of bloody mary mixers, seafood soups, seasonings, snacks, crab meat; also salt, mustard, and marinade, stoneware. Founded in 1985.
President: Pamela Barefoot
pam@baybeyond.net
VP Finance: Dawn Brasure
Marketing Director: Kelly Drummond
Sales Manager: Victoria DiLeo
Chief Operating Officer: Paul Driscoll
Purchasing: Linda Nyborg
Estimated Sales: $1-3 Million
Number Employees: 22
Square Footage: 86000
Parent Co: Bay Beyond, Inc.
Type of Packaging: Consumer
Brands:
Barnacles Snack Mix
Blue Crab Bay
Crab House Nuts
Salmonberry
Sting Ray Bloody Mary Mixer
Watts Island Trading

1471 **Blue Diamond Growers**
1802 C St.
Sacramento, CA 95811
800-987-2329
www.bluediamond.com
Processor, grower and exporter of almonds, macadamians, pistachios and hazelnuts. Two thousand almond products in many cuts, styles, sizes and shapes for use in confectionery, bakery, dairy and processed foods. In house R/D for customproducts.
President/Chief Executive Officer: Mark Jansen
Chairman of The Board: Clinton Shick
CFO: Dean LaVallee
Vice Chairman: Dale Van Groningen
Quality Assurance Lab Manager: Steven Phillips
Director, Marketing: Al Greenlee
Manager, Communications: Cassandra Keyse
Manager, Operations: Bruce Lisch
Manager, Product Development: Mike Stoddard
Senior Vice President, Procurement: David Hills
Year Founded: 1910
Estimated Sales: $709 Million
Number Employees: 1,100
Type of Packaging: Consumer, Food Service, Private Label, Bulk
Brands:
Almond Breeze
Almond Toppers
Blue Diamond
Blue Diamond Almonds
Blue Diamond Hazelnut
Blue Diamond Macadamias
Nut Thins
Smokehouse
California Nuts

1472 **Blue Dog Bakery**
3302 Fuhrman Ave E # 301
Suite 301
Seattle, WA 98102-7115
206-323-6958
Fax: 206-666-3835 888-749-7229
BlueDog@bluedogbakery.com
www.bluedogbakery.com
Company produces a variety of premium, natural, low fat dog biscuits and treats. Founded in 1998.
President/Owner: Margot Kenly
CEO: Kyle Polanski
bluedog@bluedogbakery.com
Estimated Sales: $1-3 Million
Number Employees: 1-4
Type of Packaging: Private Label
Brands:
Mariner Biscuits
Original Sesame Low Fat Crackers
Parmesan Low Fat Crackers
Sweet Onion Low Fat Crackers
Sweet Pepper Low Fat Crackers

1473 **Blue Evolution**
1528 El Camino Real
Suite 304
San Mateo, CA 94402
605-741-4074
info@blueevolution.com
www.blueevolution.com
Seaweed-infused pasta
CEO: Beau Perry
Sales Manager: Chris Elders
VP, Operations: Luke Knowles
Number of Brands: 1
Number of Products: 5
Type of Packaging: Consumer
Brands:
BLUE EVOLUTION

1474 **Blue Gold Mussels**
38 Blackmer St
P.O.Box 1803
New Bedford, MA 02744
508-993-2635
Fax: 508-994-9508 seagold01@msn.com
www.seagolddips.com
Fresh and frozen mussel products and calamari salad. Founded in 1996.
Owner: Bill Silkes
Director Marketing: Joe Jeffrey
Type of Packaging: Consumer, Food Service, Private Label
Brands:
Blue Gold

1475 **Blue Grass Quality Meat**
PO Box 17658
2648 Crescent Springs Pike
Covington, KY 41017-0658
859-331-7100
Fax: 859-331-4273
www.bluegrassqualitymeats.com
Smoked meats and sausage. Founded in 1992.
President/CEO: Paul Rice
Contact: Joan Brewer
jbrewer@bluegrassqualitymeats.com
Estimated Sales: $10-24.9 Million
Number Employees: 50-99
Type of Packaging: Consumer, Food Service, Private Label, Bulk

1476 **Blue Green Organics**
1923 Record Crossing Rd
Dallas, TX 75235
817-703-2321
bluegreenagave.com
Agave nectar and chia seeds
Number of Brands: 1
Number of Products: 3
Type of Packaging: Consumer, Food Service
Brands:
BLUE GREEN ORGANICS

1477 **Blue Harbour Cheese**
P.O. Box 46011 Novalea
Halifax, NS B3K 5V8
Canada
902-240-0305
info@blueharbourcheese.com
www.blueharbourcheese.com
Cheese
Cheese Maker: Lyndell Findlay

1478 **Blue Harvest Foods**
86 Macarthur Dr
New Bedford, MA 02740-7214
508-993-5700
Fax: 508-991-5133 www.blueharvestfisheries.com
Fresh and frozen scallops including bay and sea and fillets including flounder, cod, yellow tail and haddock; importer of cod fish and scallops; exporter of scallops
President: Albert J Santos
al@scallops-fillets.com
CEO: Linda Wisniewski
Treasurer/Vice President: Carmine Romano
Sales Manager: Patrick Moriarty
Manager: Albert Santos
al@scallops-fillets.com
Estimated Sales: $10-20 Million
Number Employees: 20-49
Square Footage: 60000
Type of Packaging: Consumer, Food Service, Private Label, Bulk
Brands:
Ding Gua Gua
Hygrade
Old Cape Harbor
Teddy's

1479 **Blue Hill Yogurt**
630 Bedford Rd.
Pocantico Hills, NY 10591
914-366-9600
www.bluehillyogurt.com
Manufacturer of yogurt.
Co-Founder, Owner: David Barber
david@bluehillfarm.com
Co-Owner: Laureen Barber
Executive Chief and Co-Owner: Dan Barber
Brands:
Blue Hill

1480 **Blue Hills Spring Water Company**
441 Quincy Avenue
Quincy, MA 02169
614-715-3900
Fax: 617-770-2720 www.bluehillswater.com
Bottled water manufacturer. Founded in 1984.
President/CEO: Mike Verrochi
COO: Mark Okum
Estimated Sales: $2.5-5 Million
Number Employees: 50-99
Brands:
Monadnock Mountain Spring Water

1481 **Blue Jay Orchards**
125 Plumtrees Rd
Bethel, CT 06801-3102
203-748-0119
Fax: 203-748-4814
Apple butter, sauce and chutney; also, pear butter. Founded in 1985.
President: Paul Patterson
pspatterson@qualityseals.com
VP: Mary Patterson
Estimated Sales: $500,000
Number Employees: 5-9
Square Footage: 40000
Type of Packaging: Consumer, Private Label
Brands:
Blue Jay Orchards

1482 **Blue Lakes Trout Farm**
133 Warm Creek Rd
Jerome, ID 83338
208-734-7151
Fax: 208-733-0325
Rainbow trout
Manager: Harold Johnson
Estimated Sales: $2.5-5 Million
Number Employees: 5-9
Type of Packaging: Consumer, Food Service

Brands:
Greene's

1483 **Blue Marble Biomaterials**
5653 Alloy S
Missoula, MT 59808
406-552-0748
Fax: 206-452-5898 800-738-0849
info@bluemarblebio.com www.bluemarblebio.com
Natural, bio-derived flavor and fragrance products including natural esters, thioesters, acids and extracts.
President/Chief Science Officer: James Stephens
Quality Research Scientist: Michalea Finnegan
Director Marketing/Communications: Melanie Calahan
Chief Business Officer: Colby Underwood
Contact: Nathan Snyder
nathan.snyder@bluemarblebio.com
Operations Manager: Wayne Smith
Electrical Systems/Production: Nate Snyder

1484 **Blue Marble Brands**
313 Iron Horse Way
Providence, RI 02908
888-534-0246
Fax: 866-402-7371
Organic, natural, specialty, ethnic and functional foods.
President: Chris Jensen
Year Founded: 2006
Estimated Sales: $16.2 Million
Number of Brands: 19
Type of Packaging: Food Service
Brands:
Woodstock®
Tumaro's®
Rising Moon Organics®
Mt. Vikos™
Mediterranean Organic™
Harvest Bay®
Natural Sea™
Field Day®
Koyo™
Mini Me's®
Fantastic World Foods®
Old Wessex™
AH!LASKA®
Asian Gourmet®
Bella Famiglia®
Haddon House®
Medford Farms®
Musette®
Tropical Pepper®

1485 **Blue Monkey**
Long Beach, CA 90831
info@bluemonkeydrinks.com
www.bluemonkeydrinks.com
Tropical fruit juices and snacks
Co-Owner: Simon Ginsberg
Co-Owner: Mary-Jane Ginsberg
Year Founded: 2010

1486 **Blue Moon Foods**
568 N Main Street
White River Junction, VT 05001-7026
802-295-1165
Fax: 802-295-2553
Ice cream and frozen desserts. Founded in 1995.
President: John Donaldson
Estimated Sales: $440,000
Number Employees: 7
Brands:
Blue Moon Tea

1487 **Blue Moose of Boulder**
1733 Majestic Dr
Unit 103
Lafayette, CO 80026
303-926-0664
customercare@bluemooseofboulder.com
bluemooseofboulder.com
Hummus, dips and spreads, pesto, salsa, and preprepared snacks.
General Manager: Bert Sartori
Year Founded: 1997
Number Employees: 11-50
Type of Packaging: Private Label

1488 **Blue Mountain Enterprise Inc**
4000 Commerce Dr
Kinston, NC 28504-7906
252-522-1544
Fax: 252-522-2599 800-522-1544
Savory flavors for the food industry, also contract manufacturing and packaging
President: William Baugher
labs@bluemoutainsflavors.com
Manager of Scientific Affairs: Jonathan Baugher
Corporate Secretay/Treasurer: Teresa Baugher
Research/Development: William Recktenwald
Quality Control: Margaret Jones
Customer Service: Maureen Suggs
Operations Manager: Laura Key
Production: Perry Price, Jr
Estimated Sales: $4 Million
Number Employees: 10-19
Number of Products: 150
Square Footage: 67775
Parent Co: Blue Mountain Enterprises
Type of Packaging: Bulk

1489 **Blue Mountain Vineyards**
7627 Grape Vine Drive
New Tripoli, PA 18066
610-298-3068
Fax: 610-298-8616 info@bluemountainwine.com
www.bluemountainwine.com
Wines
President/Owner: Joseph Greff
VP: Vickie Greff
Estimated Sales: $2.5-5 Million
Number Employees: 10-19

1490 **(HQ)Blue Pacific Flavors & Fragrances**
1354 Marion Ct
City of Industry, CA 91745
626-934-0099
www.bluepacificflavors.com
Basic manufacturer of natural flavors, extracts, essences and functional ingredients to the beverage, dairy, confectionery, baking and pharmaceutical industries. Founded in 1992.
President: Donald Wilkes
Contact: Kelly Anderson
kelly.anderson@cgtech.com
Estimated Sales: $5-9 Million
Number Employees: 20-49
Number of Brands: 5
Square Footage: 40000
Type of Packaging: Food Service, Private Label, Bulk
Other Locations:
Blue Pacific Asia
Malaysia
Blue Pacific China
Beijing, China
Blue Pacific Korea
Seoul, Korea
Brands:
Cafe Extract
Instacafe
Naturessence
Sun-Ripened
Synature

1491 **Blue Planet Foods**
9104 Apison Pike
PO Box 2178
Collegedale, TN 37315
423-396-3145
Fax: 423-396-3402 877-396-3145
sales@blueplanetfoods.net
Grain based products, granola, nutrition and granola bar components, bread bases and nutritional fillers; exporter of granola products
President: Russell McKee
Human Resources Director: Wayne White
Director of Operations: Deris Bagli
Production Manager: Cliff Myers
Plant Manager: Frank Park
Parent Co: McKee Foods Corporation
Type of Packaging: Consumer, Food Service, Private Label, Bulk
Brands:
Heartland®
Hearty Life®

1492 **Blue Point Brewing Co**
161 River Ave
Patchogue, NY 11772-3304
631-475-6944
Fax: 631-475-5252 pete@bluepointbrewing.com
www.bluepointbrewing.com
The Blue Point Brewing Company is Long Island's first currently-operating microbrewery.
Owner & President: Peter Cotter
Owner & Brewmaster: Mark Burford
getdpoint@aol.com
Chief Financial Officer: Gary Peck
Quality Control Manager: Alan Brady
Director of Branding & Communications: Curt Potter
National Sales Manager: Rob Johnson
Operations: Nick Burford
Number Employees: 20-49
Type of Packaging: Consumer

1493 **Blue Ribbon Farm Dairy Fresh**
827 Exeter Ave
Exeter, PA 18643-1728
570-655-5579
Fax: 570-655-5637 www.blueribbondairy.com
Ice cream manufacturer. Founded in 1961.
President: Ken Sorick
Estimated Sales: $5-10 Million
Number Employees: 5-9

1494 **Blue Ribbon Meats**
3316 W 67th Pl
Cleveland, OH 44102
216-631-8850
Fax: 216-631-8934 800-262-0395
www.blueribbonmeats.com
Meat and seafood.
President: Al Radis
Year Founded: 1948
Estimated Sales: $20-50 Million
Number Employees: 100-249

1495 **Blue Ridge Poultry**
396 Foundry Street
Athens, GA 30601
706-546-6767
Fresh and frozen poultry including turkey; wholesaler/distributor of poultry and eggs
President: Robert Harris
Estimated Sales: $1-3 Million
Number Employees: 5-9
Square Footage: 18000
Type of Packaging: Consumer

1496 **Blue Ridge Tea & Herb Co**
26 Woodhull St
2nd Floor Suite
Brooklyn, NY 11231-2643
718-625-3100
Fax: 718-935-1874 www.blueridgetea.com
Custom herbal and teabag formulations for private label. Also sales agent for teabags with ten vitamins; flavored. Founded in 1979.
President: Roger Rigolli
rrbrth1@aim.com
Vice President: Troy Rigolli
Estimated Sales: $4.5 Million est.
Number Employees: 10-19
Type of Packaging: Private Label
Brands:
Blue Ridge Teas

1497 **Blue Runner Foods Inc**
726 S Burnside Ave
Gonzales, LA 70737-3452
225-647-3016
Fax: 225-647-4017
customerservice@bluerunnerfoods.com
www.bluerunnerfoods.com
Processor and canner of Cajun and Creole creamed beans, peas and heat and serve entrees. Founded in 1993.
President: Richard Thomas
Vice President: Katie Thomas
kthomas@bluerunnerfoods.com
Estimated Sales: $5-10 Million
Number Employees: 20-49
Type of Packaging: Consumer, Food Service
Brands:
Blue Runner

1498 **Blue Sky Beverage Company**
550 Monica Circle
Suite 201
Corona, CA 92880
505-995-9761
Fax: 505-982-4004 800-426-7367
info@drinkbluesky.com www.drinkbluesky.com
Manufacturer and exporter of natural and energy sodas; also sparkling and artesian drinking water
Chairman/CEO: Rodney Sacks
President/COO/CFO: Hilton Schlosberg
Estimated Sales: $48,000

1499 **Blue Smoke Salsa**
119 East Main Street
PO Box 244
Ansted, WV 25812
304-658-3800
Fax: 304-658-5400 888-725-7298
bluesmokesalsa@hotmail.com
Jams and jellys, barbecue sauces, sparkling cider, honey, gourmet mustards, specialty butters, pickles, marinades and sauces, salsa, hot and spicy foods, seasonings, and dry mixes. Founded in 1992.
President: Robin Hildebrand
Estimated Sales: $300,000
Number Employees: 7

1500 **Blue Star Food Products**
3000 NW 109th Ave
Doral, FL 33172
305-836-6858
info@bluestarfoods.com
www.bluestarfoods.com
Seafood
Executive Chairman & CSO: John Keeler
jkeeler@bluestarfoods.com
Estimated Sales: $50-100 Million
Number Employees: 20-49
Number of Brands: 4
Brands:
Blue Star
Oceanica
Pacifika
Seassentials

1501 **Blue Willow Tea Co**
1200 10th St
Berkeley, CA 94710-1509
510-524-1933
Fax: 510-420-0260 800-328-0353
info@bluewillowtea.com www.bluewillowtea.com
Teas. Founded in 1994.
Owner: Ali Roth
jacqueline.rodarte@lacdc.org
Estimated Sales: Less Than $500,000
Number Employees: 1-4
Brands:
Blue Willow
Wu Wei

1502 **BlueWater Seafoods**
128 Rogers Street
Gloucester, MA 01930
978-283-3000
888-560-2539
www.bluewater.ca
Haddock and sole, shrimp temptations, five star tilapia, grill fillets, grill salmon and haddock, natural cut fillets, popcorn shrimp, classic family favorites, seasoned fillets and shrimp bowls
Number Employees: 225
Parent Co: Gortons USA
Type of Packaging: Consumer, Food Service

1503 **Blueberry Store**
PO Box 195
Grand Junction, MI 49056
269-437-6322
Fax: 269-434-6997 877-654-2400
sales@theblueberrystore.com
www.theblueberrystore.com
All natural blueberry preserve, blueberry salsa, blueberry BBQ sauce, blueberry juice, chocolate covered blueberries, blueberry syrup, blueberry mustard, blueberry vinegar and chutney
CEO: Jennifer Montgomery
CFO: Jeff Van Natter
Estimated Sales: $300,000-500,000
Number Employees: 1-4
Number of Products: 20
Parent Co: Michigan Blueberry Growers Association

1504 **Bluebird Restaurant**
19 N Main St
Logan, UT 84321-4583
435-752-3155
www.thebluebirdrestaurant.com
Candy and confectionery. Founded in 1914.
Owner: Sue Bette
sbette@bluebird-farm.com
Estimated Sales: $1-2.5 Million
Number Employees: 20-49

1505 **Bluebonnet Meat Company**
719 S. Pearl Street
Trenton, TX 75490-3111
903-989-2293
info@jackswholesalemeat.com
Beef and pork
President: Ben Buses
Vice President: Hannah Buses
Estimated Sales: $3-5 Million
Number Employees: 5-9
Type of Packaging: Consumer

1506 **Bluechip Group**
432 W 3440 S
Salt Lake City, UT 84115-4228
801-269-0997
Fax: 801-269-9666 800-878-0099
customerservice@bluechipgroup.net
Milk drinks including tofu, rice and soy
President: Mark Augason
CFO: Phil Auguson
Estimated Sales: $5 Million
Number Employees: 10-19
Number of Brands: 16
Number of Products: 160
Square Footage: 70000
Type of Packaging: Consumer, Food Service, Private Label, Bulk
Brands:
Blue Chip Baker
Blue Chip Group
Morning Moo's
Swiss Whey D'Lite

1507 **Bluegrass Brewing Company**
3929 Shelbyville Rd
Louisville, KY 40207
502-899-7070
Fax: 502-899-7051 pathagan@bbcbrew.com
www.bbcbrew.com
Brewer of ale, stout and lager. Founded in 1993.
Owner/President: Patrick Hagan
Contact: Jonathan Haeseley
haeseley@aye.net
Estimated Sales: $10-20 Million
Type of Packaging: Consumer, Food Service, Bulk
Brands:
Altbier
American Pale Ale
Bluebird Restaurant
Dark Star Porter
Nut Brown Ale

1508 **Bluegrass Dairy & Food**
1117 Cleveland Ave
Glasgow, KY 42141
Fax: 270-651-8844 800-794-4840
www.bluegrassdairy.com
Powdered ingredients for the food industry.
Plant Manager: Rick Johnson
Purchasing: Trent Walker
Other Locations:
Sprinfield Facility
Springfield KY

1509 **Bluepoint Bakery**
1721 E 58th Ave
Denver, CO 80216-1505
303-298-1100
Fax: 303-298-9797 sales@bluepointbakery.com
www.bluepointbakery.com
Manufacturer of baked goods such as croissants, cinnamon rolls, breads, muffins, scones, danishes, cakes, tarts and pies.
President: Fred Bramhall
CFO: Robb Letterman
robb@bluepointbakery.com
Vice President: Mary Clark
Estimated Sales: $20-50 Million
Number Employees: 50-99
Type of Packaging: Food Service

1510 **Blume Honey Water**
1382 Old Freeport Rd
Suite 3B
Pittsburgh, PA 15238
412-406-7391
info@blumehoneywater.com
www.blumehoneywater.com
Honey-infused water
Co-Founder: Michele Burchfield
Co-Founder: Carla Frank
Number of Brands: 1
Number of Products: 3
Type of Packaging: Consumer
Brands:
BLUME HONEY WATER

1511 **Blumenhof Vineyards-Winery**
13699 South Hwy 94
Dutzow, MO 63342
636-433-2245
Fax: 636-433-5224 800-419-2245
info@blumenhof.com www.blumenhof.com
Wine manufacturer. Founded in 1987.
President: Mark Blumenberg
Estimated Sales: $1-2.5 Million
Number Employees: 10-19

1512 **Blundell Seafoods**
11351 River Road
Richmond, BC V6X 1Z6
Canada
604-270-3300
Fax: 604-270-6513 info@blundellseafoods.com
www.blundellseafoods.com
Fresh and frozen seafood including clams, oysters, exotic fish, fin fish, freshwater fish, crustaceans, caviar
President: Ian Tak Yen Law
Vice President: Jeremy Kwun Hon Law
VP Sales: Rick Ogilvie
Manager: Bill Leung
Estimated Sales: $30 Million
Number Employees: 75
Type of Packaging: Consumer, Food Service, Private Label, Bulk

1513 **Bnutty**
Merrillville, IN 46410
844-426-8889
bnutty.com
Gourmet peanut butter
Number Employees: 1-4
Number of Products: 12
Type of Packaging: Consumer, Private Label
Brands:
Bnutty

1514 **Boar's Head**
1819 Main St
Suite 800
Sarasota, FL 34236
800-352-6277
boarshead.com
Meat products include bacon, beef, chicken, ham, pre-sliced meats, and turkey. Other products include cheese, condiments, dips, hummus, and spreads.
Year Founded: 1905
Estimated Sales: $100+ Million
Number Employees: 500-999

1515 **Boardman Foods Inc**
71320 E Columbia Ln
P.O. Box 786
Boardman, OR 97818
541-481-3000
Fax: 801-881-8999 www.boardmanfoodsinc.com
Onions including IQF and peeled
President: Brian Maag
Purchasing: Chris Bacon
Quality Control: Deanna Goodeve
VP Sales: Thomas Flaherty
VP Operations: Debbie Radie
Estimated Sales: $20-50 Million
Number Employees: 100-249
Type of Packaging: Bulk

1516 **Bob Evans Farms Inc.**
800-939-2338
BEConsumerRelations@bobevansfoods.com
www.bobevansgrocery.com
Sausage, bacon, frozen handheld breakfast items, refrigerated dinner sides, and other convenience foods.
Chairman: Mike Townsley

Year Founded: 1953
Estimated Sales: Over $1 Billion
Number Employees: 10000+
Parent Co: Post Holdings, Inc.
Type of Packaging: Consumer, Food Service
Other Locations:
Corporate Headquarters
New Albany OH
Bob Evans Farm
Rio Grande OH
Food Production
Hillsdale MI
Food Production
Xenia OH
Food Production & Distribution
Springfield OH
Food Production
Sulphur Springs TX
Brands:
Bob Evans®

1517 **Bob Gordon & Associates**
940 Linden Avenue
Oak Park, IL 60302-1349
708-524-9611
Processor and importer of green and black olives, maraschino cherries, pickled onions, pickled mushrooms and Greek pepperoncini. Founded in 1976.
President: Roberta Seefeldt
Vice President: Aaron Seefeldt
VP of Sales: Marcel Seefeldt
Controller: James Gosling
Estimated Sales: $1.2 Million
Number Employees: 10
Type of Packaging: Food Service, Private Label, Bulk
Brands:
Marquis
Splinter

1518 **Bob's Custom Cuts**
PO Box 6189
Bonnyville, AB T9N 2G8
Canada
780-826-2627
Fax: 780-826-2138
Fresh and frozen beef, pork, lamb, elk, jerky, deer, buffalo, wild boar, ostrich and game sausage
President & Board Member: Robert Belanger
Plant Manager: Ken Wychopen
Estimated Sales: A
Number Employees: 1-4
Square Footage: 19000
Parent Co: Dargis Land & Cattle
Type of Packaging: Consumer, Food Service, Private Label, Bulk

1519 **Bob's Red Mill Natural Foods**
13521 SE Pheasant Ct
Milwaukie, OR 97222-1248
503-654-3215
Fax: 503-653-1339 800-349-2173
www.bobsredmill.com
Milled whole grain flours, cereals and corn meal; also, mixes, bean flour and fat replacers
President: Bob Moore
CEO: Dennis Gilliam
CFO: John Wagner
Marketing Director: Cassidy Stockton
Head of Customer Service: Elizabeth Nawrocki
Estimated Sales: $25-50 Million
Number Employees: 250-499
Square Footage: 320000
Type of Packaging: Consumer, Food Service, Bulk
Brands:
Bob's Red Mill

1520 **Bobalu Nuts**
805-223-0919
bobalunuts.com
Flavored almonds
Owner: Scott Cummings
Number of Brands: 1
Number of Products: 6
Type of Packaging: Consumer
Brands:
BOBALU NUTS

1521 **Bobby D'S**
4737 County Road 101
Suite 222
Minnetonka, MN 55345-2634
952-278-7810
Sauces.
Owner: Robert Dechellis

1522 **Bobbysue's Nuts LLC**
65 North Bedford Rd.
Chappaqua, NY 10514
877-554-6887
getnuts@bobbysuesnuts.com
www.bobbysuesnuts.com
Combining almonds, cashews, pecas, and other nuts.
President: Barb Kobren
Contact: Adam Kobren
adam@bobbysuesnuts.com
Square Footage: 86000

1523 **Bobo's Oat Bars**
6325 Gunpark Dr
Suite B
Boulder, CO 80301
303-938-1977
info@eatbobos.com
eatbobos.com
Snack bars
Owner: Beryl Stafford
Number of Brands: 1
Number of Products: 18
Type of Packaging: Consumer
Brands:
BOBO'S

1524 **Boboli Intl. Inc.**
3439 Brookside Road
Suite 104
Stockton, CA 95219-1754
209-473-3507
Fax: 209-473-0492
Frozen bakery products including cream puffs, eclairs, pastries and breads. Founded in 1986.
CEO: Greg Helland
President/COO: Josh Helland
Estimated Sales: $12.3 Million
Number Employees: 75
Number of Brands: 6
Type of Packaging: Food Service
Brands:
Ambretta
Breadeli
Dutch Choux
Patissa™
Tulip Street Bakery
Van Dierman

1525 **Boca Bagelworks**
8177 Glades Rd # 1
Boca Raton, FL 33434-4063
561-852-8992
Fax: 561-852-5798 info@bagelworks.com
www.bagelworks.com
Owned and operated by H&L Restaurants. Processor and exporter of bagels
Owner: Paul Herman
VP: Steven Goldstein
Estimated Sales: $500,000 appx.
Number Employees: 20-49

1526 **Boca Bons East**
5190 Lake Worth Road
Greenacres, FL 33463
954-346-0494
Fax: 954-346-0497 800-314-2835
Manufacturer and exporter of a certified kosher chocolate that is a combination of a truffle, fudge, and a brownie.
President: Susan Kanter
Sales Executive: Robin Kula
Estimated Sales: $1-3 Million
Number Employees: 10-19
Square Footage: 10000
Type of Packaging: Consumer, Food Service, Private Label, Bulk
Brands:
Boca Bons

1527 **Boca Foods Company**
910 Mayer Ave
Madison, WI 53704
608-285-3311
Fax: 608-285-6741 bocaburger@kraftheinz.com
www.bocaburger.com
Meatless burgers
President: Kevin Scott
Director: Heather Fries
Brand Manager: Gary Berger
Estimated Sales: $20-50 Million
Number Employees: 35
Parent Co: Kraft Foods
Brands:
Boca®

1528 **Bodacious Foods**
339 Gennett Dr
Jasper, GA 30143-1140
706-253-1153
Fax: 706-253-1156 800-391-1979
info@bodaciousfoods.com
www.bodaciousfoods.com
Cheese straws and shortbread, gingerbread, key lime, chocolate and sugar-free brownie bites
CEO: Cathy Cunningham
cathy@bodaciousfoods.com
Shipping Manager: Anthony Russell
Purchasing Manager: Dave Hays
Estimated Sales: $1.4,000,000
Number Employees: 20-49
Square Footage: 16000
Type of Packaging: Consumer
Brands:
Geraldine's Bodacious

1529 **Bodega Chocolates**
17290 Newhope St Ste A A
Fountain Valley, CA 92708
714-432-0708
Fax: 714-432-1537 888-326-3342
Fudge truffle bars and confections
Principal: Gary Khazanovich
Owner: Martucci Angiano
Estimated Sales: Under $500,000
Number Employees: 8
Type of Packaging: Consumer, Food Service
Brands:
Fudgescotti

1530 **Bodek Kosher Produce Inc**
1294 E 8th St
Brooklyn, NY 11230-5106
718-377-4163
Fax: 718-377-0782 info@bodek.com
www.bodek.com
Grade A, California grown produce, strictly supervised from seedling to harvest to production under the Central Rabbinical Congress, OU, and Rabbi Gissinger.
Owner: Solomon Fried
sfried@bodek.com
Secretary: Zvi Gartenhouse
Vice President: Ike Rosenbluth
Estimated Sales: $1-$2,500,000
Number Employees: 5-9

1531 **Bodin Foods**
704 Avenue D
New Iberia, LA 70560-0527
337-367-1344
Fax: 337-364-4968 www.cajun-recipes.com
Frozen Cajun foods, browning/seasoning sauce, pork boudin, shrimp boudin, crawfish boudin, dressing mix, crawfish pies, meat pies, shrimp and crabmeat pies, and crawfish and crabmeat pies
Owner: Dennis Higginebotham
CEO: Madine Pacetti
Estimated Sales: $500,000
Number Employees: 5-9
Number of Brands: 2
Number of Products: 11
Square Footage: 25635
Type of Packaging: Consumer, Food Service, Private Label
Brands:
Bodin's
Brown Kwik
Cajun Bites

1532 **Body Breakthrough Inc**
561 Acorn St # I
St Unit I
Deer Park, NY 11729-3600
631-243-2443
Fax: 631-243-2464 800-924-3343
www.bodybreakthrough.com
Processor and exporter of teas including herbal, dietary and antioxidant; also, weight loss aids
President: Cori Lichter
Executive Director: Glenn Lichter
Estimated Sales: Under $800,000
Number Employees: 5-9
Square Footage: 10000
Type of Packaging: Consumer, Private Label
Brands:
Anti Oxidant Edge

Trim Maxx
Yohimbe

1533 **Bodyonics Limited**
200 Adams Blvd
Farmingdale, NY 11735-6615
516-822-1230
Fax: 516-822-1252
Sports nutrition, vitamins, herbs and supplements.
President: Mel Rich
Sales/Marketing: Andy Fishman
Number Employees: 50-99

1534 **Boeger Winery**
1709 Carson Rd
Placerville, CA 95667-5195
530-622-8094
Fax: 530-622-8112 800-655-2634
sue@boegerwinery.com www.boegerwinery.com
Wines
Owner/Secretary & Treasurer: Susan Boeger
sue@boegerwinery.com
Manager; President: Justin Boeger
Mangager: Brian Bumgarner
Marketing & Public Relations: Tara De Le Rosa
Sales Executive; Sales Mangager: Carl Keinert
Winemaker: Justin Boeger
Estimated Sales: $2-5,000,000
Number Employees: 20-49
Type of Packaging: Private Label

1535 **Boehringer Ingelheim Corp**
900 Ridgebury Rd
PO Box 368
Ridgefield, CT 06877-1058
203-798-9988
Fax: 203-431-6556 800-243-0127
webmaster@rdg.boehringer-ingelheim.com
www.us.boehringer-ingelheim.com
Organic mineral salts
President: Paul Fonteyne
Number Employees: 5000-9999

1536 **Boesl Packing Co**
2322 Belair Rd
Baltimore, MD 21213-1283
410-675-1071
Fax: 410-327-4131 800-675-1471
info@k9kraving.com www.k-9kraving.com
Manufacturer and packer of meat products including smoked frankfurters, knockwurst, bologna, salami and bacon; pig tails, neck bones and chitterlings; sausage: hot, smoked and Polish
Owner: Jeffery Burton
jburton@mr.baltimore.com
Senior Executive: J Boesl
Vice President: Robert Barrett
Estimated Sales: $3.2 Million
Number Employees: 1-4
Type of Packaging: Consumer

1537 **Boetje Foods Inc**
2736 12th Street
Rock Island, IL 61201
309-788-4352
Fax: 309-788-4365 877-726-3853
www.boetjefoodsinc.com
Gourmet mustard
President: Will Kropp
tavery@coynecollege.edu
Production Manager: Harrison Kropp
Estimated Sales: $2.5-5 Million
Number Employees: 5-9
Square Footage: 24000
Type of Packaging: Consumer, Food Service, Private Label, Bulk
Brands:
Dutch Boy

1538 **Boggiatto Produce Inc**
850 Work St # 201
Salinas, CA 93901-4378
831-424-8952
Fax: 831-424-1974 produce@boggiatto.com
Artichokes, broccoli, Brussels sprouts, cabbage, celery, cilantro, squash, lettuce, romaine lettuce hearts, kale, onions, leeks, peas, parsley, beets, green beans, rapini, spinach, etc
Owner: Kraig Kuska
Controller: Joann Glennon
Vice President: Jeffry Hitchcock
Consulting Chef: Beat Giger
Food Safety Coordinator: Jose Garcia-Canedo
Sales Manager: Kraig Kuska
kraig@boggiatto.com
Sales: Don Day
Growers & Directors: Ron & Ed Panziera
Estimated Sales: $2.5-5,000,000
Number Employees: 10-19
Type of Packaging: Consumer, Food Service
Brands:
Boggiatto
Garden Hearts

1539 **Boghosian Raisin Packing Co**
726 S 8th St
PO Box 338
Fowler, CA 93625-2506
559-834-5348
Fax: 559-834-1419
Raisins
Owner: Pete Boghosian
pboghosian@boghosianraisin.com
Owner: Paul Boghosian
Human Resource Executive: Roger Stiles
Manufacturing Supervisor: Richard Lokey
Plant Manager: Richard Lokey
Estimated Sales: $7 Million
Number Employees: 50-99
Square Footage: 33000
Type of Packaging: Consumer, Bulk

1540 **Bogland**
300 Oak Street
Pembroke, MA 02359-1984
781-829-9549
Fax: 781-829-9567
Cranberry chutney, cranberry mustard, cranberry grill sauce, cranberry cabernet vinaigrette, cranberry orange marmalade, cranberry blueberry preserves, Szechuan peanut sauce, margarita madness mustard, port mustard, seafood mustard
President: Jan Baird
Estimated Sales: $2.5-5,000,000
Number Employees: 1-4
Brands:
Bogland
Bogland By the Sea
Boglandish

1541 **Bogle Vineyards Inc**
37783 County Road 144
Clarksburg, CA 95612-5009
916-744-1030
Fax: 916-744-1187 info@boglewinery.com
www.boglewinery.com
Wine
President: Warren Bogle
Intl. Sales: Jody Bogle
VP: Ryan Bogle
Manager: Eric Aafedt
Vice President of Sales: Christopher Catterton
Human Resources Executive: Cassie Bandelyufter
Office Manager: Sue Upsite
Director of Winemaking: Christopher Smith
Estimated Sales: $2-5,000,000
Number Employees: 1-4
Type of Packaging: Private Label

1542 **Bohemian Brewery**
94 E 7200
Midvale, UT 84047
801-566-5474
Fax: 801-566-5321 info@bohemianbrewery.com
www.bohemianbrewery.com
Ale and lager
President: Joe Petras
Vice President: Helen Petras
Estimated Sales: Under $500,000
Number Employees: 10
Type of Packaging: Consumer, Food Service
Brands:
Bohemian

1543 **Boisset Family Estates**
849 Zinfandel Ln
St Helena, CA 94574-1645
707-963-6900
800-878-1123
info@boisset.com www.boissetfamilyestates.com
Wine
President: Jean-Charles Boisset
Controller: Phillip Marquand
VP: Alain Leonnet
Marketing Manager: Lisa Heisinger
Director of Consumer Marketing: Michelle Sitton
Estimated Sales: $7.8 Million
Number Employees: 5-9
Parent Co: LaFamille des Grands Vins
Brands:
Amberhill
Buena Vista Winery
California Rabbit
Deloach
Fog Mountain
Frenchie Winery
Jcb By Jean-Charles Boisset
Lockwood Vineyard
Lyeth Estate
Raymond Vineyards
Sonoma Cuvee
Bouchard Aine & Fils
Domaine De La Vougeraie
French Rabbit
J.Moreau & Fils
La Captive
Louis Bernard
Ropiteau Freres
Louis Bouillot
Beni Di Batasiolo
Neige
Idol Vodka

1544 **Boissons Miami Pomor**
704 Boulevard Guimond
Longueuil, QC J4G 1T5
Canada
450-677-3744
Fax: 450-677-7826 877-977-3744
www.boissonsmiami.com
Juices, concentrates and crystals
President: Lise Huneault
Vice President: Andre Brisebois
Vice President: Yves Brisebois
Estimated Sales: $1.4 Million
Number Employees: 9
Square Footage: 13500

1545 **Boja's Foods Inc**
13120 N Wintzell Ave
Bayou La Batre, AL 36509-2138
251-824-4186
Fax: 251-824-7339 www.bojasfoods.com
Crab meat stuffing
CFO: Nancy West
Vice President: Greg Malone
bojacrab@aol.com
Secretary: John Kramer
Manager: Donald Crammond
Estimated Sales: $1.5-2,000,000
Number Employees: 10-19
Brands:
Boja's
Boja's Chef's Delight
Paulines

1546 **Bold Coast Smokehouse**
224 County Rd
Lubec, ME 04652
207-733-8912
Fax: 207-733-8986 888-733-0807
www.boldcoastsmokehouse.com
Hot and cold smoked Atlantic salmon, smoked salmon, smoked salmon pate and lox, smoked trout pate, finnan haddie, smoked mackeral, smoked salmon kabobs, graulax, smoked lobster products, smoked mussels and smoke scallops.
President/Owner: Vinny Gartmayer
Estimated Sales: $250,000
Number Employees: 3
Type of Packaging: Consumer, Private Label

1547 **Bolner's Fiesta Spices**
426 Menchaca St
San Antonio, TX 78207
info@fiestaspices.com
www.fiestaspices.com
Processor and importer of dehydrated vegetables, liquid extracts and spices, herbs and seasonings, including: bay leaves, cinnamon, cloves, cumin, sage, nutmeg, oregano, paprika, onion salt, anise, caraway, garlic, celery and mustardseeds, black pepper.
Founder: Clifton Bolner
Plant Manager: James Morris

Estimated Sales: Under $1 Million
Number Employees: 100-249
Type of Packaging: Consumer, Food Service, Private Label, Bulk
Brands:
Fiesta
Lynwood Farms
Papa Joe's
River Road
Spice Choice
Spice Ranch
Spice Star

1548 **Bolt House Farms-Shipping Dept**
7200 E Brundage Ln
Bakersfield, CA 93307-3099
661-366-7207
Fax: 661-366-0326 800-467-4683
raust@bolthouse.com www.bolthouse.com
Vegetable and melon farming
Chairman: Andre Hdant
CEO: Jeff Dunn
Vice President: Joe Pryor
Engineering and R&D Manager: Robert Misuraca
Director, Quality Compliance: Bela Chandra
VP Marketing: Bryan Reese
VP Sales: Tim McCorkle
Contact: Anthony Abbate
aabbate@bolthouse.com
Production Manager: Aaron Corbett
Purchasing Manager: Jason Higbee
Estimated Sales: $118 Million
Number Employees: 20-49
Parent Co: Campbell Soup Co
Brands:
Earth Unt Farm
Green Gaint

1549 **Bon Courage Gourmet**
2726 Croasdaile Dr
Suite 103-C
Durham, NC 27705
919-973-0920
888-865-5841
info@boncouragegourmet.com
boncouragegourmet.com
European chocolate and confections
President: Michael Barefoot
michael@boncouragegourmet.Com
Vice President: Tim Manale
General Manager: Angela Joines
Year Founded: 2013
Brands:
Miracle Tree(c)

1550 **Bon Secour Fisheries Inc**
17449 County Road 49 S
Bon Secour, AL 36511
251-949-7411
Fax: 251-949-6478
bonsec@bonsecourfisheries.com
www.bonsecourfisheries.com
Fresh and frozen flounder, whiting, snapper, shrimp, oysters, scallops, crawfish, snow, soft shell and king crab, lobster, cod, catfish, tuna, grouper, pollock, shark, mahi, talapia, etc.; also, alligator meat.
CFO: Melani Parker
Vice President: Chris Nelson
Director, Sales: Leon Russell
Procurement Manager: Robert Eckerle
Year Founded: 1896
Estimated Sales: $25.10 Million
Number Employees: 100-249
Square Footage: 60000
Type of Packaging: Consumer, Food Service, Bulk
Brands:
Bon Secour
Nelson's

1551 **Bon Ton Products**
275 E Hintz Rd
Wheeling, IL 60090-6002
847-520-8300
Meat buyer, boxed beef and pork cuts.
Owner: George Christie
Marketing Director: Dave Centino
Human Resources Executive: Leslie Baker
Manager: James Cristy
Estimated Sales: $17 Million
Number Employees: 5-9

1552 **Bonafide Provisions**
San Diego, CA
bonafideprovisions.com
Organic bone broth
Co-Founder & CEO: Sharon Brown
Co-Founder: Alexandra Rains
Co-Founder: Reb Brown
Number of Brands: 1
Number of Products: 5
Type of Packaging: Consumer
Brands:
BONAFIDE PROVISIONS

1553 **Bonduelle North America**
540 Chemin Des Patriotes
Saint-denis-sur-richelieu
Quebec, ON J0H 1K0
Canada
450-787-3411
Fax: 450-787-3537 www.familytradition.com
Manufacturer and importer of frozen fruits and vegetables; exporter of canned corn and IQF vegetables
President/CEO: John Omstead
Number Employees: 100-249
Square Footage: 1284000
Type of Packaging: Consumer, Food Service
Other Locations:
Family Tradition Foods
Tecumseh, Ontario
Brands:
Family Traditions
John O'S

1554 **Bone Doctors' BBQ, LLC**
718 Eargil Lane
Charlottesville, VA 22902-4302
434-296-7766
Fax: 434-977-6613 sales@bonedoctorsbbq.com
www.bonedoctorsbbq.com
BBQ sauce, grilling sauces, marinades, spices.
Marketing: David Heilbronner

1555 **Bone Suckin' Sauce**
1109 Agriculture St
Suite 1
Raleigh, NC 27603
919-833-7647
Fax: 919-821-5781 bonesuckin.com
Barbecue, grilling and marinating sauces
Founder: Phil Ford
Number of Brands: 1
Number of Products: 15
Type of Packaging: Consumer
Brands:
BONE SUCKIN'

1556 **Bonert's Pies Inc**
2727 S Susan St
Santa Ana, CA 92704-5817
714-540-3535
Fax: 714-540-9615 susanm@bonertspies.com
Fruit, creme, meringue, no sugar added, and no top-ready to finish pies.
President & CEO: Michael Bonert
michaelb@bonertspies.com
CFO: Harry Kaplan
Vice President of R&D: Greg Guerra
Sales Representative: Devin Kuy
Production Manager: Laura Perez
Purchasing Agent: Jeanne Romig
Estimated Sales: $13 Million
Number Employees: 100-249

1557 **Bongard's Creameries**
250 Lake Dr E
Chanhassen, MN 55317
952-277-5500
info@bongards.com
www.bongards.com
Dairy products including cheese and whey
President/CEO: Keith Grove
CFO: Chris Freeman
Marketing Executive: Sheri Nadeau
VP, Sales & Marketing: Scott Tomes
VP, Operations: Brent Jewett
Number Employees: 50-99
Parent Co: Land O'Lakes
Type of Packaging: Consumer, Private Label

1558 **Bongiovi Brand Pasta Sauces**
PO Box 3941
Valley Village, CA 91617
434-296-7766
Fax: 434-977-6613 orders@bongiovibrand.com
www.bongiovibrand.com
Manufacturer of pasta sauces.
President: John Bongiovi
Brands:
Bongiovi Pasta Sauces

1559 **Bonk Breaker**
1810-H Berkeley St
Santa Monica, CA 90404
310-315-4129
info@bonkbreaker.com
bonkbreaker.com
Protein bars, nutrition bars and
Founder: Phil Ford
Number of Brands: 1
Number of Products: 21
Type of Packaging: Consumer
Brands:
BONK BREAKER
PROTEIN BONK BREAKER
ENERGY CHEWS
REAL HYDRATION

1560 **Bonnie & Don Flavours Inc.**
919 Kamato Dr
Mississauga, ON L4W 2R5
Canada
905-625-1813
Fax: 905-626-1824 info@bdflavours.com
www.bdflavours.com
Artifical and organic flavors and extracts
Manager Marketing & Business Development: Ken Halnan

1561 **Bonnie Baking Company**
800 Boyd Boulevard
La Porte, IN 46350-4419
219-362-4561
Fax: 219-325-0030
Breads and rolls
Manager: John West
Contact: Ben Vales
englap@lewisbakeries.com
Estimated Sales: $20-50 Million
Number Employees: 100-249

1562 **Bonnie Doon LLC**
2941 Moose Trl
Elkhart, IN 46514-8230
574-264-3390
Fax: 574-264-6208
Ice cream
President: Samuel Dugan
CEO: Sam Dugan
Vice President: Jim Otis
Office Manager: Jan Miller
Estimated Sales: $1-2 Million
Number Employees: 20-49
Type of Packaging: Food Service, Bulk

1563 **Bonnie's Ice Cream**
21 Leaman Road
Paradise, PA 17562-9660
717-687-9301
Dairy products
President: Lou Termini
Vice President: Dane Cherry
Estimated Sales: $1-2,500,000
Number Employees: 14

1564 **Bonnie's Jams**
94 Foster St
Cambridge, MA 02138-4729
617-714-5380
info@bonniesjams.com
www.bonniesjams.com
Jams, preserves and corporate gifts.
President: Bonnie Shershow
Contact: Bonnie Jams
bonnie@bonniesjams.com
Number Employees: 5-9

1565 **Bonny Doon Vineyard**
328 Ingalls Street
Santa Cruz, CA 95060
831-425-3625
888-819-6789
sales@bonnydoonvineyard.com
www.bonnydoonvineyard.com
Wines
President: Randall Grahm
Owner: Lisa Kohrf
Marketing Director: Nicholas Tucker
National Sales Manager: Keith Shulsky
Contact: Nicole Beatie
nicole@bonnydoonvineyard.com
Operations Manager: Ed Moya

Estimated Sales: $21,000,000
Number Employees: 43
Type of Packaging: Private Label

1566 Bono USA
19 Gardner Rd
Suite E
Fairfield, NJ 07004
862-485-8729
www.bonousainc.com
Extra virgin olive oil, table olives and marmalades
Year Founded: 1934

1567 Bonterra Vineyard
12625 E Side Road
Hopland, CA 95449
707-744-7575
Fax: 707-744-1844 www.bonterra.com
Wines
Vineyard Director: Dave Koball
Brands:
Bonterra

1568 Bonumose LLC
1725 Discovery Dr.
Suite 220
Charlottesville, VA 22911
erogers@bonumose.com
bonumose.com
Sugar
Co-Founder & CEO: Ed Rogers
Co-Founder & Chief Scientific Officer: Daniel Wichelecki
Engineering & Operations Manager: Mansoor Pasha
Year Founded: 2016
Type of Packaging: Private Label

1569 Bookbinder Specialties LLC
601 Beatty Rd
Media, PA 19063-1642
215-322-1305
Fax: 267-687-0112
Canned soups and broths.
President: Sean O'Neil
Contact: Colin O'Neil
colin@bookbinderspecialties.com
Brands:
Bookbinder's

1570 Boone's Butcher Shop
100 Old Bloomfield Pike
Bardstown, KY 40004
502-348-3668
Fax: 502-348-4046 888-253-3384
info@boonesbutchershop.com
www.boonesbutchershop.com
Packer of processed beef and pork products
President: Jerry Boone
boonesbutcher@bardstown.com
Estimated Sales: $6 Million
Number Employees: 20-49

1571 Booneway Farms
167 Glade Rd
Berea, KY 4043
859-986-2636
Fax: 859-986-3583
Mustards, hamburger marinades, jellies, preserves, seasonings and spices
President: Williams Arant, Jr.
Estimated Sales: $2.5-5,000,000
Number Employees: 20-49
Type of Packaging: Private Label

1572 Boordy Vineyards Inc
12820 Long Green Pike
Hydes, MD 21082-9541
410-592-5015
Fax: 410-592-5385 wine-info@boordy.com
www.boordy.com
Wines
President: Robert Deford
wine-info@deboordy.com
Owner: Julie Deford
Owner: Phillip Wagner
Vice President: Anne Deford
Accounting Director: Laurie Kregecz
Marketing Director: Susan Rayner
Public Relations: Rory Calhoun
Production Manager: Tom Burns
Estimated Sales: Under $700,000
Number Employees: 10-19
Type of Packaging: Private Label
Brands:
Boordy Vineyards

1573 Boothbay Lobster Wharf
97 Atlantic Ave
Boothbay Harbor, ME 04538-2220
207-633-4900
Fax: 207-633-4077
sales@boothbaylobsterwharf.com
Lobster
Owner: Kim Simmons
ksimmons@boothbaylobsterwharf.com
Estimated Sales: Less Than $500,000
Number Employees: 1-4

1574 Boquet's Oyster House
6645 Highway 56
Chauvin, LA 70344-2630
504-594-5574
Fax: 253-761-0504
Fresh, frozen, shucked oysters
President: Lawrenece Bouquet, Jr.

1575 Borden Canada
6890 Notre Dame Street E
Montreal, QC HIN 2E5
Canada
514-256-1601
Fax: 514-256-2537
Dairy
Quality Assurance: Daniel L'Heureux

1576 Borden Dairy
8750 N Central Expy
Suite 400
Dallas, TX 75231
214-459-1100
855-311-1583
www.bordendairy.com
Milk, cream, buttermilk, dips and sour cream, juices, teas and flavored drinks.
CEO: Steve McCormick
IT: Brad Moore
bmills@dairyfreshcorp.com
Number Employees: 100-249
Number of Brands: 1
Type of Packaging: Consumer, Food Service
Brands:
Borden Dairy

1577 Border Foods
5425 Boone Ave N
New Hope, MN 55428
763-559-7338
comments@borderfoods.com
www.borderfoods.com
Mexican food products including; green chiles, jalapenos and red jalapenos, salsas, enchilada sauces, tomatillos, chipotles, cascabellas, and red chiles.
Chief Executive Officer: Lee Engler
VP, Operations: Carol Williams
General Manager: Jeremy Poole
Year Founded: 1996
Estimated Sales: $24.7 Million
Number Employees: 150
Square Footage: 24488
Type of Packaging: Food Service, Private Label, Bulk
Other Locations:
Basic American Foods
Vacaville CA
Brands:
Classic Casserole
Golden Grill
Nature's Own
Potatoe Pearls
Quick Start
Redi Shred
Regional Recipe
Santiago

1578 Borders Sporting Goods
5876 US Route 60
Ashland, KY 41102-9508
606-928-6326
Fax: 606-928-1072
www.borderssportinggoods.com
Beef, pork, veal and lamb
Owner: Greg Borders
sales@borderssportinggoods.com
Owner: Reggie Danzhorn
Estimated Sales: $1-2.5 Million
Number Employees: 10-19
Type of Packaging: Consumer

1579 Bordoni Vineyards
Rte 4
Box 885K
Vallejo, CA 94591-9802
707-642-1504
Manufacturer of wines.
President: Jim Bordoni
Estimated Sales: $5-10,000,000
Number Employees: 1-4

1580 Borgattis Ravioli
632 E 187th St
Bronx, NY 10458
718-367-3799
Fax: 718-367-2229 www.borgattis.com/ravioli
Pasta
Owner: Mario Borgatti
Estimated Sales: $1-2,500,000
Number Employees: 1-4

1581 Borinquen Biscuit Corporation
PO Box 1607
Yauco, PR 00698
787-856-3030
Fax: 787-856-5339
oficina@galletasroyalborinquen.com
www.galletasroyalborinquen.com
Manufacturers of quality soda crackers, cookies and biscuits.
President: Antonio Rodriguez Zamora
Treasurer: Nora Rodriguez
Vice President: Antonio Morales
Secretary: Gevoveva Rodriguez
Human Relations Manager: Hircio Matey
Purchasing Manager: Antonio Rodriguez Morales
Estimated Sales: $15 Million
Number Employees: 130
Square Footage: 174000
Type of Packaging: Consumer, Private Label
Brands:
Cien En Boca
Florecitas
Rica
Royal Borinquen Export
Vanilla Imperial

1582 Bornstein Seafoods
PO Box 188
Bellingham, WA 98225
360-734-7990
Fax: 360-734-5732 www.bornstein.com
Live, fresh and frozen seafood.
CEO: Colin Bornstein
bornstein@bornstein.com
Year Founded: 1934
Estimated Sales: $20-50 Million
Number Employees: 50-99
Number of Brands: 1
Type of Packaging: Consumer, Food Service
Brands:
Bornstein

1583 Bornt & Sons Inc
2307 E US Highway 98
Holtville, CA 92250-9543
760-356-1066
Fax: 760-356-1066
Organic vegetables
Owner: Alan Bornt
borntfamilyfarms@aol.com
CFO: Mary Bornt
Vice President; Office Manager: Sandra Gaskin
VP Marketing/Sales: John Prock
Estimated Sales: $3,400,000
Number Employees: 50-99
Brands:
Bornt Family Farms
Ocean Organics

1584 Borra Vineyards
1301 E Armstrong Rd
Lodi, CA 95242-9423
209-368-2446
Fax: 209-369-5116 info@borravineyards.com
www.borravineyards.com
Wine
Owner: Steve Borra
sjb@lodiirrigation.com
CEO: Beverly Borra
VP Marketing: Gina Granlees
Estimated Sales: $1-3,000,000
Number Employees: 1-4
Type of Packaging: Private Label

Brands:
Borra

1585 **Bos Smoked Fish Inc**
1175 Patullo Avenue
Woodstock, ON N4S 7W3
Canada
519-537-5000
Fax: 519-537-5522 info@bossmokedfish.com
www.bossmokedfish.com

Smoked fish
President: Rein Bos
Sales: Chris Bruines
Sales: Kirk VanderSpek
Plant Manager: Pieter Bos
Estimated Sales: $6 Million
Number Employees: 15
Type of Packaging: Consumer, Food Service, Private Label, Bulk

1586 **Bosco Products Inc**
441 Main Rd
Towaco, NJ 07082-1201
973-334-7534
Fax: 973-334-2617 800-438-2672
Chocolate and flavored syrup and drink products
President: Steven Sanders
steven@seabreezesyrups.com
Number Employees: 50-99
Brands:
Bosco

1587 **Boscoli Foods Inc**
2254 Greenwood St
Kenner, LA 70062-7908
504-469-5500
Fax: 504-469-5548 edmontaldo@yahoo.com
www.boscoli.com

Fine Italian gourmet foods.
Owner/President: John Occhipinti
President: Sybil Klopf
Treasurer: Kathleen Occhipinti
Purchasing: Cindy Lopez
Estimated Sales: $900,000
Number Employees: 5-9

1588 **Boskovich Farms Inc**
711 Diaz Ave
PO Box 1352
Oxnard, CA 93030-7247
805-487-2299
Fax: 805-487-5189
feedback@boskovichfarms.com
www.boskovichfarms.com
Bok choy, artichokes, cilantro, endive, cebollitas, brussels sprouts, onions, lettuce, celery, carrots, cabbages, bell peppers, apples, radishes, spinach, beets, asparagus, kale, leeks, napa, parsley, radish, strawberries and sugarpeas.
President: Philip Boskovich
Co-CEO: Joseph Boskovich
Co-CEO: George Boskovich
lmartinez@boskovichfarms.com
CFO: Lynn Grayson
Sales Manager: Russ Widerburg
Human Resources Manager: Martha Mayorga
Estimated Sales: Over $1 Billion
Number Employees: 1000-4999
Type of Packaging: Consumer, Food Service
Other Locations:
Transwest Cooling
Yuma AZ
Growers Street Cooling
Salinas CA
Shipping Distribution
Oxnard CA

1589 **Boskydel Vineyard**
7501 E Otto Rd
Lake Leelanau, MI 49653-9419
231-256-7272
jim@boskydel.com
www.boskydel.com

Wines
Owner: Bernard Rink
jim@boskydel.com
Estimated Sales: Less Than $500,000
Number Employees: 1-4
Type of Packaging: Private Label
Brands:
Boskydel

1590 **Bossen**
31010 San Antonio St
Hayward, CA 94544
510-324-0168
service@bossenstore.com
bossenstore.com

Bubble tea; iced tea; juice mixes; syrup.
Co-Founder: Haber Tu
Co-Founder: Edward Shen
Year Founded: 2012
Parent Co: Leadway International, Inc.

1591 **Boston America Corporation**
325 New Boston St
Unit 17
Woburn, MA 01801
781-933-3535
Fax: 781-933-3539
customerservice@bostonamerica.com
www.bostonamerica.com

Tinned candies and cookies
President: Matthew Kavet
Contact: Jim Costa
jim.costa@bostonamerica.com
Estimated Sales: $1-3 Million
Number Employees: 20-49
Brands:
Bubblegum
Grinch
My Little Pony
Powerpuff Girls
Scooby Doo
Spider-Man
Strawberry Shortcake

1592 **Boston Beer Co Inc.**
1 Design Center Pl.
Suite 850
Boston, MA 02210
617-368-5000
Fax: 617-368-5500 888-661-2337
www.bostonbeer.com
Beer.
President/CEO: David Burwick
Chairman/Founder: C. James Koch
CFO/Treasurer: Frank Smalla
VP, Brewing: David Grinnell
Chief Sales Manager: John Geist
Year Founded: 1984
Estimated Sales: $921 Million
Number Employees: 1000-4999
Number of Brands: 5
Square Footage: 33500
Type of Packaging: Consumer, Food Service
Brands:
Angry Orchard®
Samuel Adams®
Twisted Tea®
Truly
A & S Brewing

1593 **Boston Chowda**
30 River St
Haverhill, MA 01832-5402
978-478-0500
Fax: 978-478-3588 800-992-0054
info@bostonchowda.com www.bostonchowda.com
Frozen soups and chowders
President: Richard Lamattina
Director: Paul Cassidy
Director: John Leroy
Director: Alan Katz
Manager: Michael Lamattina
Year Founded: 1987
Estimated Sales: Less Than $500,000
Number Employees: 5-9
Square Footage: 13000
Brands:
Bay State Chowda

1594 **Boston Coffee Cake**
351 Willow Street South
North Andover, MA 01845
800-434-0500
customerservice@bostoncoffeecake.com
www.bostoncoffeecake.com

Coffee cake
Founder: Mark Forman
customerservice@bostoncoffeecake.com

1595 **Boston Direct Lobsters**
207 Iris Ave
Jefferson, LA 70121-2807
504-834-6404
Fax: 504-834-6404
Lobsters
President/Owner: Earl Duke
directlobster@aol.com
Estimated Sales: $340,000
Number Employees: 1-4

1596 **Boston Fruit Slice & Confectionery Corporation**
250 Canal St
Lawrence, MA 01840
978-686-2699
Fax: 978-686-5898 rick@bostonfruitslice.com
www.bostonfruitslice.com
Jellied fruit slices
President: John Morrissey
Executive Director/Hr Manager: Richard Hiera
Purchasing: Gail Laughlin
Estimated Sales: $3.3 Million
Number Employees: 30
Brands:
Boston Fruit Slices
Polly Orchard

1597 **Boston Seafarms**
119 Marlborough Street
Boston, MA 2116
617-784-4777
Fax: 800-692-9907 bostonseafarms@gmail.com
www.bostonseafarm.com
Processor, wholesaler/distributor, importer and exporter of seafood including fish and shellfish
President/CEO: Adam Weinberg
bostonseafarms@gmail.com
Estimated Sales: $12-13,000,000
Number Employees: 5
Square Footage: 36000

1598 **Boston Spice & Tea Company**
12207 Obannons Mill Rd
Boston, VA 22713
540-547-3907
Fax: 540-547-3656 800-966-4372
Herbal tea, vinegar, seasonings, mustard, sherry-pepper hot sauce, wassil, mulling and corned beef spices and dry bean soup mixes
President/Owner: Joann Neal
Director, Marketing & Sales: Greaner Neal
Estimated Sales: $.5-1 million
Number Employees: 5-9
Type of Packaging: Consumer
Brands:
Boston Spices
Logyan's Garden
Logyn'S Garden Soups
O'Bannon's
Stews and Sauces

1599 **Boston Stoker**
10855 Engle Rd
Vandalia, OH 45377-9439
937-890-6401
Fax: 937-890-6403 www.bostonstoker.com
Coffee
President: Eckley Adams
adamse@bostonstoker.com
Secretary/Treasurer: Sally Dean
Vice President: Henry Dean
Human Resources Director: Annette Sabwani
Director Of Operation: Travis Qualls
Plant Manager: John McWilliams
Purchasing Manager: Mandi Jamison
Estimated Sales: $6,000,000
Number Employees: 10-19
Type of Packaging: Private Label

1600 **Boston Tea Company**
560 Hudson St
Suite 3
Hackensack, NJ 07601
201-440-3004
Fax: 201-440-3005 800-495-9026
www.bostontea.com
Teas
President: Andy Jacobs
Vice President: Mary Jacobs
Contact: Carleen Failla
cfailla@bostontea.com
Office Manager: Eva Kotsonas
Director of Product Development: Carleen Violante

Estimated Sales: $800,000-$1,000,000
Number Employees: 8
Brands:
Beddy By
Lemon Dew
Magic Mountain
Ming Cha
Natco
Pick O' the Bushel
Razzle Dazzle
Spice Bouquet

1601 **Boston's Best Coffee Roasters**
43 Norfolk Ave
South Easton, MA 02375-1190
508-238-8393
Fax: 508-238-6835 800-898-8393
sales@bostonsbestcoffee.com
www.bostonsbestcoffee.com
Coffee, mixers and filters
President: Jacqueline Dovner
CEO: Stephen Fortune
Director of Fundraising Sales: Erin Woodard
Contact: Mary Burke
marymb@bostonsbestcoffee.com
Production Manager: Rocky Raposa
Estimated Sales: Less Than $500,000
Number Employees: 5-9
Square Footage: 5692
Type of Packaging: Consumer, Food Service, Private Label, Bulk
Brands:
David's Gourmet Coffee
Gold Star Coffee
Premier Coffee
Tropical Coffee

1602 **Botanical Bakery, LLC**
PO Box 11083
Napa, CA 94581
707-344-8103
Fax: 707-863-8949
Shortbread cookies.
CEO: Sondra Wells

1603 **Botanical Products**
34725 Bogart Dr
Springville, CA 93265-9602
559-539-3432
Fax: 559-539-2058
Processor and exporter of tablets, capsules, extracts and powders made from yucca and melatonin
President: Gordon Bean
VP: Joyce Bean
Estimated Sales: $1-2.5 Million
Number Employees: 1-4
Square Footage: 4000
Type of Packaging: Consumer
Brands:
Desert Pride
Desert Wonder

1604 **Botsford Fisheries**
Po Box 1093
Cap Pele, NB E4N 3B3
Canada
506-577-4327
Fax: 506-577-2846 info@botsfordfisheries.com
www.botsfordfisheries.com
Processor and exporter of fresh and smoked herring
President: William LeBlanc
Export Sales Manager: Janice Ryan
Plant Manager: Clement LeBlanc
Estimated Sales: $2,500,000
Number Employees: 50-99
Square Footage: 80000
Type of Packaging: Consumer, Food Service, Private Label, Bulk

1605 **Bottle Green Drinks Company**
2375 Tedlost
Unit 1
Mississauga, ON L5A 3W7
Canada
905-273-6137
Fax: 905-273-3186 info@bottlegreen.co.uk
www.bottlegreendrinks.com
Nonalcoholic and carbonated beverages including limeflower, elderflower, cranberry and lemongrass
President: Andrew James
CFO: Corrie James
Estimated Sales: $2.3,000,000
Number Employees: 13
Number of Brands: 2
Number of Products: 9
Type of Packaging: Consumer, Food Service, Private Label
Brands:
Bottle Green

1606 **Bottom Line Foods**
15757 Pines Blvd # 302
Suite 302
Pembroke Pines, FL 33027-1207
954-843-0562
Fax: 954-843-0568
Distributor and packer, exporter for frozen foods, meats, cheese, groceries, seafood, spices, etc.
President: Rein Bos
General Manager: Brandon Koppert
Estimated Sales: $1.1 Million
Number Employees: 1-4
Square Footage: 4000
Type of Packaging: Food Service, Private Label, Bulk

1607 **Bou Brands**
135 Madison Ave
5th Floor
New York, NY 10016
858-401-3356
bouforyou.com
Bouillon cubes
General Manager: Zach Bluemer
Number of Brands: 1
Number of Products: 7
Type of Packaging: Consumer
Brands:
BOU

1608 **Bouchaine Vineyards**
1075 Buchli Station Rd
Napa, CA 94559-9716
707-252-9006
Fax: 707-252-0401 800-654-9463
www.bouchaine.com
Wines
Propietor/President: Tattiana Copeland
Proprietor/Chairman: Gerret Copeland
Vice President, Wine Production &Sales: Greg Gauthier
General Manager & Winemaker: Michael Richmond
mrichmond@bouchaine.com
Estimated Sales: $2.5-5,000,000
Number Employees: 10-19

1609 **Bouchard Family Farm**
3 Strip Rd
Fort Kent, ME 04743-1550
207-834-3237
Fax: 207-834-7422 800-239-3237
bouchard@ployes.com www.ployes.com
Processor and exporter of buckwheat pancake mixes and flour
Owner: Joseph Bouchard
bouchard@ployes.com
Director: Jane Crawford
Treasurer: Aldan Bouchard
Sales/Marketing Executive: Elaine Mininger
Estimated Sales: Under $200,000
Number Employees: 5-9
Square Footage: 110000
Type of Packaging: Consumer, Food Service
Brands:
Bouchard Family Farm

1610 **Boudreaux's Foods**
5401 Toler St
New Orleans, LA 70123
504-733-8440
Fax: 504-866-1965
Refrigerated entrees, salad dressings, breads, whole wheat pasta, soups, etc
President: Vince Hayward
Estimated Sales: $1-3,000,000
Number Employees: 1-4
Square Footage: 2000
Type of Packaging: Consumer
Brands:
Author's Choice
Boudreaux's

1611 **Boulder Beer**
2880 Wilderness Pl
Boulder, CO 80301-5401
303-444-8448
Fax: 303-444-4796 webguy@boulderbeer.com
www.boulderbeer.com
Beer and ale
President: Annie Alwin
aalwin@boulderbeer.com
Marketing Director: Dan Weltz
Area Sales Manager: Marvin Simpson
Public Relations Director: Tess McFadden
VP Brewing Operations: David Zuckerman
Estimated Sales: $6 Million
Number Employees: 50-99
Number of Brands: 9
Number of Products: 1
Square Footage: 36000

1612 **Boulder Brands, Inc.**
115 West Century Road
Suite 260
Paramus, NJ 07652-1432
201-421-3970
Ed.Bryson@fleishman.com
www.smartbalance.com
Buttery spreads
President/COO: Terrence Schulke
Chairman/CEO: Stephen Hughes
Chief Finacial Officer: Christine Sacco
EVP/General Counsel: Norman Matar
Chief Innovation Officer: Peter Dray
Contact: Michael Adamson
madamson@boulderbrands.com
Estimated Sales: $1.5 Million
Number Employees: 56
Brands:
Smart Balance®
Heart Right ®

1613 **Boulder Canyon Natural Foods**
1898 S Flatiron Court
Suite 120
Boulder, CO 80301
303-546-9939
Fax: 303-546-9133 www.bouldercanyonfoods.com
Kettle chips
Co-Founder: Don Poore
Co-Founder: Jay Poore
Year Founded: 1994
Number of Brands: 1
Number of Products: 30
Type of Packaging: Consumer
Brands:
BOULDER CANYON

1614 **Boulder Cookie**
Boulder, CO 80516
bouldercookie.com
Paleo cookies
Number of Brands: 1
Number of Products: 6
Type of Packaging: Consumer
Brands:
BOULDER COOKIE

1615 **Boulder Creek Brewing Company**
13040 Highway 9
Boulder Creek, CA 95006-9154
831-338-7882
Fax: 831-338-7583
Beer, ale, lager
Owner: Nancy Long
President: Morgan Scarborough
Estimated Sales: &500,000-1,000,000
Number Employees: 18
Brands:
Boulder Creek
Redwood Ale

1616 **Boulder Granola**
PO Box 6114
Boulder, CO 80308-6114
303-443-1136
www.bouldergranola.com
Organic granola. Gluten free and dairy free varieties available.
Contact: Jody Nagel
jody@bouldergranola.com
Type of Packaging: Consumer

1617 Boulder Homemade Inc
2935 Baseline Rd # 200
Boulder, CO 80303-2367
303-494-0366
Fax: 303-494-5589 800-691-5002
glennise@bouldericecream.com
www.bouldericecream.com
Natural and organic ice cream, gelato, sorbet, and base mixes.
Contact: Glennise Humphrey
glennise@bouldericecream.com
Number Employees: 5-9
Type of Packaging: Consumer, Bulk
Brands:
BOULDER ICE CREAM

1618 Boulder Organic Foods
6363 Horizon Lane
Niwot, CO 80503
303-530-0470
hello@boulderorganicfoods.com
boulderorganicfoods.com
Fresh soup made with organic and gluten-free ingredients. Some of their varietites include vegan, vegetarian, and dariy-free options.
Founder & President: Kate Brown
CEO: Greg Powers
Director, Marketing & Sustainability: Jen-ai Stokesbary
Plant Manager: Wyatt Miller
Year Founded: 2008
Estimated Sales: $200 Million
Number Employees: 51-200
Type of Packaging: Consumer, Food Service, Private Label, Bulk

1619 Boulder Sausage Co
513 S Pierce Ave
Louisville, CO 80027-3019
303-665-6302
Fax: 303-665-3109 866-529-0595
www.bouldersausage.com
Meat
Vice President: Tom Griffiths
bouldersausage@webaccess.net
Secretary/Treasurer: James Burton
Vice President: Donald Gullickson
Saleman Manager: Ronda Haire
Office Manager;Operations Manager: Suzanne Richards
Estimated Sales: $2.4,000,000
Number Employees: 20-49
Number of Products: 14
Type of Packaging: Consumer, Food Service, Private Label, Bulk
Brands:
Boulder Sausage Products
Private Label Products
Rocky Mountain Products

1620 Boulder Vegans LLC
4947 S Urban Ct
Morrison, CO 80465-2017
303-667-5628
info@bouldervegans.com
www.beyond-better.com
Vegan cheese and cheese products.
Owner: Kerry Behrens
Brands:
Beyond Better

1621 Boulevard Brewing
2501 Southwest Blvd
Kansas City, MO 64108-2345
816-474-7095
Fax: 816-474-1722 fineales@blvdbeer.com
www.boulevardia.com
Ale, lager, stout and seasonal beer
President: John McDonald
COO: Steve Mills
CFO: Jeff Krum
Marketing Director: Jeremy Ragonese
VP Sales: Bob Sullivan
Hr Manager: Nicole Thibodeau
Manager: Joe Palausky
Production Manager: Mike Youngquist
Estimated Sales: $27,000,000
Number Employees: 50-99
Type of Packaging: Consumer, Food Service

1622 Bouma Meats
PO Box 925
Provost, AB T0B 3S0
Canada
780-753-2092
Fax: 780-753-4939 bouma_meats@hotmail.com
www.provostnews.ca/boumameats/
Beef and pork including fresh, frozen, portion controlled, sausage and deli cuts; also, bacon and ham
Joint Owner/ Store Operator: Ben Richter
Joint Owner/ Plant Operator: Tim Rachinski
Estimated Sales: $2,000,000
Number Employees: 8
Type of Packaging: Consumer, Food Service, Private Label, Bulk
Brands:
Bouma

1623 Boundary Fish Company
225 Sigurdson Ave
Blaine, WA 98230-4004
360-332-6715
Fax: 360-332-8785 arnold@boundaryfish.com
www.boundaryfish.com
Dungeness crab, pacific salmon, halibut, black cod, dogfish.
President: Arnold Yuki
Estimated Sales: $20-50 Million
Number Employees: 20-49
Type of Packaging: Consumer, Food Service

1624 Bountiful Larder LLC
218 Butte Ave.
Crested Butte, CO 81224
303-619-8056
800-676-5057
info@jacksonshonest.com
www.jacksonshonest.com
Manufacturer of tortilla and potato chips.
Co-Founder & CEO: Megan Reamer
Social Media and Marketing: Lindsey Schauer
Director of Sales: Jessica Moore
Director of Operations: David McCormick

1625 Bountiful Pantry
PO Box 179
Nantucket, MA 02584
617-487-8019
Fax: 508-374-5850 info@bountifulpantry.com
www.bountifulpantry.com
Soup mixes, side dishes, waffle mixes, bread, roll, scone and biscuit mixes, cookie and dessert mixes and teas and coffees

1626 Bourbon Barrel Foods
1201 Story Ave # 175
Suite 175
Louisville, KY 40206-1768
502-333-6103
Fax: 502-333-6104 info@bourbonbarrelfoods.com
www.bourbonbarrelfoods.com
Gourmet foods.
President: Matt Jamie
info@bourbonbarrelfoods.com
Number Employees: 10-19

1627 Boutique Seafood Brokers
1326 White St SW
Atlanta, GA 30310-1648
404-752-8852
Fax: 404-752-6634 www.buckheadrestaurants.com
Seafood, red snapper, sea bass, lobster meat, crabmeat, grouper
President/CEO: Pano Karatassos
CFO: Christo Makrides
Senior Director of Marketing: Jennifer Parker
Director of Operations: Niko Karatassos
Estimated Sales: $4.5 Million
Number Employees: 1-4

1628 Bouvry Exports Calgary
222 58 Avenue SW
Suite 312
Calgary, AB T2H 2S3
Canada
403-253-0717
Fax: 403-259-3568
Horse meat, bison and beef
President: Claude Bouvry
CEO: John McNaughton
General Manager: Darin Sjonger
Sales: Alain Bouvry
Estimated Sales: $21.6,000,000
Number Employees: 150
Type of Packaging: Consumer, Bulk

1629 Bove's of Vermont
68 Pearl St
Burlington, VT 05403
802-862-7235
Fax: 802-651-9371 802-862-6651
sauceboy@Boves.com www.boves.com
Marinara sauce, roasted garlic sauce, chianti mushroom sauce, romano pomodoro sauce.
President: Mark Bove
sauceboy@boves.com
Vice President/Secretary/Treasurer: Richard Bove
Estimated Sales: $170,000
Number Employees: 3
Brands:
Bove's of Vermont

1630 Bow Valley Brewing Company
109 Boulder Crescent
Canmore, AB T1W 1L4
Canada
403-678-2739
Fax: 403-678-8813
Lager
President: Hugh Hancock
Treasurer: Jim Lawson
Secretary: Wayne McNeill
Number Employees: 6
Type of Packaging: Consumer, Food Service
Brands:
Bow Valley

1631 Bowery Farming Inc.
151 W 26th St.
12th Fl.
New York, NY 10001
boweryfarming.com
Leafy greens grown without pesticides and non-GMO seeds.
Co-Founder & CEO: Irving Fain
Co-Founder: Brian Falther
Co-Founder & Strategic Finance: David Golden
Marketing Director: Katie Seawell
Sales Director: Carmela Cugini
Finance & Legal Director: Darren Thompson
Year Founded: 2015
Number Employees: 51-200
Type of Packaging: Private Label

1632 Bowman & Landes Turkeys
6490 Ross Rd
New Carlisle, OH 45344-8801
937-845-9466
Fax: 937-845-9998 877-466-9466
info@bowmanlandes.com
www.bowmanlandes.com
Free range turkeys
President: Anita Bowman
anita@bowmanlandes.com
Estimated Sales: $10-20 Million
Number Employees: 100-249
Type of Packaging: Consumer, Bulk

1633 Bowness Bakery
4280-23rd Street NE
Calgary, AB T2E 6X7
Canada
403-250-9760
Fax: 403-291-9129
Specialty breads, pretzels and pizza shells
CEO: Shams Habib
Estimated Sales: $5,000,000
Number Employees: 40
Type of Packaging: Consumer, Food Service, Bulk
Brands:
Bowness Baker
Frisches Brot
Pretzeland

1634 Bowser Meat Processing
401 S Palmberg St
Meriden, KS 66512
785-484-2454
Meat including sausage
Owner: Gary Koerner
Manager: Kirsti Petesch
Estimated Sales: $140,000
Number Employees: 4
Type of Packaging: Consumer

1635 Boyajian LLC
144 Will Dr
Canton, MA 02021-3704
781-828-9966
Fax: 781-828-9922 800-965-0665
customerservice@boyajianinc.com
www.boyajianinc.com
Vinegars, infused oils and natural flavorings.
Owner/President: John Boyajian
jboyajian@boyajianinc.com
Director of Marketing: Amy Alberti
Human Resources Manager: Zovig Kanarian
General Manager: Zanig Kanarian
Estimated Sales: $1 Million
Number Employees: 10-19
Square Footage: 40000
Type of Packaging: Consumer, Food Service, Private Label, Bulk
Brands:
Boyajian

1636 (HQ)Boyd's Coffee Co
Portland, OR 97230
800-735-2878
customerservicena@farmerbros.com
www.boydscoffeestore.com
Coffees, teas, cocoa, hot and frozen beverages
Senior Sales Manager: Gabriel Dominguez
VP of Manufacturing: Mitch Karstadt
Estimated Sales: $49 Million
Number Employees: 250-499
Number of Brands: 7
Parent Co: Farmer Bros Co
Type of Packaging: Food Service
Other Locations:
Boyd's Coffee Company
Coeur D Alene ID
Brands:
Boyd's Coffee
Coffee House Roasters
Island Mist Iced Tea
Italia D'Oro Coffee
Techni-Brew
Today
Viaggio Coffee

1637 Boyd's Sausage Co
626 Highway 1 S
Washington, IA 52353-9786
319-653-5715
bls11388@gmail.com
Beef jerky, bologna and deer meat products including sausage
Owner: Brandon Statler
Estimated Sales: $270,000
Number Employees: 5-9
Square Footage: 10500
Type of Packaging: Consumer, Bulk

1638 Boyer Candy Co Inc
821 17th St
Altoona, PA 16601-2074
814-944-9401
Fax: 814-944-4923 www.boyercandies.com
Chocolate confectionery products including shell molded chocolates, cup candy and seasonal novelities
CEO: Robert Faith
rfaith@boyercandies.com
Plant Manager: Jim Lidwell
Estimated Sales: $9,000,000
Number Employees: 50-99
Number of Brands: 8
Square Footage: 150000
Type of Packaging: Consumer, Private Label, Bulk
Brands:
Bartons
Boxer
Boyer
Casanova
Hill of Westchester
Kron
Schrafft's
Winters

1639 Boyer's Coffee
7295 Washington St
Denver, CO 80229-6707
303-289-3345
Fax: 303-289-2133 800-452-5282
info@boyerscoffee.com www.boyerscoffee.com
Coffee
President: Mark Goodman
mark@boyerscoffee.com
Marketing Director: Bonnie Rine
Plant & Purchasing Manager: L Smith
Estimated Sales: $2.5-5,000,000
Number Employees: 20-49
Type of Packaging: Private Label

1640 Boylan Bottling Company
74 Lee Avenue
Haledon, NJ 07508-1202
973-790-7093
Fax: 973-790-9097 800-289-7978
Bottled soft drinks
President/CEO: Ronald Fiorina
Executive VP: Mark Fiorina
COO: David Fiorina, Jr.
Estimated Sales: $1-2,500,000
Number Employees: 20-49

1641 Boyle Meat Company
1638 Saint Louis Ave
Kansas City, MO 64101-1130
816-221-6283
Fax: 816-221-3888 800-821-3626
theresa@boylescornedbeef.com
Steaks, corn beef, pastrami and pot roast
President: Don Wendl
Special Project Manager: James Crouch
VP: Christy Chester
Estimated Sales: $20-50 Million
Number Employees: 20-49
Square Footage: 10000
Type of Packaging: Food Service, Private Label, Bulk

1642 Boyton Shellfish
RR 2
Box 85a
Ellsworth, ME 04605
207-667-8580
Fax: 619-474-6103
Shellfish
Owner: Dean Smith

1643 Bozzano Olive Ranch
6880 East Navone Road
PO Box 5009
Stockton, CA 95215
209-451-3665
Fax: 209-467-8362 info@bozzanoranch.com
www.bozzanoranch.com
Olive oils
President: Joe Bozzano
Vice President: Jack Bozzano
jack@bozzanoranch.com
Number Employees: 15

1644 Brad's Organic
7 Hoover Ave
Haverstraw, NY 10927
845-429-9080
Fax: 845-429-9089 sales@bradsorganic.com
www.bradsorganic.com
Organic, all-natural salsa, tortilla chips, honey, jams and peanut butter
Administration: Lisa Salia
Estimated Sales: $73,000
Number Employees: 2

1645 Brad's Taste of New York
P.O.Box 20475
Floral Park, NY 11002-0475
516-354-9004
Fax: 516-354-9004 bradstasteofny@aol.com
Gourmet mustard, pretzel dip, honey wheat pretzel, sourdough honey mustard nuggets, and kettle potato chips
Owner: Bradley Knese
Estimated Sales: $1-3 Million
Number Employees: 5-9

1646 Bradford Co
13500 Quincy St
Holland, MI 49424-9460
616-399-6538
Fax: 616-399-8989 info@bradfordco.com
www.bradfordco.com
Manufacturer of packaging products and material handling systems.
President: Hulda Grin
hgrin@championhealthandfitness.com
Estimated Sales: $2.5-5 Million
Number Employees: 100-249

1647 Bradley 3 Ranch
15591 Cr K
Memphis, TX 79245
806-888-1062
Fax: 806-888-1010 mmll@bradley3ranch.com
www.bradley3ranch.com
Fresh beef processing and packing
President: Mary Lou Bradley
General Manager: James Henderson
Purchasing: Kathleen Lewis
Estimated Sales: $20-50 Million
Number Employees: 50-99
Type of Packaging: Consumer, Food Service
Brands:
B 3 R
B C Natural

1648 Bradley Creek Seafood
PO Box 30446
Savannah, GA 31410
912-484-3510
Fax: 912-897-7815 www.bradleycreek.com
Crab au gratin pastries; deviled crab; and crab cakes.
President/CEO: Michael Simmons
Type of Packaging: Food Service

1649 Bradley Technologies Canada Inc.
8380 River Road
Delta, BC V4G 1B5
Canada
309-343-1124
Fax: 309-343-1126 866-508-7514
info@bradleysmoker.com
www.bradleysmoker.com
Other meat/game/pate. other sauces, seasonings and cooking enhancers, private label, cooking implements,housewares.
Marketing: Michael Tostowaryk
Estimated Sales: $2.3 Million
Number Employees: 24

1650 Bradshaw's Food Products
1425 Somerset Avenue
Dighton, MA 02715-1215
508-669-6088
Pickled beef tripe
Partner: D Bradshaw
Partner: R Bradshaw
Estimated Sales: $1-2.5 Million
Number Employees: 1-4

1651 Bradye P. Todd & Son
316 Sunburst Highway/US Route 50
Cambridge, MD 21613-1308
410-228-8633
info@toddseafood.com
www.toddseafood.com
Seafood including crabs, seafood delicatessen and restaurant
Owner: Roy Todd
Estimated Sales: $3 Million
Number Employees: 20-49
Square Footage: 12000
Parent Co: T.A. Ocean Odyssey
Type of Packaging: Consumer

1652 Bragg Live Food Products Inc
199 Winchester Canyon Rd
Goleta, CA 93117-1961
805-968-1020
Fax: 805-968-1001 800-446-1990
info@bragg.com www.bragg.com
Liquid aminos and organic apple cider vinegar and extra-virgin olive oil
Manager: Sandi Enriquez
Controller: Sandy Gooch
Estimated Sales: $5-10 Million
Number Employees: 20-49
Brands:
Bragg

1653 Braham Food Locker Service
124 Central Dr W
Braham, MN 55006
320-396-2636
Meat products including beef, goat and pork; also, smoked and cured sausage
President: Nicholas Grote
CEO: Diane Grote
Estimated Sales: $250,000
Number Employees: 5-9
Type of Packaging: Consumer

1654 **(HQ)Brakebush Brothers**
N4993 6th Dr
Westfield, WI 53964
800-933-2121
www.brakebush.com
Frozen chicken.
Research & Development Director: Jon Brakebush
Quality Assurance Manager: Donna Halbach
Marketing Manager: Steve Ross
Sales & Marketing Director: Scott Sanders
ssanders@brakebush.com
Production Manager: Steve Deery
VP, Purchasing: Chris Brakebush
Year Founded: 1925
Estimated Sales: $33.5 Million
Number Employees: 500-999
Number of Products: 200+
Square Footage: 500000
Type of Packaging: Consumer, Food Service
Brands:
Smartshapes®
Kids Klassics®
Chik'n'zips®
Global Creations®
Squawkers®
Brakebush®
Honey-Touched®
Farm Pantry®
Country Krisp®
Southern Select™
Perfect Answers®
Cayenne Kicker™
Gold'n'spice®
Tappers®
Crispy-Lishus®
Oven Lovin' Chik'n™
Wing-Ditties®
Zippity Doo-Wa Ditties®
Inferno Wings®
Chik'n Gone Wild™
Bluegrass Bourbon™ Sauce
Fiery Fingers®
Touchdown Nuggets™
Chik'n Stars™
Lil' Chicks™
Fry Stix™
Zoo Crew™
Chik'n Hoops®
Chik'n Pretzels™
Dog-Gone Chik'n®
Chik'n Giggles®
Bold Italiano™

1655 **Brand Aromatics Inc**
1600 Oak St
Lakewood, NJ 08701-5924
732-363-8080
Fax: 732-363-8041 800-363-2080
www.brandaromatics.com
Flavors and seasonings
President: Karl Brand
Co-VP: Barbara Brand
Co-VP: Dennis Shea
Sales Executive: Ed Heraty
Warehouse Manager: Mike Sernotti
Plant Manager: Vince Deangelo
Estimated Sales: $4.9 000,000
Number Employees: 20-49

1656 **Brandborg Cellars**
PO Box 506
Elkton, OR 97436-0506
510-215-9553
Fax: 415-282-6179
Wine
President: Terry Brandborg
Number Employees: 20-49

1657 **Brander Vineyard**
2401 N Refugio Rd
Santa Ynez, CA 93460
805-688-2455
Fax: 805-688-8010 800-970-9979
info@Brander.com www.brander.com
Red and white wines
Owner: Fred Brander
fred@brander.com
Sales/Marketing: Julie Hayek
Operations Assistant: Drew Horton
Office Manager: Kathy Forner
Estimated Sales: $380,000
Number Employees: 5-9
Type of Packaging: Consumer, Food Service
Brands:
Brander

1658 **Branding Iron**
1682 Sauget Business Blvd.
Sauget, IL 62206-1454
618-337-8400
Fax: 618-337-3292 800-851-4684
www.bih-us.com
Frozen high quality angus beef, pork, and veal patties
President: Mike Holten
Chairman: Jim Holten
Contact: Joe Dietrich
jdietrich@bih-us.com
CEO: Scott Hudspeth
Estimated Sales: $32 Million
Number Employees: 200
Square Footage: 50000
Type of Packaging: Food Service
Brands:
The Cloud
Thick N' Juicy
Restaurant Quality
Extra Value
Double Red Provisions

1659 **Branding Iron Meats**
245 Industrial Blvd
Sauk Rapids, MN 56379-1238
320-259-0659
Fax: 320-240-0654 800-851-4684
Manufacturer and packer of meats and meat snacks
President: James Hanson
Director, Business Dev.: Rich Blay
Director, Quality: Pat Flanigan
Director, Sales: Dave King
Manager: Paul Bravinder
pbravinder@bih-us.com
Estimated Sales: $15.3 Million
Number Employees: 50-99
Parent Co: Branding Iron Holding Company
Type of Packaging: Consumer, Private Label
Brands:
Besure
Huisken
Rg's

1660 **Brandmeyer Popcorn Co**
3785 NE 70th Ave
Ankeny, IA 50021-9734
515-262-3243
Fax: 866-631-6276 800-568-8276
www.lottapop.com
Processor and exporter of popcorn including gift boxes and specialty items
Owner: Arlie Brandmeyer
arlie@lottapop.com
Estimated Sales: $110,000
Number Employees: 1-4
Brands:
Iowa State
Lotta-Pop

1661 **Brands Within Reach**
141 Halstead Ave
2nd Floor
Mamaroneck, NY 10543
847-720-9090
contact@bwrgroup.com
bwrgroup.com
Bottled water
Brands:
Belvoir Fruit Farms
Saint Geron
Kusmi Tea
Nestea
Grand-MŠre
Lucien Georgelin
Volvic
Evian

1662 **Brandt Farms Inc**
6040 Avenue 430
P.O. Box 852
Reedley, CA 93654-9008
559-638-6961
Fax: 559-638-6964 www.brandtfarms.com
Peaches, nectarines, plums.
President: Wayne Brandt
CEO: Eleanor Brandt
COO: Jack Brandt
Sales Exec: Dave Maddux
Public Relations: Dave Maddox
davemaddux@treeripe.com
Estimated Sales: $20 Million
Number Employees: 100-249
Square Footage: 60000
Brands:
Brandt
Crystal Foods
Crystal R-Best

1663 **Brandt Mills**
607 Race Street
Mifflinville, PA 18631
570-752-4271
Fax: 570-752-8712
Flour including pastry and whole wheat
President: Richard Brandt Jr
Secretary-Treasurer: Alan Brandt
Secretary: Lisa Dunn
Retail Sales Manager: John Allen
Estimated Sales: $1.3 Million
Number Employees: 12
Square Footage: 24000

1664 **Braren Pauli Winery**
7051 N State St
Redwood Valley, CA 95470-9629
707-485-0322
Fax: 707-485-6784 800-423-6519
Wines
President: Charlie Barra
Co-Owner/CEO: Bill Pauli
Marketing Director: Larry Braren
Sales Director: Larry Braren
Winemaker: Larry Braren
Estimated Sales: $.5-1,000,000
Number Employees: 20-49
Brands:
Braren Pauli

1665 **Brass Ladle Products**
P.O.Box 39
Concordville, PA 19331
610-565-8664
Fax: 610-565-8665 800-955-2353
frontdesk@brassladle.com www.brassladle.com
All-natural gourmet cake mixes including carrot, mocha mud(chocolate) and lemon poppy seed.
Owner: Skip Achuff
Estimated Sales: $1,000,000
Number Employees: 1-4
Number of Brands: 1
Number of Products: 3
Square Footage: 6000
Type of Packaging: Consumer, Food Service, Private Label, Bulk
Brands:
Brass Ladle
Mocha Mud
Mocha Mud Cake Mix

1666 **Brasserie Brasel Brewery**
8477 Rue Cordner
Lasalle, QC H8N 2X2
Canada
514-365-5050
Fax: 514-365-2954 800-463-2728
Processor and exporter of lager beers
President: Marcel Jagermann
Managing Director: Stan Jagermann
Number Employees: 10-19
Square Footage: 24000
Type of Packaging: Consumer, Food Service, Private Label
Brands:
Brasal Bock
Brasal Legere
Brasal Special Amber
Hopps Aux Pommes
Hopps Brau

1667 **Brassica Protection Products**
250 President St # 2000
Baltimore, MD 21202-7806
410-732-1200
Fax: 410-732-1980 866-747-0001
mail@brassica.com
Food ingredients, supplements, nutraceuticals, functional foods (cander preventive products)

CEO: Antony Talalay
atalalay@mba1978.hbs.edu
National Account Manager: Shane Fantauzzo
VP Business Development: Earl Hauserman
Estimated Sales: $660,000
Number Employees: 1-4
Brands:
Brassica
Brassica Teas With Sgs
Broccosprouts

1668 **Braswell's Winery**
7556 Bankhead Highway
Dora, AL 35062-2041
205-648-8335
Fax: 205-648-8335
Wines
President: Wayne Braswell
Owner: Ruth Braswell
Estimated Sales: $1-4,9,000,000
Number Employees: 1-4

1669 **Brateka Enterprises**
15680 SW 23rd Avenue
Ocala, FL 34473-4278
352-307-5459
Fax: 352-307-5459 877-549-3227
Gourmet sauces in gift baskets
CEO: Hyacinth Thomas
Number Employees: 10-19
Brands:
Lize Jamaican Style Gourmet Bbq

1670 **Braum's Inc**
3000 NE 63rd St
P.O. Box 25429
Oklahoma City, OK 73125
405-478-1656
800-327-6455
www.braums.com
Frozen desserts, dairy and milk.
Owner: Bill Braum
President & CEO: Drew Braum
Marketing Director: Terry Holden
Purchasing Director: Kenny McDonald
Year Founded: 1933
Estimated Sales: $437 Million
Number Employees: 5000-9999
Square Footage: 260000
Type of Packaging: Food Service

1671 **Braun Seafood Co**
30840 Main Rd
Cutchogue, NY 11935-1336
631-734-6700
Fax: 631-734-7462 info@braunseafood.com
braunseafood.com
Processor and distributor of oysters
Vice President: Keith Reda
Estimated Sales: $2.5-5,000,000
Number Employees: 20-49

1672 **Bravard Vineyards & Winery**
15000 Overton Rd
Hopkinsville, KY 42240-9451
270-269-2583
Fax: 270-269-2583
Wines including dry, semi-dry, semi-sweet and sweet in white, blush, rose and red
Co-Owner: Janeth Bravard
Member: James Bravard
Estimated Sales: $32,000
Number Employees: 1-4
Square Footage: 500
Type of Packaging: Private Label
Brands:
Bravard
Countryside Red
Foch
Fruit Hill White
Lady Genevieve
Pennyroyal

1673 **Brazi Bites**
1836 NE 7th Ave
Suite 203
Portland, OR 97212
503-303-2272
brazibites.com
Brazilian cheese bread
Co-Founder: Junea Rocha
Year Founded: 2009
Number of Brands: 1
Number of Products: 4
Type of Packaging: Consumer
Brands:
BRAZI BITES

1674 **Brazilian Home Collection**
249 Monree Street
Passaic, NJ 07055
973-365-5800
Fax: 973-365-0007 bhcollection.com
Brazil handicraft.

1675 **Brazos Legends**
9087 Knight Rd
Houston, TX 77054-4305
713-795-0266
Fax: 713-795-5534 800-882-6253
sbailey@texastamale.com www.texastamale.com
Gourmet food products
President: J Boles
CEO: Shirley Bailey
sbailey@texastamali.com
Sales Director: Shirley Bailey
Operations Manager: Shirley Bailey
Plant Manager: Ana Flores
Estimated Sales: $3-5,000,000
Number Employees: 10-19
Number of Brands: 5
Number of Products: 125
Square Footage: 25000
Type of Packaging: Consumer, Food Service, Private Label, Bulk
Brands:
Brazos Legends
Red Eye

1676 **Brazos Valley Cheese**
7781 Gholson Rd
Waco, TX 76705
254-230-2535
info@brazosvalleycheese.com
Cheeses
Contact: Marc Kuehl
marc@brazosvalleycheese.com
Type of Packaging: Consumer, Food Service, Bulk

1677 **Bread & Chocolate Inc**
1538 Industrial Park
Po Box 692
Wells River, VT 05081-9806
802-429-2920
Fax: 802-429-2990 800-524-6715
info@burnhamandmills.com
Gourmet lemonade, cocoa, pancake mixes, jams, mustards and iced tea mixes
Owner: Fran Rutstein
fran@burnhamandmills.com
Vice President: Fran Rutstein
Estimated Sales: $500,000-900,000
Number Employees: 1-4
Brands:
Bear River
Bread & Chocolate
Moose Mountain
Snowman
Storytime

1678 **Bread Alone Bakery**
2121 Ulster Avenue
Lake Katrine, NY 12449
845-657-3328
Fax: 845-657-6228 800-769-3328
info@breadalone.com www.breadalone.com
Artisanal bakery.
CEO: Dan Leader
Vice President: Nels Leader
Contact: Sharon Burns-Leader
sharon@breadalone.com
Year Founded: 1985
Number Employees: 100+
Brands:
Bread Alone

1679 **Bread Box Cafe**
4711 11th St
Astoria, NY 11101-5404
Canada
718-389-9703
breadboxcafelic.com/
Bread and buns
President: Debby Andrews
Co-Owner: Irene Plaisier
Co-Owner: Dianna Careme
Contact: Tal Shuster
talshuster@yahoo.com
Estimated Sales: Less Than $500,000
Number Employees: 1-4
Square Footage: 2000
Type of Packaging: Consumer

1680 **Bread Dip Company**
PO Box 607
Maple Valley, WA 98038
425-358-7386
Fax: 425-413-2104 www.breaddipcompany.com
Gourmet spreads and dips
Contact: Jim McCaslin
jim@breaddipcompany.com
Year Founded: 1994
Number Employees: 1-4

1681 **Breads from Anna**
3007 Sierra Ct
Iowa City, IA 52240
319-354-3886
Fax: 319-358-9920 877-354-3886
info@breadsfromanna.com breadsfromanna.com
Gluten- and allergen-free baking mixes.

1682 **Breadworks**
923 Preston Ave # A
Charlottesville, VA 22903-4446
434-296-4663
Fax: 434-971-6740 info@breadworks.org
www.breadworks.org
Breads including American and French sourdough, twelve grain, Jewish rye, challah, semolina, Irish soda and baguettes; also, cookies, muffins, scones, danish, pies, cakes and deli products
Manager: Jim Baber
jsb5930@aol.com
Chairman: Marc Bridenhagen
Vice President: John Satoski
Production/Sales: Priscilla Fox
Estimated Sales: $670,000
Number Employees: 10-19
Parent Co: Worksource Enterprises
Type of Packaging: Consumer, Food Service

1683 **Breaktime Snacks**
7723 Somerset Blvd
Paramount, CA 90723
562-633-6200
Fax: 562-633-8789 800-677-1968
info@breaktimesnacks.com
www.breaktimesnacks.com
Gourmet popcorn
President/CEO: Roger Glade
Estimated Sales: $1-2,500,000
Number Employees: 5-9
Brands:
Corn Appetit

1684 **Breakwater Fisheries**
14 O'Briens Hill
St John's, NL A1B 4G4
Canada
709-754-1999
Fax: 709-754-9712
Processor and exporter of frozen snow crab, capelin, turbot, cod, mackerel, herring, squid and shrimp; importer of frozen squid
President/CEO: Randy Barnes
General Manager/Co-Owner: Lemuel White
Vice President: Ken White
Estimated Sales: $10-20 Million
Number Employees: 500
Number of Brands: 1
Square Footage: 75000
Brands:
Breakwater

1685 **Breakwater Seafoods & Chowder**
306 S F St
Aberdeen, WA 98520-4144
360-532-5693
Fax: 360-533-6488
Seafoods
Owner: Sonny Bridges
President: Lloyd Bridges
Treasurer: Jack Thompson
Vice President: Linda Mertz
Estimated Sales: Less Than $500,000
Number Employees: 5-9

1686 **Breaux Vineyards**
36888 Breaux Vineyards Ln
Purcellville, VA 20132-1748
540-668-6299
Fax: 540-668-6283 800-492-9961
jblosser@breauxvineyards.com
www.breauxvineyards.com

Wines
Owner: Paul Breaux
paul@breauxvineyards.com
Co-Owner: Alexis Breaux
Sales Director: Jennifer Breaux Blosser
paul@breauxvineyards.com
General Manager: Chris Blosser
Wine Maker: Dave Collins
Estimated Sales: $480,000
Number Employees: 10-19
Square Footage: 20000
Type of Packaging: Consumer, Private Label, Bulk

1687 **Breckenridge Brewery**
471 Kalamath St
Denver, CO 80204
303-573-0431
Fax: 303-573-4877 800-328-6723
freshbeer@breckenridgebrewery.com
www.breckenridgebrewery.com

Ale and stout
Founder/President: Edward A Cerkovnik Jr.
Brew master/Director Brewery Operations: J. Todd Usry
Controller: BJ Langton
Director of Marketing: Todd M Thibault
Director of Sales: George O'Neill
Contact: James Bartley
jamesbartley@subway.com
Director of Operations: Kurt Volker
Brew master and Director of Brewery Oper: J Usry
Estimated Sales: $14,000,000
Number Employees: 200
Parent Co: Breckenridge Brewery
Type of Packaging: Consumer, Food Service, Bulk
Brands:
Autumn Ale
Avalanche Ale
Christmas Ale
Hefe Proper
Oatmeal Stout
Pandora's Bock
Summerbright Ale
Trademark Pale Ale

1688 **Breitenbach Wine Cellars**
5934 Old Route 39 NW
Dover, OH 44622-7787
330-343-3603
Fax: 330-343-8290 www.breitenbachwine.com
Wines
President/CEO: Cynthia Bixler
info@breitenbachwine.com
Accountant: Susan Graber
Director of Sales: Jennifer Kohler
Manager: Anita Davis
Director Manufacturing: Dalton Bixler
Estimated Sales: $540,000
Number Employees: 10-19
Brands:
Breitenbach
Charming Nancy
Dardenella
Dusty Miller
Festival
First Crush
Frost Fire
Roadhouse Red
Rosebarb
Silver Seyual

1689 **Brekki**
5661 Palmer Way
Suite G
Carlsbad, CA 92010
760-487-8895
info@brekki.com
www.brekki.com

Overnight oatmeal
Co-Founder: Russell Radebaugh
Co-Founder: Greg Peyser
Number of Brands: 1
Number of Products: 5
Type of Packaging: Consumer
Brands:
BREKKI

1690 **Bremner Biscuit Company**
4600 Joliet St
Denver, CO 80239-2922
303-371-8180
Fax: 303-371-8185 866-972-6879
bremner@worldpantry.com
www.bremnerbiscuitco.com

Processor and exporter of gourmet, snack and oyster crackers
Manager: Neil Bremner
Contact: Bryan Dare
bdare@darefoods.com
Estimated Sales: $5-10 Million
Number Employees: 20-49
Square Footage: 126000
Parent Co: Dare Foods
Type of Packaging: Consumer, Food Service, Private Label, Bulk
Brands:
Bremner
Bremner Wafers
Brewski Snack

1691 **Brennan Snacks Manufacturing**
1220 W 7th Street
Bogalusa, LA 70427-3406
800-290-7486
Fax: 985-732-5397

Snacks and cotton candy
Co-Owner: Bernie Brennan, Jr.
Co-Owner: Christi Brennan
Number Employees: 20-49
Type of Packaging: Food Service, Private Label
Brands:
Oboy's

1692 **Brenntag North America**
5083 Pottsville Pike
Reading, PA 19605
610-926-6100
Fax: 610-916-3782 contactus@brenntag.com
www.brenntag.com
Ingredients & additives including; amino acids, bentonite, calcium carbonate, carotenoids, caffeine, cellulose gums, calcium oxide, magnesium oxide, enzymees, conjugated linoleic acid, precipitated silica, zinc oxide, guar gum, foamcontrol agents, magnesium carbonate, magnesium hydroxide, natural sweetener, oat ingredients, omega 3 powders, plant sterols, stearates, vegetable oils, vitamins, waxes & butters, colorants, etc.
CEO: Markus Kl,,hn
CFO: Dieter Woehrle
COO: Steven Terwindt
Estimated Sales: $160 Million
Number Employees: 135
Square Footage: 110000
Parent Co: Brenntag AG
Other Locations:
Sales Office
Norcross GA
Sales Office
Plainfield IL
Sales Office
Philadelphia PA
Sales Office
Houston TX
Sales Office
Orinda CA
Brands:
Evonik
Brenntag
Specialty Minerals
Basf
Lucarotin
Lycovit
Xangold
Vicality Albafil
Calessence
Vicron
Scora S.A.
Scoralite
Mississippi Lime
Ashland
Aqualon
Aqualon Klucel
Aqualon Benecel
Usg
Tonalin
Icl Industrial Products
Novozymes
Protamex
Alcalase
Ban
Catazyme
Celluclast
Dextranase
Dextrozyme
Flavourzyme
Fungamyl
Gluzyme
Lactozym Pure
Lecitase
Lipopan
Lipozyme
Maltogenase
Neutrase
Novo Pro D
Novoshape
Novozym
Palatase
Pentopan
Sweetzyme
Termamyl
Viscozyme L
Wacker
Silfoam
Ppg
Flo-Gard
Supercol
U.S. Zinc Votorantim Metals
Pyure Brands, Llc
Biovelop
Promoat
Proatein
Dry N-3
Vegapure
Textron
Covi-Ox
Covitol
Koster Keunen

1693 **Breslow Deli Products**
1209 N Hancock Street
Philadelphia, PA 19122-4505
215-739-4200
Fax: 215-423-4199
Beef including smoked and dried
President: Jon Breslow
Estimated Sales: $890,000
Number Employees: 6
Type of Packaging: Consumer, Food Service

1694 **Brew Dr. Kombucha**
PO Box 42291
Portland, OR 97242
760-487-8895
info@brekki.com
www.brekki.com
Kombucha
Founder & CEO: Matt Thomas
Number of Brands: 1
Number of Products: 5
Type of Packaging: Consumer
Brands:
BREW DR.

1695 **Brewers Association**
736 Pearl Street
Po Box 1679
Boulder, CO 80302
303-447-0816
Fax: 303-447-2825 888-822-6273
bob@brewersassociation.org
www.brewersassociation.com
Beer.
Marketing: Robert Pease
Contact: Katie Brown
katie@brewersassociation.org

1696 **Brewers Outlet-Chestnut Hill**
7401 Germantown Ave
Philadelphia, PA 19119-1605
215-247-1265
Fax: 215-247-1855 info@mybrewersoutlet.com
www.mybrewersoutlet.com
Craft and specialty beers
Owner: Paul Egonopoulos
Estimated Sales: $2.5-5 Million
Number Employees: 5-9
Square Footage: 15000
Parent Co: Brewers Outlet

1697 **Brewery Ommegang**
656 County Highway 33
Cooperstown, NY 13326-4737
607-286-4144
Fax: 607-547-8374 800-544-1809
info@ommegang.com www.ommegang.com

Owner: Don Feinberg
info@belgianexperts.com
Innovation Manager: Mike McManus
Number Employees: 20-49
Type of Packaging: Consumer

1698 **Brewla Inc.**
Brooklyn, NY
855-543-7677
www.brewlabars.com
Manufacturer of specialty brewed bars made from herbs, coffee, teas, and botanicals.
Co-Founder: Daniel Dengrove
Co-Founder: Rebecca Dengrove
Square Footage: 80000

1699 **(HQ)Brewster Dairy Inc**
800 Wabash Ave S
Brewster, OH 44613
330-767-3492
Fax: 330-767-3386 800-874-8874
www.brewstercheese.com
All natural swiss cheese.
Owner & CEO: Fritz Lehman
VP & Chief Financial Officer: Emil Alecusan
VP Sales & Marketing: James Straughn
Manager National Sales: Mike Walpole
flehman@brewstercheese.com
Plant Manager/Production Development: John Scott
Year Founded: 1965
Estimated Sales: $28.4 Million
Number Employees: 100-249
Square Footage: 78914
Type of Packaging: Consumer, Food Service, Private Label, Bulk
Other Locations:
Stockton Cheese, Inc.
Stockton IL
Brewster West LLC
Rupert ID

1700 **Briannas Fine Salad Dressings**
P.O. Box 2243
3015 S Blue Bell Rd
Brenham, TX 77834
979-836-5978
Fax: 979-836-6953 www.briannas.com
Gourmet salad dressings
Sales Director: Jeffrey Sadler
Number Employees: 50
Number of Products: 15
Parent Co: Del Sol Food Company Inc.
Type of Packaging: Private Label

1701 **Briceland Vineyards**
5959 Briceland Thorn Rd
Redway, CA 95560
707-923-2429
Wines and champagnes
Owner/Partner: Margaret Carey
Partner: Joe Collins
Estimated Sales: $150,000
Number Employees: 2

1702 **Brick Brewery**
400 Bimgemans Centre Drive
Kitchener, ON N2B 3X9
Canada
519-742-2732
Fax: 519-742-9874 800-505-8971
info@waterloobrewing.com
www.waterloobrewing.com
Light and dark lagers, ales, coolers, ciders, craft beers.
Chairman: Peter Schwartz
President/CEO: George Croft
CFO: David J Birch
Director Brewing, Quality and Logistics: Bill Henry
VP Marketing: Norm Pickering
VP Sales: Craig Prentice
Chief Operating Officer: Russell Tabata
Year Founded: 1984
Estimated Sales: $20-50 Million
Number Employees: 20-49
Square Footage: 45000
Type of Packaging: Consumer
Brands:
Algonquin Honeybrown
Andechs
Anniversary Bock
Brick Premium
Conners Best Bitter
Fix
Formosa Draft
Henninger Kaiser Pils
Laker Family of Beers
Pacific Real Draft
Red Baron
Red Cap
Waterloo Dark

1703 **Brickerlabs.Com**
3305 N Delaware St
Chandler, AZ 85225-1134
480-889-9450
Fax: 262-334-7651 800-274-2537
sales@brickerlabs.com
www.nutritionalmfgservices.com
Nutritional supplements
Sales/Marketing Manager: Tami Dechairo
Estimated Sales: $1-2,500,000
Number Employees: 5-9
Type of Packaging: Consumer, Food Service, Private Label, Bulk

1704 **Bridenbaugh Orchards**
316 Orchard Ln
Martinsburg, PA 16662-8145
814-793-2364
Grower and packer of apples, peaches, cherries, strawberries and raspberries; exporter of apples
Owner: Glenn Bridenbaugh
Co-Owner: David Bridenbaugh
Estimated Sales: Less Than $500,000
Number Employees: 1-4
Square Footage: 8000
Type of Packaging: Consumer, Bulk

1705 **Bridge Brands Chocolate**
286 12th St
San Francisco, CA 94103-3718
415-677-9194
Fax: 415-362-2080 888-732-4626
www.wineloverschocolate.com
Gourmet chocolates
President/Owner: Michael Litton
mike@bridgebrands.com
Number Employees: 10-19

1706 **Bridgetown Coffee**
2101 NW York St
Portland, OR 97210-2108
503-224-3330
Fax: 503-224-9529 800-726-0320
orders@bridgetowncoffee.com
www.bridgetowncoffee.com
Processor and exporter of coffee; wholesaler/distributor and exporter of tea; serving the food service market
President: Kirk Jensen
kirkj@bridgetowncoffee.com
CEO: Timothy Timmins
Treasurer: Susan Jensen
Estimated Sales: $3,000,000
Number Employees: 20-49
Number of Brands: 6
Number of Products: 21
Square Footage: 80000
Type of Packaging: Consumer, Food Service, Private Label, Bulk
Brands:
Bridgetown

1707 **Bridgeview Vineyards Winery**
4210 Holland Loop Rd
Cave Junction, OR 97523-9758
541-592-4688
Fax: 541-592-2127 877-273-4843
bvw@bridgeviewwine.com
www.bridgeviewwine.com
Wine
President: Robert Kerivan
bvw@bridgeviewwine.com
Secretary/Treasurer: Lelo Kerivan
Sales/Marketing Manager: Tim Woodhead
Estimated Sales: $610,000
Number Employees: 20-49

1708 **Bridgewell Resources LLC**
124020 SE Carpenter Dr
Clackamas, OR 97015
800-481-3557
webinfo@bridgewellres.com
Edible oils, flours, grains and pulses.
President: Pat McCauley
CEO: Pat McCauley
Chief Financial Officer: Jay Wilson
Vice President of Human Resources: Donna Lesch
Food & Agriculture General Manager: Craig Mullen
Parent Co: Bridgewell Resources
Type of Packaging: Consumer, Food Service, Private Label, Bulk

1709 **(HQ)Bridgford Foods Corp**
1308 N Patt St
Box 3773
Anaheim, CA 92801-2581
714-526-5533
Fax: 714-526-4360 800-527-2105
info@bridgford.com www.bridgford.com
Breads & rolls, ready to eat sandwiches, meat snacks, deli foods & sandwiches, and foodservice doughs and pull apart bread mixes, deli pack biscuits, sandwiches, fully baked bread and rolls, and frozen ready-to-eat meal kits
President: John V Simmons
jsimmons@bridgford.com
President: John Simmons
Executive VP CFO: Raymond Lancy
Assistant to Chief Financial Officer: Debra Morris
Sales & Marketing Executive: Martin Campbell
Director of Sales: Pat Pallarino
Human Resources Manager: L Allan
jsimmons@bridgford.com
Route Operations Manager: Danny Rossman
Plant Manager: Michael Bridgford
Number Employees: 500-999
Type of Packaging: Consumer, Food Service
Other Locations:
Frozen Rite Division
Dallas TX
Superior Foods Division
Dallas TX
Bridgford Foods of North Carolina
Statesville NC
Bridgford Foods of Illinois
Chicago IL

1710 **(HQ)Briess Malt & Ingredients Co.**
625 S Irish Road
P.O. Box 229
Chilton, WI 53014
920-849-7711
Fax: 920-849-4277 800-657-0806
info@briess.com www.briess.com
All-natural food ingredients including malts, natural sweeteners (grain and starch-based), natural colorants, tapioca maltodextrins, reduced cook-time grains, pregelatinized flakes, and toasted grains. Many are whole grain. Non-GMOKosher Certified, USDA Certified Organics.
President/COO: Gordon Lane
CEO: Monica Briess
CFO: Craig Kennedy
Research & Development: Bob Hansen
VP, Sales & Marketing: Robert O'Connell
Sales Coordinator: Ann Heus
Product Line Manager-Food Division: Shawn Kohlmeier
Purchasing: Michelle Piepenburg
Estimated Sales: $16.2 Million
Number Employees: 110
Type of Packaging: Bulk
Other Locations:
Briess Ingredients Company
Chilton WI
Waterloo WI
Brands:
Briess
Cbw
Insta Grains
Maltoferm
Maltorose

1711 **Brighams**
1328 Massachusetts Avenue
Arlington, MA 2476
781-648-9000
Fax: 781-646-0507 800-242-2423
brighams-mail@brighams.com
www.brighams.com
Ice cream, frozen yogurt, whipped cream and fudge topping
President/Coo: Charles Green
Vice President/Cfo: Greg Welch
Operations: Claudia Kost
Estimated Sales: $2.5-5 Million
Number Employees: 50
Square Footage: 330000
Type of Packaging: Consumer, Private Label, Bulk
Brands:
Brigham's
Elan

1712 **Bright Greens**
PO Box 42291
Portland, OR 97242
760-487-8895
info@brekki.com
www.brekki.com
Ready-to-drink fruit and vegetable smoothies
Founder & CEO: Brian Mitchell
Number of Brands: 1
Number of Products: 5
Type of Packaging: Consumer
Brands:
BRIGHT GREENS

1713 **Bright Harvest Sweet Potato Co**
509 E Taylor St
PO Box 528
Clarksville, AR 72830
479-754-6313
Fax: 479-754-7794 800-793-7440
sprice@brightharvest.com www.brightharvest.com
Sweet potato products including patties, mashed sweet potatoes, sweet potato sticks, center cut sweet potatoes and casseroles.
President/CEO: Rex King
rking@brightharvest.com
VP Sales: Kandy Jenkins
VP Technical Services: Jeff Hannon
Food Service Sales Manager: John Coniglio
VP Operations: Sam Winterberg
Customer Service/Logistics Manager: Sabrina Price
Estimated Sales: $20-50 Million
Number Employees: 100-249
Number of Brands: 1
Square Footage: 22000
Type of Packaging: Consumer, Food Service
Brands:
Bright Harvest

1714 **BrightFarms**
1 Bridge St.
Suite 002-4
Irvington, NY 10533
866-857-8745
www.brightfarms.com
Leafy greens, including various lettuce, kale, arugula, spinach, and basil.
CEO: Steve Platt
Year Founded: 2011
Number Employees: 11-50
Type of Packaging: Private Label

1715 **Brimhall Foods**
PO Box 34185
Bartlett, TN 38184-0185
901-377-9016
Fax: 901-377-0476 800-628-6559
brimsnacks.com
Snacks
President: Terry Brimhall
Contact: Dan Scoggin
dscoggin@brimsnacks.com
Estimated Sales: $5-10 Million
Number Employees: 100-249
Type of Packaging: Private Label

1716 **Brimstone Hill Vineyard**
61 Brimstone Hill Rd
Pine Bush, NY 12566-5400
845-744-2231
Fax: 845-744-4782 bhvwine@frontiernet.net
www.brimstonehillwinery.com
Still and sparkling wines
Owner: Richard Eldridge
bhvwine@frontiernet.net
Owner: Valerie Eldridge
Estimated Sales: $500,000-750,000
Number Employees: 1-4
Type of Packaging: Food Service
Brands:
Brimstone Hill

1717 **Briney Sea Delicaseas**
715 78th Ave SW # C
Unit 3
Tumwater, WA 98501-5700
360-956-1797
Fax: 360-956-2503 888-772-5666
www.brineysea.net
Seafood including fresh, vacuum-packed smoked salmon
President: Jay Garrison
Estimated Sales: Less than $500,000
Number Employees: 1-4
Type of Packaging: Consumer, Food Service

1718 **Brisk Coffee Co**
402 N 22nd St
Tampa, FL 33605-6086
813-248-6264
Fax: 813-248-2947 800-899-5282
customer@briskcoffee.com www.briskcoffee.com
Processor and exporter of roasted coffee; also, leasing of coffee equipment available
President/CEO: Richard Perez
VP/COO: Denise Reddick
dreddick@briskcoffee.com
Finance Executive: Julie Beck
Vice President: Mary Perez
VP, Quality Control & Manufacturing: Randy Gongalez
VP Production: Randall Gonzalez
Estimated Sales: $2.9 Million
Number Employees: 20-49
Square Footage: 40000
Type of Packaging: Food Service
Brands:
Brisk
Gold Plus
Innkeepers Choice

1719 **Bristle Ridge Vineyards**
98 NE 641
Knob Noster, MO 65336-1910
660-422-5646
800-994-9463
Producer of wines. Some of their products include Seyval Blanc, Sauterne, Mont Rose', Diamond, Burgundy, Montserrat Red, deChaunac, Hard Cider and Villard Noir.
President: Edward Smith
Co-Owner: Vickie Smith
General Manager: Todd Smith
Estimated Sales: $5-9.9,000,000
Number Employees: 5-9
Brands:
Bristle Ridge

1720 **Bristol Brewing Co**
1604 S Cascade Ave
Colorado Springs, CO 80905-2237
719-368-6120
Fax: 719-633-2145 info@bristolbrewing.com
www.bristolbrewing.com
Ale and stout
Owner: Mike Bristol
mikeb@bristolbrewing.com
Owner: Nicole Schneider
Accounting: Lynne Blesener
Marketing Guru: Amanda Bristol
Sales Guy: Alex Spinnato
mikeb@bristolbrewing.com
General Manager: Tom Zurenko
Maintenance/Problem Solving: Tad Davis
Estimated Sales: $1,400,000
Number Employees: 10-19
Type of Packaging: Consumer, Food Service, Bulk
Brands:
Beehive
Edge City Ipa
Edge City Pilsner
Laughing Lab
Mass Transit
Old No.23
Red Rocket
Scottish
Winter Warlock

1721 **Bristol-Myers Squibb Co.**
430 E. 29th St.
14th Floor
New York, NY 10016
212-546-4000
800-332-2056
www.bms.com
Pharmaceuticals and related health care products.
Chairman/CEO: Giovanni Caforio
giovanni.caforio@bms.com
Executive VP/CFO: David Elkins
Executive VP/General Counsel: Sandra Leung
Year Founded: 1887
Estimated Sales: $22.56 Billion
Number Employees: 23,300
Number of Brands: 28
Brands:
BARACLUDE®
DAKLINZA™
ELIQUIS®
EMPLICITI™
OPDIVO®
ORENCIA®
REYATAZ®
SPRYCEL®
SUSTIVA®
YERVOY®
ATRIPLA®
AZACTAM®
COUMADIN®
DROXIA®
ETOPOPHOS®
EVOTAZ®
GLUCOPHAGE®
GLUCOVANCE®
HYDREA®
KENALOG®
LYSODREN®
MEGACE®
NULOJIX®
PLAVIX®
PRAVACHOL®
VIDEX®
ZERIT®

1722 **British Aisles, LTD.**
25A Progress Avenue
Nashua, NH 03062
Fax: 603-881-3480 800-520-8565
sales@britishaisles.com www.britishaisles.com
Organic/natural, tea, non-alcoholic beverages, full-line condiments, full-line candy, ethnic sauces (soy, curry, etc), spices, full-line spreads & syrup.
Marketing: Stephanie Pressinger
Contact: D Pressinger
sales@britishaisles.com

1723 **British American Tea & Coffee**
1320 Old Oxford Road
Durham, NC 27704-2470
919-471-1357
Fax: 919-471-1357
Tea and coffee.
President: Christopher Hulbert
CFO: Elizabeth Albert
Estimated Sales: Under $500,000
Number Employees: 20-49
Square Footage: 2
Type of Packaging: Private Label

1724 **Brittle Kittle**
16285 SW 85th Ave # 101
Tigard, OR 97224-5421
503-639-9037
Fax: 615-449-6263 800-447-2128
bkettle@bellsouth.net
Peanut brittle
Owner: Christine Logue
christine@brittlekittle.com
VP: Howard Wilson
Estimated Sales: Less Than $500,000
Number Employees: 1-4
Type of Packaging: Consumer

1725 **Brix Chocolates**
590 E Western Reserve Road
PO Box 9111
Youngstown, OH 44513
330-657-5864
Fax: 330-726-0749 866-613-2749
sales@brixchocolate.com www.brixchocolate.com
Chocolate
Principal: Nicholas Proia
Partner/Sales and Marketing: Bruce Barber
Estimated Sales: $190,000
Number Employees: 2

1726 **Broad Run Vineyards**
10601 Broad Run Rd
Louisville, KY 40299-5417
502-231-0372
info@broadrunvineyards.com
www.broadrunvineyards.com
Dry table and dessert wines
Owner: Gerald J Kushner
finewine@iglou.com
Manager of Sales/Marketing: Marilyn Kushner
finewine@iglou.com
Assistant Vintner: Lloyd Hyatt
Estimated Sales: $50,000
Number Employees: 20-49
Square Footage: 4000
Type of Packaging: Food Service

Brands:
Broad Run Vineyards

1727 **Broadaway Ham Co**
500 N Culberhouse St
Jonesboro, AR 72401-1690
870-932-6688
Fax: 870-932-6683 ham-man@sbcglobal.net
Meat products including deli barbecued ham and snack sticks
Owner: Bruce Broadway
Plant Manager: John Collins
Estimated Sales: $1-3 Million
Number Employees: 1-4
Square Footage: 15000
Type of Packaging: Consumer
Brands:
Crowley Ridge

1728 **Broadbent B & B Food Products**
257 Mary Blue Rd
Kuttawa, KY 42055-6299
270-388-0609
Fax: 270-388-0613 800-841-2202
order@broadbenthams.com
www.broadbenthams.com
Cured ham, bacon and sausage
Owner: Beth Drennan
beth@broadbenthams.com
Estimated Sales: Less Than $1 Million
Number Employees: 10-19

1729 **Broadhead Brewing Co**
1680 Vimont Ct.
Unit 106
Orl,ans, ON K4A 3M3
Canada
613-830-3944
broadheadbeer.com
Microbrewed craft beer.
Co-Founder: Josh Larocque
Co-Founder: Jamie White
Head of Sales: John Buist
Head Brewer: Jon Cormier
Year Founded: 2011
Number Employees: 5-10
Type of Packaging: Consumer, Private Label

1730 **Broadleaf Venison USA Inc**
5600 S Alameda St
Vernon, CA 90058-3428
323-826-9890
Fax: 323-826-9830 800-336-3844
support@broadleafgame.com
www.broadleafgame.com
Specialty and exotic meats; Wagyu Beef, Buffalo, Cervena Venison, kurobuta Pork
Owner: Mark Mitchell
broadleaf@broadleafgame.com
CEO: Pat McGowan
CFO: Ara Temuryan
Vice President: Annie Mitchell
Sales Director: Nathan Cooney
broadleaf@broadleafgame.com
Operations Manager: Pierre La Breton
Production Manager: Randy Eves
Plant Manager: Jose Madera
Purchasing Manager: Edward Townsend
Estimated Sales: $20-30 Million
Number Employees: 50-99
Square Footage: 56000
Type of Packaging: Consumer, Food Service
Brands:
Broadleaf
Broadleaf Cervena

1731 **Broadley Vineyards**
265 S 5th St
Monroe, OR 97456-9609
541-847-5934
Fax: 541-847-6018 broadley@peak.org
www.broadleyvineyards.com
Wines
President: Craig Broadley
Estimated Sales: $110,000
Number Employees: 1-4

1732 **Brock Seed Company**
75 Richwood Rd
Finley, TN 38030-3051
731-286-2430
Fax: 760-353-1693
Manufacturer and exporter of asparagus and asparagus seed
Owner: Clark Brock
Manager: Don Brock
Estimated Sales: $210,000
Number Employees: 3
Type of Packaging: Consumer, Food Service, Private Label
Brands:
Brock

1733 **Brockmann's Chocolates**
7863 Progress Way
Delta, BC V4G 1A3
Canada
604-946-4111
Fax: 604-946-4114 888-494-2270
info@brockmannchocolate.com
www.brockmannchocolate.com
Chocolates
President: Norbert Brockmann
CEO: Marianne Brockmann
Founder: Willy Brockmann
Estimated Sales: $1.1 Million
Number Employees: 30
Type of Packaging: Private Label
Brands:
Truffini

1734 **Broken Bow Brewery**
173 Marbledale Rd.
Tuckahoe, NY 10707
914-268-0900
www.brokenbowbrewery.com
Lagers, IPAs, golden ales, porter, fruit-flavored wheat beer
Head Brewer: Michael Lamother
Head, Marketing: Kristen Stone
Head, Sales: Lyle Lamothe
Year Founded: 2013
Number of Brands: 1
Number of Products: 13
Type of Packaging: Consumer, Private Label
Brands:
Broken Bow

1735 **Brolite Products Inc**
1900 S Park Ave
Streamwood, IL 60107-2944
630-830-0340
Fax: 630-830-0356 888-276-5483
info@bakewithbrolite.com
www.bakewithbrolite.com
Flavors, stabilizers, yeast foods, dough accelerators and conditioners, egg yolk and whole egg substitutes and fudge, English muffin and bread bases; exporter of white and rye sour dough flavors
President: David Delghingaro
d.delghingaro@broliteproducts.com
R&D: Daniel Garcia
Marketing/Sales VP: Tom MacDonald
Plant Manager: Mike Koziol
Estimated Sales: $15 Million
Number Employees: 50-99
Square Footage: 108000
Type of Packaging: Bulk
Brands:
All Soft
B5000
Bro Egcellent
Bro White Sour
Brolite Ia
Brosoft
Egg-O-Lite
Fever Sours
Vita Plus

1736 **Brom Food Group**
5595 Cote De Liesse
St. Laurent, QC H4M 1V2
Canada
514-744-5152
Fax: 514-744-8195
Processor, importer and exporter of frozen foods and frozen and fresh pierogies including cheese, potato/onion, beef and chicken
Director Marketing: Tom Luczak
Director Operations: Bruce Luczak, M.B.A.
Square Footage: 36000
Type of Packaging: Consumer, Food Service, Private Label, Bulk
Brands:
Granny's
Ogi's

1737 **Brome Lake Ducks Ltd**
40 Centre Road
PO Box 3430
Knowlton, QC J0E 1VO
Canada
450-242-3825
Fax: 450-243-0497 888-956-1977
info@canardsdulacbrome.com
www.canardsdulacbrome.com
Duck products
President: Claude Trottier
CFO: Genevieve Grenier
Vice President Sales/Marketing: Bruno Giuliani
R&D Director: Jennifer Caron
Quality Control: Jennifer Caron
Marketing Coordinator: Pier-Luc Fiest
Sales Manager: Claude Cadieux
Human Resources Director: Michele Cote
Account Manager: Abraham Chien-Chung Ho
Plant Manager: Guy Ducharme
Estimated Sales: $28 Million
Number Employees: 170

1738 **Bronco Wine Co**
6342 Bystrum Rd
Ceres, CA 95307
855-874-2394
info@broncowine.com www.broncowine.com
Wine
Chief Executive Officer: Fred Franzia
Co-President/National Sales & Marketing: Joseph Franzia
Co-President: John Franzia, Jr.
Purchasing Manager: Bob Martina
Year Founded: 1973
Estimated Sales: $250 Million
Number Employees: 1,000-4,999
Square Footage: 10000
Type of Packaging: Private Label
Brands:
Charles Shaw
Estrella
Forestville
Foxhollow
Grand Cru
Hacienda
Montpellier
Napa Ridge
Rutherford Vintners
Silver Ridge

1739 **Brook Locker Plant**
243 W Main St
Brook, IN 47922-8723
219-275-2611
Meat products and fresh and frozen foods including beef, pork, chicken and veal; also, slaughtering available
Owner: Jeff Laffoon
jefflaffoon@hrblock.com
Vice President: Chris Schoonveld
Bookkeeper: Pam Chamberlin
Estimated Sales: $230,000
Number Employees: 5-9
Type of Packaging: Consumer, Bulk

1740 **Brook Meadow Meats**
716 Security Rd
Hagerstown, MD 21740-4143
301-739-3107
Pork, beef and sausage
Owner: Donald Hoffman
Estimated Sales: $5-10 Million
Number Employees: 1-4
Type of Packaging: Consumer

1741 **Brookema Company**
500 Fenton Lane
West Chicago, IL 60185-2667
630-562-2290
Fax: 630-562-2291
Dry mixes including cake, soup, cocoa, coffee and coffee creamer.
President: Dan Clery
Estimated Sales: $2.5-5 Million
Number Employees: 20-49
Type of Packaging: Bulk

1742 **Brookfield Farm**
24 Hulst Rd.
Amherst, MA 01002
413-253-7991
info@brookfieldfarm.org
www.brookfieldfarm.org

Fresh and frozen pork and beef
President/Ceo: Frank Swan
President/Ceo: Dennis Gleason
Manager: Abbe Vredenburg
abbe@brookfieldfarm.org
Estimated Sales: Less Than $500,000
Number Employees: 500-999
Type of Packaging: Consumer, Food Service

1743 **Brooklyn Bagel Company**
PO Box 120027
Staten Island, NY 10312-0027
718-349-3055
Fax: 718-349-1107 800-349-3055
Frozen bagels
Sales Manager: Stanley Silverman
Sales Manager: Arnie Lichtenstein
General Manager: Donald Santman
Estimated Sales: $1-2.5 Million
Number Employees: 20-49
Square Footage: 40000
Type of Packaging: Consumer, Food Service, Bulk

1744 **Brooklyn Baking Company**
8 John Street
Waterbury, CT 6708
203-574-9198
Baked goods including sourdough, white and rye bread and cookies
Owner: Peter Belez
Estimated Sales: $450,000
Number Employees: 5
Type of Packaging: Consumer, Bulk
Brands:
Brooklyn Baking Pumpernickel Bread
Brooklyn Baking Rye Bread

1745 **Brooklyn Bean Roastery**
7 Hanson Pl.
Brooklyn, NY 11243
908-205-0018
info@brooklynbeans.com
www.brooklynbeans.com
Coffee beans
Co-Founder: Steven Schreiber
Co-Founder: Mayer Koenig
Co-Founder: Eugene Schreiber
Brands:
Brooklyn Bean Roastery

1746 **Brooklyn Biltong**
314 Prospect Ave.
Brooklyn, NY 11215
407-538-8876
info@brooklynbiltong.com
www.brooklynbiltong.com
South African style beef jerkey
Principal CEO: Ben van den Heever
Year Founded: 2012

1747 **Brooklyn Brew Shop**
20 Jay St
Brooklyn, NY 11201
718-874-0119
info@brooklynbrewshop.com
www.brooklynbrewshop.com
Manufacturer of beer making kits.
Co-Founder: Erica Shea
Co-Founder: Stephen Valand
Contact: Sarah Blumenthal
sarahb@brooklynbrewshop.com

1748 **Brooklyn Brewery**
1 Brewers Row
79 North 11th Street
Brooklyn, NY 11249
718-486-7422
Fax: 718-486-7440 www.brooklynbrewery.com
Ale, stout and lager
Co-Founder/President: Steve Hindy
CEO: Eric Ottaway
Controller: Debbie Bascome
Quality Control Manager: Mary Wiles
Marketing Director: Ben Hudson
VP/Sales: Robin Ottaway
Operations Manager: Karl Knoop
Estimated Sales: $20-50 Million
Number Employees: 22
Type of Packaging: Consumer, Food Service, Bulk
Brands:
Brooklyn
Chimay
Duvel
Paulaner
Samuel Smith
Sierra Nevada

1749 **Brooklyn Brine Co LLC**
67 35th Street
Suite 5-1C
Brooklyn, NY 11232
347-223-4345
www.brooklynbrine.com
Manufacturer of non-GMO, Kosher pickles.
Founder: Briner Jones
Brands:
Brooklyn Brine

1750 **Brooklyn Cider House**
1100 Flushing Ave.
Brooklyn, NY 11237
347-295-0308
www.brooklynciderhouse.com
Hard dry craft ciders
Founder/Co-Owner: Peter Yi
Founder/Co-Owner: Susan Yi
Year Founded: 2014
Number of Brands: 1
Number of Products: 5
Type of Packaging: Consumer, Private Label
Brands:
Brooklyn Cider House

1751 **Brooklyn Cookie Company**
P.O. Box 170143
Brooklyn, NY 11217
347-973-0568
info@brooklyncookiecompany.com
www.brooklyncookiecompany.com
Meringue cookies
President: Cheryl Surana
Estimated Sales: Under $500,000
Number Employees: 1-4
Brands:
Just Meringues
"Mushroom" Meringues Cookies

1752 **Brooklyn Cured LLC**
326 22nd St
New York, NY 11215-6408
907-282-2221
info@brooklyncured.com
www.brooklyncured.com
Sausaged, cured and smoked meats
Founder: Scott Bridi
Year Founded: 2010

1753 **Brooklyn Delhi**
Brooklyn, NY 11230
hello@brooklyndelhi.com
brooklyndelhi.com
Condiments and sauces
Founder: Chitra Agrawal

1754 **Brooklyn Whatever LLC**
27 Cobeck Ct
Brooklyn, NY 11223
917-669-5525
brooklynwhatever.com
sugar free pickled vegetables, mixed olives, and mixed nuts.
Owner: Rachel Shamah
rachel@brooklynwhatever.com
Brands:
Shmolives
Shnuts.
Shpickles
Brooklyn Whatever

1755 **Brookmere Wine & Vineyard**
5369 SR 655
Belleville, PA 17004-9303
717-935-5380
Fax: 717-935-5349 www.brookmerewine.com
Wines
Owner: Cheryl Glick
Estimated Sales: $2.5-5,000,000
Number Employees: 5-9
Type of Packaging: Bulk

1756 **Brooks Peanut Co**
402 E Main St
Samson, AL 36477-1224
334-898-7194
Fax: 334-898-7196 www.brookspeanut.com
Peanuts
Owner: Barrett Brooks
barrettbrooks@msn.com
CEO: Fleming G. Brooks
Secretary/Treasurer: Sherry Brooks
Office Manager: Lucy Adams
Estimated Sales: $8.3 Million
Number Employees: 5-9
Type of Packaging: Bulk

1757 **Brooks Tropicals Inc**
18400 SW 256th St
Homestead, FL 33031-1892
305-247-3544
Fax: 305-242-7393 800-327-4833
maryo@brookstropicals.com
Grower, packer and shipper of papayas, avocados, starfruit, limes, passion fruit, mangos, guavas, uglyfruit and other tropical produce.
President: Pal Brooks
CEO: Greg Smith
Year Founded: 1928
Number Employees: 100-249
Type of Packaging: Bulk
Brands:
SlimCado® avocado
Caribbean Red® papaya

1758 **Brookshire Grocery Company**
PO Box 1411
Tyler, TX 75710-1411
903-534-3000
888-937-3776
www.brookshires.com
Regional supermarket chain in Texas, Louisiana and Arkansas.
Chairman/CEO: Bradley Brookshire
Year Founded: 1928
Estimated Sales: $2.5 Billion
Number Employees: 14,000+
Brands:
Brookshire's®
Full Circle®
Goldenbrook Farms®
PAWS Premium™
Tasty Bakery
Top Care®
Valu Time®
World Classics™

1759 **Brookside Foods**
17212 Miles Ave
Cleveland, OH 44128
216-991-7600
Fax: 216-991-7739
Fresh and frozen prepared salads and meats
President/Owner: Bernie Polen
CEO: Jack Lain
Sales Executive: Alisa Capriottschrei
Contact: Denis Mcguire
dmcguire@brooksidefoods.com
Office Manager: Jacke Lane
Estimated Sales: $1.3 Million
Number Employees: 12
Type of Packaging: Consumer, Food Service, Private Label
Brands:
Bosell
Brookside
Homestead

1760 **Brookside Foods**
3899 Mt. Lehman Road
Abbotsford, BC V4X 2N1
Canada
604-607-6650
Fax: 604-607-7046 800-468-1714
info@brooksidefoods.com
www.brooksidefoods.com
Base concentrates, fruit fillings, custom ice cream inclusions, confectionery coatings, and paned and deposited chocolate confections, etc. Importer of cocoa butter, cocoal powder, chocolate liquer, etc. Exporter of real fruit chipschocolate, panned and deposited chocolate confections, etc. Custom dry blending and private labeling.
President: Kenneth Shaver
Director Sales: Alan Whitteker
Estimated Sales: $26.5 Million
Number Employees: 150
Parent Co: Brookside Foods
Type of Packaging: Consumer, Private Label, Bulk

1761 **Brookview Farms**
854 Dover Road
P.O. Box 126
Manakin-Sabot, VA 23103
804-784-3131
Fax: 804-784-2697
themarket@brookviewfarm.com
www.brookviewfarm.com
Fresh and frozen meat including beef, pork, lamb and venison
President: Jack Lugbill
Estimated Sales: $5-10 Million
Number Employees: 10-19
Square Footage: 21000
Type of Packaging: Consumer, Food Service, Bulk

1762 **Brother Bru Bru's**
PO Box 2964
Venice, CA 90294-2964
310-396-9033
info@brobrubru.com
Producer of natural salt-free sauces, including Original African Hot PepperSauce, Organic Chipotle and Organic Chili Pepper Sauce.
Owner: Cynthia Riddle
Estimated Sales: $5-10,000,000
Number Employees: 50-99
Brands:
Brother Bru Bru's

1763 **Brother's Trading LLC**
P.O. Box 2234
San Gabriel, CA 91778-2234
626-378-9323
info@gemgemsweet.com
gemgemsweet.com
Ginger and citrus fruit based candy.
General Manager: Andrew Ma
Purchasing: Marlen Abolafia
Type of Packaging: Private Label
Brands:
Gem Gem

1764 **Brotherhood Winery**
100 Brotherhood Plaza Dr
P.O.Box 190
Washingtonville, NY 10992-2279
845-496-3661
Fax: 845-496-8720
contact@brotherhoodwinery.net
www.brotherhood-winery.com
wines.
President: Hernan Donoso
Co-Owner: Cesar Baeza
Vice President: Philip Dunsmore
Commercial Assistant, Marketing & Sales: Ren,e Schweizer
Production Manager: Mark Daigle
Plant Manager: Carol Tepper
Estimated Sales: $10 Million
Number Employees: 50
Type of Packaging: Consumer, Food Service, Private Label, Bulk
Brands:
Brotherhood

1765 **Brothers All Natural**
1175 Lexington Ave
Rochester, NY 14606
585-343-3007
Fax: 585-343-4218 877-842-7477
www.brothersallnatural.com
Freeze-dried fruit crisps
President & Co-CEO: Matt Betters
Co-CEO: Travis Betters
Estimated Sales: $4.1 Million
Number Employees: 22

1766 **Brothers Desserts**
2727 S Susan Street
Santa Ana, CA 92704
949-655-0080
info@brothersdesserts.com
brothersdesserts.com
Ice creams, sorbets, fruit bars and frozen desserts
President/Owner: Gary Winkler
Year Founded: 1973
Type of Packaging: Bulk
Brands:
Natural Choice
Absolute Fruit
Brothers Ice Cream

1767 **Brothers International Desserts**
2727 S Susan St
Santa Ana, CA 92704
949-655-0080
www.brothersdesserts.com
Frozen desserts, including ice cream, gelato and sorbet
President/Owner: Gary Winkler
Year Founded: 1973
Estimated Sales: C
Number Employees: 150
Number of Brands: 1
Number of Products: 15
Square Footage: 30000
Type of Packaging: Consumer
Brands:
NATURAL CHOICE
CLASSIC BON BONS
ABSOLUTE FRUIT

1768 **Brothers International Food Corporation**
1175 Lexington Ave
Rochester, NY 14606
585-343-3007
Fax: 585-343-4218
ingredients@brothersinternational.com
brothersinternational.com
Fruit ingredients
President & Co-CEO: Matt Betters
Co-CEO: Travis Betters
Estimated Sales: $6.2 Million
Number Employees: 33

1769 **Brothers Sauces**
2617 Museum Way
Fort Worth, TX 76107
817-821-3374
Fax: 877-754-3488
Gluten-free, organic/natural, BBQ sauce, dessert toppings (i.e. fudge sauce, caramel sauce, whipped cream, etc.), foodservice, private label.
Mbr: Darryl King
Manager/Mbr: Barry King
Estimated Sales: $100,000
Number Employees: 2

1770 **Broughton Foods LLC**
PO Box 961447
El Paso, TX 79996
740-373-4121
Fax: 740-373-2861 800-395-7004
www.dairypure.com
Milks, premium and homestyle ice cream, novelty ice cream, juices and fruit drinks, cottage cheese, sour cream, and chip dip.
Principle: Michael McCullum
General Manager: David Broughton
Executive Vice President: George Broughton
Manager of Sales: Neil Schilling
Plant Manager: Mike Depue
Purchasing Agent: Becci Becker
Estimated Sales: $46.6 Million
Number Employees: 100-249
Square Footage: 8000
Parent Co: Dean Foods
Type of Packaging: Consumer, Food Service, Bulk

1771 **Brown & Haley**
3500 20th St E
Suite C
Fife, WA 98424
800-426-8400
sweets@brown-haley.com www.brown-haley.com
Manufacturer and exporter of confectionery items including Almond Roca.
President & COO: John Melin
jmelin@brown-haley.com
CFO: Clarence Guimond
Year Founded: 1914
Estimated Sales: $86.9 Million
Number of Brands: 3
Type of Packaging: Consumer, Private Label, Bulk
Brands:
Mountain Bar
Roca
Zingos Mints

1772 **Brown & Jenkins TradingCompany**
286 Old Rt 15
PO Box 236
Cambridge, VT 05444-0236
802-862-2395
Fax: 802-864-7336 800-456-5282
coffee@brownjenkins.com
www.brownjenkins.com
Coffee
Owner: Sandy Riggens
Marketing Director: Sarah Squirrell
Contact: Rich Williams
rich@brownjenkins.com
Estimated Sales: $1-2,500,000
Number Employees: 1-4
Brands:
Brown & Jenkins Fresh Roasted

1773 **Brown County Winery**
4520 State Road 46 E
Nashville, IN 47448-8673
812-988-6144
Fax: 812-988-8285 888-298-2984
info@browncountywinery.com
www.browncountywinery.com
Wines
President/Manager: David Schrodt
Owner/Secretary/Treasurer: Cynthai Schrodt
Marketing Manager: Cynthia Schrodt
Estimated Sales: $525,000
Number Employees: 5-9
Square Footage: 5000
Type of Packaging: Bulk

1774 **Brown Cow Farm**
10 Burton Drive
Londonderry, NH 03053
888-429-5459
www.browncowfarm.com
Yogurt
Contact: Rosy Rodriguez
rosyr@browncowfarm.com
Estimated Sales: $3,000,000
Number Employees: 12
Number of Brands: 1
Type of Packaging: Consumer
Brands:
Brown Cow Farm

1775 **Brown Dairy Inc**
95 Browns Ln
Coalville, UT 84017-9419
435-336-5952
Fax: 435-336-5902 www.brownsdairy.com
Dairy products
Owner: Glen Brown
browndairy@hotmail.com
Number Employees: 5-9

1776 **Brown Dog Fancy**
50 Noroton Ave
Darien, CT 06820-5214
908-251-1723
info@browndogfancy.com
browndogfancy.com
Mustard and condiments
Owner/Manager: Kyle Rothschild

1777 **Brown Family Farm**
74 Cotton Mill Hl # A106
Brattleboro, VT 05301-8603
802-254-4554
Fax: 802-254-5022 866-254-8718
info@brownfamilyfarmmaple.com
www.brownfamilyfarmmaple.com
Maple products
Estimated Sales: Under $500,000
Number Employees: 10-19

1778 **Brown Foods**
3659 Atlanta Highway
PO Box 953
Dallas, GA 30132-5731
770-445-4358
Fax: 770-445-5349
Poultry, pork, seafood, produce, beef
Principal: William Brown
Owner: Graham Kirkman
Estimated Sales: $540,000
Number Employees: 4

1779 **Brown Packing Company**
One Dutch Valley Drive
P.O. Box 703
South Holland, IL 60473-8094
708-849-7990
Fax: 708-849-8094 800-832-8325
Meat products including beef carcasses and primal cuts
President: John Oedzes
Vice President: Brian Oedzes
Contact: Steven Blanton
steven@dv-foods.com
Chief Operating Officer: Bryan Scott
Estimated Sales: $10-24 Million
Number Employees: 60
Square Footage: 50000
Type of Packaging: Consumer, Bulk

1780 **Brown Produce Company**
Route 37
Farina, IL 62838
618-245-3301
Fax: 618-245-3552
Eggs and egg products including frozen, liquid, whites, whole and yolk
President: Larry Seger
Vice President: Larry Pemberton
Plant Supervisor: Larry Jahraus
Estimated Sales: $10-20 Million
Number Employees: 50-99
Square Footage: 20000000
Type of Packaging: Consumer, Bulk

1781 **Brown Thompson & Sons**
139 State Route 339 N
Fancy Farm, KY 42039
270-623-6321
Fax: 270-623-6928
Beef, beef products
Owner: Penny Lamb
Estimated Sales: $.5-1,000,000
Number Employees: 1-4

1782 **(HQ)Brown's Dairy**
1300 Baronne St
New Orleans, LA 70113-1206
504-529-2221
Fax: 504-529-9267 800-680-6455
www.brownsdairy.com
Milk
President: Kennon Davis
Cmo: Laurent Barbe
lbarbe@barbedairy.com
Sales Director: Lauren Barre
Plant Manager: John Brousard
Estimated Sales: $300,000-500,000
Number Employees: 250-499
Parent Co: Suiza Dairy Group
Type of Packaging: Consumer
Brands:
Brown's Dairy
Bulgarian Style
Hershey's Milkshake
Luzianne Ready-To-Drink
Nesquik

1783 **Brown's Ice Cream Co**
3501 Marshall St NE # 150
Suite 150
Minneapolis, MN 55418-0073
612-378-1075
Fax: 612-331-9273 info@brownsicecream.com
www.brownsicecream.com
Ice cream
Owner: Robert Nelson
browns@popp.net
Vice President: Robert Nelson
Estimated Sales: $9 Million
Number Employees: 20-49
Parent Co: Upper Lakes Foods
Type of Packaging: Consumer, Food Service, Bulk

1784 **Brown-Forman Corp**
850 Dixie Hwy.
Louisville, KY 40210
502-585-1100
Fax: 502-774-6633 brown-forman@b-f.com
www.brown-forman.com
Wine, tequila, champagne, whiskey, vodka, scotch, and liqueurs.
Chairman: Garvin Brown
President/CEO: Lawson Whiting
Executive VP/CFO: Jane Morreau
Executive VP/General Counsel/Secretary: Matthew Hamel
Senior VP/Chief Production Officer: Alejandro Alvarez
Year Founded: 1870
Estimated Sales: $3.8 Billion
Number Employees: 4,600
Number of Brands: 18
Type of Packaging: Consumer
Other Locations:
Atlanta GA
Baltimore MD
Braintree MA
Coral Gables FL
Dallas TX
Hauppauge NY
Irving TX
Jackson OH
Louisville KY
Lynchburg TN
Nashville TN
Newport Beach CA
Pleasanton CA
Brands:
Jack Daniels
Woodford Reserve
Old Forester
Early Times
Collingwood Canadian Whisky
Canadian Whiskey
Cooper's Craft
Slane Irish Whiskey
The Benriach
The Glendronach
Glenglassaugh
Herradura
El Jimador
Pepe Lopez
Finlandia
Finlandia Frost
Chambord
Korbel
Sonoma-Cutrer

1785 **Brownie Baker Inc**
4870 W Jacquelyn Ave
Fresno, CA 93722-5027
559-277-7077
Fax: 559-277-7077 800-598-6501
thebrownieb@gmail.com www.browniebaker.com
Baking products such as; muffins, cakes, brownies, cookies, danish, mexican pastries, poundcake slices and cheesecakes
CEO: Dennis Perkins
CFO: Jodi Cox
Director of Marketing: Ryan Perkins
VP Sales: Glenn Jones
VP Operations: Mike Collins
Director of Baking: Dave Robinson
Estimated Sales: $20-50 Million
Number Employees: 50-99
Square Footage: 45000
Brands:
Pro Treats
The Brownie Baker

1786 **Brownie Brittle, LLC**
2253 Vista Pkwy
Suite 8
West Palm Beach, FL 33411-2722
561-688-1890
Fax: 561-584-5881 info@browniebrittle.com
www.browniebrittle.com
Gourmet brownie mixes, cookies, chocolate, and snack foods.
Owner: Sheila Mains
Marketing Brand Manager: Barbara Riley
Brands:
Brownie Brittle

1787 **Brownie Points Inc**
5712 Westbourne Ave
Columbus, OH 43213-1400
614-860-8470
Fax: 614-860-8477 800-427-9643
info@browniepointsinc.com
www.browniepointsinc.com
Manufacturer and retailer of award-winning brownies.
Founder & Co-Owner: Lisa King
info@browniepointsinc.com
Estimated Sales: Less Than $500,000
Number Employees: 1-4

1788 **Browniepops LLC**
12008 Wenonga
Leawood, KS 66209
816-797-0715
Fax: 913-491-0788 www.berries.com
Brownies with a crisp chocolate exterior on a stick lik lollipops. Available in 11 unique flavors.
President/Owner: Marsha Pener Johnston

1789 **Browns Brewing Co**
417 River St
Troy, NY 12180-2822
518-273-2337
Fax: 518-273-4834 www.brownsbrewing.com
Beer
President: Garrett Brown
garry@brownsbrewing.com
Estimated Sales: $1-3 Million
Number Employees: 20-49
Brands:
Ales & Lagers
Brown's Ware
Revolution Hall
Taproom

1790 **Browns' Ice Cream Company**
3501 Marshall St. NE
Suite 150
Minneapolis, MN 55418
612-378-1075
info@brownsicecream.com
www.brownsicecream.com
Distributor of ice cream
President: Jerry Conder
Treasurer: William Brown
Contact: Bob Nelson
bnelson@brownsicecream.com
Estimated Sales: $8.3 Million
Number Employees: 60
Type of Packaging: Consumer, Food Service, Bulk

1791 **Bruce Baking Company**
229 Union Avenue
New Rochelle, NY 10801-6048
914-636-0808
Fax: 914-636-0808
Baked goods, macrobiotic food
Owner: Bruce Merbaum
Estimated Sales: Under $500,000
Number Employees: 5-9
Brands:
Bruce Baking
Tahini Crunch

1792 **Bruce Coffee Svc Plan USA**
77 Weston St
PO Box 987
Hartford, CT 06120-1593
860-527-7253
Fax: 860-524-9130 800-227-6638
info@baronetcoffee.com www.baronetcoffee.com
Manufacturer and importer of coffee.
President: Bruce Goldsmith
Estimated Sales: $10-20 Million
Number Employees: 10-19
Number of Brands: 1
Type of Packaging: Consumer, Food Service, Private Label
Brands:
Baronet Coffees

1793 **Bruce Cost Ginger Ale**
465 Johnson Ave.
Brooklyn, NY 11237
212-488-0661
info@brucecostgingerale.com
www.brucecostgingerale.com
Manufacturer of flavoured ginger ales.
Founder and Co-Owner: Bruce Cost
Co-Owner: Joseph Tang
Co-Owner: Terry Tang
Estimated Sales: $35.8,000,000
Number Employees: 350
Brands:
Bruce Cost Ginger Ale

1794 **Bruce Foods Corporation**
221 Southpark Plaza
PO Drawer 1030
Lafayette, LA 70508
Fax: 337-364-3742 800-299-9082
info@brucefoods.com www.brucefoods.com
Cajun and Tex Mex food products.
President/CEO: Joseph Brown
Vice President/Director: Norman Brown

Year Founded: 1928
Estimated Sales: $141.7 Million
Number Employees: 1,600
Square Footage: 295000
Type of Packaging: Consumer, Food Service, Bulk
Other Locations:
Bruce Foods Plant
El Paso TX
Bruce Foods Plant
Wilson NC
Bruce Foods Plant
Lozes LA
Bruce Foods Plant
Kerkrade, Netherlands
Brands:
Cajun Injector®
Casafiesta®
Louisiana Hot Sauce
Bruce's® Mixes
Bruce's® Yams
Cajun King®
Louisiana® Gold
Mexene® Chili
Louisiana® Wing Sauce

1795 **Bruce Tea**
info@bruceleetea.com
www.bruceleetea.com
Energy tea
VP, Sales: Jim Venia
Number of Brands: 1
Number of Products: 3
Type of Packaging: Consumer
Brands:
BRUCE TEA

1796 **Brucepac**
380 S Pacific Hwy
Woodburn, OR 97071-5931
503-982-3926
Fax: 503-769-5081 800-899-3629
sales@brucepac.com www.brucepac.com
Cooked and seasoned meats
President & CEO: Glen Golomski
Vice President: Terry Buford
National Business Development: Leo Zachman
VP, Sales & Marketing: Rick Wiser
Manager: Matt Rose
Director of Purchasing: Duane Tipton
Estimated Sales: $35 Million
Number Employees: 500-1000
Type of Packaging: Private Label
Other Locations:
Durant OK
Silverton OR
Woodburn OR
Brands:
Brucepac
City Grillers
Urban Bruce
World Kitchen's

1797 **Brucia Plant Extracts**
3855 Dividend Dr
Shingle Springs, CA 95682
530-676-2774
Fax: 530-676-0574 brucia@naturex.com
www.naturex.com
Antioxidants, colors, herbs & spices oleoresins and essential oils, and botanical extracts for the food, flavor and nutraceutical industries
CEO: Thierry Lambert
Group Marketing Director: Antoine Dauby
Sales: David Yuengniaux
Plant Manager: Chris Young
Purchasing Manager: Romain Bayzelon
Estimated Sales: $45 Million
Number Employees: 20-49
Number of Brands: 10
Number of Products: 400
Square Footage: 85000
Parent Co: Naturex
Type of Packaging: Bulk
Brands:
Theraplant

1798 **Bruegger's Bagels**
496 Main St
Melrose, MA 02176-3841
781-665-1913
Fax: 781-665-4953 www.brueggers.com
Bagels
Co-Owner: Nord Brue
Co-Owner: Mike Dressel
Number Employees: 10-19

1799 **Brum's Dairy**
631 Bruham Ave
Pembroke, ON K8A 4Z8
Canada
613-735-2325
Fax: 613-735-2068 www.ic.gc.ca
Process and distribute fresh dairy products as well as fresh juice
President: Stanley W. Brum
Manager: D.A. Fleury
Vice President: Barry D. Brum
Estimated Sales: $12.7 Million
Number Employees: 46
Square Footage: 40000
Type of Packaging: Consumer, Private Label
Brands:
Nature's Pride

1800 **Brunkow Cheese Of Wisconsin**
17975 County Road F
Darlington, WI 53530-9310
608-776-3716
Fax: 608-776-3716 www.brunkowcheese.com
Natural, cold pack and raw milk cheeses including cheddar, colby, monterey jack, mild, sharp, garlic, bacon, onion, dill, wine, jalapeno, Italian herb, smoked, etc
Owner: Karl Geissbuhler
brunchee@mhtc.net
Partner: Greg Schulte
Estimated Sales: $580,000
Number Employees: 5-9
Square Footage: 6400
Type of Packaging: Bulk
Brands:
Brunkow Cheese

1801 **Brunnett Dairy Co-Op**
11631 State Road 70
Grantsburg, WI 54840-7135
715-689-2468
Fax: 715-689-2135 715-689-2748
info@burnettdairy.com www.burnettdairy.com
Mozzarella, provolone, colby, cheddar and monterey jack
Chairman: Bill Haase
President & CEO: Dan Dowling
Year Founded: 1897
Estimated Sales: Less Than $500,000
Number Employees: 1-4
Type of Packaging: Consumer, Food Service, Private Label, Bulk
Brands:
Fancy Brand

1802 **Bruno Specialty Foods**
208 Cherry Ave
West Sayville, NY 11796-1223
631-589-1700
Fax: 631-589-6357 info@brunofoods.com
www.brunofoods.com
Frozen kosher and nonkosher Italian food products including tomato sauces, tortellini, regular and vegetable lasagnas, eggplant parmagiana, ravioli, manicotti and stuffed shells
President: Louis D'Agrosa
lrd@brunofoods.com
Quality Control: Judi D'Agrosa
Sales Executive: Amy D'Agrosa
Operations Executive: Manuel Guzman
Production Manager: Jim Harwood
Purchasing: Mike McKasty
Estimated Sales: $4.4 Million
Number Employees: 20-49
Number of Brands: 2
Number of Products: 150
Square Footage: 20000
Type of Packaging: Consumer, Food Service, Private Label, Bulk
Brands:
Bruno
Tova's Best

1803 **Brush Locker**
14505 County Road 14
Fort Morgan, CO 80701-8209
970-842-2660
Fax: 970-842-4831
Processor and packer of meat
Principal: Tyler McDonald
Plant Manager: Iram Khan
Estimated Sales: $5-10 Million
Number Employees: 10-19

1804 **Brutocao Cellars**
1400 Highway 175
Hopland, CA 95449-9754
707-744-1066
Fax: 707-744-1046 800-433-3689
www.brutocaocellars.com
Wines, gourmet foods
Owner: Leonard Brutocao
Owner/DirectorOf Winemaking: David Brutocao
National Sales Manager: Jeff Miller
brutocaocellars@pacific.net
General Manager: Aaron Niderost
Winemaker: Hoss Milone
Estimated Sales: $1,000,000
Number Employees: 20-49

1805 **Bryan Foods**
PO Box 3901
Peoria, IL 61612
800-544-3870
www.bryanfoods.com
Bacon, sausage, hot dogs, ham, corn dogs and lunchmeat

1806 **Bryant Preserving Company**
P.O.Box 367
Alma, AR 72921
800-634-2413
Fax: 479-632-2505 sales@bryantpreserving.com
www.oldsouth.com
Pickled fruits and vegetables including sweet watermelon rinds and cucumber relish, baby carrots, green tomatoes and mild and hot okra.
President: Morgan Bryant
General Manager & COO: Steve Bryant
Sales Manager: Leguetta Yates
Contact: Phillip Bryant
phillip@bryantpreserving.com
Estimated Sales: $1-2.5 Million
Number Employees: 6
Square Footage: 75000
Type of Packaging: Consumer, Food Service, Private Label, Bulk
Brands:
Old South

1807 **Bryant Vineyard**
1454 Griffitt Bend Rd
Talladega, AL 35160-7255
256-268-2638
kabryant71614@aol.com
www.bryantwines.com
Wines
Co-Owner: Kelly Bryant
Co-Owner: Dan Bryant
Estimated Sales: Less Than $500,000
Number Employees: 1-4
Brands:
Bryant Autumn Blush
Bryant Country White
Bryant Dixie Blush
Bryant Festive Red
Bryant Vineyard

1808 **Bryant's Meat Inc.**
104 Fellowship Rd
PO Box 321
Taylorsville, MS 39168-5501
601-785-6507
Fax: 601-785-6507 800-844-0507
www.bryantsmeat.com
Meat products including smoked sausage, pork and chicken
President: Robert Hunt
rrhunt@bryantsmeat.com
Secretary/Treasurer: Kay Hunt
Manager: Theresa Driskell
Estimated Sales: $2.5 Million
Number Employees: 20-49
Type of Packaging: Consumer
Brands:
River Road
Sunrise

1809 **Bt. McElrath Chocolatier**
2010 E Hennepin Ave
Suite 78
Minneapolis, MN 55413
612-331-8800
Fax: 612-331-2881 info@btmcelrath.com
www.btmcelrath.com
Chocolates
President: Brian T Mc Elrath
Partner/Chief Taster: Christine McElrath
Marketing: Nancy Gross
Estimated Sales: $3-5 Million
Number Employees: 5-9

1810 **Bubba's Fine Foods**
225 42nd Street SW
Suite C
Loveland, CO 80537
bubbasfoods.com
Gourmet chips
Co-Founder & CEO: Jeff Schmidgall
COO: Jared Menzel
Number of Brands: 1
Number of Products: 9
Type of Packaging: Consumer
Brands:
BUBBA'S FINE FOODS

1811 **Bubbies Fine Foods**
PO Box 7326
Stockton, CA 95267-0326
805-947-4622
contact@bubbies.com
bubbies.com
Kosher dill pickles, dill relish, sauerkraut and horse-radish
Co-Owner: John Gray
Co-Owner: Kathy Gray
Type of Packaging: Bulk

1812 **Bubbies Homemade Ice Cream**
99-1267 Waiua Pl # B
Aiea, HI 96701-5642
808-487-7218
Fax: 808-484-5800
bubbiesicecream@hawaii.rr.com
www.bubbiesicecream.com
Mocha ice cream
President: Keith Robbins
bubbiesicecream@hawaii.rr.com
CFO: Sandra Robbins
VP: Gertrude Robbins
Quality Control: Jayci Robbins
Marketing/Sales Director: Rick Wiser
National Sales Manager: Wayne Shervey
Public Relations: Jo Lacar
Estimated Sales: $2.9,000,000
Number Employees: 5-9
Square Footage: 18000
Type of Packaging: Bulk
Brands:
Bubbies Homemade Ice Cream
Mountain Apple
Tutus

1813 **Bubbles Baking Co**
15215 Keswick St
Van Nuys, CA 91405-1014
818-786-1700
Fax: 818-786-3617 800-777-4970
Sales@BubblesBakingco.com
Gourmet baked goods
President: Torben Jensen
Manager: Sean Naim
Manager: Armando Berument
armando@bubblesbakingco.com
Estimated Sales: 2.4 Million
Number Employees: 50-99
Number of Brands: 1
Brands:
Bubbles

1814 **Bubbles of San Francisco**
Box 7326
Stockton, CA 95209-1617
209-951-6071
Fax: 209-957-9413 info@bubbies.com
www.bubbies.com
Kosher pickle products
Co-Owner/CEO: John Gray
Co-Owner/COO: Kathy Gray
Estimated Sales: $500,000-$1,000,000
Number Employees: 1-4
Type of Packaging: Private Label, Bulk

1815 **Buccia Vineyard**
518 Gore Rd
Conneaut, OH 44030
440-593-5976
bucciwin@suite224.net
www.bucciavineyard.com
Wine
Co-Owner/President: Alfred Bucci
Co-Owner: Joanna Bucci
Estimated Sales: $80,000
Number Employees: 2
Type of Packaging: Bulk

1816 **Buchanan Hollow Nut Co**
6510 Minturn Rd
Le Grand, CA 95333-9710
209-389-4594
Fax: 209-389-4321 800-532-1500
sharleen@bhnc.com www.bhnc.com
Manufacturer and grower of organic pistachio, almonds, variety of nuts, dried fruit and candies
Owner: Sharleen Robson
sharleen@bhnc.com
Owner: Charleen Robson
Estimated Sales: $800,000
Number Employees: 20-49
Square Footage: 8000
Type of Packaging: Bulk

1817 **Buchi Kombucha**
242 Derringer Dr
Marshall, NC 28753-8909
828-394-2360
www.drinkbuchi.com
kombucha brews
Sales and Book keeper: Virginia Lancianese
Year Founded: 2009
Number Employees: 11-50

1818 **Buck's Spumoni Company**
229 Pepes Farm Rd
Milford, CT 06460
888-222-8257
bucksicecream.com
Ice cream specialties including nut roll, spumoni and tortoni
President: Charles A Buck Jr
charles.buck@bucksicecream.com
Secretary: Lois Gosselin
Vice President: Charles Buck SR
Estimated Sales: $1.1 Milion
Number Employees: 15
Type of Packaging: Food Service, Bulk

1819 **Buckeye Pretzel Company**
1253 Deerfield Drive
Williamsport, PA 17701-9307
570-547-6295
Fax: 570-547-6719 800-257-6029
Pretzels
President/Treasurer: John Best
Vice Pres-sec: Susan Best
Vice President: James Haag
Number Employees: 24
Brands:
Buckeye

1820 **Buckhead Beef**
4500 Wickersham Dr
Atlanta, GA 30337-5122
404-355-4400
Fax: 404-355-4541 800-888-5578
hf@buckheadbeef.com www.buckheadbeef.com
Fresh and frozen specialty cut meat products including beef, veal, lamb and pork
Founder/CEO: Howard Halpern
President: Chad Stine
CFO: Paul Mooring
frostypauly@yahoo.com
Vice President: Andrew Malcolm
Director of Marketing: Rick Morris
Vice President of Sales: Beverly Ham
Human Resources Executive: Sue Kozbiel
Manager: Chris Aloia
Director of Production: Raymond Morehouse
Director of Purchasing: Jason Lees
Number Employees: 500-999
Type of Packaging: Food Service

1821 **Buckhead Gourmet**
4060 Peachtree Rd NE # D-272
Atlanta, GA 30319-3020
404-256-1399
Fax: 404-256-1335 800-673-6338
Prepared sauces including fat-free gourmet, barbecue, bordeaux, hunter, peppercorn, maderia, marinades, spice ribs, salad dressings, jams, relishes and salsas
President: Stephan Gosch
CEO: Rupert Crawford
Estimated Sales: $1,000,000
Number Employees: 2
Number of Brands: 1
Number of Products: 35
Type of Packaging: Consumer, Food Service, Private Label, Bulk
Brands:
Buckhead Gourmet

1822 **Buckingham Valley Vineyards**
1521 Rte 413
Buckingham, PA 18912
215-794-7188
Fax: 215-794-3606 ask@pawine.com
www.pawine.com
Wine
Owner/Partner: Gerald Forest
Partner: Jon Forest
Partner: Kevin Forest
Partner: Kathleen Forest
Estimated Sales: $240,000
Number Employees: 5
Brands:
Buckingham

1823 **(HQ)Buckmaster Coffee Co**
4893 NW 235th Ave # 101
Hillsboro, OR 97124-5835
503-693-0796
Fax: 503-681-0944 800-962-9148
JoeS@BuckmasterCoffee.com
www.buckmastercoffee.com
Roasted whole bean gourmet coffee
President: Joe Schlichte
joes@buckmastercoffee.com
VP: Joe Schlichte
Sales Manager: Paul Hoffmann
Sales and merchandising manager: Scott Perkins
Estimated Sales: $2 Million
Number Employees: 5-9
Type of Packaging: Consumer

1824 **Budd Foods**
431 Somerville St
Manchester, NH 03103-5129
603-623-3528
Chicken pot-pies and all-in-one meals
Contact: Jenifer Bechtol
jenifer@mrsbudds.com
Number Employees: 1-4

1825 **Buddha Brands**
9600 Rue Meilleur
Suite 932
Montreal, QC H2N 2E3
Canada
514-382-3805
hello@buddhabrandscompany.com
www.buddhabrandscompany.com
Coconut water and coconut chips
Number of Brands: 1
Number of Products: 13
Type of Packaging: Consumer
Brands:
THIRSTY BUDDHA
HUNGRY BUDDHA

1826 **Buddha Teas**
5130 Avenida Encinas
Carlsbad, CA 92008
800-642-3754
service@buddhateas.com www.buddhateas.com
Loose leaf, herbal, green, black and specialty teas
Number of Brands: 1
Type of Packaging: Consumer
Brands:
BUDDHA TEAS

1827 **Buddy Fruits**
555 Theodore Fremd Ave
Suite C-306
Rye, NY 10580
914-514-2098
hello@buddyfruits.com
www.buddyfruits.com
Fruit purees
Number of Brands: 1
Number of Products: 7

Type of Packaging: Consumer
Brands:
BUDDY FRUITS
BUDDY FRUITS & VEGGIES
FRUIT TUBES

1828 Buddy Squirrel LLC
1801 E Bolivar Ave
St Francis, WI 53235-5317
414-483-4500
Fax: 414-483-4137 800-972-2658
www.buddysquirrel.com
Processor, exporter and packer of candy including regular and sugar-free boxed, chocolates, brittles, toffees, holiday, mints, molded novelties, etc.; also, nuts, nut mixes and gourmet popcorn
President: Margaret Gile
margaretg@qcbs.com
Number Employees: 100-249
Number of Brands: 2
Number of Products: 2000
Square Footage: 120000
Parent Co: Quality Candy Shoppes
Type of Packaging: Consumer, Food Service, Private Label, Bulk
Brands:
Buddy Squirrel
Fairy Food
Quality Candy

1829 Budenheim USA, Inc.
2219 Westbrooke Dr
Columbus, OH 43228-9605
614-345-2400
info@budenheim.com
www.budenheim.com/en
Supplier of ingredients for the meat, poultry, seafood, beverage, nutrition, dairy and baking industries. Primarily deals with phosphates.
Marketing: Marti Babcock
Vice President of Sales: Doug Lim
Square Footage: 5016
Parent Co: Chemische Fabrik Budenheim KG

1830 Budi Products LLC
PO Box 1325
Marblehead, MA 01945
781-990-3411
info@budibar.com
www.budibar.com
Manufacturer of bars made from superfood ingredients.
Founder: Michael McCarthy
Square Footage: 80000
Brands:
BUDIBAR

1831 Buds Kitchen
826 Gardner Center Road
New Castle, PA 16101-6020
724-654-9216
Fax: 724-654-9216 bud301@libcom.com
Hot sauce

1832 (HQ)Buedel Food Products
7661 S 78th Ave # A
Bridgeview, IL 60455-1274
708-496-3500
Fax: 708-496-8369 info@buedelfinemeats.com
Refrigerated horseradish and frozen smoked fish
Owner/President/Sales Exec: Kristyn Benson
kristynb@buedelfoods.com
Secretary/Treasurer: Kathleen Myer
Vice President: Kristin Buedel
Sales Director: Fred Buedel
COO: Darren Benson
Estimated Sales: $25,000,000
Number Employees: 20-49
Type of Packaging: Consumer, Private Label
Brands:
Prince Gourmet Foods

1833 Buehler Vineyards
820 Greenfield Rd
St Helena, CA 94574-9529
707-963-2155
Fax: 707-963-3747
Wine
President: John Buehler
john@buehlervineyard.com
Winemaker: David Cronin
Manager Sales/Marketing: Misha Chelini
Social Media and Sales: Helen Buehler
Person: Lorri Sax
Office Manager: Karan Zumalt
Vineyard and Production Manager: Raul Gloria
Estimated Sales: $2,000,000
Number Employees: 5-9
Type of Packaging: Private Label

1834 Buena Vista Historic Tstng Rm
18000 Old Winery Rd
PO Box 1842
Sonoma, CA 95476-4840
707-996-4438
Fax: 707-252-0392 800-926-1266
info@buenavistawinery.com
www.buenavistawinery.com
Manufacturer, importer and exporter of wine and also, importer of champagne
President/CEO: Harry Parsley
CFO/VP: Peter Kasper
Human Resources: Dorothy Kines
Site Manager: Starla Perez
Estimated Sales: $5-10 Million
Number Employees: 20-49
Square Footage: 240000
Type of Packaging: Consumer, Private Label
Brands:
Carneros

1835 Bueno Foods
2001 4th St SW
Albuquerque, NM 87102-4520
505-243-2722
Fax: 505-242-1680 800-888-7336
www.buenofoods.com
Frozen Mexican food including green chile and corn and flour tortillas, chile peppers, spices and dry chile powders
President: Jackie Baca
Number Employees: 100-249
Type of Packaging: Consumer, Food Service, Private Label
Brands:
Bueno
Chimayo

1836 Buff Bake
811 S Grand Avenue
Santa Ana, CA 92705
949-274-9464
info@buffbake.com
buffbake.com
Protein cookies and nut butters

1837 Buffalo Bill Brewing Company
1082 B St
Hayward, CA 94541-4108
510-886-9823
Fax: 510-886-8157 info@buffalobillsbrewery.com
www.buffalobillsbrewery.com
Ale, stout, lager and fruit flavored beers
President & CEO: Geoff Harries
Head Brewer: Mike Manty
Year Founded: 1983
Estimated Sales: $20-50 Million
Number Employees: 50-99
Type of Packaging: Consumer, Food Service, Bulk
Brands:
Alimony Ale
Billy Bock
Buffalo Brew
Pumpkin Ale
Tasmanian Devil
White Buffalo

1838 Buffalo Bills Premium Snacks
1547 Joel Dr.
P.O. Box 866
Lebanon, PA 17042
717-273-7499
Fax: 717-273-7699
customerservice@choochoorsnacks.com
www.bbjerky.com
Jerky, meat sticks, meat snacks, pickled sausages, gifts
General Manager: Paul Squires
Sales Manager: Patrick Sherburne

1839 Buffalo Trace Distillery
113 Great Buffalo Trce
Frankfort, KY 40601
502-696-5978
800-654-8471
info@buffalotrace.com
www.buffalotracedistillery.com
Bourbon and rum; importer of wine.
Marketing Services Director: Meredith Moody
Public Relations & Events Manager: Amy Preske
Year Founded: 1771
Estimated Sales: $29.3 Million
Number Employees: 100-249
Type of Packaging: Bulk

1840 Buffalo Wild Wings
600 Highway 169 S
Suite 1919
Minneapolis, MN 55426-1205
763-546-1891
Fax: 952-593-9787 info@buffalowildwings.com
www.buffalowildwings.com
Buffalo wings
Owner: Jim Disbrow
Co-Owner: Scott Lowery
Contact: Dale Gallion
dgallion@buffalowildwings.com
Estimated Sales: $300,000-500,000
Number Employees: 10-19

1841 Bull and Barrel Brewpub
988 Rte. 22
Brewster, NY 10509
845-278-2855
www.bullandbarrelbrewpub.com
IPAs and fruit-flavored Ales
Co-Owner: Rick Cipriani
Co-Owner: Wendy Wulkan
Number of Brands: 1
Number of Products: 6
Type of Packaging: Consumer, Private Label
Brands:
Bull and Barrel

1842 Bull's Head
C.P. 3151
Richmond, QC J0B 2H0
Canada
819-212-1583
info@bulls-head.com
bulls-head.com
Ginger based soda
Founder: John Bryant
Year Founded: 1986

1843 Bully Hill Vineyards
8843 Greyton H Taylor Mem Dr
Hammondsport, NY 14840
607-868-3610
Fax: 607-868-3205 info@bullyhill.com
www.bullyhillvineyards.com
Wines, champagne and grape juice
President: Lillian Taylor
VP Quality Control/Operations: Gregg Learned
Sales: Adam LaPierre
Estimated Sales: $5-9.9 Million
Number Employees: 5-9
Type of Packaging: Consumer

1844 Bumble Bee
Petco Park
900 C St
San Diego, CA 92101
858-715-4000
Fax: 858-560-6045 info@bumblebee.com
www.bumblebee.com
Canned seafood
CEO: Christopher Lischewski
Estimated Sales: $20-50 Million
Number Employees: 50-99

1845 Bumbleberry Farms LLC
119 Stauffer Rd.
Storystown, PA 15563
814-279-8083
www.bumbleberryfarms.com
Manufacturer of honey and honey products.
Founder: Karen Mosholder
Square Footage: 80000

1846 **Bunge**
1391 Timberlake Manor Pkwy.
Chesterfield, MO 63017
314-292-2000
news@bunge.com
www.bunge.com
Oilseed processing, supply milled wheat, corn and rice products to food processors, bakeries, brewers, foodservice companies and snack food producers. Offers distribution services.
CEO: Gregory Heckman
CFO: John Neppl
Chief Legal Officer: Joseph Podwika
Chief HR & Communications Officer: Deborah Borg
President, Global Operations: Raul Padilla
President, Global Supply Chain: Christos Dimopoulos
Year Founded: 1818
Number Employees: 24,000
Type of Packaging: Food Service

1847 **Bunge Canada**
2190 S. Service Road West
Oakville, ON L6L 5N1
Canada
905-825-7900
www.bungenorthamerica.com
Oil seeds, protein meals and edible oil products.
Director, Bulk Oil Sales: Steve Caloren
Brands:
Canaplus

1848 **Bunge Loders Croklaan**
24708 W Durkee Rd
Channahon, IL 60410-5249
815-730-5200
Fax: 815-730-5202 800-621-4710
blc.na@bunge.com
Fats, oils, flavored flakes, emulsifiers, dietary fiber and encapsulates, shortenings
CEO: Julian Veitch
julian.veitch@croklaan.com
CFO: Vincent Geerts
Vice President: Aaron Buettner
VP Innovation/R&D: Paul Shanahan
Quality Assurance Manager: Linda McLaren
VP Marketing: Vanessa Ballard
Director, Human Resources: Hens van Wingerden
VP of Operations: Eugenia Zorila
Facility Manager: Astrid Ackerman
Purchasing Manager: Sherry Shugart
Estimated Sales: $33.6 Million
Number Employees: 250-499
Number of Brands: 25

1849 **Bunge North America Inc.**
1391 Timberlake Manor Pkwy.
Chesterfield, MO 63017
314-292-2000
www.bungenorthamerica.com
Grain originator, processor and exporter.
CEO: Gregory Heckman
CFO: Luciano Salvatierra
Year Founded: 1918
Estimated Sales: $3.6 Billion
Parent Co: Bunge Limited
Type of Packaging: Consumer, Food Service, Private Label, Bulk
Brands:
Calrose
Kaho Mai
Maruyu
Pacific International

1850 **Bunker Foods Corp.**
79 Madison Ave
2nd Floor
New York, NY 10016
646-738-4020
info@bunkerfoodscorp.com
Importer of sunflower and chia seeds; as well as beans, chickpeas, corn, peanuts and other products.
President: Nicolas Lartitigoyen
Parent Co: Bunker Foods
Type of Packaging: Consumer, Food Service, Private Label
Brands:
Southern Ray's

1851 **Bunker Hill Cheese Co Inc**
6005 County Road 77
Millersburg, OH 44654-9045
330-893-2131
Fax: 330-893-2079 800-253-6636
info@heinis.com www.heinis.com
Processor and marketor of Heini's Brand Cheese. Products include yogurt, cultured cheese, raw milk cheeses, other natural cheeses and old fashioned churned butter.
Owner/President: Peter Dauwalder
Cmo: Lisa Troyer
ltroyer@heinis.com
Marketing Director: Bob Walker
Finance/Sales Executive: Lisa Troyer
VP Operations: Bob Troyer
Plant Manager: Eric Sheely
Purchasing Manager: Mark Schlabach
Estimated Sales: $8.6 Million
Number Employees: 50-99
Square Footage: 320000
Type of Packaging: Consumer, Bulk
Brands:
Amish Valley Farms
Heini's Brand Cheese

1852 **Bunny Bread**
Evansville, IN
bunnybread.net
Bread
Principal: Nadine Gallaway
VP: Darryl Trainer
Plant Manager: Daryl Mitchell
Estimated Sales: $90,000
Number Employees: 2
Type of Packaging: Consumer

1853 **Buns & Roses Organic Wholegrain Bakery**
6519-111th Street NW
Edmonton, AB T6H 4R5
Canada
780-438-0098
Fax: 780-437-8805
Breads and specialty baked products including organic whole grain and gluten-free
Owner: Dhammika Jayawickrama
Estimated Sales: $67,000.00
Number Employees: 1
Square Footage: 4800
Type of Packaging: Consumer, Food Service
Brands:
Buns & Roses

1854 **Buona Vita Inc**
1 S Industrial Blvd
Bridgeton, NJ 08302-3401
856-453-7972
Fax: 856-453-7978 sales@buonavitainc.com
www.buonavitainc.com
Italian specialties including meatballs, meatloaf, beef bracioli, eggplant, pasta and pizza toppings
President: Paul Infranco
pauljr@buonavitainc.com
SVP Operations: Blake Christy
Estimated Sales: $20-50 Million
Number Employees: 20-49
Square Footage: 25000
Type of Packaging: Consumer, Food Service, Private Label, Bulk
Brands:
Buona Vita
Mama Mia

1855 **Buonitalia**
75 9th Ave
New York, NY 10011
212-633-9090
Fax: 212-633-9717 info@buonitalia.com
www.buonitalia.com
Gourmet Italian foods including pasta, rice, mushrooms, truffles, flour, jams, oils, cheeses, vinegar, fruit mustard, cookies, biscuits and sweets
Owner: Mimmo Majiulo
Contact: Stacey Bonilla
staceybonilla@buonitalia.com
Manager: Scandt Zyleg
Bookkeeper: Yaribeth Dalmonte
Estimated Sales: $3.8 Million
Number Employees: 20-49
Square Footage: 20000
Parent Co: Misono Food
Type of Packaging: Consumer, Food Service, Private Label, Bulk

1856 **Burch Farms**
527 North Ave
Hilton, NY 14468-9144
585-392-2411
Fax: 585-392-4111 800-466-9668
info@burchfarms.com www.burchfarms.com
Sweet potatoes
President: Jimmy Burch
Partner: Ted Burch
Marketing Director: Jimmy Burch Jr
Contact: John Burch
john@burchfarms.com
Estimated Sales: $5,000,000
Number Employees: 5-9
Brands:
Candy Yams
Georgiana
Sugar & Spice

1857 **Burger Maker Inc**
666 16th St
Carlstadt, NJ 07072-1922
201-939-0444
Fax: 201-939-1965 www.schweidandsons.com
Hamburger patties
Owner: David Schweid
davidschweid@burgermaker.com
EVP Operations: Brad Schweld
EVP Sales: Jamie Schweld
Regional Manager: Chip Crenshaw
Regional Manager: Bill Breslin
Regional Manager: John Jernagan
davidschweid@burgermaker.com
Number Employees: 100-249

1858 **Burgers' Smokehouse**
32819 Highway 87
California, MO 65018-3227
573-796-3134
Fax: 573-796-3137 800-345-5185
service@smokehouse.com www.smokehouse.com
Producer of smoked meats, country cured ham, spare ribs, pork chops, smoked bacon, summer sausage, smoked turkey, smoked chicken, beef roasts, steaks, burgers and desserts.
President: Steven Burger
sburger@smokehouse.com
Vice President: Philip Burger
Marketing Director: Chris Mouse
Operations Manager: Keith Fletcher
Year Founded: 1952
Estimated Sales: $20-50 Million
Number Employees: 250-499
Number of Brands: 1
Square Footage: 200000
Type of Packaging: Consumer, Food Service, Private Label, Bulk
Brands:
Burgers Smokehouse

1859 **Burke Brands**
521 NE 189th St
Miami, FL 33179-3909
305-249-5628
Fax: 305-651-6018 877-436-7225
info@cafedonpablo.com www.cafedonpablo.com
Fine specialty coffee and gourmet food products.
President: Darron Burke
Vice President: Eliana Burke
Director of International Sales & Market: Thomas Stout
VP Sales: Carl Fiadini
Contact: Brian Vaughn
bvaughn@burkebrands.com
General Manager: Michele Fera
Production: Gladys Menjura
Estimated Sales: $1.8 Million
Number Employees: 19
Number of Brands: 4
Number of Products: 27
Square Footage: 10000
Type of Packaging: Consumer, Food Service, Private Label, Bulk
Other Locations:
Burke Brands
N Miami Beach FL
Brands:
Cafe Don Pablo

1860 **Burke Candy IngredientsInc**
3840 N Fratney St
Milwaukee, WI 53212-1341
414-964-7327
Fax: 414-964-7644 888-287-5350
info@burkecandy.com www.burkecandy.com
Chocolate candies and confectionery. Products are certified kosher
Owner/Chef: Julia Burke
Owner/Chef: Tim Burke
burkecandy@aol.com
Estimated Sales: Less Than $500,000
Number Employees: 1-4

1861 **Burke Corp**
1516 S D Ave
PO Box 209
Nevada, IA 50201-2708
515-382-3575
Fax: 515-382-2834 800-654-1152
sales_info@burkecorp.com www.burkecorp.com
Sausages and other prepared meats
President: William Burke Jr.
CFO: Marcy Hansen
SVP: David Weber
VP Research and Development: Casey Frye
Process and Quality Control Manager: Jim Chittenden
Marketing Director: Liz Hertz
VP Sales/Marketing: Doug Cooprider
Director: Scott Licht
VP Purchasing: Thomas Burke
Estimated Sales: $28.9 Million
Number Employees: 250-499
Type of Packaging: Food Service, Private Label, Bulk
Brands:
Burke(c)
Swiss American Sausage Co.
NaturaSelect(c)
Premoro(c)
Magnifoods(c)
Tezzata(c)

1862 **Burleigh Brothers Seafoods**
224 Burleigh Rd
Ellerslie, PE C0B 1J0
Canada
902-831-2349
Fax: 902-831-3072 tom@burleigh.pe.ca
www.burleigh.pe.ca
Fresh shellfish, mollusk, trout and smelt
CEO: Roger Burleigh
President: Proy Burleigh
Marketing Director: Tom Bradstaw
Estimated Sales: $3.2 Million
Number Employees: 16
Type of Packaging: Consumer, Food Service, Private Label, Bulk

1863 **Burleson Honey**
301 Peters St
Waxahachie, TX 75165-2855
972-937-2809
Fax: 972-937-8711 Jodie.d@burlesons-honey.com
www.burlesons-honey.com
Honey
President: T.E. Burleson Jr
Estimated Sales: $1,600,000
Number Employees: 20-49
Square Footage: 45
Type of Packaging: Private Label
Brands:
Burleson Pure Honey

1864 **Burn Brae Farms**
940 Matheson Blvd E
Mississauga, ON L4W 2R8
Canada
905-624-3600
Fax: 905-624-3363 gdowd@burnbraefarms.com
www.burnbraefarms.com
Packager of eggs
President: Joe Hudson
Marketing Director: Margaret Hudson
COO: Bob Anderson
Sales Manager: Gord Dowd
General Manager: Earl Powers
Estimated Sales: $25,000,000
Number Employees: 100
Parent Co: Burnbrae Farm
Type of Packaging: Consumer, Food Service
Brands:
Free Run
Nature's Best
Omega Pro
Organic Shell Eggs

1865 **Burnett & Son**
1420 S Myrtle Ave
Monrovia, CA 91016-4153
626-357-2165
Fax: 626-357-7115 877-632-5467
info@burnettandson.com www.burnettandson.com
Processor of meat including taco, London broil, shredded beef and pork, corned and roast beef, pot roast, steak, pork loin, etc; also, entrees including beef stew, chile, meat loaf, corned beef and cabbage, spaghetti and meatballsetc
President: Donald Burnett
Principal: David Kruse
Vice President: Derald Burnett
Year Founded: 1978
Estimated Sales: $20-50 Million
Number Employees: 50-99
Type of Packaging: Consumer, Food Service

1866 **(HQ)Burnette Foods**
701 US-31
Elk Rapids, MI 49629
231-264-8116
Fax: 231-264-9597 info@burnettefoods.com
www.burnettefoods.com
Canned fruits and vegetables including cherries, apples, plumbs, kidney beans, asparagus, green beans and potatoes.
Owner/President: Teresa Amato
CEO: John Pelizzari
CFO: Jennifer Sherman
Quality Manager/Sales Executive: Jennifer Boyer
Operations Manager: Dave Schroderus
Production Manager: Eric Rockafellow
Plant Manager: Gary Wilson
Estimated Sales: $40-$50 Million
Number Employees: 50-99
Square Footage: 12066
Type of Packaging: Consumer, Food Service
Other Locations:
Burnette Foods Plant
East Jordan MI
Burnette Foods Plant
Hartford MI
Brands:
Burnetti's
Mothers Maid
Romeo

1867 **Burnham & Morrill Co**
1 Beanpot Circle
Portland, ME 04103-5336
800-813-2165
www.bmbeans.com
Canned baked beans and brown bread
President: Kenneth Romanzi
CFO: Bruce Sherrill
Year Founded: 1867
Estimated Sales: $350,000
Number Employees: 100-249
Parent Co: B&G Foods
Type of Packaging: Consumer
Brands:
B&M Baked Beans

1868 **Burnley Vineyards**
4500 Winery Ln
Barboursville, VA 22923-1833
540-832-2828
bvwinery@gmx.com
www.burnleywines.com
Producer of wines such as Chardonnay, Cabernet Sauvignon, Cabernet Dora, Riesling, Chambourcin, Vidal and Norton.
General Manager: C.J. Reeder
Sales Manager: Patt Reeder
Tasting & Tours: Dawn Reeder
Winemaker: Lee Reeder
Estimated Sales: $5-9.9,000,000
Number Employees: 5-9
Brands:
Burnley Vineyards

1869 **Burrito Kitchens**
505 Weaver Pk Rd
Unit A
Longmont, CO 80501
720-652-9000
www.burritokitchens.com
All-natural burritos
Year Founded: 1999
Number of Products: 12

1870 **Burt Lewis Ingredients**
875 N Michigan Ave
Suite 2720
Chicago, IL 60611
312-640-8899
Fax: 312-640-8890 www.burtlewisingredients.com
Dairy products and ingredients
President: Vince Curtin
Year Founded: 1976

1871 **Burton Meat Processing**
1120 Navasota St
Burton, TX 77835-6131
979-289-4022
Fax: 978-989-4001
Beef, pork and sausage
Owner: Jerry Schultz
Estimated Sales: $2.5 Million
Number Employees: 1-4
Type of Packaging: Consumer, Bulk

1872 **Bush Brothers & Co**
800-590-3797
bushbeans.com
Baked beans
President & CEO: Al Williams
Year Founded: 1908
Estimated Sales: $100-499.9 Million
Number Employees: 1,000-4,999
Brands:
Bush's Best Baked Beans
Bush's Grilling Beans
Bush's Chili
Bush's Canned Beans

1873 **Bush Brothers ProvisionCo**
1931 N Dixie Hwy
West Palm Beach, FL 33407-6084
561-832-6666
Fax: 561-832-1460 800-327-1345
orders@bush-brothers.com
www.bush-brothers.com
Processor and exporter of fresh and frozen portion cut beef, veal, lamb, pork and poultry; wholesaler/distributor of dairy products; serving the food service market.
President: Harry Bush
sales@bushb-brothers.com
Vice President: Billy Bush
Sales Manager: Doug Bush
Operations Manager: John Bush
Estimated Sales: $13.3 Million
Number Employees: 20-49
Square Footage: 10000
Type of Packaging: Consumer, Food Service, Private Label, Bulk

1874 **Busken Bakery**
2675 Madison Rd
Cincinnati, OH 45208-1389
513-871-2114
Fax: 513-871-2662 orders@busken.com
Cookies, cakes, doughnuts, breads, rolls, pies and muffins.
Chief Executive Officer: D. Busken
Vice President: Brian Busken
Estimated Sales: $28,050,000
Number Employees: 100-249

1875 **Busseto Foods**
1090 W Church Ave
Fresno, CA 93706-3917
559-237-9591
Fax: 559-237-5745 800-628-2633
www.busseto.com
Specialty meats, salami, peperoni, prosciutto, chubs, pancetta and genoa
President & CEO: G Michael Grazier
g@busseto.com
CFO: Chuck Laizure
VP: Luca Zaniboni
Quality Assurance/quality Control Manage: Angela Gunadi
Maintenance Manager: Robert Diaz
Estimated Sales: $6.5 Million
Number Employees: 20-49
Parent Co: IBIS
Type of Packaging: Consumer, Food Service, Private Label, Bulk

Brands:
Busseto
Busseto Special Reserve

1876 **Busy Bee Yerba Mate**
www.busybeemate.com
Yerba mate
Co-Founder & CEO: Jayme Starrak
COO: Jared Yeager
Number of Brands: 1
Number of Products: 4
Type of Packaging: Consumer
Brands:
BUSY BEE

1877 **Butler Foods LLC**
P.O. Box 40
Grand Ronde, OR 97347
503-437-9133
info@butlerfoods.com
www.butlerfoods.com
Vegan products including soy curls, soy jerky, and taco crumbles
Owner: Dan Butler

1878 **Butler Winery**
6200 E Robinsion Rtd
Bloomington, IN 47408
812-332-6660
vineyard@butlerwinery.com
www.butlerwinery.com
Wine and wine making supplies
President/CEO: James Butler
Secretary/Treasurer: Susan Butler
Manager: Amy Butler
Estimated Sales: $540,000
Number Employees: 5
Brands:
Butler

1879 **Butter Baked Goods**
4907 Mackenzie Street
Vancouver, BC V6N 2G5
Canada
604-221-4333
Fax: 604-685-8563 info@butterbakedgoods.com
www.butterbakedgoods.com
Scones, muffins, cinnamon buns, cookies, bars, cupcakes, cakes, pies, tarts and mini tarts, loaves, and marshmallow
Propietor/President: Rosie Daykin
Number Employees: 1

1880 **Butter Buds Food Ingredients**
2330 Chicory Rd
Racine, WI 53403-4113
262-598-9900
Fax: 262-598-9999 800-426-1119
bbfi@bbuds.com www.bbuds.com
Processor and exporter of cholesterol-free butter flavored oils and sprays; also, natural dairy concentrates including butter, cheese and cream.
CEO: Jonh Buhler
Director of Business Development: Tom Buhler
Director of Administration: Jan Schmaus
General Manager: Bill Buhler
Estimated Sales: $5-10 Million
Number Employees: 50
Square Footage: 10000
Type of Packaging: Consumer, Food Service, Private Label, Bulk
Brands:
Alfredobuds
Butter Flo
Butterbuds
Buttermist
Cheesebuds

1881 **Butter Krust Baking Company**
1919 Flowers Circle
Thomasville, GA 31757
229-226-9110
Fax: 570-286-6975 800-282-8093
www.butterkrust.com
Bread, rolls and donuts
President: James G Apple
CFO: Brenda Swisher
Vice President: Randall Kreisher
Director of Sales: Tom Gresh
Manager: Lisa R. Hay
Plant Manager: Barry Hulfizer
Purchasing Manager: Timothy Apple
Estimated Sales: $300,000-500,000
Number Employees: 5-9
Type of Packaging: Consumer, Private Label, Bulk
Other Locations:
Northumberland PA
Brands:
Butter-Krust Country
Holsum
Milano

1882 **Butterball Farms**
1435 Buchanan Ave SW
Grand Rapids, MI 49507-1699
616-243-0105
Fax: 616-243-9169 888-828-8837
www.butterballfarms.com
Butter and margarine
President: David Riemersma
david.r@butterballfarms.com
CFO: Steve Whitteberry
Business Development Management: David Smallwood
Quality Assurance Manager: Lucia Falek
VP of Operations: Mike Craig
Plant Manager: Jim Bovee
Director of Purchasing: Ken Berry
Estimated Sales: $25.5 Million
Number Employees: 100-249
Square Footage: 125000
Type of Packaging: Food Service, Private Label
Brands:
Butterball
Figure-Maid
Pack of the Roses
Pop-Out
Sweetcorn

1883 **Butterball LLC**
1 Butterball Ln
PO Box 2389
Garner, NC 27529-5971
919-255-7900
Fax: 919-255-7973 www.butterballcorp.com
Frozen and refrigerated turkeys
President: Rodney Brenneman
CEO: Brenda Abbott
abbottb@johnstoncc.edu
SVP Research/Development: Jay Jandrain
Marketing Director: Kari Lindell
SVP Retail Sales: Dick Sarvas
Plant Manager: Jerry Lankford
Number Employees: 5000-9999
Parent Co: ConAgra Refigerated Prepared Foods
Other Locations:
Frozen Turkey Plant
Carthage MO
Prepackaging Plant
Huntsville AR
Deli Packaging Plant
Jonesboro AR
Frozen Turkey Plant
Mount Olive NC
Prepackaging Plant
Ozark AR
Brands:
Butterball

1884 **Butterfield Foods**
635 Westfield Rd
Noblesville, IN 46060-1323
317-776-4775
Fax: 317-776-4784 info@butterfield-foods.com
www.butterfield-foods.com
Prepared foods
President: Frank Violi
Estimated Sales: $30 Million
Number Employees: 150
Parent Co: Violi Foods
Type of Packaging: Consumer, Food Service, Private Label, Bulk

1885 **Butterfields**
2155 S Old Franklin Rd
Nashville, NC 27856-8952
252-459-7771
Fax: 252-459-7606 800-945-5957
Hard candy.
President: Brooks West
Estimated Sales: $670,000
Number Employees: 15

1886 **Butterfly Creek Winery**
PO Box 967
Mariposa, CA 95338
209-742-4567
Fax: 209-742-5019 www.yosemite.com
Wines
President: John Gerken
Sales: Tolleman Gorham
General Manager: Bob Gerken
Purchasing Manager: Robert Garcia
Estimated Sales: $210,000
Number Employees: 5
Type of Packaging: Private Label

1887 **Butternut Mountain Farm**
37 Industrial Park Dr
Morrisville, VT 05661-8533
Fax: 802-888-5909 800-828-2376
sales@butternutmountainfarm.com
www.butternutmountainfarm.com
Distributor and supplier of pure maple syrup and maple sugar.
Owner/Founder: David Marvin
CEO: John Kingston
Sales Manager: Stuart MacFarland
Director of Operations: Richard Harvey
Purchasing Manager: David Ellis
Square Footage: 50000
Parent Co: The Vermont Maple Syrup Company
Type of Packaging: Consumer, Food Service, Private Label, Bulk
Other Locations:
Butternut Mountain Farm Store
Johnson VT

1888 **Buttonwood Farm Winery & Vineyard**
1500 Alamo Pintado Rd
Solvang, CA 93463-9756
805-688-3032
Fax: 805-688-6168 800-715-1404
info@buttonwoodwinery.com
www.buttonwoodwinery.com
Wines
President: Bret Davenport
bret@buttonwoodwinery.com
CFO: Elizabeth Williams
VP: Seyburn Zorthian
Marketing Manager: Sherill Dugin
Secretary: Barry Zorthian
Estimated Sales: $990,000
Number Employees: 20-49

1889 **Buxton Foods**
401 Broadway
Buxton, ND 58218-4003
701-847-2110
800-726-8057
Gourmet frozen pinto beans and chili fully cooked and packaged in oven/microwaveable trays and boil-in-bags
President: Paul Siewert
CEO: Eileen Siewert
Estimated Sales: $10-20 Million
Number Employees: 1-4
Square Footage: 9000
Type of Packaging: Consumer, Food Service
Brands:
Paul's Pintos

1890 **Buywell Coffee**
4850 North Park Drive
Colorado Springs, CO 80918
719-598-7870
877-294-6246
Organic coffee
President: Segundo Guerrero
Treasurer: Benita Quevedo
Secretary: Pedro Castillo

1891 **Buzz Food Svc**
4818 Kanawha Blvd E
Charleston, WV 25306-6328
304-925-4781
Fax: 304-925-1502 info@buzzfoodsvc.com
www.buzzbutteredsteaks.com
Distributor of; beef, lamb, veal, chicken, pork, seafood, cheese, dairy, produce, canned goods, flour & baking supplies, frozen entrees and appetizers, ethnic specialties, gourmet items, beverage service, concession supplies andequipment, cleaning products and smallwares
President: Dickinson Gould
dickinson@buzzfoodsvc.com
Sales Manager: Jason Jean
General Manager: John Haddy
Operations Manager: Jeramy Kidd
Purchasing: Dennis Benson

Estimated Sales: $10.22 Million
Number Employees: 50-99
Square Footage: 90000
Type of Packaging: Consumer, Food Service
Brands:
Unipro
Fry Foods
Buzz Buttered Steaks
Code
General Mills
Haddys
Red Gold
Farmland
Reflections
Kraft
Hormel Foods
Dutch Quality House
Teays Valley
Advance
Vie De France
Gold Medal
Simplot

1892 **Buzzards Bay Trading Company**
PO Box 600
Fairhaven, MA 02719-0600
508-996-0242
Fax: 508-996-2421
Fresh and frozen seafood

1893 **Buzzn Bee Farms**
4700 N Flagler Dr
West Palm Beach, FL 33407-2907
561-881-1551
Fax: 561-881-7023 www.buzznbee.com
Honey
Owner/Beekeeper: David Rukin
Estimated Sales: $2.5-5,000,000
Number Employees: 1-4
Brands:
Buzzn Bee Farms
Sweet Squeeze

1894 **Byblos Bakery**
2479 23rd Street NE
Calgary, AB T2E 8J8
Canada
403-250-3711
Fax: 403-291-4095 info@byblosbakery.com
www.byblosbakery.com
Middle Eastern baked goods including pita bread, bagels, baklava and tortilla wraps
President: Salim Daklala
Secretary: Elias Daklala
VP: George Daklala
Estimated Sales: $5,600,000
Number Employees: 80
Number of Brands: 1
Type of Packaging: Consumer, Food Service, Private Label, Bulk
Brands:
Byblos

1895 **Byington Vineyard & Winery**
21850 Bear Creek Rd
Los Gatos, CA 95033-9438
408-354-1111
Fax: 408-354-2782 tastingroom@byington.com
www.byington.com
Wines
Manager: Frank Ashton
Secretary/Treasurer: Rod Bravo
VP: Sheryl Brissenden
Manager: Clyde Byington
c.byington@byingtonsteel.com
Manager: Frank Ashton
Estimated Sales: $510,000
Number Employees: 5-9
Square Footage: 15
Type of Packaging: Private Label
Brands:
Byington

1896 **Bylada Foods**
140 W Commercial Ave
Moonachie, NJ 07074-1703
201-933-7474
Fax: 201-933-1530 www.chefgustofoods.com
Frozen pizza and pizza bagels including regular and bite-size; exporter of pizza bagels
Vice President: Eric Silverman
eric@byladafoods.com
VP: Eric Silbeerman
Office Manager: Fay Campisi
Production Manager: Dan D'Amico
Estimated Sales: $5-10 Million
Number Employees: 10-19
Square Footage: 38000
Type of Packaging: Consumer, Food Service, Private Label
Brands:
Bocconcino

1897 **Byrd Cookie**
6700 Waters Ave
Savannah, GA 31406-2718
912-355-1716
Fax: 912-355-4431 800-291-2973
info@byrdcookiecompany.com
www.byrdcookiecompany.com
Cookies, cheese biscuits and Southern-style condiments
President: Geoff Repella
geoff@byrdcookiecompany.com
CEO: Stephanie Lindley
Chief Financial Officer: Will Brodmann
Director of Retail Operations: Stacy Jennings
Director of Operations: Jamie Lindley
Estimated Sales: $2.7 Million
Number Employees: 50-99
Number of Brands: 2
Number of Products: 75
Square Footage: 65000
Type of Packaging: Consumer, Private Label
Other Locations:
Byrd's Famous Cookies @ City Market
Savannah GA
Byrd's Famous Cookies on River St.
Savannah GA
Byrd's Famous Cookies in Pooler
Pooler GA
Brands:
Byrd's Famous Cookies
Byrd Cookies

1898 **Byrd Mill Co**
14471 Washington Hwy
Ashland, VA 23005
804-798-3627
Fax: 804-798-9357 888-897-3336
sales@byrdmill.com www.byrdmill.com
Specialty mixes including bread, pound cake, cookie, fruit cobbler, biscuit, pancake, waffle, muffin, spoon bread, shortbread, corn bread, hushpuppy, stoneground grits, etc
President: Todd Attkisson
sales@byrdmill.com
Estimated Sales: $300,000-$500,000
Number Employees: 10-19
Square Footage: 3300
Type of Packaging: Consumer, Food Service, Private Label, Bulk

1899 **Byrd's Pecans**
3 RR Box 196
Butler, MO 64730-9418
660-925-3253
866-679-5583
byrdspecans.com
Pecans
Owner: Loyle Byrd
Owner: Mary Byrd
Estimated Sales: Less than $500,000
Number Employees: 1-4
Type of Packaging: Private Label
Brands:
Byrd Missouri Grown
Byrd's Hoot Owl Pecan Ranch Pecans

1900 **Byrd's Seafood**
101 Potomac St
Crisfield, MD 21817-1448
410-968-0990
Fax: 410-968-1424 www.byrdsseafood.com
Crabmeat
Manager: Patti Marshall
Estimated Sales: $3-5,000,000
Number Employees: 5-9

1901 **Byrne & Carlson**
PO Box 789
Portsmouth, NH 03802
603-559-9778
Fax: 603-559-9778 888-559-9778
info@byrneandcarlson.com
www.byrneandcarlson.com
Chocolates and confections
Owner: Christopher Carlson
Estimated Sales: $325,000
Number Employees: 2

1902 **Byrne Dairy, Inc.**
2394 Route 11
P.O. Box 176
Syracuse, NY 13084
800-899-1535
info@byrnedairy.com www.byrnedairy.com
Dairy products including fluid milks, flavored milk drinks, ice cream mixes and custard mixes, creamers, cappuccino and mocha cappuccino drink, egg nog, orange juice, apple juice, grape juice, fruit and orange drink, lemon iced teapink lemon drink, lemonade, and heavy cream and buttermilk, whipped cream, ice cream, cheese, cottage cheese, yogurt, butter, sour cream, eggs, dips, and a recovery drink called After Byrne.
President & CEO: F. Fred Sadeghi
EVP & Treasurer: Mark Byrne
Board President & VP, Marketing: Carl Byrne
Year Founded: 1933
Estimated Sales: $44.5 Million
Number Employees: 480
Square Footage: 32000
Type of Packaging: Consumer, Food Service, Private Label, Bulk
Brands:
Byrne Dairy
After Byrne Recovery Drink

1903 **Byrnes & Kiefer Co**
131 Kline Ave
Callery, PA 16024
724-538-5200
Fax: 724-538-9292 contactus@bkcompany.com
www.bkcompany.com
Baked goods
President: Jay Thier
Chief Executive Officer: Edward Byrnes
Contact: Don Bradley
bradley@bkcompany.com
Estimated Sales: $23,000,000
Number Employees: 50
Type of Packaging: Private Label
Brands:
B&K Manufacturing
Charlie's Specialties

1904 **Byrnes & Kiefer Company**
131 Kline Avenue
Callery, PA 16024
724-538-5200
contactus@bkcompany.com
www.bkcompany.com
Bakery products, including baking supplies, fillings and icings, and read-to-eat baked goods, such as brownies, cookies, and pastries.
Year Founded: 1902
Estimated Sales: $10-20 Million
Number Employees: 20-49
Square Footage: 60000
Type of Packaging: Food Service, Private Label
Brands:
Chefmaster
Charlie's Specialties

1905 **Byrnes Packing Shed**
880 Federal Point Rd
Hastings, FL 32145-3210
904-692-1643
Fax: 904-692-2002
Grower and packer of whole potatoes
Owner: Daniel Byrnes
byrnesfarms@aol.com
Estimated Sales: $2.5-5 Million
Number Employees: 10-19
Type of Packaging: Consumer

1906 **Byron Vineyard & Winery**
5250 Tepusquet Rd.
Santa Maria, CA 93454
805-938-7365
Fax: 805-938-1581 info@byronwines.com
www.byronwines.com

Wines
Manager & Winemaker: Jonathan Nagy
Contact: Lea Brandy
lbrandy@byronwines.com
Estimated Sales: $5-10,000,000
Number Employees: 11-50
Type of Packaging: Private Label

1907 **C & C Packing Co**
1197 Highway 82
Stamps, AR 71860-9008
870-533-2251
Fax: 870-533-4309 866-365-3759
candcpackinginc@hotmail.com
www.candcpackinginc.com
Meat
Owner: Kenny Camp
kcamp@ccpacking.com
Owner/Operations Manager: Kenny Camp
Estimated Sales: Less Than $500,000
Number Employees: 5-9
Type of Packaging: Consumer

1908 **C & E Canners Inc**
1249 Mays Landing Rd
PO Box 229
Hammonton, NJ 08037-2816
609-561-1078
Fax: 609-567-2776
Processor, exporter and canner of sauces and ketchup
President: Robert Cappuccio
r.cappuccio@chi-rho.com
Corporate Secretary: Joseph Cappuccio
COO: David Cappuccio
Director Manufacturing: Stephen Cappuccio
Estimated Sales: $1.3 Million
Number Employees: 20-49
Square Footage: 320000
Type of Packaging: Consumer
Brands:
C & E Sugar
Cappuccio
Na Po'okela O Honaunau

1909 **(HQ)C & F Foods Inc**
15620 E Valley Blvd
City Of Industry, CA 91744-3926
626-723-1000
Fax: 626-723-1212 mmendoza@cnf-foods.com
www.cnf-foods.com
Dried beans, lentils, popcorn, peas and rice
President & CEO: Luis Faura
CFO: Alex Tran
VP Sales & Marketing: Paul Cromidas
Sr. Director of Operations: Mark Mendoza
Year Founded: 1975
Estimated Sales: $32.6 Million
Number Employees: 100-249
Type of Packaging: Consumer, Food Service, Private Label
Other Locations:
C&F Foods
Hansen ID
C&F Foods
Sikeston MO
C&F Foods
Manvel ND
C&F Food
Raleigh NC
Brands:
El Orgullo De Mi Tierra
Kanga Beans
Premier Fields

1910 **C & G Salsa**
PO Box 6085
Fishers, IN 46038-6085
317-569-9099
Fax: 317-569-8666 sales@cgsalsa.com
www.cgsalsa.com
Produces a variety of salsa (mild/medium/hot) and chili sauce (mild/zesty) products.
Owner: Charles Ferguson
sales@cgsalsa.com
Co-Owner: Glenda Ferguson
Number Employees: 1-4
Type of Packaging: Food Service

1911 **(HQ)C & H Sugar Co Inc**
830 Loring Ave
Crockett, CA 94525
800-773-1803
www.chsugar.com
Raw, organic and granulized sugar; sweeteners and baking sugar.
President & CEO: David Koncelik
Year Founded: 1906
Estimated Sales: $169 Million
Number Employees: 200-500
Parent Co: ASR Group
Type of Packaging: Consumer, Food Service, Private Label, Bulk
Brands:
C&H

1912 **C & J Tender Meat Co**
324 E Intl Airport Rd
Anchorage, AK 99518-1215
907-562-2838
Fax: 907-561-5846 www.cjtendermeat.com
Meats
Owner: Steve Jones
Treasurer: Arlita Jones
Estimated Sales: $1.1 Million
Number Employees: 5-9

1913 **C C Conway Seafoods**
2567 Conway Oyterhouse Road
Wicomico, VA 23184
804-642-2853
Fish and seafood
Owner/President: Christopher Conway III
Estimated Sales: $500,000-$1,000,000
Number Employees: 1-4
Type of Packaging: Food Service, Bulk

1914 **C C Pollen**
3627 E Indian School Rd # 209
Phoenix, AZ 85018-5134
602-957-0096
Fax: 602-381-3130 800-875-0096
beemail1@ccpollen.com www.beepollen.com
Bee pollen and beehive products
President: Bruce Brown
Estimated Sales: $7 Million
Number Employees: 10-19
Number of Brands: 7
Type of Packaging: Consumer, Food Service, Private Label, Bulk
Brands:
24-Hour Royal Jelly
Aller Bee-Gone
Bee Propolis
Buzz Bars
Dynamic Trio
High Desert
Pollenergy

1915 **C F Burger Creamery Co**
8101 Greenfield Rd
Detroit, MI 48228-2296
313-584-4040
Fax: 313-584-9870 info@cfburger.com
www.cfburger.com
Dairy products
President: Dean Angott
CEO: Larry Angott
langott@cfburger.com
Number Employees: 50-99
Type of Packaging: Consumer, Food Service, Private Label, Bulk
Brands:
C.F. Burger
Goody Shake
Natures Fountain

1916 **C F Gollott & Son Seafood**
9357 Central Ave
PO Box 1191
Diberville, MS 39540-5301
228-392-2747
Fax: 228-392-3701 cfgollot@gmail.com
www.gollottseafood.com
Frozen shrimp
Co-Owner: Brian Gollott
Co-Owner: Armond Gollott
Co-Owner: Dale Gollott
Co-Owner: Nicky Gollott
Plant Operations: Todd Gollott
Estimated Sales: $20-50 Million
Number Employees: 50-99
Square Footage: 7800
Type of Packaging: Consumer, Food Service, Private Label
Brands:
Treasure Chest Shrimp
Full Moon Shrimp
Gollots Brand Shrimp
Mermaid's Supreme Shrimp

1917 **C H Guenther & Son Inc**
2201 Broadway St
San Antonio, TX 78215-1135
210-227-1401
www.chg.com
Flour meal and prepared mixes; frozen bakery products.
President & CEO: Dale Tremblay
dtremblay@chguenther.com
SVP & CFO: Justin Grubbs
SVP, Corporate Services: Stephen Phillips
SVP & General Counsel: Thomas McRae
SVP & Chief Commercial Officer: Kelly Crouse
SVP & COO: Eric Stockl
Year Founded: 1851
Estimated Sales: $133.2 Million
Number Employees: 500-999
Square Footage: 22869
Type of Packaging: Consumer, Food Service, Private Label, Bulk
Other Locations:
Williams Foods
Lenexa KS
Pioneer Flour Mills
San Antonio TX
Pioneer Frozen Foods
Duncanville TX
Pioneer Frozen Foods
Prosperity SC
The Guenther House
San Antonio TX
Brands:
Pioneer
Williams
White Wings
Morrison's
Sun-Bird

1918 **C Howard Co**
1007 Station Rd
Bellport, NY 11713-1552
631-286-7940
Fax: 631-286-7947 apratz@chowardcompany.com
www.chowardsdirect.com
Confectionery products including hard candy, mints and chewing gum
President: Kenneth Pratz
inquire@chowardcompany.com
Treasurer: Gene Pratz
Vice President: Arthur Pratz
Estimated Sales: $510,000
Number Employees: 5-9
Square Footage: 20000
Type of Packaging: Consumer, Private Label
Brands:
Chowards

1919 **C J Dannemiller Co**
5300 S Hametown Rd
Norton, OH 44203-6199
330-825-7808
Fax: 330-825-3793 800-624-8671
www.cjdannemiller.com
Roasted nuts and popcorn
President: James A Dannemiller
sales@cjdannemiller.com
Secretary: TW Dannemiller
Estimated Sales: $5-10 Million
Number Employees: 20-49
Square Footage: 88000
Type of Packaging: Bulk

1920 **C J Vitner Co**
4202 W 45th St
Chicago, IL 60660-4390
773-523-7900
Fax: 773-523-9143 www.snakking.com
Potato chips, pork rinds, chesse puffs, popcorn and pretzels.
Year Founded: 1926
Estimated Sales: $20-50 Million
Number Employees: 250-499
Square Footage: 77000
Parent Co: Snak King
Type of Packaging: Consumer, Food Service, Private Label, Bulk

1921 **C Nelson Mfg Co**
265 N Lake Winds Pkwy
Oak Harbor, OH 43449-9012
419-898-3305
Fax: 419-898-4098

Manufacturer of ice cream cabinets, ice cream carts and related equipment.
Owner: Kelley Smith
nelsonoh@aol.com
Marketing/Sales: George Dunlap
Purchasing: Paul Zylka
Estimated Sales: $10-20 000,000
Number Employees: 20-49

1922 **C P Vegetable Oil**
601 SW 21st Terrace
Suite 1
Fort Lauderdale, FL 33312-2278
Canada
954-584-0420
Fax: 905-792-9461 800-398-7154
info@cpvusa.com www.cpvegoil.com
Vegetable oils
Ceo: Christian Pellerin
Manager: Giuseppe Vinci
gvinci@cpvusa.com
Number Employees: 10-19
Type of Packaging: Food Service, Bulk
Brands:
C.P.

1923 **C Roy & Sons Processing**
444 Roy Dr
Yale, MI 48097
810-387-3957
Fax: 810-387-3957 croyprocessing@hotmail.com
www.yalebologna.com
Meat products including bologna
CEO: Richard Roy
Manager: Nancy Roy
Estimated Sales: $2 Million
Number Employees: 20
Type of Packaging: Consumer

1924 **C S Steen Syrup Mill Inc**
119 N Main St
Abbeville, LA 70510-4603
337-893-1654
Fax: 337-893-2478 800-725-1654
steens@steensyrup.com www.steensyrup.com
Molasses and syrup
Owner: Charlie Steen
steens@steensyrup.com
Marketing Director: Cole Thompson
Estimated Sales: $5-10 Million
Number Employees: 20-49
Type of Packaging: Bulk
Brands:
Steen's Cane Cured Pheasant

1925 **C W Resources Inc**
200 Myrtle St
New Britain, CT 06053-4160
860-229-7700
Fax: 860-229-6847 info@cwresources.org
www.cwresources.org
Gourmet products including flavored vinegars and oils, salsas, sauces, jellies, baking mixes, dips/dip mixes, baked goods, rubs and salad dressings
President & CEO: Ronald Buccilli
Director of Finance: Marta Kuczek
VP Sales/Production: Alix Capsalors
Operations Manager: Mark Anderson
Production: Bill Blonski
Estimated Sales: $33 Million
Number Employees: 250-499
Square Footage: 100000
Type of Packaging: Consumer, Food Service, Private Label, Bulk
Brands:
B&B
Sumptuous Ions

1926 **C&J Trading**
1140 Revere Ave
San Francisco, CA 94124-3423
415-822-8910
Fax: 415-822-7526
Oriental food
Owner: C Wo
Estimated Sales: $1-2,500,000
Number Employees: 5-9
Type of Packaging: Private Label

1927 **C&P Additives**
950 Peninsula Corp Cir
Suite 3018
Boca Raton, FL 33487
561-995-7071
Fax: 561-995-7075 877-857-2623
office@cp-additives.com www.cp-additives.com
Seasonings and enzymes
Type of Packaging: Private Label, Bulk

1928 **C&S Wholesale Meat Company**
973 Confederate Ave SE
Atlanta, GA 30312
404-627-3547
Fax: 404-627-3549
Portion cut meat including pork and beef
President: Jay Bernath
CEO: Stanley D. Bernath
Chairman of the Board: Stanley Bernath
Marketing Administrator: Ronnie Berneth
Estimated Sales: $10-20 Million
Number Employees: 20-49
Type of Packaging: Food Service, Bulk
Brands:
C&S

1929 **C&T Refinery**
PO Box 9300
Minneapolis, MN 55440
804-287-1340
Fax: 804-285-9168 800-227-4455
www.cargill.com
Processor and exporter of vegetable oil
President: C Sauer
VP: Robert Holden
Parent Co: C.F. Sauer Company
Type of Packaging: Consumer, Food Service, Private Label, Bulk
Brands:
C&T

1930 **C'est Gourmet**
2 Watson Place
Framingham, MA 01701
508-877-0000
Fax: 508-877-5600 info@cestgourmet.com
Gourmet baked goods
Co-Owner: Chris Gagnon
Co-Owner: Jacques Cohen
Operations Manager: Andrea Gagnon
Number Employees: 1-4
Type of Packaging: Food Service, Private Label

1931 **C. Gould Seafoods**
PO Box 14566
Scottsdale, AZ 85267-4566
480-314-9250
Fax: 480-314-9240
Seafood
President: Carla Gould
Owner: Carlos Garcia
Secretary/Treasurer: Helen Sambrano
Vice President: Robert Llewellyn
Estimated Sales: $550,000
Number Employees: 4

1932 **C.B.S. Lobster Company**
41 Union Wharf
Portland, ME 04101
207-775-2917
Fax: 207-772-0169 www.mainelobsterdirect.com
Lobster
Owner: Lee Kressbach
CEO: Joi Kressbach
Estimated Sales: $5-10 Million
Number Employees: 20-49

1933 **C.C. Graber Company**
315 E Fourth Street
Ontario, CA 91764
909-983-1761
Fax: 909-984-2180 800-996-5483
info@graberolives.com www.graberolives.com
Manufacturer of vegetables, gourmet foods and olives.
President: Clifford Graber
Co-Owner: Robert Graber
Contact: Sue Bonetti
suebonetti@graberolives.com
Year Founded: 1894
Estimated Sales: $20-50 Million
Number Employees: 100-249
Number of Brands: 1
Brands:
Graber Olives

1934 **C.E. Fish Company**
69 Roque Bluffs Road
Jonesboro, ME 4648
207-434-2631
Fax: 207-434-6940
Soft-shelled and steamer clams
President: Barbara Fish
Treasurer: Marge Fish
Vice President: Ralph Fish
Estimated Sales: $83,000
Number Employees: 5-9
Square Footage: 10500
Type of Packaging: Consumer
Brands:
Uni

1935 **C.F. Sauer Co.**
2000 W. Broad St.
Richmond, VA 23220
800-688-5676
888-723-0052
www.cfsauer.com
Spices and mixes including cooking spices, griller seasonings, rubs, grinders, bulk spices and seasonings, baking bag mixes, microwave steamer mixes, gravy mixes, seasoning mixes, grilling marinade mixes, sauce mixes, slow cookermixes, extracts, flavorings and food colorings, mayonnaise and mustard, and BBQ sauces.
President/CEO: Conrad Sauer IV
CFO: W.N. Clemons
Vice President: Bradford Sauer
Executive VP, Sales: Mark Sauer
Year Founded: 1887
Estimated Sales: $223 Million
Number Employees: 1000-4999
Number of Brands: 7
Square Footage: 80000
Type of Packaging: Consumer, Food Service, Private Label
Other Locations:
C.F. Sauer Company
San Luis Obispo CA
Brands:
Bama
C.F. Sauer Company
Duke's Mayonaise
Gold Medal
Mrs. Filberts
Sauer's Everyday Spices
The Spice Hunter

1936 **C.J. Distributing**
P.O.Box 2344
Surf City, NC 28445
910-329-1681
Fax: 910-329-1286 800-990-2366
Peanuts and snack food items
CEO: E Howell
Number Employees: 1-4
Square Footage: 5000
Type of Packaging: Consumer, Private Label, Bulk

1937 **C.L. Deveau & Son**
PO Box 1
Salmon River, NS B0W 2Y0
Canada
902-649-2812
Fax: 902-649-2812
Salted fish and frozen herring roe
President: Irvan Paul Deveau
Number Employees: 10-19
Type of Packaging: Consumer, Food Service, Private Label, Bulk

1938 **C.W. Brown Foods, Inc.**
161 Kings Highway
Mountt Royal, NJ 08061
856-423-3700
customerservice@bottosausage.com
www.bottosausage.com
Fresh sausage, meatballs, and case ready meats
Estimated Sales: $10-20 Million
Number Employees: 50-99
Number of Brands: 1
Number of Products: 5
Type of Packaging: Consumer, Bulk
Brands:
Botto's Genuine Italian Sausage

1939 **C2O Pure Coconut Water**
4000 Cover Street
Suite 110
Long Beach, CA 90808
877-295-0873
contact@c2o-cocowater.com www.drinkC2O.com
Coconut water
Founder/President: Ronald Greene
Year Founded: 2008
Number Employees: 11-50

1940 **CA Fortune & Company**
141 Covington Dr
Bloomingdale, IL 60108-3107
630-539-3100
Fax: 608-634-2400
Dairy products, specialty foods, pizza toppings, pizza crusts and bread.
President: Ken Rzeszutko
Contact: Stephanie Anderson
stephanie.anderson@cafortune.com
Purchasing: Ralph Johnson
Estimated Sales: $1-2,500,000
Number Employees: 15
Type of Packaging: Private Label
Brands:
Burlle Meats
New Holstein Cheese
Rotella Bread

1941 **CB Beverage Corporation**
PO Box 49
Hopkins, MN 55343
952-935-9905
Fax: 952-938-2731 www.cocknbull.com
Beverages; ginger beer, sarsaparilla, sparkling juice, root beer, etc.
President: Daniel Meyers
Estimated Sales: Less than $300,000
Number Employees: 1-4

1942 **CB's Nuts**
6013 NE State Hwy 104
Kingston, WA 98346
360-297-1213
www.cbsnuts.com
Peanut butter
President & Owner: Tami Bowen
VP, Marketing: Chris Bowen
Number of Brands: 1
Number of Products: 2
Type of Packaging: Consumer
Brands:
CB'S NUTS

1943 **CBC Foods**
305 Main St
PO Box 396
Little River, KS 67457-9073
620-897-6665
Fax: 620-897-5599 800-276-4770
Manufacture frozen cookie dough
President: Carolyn Wright
carolyn@cookiehouse.com
Estimated Sales: $1,000,000
Number Employees: 5-9
Square Footage: 5000
Type of Packaging: Consumer, Food Service, Private Label, Bulk

1944 **CBP Resources**
5533 York Highway
Gastonia, NC 28052-8729
704-868-4573
Fax: 704-861-9252
Poultry processing plant.
President: JJ Smith
Principal: Paul Humphries
Estimated Sales: $20-50 Million
Number Employees: 100-249
Parent Co: Carolina By-Products Company

1945 **CBS Food Products Corporation**
2020 Fieldstone Pkwy
Suite 900-179
Franklin, TN 37069
800-216-9605
Fax: 718-452-2516 info@cbsfoods.com
www.cbsfoods.com
Shrimp burgers
President: Chaim Stein
CEO: Bernard Steinberg
Vice President: Phillip Shapiro
Purchasing Agent: Bob Green
Estimated Sales: $2 Million
Number Employees: 15
Type of Packaging: Consumer, Food Service, Private Label
Brands:
Cbs

1946 **CHO America**
204 B W YMCA Dr
Baytown, TX 77521
281-712-1549
www.cho-america.com
Organic and extra virgin olive oils and Deglet Nour dates
CEO: Wajih Rekik

1947 **CHR Foods**
P.O.Box 608
Watsonville, CA 95077-0608
831-728-0157
Fax: 831-728-0459
Frozen mixed vegetables and strawberries including whole and puree
President/CEO: Ray Rodriguez
CFO: Julis Skelton
Estimated Sales: $5-10,000,000
Number Employees: 5-9
Type of Packaging: Food Service
Brands:
Chr
New Harvest Foods

1948 **CHS Inc.**
5500 Cenex Dr.
Inver Grove Hts., MN 55077
651-355-6000
800-328-6539
www.chsinc.com
Agriculture, energy, transportation and business services company, with food products through subsidiary Ventura Foods.
President/CEO: Jay Debertin
Executive VP/CFO: Olivia Nelligan
Executive VP/General Counsel: Jim Zappa
Estimated Sales: $32.6 Billion
Number Employees: 10000+
Type of Packaging: Consumer, Food Service, Private Label, Bulk

1949 **CHS Sunflower**
220 Clement Ave
Grandin, ND 58038-4017
701-484-5313
Fax: 701-484-5657 sunflower@chsinc.com
www.chssunflower.com
Sunflower kernels, in-shell sunflower, flax, millet, buckwheat, pumpkin seeds, and soybean.
President/CEO: James Krogh
james.krogh@chsinc.com
Research & Development: Joel Schaefer
Sales Director: Wes Dick
Sales Director: Bruce Fjelde
Plant Superintendent: Arvid Terry
Controller: Chuck Schmidt
Number Employees: 100-249
Parent Co: CHS, Inc.
Type of Packaging: Consumer, Food Service, Private Label, Bulk

1950 **CHS Sunprairie**
1800 13th St SE
Minot, ND 58701-6061
Canada
701-852-1429
Fax: 701-852-2755 800-556-6807
Organic flour, pancake mixes and hot breakfast cereals; exporter of hot organic breakfast cereals, bars and herbal supplements
Member: Peggy Lesueur-Brymer
Broker Sales Manager: Pat Maloney
Sales Coordinator: Sarah Sanders
Manager: Brad Haugeberg
brad.haugegerg@chsinc.com
Operations Manager: Curt Currie
Estimated Sales: $17,500,000
Number Employees: 20-49
Type of Packaging: Consumer, Food Service
Brands:
Golden Loaf
Prairie Sun
Rosebud
Sunny Boy

1951 **CHiKPRO**
417-708-0988
www.chikpro.com
Chicken protein powder
Number of Brands: 1
Number of Products: 26
Type of Packaging: Consumer
Brands:
REAL CLEAN PROTEIN
BIN CHXN

1952 **CJ America**
3530 Wilshire Blvd.,
Suite 1220
Los Angeles, CA 90010
213-427-5566
Fax: 213-427-7878 www.cjamerica.com
Manufacturer of amino acids, flavor enhancers and sweeteners.
President: Joonmo Suh
Vice President: Stephen Chang
Food Ingredients Sales Manager: Cecilia Kim
Product Manager: Chris Lee
Purchasing Agent: Jane Cho
Estimated Sales: $.5-1 million
Number Employees: 10
Square Footage: 31304
Parent Co: Cheiljedang
Type of Packaging: Consumer, Food Service, Private Label, Bulk

1953 **CJ Foods**
4 Centerpointe Dr
Suite 100
La Palma, CA 90623
714-367-7200
Fax: 714-367-7192 info@cjfoods.com
cjfoods.com
Natural, gourmet Pan-Asian foods and sauces including sauces and pastes, condiments, ingredients, cooked rice, seaweed snacks, potstickers and mini wontons.
President: Sung Shin
CEO & Chairman: Tod Morgan
Contact: Brad Schulz
bradschulz@cj.net
Purchasing Manager: Jason Baik
Estimated Sales: $2.1 Million
Type of Packaging: Consumer, Bulk
Brands:
bibigo
Annie Chun's
Cheiljedang

1954 **CJ Omni**
4591 Firestone Blvd
South Gate, CA 90280
323-567-8171
Korean foods; specialize in mini wontons and korean sauces
President: James Chae
Estimated Sales: $3.5 Million
Number Employees: 50

1955 **CJ's Seafood**
125 Dixie Drive
Des Allemands, LA 70030-3320
985-758-1237
Fresh and frozen catfish
President: Curtis Matherne
Number Employees: 1-4
Square Footage: 560
Type of Packaging: Consumer, Food Service

1956 **CK Living LLC**
606 Kinderkarmack Rd Bsmt
River Edge, NJ 07661-2143
201-261-2078
contactus@crazykoreancooking.com
crazykoreancooking.com
Korean preprepared meals; soups; soy sauce; curry
CEO: Grace Lewis
Type of Packaging: Food Service, Private Label

1957 **CMA Global Partners/German Foods LLC**
719 6th St
NW Washington, DC 20001
301-365-5043
Fax: 202-467-5440 800-881-6419
info@germanfoods.org
Baking mixes; cake decorations; baking ingredients; hot chocolate powders; confections; curred meats; spreads and jellies.

Managing Partner: Arnim von Friedeburg
Year Founded: 2009
Number Employees: 1-10
Type of Packaging: Food Service, Private Label
Brands:
Brandt
Dallmayr
Favorit Swiss Premium
Grafschafter
Hela
Hengstenberg
Kathi
Manner
Meica
Niederegger Lubeck
Scho-ko-lade
Seitenbacher

1958 **CMS Fine Foods**
4791 Dry Creek Rd
Healdsburg, CA 95448
707-473-9561
Fax: 707-473-9765 www.cmsfinefoods.com
sauces, dressings, mustards, marinades and other condiments; offers co-packing and private label services.
Type of Packaging: Consumer, Food Service, Private Label, Bulk

1959 **CNS Confectionery Products**
33 Hook Rd
Bayonne, NJ 07002-5006
201-823-1400
Fax: 201-823-2452 888-823-4330
sales@cnscoinc.com www.cnscoinc.com
Importer, processor and national distributor of sweetened, toasted and desiccated coconut as well as other sweet, dry baking ingredients. Certified kosher.
Owner: Eva Deutsch
e.deutsch@cnscoinc.com
CFO: Irene Fishman
VP Sales: Miriam Gross
e.deutsch@cnscoinc.com
Chief, Production/Purchasing: Eva Deutsch
Estimated Sales: $1-2.5 Million
Number Employees: 10-19
Type of Packaging: Private Label
Brands:
Cns

1960 **CO YO**
Albuquerque, NM 87107
505-247-0012
info@coyo.us
coyo.com
Coconut yogurt
Founder: Henry Gosling
Brands:
CO YO

1961 **COnut Butter**
727 Lyons St
New Orleans, LA 70115
info@COnutButter.com
www.COnutButter.com
Nut butters
Owner: Alexandra Pericak
Year Founded: 2015

1962 **CP Kelco**
Cumberland Center II
3100 Cumberland Blvd, Suite 600
Atlanta, GA 30339
678-247-7300
800-535-2687
www.cpkelco.com
Texturizing and stabilizing ingredients.
President & CEO: Dieder Viala
Year Founded: 1929
Estimated Sales: $370.5 Million
Number Employees: 2,200
Number of Brands: 10
Number of Products: 24
Parent Co: J.M. Huber Company
Other Locations:
CP Kelco Production Plant
Okmulgee OK
CP Kelco Production Plant
San Diego CA
Brands:
Cekol
Genu
Genu Plus
Genugel
Genulacta
Genulacta
Genutine
Genuvisco
Kelcogel
Kelgum
Keltrol
Simplesse
Splendid

1963 **CROPP Cooperative**
One Organic Way
La Farge, WI 54639
Fax: 608-625-2600 888-444-6455
contact.us@organicvalley.coop www.farmers.coop
Organic products including dried and fresh cheeses, eggs, yogurt, milk and butter; also, organic vegetables and certified organic pork, beef and chicken; importer of certified organic bananas.
CEO: Robert Kirchoff
Project Advisor: Mike Bedessem
Executive VP, Marketing: Lewis Goldstein
Year Founded: 1988
Estimated Sales: $1.157 Billion
Number Employees: 932
Number of Brands: 2
Square Footage: 10000
Type of Packaging: Consumer, Food Service, Private Label, Bulk
Brands:
Organic Valley
Organic Prairie
Mighty Organic

1964 **CTC Manufacturing**
416 Meridian Road SE
Suite B12
Calgary, AB T2A 1X2
Canada
403-235-2428
Fax: 403-272-9558 800-668-7677
Lollypops
President: G Paul Allen
Sales Manager: David Skultety
Plant Manager: Malcolm Steel
Number Employees: 10-19
Square Footage: 6900
Parent Co: Candy Tree Company
Type of Packaging: Consumer, Food Service, Private Label
Brands:
The Candy Tree

1965 **CTI Foods**
22303 Hwy 95
Wilder, ID 83676
208-482-7844
info@ctifoods.com
www.ctifoods.com
Processes meat to beef patties, fajitas, taco meat and others.
CEO: Mike Buccheri
Estimated Sales: $134 Million
Number Employees: 500
Parent Co: CTI Foods Holding Co., LLC
Other Locations:
Plant
Azusa CA
Plant
Signaw TX
Plant
Owingsville KY
Plant
King of Prussia PA

1966 **CTL Foods**
514 Main St
Colfax, WI 54730
715-962-3121
Fax: 715-962-4030 800-962-5227
foods@ctlcolfax.com www.ctlcolfax.com
Malted milk powder, dry-form syrup bases and flavored slush drinks and bases; manufacturer of dry powder dispensers; also, custom blending and packaging services available
President: Michael Bean
Estimated Sales: $1.5 Million
Number Employees: 5-9
Square Footage: 40000
Type of Packaging: Food Service, Private Label
Brands:
Glacier Ice
Soda Fountain

1967 **CVC4Health**
4510 S Boyle Ave
Vernon, CA 90058
323-581-0176
Fax: 323-589-6667 800-421-6175
www.cvc4health.com
Vitamins
President: William Ballard
Treasurer: Lillian Beckenfield
VP: Harvey Monastirsky
VP Sales and Marketing: Greg Faull
Contact: Ronald Beckenfeld
ron@cvc4health.com
Estimated Sales: $12.3 Million
Number Employees: 60
Brands:
Cvc Specialsties
Superior Source

1968 **CVP Systems Inc**
2518 Wisconsin Ave
Downers Grove, IL 60515-4230
630-852-1190
Fax: 630-852-1386 800-422-4720
sales@cvpsystems.com www.cvpsystems.com
Owner/CEO: Wes Bork
COO: Chris Van Wandelen
Estimated Sales: $10-20 Million
Number Employees: 20-49
Brands:
C.V.P. Systems

1969 **Cable Car Beverage Corporation**
555 17th Street
Denver, CO 80202-3950
303-298-9038
Fax: 303-298-1150
Beverages
Chairman/President: Samuel Simpson
ssimpson@hollandhart.com
Number Employees: 20-49

1970 **Cabo Chips**
Cypress, CA 90630
www.cabochips.com
Tortillas and tortilla chips

1971 **Cabo Rojo Enterprises**
3301 Combate
Boqueron, PR 622
787-254-0015
Fax: 787-254-2048
Processor and importer of salt
President: Jeffrey Padilla Montero
Treasurer: Edwin Almodovar
Secretary: Lourdes Collado
Estimated Sales: $380,000
Number Employees: 5
Type of Packaging: Consumer

1972 **Cabot Creamery Co-Op**
193 Home Farm Way
Waitsfield, VT 05673-7512
802-496-1200
Fax: 802-371-1200 888-792-2268
info@cabotcheese.com www.cabotcheese.com
Cheese and other dairy products
President/CEO: Rich Stammer
Master Cheddar Maker: Marcel Gravel
CFO: Margaret Bertolino
Senior VP: David Hill
david.hill@cabotcheese.com
Director of Q/C: May Leach
Senior VP of Marketing: Roberta Macdonald
Sales & Marketing Manager: Sara Wing
Public Relations Manager: Bob Schiers
VP of Operations: Dick Gilangworthy
Plant Manager: Chris Pearl
Purchasing Manager: Kathleen McDonnell
Estimated Sales: $300 Million
Number Employees: 50-99
Square Footage: 450000
Parent Co: Agri-Mark
Type of Packaging: Consumer, Food Service, Private Label, Bulk
Brands:
Cabot
Cabot Cheeses

1973 **Cacao Prieto**
218 Conover Street
Brooklyn, NY 11231
347-225-0130
www.cacaoprieto.com

Fine chocolates
President/CEO: Dan Preston
VP & Art Director: Michele Clark
Sales Director: Mike Dirksen
Contact: Michele Clark
michele@cacaoholdings.com
Chief Operating Officer: Dennis Walsh
Number Employees: 20

1974 **Cachafaz US**
3325 NW 70th Ave
Miami, FL 33122
305-779-6340
cachafaz.us
Vegan and gluten-free chocolate, cookies, and spreads.
Manager: Juan Mandayo
Year Founded: 2001
Number Employees: 10-19

1975 **Cache Cellars**
RR 2 Box 2780
Davis, CA 95616-9604
530-756-6068
Fax: 530-756-6463
Wines
President: Charles Lowe
Estimated Sales: $1-2,500,000
Number Employees: 5-9
Type of Packaging: Private Label

1976 **Cache Creek Foods LLC**
411 N Pioneer Ave
Woodland, CA 95776-6122
530-662-1764
Fax: 530-662-2529 www.cachecreekfoods.com
Custom flavoring and wholesale manufacturing of almond, cashew, pistachio, nut products and nut butters
President: Nicholas Celek
ncelek@thelabb.com
CEO: Matthew Morehart
Sales and Marketing Executive: Mike Leonard
Office Manager: Connie Stephens
Production: Ana Contreras
Estimated Sales: $10 Million
Number Employees: 20-49
Number of Products: 75
Square Footage: 60000
Type of Packaging: Consumer, Food Service, Private Label, Bulk
Brands:
Private Label

1977 **(HQ)Cacique**
800 Royal Oaks Dr
Suite 200
Monrovia, CA 91017
626-961-3399
Fax: 626-369-8083 800-521-6987
www.caciqueinc.com
Processor and exporter of mozzarella and fresco cheeses, beef chorizo, pork choriso, soy choriso, mexican cremes, yogurts and beverages.
President: Gilbert Decardenas
Manager: Margarita Hodge
Estimated Sales: $50-100 Million
Number Employees: 325
Number of Brands: 5
Square Footage: 200000
Other Locations:
Cacique
Cedar City UT
Brands:
Black & Gold
Cacique
Nochebuena
Ranchero
Yonique

1978 **Cacoco**
hello@drinkcacoco.com
drinkcacoco.com
Drinking chocolate
Co-Founder & CEO: Tony Portugal
Co-Founder & COO: Liam Blackmon
Number of Brands: 1
Number of Products: 5
Type of Packaging: Consumer
Brands:
CACOCO

1979 **CactuLife, LLC**
PO Box 349
Corona Del Mar, CA 92625-0349
949-640-8991
Fax: 949-640-8992 800-500-1713
info@cactulife.com www.cactulife.com
Health food supplements
President: Jeff Leibfreid
Estimated Sales: $500,000
Number Employees: 1-4
Brands:
Cactu Life

1980 **Cadbury Adams**
5000 Yonge Street
Toronto, ON M2N 7E9
Canada
416-590-5000
Fax: 416-590-5600
consumer.relations@brandspeoplelove.com
www.kraftfoodsgroup.com
A variety of confectionery products.
President/ Canada: Dino Bianco
Chief Executive Officer: Todd Stitzer
Chief Financial Officer: Ken Hanna
Chief Legal Officer: Michael Clark
Chief Science & Technology Officer: David MacNair
President Americas Beverages: Gil Cassagne
President Europe/Middle East/Africa: Matt Shattock
Group Strategy Director: Mark Reckitt
Chief Legal Officer: Hank Udow
Chief Human Resources Officer: Bob Stack
Group Secretary: Hester Blanks
President Americas Confectionery: Jim Chambers
President Global Supply Chain: Steve Drive
Number Employees: 1,000-4,999
Parent Co: Cadbury Schweppes
Type of Packaging: Consumer, Food Service, Bulk
Brands:
Bubbilicious Bubble Gum
Certs Breath Mints
Certs Cool Mint Drops
Certs Powerful Mints
Chiclets Gum
Clorets Breath Freshener
Dentyne Fire Gum
Dentyne Ice
Dentyne Tango

1981 **Cadbury Beverages Canada**
30 Eglinton Avenue W
Mississauga, ON L5R 3E7
Canada
905-712-4121
Fax: 905-712-8635
consumer.relations@brandspeoplelove.com
www.mondelezinternational.com
Beverage brands include 7 UP, Canada Dry, Clamato, Dr. Pepper, Hawaiian Punch, Mott's, Schweppes and Snapple.
President/CEO: Irene Rosenfeld
Chief Financial Officer: Ken Hanna
Vice President/ CFO: David Brearton
Chief Science & Technology Officer: David MacNair
President Americas Beverages: Gil Cassagne
President Europe/Middle East/Africa: Matt Shattock
Group Strategy Director: Mark Reckitt
Chief Legal Officer: Hank Udow
Chief Human Resources Officer: Bob Stack
Group Secretary: Hester Blanks
President Americas Confectionery: Jim Chambers
President Global Supply Chain: Steve Drive
Number Employees: 1,000-4,999
Parent Co: Cadbury Schweppes
Type of Packaging: Consumer, Food Service, Bulk
Brands:
Cadbury Chocolate
Cadbury Dairy Milk
Cadbury Dark
Cadbury Favourites
Cadbury Thins
Caramilk

1982 **(HQ)Cadbury Trebor Allan**
850 Industrial Boulevard
Granby, QC J2J 1B8
Canada
450-372-1080
Fax: 450-378-4256 800-387-3267
consumer.relations@brandspeoplelove.com
www.cadburyschweppes.com
Candy including hard, filled hard, toffee, mints, licorice, gums, taffy kisses, penny goods, cough drops, jellies and lollypops, chocolates
Chairman And Ceo: Irene Rosenfeld
Number Employees: 3030
Parent Co: Cadbury Schweppes PLC
Type of Packaging: Consumer, Food Service, Private Label, Bulk
Brands:
Trebor

1983 **Caddo Packing Co**
609 S Washington Ave
Marshall, TX 75670-5327
903-935-2211
Processors and butchers of beef and pork.
President: Pat Parrish
Secretary/Treasurer: Judy Parrish
Estimated Sales: $1.5 Million
Number Employees: 10-19
Type of Packaging: Consumer

1984 **Cadillac Coffee Co**
7221 Innovation Blvd.
Ft. Wayne, IN 46818
248-545-2266
Fax: 248-584-4184 800-438-6900
info@cadillaccoffee.com www.cadillaccoffee.com
Coffee, specialty teas, iced teas, flavored syrups, blended drink mixes, iced cappuccino and more.
President: Guy Gehlert
Chairman: John Gehlert
VP Finance: Timothy Mantyla
Contact: Lisa Adkins
l.adkins@cadillaccoffee.com
VP Operations: Doug Bachman
Purchasing Director: John Hunter
Estimated Sales: Less Than $500,000
Number Employees: 5-9
Square Footage: 6580
Type of Packaging: Consumer, Food Service, Private Label, Bulk
Brands:
Cadillac Coffee

1985 **Cady Cheese Factory**
126 Hwy. 128
Wilson, WI 54027
715-772-4218
Fax: 715-772-4224 info@cadycheese.com
www.cadycheese.com
Producer of different varieties and flavors of longhorn cheese. Products are 100% natural and include Colby, Monterey Jack, Gold'n Jack and Veg'y Jack. Cady Cheese company also makes flavored cheeses such as Hot Pepper Jack, SalsaCheddar, Garlic Jack, Roasted Garlic Jack, Bacon and Onion Colby, Jack and Dill, and many more.
Plant Manager, Control: Sandy Lee
Estimated Sales: $5.8,000,000
Number Employees: 45
Type of Packaging: Private Label, Bulk
Brands:
Cady Creek Farms

1986 **Caesar's Pasta**
1001 Lower Landing Rd
Suite 302
Blackwood, NJ 08012
888-432-2372
www.caesarskitchen.com
Frozen pre-cooked and raw pasta specialties including ravioli, stuffed shells, manicotti with crepes, gnocchi, cavatelli, spaghetti, fettuccine, linguine, angel hair, agnolotti, ravioletti, tortelloni, cheese lasagna, etc
President/CEO: Michael Lodato
Secretary/Treasurer/VP of Sales: Raymond Lodato
VP: Ronald R. Lodato
Director of Sales: Michelle Hennessy
General Manager: Ronald P. Ladato
Purchasing Manager: Ronald Lodato
raylodato@caesarspasta.com
Estimated Sales: $1-2.5 Million
Number Employees: 20-49
Number of Products: 15
Square Footage: 60000
Type of Packaging: Consumer, Food Service, Private Label, Bulk
Brands:
Caesar's Kitchen

1987 **Cafe Altura**
760 East Santa Maria Street
Santa Paula, CA 93060
805-933-3027
Fax: 805-933-9367 800-526-8328
www.cafealtura.com
Processor, importer and exporter of organic coffee
President: Chris Shepard
Sales Manager: Elizabeth Blatz
Estimated Sales: $2.5-5 Million
Number Employees: 5-9
Square Footage: 4000
Parent Co: Clean Foods
Brands:
Cafe Altura

1988 **Cafe Bustelo**
5605 Nw 82nd Avenue
Miami, FL 33166
786-336-8048
Fax: 305-594-7603 800-990-9039
www.javacabana.com
Roasted coffee
President: Jose Souto
Marketing: Fernando Acosta
Estimated Sales: $2.5-5 000,000
Number Employees: 5-9

1989 **Cafe Cartago**
3835 Elm St Ste D
Denver, CO 80207
303-297-1212
Fax: 303-316-3325 800-443-8666
Coffee
Owner: Steve Larsen
Partner: Chuck Ask
Purchasing Manager: Steve Larsen
Estimated Sales: $2.5-5,000,000
Number Employees: 5-9
Type of Packaging: Private Label, Bulk

1990 **Cafe Chilku**
433 Bar Road, Unit 2
Colchester, VT 05446-7916
802-878-4645
Producer of BBQ sauces and dipping sauce
Owner: Chilku Yi

1991 **Cafe Del Mundo**
229 E 51st Ave
Anchorage, AK 99503
907-562-2326
Fax: 907-562-3278 800-770-2326
www.cafedelmundo.com
Coffee, espresso equipment
Owner: Perry Merkel
Manager: Monique Johnston
Purchasing: Perry Merkel
Estimated Sales: $800,000
Number Employees: 12
Type of Packaging: Private Label, Bulk
Brands:
Cafe Del Mundo

1992 **Cafe Descafeinado de Chiapas**
3625 NW 82nd Avenue
Suite 404
Doral, FL 33166-7602
305-499-9775
Fax: 305-499-9776
Coffee importers
President: Daniel Robles
Director: Arandio Muguira
Director: Luis Demetrio
Estimated Sales: $500,000-$1,000,000
Number Employees: 1-4
Type of Packaging: Private Label

1993 **Cafe Du Monde Coffee Stand**
1039 Decatur St
New Orleans, LA 70116-3309
504-581-2914
Fax: 504-587-0847 800-772-2927
office@cafedumonde.com www.cafedumonde.com
Processor and exporter of beignet doughnut mix, coffee and roasted chicory for coffee flavoring
CFO: J Roman
burt@cafedumonde.com
Manager: Burt Benrud
burt@cafedumonde.com
Manager: Robert Maher
Estimated Sales: $500,000 appx.
Number Employees: 10-19
Square Footage: 30000
Other Locations:
Cafe Du Monde-French Market
New Orleans LA
Cafe Du Monde-Riverwalk Marketplace
New Orleans LA
Care Du Monde-New Orleans Centre
New Orleans LA
Cafe Du Monde-Oakwood Mall
Gretna LA
Cafe Du Monde-Lakeside Mall
Metairie LA
Cafe Du Monde-Esplanade Mall
Kenner LA
Cafe Du Monde-Veterans Boulevard
Metairie LA
Brands:
Cafe Du Monde

1994 **Cafe Fanny**
1619 5th St
Berkeley, CA 94710-1714
510-526-7664
Fax: 510-526-7486 800-441-5413
shop@cafefanny.com www.cafefanny.com
Organic granola.
Owner: James Maser
Contact: Melody Elliott
melliott@cafefanny.com
Manager: Leslie Wilson
Estimated Sales: $1-2,500,000
Number Employees: 20-49

1995 **Cafe Grumpy**
199 Diamond St
Brooklyn, NY 11222
718-383-0748
info@cafegrumpy.com
cafegrumpy.com
Coffee roasters
Co-Owner: Chris Timbrell
Co-Owner: Caroline Bell
Head Roaster: Chris Cross
Buyer: Cheryl Kingan
Year Founded: 2005
Type of Packaging: Consumer, Private Label

1996 **Cafe Kreyol**
Manassas, VA 20109
www.coffeehunterproject.com
Organic specialty coffee

1997 **Cafe La Semeuse**
55 Nassau Ave
Brooklyn, NY 11222-3143
718-387-9696
Fax: 718-782-2471 800-242-6333
www.cafelasemeuse.com
Coffee
Manager: Andi Billow
Contact: Marc Greenberg
marc@cafelasemeuse.com
Estimated Sales: Under $500,000
Number Employees: 1-4
Brands:
Cafe La Semeuse
Classique
Espresso

1998 **Cafe Moak**
509 E Division Street
Rockford, MI 49341-1342
616-866-7625
Fax: 616-866-6422
Bread sticks, subs, pizzas and coffee; importer of coffee
Owner: Sal Russo
Administrative Assistant: Becky Fate
Brands:
Russo's

1999 **Cafe Moto**
2619 National Ave
San Diego, CA 92113-3617
619-239-6686
Fax: 619-239-9344 800-818-3363
www.cafemoto.com
Imported tea and roasted coffee
President: Torrey Lee
CFO: Kimberly Lee
Manager: Chris Peters
Production Manager: Michael Figgins
Estimated Sales: Under $500,000
Number Employees: 20-49
Type of Packaging: Private Label

2000 **Cafe Sark's Gourmet Coffee**
22800 Savi Ranch Parkway
Yorba Linda, CA 92887-4623
626-579-6000
Gourmet coffee
President: Jeff Shamburger
Estimated Sales: Under $500,000
Number Employees: 5-9

2001 **Cafe Society Coffee Company**
2910 N Hall St
Dallas, TX 75204
214-922-8888
Fax: 214-922-0280 800-717-6000
Flavored and organic coffee and tea
President: Lauri Sanderfer
Sales Representative: Byron Laszlo
General Manager: Jessie Nickerson
Estimated Sales: $1-$1.4,000,000
Number Employees: 11
Type of Packaging: Private Label

2002 **Cafe Spice**
677 Little Britain Rd
New Windsor, NY 12553
845-863-0910
info@cafespice.com
cafespice.com
Preprepared meals including Indian and Thai foods; soups; frozen appetizers; sauces; and rice.
Culinary Director: Hari Nayak
R&D Manager: Deepak Rajamani
Year Founded: 2000
Number Employees: 51-200
Type of Packaging: Food Service, Private Label

2003 **Cafe Tequila**
967 N Point Street
San Francisco, CA 94109-1111
415-264-0106
Fax: 415-674-1740 www.cafetequila.com
Tequila sauces
President/CEO: John Fielder
Sales/Marketing Executive: Julie Fielder
Number Employees: 1-4
Type of Packaging: Consumer, Food Service
Brands:
Cafe Tequila

2004 **Cafe Yaucono/Jimenez & Fernandez**
1103 Avenue Fernandez Juncos
Po Box 13097
San Juan, PR 00908-3097
787-721-3337
Fax: 787-722-5590 info@yaucono.com
www.yaucono.com
Coffee
President: Jose Jimenez
VP/Comp/Treasurer: Julio Torres
Marketing Manager: Joaquin Class
Number Employees: 20
Square Footage: 75000
Type of Packaging: Consumer
Brands:
Yaucono

2005 **Caffe Appassionato Coffee**
4001 21st Ave W
Seattle, WA 98199-1201
206-281-8040
Fax: 206-282-5218 888-502-2333
www.caffeappassionato.com
Coffee
President/CEO: Phil Sancken
CFO: Tim Schondelmayer
Sales Exec: Tucker McHugh
tucker@caffeappassionato.com
Roastmaster: Richard Oakes
Production Manager: David Crumb
Estimated Sales: $5-10,000,000
Number Employees: 50-99
Type of Packaging: Private Label
Brands:
Cafe Appassionato

2006 **Caffe D'Amore**
3400 Milington Road
Beloit, WI 53511
626-792-9146
Fax: 626-932-0152 800-999-0171
support@caffedamore.com www.caffedamore.com
Instant cappuccino

President: Chris Julius
Director Marketing: Cheri Hays
National Sales & Marketing Manager: Adelina Mirzakhanyan
Regional Sales Manager: Jill Zimmerman
Estimated Sales: $1-3,000,000
Number Employees: 20-49
Type of Packaging: Consumer, Food Service

2007 **Caffe D'Amore Gourmet Beverages**
5400 Butler St
Pittsburgh, PA 15201
626-792-9146
Fax: 626-792-4382 800-999-0171
www.caffedamorepgh.com
Specialty coffee beverages
President: Paul Comi
p.comi@caffedamore.com
Marketing Director: Adelina Mirzakhanyan
Regional Sales Manager: Jill Zimmerman
Estimated Sales: $30-50 Million
Number Employees: 50-99
Parent Co: Kerry

2008 **Caffe D'Oro**
14020 Central Avenue
Suite 580
Chino, CA 91710-5524
909-591-9493
Fax: 909-522-8844 800-200-5005
Specialty coffee and cappuccino
President: Pamela Abbadessa
V P Marketing: Frank Abbadessa
Number Employees: 5-9
Parent Co: Brad Barry Company
Type of Packaging: Private Label
Brands:
Caffe D'Oro Cappuccino & Cocoa

2009 **Caffe D'Vita**
14020 Central Avenue
Suite 580
Chino, CA 91710-5524
909-591-9493
Fax: 909-627-3747 800-200-5005
info@caffedvita.com www.caffedvita.com
Instant cappuccino, smoothies, frappes, iced coffees, cocoas and sugar-free products
President & CEO: Bob Greene
Vice President: Frank Abbadessa
Marketing Director: Frank Greene
Operations Manager: Frank Abbadessa
Estimated Sales: Under $500,000
Number Employees: 20-49
Parent Co: Brad Barry Company
Type of Packaging: Consumer, Food Service, Private Label, Bulk
Brands:
Caffe D'Vita
Baristatude

2010 **Caffe Darte**
33926 9th Ave S
Federal Way, WA 98003-6708
253-252-7050
Fax: 206-763-4665 800-999-5334
sales@caffedarte.com www.caffedarte.com
Processor of coffee beans.
General Manager: Joe Mancuso
jmancuso@caffedarte.com
National Sales Manager: Tim Fleming
Director of Operations: John Virden
Estimated Sales: $5-10,000,000
Number Employees: 20-49
Other Locations:
Boise Caff,
Boise ID
Bonney Lake Caff,
Tehaleh WA
Portland Caff,
Portland OR
Seattle Caff,-1st & Yesler
Seattle WA
Brands:
Campania(c)
Capri(c)
Fabriano(c)
Firenze(c)
Meaning of Life(c)
Parioli(c)
Taormina(c)
Velletri(c)
and more

2011 **Caffe Ibis Gallery Deli**
52 Federal Ave
Logan, UT 84321-4641
435-753-4777
Fax: 435-755-9139 888-740-4777
www.caffeibis.com
Artisan custom coffee roasting house. Focus is on Triple Certified, Organic, Fair Trade, and Smithsonian Shade Grown "Bird-Friendly" coffee from around the world.
Owner: Sally Sears
sally@caffeibis.com
Co-Owner & Roastmaster: Randy Wirth
Number Employees: 20-49
Type of Packaging: Consumer

2012 **Caffe Luca Coffee Roaste**
1025 Industry Drive
Seattle, WA 98188
206-466-5579
Fax: 206-575-0537 800-728-9116
info@caffeluca.com www.caffeluca.com
Processor, exporter and importer of espresso and blended coffee; also, custom roasting available
Owner: Carol Dema
caroldema@caffeluca.com
Estimated Sales: $380,000
Number Employees: 5
Square Footage: 4000
Type of Packaging: Consumer, Food Service
Brands:
Antonio
Casa Luca
Giovanni
Gregorio
Leonardo
Misto
Misto Dark

2013 **Caffe Trieste**
1465 25th St
San Francisco, CA 94107-3403
415-550-1107
Fax: 415-550-1239 CaffeTrieste56@aol.com
Coffee
President: Fabio Giotta
postmaster@caffetrieste.com
Secretary: Sonia Panaleo
Estimated Sales: $2,760,000
Number Employees: 5-9
Type of Packaging: Private Label
Brands:
Caffe Trieste Coffee Beans

2014 **Cahoon Farms**
10941 Lummisville Rd
Wolcott, NY 14590-9549
315-594-9610
Fax: 315-594-1678
customerservice@cahoonfarms.com
www.cahoonfarms.com
Frozen apples and cherries
Owner: Duane Cahoon
Controller: Jolene Green
Vice President: William B. Cahoon
Quality Control: Kristy Watson
Sales Manager: Chuck Frederick
customerservice@cahoonfarms.com
Operations Manager: Dave Green
Production Manager: Joe Cahoon
Plant Manager: Robert Cahoon
Estimated Sales: $940,000
Number Employees: 100-249
Type of Packaging: Consumer

2015 **Cain Vineyard & Winery**
3800 Langtry Rd
St Helena, CA 94574-9772
707-963-1616
Fax: 707-963-7952 winery@cainfive.com
www.cainfive.com
Producer of wines.
Owner: James Meadlock
Owner: Nancy Meadlock
Director of Sales & Marketing: Katie Lazar
Operations Manager: J.J. McCarthy
Production Manager: Francois Bugue
Estimated Sales: $5-10,000,000
Number Employees: 20-49
Number of Brands: 3
Brands:
Cain Concept
Cain Cuv,e
Cain Five

2016 **Caito Fisheries Inc**
19400 Harbor Ave
PO Box 1370
Fort Bragg, CA 95437-5615
707-964-6368
Fax: 707-964-6439 caitofsh@mcn.org
www.caitofisheries.com
Fresh and frozen fish such as albacore, sole, and flounder, dudungeousness crab, shark, octopus, acallops, prawns, rock shrimp, oysters, clams, swwordfish and salmon.
President: Joe Caito
caito@mcn.org
Estimated Sales: $20-50 Million
Number Employees: 100-249
Type of Packaging: Consumer, Food Service, Private Label, Bulk
Brands:
Caito

2017 **Cajohn's Fiery Foods Co**
816 Green Crest Dr
Westerville, OH 43081-2839
614-776-5356
Fax: 614-418-0800 888-703-3473
cajohns@cajohns.com www.cajohns.com
Salsas, hot sauce, barbecue sauce, rubs, spice blends, mixes and mustards.
President/Owner: John Hard
cajohn@cajohns.com
Secretary: Wanza Hard
Director of Operations: Jeremy Priwer
Estimated Sales: $125,000
Number Employees: 5-9
Brands:
Cajohns
Nate Dog's

2018 **Cajun Boy's Louisiana Products**
136 Austin Dr
Church Point, LA 70525
337-207-2391
Fax: 225-357-6888 800-880-9575
datcajunboysco@aol.com
datcajunboysco.com/products
Seasoned beans, blended seasonings and mixes.
Owner/President: Gerald Hicks
Number Employees: 1-4
Type of Packaging: Consumer
Brands:
Cajun Boy's Louisiana

2019 **Cajun Brands**
2511 Sugar Mill Rd
New Iberia, LA 70560
504-408-2252
info@cajunbrands.com
www.cajunbrands.com
Peppers including pickled, sport, tobasco, cherry, jalapeno, yellow chile, banana and serrano; also, prepared mustard, pure and imitation pepper and flavoring extracts, pickled okra and tomatoes and sauces including hotworcestershire, etc.
Estimated Sales: $9.2 Million
Number Employees: 90
Type of Packaging: Consumer, Food Service, Private Label, Bulk
Brands:
Big Chief
Cajun Chef
Evangeline
Andy Roo's
Bird Brine
Bon Ca Ca
Bruce Foods
Cajun Blast
Cajun Flip N Fry
Cajun Land
Louisiana Mixes
Mello Joy
Mossy Bayou
Panola Pepper Corp
Papa Scotts
Pepperdoux
Poche's
Savoie's
Slap Ya Mama
Southern
Steens

2020 **Cajun Crawfish Distributors**
379 Industrial Blvd
PO Box 393
Branch, LA 70516
Fax: 337-334-8477 888-254-8626
boudreaux@cajuncrawfish.com
www.cajuncrawfish.com
Live crawfish, cooked crawfish, gumbos, Cajun meats, turducken
Co-Owner: Mark Fruge
Co-Owner: Michael Fruge
Administration: Pam Estes
Marketing Director: Courtney Fruge
Sales Manager: Richard Hotard
Public Relations: Carol Schultz
Operations Manager: Ed Guidry
Year Founded: 1972
Estimated Sales: $30 Million
Number Employees: 4

2021 **Cajun Creole Products Inc**
5610 Daspit Rd
New Iberia, LA 70563-8961
337-229-8464
Fax: 337-229-4814 800-946-8688
info@cajuncreole.com www.cajuncreole.com
Coffee, peanuts and seasoning
President/Manager: Joel Wallins
Secretary/Treasurer: Sandra Wallins
Estimated Sales: $300,000
Number Employees: 5-9
Type of Packaging: Consumer, Food Service, Bulk
Brands:
Cajun Creole
Cajun Creole Coffee
Cajun Creole Hot Nuts
Cajun Creole Jalapeanuts
Jalapeanuts

2022 **Cajun Fry Co Inc**
107 Mike St
Pierre Part, LA 70339-4415
985-252-6438
Fax: 985-252-8010 888-272-2586
cajunfrycompany@aol.com www.cajunfry.com
Cajun rice mixes, jambalaya, spices
President: Clarence Cavalier Jr
Vice President: Marilyn Cavalier
Estimated Sales: $1-2,500,000
Number Employees: 1-4
Brands:
Cajun Creole Coffee & Chicory
Jalapeanuts
Smokeless Blackened Seasoning

2023 **Cajun Original Foods Inc**
704 Avenue D
New Iberia, LA 70560-0527
337-367-1344
Fax: 337-364-4968 www.cajunoriginal.com
Processor and exporter of liquid injectable marinades for poultry and red meats, and dry seasonings
President/CEO: Dennis Higginbotham
cajunoriginal@bellsouth.net
Estimated Sales: $1-2.5 Million
Number Employees: 10-19
Square Footage: 54400
Type of Packaging: Consumer, Bulk
Brands:
Cajun Aujus
Cajun Injector
Cajun Poultry Marinade
Cajunshake

2024 **Cajun Seafood Enterprises**
9650 Highway 52 E
Murrayville, GA 30564-6901
706-864-9688
Fax: 706-864-9688
Seafood

2025 **Cakebread Cellars**
8300 Saint Helena Hwy
PO Box 216
Rutherford, CA 94573
707-963-5221
Fax: 707-967-8620 800-588-0298
cellars@cakebread.com www.cakebread.com
Manufacturer of fine wines.
Founder/Chairman/CEO: Jack Cakebread
President/COO: Bruce Cakebread
SVP, Sales & Marketing: Dennis Cakebread
Contact: Samantha Arnold
arnold@cakebread.com
Director, Vineyard Operations: Toby Halkovich
Estimated Sales: $20-50 Million
Number Employees: 50-99
Number of Brands: 1
Brands:
Cakebread

2026 **Cal Harvest Marketing Inc**
8700 Fargo Ave
Hanford, CA 93230-9771
559-582-4494
Fax: 559-582-0683 www.calharvest.com
Fresh fruits and vegetables
President: John Fagundes IV
johnf2006@hughes.net
Purchasing: John Fagundes
Estimated Sales: $2 Million
Number Employees: 5-9
Type of Packaging: Consumer, Private Label, Bulk
Brands:
Cal-King
Fresh Harvest
Golden Harvest

2027 **Cal India Foods Inc**
13591 Yorba Ave
Chino, CA 91710-5071
909-613-1660
Fax: 909-613-1663
www.systemicenzymetherapy.com
Fruit juices, purees and concentrates
President: Vic Rathi
info@4enzymes.com
Quality Control: Vilas Amin
Purchasing Agent: Priscilla Ferreri
Estimated Sales: $5-7 Million
Number Employees: 20-49
Square Footage: 24000
Parent Co: Specialty Enzymes and Biochemicals Company
Type of Packaging: Bulk
Brands:
Cal India

2028 **Cal Ranch**
2628 Concord Blvd
Concord, CA 94519
925-429-2900
Fax: 925-476-2017 info@calranchfood.com
calranchfood.com
Dried fruits and nuts
President/Owner: Juliana Colline
Type of Packaging: Consumer, Food Service

2029 **Cal-Grown Nut Company**
8616 E. Whitmore
Hughson, CA 95326-0069
209-883-4081
Fax: 209-883-0305 www.californiagrown.com
Processor and exporter of almonds
President: Frank Assali
frankassali@californiagrown.com
Vice President: Marie Assali
Office Manager: Linda Thomas
Estimated Sales: $.5-1 million
Number Employees: 5-9

2030 **Cal-Java International Inc**
19519 Business Center Dr
Northridge, CA 91324
818-718-2707
Fax: 818-718-2715 800-207-2750
sales@caljavaonline.com caljavaonline.com
Cake decorating supplies
Owner: Daniel Budiman
caljava@aol.com
Vice President: Laurie Budiman
Estimated Sales: $9 Million
Number Employees: 10-19

2031 **Cal-Maine Foods Inc.**
3320 Woodrow Wilson Dr.
Jackson, MS 39209
601-948-6813
Fax: 601-969-0905 ir@cmfoods.com
www.calmainefoods.com
Shell eggs.
CEO/Chairman: Adolphus Baker
abaker@cmfoods.com
Chairman Emeritus: Fred Adams
VP/CFO/Treasurer/Secretary/Director: Max Bowman
Vice President/General Counsel: Rob Holladay
VP Sales: Jeff Hardin
VP, Controller: Mike Castleberry
President/COO/Director: Sherman Miller
Year Founded: 1969
Estimated Sales: $1.037 Billion
Number Employees: 1000-4999
Number of Brands: 3
Type of Packaging: Food Service, Private Label, Bulk
Brands:
Egg-Land's Best™
Farmhouse™
4-Grain™

2032 **Cal-Tex Citrus Juice LP**
402 Yale St
Houston, TX 77007-2530
713-869-3471
Fax: 713-869-3277 800-231-0133
gary.van.liew@cal-texjuice.com
www.cal-texjuice.com
Fresh and frozen concentrate citrus juices
CEO: Ronald Peterson
Quality Control: Alvaro Falquez
National Sales Manager: Vicki White
Operations: Danny Teague
Purchasing: Kory Mason
Estimated Sales: $40 Million
Number Employees: 100-249
Number of Brands: 3
Number of Products: 63
Parent Co: Country Pure Foods
Type of Packaging: Consumer, Food Service, Private Label
Brands:
Cal-Tex
Citrus Pride
Vita-Fresh
Vita-Most

2033 **Calabro Cheese Corp**
580 Coe Ave
East Haven, CT 06512
203-469-1311
Fax: 203-469-6929 www.calabrocheese.com
Ricotta, mozzarella and grated cheese
President & CEO: Frank Angeloni
CFO: Sara Estrom
Vice President: Salvatore Calabro
Estimated Sales: $170,000
Number Employees: 50-99
Type of Packaging: Consumer, Food Service, Private Label, Bulk
Brands:
Calabro

2034 **Calafia Cellars**
629 Fulton Ln
St Helena, CA 94574-1014
707-963-0114
Fax: 707-963-0114 randle@calafiacellars.com
www.calafiacellars.com
Wines
Owner: Randall Johnson
marylee53@comcast.net
VP Marketing: Mary Lee Johnson
Estimated Sales: Less Than $500,000
Number Employees: 1-4
Brands:
Calafia Wines

2035 **Calamondin Cafe**
4600 Summerlin Rd C-2
Fort Myers, FL 33907
239-288-5535
Fax: 239-288-5534 info@calamondincafe.com
www.calamondincafe.com
Cakes, jams, teacakes and coulis.
Founder & CEO: Laurie Gutstein

2036 **Calapooia Brewing Co**
140 NE Hill St
Albany, OR 97321-3002
541-928-1931
Fax: 541-928-4131 web@calapooiabrewing.com
www.calapooiabrewing.com
Beer

Owner: Mark Martin
Treasurer: Nancy Coleman
Estimated Sales: Below $5 Million
Number Employees: 10-19
Brands:
Oregon Brewers

2037 Calavo Growers
1141A Cummings Rd
Santa Paula, CA 93060
805-525-1245
Fax: 805-921-3232 www.calavo.com
Growers and processors of pineapples, papayas, and avocados; Manufacturer of; salsa and corn chips
Chairman/President/CEO: Lecil Cole
lecilc@calavo.com
CEO: Robin Osterhues
COO/CFO/Corporate Secretary: Arthur Bruno
VP/Fresh Sales & Marketing: Rob Wedin
Quality Assurance Manager: Diane Valine
Vice President, Sales & Marketing: Alan Ahmer
Fresh Operations: Mike Browne
Plant Manager: Brett Viera
Purchasing Agent: Bruce Spurrell
Estimated Sales: $551 Million
Number Employees: 1000-4999
Type of Packaging: Consumer, Food Service, Bulk
Other Locations:
Temecula Packinghouse
Temecula CA
Santa Paula Packinghouse
Santa Paula CA
Calavo Processing Plant
Santa Paula CA
Brands:
Calavo

2038 Calbee America Inc
2600 Maxwell Way
Fairfield, CA 94534-1915
707-427-2500
Fax: 707-428-2900
Processor and exporter of potato chips
President/Ceo: Masanori Yasunaga
Vice President: Doug Warner
Manager Sales and Marketing: Takashi Katsunoi
VP Human Resources: Yoshi Ishiquro
IT Executive: Masa Suito
msaito@calbeeamerica.com
Estimated Sales: $15 Million
Number Employees: 100-249

2039 Calcium Springs Water Company
2442 Lily Langtree Ct
Park City, UT 84060
435-615-7600
Fax: 435-615-7600
Water
Owner: Lavelle Klobes

2040 Calco of Calgary
Bay C 1007 55th Avenue NE
Calgary, AB T2E 6W1
Canada
403-295-3578
Fax: 403-516-0286 www.calcoofcalgary.com
Processor and packer of bean sprouts, pre-cut vegetables, frozen Chinese dumplings, spring and egg rolls and steamed noodles
President: Wing Tam
General Manager: May Yu
Production: Grace Tam
Number Employees: 10-19
Parent Co: Fung Nin Fine Foods
Type of Packaging: Consumer, Food Service
Brands:
Calgo
Mr. Egg Roll
Noodle Delights

2041 Caldic USA Inc
2425 Alft Ln
Elgin, IL 60124-7864
847-468-0001
customerservice@caldic.us
Sourcing, R&D, processing, warehousing and distribution of ingredients.
Owner: Bob Leonard
bleonard@nealanders.com
Number Employees: 10-19
Parent Co: Caldic

2042 Caleb Haley & Co LLC
800 Food Center Dr # 110
Suite 110
Bronx, NY 10474-1259
718-617-7474
Fax: 718-617-7477 www.calebhaley.com
Wholesale provider in both fresh and frozen seafood.
President: Neil Smith
neil@calebhaley.com
Vice President: Michael Driansky
Office Manager: Robby De Vincenzi
Year Founded: 1859
Estimated Sales: $20-50 Million
Number Employees: 20-49
Brands:
Angel
Callaway
Ocean Harvest

2043 Calendar Islands Maine Lobster LLC
6a Portland Fish Pier
Portland, ME 04101
207-541-9140
Fax: 207-518-9049
Hors d'oeuvres/appetizers, ready meals/pizza/soup, full-line soups, stews, beans, shellfish.
Marketing: Emily Lane

2044 Calera Wine Co
11300 Cienega Rd
Hollister, CA 95023-9619
831-637-9170
Fax: 831-637-9070 info@calerawine.com
Wines
President: Josh Jensen
info@calerawine.com
COO: Diana Vita
Number Employees: 10-19
Brands:
Calera
Central Coast
Doe Mill
Mills
Mt. Harlan
Reed
Selleck
Viognier

2045 Calgary Italian Bakery
5310 5th Street SE
Calgary, AB T2H 1L2
Canada
403-255-3515
Fax: 403-255-7016 800-661-6868
contact@cibl.com www.cibl.com
Baked goods including bread, buns, pastries and English muffins
CEO: Luigi Bontorin
Marketing Manager: Ralph Knipsthilb
Office Manager: Louis Bontorin
Plant Manager: Dave Bontorin
Estimated Sales: D
Number Employees: 50-99
Square Footage: 60000
Type of Packaging: Consumer, Food Service
Brands:
Calgary Italian
Country Boy
Golden Rich

2046 Calhoun Bend Mill
PO BOX 520
Libuse, LA 71348
318-640-0060
Fax: 318-339-9099 800-519-6455
sales@calhounbendmill.com
www.calhounbendmill.com
Fruit cobbler mixes, cornmeal and seafood coating.
President/CEO: Patrick Calhoun
Treasurer: Monica Calhoun
Vice President: Nathan Martin
Sales Manager: Emma Cash
Corporate Secretary: Martie Hoover
Estimated Sales: $400,000
Number Employees: 5
Number of Brands: 2
Number of Products: 25
Square Footage: 34000
Type of Packaging: Consumer, Food Service, Private Label, Bulk
Brands:
Calhoun Bend Mill
Orchard Mills

2047 Cali'flour Foods
1057 Village Lane
Chico, CA 95926
866-422-3568
www.califlourfoods.com
Cauliflower pizza crusts
Founder/Owner: Amy Lacey

2048 Calico Cottage
210 New Hwy
Amityville, NY 11701-1116
631-841-2100
Fax: 631-841-2401 800-645-5345
www.calicocottage.com
Fudge mixes, flavors and colorings.
President & CEO: Mark Wurzel
m.wurzel@calicocottage.com
Chief Financial Officer: Michael Lobaccaro
Vice President: Larry Wurzel
Executive VP, Sales & Marketing: David Sank
Director, Human Resources & Admin: Barbara Stone-Carroll
Sr. VP, Operations & Technology: Thomas Montoya
Estimated Sales: $5 Million
Number Employees: 50-99
Square Footage: 45000
Type of Packaging: Consumer
Brands:
Calico Cottage Fudge Mix
Mister Fudge

2049 Calidad Foods
1313 Avenue R
Grand Prairie, TX 75053-5008
214-521-7999
Tortillas and other mexican food products.
CEO/President: Bing Graffunder
CFO: Sam Hillin
V.P Sales/Marketing: Gary Fraizer
Estimated Sales: $25,000,000
Number Employees: 250

2050 Calif Snack Foods
2131 Tyler Ave
South El Monte, CA 91733-2754
626-454-4099
Fax: 626-579-3038
info@californiasnackfoods.com
www.caltreats.com
Manufacturer of snack food such as popcorn, candy coated apples, cotton candy and freezies.
President: Steve Nelson
Secretary: Mary Nelson
Vice President: Paul Mullen
Manager: Alva Dallas
Production Manager: John Ohms
Estimated Sales: $5.3,000,000
Number Employees: 20-49
Brands:
Karm'l Dapples
Ice Tickles

2051 Calif Watercress Inc
550 E Telegraph Rd
Fillmore, CA 93015-9667
805-524-4808
Fax: 805-524-5295
Herbal supplements and herbs including cilantro and chives; also, vegetables including mixed, watercress and leeks
President/Treasurer: Alfred Beserra
Accounting: Catherine King
cah2ocress@aol.com
Human Resource Director: Susan Barbera
Secretary: Teresa Beserra
Estimated Sales: $5 Million
Number Employees: 50-99
Type of Packaging: Consumer, Food Service, Bulk
Brands:
Al's Best

2052 Califia Farms
1095 E Green St
Pasadena, CA 91106
844-237-4779
califiafarms.com
Plant and fruit based creamers and espresso blends.
Founder: Greg Steltenpohl
Year Founded: 2010
Type of Packaging: Private Label

2053 **California Almond Packers**
1150 Ninth Street
Suite 1500
Modesto, CA 95354
209-549-8262
Fax: 209-549-8267
Almonds
Manager: Mathieu Esteve
Finance Executive: Chuck Niehues
Human Resources Executive: Mabel Kindel
Estimated Sales: Less than $500,000
Number Employees: 50-99
Brands:
California Almond

2054 **California Balsamic Inc**
966 Mazzoni St
Ukiah, CA 95482-3475
707-463-2646
Fax: 707-463-2299 888-644-5127
www.californiabalsamic.com
Gourmet cooking, sauces, dipping oils, dessert sauces and herbed wine vinegars
Owner: Thomas Allen
balsamics@tresclassique.com
Estimated Sales: Under 500,000
Number Employees: 1-4
Number of Products: 38
Type of Packaging: Food Service, Private Label, Bulk
Brands:
Lemon Splash
Splash

2055 **California Blending Co**
2603 Seaman Ave
El Monte, CA 91733-1929
626-448-1918
Fax: 626-448-1998
Pizza spices, dough mixes, dressing mixes, steak salts, and garlic blends. Also provided; custom blending
President: Bill Morehart
calblending@aol.com
Vice President: Roger Morehart
Estimated Sales: Less Than $500,000
Number Employees: 1-4
Square Footage: 14600
Type of Packaging: Private Label, Bulk

2056 **California Cereal Products**
1267 14th St
Oakland, CA 94607-2246
510-452-4500
Fax: 510-452-4545 californiacereal.com
Gluten-free cereal ingredients, including rice, cereal and flour products.
President: Mark Graham
Co-Founder/Chairman/CEO: Robert Sterling Savely
Accounting: Richard O'Connor
Estimated Sales: $13.9 Million
Number Employees: 75
Square Footage: 600000
Type of Packaging: Consumer, Private Label, Bulk
Other Locations:
Manufacturing Facility
Macon GA

2057 **California Citrus Producers**
525 E Lindmore St
Lindsay, CA 93247-2559
559-562-5169
Fax: 559-562-5691
Producer of orange juice concentrates.
President: Tommy Elliott
CEO: John Barkley
Estimated Sales: $9,000,000
Number Employees: 20-49
Square Footage: 40000

2058 **California Coast Naturals**
12477 Calle Real
Santa Barbara, CA 93117
805-685-2076
cacoastnaturals.com
Olives and olive oil
CEO: Craig Makela
Number of Brands: 1
Number of Products: 15
Type of Packaging: Consumer
Brands:
CALIFORNIA COAST NATURALS

2059 **California Custom Foods**
2325 Moore Ave
Fullerton, CA 92833-2510
714-870-0490
Fax: 714-870-5609 gilbertj@vanlaw.com
www.vanlaw.com
Processor and exporter of refrigerated and shelf stable salad dressings, pancake yrup, syrup concentrates, flavorings, extracts, colorings, ice cream toppings and barbecue and teriyaki sauces; importer of romano and parmesan cheeseolive oil and balsamic vinegar
Owner: Matthew Jones
jonesm@vanlaw.com
Director of Quality Assurance: Anna Tran
VP Sales/Marketing: John Gilbert
jonesm@vanlaw.com
Estimated Sales: $.5-1 million
Number Employees: 100-249
Square Footage: 520000
Type of Packaging: Consumer, Food Service, Private Label
Brands:
California Classics
Sunfruit
Zito

2060 **California Custom Fruits**
15800 Tapia St
Baldwin Park, CA 91706-2178
626-736-4130
Fax: 626-736-4145 877-558-0056
info@ccff.com www.ccff.com
Fruit products and flavors
Owner: Monica Ahuero
President: Mike Mulhausen
CFO: Jim Fragnoli
Marketing Manager: Christine Long
Director Operations: Jack Miller
Production Manager: Eric Nielsen
Director of Flavor Development: Phillip Barone
Purchasing Director: Phyllis Ferguson
Estimated Sales: $20-35 Million
Number Employees: 100-249
Square Footage: 33000
Type of Packaging: Bulk
Brands:
B2b
Ccff
Private Label

2061 **California Dairies Inc.**
2000 N. Plaza Dr.
Visalia, CA 93291
559-625-2200
Fax: 559-625-5433 info@californiadairies.com
www.californiadairies.com
Dairy products.
Chairman: Simon Vander Woude
President/CEO: Brad Anderson
Year Founded: 1999
Estimated Sales: Over $1 Billion
Number Employees: 500-999
Type of Packaging: Consumer, Food Service, Bulk
Other Locations:
Artesia CA
Fresno CA
Los Banos CA
Tipton CA
Turlock CA
Brands:
Challenge Dairy Products
DairyAmerica

2062 **California Fruit**
8385 Miramar Mall Road
San Diego, CA 92121
559-266-7117
Fax: 559-266-0988 877-378-4811
admin@californiafruit.com
www.californiafruit.com
Dried apricots, prunes, pears and nectarines
President: Mark Melkonian
Contact: Marshal Dohoney
m.dohoney@caconstructionconcepts.com
Estimated Sales: $2.5-5 Million
Number Employees: 10-19
Type of Packaging: Bulk

2063 **California Fruit & Nut**
295 South Avenue
Gustine, CA 95322-1235
209-854-1819
Fax: 209-854-1819 888-747-8224
Flavored nuts including pistachios, peanuts and cashews; also, dried fruit and fruit rolls including apricot
President: Zaher Shahbaz
z.shahbaz@fruitnnut.com
Estimated Sales: Less than $500,000
Number Employees: 5-9
Square Footage: 10800
Type of Packaging: Consumer, Food Service
Brands:
Cal-Fruit

2064 **California Fruit Processors**
2851 Bozzano Rd
Stockton, CA 95215-9152
209-931-1760
Fax: 209-931-0784 www.cafruitprocessors.com
Brined cherries
President: Alan Corradi
acorradi@cafruitprocessors.com
Office Manager: Cindy Haddad
Estimated Sales: $1,500,000
Number Employees: 50-99

2065 **California Fruit and Tomato Kitchens**
3800 Leckron Road
Modesto, CA 95357
209-574-9407
Fax: 209-529-1340
Canned goods including tomato products and peaches
President: Barbara Langum
Marketing: Nick Kastle
Product Sales: Greg Wuttke
Product Sales: Kelly Hayward
Plant Manager: Ed Harmon
Estimated Sales: $10-20 Million
Number Employees: 20-49
Type of Packaging: Food Service, Private Label
Brands:
Dinapoli
Flotta
Paradise

2066 **California Garden Products**
31642 Avenida Los Cerritos
San Juan Capistrano, CA 92675
949-215-0000
Fax: 949-215-0965 felabd@californiagarden.com
www.californiagarden.com
Canned beans
President: Fouad El-Abd
Estimated Sales: $5-9.9,000,000
Number Employees: 11-50

2067 **California Garlic Co**
2707 Boston Avenue
San Diego, CA 92113
951-506-8883
Fax: 951-699-9155 info@garlicking.net
www.garlicking.net
Garlic, ginger, shallots, green onion, herbs and other
President: John Rosingana
Vice President: Peter Tarantino
Quality Control/Production: Larry George
Marketing: Jeff Crace
Estimated Sales: $1 Million
Number Employees: 35
Number of Brands: 4
Number of Products: 60
Square Footage: 24000
Type of Packaging: Consumer, Food Service, Private Label, Bulk

2068 **California Independent Almond Growers**
13000 Newport Road
Merced, CA 95303-9704
209-667-4855
Fax: 209-667-4854
Growers, packers, processors and shippers worldwide. California grown whole natural almonds direct from the source. State-of-the-art equipment
President: Karen Barstow
Estimated Sales: $2.5-5 Million
Number Employees: 50-99
Square Footage: 60000
Type of Packaging: Consumer, Food Service, Private Label, Bulk
Brands:
California Independent Brand

2069 **California Juice Co.**
Santa Barbara, CA 93101
805-738-8723
info@caljuiceco.com
caljuiceco.com
Organic cold-pressed juice shots

2070 **California Lavash**
101 Leavesley Rd
Gilroy, CA 95020-3604
408-846-7705
info@californialavash.com
www.californialavash.com
Manufacturer of flatbreads.
Marketing Associate: Julia Voyvodich
Sales Director: Lilea Eshoo
leshoo@californialavash.com

2071 **California Natural Products**
1250 Lathrop Rd
Lathrop, CA 95330-9709
209-858-2525
Fax: 209-858-4076 marci.howe@cnp.com
www.cnp.com
Organic food ingredients, rice and soy beverages, nutritional drinks, soups, broths, teas and wine.
President: Robert Hatch
CEO/Owner: Pat Mitchell
patm@californianatural.com
Vice President of Finance: Gene Guelfo
Vice President: Kevin Haslebacher
Vice President of R&D: Khalid Shammet
Quality Regulatory: Connie Gutierrez
Technical Sales Manager: John Ashby
Director of Human Resources: Skip Lindstrom
Operations Manager: Emil Skaria
Purchasing Manager: Chirs Mifsud
Estimated Sales: $42 Million
Number Employees: 250-499
Type of Packaging: Private Label
Brands:
Dacopa

2072 **California Nuggets Inc**
23073 S Frederick Rd
Ripon, CA 95366-9616
209-599-7131
Fax: 209-599-1531 www.californianuggets.com
Roasted nuts and peanut butter manufacturer
Owner: Steve Gikas
steve@californianuggets.com
Secretary/Treasurer: Barbara Bain
Marketing Director: Terry Wells-Brown
Sales Executive: Brenda Orlando
Estimated Sales: $2.6 Million
Number Employees: 50-99
Brands:
California Nuggets

2073 **California Oils Corp**
1145 Harbour Way S
Richmond, CA 94804-3618
510-233-7660
Fax: 510-233-1329 800-225-6457
www.caloils.com
Vegetable oils and meal; exporter of corn and safflower oils
CEO: Sihira Ito
Controller: Masako Hirose
Vice President/Sales Executive: Joevic Fabregas
Sales and Marketing Manager: Karol Sop
Number Employees: 20-49
Parent Co: Mitsubishi

2074 **California Olive Growers**
8427 N Millbrook Avenue
Suite 101
Fresno, CA 93720-2197
559-674-8741
Fax: 559-673-3960 888-965-4837
www.californiaolivegrowers.com
Packer of canned California ripe olives, olive oil, tomatoes and pizza sauce
President: Lewis Johnson
CEO: Tom Lindemann
CEO: Fred Avalli
Quality Control: Larry Newby
Production Manager: Bob Marshall
Estimated Sales: $10 Million
Number Employees: 100-249
Number of Brands: 2
Number of Products: 10
Square Footage: 600000
Type of Packaging: Consumer, Food Service, Private Label, Bulk
Brands:
Madera
Oberti

2075 **California Olive Oil Council**
801 Camelia St # D
Suite D
Berkeley, CA 94710-1459
510-524-4523
Fax: 510-898-1530 888-718-9830
oliveoil@cooc.com www.cooc.com
Processor and exporter of oils including garlic, sesame, peanut, olive, canola, mineral, soybean, citrus, infused, organic, cold pressed and unrefined; also, balsamic vinegar and cooking wines; importer of kosher certified soy sauce
Owner: Claudia Siniawski
Vice President: Robert Mandia
CFO: Dave Lofgren
VP Sales/Marketing: Mark Moffitt
Contact: Alison Altomari
alison@cooc.com
Executive Director: Patricia Darragh
Estimated Sales: $420,980
Number Employees: 5-9
Square Footage: 76000
Parent Co: East Coast Olive Corporation
Type of Packaging: Consumer, Food Service, Private Label, Bulk
Brands:
California Classics
Montebello
Oishii
Virginia

2076 **California Olive Ranch**
1367 E Lassen Ave
Suite A1
Chico, CA 95973-7881
530-592-3700
Fax: 530-592-3275 cor@cal-olive.com
Olive oil
CEO: Gregory Kelly
Estimated Sales: 5,300,000
Number Employees: 10-19

2077 **California Packing Company**
1309 Melody Rd
Olivehurst, CA 95961
530-740-1040
Fax: 530-740-1044 info@calprune.com
www.calprune.com
Prunes in consumer and bulk packs.
Number Employees: 10
Type of Packaging: Private Label

2078 **California Shellfish Company**
505 Beach St
Suite 200
San Francisco, CA 94133-1131
415-923-7400
Fax: 415-923-1677
Crab, smoked salmon, halibut and snapper
President: Eugene Bugatto
CFO/Secretary/Treasurer: David Zellar
Manager: Richard Amundsen
Estimated Sales: $75.4 Million
Number Employees: 723
Type of Packaging: Consumer, Food Service, Private Label, Bulk

2079 **California Smart Foods**
2565 3rd St # 341
Suite 342
San Francisco, CA 94107-3159
415-826-0449
Fax: 415-826-0435 calsmartfds@att.net
Baked goods including breads, rolls, cakes, cookies, muffins, scones, danishes, tarts and pastries.
Owner: Helaine Melnitzer
calsmartfds@att.net
Estimated Sales: $20-50 Million
Number Employees: 20-49

2080 **California Walnut Co**
24490 Joseph Ave
Los Molinos, CA 96055-9663
530-527-2616
Fax: 530-527-7991
www.californiawalnutcompany.com
Walnuts
President: Brendon Flynn
brendon@californiawalnutcompany.com
Vice President: Ginger Gilchrist
Estimated Sales: $5 Million
Number Employees: 20-49

2081 **California Wholesale Nut**
1925 Manzanita Ave
Chico, CA 95926
530-895-0512
Fax: 530-345-1263
Nuts
Owner: Naomi Mc Dermott
Estimated Sales: $100,000
Number Employees: 1

2082 **California Wild Rice Growers**
41577 Osprey Rd
Fall River Mills, CA 96028-9750
530-336-5222
Fax: 530-336-5265 800-626-4366
www.frwr.com
Wild Rice
General Manager: Walt Oiler
Manager: Hiram Oilar
PLant Manager: Tony Knight
Estimated Sales: $420,000
Number Employees: 4
Brands:
Fall River

2083 **California-Antilles Trading**
3735 Adams Ave
San Diego, CA 92116-2220
619-283-4834
Fax: 619-283-4834 800-330-6450
www.calantilles.com
Hot sauces, salsas, barbecue sauces
President: Richard E Gardner
irina.profosovitskaya@kp.org
Operations: Tevor Dyer
Production: Robert Davis
Estimated Sales: $2.5-5,000,000
Number Employees: 1-4
Number of Brands: 2
Number of Products: 25
Type of Packaging: Consumer, Private Label

2084 **Calihan Pork ProcessorsInc**
1 South St
Peoria, IL 61602
309-674-9175
Fax: 309-674-3003 www.calihanpork.com
Pork products including pre-rigor, boneless hams, Canadian bacon, spareribs, boneless pork tenderloins, pork riblets, pork hearts and pork tongue
President: Tom Landon
CFO: Al Schmid
General Manager: Jason Jones
Plant Manager: Ben Elbert
Year Founded: 1937
Estimated Sales: $20 Million
Number Employees: 50-99
Type of Packaging: Bulk

2085 **Calio Groves**
58 Calvert Court
Piedmont, CA 94611
707-402-4700
Fax: 707-402-4747 800-865-4836
Olive oil and extra virgin olive oil; importer of olive oil
President: Brendan Frasier
VP Production & Farming: Bob Singletary
Estimated Sales: $20-50 Million
Number Employees: 20-49
Parent Co: NVK Realty
Type of Packaging: Consumer, Food Service, Private Label, Bulk
Brands:
Calio Groves
Evo
Olio Santo
Stutz Olive Oil
Vg Buck California Foods

2086 **Calise & Sons Bakery Inc**
2 Quality Dr
Lincoln, RI 02865-4266
401-334-3444
Fax: 401-334-0938 800-225-4737
Info@calisebakery.com www.calisebakery.com
Fresh Italian bread, rolls and pizza shells.

President: Michael Calise
Treasurer: Joseph Calise
CEO: Peter Petrocelli
VP Sales: Michael J. Pritchard
Production Manager: James Fontaine
Purchasing Manager: Anthony Capuzli
Estimated Sales: $34.8 Million
Number Employees: 100-249
Number of Products: 150
Square Footage: 210000
Type of Packaging: Consumer, Food Service, Private Label
Brands:
Calise
Sun Ray

2087 **Calistoga Food Company**
171 E 74th Street
New York, NY 10021-3221
212-879-4940
Fax: 212-879-5005
President: Martin Kreinik
Estimated Sales: $2.5-5,000,000
Number Employees: 5-9
Brands:
Calistoga Food

2088 **Calivirgin Olive Oils**
13950 N Thornton Rd
Lodi, CA 95242
209-210-3142
calivirgin.com
Olive oil
Accounting: Julie Coldani
Year Founded: 2007
Type of Packaging: Food Service, Private Label

2089 **Calkins & Burke**
#800-1500 Georgia St
Vancouver, BC V6G 2Z6
Canada
604-669-3741
Fax: 604-699-9732 800-669-7992
www.calbur.com
Fresh and frozen halibut, salmon and crab
President: David Calkins
Secretary: Micheal Calkins
VP: Micheal Kolinn
Head of Marketing: Ken Jonn
Estimated Sales: $11.95
Number Employees: 60
Type of Packaging: Consumer, Food Service, Private Label
Brands:
Astra
Norden
Royal Canadian

2090 **Callaway Packing Inc**
663 W 4th St
Delta, CO 81416-1534
970-874-9743
Fax: 970-874-7842
Fresh meat packer of beef, pork and lamb
President: David Dillie
callaway@kaycee.net
Estimated Sales: $20-50 Million
Number Employees: 10-19
Type of Packaging: Consumer

2091 **Callaway Vineyards & Winery**
32720 Rancho California Road
Temecula, CA 92591
951-676-4001
Fax: 951-676-5209 800-472-2377
info@callawaywinery.com
www.callawaywinery.com
Red and white wine
President: Mike Jellison
Director: Lori Lyn Narlock
VP/Winemaker: Dwayne Helmuth
Associate Public Relations Manager: Kelly Keagy
Vineyard Manager: Craig Weaver
Cellar Foreman: Joe Vera
Plant Manager: Jose Ceja
Estimated Sales: $20-50 Million
Number Employees: 50-99
Parent Co: Hiram Walker-Allied Domeq.
Type of Packaging: Consumer, Food Service

2092 **Callie's Charleston Biscuits**
1895 Avenue F
North Charleston, SC 29405-1914
843-577-1198
carrie@calliesbiscuits.com
www.calliesbiscuits.com
Bread/biscuits, cakes/pastries, full line of baked goods and frozen desserts.
Owner: Carrie Bailey-Morey
carrie@calliesbiscuits.com
Estimated Sales: Less Than $500,000
Number Employees: 1-4

2093 **Callis Seafood**
353 Callis Road
Lancaster, VA 22503-4112
804-462-7634
Fax: 804-435-6808
Oysters, crabs and frozen shrimp
President: Diane Callis-Haydon
CEO/VP: Diane Haydon
Pres-treas: Terry Haydon
Estimated Sales: $200,000
Number Employees: 2
Type of Packaging: Consumer

2094 **Calmar Bakery**
4906 50 Ave
Calmar, AB T0C 0V0
Canada
780-985-3583
Fax: 780-985-3583
Baked goods including fruit cakes and Danish almond rings and wedding cakes
CEO: Doug Campbell
Secretary/Treasurer: Marlene Campbell
Manager: Tork Kristiansen
Estimated Sales: $99,590
Number Employees: 2
Type of Packaging: Consumer, Food Service
Brands:
Calmar Bakery

2095 **Calpro Ingredients**
1787 Pomona Road
Corona, CA 951-735-59
909-493-4890
Fax: 909-493-4845 www.calprofoods.com
Whey protein concentrates
President: Garry Johns
Operations: Carole Northup
Number Employees: 5-9
Square Footage: 6000
Parent Co: Golden Cheese Company of California
Type of Packaging: Bulk
Brands:
Calpro

2096 **Caltex Foods**
9045-A Eton Ave
Canoga Park, CA 91304
818-700-8657
Fax: 818-700-0285 800-522-5839
www.aasanfoods.com
Ready made meals, Kosher ready made foods, Halal ready made foods, Mediterrenean foods, Middle Eastern Foods.
President/Secretary: Mehrdad Pakravan
Estimated Sales: $3 Million
Number Employees: 8
Square Footage: 10000
Parent Co: Caltex Trading
Type of Packaging: Consumer, Private Label
Brands:
Aasan
Aviva
Beit Hashita
Jaffer

2097 **Calumet Diversified Meats Company**
Ten Thousand 80th Avenue
Pleasant Prairie, WI 53158
262-947-7200
Fax: 262-947-7209 800-752-7427
info@porkchops.com www.porkchops.com
Pork including cutlets, loin, barbecued ribs, tenderloins, chops, etc
CEO & President: Andrew Becker
Chief Financial Officer: Tina Novosel
Vice President: Larry Becker
VP Business Development: Russell Findlay
EVP Sales/Marketing: Joy Huskey
VP Operations: Chidel Taylor
Estimated Sales: $24 Million
Number Employees: 125

2098 **Calvert's**
PO Box 1761
El Paso, TX 79949
915-544-3434
Fax: 915-533-0026 888-472-5727
www.desertpepper.com
Lemonade mix
Owner: William Parker
Estimated Sales: $10-20 Million
Number Employees: 20-49

2099 **Calvisius Caviar**
444 Madison Ave
Suite 1206
New York, NY 10022-6957
212-207-8222
Fax: 212-207-8333 www.calvisius.com
Caviar; smoked fish; and gift baskets.
Vice President: John Knierim
john.knierim@calvisius.com
Year Founded: 1977
Number Employees: 1-10
Type of Packaging: Food Service

2100 **Camas Prairie Winery**
110 S Main St
Moscow, ID 83843-2806
208-882-0214
Fax: 208-882-0214 800-616-0214
www.camasprairiewinery.com
Wine
Co-Owner/President: Stuart Scott
Co-Owner/CFO: Susan Scott
Contact: Jeremy Ritter
tastingroom@camasprairiewinery.com
Estimated Sales: $120,000
Number Employees: 2
Number of Products: 22
Type of Packaging: Private Label
Brands:
Camas

2101 **Cambria Winery**
5475 Chardonnay Ln
Santa Maria, CA 93454-9600
805-937-8091
Fax: 805-934-3589 888-339-9463
info@cambriawines.com www.cambriawines.com
Producer of wines such as Chardonnay, Pinot Noir, Pinot Gris, Syrah and Viognier.
President: Barbara Banke
Marketing: Holly Evans
Customer Relations: Karen Readey
General Manager: Keith Moak
Vineyard Manager: Matt Mahoney
Winemaker: Denise Shurtleff
Estimated Sales: $5-10,000,000
Number Employees: 50-99
Brands:
Cambria

2102 **Cambridge Brands Inc**
810 Main St
Cambridge, MA 02139-3588
617-491-2500
Fax: 617-547-2381 www.tootsie.com
Candy: bagged, bars, caramels, chocolate, chocolate covered cherries, fudge, holiday, gums and jellies, hard, jelly beans, licorice, lollypops, mints, nougats and coated nuts; also, chocolate and cocoa products for bakersconfectioners, etc.
President: Ellen Gordon
Director of Quality Control: John Zhang
Director of Human Resources: Jon Kopera
Manager: Paul Murphy
Prod Superintedent: Val Ponte
Plant Manager: Gerald Chesser
Number Employees: 100-249
Parent Co: Tootsie Roll Industries
Type of Packaging: Consumer, Food Service
Brands:
Charleston Chew
Chuckles
Junior Mints,
Pearson
Pom Poms
Sugar Babies
Sugar Daddy
Sugar Mama

2103 Cambridge Food
2801 Salinas Hwy # F
Monterey, CA 93940-6240
831-373-2300
Fax: 866-373-0369 800-433-2584
info@cambridgedietusa.com
www.cambridgedietusa.com
Meal replacement formulas, cereals, soups, nutrition bars
Manager: Janet Bishop
Research & Development: Dr Robert Nesheim
Estimated Sales: $300,000-500,000
Number Employees: 1-4
Brands:
Cambridge Food

2104 Cambridge Packing Company
41 Foodmart Road
Boston, MA 02118
617-269-6700
Fax: 617-269-0266 800-722-6726
salesinfo@cambridgepacking.com
www.cambridgepacking.com
Fine meats and seafoods including beef, lamb, pork, chicken, fish and shellfish
President/CEO: Bruce Rodman
Co-CEO: Alan Roberts
CFO: Wendy DeMonico
Operations: Paul Dias
Year Founded: 1923
Estimated Sales: $45 Million
Number Employees: 62
Square Footage: 30000

2105 Camellia Beans
5401 Toler Street
Harahan, LA 70183
504-733-8480
Fax: 504-733-8155 info@camelliabeans.com
www.camelliabrand.com
Dried beans, peas and lentils
Partner: Ken Hayward
Partner: Connely Hayward
Estimated Sales: $10-20 Million
Number Employees: 20-49
Type of Packaging: Consumer, Food Service, Bulk
Brands:
Camellia

2106 Camellia General Provision Co
1333 Genesee St
Buffalo, NY 14211-2227
716-893-5352
Fax: 716-895-7713 contact@camelliafoods.com
www.camelliafoods.com
Meat including smoked, sausage and ham
Owner: Adam Cichocki
adam@camelliafoods.com
Vice President: Patrick Cichocki
Vice President: Eric Cichocki
Office Manager: Joell Gilley
Estimated Sales: $5 Million
Number Employees: 20-49

2107 Cameo Confections
543 Juneway Drive
Bay Village, OH 44140-2606
440-871-5732
Fax: 440-892-8656
Confections
President: Gail Barker

2108 Cameron Birch Syrup & Confections
951 Hermon Road
Suite 6
Wasilla, AK 99654-7379
907-373-6275
Fax: 907-373-6274 800-962-4724
Birch syrup, marinades, salad dressing and candy
President: Marlene Cameron
Number Employees: 1-4
Square Footage: 2500
Type of Packaging: Consumer, Food Service, Private Label, Bulk
Brands:
Birch Bark
Birch Logs
Black Tie
Cameron
Cameron's
Sesame Birch Sticks

2109 Cameron Seafood Processors
PO Box 1228
Cameron, LA 70631-1228
318-775-5510
Fax: 318-755-5529
Seafood
President: Bruce Bang

2110 Camilla Pecan Company
P.O.Box 508
275 Industrial Blvd
Camilla, GA 31730-3911
229-336-7282
Fax: 229-336-1177 800-526-8770
info@harrellnut.com
Pecans
President/CEO: Marty Harrell
CFO: Paula Johnson
General Corporate Management: David Stanfield
Estimated Sales: $43,000,000
Number Employees: 250
Number of Brands: 3
Brands:
Camilla Pecan
Harrell Nut
Ole' Henry's Nuthouse

2111 Camino Real Foods Inc
2638 E Vernon Ave
Vernon, CA 90058-1825
323-585-6599
Fax: 323-585-5420 800-421-6201
www.chicknwraps.com
Frozen burritos and stuffed microwaveable sandwiches
President: Robert Cross
rcross@crfoods.com
CFO: Richard Lunsford
Vice President: Juan Salazar
Marketing: Clark Metcalf
VP Sales: Terry McMartin
Human Resource Compliance & Regulatory: Lulu Saiden
Manager: Jim Gatten
Estimated Sales: $40 Million
Number Employees: 250-499
Parent Co: Nissan Foods
Type of Packaging: Consumer, Food Service
Brands:
Taxco
Tina's Las Campanas

2112 Campagana Winery
10950 West Road
Redwood Valley, CA 95470-9741
707-485-1221
Fax: 707-485-1225 www.winesandromance.com
Winery
Chairman: Joseph Campagna
CEO: Tony Coturri
CFO/COO: George Pruden
Marketing Director: Paul White
Sales Director: Paul White
Production Manager: Nic Coturri
Estimated Sales: $3,000,000
Number Employees: 8
Type of Packaging: Private Label
Brands:
Gabrielli
Gabrielli Winery

2113 Campagna Distinct Flavor
40759 Mcdowell Creek Drive
Lebanon, OR 97355-0995
541-258-6806
Fax: 541-258-7806 800-959-4372
Cooking sauces, fruit, savory, and mustard flavors; hot pepper and garlic jellies
President: Marlene Peterson
CFO: Joseph Peterson
Estimated Sales: $660,000
Number Employees: 7
Type of Packaging: Private Label

2114 Campari
55 E 59th St
Suite 9
New York, NY 10022-1112
212-891-3600
Fax: 212-891-3661 www.campari.com
Alcoholic beverages
CEO: Bob Kunze-Concewitz
General Manager: Gennaro Miccoli
Estimated Sales: $2.5-5,000,000
Number Employees: 10-19
Parent Co: Campari
Brands:
Campari
Cinzano
Skyy
Aperoi
Glen Grant
Wild Turkey

2115 Campbell Company of Canada
2845 Matheson Blvd E
Toronto, ON L4W 5J8
Canada
800-410-7687
www.campbellsoup.ca
Canned foods including condensed soups, broth, chili and ready to serve soups.
President: Julio Gomez
Year Founded: 1930
Estimated Sales: $224 Million
Number Employees: 700
Type of Packaging: Consumer, Food Service, Private Label
Brands:
Bisto
Broths
Campbells Ready To Enjoy Soups
Campbells Soup At Hand
Chunky Ready To Go Bowls
Chunky Ready To Serve Soups/Chili
Gardennay
Godiva
Habitant
Healthy Request Ready To Serve Soup
Pace
Pepperidge Farm
Red & White Condensed Soups
V8
V8 Splash
V8 Vgo

2116 Campbell Soup Co.
1 Campbell Pl.
Camden, NJ 08103-1701
856-342-4800
Fax: 856-342-3878 800-257-8443
www.campbellsoupcompany.com
Soups, snacks, beverages and simple meals.
President/CEO: Mark Clouse
Executive VP/CFO: Mick Beekhuizen
Executive VP/General Counsel: Adam Ciongoli
Executive VP, Global R&D: Craig Slavtcheff
Executive VP, Global Supply Chain: Bob Furbee
Year Founded: 1869
Estimated Sales: Over $1 Billion
Number Employees: 18,000
Number of Brands: 21
Type of Packaging: Consumer, Food Service, Bulk
Other Locations:
Toronto, Canada
Corporate Headquarters
Camden NJ
Pepperidge Farm Headquarters
Norwalk CT
Bolthouse Farms Headquarters
Bakersfield CA
Norre Snede, Denmark
Selangor, Malaysia
Bekasi, Indonesia
Arnott's Headquarters
Homebush, Australia
New Market, New Zealand
Brands:
Campbells
Campbells Foodservice
Campbells Canada
Campbells Chunky
Cape Cod
Goldfish
Kettle Brand
Lance
Late July Snacks
Milano
Pace
Pacific Foods
Pepperidge Farm
Plum Organics
Prego
Snack Factory Pretzel Crisps
Snyder's of Hanover
SpaghettiOs
Swanson

V8 Beverages
Well Yes

2117 **Campbell's Quality Cuts**
2551 Michigan St
Sidney, OH 45365-9083
937-492-2194
Fax: 937-492-4044
Lamb, beef and pork
Owner: Dennis Campbell
Estimated Sales: $380,000
Number Employees: 5
Type of Packaging: Consumer, Bulk

2118 **Camrose Packers**
5320 47th Street
Camrose, AB T4V 1K6
Canada
780-672-4887
Fresh beef and pork and wild game including deer, elk and moose
Owner: Andrew Anderson
Manager: Debilyn Witvoet Parent
Treasurer/Secretary: Sharon Miller
Estimated Sales: $1,600,000
Number Employees: 5
Type of Packaging: Consumer
Brands:
Camrose

2119 **Can Am Seafood**
972 County Road
Lubec, ME 04652
207-733-2267
Fax: 207-733-0927
Seafood
President: William Jackson
Estimated Sales: $200,000
Number Employees: 1

2120 **CanAmera Foods**
14711-128th Avenue
Edmonton, AL T5L 3H3
Canada
780-447-6960
Fax: 780-452-0541 canamera.lookchem.com
Shortenings, margarines, oils, lard, whipped toppings, stabilizers and emulsifiers including lecithin
President: Murray Davis

2121 **Canada Bread Co, Ltd**
10 Four Seasons Place
Etobicoke, ON M9B 6H7
Canada
416-622-2040
800-465-5515
www.canadabread.com
Baked goods, snacks and bread company.
President: Joseph McCarthy
Year Founded: 1911
Estimated Sales: $1.3 Billion
Number Employees: 4,175
Number of Brands: 7
Number of Products: 1K+
Parent Co: Grupo Bimbo
Type of Packaging: Consumer, Food Service, Private Label, Bulk
Brands:
Villaggio®
Stonemill®
POM®
Dempster's®
Bon Matin®
Vachon®
Ben's®

2122 **Canadian Fish Exporters**
134 Rumford Ave # 202
Suite 202
Auburndale, MA 02466-1377
617-916-0900
Fax: 617-926-8214 800-225-4215
cfe@cfeboston.com www.cfeboston.com
Saltfish including bacalao, pollock, hake, cusk, haddock, herring, mackerel and cod; importer of Italian cheeses and canned tomatoes
CEO: Robert Metafora
CFO/Treasurer: Janelle Calamari
VP: James Scannell
Estimated Sales: $10-20 Million
Number Employees: 10-19
Type of Packaging: Consumer, Private Label, Bulk
Brands:
Bacala Rico
Buena Ventura
Cristobal

2123 **Canadian Harvest-U.S.A.**
7301 Ohms Lane
Suite 600
Edina, MN 55439
952-820-2518
Fax: 952-835-1991 888-689-5800
miker@skypoint.com www.sunopta.com
Fiber ingredients including bleached oat fibers, red and white wheat brans, corn brans, oat blends, wheat germs and customized grain blends
President: David Belaney
Marketing Manager: Mike Rudquist
General Manager: John White
Plant Manager: Paul Empanger
Estimated Sales: $4 Million
Number Employees: 40
Other Locations:
Canadian Harvest
St. Thomas ON
Brands:
Snowite

2124 **Canadian Mist Distillers**
202 MacDonald Road
Collingwood, ON L9Y 4J2
Canada
705-445-4690
Fax: 705-445-7948 www.canadianmist.com
Processor and exporter of whiskey
Officer: Pat Sullivan
Manager Admin./Commodities: Steve Sly
Manager Production: Don Jaques
Plant Manager: Harold Ferguson
Estimated Sales: $24.4 Million
Number Employees: 35
Square Footage: 1000000
Parent Co: Brown-Forman Corporation
Type of Packaging: Consumer, Food Service
Brands:
Canadian Mist

2125 **Canaf Foods International**
405 Queen Street S
Po Box 75047
Bolton, ON L7E 2B0
Canada
905-362-0524
Fax: 905-362-0526 info@canaffoods.com
www.canaffoods.com
Bread/biscuits, cakes/pastries, frozen baked goods, frozen desserts, foodservice, private label.
Marketing: Giovanni Bartolomeo

2126 **Canal Fulton Provision**
2014 Locust St S
Canal Fulton, OH 44614-9477
330-854-3502
Fax: 330-854-3502 800-321-3502
www.canalfultonpro.com
Portion cut poultry and meats including beef, lamb and pork
President: George Mizarek
jmizarek@aol.com
Estimated Sales: $4.5 Million
Number Employees: 20-49
Square Footage: 81000
Type of Packaging: Consumer, Food Service, Private Label, Bulk
Brands:
Corn King
Flavor Pack
Weaver

2127 **Canarino**
267 Libbey Parkway
Weymouth, MA 02189
Fax: 781-413-8999 800-510-4202
www.canarino.com
Hot lemon beverage

2128 **Candelari's Specialty Sausage**
6002 Washington Ave
Houston, TX 77007-5015
832-200-1474
Fax: 281-568-8098 800-953-5343
emaillist@candelaris.com www.candelaris.com
Sausage
President: Michael May
michael@candelaris.com
CFO: Michael Freeman
Estimated Sales: $500,000-$1,000,000
Number Employees: 5-9
Type of Packaging: Private Label
Brands:
Candelari's

2129 **Cando Pasta**
1301 5th Ave
PO Box 689
Cando, ND 58324-6603
701-968-4401
www.candopasta.weebly.com
Producer of dry pasta products.
Owner: Jim Gibbens
Owner: Bruce Gibbens
Estimated Sales: Less than $500,000
Number Employees: 20-49
Number of Brands: 1
Square Footage: 80000
Type of Packaging: Consumer, Bulk
Brands:
Cando Pasta

2130 **Candy Basket Inc**
1924 NE 181st Ave
Portland, OR 97230
503-666-2000
Fax: 503-666-6400 800-864-1924
candybasket@comcast.net
Milk, dark and white chocolate. Truffles, nuts, chews, turtles, creams, toffee's, barks, corns and brittles.
President/Owner: Dale Fuhr
Contact: Amber Allan
aallan-candybasket@comcast.net
Estimated Sales: $4.5 Million
Number Employees: 35

2131 **Candy Bouquet of Elko**
3362 Dux Avenue
Elko, NV 89801-4432
775-777-9866
Fax: 775-777-3200 888-855-3391
hopkins@sierra.net
Candy bouquets
Co-Owner: Judy Hopkins
Co-Owner: Diane Noble
Manager: Angie Demars
Number Employees: 1-4

2132 **Candy Central**
905 Murray Rd
East Hanover, NJ 07936
www.candycentral.com
Candy and confections
Year Founded: 1937
Estimated Sales: Less Than $500,000
Number Employees: 50-249
Number of Brands: 70
Parent Co: Consolidated Service Distributors, Inc
Brands:
100 Grand(c)
3 Musketeers(c)
Adams & Brooks, Inc
Airheads
Almond Joy
Altoids
American Licorice Co.
Andre Prost, Inc.
Atomic Fireball
Au'some
Baby Ruth
Basic Promotions
Big League Chew
Bonomo
Boston America Corp
Bottle Caps
BreathSavers
Bubblicious Bubble Gum
Butterfinger
C Howard Co.
Candyrific
Charleston Chew
Charms Co.
Chuckles
Cold Stone Creamery
Colombina
Cry Baby
Dentyne
Dryden & Palmer
Dubble Bubble
Dum Dums(c) Pops
Ferrara Candy Co.
Fluffy Stuff
Frankford Candy
Frooties

Gerrit J. Verburg Co.
Gobstopper
Haribo
Heath
Hello Kitty
Hershey's(c)
Hilco Corporation
Hospitality Mints
Hubba Bubba(c)
Ice Breakers
Icee
Impact Confections
Jolly Rancher
Just Born, Inc
Kidsmania Inc
KIT KAT(c)
Koko's Confectionary & Novelty
Laffy Taffy
M & M's
Mars, Inc
Mentos
MILKY WAY(c)
Minions
Mondelez International
My M&Ms
NECCO
Nerds
Nestl,
Novelty Specialties
Nutella(c)
Orbit Gum
Pez Candy
Nutella(c)
Orbit Gum
Pez Candy
Pixy Stix
Pop Rocks
Push Pop Candy

2133 **Candy Cottage Company**
465 Pike Rd Ste 103
Huntingdon Valley, PA 19006
215-953-8288
Fax: 215-357-3035 thecandycottageco@gmail.com
Chocolate covered pretzels
Co-Owner: Al Palagruto
Co-Owner: Joan Palagruto
Estimated Sales: Under $500,000
Number Employees: 3
Type of Packaging: Consumer, Food Service, Private Label, Bulk
Brands:
Ultimate Petite Pretzels
Ultimate Pretzel
Ultimate Pretzel Rods
Ultimate Pretzel Sculptures

2134 **(HQ)Candy Flowers**
9286 Mercantile Drive
Mentor, OH 44060-4525
440-974-1333
Fax: 440-974-1338
Chocolate and candy flowers, chocolate covered pretzels, coffee spoons and cookies and theme wrapped chocolate bars; exporter of candy flowers; importer of chocolates
President: Joanne Henry
Marketing: Anthony Henry
Estimated Sales: $5-10,000,000
Number Employees: 20-49
Square Footage: 42000
Type of Packaging: Food Service
Brands:
Candy Flower Bouquets
Spoonful of Flavors
Sweet Blossoms

2135 **Candy Mountain Sweets & Treats**
1484 Atlanta Industrial Dr NW
Suite A
Atlanta, GA 30331-1031
404-505-7332
Fax: 404-696-4003 800-621-1954
www.tootarts.com
Sugar free candy
President & CEO: Armand Hammer
VP Purchasing: Bob Davis
VP Sales: Al Silva
Estimated Sales: $20-50 Million
Number Employees: 50-99
Brands:
Tpp Tarts Kids Kandy

2136 **Candyrific**
3738 Lexington Rd
Louisville, KY 40207-3010
502-893-3626
Fax: 502-893-3951 sales@candyrific.com
www.candyrific.com
Candy
President: Rob Auerbach
robr@candyrific.com
Vice President: Paul Roberts
Vice President: Mike Roberts
Quality Assurance Manager: Joshua Boone
V.P. of Sales: Larry Lindenbaum
Customer Service: Rebecca Raymond
Estimated Sales: $34.9 Million
Number Employees: 20
Brands:
Cool Pops
Crayola
Etch-A-Sketch
Marvel
Peeps
Slinky Brand Candy

2137 **Canelake's Candy**
414 Chestnut St
Virginia, MN 55792-2526
218-741-1557
Fax: 218-741-1557 888-928-8889
Processor and exporter of candies and chocolates; importer of nuts
President: James Cina
candy@canelakes.com
Estimated Sales: Less Than $500,000
Number Employees: 5-9
Square Footage: 6000
Type of Packaging: Consumer

2138 **Cangel**
60 Paton Road
Toronto, ON M6H 1R8
Canada
416-532-5111
Fax: 416-532-6231 800-267-4795
Manufacturer and exporter of food, hydrolyzed and technical gelatins
President: Richard Manka
Number Employees: 2
Square Footage: 160000
Type of Packaging: Bulk

2139 **Cannoli Factory**
75 Wyandanch Ave
Wyandanch, NY 11798-4441
631-643-2700
Fax: 631-643-2777 sales@cannolifactory.com
www.cannolifactory.com
Processor and exporter of Italian and New York style cheesecake, tiramisu, lobster tail pastries and cannoli products including chocolate covered shells, cream and tarts
Owner: Michael Zucaro
Contact: John Edwards
johne@cannolifactory.com
Estimated Sales: $4 Million
Number Employees: 50-99
Type of Packaging: Food Service

2140 **Cannon's Sweets Hots**
645.S Almada
Las Cruces, NM 880005
575-523-1447
Fax: 575-523-1447 800-214-6639
sweethot@sweethots.com www.sweethots.com
Hot sauces and chili
Co-Owner/President: John Cannon
Co-Owner/CEO: Diane Cannon
Estimated Sales: Under $500,000
Number Employees: 1-4

2141 **Canoe Lagoon Oyster Company**
118 Bayview Ave
Coffman Cove, AK 99918
907-329-2253
Fax: 425-643-7266
Oyster
Owner: Sharon Gray
Owner: Don Nicholson
Estimated Sales: $310,000
Number Employees: 2
Type of Packaging: Consumer, Food Service, Bulk

2142 **Canoe Ridge Vineyard**
1102 W Cherry St
Walla Walla, WA 99362-1746
509-527-0885
Fax: 509-527-0886 www.canoeridgevineyard.com
Wines
Manager: Sue Bridwell
sueb@preceptwine.com
Estimated Sales: $500,000-$1 Million
Number Employees: 10-19
Parent Co: Chalone Wine Group

2143 **Canon Potato Company**
P.O.Box 880
Center, CO 81125-0880
719-754-3445
Potato packer and shipper
President: David Tonso
d.tonso@canonpotato.com
Estimated Sales: $2,689,000
Number Employees: 40
Parent Co: Woerner Holdings, L.P.
Type of Packaging: Private Label

2144 **Canton Noodle Corporation**
101 Mott St
New York, NY 10013
212-226-3276
Fax: 212-226-8037
Chinese canned noodles
Principal: James Eng
Estimated Sales: $610,000
Number Employees: 8
Type of Packaging: Consumer

2145 **Cantrell's Seafood**
Sabino Road
Bath, ME 04530
207-442-7261
Fax: 207-770-1600
Seafood
President: S C Cantrell

2146 **Canyon Bakehouse LLC**
1510 E 11th St
Loveland, CO 80537-5049
970-461-3844
www.canyonglutenfree.com
Gluten free baked goods
Co-Founder: Christi Skow
Co-Founder: Josh Skow
jskow@canyonbakehouse.com
Co-Founder: Ed Miknevicius
Estimated Sales: Less Than $500,000
Number Employees: 1-4

2147 **Canyon Specialty Foods**
11035 Switzer Ave
Dallas, TX 75238-1333
214-352-1771
Fax: 214-352-3118 aconally@canyonfoods.com
www.frankievskitchen.com
Gourmet shelf and frozen food, salsa and sauces
Owner, President: Anne Connally
aconnally@canyonspecialtyfoods.com
Estimated Sales: $1,100,000
Number Employees: 10-19
Parent Co: 321 Capital Partners LLC
Type of Packaging: Private Label

2148 **Cap Candy**
50 Technology Court
Napa, CA 94558-7519
707-251-9321
Fax: 707-251-9482
Candy
VP of Marketing: Deirdre Gonzalez
General Manager: Tom Pritchard
Number Employees: 250-499
Parent Co: Hasbro

2149 **Capa Di Roma Inc**
358 Burnside Ave
East Hartford, CT 06108-2426
860-282-0298
Fax: 860-289-6211 email@capadiroma.com
www.capadiroma.com
Olive oil, balsamic vinegar, pasta sauce.
Presidnet: Frank Capaccio
frank@capadiroma.com
VP, Marketing: Emilia Capaccio
Estimated Sales: $150,000
Number Employees: 2

2150 Capalbo's Fruit Baskets
350 Allwood Rd
Clifton, NJ 07012-1701
973-667-6262
Fax: 973-450-1199 800-252-6262
service@capalbosonline.com
www.capalbosonline.com
Produces gift baskets for the specialty food industry.
President: Frank Capalbo
Vice President: Susan Capalbo
Digital Marketing Manager: Joe Wilson
Estimated Sales: $4.8,000,000
Number Employees: 50-99
Type of Packaging: Food Service
Brands:
Capalbo's

2151 Caparone Winery LLC
2280 San Marcos Rd
Paso Robles, CA 93446-5322
805-610-5308
info@caparone.com
www.caparone.com
Wines
President: Mark Caparone
Partner: David Caparone
Estimated Sales: $100,000
Number Employees: 1-4

2152 Capay Canyon Ranch
P.O.Box 508
Esparto, CA 95627-0508
530-662-2372
Fax: 530-662-2306 capaycanyonranch.com
Processor and exporter of almonds, walnuts and grapes, and inshell chandler walnuts.
Sales Director: Leslie Barth
Contact: Stan Barth
stan@capaycanyon.com
Plant Operations: Todd Barth
Estimated Sales: $1-2,499 Million
Number Employees: 4
Number of Brands: 2
Number of Products: 8
Square Footage: 10000
Type of Packaging: Bulk
Brands:
Capay Canyon Ranch
Stan Barth Farms

2153 Capco Enterprises
34 Deforest Ave # 3
East Hanover, NJ 07936-2832
973-884-0044
Fax: 973-884-8711 800-252-1011
www.capcoenterprisesinc.com
Almonds, licorice, baked beans, sugar-coated pistachios and chick peas
President/CEO: Carole Lapone
clapone@capcoenterprisesinc.com
Operations Executive: James Ventola
Plant Manager: Daniel Rivera
Estimated Sales: $1 Million
Number Employees: 5-9

2154 Cape Ann Seafood
44 Grapevine Road
Gloucester, MA 01930-4241
978-283-0687
Fax: 978-282-1870
President: Nickolas Avelis
Treasurer: Faith Avelis
Vice President: James Douglass
Estimated Sales: $2.0 Million
Number Employees: 2

2155 Cape Cod Coffee Roasters
348 Main St
Mashpee, MA 02649-2045
508-477-2400
Fax: 508-477-2989 www.capecodcoffee.com
Coffee
Owner: Demos Young
demos@capecodroasters.com
Office Manager: Bonnie Cohen
Estimated Sales: $340,000
Number Employees: 5-9

2156 Cape Cod Potato Chips
100 Breeds Hill Rd
Hyannis, MA 02601-1886
508-775-3358
Fax: 508-775-2808 800-438-1880
www.capecodchips.com
Popcorn including white cheddar cheese, natural and butter; also, kettle-cooked potato chips
President: Margaret Wicklund
Chief Executive Officer: Roger Gray
Sr Vice President: Dan Collins
Vice President: Chuck Fisher
Estimated Sales: $20-50 Million
Number Employees: 100-249
Square Footage: 30000
Parent Co: Snyder's Lance
Type of Packaging: Consumer
Brands:
Cape Cod

2157 Cape Cod Provisions
31 Jonathan Bourne Dr # 1
Unit 1
Pocasset, MA 02559-4919
508-564-5840
Fax: 508-564-5844
customerservice@capecodprovisions.com
Chocolate covered cranberries, chocolate covered fruit, fruit truffles
Owner/President/Quality Control: Susan Faria
Finance Manager: Rick Ottaviano
Director of Sales and Marketing: Kristin McGillicuddy
Sales Representative: Erin Mancinelli
Estimated Sales: $1.2 Million
Number Employees: 10-19

2158 Cape Cod Specialty Foods
11 Cranberry Hwy
P.O. Box 519
Sagamore, MA 2561
508-888-7099
Fax: 508-888-6616 orders@ccsfoods.com
Wholesaler/distributor of gourmet condiments including lemon pepper mustard, cranberry chutney, relish and sauces, schnappy peach preserves, chocolate covered cranberries, bog beans, etc.; also mail order available
Owner: Michael Duryea
bogbeans@verizon.net
Estimated Sales: $160,000
Number Employees: 5-9
Square Footage: 2000
Type of Packaging: Consumer, Food Service

2159 Cape Cod Sweets, LLC
31 Jonathan Bourne Dr
Suite 1
Pocasset, MA 02559-4919
508-564-5840
Fax: 508-564-5844
Chocolate, candy, and fruit confections.
Founder: Sue Faria
Year Founded: 1996
Number Employees: 5-9
Brands:
Harvest Sweets
Cape Cod Cranberry Candy
Sweet Cravings

2160 Capital Brewery & Beer Garden
7734 Terrace Ave
Middleton, WI 53562-3163
608-836-7100
Fax: 608-831-9155 capbrew@capitalbrewery.com
Brewer of lager and ale
President, CEO: Carl Nolen
Brew master: Kirby Nelson
Estimated Sales: $5-10,000,000
Number Employees: 20-49
Type of Packaging: Consumer, Food Service, Bulk
Brands:
Gartenbrau

2161 Capital City Processors
P.O. Box 3588
Winchester, VA 22604-2586
540-877-2590
Fax: 540-877-3215 800-473-2731
www.valleyproteins.com
Cooking oils
President: Gerald Smith
Owner: Mike Smith
Estimated Sales: $20-50 Million
Number Employees: 10-19
Type of Packaging: Bulk

2162 Capital Packers Inc
12907-57th Street
Edmonton, AB T5A 0E7
Canada
780-476-1391
Fax: 780-478-0083 800-272-8868
info@capitalpackers.ca www.capitalpackers.ca
Cooked and smoked meats including beef, pork and veal
President: Brent Komarnicki
Vice President: Augustine Komarnicki
Sales Manager: Peter Andreassen
Plant Manager: Cor Van Miltenburg
Estimated Sales: $20.6,000,000
Number Employees: 120
Number of Brands: 3
Number of Products: 850
Type of Packaging: Food Service, Private Label, Bulk
Brands:
Bavarian Brand Sausage
Cajun Brand Sausage
Ham Sausage
Polish Sausage

2163 Capital Produce II Inc
8005 Rappahanock Ave
Jessup, MD 20794-9438
443-755-1733
Fax: 443-755-0282 www.capitalseaboard.com
Seafood
Owner: Tom Alascio
tom@capitalseaboard.com
Vice President: Steve Hanson
Estimated Sales: $3.7 Million
Number Employees: 50-99

2164 Capitol Foods
PO Box 751541
Memphis, TN 38175-1541
662-781-9021
Fax: 662-781-0697
Canned vegetables, diced peaches, mixed fruits and edible oils; exporter of canned vegetables; wholesaler/distributor of bakery, dairy and grocery products, soups and bases, produce, syrups, oils, pasta, meats; serving the food servicemarkets
President: Kenneth Porter
CFO: Phillip Duncan
Number Employees: 134
Square Footage: 20000
Type of Packaging: Consumer, Food Service
Brands:
Capitol Foods
Orchard Naturals

2165 Capolla Food Inc
25 Lepage Court
North York, ON M3J 3M3
Canada
416-633-0389
Fax: 416-633-7718 www.cappolafood.com
Packaged luncheon meats including beef and pork
CEO: Rick De Vincenzo
Marketing Director: Francefca Ivas
Sales/Marketing: Dion McGuire
Purchasing Agent: John Capolla
Number Employees: 50-99
Parent Co: J.M. Schneider
Type of Packaging: Consumer
Brands:
Capolla Foods

2166 Capone Foods
14 Bow St. Union Square
Somerville, MA 02143
617-629-2296
Fax: 617-776-0318 albert@caponefoods.com
www.caponefoods.com
Producer of pasta and sauces. Some of their products include fresh pasta, ravioli, tortellini, gnocchi, pizza, entr,es, meatballs, sausage, empanadas and many more items. Their products can be found in several store locationsthroughout Massachusetts, such as Bedford, Boston, Brighton, Brookline, Cambridge, Concord, and other locations.
Owner: Albert Capone
Manager: Jennifer Capone
Estimated Sales: $320,000
Number Employees: 7
Brands:
Capone Foods

2167 **Caporale Winery**
910 Enterprise Way
Napa, CA 94558-6209
707-253-9230
Fax: 707-253-9232
Wines
President: Mark Caporale
Estimated Sales: $500,000- 1,000,000
Number Employees: 20-49

2168 **Cappello's**
PO Box 11757
Denver, CO 80211
844-353-2863
talk@cappellos.com cappellos.com
Gluten-free, grain-free cookie dough, pasta and pizza
Co-Founder: Stacey Marcellus
Co-Founder: Benjamin Frohlichstein
Year Founded: 2011

2169 **Cappo Drinks**
15011 Badillo St.
Baldwin Park, CA 91706
626-813-1006
sales@cappodrinks.com
www.cappodrinks.com
Manufacturer and exporter of smoothie mixes.
CEO: Scott Berberian
Contact: Ara Berberian
aberberian@cappodrinks.com
Brands:
Cappo

2170 **Cappola Foods**
25 Lappage Ct
Toronto, ON M3J 3M3
Canada
416-633-0389
Fax: 416-787-1535 sales@cappolafood.com
www.cappolafood.com
Processor and exporter of Italian flavored ices
Owner: Dom Cappola
Type of Packaging: Consumer, Food Service

2171 **Cappuccine**
375 Klug Cir
Corona, CA 92880-5408
760-864-7355
Fax: 760-864-7360 800-511-3127
www.cappuccine.net
Manufacturer of gourmet instant powder beverage mixes in chai, vanilla, chocolate, fruit, toffe and coconut flavors. Some of these flavors include Caramel Latte, Double Fudge Mocha, Java Chip, Mocha Glacier, Dark Chocolate Chip, LemonVelvet, Tart Culture Smoothie, Indian Chai Latte and many more.
Founder, Owner & CEO: Michael Rubin
Chief Financial Officer: Lawrence Lathrop
Executive VP: Charles Jennings
chuck@cappuccine.net
Estimated Sales: $5,000,000
Number Employees: 10-19
Number of Brands: 1
Number of Products: 18
Square Footage: 3600
Type of Packaging: Consumer, Food Service, Private Label, Bulk
Brands:
Cappuccine

2172 **Capri Bagel & Pizza Corporation**
215 Moore St
Brooklyn, NY 11206-3745
718-497-4431
Fax: 718-497-7567
Manufacturer and exporter of pizza, pizza bagels and mini pizzas
President: Adrian Cooper
Plant Manager: Ikey Tuachi
Estimated Sales: $500,000-$1,000,000
Number Employees: 20-49
Square Footage: 31000
Type of Packaging: Consumer, Food Service, Private Label
Brands:
Big Time
Boardwalk

2173 **Capri Sun**
2901 State St
Granite City, IL 62040
parents.caprisun.com
Flavoring, extracts and beverages
CEO: Roland Weening
Estimated Sales: $100+ Million
Parent Co: Kraft Foods

2174 **Capriccio**
10021 1/2 Canoga Avenue
Chatsworth, CA 91311-0981
818-718-7620
Fax: 818-718-0204
Manufacturer and exporter of food ingredients
CEO: Jack Barsoumian
Estimated Sales: $500,000-$1,000,000
Number Employees: 1-4
Type of Packaging: Food Service

2175 **Capricorn Coffees Inc**
353 10th St
San Francisco, CA 94103-3804
415-621-8500
Fax: 415-621-9875 800-541-0758
www.capricorncoffees.com
Coffee, Tea, Accessories
Manager: Annie Ngo
Manager: Rachel Akins
rachel.akins@capricorncoffees.com
Estimated Sales: $1-2.5 Million
Number Employees: 10-19
Type of Packaging: Private Label

2176 **Caprine Estates**
3669 Centerville Road
Bellbrook, OH 45305-0307
937-848-7406
Fax: 937-848-7437
Goat milk cheese, fudge and bottled milk
President: Dennis Dean
VP: Patti Dean
Sales/Marketing VP: Ron Best
Estimated Sales: $250,000
Number Employees: 5
Square Footage: 15000
Type of Packaging: Consumer, Food Service, Private Label, Bulk

2177 **Capriole Inc**
10329 New Cut Rd
Greenville, IN 47124-9202
812-923-9408
Fax: 812-923-8901
cheese@capriolegoatcheese.com
www.capriolegoatcheese.com
Cheese
President: Judy Schad
judygoat@aol.com
Estimated Sales: Less Than $500,000
Number Employees: 5-9

2178 **Caprock Winery Inc**
408 E Woodrow Rd
Lubbock, TX 79423-7809
806-863-2704
Fax: 806-863-2712 800-546-9463
www.caprockwinery.com
Wines
President: Don Roark
CEO: Phillip Anderson
phillip@caprockwinery.com
Manager: Jason Butler
Plant Manager: Kim McPherson
Estimated Sales: $1,000,000
Number Employees: 5-9
Type of Packaging: Private Label

2179 **Capsule Works**
2100 Smithtown Avenue
Ronkonkoma, NY 11779
Fax: 631-472-2817 877-435-2277
Vitamins
President: Kazuo Kawabata
CFO: Jean-Marc Hu%t
Estimated Sales: $10-20 Million
Number Employees: 20-49
Brands:
Capsule Works

2180 **Capt Collier Seafood**
14733 Tom Johnson Ave
Coden, AL 36523-3116
251-824-4925
Fax: 251-824-2374
Seafood
Owner: Phil Brannon
brannonmerle@aol.com
Estimated Sales: $3-5 Million
Number Employees: 5-9

2181 **Capt Joe & Sons Inc**
95 E Main St
Gloucester, MA 01930-3860
978-283-1454
Fax: 978-283-1466 captijoe06@yahoo.com
Seafood
President: Benjamin Ciaramitaro
Treasurer/Clerk: Charles Ciaramitaro
Vice President: Frank Ciaramitaro
Manager: Joe Ciaramitaro
Estimated Sales: Less Than $500,000
Number Employees: 1-4

2182 **Captain Alex Seafoods**
8874 N Milwaukee Ave
Niles, IL 60714-1752
847-803-8833
Fax: 847-803-9854 www.fishandseafoodniles.com
Seafood
President/Secretary: Alex Malidis
Vice President: Matthew Mallidis
Office Manager: Ilir Veliu
Estimated Sales: $530,000
Number Employees: 5-9

2183 **Captain Bob's Jet Fuel**
2216 Ladue Ln
Fort Wayne, IN 46804-2794
260-436-3895
877-486-6468
Hot sauces including habanero-garlic, smoked serrano jalapeno and chile de arbol; also, hot barbecue sauces
President: Robert Kitto
Contact: Bob Kitto
bkitto@captainbobs.net
Estimated Sales: $1-2,500,000
Number Employees: 1-4
Brands:
Captain Bob's Jet Fuel

2184 **Captain Cook Coffee Company**
79-7415 Mamalahoa Hwy.
Kealakekua, HI 96750
650-766-9149
Fax: 808-322-2087 info@captaincookkona.com
captaincookkona.stores.yahoo.net
Manufacturer of Kona coffee.
Owner: Steven McLaughlin
Estimated Sales: $5-10,000,000
Number Employees: 10-19
Brands:
Captain Cook Coffee

2185 **Captain Foods, Inc.**
2732 Hibiscus Dr
Edgewater, FL 32141-5404
Fax: 386-428-9988 800-749-5047
www.captainfoods.com
BBQ sauces and seasonings; grilling sauces.
Sice President of Sales: Chris Feindt
Type of Packaging: Private Label

2186 **Captain Ken's Foods Inc**
344 Robert St S
St Paul, MN 55107-2200
651-298-0071
Fax: 651-298-0849 800-510-3811
jtraxler@captainkens.com www.captainkens.com
Frozen foods including chili, oven baked beans and au gratin potatoes, taco meat, meatloaf, macaroni and beef
President: John Traxler
jtraxler@captainkens.com
Chairman, Owner: Mike Traxler
Controller: Linda Traxler
VP Business Development/Sales: Tom Traxler
Operations Manager: Kevin Kosel
Plant Manager: Richard Gavin
Estimated Sales: $1.9 Million
Number Employees: 10-19
Square Footage: 124000
Type of Packaging: Consumer, Food Service
Brands:
Captain Ken's

2187 **Captain Lawrence Brewing Co**
444 Saw Mill River Rd # 100
Elmsford, NY 10523-1031
914-741-2337
www.captainlawrencebrewing.com

Craft beer.
Owner/Brewer: Scott Vaccaro
scott@captainlawrencebrewing.com
CFO: Vince Vaccaro
Quality Control Manager: Jim Elliot
Sales Manager: Keith Feckete
Number Employees: 1-4
Type of Packaging: Consumer

2188 **Captain Little Seafood**
413 Central Port Mouton Td.
Queens County, NS B0T1T0
Canada
902-947-2087
Fax: 902-947-2088 www.scotiafish.com
Lobster, Atlantic sea cucumber, red sea cucumber, sea urchin, snow crab, Jonah crab, salmon caviar, halibut, herring, capelin fish, whelk, cold water shrimp, tuna, scallops
Procurement: Steven Shi
Square Footage: 72500

2189 **Captain's Choice**
29629 11th Pl S
Federal Way, WA 98003-3727
253-941-1184
Fax: 253-946-2852
info@captainschoicesalmon.com
www.captainschoicesalmon.com
Honey brine smoked salmon products and gift packages
President: Donald Buchanan
d.buchanan@captains-choice.com
Treasurer/Secretary: Rosalie Buchanan
Estimated Sales: Less Than $500,000
Number Employees: 1-4
Type of Packaging: Consumer, Food Service, Private Label
Brands:
Captain's Choice Honey Brine
Smoked Salmon
Smoked Spices

2190 **Captiva Limited Inc**
45 Us Highway 206 Ste 104
Augusta, NJ 7822
973-579-7883
Fax: 973-579-2509
Processor and exporter of bottled water including stilled, carbonated and flavored; also, sports/health drinks
Owner: Don Destefano
VP: Mary Ann Bell
Estimated Sales: $3-5 Million
Number Employees: 1-4
Square Footage: 6000
Type of Packaging: Consumer, Food Service, Private Label, Bulk
Brands:
Nature's Mist
Pro-Life

2191 **Caputo Cheese**
1931 N 15th Ave
Melrose Park, IL 60160-1402
708-450-0074
Fax: 708-450-1670 sales@caputocheese.com
www.caputocheese.com
Dairy and cheese products, including fresh and greated cheeses.
President: Natale Caputo
Sales Manager: Renzo Berardi
General Manager: Brett Piccioni
Type of Packaging: Consumer, Food Service, Private Label, Bulk

2192 **Caracolillo Coffee Mills**
4419 N Hesperides St
Tampa, FL 33614-7618
813-876-0302
Fax: 813-875-6407 800-682-0023
info@ccmcoffee.com www.ccmcoffee.com
Coffee
President: Julian Faedo
info@ccmcoffee.com
Estimated Sales: $3-5 Million
Number Employees: 5-9
Type of Packaging: Consumer, Food Service, Private Label
Brands:
Cafe Quisqueva
Cafe Caracolillo Decafe
Cafe Caracolillo Expresso
Cafe Caracolillo Gourmet
Cafe Regil
Cafe Rico Rico
Cafe Riquisimo

2193 **Carando Gourmet Frozen Foods**
175 Main St
Agawam, MA 01001-1804
413-737-0183
Fax: 413-789-1653 888-227-2636
www.carandogourmet.com
Frozen food and entrees including roast beef, corned beef, pastrami, sauces, Italian stuffed pastas, gourmet meatballs, cabbage and sweet peppers
President/CEO/Chairman: Peter Carando Jr
CFO: Len Lumber
Director Sales: Brian Kelly
Plant Manager: Miguel Velez
Estimated Sales: $3.9 Million
Number Employees: 100-249
Parent Co: Carando Gourmet
Type of Packaging: Consumer, Food Service, Private Label, Bulk
Brands:
Carando Gourmet

2194 **Caraquet Ice Company**
20 Rue Du Quai
Caraquet, NB E1W 1B6
Canada
506-727-7211
Fax: 506-727-6769
Fresh and frozen seafood
President: Richard Albert
Type of Packaging: Bulk
Brands:
Caraquet

2195 **Caravan Company**
237 Chandler St
Worcester, MA 01609
508-752-3777
Fax: 508-753-4717
Coffee
President/Treasurer: George Drapos
Vice President: Arthur Drapos
Clerk: Alex Drapos
Estimated Sales: $2.1 Million
Number Employees: 17

2196 **CarbRite Diet**
3 Terminal Rd
New Brunswick, NJ 08901
732-545-3130
Fax: 732-509-0458 800-872-0101
info@carbritediet.com www.carbritediet.com
Low-carb snack bars and brownies
President: Danny Keller
VP: Robert Gluckin
Year Founded: 2000
Parent Co: Universal Nutrition

2197 **Carbon's Golden Malted**
4101 William Richardson Dr
South Bend, IN 46628
574-247-2270
Fax: 574-247-2280 800-253-0590
retail@goldenmalted.com www.goldenmalted.com
Manufacturer and market flour mix for pancakes and waffles
President: Rick Mc Keel
Chief Financial Officer: Brian Coyne
VP Sales and Marketing: Robert A. Coquillard
National and International Sales Manager: Tom McVey
Vice President of Operations: Mike McKeel
Number Employees: 1-4

2198 **Carborator Rental Svc**
6500 Eastwick Ave
PO Box 33327
Philadelphia, PA 19142-3399
215-726-8000
Fax: 215-726-6367 800-220-3556
info@carbonatorrental.com
www.carbonatorrental.com
Soda water syrups and bar mixes; wholesaler/distributor of beverage dispensing equipment
President: Andy Pincus
andy@carbonatorrental.com
Chairman: Herbert Pincus
Corporate Secretary: Susan Pincus
Vice President: Leatrice Pincus
Manager: Thomas Moreno
Production: George Rossi
Estimated Sales: $3.7 Million
Number Employees: 20-49
Square Footage: 80000

2199 **Cardi Foods**
1003 Sethcreek Drive
Fuquay Varina, NC 27526-5156
919-557-3866
schwescs@cs.com
Yeast extracts, kosher flavors
Vice President: Charles Schweizer
Estimated Sales: $150,000
Number Employees: 1
Number of Brands: 5
Number of Products: 10
Type of Packaging: Consumer, Food Service
Brands:
Cardi C

2200 **Cardinal Meat Specialists**
155 Hedgedale Road
Brampton, ON L6T 5P3
Canada
905-459-4436
Fax: 905-459-8099 800-363-1439
www.cardinalmeats.com
Hamburger patties and steaks
President: Brent Cator
Estimated Sales: $5-10 Million
Number Employees: 35
Type of Packaging: Food Service
Brands:
Cardinal Kettle
Roadhouse

2201 **Cardinale Winery**
7600 St Helena Hwy
Oakville, CA 94562
707-948-2643
Fax: 707-944-2824 800-588-0279
info@cardinale.com www.cardinale.com
Cabernet Sauvignon
Winemaker: Christopher Carpenter
ccarpenter@cardinale.com
Vineyard Manager: Pete Richmond
Estimated Sales: $20-50 Million
Number Employees: 50-99

2202 **Care Foods International**
4715 33rd St
Long Island, NY 11101-2407
718-392-3355
Fax: 718-392-2072
Coconut water and packaged dried fruit chips.
Vice President: Brian Lee
Type of Packaging: Private Label
Brands:
CoCo Well

2203 **Caremoli USA**
23959 580th Ave
Ames, IA 50010-9390
515-233-1255
Fax: 515-233-2933 www.caremoligroup.com
Ingredients of naturally processed grains, flours and fibers
President: Andrea Caremoli
a.caremoli@caremoli-usa.com
Quality Manager: Bethany Christensen
VP Sales/Marketing: Devin Miller
Sales Manager, North & South America: Carolina Calvert
Estimated Sales: $24 Million
Number Employees: 20-49

2204 **(HQ)Cargill Inc.**
P.O. Box 9300
Minneapolis, MN 55440-9300
800-227-4455
www.cargill.com
Stores, trades, processes and distributes grains, oilseeds, vegetable oils and meals; raises livestock and produces animal feed; produces food ingredients such as starches, glucose syrups, oils and fats.
Chairman/CEO: David MacLennan
CFO: David Dines
Chief Compliance Officer/General Counsel: Anna Richo
Cheif Human Resources Officer: LeighAnne Baker
Business Operations & Supply Chain: Ruth Kimmelshue
Year Founded: 1865
Estimated Sales: $114.6 Billion
Number Employees: 166,000

Type of Packaging: Bulk

2205 **Cargill Kitchen Solutions Inc.**
15407 McGinty Rd. W.
Wayzata, MN 55391
833-535-5205
CustomerService_Protein@Cargill.com
www.sunnyfresh.com
Eggs and breakfast products for foodservice operatos, convenience stores, chain restaurants, healthcare foodservice facilities, and schools.
Parent Co: Cargill Inc.
Type of Packaging: Bulk
Brands:
Sunny Fresh™

2206 **Cargill Protein**
825 E Douglas
Wichita, KS 67202
consumer_affairs@cargill.com
www.cargill.com/meat-poultry/protein-north-america
Beef, turkey, and swine products.
Chief Risk Officer, Protein & Salt: Brian Sikes
Number Employees: 28,000
Parent Co: Cargill Inc.
Type of Packaging: Food Service, Bulk

2207 **Caribbean Coffee Co**
495 Pine Ave # A
Goleta, CA 93117-3709
805-692-2200
Fax: 805-962-5074 800-932-5282
info@caribbeancoffee.com
www.caribbeancoffee.com
Over 100 varieties of specialty coffees and teas.
President: John Goerke
john@caribbeancoffee.com
Marketing Manager: Putnam Fairbanks
Estimated Sales: $20-50 Million
Number Employees: 10-19
Type of Packaging: Private Label

2208 **Caribbean Cookie Company**
515 Central Drive
Suite 103
Virginia Beach, VA 23454-5274
757-631-6767
Fax: 757-631-1725 800-326-5200
Gourmet cookies
President: Charles Phelps
Marketing Director: Leo Palomo
Estimated Sales: $1-2,500,000
Number Employees: 10-19

2209 **Caribbean Food DelightsInc**
117 Route 303 # B
Suite B
Tappan, NY 10983-2136
845-398-3000
Fax: 845-398-2316
info@caribbeanfooddelights.com
www.caribbeanfooddelights.com
Manufacturer and exporter of Jamaican baked goods including breads, fruit cakes and buns; also, beef, chicken and vegetable patties, jerk chicken, sausage, curried goat, rice, peas, etc
President/CEO: Vincent HoSang
CEO: Vincent Hosang
Estimated Sales: $10-20 Million
Number Employees: 50-99
Square Footage: 120000
Parent Co: Royal Caribbean Bakery
Type of Packaging: Consumer, Food Service, Private Label, Bulk

2210 **Caribbean Products**
3624 Falls Rd Ste 2
Baltimore, MD 21211
410-235-7700
Fax: 410-235-1513
Manufacturer and also processor and packager of beef and pork products.
President: Brian Hartman
bhartman@caribbeanproductsltd.com
Controller: Alan Wilner
Vice President: Mark Sheubrooks
Sales & Marketing Executive: Brad Ambill
Sales Executive: Jim Vogtman
Plant Manager: Scott Sheubrooks
Estimated Sales: $7.1 Million
Number Employees: 46
Type of Packaging: Consumer, Food Service

2211 **Caribou Coffee Co Inc**
Minneapolis, MN 55429
888-227-4268
www.cariboucoffee.com
Coffee
President & CEO: John Butcher
CFO: Mike Jensen
Brand Marketing Leader: Michelle Chester
Year Founded: 1992
Estimated Sales: $250,904,568
Number Employees: 5,000-9,999
Number of Brands: 1
Parent Co: JAB Holding Company

2212 **Carl Buddig & Co.**
950 W. 175th St.
Homewood, IL 60430
708-798-0900
Fax: 708-798-1284 888-633-5684
www.buddig.com
Luncheon meats including chipped beef, ham, turkey, chicken, pastrami and turkey ham; also, specialty sausage and meat snacks.
President: John Buddig
CEO: Robert Buddig
rbuddig@buddig.com
CFO: Peter Maciekewski
Executive VP: Thomas Buddig
Year Founded: 1886
Estimated Sales: $162 Million
Number Employees: 500-999
Number of Brands: 5
Square Footage: 15000
Type of Packaging: Consumer, Food Service, Private Label, Bulk
Brands:
Buddig Original
Deli Cuts
Fix Quix
Old Wisconsin
Carl Buddig Meats

2213 **Carl Rittberger Sr Inc**
1900 Lutz Ln
Zanesville, OH 43701-9260
740-452-2767
Fax: 740-452-6001 info@rittbergermeats.com
www.rittbergers.com
Beef and pork
President: Mark Mccabe
markmccabe@rittbergers.com
VP: George Rittberger
VP Sales: Mark McCabe
Estimated Sales: $4.5 Million
Number Employees: 10-19
Square Footage: 400000
Type of Packaging: Consumer, Bulk

2214 **Carl Venezia Fresh Meats**
1007 Germantown Pike
Plymouth Meeting, PA 19462-2449
610-239-6750
Fax: 610-239-6751 www.carlveneziameats.com
Processor and packer of meat
President: Carl Venezia
carlveneziameats@gmail.com
Sales Manager: Don Venezia
Estimated Sales: $500,000
Number Employees: 1-4

2215 **Carla's Pasta**
50 Talbot Ln
South Windsor, CT 06074
860-436-4042
www.carlaspasta.com
Pasta sauces and frozen pastas, including ravioli and lasagna.
Founder & President: Carla Squatrito
sergio@carlaspasta.com
VP, Business Development: Sandro Squatrito
VP, Operations: Sergio Squatrito
Year Founded: 1978
Estimated Sales: $21.20 Million
Number Employees: 50-99
Square Footage: 100000
Type of Packaging: Food Service, Private Label, Bulk

2216 **Carlisle Cereal Company**
PO Box 2775
Bismarck, ND 58502
701-222-3531
Fax: 701-222-3531 800-809-6018
Cereal
President: Charles Fleming
Estimated Sales: $1 Million
Number Employees: 5-9
Type of Packaging: Private Label
Brands:
Hometown Stars

2217 **Carlson Vineyards Winery**
461 35 Rd
Palisade, CO 81526-9518
970-464-5554
Fax: 970-464-5542 888-464-5554
www.carlsonvineyards.com
Wines
Owner: Garrett Portra
info@carlsonvineyards.com
Estimated Sales: $1-2.5 Million
Number Employees: 5-9

2218 **Carlton Farms**
P.O.Box 580
Carlton, OR 97111
503-852-7166
Fax: 503-852-6263 800-932-0946
rita@carltonfarms.com www.carltonfarms.com
Meats
President/CEO: Rita Duyn
Estimated Sales: $13 Million
Number Employees: 75

2219 **Carmadhy's Foods**
282 Marsland Drive
Waterloo, ON N2J 3Z1
Canada
519-746-0551
Fax: 519-746-0280
Flavored popcorn including caramel, butter, cheese, white cheddar, pizza, barbecue, ranch, salt and vinegar, sour cream and onion, dill pickle, jalapeno, custom packaging and popcorn seasoning
Proprietor: Dave Charlton
Number Employees: 5-9
Square Footage: 18000
Type of Packaging: Consumer, Private Label, Bulk
Brands:
Country Style
Olde Fashioned

2220 **Carmela's Gourmet**
415 English Ave
Monterey, CA 93940-3810
831-373-6291
Fax: 831-375-5313
Salad dressings
Owner: Carmela Cantisani
Co-Owner: Carmela Cantisani
Estimated Sales: Under $500,000
Number Employees: 1-4
Type of Packaging: Private Label
Brands:
Carmela's

2221 **Carmelita Provisions Company**
2901 W Floral Dr
Monterey Park, CA 91754-3626
323-262-6751
Fax: 323-262-3503
Pigs' feet including crackling and pickled; also, chorizo
Owner: Mario Lopez
Estimated Sales: $.5-1 million
Number Employees: 20-49
Type of Packaging: Consumer, Food Service

2222 **Carmenet Winery**
1680 Moon Mountain Rd
Sonoma, CA 95476-3087
707-996-3526
Fax: 707-996-5302
Wines
President: Tom Selfridge
CFO: Paul Ogarzelec
Public Relations: Lisa Yaple
General Manager: Paula Conwell
Estimated Sales: $5-10 Million
Number Employees: 10-19
Parent Co: Chalone Wine Group

2223 **(HQ)Carmi Flavor & Fragrance Company**
6030 Scott Way
Commerce, CA 90040-3516
323-888-9240
Fax: 323-888-9339 800-421-9647
sales@carmiflavors.com www.carmiflavors.com
High quality natural and artificial flavors in liquid or powder form; supplier of packaging products.
President: Eliot Carmi
CEO: Eliot Carmi
Chief Operating Officer: Dan Carmi
Estimated Sales: $12 Million
Number Employees: 40
Number of Brands: 1
Number of Products: 500
Square Footage: 60000
Type of Packaging: Private Label, Bulk
Other Locations:
Carmi Flavor & Fragrance
Port Coquitlam, Canada
Midwest Office & Manufacturing
Waverly IA
Southern Office & Warehouse
Lawrenceville GA
Brands:
Carmi Flavors
Flavor Depot

2224 **Carmine's Bakery**
2100 Country Club Road
Sanford, FL 32771-4051
407-328-4141
Fax: 407-324-1209 marlafrede@aol.com
Baked goods
Principal: John Schlater
Number Employees: 250 to 500

2225 **Carneros Creek Winery**
PO Box 8090
Napa, CA 94559
707-253-9464
Fax: 707-253-9465 www.mahoneyvineyards.com
Wines
President: Francis Mahoney
Winemaker: Ken Foster
Vice President: Scot Rich
Sales Director: Hadden Guridie
Plant Manager: Greg Opitz
Estimated Sales: $5-10 Million
Number Employees: 10-19
Type of Packaging: Bulk
Brands:
Carneros
Carneros Creek
Cote De Carneros
Fleur De Carneros

2226 **Carnival Brands Mfg**
5900 S Front St
New Orleans, LA 70115-2152
504-897-5454
Fax: 504-734-5886 800-925-2774
gumboking@aol.com www.carnivalbrands.com
French bisques, alligator sauce piquante, dry seasoning, boneless stuffed chicken, sauce mix and seafood entrees including gumbo, crab and shrimp cakes, shrimp Creole and crawfish etouffee
President: Raymond Rathle Jr
Vice President: Stephen Scott
Marketing: E Alexander Stafford
Public Relations: Simone Rathle
Estimated Sales: $1-2.5 Million
Number Employees: 5-9
Square Footage: 28000
Type of Packaging: Consumer, Food Service
Brands:
Baby Cakes
Carnival Cajun Classics
Chef Creole
Zipp

2227 **Caro Foods**
2324 Bayou Blue Rd
Houma, LA 70364
985-872-1483
Fax: 985-876-0825 800-395-2276
Fresh meat and produce, canned and dry goods.
Parent Co: Performance Food Group Company
Brands:
Heritage Ovens

2228 **Carob Tree**
1008 N Santa Anita Ave
Arcadia, CA 91006
626-445-0215
Fax: 626-445-0215
Natural groceries and vitamins
Owner: Hyun Chung
Estimated Sales: $160,000
Number Employees: 1-4
Type of Packaging: Consumer, Bulk

2229 **Carol Hall's Hot PepperJelly**
330 North Main Street
Fort Bragg, CA 95437
707-961-1899
Fax: 707-961-0879 866-737-7379
hall@mcn.org www.hotpepperjelly.com
Jams and condiments
President: Carol Hall
CFO: Albert Hall
Marketing Director: John Temples
Contact: William Hall
edward.getty@na.cokecce.com
Production Manager: Bill Hall
Estimated Sales: $1-2.5 Million
Number Employees: 5-9
Type of Packaging: Private Label

2230 **Carol Lee Donuts**
104 S 5th St
Salina, KS 67401-2804
785-827-2402
www.carolleedonutssalina.com
Blended mixes for bakery products including yeast raised and cake doughnuts, danish, breads and cookies
Owner: Hong Kim
carolleedonutssalina@gmail.com
VP: Agnes Scott
Estimated Sales: Less Than $500,000
Number Employees: 1-4
Square Footage: 27990
Type of Packaging: Consumer
Brands:
Carol Lee

2231 **Carol's Country Cuisine**
2546 Warm Springs Road
Glen Ellen, CA 95442-8712
707-996-1124
Fax: 707-996-1124 carolco@vom.com
Marinades, dressings, sauces
Partner & Production Manager: Carol Frankenfield
carolco@vom.com
Sales Director: Susan Wise
Estimated Sales: $5-10 Million
Number Employees: 5-9
Type of Packaging: Private Label

2232 **Carole's Cheesecake Company**
1275 Castlefield Ave
Toronto, ON M6B 1G3
Canada
416-256-0000
Fax: 416-256-0001 www.carolescheesecake.com
cheesecakes including praline, lemon, blueberry, raspberry and strawberry; also, pies, low-fat salad dressings, pasta sauces and toppings for cakes and ice cream.
President: Edison Carbajal
CEO: Carole Ogus
Executive VP: Michael Ogus
Estimated Sales: $1-5 Million
Number Employees: 30
Number of Brands: 2
Number of Products: 160
Square Footage: 60000
Type of Packaging: Consumer, Food Service, Private Label
Brands:
Carole's
Carole's Tops
Positively Blueberry
Positively Pralines
Positively Strawberry

2233 **Carolina Atlantic Seafood Enterprises**
PO Box 158
Beaufort, NC 28516-0158
252-504-2663
Fax: 252-726-7097
Frozen seafood
President: Doug Brady
CEO: Walter C Brady
Estimated Sales: $5-10,000,000
Number Employees: 10-19
Type of Packaging: Private Label
Brands:
Carolina Atlantic Seafood

2234 **(HQ)Carolina Beverage Corp**
1413 Jake Alexander Blvd S
Salisbury, NC 28146-8359
704-633-4550
Fax: 704-633-7491 custserv@cheerwine.com
www.cheerwine.com
Syrups and beverage concentrates; exporter of soft drinks and concentrates; wholesaler/distributor of soft drinks and water
President: Clift Ritchie
critchie@carolinabottlingcompanyinc.com
CFO: Tommy Page
CIO: Bill Barten
VP Operations: David Swaim
Estimated Sales: $10-20 Million
Number Employees: 20-49
Square Footage: 75000
Parent Co: Cheerwine & Diet Cheerwine
Type of Packaging: Consumer
Other Locations:
Carolina Beverage Corp.
Hickory NC
Carolina Beverage Corp.
Greenville SC
Brands:
Cheerwine
Cheerwine Soft Drink
Diet Cheerwine
Savage Energy

2235 **Carolina Blueberry Co-Op Assn**
11421 US Highway 701 N
P.O. Box 368
Garland, NC 28441-9642
910-588-4220
Fax: 910-588-4297 www.carolinablueberry.com
Fresh and frozen blueberries
General Manager: Rod Bangert
rbangert@carolinablueberry.com
Process Facility Manager: Sonny Parker
Estimated Sales: Less Than $500,000
Number Employees: 1-4
Type of Packaging: Consumer, Food Service, Bulk
Brands:
Bonnie Blue

2236 **Carolina Brewery**
460 W Franklin St
Chapel Hill, NC 27516-2313
919-942-1800
Fax: 919-942-1809 www.carolinabrewery.com
Ale, stout and lager
Owner: Robert Poitras
rcpoitras@aol.com
Co-Owner: Chris Rice
Estimated Sales: $2.5-5 Million
Number Employees: 50-99
Square Footage: 32000
Type of Packaging: Consumer, Food Service, Bulk
Brands:
Copperline Amber
Franklin Street
Old North State

2237 **Carolina Classics Catfish Inc**
7178 NC 11 S
P.O. Box 10
Ayden, NC 28513-8404
252-746-2818
Fax: 252-746-3947 www.cccatfish.com
Fresh and frozen catfish
President: Robert Mayo
rmayo@cccatfish.com
Accounting Manager: Mike Walker
Sales Manager: Doug Doering
Sales Manager: Jeff Betcher
VP Operations: Mike McCready
Controller: Mark Lomis
Estimated Sales: $20-50 Million
Number Employees: 100-249
Type of Packaging: Consumer, Food Service
Brands:
Carolina Classics

2238 **Carolina Cookie Co**
1010 Arnold St
Greensboro, NC 27405-7102
336-294-2100
Fax: 336-294-9537 800-447-5797
gary@carolinacookie.com
www.carolinacookie.com
Cookies
Owner: Chris Belton
chris@carolinacookie.com
Estimated Sales: $3,000,000
Number Employees: 100-249
Square Footage: 24000

2239 **Carolina Cracker**
P.O.Box 374
Garner, NC 27529-0374
919-779-6899
Fax: 919-779-6899 www.carolinacracker.net
Nut crackers for soft shell nuts, shelled pecans in bulk
President: Dot Woodruff
CEO: Harold Woodruff
Estimated Sales: $1-2.5 Million
Number Employees: 10-19
Number of Brands: 3
Square Footage: 4
Type of Packaging: Bulk
Brands:
The Carolina Cracker

2240 **Carolina Fine Snacks**
209 Citation Ct
Greensboro, NC 27409-9026
336-605-0773
Fax: 336-605-0721
Nutrional snacks
Owner: Echo Frye
echo@carolinafinesnacks.com
Estimated Sales: $2.5-5,000,000
Number Employees: 20-49

2241 **Carolina Food Company**
3642 South 106th East Place
Tulsa, OK 74146
918-519-9338
toastedyum@hotmail.com
www.toastedwinespreads.com
Manufacturer of wine and fruit flavored spread.
Founder: Corey Carolina
corey.carolina@hotmail.com

2242 **Carolina Foods Inc**
1807 S Tryon St
Charlotte, NC 28203
704-333-9812
800-234-0441
www.carolinafoodsinc.com
Baked goods including sweet rolls, fresh and frozen fried pies, yeast raised doughnuts and cakes, fruit turnovers and pie dough
President: Paul Scarborough
proach@carolinafoods.com
VP of Operations: Kent Byrom
Estimated Sales: $20-50 Million
Number Employees: 250-499
Number of Brands: 3
Square Footage: 110000
Type of Packaging: Consumer, Food Service, Private Label
Brands:
Duchess
O'Boy
Sunbeam

2243 **Carolina Ingredients Inc**
1595 Cedar Lane Dr
Rock Hill, SC 29730
803-323-6550
Fax: 803-323-6535 www.carolinaingredients.com
Ingredients
President: Doug Meyer-Cuno
Manager of Sales: Kyle Jones
Contact: Mike Cantore
mcantore@carolinaingredients.com
Production Manager: Richard Dawes
Purchasing Director: Glenn Shishido
Number Employees: 5-9

2244 **Carolina Innovative Food Ingredients, Inc.**
4626 Coleman Dr
Nashville, NC 27856
252-462-1551
info@cifi1.com
cifingredients.com
Domestic manufacturer of sweet potato juice concentrates and dehydrated sweet potato ingredients.
President: Jim Nagey
CEO: John Kimber

2245 **Carolina Packers Inc**
2999 S Brightleaf Blvd
Smithfield, NC 27577
800-682-7675
info@carolinapackers.com
www.carolinapackers.com
Hot dogs, bologna, smoked sausage, ham and chili
President: Kent Denning
kdenning@carolinapackers.com
Year Founded: 1940
Estimated Sales: $20-50 Million
Number Employees: 100-249
Number of Brands: 1
Type of Packaging: Consumer, Bulk
Brands:
Bright Leaf

2246 **Carolina Pride Foods**
1 Packer Ave.
Greenwood, SC 29646
864-229-5611
Fax: 864-229-0541 www.carolinapride.com
Fresh pork and bacon, smoked meats and processed luncheon meats including deli loaves and bologna; exporter of skinned jowls, pork kidneys, liver and stomachs, flat belly skins, etc.
President: Michael Cox
CFO: Mark Litts
Year Founded: 1920
Estimated Sales: $185 Million
Number Employees: 500-999
Number of Brands: 1
Square Footage: 250000
Type of Packaging: Consumer, Food Service, Private Label, Bulk
Brands:
Carolina Pride

2247 **Carolina Pride Products**
24488 Nc Highway 561
Enfield, NC 27823
252-445-3154
Fax: 252-445-1033
Sweet potatoes
President: Jake Taylor
Estimated Sales: $1-2.5 Million
Number Employees: 1-4
Brands:
Carolina Pride

2248 **Carolina Products**
5519 W. Idlewild Ave.
Tampa, FL 33634
813-313-1800
Fax: 813-881-1926 info@cott.com
www.cliffstar.com
Bottled apple juice
President, CEO: Steven Kitching
Chief Executive Officer: Jerry Fowden
Chief Financial Officer: Jay Wells
Senior Vice President: Gregory Leiter
Quality Control: Angela Lewis
VP Human Resources: Michael Creamer
VP General Counsel: Marni Morgan Poe
Purchasing: Dennis Jones
Estimated Sales: $10-20 Million
Number Employees: 20-49
Square Footage: 58000
Parent Co: Cliffstar
Type of Packaging: Consumer, Private Label
Brands:
Carolina Gold

2249 **Carolina Summit Mountain Spring Water**
6557 Garden Road
Unit 9
Riviera Beach, FL 33404-6307
561-841-8841
Fax: 828-743-5483 water123@bellsouth.net
bottledwater123.com
Bottled water
President: Tom Mitchell
Estimated Sales: $1-2.5 Million
Number Employees: 10-19
Parent Co: Mountain Valley Spring Company

2250 **Carolina Treet**
Po Box 1017
Wilmington, NC 28402
910-762-1950
Fax: 910-762-1438 800-616-6344
info@carolinatreet.com www.carolinatreet.com
Processor and importer of barbecue sauce, condiments, syrups, brewed tea, bar mixes and beverage concentrates
President: Joe King
Vice President: Lenwood King
General Manager: Allen Finberg
Estimated Sales: $1.4 Million
Number Employees: 13
Number of Brands: 5
Number of Products: 20
Square Footage: 80000
Type of Packaging: Consumer, Food Service, Private Label, Bulk
Brands:
Aunt Bertie's
Carolina Treet

2251 **Carolyn's Gourmet**
40 Beharrell St Ste 2
Concord, MA 01742
978-369-2940
Fax: 978-371-0639 800-656-2940
Pecans, walnuts, peanuts, English toffee, chocolate bars
President: Hans van Putten
Executive VP: Tracey van Putten
Estimated Sales: $5-10 Million
Number Employees: 5-9
Parent Co: 40ParkLake, LLC
Type of Packaging: Consumer, Private Label, Bulk
Brands:
Tulip

2252 **Carousel Cakes**
5 Seeger Dr
Suite 3
Nanuet, NY 10954-2332
845-627-2323
Fax: 845-627-0258 800-659-2253
info@carouselcakes.com www.carouselcakes.com
Fresh and frozen cakes, mousse, cheesecakes and pies, kosher pdairy and non-dairy products
Owner: David Finkelstein
david@carouselcakes.com
Estimated Sales: $500,000-$1 Million
Number Employees: 10-19
Type of Packaging: Consumer, Food Service
Brands:
Carousel Cakes

2253 **Carousel Candies**
2248 Gary Ln
Geneva, IL 60134-2519
630-232-2500
Fax: 708-656-0010 888-656-1552
info@silvestrisweets.com
Candy including caramel, caramel apples, caramel sauce, chocolates, chocolate covered strawberries, gift boxes, gift baskets, assortments, bulk, and special occasion gift bags for holidays and special events.
President: Andy Silvestri
andy@carouselcandy.com
Vice President: Andy Silvestri
Estimated Sales: $2.5-5 Million
Number Employees: 10-19
Type of Packaging: Food Service, Bulk
Brands:
Carousel

2254 **Carr Cheese Factory/GileCheese Company**
116 North Main Street
Cuba City, WI 53807
608-744-8455
Fax: 608-744-3457 www.gilecheese.com
Cheese and cheese products
Owner: John Gile
Owner: Diane Gile
Contact: Tim Gile
tim@gilecheese.com
Estimated Sales: $2.5-5 Million
Number Employees: 1-4

2255 **Carr Valley Cheese**
1675 Lincoln Ave
Fennimore, WI 53809-2101
608-822-6416
Fax: 608-822-3505 800-462-7258
www.carrvalleycheese.com

Cheese
National Sales Manager: Beth Wyttenbach
Manager: Sid Cook
sid@carrvalleycheese.com
Manager: Linda Parrish
Estimated Sales: $2.5-5 Million
Number Employees: 10-19
Type of Packaging: Consumer, Private Label, Bulk
Brands:
Bahl Baby

2256 **Carr Valley Cheese Company**
S3797 County G
La Valle, WI 53941
608-986-2781
Fax: 608-986-2906 800-462-7258
www.carrvalleycheese.com

Monterey jack, cheddar and colby cheese, butter, jams, jellies and sausage.
President: Sid Cook
National Sales Manager: Beth Wyttenbach
Estimated Sales: $15 Million
Number Employees: 25
Number of Brands: 1
Brands:
Carr Valley

2257 **Carrabassett Coffee Roasters**
2 Mountain View Rd
North Main St.
Kingfield, ME 4947
207-265-2326
Fax: 207-265-3527 888-292-2326
carrcoff@tdstelme.net
www.carrabassettcoffee.com

Roaster and wholesaler of coffee
Owner: Tom Hildreth
carrcoff@tds.com
CEO: Steve Skaling
Estimated Sales: Less Than $500,000
Number Employees: 5-9
Number of Brands: 35
Number of Products: 1
Square Footage: 7200
Type of Packaging: Bulk
Brands:
35

2258 **Carriage House Foods**
1131 Dayton Ave
Ames, IA 50010
515-232-2273
Fax: 515-232-3003

Frozen meat products
President: Jerry Grauf
Plant Manager: Jim Ringelstetter
Estimated Sales: $7.5 Million
Number Employees: 35
Type of Packaging: Consumer, Food Service, Private Label
Brands:
Carriage House

2259 **Carrie's Chocolates**
9216-63 Avenue
Edmonton, AB T6E 0G3
Canada
780-435-7900
877-778-2462

Processor and exporter of handmade novelty and gift chocolates, promotional bars, and wedding candy
Owner: Carrie MacKenzie
Number Employees: 2
Square Footage: 1800
Type of Packaging: Consumer, Food Service, Private Label, Bulk

2260 **Carriere Foods Inc**
540 Chemin Des Patriotes
Saint-Denis-Sur-Richelie, QC J0H 1K0
Canada
450-787-3411
Fax: 450-787-3537 marketing@carrierefoods.com
www.bonduelle.ca

Manufacturer and exporter of frozen and canned vegetables and fruits including peas, waxed beans, chick peas, green beans, asparagus and corn, dried beans, blueberries, cranberries, rasberries, rhubarb, strawberries, soups and sauces;importer of asparagus, carrots and spinach
President: Marcel Ostiguy
Number Employees: 250-499
Type of Packaging: Consumer, Private Label
Brands:
Arctica Gardens
Avon
Carriere
Festino
Graves
Paula
Sunny Farm
Stokely

2261 **Carrington Foods Co Inc**
200 Jacintoport Blvd
PO Box 509
Saraland, AL 36571-3397
251-675-9700
Fax: 251-679-8721 www.carringtonfoods.com

Frozen seafood including stuffed flounder, crab and shrimp
President: David Carrington Sr
Secretary: Sally Carrington
IT: Joshua Boozer
joshua@carringtonfoods.com
Estimated Sales: $10-20 Million
Number Employees: 100-249
Type of Packaging: Consumer, Food Service
Brands:
Miss Sally's

2262 **Carrington Tea Co.**
PO Box 102
Closter, NJ 07624
800-505-9546
support@carringtontea.com

Green, black, herbal and organic teas
Number of Brands: 1
Number of Products: 4
Type of Packaging: Consumer
Brands:
CARRINGTON TEA

2263 **Carrousel Cellars**
2825 Day Road
Gilroy, CA 95020-8827
408-847-2060
Fax: 831-424-1077

Wines
Winemaker: John DeSantis
Number Employees: 20-49

2264 **Carson City Pickle Company**
7451 S Garlock Rd
Carson City, MI 48811
989-584-3148
Fax: 517-879-2146

Produce including cucumbers, pickles and pickled and brined vegetables
Manager: Mike Zwerk
Contact: Wyatt Waldron
police@carsoncitymi.com
Manager: Rudy Montoya
Estimated Sales: $1-2.5 Million
Number Employees: 1-4
Parent Co: Funk Enterprises
Type of Packaging: Consumer, Food Service, Bulk

2265 **Carta Blanca**
3912 Frutas Ave
El Paso, TX 79905-1316
915-544-6367
Fax: 915-544-0109

Beer
Manager: Carmen Bitar
Contact: Elias Ceballos
elias.ceballos@grupodelavega.com
General Manager: Miriam De La Vega
Estimated Sales: $1-3,000,000
Number Employees: 1-4

2266 **Carve Nutrition**
114 Washington Blvd
Suite B
Marina Del Rey, CA 90292
310-905-8100
hello@carvenutrition.com
carvenutrition.com

Cookie alternative
CEO: Joey Adler
Number of Brands: 1
Number of Products: 4
Type of Packaging: Consumer
Brands:
CARVE COOKIE

2267 **Cary Randall's Sauces & Dressings**
PO Box 363
Highlands, NJ 07732-0363
732-872-6353
Fax: 732-872-2035

Fat-free all natural salad dressing, hot sauce
Contact: Cary Lazon
Estimated Sales: Under $500,000
Number Employees: 1-4

2268 **Cary's of Oregon**
413 Union Ave
Grants Pass, OR 97527-5541
541-474-0030
Fax: 541-474-5924 888-822-9300

English toffee in 7 different flavors.
Number Employees: 10-19

2269 **Casa Di Lisio Products Inc**
486 Lexington Ave # 3
Mt Kisco, NY 10549-2779
914-666-5021
Fax: 914-666-7209 800-247-4199
info@casadilisio.com www.casadilisio.com

Frozen Italian sauces including walnut and sun dried tomato pesto, clam, marinara, puttanesca, basil pesto, cilantro pesto provencal,alfredo and roasted red peppers pest
Owner: Linda DiLisio
ldilisio@kitchencooked.net
VP: Lucy DiLisio
Year Founded: 1973
Estimated Sales: $20-50 Million
Number Employees: 50-99
Number of Brands: 1
Number of Products: 25
Square Footage: 4000
Type of Packaging: Consumer, Food Service, Private Label, Bulk
Brands:
Casa Dilisio

2270 **Casa Larga Vineyards**
2287 Turk Hill Rd
Fairport, NY 14450-9579
585-223-4210
Fax: 585-223-8899 info@casalarga.com
www.casalarga.com

Wines
President: Andrew Colaruotolo
acolaruotolo@casalarga.com
Wine-Making Director: John Colaruotolo
Director, Accounting/IT: Mary Jo Colaruotolo
Marketing Director: Andrea Colaruotolo
Estimated Sales: $1-9 Million
Number Employees: 20-49
Square Footage: 20
Type of Packaging: Private Label

2271 **Casa Nuestra Winery & Vineyard**
3451 Silverado Trl N
St Helena, CA 94574-9662
707-963-5783
Fax: 707-963-3174 866-844-9463
info@casanuestra.com

Wine
Owner: Shane Brown
brownshane@commission-tracker.com
Co-owner: Cody Gillette Kirkham
General Manager: Katrina Kirkham
Marketing Manager/Apprentice Winemaker: Stephanie Zacharia
Chief Winemaker: Allen Price
Production Assistant: Hector Ortiz
Estimated Sales: $500,000
Number Employees: 5-9
Brands:
Casa Nuestra

2272 **Casa Sanchez Foods**
P.O. Box 12582
San Francisco, CA 94112
650-697-7525
Fax: 650-697-1810 877-227-2726
info@casasanchez.com
www.casasanchez.com/index.html
Guacamole and salsas
Contact: Roger Esponilla
roger@casasanchez.com

2273 **Casa Valdez Inc**
502 E Chicago St
Caldwell, ID 83605-3337
208-459-6461
Fax: 208-459-4154 www.casavaldez.com
Corn and flour tortillas
Owner: Jose Valdez
joejr@casavaldez.com
Sales/Marketting: Joe Romero
Estimated Sales: $2 Million
Number Employees: 20-49

2274 **(HQ)Casa Visco**
819 Kings Rd
Schenectady, NY 12303-2627
518-377-8814
Fax: 518-377-8269 888-607-2823
www.casavisco.com
Kosher products including spaghetti and barbecue sauces, salsa and mustard; exporter of spaghetti sauce
Owner: Joe Viscusi
info@casavisco.com
VP: Michael Viscusi
Sales & Marketing: Adine Gallo
Production Manager: Michael Viscusi, Jr.
Estimated Sales: $1-2.5 Million
Number Employees: 5-9
Square Footage: 100000
Parent Co: Casa Visco Finer Food
Type of Packaging: Consumer, Food Service, Private Label, Bulk
Brands:
Casa Visco
My Country Sweet
Schabers

2275 **Casa di Carfagna**
1405 E Dublin Granville Rd
Columbus, OH 43229-3357
614-846-6340
Fax: 614-846-0937 www.carfagnas.com
Italian sausages, frozen Italian meals and sauces
President: Sam Carfagna
Estimated Sales: $5-10 Million
Number Employees: 50-99
Brands:
Carfagna

2276 **Casablanca Foods LLC**
P.O. Box 287447
New York, NY 10128-0025
212-317-1111
Fax: 866-530-3110 contact@casablancafoods.com
www.casablancafoods.com
Moroccan inspired spices and sauces.
Founder: Mina Kallamni
Estimated Sales: $100,000
Number Employees: 8
Type of Packaging: Private Label
Brands:
Mina

2277 **Casablanca Market**
8430 Central Ave
Suite 3A
Newark, CA 94560-3446
650-964-3000
info@casablancamarket.com
casablancamarket.com
Soy sauce; curry; spreads; marinades; olives; pickles and pickled vegetables
President: Katia Essyad
Type of Packaging: Private Label

2278 **Casados Farms**
201 State Road 582
Ohkay Owingeh, NM 87566
505-852-2433
Dried and dehydrated fruits
President: Peter Casados
Estimated Sales: $200,000
Number Employees: 10-19

Type of Packaging: Consumer

2279 **Casani Candy Company**
7905 Browning Rd.
Ste. 208
Pennsauken, NJ 08109
856-488-0045
Fax: 456-488-2645 www.casanicandyco.com
Confectionery ingredients
Chairman: John Lees
President: Joey Traynor
VP: Joseph Lees
Contact: Joe Lees
jlees55@comcast.net
Manager: John Lees
Estimated Sales: $2.5-5 000,000
Number Employees: 10-19

2280 **Cascade Cheese Co**
302 E Water St
Cascade, WI 53011-1606
920-528-8221
Fax: 920-528-7473 trade.eatwisconsincheese.com
Provolone, mozzarella
Owner: Joel Narges
jnarges@wmmb.com
Treasurer: Elizabeth Babler
Estimated Sales: $2.4 Million
Number Employees: 20-49

2281 **Cascade Clear Water**
4804 NW Bethany Blvd
I-2, #228
Portland, OR 97229
800-888-3879
Fax: 503-616-7971 www.cascadeh2o.com
Clear water
President, CEO: Douglas Mason
Managing Director International Div: Robert Allen
Estimated Sales: $2.5-5 Million
Number Employees: 20-49
Parent Co: Cleary Canadian Beverage Company

2282 **Cascade Coffee**
1525 75th St SW # 100
Suite 100
Everett, WA 98203-7007
425-347-3995
Fax: 425-347-5076 800-995-9655
info@cascadecoffee.com www.cascadecoffee.com
Custom coffee roasting and packaging.
President: Kelly Johnson
Chairman/Chief Executive Officer: Phil Johnson
Chief Financial Officer: Nick Jonson
VP, Product Development: Patrick Lyon
Director, Quality Assurance: Nichole Hyde
Director, Engineering & Maintenance: Jerry Klobertanz
Plant Manager: Todd Larson
Estimated Sales: $20-50 Million
Number Employees: 100-249
Type of Packaging: Private Label
Brands:
Organic Altura
Organic Mexican Altura
Organic Sierra Madre Blend

2283 **Cascade Fresh**
14300 Greenwood Ave N Ste E
Seattle, WA 98133
206-363-0991
Fax: 206-363-8191 800-511-0057
yogurt@cascadefresh.com
Fat free, low fat and whole milk yogurts, as well as Greek and Mediterranean style yogurts, sour cream and açaí, peach, raspberry and strawberry smoothies.
President: Satshakti Khalsa
Estimated Sales: $2,600,000
Number Employees: 10-19
Brands:
Cascade Fresh

2284 **Cascade Mountain Winery**
835 Cascade Road
Amenia, NY 12501
845-373-9021
Fax: 845-373-7869 info@cascademt.com
www.cascademt.com
Processor and exporter of dry and semi-dry and nonsweet table wines
Owner: William Wathmore
CEO: Margaret Wetmore
Estimated Sales: $3-5 Million
Number Employees: 5-9

Number of Products: 8
Square Footage: 24000
Type of Packaging: Consumer

2285 **Cascade Specialties, Inc.**
1 Cascade Way
Boardman, OR 97818
541-481-2522
Fax: 541-481-2640 www.cascadespec.com
Dehydrated onion products.
Owner: Fraser Hawley
CEO: Suvan Sharma
Director of Quality: Tina Kovscek
General Manager: Carl Hearn
Production Manager: Jerry Dyer
Estimated Sales: $5-10 Million
Number Employees: 20-49
Parent Co: JAIN
Other Locations:
Port Warehouse
Boardman OR
Brands:
Cascade Specialties

2286 **Cascadian Farm Inc**
719 Metcalf St
Sedro Woolley, WA 98284-1456
360-855-0542
Fax: 360-855-0444 www.cascadianfarm.com
Processor, importer, manufacturer and marketer of frozen organic foods including fruits, vegetables and juice concentrates; also pickles and fruit spreads.
President: Maria Morgan
CEO: Steve Sanger
Estimated Sales: $10-20 Million
Number Employees: 50-99
Square Footage: 28930
Parent Co: Small Planet Foods
Type of Packaging: Consumer, Food Service, Bulk
Other Locations:
Cascadian Farm
Napa CA
Brands:
Cascadian Farm
Fantastic Foods
Muir Glen
Small Planet Foods

2287 **(HQ)Case Farms**
385 Pilch Rd
Troutman, NC 28166
704-528-4501
Fax: 704-528-4277 www.casefarms.com
Fresh, partially-cooked and frozen-for-export poultry products.
Chairman & CEO: Tom Shelton
President & COO: Kevin Phillips
Year Founded: 1986
Estimated Sales: $138.4 Million
Number Employees: 3,200
Other Locations:
Dudley NC
Winesburg OH
Goldsboro NC
Morganton NC
Strasburg OH
Mt. Olive NC
Shelby NC
Massillon OH
Troutman NC

2288 **Case Farms Ohio Division**
1818 County Road 160
Winesburg, OH 44690
330-359-7141
www.casefarms.com
Fresh, partially-cooked and frozen-for-export poultry products.
Parent Co: Case Farms
Type of Packaging: Private Label
Brands:
Case Farms Amish Country

2289 **Case Side Holdings Company**
37 Garden Dr
Kensington, PE C0B 1M0
Canada
902-836-4214
Fax: 902-836-3297
Bread, muffins, biscuits, scones, doughnuts, cookies, pastries, cakes and pies
President: Don Caseley
VP & Manager Director: Trudy Caseley
Secretary: Roy Hogan
Estimated Sales: $752,000
Number Employees: 15

Type of Packaging: Private Label

2290 **Casey Fisheries**
PO Box 86
Digby, NS B0V 1A0
Canada
902-245-5801
Fax: 902-245-5552 info@caseyfisheries.com
www.caseyfisheries.com
Processor and exporter of fresh and frozen scallops and salmon
President: Joseph Casey
Plant Manager: Duncan Casey
Estimated Sales: $1.6 Million
Number Employees: 15
Type of Packaging: Consumer, Food Service, Private Label, Bulk

2291 **Casey's Seafood Inc**
807 Jefferson Ave
Newport News, VA 23607-6117
757-928-1979
Fax: 757-928-0257 www.caseysseafood.com
Canned and frozen blue crab meat; also, heat and serve gourmet crab cakes and deviled crabs and crawfish cakes
Owner: Jim Casey
jim@caseysseafood.com
Marketing Director: Mike Casey
Estimated Sales: $3 Million
Number Employees: 50-99
Square Footage: 40000
Type of Packaging: Consumer, Food Service
Brands:
Casey's
Chesapeake Bay's Finest

2292 **Casino Bakery**
2726 N 36th St
Tampa, FL 33605-3126
813-242-0311
Fax: 813-242-4691
Cuban bread
Owner: Mark N Muhsen
Estimated Sales: $1-2.5 Million
Number Employees: 10-19
Type of Packaging: Consumer, Food Service

2293 **Casper Foodservice Company**
310 N Green St
Chicago, IL 60607-1300
312-226-2265
Fax: 312-226-2686
President: Thomas Casper
Estimated Sales: $1-3 Million
Number Employees: 10-19

2294 **Casper's Ice Cream**
11805 N 200 E
Richmond, UT 84333-1408
435-258-2477
Fax: 435-258-5633 800-772-4182
fatboy@fatboyicecream.com
Ice cream novelties including sandwiches and nut sundaes on a stick
President: Kyle Smith
CEO: Paul Merrill
Vice President: Shane Petersen
Vice President: Keith Lawes
Estimated Sales: $35 Million
Number Employees: 175
Square Footage: 184000
Type of Packaging: Consumer, Food Service, Private Label, Bulk
Brands:
Fat Boy

2295 **Cass-Clay Creamery**
200 20th St N
PO Box 3126
Fargo, ND 58102-4136
701-293-6455
Fax: 701-241-9154
Liquid milk, ice cream, dips, sour cream, cream & butter, juice, cottage cheese, and yogurt.
Cio/Cto: Kurt Quiggle
kurtquig@msn.com
Marketing: Rachel Kyllo
Sales Manager: Brian Day
Plant Manager: Troy Anderson
Purchasing: Brenda Hartmann
Estimated Sales: $28.9 Million
Number Employees: 320
Number of Brands: 1
Square Footage: 5000
Parent Co: Kemps LLC
Type of Packaging: Consumer, Food Service, Private Label, Bulk
Brands:
Cass-Clay

2296 **Cassandra's Gourmet Classics/Island Treasures Gourmet**
10681 Wakeman Ct.
Manassas, VA 20110
703-590-7900
www.cassandrasgourmet.com
Manufacturer of rum cakes.
President: Cassandra Craig
General Manager: Pam Brewster
VP/Sales Manager: Ken Craig
Type of Packaging: Private Label
Brands:
Island Treasures Gourmet

2297 **Castella Imports Inc**
120 A Wilshire Blvd
Brentwood, NY 11717
631-231-5500
Cheeses, spices, olives and olive oils
Estimated Sales: $100+ Million
Number Employees: 250-499
Square Footage: 66000

2298 **(HQ)Castellini Group**
PO Box 721610
Newport, KY 41072-1610
800-233-8560
info@castellinicompany.com
www.castellinicompany.com
Produce; private labeling and custom packaging; also, transportation company offering a 48 state authority of transporting
CEO: Brian Kocher
Number Employees: 250-499
Type of Packaging: Consumer, Food Service, Private Label, Bulk
Brands:
Castellini
Club Chef
Crosset Company
General Produce
Grant County Foods
RWI Logistics

2299 **Castello di Borghese Vineyard**
17150 Rte 48
Cutchogue, NY 11935
631-734-5111
Fax: 631-734-5485 info@castellodiborghese.com
castellodiborghese.com
Vineyard and winery
Owner: Marco Borghese
Owner: Ann Marie Borghese
Estimated Sales: $500-1 Million appx.
Number Employees: 10-19
Type of Packaging: Private Label
Brands:
Hargrave Vineyards

2300 **Castle Beverages Inc**
105 Myrtle Ave
Ansonia, CT 06401-2099
203-734-0883
Carbonated beverages
President & General Manager: David Pantalone
Estimated Sales: $2.5-5,000,000
Number Employees: 5-9
Brands:
Castle Beverages
Castle Carbonated Beverages

2301 **(HQ)Castle Cheese**
2850 Perry Hwy
Slippery Rock, PA 16057
724-368-3022
Fax: 724-368-9456 800-252-4373
Processor and exporter of cheese foods including substitutes, imitation and natural blends
President: George Myrter
Purchasing Manager: Michelle Sabol
Estimated Sales: $370,000
Number Employees: 2
Square Footage: 13112
Type of Packaging: Consumer, Food Service, Private Label, Bulk
Other Locations:
Castle Cheese
Vernon BC
Brands:
Castle Cheese
Vernon Bc

2302 **Castle Hill Lobster**
333 Linebrook Rd
Suite R
Ipswich, MA 01938-1146
978-356-3947
Fax: 978-356-9883
Whole seafoods; lobsters
Owner: Robert Marcaurelle
Contact: Dennis Wilke
dennis.wilke@castlehillco.com
Estimated Sales: $2 Million
Number Employees: 1-4
Type of Packaging: Food Service

2303 **Castle Rock Meats**
707 E 50th Ave
Denver, CO 80216-2006
303-292-0855
Fax: 303-292-0680
Meats
President: Michael Andrade
Plant Manager: Allen Rigby
Estimated Sales: $20-50 Million
Number Employees: 20-49

2304 **Castor River Farms**
Dexter, MO 63841
castorriverfarms.com
Long grain white and brown rice
Principal: Johnny Hunter

Brands:
Castor River Farms

2305 **Casual Gourmet Foods**
4500 140th Avenue N
Suite 113
Clearwater, FL 33762-3827
727-298-8307
Fax: 727-298-0616 info@cgfoods.com
www.cgfoods.com
Fully-cooked, all-natural chicken sausages and chicken burgers. Turkey sausage
Marketing/Sales: David Canarelli
Public Relations: Ben Rizzo
Operations/Production/Plant Manager: Robert Hapanowicz
Number Employees: 5-9

2306 **Casually Gourmet**
PO Box 143
New Haven, VT 5472
80- 63- 760
Fax: 802-870-3061 800-639-7604
info@casuallygourmet.com www.gormlys.com
Pancake and scone mixes, jellies, preserves, mustards, barbecue sauce and spiced apple cider concentrate
President: Bill Gormly
Estimated Sales: $500,000 appx.
Number Employees: 5-9
Square Footage: 19000
Type of Packaging: Consumer, Food Service, Private Label

2307 **Catamount Specialties of Vermont**
8053 US Route 2
PO BOX 275
Plainfield, VT 05667
802-253-4525
Fax: 802-253-6933 800-639-2406
debhillld@myfairpoint.net
www.catamountspecialties.com
Produces mustards, salsas, BBQ sauces, pepper jellies, pasta sauces and seasonings
Co-Owner: Don Mugford
Co-Owner: George Gooss
Estimated Sales: $.5-1 million
Number Employees: 1-4

2308 **Catania Bakery**
1404 N Capitol St NW
Washington, DC 20002-3342
202-332-5135
info@cataniabakery.com
www.cataniabakery.com
Italian bread and biscotti

President: Nicole Tramonte
General Manager: Carolyn Craig
Estimated Sales: $630,000
Number Employees: 5-9

2309 Catania Hospitality Group
141 Falmouth Rd
Hyannis, MA 02601-2755
508-771-0040
Fax: 508-771-0883 888-774-5511
info@cataniahospitalitygroup.com
www.cataniahospitalitygroup.com
Fresh and frozen soups and chowders
President: William Catania
william@cataniahospitalitygroup.com
VP: Richard Catonia
Estimated Sales: $500,000-$1,000,000
Number Employees: 500-999
Type of Packaging: Private Label
Brands:
Cape Cod Clam Chowder
Cape Cod Lobster Bisque
Cape Cod Lobster Chowder
Lobster Chowder
Minestrone

2310 Catania Oils
3 Nemco Way
Ayer, MA 01432
978-772-7900
Fax: 978-722-7970 cataniaoils.com
Specialty oils
Exec. VP, Sales & Marketing: Stephen Basile
Number of Brands: 1
Type of Packaging: Consumer, Food Service, Private Label, Bulk

2311 Catawissa Bottling Co
450 Fisher Ave
PO Box 27
Catawissa, PA 17820-1022
570-356-2301
Fax: 570-356-2304 800-892-4419
www.catawissabottling.com
Soft drinks.
Owner: Michael Gregorowicz
bigbens1926@peoplepc.com
Plant Manager: Stephen Gregorowicz
Purchasing: Paula Clark
Estimated Sales: $10-20 Million
Number Employees: 20-49
Number of Brands: 2
Brands:
Big Ben
Moxie

2312 Catch Up Logistics
5711 Friendship Ave
Pittsburgh, PA 15206-3616
412-441-9512
Fax: 412-441-9517 catchup@bellatlantic.net
www.catchuplogistics.com
Processor and exporter of plain and kosher frozen pizza; also, Italian specialties including pasta
Owner: Ronald Pasekoff
ronald.pasekoff@catchuplogistics.com
COO: Donald Paskoff
Estimated Sales: $2.5-5 Million
Number Employees: 5-9
Type of Packaging: Consumer, Food Service, Private Label, Bulk
Brands:
Cholov Yisrael
Tambellini

2313 Catelli Brothers Inc
50 Ferry Ave
Collingswood, NJ 08103-3006
856-869-9293
Fax: 856-869-9488 jresnick@catellibrothers.com
www.catellibrothers.com
Veal and lamb
CEO: Anthony Catelli
acatelli@catellibrothers.com
CFO: Norm Gunn
Quality Control Manager: Cheryl Edwards
Director of Marketing: Doug Buchanan
VP of Sales: Anthony Longino
Human Resources: Vanessa Vogt
Purchasing Manager: Harry Edwards
Estimated Sales: $20.4 Million
Number Employees: 250-499
Other Locations:
Shrewsbury NJ
Brands:
American Lamb
Ami
Namp

2314 Cateraid Inc
1167 Fendt Dr
Howell, MI 48843-6501
517-546-8217
Fax: 517-546-8674 800-508-8217
cateraid@sbcglobal.net www.cateraidinc.com
Frozen European style tortes, cakes, cheesecakes, miniature pastries and hors d'oeuvres
Owner: Rob Katz
cateraidinc@provide.net
Vice President, Director of Marketing: Rob Katz
Estimated Sales: $2.5-5 Million
Number Employees: 20-49
Number of Brands: 2
Number of Products: 85
Square Footage: 68000
Type of Packaging: Food Service, Private Label
Brands:
Cateraid
Catered Gourmet

2315 Cates Addis Company
2640 McLver Road
Parkton, NC 28371
910-858-3439
Fax: 910-858-3074 800-423-1883
Grower of fresh vegetables for pre-prepared salads and food services.
President: Curtiss Cates
Estimated Sales: $3-5 Million
Number Employees: 7
Type of Packaging: Bulk

2316 Catfish Wholesale
P.O.Box 759
Abbeville, LA 70511
337-643-6700
Fax: 337-643-1396 800-334-7292
Processor and distributor of catfish, garfish, crawfish, shrimp, crabs, flounder and trout
President: James Rich
Sales Executive: Shab Calahan
Sales Manager: David Lowery
Estimated Sales: $2.5 Million
Number Employees: 60
Number of Brands: 1
Square Footage: 32000
Type of Packaging: Consumer, Food Service, Private Label, Bulk

2317 Cathay Foods Corporation
960 Massachusetts Ave
Boston, MA 02118-2620
617-427-1507
Fax: 617-427-4083
Frozen spring, cocktail and full sized egg rolls including shrimp, lobster, vegetable, pizza, spinach and cheese; also, egg roll wrappers and crab rangoons
President: Victor Wong
Sales: Nancy Tashjian
Estimated Sales: $5-10 Million
Number Employees: 20-49
Square Footage: 36000
Type of Packaging: Consumer, Food Service, Private Label, Bulk
Brands:
Cathay Foods

2318 Catherych
141 Mountainview Rd
Warren, NJ 07059
732-566-6625
Fax: 732-566-6392 info@catherych.com
www.catherych.com
Bulk ingredient supplier to the nutraceutical industry
Type of Packaging: Bulk

2319 Catoctin Vineyards
805 Greenbridge Rd
Brookeville, MD 20833
301-774-2310
Fax: 301-774-2310
Wines
President: Bob Lyon
Estimated Sales: Less than $500,000
Number Employees: 1

2320 Catoris Candies Inc
981 5th Ave
New Kensington, PA 15068-6307
724-335-4371
Fax: 724-335-1759 www.catoriscandies.com
Confectionery items
Owner: John Gentile
Estimated Sales: $5-10 Million
Number Employees: 10-19
Type of Packaging: Consumer

2321 Catskill Brewery
672 Old Rte. 17
Livingston Manor, NY 12758
845-439-1232
info@catskillbrewery.com
www.catskillbrewery.com
IPA, Pilsner, Lager, Stout and sour beer
Founder: Ramsay Adams
Number of Brands: 1
Number of Products: 14
Type of Packaging: Consumer, Private Label
Brands:
Catskill Brewery

2322 Catskill Distilling Company
2037 Rte. 17B
Bethel, NY 12720
845-583-3141
www.catskilldistilling.com
Vodka, gin, grappa, whiskey, bourbon and rye
Owner/Distiller: Monte Sachs
Year Founded: 2008
Number of Brands: 1
Number of Products: 8
Brands:
Catskill Distilling Company

2323 Catskill Mountain Specialties
1411 Route 212
Saugerties, NY 12477-3040
845-246-0900
Fax: 845-246-5313 800-311-3473
www.newworldhomecooking.com
Condiments including roasted habanero, chipotle, barbecue, Jamaican jerk, etc.; importer of hot peppers, spices, etc.; also, co-packer of acidified foods
Owner: Liz Corrado
VP: Edward Palluth
Number Employees: 1-4
Square Footage: 8000
Type of Packaging: Consumer, Food Service, Private Label, Bulk
Brands:
Mountainman
New World Home Cooking Co.

2324 Cattaneo Brothers Inc
797 Caudill Streey
San Luis Obispo, CA 93401
800-243-8537
info@cattaneobros.com www.cattaneobros.com
Jerky, pepperoni sticks and sausage
Owner: Kaitlyn Kaney
Marketing Director: Katelyn Kaney
Estimated Sales: $2.5-5 Million
Number Employees: 20-49
Number of Brands: 1
Number of Products: 50
Square Footage: 34000
Type of Packaging: Consumer, Food Service, Private Label
Brands:
Cattaneo Brothers

2325 Cattle Boyz Foods
Suite 314, #14
900 Village Lane
Okotoks, Alberta,, CA T1S 1Z6
Canada
403-995-2279
Fax: 403-995-2056 888-662-9366
sales@cattleboyz.com www.CattleBoyZ.com
Manufacturer and exporter of unique latchtop bottle containing versatile gourmet sauces for barbecuing, marinades, glaze for all meats and seafoods. Available in 17 and 35 oz. sizes
Managing Partner/Owner: Karen Hope
Managing Partner: Joe Ternes
Quality Control: Roxanne Quest
Sales: Karen Hope
Number Employees: 1-4
Number of Brands: 1
Number of Products: 4

Type of Packaging: Consumer, Food Service, Private Label, Bulk
Brands:
Cattle Boyz

2326 **Cattleman Meat & Produce**
11400 Telegraph Rd
Taylor, MI 48180-4078
734-287-8260
Fax: 734-287-8368 www.cattlemansmeats.com
Fresh and frozen beef and meat products.
Owner: Peter Synoweic
Number Employees: 20-49
Type of Packaging: Bulk
Brands:
Cattleman's

2327 **Caughman's Meat Plant**
164 Meat Plant Rd
Lexington, SC 29073-8911
803-356-0076
Established in 1955. Manufacturer of sausage, poulty, beef, pork, liver pudding, barbecue hash and beef chili.
President: Marguerite Caughman
VP: Ronald Caughman
Estimated Sales: $20-50 Million
Number Employees: 20-49
Type of Packaging: Consumer
Brands:
Lexington

2328 **Caulipower**
Encino, CA 91436
844-422-8544
info@eatcaulipower.com www.eatcaulipower.com
Cauliflower flour-based tortillas, pizzas and baking mixes
Founder & CEO: Gail Becker

2329 **Cave Shake**
Los Angeles, CA 90065
hi@caveshake.com
eatspaceshake.com
Keto, paleo and vegan meal replacements
CEO: Holly Heath

2330 **Caveman Foods**
3595 Mt. Diablo Blvd
Suite 200
Lafayette, CA 94549
925-979-9515
www.cavemanfoods.com
Paleo-friendly snack bars and chicken jerky
Number of Brands: 1
Number of Products: 4
Type of Packaging: Consumer

2331 **Cavender Castle Winery**
142 Mitchell Street SW
Suite 300
Atlanta, GA 30303-3432
706-864-4759
Wines
Vineyard Manager: Gerry Carty
Number Employees: 20-49

2332 **Cavendish Farms**
100 Midland Dr.
Dieppe, NB E1A 6X4
Canada
506-858-7710
Fax: 506-858-7708 www.cavendishfarms.com
Potato products.
President: Robert Irving
Vice President, Sales: Gerald Toews
Year Founded: 1980
Estimated Sales: $294 Million
Number Employees: 16,000
Parent Co: Cavendish Farms Corporation
Brands:
FreshCut
Cavendish Farms®
Double R®
FlavourCrisp®
Clear Coat
Fine Coat®
Jersey Shore®

2333 **Cavens Meats**
US Route 36
Conover, OH 45317-0400
937-368-3841
Fax: 937-368-3849
Processor and wholesaler/distributor of meat products; serving the food service market
President: Victor Caven
VP: Dean Caven
Estimated Sales: $10-20 Million
Number Employees: 10-19
Square Footage: 45000
Type of Packaging: Consumer, Food Service

2334 **Caves Of Faribault/SwissValley**
222 3rd St NE
Faribault, MN 55021
507-334-5260
Fax: 507-332-9011 jeff.jirik@cavesoffaribault.com
www.faribaultdairy.com
Cheese
President/Owner: Sarah Arhameault
CEO: Jeff Jirik
VP: Michael Gilbertson
Estimated Sales: $3.5 Million
Number Employees: 21

2335 **Caviness Beef Packers LTD**
3255 W Highway 60
P.O. Box 790
Hereford, TX 79045
806-357-2333
Fax: 806-357-2377 www.cavinessbeefpackers.com
Meat products; slaughtering services available.
President: Trevor Caviness
Year Founded: 1962
Estimated Sales: $28.2 Million
Number Employees: 500-999
Square Footage: 100000
Other Locations:
Manufacturing Plant
Amarillo TX

2336 **Caviness Beef Packers LTD**
4206 Amarillo Blvd E
P.O. Box 31117
Amarillo, TX 79120
806-372-5781
Fax: 806-372-1215 www.cavinessbeefpackers.com
Meat products; slaughtering services available.
President: Trevor Caviness
Year Founded: 1962
Estimated Sales: $20-50 Million
Number Employees: 500-999

2337 **Cawston Press**
Pittsburgh, PA 15241
info@cawstonpress.com
cawstonpress.com
Sparkling fruit soft drinks
Managing Director: Steve Kearns
Number of Products: 4

2338 **Cawy Bottling Co**
2440 NW 21st Ter
Miami, FL 33142-7182
305-634-2291
Fax: 305-634-2291 877-917-2299
cawy@cawy.net www.cawy.net
Soft drinks
CEO/VP/Public Relations: Vincent Cossio
Quality Control: Ramon Mesa
Sales Director: Harris Padron
Operations Manager: Mayra Alfonsin
Production Manager: Carlos Garcia
Estimated Sales: $10-20 Million
Number Employees: 20-49
Square Footage: 120000
Type of Packaging: Consumer, Food Service
Brands:
Cawy Cc
Cawy Lemon-Lime
Cawy Watermelon
Champ's Cola
Coco Solo
Jupina
Malta Cawy
Malta Rica
Materva
Quinabeer
Rica Malt Tonic
Trimalta

2339 **Caymus Vineyards**
8700 Conn Creek Rd
Rutherford, CA 94573
707-967-3010
Fax: 707-963-5958 reception@caymus.com
www.caymus.com
Wines
President: Chuck Wagner
VP: Karen Perry
Public Relations: Phyllis Turner
Estimated Sales: $300,000-500,000
Number Employees: 20-49
Number of Brands: 1
Number of Products: 2
Brands:
Caymus

2340 **Cayuga Pure Organics**
18 Banks Rd
Brooktondale, NY 14817-9752
607-273-2621
www.cporganics.com
Grain
Farm Owner/Founder: Erick Smith
erick@cporganics.com
Office Mgr / NYC Operations: Amy Martin
Estimated Sales: Less Than $500,000
Number Employees: 1-4
Type of Packaging: Food Service, Bulk

2341 **Cayuga Ridge Estate Winery**
6800 State Route 89
Ovid, NY 14521-9599
607-869-5158
Fax: 607-869-3412 800-598-9463
www.cayugaridgewinery.com
Wines
Owner: Tom Challen
crew@flpg.net
Owner: Susie Challen
Estimated Sales: Less Than $500,000
Number Employees: 1-4

2342 **Cebro Frozen Food**
2100 Orestimba Rd
Newman, CA 95360-9788
209-862-0150
Fax: 209-862-0717 www.cebrofrozenfoods.com
Frozen foods
President: William Cerutti
wcerutti@cebrofrozenfood.com
Estimated Sales: $2.5-5 Million
Number Employees: 10-19

2343 **Cecchetti Sebastiani Cellar**
389 Fourth Street East
Sonoma, CA 95476-1607
707-933-3230
Fax: 707-996-0424 www.sebastiani.com
Wine
President/CEO: Mary Ann Sebastiani-Cuneo
SVP Sales: Jim O'Connor
SVP/Winemaker: Bob Broman
Number Employees: 1-4
Type of Packaging: Private Label
Brands:
Brandy
Cecchetti Sebastiani Napa Valley
Pepperwood Grove
Quatro
Wines

2344 **Cece's Veggie Co.**
3714 Bluestein Dr
Suite 650
Austin, TX 78721
512-200-3337
info@cecesveggieco.com
www.cecesveggieco.com
Organic vegetable spirals
Founder: Mason Arnold
Number of Brands: 1
Number of Products: 9
Type of Packaging: Consumer
Brands:
CECE'S VEGGIE NOODLE CO.

2345 **Cedar Creek Winery**
N70 W6340 Bridge Rd
Cedarburg, WI 53012
262-377-8020
Fax: 262-375-9428 800-827-8020
info@cedarcreekwinery.com
www.cedarcreekwinery.com
Bottler of wine
Manager: Steve Danner
Estimated Sales: $5-9.9 Million
Number Employees: 10-19
Square Footage: 48000
Type of Packaging: Consumer, Food Service, Private Label

Brands:
Cedar Creek

2346 Cedar Crest Specialties
7269 Hwy. 60
P.O. Box 260
Cedarburg, WI 53012
262-377-7252
Fax: 262-377-5554 800-877-8341
info@cedarcresticecream.com
www.cedarcresticecream.com
Premium ice cream and no-fat ice cream, frozen yogurt, sherbet and Tom and Jerry mix
President: Ken Kohlwey
CEO: Bill Kohlwey
VP: Robert Kohlwey
Marketing Manager: Charlene Leach
Sales: Robert Kohlwey
Purchasing: Nadine Schmitt
Estimated Sales: $16 Million
Number Employees: 50-99
Number of Brands: 2
Number of Products: 400
Square Footage: 135000
Parent Co: Cedar Crest Specialties
Type of Packaging: Consumer, Food Service, Private Label, Bulk
Brands:
Cedar Crest
Gustafson's

2347 Cedar Grove Cheese Inc
E5904 Mill Rd
PO Box 185
Plain, WI 53577-9674
608-546-5284
Fax: 608-546-2805 800-200-6020
info@cedargrovecheese.com
www.cedargrovecheese.com
Organic cheese and specialty artisan crafted cheese
Owner: Bob Wills
bob@cedargrovecheese.com
Vice President: Beth Nachreiner
Marketing Director: Robert Wills
General Manager: Peter DeWaard
Estimated Sales: $2.5-5 Million
Number Employees: 20-49
Number of Brands: 3
Number of Products: 50
Type of Packaging: Consumer, Food Service, Private Label, Bulk
Brands:
Cedar Grove
Family Farmer
Squeaks

2348 Cedar Hill Seasonings
P.O.Box 4055
Edmond, OK 73034
405-340-1119
Fax: 405-340-7673 800-342-1986
info@cedarhillseasonings.com
www.cedarhillseasonings.com
Seasonings, bottled products and packaged mixes, Cedar Hill Seasonings produces a variety of food items including taco mixes; dip mix with seasonings; cheese ball mixes; marinara and sauce mixes, in addition to offering gift packagesand combo samplers.
Co-Owner: Felicia Schaefer
info@cedarhillseasonings.com
Co-Owner: Helen Schaefer
Type of Packaging: Food Service

2349 Cedar Key Aquaculture Farms
11227 Riverview Dr
Riverview, FL 33578-4471
813-681-5796
Fax: 352-543-9132 888-252-6735
custserv@cedarkeyclams.com
www.cedarkeyclams.com
Fresh and frozen clams including hors d'oeuvres
President: Dan Solano
Operations Manager: Mike Smith
Contact: Stephen Jaeb
stephen.j@cedarkeyclams.com
Estimated Sales: Less Than $500,000
Number Employees: 1-4
Type of Packaging: Food Service

2350 Cedar Lake Foods
5333 Quarter Line Rd
Cedar Lake, MI 48812
989-427-5143
Fax: 989-427-5392 800-246-5039
www.cedarlakefoods.com
Processor and exporter of canned and frozen vegetable protein entrees including meat analogs; also, dry soy milk and vegetarian foods
President: Alejo Pizzaro
Contact: Cheri Graves
Production Manager: John Sias
Plant Manager: John Sias
Purchasing Manager: Ann Britten
Estimated Sales: $5-9.9 Million
Number Employees: 20-49
Type of Packaging: Consumer, Food Service, Private Label, Bulk
Brands:
Cedar Lake
Mgm

2351 Cedar Mountain Winery
7000 Tesla Rd
Livermore, CA 94550
925-373-6636
Fax: 925-373-6694 cedarmtn@wt.net
www.cedarmountainwinery.com
Wines
Owner: Linda Ault
Owner: Earl Ault
Co-Owner: Earl Ault
Marketing Manager: Sigrid Laing
VP Operations/Production Manager: R Michael Hasbrouck
Estimated Sales: $840,000
Number Employees: 12
Type of Packaging: Private Label
Brands:
Cedar Grove
Cedar Mountain

2352 Cedar Valley Cheese Store
W3115 Jay Rd
Belgium, WI 53004-9769
920-994-9500
Fax: 920-994-2317
www.cedarvalleycheesestore.com
Cheese
Owner: Tracy Hiller
tracy@cedarvalleycheese.com
Sec: William Peterson
Estimated Sales: $6.5 Million
Number Employees: 5-9

2353 Cedar Valley Fish Market
218 Division St
Waterloo, IA 50703
319-236-2965
Fax: 253-761-0504
Seafood
Owner: Marilyn Ruvino
Estimated Sales: $370,000
Number Employees: 5-9

2354 Cedar's Mediterranean Foods
50 Foundation Ave
Ward Hill, MA 01835
978-372-8010
www.cedarsfoods.com
Mediterranean foods, including hommus, tzatziki, salads, dips, salsa and pita chips
President & CEO: Charlie Hanna
VP: Bruce Rubin
Number of Brands: 1
Type of Packaging: Consumer
Brands:
CEDAR'S

2355 Cedarlane Foods
1135 E Artesia Blvd
Carson, CA 90746-1602
310-886-7720
Fax: 310-886-7733 800-826-3322
feedback@cedarlanefoods.com
www.cedarlanefoods.com
Natural refrigerated and frozen foods including enchiladas, burritos, pot pies, tortillas, specialty breads, pizza and lasagna; varieties include vegetarian, low-fat and cholesterol and lactose-free
Founder, President: Robert Atallah
terry@franklyfresh.com
Vice President: Terry Mayo
Sales Exec: Terry Mayo
Number Employees: 250-499
Square Footage: 64000
Type of Packaging: Consumer, Food Service, Private Label
Brands:
Cedarlane
Soypreme

2356 Cedarlane Natural FoodsToc
1135 E Artesia Blvd
Carson, CA 90746-1602
310-527-7833
www.cedarlanefoods.com
Breakfast selections, tamales and vegetarian foods
CEO: Robert Atallah
ktorosyan@franklyfresh.com
Number Employees: 5-9
Type of Packaging: Private Label

2357 Cedarvale Food Products
11 Wiltshire Avenue
Toronto, ON M6N 2V7
Canada
416-656-3330
Fax: 416-656-6803 lounsbury@lounsbury.ca
Mustard and sauces including horseradish, cocktail, mint and tartar; importer of tomato paste
VP: David Higgins
Manager Export Sales/Marketing: Tim Higgins
General Manager: Gil Marks
Estimated Sales: $487,000
Number Employees: 12
Square Footage: 60000
Parent Co: Lounsbury Foods
Type of Packaging: Consumer, Food Service, Private Label, Bulk
Brands:
Cedarvale
Lounsbury
Wiltshire

2358 Ceilidh Fisherman's Cooperative
158 Main St
Port Hood, NS B0E 2W0
Canada
902-787-2666
Fax: 902-787-2388 www.ceilidhlobster.ca
Processor and exporter of salted cod, live lobster and crab.
General Manager: Bernie MacDonald
Year Founded: 1985
Estimated Sales: $6 Million
Number Employees: 35
Type of Packaging: Consumer, Food Service, Private Label, Bulk

2359 Celebrity Cheesecake
655 Nova Drive
Suite 304
Davie, FL 33317
877-986-2253
Cheesecakes, pies, cakes
Owner: Anita Phillips
President: Susie Bernstein
Estimated Sales: $500,000-$1 Million
Number Employees: 10-19
Square Footage: 24000
Brands:
Celebrity Cheesecakes

2360 Celebrity Tea, LLC
7010 East Adamo Drive
Building C Unit 1
Tampa, FL 33619
813-600-3317
Ready-to-drink teas made from natural and USDA-certified organic ingredients.
Type of Packaging: Consumer
Brands:
CELEBRI TEA

2361 Cell-Nique
65 East Avenue, 3rd Floor
Norwalk, CT 06851
888-417-9343
dan@cell-nique.com www.cell-nique.com
Organic Super Green drinks made with foods such as Spirulina, Chlorella and Blue-green algae as well as cereal grass juices and sprouts like barley, wheat, oats and alfalfa. Cell-nique also contains the high anti-oxidant Super Fruitslike Noni, Goji berry, and Açaí.

Co-founder, CEO and CFO: Dan Ratner
Co-Founder and CMO: Donna Ratner
Contact: Candi Sterling
candi@healthybrandsco.com
National Operations Manager: Shaun Conners
Warehouse & Distribution: Victor Pinto
Type of Packaging: Consumer

2362 **Cellone Bakery Inc**
193 Chartiers Ave
Pittsburgh, PA 15205-3321
412-922-5335
Fax: 412-922-6940 800-334-8438
info@Cellones.com www.cellones.com
Bread and rolls
Owner: Brandon Cellone
Owner: Randy Cellone
Management Info Systems Manager: Lori Edward
bcellone@cellonebakery.net
Operations Manager: Gary Cellone
Production Manager: Dean Cellone
Estimated Sales: Less Than $500,000
Number Employees: 5-9
Type of Packaging: Private Label

2363 **Cellucon Inc**
19994 Meredith Dr
Strathmore, CA 93267
559-568-0190
Fax: 559-568-0271 www.cellucon.com
Natural yucca extract
Owner: John Yale
Manager: Carol Hilty
Administrative Assistant: Kelly Smith
Estimated Sales: $1-3 Million
Number Employees: 10-19
Square Footage: 40000

2364 **Celsius**
2424 North Federal Hwy
Boca Raton, FL 33431
866-423-5748
www.celsius.com
Fitness drink
Interim President & CEO: John Fieldly
EVP, Marketing & Innovation: Vanessa Walker
SVP, Sales-North America: Jon McKillop
Number of Brands: 1
Number of Products: 23
Type of Packaging: Consumer
Brands:
CELSIUS LIVE FIT
CELSIUS HEAT

2365 **Celtic Sea Salt**
Arden, NC 28704
800-867-7258
www.celticseasalt.com
Sea salt

2366 **Centennial Farms**
199 Jackson St
Augusta, MO 63332-1721
636-228-4338
centfarmaug@aol.com
www.centennialfarms.biz
Apple butters
Owner: Robert Knoernschild
Estimated Sales: Less Than $500,000
Number Employees: 5-9
Number of Brands: 1
Number of Products: 8
Type of Packaging: Consumer, Private Label

2367 **(HQ)Centennial Food Corporation**
4412 Manilla Rd
Calgary, AB T2G 4A7
Canada
403-214-0044
Fax: 403-214-1656
www.centennialfoodservice.com
Processor and exporter of fresh and frozen meat products including spiced and formed ground beef, beef patties, battered and breaded steaks and cutlets, vacuum sealed and aged beef cuts, bacon wrapped scallops and marinated short ribs;importer of beef and seafood
Chairman: Ron Kovitz
CEO/President: J Kalef
VP/General Manager: Nashir Vasanji
Number Employees: 250-499
Type of Packaging: Consumer, Food Service, Private Label, Bulk
Other Locations:
Centennial Food Corp.
Calgary AB
Brands:
Canadian Gourmet
Centennial
Mastercut

2368 **Centennial Mills**
601 1st St
Cheney, WA 99004-1653
509-235-6216
Fax: 509-235-2144
Flour
Manager: Luke Burger
Estimated Sales: Under $500,000
Number Employees: 10-19
Parent Co: Archer Daniels Midland Company
Type of Packaging: Consumer, Food Service, Bulk

2369 **Center Locker Svc**
107 S Public St
Center, MO 63436-1217
573-267-3343
Fax: 573-267-3392 800-884-0737
centerlocker@att.net www.centerlocker.com
Beef, pork, sausage and meat and meat products
Owner: Dennis McMillen
Co-Owner: Debby McMillen
Estimated Sales: $500,000-$1 Million
Number Employees: 1-4
Type of Packaging: Food Service, Bulk

2370 **Centerchem, Inc.**
20 Glover Ave # 4n
Norwalk, CT 06850-1234
203-822-9800
Fax: 203-822-9820 orders@centerchem.com
www.centerchem.com
Manufacturer & distributor of pectin, bittering agents, essential oils, polishing and glazing agents, waxes, release agents & encapsulated specialty ingredients.
President: Jon Packer
Chief Financial Officer & Treasurer: Mary Fcc
Vice President: John Dondero
Marketing Coordinator: Claude Dougherty
Vice President Sales: Ray Sourial
Tech. Sales Rep.: Jennifer Czerner
Estimated Sales: $6.7 Million
Brands:
Capol®
Maxinvert®
Candurin®
Rapidase®
Pearex®
Hazyme®
Klerzyme®

2371 **Centflor Manufacturing Co**
545 W 45th St # L1
New York, NY 10036-3490
212-246-8307
Fax: 212-262-9717 www.mcmahonmed.com
Processor and exporter of essential oils and aromatic chemicals
President: Robert Beller
robjbeller@gmail.com
General Manager: Gloria Rose
Estimated Sales: $1.5 Million
Number Employees: 5-9
Square Footage: 48000

2372 **Cento Fine Foods**
100 Cento Blvd
West Deptford, NJ 08086-2133
856-853-5445
Fax: 856-853-2843 www.cento.com
Manufacturer of over 1,000 Italian products, including tomato brand products, oils, and vinegars.
President: Rick Ciccotelli
sales4@cento.com
National Sales Manager: Bart Ricci
sales4@cento.com
Number Employees: 100-249

2373 **Central Bakery**
711 Pleasant St
Fall River, MA 02723
508-675-7620
Fax: 508-677-4523
Bread & other bakery products
Owner: Tibeiro Lopes
Contact: David Lopes
dlopes@centralbakery.com
Estimated Sales: $2.3,000,000
Number Employees: 10-19

2374 **Central Bean Co**
815 E St SW
Quincy, WA 98848-1073
509-787-1544
Fax: 509-787-4040 info@centralbean.com
www.centralbean.com
Dry bean supplier to canneries and packagers.
President: Tom Grebb
tom@centralbean.com
Estimated Sales: G
Number Employees: 10-19
Type of Packaging: Consumer, Food Service, Private Label, Bulk

2375 **Central California Raisin Packing Co, Inc.**
5316 S Del Rey Ave
Del Rey, CA 93616
559-888-2195
Dried apricots, mixed fruit, peaches, prunes, raisins
President: Dan Milinovich
Estimated Sales: $1.5 Million
Number Employees: 10
Number of Brands: 1
Brands:
Del Cara

2376 **(HQ)Central Coast Seafood**
5495 Traffic Way
Atascadero, CA 93422-4246
805-462-3474
Fax: 805-466-6613 800-273-4741
www.ccseafood.com
Wholesaler/distributor and exporter of fresh seafood; serving the food service market in California
CEO: Giovanni Comin
VP Sales/Marketing: Nancy Osorio
Estimated Sales: $5.9 Million
Number Employees: 5-9
Square Footage: 40000
Other Locations:
Central Coast Seafoods
Morro Bay CA

2377 **Central Dairies**
PO Box 8588
Station A
St Johns, NL A1B 3P2
Canada
709-364-7531
Fax: 709-364-8714 800-563-6455
www.centraldairies.com
Milk, cultured products, frozen desserts, cheese, spreads, juices and drinks
VP: Deve Collins
CEO: Kennetch Peacock
VP/General Manager: David Collins
Manager Sales/Marketing: Ron Croke
Plant Manager: Clarence Chaytor
Parent Co: Farmers Co-op Dairy
Type of Packaging: Consumer
Brands:
Farmers Ice Cream
Flavoured Milk

2378 **Central Dairy**
610 Madison St
Jefferson City, MO 65101-3199
573-635-6148
Fax: 573-634-3028 www.centraldairy.biz
Milk, egg nogs, half and half, sour cream. onion dips, cottage cheese, orange juice, bottled water, and ice cream.
President: Gale Hackman
CEO: Chris Hackman
VP: Steve Raithel
Controller: Mike Fennewald
Estimated Sales: $20-50 Million
Number Employees: 50-99

2379 **Central Meat & Provision**
1603 National Ave
San Diego, CA 92113-1008
619-239-1391
Fax: 619-239-1634 www.centralmeatco.com
Beef, pork and veal
Owner/President: Robert Kuhlken
rkuhlken@centralmeat-market.com
VP Key Accounts: Kevin Gawle
Sales Manager: John Kuhlken
VP Operations: Bert Risley

Estimated Sales: $10-20 Million
Number Employees: 20-49

2380 Central Meat Market
113 Gano St
Providence, RI 02906-3822
401-751-6935
Fax: 401-223-0125 www.centralmeatmarket.com
Portuguese sausages
Owner: Tony Cabaral
cabaraltony@centralmeat-market.com
Estimated Sales: $510,000
Number Employees: 5-9

2381 Central Milling Co
122 E Center St
Logan, UT 84321-4607
435-752-6625
Fax: 435-753-7960 reception@centralmilling.com
www.centralmilling.com
Pancake flour, Golden West All Purpose Flour, Red Rose All Purpose Flour, whole wheat flour, and Germade.
President: H Roscoe Weston
Controller: Shaun Owen
Quality Control: Jeff Daniels
Mill Manager: Manuel Solis
Mill Manager: Nathan Shumway
Mill Manager: Melvin Alberta
Secretary: James Weston
Mill Manager/Electrician: Kurtis Williams
Plant Manager: Fred Weston
Estimated Sales: $10-20 Million
Number Employees: 10-19
Type of Packaging: Consumer, Food Service
Brands:
Golden West
Red Rose

2382 Central Snacks
1700 N Pearl St
Carthage, MS 39051-8635
601-267-3112
Fax: 601-267-5249 porkskin@aol.com
www.centralsnacks.com
Pork skins
President: Randy Carson
porkskin@aol.com
Estimated Sales: $2.5-5,000,000
Number Employees: 10-19

2383 Central Soyfoods
710 East 22nd Street
Suite C
Lawrence, KS 66046
785-312-8698
Soybean oil manufacturer
General Partner: Jim Cooley
Plant Manager: Lori Kruger
Estimated Sales: $700,000
Number Employees: 12

2384 Centreside Dairy
61 Lorne Street North
Renfrew, ON K7V 1K8
Canada
613-432-2914
Fax: 613-432-5157 800-889-9974
info@traceysicecream.ca traceysicecream.ca
Ice cream; wholesaler/distributor of dairy products
President: Mark Tracey
General Manager: Melany Tracey
Estimated Sales: $2 Million
Number Employees: 15
Type of Packaging: Consumer, Food Service, Private Label
Brands:
Economy
Premium
Tracey's

2385 Century Agricultural Products LLC
7085 Morganton Rd
Greenback, TN 37742
865-980-8522
Beef; pickles and preserves
Co-Owner: Christopher Burger
Co-Owner: Shona Burger
Admistrator: Dana Couch
Type of Packaging: Food Service, Bulk
Brands:
Century Harvest Farms

2386 (HQ)Century Blends LLC
11110 Pepper Rd # A
Hunt Valley, MD 21031-1204
410-771-6606
Fax: 410-771-6608 jwaynewheeler@sun-ripe.com
Processor and exporter of bakery and confectionery supplies and mixes including dry bar, salad dressings and sauces
Owner: J Wayne Wheeler
Production Manager: Tim Wheeler
Estimated Sales: $1,000,000
Number Employees: 5-9
Type of Packaging: Food Service, Bulk
Brands:
Coag-U-Loid
Condex
Pie Rite
Sun-Ripe
T.H. Angermeier
Veg-A-Loid

2387 Century Foods Intl LLC
400 Century Ct
Sparta, WI 54656-2468
608-269-1900
Fax: 608-269-1910 800-269-1901
www.centuryfoods.com
Century Foods International is a manufacturer of nutritional powders and ready-to-drink beverages under private label and contract manufacturing agreements for food, sports, health and nutritional supplement industries. Other servicesprovided include agglomeration, blending and instantizing, research and development, analytical testing, and packaging from bulk to consumer size.
President: Tom Miskowski
VP R&D: Julie Wagner
VP Sales/Marketing: Gene Quast
VP Operations: Wade Nolte
Number Employees: 250-499
Square Footage: 1680000
Parent Co: Hormel Foods Corporation
Type of Packaging: Private Label, Bulk
Brands:
Cenprem
Lacey Delite
Pizazz
Ready Cheese

2388 Cereal Food Processors
425 West 500 South Street
Salt Lake City, UT 84101
801-355-2981
info@cerealfood.com
Wheat flour
President: J. Breck Barton
VP: J. Brent Wall
SVP, Sales: Timothy S. Miller
VP, Operations: John C. Erker
Plant Manager: Rick Thomas
Plant Superintendant: Max Horrocks
Estimated Sales: $10-24.9 Million
Number Employees: 10-19
Parent Co: Cereal Food Processors

2389 Cereal Food Processors Inc
416 N Main St
Mcpherson, KS 67460-3404
620-241-2410
Fax: 620-241-7167 800-835-2067
b.wall@cerealfood.com www.cerealfood.com
Miller of flour including, bakery, bread, all-purpose and self-rising; also, pancake and waffle mix, wheat bran and mill feeds
President: J. Breck Barton
Chairman: Fred Merrill
EVP, Finance & Admin: Steven J. Heeney
Vice President: Greg Edelblute
Plant Superintendent: Kendall Allison
SVP, Sales: Timothy S. Miller
Vice President of Operations: John C. Erker
Vice President: Wayne Ford
Plant Manager: Max Streit
Estimated Sales: $10-20 Million
Number Employees: 20-49
Square Footage: 123810
Type of Packaging: Consumer, Food Service, Private Label, Bulk
Brands:
America's Best
Bake-Rite H & R
Kansas Sun
Utility
W-R

2390 (HQ)Cereal Food Processors Inc
2001 Shawnee Mission Pkwy #110
Mission Woods, KS 66205-2097
913-890-6300
Fax: 913-890-6382 info@cerealfood.com
Manufacturer and exporter of flour.
President: J. Breck Barton
Executive VP: Mark L Dobbins
m.dobbins@cerealfoods.com
Year Founded: 1972
Estimated Sales: $20-50 Million
Number Employees: 20-49
Type of Packaging: Consumer
Other Locations:
Cereal Food Processors Plant
Los Angeles CA
Cereal Food Processors Plant
Kansas City MO
Cereal Food Processors Plant
McPherson KS
Cereal Food Processors Plant
Billings MT
Cereal Food Processors Plant
Great Falls MT
Cereal Food Processors Plant
Cleveland OH
Cereal Food Processors Plant
Portland OR
Cereal Food Processors Plant
Ogden UT
Cereal Food Processors Plant
Salt Lake City UT
Cereal Food Processors Plant
Montreal QC

2391 Cereal Ingredients, Inc.
4720 S 13th St
Leavenworth, KS 66048-5585
913-727-3434
Fax: 913-727-3681 info@cerealingredients.com
www.cerealingredients.com
specialized ingredients developed from wheat fiber concentrates.
Chairman, CEO: Bob Hatch
Vice President: Bruce Hoffmann
Estimated Sales: $1-2.5 Million
Number Employees: 50-99

2392 Ceres Fruit Juices
6370 Lusk Blvd
8th Floor
San Diego, CA 92121B9
800-778-6498
info@ceresjuices.com www.ceresjuices.com
Fruit juices

2393 Cericola Farms
Bradford, ON L3Z 2A4
Canada
905-939-2962
www.cericola.com
Organic, antibiotic-free chicken producer.
President: Amedeo Cericola
VP: Anthony Cericola
Co-Owner/VP: Mary Cericola
Marketing Director: Amedeo Cericola
Type of Packaging: Consumer, Food Service, Private Label, Bulk
Brands:
Surefresh Foods

2394 Certi Fresh Foods Inc
842 Flint Ave
Wilmington, CA 90744-3739
310-221-6262
Fax: 310-427-6061 sobel@certi-fresh.com
www.certi-fresh.com
Seafood processing and distribution
Owner: Antonino Palma
CFO/COO: Scott Obel
Quality Control: Michael Jamehdor
VP of Sales & Marketing: Maria White
Director of Sales: Pete Palma
apalma@certi-fresh.com
Operator Specialist: Mario Galaz
Plant Manager: Tom Dukescherer
Purchasing: Revi Ayla
Number Employees: 50-99
Type of Packaging: Consumer, Food Service
Brands:
Certi-Fresh

2395 **Certi-Fresh Foods, Inc**
842 Flint Ave
Wilmington, CA 90744
910-221-6262
Fax: 310-427-6060 www.certi-fresh.com
Seafood
CEO/Owner: Nino Palma
President/COO/Owner: Pete Palma
US Sales Manager: Mario Galaz
International And Domestic Procurement: Ramiro Ayala

2396 **Certified Piedmontese Beef**
100 West Harvest Drive
PO Box 82545
Lincoln, NE 68521
402-458-4442
Fax: 402-458-4531 800-414-3487
info@piedmontese.com www.piedmontese.com
Prime cuts of beef
President: Billy Swain

2397 **Cervantes Food ProductsInc**
1125 Arizona St SE
Albuquerque, NM 87108-4829
505-254-9414
Fax: 505-256-1789 877-982-4453
www.cervantessalsa.com
Chiles: red and green; fresh, dried, canned, frozen
Owner: Richard Gonzales
richard@cervantessalsa.com
Estimated Sales: $1-3 Million
Number Employees: 5-9

2398 **Chacewater Winery and Olive Mill**
5625 Gabby Lane
Kelseyville, CA 95451
707-279-2995
Fax: 707-279-1972 info@chacewaterwine.com
www.chacewaterwine.com
Fine wines, olive oils, and soaps
Owner/General Manager: Paul Manuel
Mill Master: Emilio De La Cruz
Winemaker: Mark Burch
Number Employees: 10

2399 **Chaddsford Winery**
632 Baltimore Pike
Chadds Ford, PA 19317-9305
610-388-6221
Fax: 610-388-0360 info@chaddsford.com
www.chaddsford.com
Wines
Owner: Eric Miller
Special Events Planner: Betsie Williamson
Marketing Director: Lee Miller
Sales Director: William Harris
Public Relations: Larry D'Antonio
Operations Manager: James Osborn
Estimated Sales: $1-2.5 Million
Number Employees: 20-49
Type of Packaging: Private Label
Brands:
Chaddsford

2400 **Chai Diaries**
23052 H Alicia Pkwy
Suite 603
Mission Viejo, CA 92692
917-460-6828
cs@mychaidiaries.com
www.mychaidiaries.com
Premium organic teas
Principal: Ami Bhansali
Year Founded: 2013

2401 **Chalet Cheese Co-Op**
N4858 County Road N
Monroe, WI 53566-9355
608-325-4343
Fax: 608-325-4409
Cheese
Manager: Myron Olson
chalet@cppweb.com
Owner: Hans Wampfler
Estimated Sales: $2.5 Million
Number Employees: 20-49
Type of Packaging: Private Label

2402 **Chalet Debonne Vineyards**
7743 Doty Rd
Madison, OH 44057
440-466-3485
Fax: 440-466-6753 info@debonne.com
www.debonne.com
Wines and vineyard
Owner: Anthony Debevc
Treasurer: Rose Debevc
Vice President: Tony Debevec
Contact: Beth Debevc
bdebevc@debonne.com
Estimated Sales: $2.5-5 Million
Number Employees: 10-19

2403 **Chalk Hill Estate Winery**
10300 Chalk Hill Rd
Healdsburg, CA 95448-9558
707-657-4839
Fax: 707-838-9687 concierge@chalkhill.com
www.chalkhill.com
Wines
Vice President: Mark Lingenfelder
Head Winemaker: Steve Nelson
Estimated Sales: $10-20 Million
Number Employees: 50-99
Number of Brands: 2
Type of Packaging: Private Label
Brands:
Chalk Hill Estate Bottled
Chalk Hill Estate Selection

2404 **Challenge Dairy Products, Inc.**
6701 Donion Way
Dublin, CA 94568
877-883-2479
Fax: 925-551-7591 800-733-2479
consumerinfo@challengedairy.com
www.challengedairy.com
Processor and exporter of butter and dehydrated milk; wholesaler/distributor of butter and frozen foods.
President, CEO: Irv Holmes
Controller: Geoffrey Uy
SR VP Retail & Foodservice: Tim Anderson
EDI Coordinator: Michael Jenkins
Office Manager: Daisrea Smith
Estimated Sales: $500 Thousand
Number Employees: 175
Number of Brands: 2
Square Footage: 8500
Type of Packaging: Consumer, Food Service, Private Label, Bulk
Brands:
Challenge
Challenge Danish

2405 **Chalone Vineyard**
32020 Stonewall Canyon Rd
Soledad, CA 93960
831-678-1717
Fax: 831-678-2742 www.chalonevineyard.com
Wines
Manager: Robert Cook
robert.cook@biateo.com
Public Relations: Lynn Johnston
General Manager/Winemaker: Dan Karlsen
Estimated Sales: $5-10 Million
Number Employees: 5-9
Parent Co: Chalone Wine Group

2406 **Cham Cold Brew Tea**
300 Park Ave
New York, NY 10022
646-926-0206
www.drinkcham.com
Cold brewed teas
Co-Founder & CEO: Niko Nikolaou
Number of Brands: 1
Number of Products: 3
Type of Packaging: Consumer
Brands:
CHAM COLD BREW TEA

2407 **Chambord**
850 Dixie Highway
Louisville, KY 40210
215-425-9300
Fax: 215-425-9438 800-523-3811
Brown-Forman@b-f.com
www.chambordchannel.com
Raspberry liquor
CEO: Lawson Whiting
CFO: Jane Morreau
External Communications: Elizabeth Conway
Estimated Sales: $26 Million
Number Employees: 120
Square Footage: 188000
Parent Co: Brown-Forman
Type of Packaging: Private Label
Brands:
Chambord

2408 **Chameleon Cold Brew**
P.O. Box 4518
Austin, TX 78765-4518
chameleoncoldbrew.com
Cold brewed coffee; organic; instant; and concentrates.
Co-Founder: Chris Campbell
Co-Founder: Steve Williams
Year Founded: 2010
Number Employees: 40
Type of Packaging: Food Service, Private Label

2409 **Champignon North America Inc**
456 Sylvan Ave
Suite 4
Englewood Cliffs, NJ 07632-2707
201-871-7211
Fax: 201-871-7214 info@champignon-usa.com
www.champignon-international.com
Gourmet cheeses.
President: Birgit Bernhard
VP: Olaf Glaser
Estimated Sales: $8 Million
Number Employees: 1-4
Number of Brands: 2
Brands:
Brie W/Garlic De Luxe
Cambozola
Champignon
Hofmeister
Mirabo
Montagnolo
Rougette
Royal Bavarian

2410 **Champion Beverages**
44 Talmadge Hill Road
Darien, CT 06820-2125
203-655-9026
Fax: 203-655-0676
Beer, dairy drinks
President/CEO: Joseph Tighe
COO: Elaine Tighe
Estimated Sales: Under $500,000
Number Employees: 1-4
Brands:
Erin's Rock Amber and Stout
Smoothie Sparkling Choc.Egg Cream
Stallion X Malt Liquor

2411 **Champion Nutrition Inc**
1301 Sawgrass Corporate Pkwy
Sunrise, FL 33323-2813
954-233-3300
Fax: 925-689-0821 800-225-4831
www.champion-nutrition.com
Processor and exporter of sports nutrition supplements
Owner: Malcolm Borg
VP Finance: Jannie Motta
Industry Contact: Christy Olson
Estimated Sales: Less Than $500,000
Number Employees: 1-4
Square Footage: 18188
Brands:
Heavyweight Gainer 900
Met-Max
Metabolol
Muscle Nitro
Oxi Pro Metabolol
Revenge

2412 **Champlain Valley Apiaries**
504 Washington Street Ext
Middlebury, VT 05753-8878
802-388-7724
Fax: 802-388-1653 800-841-7334
cva@together.net
www.champlainvalleyhoney.com
Liquid and natural crystallized honey

Owner: Charles Mraz
cva@together.net
Office Manager: Sue Synder
Bee Keeper: James Gabriel
Estimated Sales: $2.5-5 Million
Number Employees: 1-4
Type of Packaging: Consumer

2413 **Champlain Valley Milling Corp**
6679 Main St
Westport, NY 12993
518-962-4711
Fax: 518-962-8799
info@champlainvalleymilling.com
Organic and kosher whole grain flour including spring wheat, stone ground, soy, rye, white, whole pastry, pancake, etc
President: Sam Sherman
samsherman@champlainvalleymilling.com
Vice President: Paul Barton
Operations Manager: Donald White
Estimated Sales: $5-9.9 Million
Number Employees: 5-9
Type of Packaging: Private Label
Brands:
Champ

2414 **Champoeg Wine Cellars Inc**
10375 Champoeg Rd NE
Aurora, OR 97002-8657
503-678-2144
Fax: 503-678-1024
champoeg@champoegwine.com
www.champoegwine.com
Wines
Owner: Lounna Eggert
leggert@champoegwine.com
Estimated Sales: Less Than $500,000
Number Employees: 1-4

2415 **Champs Chicken**
170 Commerce Dr
PO Box 160
Holts Summit, MO 65043-1098
573-896-2500
Fax: 573-896-9583 888-581-9188
customer.service@PFSbrands.com
www.champschicken.com
Chicken products
CEO: Shawn Burcham
CFO: Trevor Monnig
VP, Human Resources: Carla Dowden
VP, Marketing: Carl Christenson
VP, Operations: Brock Blaise
Number Employees: 50-99

2416 **Chandler Foods Inc**
Greensboro, NC 27407
336-299-1934
Fax: 336-854-4649 800-537-6219
cfoods@chandlerfoodsinc.com
www.chandlerfoodsinc.com
Barbecue products including pork, chicken and beef; also, chili products including frozen, hot dog and con carne
President: Jeff Chandler
jeffc@chandlerfoodsinc.com
Estimated Sales: $5-9.9 Million
Number Employees: 20-49
Square Footage: 159600
Type of Packaging: Food Service
Brands:
Carolina Barbecue
Chandler Foods

2417 **Chang Food Company**
13941 Nautilus Dr
Garden Grove, CA 92843-4026
714-265-9990
Fax: 714-265-9996 www.changs.com
Process frozen egg rolls, spring rolls, soba noodle, egg noodle bowls (stir fried tofu, vegetable, etc)
President: Van Nguyen
service@changs.com
Manager: Nhuan Nguyen
Estimated Sales: $2.5-$3 Million
Number Employees: 21
Square Footage: 19600
Type of Packaging: Consumer, Food Service, Private Label, Bulk
Brands:
Chang Food

2418 **Channel Fish ProcessingCo Inc**
18 Food Mart Rd
Boston, MA 02118-2802
617-464-3366
Fax: 617-464-3377 800-536-3474
t.zaffiro@channelfish.com www.channelfish.com
Fresh and frozen seafood.
President: John Zaffiro
Owner: Roy Zaffiro
Director, Business Development: Thomas Zaffiro
Estimated Sales: $45 Million
Number Employees: 50-99
Number of Brands: 3
Type of Packaging: Consumer, Food Service, Private Label
Other Locations:
Gloucester MA
Brands:
Channel
Fish Crunchies
North Atlantic

2419 **Channel Fish Processing**
88 Commercial St
Gloucester, MA 01930-5096
978-283-4121
Fax: 978-283-5948 800-457-0054
t.zaffiro@channelfish.com
Processor and exporter of frozen catfish, cod, halibut, herring, smelt, squid, shrimp, scallops and whiting; portion-controlled breaded and prepared seafood
President: Frank Cefalo
Sales Manager: Joe Bertolino
Contact: Jim Cross
jcross@channelfish.com
Operations Manager: James Stuart
Estimated Sales: $4.20 Million
Number Employees: 20-49
Square Footage: 160000
Type of Packaging: Consumer, Food Service
Brands:
Better Buy
Courageous Captain's
North Atlantic

2420 **Channing Rudd Cellars**
PO Box 426
Middletown, CA 95461-0426
707-987-2209
Wines
President: J Rudd
Sales: Reese Grandstaff
Sales: Darrel Burns
Number Employees: 20-49

2421 **Chaparral Gardens**
16422 Morro Rd
Atascadero, CA 93422-1017
USA
805-703-0829
Fax: 805-461-1099
artisans@chaparralgardens.com
www.cgvinegar.com
Marinades, balsamic vinegar, olive oil
Owners/Founders: Craig & Cari Clark
craig@chaparralgardens.com
Estimated Sales: 230,000
Number Employees: 4

2422 **Chappaqua Crunch**
65 Tedesco St
Marblehead, MA 01945-1039
781-631-8118
Fax: 781-631-8113
Granola, snack foods
President: Debbie Waugh
Estimated Sales: Under $500,000
Number Employees: 1-4

2423 **Chappellet Winery**
1581 Sage Canyon Rd
St Helena, CA 94574-9628
707-963-7136
Fax: 707-963-7445 800-494-6379
customerservice@chappellet.com
www.chappellet.com
Wines
Owner: Swetha Anbarasan
Founder: Molly Chappallet
Owner: Jon-Mark Chappellet
Marketing/Sales: Cyril Chappellet
Director National Sales: Steve Tamburelli
sanbarasan@cisco.com
Winery/Vineyard Operations: Jon Mark
Winemaker: Phillip Corallo-Titus
Vineyard Manager: David Pirio
Purchasing Manager: Carissa Chappellet
Estimated Sales: $2.5 Million
Number Employees: 20-49
Type of Packaging: Private Label
Brands:
Chappallet

2424 **Char Crust**
3017 North Lincoln Avenue
Chicago, IL 60657-4242
773-528-0600
Fax: 773-472-1101 800-311-9884
customerservice@charcrust.com
Dry-rub seasonings for all meat and fish
Founder/President: Bernard Silver
Director/Marketing: Susan Eriksen
Estimated Sales: $500,000-$1 Million
Number Employees: 5-9
Brands:
Char Crust

2425 **Char-Wil Canning Company**
5620 Landing Neck Road
Trappe, MD 21643-3318
410-476-3167
Fax: 410-943-3580
Processor and canner of whole and peeled tomatoes
Owner/Partner: Charles Adams
Number Employees: 6
Type of Packaging: Consumer, Food Service, Private Label, Bulk
Brands:
Char-Wil

2426 **Charcuterie LaTour Eiffel**
1020, boul. MichŠle-Bohec
Blainville, QC J7C 5E2
Canada
418-687-2840
Fax: 418-688-9558 800-361-0001
www.toureiffel.ca
Processor and exporter of fresh and frozen pork
Marketing Director: Francois Couture
Parent Co: McCain Foods USA
Type of Packaging: Bulk
Brands:
Bilopage
Tour Eiffel

2427 **Charissa**
8595 Cox Ln
Unit 3
Cutchogue, NY 11935
631-734-8878
charissaspice.com
Morrocan seasonings
Co-Founder: Earl Fultz
Co-Founder: Gloria Fultz
Number Employees: 4
Type of Packaging: Private Label

2428 **Charles B. Mitchell Vineyards**
8221 Stoney Creek Road Fair Play
Somerset, CA 95684
530-620-3467
Fax: 530-620-1005 800-704-9463
info@charlesbmitchell.com
www.charlesbmitchell.com
Wine
Owner: Michael Conti
Estimated Sales: $2.5-5 Million
Number Employees: 5-9
Type of Packaging: Private Label

2429 **Charles Chocolates**
535 Florida St
San Francisco, CA 94110
www.charleschocolates.com
Handmade chocolates
Founder: Chuck Siegel

2430 **Charles H Baldwin & Sons**
1 Center St
P.O.Box 372
West Stockbridge, MA 01266-9502
413-232-7785
Fax: 413-232-0114 www.baldwinextracts.com
Flavoring extracts and flavors, maple table syrup and supplier of baking supplies.
Owner: Jackie Moffatt
jackie@baldwinextracts.com
Estimated Sales: $500,000-$1 Million
Number Employees: 1-4
Brands:
Baldwin

2431 **Charles H. Parks & Company**
2405 Hoopers Island Rd
Fishing Creek, MD 21634
410-397-3400
Fax: 410-397-3400
Fresh, canned and pasteurized crabmeat; also, fresh crabs
President: Virgil Ruark Jr
Estimated Sales: $3-5 Million
Number Employees: 10-19
Square Footage: 9000
Type of Packaging: Consumer
Brands:
Captain Charlie

2432 **Charles Krug Winery**
2800 Main St
St Helena, CA 94574-9502
707-967-2200
Fax: 707-967-2291 www.charleskrug.com
Fine wines
Winemaker, CK Mondavi Vineyards: Marc Mondavi
Winemaker, Charles Krug: Peter Mondavi
Year Founded: 1861
Number Employees: 100-249
Brands:
Charles Krug
CK Mondavi

2433 **Charles Poultry Company**
2943 Charlestown Road
Lancaster, PA 17603-9758
717-872-7621
Fax: 717-872-9570
Free range and all natural chicken and turkey including whole cut up, cutlets, legs, wings, whole breasts, drums, thighs, etc
President: Ken Charles
VP: Richard Charles
Estimated Sales: $20-50 Million
Number Employees: 20-49
Square Footage: 9000
Parent Co: Charles Poultry Live Broker
Type of Packaging: Consumer, Food Service, Private Label, Bulk

2434 **Charles Rockel & Son**
4303 Smith Rd
Cincinnati, OH 45212-4236
513-631-3009
Fax: 513-631-3083
Food brokers of dairy/deli products, frozen foods, general merchandise, groceries, industrial ingredients, etc
President: Charles Rockel
CFO: Don Rockel
Estimated Sales: $2.5-5 Million
Number Employees: 3

2435 **Charles Spinetta Winery**
12557 Steiner Rd
PO Box 717
Plymouth, CA 95669-9510
209-245-3384
Fax: 209-245-3386
www.charlesspinettawinery.com
Table wine including wines for bulk market
Owner: Charles Spinetta
Estimated Sales: $1-2.5 Million
Number Employees: 1-4
Brands:
Charles Spinetta Barbera
Charles Spinetta Primitivo
Charles Spinetta Zinfanel

2436 **Charles Walker North America**
2901 Stanley Ave
Fort Worth, TX 76110
817-922-9834
Fax: 817-922-9854 cissy@charlesalaninc.com
www.charlesalanfurniture.com
Furniture manufacturer
Owner: Margaret Sevadjian
Vice President: Jim Boston
Operations Manager: Steve McDonald
Square Footage: 120
Brands:
Waiker Conveyor Belt & Equipment

2437 **Charleston Tea Plantation**
6617 Maybank Hwy
Wadmalaw Island, SC 29487-7006
843-559-0383
Fax: 843-559-3049 800-443-5987
www.charlestonteaplantation.com
Tea
Owner: William Hall
lfasig@rcbigelow.com
Estimated Sales: $2,900,000
Number Employees: 5-9
Brands:
American Classic Tea

2438 **Charlie Beigg's Sauce Company**
4 Heritage Lane
Windham, ME 04062-4984
888-502-8595
sales@charliebeiggs.com
BBQ sauce and salsa.
Head of Sales/Marketing: Paula Standley
Parent Co: Equitythink Holdings, LLC

2439 **Charlie Palmer Group**
420 Lexington Avenue
Suite 850
New York, NY 10170
212-967-6942
Fax: 212-750-8613 866-458-7224
info@charliepalmer.com www.charliepalmer.com
Pan sauces, dessert sauces
Owner: Charlie Lee
VP, HR: Sabrina Orque
Marketing Manager: Christie Sheffield
Corporate Sales Director: Rick Becker
Estimated Sales: $2.5-5 Million
Number Employees: 50-99
Brands:
Charlie Palmer

2440 **Charlie's Country Sausage**
4005 Burdick Expy E
Minot, ND 58701-5462
701-838-6302
Meat products including salami, honey ham and sausage
Owner: Rod Lynch
Estimated Sales: $1-2.5 Million
Number Employees: 5-9

2441 **Charlie's Pride**
2650 Leonis Boulevard
Vernon, CA 90058
Fax: 323-587-7317 877-866-0992
www.charliespride.com
Prepared meats manufacturer founded in 1969.
Co-CEO: Jim Dickman
Co-CEO: Robert Dickman
CFO: Ted Murphy
VP, Sales: Peter Goldsberry
Plant Manager: Krystal Valle
Purchasing Manager: Yahaira Martinez
Number Employees: 140
Square Footage: 60000
Type of Packaging: Consumer, Food Service, Private Label, Bulk

2442 **Charlie's Specialties Inc**
2500 Freedland Rd
Hermitage, PA 16148-9022
724-346-2350
Fax: 724-346-1110 contactus@bkcompany.com
www.bkcompany.com
Fancy cookies
President: Jay Thier
jthier@charliesusa.com
Owner: E.G. Byrnes, Jr.
Sales: Stacy Rouse
Plant Manager: Frank Keck
Purchasing: Thomas Byrnes
Estimated Sales: $5-10 Million
Number Employees: 100-249
Number of Products: 45
Square Footage: 96000
Parent Co: Byrnes Kitchen Company

2443 **Charlito's Cocina**
21-09 Borden Avenue
Brooklyn, NY
718-482-7890
info@charlitoscocina.com
www.charlitoscocina.com
Cured meats.
Founder: Charles Wekselbaum

2444 **Charlotte's Confections**
1395 El Camino Real
Millbrae, CA 94030-1410
650-589-1126
Fax: 650-589-1923 800-798-2427
lisa@charlottesconfections.com
www.charlottesconfections.com
Boxed chocolates, taffy, caramel, brittle, fudge, marshmallow, and holiday specialties.
President: Jeffrey Sosnick
Vice President: Sean Callaway
Marketing Director: Susan Muniak
Contact: Lisa Olswing
lisa@charlottesconfections.com
Production Coordinator: Jim Macintire
Purchasing Manager: Jim Macintire
Estimated Sales: $5 Million
Number Employees: 50-99
Square Footage: 96000
Type of Packaging: Consumer, Food Service, Private Label, Bulk

2445 **Charlton Charters**
P.O.Box 637
Warrenton, OR 97146-0637
503-338-0569
Fax: 503-861-3229 dscharters@qwestoffice.net
Seafood, including halibut, salmon, sturgeon, tuna, bottomfish
President: Mark Charlton
Estimated Sales: $2.5-5 Million
Number Employees: 1-4

2446 **Charlton Natural Foods, Inc.**
8277 Kendall Dr
Huntington Beach, CA 92646-6932
888-611-7753
www.charltonfoods.com
Snack chips; pellets and granules; quinoa; chocolate covered dried fruit.
Director: Norman Suh
norman_suh@charltonfoods.com
Type of Packaging: Private Label

2447 **Chartreuse Organic Tea**
2837 W Jefferson Ave
Trenton, MI 48183
734-671-3006
Fax: 734-671-3953 866-315-7832
Aromatic herbal teas made with all organic herbs. Created using the leaves, stems, roots, berries and flowers from different plants, containing no actual tealeaves. 90% of the herbs used are USA and USDA certified organic with noneof the herbs coming from China, Sri Lanka or India
Owner: Linda Shannon
Type of Packaging: Consumer

2448 **Chas Boggini Co.**
733 Bread & Milk Street
Coventry, CT 06238
860-742-2652
Fax: 860-742-7903 glen@bogginicola.com
www.bogginicola.com
Manufacturer and exporter of flavoring extracts
President: Glen Boggini
VP: David Boggini
Estimated Sales: $5-10 Million
Number Employees: 5-9
Type of Packaging: Consumer

2449 **Chase & Poe Candy Co**
1307 S 59th St
PO Box 698
St Joseph, MO 64507-8124
816-279-1625
Fax: 816-279-1997 800-786-1625
info@cherrymash.com www.cherrymash.com

Candy including bagged, bar, brittle, chocolate, coconut, fund raising, multi-pack, vending, Christmas, Easter, Halloween and Valentine
President: Barry Yantis
Contact: Chris Adams
cadams@cherrymash.com
Estimated Sales: $10-20 Million
Number Employees: 20-49
Square Footage: 60000
Type of Packaging: Consumer, Bulk
Brands:
Cherry Mash
Poe Brands

2450 **Chase Brothers Dairy**
595 S Wolff Rd
Oxnard, CA 93033-2101
805-487-4981
Fax: 805-487-2529 800-438-6455
Milk and related products including fluid, half and half, chocolate, low-fat, nonfat, buttermilk, eggnog and shakes; also, juices, concentrates and drinks including orange, etc
President: Glywn Chase Jr
Vice President: S Chase
Contact: Danny Lopez
dlopez262006@yahoo.com
Estimated Sales: $5-10 Million
Number Employees: 20-49
Square Footage: 28000
Parent Co: Hailwood
Type of Packaging: Consumer, Food Service
Brands:
Chase Brothers
Gold Coast

2451 **Chases Lobster Pound**
7935 Hwy 6
PO Box 1
Port Howe, NS B0K 1K0
Canada
902-243-2408
Fax: 902-243-3334 www.chaseslobsterltd.ca
Processor and exporter of fresh and frozen lobster
Owner/Manager: Earl Chase
Number Employees: 10-19
Type of Packaging: Consumer, Food Service, Private Label, Bulk

2452 **Chasquis Natural Foods**
35 Yale Cres
Unit 300G
St. Catharines, ON L2R 2Y6
Canada
info@chasquisnaturalfoods.com
www.chasquisnaturalfoods.com
Quinoa-based snacks
President: Dave Orosz
Brands:
Quinoa Krunch

2453 **Chateau Anne Marie**
6580 NE Mineral Springs Road
Carlton, OR 97111
503-864-2991
Fax: 503-864-2203 www.anneamie.com
Wines
Owner: Robert Pamplin Jr
Director, Sales & Marketing: Kim McLeod
Director of Operations: Tim Lamers
Estimated Sales: $5-10 Million
Number Employees: 20-49

2454 **Chateau Boswell Winery**
3468 Silverado Trl N
St Helena, CA 94574-9662
707-963-5472
josh@chateauboswellwinery.com
www.chateauboswell.com
Wines
Owner: Susan Boswell
susan@chateauboswellwinery.com
COO: Susan Boswell
Operations Manager: Joshua Peeples
Estimated Sales: Less Than $500,000
Number Employees: 1-4
Type of Packaging: Consumer
Brands:
Chateau Boswell
Chateau Boswell Estate
Jacquelynn Cuv'e
Jacquelynn Syrah

2455 **Chateau Chevre Winery**
2030 Hoffman Ln
Napa, CA 94558
707-944-2184
Fax: 707-944-2408
Wines
Owner: Jerry Hazen
Estimated Sales: Less than $100,000
Number Employees: 1-4
Type of Packaging: Private Label

2456 **Chateau Diana Winery**
6195 Dry Creek Rd
Healdsburg, CA 95448-8100
707-433-6992
Fax: 707-433-0743 info@chateaud.com
www.chateaud.com
Wines
President: Jose Arreola
josea@chateaud.com
Co-Owner & President of Sales: Dawn Manning
CFO: Donna Gibson
Quality Control Manager: Andrew Moore
Production Manager: Jos, Arreola
Estimated Sales: $5-10 Million
Number Employees: 20-49
Brands:
Chateau Diana

2457 **Chateau Food Products Inc**
6137 W Cermak Rd
Cicero, IL 60804-2024
708-863-4207
Fax: 708-863-5806 www.chateaufoods.com
Frozen potato and bread dumplings
President: Donald Shotola
don.shotola@gmail.com
VP: Anita Shotola
Production: Jon Shotola
Estimated Sales: $1 Million
Number Employees: 5-9
Square Footage: 40000
Type of Packaging: Consumer, Food Service
Brands:
Chateau
Mihel

2458 **Chateau Grand Traverse Winery**
12239 Center Rd
Traverse City, MI 49686-8558
231-938-6120
Fax: 231-223-4105 www.cgtwines.com
Wines
Owner: Ed O' Keefe
Founder/Chairma: Edward O'Keefe, Sr
VP: Sean O'Keefe
Marketing Coordinator: Elizabeth Smith
NSM: Rhonda Riebow
edokeefe@cgtwines.com
Operations Manager/Controller: Terrie McClelland
Bottling Production Manager: Peter Francisco
Purchasing Manager: Mark Groenevelt
Estimated Sales: $2.5-5 Million
Number Employees: 50-99

2459 **Chateau Julien Winery**
8940 Carmel Valley Road
Carmel, CA 93923
831-624-2600
Fax: 831-624-6138
Wines
Owner: Robert Brower
Assistant Director of Marketing: Shonda Kroll
National Sales Manager: Bobby Brower
Contact: Fina Dominquez
dominquez@chateaujulien.com
VP Production: Bill Anderson
Estimated Sales: $1-2.5 Million
Number Employees: 10-19
Brands:
Chateau Julien
Emerald Bay Coastak
Garland Ranch

2460 **Chateau LA Fayette Reneau**
5081 State Route 414
Hector, NY 14841
607-546-2062
Fax: 607-546-2069 800-469-9463
info@clrwine.com www.clrwine.com
Wine
Owner/Purchasing Manager: Dick Reno
clrwine@aol.com
VP: Betty Reno
General Manager: Heather Lodge
Estimated Sales: $1.4 Million
Number Employees: 20-49
Type of Packaging: Private Label

2461 **Chateau Montelena Winery**
1429 Tubbs Ln
Calistoga, CA 94515-9726
707-942-5105
Fax: 707-942-4221
customer-service@montelena.com
www.montelena.com
Wines
General Partner: James Barrett
Partner: Bo Barrett
Vice President, Sales/Marketing: Brian Baker
Estimated Sales: $35 Million
Number Employees: 20-49
Number of Brands: 2
Brands:
Chateau Montelena
Silverado Cellars

2462 **Chateau Morrisette Winery**
287 Winery Rd SW
Floyd, VA 24091-4033
540-593-2865
info@thedogs.com
www.thedogs.com
Wines
President: David Morrisette
Marketing Director: Keith Toler
Estimated Sales: $10-20 Million
Number Employees: 20-49

2463 **Chateau Potelle Winery**
1200 Dowdell Ln
St Helena, CA 94574 1407
707-255-9440
Fax: 707-963-3031 info@chateaupotelle.com
www.vgschateaupotelle.com
Wines
Owner: Jean-Noel Fourmeaux
jean-noel@chateaupotelle.com
Purchasing Manager: Ulysses Montre
Estimated Sales: $2.5-5 Million
Number Employees: 5-9
Brands:
Chateau Potelle

2464 **Chateau Ra-Ha**
301 Commerce Blvd
Jerseyville, IL 62052
618-639-4841
Fax: 618-639-0510 866-639-4832
info@gtec.net www.gtec.com
Wines
Owner: Paul Arnold
Estimated Sales: $500,000-$1 Million
Number Employees: 1-4

2465 **Chateau Souverain**
26150 Asti Road
PO Box 245
Cloverdale, CA 95425-245
707-302-7722
Fax: 707-433-5174 877-687-9463
shawna.hernandez@tweglobal.com
www.souverain.com
Cabernet sauvignon, merlot, sauvignon blanc, chardonnay and zinfandel
President: Dan Leese
Event Manager: Shawna Hernandez
Purchasing Manager: John Peavey
Estimated Sales: $20-50 Million
Number Employees: 50-99
Parent Co: E&J Gallo
Type of Packaging: Private Label
Brands:
Chateau Souverain

2466 **Chateau St Jean Winery**
8555 Sonoma Hwy
P.O.Box 293
Kenwood, CA 95452-9026
707-833-4134
Fax: 707-833-4200 www.chateaustjean.com
Table wine

Manager: Margo Van Stafvaren
margo.vanstafvaren@scatecsolar.com
Winemaker/Operation Director: Margo Anstaavern
Public Relations Manager: Nicole Breier
Wine Maker: Steven Reeder
Estimated Sales: $10-24.9 Million
Number Employees: 50-99
Parent Co: Beringer Wine Estates
Type of Packaging: Consumer

2467 **Chateau des Charmes Wines**
PO Box 280
St. Davids, ON L0S 1P0
Canada
905-262-4219
Fax: 905-262-5548 800-263-2541
www.chateaudescharmes.com
Wines and champagnes, ice wine
President: Paul Bosc
Secretary: Rodger Gordon
Director Marketing: Paul-Andre Bosc
Estimated Sales: $1-2.5 Million
Number Employees: 100-249

2468 **Chatila's**
254 N Broadway
Salem, NH 03079-2132
603-898-5459
Fax: 603-893-1586
customercare@chatilasbakery.com
www.chatilasbakery.com
All sugar-free items. Chatila's muffins, cookies, pastries, cheesecakes, donuts, bagels, pies, breads, chocolates and ice cream. All items sweetend with Splenda and/or Melltitol, low carb, low cal, low fat, low cholestrol, notrans-fat.
President: Mohamad Chatila
cutomercare@chatilas.com
Sales: Jennifer Marks
Estimated Sales: Less Than $500,000
Number Employees: 1-4
Number of Brands: 1
Number of Products: 100+
Square Footage: 24000
Type of Packaging: Consumer, Food Service, Private Label, Bulk

2469 **Chatom Vineyards Inc**
7449 Esmeralda Rd
San Andreas, CA 95249-9641
209-736-4604
Fax: 209-736-6507 800-435-8852
www.chatomvineyards.com
Wines
Owner: Gay Callan
info@chatomvineyards.com
Director: Nikki FYFE
Production Manager: Scott Klann
Purchasing Manager: Mari Wells
Estimated Sales: Less Than $500,000
Number Employees: 1-4
Number of Products: 7
Square Footage: 16800
Brands:
Sangiovese
Syrah

2470 **Chattanooga Bakery Inc**
900 Manufacturers Rd # 101
Chattanooga, TN 37405-3763
423-267-3351
Fax: 423-266-2169 800-251-3404
moonpiedirect@moonpie.com
Chattanooga Bakery was founded in 1902. An independent bakery offering snack cake and cookie products, including moon pies, pecan pies, coconut pies and marshmallow treats.
President/CEO: Sam Campbell
CFO: Keith Holt
keith@moonpie.com
VP Marketing: Tory Johnston
VP Sales: John Campbell
VP Operations: Guy Callahan
Estimated Sales: $20-50 Million
Number Employees: 100-249
Number of Brands: 1
Type of Packaging: Consumer
Brands:
MoonPie

2471 **Chattem Chemicals Inc**
3708 Saint Elmo Ave
Chattanooga, TN 37409-1235
423-822-5000
Fax: 423-825-0507
eva.edwards@chattemchemicals.com
www.chattemchemicals.com
Glycine and creatine monohydrate
President: Jitendra Doshi
Cmo: Herman Echeverri
herman.echeverri@chattemchemicals.com
CFO: Ed Rusk
VP/General Manager: Jason Allen
Research & Development: Nilesh Patel
Quality Assurance/Quality Control: Frank Seymour
Sales/Marketing Hamposyl Surfactants: Art Pavlidis
Sales/Marketing Rheology Modifiers/APIs: Herman Echeverri
VP Operations/Production/Manufacturing: Ray Smith
Manufacturing Director: Scott Newton
Purchasing/ Traffic: Bill Grant
Estimated Sales: $5-10 Million
Number Employees: 50-99
Square Footage: 51948
Parent Co: Elcat
Type of Packaging: Bulk

2472 **Chatz Roasting Co**
4221 Brew Master Dr # 13
Suite 13
Ceres, CA 95307-7590
209-541-1100
Fax: 209-541-1131 chatzcoffee@yahoo.com
Gourmet coffee, tea and cocoa.
President: Linda Blaney
Partner: Linda Blaney
Estimated Sales: $10-20 Million
Number Employees: 1-4
Brands:
Chatz

2473 **Chaucer Consumer Solutions**
Calabasas, CA 91302
info@crunchiesfood.com
www.crunchiesfood.com
Chocolate-covered freeze-dried fruit snacks
President & CEO: Scott Jacobson

2474 **Chaucer Foods, Inc. USA**
2238 Yew St
Forest Grove, OR 97116
www.chaucergroup.co.uk
Manufacturers freeze dried ingredients and specialty bread products.
CEO: Andy Ducker
Number Employees: 5-9
Parent Co: Chaucer Foods Ltd

2475 **Chauvin Coffee Corporation**
4160 Meramec St
Saint Louis, MO 63116
314-772-0700
Fax: 314-772-0722 800-455-5282
info@chauvincoffee.com www.chauvincoffee.com
Coffee
President: Bonnie Charleville
VP: Mike Charleville
Marketing Manager: Verner Earls
Sales Manager: Sonya Miller
Contact: Lisa Contestabile
l.contestabile@chauvincoffee.com
Estimated Sales: $1-3 Million
Number Employees: 10-19
Type of Packaging: Private Label

2476 **Chazy Orchards**
9486 State Route 9
Chazy, NY 12921
518-846-7171
Fax: 518-846-8171
customerservice@chazyorchards.com
www.chazy.com
Grower of apples
Operations Manager: Craig Reyell
Estimated Sales: $5-10 Million
Number Employees: 20-49
Parent Co: Giroux's Poultry Farm
Brands:
SweeTango ™

2477 **Cheating Gourmet**
PO Box 1537
Auburn, ME 04211
800-239-9731
www.scottandjons.com
Flash frozen shrimp bowls
Founder: Scott Demers
Founder: Jon Demers
Number of Products: 10
Brands:
Scott & Jon's

2478 **Chebe Bread Products**
1840 Lundberg Dr W
Spirit Lake, IA 51360-7661
712-336-4211
www.chebe.com
Gluten free dry mixes and frozen bread
Owner: Richard Reed
dreed@chebe.com
Number Employees: 5-9

2479 **Cheddar Box Cheese House**
264 Alpine Dr
Shawano, WI 54166
715-526-5411
Fax: 715-524-9930
Cheese spreads
President: James O'Betts
Estimated Sales: $400,000
Number Employees: 1-4
Brands:
Cheddar Box Cheese

2480 **Cheese Factory**
4856 Lake Ave
Buffalo, NY 14219-1314
716-828-0178
Fax: 716-828-0179
President: Edwin Hildebrand
e.hildebrand@cheesefactory.com
Estimated Sales: Less Than $500,000
Number Employees: 1-4
Parent Co: Cheese Factory

2481 **Cheese Merchants of America**
248 Tubeway Dr
Carol Stream, IL 60188
630-768-0317
Fax: 630-221-0584 johnp@cheesemerchants.com
www.cheesemerchants.com
Processors of custom blends of Italian cheeses, converters of hard Italian cheeses to grated, shredded, and shaved.
EVP/Managing Partner: Robert Greco
Director Purchasing/Quality Assurance: Paul DelleGrazie
Central Regional Sales Manager: Mark Lewis
EVP Sales: Jim Smart
Contact: Brian Barrett
brianb@cheesemerchants.com
Estimated Sales: $19.3 Million
Number Employees: 90
Square Footage: 105000
Type of Packaging: Consumer, Food Service, Bulk

2482 **Cheese Straws & More**
5717 Desiard Street
Monroe, LA 71203-4793
318-343-4666
Fax: 318-343-6333 800-997-1921
Straws including Cajun cheese and southern tea; also, pecan pralines, candied pecans and pecan brittle
President: Brenda Schwab
Number Employees: 1-4

2483 **CheeseLand**
P.O.Box 22230
Seattle, WA 98122-0230
206-709-1220
Fax: 206-709-1818
Cheese
President: Jan Kos
Contact: Mark Roeland
info@cheeselandinc.com
Estimated Sales: $1-2,500,000
Number Employees: 1-4

2484 **Cheesecake Etc Desserts**
400 Swallow Dr
Miami Springs, FL 33166-4432
305-887-0258
Fax: 305-888-5463

Cheesecakes, key lime pies, diner style layer cakes, individual dessert cups; including all varieties of layer cakes, cheesecake, and key lime pie
Owner: Frank Romano
cheesecakeemail@aol.com
VP: MILO IRSULA
Office Manager: Rachelle Romano
Estimated Sales: Under $500,000
Number Employees: 1-4
Number of Brands: 3
Number of Products: 25
Square Footage: 40000
Parent Co: Obem Foods, Inc
Type of Packaging: Food Service
Brands:
Florida Key Lime Pie

2485 **Cheesecake Factory Inc.**
26901 Malibu Hills Rd.
Calabasas Hills, CA 91301
818-871-3000
Fax: 818-871-3100
www.thecheesecakefactory.com
Restaurant chain and dessert distributor, specializing in cheesecakes.
President: David Gordon
Chairman/CEO: David Overton
doverton@thecheesecakefactory.com
Executive VP/CFO: Matthew Clark
Executive V/General Counsel: Scarlett May
Year Founded: 1972
Estimated Sales: $2.26 Billion
Number Employees: 38,800
Brands:
Cheesecake Factory®

2486 **Cheesecake Momma**
200 W Henry St
Ukiah, CA 95482
707-462-2253
Fax: 707-468-9056 momma@pacific.net
Processor and wholesaler of cheesecake including all natural and 100% organic
President: Robin Collier
Vice President: Alana Rouse
Estimated Sales: $2.5-5 Million
Number Employees: 20-49

2487 **Cheeze Kurls**
2915 Walkent Drive NW
Grand Rapids, MI 49544-9745
616-784-6095
Fax: 616-784-7445
Snack foods including popcorn and cheese curls
President: Tim DeDinas
VP: Bob Franzak
Vice President, Marketing: Dave Krombeen
Contact: Christopher Dedinas
cdedinas@cksnacks.com
Number Employees: 20-49
Square Footage: 120000
Type of Packaging: Consumer, Food Service, Private Label, Bulk
Brands:
Ck

2488 **Chef America**
9601 Canoga Ave
Chatsworth, CA 91311
818-718-8111
www.chefamerica.com
Prepared frozen foods including stuffed sandwiches and croissants, pizza snacks and waffles
CEO: Paul Merage
CFO: Glenn Lee
VP: Larry Johnson
Research & Development: Phil Mason
V P Finance: Glenn Lee
Contact: John Mccarthy
john.mccarthy@us.nestle.com
Purchasing Director: George Turner
Purchasing Manager: Russ Shroyer
Plant Manager: Mike Crawford
Number Employees: 500-999
Type of Packaging: Consumer, Food Service

2489 **Chef Hans' Gourmet Foods**
310 Walnut St
Monroe, LA 71201-6712
318-322-2334
Fax: 318-322-2340 800-890-4267
ckorrodi@bayou.com
www.chefhansgourmetfoods.com
Processor and exporter of soup bases, batter, spices, seafood, breading, seasonings, wild rice pilaf, rice, desserts, bran, jambalaya, gumbo, etouffee, etc.
President: Hans Korrodi
ckorrodi@bayou.com
Estimated Sales: $1-2.5 Million
Number Employees: 1-4
Square Footage: 88000
Brands:
Chef Hans

2490 **Chef Merito Inc**
7915 Sepulveda Blvd
Van Nuys, CA 91405-1032
818-787-0100
Fax: 818-787-5900 800-637-4861
info@chefmerito.com www.chefmerito.com
Processor, importer and exporter of dried spices, seasonings, seasoned rice, batters, breading mixes, soups and sauces
President/CEO: Plinio Garcia, Jr
Project Manager: Sara Nicholson
Estimated Sales: $10-20 Million
Number Employees: 50-99
Number of Brands: 4
Square Footage: 30000
Type of Packaging: Consumer, Food Service, Bulk
Brands:
Chef Merito
Pikos Pikosos
Ppeppers
Sabrosito

2491 **Chef Paul Prudhomme's Magic Seasonings Blends**
PO Box 23342
New Orleans, LA 70183-0342
504-731-3590
Fax: 504-731-3576 800-457-2857
info@chefpaul.com www.chefpaul.com
Seasonings and spices.
President/CEO: Shawn McBride
CFO: Tiffanie Roppolo
VP, Sales & Marketing: John McBride
International Sales & Marketing: Anna Zuniga
Contact: Wade Anderson
wanderson@chefpaul.com
Director, Operations: Joey Duplechain
VP, Manufacturing: David Hickey
Plant Manager: Buddy Duplechain
Estimated Sales: $10-20 Million
Number Employees: 50-99
Number of Brands: 1
Square Footage: 30000
Type of Packaging: Private Label
Brands:
Chef Paul Prudhomme's

2492 **Chef Philippe LLC**
715 Ryan Plaza Drive
Suite Ai
Arlington, TX 76011-1714
817-461-9049
Fax: 817-460-0309
www.ChefPhilipeesKitchen.com
Sauces such as pepper brandy sauce, roasted garlic sauce, rosemary sauce, truffle red wine sauce, seafood white wine cream sauce, lingonberry pepper sauce, and apple cider sauce
Estimated Sales: $.5-1 million
Number Employees: 5-9

2493 **Chef Salt**
6025 Vera Cruz Road
Center Valley, PA 18034
215-782-1730
www.chefsalt.com
Manufacturer of salts.
Co-Founder: David Joachim
Co-Founder: Andrew Schloss
Co-Founder: Mark Bitterman

2494 **Chef Shamy Gourmet**
Salt Lake City, UT 84104
chefshamy.com
Gourmet garlic butter
Founder: David Shamy

2495 **Chef Shells Catering & Roadside Cafe**
324 Superior Mall
Downtown Port Huron, MI 48060
810-966-8371
Fax: 810-966-8372 info@chefshells.com
www.chefshells.com
Wine vinaigrettes, sauces, seasonings and dip mixes; gourmet catering available
Owner: Shell Wrubel
Owner: Mark Wrubel
Estimated Sales: $38,000
Number of Products: 45
Square Footage: 7200
Type of Packaging: Consumer, Food Service, Private Label, Bulk

2496 **Chef Silvio's of Wooster Street**
69 Brookward Road
Guilford, CT 06437-1804
203-453-1064
Fax: 203-453-1064 newmedfoods@aol.com
www.chefsilvios.com
Gourmet foods and sauces.

2497 **Chef Soraya**
6350 Gunpark Dr
Boulder, CO 80301
800-677-7423
info@chefsoraya.com www.chefsoraya.com
Prepared rice bowls
CEO: Soraya Fouladi
Number of Brands: 1
Number of Products: 6
Type of Packaging: Consumer
Brands:
EAT A BOWL

2498 **Chef Tim Foods, LLC**
65 Sam Snead Circle
Etters, PA 17319-9565
717-802-0350
cheftim@ptd.net
www.cheftimfoods.com
Gluten-free, kosher, organic/natural, salad dressing, marinades, other sauces, seasonings and cooking enhancers.
Contact: Sabrena Jutzi
sabrena@cheftimfoods.com

2499 **Chef Zachary's Gourmet Blended Spices**
PO Box 24115
Detroit, MI 48224
313-226-0000
Fax: 313-226-0000 zach4spice@aol.com
Natural, gourmet spice blends
Owner/President: Chef Zachary Smith
Estimated Sales: $300,000-500,000
Number Employees: 1-4
Type of Packaging: Consumer
Brands:
Blackening Spice
Chelsea Spice
Mediterranean
Shana Spice

2500 **Chef's Cut: Real Jerky**
PO Box 110871
Naples, FL 34108-0115
USA
586-615-0329
www.chefscutrealjerky.com
Jerky, cured meats: prosciutto, bacon
Owner/Chef: Blair Swiler
CEO: Bart Silvestro
Owner: Dennis Riedel
Contact: Nancy Mancini
nancy@chefscutrealjerky.com
Number Employees: 20-49

2501 **Chef's Pride Gifts LLC**
21740 Trolley Industrial # 1
Taylor, MI 48180-1875
313-295-1800
Fax: 313-295-0448 800-878-1800
www.chefspride.com
Fresh and frozen sandwiches; also, salads, desserts and gourmet cinnamon rolls
President/CEO/Owner: Neil Sloman
Manager: Mike Parks
mike@chefspride.com

Estimated Sales: Less Than $500,000
Number Employees: 1-4
Square Footage: 200000
Type of Packaging: Consumer, Private Label
Brands:
Honeybake Farms

2502 **Chef's Requested Foods**
2600 Exchange Ave
Oklahoma City, OK 73108-2448
405-239-2610
Fax: 405-239-2616
Processor of fresh and frozen meats, including pork, beef and poultry.
President: John Williams
Manager, IT: Jody Lankford
Director, Marketing: John Brewster
VP of Sales/Marketing: Steven Folenius
VP of Operations: Justin Williams
Estimated Sales: $38 Million
Number Employees: 100-249
Type of Packaging: Food Service

2503 **Chef-A-Roni Fancy Foods**
2832 S County Trl
East Greenwich, RI 02818-1742
401-884-8798
Fax: 401-884-3552 www.chefaroni.com
Spaghetti sauce
President: Henry Caniglia
h.caniglia@chefaroni.com
Vice President: Lillian Caniglia
Estimated Sales: $500,000-$1 Million
Number Employees: 1-4
Type of Packaging: Consumer, Food Service
Brands:
Chef-A-Roni

2504 **Chefwise**
2200 NW 102nd Ave # 2
Unit 2
Doral, FL 33172-2225
786-845-3884
Fax: 786-845-9997 866-254-CHEF
chefwise@hotmail.com www.chefwise.com
Au jus, desserts, sauces, soups and stocks
Owner: Daniel Durand
ddurand@chefwise.com
Chef: Daniel Durand
Number Employees: 1-4

2505 **Chelan Fresh Marketing**
PO Box 669
Chelan, WA 98816
509-682-2591
Fax: 509-682-4620 www.chelanfresh.com
Apples, pears and cherries from Washington state.
Domestic Sales Manager: Daniel Gebbers
General Manager: Tom Riggan
Type of Packaging: Consumer, Bulk
Brands:
Crunch Pak®
Cascade Crest Organics

2506 **Chella's Dutch Delicacies**
333 2nd St
Lake Oswego, OR 97034-0000
503-534-9888
Fax: 503-635-1399 800-458-3331
Shortbread pastry and bread
President: Ron Kirk
Purchasing Agent: Jake Raymond
Estimated Sales: $10-20 Million
Number Employees: 10-19

2507 **Chelsea Flower Market**
75 9th Ave
New York, NY 10011-7006
212-727-1111
Fax: 212-727-1778 888-727-7887
info@chelseamarketbaskets.com
www.chelseamarketbasket.com
Custom made gift baskets for various occasions
Owner: David Porat
Contact: Bhago Ramprashad
andy@chelseamarketbaskets.com
Estimated Sales: $500,000-$1 Million
Number Employees: 1-4
Brands:
Chelsea Market Baskets
Cottage Delight
Shortbread Housf

2508 **Chelsea Milling Co.**
201 W. North St.
P.O. Box 460
Chelsea, MI 48118-0460
734-475-1361
Fax: 734-475-4630 800-727-2460
www.jiffymix.com
Prepared baking mixes including cake, frosting, muffin, brownie, pizza crust, biscuit, etc.
President/Chief Executive Officer: Howard Holmes
Vice President/Chief Financial Officer: John Powers
Vice President, Sales: William McCreadie
Year Founded: 1901
Estimated Sales: $124 Million
Number Employees: 300
Number of Brands: 1
Number of Products: 7
Type of Packaging: Consumer
Other Locations:
Chelsea Milling Co.
Marshall MI
Brands:
Jiffy Mix

2509 **Chelten House Products**
607 Heron Dr
Swedesboro, NJ 08085
info@cheltenhouse.com
www.cheltenhouse.com
Organic and all-natural dressings, sauces, marinades, salsa and ketchup. QAI certified and OU approved.
President & COO: Jason Dabrow
Chairman & CEO: Steve Dabrow
CFO: Ken Pawloski
VP, Business Development: David Elchynski
VP, Operations: Jeff Skirvin
Estimated Sales: $40 Million
Number Employees: 50-99
Number of Brands: 3
Square Footage: 150000
Type of Packaging: Consumer, Food Service, Private Label
Brands:
Chelten House
Marinade Bay
Simply Natural

2510 **Chempacific Corp**
6200 Seaforth St # 6200
Baltimore, MD 21224-6536
410-633-5771
Fax: 410-633-5808 sales@chempacific.com
www.chempacific.com
President: Dr Dean Wei
Vice President Of Operations And Co- Fou: Tony Liang
VP, QA/QC Global and Co-Founder: Rebecca Chiu
Chief Technical Officer: Jian Huang
VP Sales/Marketing: Jim Havlin
Vice President Of Operations And Co- Fou: Tony Liang
Director of Production: Wuyi Wang
Estimated Sales: $3-5 Million
Number Employees: 20-49

2511 **Cher-Make Sausage Co**
2915 Calumet Avenue
Manitowoc, WI 54220
Fax: 920-683-5990 800-242-7679
www.cher-make.com
Processor and exporter of kippered beef, sausage and meat snacks; importer of frozen meat.
Founder: Art Chermak
Director Finance/Vp Fin: Lawrence Franke
VP of Operations: Chuck Hoefner
Plant Manager: Chuck Hoefner
Purchasing Manager: Jim Coulson
Estimated Sales: $10-20 Million
Number Employees: 100-249
Square Footage: 80000
Type of Packaging: Consumer, Private Label
Brands:
Cher-Make Sausage
Home Game
Smokey Mesquite
Smoky Valley

2512 **Cheraw Packing Plant**
578 Highway 1 S
Cheraw, SC 29520-3812
843-537-7426
Beef and pork
Estimated Sales: $5-10 Million
Number Employees: 10-19

Type of Packaging: Consumer, Food Service, Private Label, Bulk

2513 **Cherbogue Fisheries**
98 Cliff St
Yarmouth, NS B5A 4B3
Canada
902-742-9157
Fax: 902-742-7708
Processor and exporter of fresh and frozen seafood
President/ Founder: Alfred Le Blanc
VP: Alfred LeBlanc
Number Employees: 20-49
Type of Packaging: Bulk

2514 **Cherchies**
One Bacton Hill Rd. North
Suite 109
Malvern, PA 19355
610-640-9440
Fax: 610-644-7937 800-644-1980
info@cherchies.com www.cherchies.com
Gourmet foods including mustard, peppers, pepper jellies, sauces, soups, chowders, preserves and seasonings; also, chili and freeze-dried soup and chowder mixes
President: Anthony Spallone
VP: Patti Spallone
Marketing: Joe Shrum
Contact: Rose Engleka
rose.engleka@cherchies.com
Operations: Lori Hughes
Purchasing: Gayle Snyder
Estimated Sales: $1-2.5 Million
Number Employees: 10-19
Number of Brands: 1
Number of Products: 60
Square Footage: 5600
Type of Packaging: Consumer, Food Service, Private Label
Brands:
Cherchies

2515 **Cheri's Desert Harvest**
1840 E Winsett St
Tucson, AZ 85719-6548
520-623-4141
Fax: 520-623-7741 800-743-1141
www.cherisdesertharvest.com
Jellies, marmalade, bread, candies, syrup
Owner: Cheri Romanoski
cheri@cherisdesertharvest.com
Vice President: Jon Romanaski
Production Manager: Nancy Howes
Purchasing Manager: Cheryl Romanaski
Estimated Sales: $1-2.5 Million
Number Employees: 5-9
Brands:
Cheri's Desert Harvest

2516 **Cheribundi**
500 Technology Farm Drive
Geneva, NY 14456
315-781-7308
Fax: 315-282-2317 800-699-0460
www.cheribundi.com
Juice/cider.
President: Brian Ross
Contact: Mary Baggott
maryruth@cheribundi.com

2517 **Cherith Valley Gardens**
4009 Eloop 820 South
Suite B
Fort Worth, TX 76119
817-466-0600
Fax: 817-446-0602 800-610-9813
terriw@cherithvalley.com
Processor, importer and exporter of gourmet pickles, pickled vegetables, salsas, jellies, fruit toppings, peppers, relishes and hors d'oeuvres
President: Alan Werner
Public Relations: Terri Werner
Operations Manager: Christa Werner
Estimated Sales: $5-10 Million
Number Employees: 10-19
Square Footage: 24000
Type of Packaging: Consumer, Food Service
Brands:
Cherith Valley Gardens

2518 **Cherry Central Cooperative, Inc.**
1771 N. US Highway 31 S.
Traverse City, MI 49684
231-946-1860
Fax: 231-941-4167 info@cherrycentral.com
www.cherrycentral.com
Red tart cherries, apples and blueberries and also a major supplier of cranberries, strawberries, pomegranate arils and asparagus. Supplier to major manufacturers for dried, frozen, canned and custom products.
President/CEO: Steve Eisler
Director, Food Service: David Barger
Retail National Sales Manager: Vince Higgs
Director, Private/Custom Label: Frank Wolff
Year Founded: 1973
Estimated Sales: $154 Million
Number Employees: 100-249
Square Footage: 15500
Type of Packaging: Consumer, Food Service, Private Label, Bulk
Brands:
Cherry Central
Traverse Bay Fruit Co
Indian Summer

2519 **Cherry Hill Orchards**
400 Long Lane
Lancaster, PA 17603
717-872-9311
www.cherryhillorchards.com
Processor and packer of fresh cherries, nectarines, peaches, apricots, sweet corn, and pumpkins.
Owner: Tom Haas
cherryhillorchards@verizon.net
Plant Manager: Stephen Haun
Year Founded: 1971
Number Employees: 20-49
Square Footage: 100000
Type of Packaging: Consumer, Food Service
Brands:
Tree Ripe

2520 **Cherry Hut**
2345 Munson Ave. (North US-31 North)
Traverse City, MI 49686-3755
231-938-8888
Fax: 231-938-3333 888-882-4431
www.cherrytreeinn.com
Products made from cherries, including sauces, jams, jellies, conserves, preserves
General Manager: Jonathan Pack
Owner: Brenda Case
Production VP: Leonard Case
Estimated Sales: Less than $500,000
Number Employees: 1-4

2521 **Cherry Lane Frozen Fruits**
4230 Victoria Avenue
Vineland Station, ON L0R 2E0
Canada
905-562-4337
Fax: 905-562-5577 877-243-7796
www.cherrylane.net
Cherries and peaches
President: John Smith
Number Employees: 100
Type of Packaging: Consumer, Food Service

2522 **Cherry Moon Farms**
4840 Eastgate Mall
San Diego, CA 92121
858-729-2800
800-580-2913
wecare@customercare.cherrymoonfarms.com
Fruit baskets, gift baskets wth chocolates and treats, and spa baskets
President/COO: Abe Wynperle
VP Finance: Rex Bosen
VP/General Counsel: Blake Bilstad

2523 **Cherrybrook Kitchen**
20 Mall Rd # 410
Suite 410
Burlington, MA 01803-4129
781-272-4460
Fax: 781-272-4460 866-458-8225
info@cherrybrookkitchen.com
www.cherrybrookkitchen.com
Peanut free, dairy free, egg free and nut free cake, cookie and brownie mixes, cookies, frostings, breakfast mixes, and wheat free and gluten free mixes
President/CEO: Chip Rosenberg
Founder: Patsy Rosenberg
VP Marketing: Laura Kuykendall
VP Sales: Sallie Bowling
Finance/HR Manager: Sue Giannetti
Estimated Sales: Less Than $500,000
Number Employees: 5-9

2524 **Cherryfield Foods**
320 Ridge Rd
Cherryfield, ME 04622-4030
207-546-7573
Fax: 207-546-2713 sales@oxfordfrozenfoods.com
www.oxfordfrozenfoods.com
Blueberries
COO: Jeff Vose
Estimated Sales: $50-100 Million
Number Employees: 100-249
Parent Co: Oxford Frozen Foods

2525 **Cherryvale Farms**
310-910-1124
info@cherryvalefarms.com
www.cherryvalefarms.com
Cookie, brownie and muffin mixes
CEO: Lindsey Rosenberg
Number of Brands: 1
Number of Products: 9
Type of Packaging: Consumer
Brands:
EVERYTHING BUT THE...
INSTANT INDULGENCE

2526 **Cheryl's Cookies**
646 Mccorkle Blvd
Westerville, OH 43082-8778
614-776-1500
Fax: 614-891-8599 800-443-8124
www.cheryls.com
Cookies and baked goods
President: Cheryl Krueger
CFO/COO: Dennis Hicks
dhicks@cherylandco.com
Quality Assurance Director: Sara Reed
VP Creative Services: Lisa Henry
Estimated Sales: $25.5 Million
Number Employees: 250-499
Square Footage: 23103
Parent Co: 1-800-Flowers
Brands:
Cheryl & Co.

2527 **Chesapeake Bay Crab Cakes & More**
10711 Red Run Blvd
Owings Mills, MD 21117
800-282-2722
Fax: 800-858-6547 www.cbcrabcakes.com
Crab cakes and gourmet seafood products.
President: Laura McManus
Estimated Sales: $20-50 Million
Number Employees: 20-49
Square Footage: 35000
Parent Co: Chesapeake Fine Food Group
Type of Packaging: Consumer

2528 **Chesapeake Spice Company**
4613 Mercedes Dr
Belcamp, MD 21017-1224
410-272-6100
Fax: 410-273-2122 www.chesapeakespice.com
Processor and importers of spices and seasonings, including anise, cumin, sage, sage oil, black pepper, paprika, cinnamon, saffron, thyme and ginger.
President: Larry Lessans
Vice President: David Lessans
Estimated Sales: $5-10 Million
Number Employees: 20-49
Square Footage: 200000
Type of Packaging: Bulk
Other Locations:
Chesapeake Spice Company-Reno
Reno NV

2529 **Chester Dairy Co**
1915 State St
Chester, IL 62233-1115
618-826-2394
Fax: 618-826-2395 www.chesterillinois.com
Dairy
President: Jason Ohlau
Estimated Sales: $10-20 Million
Number Employees: 20-49

2530 **Chester Inc Information**
555 Eastport Centre Dr
Valparaiso, IN 46383-2911
219-465-7555
Fax: 219-462-2652 800-778-1131
clark@chesterinc.com www.chesterinc.com
Processor and exporter of popcorn
Chairman/CEO: Peter Peuquet
President: Larry Holt
EVP: Leonard Clark
Contact: James Chester
jchester@chestertech.com
Estimated Sales: $5-10 Million
Number Employees: 5-9
Type of Packaging: Consumer, Private Label
Other Locations:
Francesville IN
Gary IN
Troy MI
Brands:
Chester Farms
Chester Farms Popping Corn
Golden

2531 **Chester River Clam Co**
305 Roe Ingleside Rd
Centreville, MD 21617-2012
410-758-3810
Fax: 410-758-4089
Clams
Owner: Mel Hickman
mhickman@chesterriverhealth.org
Estimated Sales: $2,100,000
Number Employees: 5-9

2532 **Chester W. Howeth & Brother**
P.O.Box 446
Crisfield, MD 21817-0446
410-968-1398
Fax: 410-968-0670
Fresh and frozen seafood
Manager: Arthur Tawes
Estimated Sales: $5-10 Million
Number Employees: 20-49
Square Footage: 8400
Type of Packaging: Food Service
Brands:
Chas. W. Howeth & Bro.

2533 **Chester's International, LLC**
2020 Cahaba Rd
Suite 325
Mountain Brook, AL 35223-1179
205-949-4690
Fax: 205-298-0332 800-288-1555
info@chestersinternational.com
www.chestersinternational.com
Manufacturer and exporter of fried chicken products including breading mixes, seasonings, packaging supplies, deep fryers, fry kettles, marinades, warmers, breading tables, etc
President: Blue Akers
bluea@chestersinternational.com
CFO: Wade King
Director of Operations: Jamees Venable
Estimated Sales: $5.9 Million
Number Employees: 5-9
Brands:
Chester Fried Chicken
Chesterfried

2534 **(HQ)Chester-Jensen Co., Inc.**
345 Tilghman St
Chester, PA 19013-3432
610-876-6276
Fax: 610-876-0485 800-685-3750
htxchng@chester-jensen.com
www.chester-jensen.com
stainless steel food processing equipment, including sanitary chillers, ice builders (thermal storage), batch mixing processors, plate heat exchangers & cook-chill equipment.
President: Richard Miller
CEO: Steven Miller
Sales Director: Robert Skoog
Estimated Sales: $10-20 Million
Square Footage: 76000
Type of Packaging: Consumer, Food Service, Private Label, Bulk
Other Locations:
Chester-Jensen Company
Cattaraugus NY

2535 **Chestertown Natural Foods**
303 Cannon St
Chestertown, MD 21620-1327
410-778-1677
Fax: 410-778-6386
www.chestertownnaturalfoods.biz
Poultry
Owner: Trish Young-Gruber
CEO: Louis Rothman
Vice President: William Schroeder
Manager Industrial Sales: Michael Carrow
Plant Manager: Jack Laird
Estimated Sales: $5-10 Million
Number Employees: 5-9
Type of Packaging: Private Label
Brands:
Chestertown

2536 **Chestnut Mountain Winery**
1123 Highway 124
Hoschton, GA 30548-3421
770-867-6914
Fax: 770-867-6914
Wines
President: James Laikam
General Manager: Jim O'Dell
Estimated Sales: $1-2,500,000
Number Employees: 1-4

2537 **Chevalier Chocolates**
39 Eastgate Lane
Enfield, CT 06082-6213
860-741-3330
Belgian chocolates, pralines, truffles, mints, also chocolate, cordial, and brandy covered cherries
President: Linda Chevalier
linda@chevalier.ws
Brands:
Chevalier Chocolates

2538 **Chewys Rugulach**
7795 Arjons Dr
San Diego, CA 92126-4366
858-271-1234
Fax: 858-271-1346 800-241-3456
chewyssales@aol.com www.chewys.com
Filled rugulach including baked, unbaked and frozen
President: Ahmad Paksima
chewys123@aol.com
Vice President: Emily Paksima
Marketing Director: Shahriar Paksima
Estimated Sales: $2.5-5 Million
Number Employees: 20-49
Square Footage: 24960
Parent Co: Ahuramazda
Type of Packaging: Consumer, Food Service, Private Label, Bulk
Brands:
Chewy's

2539 **Chex Finer Foods Inc**
71 Hampden Rd # 100
Mansfield, MA 02048-1807
508-226-0660
Fax: 508-226-7060 800-227-8114
info@chexfoods.com www.chexfoods.com
Processor and importer of gourmet foods including biscuits, confectionery items, specialties, etc
President: David Isenberg
Controller: Donald Robillard
Purchasing: Dan Powers
Estimated Sales: $10-20 Million
Number Employees: 20-49
Type of Packaging: Consumer

2540 **Chic Naturals**
PO Box 11541
Lahaina, HI 96761
808-463-7878
www.chicnaturals.com
Chickpea snacks, chocolate and spice blends from Hawaii

2541 **Chicago 58 Food Products**
135 Haist Ave
Woodbridge, ON L4L 5V6
Canada
416-603-4244
Fax: 905-265-0566
chicago58foodproducts@bellnet.ca
Meat products including beef, pastrami, smoked salami, frankfurters; also, herring, condiments and cheese; importer of beef cuts
President and Production Manager: Mosho Ami
Secretary and Sales Director: Ted Bernholtz
VP: Shane Reiken
Estimated Sales: $6.8 Million
Number Employees: 12
Square Footage: 60000
Type of Packaging: Consumer, Food Service, Private Label, Bulk
Brands:
Chicago 58
Deli-Dogs
Lanky Franky

2542 **Chicago Avenue Pizza**
1376 W Hubbard St # 1378
Chicago, IL 60642-6453
312-421-3000
Fax: 312-421-0774 800-244-8935
www.iltaco.com
Frozen pizza, pizza puffs, pasta with marinara sauce, burritos, tamales and taco puffs
President: Warren Shabaz
warren@iltaco.com
Estimated Sales: $10-20 Million
Number Employees: 50-99
Type of Packaging: Consumer, Food Service, Private Label
Brands:
Iltaco

2543 **Chicago Coffee Roastery**
11880 Smith Court
Huntley, IL 60142
847-669-1156
Fax: 847-669-1114 800-762-5402
sales@chicagocoffee.com www.chicagocoffee.com
Coffee, instant cocoa, instant cappuccio, tea
Owner: Sandra Knight
sknight@coffeemasters.com
Vice President: Brian Gosell
Purchasing Manager: Brian Gosell
Estimated Sales: $2 Million
Number Employees: 5-9
Square Footage: 32000
Type of Packaging: Consumer, Food Service, Private Label, Bulk

2544 **Chicago Food Market**
2245 S Wentworth Ave
Chicago, IL 60616-2011
312-842-4361
Fax: 312-842-6448
President: Matthew Chan
Estimated Sales: $2,500,000
Number Employees: 10-19

2545 **Chicago Gourmet Steaks**
PO Box 09094
Chicago, IL 60609
773-254-3384
Fax: 773-254-4355 800-997-8325
sales@cgsteaks.com
Steaks
Contact: Gail Glowacki
gail@cgsteaks.com

2546 **Chicago Meat Authority Inc**
1120 W 47th Pl
Chicago, IL 60609
773-254-3811
Fax: 773-254-5851 800-383-3811
info@chicagomeat.com www.chicagomeat.com
Pork and pork products as well as beef and beef products.
Founder/Owner/President: Jordan Dorfman
jdorfman@chicagomeat.com
Quality Control Manager: Charles Clayton
Year Founded: 1990
Estimated Sales: $29.7 Million
Number Employees: 250
Square Footage: 50000
Type of Packaging: Consumer, Food Service, Private Label, Bulk

2547 **Chicago Pastry**
142 N Bloomingdale Rd
Bloomingdale, IL 60108-1017
630-529-6391
Fax: 630-529-4824 www.chicagopastry.com
Bread including rye, wheat and white; also, pastries, Italian cookies and danish including prune, strawberry and blueberry
President: Renato Turano
Contact: Pete Turano
pturano@chicagopastry.com
Number Employees: 5-9
Type of Packaging: Consumer, Food Service

2548 **Chicago Premier Meats**
822 W Exchange Ave
Chicago, IL 60609-2507
773-847-3364
Fax: 773-847-3364 800-385-0661
tschicagosteak@aol.com www.chicagosteaks.com
Meat packing
President/CEO/Treasurer: Tom Summers
CEO/Principal: Thomas Campbell
Vice President: Rick Allison
Estimated Sales: $5.50 Million
Number Employees: 10-19

2549 **Chicago Steaks**
Chicago, IL
773-847-5400
www.chicagosteaks.com
Meat products, value added products, and gift steaks
Estimated Sales: $9 Million
Number Employees: 20-49
Number of Brands: 5
Square Footage: 6560
Type of Packaging: Food Service, Private Label
Brands:
Chicago Steak

2550 **Chicago Vegan Foods**
905 N Ridge Ave
Suite 7
Lombard, IL 60148
630-629-9667
info@chicagoveganfoods.com
chicagoveganfoods.com
Vegan alternatives to marshmallows, cheese and ice cream
Co-Founder: Ryan Howard
Co-Founder: Dan Ziegler
Number of Brands: 3
Number of Products: 3
Type of Packaging: Consumer
Brands:
DANDIES MARSHMALLOWS
TEESE VEGAN CHEESE
TEMPTATION ICE CREAM

2551 **Chicama Vineyards**
PO Box 430
West Tisbury, MA 02575-0430
508-693-0309
Fax: 508-693-5628 888-244-2262
Wines, vinegar and dressings
President: Catherine Mathiesen
Co-Owner: George Mathiesen
Purchasing Manager: Catherine Mathiesen
Estimated Sales: $5-9.9 Million
Number Employees: 1-4
Brands:
Chicama

2552 **Chick-Fil-A Inc.**
5200 Buffington Rd.
Atlanta, GA 30349
866-232-2040
www.chick-fil-a.com
American fast food restaurant chain specializing in chicken.
President/COO: Tim Tassopoulos
Chairman/CEO: Dan Cathy
Senior VP/CFO: Brent Ragsdale
Year Founded: 1946
Estimated Sales: $10.5 Billion
Brands:
Chick-Fil-A®

2553 **Chickapea**
Collingwood, ON L9Y 3L6
Canada
888-868-9968
hello@choosechickapea.com choosechickapea.com
Chickpea and lentil pasta
Founder: Shelby Taylor
Year Founded: 2015
Number of Brands: 1
Number of Products: 6
Type of Packaging: Consumer
Brands:
CHICKAPEA
CHICKAPEA PASTA

2554 **Chickasaw Trading Company**
PO Box 1418
Denver City, TX 79323
806-592-3515
Fax: 806-592-3460 800-848-3515
Processor and exporter of lean beef jerky and smoked turkey breast strips
Co-Owner: Linda Kay
Co-Owner: Joe Kay
Number Employees: 1-4
Square Footage: 10000
Type of Packaging: Private Label
Brands:
Texas Lean

2555 **Chicken Of The Sea**
2150 E. Grand Ave.
El Segundo, CA 90245
844-267-8862
www.chickenofthesea.com
Tuna, salmon, shrimp, crab, oysters, clams, mackerel and sardines.
CEO, Chicken of the Sea International: Valentin Ramirez
Year Founded: 1917
Estimated Sales: $600 Million
Number Employees: 1000-4999
Parent Co: Thai Union Group
Type of Packaging: Consumer, Food Service, Private Label
Brands:
Chicken of the Sea
Chicken of the Sea Singles
Chicken of the Sea Tuna Salad Kit
Genova Tonno
Jack Mackerel

2556 **Chicken Salad Chick**
724 North Dean Road
Suite 100
Auburn, AL 36830
334-275-4578
Fax: 334-209-0251 www.chickensaladchick.com
Chicken salads, sandwiches, and side dishes
Founder/President/VP, Brand Development: Stacy Brown
Chief Executive Officer: Scott Deviney
Chief Financial Officer: David Ostrander
Founder: Kevin Brown
Controller: Shawn Jones
Director of Marketing: Ali Rauch
Human Resources Manager: Angela Hands
Director of Operations: Paul Grilli
Construction Project Manager: Miles Coggins
Year Founded: 2008
Number Employees: 40

2557 **Chico Nut Company**
2020 Esplanade
Chico, CA 95926
530-891-1493
Fax: 530-893-5381 almonds@chiconut.com
Processor, exporter and packer of almonds
Owner: Peter D Peterson
Contact: Cheri Azevedo
azevedoc@chiconut.com
Estimated Sales: $3-5 Million
Number Employees: 20-49
Type of Packaging: Bulk

2558 **Chico Pops**
24 Hanover Lane
Suite B
Chico, CA 95973
530-895-1290
Fax: 530-895-1266 844-467-7677
contactus@chicopops.com www.chicopops.com
A gourmet popcorn and nut manufacturer
COO/Brand Manager: Anna Ashley

2559 **Chicopee Provision Co Inc**
19 Sitarz Ave
Chicopee, MA 01013
800-924-6328
gary@bluesealkielbasa.com
www.bluesealkielbasa.com
Kielbasa and table ready meats, including polish kielbasa, cheese, hot dogs, cold cuts, and sausage
President: Gary Bernatowicz
Estimated Sales: $4.5 Million
Number Employees: 20-49
Number of Brands: 220
Number of Products: 610
Square Footage: 96000
Type of Packaging: Consumer, Food Service, Private Label, Bulk
Brands:
Blue Seal
Chicopee Provision
F Domin and Sons
Friendship Diaries
Hatfield

2560 **Chief Wenatchee**
1705 N Miller St
Wenatchee, WA 98801-1585
509-662-5197
Fax: 509-662-9415
Grower and exporter of apples, cherries and pears
President: Brian Birsall
Operations Manager: Skip Coonfield
Number Employees: 250 to 499
Type of Packaging: Bulk
Brands:
Chief Chelan
Chief Supreme
Chief Wenatchee
Wenatchee Gold

2561 **Chieftain Wild Rice**
PO Box 550
1210 Basswood Ave
Spooner, WI 54801-0550
715-635-6401
Fax: 715-635-6415 800-262-6368
www.chieftainwildrice.com
Wild rice and wild rice blends
President: Donald Richards
General Manager: Joan Gerland
Marketing: Lisa Johnson
Operations Manager: Jim Deutsch
Estimated Sales: $1.6 Million
Number Employees: 25
Number of Brands: 1
Type of Packaging: Private Label
Brands:
Chieftain(c)

2562 **Chihon Biotechnology Co., Ltd.**
2220 Glouceston Lane
Naperville, IL 60564
630-670-5701
jeff@chihonbio.com
www.chihonbio.com
A leading manufacturer of natamycin and nisin.
US Contact: Jeffrey Liu

2563 **Childlife**
8690 Hayden Pl
Culver City, CA 90232-2902
310-853-4300
Fax: 310-305-4680 800-993-0332
mailroom@childlife.net www.childlife.net
Liquid supplements & vitamins for infants to children up to twelve years old
President: Murray Clarke
VP: Helen Mauchi
Estimated Sales: $300,000-500,000
Number Employees: 5-9
Number of Products: 9

2564 **Chili-Mex**
1450 Lake Robbins Dr
Spring, TX 77380-3258
281-298-5364
Fax: 281-364-8452
Estimated Sales: $1-3 Million
Number Employees: 5-9

2565 **Chili Dude**
745 Kirkwood Dr
Dallas, TX 75218
214-354-9906
Chili
Director: Corrine Lovato
Brands:
Chili Dude

2566 **Chill & Moore**
3221 May Street
Fort Worth, TX 76110-4124
505-769-2649
Fax: 505-762-0571 800-676-3055
Frozen ices
Sales Manager (Food Service): Bob Moore
Sales Manager (Retail): Jay Jackson
Type of Packaging: Consumer, Food Service

2567 **Chill Pop**
PO Box 19092
Cleveland, OH 44119
info@chillpopshop.com
chillpopshop.com
Frozen fruit pops
Co-Founder: Elizabeth Pryor
Co-Founder: Maggie Pryor

2568 **Chimayo To Go / Cibolo Junction**
500 Broadway SE
Albuquerque, NM 87102
800-683-9628
info@chimayotogo.com www.chimayotogo.com
Soup, stew and bread mixes, salsas, pretzels, herbs, spices and seasonings.
President: Brian McKinsey
Vice President: Susan McKinsey
Type of Packaging: Private Label

2569 **Chimere Winery**
1800 Sequoia Dr
Santa Maria, CA 93454-7645
805-928-5611
Fax: 805-922-9143 www.vinarium-usa.com
Wines
Owner: Gary R Mosby
gmosby@ymail.com
Estimated Sales: Less Than $500,000
Number Employees: 1-4

2570 **China Mist Brands**
7435 E Tierra Buena Ln
Scottsdale, AZ 85260-1608
480-998-8807
Fax: 480-443-8384 800-242-8807
info@chinamist.com www.organichotteas.com
China mist and leaves pure teas
President: Rommie Flammer
rommie@chinamist.com
CEO. John Martinson
President/CEO/Finance Executive: Rommie Flammer
Marketing Coordinator: Kiley Biggins
Director of Retail Sales: Ed Baird
Human Resource Manager: Wade McKesson
rommie@chinamist.com
Plant Manager: Kevin McCullough
Estimated Sales: $3.8 Million
Number Employees: 20-49
Square Footage: 70000
Brands:
China Mist
Frenzy Mist
Green Star

2571 **China Pharmaceutical Enterprises**
8323 Ohara Court
Baton Rouge, LA 70806-6513
225-924-1423
Fax: 225-924-4154 800-345-1658
Processor and importer of ascorbic acid, caffeine anhydrous and vitamin B-12
Office Manager: Susan Giska
Type of Packaging: Bulk

2572 **(HQ)Chincoteague Seafood CoInc**
7056 Forest Grove Rd
PO Box 88
Parsonsburg, MD 21849-2096
443-260-4800
Fax: 443-260-4900 gourmetsoups@hotmail.com
www.chincoteagueseafood.com
Processor and distributor of gourmet specialty seafood items: canned and frozen products including fried clams, stuffed clams, New England/Manhattan clam chowders, corn chowder, lobster/clam/shrimp/lobster and cheddar bisques, cream ofcrab/vegetable crab/crab and cheddar soups, white/red clam sauces, chopped clams, clam juice
Owner: Leonard Rubin
lrubin60@aol.com
CEO: Bernard Rubin
CFO: Toby Rubin
Estimated Sales: $1-2.5 Million
Number Employees: 5-9
Number of Brands: 4
Number of Products: 25
Square Footage: 24000
Type of Packaging: Consumer, Food Service, Private Label, Bulk
Brands:
Cape Cod
Capt'n Don's

Capt'n Eds
Chinoteaque

2573 **Chinese Spaghetti Factory**
83 Newmarket Sq
Boston, MA 02118-2619
617-445-7714
Fax: 617-427-5918 www.chinese-spaghetti.com
Peking ravioli, chicken and pork dumplings, scallops with bacon and shrimp spring rolls
Owner: David Sou
dsou@chinese-spaghetti.com
General Manager: Henry Moy
Operations Manager: Ken Moy
Estimated Sales: $1 Million
Number Employees: 20-49
Square Footage: 64000
Type of Packaging: Consumer, Food Service, Private Label, Bulk

2574 **Chino Meat Provision Corporation**
13564 Central Ave
Chino, CA 91710-5105
909-627-1997
Fax: 909-628-5147
Processor and packer of meat products
Owner: Orestes Blanco
Estimated Sales: $2.5-5 Million
Number Employees: 10-19
Square Footage: 12000
Brands:
El Paso

2575 **Chino Valley Dairy**
12000 Eastend Ave
Chino, CA 91710-1565
909-628-8516
Fax: 909-591-4292 800-324-7948
sales@scottbrothers.com www.scottbrothers.com
Dairy products
Heardsman: Stan Scott
Heardsman: Brad Scott
Heardsman: Bruce Scott
General Manager: Rene Peauroi
General Manager: Michael Peauroi
General Manager: Vince Sartain
Manager: Ryan Blair
ryan@sbdfarms.com
Number Employees: 50-99

2576 **Chino Valley Ranchers**
331 W Citrus Street
Colton, CA 92324
626-652-0890
Fax: 626-652-0893 800-354-4503
info@chinovalleyranchers.com
www.chinovalleyranchers.com
Fresh organic, cage free, free range and fertile white and brown eggs
Marketing Director: David Will
Plant Manager: Mario Gonzalez
Type of Packaging: Consumer, Food Service, Private Label
Brands:
Chino Valley
Humane Harvest
Mothers Free Range
Nutrifresh
Veg-A-Fed

2577 **Chip Steak & Provision Co**
232 Dewey St
Mankato, MN 56001-2393
507-388-6277
Fax: 507-388-6279
Wholesales meat & meat products; wholesales packaged frozen foods
President: Michael Miller
ddi95@yahoo.com
Estimated Sales: $5-9.9 Million
Number Employees: 5-9
Square Footage: 16000
Type of Packaging: Consumer, Food Service, Bulk

2578 **Chip'n Dipped Cookie Co**
342 New York Ave # 2
Huntington, NY 11743-3567
631-470-2579
questions@chipndipped.com
www.chipndipped.com
Manufacturer of cookies and chocolate.
Foudner and Owner: Peter Goldfarb
peter@chipndipped.com

Estimated Sales: Less Than $500,000
Number Employees: 1-4
Square Footage: 80000

2579 **Chipper Snax**
1750 S 500 W Ste 700
Salt Lake City, UT 84115
801-977-0742
Fax: 801-977-0743
Beef jerky
Manager: Jeffrey Labrum
Executive Vice President: Jeffrey Labrum
National Sales Manager: Steve Pich
Estimated Sales: $10-20 Million
Number Employees: 20-49
Brands:
Chipper Beef Jerky

2580 **Chiquita Brands LLC.**
DCOTA Office Center
1855 Griffin Rd., Suite C-346
Fort Lauderdale, FL 33004-2275
954-924-5700
www.chiquita.com
Fruit and vegetable grower and producer of fresh and prepared food products.
President: Carlos Lopez Flores
VP: Chris Dugan
Year Founded: 1899
Estimated Sales: $3 Billion
Number Employees: 20,000
Number of Brands: 3
Parent Co: Cutrale-Safra
Type of Packaging: Consumer, Food Service, Private Label, Bulk
Brands:
Chiquita®
Fresh Express®
Bites

2581 **Chisesi Brothers Meat Packing**
5221 Jefferson Hwy
New Orleans, LA 70123-5300
504-822-3550
Fax: 504-822-3916 800-966-3550
www.chisesibros.com
Hams, frankforters, and sausage
President: Donald Bordelon
donald@chisesibros.com
Estimated Sales: $15-20 Million
Number Employees: 100-249
Type of Packaging: Consumer, Food Service

2582 **Chisholm Bakery**
128 8th Street NW
Chisholm, MN 55719-1656
218-254-4006
Baked goods
Owner: Todd Renke
Estimated Sales: $500,000-$1,000,000
Number Employees: 5-9

2583 **Chloe's Fruit**
New York, NY 10011
646-442-8000
www.chloesfruit.com
Frozen fruit pops
Founder: Chloe Epstein

2584 **Chmura's Bakery**
14 Pulaski St
Indian Orchard, MA 01151-2215
413-543-2521
Fax: 413-543-2507 www.aawindowcleaning.com
Rye bread and bakery products
CEO: Joe Albes
Estimated Sales: $1-2,500,000
Number Employees: 10-19

2585 **Chobani, Inc.**
Norwich, NY
www.chobani.com
Strained yogurt, including Greek, plain, blended, smoothies, snack packs and non-Greek yogurts.
Founder & CEO: Hamdi Ulukaya
Year Founded: 2005
Number Employees: 3,000
Number of Brands: 2
Type of Packaging: Consumer

2586 **ChocAlive**
16 Mt Ebo Road South
Brewster, NY 10509
845-279-1715
orderchocalive@verizon.net
Gluten free, vegan and raw truffles

2587 **Chock Full O'Nuts**
888-246-2598
www.chockfullonuts.com
Regular and decaffeinated, ground, instant, and flavoured coffees
Estimated Sales: $67,000
Square Footage: 8984
Parent Co: Massimo Zanetti Beverage
Type of Packaging: Consumer, Food Service, Private Label
Other Locations:
Chock Full O'Nuts Corp.
Brooklyn NY
Brands:
Chock Full O'Nuts
New York Classics

2588 **Choclatique**
11030 Santa Monica Blvd
#301
Los Angeles, CA 90025-7530
310-479-3849
Fax: 310-479-8448 www.choclatique.com
Chocolates, bars, marshmallows, nuts and novelties, sauces, ganaches and beverages, and baking ingredients
Co-Founder: Ed Engoron
Co-Founder: Joan Vieweger
Marketing: Joan Vieweger

2589 **Choco Finesse, LLC**
5019 N Meridian St
Indianapolis, IN 46208
317-476-6034
epogee.net
Developer and manufacturer of Epogee Fat Replacement, a low-calorie solid fat replacement.
Founder/CEO: David Rowe
Sr Product & Process Development Advisor: Leo Strecker
Sr Regulatory & Toxicology Advisor: David Bechtel
Head of Manufacturing: Chess Mizell

2590 **ChocoME US LLC**
25241 Derby Circle
Laguna Hills, CA 92653
949-500-8837
Fax: 949-500-8837 www.chocome.us
Manufacturer of chocolates.
Founder and Owner: Gabor Meszaros
Square Footage: 80000

2591 **Chocoholics Divine Desserts**
14400 E Highway 26
Linden, CA 95236-9744
Fax: 209-759-3350 800-760-2462
info@gourmetchocolate.com
Chocolate dessert toppings, carmel sauces, double fudge cookies, truffles and chocolate novelties
President: Ernie Schenone
VP Sales & Operations: Mary Schenone
Estimated Sales: $5-10 Million
Number Employees: 10-19
Type of Packaging: Private Label

2592 **Chocolat**
2039 Bellevue Sq
Bellevue, WA 98004-5028
425-452-1141
Fax: 425-452-1142 800-808-2462
Beverages
President: Will Deeg
Director Marketing: Rob Scott
Brands:
Neuhaus
Teuscher

2593 **Chocolat Belge Heyez**
16 Ch De La Rabastaliere E
St-Lazare-De-Bellechasse, QC J3V 2A5
Canada
450-653-5616
Fax: 450-653-1445
Processor and importer of chocolates
Chairman: Bernard Falmagne
VP: Marc Voyer
Treasurer: Dominique Tran
Secretary: Claude Leblanc
Administrator: Sharmila Amin
Estimated Sales: $371,000
Number Employees: 6
Square Footage: 16000
Type of Packaging: Consumer, Private Label

2594 **Chocolat Jean Talon**
4620 Boul Thimens
Montreal, QC H4R 2B2
Canada
514-333-8540
Fax: 514-333-8540 888-333-8540
info@jtalon.ca
Molded hollow chocolates for Easter
President: Robert Poirier
VP/Marketing: Richard Poirier
Sales Manager: Johanne Lavallee
Plant Manager: Lyne Lacharite
Purchasing Manager: Marc Plante
Estimated Sales: $6 Million
Number Employees: 93
Number of Products: 100
Square Footage: 220000
Type of Packaging: Food Service
Brands:
Chocolat Jean Talon

2595 **Chocolat Michel Cluizel**
199 Madison Ave
New York, NY 10016-4305
646-415-9126
madison@cluizel.us
www.cluizel.us
Chocolates, calissons, candies and caramels
Contact: Michele Laurent
mlaurent@cluizel.us
Number Employees: 10-19

2596 **Chocolat Moderne, LLC.**
27 W. 20th St.
Suite 904
New York, NY 10011
212-229-4797
orders@chocolatmoderne.com
www.chocolatmoderne.com
Manufacturer of gourmet chocolate.
Founder and President: Joan Coukos
Contact: Jake Ben-Ami
jake@chocolatmoderne.com
Square Footage: 80000

2597 **Chocolate By Design Inc**
700 Union Pkwy # 4
Ronkonkoma, NY 11779-7427
631-737-0082
Fax: 631-737-0188 800-536-3618
chocobd@aol.com
Gourmet chocolate novelties and coins; also, custom molding available
President: Ellen Motlin
CEO: Richard Motlin
chocobd@aol.com
Estimated Sales: $500,000
Number Employees: 10-19
Number of Products: 350
Square Footage: 20000
Type of Packaging: Consumer, Private Label

2598 **Chocolate By Design Inc**
700 Union Pkwy # 4
Ronkonkoma, NY 11779-7427
631-737-0082
Fax: 631-737-0188
Confectionery
Owner: Richard Motlin
chocobd@aol.com
Estimated Sales: $500,000-$1 Million
Number Employees: 10-19
Type of Packaging: Private Label
Brands:
Chocolate By Design

2599 **Chocolate Chix**
501 N College Street
Waxahachie, TX 75165-3361
214-744-2442
Fax: 214-744-2449 csurana@chocolatechix.com
www.chocolatechix.com
Meringue cookies
President: Cheryl Surana
Estimated Sales: Less than $500,000
Number Employees: 1-4
Brands:
Just Meringues
Mushroom Meringue Cookies

2600 **Chocolate Chocolate Chocolate**
5025 Pattison Ave
St Louis, MO 63110-2037
314-338-3501
Fax: 314-832-2299 www.chocolatechocolate.com
Manufacturer of handcrafted, premium chocolate.
President: Dan Abel
Number Employees: 10-19
Square Footage: 80000

2601 **Chocolate Creations**
3465 Brodhead Rd # 4
Monaca, PA 15061-3144
724-774-7675
Fax: 724-774-7675 chocolatecreations@msn.com
Full line of specialty and seasonal chocolate gifts
Owner: Tony Unterberger
tunterberger@duquesnelight.com
Estimated Sales: $5-10 Million
Number Employees: 1-4

2602 **Chocolate Delivery Systems Inc**
85 River Rock Dr
Suite 202
Buffalo, NY 14207-2170
716-854-6050
Fax: 716-854-7363 www.tomric.com
Manufacturer of chocolates.
President: Tim Thill
CFO: Jim Heron
Quality Manager: Robert Short
t.elsinghorst@tomric.com
Number Employees: 10-19
Square Footage: 80000

2603 **Chocolate Fantasies**
340 Shore Drive
Burr Ridge, IL 60527
630-572-0045
Fax: 630-572-0039 contactus@espressosecrets.net
All natural dark chocolate confections married to rich espresso coffee.
CEO: Leonard Defranco

2604 **Chocolate House**
4121 South 35th Street
Milwaukee, WI 53221
414-281-7803
Fax: 414-423-2484 800-236-2022
Manufacturer and exporter of chocolate
Manager: Irene Hyducki
Executive Vice President: Gary Winder
Estimated Sales: $10-20 Million
Number Employees: 50-99
Type of Packaging: Consumer
Brands:
Absolutely Almond
Chocolate Mint Meltaways
Fudgie Bears
Positively Pecan

2605 **Chocolate Maven**
Chocolate Maven Bakery & Cafe 821
W. San Mateo Rd
Santa Fe, NM 87505
505-984-1980
www.chocolatemaven.com
Pastries and baked goods

2606 **Chocolate Moon**
2002 Riverside Drive
42F
Asheville, NC 28804
828-253-6060
Fax: 828-253-1020 800-723-1236
info@bluemoonwater.com
www.bluemoonwater.com
Chocolate covered dried cherries, blueberries and apricots, toffee, cocoa and cappuccino chocolate almonds and pistachios
Owner: Chris Mathis
Operations Manager: Jennifer Donnell
Purchasing Manager: Jennifer Donnell
Estimated Sales: $1-2.5 Million
Number Employees: 10-19
Brands:
Davinci Gourmet
Ghiardelli
Guittard
Lindt
Marich
Oregon Chai

2607 **Chocolate Shoppe Ice Cream Co**
2221 Daniels St
Madison, WI 53718-6745
608-221-8640
Fax: 608-221-8650 800-466-8043
www.chocolateshoppeicecream.com
Frozen desserts
Owner: Chuck Deadman
dave@chocolateshoppeicecream.com
Vice President: Dave Deadman
Purchasing Manager: Dave Deadman
Estimated Sales: $2.5-5 Million
Number Employees: 20-49

2608 **Chocolate Signatures LP**
166 Norseman St
Toronto, ON M8Z 2R4
Canada
416-234-8528
Fax: 416-234-0627
www.chocolatesignaturesinc.com
Chocolate bars, truffles, toffee, caramel candy
Sales/Corporate: Dina Gama
Brand Manager: Heather Chu

2609 **Chocolate Smith**
851 Cerrillos Rd # A
Santa Fe, NM 87505-3005
505-473-2111
Fax: 505-982-6897 www.chocolatesmith.com
Chocolates
Owner: Kari Keenan
contact@chocolatesmith.com
Estimated Sales: Less Than $500,000
Number Employees: 5-9

2610 **Chocolate Soup**
2300 Mount Werner Circle
Unit C-1
Steamboat Springs, CO 80487
970-870-0224
Fax: 970-870-0378
Organic/natural, cakes/pastries, cookies, crackers, other baked goods, other chocolate, other snacks, private label.
Marketing: Lisa Ciraldo

2611 **Chocolate Street of Hartville**
114 South Prospect Avenue
Hartville, OH 44632-1010
330-877-1999
Fax: 330-877-1100 888-853-5904
www.discoverhartville.com
Custom chocolate products including 3-D corporate logos, bars and personalized gold foil wrapped coins; also, private label available; exporter of chocolate processing equipment including cooling tunnels, vibration tables, measuringpumps, etc
General Manager: Robert Barton
Estimated Sales: $10-20 Million
Number Employees: 20-49
Square Footage: 26000
Type of Packaging: Consumer, Food Service, Private Label, Bulk
Brands:
Chocolate Street of Hartville

2612 **Chocolate Studio**
142 W Germantown Pike
Unit A
Norristown, PA 19401
610-272-3872
Fax: 610-272-3872
Chocolates
Owner: John Giaimo
Estimated Sales: $2.5-5 Million
Number Employees: 5-9
Type of Packaging: Consumer, Bulk

2613 **Chocolate Works**
114 Church St
Freeport, NY 11520
info@chocolateworks.com
www.chocolateworks.com
Chocolate
Founder: Joe Whaley

2614 **Chocolaterie Bernard Callebaut**
133 1st Street SE
Calgary, AB T2G 5L1
Canada
403-265-5777
Fax: 403-265-7738 800-661-8367
www.bernardcallebaut.com

Processor and exporter of quality chocolates and chocolate products, including spreads, sauces and ice cream bars
President/CEO: Bernard Callebaut
Number Employees: 20-49
Type of Packaging: Consumer, Private Label
Brands:
Chocolaterie Bernard Callebaut

2615 **Chocolaterie Stam**
2814 Ingersoll Ave
Des Moines, IA 50312-4013
515-282-9575
Fax: 515-282-9763 877-782-6246
ton@stamchocolate.com www.stamchocolate.com
Quality Dutch chocolates
President: Ton Stam
ton@stamchocolate.com
Estimated Sales: $500,000-$1 Million
Number Employees: 10-19
Brands:
Stam

2616 **Chocolates By Mr Roberts**
505 NE 20th St
Boca Raton, FL 33431-8141
561-392-3007
Fax: 561-392-3014
chocbymrroberts@bellsouth.net
www.chocolatesbymrroberts.com
Fine chocolates and truffles, chocolate-covered fruit
Owner: Heinz Robert Goldschneider
CEO: Michelle Zander
Contact: Robert Goldschmider
chocbymrroberts@bellsouth.net
Estimated Sales: Less Than $500,000
Number Employees: 1-4

2617 **Chocolates El Rey, Inc**
1324 West Clay
Houston, TX 77019
800-357-3999
Info@ChocolatesElRey.com
Premium chocolates. Retail/wholesale, block, discos and chips
President: Randall Turner
Contact: Cody Bollig
bolligcody@chocolate.com.ve
Estimated Sales: $2.5-5 Million
Number Employees: 1-4
Brands:
Carenero
El Rey
Rio Caribe

2618 **Chocolates Turin**
Granite Parkway
Suite 200
Plano, TX 75024
972-731-6771
Fax: 972-731-6774 www.turin.com.mx
Chocolates
National Sales Manager: Jim Hutchins

2619 **Chocolates a La Carte**
24836 Avenue Rockefeller
Valencia, CA 91355
661-257-3700
Fax: 661-257-4999 800-818-2462
orders@candymaker.com www.candymaker.com
Processor, importer and exporter of chocolate designs for desserts, amenities and gifts including pianos, swans, sea shells, etc
President: Rena Pocrass
CEO/VP: Richard Pocrass
VP Finance and Administration: Michael Pocrass
Marketing Manager: Diane Rudman
Contact: Tony Aguirre
taguirre@candymaker.com
EVP/Head of Operations: Frank Geukens
Estimated Sales: $26 Million
Number Employees: 165
Square Footage: 110000
Type of Packaging: Food Service
Brands:
Chocolates a La Carte

2620 **Chocolates by Mark**
2100 Space Park Drive
Suite 102
Houston, TX 77058
832-736-2626
Fax: 603-925-8000 www.chocolatesbymark.com
Custom chocolate wedding/party favors, gifts
President: Mark Caffey
Number Employees: 1-4
Square Footage: 8800
Type of Packaging: Private Label, Bulk

2621 **Chocolati Handmade Chocolates**
7708 Aurora Ave N
Seattle, WA 98103-4752
206-784-5212
Fax: 206-525-4574 information@chocolati.com
www.chocolati.com
Candy including mint truffles
Owner: Christian Wong
VP: John Berg
Estimated Sales: $100000
Number Employees: 5-9
Square Footage: 20400
Type of Packaging: Consumer, Private Label, Bulk

2622 **Chocolatier**
27 Water St
Exeter, NH 03833-2440
603-772-5253
Fax: 603-772-0793 888-246-5528
www.the-chocolatier.com
Molded corporate chocolate candy
Owner: Jason Martone
jmartone@the-chocolatier.com
Estimated Sales: $220,000
Number Employees: 5-9

2623 **Chocolove**
PO Box 18357
Boulder, CO 80308
303-786-7888
Fax: 303-440-8850 888-246-2656
margaret@chocolove.com www.chocolove.com
Belgian chocolate bars
Founder, Owner: Timothy Moley
Marketing: Kerri Gedert
Estimated Sales: $2.5-5 Million
Number Employees: 5-9
Brands:
Chocolove

2624 **Chocomize**
30-10 41st Ave.
4th Floor
Long Island City, NY 11101
800-621-3294
info@chocomize.com
www.chocomize.com
Manufacturer of chocolate bars and pieces.
Co-Founder: Eric Heinbockel
Co-Founder: Fabian Kaempfer
Contact: Jeleisa Forbes-Lowry
jeleisa@chocomize.com
Square Footage: 80000

2625 **Chocopologie By Knipschildt**
12 S Main St
Norwalk, CT 06854-2978
203-854-4754
Fax: 203-838-3137 info@knipschildt.com
www.chocopologie.com
Chocolates
President/Owner: Fritz Knipschildt
chocopologie@gmail.com
Marketing: Amanda Ciaszki
Number Employees: 10-19

2626 **Choctal**
1 W Mountain St # 12
Pasadena, CA 91103-3070
USA
626-798-1351
www.choctal.com
Ice cream
CEO: Michael Leb
COO: Robert Michero
Chief Strategy Officer: Nancy Hytone Leb
Contact: Marlene Munoz
marlene.munoz@choctal.com
Operations Manager: Marlene Munoz
Estimated Sales: 250,000
Number Employees: 1-4

2627 **Choctaw Maid Farms**
Old Highway 15 N
Jackson, MS 39209
601-683-4000
Fax: 601-298-5497
Processor, importer and exporter of fresh and frozen chicken parts
Owner: Tammy Etheridge
Purchasing Agent: Ruthie Harper
Number Employees: 250-499
Type of Packaging: Bulk

2628 **Choice Food Distributors LLC**
6167 Cockrill Bend Cir
Nashville, TN 37209-1051
615-350-6070
Fax: 615-350-6862 www.thechoicefood.com
Manufacturer and marketer of shelf-stable and prepared foods including muffin and baking mixes, salad dressings, sauces, spices and herbs
Chairman: Michael Shmerling
CEO: Jerry Walker
jwalker@thechoicefood.com
CFO: Mark Johnson
National Accounts Sales Manager: Beth Eaton
Estimated Sales: $4.2 Million
Number Employees: 50-99
Brands:
Mayberry's Finest
O'Charley's
Lamont's

2629 **Choice Food Group Inc**
618 Church St # 220
Nashville, TN 37219-2453
615-248-9255
www.choicefood.com
Shelf-stable and prepared foods
Number Employees: 1-4
Type of Packaging: Consumer, Private Label

2630 **Choice Organic Teas**
600 S Brandon St
Seattle, WA 98108-2240
206-525-0051
Fax: 206-523-9750 866-972-6879
choiceorganicteas@worldpantry.com
www.choiceorganicteas.com
Processor and exporter of organic teas including black, green and herbal
Founder: Blake Rankin
Estimated Sales: $1-$2.5 Million
Number Employees: 20-49
Parent Co: Granum Inc
Type of Packaging: Consumer, Food Service, Private Label, Bulk
Brands:
Choice
Choice Organic Teas
Granum
Kaiseki Select
Mitoku Macrobiotic
Sound Sea Vegetables

2631 **Choice of Vermont**
305 Tequesta Drive
Destin, FL 32541-5715
802-888-6261
Fax: 802-888-6244 800-444-6261
Mustard, hummus, black bean salsa, bruschetta toppings, maple pumpkin butter, pesto sauce and horseradish jam
President: Jim Peterson
Sales Director: Kevin Butler
Operations Manager: Robert Nelson
Estimated Sales: $1 Million
Number Employees: 5-9
Number of Brands: 1
Number of Products: 28
Square Footage: 40000
Type of Packaging: Consumer, Food Service, Private Label
Brands:
Choice of Vermont

2632 **Chomps**
465 Bayfront Place
Naples, FL 34102
team@chomps.com
chomps.com
Beef chews
Number of Brands: 1
Number of Products: 4
Type of Packaging: Consumer
Brands:
CHOMPS

2633 Chong Mei Trading
1130 Oakleigh Dr
East Point, GA 30344
404-768-3838
Fax: 404-768-0008
Pork, beef, seafood, chicken, dry goods, dairy, produce, Oriental grocery items
President: Kai Chen Wong
Estimated Sales: $1-3 Million
Number Employees: 10-19

2634 Chooljian Bros Packing Co
3192 S Indianola Avenue
PO Box 395
Sanger, CA 93657
559-875-5501
Fax: 559-875-1582
k.elliott@chooljianbrothers.com
www.chooljianbrothers.com
Processor and exporter of raisins; also, custom packaging services
President: Michael Chooljian
mchooljian@chooljianbrothers.com
Estimated Sales: $500,000
Number Employees: 50-99
Parent Co: Chooljian Brothers Packing Company
Type of Packaging: Consumer, Food Service, Private Label, Bulk
Brands:
Chooljian
Prize

2635 Chops Snacks
5101 Old Highway 5
Suite 440
Lebanon, GA 30146
Fax: 718-210-2746 888-571-4442
info@chopssnacks.com topchops.com
Beef jerky
Co-Founder: Luke Sellers
Co-Founder: Dusty Jaquins
Marketing: Carole Gervasi
Number of Brands: 1
Number of Products: 4
Type of Packaging: Consumer
Brands:
T.O.P. Chops

2636 Chosen Foods, Inc.
453 54th St
Suite 102
San Diego, CA 92114-2220
USA
877-674-2244
Fax: 888-503-6591 www.chosen-foods.com
Grain, cereal, pasta, spreads, syrups, oils
President: George Todd
Chief Executive Officer: Carsten Hagen
Contact: Ardith Alexander
ardith@chosen-foods.com
Estimated Sales: 1,200,000
Number Employees: 12

2637 Chouinard Vineyards & Winery
33853 Palomares Rd
Castro Valley, CA 94552-9616
510-582-9900
Fax: 510-733-6274 chouinard@chouinard.com
www.chouinard.com
Wines
Owner: Damian Chouinard
mamachouinard@gmail.com
Estimated Sales: $1-2.5 Million
Number Employees: 1-4
Brands:
Alicante Bouschet
California Champagne
Central Coast Chardonnay
Chouinard Red
Chouinard Rose
Granny Smith Apple
Lodi Zinfandel
Monterey Cabernet Sauvignon
Monterey Chardonnay
Monterey Petite Syrah
Paso Robles Cabernet Sauvignon
Paso Robles Orange Muscat

2638 Choyce Produce
3140 Ualena St
Suite 206
Honolulu, HI 96819-1965
808-839-1502
President: Edmund Choy
Contact: Annette Forness
aforness@choycehi.com
Estimated Sales: $5-10 Million
Number Employees: 5-9

2639 Chozen Ice Cream
171 W 12th Street
Suite 6C
New York, NY 10011-8210
212-675-4191
Fax: 212-675-4191
Kosher, organic/natural, frozen desserts. ice cream/sorbet.
Marketing: Meredith Fisher

2640 Chr Hansen Inc
9015 W Maple St
Milwaukee, WI 53214
414-607-5700
Fax: 414-607-5959 usinfo@chr-hansen.com
www.chr-hansen.com
Health nutritionals and savory, sweet, dairy, and compound blend flavors.
President & CEO: Mauricio Graber
EVP & CFO: Soren Westh Lonning
EVP & CSO: Thomas Schafer
EVP, Global Operations: Torsten Steenholt
Estimated Sales: $100-499.9 Million
Number Employees: 100-249

2641 Chris Candies Inc
1557 Spring Garden Ave
Pittsburgh, PA 15212-3632
412-322-9400
Fax: 412-322-9402 sales@chriscandies.com
Chocolate bars and novelties; also, custom molds, labels and imprints available. Organic and kosher certified
President: Mark Davis
mark.davis@chriscandies.com
VP/CIO: Dave Byard
Human Resources Manager: Lori Cipkins
mark.davis@chriscandies.com
Operations Executive: Mike Gefert
Estimated Sales: $5-9.9 Million
Number Employees: 50-99
Square Footage: 128000
Type of Packaging: Consumer, Food Service, Private Label

2642 Chris Hansen Seafood
134 Chris Ln
Port Sulphur, LA 70083-2814
504-564-2888
Seafood
Owner: Chris Hansen
Estimated Sales: Less Than $500,000
Number Employees: 1-4

2643 Chris' Farm Stand
Stasinos Farm
11 Lake Street
Peabody, MA 01960
978-994-4315
stasinosma@gmail.com
www.chrisfarmstand.com
Organic produce and jams and jellies
President: Thomas Holopainen
Estimated Sales: Less than $500,000
Number Employees: 5-9
Type of Packaging: Consumer

2644 Chris's Cookies
100 Hollister Rd # 5
Unic C-1
Teterboro, NJ 07608-1139
201-288-8881
Fax: 201-438-8444
customerservice@chriscookies.com
www.chriscookies.com
Manufacturer of cookies, brownies, and pastries.
Co-Founder: Chris Gargiulo
CEO and Co-Founder: Manish Wadia
EVP: Betty Osmanoglu
Quality Assurance Manager: Kapila Devkota
Number Employees: 50-99
Square Footage: 80000

2645 Christensen Ridge Winery
HCR 02,
Box 459
Madison, VA 22727
540-923-4800
Wine
President/Owner: J D Hartman
Estimated Sales: $3-5 Million
Number Employees: 5-9

2646 Christie Cookie
1205 3rd Ave N
Nashville, TN 37208-2703
615-242-3817
Fax: 615-242-5572 800-458-2447
www.christiecookies.com
Gourmet cookies and frozen ready to bake dough.
President: Fleming Wilt
fleming.wilt@christiecookies.com
VP, Sales: Jay McKnight
Director, New Business Development: Charles Tommolino
Marketing Manager: Caroline Sloan
Estimated Sales: $10-20 Million
Number Employees: 20-49
Type of Packaging: Food Service

2647 Christie's
220 Canton Street
Stroughton, MA 02072
781-341-3341
Fax: 781-341-3340 info@avonfood.com
avonfood.com
Processor and contract packager salad dressings and marinades
Estimated Sales: $1-2.5 Million
Number Employees: 20-49
Square Footage: 120000
Parent Co: Avon Food Company
Type of Packaging: Consumer, Food Service, Private Label, Bulk
Brands:
Christie's Instant-Chef

2648 Christie-Brown
200 Deforest Avenue
East Hanover, NJ 07936-2833
973-503-4000
Fax: 973-503-3660
CEO: Chip Clothier
Estimated Sales: Under $500,000
Number Employees: 5-9

2649 Christine & Rob's Inc
41103 Stayton Scio Rd SE
Stayton, OR 97383-9400
503-769-2993
Fax: 503-769-1291 bartell@wvi.com
www.christineandrobs.com
Old-fashioned oatmeal and preserves
Owner: Christine Bartell
Owner: Rob Bartell
bartell@wvi.com
Estimated Sales: Less Than $500,000
Number Employees: 1-4

2650 Christine Woods Winery
3155 Highway 128
Philo, CA 95466
707-895-2115
Fax: 707-895-2748 www.christinewoods.com
Wines
Owner: Vernon Rose
Owner: Jo Rose
Partner: Edward Rose
Partner: Lisa Rose
Estimated Sales: $500,000-$1 Million
Number Employees: 1-4
Type of Packaging: Private Label

2651 Christmas Point Wild Rice Co
14803 Edgewood Dr
Baxter, MN 56425-8455
218-828-0603
Fax: 218-828-0543 info@christmaspoint.com
www.christmaspoint.com
Wild rice products
Manager: Scott Goehring
info@christmaspoint.com
Estimated Sales: $500,000-$1 Million
Number Employees: 20-49

2652 Christopher Creek Winery
641 Limerick Ln
Healdsburg, CA 95448-9586
707-433-2001
Fax: 707-431-0183 www.christophercreek.com
Wines

Owner: Juan Escudero
juan@ea.com
Owner: Fred Wasserman
Estimated Sales: $500,000
Number Employees: 5-9
Square Footage: 12
Type of Packaging: Private Label

2653 **Christopher Joseph Brewing Company**
6812 E Valley Vista Ln
Paradise Valley, AZ 85253
480-948-7882
Beer
President: Joseph Mocca
Estimated Sales: Under $500,000
Number Employees: 10-19
Brands:
Bandersnatch Milk Stout
Big Horn Premium
Cardinal Pale Ale

2654 **Christopher Norman Chocolates**
PO Box 1145
Hudson, NY 12534
518-822-0300
Fax: 877-220-5751
Manufacturers of hand made chocolates
Founder/Owner: John Down
Estimated Sales: $300,000-500,000
Number Employees: 1-4
Brands:
Christopher Norman Chocolates

2655 **Christopher Ranch LLC**
305 Bloomfield Ave.
Gilroy, CA 95020
408-847-1100
Fax: 408-847-5488 Info@christopherranch.com
www.christopherranch.com
Garlic. Varieties include fresh peeled, fresh roasted, whole fresh, chopped and crushed in oil, chopped and minced in water, pickled garlic, elephant garlic, fresh ginger, fresh shallots, specialty onions, sun dried tomatoes, cherriespeeled specialty onions, horseradish, sweet corn, organic, and dried chiles.
President/CEO: Bill Christopher
Year Founded: 1956
Estimated Sales: $135 Million
Number Employees: 1000-4999
Square Footage: 220000
Type of Packaging: Consumer, Food Service, Bulk

2656 **Christopher's Herb Shop**
188 S Main St
Springville, UT 84663-1849
801-489-4500
Fax: 801-489-4814 888-372-4372
www.drchristophersherbshop.com
Food supplements manufacturer, private label items, herbs and health foods
President: David Christopher
Vice President: Ruth Christopher Bacalla
Manager: Bobbie Henderson
manager@drchristopherhersherbshop.com
Production Manager: James Webster
Purchasing Manager: Josh Bruni
Estimated Sales: Less Than $500,000
Number Employees: 5-9
Square Footage: 15000
Type of Packaging: Private Label

2657 **Christy Wild Blueberry Farms**
1167 Southhampton Road
Amherst, NS B4H 3Y4
Canada
902-667-3013
Fax: 902-667-0350 chrisgaklis@comcast.net
christywildblueberryfarms.com/
Processor and exporter of IQF wild blueberries
President: Chris Gaklis
Estimated Sales: $1.95 Million
Number Employees: 15
Parent Co: International Food Trade
Brands:
Blue Boy
Christy Crops

2658 **Chuao Chocolatier**
2345 Camino Vida Roble
Carlsbad, CA 92011
760-476-1668
Fax: 760-476-1355 888-635-1444
sales@chuaochocolatier.com
www.chuaochocolatier.com
Chocolates
President: Michael Antonorsi
Ceo: Sergio Alvarez
Chairman: Richard Antonorsi
Marketing: Thomas Pineda
Number Employees: 30

2659 **Chuck's Seafoods**
91135 Cape Arago Hwy
Charleston, OR 97420
541-888-5525
Fax: 541-888-2121 www.chucksseafood.com
Processor and canner of seafood including salmon, tuna, clams, crabs and shrimp
President: Jack Hampel
Secretary: Diana Hampel
Estimated Sales: $5-10 Million
Number Employees: 5-9
Type of Packaging: Consumer
Brands:
Vandon Sea-Pack

2660 **Chudabeef Jerky Co.**
Long Beach, CA 90804
chastian@chudabeef.com
www.chudabeef.com
Beef jerky
Founder: Kevin Casey

2661 **Chudleigh's**
8501 Chudleigh Way
Milton, ON L9T 0L9
Canada
905-878-8781
Fax: 905-878-6979 800-387-4028
farm@chudleighs.com www.chudleighs.com
Fresh fruit pies and baked fruits
President: Dean Chudleigh
VP: Scott Chudleigh
Estimated Sales: $4.8 Million
Number Employees: 120
Brands:
Chudleigh's

2662 **Chugwater Chili**
210 1st St
Chugwater, WY 82210
307-422-3345
Fax: 307-422-3357 800-972-4454
chugchili@direcway.com
www.chugwaterchili.com
Chili products including dip and dressing mixes, chili nuts red pepper jelly and ingredients including spices, seasoning blends and peppers, and also steak rub which is new.
Owner: Marcelyn Brown
chugchili@chugwaterchili.com
CEO: Del Ficanz
VP: Karl Wilkerson
Marketing Director: Raece Wilkerson
Sales Director: Raece Wilkerson
chugchili@chugwaterchili.com
Public Relations: Marcelyn Brown
Estimated Sales: $2.5-5 Million
Number Employees: 10-19
Number of Brands: 1
Number of Products: 5
Square Footage: 10240
Type of Packaging: Consumer, Food Service
Brands:
Chugwater Chili

2663 **Chukar Cherries**
320 Wine Country Rd
P.O. Box 510
Prosser, WA 99350-9797
509-786-2055
Fax: 509-786-2591 800-624-9544
sales@chukar.com www.chukar.com
Cherries, dried fruit, trail mixes, chocolates, preserves, sauces, baking mixes, tea and fresh cherries
President: Pam Auld
pam@chukar.com
Chief Financial Officer: JT Montgomery
Head of Production: Kathlene Yound
Estimated Sales: $20-50 Million
Number Employees: 20-49

2664 **Chunco Foods Inc**
1400 E 2nd St
Kansas City, MO 64106-1301
816-283-0716
Fax: 816-472-7779
Fresh tofu, mung bean sprouts, alfalfa sprouts, radish sprouts, authentic koream kim chee, broccoli sprouts, onion sprouts, crispy sprouts and soy milk
Owner: Peter Chun Jr
Estimated Sales: $660,000
Number Employees: 5-9
Square Footage: 8000
Type of Packaging: Food Service

2665 **Chungs Gourmet Foods**
3907 Dennis St
Houston, TX 77004-2520
713-741-2118
Fax: 713-741-2330 www.chungsfoods.com
Producer of Asian food products, including egg rolls, sprin rolls, potstickers and ready-to-eat entrees.
President: Vreij "Reg" Kolandjian
CEO: Danny Bell
dbell@chungsfoods.com
Number Employees: 250-499
Parent Co: Yellowstone Brands
Type of Packaging: Consumer, Food Service, Private Label
Brands:
Chung's

2666 **Church & Dwight Co., Inc.**
Princeton South Corporate Center
500 Charles Ewing Boulevard
Ewing, NJ 08628
609-806-1200
800-833-9532
www.churchdwight.com
Personal care, household cleaning, fabric care, and health and well-being products for the consumer market. Manufacturer of Arm & Hammer brand sodium bicarbonate (baking soda), and other leavening products for the baking industry.
Chairman/President/CEO: Matthew Farrell
Executive VP/CFO: Rick Dierker
Executive VP/General Counsel/Secretary: Patrick de Maynadier
Executive V, Global R&D: Carlos Linares
Executive VP/CMO: Britta Bomhard
Executive VP, U.S. Sales: Paul Wood
Executive VP, Global Operations: Rick Spann
Year Founded: 1846
Estimated Sales: $4.15 Billion
Number Employees: 4,700
Number of Brands: 34
Type of Packaging: Consumer, Food Service, Bulk
Brands:
ARM & HAMMER
Arrid
Answer
AIM
Batiste Dry Shampoo
Close-Up
Delicare
Feline Pine
First Response
KABOOM
Lady's Choice
Legatin
L'il Critters
Nair
Orajel
Orange Glo
OxiClean
PB 8
Pepsodent
Pre-Seed
RepHresh
Replens
Simply Saline
Spinbrush
Toppik
Trojan
Truly Radient
vitafusion
Viviscal
Waterpik
Wellgate
XTRA

2667 (HQ)Churny Company
705 W Fulton St
Waupaca, WI 54981
715-258-4040
Fax: 715-258-4046 www.churnyfoodservice.com
Cheese
President/CEO: William Gifford
Sr Vice President: Pascal Fernandez
Vice President, General Manager: Cliff Fleet
Contact: Laura Ruzzo
lruzzo@atwoodcherny.com
Asset Manager: Dave Edel
Operations/Plant Manager: Michael Spence
Estimated Sales: $10-20 Million
Number Employees: 100-249
Square Footage: 126000
Parent Co: Kraft Foods
Type of Packaging: Consumer, Food Service, Private Label
Brands:
Hoffmans
Polly-O
Athenos
Digiorno

2668 Churny Company
114 Waukegan Rd,
Glenview, IL 60025
847-646-5500
Fax: 847-646-5588 www.athenos.com
Feta cheese
Sales: John Curran
Marketing Director: Roy Lubetkin
Manager: Mary Kay Haben
Estimated Sales: $1-2.5 Million
Number Employees: 50-99
Parent Co: Kraft Foods

2669 (HQ)Ciao Bella Gelato Company
25 Vreeland Rd, #A-104
Irvington, NJ 07040
973-373-1200
Fax: 973-373-1224 800-435-2863
info@ciaobellagelato.com
www.ciaobellagelato.com
Gelato and sorbet
CFO: Stan Fabian
VP, Finance: Ray Bialick
Estimated Sales: $5-10 Million
Number Employees: 50
Square Footage: 40000
Type of Packaging: Consumer, Food Service, Private Label, Bulk
Other Locations:
Ciao Bella Gelato Co.
San Francisco CA
Ciao Bella Gelato Co.
Los Angeles CA
Brands:
Ciao Bella
Gelato
Gotham Dairy
Sarabeth's
Ciao Bella Sorbet

2670 Cibao Meat Products Inc
630 Saint Anns Ave
Bronx, NY 10455-1404
718-993-5072
Fax: 718-993-5638 info@cibaomeat.com
www.cibaomeat.com
Processor and exporter of Spanish sausage and salami.
President: Lutzi Vieluf
CEO: Heinz Vielus
Estimated Sales: $5-10 Million
Number Employees: 50-99
Type of Packaging: Food Service, Bulk
Brands:
Campesino Jamoneta
Don Pedro Jamonada
Induveca
Longaniza Cibao
Pavolami
Salami Campesino
Salami Del Pueblo
Salami Sosua
Salapeno Salami
Ver-Mex
Villa Mella

2671 Cibaria International
705 Columbia Ave
Riverside, CA 92507
951-823-8490
Fax: 951-823-8495 www.cibaria-intl.com
Oils, vinegars and accessories
Founder: Kathy Griset
Square Footage: 55000
Type of Packaging: Food Service, Private Label, Bulk

2672 Cibo Vita
12 Vreeland Ave
Totowa, NJ 07512
862-238-8020
info@cibovita.com
www.cibovita.com
Natural and organic snacks and chocolate-covered fruits and nuts
Owner: Ahmet Celik

2673 CideRoad, LLC
P.O. Box 520
Mendham, NJ 07945-0520
973-543-9003
www.cideroad.com
Organic switchel
CEO: Kevin Duffy
Brand Manager: Noelle Shea
Year Founded: 2013
Type of Packaging: Private Label

2674 Cielo Foods
9238 Bally Ct
Rancho Cucamonga, CA 91730-5313
909-945-2323
Fax: 909-945-9090 877-652-4356
www.cielousa.com
Frozen yogurt
Owner: Dan Kim
info@cielousa.com
Number Employees: 5-9

2675 Cienega Valley Winery/DeRose
9970 Cienega Road
Hollister, CA 95023
831-636-9143
Fax: 831-636-1435 info@derosewine.com
www.derosewine.com
Producers of red, white and port wines.
Owner: Pat De Rose
Winemaker: Al DeRose
Assistant Winemaker: Ralph Hurd
Estimated Sales: $500,000-1 Million
Number Employees: 1-4
Type of Packaging: Private Label
Brands:
De Rose Vineyards

2676 Cifelli & Sons Inc
38 Obert St
PO Box 538
South River, NJ 08882-1235
732-238-0090
Fax: 732-238-7768
Italian sausage
Owner: Anthony Cifelli
Estimated Sales: $2.5 Million
Number Employees: 10-19
Square Footage: 14000
Type of Packaging: Private Label

2677 Cimarron Cellars
P.O.Box 8
Caney, OK 74533
580-889-5997
Fax: 580-889-6312
Wine
Owner/Winemaker: Dwayne Pool
Owner: Suze Pool
President: Linda Pool
Estimated Sales: $1-2,500,000
Number Employees: 1-4
Brands:
Cimarron Cellars

2678 Cimpl Meats
1000 Cattle Dr.
Yankton, SD 57078
605-665-1665
Fax: 605-665-8908
Sausage and beef.
President: Gary Becker
Senior Vice President: Charleen Ward
Year Founded: 1940
Estimated Sales: $152.3 Million
Number Employees: 2,000
Square Footage: 25265

2679 Cincinnati Preserving Co
3015 E Kemper Rd
Cincinnati, OH 45241-1514
513-771-2000
Fax: 513-771-8381 800-222-9966
www.clearbrookfarms.com
Fruit preserves ,jams,jellies,canned fruit,pie fillings,fruit pie mixes.
Owner/CFO: Andrew Liscow
VP: Dan Cohen
Contact: Joe Heinrich
joe@clearbrookfarms.com
Estimated Sales: 1.8 Million
Number Employees: 18
Square Footage: 120000
Parent Co: Cincinatti Preserving Company
Type of Packaging: Consumer
Brands:
Clearbrook Frams
Spreadable Fruit

2680 Cinderella Cheese Cake Co
208 N Fairview St
PO Box 36
Riverside, NJ 08075-3113
856-461-6302
Fax: 856-461-5813 800-521-1171
Processor/Manufacturer of frozen cheesecake
President/CEO: Joseph Makin
Founder: Alfred Rezende
Estimated Sales: $1 Million
Number Employees: 10-19
Square Footage: 80000
Type of Packaging: Consumer, Food Service
Brands:
Cinderella

2681 Cinnabar Specialty Foods Inc
1134 Haining St # C
Prescott, AZ 86305-1693
928-778-3687
Fax: 928-778-4289 866-293-6433
info@cinnabarfoods.com www.cinnabarfoods.com
Processor and exporter of sauces including ethnic and barbecue; also, fruit chutneys, dry spice blends, Caribbean salsa, kashmiri marinade, rice mixes, soup enhancers, etc
Owner: Alana Morrison
sales@cinnabarfoods.com
Vice President: Ted Schleicher
Estimated Sales: $1-4.9 Million
Number Employees: 1-4
Square Footage: 4000
Type of Packaging: Consumer, Food Service, Private Label, Bulk
Brands:
Cinnabar Specialty Foods
Neera's

2682 Cinnabar Winery
14612 Big Basin Way # A
Saratoga, CA 95070-6085
408-867-1010
Fax: 408-741-5860
Wines
President: Suzanne Frontz
General Manager: Suzan Franz
Estimated Sales: $2.5-5 Million
Number Employees: 10-19

2683 Cinnamon Bakery
121 Hancock Street
Braintree, MA 02184-7040
781-843-2867
Fax: 781-849-0015 800-886-2867
cinbak@aol.com
Cinnamon, raspberry and chocolate sticks, pecan sticky buns and cinnamon rolls
President: Tom Pattavina
Treasurer: Frances Pattavina
Estimated Sales: $2.5-5 Million
Number Employees: 5-9
Brands:
Boston Bakers Exchange
Cinnamon Bakery

2684 **Cipriani's Spaghetti & Sauce Company**
1025 West End Avenue
Chicago Heights, IL 60411-2742
708-755-6212
Fax: 708-755-6272
Processor and exporter of pasta including angel hair, vermicelli, linguine, fettuccine, lasagna, spinach, etc.; also, pasta sauces
President/Purchasing Manager: Annette Johnson
Executive VP: Arthur Petrarca
Estimated Sales: $5-10 Million
Number Employees: 10-19
Square Footage: 43572
Type of Packaging: Consumer, Food Service, Private Label, Bulk
Brands:
Cipriani's Classic Italian
Cipriani's Premium

2685 **Circle B Ranch**
RR2 Box 2824
Seymour, MO 65746
417-683-0271
www.circlebranchpork.com
Pork products, bacon, meat sticks, sauces, chutneys, and gluten free Bloody Mary mix
Owner: Marina Backes
Owner: John Backes

2686 **Circle R Ranch**
5901 Cross Timbers Rd
Flower Mound, TX 75022-3142
817-430-1561
Fax: 817-430-8108 800-247-3077
www.circlerranch.org
Sauces including black bean salsa, jalapeno jelly, green chili salsa, cheese and spice blend, corn relish and mesquite barbecue; also, snacks including jalapeno popcorn, habanero popcorn and snack mix
Owner: Jason Roberts
jasonroberts@circlerranch.org
CEO: Alan Powdermaker
Chief Financial Officer: Laura Johnson
Sales manager: Robyn Lacasse
jasonroberts@circlerranch.org
Director of Events: Blair Green
Event Services Manager: Ocean Martinez
Estimated Sales: Less than $500,000
Number Employees: 10-19
Parent Co: Sunset Trails
Type of Packaging: Consumer, Private Label
Brands:
Circle R Gourmet Foods

2687 **Circle V Meats**
609 Arrowhead Trl
Spanish Fork, UT 84660-9237
801-798-3081
Fax: 801-798-8671 www.circlevmeat.com
Beef and pork including roasts, ham and bacon
Owner: Cliff Voorhees
admin@circlevmeat.com
Estimated Sales: $3 Million
Number Employees: 10-19

2688 **Circle Valley Produce LLC**
1370 Burgess St
Idaho Falls, ID 83402-1825
208-524-2628
Fax: 208-524-2630 www.idahopotato.com
Processor and exporter of potatoes
President: Kent Cornelison
Communications: Kirk Hart
Purchasing: Dave Owens
Estimated Sales: $8.8 Million
Number Employees: 50-99
Type of Packaging: Consumer, Bulk
Brands:
Throughbred
Valley Gold

2689 **Circus Man Ice Cream Corporation**
1000 Fulton St
Farmingdale, NY 11735-4245
516-249-4400
Fax: 516-249-4435
Ice cream
Owner: Blaise Graziano
Estimated Sales: $1.8,000,000
Number Employees: 10-19
Brands:
Circus Man

2690 **Ciro Foods**
PO Box 44096
Pittsburgh, PA 15205-0296
412-771-9018
Fax: 412-771-9018 cirofoods@usa.net
Roasted red pepper spread, Italian salsa, sauces including pizza, barbecue and cooking and hot honey mustard; wholesaler/distributor of hot pepper sauce; serving the food service market; importer of vinegar; exporter of hot honeymustard
President: Robert Pasquarelli
VP: Josephine Proto
Marketing Executive: Armand Pasquarelli
Number Employees: 20
Type of Packaging: Consumer, Food Service, Private Label

2691 **Cisco Brewers**
5 Bartlett Farm Rd
Nantucket, MA 02554-4341
508-325-5929
Fax: 508-325-5209 tracy@ciscobrewers.com
www.ciscobrewers.com
Producer of ale and lager beers
Owner: Randy Hudson
randy@ciscobrewers.com
CEO: Jay Harman
Web And Social Media Manager: Kristen V Hull
randy@ciscobrewers.com
Estimated Sales: $600,000
Number Employees: 1-4
Square Footage: 12800
Type of Packaging: Consumer
Brands:
Baggywrinkle
Bailey's
Captain Swain's Extra
Celebration Libation
Dubbel Felix Caspian
Moor
Nobadeer Ginger
Summer of Lager
Whale's Tale

2692 **Cisse Trading Co**
129 Halstead Ave
Mamaroneck, NY 10543-5608
914-381-5555
info@cissetrading.com
www.cissecocoa.com
Baking mixes, hot cocoa, and super thin brownie thins.
Founder: Diana Lovett
Number Employees: 10-19
Brands:
Super THINS

2693 **(HQ)Citadelle Maple Syrup Producers' Cooperative**
2100 St-Laurent, CP 310
Plessisville, QC G6L 2Y8
Canada
819-362-3241
Fax: 819-362-2830 citadelle@citadelle.coop
www.citadelle.coop
Processor and exporter of fruit spreads, honey, pure maple syrup and maple sugar.
CEO: Martin Plante
Director Financial Services & Treasurer: Patrick Fleurent, CPA, CMA
Dir. of Corporate Affairs & Secretary: Jean-Marie Chouinard
Director of Marketing: Sylvie Chapron
Princial Sales Director: Stephane Vachon, M.Sc.
Human Resources Director: Richard Cote
Director Operations & Quality: Remi Fortin, ing. MBA
Number Employees: 150
Square Footage: 360000
Type of Packaging: Consumer, Food Service, Private Label, Bulk
Other Locations:
La Guadeloupe Facility
Guadeloupe QC
Restigouche Brand Inc
Saint-Quentin NB
Facility & Distribution Centre
Plessisville QC
Tertiary Transformation Facility
Plessisville QC
Cranberry Transformation Facility
Aston-Jonction QC
Brands:
Camp
Canada Gold
Citadelle
O'Canada

2694 **Citrico**
155 Revere Dr # 1
Northbrook, IL 60062-1558
847-835-4368
Fax: 847-945-7405 800-445-2171
www.creativeimpactgroup.com
An independent manufacturer of citrus products for the food, beverage, pharmaceutical and nutraceutical industries.
Owner: Joanne Brooks
VP Technical Sales: Robert Vieregg
Sales: Timothy Grano
Contact: Todd Heinz
th@citico.com
Estimated Sales: $4.8 Million
Number Employees: 10-19
Number of Brands: 20
Parent Co: Citrico International
Brands:
Citrico

2695 **Citromax Flavors Inc**
444 Washington Ave
Carlstadt, NJ 07072-2806
201-933-8405
Fax: 201-549-1261 www.citromax.com
Grower of lemons and producer of oils, juices and lemon by-products such as essential oils, cloudy and clarified concentrated juices and dehydrated peel. Flavors are used in beverages, confection, dairy and baked goods.
President: Angela Begley
angelabegley@citromaxflavors.com
Quality Control Chemist: Joseph Clark
Directory Of Operations/Plant Manager: Max Van Der Linden
Estimated Sales: $560,000
Number Employees: 1-4
Square Footage: 4599

2696 **Citrop Inc**
5707 W Sligh Ave
Tampa, FL 33634-4435
813-249-5955
Fax: 813-249-5956
Natural flavoring
President/CEO: Jorge Figueredo
Estimated Sales: $1-2.5 000,000
Number Employees: 1-4

2697 **Citrosuco North AmericaInc**
5937 State Road 60 E
Lake Wales, FL 33898-9279
863-696-7400
Fax: 863-696-1303 800-356-4592
citrosuco@citrosuco.com.br www.citrosuco.com
Orange juice and concentrates; importer of frozen orange and apple concentrates and not from concentrate orange juice; exporter of frozen orange juice concentrates and not from concentrate orange juice
President: Nick Emanuel
CEO: Kathy Baker
kbaker@citrosuco.com
CFO: Dennis Helms
Sales Manager: Michael DuBrul
Plant Manager: Jim Bolden
Purchasing Manager: Gary Brundage
Estimated Sales: Less Than $500,000
Number Employees: 1-4
Square Footage: 38200
Parent Co: Citrosuco
Type of Packaging: Bulk

2698 **Citrus International**
210 Salvador Sq
Winter Park, FL 32789-5619
407-629-8037
Fax: 407-629-8195
Citrus juice
President: Brian Albertson
Estimated Sales: Under $500,000
Number Employees: 1-4

2699 **Citrus Service**
120 S Dillard St
Winter Garden, FL 34787
407-656-4999
Fax: 407-656-4999 beroper@iag.net
Manufacturer and exporter of frozen organic citrus juices and frozen juice concentrates

President: Bert Roper
CEO: Charles Roper
Estimated Sales: $4 Million
Number Employees: 20-49
Square Footage: 42000
Type of Packaging: Bulk
Brands:
Grove Sweet

2700 Citrus and Allied Essences
3000 Marcus Ave, Ste 3e11
New Hyde Park, NY 11042
516-354-1200
Fax: 516-354-1502 www.citrusandallied.com
Supplier of essential oils, oleoresins, aromatic chemicals and specialty flavor ingredients.
President/CEO/Owner: Richard Pisano Jr.
Executive Vice President: Stephen Pisano
Sales Manager: Ann Heller
Contact: Jodi Adams
jadams@citrusandallied.com
Director Purchasing: Rob Haedrich
Number Employees: 100+
Type of Packaging: Food Service, Bulk

2701 Citterio USA
2008 State Route 940
Freeland, PA 18224-3256
570-636-3171
Fax: 570-636-1267 800-435-8888
sales@citteriousa.com www.citteriousa.com
Processor and importer of Italian Speciality deli meat products
President/COO: Osvaldo Vanucci
CEO: Michelle Basista
mbasista@citteriousa.com
CEO: Nick Dei Tos
VP Sales: Joseph Petruce
VP Manufacturing: Michael Zieminski
Estimated Sales: $5-10 Million
Number Employees: 100-249
Parent Co: Giuseppe Citterio Spa
Type of Packaging: Consumer, Food Service, Private Label, Bulk
Brands:
Citterio

2702 City Bakery
3 W 18th St # 1
New York, NY 10011-4610
212-366-1414
Fax: 212-645-0810 info@thecitybakery.com
www.thecitybakery.com
Pretzel croissants and other baked goods.
Owner: Maury Rubin
citybakerysara@mac.com
Number Employees: 20-49

2703 City Bakery Cafe
60 Biltmore Ave # 1
Asheville, NC 28801-3643
828-252-4426
Fax: 212-645-0810 877-328-3687
info@thecitybakery.com www.citybakery.net
Pretzel croissants and other baked goods.
Owner: Maury R Rubin
Marketing: Allison Dees
Manager: Craig Peters
citybakery@bellsouth.net
Estimated Sales: Less Than $500,000
Number Employees: 5-9
Brands:
Maury's Cookie Dough
The City Bakery

2704 City Bean
5051 W Jefferson Blvd
Los Angeles, CA 90016-3940
323-734-0828
Fax: 310-208-4554 888-248-9232
info@citybean.com www.citybean.com
Coffee, tea
Owner: Gary Salzer
Estimated Sales: $500,000-$1 Million
Number Employees: 5-9

2705 City Brewing Company
925 S 3rd St
La Crosse, WI 54601
608-785-4200
inquiries@citybrewery.com
www.citybrewery.com
Manufacturer/processor of beer for major and private label brands.
VP & Chief Financial Officer: Gregory Inda
Director, Supply Chain: Jeff Glynn
Year Founded: 1939
Estimated Sales: $38 Million
Number Employees: 400
Type of Packaging: Consumer
Other Locations:
Latrobe PA
Memphis TN
Brands:
City Lager
City Light
City Slicker
Kul
Lacrosse Lager
Lacrosse Light

2706 City Cafe & Bakery
215 Glynn St S
Fayetteville, GA 30214-2039
770-461-6800
Fax: 770-461-2161 www.citycafeandbakery.com
Bakery products
Owner: Jorg Schatte
citycafebakery@bellsouth.net
Estimated Sales: $3-5 Million
Number Employees: 20-49

2707 City Farm/Rocky Peanut Company
1545 Clay Street
Detroit, MI 48211-1911
313-871-5100
Fax: 313-871-5106 800-437-6825
rocky-peanut.com/city-farm.com
Holiday snack items
President: Joe Russo
Estimated Sales: $2.5-5 Million
Number Employees: 5-9

2708 City Foods Inc
4230 S Racine Ave
Chicago, IL 60609-2526
773-523-1566
Fax: 773-523-1414 info@beasbest.com
www.beasbest.com
Processor, importer and exporter of frozen beef products including corned beef brisket, short ribs, corned, sliced, roast beef, pastrami,and beef bacon
President: Kenneth Kohn
CEO: John Campbell
john@beasbest.com
Information Technology Manager: Chris Humberg
Sales Manager: Scott Weiss
Director Of Purchasing: John Campbell
Estimated Sales: $48 Million
Number Employees: 50-99
Number of Brands: 3
Square Footage: 43000
Type of Packaging: Consumer, Food Service, Private Label, Bulk
Brands:
Bea's Best
Chef's Pride
Silver Label

2709 City Market
1508 Gloucester St
Brunswick, GA 31520-7143
912-265-4430
Fax: 912-261-2191 www.citymarketseafood.com
Fish and seafood
Owner: Michael Howell
m.howell@citymarket.com
Manager: Frank Owens
Estimated Sales: $3,500,000
Number Employees: 5-9

2710 City Saucery
37 Laconia Ave.
Staten Island, NY 11215
718-753-4006
info@citysaucery.com
www.citysaucery.com
A variety of tomato products including tomato sauce, paste, and preserved tomatoes.
Owner and Co-Founder: Michael Marino
Owner and Co-Founder: Jorge Moret

2711 Clabber Girl Corporation
900 Wabash Ave
Terre Haute, IN 47807-3208
812-232-9446
Fax: 812-232-2397 www.clabbergirl.com
Manufacturer of baking powder, baking soda, dessert mixes and corn starch for retail, food service and industrial customers.
National Sales Manager: Mark Rice
Type of Packaging: Consumer, Food Service, Private Label, Bulk
Brands:
Clabber Girl®
Rumford®
Rex Coffee
Hearth Club
Davis®
Fleischmann's Baking Powder
Royal®
InnovaPhase™

2712 Claeys Candy Inc
525 S Taylor St
South Bend, IN 46601-2744
574-287-1818
Fax: 574-287-4184
customerservice@claeyscandy.com
www.claeyscandy.com
Candy, old fashioned hard candies, cream fudge, gourmet peanut brittle, chocolate charlie gift boxes, bulk, private label
President: Gregg Claeys
gclaeys@claeyscandy.com
Plant Manager: Brian Machalleck
Estimated Sales: $10-20 Million
Number Employees: 20-49
Number of Brands: 4
Type of Packaging: Consumer, Private Label, Bulk
Brands:
Chocolate Charlie
Claeys Gourmet Cream Fudge
Claeys Gourmet Peanut Brittle
Claeys Old Fashion Hards Candies

2713 Claiborne & Churchill Vintners
2649 Carpenter Canyon Rd
San Luis Obispo, CA 93401-8934
805-544-4066
Fax: 805-544-7012 info@claibornechurchill.com
www.claibornechurchill.com
Wines
Owner: Clay Thompson
Owner/CEO: Fredericka Churchill
Marketing Manager: Angela Gloeckler
Estimated Sales: $500,000-$1 Million
Number Employees: 1-4
Brands:
Claiborne & Churchill

2714 Clara Foods
100 First Avenue SE
Clara City, MN 56222-0457
320-847-3680
Fax: 320-847-3939 888-844-8518
Snack foods, pretzels, cereal, baking ingredients and extruded products
President: Massoud Kazemzadeh
VP Sales/Marketing: Tom Condon
Research & Development: Massoud Kazemzadeh
Purchasing Manager: Joe Jeanotte
Estimated Sales: $1.5 Million
Number Employees: 40

2715 Clara Foods
One Tower Pl.
Ste. 800
San Francisco, CA 94080
info@clarafoods.com
www.clarafoods.com
Egg whites, egg replacers, baking products, food and beverage ingredients, nutritional supplements, animal-free protein.
CEO: Arturo Elizondo
VP, Product: Harshal Kshirsagar
VP, Tech: Joel Kreps
Year Founded: 2014
Number Employees: 11-50
Type of Packaging: Consumer, Food Service

2716 Clarendon Flavor Engineering
2500 Stanley Gault Parkway
Louisville, KY 40223
502-634-9215
Fax: 502-634-1438 www.clarendonflavors.com
Manufactures natural and artificial flavors to food and beverage industry. Specializes in natural soft drinks, juice added and flavored sparkling waters
President: Richard Rigney

Estimated Sales: $5-10 Million
Number Employees: 6
Square Footage: 80000
Type of Packaging: Bulk

2717 Clariant
4000 Monroe Rd
Charlotte, NC 28205
704-331-7000
Fax: 704-377-1063 www.clariant.com
Chemical and ingredient manufacturer.
CEO: Hariolf Kottmann

2718 Clark Spring Water Co
319 Clark Street
Pueblo, CO 81003
719-543-1594
ar@clarkspringwater.com
www.clarkspringwater.com
Processor and bottler of water
Founder: Silas Clark
Estimated Sales: Less Than $500,000
Number Employees: 5-9
Type of Packaging: Consumer
Brands:
Alpine

2719 Clarke J F Corp
173 Franklin Ave
Franklin Square, NY 11010-1441
516-328-8333
Fax: 516-328-8346 800-229-7474
jclarke@jfclarke.com www.jfclarke.com
Frozen shrimp and seafood
President: James Clarke
jclarke@jfclarke.com
Estimated Sales: $5-10 Million
Number Employees: 1-4
Type of Packaging: Food Service
Brands:
Amazonas
Avila
Bee Gee
Fresh Cargo
Yutaka

2720 Clarkson Scottish Bakery
1715 Lakeshore Road West
Mississauga, ON L5J 1J4
Canada
905-823-1500
Scottish baked goods including pies, pastries and breads; importer of Scottish and English meats, candies and chocolates
Proprietor: Catherine Whitelaw
Number Employees: 1-4
Square Footage: 1800

2721 Clarmil Manufacturing Corp
30865 San Clemente St
Hayward, CA 94544-7136
510-476-0700
Fax: 510-476-0707 888-252-7645
customerservice@goldilocks-usa.com
Manufacturers a full line of breads, rolls, buns, filled buns and pies, pastries, sweet goods, cookies, crackers and snack items. Cakes-pound cake, sponge, devil, chiffon, snack cakes and other specialty cake items. Processes soupsauces, side dishes, stews, processed meat products, meat and vegetable fillings, hors d'ouvers, specialty snacks and appetizers.
President: Marion Ortiz Luis
myoritz-lus@clarmilmfg.com
Estimated Sales: Less than $500,000
Number Employees: 100-249
Number of Products: 200+
Square Footage: 228000
Type of Packaging: Consumer, Food Service, Private Label, Bulk

2722 Clasen Quality Chocolate
5126 W Terrace Dr # 100
Suite 100
Madison, WI 53718-8346
608-467-1130
Fax: 608-249-4573 877-459-4500
info@clasen.us www.clasen.us
Pure chocolate and confectionery coatings, including milk, dark, white, yogurt, peanut, colored and flavored coatings.
President: Jay Jensen
CFO: Andy Gitter
VP: Dennis Tagarelli
Vice President of Sales and Marketing: Joe Lucas
Estimated Sales: Under $500,000
Number Employees: 5-9
Square Footage: 11228
Type of Packaging: Consumer, Bulk
Brands:
Clasen

2723 Classic Commissary
126 E Arterial Highway
Binghamton, NY 13901-1656
800-929-3486
Fax: 607-722-1415 classiccommissary@aol.com
Fresh salads and fruits; also, frozen dinners, sandwiches and bagels; for the vending and convenience food industry
Owner: Tara Gianfrate
Contact: Cataldo Gianfrate
cataldo.gianfrate@classiccatering.com
Manager: Cataldo Gianfrate
Number Employees: 50-99
Number of Products: 125
Square Footage: 88000
Type of Packaging: Food Service, Private Label, Bulk
Brands:
Classic Commissary

2724 Classic Confectionery
PO Box 573
Fort Worth, TX 76101-0573
847-674-4490
Fax: 847-674-4435 800-674-4435
TomDetective@yahoo.com
www.candydetective.com
Candy and confectionery
President: Cory Rogin
Co-Founder: Thomas Allen
President: Gail Robinson
General Manager: Trevor Toppen
Number Employees: 50-99

2725 Classic Cookings, LLC
165-35 145th Drive
Jamaica, NY 11434
718-439-0200
www.classiccooking.com
Manufacturer of souffles, quiches, and hearty soups.
Contact: Elliot Huss
elliot@classiccooking.com
Square Footage: 80000

2726 Classic Delight Inc
310 S Park Dr
P.O.Box 367
St Marys, OH 45885-9688
419-394-7955
Fax: 419-394-3199 800-274-9828
orders@classicdelight.com
www.classicdelight.com
Processor and co-packer of USDA and FDA frozen and refrigerated sandwiches, meat and entrees
Owner: Darl Harkleroad
darl@classicdelight.com
Estimated Sales: $5 Million
Number Employees: 50-99
Number of Brands: 25
Number of Products: 60
Square Footage: 74000
Type of Packaging: Consumer, Food Service, Private Label, Bulk
Brands:
Classic Delight
Express Delights
Sensible Delights

2727 Classic Flavors & Fragrances
878 W End Ave Apt 12b
New York, NY 10025
212-777-0004
Fax: 212-353-0404 cffi125@aol.com
Manufacturer, importer and exporter of flavors, essential oils, aromatics, etc
CEO: George Ivolin
Estimated Sales: $2.5-5 Million
Number Employees: 5-9
Square Footage: 3600
Type of Packaging: Bulk

2728 Classic Foods
1592 Union Street
49
San Francisco, CA 94123-4531
800-574-8122
Fax: 866-235-9993
Family owned manufacturer of top quality branded snack foods distributed throughout the United States and Canada.
President: Florencio Cuetara
VP of Sales-Food Service: Shane Gray
Director of Sales-Vending: Lynn Marie Robles
Contact: Jeff Rynearson
jeffr_ims@yahoo.com
Estimated Sales: $5-10 Million
Number Employees: 100-249
Brands:
Baked Classics
Kettle Classics
Kids Klassics
Stoned Classics

2729 (HQ)Classic Tea
649 Innsbruck Court
Libertyville, IL 60048-1845
630-680-9934
Processor, importer and exporter of ceylon (black) tea, liquid tea syrup and iced tea concentrates
Managing Director: Thomas Rielly
Director: F Court Bailey
Number Employees: 20-49
Square Footage: 80000
Type of Packaging: Consumer, Food Service, Private Label, Bulk
Other Locations:
Classic Tea Ltd.
Chicago IL
Brands:
Ceylon Classic
Classic Ceylon
Pearl

2730 Classy Delites
P.O.Box 340189
Austin, TX 78734-0004
512-266-7157
Fax: 512-266-7198 800-440-2648
All-natural, artichoke marvelous melody, basalmic bean sauce, reduced carbs tweed tortilla chips, jamaican sauce, spinach-avacado sauce and portabella sauce.
Owner: Debbie Westbrook
CEO: Drew Westbrook
drew@classydelites.com
Estimated Sales: $1-2.5 Million
Number Employees: 1-4
Type of Packaging: Consumer
Brands:
Classy Delites

2731 Claudia B Chocolates
663 W Rhapsody Dr
San Antonio, TX 78216-2608
210-366-4602
Fax: 800-375-4602 800-725-4602
sales@claudiab.com www.claudiab.com
Chocolates
President: Don Bankler
sales@claudiab.com
Estimated Sales: Less Than $500,000
Number Employees: 1-4
Square Footage: 8000
Type of Packaging: Consumer, Private Label, Bulk

2732 Claxton Bakery Inc
203 W Main St
PO Box 367
Claxton, GA 30417-1705
912-739-3097
Fax: 912-739-3097 800-841-4211
service@claxtonfruitcake.com
www.claxtonfruitcake.com
Established in 1910. Manufacturer and exporter of fruit cake, pecans, candies, and dressings.
Vice President: Paul Parker
ppgolf912@bellsouth.net
Estimated Sales: $20-50 Million
Number Employees: 100-249
Type of Packaging: Consumer
Brands:
Claxton

2733 Clay Center Locker Plant
212 6th St
Clay Center, KS 67432-3312
785-632-5550
Fax: 785-632-5550 800-466-5543
brad@claycenterlocker.com
www.claycenterlocker.com
Beef, pork, lamb, buffalo and ostrich

Owner: Brad Dieckmann
claycorod@claycountykansas.org
Estimated Sales: $3-5 Million
Number Employees: 5-9
Type of Packaging: Consumer, Food Service

2734 Clayton Coffee & Tea
502 10th St
Modesto, CA 95354-3504
209-576-1120
Fax: 209-576-1123 sales@claytoncoffee.com
www.claytoncoffee.com
Coffee and tea
Owner: Gretchen Peek
billkuhn@claytoncoffe.com
Estimated Sales: $1-2.5 Million
Number Employees: 1-4
Type of Packaging: Bulk
Brands:
Clayton Coffee & Tea

2735 Clayton's Crab Co
5775 US Highway 1
Rockledge, FL 32955-5729
321-636-6673
Fax: 321-636-4631
www.claytonscrabcompany.com
Crab meat; wholesaler/distributor of fresh, frozen and canned seafood and meat; serving the food service market
Owner: Janet Walker
claytoncrabjan@cfl.rr.com
Estimated Sales: $1-3 Million
Number Employees: 10-19

2736 Cleanfish Inc
450 Bay St
San Francisco, CA 94133-1820
415-626-3500
Fax: 415-626-2505 annette@cleanfish.com
www.cleanfish.com
Fresh seafood
Owner: Gakhan Perain
gpercin@cadence.com
CEO: Tim o'Shea
Controller: Annette Lee
Bay Area Dealer: Kendrick Wu
Number Employees: 10-19

2737 Clear Creek Distillery
2389 NW Wilson St
Portland, OR 97210-2319
503-248-9470
Fax: 503-248-0490 info@clearcreekdistillery.com
www.clearcreekdistillery.com
Wine and liquor
President: Stephen R Mc Carthy
Vice President: Rachel Showaiter
Estimated Sales: $700,000
Number Employees: 5-9
Type of Packaging: Private Label
Brands:
Bartlett
Blue Plumb Brandy
Clear Creek Grappas
Flamboise
Kirschwasser (Cherry Brandy)
McCarthy's Oregon Single Malt
Pear Brandy
Pure Fruite

2738 Clear Mountain Coffee Company
9155 Brookville Rd
Silver Spring, MD 20910
301-587-2233
Fax: 301-587-7158
Fourteen varieties of organic and wood roasted coffees, syrups, Choice Tea, Ghiradelli Chocolate
President: Robert Dasilva
Estimated Sales: $1-2.5 Million
Number Employees: 10-19
Number of Brands: 10
Brands:
10

2739 Clear Products Inc.
6156 Mission Gorge Rd
Suite C
San Diego, CA 92120
619-521-0327
Fax: 619-283-3913 888-257-2532
mail@clearproductsinc.com
www.clearproductsinc.com
Manufacturing

Owner: Del Neville
Estimated Sales: $300,000-500,000
Number Employees: 1-4

2740 Clear Springs Foods Inc.
1500 E. 4424 N. Clear Lakes Rd.
PO Box 712
Buhl, ID 83316
208-543-4316
800-635-8211
csfsales@clearsprings.com www.clearsprings.com
Fresh and frozen rainbow trout, breaded trout portions, shapes and melts.
CEO: Kurt Meyers
COO: Jeff Jermunson
Year Founded: 1991
Estimated Sales: $130 Million
Number Employees: 250-499
Number of Brands: 4
Square Footage: 7200
Type of Packaging: Consumer, Food Service, Private Label
Brands:
Clear Springs Kitchen®
Clear Springs®
ClearùCuts®
Splash®

2741 Clear-Vu Industries
200 Homer Avenue
Suite 3
Ashland, MA 01721-1716
508-881-9100
Fax: 508-881-9111 www.clear-vu.com
Bulk Candy System
President: Robert McCann
Estimated Sales: $1-2.5 Million
Number Employees: 10-19

2742 Clearly Canadian Beverage Corporation
220 Viceroy Rd
Units 11/12
Vanghan, ON L4K 3CA
Canada
905-761-0597
Fax: 607-742-5301 866-414-2326
www.clearly.ca
Processor and exporter of water including sparkling fruit, carbonated mineral and artesian
President: David Reingold
CEO: Roy Hessel
CFO: Craig Lennox
Director of Business Intelligence & FP&A: Ibrahim Kamar
Director, Human Resources: Nancy Savard
COO: Nancy Morison
Estimated Sales: $10.62million
Number Employees: 20
Type of Packaging: Consumer, Food Service
Brands:
Clearly Canadian
Clearly Canadian O+2
Orbitz
Quencher
Tre' Limone

2743 Clearly Kombucha
San Francisco, CA 94533
www.clearlykombucha.com
Sparkling teas
Co-Founder: Alison Zarrow
Co-Founder: Caleb Cargle
Number of Brands: 1
Number of Products: 6
Type of Packaging: Consumer
Brands:
CLEARLY KOMBUCHA

2744 Clearwater Coffee Company
711 Rose Rd
Lake Zurich, IL 60047-1542
847-540-7711
Fax: 847-540-7719
Coffee
President: Jim Ludwig

2745 Clearwater Fine Foods
757 Bedford Highway
Bedford, NS B4A 3Z7
Canada
902-443-0550
Fax: 902-443-8367 www.clearwater.ca

Processor and exporter of frozen shrimp, lobster, scallops, crabs and clams
Chairman: Colin MacDonald
CEO: Ian Smith
Number Employees: 100-249
Type of Packaging: Consumer, Food Service

2746 Clem Becker Meats
2720 Lincoln Ave
Two Rivers, WI 54241
920-793-1391
Fax: 920-793-1393 clembeckerinc@lakefield.net
Smoked pork products
President: Peter Becker
VP: Oliver Skrivanie
Business Manager: Jan Eycke
Estimated Sales: $5-10 Million
Number Employees: 25
Type of Packaging: Consumer, Food Service, Private Label

2747 Clem's Seafood & Specialties
4505 Mattingly Ct
Buckner, KY 40010-8830
502-222-7571
Fax: 502-222-7598
Seafood
Owner: Michael McAlister
Estimated Sales: $3-5 Million
Number Employees: 1-4

2748 Clemens Family Corporation
2700 Clemens Rd
Hatfield, PA 19440-0902
800-523-5291
www.clemensfamilycorp.com
Pork products
CEO: Douglas C. Clemens
Contact: Michelle Alldred
malldred@cvff.com

2749 Clement's Pastry Shops Inc
3355 52nd Ave # B
Hyattsville, MD 20781-1033
301-277-6300
Fax: 301-277-2897 office@clementspastry.com
www.clementspastry.com
Custom manufacturing of specialty dessert and pastry items.
President: Richard Barrazotto
Co-Owner: Matthew Barrazotto
VP: John Barrazotto
Estimated Sales: $11 Million
Number Employees: 100-249
Number of Brands: 1
Number of Products: 200
Type of Packaging: Food Service, Private Label
Brands:
Clements Pastry Shop

2750 (HQ)Clements Foods Co
6601 N Harvey Pl
Oklahoma City, OK 73116
405-842-3308
Fax: 405-843-6894 800-654-8355
clementsfoodscompany.com
Apple butter, preserves, jellies, salad dressings, pie fillings, mayonnaise, mustard, sauces, syrups, vinegar, peanut butter and imitation vanilla; exporter of salad dressings and mustards
President: Edward Clements
Executive Vice President: Robert Clements
Year Founded: 1952
Estimated Sales: $61 Million
Number Employees: 100-249
Number of Brands: 8
Square Footage: 150000
Type of Packaging: Consumer, Food Service, Private Label
Other Locations:
Clements Foods Company
Lewisville TX
Brands:
American
Delicious
Dorcheste
Garden Club
Little Pig
Par
Savory
Win You

2751 **Clemmy's**
PO Box 1746
Randcho Mirage, CA 92270
877-253-6698
www.clemmysicecream.com
Lactose free, 100% sugar free and gluten free ice cream.
Founder/Owner: Jon Gordon
Number Employees: 6
Square Footage: 4374
Type of Packaging: Consumer

2752 **Clemson Bros. Brewery**
22 Cottage St.
Middletown, NY 10940
845-775-4638
info@clemsonbrewing.com
www.clemsonbrewing.com
Flavored ale, IPA, Belgian-style wheat beer, fruit wheat beers, stout & porter
Co-Owner: Kenan Porter
Number of Brands: 1
Number of Products: 19
Type of Packaging: Consumer, Private Label
Brands:
Clemson Bros.

2753 **Cleveland Kraut**
4700 Lakeside Ave
Suite 19-1C
Cleveland, OH 44114
216-264-6895
sales@clevelandkraut.com
clevelandkraut.com
Unpasteurized kraut
Co-Founder: Luke Visnic
Estimated Sales: Less than $500,000
Number Employees: 4
Type of Packaging: Private Label

2754 **Cleveland Syrup Corporation**
4999 Mead Avenue
Cleveland, OH 44127-1107
216-883-1845
Fax: 216-883-6204
Syrup and powdered sugar
Vice President: James Chaney
General Manager: Jim Chaney
President: Virginia Chaney
Estimated Sales: $1-2.5 Million
Number Employees: 1 to 4
Type of Packaging: Food Service, Bulk

2755 **Clic International Inc**
2185 Av. Francis Hugues
Laval, QC H7S 1N5
Canada
450-669-2663
Fax: 450-667-6799 agtclic@agtclic.com
www.agtclic.com
Grains, rices, beverages, condiments, pasta, dairy products, dried fruit and nuts, and more.
Estimated Sales: $24.5
Number Employees: 123

2756 **Clif Bar & Co**
1451 66th St
Emeryville, CA 94608-1004
510-547-1144
Fax: 510-558-7872 802-254-3227
www.clifbar.com
Energy bars, nutrition bars, protein bars, energy chews, energy granolas, energy gel, protein drink mixes, and electrolyte drink mixes
CEO: Kevin Cleary
Founder/Owner & Co-CVO: Gary Erickson
Owner & Co-CVO: Kit Crawford
EVP Food & Innovation: Michelle Ferguson
Marketing Director: Joey Steger
Year Founded: 1992
Estimated Sales: $500 Million-$1 Billion
Number Employees: 1200
Type of Packaging: Consumer, Private Label
Brands:
CLIF BAR
CLIF KID
LUNA
CLIF SHOT
CLIF BUILDER'S
CLIF CRUNCH
CLIF MOJO

2757 **Cliff Lede Vineyards**
1473 Yountville Cross Rd
Yountville, CA 94599-9471
707-944-8642
Fax: 707-944-8020 800-428-2259
info@CliffLedeVineyards.com
www.cliffledevineyards.com
Wines and champagne
Owner: Cliff Lede
CEO: John Anderson
Vice President of Operations: Remi Cohen
Marketing Manager: Alfred Andreson
Sales Manager: Peter Vanm
Estimated Sales: $430,000
Number Employees: 20-49
Type of Packaging: Consumer, Food Service

2758 **Clifty Farm Country Meats**
P.O. Box 1146
Paris, TN 38242
731-642-9740
Fax: 731-642-7129 800-486-4267
www.cliftyfarm.com
Frozen portion cuts of bacon, ham and barbecue pork and turkey
President & CEO: Dan Murphey
Marketing & Sales Manager: Adrian Harrod
Number Employees: 100
Square Footage: 800000
Type of Packaging: Consumer, Food Service
Brands:
Clifty Farm

2759 **Cline Cellars**
24737 Arnold Dr
Sonoma, CA 95476-9216
707-940-4030
Fax: 707-931-7118 800-543-2070
www.mizpahhotel.info
Wines
Owner: Laura Feinstein
lauracfeinstein@gmail.com
CFO: Nancy Cline
Event Planner: Jennifer Alvarez
Production Manager: Matt Cline
Estimated Sales: Under $500,000
Number Employees: 1-4
Type of Packaging: Private Label
Brands:
Cline Cellars

2760 **Clinton St Baking Co**
4 Clinton St
New York, NY 10002-1703
646-602-6263
dede@clintonstreetbaking.com
www.clintonstreetbaking.com
Baked goods
Owner: Neal Kleinberg
graybiscuits@earthlink.net
Estimated Sales: Less Than $500,000
Number Employees: 1-4

2761 **Clinton Vineyards Inc**
450 Schultzville Rd
Clinton Corners, NY 12514-2402
845-266-5372
Fax: 845-266-3395 clintonwine@gmail.com
www.dutchesswinetrail.com
Producer of estate bottled champagnes, white wines & dessert wines.
Owner: Phyllis Feder
info@clintonvineyards.com
Marketing Director: Rita Flood
Public Relations: Debbie Groduindo
General Manager: Chris Stuart
Plant Manager: Bill Wentzel
Estimated Sales: Less Than $500,000
Number Employees: 1-4
Type of Packaging: Consumer
Brands:
Clinton Victory
Duet
Embrace
Nuit
Peach Gal
Romance
Seyval Blanc
Seyval Naturel

2762 **Clio Snacks**
Roselle, NJ 07203
info@cliosnacks.com
www.cliosnacks.com
Chocolate-covered Greek yogurt bars
General Manager: Heather MacNeil Cox
Marketing Director: Rachel Moore
Estimated Sales: $6 Million

2763 **Clipper City Brewing**
4615 Hollins Ferry Rd
Halethorpe, MD 21227
410-247-7822
Fax: 410-247-7829 www.hsbeer.com
Brewer of beer and ale
Owner: Hugh Sisson
Sales Manager: Joe Gold
Contact: J Hugh
hugh@ccbeer.com
Southern Territory Manager: Kevin Fox
Packaging Manager: John Eugeni
Estimated Sales: $2 Million
Number Employees: 20
Type of Packaging: Consumer, Food Service
Brands:
Loose Cannon
Heavy Seas Marzen
Great Pumpkin
Aarsh
Big Dipa
Hang Ten
Holy Sheet
Letter of Marquee 2010
Letter of Marquee 2011
Plank 1
Yule Tide

2764 **(HQ)Clofine Dairy Products Inc**
1407 New Rd
P.O. Box 335
Linwood, NJ 08221
609-653-1000
Fax: 609-653-0127 info@clofinedairy.com
www.clofinedairy.com
Fluid and dried dairy products; proteins, cheeses, milk replacement blends, tofu and soymilk powders, vital wheat gluten, etc.
Chairman: Larry Clofine
lclofine@clofinedairy.com
President & CEO: Frederick Smith
CFO: Butch Harmon
Warehouse Coordinator: Pamela Gerety
Estimated Sales: $20-50 Million
Number Employees: 10-19
Number of Brands: 2
Number of Products: 100
Type of Packaging: Food Service, Private Label, Bulk
Other Locations:
Midwest Officer
Chicago IL
Brands:
Fine-Mix Dairy
Food Blends
Soy Products
Soyfine
Soymilk

2765 **Cloister Honey LLC**
3818 Warrington Dr
Charlotte, NC 28211-3956
704-517-6190
www.cloisterhoney.com
Manufacturer of natural honey.
Owner: Joanne Young
Manager: Randall York
randall@cloisterhoney.com
Number Employees: 1-4

2766 **Clorox Company**
1221 Broadway
Oakland, CA 94612
510-271-7000
corporate.communications@clorox.com
www.thecloroxcompany.com
Dips, dip mixes, bbq sauces, marinades, and dressings; plastic bags and wrap; disinfectants.
Chairman/CEO: Benno Dorer
EVP/General Counsel: Laura Stein
SVP, Corporate Business Development: Bill Bailey
SVP/Chief Innovation Officer: Denise Garner
SVP/Chief Financial Officer: Kevin Jacobsen
SVP/Chief Customer Officer: Troy Dratcher
SVP/Chief People Officer: Kirsten Marriner
SVP/Chief Product Supply Officer: Andy Lowery
EVP, Household & Lifestyle: Eric Reynolds
Year Founded: 1913
Estimated Sales: $6.2 Billion
Number Employees: 8,800

Brands:
Brita
Clorox
Glad Bags
Kitchen Bouquet
Hidden Valley
Masterpiece
Burt's Bees
Chux
Ever Clean
409
Fresh Step
Green Works
Kings Ford
Liquid PlumR
Poett
Renew Life
Scoop Away
S.O.S.
Tilex

2767 **Clos Du Bois Winery**
19410 Geyserville Ave
Geyserville, CA 95441-9603
707-857-3164
Fax: 707-857-1667 800-222-3189
www.closdubois.com
Wine
President: Jon Moramarco
CFO: Kimberly Hernandez
Vice President: Barbara Adair
barbara.adair@cwine.com
VP Operations: Chase Cambron
Estimated Sales: $7 Million
Number Employees: 100-249

2768 **Clos Du Lac Cellars**
3151 Highway 88
3151 Hwy 88
Ione, CA 95640
209-274-2238
Fax: 209-274-4147 cdltr@earthlink.net
www.closdulac.com
Wines
Owner: Tim Evans
cdltr@earthlink.net
CFO: Robert Neumann
Vice President: Peter Evans
Winemaker: Francois Cardesse
Cellar Manager: Kelly Evans
Estimated Sales: $2.5-5 Million
Number Employees: 10-19

2769 **Clos Du Val Co LTD**
5330 Silverado Trl
Napa, CA 94558-9410
707-261-5200
Fax: 707-252-6125 cdv@closduval.com
www.closduval.com
Producer and exporter of wines
President: Steve Tamburelli
COO: Lazaro Cardenas
lazaro.cardenas@dgs.ca.gov
Director of Operations: Jon-Mark Chappellet
Estimated Sales: $5.2 Million
Number Employees: 50-99
Square Footage: 128000
Brands:
Clos Du Val

2770 **Clos Pegase Winery**
1060 Dunaweal Ln
Calistoga, CA 94515-9642
707-942-4981
Fax: 707-942-4993 800-866-8583
www.clospegase.com
Wines
President: Jon Shrem
Controller/Business Manager: Abbe Bailon
VP: Theodore Sanford
Sales Director: Shannon Beglin
Manager: Jeremy Anderson
jeremy_anderson@clospegase.com
Winemaker: Steven Rogstad
Purchsing Manager: Theodore Sanford
Estimated Sales: $5-10 Million
Number Employees: 20-49
Brands:
Hommage Chardonnay
Hommage Cabernet
Mitsuko's Vineyard
Napa Valley
Dunaweal Vineyard
Late Harvest

2771 **Clos Saint-Denis**
1150 chemin des Patriotes
Richelieu, QC J0H 1K0
Canada
450-645-9777
Fax: 450-645-3060
Fine apple ciders
President/Owner: Roland Prud'homme
Estimated Sales: $2.59 Million
Number Employees: 15

2772 **Cloud Nine**
216 W. Second Street
Claremont, CA 91711
909-624-3147
Fax: 909-624-3951 cloudninepaper@hotmail.com
www.cloudninepaper.com
Processor and exporter of hard candy, organic breath mints, caramel popcorn and natural, gourmet, dairy, nondairy, low-fat and organic chocolate bars
President: Josh Taylor
CFO: Lana Nguyen
Marketing Director: Robert Wagg
Sales Director: Sharon Desser
Director Operations: Andrew Spector
Number Employees: 10-19
Square Footage: 8000
Type of Packaging: Consumer, Private Label
Brands:
Cloud Nine
Cloud Nine All-Natural Chocolate Environments
Sorrento Valley Organics
Tropical Source
Tropical Source Dairy-Free Gourmet
Tropical Source Organic

2773 **Cloud Top**
556 S. Fair Oaks Ave
#101-1
Pasadena, CA 91105
Fax: 626-628-3340 888-263-1778
kathy@cloudtopyogurt.com
www.cloudtopyogurt.com
Organic frozen yogurt made from scratch. Cloud Top is available coast to coast, including the Hawaiian Islands, through distributors. If you are a distributor, please email distributorsales@cloudtopyogurt.com for more information.
Founder: Kathy Kim
kathy@cloudtopyogurt.com
Type of Packaging: Bulk

2774 **Cloud's Meat Processing**
2051 S Paradise Ln
Carthage, MO 64836-8452
417-358-5855
Fax: 417-358-7639 www.cloudsmeats.com
Smoked meat; slaughtering services available
Marketing Director: Mike Cloud
mcloud@4state.com
Estimated Sales: $5-10 Million
Number Employees: 20-49

2775 **Cloudstone Vineyards**
27345 Deer Springs Way
Los Altos Hills, CA 94022-4352
650-948-8621
Wines
President: Peter Wolken
CEO: Judith Wolken
Number Employees: 1-4

2776 **Clougherty Packing LLC**
3049 E. Vernon Ave.
Los Angeles, CA 90058
800-846-7635
www.farmerjohn.com
Bacon, breakfast sausage, fresh pork, ham, hot dogs, lunch meat, and smoked sausage.
Year Founded: 1931
Estimated Sales: $156.6 Million
Number Employees: 1,300
Square Footage: 1000000
Parent Co: Smithfield Foods
Type of Packaging: Consumer, Bulk
Brands:
Farmer John
Farmer John Meats

2777 **Clover Blossom Honey**
7597 E State Road 218
La Fontaine, IN 46940
765-981-4443
Fax: 765-981-4086
Honey
President/Co-Owner: David Shenefield
VP/Co-Owner: Don Shenefield
Estimated Sales: $5-10 Million
Number Employees: 5-9
Type of Packaging: Consumer, Food Service, Private Label, Bulk

2778 **Clover Farms Dairy Co Inc**
3300 Pottsville Pike
Reading, PA 19605
610-929-6981
Fax: 610-921-9913 800-323-0123
www.cloverfarms.com
Milk, juice and other dairy products including buttermilk, cottage cheese, half & half, non-dairy creamers, sour cream, heavy cream, and iced tea.
President/CEO: Richard Hartman
Treasurer: John Rothenberger
VP, Sales: Thomas Mullery
VP, Operations: Dennis Dietrich
Estimated Sales: $48.8 Million
Number Employees: 100-249
Number of Brands: 1
Type of Packaging: Private Label
Brands:
Clover Farms

2779 **Clover Hill Vineyards &Winery**
9850 Newtown Rd
Breinigsville, PA 18031-1808
610-395-2468
Fax: 610-366-1246 800-256-8374
www.cloverhillwinery.com
Wines
Owner: Kari Skrip
kari@cloverhillwinery.com
Owner: Pat Skrip
Estimated Sales: $2.5-5 Million
Number Employees: 10-19
Brands:
Clover Hill Rose
Clover Hill Pinot Noir
Clover Hill Cuvee

2780 **Clover Leaf Cheese**
1201 45th Avenue NE
Calgary, AB T2E 2P2
Canada
403-250-3780
Fax: 888-835-0127 888-835-0126
www.cloverleafcheese.ca
Packer and wholesaler/distributor of cheese
President: John Downey
Sales Manager: Chris Cameron
Plant Manager: Brad Lake
Estimated Sales: F
Number Employees: 50-99

2781 **Clover Sonoma**
Petaluma, CA 94954
800-237-3315
cloversonoma.com
Dairy products
President: Ken Gott

2782 **Clover Stornetta Farms Inc**
91 Lakeville St
Petaluma, CA 94952-3163
707-778-8448
800-237-3315
askclo@cloverstornetta.com
www.cloverpetaluma.com
Dairy products including milk and cream, yogurt, cheese, cottage cheese, sour cream, butter, cage free eggs and kefir.
President/CEO: Marcus Benedetti
Chief Sourcing Officer: Mkulima Britt
Director, Plant Operations: Michael Benedetti
Estimated Sales: $34.6 Million
Number Employees: 250-499
Number of Brands: 1
Type of Packaging: Consumer
Brands:
Clover Farms

2783 **(HQ)Cloverdale Foods**
3015 34th St NW
Mandan, ND 58554
800-669-9511
www.cloverdalefoods.com
Manufacturer and wholesaler/distributor of meat products including hickory smoked franks, bacon, ham and sausages, along with other quality pork products.
President & CEO: Scott Russell
Estimated Sales: $49 Million
Number Employees: 250-499
Number of Brands: 2
Square Footage: 61000
Type of Packaging: Consumer, Food Service, Private Label, Bulk
Other Locations:
Cloverdale Foods Plant
Minot ND
Brands:
Cloverdale
Teardrop

2784 **Cloverhill Bakery-Vend Corporation**
2035 N Narragansett Ave
Chicago, IL 60639-3842
773-745-9800
Fax: 773-745-1647 www.cloverhill.com
Processor and exporter of sweet goods, doughnuts, cakes, muffins, danishes and cinnamon rolls.
President: William Gee
Executive VP: Edward Gee
Quality Control: Dan Gee
VP Sales: Robert Gee
Production Manager: Joe Perez
Year Founded: 1961
Estimated Sales: $20-50 Million
Number Employees: 100-249
Square Footage: 140000
Parent Co: Hostess
Type of Packaging: Consumer, Food Service
Brands:
Clover Hill

2785 **Cloverland Dairy**
PO Box 329
Saint Clairsville, OH 43950-0329
740-699-0509
www.cloverlanddairy.com
Portion controlled butter and buttermilk
President: Robert Hyest
Estimated Sales: $.5-1 million
Number Employees: 300
Type of Packaging: Consumer, Private Label, Bulk

2786 **Cloverland/Green Spring Dairy**
2701 Loch Raven Rd
Baltimore, MD 21218
410-235-4477
Fax: 410-889-3690 800-876-6455
www.cloverlanddairy.com
Fluid milk and dairy products
President: Michael Marcus
Controller: Greg Stech
SVP Research, Development & Engineering: Edward Kennedy
Contact: Kory Carroll
kcarroll@cloverlanddairy.com
Operations Executive: Robert Glessner
Distribution Supervisor: Norman Maxwell
Estimated Sales: $1.3 Million
Brands:
Cloverland

2787 **Clovervale Farms**
1833 Cooper Foster Park Rd
Amherst, OH 44001
440-960-0146
Fax: 440-960-2358 800-433-0146
Individual portioned servings of entrees, vegetables, sandwiches, fruits, cobblers, butter and jelly bars, frozen yogurts, sherberts, italian ices, frozen juice pops and milk
President: Richard Cawrse Jr
CEO: Don Russel
Marketing/Sales Manager: Ray Kautzman
VP Sales: Anne Williams
Purchasing Manager: Angela Viglas
Estimated Sales: $20-50 Million
Number Employees: 100
Brands:
Chef's Pastry
Cloverdale

2788 **Clown Global Brands**
3184 Doolittle Dr
Northbrook, IL 60062-2409
847-498-4696
Fax: 847-564-9076 800-323-5778
info@clown-gysin.com
www.clownglobalbrands.com
Producer and importer of marshmallows, snack foods, breadsticks, toasted onion bits, sesame dots, confectionery, and caramel apple dip items; importer of toasted onion bits and breadsticks
President: Herb Horn
Contact: Martin Haver
mhaver@clownglobalbrands.com
Estimated Sales: $7-10 Million
Number Employees: 5-9
Number of Brands: 2
Square Footage: 8000
Parent Co: Food Network
Type of Packaging: Food Service

2789 **Club Chef LLC**
3776 Lake Park Dr # 1
Covington, KY 41017-8171
859-578-3100
Fax: 859-578-3374 info@clubchef.com
www.clubchef.com
Wet and dry chopped salad items including lettuce, onions and cabbage
Vice President: Jeff Klare
jtklare@clubchef.com
Estimated Sales: $1-2.5 Million
Number Employees: 100-249
Square Footage: 360000
Parent Co: Castellini Company
Type of Packaging: Consumer, Food Service, Private Label, Bulk
Brands:
Club Chef
Farm Fresh
Readypac

2790 **Clutter Farms**
7283 Millersburg Rd
Gambier, OH 43022-9775
740-427-3515
www.bulkwholesalepopcorn.com
Popcorn including microwaveable
President: Gordon Clutter
V.P.: Larry Clutter
Number Employees: 5-9
Square Footage: 14000
Type of Packaging: Consumer
Brands:
Clutters Indian Fields

2791 **Clyde's Delicious Donuts**
1120 W Fullerton Ave
Addison, IL 60101-4304
630-628-6555
Fax: 630-628-6838 info@clydesdonuts.com
www.clydesdonuts.com
Baked goods including bagels, danishes, coffee cakes, sweet rolls, frozen and fresh yeast and cake doughnuts, and apple, blueberry, maple, and cherry fritters.
President: Kent Bickford
CEO: Kim Bickford
SVP, Sales & Marketing: David Bennett
VP, Business Development: John Cheesman
Marketing Director: Sue Nieves
Purchasing Manager: Dave Kells
Estimated Sales: $16-20 Million
Number Employees: 100-249
Number of Brands: 1
Number of Products: 125
Square Footage: 56000
Type of Packaging: Consumer, Food Service, Private Label, Bulk
Brands:
Clyde's

2792 **Clyde's Italian & German Sausage**
3655 Inca St
Denver, CO 80211-3030
303-433-8744
Italian and German sausage
President: Michael Tricarco
Estimated Sales: $10 Milion
Number Employees: 1-4
Type of Packaging: Consumer

2793 **Coach Farm Enterprises**
105 Mill Hill Rd
Pine Plains, NY 12567
518-398-5325
Fax: 518-398-5329 800-999-4628
info@coachfarm.com www.coachfarm.com
Goat's milk products including soft cheese and yogurt
President: Miles Cahn
m.cahn@coachfarm.com
Marketing: Steve Margarites
General Manager: Phil Peeples
Plant Manager: Rosie Parsons
Estimated Sales: $10-20 Million
Number Employees: 20-49
Type of Packaging: Private Label
Brands:
Coach Farm
Yo-Goat

2794 **Coach Sposato's Bar-B-Que**
P.O. Box 957
Lincoln, AR 72744
479-824-3300
Fax: 870-910-0619 800-264-7535
coachbbq@pgtc.com
Barbecue sauce
Chairman: Beth Couch
General Manager: Sharon Spurlock
Estimated Sales: $.5-1 million
Number Employees: 20-49
Square Footage: 24800
Brands:
Couch's Original

2795 **Coach's Oats**
22735 LA Palma Ave
Yorba Linda, CA 92887-4772
714-692-6885
Fax: 714-692-6887 coachsoats@coachsoats.com
www.coachsoats.com
Oats
Owner: Lynn Rogers
coachsoats@coachsoats.com
Estimated Sales: $1-3 Million
Number Employees: 5-9

2796 **Coast Packing Co**
3275 E Vernon Avenue
Vernon, CA 90058
323-277-7700
www.coastpacking.com
Quality shortening products for the restaurant, baking, and food industries. A supplier of animal fat and vegetable oil shortenings.
President: Ronald Gustafson
ronald.gustafson@coastpacking.com
CEO: Eric Gustafson
HR Manager: Washington Paredes
Director of Operations: Chavis Ferguson
Number Employees: 50-99
Type of Packaging: Consumer, Food Service
Brands:
Bake Lite All Soy
Bake Lite Soy/Cotton
Coast Refined Lard
Flavor King Blue
Flavor King Red
Gold Coast
Golden Bake
Supreme
Viva Lard
VIVA Manteca Mixta
Viva Retail Lard

2797 **Coast Seafoods Company**
14711 NE 29th Pl Ste 111
Bellevue, WA 98007
425-702-8800
Fax: 425-702-0400 800-423-2303
info@coastseafoods.com www.coastseafoods.com
Processor and exporter of fresh oysters and clams
President: John Petrie
CFO: Kay Christopher
Contact: Sharon Adams
sharon@cni.org
Manager: Jim Donaldson
Estimated Sales: $2.5-5 Million
Number Employees: 1-4
Parent Co: Coast Seafoods Company

Type of Packaging: Consumer, Food Service

2798 Coastal Classics
380 Church St
Duxbury, MA 02332
508-746-6058
Fax: 508-746-6063
Cranberry chutney, cranberry mustard, cranberry preserves, cranberry hot sauce, cranberry orange marmalade, cranberry blueberry grilling sauce, peanut sauce
President: Jan Baird
Brands:
Bogland
Bogland By the Sea
Coastal Gourmet

2799 Coastal Cocktails
18242 McDurmott Street
Irvine, CA 92614
949-250-8951
Fax: 949-250-9787 bbartels@coastalcocktails.com
Cocktail mixers
Contact: Jeff Dun
dun@coastpacificbuilders.com
Brands:
Ultimate Bartender
Martini Party

2800 Coastal Goods
44 Old Jail Ln
Barnstable, MA 02630-1418
508-375-1050
Fax: 508-375-1052
customerservice@coastalgoods.com
www.coastalgoods.com
Salt, peppers, rubs and spices.
Co-Founder: Nigel Dyche
Co-Founder: Sarah Chase
Number Employees: 1-4

2801 Coastal Promotions, Inc.
128 Indian Bayou Dr
Destin, FL 32541
850-460-2328
info@tasteoffl.com
www.tasteoffl.com
Cocktail mixers
Founder & CEO: Doug McWhorter
General Manager: Brian Todd
Number of Brands: 3
Number of Products: 21
Type of Packaging: Consumer, Food Service, Private Label, Bulk
Brands:
Taste of Florida
Wild Olive

2802 Coastal Seafood Partners
2939 West Grand Avenue
Chicago, IL 60622
773-235-4000
Fax: 773-989-7799
Seafood
President: Chris Costello
Estimated Sales: $1-3 Million
Number Employees: 20-49

2803 Coastal Seafood Processors
134 Brookhollow Esplanade
Harahan, LA 70123
504-734-9444
Fax: 504-736-9447
Seafood
President: Brian Quartano

2804 Coastal Seafoods
39 Acre Ln
Ridgefield, CT 06877-5501
203-431-0453
Fax: 203-438-7099
Seafood
President: Robert Iseley
CFO/Secretary: Linda Iseley
Operations: Manuel Reyes
Estimated Sales: $2.5-5 Million
Number Employees: 10-19
Square Footage: 5000
Type of Packaging: Food Service, Private Label

2805 Coastlog Industries
46755 Magellan Drive
Novi, MI 48375-3000
248-344-9556
Fax: 248-344-9559
Aseptic shelf stable juice and milk products
President: R K Sridharan
VP Sales: Andy Larkin
Type of Packaging: Food Service
Brands:
Coastlog

2806 Coastside Lobster Company
PO Box 151
Stonington, ME 04681-0151
207-367-2297
Fax: 207-367-5929
Lobster
President: Peter Collin
Purchsing Director: Karen Rains
Number Employees: 5-9

2807 Cobb Hill Cheese
5 Linden Rd
Hartland, VT 05048-8104
802-436-1612
802-436-4360
info@cobbhillcheese.com
www.cobbhillcheese.com
Cheese
President: Gail Holmes
Contact: Jeannine Kilbride
cobbhillcheese@gmail.com
Estimated Sales: Less Than $500,000
Number Employees: 1-4

2808 Cobraz Brazilian Coffee
450 Park Ave
New York, NY 10022-2644
212-759-7700
Fax: 212-725-1170
Coffee
Managing Director: Francisco Barreto
Estimated Sales: $500,000-$1,000,000
Number Employees: 5-9

2809 Cobscook Bay Seafood
PO Box 252
Perry, ME 04667-0252
207-853-2890
Fax: 208-459-3712
Seafood
President: Joyce Pottle

2810 (HQ)Coby's Cookies
17 Vickers Rd
Toronto, ON M9B 1C1
Canada
416-633-1567
Fax: 416-633-9812
Processor and exporter of frozen cookie dough, muffin and brownie batter; also, retail pack rice crispy squares and brownies
President: Michael Topolinkski
Executive VP: Jay Punwasee
Estimated Sales: $9.3 Million
Number Employees: 150
Square Footage: 60000
Type of Packaging: Consumer, Food Service, Private Label
Other Locations:
Coby's Cookies
Downsview ON
Brands:
Coby's Cookies, Inc.
Just Great Bakers, Inc.

2811 Coca-Cola Beverages Northeast
1 Executive Park Drive
Suite 330
Bedford, NH 03110
603-627-7871
844-619-3388
www.cokenortheast.com
Sparkling soft drinks, still beverages, and emerging brands such as vitamin water
President: Mark Francoeur
VP, Sales Center Operations: Steve Perrelli
VP, Sales & Marketing: Andrew Marchesseault
VP, Operations: David Dumont
Year Founded: 1977
Number Employees: 3,500
Parent Co: Kirin Brewery Company, Ltd.
Type of Packaging: Consumer, Food Service, Bulk
Brands:
Barq's
Canada Dry
Coca-Cola
Core Power
Dasani
Dr Pepper
Dunkin Donuts
Fanta
Fresca
Fuze
Gold Peak
Honest Tea
Hubert's Lemonade
McCaf,
Mello Yello
Minute Maid
Monster Energy
NOS
Peace Tea
Powerade
Reign
Smartwater
Sprite
Vitamin Water
Yup!
Zico

2812 Coca-Cola Bottling Co. Consolidated
PO Box 31487
Charlotte, NC 28231
800-866-2653
www.cokeconsolidated.com
Bottled soft drinks and fountain syrup.
Chairman/CEO: J Frank Harrison, III
Year Founded: 1902
Estimated Sales: $4.3 Billion
Number Employees: 15,500
Number of Brands: 300
Type of Packaging: Consumer, Food Service, Bulk

2813 Coca-Cola Bottling Company UNITED, Inc.
46090 East Lake Boulevard
Dirmingham, AB 35217
205-841-2653
800-844-2653
cocacolaunited.com
Bottled soft drinks and fountain syrup.
Chairman: Claude Nielsen
President & CEO: John Sherman, III
Executive VP/CAO/CFO: Hafiz Chandiwala
General Counsel/VP: Lucas Gambino
VP, Supply Chain & Operations: Stanley Ellington
VP/Controller/CIO: Eric Steadman
Year Founded: 1902
Estimated Sales: $2.81 Billion
Number Employees: 10,000
Type of Packaging: Consumer, Food Service, Bulk

2814 Coca-Cola Co.
PO Box 1734
Atlanta, GA 30301
404-676-2121
800-438-2653
consumer.relations@coca-cola.com
www.coca-colacompany.com
Non-alcoholic beverage concentrates and syrups.
Chairman/CEO: James Quincey
jaquincey@coca-cola.com
President/COO: Brian Smith
Executive VP/CFO: John Murphy
Senior VP/Chief Innovation Officer: Robert Long
Senior VP/Chief Communications Officer: Beatriz Perez
Year Founded: 1892
Estimated Sales: $31.8 Billion
Number Employees: 62,600
Number of Brands: 500
Number of Products: 4300
Type of Packaging: Consumer, Food Service
Other Locations:
Bottling Facility
Honolulu HI
Bottling Facility
Kapolei HI
Bottling Facility
Charlotte NC
Bottling Facility
Lenexa KS
Bottling Facility
El Paso TX
Bottling Facility
West Memphis AZ
Bottling Facility
Columbus OH
Brands:
Coca-Cola
Coca-Cola Zero
DASANI

Diet Coke
Fanta
glac,au vitaminwater
Minute Maid
Odwalla
POWERADE
Sprite
Simply Orange
Sprite
Del Valle
Ciel
Fa!rlife
Georgia
Gold Peak Tea
Honest
Mello Yello
Surge
Costa Coffee
Zico
glac,au smart water

2815 Coca-Cola European Partners
Pemberton House
Bakers Road
Uxbridge, Middx, UB8 1EZ
UK
800-418-4223
comms@ccep.com www.cocacolaep.com
Coca-Cola brands products.
Chairman: Sol Daurella
CEO: Damian Gammell
CFO: Nik Jhangiani
Chief Public Affairs Officer: Lauren Sayeski
Estimated Sales: $10.9 Billion
Number Employees: 23,300
Number of Brands: 44
Type of Packaging: Consumer, Food Service, Bulk
Brands:
5-Alive
Abbey Well
Apollinaris
Appletiser
aquaBona
Aquarius
Bonaqua
Burn
Capri-Sun
Chaqwa
Chaidfontaine
Coca-Cola
Coca-Cola Light/Diet
Coca-Cola Zero
Dr. Pepper
Fanta Still
Fanta Zero
Fanta
Fernandes
Finley
Fruit & Nadia
Fruitopia
Glaceau vitamin water
Glaceau smart water
Kia Ora
Kinley
Krystal
Kuli
Lift
Lilt
MER
Mezzo Mix
Minute Maid
Monster Energy
Nalu
Nestea
Nordic
Oasis
Ocean Spray
Powerade
Relentless Energy Drink
Rosport Blue
Schuss
Schwepps
Seagram's
Sprite
TAB X-tra
Toscal
Urge
Vilas del Turbon
ViO
ViO BiO LiMO
Viva

2816 Cocina De Mino
6022 S Western Ave
Oklahoma City, OK 73139-1602
405-632-1036
Fax: 405-632-1394 www.cocinademino.com
Ethnic foods
Owner: Tim Wagner
Marketing Manager: Emeleo Perez
Estimated Sales: $1-3 Million
Number Employees: 10-19
Brands:
Cocina De Mino

2817 Cocktail Crate
23-23 Borden Ave.
Long Island City, NY 11101
718-316-2033
info@cocktailcrate.com
www.cocktailcrate.com
Manufacturer of cocktail mixes.
Founder: Alex Boyd
alex@cocktailcrate.com

2818 Cocktail Kits 2 Go LLC
205 W 95th St
Apt 5A
New York, NY 10025-6324
917-750-3998
cocktailkits2go.com
Premade cocktail mixes
Owner: Justin Durling
Type of Packaging: Private Label

2819 Coco International
6 Highpoint Dr
Suite 1
Wayne, NJ 07470-7423
973-694-1200
Fax: 973-694-1242 info@cocofoods.com
www.cocofoods.com
Manufacturer of energy bars and other snacks.
Contact: Michael Kim
ykim@cocofoods.com
Number Employees: 5-9

2820 Coco Lopez Inc
3401 SW 160th Ave # 350
Miramar, FL 33027-6306
954-450-3111
Fax: 954-450-3111 800-341-2242
customerservice@cocolopez.com
www.cocolopez.com
Canned fruits and vegetables, preserves, jams and jellie. Also manufacturer of cream of coconut, coconut milk, and coconut juice.
President: Leonardo Vargas
VP: Gisela Sanchez
Manager: Nicole Bennett
nbennett@kaplanuniversity.edu
Estimated Sales: $1,888,884
Number Employees: 10-19
Brands:
Coco Lopez

2821 Coco Polo
320 Cleveland Ave
Highland Park, NJ 08904-1845
732-249-4847
Fax: 732-545-4494 800-433-2462
so@cocopolo.com www.cocopolo.com
Stevia-sweetened, milk chocolate bars.
President: Diane Yamate

2822 Cocoa Metro
929 W Sunset Blvd
Suite 21
St. George, UT 84770-4867
888-676-1527
www.cocoametro.com
Chocolate milk and drinking chocolate
CEO: Mike Dunford
Number of Brands: 1
Number of Products: 6
Type of Packaging: Consumer
Brands:
COCOA METRO

2823 Cocoa Parlor
31161 Niguel Rd
Suite A
Laguna Niguel, CA 92672
949-877-9549
info@tonicscene.com
cocoaparlor.com
Organic chocolate bars
CEO: Richard Pascall
Type of Packaging: Consumer, Private Label

2824 CocoaPlanet Inc.
1198 Ingram Dr
Sonoma, CA 95476-7680
650-454-0757
Fax: 707-721-1338 info@cocoaplanet.com
cocoaplanet.com
Dark chocolate; hot chocolate powders; and chocolate products.
Founder & CEO: Anne McKibben
anne@cocoaplanet.com
Year Founded: 2012
Estimated Sales: Less than $500,000
Number Employees: 5
Type of Packaging: Consumer, Food Service

2825 Cocolalla Winery
463254 Highway 95 N
Cocolalla, ID 83813
208-263-3774
Fax: 208-263-7605
Wines
President/Owner: Mike Wagoner
VP: Vivian Merkeley
Estimated Sales: $1-4.9,000,000
Number Employees: 1-4
Brands:
Cocolalla

2826 Cocomels by JJ's Sweets
PO Box 3312
Boulder, CO 80307
303-800-6492
www.cocomels.com
Coconut milk caramels
Founder and Owner: JJ Rademaekers
Vice President of Sales: Rasa Kumar
Square Footage: 80000
Brands:
Cocomels

2827 Cocomira Confections
321 Evans Avenue
Toronto, ON M8Z 1K2
Canada
416-253-4867
Fax: 416-946-1749 866-413-9049
info@cocomira.com www.cocomira.com
Chocolates, hazelnut crunch, dark chocolate crunch, espresso crunch and maple crunch.
President/Owner: Anna Janes
Director of Sales: Betty Baran

2828 Coconut Beach
PO Box 1949
Bonita, CA 91908-1949
info@coconutbeach.com
www.coconutbeach.com
Coconut oil, water and chips
Number of Brands: 1
Number of Products: 11
Type of Packaging: Consumer
Brands:
COCONUT BEACH

2829 Coconut Bliss
PO Box 288
Eugene, OR 97440
541-345-0020
844-305-5441
coconutbliss.com
Dairy-free frozen desserts
Co-Founder: Larry Kaplowitz
Number of Brands: 1
Number of Products: 21
Type of Packaging: Consumer
Brands:
COCONUT BLISS

2830 Coconut Collaborative
coconutcollaborative.com
Coconut milk-based yogurt
Number of Brands: 1
Number of Products: 3
Type of Packaging: Consumer
Brands:
THE COCONUT COLLABORATIVE

2831 **Codinos Food Inc**
704 Corporation Park # 5
Suite 5
Scotia, NY 12302-1091
518-372-3308
Fax: 518-372-2787 800-246-8908
info@codinos.com www.codinos.com
Frozen pasta including lasagna, manicotti, stuffed shells and rigatoni, ravioli, gnocchi and cavatelli
Owner: Leno Codino
scott@codinos.com
Marketing Director: Scott DeVantier
Sales Exec: Scott Devantier
Estimated Sales: $5-10 Million
Number Employees: 20-49
Type of Packaging: Consumer, Food Service, Private Label, Bulk
Brands:
Poppy's Pierogies

2832 **Coffee Associates**
178 Old River Rd
Edgewater, NJ 07020
201-945-1060
Fax: 201-945-4887 info@coffeeassociates.com
www.coffeeassociates.com
Coffee
Parent Co: Coffee Associates

2833 **Coffee Barrel**
2237 Aurelius Rd # 1
Holt, MI 48842-6323
517-694-9000
Fax: 517-694-9001 coffeebarrel@gmail.com
www.thecoffeebarrel.com
Coffee
President: William DeGrow
Manager: Mary Vegrow
CEO: Tim Brenner
Estimated Sales: Less Than $500,000
Number Employees: 5-9
Type of Packaging: Private Label
Brands:
Bis Train
David Rio
Ghiradelli Syrup
Guidparg Chocolates
Stirling Syrup

2834 **Coffee Bean**
1630 W Evans Ave
Englewood, CO 80110-1098
303-922-1238
Fax: 303-937-6336
Coffee
Owner: Carlo Rondn
Estimated Sales: Under $500,000
Number Employees: 1-4
Brands:
Country Spice Tea
Panache Cocoa and Blender Mix
Panache Gourmet Coffee
Xanadu Exotic Tea

2835 **(HQ)Coffee Bean & Tea Leaf**
2000 NE Court
Bloomington, MN 55425-5506
952-853-1148
Fax: 952-853-0590 www.coffeebean.com
Coffee and tea
Owner: Jim Cone
coffeeandtealtd@aol.com
Vice President: Jim Cone
Estimated Sales: Less Than $500,000
Number Employees: 5-9
Type of Packaging: Private Label

2836 **Coffee Bean Intl**
9120 NE Alderwood Rd
Portland, OR 97220-1366
503-227-4490
Fax: 503-225-9604 800-877-0474
info@coffeebeanintl.com www.coffeebeanintl.com
Roaated coffee, tea, cocoa, syrups, and confectionary products; manufacturer of coffee equipment, importer of coffee beans and teas.
President & CEO: Patrick Criteser
pcriteser@coffeebeanintl.com
VP Product Development & Training: Bruce Mullins
Creative Director: Audrey Crespo
Vice President of Marketing: Joe Prewett
Vice President of Sales: Rich Sermone
Manager of Internet Marketing: Vickie Grimes
Operations Executive: Les McDonald
Roastmaster: Paul Thornton
Purchasing Manager: Mark Peldyak
Estimated Sales: $29.3 Million
Number Employees: 100-249
Square Footage: 500000
Parent Co: Farmer Brothers Company
Type of Packaging: Consumer, Food Service, Private Label, Bulk

2837 **Coffee Bean of Leesburg**
110 S King St # A
Leesburg, VA 20175-3009
703-777-9556
Fax: 703-777-4515 800-232-6872
www.beanusa.com
Coffee
Manager: Juanita Frye
Estimated Sales: $250,000
Number Employees: 5-9

2838 **Coffee Beanery LTD**
3429 Pierson Pl
Flushing, MI 48433-2498
810-733-1020
Fax: 810-733-1536 800-441-2255
info@beanerysupport.com
www.coffeebeanery.com
Began in 1976. Manufacturer of coffees, teas, syrups, dessert drink mixes and coffee accessories such as mugs, coffee grinders and canisters.
President/CEO: JoAnne Shaw
Chairman: Julius Shaw
COO: Laurie Shaw
VP, Development: Kevin Shaw
VP, Franchise Sales: Kurt Shaw
Marketing Manager: Patti Tushim
Operations Manager: Bob Ashley
Estimated Sales: $20 Million
Number Employees: 100-249
Number of Brands: 1
Square Footage: 45000
Type of Packaging: Private Label
Brands:
Coffee Beanery Franchise

2839 **Coffee Brothers Inc**
1204 Via Roma
Colton, CA 92324-3909
909-370-1100
Fax: 909-370-1101 888-443-5282
info@coffeebrothers.com www.coffeebrothers.com
Coffee and espresso; importer and wholesaler/distributor of espresso machines
Owner: Cal Amodemo
cal@coffeebrothers.com
General Manager: Max Amodeo
Estimated Sales: $2.5-5 Million
Number Employees: 1-4
Square Footage: 44000
Type of Packaging: Private Label, Bulk
Brands:
Coffee Brothers
Il Caffe
Sigma

2840 **Coffee Butler Service**
3660 Wheeler Avenue
Alexandria, VA 22304-6403
703-823-0028
Fax: 703-823-6943
Coffee
President: H Steve Swink, Ph.D.
COO: Mike Kelsey

2841 **Coffee Culture-A House**
1311 O Street
Lincoln, NE 68508-1512
402-438-8456
Fax: 402-474-3535
Coffee
General Manager: Terrance Alan Reis
Operations Manager: Gregory Looney
Estimated Sales: Less than $500,000
Number Employees: 1-4

2842 **Coffee Enterprises**
32 Lakeside Ave
Burlington, VT 05401-5242
802-865-4480
Fax: 802-865-3364 800-375-3398
www.coffeeenterprises.com
Coffee extracts and chilled coffee-based beverage concentrates; laboratory specializing in the testing and analyzing services for coffee; consultant specializing in the marketing and promotion of coffee
Owner/President: Daniel C Cox
dancox@coffee-ent.com
Administrative Assistant: Christine Hibma
Office Manager: Judy Mammorella
Estimated Sales: $1-3 Million
Number Employees: 10-19
Square Footage: 14000
Type of Packaging: Bulk

2843 **Coffee Exchange**
207 Wickenden St Uppr
Providence, RI 02903-4348
401-273-1198
Fax: 401-273-4440 877-263-3334
info@thecoffeeexchange.com
www.thecoffeeexchange.com
Processor and importer of regular and decaffeinated whole bean organic coffee; gift baskets available
Owner: Charles Fishbein
charlie@mailordercoffee.com
CEO: Susan Wood
Cafe Manager: Tania Montenegro
Estimated Sales: $1-2.5 Million
Number Employees: 20-49
Brands:
Coffee Exchange
Mel's

2844 **Coffee Express RoastingCo**
47722 Clipper St
Plymouth, MI 48170-2437
734-459-4900
Fax: 734-459-5511 800-466-9000
info@coffeeexpressco.com
www.coffeeexpressco.com
Wholesaler roaster of specialty coffees; distributors of associated products.
President: Tom Isaia
Office Manager: Joyce Novak
Contact: Genevieve Boss
g.boss@coffeeexpressco.com
Production: Scott Novak
Estimated Sales: Less Than $500,000
Number Employees: 1-4
Number of Brands: 8
Number of Products: 20
Square Footage: 32000
Type of Packaging: Consumer, Food Service, Private Label, Bulk
Brands:
Coffee Express
Mountain Country

2845 **Coffee Globe LLC**
1118 Pacific Coast Hwy
Suite A-441
Huntington Beach, CA 92648
587-966-1171
Ground, instant, and whole bean coffee
Founder & CEO: Alexandra Mogilevskaya
alex@Coffeeglobe.co
Sales Director: Svetlana Fedoseeva
Number Employees: 11-19
Type of Packaging: Private Label
Brands:
Evo Coffee

2846 **Coffee Grounds**
1579 Hamline Ave N
Falcon Heights, MN 55108-2107
651-644-9959
Fax: 651-776-1143
undergroundcafecommander@gmail.com
www.thecoffeegrounds.net
Coffee flavorings
Owner: David Lawrence
Estimated Sales: $420,000
Number Employees: 5-9

2847 **Coffee Holding Co Inc**
3475 Victory Blvd
Staten Island, NY 10314
718-832-0800
Fax: 718-832-0892 800-458-2233
info@coffeeholding.com www.coffeeholding.com
Roaster, vemdor and packer of regular and green coffee; also, packer of instant coffees.
Founder: Sterling Gordon
President & CEO: Andrew Gordon
EVP & COO: David Gordon
EVP of Sales: Erik Hansen
Year Founded: 1971
Estimated Sales: $25 Million
Number Employees: 50-99
Number of Brands: 3
Square Footage: 22000
Type of Packaging: Consumer, Food Service, Private Label, Bulk
Other Locations:
Harmoney Bay Coffee
Andover MA
Organic Products Trading Co.
Vancouver WA
Sonofresco
Burlington WA
Brands:
5th Avenue
Cafe Caribe
Cafe Supremo
Don Manuel 100% Colombian
S&W
Via Roma

2848 **Coffee Masters**
P.O.Box 460
Spring Grove, IL 60081
815-675-0088
Fax: 815-675-3166 800-334-6485
cmaster@coffeemasters.com
www.coffeemasters.com
Gourmet coffee, tea and cocoa
President: Mike Ebert
Marketing Director: Betsy Summers
Sales Director: Alan Denek
Operations Manager: Tony Nowak
Number Employees: 50-99
Square Footage: 186000
Type of Packaging: Consumer, Food Service, Private Label, Bulk
Brands:
Ashby's Iced Teas
Ashby's Teas of London
Bella Crema
Brew-A-Cup: Perfect Potfuls
Cocoa Amore
Coffee Masters

2849 **Coffee Mill Roastery**
108 Branchwood Drive
Elon, NC 27244-9384
919-929-1727
Fax: 919-929-5899 800-729-1727
Coffee and tea
Owner: Jan Lawrence
Estimated Sales: $1-2,500,000
Number Employees: 10-19
Type of Packaging: Private Label

2850 **Coffee Mill Roasting Company**
598 Falconbridge Road
Sudbury, ON P3A 5K6
Canada
705-525-2700
Fax: 705-525-2790
Processor and packer of coffee
President: Geoff Hong
Number Employees: 1-4
Type of Packaging: Food Service
Brands:
The Coffee Mill

2851 **Coffee Millers & Roasters**
2924 Del Prado Boulevard S
Suite 5
Cape Coral, FL 33904-7224
941-542-1215
Coffee
President: Edward Miller
Estimated Sales: Less than $500,000
Number Employees: 1-4
Parent Co: Spices of Life Gourmet Coffee

2852 **Coffee Millers & Roasting**
926 SE 9th Ln # B
Cape Coral, FL 33990-3121
239-573-6800
Fax: 239-573-3693
Domestic and European coffees and blends. Over 150 varieties
President: Marcell Miller
Estimated Sales: $1-2.5 Million
Number Employees: 1-4

2853 **Coffee People**
4130 SW 117th Ave Ste P
Beaverton, OR 97005
503-643-3053
Fax: 503-672-9013 800-354-5282
customerservice@coffeepeople.com
Specialty coffees and teas
Customer Service: Patti Graves
Estimated Sales: $.5-1 million
Parent Co: Diedrich Coffee

2854 **Coffee Process**
6005 N Shepherd Dr # G1
Houston, TX 77091-4253
713-695-8483
Fax: 713-695-7530
Coffee
Owner: Carlos DE Aldecoa
CFO: Larissa De Aldeco
Vice President: Maria Carmen De Aldecoa
Estimated Sales: $1-2.5 Million
Number Employees: 10-19
Type of Packaging: Private Label
Brands:
Uvvw Decaff

2855 **Coffee Reserve**
2030 W Quail Ave
Phoenix, AZ 85027-2610
623-201-1400
Fax: 623-434-0946 888-755-6789
www.crescendobev.com
Coffee roasting
President & Chief Executive Officer: Rick C. Grayson, Jr.
Account Executive: Debbie Teichmann
VP of Operations & Green Coffee Buyer: John Gozbekian
Director of Business Development: Ted Pearson
Manager: Mick Sampson
mick@coffeereserve.com
COO: John Nugent
Production Manager: Jeff Jackson
Estimated Sales: $5-10 Million
Number Employees: 20-49
Type of Packaging: Bulk

2856 **Coffee Roasters Inc**
29 Edison Ave # 2a
Oakland, NJ 07436-1311
201-337-8221
Fax: 201-337-0622 800-285-2445
info@coffeeroastersinc.com
www.coffeeroastersinc.com
Coffees
President: Lance Wetzel
Founder, Chief Executive Officer: Gerald Comiskey
Vice President: Leonard Grasser
Estimated Sales: $1,300,000
Number Employees: 5-9

2857 **Coffee Roasters Of New Orleans**
1001 Industry Rd # A
Kenner, LA 70062-6880
504-712-4966
Fax: 504-827-0818 800-737-5464
www.orleanscoffee.com
Coffees including flavored, regular and decaffeinated; also, grinders, coffee makers and tea
Owner: William Siemers
wholesale@coffeeroastersofneworleans.com
Co Owner: Bob Arceneaux
Owner: Kathleen Siemers
Estimated Sales: Less than $500,000
Number Employees: 20-49
Square Footage: 12000
Type of Packaging: Consumer, Private Label, Bulk

2858 **Coffee Roasters of New Orleans**
712 Orleans Avenue
New Orleans, LA 70116-3111
504-827-0878
Fax: 800-743-5711 800-737-5464
www.orleanscoffee.com
Coffee
Owner: Bob Arceneaux
Director Sales/Marketing: Kathleen Siemers
General Manager: William Siemers
Production Supervisor: Robert Arceneaux
Estimated Sales: $5-9.9 Million
Number Employees: 5-9

2859 **Coffee Up**
2201 S Halsted Street
Chicago, IL 60608-4585
847-288-9330
Fax: 847-288-9334
Coffee
President: Chris Chacko
Estimated Sales: Under $500,000
Number Employees: 1-4

2860 **Coffee Works**
3418 Folsom Blvd
Sacramento, CA 95816-5312
916-452-1086
Fax: 916-452-9134 800-275-3335
info@coffeeworks.com www.coffeeworks.com
Coffee
President: John Shahabian
General Manager: Edwin Alagozian
alagozian@coffeeworks.com
Director: Alexandria Shahabian
Estimated Sales: Less Than $500,000
Number Employees: 5-9
Brands:
Balthazar's Blend
Dark Star
Jump Start
Sweetfire

2861 **Cognis**
4900 Este Ave
Cincinnati, OH 45232
973-245-6000
Fax: 513-482-5503 800-526-1072
Suppliers of bulk nutritional raw materials for the food industry
CEO: Antonio Trius
CFO: Klaus Edelmann
Executive Vice President, President of B: Beate Ehle
Managing Director: Paul Allen
Estimated Sales: $1-2.5 Million
Number Employees: 500-999

2862 **Cohen's Bakery**
89 Center Street
Ellenville, NY 12428
845-647-2200
cohens1920@gmail.com
www.cohensbakery.cafe
Fresh bread, rolls and pastries, cookies, danishes, and muffins; also, frozen raw bread, pizza and roll dough
Owner: Bill Tochterman
info@cohensbakery.com
Number Employees: 1-4
Square Footage: 100000
Brands:
Al Cohen's

2863 **Cohen's Original Tasty Coddie**
6639 Chippewa Dr
Baltimore, MD 21209-1542
410-539-0111
Snack foods including potato chips.
President: Esther Cohen
Estimated Sales: Under $500,000
Number Employees: 1-4

2864 **Colavita USA**
1 Runyons Ln
Edison, NJ 08817-2219
732-404-8300
Fax: 732-287-9401 888-265-2848
usa@colavita.com www.colavita.com
Grains and oils including; extra virgin olive oil, vinegar, pasta, sauces, gnocchi, polenta, rice, marinated vegetables, and gift baskets and foodservice bulk supply

President: Sophia Aspromatis
sophiaa@colavita.com
CEO: Giovanni Colavita
VP Quality Control: Anthony Profaci
VP of Sales: Tom Marrone
VP Sales & Marketing: John Profaci
Director of Marketing: Nicole Jeannette
Plant Manager: Les Horowitz
VP Purchasing: Robert Profaci
Estimated Sales: $15 Million
Number Employees: 50-99
Brands:
Colavita 25-Star Gran Riserva Vin.
Colavita Balsamic Vinegar
Colavita Classic Hot Sauce
Colavita Extra Virgin Olive Oil
Colavita Fat Free Classic Hot Sauce
Colavita Fat Free Garden Style Sau.
Colavita Fat Free Marinara Sauce
Colavita Fat Free Mushroom Sauce
Colavita Garden Style Sauce
Colavita Healthy Sauce
Colavita Marinara Sauce
Colavita Marinated Vegetables
Colavita Mushroom Sauce
Colavita Pasta
Colavita Pasta Plus
Colavita Puttanesca Sauce
Colavita Red Clam Sauce
Colavita White Clam Sauce

2865 **Colchester Bakery**
96 Lebanon Ave
Colchester, CT 06415
860-537-2415
Fax: 860-537-4742
Baked breads
Owner: Ursula Paredes
Estimated Sales: $1-2.5 Million
Number Employees: 20-49
Type of Packaging: Consumer

2866 **Colchester Foods**
17 Schwartz Rd
Bozrah, CT 6334
860-886-2445
Fax: 860-886-1138 800-243-0469
Processor and exporter of brown and white eggs
VP: Kevin O'Brien
Number Employees: 20-49
Parent Co: Kofkoff Egg Farm
Type of Packaging: Consumer, Food Service, Private Label
Brands:
New England Farms Eggs

2867 **Cold Brew EvyTea**
253 Amory St
Boston, MA 02130-2337
617-429-5229
evytea.com
Cold brewed tea
Founder: Evy Chen
Year Founded: 2014
Number Employees: 6

2868 **Cold Fusion Foods**
8787 Shoreham Drive
Apt 308
West Hollywood, CA 90069-2227
310-287-3244
Fax: 310-287-3242
Protein enriched frozen juice bars
President: Collin Madden

2869 **Cold Hollow Cider Mill**
3600 Waterbury-Stowe Rd
PO Box 420
Waterbury Center, VT 05677-8020
802-244-8771
Fax: 802-244-7212 800-327-7537
info@coldhollow.com www.coldhollow.com
Apple products including cider, cider jelly, butters, syrup, sauce, preserves and juices; exporter of cider jelly; wholesaler/distributor of health and specialty foods, general merchandise, private label items and produce
Owner: Paul Brown
Vice President: Gayle Brown
Estimated Sales: $5-10 Million
Number Employees: 20-49
Square Footage: 40000
Type of Packaging: Consumer, Food Service, Bulk
Brands:
Cold Hollow Cider Mill

2870 **Cold Spring Bakery Inc**
308 Main St
Cold Spring, MN 56320-2597
320-685-8681
Fax: 320-685-3634 csb@coldspringbakery.com
www.coldspringbakery.com
Bakery goods
Owner: Phillip Brown
pbrown@globeuniversity.edu
Vice President: Brian Schurman
Estimated Sales: $2.2 Million
Number Employees: 50-99

2871 **Coldani Olive Ranch LLC**
13950 North Thornton Road
Lodi, CA 95242
209-334-0527
www.calivirgin.com
Manufacturer of olive oils, balsamic vinegar, and other oils.
Owner: Gina Sans
Square Footage: 80000

2872 **Coldwater Fish Farms**
PO Box 1
Lisco, NE 69148-0001
308-772-3474
Fax: 308-772-3845 800-658-4450
coldwaterfarms.al@gmail.com
Fish
President: Walter Queen
Sales Director: Molly Vogler
Production Manager: Lloyd Harding
Estimated Sales: $5-10 Million
Number Employees: 20-49
Type of Packaging: Private Label

2873 **Cole's Quality Foods**
4079 Park East Ct
Grand Rapids, MI 49546
616-975-0081
Fax: 616-975-0267 info@coles.com
www.coles.com
Fresh and frozen garlic bread, baguettes, garlic toast, breadsticks, cheesesticks, and cinnamonsticks.
Brand Manager: Alexis Reininger
Year Founded: 1943
Estimated Sales: $76 Million
Number Employees: 200
Type of Packaging: Consumer, Food Service
Brands:
Home Style

2874 **Colectivo Coffee**
Milwaukee, WI
414-273-3747
info@colectivocoffee.com
Independent coffee roaster.
Owner: Paul Lincoln Ward
Square Footage: 24000
Brands:
Session Roasted coffees
Letterbox Fine Tea
Colectivo Keg Company beers
Troubadour artisan breads

2875 **(HQ)Coleman Natural**
PO Box 768
Kings Mountain, NC 28086
303-468-2920
Fax: 303-277-9263 800-442-8666
info@colemannatural.com
www.colemannatural.com
Premium natural and organic poultry, pork, and prepared foods. No antibiotics or growth hormones, 100% vegetarian diets and no animal byproducts.
Ceo: Mark McKay
Vice President Of Marketing: Gudjon Olafsson
Vice President Of National Sales: Hans Liebl
Vice President Of Operations: Bart Vittori
Plant Manager: George Lofink
Purchasing Manager: Kevin Rafferty
Estimated Sales: $1 million
Number Employees: 2,300
Square Footage: 50000
Type of Packaging: Food Service
Brands:
COLEMAN NATURAL
COLEMAN ORGANIC

2876 **Colgin Co**
4111 Mint Way
Dallas, TX 75237
Fax: 214-951-8668 888-226-5446
www.colgin.com
Barbecue sauces including mesquite, apple and hickory liquid smoke
Vice President: Mark Gardner
Estimated Sales: $2.5-5 Million
Number Employees: 5-9
Type of Packaging: Consumer, Bulk
Brands:
Colgin
Liquid Smoke

2877 **Colibri Pepper Company**
21 Burrough Cemetery Rd
Elmer, LA 71424
316-730-6528
millereric@bellsouth.net
Pepper sauce
President: Eric Miller
Estimated Sales: $25,000
Number Employees: 2
Number of Brands: 1
Number of Products: 1
Square Footage: 1400
Type of Packaging: Consumer

2878 **Colin Ingram**
P.O.Box 146
Comptche, CA 95427-0146
707-937-1824
Fax: 707-937-5834
Manufacturer, importer and exporter of essential oils
President: John Weir
bill.lechtner@petco.com
Estimated Sales: $2.5-5 Million
Number Employees: 1-4
Type of Packaging: Consumer, Food Service, Private Label, Bulk

2879 **Collaborative Advantage Marketing**
2987 Franklin St
Detroit, MI 48207
248-723-0793
info@camtrade.com
camtrade.com
Sea salt; beans; pasta sauce; soups
President: Catherine Hanson
Year Founded: 1999
Estimated Sales: $106,300,00
Number Employees: 15
Brands:
Jack's Beans
Falk Salt

2880 **College Coffee Roaster**
115 N Donerville Rd # I
Mountville, PA 17554-1512
717-285-9561
Fax: 717-872-8554
Coffee
President/Owner: Susan Lithgoe
collegecoffeeroasters@dejazzd.com
VP: George Kerekgyarto
Estimated Sales: Less than $500,000
Number Employees: 1-4

2881 **Collin Street Bakery**
Corsicana, TX 75110
800-267-4657
www.collinstreet.com
Pecan cakes, coffees, cheesecake, cookies, cakes, pecan pies, breads, muffins and candies
Chief Marketing Officer: Hayden Crawford
Plant Manager: Debbie Watson
Purchasing Manager: Marcia Longo
Year Founded: 1896
Estimated Sales: $20-50 Million
Number Employees: 600
Square Footage: 125000
Type of Packaging: Consumer
Brands:
Apple Cinnamon Pecan Cake
Apricot Pecan Cake
Brittle Duet
Cheesecake Slicer
Cinchona Coffee
Deep Dish Pecan Pike
DeLuxe Fruitcake®
Double Deep Fudge Pecan Pie
Golden Rum Cake

Key Lime Cheesecake
Lemon Poppy Seed Cake
New York Style Cheesecake
Orange Paradise Cake
Pecan Coffee Cake
Pecan Duet
Pecan Halves & Pieces
Pineapple Pecan Cake
Praline Pecan Cheesecake
Trio of Cheesecake
Triple Chocolate Cake

2882 Collins Cavier Co
113 York St
Michigan City, IN 46360-3653
219-809-8100
Fax: 219-809-8105 cavco@collinscaviar.com
www.collinscaviar.com
American freshwater caviar, caviar creme spreads and custom compound butters
Owner: Rachel Collins
cavco@collinscavier.com
VP: Rachel Collins
Estimated Sales: $500,000-$1 Million
Number Employees: 1-4
Type of Packaging: Private Label

2883 Coloma Frozen Foods Inc
4145 Coloma Rd
Coloma, MI 49038-8967
269-944-1421
Fax: 269-944-3291 800-642-2723
www.colomafrozen.com
Frozen fruits, vegetables, juices and juice concentrates.
President: Brad Wendzel
CFO: Doug Singleton
Estimated Sales: $25 Million
Number Employees: 50-99
Type of Packaging: Food Service, Bulk
Brands:
Coloma

2884 Colombo Bakery
1329 Fee Dr
Sacramento, CA 95815-3911
916-648-1011
Fax: 916-649-2534
Bread, buns and rolls
Plant Manager: Paul Gonzalez
Estimated Sales: $300,000-500,000
Number Employees: 5-9
Parent Co: Metz Group
Type of Packaging: Consumer, Food Service, Private Label, Bulk

2885 Colonial Coffee Roasters Inc
3250 NW 60th St
Miami, FL 33142-2125
305-638-0885
Fax: 305-634-2538 info@colonialcoffee.com
Coffee roaster
Owner/President: Rafael Acevedo
main@colonialcoffee.com
Vice President: Melvin Weinkle
Operations Manager: Al Reyes
Estimated Sales: $6 Million
Number Employees: 10-19
Number of Brands: 3
Square Footage: 120000
Type of Packaging: Food Service, Private Label, Bulk
Brands:
Cafe Europa
Cafe Latino
Colonial International

2886 Colonial Cookies, Ltd
135 Otonabee Drive
Kitchener, ON N2C 1L7
Canada
519-893-6400
Fax: 519-893-9223 800-265-6508
info@colonialcookies.ca
Cookies
President, Bakery Division: Ray Kingdon
President: John Stephens
Senior VP Finance Bakery Division: Brian Paluch
VP Sales: Richard Bordwell
VP Sales/Marketing: Ted Clarke
Number Employees: 500-999
Parent Co: Parmalat Bakery Group North America
Type of Packaging: Consumer

Brands:
A & M Cookie

2887 Colonna Brothers Inc
4102 Bergen Tpke
North Bergen, NJ 07047-2510
201-864-1115
Fax: 201-864-0144
customerservice@colonnabrothers.com
www.colonnabrothers.com
Bread crumbs, grated cheese, sauces, olive oil & vinegar, soups, stuffing mix, roasted peppers, marinated mushrooms, pepperoncini, chopped garlic, artichoke hearts and bread sticks
President: Peter Colonna
cvifoods@aol.com
Estimated Sales: $5.6 Million
Number Employees: 100-249
Type of Packaging: Consumer, Food Service
Brands:
Colonna

2888 Colony Brands Inc
1112 7th Ave
Monroe, WI 53566-1364
608-328-8400
Fax: 608-328-8457 800-544-9036
www.colonybrands.com
Cakes, tortes & pies; cookies & bars; pastries; petits fours; candy & chocolate; boxed assortments of all kinds; cheeses; sausage, ham and other meats; nuts & pre-mixed snacks; home furniture; home d,cor; electronics; jewelry; fitnessequipment; unisex apparel; small appliances
CEO: John Baumann
Chairman: Pat Kubly
VP/CIO: Steve Cretney
Content Marketing Manager: Matt Stetler
Director of Strategic Planning: Ryan Kubly
Number Employees: 1000-4999
Square Footage: 13236
Parent Co: Colony Brands, Inc.
Brands:
Swiss Colony Foods

2889 Colony Foods
439 Haverhill St
Lawrence, MA 01841
978-682-9677
Fax: 978-687-8448
Frozen, fresh and special order food items.
President: Dereck Barbagallo
Contact: George Abdallah
georgeabdallah@colonyfoods.com
Estimated Sales: $10-20 Million
Number Employees: 20-49

2890 Color Garden
1300 Hancock St
Anaheim, CA 92807
714-572-0444
Fax: 714-572-0999 inquire@colormaker.com
Plant-based food colorings
Type of Packaging: Consumer
Brands:
COLOR GARDEN

2891 ColorKitchen
740 NE 3rd Street
Suite 3-143
Bend, OR 97701
510-227-6174
info@colorkitchenfoods.com
www.colorkitchenfoods.com
Plant-based food colorings
Founder: Ashley Phelps
Type of Packaging: Consumer

2892 ColorMaker, Inc.
1300 N Hancock St # A
Anaheim, CA 92807-1928
714-572-0444
Fax: 714-572-0999 inquire@colormaker.com
www.colorgarden.net
custom natural color blends compatible with product, process and package requirements. Products include free-flowing powders, liquid concentrates, liquid emulsions or viscous pastes.
CEO: Stephen Lauro
stephenl@colormaker.com
Accounting: Shannon Lauro
Research & Development Manager: Dr. Gabriel Lauro
Marketing & Social Media Manager: Dan Wegrzyn
Office Manager: Christine White
Production Manager: Carlos Pena
Number Employees: 5-9
Type of Packaging: Bulk

2893 Colorado Cellars
3553 E Rd
Palisade, CO 81526-9558
970-464-7921
Fax: 970-464-0574 info@coloradocellars.com
www.coloradocellars.com
Wines
President: Richard Turley
rturley@vineland.com
Treasurer: Padte Turley
Estimated Sales: Less Than $500,000
Number Employees: 1-4

2894 Colorado Hemp Honey
Frangiosa Farms
41322 London Dr
Parker, CO 80138
833-233-2256
info@frangiosafarms.com
coloradohemphoney.com
Honey with hemp extract
Founder: Nick French
Business Development: Ali French
Brand and Marketing Manager: Matt Seres
Production Lead: Eric Peter
Facilities and Shipping Manager: James Cole

2895 Colorado Mountain Jams & Jellies
3573 G Rd
Palisade, CO 81526
970-464-0745
www.plumdaisy.com
Fruit jams and wine jellies

2896 Colorado Nut Co
2 Kalamath St
Denver, CO 80223-1550
303-733-7311
800-876-1625
sales@coloradonutco.com
www.coloradonutco.com
Manufactures and Imports candies, chocolates, unique trail mixes, snack mixes, dried fruits and gift baskets for any occasion. Also roast nuts on site. Also offer products with private labeling and customized logos for a variety ofspecialized events.
Owner: Mark Goodman
mgoodman@coloradonutco.com
Owner: Roger Renaud
Estimated Sales: Less Than $500,000
Number Employees: 5-9
Type of Packaging: Consumer, Private Label

2897 Colorado Popcorn Co
320 Oak St
Sterling, CO 80751-3306
970-522-7612
Fax: 970-522-8630 866-491-2676
www.coloradopopcorn.com
Gourmet popcorn
Owner: Kathy Littler
coloradopopcorn@bresnan.net
Estimated Sales: Less Than $500,000
Number Employees: 1-4
Number of Products: 13
Type of Packaging: Consumer, Food Service

2898 Colorado Salsa Company
1228 W Littleton Blvd
Littleton, CO 80120-5800
303-932-2617
Fax: 303-297-7752
info_salsacolorado@yahoo.com
Salsa
Owner: David Karas
CEO: Patricia Parkos
Estimated Sales: $1-2.5 Million
Number Employees: 1-4
Square Footage: 6000
Type of Packaging: Consumer
Brands:
Denver

2899 **Colorado Spice Co**
6350 Gunpark Dr
Boulder, CO 80301-3588
303-581-9586
Fax: 303-581-9288 800-677-7423
tzieglerne@prodigy.net www.coloradospice.com
Custom packed spice and herb blends; also, tea and tea blends
President: Tomas Amo
tomas@coloradospice.com
CEO: Rod Smith
Estimated Sales: $900,000 appx.
Number Employees: 1-4
Square Footage: 20400
Type of Packaging: Food Service, Private Label, Bulk
Brands:
Cinnamon Ridge
Shadow Mountain Foods, Inc.
The Colorado Spice Co.
The Spice Box
The Spice Co.

2900 **Colorado Sweet Gold**
1722 S Golden Road
Lakewood, CO 80401
303-384-1101
Fax: 303-384-1118 www.coloradosweetgold.com
Manufacturers of sweeteners and food ingredients
President: Charlie Gilbert
Executive: Tom Herrmann
Estimated Sales: $500,000-$1 Million
Number Employees: 1-4
Number of Products: 6
Type of Packaging: Private Label

2901 **Colors Gourmet Pizza**
2349 LA Mirada Dr
Vista, CA 92081-7863
760-597-1400
Fax: 760-431-0914 info@colorspizza.com
www.colorspizza.com
Gourmet pizza, handmade crusts, focaccia and panini bread
Chef, Owner: Martial Bricnet
martialb@colorspizza.com
Director of Sales/Distribution: James Tuckwell
Estimated Sales: $1-3 Million
Number Employees: 20-49
Square Footage: 30000
Brands:
Colors Gourmet Pizza

2902 **Colteryahn Dairy**
1601 Brownsville Rd
Pittsburgh, PA 15210-3903
412-881-1408
Fax: 412-881-0460
Milk, cream and juices
Owner: Carl Colteryahn
ccolteryahn@colteryahndairy.com
Director: Frank Dean
Estimated Sales: $1 Million
Number Employees: 50-99

2903 **Colts Chocolates**
609 Overton St
Nashville, TN 37203-4149
615-251-0100
Fax: 615-251-0120
information@coltschocolates.com
www.coltschocolates.com
Chocolate candy and pies
Owner: Mackenzie Colt
coltsbolts@aol.com
Estimated Sales: $1-2.5 Million
Number Employees: 20-49
Brands:
Animal Crackers
Brownies & Roses
Butter Grahams
Chocolate Covered Marshmallows
Colts Bolts
Gooey Butter Bar, New!
Happy Trails T-Shirts
Marie McGhee's
Roy Rogers Happy Trails
Truffle Babies

2904 **Coltsfoot/Golden Eagle Herb**
PO Box 5205
Grants Pass, OR 97528
541-476-8267
Fax: 541-476-0205 800-736-8749
sales@goldeneaglechew.com
www.goldeneaglechew.com
Herbs
Owner: Robert Anderson
Owner: Joni Anderson
Estimated Sales: $3-5 Million
Number Employees: 5-9

2905 **(HQ)Columbia Empire Farms Inc**
31461 NE Bell Rd
Sherwood, OR 97140-8504
503-538-2156
Fax: 503-538-2156
moreinfo@columbiaempirefarms.com
www.columbiaempirefarms.com
Salted and roasted hazelnuts
President: Floyd Aylor
Owner: Robert Pamplin
Director Information Technology: Janet Pendergrass
Director of Marketing: Linda Strand
Estimated Sales: $4.4 Million
Number Employees: 20-49
Type of Packaging: Private Label
Brands:
America's Northwest
Chateau Beniot
Columbia Empire Farms
Doodleberry
Northwest Gourmet
Nutworld

2906 **Columbia Packing Co Inc**
Dallas, TX 75203
214-946-8171
www.columbiapacking.com
Meat packers, cattle and hog slaughterers and distributors of boxed beef, boxed pork and sausage items
President: Amber Ondrusek
Vice President: Rusty Ondrusek
Year Founded: 1913
Estimated Sales: $20-50 Million
Number Employees: 50-99

2907 **Columbia Phyto Technology**
250 Steelhead Way
The Dalles, OR 97058-3570
541-298-4800
Fax: 888-765-1720 sales@powderpure.com
www.columbiaphytotechnology.com
Producer of high quality fruit and vegetable powders. Certified organic, Kosher and all non-GMO.
Contact: Travis Aerni
travis@columbiaphytotechnology.com

2908 **Columbia Valley Farms Inc.**
P.O. Box 2563
911 Crestloch Ln
Pasco, WA 99302-2563
855-261-6395
www.fostersasparagus.com
Pickled asparagus, green beans, and carrots.
President/CFO: Kevin Filbrun
VP/Sales & Marketing: Bryan Lynch
Customer Relations: Sandy Lehrman
Operations Manager: Ryan Brovont
Year Founded: 1984
Estimated Sales: $611,416,00
Number Employees: 7
Type of Packaging: Private Label
Brands:
Foster's

2909 **Columbia Winery**
14030 NE 145th St
Woodinville, WA 98072-6994
425-488-2776
Fax: 425-488-3460 www.columbiawinery.com
Producers of various red, white and blush wines.
CEO: Andrew Browne
Vice President: Glenn Coogan
Year Founded: 1962
Estimated Sales: $270,000
Number Employees: 50-99
Brands:
Alder Ridge
Battle Creek
Sawtooth
Zefina

2910 **Columbine Confections LLC**
701 Automation Dr
Windsor, CO 80550-3142
970-377-2293
Fax: 970-225-0910
orders@ferncreekconfections.com
www.ferncreekconfections.com
Manufacturer of gourmet sweets, treats, and chocolates.
Estimated Sales: Less Than $500,000
Number Employees: 1-4
Square Footage: 80000

2911 **Columbus Brewing Co**
525 Short St
Columbus, OH 43215-5614
614-464-2739
Fax: 614-464-0347 www.dinecbccolumbus.com
Beer
Owner: Mike Campbell
Owner: Doug Griggs
dgriggs@columbusbrewingco.com
Vice President: Ben Pridgeon
Estimated Sales: $500,000-$1 Million
Number Employees: 20-49
Brands:
1859 Porter
Apricot Ale
Columbus Pale Ale
Nut Brown Ale

2912 **Columbus Salame**
30977 San Antonio Road
Hayward, CA 94544
www.columbussalame.com
Salame and meat products
Contact: Valeria Fiorito
vfiorito@columco.com

2913 **Columbus Vegetable Oils**
30 E Oakton St
Des Plaines, IL 60018-1945
847-257-8920
Fax: 773-265-6985 www.cvoils.com
A producer of quality oils, fats, and shortenings. Products range from highly competitive commodity oils to exotic specialty oils.
President: Paulette Gagliardo
Production Manager: Benjamin Caffrey
Estimated Sales: Over $1 Billion
Number Employees: 50-99
Parent Co: CFC Inc.

2914 **Comanche Tortilla Factory**
107 S Nelson St
Fort Stockton, TX 79735-6707
432-336-3245
www.comanche-tortilla-factory.dinehere.us
Mexican products including peppers, tortillas and tamales
Owner: Joe Ben Gallegos
Number Employees: 1-4
Type of Packaging: Consumer

2915 **Comanzo & Company Specialty Bakers**
10 Industrial Dr
Smithfield, RI 02917-1500
401-231-2361
Fax: 401-232-9826 888-352-5455
Biscotti, European style shortbread
President: Liz Walker
Estimated Sales: Less than $500,000
Number Employees: 1-4

2916 **Comax Flavors**
130 Baylis Rd
Melville, NY 11747-3808
631-420-0073
Fax: 631-249-9255 800-992-0629
info@comaxflavors.com www.comaxflavors.com
Supplier of flavors
President: Weisz Agneta
CEO: Peter Calabretta
CFO: Virginia Wyan
Vice President: Paul Calabretta
Sr. Flavor Chemist: Mike Crain
Quality Control: Frank Vollaro
EVP Sales & Marketing: Bill Graham
PR/Communications Manager: Laura Ferrante
VP Operations: Joe Piazza
Production Manager: Jorge Quintanilla
Plant Manager: Marion Cunningham
Purchasing Manager: Michael Keppel

Estimated Sales: $15 Million
Number Employees: 250-499

2917 Comeau's Seafoods
60 Saulnierville Rd
Saulnierville, NS B0W 2Z0
Canada
902-769-2101
info@comeausea.com
www.comeauseafoods.com
Fresh, frozen and processed seafoods, herring, smoked salmon.
President & CEO: Noel Despres
Vice President & General Manager: Kim d'Entremont
Estimated Sales: $50-100 Million
Number Employees: 375
Type of Packaging: Consumer, Food Service, Private Label, Bulk

2918 Comeaux's
116 Alley 3
Lafayette, LA 70506
337-332-0720
Fax: 337-507-3343 888-264-5460
Kelly@comeaux.com www.comeaux.com
Vacuum packed seafood including crawfish boudin, oysters, seafood boudin, shrimp, pork and tasso
Owner: Ray Comeaux
Co-Owner: Sonja Comeaux
Estimated Sales: $570,000
Number Employees: 8
Type of Packaging: Consumer, Food Service
Brands:
Comeaux's Andouille Sausage
Comeaux's Crawfish Tails
Comeaux's Tasso

2919 Comfort Foods
9900 Montgomery Blvd Ne
Suite A
Albuquerque, NM 87111
505-281-7083
Fax: 505-323-8721 800-460-5803
www.comfortfoods.com
Soups and dip mixes
President/CEO: Mark Harden
VP: Dawn Johnson
Handles Marketing/Sales: Matthew Coxler
Plant Manager: Debbie Holm
Estimated Sales: $4 Million
Number Employees: 24
Number of Brands: 2
Number of Products: 80
Square Footage: 140000
Type of Packaging: Private Label
Brands:
Country Gardens Cuisine
Desert Gardens Chile and Spice

2920 Commercial Bakeries
45 Torbarrie Rd
Toronto, ON M3L 1G5
Canada
416-247-5478
Fax: 416-242-4129 info@commercialbakeries.com
commercialbakeries.com
Private label cookie manufacturer
President/Owner: Anthony Fusco
CFO: Sam Palermo
Quality Control: Sahar Maftoon
Plant Manager: Steve Brain
Type of Packaging: Private Label

2921 Commercial Creamery Co
159 S Cedar St
Spokane, WA 99201
509-747-4131
sales@cheesepowder.com
www.cheesepowder.com
Dried cheese and yogurt powders; processor and exporter of snack seasoning and spray dried dairy flavors
Owner/VP Sales & Marketing: Megan Boell
mboell@cheesepowder.com
Year Founded: 1908
Estimated Sales: $28 Million
Number Employees: 5-9

2922 Commissariat Imports
PO Box 643025
Los Angeles, CA 90064-0271
310-475-5628
Fax: 310-475-8246 info@bombaybrand.com
Processor, importer and exporter of indian chutneys, pickles, curry powder and pastes including curry, biryani, ginger, garlic and tandoori; certified kosher available
President/CEO: Parvez Commissariat
VP: Aban Commissariat
Estimated Sales: Over $500,000
Number Employees: 2
Type of Packaging: Food Service, Private Label
Brands:
Bombay

2923 Commodities Marketing Inc
6 Stone Tavern Dr
Clarksburg, NJ 08510
732-516-0700
Fax: 732-516-0600 weldonrice@usa.net
www.weldonfoods.com
Jasmine rice, Basmati rice, Coconut drinks, Coconut milk, Fruits, Beans, Guar gum, Fruit juices and Cashews, Almonds, Saffron (Spain) White Rice/Parboiled Rice.
President: Herbander Sahni
herbandersahni@weldonfoods.com
CEO: Gagandeep Sahni
CFO: Soena Sahni
VP: Avneet Sodhi
R&D: Manoj Hedge
Marketing: Harbinder Singh Sahni & Dee Mirchandai
Sales: Avneet Sodhi
Public Relations: Mr. Dough & Harshida Shaw
Operations: Harshida Shah
Production: Mr Nobpsaul
Plant Manager: Mr Chandej
Estimated Sales: $25 Million
Number Employees: 5-9
Number of Brands: 3
Number of Products: 6
Square Footage: 3000
Type of Packaging: Consumer, Food Service, Private Label, Bulk
Brands:
Meher
Weldon

2924 Common Folk Farm
PO Box 141
Naples, ME 04055-0141
207-787-2764
Fax: 207-787-3894
Processor and exporter of herbal teas, seasonings and culinary mixes
Owner: Betz Golon
Owner: Dale Golon
Type of Packaging: Consumer, Private Label, Bulk
Brands:
Common Folk Farm, Inc.

2925 Community Bakeries
3250 Lacey Rd.
Suite 600
Downers Grove, IL 60515
630-455-5200
Fax: 630-455-5202 800-952-5754
Muffins
President: Charles Huber Jr.
CFO: James Wojciechowski
VP Retail Sales and Marketing: Mark Leopold
Number Employees: 3000
Brands:
Community Bakeries

2926 Community Coffee Co.
3332 Partridge Ln.
Building A
Baton Rouge, LA 70809
800-884-5282
Fax: 800-643-8199
customerservice@communitycoffee.com
www.communitycoffee.com
Coffee and tea; importer of green coffee; and wholesaler/distributor of coffee creamer.
President/CEO: David Belanger
dbelanger@communitycoffee.com
Chairman: Matthew Saurage
CFO: Annette Vaccaro
Year Founded: 1919
Estimated Sales: $195 Million
Number Employees: 1000-4999
Type of Packaging: Consumer, Food Service, Private Label, Bulk
Brands:
Community Coffee

2927 Community Mill & Bean
267 State Route 89
Savannah, NY 13146-9711
315-365-2664
Fax: 315-365-2690 800-755-0554
Organic flour milling
CEO: Richard Corichi
Estimated Sales: $1-2.5 Million
Number Employees: 1-4

2928 Community Orchards
2237 160th St
Fort Dodge, IA 50501-8547
515-573-8212
Fax: 515-576-0489 888-573-8212
mail@communityorchards.com
Apple cider, pie and dumplings
President: Greg Baedke
VP: Bev Baedke
Estimated Sales: $678,000
Number Employees: 20-49

2929 Company of a Philadelphia Gentleman
2824 N 2nd St
Philadelphia, PA 19133-3515
215-427-2827
Fax: 215-739-0871 sim4033@aol.com
Teas
Owner: Morton Simkins
Estimated Sales: $500,000-$1 Million
Number Employees: 6
Square Footage: 160000

2930 Compass Minerals
9900 W 109th St
Suite 100
Overland Park, KS 66210
913-344-9200
www.compassminerals.com
Food grade salt products.
President & CEO: Kevin Crutchfield
Chief Financial Officer: Jamie Standen
Chief Legal & Administrative Officer: Mary Frontczak
Chief Commercial Officer: Brad Griffith
Chief Operating Officer: George Schuller
Year Founded: 1844
Estimated Sales: Over $1 Billion
Number Employees: 3,500
Type of Packaging: Consumer, Food Service, Private Label, Bulk

2931 Compton Dairy
25 Walker Street
Shelbyville, IN 46176-1332
317-398-8621
Fax: 317-392-9777
Milk, dairy products-noncheese
President: Dan Compton
Estimated Sales: $2.5-5 Million
Number Employees: 10-19

2932 Comte Cheese Association
152 West 36th Street
Suite 601
New York, NY 10018
646-515-9209
www.comte.com
Cheese, agency/trade organization.

2933 Comvita USA
Santa Barbara, CA 93101
855-449-2201
usacustomerservice@comvita.com
www.comvita.com
Manuka honey and apple cider vinegar
SVP & General Manager: Corey Blick

2934 Con Agra Foods Inc
801 Dye Mill Rd
Troy, OH 45373-4223
937-335-2115
Fax: 937-339-6930 www.conagrafoods.com
Pizza
Plant Manager: Scott Adkins
Estimated Sales: $10-20 Million
Number Employees: 250-499
Parent Co: A.M. Gilardi & Sons

2935 Con Agra Snack Foods
2301 Washington St
Hamburg, IA 51640-1835
712-382-2202
Fax: 712-382-1357 800-831-5818
www.vogelpopcorn.com
Processor and exporter of popcorn and popping oils; importer of popcorn and popcorn seeds.
President/CEO: Sean Connolly
Estimated Sales: $20-50 Million
Number Employees: 50-99
Number of Brands: 2
Parent Co: ConAgra Foods
Type of Packaging: Consumer, Food Service, Private Label, Bulk
Brands:
Act II
Vogel

2936 Con Yeager Spice Co
144 Magill Rd
Zelienople, PA 16063-3424
724-452-4120
Fax: 724-452-6171 800-222-2460
www.conyeagerspice.com
Seasonings and meat cures and binders; wholesaler/distributor of meat casings and spices
Owner: Bill Kreuer
VP: Rodney Schaffer
Sales Rep.: Rod Schaffer
rschaffer@conyeagermail.com
Production Manager: William Wolford
Estimated Sales: $2.8 Million
Number Employees: 10-19
Square Footage: 54000
Type of Packaging: Consumer, Food Service, Private Label, Bulk
Brands:
Con Yeager Spices

2937 ConSup North America
170 Beaverbrook Rd
Unit 2
Lincoln Park, NJ 07035-1441
973-628-7330
Fax: 973-628-2919 customerservice@consup.us
www.consupna.com
Importer of German food brands
Owner: Martin Moog
m.moog@consup.us
Marketing: Russ Harlock
Estimated Sales: $5-10 Million
Number Employees: 5-9

2938 Conagra Brands Canada
5055 Satellite Drive
Mississauga, ON L4W 5K7
Canada
416-679-4200
800-461-4556
www.conagrabrands.ca
Consumer brands.
VP/General Manager: Ian Roberts
Number Employees: 500
Square Footage: 20000
Parent Co: Conagra Brands
Type of Packaging: Consumer, Food Service
Other Locations:
Boisbriand Office
Boisbriand QC

2939 (HQ)Conagra Brands Inc
222 W. Merchandise Mart Plaza
Chicago, IL 60654
312-549-5000
877-266-2472
www.conagrafoods.com
Consumer brands.
President & CEO: Sean Connolly
Executive VP/CFO: David Marberger
Executive Vice President: Colleen Batcheler
Executive VP/Co-COO: Tom McGough
Estimated Sales: $11 Billion
Number Employees: 18,000
Number of Brands: 70
Type of Packaging: Consumer, Food Service, Bulk
Brands:
ACT II®
Alexia®
Andy Capp's®
Angie's BOOMCHICKAPOP®
Armour Star®
Aunt Jemima®
Banquet®
Bernstein's®
Bertoli®
BIGS®
Birds Eye®
Birds Eye C&W
Birds Eye Voila
Blake's®
Blue Bonnet®
Brooks®
Celeste® Pizza for One
Chef Boyardee®
Crunch 'n Munch®
DAVID® Seeds
Dennison's®
Duke's®
Duncan Hines®
Duncan Hines Comstock®
Duncan Hies Wilderness®
Earth Balance®
Egg Beaters®
Erin's®
EVOL®
Fiddle Faddle®
Fleischmann's®
Frontera®
Gardein®
Glutino®
Gulden's®
H.K. Anderson®
Hawaiian Snacks®
Healthy Choice®
Hebrew National®
Hungry-Man®
Hunt's®
Husman's®
Jiffy Pop®
Kangaroo®
Kid Cuisine®
La Choy®
Lender's®
Libby's®
Log Cabin®
Manwich®
Marie Callender's®
Mrs.Butterworth's®
Mrs.Paul's®
Nalley®
Odom's Tennessee Pride®
Open Pit®
Orville Redencacher'S®
P.F. Chang's Home Menu®
PAM®
Parkay®
Penrose®
Peter Pan®
Poppycock®
Ranch Style Beans®
Reddi-wip®
RO*TEL®
Rosarita®
Reddi-wip®
RO*TEL®
Rosarita®
Sandwhich Bros. of Wisconsin®
Slim Jim®
Smart Balance®

2940 Conagra Foodservice
222 W. Merchandise Mart Plaza
Suite 1300
Chicago, IL 60654
312-549-5000
877-266-2472
www.conagrabrands.com
Supplies restaurants, retailers, commercial customers and other foodservice suppliers.
President/CEO: Sean Connolly
Executive VP/CFO: David Marberger
Executive VP/General Counsel: Colleen Batcheler
Executive VP/Co-COO: Tom McGough
Estimated Sales: K
Number Employees: 10,000+
Number of Brands: 70
Square Footage: 11042
Parent Co: Conagra Brands
Type of Packaging: Consumer, Food Service, Bulk
Other Locations:
ConAgra Headquarters
Kennewick WA
ConAgra Headquarters
Naperville IL
Sales Office
Anaheim CA
Sales Office
Mesa AR
Sales Office
San Antonio TX
Sales Office
Plano TX
Sales Office
Tampa FL
Sales Office
Baltimore MD
Sales Office
Mason OH
Sales Office
Troy OH
Brands:
ACT II®
Alexia®
Andy Capp's®
Angie's BOOMCHICKAPOP®
Armour Star®
Aunt Jemima®
Banquet®
Bernstein's®
Bertoli®
BIGS®
Birds Eye®
Birds Eye C&W
Birds Eye Voila
Blake's®
Blue Bonnet®
Brooks®
Celeste® Pizza for One
Chef Boyardee®
Crunch 'n Munch®
DAVID® Seeds
Dennison's®
Duke's®
Duncan Hines®
Duncan Hines Comstock®
Duncan Hies Wilderness®
Earth Balance®
Egg Beaters®
Erin's®
EVOL®
Fiddle Faddle®
Fleischmann's®
Frontera®
Gardein®
Glutino®
Gulden's®
H.K. Anderson®
Hawaiian Snacks®
Healthy Choice®
Hebrew National®
Hungry-Man®
Hunt's®
Husman's®
Jiffy Pop®
Kangaroo®
Kid Cuisine®
La Choy®
Lender's®
Libby's®
Log Cabin®
Manwich®
Marie Callender's®
Mrs.Butterworth's®
Mrs.Paul's®
Nalley®
Odom's Tennessee Pride®
Open Pit®
Orville Redencacher'S®
P.F. Chang's Home Menu®
PAM®
Parkay®
Penrose®
Peter Pan®
Poppycock®
Ranch Style Beans®
Reddi-wip®
RO*TEL®
Rosarita®
Reddi-wip®
RO*TEL®
Rosarita®
Sandwhich Bros. of Wisconsin®
Slim Jim®
Smart Balance®

2941 Concannon Vineyard
4590 Tesla Rd
Livermore, CA 94550-9002
925-456-2505
Fax: 925-583-1160 800-258-9866
info@concannonvineyard.com
www.concannonvineyard.com

Processor and exporter of bottled wines; grower of grapes
CFO: Jim Page
Estimated Sales: $1.6 Million
Number Employees: 50-99
Square Footage: 29912
Parent Co: Wine Group
Type of Packaging: Consumer, Private Label
Brands:
Concannon Vineyard

2942 **Concord Farms**
2811 Faber St
Union City, CA 94587-1203
510-429-8855
Fax: 510-429-8844 www.concordtapes.com
Grower of fresh shiitake and oyster mushrooms
Owner/President: David Tung
dtung@concordfarms.com
VP: Grace Tung
Estimated Sales: $1.9 Million
Number Employees: 5-9
Type of Packaging: Consumer, Private Label, Bulk
Brands:
Oringer
Reddy Glaze

2943 **Concord Foods, LLC**
10 Minuteman Way
Brockton, MA 02301-7508
508-580-1700
Fax: 508-584-9425 www.concordfoods.com
Supplier of retail food products and custom ingredients. The retail line includes companian items for fresh produce (juices, produce seasoning mixes, smoothie mixes, fresh desserts, dips, etc) and seasoning mixes for ground beefpoultry and seafood. The business ingredients division supplies beverage bases, fountain syrups, toppings, caramels, fruit purees and chocolate products, breadings and batters, and pancake and baking mixes. Recapitalized by Arbor Investments in2015.
President/CEO: Peter Neville
pneville@concordfoods.com
VP: Rich Renna
Marketing Manager: Samantha McCaul
Production Supervisor: Michelle Marvel
Warehouse Team Leader: Gabriel Alves
Estimated Sales: $38 Million
Number Employees: 100-249
Number of Brands: 4
Square Footage: 190000
Parent Co: Arbor Investments
Type of Packaging: Consumer, Food Service, Bulk
Brands:
Concord Foods
Tempo
Oringer
Red E Made

2944 **Conecuh Sausage Co**
200 Industrial Park
PO Box 327
Evergreen, AL 36401-1807
251-578-3380
Fax: 251-578-5408 800-726-0507
sales@conecuhsausage.com
www.conecuhsausage.com
Meat products including sausage
President/CEO/Owner: John Sessions
relliott@conecuhsausageco.com
Site Manager: Ronnie Elliott
relliott@conecuhsausageco.com
Estimated Sales: $5.6 Million
Number Employees: 50-99
Type of Packaging: Consumer
Brands:
Cajun Smoked Sausage
Hickory Smoked Sausage
Original Smoked Sausage
Spicy and Hot Hickory Sausage

2945 **Coney Island Classics**
65 Roosevelt Ave
Suite 107
Valley Stream, NY 11581
516-823-3001
Fax: 516-823-3003 www.coneyislandclassics.com
Kettle corn, potato chips and cookies

2946 **Confection Art Inc**
3636 North Williams Avenue
Portland, OR 97227
503-505-0481
info@chocolatecraftkits.com
www.chocolatecraftkits.com
Molded chocolates
President: Nancy Baggett
Master Pastry Chef: Pierre Herme
Number Employees: 8

2947 **Confectionately Yours LTD**
160 Lexington Dr
Suite D
Buffalo Grove, IL 60089-6929
847-537-5761
Fax: 847-537-7178 800-875-6978
conyrs@sbcglobal.net
Pretzel rods, English toffee and other homemade style candies
President: Kathy Fish
info@confectionately-yours.com
VP: Tom Fish
Estimated Sales: $600,000
Number Employees: 1-4
Number of Products: 35
Square Footage: 16000
Type of Packaging: Consumer, Food Service, Private Label, Bulk
Brands:
Big Yummy
Blasting Powder
Bola Pop's
Fizz Wiz
Fun Stuff
Joy Stiks
Lumpy Logs
Lumpy Lous
Monster
Monster Chews
Nasty Tricks
Ninja Sticks
Oogly Eyes
Rock 'n Roll Chews
Stickers
Sweet Stirrings
Tuesday Toffee

2948 **Confoco USA, Inc.**
1139 E Jersey St
Suite 415
Elizabeth, NJ 07201
908-659-0566
Fax: 908-659-9339 confocosales@confoco.com
www.confoco.com
Manufacturer and distributor of fruit and vegetable flakes, powder and essences as well as aseptic banana puree. Kosher & Halal Certified products
General Manager: Edwardo Chiriboga
Contact: Francisco Larrea
flarrea@confoco.com
Type of Packaging: Food Service, Bulk

2949 **Congdon Orchards Inc.**
P.O. Box 2725
Yakima, WA 98907
509-966-4440
Fax: 509-966-4447 www.congdonorchards.com
Apples and pears.
President/CEO: Dick Woodin
CFO: Bob Martin
General Manager: Mark Blore
mblore@congdonorchards.com
Estimated Sales: $1.1 Million
Number Employees: 20-49
Type of Packaging: Consumer, Food Service

2950 **Conifer Foods**
Medina, WA 98039
425-486-3334
Fax: 425-398-0301 800-588-9160
pgimness@conifer-inc.com conifer-inc.com
Gourmet convenience foods
President/Chief Executive Officer: Mike Maher
Director, Quality: Kurt Larson
Vice President, Marketing: Joanne Ramsay
Vice President, Sales/Marketing: Harry Forsberg
Contact: Bob Benson
rbenson@conifer-inc.com
Plant Manager: Jesse Riojas
Estimated Sales: $40 Million
Number Employees: 32
Number of Brands: 4
Brands:
Canterbury Naturals
CrockPot
Fisher Scones
Starbucks Hot Cocoa

2951 **Conifer Specialties Inc**
15500 Woodinville-Redmond Rd
Suite C-400
Woodinville, WA 98072
425-486-3334
Fax: 425-398-0301 800-588-9160
pgimness@conifer-inc.com www.conifer-inc.com
Soups, breads, desserts and Fisher scones
CEO: Mike Maher
Estimated Sales: $2.7 Million
Number Employees: 75

2952 **(HQ)Conn's Potato Chips**
1805 Kemper Ct
Zanesville, OH 43701-4634
740-452-4615
Fax: 740-452-9272 sales@connschips.com
www.connschips.com
Manufacturer of potato chips and snack foods.
President: Montie Hunter
Founder: Ida Conn
Estimated Sales: $20-50 Million
Number Employees: 20-49
Type of Packaging: Private Label
Brands:
Conn's Bbq Pork Rinds
Conn's Bean Dip
Conn's Caramel Popcorn
Conn's Cheese Corn Popcorn
Conn's Cheese Curls
Conn's Cheese Dip
Conn's Corn Chips
Conn's Corn Pops Popcorn
Conn's Green Onion
Conn's Honey Bbq Jerky
Conn's Honey Mustard Dip
Conn's Jalapeno Dip
Conn's Nacho Tortilla Chips
Conn's Oat Bran Pretzels
Conn's Original
Conn's Original Beef Jerky
Conn's Party Mix
Conn's Picante Dip
Conn's Pork Rinds
Conn's Pretzel Rods
Conn's Pretzel Sticks
Conn's Pretzel Thins
Conn's Pretzel Twists
Conn's Restaurant Tortilla Chips
Conn's Round Tortilla Chips
Conn's Salsa Supreme Dip
Conn's Salt & Vinegar
Conn's Sour Cream
Conn's Wavy

2953 **Conneaut Cellars Winery LLC**
12005 Conneaut Lake Rd
Conneaut Lake, PA 16316
814-382-3999
Fax: 814-382-6151 877-229-9463
www.conneautcellarsdistillery.com
Wines
President: Joel Wolf
Sales/Office Manager: Jackie Elliot
Estimated Sales: $2.5-5 Million
Number Employees: 5-9

2954 **Connors Aquaculture**
Estes Head
Eastport, ME 04631
207-853-6081
Fax: 207-853-6056
Fish hatchery
President: Ken Hirtle
Treasurer: Charles Crowe
Estimated Sales: $6.9 Million
Number Employees: 150

2955 **Conoley Citrus Packers Inc**
12488 W Colonial Dr
Winter Garden, FL 34787-4121
407-656-3300
Fax: 407-656-1168 www.conoleyfruit.com
Frozen citrus fruits
President: E. Conoley
CFO: Bill Lewin
bill@conoleyfruit.com
General Manager: Kevin Paffrath

Estimated Sales: $11.8 Million
Number Employees: 50-99
Type of Packaging: Private Label

2956 Conrad Rice Mill Inc
P.O. Box 10640
New Iberia, LA 70562-0640
337-364-7242
Fax: 337-365-5806 800-551-3245
sales@conradricemill.com www.conradrice.com
Packed rice including yellow, herb, curry, ranch and wild; also, rice mixes including paella, long grain and wild.
President: Michael Davis
mikedavis@conradricemill.com
Estimated Sales: $20-50 Million
Number Employees: 10-19
Type of Packaging: Consumer, Food Service
Brands:
Conrad-Davis
Hol Grain
Konriko
R.M.Quiggs

2957 Conrotto A. Winery
1690 Hecker Pass Road
Gilroy, CA 95020-8800
408-847-2233
Wine
President: James Burr
Estimated Sales: $1-2.5 Million
Number Employees: 1-4

2958 Conroy Foods
100 Chapel Harbor Dr # 2
Suite 2
Pittsburgh, PA 15238-4163
412-781-0977
Fax: 412-781-1409 beanos@conroyfoods.com
Deli and seafood condiments
Owner: Jim Conroy
jlc@conroyfoods.com
CEO: William Conroy
Treasurer: Leslee Conroy
Estimated Sales: $1.8 Million
Number Employees: 10-19
Brands:
Beanos's

2959 Conscious Choice Foods
1620 E. Highway 121
Building C, Suite 700
Lewisville, TX 75056
877-898-6158
Fax: 214-550-2682
consciouschoicefoods@gmail.com
www.consciouschoicefoods.com
Manufacturer of pickles.
CEO: Harold Callaway
Square Footage: 80000

2960 Consolidated Biscuit Company
312 Rader Rd
McComb, OH 45858
info@cbiscuits.com
www.cbiscuits.com
Cookies and crackers.
Estimated Sales: $400 Million
Number Employees: 2,500
Number of Brands: 4
Parent Co: Consolidated Biscuit Co. Ltd.
Brands:
Healthline
Devon
Tal-furnar
Sunshine Snacks

2961 Consolidated Catfish Co LLC
299 S St
P.O. Box 271
Isola, MS 38754
662-962-3101
Fax: 662-962-0114 sales@countryselect.com
www.countryselect.com
Seafood
President: Dick Stevens
dstevens@countryselect.com
VP of Controller: David Gray
VP: David Allen
VP of Marketing: Jack Perkins
VP of Sales: Joe Forrester
VP of Operations: Lee Parker
Year Founded: 1967
Estimated Sales: $123 Million
Number Employees: 250-499
Number of Brands: 1
Square Footage: 960000
Brands:
Country Select

2962 Consolidated Mills Inc
7190 Brittmoore Road
Suite 150
Houston, TX 77041
713-896-4196
Fax: 713-896-4199 Info@cmillsinc.com
www.consolidatedmills.com
Specializing in contract packaging and product solutions. Products include frozen drink bases, slush flavors, flavoring extracts, sundae toppings, sno-cone syrups and custom spice blends
President: Scott Vrana
cordner@cmillsinc.com
Executive Vice President: Keith Vrana
Director of Quality Assurances: Cheryl Meche
Customer Service Supervisor: Carol Kirchhoff
Purchasing/Acct. Receivables/Payables: Jo Piercy
Estimated Sales: $3 Million
Number Employees: 20-49
Square Footage: 60000
Parent Co: Consolidated Mills
Type of Packaging: Consumer, Food Service

2963 Consolidated Sea Products
250 N Water St
Suite 112
Mobile, AL 36602-4000
251-433-3240
Fax: 251-433-6721
Seafood
Owner/President: Paul William
Estimated Sales: $740k
Number Employees: 4

2964 Consumer Guild Foods Inc
5035 Enterprise Blvd
Toledo, OH 43612-3839
419-726-3406
Fax: 419-726-8771
Salad dressings and oils, mayonnaise, condiments and relishes
President: Wilbur Ascham
VP: Robert Petrick
Estimated Sales: $2.7 Million
Number Employees: 20-49
Type of Packaging: Consumer, Food Service, Private Label, Bulk
Brands:
Amhurst Kitchens
Annie's Supreme
Cg Supreme

2965 Consumers Packing Co
1301 Carson Dr
Melrose Park, IL 60160-2970
708-345-6780
Fax: 708-345-9052 800-356-9876
www.consumerspacking.com
Meat products
President: William Schutz
Finance Executive: Anthony Barone
VP Sales and Marketing: Mike Gale
Estimated Sales: $17 Million
Number Employees: 100-249

2966 Consumers Vinegar & Spice Co
4723 S Washtenaw Ave
Chicago, IL 60632
773-376-4100
info@cvsco.com
www.cvsco.com
Vinegar, spices and dehydrated garlic and onion
Estimated Sales: $5-10 Million
Number Employees: 10-19
Square Footage: 160000
Type of Packaging: Consumer, Food Service, Private Label, Bulk
Brands:
Burma
Consumers

2967 Conte's Pasta Co.
310 Wheat Rd
Vineland, NJ 08360
Fax: 856-697-1757 800-211-6607
customerservice@contespasta.com
contespasta.com
Pasta; sauce; and soup
Founder: Angela Conte
Year Founded: 1970
Number Employees: 11-50
Type of Packaging: Food Service, Private Label

2968 Continental Carbonic Products
2985 East Harrison Avenue
Decatur, IL 62526
217-428-2068
Fax: 217-424-2325 800-379-4232
www.continentalcarbonic.com
Specializes in the manufacture and distribution of dry ice and liquid carbon dioxide, along with sales and rental of dry ice blasting equipment.
President: John Funk
Vice President/Chief Financial Officer: Randy Spitz
General Manager, Manufacturing: Phil Wood
Vice President, Business Development: David Butts
Vice President, Distribution: Jason Taulbee
VP, Manufacturing & Distribution: Mark Hatton

2969 Continental Coffee Products Company
235 N Norwood St
Houston, TX 77011-2311
713-928-6281
Fax: 713-924-9870 800-323-6178
Coffee, tea
President: Peter JW Roorda
Sales Manager: Scott Kolber
Plant Manager: Dan Hickman
Number Employees: 175

2970 Continental Grain Company
787 5th Ave
15th Fl
New York, NY 10153-0015
212-207-5100
information@conti.com
www.continentalgrain.com
Grain, poultry, pork, beef, animal feed, aquaculture, and flour milling.
Directeur General: Charles Fribourg
Chairman & CEO: Paul J. Fribourg
CFO: Frank Baier
General Counsel: Michael Mayberry
Executive Vice President: David Tanner
COO: Robert Golden
Estimated Sales: $2.5 Billion
Number Employees: 11,000
Type of Packaging: Consumer, Bulk
Brands:
Chiatai Conti Group
Conti
ContiParaguay
Les Moulins D'Haiti
Moderna Alimentos
Molinos Champion S.A.
Santa Elena
Wayne Farms

2971 Continental Mills Inc
18100 Andover Park W
Tukwila, WA 98188-4703
206-816-7000
Fax: 253-872-7954 www.continentalmills.com
Manufacturer and exporter of baking products including dry flour mixes. Continental Mills has acquired the Pillsbury foodservice small package dry mix business from Best Brands Corporation
President: John Heily
CEO: John M Heily
jheily@continentalmills.com
CFO: Michael Castle
Vice President: Bob Wallach
Research & Development: Dan Donahue
Quality Control: Christy Johnson
Marketing Director: Steve Donley
Sales Director: Steve Giuditta
Public Relations: Clyde Walker
Operations Manager: Mark Harris
Production Manager: Mike Meredith
Year Founded: 1932
Estimated Sales: $43.2 Million
Number Employees: 100-249
Number of Brands: 10
Square Footage: 300000
Parent Co: Pillsbury Food Service
Type of Packaging: Consumer, Food Service, Private Label, Bulk
Brands:
Albers
Alpine
Ghirardelli

Kretschmer
Krusteaz
Krusteaz Professional
Old Country Store
Red Lobster
Snowqualmie Falls Lodge
Wild Roots

2972 Continental Sausage
911 E 75th Ave
Denver, CO 80229-6401
303-288-9787
Fax: 303-288-9789 866-794-7727
www.continentalsausage.com
Meats, sausage
Owner: Duane Garrison
dgarrison@llbean.com
Vice President/Treasurer: Ursula Gutknecht
Purchasing Manager: Eric Gutknecht
Estimated Sales: $2.5 Million
Number Employees: 5-9

2973 Continental Seasoning
1700 Palisade Ave
Teaneck, NJ 07666
201-837-6111
Fax: 201-837-9248 800-631-1564
Processor, importer and exporter of sauces, spices, seasonings and food additives
President: Pete Federer
CFO: Jeffrey Bovit
Vice President: Edward Levine
Quality Control: Marty Haas
VP Production: Ann Davis
Plant Manager: Steve Wagner
Estimated Sales: $5 Million
Number Employees: 50
Square Footage: 80000
Type of Packaging: Food Service, Private Label, Bulk

2974 Continental Yogurt
1358 E Colorado Street
Glendale, CA 91205-1474
818-240-7400
Fax: 818-243-3601
Yogurt
Principal: Martha Frazier
Sales Manager: Gary Correll
Purchasing Agent: Juan Garcia
Estimated Sales: $1-3 Million
Number Employees: 10-19
Type of Packaging: Food Service

2975 Conway Import Co Inc
11051 Addison Street
Franklin Park, IL 60131
800-323-8801
info@conwaydressings.com
www.conwaydressings.com
High quality salad dressing and sauce pods for the finest hoels, airlines, cruiselines, and restaurants.
Owner/Vice President, Operations: Gregg Heineman
conwaydressings@mindspring.com
Founder: Albert Heineman
VP Marketing & Sales: Robert Burns
Number Employees: 50-99
Number of Products: 370+
Square Footage: 240000
Type of Packaging: Food Service, Private Label, Bulk

2976 Cook Inlet Processing
909 W 9th Ave
Anchorage, AK 99501-3322
907-243-1166
Fax: 907-243-4231
Manufacturer of fresh seafood, frozen seafood, and canned seafood
Sales Manager: Mike Shupe
VP Operations: Tim Blott
Year Founded: 1977
Estimated Sales: $1-3 Million
Number Employees: 1-4

2977 Cook Natural Products
260 Lafayette Circle
Lafayette, CA 94549
925-283-6897
Fax: 925-283-6086 800-537-7589
www.cooknaturally.com
Organic flour, grains, seeds, beans
President: Brenda McEntee
Estimated Sales: $12 Million
Number Employees: 10-19

2978 Cook's Gourmet Foods
5821 Wilderness Avenue
Riverside, CA 92504
951-352-5700
Fax: 951-352-5710
Co-packers of gourmet foods
President: Tom Harris Jr
General Manager: Tommy Harris
Vice President: Richard Harris
Production Planner: Mike Elsman
Plant Supervisor: Ken Lujan
Estimated Sales: $500,000-$1 Million
Number Employees: 50-99

2979 Cook's Pantry
4125 Market St
Suite 1
Ventura, CA 93003
805-947-4622
cookspantry.com
Spreads, sauces, sauerkrauts and pickles
President/Owner: Matt Hately
Number of Brands: 1
Number of Products: 20
Type of Packaging: Consumer
Brands:
COOK'S PANTRY ORGANIC

2980 Cook-In-The-Kitchen
PO Box 8
Hampden, ME 04444
207-848-4900
Fax: 207-848-4988 www.cookinthekitchen.com
All natural pancake, bakery and soup mixes.
President: Mary Spata
VP/General Manager: Murray Burk
Estimated Sales: $1-2.5 Million
Number Employees: 3
Number of Products: 20
Type of Packaging: Consumer, Private Label

2981 Cooke Aguaculture
874 Main Street
Blacks Harbour, NB E5H-1E6
Canada
506-456-6600
Fax: 506-456-6652 nhalse@cookeaqua.com
www.cookeaqua.com
Distributor of fresh and smoked salmon.
CEO: Glenn Cooke
CFO: Peter Buck
VP Marketing: Jean Lamontagne
VP Sales: Alan Craig
VP Public Relations/Communications: Neil Halse
Purchasing Director: Don Bourque
Number Employees: 20-49
Number of Brands: 3
Number of Products: 60
Square Footage: 10000
Brands:
Appledore
Horton's

2982 Cooke Tavern LTD
4158 Penns Valley Rd
Spring Mills, PA 16875-8306
814-422-7687
Fax: 814-422-8752 866-422-7687
gregw@cooketavernsoups.com
www.cooketavernsoups.com
Soups
President/Owner: Greg Williams
gregw@cooketavernsoups.com
Estimated Sales: Less Than $500,000
Number Employees: 5-9

2983 Cookie Factory
1844 Givan Ave
Bronx, NY 10469-3155
718-379-6223
Fax: 718-379-4417 ggcookies@aol.com
www.thecookiefactory.com
Cookies, cakes and Italian pastries
President: Rose Florio
ggcookies@aol.com
VP: Salvatore Florio Jr
VP Sales: Sal Florio
Finance Executive: Pete Russo
VP Production: Joan Florio
Estimated Sales: $2.5-5 Million
Number Employees: 20-49
Brands:
Mama Rose

2984 Cookie Kingdom
1201 E Walnut St
Oglesby, IL 61348-1344
815-883-3331
Fax: 815-883-3332 ckingdomoffice@gmail.com
www.cookiekingdom.com
Manufacturer of cookies, ice cream wafers and dairy inclusions; co-packer for private label companies; and builder and upgrader of dairy equipment for lease or purchase.
President: Cliff Sheppard
ckingdom@ivnet.com
Director: Patty Smith
Estimated Sales: $13 Million
Number Employees: 100-249
Type of Packaging: Consumer, Private Label, Bulk

2985 Cookie Specialties Inc
482 N Milwaukee Ave
Wheeling, IL 60090-3067
847-537-3888
Fax: 847-537-6709 matt@mattscookies.com
www.mattscookies.info
Cookies
President: Grant Pierce
VP: Matthew Pierce
Contact: Fran Burke
franburke@mattscookies.info
Estimated Sales: $10-20 Million
Number Employees: 10-19
Type of Packaging: Consumer, Food Service, Private Label
Brands:
Matt's Cookies

2986 Cookie Tree Bakeries
4010 W Advantage Circle
Salt Lake City, UT 84104
801-268-2253
www.cookietree.com
Frozen gourmet cookies and cookie dough; also, fat-free available.
Purchasing: Wayne Davis
Year Founded: 1981
Estimated Sales: $20-50 Million
Type of Packaging: Consumer, Food Service, Private Label, Bulk
Brands:
Cookietree Bakeries

2987 Cookies By Design Inc
1865 Summit Ave # 607
Plano, TX 75074-8185
972-398-9536
Fax: 972-398-9542 888-675-1453
customerservice@cookiesbydesign.com
www.cookiesbydesign.com
Cookies and baked goods
Founder: Gwen Wilhite
Contact: Jolene Day
jday@cookiesbydesign.com
Number Employees: 20-49

2988 Cookies Food Products
PO Box 458
Wall Lake, IA 51466
712-664-2437
Fax: 712-664-2675 800-331-4995
www.cookiesbbq.com
Barbecue and taco sauces
President: Speed Herrig
Purchasing Manager: Jeff Herrig
Estimated Sales: $10-20 Million
Number Employees: 10-19
Square Footage: 122000
Type of Packaging: Consumer, Food Service
Brands:
Cookies

2989 Cookies United
141 Freeman Ave
Islip, NY 11751-1428
631-581-4000
Fax: 631-581-4510 info@cookiesunited.com
Manufacturer and national marketer of branded and private label baked goods.
President: Joseph Vitarelli
joseph@silverlakecookie.com
Number Employees: 250-499
Type of Packaging: Consumer, Food Service, Private Label, Bulk

2990 Cookiezen, LLC
Po Box 2519
Falls Church, VA 22042-0519
703-389-9274
Fax: 866-496-6034
Cookies
Marketing: Laura Englander
Contact: Emma May
emmamay@cookiezen.com

2991 Cookshack
2304 N Ash St
Ponca City, OK 74601-1109
580-765-3669
Fax: 580-765-2223 800-423-0698
info@cookshack.com www.cookshack.com
Sauces & spices, smoking wood accessories for better barbeque, Cookshack smoked foods cookbooks, electric smoker ovens, pellet fired smokes, charbroilers, pellet grills
President: Brent Matthews
CEO: Sara Birch
j.kenney@varde.com
VP: Edward Aguiar Jr
Marketing Coordinator: Cayley Armstrong
Finance/Marketing/Sales Manager: John Shiflet
General Manager: Stuart Powell
Production Manager: Jim Linnebur
Estimated Sales: $4 Million
Number Employees: 20-49
Number of Brands: 2
Number of Products: 1
Square Footage: 44000
Type of Packaging: Consumer, Food Service, Private Label, Bulk
Brands:
Fast Eddy's

2992 Cool
801 E Campbell Rd # 348
Richardson, TX 75081-1866
972-437-9352
Fax: 972-644-7231
Sodas and sports drinks
Manager: Dan C Cole
Estimated Sales: $500-1,000,000 appx.
Number Employees: 1-4
Brands:
Cool Natural Sodas
Cool Quencher Sports

2993 (HQ)Cool Brands International
4175 Veteran's Memorial Highway
3rd Floor
Ronkonkoma, NY 11779
631-737-9700
Fax: 631-737-9792
Ice cream and ice cream novelties
President/CEO: David Kewer
General Manager: Antonio Brooks
Number Employees: 20-49
Parent Co: CoolBrands International

2994 Cool Mountain BeveragesInc
1065 E Prairie Ave
Des Plaines, IL 60016-3341
847-759-9330
Fax: 847-789-8575 888-838-7632
coolmountn@aol.com www.coolmountain.com
Produces gourmet flavored sodas.
President: Bill Daker
Estimated Sales: $3-5 Million
Number Employees: 5-9
Brands:
Cool Mountain Gourmet Soda

2995 Coolhaus
8588 Washington Blvd
Culver City, CA 90232
310-853-8995
info@cool.haus
cool.haus
Premium ice cream and ice cream sandwiches
Owner: Natasha Case
Owner: Freya Estreller
Estimated Sales: Less Than $500,000
Number Employees: 5-9

2996 Coombs Family Farm
P.O. Box 117
Brattleboro, VT 05302
888-266-6271
coombsfamilyfarms.com
Maple syrup, sugar, candy, baking mixes, and gift baskets.
Co-Owner: Bruce Bascom
Co-Owner: Arnold Coombs
Estimated Sales: $30 Million
Number Employees: 10-19
Type of Packaging: Private Label

2997 Coon Creek Winery
8711 Silverado Trl S
St Helena, CA 94574-9577
707-963-5133
Fax: 707-963-7840 800-793-7960
info@conncreek.com www.conncreek.com
Wines
Director: Donna Duncanson
COO: David Lawrence
Manager: Paul Asikainen
paul.asikainen@conncreek.com
Number Employees: 10-19

2998 Cooper Farms Cooked Meats
6793 US Route 127
Van Wert, OH 45891-9601
419-238-4056
Fax: 419-238-1587 www.cooperfarms.com
Fresh turkey products
Chief Executive Officer: James Cooper
Treasurer: Anada Cooper
Chief Operating Officer: Gary Cooper
Estimated Sales: $500,000-999,999 Thousand
Number Employees: 100-249

2999 Cooper Lake Farm LLC
203 Cooper Lake Rd
Bearsville, NY 12409
845-679-7822
cooperlakefarm.com
Brittles and cheese
Owner: Gayle Burbank
gayleburbank@gmail.com
Owner: Ken Cohen

3000 Cooper Mountain Vineyards
9480 SW Grabhorn Road
Beaverton, OR 97007
503-649-0027
Fax: 503-649-0702
info@coopermountainwine.com
www.coopermountainwine.com
Wines
Owner: Robert J. Gross
Sales & Marketing Manager: Barbara Gross
Sales Director: Susan Baltus
Winemaker: Rich Cushman
Estimated Sales: $1-2.5 Million
Number Employees: 5-9
Type of Packaging: Private Label

3001 Cooper Street Cookies
320 Martin St
Suite 100
Birmingham, MI 48009
248-283-7700
info@cooperstreetcookies.com
cooperstreetcookies.com
Cookies
President: Max Surnow
Year Founded: 2011
Estimated Sales: $450,000,00
Number Employees: 25
Type of Packaging: Private Label

3002 Cooper Vineyards
13372 Shannon Hill Rd
Louisa, VA 23093-3929
540-894-5474
Fax: 804-285-8773 Info@CooperVineyards.com
www.coopervineyards.com
Wine
Co-Owner: Jaque P. Hogge
Partner: Jacque Hogge
Estimated Sales: Less Than $500,000
Number Employees: 1-4

3003 Cooperative Elevator Co
7211 E Michigan Ave
Pigeon, MI 48755
989-453-3120
Fax: 989-453-3942 800-968-0601
www.coopelev.com
Dried beans
President/CEO: Pat Anderson
panderson@coopelev.com
Chairman: Kurt Ewald
VP Of Finance & Board Treasurer: Mike Wehner
VP of IT & Assistant Board Secretary: Barry Albrecht
Estimated Sales: $500,000-$1 Million
Number Employees: 100-249

3004 Cooperstown Cookie Company
P.O.Box 64
Cooperstown, NY 13326
888-269-7315
Fax: 607-547-2673 888-269-7315
www.cooperstowncookie.com
Baseball cookies
President/Owner: Pati Grady

3005 Copak Solutions
103b Somerset Dr NW
Conover, NC 28613-9217
828-261-0255
Fax: 828-261-0256
Manufacturer of chips.
President: Larry Deal
larry@copaksolutionsinc.net
Number Employees: 20-49
Square Footage: 80000

3006 Copper Hills Fruit Sales
4337 N Golden State Boulevard
Suite 102
Fresno, CA 93722-3801
559-432-5400
Fax: 559-432-5620
Packers of peaches, plums, nectarines, apricots, pomegranates, and persimmons
Managing Member: Wilma J. Deniz

3007 Copper Moon Coffee LLC
1503 Veterans Memorial Parkway East
Lafayette, IN 47905
317-541-9000
Fax: 317-543-0757 www.coppermooncoffee.com
Manufacturer of world coffee blends.
CEO: Brad Gutwein
Square Footage: 80000

3008 Copper Tank Brewing Company
504 Trinity Street
Austin, TX 78701-3714
512-854-9380
Fax: 512-478-1832
Seasonal beer, ale, stout, lager and porter
President: Aaron Scharff
Purchasing: Patrick Bradshaw
Estimated Sales: $2.5-5 Million
Number Employees: 50-99
Type of Packaging: Food Service

3009 Cora Italian Specialties
9630 Joliet Rd
Countryside, IL 60525-4138
708-482-4660
Fax: 708-482-4663 800-696-2672
info@corainc.com www.corainc.com
Monin syrups, Oregon chai, Guitiard and Ghirardelli chocolates, Mocafe, Jet tea etc
President: John Cora
jcora@corainc.com
Sales: Paul Rekstad
Estimated Sales: 1.80 Million
Number Employees: 10-19
Square Footage: 60000
Type of Packaging: Food Service
Brands:
Danesi
Dolce
Ghirardelli
Guittard
Jet Tea
Mocafe
Monin
Musetti
Nikola's Biscotti
Numi Tea
Oregon Chai
Soy Dream
White Wave

3010 **Cora Texas Mfg Co Inc**
32505 Highway 1
White Castle, LA 70788-3638
225-545-3679
Fax: 225-545-8360 info@coratexas.com
www.coratexas.com
Manufacturer of Louisiana raw sugar and molasses.
President/CEO: Paul Buckley Kessler
Chief Operating Officer/Secretary: Charles Schudmak
Year Founded: 1817
Estimated Sales: $20-50 Million
Number Employees: 100-249
Type of Packaging: Bulk

3011 **Coral LLC**
5576 Bighorn Dr # B
Carson City, NV 89701-1474
775-883-9853
Fax: 775-883-9858 800-882-9577
sales@coralcalcium.com www.coralcalcium.com
Natural minerals
Sales Director: Alberto Galdamez
Contact: Matt Cuhadar
matt@coralcalcium.com
Number Employees: 5-9

3012 **Corazonas Foods, Inc**
11900 West Olympic Boulevard
Suite 630
Los Angeles, CA 90064
310-622-9550
Fax: 310-622-9551 800-967-2451
Chips
Contact: Greg Fry
gfry@corazonas.com

3013 **Corbin Foods-Edibowls**
P.O.Box 28139
Santa Ana, CA 92799-8139
714-966-6695
Fax: 949-640-0279 800-695-5655
www.edibowls.com
Processor and exporter of edible bowls for salads, desserts and tarts; club packs available
Manager: R J Hill
Estimated Sales: $5-10 Million
Number Employees: 5-9
Square Footage: 400000
Type of Packaging: Consumer, Food Service, Bulk
Brands:
Edibowl

3014 **(HQ)Corbion**
7905 Quivira Rd
Lenexa, KS 66215-2732
913-890-5500
Fax: 913-888-4970 800-669-4092
foodsus@corbion.com www.corbion.com
Lactic acid, lactic acid derivatives and lactides; functional blends containing enzymes, emulsifiers, minerals, and vitamins; biobased products made from renewable resources and applied in global markets such as bakery, meat, food andbeverages.
CEO: Tjerk de Ruiter
Chief Financial Officer: Eddy van Rhede van der Kloot
Executive VP Biobased Ingredients: Andy Muller
Chief Technology Officer: Marcel Wubbolts
Vice President of Human Resources: Johan van der Hel
Executive Vice President of Operations: Jacqueline van Lemmen
Number Employees: 50-99
Parent Co: Corbion
Other Locations:
Manufacturing & Product Development
Totowa NJ
Manufacturing Facility
Grandview MO
Manufacturing Facility
East Rutherford NJ
Manufacturing Facility
Dolton IL
Manufacturing Facility
Blair NE
Manufacturing Facility
Tucker GA

3015 **Corbion**
100 Adams Dr
Totowa, NJ 07512
973-256-8886
800-526-5261
www.corbion.com
Lactic acid, lactic acid derivatives and lactides; functional blends containing enzymes, emulsifiers, minerals, and vitamins; biobased products made from renewable resources and applied in global markets such as bakery, meat, food andbeverages.

3016 **Corbion**
13830 Botts Rd
Grandview, MO 64030
816-763-8377
www.corbion.com
Lactic acid, lactic acid derivatives and lactides; functional blends containing enzymes, emulsifiers, minerals, and vitamins; biobased products made from renewable resources and applied in global markets such as bakery, meat, food andbeverages.

3017 **Corbion**
96 E Union Ave
East Rutherford, NJ 07073
800-526-5261
www.corbion.com
Lactic acid, lactic acid derivatives and lactides; functional blends containing enzymes, emulsifiers, minerals, and vitamins; biobased products made from renewable resources and applied in global markets such as bakery, meat, food andbeverages.

3018 **Corbion**
14622 Lakeside Ave
Dolton, IL 60419
708-849-8590
Fax: 708-849-3114 www.corbion.com
Lactic acid, lactic acid derivatives and lactides; functional blends containing enzymes, emulsifiers, minerals, and vitamins; biobased products made from renewable resources and applied in global markets such as bakery, meat, food andbeverages.

3019 **Corbion**
650 Industrial Park Dr
P.O. Box 38
Blair, NE 68008
402-426-0377
Fax: 402-533-1801 www.corbion.com
Lactic acid, lactic acid derivatives and lactides; functional blends containing enzymes, emulsifiers, minerals, and vitamins; biobased products made from renewable resources and applied in global markets such as bakery, meat, food andbeverages.

3020 **Corbion**
5150 N Royal Atlanta Dr
Tucker, GA 30084
470-545-7100
Fax: 470-545-7098 www.corbion.com
Lactic acid, lactic acid derivatives and lactides; functional blends containing enzymes, emulsifiers, minerals, and vitamins; biobased products made from renewable resources and applied in global markets such as bakery, meat, food andbeverages.

3021 **Corbion**
One Tower Place
Suite 6, 6th Floor
S San Francisco, CA 94080
www.corbion.com
Lactic acid, lactic acid derivatives and lactides; functional blends containing enzymes, emulsifiers, minerals, and vitamins; biobased products made from renewable resources and applied in global markets such as bakery, meat, food andbeverages.

3022 **Corbion**
2500 Meadowpine Blvd
Unit 3
Mississauga, ON L5N 6C4
Canada
905-826-1089
Fax: 905-826-8432 800-324-8802
www.corbion.com
Lactic acid, lactic acid derivatives and lactides; functional blends containing enzymes, emulsifiers, minerals, and vitamins; biobased products made from renewable resources and applied in global markets such as bakery, meat, food andbeverages.

3023 **Corbion**
Av. Insurgentes Sur 1787 Piso 8
Col. Guadalupe Inn
Ciudad de Mexico, CP., 01020
Mexico
pmx@corbion.com
www.corbion.com
Lactic acid, lactic acid derivatives and lactides; functional blends containing enzymes, emulsifiers, minerals, and vitamins; biobased products made from renewable resources and applied in global markets such as bakery, meat, food andbeverages.

3024 **Corby Distilleries**
225 King Street West
Suite 1100
Toronto, ON M5V 3M2
Canada
416-479-2400
Fax: 416-369-9809 800-367-9079
corbyweb@adsw.com www.corby.ca
Whiskey, Scotch whiskey, Irish whiskey, bourbon, rum, gin, vodka, tequila, cognac and brandy.
President/CEO: Patrick O'Driscoll
VP/CFO: Thierry Pourchet
VP Marketing: Jeff Agdern
VP Sales: Andy Alexander
VP SP/Customer Service: Chris Chan
VP Production: Jim Stanski
Number Employees: 100-249
Number of Brands: 45
Parent Co: Allied Lyons
Type of Packaging: Consumer, Food Service
Brands:
Ballantine's Finest
Barclay's
Beefeater Dry
Belvedere
Canadian Club
Chopin
Courvoisier
D'Eaubonne Vsop Napoleon
De Kuyper Geneva
Glendronach
Hornitos Sauza
Lamb's Navy
Lamb's Palm Breeze
Lamb's White
Laphroaig
Lemon Hart
Maker's Mark
Malibu Coconut Rum
Polar Ice Tassel
Revelstoke
Royal Reserve
Sauza Commemorativo
Sauza Extra Gold
Sauza Silver
Sauza Triada
Scapa Single Malt
Silk Tassel
Special Old
Stolichnaya
Stolichnaya Razberi
Stolichnaya Red
Stolichnaya Vanil
Teacher's Highland Cream
Tres Generaciones
Tullamore Dew
Wiser's Deluxe
Wiser's Special Blend
Wiser's Very Old

3025 **Cordoba Foods LLC**
15912 NW 48th Avenue
Hialeah, FL 33014-6410
786-202-2988
sales@gauchoranchfoods.com
www.gauchoranchfoods.com
Condiments, BBQ sauce, ethnic sauces (soy, curry, etc.), grilling sauces, marinades, other sauces, seasonings and cooking enhancers, dessert toppings (i.e. fudge sauce, caramel sauce, whipped cream, etc.) other spreads & syrup.

3026 **Cordon Bleu International**
8383 Rue J Rene Ouimet
Anjou, QC H1J 2P8
Canada
514-352-3000
Fax: 514-352-3226 800-363-1182
info@cordonbleu.ca www.cordonbleu.ca
Processor and exporter of pickled food products, sauces, gravies, chicken broth, meat pates, beef and chicken entrees and red kidney beans in tomato sauce.
Director Advertising/Promotions: Michelle Guibord
Director Sales: Jacques LeGare
Purchasing: Kristen Gerard
Number Employees: 100-249
Parent Co: J-R Ouimet

Type of Packaging: Consumer, Private Label

3027 **Corea Lobster Cooperative**
191 Crowley Island Rd
Corea, ME 04624
207-963-7936
Fax: 207-963-5952
Processors of lobsters
President: Michael Hunt
Treasurer: F.D. Rodgers
VP: Gary Moore
Estimated Sales: $1.5 Million
Number Employees: 4

3028 **(HQ)Corfu Foods Inc**
755 Thomas Dr
Bensenville, IL 60106-1624
630-595-2510
Fax: 630-595-3884 info@corfufoods.com
www.corfufoods.com
Processor and exporter of pita bread, honey mustard sauce and beef and chicken gyro products including cones, patties, deli kits, sauce and loaves; importer of cheese, olives and stuffed grape leaves.
President: Vasilios Memmos
vmemmos@corfufoods.com
VP: Sophie Maroulis
Purchasing Agent: Ron Fallot
Estimated Sales: $10-20 Million
Number Employees: 50-99
Square Footage: 140000
Other Locations:
Corfu Foods
Long Island City NY
Brands:
Corfu
Gyros Usa
Omega
Tasty

3029 **Corfu Foods Inc**
755 Thomas Dr
Bensenville, IL 60106-1624
630-595-2510
Fax: 630-595-3884 800-874-9767
www.corfufoods.com
Gyros
President: Vasilios Memmos
vmemmos@corfufoods.com
Estimated Sales: $10-20 Million
Number Employees: 50-99

3030 **Corim Industries Inc**
1112 Industrial Pkwy
Brick, NJ 08724-2508
732-840-1640
Fax: 732-840-1608 800-942-4201
sales@corimindustries.com
www.corimindustries.com
Manufacturer, wholesaler and exporter of gourmet coffees, custom printed sugar packets, instant cappuccino, chai, and soluble milk for vending machines, custom blending and supplies, and also custom branding for private labelsuppliers.
President: Nathan Teren
nathan.teren@marinemax.com
CEO: Sam Teren
Treasurer/Controller: Nathan Teren
Estimated Sales: $2.1 Million
Number Employees: 20-49
Square Footage: 41672
Type of Packaging: Consumer, Food Service, Private Label, Bulk

3031 **Corine's Cuisine**
Sparks, MD 21152
www.corinescuisine.com
Gourmet sauces
Owner: Corine Parish
Type of Packaging: Private Label

3032 **Corky's Ribs & BBQ**
3584 Parkway
Pigeon Forge, TN 37863
865-453-7427
www.corkysbbq.com
Frozen barbecue ribs, pork shoulders and beef brisket
Owner: Barry Pelts
barry@corkysbbq.com
CEO: Andrew Woodman
Principal: Don Pelts
Estimated Sales: $5-10 Million
Number Employees: 100-249
Type of Packaging: Consumer, Food Service

3033 **Cormier Rice Milling CoInc**
501 W 3rd St
De Witt, AR 72042-2500
870-946-3561
Fax: 870-946-3029 www.cormierrice.com
Processor and exporter of long and medium grain, milled, brown and organic brown rice
Owner: Robert Ellis
robert@cormierrice.com
Vice President: Julie Simpson
VP: J Ferguson
Estimated Sales: $10-20 Million
Number Employees: 10-19
Type of Packaging: Consumer, Food Service, Private Label, Bulk
Brands:
Lone Pine
Regal
Snow Goose

3034 **Corn Popper**
5584 S Garnett Rd
Tulsa, OK 74146-6814
918-250-9317
Fax: 918-250-7148 www.cornpopper.com
Flavored, organic and plain popcorn.
Owner: Brad Berry
brad@cornpopper.com
CFO: Betty Melton
General Manager: Jose Alves
Estimated Sales: Less Than $500,000
Number Employees: 1-4
Parent Co: Corn Poppers
Brands:
Popcorn Dippers

3035 **Cornabys**
421 S 200 E
Spanish Fork, UT 84660-2418
801-830-4530
Fax: 801-423-7838 janetstocks@cornabys.com
www.fruitivia.com
Jams & jellies.
Marketing: Janet Stocks

3036 **Cornell Beverages Inc**
105 Harrison Pl
Brooklyn, NY 11237-1403
718-381-3000
Fax: 718-381-3001
Carbonated soft drinks
President: Allan Hoffman
allan@cornellbev.com
Treasurer: Donna Hoffman
Purchasing: Jim Dehaan
Estimated Sales: $850,000
Number Employees: 20-49
Brands:
Cornell Beverages

3037 **Cornfields Inc**
3898 Sunset Ave
Waukegan, IL 60087-3258
847-263-7000
Fax: 847-263-7090 jbweiler@cornfieldsinc.com
www.cornfieldsinc.com
Chips, nuts, popcorn, pretzels, puffed snacks.
Sales/Marketing: J.B. Weiler
Manager: Henry Cretors
ccretors@cornfieldsinc.com
Number Employees: 1-4

3038 **Corning Olive Oil Company**
721 Fig Lane
Corning, CA 90621
530-824-5447
Fax: 530-824-5862 sales@corningoliveoil.com
www.corningoliveoil.com
Olive oils
President: John Psyllos
Number Employees: 12

3039 **Corona College Heights**
8000 Lincoln Ave
Riverside, CA 92504-4343
951-351-7880
Fax: 951-689-5115 www.cchcitrus.org
Processor and exporter of oranges, lemons and grapefruit.
Director: Thomas Chao
Vice President, Field Operations: Ruben Gutierrez
Export Sales Manager: Jessica Chavez
Plant Manager: Brad Tilden
Estimated Sales: $35 Million
Number Employees: 100-249
Square Footage: 180000
Type of Packaging: Consumer, Bulk

3040 **Corrin Produce Sales**
23667 E Dinuba Ave
Dinuba, CA 93618
559-596-0517
Fax: 559-638-8508
Grower and exporter of fresh fruit including peaches, plums, nectarines and table grapes; also, raisins
President: Harold Seitz
CFO: Robert Greiner
Manager: Lisa Macedo
Estimated Sales: $400,000
Number Employees: 5
Type of Packaging: Bulk

3041 **Corsair Pepper Sauce**
1110 42nd Avenue
Gulfport, MS 39501-2663
228-452-0311
Fax: 228-452-0152
Pickled fruits and vegetables, vegetable sauces and seasonings and salad dressings.
President: Martha Murphy
Estimated Sales: $120,000
Number Employees: 2

3042 **Corsetti's Pasta Products**
1001 N Evergreen Ave
Woodbury, NJ 08096-3557
856-853-0999
Fax: 856-853-7438 800-989-1188
Various pasta products such as lasagna and spaghetti.
Owner: Dan Pellegrino
Plant & Purchasing Manager: Michael Corsetti
Estimated Sales: $2.5-5,000,000
Number Employees: 5-9
Type of Packaging: Bulk

3043 **Corso's Cookies**
314 Lakeside Rd
Syracuse, NY 13209-9729
315-487-2111
Fax: 315-487-4208 800-465-7775
customerservice@corsoscookies.com
www.corsoscookies.com
Cookies and baked goods
CEO: Peter Hess
peter@corsoscookies.com
Number Employees: 20-49

3044 **Corteva Agriscience**
P.O. Box 80735
Chestnut Run Plaza 735
Wilmington, DE 19805-0735
302-485-3000
www.corteva.com
Agricultural chemicals, seeds and software/digital solutions for farmers.
CEO: James Collins
Executive VP/CFO: Greg Friedman
Senior VP/General Counsel: Cornel Fuerer
Executive VP/Chief Commercial Officer: Tim Glenn
Senior VP, Enterprise Operations: Susan Lewis
Year Founded: 2019
Estimated Sales: $14 Billion
Parent Co: Corteva Agriscience

3045 **Cosco International**
1826 N Lorel Ave
Chicago, IL 60639-4376
773-889-1400
Fax: 773-889-0854 800-621-4549
Flavors.
President: Patrick Carney
CFO: Joe Hughes
Purchasing Agent: Ken Ciukowski
Estimated Sales: $1-$2.5 Million
Number Employees: 20-49
Brands:
Apple Sidra
Cosco Flavors

3046 **Cosentino Winery**
7415 Saint Helena Highway
Napa, CA 94558
707-921-2809
Fax: 707-944-2609 800-764-1220
finewines@cosentinowinery.com
www.cosentinowinery.com
Fine red and white wines.
President: Mitch Cosentino
CEO: Larry Soldinger
Marketing Director: Shawn Lutwalla
Public Relations: Julie Weinstock
Estimated Sales: $5-10 Million
Number Employees: 25
Type of Packaging: Private Label

3047 **Cosgrove Distributors Inc**
120 S Greenwood St
Spring Valley, IL 61362-2014
815-664-4121
Fax: 815-663-1433 800-347-3071
www.cosgrovedistributors.com
Wholesaler/distributor of general line products; serving the food service market.
President: Nora Cosgrove
cosgroves@insightbb.com
Estimated Sales: $2.5-5 Million
Number Employees: 20-49

3048 **Cosmo Food Products**
200 Callegari Dr
P.O. Box 256
West Haven, CT 06516-6234
203-933-9323
Fax: 203-937-7283 800-942-6766
claudano@cosmosfoods.com
www.cosmosfoods.com
Processor, packer and importer of olives, artichokes, capers, peppers, marinated mushrooms and roasted peppers; also, sun-dried tomatoes, hot cherry peppers, pepperoncini and garlic.
President: Cosmo Laudano
claudano@cosmosfoods.com
VP: Lisa Laudano
Sales Manager: Mario Laudano
Production: Peter Merola
Estimated Sales: $5-10 Million
Number Employees: 20-49
Number of Products: 39
Square Footage: 90000
Type of Packaging: Consumer, Food Service, Private Label, Bulk
Brands:
Cosmo's

3049 **Cosmopolitan Foods**
138 Essex Avenue
Glen Ridge, NJ 07028-2409
973-680-4560
Sauces such as BBQ, Worcestershire and Spaghetti
President: Nick Ten Velde
Purchasing Manager: Nick Ten Velde
Number Employees: 5-9

3050 **Costa Deano's Gourmet Foods**
PO Box 6367
Canton, OH 44706-0367
330-453-1555
Fax: 330-453-9766 800-337-2823
Processor and exporter of gourmet pasta sauces
President: Dean Bacopoulos
VP: Bill Bacopoulos
Number Employees: 5-9
Square Footage: 60000
Parent Co: Costa Deano's Enterprises
Type of Packaging: Consumer, Food Service, Private Label, Bulk
Brands:
Costa Deano's

3051 **Costa Macaroni Manufacturing**
PO Box 32308
Los Angeles, CA 90032-0308
Fax: 323-225-1667 800-433-7785
www.costapasta.com
Homemade various shapes and sizes of pastas
West Coast Sales Manager: Stephen Zoccoli
VP Foodservice Sales: Buzz Weisman
Estimated Sales: $5-10 Million
Number Employees: 20-49
Type of Packaging: Food Service, Bulk
Brands:
Costa

3052 **CostaDeano's Enterprises**
PO Box 6367
Canton, OH 44706-0367
330-453-1555
Fax: 330-493-9766
Producer of gourmet foods.
President: Dean Bacopoulos
Estimated Sales: $5-10,000,000
Number Employees: 20-49
Square Footage: 10
Type of Packaging: Private Label
Brands:
Costadeanos Gourmet

3053 **Costas Pasta**
2045 Attic Pkwy NW
Kennesaw, GA 30152-7610
770-514-8814
Fax: 770-514-9766
Fresh pasta
Owner: Joseph Costa
CFO: Joe Costa
Vice President: Stephen Zoccoli
Sales Director: Stephen Saferite
joe@costapasta.com
Estimated Sales: $2.5-5 Million
Number Employees: 5-9
Brands:
Costa's Pasta

3054 **Cotswold Cottage Foods**
9820 W 60th Ave
Arvada, CO 80004
303-423-2987
Fax: 303-423-2987 800-208-1977
cotscotfds@aol.com
Scone mixes, gingerbread mixes, stuffing mixes, lemon curd, jams, and tea
President: Tricia Mackell
Estimated Sales: $300,000-500,000
Number Employees: 5-9
Type of Packaging: Consumer

3055 **Cottage Street Pasta**
167 S Main Street
Barre, VT 05641-4813
802-476-4024
pastajules@aol.com
Fresh pasta and ravioli.
Purchasing Agent: Karen Gordon
Estimated Sales: $300,000-500,000
Number Employees: 1-4

3056 **Cotton Baking Company**
3400 S. Macarthur Drive
Alexandria, LA 71302
318-448-6600
Fax: 318-747-0118
Manufacturer of baked products.
Plant Manager: Don Thomas
Sales Manager: Slade Cooper
Estimated Sales: $20-50 Million
Number Employees: 20-49
Type of Packaging: Consumer
Brands:
Holsum Bread
Wonder Bread

3057 **Cottonwood Canyon Vineyard**
3940 Dominion Rd
Santa Maria, CA 93454-9678
805-937-8463
Fax: 805-937-8418 info@cottonwoodcanyon.com
www.cottonwoodcanyon.com
Wine
Owner/Winemaker: Norman Beko
xlntpno@earthlink.net
VP: Stephen Beko
Estimated Sales: $1-2.5 Million
Number Employees: 10-19
Number of Products: 24
Brands:
Cottonwood Canyon

3058 **Couch's Country Style Sausages**
4750 Osborn Rd
Cleveland, OH 44128-3138
216-823-2332
Fax: 216-663-3311
Sausage including pork, beef and turkey
President: Ludie Couch
Manager: Stanley Redd
Estimated Sales: $500,000-$1 Million
Number Employees: 1 to 4
Square Footage: 10500
Type of Packaging: Consumer, Bulk

3059 **Cougar Mountain Baking Co**
4224 24th Ave W
Seattle, WA 98199-1216
206-467-5044
Fax: 206-467-0993 877-328-2622
comments@cougar-mountain.com
www.cookieman.com
Producers of bakery products.
Owner: David Saulnier
david@cougar-mountain.com
Customer Service: Dana Pantley
Estimated Sales: $300,000-500,000
Number Employees: 20-49
Brands:
Cougar Mountain

3060 **Coulter Giufre & Co Inc**
8579 Lakeport Rd
Chittenango, NY 13037-9577
315-687-6510
Fax: 315-687-6637
Processor and exporter of produce including onions and turf grass
Owner: Chris Coulter
Estimated Sales: $3-5 Million
Number Employees: 5-9
Brands:
Bulls Eye

3061 **Counter Culture Coffee**
812 Mallard Ave
Durham, NC 27701
919-361-5282
888-238-5282
counterculturecoffee.com
Coffee
Coffee Buyer: Chelsea Thoumsin
Year Founded: 1995

3062 **Countertop Productions**
Alexandria, VA 22304
www.sparkbites.net
Vegan protein bars
Founder: Warren Brown
Number of Products: 5
Brands:
Spark Bites

3063 **Country Archer Jerky Co.**
379 E Industrial Rd
San Bernardino, CA 92408
909-370-0155
info@countryarcher.com
www.countryarcher.com
Beef jerky and protein bars
Co-Founder: Eugene Kang
Co-Founder: Susan Kang
Marketing Director: Mathew Thalakotur
VP, Sales: Tim Bateman
COO/CFO: Jeremy White
Year Founded: 1977
Number of Brands: 1
Number of Products: 15
Type of Packaging: Consumer
Brands:
COUNTRY ARCHER BEEF JERKY

3064 **Country Bob's Inc**
24000 N US Highway 51
Centralia, IL 62801-8992
618-533-2375
Fax: 618-533-7828 800-373-2140
www.countrybobs.com
Producers of sauces and seasonings.
President: Nate Edison
nate@countrybobs.com
Estimated Sales: $2.5-5 Million
Number Employees: 10-19

3065 **Country Butcher Shop**
286 Mcallister Church Rd
Carlisle, PA 17015-9504
717-249-4691
Fax: 573-769-4652 800-272-9223
www.countrybutchershopinc.com
Processor and distributor of lamb, beef and pork.
Owner: Mary Finkenbinder
finkenbinder@socket.net

Estimated Sales: $10-20 Million
Number Employees: 5-9
Type of Packaging: Private Label

3066 Country Choice Organic
9531 W 78th St # 230
Eden Prairie, MN 55344-8000
952-829-8824
Fax: 952-833-2090
jocelyneg@countrychoiceorganic.com
www.countrychoiceorganic.com
Organic hot cereals, cookies and cocoas.
Chief Cookie Officer: John DePaolis
Director of R&D: Sharon Herzog
Sales Director: Jocelyne Gregg
Contact: Dawn Braam
dawnb@countrychoiceorganic.com
Number of Brands: 1
Number of Products: 35
Type of Packaging: Consumer
Brands:
Country Choice

3067 Country Club Bakery
1211 Country Club Rd
Fairmont, WV 26554-2318
304-363-5690
Fax: 304-363-6099 www.hollyeats.com
Bread, sandwich rolls, hoagie buns and pepperoni rolls
Owner: Chris Pallotta
Estimated Sales: $5-10 Million
Number Employees: 5-9
Type of Packaging: Consumer, Food Service

3068 Country Clubs Famous Desserts
83 Bustleton Pike
Feasterville Trevose, PA 19053-6465
215-322-0700
Fax: 215-322-1534 800-843-2253
Desserts
Owner: Brian Rothaus
Marketing Executive: Steve Merchant
VP Sales: Bruce Davidsen
Estimated Sales: $20-50 Million
Number Employees: 50-99

3069 Country Cupboard
101 Hafer Rd
Lewisburg, PA 17837-7408
570-523-3211
Fax: 570-524-9299 info@countrycupboardinc.com
www.mattyssporthouse.com
Dehydrated soups, pastas, rices, sauces, relish, jams, beans, sugar-free chocolates, cornbread, honey and salsa, among other products.
Owner: Nicole Edinger
nicicci@dejazzd.com
CEO: Chris Baylor
General Manager: Steve Kulhavy
Events Coordinator: Melissa Swartz
Estimated Sales: $5-10 Million
Number Employees: 250-499

3070 Country Delite Farms LLC
1401 Church St
Nashville, TN 37203-3428
615-320-1440
Fax: 615-329-3017 800-232-4791
www.deanfoods.com
Dairy products
General Manager: Mark Ezell
Marketing Director: Jim Greaving
Public Relations: Royce McClintock
Operations Manager: Charles Hilton
Plant Manager: Eric Steer
Estimated Sales: $25-49.9 Million
Number Employees: 100-249
Brands:
Country Delight

3071 Country Estate Pecans
1020 West Front Street
Goldwaite, TX 76844
325-648-2200
800-473-2267
retail@pecans.com www.pecans.com
Fresh shelled pecans, inshell pecans, gourmet pecans, and many other unique items
President: Liz Alexander
General Manager: DeWayne McCasland
Year Founded: 1972
Estimated Sales: $20-50 Million
Number Employees: 4
Parent Co: Fermers Investment
Type of Packaging: Private Label

3072 Country Foods
46835 US Highway 93
Polson, MT 59860-7586
406-883-4384
Fax: 406-883-3275 info@countrypasta.com
Manufacturers of pasta.
President: Heather Knutson
knutsonheather@hotmail.com
Vice President: Linda Knutson
Marketing Director: Dan Johnson
Operations Manager: Gary Ivory
Estimated Sales: $2.5-5 Million
Number Employees: 20-49
Type of Packaging: Private Label
Brands:
Country Pasta

3073 Country Fresh
2555 Buchanan Ave SW
Grand Rapids, MI 49548
616-243-0173
www.enjoycountryfresh.com
Milk, flavored milk, teas & juices, cream, cottage cheese, sour cream & dips, ice cream & frozen novelties.
CEO, Dean Foods Company: Ralph Scozzafava
Year Founded: 1946
Parent Co: Dean Foods Company
Type of Packaging: Consumer, Private Label

3074 (HQ)Country Fresh Farms
432 W 3440 S
Salt Lake City, UT 84115
801-263-6667
Fax: 801-269-9666 800-878-0099
www.bluechipgroup.net
Producers of whey drinks, dairy products and dry mixes.
President: George Moo
CFO: Mike Leonard
Contact: Samuel Howard
howards@domo.com
Estimated Sales: $5 Million
Number Employees: 23
Square Footage: 42400
Type of Packaging: Consumer, Food Service, Private Label, Bulk
Other Locations:
Country Fresh Farms
Livonia MI
Country Fresh Farms
Grand Rapids MI
Brands:
Country Fresh Farms
Swiss Whey D'Lite

3075 Country Fresh Food & Confections, Inc.
405 Main Street
Po Box 604
Oliver Springs, TN 37840
865-435-2655
Fax: 865-435-1930 800-545-8782
info@countryfreshfood.com
www.countryfreshfood.com
Country Fresh Fudge, regular & sugar-free, Pamela Ann Classic Confections, Jim Bean Fudge, Kahula Fudge, Papa Joe's Downhome Gourmet.
President: Edward Stockton
Estimated Sales: $1-2.5 Million
Number Employees: 20-49
Number of Brands: 6
Number of Products: 150
Square Footage: 32000
Type of Packaging: Consumer, Food Service, Private Label, Bulk
Brands:
Country Fresh
Country Fresh Fudge
Papa Joe's Downhome

3076 Country Fresh Inc
3200 Research Forest Dr
Spring, TX 77381
281-453-3300
Fax: 281-453-3304
customerservice@countryfreshinc.com
www.countryfreshinc.com
Fresh-cut fruit, apple slices, vegetable and snacks.
Owner: Bryan Herr
Number Employees: 50
Type of Packaging: Consumer, Private Label

3077 Country Fresh Mushroom Co
289 Chambers Rd
PO Box 490
Toughkenamon, PA 19374
610-268-3033
Fax: 610-268-0479 bbesix@cfmushroom.com
www.cfmushroom.com
Processor of mushrooms including exotic, fresh, processed, whole and sliced.
Chairman/CEO: Edward Leo
President/COO: Laura Matar
SVP, Sales & Marketing: Bob Besix
Director, Warehouse Operations: Dan Tobin
Year Founded: 1925
Estimated Sales: $20-50 Million
Number Employees: 100-249
Number of Brands: 1
Square Footage: 60000
Type of Packaging: Consumer, Food Service, Private Label, Bulk
Brands:
Country Fresh

3078 Country Home Bakers
720 Metropolitan Pkwy SW
Atlanta, GA 30310
404-215-5540
Fax: 404-527-6690 800-241-6445
Frozen dough including danish, doughnut, roll and cookie; Frozen bread dough including jalapeno/cheese, salsa, spinach/mushroom/cheese, vegetable, focaccia, etc.; also, frozen baked and unbaked pies, frozen cakes, toppings, ice creamand candy
President: Gary Schreiber
Purchasing Executive: Robert Brooks
Regional Sales Manager: Jim Rasmussen
General Manager: Roy Lowery
Plant Manager: Mike Harvison
Year Founded: 2004
Estimated Sales: $20-50 Million
Number Employees: 100-249
Square Footage: 80000
Parent Co: J&J Snack Foods
Type of Packaging: Consumer, Food Service, Private Label, Bulk
Other Locations:
Country Home Bakers
Highland Park MI
Brands:
Chop Block Breads
Country Home Bakers
Jessie Lord, Inc.
Sanders
Warme Bakker

3079 Country Home Creations Inc
5132 Richfield Rd
Flint, MI 48506-2121
810-244-7348
Fax: 810-244-5348 800-457-3477
chcdips@countryhomecreations.com
Processor and exporter of mixes including cheesecake, cookie, dip and soup.
Owner: Shirley Kautman Jones
chcdips@countryhomecreations.com
Estimated Sales: $-5 Million
Number Employees: 20-49
Square Footage: 40000
Type of Packaging: Consumer, Private Label
Brands:
Camp Mixes
Classic Country
Country Home Creations
Ginger Kids
My Mom's Mixes
Perfect Party Mixes

3080 Country Life
101 Corporate Dr
Hauppauge, NY 11788
631-231-1031
Fax: 631-231-2331 800-645-5768
www.country-life.com
Supplements and health beverages
CEO: Halbert Drexler
Contact: Ramsook Alexis
aramsook-purpura@countrylifevitamins.com
Estimated Sales: $10-20 Million
Number Employees: 100-249
Brands:
Biochem

Country Life
Iron-Tek
Long Life Beverages
Natural Personal Care

3081 **Country Maid Inc**
1919 S Kinnickinnic Ave
Milwaukee, WI 53204-4000
414-383-3970
Fax: 414-383-9809 800-628-4354
www.countrymaid.com
Refrigerated salads, entrees and desserts
President: Ashley Akridge
ashley@countrymaid.com
CFO: Jordan Plotkin
Office Manager: Pat Plotkin
Estimated Sales: $6.7 Million
Number Employees: 50-99
Square Footage: 160000
Type of Packaging: Consumer, Food Service, Private Label
Brands:
Country Maid

3082 **Country Oven Bakery**
2840 Pioneer Dr
Bowling Green, KY 42101-4053
270-782-3203
Fax: 270-782-7170 www.giftagift.com
Pizza dough and pizza shells.
President: Roger Bullion
Cio/Cto: Sam Grado
sam.grado@kroger.com
COO: Jim Bennett
Director Manufacturing: John Madison
Director Engineering: Rick Noall
Plant Manager: Roger Bullion
Purchasing Manager: Wayne Miller
Estimated Sales: $25-49.9 Million
Number Employees: 250-499
Parent Co: Kroger Company

3083 **(HQ)Country Pure Foods Inc**
222 S Main St
Suite 401
Akron, OH 44308
330-753-2293
Fax: 330-848-4287 877-995-8423
info@juice4u.com www.juice4u.com
Fruit drinks, bottled spring water and juices including apple, orange, grape and pineapple.
Chief Executive Officer: Kenny Sadai
VP, Marketing: Joe Koch
VP, Retail Sales: Jon Hanley
SVP, Operations: Paul Sukalich
Estimated Sales: $44.7 Million
Number Employees: 250-499
Square Footage: 100000
Type of Packaging: Consumer, Food Service, Private Label
Other Locations:
Ellington CT
Deland FL
Brands:
Ardmore Farms®
Natural Country®
Glacier Valley®

3084 **Country Pure Foods Inc**
58 West Rd
Ellington, CT 06029
877-995-8423
info@juice4u.com www.juice4u.com
Fruit drinks, bottled spring water and juices including apple, orange, grape and pineapple.
Number Employees: 100-249
Square Footage: 51266
Type of Packaging: Consumer, Food Service, Private Label
Brands:
Glacier Valley
Natural Country
Sunflo
Sunny Lea

3085 **Country Pure Foods Inc**
681 W Waterloo Rd
Akron, OH 44314
877-995-8423
info@juice4u.com www.juice4u.com
Fruit drinks, bottled spring water and juices including apple, orange, grape and pineapple.
Type of Packaging: Consumer, Private Label

3086 **Country Pure Foods Inc**
1915 N Woodland Blvd
Deland, FL 32724
877-995-8423
info@juice4u.com www.juice4u.com
Fruit drinks, bottled spring water and juices including apple, orange, grape and pineapple.
Type of Packaging: Consumer, Private Label

3087 **Country Pure Foods Inc**
402 Yale St
Houston, TX 77007
877-995-8423
info@juice4u.com www.juice4u.com
Fruit drinks, bottled spring water and juices including apple, orange, grape and pineapple.
Type of Packaging: Consumer, Private Label

3088 **Country Smoked Meats**
510 Napolean Road
Bowling Green, OH 43402-0171
419-353-0783
Fax: 419-352-7330 800-321-4766
Processor and exporter of chunked, sliced and deli style Canadian bacon, smoked sausage, pork loins, hocks, turkey parts and ham, pepperoni, bratwurst, kielbasa, chorizos, egg and muffin sandwiches, fresh link sausage and freshboneless pork loins and ten
National Sales Manager: Bruce Schroeder
Estimated Sales: $2.5-5 Million
Number Employees: 20-49
Square Footage: 84000
Type of Packaging: Consumer, Food Service, Private Label, Bulk

3089 **Country Village Meats Inc**
401 N Pennsylvania St
Sublette, IL 61367-9400
815-849-5532
800-700-4545
www.countryvillagemeats.com
Beef, pork, lamb, veal, sausage, hot dogs, etc.; slaughtering services available
Co-Owner: Edward Morrissey
Estimated Sales: $1-2.5 Million
Number Employees: 1-4
Type of Packaging: Consumer, Bulk

3090 **County Gourmet Foods, LLC**
751 Chestnut Road
Sewickley, PA 15143-1143
412-741-8902
Fax: 412-741-9176
Gourmet foods
Quality Control: Thomas MacMurray, Ph.D.

3091 **Coupla Guys Foods**
401 N Racine Ave
Chicago, IL 60642
312-829-2332
Fax: 312-829-8866
Pasta sauces including: sesame; arrabiata; puttanesca; tapenade; buoy base; marinara; and creme de la crimini sauce.
General Manager: Joe Rowley
Sales Manager: Ute Rowley
Contact: Joe Coupla
joe@bbfdirect.com
Type of Packaging: Food Service

3092 **Coutts Specialty Foods Inc**
1190 Liberty Square Rd
Boxborough, MA 01719-1115
978-263-2952
Fax: 978-263-2953 800-919-2952
csf@couttsspecialtyfoods.com
www.couttsspecialtyfoods.com
Mother's Prize-sweet red pepper, hot sweet red pepper, corn, picclilli relishes, apple butter, and applesauce (with and with no sugar). No preservatives or fillers are added to any of our products. Mother's Pure Preserves-jamsjellies, and marmalades
Owner: Alison Chateauneuf
acouttsspecialty@aol.com
Estimated Sales: $3-5 Million
Number Employees: 1-4
Number of Brands: 2
Number of Products: 38
Type of Packaging: Consumer, Food Service
Brands:
Mother's Prize
Mother's Pure Preserves

3093 **Couture Farms**
30650 Quebec Ave
Kettleman City, CA 93239
559-386-9865
Fax: 559-386-4365
Processor and importer of asparagus, pistachios and mixed melons
Co-Partner: Steve Couture
Co-Partner: Christina Couture
stcou@aol.com
Partner: Chris Couture
stcou@aol.com
Estimated Sales: $2.2 Million
Number Employees: 20-49
Square Footage: 8640
Type of Packaging: Consumer, Food Service, Private Label, Bulk

3094 **Couture's Maple Shop/B & B**
560 VT Route 100
Westfield, VT 05874-9791
802-744-2733
Fax: 802-744-6275 800-845-2733
www.maplesyrupvermont.com
Maple syrup and candy
Co-Owner: Jacques Couture
Co-Owner: Pauline Couture
jcouture@maplesyrupvt.net
Estimated Sales: Less Than $500,000
Number Employees: 1-4

3095 **Couturier Na Inc**
2986 US Route 9
Hudson, NY 12534-4407
518-851-2570
Fax: 518-851-2574
Cheese.
President: Alain Foster
afoster@couturierna.com
Marketing: Dominique Penicaud
Number Employees: 5-9

3096 **Covered Bridge Potato Chip Company**
35 Alwright Ct
Waterville, NB E7P 0A5
Canada
506-375-2447
Fax: 506-375-2448 info@coveredbridgechips.com
www.coveredbridgechips.com
Old fashioned kettle style potato chips
Marketing Manager: Krysten Scott
Production: Mike McCartney
Estimated Sales: $2 Million
Number Employees: 14

3097 **Cowart Seafood Corp**
755 Lake Landing Dr
Lottsburg, VA 22511-2503
804-529-6101
Fax: 804-529-7374 www.gmail.com
Seafood including fresh, frozen, and breaded oysters, frozen softshell crabs, and canned herring roe
President: S Cowart
cowartsfd@gmail.com
VP: Lake Cowart Jr
Estimated Sales: $10-20 Million
Number Employees: 50-99
Square Footage: 30000
Type of Packaging: Food Service, Private Label
Brands:
Chesapeake Pride
Mannings
Sea Mist

3098 **Cowboy Caviar**
169 Fairlawn Dr
Berkeley, CA 94708
510-841-0635
Fax: 510-594-8058 877-509-1796
Spreads and chunky marinara sauces
President: Gary Forbes
Estimated Sales: $1-2,500,000
Number Employees: 1-4
Type of Packaging: Private Label

3099 **Cowboy Food & Drink**
8586 Washington St
Chagrin Falls, OH 44023-5369
440-708-1011
Fax: 406-522-9337 800-759-5489
hucklebuddy@hotmail.com
www.cowboyfoodanddrink.com

Natural barley without hulls; also, barbecue and bean sauces, bean soups, pancake, bread and baking mixes, flours, cereals and whole grains canning fruits and vegies,prepares flour,grain, and mill products.
Co-Ownert/President: Jean Clem
Co-Owner: Bud Clem
Estimated Sales: Less Than $500,000
Number Employees: 10-19
Number of Products: 30
Square Footage: 11200
Type of Packaging: Consumer, Food Service, Bulk
Brands:
Cowboy Foods

3100 **Cowgirl Chocolates**
428 W 3rd St # 3
#3 corner of 3rd and Lilly
Moscow, ID 83843-2284
208-882-4098
Fax: 208-882-0265 888-882-4098
cowgirl@cowgirlchocolates.com
www.cowgirlchocolates.com
Manufacturers of chocolate candies.
Manager: Marilyn Coates
cowgirl@cowgirlchocolates.com
Estimated Sales: Less Than $500,000
Number Employees: 1-4
Brands:
Cowgirl Chocolates

3101 **Cowgirl Creamery**
80 Fourth St
Point Reyes Station, CA 94956
415-663-9335
Fax: 415-663-5418 www.cowgirlcreamery.com
Artisan organic cheese
Contact: Becky Birkmann
mailorder@cowgirlcreamery.com

3102 **Cowie Wine Cellars & Vineyards**
101 N Carbon City Rd
Paris, AR 72855-4630
479-963-3990
Fax: 479-963-3990 cowie@cswnet.com
www.cowiewinecellars.com
Wines
President: Robert Cowie
cowie@cswnet.com
Sales Room Manager: Katie Cowie
Estimated Sales: Less than $50,000
Number Employees: 1-4
Brands:
Cowie

3103 **Cozy Harbor Seafood Inc**
75 Saint John St
Portland, ME 04102-3013
207-879-2665
Fax: 207-879-2666 800-225-2586
jnorton@cozyharbor.com www.cozyharbor.com
Buys, processes and distributes premium quality seafood products
Founder and President: John Norton
CEO: John S Norton
jnorton@cozyharbor.com
CFO: Mark Lannon
Co-founder and Technical Manager: Joe Donovan
Domestic and Intl Shrimp Lobster Sales: Tom Keegan
Operations VP: Joseph Donovan Norton
Plant/Production Manager: Roland Jacques
Estimated Sales: $.5-1 million
Number Employees: 100-249
Type of Packaging: Consumer, Food Service, Bulk

3104 **Crab Quarters**
2909 Eastern Ave
Baltimore, MD 21224-3812
410-686-2222
Fax: 410-686-0343
Fresh crab
Owner: Jim Myrick
Estimated Sales: $1-3 Million
Number Employees: 20-49

3105 **Craby's Fish Market**
303 S Black Horse Pike
Blackwood, NJ 08012-2893
856-227-9743
Seafood
Manager: Stephen Palo
Estimated Sales: Less than $500,000
Number Employees: 1-4

3106 **Cracked Candy LLC**
549 10th St
Suite 1
Brooklyn, NY 11215-4401
646-543-1405
hello@crackedcandy.com
www.crackedcandy.com
Sugar-free candy, mints and chips.
Founder: Flora Pringle
Type of Packaging: Private Label

3107 **Craft Brew Alliance**
929 N Russell St
Portland, OR 97227
503-331-7270
contact@craftbrew.com
craftbrew.com
Beer
CEO: Andy Thomas
Number of Brands: 8
Type of Packaging: Private Label
Brands:
Hefeweizer
Okio
Widmer Brothers

3108 **Craft Distillers**
108 W Clay St
Ukiah, CA 95482-5420
707-468-7899
Fax: 707-462-8103 800-782-8145
Distiller and exporter of brandy and specialty spirits
President: Ansley J Coale Jr
VP,CFO: Denise Niderost
Estimated Sales: $1-2,500,000
Number Employees: 5-9
Square Footage: 40000
Type of Packaging: Consumer, Private Label

3109 **Crafty Counter**
PO Box 160361
Austin, TX 78716
512-643-2412
hello@craftycounter.com
www.craftycounter.com
All natural chicken nuggets
Founder: Hema Reddy
CFO: Alejandro Navarro
Marketing: Usha Rao
Operations: Jennifer Martinez
Brands:
Wundernuggets

3110 **Crain Ranch**
10660 Bryne Ave
Los Molinos, CA 96055-9560
530-527-1077
Fax: 530-529-4143 billcrain@crainranch.com
www.crainranch.com
Processor, grower and exporter of walnuts in the shell.
Owner: Charles R Crain
charles@crainranch.com
Business Office: Kerry Crain
Production: Hal Crain
Estimated Sales: $300,000-500,000
Number Employees: 10-19
Square Footage: 320000
Type of Packaging: Consumer, Private Label, Bulk
Brands:
Crain Ranch

3111 **Crain Walnut Shelling, Inc.**
10695 Decker Ave
Los Molinos, CA 96055-9628
530-529-1585
Fax: 530-529-1458 crainwalnut@crainwalnut.com
www.crainwalnut.com
Shelled walnuts supplying industrial ingredient needs.
President: Grant Skognes
gskognes@ridefox.com
Owner: Harold Crain
Vice President of Sales & Logistics: Vicki Lapera
Quality Assurance: Devan Wilson
Sales Administrator: Kimberly Gonsalves
Number Employees: 100-249
Type of Packaging: Bulk

3112 **Cramer's Bakery**
14 East Afton Ave.
Yardley, PA 19067
215-493-2760
www.cramerbakery.com
Cakes, pastries, pies, breads and rolls
Founder: John E. Cramer, Jr.

3113 **Cranberry Isles Fisherman's**
1 Water St
Islesford, ME 4646
207-244-5438
Fax: 207-244-9479
Manager: Mark Neighman
Estimated Sales: $.5-1 million
Number Employees: 1-4

3114 **Cranberry Sweets Co**
1005 Newmark Ave
Coos Bay, OR 97420-3102
541-888-9824
Fax: 541-888-2824 800-527-5748
www.cranberrysweets.com
Manufacturers of cranberries, jellies and candies.
Owner: Clayton Shaw
cranberrysweets@frontier.com
Estimated Sales: $1-2.5 Million
Number Employees: 20-49
Brands:
Cranberry Sweets
Oregon Berries
Sweet Basics

3115 **Crane & Crane Inc**
100 Crane Orchard Rd
PO Box 277
Brewster, WA 98812
509-689-3447
Fax: 509-689-2214
Grower and exporter of apples
President: Meg Spellman
meg@craneandcrane.com
Secretary/Treasurer: Margaret Crane
Vice President: Robert Reimmer
Estimated Sales: $930,000
Number Employees: 100-249
Square Footage: 196000
Type of Packaging: Consumer, Food Service, Private Label, Bulk
Brands:
Crane's Aqua Line
Crane's Blue Line
Crane's Gray Line
Crane's Maroon Line
Crane's Red Line

3116 **Crane's Pie Pantry Restaurant**
6054 124th Ave
Fennville, MI 49408-9440
269-561-2297
Fax: 269-561-5545 contact@cranespiepantry.com
www.cranespiepantry.com
Pies and wine
Owner: Beckey Crane-Hagger
contact@cranespiepantry.com
Owner: Lue Crane
Winemaker: Rob Crane
Estimated Sales: Less Than $500,000
Number Employees: 10-19

3117 **Crater Meat Co Inc**
2811 Biddle Rd
Medford, OR 97504-4114
541-772-6966
Meat products
Owner: James K Cearley
Estimated Sales: Less Than $500,000
Number Employees: 1-4
Type of Packaging: Consumer
Brands:
Crater's Meats

3118 **Crave Natural Foods**
2043 Imperial Street
Los Angeles, CA 90021
213-627-8887
877-425-2599
www.cravefoods.com
Nondairy whipped cream, dressings, ice cream and cheese sauce
Owner: Sally A Conway
Contact: Shaheda Sayed
shaheda@cravefoods.com
Number Employees: 1-4
Square Footage: 1600
Type of Packaging: Consumer

3119 **Craven Crab Company**
PO Box 3321
New Bern, NC 28564-3321
252-637-3562
Fax: 252-637-3562
Crab
President: Gaston Fulcher
Brands:
Craven Crab

3120 **Craveright**
5902 Mount Eagle Dr
Alexandria, VA 22303-2513
703-888-3796
info@craveright.com
www.craveright.com
Gluten free treats.
Owner: Darioush Danaei
ddanaei@craveright.com
Estimated Sales: Less Than $500,000
Number Employees: 1-4

3121 **Crawford Sausage Co Inc**
2310 S Pulaski Rd
Chicago, IL 60623
773-277-3095
judy@daisybrandsausage.net
www.daisybrandsausage.net
Bratwursts, frankfurters, polish sausage, other linked sausage, sliced lunchmeats, fresh sausages, smoked meats and gift boxes.
Year Founded: 1925
Estimated Sales: $5-10 Million
Number Employees: 20-49
Type of Packaging: Consumer, Food Service, Bulk
Brands:
Daisy Brand Meat Products

3122 **Crazy Go Nuts**
Fower, CA 93291
www.crazygonutswalnuts.com
Walnut snacks
Founder: Courtney Carini

3123 **Crazy Jerrys Inc Kahuna-Sauces**
721 Bascomb Commercial Pkwy
Woodstock, GA 30189-2466
770-993-0651
Fax: 770-993-8201 800-347-2823
Sauces, can mixed nuts, garlic mushrooms, maters in spicy vermouth, stuffed olives, can beef stew, soup mix and gumbo mix
President: Jerry Gualtieri
jgualt9817@aol.com
Estimated Sales: $1 Million
Number Employees: 1-4
Type of Packaging: Private Label
Brands:
Crazy Jerry's

3124 **Crazy Mary's**
300 E. 34th Street
36th Floor
New York, NY 10016
212-889-8124
CrazyMary@CrazyMary.com
www.crazymary.com

3125 **Crazy Richard's**
P.O. Box 715
Dublin, OH 43017
614-889-4824
info@crazyrichards.com
www.crazyrichards.com
Natural peanut butter, almond butter, cashew butter, peanut powder, and protein snack balls
President & Owner: Kimmi Wernli

3126 **Crea Fill Fibers Corp**
10200 Worton Rd
Chestertown, MD 21620-3545
410-810-0779
Fax: 410-810-0793 800-832-4662
fiber@creafill.com www.creafill.com
Processor and exporter of powdered cellulose and pure vegetable fibers
President: Paolo Fezzi
pfezzi@creafill.com
Sales Associate: Sara Emgland
Estimated Sales: $5.5 Million
Number Employees: 20-49
Type of Packaging: Bulk
Brands:
Qc Fibers
Sc Fibers

3127 **Creagri Inc**
25565 Whitesell St
Hayward, CA 94545-3614
510-732-6478
Fax: 510-732-6493 info@creagri.com
www.creagri.com
Extra virgin olive oil
Founder/Chairman: Roberto Crea
rcrea@creagri.com
VP: Paolo Pontoniere
Estimated Sales: $1 Million
Number Employees: 5-9
Type of Packaging: Consumer, Food Service, Bulk
Brands:
Integrale
Supremo

3128 **Cream Crock Distributors**
50 Worcester Rd
Sterling, MA 01564-1466
978-422-3500
Fax: 978-422-6699 800-423-2736
Ice cream
President: Gary Jonaitis
Estimated Sales: $2.5-5 Million
Number Employees: 5-9

3129 **Cream Hill Estates**
9633 rue Clement
LaSalle, QC H8R 4B4
Canada
514-363-2066
Fax: 514-363-1614 866-727-3628
info@creamhillestates.com
Producer and distributor of guaranteed pure oats

3130 **Cream Of The West**
408 Wheatland Ave S
Harlowton, MT 59036-5199
406-632-4804
800-477-2383
cotw@mtintouch.net www.creamofthewest.com
Company products line includes cereals, pancake mixes, jams and jellies, honey, coffee and gift baskets.
Manager: Freida Robertson
Manager: Lian Kent
cotw@itstriangle.com
Production Manager: Bobby Lewis
Estimated Sales: $1-2.5 Million
Number Employees: 5-9
Square Footage: 24000
Type of Packaging: Consumer, Food Service, Bulk
Brands:
Cream of the West

3131 **Creamland Dairies Inc**
10 Indian School Rd NW
Albuquerque, NM 87105
505-247-0721
Fax: 505-246-9696
Dairy products including ice cream, milk, cultured, cottage cheese, sour cream and dips.
CEO: Howard Miller
CEO: Howard Miller
Public Relations: Connie Holdren
Number Employees: 20-49
Parent Co: Dean Foods Company
Type of Packaging: Consumer
Brands:
Creamland
Dean's

3132 **Creation Nation**
Calabasas, CA 91301
424-234-5800
hi@foodcreationnation.com
proteinbarmix.com
Protein balls, bars and bites
Founder & CEO: Karen Nation
Year Founded: 2014
Number of Brands: 1
Number of Products: 5
Type of Packaging: Consumer
Brands:
CREATION NATION

3133 **Creative Cotton**
945 Bermuda Dunes Pl
Northbrook, IL 60062-3125
847-291-4128
alicia@creativeconfections.net
www.creativeconfections.net
Gourmet candy including chocolate and English toffee
President: Alicia Russell
Vice President: Bert Gideon
Estimated Sales: $1-3 Million
Number Employees: 5-9
Type of Packaging: Consumer
Brands:
Creative Confections

3134 **Creative Flavors & Specialties LLP**
991 E Linden Ave
Linden, NJ 07036
908-862-4678
Fax: 908-862-7458
Flavors for coffee, candy, fruit drinks, bagels, ice cream, ice tea, coffee syrups, snack seasonings, spices and much more. We also customize any flavors, spray drieds and blending
President: Esther Baita
CEO: Mike DiPierro
VP: Danielle Lau
Quality Control: Esther Baita
Production: Fredy Lau
Estimated Sales: $100,000
Number Employees: 5
Number of Products: 5000
Square Footage: 5000
Type of Packaging: Bulk

3135 **Creative Flavors Inc**
16686 Hilltop Park Pl
Chagrin Falls, OH 44023-4500
440-543-9881
Fax: 440-543-8707 800-848-9043
www.creativeflavorsinc.com
Flavors and ingredients for the dairy industry including cherries, flavors and core powders for novelty bars and sour cream dip bases
President: Michael Ramsey
Public Relations: Cindy Ramsey
Estimated Sales: $2.5-5 Million
Number Employees: 5-9

3136 **Creative Food Ingredients**
1 Lincoln Ave
Perry, NY 14530
585-237-2213
Fax: 585-237-2735 www.creativefoods.com
Cookies, creme filled cookies, crumble toppings and crushed cookies
President & CEO: Michael O'Flaherty
moflaherty@creativefoods.com
CFO: Jeffrey Arcand
Executive Director, Quality Research: David Humberstone
Executive Director, Operations: Michael Humberstone
Executive Director, Supply Chain: Rodney Smith
Estimated Sales: $100+ Million
Number Employees: 100-249
Brands:
Creative Foods

3137 **Creative Foodworks Inc**
1011 S Acme Rd
San Antonio, TX 78237-3218
210-212-4761
Fax: 210-212-4919
Private label condiments
President: Dee Dee Garcia
dgarcia@creativefoodworks.com
Quality Control: Michael Billings
Operations Manager: Emilio Herrera
Plant Manager: Norman Diggec
Purchasing Manager: Chris Boynton
Estimated Sales: $5-10 Million
Number Employees: 5-9
Type of Packaging: Consumer, Food Service, Private Label, Bulk

3138 **Creative Seasonings**
34 Audubon Road
Wakefield, MA 01880-1203
617-246-1461
Fax: 617-246-5381 www.conagrafoods.com
Seasonings

President/CEO: Greg Heckman
CEO: Gary Rodkin

3139 Creative Snacks Co LLC
241 Burgess Rd
Suite B
Greensboro, NC 27409-9333
336-668-4151
Manufacturer of snack foods, ranging from coconut chips to chocolate pretzels and almonds.
Founder and CEO: Marius Andersen
VP of Sales: Scott Feldman
Director of Operations: Zachary Breeden
zacharybreeden@creativesnacks.com
Number Employees: 20-49
Brands:
CREATIVE SNACKS CO.

3140 Creative Spices
33436 Western Avenue
Union City, CA 94587-3202
510-471-4956
Fax: 510-471-9174
Bread and bakery products
President: Carmella Hagman
Treasurer: Virginia Holmes
VP: Donna Hagman
Contact: Donna Hageman
donna@iconnex.com
Estimated Sales: $10-24.9,000,000
Number Employees: 20-49
Brands:
Creative Spices

3141 Creemore Springs Brewery
139 Mill St
Creemore, ON L0M 1G0
Canada
705-466-2240
Fax: 705-466-3306 800-267-2240
thefolks@creemoresprings.com
www.creemoresprings.com
Lager beer
President/CEO: Jason Moore
Estimated Sales: $6.9 Million
Number Employees: 90
Type of Packaging: Consumer, Food Service
Brands:
Creemore Springs Premium Lager
Creemore Springs Urbock

3142 Creighton Brothers
4217 W Old Road 30
Warsaw, IN 46580-6842
574-267-3101
Fax: 574-267-6446 www.creightonbrothersllc.com
Established in 1925. Processor of fresh, frozen, and hard cooked eggs.
President: Ron Truex
ron@creightonbrothersllc.com
Co-Founder: Russell Creighton
Co-Founder: Hobart Creighton
Estimated Sales: $20,800,000
Number Employees: 100-249
Type of Packaging: Consumer, Food Service, Private Label, Bulk
Brands:
Good News Eggs
Grandpa's Choice

3143 Creme Curls
5292 Lawndale Ave
PO Box 276
Hudsonville, MI 49426-1213
616-669-2468
Fax: 616-669-2468 800-466-1219
www.cremecurls.com
Creme horns, eclairs and cream puffs, strudel and turnovers, and pie dough
President: Gary Bierling
gary@cremecurls.com
CFO: Lee Deboer
Vice President: Paul Bierling
VP Sales: Michael Burkett
Estimated Sales: $11.7 Million
Number Employees: 100-249
Square Footage: 66000
Type of Packaging: Consumer, Food Service, Private Label, Bulk
Brands:
Creme Curls

3144 Creme D'Lite
2366 Hill N Dale Dr
Irving, TX 75038-5619
972-255-7255
A frozen nondairy cream beverage
President: Don Allen
Estimated Sales: $99,000
Number Employees: 2
Square Footage: 10000
Type of Packaging: Consumer, Food Service, Private Label, Bulk
Brands:
Creme D'Lite
Tropic D'Lite

3145 Creme Unlimited
600 Holiday Plaza Dr # 520
Matteson, IL 60443-2238
708-748-1336
Fax: 708-748-4985 800-227-3637
Non-dairy whipped toppings and icings
Manager: John Evans
Manager: Cher Vivich
cvicich@cremesunlimited.com
Estimated Sales: $10-20 000,000
Number Employees: 5-9
Brands:
Cremes

3146 Creminelli Fine Meats
310 N Wright Brothers Dr
Salt Lake City, UT 84116-2881
801-428-1820
Fax: 202-478-0434 www.creminelli.com
Organic/natural, cured meats i.e. prociutto/bacon, other meat/game/pate.
Manager: Samantha Smith
Number Employees: 20-49

3147 Creole Delicacies Gourmet Shop
533 Saint Ann St
New Orleans, LA 70116-3387
504-525-9508
Fax: 504-288-0042 lisette@cookincajun.com
Pralines
President: Lisette Sutton
lisette@cookincajun.com
Estimated Sales: Less Than $500,000
Number Employees: 5-9
Type of Packaging: Consumer
Brands:
Cookin' Cajun ·
Creole Delicacies

3148 Creole Fermentation Indu
7331 Ben Frederick Rd
Abbeville, LA 70510
337-898-9377
Fax: 337-898-9376
Vinegar including white distilled; manufacturer of vinegar production equipment
President: Albert Steen
General Manager: Bill Tribados
Plant Manager: Bill Tribaldos
Estimated Sales: $5-10 Million
Number Employees: 5-9
Type of Packaging: Bulk

3149 Crepini
101 Castleton Street
Pleasantville, NY 10570
914-533-6645
Fax: 914-206-4848
Organic crepes
Production Manager: Mike McCartney
Estimated Sales: A
Number Employees: 1-4

3150 Crepini & The Crepe Team
5600 1st Ave
Brooklyn, NY 11220-2550
USA
718-372-0505
Fax: 914-206-4848 www.crepini.com
Grain, cereal, pasta, cakes, pastries
Executive Officer: Paula Rimer
Contact: Phil Campo
phil@crepini.com

3151 Crescent Duck Farm
10 Edagr Ave
PO Box 500
Aquebogue LI, NY 11931-0500
631-722-8000
www.crescentduck.com
Processor and exporter of fresh and frozen duck. Founded in 1908.
President: Douglas Corwin
Controller: Janet Corwin Wedel
Maintenance Engineer and Manager: Jeffrey Corwin
Plant Manager: Arnold Tilton
Estimated Sales: $7 Million
Number Employees: 50-99
Type of Packaging: Consumer, Food Service
Brands:
Crescent

3152 Crescent Foods
4343 W 44th Place
Chicago, IL 60632
800-939-6268
communications@crescentfoods.com
www.crescentfoods.com
Halal beef and poultry
President & CEO: Ahmad Adam
VP: Ibrahim Abed
Director of Sales & Marketing: Amna Haq
VP Human Resources: Muneeza Arjmand
Year Founded: 1995
Number Employees: 50-99

3153 Crescent Ridge Dairy
355 Bay Rd
Sharon, MA 02067-1399
781-784-2740
Fax: 781-784-8446 800-660-2740
info@crescentridge.com www.crescentridge.com
Milk
President: Mark Parrish
VP: Jim Carroll
Estimated Sales: $2.5-5 Million
Number Employees: 50-99
Type of Packaging: Private Label
Brands:
Crescent Ridge Dairy

3154 Crescini Wines
PO Box 216
Soquel, CA 95073-0216
831-462-1466
Wines
President: Richard Crescini
Co-Owner: Paula Crescini
Estimated Sales: $1-2,500,000
Number Employees: 5-9
Square Footage: 3
Type of Packaging: Private Label

3155 Crest Foods Inc
905 Main St.
Ashton, IL 61006
877-273-7893
www.crestfoods.com
Established in 1941. Processor of food ingredients including emulsifying agents, proteins, caseinates, whey, stabilizers and flavors for dips, bases and seasonings; contract packaging available
President: Jeff Meiners
VP of Corporate Sales: Steve Meiners
VP Manufacturing: Mike Meiners
Contact: Rebecca Henson
bhenson@crestfoods.com
Estimated Sales: $20-50 Million
Number Employees: 250-499
Type of Packaging: Consumer, Food Service, Private Label

3156 Crest International Corporation
P.O.Box 83309
San Diego, CA 92138-3309
619-296-4300
Fax: 619-296-3624 800-548-1232
www.crestinternational.com
Fresh or frozen fish and seafoods, fresh and frozen packaged seafood
Owner/President: Stephen Willis
Corporate Secretary: Lourdes Garber
Estimated Sales: $2 Million
Number Employees: 10
Type of Packaging: Food Service, Bulk

3157 **Crestar Crusts**
1104 Clinton Ave.
Washington Court House, OH 43160-1215
740-335-4813
Fax: 781-767-1751 www.richelieufoods.com
Frozen pizza crusts and pizzas
President/CEO: Robbie Jamieson
Director Sales Administration: Steve Deveau
VP Sales: Phillip Scolley
Plant Manager: Jason Yoakum
Estimated Sales: $20-50 Million
Number Employees: 400
Parent Co: Richelieu Foods Inc.

3158 **Crestmont Enterprises**
1420 Crestmont Ave
Camden, NJ 8103
856-966-0700
Fax: 856-966-6137
Flavors and extracts
President: Amy Baskin
VP: Joseph Shediack, Jr.
VP: Annette Rapaport
Estimated Sales: $5-10 Million
Number Employees: 10-19

3159 **Creuzebergers Meats**
3001 6th Avenue
Duncansville, PA 16635
814-695-3061
Meat processing
Owner: Sieglinde Creuzberger
Estimated Sales: Less than $500,000
Number Employees: 1-4

3160 **Crevettes Du Nord**
139 Rue De La Reine
C.P. 6380
Gaspe, QC G4X 2R8
Canada
418-368-1414
Fax: 418-368-1812 gesco@globetrotter.qc.ca
Processor and exporter of fresh and frozen shrimp
President: Amedee La Pierre
Number Employees: 50-99
Type of Packaging: Bulk

3161 **Cribari Vineyard Inc**
4180 W Alamos Ave # 108
Suite 108
Fresno, CA 93722-3943
559-277-9000
Fax: 559-277-2420 800-277-9095
bulk@cribari.net www.sacramentalwines.com
Processor and exporter of high quality California bulk wine
CEO & CFO: John F. Cribari
Sales: Ben Cribari
Estimated Sales: $730,000
Number Employees: 1-4
Number of Brands: 7
Type of Packaging: Bulk
Brands:
Cvi Bulk Wines

3162 **Crickle Company**
90 Genesis Pkwy
Thomasville, GA 31792
229-225-1902
Fax: 229-225-2116 800-237-8689
www.crickle.com
Brittle and popcorn
President/Owner: Harry Jones
VP: Jerry Hunter
Number Employees: 12

3163 **Cricklewood Soyfoods**
250 Sally Ann Furnace Road
Mertztown, PA 19539-9036
610-682-4109
Fax: 717-484-4789
Kosher vegetarian soy-based foods including burgers and low-fat three bean, organic soy and three grain tempeh, organic and GMO free foods
President: Renate Krummenoehl
Estimated Sales: $380,000
Number Employees: 4
Number of Products: 5
Square Footage: 2400
Type of Packaging: Consumer, Food Service, Bulk
Brands:
Cricklewood Soyfoods
Cricklewood Soyfoods

3164 **Criders Poultry**
1 Plant Avenue
PO Box 398
Stillmore, GA 30464-0398
912-562-4435
Fax: 912-562-4168 800-342-3851
info@criderinc.com www.cridercorp.com
Fresh, frozen, canned and further processed chicken
Owner/CEO: William Crider Jr
CFO: Max Harrell
Research & Development: Phil Hudspeth
Quality Control: Stan Wallen
Operations: Lee Thompkins
Plant Manager: Kenneth Houghton
Purchasing: Ritchie Young
Estimated Sales: $20-50 Million
Number Employees: 400
Type of Packaging: Food Service, Private Label, Bulk
Brands:
Crider

3165 **Crillon Importers LTD**
80 E State Rt 4 # 108
Paramus, NJ 07652-2657
201-368-8878
Fax: 201-368-4450 support@crillonimporters.com
www.crillonimporters.com
Wines and liquors
Owner: Michel Roux
roux@crillonimporters.com
Estimated Sales: $10-20 Million
Number Employees: 5-9
Brands:
Absente
Agavero
Aquavits
Douce Provence
Elisir Mp Roux
Hb Pastis
Magellin Gin
Rhum Barbancourt
Rinquinquin
Talapa Mezcal
Unicum Zwack

3166 **Crispy Green Inc.**
144 Fairfield Rd
Fairfield, NJ 07004
973-679-4515
Fax: 973-755-0358 info@crispygreen.com
www.crispygreen.com
Freeze-dried fruits, including all natural and 100-calorie
Chief Executive Officer: Angela Liu
Contact: Kim Driggs
driggs@crispygreen.com
Estimated Sales: $680,000
Number Employees: 7

3167 **Cristom Vineyards**
6905 Spring Valley Rd NW
Salem, OR 97304-9779
503-375-3068
Fax: 503-391-7057 jeri@cristomwines.com
www.cristomvineyards.com
Wines
Owner: Tom Gerrie
tom@cristomvineyards.com
Co-Owner: Eileen Gerrie
Estimated Sales: $2.5-5 Million
Number Employees: 10-19
Type of Packaging: Private Label

3168 **Critchfield Meats Inc**
2220 Nicholasville Rd # 166
STE 166
Lexington, KY 40503-2400
859-276-4965
Fax: 859-278-4965 800-866-2901
orders@critchfieldmeats.com
www.critchfieldmeats.com
Meats
President: Mark Critchfield
CEO: Larry McMillan
Secretary/Treasurer: Mike Critchfield
Vice President: Larry Critchfield
ldcritchfield@critchfieldmeats.com
Number Employees: 10-19
Brands:
Critchfield Meats

3169 **Critelli Olive Oil**
2445 South Watney Way, Ste D
Fairfield, CA 94533-6721
707-426-3400
Fax: 707-426-3423 800-865-4836
www.critelli.com
Manufacturer of organic olive oil and dipping oil. Importer of culinary oil, Balsamic, Varietal Wine, and flavored vinegars from around the world.
Director Food Service: Mike Brossier
Director Of Operations: Brian Witbracht
Type of Packaging: Food Service, Private Label
Brands:
Critelli

3170 **Criterion Chocolates Inc**
125 Lewis St
Eatontown, NJ 07724-3454
732-542-7847
Fax: 732-542-0045 800-804-6060
info@criterionchocolates.com
www.criterionchocolates.com
Chocolates
Owner: George Karagias
criterion@criterionchocolates.com
VP: James Samaras
Marketing Director: Ron Boyadjian
Estimated Sales: $5-10 Million
Number Employees: 20-49
Brands:
Criterion

3171 **Criveller California Corp**
185 Grant Ave
Healdsburg, CA 95448-9539
Canada
707-431-2211
Fax: 707-431-2216 888-849-2266
info@criveller.com www.criveller.com
Ale and lager beer
President: Bruce McCubbin
Marketing Director: Matt Johnson
Manager: Barbara Criveller
Number Employees: 5-9
Square Footage: 24000
Type of Packaging: Consumer, Food Service
Brands:
Eisbock
Gritstone
Honey Brown
Millstone
Niagara
Paleao

3172 **Crocetti's Oakdale Packing Co**
378 Pleasant St
East Bridgewater, MA 02333-1349
508-587-0035
Fax: 508-587-8758 www.crocettis.com
Packer of hamburger meat and sausage
Marketing Director & CFO: Carl Crocetti
Estimated Sales: $5-10 Million
Number Employees: 20-49
Type of Packaging: Consumer, Food Service, Bulk

3173 **Crockett Honey**
1040 W Alameda Dr
Tempe, AZ 85282-3332
480-731-3936
Fax: 480-731-3938 800-291-3969
bnipper@crocketthoney.com
www.crocketthoney.com
Processor and exporter of honey
Owner: Brian Nipper
Secretary: Linda Nipper
VP: Brian Nipper
Estimated Sales: $5-10 Million
Number Employees: 5-9
Square Footage: 48000
Type of Packaging: Consumer, Food Service, Bulk
Brands:
Crockett's
Mrs. Crockett's

3174 **Croda Inc**
300 Columbus Cir # A
Edison, NJ 08837-3907
732-417-0800
Fax: 732-417-0804 marketing-usa@croda.com
www.crodausa.com
Super refined marine and plant oils, proteins, and peptides for nutraceuticals, functional foods and dietary supplements.

President: Sandra Breene
Vice President: Esther Horowitz
ehorowitz@itsadeal.ie
Estimated Sales: $20-50 Million
Number Employees: 100-249
Square Footage: 45000
Parent Co: Croda International P/C

3175 **Croft's Crackers**
504 14th Avenue
Monroe, WI 53566-1140
608-325-1223
Fax: 608-325-1289 crofts@mail.tds.net
Crackers, granola, cookies
President: John King
Public Relations: John or Kathy King
Estimated Sales: $500,000-$1,000,000
Number Employees: 1-4

3176 **Crofter's Food**
7 Great North Rd
Parry Sound, ON P2A 2X8
Canada
705-746-6301
www.croftersorganic.com
Organic fruit spreads
Year Founded: 1989
Number of Brands: 1
Number of Products: 26
Type of Packaging: Consumer
Brands:
CROFTER'S
CROFTER'S SUPERFRUIT
CROFTER'S JUST FRUIT

3177 **Crofton & Sons Inc**
10250 Woodberry Rd
Tampa, FL 33619-8008
813-685-7745
Fax: 813-689-4535 800-878-7675
debbie@unclejohnspride.com
www.unclejohnspride.com
Beef and pork smoked sausage, Italian sausage and smoked turkey links; also, full line of smoked meats
President: Kevin Crofton
kevin@unclejohnspride.com
Co-Owner: Noble Crofton
Estimated Sales: $8 Million
Number Employees: 50-99
Square Footage: 160000
Type of Packaging: Consumer, Food Service, Private Label, Bulk
Brands:
Bean Brothers
Smokehouse Favorite
Uncle John's Pride

3178 **Crompton Corporation**
One American Lane
Greenwich, CT 06831-2560
203-573-2000
Fax: 203-552-2010 800-295-2392
Chemical ingredients and food additives
Chairman/ President/ CEO: Craig A. Rogerson
CFO/ SVP: Stephen C. Forsyth
VP/ Corporate Controller/ Principal Acco: Laurence Orton
Global Market Manager: Bob Ruckle
Sales Director: Rick Beitel
Contact: Paul Ellis
paul.ellis@chemtura.com
Number Employees: 20-49

3179 **Cronin Vineyards**
11 Old La Honda Road
Woodside, CA 94062-2604
650-851-1452
Fax: 650-851-5696
Wines
Prorietor: Duane Cronin
VP: Mora Cronin
Estimated Sales: $300,000
Number Employees: 1-4
Type of Packaging: Consumer
Brands:
Cizonin Vineyards
Portola Hills

3180 **Crooked River Brewing Company**
1101 Center St
Cleveland, OH 44113-2405
216-771-2337
Fax: 216-771-7990
Beer, ale, stout, lager and porter
Owner: Stephen Danckers
Co-Owner: Stuart Sheridan
Estimated Sales: $5-9.9 Million
Number Employees: 10-19
Type of Packaging: Consumer, Food Service, Bulk
Brands:
Cool Mule
Crooked River Brewing
Lighthouse Gold

3181 **Crooked Vine/Stony Ridge Wnry**
4948 Tesla Rd
Livermore, CA 94550-9530
925-449-0458
Fax: 925-449-0646
bacchus@stonyridgewinery.com
Wines
Owner: Rick Corbett
rick@crookedvine.com
Winemaker: Dale Vaughn-Bowen
Estimated Sales: Below $5 Million
Number Employees: 5-9
Brands:
Orobianco-California Nv

3182 **Crookston Bean**
1600 S Main St
Crookston, MN 56716-2445
218-281-2567
Fax: 218-281-2567 www.eteamz.com
Processor and exporter of dried edible beans
President: Paul Biermaier
paul.biermaier@crookston.mn.us
Manager: Dave Seaver
Estimated Sales: $10-20 Million
Number Employees: 5-9
Type of Packaging: Private Label, Bulk

3183 **Crop One**
2201 Broadway
Oakland, CA 94612
media@cropone.ag
cropone.ag
Leafy greens produced with 95-99% less water than traditional growers and packaged in 100% recycled materials.
CEO: Sonia Lo
Chief Scientific Officer: Dr. Deane Falcone
CFO & SVP of Strategy: Dave Vosburg
Number of Brands: 1
Type of Packaging: Consumer, Private Label
Brands:
FreshBox Farms

3184 **Crop Pharms, LLC**
59 Walnut Lane
Staatsburg, NY 12580
845-266-8999
www.currantc.com
Commercial currant farm; developer, marketer and seller of Black Currant products under CurrantC brand. Products include preserves, syrups and frozen currants
Founder/CEO: Greg Quinn
Year Founded: 1999
Number of Brands: 1
Number of Products: 6
Type of Packaging: Private Label
Brands:
CurrantC

3185 **Crosby Molasses Company**
327 Rothesay Avenue
Saint John, NB E2J 2C3
Canada
506-634-7515
Fax: 506-634-1724 800-561-2206
feedback@crosbys.com www.crosbys.com
Molasses, corn syrup, and glucose for co-manufactured retail and food service.
President: James Crosby
Senior Vice President: Lorne Goodman
Director of Sales & Marketing: William Crosby
VP of Operations: Jeanette Howley
Estimated Sales: $7.8 Million
Number Employees: 60
Type of Packaging: Consumer, Food Service, Private Label, Bulk
Brands:
Crosby

3186 **Crossings Winery**
1289 W Madison Ave
Glenns Ferry, ID 83623-2335
208-366-2539
Fax: 208-366-2458 carmelavineyards@rtci.net
www.carmelavineyards.com
Wines
Winemaker: Neil Glancy
Estimated Sales: $1-2.5 Million
Number Employees: 20-49

3187 **Crowley Beverage Corporation**
526 Boston Post Road
Wayland, MA 01778-1835
508-358-7177
Fax: 978-358-0057 800-997-3337
Soft drinks
President/CEO: Jill Crowley
Chairman: Edward Crowley
Estimated Sales: $3,000,000
Number Employees: 10-19
Brands:
Razcal

3188 **Crowley Cheese Inc**
14 Crowley Ln
Mt Holly, VT 05758-9656
802-259-2340
Fax: 802-259-2347 800-683-2606
sales@crowleycheese.com
www.crowleycheese.com
Cheese including colby, sage, pepper, smoked, dill, garlic and caraway
Manager: Cindy Dawley
rawmilk@vermontel.net
Principal: Jill Jones
President: Galen Jones
Estimated Sales: Less Than $500,000
Number Employees: 5-9
Type of Packaging: Consumer, Food Service, Private Label, Bulk
Brands:
Crowley

3189 **Crown Candy Corp**
4145 Mead Rd
Macon, GA 31206
478-781-4911
800-241-3529
info@crowncandy.com www.crowncandy.com
Processor and exporter of confectionery products including brittles, chocolate, coconut, peanut and pecan candies and fudge.
CEO: James Weatherford
jweatherford@crowncandy.com
Estimated Sales: $10-24.9 Million
Number Employees: 100-249
Type of Packaging: Consumer, Private Label, Bulk
Brands:
Delights
Royal Recipe

3190 **Crown Holdings, Inc.**
770 Township Line Rd.
Yardley, PA 19067
215-698-5100
ir@crowncork.com
www.crowncork.com
Bottle caps, can tops, crowns and cans including tin, beer and ale; also, bottling machinery
Chairman: John Conway
President/CEO: Timothy Donahue
Senior VP/CFO: Thomas Kelly
VP/Treasurer: Kevin Clothier
Executive VP/COO: Gerard Gifford
Year Founded: 1892
Estimated Sales: $11.7 Billion
Number Employees: 33,000
Type of Packaging: Consumer, Food Service, Private Label, Bulk
Other Locations:
Crown Cork & Seal Co.
Apopka FL

3191 **Crown Maple Syrup**
47 Mccourt Rd
Dover Plains, NY 12522-5734
USA
845-877-0640
Fax: 845-675-5044 www.crownmaple.com
Maple syrup, baking mixes

Owner: Rob Turner
Chief Executive Officer: Compton Chase-Lansdale
Contact: Terriann Albrecht
terriann@crownmaple.com
Estimated Sales: Less Than $500,000
Number Employees: 1-4

3192 Crown Pacific Fine Foods
8809 S 190th St
Kent, WA 98031-1270
425-251-8750
Fax: 425-251-8802 info@cpff.net
www.crownpacificfinefoods.com
Asian foods, baking and pancake mixes, baking goods, chocolates, condiments, and sauces
President/CEO/Founder: Tony Ataee
tony@cpff.net
Year Founded: 1982
Estimated Sales: $20-50 Million
Number Employees: 50-99

3193 (HQ)Crown Packing Company
5 Foster Road
Salinas, CA 93908-9339
831-424-2067
Fax: 831-424-7812
Grower and packer of lettuce, celery and cauliflower; exporter of lettuce and celery
President: Chris Bunn
Sales Manager: Rob Steitz
Sales: Tonya Tempalski
Estimated Sales: $3-5 Million
Number Employees: 2
Type of Packaging: Consumer, Food Service, Private Label, Bulk
Brands:
Bunny

3194 Crown Prince Inc
18581 Railroad St
City Of Industry, CA 91748-1316
626-912-3700
Fax: 626-854-0350 sales@crownprince.com
www.crownprince.com
Processors and packers of specialty canned seafood.
President: Dustan Hoffman
dhoffman@crownprince.com
Chief Executive Officer: Robert Hoffman
Chief Financial Officer: Chris Bruno
Marketing Manager: Denise Hines
National Sales Manager: Gary Gruettner
Director, Operations: Jeanmarye Stobaugh
Warehouse Manager: John Brassell
Estimated Sales: $20-50 Million
Number Employees: 20-49
Number of Brands: 3
Type of Packaging: Consumer, Private Label
Brands:
Crown Prince Natural
Crown Prince Seafood
Ocean Prince Seafood

3195 Crown Processing Company
10754 Artesia Blvd
Cerritos, CA 90703-2650
562-865-0293
Processor, importer and exporter of citrus rinds including graded, sliced, cooked, canned, made into marmalade. Founded in 1960.
President: John Bowen
Estimated Sales: $5-10 Million
Number Employees: 20-49
Square Footage: 108000
Type of Packaging: Food Service
Brands:
Crown

3196 Crown Regal Wine Cellars
586 Montgomery St
Brooklyn, NY 11225-3130
718-604-1430
Fax: 718-384-1336 ywine@hotmail.com
Wine and grape juice
Owner: Joseph Baycount
Estimated Sales: $2.5-5,000,000
Number Employees: 5-9

3197 Crown Valley Food Service
550 East First Street
PO Box 2101
Beaumont, CA 92223-1001
951-769-8786
Fax: 951-769-8788
Prepared specialty foods

President: Sheldon Zaritsky
CEO: Mike Cavanaugh
Estimated Sales: $1-3 Million
Number Employees: 10-19

3198 Crum Creek Mils
700 Old Marple Rd
Springfield, PA 19064-1236
610-604-0505
Fax: 413-581-3501 888-607-3500
info@crumcreek.com www.crumcreek.com
Soy-based pastas, breadsticks and soy powders
President: Dr Ara Yeramyan
Contact: Richard Walton
info@crumcreek.com

3199 Crumbs Bake Shop
110 W 40th Street
Suite 2100
New York, NY 10018
877-278-6270
Cupcakes
President: Jason Bauer
Owner/VP: Mia Bauer

3200 Crunch-A-Mame
PO Box 539
Mulberry, AR 72947
hello@crunchamame.com
crunchamame.com
Organic edamame puffs
Number of Brands: 1
Number of Products: 4
Type of Packaging: Consumer
Brands:
CRUNCH-A-MAME

3201 Crunchies Natural Food Company
733 Lakefield Dr
Suite B
Westlake Village, CA 91361
888-997-1866
crunchiesfood.com
Dried fruit and vegetable snacks
President & CEO: Scott Jacobson
Year Founded: 2004
Number Employees: 11-50
Type of Packaging: Private Label

3202 Crunchsters
303-545-9000
sales@crunchsters.com
www.crunchsters.com
Organic superfood snack
Founder: Frank Lambert
Sales & Marketing: Gina Lambert
Number of Brands: 1
Number of Products: 3
Type of Packaging: Consumer
Brands:
CRUNCHSTERS

3203 Crunchy Rollers
Dallas, TX 75233
info@crunchyrollers.com
crunchyrollers.com
Organic rice snack bars
Founder: Brian Park

3204 Cruse Vineyards
2883 Lakeshore Dr
Chester, SC 29706
803-377-3944
Wines
Owner: Kenneth Cruse
Owner: susan Cruse
Estimated Sales: $1-4.9,000,000
Number Employees: 1-4
Brands:
Cruse Vineyards
Red Vines

3205 Crush Foods Service
Westlake Village, CA 91361
818-699-6381
www.crushfoodservice.com
Portioned herbs, butters and sauces
VP, Business Development: Jon Startz
Type of Packaging: Consumer, Food Service

3206 Crusoe Seafood LLC
9500 El Dorado Avenue
Sun Valley, CA 91352-1339
866-343-7629
Fax: 818-768-2366 jcohen@sugarfoods.com
Seafood.

3207 Crustacean Foods
5369 W Pico Blvd
Los Angeles, CA 90019-4037
323-460-4387
Fax: 323-933-4863 866-263-2625
Gourmet sauces.
Owner: Elizabeth An
Estimated Sales: $300,000-500,000
Number Employees: 5-9

3208 Crusty Bakery Inc
60 Broad St # 35
Suite 3502
New York, NY 10004-2306
917-733-6396
Fax: 646-349-2240
Baked goods.
President: David Banet
Estimated Sales: Less Than $500,000
Number Employees: 5-9

3209 Crystal & Vigor Beverages
174 Sanford Ave
Kearny, NJ 07032-5920
201-991-2342
Fax: 201-991-1882
Alcoholic and non-alcoholic beverages
Owner: Martinho Oliveira
Estimated Sales: $2.5-5,000,000
Number Employees: 10-19
Type of Packaging: Private Label

3210 Crystal Creamery
529 Kansas Ave
Modesto, CA 95351
209-576-3400
866-225-4821
crystalcreamery.com
Milk.
President & CEO: Martin Devine
CFO: Bonnie Chan
VP, Human Resources: Walter Mendez
VP, Manufacturing: Hugo Andrade
Year Founded: 1901
Estimated Sales: $160 Million
Number Employees: 500-999
Type of Packaging: Consumer, Food Service, Private Label, Bulk
Other Locations:
Crystal Cream & Butter Co.
Sacramento CA
Brands:
Crystal

3211 Crystal Farms Dairy Company
Minnetonka, MN
800-672-8260
info@crystalfarms.com www.crystalfarms.com
Cheese and dairy products, including shredded and spreadable cheeses.
VP of Sales: Jason Krzewinski
Supply Chain Leader: John Larson
Number Employees: 30
Square Footage: 92000
Type of Packaging: Consumer
Brands:
Crystal Farms
Better'n EGGS

3212 Crystal Geyser Water Co.
Burlingame, CA 94010
800-443-9737
cgwconsumers@crystalgeyser.com
www.crystalgeyser.com
America's first domestic sparkling water
CEO: Yasumasa Iwamoto
VP, Finance: Kevin Moloughney
VP, Sales: Rob Bulot
Operations: Josh Butt
Year Founded: 1977
Number Employees: 50-99

3213 (HQ)Crystal Lake Farms
1200 E Roller Ave
Decatur, AR 72722
479-752-8274
800-382-4425
Processor and exporter of chicken

Manager: Daryl Hopkins
Vice President: Lisa Garrett
lisa@crystallakefarms.com
Sr Director, Commodity Sales: Bruce Bayley
VP Human Resources: Janet Wilkerson
Sr VP, Development: Dennis Martin
Estimated Sales: $500,000-$1 Million
Number Employees: 1000-4999
Type of Packaging: Food Service, Private Label, Bulk
Other Locations:
Crystal Lake
North Kansas City MO
Brands:
Crystal Lake

3214 **Crystal Lake LLC**
6500 W Crystal Lake Rd
Warsaw, IN 46580-8986
574-858-2514
Fax: 574-858-9886 info@crystallakellc.net
Liquid, frozen and cooked egg products.
President: Ron Truex
Sales Manager: Brian Hayward
Contact: Jeff Johnson
jeff.johnson@crystallakellc.net
Plant Manager: Jason Nichols
Estimated Sales: $10-20 Million
Number Employees: 1-4
Type of Packaging: Food Service, Private Label, Bulk

3215 **Crystal Noodle**
369 Van Ness Way
Suite 707
Torrance, CA 90501
310-781-9734
Fax: 310-212-6768 www.crystalnoodle.com
Manufacturer of freeze-dried soups.
President/Owner: Masaki Mizuhashi

3216 **Crystal Potato Seed Co**
652 6th St
Crystal, ND 58222-4021
701-657-2143
Fax: 701-657-2366
Seed potatoes
President: Bruce Otto
Partner: Robert Otto
Estimated Sales: $600,000
Number Employees: 1-4
Type of Packaging: Consumer
Brands:
Dr. Red Norland
Goldrush
Norchip
Red Lasoda
Shephody
Snowden

3217 **Crystal Rock LLC**
1050 Buckingham St
Watertown, CT 06795-6602
860-945-0661
Fax: 860-274-0397 800-525-0070
www.crystalrock.com
Spring water; also, office coffee service
President: Jack Baker
CEO: Peter Baker
VP of Finance: David Jurasek
VP Sales/Marketing: Peter Guildner
VP of Procurement: Tim Descoteaux
Estimated Sales: $10.7 Million
Number Employees: 100-249
Type of Packaging: Consumer
Brands:
Crystal Rock Water
Vermont Pure Water
Cool Beans Coffee

3218 **Crystal Springs**
1200 Britannia Road East
Mississauga, ON L4W 4T5
Canada
905-795-6500
Fax: 905-670-3628 800-822-5889
www.crystalsprings.ca
Bottled water
Marketing Manager: Jeff Smith
Retail Manager: Steve Bondmini
General Manager: Paul Elliot
Production Manager: Eric Chastain
Estimated Sales: $5-10 Million
Number Employees: 100-249
Type of Packaging: Private Label
Brands:
Crystal Springs
Value Glacier

3219 **Crystal Springs Bottled Water**
200 Eagles Landing Blvd
Lakeland, FL 33810
800-728-5508
www.crystal-springs.com
Bottled water
VP/GM Mid-Atlantic Region: Edward Gemind
Estimated Sales: F
Number Employees: 50-99
Number of Brands: 1
Parent Co: DS Services Of America Inc.

3220 **Crystal Springs Water Company**
200 Eagles Landing Blvd
Lakeland, FL 33810
800-728-5508
www.crystal-springs.com
Bottled, spring, purified, distilled and fluoridated drinking water.
President & CEO: Jeff Vinyard
Year Founded: 1921
Estimated Sales: $20-50 Million
Number Employees: 100-249
Number of Brands: 11
Parent Co: DS Services
Brands:
Alhambra®
Athena®
Belmont Springs®
Crystal Springs®
Deep Rock®
Hinckley Springs®
Kentwood Springs®
Mount Olympus®
Nursery®
Sierra Springs®
Sparkletts®

3221 **Crystal Star Herbal Nutrition**
1542 N Sanborn Rd
Salinas, CA 93905-4760
831-422-7500
Fax: 800-260-4349 www.crystalstar.com
Processor, importer and exporter of herbal extracts, capsules, teas, powdered drink mixes and sports nutrition products
Manager: Julie Lu
Founder: Linda Page PhD
VP Sales: Scott Seabaugh
VP Operations: Glenn Korando
Estimated Sales: Less than $500,000
Number Employees: 1-4
Square Footage: 40000
Parent Co: Jones Products International
Type of Packaging: Consumer, Bulk

3222 **Crystal Temptations**
67 Porete Ave
North Arlington, NJ 07031
201-246-7990
Fax: 201-246-7995 info@crystaltemptations.com
crystaltemptations.com
Gourmet popcorn and confections
Manager: Ari Green
VP, Operations: Solomon Green
Year Founded: 1995
Estimated Sales: $170 Million
Number Employees: 50
Type of Packaging: Private Label

3223 **Cucina & Amore**
2100 Atlas Rd
Unit F01
San Pablo, CA 94806
510-964-4838
info@cucinaandamore.com
www.cucinaandamore.com
Specialty foods, including gnocchi, oils, vinaigrettes and sauces
Founder & Chairman: Ruth Wilkinson
CEO: Hossein Banejad
Operations: Dean Wilkinson
Year Founded: 2007
Type of Packaging: Consumer
Brands:
CUCINA & AMORE

3224 **Cucina Antica Foods Corp**
333 N Bedford Rd # 118
Mt Kisco, NY 10549-1160
914-244-9700
Fax: 914-244-1794 877-728-2462
info@cucina-antica.com www.montebene.com
Italian sauces
Owner: Niel Fusco
neil@cucina-antica.com
Estimated Sales: $5-10 Million
Number Employees: 1-4

3225 **Cudlin's Meat Market**
8 Cox Rd
Newfield, NY 14867-9420
607-564-3443
Meat products; also, slaughtering services available
President: Vince Distefano
Estimated Sales: Less Than $500,000
Number Employees: 1-4
Type of Packaging: Consumer

3226 **Cugino's Gourmet Foods**
1000 Meyer Dr
Crystal Lake, IL 60014
815-455-7242
Fax: 815-455-1948 888-592-8446
dhochstatter@cuginos.com www.cuginos.com
Garlic bread spread, gourmet soups, pasta sauce, BBQ sauce and marinades
Owner: Daniel Hochstatter
Estimated Sales: $10-20 Million
Number Employees: 10-19

3227 **Cuisine International**
1920 Swarthmore Ave
Suite 1
Lakewood, NJ 08701-4589
732-367-2145
Fax: 732-730-9913 info@cuisinellc.com
www.cuisinellc.com
Frozen hors d'oeuvres
Estimated Sales: Less Than $500,000
Number Employees: 5-9
Type of Packaging: Consumer, Food Service

3228 **Cuisine Perel**
1001 Canal Blvd Ste A
Richmond, CA 94804
510-232-0343
Fax: 510-232-0321 800-887-3735
info@cuisineperel.com www.cuisineperel.com
Chocolate, salad dressings, flavored grapeseed oil, mayonnaise, pasta and barbecue sauces, dry pastas and mustard; private label available
Owner: Mark Birchall
mark@cuisineperel.com
Estimated Sales: $2.5-5 Million
Number Employees: 5-9
Square Footage: 24000
Type of Packaging: Private Label

3229 **Cuisine Solutions Inc**
1501 Moran Rd # 100
Suite 100
Sterling, VA 20166-9338
703-270-2900
Fax: 703-750-1158 888-285-4679
information@cuisinesolutions.com
www.cuisinesolutions.com
Prepared foods including beef meals, lamb, pork, veal, poultry, rice, pasta, sauces, seafood and vegetarian meals.
Chairman/CEO: Stanislas Vilgrain
President: Felipe Hasselmann
Vice President: Martha Anderson
manderson@jchs.edu
Estimated Sales: $29.2 Million
Number Employees: 250-499
Number of Brands: 2
Square Footage: 58000
Type of Packaging: Food Service
Brands:
Cuisine Solutions
Five Leaf

3230 **Cuizina Food Company**
18565 142nd Ave NE
Woodinville, WA 98072-8523
425-486-7000
Fax: 425-486-1148

Sauces including alfredo, marinara, primavera and spaghetti; also, minestrone and croppino soup and pastas including frozen, filled, extruded and vegetable blends.
President: Ric Ferrera
Contact: Arnold Alvarado
aalvarado@cuizina.com
Estimated Sales: $5 Million
Number Employees: 35
Square Footage: 40000
Type of Packaging: Consumer, Food Service, Private Label, Bulk
Brands:
Cuizina Italia

3231 **Culina**
Austin, TX 78701
www.culinayogurt.com
Botanical yogurt alternative
Type of Packaging: Consumer, Food Service

3232 **Culinaire**
1111 W Exposition Ave
Denver, CO 80223-2335
303-592-9100
Fax: 303-592-7619 877-502-9100
leo@culinairefoods.com www.culinairefoods.com
Hand made gourmet hors d oeuvres and entrees. Custom production available
President: Leo Reiff
Number Employees: 10-19
Number of Brands: 2
Number of Products: 110+
Square Footage: 20000
Type of Packaging: Consumer, Food Service, Private Label
Brands:
Bistro Faire
Culinaire

3233 **Culinar Canada**
58 Av William-Dobell
Baie-Comeau, QC G4Z 1T7
Canada
418-296-4395
Fax: 418-296-4395
Cakes
Head Culinary Chef: Will Franz
Number Employees: 500-999
Parent Co: Culinar Canada
Brands:
Frenzi

3234 **Culinary Farms Inc**
1244 E Beamer St
Woodland, CA 95776-6002
916-375-3000
Fax: 916-375-3010 888-383-2767
info@culinaryfarms.com www.culinaryfarms.com
Processors of dried tomatoes, tomato paste and mexican chile peppers.
President: Mohammad Azam
drazam@culinaryfarms.com
CFO: Bal Pattar
National Sales Manager: Deepak Singh
Estimated Sales: $5-10 Million
Number Employees: 10-19
Square Footage: 24000
Type of Packaging: Bulk

3235 **Culinary Institute Lenotre**
7070 Allensby St
Houston, TX 77022-4322
713-692-0077
Fax: 713-692-7399 888-536-6873
Processor, importer and exporter of frozen strudel, muffins, cakes, cookies, danish, etc
Owner: Alain Lenotre
alenotre@culinaryinstitute.edu
VP: Marie Le Notre
Estimated Sales: $2 Million
Number Employees: 50-99
Square Footage: 120000
Type of Packaging: Private Label

3236 **Culinary Masters Corporation**
69 Brandywine Trl
Suite 109
Alpharetta, GA 30005
770-667-1688
Fax: 770-667-1682 800-261-5261
www.culinarymasters.com
Wholesaler/distributor and importer of specialty foods, baked goods, equipment and tools; serving the food service market; exporter of spices, blends and specialty equipment
Master Chef/President: Helmut Holzer
Controller: Beth Ann Jackson
Vice President: Sara Jane Holzer
Sales: Michelle Brayley
Estimated Sales: $3-5 Million
Number Employees: 5-9
Square Footage: 16000
Type of Packaging: Food Service, Private Label
Brands:
Affiorato
Dreimeister
Ravifruit
Stubi
Symphony Pastries
Vincotto

3237 **Culinary Revolution**
1320 Inspiration Drive
La Jolla, CA 92037-6810
858-454-4390
Fax: 323-939-4844 chefakasha@aol.com
Organic and diet food
Owner: Harry Coplan

3238 **Culligan International Co**
9399 W Higgins Rd # 1100
Suite 1100
Rosemont, IL 60018-4940
847-430-2800
Fax: 732-512-0166 800-231-9283
www.culligan.com
Water Systems, Water
Manager: Bob Prigen
President: Scoot Levy
Chairman: Peter Dixon
Estimated Sales: Under $500,000
Number Employees: 5000-9999
Parent Co: Culligan Water Technologies

3239 **Culligan International Company**
9399 West Higgins Road
Suite 1100
Rosemont, IL 60018
847-205-6000
Fax: 847-205-6030 www.culligan.com
Water softeners, filtration systems, drinking water systems, commercial and industrial water treatment solutions, whole-house filtration systems and bottled water delivery
Chairman: George Tamke
CEO: Mark Seals
VP Marketing: Eric Rosenthal
VP Sales North America, Comm & Indust: Rod McNelly
Media Contact: Jennifer Griffin
Operations Manager: Jackie McCaleb
Plant Manager: Seth Lewis
Estimated Sales: $26.2 Million
Number Employees: 2000
Brands:
Culligan

3240 **Culture**
60 W 8th St
New York, NY 10011
718-499-0207
cultureny.com
Yogurt
Founder: Jenny Ammirati
Type of Packaging: Consumer

3241 **Culture Republick**
Englewood Cliffs, NJ 07632
800-662-0348
www.culturerepublick.com
Probiotic ice cream
Marketing: Leslie Miller
Number of Products: 7
Type of Packaging: Consumer, Food Service

3242 **Culture Systems Inc**
3224 N Home St
Mishawaka, IN 46545-4436
574-258-0602
Fax: 574-258-1136 info@culturesystemsinc.com
www.culturesystemsinc.com
Processor, exporter and wholesaler/distributor of dairy ingredients; also, researcher for the food industry
President: David Kim
dhyungkim@aol.com
Estimated Sales: $1-2.5 Million
Number Employees: 10-19
Square Footage: 16000

3243 **Cultures for Health**
200 Innovation Ave
Suite 150
Morrisville, NC 27560
www.culturesforhealth.com
Starter cultures for cultured and fermented food
Co-Founder: Julie Feickert
Co-Founder: Eric Feickert

3244 **Culver Duck Farms Inc**
12215 County Road 10
PO Box 910
Middlebury, IN 46540-9694
574-825-9537
Fax: 574-825-2613 800-825-9225
info@culverduck.com www.culverduck.com
Duck, chicken and sausage products.
President: John Metzger
Year Founded: 1858
Estimated Sales: $20-50 Million
Number Employees: 100-249
Square Footage: 30000
Type of Packaging: Food Service
Brands:
Culver Duck

3245 **Culver Fish Farm**
1316 W Kansas Ave
Mcpherson, KS 67460-6053
620-241-5200
Fax: 620-241-5202 800-241-5205
Fish
Owner: Brent Culver
culverfish@gmail.com
Estimated Sales: Less Than $500,000
Number Employees: 1-4

3246 **Cumberland Creamery**
4350 Hurricane Creek Blvd
Antioch, TN 37013-2223
615-641-1027
Fax: 615-641-7038
Dairy
Operations Manager: Jim Monteleone
General Manager: David Moss
Plant Manager: Bill Merrick
Estimated Sales: Under $500,000
Number Employees: 50-99
Parent Co: Suiza Foods

3247 **Cumberland Dairy**
899 Landis Ave
Rosenhayn, NJ 08352
856-451-1300
Fax: 856-451-1332 800-257-8484
sales@cumberlanddairy.com
www.cumberlanddairy.com
Ice cream mixes, juices, soy products and milk including whole, skim, 1% and 2%; processor of ice cream
President: Carmine Catalana
CFO: Stan Fronczkowski
Director of Research & Development: John Contino
Director of Quality: Richard Grigsby
VP Sales: David A Catalana
VP Operations: Frank Catalana
Year Founded: 1932
Estimated Sales: $20-50 Million
Number Employees: 100-249
Type of Packaging: Consumer, Food Service, Private Label, Bulk
Brands:
Cumberland Dairy

3248 **Cumberland Gap Provision Company**
South 23rd Street
PO Box 1797
Middlesboro, KY 40965
606-248-3311
Fax: 606-248-6517 855-411-7675
consumeraffairs@smithfield.com
www.cumberlandgapprovision.com
Fresh smoked sausages and hams

President/CEO: Ray Mc Gregor
Vice President: Patrick Flanagan
Quality Control: Kim Treiter
Sales Director: Tim Kreiter
Contact: Michael Bailey
michael.bailey@johnmorrell.com
Purchasing Manager: Gary Evans
Estimated Sales: $20-50 Million
Number Employees: 320
Parent Co: Smithfield Foods
Type of Packaging: Consumer, Food Service, Private Label
Brands:
Cumberland Gap
Hickory Hills
Old Kentucky

3249 **Cummings Studio Chocolates**
679 E 900 S
Salt Lake City, UT 84105-1128
801-328-4858
Fax: 801-328-4801 800-537-3957
candy@CummingsStudioChocolates.com
www.cummingsstudiochocolates.com
Processors of candy including chocolates
President/CEO: Marion Cummings
marion@cummingsstudiochocolates.com
Marketing Manager: Jolend Proter
Estimated Sales: $2.5-5 Million
Number Employees: 50-99
Square Footage: 28000

3250 **Cuneo Cellars**
9360 SE Eola Hills Road
Amity, OR 97101-2416
503-835-2782
Wines
Partner: Gino Cuneo
Estimated Sales: Less than $500,000
Number Employees: 1-4

3251 **Cup 4 Cup LLC**
6540 Washington Street
Yountville, CA 94599
833-287-4287
www.cup4cup.com
Gluten free flour, baking mixes
Owner/Chef: Lena Kwak
Co-Founder: Thomas Keller
National Sales Director: Sarah Robinson
Contact: Magali Delgado
magalidelgado@cup4cup.com

3252 **Cup 4 Cup LLC**
840 Latour Ct
Suite B
Napa, CA 94558-6286
707-754-4263
Fax: 707-927-0130 www.cup4cup.com
Gluten-free baking mixes, flour and other ingredients.
General Manager: Dave Mogridge
Year Founded: 2010
Number Employees: 11-50

3253 **Cupid Candies**
7637 S Western Ave
Chicago, IL 60620-5871
773-925-8191
Fax: 773-925-7736
Candy
President: John Stefanos
cupidcandiesinc@yahoo.com
Estimated Sales: $3 Million
Number Employees: 20-49
Square Footage: 28512
Type of Packaging: Consumer, Private Label

3254 **Cupoladua Oven**
PO Box 266
Wexford, PA 15090
412-592-5378
info@cupoladuaoven.com
www.cupoladuaoven.com
All natural baked goods, sweet treats and savory snacks.

3255 **(HQ)Cupper's Coffee Company**
1502C 3rd Avenu South
Lethbridge, AB T1J 0K8
Canada
403-380-4555
Fax: 403-328-8004 cuppercoffee@gmil.com
Importer and exporter of coffee

President: Al Anctil
Number Employees: 20-49

3256 **Curaleaf**
301 Edgewater Pl
Suite 405
Wakefield, MA 01880
833-760-4367
info@curaleafhemp.com curaleafhemp.com
Hemp-based CBD products including tinctures, topical creams and vape pens
President and CEO: Joe Lusardi

3257 **Curley's Custom Meats**
315 East St
Jackson Center, OH 45334-5078
937-596-6518
Fax: 937-596-6518 www.curlysmeats.com
Meats
President: Larry Edwards
lawrence@curlysjerky.com
Estimated Sales: $2.5-5,000,000
Number Employees: 1-4

3258 **Curly's Foods Inc**
5201 Eden Ave # 181
Suite 370
Edina, MN 55436-2449
612-920-3400
Fax: 612-920-9889 www.curlys.com
Beef including roast, corned, barbecued and cooked and frozen ribs.
President: John Pauley
Vice President: Ken Fineberg
Manager, R&D: Brian Quandt
Estimated Sales: $22 Million
Number Employees: 500-999
Number of Brands: 1
Square Footage: 100000
Parent Co: John Morrell/Smithfield Foods
Type of Packaging: Consumer, Food Service, Private Label, Bulk
Brands:
Curly's

3259 **Curran's Cheese Plant Inc**
W8850 Davis Rd
Browntown, WI 53522-9741
608-966-3361
Fax: 608-966-3309
Cheese products
Owner: Jim Curran
Estimated Sales: Less Than $500,000
Number Employees: 5-9
Brands:
Curran Cheese

3260 **Curry King Corporation**
34 West Prospect St
Waldwick, NJ 07463
201-652-6228
Fax: 201-447-3291 800-287-7987
info@curryking.com www.curryking.com
Processor and importer of curry, balti and tandoori sauce; also, mango chutney; exporter of curry sauce
President: Lall Kwatra
lall@addesign.net
Vice President: Pamela Kwatra
Estimated Sales: Under $500,000
Number Employees: 3
Square Footage: 10000
Type of Packaging: Food Service, Private Label, Bulk
Brands:
Curry King

3261 **Curtice Burns Foods**
11 Clark St
Shortsville, NY 14548-9755
585-289-4414
Fax: 585-289-4280
Canned fruits and vegetables
Chief Financial Officer: Tom Palmer
Manager: Luke Plamondon
Estimated Sales: $1-3 Million
Number Employees: 40
Parent Co: Curtice Burns
Type of Packaging: Consumer, Food Service, Private Label

3262 **Curtis Packing Co**
2416 Randolph Ave
Greensboro, NC 27406-2910
336-275-7684
Fax: 336-275-1901
www.curtispackingcompany.com
Packer of meat products including frankfurters, bologna, bacon, ham, beef and fresh pork
President: Douglas Curtis
douglas.curtis@curtispackingcompany.com
Sales Executive: John Curtis
Estimated Sales: $18 Million
Number Employees: 50-99
Number of Brands: 6
Square Footage: 40000
Type of Packaging: Consumer
Brands:
Beef Master
Curtis
Ibp
Mbpxl
Monfort
Porter House

3263 **Cusa Tea**
1823 Folsom St
Boulder, CO 80302
cusatea.com
Premium instant teas
Founder: Jim Lamancusa
Number of Brands: 1
Number of Products: 6
Type of Packaging: Consumer
Brands:
CUSA TEA

3264 **Cusack Meats**
301 SW 12th St
Oklahoma City, OK 73109
Fax: 405-232-2127 800-241-6328
cusack@cusackmeats.com www.cusackmeats.com
Beef, pork, lamb, veal and poultry
Owner: Donnie Cusack
General Manager: Al Cusack
Year Founded: 1933
Estimated Sales: $20-50 Million
Number Employees: 20-49
Type of Packaging: Food Service

3265 **Cusano's Baking Company**
2798 SW 32nd Ave
Hallandale, FL 33009
954-458-1010
Fax: 954-458-1052 sales@cusanosbakery.com
www.cusanosbakery.com
Italian bread and bakery products
Owner: Michael Grecco
Co-Owner: Sal Grecco
Director: Mike Hernandez
General Manager: Sal Grego
Estimated Sales: $5-10 Million
Number Employees: 79
Brands:
Cusano's

3266 **Cushner Seafoods Inc**
4141 Amos Ave
Baltimore, MD 21215-3309
410-358-5564
Fax: 410-358-5558
Fish & Seafood
Owner: Jack Deckelbaum
Estimated Sales: $1,600,000
Number Employees: 5-9

3267 **(HQ)Custom Coffee Plan**
20333 Normandie Ave
Torrance, CA 90502-1215
310-787-5200
Fax: 310-787-5394 800-841-5949
dsdcustomerservice@farmerbros.com
Manufacturer, wholesaler and distributor of coffee, tea, and culinary products.
District Sales Manager: Mike Zankich
Manager: Jon Smith
jsmith@ccpusa.net
Number Employees: 100-249
Type of Packaging: Food Service

3268 **Custom Confections & More**
PO Box 62
Algonquin, IL 60102-0062
832-420-5944
Fax: 208-342-5996

Hard candy, lollipops
President: Lowell Fugal
Estimated Sales: $5-10 Million
Number Employees: 20-49

3269 **Custom Culinary Inc.**
1000 E. State Pkwy.
Suite 1
Schaumberg, IL 60173-4569
866-878-3827
800-621-8827
www.customculinary.com
Gravy mixes, soup bases, soup mixes and sauce & gravy concentrates.
Regional Manager: Tom Nemanich
Vice President Operations: David Love
Year Founded: 1945
Estimated Sales: $100 Million
Number Employees: 100-249
Number of Brands: 3
Square Footage: 75000
Parent Co: Griffith Laboratories, Inc.
Type of Packaging: Food Service, Bulk
Brands:
Gold Label
Master's Touch
Panroast

3270 **Custom Food Solutions LLC**
2505 Data Dr
Louisville, KY 40299-2517
502-671-6966
Fax: 502-671-6906 800-767-2993
www.customfoodsolutions.com
A USDA, FDA and AIB inspected food manufacturing facility specializing in custom batch, fresh ingredient production of soups, sauces, fillings and Sous Vide cooked proteins in flexible sized pouches.
Sales: Karen Reid
Facilities: Chris Smith
Number Employees: 20-49
Number of Products: 50
Square Footage: 130000
Type of Packaging: Food Service

3271 **Custom Foods Inc**
9101 Commerce Dr
De Soto, KS 66018-8410
913-585-1900
Fax: 913-585-1470 www.customfoodsinc.com
Frozen bakery products
Number Employees: 20-49

3272 **Custom House Seafoods**
PO Box 7112
Portland, ME 04112
207-773-2778
Fax: 207-761-9458
Fish and seafood.
President: Craig Johnson
Estimated Sales: $820,000
Number Employees: 1-4

3273 **Custom Ingredients Inc**
1614 N Interstate 35
New Braunfels, TX 78130-2502
830-608-0915
Fax: 830-625-7914 800-457-8935
info@customingredients.com
www.customingredients.com
Ingredients, snacks, dips, bakery, sauces, tortilla
President: James Curry
brcurry@customingredientsinc.com
Marketing: D Ames
Operations: Grey Baker
Production: R Nahn
Estimated Sales: $2.5-5 Million
Number Employees: 10-19
Type of Packaging: Bulk

3274 **Custom Produce Sales**
13475 E Progress Dr
Parlier, CA 93648-9674
559-254-5800
Fax: 559-646-1003
Peaches, nectarines, blueberries, apricots, plums and grapes
Manager: Bob Melenbacker
Number Employees: 100-249
Brands:
River Island
River Valley Farms

3275 **Custom-Pak Meats**
2013 Dutch Valley Road
Knoxville, TN 37918
615-687-0871
Packer of meat
President: C Hobbs
Executive VP: Christopher Satterfield
Number Employees: 42
Square Footage: 99200
Type of Packaging: Food Service
Brands:
Nugget
Pocahontas

3276 **Cutie Pie Corp**
443 W 400 N
Salt Lake City, UT 84103-1227
801-533-9550
Fax: 801-355-8021 800-453-4575
www.getcutiepie.com
Processor and exporter of frozen fruit snack pies
Principal: Bob Sharp
CFO: Lee Rucker
Director: Lee Wacker
Manager: Williams Arroyo
arroyo@horizonsnackfoods.com
Estimated Sales: Under $500,000
Number Employees: 50-99
Type of Packaging: Consumer, Food Service
Brands:
Cutie Pies

3277 **Cutone Specialty Foods**
145 Market Street
Chelsea, MA 02150
617-889-1122
Fax: 617-884-3944
customerservice@cutonespecialtyfoods.com
www.cutonespecialtyfoods.com
Marinated and blanched mushrooms
President/Owner: Mario Cutone

3278 **Cutrale Citrus Juices**
602 McKean St.
Auburndale, FL 33823-4070
863-965-5000
Fax: 863-965-5311 www.cutrale.com
Grapefruit and orange juices.
President: Hugh Thompson
Year Founded: 1996
Estimated Sales: $173 Million
Number Employees: 400
Square Footage: 16252
Parent Co: Sucocitrico Cutrale Ltda.
Type of Packaging: Consumer, Food Service, Private Label, Bulk

3279 **Cutting Edge Beverages**
2424 N Federal Hwy
#101
Boca Raton, FL 33431-7796
561-347-5860
Manufacturer of juices, sparkling juices, juice drinks and flavoured waters.
Estimated Sales: $5-10 Million
Number Employees: 5-9
Number of Brands: 4
Parent Co: Whitlock Packaging Corporation
Brands:
Juice Bowl
JB'S Extreme
Fruit Wave H2O
Juice Bowl Sparkling Juice

3280 **Cuvaison Winery**
4550 Silverado Trl
Calistoga, CA 94515-9604
707-942-6266
Fax: 707-942-5732 www.cuvaison.com
Red and white wines.
President: Jay Schuppert
jschuppert@cuvaison.com
CFO: Bonnie Schoch
Dir. Of Consumer Sales & Marketing: Mary Pencek
National Sales Manager: Steve Richards
Estimated Sales: $10-20 Million
Number Employees: 20-49
Type of Packaging: Consumer, Food Service
Brands:
Cuvaison

3281 **Cyanotech Corp**
73-4460 Queen Kaahumanu
Suite 102
Kailua Kona, HI 96740-2637
808-326-1353
Fax: 808-329-4533 800-395-1353
info@cyanotech.com www.cyanotech.com
Cyanotech Corporation, the world's leader in microalgae technology, produces high-value natural products from microalgae, and is the world's largest commercial producer of natural astaxanthin from microalgae. Products include HawaiiamSpirulina Pacifica, a nutrient-rich dietary supplement; BioAstin, a natural astaxanthin, a powerful antioxidant with expanding applications as a human nutraceutical
CEO: Gerald R Cysewski
gcysewski@cyanotech.com
VP Sales/Marketing: Robert Capelli
Sales Manager: Jeane Vinson
Estimated Sales: F
Number Employees: 100-249
Number of Brands: 3
Number of Products: 2
Square Footage: 1306800
Parent Co: Cyanotech Corporation
Type of Packaging: Consumer, Private Label, Bulk
Brands:
Bioastin Natural Astaxanthin
Spirulina Hawaiian Spirulina

3282 **Cybele's Free To Eat**
Los Angeles, CA 90046
877-895-3729
info@cybelesfreetoeat.com cybelesfreetoeat.com
Vegan cookies and superfood veggie pastas
President & CEO: Cybele Pascal
Number of Brands: 1
Number of Products: 9
Type of Packaging: Consumer
Brands:
CYBELE'S FREE TO EAT

3283 **Cybros**
P.O.Box 851
Waukesha, WI 53187-0851
262-547-1821
Fax: 262-547-8946 800-876-2253
Fine breads, rolls, cookies and other products
Owner: Debbie Brooks
General Manager: Paul Geboy
Estimated Sales: $2.5-5 Million
Number Employees: 10-19
Square Footage: 32000

3284 **Cyclone Enterprises Inc**
146 Knobcrest Dr
Houston, TX 77060-1213
281-872-0087
Fax: 281-872-7645 www.cyclone-ent.com
Processor and importer of Mexican food including hot sauce and peppers. Distributors of dry, canned, processed and frozen grocery items including juices, drinks, dairy products, meats, cheeses, deli products, specialty foods, herbsspices, candy and snac
Owner: Mike Germany
Sales: Jim Petree
mgermany@cyclone-ent.com
Customer Support: Dora Mendoza
General Information: Martha Gibbs
Purchasing: Lam Townsend
Estimated Sales: $2.5-5 Million
Number Employees: 100-249
Type of Packaging: Consumer, Food Service, Private Label

3285 **Cygnet Cellars**
PO Box 1956
Hollister, CA 95024-1956
831-637-7559
Wine
Partner: Jim Johnson
Estimated Sales: $500,000 appx.
Number Employees: 1-4
Brands:
Cygnet

3286 **Cypress Grove**
1330 Q St
Arcata, CA 95521
707-825-1100
Fax: 707-825-1101 info@cypressgrovecheese.com
cypressgrovecheese.com
Goat cheeses

Founder: Mary Keehn
President: Pamela Dressler
Year Founded: 1983
Estimated Sales: $9317243
Number Employees: 51-200
Type of Packaging: Private Label

3287 **Cypress Point Creamery**
18825 SE 24th Ave
Hawthorne, FL 32640
352-481-2806
www.cypresspointcreamery.com
Cheese

3288 **(HQ)Cyrils Bakery**
2890 W State Road 84 # 103
Unit 103
Fort Lauderdale, FL 33312-4828
954-797-1832
Fax: 413-473-9708 800-929-7457
sales@cyrils.com www.cyrils.com
Frozen bakery products including breads and pastries.
President: Cyril Cohen
CEO: Adam Weizer
adam@servistree.com
VP: Adam Weizer
Estimated Sales: Less Than $500,000
Number Employees: 1-4
Number of Brands: 1
Number of Products: 75
Type of Packaging: Consumer, Food Service

3289 **Czech Stop Grocery & Deli**
105 N College Ave
105 N. College St.
West, TX 76691-1455
254-826-4161
Fax: 254-826-5117 Info@CzechStop.net
www.czechstop.net
Baked goods
President: Bill Polk
Number Employees: 50-99

3290 **Czepiel Millers Dairy**
PO Box 277
Ludlow, MA 01056-0277
413-589-0828
Fax: 413-589-0828
Dairy
President: Stanly Czepiel

3291 **Czimer's Game & Seafoods**
13136 W 159th St
Homer Glen, IL 60491
708-301-0500
888-294-6377
www.czimers.com
Meat and fish
Owner: Richard Czimer Jr
Estimated Sales: $300,000
Number Employees: 1-4

3292 **D & D Foods Inc**
5820 Weston Parkway
West Des Moines, IA 50266
515-267-2800
800-772-4098
productinquiry@hy-vee.com www.hy-vee.com
Barbecue sauces, marinades and salad dressings; also, contract packaging available
President: Fred Dodelin
fdodelin@hy-vee.com
CFO: Fred Dodelin
Estimated Sales: $3-5 Million
Number Employees: 5-9
Type of Packaging: Consumer, Food Service, Private Label, Bulk
Brands:
Foy's B.B.Q. Sauce

3293 **D & D Sugarwoods Farm**
2287 Glover St
Glover, VT 05839-9356
802-525-3718
Fax: 802-525-4103 800-245-3718
SugarwoodsFarm@comcast.net
Produces Vermont maple syrup, maple candy, maple cream and all natural pancake mixes.
Estimated Sales: Less Than $500,000
Number Employees: 5-9
Type of Packaging: Consumer, Food Service, Private Label

3294 **D D Williamson & Co Inc**
1901 Payne St
Louisville, KY 40206-1902
502-895-2438
Fax: 502-895-7381
Global manufacturer of natural colour for the food and beverage industries with facilities in Africa, Asia, Europe and North and South America.
Chairman & CEO: Ted Nixon
Type of Packaging: Bulk

3295 **D F Ingredients Inc**
127 Elm St # 200
Suite 200
Washington, MO 63090-2140
636-583-0802
Fax: 630-583-4877 888-583-0802
michael@dfingredients.com
www.dfingredients.com
Ingredients and dairy products
President: Michael Husmann
Vice President: Larry Rice
Sales Rep: Richard Kuddes
Sales Rep: Kenneth Johnson
Sales Rep: Jim Wesselschmidt
Manager: Megan Bade
megan@dfingredients.com
Number Employees: 1-4

3296 **D I Mfg LLC**
13335 C St
Omaha, NE 68144-3601
402-330-5650
info@dimanufacturing.com
www.dimanufacturing.com
Specialty food products including gluten free foods, garlic bread, wrapped breads, pizza, cookie dough
Contact: Zack Best
zbest@dimanufacturing.com
Number Employees: 10-19
Type of Packaging: Food Service, Bulk

3297 **D Seafood**
2723 S Poplar Avenue
Chicago, IL 60608-5915
312-808-1086
Fax: 312-808-0869
Seafood
Owner: De Trinh

3298 **D Steengrafe Co Inc**
1726 Main St
Pleasant Valley, NY 12569-5611
845-635-4067
Fax: 845-635-4239
Manufacturer and importer of beeswax, botanicals, kola nuts and nut powder, quassia chips, dried ginger and spices
VP: Margot Nordenholt
m_nordenholt@yahoo.com
VP: Carl Schmidt
Estimated Sales: $5 Million
Number Employees: 1-4
Type of Packaging: Bulk

3299 **D Waybret & Sons Fisheries**
3 Clam Point
Shelburne, NS B0T 1W0
Canada
902-745-3477
Fax: 902-745-2112
Manufacturer and exporter of fresh and salted haddock, cod, halibut and hake; also, fresh lobster
President/Co-Owner: Dewey Waybret
Manager/Co-Owner: Cecil Waybret
Number Employees: 50
Type of Packaging: Bulk

3300 **D&M Seafood**
135 N King St # 2b
Honolulu, HI 96817-5084
808-531-0687
Fax: 808-531-4947
Seafood
Owner: Hansen Chong

3301 **D'Arrigo Brothers Company of California**
21777 Harris Rd
Salinas, CA 93908
831-455-4500
Fax: 831-455-4445 bcoleman@darrigo.com
www.andyboy.com
Vegetables: broccoli, fennel, hearts of romaine, broccoli rabe, cauliflower and cactus pear
President & CEO: John D'Arrigo
Chairman: Andy D'Arrigo
VP, Sales & Business Development: Chad Amaral
Director, Business Development: Matt Amaral
Director, Marketing & Culinary: Claudia Villalobos
VP, Sales: Dave Martinez
Director, Sales: John Scherpinski
Estimated Sales: $22 Million
Type of Packaging: Consumer, Bulk
Brands:
Andy Boy
Green Head

3302 **D'Artagnan**
600 Green Ln
Union, NJ 07083-8074
973-344-0565
Fax: 973-465-1870 800-327-8246
www.dartagnan.com
Gourmet foods: beef, duck, lamb
Owner: Lily Hodge
lilyh@unionleague.org
Number Employees: 100-249

3303 **D'Oni Enterprises**
PO Box 962
San Juan Capistrano, CA 92693-0962
949-240-3053
Fax: 949-240-3086 800-809-8298
www.d-0ni.com
Sauces
President: Greg Bloom
Vice President: David Dallesandro
Vice President: David Bloom
Shipping/Receiving: Linda Trudeau

3304 **D-Liteful Baking Company**
9012 NW 105 Way
Medley, FL 33178
305-883-6449
Fax: 305-883-8797
Product line includes that of Heavenly Desserts featuring a variety of sugar free products such as cheesecakes and meringues available in vanilla, chocolate, cappuccino, strawberry and lemon flavors. Their Heavenly Harvest lineincludes sugar free baked products such as sesame and wheat crackers.
Founder: Jorge Guevara
Type of Packaging: Food Service

3305 **D2 Ingredients, LP.**
1244 Enterprise Dr
De Pere, WI 54115
920-425-8870
Fax: 920-964-0116 info@d2ingredients.com
d2ingredients.com
Functional ingredients and products, including smoke flavorings, alginate products, extrudable yeast-less doughs and savory fillings; spice blends, caramelized sugars and commodities; injection and tumbling products for poulty andmeat. Also provide
Vice President of Sales & Marketing: Dan Rose
Type of Packaging: Private Label, Bulk

3306 **DAGOBA Organic Chocolate**
1105 Benson Way
Ashland, OR 97520-9540
541-482-2001
Fax: 541-482-5661 866-972-6879
dagoba@worldpantry.com
www.dagobachocolate.com
Organic chocolate bars, drinking chocolate, baking products, tasting squares, and professional products.
Estimated Sales: $10-20 Million
Number Employees: 20-49
Type of Packaging: Consumer
Brands:
Dagoba Organic Chocolate

3307 **DB Kenney Fisheries**
301 Water Street
PO Box 1210
Westport, NS B0V 1H0
Canada
902-839-2023
Fax: 902-839-2070
dbkenney@dbkenneyfisheries.com
www.dbkenneyfisheries.com
Manufacturer and exporter of scallops, lobster, cod and haddock

President: Daniel Kenney Jr
Controller: Steven Lombard
Sales Manager: Dave Titus
Operations manager: Glenn Wadman
Number Employees: 50-99
Type of Packaging: Bulk

3308 **DDW: The Color House**
1901 Payne Street
Louisville, KY 40206
502-895-2438
Fax: 502-895-7381 www.ddwcolor.com
Natural colors, coloring foods, caramel colors and burnt sugars.
President: Elaine Gravatte
CEO: Ted Nixon
Chief Financial Officer: Ann Joseph
VP Global Human Resources: Ute Purschke-Hamdani
Chief Operating Officer: Elaine Gravatte
Other Locations:
DDW Global Support Center
Louisville KY
D.D. Williamson Colors, LLC
Port Washington WI

3309 **DF Mavens**
24-20 49th St
Astoria, NY 11103
347-813-4705
info@falfoodsworldwide.com
dfmavens.com
Fruit based frozen deserts
President: Malcom Stogo
Marketing Manager: Maria Correa
Year Founded: 2013
Estimated Sales: $970000
Number Employees: 20
Type of Packaging: Private Label

3310 **DG Yuengling & Son, Inc.**
420 Mahantongo St
Pottsville, PA 17901
570-628-4890
marketing@yuengling.com
www.yuengling.com
Beer including ale, porter, lager and light.
President & Owner: Dick Yuengling, Jr.
Chief Operating Officer: David Casinelli
Chief Administrative Officer: Wendy Yuengling
Quality Manager: Joe Frinzi
Sales Administration & Pricing Manager: Debbie Yuengling
Vice President, Operations: Jennifer Yuengling
Order Services: Sheryl Yuengling
Year Founded: 1829
Estimated Sales: $37.7 Million
Number Employees: 185
Square Footage: 36000
Other Locations:
Yuengling Beer Company
Pottsville PA
Yuengling Beer Co of Tampa, Inc
Tampa FL
Brands:
Yuengling

3311 **DGZ Chocolate**
6909 Ashcroft Dr # 315
Suite 315
Houston, TX 77081-5819
713-777-3444
Fax: 713-777-9444 877-949-9444
Chocolates, caramel apples, popcorn covered in chocolate and caramel
Owner: Debbie Zissman
debbie@dgzchocolate.com
Estimated Sales: $5-10 Million
Number Employees: 1-4
Brands:
Applerazzi
Poparazzi
Toffarassi
Turtlerazzi

3312 **DIP Seafood Mudbugs**
1870 Dauphin Island Pkwy
Mobile, AL 36605-3000
251-479-0123
Fax: 251-479-9869 info@dipseafoodmudbugs.com
www.dipseafoodmudbugs.com
Seafood
Owner: Phan Nguyen
Estimated Sales: Less Than $500,000
Number Employees: 1-4

3313 **DMH Ingredients Inc**
1228 American Way
Libertyville, IL 60048-3936
847-362-9977
Fax: 847-362-9977
customerservice@dmhingredients.com
www.dmhingredients.com
Confectionery, gums and stabilizers, cheese and dairy powders, fruit and vegetable products, powdered cellulose, savory flavors, flavor enhancers, sweet flavors, coffee, tea and botanicals, vitamins, amino acids and food chemicalsgrain products, meat aspartame
President: David Damlich
ddamlich@dmhingredients.com
Estimated Sales: $5-10 Million
Number Employees: 10-19

3314 **DNE World Fruit Sales**
1900 N Old Dixie Hwy
Fort Pierce, FL 34946
Fax: 772-465-1181 800-327-6676
www.dneworld.com
Grower, packer, marketer, and importer of citrus fruit including navel oranges, clementines, lemons and limes; exporter of grapefruit, oranges, tangerines and juice.
Senior Director, Sales: Mark Hanks
Sales: Kevin Carroll
Year Founded: 1914
Estimated Sales: $20-50 Million
Number Employees: 50-99
Parent Co: Wonderful Packing LLC
Type of Packaging: Consumer, Food Service, Private Label, Bulk
Brands:
Indian River Pride
Ocean Spray
Pride

3315 **DNO Inc**
3650 E 5th Avenue
Columbus, OH 43219
614-231-3601
dno@dnoproduce.com
www.dnoinc.com
Pre-cut prepackaged fresh fruit and vegetables
Founder/Owner: Tony DiNovo
tdinovo@dnoproduce.com
President/COO: Alex DiNovo
Purchasing Manager: Tony DiNovo
Estimated Sales: $10-20 Million
Number Employees: 20-49
Square Footage: 10000
Type of Packaging: Consumer, Food Service, Private Label, Bulk
Brands:
Fresh Health
Fresh Health Kids
OHganics

3316 **DNX Foods**
120 S Houghton Rd
Suite 138-273
Tucson, AZ 85748
888-612-5037
info@dnxbar.com www.dnxbar.com
Nutrition bars made from meat and superfoods
Founder/CEO: John Rooney
CFO: Josh Nelson
VP Sales: Tim Larsen
Year Founded: 2015

3317 **DO, Cookie Dough Confections**
550 LaGuardia Pl
New York, NY 10012
646-892-3600
cookiedonyc.com
Cookie dough; baking mixes; frozen desserts
Operations Manager: Nadalyn McNichols
Year Founded: 2014
Number Employees: 1-10

3318 **DRY Soda Co.**
506 2nd Ave
Suite 1200
Seattle, WA 98104
888-379-7632
drysparkling.com
Sparkling sodas
Founder & CEO: Sharelle Klaus
VP of Marketing: BreeAnna Marchitto
Year Founded: 2005
Number Employees: 11-50
Type of Packaging: Food Service, Private Label

3319 **DS Services of America**
200 Eagles Landing Blvd.
Lakeland, FL 33810
800-728-5508
www.water.com
Bottled water, water filtration coolers, spring water, purified drinking water, distilled drinking water, and more.
President: Dave Muscato
CEO: Tom Harrington
CFO: Jerry Hoyle
General Manager: Mike Garrity
Year Founded: 1985
Estimated Sales: $787 Million
Number Employees: 5300
Type of Packaging: Consumer, Food Service, Private Label, Bulk
Brands:
Alhambra®
Abita Springs®
Athena®
Belmont Springs®
Crystal Springs®
Deep Rock®
Hinckley Springs®
Kentwood Springs®
Mount Olympus®
Nursery® Water
Sierra Springs®
Sparkletts®
Standard Coffee®
My Utapia®

3320 **(HQ)DSM**
Het Overloon 1
6411 TE
Heerlen,
Netherlands
info@dsm.com
www.dsm.com
Nutrition, health and materials industries, such as food enzymes, cultures and savory ingredients to food and beverage manufacturers.
Co-CEO: Dimitri de Vreeze
Co-CEO: Geraldine Matchett
Chairman, Supervising Board: Rob Routs
Year Founded: 1902
Estimated Sales: $9 Billion
Number Employees: 21,000
Number of Brands: 82
Brands:
AgiSyn™
Akulon®
ALL-Q™
ALPAFLOR®
AMPHISOL®
Arnite®
Arnitel®
Bionate®
BioSpan®
Brewers Clarex®
CakeZyme®
CarboSil®
CaroCare®
CAROPHYLL®
ComfortCoat®
CRINA®
CYLACTIN®
Decovery®
Delvo®Cheese
Delvo®Fresh
Delvotest®
DeSolite® Supercoatings
DHAgold™
Dyneema Purity®
Dyneema®
EcoPaXX®
Elasthane™
elaVida™
Epi-Guide®
Fabuless®
FloraGLO® LUTEIN
ForTii®
Fortitech® Premixes
Fruitflow®
geniVida®
Haloflex™
Hy-D®
life's DHA®
life's™ARA
life's™GLA
life's™OMEGA

Maxilact®
Maxiren®
Medeor® Matrix
MEG-3®
Meso BioMatrix®
Multirome®
NeoCryl®
NeoPac™
NeoRad™
NeoRez™
Niaga®
Novamid®
OatWell®
OPTISHARP® Zeaxanthin
OPTRIX®
OsseoFit™
OVN™
Pack-Age®
Panamore®
PARSOL®
PeptoPro®
PurSil®
Quali®-Carotene
Rapidase®
redivivo® Lycopene
resVida®
Rapidase®
redivivo® Lycopene
resVida®
Ronozyme®
Rovimix®
Skins®

3321 DSM Food Specialties
45 Waterview Blvd
Parsippany, NJ 07054
info@dsm.com
www.dsm.com/corporate/about/businesses/dsm-food-specialties.html
DSM Food Specialties is a producer of value-added ingredient solutions for the international food, feed and beverage industries.
President: Patrick Niels
Estimated Sales: K
Number Employees: 10,000+
Parent Co: Koninklijke DSM N.V.

3322 DSM Fortitech Premixes
2105 Technology Dr
Schenectady, NY 12308-1151
info@dsm.com
www.dsm.com
Vitamin and mineral pre mixes, amino acids, nucleotides, nutraceuticals and herbs
VP & CFO: Brian Wilcox
SEVP & Chief Scientific Officer: Ram Chaudhari
Senior QC Specialist: Cindy Grimm
International Project Manager: Dominic Kwiatkowski
Director, Human Resources: Joanne Murphy
Director, Manufacturing: Ed Webster
Purchasing Manager, North America: Thomas Morba
Estimated Sales: K
Number Employees: 10,000+
Square Footage: 68000
Parent Co: DSM
Type of Packaging: Food Service
Other Locations:
Fortitech
Europe
Fortitech
South America
Fortitech
Mexico

3323 DWC Specialities
710 Oak Ln
Horicon, WI 53032
920-485-4550
Fax: 920-485-4035 800-383-8808
www.dwcspecialties.com
Frozen bakery products, organic cookies and bread/specialty distributor of food products and supply goods 80% of WI/Chicago
President: Robert Scott
VP: Kim Gassner
Contact: Brett Anfinson
brett@dwcspecialties.com
Estimated Sales: $500,000-$1 Million
Number Employees: 11
Square Footage: 128000

3324 Daabon Organic USA, Inc.
1110 Brickell Ave
#212
Miami, FL 33131
305-358-7667
Producer of palm oil, and palm oil products including shortenings, hard fats, fry oils, soaps, glycerin and custom oil blends.
President/Owner: Raul Arenas
Vice President: Sergio Espinosa
Sales, North America: Esther Meima
Parent Co: Daabon Organic
Other Locations:
Daabon Europa GmbH
Pulheim, Germany
Daabon Organic Australia Pty Ltd.
New South Wales
Daabon Organic Japan Co., Ltd.
Tokyo

3325 Dabruzzi's Italian Foods
417 2nd St
Hudson, WI 54016-1509
715-386-3653
Fax: 715-549-5202
Ravioli, garlic butter bread and red and white sauces
Owner: Sharon Ellstrom
dabruzzis@earthlink.net
Manager: Nancy Cramer
Estimated Sales: $1-2,500,000
Number Employees: 5-9

3326 Dahlicious
320 Hamilton St
Leominster, MA 01453
www.dahlicious.com
Organic India-styled yogurt drinks
Number of Brands: 1
Number of Products: 5
Type of Packaging: Consumer
Brands:
DAHLICIOUS

3327 Daily Crave, The
Natural Intentions, Inc.
PO Box 6688
Folsom, CA 95763
thedailycrave.com
Quinoa, lentil and veggie chips and straws
Founder: Hassan Alireza

3328 Daily Greens LLC
PO Box 1437
Austin, TX 78767-1437
512-524-1500
Fax: 512-532-6499 www.drinkdailygreens.com
Juice
Owner/Founder: Shauna Martin
shauna@drinkdailygreens.com
Marketing Manager: Yoshie Yanno-Pennings

3329 Daily Nutrition
120 S Houghton Rd
Suite 138-273
Tucson, AZ 85748
888-612-5037
info@dnxbar.com
Grass-fed meat snack bars
Founder & CEO: John Rooney
CFO: Josh Nelson
Sales: Ali Shouman
Number of Brands: 1
Number of Products: 5
Type of Packaging: Consumer
Brands:
DNX

3330 Daily Soup
134 E 43rd St # 1
New York, NY 10017-4019
212-949-7687
Fax: 212-687-7839 888-393-7687
Fresh soups
Owner: Young Yoon
Executive Chef: Leslie Kaul
Estimated Sales: Less than $500,000
Number Employees: 10-19
Brands:
Daily Made

3331 Dailys Premium Meats
3535 S 500 W
Salt Lake City, UT 84115-4205
801-269-1998
Fax: 801-269-1409 800-328-7695
info@dailysmeats.com
A variety of premium meat products, including bacon, hams and breakfast sausages.
President: Samantha Ames
sames@dailysmeats.com
Marketing Manager: John Garlinghouse
VP Sales: Sig Skarland
Production Manager: Dave Caron
Plant Manager: Jeff Lubbers
Number Employees: 250-499
Parent Co: Seaboard Foods
Type of Packaging: Consumer, Food Service
Other Locations:
Missoula MT
Brands:
Daily Foods

3332 Dainty Confections
725 Broadway St.
Windsor, ON N9C 0C1
Canada
519-972-8888
Fax: 519-966-3298 800-268-0222
jones@dainty.ca www.daintyrice.com
Candy
President: Catherine Diehl
Marketing: Sherry Jones

3333 Dairiconcepts
3253 E Chestnut Expy
Springfield, MO 65802-2540
417-829-3400
Fax: 417-829-3401 877-596-4374
dcinfo@dairiconcepts.com
www.dairiconcepts.com
Dairy powders and replacement systems, cheese powders and cheese concentrates, block and grated Italian cheeses.
CEO: Jeff Miyake
jeffmiyake@dairiconcepts.com
Number Employees: 1-4

3334 Dairy Connection Inc
501 Tasman St # B
Suite B
Madison, WI 53714-3173
608-242-9030
Fax: 608-242-9036 info@dairyconnection.com
www.dairyconnection.com
Cheese cultures
President: Cathy Potter
getculture@dairyconnection.com
VP/Technical Manager: Dave Potter
Technical Specialist: Sandy S
Customer Service Specialist: Patrick C
Number Employees: 10-19

3335 Dairy Farmers Of America
1405 N. 98th St.
Kansas City, KS 66111
816-801-6455
888-332-6455
webmail@dfamilk.com www.dfamilk.com
Milk, cheese, butter and dairy ingredients.
President/CEO: Rick Smith
rsmith@dfamilk.com
CFO: Greg Wickham
Year Founded: 1998
Estimated Sales: $13.5 Billion
Number Employees: 6,000
Number of Brands: 9
Type of Packaging: Private Label, Bulk
Brands:
Borden® Cheese
Cache Valley® Cheese
Keller's® Creamery Butter
Plugra® Butter
Sport Shake
Kemps®
Guida's Dairy
La Vaquita®
Dairy Maid Dairy®

3336 (HQ)Dairy Fresh Foods Inc
21405 Trolley Industrial Dr
Taylor, MI 48180-1811
313-299-0735
Fax: 313-295-6950

Beverages, cheeses, deli foods and frozen foods; importer of cheese and meats including corned beef and ham; exporter of cheese
Co-President: Alan Must
amust@dairyfreshfoods.com
Co-President: Joel Must
Number Employees: 100-249
Square Footage: 800000
Type of Packaging: Consumer, Food Service, Bulk
Brands:
Brittnia
Dairy Fresh
Deli-Fresh
Gourmet
Marla
Oceen Fresh
Pure Maid

3337 **Dairy Group**
366 N Broadway # 410
Jericho, NY 11753-2000
516-433-0080
Fax: 516-433-7657
Cheese
President: Ned Dorman
ndorman@thedairygroup.com
Estimated Sales: $1-3 Million
Number Employees: 1-4
Brands:
Dairy Group

3338 **Dairy House**
150 Larkin Williams Ind Ct
Fenton, MO 63026
636-343-5444
Fax: 314-772-4280
Manufacturer and suppliers of cocoa, chocolate dairy powders and beverage flavors.
President: Carl Fitzwater
Vice President: John Hutchinson
Contact: Devine Allen
allen@dairy-house.com
Estimated Sales: 4.6 Million
Number Employees: 30

3339 **Dairy King Milk Farms/Foodservice**
PO Box 1259
11954 East Washington Blvd
Whitter, CA 90606
818-243-6455
Fax: 818-243-2455 800-900-6455
www.dairyberries.com
Dairy products, frozen vegetables and dry goods; wholesaler/distributor of frozen foods, general merchandise, general line products, produce, meats and seafood; serving the food service market
VP: Joseph Goldstein
Number Employees: 50-99
Square Footage: 280000
Type of Packaging: Consumer

3340 **Dairy Maid Dairy LLC**
259 E 7th St
Frederick, MD 21701-5227
301-663-5114
Fax: 301-695-0431 www.dairymaiddairy.com
Milk, buttermilk, eggnog, whipping cream, creamer, juices and drinks.
Co-President: Jody Vona
Co-President: Jimmy Vona
jvona@dairymaiddairy.com
General Manager: David Staz
Transportation Manager: Bill Fulmer
Plant Manager: Ilir Emini
Estimated Sales: $20-50 Million
Number Employees: 100-249
Number of Brands: 1
Parent Co: Dairy Farmers of America
Type of Packaging: Consumer
Brands:
Dairy Maid Dairy

3341 **Dairy Maid Ravioli Mfg Co**
216 Avenue U
Brooklyn, NY 11223-3825
718-449-2620
Fax: 718-449-3206 866-777-3661
dairymaid1@aol.com
Manufacturer and distributor of pasta products including ravioli and tortellini
President/Co-Owner: Louis Ballarino
dairymaid1@aol.com
Co-Owner: Salvatore Ballarino
Vice President: Anthony Ballarino
Estimated Sales: $1-2.5 Million appx.
Number Employees: 5-9
Square Footage: 44000
Type of Packaging: Consumer, Private Label, Bulk
Brands:
Dairy Maid

3342 **Dairy Management Inc**
10255 W Higgins Rd # 900
Suite 900
Rosemont, IL 60018-5638
847-803-2000
Fax: 847-803-2077 800-853-2479
www.dairy.org
Bleaching compounds, chocolate, cultures, dairy powders, nonfat dry milk, milk, protiens, vegetable, sweetners
CEO: Thomas Gallagher
thomas.g@rosedmi.com
SVP Nutrition/Product Innovation: Greg Miller, PhD, FACN
VP Nutrition Research: Doug DiRenzom, PhD, FACN
Brand Development Director: Jose Cubillos
Number Employees: 100-249
Parent Co: National Dairy Council

3343 **Dairy State Foods Inc**
6035 N Baker Rd
Milwaukee, WI 53209-3701
414-228-1240
Fax: 414-228-9747 800-435-4499
sales@dairystatefoods.com
www.dairystatefoods.com
Manufacturer and exporter of juvenile cookies and animal, oyster crackers, also contract packaging available
President: Larry Rabin
rabin@dairystatefoods.com
Estimated Sales: $1-2.5 Million
Number Employees: 20-49
Square Footage: 120000
Type of Packaging: Consumer, Food Service, Private Label
Brands:
Alphabet Cookies
Circus Wagon Animal Crackers
Toy Bus Animal Crackers
Wild Jungle Animal Crackers

3344 **(HQ)Dairy-Mix Inc**
3020 46th Ave N
St Petersburg, FL 33714-3863
727-525-6101
Fax: 727-522-0769 800-955-6101
ecoryn@dairymix.com www.dairymix.com
Manufacturer and exporter of ice cream, ice milk and milk shake mixes, frozen dessert
President: Edward Coryn
ecoryn@dairymix.com
Corporate VP: John Coryn
Sales/Marketing: Mike Costello
Plant Manager: Jerry Maine
Estimated Sales: $8 Million
Number Employees: 10-19
Type of Packaging: Food Service, Bulk

3345 **DairyAmerica**
4974 E Clinton Way
Suite C-121
Fresno, CA 93727
559-251-0992
Fax: 559-251-1078 800-722-3110
webmaster@dairyamerica.com
www.dairyamerica.com
Manufacturer and exporter of milk including low heat, medium heat, high heat, whole and dry buttermilk
President/SVP: Keith Gomes
CEO: Hoyt Huffman
Controller: Jean McAbee
CEO: Rich Lewis
Director Sales/Marketing: Dan Block
International Sales: Steve Gulley
Contact: Craig Alexander
acraig@dairyamerica.com
Operations Manager: Frances Zapanta
Estimated Sales: $1-2,500,000
Number Employees: 20-49
Type of Packaging: Bulk
Other Locations:
Manufacturing Plant
Los Banos CA
Manufacturing Facility
Turlock CA
Manufacturing Facility
Visalia CA
Manufacturing Facility
Artesia CA
Manufacturing Facility
Bactavia NY
Brands:
Dairyamerica

3346 **DairyChem Inc.**
9120 Technology Ln
Fishers, IN 46038-2839
317-849-8400
Fax: 317-849-8213 cservice@dairychem.com
www.dairychem.com
Manufacturer and exporter of natural dairy flavors including butter, cream, buttermilk, sour cream, cream cheese, cultured dairy, yogurt, milk, starter distillate and starter flavors.
Owner: Grant Church
VP: Diana Church
Sales Manager: Travis McMahan
gchurch@dairychem.com
Operations Manager/Purchasing: Paul Hampton
Estimated Sales: $1 Million
Number Employees: 10-19
Square Footage: 33400
Type of Packaging: Private Label, Bulk

3347 **DairyPure**
P.O. Box 961447
El Paso, TX 79996
800-395-7004
deanfoods@casupport.com www.dairypure.com
Dairy products; including lowfat milk, lactose free milk, creamers, sour creams, and flavour mixes.
CEO, Dean Foods Company: Ralph Scozzafava
Year Founded: 1931
Number Employees: 1,600
Parent Co: Dean Foods Company
Type of Packaging: Consumer, Private Label

3348 **Dairyfood USA Inc**
2819 County Highway F
Blue Mounds, WI 53517
608-437-5598
Fax: 608-437-8850 800-236-3300
customerservice@dairyfoodusa.com
www.dairyfoodusa.com
Cheeses, as well as candies, coffees, sausages and crackers
President/Owner: Daniel Culligan
Human Resources Manager: Teddy White
Purchasing: Vicki Mosure
Estimated Sales: $14.2 Million
Number Employees: 100

3349 **Dairytown Products Ltd**
49 Milk Board Road
Sussex, NB E4E 5L2
Canada
506-432-1950
Fax: 506-432-1940 800-561-5598
admin@dairytown.com www.dairytown.com
Butter and skim milk, whole milk and buttermilk powders
CEO: Derek Roberts
Quality Assurance: Wendy Palmer
VP Sales/Marketing: George MacPhee
Operations Manager: Lynn McLaughlin
Type of Packaging: Private Label

3350 **Daisy Brand**
12750 Merit Dr.
Suite 600
Dallas, TX 75251
877-292-9830
www.daisybrand.com
Sour cream and cottage cheese.
President: David Sokolsky
Director, Human Resources: Julie King
Year Founded: 1917
Estimated Sales: $171 Million
Number Employees: 300
Square Footage: 12000
Type of Packaging: Consumer, Food Service, Private Label, Bulk
Brands:
Daisy Light Sour Cream
Daisey Sour Cream

Daisy Cottage Cheese
Daisy Low Fat Cottage Cheese

3351 **Daiya Foods**
2768 Rupert St
Vancouver, BC V5M 3T7
Canada
877-324-9211
cr@daiyafoods.com daiyafoods.com
Dairy-free cheeze shreds, slices and blocks, dressings and meatless pizza.
Vice President: Michael Lynch

3352 **Dakota**
4850 Hahns Peak Drive, Ste 240
Loveland, CO 80538
888-586-2209
DBcustomers@dakotaorganic.com
www.grassfedbeef.com
Meat, beef

3353 **(HQ)Dakota Brands Intl**
2121 13th St NE
Jamestown, ND 58401-3568
701-252-5073
Fax: 701-251-1047 800-844-5073
www.dakotabrands.com
Bagels, rolls and frozen roll dough
President: Rex King
rking@daktel.com
CEO: Donald Kerr
Vice President: Kandy Jenkins
R&D/QA Manager: Colleen Krapp
National Sales Manager: Dick Earle
VP Operations: Darvin Becker
Estimated Sales: $2.5-5 Million
Number Employees: 50-99
Number of Products: 60
Square Footage: 21000
Type of Packaging: Consumer, Food Service, Private Label, Bulk
Brands:
Bagels
Bakeable
Dakota

3354 **Dakota Gourmet**
896 22nd Ave N
Wahpeton, ND 58075
701-642-3068
Fax: 701-642-9403 800-727-6663
www.dakotagourmet.com
Roasted sunflower nuts, soynuts, and toasted corn
Manager: Lucy Spiekermeier
General Manager: Lucy Spiekermeier
Estimated Sales: $2.5-5,000,000
Number Employees: 20-49
Square Footage: 40000
Parent Co: Sonne
Type of Packaging: Consumer, Food Service, Private Label, Bulk
Brands:
Giants

3355 **Dakota Specialty Milling, Inc.**
4014 15th Ave N
Fargo, ND 58102-2833
844-633-2746
sales@dakotaspecialtymilling.com
www.dakotaspecialtymilling.com
Producer of grain-based mixes and ingredients.
President: Peter Matthaei
Vice President of Sales & Marketing: Brian Andrews
Senior Director of Sales: Richard Karnemaat
Manager of Customer Logistics: Bernadine King
Director of Milling Operations: Brian Sorenson
bsorenson@dakotaspecialtymilling.com
Director of Technical Services: Bob Meyer
VP of Engineering & Manufacturing: Daryl Bashor
Estimated Sales: $15,000,000
Number Employees: 50-99
Type of Packaging: Consumer, Food Service, Private Label, Bulk

3356 **Dakota Style**
211 Industrial Dr
Clark, SD 57225-1595
605-532-5278
Fax: 605-532-3599 800-446-2779
www.dakotastyle.com
Kettle cooked potato chips, sunflower seeds
Contact: Riley Dandurand
riley@dakotastyle.com

Number Employees: 5-9

3357 **Dale & Thomas Popcorn**
1 Cedar Ln
Englewood, NJ 07631-4802
201-645-4586
Fax: 201-645-4848 800-767-4444
Flavored popcorn
Founder: Richard Demb
Estimated Sales: $40.8 Million
Number Employees: 10-19

3358 **(HQ)Dale T Smith & Sons Inc**
12450 S Pony Express Rd
Draper, UT 84020-9510
801-571-3611
Fax: 801-571-3685 mail@smithmeats.com
Beef processor.
President: Dale Smith
Vice President: Dennis Smith
Production Manager: Roger McNicol
Number Employees: 50-99
Type of Packaging: Consumer, Food Service

3359 **Daley Brothers ltd.**
215 Water Street, Suite 301
St John's, NL A1C 6C9
Canada
709-364-8844
Fax: 709-364-7216
Manufacturer and exporter of fresh and frozen seafood
President: Terry Daley
CEO: Steve Hoskins
Sales Manager: Rosemary Buckingham
Number Employees: 20-49
Type of Packaging: Bulk

3360 **Dalian Xinfeng International Industry & Trade Co.**
1114 Zane Ave N
Golden Valley, MN 55422-4606
612-964-7391
Fax: 612-486-8895
Organic rice, beans, and grains.
Vice President: David Su
Year Founded: 1997
Type of Packaging: Food Service, Private Label

3361 **Dalla Valle Vineyards**
7776 Silverado Trl
Napa, CA 94558-9739
707-944-2676
Fax: 707-944-8411 info@dallavallevineyards.com
www.dallavallevineyards.com
Wines
President: Naoko Dalla Valle
info@dallavallevineyards.com
Vineyard Manager: Fausto Sanchez
Winemaker: Andy Erikksion
Estimated Sales: $2.5-5,000,000
Number Employees: 10-19
Type of Packaging: Private Label
Brands:
Dalla

3362 **Dallis Brothers**
11-22 44th Road
Suite 301
Long Island City, NY 11101
718-845-3010
Fax: 718-843-0178 info@dallisbroscoffee.com
www.dallisbroscoffee.com
Manufacturer of coffee.
Director, Sales Technology: Marcelo Crescente
Director, Specialty Coffee: Jon Phillips
Year Founded: 1913
Estimated Sales: $20-50 Million
Number Employees: 20-49
Number of Brands: 1
Parent Co: Lacas Coffee Company
Type of Packaging: Private Label
Other Locations:
Pennsauken NJ
Brands:
Dallis Bros. Coffee

3363 **Damascus Bakery**
56 Gold St
Brooklyn, NY 11201-1297
USA
718-855-1456
Fax: 718-403-0948
Paninis and pita and lavash breads

President/Owner: Edward Mafoud
edward@damascusbakery.com
Sales Executive: Dave Martz
Number Employees: 100-249

3364 **Damiani Wine Cellars LLC**
4704 State Route 414
Burdett, NY 14818-9779
607-546-5557
info@damianiwinecellars.com
www.damianiwinecellars.com
Wines
Owner/Winemaker: Lou Damiani
Wine Grower/Maker: Phil Davis
Manager: Michael Cimino
Number Employees: 5-9

3365 **Damon Industries**
822 Packer Way
Sparks, NV 89431-6445
775-331-3200
Fax: 775-331-3980 800-225-3046
info@fruitful.com www.fruitful.com
Shelf stable juice and beverage concentrates
President: Jeff Baldridge
info@fruitful.com
Quality Control: Richard Johnson
Sales Manager: Larry Grant
Productions: Gary Messerli
Estimated Sales: $5-10,000,000
Number Employees: 20-49
Brands:
Fruitful Juice Products
Juice Direct

3366 **Damron Corp**
4433 W Ohio St
Chicago, IL 60624-1054
773-826-6001
Fax: 773-826-6004 800-333-1860
info@damrontea.com www.damronplg.com
Tea
President/CEO: Ronald Damper
damrontea@aol.com
General Manager: Gina Gatta
Estimated Sales: $3,000,000
Number Employees: 20-49
Type of Packaging: Bulk
Brands:
Damron
Harvest Delighta

3367 **Dan Carter**
3018 Helsan Drive
PO Box 282
Richfield, WI 53076-0282
262-677-3407
Fax: 262-677-3806 800-782-0741
www.dcicheeseco.com
Cheese
President: Timothy Omer
Estimated Sales: $500,000-$1,000,000
Number Employees: 20-49
Brands:
Dan Carter

3368 **Dan-D Foods Ltd**
11760 Machrina Way
Richmond, BC V7A 4V1
Canada
604-274-3263
Fax: 604-274-3268 800-633-4788
www.dan-d-pak.com
Fine food importer, manufacturer and distributor of cashews, dried fruits, rice crackers, snack foods, spices etc. from around the world.
Chairman/President/CEO/Founder: Dan On
Number Employees: 500
Type of Packaging: Food Service, Bulk

3369 **Dancing Deer Baking Company**
65 Sprague Street
Building-west A
Boston, MA 02136
617-442-7300
Fax: 617-442-8118 888-699-3337
info@dancingdeer.com www.dancingdeer.com
Natural cakes and cookies

President/CEO: Patricia Karter
CFO: James Tyson
Marketing: Duane Lefevre
Sales: Dave Lamlein
Contact: Craig Drinkwater
cdrinkwater@dancingdeer.com
Production: Lissa McBurney
Estimated Sales: $59,000
Number Employees: 2
Number of Brands: 1
Number of Products: 25
Square Footage: 14000
Type of Packaging: Consumer, Food Service, Private Label, Bulk

3370 **Dandelion Chocolate**
740 Valencia St
San Francisco, CA 94110-1735
415-349-0942
800-785-2301
www.dandelionchocolate.com
Chocolates
Owner: Maggi Mcconnell
maggi.m@gmail.com
CEO: Todd Masonis
Number Employees: 5-9

3371 **Dang Foods**
3254 Adeline St
Suite 210
Berkeley, CA 94703
510-338-3345
Fax: 888-645-6065 hello@dangfoods.com
www.dangfoods.com
Coconut and sticky-rice chips
President/Owner: Vincent Kitirattragarn
vincent.kit@gmail.com
Number Employees: 1-4

3372 **Daniel Le Chocolat Belge**
88 East 7th Ave
Vancouver, BC V5T 1M2
Canada
604-879-7782
Fax: 604-879-7260 info@danielchocolates.com
www.danielchocolates.com
Fine chocolates and chocolate products including boxed chocolates, chocolate bars, and pastries
Owner: Daniel Poncelet
Secretary/Owner: Monique Poncelet
Estimated Sales: $2.49 Million
Number Employees: 30
Type of Packaging: Consumer, Food Service, Private Label, Bulk

3373 **Daniel's Bagel & Baguette Corporation**
414 36th Avenue SE
Calgary, AB T2G 1W4
Canada
403-243-3207
www.danielsbagel.foodpages.ca
Baked goods including specialty breads, bagels and pretzels
President: D Oppenheim
Estimated Sales: A
Number Employees: 6
Type of Packaging: Consumer, Food Service

3374 **Daniele Inc**
105 Davis Dr
Pascoag, RI 02859-3507
401-568-6228
Fax: 401-568-4788 800-451-2535
www.danielefoods.com
Manufacturer of dry-cured delicacies and other gourmet Italian products.
Co-Owner: Stefano Dukcevich
Co-Owner: Davide Dukcevich
Number Employees: 50-99

3375 **Danisco-Cultor**
430 Saw Mill River Rd
Ardsley, NY 10502-2605
914-674-6300
Fax: 914-674-6538 www.danisco.com
Ingredients for beverage products, including flavor enhancers, and functional botanicals, xylitol, industrial enzymes, sugar
President: Robert Mayer
CEO: Tom Knutzen
VP: Philippe Lavielle
Estimated Sales: $5-10 000,000
Number Employees: 20-49

3376 **Danish Maid Butter Co**
8512 S Commercial Ave
Chicago, IL 60617-2533
773-731-8787
Fax: 773-731-9812
danishmaidbutter@hotmail.com
www.danishmaid.com
Dairy products including anhydrous milkfat, butter oil and regular and whipped butter; also, packaging services available
President: Susie Wagner
Plant Manager: Matthew Wagner
Estimated Sales: $5 Million
Number Employees: 10-19
Square Footage: 36000
Type of Packaging: Consumer, Food Service, Private Label, Bulk

3377 **(HQ)Dannon Company**
P.O. Box 90296
Allentown, PA 18109-0296
877-326-6668
Fax: 914-366-2805 877-326-6668
mediainquiries@dannon.com www.dannon.com
Yogurt products
President & CEO: Guastavo Valle
VP Finance, CFO: Antoine Remy
VP Human Resources: Tony Cicio
VP Research & Development North America: Stewart Townsend
VP Quality: Christian Maisonneuve
SVP Marketing: Sergio Fuster
SVP Sales: Lucho Lopez-May
Contact: Jason Moloff
jason.moloff@dannon.com
VP Operations: Fernando Lafuente
Estimated Sales: $198.1 Million
Number Employees: 900
Parent Co: Dannone
Other Locations:
- Dannon Company Plant West Jordan UT
- Dannon Company Plant Fort Worth TX
- Dannon Company Plant Minster OH

Brands:
- Dannon
- Activia
- Danimals
- La Creme
- Light and Fit

3378 **Dannon Yo Cream**
5858 NE 87th Ave
Portland, OR 97220
800-962-7326
info@yocream.com www.yocream.com
Frozen dessert, snacks and beverages
CFO: W. Douglas Caudell
Estimated Sales: $70 Million
Number Employees: 100-249
Number of Brands: 4
Parent Co: The Dannon Company
Type of Packaging: Consumer, Food Service, Private Label, Bulk
Brands:
- Sorbet By Yo Cream
- The Yogurt Stand
- Yo Cream
- Yo Cream Smoothies

3379 **Danone North America**
12002 Airport Way
Broomfield, CO 80021
303-635-4000
michael.neuwirth@danone.com
www.danonenorthamerica.com
Organic dairy; fresh dairy; plant-based; coffee creamers & beverages
Year Founded: 2017
Number Employees: 6000
Brands:
- Activia
- DanActive
- Danimals
- Dannon
- Earthbound Farm
- Horizon Organic
- International Delight
- Left Field Farms
- Light & Fit
- Oikos
- Silk
- So Delicious
- Stok
- Vega
- Wallaby Organic
- YoCrunch
- YoCream

3380 **Daphne's Creamery**
707-762-1760
Fax: 707-542-9601 sales@daphnecreamery.com
daphnecreamery.com
Artisanal cheese and butter
Co-Founder & CEO: George Gavros
Number of Brands: 1
Number of Products: 7
Type of Packaging: Consumer
Brands:
- DAPHNE'S CREAMERY

3381 **Daprano & Company**
Po Box 49228
Charlotte, NC 28277
704-927-0590
Fax: 704-927-0591 877-365-2337
sales@daprano.com www.daprano.com
Designer chocolates, bonbons, novelties, Italian cookies, biscotti, madeleines, shortbread
President: Angelo Daprano
Brands:
- Amaretti Virginia
- Bonbon Barnier
- Caffarel
- Cantatti
- Flamigni
- Gatsby's/Pierre Koenig
- Jila & Jols
- Reinhardt

3382 **Dardimans California**
7842 Willis Ave
Panorama City, CA 91402
818-849-5770
dardimans.com
California fruit crisps
CEO: Annie Babayan
Number of Brands: 1
Type of Packaging: Consumer
Brands:
- DARDIMANS

3383 **Dare Foods**
3750 N. Blackstock Rd
Spartanburg, SC 29303
781-639-1808
Fax: 781-639-2286 800-668-3273
www.darefoods.com
Cookies, candies and crackers; also, ground cookie ingredients
National Sales Manager: Neil S Voutt
Number Employees: 60
Type of Packaging: Bulk

3384 **Dare Foods Incorporated**
2481 Kingway Drive
PO Box 1058
Kitchener, ON N2C 1A6
Canada
519-893-5500
Fax: 519-893-2644 800-668-3273
www.darefoods.com
Cookies, crackers, fine breads and candy
Number Employees: 1300
Square Footage: 240487
Brands:
- Breaktime
- Dare Creme Cookies
- Pure Chocolate Whippet
- Breton Minis
- Vinta
- Cabaret
- Grainsfirst
- Vivant
- Water Crackers
- Breton
- Bremner Wafers
- Dare Realfruit Candies

3385 **Daregal**
100 Overlook Ctr
2nd Floor Suite 2014
Princeton, NJ 08540-7814
609-375-2312
Fax: 609-375-2402
Frozen chopped herbs

Contact: Christine Cooney
christine@daregalgourmet.com

3386 **Darifair Foods**
4131 Sunbeam Rd
Jacksonville, FL 32257-6027
904-268-9916
Fax: 904-268-8666 sales@darifair.com
www.darifair.com
Cultured dairy ice cream and dessert
President: Andrew Block
CEO: Christiaan Avonda
h.hammond@mpls-synod.org
CFO: William Block
VP Business Development: Jeffrey Block
VP Marketing: Michele Block
VP Operations: Ed Stevens
Executive Chief/VP: John Penland
Estimated Sales: $2.5-5,000,000
Number Employees: 20-49
Type of Packaging: Private Label
Brands:
Dairfair

3387 **Darigold**
5601 6th Ave. S.
Suite 300
Seattle, WA 98108
800-333-6455
www.darigold.com
Milk, butter, cottage cheese, cheese, whipping cream, yogurt and sour cream.
President/CEO: Stan Ryan
stan.ryan@darigold.com
Year Founded: 1918
Estimated Sales: Over $1 Billion
Type of Packaging: Consumer, Food Service, Private Label, Bulk
Other Locations:
Powdered Milk/Butter
Caldwell ID
Milk & Cultured
Boise ID
Condensed, Powdered Milk
Jerome ID
HTST Milk
Medford OR
HTST Milk
Salt Lake UT
HTST Milk
Bozeman MT
UP Milk
Portland OR
Powdered Milk
Chehalis WA
HTST Milk
Seattle WA
HTST Milk
Spokane WA
Cheese
Sunnyside WA
Cultured/Butter
Issaquah WA
Powdered Milk
Lynden WA
Brands:
Fred Meyer
Haggen
Safeway
Sysco Products
Western Family

3388 **Dark Dog**
3921 Alton Rd
Suite 242
Miami Beach, FL 33140
www.darkdog-organic.com
Organic energy drinks
Year Founded: 1995
Number of Brands: 1
Number of Products: 4
Type of Packaging: Consumer
Brands:
DARK DOG ORGANIC

3389 **Dark Tickle Company**
75 Main St.
PO Box 160
St Lunaire-Griquet, NL A0K 2X0
Canada
709-623-2354
Fax: 709-623-2354 www.darktickle.com
Wild berry jams, toppings, beverage concentrate, relish and vinegars
President: Stephen Knudsen
Number Employees: 5-9
Square Footage: 5000
Type of Packaging: Consumer
Brands:
Dark Tickle

3390 **Darling Ingredients Inc.**
5601 N MacArthur Blvd.
Irving, TX 75038
927-717-0300
800-800-4841
info@darlingii.com www.darlingii.com
Repurposed beef, poultry and pork by-products into specialty ingredients for use in the pharmaceutical, food, pet food, feed, fuel and fertilizer industries.
CEO: Randall Stuewe
Executive VP/CFO: Brad Phillips
Executive VP/General Counsel: John Sterling
Executive VP/CAO: John Muse
Estimated Sales: $3.4 Billion
Number Employees: 10,000
Number of Brands: 16
Type of Packaging: Private Label, Bulk
Brands:
Bakery Feeds
EnviroFlight
CTH
Dar Pro Bioenergy
Dar Pro Ingredients
Dar Pro Solutions
Diamond Green Diesel
Ecoson
Hepac
Laru
NatureSafe
Peptan
Rousselot
Sonac
Rendac
Rothsay

3391 **Das Foods**
2041 W Carroll Avenue
Chicago, IL 60612
312-224-8590
Fax: 800-861-1336 www.dasfoods.com
Gourmet salts, caramels, lollipops and other treats
President: Katie Das
Member: Dhurba Das
Estimated Sales: $500,000-1 Million
Number Employees: 1-4

3392 **Date Lady Inc.**
900 W Commercial St
Springfield, MO 65803
417-414-2282
info@ilovedatelady.com
ilovedatelady.com
Manufacturer of organic dates, date syrup, and other sauces and syrups sweeteened with dates.
Founder: Colleen Sundlie
Co-Founder: Ryan Sundlie

3393 **Dave's Gourmet**
4314 Redwood Hwy
Suite 200
San Rafael, CA 94903
Fax: 415-401-9107 800-758-0372
info@davesgourmet.com www.davesgourmet.com
Trail mixes, gourmet hot sauce, salsa, seasoned pretzels, dried chiles and chile powders
Owner: Dave Hirschkop
info@davesgourmet.com
VP: David Lipson
Purchasing Manager: David Lipson
Estimated Sales: $1-2.5 Million
Number Employees: 5-9
Square Footage: 28000
Type of Packaging: Consumer, Food Service
Brands:
Chile
Fire Nugget
Smoked Habanero Pretzels

3394 **Dave's Gourmet Albacore**
10 Hangar Way
Watsonville, CA 95076
206-999-5517
info.davesalbacore@gmail.com
www.davesalbacore.com
Salmon, albacore tuna, rainbow trout, oysters, dungeness crab, shrimp, pates and mousses
President: Thad Pound
Sales Manager: Lindsay Turner
Contact: Debbie Driessche
davesalbacore@aol.com
Estimated Sales: $1 Million
Number Employees: 1-4
Square Footage: 10000
Type of Packaging: Consumer, Private Label, Bulk
Brands:
Alder Cove

3395 **Dave's Killer Bread**
5209 SE International Way
Milwaukie, OR 97222
503-335-8077
www.daveskillerbread.com
Organic sliced bread

3396 **David Bradley Chocolatier**
92 N Main St # 19
Bldg 19
Windsor, NJ 08561-3209
609-443-4747
Fax: 609-443-8762 877-289-7933
david@dbchocolate.com www.dbchocolate.com
Confectionery
Owner: Robert Hicks
admin@dbchocolate.com
Vice President: Marcy Hicks
Estimated Sales: $1-3 000,000
Number Employees: 10-19
Type of Packaging: Private Label
Brands:
Gourmet Snack Bags
Sophisticated Chocol
Zany Pretzels

3397 **David Mosner Meat Products**
355 Food Center Dr
Bronx, NY 10474
718-328-5600
866-928-6428
info@davidmosner.com www.davidmosner.com
Packer of veal and lamb.
President: Michael Mosner
VP, Business Development: Benjamin Mosner
Sales: Neil Harris
Year Founded: 1957
Estimated Sales: $20-50 Million
Number Employees: 20-49
Type of Packaging: Consumer, Food Service, Private Label
Brands:
Mvp

3398 **David Rio**
PO Box 885462
San Francisco, CA 94188
415-543-2733
Fax: 415-543-2749 800-454-9605
chai@davidrio.com www.davidrio.com
Chai and loose leaf teas
Co-Founder, President and CEO: David Scott Lowe
Co-Founder: Rio H. Miura
Chief Operating Officer: Ai Okuba
Director of Sales: Erin-Kate Whitcomb
Contact: Linda Avilla
lavilla@davidrio.com
Estimated Sales: $2,000,000
Number Employees: 10-19
Number of Brands: 2
Number of Products: 20
Square Footage: 3150
Parent Co: David Rio San Francisco
Type of Packaging: Consumer, Food Service, Private Label, Bulk
Brands:
David Rio Chai

3399 **David's Cookies**
11 Cliffside Dr
Cedar Grove, NJ 07009
800-500-2800
custserv@davidscookies.com
www.davidscookies.com
Thaw and serve tarts, layer cakes and single serve desserts, cookies, cookie dough, scones, crumbcake, ruggalach, butter cookies, brownies and mini-muffins
President: Ari Margulies
Vice President: Michael Zuckerman
Year Founded: 1979
Estimated Sales: $90 Million+
Number Employees: 350

Number of Brands: 2
Square Footage: 160000
Parent Co: Fairfield Gourmet Foods Corp.
Type of Packaging: Consumer, Food Service
Brands:
Cookie Cupboard
David's Cookies

3400 Davidson's Organics
PO Box 11214
Reno, NV 89510-1214
775-356-1690
Fax: 775-356-3713 800-882-5888
www.davidsonstea.com
Teas, herbs, cocoa, spices, and accessories for the specialty trade and retail use
Estimated Sales: $5-10 Million
Number Employees: 10-19
Square Footage: 50000
Brands:
Davidson's Inc

3401 Davidson's Safest Choice Eggs
2963 Bernice Road
Lansing, IL 60438
708-418-8500
Fax: 708-418-1235 800-410-7619
info@safeeggs.com www.safeeggs.com
Pasteurized eggs
President: Greg West
CFO: Michael Smith

3402 Davinci Gourmet LTD
7224 1st Ave S
Seattle, WA 98108-4103
206-768-7401
Fax: 206-768-1855 800-640-6779
info@davinci-gourmet.com www.kerry.com
Manufacturers flavored syrups, gourmet sauces, and confections
Manager: Gary Sletten
Manager: Greg Desbien
greg@davincigourmet.com
Estimated Sales: $14 Million
Number Employees: 50-99
Number of Products: 120+
Square Footage: 130000
Type of Packaging: Consumer, Food Service, Private Label, Bulk

3403 Davis & Davis Gourmet Foods
3614 William Flynn Hwy
Allison Park, PA 15101-3722
412-487-7770
customerrelations@davisanddavisonline.com
www.davisanddavisonline.com
Manufacturer of gourmet foods including cocktails, seasonings and mixes.
Founder and President: Kenneth Davis
Number Employees: 20-49

3404 Davis Bakery & Delicatessen
28700 Chagrin Blvd # 1
Cleveland, OH 44122-4560
216-292-3060
Fax: 216-292-4588 www.davisbakery.net
Specialty baked goods including cakes, doughnuts and low-sodium
President: Joel Davis
VP Treasurer: Sheldon Davis
Supervisor Sales: Janice Davis
Manager: John Stapleton
jdowling@aspenonnet.com
VP Deli Operations: Sam Perkul
Estimated Sales: $1-2.5 Million
Number Employees: 10-19
Brands:
Kiddie Kakes
Sodex

3405 Davis Bread & Desserts
#O, 720 Olive Dr.
Davis, CA 95616
530-220-4375
tomthebaker@gmail.com
www.davisbreadanddesserts.com
Producer of breads, rolls and desserts. Food items for sale include Cinnamon Rolls, European Danish, Cinnamon Crisps, Raspberry Cheese Pockets, Frosted Brownie, and more. The company sells its products at several farmer's marketsthroughout the Northern California and Nevada area.
Owner: Tom Kilbourn
Estimated Sales: $320,000
Number Employees: 10
Brands:
Davis Bread

3406 Davis Bynum Winery
8075 Westside Rd.
Healdsburg, CA 95448-3445
866-442-7547
Fax: 707-433-0939 800-826-1073
info@davisbynum.com www.davisbynum.com
Wines
President: Lindley Bynum
GM: Susie Bynum
CFO: Susie Bynum
Contact: Davis Bynum
d.bynum@davisbynum.com
Purchasing: Hampton Bynum
Estimated Sales: $2.5-5,000,000
Number Employees: 10-19
Number of Brands: 2
Type of Packaging: Private Label
Brands:
Davis Bynum
River Bend

3407 Davis Food Company
P.O.Box 16118
Plantation, FL 33318-6118
954-791-5868
Fax: 440-461-2261 www.stadiummustard.com
Mustard
President: Peggy D Davis
Estimated Sales: $1-2,500,000
Number Employees: 1-4
Brands:
Stadium Mustard

3408 Davis Strait Fisheries
71 McQuade Lake Crescent
Halifax, NS B3S 1C4
Canada
902-450-5115
Fax: 902-450-5006 john@davisstrait.com
Seafood products such as northern shrimp, scallops, clams, cod, haddock, and pollack fish
President: Grant Stonehouse
Marketing Director: John Andrews
Operations Manager: Grant Stonehouse
Year Founded: 1991
Estimated Sales: $32 Million
Number Employees: 82
Type of Packaging: Bulk
Brands:
Davis Strait Fisheries Ltd

3409 Davis Street Fish Market
501 Davis Street
Evanston, IL 60201
847-869-3474
Fax: 847-869-6435 davisstreetfish@gmail.com
Seafood
Contact: Ed Huelke
ehuelke@cleanplate.net
Manager: Ed Heulke
Estimated Sales: $3-5 Million
Number Employees: 50-99

3410 Davisco Foods International
11000 W 78th St # 210
Eden Prairie, MN 55344-8012
952-914-0400
Fax: 952-914-0887 800-757-7611
polly@daviscofoods.com www.daviscofoods.com
Whey proteins
Manager: Dana Bellanger
CFO: Jim Ward
VP Finance/Business Administration: John Velgersdyk
Director Quality Assurance: Matt Davis
VP Sales/Marketing/Business Development: Pauline Olson
Contact: Maher Ahmad
maher.ahmad@daviscofoods.com
General Manager: Martin Davis
Estimated Sales: $10-20 000,000
Number Employees: 20-49

3411 Dawes Hill Honey Company
12 S State St
Po Box 429
Nunda, NY 14517
585-468-2535
Fax: 585-468-5995 888-800-8075
info@onceagainnutbutter.com
www.onceagainnutbutter.com
Honey, royal jelly and fruit honey cream spread
Owner: Sandi Alexander
Comptroller: Sandra Alexander
Purchasing Agent: Lloyd Kirwan
Estimated Sales: $10-20 Million
Number Employees: 10-19
Square Footage: 40000
Parent Co: Once Again Nut Butter
Type of Packaging: Consumer, Private Label, Bulk
Brands:
Bee Supreme

3412 Dawn Food Products, Inc
3333 Sargent Rd
Jackson, MI 49201
517-789-4400
800-248-1144
questions@dawnfoods.com www.dawnfoods.com
Doughnut, cake, brownie and other dry mixes, icings and fillings, frozen products.
Chief Executive Officer: Carrie Jones-Barber
Chief Financial Officer: Karl Brown
Chief Legal Officer & Secretary: Scott Thayer
Chief Human Resources Officer: Jason Lioy
Year Founded: 1929
Estimated Sales: Over $1 Billion
Number Employees: 4,000
Square Footage: 95000
Type of Packaging: Consumer, Food Service
Other Locations:
Manufacturing Facilities
Atlanta GA
Baltimore MD
Boston MA
Buffalo NY
Chicago IL
Cleveland OH
Columbus OH
Dallas TX
Denver CO
Las Vegas NV
Little Rock AK
Los Angeles CA
Seattle WA
Brands:
Weight Watchers® Baked Goods
Velvetop™
But-R-Creme™

3413 Dawn's Foods
1530 LaDawn Dr
Portage, WI 53901-8823
608-742-2494
Fax: 608-742-1806 800-993-2967
rrehlinger@dawnsfoods.com
www.dawnsfoodsinc.com
Potato salad, coleslaw, homestyle salads, pasta salads, dips and spreads, quiche, puddings and desserts
President: Greg Drewsen
VP Quality, Food Safety, Training: Dan Waite
VP Sales: Ron Rehlinger
Estimated Sales: $20-50 Million
Number Employees: 20-49
Brands:
Dawn's Foods

3414 Day Foods Company
1901 Durand Ave
Racine, WI 53403
262-634-2164
Fax: 262-634-9929
Frozen pizzas
Manager: Brian Ehmcke
Plant Manager: Ron Harter
Estimated Sales: $10-20 Million
Number Employees: 10-19
Parent Co: Pride of Italy

3415 Day Spring Enterprises
45 Benbro Dr
Cheektowaga, NY 14225-4805
716-685-4340
Fax: 716-685-0810 800-879-7677
www.rainbowpops.com
Hard candy and lollypops; also, seasonal items available

President: Linda Zangerie
Sales Manager: Jeff Baran
Plant Manager: George Sparks
Estimated Sales: $50,000
Number Employees: 1
Square Footage: 32000
Type of Packaging: Consumer, Food Service, Private Label, Bulk
Brands:
Rainbow Pops

3416 **Day-Lee Foods, Inc.**
10350 Heritage Park Dr
Suite 111
Santa Fe Springs, CA 90670
562-903-3020
Fax: 562-906-5080 800-329-5331
info@day-lee.com www.day-lee.com
Meats and poultry
President/CEO: Sumio Somura
Vice President: Kiyoshi Zobe
Marketing: Dan Van Gompel
VP Finance: Misako Ipavec
Contact: Daniel Aigner
daniel.aigner@shopgate.com
General Manager: Yasushi Yokozeki
Director Manufacturing: Toshiyuki Iho
Square Footage: 286240
Parent Co: Nippon Meat Packers
Other Locations:
Hayward CA
Santa Fe Springs CA
Brands:
Day-Lee Foods

3417 **Daybreak Coffee Roasters**
2377 Main St # C
Glastonbury, CT 06033-4063
860-657-4466
Fax: 860-633-6614 800-882-5282
freshcoffee@daybreakcoffee.com
www.daybreakcoffee.com
Coffee
President: Thomas Clarke
Vice President: Linda Kenneman
admin@daybreakcoffee.com
Sales: Cathy Reynolds
Estimated Sales: $500,000-$1,000,000
Number Employees: 10-19
Brands:
Daybreak

3418 **Daybreak Foods Inc**
609 6th St NE
Long Prairie, MN 56347-1003
320-732-2966
Fax: 320-732-3690 www.daybreakfoods.com
Egg products
President: Robert Rehm
CEO: Brent Rehm
Finance Manager: Tom Bandevencer
Manager: Tom Vandeventer
tom@daybreakfoods.com
Plant Manager: Steven Masia
Estimated Sales: $10,000,000
Number Employees: 50-99
Type of Packaging: Bulk
Brands:
Daybreak Foods

3419 **Daybrook Fisheries**
365 Canal Place
Suite 2300
New Orleans, LA 70130
504-561-6163
Fax: 504-636-4993 www.daybrook.com
Menhaden fishmeal and fish oil.
President: Gregory Holt
CFO: Stephen Morganstern
Executive Vice President: W. Borden Wallace
Senior Vice President, Operations: Lee Alexander
Year Founded: 1898
Estimated Sales: $324.4 Million
Number Employees: 400
Parent Co: Oceana Group
Type of Packaging: Bulk

3420 **Daymar Select Fine Coffees**
460 Cypress Ln # B
El Cajon, CA 92020-1647
619-444-1155
Fax: 619-444-1985 800-466-7590
info@daymarcoffee.com www.daymarcoffee.com
Chocolates, syrups, teas and coffees including flavored, organic, roast, ground, whole beans and instant
President: Roy Gallegos
roy@daymarcoffee.com
Secretary: Diana Gallegos
Estimated Sales: $5-10 Million
Number Employees: 10-19
Type of Packaging: Consumer, Food Service, Private Label, Bulk
Brands:
Cafe El Marino

3421 **Dayton Nut Specialties**
45 N Pioneer Bld
Springboro, OH 45066
937-743-4377
candyandnutstore.com
Confectionery and nuts
President: Stanley Maschino
Estimated Sales: $2,000,000
Number Employees: 46
Number of Brands: 3
Type of Packaging: Private Label
Brands:
Dayton Nut Specialties
Friesinger's Fine Chocolates
Candy Farm

3422 **Dazbog Coffee Co**
1090 Yuma St
Denver, CO 80204-3838
303-892-9999
Fax: 303-893-9999 coffee@dazbog.com
www.dazbog.com
Manufacturer of coffee and tea.
Co-Founder: Anatoly Yuffa
Co-Founder: Leonid Yuffa
coffee@dazbog.com
Number Employees: 10-19

3423 **De Boles Nutritional Foods**
104 N Common St
Shreveport, LA 71101-2614
318-222-6857
Fax: 318-221-7815
Organic and all natural pastas
President: William Robertson
Vice President: Pete Holcombe
Plant Manager: Monty Phares
Estimated Sales: Under $500,000
Number Employees: 20-49
Parent Co: DeBoles Nutritional Foods

3424 **De Bruyn Produce Company**
709 NW 12th Ter
Ponpano Beach, FL 33069-2041
954-788-6707
Fax: 954-788-6340 800-733-9177
Onions an carrots
President: Margret DeBruyn
CEO: Mike Diaz
EVP: Ralph Diaz
Sales/Marketing: Betty Aquire
Operations Manager: Kevin Hubbard
Type of Packaging: Consumer, Food Service
Other Locations:
Cooling And Manufacturing Plant
Byron Center MI
Carrot Manufacturing Plant
Weslaco TX
Onion Manufacturing Plant
Farmersville TX
Vegetable Cooling Plant
Tifton GA
Spanish Onion Manufacturing
Ontario OR
Brands:
Citation
Debco
Gold Rim
Gulf

3425 **De Coty Coffee Co**
1920 Austin St
San Angelo, TX 76903-8704
325-655-5607
Fax: 325-655-6837 800-588-8001
eric@decoty.com www.decoty.com
Importer, Roaster, & Distributor of coffe. Manufacturer of coffee, tea, spices & seasonings.
CEO/President: Michael Agan
agan@decoty.com
Sales/Marketing: Bryan Baker
Operations: Ronnie Wallace
Production Manager: Eric Fischer
Purchasing: Teresa Rocha
Estimated Sales: $12 Million
Number Employees: 50-99
Square Footage: 50000
Type of Packaging: Food Service, Private Label, Bulk

3426 **De Fluri's Fine Chocolate**
130 N Queen St
Martinsburg, WV 25401-3312
304-264-3698
Fax: 304-264-3698 sales@defluris.com
www.defluris.com
Truffles, nuts, crunches and chews, creams
President/Owner: Brenda Casabona
sales@defluris.com
Estimated Sales: Less Than $500,000
Number Employees: 1-4

3427 **De Iorio's Foods Inc**
2200 Bleecker St
Utica, NY 13501-1739
315-732-7612
Fax: 315-732-7621 800-649-7612
www.deiorios.com
Manufacturer of dough products. Products include dough balls, flats, shells, self rise, breads and sub rolls, breadsticks, and more.
Chairman & CEO: Robert Ragusa
VP, Business Development: Robert Horth
Manager: Fabio Faro
ffaro@deiorios.com
Manager: Donald King
Estimated Sales: $5-10,000,000
Number Employees: 100-249
Number of Brands: 1
Number of Products: 87
Type of Packaging: Consumer, Food Service, Private Label
Other Locations:
De-Iorio's Frozen Dough
Utica NY
Brands:
DeIorio's

3428 **De Iorios Frozen Dough Co Inc**
2200 Bleecker St
Utica, NY 13501-1739
315-724-2401
Fax: 315-732-7621 800-649-7612
www.deiorios.com
Frozen dough
President & CEO: Robert J. Ragusa
bhorth@deiorios.com
VP, Business Development: Robert Horth
Sales Exec: Bob Horth
Number Employees: 100-249

3429 **De Maria's Seafood**
12544 Warwick Blvd
Newport News, VA 23606-2644
757-930-3474
Fax: 757-930-4847
Catfish, cod, flounder, haddock, halibut, mackerel, perch, salmon, shad, tuna, monkfish fillets, blue crabmeat, clams, shrimp
Owner: John DE Maria
oyster1@cox.net
Estimated Sales: $500,000-$1,000,000
Number Employees: 5-9
Brands:
Demaria Seafood

3430 **De Met's Candy Co**
30 Buxton Farm Rd
Stamford, CT 06905-1224
203-329-4545
Fax: 203-329-4555 800-872-7622
www.demetscandy.com
Popcorn snacks
President/CEO: Hendrick Hartong
CEO: David Clarke
CFO: Joanne Prier
CEO: David Clarke
Estimated Sales: $3-5 Million
Number Employees: 5-9
Type of Packaging: Consumer
Brands:
Fiddle Faddle

Golden Gourmet Nuts
Poppycock

3431 **De Nigris**
31 Vreeland Ave
Totowa, NJ 07512
973-837-6791
Fax: 973-837-6794
Tomato sauce, bruschetta toppings, olive oil, vinegars
CEO Partner: Helena Dane

3432 **De Souza's**
4092 W Ramsey St
Banning, CA 92220-3518
951-849-5172
Fax: 951-849-1348 800-373-5171
info@desouzas.com www.desouzas.com
Solar-dried sea salt; also, chlorophyll liquid, tablets and capsules
President/CEO: Rosalie DeSouza
VP Operations: K Hill
Estimated Sales: $1-2.5 Million
Number Employees: 1-4
Square Footage: 32000
Type of Packaging: Private Label

3433 **DeBeukelaer Cookie Co**
228 Industrial Dr N
PO Box 1697
Madison, MS 39110-9481
601-856-7454
Fax: 601-856-1462 www.pirouline.com
Cookies
Founder: Peter DeBeukelaer
Founder: Mireilla DeBeukelaer
SVP Sales: Tim Sullivan
Human Resources Manager: Ana Robinson
Estimated Sales: $22 Million
Number Employees: 100-249
Square Footage: 100000
Brands:
De Beukelaer

3434 **DeBeukelaer Corp**
P.O. Box 456
Madison, MS 39130
601-856-7454
swirlmaster@pirouline.com
Cookies
Founder: Peter De Beukelaer
Senior VP of Sales: Tim Sullivan
Year Founded: 1984
Estimated Sales: $23273178
Number Employees: 100
Type of Packaging: Food Service, Private Label

3435 **DeLallo Foods**
1 DeLallo Way
Mount Pleasant, PA 15666
877-355-2556
www.delallo.com
Organic pasta, sauces and olive oil
VP: Anthony DiPietro
Operations: Jeff Latimer

3436 **DeLallo Italian Foods**
6390 Route 30
Jeannette, PA 15644-3193
724-523-6577
Fax: 724-853-0141 800-433-9100
www.delallo.com
Olives, antipasti, sauces, pasta, oils & vinegars
Owner: Francis DeLallo
VP Marketing: Robert Lubic
Type of Packaging: Consumer

3437 **DeLima Coffee**
7546 Morgan Rd
Liverpool, NY 13090
315-457-3725
Fax: 315-457-3730 800-962-8864
info@delimacoffee.com www.delimacoffee.com
Coffee
Principle: Paul Lima
President: Michael Garlick
CFO: Steve Zaremba
Vice President Sales: Donald Hughes
dhughes@delimacoffee.com
VP Human Resources: Peter Sansone
Purchasing Agent: Lisa Priest
Type of Packaging: Consumer, Food Service

3438 **DeLuscious Cookies**
829 N Highland Ave
Los Angeles, CA 90038
323-460-2370
Fax: 323-460-6301 info@delusciouscookies.com
www.delusciouscookies.com
Gourmet cookies
Owner: Lydia Shayne
Year Founded: 2002
Number of Brands: 1
Number of Products: 11
Type of Packaging: Consumer
Brands:
DELUSCIOUS

3439 **(HQ)DeMedici Imports**
One Atalanta Plaza
Elizabeth, NJ 07206
908-372-0965
Fax: 908-372-0960 info@demedici.com
www.demedici.com
Gourmet specialty foods
President: Paul Farber
Contact: Steven Kaufman
sbk@demedici.com
Operations: Marilym O'Daniels
Estimated Sales: $5-10 Million
Number Employees: 5-9
Type of Packaging: Private Label
Brands:
Colonna

3440 **Dean & De Luca Inc**
383 Kalaimoku St
Honolulu, HI 96815
808-729-9720
customercare@deandeluca.com
www.deandeluca.com
Coffee beans
Estimated Sales: $80,000,000
Brands:
Dean & Deluca

3441 **Dean Distributors, Inc.**
1350 Bayshore Highway
Suite 400
Burlingame, CA 94010
800-792-0816
corporate@deandistributors.com
www.deandistributors.com
Specialty food products including sauces, kosher and Mexican soups and gravy bases, tenderizers and aid, consomme, smoke and cheese flavors, syrups, extracts and nutritional supplements
President: Ralph Schulz
Controller: Stacey Rusley
VP: Mark Schulz
Director Sales/Marketing: Mark Schulz
Contact: David Mojarro
dmojarro@deandistributors.com
Estimated Sales: $15 Million
Number Employees: 5-9
Square Footage: 140000
Parent Co: Dean Distributors
Type of Packaging: Food Service
Brands:
Bernard Fine Foods
Dean
Flavor-Glow

3442 **(HQ)Dean Foods Co.**
2711 N. Haskell Ave.
Suite 3400
Dallas, TX 75204
800-395-7004
deanfoods@casupport.com www.deanfoods.com
Milk, ice cream, cultured dairy products, juices, teas and bottled water.
President/CEO: Eric Beringause
Interim CFO/SVP, Finance & Strategy: Gary Rahlfs
SVP/General Counsel: Kristy Waterman
SVP/Chief Commercial Officer: Thomas Murray
Year Founded: 1925
Estimated Sales: $7.7 Billion
Number Employees: 16,000+
Number of Brands: 35
Type of Packaging: Food Service, Private Label
Brands:
Alta Dena
Barber's®
Berkeley Farms
Broughton®
Brown's Dairy®
Country Fresh™
Creamland
Dairy Pure®
Dean's™
Friendly's®
Fruit Rush™
Gandy's
Garelick Farms®
Hygeia®
Jilbert
Land O Lakes®
Lehigh Valley®
Mayfield Creamery™
Mayfield®
McArthur Dairy®
Meadow Brook®
Meadow Gold®
Model Dairy
Oak Farms Dairy
Orchard Pure™
PET®
Price's
Purity
Ready Leaf
Reiter Dairy™
Swiss Premium®
T.G. Lee
TruMoo
Tuscan™
Uncle Matt's®

3443 **Dean Sausage Co Inc**
3750 Pleasant Valley Rd
P.O. Drawer 750
Attalla, AL 35954-5606
256-538-6082
Fax: 256-538-2584 800-228-0704
deansausage@deansausage.com
www.deansausage.com
Sausage
President/Treasurer: Marsue Lancaster
Secretary: Jane Moore
Vice President: Garry Shirley
Marketing Director: Hugh Miller
Estimated Sales: $10-20 Million
Number Employees: 100-249
Square Footage: 75000
Type of Packaging: Consumer, Food Service, Private Label
Brands:
Dean's Country
Kentucky Farm

3444 **Deanna's Gluten Free Baking Co.**
2250 S Escondido Blvd
Suite 110
Escondido, CA 92025
760-432-6100
info@deannasgf.com
deannasglutenfree.com
Gluten free baked goods

3445 **Dear North**
9301 Glacier Hwy
Suite 200
Juneau, AK 99801-9380
907-789-8500
Fax: 907-789-7896
customercervice@dearnorth.com
dearnorth.com
Smoked seafood; pft,; dried salmon snacks.
Director of Marketing: Ruth Banaszak
Vice President of Sales: Timothy Meskill
Year Founded: 2016
Parent Co: Huna Totem Corporation
Type of Packaging: Private Label

3446 **Dearborn Sausage Co Inc**
2450 Wyoming St
Dearborn, MI 48120-1518
313-842-2375
Fax: 313-842-2640 866-900-4426
info@dearbornbrand.com
www.dearbornsausage.com
Sausage
Chief Executive Officer: Donald Kosch
Chief Financial Officer: Elizabeth Cooley
Vice President: Michael Kosch
Manager: Mary Kral
mkral45@comcast.net
Estimated Sales: $6,845,000
Number Employees: 50-99
Number of Brands: 1
Brands:
Dearborn Sausage

3447 Deaver Vineyards
12455 Steiner Rd
Plymouth, CA 95669-9504
209-245-4099
Fax: 209-245-4097
deaverwinery@deavervineyard.com
www.deavervineyards.com
Wines
President/Marketing Manager: Ken Deaver
Estimated Sales: $2.5-5,000,000
Number Employees: 5-9
Number of Brands: 19
Number of Products: 1
Type of Packaging: Private Label
Brands:
19
Deaver Vineyards Wine

3448 Debbie D's Jerky & Sausage
2210 Main Ave N
Tillamook, OR 97141-7724
503-842-2622
debbie@debbiedssausage.com
www.debbiedssausage.com
Smoked beef jerky and sausage
President: Debbie Downie
debbie.downie@oregoncoast.com
Estimated Sales: Less Than $500,000
Number Employees: 1-4
Type of Packaging: Consumer, Bulk
Brands:
Debbie D'S

3449 Debel Food Products
2 Papetti Plz
Elizabeth, NJ 07206-1421
908-351-0330
Fax: 908-351-0334 800-421-3447
info@debelfoods.com www.debelfoods.com
Egg products
President: Elliott Gibber
Manager: John Mckay
jmckay@debelfoods.com
Estimated Sales: $48.3 Million
Number Employees: 50-99
Number of Brands: 2
Square Footage: 75000
Brands:
Just Whites
Scramblettes

3450 Deborah's Kitchen Inc.
147 King Street
Suite 406
Littleton, MA 01460
617-216-9908
Fax: 413-552-3259 deborah@deborahskitchen.com
www.deborahskitchen.com
All natural, low-sugar spreadable fruit and relish.
Owner: Deborah Taylore
beborah@deborahskitchen.com
Type of Packaging: Food Service, Private Label

3451 Debragga & Spitler
65-77 Amity St
Jersey City, NJ 07304-3509
info@debragga.com
www.debragga.com
Prime cuts of beef, lamb and pork; wholesaler/distributor of further processed beef, veal, lamb and pork.
President & CEO: Marc John Sarrazin
Year Founded: 1920
Estimated Sales: $20-50 Million
Number Employees: 50-99
Number of Brands: 1
Type of Packaging: Food Service, Bulk
Brands:
Natural Certified Angus Beef

3452 Debrand Chocolatier
10105 Auburn Park Dr
Fort Wayne, IN 46825-2388
260-969-8333
Fax: 260-969-8334 customerservice@debrand.com
www.debrand.com
Chocolate bars, chocolate truffles, full-line chocolate, other chocolate, toffee.
Owner: Timothy Beere
tbeere@debrand.com
Marketing: Cathy Brand-Beere
Number Employees: 20-49

3453 Deca & Otto Farms
7953 NW 21st Street
Miami, FL 33122
305-629-9335
www.decaotto.com
Buffalo milk yogurts and cheeses
President: Alberto Sasson

3454 Decadence Cheese Cakes
2591 Legacy Way
Grand Junction, CO 81503
970-256-4688
www.decadencecheesecakes.com
Cheese cake
Contact: Lee Mathis
decadencecheesecakes@mindspring.com

3455 Decadent Desserts
831 10th Ave SW
Calgary, AB T2R 0B4
Canada
403-245-5535
Cakes including cheese and wedding; also, pies and cookies
President: Pamela Fortier
Estimated Sales: B
Number Employees: 6
Type of Packaging: Consumer, Food Service

3456 Decas Cranberry Sales Inc
4 Old Forge Way # 1
Carver, MA 02330-1765
508-866-8506
Fax: 508-866-9020 800-649-9811
www.decascranberry.com
All-natural cranberry and fruit products
President/CEO: John Decas
CEO: Charles B Dillon
cdillon@decascranberry.com
VP Sales: Nick Decas
Estimated Sales: $5-10 000,000
Number Employees: 250-499

3457 Decatur Dairy
W1668 Hwy F
Brodhead, WI 53520-9505
608-897-8661
Fax: 608-897-4587 www.decaturdairy.com
Brick, muenster, farmer cheese, pavarti
President: Steven Stettler
Estimated Sales: $500,000-$1,000,000
Number Employees: 10-19
Brands:
Decatur Dairy

3458 Decker Farms Inc
12475 SW River Rd
Hillsboro, OR 97123-9314
503-628-1532
Fax: 503-628-3696 info@deckerfarm.com
www.deckerfarm.com
Frozen fruits including red and black raspberries and strawberries; also, frozen filberts and hazelnuts
Owner: Priscilla Decker
deckerfarms@frontier.net
Number Employees: 5-9
Type of Packaging: Bulk
Brands:
Decker Farms Finest

3459 Decker Food Company
3200 W Kingsley Road
Garland, TX 75041-2204
972-278-6192
Fax: 972-278-1983
Meat products
President/CEO: R Belsito
Brand Manager: Mike Rook
Vice President: Dennis Swingle
Sales Director: Denny Swingle
VP Marketing/Sales: Paul Wood
Chief Engineer: Jerry Rhubert
Plant Manager: John Vincent
Estimated Sales: $10-20 Million
Number Employees: 5-9
Parent Co: ConAgra Foods
Type of Packaging: Private Label

3460 Decko Products Inc
2105 Superior St
Sandusky, OH 44870-1891
419-626-5757
Fax: 419-626-3135 800-537-6143
shumphrey@decko.com www.decko.com
Edible cake and candy decorations and packaged rings, gels
President: F William Niggemyer
Marketing Director: Sara Humphrey
Estimated Sales: $10 Million
Number Employees: 50-99
Square Footage: 105000
Type of Packaging: Private Label
Brands:
Royal Icing Decoration

3461 Deconna Ice Cream
6300 W Highway 318
Reddick, FL 32686-2334
352-591-1530
Fax: 352-591-4418 800-824-8254
sales@deconna.com www.deconna.com
Ice cream
President: Vince Deconna
v.conna@deconna.com
Estimated Sales: $36,000,000
Number Employees: 50-99
Number of Brands: 1
Type of Packaging: Bulk
Brands:
Deconna

3462 DeeBee's Organics
6-798 Fairview Rd
Victoria, BC V9A 5V1
Canada
778-265-8327
Fax: 778-433-8327 855-515-8327
www.deebeesorganics.com
Organic fruit popsicles
Founder: Dr. Dionne Baker

3463 Deen Meat & Cooked Foods
813 E Northside Dr
PO Box 4155
Fort Worth, TX 76102-1017
817-335-2257
Fax: 817-338-9256 800-333-3953
www.deenmeat.com
Meat
President: Danny Deen
danny77@deenmeat.com
VP: Craig Deen
VP: Matthew Deen
Business Development Manager: Steve Dumas
Quality Assurance/ R&D: Marc de Plante
Director of Partner Development: Pat Harrington
VP Operations: Joe Cholopisa
VP, Purchase: Mike Pritchard
Number Employees: 100-249
Brands:
Deen
Double L

3464 Deep Creek Custom Packing
Mile 137 Sterling Highway
PO Box 39752
Ninilchik, AK 99639
907-567-3395
Fax: 907-567-3579 800-764-0078
dccp@ptialaska.net
Alaska smoked salmon, halibut, canned giftpacks, custom processing and gourmet seafood
CEO: Jeff Berger
Plant Manager: Chris Baobo
Estimated Sales: $7 Million
Number Employees: 20-49
Square Footage: 24000

3465 Deep Foods Inc
1090 Springfield Rd
Suite 1
Union, NJ 07083-8147
908-810-7500
Fax: 908-810-8482 www.deepfoods.com
Indian foods such as snacks, frozen meals, ice creams and others.
Vice President: Pravin Amin
deepfoods@aol.com
VP Marketing: Archit Amin
Sales Director: Chintam Trivedi
Estimated Sales: $5-10 Million
Number Employees: 50-99
Square Footage: 120000
Type of Packaging: Consumer, Food Service, Bulk
Other Locations:
Deep Foods
Mississagua, CANADA ON
Brands:
Babu's Pocket Sandwiches

Bansi
Deep
Deep Dairy
Gujarati
Hot Mix
Hot Wok
Mirch Masala
Reena's
Tandoor Chef
Udupi

3466 **Deep River Snacks**
PO Box 1127
Deep River, CT 06417
860-434-7347
Fax: 860-434-7512 info@deepriversnacks.com
www.deepriversnacks.com
Chips and popcorn
President: James Goldberg
info@deepriversnacks.com
Estimated Sales: $2 Million
Number Employees: 5-9
Brands:
Deep River Snacks
Honchos

3467 **Deep Valley**
New York, NY
917-673-5121
Fax: 929-250-2856 www.deepvalleycoffee.com
Organic coffee
Number of Brands: 1
Number of Products: 2
Type of Packaging: Consumer
Brands:
DEEP VALLEY

3468 **Deer Creek Honey Farms LTD**
551 E High St
London, OH 43140-9521
740-852-0899
Fax: 740-852-4530 www.deercreekhoney.com
Kosher certified honey and molasses
President: Chris Dunham
chris@deercreekhoney.com
Estimated Sales: $650,000
Number Employees: 5-9
Square Footage: 44000
Type of Packaging: Consumer, Food Service, Private Label, Bulk
Brands:
Deer Creek

3469 **Deer Park Spring Water Co**
925 Cavalier Blvd # D
Chesapeake, VA 23323-1549
757-485-3200
Fax: 757-487-4970 800-832-0271
deerparkwater.com
Bottled spring and distilled water
CFO: Kim Jefferies
General Manager: Michael Difrancesco
Plant Manager: Edgar Gaskins
Estimated Sales: $3-5 Million
Number Employees: 20-49
Square Footage: 146000
Type of Packaging: Consumer, Food Service
Brands:
A&D Water Care
Culligan
Diamond Springs
H2o To Go
Hydrologix
Miller's
The Water Fountain
Water & Health
Water Fountain of Edenton
Yoder Dairies

3470 **Deerfield Bakery**
201 N Buffalo Grove Rd
Buffalo Grove, IL 60089-1748
847-520-0068
Fax: 847-520-0135 sheila@deerfieldbakery.com
www.deerfieldsbakery.com
Cakes and full service bakery
Owner: Kurt Schmitt
Contact: Paula Schmitt
paula@bodnardesign.com
Estimated Sales: Less than $500,000
Number Employees: 100-249
Type of Packaging: Private Label
Brands:
Deerfield

3471 **(HQ)Deerland Probiotics & Enzymes**
3800 Cobb International Blvd.
Kennesaw, GA 30152
Fax: 770-919-1194 800-697-8179
www.deerland.com
Manufacturer and exporter of digestive enzymes and nutritional supplements
Chief Executive Officer: Scott Ravech
VP, Science & Technology: John Deaton
Director, Innovation & Education: John Davidson
Director, Quality Assurance & Control: Maggie Leroux
VP, Marketing & Strategy: Sam Michini
Estimated Sales: $20-50 Million
Number Employees: 50-99
Type of Packaging: Private Label, Bulk
Brands:
Eds
Nozimes

3472 **Deerland Probiotics & Enzymes**
15366 US Highway 160
Forsyth, MO 65653-8107
800-825-8545
www.deerland.com
Manufacturer and exporter of digestive enzymes and nutritional supplements
Type of Packaging: Private Label, Bulk

3473 **(HQ)Deerwood Rice & Grain Procng**
21926 County Road 10
Deerwood, MN 56444-8486
218-534-3762
Fax: 218-534-3802
Wild rice
President: Dan Mohs
Estimated Sales: $1.20 Million
Number Employees: 20-49
Square Footage: 117000
Type of Packaging: Consumer, Bulk

3474 **Dehydrates Inc**
1251 Peninsula Blvd
Hewlett, NY 11557-1223
516-295-3700
Fax: 516-295-3777 800-983-4443
dehydrates123@hotmail.com
www.dehydratesinc.com
Dehydrated fruits, vegetables and herbs
President: Steven Reich
Marketing: Gail Whiteford
Public Relations: Lori Zahler
Estimated Sales: $1.5 Million
Number Employees: 1-4
Square Footage: 80000
Type of Packaging: Food Service, Private Label, Bulk
Brands:
Dehydrates

3475 **Dei Fratelli**
411 Lemoyne Road
Toledo, OH 43619
416-693-0531
Fax: 419-693-0744 800-837-1631
info@hirzel.com www.deifratelli.com
Salsas, tomatoes, tomato juice, pasta sauces
President: Joe Hirzel
Research & Development: Karl Hirzel
Retail Sales: Herb Milem
Human Resources: Sara Monhollen
Square Footage: 250000
Type of Packaging: Consumer

3476 **Deko International Company**
4283 Shoreline Dr
Earth City, MO 63045-1209
314-298-0910
Fax: 314-298-0081 dekointl@aol.com
www.dekointl.com
Distributor of products and ingredients for the food service industry.
President/CEO: Peter Dekointl
Vice President: Nung Kuo
Sales Coordinator: Jennifer Suen
Customer Service: Johnny Liu
Vice President of Operations: Art Chung
Purchasing Manager: Sarah Zhang
Number Employees: 10-19
Type of Packaging: Food Service
Other Locations:
Rancho Cucamonga CA
Clifton NJ
Norcross GA

3477 **Del Mar Food Products Corp**
1720 Beach Rd
P.O. Box 891
Watsonville, CA 95077
831-722-3516
Fax: 831-722-7690 www.delmarfoods.com
Apricots, blackberries, peaches, strawberries, brussel sprouts, red bell peppers and spinach
President: P.J. Mecozzi
Vice President, Operations: Lee Haskin
Estimated Sales: $50-99 Million
Number Employees: 500
Number of Brands: 1
Square Footage: 53408
Brands:
Del Mar

3478 **Del Monte Foods Inc.**
3003 Oak Rd.
Walnut Creek, CA 94598
www.delmonte.com
Canned fruits and vegetables. Not affiliated with Del Monte Fresh Produce.
President & CEO: Gregory Longstreet
CFO: Gene Allen
General Counsel/Chief Compliance Officer: William Sawyers
Chief Marketing Officer: Bibie Wu
Contact: Gerald Abele
gerald.abele@delmontefoods.com
Year Founded: 1886
Estimated Sales: $3.8 Billion
Number Employees: 7,800
Number of Brands: 7
Parent Co: Del Monte Pacific, Ltd.
Type of Packaging: Consumer, Food Service, Private Label
Other Locations:
Del Monte Foods
Cambria WI
Brands:
Del Monte®
Contadina®
College Inn®
S&W®
Fruit & Chia™
Fruit & Oats™
Fruit Refreshers®

3479 **(HQ)Del Monte Fresh Produce Inc.**
PO Box 149222
Coral Gables, FL 33114-9222
305-520-8400
Fax: 305-567-0320 800-950-3683
contact-us-executive-office@freshdelmonte.com
www.freshdelmonte.com
Fresh and fresh-cut fruit and vegetables.
President/COO: Youssef Zakharia
Chairman/CEO: Mohammad Abu-Ghazaleh
mabughazaleh@freshdelmonte.com
Senior VP/CFO: Eduardo Bezerra
Senior VP/General Counsel/Secretary: Marlene Gordon
Senior VP, North America Operations: Annunciata Cerioli
Year Founded: 1886
Estimated Sales: $3.9 Billion
Number Employees: 45,000
Number of Brands: 11
Type of Packaging: Consumer, Food Service
Other Locations:
Del Monte Fresh Plant
Forest Park GA
Del Monte Fresh Plant
Kankakee IL
Del Monte Fresh Plant
Jessup MD
Del Monte Fresh Plant
Kansas City MO
Del Monte Fresh Plant
Bloomfield NJ
Del Monte Fresh Plant
Mappsville VA
Del Monte Fresh Plant
Canton MA
Del Monte Fresh Plant
Mulberry FL
Del Monte Fresh Plant
Richmond CA
Del Monte Fresh Plant
Eddystone PA
Del Monte Fresh Plant

Chicago IL
Del Monte Fresh Plant
Plant City FL
Del Monte Fresh Plant
Columbus OH
Brands:
Del Monte Fresh®
Mann's®
Rosy®
Fruitini
Golden Ripe®
Just Juice
Mission®
MAG® Melon
UTC®
National Poultry Company
De L'Ora®

3480 **Del Rey Packing**
5287 S Del Rey Ave
P.O. Box 160
Del Rey, CA 93616
559-888-2031
Fax: 559-888-2715
gchooljian@delreypacking.com
www.delreypacking.com
Manufacturer and exporter of raisins.
President: Gerald Chooljian
gchooljian@delreypacking.com
Vice President: Kathy Merlo
Estimated Sales: $20-50 Million
Number Employees: 50-99
Number of Brands: 2
Type of Packaging: Consumer, Food Service, Private Label, Bulk
Brands:
Deluxe
Regent

3481 **Del Rio Nut Company**
15391 Vinewood Circle
P.O. Box 396
Livingston, CA 95334
209-394-7945
Fax: 209-394-7955 david@delrionut.com
www.delrionut.com
Natural almonds
President/ Marketing Director: David Arakelian
Contact: Barret Arakelian
arakelianbarret@delrionut.com
Operations Manager: Mona Menezes
Estimated Sales: $3-5 Million
Number Employees: 20-49
Square Footage: 36000
Type of Packaging: Consumer, Food Service, Private Label, Bulk
Brands:
Del Rio

3482 **Del's Lemonade & Refreshments**
1260 Oaklawn Ave
Cranston, RI 02920-2628
401-463-6190
Fax: 401-463-7931 dels@dels.com
www.dels.com
Lemonade
Owner: Bruce DE Lucia
dels@dels.com
VP: Joe Padula
Estimated Sales: $3 Million
Number Employees: 20-49
Brands:
Del's
Del's Italian Ices
Del's Lemonade

3483 **Del's Pastry**
344 Bering Avenue
Toronto, ON M8Z 3A7
Canada
416-231-4383
Fax: 416-231-3254 800-461-0663
dels@delspastry.com www.delspastry.com
Muffins, turnovers, pies, tea biscuits, cakes and danish
President: Benno Mattes
Vice President: Tom Mattes
Estimated Sales: $9 Million
Number Employees: 170

3484 **Del's Seaway Shrimp & Oyster Company**
PO Box 648
Biloxi, MS 39533-0648
228-432-2604
Fax: 228-432-8919
Frozen shrimp
President: George Higginbotham
Executive VP: Paul Delcambre
Estimated Sales: $10-20,000,000
Number Employees: 50-99
Type of Packaging: Consumer, Food Service
Brands:
Seaway

3485 **DelGrosso Foods**
Old Route 220
Tipton, PA 16684
814-684-5880
Fax: 814-684-3943 800-521-5880
info@delgrossos.com www.delgrossos.com
Spaghetti sauce, pizza sauce, salsa, sloppy joe sauce and meatballs.
President: James DelGrosso
VP Global Sales/Marketing: Michael DelGrosso
VP Operations: Joseph DelGrosso
Number Employees: 68
Square Footage: 270000
Type of Packaging: Consumer

3486 **DelGrosso Foods**
632 Sauce Factory Dr
Tipton, PA 16684
814-684-5880
800-521-5880
info@delgrossosauce.com
www.delgrossofoods.com
Spaghetti sauces, salsas, and Italian-style meatballs
President: James DelGrosso
VP Global Sales & Marketing: Michael DelGrosso
Operations Director: James Mayall
Purchasing Director: Lisa Pier
Estimated Sales: $22 Million
Number Employees: 68
Square Footage: 135000

3487 **Delallo's Italian Store**
6390 State Route 30
Jeannette, PA 15644-3193
724-523-5000
Fax: 724-523-0981 info@DeLallo.com
www.delallo.com
Olives
Manager: Eric Baker
Manager: Chuck Glona
chuckg@delallo.com
Estimated Sales: $2.5-5 Million
Number Employees: 100-249
Brands:
Delallo

3488 **Delancey Dessert Company**
573 Grand St
New York, NY 10002-4381
914-393-5209
Fax: 914-574-5270 800-254-5254
Candy and confectionery
Owner: Zvia Levi
Estimated Sales: $1-2.5 Million
Number Employees: 1-4
Brands:
Delancey Dessert

3489 **(HQ)Delano Growers Grape Products**
32351 Bassett Ave
Delano, CA 93215-9699
661-725-3255
Fax: 661-725-0279
White grape juice concentrate
President: Ray Cox
ray@delanogrowers.com
R&D: Rick Lord
Sales: Ray Cox
Production: Rick Lord
Estimated Sales: $26.30 Million
Number Employees: 50-99
Type of Packaging: Bulk

3490 **Delaviuda USA Inc**
2100 Salzedo St
Suite 201
Coral Gables, FL 33134
786-599-9814
delaviuda.com
Confections
Marketing development Director: Alvaro Potente
apotente@Delaviuda.com
Year Founded: 1973
Brands:
El Almendro
Delaviuda

3491 **Delaware Valley Fish Co**
108 W Basin St
Norristown, PA 19401-3859
610-277-4900
Fax: 610-277-4051 info@dvfish.com
www.dvfish.com
Farm raised shellfish, fish, and delicacies
Owner: Barry Kratchman
delvalfish@aol.com
Number Employees: 5-9

3492 **Delectable Gourmet LLC**
1095 Long Island Ave
Deer Park, NY 11729
631-957-1350
Fax: 631-957-1013 800-696-1350
jeremy@icbakers.com
www.worldsbestcranberries.com
Pesto, cranberry sauce, and gourmet cranberry juice
President: Ted Heim Sr
Estimated Sales: $20-50 Million
Number Employees: 50-99

3493 **Delftree Corp**
234 Union St
North Adams, MA 01247-3522
413-664-4907
Fax: 413-664-4908 800-243-3742
Gourmet foods and vegetables
Manager: Lori Garvey
selfstorage@delftree.com
VP: Steve Rich
Estimated Sales: $2.5-5,000,000
Number Employees: 10-19
Brands:
Delftree

3494 **Delgrosso Foods Inc.**
632 Sauce Factory Drive
Tipton, PA 16684
814-684-5880
Fax: 814-684-3943 800-521-5880
michaeld@delgrossofoods.com
www.delgrossofoods.com
Manufacturer and importer of traditional spaghetti sauce, pizza sauce, salsa, sloppy joe sauce, country garden spaghetti sauce and meatballs.
President: James Del Grosso
R&D: Sean Etters
Quality Control: Fredrick Del Grosso
Marketing: Michael Del Grosso
Sales Manager: Robert DelGrosso
Public Relations: Sean Albright
Manager: Joseph Del Grosso
Estimated Sales: $10-20 Million
Number Employees: 50-99
Square Footage: 315000
Type of Packaging: Consumer, Food Service
Brands:
Del Grosso

3495 **Delia's Food Co**
313 Hilton Pl
Cincinnati, OH 45219-2604
513-221-4322
Fax: 360-248-6677
www.daeliasbiscuitsforcheese.com
Crackers.
Site Manager: Maria Walley
Number Employees: 1-4

3496 **Delicae Gourmet**
1310 E Lake Dr
Tarpon Springs, FL 34688-8110
727-942-2502
Fax: 727-942-1837 800-942-2502
sales@delicaegourmet.com
www.delicaegourmet.com

Bread topppers, slow cooker meals, spice rubs, mustards, relishes, chutneys, jams, jellies, spices, infused oils and vinegars.
Owner/CEO: Barbara Macaluso
sales@delicaegourmet.com
CFO: Linda Parish
VP: Leonard Macaluso
R&D: Eugene Mann
Quality Control: James Parish
Marketing: Janice Strayer
Sales: Janice Strayer
Operations: James Parish
Production: Scott Shepard
Estimated Sales: $1,500,000
Number Employees: 10-19
Number of Brands: 1
Number of Products: 120
Square Footage: 20000
Type of Packaging: Consumer, Food Service, Private Label, Bulk

3497 **(HQ)Delicato Family Vineyards**
455 Devlin Rd
Suite 201
Napa, CA 94558
707-265-1700
Fax: 707-253-1471 intlmrktg@dfvwines.com
www.delicatofamilyvineyards.com
Wines.
President & CEO: Chris Indelicato
SVP, Operations: Jay Indelicato
VP, Exclusive Brands & Innovation: Jim Ferguson
Regional Accounts Manager: Adam Basala
abasala@dfvwines.com
Year Founded: 1924
Estimated Sales: $29.5 Million
Number Employees: 250-499
Square Footage: 12000
Type of Packaging: Consumer, Food Service, Private Label, Bulk
Brands:
Delicato

3498 **Delicious Desserts**
785 5th Ave
Brooklyn, NY 11232-1750
718-680-1156
Fax: 718-369-6665
Italian desserts including spumoni, tartufo, tortoni, tiramisu, cannolis and cakes; importer of fruit sorbet and Italian cakes
President: Joe Fusceo
Contact: D Lisa
lisa@deliciousdesserts.net
Estimated Sales: Less Than $500,000
Number Employees: 1-4
Square Footage: 8000
Type of Packaging: Private Label

3499 **Delicious Frookie**
2070 Maple Street
Des Plaines, IL 60018-3019
847-699-3200
Fax: 847-699-3201
Cookies.
President: Phil Roos

3500 **Delicious Frookie Company**
5520 N Northwest Highway
Chicago, IL 60630-1116
773-763-5553
Cookies, crackers
President/CEO: M Kirby
Estimated Sales: $500,000 appx.
Number Employees: 1-4
Parent Co: Delicious Frookie Company

3501 **Delicious Popcorn**
300 DE Lish US Ave
Waupaca, WI 54981-1260
715-258-7683
Fax: 715-258-1514 www.wisnack.com
Potato chips and popcorn; wholesaler/distributor of pretzels, tostados, tortillas, baked and fried corn curls, party snack mix, corn chips, raw popcorn and popping oil and gourmet popcorn products
President/Co-Owner: James Hollnbacher
CEO/Co-Owner: Jeff Hollnbacher
Marketing/Sales: Jeff Hollnbacher
Production Manager: James Hollnbacher
Purchasing Manager: James Hollnbacher
Estimated Sales: $2-5 Million
Number Employees: 10-19
Type of Packaging: Consumer, Food Service, Private Label, Bulk
Brands:
De-Lish-Us
Wisnack

3502 **Delicious Valley Frozen Foods**
1200 E Ridge Rd # 9
McAllen, TX 78503-1528
956-631-7177
Fax: 956-630-1757
Frozen foods
Manager: Sylvia Villarreal
Estimated Sales: $.5-1,000,000
Number Employees: 1-4

3503 **Delicious Without Gluten**
90 Brunswick Blvd
Dollard Des Ormeaux, QC H9B 2C5
Canada
514-542-3943
info@deliciouswithout.com
deliciouswithout.com
Baked goods; pizza; cookies
Founder: Miriam Pearl
Number Employees: 5-9

3504 **Delighted By**
delightedbyhummus.com
Dessert hummus
Founder: Makenzie Marzluff
Number of Brands: 1
Number of Products: 4
Type of Packaging: Consumer
Brands:
DELIGHTED BY

3505 **Delizza**
6610 Corporation Pkwy
Battleboro, NC 27809-9804
252-442-0270
info@delizza.us
delizza.us
Frozen pastries
Contact: Ken Martin
kmartin@delizza.us
Estimated Sales: Less Than $500,000
Number Employees: 1-4

3506 **Dell'Amore Enterprises**
PO BOX 974
Colchester, VT 05446
802-655-6264
Fax: 802-655-6262 800-962-6673
www.dellamore.com
All natural pasta sauces
President: Frank Dell'amore
VP: David Dell'Amore
Estimated Sales: $2.5-5 Million
Number Employees: 5-9
Type of Packaging: Private Label

3507 **Dellaco Classic Confections**
8002 352nd Ave
Burlington, WI 53105
262-843-1604
Fax: 262-843-1604 866-537-2656
www.pamperedpetscatalog.com
Confections and nuts
Chairman: Cynthia Delligatti
President: Laura Delligatti
Sales/Marketing: Margaret Delligatti
Estimated Sales: $2.5-5 Million
Number Employees: 10-19

3508 **(HQ)Delmonaco Winery & Vineyards**
600 Lance Dr
Baxter, TN 38544-3530
931-858-1177
barbara@delmonacowinery.com
www.delmonacowinery.com
Wines
President/Winemaker: David Delmonaco
david@delmonacowinery.com
Vice President: Barbara Delmonaco
Estimated Sales: $3 Million
Number Employees: 1-4
Type of Packaging: Bulk

3509 **Deloach Vineyards**
1791 Olivet Rd
Santa Rosa, CA 95401-3898
707-755-3300
Fax: 707-526-4151
customerservice@deloachvineyards.com
www.deloachvineyards.com
Wines
Vice President: Lisa Heisinger
lisaheisinger@deloachvineyards.com
VP: Christine DeLoach
Winemaker: Cecil DeLoach
Production Manager: Rob Cooper
Estimated Sales: $20-50 Million
Number Employees: 20-49
Brands:
De Loach

3510 **Delorimier Winery**
2001 Highway 128
Geyserville, CA 95441-9489
707-857-2000
Fax: 707-857-3262 800-546-7718
www.delorimierwinery.com
Wines
President: Alfred De Lorimier
Marketing: John Woodward
Estimated Sales: $2.5-5,000,000
Number Employees: 10-19
Number of Brands: 1
Number of Products: 10
Type of Packaging: Private Label
Brands:
De Lorimeir

3511 **Delphos Poultry Products**
205 S Pierce St
Delphos, OH 45833
419-692-5816
Fax: 419-692-1606
Chicken products including marinated breasts, breaded, breast fillets, hot wings, wingettes and gizzards
President: Thomas J Schimmoller
Estimated Sales: $1-2.5 Million
Number Employees: 10-19
Square Footage: 21000
Type of Packaging: Consumer, Food Service, Private Label, Bulk
Brands:
Volcano Wings

3512 **Delta Catfish Products**
602 E Lee St
PO Box 99
Eudora, AR 71640
870-355-4192
Fax: 714-778-0998
Catfish
President/CEO: Thomas Marshall

3513 **Delta Food Products**
10557 114th Street NW
Edmonton, AB T5H 3J6
Canada
780-424-3636
Fax: 780-424-1536
Frozen Chinese dim sum, fresh noodles, egg and spring rolls, microwaveable Oriental dinners and green onion cakes
President: Gordon Becker
Manager: Mei-ling Chan
Estimated Sales: $1.8 Million
Number Employees: 22
Square Footage: 60000
Type of Packaging: Consumer, Food Service, Private Label
Brands:
Delta Foods
Wok Menu

3514 **Delta Pacific Seafoods**
6001-60 Ave
Delta, BC V4K 4E2
Canada
604-946-5160
www.deltapacific.ca
Fresh and frozen salmon, hake, sardines, halibut
General Manager: Paul Edgett
Estimated Sales: $8 Million
Number Employees: 20
Type of Packaging: Consumer, Food Service

3515 **Delta Packing**
6021 E Kettleman Ln
Lodi, CA 95240-6400
209-334-1023
Fax: 209-334-0811 www.deltapacking.com
Grower, packer and shipper of cherries, wine grapes, grape juice, pears, asparagus and bell peppers.
Manager: Carl Elkins
Manager: Berton Costamagna
Year Founded: 1976
Number Employees: 10-19
Type of Packaging: Consumer, Food Service, Private Label
Brands:
Delta Fresh

3516 **Delta Pride Catfish**
1301 Industrial Parkway
Indianola, MS 38751
662-887-5401
Fax: 662-887-5950 800-228-3474
sales@deltapride.com www.deltapride.com
Manufacturer of farm-raised catfish and wholesaler/distributor of fresh and frozen farm raised catfish and hush puppies.
President and CEO: Steve Osso
Owner: Adrian Percy
Contact: Darry Adams
dadams@deltapride.com
Year Founded: 1981
Estimated Sales: $30 Million
Number Employees: 450
Parent Co: Delta Pride Catfish

3517 **Deluxe Delight**
10700 Santa Monica Blvd
Suite 207
Lost Angeles, CA 90025
424-230-3664
Mediterranean pastries
Owner: Mohamad El Halabi
Year Founded: 1919
Number Employees: 1-10

3518 **Demitri's Bloody Mary Seasonings**
PO Box 84123
Seattle, WA 98124
206-764-6006
Fax: 206-764-3163 800-627-9649
www.demitris.com
Concentrated Bloody Mary seasonings
President: Demitri Pallis
Contact: Dillon Holmes
dillon@demitris.com
Estimated Sales: Under $300,000
Number Employees: 1-4
Square Footage: 4800
Parent Co: Gourmet Mixes
Type of Packaging: Consumer, Food Service, Bulk
Brands:
Demitri's Bloody Mary Seasonings

3519 **Dempsey's Restaurant & Brewery**
50 E Washington St
Petaluma, CA 94952-3115
707-765-9694
Fax: 707-762-1259 www.dempseys.com
Beer
Owner: Peter Burrell
redroosteraile@att.net
CFO: Peter Burrell
Estimated Sales: $1-2.5 Million
Number Employees: 20-49
Square Footage: 24000
Brands:
Golden Eagle Ale
Red Rooster Ale
Sonoma Brewing
Ugly Dog Stout

3520 **Den's Hot Dogs**
105 Oceana Dr E
Suite 4E
Brooklyn, NY 11235-6682
718-355-9636
Fax: 718-355-9636 www.denshotdogs.com
Hot dog sandwhiches and condiments
President: Denys Gorbatiuk
Year Founded: 2011
Estimated Sales: $250000
Number Employees: 3
Type of Packaging: Private Label

3521 **Denatale Vineyards**
11020 Eastside Road
Healdsburg, CA 95448-9487
707-431-8460
Fax: 707-431-8736
Wines
President: Ron DeNatale
Owner: Sandy De Natale
Estimated Sales: $98,000
Number Employees: 2

3522 **Deneen Foods**
33859 United Avenue
Santa Fe, NM 81001
505-332-2000
Fax: 505-323-7100 800-866-4695
www.santafeseasons.com
Sauces and spice blends
President: Greg Deneen
VP: Edith Deneen
Estimated Sales: $1-2.5 Million
Number Employees: 39009
Number of Brands: 3+
Number of Products: 5+
Square Footage: 68000
Type of Packaging: Consumer, Food Service, Private Label, Bulk
Brands:
Coyote Cocina
Santa Fe Seasons
Go Salsa

3523 **Denning's Point Distillery, LLC**
10 N. Chestnut St.
Beacon, NY 12508
845-476-8413
info@denningspoint.com
www.denningspointdistillery.com
Brandy, bourbon, whiskey, gin and vodka
Co-Founder: Karl Johnson
Co-Founder: Susan Keramedjian
Year Founded: 2014
Number Employees: 5-9
Number of Brands: 1
Number of Products: 6
Type of Packaging: Private Label

3524 **Dennison Meat Locker**
109 Farm Rd
Dennison, MN 55018-4108
507-645-8734
dogoods@hotmail.com
www.dennisonmeatlocker.com
Frankfurters and sausage
Owner: Dori Gregory
Estimated Sales: $1-3 Million
Number Employees: 1-4
Type of Packaging: Consumer

3525 **Denny's 5th Avenue Bakery**
7840 5th Avenue S
Bloomington, MN 55420
952-881-4445
Fax: 952-881-5321 www.dennysbakery.com
Bakery products
Estimated Sales: $1-2.5 Million
Number Employees: 20-49

3526 **Denomega Pure Health**
992S,4th Ave
Brighton, CO 80601
479-181-2845
Fax: 303-581-9005 jennifer.kibel@denomega.com
www.denomega.com
Edible fats and oils, Omega-3
General Manager: Harold Ranneberg
CEO: Thomas Grys
Marketing Director: Mike OShea
Vice President of Operations: Jarle Wikeby

3527 **Denzer's Food Products**
PO Box 5632
Baltimore, MD 21210-0632
410-889-1500
Fax: 410-235-7032 jake@denzer.com
Conch chowder, crab soup, lima bean soup, peanut soup. Southeastern and US regional foods
President: Jacob Slagle
Estimated Sales: $1-3,000,000
Number Employees: 1-4
Type of Packaging: Consumer

3528 **Deosen USA**
1140 Stelton Rd # 205
Suite 205
Piscataway, NJ 08854-5291
908-292-1165
Fax: 908-292-1165 www.deosenusa.com
Ziboxan Xanthan gum.
CEO: Lawrence Herbolsheimer
Director of Sales: John Fritz

3529 **Deppeler Cheese Factory**
W6805 Deppeler Rd
West 6805 Deppeler Road
Monroe, WI 53566-9709
608-325-6311
Fax: 608-325-6935
Cheese and cheese products
Manager: Silvan Blum
Estimated Sales: Less Than $500,000
Number Employees: 1-4
Type of Packaging: Private Label

3530 **Derco Foods Intl**
2670 W Shaw Ln # 101
Fresno, CA 93711-2772
559-435-2664
Fax: 559-435-8520 derco@dercofoods.com
www.dercofoods.com
Dried fruits, nuts, specialty foods, pineapple, mushrooms, canned fruit, caned fruit, beans and popcorn
President: Leon Dermenjian
leon@dercofoods.com
Quality Control: Debbie McMillan
VP Sales/Purchasing: Ago Dermanjian
Sales/Marketing: Jeff Margarian
Estimated Sales: $20-50 Million
Number Employees: 10-19
Square Footage: 6000
Brands:
Derco

3531 **Dere Street**
5 Shelter Rock Road
Unit 5D
Danbury, CT 06810
203-797-9386
Fax: 203-797-0714 www.derestreet.com
Scones and shortbread
President: David Dere
Vice President: Robin Dere

3532 **Derlea Foods**
1739 Orangebrook Court
Pickering, ON L1W 3G8
Canada
905-839-7212
Fax: 905-839-7217 888-430-7777
sales@derlea.com www.derlea.com
Fresh garlic
President: Salvatore Geraci
Estimated Sales: $1.2 Million
Number Employees: 30
Type of Packaging: Consumer, Food Service, Private Label, Bulk

3533 **Deschutes Brewery**
901 SW Simpson Ave
Bend, OR 97702-3118
541-385-8606
Fax: 541-383-4505 www.deschutesbrewery.com
Seasonal beer, ale, stout, lager and porter
President & CEO: Michael LaLonde
Estimated Sales: $44 Million
Number Employees: 100-249
Type of Packaging: Consumer, Food Service
Brands:
Black Butte
Cascade Ale
Mirror Pond Pale Ale
Obsidian Stout

3534 **Deseret Dairy Products**
784 W 700 S
Salt Lake City, UT 84104-1415
801-240-7350
Fax: 801-240-7352
Milk and cheese producer; social service and welfare organization.
Manager: Bill Beane
Manager: Pmp Anderson
pranderson@ldschurch.org
Production Supervisor: Curtis Frame
Estimated Sales: $10-25 Million
Number Employees: 20-49

Parent Co: The Church of Jesus Christ of Latter-day Saints
Type of Packaging: Food Service

3535 **Desert Farms Inc**
2708 Wilshire Blvd # 380
Santa Monica, CA 90403-4706
310-430-2096
press@desertfarms.com
www.desertfarms.com
Camel milk
Contact: Walid Abdul-Wahab
walid@desertfarms.com
Number Employees: 5-9

3536 **Desert King International**
7024 Manya Cir
San Diego, CA 92154-4711
619-429-5222
Fax: 619-429-5001 800-982-2235
info@desertking.com www.desertking.com
Quillaja and yucca extracts for root beer and oil flavors
President: Paul Hiley
philey@desertking.com
VP: Joel Powers
Regional Sales Manager: Raymond Kramer
Estimated Sales: $3-5 Million
Number Employees: 10-19
Square Footage: 60000
Type of Packaging: Private Label, Bulk
Brands:
Foamation

3537 **Desert Pepper Trading Co**
PO Box 1761
El Paso, TX 79949
915-533-0008
Fax: 915-533-0026 888-472-5727
www.desertpepper.com
Salsas, condiments, dips and sauces.
Founder: W Park Kerr
Estimated Sales: $3 Million
Number Employees: 37
Type of Packaging: Private Label
Brands:
Daddy-Q
Desert Pepper
Ol' Smokey
Salsa Del Rio
Salsa Diablo
Salsa Divino
XXX Habanero

3538 **Desert Valley Date**
86740 Industrial Way
Coachella, CA 92236-2718
760-398-0999
Fax: 760-398-1514 sales@desertvalleydate.com
Dates
President: George Kirkjan
georgekirkjan@desertvalleydate.com
Estimated Sales: $10-20 Million
Number Employees: 50-99

3539 **Designed Nutritional Products**
1199 South 1480 West
Orem, UT 84058-4907
801-224-4518
Fax: 801-434-8270 info@designednutritional.com
www.designednutritional.com
Dietary supplements including organic germanium, saw palmetto extracts, ascorbigen, melatonin and indole-3-carbinol; exporter of melatonin, gramine, bisindolylmethance and glycogen
President: David Parish
Marketing: Omar Filippelli
Contact: Gus Diaz
customerservice@designednutritional.com
Purchasing Director: Craig Hansen
Estimated Sales: $10-20 Million
Number Employees: 5-9
Square Footage: 10000
Type of Packaging: Bulk

3540 **Designer Protein**
PO Box 2469
Carlsbad, CA 92018
800-337-4463
info@designerprotein.com designerprotein.com
Whole egg protein powder
CEO: Grace Jeon
Year Founded: 1993
Number of Brands: 1
Number of Products: 10
Type of Packaging: Consumer
Brands:
DESIGNER WHEY
ARIA
SUSTAINED ENERGY
ESSENTIAL 10
LITE
TOTALLY EGG
SUNSHINE
ORGANIC PRO 30

3541 **Dessert Innovations Inc**
25 Enterprise Blvd SW # B
Atlanta, GA 30336-2131
404-691-5000
Fax: 404-691-5001 800-359-7351
sales@dessertinnovations.com
www.classicconfections.com
Industrial dessert manufacturer; barcakes, cupcakes, parfaits, layer cakes, and petit fours
President: Tony Ereiddia
tony@dessertinnovations.com
VP Finance/Operations: Rolf Schittli
General Manager: Tim Guidry
senior sales manager: Bob Lunde
Production Manager: Ralph Ferdinand
Estimated Sales: $10-20 Million
Number Employees: 20-49
Square Footage: 96000
Brands:
Classic Confections
Custom Up Cakes
Singel Serving Sundae

3542 **Desserts Of Distinction**
14345 SW Pacific Hwy
Tigard, OR 97224-3647
503-654-8370
Fax: 503-654-1322
customerservice@dessertsofdistinction.com
www.dessertsofdistinction.com
Baked goods including frozen cheesecake
Owner: Sue Sanders
ssanders@dessertsofdistinction.com
Estimated Sales: $2.1 Million
Number Employees: 5-9
Type of Packaging: Food Service

3543 **Desserts On Us Inc**
57 Belle Falor Ct
Arcata, CA 95521-9234
707-822-0160
Fax: 707-822-5908 desonus@aol.com
www.dessertsonus.com
Cookies.
Owner: Emren Essa
desonus@aol.com
Number Employees: 10-19

3544 **Desserts by David Glass**
400 Chapel Road
Unit 2d Bissell Commons
South Windsor, CT 6074
860-462-7520
Fax: 860-242-4408
Desserts including chocolate truffle cake, cheesecake and chocolate mousse balls
President: David Glass
Estimated Sales: $10-20 Million
Number Employees: 20-49
Square Footage: 20000
Type of Packaging: Consumer, Food Service
Brands:
Desserts By David Glass

3545 **Destileria Serralles Inc**
P.O. Box 198
Mercedita, PR 00715-0198
787-840-1000
Fax: 787-840-1155
Rum, vodka, gin, cordials and wine; importer of scotch; exporter of rum; wholesaler/distributor of general merchandise
President & CEO: Felix Serralles, Jr.
Chief Financial Officer: Jorge Vazquez
Product Quality Director: Roberto Pantoja
Chief Marketing Officer: Gabriela Ripepi
State Manager: Vanessa Gehl
Human Resources Director: Daniel Beautista
Estimated Sales: $28.5 Million
Number Employees: 370
Square Footage: 18777
Type of Packaging: Consumer, Private Label, Bulk
Brands:
Donq Gold
Donq Cristal
Donq Limon
Donq Pasion
Donq Coco
Donq Mojito
Donq Anejo
Donq Grand Anejo
Ron Palo Viejo
Ron Granado
Ron Llave
Ron Rico
Ginebra Calvert
Vodka Nikolai
Alcoholado Superior 70
Alcoholado Baluarte
Blue Curacao
Crema De Cacao
Garandina
Triple Sec
Captain Morgan
Parrot Bay
Cutty Sark
Glenrothes
Glenlivet
Raynal
Aguardiente Caldas
Jim Beam
El Jimador
Cinzano
Skyy Vodka
Roederer Estate
Corbett Canyon
Justin Vineyard
Sterling Vinyards
Trave Amaretto
Kamora
Trave Amaretto-Decanter
Anis Paloma
Sambuca Molinari
Aqua Best
Crema De Coco
Guayabita Best-Pasta De Guayaba
Sense
Pares Baltas
Villaformosa
Tilenus
Casa De La Ermita
Monasterio Sta. Ana Monte
Condado De Almara
Priorato-Mas D' En Gil
Rias Baixas
Ribera Del Duero
Rioja
Montesierra
Pirineo
Pirineos
Senorio De Lazan
Camparron
Cano Cosecha
Bajoz
Ovacion
Casa Blanco
Casa Tinto
Senorio De Los Llanos
Pata Negra
Sandeman Don Fino
Senorio De Los Llanos
Pata Negra
Sandeman Don Fino
Sandeman Character Oloroso
Louis Roederer-Remis
Perrier Jouet-Epernay

3546 **Detoxwater**
212 7th Street
Brooklyn, NY 11215
888-887-4318
info@detoxwater.com detoxwater.com
Aloe-infused water
Founder: Kenneth Park
Number of Brands: 1
Number of Products: 6
Type of Packaging: Consumer
Brands:
DETOXWATER

3547 **Detroit Chili Co**
21400 Telegraph Rd
Southfield, MI 48033-4245
248-440-5933
Fax: 248-440-5945 www.dtigroup.biz
Frozen chili
Owner: Tim Keros
Purchasing Agent: Terry Keros
Estimated Sales: $500,000-$1 Million
Number Employees: 5-9
Square Footage: 20000
Type of Packaging: Consumer, Food Service

3548 **Devansoy Farms**
206 W 7th St
PO Box 885
Carroll, IA 51401-2317
712-792-9665
Fax: 712-792-2712 800-747-8605
info@devansoy.com www.devansoy.com
Powdered and liquid soy milk and soy flours;. Organic and parve available
President: Elmer Schettler
eschettler@devansoy.com
VP/Sales & Mktg: Montgomery Kilburn
VP/Operations: Deb Wycoff
Estimated Sales: $510,000
Number Employees: 1-4
Number of Products: 8
Type of Packaging: Food Service, Private Label, Bulk
Brands:
Enzact
Soy Roast

3549 **Devault Foods**
1 Deveault Lane
Devault, PA 19432
610-644-2536
800 426 2874
info@devaultfoods.com www.devaultfoods.com
Fresh and frozen portion controlled ground beef, hamburgers, pre-cooked meat balls and Philadelphia-style sandwich steaks
President/CEO: Thomas Fillippo
Chief Financial Officer: Carl Sorzano
Vice President, Sales & Marketing: Bill Irwin
COO: Brett Black
Estimated Sales: $41 Million
Number Employees: 120
Number of Brands: 4
Square Footage: 114000
Type of Packaging: Food Service, Private Label, Bulk
Brands:
Minute Menu
Mrs Difillippo's
Steakwich
Steakwich Lite

3550 **Devine Foods**
8 S Plum St
Elwyn, PA 19063-3309
610-566-2400
888-338-4631
denise@devinefoods.com
Beverages, frozen confections
President: Denise Devine
Operations: Jerome Renners
Estimated Sales: $5-10 Million
Number Employees: 5-9
Brands:
Devine Nectar
Fibrymid
Fruice
Simply Devine

3551 **Devlin Wine Cellars**
PO Box 728
Soquel, CA 95073-0728
831-476-7288
Fax: 831-479-9043 www.webwinery.com/devlin
Wines
President: Cheryl Devlin
Estimated Sales: Less than $500,000
Number Employees: 1-4
Type of Packaging: Private Label

3552 **Devro Inc**
785 Old Swamp Rd
Sandy Run
Swansea, SC 29160-8387
803-796-9730
Fax: 803-796-1636 www.devro.com
Casings for sausages, hams, salami and other meat products.
VP Product Management: Paul Tutt
Quality Manager: Rocco Del Priore
Business Development Manager: Marco Hobi
Purchasing Agent: Bobbie Fallaw
Estimated Sales: $28.8 Million
Number Employees: 250-499
Number of Brands: 1
Type of Packaging: Consumer
Brands:
Devro

3553 **Dewey's Bakery**
100 Vinegar Hill Rd
Winston-Salem, NC 27104-5068
336-765-2095
Fax: 336-748-0501 877-339-3974
mike@deweys.com www.deweys.com
Bakery products
Owner/President: Guy Wilkerson
Estimated Sales: $57,000
Number Employees: 2

3554 **(HQ)Dewied International Inc**
5010 Interstate 10 E
San Antonio, TX 78219-3352
210-661-6161
Fax: 210-662-6112 800-992-5600
www.dewied.com
Natural and synthetic sausage casings specializing in hog, sheep and beef casings
President: Phil Bohlender
philb@dewiedint.com
VP Sales: George Burt
Estimated Sales: $10-20 Million
Number Employees: 50-99
Brands:
Dewied

3555 **Dewig Brothers Packing Company**
100 Maple Street
Haubstadt, IN 47639-0186
812-768-6208
Fax: 812-768-6220 www.dewigmeats.com
Country style meats
President: Thomas Dewig
Finance Executive: Tom Dewig
Estimated Sales: $3,501,748
Number Employees: 35

3556 **Dexpa**
5503 Kingsley Mnr
Cumming, GA 30041-6119
USA
770-887-7412
Fax: 770-887-8864
Cheese

3557 **Dharma Bars**
sales@dharmabars.com
www.dharmabars.com
Organic, gluten free, and vegan energy bars
Founder: James Ricciuti

3558 **Dhidow Enterprises**
PO Box 285
Oxford, PA 19363-0285
610-932-7868
Fax: 509-753-0570
Nonvinegar based hot sauces
President: Dhidow Stephens
CEO: Paulette Colman
Estimated Sales: $300,000
Number Employees: 2
Type of Packaging: Consumer, Food Service, Bulk
Brands:
Dhidow Enterprise 150x
Dhidow Enterprise 20x
Dhidow Enterprise 50x
Dhidow Enterprise Zero

3559 **Di Alfredo Foods**
3060 Plaza Dr
Suite 108
Garnet Valley, PA 19060
610-558-2802
dialfredo.com
Pasta; olive oil; vinegar; balsamic glaze; jams and jellies; cookies; crackers; truffles
Director of Sales & Marketing: Thomas Sheridan
tom@dialfredo.com
Type of Packaging: Private Label, Bulk

3560 **Di Bruno Bros**
930 S 9th St
Philadelphia, PA 19147-3994
215-922-2876
Fax: 215-922-2080 www.dibruno.com
Manufacturer of cured meats, cheeses, and specialty foods such as oils and mixers.
VP of Culinary Pioneering: Emilio Mignucci
Number Employees: 5-9

3561 **Di Camillo Baking Co**
811 Linwood Ave
Niagara Falls, NY 14305-2517
716-282-2341
Fax: 716-282-2596 800-634-4363
info@dicamillobakery.com
www.dicamillobakery.com
Cakes, biscuits, biscotti, cookies, crispbreads and flatbreads, jams, honey, and confectionary
President: David Di Camillo
dcamillo@dicamillobakery.com
VP: Skip Di Camillo
VP: Tom Di Camillo
VP Marketing: Michael Di Camillo
Year Founded: 1920
Estimated Sales: $20-50 Million
Number Employees: 50-99

3562 **Di Cola's Seafood**
10754 S Western Ave
Chicago, IL 60643-3199
773-238-7071
Fax: 773-238-8337
www.dicolasseafoodbeverly.com
Seafood
Owner: Robert Di Cola
Estimated Sales: $5-10 Million
Number Employees: 20-49

3563 **Di Fiore Pasta Co**
556 Franklin Ave
Hartford, CT 06114-3024
860-296-1077
Fax: 860-296-5635
Pasta
Owner: Louise Di Fiore
Manager: Andrea Di Fiore
Estimated Sales: $1-2,500,000
Number Employees: 5-9
Brands:
Difiore Pasta

3564 **Di Lusso & Be Bop Baskote LLC**
1950 SW Badger Ave
Suite 105
Redmond, OR 97756
541-388-8164
Fax: 541-389-6185 888-545-7487
orders@be-bop.net www.be-bop.net
Biscotti and specialty roasted coffees
Owner: Bob Golden
bgolden@dilusso.com
Roastmaster: Dona Houtz
Vice President: M Lee
Sales Representative: Abbie Keenan
Estimated Sales: $20-50 Million
Number Employees: 50-99
Square Footage: 6000
Type of Packaging: Consumer, Food Service
Brands:
Royal Blend

3565 **(HQ)Di Mare Fresh Inc**
4629 Diplomacy Rd
Fort Worth, TX 76155-2621
817-385-3000
Fax: 817-385-3015 www.dimarefresh.com
Growers, packers and distributors of fresh fruits and vegetables.
President: Paul DiMare
CFO: Cheryl Taylor
cheryl.taylor@dimarefresh.com
Year Founded: 1930
Number Employees: 50-99
Type of Packaging: Consumer, Food Service, Private Label, Bulk
Brands:
Bermuda Dunes
Di-Mare Gold Label
Rancho Palm Springs
Sea View

3566 **DiBella Baking Company**
3524 Seagate Way
Suite 110
Oceanside, CA 92056
888-857-6151
www.dibellafamiglia.com
Cookies, biscotti and cookie brittle
Number of Brands: 1
Number of Products: 30
Type of Packaging: Consumer
Brands:
DIBELLA

3567 **DiGregorio Food Products**
5200 Daggett Ave
St Louis, MO 63110
314-776-1062
Fax: 314-776-3954 www.digregoriofoods.com
Sausage, meat balls and spaghetti sauce
President: Dora Di Gregorio
d.digregorio@digregoriofoods.com
CEO: John DiGregorio
Estimated Sales: $.5-1 million
Number Employees: 20-49
Square Footage: 200000
Type of Packaging: Food Service, Private Label

3568 **DiMario Foods**
56 Windsor Dr
Oak Brook, IL 60523-2365
630-581-5250
Fax: 630-581-5250 www.dimariofoods.com
Gourmet pork sticks
Co-Owner: Laura DeBartolo
Co-Owner: Nick DeBartolo
Year Founded: 2014
Number Employees: 8
Type of Packaging: Private Label

3569 **Diageo Canada Inc.**
401 The West Mall
Suite 800
Toronto, ON M9C 5P8
Canada
416-626-2000
Fax: 416-626-2688 www.diageo.com
Processor and exporter of gin and wine
President/Board Member: John Kennedy
Head of Corporate Communications: Rowan Pearman
Parent Co: Grand Metropolitan
Type of Packaging: Consumer, Food Service

3570 **(HQ)Diageo North America Inc**
801 Main Ave
Norwalk, CT 06851-1163
203-229-2100
Fax: 203-229-8925 www.diageo.com
Distilled liquors, spirits and wines
President: Deirdre Mahlan
deirdre.mahlan@diageo.com
Senior VP: John Adams
Marketing Manager: James Thomson
Number Employees: 1000-4999
Brands:
Asbach Brandy
Bell's Scotch
Black & White
Canard Duchene
Cardhu
Classic Malts
Dewar's White Label
Dom Perignon
George Dickel Whiske
Glen Ord Scotch
Gordon's Gin
Gordon's Vodka
Gordon's Vodka
Haig
Hennessy Cognacs
Hine Cognac
I.W. Harper Bourbon
Johnny Walker Scotch
Mercier Champagnes
Safari
Scoresby Scotch
Tanqueray Gin
The Dimple
Vat 69
Veuve Cliquot
Weller Bourbon
White Horse

3571 **(HQ)Diamond Bakery Co LTD**
756 Moowaa St
Honolulu, HI 96817-4405
808-847-3551
Fax: 808-847-7482 www.diamondbakery.com
Crackers and cookies, including all natural crackers.
President: Gary Yoshioka
Manager: Katy Leung
kleung@diamondbakery.com
Year Founded: 1921
Estimated Sales: Less Than $500,000
Number Employees: 5-9
Number of Products: 50+
Square Footage: 50500
Type of Packaging: Consumer, Food Service, Private Label, Bulk
Brands:
Diamond Bakery

3572 **Diamond Blueberry Inc**
548 Pleasant Mills Rd
Hammonton, NJ 08037-8931
609-561-3661
Fax: 609-567-4423
Fresh and frozen blueberries
Owner: David Berger
Sales: Tim Wetherbee
david@driscolls.com
Manager: Tim Wetherbee
Estimated Sales: $500,000-$1 Million
Number Employees: 20-49
Brands:
Diamond

3573 **Diamond Creek Vineyards**
1500 Diamond Mountain Rd
Calistoga, CA 94515-9669
707-942-6926
Fax: 707-942-6936
info@diamondcreekvineyards.com
www.diamondcreekvineyards.com
Wines
President: Al Brounstein
Estimated Sales: $2.5-5 Million
Number Employees: 5-9
Type of Packaging: Private Label

3574 **Diamond Crystal Brands Inc**
3000 Tremont Rd
Savannah, GA 31405
800-654-5115
www.dcbrands.com
Low-sodium mixes including soup, milk shake, ice cream, sauce, sugar-free dessert and fruit drink; also, instant breakfast beverages, cookies, nutritional chocolate bars and portion packed condiments including jelly, mustard, etc.
President & CEO: Tony Muscato
Director, Information Technology: Arlete Bacon
Year Founded: 1966
Estimated Sales: $45.2 Million
Number Employees: 250-499
Number of Brands: 12
Square Footage: 1200000
Parent Co: Peak Rock Capital of Austin
Type of Packaging: Food Service, Private Label
Other Locations:
Diamond Crystal Specialty Foo
Aurora ON
Brands:
Skippy
Treemont Farms
Salt for Life
True Citrus
Flavor Fresh
Chef's Seasoning
Chef'S Companion
House Blend
Single Serv
Lakeland Dairies
Caf, Delight Premium Drink Mixes
Caf, Delight Certified Sweeteners

3575 **Diamond Foods**
2200 Delaware Avenue
Santa Cruz, CA 95060
831-457-3200
Fax: 831-460-9407 www.emeraldnuts.com
Processor and exporter of gummys, jelly beans, gels, yogurt, chocolate confections and sugar-free and natural candies; also, dried fruit, banana chips and snack and trail mixes
Cfo: Dennis Barrow
Vice President: Dennis Daniels
Estimated Sales: $1-2.5 Million
Number Employees: 100-249
Square Footage: 600000
Type of Packaging: Consumer, Food Service, Private Label, Bulk
Brands:
Bold Beans
Harmony Snacks
Planet Harmony
Emerald Nuts

3576 **Diamond Fruit Growers**
3515 Chevron Dr
Hood River, OR 97044
541-354-5300
Fax: 541-354-5394 www.diamondfruit.com
Cooperative grower, packer, shipper and exporter of apples, pears and cherries.
President & CEO: David Garcia
Controller: Linda Gray
Field Representative: Grady Leiblein
Food Safety Coordinator: Corey Yasui
VP, Operations: Bob Wymore
VP, Raw Product: Chad Wimmers
Purchasing Coordinator: Wes Bailey
Year Founded: 1913
Estimated Sales: $20-50 Million
Number Employees: 100-249
Type of Packaging: Bulk

3577 **Diamond Seafood**
204 N Edgewood Avenue
Wood Dale, IL 60191-1610
630-787-1100
Fax: 630-787-1309
Seafood
President: Thomas Hannagan
Contact: Thomas Hanigan
diamondseafood@yahoo.com
Estimated Sales: $5-10 Million
Number Employees: 10-19

3578 **Diamond Water Bottling Fclty**
181 Cedar St
Hot Springs, AR 71901
501-623-1251
Fax: 501-623-2648
Bottled spring water
President: Tom Mitchell
Plant Manager: Brian Hinds
Estimated Sales: $5-10 Million
Number Employees: 10-19
Parent Co: Mountain Valley Water
Type of Packaging: Consumer

3579 **Diamond of California**
600 Montgomery Street
13th Floor
San Francisco, CA 94111
415-912-3180
Fax: 925-251-3820 www.diamondfoods.com
Nuts
President/CEO: Michael Mendes
CFO: Seth Halio
VP: Mario Alioto
Sales: Frank Morgan
Public Relations Manager: Vicki Zeigler

3580 **Diana Naturals**
250 Pehle Ave Concourse Level
Plaza 1, #207
Saddle Brook, NJ 07663
845-729-0942
www.diana-food.com
Producer of natural ingredients.
President: Yannick Riou
Applications Group Manager: Vinifer Dutia
Sweet & Beverage Category Manager: Teresa Kilgore
Parent Co: Diana Naturals

3581 **Diana's Specialty Foods**
2305 Aurora Dr
Pingree Grove, IL 60140-6442
847-683-1200
Fax: 847-683-1207
Vinegar, fancy gifts, Italian riviera and provencial bread dippers, grapeseed oils, miniature bread dipping oils, salsa, jams, jelly, mustard, herb mayonnaise, and olive oil
Manager: Mark Pagnoni
Estimated Sales: $12,000
Number Employees: 10-19
Square Footage: 3000

Type of Packaging: Private Label

3582 **Diane's Signature Products**
PO Box 2705
Edmond, OK 73083
405-509-3311
sales@dianessignatureproducts.com
www.dianessignatureproducts.com
Manufacturer of signature dressings for salads.
Owner: Brooke Franklin

3583 **Diane's Sweet Heat**
McKinleyville, CA
dianessweetheat.com
Habanero pepper-infused fruit jams
Owner: Diane Hunt
Year Founded: 2007
Number of Brands: 1
Number of Products: 8
Type of Packaging: Consumer
Brands:
DIANE'S SWEET HEAT

3584 **Diaz Foods**
5501 Fulton Industrial Blvd
Atlanta, GA 30336
404-344-5421
Fax: 404-344-3003 www.diazfoods.com
Dry, refrigerated and frozen products

3585 **Diazteca Inc**
993 E Frontage Rd
Rio Rico, AZ 85648-6234
520-761-4621
Fax: 520-281-1024 www.diazteca.com
Processor and distributor of Mexican fresh mangos, fresh hot peppers, granulated cane sugar, refrigerated and frozen lean beef, frozen shrimp, frozen IQF fruits and vegetables, aseptic fruit purees and other food products.
Owner/President: Ismael Diaz
Vice President: Roderigo Diaz
Estimated Sales: Less Than $500,000
Number Employees: 5-9
Type of Packaging: Consumer, Private Label, Bulk

3586 **Dick Garber Company**
2295 Parklake Dr NE Ste 165
Atlanta, GA 30345
770-414-0500
Fax: 770-414-9484 m.gokel@inetmail.att.net
Vice President: Mike Goeckel
Estimated Sales: $5-10 Million
Number Employees: 5-9
Parent Co: Dick Garber Company

3587 **Dick Garber Company**
1202 Tech Blvd
Tampa, FL 33619
813-621-8634
Fax: 813-627-9115 r.i.reynolds@inetmail.att.net
Groceries
President: Dick Garber
Vice President: Bob Reynolds
Contact: Robert Reynolds
r.reynolds@pinnaclefoodsales.com
Estimated Sales: $20-50 Million
Number Employees: 20-49
Parent Co: Dick Garber Company

3588 **Dickinson Frozen Foods**
1205 Iron Eagle Dr.
Suite B
Eagle, ID 83616
208-452-5200
Fax: 208-452-5365 800-886-4326
customerservice@df-foods.com
www.df-foods.com
Frozen onions, potatoes, and bell peppers
President & CEO: Paul Fox
CFO: Doug Reader
Quality Assurance Manager: George Condie
Director of Sales & Marketing: Aaron Mann
VP Sales: Bruce Robinson
Contact: Lynae Addy
laddy@dickinsonfrozenfoods.com
Director of Operations: Todd Campbell
Plant Manager: Todd Campbell
Purchasing Manager: Tim Burnett
Estimated Sales: $24.1 Million
Number Employees: 462
Square Footage: 100000
Type of Packaging: Consumer, Food Service, Private Label
Brands:
Dickinson Frozen Foods

3589 **Dickson's Pure Honey**
4331 Hatchery Road
San Angelo, TX 76903-1513
915-655-9233
Pure honey
President: Andrew Dickson
Estimated Sales: $1-2,500,000 appx.
Number Employees: 1
Brands:
Dickson's Pure Honey

3590 **Didion Milling Inc**
520 Hartwig Blvd # C
Johnson Creek, WI 53038-9315
920-348-6816
Fax: 920-699-3628 jdillon@didionmilling.com
www.didionmilling.com
Dry corn miller, corn products
President: Dow Didion
CEO: John Didion
jdidion@didionmilling.com
Vice President: Dow Drachenberg
Vice President of Sales & Marketing: Jeff Dillon
Number Employees: 10-19

3591 **Diedrich Coffee**
28 Executive Park, Ste 200
Irvine, CA 92614
949-260-1600
Fax: 949-260-1610 800-354-5282
java@diedrich.com
Coffee
President/CFO: Sean McCarthy
Contact: Anthony Barr
barr@gloriajeans.com
Estimated Sales: $18.4 Million
Number Employees: 500
Square Footage: 17620
Parent Co: Green Mountain Coffee
Brands:
Coffee People
Diedrich Coffee
Gloria Jeans

3592 **Dieffenbach's Potato Chips**
51 Host Rd
Womelsdorf, PA 19567-9421
610-589-2385
Fax: 610-589-2866 www.dieffenbachs.com
Dieffenbach's Old Fashioned Potato Chips; Uglies Kettle-Cooked Chips, which are made from potatoes that do not adhere to USDA cosmetic regulations for produce
President & CEO: Nevin Dieffenbach
VP, Business Development: Dwight Zimmerman
Chief Operating Officer: Michael Marlowe
Estimated Sales: $5-10 Million
Number Employees: 10-19
Number of Brands: 2
Type of Packaging: Consumer, Private Label
Other Locations:
Factory Outlet Store
Womelsdorf PA
Brands:
Dieffenbach's
Uglies

3593 **Diehl Food Ingredients**
136 Fox Run Dr
Defiance, OH 43512
419-782-5010
Fax: 419-783-4319 800-251-3033
Lactose free beverages, powdered fat, coffee creamers and whip topping bases.
President: Charles Nicolais
CFO: Darren Lane
CEO: Peter Diehl
Research & Development: Joan Hasselman
Quality Control: Kelly Roach
Marketing Director: Dennis Reid
Sales Director: Jim Holdrieth
Number Employees: 100-249
Parent Co: Diehl
Type of Packaging: Consumer, Food Service, Bulk
Brands:
Chocomite
Vitamite

3594 **Diestel Family Turkey Ranch**
209-532-4950
info@diestelturkey.com
diestelturkey.com
Turkey, ham and beef products
Marketing: Heidi Diestel
Year Founded: 1949
Number of Brands: 1
Type of Packaging: Consumer
Brands:
DIESTEL TURKEY RANCH

3595 **Dietz & Watson Inc.**
5701 Tacony St.
Philadelphia, PA 19135
215-831-9000
Fax: 215-831-1044 www.dietzandwatson.com
Meats and cheeses, including kielbasa, scrapple, bacon, ham fillets, franks, grillers, chicken sausages, natural casing sausages, resealable deli meats, sauces and dressings, potato and eggsalad, cole slaw, macaroni salad, greek pastasalad, bruschetta, oriental noodle, pasta parm, pasta primavera, totellini, spinesto, antibasto, black bean, edamame, ambrosia, salami, italian sausage (hot or sweet), pepperoni, etc.
President/CEO: Louis Eni
CFO: Cindy Eni Yingling
COO: Christophe Eni
Year Founded: 1939
Estimated Sales: $245 Million
Number Employees: 500-999
Number of Brands: 1
Square Footage: 180000
Type of Packaging: Consumer, Bulk
Other Locations:
Black Bear Distribution
Delanco NJ
Dietz & Watson
Baltimore MD
Brands:
Dietz & Watson

3596 **(HQ)Diggs Packing Company**
1207 Rogers St
Columbia, MO 65201-4796
573-449-2995
Fax: 573-449-3163
Beef, ham, sausage, meat packing services, distributes fresh meat, provides slaughtering
Owner: Dale Diggs
Public Relations: Dan Reynolds
Estimated Sales: $14.10 Million
Number Employees: 20-49
Type of Packaging: Consumer

3597 **Digrazia Vineyards**
131 Tower Rd
Brookfield, CT 06804-3654
203-775-1616
Fax: 203-775-3195 800-230-8853
info@digraziavineyards.com
www.digraziavineyards.com
Wine, wholesale & retaile; Altar wine for Church use; winery tours and group events.
Owner: Christopher Kelly
christopherkelly@digrazia.com
Vice President: Mark Longford
Plant Manager: Aaron Cox
Estimated Sales: Less Than $500,000
Number Employees: 1-4
Brands:
Convetual Franciscan Friars
Di Grazia Vineyards

3598 **Dilettante Chocolates**
19016 72nd Avenue South
Kent, WA 98032
425-656-9076
Fax: 425-656-8059 800-800-9490
www.seattlegourmetfoods.com
Candy and confectionery
President: David Taylor
sales@seattlegourmetfoods.com
CEO: Brian Davenport
Director Sales/Marketing: Tom Davis
Sales Manager: Chris Ratliff
Production Manager: Brian Hubbard
Estimated Sales: $1-2.5 Million
Number Employees: 5-9

3599 **Dillanos Coffee Roasters**
1607 45th St E
Sumner, WA 98390-2202
253-826-1807
Fax: 253-826-1827 800-234-5282
www.dillanos.com
Coffee

Owner: Chris Heyer
chrish@dillanos.com
CFO: Rand Hill
Estimated Sales: $3 Million
Number Employees: 50-99
Type of Packaging: Food Service

3600 Dillard's Bar-B-Q Sauce
1058 W Club Boulevard
Ste. 6672
Durham, NC 27701
919-286-1080
Fax: 919-361-3410 sales@carolinasauce.com
Barbecue sauce
Co-Partner: Geneva Dillard
Co-Partner/General Manager: Wilma Dillard
Estimated Sales: Less than $500,000
Number Employees: 10-19
Type of Packaging: Consumer
Brands:
Dillard's

3601 Dillman Farm Inc
4955 W State Road 45
Bloomington, IN 47403-9362
812-825-8118
Fax: 812-825-4650 800-359-1362
dillman@dillmanfarm.com www.dillmanfarm.com
Fruit butters, preserves, jellies, salsa, mustard, bbq, no preservatives, cane sugar or grape juice to sweeten products
President: Cary Dillman
carydillman@dillmanfarm.com
Treassurer: Amy Dillman
Director of Sales: Jean Brook
Estimated Sales: $820,000
Number Employees: 5-9
Square Footage: 60000
Brands:
Dillman Farm
Dillman's All Natural

3602 Dillon Candy Co
19927 US Highway 84 E
Boston, GA 31626-2666
229-498-2051
Fax: 229-498-2201 800-382-8338
Candy including peanut and pecan log rolls, sand brittles, divinity, coated pecans, pralines and pecan puffs
Owner: Tom Cook
Sales: Michele Tull
dcc@dilloncandy.com
Estimated Sales: $10-20 Million
Number Employees: 20-49
Type of Packaging: Consumer

3603 Dimitria Delights Baking Co
81 Creeper Hill Rd
North Grafton, MA 01536-1421
508-839-1638
Fax: 508-839-1685 800-763-1113
sales@dimitriadelights.com
www.dimitriadelights.com
Frozen baked and nonbaked desserts including spinach pies, puff pastries, fruit strudels, regular and filled danish and croissant dough
President/Production Manager: John Colorio
Vice President: Mary Colorio
Estimated Sales: $10-20 Million
Number Employees: 50-99
Square Footage: 70000
Type of Packaging: Consumer, Food Service, Private Label
Brands:
Mary's
Pita
Strudelkins

3604 Dimock Dairy Products
400 S Main St
Dimock, SD 57331
605-928-3833
Fax: 605-928-3390 dimockdairy@santel.net
www.dimockdairy.com
Cheese
GM: Roger Swemby
Manager: Roger Swenby
rogerswenby@dimockdairy.com
Manager: Mike Royston
Estimated Sales: $5-10 Million
Number Employees: 5-9
Square Footage: 18000
Type of Packaging: Consumer

3605 Dimond Tager Company Products
2801 E Hillsborough Ave
Tampa, FL 33610-4410
813-238-3111
Fax: 813-238-3114
Manufacturer and wholesaler/distributor of produce
President: Raymond Charlton
Estimated Sales: $1.7 Million
Number Employees: 10
Square Footage: 16000
Type of Packaging: Consumer, Food Service, Bulk

3606 Dimpflmeier Bakery
26-36 Advance Road
Toronto, ON M8Z 2T4
Canada
416-236-2701
Fax: 416-239-5370 800-268-2421
orders@dimpflmeierbakery.com
www.dimpflmeierbakery.com
German-style breads including rye, pumpernickel, sourdough and monastery; also, rolls and buns
President: Alfonse Dimpflmier
Number Employees: 170
Type of Packaging: Consumer, Food Service
Brands:
Holzofen
Klosterbrot
Muenchner/Stadtbrot

3607 Dina's Organic Chocolate
4 Smith Avenue
Mt Kisco, NY 10549
914-242-0124
Fax: 914-242-5289 888-625-2008
www.dinakhader.com
Line of 74 percent organic dark chocolate products including goji, green tea, omega 3 flax and almond. Also available are 74 percent dark chocolate truffels and rasberry truffles whole line is gluten and dairy free.
President/Owner: Dina Khader
Sales/Marketing/Purchasing: Andre Avdant
Number Employees: 7
Square Footage: 6600

3608 Ding Hau Food Co, Ltd
12760 Bathgate Way
Suite 6
Richmond, BC V6V 1Z4
Canada
604-273-1188
Fax: 604-273-9288
Frozen prepared meals
Owner/President: Yu Lang Chang
Estimated Sales: $3.19 Million
Number Employees: 7
Type of Packaging: Food Service, Private Label, Bulk

3609 Dinkel's Bakery Inc
3329 N Lincoln Ave
Chicago, IL 60657-1107
773-281-7300
Fax: 773-281-6169 800-822-8817
www.dinkels.com
Baked goods including chocolate chip butter cookies, cakes, pecan fudge brownies and snacks; contract baking available
President: N Dinkel
norm@dinkels.com
Controller/Treasurer: Holly Dinkel
General Manager: Luke Karl
Human Resource Manager: J Norman
norm@dinkels.com
Estimated Sales: $870,000
Number Employees: 20-49
Square Footage: 60000
Type of Packaging: Consumer, Food Service, Private Label, Bulk
Brands:
Dinkel's
Dinkel's Famous Stollen
Dinkel's Sip'n
Dinkel's Southern Double

3610 Dinner Bell Meat Product
1700 17th Street
Lynchburg, VA 24501
434-847-7766
Fax: 434-847-6305
Sausage
President: Butch Anderson
Estimated Sales: $10-20 Million
Number Employees: 10-19
Type of Packaging: Consumer

3611 Dino's Sausage & Meat Co Inc
722 Catherine St
Utica, NY 13501-1304
315-732-2661
Fax: 315-732-3094 www.dinossausage.com
Sausage and beef products; wholesaler/distributor of bacon, ham, pork, lamb, etc
President: Chris Houser
fchousercpa@yahoo.com
Vice President: Anthony Ferrucci
Estimated Sales: $10-20 Million
Number Employees: 10-19
Type of Packaging: Consumer
Brands:
Dino's

3612 Dino-Meat Company
PO Box 95
White House, TN 37188-0095
615-643-1022
Fax: 615-643-1022 877-557-6493
Emu meat including steaks, ground, breakfast sausage, summer sausage, hot dogs, hot links, meat balls, snack sticks and jerky. Also emu oil and emu oil products
President: Neil Williams
Type of Packaging: Consumer, Food Service
Brands:
Back Country Emu Products
Dine-Meat Emu Products

3613 Dion Herbs & Spices
801 Montee St. Nicolas
St-Jerome, QC J7Y 4C7
Canada
450-569-8001
Fax: 450-569-0062 877-569-8001
gaston@alimentsgdion.com
www.alimentsgdion.com
Extracts, herbs, salt, spices, private label.
Marketing: Gaston Dion

3614 Dipaolo Baking Co Inc
598 Plymouth Ave N
Rochester, NY 14608-1629
585-232-3510
Fax: 585-423-5975 sales@dipaolobread.com
Breads, rolls and pastries.
Owner: Jim Acquilano
President/CEO: Dominick Massa
dominick@dipaolobread.com
Estimated Sales: $10-20 Million
Number Employees: 20-49
Type of Packaging: Food Service

3615 Dipasa USA Inc
6600 Ruben Torres Sr Blvd # B
Brownsville, TX 78526-6954
956-831-4072
Fax: 956-831-5893 info@dipasausa.com
www.dipasausa.com
Tahini and sesame seeds, raisins, oil, flour and candy; wholesaler/distributor of onion and cheese breadsticks, baked snacks, halvah and confectionery items, natural colors, oleoresins
Vice President: Garry Lowder
garrylowder@dipasausa.com
Vice President: Garry Lowder
garrylowder@dipasausa.com
Vice President, Marketing: Garry Lowder
Estimated Sales: $8 Million
Number Employees: 10-19
Number of Brands: 2
Number of Products: 10
Square Footage: 80000
Type of Packaging: Consumer, Food Service, Private Label, Bulk
Brands:
Biladi
Biladi Tohina
De Champaque Bakery Snacks
Dipasa Biladi
Dipasa De Champagne
Dipasa Usa
Sesamin

3616 Dippin' Dots LLC
5101 Charter Oak Dr
Paducah, KY 42001-5209
270-443-8994
Fax: 270-443-8997 sales@dippindots.com
www.dippindots.com
Ice cream, yogurt, flavored ices and sherbets
CEO: Scott Fischer
President: Tom Leonard
CFO: Sheri Dikin
Chief Marketing & Sales Officer: Michael Barrette
Public Relations: Terry Reeves
Director Operations: Rick Noble
Estimated Sales: $20-50 Million
Number Employees: 1-4
Brands:
Dippin' Dots

3617 Dippy Foods
10554 Progress Way Ste K
Cypress, CA 90630
714-816-0150
Fax: 714-816-0153 800-819-8551
Single-serving meals to schools and other institutional food servers
President: Jon Stevenson
VP: Erin Stevenson
Brands:
Earth's Best
Hain Kidz
Health Valley

3618 Discovery Foods
2395 American Ave
Hayward, CA 94545
510-780-9238
Fax: 510-293-1830
Asian inspired frozen foods
President & Founder: Clarence Mou
Founder: Alfred Mou
Contact: John Cotts
jcotts@dfcusa.com
Year Founded: 1996
Estimated Sales: $20-50 Million
Number Employees: 100-249

3619 Dismat Corporation
336 N Westwood Ave
Toledo, OH 43607
419-531-8963
Fax: 419-531-8965
Powdered soup mixes and seasonings
President: John Donofrio
mckayssoupmix@bex.net
Operations VP: Sandra Lee Jones
Estimated Sales: $1-$2 Million
Number Employees: 5-9
Number of Brands: 1
Number of Products: 3
Square Footage: 48000
Type of Packaging: Consumer, Bulk
Brands:
McKay's

3620 Distant Lands Coffee Roaster
801 Houser Way N
Renton, WA 98057
903-592-9771
Fax: 903-593-2699 800-758-4437
info@dlcoffee.com www.dlcoffee.com
Roasters of organic, flavored and fair-trade coffees.
President: Bill McAlpin
Marketing: Kristin Jones
VP Sales: Todd Hughes
Contact: Chris Ashby
ashbyc@dlcoffee.com
Estimated Sales: $5 Million
Number Employees: 50
Type of Packaging: Private Label, Bulk
Brands:
Country Coffee

3621 Distillata
1608 E 24th Street
Cleveland, OH 44114
800-999-2906
www.distillata.com
Bottler of spring and distilled water, as well as water filtration systems, water coolers, water fountains, and pool filling services.
Owner: Kevin Schroeder
Head of Sales: Adam Schroeder
Operations Manager: Heather Schroeder
Estimated Sales: $10-20 Million
Number Employees: 100-249
Type of Packaging: Consumer, Food Service, Private Label, Bulk
Brands:
Distillata

3622 Diversified Avocado Products
25950 Acero Street
Suite 360
Mission Viejo, CA 92691-7900
949-837-6464
Fax: 949-837-6464 800-879-2555
Frozen guacamole and fresh avocados
Account Executive: Alberto Castro
Director Sales/Marketing: Ray Flores
Contact: Sam Carson
scarson@dapguacamole.com
Estimated Sales: $500,000- 1 Million
Number Employees: 5-9
Square Footage: 400000
Type of Packaging: Consumer, Food Service

3623 Diversified Foods & Seasonings
1404 Greengate Dr.
Suite 300
Covington, LA 70433
985-809-3600
Fax: 504-834-0395 800-914-2382
sales@diversified-foods.com
www.diversified-foods.com
Frozen specialty foods such as beans, bbq sauces, creole sauces, marinara sauces, side dishes of macaroni and cheese, spinach and artichoke dips, collard greens, soups and chilis, gumbo, rice seasonings, dry marinades, breadings, drygravies, biscuit mixes and custom cheesecakes.
Chairman: Al Copeland Jr.
President & CEO: Peter Smith
CFO: Frank Parent
VP Research & Development: David Smith
Chief Mangement Officer: William Marvin
Estimated Sales: $20-50 Million
Number Employees: 1-4
Parent Co: A.L. Copeland
Type of Packaging: Food Service, Private Label
Brands:
Chief's Creations

3624 Divine Chocolate
418 7th St SE
Washington, DC 20003
202-332-8913
Fax: 202-332-8916 www.divinechocolateusa.com
Chocolate bars
Ceo: Erin Gorman
Marketing: Niki Lagos
Contact: Amanda White
amanda@divinechocolateusa.com
Estimated Sales: $1 Million
Number Employees: 3

3625 Divine Delights
1250 Holm Rd
Petaluma, CA 94954-1106
707-559-7099
Fax: 707-559-7098 800-443-2836
customerservice@divinedelights.com
www.divinedelights.com
Premium petit fours and petite confections
President: Angelique Fry
Co-owner: Bill Fry
bill@divinedelights.com
Estimated Sales: $5-10 Million
Number Employees: 10-19
Type of Packaging: Private Label, Bulk
Brands:
Checkerbites
Divine Delights
Mice-A-Fours
Trufflecots

3626 Divine Foods
Po Box 490
Elizabethtown, NC 28337-0490
910-862-2576
Fax: 910-862-2799
Functional (antioxidants), bread/bisucits, juice/cider, wine, salsa/dips, jams, jellies.
Marketing: Miller Taylor

3627 Divine Organics
209-532-4950
www.divineorganics.com
Organic superfoods
Founder: David Kaplan
Number of Brands: 1
Type of Packaging: Consumer
Brands:
DIVINE ORGANICS

3628 Divvies
700 Oakridge Cmns
South Salem, NY 10590-2440
914-533-2804
www.divvies.com
Dairy free, egg free, peanut free, tree nut free food snacks
Owner: Mark Sandler
mark@divvies.com
Number Employees: 10-19

3629 Dixie Dew Prods Co
1360 Jamike Ave
P.O.Box 18310
Erlanger, KY 41018-3114
859-283-1050
Fax: 859-282-3781 800-867-8548
info@dixiedewproducts.com
Fruit glazes, dips, puddings, toppings, day blends and specialty sauces; contract processing and packaging available
Managing Director: Robert Carl
Quality Controll: Glen Delong
Contact: Margaret Carl
margaretc@dixiedewproducts.com
Estimated Sales: Less Than $500,000
Number Employees: 1-4
Square Footage: 160000
Type of Packaging: Consumer, Food Service, Private Label, Bulk
Brands:
Classic Traditions
Harry's Choice
Heritage Fancy Foods

3630 Dixie Egg Co
5139 Edgewood Ct
Jacksonville, FL 32254-3601
904-783-0950
Fax: 904-786-6227 800-394-3447
kjkeggs@aol.com www.dixieegg.com
Fresh shell eggs
President: Jacques Klempf
CEO: Edward Klempf
sshimoda@dixieegg.com
Controller: Paul Stevenson
IT: Steve Slayter
Feed/Production Manager: Dennis Hughes
Number Employees: 250-499
Parent Co: Foodonics International
Type of Packaging: Consumer, Bulk

3631 Dixie Rice
600 Pasquiere St
Gueydan, LA 70542
337-536-9276
Fax: 337-536-5099
Rice
President: Steven Watson
Chairman: Harold Simmons
Estimated Sales: $460,000
Number Employees: 8
Square Footage: 12000
Brands:
Dixie

3632 Dixie Trail Farms
PO Box 4082
Wilmington, NC 28406-1082
800-665-3968
Fax: 800-765-7482
Grilling sauces and marinades

3633 Dixie USA
P.O. Box 1969
Tomball, TX 77377
832-616-3366
Fax: 832-201-0765 800-233-3668
info@dixieusa.com www.dixiediner.com
Meat analogs, tofu, soy products and low carb products; exporter of soy
President: Brenda K. Oswalt
Chairman, Founder: Bob Beeley
EVP: Jim Oswalt
Estimated Sales: $5-10 Million
Number Employees: 20-49
Square Footage: 120000

Type of Packaging: Consumer, Food Service, Private Label, Bulk
Brands:
Beef Not
Chicken Not
Dutlettes

3634 **Dixon's Fisheries**
1807 N Main St
East Peoria, IL 61611-2193
800-373-1457
Fax: 309-694-0539 800-373-1457
internetsales@dixonsseafood.com
www.dixonsseafood.com
Appetizers, caviar, squid, dips, spreads, marinades, sauces, fresh fish & shellfish, frozen fish & shellfish, smoked fish, exotic meats
President: Robert Dixon
Principal: James Dixon
Estimated Sales: $20-50 Million
Number Employees: 5-9

3635 **Dizzy Pig BBQ Co**
8763 Virginia Meadows Dr
Manassas, VA 20109-7826
571-379-4884
Fax: 206-984-3736 chris.capell@dizzypigbbq.com
dizzypigbbq.com
Other condiments, rubs, spices, foodservice, gift packs.
Owner: Chris Capell
chris@dizzypigbbq.com
Marketing: Chris Capell
Number Employees: 10-19

3636 **Djerdan Burek Corp**
9E Wesley St
South Hackensack, NJ 07606
888-462-8735
info@djerdan.com
djerdan.com
Packed bread rolls; stuffed bread sticks
President/Owner: Selma Medunjanin-Ismajli
Year Founded: 1997
Estimated Sales: Less than $500,000
Number Employees: 8
Type of Packaging: Consumer, Food Service, Private Label

3637 **Dl Geary Brewing**
38 Evergreen Dr
Portland, ME 04103-1066
207-878-2337
Fax: 207-878-2388 info@gearybrewing.com
www.gearybrewing.com
Beers
President: David Geary
Marketing: Kelly Lucas
Operations: Kelly Lucas
Estimated Sales: $2 Million
Number Employees: 20-49
Brands:
Dl Geary Brewing

3638 **Do Anything Foods**
New York, NY 10007
hello@doanythingfoods.com
www.doanythingfoods.com
Vegetable-based sauces

3639 **Dobake**
810 81st Avenue
Oakland, CA 94621-2510
510-834-3134
Fax: 510-834-4408 800-834-3134
dobeinc@aol.com
Gourmet and premium baked sweet goods.
President: Dan Giraudo
Marketing Manager: Lynn Knott
Vice President of Sales: Ron Tallia
Contact: Cecilia Bracamonte
cbracamonte@dobake.com
Number Employees: 100-249
Brands:
Dobake

3640 **Dockside Market**
PO Box 1002
Key Largo, FL 33037
305-283-6678
Fax: 305-397-2389 800-813-2253
donna@docksidemarket.com
www.docksidemarket.com
Cakes, cookies, salsa, sauces, hot sauces, coffee & tea

3641 **Doctor Dread's Jerk**
PO Box 740
Glen Echo, MD 20812
301-908-9450
gary@doctordreadsjerk.com
Manufacturer of jerk chicken, fish and salmon burgers.
Owner: Gary Himelfarb
Brands:
Doctor Dread's

3642 **Doctor's Best Inc**
197 Avenida LA Pata # A
Suite A
San Clemente, CA 92673-6307
949-498-3628
Fax: 949-498-3952 800-333-6977
info@drbvitamins.com www.drbvitamins.com
Food supplements
President: Ken Halvorsrude
Cmo: Erin O Gehan
eri@drbvitamins.com
VP Operations: Ranate Halvorsrude
Estimated Sales: $1-2.5 Million
Number Employees: 20-49
Square Footage: 20000

3643 **(HQ)Doerle Food Svc LLC**
113 Kol Dr
Broussard, LA 70518-3825
337-252-8551
Fax: 337-252-8558 800-256-1631
www.doerlefoods.com
Fresh and frozen meats and poultry, a wide variety of beverages and chemical supplies, also includes seafood, gourmet foods, fresh produce, dry groceries, dairy products, disposables, small ware and table top items, specialtyhealthcare products and janitorial supplies
President & CEO: Allen Boudreaux
VP Operations & Transportation: John Romero
VP Sales & Marketing: Charlie Martin
VP Purchasing & Merchandising: Rick Blum
Year Founded: 1950
Estimated Sales: $20-50 Million
Number Employees: 100-249
Other Locations:
Doerle Food Service
Shreveport LA

3644 **Dogfish Head Craft Brewery**
105 Savannah Rd
Lewes, DE 19958
302-644-8292
888-834-3474
info@dogfish.com www.dogfish.com
Beer
President & COO: George Pastrana
Vice President: Mariah Calagione
Inventory Coordinator: James Cosby
Year Founded: 1995
Estimated Sales: $226 Million
Number Employees: 150
Number of Brands: 5
Type of Packaging: Consumer, Private Label
Brands:
Chicory Stout
Immort Ale
Indian Brown Ale
Raison D'Etre
Shelter Pale Ale

3645 **Dogswell LLC**
1964 Westwood Boulevard
Suite 350
Los Angeles, CA 90025
310-651-5200
Fax: 877-327-3145 888-559-8833
info@dogswell.com www.dogswell.com
Functional (antioxidants), other lifestyle, pet food.
Marketing: Marco Giannini

3646 **Dogwood Brewing Company**
1222 Logan Cir NW
Atlanta, GA 30318
404-367-0500
Fax: 404-367-0505
Ale and stout beers
President: Crawford Moran
Estimated Sales: $1-2.5 Million
Number Employees: 1-4
Type of Packaging: Consumer, Food Service
Brands:
Dogwood

3647 **Dohar Meats Inc**
1979 W 25th St
Cleveland, OH 44113-3455
216-241-4197
Fax: 216-664-3390
ADempsey@city.cleveland.oh.us
westsidemarket.org/vendor/dohar-lovaszy-meats/?portfolioID=955
Pork including sausage and deli meats
Owner: Angela Dohar
Manager: Mike Szucs
Estimated Sales: Less than $500,000
Number Employees: 1-4
Type of Packaging: Consumer, Bulk

3648 **Dohler-Milne Aseptics LLC**
804 Bennett Ave
PO Box 111
Prosser, WA 99350-1267
509-786-2240
Fax: 630-797-2001
Flavoring extracts and syrups
Manager: Dan Villarreal
danv@dmaseptics.com
Controller: Joe Stoops
Estimated Sales: $1.2 Million
Number Employees: 1-4

3649 **Dol Cice' Gelato Company**
PO Box 343
Yardley, PA 19067
215-499-5661
Fax: 215-493-6348 Info@DolCice.com
www.dolcice.com
Italian water ices
President: Laurence Dobelle
Type of Packaging: Food Service, Private Label

3650 **Dolce Nonna**
162-43 12th Avenue
Whitestone, NY 11357
718-767-3501
Fax: 718-767-3501
Marinated string beans, agri-dolce peppers and marinated eggplant
President/Owner: Gisella Civale

3651 **Dolci Gelati**
5766 2nd St NE
Washington, DC 20011-2524
202-257-5323
Fax: 202-526-8064 www.dolcigelati.net
Frozen desserts, ice cream/sorbet, co-packing, private label.
President: Gianluigi Dellaccio
dolcigelati@gmail.com
Number Employees: 1-4

3652 **Dold Foods**
2929 N Ohio St
Wichita, KS 67219
316-838-9101
Fax: 316-838-9053 www.hormel.com
Fresh and frozen ham and bacon
Manager: Terry W Hadden
Contact: Brad Blum
brad.blum@hormel.com
Plant Manager: Mark Coffey
Number Employees: 250-499
Square Footage: 400000
Parent Co: Hormel Foods Corporation
Type of Packaging: Consumer

3653 **(HQ)Dole & Bailey Inc**
16 Conn St
Woburn, MA 01801-5699
781-935-1234
Fax: 781-935-9085 sales@doleandbailey.com
www.doleandbailey.com
Meats such as lamb, sheep, beef, poultry and pork, as well as maple syrups, cheeses, breads and desserts.
President/CEO: Nancy Matheson-Burns
nancymb@doleandbailey.com
Founder: Cyprus Dole
Co-Founder: Frank Bailey
Vice President: Bill Burns
General Manager/Corporate Chef: Ed Brylczyk
Year Founded: 1868
Estimated Sales: $25 Million
Number Employees: 100-249

Brands:
Chef's Signature
Northeast Family Farms

3654 Dole Food Company, Inc.
PO Box 5700
Thousand Oaks, CA 91359-5700
800-356-3111
www.dole.com
Fresh fruit, vegetables, prepared foods and salads.
Chairman: David Murdock
President/CEO: Johan Linden
Vice President/CFO: Johan Malmqvist
President, Dole Fresh Vegetables: Michael Solomon
Year Founded: 1851
Estimated Sales: $4.5 Billion
Number Employees: 59,000
Type of Packaging: Consumer, Food Service, Private Label, Bulk
Other Locations:
Dole Manufacturing Facility
(9) Arizona
Dole Manufacturing Facility
(11) California
Dole Manufacturing Facility
(25) Delaware
Dole Manufacturing Faciltiy
(27) Florida
Dole Manufacturing Facility
(29) Hawaii
Dole Manufacturing Facility
(33) Michigan
Dole Manufacturing Facility
(35) North Carolina
Dole Manufacturing Facility
(37) Ohio
Dole Manufacturing Facility
(38) Texas
Dole Manufacturing Facility
(39) Obtario, Canada

3655 Dole Pond Maple Products
PO Box 841
Jackman, ME 04945
418-653-5322
Fax: 418-653-5322 jcpare@xplornet.com
www.dolepondmapleproducts.com
Maple syrup
President: Jean-Claude Pare
Number Employees: 1-4

3656 Dolisos America
1710 Whitney Mesa Dr
Henderson, NV 89014-2055
702-871-7153
Fax: 702-871-9670 800-365-4767
Homeopathic medicines.
President/CEO: Luc Clouatre

3657 Dollar Food Manufacturing
1410 Odlum Drive
Vancouver, BC V5L 4X7
Canada
604-253-1422
Fax: 604-253-2226 dollarfood@telus.net
Salted and/or dried salmon, sausage cured, golden pork hock. Founded in 1983.
President: Kelly Chow
Data Provider: Louisa Fung
Number Employees: 35
Type of Packaging: Consumer, Food Service

3658 Dolores Canning Co Inc
1020 N Eastern Ave
Los Angeles, CA 90063-3214
323-263-9155
Fax: 323-269-4876 sales@dolorescanning.com
Pickled pork products, chili bricks and specialty Mexican items
President, Co-Founder: Steve Munoz
Co-Founder: Augustine L. Munoz
Marketing: David Munoz
Sales: Bert Munoz
Estimated Sales: $1 Million
Number Employees: 20-49
Type of Packaging: Consumer, Food Service, Private Label
Brands:
Dolores

3659 Dolphin Natural Chocolates
1975 Woodview Avenue
Cambria, CA 93428-5168
805-927-7103
Fax: 831-722-0318 800-236-5744
Sugar and dairy-free chocolates; also, chocolate dipped apricots, papaya and pineapple
Owner: Henry McKowen
Estimated Sales: $2.5-5 Million
Number Employees: 5-9
Square Footage: 4000
Type of Packaging: Consumer
Brands:
Dolphin Natural

3660 Dom's Sausage Co Inc
10 Riverside Park
Malden, MA 02148-6781
781-324-6390
Fax: 781-322-6776 info@domsausage.com
www.domsausage.com
Meats including beef, pork, chicken, lamb and sausages.
President: Angelo Botticelli
CEO: Dominic Botticelli
summerman9@aol.com
Estimated Sales: $15 Million
Number Employees: 20-49
Number of Brands: 1
Type of Packaging: Bulk
Brands:
Dom's

3661 Domaine Chandon
1 California Dr
Yountville, CA 94599
888-242-6366
clubchandonwine@chandon.com
www.chandon.com
Sparkling and aperitif wines.
Engineer: Mike Morris
Year Founded: 1973
Estimated Sales: $20-50 Million
Number Employees: 250-499
Type of Packaging: Consumer
Brands:
Blanc De Noirs
Brut Classic
Chardonnay
Mt. Veeder Blanc De Blancs
Pinot Meunier
Pinot Noir
Reserve Brut
Reserve Brut Rose
Riche
Vintage

3662 Domaine St George Winery
1141 Grant Ave
Healdsburg, CA 95448-9570
707-433-5508
Fax: 707-433-5736 dswines@domstgeo.com
www.domainestgeorge.com
Wines
President: Somchai Likitprakong
dswines@domstgeo.com
Chairman: Yu Yee
Estimated Sales: $5-10 Million
Number Employees: 20-49
Type of Packaging: Private Label
Brands:
Domaine St. George

3663 Domata Living Flour
P.O. Box 24074
Minneapolis, MN 55424
952-303-5484
Fax: 952-303-5955 855-DOM-TA1
domataglutenfree.com
Gluten free flour
Co-Owner: David Madison

3664 Dominex
P.O.Box 5069
St Augustine, FL 32085
904-810-2132
Fax: 904-810-9852 sales@dominexeggplant.com
www.dominexeggplant.com
Eggplant cutlets and appetizers; including peeled, breaded, battered, deep fried and IQF. All natural fully cooked breaded in italian crumbs, eggplant appetizers and cutlets
President: John McGarvey
Director- Sales and Marketing: Miranda Chalke
chalke@dominexeggplant.com
Estimated Sales: 10-19
Number Employees: 50-99
Number of Brands: 10
Number of Products: 145
Type of Packaging: Food Service, Private Label, Bulk
Brands:
Dominex

3665 Dominion Wine Cellars
PO Box 1057
Culpeper, VA 22701-1057
540-825-8772
Fax: 540-829-0377
Wine
President: Wade D Sampson

3666 Domino Specialty Ingredients
One N Clematis St
West Palm Beach, FL 33401
info@dominospecialtyingredients.com
www.dominospecialtyingredients.com
Organic sugars, tapioca syrup, molasses, malt, honey, rice, rice syrup, rice bran, rice flour, sugar, icing and fondant.
EVP & CFO: Jeff Lawrence
Estimated Sales: $100+ Million
Parent Co: Domino Foods Inc
Brands:
Florida Crystals
Domino Sugar
C&H Sugar
Redpath Sugar
Tate+Lyle
Lyle's Golden Syrup
Zing
Sidul

3667 Don Alfonso Foods
7218 McNeil Drive
Austin, TX 78729-7980
512-335-2370
Fax: 512-335-0636 800-456-6100
Mexican food ingredients (prepared moles) dried chiles, spices and sauces
President: Jose Marmolejo
Brands:
Don Alfonso

3668 Don Bugito
San Francisco, CA 94110
www.donbugito.com
Pre-Columbian Mexican snack foods
Founder: Monica Martinez

3669 Don Hilario Estate Coffee
300 State Street East
Suite 226
Oldsmar, FL 34677
813-814-2888
Fax: 813-814-1788 800-799-1903
info@donhilario.com
Coffee
CEO/Marketing Director: Russell Versaggi
Estimated Sales: $2.5-5 Million
Number Employees: 1-4
Type of Packaging: Private Label
Brands:
Don Hilario Estate Coffee

3670 Don Jose Foods
8906 N 84th Way
Scottsdale, AZ 85258-2434
480-443-1000
Fax: 480-443-1216 www.donjosefoods.com
Fruit and juice beverages, chocolate drinks and assorted non-dairy items
President: Chuck Kuhlman
Vice President: Robby Kuhlman
Sales Manager: Enrique Ibarra
Number Employees: 1-4
Parent Co: Paradise Valley Foods
Type of Packaging: Private Label
Brands:
Cereal Match
Choco D' Lite
Don Jose Horchata

3671 Don Lee Farms
812 S 5th Ave
Mansfield, TX 76063
817-453-3180
sales@donleefarms.com
www.donleefarms.com
Fully cooked fresh and frozen foods manufacturers.
Type of Packaging: Consumer, Private Label

3672 **Don Sebastiani & Sons**
19150 Highway 12
Sonoma, CA 95476-5412
707-224-0410
Fax: 707-939-7115 hbast@donandsons.com
www.projectpaso.com
Wine
President: Sarah Anderson
sanderson@donandsons.com
VP: Don Staaveren
VP Marketing: Robert Carroll
Account Manager: Mike Wangbickler
President/COO: Mike Holden
Estimated Sales: $9.4 Million
Number Employees: 50-99

3673 **Don's Dock Seafood Market**
1220 E Northwest Hwy
Des Plaines, IL 60016-3391
847-827-1817
Fax: 847-827-1846 donsdockinc@yahoo.com
Fresh seafood
Owner: Andy Johnson
dkarr4604@yahoo.com
Co-Owner: George Johnson
Co-Owner: Don Johnson
Estimated Sales: $3-5 Million
Number Employees: 10-19

3674 **Don's Food Products**
4461 Township Line Road
Schwenksville, PA 19473
888-321-3667
www.donssalads.com
Salads, cream cheeses, commodity salads, soups and desserts
President/Owner: Victor Skloff
Contact: Ronnie Carter
rcarter@donssalads.com

3675 **Don't Go Nuts**
Salida, CO 81201
855-666-8826
dontgonuts.com
Whole grain snack bars and plant-based protein spreads
Co-Founder: Doug Pinto
Co-Founder: Jane Pinto
Number of Brands: 1
Number of Products: 8
Type of Packaging: Consumer
Brands:
DON'T GO NUTS

3676 **Dona Yiya Foods**
P.O.Box 1623
San Sebastian, PR 00685
787-896-4007
Fax: 787-280-1430 jd@donayiya.com
www.donayiya.com
Manufacturer, exporter and importer of spices and seasonings including garlic in oil or water, soffritto, condiments and tropical candies
President: Javier Quinones
Plant Manager: Luis Denis
Estimated Sales: $3.1 Million
Number Employees: 12
Number of Brands: 2
Number of Products: 23
Square Footage: 40000
Type of Packaging: Consumer, Food Service, Private Label, Bulk

3677 **Donald E Hunter Meats**
4612 Turkey Rd
Hillsboro, OH 45133-7044
937-466-2311
Beef
Owner: Betty Hunter
Estimated Sales: $1-2.5 Million
Number Employees: 1-4
Type of Packaging: Consumer

3678 **Donaldson's Finer Chocolates**
600 S State Road 39
Lebanon, IN 46052-9401
765-482-3334
Fax: 765-482-7994 800-975-7236
www.donaldsonschocolates.com
Chocolates and candy
President: George Donaldson
george@donaldsonschocolates.com
Estimated Sales: $5-10 Million
Number Employees: 5-9
Type of Packaging: Consumer

3679 **Donatoni Winery**
10604 S La Cienega Boulevard
Inglewood, CA 90304-1115
310-645-5445
Fax: 310-645-5445
Wines
President/CEO: Mark Donatoni
Manager Sales: Tina Donatoni
Estimated Sales: Less than $500,000
Number Employees: 1-4
Brands:
Donatoni

3680 **Donells Candies**
201 E 2nd St # 2
Casper, WY 82601-2576
307-234-6283
Fax: 307-235-9119 877-461-2009
www.donellschocolates.com
Confectionery products including hand-dipped chocolates and fudge
Owner: Mike Stepp
mike@donellschocolates.com
President: Mike Stepp
Estimated Sales: $1-2.5 Million
Number Employees: 5-9
Type of Packaging: Consumer

3681 **Dong Kee Company**
2252 S Wentworth Ave
Chicago, IL 60616-2042
312-225-6340
Fax: 312-567-9119
Canned Chinese products including egg rolls, water chestnuts, bamboo shoots, mushrooms and fortune and almond cookies
President: Betty Wong
Owner: Herman Wong
Estimated Sales: $500,000-$1 Million
Number Employees: 5-9
Type of Packaging: Consumer, Food Service

3682 **Dong Phuong Oriental Bakery**
14207 Chef Menteur Hwy
New Orleans, LA 70129
504-254-0214
Fax: 504-254-1744 info@dpbanhmi.com
Baked goods

3683 **Dong Us I**
2590 Main St
Irvine, CA 92614-6227
949-251-1768
Fax: 949-251-8865 888-580-0088
info@dongyu.us www.dongyu.us
Manufacturer and distributor of L-Carnitine products, amino acids, vitamins, sweeteners, sports nutrition ingredients, food and beverage ingredients
Manager: Weili Zhang
Number Employees: 10-19
Square Footage: 40000

3684 **Donna & Company**
505 Orange Avenue
Cranford, NJ 07016-2047
908-272-4380
bob@shopdonna.com
www.shopdonna.com
Chocolate bars, chocolate truffles, full-line chocolate, other chocolate, toffee.
Marketing: Robert Koshinskie
Contact: Don Kidd
d.kidd@donna-art.com

3685 **Donnelly Fine Chocolates**
1509 Mission St
Santa Cruz, CA 95060-4740
831-458-4214
Fax: 831-425-0678 888-685-1871
info@donnellychocolates.com
www.donnellychocolates.com
Chocolate, dessert sauces and mixes; gift boxes available
Owner: Richard Donnelly
donnellyr@donnellychocolates.com
Estimated Sales: Less than $500,000
Number Employees: 1-4
Type of Packaging: Private Label
Brands:
Donnelly Chocolates

3686 **Donsuemor Madeleines**
2080 N Loop Rd
Alameda, CA 94502-8012
510-865-6406
Fax: 510-865-6947 888-420-4441
remember@donsuemor.com www.donsuemor.com
Gourmet French madeleine cookies
CEO: Susan Davis
susan@donsuemor.com
Number Employees: 50-99

3687 **Donut Farm**
6037 San Pablo
Oakland, CA 94608
510-338-6319
www.vegandonut.farm
Organic, vegan donuts
Founder: Josh Levine
Year Founded: 2007

3688 **Donut Whole**
1720 E Douglas Ave
Wichita, KS 67214-4212
316-262-3700
www.thedonutwhole.com
Natural donuts, coffehouse
Owner: Donni Wempen
donniwempen@hotmail.com
Estimated Sales: Less Than $500,000
Number Employees: 1-4

3689 **Doodles Cookies**
1748 Rosebud Lane
Aurora, IL 60504
630-701-0847
info@doodlescookies.com
Cookies

3690 **Door County Fish Market**
2831 Dundee Rd
Northbrook, IL 60062-2501
847-559-9229
Fax: 847-559-9273
Seafood
President: Steven Messner
Secretary/Treasurer: Jeannie Lindwall
Estimated Sales: $1 Million
Number Employees: 6

3691 **Door County Potato Chips**
3840 N Fratney St
Milwaukee, WI 53212-1341
414-964-1428
Fax: 414-964-1484
Potato chips and pasta and contract packaging
Owner: Jamie Swisher
Number Employees: 1-4
Brands:
Door County Potato Chips
Strendge Pasta

3692 **Door Peninsula Winery**
5806 State Highway 42
Sturgeon Bay, WI 54235-9767
920-743-7431
Fax: 920-743-5999 800-551-5049
DPW@DCwis.com www.dcwine.com
Wines
Owner: Bob Polman
dpw@dcwis.com
VP/Marketing: Bob Pollman
Estimated Sales: $2.5-5 Million
Number Employees: 10-19
Square Footage: 32
Type of Packaging: Private Label
Brands:
Door-Peninsula

3693 **Doral International**
215-10 42nd Avenue
Bayside, NY 11361
718-224-7413
Fax: 718-224-7429
Organic/natural, cakes/pastries. cookies, balsamic vinegar, full-line chocolate, gummies/jellies/pates de fruits, pasta (dry), other sauces, seasonings and cooking enhancers.
Marketing: Dora Lara Bonaccolta

3694 **(HQ)Dorchester Crab Co**
2076 Wingate Bishops Head Rd
Wingate, MD 21675-2015
410-397-8103
Fax: 410-376-3179

Fresh and frozen seafood, shellfish including crabs and crab meat
President: Louis K Woodland
Owner: Zach Seaman
Estimated Sales: $1.70 Million
Number Employees: 5-9
Type of Packaging: Consumer, Bulk

3695 **(HQ)Dorina So-Good Inc**
17400 Jefferson St
Union, IL 60180-9705
815-923-2144
Fax: 815-923-2151
Manufacturer and exporter of shelf stable barbecue beef and pork; also, mustard, sauces, salsa, salad dressings, chip dips, olive salad and cheesespreads
President: Tim Young
CEO: Darwin Young
Estimated Sales: $.5-1 Million
Number Employees: 20-49
Square Footage: 24000
Type of Packaging: Consumer, Food Service, Private Label, Bulk
Brands:
Bar-B-Q Fiesta
Bar-B-Q Treat
Coney Island
Duffy
Farm Country
Old West Bar-B-Q Delight
So-Good Bar-B-Q Delight
So-Good Pork Bar-B-Q
Super
Young's Breading

3696 **Dorothy Dawson Food Products**
251 W Euclid Ave
Jackson, MI 49203-4101
517-788-9830
Fax: 517-788-7852 info@dawsonfoods.com
www.dawsonfoods.com
All-natural, ready-to-use frozen soups, sauces, batters, breadings and mixes including soup, marinade and steak au jus; also, pizza products including sauces, mixes and seasoning blends
President: Laura Bommarito
bbommarito@jacksondawson.com
VP: Brett Crosthwaite
Purchasing: Troy Ghent
Estimated Sales: $10-20 Million
Number Employees: 20-49
Type of Packaging: Food Service, Private Label, Bulk
Brands:
Emily's Gourmet
Freshdry
Kettle Gourmet
Simon's
Starters
Zip

3697 **Dorothy Timberlake Candies**
2351 Eaton Rd
Madison, NH 03849
603-447-2221
Fax: 603-447-2221 www.timberlakecandies.com
Hard candy and lollipops
President: William Timberlake
Estimated Sales: $1-2.5 Million
Number Employees: 1-4
Brands:
Dorothy

3698 **Dorset Fisheries**
215 Water St
Suite 302
St Josephs, NL A1C 6C9
Canada
709-739-7147
Fax: 709-739-0586
Manufacturer and exporter of fresh lobster and cod
President: Derick Philpott
Estimated Sales: $5 Million
Number Employees: 30
Type of Packaging: Bulk

3699 **Doscher's Candies Co.**
24 W Court St
Cincinnati, OH 45244
513-381-8656
greg@doscherscandies.com
www.doscherscandies.com
Candy including bars, canes and taffy products. Founded in 1871.
Chairman: Chip Nielson
VP, Operations: Kevin Gilligan
Estimated Sales: $1-2.5 Million
Number Employees: 5-9
Square Footage: 33600
Type of Packaging: Consumer
Brands:
French Chew
Gourmet French Chew

3700 **Double B Distributors**
1031 W New Circle Rd
Lexington, KY 40511-1843
859-255-8822
Fax: 859-233-1241
Meat snack foods
Owner: Bob Heim
bbdis@aol.com
Estimated Sales: $5-10 Million
Number Employees: 10-19

3701 **Double B Foods Inc**
800 W Arbrook Blvd # 210
Suite 210
Arlington, TX 76015-4393
469-567-6000
Fax: 817-472-8330 800-679-0349
www.doubleb.com
Chicken, eggs, frankfurters and Mexican foods
President: Kevin Macdal
kmacdal@doubleb.com
Chief Executive Officer: Patrick O'Ray
Chief Financial Officer: Don Wall
Year Founded: 1971
Estimated Sales: $25-49.9 Million
Number Employees: 250-499

3702 **Double Date Packing**
86301 Industrial Way
Coachella, CA 92236
760-398-8900
www.doubledatepacking.com
Medjool dates
CEO: Steven Gilfenbain
General Manager: Rob Carian

3703 **Double Good**
16W030 83rd St
Burr Ridge, IL 60527
630-568-5544
www.doublegood.com
Popcorn and snacks
Supply Chain & Operations: Justin Barnes
Year Founded: 1998
Estimated Sales: Less Than $500,000
Number Employees: 11-50
Square Footage: 12000

3704 **Double Play Foods**
500 E 77th Street
Apt 3525
New York, NY 10162-0011
212-682-4611
Fax: 212-570-4488
Peanut butter cups

3705 **Double Premium Confections**
6630 Kirkley Ave
McLean, VA 22101
202-495-1884
info@dpconfections.com
dpconfections.com
Manufacturer of chocolates, candies, and confections.
Owner: Bailey Kasten

3706 **Double Rainbow Gourmet Ice Cream**
275 S Van Ness Ave
San Francisco, CA 94103-3733
415-861-5858
Fax: 415-861-5872 800-489-3580
Manufacturers of ice cream and nondairy desserts
President: Steve Fink
CEO: Jeffrey Ross
jeffrey.ross@riverbed.com
Number Employees: 10-19

3707 **Double-Cola Company**
537 Market Street
Suite 100
Chattanooga, TN 37402
423-267-5691
Fax: 423-267-0793 info@double-cola.com
www.double-cola.com
Soft drinks
President: Alnoor Dhanini
VP Sales/Marketing: Gilford Thomas
Contact: Ramey Arnold
ramey.arnold@double-cola.com
Production: Roy Chisenall
Estimated Sales: $5-10 Million
Number Employees: 5-9
Brands:
Chaser
Diet Chaser
Diet Double-Cola
Diet Ski
Double Dry Gingerale
Double-Cola
Double-Dry Mixers
Jumbo Flavors
Ski

3708 **Doug Hardy Company**
Mountainville Rd
Deer Isle, ME 04627
207-348-6604
Fax: 207-348-6100
Seafood
Owner: Doug Hardy
Estimated Sales: $3-5 Million
Number Employees: 5-9

3709 **Dough-To-Go**
3535 DE LA Cruz Blvd
Santa Clara, CA 95054-2112
408-727-4094
Fax: 408-727-4095 betsyl@doughtogo.com
www.dough-to-go.com
Frozen raw dough and cookies, scones and brownies
President: Betsy Lee
Vice President: Rosel Witt
Contact: Lee Betsy
l.betsy@dough-to-go.com
Plant & Purchasing Manager: Tom Natusch
Estimated Sales: $2 Million
Number Employees: 15
Square Footage: 40000
Type of Packaging: Food Service
Brands:
Dough-To-Go
Jane Dough

3710 **Douglas Cross Enterprises**
2030 5th Ave
Seattle, WA 98121-2505
206-448-1193
Fax: 206-448-1979 office@tomdouglas.com
www.tomdouglas.com
BBQ Sauces
Owner: Mauricio Lopez
calimolo209@gmail.com
Estimated Sales: $5-10 Million
Number Employees: 10-19

3711 **Douglas Machines Corp**
2101 Calumet St
Clearwater, FL 33765-1310
727-461-3477
Fax: 727-449-0029 800-331-6870
info@dougmac.com www.dougmac.com
Douglas Machines Corporation specializes in the design and manufacture of automated industrial and commercial washers and sanitizing equipment for all containers commonly found in the Bakery, Food Processing, Food Service andDistribution industries.
President: Gerri Boyce
boyce@jea.com
Executive Vice President: Kevin Lemen
Vice President Finance & Accounting: Susan Mader
Engineering Manager: Josef Weinberger
Service Manager: Dale Breedlove
Sales & Marketing Coordinator: Rosie Rachel
Operations Manager: Jim Beadling
Technical Support Specialist: John Jurski
Purchasing Manager: Karen McCrae
Number Employees: 50-99

3712 **Douknie Winery**
14727 Mountain Rd
Purcellville, VA 20132-3638
540-668-6464
Fax: 540-668-7679 info@DoukenieWinery.com
Wines
Owner: Hope Bazaco
hbazaco@doukeniewinery.com
Public Relations: Denise Benoi
Number Employees: 10-19

3713 **Doumak Inc**
2201 Touhy Avenue
Elk Grove Village, IL 60007
800-323-0318
customerservice@doumak.com www.doumak.com
Manufacturer of marshmallows.
CFO: Tim Etzkorn
Director of Operations: Brent Lyons
Estimated Sales: $2.5-5 Million
Number Employees: 50-99
Square Footage: 160000
Type of Packaging: Consumer, Food Service, Private Label
Brands:
Campfire

3714 **Douwe Egberts**
771 Dearborn Park Lane
Suite B
Worthington, OH 43085
614-436-6112
Fax: 888-886-1533 800-582-6617
support@enjoybettercoffee.com
www.enjoybettercoffee.com
Coffee
Sales Director: Victor Borsukevich
International Marketing Director: Kerry Owens
Brands:
Dallmayr
Jacobs
Tchibo
Idee
Helmut
Sachers

3715 **Doves and Figs LLC**
89 Falmouth Rd W
Arlington, MA 02474-1007
781-646-2272
Fax: 866-903-7912 www.dovesandfigs.com
Jams; chutneys; and fruit mustards
Owner: Robin Cohen
Year Founded: 2011
Number Employees: 3
Type of Packaging: Private Label

3716 **Dow AgroSciences Canada**
450 1st St SW
Suite 2100
Calgary, AB T2P 5H1
Canada
403-735-8800
Fax: 403-735-8841 info@dow.com
www.omega-9oils.com
Omega-9 oils
President/Chief Executive Officer: Jim Wispinski
Estimated Sales: $25.36 Million
Number Employees: 60
Parent Co: DOW Chemical Company
Type of Packaging: Food Service, Bulk

3717 **Dow Distribution**
524 Ohohia St
Honolulu, HI 96819-1934
808-836-3511
Fax: 808-833-3634
Fish and seafood
President: Craig Mitchell
cmitch@hawaii.rr.com
Estimated Sales: $10-20 Million
Number Employees: 10-19

3718 **Dowd & Rogers**
1403 N
El Camino Real
San Clemente, CA 92672
916-451-6480
Fax: 800-767-8514 800-232-8619
Premium wheat free and gluten free products
President: Derek Dowd
Number of Brands: 2
Number of Products: 8
Type of Packaging: Consumer, Food Service, Private Label, Bulk
Brands:
Dowd and Rogers

3719 **Down East Specialty Products/Cape Bald Packers**
P.O. Box 9739
Suite 1200
Portland, ME 04103
207-878-9170
Fax: 207-878-9104 800-369-6327
www.capebaldpackers.com
Lobster, mussels, rock crab and red crab
Manager: Kathy Nally
Manager: Patrice Landry
Estimated Sales: $1-3 Million
Number Employees: 1-4
Parent Co: Cape Bald Packers
Type of Packaging: Private Label
Brands:
Downeast

3720 **Downeast Candies**
P.O.Box 25
Boothbay Harbor, ME 4538
207-633-5178
Fudges and taffy
President: David Carmolli
VP: Elaine Miller
Production Manager: Rick Carmolli
Estimated Sales: $1-2.5 Million
Number Employees: 1-4
Type of Packaging: Consumer, Private Label, Bulk
Brands:
Downeast Candies

3721 **Downeast Cider House**
256 Marginal Street
Suite 32
East Boston, MA 02128
857-301-8881
info@downeastcider.com
downeastcider.com
Craft hard cider
Co-Founder: Ross Brockman
Co-Founder: Tyler Mosher
Co-Founder: Ben Manter
Co-Founder: Matt Brockman
Year Founded: 2011
Number Employees: 51-200
Number of Brands: 10
Type of Packaging: Consumer

3722 **Downeast Coffee Roasters**
259 East Ave
Pawtucket, RI 02860-3801
401-724-6393
Fax: 401-724-0560 800-345-2007
www.downeastcoffee.com
Roasted coffees.
President/CEO: William Kapos
wkapos@excellentcoffee.com
Vice President: Michael Kapos
VP, Retail Sales: Keith McClain
Estimated Sales: $16 Million
Number Employees: 100-249
Number of Brands: 2
Type of Packaging: Private Label
Brands:
Downeast Coffee
Ocean Coffee Roasters

3723 **Doyon**
Canada
800-265-2600
www.mieldoyon.com
Beeswax and honey; exporter of honey; importer of pollen
President: Paul Doyon
CEO: David Sugarman
Number Employees: 15
Square Footage: 60000
Parent Co: McCormick & Co.
Type of Packaging: Consumer, Food Service, Bulk

3724 **Dr Konstantin Frank's Vinifera**
9749 Middle Rd
Hammondsport, NY 14840-9612
800-320-0735
Fax: 607-868-4888 800-320-0735
info@drfrankwines.com www.drfrankwines.com
Manufacturer and exporter of table wine and champagne
President: Fred Frank
VP & Vineyard Manager: Eric Volz
Consulting Winemaker & Regional Sales Ma: Barbara Frank
Contact: Peter Bell
pbell@spidergraphics.com
Estimated Sales: $5-10 Million
Number Employees: 5-9
Type of Packaging: Consumer
Brands:
Chateau Frank Champagne Cellars
Dr. Konstantin Frank

3725 **Dr Pepper Snapple Group**
5301 Legacy Dr.
Plano, TX 75024
800-696-5891
www.drpeppersnapplegroup.com
Fruit juices, soft drink, and more.
CEO: Robert Gamgort
CFO: Ozan Dokmecioglu
Chief Legal Officer/General Counsel: Jim Baldwin
Chief Research & Development Officer: David Thomas
Chief Marketing Officer: Andrew Springate
Year Founded: 2008
Estimated Sales: $11 Billion
Number Employees: 21,000
Number of Brands: 34
Parent Co: Keurig Dr Pepper
Type of Packaging: Consumer, Food Service, Bulk
Brands:
7UP®
All Sport®
A&W Root Beer®
Bai®
Big Red®
Canada Dry®
Clamato®
Crush®
Deja Blue®
Diet Rite®
Dr Pepper®
Hawaiian Punch®
Hires®
IBC Root Beer®
Margaritaville®
Mott's®
Mr. & Mrs. T®
Nantucket Nectars®
Orangina®
Penafiel®
RC Cola®
ReaLemon®
ReaLime®
Rose's®
Schweppes®
Snapple®
Squirt®
Straight Up Tea®
Stewarts®
Sun Drop®
Sunkist®
Vemon Energy®
Vernors®
Yoohoo®

3726 **Dr Pete's**
P.O. Box 24089
Savannah, GA 31403
912-233-3035
Fax: 912-233-0001 888-599-0047
info@dr-petes.com www.dr-petes.com
Sauces, marinades and dressings
CEO: Joel Coffee
Estimated Sales: $600,000
Number Employees: 5-9
Type of Packaging: Consumer, Food Service
Brands:
Dr. Pete's

3727 **Dr Praeger's Sensible Foods**
9 Boumar Pl
Elmwood Park, NJ 07407-2615
201-703-1300
877-772-3437
www.dpsensiblefood.net
Kosher natural frozen products such as veggie burgers, fish sticks and potato pancakes
President: Dr Peter Praeger
CEO: Larry Praeger
larry@drpraegers.com
Director Sales/Marketing: Larry Praeger

Estimated Sales: $20-50 Million
Number Employees: 50-99
Type of Packaging: Food Service
Brands:
Dr Praeger's
Ungar's

3728 **Dr. B's Beverages, LLC**
4325 Gerrardstown Rd.
Inwood, WV 25428
304-283-2257
www.docstea.com
Manufacturer of drinks made with tea.
Co-Founder: Ken Banks
Co-Founder: Christopher Banks
Co-Founder: Sarah Banks

3729 **Dr. Christopher's Herbal Supplements**
155 W 2050 N
Spanish Fork, UT 84660
801-453-1406
Fax: 801-794-6801 800-453-1406
www.drchristopher.com
Supplements and herbal formulas
Sales/Marketing: Troy Fukumitsu
Contact: Robert Scott
rscott@drchristopher.com
Estimated Sales: $20-50 Million
Number Employees: 20-49
Type of Packaging: Consumer, Private Label, Bulk

3730 **Dr. Cookie**
2112 6th Ave
Seattle, WA 98121-2513
206-389-9321
www.drcookie.com
Cookies, breads, rolls
Manager: Steve Krendall
Estimated Sales: $1-5 Million appx.
Number Employees: 1-4
Brands:
Dr Cookie

3731 **Dr. In The Kitchen**
P.O. Box 24868
Minneapolis, MN 55424
952-746-3007
orders@drinthekitchen.com
www.drinthekitchen.com
Snack bars and crackers made with seeds.
Co-Founder: Alison Levitt
Co-Founder: Donna Kelly
Year Founded: 2007
Estimated Sales: $610000
Number Employees: 8
Type of Packaging: Private Label

3732 **Dr. Lucy's LLC**
930 Denison Ave.
Suite 101-A
Norfolk, VA 23513
757-233-9495
Fax: 757-233-9398 info@drlucys.com
www.drlucys.com
Cookies baked without wheat, gluten, dairy milk, butter, eggs, casein, peanuts or tree nuts.
President/Owner: Lucy Gibney
Contact: Megan Hallman
megan@drlucys.com

3733 **Dr. McDougall's Right Foods**
Woodland, CA
866-972-6879
www.rightfoods.com
Vegan prepared foods
Founder: Dr. John McDougall
Type of Packaging: Consumer
Brands:
DR. MCDOUGALL'S

3734 **Dr. Oetker Canada Ltd.**
2229 Drew Road
Mississauga, ON L5S 1E5
Canada
905-678-1311
Fax: 905-678-9334 800-387-6939
www.oetker.ca
Cake and muffin mixes, mashed potatoes, drink crystals
Chairman: Dr August Oetker
Brands:
Dr Oetker

3735 **Dr. Paul Lohmann Inc.**
1757-10 Veterans Memorial Hwy
Islandia, NY 11749
631-851-8810
Fax: 631-851-8815
Specialty mineral salts

3736 **Dr. Pete's**
2224 Gamble Rd
PO Box 24089
Savannah, GA 31403
912-233-3035
Fax: 912-233-0001 info@dr-petes.com
www.dr-petes.com
Sauces, marinades, dressings, baking mixes
CEO: Joel Coffee
VP: Jan Coffee
Number Employees: 5

3737 **Dr. Pete's/J.C. Specialty Foods**
P.O.Box 24089
Savannah, GA 31403-4089
912-233-3035
Fax: 912-233-0001 info@dr-petes.com
www.dr-petes.com
Products that complement meats, vegetables and salads, marinades, glazes, salad dressings
Owner: Joel Coffee
Estimated Sales: $2.5-5 Million
Number Employees: 1-4

3738 **Dr. Schar USA**
1050 Wall Street West
Suite 370
Lyndhurst, NJ 7071
201-355-8470
Fax: 201-355-8624 info.us@drschar.com
www.drschaer.com/en/company/locations/usa/
Gluten free products
Contact: Paul Altieri
paul.altieri@schar.com

3739 **Dr. Smoothie Brands**
1730 Raymer Avenue
Fullerton, CA 92833
714-449-9787
Fax: 714-449-9474 888-466-9941
info@drsmoothie.com www.drsmoothie.com or www.cafeessentials.com
Dr. Smoothie Brands is a full line beverage company manufacturing shelf-stable , liquid natural fruit smoothies and powdered cocoa, mocha, latte, and chai blends. Manufactures nutritional blends ranging from raw, whole food nutritionbars to a full range of botanicals, including medically endorsed products like The Complete Meal, and Amino line.
Contact: Megan Wood
meganwood@inewsource.org
Number of Brands: 6
Number of Products: 93
Type of Packaging: Consumer, Food Service

3740 **Dr. Tima Natural Products**
131 Groverton Pl
Los Angeles, CA 90077-3732
310-472-2181
Fax: 310-652-9884
Natural health products and soda
Owner: Potito Depaolis
VP: Mary Caronna
Estimated Sales: $2.5-5,000,000
Number Employees: 5-9
Brands:
Dr Tima

3741 **Draco Natural Products Inc**
539 Parrott St
San Jose, CA 95112-4121
408-287-7871
Fax: 408-287-8838 info@dracoherbs.com
www.draconatural.com
Wholesales herbal extracts
CEO: Jerry Wu
Sales: Ed Schack
Estimated Sales: $3 Million
Number Employees: 10-19

3742 **Drader Manufacturing Industries**
5750-50 Street NW
Edmonton, AB T6B 2Z8
Canada
780-440-2231
Fax: 780-440-2244 800-661-4122
bakery@drader.com www.drader.com
Custom carriers, bread baskets, bakery trays, hand trucks, dollies and bakery shelving
President/General Manager: Gordon McTavish
Account Manager: Chris Gaucher
Operations Manager: Jeff McTavish
Manager: Glenn Eckert
Number Employees: 60
Square Footage: 140000

3743 **Dragnet Fisheries**
4141 B St
Anchorage, AK 99503-5940
907-276-4551
Fax: 907-274-3617
Fresh and frozen herring, black cod, halibut and salmon
President: Jay Cherrier
Estimated Sales: Less than $500,000
Number Employees: 1-4
Type of Packaging: Consumer, Food Service
Brands:
Dragnet

3744 **Dragunara LLC**
Po Box 1111
Palos Verdes Estate, CA 90274
310-618-8818
info@dragunara.com
www.dragunara.com
Other lifestyle, full-line condiments, BBQ sauce, ethnic sauces (soy, curry, etc.), full-line spices, marinades, other sauces, seasonings and cooking enhancers, rubs.

3745 **Drake Bakeries**
P.O. Box 750
Collegedale, TN 37315
855-403-7253
drakescake.com
Baked goods including snack cakes.
Chief Executive Officer: Mike McKee
Year Founded: 1896
Estimated Sales: $20-50 Million
Number Employees: 50-99
Parent Co: McKee Foods

3746 **Drakes Brewing Co**
1933 Davis St # 177
Building 177
San Leandro, CA 94577-1256
510-568-2739
Fax: 510-568-9857 drinkdrakes@jbrfoods.com
www.drinkdrakes.com
Beer
Principal: Adolfo Carrera
CFO: Peter Rogers
Manager: John Gittins
john.gittins@drakesbrewing.com
Director Manufacturing: Roger Lind
Estimated Sales: $1-2.5 Million
Number Employees: 1-4
Brands:
Autumn Fest
Blood Red
Chocolate Milk Stout
Drakes Amber Ale
Drakes Blond Ale
Drakes Hefe-Weizen
Drakes Ipa
Expedition
Harvest Ale British Esb
Imperial Ipa Black Pilsner
Imperial Ipa Pilsner
Imperial Stout
Jolly Rogers
Sir Francis Stout
Zatec Pilsner

3747 **Drakes Fresh Pasta Co**
636 Southwest St
High Point, NC 27260-8107
336-861-5454
Fax: 336-861-4823 800-737-2782
info@drakesfreshpasta.com
Pasta products
President: Richard Drake
rdrake@drakesfreshpasta.com
Vice President: Simone Drake
Sales: Ginger Edward
Estimated Sales: $5 Million
Number Employees: 20-49
Brands:
Drakes Fresh

3748 **Drangle Foods**
300 S Riverside Dr
Gilman, WI 54433
715-447-8241
Fax: 715-447-8242
Flavored processed cheese
President: Tom Hand
Office Manager: Char Hand
Estimated Sales: $1 Million
Number Employees: 80
Square Footage: 80
Type of Packaging: Private Label
Brands:
Drangle

3749 **Draper Valley Farms**
1000 Jason Ln
Mt Vernon, WA 98273-2490
360-748-9466
Fax: 360-424-1666 800-562-2012
www.drapervalleyfarms.com
Free range chicken
Vice President: Jeff Power
CFO: Richard Koplowitz
VP & General Manager: Bob Wolfe
Sales & Marketing Manager: Vicki Knutson
Human Resources Manager: Colleen Helgeson
Plant Manager: John Michalak
Head of Purchasing: Jody Dethman
Number Employees: 250-499
Square Footage: 131196
Type of Packaging: Consumer, Food Service

3750 **(HQ)Dream Confectioners LTD**
540 Cedar Ln
Teaneck, NJ 07666-1742
201-836-9000
Fax: 201-836-9015
Manufacturer and exporter of pretzels
President: Joseph Podolski
Estimated Sales: $2.5-5 Million
Number Employees: 1-4
Type of Packaging: Consumer, Private Label, Bulk
Brands:
Great

3751 **Dream Foods Intl**
2116 Wilshire Blvd
Suite 355
Santa Monica, CA 90403-5750
310-315-5739
Fax: 310-388-1322
Dairy-free, functional (antioxidants), gluten-free, kosher, organic/natural, USDA, juice/cider.
Owner: Adriana Kahane
adk@dreamfoods.com
Marketing: Adriana Kahane
Number Employees: 5-9

3752 **Dream Pretzels**
260 Madison Ave
New York, NY 10016
877-966-8434
www.pressels.com
New York deli-style pretzels
Number of Brands: 1
Number of Products: 4
Type of Packaging: Consumer
Brands:
DREAM PRETZELS

3753 **DreamPak LLC**
4717 Eisenhower Avenue
Alexandria, VA 22304
703-751-3511
877-687-4662
info@dreampak.com www.dreampak.com
On-the-go beverages
President/CEO: Dr. Aly Gamay
Executive Vice President: Terry Schneider
Contact: Taufeeque Ali
tali@dreampak.com
Vice President, Operations: Randy Cook
Brands:
Fruitslim
Soluflex
Dogflex
Trimma
Enhance To Go
Joker's Wild Energy
Chocolate Slim
Zeniht

3754 **DreamTime, Inc**
1115 Thompson Ave
#5
Santa Cruz, CA 95062
831-464-6702
Fax: 831-464-6703 877-464-6702
info@dreamtimeinc.com www.dreamtimeinc.com
Natural ingredient health products
Founder/CEO: Judy Day
Contact: Judy Dy
judy.day@dreamtimeinc.com
Estimated Sales: $1-3 Million
Number Employees: 15

3755 **Dreaming Cow**
www.dreamingcow.com
Grass-based whole milk yogurt and yogurt drinks
Number of Brands: 1
Number of Products: 12
Type of Packaging: Consumer
Brands:
LUSH
DREAMING COW

3756 **Dresden Stollen Co USA**
7 Heathcote Dr
Albertson, NY 11507-2224
516-746-5802
Fax: 516-746-5918 http://www.dresdenstollen.com
Gourmet foods
President/Owner: Joan Greenfield
Estimated Sales: A
Number Employees: 5-9

3757 **(HQ)Dressel Collins Fish Company**
5131 S Director St
Seattle, WA 98118
206-725-0121
Fax: 206-725-1354
Canned and smoked salmon
President: Mike Bonney
Estimated Sales: $10 Million
Number Employees: 1-4
Type of Packaging: Consumer, Food Service

3758 **Drew's Organics**
926 VT Route 103 S
Chester, VT 05143-8461
802-875-1184
Fax: 802-875-5126 800-228-2980
info@chefdrew.com www.drewsorganics.com
All-natural salad dressings and salsa. Certified Organic.
President/CEO: Andrew Starkweather
Assistant Controller: Rob Feakes
Manager: John Cummings
johnc@chefdrew.com
Plant Manager: Joe Brent
Estimated Sales: $1.5 Million
Number Employees: 20-49
Type of Packaging: Consumer, Private Label
Brands:
Drew's All Natural

3759 **Dreyer Sonoma**
161 Fox Hollow Rd
Woodside, CA 94062-3607
650-851-9448
Fax: 650-851-3268 jdreyer@dreyerwine.com
www.dreyerwine.com
Wines
Co-Owner: Walter Dreyer
Co-Owner: Bettina Dreyer
General Manager: Jonathan Dreyer
Estimated Sales: $2.5-5 Million
Number Employees: 5-9
Brands:
Dreyer Wine

3760 **Dreyer's Grand Ice Cream Inc.**
5929 College Ave.
Oakland, CA 94618
877-437-3937
www.dreyers.com
Premium ice creams.
CEO: Kim Peddle Rguem
Year Founded: 1928
Estimated Sales: $1.5 Billion
Number Employees: 10,000
Number of Brands: 28
Parent Co: Nestl, USA
Type of Packaging: Consumer, Food Service
Other Locations:
Dreyer's Grand Ice Cream
Fort Wayne IN
Brands:
Dreyer's
Edy's

3761 **Dreymiller & KRAY Inc**
140 S State St
Hampshire, IL 60140-7000
847-683-2271
Fax: 847-683-2272 www.dreymillerandkray.com
Packer/processor of sausage, ham and bacon
President: Ed Reiser
dreymillerandkray@gmail.com
Estimated Sales: $500,000-$1 Million
Number Employees: 5-9
Type of Packaging: Consumer

3762 **Dried Ingredients, LLC.**
9010 NW 105th Way
Miami, FL 33178
786-999-8499
Fax: 888-893-6595 info@driedingredients.com
www.driedingredients.com
Maufacturer of organic, precooked pulses (beans, lentils, peas); also teas, tea ingredients, herbs, spices, essential oils & dried vegetables. Provide product development & logistics services.
President: Armin Dilles
armin.dilles@driedingredients.com
Sales Manager: Maria Rosello
Parent Co: Dried Ingredients GmbH
Type of Packaging: Food Service, Bulk

3763 **Drier's Meats**
14 S Elm Street
Three Oaks, MI 49128
269-756-3101
Fax: 269-756-9285 info@driers.com
www.driers.com
Smoked meats
Owner: Carolyn Drier
Estimated Sales: Less than $500,000
Number Employees: 1-4
Brands:
Drier Meats

3764 **Driftwood Dairy**
10724 E. Lower Azusa Rd.
El Monte, CA 91731
626-444-9591
www.driftwooddairy.com
Dairy products.
President: Mac Berry
macb@driftwooddairy.com
CEO: James Dolan
Year Founded: 1946
Estimated Sales: $100+ Million
Number Employees: 250-499
Type of Packaging: Consumer, Food Service, Bulk

3765 **Driscoll Strawberry Assoc Inc**
345 Westridge Dr
Watsonville, CA 95076-4169
831-424-0506
Fax: 831-761-1090 www.driscolls.com
Grower of premium berries.
Chairman & CEO: Miles Reiter
Manager: J M Reiter
jm.reiter@driscolls.com
Number Employees: 50-99
Brands:
Associates
Driscoll's
Dsa
Islander

3766 **Driscoll's**
PO Box 50045
Watsonville, CA 95077-5045
800-871-3333
driscolls@allisonpr.com www.driscolls.com
Supplier of fresh berries
Contact: Saumya Lanka
saumya.lanka@driscolls.com

3767 **Droga Chocolates**
401 East Las Olas Blvd
Suite 800
Fort Lauderdale, FL 33301
800-213-0754
drogachocolates.com
Caramels sweetened with honey

President: Michelle Crochet
Partner: Lisa Albani
Contact: Lisa Albani
lisa@drogachocolates.com
Year Founded: 2007
Estimated Sales: B
Number Employees: 5-9
Number of Products: 4
Brands:
Money on Honey

3768 **Droubi's Imports**
2721 Hillcroft Street
Houston, TX 77057-5003
713-334-1829
Fax: 713-988-9506
Manufacturer, importer and wholesaler/distributor of tea and coffee
President: A Droubi
VP: Sharon Droubi
Estimated Sales: $1-2.5 Million
Number Employees: 20-49
Square Footage: 48000
Parent Co: Droubi's Bakery & Delicatessen
Brands:
Gold Star

3769 **Drum Rock Specialty Co Inc**
44 Fullerton Rd
Warwick, RI 02886-1422
401-737-5165
Fax: 401-737-5060
marketing@drumrockproducts.com
www.drumrockproducts.com
Manufacturer and exporter of fritter breading and batter mixes for vegetables, seafood and poultry; also, custom dry blending and mixing and private labeling services available
President: Stephen Hinger
Sales Manager: Paul Skorupa
Estimated Sales: $1-2.5 Million
Number Employees: 5-9
Type of Packaging: Food Service, Private Label, Bulk
Brands:
Fis-Chic Wonder Batter

3770 **Drusilla Seafood**
3482 Drusilla Ln # D
Baton Rouge, LA 70809-1800
225-923-0896
Fax: 225-928-4936 800-364-8844
info@drusillaplace.com www.drusillaplace.com
Manufacturer and packer of seafood, spices, salad dressings and breading mixes
President: James Zito
Cio/Cto: Brad Bito
bradb@drusillaseafood.com
VP: Don Zito
Marketing Manager: Nancy Zito
Estimated Sales: $300,000-$500,000
Number Employees: 100-249
Square Footage: 10000
Parent Co: Seafood Restaurant
Brands:
Drusilla

3771 **Dry Creek Vineyard**
3770 Lambert Bridge Rd
Healdsburg, CA 95448-9713
707-433-1000
Fax: 707-433-5329 800-864-9463
dcv@drycreekvineyard.com
www.drycreekvineyard.com
Wines
President: Lynda Abbott
traceyrathjen@cabainc.com
CFO: Dru Cochran
VP: Don Wallace
Consumer Manager: Michael Longerbeam
traceyrathjen@cabainc.com
Estimated Sales: $10-20 Million
Number Employees: 20-49
Type of Packaging: Consumer, Food Service
Brands:
Dry Creek
Meritage
Regatta
Soleil-Late Harvest Sauvignon

3772 **Dryden Provision Co Inc**
1016 E Washington St
Louisville, KY 40206-1821
502-583-1777
Fax: 502-583-3006 www.drydenprovidin.com
Meat distributor of pork, poultry, beef, lamb, veal and seafood
President: John Dryden
Co-Owner: Janinne Agee
Manager: Bobby Pound
john@drydenprovidin.com
Estimated Sales: $3 Million
Number Employees: 10-19
Brands:
Dryden

3773 **DuPont Nutrition & Biosciences**
4 New Century Pkwy
New Century, KS 66031
913-764-8100
www.food.dupont.com
Ingredients for baking, bars, beverages, confectionery, culinary, diary, frozen desserts, fruit applications, meat alternatives, meat/poultry/seafood, oils and fats, and pet food
President, Nutrition & Biosciences: Mathhias Heinzel
Estimated Sales: $4.4 Billion
Number Employees: 10,000
Parent Co: DuPont
Type of Packaging: Consumer, Bulk
Other Locations:
Central Soya Company-Processing
Decatur IN
Central Soya Company-Processing
Gibson City IL
Central Soya Company-Processing
Marion OH
Central Soya Company-Grain Plant
Indianapolis IN
Central Soya Company-Processing
Bellevue OH
Central Soya Company-Grain Plant
Cincinnati OH
Central Soya Company-Processing
Delphos OH
Central Soya Company-Mfg
Remington IN
Central Soya Company-Processing
Morristown IN
Central Soya Company-Grain
Jeffersonville OH
Central Soya Company-Grain
Waterloo IN
Central Soya Company-Bulk Oil
Pawtucket RI
Central Soya Company-Mfg
New Bremen OH
Brands:
Fibrim
Solae
V8 Splash
Gardenburgers
Mori-Nu
Yves Veggie Cuisine
Medifast

3774 **DuPont Pioneer**
7100 NW 62nd Ave
P.O. Box 1150
Johnston, IA 50131-941
515-535-5954
www.pioneer.com
Producer of hybrid seeds and other GMO products, focusing on corn, soybeans, alfalfa, sorghum, sunflowers, canola and wheat.
Chairman/CEO: Edward Breen
Chief Financial Officer: Nicholas Fanandakis
Executive Vice President: James Collins Jr.
Senior Marketing Manager: David Tegeder
Sr. VP of Human Resources: Benito Cachinero-Sanchez
Parent Co: DuPont

3775 **DuPont Pioneer**
P.O. Box 1000
Johnston, IA 50131-0184
515-535-3200
www.pioneer.com
Hybrid and genetically modified seeds.
CEO, Corteva Agriscience: James Collins
Year Founded: 1926
Estimated Sales: $4.3 Billion
Number Employees: 12,300
Number of Brands: 6
Parent Co: Corteva Agriscience
Type of Packaging: Consumer, Food Service, Bulk
Brands:
Pioneer®
Plenish™
Optimum®
AcreMax®
AQUAmax™

3776 **DuPont Tate & Lyle BioProducts Company, LLC.**
198 Blair Bend Dr
Loudon, TN 37774
866-404-7933
www.duponttateandlyle.com
Producer of bio-based 1,30-propanediol.
President: Todd Sutton
Chief Financial Officer: Jennifer Moss
Vice President, Technology: Jim Zahn, Ph.D
Vice President, Marketing & Sales: Stephen Hurff
Vice President, Operations: Sukh Rabeendran
Product Director: Colton Reid

3777 **Dubois Seafood**
285 Saint Peter St
Houma, LA 70363
985-876-2514
Fax: 985-851-6147
Seafood wholesalers
President: Kerry Dubois
Estimated Sales: $6 Million
Number Employees: 5

3778 **Duck Pond Cellars**
23145 N Highway 99w
PO Box 429
Dundee, OR 97115-9126
503-538-3199
Fax: 503-538-3190 800-437-3213
dpinfo@duckpondcellars.com
www.duckpondcellars.com
Wines
Owner: Douglas Fries
CFO: Jo Ann Fries
Sales: Scott Jenkins
douglasf@duckpondcellars.com
Wine Club Director: Kathy Wildman
VP Operations: Lisa Jenkins
Estimated Sales: $1-2.5 Million
Number Employees: 10-19
Type of Packaging: Private Label
Brands:
Duck Pond Cellars

3779 **Duckhorn Vineyards**
1000 Lodi Ln
St Helena, CA 94574-9410
707-963-7108
Fax: 707-963-7078 888-354-8885
customerservice@duckhorn.com
www.duckhorn.com
Wines
Chairman/Co-Founder: Daniel Duckhorn
President/Chief Executive Officer: Alex Ryan
alex@duckhorn.com
Vice President: Neil Bernardi
Chief Operations Officer: Zach Rasmuson
Estimated Sales: $10-20 Million
Number Employees: 100-249
Number of Brands: 6
Parent Co: GI Manager L.P
Brands:
Canvasback
Decoy
Duckhorn Vineyards
Goldeneye
Migration
Paraduxx

3780 **Ducktrap River Of Maine**
57 Little River Dr
Belfast, ME 04915-6035
207-338-6280
Fax: 207-338-6288 800-434-8727
ducktrap.sales@marineharvest.com
www.ducktrap.com
Pate and smoked seafood including trout fillets, Atlantic salmon, peppered and herb mackerel, mussels, scallops and shrimp
CEO: Alf-Helge Aarskog
General Manager: Don Cynewski
Estimated Sales: $20-50 Million
Number Employees: 100-249
Square Footage: 25000
Type of Packaging: Consumer, Food Service, Bulk

Brands:
Ducktrap
Kendall Brook
Spruce Point
Winter Harbor

3781 Duda Farm Fresh Foods Inc
1200 Duda Trl
Oviedo, FL 32765-4507
407-365-2111
Fax: 407-365-2010 www.dudafresh.com
Fruits and vegetables
Chief Executive Officer: David Duda
Chief Financial Officer: Mark Engwall
Senior Vice President, Corporate Affairs: Rick Hanas
Senior VP, Real Estate/General Counsel: Tracy Duda Chapman
Senior Vice President, Fresh Operations: Dan Duda
Senior Vice President, Duda Ranches: Drew Duda
Sales Exec: Dan Duda
joseph.duda@duda.com
SVP, Mergers & Acquisitions: Tom Duda
Chief Operating Officer: Barton Weeks
Lease Manager: Patrick Schmidt
Number Employees: 20-49
Parent Co: DUDA
Brands:
Dandy(c)

3782 Dufflet Pastries
166 Norseman St
Toronto, ON M8Z ZR4
Canada
416-536-1330
Fax: 416-538-2366 866-238-0899
info@dufflet.com www.dufflet.com
Cakes, tortes, pies, flan, tarts, brownies, cookies, etc.
President: Daniele Bertrand
CEO: Dufflet Rosenberg
Estimated Sales: $11 Million
Number Employees: 65
Number of Products: 100
Square Footage: 40000
Type of Packaging: Consumer, Food Service

3783 Dufour Pastry Kitchens Inc
251 Locust Ave
Bronx, NY 10454-2004
718-402-8800
Fax: 718-402-7002 800-439-1282
info@dufourpastrykitchens.com
www.dufourpastrykitchens.com
Manufacturer of frozen puff pastry products including hors d'oeuvres, doughs, snacks, lunch products, tart shells, etc.
Owner: Felicia Forster
forster@convertmedia.com
CEO: Judi Arnold
Year Founded: 1984
Number Employees: 50-99
Type of Packaging: Consumer, Food Service, Bulk
Brands:
Dufour Pastry Kitchens

3784 Dugdale Beef Company
4420 Stout Field North Dr.
Indianapolis, IN 46241
317-520-9981
Fax: 317-298-7608 jeff@dugdalefoods.com
www.dugdalefoods.com
Fine meats, seafood, poultry, cheese, salads, breads, desserts
President: Jean Deering
Founder: Eleanor Dugdale
Contact: Joe Dugdale
joe@dugdalefoods.com
Year Founded: 1975
Estimated Sales: $20-50 Million
Number Employees: 20-49
Type of Packaging: Consumer

3785 Duguay Fish Packers
1062 Bas-Cap-Pele Ch
Cap-Pele, NB E4N 1K9
Canada
506-577-2287
Fax: 506-577-1995
Seafood product preparation and packaging
President: Omer Duguay
Board Member: Alfreda Duguay
Estimated Sales: $3 Million
Number Employees: 20
Type of Packaging: Food Service

3786 (HQ)Duis Meat Processing
1991 E 6th St
Concordia, KS 66901-2621
785-243-7850
800-281-4295
kgduis@aol.com www.duismeatprocessing.com
Quality services for all deer and meat processing needs
Owner: Toby Duis
kgduis@aol.com
CEO: Keith Duis
VP: Toby Duis
Estimated Sales: $1-3 Million
Number Employees: 5-9
Square Footage: 12800
Type of Packaging: Consumer, Food Service, Private Label, Bulk
Other Locations:
Duis Meat Processing
Salina KS

3787 Duke's
dukesmeats.com
Dried sausages and beef brisket strips
Founder: Justin Havlick
Number of Brands: 2
Number of Products: 15
Type of Packaging: Consumer
Brands:
DUKE'S
DUKE'S SMOKED SHORTY

3788 Dulce de Leche DelcampoProducts
15908 NW 48th Ave
Miami, FL 33014
305-620-1444
Fax: 305-624-2728 877-472-9408
Dulce de leche, cholesterol-free white cheese, guava spread and filling
President: Carlos Ruiz DeLuque
Estimated Sales: $37,000
Number Employees: 7
Type of Packaging: Consumer, Food Service, Private Label, Bulk
Brands:
Del Campo

3789 Dulcette Technologies
2 Hicks Street
Lindenhurst, NY 11757
631-752-8700
Fax: 631-752-8117 sales@dulcettetech.com
Sweeteners, nutraceuticals & antioxidants
CEO: M Blum
Quality Control: M Samuels
Marketing: E Saltsberg
Sales: Luke Verdet
Estimated Sales: $500,000-1 Million
Number Employees: 7

3790 Duma Meats Inc
857 Randolph Rd
Mogadore, OH 44260-9343
330-628-3438
Fax: 330-628-2172 d.duma@sbcglobal.net
www.dumameats.com
Supplier of all kinds of cuts of meat and cheeses
President: David Duma Jr
beverley@dumameatsfarmmarket.com
Treasurer: Beverley Duma
Estimated Sales: $840,000
Number Employees: 20-49
Type of Packaging: Consumer, Food Service, Bulk

3791 Dumbee Gourmet Foods
PO Box 70159
Albany, GA 31708-0159
229-435-4800
Fax: 229-420-4108 800-569-1657
Gourmet foods
Owner: Steve Barber
President: Tammy Barber
Estimated Sales: Under $500,000
Number Employees: 1
Brands:
Dummbee Gourmet

3792 Dunbar Foods Corp
1000 S Fayetteville Ave
Dunn, NC 28334-6213
910-892-3175
Fax: 910-892-6311 www.moodydunbar.com
Processor of bell peppers, pimientos and sweet potatoes; products are certified kosher.
President: Jeff Lucas
jeff@moodydunbar.com
Estimated Sales: $10-20 Million
Number Employees: 250-499
Parent Co: Moody Dunbar, Inc.

3793 Duncan Peak Vineyards
PO Box 1473
Lafayette, CA 94549
925-283-3632
www.duncanpeak.com
Wines
President: Hubert Lenczowski
Estimated Sales: Less than $500,000
Number Employees: 2
Type of Packaging: Private Label
Brands:
Duncan

3794 Dundee Brandied Fruit Co
PO Box 445
Dundee, OR 97115-0445
503-537-2500
Fax: 503-538-8599
Brandied fruit
Owner: Richard Sadler
Estimated Sales: Under $500,000
Number Employees: 5-9
Brands:
Dundee Brandied

3795 Dundee Candy Shop
2112 Bardstown Rd
Louisville, KY 40205-1916
502-452-9266
Fax: 502-459-7981 866-877-9266
www.dundeecandy.com
Candy
Owner: Maria Moore
Estimated Sales: $390,000
Number Employees: 5-9
Brands:
Dundee Candy Shop

3796 Dundee Citrus Growers Assn
111 1st St N
Dundee, FL 33838-4002
863-439-1574
Fax: 863-439-1535 800-447-1574
info@dun-d.com www.dun-d.com
Florida citrus fruits including oranges, grapefruit, tangerines and red grapefruit
President & Chairman: W. Lindsay Raley Jr.
Executive VP & CEO: Steve B. Callaham
CFO: Mary Schaal
Quality Control Manager: Mike Mobley
Vice President of Sales: Bobby Finch
VP Human Resource: Missy McGuiness
COO: Greg Dunnahoe
VP Harvesting & Fruit Procurement: Adam Pate
Plant Manager: James Giddens
Purchasing Manager: Nyago Summers
Estimated Sales: $14.9 Million
Number Employees: 500-999
Square Footage: 375000
Type of Packaging: Consumer, Food Service
Brands:
Dun-D

3797 Dundee Groves
28421 US Highway 27
PO Box 829
Dundee, FL 33838
863-439-2284
Fax: 863-439-5049 800-294-2266
info@dundeegroves.com
www.davidsonofdundee.com
Fresh citrus fruit including; oranges, ruby red grapefruits, all natural citrus candies, coconut patties, citrus marmalades, citrus jellies, butters and orange blossom honey. Gift baskets available
President: Glen Davidson
CEO: Susan Davidson
Estimated Sales: $6 Million
Number Employees: 100-249
Number of Brands: 1
Number of Products: 112
Square Footage: 450000
Type of Packaging: Consumer, Private Label

3798 **Dundee Wine Company**
691 Highway 99W
PO Box 280
Dundee, OR 97115-0220
503-538-3922
Fax: 503-538-2055 888-427-4953
wine@argylewinery.com www.argylewinery.com
Wines
Executive Manager: Valeri Cetz
Director of Marketing: Craig Eastman
Estimated Sales: $5 Million
Number Employees: 60
Type of Packaging: Private Label
Brands:
Dundee

3799 **Dunford Bakers**
8556 S 2940 W
West Jordan, UT 84088-9660
801-304-0400
Fax: 801-304-0511 800-748-4335
donuts@dunfordbakers.com
www.dunfordbakers.com
Pastries and breads
President: Ron Stevens
Vice President: John R Stevens
VP: Gary E Gottfred
Plant Manager: Dale Hatch
Estimated Sales: $5-10 Million
Number Employees: 100-249
Type of Packaging: Consumer, Private Label, Bulk

3800 **Dungeness Development Associates**
12969 74th PL. NE
Kirkland, WA 98034
425-823-0770
Fax: 425-823-5049
Producer and importer of Dungeness Crab and Pacific Tiny Shrip
Owner: Joel Van Ornun
Contact: Tena Boggs
tenab@dungenessassoc.com
Plant Manager: Mel Corbitt
Estimated Sales: $5-10 Million
Number Employees: 20-49

3801 **Dunham's Lobster Pot**
60 Mt Blue Pond Rd
Avon, ME 04966-3301
207-639-2815
Fax: 207-639-2815
Fresh seafood including fish, clams, haddock, scallops, crab meat, mussels, oysters, shrimp, lobster and rib-eye steaks
Owner: Bruce Dunham
Co-Owner: Mary Dunham
Estimated Sales: $220 Thousand
Number Employees: 2
Type of Packaging: Food Service, Bulk

3802 **Dunham's Meats**
12907 E Wellesley Ave
Spokane Valley
Urbana, WA 99216
509-924-9821
Fax: 937-834-2411 www.dunhammeats.com
Meat products; also, slaughtering services available
Owner/VP: Barry Dunham
Estimated Sales: $1-2.5 Million
Number Employees: 5-9
Type of Packaging: Consumer, Bulk

3803 **Dunkin' Brands Inc.**
130 Royall St.
Canton, MA 02021
781-737-3000
800-859-5339
www.dunkinbrands.com
Coffee, baked goods and premium ice cream.
President/CEO: David Hoffmann
CFO: Kate Jaspon
Chief Marketing Officer: Tony Weisman
Chief Operating Officer: Scott Murphy
Year Founded: 2004
Estimated Sales: $860 Million
Number Employees: 1,163
Number of Brands: 2
Type of Packaging: Food Service
Brands:
Baskin-Robbins®
Dunkin' Donuts®

3804 **Dunn Vineyards**
805 White Cottage Rd N
Angwin, CA 94508-9616
707-965-3642
Fax: 707-965-3805 dunnvineyards@sbcglobal.net
www.dunnvineyards.com
Wines
Owner: Randy Dunn
dundineyards@sdglobal.net
Director of Marketing: Christina Dunne
Estimated Sales: $390,000
Number Employees: 1-4
Brands:
Dunn

3805 **Duplin Wine Cellars**
505 N Sycamore Street
Rose Hill, NC 28458
910-289-3888
Fax: 910-289-3094 800-774-9634
info@duplinwinery.com www.duplinwinery.com
Wines
Owner: David Fussell Jr
Director of Sales: Tabitha Fussell
Contact: Jonathan Fussell
jonathan@duplinwinery.com
Estimated Sales: $5-10 Million
Number Employees: 50
Type of Packaging: Private Label
Brands:
Duplin

3806 **Dupont Cheese**
N10140 Hwy 110
Marion, WI 54950
715-754-5424
Fax: 715-754-1313 800-895-2873
info@dupontcheeseinc.com
www.dupontcheeseinc.com
Cheese including colby, mini-horus and longhorn
President: Fred Laack
Estimated Sales: $10-20 Million
Number Employees: 20-49
Type of Packaging: Consumer

3807 **Durango Brewing Co**
3000 Main Ave
Durango, CO 81301-4245
970-247-3396
scott@durangobrewing.com
www.durangobrewing.com
Beer
Owner: Bob Beardsley
bbeardsley@durangobrewing.com
Estimated Sales: $1-2.5 Million
Number Employees: 5-9
Brands:
Durango

3808 **Durey-Libby Edible Nuts**
100 Industrial Rd
Carlstadt, NJ 07072
201-939-2775
Fax: 201-939-0386 800-332-6887
Custom roasted nuts
President: Wendy Dicker
CEO: Billy Dicker
Contact: William Dicker
billythenutman@msn.com
Estimated Sales: $1-2.5 Million
Number Employees: 20-49
Square Footage: 120000
Type of Packaging: Bulk

3809 **Durham Ellis Pecan Co**
308 S Houston St
Comanche, TX 76442-3237
325-356-5291
Fax: 325-356-3974 800-732-2629
www.durhams.com
Pecans and other nuts
Owner: Hl Dollins
hl.dollins@durhams.com
Estimated Sales: $4 Million
Number Employees: 50-99

3810 **Durkee-Mower**
2 Empire Street
Lynn, MA 01902
781-593-8007
www.marshmallowfluff.com
Manufacturer and exporter of marshmallow creme
Estimated Sales: $5-10 Million
Number Employees: 24
Square Footage: 140000
Type of Packaging: Consumer, Food Service
Brands:
Marshmallow Fluff

3811 **Dutch Ann Foods Company**
28 Col John Pitchford Pkwy
Natchez, MS 39120
601-445-5566
Fax: 601-445-8738
Frozen pie crusts
President: William Jones
Estimated Sales: $1-3 Million
Number Employees: 35
Type of Packaging: Consumer, Food Service, Private Label
Brands:
Best Way
Dutch Ann

3812 **Dutch Cheese Makers Corp**
585 Stewart Ave
Suite 318
Garden City, NY 11530-4701
631-533-9202
Fax: 631-342-8091 www.dutchcheesemakers.com
Dutch cheese
CEO: Steve Margarites
National Sales Director: Tim Sirera
Estimated Sales: $122782
Number Employees: 1-4
Type of Packaging: Private Label

3813 **Dutch Farms Inc**
700 E 107th St
Chicago, IL 60628-3806
773-660-0900
Fax: 773-660-1044 800-637-3447
support@dutchfarms.com www.dutchfarms.com
Manufacturer/processor of eggs, cheeses, dairy products, deli, bakery and meat items.
Owner: Brian Boomsma
bboomsma@dutchfarms.com
Controller: Kurt Gilbertson
VP: Rachelle Knapper
Marketing Executive: Kevin De Vries
Estimated Sales: $38 Milliom
Number Employees: 100-249
Type of Packaging: Food Service

3814 **Dutch Girl Donut Co**
19000 Woodward Ave
Detroit, MI 48203-1903
313-368-3020
Doughnuts
Owner: Cecilia Voss
Partner: Gene Timmer
Estimated Sales: $430,000
Number Employees: 10-19

3815 **(HQ)Dutch Gold Honey Inc**
2220 Dutch Gold Dr
Lancaster, PA 17601
717-393-1716
Fax: 717-393-8687 800-338-0587
info@dutchgoldhoney.com
www.dutchgoldhoney.com
Honey and honey products
VP Finance & Administration: Charles Schatzman
Operations Manager: Jody Gable
Year Founded: 1946
Estimated Sales: $20-50 Million
Number Employees: 20-49
Number of Brands: 4
Square Footage: 100000
Type of Packaging: Consumer, Food Service, Private Label, Bulk
Other Locations:
Dutch Gold Honey
Littleton NH
Brands:
Blossom Hill
Dutch Gold
Honey In the Rough
McLure's Maple

3816 **Dutch Henry Winery**
4300 Silverado Trl
Calistoga, CA 94515-9603
707-942-5771
Fax: 707-942-5512 888-224-5879
info@dutchhenry.com
Wines

Owner: Scott Chafen
info@dutchhenry.com
Customer Service: Less Chafen
Estimated Sales: $2.5-5 Million
Number Employees: 5-9
Type of Packaging: Private Label
Brands:
Dutch Henry

3817 Dutch Kitchen Bake Shop& Deli
12 John Fitch Hwy
Fitchburg, MA 01420-5902
978-345-1393
Fax: 978-345-6651 peter.raimo@yahoo.com
www.dutchkitchenbakery.com
Breads, rolls, cakes and pastries
Owner: Joe Raimo
VP: Mary Raimo
Sales Manager: Chris Raimo
peter.raimo@yahoo.com
Estimated Sales: $1.50 Million
Number Employees: 20-49
Brands:
Dutch Kitchen

3818 Dutch Packing Co., Inc.
2800 NW 112th Ave
Doral, FL 33172
305-871-3640
Fax: 305-871-3668 800-723-9249
garciasausagebrand.com
Sausage
President: Raul Rodriguez
Vice President Sales: William Rodriquez
VP Production: Victor Rodriguez
Estimated Sales: $5.2 Million
Number Employees: 36
Type of Packaging: Consumer, Food Service
Brands:
Garcia Brand

3819 Dutchess Bakery
715 Bigley Ave
Charleston, WV 25302
304-346-4237
Cookies
Owner: Edward S Rada Iii
Estimated Sales: $500,000-$1 Million
Number Employees: 5-9
Type of Packaging: Consumer

3820 Dutchland Frozen Foods
205 Main St
PO Box 148
Lester, IA 51242-7701
712-478-4349
Fax: 712-478-4554 888-497-7243
Pastry puffs and euro classic pastries
Owner: Wayne Van Wyne
CEO: Peter Van Wyhe
pvw@dutchlandfrozenfoods.com
VP: Pete Van Wyne
Number Employees: 20-49

3821 Dutterer's Home Food Service
2700 Lord Baltimore Drive
Baltimore, MD 21244-2648
410-298-3663
Fax: 410-298-1625
Food transporters of meat and refrigerated food
President: Mark Mules
Estimated Sales: $10-20 Million
Number Employees: 6
Type of Packaging: Consumer, Private Label

3822 Duval Bakery Products
1733 Evergreen Ave
Jacksonville, FL 32206-4730
904-354-7878
Fax: 904-354-7828
Stuffing and bread crumbs
Owner: Bob Gorsuch
robertgorsuch@duvalbakeryproducts.com
Plant Manager: Jim Gorsuch
Estimated Sales: $310,000
Number Employees: 5-9
Square Footage: 24000
Type of Packaging: Food Service, Private Label, Bulk

3823 Duverger
Oxnard, CA 93033
www.duvergermacarons.com
Macarons

Founder: Claire Becker

3824 Duxbury Mussel & Seafood Corporation
8 Joseph St # B
Kingston, MA 02364-1122
781-585-5517
Fax: 781-585-2976
Wholesale seafood
President: Robert Marconi

3825 Dwayne Keith Brooks Company
6628 Fiesta Ln
Orangevale, CA 95662-3554
916-988-1030
Fax: 916-988-4442
School and institutional frozen foods
President: Dwayne Brooks
Estimated Sales: $500,000
Number Employees: 2
Square Footage: 7200
Parent Co: SA Products Company
Type of Packaging: Food Service, Bulk

3826 DyStar Hilton Davis/DyStar Foam Control
2020 Front St
Cuyahoga Falls, OH 44221
330-916-6726
Dystar LP manufactures food color & process aids with two divisions focused on the food industry: DyStar Hilton Davis manufactures FD&C Dyes and Lake Color; Dystar Foam Control manufacturers Foam Blast Defoamers.
CEO/Head of Global Sales & Marketing: Eric Hopman
CFO/Vice President of Group Finance: Victor Leendertz
VP, Global Quality & Compliance Mgmt: Kevin Tan
VP, Global Human Resources: Kevin Tan
VP, Global Procurement-North Asia: Vera Huang
VP, Global Manufacturing & Supply Chain: Gerald Talhoff
Parent Co: DyStar Group

3827 Dylan's Candy Bar
1011 Third Ave, 60th St
New York, NY
866-939-5267
customerservice@dylanscandybar.com
www.dylanscandybar.com
Candy, confections

3828 Dyna Tabs LLC
1933 E 12th St
Brooklyn, NY 11229-2703
718-376-6084
sales@dynatabs.com
www.dynatabs.com
Health, wellness, beauty products including oral edible strips, aloe vera drinking gel and passion punch.
Executive Director: Harold Baum
hbaum@dynatabs.com
CFO: Setty Baum
Estimated Sales: $830,000
Number Employees: 10-19
Parent Co: Baum International, Inc
Type of Packaging: Consumer, Private Label

3829 Dynamic Confections
1050 S. 200 West
Salt Lake City, UT 84101-3003
801-355-4422
Fax: 801-355-5546
Quality chocolates
CEO: Taz Murray
President: Keith Elliot
CFO: Jim Loveridge
Executive Assistant: Bonnie Labrum
Estimated Sales: $28 Million
Number Employees: 5

3830 Dynamic Foods
1001 E 33rd St
Lubbock, TX 79404-1816
806-723-5600
Fax: 806-723-5680 jsullivan@dynamicfoods.com
www.dynamicfoods.com
Baked goods, cakes, muffins, cornbread, pies, cobblers, frozen dinner rolls, casseroles, side dishes, soups, sauces, glazes, mexican foods, breaded fish, bread sticks

President: Mike Blasdell
Executive Manager: Gabriel Olivarez
Estimated Sales: $4 Million
Number Employees: 100-249
Number of Brands: 2
Number of Products: 100+
Square Footage: 225000
Type of Packaging: Food Service, Private Label
Brands:
Dynamic Foods
Private Label

3831 Dynamic Health Laboratories Inc.
110 Bridge St
Brooklyn, NY 11201
718-472-4009
Fax: 718-392-9301 800-396-2114
info@dynamichealth.com
www.dynamichealth.com
Liquid health products
President: Bruce Burwick
VP: Dan Gombo
Sales Manager: Jane Medress
Contact: Dennis Amaral
dennis@marathonconsulting.com
Estimated Sales: $18 Million
Number Employees: 30

3832 Dynapro International
451 N Main St
Kaysville, UT 84037-1114
801-621-1413
Fax: 801-621-8258 800-877-1413
sales@dynaprointernational.com
www.dynaprointernational.com
Manufacturer and exporter of vitamins and herbal supplements
Owner: Bailey Hall
sales@dynaprointernational.com
Marketing Director: Gary Hoffman
Estimated Sales: Less Than $500,000
Number Employees: 5-9
Square Footage: 15600

3833 (HQ)Dynic USA Corp
4750 NE Dawson Creek Dr
Hillsboro, OR 97124-5799
503-693-1070
Fax: 503-648-1185 800-326-1249
enrique@dynic.com www.dynic.com
Labeling and printing products
President: Gwen Robinson
leej@smccd.edu
CEO/President: Shigeru Tamura
Director of Marketing: Mindy Nybert
Sales Engineer: Cesar Santa
Customer Service Rep: James Brandow
Estimated Sales: $25 Million
Number Employees: 50-99
Parent Co: Dynic Corporation
Other Locations:
Dynic UK Ltd
Cardiff, South Wales UK
Dynic Corporation
Minatoku, Tokyo, Japan HK
Brands:
Cabin Air Filters
Cetus Textile Fabrics
Oled Desiccant
Sirius Ttr

3834 (HQ)E & J Gallo Winery
600 Yosemite Blvd.
Modesto, CA 95354-2760
877-687-9463
www.gallo.com
Wines, brandy and sparkling wine.
Chief Marketing Officer: Stephanie Gallo
Year Founded: 1933
Estimated Sales: Over $1 Billion
Number Employees: 5000-9999
Type of Packaging: Consumer, Food Service
Other Locations:
E&J Gallo Winery
Mississauga ON
E&J Gallo Winery
Fresno CA
E&J Gallo Winery
Livingston CA
Brands:
Argiano®
Allegrini
Alamos®
Andre®
Apothic®

Barefoot Bubbly®
Barefoot®
Bear Flag®
Ballatore®
Bartles & Jaymes®
Boone's Farm®
Brancaia®
Bridlewood Estate Winery®
Bella Sera®
Carnivor®
Clarendon Hills®
Maso Canali®
Columbia Winery®
Covey Run Winery®
Carlo Rossi®
Canyon Road®
Davinci®
Dancing Bull®
Dark Horse®
Don Miguel Gascon®
Ecco Domani®
Gallo Family Vineyards®
Edna Valley Vineyard®
Copper Ridge Vineyards®
Livingston Cellars®
Ghost Pines®
Jermann®
J Vineyards & Winery®
La Marca®
Las Rocas®
Liberty Creek®
Louis M. Martini®
Laguna®
MacMurray Estate®
Martin Codax®
Dolcea®
Madria Sangria®
Mirassou®
Orin Swift Cellars®
Polka Dot®
Prophecy®
Pieropan®
Peter Vella®
Frei Brothers Reserve®
Renato Ratti®
Red Rock Winery®
Redwood Creek®
Starborough®
Saint Clair Family Estate®
Storypoint®
Fleur de Mer®
Souverain®
Talbott Vineyards®
Tisdale Vineyards®
Turning Leaf®
The Naked Grape®
Tott's®
Tornatore®
Vin Vault®
William Hill Estate®
Whitehaven®
Wild Vines®
William Hill Estate®
Whitehaven®
Wild Vines®
WM. Wycliff Vineyards®
Rancho Zabaco®

3835 E & J Gallo Winery

3387 Dry Creek Rd.
Healdsburg, CA 95448

707-431-1946
www.gallo.com

Wines
Estimated Sales: $1-2.5 Million
Number Employees: 1-4
Parent Co: E & J Gallo Winery

3836 E A Sween Co

16101 W 78th St
Eden Prairie, MN 55344-5798

952-937-9440
Fax: 952-937-0186 800-328-8184
tsween@deliexpress.com www.deliexpress.com

Prepackaged individual sandwiches
President/CEO: Tom Sween
tom.sween@easween.com
CFO: Dick Pearson
Sr. Vice President of Foodservice Sales: Bill Bastian
R&D: Grant Nellis
VP Product Safety: Lavonne Kucera
Marketing: Cheryl Peterson
Vice President of Operations: Tim Engmark
Production: Curt Karger
Plant Manager: Curt Karger
Purchasing: Janet Robling
Estimated Sales: $150,000
Number Employees: 1-4
Parent Co: E.A. Sween Company
Type of Packaging: Consumer
Brands:
Deli Express
Sensible Carbs

3837 E L K Run Vineyards

15113 Liberty Rd
Mt Airy, MD 21771-9502

301-363-3156
Fax: 410-875-2009 800-414-2513
elk_run@msn.com www.elkrun.com

Wines
President: Neil Bassford
neil@elkrun.com
Treasurer: Neil Bassford
Marketing Director: Carol Wilson
Estimated Sales: $1-2.5 Million
Number Employees: 1-4
Type of Packaging: Private Label
Brands:
Elk Run

3838 E Waldo Ward & Son Marmalades

273 E Highland Ave
Sierra Madre, CA 91024-2014

626-355-1218
Fax: 626-355-5292 800-355-9273
service@waldoward.com www.waldoward.com

Manufacturer and importer of gourmet foods including olives, preserves, jellies, marmalades, brandied fruits and sauces including meat, relish and seafood cocktail; exporter of marmalades. Services, private labeling and anufacturing tolarge and small companies. Also offers consulting services
Owner: Richard Ward
richard@waldoward.com
VP: Jeffrey Ward
Estimated Sales: $810,000
Number Employees: 10-19
Number of Brands: 2
Number of Products: 150
Square Footage: 40000
Type of Packaging: Consumer, Private Label
Brands:
E. Waldo Ward
Sierra Madre Brand

3839 E&H Packing Company

2453 Riopelle St
Detroit, MI 48207

313-567-8286
Fax: 313-567-8287

Beef
Owner/President: Robert Buzar
Treasurer: Bob Buzar
Estimated Sales: $670,000
Number Employees: 5
Type of Packaging: Consumer, Food Service

3840 E-Fish-Ent Fish Company

1941 Goodridge Road
Sooke, BC V0S 0C6
Canada

250-642-4007
Fax: 250-642-4057 www.e-fish-ent.ca

Manufacturer and exporter of smoked salmon in retort pouch; meat products in pouch, stews, chili, curry.
President: Bryan Mooney
VP: Linda Mooney
Number Employees: 4
Square Footage: 32000
Type of Packaging: Private Label

3841 E. Gagnon & Fils

405 Rte 102
St Therese-De-Gaspe, QC G0C 3B0
Canada

418-385-3011
Fax: 418-385-3021

Manufacturer and exporter of frozen snow crabs, crab
President: Roger Gagnon
Estimated Sales: $2.3 Million
Number Employees: 5
Type of Packaging: Food Service

3842 E. H. Gourmet

575 Lynnhaven Pkwy
Suite 300
Virginia Beach, VA 23452

757-431-1996
info@ehgourmet.com
ehgourmet.com

Hot sauces; sea salt; seasonings; cocktail mixes
Co-Owner: Kerry Takach
Type of Packaging: Private Label

3843 E.C. Phillips & Son

PO Box 7090
Ketchikan, AK 99901-3235

907-247-7975
Fax: 907-225-7250 ecp@ecphillipsalaska.com
www.ecphillipsalaska.com

Buyers and processors of salmon
Owner: Colleen Picillo
CEO: Larry Elliot
VP: Michael Cusack
Estimated Sales: $10-20 Million
Number Employees: 60
Type of Packaging: Consumer

3844 E.D. Smith Foods Ltd

8 Burford Rd
Hamilton, ON L8E 5B1
Canada

905-573-1207
inquiry@edsmith.com
www.edsmith.com

Manufacturer and exporter of jams, ketchup, pie fillings, barbecue and pasta sauces, fruit toppings, salsas and syrups
President/CEO: Michael Burrows
VP Finance: David Smith
VP Operations: Dorothy Pethick
Type of Packaging: Consumer, Food Service, Private Label, Bulk
Brands:
E.D. Smith
Habitant
Lea & Perrins

3845 E.F. Lane & Son

744 Kevin Ct
Oakland, CA 94621

510-569-8980
Fax: 510-569-0240

Manufacturer and exporter of honey and peanut products
Manager: Phyllis Tut
Estimated Sales: $500,000-$1 Million
Number Employees: 1-4
Type of Packaging: Consumer, Food Service, Private Label, Bulk

3846 E.W. Bowker Company

581 New Lasbon
Pemberton, NJ 08068

609-894-9508
Fax: 609-894-2165 ewbowker@yahoo.com

Fresh cranberries and blueberries
President: Ernest Bowker
Estimated Sales: $210,000
Number Employees: 3
Type of Packaging: Consumer, Food Service, Bulk

3847 (HQ)E.W. Knauss & Son

625 East Broad Street
Quakertown, PA 18951-1713

215-536-4220
Fax: 215-536-1129 800-648-4220
www.knaussfoods.com

Sliced dried beef products including beefsticks, beef jerky, hot sausage and pickled meat products.
CEO: Robert Longacre
VP Sales: William Carter
Estimated Sales: $20-50 Million
Number Employees: 50-99

Number of Brands: 2
Square Footage: 100000
Type of Packaging: Consumer, Food Service, Private Label, Bulk
Brands:
Carson's
Knauss

3848 **ECOM Agroindustrial Corporation Ltd**
Av Etienne Guillemin 16
PO Box 64
Pully, CH-1009
Switzerland
www.ecomtrading.com
Cotton, cocoa, coffee and sugar.
CFO: Daniel Willett
Year Founded: 1849
Estimated Sales: $5.1 Billion
Number Employees: 6,000
Type of Packaging: Consumer, Food Service, Private Label, Bulk

3849 **EDCO Food Products Inc**
2815 Packerland Dr # 23
P.O. Box 12511
Hobart, WI 54313-6182
920-499-7651
Fax: 920-499-8023 800-255-3768
sales@edcofood.com www.edcofood.biz
Processor and importer of peppers including jalapeno, serrano, sport and cascabella; also, cauliflower buttons, chipotle powder and pickled vegetables
President: James Manning
accounting@edcofood.com
VP: Edward Manning
VP: Sylvia Roman
Business Development: David J. Sinkula
Customer Service & Logistics: James Gumtow
Estimated Sales: $3-5 Million
Number Employees: 5-9
Square Footage: 64000
Type of Packaging: Food Service, Private Label, Bulk

3850 **EFCO Products Inc**
130 Smith St
Poughkeepsie, NY 12601
800-284-3326
info@efcoproducts.com www.efcoproducts.com
Leading supplier of mixes, fruit and creme style fillings, jellies, jams and concentrated icing fruits to the baking industry.
CEO: David Miller
Vice President: Andy Herzing
Senior Director of Sales & Marketing: Mark Lowman
Director of Manufacturing Operations: Veronica Miller
Year Founded: 1903
Estimated Sales: $2.5-5 Million
Number Employees: 50-99

3851 **EFFi Foods**
11620 Wilshire Blvd
Suite 900
Los Angeles, CA 90025
310-582-5938
Fax: 310-388-8798 www.effifoods.com
Chickpea granola
Co-Founder & CEO: Johnny Fayad
Co-Founder & COO: Ali Kothari
Type of Packaging: Consumer
Brands:
EFFI

3852 **EIWA America Inc.**
19301 Pacific Gateway Dr
Suite 210
Torrance, CA 90502
310-327-7222
Fax: 310-327-7352 eiwamm.co.jp
Marshmellows and candy
CEO: Hiroya Miyajima
Year Founded: 2010
Estimated Sales: $150000
Number Employees: 3
Type of Packaging: Private Label
Brands:
Hello Kitty
Heart
EIWA
Suzuki Eikodo
Ginbis

3853 **EJZ Foods**
Winston-Salem, NC 27106
tryzen.com
Hazelnut milk chocolate pudding

3854 **ELP Inc**
366 Grant St
Elizabeth, CO 80107
303-688-2240
Fax: 303-688-2240
Packer of meat including beef, lamb, goat and pork
President: Mike Hundley
VP: Robert Hundley
Estimated Sales: $1-2.5 Million
Number Employees: 10-19
Type of Packaging: Consumer

3855 **EMD Performance Materials**
One International Plaza
#300
Philadelphia, PA 19113
908-591-7496
Fax: 484-652-5749 888-367-3275
Specialty testing products for the Food and Beverage industry including Microbiology Culture Media featuring granulated media for safety and convenience; the MAS-100 Eco, a lightweight, portable air sampling instrument; the HYLiTE 2system, a portable system for determining the cleanliness of surfaces and work spaces; and Test Strip Kits for rapid testing of Ions and pH measurement. Manufactures a mineral based line of colors for use in foods, dietary supplements and drugs.
President/CEO: Meiken Krebs
Contact: Matthew Girard
mgirard@emdchemicals.com
CFO: Klaus Rueth
Vice President: Octavio Diaz
Research & Development: Jim Morgera
Quality Control: Stephen Bates
Marketing Director: Rebecca Vaiarelli
Key Account Manager: Taina Franke
Public Relations: Rina Spatafore
Operations Manager: Thorsten Hartis
Production Manager: John Alestra
Plant Manager: Bob Jones
Purchasing Manager: Ron Wisda
Estimated Sales: $10-25 Million
Number Employees: 500-999
Parent Co: Merck KgaA Darmstadt

3856 **EMD Sales Inc**
2010 Washington Blvd
Baltimore, MD 21230-1736
410-385-3023
Fax: 301-322-4504 emdsales@aol.com
www.emdsalesinc.com
International foods distributors of spices, cheeses, groceries, candies, refrigerated and frozen products
Contact: Arly Aguirre
arly.aguirre@emdsalesinc.com
Estimated Sales: $640,000
Number Employees: 50-99

3857 **EOS Estate Winery**
2300 Airport Rd
Paso Robles, CA 93446-8549
805-591-8050
Fax: 805-239-2317 800-249-9463
customerservice@eosvintage.com
www.eosvintage.com
Wines
Partner: Frank Arciero Jr
Partner: Fern Underwood
CFO: Pati Withers
Marketing: Christopher Vix
Sales: Luis Cota
Public Relations: Denise McLean
Operations: Steve Felten
Production: Leslie Melendez
Plant Manager: Gary Cargill
Purchase Manager: Pat Withers
Estimated Sales: Less Than $500,000
Number Employees: 1-4
Number of Brands: 4
Type of Packaging: Private Label
Brands:
Aruero
Cupagranols
Eos
Novella

3858 **ERBL**
2525 Commerce Way
Vista, CA 92081
760-599-6088
Fax: 760-599-6089 800-275-3725
support@coromega.com www.coromega.com
Omega-3 dietary supplements.
Manager: Suzanne Goodrich
President, Chief Operating Officer: Frank Morley
Estimated Sales: $5-10 Million
Number Employees: 10-19

3859 **Eagle Brand**
1 Strawberry Lane
Orrville, OH 44667-0280
888-656-3245
www.eaglebrand.com
Sweetened, condensed milk

3860 **(HQ)Eagle Coffee Co Inc**
1027 Hillen St
Baltimore, MD 21202-4132
410-685-5893
Fax: 410-528-0369 contactus@eaglecoffee.com
www.eaglecoffee.com
Restaurant and gourmet coffees, coffee machines and grinders and coffee beans; serving the food service market
Owner: Nick Constantine
eaglecoffee@aol.com
Controller: Tom Brooks
VP: Jacqueline Parris
Estimated Sales: $1.6 Million
Number Employees: 10-19
Square Footage: 120000
Type of Packaging: Food Service, Private Label
Other Locations:
Eagle Coffee Co.
Baltimore MD

3861 **Eagle Crest Vineyards LLC**
7107 Vineyard Rd
Conesus, NY 14435-9521
585-346-2321
Fax: 585-346-2322 800-977-7117
will@onehda.com www.eaglecrestvineyards.com
Sacramental and table wine
VP: Bob Quinn
Production Manager: Rose Michaels
Estimated Sales: $2.5-5 Million
Number Employees: 5-9

3862 **Eagle Family Foods**
4020 Kinross Lakes Pkwy
Richfield, OH 44286
888-656-3245
eaglefoods.com
Snack foods, sweetened condensed milk and evaporated milk products
CEO: Bernard Kreilman
CFO: Joe Sinicropi
Vice President, Finance: Dan Gentile
Vice President, Marketing: Corinne Kelly
Vice President, Sales: Bill Iggins
Vice President, Operations: Rob Miller
Year Founded: 2016
Number Employees: 48
Brands:
Eagle Brand
Borden
PET
Milnot
G.H. Cretors
Skinny Sticks
Popcorn, Indiana

3863 **Eagle Ice Cream Company**
90 Broadway Avenue
Cleveland, OH 44146-2059
440-232-0085
Fax: 216-591-2966
Ice Cream
VP: Richard Nye
Estimated Sales: $2.5-5 Million
Number Employees: 20-49
Parent Co: Riser Foods

3864 **Eagle Rock Food Co**
1225 12th St NW
Albuquerque, NM 87104-2113
505-323-1183
Meat processing
Owner: Mike Perea
Estimated Sales: $1-3 Million
Number Employees: 1-4

3865 **Eagle Seafood Producers**
56 N 3rd Street
Brooklyn, NY 11211-3925
718-963-0939
Fax: 718-963-1306
Fresh and frozen seafood
President: Mark Rudes
VP: Donald Draghi
Estimated Sales: $10-20 Million
Number Employees: 20-49
Type of Packaging: Food Service

3866 **Earnest Eats**
444 S Cedros Ave
Suite 175
Solana Beach, CA 92075
858-299-4238
Fax: 858-793-3662 earnesteats.com
Superfood cereal, oatmeal and bars
Co-Founder & President: Andrew Aussie
Sales: Andrew Brayton
Year Founded: 2007
Type of Packaging: Consumer
Brands:
EARNEST EATS

3867 **Earth & Vine ProvisionsInc**
160 Flocchini Cir
Lincoln, CA 95648-1700
916-434-8399
Fax: 916-434-8398 888-723-8463
customerservice@earthnvine.com
www.earthnvine.com
Jams, sauces, beverage elixirs and dressings
Owner: Tressa Cooper
earthnvine@yahoo.com
CEO: Ron Cooper
Number Employees: 10-19

3868 **Earth Balance**
1600 Pearl St
Suite 300
Boulder, CO 80302
866-234-6429
www.earthbalancenatural.com
Spreads, nut butters, dressings, crackers and snacks
Parent Co: Boulder Brands
Type of Packaging: Consumer
Brands:
EARTH BALANCE

3869 **Earth Circle Organics**
12745 Earhart Ave
Auburn, CA 95602
877-922-3663
earthcircleorganics.com
Organic ingredients
President & COO: Herb Heller
Founder & CEO: Eric Botner
Vice President, Sales & Marketing: Claire Modjeski
Type of Packaging: Consumer, Bulk

3870 **Earth Island**
9201 Owensmouth Ave
Chatsworth, CA 91311-5854
818-725-2820
Fax: 818-725-2812 888-394-3949
info@followyourheart.com
www.betterthanmayo.com
Vegan mayonnaise, dips, cheeses, and salad dressings.
Owner: Robert Goldberg
bob@followyourheart.com
Co-Owner: Paul Lewin
Estimated Sales: $1-3 Million
Number Employees: 50-99
Square Footage: 12000
Type of Packaging: Consumer, Food Service, Private Label, Bulk
Brands:
VEGENAISE
VEGAN GOURMET
FOLLOW YOUR HEART

3871 **Earth Science**
475 N Sheridan St
Corona, CA 92880
951-371-7565
Fax: 909-371-0509
Vitamin C products
President: Kristine Schoenauer
VP: Michael Rutledge
Contract Sales Manager: Diane Smart
Contact: Sergio Aguirre
saguirre@cosmedxscience.com
Number Employees: 100-249
Square Footage: 160000
Type of Packaging: Consumer, Bulk

3872 **Earth Song Whole Foods**
4880 San Juan Avenue
Suite 216
Fair Oaks, CA 95628-4719
916-332-1355
Fax: 916-332-1355 877-327-8476
Vegan natural food products
Owner: Julie Rogers
Estimated Sales: $300,000-500,000
Number Employees: 1-4
Brands:
Earth Song Whole Food Bars
Grandpa's Secret Omega-3 Muesli

3873 **Earth Source Organics**
1370 Decision Street
Suite C
Vista, CA 92081
760-734-1867
Fax: 760-734-1576
www.righteouslyrawchocolate.com
Chocolate
Contact: Brittany England
brittany@earthsourceorganics.com

3874 **Earth Source Organics**
1235 Activity Drive, Suite E
Vista, CA 92081
760-734-1867
Fax: 760-734-1576 info@earthsourceorganics.com
www.righteouslyrawchocolate.com
Gourmet organic raw chocolate bars. Earth Source Organics provides contract food packaging services exclusively for Certified Organic, Vegan, and Kosher raw foods that are Non-GMO, Allergen Free, Nut Free, and Gluten Free.
President: Audrey Darrow
Contact: Dan England
dan@earthsourceorganics.com
Type of Packaging: Consumer
Brands:
RIGHTEOUSLY RAW CHOCOLATE

3875 **Earthbound Farm**
1721 San Juan Hwy
San Jn Bautista, CA 95045-9780
831-623-7881
800-690-3200
www.earthboundfarm.com
Organic salads, vegetables, frozen fruit, herbs, frozen vegetables, fruit, dried fruit, and snacks.
President: Myra Rubin
myra@ebfarm.com
CEO: Charles Sweat
Chief Financial Officer: Jeff Cook
VP, Product Innovation: Nathalie Fontanilla
Chief Customer & Marketing Officer: Craig Hope
VP, Sales/Customer Service & Product Mgm: Steve Koran
Sr VP, Operations & Organic Integrity: Will Daniels
Chief Production Officer: Otto Kramm
Senior Vice President, Supply Management: Todd Kodet
Number Employees: 1000-4999
Type of Packaging: Consumer

3876 **Earthrise Nutritionals**
2151 Michelson Dr # 258
Suite 258
Irvine, CA 92612-1382
949-623-0980
Fax: 949-623-0990 800-949-7473
www.earthrise.com
Spirulina based green food nutritional products
President: Hiroyuki Mochizuki
CEO: Sumi Hitoshi
Controller: Adrian Hsu
VP: Rob Kelly
Sales & Marketing Division Manager: Lee Crockett
National Sales: Shiro Nobunaga
COO: Taro Ichimoto
Facility Production Mgr: Antonio Flores
Estimated Sales: Less Than $500,000
Number Employees: 1-4
Type of Packaging: Private Label

3877 **Easley Winery**
205 N College Ave
Indianapolis, IN 46202-3799
317-636-4516
Fax: 317-974-0128 info@easleywinery.com
www.easleywinery.com
Table wine
President/Winemaker: Mark Easley
measley@500festival.com
Banquet Manager: Meredit Easley
Estimated Sales: $2.6 Million
Number Employees: 10-19
Type of Packaging: Consumer, Food Service, Private Label, Bulk
Brands:
Cape Sandy Vineyards
Easley's

3878 **(HQ)East Balt Commissary Inc**
1801 W 31st Pl
Chicago, IL 60608-6199
773-376-4444
Fax: 773-376-8137 800-621-8555
www.eastbalt.com
Classic buns, ciabatta breads, and specialty breads
CEO: Mark Bendix
EVP US Region: Lianying "Kelley" Wang
EVP Research & Development: Joe McDilda
VP Global Quality: Mike LaBosky
VP Sales: Daniel Harrison
Estimated Sales: $20-50 Million
Number Employees: 100-249
Type of Packaging: Private Label

3879 **East Coast Fresh Cuts Inc**
9001 Whiskey Bottom Rd
Laurel, MD 20723
www.eastcoastfresh.com
Fresh cut vegetables including onions, peppers, carrots, celery, etc
CEO: John Corso
CFO: Bob Lahmann
VP, Sales: Jim McWhorter
VP, Customer Care: Tracy Moore
VP, Purchasing: Jason Lambros
Year Founded: 1997
Estimated Sales: $53.35 Million
Number Employees: 300
Square Footage: 330000
Parent Co: Coastal Sun Belt
Type of Packaging: Food Service, Private Label, Bulk

3880 **East Dayton Meat & Poultry**
1546 Keystone Ave
Dayton, OH 45403
937-253-6185
Fax: 937-253-1040 www.eastdaytonmeat.com
Beef, pork and deer; fresh cut meat, marinades, seasonings, spices, rubs, cheeses, vegetables and salads
Owner: Mike Lakey
Year Founded: 1944
Estimated Sales: $20-50 Million
Number Employees: 5-9
Type of Packaging: Consumer, Food Service

3881 **East Indies Coffee & Tea Co**
7 Keystone Dr
Lebanon, PA 17042-9791
717-228-2000
Fax: 717-228-2540 800-220-2326
wprog@eastindiescoffeeandtea.com
www.eastindiescoffeeandtea.com
Gourmet and flavored coffees and teas
Owner: Philip Auman
pauman@eastindiescoffeeandtea.com
VP: Mim Enck
Estimated Sales: Less Than $500,000
Number Employees: 1-4

3882 **East Kentucky Foods**
739 Ecton Road
Winchester, KY 40391
859-744-2218
Fax: 859-744-8511
Packaged frozen goods
President: Greg Ginter
Estimated Sales: $1.4 Million
Number Employees: 7

3883 **East Point Seafood Company**
350 Blake Street
Raymond, WA 98586
360-875-5507
Fax: 360-875-5417 888-317-8459
onlinesales@eastpointseafood.com
www.eastpointseafood.com
Seafood
Owner: Joel Van Ornun
onlinesales@eastpointseafood.com
Estimated Sales: $1-3 Million
Number Employees: 5-9
Type of Packaging: Private Label

3884 **East Poultry Co**
2615 E 6th St
Austin, TX 78702-3900
512-476-5367
Fax: 512-476-5360 www.eastpoultry.com
Poultry and eggs
President: Ken Aune
eastpoultry@austin.rr.com
Estimated Sales: $4.10 Million
Number Employees: 10-19
Square Footage: 54000
Type of Packaging: Food Service, Bulk

3885 **East Shore Specialty Foods**
643 Cardinal Ln
Po Box 379
Hartland, WI 53029-2316
262-367-8988
Fax: 262-367-9081 800-236-1069
customerservice@eastshorefoods.com
www.eastshorefoods.com
Gourmet mustards, pretzels, chocolate sauces
Owner: Jeri Mesching
jeri@eastshorefoods.com
CEO: Khristian Graves
Manager: Greg Seales
Marketing: Kristin Graves
Estimated Sales: $760,000
Number Employees: 10-19
Type of Packaging: Private Label

3886 **East Side Winery/Oak Ridge Vineyards**
6100 E Hwy 12 (Victor Rd)
Lodi, CA 95240
209-369-4758
Fax: 209-369-0202
orderprocessing@oakridgewinery.com
www.oakridgewinery.com
Bottled wines
Owner: Rudy Maggio
Director of Marketing: Marc Lohnes
Director of U.S. Sales and Marketing: Marc M. Lohnes
Estimated Sales: $10-20 Million
Number Employees: 20-49
Type of Packaging: Consumer, Food Service, Private Label, Bulk

3887 **East Wind Inc**
1361 County Road 547
Tecumseh, MO 65760-7310
417-679-4682
Fax: 417-679-4684 www.eastwind.org
Peanut and organic peanut butters; also, cashew and almond butters and tahini
Manager: Lena Berglund
Sales & Marketing: Shaya Kraut
Sales Director: Sam Lucas
Contact: Virgil Carpenter
virgil.eastwind@gmail.com
Purchasing: Jaime Escobedo
Estimated Sales: $2 Million
Number Employees: 50-99
Square Footage: 28000
Parent Co: East Wind Community
Type of Packaging: Consumer, Food Service, Private Label
Brands:
East Wind
East Wind Almond
East Wind Cashew
East Wind Organic Peanut Butter
East Wind Peanut
East Wind Tahini

3888 **Eastern Brewing Corporation**
PO Box 497
Hammonton, NJ 08037
609-561-2700
Fax: 609-561-9441
Beer
President: Louis Fatatm
Treasurer: James Penza Jr
Estimated Sales: Less than $500,000
Number Employees: 2

3889 **(HQ)Eastern Fish Company**
Glennpointe Centre East
300 Frank W Burr Blvd Ste 30
Teaneck, NJ 07666
201-801-0800
Fax: 201-801-0802 800-526-9066
www.easternfish.com
Manufacturer and importer of farm raised shrimp and other seafood, bay and sea scallops, lobster, king crab legs and claws, snow crab clusters, yellow fin tuna
Founder: Bill Bloom
President: Eric Bloom
Secretary: Charna Bloom
Vice President: Lee Bloom
Estimated Sales: $6.7 Million
Number Employees: 30
Square Footage: 18000
Type of Packaging: Private Label
Other Locations:
Norwestern Sales Office
Kingston WA
Western Sales Office
Anaheim CA
Northeastern Sales Office
Gloucester MA
Southeastern Sales Office
Coral Springs FL
Brands:
Sail

3890 **Eastern Food IndustriesInc**
2832 S County Trl
East Greenwich, RI 02818-1742
401-884-8798
Fax: 401-884-3552 www.chefaroni.com
Pasta sauces
President: Henry Caniglia
h.caniglia@chefaroni.com
VP: Stephen Caniglia
Estimated Sales: $525,000
Number Employees: 5-9

3891 **Eastern Sea Products**
11 Addison Avenue
Scoudouc, NB E4P 3N3
Canada
506-532-6111
Fax: 506-532-9111 800-565-6364
maurice@easternsea.ca
Manufacturer and exporter of salted and smoked seafood: herring, mackerel, salmon
President: Maurice Allain
Director: Joanne Allain
Estimated Sales: $1.3 Million
Number Employees: 10
Number of Brands: 2
Number of Products: 10
Square Footage: 48000
Type of Packaging: Consumer, Private Label
Brands:
Cape Royal
Seapro

3892 **Eastern Seafood Co**
1020 W Hubbard St
Chicago, IL 60642-6526
312-243-2090
Fax: 312-243-9467
Seafood
President: Mario Falco
easternseafood@att.net
Estimated Sales: $730 Thousand
Number Employees: 5-9

3893 **Eastern Shore Tea**
9 W Aylesbury Rd # T
Lutherville, MD 21093-4121
410-561-5079
Fax: 410-561-4816 800-823-1408
bct@baltcoffee.com
Tea including whole leaf and bagged
President: Stanley Constantine
sconstantine@easternshoretea.com
CEO: Janice Burns
Estimated Sales: $5-9.9 Million
Number Employees: 5-9
Type of Packaging: Consumer
Brands:
Baltimore Tea

3894 **Eastern Tea Corp**
1 Engelhard Dr
Monroe Twp, NJ 08831-3722
609-860-1100
Fax: 609-860-1105 800-221-0865
www.bromleytea.com
Manufacturer, importer and exporter of packaged and loose tea; also, tea bags and tapioca
President: Paul Barbakoff
paul@bromleytea.com
Vice President: Ira Barbakoff
VP of Manufacturing: Glenn Barbakoff
Estimated Sales: $5-10 Million
Number Employees: 50-99
Square Footage: 360000
Type of Packaging: Consumer, Food Service, Private Label

3895 **Eastrise Trading Corp.**
16025 Arrow Hwy Ste A
Baldwin Park, CA 91706-2063
Fax: 626-330-0205 info@eastriseteas.com
www.eastriseteas.com
Certified organic teas
Owner: Stephen Chau
Treasurer: Lydia Chao
Contact: Stephen Chal
info@foojoyteas.com
Estimated Sales: $1-2.5 Million
Number Employees: 8
Brands:
Rare Teas

3896 **Eastside Deli Supply**
2601 W Main St
Lansing, MI 48917
517-485-4630
Fax: 517-485-7904 800-349-6694
products@eastsidedeli.com
Fresh prepared deli sandwiches and beef jerky
President: Jeffrey Jacobs
Route Sales Manager: Kevin Hedley
Contact: Jeff Jacobs
jjacobs@eastsidedeli.com
Estimated Sales: $7.5 Million
Number Employees: 50
Square Footage: 10000
Type of Packaging: Food Service
Brands:
Eastside Deli
Fresh From the Deli
Tillamook Country Smoker

3897 **Eastside Seafood**
1248 Jeffersonville Rd
Macon, GA 31217-4335
478-743-1888
Fax: 478-272-5800
Seafood
Owner: Riccardo Del Mastro
Estimated Sales: Less Than $500,000
Number Employees: 1-4

3898 **Easy Lift Equipment Co Inc**
2 Mill Park Ct
Newark, DE 19713-1986
302-737-8784
Fax: 302-737-7333 800-233-1800
sales@easylifteqpt.com www.easylifteqpt.com
Manufacturers of Drum & Roll handling Equipment
President: Lorea Eastbrun
eastbrun@easylifteqpt.com
Estimated Sales: $5-10 Million
Number Employees: 5-9

3899 **Eat Dutch Waffles, LLC**
69 W. 500 S.
Orem, UT 84058
801-319-4788
www.eatdutchwaffles.com
Manufacturer of stroopwafels.
Founder: Joost Kling

3900 **Eat It Corporation**
4002 2nd Avenue
Brooklyn, NY 11232
718-768-7950
Fax: 718-832-0406 eatitcorp@aol.com
Soft drinks
President: John Ra
General Manager: Antonio Pichardo

3901 **Eat My Waffles**
Cardiff By The Sea, CA 92007
www.eatmywaffles.com
Waffle mix

3902 **Eat Real Snacks USA**
1860 Sandy Plains Rd
Suite 204-125
Marietta, GA 30066
404-432-0842
sales@cofresh.co.uk
eatrealsnacks.com
Organic chips
Director: Priyesh Patel
Type of Packaging: Private Label
Other Locations:
Headquarters
Leicester UK

3903 **Eat This**
75 Headquarters Rd.
Erwinna, PA 18920
215-391-5807
info@eatthisyum.com
www.eatthisyum.com
Manufacturer of sweet jams and marmalades.
Founder: Gino Schrijver

3904 **Eat Your Coffee**
333 Newbury St
Unit 2B
Boston, MA 02115
info@eatyour.coffee
www.eatyour.coffee
Naturally-caffeinated snacks
Co-Founder & CEO: Johnny Fayad
Co-Founder & COO: Ali Kothari
Type of Packaging: Consumer
Brands:
EAT YOUR COFFEE

3905 **Eat Zi's Market & Bakery**
3403 Oak Lawn Ave
Dallas, TX 75219-4215
214-526-1515
Fax: 214-526-1540 feedback@eatzis.com
www.eatzis.com
Market and bakery
Founder: Phil Romano
CEO: Adam Romo
Vice President: Barry Partos
bpartos@eatzis.com
Number Employees: 100-249

3906 **EatKeenwa, Inc.**
179 Beacon Ave.
Jersey City, NJ 07306
855-453-3692
Manufacturer of quinoa cluster snacks.
Founder: Blake Niemann
Brands:
Keenwa Krunch

3907 **EatPastry LLC**
11545 Sorrento Valley Rd
San Diego, CA 92121
858-755-7456
info@eatpastry.com
www.eatpastry.com
vegan cookie dough and baking mixes; gluten free products.
Co-founder: Alfredo Elias
Co-founder: Jessie Williams
Type of Packaging: Consumer

3908 **Eatem Foods Co**
1829 Gallagher Dr
Vineland, NJ 08360-1548
856-692-1663
Fax: 856-692-0847 800-683-2836
sales@eatemfoods.com www.eatemfoods.com
Food base manufacturing; supplier of savory flavor systems, flavor concentrates, broth concentrates and seasoning bases.
Vice President: Gerrie Bouchard
gerriebouchard@gmail.com
Chief Technical Officer: John Randazzi
Chief Financial Officer: Danine Freeman
Vice President, Treasurer: Mario Riviello
Director, R&D: Bill Cawley
Marketing Manager: Gerrie Bouchard
Vice President, Sales: Don Witherspoon
Director of Operations: Jerry Santo
Estimated Sales: $14 Million
Number Employees: 50-99
Square Footage: 12916
Type of Packaging: Consumer, Food Service, Bulk
Brands:
Eatem

3909 **Eating Evolved**
Setauket, NY 11733
631-675-2440
eatingevolved.com
Keto-friendly snack cups and bars
Co-Founder: Rick Gusmano
Co-Founder: Christine Cusano
Brands:
Keto Cups
Primal Chocolate

3910 **Eau Galle Cheese Factory Shop**
N6765 State Highway 25
Durand, WI 54736-4209
715-283-4211
Fax: 715-283-0711 www.eaugallecheese.com
Cheeses.
President: John Buhlman
Estimated Sales: $10-20 Million
Number Employees: 20-49
Number of Brands: 1
Brands:
Eau Galle Cheese

3911 **Eberhard Creamery**
235 S.W. Evergreen Ave
P.O. Box 845
Redmond, OR 97756
541-548-5181
Fax: 541-548-7009 ebdairy@eberhardsdairy.com
www.eberhardsdairy.com
Dairy products and frozen foods
President: John Eberhard
Vice President: Ted Eberhard
Manager: Mike Prom
Manager: Ron Jackson
Estimated Sales: $4 Million
Number Employees: 40
Type of Packaging: Consumer, Food Service

3912 **Eberle Winery**
3810 E Highway 46
Paso Robles, CA 93446-7044
805-238-9607
Fax: 805-237-0344 sales@eberlewinery.com
www.eberlewinery.com
Wine
Owner: Gary Eberle
gary@eberlewinery.com
Estimated Sales: $5-10 Million
Number Employees: 20-49

3913 **Eberly Poultry, Inc.**
1095 Mount Airy Rd
Stevens, PA 17578
717-336-6440
Fax: 717-336-6905
Organic and specialty poultry.
President: Robert Eberly
Supervisor: Joe Hoover
Manager: Tom Mikus
Contact: Melody Eckenroth
meckenroth@eberlypoultry.com
Estimated Sales: $10-20 Million
Number Employees: 75
Type of Packaging: Consumer

3914 **Ebro Foods**
1330 W 43rd St
Chicago, IL 60609-3308
773-696-0150
Fax: 773-696-0151 info@ebrofoods.com
www.ebrofoods.com
Manufacturer of Hispanic foods.
VP, Sales & Marketing: Pedro Morales
Manager: Silvio Vega
silvio.vega@ebrofoods.com
Estimated Sales: $14 Million
Number Employees: 10-19
Number of Brands: 1
Type of Packaging: Consumer
Brands:
Ebro

3915 **Echo Farms Puddings**
573 Chesterfield Rd
Hinsdale, NH 03451-2210
603-336-7706
Fax: 603-336-5964 866-488-3246
www.echofarmpuddings.com
Desserts, pudding
Owner: Robert Hodge
VP: Shelley Schofield
Contact: Beth Hodge
beth@echofarmpuddings.com
Estimated Sales: $1 Million
Number Employees: 12
Brands:
Echo Farm Pudding

3916 **Echo Lake Foods, Inc.**
340 West Grove
Burlington, WI 53105
262-763-9551
Fax: 262-763-4593 info@echolakefoods.com
www.echoforeggs.com
Frozen and liquid egg processing, pancakes, French toast, waffle, omelets, egg pattys, bread rolls, mini pancakes, flavored waffles and pancakes.
Vice President: Jerry Warntjes
VP: Jerry Warntjes
Sales Director: Scott Hall
Retail Sales: Justin Milbradt
Year Founded: 1941
Estimated Sales: $150 Million
Number Employees: 800
Type of Packaging: Consumer, Food Service, Private Label, Bulk

3917 **Echo Spring Dairy**
706 Oscar St
Eugene, OR 97402
541-342-1291
Fax: 541-342-8379
Dairy products
Manager: Mike Miller
Estimated Sales: $10-20 Million
Number Employees: 20-49
Parent Co: Darigold
Type of Packaging: Consumer, Food Service

3918 **Eckert Cold Storage**
757 Moffat Blvd
Manteca, CA 95336-5819
209-823-3181
Fax: 209-823-2499
IQF red, green and yellow bell and jalapeno peppers, cabbage leaves, diced cabbage, bok choy, kabocha and mangos
President & CEO: Kevin Mills
CFO: Jack Higgins
HR Executive: Steve West
steve@eckertcoldstorage.com
Researcher: Jason Crichton
Director of Brand Communications: Kevin Kampwerth
Sales & Marketing Manager: Craig West
Purchasing Supervisor: Deborah Haas
Number Employees: 250-499
Square Footage: 77168
Type of Packaging: Bulk

3919 **(HQ)Eckhart Corporation**
7110 Redwood Blvd Ste A
Novato, CA 94945
415-898-9528
Fax: 415-898-1917 800-200-4201
info@eckhartcorp.com www.eckhartcorp.com
Manufacturer and exporter of vitamins, food supplements and diet aids
President: Deepak Chopra
VP/Latin America: Arnoldo Rosas
Estimated Sales: $500,000-1 Million
Number Employees: 8
Square Footage: 640000
Type of Packaging: Consumer, Food Service, Private Label, Bulk
Brands:
Nature's Edge
Stay Well

3920 **Eckhart Seed Company**
531 Eckhart Road
Salinas, CA 93908
831-758-0925
Fax: 831-758-0388 rene@eckhartseed.com
www.eckhartseed.com

Dried beans
President: Richard Eckhart
Secretary: Connie Lord
VP: James Eckhart
Contact: Ed Acrey
beaney12@aol.com
Estimated Sales: $710,000
Number Employees: 12
Type of Packaging: Bulk

3921 **Eckroat Seed Company**
1106 Martin Luther King Avenue
Oklahoma City, OK 73117
405-427-2484
Fax: 405-427-7174 800-331-7333
www.eckroatseed.com
Manufacturer, importer and exporter of mung beans
President: Robert Eckroat
VP: Don Eckroat
Estimated Sales: $5-10 Million
Number Employees: 10-19
Square Footage: 400000
Type of Packaging: Consumer, Food Service, Private Label, Bulk
Brands:
Green Dragon

3922 **Eclat Chocolate**
24 S High St
West Chester, PA 19382-3225
610-692-5206
Fax: 610-692-5207 info@eclatchocolate.com
www.eclatchocolate.com

Chocolate
Owner: Christopher Curtin
info@eclatchoclate.com
Estimated Sales: $510,000
Number Employees: 5-9

3923 **Eclectic Institute**
36350 Industrial Way
Sandy, OR 97055-7377
503-668-4120
Fax: 503-668-3227
customerservice@eclecticherb.com
www.alstat.com
Organic alcohol extracts, alcohol free glycerins and nutritional supplements.
Owner: Edward Alstat
ealstat@eclecticherb.com
Estimated Sales: $5-10 Million
Number Employees: 50-99

3924 **Eco-Planet Cookies**
2516 California Ave
Santa Monica, CA 90403
310-829-9050
Fax: 310-829-6745
Croutons, breadcrumbs, breadsticks and cookies including seasonal, butter, natural, wheat-free, fat-free and special dietary baked without refined sugar; also, gingerbread houses and cookies. We also do private label
President: Tom Mosk
Estimated Sales: $2 Million approx.
Number Employees: 1-4
Square Footage: 80000
Type of Packaging: Private Label
Brands:
Heaven Scent Windmill Cookies
Heaven Scent
Heaven Scent Butter Cookies
Heaven Scent Croutons
Heaven Scent Fat Free Cookies
Heaven Scent Natural Foods

3925 **EcoNatural Solutions**
997 Dixon Rd
Boulder, CO 80302
303-357-5682
Fax: 303-358-4111 sales@stclaires.com
www.stclaires.com
Manufacturer and exporter of organic sweets
CEO: Debra St Claire
d.stclaire@stclaires.com
Estimated Sales: $2.5-5 Million
Number Employees: 5-9
Type of Packaging: Consumer
Brands:
St. Claire

3926 **Ecom Manufacturing Corporation**
80 Telson Road
Markham, ON L3R 1E5
Canada
905-477-2441
Fax: 905-477-2551 dsoknacki@ecomcanada.com
www.ecomcanada.com
Natural colors and flavors including garlic, onion, rosemary, allspice, turmeric, jalapeno, cilantro and nutmeg extracts,capsicum,enhancers.
President: David Soknacki
Sales/Marketing: Kan Husband
Estimated Sales: $249,000
Number Employees: 5
Square Footage: 160000
Type of Packaging: Bulk

3927 **Ed & Don's Of Hawaii Inc**
4462 Malaai St
Honolulu, HI 96818-3134
808-423-8200
Fax: 808-423-0550 sales@edanddons.com
www.edanddons.com

Chocolate candies
President: Vladimir Grave
VP: Earl Kurisu
Marketing: Mark Honda
Estimated Sales: $13 Million
Number Employees: 20-49
Parent Co: Oritz Corporation
Type of Packaging: Private Label
Brands:
Ed & Don's Chocolate Macadamias
Ed & Don's Macadamia Brittles
Ed & Don's Macadamia Chews

3928 **(HQ)Ed Miniat Inc**
16250 Vincennes Ave
South Holland, IL 60473-1260
708-589-2400
Fax: 708-589-2525 info@miniat.com
www.miniat.com
Frozen prepared meats
President: David Miniat
Chairman: Ronald Miniat
CFO: David Boyle
Executive VP: Michael Miniat
Marketing Manager: Eugene Matern
Sales Manager: Chuck Nalon
Operations Executive: David Jackson
Plant Manager: Darryl Hood
Estimated Sales: $23 Million
Number Employees: 10-19

3929 **Ed Miniat Inc**
16250 Vincennes Ave
South Holland, IL 60473-1260
708-589-2400
Fax: 708-589-2525 info@miniat.com
www.miniat.com
Prepared frozen meats
President: David Miniat
Director Sales/Marketing: Chuck Nalon
Director Operations: Neil Braderick
Production Manager: Lucio Fragoso
Plant Manager: John Nault
Estimated Sales: $5-10 Million
Number Employees: 10-19
Parent Co: Ed Miniat

3930 **Ed Oliveira Winery**
155 Center Street
Arcata, CA 95521-6056
707-822-3023
Wines
Owner: Douglas Oliveira
President: Catty Oliveira
Estimated Sales: $62,000
Number Employees: 2

3931 **Ed Roller Inc**
1115 Ridgeway Ave # 2
Suite 2
Rochester, NY 14615-3755
585-458-8020
Fax: 585-458-8169
Condiments including horseradish and cocktail sauces
Owner: Mike Mendick
edroller@rochester.rr.com
Estimated Sales: $1-2,500,000
Number Employees: 1-4
Number of Products: 2
Square Footage: 10000
Type of Packaging: Consumer, Food Service, Private Label, Bulk
Brands:
Private Labels
Rollers

3932 **Ed's Honey Co**
497 10th Ave SE
Dickinson, ND 58601-7421
701-225-9223
Honey
Owner: Ed Fetch
Estimated Sales: $150,000
Number Employees: 1-4
Type of Packaging: Consumer

3933 **Ed's Kasilof Seafoods**
26085 Williamson Ln
Kasilof, AK 99610
907-262-7295
Fax: 907-262-1617 800-982-2377
eks@alaska.net www.kasilofseafoods.com
Seafood
President: James Trujillo
eks@alaska.net
Estimated Sales: $960 Thousand
Number Employees: 20-49

3934 **Eda's Sugar Free**
4900 N 20th St
Philadelphia, PA 19144-2402
215-324-3412
Fax: 888-626-7785 brianberry44@gmail.com
www.edassugarfree.com
Manufacturer, processor and exporter of sugar free hard candies.
Owner: Mike Bernert
mbernert@edassugarfree.com
Estimated Sales: Less Than $500,000
Number Employees: 1-4
Number of Brands: 1
Number of Products: 28
Square Footage: 80000
Type of Packaging: Consumer, Food Service, Private Label, Bulk
Brands:
Eda Sugarfree Hard Candies

3935 **Eddy's Bakery**
380 N Five Mile Rd
Boise, ID 83713-8959
208-377-8100
Fax: 208-322-7823
Manfuacturer of baked goods including bread and cakes
General Manager: Chris Smith
Sales Director: Roy Schmidt
Estimated Sales: $3-5 Million
Number Employees: 1-4
Type of Packaging: Consumer

3936 **Edelman Meats Inc**
1128 1st Ave
Antigo, WI 54409-1606
715-623-7686
Fax: 715-623-7688
Beef, pork, chicken, fish, etc.
Owner: Joe Edelman
carmin@edelmanmeats.com
President/CEO: Joseph Edelman
Estimated Sales: $20-50 Million
Number Employees: 10-19
Type of Packaging: Food Service

3937 **(HQ)Edelmann Provision Company**
10000 Martins Way
Harrison, OH 45030
513-881-5800
g.basham@freshsausage.com
www.freshsausage.com

Fresh sausage
President: James Frondorf
jfrondorf@freshsausage.com
Vice President: James Burke
Controller: Casey Flick
Quality Control Manager: Jennifer Stone
Estimated Sales: $17.2 Million
Number Employees: 80

3938 Edelweiss Patisserie
19 Blake St
Medford, MA 02155-4921
781-628-0225
Fax: 781-628-0208 sales@edelweisspastry.com
www.edelweisspastry.com
Baked goods including cakes, pastries, muffins, croissants, pullman and tea loaves, rustic breads, cookies, etc
Owner: Elliott Thompson
Owner: Rifat Cebi
Account Manager: Colleen Scribner
Estimated Sales: Less Than $500,000
Number Employees: 5-9
Type of Packaging: Food Service

3939 Eden Creamery
Los Angeles, CA
info@halotop.com
www.halotop.com
Low calorie ice cream
Co-Founder: Justin Woolverton
Co-Founder: Douglas Bouton
Brands:
Halo Top

3940 Eden Foods Inc
701 Tecumseh Rd
Clinton, MI 49236-9599
517-456-7424
Fax: 517-456-6075 888-424-3336
info@edenfoods.com
Established in 1969. Natural and organic foods including pasta, soymilk, green tea, beans, tomatoes, spaghetti sauce, etc
President/CEO: Michael Potter
CEO: Manuela Della
manueladella@hfhs.org
CFO: Jay Hughes
Vice President: Jim Fox
Quality Control: Jon Solomon
VP Marketing & Sales: Sue Becker
VP Operations: William Swaney
Estimated Sales: $20-50 Million
Number Employees: 100-249
Type of Packaging: Food Service
Brands:
Eden
Eden Organic
Edenbalance
Edenblend
Edensoy
Edensoy Extra

3941 Eden Organic Pasta Company
701 Tecumseh Road
Clinton, MI 49236
517-456-7424
Fax: 517-456-6075 888-424-3336
info@edenfoods.com www.edenfoods.com
Organic and vegetable pastas
President/CEO: Michael Potter
Chief Financial Officer: Jay Hughes
General Manager: Steve Swaney
VP/Marketing: Sue Anne Becker
Manager: Massimo D'Amore
Estimated Sales: $44 Million
Number Employees: 117
Parent Co: Eden Foods
Type of Packaging: Food Service
Other Locations:
Eden Foods Plant
Detroit MI
Eden Foods Plant
Union City CA
Brands:
Eden's

3942 Eden Processing
100 East St
Poplar Grove, IL 61065
815-765-2000
Fax: 815-765-2777
Bakers' and confectioners' supplies including maraschino cherries, sweetened coconut, mince meat pie fillings, orange, lemon, melon, grapefruit and citron peels, etc
President, CEO: Louis Tenore, Jr.
Marketing Director: Pam McDowell
Contact: Pam Mcdowell
cherryboss@msn.com
Estimated Sales: $700,000
Number Employees: 14
Square Footage: 220000
Type of Packaging: Bulk
Brands:
True Blue

3943 Eden Vineyards Winery
19709 Little Ln
Alva, FL 33920
239-728-9463
Fax: 239-728-9463 info@edenwinery.com
www.edenwinery.com
Wines
President: Earl Kiser
VP: Michael Kiser
Estimated Sales: $520,000
Number Employees: 3

3944 Eden's Market
99 Alfred St
Pittsburgh, PA 15228-2309
412-343-1802
Fax: 412-343-1803
edensdownunder@edens-market.com
www.edens-market.com
Gluten free
Owner: Jeff Weiner
edensdownunder@yahoo.com
Estimated Sales: Less Than $500,000
Number Employees: 1-4

3945 Edgar A Weber & Co
549 Palwaukee Dr
Wheeling, IL 60090-6049
847-215-1980
Fax: 847-215-2073 800-558-9078
info@weberflavors.com www.weberflavors.com
Manufacturer and exporter of flavoring extracts for wine, liquor, baked goods and ice cream
Owner: Pam Grossman
pamg@weberflavors.com
CFO: Judith Turyna
Marketing Manager: Roger Passaglia
Plant Manager: Mike Sciore
Purchasing: Carol Myers
Estimated Sales: $3 Million
Number Employees: 50-99
Square Footage: 20000
Brands:
Hy Van
Simply Natural
Simply Natural-Like

3946 Edgewood Estate Winery
607 Airpark Road
Napa, CA 94558-6272
800-755-2374
Fax: 707-254-4920
Wines
CEO: Jeff O'Neill
CFO: John Kelleher
Sales: Steve Lindsay
Purchasing: David Weckerle
Estimated Sales: $1-2.5 Million
Number Employees: 7
Number of Brands: 1
Number of Products: 14
Square Footage: 280000
Parent Co: Golden State Vintners
Type of Packaging: Consumer, Private Label
Brands:
Edgewood Estate

3947 Edison Grainery
Benicia, CA 94510
510-382-0202
Fax: 510-263-5778 service@edisongrainery.com
edisongrainery.com
Beans, grains, seeds, cereals, super foods, pastas, flours and sweets.
Co-founder: Jeffrey Barnes
Co-founder: Amy Barnes

3948 (HQ)Edlong Corporation
225 Scott St
Elk Grove Village, IL 60007-1299
847-631-6700
info@edlong.com
www.edlong.com
Cheese, butter, milk & cream, cultured, sweet and functional flavors. Concentrated dairy flavors.
President & CEO: Laurette Rondenet
CFO: David Starr
Vice President, Global R&D: Laura Enriquez
Vice President, Operations: Ken Mack
Square Footage: 360000
Type of Packaging: Food Service, Private Label, Bulk
Other Locations:
Edlong Dairy Flavors
Suffolk
Edlong Dairy Flavors
United Kingdom
Edlong Dairy Flavors
Mexico City
Brands:
Capsulong
Cheolong
Ed-Vance
Vision

3949 Edmond's Chile Co
3236 Oregon Ave
St Louis, MO 63118-3004
314-772-1499
Fax: 314-664-7735
Sliced pork and gravy, sliced beef and gravy, beef au jus, vegetable soup, beef stew, meat sauce, beef chili, chili con carne, beef patties and tamales
President: Mark Adelman
edmondschile@yahoo.com
Estimated Sales: $2.5-5 Million
Number Employees: 10-19
Type of Packaging: Consumer

3950 Edmonton Potato Growers
12220-170 Street
Edmonton, AB T5V 1L7
Canada
780-447-1860
Fax: 780-447-1899 admin@epg.ab.ca
www.epg.ab.ca
Manufacturer and exmporter of potatoes including table, seed and processed, onions
President: Wayne Groot
VP: Ernie Van Boom
Sales: Darcy Olson
General Manager: Bob Jensen
Estimated Sales: $13 Million
Number Employees: 23
Type of Packaging: Consumer, Food Service, Bulk
Brands:
Canada Goose

3951 Edmunds St. John
1331 Walnut St
Berkeley, CA 94709
510-981-1510
Fax: 510-981-1610 info@edmundsstjohn.com
www.edmundsstjohn.com
Wine
President: Steve Edmunds
s.edmunds@edmundsstjohn.com
Estimated Sales: $1-2.5 Million
Number Employees: 1-4

3952 Edna Valley Vineyard
2585 Biddle Ranch Rd
San Luis Obispo, CA 93401
805-544-5855
Fax: 805-544-0112 866-979-8477
www.ednavalley.com
Table wines including Chardonnay and Pinot Noir
Winemaker: Josh Baker
CEO: Tom Selfridge
Marketing and Customer service: Rebecca Tincher
Sales Manager: Marty Taylor
Contact: Mark Cave
info@ednavalley.com
Plant Manager: Randy Weaver
Estimated Sales: $4 Million
Number Employees: 45
Square Footage: 240000
Parent Co: E&J Gallo Winery
Type of Packaging: Consumer, Food Service, Private Label
Brands:
Edna Valley
Videyards

3953 Edner Corporation
1200 Zephyr Ave
Hayward, CA 94544
510-441-8504
Fax: 510-441-9395
Breads (specialty), cakes, cookies, croissants (filled and unfilled), muffins, pastries, & scones (filled and unfilled)
President: Ed Kirschner
VP Technical Sales: Mark Aquilar
Manager: Sandy Caires

Estimated Sales: $2 Million
Number Employees: 30
Parent Co: Edner Corporation
Type of Packaging: Consumer, Food Service, Private Label, Bulk
Brands:
Edna Foods
Extreme
Huckleberry
Jonathan International Foods
La Patisserie
Warfarers

3954 **(HQ)Edom Labs Inc**
100 E Jefryn Blvd
Suite M
Deer Park, NY 11729-5729
631-586-2266
Fax: 631-586-2385 800-723-3366
info@edomlaboratories.com
www.edomlaboratories.com
Vitamins and dietary supplements
Owner: Eric Pollack

Estimated Sales: Less Than $500,000
Number Employees: 1-4
Type of Packaging: Consumer, Private Label, Bulk

3955 **Edoughble**
Los Angeles, CA 90034
www.edoughble.com
Edible cookie dough dessert
Founder: Rana Lustyan

3956 **Edward & Sons Trading Co**
4420 Via Real
Suite C
Carpinteria, CA 93013-1635
805-684-8500
Fax: 805-684-8220 www.edwardandsons.com
Manufacturer, importer and exporter of natural, organic and specialty foods: condiments, confectionery products, crackers, vegetarian soup mixes, snack foods, canned organic vegetables, vegetarian bouillon cubes, cake decorationsorganic coconut milk
President: Joel Dee
edwardsons@aol.com
Vice President: Alison Cox
Estimated Sales: $1 Million
Number Employees: 10-19
Type of Packaging: Consumer, Food Service, Private Label
Brands:
Edward&Sons
Heritage Soups
Let's Do
Let's Do Organic
Native Forest
Organic Country
Premier Japan
Rainforest Organic
Troy's
Wizards

3957 **Edward Johnson's Salsa**
Flemington, NJ 08822
customerservice@ejsalsa.com
ejsalsa.com
Gourmet salsa
Owner: Edward Johnson III
Year Founded: 2014
Number Employees: 1-10
Type of Packaging: Private Label
Brands:
All-American Squeeze-Salsa

3958 **Edward Marc Brands**
55 38th St
Pittsburgh, PA 15201
877-488-1808
edwardmarc.com
Chocolate; confections; and milk shakes
CEO: Mark Edwards
VP of Operations: Steve Brown
Year Founded: 1914
Number Employees: 50-200
Type of Packaging: Food Service, Private Label
Brands:
MilkShake Factory
Eward Marc Chocolatier
Snappers

3959 **Edwards Baking Company**
115 West College Dr.
Marshall, MN 56258
404-377-0511
Fax: 404-378-2074 866-739-2328
www.edwardsdesserts.com
Frozen dessert pies
CEO: Dimitrios Smyrnios
Manufacturing Director: Mark Glennon
Estimated Sales: $20-50 Million
Number Employees: 432
Parent Co: Schwan's

3960 **Edwards Mill**
PO Box 205
Hollister, MO 65673
417-334-6411
Fax: 417-335-2618 800-222-0525
Josh@StateoftheOzarks.net
www.stateoftheozarks.net
Whole grains that are blended into mixes; pancake, waffle, biscuit, muffin, fruitcakes, jams, jelly, preserves, apple butter
President: Jerry Davis

3961 **Edy's Grand Ice Cream**
PO Box 2178
Wilkes-Barre, PA 18703
888-590-3397
Fax: 570-301-4538 www.edys.com
Ice cream

3962 **Efco Products Inc**
130 Smith St
Poughkeepsie, NY 12601-2109
845-452-4715
Fax: 845-452-5607 800-284-3326
info@efcoproducts.com www.efcoproducts.com
Bakery mixes and ingredients, fruit and creme-style fillings, jellies, jams, and concentrated icing fruits
Owner: Ira Effron
ieffron@efcoproducts.com
VP/Controller: Kevin Laffin
VP Sales & Marketing: David A. Miller
VP Operations: Andy Herzing
Estimated Sales: $2.5-5 Million
Number Employees: 50-99

3963 **Effies Homemade**
1 Westinghouse Plz
Hyde Park, MA 02136-2075
617-364-9300
Fax: 617-364-9333 effie@effieshomemade.com
www.effieshomemade.com
All natural oatcakes and crispy corncakes
Owner: Joan Mac Issac
effie@effieshomemade.com
Partner: Joan MacIsaac
Number Employees: 1-4

3964 **Egg Cream America Inc**
633 Skokie Blvd
Suite 200
Northbrook, IL 60062-2824
847-559-2703
Fax: 847-559-2709 getcreamed@aol.com
www.getcreamed.com
Dairy based carbonated beverages
President: Adam Kurlander
CEO: John Beslow
Estimated Sales: Less Than $500,000
Number Employees: 1-4

3965 **Egg Innovations**
PO Box 1275
Warsaw, IN 46581-1275
Fax: 574-267-7305 800-337-1951
info@egginnovations.com
www.egginnovations.com
Free-range organic eggs
President & CEO: John Brunnquell
VP, Finance: Wes LaRue
VP, Sales & Marketing: Steve Hagopian

3966 **Egg Low Farms**
35 West State Street
Sherburne, NY 13460
607-674-4653
Fax: 607-674-9216
Fresh eggs including diced and scrambled. Also salad ready diced eggs and tray ready scrambled eggs; all fresh
President: Helen A. Dunckel
CEO: David Dunckel
VP: David L. Dunckel
Estimated Sales: $850,000
Number Employees: 10
Square Footage: 160000
Type of Packaging: Food Service, Private Label
Brands:
Egg Low Farms
The Unbeatable Eatable Egg

3967 **Egg Roll Fantasy**
PO Box 7895
Auburn, CA 95604-7895
530-887-9197
Fax: 530-887-9199
Gourmet egg rolls
President: Louie Buendia
VP: Robert DiMiceli
Estimated Sales: $500,000-$1 Million
Number Employees: 10
Number of Brands: 3
Number of Products: 20
Square Footage: 16000
Type of Packaging: Consumer, Food Service, Private Label, Bulk

3968 **Eggland's Best Eggs**
70 East Sweedsford Road
Suite 150
Malvern, PA 19355
800-922-3447
www.egglandsbest.com
Dairy, organic eggs.
President/CEO: Charles Lanktree
Director of Quality Assurance: Bart Slaugh
bbarnes@eggland.com
Contact: Barb Barnes
bbarnes@eggland.com
Estimated Sales: $10-20 Million
Number Employees: 10-19
Number of Brands: 1
Type of Packaging: Consumer, Private Label
Brands:
Eggland's Best

3969 **Eggology**
6728 Eton Ave
Canoga Park, CA 91303-2813
818-610-2222
Fax: 818-610-2223 ninag@eggology.com
www.eggology.com
Pure liquid egg whites
President: Brad Halpern
VP: Robyn Mitofsky
Manager: Jose Cardenas
josec@eggology.com
Estimated Sales: $1 Million
Number Employees: 10-19

3970 **Egypt Star Bakery Inc**
608 N Front St
Allentown, PA 18102-5125
610-434-8516
Fax: 610-443-1915
Breads, rolls
President: Esther Erdossy
eerdossy@egyptstarbakery.com
VP: Steven Zdrofcoff
Estimated Sales: $3 Million
Number Employees: 20-49

3971 **Ehresman Packaging Co**
912 E Fulton St
Garden City, KS 67846-6042
620-276-3791
Fax: 620-276-1916
Meat products; also, custom butchering available
Owner: Mike Plankenhorn
velda.epc@gmail.com
Co-Owner: Velda Plankenhorn
Estimated Sales: $49,000
Number Employees: 10-19
Type of Packaging: Consumer, Private Label

3972 **Eickman's Processing Co**
3226 S Pecatonica Rd
PO Box 118
Seward, IL 61077
815-247-8451
Fax: 815-247-8463 www.eickmans.com
Beef, pork, lamb and wild game
President: Michael Eickman
redtail15@aol.com

Estimated Sales: $3 Million
Number Employees: 20-49
Type of Packaging: Consumer, Food Service

3973 Eidon
12330 Stowe Dr
Poway, CA 92064-6802
858-668-0804
Fax: 858-668-3593 800-700-1169
www.eidon.com
Mineral supplements
Manager: Deborah Stewart
CEO: Rick Wagner
info1@eidon.com
VP: Fred Elsner
Production Manager: Cory Wagner
Estimated Sales: $1 Million
Number Employees: 10-19
Number of Brands: 1
Number of Products: 30
Square Footage: 23000
Type of Packaging: Consumer, Private Label, Bulk

3974 Eight O'Clock Coffee Company
5901 West Side Avenue
4th Floor
North Bergen, NJ 07645
800-299-2739
www.eightoclock.com
Roasted coffee.
CFO: Tom Corcoran
SVP, Sales & Marketing: David Allen
Director, Trade Marketing: Robert Hodge
VP, Human Resources: Liesel Bell
Brand Manager: Michael Scalera
Estimated Sales: $44.4 Million
Number Employees: 215
Number of Brands: 1
Parent Co: Tata Coffee Limited
Type of Packaging: Consumer
Other Locations:
New Providence NJ
Brands:
Eight O'Clock

3975 Eilenberger Bakeries
512 N John St
Palestine, TX 75801-2725
903-729-0881
Fax: 903-723-2915 800-831-2544
Gourmet cakes and brownies
Owner: Terresa Smith
sales@eilenbergerbakery.com
VP: Stephen Smith
VP/Marketing: Sarah Pryor
Estimated Sales: $720,000
Number Employees: 20-49

3976 Eiserman Meats
401 12 St SE
Slave Lake, AB T0G 2A3
Canada
780-849-5507
Fax: 780-849-6097 info@eisermanmeats.com
www.eisermanmeats.com
Fresh beef, pork, sausage and wild game; also, beef jerky; slaughtering services available
President/Co-Owner: Russell Eiserman
Co-Owner: Annellen Eiserman
Estimated Sales: $527,000
Number Employees: 4
Type of Packaging: Consumer

3977 El Brands
323 Van Heusen Drive
Ozark, AL 36360-1054
334-445-2828
Fax: 334-352-7263
Peanuts
CEO: Ed Lindley
VP Sales/Marketing: Steve Ratliff

3978 El Charro Mexican Food Ind
1711 S Virginia Ave
Roswell, NM 88203-1829
575-622-8590
Fax: 575-622-8590 ectortilla@yahoo.com
Manufacturer and exporter of chili sauce and tortilla chips
Owner: Micheal Trujillo
Owner: Mireya Trujillo
Estimated Sales: $5-10 Million
Number Employees: 10-19
Type of Packaging: Consumer, Food Service, Private Label, Bulk
Brands:
El Charro
La Pablanita

3979 El Grano De Oro
1710 Francisco Blvd
Pacifica, CA 94044-2515
650-355-8417
Fax: 650-355-7705 www.hotelgranodeoro.com
Mexican Restaurant
Owner: Mauricio Garcia
Co-Owner: Oscar Garcia
Estimated Sales: $470,000
Number Employees: 10-19

3980 El Jay Poultry Corporation
1010 Haddonfield Berlin # 402
Voorhees, NJ 08043-3514
856-435-0900
Fax: 856-435-3019
Poultry
President: Leo Rubin
Co-Owner: Joseph Milgrim
Estimated Sales: $5-10 Million
Number Employees: 5 to 9
Brands:
Oak Valley Farms

3981 El Matador Foods
7201 Bayway Dr
Baytown, TX 77520-1303
281-424-0350
Fax: 281-838-1375 800-470-2447
info@elmatadorfoods.com
www.elmatadorfoods.com
Tortilla chips
Owner: Erick Ybarra
elmatador@huston.rr.com
Estimated Sales: $5-10 Million
Number Employees: 20-49
Brands:
El Matador Tortilla Chip

3982 El Milagro
3050 W 26th St
Chicago, IL 60623-4130
773-579-6120
www.el-milagro.com
Corn and flour tortilla manufacturer in the Midwest.
President: Raphael Lopez
Contact: Phil Crookham
pcrookham@el-milagro.com
Year Founded: 1942
Estimated Sales: Less Than $500,000
Number Employees: 5-9
Type of Packaging: Consumer, Food Service

3983 El Molino Winery
3315 Saint Helena Hwy N
St Helena, CA 94574-9660
707-963-3632
Fax: 707-963-1647 wine@elmolinowinery.com
www.elmolinowinery.com
Wine
Owner: Lily Oliver Berlin
Co-Owner: Jon Berlin
Sales/Marketing: Mimi Buttenheim
Labelling/Foiling Wines: Altagracia Rincon
Estimated Sales: Less Than $500,000
Number Employees: 1-4

3984 El Paso Meat Co
1523 Myrtle Ave
El Paso, TX 79901-1796
915-838-8600
Fax: 915-533-3997
Fresh and frozen beef and pork; slaughtering services available
Owner: Francis Ramos
General Manager: Javier Garcia
Estimated Sales: $3-5 Million
Number Employees: 20-49
Type of Packaging: Consumer, Food Service

3985 El Paso Winery
742 Broadway Route 9 West
Ulster Park, NY 12487
845-331-8642
marylvogel@aol.com
www.elpasowinery.com
Red, white and rose wines
Owner: Maryl Vogel
Operations Manager: Felipe Beltra
Estimated Sales: Less than $500,000
Number Employees: 2
Type of Packaging: Consumer, Food Service

3986 El Perico Charro
204 N 7th St
Garden City, KS 67846-5519
620-275-6454
Manufacturer and retailers of Mexican foods, tortillas
President/CEO: Natividad Hernandez
Estimated Sales: $500,000-$1 Million
Number Employees: 1-4
Number of Products: 2
Type of Packaging: Consumer, Food Service

3987 El Peto Products
65 Saltsman Drive
Cambridge, ON N3H 4R7
Canada
519-650-4614
Fax: 519-650-5692 800-387-4064
info@elpeto.com www.elpeto.com
Manufacturer and exporter of wheat, gluten and milk-free products including baking mixes, breads, muffins, cakes, buns, pies, cookies, frozen doughs and batters, pastas, soups and specialty flours
President: Elisabeth Riesen
VP: Peter Riesen
Estimated Sales: $3 Million
Number Employees: 18
Number of Brands: 3
Square Footage: 18000
Type of Packaging: Consumer, Food Service, Bulk
Brands:
El Peto

3988 El Rancho Tortilla
623 New Laredo Hwy
San Antonio, TX 78211
210-922-8411
Fax: 210-922 9159
Corn and flour tortillas, tostadas, taco shells and picante sauce
Owner: Ruben Martinez
Estimated Sales: $2.5-5 Million
Number Employees: 20
Type of Packaging: Consumer

3989 El Rey Cooked Meats
6190 Bermuda Dr
St Louis, MO 63135-3298
314-521-3113
dryan@elreycookedmeats.com
www.elreycookedmeats.com
Manufacturer and exporter of frozen foods including chili, tamales, roast and barbecued beef, taco meat and pork; also, barbecue sauce
Owner: Joseph Frisella
elreyfoods@aol.com
VP, Sales: Don Ryan
Estimated Sales: $10-20 Million
Number Employees: 5-9
Square Footage: 6000
Type of Packaging: Consumer, Food Service
Brands:
Chef's Helper
Menu a La Carte

3990 El Toro Brew Pub
17605 Monterey St
Morgan Hill, CA 95037-3620
408-782-2739
Fax: 408-782-0171
Beer
Owner: Geno Acevedo
Estimated Sales: Less Than $500,000
Number Employees: 1-4

3991 El Toro Food Products
504 El Rio Street
Watsonville, CA 95076-3540
831-728-9266
Fax: 831-688-8766
Manufacture of canned salsas varieties including sauces and vegetables
President: Richard Thomas
Estimated Sales: $5-10 Million
Number Employees: 5-9
Number of Brands: 6
Number of Products: 10
Square Footage: 24000
Type of Packaging: Food Service, Private Label, Bulk

3992 **Elaine's Toffee Co.**
PO Box 38
Clayton, CA 94517
925-524-0000
Fax: 925-524-9000 800-883-3050
info@elainestoffee.com www.elainestoffee.com
Kosher, sugar-free, chocolate bars, other chcoolate, toffee, other snacksprivate label.
President: Janet Long
Estimated Sales: $300,000
Number Employees: 7

3993 **Elan Vanilla Co**
268 Doremus Ave
Newark, NJ 07105-4879
973-344-8014
Fax: 973-344-5880 www.elanvanilla.com
Organic kosher certified vanilla extract, flavoring and synthetic and natural aromatic chemicals
President: Jocelyn Manship
jmanship@elan-chemical.com
Quality Control Manager: Phil Kapp
VP Sales: David Pimentel
Director of Customer Service: Marilyn Santiago
Estimated Sales: $20-50 Million
Number Employees: 50-99
Type of Packaging: Bulk

3994 **Elba Custom Meats**
405 Alabama Highway 203
Elba, AL 36323-4217
334-897-2007
Meat products
Owner: Billy F Hudson
VP: Douglas Hudson
Estimated Sales: $140,000
Number Employees: 3
Type of Packaging: Consumer

3995 **Elco Fine Foods**
233 Alden Road
Markham, ON L4B 1G5
Canada
905-731-7337
Fax: 905-731-2391 info@elcofinefoods.com
www.elcofinefoods.com
Distributor of premium confectionery, food and beverage products
CEO: Moe Cussen
Number Employees: 100
Square Footage: 270000

3996 **(HQ)Eldorado Artesian Springs Inc**
1783 Dogwood St
Louisville, CO 80027-3085
303-499-1316
Fax: 303-499-1339 info@eldoradosprings.com
www.eldoradosprings.com
Bottled water
President/CEO: Douglas Larson
doug@eldoradosprings.com
VP Marketing: Jeremy Martin
VP Operations: Kevin Sipple
Estimated Sales: $5.3 Million
Number Employees: 50-99
Type of Packaging: Private Label
Brands:
Eldorado Natural Spring Water
Eldorado Spring Water

3997 **Eldorado Coffee Distributors**
5675 49th St
Flushing, NY 11378-2012
718-418-4100
Fax: 718-418-4500 800-635-2566
www.eldoradocoffee.com
Established in 1980. Manufacturer and roaster of coffee.
Founder: Segunda Martin
eldoradon1@aol.com
VP: Juan Martin
VP of Sales: Albert Valdes
Estimated Sales: $20-50 Million
Number Employees: 20-49
Type of Packaging: Consumer, Food Service, Private Label
Brands:
El Dorado Coffee Roasters

3998 **Eldorado Seafood Inc**
27 Cambridge Street
Burlington, MA 01803
781-270-4290
Fax: 781-270-4242 800-416-5656
Shrimp including breaded, cooked, peeled and deveined
President: Christinne Randazzo
VP: Laura Randazzo
Estimated Sales: $2.5-5 Million
Number Employees: 1-4
Type of Packaging: Consumer, Food Service, Private Label
Brands:
Eldorado
Max-Sea

3999 **Eleanor's Best LLC**
PO Box 9
Garrison, NY 10524
646-296-6870
info@eleanorsbest.com
www.eleanorsbest.com
Handmade, vegan, gluten jams and marmalades, maple syrup, wildflower honey
Founder/Owner: Jennifer Mercurio
Year Founded: 2013
Number Employees: 10
Number of Brands: 1
Number of Products: 16
Type of Packaging: Consumer, Private Label
Brands:
Eleanor's Best

4000 **Elegant Desserts**
275 Warren St
Lyndhurst, NJ 07071-2017
201-933-0770
Fax: 201-933-7309 info@elegantdesserts.com
www.elegantdesserts.com
Manufacturer and wholesaler/distributor of pastries including tarts and miniature grand viennas
President: John Mazur
jjmazur@bellatlantic.net
Estimated Sales: $2 Million
Number Employees: 20-49
Type of Packaging: Food Service, Private Label

4001 **Elegant Edibles**
3311 Mercer St
Houston, TX 77027-6019
713-522-2884
Fax: 713-522-1777 800-227-3226
info@elegantedibles.com www.elegantedibles.com
All natural, gourmet confections, snacks, and recipe ready ingredients
Owner: Diane Dagostino
info@elegantedibles.com
R&D: Francis Jacquinet
Operations: Lori Lake
Production: Amanda Stults
Plant Manager: Ana Olmedo
Estimated Sales: Less than $500,000
Number Employees: 5-9
Number of Brands: 8
Type of Packaging: Consumer, Food Service, Private Label, Bulk
Brands:
Mrs. Powell's Gourmet

4002 **Element Snacks**
153 W 27th St
Suite 302
New York, NY 10001-6259
212-966-7696
Fax: 212-994-0392 elementsnacks.com
chocolate covered rice cakes
Founder: Nadia Leonelli
Year Founded: 2012
Estimated Sales: $675000
Number Employees: 1-10
Type of Packaging: Private Label

4003 **Elemental Superfood**
Torrance, CA 90501
tryzen.com
Organic seedbars and crumble
Founder: Nicole Anderson

4004 **Elements Truffles**
78 John Miller Way
Kearny, NJ 07032
917-836-2819
we@elementstruffles.com
Chocolate bars and truffles
President: Alak Vasa
Estimated Sales: $74425
Number Employees: 1-4
Type of Packaging: Private Label

4005 **Elena's**
2650 Paldan
Auburn Hills, MI 48326
248-373-1100
Fax: 248-373-1120 800-723-5362
info@elenas.com www.elenas.com
Manufacturer and exporter of pasta, pasta sauce and pasta salad
President: Elena Houlihan
VP Finance: Caroline Moose
VP Operations: John Houlihan
Estimated Sales: $2.5-5 Million
Number Employees: 20-49
Parent Co: Houlihan's Culinary Traditions
Type of Packaging: Food Service, Private Label, Bulk
Brands:
Bella Mercato
Bruschetta

4006 **Elena's Food Specialties**
405 Allerton Ave
S San Francisco, CA 94080-4818
650-871-8700
Fax: 650-871-0502 800-376-5368
Frozen Mexican foods including enchiladas and burritos
President: Peter Sartorio
VP Product Development: Nathan Steck
R&D Manager: Mark Cooley
Eastern Regional Sales Manager: Alice Pager
Contact: Don Anderson
don@elenasfoods.com
Plant Manager: Manuel Lara
Office Manager: Crystal Snearing
Estimated Sales: $5-10 Million
Number Employees: 50-99
Type of Packaging: Consumer, Food Service

4007 **Eleni's Cookies**
75 Ninth Avenue
New York, NY 10011-7006
Fax: 800-283-3074 888-435-3647
sales@elenis.com www.elenis.com
Nut-free cookies
Owner: Eleni Giamopulos
Contact: Nicholas Colloton
ncolloton@elenis.com
Estimated Sales: $300,000-500,000
Number Employees: 5-9

4008 **Elgin Dairy Foods**
3707 W Harrison St
Chicago, IL 60624-3622
773-722-7100
Fax: 773-722-3230 800-786-9900
Ice cream, frozen yogurt, dairy and nondairy whipped toppings, sour cream and dairy mixes
President: Edward Gignac
EVP Sales: James Cignac
Marketing Manager: Nathan Langer
Estimated Sales: $12 Million
Number Employees: 95
Square Footage: 58000
Brands:
Flav'r Top
Freeze-Thaw

4009 **Eli's Bread Inc**
403 E 91st St # 1
New York, NY 10128-6800
212-831-4800
Fax: 212-423-9078 866-354-3547
customerservice@elizabar.com www.elizabar.com
Hearth-baked European-style breads, rolls, bagels and crisps based on traditional European recipes
Owner: Eli Zabar
Administrative Executive: Uzziah Phillips
Director Sales: Mark Stewart
Manager: Mark Stewart
mstewart@elizabar.com
Estimated Sales: $5-10 Million
Number Employees: 100-249
Square Footage: 30000

4010 **Eli's Cheesecake**
6701 W Forest Preserve Drive
Chicago, IL 60634
773-308-7000
Fax: 773-736-1169 800-354-2253
info@elicheesecake.com www.elicheesecake.com
Manufacturer of cheesecakes and desserts sold in Illinois, Indiana, Michigan, Minnesota, Missouri, Ohio and Wisconsin.
President: Marc Schulman
Square Footage: 62000
Type of Packaging: Consumer
Brands:
Eli's

4011 **Eliot's Adult Nut Butters**
503-847-9457
info@eliotsadultnutbutters.com
eliotsadultnutbutters.com
Nut butters
Founder: Michael Kanter
Number of Brands: 1
Number of Products: 7
Type of Packaging: Consumer
Brands:
ELIOT'S ADULT NUT BUTTERS

4012 **Elite Spice Inc**
7151 Montevideo Rd
Jessup, MD 20794-9308
410-796-1900
Fax: 410-379-6933 800-232-3531
jbrandt@elitespice.com www.elitespice.com
Spice, seasoning, capsicum, oil & oleoresin, and dehydrated vegetable producer.
President & CEO: Isaac Samuel
CFO/Human Resources Director: Debbie Ingle
R&D Director: Leslie Krause
Quality Control Directory: Dave Anthony
Marketing Executive: Kathy Lyons
VP, Sales: Paul Kurpe
VP/Plant Manager: George Mayer
Purchasing Manager: Margie Schneidman
Year Founded: 1988
Estimated Sales: $20-50 Million
Number Employees: 100-249
Square Footage: 11000
Type of Packaging: Private Label

4013 **Elk Cove Vineyards**
27751 NW Olson Rd
Gaston, OR 97119-8042
503-985-7760
Fax: 503-985-3525 877-355-2683
info@elkcove.com www.elkcove.com
Wines
Owner: Adam Campbell
Founder/CEO: Patricia Campbell
Controller: Robert Verant
Sales Manager: Shirley Brooks
adam@elkcove.com
Hospitality Coordinator: Kathy Kennedy
Vineyard Manager: Travis Watson
Estimated Sales: $5-10 Million
Number Employees: 10-19

4014 **Elki Coporation**
6101 23rd Dr W
Everett, WA 98203
425-261-1002
Fax: 425-261-1006 info@elki.com
elki.com
Bruschettas; jams and preserves; dips; pesto; crostinis; gluten-free snacks; grilled vegetables; tomato sauce
President/Owner: Elizabeth Lie
Year Founded: 1984
Number Employees: 1-4

4015 **Ella's Flats**
5811 Pelican Bay Blvd
Naples, FL 34106
ellen@ellasflats.com
www.ellasflats.com
Seed crisps
Owner: Ellen Macks

4016 **Ella's Kitchen**
1209 Orange St
New Castle, DE 19801
800-685-7799
www.ellaskitchen.com
Organic baby food and kids' food
Founder: Paul Lindley
CEO: Mark Cuddigan
Year Founded: 2009
Parent Co: Hain Celestial

4017 **Ellenbee-Leggett Co Inc**
3765 Port Union Rd
Fairfield, OH 45014-2207
513-874-3200
Fax: 513-874-3323 800-536-1613
service@ellenbee.com www.ellenbee.com
Distributor of premium foodservice products
President: James Kite
jkite@ellenbee.com
Number Employees: 100-249

4018 **Ellenos**
5707 Airport Way S
Seattle, WA 98108
206-535-7562
hello@ellenos.com
www.ellenos.com
Greek yogurt
CEO: John Tucker
Vice President, Finance: Adam Karnofski
Vice President, Marketing: Ben Garnero

4019 **Ellie's Country Delights**
PO Box 1059
Wainscott, NY 11975
631-478-5200
Fax: 631-604-1076
Ratatouille
President: Ellenka Baumrind

4020 **Ellio's Pizza**
10000 Midlantic Drive
Suite 107W
Mt. Laurel, NJ 8054
866-435-5467
www.ellios.com
Frozen Pizza

4021 **Elliott Bay Baking Co.**
5601 1st Avenue South
Seattle, WA 98108-3951
206-545-3804
Fax: 206-767-1176
marketing@essentialbaking.com
www.essentialbaking.com
Biscotti bites, java mocha cookies, European tea biscuits
President: Paula Lukoff
Estimated Sales: $2.5-5 Million
Number Employees: 20-49
Brands:
Ii Biscotto Della Nonna
My Bubby's

4022 **Elliott Seafood Company**
53 Stevens Ln
Cushing, ME 04563
207-354-2533
Fax: 207-354-2533
Seafood
President: Stan Elliott

4023 **Ellis Coffee Co**
2835 Bridge St
Philadelphia, PA 19137-1895
215-537-9500
Fax: 215-534-5311 800-822-3984
www.elliscoffee.com
Coffee
President: Eugene Kestenbaum
Chairman: William Strauss
CFO: Tom McElwee
Executive VP: Frank Parker
VP Sales/Marketing: James O'Ferrell
Estimated Sales: Less Than $500,000
Number Employees: 5-9

4024 **Ellison Bakery, Inc.**
4108 W Ferguson Rd
Fort Wayne, IN 46899
www.ebakery.com
Cookies, ice-cream sandwich wafers, crunch toppings and inclusion products.
CEO: Stephanie Chattilion
COO: Todd Wallin
todd.wallin@ebakery.com
Production Manager: Matthew Barton
Year Founded: 1945
Estimated Sales: $20-50 Million
Number Employees: 50-99
Number of Brands: 2
Type of Packaging: Consumer, Food Service, Private Label, Bulk
Brands:
Ella's Oven™
Ellison

4025 **Ellison Milling Company**
PO Box 400
Lethbridge, AB T1J 3Z2
Canada
403-328-6622
Fax: 403-327-3772
Durum Semolina, Hard and Soft Wheat Flours
President: Michael Greer
Quality Control: Paolo Santangelo
Marketing Director: Bob Grebinsky
Plant Manager: B McConnell
Number Employees: 65
Parent Co: Parrish & Heimbecker
Type of Packaging: Food Service, Private Label, Bulk
Brands:
Alebrta
Baker's Gold
Dream
Ellison's
Royal Pastry
U-Bake

4026 **Elliston Vineyards**
463 Kilkare Rd
Sunol, CA 94586-9415
925-862-2377
Fax: 925-862-0316 info@elliston.com
www.elliston.com
Wines
Vice President: Mark Piche
info@elliston.com
VP: Keith Flavetta
Manager: Catherine Neufeld
info@elliston.com
Estimated Sales: $5 Million
Number Employees: 1-4
Type of Packaging: Private Label

4027 **Ello Raw**
hello@elloraw.com
www.elloraw.com
Superfood snack bites
Founder & CEO: Rebecca Holmes
Number of Brands: 1
Number of Products: 4
Type of Packaging: Consumer
Brands:
ELLO RAW

4028 **Ellsworth Cooperative Creamery**
232 N. Wallace St.
PO Box 610
Ellsworth, WI 54011
715-273-4311
Fax: 715-273-5318 www.ellsworthcheese.com
Cheese curds, also available in flavors such as garlic, taco, cajun, natural, premium cheddar and ranch, also breaded and vacuum sealed/freezable.
President/Director: Albert Knegendorf
CEO/Manager: Paul Bauer
paulb@ellsworthcreamery.net
Vice President, Sales/Marketing: Jim Grande
Year Founded: 1910
Estimated Sales: $145 Million
Number Employees: 100-249
Number of Brands: 5
Square Footage: 120000
Type of Packaging: Consumer, Private Label, Bulk
Brands:
Antonella
Blaser's
Ellsworth
Ellsworth Valley
Kammerude

4029 **Ellsworth Foods**
1510 Eastman Dr
Tifton, GA 31793-8228
229-386-8448
Fax: 229-387-9749 www.ellsworthfoods.com
Grocery products
Owner: Ken Ellsworth Jr
kellsworth@ellsworthfoods.com
VP: Rebecca Ellsworth

Estimated Sales: $5 Million
Number Employees: 20-49

4030 Ellsworth Locker
317 S Broadway St
Ellsworth, MN 56129-1092
507-967-2544
www.ellsworthamerican.com
Sausage, beef, pork and venison
Owner: Brian Chapa
Co-Owner: Kathy Chapa
Estimated Sales: $1-2.5 Million
Number Employees: 5-9
Type of Packaging: Consumer

4031 Elm City Cheese Co Inc
2240 State St
Hamden, CT 06517-3798
203-865-5768
Fax: 203-865-8303 www.elmcitycheese.com
Grated parmesan cheese
President: Weinstein Margie
wmargie@elmcitycheese.com
Vice President: Marge Weinstein
Estimated Sales: $1.4 Million
Number Employees: 10-19
Type of Packaging: Consumer

4032 Elmer Chocolate®
401 N 5th St
Ponchatoula, LA 70454
985-386-6166
800-843-9537
www.elmerchocolate.com
Only one Elmer Chocolate product can be purchased year-round, which is Gold Brick Topping, also manufactures Christmas, Valentine's and Easter chocolates.
Chairman & CEO: Robert Nelson
Safety Manager: Jeffrey Bell
Year Founded: 1914
Estimated Sales: $26.7 Million
Number Employees: 300
Square Footage: 250000
Type of Packaging: Consumer
Brands:
Fiddlers
Gold Brick
Heavenly Hash
Just Nuts
Small Talk Conversation Hearts
Sweet Occasion

4033 Elmers Fine Foods Inc
2404 Port St
New Orleans, LA 70117-7418
504-949-2716
Fax: 504-948-2537 888-570-0764
sales@elmerscheewees.com
www.elmerscheewees.com
Snack foods including potato chips, popcorn and cheese curls
President: Alan Elmer
alan@elmerscheewees.com
Treasurer: Paul Elmer
VP: Stephen M Elmer
Director of Sales: Gary Langlois
Estimated Sales: $1 Million
Number Employees: 20-49
Type of Packaging: Consumer

4034 Elmhurst Milked
1150 Maple Rd
Elma, NY 14059
888-356-1925
cs@elmhurst1925.com
elmhurst1925.com
Plant-based milks
President: Henry Schwartz
Vice President of Sales: Mike Brown
Year Founded: 1925
Number of Brands: 1
Type of Packaging: Consumer, Food Service
Brands:
ELMHURST MILKED

4035 Elmwood Locker Svc
214 S Magnolia St
Elmwood, IL 61529-7902
309-742-8929
Fax: 309-742-7071
john@elmwoodmeatlocker.com
Custom butchering and processing. Manufacturer of sausage jerky, beef sticks and bratwurst
Owner: John Powers
Estimated Sales: $500,000-$1 Million
Number Employees: 1-4
Type of Packaging: Consumer, Bulk
Brands:
J & J

4036 Elmwood Pastry Shop
1136 New Britain Ave
West Hartford, CT 06110-2413
860-233-2029
Fax: 203-865-8303 www.elmwoodpastryshop.com
Hard rolls, bread, doughnuts, cakes and cookies
President: Richard S Winalski Jr
richard.winalski@elmwoodpastryshop.com
Estimated Sales: $500,000-$1 Million
Number Employees: 10-19
Type of Packaging: Consumer

4037 (HQ)Elore Enterprises Inc
1055 NW 159th Dr
Miami Gardens, FL 33169-5805
305-477-1650
Fax: 305-477-2291 www.quijotefoods.com
Spanish sausage
President: Joe Alanso
VP: Juan Alanso
Manager: Sergio Pires
elore@bellsouth.net
Estimated Sales: $1-2.5 Million
Number Employees: 20-49
Type of Packaging: Consumer, Food Service

4038 Elwood International Inc
89 Hudson St
Copiague, NY 11726-1505
631-842-6600
Fax: 631-842-6603 info@elwoodintl.com
Manufacturer and exporter of regular and dietetic portion controlled condiments including dressings, jellies, mayonnaise, mustard, ketchup, peanut butter, table syrups, private label and contract packaging
President: Stuart Roll
Vice President: Richard Roll
IT: Anna Marx
anna@elwoodintl.com
Estimated Sales: $2.90 Million
Number Employees: 10-19
Number of Brands: 3
Number of Products: 40
Square Footage: 92000
Type of Packaging: Consumer, Food Service, Private Label, Bulk
Brands:
Elwood
Renaissance
Winston

4039 Embassy Flavours Ltd.
5 Intermodal Drive
Unit 1
Brampton, ON L6T 5V9
Canada
905-789-3200
Fax: 905-789-3201 800-334-3371
info@embassyflavours.com
www.embassyflavours.com
Manufacturer and exporter of extracts, flavors, colors, essential oils, bases and mixes including cake, pastry and bread. Certifications include BRC, Canadian Celiac Association, Kosher and Halal. Facility is peanut free.
President: Martino Brambilla
R&D: Anne Klingerman
National Sales/Marketing Manager: Mike Taras
Estimated Sales: $1.7 Million
Number Employees: 38
Square Footage: 57600
Type of Packaging: Consumer, Food Service, Private Label, Bulk
Brands:
Batter-Moist
Elite
Embassy
Prairie Sun

4040 Embria Health Sciences
2105 SE Creekview Dr
Ankeny, IA 50021-8899
515-963-9100
Fax: 515-964-9004 877-362-7421
info@embriahealth.com www.epicorimmune.com
EpiCor® and eXselen®, immune health ingredients for use in all food, beverage and nutritional supplement applications.
President/CEO: Paul Faganel
Research & Development: Larry Robinson
Quality Control Manager: Gayle Kittelson
Marketing Director: Cheryl Sturm
Regional Sales Rep: Naz Kalantari
Regional Sales Rep: Doug Reyes
Director of Operations: Mark Joyner
Estimated Sales: $500,000-1 Million
Number Employees: 10-19

4041 Emerald Hilton Davis LLC
2235 Langdon Farm Rd
Cincinnati, OH 45237-4712
513-841-0057
Fax: 513-841-3771 www.emeraldmaterials.com
Applications for the food and beverage industry.
President/CEO: Jim Donnelly
jimdonnelly@emeraldperformancematerials.com
VP/CFO: Pat McGill
R&D: Joe Uern
Environmental/Safety Manager: Peggy Roundtree
Marketing: Kelly Schaeffer
Sales/Marketing Manager: Bobby Gruber
VP Human Resourced: Thomas Nelson
Plant Manager: Doug Jackson
Purchasing: Jerry McCluskey
Number Employees: 100-249

4042 Emerald Kalama Chemical, LLC
1296 Third Street, N.W.
Kalama, WA 98625
360-673-2550
Fax: 360-673-3564 800-223-0035
kalama@emeraldmaterials.com
www.emeraldmaterials.com/epm/kalama
Manufacturer and exporter of specialty chemicals including benzaldehyde, cinnamic aldehyde, benzyl benzoate, benzyl alcohol, benzylacetate, potassium benzoate, benzoic acid and sodium benzoate
President: Edward T. Gotch
Sr. Vice President, Finance: Daniel Emmett
Vice President Operations and HS&E: Brian A. Denison
Number Employees: 175
Parent Co: Emerald Performance Materials

4043 Emerald Performance Materials
2020 Front St
Cuyahoga Falls, OH 44221-3257
330-916-6700
Fax: 330-916-6734
corporate@emeraldmaterials.com
www.emeraldmaterials.com
Produces and markets technologically advanced speciality chemicals for a broad range of food and industrial applications
President: Carrington Don
carrington.don@winwholesale.com
VP/CFO: Candace Wagner
Number Employees: 500-999

4044 Emerling International Foods
2381 Fillmore Ave
Suite 1
Buffalo, NY 14214-2197
716-833-7381
Fax: 716-833-7386 pemerling@emerfood.com
www.emerlinginternational.com
Bulk ingredients including: Fruits & Vegetables; Juice Concentrates; Herbs & Spices; Oils & Vinegars; Flavors & Colors; Honey & Molasses. Also produces pure maple syrup.
President: J Emerling
jemerling@emerfood.com
Sales: Peter Emerling
Public Relations: Jenn Burke
Year Founded: 1988
Estimated Sales: $10-20 Million
Number Employees: 20-49
Square Footage: 500000

4045 Emery Smith Fisheries Limited
5309 Hwy 3
Shag Harbour, NS B0W 3B0
Canada
902-723-2115
Fax: 902-723-2372
Manufacturer and exporter of salt fish
President: Emery Smith
Estimated Sales: $12 Million
Number Employees: 25

Type of Packaging: Bulk

4046 **Emkay Trading Corporation**
250 Clearbrook Road
PO Box 504
Elmsford, NY 10523
914-592-9000
Fax: 914-347-3616 hkpilot@aol.com
Manufacturer and distributor of cheese including cream, bakers, neuchatel, lite, tvorog (Russian style soft cheese) and quark, also, bulk cream, custom fluid diary blends, bulk skim, sour cream, bulk cultured buttermilk and condensedskim milk
Owner: Howard Kravitz
tlindquistturner@limitedbrands.com
Vice President: Ruth Kravitz
Estimated Sales: $2 Million
Number Employees: 30
Square Footage: 800000
Type of Packaging: Consumer, Food Service, Private Label, Bulk
Brands:
Emkay

4047 **Emmi Roth USA**
657 2nd St
Monroe, WI 53566-1013
608-845-5796
www.emmiusa.com
Swiss cheese
Brand Manager: Alison Lacey
Managing Director: Tim Omer
Estimated Sales: Less than $500,000
Number Employees: 5-9
Type of Packaging: Food Service, Private Label

4048 **Emmy's Candy from Belgium**
9816 Emerald Point Drive
Unit 3
Charlotte, NC 28278-6536
205-879-1901
Fax: 205-879-1903 866-879-1901
Candies
President: Emmy Verchecke

4049 **Emmy's Organics**
629 West Buffalo St
Ithaca, NY 14850
855-463-6697
info@emmysorganics.com
emmysorganics.com
Buckwheat-based cereals
Co-Founder: Ian Gaffney
Co-Founder: Samantha Abrams

4050 **Empact Bars**
885 Arapahoe Ave
Boulder, CO 80302
877-836-7228
info@empactbars.com empactbars.com
Superfood snack bars
Co-Founder: Melonie Derose
Co-Founder: Zeke Derose
Number of Brands: 1
Number of Products: 3
Type of Packaging: Consumer
Brands:
EMPACT

4051 **Empire Coffee Company**
106 Purdy Ave
Port Chester, NY 10573
914-934-1100
Fax: 914-934-1190 800-642-1100
Coffee
Founder & CEO: Robert Richter
VP of Operations: Todd Good
Year Founded: 1984
Square Footage: 40000
Type of Packaging: Private Label

4052 **Empire Kosher Foods**
247 Empire Dr
Mifflintown, PA 17059
717-436-5921
800-367-4734
www.empirekosher.com
Kosher poultry
President & CEO: Jeff Brown
Director of Quality Assurance: Ahern Tim
VP of Sales: Lisa Nelson
Year Founded: 1938
Estimated Sales: $179.9 Million
Number Employees: 1,000
Square Footage: 240000
Type of Packaging: Private Label
Brands:
Empire Kosher Poultry Products

4053 **Empire Mayonnaise Company, LLC.**
564 Vanderbilt Ave.
Brooklyn, NY 11238
718-636-2069
Manufacturer of mayonnaise.
Co-Founder: Sam Mason
Co-Founder: Eilzabeth Valleau

4054 **Empire Spice Mills**
908 William Avenue
Winnipeg, NB R3E 0Z8
Canada
204-786-1594
Fax: 204-783-2847
Flavoring extracts and whole ground and blended spices, herbs and seeds, seasonings
President: Don Ramage
Estimated Sales: $1 Million
Number Employees: 10
Square Footage: 64000
Type of Packaging: Consumer, Food Service, Private Label, Bulk
Brands:
Empire's Best

4055 **Empire Tea Svc**
1965 St James Pl
Columbus, IN 47201-2805
812-375-1937
Fax: 812-376-7382 800-790-0246
sales@empiretea.com www.empiretea.com
Importer of tea in tins, black tea, green tea, herb tea bulk tea, tea bags in wood boxes and various forms of packing
President: Lalith Guy Paranavitana
info@empiretea.com
Plant Manager: Cheryl Paranavitana
Estimated Sales: $250,000
Number Employees: 1-4
Number of Brands: 3
Number of Products: 27
Square Footage: 8000
Type of Packaging: Consumer, Food Service, Private Label, Bulk
Brands:
Guy's Tea
Tea Temptations

4056 **Empresa La Famosa**
PO Box 51968
Toa Baja, PR 00950-1968
787-251-0060
Fax: 787-251-2270
Juice
President: Jose Corripio
VP Operations: Sandy Martin
Purchasing Supervisor: Carmen Menes
Estimated Sales: $5 Million
Number Employees: 61

4057 **(HQ)Empresas La Famosa**
PO Box 51968
Toa Baja, PR 00950-1968
787-251-0060
Fax: 787-251-2270
Fruit juices, coconut, cream & milk, beans and tomato willow
President: Jose Corripio
Purchasing Supervisor: Carmen Menes
Estimated Sales: $5.6 Million
Number Employees: 61
Square Footage: 960000
Brands:
Coco Lopez, Usa

4058 **Empress Chocolate Company**
5518 Avenue N
Brooklyn, NY 11234
718-951-2251
Fax: 718-951-2254 800-793-3809
Manufacturer and exporter of custom and stock molded chocolate novelties, cream filled chocolates, truffles and gift boxes
President: Jack Grunhut
VP: Ernest Grunhut
Sales Director: Jerry Sumner
Estimated Sales: $3 Million
Number Employees: 35
Square Footage: 80000
Parent Co: Ernex Corporation
Type of Packaging: Consumer, Private Label
Brands:
Empress Chocolates

4059 **En Garde Health Products, Inc.**
7702 Balboa Blvd
#9
Van Nuys, CA 91406
818-970-9444
Fax: 818-757-0773 800-955-4633
info@engardehealth.com www.engardehealth.com
Health products
President: Hy Null Levy
CEO: Roberta Gabor
Contact: Roberta Chaplanp
roberta@engardehealth.com
Estimated Sales: $410 Thousand
Number Employees: 4

4060 **Endangered Species Chocolate**
5846 W 73rd St
Indianapolis, IN 46278-1742
317-387-4372
Fax: 317-844-4951 800-293-0160
info@chocolatebar.com www.chocolatebar.com
Gourmet Belgian chocolate, chocolate squares
Co-owner: Wayne Zink
CEO: Curt Meer
Director Finance: Carl Dodds
Operations: Bryan Fuller
Estimated Sales: $9 Million
Number Employees: 50-99
Brands:
Bug Bites
Endangered Species Chocolate Bars

4061 **Endico Potatoes Inc**
160 N Macquesten Pkwy
Mt Vernon, NY 10550-1099
914-664-1151
Fax: 914-664-9267 www.endicopotatoes.com
Frozen potato, vegetable, chicken and appetizer products.
CEO: Mike Edwards
Manager: Mike Acocella
michael.roff@gmail.com
Estimated Sales: $860,000
Number Employees: 20-49
Square Footage: 240000
Type of Packaging: Consumer, Food Service
Brands:
McCain®
Sally Sherman Foods
Tyson®
Moore's®
Lambweston®

4062 **(HQ)Ener-G Foods**
5960 1st Ave S
Seattle, WA 98108-3248
206-767-3928
Fax: 206-764-3398 800-331-5222
samiii@ener-g.com
Manufacturer and exporter of wheat free and gluten free, dairy free, nut free; bread, hamburger buns, cereals, cookies, pasta, mixes, etc.; also allergy-free foods; importer of gluten-free pasta and starches, Medical and diet foodsand low protein foods for PKU.
President: Sam Wylde III
cje@ener-g.com
Marketing/Sales: Jerry Colburn
Sales Exec: Jerry Colburn
Production Manager: Roger Traynor
Purchasing Manager: Sabina Milovic
Estimated Sales: $10 Milion
Number Employees: 20-49
Number of Brands: 2
Number of Products: 200
Square Footage: 40000
Type of Packaging: Consumer, Food Service, Private Label
Brands:
Ener-G
Old World

4063 **(HQ)Energen Products Inc**
14631 Best Ave
Norwalk, CA 90650-5258
562-926-5522
Fax: 562-921-0039 800-423-8837
Manufacturer and exporter of vitamins, wheat germ oil and brewers' yeast
President: Joseph Bensler
energen@ix.netcom.com
Estimated Sales: $3 Million
Number Employees: 20-49
Number of Brands: 13
Number of Products: 250
Square Footage: 300000
Type of Packaging: Food Service, Private Label
Brands:
American Dietary
Real Life
The Pierson Company
Vegetrates

4064 **Energenetics International**
P.O.Box 845
Keokuk, IA 52632
319-535-0760
Corn-based protein
President: Sammy Pierce
VP: Vincent James
Secretary: Gary Staggs
Number Employees: 5-9

4065 **Energique**
P.O. Box 121
201 Apple Boulevard
Woodbine, IA 51579
712-647-2499
Fax: 800-503-2588 800-869-8078
inquiry@energiqueherbal.com
Liquefied herbal extracts
President: Scott Beach
CEO/Owner: Jesse Rettig
Sales Manager: Dean Dobmeier
Contact: Joyce Beach
info@energiqueherbal.com
Estimated Sales: $3-5 Million
Number Employees: 10-19
Type of Packaging: Private Label, Bulk
Brands:
Energique®

4066 **Energy Brands/Haute Source**
1720 Whitestone Expy
Flushing, NY 11357-3000
718-746-0087
Fax: 718-747-5900 800-746-0087
ebi@energybrands.com
Distilled water
President/CEO: Brent Hastie
SVP Finance: Wadih Khayat
CMO: Rohan Oza
Contact: Charles Alfaro
calfaro@glaceau.com
COO: Glen Ricks
Estimated Sales: Less than $500,000
Number Employees: 1-4
Type of Packaging: Consumer, Food Service
Brands:
Fruit Water
Glaceau Vitaminwater
Go-Go Drinks
Smart Water
Soy Water
Vitamin Water

4067 **Energy Foods Intl.**
9300 South Dadeland Blvd
Suite 600
Miami, FL 33156
844-772-6622
info@energyfoodsintl.com
www.energyfoodsintl.com
Raw, organic fruit powders
CEO: Laercio Goncalves
Number of Products: 4

4068 **Enfield Farms Inc**
1064 Birch Bay Lynden Rd
Lynden, WA 98264-9490
360-354-2919
Fax: 360-354-0503 info@enfieldfarms.com
www.nwplant.com
Manufacturer and packer of frozen red raspberries and blueberries
Owner: Marv Enfield
Chairman: Adam Enfield
Secretary/Treasurer: Linda Enfield
Sales Manager: Mike Haveman
menfield@enfieldfarms.com
Human Resources Compliance & Regulatory: Karin Myhre
Estimated Sales: $1.3 Million
Number Employees: 250-499
Square Footage: 17444
Type of Packaging: Food Service, Private Label, Bulk
Brands:
Enfield Farms

4069 **Engel's Bakeries**
4709 14 Street NE
Bay 6
Calgary, AB T2E 6S4
Canada
403-250-9560
Fax: 403-250-5381 www.engelsbakeriesltd.ca
Baked and frozen ready-to-bake products including breads, pastries, sausage rolls, cakes, etc
President: Mithoo Gillani
R&D: Brian Hinton
Marketing/Sales: Ron Clappison
Sales Manager: Aaron Goss
Production Manager: Greg Zub
Purchasing: Danoz McKinnon
Estimated Sales: $5 Million
Number Employees: 70
Square Footage: 64000
Type of Packaging: Food Service

4070 **English Bay Batter Us Inc**
2241 Citygate Dr
Columbus, OH 43219-3564
614-471-9994
Fax: 614-890-9992 800-253-6844
www.englishbaycookies.com
Frozen batter and baked goods
Manager: Dan Rudd
Estimated Sales: $5-10 Million
Number Employees: 20-49
Parent Co: English Bay Batter
Type of Packaging: Consumer, Food Service, Private Label, Bulk
Brands:
English Batter

4071 **Enjoy Foods International**
10601 Beech Ave
Fontana, CA 92337
909-823-2228
Fax: 909-355-1573 info@EnjoyBeefJerky.com
www.enjoybeefjerky.com
Manufacturer and exporter of beef and turkey jerky and meat snacks; exporter of steak kabobs
Chairman: Waleed Saab
VP: Mohamad Kabab
Marketing/Sales: Pierre Taylor
Contact: Walter Dorrouh
waleed@enjoybeefjerky.com
Plant Manager: Dennis Quinzon
Estimated Sales: $6.3 Million
Number Employees: 40
Square Footage: 40584
Type of Packaging: Consumer

4072 **Enjoy Life Foods**
8770 W Bryn Mawr Ave
Suite 1100
Chicago, IL 60631
888-503-6569
enjoylifefoods.com
Gluten-free cookies, snacks, granola and bagels.
President: Federico Meade
Founder/CEO: Scott Mandell
CFO: Bert Cohen
Senior Manager of R&D/Innovation: Lindsey Herman
Quality Assurance Director: Sandy Kasten
Chief Marketing Officer: Joel Warady
Senior Director of Sales: Patricia Marko
Contact: Courtney Benavides
cbenavides@enjoylifefoods.com
Operations Manager: Marvin Rea
Estimated Sales: $6 Million
Number Employees: 50
Square Footage: 60000

4073 **Enlightened**
101 Lincoln Ave
Suite 100
Bronx, NY 10454-4415
212-888-1120
www.eatenlightened.com
Ice cream and ice cream bars
CEO: Michael Shoretz
Year Founded: 2013
Estimated Sales: Less than $500,000
Number Employees: 1-4
Type of Packaging: Food Service, Private Label

4074 **Enray, Inc**
6999 Southfront Road
Suite D
Livermore, CA 94551
925-218-2205
Fax: 925-365-0587 800-288-3637
www.truroots.com
Full-line grains, cereal and pasta.
Marketing: Esha Ray
Contact: Steve Fischer
steve@fischer-creative.com

4075 **Enrico Biscotti Co**
2022 Penn Ave
Pittsburgh, PA 15222-4418
412-281-2602
www.enricobiscotti.com
Italian cookie/biscotti
Owner: Larry Lagattuta
Estimated Sales: Less Than $500,000
Number Employees: 10-19

4076 **Enrico's/Ventre Packing**
6050 Court Street Rd
Syracuse, NY 13206-1711
315-463-2384
Fax: 315-463-5897 888-472-8237
Sauces and salsas.
President: Marty Ventre
Manager Quality Control: Kurt Alpha
Eastern Regional Sales Manager: Rick Alesia
Estimated Sales: $10-20 Million
Number Employees: 10-19

4077 **Ensemble Beverages**
600 S Court Street
Suite 460
Montgomery, AL 36104-4106
334-324-7719
Manufacturer, importer and exporter of beverages including carbonated, sports drinks, nutritional shakes, iced tea and powders
President: James Harris
CFO: Cornelius Blanding, Jr
Number Employees: 10-19

4078 **Enslin & Son Packing Company**
2500 Glendale Ave
Hattiesburg, MS 39401
601-582-9300
Fax: 601-544-2010 800-898-4687
Manufacturer, packer and wholesaler/distributor of sausage
President: August Enslin
Estimated Sales: $4 Million
Number Employees: 30
Square Footage: 32000
Type of Packaging: Consumer, Private Label, Bulk
Brands:
Bowie River
Country Morning
Glendale
Hickory

4079 **Enstrom Candies, Inc.**
701 Colorado Ave
Grand Junction, CO 81501
Fax: 970-683-1011 800-367-8766
www.enstrom.com
Manufacturing and sales of confectionery products, including Almond Toffee, Truffles, Chocolates, Brittles, Fudges.

Owner: Doug Simons
Secretary/Treasurer & VP, Marketing: Jamee Simons
Quality Control Manager: Ginny Ansbaugh
National Sales Director: Bob Jackson
Contact Center Manager: Wendy Hanway
wendy@enstrom.com
Chief Technology Officer: Daniel Lively
Manufacturing Director: Doug Tuttle
Buyer: Diana Wilsey
Year Founded: 1929
Estimated Sales: $25 Million
Number Employees: 107
Number of Brands: 1
Square Footage: 19360
Type of Packaging: Consumer
Other Locations:
Enstrom Candies
Denver CO
Brands:
Denver Co
Enstrom Candies

4080 Entenmann's
930 Riverview Dr
Totowa, NJ 07511
973-785-7601
Fax: 973-785-0009 www.entenmanns.com
Baked goods
Parent Co: Bimbo Bakeries USA

4081 Enterprise Foods
5315 Tulane Dr SW Ste D
Atlanta, GA 30336
404-351-2251
Fax: 404-351-3969
Wholesale bakery ingredients and emulsifiers, dough conditioners, bromate replacers
President: Gerald Anderson
Estimated Sales: $1 Million
Number Employees: 10-19
Number of Brands: 1
Number of Products: 10
Square Footage: 300000
Type of Packaging: Bulk
Brands:
Enterprise
Sip
Zeelanco

4082 Enterprises Pates et Croutes
14 Rue De Montgolfier
Boucherville, QC J4B 7Y4
Canada
450-655-7790
Fax: 450-655-8037 800-265-7790
patesetcroutes.com
Manufacturer and exporter of frozen pie dough and shells; processor of baked muffins,bakery products,pastry products,and food product machinery.
President: Francine Benoit
Estimated Sales: 3.8 Million
Number Employees: 40
Type of Packaging: Consumer, Food Service

4083 Entner-Stuart Premium Syrups
1852 Fescue St SE
Albany, OR 97322-7075
541-812-8000
Fax: 541-812-8010 800-926-6886
sales@allanbroscoffee.com
www.allanbroscoffee.com
Tea and coffee syrups
President/CEO: Allan Stuart
Estimated Sales: $5-10 Million
Number Employees: 10-19

4084 Enz Vineyards
1781 Limekiln Rd
Hollister, CA 95023-9172
831-637-6443
Fax: 831-637-9382 www.vinarium-usa.com
Wines
Owner: Robert Enz
Partner: Susan Enz
Estimated Sales: $500,000-$1 Million
Number Employees: 1-4

4085 Enzo Olive Oil Co.
7770 Road 33
Madera, CA 93638
559-299-7278
Fax: 559-299-7292 info@enzooliveoil.com
enzooliveoil.com
Balsamic vinegars and olive oils
Owner: Pat Ricchiuti
Number of Brands: 3
Number of Products: 13
Type of Packaging: Consumer
Brands:
ENZO ORGANIC OLIVE OIL
ENZO ORGANIC BALSAMIC VINEGAR
ENZO'S TABLE

4086 Enzymatic Therapy Inc
825 Challenger Dr
Green Bay, WI 54311
Fax: 920-469-4444 800-783-2286
www.enzymatictherapy.com
Nutritional supplements
President & CEO: Randy Rose
Territory Sales Manager: Ben Bechtolt
pbechtolt@enzy.com
Estimated Sales: $100-499 Million
Number Employees: 250-499
Number of Products: 350
Parent Co: Nature's Way Holding Co.
Type of Packaging: Consumer, Private Label
Brands:
Acidoplius Pearls
Remifemin
Vitaline CoQ10
Whole Body Cleanse

4087 Enzyme Development Corporation
505 Eighth Avenue
Suite 500
New York, NY 10018
212-736-1580
Fax: 212-279-0056
info@enzymedevelopment.com
www.enzymedevelopment.com
Manufacturer, importer and exporter of industrial and specialty enzymes.
Technical Sales Representative: Christina Barsa
Contact: Bobby Gau
bobby.gau@scinopharm.com
Type of Packaging: Bulk
Brands:
Enzeco®

4088 Enzyme Formulations Inc
6421 Enterprise Ln
Madison, WI 53719-1116
608-273-8100
Fax: 608-273-8111 800-614-4400
www.naturalenzymes.com
Supplements
Owner: Polly Fleming
pfleming@enzymeformulations.com

4089 Enzyme Innovation
13591 Yorba Ave
Chino, CA 91710-5071
909-203-4620
adm@enzymeinnovation.com
www.enzymeinnovation.com
Enzymes.
Vice President: Dipak Roda
Estimated Sales: Below $1 Million
Number Employees: 1-4

4090 Eola Hills Wine Cellars
501 S Pacific Hwy
Rickreall, OR 97371-9728
503-623-2405
Fax: 503-623-0350 800-291-6730
www.eolahillswinery.com
Wines
President: Tom Huggins
tom-huggins@eolahillswinery.com
CEO: Eric Rogers
CFO: Cherie Haines
Marketing: Michael Connell
Estimated Sales: $4 Million
Number Employees: 20-49

4091 Epi De France Bakery
1749 Tullie Circle NE
Atlanta, GA 30329
404-325-1016
Fax: 404-325-0735 800-325-1014
bdoan@epibreads.com www.epibreads.com
Fresh and frozen bread, hoagies, table breads, baguettes, buns and rolls, sliced loaves, and ciabattas.
President: Nic Mulliez
CEO: Hugh Sullins
Sales Manager: B Doan
Estimated Sales: $20-50 Million
Square Footage: 42500
Type of Packaging: Consumer, Food Service, Private Label, Bulk
Brands:
Epi De France
Graines De Vie

4092 Epic Provisions
PO Box 684581
Austin, TX 78768
512-944-8502
Fax: 512-900-7982 eatepic@epicbar.com
epicprovisions.com
Protein bars and snacks; duck fat; cured meats; smoked seafood.
Co-Founder: Taylor Collins
Co-Founder: Katie Forrest
Sales Director: Martha Siskron
marth@epicbar.com
Year Founded: 2012
Estimated Sales: $4 Million
Number Employees: 11-50
Type of Packaging: Private Label

4093 Epic Source Food
PO Box 2244
Frisco, TX 75034
214-407-7154
epicsourcefoods.com
Goat cheese products and ice cream
CEO & National Sales Manager: Tim Millson
tmillson@epicsourcefoods.com
Sales & Marketing Support: Gayle Franks
Estimated Sales: $2-3 Million
Number Employees: 2-10
Brands:
Funny Farm
Laloo's(c)
Nutritional Noodle
Planet Harvest

4094 (HQ)Epicurean Butter
9355 Elm Ct
Federal Heights, CO 80260-5211
303-427-5527
Fax: 303-254-5381 epicureanbutter@msn.com
www.epicureanbutter.com
Compound butters, both sweet and savory.
President: Carlos Garcia
carlos@epicureanbutter.com
VP: Janey Hubschman
Estimated Sales: $6.4 Million
Number Employees: 20-49

4095 Epogee
Indianapolis, IN 46208
www.epogeefoods.com
An alternative ingredient to fat, GMO-free and free of vegetable oils.
CEO: Tom Burrows
Founder & Chief Technology Officer: David Rowe
Chief Commercial Officer: Jayme Caruso
Sr. Director, Marketing: Sarah Malenich
Year Founded: 2011
Number Employees: 10
Type of Packaging: Food Service

4096 (HQ)Equal Exchange Inc
50 United Dr
West Bridgewater, MA 02379-1026
774-776-7400
Fax: 508-587-0088 orders@equalexchange.coop
www.equalexchange.coop
Organic coffee, tea, chocolate, and nuts
Co-Executive Director: Rink Dickinson
Co-Executive Director: Rob Everts
dabbott@equalexchange.coop
Marketing: Bruce McKinnon
Sales: Mark Sweet
Director Operations: Denise Abbott
Estimated Sales: $20-50 Million
Number Employees: 50-99
Square Footage: 10000
Type of Packaging: Bulk

4097 Equal Exchange Inc
15 Campanelli Circle
Canton, MA 02021
orders@equalexchange.coop
www.equalexchange.coop
Organic coffees
Type of Packaging: Bulk

4098 **Equal Exchange Inc**
3460 NW Industrial St.
Portland, OR 97210
503-847-2000
orders@equalexchange.coop
www.equalexchange.coop
Organic coffees
Type of Packaging: Bulk

4099 **Equal Exchange Inc**
744 Vandalia St.
St. Paul, MN 55114
651-379-5020
Fax: 651-379-5023 orders@equalexchange.coop
www.equalexchange.coop
Organic coffees
Type of Packaging: Bulk

4100 **Equal Exchange Inc**
23400 Aurora Rd.
Unit 4
Bedford Heights, OH 44146
440-945-6875
orders@equalexchange.coop
www.equalexchange.coop
Organic coffees
Type of Packaging: Bulk

4101 **Equator Coffees & Teas**
115 Jordan St
San Rafael, CA 94901-3919
415-485-2213
800-809-7687
orders@equatorcoffees.com
www.equatorcoffees.com
Coffees and teas
Owner: Helen Russell
hrussell@equatorcoffees.com
Number Employees: 20-49

4102 **Eragrain**
208-867-8416
info@eragrain.com
www.eragrain.com
Ivory and Brown teff.
Brands:
Eragrain(c)

4103 **Erath Vineyards Winery**
9409 NE Worden Hill Road
Dundee, OR 97115
503-538-3318
Fax: 503-538-1074 800-539-5463
info@erath.com www.erath.com
Wines
Founder: Dick Erath
Accounting Manager: Doug Moe
Marketing/Sales Manager: Steve Vuylsteke
Contact: Mayo Alba
malba@erath.com
Estimated Sales: $5-10 Million
Number Employees: 20-49
Number of Brands: 1
Number of Products: 1
Type of Packaging: Private Label, Bulk

4104 **(HQ)Erba Food Products**
2 Metro Tech Ctr. Ste 2000
Brooklyn, NY 11201-3838
718-272-7700
Fax: 718-272-7711
Manufacturer, importer and exporter of kosher foods including vegetables, juices, coffee, spices, seasonings, baked goods, fruits, condiments, fish, nuts, oils, etc
Manager: Heeren Patel
VP of Marketing: Abraham Perkowski
Sales: Jen O'Connor
Number Employees: 10-19
Type of Packaging: Consumer, Food Service
Brands:
Embassy Wines
Haddar

4105 **Ericas Rugelach & Baking Co**
389 4th St
Brooklyn, NY 11215-2901
718-965-3657
Fax: 718-832-6160 ericasrugelach@aol.com
www.ericasrugelach.com
Cookies and rugelach
CEO: Erica Kalick
ekalick@nyc.rr.com
Estimated Sales: Less Than $500,000
Number Employees: 1-4
Brands:
Erica's Rugelach

4106 **Erick Schat's Bakery**
763 N Main St
Bishop, CA 93514-2427
760-873-7156
Fax: 760-872-4932 866-323-5854
schatsbakery@mindspring.com
www.schatsbakery.com
Baked goods
Number Employees: 50-99

4107 **(HQ)Erie Foods Intl Inc**
401 7th Ave
PO Box 648
Erie, IL 61250
309-659-2233
Fax: 309-659-2822 glindsey@eriefoods.com
www.eriefoods.com
Co-dried and concentrated milk proteins; also sodium, calcium, combination and acid-stable caseinates and dairy blends; importer of milk proteins
President/CEO: David Reisenbigler
dreisenbigler@eriefoods.com
CFO: Mark Delaney
COO: Jim Klein
Technical Services Manager: Craig Air
Quality Manager: Rene Perla
Purchasing Manager: Jake VanDeWostine
Process Development Manager: Jim Jacoby
Purchasing Manager: Shawn Larson
Estimated Sales: $1-2.5 Million
Number Employees: 10-19
Square Footage: 120000
Parent Co: Erie Foods International Inc
Type of Packaging: Bulk
Other Locations:
Erie Foods International
Beenleigh QLD
Brands:
Ecco
Erie

4108 **Erivan Dairy**
105 Allison Rd
Oreland, PA 19075-1808
215-887-2009
Fax: 215-885-3679 www.erivandairy.com
Yogurt
President: Harry Fereshetian
Plant Manager: Paul Fereshetian
Estimated Sales: $1-2.5 Million
Number Employees: 20-49
Type of Packaging: Consumer

4109 **Errol's Cajun Foods**
6801 Highway 1001
Belle Rose, LA 70341-5405
225-746-1002
Fax: 225-746-1004 866-746-6003
www.errolscajunfoods.com
Stuffed and frozen jalapeno peppers and value added seafood products including crab and shrimp; also, seafood gumbo and shrimp etouffee and patties
Owner: Errol Perera
bmtheriot@yahoo.com
Estimated Sales: $2.5-5 Million
Number Employees: 10-19
Type of Packaging: Consumer, Food Service

4110 **Escalade Limited**
37 W Shore Rd # 2
Huntington, NY 11743-7206
631-659-3373
Fax: 631-659-3376 latitudeltd@aol.com
www.latitudeltdusa.com
Ingredients and additives, including anti-oxidants, preservatives, sweeteners and minerals
President: Lourel Mandel
VP: Dedi Avner
Contact: Dedi Avner
escalade@bezeqint.net
Estimated Sales: $500,000- 1 Million
Number Employees: 8

4111 **Escalon Premier Brand**
1905 McHenry Ave
Escalon, CA 95320
209-838-7341
Fax: 209-838-6206 www.escalon.net
Canned tomatoes and tomato products including sauces
Controller: Steve Kelly
Human Resource Executive: Susan McCready
Product Manager: Dan Milazzo
Plant Manager: John Raggio
Purchasing Agent: Tom Muller
Number Employees: 100-249
Parent Co: Heinz USA
Type of Packaging: Consumer, Food Service
Brands:
6-In-1
Bell 'orto
Bella Rosa
Christina's Organic
Heniz
Mama Linda

4112 **Eschete's Seafood**
229 New Orleans Blvd
Houma, LA 70364-3345
985-872-4120
Fax: 504-851-6147
Seafood
Owner: John Eschete
Estimated Sales: $300,000-500,000
Number Employees: 1-4

4113 **(HQ)Esco Foods Inc**
131 Russ St
San Francisco, CA 94103-4009
415-864-2147
info@escofoods.com
www.escofoods.com
Syrups, toppings, salad dressings, marinades, bbq sauce, flavors
President: Marc Bosschart
Contact: Michele Bosschart
info@escofoods.com
Estimated Sales: $2.5-5 Million
Number Employees: 5-9

4114 **Eskimo Candy Inc**
2665 Wai Wai Pl
Kihei, HI 96753-8178
808-879-5686
Fax: 808-874-0504 www.eskimocandy.com
Seafood and other fine foods.
Owner: Jeff Hansen
eskimo@maui.net
Estimated Sales: $10-20 Million
Number Employees: 20-49

4115 **(HQ)Esper Products DeLuxe**
2793 N Orange Blossom Trl
Kissimmee, FL 34744-1375
407-847-3726
800-268-0892
colleen1014@webtv.com
Jellies and preserves
President: Andrew McFarland
Estimated Sales: $2.5-5,000,000
Number Employees: 5-9
Brands:
Esper Deluxe

4116 **Espresso Vivace**
901 E Denny Way Ste 100
Seattle, WA 98122
206-860-5869
Fax: 206-860-1567 info@espressovivace.com
www.espressovivace.com
Coffee
Founder: David Schomer
Estimated Sales: $1-2.5 Million
Number Employees: 20-49

4117 **Espro Manufacturing**
2800 Ayers Avenue
Vernon, CA 90058
323-415-8544
Fax: 323-268-4060
Manufacturer and packager of food ingredients, including custom dry powder blends.
Contact: Blas Tiangson
blas.tiangson@kp.org

4118 **Essen Nutrition Corp**
1414 Sherman Rd
Romeoville, IL 60446-4046
630-739-6700
Fax: 630-739-6464 800-582-6064
sales@essen-nutrition.com
www.essen-nutrition.com

Dietary and health foods
President: Madhavan Anirudhan
manirudhan@essennutritioncorp.com
Vice President: Mike Holland
VP Operations: Tom Grandys
Estimated Sales: $4 Million
Number Employees: 20-49
Type of Packaging: Private Label

4119 **Essentia Protein Solutions**
2425 SE Oak Tree Court
Ankeny, IA 50021
515-289-5100
Fax: 515-289-5110 essentiaproteins.com
Essentia manufactures functional proteins that improve the taste and texture of commercial food products. It is a global company with operations in the United States, South America, Europe and Asia.
COO: Asger Jacobsen
Executive VP, Global Sales: Moises Contreras
Parent Co: Lauridsen Group
Brands:
ScanPro™
APro™
ExcelPro™
ExcelPro™ Plus
Drinde™
ProBase™
ProFlavor™

4120 **Essentia Water**
22833 Bthell Everett Hwy
Street 220
Bothell, WA 98021
425-402-9555
877-293-2239
customerservice@essentiawater.com
www.essentiawater.com
Purifying drinking water
President: Ken Uptain
CFO: Keith Huetson
Estimated Sales: $2 Million
Number Employees: 1-4

4121 **Essential Baking Co, The**
5601 1st Avenue South
Seattle, WA 98108
206-545-3804
Fax: 206-767-1176
marketing@essentialbaking.com
essentialbaking.com
Artisan breads, pastries and desserts
Chairman: Peter Miller
President & CEO: Tom Campanile
Marketing Manager: Kuanny Yin
HR Generalist: Kanjarin Hiranworawuthikul
Purchasing Manager: Alec Norman
Estimated Sales: $25-50 Million
Number Employees: 200-500
Brands:
The Essential Baking Company

4122 **Essential Flavors & Fragrances**
1521 Commerce St
Corona, CA 92880-1730
951-737-3889
Fax: 951-737-4237 888-333-9935
customerservice@essentialflavors.com
www.essentialflavors.com
Drink based concentrates, flavorings, herbal extracts and body building formulas
President: Michael Gulan
mpgro@juno.com
Vice President: Richard Staley
Office Manager: Susan Wakeling
Estimated Sales: $630,000
Number Employees: 5-9
Type of Packaging: Bulk

4123 **Essential Living Foods**
Torrance, CA 90503
310-319-1555
essentiallivingfoods.com
Trail mixes and smoothie blends

4124 **Essential Nutrients Inc**
174 E 400 S
Emery, UT 84522
435-286-2460
Fax: 435-286-2471
vickie@essentialnutrientsinc.com
www.essentialnutrientsinc.com
Nutrients
President: Randy Haringa
Vice President: Vicki Heringa
Estimated Sales: $58,000
Number Employees: 1-4
Type of Packaging: Private Label
Brands:
Super Kmh

4125 **Essential Products of America**
6710 Benjamin Road
Suite 700
Tampa, FL 33634-4314
813-886-9698
Fax: 813-886-9661 800-822-9698
Manufacturer, importer and exporter of essential oils
President: Michael Alexander
Estimated Sales: $2.5-5 Million
Number Employees: 5
Square Footage: 4800
Type of Packaging: Consumer, Private Label, Bulk
Brands:
Whole Spectrum

4126 **Essiac Canada International**
164 Richmond Rd
Ottawa, ON K1Z 6W2
Canada
514-695-2299
888-900-2299
www.essiaccanadainternational.com
Manufacturer and exporter of herbal dietary supplements
President: Terrence Maloney
Estimated Sales: $975,000
Number Employees: 6
Number of Brands: 2
Number of Products: 2
Parent Co: Essiac Canada International
Type of Packaging: Consumer, Food Service
Brands:
Essiac (Extract)
Essiac (Powder)

4127 **Esteem Products**
1800 136th Pl NE
Ste 5
Bellevue, WA 98005
425-562-1281
Fax: 425-562-1284 800-255-7631
customerservice@esteemproducts.com
www.esteemproducts.com
Manufacturer, wholesaler/distributor and exporter of nutritional supplements and specialty vitamins. All combination formulas for consumer simplicity
CEO/President: John Sheaffer
VP: Linda Sheaffer
Marketing: Amy Braisford
Contact: Chana Madsen
chana@esteemproducts.com
Estimated Sales: $500,000-$1 Million
Number Employees: 5-9
Square Footage: 20000
Brands:
Artho Life
Cardio Life
Esteem Plus
Golden Life
Immune Life
Super Life
Total Man
Total Woman
Trim & Firm Am/Pm

4128 **Esterlina Vineyard & Winery**
435 West Dry Creek Road
Healdsburg, CA 95448
707-895-2920
Fax: 707-895-2972 888-474-7456
Wines
President: Craig Sterling
CEO: Eric Sterling
Marketing Manager: Steve Sterling
Estimated Sales: Under $500,000
Number Employees: 5-9
Brands:
Esterlina

4129 **Esther Price Candies & Gifts**
1709 Wayne Ave
Dayton, OH 45410-1711
937-253-2121
Fax: 937-253-6034 855-337-8437
customerservice@epcandies.com
www.estherprice.com
Chocolates
President: James Day
james@epcandies.com
Manager: Barb Dressman
Estimated Sales: Under $500,000
Number Employees: 100-249
Type of Packaging: Consumer, Private Label

4130 **Etchandy Farms**
Anaheim, CA
Strawberries
President/Owner: Mike Etchandy
Year Founded: 1947
Type of Packaging: Consumer, Private Label

4131 **Eternal Water**
2950 Buskirk Ave
Suite 312
Walnut Creek, CA 94597
877-854-5494
info@eternalwater.com www.eternalwater.com
Sparkling spring water
Founder & CEO: Karim Mashouf

4132 **Ethan's**
939 Pearl St
Boulder, CO 80302
720-432-8384
info@ethans.com
www.ethans.com
Apple cider vinegar shots
Founder: Ethan Hirshberg
Number of Brands: 1
Number of Products: 6
Type of Packaging: Consumer
Brands:
ETHAN'S

4133 **Ethel M Chocolates**
1 Sunset Way
Henderson, NV 89014
800-438-4356
www.ethelm.com
Chocolate.
Sales Director: Viviana Strahl Dickieson
Estimated Sales: $100-500 Million
Number Employees: 5-9
Parent Co: Mars

4134 **Ethel's Baking Co.**
22314 Harper Ave
St. Clair Shores, MI 48080
586-552-5110
ethelsbaking.com
Gluten-free dessert bars and cookies
Founder: Jill Bommarito
Year Founded: 2011
Number of Brands: 1
Number of Products: 10
Type of Packaging: Consumer
Brands:
ETHEL'S BAKING

4135 **Ethical Bean Coffee**
1315 Kootenay St
Vancouver, BC V5K 4Y3
Canada
604-431-3830
Fax: 604-431-3834 877-431-3830
ethicalbean.com
Roasted coffee beans
Co-Founder: Lloyd Bernhardt
Co-Founder: Kim Schachte
Sales Development & Marketing: Lauren Archibald
Year Founded: 2003
Estimated Sales: $6,000,000
Number Employees: 25
Type of Packaging: Private Label

4136 **Ethical Naturals**
330 H Sir Francis Drake Blvd
Suite F
San Anselmo, CA 94960
415-459-4454
866-459-4454
info@ethicalnaturals.com
www.ethicalnaturals.com
Natural ingredients and flavors
President: Cal Bewicke
Estimated Sales: Under $500,000
Number Employees: 1

4137 Ethnic Edibles
2186 5th Avenue
Apt 17a
New York, NY 10037-2720
718-320-0147
Fax: 718-320-0147 info@ethnicedibles.com
www.ethnicedibles.com
Cookies and cookie cutters with African and Puerto Rico themes
President: Heather McCartney
Contact: Heather Mccartney
heathermccartney@msn.com
Brands:
Coqui Cookies
Ethnic Edibles

4138 Ethnic Gourmet Foods
4600 Sleepytime Drive
Boulder, CO 80301
610-692-7575
Fax: 610-719-6399 800-434-4246
www.ethnicgourmet.com
Frozen gourmet foods
Manager: Richard Alexander
Estimated Sales: $20 Million
Number Employees: 50-99
Parent Co: Hain Celestial Group

4139 Etna Brewing Co
131 Callahan St
Etna, CA 96027
530-467-5277
Fax: 530-567-3083 etnabrew@gmail.com
www.etnabrew.com
Beer
Owner: Dave Krell
Brewer: Luke Hurlimann
Estimated Sales: $500,000-$1 Million
Number Employees: 10-19
Brands:
Dark Lager
Etna Ale
Etna Bock
Etna Doppelbock
Etna Oktoberfest
Etna Weizen
Export Lager

4140 (HQ)Ettlinger Corp
175 Olde Half Day Rd # 247
Lincolnshire, IL 60069-3063
847-564-5020
Fax: 847-564-0802
Cereal grains, barley & wheat, reduced lactose whey
President: Peter Ettlinger
peter@ettlingercorp.com
Estimated Sales: $1-2.5 Million
Number Employees: 5-9
Type of Packaging: Food Service, Bulk

4141 Euphoria Chocolate Company
4090 Stewart Rd
Eugene, OR 97402
541-344-4914
Fax: 541-344-5223 www.euphoriachocolate.com
Chocolate truffles, trail mix
President/CEO: Bob Bury
Contact: Lorrie Betty
lorrie@euphoriachocolate.com
Estimated Sales: Less than $500,000
Number Employees: 1-4

4142 Eureka Locker Inc
110 4h Park Rd
Eureka, IL 61530-1706
309-467-2731
Fax: 309-467-2731 www.bittnersmeatco.com
Beef, pork and lamb
President: Scott Bittner
Estimated Sales: $500,000-$1 Million
Number Employees: 1-4
Type of Packaging: Consumer

4143 Eureka Water Co
729 SW 3rd St
Oklahoma City, OK 73109-1100
405-235-8474
Fax: 405-235-6344 800-310-8474
info@ozarkah2o.com
Bottled water
President: Bl Carter
blc@ozarkah2o.com
Plant Manager: Robert DeShazo
Estimated Sales: $5-10 Million
Number Employees: 100-249
Type of Packaging: Consumer, Private Label, Bulk
Brands:
Mountain Valley
Ozarka
Shamrock

4144 Euro Cafe
1150 University Ave # 8
Rochester, NY 14607-1663
585-244-3140
Fax: 585-461-2234 800-298-9410
Biscotti, chocolate, espresso, flavoring. Distributors of cafe and restaurant products
Owner: Barb Campbell
Public Relations: Danny Daniele
Estimated Sales: $1-2.5 000,000
Number Employees: 5-9

4145 Euro Chocolate Fountain
2647 Ariane Dr
San Diego, CA 92117-3422
858-270-9863
Fax: 858-270-6801 800-423-9303
info@eurochocolate.com
Bakery products, chocolate confections and specialty baking
Owner: Urs Huwyler
VP: Don Rein
Estimated Sales: Less Than $500,000
Number Employees: 1-4
Brands:
Euro Chocolate

4146 Euro Source Gourmet
220 Little Falls Road
Unit 2
Cedar Grove, NJ 07009-1255
973-857-6000
Fax: 973-857-8862 tjvambass@aol.com
Gourmet foods
Owner: Thomas Calvaruso
Sales: Janka Delatte

4147 Euroam Importers Inc
1302 S 293rd Pl
Auburn, WA 98003-3756
253-839-5240
Fax: 253-839-4171 888-839-2702
euroaminc1@aol.com
Coffee
President: Vito Rizzo
euroaminc1@aol.com
VP: Anita Goransson
Estimated Sales: $270,000
Number Employees: 1-4
Number of Brands: 10
Number of Products: 20
Square Footage: 7200
Parent Co: Euro Am Imports

4148 Eurobubblies
58 Union Street
Ashland, MA 01721
508-881-9900
800-273-0750
christian@eurobubblies.com
www.eurobubblies.com
Beverage and food products from Europe
President: Pascal Benichou
Estimated Sales: Under $500,000
Number Employees: 5-9
Type of Packaging: Consumer, Food Service, Private Label, Bulk
Brands:
Basilic Pistou
Bel Normande-Spritzers
Clos Normand
Dupont D'Isigny-Candies
Eat Natural
Efferve
Eurobubblies
Eurosupreme
Harrgate
Hobgoblin-Beer
Joker-Fruit Juice
Lorina-Lemonade
Pampryl
Primel
Seasoning Salt
Siracuse
Spoonty
St Peter's
Terrafood
Wychwood

4149 Eurocaribe Packing Company
Vega Baja, PR
787-793-6900
www.matosantos.com/manufacturingsubsidiaries-eurocaribe.htm
Smoked meats
President: Jose Casanova
CFO: John Erickson
Purchasing: Hiram Morales
Estimated Sales: $10-20,000,000
Number Employees: 160
Parent Co: Matosantos Commercial Corp.
Type of Packaging: Private Label, Bulk
Other Locations:
Zona Industrial
Carolina PR

4150 Europa Sports Products
11401 Granite St
Charlotte, NC 28273
800-447-4795
sales@europasports.com www.europasports.com
Sports food and nutrition.
CEO: Eric Hillman
erichillman@europasports.com
CFO: Anthony Todaro
COO: Robbie Duncan
Year Founded: 1990
Estimated Sales: $100-499 Million
Number Employees: 250-499
Number of Brands: 280
Brands:
ABB
ABN
Absolute Nutrition
AccuFitness
Basic Research
Best Bar Ever
Bpi
Caveman Foods
Cellucor
Cytosport
Designer Protein
Eat The Bear
EFX Sports
Fitmark
FRS Company
Clif Bar
Gatorade
Hydroxycut
Jack Links
Jelly Belly Candy Company
Kind Snacks
Mancakes
Paleo People
Pure Protein
Quest Nutrition

4151 European Bakers
5055 S Royal Atlanta Dr
Tucker, GA 30084-3097
770-723-6180
Fax: 770-939-6632 www.europeanbakers.com
Baked goods including breads and buns
President: James Allen
Estimated Sales: $10-20 Million
Number Employees: 100-249
Square Footage: 260000
Parent Co: Flowers Baking Company
Type of Packaging: Consumer

4152 European Coffee
13925 58th Street North
Clearwater, FL 33760
727-535-2111
Fax: 856-428-7262 888-635-4882
ConsumerRelations@melitta.com
www.melitta.com
Coffee
President/CEO: H Radtke
Finance Mananger: Scott Landem
VP: John Masters
Director: Jay Burdette
Operations Manager: Timm Rose
Plant Manager: Vincent Tagliaferro
Estimated Sales: $5-10 Million
Number Employees: 20-49
Brands:
Frac-Packs

4153 European Egg Noodle Manufacturing
14815 Yellowhead Trail Nw
Edmonton, AB T5L 3C4
Canada
780-453-6767
Fax: 780-453-6769
Frozen pastas, sauces, sausages and pizzas
President/Sales: Fausto Chinellato
Operations: Dorothy Chinellato
Estimated Sales: $743,000
Number Employees: 5
Type of Packaging: Consumer
Brands:
Bella Festa
Pasta Time

4154 European Roasterie
250 W Bradshaw St
Le Center, MN 56057-1121
507-357-2272
Fax: 507-357-4478 888-588-5282
www.euroroast.com
Coffees and teas
President/CEO: Timothy Tulloch
timothy@euroroast.com
Sales: Cindy Dorzinski
Operations: Thomas Dotray
Estimated Sales: $20-50 Million
Number Employees: 20-49
Type of Packaging: Private Label

4155 European Style Bakery
112 N Hamilton Drive
Unit 107
Beverly Hills, CA 90211-2279
818-368-6876
Blueberry filling, cakes and bakery items
President: Vladimir Landa
vladimir.landa@europeanpastry.com
Estimated Sales: Less than $500,000
Number Employees: 5-9

4156 Eva Gates Homemade Preserves
456 Electric Ave
Bigfork, MT 59911-3641
406-837-4356
Fax: 406-837-4376 800-682-4283
info@evagates.com www.evagates.com
Fruit preserves and fruit syrups
President: Gretchen Gates
Estimated Sales: Less Than $500,000
Number Employees: 1-4
Type of Packaging: Private Label

4157 Evans Creole Candy
848 Decatur St
New Orleans, LA 70116-3375
504-522-7111
Fax: 504-522-7113 800-637-6675
Praline, chocolate candy and syrup
President: Jaye Cuccia
evanscc@bellsouth.net
Estimated Sales: $1-2.5 Million
Number Employees: 5-9
Type of Packaging: Bulk

4158 Evans Food Group LTD
4118 S Halsted St
Chicago, IL 60609-2693
773-254-7400
Fax: 773-254-7791 866-254-7400
www.evansfood.com
Manufacturer and exporter of rendered pork rinds.
Chairman/CEO: Jose Luis Prado
Purchasing: Ed McKenna
Estimated Sales: $20-50 Million
Number Employees: 100-249
Number of Brands: 4
Square Footage: 104000
Type of Packaging: Consumer, Private Label
Brands:
Bill's
La Tonita
Macs
Porkies

4159 Evans Properties
#301, 660 Beachland Blvd.
Vero Beach, FL 32963
772-234-2410
www.evansprop.com
Agricultural and land-management company. This company has 8 land holdings across Florida, and are responsible for growing citrus.
Chairman of the Board: Jimmy Evans, Jr.
President & CEO: Ronald Edwards
VP, Chief Financial Officer: Jerry Beasman
Vice President: Emmett Evans, III
Estimated Sales: $5-10,000,000
Number Employees: 5-9

4160 Eve Sales Corp
945 Close Ave
Bronx, NY 10473
718-589-6800
Fax: 718-617-6717 executiveoffice@evesales.com
Juice; instant coffee; tea; concentrates and powders; BBQ sauce; marinades; seasonings; and chips
Vice President: Stuart Gale
Year Founded: 1965
Estimated Sales: $299531
Number Employees: 13
Type of Packaging: Private Label

4161 Evensen Vineyards
PO Box 127
Oakville, CA 94562-0127
707-944-2396
Wines
President: Richard Evensen

4162 Ever Fresh Fruit Co
35855 SE Kelso Rd
PO Box 1177
Boring, OR 97009-7064
503-668-8026
Fax: 503-668-5823 800-239-8026
www.everfreshfruit.com
Apples
Owner: Brittany Beem
brittany@everfreshfruit.com
VP: LeAnn Miller
Estimated Sales: $10-20 Million
Number Employees: 50-99
Type of Packaging: Consumer, Food Service, Private Label
Brands:
Nature's Quest

4163 Everfresh Beverages
6600 E 9 Mile Rd
Warren, MI 48091-2673
586-755-9500
Fax: 586-755-9587 800-323-3416
www.everfreshjuice.com
Manufacturer and exporter of soft drinks and fruit juices including orange and grape
President/CEO: Stan Sheridan
Telecommunications: Ray Laurinaitis
Operations: Dave Piontkowski
Plant Manager: Matt Filipovitch
Purchasing Director: Walter Koziara
Number Employees: 50-99
Square Footage: 500000
Parent Co: National Beverages Corporation
Type of Packaging: Consumer, Private Label
Brands:
Everfresh
Lacroix

4164 Everfresh Food Corporation
501 Huron Blvd SE
Minneapolis, MN 55414
612-331-6393
Fax: 612-331-1172 george_edgar@yahoo.com
Chow mein noodles and vanilla including pure and imitation; importer of bamboo shoots and water chesnuts including whole and sliced
VP: Rita Sorsveen
Estimated Sales: $5-10 Million
Number Employees: 10-19
Type of Packaging: Consumer, Food Service, Private Label, Bulk
Brands:
China Boy

4165 Everglades Foods
441 Webster Turn Drive
Sebring, FL 33870
Fax: 863-655-2214 800-689-2221
sales@evergladesseasoning.com
Seasonings
President: Seth Howard
Owner: Chris Sebring
Marketing Director: Kelli Bronson
Sales: Jenna Buchanan
Estimated Sales: $1-2.5 Million
Number Employees: 5-9
Type of Packaging: Consumer, Food Service
Brands:
Everglades
Everglades Heat
Everglades Original

4166 Evergood Fine Foods
1389 Underwood Ave
San Francisco, CA 94124-3308
415-822-4660
Fax: 415-822-1066 800-253-6733
info@evergoodfoods.com evergoodfoods.com
Sausage manufacturer founded in 1926.
General Manager: Harlan Miller
VP, Sales & Marketing: Don Miller
Estimated Sales: $20-50 Million
Number Employees: 50-99
Type of Packaging: Consumer

4167 Evergreen Juices Inc.
Po Box 1
Don Mills, ON M3C 2R6
Canada
905-886-8090
Fax: 905-886-5633 877-915-8423
info@evergreenjuices.com
www.evergreenjuices.com
Juice
President: Don Mills
Treasurer: Robert MacIntosh

4168 Evergreen Sweeteners, Inc
1936 Hollywood Blvd
Suite 200
Hollywood, FL 33020
954-381-7776
Fax: 954-458-5793 www.esweeteners.com
Bulk liquid sweeteners and bagged sweeteners
President: Arthur Green
Year Founded: 1925
Estimated Sales: $55 Million
Number Employees: 50+
Number of Products: 40
Square Footage: 150000
Type of Packaging: Food Service, Bulk
Other Locations:
Evergreen Sweeteners, Inc.
Atlanta GA
Evergreen Sweeteners, Inc.
Sanford FL
Evergreen Sweeteners, Inc.
Miami FL

4169 Everland Foods
7442 Fraser Park Dr
Burnaby, BC V5J 5B9
Canada
info@everland.ca
everland.ca
Organic, kosher health foods
CEO: Rajinder Bagga
Type of Packaging: Food Service, Private Label

4170 Everland Parks
7442 Fraser Park Dr
Burnaby, BC V5J 5B9
Canada
info@everland.ca
everland.ca
Oils, nuts and nut butters
President & CEO: Kulwant Bagga
Year Founded: 2005
Number of Brands: 1
Number of Products: 400+
Type of Packaging: Consumer
Brands:
EVERLAND

4171 Everson Spice Co
2667 Gundry Ave
Signal Hill, CA 90755-1808
562-595-4785
Fax: 562-988-0219 800-421-3753
customerservice@eversonspice.com
www.eversonspice.com
Seasonings, dry rubs, stuffing mixes and marinades

Owner: Tom Everson
tomeverson@eversonspice.com
President: Ken Hopkins
CEO: Kim Everson
Estimated Sales: $2.5-5 Million
Number Employees: 50-99
Type of Packaging: Food Service

4172 Everspring Farms
Seaforth, ON N0K 1W0
Canada
519-527-0990
sales@everspringfarms.ca
www.everspringfarms.ca
Sprouted grains, seeds and beans
Co-Founder: Dale Donaldson
Co-Founder: Marianne Donaldson

4173 Everything Yogurt
1100 Pennsylvania Ave NW
Washington, DC 20004-2501
202-842-2990
Yogurt, salad products
Owner: January Kwak
Estimated Sales: Under $500,000
Number Employees: 20-49

4174 Evo Hemp
Boulder, CO
evohemp.com
Hemp extracts, bars, snacks, seeds and seed oil
Type of Packaging: Consumer
Brands:
EVO HEMP

4175 Evol Foods
1600 Pearl St # 300
Boulder, CO 80302-5457
303-554-7000
www.evolfoods.com
Frozen foods
Sales: Marcus Seiden
Number Employees: 20-49

4176 Evolution Fresh
Seattle, WA 98134
800-794-9986
info@evolutionfresh.com
www.evolutionfresh.com
Cold-pressed juices and smoothies
Founder: Jimmy Rosenberg
Number of Brands: 1
Number of Products: 24
Type of Packaging: Consumer
Brands:
EVOLUTION FRESH

4177 Evolution Salt Co.
3310 W Braker Ln
Suite 300-234
Austin, TX 78758-7853
877-868-7979
Fax: 512-828-8789 www.evolutionsalt.com
Himalayan salt producsts
Owner: Hayden Nasir
VP of Sales: Jordan Holtz
Number Employees: 1-10
Type of Packaging: Food Service, Private Label

4178 Evolve
1340 Treat Blvd
Suite 350
Walnut Creek, CA 94597
888-298-6629
www.drinkevolve.com
Protein bars and shakes

4179 Evy Tea
Boston, MA 02130
www.evytea.com
Ready-to-drink cold brew tea
Founder: Evy Chen

4180 Eweberry Farms
30377 Brownsville Rd
Brownsville, OR 97327-9525
541-466-3470
Gourmet jams and syrups
Owner: John Morrison
Estimated Sales: Less Than $500,000
Number Employees: 1-4

4181 Ex Drinks
1879 Whitney Mesa Dr
Henderson, NV 89014
702-949-6555
Fax: 702-949-6556 866-753-4929
hq@exdrinks.com
Energy drinks and vitamin water
Headquarters Manager: Natasha Platin
Senior Director of Business Development: Clark Wright
Director of Strategic Planning: Kristen Hirtz
Marketing: Travis Arnesen
Contact: Travis Arnesen
tarnesen@exdrinks.com
Estimated Sales: $500,000- 1 Million
Number Employees: 5-9

4182 Excalibur Seasoning
1800 Riverway Dr
Pekin, IL 61554-9307
309-347-1221
Fax: 309-347-9086 800-444-2169
sales@excaliburseasoning.com
www.excaliburseasoning.com
Seasoning
President: Jay Hall
CEO: Blake Taylor
btaylor@lumc.edu
Estimated Sales: $5-10 Million
Number Employees: 50-99

4183 Exceldor Cooperative
5700 Rue J.B.Michaud
Bureau 500
Levis, QC G6V 0B1
Canada
418-830-5600
info@exceldor.com
www.exceldor.ca
Manufacturer and exporter of fresh and frozen chicken.
President & CEO: René Proulx
VP, Operations: □É□ric Cadoret
VP, Finance: Christian Jacques
VP, Quality Assurance & R&D: Geneviève Arsenault
VP, Communications & Marketing: Isabelle Drouin
VP, Sales: Luc Gagnon
VP, Human Resources: Clémence Drouin
SVP, Chicken Division: Joël Cormier
SVP, Turkey Division: Anthony Tavares
Year Founded: 1945
Estimated Sales: $229 Million
Number Employees: 1400
Square Footage: 7502
Type of Packaging: Consumer, Private Label, Bulk
Brands:
Exceldor Express

4184 Excellentia Intl.
30 Stewart Place
Fairfield, NJ 07004
737-749-9840
excellentiainternational.com
Ingredient supplier
President/Owner: Tom Buco

4185 Exeter Produce
215 Thames Road West
Exeter, ON N0M 1S3
Canada
519-235-0141
info@exeterproduce.com
exeterproduce.com
Grower, packer and shipper of beans, peppers, lettuce, cabbage and other hydroponic and field produce.
President: Leonard Veri
Director: James Veri
Director: Michael Veri
Year Founded: 1951
Type of Packaging: Bulk
Brands:
VeriFine

4186 Exo Inc.
94 South 4th Street
Apt. 4
Brooklyn, NY 11249
818-744-4140
exoprotein.com
Protein bars and bites made with cricket flour
Co-Founder: Gabi Lewis
Co-Founder: Greg Sewitz
Year Founded: 2012
Number of Brands: 1
Number of Products: 6
Type of Packaging: Consumer
Brands:
EXO

4187 Explore Cuisine
308-157 Broad St
Red Bank, NJ 07701
info@explorecuisine.com
www.explorecuisine.com
Bean and pulse pastas
Number of Brands: 1
Number of Products: 15
Type of Packaging: Consumer
Brands:
EXPLORE CUISINE

4188 Expro Manufacturing
2800 Ayers Avenue
Vernon, CA 90058
323-415-8544
Fax: 323-268-4060
Manufacturer and packager of food ingredients, including custom dry powder blends
President: Peter Ernster
CEO: Douglas Kantner
R&D: Greg Rowland
VP Sales: Michele Mullen
Contact: Daniel Diaz
ddiaz@expromfg.com
Purchasing: James Ernster
Number Employees: 20

4189 Exquisita Tortillas Inc
700 W Chapin St
Edinburg, TX 78541-2416
956-383-6712
Fax: 956-383-1012 info@exquisitatortillas.com
www.exquisitatortillas.com
Corn and flour tortillas, chips, taco & challupa shells, pork skins
Owner: Humberto Rodriguez
hrodriguez@exquisitatortillasinc.com
President & CEO: J Rodriguez
COO: Bill Guerra
Estimated Sales: $26.6 Million
Number Employees: 100-249
Square Footage: 46000
Brands:
Exquisita

4190 Extracts and Ingredients Ltd
One Gary Road
Union, NJ 07083-5527
908-688-9009
Fax: 908-688-9005 www.morretec.com
Supplier of natural specialty ingredients to the food, nutraceutical and personal care markets. Offer organic specialty oils, Oregano Extract as a natural preservative, Indian spice oleoresins and essential oils, fruit concentratescarrageenans and water-soluble vitamins A, D & E. Manufacture and supply micronized particle powders of TCP, DCP, bran, phytosterols etc. using a patented Vortex milling technology. Also a major distributor of Magnesium, Potassium, and Calciumchlorides.
President: Leonard Glass
Quality Assurance Manager: Anzorena Ramirez
Marketing Coordinator: Melissa Bevilaque
VP Sales/Marketing: David Fondots
Contact: D Fondots
dfondots@morretec.com
VP Administration/Operations: Paul Caskey
Parent Co: Morre-Tec Industries, Inc

4191 Extravagonzo Gourmet Foods
P.O. Box 6346
Boise, ID 83707
208-639-2926
garlic@extravagonzofoods.com
extravagonzofoods.com
Vinegar; olive oil; cooking sauces and seasonings
President: Tom Stevens
Brand Manager: Leah Ryneer
Type of Packaging: Food Service, Private Label

4192 Extreme Creations
4970 Windplay Dr Ste C5
El Dorado Hills, CA 95762
916-941-0444
Fax: 916-941-1777
Jellied lollipops

Manager: Kamal Naim
Estimated Sales: $.5-1 million
Number Employees: 1-4

4193 **Eyrie Vineyards**
935 NE 10th Ave
Mcminnville, OR 97128-4003
503-472-6315
Fax: 503-472-5124 888-440-4970
info@eyrievineyards.com
www.eyrievineyards.com
Wines
Owner: Jason Lett
info@eyrievineyards.com
Vice President: Diana Lett
Estimated Sales: $5-10 Million
Number Employees: 20-49

4194 **Ezzo Sausage Company**
PO Box 7784
Columbus, OH 43207
614-445-8841
Fax: 614-445-8843 800-558-8841
www.ezzo.com
Sausage, pepperoni
Owner: Bill Ezzo
Contact: Mike Spicer
mspicer@ezzo.com
Plant Manager of Operation: Mike Spicer
Number Employees: 10-19

4195 **F & A Dairy Products Inc**
212 State Road 35 S
Dresser, WI 54009
715-755-3485
Fax: 715-755-3480 800-657-8582
info@fadairy.com www.fadairy.com
Cheese including mozzarella, provolone, romano and parmesan; importer of pecorino romano
President: Chuck Engdahl
chuck@fadairy.net
Controller: Clyde Loch
CFO: Jay Benusa
QC: Ralph Ramos
Sales: Chris Slavek
Sales: Renzo Sciortino
Human Resources: Carl Gutierrez
VP Wisconsin Operations: Mike Breault
VP New Mexico Operations: Bob Snyder
Estimated Sales: $10-24.9 Million
Number Employees: 50-99
Type of Packaging: Food Service
Other Locations:
F&A Dairy Products
Las Cruces NM
Brands:
F&A

4196 **F & S Produce Co Inc**
500 W Elmer Rd
Vineland, NJ 08360
800-886-3316
www.freshcutproduce.com
Fresh, whole and pre-cut produce including peppers, onions, lettuce, carrots, spinach, cabbage, tomatoes and cucumbers; brine products including vegetables, cherry and bell peppers, onions and jalapenos; also, salad, vegetable traysand fruit snacks
President: Salvatore Pipitone
CFO: Maddalena Lori
Purchasing Agent: Ted Brode
Estimated Sales: $85 Million
Number Employees: 100-249
Square Footage: 650000
Type of Packaging: Consumer, Food Service, Private Label, Bulk

4197 **F B Purnell Sausage Co Inc**
6931 Shelbyville Rd
Simpsonville, KY 40067-6511
502-722-5626
Fax: 502-722-5586 800-626-1512
Sausage links, patties and slices.
President: Todd Purnell
tpurnell@itsgood.com
Chairman/CEO: Allen Purnell Jr.
Controller: Dave Fowler
Estimated Sales: $39 Million
Number Employees: 100-249
Number of Brands: 1
Type of Packaging: Consumer, Food Service
Brands:
Old Folks

4198 **(HQ)F B Washburn Candy Corp**
137 Perkins Ave
P.O. Box 3277
Brockton, MA 02302-3891
508-588-0820
Fax: 508-588-2205 www.fbwashburncandy.com
Manufactured and distributor of hard candies, specializing in ribbon candies; offer rebagging, private label and wrapping services.
President: James Gilson
jamesgilson@fbwashburncandy.com
Treasurer: Douglas Gilson
Estimated Sales: $10 Million
Number Employees: 20-49
Number of Brands: 2
Square Footage: 150000
Type of Packaging: Consumer, Private Label
Brands:
Sevigny
Washburn

4199 **F C C**
700 NE Highway 99w
Mcminnville, OR 97128-2711
503-472-2157
Fax: 503-472-3821
Milk, butter and powdered milk
President: Dan Bansen
CEO: Michael Anderson
manderson@farmerscoop.org
Estimated Sales: $4.9 Million
Number Employees: 5-9
Square Footage: 224000
Type of Packaging: Consumer, Food Service, Bulk

4200 **F W Bryce Inc**
8 Pond Rd
Gloucester, MA 01930-1833
978-283-7080
Fax: 978-283-7647 fwbryce@fwbryce.com
www.fwbryce.com
Frozen seafood
President: Kerry Amero
kerryamero@fwbryce.com
CFO: Paul Cantrell
General Counsel: Ian Moores
Logistics Manager: Frank Souza
Quality Assurance Manager: Justin Moores
Director Sales: Glenn Hale
VP Sales: Joe Flammia
Operations Manager: Frank Souza
Warehousing/Logistics: Ralph Pierce
Number Employees: 10-19
Square Footage: 26000

4201 **F&Y Enterprises**
1205 Karl Ct
Suite 115
Wauconda, IL 60084-1090
847-526-0620
Manufacturer and exporter of hickory smoked meat snacks including sausage sticks and beef jerky
President: Frank Vitek
VP: Bonnie Vitek
Estimated Sales: $2 Million
Number Employees: 40
Parent Co: F&Y Enterprises
Type of Packaging: Consumer, Food Service, Private Label
Brands:
Texas Brand

4202 **F. Gavina & Sons**
2700 Fruitland Ave
Vernon, CA 90058
800-428-4627
hello@gavina.com www.gavina.com
Gourmet coffee
CEO: Pedro Gavina
VP, Marketing: Leonor Gavina-Valls
VP, Operations: Carlos Fandino
Brands:
Gavina
Don Francisco's
Caffe La Llave

4203 **FAGE USA Dairy Ind Inc**
1 Opportunity Dr
Johnstown Industrial Park
Johnstown, NY 12095
518-762-5912
Fax: 518-762-5918 866-962-5912
usa.fage
Greek yogurt and feta cheese
Manager: Antonios Maridakis
Vice President: Ioannis Ravanis
info@fageusa.com
Number Employees: 250-499
Type of Packaging: Consumer

4204 **FBC Industries**
1933 N Meacham Rd # 550
Suite 550
Schaumburg, IL 60173-4342
847-839-0880
Fax: 847-839-0884 888-322-4637
sales@fbcindustries.com www.fbcindustries.com
Industrial ingredients including dipotassium phosphate, calcium chloride, sodium and potassuim citrates, lactates and benzoates used as buffering agents, emulsifers, firming agents, preservatives, antioxidants, flavorings, etc
President: Robert Bloom
rbloom@fbcindustries.com
VP: John Tramontana
Estimated Sales: $1-3 Million
Number Employees: 10-19
Type of Packaging: Bulk

4205 **FDI Inc**
5440 Saint Charles Rd
Suite 201
Berkeley, IL 60163-1231
708-544-1880
Fax: 708-544-4117 info@fdiusa.net
www.fdiusa.net
Canned and frozen foods; uses freeze-drying to preserve herbs, fruits, vegetables, spices, meat, pasta and fish
President: Joseph Lucas
National Sales Manager: Barbara Laffey
Manager: Terry Bliudzius
info@fdiusa.net
Estimated Sales: $1.3 Million
Number Employees: 10-19
Parent Co: Groneweg Group
Type of Packaging: Consumer

4206 **FIFO Innovations**
107-2999 Underhill Ave
Burnaby, BC V5A 3C2
Canada
778-383-6200
800-453-3436
sales@fifobottle.com www.fifobottle.com
Sauce dispensing solutions for restaurants
General Manager: Katie Third

4207 **FLAT Tech Inc.**
1 North Wacker Dr
Suite 4400
Chicago, IL 60606-2833
855-999-3528
www.flattech.com
Table-stabilising technology
Managing Director: Mike Drake
CFO: Barry Mancell
COO: Ozcan Ozagir
Brands:
FLAT

4208 **FNI Group LLC**
188 Lake Street
Sherborn, MA 01770-1606
508-655-4175
Fax: 508-655-8816
All natural cookies that are cholesterol and lactose free
President/Founder: Josephine Ho
Estimated Sales: $200.00 K
Number Employees: 2
Brands:
Essen Smart Gluten Free
Essen Smart Single Cookie 2
Essen Smart Single Cookie 3
Essen Smart Soy Cookies

4209 **FODY Food Co.**
376 Victoria Ave
Suite 220
Westmount, QC H3Z 1C3
Canada
818-835-1850
flavorproducers.com
Low FODMAP products for people with irritable bowel syndrome
Founder & CEO: Steven Singer
COO: Sean Surkis

Year Founded: 2016
Number of Brands: 1
Number of Products: 24
Type of Packaging: Consumer
Brands:
FODY

4210 **FOND Bone Broth**
San Antonio, TX 78220
www.fondbonebroth.com
Bone broth tonics
Founder: Alysa Seeland

4211 **FW Thurston**
2 Steamboat Wharf Road
11 Thurston Rd.
Bernard, ME 04612-0178
207-244-3320
Fax: 207-244-3320
Fresh lobster
President: Michael Radcliffe
Estimated Sales: $3-5 Million
Number Employees: 20-49

4212 **Fa Lu Cioli**
553 Lehigh Ave
Union, NJ 07083-7976
908-258-8651
Manufacturer of a variety of meats.
Number Employees: 1-4

4213 **Fabbri Sausage Mfg Co**
166 N Aberdeen St
Chicago, IL 60607-1606
312-829-6363
Fax: 312-829-0396 info@fabbrisausage.com
www.fabbrisausage.com
Italian meats and other pizza supplies including italian sausage, meatballs, italian roast beef, italian style gravy, italian chili.
President: Ray Fabbri
info@fabbrisausage.com
Estimated Sales: $2.5-5 Million
Number Employees: 20-49
Square Footage: 100000
Type of Packaging: Consumer, Food Service, Private Label, Bulk

4214 **Faber Foods and Aeronautics**
1153 Evergreen Parkway
Suite M105
Evergreen, CO 80439-9501
800-237-3255
Fax: 303-670-0971
Low-fat muesli cereal including strawberry/banana, cranberry/apricot, papaya/peach, blueberry/peach, raspberry/apple, etc.; also, custom blend cereals; exporter of extruded crisp rice, edible seeds, canned oats dried fruit raisins andnuts
President: Maria Faber
Estimated Sales: $300,000-500,000
Number Employees: 10-19
Square Footage: 40000
Type of Packaging: Consumer, Food Service, Private Label, Bulk
Brands:
Low Fat Body Mueslix

4215 **Fabio Imports**
6048 De La Rosa Ln
Oceanside, CA 92057-2101
760-726-7040
Fax: 760-726-5731
Italian specialties
Owner/President: Fabio Peraro
Estimated Sales: $1 Million
Number Employees: 35
Square Footage: 12000

4216 **Fabrique Delices**
1610 Delta Ct
Suite 1
Hayward, CA 94544-7043
510-441-9500
Fax: 510-441-9700 vanessa@fabriquedelices.com
www.fabriquedelices.com
Foie gras, terrine, block and mousse, smoked meats, mousses
President & Co-Owner: Marc Poinsignon
Co-Owner: Antonio Pinheiro
VP, Sales & Marketing: Sebastien Espinasse
Estimated Sales: $2.5-5 Million
Number Employees: 20-49

4217 **Faidley Seafood**
203 North Paca St
Baltimore, MD 21201
410-727-4898
Fax: 410-837-6495 faidleysseafood@gmail.com
www.faidleyscrabcakes.com
Seafood
President: Nancy Devine
Estimated Sales: $3-5 Million
Number Employees: 10-19

4218 **Fair Oaks Farms LLC**
7600 95th St
Pleasant Prairie, WI 53158
262-947-0320
Fax: 262-947-0348 800-528-8615
fofcontact@fairoaksfarms.com
www.fairoaksfarms.com
Fresh, ready-to-cook or fully cooked meats including; sausage patties, links & crumbles; bacon strips and bits; hot dogs & smoked sausages; ready-to-cook beef patties, fully-cooked beef patties; pork ribbette and chopette; chickenbreasts, strips and nuggets; salisbury steak; meat loaf
President & CEO: Michael Thompson
Senior Vice President: Joseph Freda
Vice President: Michael Thompson
R&D Manager: Jeannette Falls
Production Supervisor: Sonia Valle
Year Founded: 1985
Estimated Sales: $111.5 Million
Number Employees: 100-249
Square Footage: 55000

4219 **Fair Scones**
P.O.Box 177
Medina, WA 98039-0177
425-486-3334
Fax: 425-398-0301 800-588-9160
pgimness@conifer-inc.com www.conifer-inc.com
Bean soup and chili mixes, bread, breakfast, dessert and beverage mixes
President: Michael Maher
Contact: John Weber
jweber@conifer-inc.com
Estimated Sales: $10-20 Million
Number Employees: 20-49

4220 **Fairbury Food Products**
601 2nd St
Fairbury, NE 68352
402-729-3379
Fax: 402-729-2437
Bacon bits
President: Arden Schacht
Number Employees: 20-49
Parent Co: Fairbury Food
Type of Packaging: Food Service, Private Label

4221 **Fairchester Snacks Corp**
100 Lafayette Ave
White Plains, NY 10603-1612
914-761-2824
www.nysnacks.com
Salty biscuts
Owner: John Barisano
Estimated Sales: $300,000-500,000
Number Employees: 5-9

4222 **Fairfield Farm Kitchens**
309 Battles Street
Brockton, MA 02301
508-584-9300
Fax: 508-580-9910
Frozen organic soups, entrees, side dishes, sauces, gravies, layer, sheet and pound cakes, etc
Founder/Chairman: Norman Cloutier
Contact: Stephen Korotsky
skorotsky@fairfieldfarmkitchens.com
Year Founded: 2001
Estimated Sales: $20-50 Million
Number Employees: 100-249
Square Footage: 170000
Brands:
Basic American Frozen Foods
Fairfield Farm

4223 **Fairhaven Cooperative Flour Mill**
1115 Railroad Ave
Bellingham, WA 98225-5007
360-757-9947
Fax: 360-734-9947 fairhavenflour@q.com
www.fairhavenflour.com
Manufacturer and exporter of flour including whole grain, wheat, rye, corn, buckwheat, rice, etc
Manager: Bill Distler
Estimated Sales: $1-2.5 Million
Number Employees: 1-4
Type of Packaging: Consumer, Bulk

4224 **Fairlife**
1001 W Adams St.
Chicago, IL 60607
fairlife.com
Milk and milk products including creamers and protein shakes.
CEO: Tim Doelman
Year Founded: 2012
Parent Co: Coca-Cola Co.
Type of Packaging: Private Label

4225 **Fairmont Foods Of Minnesota**
905 E 4th St
Fairmont, MN 56031-4014
507-238-9001
Fax: 507-238-9560 www.downsfoodgroup.com
Frozen meals including; entrees, side dishes, soups, sauces and meal kits
President: William Bosshard
william.bosshard@fairmontfoods.com
CEO: Larry McGuire
CFO: William Bosshard
Director Quality Assurance: John Heuer
VP of Operations: Jerald Nasalroad
Production Manager: Pat Meschke
Purchasing: Greg Korth
Estimated Sales: $25.5 Million
Number Employees: 250-499
Square Footage: 152000

4226 **Fairmont Snacks Group**
6133 Rockside Rd
Suite 208
Independence, OH 44131-2244
216-642-3336
Potato chips, peanuts and snack items
Owner: E. Kelley
Contact: Mark Johnson
mark.johnson@fornuts.com
Estimated Sales: $59,000
Number Employees: 2

4227 **Fairview Dairy Inc**
1562 Mission Rd
Latrobe, PA 15650-2845
724-537-7111
Fax: 724-537-7249 mblystone@valleydairy.net
www.valleydairy.net
Processor and wholesaler/distributor of ice cream; serving the food service market
President: Melissa Blystone
Vice President: Melissa Blystone
Marketing Director: Virgina Greubel
Contact: Lujean Wasnesky
lwasnesky@valleydairy.net
Director of Operations: Tom Webb
Plant Manager: Ray Sneets
Number Employees: 250-499
Square Footage: 24000
Parent Co: Fairview Dairy
Type of Packaging: Consumer, Food Service
Brands:
Ice Cream Joe
Valley Dairy

4228 **Fairview Swiss Cheese**
1734 Perry Hwy
Fredonia, PA 16124-2720
724-475-4154
Fax: 724-475-4777 www.fairviewswisscheese.com
Cheeses
President: Richard Koller
rkoller54@aol.com
Estimated Sales: $2 Million
Number Employees: 10-19
Square Footage: 80000
Parent Co: John Koller and Son, Inc
Type of Packaging: Consumer, Food Service, Private Label, Bulk

4229 **Fairwinds Gourmet Coffee**
1731 Aviation Blvd.
Lincoln, CA 95648
916-543-0493
Fax: 603-668-0888 800-829-1300
rogers_service@rogersfamilyco.com
Gourmet Coffee and tea

President: Kathy Hybsch
Estimated Sales: $2.5-5 Million
Number Employees: 1-4
Parent Co: JBR Gourmet Foods
Type of Packaging: Bulk
Brands:
East India Coffee and Tea
Fairwinds Coffee
Organic Coffee Co

4230 **Fairytale Brownies**
4610 E Cotton Center Blvd
Suite #100
Phoenix, AZ 85040-8898
602-489-5100
Fax: 602-489-5133 800-324-7982
julieg@brownies.com www.brownies.com
Brownies, cookies
Co- Founder: Eileen Spitalny
Marketing: Julie Gaffney
Manager: Kim Silva
Number Employees: 20-49

4231 **Falafel Republic**
800 Hingham St Rockland
Needham Heights, MA 02494
781-878-6027
Fax: 781-444-1420 nancy@originalrangoon.com
Dairy-free, gluten-free, vegetarian, helath, fitness and energy bars, other snacks, foodservice.
Marketing: Greg Bukuras

4232 **Falcon Rice Mill Inc**
600 S Avenue D
PO Box 771
Crowley, LA 70526-5606
337-783-3825
Fax: 337-783-1568 800-738-7423
www.falconrice.com
Long and medium grain rice, jasmine rice, popcorn rice.
President: Mona Trahan
CFO: Robert Trahan
VP, Sales: Charles Trahan
General Manager: Tom Dew
Estimated Sales: $20-50 Million
Number Employees: 20-49
Number of Brands: 6
Type of Packaging: Consumer, Food Service, Private Label, Bulk
Brands:
Cajun Country
Falcon
Home Country
Jackpot
Laredo
Toro

4233 **Falcone's Cookie Land LTD**
1632 61st St
Brooklyn, NY 11204-2109
718-236-4200
Fax: 718-259-6133 www.falconebaking.com
Regular and dietetic cookies; also, crackers, biscuits, breadsticks and flatbread
Owner: Angelo Falcone
falconecookie@aol.com
Vice President: Angelo Falcone
Estimated Sales: $5-9.9 Million
Number Employees: 50-99
Type of Packaging: Consumer, Food Service, Private Label, Bulk
Brands:
Falcone's
Falcone's Baked Goods
Falcone's Cookies
Falcone's Flatbread

4234 **Fall Creek Vineyards**
1402 San Antonio St # 200
Austin, TX 78701-1623
512-476-4477
Fax: 512-476-6116 www.fcv.com
Wine
Owner: Ed Auler
ed@fcv.com
Co-founder: Susan Auler
Corporate Accountant: Suzette Kramer
VP: Chad Auler
VP Marketting: Chad Auler
VP Sales: Dani Seelig
ed@fcv.com
Operations Manager: Roy Nobles
Estimated Sales: $3-5 Million
Number Employees: 5-9
Type of Packaging: Bulk

4235 **Fall River Wild Rice**
41577 Osprey Road
Fall River Mills, CA 96028
530-336-5222
Fax: 530-336-5265 800-626-4366
www.frwr.com
Wild rice
General Manager: Walt Oiler
Estimated Sales: $420,000
Number Employees: 4
Square Footage: 56000
Brands:
Fall River

4236 **(HQ)Falla Imports**
PO Box 1532
Greenville, ME 04441-1532
609-476-4106
Fax: 609-476-0412
Importers of coffee
President: Roderick Falla
Number Employees: 1-4

4237 **Fallwood Corp**
75 S Broadway
Suite 494
White Plains, NY 10601-4413
914-304-4065
Fax: 914-304-4063 ana@fallwoodcorp.com
www.fallwoodcorp.com
Manufacturer and supplier of all natural nutraceutical ingredients and raw materials. All glanulars-Bovine and Porcine Enzymes
President/CEO: Jorge Millan
Vice President: Graciela Rocchia
Sales: Wayne Battenfield
Manager: Anne-Marie Rodriguez
anna@fallwoodcorp.com
Adminstration: Anne Marie Rodriguez
Estimated Sales: Under $500,000
Number Employees: 1-4
Parent Co: Loboratorio Opoterapico Argentino

4238 **Fama Sales Co**
450 W 44th St
New York, NY 10036-5205
212-757-9433
Fax: 212-765-4193 800-682-0425
Food products
Owner: Ugo R Quazzo
famasales@aol.com
Estimated Sales: $1-2.5 Million
Number Employees: 10-19

4239 **Famarco Limited**
1381 Air Rail Ave
Virginia Beach, VA 23455-3301
757-460-3573
Fax: 757-460-2621
Raw material importer and processor for spice, botanicals and carob
President: Bruce Martin
bruce@famarco.com
VP: Ken Hartfelder
Quality Control: Darrick Bargher
Marketing: Mark Herrick
Plant Manager: James O'Neil
Estimated Sales: $10 Million
Number Employees: 20-49
Square Footage: 80000
Parent Co: B&K International
Type of Packaging: Private Label, Bulk
Brands:
Martin's Virginia Roast
Virginia Roast

4240 **Family Food Company**
6801 De Bie Dr
Paramount, CA 90723-2027
310-715-2698
Fax: 562-272-8585
Salads; jams; coffee; sugar; sauces; liquid smoke
Type of Packaging: Private Label

4241 **Family Sweets Candy Company**
1099 Pratt Boulevard
Elk Grove Village, IL 60007-5120
336-788-5068
Fax: 336-784-6708 800-334-1607
Candy
President: LeRoy Mansson

4242 **Family Tree Farms**
41646 Road 62
Reedley, CA 93654-9124
559-591-8394
Fax: 559-595-7795 866-352-8671
www.familytreefarms.com
Plumcots, white peaches and nectarines, donut peaches and nectarines, yellow peaches and nectarines, apricuts, apriums, plums, blueberries, cherries, satsumas
President: David Jackson
djackson@familytreefarms.com
CFO: Dan Clenney
Executive Director of Global Development: Gerome Raco
Director of Research & Development: Eric Wuhl
Quality Control: Mary Ortiz
Director of Marketing: Don Goforth
Estimated Sales: $20-50 Million
Number Employees: 250-499
Brands:
Eat Smart
Great Whites
Flavor Safari
Farmers Market
Summerripe
River Run

4243 **Famous Chili Inc**
1421 N 7th St
Fort Smith, AR 72901-1320
479-782-0096
Fax: 501-782-6825 www.famouschili.com
Chili and salsa
President: David Korkames
famouschili@earthlink.net
Estimated Sales: $5-10 Million
Number Employees: 5-9
Square Footage: 20000
Type of Packaging: Consumer, Food Service, Private Label
Brands:
Famous
Four Star
Heat & Serve
Star

4244 **Famous Specialties Co**
55 Saratoga Blvd # B
Island Park, NY 11558-1114
516-889-9099
Fax: 516-889-9099 800-894-9218
famousspecialties@gmail.com
Raw prepared strudel dough
President: Craig Tropp
ctropp@famousspecialties.com
Estimated Sales: $2.5-5 Million
Number Employees: 1-4
Square Footage: 7500
Brands:
Barney's Town & Country
Beef International
Blue Ridge Farms
Brandt
Caesar's
Creative Bakers
Fancy Foods
Fancy's Finest
Fantasia
Gilda
Heath & Heather
High Meadows
Leaves
Redi Prep Strudel
Silver Lake
Stahl Meyer
Sweet Street

4245 **Fancy Farms Popcorn**
2893 County Road 675
Bernie, MO 63822
573-276-3315
Fax: 573-276-2287 800-833-8154
sales@fancyfarmpopcorn.com
www.fancyfarmpopcorn.com
Portion-packed popcorn
President: Chris Tanner
Sales: J Smith
Estimated Sales: $500,000-$1 Million
Number Employees: 5-9
Parent Co: St. Francis River Farming
Type of Packaging: Food Service, Bulk

Brands:
Fancy Farm

4246 **Fancy Lebanese Bakery**
2573 Agricola St
Halifax, NS B3K 4C4
Canada
902-429-0400
Fax: 902-429-0403 fancylebanese@eastlink.ca
fancylebanesebakery.com
Pita bread and submarine sandwich buns
President: Mary Laba
Manager: Maura Fougere
Estimated Sales: $2.6 Million
Number Employees: 20
Type of Packaging: Consumer, Food Service, Private Label
Brands:
Fancy Lebanese Bakery
Flb

4247 **Fancy's Candy's**
5601 Twin Creeks Trl
Rougemont, NC 27572-8657
919-644-2573
Fax: 919-732-2070 888-403-2629
www.sininatin.com
Toffee, milk chocolate, dark chocolate, hazelnuts, white chocolate, and pecans
President: Anne Keller
anne.keller@fancyscandys.com
Estimated Sales: $1-3 Million
Number Employees: 1-4

4248 **Fancypants Bakery**
160 Elm St # 2
Unit 2
Walpole, MA 02081-1934
508-660-1140
Manufacturer of cookies.
Principal Owner: Justin Housman
President: Maura Duggan
Number Employees: 20-49

4249 **(HQ)Fanestil Packing Company**
1542 S Highway 99
Emporia, KS 66801
620-342-6354
Fax: 620-342-8190 800-658-1652
www.fanestils.com
Sausage, ham and bacon
President: Scott Sanders
CEO: Dan Smoots
General Manager: Jan Smoots
Estimated Sales: 25,948,000
Number Employees: 52
Type of Packaging: Consumer, Food Service
Brands:
Fanestil

4250 **Fannie May Fine Chocolate**
2457 W. North Avenue
Melrose Park, IL 60160
Oakdale, MN 55128
80- 33- 362
800-999-3629
customerservice@fanniemay.com
www.fanniemay.com
Chocolates
President: Terry Mitchell
CEO: David Taiclet
Partner: Michael Givens
Partner: Ulysses Bridgeman
Partner: Rodney Burwell
Number Employees: 5-9
Parent Co: Archibald Candy Corporation
Other Locations:
Fanny May Fine Chocolates
Bloomington IN
Fanny May Fine Chocolates
Champaign IL
Fanny May Fine Chocolates
Peoria IL
Fanny May Fine Chocolates
Rockford IL
Fanny May Fine Chocolates
Indianapolis IN
Fanny May Fine Chocolates
Greenwood IN
Fanny May Fine Chocolates
Avon IN
Fanny May Fine Chocolates
Terr Haute IN
Fanny May Fine Chocolates
Davenport IA
Fanny May Fine Chocolates
Springfield IL
Fanny May Fine Chocolates
Bourbonnais IL
Fanny May Fine Chocolates
Portage MI
Fanny May Fine Chocolates
Janesville WI
Brands:
Fanny May Fine Chocolates
Harry London
Fanny Farmer

4251 **Fantasia**
PO Box 1267
Sedalia, MO 65302-1267
660-827-1172
Fax: 660-827-3653
Frozen cakes
President: Robert Wright
VP Sales: Thad Bagnato
Plant Manager: Trent Wanamaker
Purchasing Agent: Mike Mallory
Estimated Sales: $10-20,000,000
Number Employees: 150

4252 **Fantastic World Foods**
313 Iron Horse Way
Providence, RI 02908
www.fantasticfoods.com
Vegetarian convenience foods including soups and rice; importer of rice.
Estimated Sales: $20-50 Million
Number Employees: 30
Square Footage: 150000
Type of Packaging: Consumer
Brands:
Fantastic
Jumping Black Beans
Nature's Burger Mix
Tabouli Salad Mix
Tofu Burger Mix
Tofu Scrambler Mix

4253 **Fantasy Chocolates**
2045 High Ridge Rd
Boynton Beach, FL 33426-8713
561-276-9007
Fax: 561-265-0027 800-804-4962
fantasychocolate@aol.com
www.williamsandbennett.com
Manufacturer and exporter of chocolate novelties and gourmet pretzels including chocolate, keylime, chocolate pizza, caramel and chocolate apple
President: Becky Gardner
Contact: Bill Gardner
b.gardner@williamsandbennett.com
Products: Bill Gardner
Estimated Sales: $1.2,000,000
Number Employees: 1-4
Type of Packaging: Consumer, Private Label, Bulk
Brands:
Chocolate Oreos
Chocolate Pizza
Forbidden Fruit
Keylime Graham Crackers
Logo Chocolates
Novelty Chocolates
Party Pretzels
Peanut Butter Dream

4254 **Fantasy Cookie Company**
12800 Arroyo Street
Sylmar, CA 91342-5318
818-361-6901
Fax: 818-365-0040 800-354-4488
www.fantasycookie.com
Cookies including low fat, fruit juice sweetened and holiday; also, gingerbread houses
President/CEO: Joseph Semder
VP Sales: Richard Semder
Estimated Sales: $2.5-5 Million
Number Employees: 5-9
Type of Packaging: Private Label, Bulk

4255 **Fantazzmo Fun Stuff**
425 N Martingale Road
Suite 1680
Schaumburg, IL 60173-2214
847-413-4036
Fax: 847-413-0500
Novelty candy
VP Marketing: Deirdre Gonzalez
Brands:
Candy Whistler
Slide Pops
Sport Totoe 'ems
Tote 'ems
Wonka
Wonka Pixy Stix Mixers
Xtreme Nerds

4256 **Fantini Baking Co Inc**
375 Washington St
Haverhill, MA 01832-5377
978-891-5205
Fax: 978-373-6250 800-343-2110
www.fantinibakery.com
Breads
President: Robert Fantini
robert@fantinibakery.com
Chief Marketing Officer: Joe Fantini
Estimated Sales: $1-2,500,000
Number Employees: 100-249

4257 **Fantis Foods Inc**
60 Triangle Blvd
Carlstadt, NJ 07072-2701
201-933-6200
Fax: 201-933-8797 info@fantisfoods.com
www.fantisfoods.com
Olive oil, olives, cheese, seafood, gourmet, pasta, mineral water, cookies and baked goods, gyros, frozen pastries, herbs and spices, confectionary, bean and rice, drinks
President: George Makris
fantisfoods@aol.com
VP/CFO: Jerry Makris
VP/Manager: Steve Makris
Sales Executive/Sales Manager: Bill Paelekanos
Estimated Sales: $6 Million
Number Employees: 20-49
Square Footage: 210000
Type of Packaging: Consumer

4258 **Far Niente Winery**
1350 Acacia Dr
Oakville, CA 94562
707-944-2861
Fax: 707-944-2312 info@farniente.com
www.farniente.com
Wines
Partner: Beth Nickel
Partner: Erik Nickel
Contact: Aaron Fishleder
afishleder@farniente.com
Estimated Sales: $10-20,000,000
Number Employees: 100-249
Parent Co: GI Manager L.P.
Brands:
Bella Union
Dolce
Enroute
Far Niente
Nickel & Nickel

4259 **Far West Meats**
7759 Victoria Ave
PO Box 248
Highland, CA 92346-5637
909-864-1990
Fax: 909-864-0554
Processor and exporter of meat products including smoked sausage, knockwurst, bologna, salami, bratwurst, frankfurters, kielbasa, beef, pork and smoked pork and turkey parts
Owner: Tom Serrato
raemica@pacbell.net
President: Michael Serrato
CFO/Vice President: Wade Snyder
Estimated Sales: $13 Million
Number Employees: 50-99
Square Footage: 50000
Type of Packaging: Consumer, Private Label, Bulk
Brands:
Far West Meats

4260 **Far West Rice Inc**
3455 Nelson Road
Nelson, CA 95938
530-891-1339
Fax: 530-891-0723 sales@farwestrice.com
www.farwestrice.com
Mill, paakage and market rice for food service and retail demands.
President: C W Johnson
Owner: Greg Johnson
Research & Development: Steve Ross
Marketing Director: Greg Johnson
Operations Manager: Steve Ross

Estimated Sales: $10 Million
Number Employees: 50
Number of Brands: 10
Number of Products: 100
Type of Packaging: Consumer, Food Service, Private Label, Bulk
Brands:
Calrose Rice
Fukusuke Rice
Komachi Premium Rice
Valley Sun Organic Brown Rice

4261 **Farallon Fisheries Co**
207 S Maple Ave
S San Francisco, CA 94080-6305
650-583-3474
Fax: 650-583-0137
Seafood
Manager: Juan De Alva
Contact: Aiden Coburn
Manager: Juan De
juande@farallonfisheries.com
Estimated Sales: $500,000-$1,000,000
Number Employees: 5-9
Brands:
Farallon Foods

4262 **Farbest Foods Inc**
1155 W 12th Ave
Jasper, IN 47546
812-683-4200
rdownes@farbestfoods.com
www.farbestfoods.com
Turkey and turkey products
Quality Assurance Director: Shawn Archie
Sales & Marketing: Ryan Downes
Plant Manager: Jean Munger
Estimated Sales: $85 Million
Number Employees: 500-999
Number of Brands: 3
Type of Packaging: Consumer, Food Service, Private Label, Bulk
Brands:
Country Festival
Farbest Foods
Heritage Pride

4263 **(HQ)Farbest-Tallman Foods Corp**
160 Summit Ave # 2
#3101
Montvale, NJ 07645-1721
201-573-4900
Fax: 201-573-0404 www.farbest.com
Manufacturer of dairy and soy proteins, carotenoids, vitamins, sweeteners and nutraceuticals.
President/Chairman: Daniel Meloro
dmeloro@farbest.com
Senior Vice President: Bob Claire
Senior Vice President: Chip Jackson
Vice President: Brent Lambert
Vice President: Paul Guzman
Quality Assurance & Compliance Manager: Shakirul Alom
Sales Director: Michael Sepela
Human Resources Manager: Teresa Lauricella
Director of Operations: Frank Volpe
Dir. Product Management & Supply Chain: Kevin Burke
Estimated Sales: $20-50 Million
Number Employees: 20-49
Number of Brands: 1
Type of Packaging: Consumer, Bulk
Other Locations:
Kentucky Office
Louisville KY
California Office
Huntington Beach CA
Farbest Brands Warehousing Center
Edison NJ
Farbest Brands Warehousing Center
Columbus OH
Farbest Brands Warehousing Center
Carson CA
Brands:
Farbest

4264 **Fare Foods Corp**
208 Cherry Lake Rd
Du Quoin, IL 62832-1248
618-542-2155
Fax: 618-542-2396 www.farefoods.com
Fresh fruits and vegetables
President: Ron Porter
rporter@farefoods.com

Estimated Sales: $10-20 Million
Number Employees: 20-49

4265 **Farella-Park Vineyards**
2222 N 3rd Ave
Napa, CA 94558-3840
707-254-9489
info@farella.com
www.farella.com
Wines
Owner: Tom Farella
Winemaker/Farm Manager: Tom Farella
Estimated Sales: Less Than $500,000
Number Employees: 1-4

4266 **Farfelu Vineyards**
13058 Crest Hill Road
Flint Hill, VA 22627-1814
540-364-2930
Fax: 540-364-3930
Wines
Owner: C Raney
Estimated Sales: $500,000-$1,000,000
Number Employees: 1-4

4267 **Faribault Foods, Inc.**
3401 Park Ave. NW
Fairbault, MN 55021
507-331-1400
ConsumeResponse@faribaultfoods.com
www.faribaultfoods.com
Canned vegetables, sauced beans, refried beans, baked beans, pasta, soup, chili, and organic and Mexican specialties.
President/CEO: Reid MacDonald
CFO: Mike Weber
Executive VP, Sales/Marketing: Frank Lynch
Year Founded: 1888
Estimated Sales: $164 Million
Number Employees: 5
Number of Brands: 8
Parent Co: Arizona Canning Company, LLC
Type of Packaging: Consumer, Private Label, Bulk
Other Locations:
Faribault Foods Distribution
Faribault MN
Faribault Foods Plant
Cokato MN
Brands:
Butter Kernel®
Chilliman®
Kuner's®
Luck's®
Mrs. Grimes®
SunVista®
Pride®
S & W Beans®

4268 **Farm & Oven Snacks**
Boulder, CO 80304
info@farmandoven.com
farmandoven.com
Vegetable brownies, muffins and cakes
Co-Founder: Kay Allison
Co-Founder: Mike Senackerib
Number of Products: 8

4269 **Farm 2 Market**
Pier 45 Shed B
San Francisco, CA 94118
Fax: 866-821-9598 800-447-2967
www.farm-2-market.com
Seafood including farm raised shrimp, freshwater prawns, scallops, crawfish and oysters; importer of Australian crawfish and freshwater prawns
President: Marshall Schnider
Estimated Sales: $3-5 Million
Number Employees: 10-19
Type of Packaging: Consumer, Food Service
Brands:
Sweet-Water

4270 **(HQ)Farm Boy Food Svc**
2761 N Kentucky Ave
Evansville, IN 47711-6203
812-428-8436
Fax: 812-428-8432 800-852-3976
www.farmboy-foodservice.com
Established in 1952. Manufacturer of beef and pork; wholesaler/distributor of frozen, refrigerated and dry food products, meat, equipment and fixtures. Specializes in pizza toppings and equipment.
President/Co-Owner: Robert Bonenberger
VP/Co-Owner: Richard Bonenberger

Estimated Sales: $38 Million
Number Employees: 50-99
Type of Packaging: Consumer, Food Service, Private Label

4271 **Farm Fresh to You**
2970 E La Palma Ave Q
Anaheim, CA 92806
800-796-6009
contactus@farmfreshtoyou.com
www.farmfreshtoyou.com
Organic fruits and vegetables

4272 **Farm Pak Products Inc**
7840 Old Bailey Hwy
Spring Hope, NC 27882
252-459-3101
Fax: 252-459-9020 800-367-2799
sales@farmpak.com www.farmpak.com
Produce including sweet potatoes.
Vice President: Johnny Barnes
International Sales Manager: Jose "Pepe" Calderon
Packing House Supervisor: Frank Salinas
Year Founded: 1969
Estimated Sales: $20-50 Million
Number Employees: 100-249
Type of Packaging: Consumer, Bulk

4273 **FarmGro Organic Foods**
101-2445 13th Avenue
Regina, SK S4P 0W1
Canada
306-751-2449
Fax: 306-721-3130
Organic food
President: Bruce Johnson
CFO: Dennis Puff
Purchase Manager: Tim Beard

4274 **FarmSoy Company**
116 Second Road
Summertown, TN 38483
931-964-2411
www.farmsoy.com
Soymilk and tofu
President: Thomas Elliot
VP: Barbara Elliot
Estimated Sales: $50,000
Number Employees: 7
Square Footage: 1200

4275 **Farmdale Creamery Inc**
1049 W Base Line St
San Bernardino, CA 92411-2310
909-889-3002
Fax: 909-888-2541 800-346-7306
www.farmdale.net
Dairy products including sour cream, sour cream dressing, buttermilk, cheese, whey, cream and butter
Owner: Nick Sibilio
VP & General Manager: Michael Shotts
Customer Service: Wendy Zimmerman
Quality Assurance Manager: Josie Emery
Human Resource Manager: Sam Jimenez
nicksibilio@farmdale.net
VP of Operations: Norman Shotts
nicksibilio@farmdale.net
Production Manager: Shannon Shunk
Planning & Procurement: Norman Crow
Estimated Sales: $8 Million
Number Employees: 50-99
Square Footage: 440000
Type of Packaging: Consumer, Food Service, Private Label, Bulk

4276 **Farmer Brothers Company**
1912 Farmer Brothers Dr
Northlake, TX 76226
682-549-6600
www.farmerbros.com
Coffee, tea, and culinary products.
President, CEO & Director: Michael Keown
Chairman: Randy Clark
Treasurer & Chief Financial Officer: David Robson
SVP & General Manager, Direct Ship: Scott Siers
General Counsel & Assistant Secretary: Thomas Mattei, Jr.
Secretary: Teri Witteman
Chief Operating Officer: Ellen Iobst
Year Founded: 1912
Estimated Sales: $545.9 Million
Number Employees: 1,800
Type of Packaging: Food Service
Other Locations:
Farmer Brothers Company

Central Point OR
Farmer Brothers Company
Oklahoma City OK
Farmer Brothers Foodservice Plant
Torrance CA
Brands:
Farmer Brothers
Spice Products
Custom Coffee Plan
Coffee Bean

4277 Farmer Direct Organic
12011 Wascana Heights
Regina, SK S4V 3E2
Canada
306-563-7815
contact@fdorganic.com
www.fdorganic.com
Organic grains, seeds and legumes
Type of Packaging: Consumer

4278 Farmer's Hen House
1956 520th St SW
Kalona, IA 52247-9173
319-683-2206
Fax: 319-683-2256 ryan@farmershenhouse.com
www.farmershenhouse.com
Eggs; commercial, organic and cage free
Owner: Laura Frank
laura@farmershenhouse.com
Estimated Sales: $10-20 Million
Number Employees: 10-19
Brands:
Farmers Hen House

4279 (HQ)Farmers Cooperative Dairy
4600 Armand-Frappier St
Saint-Hubert, QC
Canada
450-878-2333
800-501-1150
www.farmersdairy.ca
Dairy products including milk, yogurt, ice cream, cheese, sour cream, etc.
President: Roger Massicotte
Estimated Sales: $110.64 Million
Number Employees: 550
Square Footage: 140221
Type of Packaging: Consumer, Food Service, Private Label
Other Locations:
Brands:
Farmers
Lacteeze

4280 Farmers Cooperative Grain Co
338 Main St
Kinde, MI 48445-7711
989-874-4200
Fax: 989-874-5793 kindecoop@centurytel.net
www.kindecoop.com
Dried beans
President: Henry Ziel
CEO: Dan Gottschalk
Marketing Director: David Gage
Manager: Adam Farmer
afarmer@kindecoop.com
Estimated Sales: $10-20 Million
Number Employees: 20-49
Type of Packaging: Consumer

4281 Farmers Dairies
7321 N Loop Dr
El Paso, TX 79915
915-772-2736
Fax: 915-772-0907
Dairy products
Partner: Adalberto Navar
Partner: Miguel Navar
Office Manager: Monica Navar
Contact: Ovidio Matamores
ovidiom@mvtvwireless.com
Estimated Sales: $19,000,000
Number Employees: 108

4282 Farmers Meat Market
5213 50 St
Viking, AB T0B 4N0
Canada
780-336-3241
Fax: 780-336-0180
Bologna, cured meats and wild game including deer, elk and moose, famous original viking wieners
President: Eugene Miskew
Sales: Shirley Miskewn
Purchasing Manager: Chris Ferguson
Estimated Sales: $150,000
Number Employees: 3
Type of Packaging: Private Label

4283 Farmers Produce
103 Melby Ave
Ashby, MN 56309-4707
218-747-2749
Chicken
Owner: Gerry Molter
Estimated Sales: $3-5 Million
Number Employees: 10-19
Type of Packaging: Consumer

4284 Farmers Rice Milling Co
3211 Highway 397 S
Lake Charles, LA 70615
337-433-5205
Fax: 337-433-1735 sales@FRMCO.com
www.frmco.com
Processor and grower of rice
General Manager: Philip Bertrand
CEO: Jamie Warshaw
jamiew@frmco.com
By-Product Sales: Jerry Sonnier
Year Founded: 1917
Number Employees: 50-99
Parent Co: The Powell Group
Type of Packaging: Consumer, Food Service

4285 Farmers Seafood Co Wholesale
1192 Hawn Ave
Shreveport, LA 71107-6699
318-222-9504
Fax: 318-424-2029 800-874-0203
farmersseafood@aol.com
www.farmersseafood.com
Wholesaler/distributor of groceries, dairy products and seafood; serving the food service market
Owner: Alex Mijalis
farmersseafood@aol.com
Estimated Sales: $5-10 Million
Number Employees: 50-99

4286 Farmers Way
info@farmerswayus.com
farmerswayus.com
Grains, flours and smoothie blends
Number of Brands: 1
Type of Packaging: Consumer
Brands:
FARMERS WAY

4287 Farmgate Cheese LLC
3627 1/2 Midvale Ave
Los Angelse, CA 90034-6608
310-733-6853
usa@farmgatecheese.com
www.farmgatecheese.com
Cheese; condiments; jams and preserves.
Owner: Travis Sanders
Year Founded: 2010
Type of Packaging: Private Label
Other Locations:
Warehouse
Oakleigh, Australia

4288 Farmhouse Culture
182 Lewis Road
Watsonville, CA 95076
831-466-0499
info@farmhouseculture.com
www.farmhouseculture.com
Manufacturer of organic kraut and kimchi.
CEO: John Tucker
Founder: Kathryn Lukas
COO: Capp Culver
Director of Sales: Heather Dean
Brands:
Farmhouse Culture

4289 Farmington Foods Inc
7419 West Franklin St
Forest Park, IL 60130-1016
708-771-3600
Fax: 708-771-4140 800-609-3276
info@farmingtonfoods.com
www.farmingtonfoods.com
Pork chops, boneless pork, baby back ribs, St. Louis-style spareribs, pre-packaged kabobs made with beef, chicken and pork, frenched pork racks, and seasoned port tenderloins and roasts
President: Tony Dijohn
tony.dijohn@farmingtonfoods.com
CFO: Albert LaValle
Quality Assurance: Marnie Adamski
Sales Manager: Tony DiJohn
Plant Manager/Director Operations: Dan Bernkopf
Warehouse Manager: Ram McKee
Estimated Sales: $30 Million
Number Employees: 100-249
Square Footage: 55000

4290 Farmland Dairies
520 Main Avenue
Wallington, NJ 07057
973-777-2500
Fax: 973-777-7648 888-727-6252
www.farmlanddairies.com
Milk, ice cream, yogurt, juice and ice tea
President/CEO: Martin Margherio
VP Finance: Anthony Mayzun
Contact: Mayra Olvera
molvera@bordendairy.com
Estimated Sales: $39.4 Million
Number Employees: 490
Square Footage: 150000
Parent Co: Groupo LALA/LALA National Dairy Group
Type of Packaging: Consumer, Food Service
Other Locations:
Farmland Dairies Facility
Wallington NJ
Farmland Dairies Facility
Newark NJ
Farmland Dairies Facility
Grand Rapids MI
Brands:
Altanta Dairy
Clinton's
Farmland Dairies
Farmland Dairies Special Request
School Milk!
Skim Plus
Sunnydale Farms
Welsh Farms

4291 Farmland Fresh Dairies
802-814 Bergens St
Newark, NJ 07108
973-961-2500
sales@farmlandmilk.com
farmlandmilk.com
Milk; dairy products
Director of Customer Service: Gabrielle Romeo
Year Founded: 1914
Number Employees: 500-1000
Type of Packaging: Private Label

4292 Farms For City Kids Foundation, Inc.
734 Caper Hill Rd.
Reading, VT 05062
802-484-1236
info@farmsforcitykids.org
www.farmsforcitykids.org
Manufacturer of cheese.
Marketing Manager: Larry Ference
Sales Manager: Cristi Menard
Contact: Curt Allen
curt@farmsforcitychildren.org
Operations Manager: Gary Wojdyla

4293 Farmstead At Long Meadow Ranch
738 Main St
St Helena, CA 94574-2005
707-963-4555
Fax: 707-963-1956 877-627-2645
info@longmeadowranch.com
www.longmeadowranch.com
Olive oils, fine wines, and grass fed beef
President/General Manager: Ted Hall
tedhall@longmeadowranch.com
Director/Chairman: Les Denend
Chief Financial Officer: Devonna Smith
VP/General Manager: Chris Hall
Director of Winemaking: Ashley Heisley
Cellarmaster-Red Wine: Hans Van Dale
Cellarmaster-White Wine: Jeff Restell
Operations Manager: Tony Fernandez
Estimated Sales: $20 Million
Number Employees: 100-249

4294 **Farmtrue**
81 Norwich Westerly Rd
North Stonington, CT 06359
401-474-5073
860-495-2231
info@farmtrue.com www.farmtrue.com
Ghee (clarified butter), ghee-nut butter, tea, spices
Co-Founder: Kim Welch
Co-Founder: Lynn Goodwin

4295 **Farmwise LLC**
P.O. Box 812428
Wellesley, MA 02482
508-401-7040
Fax: 508-401-7430 eatveggiefries.com
Veggie fries, tots and rings.
Co-Founder & CEO: David Peters
Co-Founder: Christina Peters
Estimated Sales: $1.6 Million
Type of Packaging: Private Label
Brands:
Veggie Fries
Veggie Tots
Veggie Rings

4296 **Faroh Candies**
7223 Pearl Rd
Middleburg Heights, OH 44130
440-888-9866
Fax: 440-842-4013
Confectionery products including boxed chocolates, chocolate cherries and popcorn specialties.
Owner: George Faroh
Purchasing: Donna Parrot
Estimated Sales: $5-10 Million
Number Employees: 20-49
Type of Packaging: Consumer

4297 **Farr Candy Company**
345 D Street
Idaho Falls, ID 83402
208-522-8215
Fax: 208-523-3307 www.farrcandy.com
Confectionery products including cherry cordials, peanut clusters and malo nuts; also, ice cream
President/Owner: Kevin W. Call
Estimated Sales: $3-5 Million
Number Employees: 10-19

4298 **Farrell Baking Company**
26 Stefanak Dr
West Middlesex, PA 16159-3138
724-342-7906
Bread and bakery products
President: Richard Vatavuk
Owner: Richard Vatavuk
Estimated Sales: $1-2,500,000
Number Employees: 10-19
Brands:
Farrell Baking

4299 **Fashion Snackz**
3201 W Temple Ave
Suite 275
Pomona, CA 91768
909-598-0880
info.fashionsnackz@gmail.com
www.fashionsnackz.com
Gluten-free fruit and nut clusters
Type of Packaging: Consumer
Brands:
DEEZ NUTZ

4300 **Fast Fixing Foods**
1481 US Highway 431
Boaz, AL 35957-1552
256-593-7221
Fax: 256-593-7208 800-317-4232
www.fastfixinfoods.com
Fast foods
Owner: Eugene Davis
eugene.davis@fastfixin.com
Estimated Sales: $10-20 Million
Number Employees: 10-19

4301 **Fastachi**
598 Mount Auburn St
Watertown, MA 02472-4124
617-924-8787
Fax: 617-924-8844 800-466-3022
Almonds, cashews, pistachios, hazelnuts, peanuts and sunflower seeds; also, gift baskets available
Owner: Souren Etyemezian
sourene@fastachi.com
Estimated Sales: Less Than $500,000
Number Employees: 1-4
Brands:
Fastachi

4302 **(HQ)Fasweet Co**
215 N Culberhouse St
Jonesboro, AR 72401-1998
870-932-1562
Fax: 870-932-1114 888-223-6693
www.fasweet.com
Sugar substitutes
President: Jake Morse
Estimated Sales: $5-10 Million
Number Employees: 5-9
Square Footage: 30000
Parent Co: Morse Company
Type of Packaging: Consumer, Food Service
Brands:
Fasweet

4303 **Fat Snax**
Brooklyn, NY 11206
347-496-5834
fatsnax.com
Low-carb, keto-friendly cookies and teas
Type of Packaging: Consumer
Brands:
Fat Snax
Fat Tea

4304 **Fat Toad Farm**
787 Kibbee Rd
Brookfield, VT 05036-9615
802-279-0098
info@fattoadfarm.com
www.fattoadfarm.com
Manufacturer of goat's milk.
Co-Owner: Steve Reid
Co-Owner: Judith Irving
Co-Owner: Calley Hastings
Contact: Calley Hastings
calley@fattoadfarm.com
Number Employees: 1-4

4305 **FatBoy's Cookie Company**
18-01 River Road
Fair Lawn, NJ 07410
201-796-1000
Fax: 201-475-3501 888-328-2690
fatboycookies@aol.com
Cookie dough
President: Joel Ansh

4306 **Father Sam's Bakery**
105 Msgr Valente Dr
Buffalo, NY 14206-1815
716-853-1071
Fax: 716-853-1062 800-521-6719
www.fathersams.com
Flatbreads, tortilla shells, and flavored wraps.
President: William Sam
Sales: Glenn Povitz
Estimated Sales: $20-50 Million
Number Employees: 50-99
Square Footage: 40000
Type of Packaging: Consumer, Food Service, Private Label
Brands:
Father Sam's Pocket Breads
Father Sam's Tortillas
Father Sam's Wraps

4307 **Father's Country Hams**
P.O.Box 99 6323 St. Rt 81
Bremen, KY 42325
270-525-3554
Fax: 270-525-3333 info@fatherscountryhams.com
www.fatherscountryhams.com
Ham, bacon, and smoked sausage
President: Charles Gatton Jr
Estimated Sales: $.5-1 million
Number Employees: 5-9

4308 **Father's Table Inc**
2100 Country Club Rd
P.O. Box 1509
Sanford, FL 32771-4051
407-324-1200
Fax: 407-324-1228 www.thefatherstable.com
Desserts, pizza cheesecake
President: Tim Lambert
tim.lambert@thefatherstable.com
Number Employees: 100-249

4309 **Fatty Sundays**
630 Flushing Ave
5th Fl
Brooklyn, NY 11206-5026
646-762-2555
Fax: 646-762-2554 info@fattysundays.com
www.fattysundays.com
Gluten-free baked goods; candy; and pretzels.
Co-Founder: Lauren Borowick
Co-Founder: Ali Borowick
Year Founded: 2011
Type of Packaging: Food Service, Private Label

4310 **Fatworks**
Niwot, CO 80544
fatworksfoods.com
Cooking oils
Number of Brands: 1
Number of Products: 4
Type of Packaging: Consumer
Brands:
FATWORKS

4311 **Favorite Foods**
6934 Greenwood Street
Burnaby, BC V5A 1X8
Canada
604-420-5100
Fax: 604-420-9116 www.favoritefoods.com
Manufacturer and exporter of sauces including light and dark soy, oyster, teriyaki, marinade, barbecue, black bean, stir fry, Szechuan spicy hot and plum
President: Chris Barstow
VP of Sales: Chris Langella
Sr. Marketing Manager: Pearl Lyman
Chief Operating Officer: John Libby
Category Managers/Purchasing: Steve Gerasimchik
Estimated Sales: $1-5 million
Number Employees: 24
Square Footage: 70000
Type of Packaging: Consumer, Food Service, Private Label, Bulk
Brands:
Golden Dragon

4312 **Fawen**
134 N 4th
2nd Floor
Brooklyn, NY 11249
888-737-7052
drinkfawen.com
Ready-to-drink soups
Number of Brands: 1
Number of Products: 3
Type of Packaging: Consumer
Brands:
FAWEN

4313 **Fayes Bakery Products**
216 E McCollum Street
Dexter, MO 63841-1222
573-624-4920
Bakery products
Owner: Dale Parks
Estimated Sales: $.5-1,000,000
Number Employees: 1-4

4314 **Faygo Beverages Inc**
3579 Gratiot Ave
Detroit, MI 48207
313-925-1600
www.faygo.com
Carbonated soft drinks
President: Alan Chittaro
Controller: Lynn Beauvais
Estimated Sales: $25,000,000-$100,000,000
Number Employees: 500-999
Parent Co: National Beverage Company
Type of Packaging: Consumer, Private Label

4315 **Fayter Farms Produce**
69400 Jolon Rd
Bradley, CA 93426-9676
831-385-8515
Fax: 831-385-0833
Fresh herbicide pesticide-free Kiss of Burgundy globe artichokes.
President: Thomas Fayter
Estimated Sales: $300,000-500,000
Number Employees: 1-4
Type of Packaging: Private Label, Bulk
Other Locations:
Fayter Farms Produce
Bradley CA

Brands:
Globe Artichoke
Kiss of Burgundy

4316 **Fazio's Bakery**
1717 Sublette Ave
St Louis, MO 63110-1926
314-645-6239
Fax: 314-645-2410 fazioinfo@faziosbakery.com
Bakery products
President: Charles Fazio
charles@faziosbakery.com
Estimated Sales: Below $5 Million
Number Employees: 100-249
Brands:
Fazio's

4317 **Feature Foods**
30 Finley Rd.
Brampton, ON L6T 1A9
Canada
905-452-7741
Fax: 905-452-9210 info@featurefoods.com
www.featurefoods.com
Manufacturer and exporter of pickled eggs and herring; also, herb horseradish
President: Lorne Krongold
Number Employees: 20-49
Type of Packaging: Consumer

4318 **Federal Pretzel Baking Company**
300 Eagle Court
Bridgeport, NJ 08014
215-467-0505
Fax: 215-467-3153 www.federalpretzel.biz
Pretzels, cookies
President: Florence Sciambi
Plant Manager: Rich Bezila
Estimated Sales: $1-2,500,000
Number Employees: 20-49
Brands:
Federal Pretzel

4319 **Federation-Southern Cprtvs**
2769 Church St
Atlanta, GA 30344-3258
404-765-0991
Fax: 404-765-9178 fsc@federation.coop
www.federationsoutherncoop.com
Manufacturer and exporter of fresh vegetables
Chairman: Shirley Williams Blakely
Vice Chair: Daniel Bustamante
Secretary: Satina James
Treasurer: Carrie Fulghum
Estimated Sales: $500,000-$1 Million
Number Employees: 20-49
Type of Packaging: Consumer, Bulk

4320 **Fee Brothers**
453 Portland Ave
Rochester, NY 14605-1597
585-544-9530
Fax: 585-544-9530 800-961-3337
info@feebrothers.com www.feebrothers.com
Manufacturer and exporter of cocktail mixes including whiskey sour, daiquiri, margarita, pina colada, etc.; also, slush bases, bitters, nonalcoholic cordials, tea and juice concentrates, grenadine, coffee flavoring syrups, maraschinocherries, olives, cocktail
President: John Fee
CEO: Ellen Fee
Treasurer: Joe Fee
Estimated Sales: $1 Million
Number Employees: 10-19
Number of Brands: 1
Number of Products: 90
Square Footage: 96000
Type of Packaging: Food Service, Private Label, Bulk
Brands:
Fee Brothers

4321 **Feed The Party**
2055 Nelson Miller Pkwy
Louisville, KY 40223
partyon@feedtheparty.com
feedtheparty.com
Supplier of the finest butcher shop quality meats, including steak, pork, chicken, and lamb.
President & Founder: Matt Kenney
Estimated Sales: $100+ Million
Number Employees: 2-10
Square Footage: 89000
Type of Packaging: Food Service, Bulk

Brands:
A. Thomas Meats
Berkwood Farms
Border Springs Farm Lamb
Shire Gate
Shuckman's Fish Co. & Smokery, Inc.
Joyce Farms
Big Fork

4322 **Feeding the Turkeys, Inc.**
745 Atlantic Ave
Suite 327
Boston, MA 02111-2735
207-712-4034
www.eatvicecream.com
Ice cream
Founder: Dan Schorr
Senior Marketing Manager: Molly DeLong
Year Founded: 2016
Number Employees: 1-4
Type of Packaging: Food Service, Private Label

4323 **Feel Good Foods**
220 36th St
Unit 22
Brooklyn, NY 11232
800-638-8949
tryg@feelgf.com feel-good-foods.com
Gluten-free meals
Contact: Carrie Mcquade
carrie@feelgf.com

4324 **Felbro Food Products**
5700 W Adams Blvd
Los Angeles, CA 90016
323-936-5266
Fax: 323-936-5946 www.felbro.com
Manufacturer, importer and exporter of fountain syrups, sno cone syrups, dessert toppings, fillings, puddings, sauces, dressings and drink bases for shakes, punches and slushies.
CEO: Mike Feldmar
CFO: Brian Seigel
Business Development Manager: Jim DeBiase
COO: Daniel Feldmar
Year Founded: 1946
Estimated Sales: $20-50 Million
Number Employees: 20-49
Number of Brands: 4
Square Footage: 80000
Type of Packaging: Consumer, Food Service, Private Label, Bulk
Brands:
Coffee Express
Felbro
Food Tone
Marsa

4325 **Felix Custom Smoking**
17461 147th St SE # 2a
Monroe, WA 98272-1070
425-485-2439
Fax: 425-485-2439 felixcustom@aol.com
Albacore Tuna to Yukon Wild Chum Salmon, smoked seafoods, salmon sausages, dips, ready to eat, etc. Mostly custom work for fisher person.
Owner: Diane Zollinger
felixcustom@aol.com
Plant Manager: Tony Newman
Estimated Sales: More than $500,000
Number Employees: 5-9
Square Footage: 12000
Type of Packaging: Private Label

4326 **Felix Roma & Son Inc**
2 S Page Ave
Endicott, NY 13760-4693
607-748-3336
Fax: 607-748-3607 www.felixroma.com
Breads, rolls and pizza dough
President: Brian Bertoni
brian@felixroma.com
VP: Barry Roma
VP/Sales Manager: Anthony Roma
Office Manager: Mary Consentio
brian@felixroma.com
Bakery General Manager: James Wasley
VP/Frozen Foods Manager: Michael Roma
Production Manager: Brian Bertoni
Plant Manager: Eugene Roma
brian@felixroma.com
Estimated Sales: $4.3 Million
Number Employees: 50-99
Square Footage: 86000
Type of Packaging: Consumer, Food Service, Private Label, Bulk
Brands:
Felix Roma

4327 **Fenchem Inc**
15308 El Prado Rd
Building 8
Chino, CA 91710-7659
909-597-1113
Fax: 909-597-1113 sales@fenchem.com
www.fenchem.com
Manufactures natural ingredients for nutrition supplements and functional foods
President: Yanyan Zhu
Contact: Jason Betts
jasonb@fenchem.com
Estimated Sales: 5-9

4328 **Fendall Ice Cream Company**
470 South 700 East
Salt Lake City, UT 84102
801-355-3583
Fax: 801-521-0133 sales@fendalls.com
Manufacturer and wholesaler/distributor of ice cream, sherbet, water ices, sorbets and frozen yogurt
Owner: Carol Radinger
Contact: Gunter Radinger
gunter@fendalls.com
Estimated Sales: $1-2.5 Million
Number Employees: 5-9
Type of Packaging: Consumer
Brands:
Cream of Weber
Fendall's

4329 **Fenestra Winery**
83 Vallecitos Rd
Livermore, CA 94550-9603
925-447-5246
Fax: 925-447-4655 800-789-9463
www.fenestrawinery.com
Wines
Owner: Lanny Replogle
l.r@fenestrawinery.com
Estimated Sales: $500,000-$1,000,000
Number Employees: 1-4
Type of Packaging: Private Label
Brands:
Fenestra Winery

4330 **(HQ)Fenn Valley Vineyards**
6130 122nd Ave
Fennville, MI 49408-9457
269-561-2396
Fax: 269-561-2973 800-432-6265
winery@fennvalley.com www.fennvalley.com
Wines
President: Vernon Jenewein
vernon@fennvalley.com
Estimated Sales: $500,000-$1,000,000
Number Employees: 10-19

4331 **Fenn Valley Vineyards**
6130 122nd Ave
Fennville, MI 49408
269-561-2396
www.fennvalley.com
Wines
Asst. Manager, Tasting Room: Chelsea Hundey

4332 **Fentimans North America**
2286 Holdom Ave
Burnaby, BC V5B 4Y5
Canada
877-326-3248
info@drinkfentimans.com
www.drinkfentimans.com
Botanically brewed beverages-natural sodas
President: Nap Veltri
CEO: Craig James
Marketing: Craig L'Heureux
Sales: Craig James
Public Relations: Samantha James
Year Founded: 1905

4333 **Fenton & Lee Chocolatiers**
35 E 8th Avenue
Eugene, OR 97401-2906
541-343-7629
Fax: 541-343-6385 800-336-8661
Chocolates and confections
President: Janele Smith

Estimated Sales: $2.5-5,000,000
Number Employees: 5-9

4334 **Feridies**
PO Box 186
28285 Mill Creek Dr
Courtland, VA 23837
800-544-0896
customerservice@feridies.com www.feridies.com
Gluten-free, kosher, organic/natural, other candy, hors d'oeuvres/appetizers, nuts, other snacks, gift packs.
Marketing: Jane Riddick-Fries

4335 **Feridies**
28285 Mill Creek Dr
Courtland, VA 23837
866-732-6883
www.feridies.com
Virginia peanuts and trail mix
Year Founded: 1973
Type of Packaging: Consumer
Brands:
FERIDIES

4336 **Fermalife**
fermalife.com
Fermented soy beverage mix
Type of Packaging: Consumer
Brands:
FERMALIFE

4337 **Ferme Ostreicole Dugas**
675 St-Pierre Blvd W
Caraquet, NB E1W 1A2
Canada
506-727-3226
Fax: 506-727-4950
Fresh oysters
President: Gaetan Dugas
Estimated Sales: $520,000
Number Employees: 6
Type of Packaging: Consumer, Food Service

4338 **Fermenting Fairy**
Santa Monica Blvd
Santa Monica, CA 90403
fatsnax.com
Probiotic foods and beverages
Founder: Lauren Mones

4339 **Fernandez Chili Co**
8267 County Road 10 S
Alamosa, CO 81101-9176
719-589-6043
Fax: 719-587-0485
Manufacturer and importer of chili and taco sauces, spices and prepared chili mixes; also, Mexican corn products
Vice President: Blair Fernandez
VP: Blair Fernandez
Estimated Sales: $5-10 Million
Number Employees: 5-9
Square Footage: 45000
Type of Packaging: Consumer, Food Service, Bulk

4340 **Fernando C Pujals & Bros**
B St Cntro De Dist Amlia St
Guaynabo, PR 00968
787-792-3080
Fax: 787-792-8797
Candy
President: Fernando Pujals
Estimated Sales: $24 Million
Number Employees: 80

4341 **Ferncreek Confections LLC**
2720 Council Tree Ave Ste 224
Fort Collins, CO 80525-6329
970-377-2293
Fax: 970-229-0910
www.ferncreekconfections.com
Confections: toffee
Sales Manager: Dawn Wittstruck

4342 **Ferolito Vultaggio & Sons**
60 Crossways Park Dr W # 400
Woodbury, NY 11797-2003
516-812-0300
Fax: 516-326-4988 800-832-3775
Beverages, general grocery
President: John Ferolito
CEO: Rick Adonailo
VP Corporate Communications: Francie Patton
Estimated Sales: $10-100,000,000
Number Employees: 500-999
Type of Packaging: Private Label
Brands:
Arizona Iced Tea
Ferolito Vultaggio

4343 **Ferrante Winery & Ristorante**
5585 State Route 307
Geneva, OH 44041
440-466-6046
Fax: 440-466-7370 www.ferrantewinery.com
Wines
Manager: Bob Strickland
Estimated Sales: $2,000,000
Number Employees: 20-49
Brands:
Ferrante

4344 **Ferrara Bakery & Cafe**
195 Grand St
b/w Mulberry & Mott St
New York, NY 10013-3717
212-226-6150
Fax: 212-226-0667 information@ferraracafe.com
www.ferraranyc.com
Manufacturer and importer of confectionery products including candies, novelties, Italian and seasonal products; also, syrups, coffee and baked goods
Owner: Ernest Lepore
ernestl@ferraracafe.com
Owner/CEO: Peter Lepore
Estimated Sales: $5-10 Million
Number Employees: 100-249
Type of Packaging: Consumer, Private Label

4345 **Ferrara Candy Co Inc**
404 W Harrison St
Suite 650
Chicago, IL 60607
800-323-1768
talktous@ferrarausa.com www.ferrarausa.com
Candy including butterscotch, caramels, chocolate, jelly beans, hard, licorice, lollypops, mints, marshmallows, nougats, etc.
CEO: Todd Siwak
CFO: Maurizio Ficarra
VP, Business Development: Willy Pfenning
Chief Customer Officer: Mike Sayles
COO: Michael Murray
Estimated Sales: $50 Million
Number Employees: 500-999
Number of Brands: 18
Square Footage: 365000
Parent Co: Catterton Management Company
Type of Packaging: Food Service, Private Label, Bulk
Other Locations:
Farley's & Sathers-Distribution
Chattanooga TN
Farley's & Sathers-Manufacturing
Des Plaines IL
Farley's & Sathers-Manufacturing
Reynosa MX
Brands:
Atomic FireBall
Black Forest Organic
Bob's
Boston Baked Beans
Brach's
Chuckles
Fruit Stripe
Now and Later
Jaw Busters
Jujyfruits
Lemonhead
Now & Later
Sweet Stripes
Rainblo
Redhots
Sathers
Super Bubble
Trolli

4346 **Ferrara Winery**
1120 W 15th Ave
Escondido, CA 92025
760-745-7632
Wines
Owner: Gasper D Ferrara
CEO: Vera Ferrara
Estimated Sales: $1-2,500,000
Number Employees: 5-9
Brands:
Ferrara

4347 **Ferrari-Carano**
8761 Dry Creek Rd
P.O. Box 1549
Healdsburg, CA 95448-9133
707-433-6700
Fax: 707-431-1742 800-831-0381
info@ferrari-carano.com www.ferrari-carano.com
Wines
President: Don Carano
d.carano@ferrari-carano.com
Co-Owner/Vice President: Rhonda Carano
Director, Vineyard Operations: Steve Domenichelli
Sr. Winemaker: Aaron Piotter
Estimated Sales: $20-50 Million
Number Employees: 100-249
Type of Packaging: Private Label

4348 **Ferrero USA Inc**
600 Cottontail Ln
Somerset, NJ 08873-1233
732-764-9300
Fax: 732-764-2700 800-337-7376
www.ferrerousa.com
Confectionery items including breath mints, chocolates, chocolate and hazelnut wafers and spread; also, chocolate espresso coffee
Owner: Luigi Cavalotto
CEO: Michael Gilmore
Vice President: F Veglio
VP Of Marketing: Leonardo Limitone
Director of Sales: John Kennington
Estimated Sales: $10-20 Million
Number Employees: 100-249
Parent Co: Ferrero, SPA
Type of Packaging: Consumer
Brands:
Mon Cheri
Raffaello
Rocher
Silvers
Tic Tac

4349 **Ferrigno Vineyards & Wine**
17301 State Route B
St James, MO 65559-8583
573-265-7742
www.ferrignovineyards.com
Wines
CEO: Richard Ferrigno
Estimated Sales: $150,000
Number Employees: 9
Type of Packaging: Private Label
Brands:
Ferrigno

4350 **Ferris Organic Farms**
3565 Onondaga Rd
Eaton Rapids, MI 48827-9608
517-628-2506
Fax: 517-628-8257 800-628-8736
ferrisorganicfarm@gmail.com
www.ferrisorganicfarm.com
Manufacturer, grower and exporter of organic beans including black, soy, black turtle and pinto; also, grains including wheat and barley; wholesaler/distributor of organic natural foods
Co-Owner: Richard Ferris
ferrisorganicfarm@excite.com
Estimated Sales: $1-2.5 Million
Number Employees: 1-4
Square Footage: 14000
Type of Packaging: Bulk

4351 **(HQ)Ferris, Stahl-Meyer**
2071 Lemoine Ave
Suite 202
Fort Lee, NJ 07024
201-242-5500
Fax: 201-242-5516 www.stahlmeyer.com
Cold cuts and frankfurters including; smoked meats, spanish products, beef bacon, cooked hams & deli meats, corned beef & pastrami, and roast beef. Frankfurters include beef, chicken, hot dogs, knockwurst, smoked sausage, andturkey.
President & CEO: Guillermo Gonzalez
Number Employees: 100-249
Number of Brands: 5
Type of Packaging: Consumer, Food Service, Private Label, Bulk
Brands:
Ferris
Stahl-Meyer
Sweet Meadow Farms

El Taino
El Conquistador

4352 Ferroclad Fishery
Mamainse Pt
Batchawana Bay, ON P0S 1A0
Canada
705-882-2295
Fax: 705-882-2297
Manufacturer, importer and exporter of herring, trout, whitefish and caviar
Owner: Gary Symons
Number Employees: 20-49
Parent Co: Presteve Foods Limited
Type of Packaging: Consumer, Food Service

4353 Fess Parker Winery
6200 Foxen Canyon Rd
Los Olivos, CA 93441
805-688-1545
Fax: 805-686-1130 800-841-1104
infowinery@fessparker.com www.fessparker.com
Producer of wines
CEO: Eli Parker
Estimated Sales: $110,000
Number Employees: 11-50
Square Footage: 9
Brands:
American Tradition Reserve
Pinot Noir Santa Barbara County
Santa Barbara County
Syrah Santa Barbara County
Viognier Santa Barbara County
and more

4354 Festive Foods
389 Edwin Dr # 100
Virginia Beach, VA 23462-4548
757-490-9186
Fax: 757-490-9494 www.festivefoods.com
Sauces including spicy and extra spicy
President: Bobby Cannon
bcannon@festivefoods.com
Purchasing: Robert Buchanan
Estimated Sales: $.5-1,000,000
Number Employees: 1-4
Type of Packaging: Consumer
Brands:
Buffalo Bob's Everything Sauce

4355 Fetzer Vineyards
12901 Old River Rd
Hopland, CA 95449
707-744-1250
www.fetzer.com
Wines
CEO: Giancarlo Bianchetti
CFO: Jorge Lyng Benitez
COO: Cindy DeVries
SVP Sales & Distribution: Barry Marek
Year Founded: 1968
Estimated Sales: $20-50 Million
Number Employees: 100-249

4356 Fiberstar
713 Saint Croix St
River Falls, WI 54022-3600
715-425-7550
Fax: 715-425-7572 sales@fiberstar.net
www.fiberstaringredients.com
Food ingredients and additives
President/CEO: Dale Lindquist
CEO: Greg Aronson
gregaronson@fiberstar.net
VP Technology: Brock Lundberg
Number Employees: 20-49

4357 Fibred
10900 Day Rd SE
Cumberland, MD 21502-8638
301-724-6050
Fax: 301-722-7131 800-598-8894
Customerservice@fibred.com www.fibred.com
Soy fiber
President: Kim Alkire
kim@fibred.com
Quality Assurance Manager: Rhonda Niland
VP Sales: Karen Ort
Estimated Sales: $10-20 Million
Number Employees: 20-49
Type of Packaging: Bulk
Brands:
F1-1 Soy Fibre

4358 Ficklin Vineyards Winery
30246 Avenue 7 1/2
Madera, CA 93637-9198
559-674-4598
www.ficklin.com
Wines
President: Peter Ficklin
Assistant Winemaker: Paige Diffenderfer
Marketing: Rick Wilcox
PR/Media, Brand Management and Retail Op: Liz Wilcox
Administrative Manager: Kellie Murpfy
Winemaker: Robeart Simons
Estimated Sales: $500,000-$1,000,000
Number Employees: 5-9

4359 Ficks & Co.
2662 Bush St
San Francisco, CA 94115
ficksdrink.com
Hard seltzers and cocktail mixes
CEO: Ron Alvarado
COO: Mike Williamson
Number of Brands: 1
Number of Products: 8
Type of Packaging: Consumer
Brands:
FICKS

4360 Ficon
10630 Midwest Industrial Blvd
St Louis, MO 63132-1221
314-427-4099
Fax: 314-427-6646 888-569-4099
www.ficoninc.com
Confectioneries
President: Charlie Hirschi
chirschi@ficoninc.com
Secretary / Treasurer: Gary Sauer
Vice President: Jim Sauer
Estimated Sales: $1-2.5 Million
Number Employees: 1-4

4361 Fidalgo Bay Roasting Co
856 N Hill Blvd
Burlington, WA 98233-4640
360-757-8818
Fax: 360-757-8810 800-310-5540
www.fidalgobaycoffee.com
Coffee
Owner: Gary Swoyer
gary@fidalgobaycoffee.com
CEO: David Evans
VP Sales & Marketing: Darryl Miller
gary@fidalgobaycoffee.com
Purchasing: Gary Sawyer
Estimated Sales: $1-2,500,000
Number Employees: 20-49

4362 Fiddlers Green Farm
16 Mayo St
PO Box 1
North Vassalboro, ME 4962
207-877-7445
Fax: 207-338-3872 800-729-7935
info@fiddlersgreenfarm.com
www.fiddlersgreenfarm.com
Organic and stone ground grains, flour and corn meal
Owner: Marada Cook
Owner: Leah Cook
Vice President: Laine Alexander
Estimated Sales: Under $500,000
Number Employees: 1-4
Square Footage: 600
Type of Packaging: Consumer, Food Service
Brands:
Belleweather
Bertha's
Bread & Biscuits
Fiddle Cakes
Fiddlers Green Farms
Islander's Choice
Oatbran & Brown Rice
Penobscot Porridge
Spice
Toasted Buckwheat

4363 Field Coffee
6700 Dawson Blvd
Building 3
Norcross, GA 30093
844-343-5326
fieldcoffee.net
Coffee
President: Geoffrey Paul
Controller: Jodi Burkett
Sales Manager: Daniel Lane
Estimated Sales: $10-20 Million
Number Employees: 84
Parent Co: Excelso

4364 Field Roast
3901 7th Ave South
Seattle, WA 98108
800-311-9497
fieldroast.com
Sausages, burgers, deli slices, appetizers and entr,es
Founder: David Lee
Year Founded: 1997
Number of Brands: 1
Number of Products: 20
Type of Packaging: Consumer
Brands:
FIELD ROAST

4365 Field Stone Winery
10075 Highway 128
Healdsburg, CA 95448-9025
707-433-7266
Fax: 707-433-2231 800-544-7273
Wines
Owner: Roger Hull
soconnor@corvel.com
General and Vineyard Manager: Ben Staten
Owner: Katrina Staten
Tasting Room Manager: Helen Weber
Public Relations: Roger Hull
Estimated Sales: $2.5-5,000,000
Number Employees: 10-19

4366 Field Trip Jerky
630 Flushing Ave
Suite 4
Brooklyn, NY 11206-5026
315-491-8240
Fax: 646-233-0638 www.fieldtripjerky.com
Manufacturer of all natural jerky.
Co-Founder: Matthew Levey
Co-Founder: Tom Donigan
tom@fieldtripjerky.com
Co-Founder: Scott Fiesinger
Estimated Sales: Less Than $500,000
Number Employees: 1-4
Brands:
FIELD Trip

4367 Field's Pies
100 Fields Row
Pauls Valley, OK 73075-9600
405-238-7381
Fax: 405-238-5075 800-286-7501
fields@fieldspies.com www.fieldspies.com
Manufacturer of frozen pies including pecan, German chocolate, lemon chess and pumpkin.
President: Chris Field
Vice President: Jenny Wallace
Year Founded: 1975
Estimated Sales: G
Number Employees: 20-49
Square Footage: 12500
Type of Packaging: Consumer, Food Service, Private Label, Bulk
Brands:
Field's

4368 Fieldale Farms
P.O. Box 558
Baldwin, GA 30511
800-241-5400
www.fieldale.com
Fresh and frozen chicken.
President: Thomas Hensley
General Manager, Further Processing: David Stevens
Year Founded: 1972
Estimated Sales: $473.5 Million
Number Employees: 5,000+
Square Footage: 21000
Type of Packaging: Consumer, Food Service, Private Label, Bulk

4369 **Fieldbrook Foods Corp.**
1 Ice Cream Dr.
P.O. Box 1318
Dunkirk, NY 14048
716-366-5400
Fax: 716-366-3588 800-333-0805
www.fieldbrookfoods.com
Ice cream, frozen yogurt, sherbert and sorbet, sandwiches, ice cream/fudge bars, ice pops, juice and fruit bars, cones, cups, sorbet bars, etc.
President/Chief Executive Officer: Robin Galloway
Chief Financial Officer: Derek Kamholz
Senior VP, Sales & Marketing: James Masood
COO: Mark McLenithan
Vice President, Purchasing: Robert Griewisch
Year Founded: 2001
Estimated Sales: $101 Million
Number Employees: 250-499
Number of Brands: 3
Square Footage: 280000
Type of Packaging: Consumer, Food Service, Private Label, Bulk
Other Locations:
Fieldbrook Farms
Columbus GA
Brands:
Deering
Howard Johnson
My Favorite

4370 **Fieldbrook Valley Winery**
4241 Fieldbrook Rd
Mckinleyville, CA 95519-8130
707-839-4140
Fax: 707-839-2278 www.fieldbrookwinery.com
Wines
Owner: Robert Hodgson
COO: Judith Hodgson
Estimated Sales: Less Than $500,000
Number Employees: 1-4

4371 **Fiera Foods**
50 Marmora St
Toronto, ON M9M 2X5
Canada
800-675-6356
info@fierafoods.com www.fierafoods.com
French pastries including croissants, danish and turnovers; also, muffin mixes.
President & CEO: Boris Serebryany
COO: Alex Garber
Year Founded: 1987
Estimated Sales: $188.48 Million
Number Employees: 1,200
Square Footage: 200000
Type of Packaging: Food Service

4372 **Fiesta Candy Company**
25 Old Dover Rd
Suite 1
Rochester, NH 03867
603-335-0003
Fax: 603-994-0333 800-285-9735
Candy
Managing Director: Jose Mayoral
jmayoral@fiestacandy.com
Estimated Sales: $5-10 Million
Number Employees: 5-9

4373 **Fiesta Canning Co**
1480 E Bethany Home Rd # 110
Suite 110
Phoenix, AZ 85014-2074
602-212-2424
Fax: 602-343-5141
SalesCoordinator@Fiestacan.com
Canned chili pepper paste
President: Gary Johnson
Director: Bob Godfrey
CFO: Bob Myers
bob@fiestacan.com
VP: Stephen Johnson
Marketing: Ernie Jayme
Sales Executive: Iris Marin
Manufacturing Executive: Jesus Ayala
Plant Manager: Bob Godfrey
Number Employees: 5-9
Square Footage: 20000
Brands:
Cochise Farms
Fiesta Del Sole
Macayo Mexican Foods

4374 **Fiesta Farms**
200 Christie St.
Toronto, ON M6G 3B6
Canada
416-537-1235
Fax: 416-537-1244 www.fiestafarms.ca
Onions including red, yellow and white
President: Garry Bybee
Secretary: Tamara Bybee
VP: Marc Bybee
Estimated Sales: $10-20 Million
Number Employees: 20-49
Type of Packaging: Consumer, Food Service, Private Label, Bulk
Brands:
Bloombuilder
Bybee's
Ff
Ru-Bee
Zoombees

4375 **Fiesta Gourmet of Tejas**
42 Oak Villa Road
Canyon Lake, TX 78133-3102
210-212-5233
Fax: 210-212-5240 800-585-8250
Manufacturer and exporter of Texas-made wines, chiles, salsas, sauces, jellies, oils, coffees and teas; custom-made gift baskets available
Owner: Maricela Smith
Estimated Sales: Less than $500,000
Number Employees: 1-4
Square Footage: 4000
Parent Co: Fiesta Gourmet del Sol
Type of Packaging: Consumer, Food Service, Private Label
Brands:
Fiesta Del Sol
Poblanos
Serranos
Tejas Sizzle

4376 **Fiesta Mexican Foods**
979 G St
Brawley, CA 92227-2615
760-344-3580
Fax: 760-344-3580 www.chexfoods.com
Tortillas
President: Raymond Armenta
raymond.armenta@chexfoods.com
Estimated Sales: $3,000,000
Number Employees: 20-49

4377 **Fife Vineyards**
3620 Road B
Redwood Valley, CA 95470
707-485-0323
Fax: 707-485-0832 info@fifevineyards.com
Wines
President: Dennis Fife
Owner: Karen MacNeil
Estimated Sales: $2.5-5,000,000
Number Employees: 5-9

4378 **Fig Food Co.**
PO Box 265
New York, NY 10014
855-344-3663
figfood.com
Fig Food offers four ready-to-eat varieties and three condensed varieties of soup. 100% plant-based recipes made with fresh, organic ingredients.
Contact: Joel Henry
joel@figfood.com
Type of Packaging: Consumer
Brands:
FIG FOOD CO.

4379 **Fig Garden Packing Inc**
5545 W Dakota Ave
Fresno, CA 93722-9749
559-271-9000
Fax: 559-271-1332
Manufacturer, exporter and packer of dried and diced figs and fig paste including regular and crushed seed
President: Michael Jura
Partner: Lisa Jura
lisa@figgardenpacking.com
Marketing Executive: Bert Zigenman
Estimated Sales: $1.3 Million
Number Employees: 50-99
Square Footage: 9646

4380 **Figamajigs**
20 North San Mateo Drive
Suite 2
San Mateo, CA 94401
650-227-3830
Fax: 707-581-1753
All natural, gluten free, low fat, kosher fig bars and fig pieces covered in chocolate
Founder: Mel Lefer

4381 **Figaro Company**
3601 Executive Blvd
Mesquite, TX 75149
972-288-3587
Fax: 972-288-1887
Manufacturer and exporter of hickory liquid smoke, mesquite liquid smoke, fajita marinade, brisket cooking sauce
Owner: J K Mc Kenney
CEO: Dave McCormack
Sales: Dave McCormack
Public Relations: Linda Willett
Operations: Anita Watson
Production: C Platero
Number Employees: 10-19
Number of Products: 6
Square Footage: 42000
Type of Packaging: Consumer, Food Service, Private Label
Brands:
Figaro

4382 **Figueroa Brothers**
1740 Hurd Dr
Irving, TX 75038-4324
972-714-0985
Fax: 214-351-9061 800-886-6354
greg@figbros.com www.figbros.com
Habanero pepper sauce
Owner: Greg Figueroa
CEO: Greg P. Figueroa
VP of Sales: Kevin Anderson
greg@figbros.com
Number Employees: 20-49
Brands:
Melinda's
Original Habanero Pepper Sauce

4383 **Figuerola Laboratories**
PO Box 1569
Santa Ynez, CA 93460-1569
805-688-6626
Fax: 805-688-8099 800-219-1147
customerservice@figuerola.net
Dietary supplements
President: Rossana Figuerola
rossana@figuerola.net
Executive Marketing Director: Antonio Figuerola
Number Employees: 5-9
Brands:
Figuerola

4384 **Fiji Water Co LLC**
11444 W Olympic Blvd # 210
2nd Floor
Los Angeles, CA 90064-1559
310-312-2850
Fax: 310-312-2828 888-426-3454
info@fijiwater.com www.fijiwater.com
Bottled water
President: James Ahn
james.ahn@mattel.com
CEO: Doug Carlson
SVP: Grace Jeon
SVP Sustainable Growth: Thomas Mooney
Number Employees: 50-99
Parent Co: Roll International Corporation
Brands:
Fiji

4385 **Filfil Foods LLC**
457 MacDonough St
Brooklyn, NY 11233-1509
917-971-3493
contact@filfilfoods.com
filfilfoods.com
Vegan spreads, jams, hot sauces, garlic condiments
Co-Founder: Einav Sharon
Co-Founder: Jeff Silva
Year Founded: 2012
Number Employees: 1-4
Type of Packaging: Food Service, Private Label

4386 **Filippo Berio Brand**
9 Polito Ave # 10
Floor 10
Lyndhurst, NJ 07071-3406
201-525-2900
Fax: 201-525-0805 www.filippoberio.com
Olive oil
President: Tom Mueller
Chief Executive Officer: Tonghong Wu
Vice President: Alberto Fontana
Estimated Sales: $10-20,000,000
Number Employees: 10-19
Number of Brands: 11
Parent Co: Societa' Per Azioni Lucchese Olii E Vini
Brands:
Casale Degli Ulivi
Centanni
Filippo Berio Extra Virgin
Tiger Brand
Sagri
Francesconi
Filippo Berio Green
Farmhouse
Fattoria Dell'ulivo
Filippo Berio
Filippo Berio Olive

4387 **Fillmore Piru Citrus**
357 N Main St
P.O. Box 350
Piru, CA 93040
805-521-1781
Fax: 805-521-0990 www.fillmorepirucitrus.com
Oranges, lemons and avocados
President: Brett Kirkpatrick
brett@fpcitrus.com
CFO: Christina Morris
Sales Manager: Lupita Fernandez
VP, Operations: Tim Shugrue
Grower Relations: Samuel Orozco
Plant Supervisor: Antonio Martinez
Year Founded: 1897
Estimated Sales: $20-50 Million
Number Employees: 50-99
Type of Packaging: Consumer, Food Service
Brands:
Airship
Belle of Piru
Cupid
Cycle
Desirable
Glider
Home of Ramona
Mansion
Oriole
Weaver

4388 **Fillo Factory, The**
Northvale, NJ 07647
201-439-1036
Fax: 201-385-0012 800-653-4556
ronrex@bellatlantic.net www.fillofactory.com
Gourmet appetizers, baklava, strudel, pastries and fillo dough; importer of dough
President: Ron Rexroth
VP Marketing: Tony Falletta
Contact: Tim Bennett
t.bennett@fillofactory.com
Estimated Sales: $1-3 Million
Number Employees: 60
Square Footage: 12000
Type of Packaging: Consumer, Food Service, Private Label, Bulk
Brands:
Fillo Factory

4389 **Filsinger Vineyards & Winery**
39050 De Portola Road
Temecula, CA 92592
951-302-6363
Fax: 877-801-8088 www.filsingerwinery.com
Wines
President: Robert Olson
Contact: William Filsinger
wfilsinger@aol.com
Estimated Sales: $500-1,000,000 appx.
Number Employees: 5-9

4390 **Finchville Farms Country Ham**
5157 Taylorsville Rd
P.O. Box 56
Finchville, KY 40022-6771
502-834-7952
Fax: 502-834-7095 800-678-1521
www.finchvillefarms.com
Manuafacturer of country ham
Dir: Nathan Arvin
Estimated Sales: $1 Million
Number Employees: 10-19
Type of Packaging: Consumer

4391 **Finding Home Farms**
140 Eatontown Rd.
Middletown, NY 10940
845-355-4335
www.findinghomefarms.com
Organic maple syrup, waffle and pancake mix, maple mustard and maple candy
Founder/Co-Owner: Laura Putnam
Founder/Co-Owner: Dana Putnam
Year Founded: 2013
Number of Brands: 1
Number of Products: 5
Type of Packaging: Consumer, Private Label
Brands:
Finding Home Farms

4392 **Fine & Raw Chocolate**
Brooklyn, NY 11206
718-366-3633
factory@fineandraw.com
www.fineandraw.com
Truffles, chocolate bars, butters and spreads
Owner: Daniel Sklaar

4393 **Fine Choice Foods**
23111 Fraserwood Way
Richmond, BC V6V 1B3
Canada
604-522-3110
Fax: 866-372-7744 866-760-0888
info@finechoicefoods.com
www.finechoicefoods.com
Dim sum, frozen Chinese entrees and egg rolls
President: Charles Lui
Operations Manager: Christina Lui
Estimated Sales: $5.9 Million
Number Employees: 20-49
Square Footage: 20000
Type of Packaging: Consumer, Food Service, Private Label, Bulk

4394 **Fine Dried Foods Intl**
2553 Mission St # A
Santa Cruz, CA 95060-5745
831-426-1413
Fax: 831-426-0870 awesomefruit@yahoo.com
www.finedriedfoods.com
Fine Dried Foods International specializes in fresh dried, high quality tropical fruits.
President: Rusty Brown
fdfi@pacbell.net
Estimated Sales: $2.5-5,000,000
Number Employees: 5-9
Type of Packaging: Private Label
Brands:
True Fruit

4395 **Fine Foods Intl**
9907 Baptist Church Rd
St Louis, MO 63123-4903
314-842-4473
Fax: 314-843-8846 ffinylp@aol.com
www.dek.de
Tea and coffee industry bags (brick packs), coffee and cappuccino mixes
Manager: Carole Garnett
cagarnett1@aol.com
VP: Keith Sheller
Operations: Carole Garnett
Estimated Sales: Less Than $500,000
Number Employees: 1-4
Type of Packaging: Bulk

4396 **Fine Foods Of America Inc**
11700 Manor Rd
Leawood, KS 66211-3010
913-451-2525
info@firehook.com
Manufacturer of different types of ketchups.
Owner: Bruce Steinberg
sales@finefoodsofamerica.com

Number Employees: 10-19
Brands:
Fine Vines

4397 **Fine Foods Trading Company**
801 New York Ave
Union City, NJ 07087-4115
973-772-2221
Fax: 973-767-2514 info@finecaviar.com
www.finecaviar.com
Caviar
Co-Owner: Irina Walinsky
Year Founded: 1998
Type of Packaging: Consumer, Food Service

4398 **Fine Line Seafood**
194 Thompson Mill Rd
Newtown, PA 18940-3102
215-598-3359
Fax: 215-598-7235
Producer of fish and seafood.
President: Herbert Young
Estimated Sales: Under $500,000
Number Employees: 1-4

4399 **(HQ)Fineberg Packing Company**
2875 Starling Place
P.O.Box 80432
Memphis, TN 38108
901-458-2622
Fax: 901-458-7449 katey@finebergpacking.com
www.finebergpacking.com
Meat products: boloney, hot dogs, bacon, smoked hams, packing services available
President: Richard Freudenberg
General Manager: Kay Scott
Estimated Sales: $13.8 Million
Number Employees: 50-99

4400 **Finer Foods Inc**
3100 W 36th St
Chicago, IL 60632-2304
773-579-3870
Fax: 773-890-1115 finerfoods@aol.com
www.midwestfoods.com
Frozen foods
President: James Fitzgerald
mfitzg3580@aol.com
Estimated Sales: $10-20 Million
Number Employees: 50-99
Square Footage: 100

4401 **Finest Call**
810 Progress Blvd
New Albany, IN 47150
812-944-3585
finestcallinfo@abmcocktails.com
www.finestcall.com
Alcoholic and nonalcoholic cocktail mixes.
Estimated Sales: $20-50 Million
Number Employees: 50-99
Square Footage: 110000
Type of Packaging: Consumer, Food Service, Private Label
Other Locations:
American Beverage Marketers
Overland Park KS
Brands:
Finest Call
Master of Mixes

4402 **Finestkind Fish Market**
855 US Route 1
York, ME 03909-5835
207-363-5000
Fax: 207-363-2664 800-288-8154
Manufacturer and Wholesaler full service seafood company.
Owner: Michael Goslin
Estimated Sales: $2.2 Million
Number Employees: 5

4403 **Finger Lakes Coffee Roasters**
7330 Route 251
Victor, NY 14564
585-742-6210
Fax: 585-742-6211 800-420-6154
service@fingerlakescoffee.com
www.fingerlakescoffee.com
Fresh roasted coffee
Manager: Kierna McGhan
Co-Owner: Robert Cowdery
Estimated Sales: Less than $500,000
Number Employees: 10-19
Square Footage: 1100

Brands:
Canandaigua Blend
Lake Blend
Seneca Blend

4404 **Finkemeier Bakery**
3103 Strong Avenue
Kansas City, KS 66106-2113
913-831-3103
Bakery products
President: Bill Crum
Estimated Sales: $500,000 appx.
Number Employees: 5-9

4405 **(HQ)Finlandia Cheese**
2001 US Highway 46
Suite 303
Parsippany, NJ 07054-1315
973-316-6609
Fax: 973-316-6609 www.finlandiacheese.com
Producer and supplier of cheeses and butter. Some of their customers include supermarkets, delis, cheese shops and restaurants. Some of their cheeses include Swiss, Colby Jack, Gouda, Monterey Jack, Harvati, American, Pepper Jack andmany more.
President: Sam Aquino
samaquino@finlandiacheese.com
CEO: Emma Aer
Director, Marketing: Judy Lofgren
Estimated Sales: $5-10,000,000
Number Employees: 10-19
Parent Co: Valio International USA
Brands:
Finlandia Lappi
Finlandia Naturals
Finlandia Swiss
Heavenly Light
Muenster
Sandwich Naturals

4406 **Finlay Extracts & Ingredients USA, Inc.**
23 Vreeland Road
Suite 201
Florham Park, NJ 07932-1510
973-539-8030
Fax: 973-539-4816 800-288-6272
infoUSA@finlays.net www.finlayusa.com
Bleding facility for tea and tea products.
Chief Executive Officer: Dushanth Ratwatte
HR Director, Extracts & Ingredients: Tamie Hutchins
Vice President, R&D: Catherine Robinson
NJ Contact: Steve Olyha
Estimated Sales: $10-20 000,000
Number Employees: 5-9
Parent Co: Finlays
Type of Packaging: Bulk
Other Locations:
Manufacturing Facilty
Lincoln RI

4407 **(HQ)Finlays**
10 Blackstone Valley Place
Lincoln, RI 02865
401-333-3300
800-288-6272
americas@finlays.net www.finlays.net
Roaster and extractor of gourmet coffee and tea; also, coffee extracts, syrups, concentrates, iced cappuccino, iced coffee, espresso and smoothies available; services include retail, distributor, OCS, food service and foodingredients
Managing Director: Guy Chambers
Finance Director: Julian Rutherford
Technical Director: Wolfgang Tosch
Year Founded: 1895
Number Employees: 100-249
Square Footage: 180000
Parent Co: Swire
Type of Packaging: Consumer, Food Service, Private Label
Brands:
Autocrat
Eclipse
Newport Coffee Traders

4408 **Fiore Di Pasta**
4776 E Jensen Ave
Fresno, CA 93725-1704
559-457-0431
Fax: 559-457-0164 info@fioredipasta.com
www.fioredipasta.com
Fresh and frozen organic pastas, sauces, and entrees
Owner: Shanaz Ahmed
ahmed.sarah81@gmail.com
Chief Operating Officer: Benedetta Primavera
Vice President: Anthony Primavera
Purchasing Director: John Day
Number Employees: 20-49
Square Footage: 120000

4409 **Fiore Winery**
3026 Whiteford Rd
Pylesville, MD 21132-1212
410-452-0132
Fax: 410-879-4926 contact@fiorewinery.com
www.fiorewinery.com
Wines
Owner: Mike Fiore
mike.fiore@fiorewinery.com
VP: Erich Fiore
Estimated Sales: $1-2,500,000
Number Employees: 5-9

4410 **Fiori Bruna Pasta Products**
5340 NW 163rd St
Miami Lakes, FL 33014-6228
305-705-2534
Fax: 305-621-4997 info@fioribruna.com
www.fioribruna.com
Manufacturer and exporter of frozen cheese tortellini, ravioli, cavatelli and potato gnocchi; also, dry egg fettuccine and linguine
President: Romano Fiori
fiori@bellsouth.net
VP Sales/Co-Founder: Cesare Bruna
Estimated Sales: $2.5-5 Million
Number Employees: 10-19
Square Footage: 20000
Type of Packaging: Consumer, Food Service, Private Label, Bulk
Brands:
Fiori-Bruna

4411 **Fiorucci Foods USA Inc**
1800 Ruffin Mill Rd
S Chesterfield, VA 23834-5910
804-520-8392
Fax: 804-520-7180 800-524-7775
marketing@cfg-america.com
www.fioruccifoods.com
Manufacturer and exporter of Italian speciality meats including prosciutto, salami, regional specialty meats, pre-sliced, diced, small salamis, pepperoni, balsamic vinegar
President/CEO: Claudio Colmignoli
CEO: Chris Maze
Finance Executive: Mark Morrison
Quality Assurance Manager: Richard Wilson
Marketing: Keith Amrhein
VP Sales/Marketing: John Jack
Human Resources Manager: Carey Tillett
VP Operations: Oliviero Colmignoli
Plant Manager: Mark Bragalone
Purchasing Manager: Jennifer Erdelyi
Estimated Sales: $10-20 Million
Number Employees: 1-4
Square Footage: 280000
Parent Co: Cesare Fiorucci
Type of Packaging: Consumer, Food Service, Private Label, Bulk
Brands:
Colosseum
Fiorucci

4412 **Fire Fruits International**
5036 Dr Phillips Blvd
Suite 198
Orlando, FL 32819-3310
407-480-6580
Fax: 321-396-7548 www.firefruits.com
Fruit based hot sauces and condiments.
Founder: Francisco Brignoni
Estimated Sales: $127,346
Number Employees: 2
Type of Packaging: Food Service, Private Label

4413 **Firebird Artisan Mills**
500 North St W
Harvey, ND 58341-1012
701-324-4330
Fax: 701-324-4334 www.firebirdmills.com
Manufactuere of gluten free flour and mixes; custom blending available.
President Sales & Procurement: Chris Cairo
Plant Manager: Don Franke
Number Employees: 20-49
Parent Co: Agspring LLC
Type of Packaging: Consumer, Food Service, Private Label, Bulk

4414 **Firefly Fandango**
3401 Rainier Ave S
Seattle, WA 98144
206-760-3700
Fax: 206-721-0909
Chocolate and cookies
Estimated Sales: $300,000-500,000
Number Employees: 5-9

4415 **Firehook Bakery & Coffeehouse**
14701 Flint Lee Rd
Chantilly, VA 20151-1505
703-263-2253
info@firehook.com
www.firehook.com
Manufacturer of baked goods.
Owner: Bruce Steinberg
Estimated Sales: Less Than $500,000
Number Employees: 1-4

4416 **Firelands Winery**
917 Bardshar Rd
Sandusky, OH 44870-1507
419-625-5474
Fax: 419-625-4887 800-548-9463
info@firelandswinery.com
www.firelandswinery.com
Producer of wines. Products include chardonnay, riesling, ice wine, merlot, pinot noir, dolcetto, brut champagne and more.
Owner: Adrian Salvador
asalvador@firelandswinery.com
Sales Manager: David Blankenbeker
Office Manager: Vicky Rogers
Estimated Sales: $5-10,000,000
Number Employees: 10-19
Parent Co: Paramount Distillers

4417 **Fireside Kitchen**
3430 Prescott Street
Halifax, NS B3K 4Y4
Canada
902-454-7387
Fax: 902-453-0275 www.prescottgroup.ca
Natural jams, marmalades, cranberry sauce, cookies, muffins and fruit cakes; also, available in gift packs
Executive Director: Susan Slaunwhite
Sales Coordinator: Cindy Kingwell
Production Supervisor: Dorothy O'Reilly
Brands:
Fireside Kitchen

4418 **Firestone Pacific FoodsCo**
4211 Fruit Valley Rd
Vancouver, WA 98660-1280
360-695-9484
Fax: 360-695-0040
sales@firestonepacificfoods.com
www.firestonepacificfoods.com
Wine
Owner: Stan Firestone
stan@firestonepacking.com
Estimated Sales: $2.5-5,000,000
Number Employees: 100-249

4419 **Firestone Vineyard**
5017 Zaca Station Rd
Los Olivos, CA 93441
805-688-3940
Fax: 805-686-1256 info@firestonewine.com
www.firestonewine.com
Wines
Owner: William Foley
Estimated Sales: $8,725,246
Number Employees: 20-49
Parent Co: Foley Family Wines, Inc

4420 **Firmenich Inc.**
250 Plainsboro Rd.
Plainsboro, NJ 08536
609-452-1000
Fax: 609-520-9780 800-257-9591
www.firmenich.com
Flavors and fragrances.

Chairman: Patrick Firmenich
CEO: Gilbert Ghostine
President, Perfumery & Ingredients: Armand de Villoutreys
Chief Research Officer: Genevieve Berger
President, Flavors: Emmanuel Butstraen
COO: Eric Nicolas
Chief Supply Chain Officer: Boet Brinkgreve
Year Founded: 1895
Estimated Sales: $4 Billion
Number Employees: 8,000
Other Locations:
Firmenich Chemical Plant
Newark NJ
Fermenich Citrus Center
Safety Harbor FL

4421 **First Choice Ingredients**
N112 W19528 Mequon Rd
Germantown, WI 53022
262-251-4322
Fax: 262-251-3881 roddyt@fcingredients.com
www.fcingredients.com
Food flavor and ingredients manufacturers; including cheese powders & pasts, dairy powders, meat flavors, savory flavors, bakery flavors, and beverage liquids & powders
President: Jim Pekar
EVP: Roger Mullins
Sales Manager: Natalie Moore
Contact: Lucas Lieffring
llieffring@fcingredients.com
Estimated Sales: $3 Million
Number Employees: 20

4422 **(HQ)First Colony Coffee & Tea Company**
204 W 22nd Street
Po Box 11005
Norfolk, VA 23517-2231
757-622-2224
Fax: 757-623-2391 800-446-8555
Processor, importer and exporter of teas and coffees including varietal, blends and flavored
President/CEO: Bruce Grembowitz
Marketing Director: Julie Anderson
National Sales Director: Joyce Jordan
Contact: John Bergsten
john.bergsten@orbitalatk.com
Production Manager: Justin Goodman
Estimated Sales: $13 Million
Number Employees: 80
Square Footage: 94000
Type of Packaging: Consumer, Food Service, Private Label, Bulk
Brands:
Bencheley
Carolan's
First Colony
Frangelico
Ghirardelli
Jack Daniel's
Southern Comfort

4423 **First Colony Winery**
1650 Harris Creek Rd
Charlottesville, VA 22902-7820
434-979-7105
Fax: 434-293-2054 877-979-7105
info@firstcolonywinery.com
www.firstcolonywinery.com
Wine
Owner: Heather A. Spiess
Owner: Bruce D. Spiess (MD)
Owner: Jeffrey W. Miller
General Manager: Martha Hayman
Estimated Sales: $3-5 Million
Number Employees: 5-9

4424 **First District Association**
101 S. Swift Ave.
Litchfield, MN 55355
320-693-3236
info@firstdistrict.com
www.firstdistrict.com
Dairy products including lactose blends and mixes, specialty cheeses, cream, wheys, whey protein concentrates and milk powders.
President/CEO: Clinton Fall
cfall@firstdistrict.com
Director, Quality Assurance: Dawn Raymond
Director, Sales/Marketing: Glenn Kaping
Director, Operations: Doug Anderson

Year Founded: 1894
Estimated Sales: $476.6 Million
Number Employees: 100-249
Square Footage: 100000
Brands:
Fieldgate

4425 **First Food Co**
4561 Leston St
4561 Leston Street
Dallas, TX 75247-5709
214-637-0214
Fax: 214-905-0605 800-527-1866
service@firstfoodco.com www.firstfoodco.com
Gelatins for desserts, salads, etc
Owner: Brooke Hogan
mhogan@fqfood.com
Estimated Sales: $5-10,000,000
Number Employees: 50-99
Type of Packaging: Consumer, Food Service, Private Label, Bulk

4426 **First Food International**
333 Cantor Ave
Linden, NJ 07036
908-862-5558
Fax: 908-474-1119
Oilseed production (coconut, peanut, soybean and sunflower)
President: Tony Chiang
Estimated Sales: 1-2.5 Million
Number Employees: 7

4427 **First Oriental Market**
2774 E Ponce DE Leon Ave
Decatur, GA 30030-2715
404-377-6950
Fax: 404-377-7505
Tilapia, flounder, catfish, mackerel, oriental food items
Owner: Diane Bounngaseng
Estimated Sales: $5-10 Million
Number Employees: 5-9

4428 **First Original Texas Chili Company**
3313 N. Jones
Fort Worth, TX 76164-0281
817-626-0983
Fax: 817-626-9105 800-507-0009
www.texaschili.com
Frozen chili con carne, chili sauce and beef taco filling
President: Danny Owens
Estimated Sales: $5-10,000,000
Number Employees: 5-9
Type of Packaging: Consumer, Food Service, Private Label
Brands:
Our Famous Texas Chili
Sloppy Joe
Tex-O-Gold
Texas One Step

4429 **First Roasters of Central Florida**
863 N Highway 17/92
Longwood, FL 32750-3167
407-699-6364
Fax: 407-699-6301
Coffee
Manager: Leonardo Lamastus
Estimated Sales: $2.5-5,000,000
Number Employees: 1-4
Brands:
First Roasters of Central Florida

4430 **(HQ)First Spice Mixing Co**
3333 Greenpoint Ave
Long Island City, NY 11101-2084
718-361-2556
Fax: 718-361-2515 800-221-1105
www.firstspice.com
Seasonings, binders and curing compounds; also, textured vegetable protein, hydrolyzed dairy products, nonfat dry milk, curing ingredients, phosphate compounds, MSG-flavor boosters and spices
President: Peter Epstein
peter@firstspice.com
CEO: Wendy Epstein
Vice President: Vicki Miller
Research & Development: Marcy Epstein
Estimated Sales: $5-10 Million
Number Employees: 10-19

Other Locations:
First Spice Mixing Company
San Francisco CA
Brands:
Albunate
Flavolin
Flavor 86
Savorlok
Texite
Tietolin
Vegolin Hvp
Vita-Curaid
Vitaphos

4431 **Firth Maple Products**
22418 Firth Rd
Spartansburg, PA 16434-3222
814-654-2435
Fax: 814-654-7265 guy.dunkel@gmail.com
www.foundationforsustainableforests.org
Maple syrup
Owner: Troy Firth
firthmaple@aol.com
Estimated Sales: $720,000
Number Employees: 20-49

4432 **Fischer & Wieser Spec Foods**
411 S Lincoln St
Fredericksburg, TX 78624-4502
830-997-7194
Fax: 830-997-0455 877-861-0260
info@jelly.com
Jams, jellies, preserves, marmalades, mustard, sauces, salsa, syrup, honey and snacks
President: Case Fischer
info@jelly.com
President/CEO: Case D Fischer
Director Quality Assurance & Product Dev: Ashley Seelig
Chief Marketing Officer: Deanna Fischer
Sales Director: Mary Llanes Guevera
Director Customer Service: Yvonne Fox
COO: Jenny Wieser Ph.D.
Purchasing: Jenny Wieser
Estimated Sales: $1-3,000,000
Number Employees: 50-99
Type of Packaging: Consumer, Food Service, Private Label
Brands:
Fischer & Wieser
Mom's
Old Chisholm Trail

4433 **Fischer Honey Company**
2001 N Poplar Street
North Little Rock, AR 72114-2999
501-758-1123
Fax: 501-758-8601 fischerhoney@att.net
www.fischerhoney.com
Honey including table, creamed and bakers
Year Founded: 1935
Estimated Sales: $5-10 Million
Number Employees: 5-9
Square Footage: 100000
Type of Packaging: Consumer, Food Service, Private Label, Bulk
Brands:
Fischer's

4434 **Fischer Meats**
85 Front St N
Issaquah, WA 98027-3237
425-392-3131
Fax: 425-392-0168 www.fischermeatsnw.com
Meat
Owner: Chris Chiechi
fischermeats@gmail.com
Estimated Sales: Less Than $500,000
Number Employees: 5-9
Type of Packaging: Consumer, Food Service

4435 **Fish Breeders of Idaho**
18374 Hwy 30
Hagerman, ID 83332
208-837-6114
Fax: 208-837-6254 fpi@fishbreedersofidaho.com
www.fishbreedersofidaho.com
Breeders of fish. Varieties include trout, sturgeon, catfish, tilapia, and tropical aquarium fish.
Owner: Leo Ray
Vice President: Tod Ray
Sales: Netty Marino
Contact: Judith Ay
judith.ray@alaskasbest.com
Production Manager: Starla Barnes

Estimated Sales: $5-10 Million
Number Employees: 2-10
Brands:
Pride of Idaho

4436 **Fish Brothers**
203 Taylor Way
PO Box 416
Blue Lake, CA 95525
707-668-9700
Fax: 707-668-9701 800-244-0583
www.fishbrothers.com
Smoked fish including, salmon, nova lox and albacore
Owner: Scott Bradshaw
fishbro@fishbrothers.com
Estimated Sales: $500,000-1 Million
Number Employees: 10-19
Square Footage: 5000
Type of Packaging: Consumer, Food Service, Private Label, Bulk
Brands:
Fish Brothers

4437 **Fish Express**
3343 Kuhio Hwy # 10
Suite 10
Lihue, HI 96766
808-245-9918
Fax: 808-246-9188
Seafood
Principal: David Wada
Estimated Sales: $3-5 Million
Number Employees: 10-19

4438 **Fish Hopper**
700 Cannery Row # K
Monterey, CA 93940-1036
831-372-3406
Fax: 831-372-2026 www.fishhopper.com
Canned clam chowder
CEO: Sabu Shake Jr
Estimated Sales: $2.5-5 Million
Number Employees: 50-99
Type of Packaging: Private Label

4439 **Fish King**
722 N Glendale Ave
Glendale, CA 91206-2198
818-244-2161
Fax: 818-244-2115 fishkingsfd@aol.com
www.fishkingseafood.com
Seafood including breaded and IQF scallops, shrimp and calamari
President: Tom Furuckawa
Manager: Robert Sperry
fishkingsfd@aol.com
Number Employees: 20-49
Type of Packaging: Consumer, Food Service

4440 **Fish King Processors**
1 King & Prince Blvd
Brunswick, GA 31520
360-733-9090
Fax: 360-733-9152 800-841-0205
www.kpseafood.com
Smoked salmon
CEO: Terrill Beck
Estimated Sales: $10-20,000,000
Number Employees: 20-49
Parent Co: Unisea Foods
Type of Packaging: Consumer, Food Service
Brands:
Pride of Alaska
Salmon Bay

4441 **Fish Market Inc**
1406 W Chestnut St
Louisville, KY 40203-1776
502-587-7474
Fax: 502-587-7503
Frozen seafood
President: Steven Smith
sseafoods@aol.com
Estimated Sales: $5-10,000,000
Number Employees: 20-49
Square Footage: 14000
Type of Packaging: Consumer, Food Service, Private Label
Brands:
Fishmarket Seafoods

4442 **Fish Market Inc**
1406 W Chestnut St
Louisville, KY 40203-1776
502-587-7474
Fax: 502-587-7503
Seafood
President: Steven Smith
sseafoods@aol.com
Estimated Sales: $10 Million
Number Employees: 20-49

4443 **Fisher Honey Co**
1 Belle Ave # 21
Lewistown, PA 17044-2433
717-242-4373
Fax: 717-242-3978 fisherhoney@fisherhoney.com
www.fisherhoney.com
Manufacturer and exporter of honey, beeswax, beekeepers supplies, containers, glass, metal and plastic
Owner: Scott Fisher
fisherhoney@fisherhoney.com
Plant Supervisor: Scott Fisher
Estimated Sales: $1-2 Million
Number Employees: 1-4
Square Footage: 40000
Type of Packaging: Consumer, Food Service, Private Label, Bulk
Brands:
Fisher Honey
Stewarts Honey

4444 **Fisher Ridge Wine Co Inc**
529 Sheridan Cir
Charleston, WV 25314-1054
304-342-8702
Wines
Owner: Wilson Ward
Estimated Sales: $1-2,500,000
Number Employees: 1-4

4445 **Fisher Vineyards**
6200 Saint Helena Rd
Santa Rosa, CA 95404-9692
707-539-7511
Fax: 707-539-3601 info@fishervineyards.com
www.fishervineyards.com
Wines
President: Fred Fisher
ffisher@fishervineyards.com
Vice President: Juelle Fisher
Sales/Marketing: Cameron Fisher
General Manager: Robert Fisher
Winemaker: Whitney Fisher
Estimated Sales: $500,000
Number Employees: 10-19
Type of Packaging: Private Label

4446 **Fisher's Popcorn**
200 S Boardwalk
Ocean City, MD 21842
410-289-5638
Fax: 410-289-1720 888-395-0335
www.fisherspopcorn.com
Caramel-coated popcorn
Owner: Donald Fisher
Marketing: Ben Bauer
Number Employees: 50-99

4447 **Fisherman's Market International**
607 Bedford Highway
Halifax, NS B3M 2L6
Canada
902-445-3474
Fax: 902-443-5561 retail@fishermansmarket.com
www.fishermansmarket.ca
Live lobster and fresh or frozen seafood
President: Fred Greene
Director International Marketing: Gino Nadalini
Sales: Scott Thompson
General Manager: Monte Snow
Plant Manager: Bill Langdon
Estimated Sales: $20+ Million
Number Employees: 150
Square Footage: 20000
Type of Packaging: Consumer, Food Service, Private Label

4448 **Fisherman's Reef Shrimp Company**
5192 Fannett Rd
Beaumont, TX 77705
409-842-9520
Fax: 409-842-1212
Frozen domestic shrimp
Owner: Vikki Jones
VP: Trudy Verdine
Contact: Vicki Jones
vsj42@aol.com
Number Employees: 100-249
Parent Co: Farmer Boys Catfish International
Type of Packaging: Food Service, Private Label
Brands:
Fisherman's Reef

4449 **Fishermens Net**
849 Forest Ave
Portland, ME 04103-4162
207-772-3565
Fax: 207-828-1726
Seafood
Owner: Benjamin Lindner
Estimated Sales: Less Than $500,000
Number Employees: 1-4

4450 **Fishhawk Fisheries**
1 4th St
Astoria, OR 97103-4339
503-325-5252
Fax: 503-325-8786
Crab, shrimp, canned fish, salmon, sturgeon, shad, smelt, halibut and black cod
Owner: Steve Fick
fishhawk@ideal-web.com
Director: Carol Fratt
Estimated Sales: $1 Million
Number Employees: 10-19
Square Footage: 12000
Type of Packaging: Bulk
Brands:
Fishhawk

4451 **Fishland Market**
117 Ahui Street
Suite C
Honolulu, HI 96813
808-523-6902
Fax: 808-523-6905
Bottomfish, reef fish, Kona crab, white crab, Hawaiian crab
President: Paul Nishimoto

4452 **Fishpeople**
2540 NE M L King Blvd
Portland, OR 97212
503-342-2424
info@fishpeopleseafood.com
fishpeopleseafood.com
Sustainable seafood
Co-Founder: Duncan Berry
Co-Founder: Kipp Baratoff
Year Founded: 2012
Type of Packaging: Food Service

4453 **FitPro USA**
2333 Courage Dr
Fairfield, CA 94533
Fax: 707-419-4845 877-645-5776
info@teamfitpro.com www.fitprousa.com
Protein shakes and vitamin supplements
CEO: Gus Malliarodakis
COO: Mike Zumpano
Number of Brands: 1
Number of Products: 8
Type of Packaging: Consumer
Brands:
FITPRO GO
EVO

4454 **Fitzkee's Candies Inc**
2352 S Queen St
York, PA 17402-4939
717-741-1031
Fax: 717-741-5176
Assorted chocolates
President: Robert Fitzkee
Estimated Sales: $2.5-5 Million
Number Employees: 10-19
Type of Packaging: Consumer

4455 **Fitzpatrick Winery & Lodge**
7740 Fairplay Rd
Somerset, CA 95684-9208
530-620-3248
Fax: 530-620-6838 800-245-9166
Wines

Owner: Brian Fitzpatrick
brian@fitzpatrickwinery.com
VP: Diana Fitzpatrick
Estimated Sales: $500,000-$1,000,000
Number Employees: 1-4
Brands:
Fitzpatrick

4456 **Five Acre Farms**
44 Court Street
Brooklyn, NY 11201
718-522-3819
info@fiveacrefarms.com
fiveacrefarms.com
Milk; eggs; and apple cider.
CEO: Daniel Horan
Director of Sales: Jill Bellville
Director of Operations: Patrick Horan
Year Founded: 2011
Estimated Sales: $381,313
Number Employees: 6
Type of Packaging: Food Service, Private Label

4457 **Five Ponds Farm**
1933 E Mill Rd
Lineville, AL 36266
256-396-5217
Fax: 256-386-5899
Fruits and vegetables
President: Edward Donlon

4458 **Five Star Food Base Company**
865 Pierce Butler Rte
St Paul, MN 55104-3073
651-488-2300
Fax: 651-488-2094 800-505-7827
Soup bases and blended seasonings
Owner: Sid Larson
Estimated Sales: $5-10 000,000
Number Employees: 10-19

4459 **Five Star Foodies**
3101 Clifton Ave
Cincinnati, OH 45220
info@fivestarfoodies.com
foodiesvegan.com
Vegan burger patties and cold pressed juices
CEO: Valerie Williams
Number of Brands: 1
Number of Products: 8
Type of Packaging: Consumer
Brands:
FOODIES

4460 **Five Star Home Foods, Inc.**
234 Mall Boulevard
Suite 140
King of Prussia, PA 19406
610-337-9004
800-246-5405
www.fivestarhomefoods.com
Prepared meals, organic vegetables, and juices
President/Owner: Chef Dan
Contact: Gabrielle Delconte
gdelconte@fivestarhomefoods.com
Estimated Sales: $5-10 Million
Number Employees: 9

4461 **FiveStar Gourmet Foods**
3880 E Ebony Street
Ontario, CA 91761
909-390-0032
info@fivestargourmetfoods.com
fivestargourmetfoods.com
Sustainable seafood
Co-Founder: Duncan Berry
Co-Founder: Kipp Baratoff
Type of Packaging: Food Service
Brands:
Simply Fresh

4462 **Fizz-O Water Co**
809 N Lewis Ave
Tulsa, OK 74110-5365
918-834-3691
Fax: 918-832-0899 water@fizzowater.com
www.fizzowater.com
Bottler and wholesaler/distributor of spring, drinking and distilled water
President: Harry R Doerner
fizzowater@att.net
Owner: Hency Doerner
Owner: Rick Doerner
Plant Manager: Rick Malkey
Estimated Sales: $1-3 Million
Number Employees: 20-49
Number of Brands: 4
Square Footage: 30000
Type of Packaging: Consumer
Brands:
Doublepure Distilled
Mountain Valley
Ozarka
Spring House

4463 **Fizzle Flat Farm, L.L.C.**
18773 E 1600th Avenue
Yale, IL 62448
618-793-2060
Fax: 618-793-2060 mcmanges@fizzleflatfarm.com
www.fizzleflatfarm.com
Organic popcorn and food grade certified organic grains including white, yellow and blue corn, wheat, soybeans, buckwheat. Grass fed beef raised on certified organic pastures (pasture-raised).
Owner/Manager: Marvin Manges
Owner/Manager: Lori Wells
Estimated Sales: $1-3 Million
Number Employees: 4
Square Footage: 8750
Type of Packaging: Bulk
Brands:
Fizzle Flat Farm

4464 **Fizzy Lizzy**
64 Wayne Street
Suite D20
Jersey City, NJ 07302
212-966-3232
Fax: 888-680-2444 800-203-9336
info@fizzylizzy.com
Whole fruit juice and sparkling water.
CEO: Aaron Morrill
VP: Amy Drown
Estimated Sales: $1.1 Million
Number Employees: 5

4465 **Flackers**
Minneapolis, MN 55424-0868
hello@flackers.com
flackers.com
Organic flaxseed crackers
Co-Founder: Dr. Alison Levitt
Year Founded: 2008

4466 **Flagstaff Brewing Co**
16 E Route 66 # 1
Flagstaff, AZ 86001-5792
928-773-1442
www.flagbrew.com
Beer
President: Jeff Thorsett
jefft@flagbrew.com
Estimated Sales: $8,722,990
Number Employees: 20-49
Brands:
Agassiz Amber
Bitterroot Extra Special Bitter
Blackbird Porter
Bubbaganouj Ipa
Great Golden Ale
Sasquatch Stout
Three-Pin Pale Ale

4467 **Flaherty Inc**
9047 Terminal Ave
Skokie, IL 60077-1570
847-966-1005
Fax: 847-966-1072
Producer of mustard.
Owner: Catherine Flaharty
Finance Manager: Deirdre Flaherty
General Manager: Bridget Flaherty
Estimated Sales: $5-10,000,000
Number Employees: 5-9

4468 **Flamin' Red's Woodfired**
Robinson Hill Rd
Pawlet, VT 05761
802-325-3641
Fax: 802-325-3641 woodfire@vermontel.net
Pizza crusts made with organic flour
Owner: Carson Lake
Estimated Sales: $300,000-500,000
Number Employees: 1-4

4469 **(HQ)Flamm Pickle & Packing**
4502 Hipps Hollow Rd
PO Box 500
Eau Claire, MI 49111
269-461-6916
Fax: 269-461-6166 800-742-5531
pickles@flammpickle.com www.flammpickle.com
Sweet pickle relish, dill pickle relish and pickle brine used in salad dressings
President/General Manager: Gina Flamm
Year Founded: 1917
Estimated Sales: $4.20 Million
Number Employees: 10-19
Square Footage: 120000
Type of Packaging: Food Service, Bulk
Brands:
Flamm's

4470 **Flamous Brands**
1801 Highland Ave # C
Suite C
Duarte, CA 91010-2833
626-799-7909
Fax: 626-551-3088 www.flamousbrands.com
Falafel Chips and dip.
Manager: Alejandra Lopez
alejandra@flamousbrands.com
Number Employees: 5-9
Type of Packaging: Consumer

4471 **(HQ)Flanders**
1104 Gilmore St
Waycross, GA 31501-1307
912-283-5191
Fax: 912-283-6228 info@flandersburgers.com
www.flandersprovision.com
Manufacturer, distributor and packager of beef patties
President/CEO: Huey Dubberly
CEO: Chris Huff
chuff@flandersprovision.com
CEO/Chief Financial Officer: Chris Huff
Quality Assurance Manager: Michael Denton
Sales: Hollis Yarn
Operations Manager: Rusty Rainey
Year Founded: 1958
Estimated Sales: $36.80 Million
Number Employees: 100-249

4472 **Flanigan Farms**
9522 Jefferson Blvd
PO Box 347
Culver City, CA 90232
310-836-8437
Fax: 310-838-0743 800-525-0228
www.flaniganfarms.com
Nut mixes and dried organic persimmons
Owner: Patsy Flanigan
Operations: C Flanigan
Estimated Sales: $3 Million
Number Employees: 10-19
Number of Products: 42
Square Footage: 24000
Type of Packaging: Consumer, Food Service, Private Label
Brands:
Nuts 'n' Fruit
Nuts 'n' Things

4473 **FlapJacked**
960 W 124th Ave
Suite 100
Westminster, CO 80234
720-476-4758
info@flapjacked.com
www.flapjacked.com
Pancake, muffin and cookie mixes
Co-Founder: Jennifer Bacon
Co-Founder: Dave Bacon
Number of Brands: 1
Number of Products: 18
Type of Packaging: Consumer
Brands:
FLAPJACKED

4474 **Flat Cracker Inc.**
143 Washington Ave.
Lawrence, NY 11559-1613
347-223-2587
Fax: 516-812-9325
Manufacturer of crackers.
Founder: Nicole Dawes

4475 **(HQ)Flat Tire Bike Shop**
6033 E Cave Creek Rd
Cave Creek, AZ 85331-8510
480-488-5261
Fax: 480-577-0177 www.flattirebike.com
Coffee
Owner: David Thompson
Co-Owner/Roastmaster: David Anderson
Estimated Sales: $5-10 Million
Number Employees: 1-4

4476 **Flathau's Fine Foods**
211 Greenwood Place
Hattiesburg, MS 39402
601-582-9629
Fax: 601-544-2333 888-263-1299
info@flathausfinefoods.com
www.flathausfinefoods.com
Flavored shortbread cookies covered with powdered sugar

4477 **Flatout Inc**
1422 Woodland Dr
Saline, MI 48176-1633
734-944-5445
Fax: 734-944-5115 866-944-5445
feedback@flatoutbread.com
www.flatoutbread.com
Flatbreads
Owner: Stacey Marsh
Co-Owner: Mike Marsh
Sales/Marketing: Bob Palotta
Number Employees: 100-249

4478 **Flaum Appetizing**
288 Scholes St
Brooklyn, NY 11206-1728
718-821-1970
Fax: 718-821-9051 info@flaums.com
www.flaumsappetizing.com
Sour pickles, sauerkraut, pickled herring, cole slaw, lox spreads and potato, whitefish, tuna and eggplant salads
Owner: Joel Stern
joel@flaums.com
Production Manager: Salomon Benatar
Estimated Sales: Less than $500,000
Number Employees: 20-49
Square Footage: 50000
Parent Co: M&M Food Products
Type of Packaging: Consumer, Food Service, Private Label, Bulk

4479 **(HQ)Flavor & Fragrance Specialties**
3 Industrial Ave
Mahwah, NJ 07430-3595
201-825-0352
Fax: 201-825-4785 800-998-4337
customer.care@ffs.com www.ffs.com
Flavor concentrates and fragrance extracts
President: Michael Bloom
m.bloom@ffs.com
Executive Vice President: William Palmer
Director, Sales: Robert C. Frantzen
Estimated Sales: $2.5-5 Million
Number Employees: 20-49
Square Footage: 120000
Type of Packaging: Bulk
Brands:
Ammonia Guard
E.O.C.
High Impact

4480 **Flavor Dynamics Two**
640 Montrose Ave
South Plainfield, NJ 07080-2602
908-822-8855
Fax: 908-822-8547 888-271-8424
customercare@flavordynamics.com
Food and beverage flavors
President: Dolf DeRovira
R&D Director: Norma Schwarz
Estimated Sales: 20.5 Million
Number Employees: 20-49
Square Footage: 29000
Type of Packaging: Food Service, Private Label, Bulk
Other Locations:
Flavor Dynamics
Glenview IL
Flavor Dynamics
Corona Del Mar CA
Flavor Dynamics
Cape Charles VA

4481 **Flavor House, Inc.**
9516 Commerce Way
Adelanto, CA 92301-3947
760-246-9131
Fax: 760-246-8431 flavorhouseinc.com
Manufacturer and exporter of flavor concentrates including meat, poultry and seafood; also, hydrolyzed vegetable proteins and liquid and dry soy sauce.
Estimated Sales: $4 Million
Number Employees: 20-49
Square Footage: 84000
Type of Packaging: Bulk

4482 **Flavor Producers**
8521 Fallbrook Ave
Suite 380
West Hills, CA 91304
818-835-1850
sales@flavorproducers.com
flavorproducers.com
Custom flavors for food and beverage manufacturers
Year Founded: 1981
Type of Packaging: Consumer

4483 **Flavor Right Foods Group**
2517 E Chambers
St Phoenix, AZ 85040
602-232-2570
Fax: 602-232-2569 888-464-3734
info@flavorright.com
Dessert and pastry toppings and icings, frozen dessert mixes.
President: Doug Smith
Vice President: Rick Warf
Contact: Ivygalliher Galliher
ivygalliher@flavorright.com
Estimated Sales: $5-10 Million
Number Employees: 10-19
Brands:
Festejos
Whip N Ice
Whip N Top

4484 **(HQ)Flavor Sciences Inc**
652 Nuway Cir
Lenoir, NC 28645-3646
828-758-2525
Fax: 828-758-2424 800-535-2867
information@flavorsciences.com
Natural and artificial flavors and essential oils; exporter of natural and artificial flavors and extracts
President: Roger Kiley
rogerkiley@gmail.com
Vice President: Joyce Kiley
Estimated Sales: $3-5 Million
Number Employees: 5-9

4485 **Flavor Systems Intl.**
10139 Commerce Park Dr
Cincinnati, OH 45246
513-870-4900
Fax: 513-870-4909 800-498-2783
info@flavorsystems.com
Custom flavorings and specialty food systems
President: William Wasz
Owner: Bob Bahoshy
VP: William Baker
R&D: Angie Lantman
Quality Control: Alan Baker
Contact: Bill Baker
bill.baker@flavorsystems.com
Plant Manager: Rick Messinger
Purchasing: Roger Sage
Estimated Sales: $20 Million
Number Employees: 55
Square Footage: 25000
Type of Packaging: Bulk

4486 **FlavorHealth**
685 US Hwy 1
North Brunswick, NJ 08902
732-875-4799
Fax: 732-565-1183 info@flavorhealth.com
www.flavorhealth.com
Use natural ingredients to create bitter balancing, sodium reduction and sweet enhancement solutions.
CEO: Christian Kopfli
Senior Director of Finance: Deborah Beckwith
Vice President, Flavor Sciences: Dennis Sawchuk
Vice President, Commerical Development: Shari Joslin

4487 **Flavorbank Company**
6372 E Broadway Blvd
Tucson, AZ 85710-3538
520-747-5431
Fax: 520-790-9469 800-835-7603
Spices and seasonings
Owner: Jennifer English
Public Relations: Jan Jorden
Operations: Jackie Brooks
Production: James Husser
Plant Manager: Ramona Flores
Estimated Sales: $1-2,500,000
Number Employees: 1-4
Type of Packaging: Private Label
Brands:
Daniel Orr
Flavorbank

4488 **Flavorchem Corp**
1525 Brook Dr
Downers Grove, IL 60515-1024
630-932-8100
Fax: 630-932-4626 800-435-2867
www.flavorchem.com
Manufacturer and exporter of flavorings and food colorings; processor of pure vanilla extract; importer of fine chemicals and essential oils.
President: Ken Malinowski
kmalinowski@flavorchem.com
Year Founded: 1971
Number Employees: 100-249
Square Footage: 215000
Type of Packaging: Consumer, Food Service, Private Label, Bulk
Other Locations:
Headquarters
Downers Grove IL
Flavorchem West
San Clemente CA
Flavorchem Europe
Kerepes, Hungary
Brands:
Splcery Shoppe Natural

4489 **Flavorganics**
268 Doremus Ave
Newark, NJ 07105-4875
973-344-8014
Fax: 973-344-1948 866-972-6879
flavorganics@worldpantry.com
www.flavorganics.com
Organic extracts including vanilla, almond, peppermint, lemon and orange
President: Jocelyn Manship
Contact: Jenny Fagundes
jenny@ecsalesco.com
Estimated Sales: $20-50 Million
Number Employees: 50-99
Parent Co: Elan
Type of Packaging: Private Label, Bulk
Brands:
Flavorganics
Kogee

4490 **(HQ)Flavormatic Industries**
230 All Angels Hill Rd
Wappingers Falls, NY 12590
845-297-9100
Fax: 845-297-2881 sales@flavormatic.com
www.flavormatic.com
Manufacturer, importer and exporter of flavors, fragrances and essential oils
President: Judith Back
Executive VP: Ronald Black
Sales: Frank Wells
Operation Manager: Richard Febles
Estimated Sales: $2.5 Million
Number Employees: 20-49
Square Footage: 63000
Type of Packaging: Bulk
Other Locations:

4491 **Flavors and Color**
20653 Lycoming St
Unit A9
Walnut, CA 91789
909-598-4441
Fax: 909-598-7740 flavorsandcolor.com
Flavorings, colorings and other food ingredients.

4492 **Flavors from Florida**
203 Bartow Municipal Arprt
Bartow, FL 33830
863-533-0408
Fax: 863-533-9478 800-888-0409

Ice cream, sherbert, drink base flavoring, flavoring extracts and syrups
President: Robert K Prendes
Contact: Wendy Arsenault
wendy.arsenault@agrana.com
Year Founded: 1971
Estimated Sales: $25-50 Million
Number Employees: 20-49

4493 **Flavors of Hawaii Inc**
945 Waimanu St
Honolulu, HI 96814-3319
808-597-1727
Fax: 808-597-1728
Coconut syrup, guava syrup, cocopine syrup
President: Alexander Lee
Vice President: Violet Mau
Estimated Sales: $650,000
Number Employees: 5-9
Brands:
Hawaii

4494 **Flavors of the Heartland**
201 2nd St
Rocheport, MO 65279
573-698-2063
800-269-3210
Gourmet foods
Manager: Roger Pilkinton
Estimated Sales: Less than $500,000
Number Employees: 1-4
Brands:
Flavors of the Heartland

4495 **Flavouressence Products**
1-6750 Davand Drive
Mississauga, ON L5T 2L8
Canada
905-795-0318
Fax: 905-795-0317 866-209-7778
backbaytrading.com
Beverage syrups, juices, bar mixes and slush; exporter of juices, bar mixes and beverage syrups
President/CEO: Mark Weber
CFO: Brain Ferry
Marketing: Bob Graham
Sales: Jolene Davies
Plant Manager: David Milner
Estimated Sales: $5 Million
Number Employees: 5-9
Square Footage: 21000
Type of Packaging: Food Service, Private Label, Bulk

4496 **Flax4Life**
468 W Horton Rd
Bellingham, WA 98226
360-715-1944
Fax: 360-233-1212 877-352-9487
www.flax4life.net
Flax-based baked goods
General Manager: Kasondra Shippen
Marketing Coordinator: Sarah Bishop
Vice President, Sales: Bob Johnston
Production Manager: Jen Bishop

4497 **Fleet Fisheries Inc**
20 Blackmer St
New Bedford, MA 02744-2614
508-910-2100
Fax: 508-996-3785 www.fleetfisheries.com
Scallops
President: Lars Vinjerud
lars@oceansfleet.com
Vice President: Rick Miller
Quality Control: Rick Tavis
Operations: Shaun Souza
Accounts Receivable: Dan Pacheco
Plant Manager: Chris Brown
Estimated Sales: $5-10 Million
Number Employees: 10-19

4498 **Fleischer's Bagels**
1688 N Wayneport Rd
Macedon, NY 14502-8765
315-986-9999
Fax: 315-986-7200 mark@fleischersbagels.com
Fresh, frozen and refrigerated bagels
President: Robert Drago
SVP Operations/CFO: Keith Bleier
Quality Assurance Manager: George Sparks
VP Sales/Marketing: Robert Pim
Contact: Marc Fleischer
mfleischer@fleischersbagels.com
Production Manager: Mike O'Hara
Estimated Sales: $6 Million
Number Employees: 135
Square Footage: 85370
Type of Packaging: Consumer, Food Service, Private Label, Bulk
Brands:
Fleischer's

4499 **Fleischmann's Vinegar Co Inc**
12604 Hiddencreek Way
Suite A
Cerritos, CA 90703-2137
Canada
562-483-4600
Fax: 562-483-4644 800-443-1067
sales@fvinegar.com
www.fleischmannsvinegar.com
Vinegar
President/CEO: Ken Simril
CEO: Butch Daugherty
butch.daugherty@fvinegar.com
CFO: Larry McKeown
VP: Sylvain Norton
VP Sales: Roger Arnold
Number Employees: 100-249
Parent Co: Burns Philp Foods
Type of Packaging: Consumer, Food Service, Private Label, Bulk
Brands:
Allens
Fleischann's
Spice Islands

4500 **Fleischmann's Yeast**
Chesterfield, MO 63017
800-777-4959
info@fleischmannsyeast.com
www.breadworld.com
Active and inactive yeasts, vinegars, leaveners and mold inhibitors; also, technical consulting for bakeries available
Estimated Sales: $50-100 Million
Number Employees: 74
Number of Brands: 1
Parent Co: Garfield Weston Foundation
Type of Packaging: Food Service, Bulk
Brands:
Fleischmann's Yeast

4501 **Fletcher's Fine Foods**
502 Boundary Blvd
Auburn, WA 98001-6503
Canada
253-735-0800
www.fletchers.com
Manufacturer and exporter of pork and by-products
President/CEO: Fred Knoedler
President: Michael Lattifi
Manager: Ed Clark
clark@fletchers.com
Number Employees: 100-249
Parent Co: Fletcher's Fine Foods
Type of Packaging: Food Service, Bulk
Brands:
Fletcher's
Goodlife

4502 **Fleur De Lait Foods Inc**
400 S Custer Ave
New Holland, PA 17557-9220
717-355-8580
Fax: 717-355-8561 800-322-2743
alouetteculinary@savenciacheeseusa.com
www.savenciafoodserviceusa.com
Cheese manufacturer
President & CEO: Dominique Huth
National Sales: Larry Rosenberg
Year Founded: 1990
Estimated Sales: $20-50 Million
Number Employees: 250-499

4503 **Fleurchem Inc**
33 Sprague Ave
Middletown, NY 10940-5128
845-341-2100
Fax: 845-341-2121 info@fleurchem.com
www.fleurchem.com
Natural and synthetic flavoring agents and fragrances including acidulants, anethole, citronellal, eucalyptol, furfural, geraniol, heptanal, methyl actetate, etc
CEO: Charles Barton
cbarton@fleurchem.com
CEO: George Gluck
CFO: Sara Gluck
CEO: Rochele Gluck
Quality Control: Brian Merdler
VP Marketing: Jack Snicolo
Operations Manager: Louis Mercun
Production: Larry Costa
Purchasing Manager: Angie Roman
Estimated Sales: $10-20 Million
Number Employees: 20-49
Square Footage: 400000
Type of Packaging: Private Label, Bulk

4504 **Flex Pack USA**
6321 Emperor Dr
Orlando, FL 32809-5513
407-857-2883
Fax: 407-857-6970
Packaging/bags
Owner: Mark Dorey
Estimated Sales: $5-10 Million
Number Employees: 50-99

4505 **Fliinko**
PO Box 80102
South Dartmouth, MA 02748-0102
508-996-9609
Fax: 508-990-1281 800-266-9609
fliinko@ultranet.com
Manufacturer of all natural instant drink mixes.
President: Ingrid Flynn
Treasurer: Thomas Flynn
Estimated Sales: $1-22,500,000
Number Employees: 1-4
Type of Packaging: Private Label
Brands:
Nectarade

4506 **Flippin-Seaman Inc**
5529 Crabtree Falls Hwy
Tyro, VA 22976-3103
434-277-5828
Fax: 434-277-9057
Growers, packer and shippers of fine fruit.
Owner: Bill Flippin
Owner: Richard Seaman
info@flippin-seaman.com
Estimated Sales: $10-20 Million
Number Employees: 20-49
Brands:
Seaman Orchard
Silver Creek

4507 **Flix Candy**
6401 W Gross Point Rd
Niles, IL 60714-4507
847-647-1370
Fax: 847-647-0633 info@flixcandy.com
www.flixcandy.com
Candy
President: Sidney Diamond
VP Sales: Jeff Grossman
Contact: Jennifer Baldwin
jenniferb@flixcandy.com
Estimated Sales: Less Than $500,000
Number Employees: 1-4
Brands:
Disney Princess
Mickey Mouse
Rudolph the Red Nosed Reindeer
Toy Story
Dippin' Candy

4508 **Floating Leaf Fine Foods**
28 Christopher St
Winnipeg, MB R2C 2Z2
Canada
204-989-7696
Fax: 204-943-4719 866-989-7696
info@slwr.com eatwildrice.ca
Wild rice
President: Murray Ratuski
murray@slwr.com
Director of Sales: Matthew Ratuski
Coordinator: Sheldon Ratuski
Number Employees: 1-4
Type of Packaging: Food Service, Private Label, Bulk

Brands:
Canadian Wild Rice
Floating Leaf
Canoe
Oh Canada

4509 Flora Inc
805 E Badger Rd
PO Box 73
Lynden, WA 98264-9502
360-354-2110
Fax: 360-354-5355 800-446-2110
info@florahealth.com www.florahealth.com
Digestive enzymes, herbal extracts, herbal teas, herbal tonics, nutritional oils, nutritional supplements, organic chocolates, probiotics and whole foods.
President/Owner: Thomas Greither
Cmo: Gabrial Lightfriend
glightfriend@florahealth.com
Marketing Manager: Gabriel Lightfriend
Estimated Sales: $10-20 Million
Number Employees: 50-99
Type of Packaging: Consumer
Other Locations:
Flora Manufacturing Facility
Burnaby BC
Brands:
Flor-Essence
Flora

4510 Flora Springs Winery
1978 Zinfandel Ln
St Helena, CA 94574-1611
707-963-5711
Fax: 707-963-7518 info@florasprings.com
www.florasprings.com
Wines
President: John Komes
jkomes@florasprings.com
Finance: Ronette Aiello
Estimated Sales: $1,8,000,000
Number Employees: 10-19

4511 Florence Macaroni Manufacturing
4334 W Chicago Ave
Chicago, IL 60651-3422
773-252-6113
Fax: 773-252-7085 800-647-2782
Macaroni products including regular/orangic semolina and whole wheat
President: Roy Pier Dominici
Sales Executive: Gino Ricciardi
Contact: Tom Behnke
tbenhke@florenceal.org
Manager: Tom Behnke
Plant Manager: Thomas Benhke
Estimated Sales: $3.3 Million
Number Employees: 25
Type of Packaging: Consumer, Food Service, Private Label, Bulk

4512 Florence Pasta & Cheese
115 W College Drive
Marshall, MN 56258-1747
800-533-5290
Fax: 507-537-8159 www.foodpros.com
Frozen pasta and dehydrated cheese
President: Alfred Schwan
Parent Co: Schwann's Sales
Type of Packaging: Consumer, Food Service, Bulk

4513 Florentyna's Fresh Pasta Factory
1864 E 22nd St
Los angles, CA 90058
213-742-9374
Fax: 310-677-2782 800-747-2782
jascha@freshpasta.com www.freshpasta.com
Fresh and fresh frozen pasta products for the food service industry
Manager: Jascha Smuloviez
Contact: Pat Brophy
brophypat@freshpasta.com
Estimated Sales: $1-4.9,000,000
Number Employees: 20-49
Number of Products: 60
Type of Packaging: Food Service, Private Label, Bulk

4514 Florida Brewery
202 Gandy Rd
Auburndale, FL 33823-2726
863-965-1825
Fax: 863-967-6965
Beer
Owner: Ming Tseng
ming@floridabrewery.com
Controller: Julie Williams
Operations: Erich Schalk
Estimated Sales: $3,000,000
Number Employees: 20-49
Square Footage: 62
Type of Packaging: Private Label

4515 Florida Caribbean Distillers
530 Dakota Ave
Lake Alfred, FL 33850
863-956-2002
Fax: 863-956-3979 www.floridadistillers.com
Beverages including wines and spirits
Director Of Bottling Operations: Mike Ryan
Contact: Jacob Call
jacob.call@floridadistillers.com
Estimated Sales: $14.3 Million
Number Employees: 99
Number of Brands: 13
Type of Packaging: Consumer, Bulk
Other Locations:
Bottling Operations
Auburndale FL
Storage/Rum Aging Facility
Winter Haven FL
Brands:
Capriccio
Club Caribe
Black Roberts
James Harbour
Florida Old Reserve
Minski
Mad Dragon
Kentucky's Old Reserve
Deauville
Shotball
Express Load
Sonavavitch
Ron Carlos

4516 Florida Citrus
Po Box 9010
Bartow, FL 33831-9010
863-537-3999
Fax: 877-352-2487 www.floridajuice.com
Fruit cocktails, juice and syrup. Product categories are vegetables, canned fruits and fresh fruits
VP: John Roberts
VP: Scott Stallard
Contact: Murat Azik
mazik@citrus.state.fl.us
Estimated Sales: $5-10 Million
Number Employees: 1-4
Type of Packaging: Consumer

4517 Florida Crystals Corporation
1 North Clematis St.
Suite 200
West Palm Beach, FL 33401
561-366-5100
Fax: 561-366-5158 844-344-9497
info@floridacrystals.com www.floridacrystals.com
Sugar, including certified organic, granulated, powdered, and brown sugar, and agave nectar.
Chairman/COO/President: Jose Fanjul
Chairman/CEO: Alfonso Fanjul
Executive VP/CFO: Luis Fernandez
Year Founded: 1960
Estimated Sales: $213.5 Million
Number Employees: 2,000
Number of Brands: 4
Square Footage: 10266
Type of Packaging: Consumer, Bulk
Brands:
Florida Crystals
Domino
C&H
Redpath

4518 (HQ)Florida Food Products Inc
2231 W County Road 44 # 1
Eustis, FL 32726-2628
352-357-4141
Fax: 352-483-3192 800-874-2331
contact@floridafood.com www.floridafood.com
Vegetable juice concentrates, aloe vera gel, fruit juice powders, vegetable juice powders
President: Jerry Brown
jbrown@floridafood.com
Vice President: Tom Brown
Research & Development: Scott Ruppe
VP Marketing: Thomas Brown
Sales Manager: Mike McIntyre
National Accounts Manager: Randy Blackmar
VP Operations & Manufacturing: Charles Hamrick
Plant Manager: Keith Burt
Purchasing Manager: James Arnett
Estimated Sales: $15-20 Million
Number Employees: 50-99
Square Footage: 300000
Other Locations:
Florida Food Products
Sabila
Brands:
Florida Food Products
Veg Con Beet
Veg Con Carrot
Veg Con Celery

4519 Florida Fruit Juices
7001 W 62nd St
Chicago, IL 60638-3924
773-586-6200
Fax: 773-586-6651 www.puredelitebev.com
Fruit juices including apple, grape, orange, grapefruit, pineapple, etc
President: Donald Franko
clivanos@dupageco.org
VP: Don Franko
VP: Don Franko, Jr.
Estimated Sales: $5-10 Million
Number Employees: 20-49
Type of Packaging: Consumer, Food Service, Private Label

4520 Florida Key West
5470 Division Dr
Fort Myers, FL 33905
239-694-8787
Fax: 239-694-0402 juice@florida-juice.com
Lemon and key lime juices
Owner: Earl Tanner
Director of Sales and Marketing: Sandra Tanner
Estimated Sales: $1-2,500,000
Number Employees: 5-9
Type of Packaging: Consumer, Food Service, Private Label, Bulk
Brands:
Florida Key West

4521 Florida Natural Flavors
180 Lyman Rd # 120
Casselberry, FL 32707-2805
407-834-5979
Fax: 407-834-6333 800-872-5979
info@floridanaturalflavors.com
www.barcontrolsofflorida.com
Manufacturer, exporter and importer of juice and beverage concentrates including carbonated, noncarbonated and frozen products
Vice President: Garry Erdman
gerdman@floridanaturalflavors.com
COO: Gary Erdman
Manager: Leonard Combs
Estimated Sales: $4,000,000
Number Employees: 20-49
Parent Co: Florida Natural Flavors
Type of Packaging: Private Label
Brands:
Diet Rite
Davy's Mix
Juicemaster
Mistic Iced Tea
Nehi Flavors
Polynesian Pleasure
R-Own Cola
Stewart's
Tropical Pleasure

4522 Florida Veal Processors
6712 State Road 674
Wimauma, FL 33598
813-634-5545
Fax: 813-633-1405
Fresh and frozen veal
President: Richard Nusman
Co-Owner: Max Nusman
Estimated Sales: $5.70 Million
Number Employees: 15
Type of Packaging: Consumer, Food Service

4523 **Florida's Natural Growers**
20205 US Hwy. 27 N.
Lake Wales, FL 33853
863-676-1411
Fax: 863-676-1640 888-657-6600
www.floridasnatural.com
Fresh and frozen fruit juices, concentrates and blends including grapefruit, orange, lemonade, lime, apple and grape.
Owner/President: Frank Hunt
CEO: Bob Behr
CFO: William Hendry
chip.hendry@citrusworld.com
Year Founded: 1933
Estimated Sales: $105 Million
Number Employees: 1,100
Type of Packaging: Consumer, Food Service, Private Label
Brands:
Florida's Natural

4524 **Floron Food Services**
2545 96th Street
Edmonton, AB T6N 1E3
Canada
780-438-9300
Fax: 780-438-9200 www.floron.com
Manufacturer of mozzarella and cheddar cheese, manufacturer of private label pasta sauce, full line distribution
President: Ronald Coyle
VP: Stephen Robbins
Year Founded: 1984
Estimated Sales: $20 Million
Number Employees: 40
Square Footage: 20000
Type of Packaging: Consumer, Food Service

4525 **Flower Essence Svc**
13139 Daisy Blue Mine Rd
Nevada City, CA 95959-9708
530-265-0258
Fax: 530-265-6467 800-548-0075
info@fesflowers.com www.fesflowers.com
Manufactuer of flower essences
Owner: Richard Katz
rkatz@fesflowers.com
Estimated Sales: $1-3 Million
Number Employees: 10-19

4526 **Flowers Baking Co**
900 16th St N
Birmingham, AL 35203-1017
205-252-1161
Fax: 205-323-7610 www.flowersfoods.com
Manufacturer and exporter of hamburger buns
President: Carter Wood
carter_wood@flocorp.com
Vice President of Marketing: Janice Anderson
Chief Engineer: Richard Davis
Estimated Sales: $10-20 Million
Number Employees: 250-499
Square Footage: 195000
Parent Co: Flowers Baking Company
Type of Packaging: Consumer

4527 **Flowers Baking Co**
301 Dallas St
El Paso, TX 79901-1821
915-533-8434
Fax: 915-534-0043 800-328-6111
Baked products including bread, rolls, buns and cake
VP Sales: Jef Dunigan
VP Sales: Tony Ruiz
Number Employees: 20-49
Square Footage: 320000
Parent Co: Flowers Industries
Brands:
Sunbeam

4528 **Flowers Baking Co**
546 15th St
Tuscaloosa, AL 35401-4708
205-752-5586
Fax: 205-752-1780
Baked goods including breads, buns and rolls.
President: Keith Singletary
keith_@flocorp.com
CEO: Joe Tashie
Estimated Sales: $.5-1 million
Number Employees: 100-249
Parent Co: Flowers Baking Company
Type of Packaging: Consumer

4529 **Flowers Foods Inc.**
1919 Flowers Circle
Thomasville, GA 31757
229-226-9110
Fax: 229-225-3823 www.flowersfoods.com
Packaged bakery foods.
President/CEO: A. Ryals McMullian
CFO/Chief Administrative Officer: R. Steve Kinsey
Senior VP/Chief Accounting Officer: Karyl Lauder
Chief Marketing Officer: Debo Mukherjee
Chief Sales Officer: D. Keith Wheeler
COO: Bradley Alexander
Year Founded: 1919
Estimated Sales: Over $1 Billion
Number Employees: 9,800
Number of Brands: 12
Type of Packaging: Consumer, Food Service
Brands:
Nature's Own
Tastykake
Dave's Killer Bread
Wonder
Cobblestone Bread Co.
Canyon Bakehouse
Mrs. Freshley's
Alpine Valley Bakery
Sunbeam Bread
Merita
Captain John's Derst's
Butternut Breads
Mi Casa
Bunny Bread
European Bakers
Home Pride

4530 **Floyd**
131 Atlantic Ave
Brooklyn, NY 11201-5504
718-858-5810
info@floydny.com
www.floydny.com
Manufacturer beer cheese and crackers.
Co-Founder: Jim Carden
cardenjim@gmail.com
Co-Founder: Andrew Templar
Co-Founder: Kevin Avanzato
Estimated Sales: Less Than $500,000
Number Employees: 1-4

4531 **Flurowater, Inc.**
12424 Wilshire Blvd.
Suite 850
Los Angeles, CA 90025
www.wanuwater.com
Manufacturer of flavored water.
Founder & President: Todd O'Gara
CEO: Steve Dollase
CFO: Danelle Larsen
CMO: Jacqueline Gonzalez

4532 **Flying Bird Botanicals LLC**
905 Squalicum Way Ste 106
Bellingham, WA 98225-2076
USA
360-366-8013
Fax: 360-933-8050 www.flyingbirdbotanicals.com
Tea
Owner/Founder: Scout Urling

4533 **Flying Burrito Co**
3200 N College Ave
Fayetteville, AR 72703-3565
479-527-0400
Fax: 479-527-0401 arch@flyingburritoco.com
www.flyingburritoco.com
Mexican restaurants serving burritos, tacos, quesadillas, nachos, and salads.
Owner: Mike Rohrbach
mike@flyingburritoco.com
Partner: Archie Schaffer
Estimated Sales: $600,000
Number Employees: 13

4534 **Flying Dog Brewery**
4607 Wedgewood Blvd
Frederick, MD 21703-7120
301-694-7899
www.flyingdogales.com
Manufacturer and exporter of beer, ale, stout, lager and porter.
President/CFO: Kelly McElroy
CEO: Jim Caruso
jimcaruso@flyingdogales.com
COO: Matt Brophy
CMO: Ben Savage
VP Sales: John Stolins
VP Plant Operations: Mark Matovich
Director, Packaging & Logistics: Christopher Farley
Estimated Sales: $7 Million
Number Employees: 50-99
Square Footage: 114000
Type of Packaging: Consumer, Food Service, Private Label

4535 **Flying Embers**
Ventura, CA 93003
flyingembers.com
Hard kombucha
Founder & CEO: Bill Moses

4536 **Flynn Vineyards Winery**
2200 N Pacific Hwy W
Rickreall, OR 97371-9774
503-623-8683
Fax: 503-623-0908 888-427-4953
Producer of wines. Products include Pinot Noir, Chardonnay and Pinot Gris.
President: Howard Rossbach
Estimated Sales: $5-10,000,000
Number Employees: 5-9
Type of Packaging: Private Label

4537 **(HQ)Fmali Herb**
831 Almar Avenue
Santa Cruz, CA 95060-5899
831-423-7913
Fax: 831-429-5173 sales@fmali.com
Manufacturer and contract packager of ginseng, hibiscus flowers, orange and lemon peels, herbal, green and black teas and chamomile; importer of ginseng, royal jelly and panax extractum; exporter of herbal teas and orange and lemonpeels
President/Co-Founder: Ben Zaricor
Executive VP/Co-Founder: Louise Veninga
Contact: Roberto Avila
ravila@goodearthteas.com
Estimated Sales: $14.0 Million
Number Employees: 50-99
Square Footage: 84000
Type of Packaging: Consumer, Food Service, Private Label, Bulk
Brands:
Famli
Good Earth
Wildcraft

4538 **Focus Foodservice**
300 Knightsbridge Pkwy
Lincolnshire, IL 60069
Fax: 800-968-4129 800-968-3918
info@focusfoodservice.com
Bakeware, smallwares and storage and transportation solutions
Brands:
FOCUS FOODSERVICE
FOCUS FOODSERVICE BAKEWARE
WEST BEND
SWING-A-WAY

4539 **Foell Packing Company**
PO Box 4595
Naperville, IL 60567-4595
919-776-0592
Fax: 919-774-1627 www.foellpacking.com
Manufacturer and exporter of canned meats including tripe, Vienna sausage and pork brains; also, contract packaging available
President: D Johnson
Vice President: T O'Shea
Estimated Sales: $5-10 Million
Number Employees: 20-49
Square Footage: 108000
Type of Packaging: Consumer, Private Label
Brands:
Beverly
Rose

4540 **Fogo Island Cooperative Society**
P.O. Box 70
Seldom Fogo Island, NL A0G 3Z0
Canada
709-627-3452
Fax: 709-627-3495 fogoislandcoop@nf.aibn.com
www.fogoislandcoop.com

Manufacturer and exporter of live and frozen crabs
President: Roy Freake
General Manager: Keith Watts
Estimated Sales: $1.4,000,000
Number Employees: 10
Type of Packaging: Consumer, Food Service, Bulk

4541 **Foley Estates Vineyard**
6121 E Highway 246
Lompoc, CA 93436-9679
805-737-6222
Fax: 805-737-6923 www.foleywines.com
Wines
President: Robert Lidquist
Marketing Manager: Lisa Schaeffer
Sales: Mike Keonig
Manager: Lisa Kekuewa
lkekuewa@foleywines.com
Production Manager: Norm Yost
Estimated Sales: $2.5-5,000,000
Number Employees: 10-19
Type of Packaging: Private Label

4542 **Foley's Chocolates & Candies**
11520 Horseshoe Way
Richmond, BC V7A 4V5
Canada
604-274-2131
Fax: 604-275-1682 888-236-5397
info@foleyscandies.com
www.foleyschocolates.com
Chocolate and confectionery products including wafers, blocks, chips, almond barks, squares, mints, yogurt covered almonds, raisins, peanuts and coffee beans
Co-Founder: Wade Pugh
Co-Founder: Richard Foley
Number Employees: 20-49
Type of Packaging: Private Label, Bulk

4543 **(HQ)Folgers Coffee Co**
1 Strawberry Ln
Orrville, OH 44667-0208
800-937-9745
www.folgerscoffee.com
Roasted, ground, regular and decaffeinated coffee. Also, Folgers is the licensed manufacturer and distributor of Dunkin' Donuts retail coffee brand.
Chief Executive Officer: Richard Smucker
SVP/Chief Financial Officer: Mark Belgya
Chief Operating Officer: Vincent Byrd
VP/Controller: John Denman
VP/General Counsel: Jeannette Knudsen
SVP/Corporate Communications: Christopher Resweber
Logistics Leader/Operations Manager: Shane Boddie
Number Employees: 100-249
Parent Co: J.M Smucker Company
Type of Packaging: Consumer
Brands:
Black Silk
Classic Complements
Folger's Filter Pack
Folger's Flavor
Folger's Instant
Folger's Simply Smooth
Gourmet Selections
K-Cup Packs
Mountain Grown

4544 **Folie ... Deux Winery**
7481 St. Helena Highway
Oakville, CA 94562
707-944-2565
Fax: 707-944-0250 800-535-6400
fadinfo@folieadeux.com www.folieadeux.com
Wines
Manager: Paul Scholfield
CEO: Richard Peterson
CFO: George Schofield
Marketing: Cardace Guridi
Public Relations: David Foster
Operations: Carla Clift
Production: Alejandro Pantoja
Purchasing: Marc Norwood
Number Employees: 10-19
Number of Brands: 3
Type of Packaging: Consumer
Brands:
Fantaisie
Folie a Deux
La Grande Folie
La Petite Folie

4545 **Folklore Foods**
2011 Hwy 12 & 83
PO Box 104
Selby, SD 57472
605-649-1144
Fax: 509-865-7363 www.folklorefoods.com
Manufacturer and exporter of espresso syrups and granita concentrate
President/CEO: Daniel Hanson
VP: Chris Hanson
Estimated Sales: $690,000
Number Employees: 5
Square Footage: 22000
Type of Packaging: Consumer, Food Service, Private Label
Brands:
Folklore
Folklore Cream Soda
Folklore Gourmet Syrups
Folklore Sasaparilla
Folklore Sparkling Beverages

4546 **Follmer Development, Inc**
884 Tourmaline Dr
Newbury Park, CA 91320-1205
805-498-4531
Fax: 805-499-4668 fdi@follmerdevelopment.com
www.follmerdevelopment.com
Aerosol cooking, baking and flavoring sprays.
President: Garrett Follmer
Estimated Sales: $9,000,000
Number Employees: 11-50
Type of Packaging: Consumer, Food Service, Private Label

4547 **Follow Your Heart**
9201 Owensmouth Ave
Chatsworth, CA 91311-5854
818-725-2820
Fax: 818-725-2812 www.followyourheart.com
Organic condiments, sauces, spreads
Owner/Founder: Michael Besancon
Chief Executive Officer: Bob Goldberg
Contact: Pamela Bluestein
pbluestein@followyourheart.com
Purchasing Executive: Lauren Hollenspein
Estimated Sales: F
Number Employees: 50-99

4548 **Fona International**
1900 Averill Rd
Geneva, IL 60134
630-578-8600
Fax: 630-578-8601 www.fona.com
Flavoring extracts and syrups.
Founder, Chairman & CEO: Joe Slawek
jslawek@fona.com
VP, Accounting & Finance: Chad Hall
EVP: TJ Widuch
EVP: Manon Daoust
COO: Jeremy Thompson
Estimated Sales: $100-500 Million
Number Employees: 100-249

4549 **Fontana Flavors Inc**
2342 Fulton St
Janesville, WI 53546-1004
608-754-9668
Fax: 608-754-9655
customerservice@fontanaflavors.com
www.fontanaflavors.com
Flavors manufacturer for seafood, meats, prepared foods and vegetarian products
President: Julie Eicksteadt
jeicksteadt@fontanaflavors.com
Estimated Sales: $4 Million
Number Employees: 1-4

4550 **Fontanini Italian Meats**
8751 W 50th St
McCook, IL 60525-3132
708-485-4800
Fax: 708-485-9600 800-331-6328
webinfo@fontanini.com www.fontanini.com
Meatballs, breakfast items, pizza toppings, beef
President: Joanne Fontanini
CEO: Eugene Fontanini
Account Executive: Rita Rufo
Controller Midwest: Eric Divelbiss
Director QC: Anthony Pavel
General Manager: Charles Brown
Regional Manager: Jim Doherty
West Coast Regional Manager: Gene Borgomainero
Director Operations: Mike Catania
Estimated Sales: $46 Million
Number Employees: 5-9
Square Footage: 240000
Parent Co: Hormel Foods Corporation
Type of Packaging: Consumer, Food Service
Brands:
Mama Ranne

4551 **Fontazzi/Metrovox Snacks**
612 N. Eckhoff St
Orange, CA 92868
714-634-3478
Fax: 714-634-4424 800-428-0522
questions@giftbasketsupplies.com
www.giftbasketsupplies.com
Popcorn, pretzels, snack mixes, gift packs, gift boxes, sourdough truffles
President: Paul Voxrand
Estimated Sales: $300,000-500,000
Number Employees: 1-4

4552 **Fonterra Co-operative Group Limited**
8700 W Bryn Mawr Ave
Chicago, IL 60631
888-869-6455
FUSA@fonterra.com www.fonterra.com
Dairy exporter based in New Zealand.
CEO: Miles Hurrell
CFO: Marc Rivers
CEO, Americas: Kelvin Wickham
COO: Fraser Whineray
Year Founded: 2001
Estimated Sales: $19.2 Billion
Number Employees: 21,400
Type of Packaging: Consumer, Food Service
Brands:
Anchor®
De Winkel®
Fresh 'n Fruity®
Kapiti®
Mainland®
Mammoth®
Perfect Italiano®
Piako®
Primo®
Symbio®
Tip Top®
NZMP™

4553 **Food & Vine Inc.**
68 Coombs St
Suite 2
Napa, CA 94559-3966
707-251-3900
Fax: 707-251-3939 info@grapeseedoil.com
grapeseedoil.com
Grapeseed oil and flour
President/CEO: Valentin Humer
valentin@grapeseedoil.com
Owner: Nanette Humer
Estimated Sales: $620,000
Number Employees: 1-4

4554 **Food City Pickle Company**
13760 Verona Road
Battle Creek, MI 49014-8920
269-781-9135
Fax: 616-781-3422
Sweet relish, dill relish, whole dill pickles, dill slices, sweet pickles, pepperoncini and peppers including hot and mild banana
President: Ron DeRuiter
Estimated Sales: $2.5-5 Million
Number Employees: 5-9
Square Footage: 44000
Type of Packaging: Consumer, Food Service, Private Label, Bulk
Brands:
King's Choice

4555 **Food City USA**
4752 W 60th Ave # A
Suite A
Arvada, CO 80003-6900
303-321-4447
Fax: 303-428-4143 joan@grandmaspasta.com
www.grandmaspasta.com
Fresh and frozen pre-cooked pasta including wide egg noodles, linguini, fettuccine and angel hair
Owner: Moni Piz-Wilson
president@grandmaspasta.com

Estimated Sales: $3-5 Million
Number Employees: 5-9
Parent Co: Grandma's Pasta Products
Type of Packaging: Consumer, Food Service
Brands:
Grandma's

4556 **Food Concentrate Corporation**
921 NW 72nd St
Oklahoma City, OK 73116
405-840-5633
Fax: 405-843-6832
Barbecue sauce concentrate and muffin and seasoning mixes
Owner: Walter Satterman
Estimated Sales: $2.5-5 Million
Number Employees: 6
Square Footage: 8000
Type of Packaging: Consumer, Food Service, Private Label
Brands:
Food Concentrate Corp.
Oat-N-Bran
Uncle Walter's

4557 **Food Factory**
875 Waimanu St
Suite 535
Honolulu, HI 96813
808-593-2633
Fax: 808-591-2943
Frozen foods
President: David Phillips
Estimated Sales: $300,000-500,000
Number Employees: 5-9

4558 **Food First**
PO Box 499
Walhalla, ND 58282
701-549-3864
800-241-0799
info@probiotein.com foodfirstllc.com
Prebiotic fiber and protein blend
Type of Packaging: Consumer

4559 **Food For Thought Inc**
10704 Oviatt Rd
Honor, MI 49640-9546
231-326-5444
Fax: 231-326-2649 sales@foodforthought.net
www.foodforthought.net
Organic and fair trade preserves, salsa, maple syrup, hot sauce, and mustard.
President: Timothy Young
sales@foodforthought.net
Number Employees: 10-19
Type of Packaging: Consumer, Private Label

4560 **Food Ingredient Solutions**
10 Malcolm Ave
Suite 1
Teterboro, NJ 07608
917-449-9558
Fax: 201-440-4211 jgreaves@foodcolor.com
www.foodcolor.com
Manufacturer and distributor of ingredients for barbeque sauces, spices, seasonings, colors, flavors, gums
CEO: Jeff Greaves
jeffgreaves@earthlink.net
VP, Operations: Helen Greaves
Estimated Sales: $6 Million
Number Employees: 10-19
Number of Brands: 2
Number of Products: 80
Type of Packaging: Food Service, Private Label, Bulk
Other Locations:
Food Ingredients Solutions
Signal Hill CA
Brands:
Grill-In-A-Bottle
Safrante

4561 **Food Ingredient Specialties**
30003 Bainbridge Road
Solon, OH 44139-2205
440-248-1820
Fax: 440-349-3334
Liquid seasonings and food bases
President/CEO: Gary Tortorelli
Parent Co: Nestle USA

4562 **Food Masters**
PO Box 1565
Griffin, GA 30223-1565
770-227-0330
Fax: 770-228-4281 888-715-4394
foodmasters@hotmail.com www.foodmasters.com
Mesquite BBQ sauce, Caesar, cucumber dressing and dip, sea sauce, honey mustard, dill delight, vinaigrette, poppy seed
Owner: Pradeep Kumarhia
Estimated Sales: $1-2,500,000
Number Employees: 5-9

4563 **Food Matters Again**
21 Provost St
Brooklyn, NY 11222
718-361-3183
info@foodmattersagain.com
foodmattersagain.com
Cheese; butter; cured meats; olives and olive oil; honey.
Founder: Brad Dube
Year Founded: 2009
Estimated Sales: $300,000
Number Employees: 6
Type of Packaging: Private Label

4564 **Food Mill**
3033 Macarthur Blvd
Oakland, CA 94602-3299
510-482-3848
Fax: 510-482-0344
Nut butter, cookies and breads
President/Co-Owner: Kirk Watkins
kkcwatkins@yahoo.com
Treasurer/Co-Owner: Arthur Watkins
Sales Exec: Ken Watkins
Estimated Sales: $1-2.5 Million
Number Employees: 10-19
Square Footage: 36000
Type of Packaging: Consumer, Bulk
Brands:
Food Mill

4565 **Food Processor of New Mexico**
PO Box 3672
Albuquerque, NM 87190-3672
505-881-4921
Fax: 505-797-2505 877-634-3772
Bar-b-que sauces, green chile, red chile, habanero
Co-Owner: Phillip Clark
Co-Owner: Wanda Clark

4566 **Food Products Corporation**
3121 E Washington St
Phoenix, AZ 85034
602-273-7139
Fax: 602-275-9429
Mexican foods including flour and corn tortillas, tortilla chips and masa
CEO: David Brennan
Plant Manager: Joaquin Amaro
Estimated Sales: $5-10 Million
Number Employees: 50-99
Square Footage: 120000
Parent Co: Sparta Foods
Type of Packaging: Consumer, Food Service, Private Label, Bulk
Brands:
Arizona

4567 **Food Sciences Corp**
821 E Gate Dr
Mt Laurel, NJ 08054-1239
856-924-5185
Fax: 856-778-4192 800-346-4422
www.foodsciences.com
Nutritional shakes, puddings; protein snack bars, chips; soups, pastas, hot beverages, other nutritional food supplements
President: Robert Schwartz
Estimated Sales: $10-20 Million
Number Employees: 50-99

4568 **Food Should Taste Good**
PO Box 9452
Denver, CO 80218
877-588-3784
www.foodshouldtastegood.com
Flavored tortilla chips
Founder: Pete Lescoe
VP, Finance: Bob Craig
VP, Marketing: James Borteck
Contact: Amanda Barrasso
amanda@foodshouldtastegood.com
Estimated Sales: $5 Million
Number Employees: 8

4569 **Food Source Company**
1335 Fewster Drive
Mississauga, ON L4W 1A2
Canada
905-625-8404
Fax: 905-238-9160
Manufacturer, exporter and importer of salad dressings, sauces and fat-free mayonnaise
President: Ralph Murray
Estimated Sales: $2,000,000
Number Employees: 18
Square Footage: 40000
Type of Packaging: Consumer, Food Service, Private Label

4570 **Food for Life Baking**
Corona, CA 92879
800-797-5090
www.foodforlife.com
Breads, buns, cereals, pasta, tortillas and waffles
CFO: Scott Kraus
Marketing Manager: Gary Torres
Type of Packaging: Consumer
Brands:
FOOD FOR LIFE

4571 **Food of Our Own Design**
1988 Springfield Ave
Maplewood, NJ 7040
973-762-0985
Fax: 973-762-7895
Cakes, pastries, brownies and crunch bars
Owner: Timothy Quickel
VP Sales/Operations: Tisha Jackson
Estimated Sales: $10-20 Million
Number Employees: 10-19
Square Footage: 8000

4572 **FoodMatch Inc**
575 Eight Avenue
Fl 23
New York, NY 10018
212-244-5050
Fax: 212-334-5042 800-350-3411
info@foodmatch.com www.foodmatch.com
Olives, fig spreads and dolmas
President: Philip Meldrum
President: Phil Meldrum
Contact: Emma Archbold
emma.archbold@foodmatch.com
Estimated Sales: $2.5 Million
Number Employees: 23

4573 **Foodie Fuel**
Boulder, CO 80303
foodiefuel.com
Organic, gluten-free energy snacks
CEO: John Herbers
Number of Brands: 1
Number of Products: 4
Type of Packaging: Consumer
Brands:
FUEL SNACKS

4574 **Foods Alive**
300 Industrial Dr
Suite C
Angola, IN 46703
260-488-4497
foodsalive.com
Flax crackers, artisan cold-pressed oils, super dressings, super foods and hemp foods. Organic, vegan, kosher & gluten-free.
President/Owner: Ellen Moor
info@foodslive.com
CEO: Michael Moor
Operations: Matt Alvord
Number Employees: 5-9
Type of Packaging: Consumer

4575 **Foodscience Corp**
20 New England Dr
PO Box 1
Essex Junction, VT 05452-2896
802-878-5508
Fax: 802-878-0549 800-874-9444
international@foodsciencecorp.com
www.foodsciencecorp.com
Manufacturer and exporter of vitamin supplements, joint and immune support supplements and specialty nutritional formulas
President: Dom Orlandi
CEO: Dale Metz
Financial Executive: Tricia Wunsch
Director of Strategic Planning: Mary Helrich
VP Marketing: Mark Ducharme
Operations: Sarah Oliveira
Estimated Sales: $300,000-500,000
Number Employees: 100-249
Parent Co: FoodScience Corporation
Brands:
Aangamik Dmg
Chitolean
Discovery
Herb Alchemy

4576 **Foodstirs**
Santa Monica, CA
844-250-3332
foodstirs.com
Organic baking kits and mixes
CEO: Galit Laibow
Type of Packaging: Consumer
Brands:
FOODSTIRS

4577 **Fool Proof Gourmet Products**
1813 Parkwood Dr.
Grapevine, TX 76051
817-329-1839
Fax: 817-329-1819
Manufacturer and exporter of gourmet seasonings, spices, sauces, etc
President: Mark Pierce
VP: Jeff Covington
Estimated Sales: $1-3,000,000
Number Employees: 5-9
Square Footage: 20000
Parent Co: Coulton Associates
Type of Packaging: Consumer, Food Service
Brands:
Fool Proof Gourmet

4578 **(HQ)Foothills Creamery**
2825 Bonnybrook Rd. SE
Calgary, AB T2G 4N1
Canada
403-263-7725
Fax: 403-237-5051 800-661-4909
www.foothillscreamery.com
Ice cream, unique cones, various novelties, frozen yogurt, and butter
President: Don Bayrack
Vice President: Barry Northfield
Sales Manager: Randy Wagner
Year Founded: 1969
Estimated Sales: $24 Million
Number Employees: 700
Number of Brands: 3
Number of Products: 24
Type of Packaging: Consumer, Food Service, Private Label, Bulk
Brands:
Jersey Supreme
Lone Pine Country
Rocky Mountain

4579 **Foppiano Vineyards**
12707 Old Redwood Hwy
PO Box 606
Healdsburg, CA 95448-9241
707-433-7272
Fax: 707-433-0565 info@foppiano.com
www.foppiano.com
Manufacturer and exporter of wines
President: Louis Foppiano
louis@foppiano.com
Winemaker: Bill Regan
Estimated Sales: $10-20 Million
Number Employees: 20-49
Type of Packaging: Consumer
Brands:
Foppiano
Fox Mountain
Riverside

4580 **Fora Foods**
Brooklyn, NY 11206
info@forafoods.com
forafoods.com
Dairy-free butter
Co-Founder & CEO: Aidan Altman
Co-Founder & CFO: Andrew McClure

4581 **Forager Project**
San Francisco, CA 94111
foragerproject.com
Cashew-based yogurt and milk
Founder & CEO: Stephen Williamson
Founder & COO: John-Charles Hanley
Number of Brands: 1
Number of Products: 22
Type of Packaging: Consumer
Brands:
FORAGER PROJECT

4582 **Foran Spice Inc**
7616 S 6th St
P.O. Box 109
Oak Creek, WI 53154-2049
414-764-1220
Fax: 414-764-8803 800-558-6030
email@asenzya.com www.asenzya.com
Re-cleaned and sterilized spices, custom engineered seasonings, and value-added food products
President: Patty Goto
patty.goto@foranspice.com
CFO: Andy Gitter
Vice President: Joy Hauser
VP of Business Development & Marketing: Chris Anderson
VP Sales: Paul Duddleston
Engineer: Alan Goto
Estimated Sales: $19 Million
Number Employees: 100-249
Square Footage: 213000
Type of Packaging: Food Service, Private Label, Bulk

4583 **Forbes Candies**
1300 Taylor Farm Road
Virginia Beach, VA 23453-3141
757-468-6602
Fax: 757-486-0646 800-626-5898
www.forbescandies.com
Confectionery products including salt water taffy, fudge, assorted brittle, and peanuts.
Owner: Jody Crosswhite
CEO: William M. Lawton
Sales Manager: Lynn Watson
Contact: Joanne Friedenson
jo.friedenson@atkinsonrealty.com
Estimated Sales: $5-10 Million
Number Employees: 20-49
Type of Packaging: Consumer

4584 **Forbes Chocolate BP**
800 Ken Mar Industrial Pkwy
Broadview Hts, OH 44147
440-838-4400
Fax: 440-838-4438 info@forbeschocolate.com
www.forbeschocolate.com
Manufacturer and exporter of cocoa and flavor powders for dairies. Chocolate ,mocha, strawberry, vanilla, orange cream, root beer, banana, mango and others
Owner: Keith Geringer
kgeringer@forbeschocolate.com
VP: Douglas Geringer
Quality Control: Ellon Waters
Director of Marketing: Rick Stunek
Sales: Mike Richter
Estimated Sales: $1.4 Million
Number Employees: 10-19
Square Footage: 17000
Type of Packaging: Bulk

4585 **Forbes Co**
4855 Kendrick St SE
Grand Rapids, MI 49512-9602
616-940-9900
Fax: 616-940-2028
Magazine publisher
Manager: Bret Foster
Estimated Sales: $3-5 Million
Number Employees: 5-9
Parent Co: Volk Corporation

4586 **Ford Gum & Mach Co Inc**
18 Newton Ave
Akron, NY 14001-1099
716-542-4561
Fax: 716-542-4610 fordgum@fordgum.com
www.fordgum.com
Manufacturer and distributor of gum balls and gum ball machines.
President: Lindsey Barnick
lbarnick@harrisbeach.com
Sr. Vice President: Steve Greene
Year Founded: 1913
Number Employees: 5-9
Type of Packaging: Consumer, Food Service, Private Label, Bulk
Brands:
Carousel
Chunk a Chew
Yowser!!

4587 **Ford's Gourmet Foods**
1109 Agriculture St # 1
Raleigh, NC 27603-2371
919-833-7647
Fax: 919-821-5781 800-446-0947
sales@bonesuckin.com www.bonesuckin.com
Producer of sauces, mustards, salsa and nuts. Some of their products include Bone Suckin Sauce, Bone Suckin Mustard, Bone Suckin Hiccuppin Hot, Bone Suckin Seasoning and Bone Suckin Yaki Sauce.
President: Connie Ford
Vice President: Patrick Ford
Estimated Sales: $11.6,000,000
Number Employees: 50-99
Type of Packaging: Private Label
Brands:
Big Chunks Salsa
Blessing's Mustard
Bone Suckin' Sauce
Ford's Foods
Hiccuppin' Hot Sauce
J. Berrie Brown Wine Nuts
We're Talking Serious Salsa

4588 **Ford's Gourmet Foods**
1109 Agriculture St # 1
Raleigh, NC 27603-2371
919-833-7647
Fax: 919-821-5781 800-446-0947
Sales@BoneSuckin.com www.bonesuckin.com
Sauces, marinades, mustards, and nuts
Owner: Sandi Ford
sandi@bonesuckin.com
VP: Patrick Ford
Number Employees: 50-99

4589 **Foreign Candy Company**
1 Foreign Candy Dr
Hull, IA 51239-7499
712-439-1496
Fax: 712-439-3207 800-831-8541
www.foreigncandy.com
Developer and distributor of candy.
CEO, President & Owner: Peter De Yager
VP, Marketing & Sales: Bill Lange
HR Manager: Bethany Bosma
Estimated Sales: $5-10 Million
Number Employees: 11-50
Type of Packaging: Private Label
Brands:
Mega Warheads
Rips Toll

4590 **Foreign Domestic Chemicals**
3 Post Rd
Oakland, NJ 07436-1609
201-651-9700
Fax: 201-651-9703
Manufactures ingredients and additives
President: Heinrich Dieseldorff
Estimated Sales: $500,000-1 Million
Number Employees: 1-4

4591 **Foremost Farms USA**
E10889 Penny Lane
Baraboo, WI 53913-8115
608-355-8700
800-362-9196
www.foremostfarms.com
Dairy products including cheeses, fresh milk, butter, and whey ingredients.

President/CEO: Greg Schlafer
Senior VP/CFO: Bob Bascom
VP, Milk Division & Risk Management: Darin Hanson
Manager: Wally Heil
Year Founded: 1994
Estimated Sales: Over $1 Billion
Number Employees: 1000-4999
Number of Brands: 2
Number of Products: 10
Type of Packaging: Consumer, Food Service, Private Label, Bulk
Brands:
1950 127 Brand
Formost Farms USA

4592 **Forever Green Food Inc.**
5700 E Oplympic Blvd
Commerce, CA 90022-5115
323-721-9928
Fax: 323-721-1487 info@forevergreenfood.com
forevergreenfood.com
Butter cookies; fruit snacks; crackers; assorted chocolates; pumpkin seeds;
President: John Ren
Director of Sales: Luis Gonzalez
Type of Packaging: Private Label
Brands:
Bahlsen
SQUE'EASY
Hawaiian Host

4593 **Forge Mountain Foods**
1215 Greenville Hwy
Hendersonville, NC 28792
828-692-9470
Fax: 828-692-9917 800-823-6743
Specialty foods company with over 250 varieties of old timey food products; jams and jellies, pickles and relishes and more
Owner: Brian Pawling
VP Sales/Marketing: Paul Brim
Estimated Sales: $500,000-$1,000,000
Number Employees: 5-9
Number of Products: 250+
Brands:
Forge Mountain

4594 **Foris Vineyards**
654 Kendall Rd
Cave Junction, OR 97523-9721
541-592-3752
Fax: 541-592-4424 foris@foriswine.com
www.foriswine.com
Wines
Owner: Ted Gerber
Estimated Sales: $2.5-5,000,000
Number Employees: 10-19
Number of Brands: 10
Type of Packaging: Private Label

4595 **Fork & Goode**
Brooklyn, NY
hello@forkngoode.com
www.forkandgoode.com
Pork and other meat products.
CEO: Niyati Gupta
CSO: Gabor Forgacs
Number Employees: 1-4

4596 **Forkless Gourmet Inc**
10 S Riverside Plz
Chicago, IL 60606-3728
312-474-5746
Fax: 312-474-6127
Manufacturers forkless bun meals available in several varieties including: chicken sesame teriyaki; thai style chicken; beef & broccoli; pork & vegetables with Five Fortune BBQ Sauce; kung pao shrimp (spicy); vegetarian feast withtofu & edamame; chipotle chicken (spicy); margarita chicken; beef asada; pork & vegetable with Ancho Honey BBQ Sauce, and black bean adobo.
President: Gregory Stahl
CFO: Steven Spiegel
VP: Katie Torres
Type of Packaging: Food Service

4597 **Forman Vineyard**
1501 Big Rock Rd
St Helena, CA 94574-9613
707-963-3900
Fax: 707-963-5384 www.formanvineyard.com
Wines, grow produce & bottle cabernet savignon & chardonnay
President/Operations/Prod./Mgr: Ric Forman
forman@sonic.net
Vice President/Operations/Prod./Mgr: Toby Forman
Marketing/Sales/Pub Relations Director: Margaret Hatte
Estimated Sales: $1.8 Million
Number Employees: 5-9
Square Footage: 36000

4598 **Formosa Enterprises Inc**
111 N Market St
Suite 460
San Jose, CA 95113-1112
408-297-3300
Fax: 408-297-3311 info@formosasauce.com
www.formosasauce.com
Manufacturer of different sauces.
Owner: Julio Lopez
julio@formosasauce.com
Number Employees: 1-4

4599 **Formost Friedman Company**
152 Frankel Boulevard
Merrick, NY 11566-4033
516-378-4919
Fax: 516-379-8301
General grocery
President: William MacMelville
Estimated Sales: $1-2,500,000
Number Employees: 1-4

4600 **Fort Boise Produce Company**
103 Main St
Nyssa, OR 97913
541-372-5174
Fax: 541-372-3326
Packed onions
President: Thomas Stephens
Estimated Sales: $1-2,500,000
Number Employees: 50-99

4601 **Fort Garry Brewing Company**
130 Lowson Crescent
Winnipeg, MB R3P 2H8
Canada
204-487-3678
Fax: 204-487-0839 info@fortgarry.com
www.fortgarry.com
Beer
President/CEO: Doug Saville
CFO: Denis Chabbert
General Manager: Orest Horechko
Corporate Controller: Maria Nemeth
Sales: Wayne Vanlandeghem
Customer Service: Cathy Di Stefano
Estimated Sales: B
Number Employees: 23
Number of Brands: 13
Number of Products: 1
Square Footage: 50000
Type of Packaging: Private Label, Bulk

4602 **Forte Gelato**
PO Box 327
Greens Farms, CT 06838
203-764-1826
Fax: 203-254-3080 info@tasteforte.com
www.tasteforte.com
Manufacturer of low fat, high protein gelato.
Founder: Adrian Pace

4603 **Forte Stromboli Company**
3129 S 13th Street
Philadelphia, PA 19148-5234
215-463-6336
Fax: 215-463-8616
Frozen stromboli
President: Ronald Conti
Estimated Sales: $5-10,000,000
Number Employees: 5-9
Type of Packaging: Consumer, Food Service

4604 **Fortella Fortune Cookies**
214 W 26th St
Chicago, IL 60616-2204
312-567-9000
Fax: 312-567-9119
Fortune, almond and specialty cookies
Owner: Jatico Francis
bjatico@yahoo.com
Company Manager: Brenda Wong
Estimated Sales: $1-2.5 Million
Number Employees: 10-19
Type of Packaging: Consumer, Food Service

4605 **Fortenberry Mini-Storage**
3128 Fortenberry Rd
Kodak, TN 37764-2020
865-933-2568
Fax: 865-933-2568
Ice, cheese and dairy products.
Owner: Regina Underwood
Estimated Sales: Less Than $500,000
Number Employees: 1-4
Type of Packaging: Consumer
Other Locations:
Fortenberry Ice Company
Kodak TN

4606 **Fortino Winery**
4525 Hecker Pass Rd
Gilroy, CA 95020-8807
408-842-3305
Fax: 408-842-8636 888-617-6606
gino@fortinowinery.com www.fortinowinery.com
Wines
Owner: Gino Fortino
gino@fortinowinery.com
Tasting Room Manager: Jill Fortino
Wine-Club Director & Admin. Assistant: Dawn Jackson
Outside Sales Representative: Bertha Valenzula
Estimated Sales: $900,000
Number Employees: 5-9

4607 **Fortitude Brands LLC**
6925 Almansa Street
Coral Gables, FL 33146-3809
305-661-8198
Fax: 305-662-4977
Manufacturer and importer of exotic and natural tropical food products
Principal: Franco Stanzione
CFO: Juan Serna
Marketing: Robert Hunt
Sales: Bob Ottmar
Public Relations: Renee Morales
Estimated Sales: $400,000
Number Employees: 21
Number of Brands: 5
Number of Products: 14
Type of Packaging: Consumer
Brands:
Casabe Rainforest Crackers
Isabo Hearts of Palm
Samai

4608 **Forto Coffee**
New York, NY 10004
844-450-7575
fortocoffee.com
Coffee shots
Founder & CEO: Neel Premkumar
Number of Brands: 1
Number of Products: 6
Type of Packaging: Consumer
Brands:
FORTO

4609 **Fortress Systems LLC**
2132 S 156th Cir
Omaha, NE 68130-2503
402-333-3532
Fax: 402-333-3536 888-331-6601
Dietary supplements
CEO: Mike Carnazzo
VP/R&D: Joseph Carnazzo
Consultant: Dr Martha Garcia
Consultant: Dr Brian Sakurada
Number Employees: 1-4
Parent Co: FSI Nutrition

4610 **Fortuna Cellars**
2124 Fortuna Court
Davis, CA 95616-0603
530-756-6686
Wines
President: Gerald Bowes

4611 **Fortunate Cookie**
PO Box 1386
Stowe, VT 05672-1386
802-888-5706
Fax: 802-888-5563 866-266-5337
portico@stowevt.net www.thefortunatecookie.com

Specialty cookies/gift baskets made from scratch and to order signature offering: fortune cookies in 4 sizes and 19 flavors
Owner/CEO: Portia Arthur
Type of Packaging: Consumer

4612 Fortune Cookie Factory
261 12th St
Oakland, CA 94607-4440
510-832-5552
Fax: 510-832-2565
Personalized fortune cookies
President: Andrew Wong
fcf261@yahoo.com
Estimated Sales: $2.5-5 Million
Number Employees: 5-9

4613 Fortune Seas
42 Rogers Street
Gloucester, MA 01930-5000
978-281-6666
Fax: 978-281-8519
Seafood
President/CEO: Donald Short
VP Sales: Charles Bencal
Brands:
Fortune's Catch
Ocean Deli

4614 Fortunes International Teas
11 Tunnel Way
Mc Kees Rocks, PA 15136
412-771-7767
Fax: 412-771-2122 www.fortunescoffee.com
Black, green and herbal teas
Owner: Richard Cefola Sr
r.cefolasr@fortunescoffee.com
VP Marketing: Michael Brunk
Estimated Sales: $500,000-$1,000,000
Number Employees: 1-4
Type of Packaging: Private Label
Brands:
Commonwealth
Fortunes
London Herb & Spice
Ridgways

4615 Forty Second Street Bagel Cafe
733 W. Westfoot Blvd.
Upland, CA 91786-5603
909-949-7334
Fax: 909-949-0721
Bagels and rolls
Owner: Robert Hall
Estimated Sales: $3-5,000,000
Number Employees: 5-9

4616 Fort, Products
4801 Main St
Suite 205
Kansas City, MO 64112
816-741-3000
www.forteproducts.com
Retail fixtures for the food service industry
CFO: Scott Morris

4617 Fosselman's Ice Cream Co
1824 W Main St
Alhambra, CA 91801-1897
626-282-6533
Fax: 626-282-0246 www.fosselmans.com
Ice cream, sherbet
Owner: Anna Fosselman
acfosselman@charter.net
VP: Christian Fosseleman
Estimated Sales: $2.5-5,000,000
Number Employees: 20-49
Type of Packaging: Consumer, Bulk

4618 Fossil Farms
81 Fulton St
Boonton, NJ 07005-1909
973-917-3155
Fax: 973-917-3156 sales@fossilfarms.com
www.fossilfarms.com
Farm raised game and all natural meats
CEO/Co-Owner: Lance Appelbaum
lance@fassilfarms.com
Accounts Payable/Receivable: Denise Polizzotto
Sales Manager: Sturgess Spanos
Customer Service: Kristyn Behnke
COO/Co-Owner: Todd Appelbaum
Warehouse Manager: Jose Rivera
Estimated Sales: $1.1 Million
Number Employees: 20-49

4619 Foster Family Farm
90 Foster St
South Windsor, CT 06074-3873
860-648-9366
www.fosterfarms.com
Manufacturer and exporter of pickled asparagus and beans
Principal: Chris Foster
Co-Owner/Member: Teresa Robertson
Partner: Alexandra Palmer
alexandrapalmer@fosterfarm.com
Estimated Sales: $10-20 Million
Number Employees: 10-19

4620 Foster Fams
P.O. Box 52
Kelso, WA 98626
800-255-7227
www.fosterfarms.com
Chicken and turkey

4621 Foster Farms Inc.
1000 Davis St.
PO Box 306
Livingston, CA 95334
800-255-7227
www.fosterfarms.com
Poultry producer.
CEO: Dan Huber
Estimated Sales: Over $1 Billion
Number Employees: 10000+
Number of Brands: 6
Type of Packaging: Consumer, Food Service, Private Label, Bulk
Brands:
Foster Farms Fresh & Natural
Foster Farms Naturally Seasoned
Foster Farms Simply Raised
Foster Farms Organic
Foster Farms Always Natural
Foster Farms Saut, Ready

4622 Fountain Shakes/MS Foods
13508 Orchard Road
Minnetonka, MN 55305
952-988-6940
Fax: 952-988-6941
Fountain shake in six flavors: chocolate malt, cappuccino, strawberry, vanilla, banana and chocolate
Owner: Alan B Stone
Marketing: Lou Ann Stone
Contact: Alan Stone
astone2454@aol.com
Parent Co: MS Foods
Type of Packaging: Consumer, Bulk
Brands:
Fountain Shake

4623 (HQ)Fountain Valley Foods
2175 N Academy Circle # 201
PO Box 9882
Colorado Springs, CO 80932
719-573-6012
Fax: 719-573-5192 www.fountainvalleyfoods.com
Salsa, ketchup, bean dip and specialty chili products; Importer/Distributor of cheese sauce, jalapeno peppers, banana peppers, chipotle peppers, green chile.
President: James Loyacono
Contact: Ginger Steineke
ginger@fountainvalleyfoods.com
Estimated Sales: $4.9 Million
Number Employees: 4
Square Footage: 20000
Type of Packaging: Consumer, Food Service, Private Label, Bulk
Other Locations:
Den-Mar Products
Trinidad CO
Brands:
Lone Tree Farm
Nacho Grande

4624 Four Barrel Coffee
375 Valencia St
San Francisco, CA 94103-3504
415-252-0800
info@fourbarrelcoffee.com
fourbarrelcoffee.com
Coffee
Owner: Jeremy Tooker
jtooker@fourbarrelcoffee.com
Number Employees: 20-49

4625 Four Chimneys Farm Winery Trust
211 Hall Rd
Himrod, NY 14842
607-243-7502
Fax: 607-243-8156
Organically grown grape juice, wine, cooking wine and vinegar
Owner: Scott Smith
ssmith@htva.net
Sales Manager: W Daniel
Estimated Sales: Less than $500,000
Number Employees: 5-9
Type of Packaging: Consumer, Bulk

4626 Four Percent Company
16145 Hamilton Ave
Highland Park, MI 48203-2615
313-345-5880
Fax: 313-345-8686
Flavors
Owner: Harold Samhat
Estimated Sales: $500,000-$1,000,000
Number Employees: 1-4
Type of Packaging: Food Service, Private Label
Brands:
Seely

4627 Four Seasons Produce Inc
400 Wabash Rd
PO Box 788
Ephrata, PA 17522-9100
717-721-2800
Fax: 717-721-2597 800-422-8384
www.sunrisetransportinc.com
Fruits and vegetables
Owner: David Hollinger
VP Finance: Loretta Radanovic
Quality Manager: Daniel Oloro
National Sales Manager: Stan Paluszewski
davidh@fsproduce.com
VP/General Manager: Rob Kurtz
Number Employees: 500-999
Square Footage: 261000

4628 Four Sigmatic
1629 Abbot Kinney Blvd
Venice, CA 90291
us.foursigmatic.com
Mushroom coffees, elixirs and cacaos
Type of Packaging: Consumer
Brands:
FOUR SIGMATIC

4629 Four Sisters Winery
783 County Road 519
Belvidere, NJ 07823
908-475-3671
Fax: 908-475-3555 mattyfla@gmail.com
www.foursisterswinery.com
Wines
Owner: Robert Matarazzo
Manager: Valerie Tishuk
Estimated Sales: $1-2,500,000
Number Employees: 5-9
Type of Packaging: Private Label

4630 Four Star Beef
Omaha, NE
www.fourstarbeef.com
Beef
Parent Co: JBS USA, LLC.
Other Locations:
Tolleson AZ
Green Bay WI
Plainwell MI
Souderton PA

4631 Fournier R & Sons Seafood
14147 Old Highway 67
Biloxi, MS 39532-8803
228-392-4293
Fax: 228-392-7130
Seafood
Owner: Doty Fournier
Secretary: Barbara Fournier
Estimated Sales: $2.5-5 000,000
Number Employees: 20-49

4632 **Fowler Farms**
10273 Lummisville Rd
Wolcott, NY 14590
315-594-8068
Fax: 315-594-8060 800-836-9537
www.fowlerfarms.com
Apples.
Director, Business Development: Mark Sharp
VP, Sales & Marketing: Dave Williams
Sales Assitant: Jennifer Sutton
Year Founded: 1858
Estimated Sales: $100-500 Million
Number Employees: 250-499

4633 **Fowler Packing Co**
8570 S Cedar Ave
Fresno, CA 93725-8905
559-834-5911
Fax: 559-834-5272 erin@fowlerpacking.com
www.fowlerpacking.com
Table grapes, sorbet grapes, and mandarins
President: Leland Parnagian
CEO: Justin Parnagian
Sales: Chad Nelsen
Year Founded: 1935
Estimated Sales: $20-50 Million
Number Employees: 50-99
Brands:
Golden State Hops
SamSonS
Halos

4634 **Fox Deluxe Inc**
370 N Morgan St
Chicago, IL 60607
312-421-3737
Fax: 312-421-8067 www.foxdeluxefoods.com
Wholesale frozen meats
Owner: Sam Samano
Estimated Sales: $50-100 Million
Number Employees: 50-99

4635 **Fox Hollow**
8909 Highway 329
Crestwood, KY 40014-9596
502-241-8621
foxhollow.com
Manufacturer sweet and spicy mustard sauce used as a glaze, marinade and a mustard on meat, fish, chicken and sandwiches
President: Phyllis Fox
Estimated Sales: $500,000-$1 Million
Number Employees: 10-19
Type of Packaging: Consumer
Brands:
Fox Hollow Farm Mustard
Fox-More Than a Mustard

4636 **Fox Iv Technologies**
6011 Enterprise Dr
Export, PA 15632-8969
724-387-3500
Fax: 724-387-3516 877-436-2434
www.foxiv.com
Labels and packing supplies
President/CEO: Rick Fox
Estimated Sales: $10-20 Million
Number Employees: 20-49

4637 **Fox Meadow Farm**
1439 Clover Mill Road
Chester Springs, PA 19425-1108
610-827-9731
Wines
President: Harry Mandell, Jr.
Estimated Sales: $500,000 appx.
Number Employees: 1-4

4638 **Fox Meadow Farm of Vermont**
135 N Main St
Suite 5
Rutland, VT 05701-3238
802-259-7805
Fax: 802-773-2242 888-754-4204
www.foxmeadowfarmvt.com
Dry seasoning and herb blends, dry mixes
President: James Harrison
Estimated Sales: $300,000-500,000
Number Employees: 1-4

4639 **Fox N Hare Brewing Co.**
46 Front St.
Port Jervis, NY 12771
845-672-0100
www.foxnhare-brewing.com
IPAs and American ales; fruit-flavored beers
Co-Owner: Sean Donnelly
Co-Owner: David Krantz
Number of Brands: 1
Number of Products: 9
Type of Packaging: Consumer, Private Label
Brands:
Fox N Hare

4640 **Fox Run Vineyards**
670 State Route 14
Penn Yan, NY 14527-9622
315-536-4616
Fax: 315-536-1383 800-636-9786
info@foxrunvineyards.com
www.foxrunvineyards.com
Winery, producing riesling, chardonnay, gewurztraminer, lemberger, cabernet franc and pinot noir.
President/Co-Owner: Scott Osborn
Co-Owner: Albert Zafonte
Co-Owner: Kathy Zafonte
Vice President/Co-Owner: Ruth Osborn
Marketing & Events: Kelli Shaffner
Sales Manager: Dan Mitchell
Vineyard Manager: John Kaiser
Winemaker: Peter Bell
Crush Operations & Inventory: Pete Howe
Estimated Sales: $3.8 Million
Number Employees: 10-19
Number of Brands: 1
Type of Packaging: Consumer
Brands:
Fox Run

4641 **Fox Vineyards & Winery**
225 Highway 11 S
Social Circle, GA 30025-5003
770-787-5402
Fax: 770-787-5402 www.foxvinwinery.com
Wines
Owner: John Fuchs
Estimated Sales: $1-2,500,000
Number Employees: 1-4

4642 **Fox's Fine Foods**
303 Broadway St Ste 106
Laguna Beach, CA 92651
949-497-8910
Fax: 949-497-1763 888-522-3697
Pestos, relishes, condiments, soups
President: Kim Fox
Estimated Sales: Under $500,000
Number Employees: 5-9
Type of Packaging: Private Label

4643 **Foxen Foxen 7200**
7200 Foxen Canyon Rd
Santa Maria, CA 93454-9581
805-937-4251
Fax: 805-937-0415 www.foxenvineyard.com
Wines
Owner: Richard Dore
Contact: Jesse Cloutier
jesse@foxenvineyard.com
Estimated Sales: $1-2,500,000
Number Employees: 5-9

4644 **Foxtail Foods**
6880 Fairfield Business Ctr
Fairfield, OH 45014-5476
513-881-7900
Fax: 513-881-7910 800-487-2253
customerservice@foxtailfoods.com
www.foxtailfoods.com
Pies, cookies, muffin batter, mixes and syrups and specialty products
President: Lonnie Howard
VP: Matt Daniel
Director of R&D: Doug Snedden
VP Sales/Marketing: Athos Rostan
Manager: Joe Reinhardt
Purchasing Agent: Rich Frysinger
Estimated Sales: $10-20 Million
Number Employees: 100-249
Square Footage: 179055
Parent Co: Perkins
Type of Packaging: Consumer, Food Service, Private Label, Bulk
Other Locations:
Foxtail Foods-Corporate
Memphis
Foxtail Foods-Corporate
Tennesse
Foxtail Foods-R&D
Cincinnati
Brands:
Foxtail

4645 **Fralinger's**
1325 Boardwalk # 1
Atlantic City, NJ 08401-7287
609-344-0758
Fax: 609-344-0758 800-938-2339
comments@jamescandy.com
www.jamescandy.com
Taffy and candy
President: Frank Glaser
frank.glaser@jamescandy.com
Controller: Rose Gedicke
VP/Internet Technology: Arthur Gager
EVP Marketing/Sales: Lisa Glaser-Whitney
Sales: Alan Green
VP Operations/Manufacturing: Rob Fisher
Number Employees: 1-4
Type of Packaging: Private Label
Other Locations:
Fralinger's-Bally's Park
Atlantic City NJ
Fralinger's-Tennesee Ave
Atlantic City NJ
Fralinger's-Ocean City
Atlantic City NJ
Fralinger's-Cape May
Cape May NJ
Brands:
Fralinger's
Bayard's
James'

4646 **Fran's Chocolates**
1300 East Pike St
Seattle, WA 98122
206-322-0233
Fax: 203-322-0452 800-422-3726
orders@franschocolates.com
www.franschocolates.com
Chocolates
Owner: Fran Bigelow
Marketing: Adriana Bigelow
Contact: Keita Horn
keitah@franschocolates.com
Estimated Sales: $5 Million
Number Employees: 30

4647 **Fran's Healthy Helpings**
840 Hinckley Road
Suite 128
Burlingame, CA 94010-1505
650-652-5772
Fax: 650-652-5773
Health foods
President: Fran Lent
VP Operations: Ada Chang
Estimated Sales: $1-2,500,000
Number Employees: 5-9
Brands:
Fran's Healthy Helpings

4648 **France Delices**
5065 Rue Ontario E
Montreal, QC H1V 3V2
Canada
514-259-2291
Fax: 514-259-1788 800-663-1365
information@francedelices.com
www.francedelices.com
Manufacturer and exporter of cakes including fresh, frozen and gourmet
President: Colette Durot
VP: Laurent Durot
Estimated Sales: $13million
Number Employees: 3
Square Footage: 100000
Type of Packaging: Consumer, Food Service

4649 **Franciscan Estate**
1178 Galleron Road at Highway 29
St. Helena, CA 94574
707-967-3830
www.franciscan.com
Winemaker
Director of Winemaking: Janet Myers
Type of Packaging: Consumer

Brands:
Estancia
Franciscan Oakville Estate
Mt Veeder
Quintessa
Simi Ravenswood
Veramonte
Magnificat
Cuvee Sauvage
Napa Valley
Stylus
Clos Reserve
Oakville
Winemakers Reserve
Fountain Court
Rose

4650 **Franco's Cocktail Mixes**
121 SW 5th Ct
Pompano Beach, FL 33060-7909
954-782-7491
Fax: 954-786-9253 800-782-4508
Francocktl@aol.com
www.francoscocktailmixes.com
Manufacturer and exporter of liquid and dry cocktail mixes; also, colored margarita salt and colored rimming sugars
Owner: Michael A Pitino
Quality Control: Guy Haret
Manager: Laura Schnell
michael@francoscocktailmixes.com
Estimated Sales: $10-24.9 Million
Number Employees: 5-9
Number of Brands: 12
Number of Products: 100+
Square Footage: 50000
Type of Packaging: Food Service, Private Label
Brands:
Crown's Pride
Florida Straits Rum Runner
Florida's Gold Cocktail
Florida's Pride
Franco's Margarita Salt Sombrero
Jose Cuervo Margarita Salt Sombrero
Pat O'Brien's
Sauza Margarita Salt With Juicer
Tout Fini Cocktail Mixes

4651 **Frank & Dean's Cocktail Mixes**
1395 Coronet Avenue
Pasadena, CA 91107-1639
626-351-4272
Fax: 909-596-4640
Bloody Mary, margarita, pina colada, mai tai, strawberry margarita, lime juice and grenadine
President: Frank Abbadessa
CFO: John Kennick
VP: Dean Carbone
Number Employees: 1-4
Type of Packaging: Private Label
Brands:
Frank & Dean's Cocktail Mixes

4652 **Frank Brunckhorst Company**
1819 Main St.
Suite 800
Sarasota, FL 34236
804-722-4100
Fax: 804-863-1409 www.boarshead.com
Boar's Head brands of deli meats and cheeses.
Year Founded: 1905
Estimated Sales: $500+ Million
Number Employees: 250-500
Parent Co: Boar's Head
Brands:
Boar's Head

4653 **Frank Family Vineyards**
1091 Larkmead Ln
Calistoga, CA 94515-9675
707-942-0859
Fax: 707-942-2581 880-574-9463
info@frankfamilyvineyards.com
www.frankfamilyvineyards.com
Wines
Owner: Richard Frank
info@frankfamilyvineyards.com
Estimated Sales: $10-20 000,000
Number Employees: 20-49
Type of Packaging: Private Label

4654 **Frank Korinek & Co**
4828 W 25th St
Cicero, IL 60804-3489
708-652-2870
Fax: 773-242-1917
Pastry fillings, fruit pie filling, donut mixes
President: George Korinek
g.korinek@frankkorinek.com
Estimated Sales: $1-2,500,000
Number Employees: 5-9
Brands:
Bohemian Maid
Korinek

4655 **Frank Mattes & Sons Reliable Seafood**
2327 Edwards Lane
Bel Air, MD 21015-5001
410-879-5444
Fax: 410-734-6061
Seafood

4656 **Frank Pagano Company**
1513 S State Street
Lockport, IL 60441-3550
815-838-0303
Fax: 815-723-9861
Quality meats
President/CEO: Frank Pagano

4657 **Frank Wardynski & Sons Inc**
336 Peckham St
PO Box 336
Buffalo, NY 14206-1717
716-854-6083
Fax: 716-854-4887 www.wardynski.com
Smoked polish sausage, italian sausage, natural casing wieners, tender casing weiners, skinless weiners, knockwurst, bologna, cooked salami, liver sausage, kiska, blood tongue, sweet or sour head cheese.
Chairman/President: Raymond Wardynski
rmwardynski@wardynski.com
Estimated Sales: $5-10 Million
Number Employees: 20-49
Square Footage: 105000

4658 **Frank-Lin Distributors**
2455 Huntington Dr
Fairfield, CA 94533-9734
707-437-1264
Fax: 408-258-9527 800-922-9363
humanresources@frank-lin.com
www.frank-lin.com
Leading producer of wines and distilled spirits
Owner: Frank Lin
bottling@frank-lin.com
President/CEO: Frank Maestri
VP Brand Development: Michael Wasteney
VP Sales/Marketing: Mark Pechusick
Marketing Director: Christina Maestri
VP Sales: David Covello
bottling@frank-lin.com
Estimated Sales: $3-5,000,000
Number Employees: 5-9
Square Footage: 45000
Type of Packaging: Bulk
Brands:
8 Seconds Canadian Whiskey
Beyond Vodka
Buck
Bellringer
Puerto Vallarta

4659 **Frankford Candy & Chocolate Co**
9300 Ashton Rd
Philadelphia, PA 19114-3532
215-735-5200
Fax: 215-735-0721 800-523-9090
info@frankfordcandy.com
Processor of solid, hollow chocolate molded novelties and nonchocolate candies for Christmas, Easter, Halloween and Valentine's Day.
CEO: Morgan Brehm
mbrehm@inmetco.com
CEO: Stuart Selarnik
Executive VP: Nathan Hoffman
Director, Marketing: Molly Jacobson
Year Founded: 1947
Estimated Sales: $20-50 Million
Number Employees: 250-499
Number of Brands: 7
Square Footage: 65000
Type of Packaging: Bulk
Brands:
Disney
Frankford
Hello Kitty
Marvel
Nickelodeon
SpongeBob SquarePants
Welchs

4660 **Frankfort Cheese**
F1705 County Rd N
Edgar, WI 54426-9648
715-352-2345
Fax: 715-352-2346
Cheese
President: Dennis Telschow
Estimated Sales: Less than $500,000
Number Employees: 5-9

4661 **Franklin Baker Company**
275 Tournament Drive
Southwind Office Center B, Suite 305
Memphis, TN 38125
901-881-6681
Fax: 901-881-6682 www.franklinbaker.com
Baked goods using coconut
President & CEO: Jerry Lorenzo
SVP, Finance: Jim Laurian
SVP, Sales, Marketing & Operations: Ken Gibson
SVP, Operations: Cesar Galvez

4662 **Franklin Baking Co.**
500 W. Grantham St.
Goldsboro, NC 27530
919-735-0344
Fax: 919-705-2029
Fresh breads and cakes in eastern North Carolina.
President/CEO, Flowers Foods: Allen Shiver
Year Founded: 2000
Estimated Sales: $100-500 Million
Number Employees: 250-499
Parent Co: Flowers Foods
Type of Packaging: Consumer
Brands:
Sunbeam
Nature's Own
Cobblestone Mill
Bluebird
Mi Casa

4663 **Franklin Baking Company**
2004 N Queen Street
Kinston, NC 28501-1621
252-527-1155
Fax: 252-527-9871 800-248-7494
Bakery items
President: Eugene Franklin
Production: Randy Brock
Estimated Sales: $10-24.9,000,000
Number Employees: 100-249

4664 **Franklin Farms**
222 New Road
Parsippany, NJ 07054
www.franklinfarms.com
Veggie burgers, edamame and veggie breakfast foods
President: Wilhelm Meya
Estimated Sales: $100+ Million
Number Employees: 600
Square Footage: 400000
Brands:
Veggiballs
Veggiburger
Veggidogs
Vegginuggets

4665 **Franklin Foods**
68 East St
P.O. Box 486
Enosburg Falls, VT 05450
802-933-4338
Fax: 802-933-4039 800-933-6114
info@franklinfoods.com www.franklinfoods.com
Yogurt and cream cheese
VP of Marketing: Rocco Cardinale
Estimated Sales: $25-49.9 Million
Number Employees: 100-249
Number of Brands: 4
Square Footage: 43000
Type of Packaging: Consumer, Food Service, Private Label, Bulk
Brands:
All Season's Kitchen

Green Mountain Farms
Hahn's
Lombardi's Italian Classics

4666 **Franklin Hill Vineyards**
7833 Franklin Hill Rd
Bangor, PA 18013-4039
610-588-8708
Fax: 610-588-8158 888-887-2839
franklinhill@enter.net
www.franklinhillvineyards.com
Wines
Owner: Elaine Pivinski
elaine@franklinhillvineyards.com
Estimated Sales: $2.5-5,000,000
Number Employees: 10-19
Type of Packaging: Private Label

4667 **Franklin's Cheese**
PO Box 8
Los Banos, CA 93635
209-826-6259
Fax: 209-826-8781 franklinsteleme@gmail.com
franklinscheesedotcom.wordpress.com
Rice flour coated Teleme cheese.
President: Franklin Peluso
Year Founded: 1980
Estimated Sales: $20-50 Million
Number Employees: 20-49

4668 **Frankly Natural Bakers**
7740 Formula Pl
San Diego, CA 92121-2419
858-536-5910
Fax: 858-536-5911 800-727-7229
info@franklynatural.com www.franklynatural.com
Brownies, cookies, energy bars, etc
Owner: Jerry Sarnow
jerry@franklynatural.com
Estimated Sales: $3-5 Million
Number Employees: 10-19
Number of Brands: 3
Number of Products: 26
Square Footage: 20000
Type of Packaging: Consumer, Private Label, Bulk
Brands:
98% Fat-Free
Amazingly Tasty
Beach
Coast
Frankly Natural3
Frankly Organic
Rice Crunchies
Vegan Decadence

4669 **Franz Bakery Outlet Store**
340 NE 11th St
Portland, OR 97293
503-232-2191
www.franzbakery.com
Bakery products.
President & CEO: Bob Albers
CFO: Jerry Boness
VP, Human Resources: Forrest Clayton
Corporate Controller: Keith VanEmmerik
VP, National Sales: Kim Nisbet
Product Wrapper: Sonja Abel
Year Founded: 1906
Estimated Sales: $100-500 Million
Number Employees: 1,000-4,999

4670 **Franzia Winery**
17000 E State Highway 120
Ripon, CA 95366
209-599-4111
Fax: 209-599-5892 info@franzia.com
www.franzia.com
Wines
CEO: Fred Franzia
CFO: Jim Page
General Manager: Dan Leonard
Sales Executive: Steve Hughs
Head of Operations: Jim Carter
Manufacturing Executive: Lou Dambrosio
Purchasing Executive: Beth Kirkpatrick
Number Employees: 20
Square Footage: 6174
Type of Packaging: Consumer, Food Service, Private Label
Brands:
Franzia

4671 **Fratelli Beretta USA**
750 Clark Dr
Mount Olive, NJ 07828
201-438-0723
info@fratelliberettausa.com
www.fratelliberettausa.com
Italian and Spanish meat specialties
President: Lorenzo Beretta
Contact: Simone Bocchina
s.bocchina@fratelliberettausa.com
Estimated Sales: $5-10 Million
Number Employees: 20-49

4672 **Fratelli Mantova**
2608 Flagstone Circle
Naperville, IL 60564
630-904-0002
Fax: 630-904-0003 info@fineitalianfood.com
www.fineitalianfood.com
Italian foods, including oils, vinegar, pasta, condiments and espresso
Year Founded: 1905

4673 **Fratelli Perata**
1595 Arbor Rd
Paso Robles, CA 93446-9669
805-238-2809
Fax: 805-238-2809 carol@fratelliperata.com
www.fratelliperata.com
Wines
Owner: Liao Hsinchao
philliao@alum.mit.edu
Estimated Sales: Under $500,000
Number Employees: 1-4

4674 **Fratello Coffee Roasters**
4021 9th Street SE
Calgary, AB T2G 3C7
Canada
403-265-2112
Fax: 403-263-3255 800-465-7227
info@fratellocoffee.com www.fratellocoffee.com
Gourmet coffee
President: Henry Kutarna
VP: Jason Prefontaine
Marketing Director: David Selley
Number Employees: 20-49
Type of Packaging: Consumer, Food Service
Brands:
Fratello

4675 **Frazier Nut Farms Inc**
10830 Yosemite Blvd
Waterford, CA 95386-9637
209-522-1406
Fax: 209-874-9638 fraznut@aol.com
www.fraziernut.com
Manufacturer and exporter of nuts including shelled and in-shell English walnuts and shelled almonds
President: Jim Frazier
jfrazier@fraziernut.com
VP: Steve Slacks
Estimated Sales: $2.5-5 Million
Number Employees: 100-249
Type of Packaging: Bulk
Brands:
Frazier's Finest

4676 **Fred Usinger Inc**
1030 N Old World 3rd St
Milwaukee, WI 53203-1300
414-276-9100
Fax: 414-291-5277 800-558-9998
info@usinger.com www.usinger.com
Sausages
President: Fritz Usinger
Vice President: Debra Usinger
VP Marketing/Sales: John Gabe
Estimated Sales: $20-50 Million
Number Employees: 100-249
Brands:
Sausage a La Carte

4677 **Frederick Wildman & Sons LTD**
307 E 53rd St # 3
New York, NY 10022-4985
212-355-0700
Fax: 212-355-4719 800-733-9463
info@frederickwildman.com
www.frederickwildman.com
Manufacturer, importer and distributor of fine wines.
President: John Sellar
CEO: Davide Mascalzoni
d.mascalzoni@frederickwildman.com
VP, Finance: James DiCicco
VP/Director, Marketing: Martin Sinkoff
VP/National Sales Manager: Bill Seawright
Assistant VP/Director, Public Relations: Odila Galer-Noel
Year Founded: 1934
Estimated Sales: $20-50 Million
Number Employees: 100-249
Number of Brands: 26
Type of Packaging: Consumer, Food Service
Brands:
Kanonkop
Pol Roger
Chateau Fuisse
Domaine Armand Rousseau
Hugo Et Fils
Marc Roman
Olivier Leflaive
Pascal Jolivet
Potel Aviron
Egon Muller
Weingut Wittman
Grooner
Astica
Michel Torino
Ca Bianca
Ca Donini
Castello Monachi
Lamberti
Churchills Ports
Baron De Ley
El Coto De Rioja
Maximo
Museum
Cartreuse Liqueur
Edinburgh Gin
Illegal Mezcal

4678 **Fredericksburg Herb Farm**
405 Whitney St
Fredericksburg, TX 78624-3785
830-997-8615
Fax: 830-997-5069 800-259-4372
information@fredericksburgherbfarm.com
www.fredericksburgherbfarm.com
Gourmet herbs and vinegars
President: Bill Varney
info@fredericksburgherbfarm.com
Estimated Sales: $1-2.5 Million
Number Employees: 20-49

4679 **Free2b Foods**
6880 Winchester Circle
Unit E
Boulder, CO 80301
hey@free2bfoods.com
free2bfoods.com
Allergen-free snacks
Type of Packaging: Consumer
Brands:
free2b

4680 **FreeYumm**
54 E 69th Ave
Vancouver, BC V5X 4R2
Canada
info@freeyumm.com
www.freeyumm.com
Allergen- and gluten-free snacks
President/Owner: Sarah Clarke
Number of Brands: 1
Number of Products: 8
Type of Packaging: Consumer
Brands:
FREEYUMM

4681 **Freed, Teller & Freed**
436 N Canal Street
Suite 2
South San Francisco, CA 94080-4668
650-589-8500
Fax: 650-589-0711 800-370-7371
Tea, coffee, preserves, condiments and sugars
President: A J Techeira Jr.
Estimated Sales: $570,000
Number Employees: 7
Number of Brands: 10
Number of Products: 275
Type of Packaging: Consumer, Private Label, Bulk
Brands:
Dependable

Freed's
Freed, Teller & Fredd

4682 **Freeda Vitamins Inc**
4725 34th St # 301
Long Island City, NY 11101-2436
718-433-4337
Fax: 212-685-7297 800-777-3737
info@freedavitamins.com
www.freedavitamins.com
Manufacturer and exporter of kosher yeast-free vitamins and supplements including garlic. Our products are also gluten free, dairy free, and free of artificial colors & flavors.
President/CEO: Eliyahu Zimmerman
Estimated Sales: $2.5 Million
Number Employees: 20-49
Number of Brands: 1
Number of Products: 200
Square Footage: 9150
Type of Packaging: Consumer
Brands:
Freeda

4683 **Freedman's Bakery**
803 Main St
Belmar, NJ 07719
732-681-2334
Fax: 732-681-1269
Bakery items
President: Herb Freedman
Contact: Herbert Freedman
herb@apex-equip.com
Estimated Sales: $500,000-$1,000,000
Number Employees: 100-249

4684 **Freedom Foods LLC**
300 Beanville Rd
Randolph, VM 05060
802-728-0070
info@freedom-foods.com
freedom-foods.com
Baked goods; baking mixes and ingredients; soft drinks; snacks; and condiments
President: Eric Woller
Compliance Coordinator: Tara Matthews
Estimated Sales: $2.5-5 Million
Number Employees: 30
Type of Packaging: Private Label

4685 **Freekehlicious**
P.O. Box 103
Norwood, NJ 07628
201-297-7957
Fax: 201-322-3127 info@freekehlicious.com
freekehlicious.com
Granola; cereal; and pasta
CEO: Barbara Fanelli
Year Founded: 2010
Type of Packaging: Food Service, Private Label

4686 **Freeland Bean & Grain Inc**
1000 E Washington
PO Box 515
Freeland, MI 48623-8439
989-695-9131
Fax: 989-695-5241 800-447-9131
freeland.i@att.net www.freelandbeanandgrain.com
Manufacturer and exporter of dried beans and grains
Owner: John Hupfer
freeland.i@att.net
VP: Elenor Hupfer
Estimated Sales: $3.8 Million
Number Employees: 5-9
Type of Packaging: Bulk

4687 **Freeman Industries**
100 Marbledale Rd
Tuckahoe, NY 10707
914-961-2100
Fax: 914-961-5793 800-666-6454
freeman@lanline.com www.freemanllc.com
Dairy vitamin concentrates and zein. Importer and exporter of dried fruits and vegetables, pectin, herbal extracts and natural colors. Processor of citrus bioflavonoids and rice bran and rice bran derivates
President/CEO: Joel G Freeman
VP: Paul Freeman
Contact: Joel Freeman
joelfreeman@freemanb2b.com
Estimated Sales: $1-3 Million
Number Employees: 10-19
Square Footage: 10000
Type of Packaging: Bulk

Brands:
A/D/F
D' Sol

4688 **Freemark Abbey Winery**
3022 Saint Helena Hwy N # 5
St Helena, CA 94574-9652
707-963-9698
Fax: 707-963-7633 800-963-9698
info@freemarkabbey.com
www.freemarkabbey.com
Manufacturer and exporter of wines including cabernet sauvignon, chardonnay and johannisberg riesling
Director of Winemaking: Ted Edwards
wineinfo@freemarkabbey.com
Estimated Sales: $5-9.9 Million
Number Employees: 20-49
Type of Packaging: Food Service
Brands:
Freemark Abbey

4689 **Freestone Pickle Co**
610 N Center St
Bangor, MI 49013-1434
269-427-7702
Fax: 269-427-5542 877-874-2553
info@freestonepickles.com
www.freestonepickles.com
Pickles, relish and pickled peppers and cauliflower
Owner: Mike Hescott
info@freestonepickles.com
Estimated Sales: $10-20,000,000
Number Employees: 20-49
Type of Packaging: Consumer, Food Service, Private Label, Bulk
Brands:
Freestone
Holiday Royal
Partetime

4690 **Freeze-Dry Foods Inc**
111 West Ave # 4
Albion, NY 14411-1500
585-589-6399
Fax: 585-589-6402 info@freeze-dry.com
www.freeze-dry.com
Freeze dried ingredients specializing in meat, seafood and protein items
President: Karen Richardson
krichardson@freeze-dry.com
Business Development: Lisa Horvath
Estimated Sales: $4.5 Million
Number Employees: 20-49
Type of Packaging: Consumer

4691 **Freeze-Dry Ingredients**
188 W Industrial Dr
Suite 200
Elmhurst, IL 60126
630-530-1880
info@fdiusa.net
www.fdiusa.net
Freeze-dried ingredients

4692 **Freirich Foods**
P.O. Box 1529
Salisbury, NC 28145
800-221-1315
www.freirich.com
Marinated beef and pork, corned beef, roast beef, pastrami, rib roasts, pot roasts, beef sirloin and beef ribs.
President & CEO: Paul Bardinas
CFO & VP of Finance: Doug Sokolowski
VP of Sales & Marketing: Phil Percoco
COO & VP of Operations: Dennis Arrasmith
Estimated Sales: $25 Million
Number Employees: 50-99
Number of Brands: 2
Square Footage: 35000
Type of Packaging: Consumer, Food Service
Brands:
Freirich Porkette®
Regal Chef

4693 **(HQ)Freixenet USA Inc**
967 Broadway
Sonoma, CA 95476-7403
707-996-4981
Fax: 707-996-0720 info@freixenetusa.com
www.gloriaferrer.com
Manufacturer and importer of Spanish champagnes and wines; also, processor of California wines
President: Robert Abel
robert.abel@freixenetusa.com
Number Employees: 50-99
Parent Co: Freixenet SA
Type of Packaging: Consumer
Brands:
Castellblanch
Freixenet Spanish Wines
Freixenet Wines
Gloria Ferrer
Henri Abele
Rene Barbier
Segura Viudas

4694 **Fremont Authentic Brands**
802 N Front St
Fremont, OH 43420-1917
419-334-8995
Fax: 419-334-8120 info@fremontcompany.com
www.fremontfoodservice.com
Tomatoes, sauerkraut, salsa and barbecue sauces.
Logistics Manager: Pam Hufford
Year Founded: 1905
Estimated Sales: $28 Million
Number Employees: 250-499
Square Footage: 250000
Type of Packaging: Consumer, Food Service, Private Label
Brands:
Paisley Farm
Frank's Kraut

4695 **Fremont Beef Co**
960 Schneider St
Fremont, NE 68025-6134
402-727-7200
Fax: 402-727-0907 800-331-4788
www.fremontbeef.com
Beef tongue, outside skirts, calf and cow livers
President: Les Leech
Vice President: Jim Pomrenke
Director, Marketing and Sales: Laun Hinkle
Year Founded: 1990
Estimated Sales: $20-50 Million
Number Employees: 100-249

4696 **French & Brawn Marketplace**
1 Elm St
Camden, ME 04843-1902
207-236-3361
Fax: 207-236-4880 todd@frenchandbrawn.com
www.frenchandbrawn.com
Choice meats, lobsters, soups and sandwiches
Owner: Todd Anderson
todd@frenchandbrawn.com
Estimated Sales: $5-10 Million
Number Employees: 20-49

4697 **French Creek Seafood**
1097 Lee Road
Parksville, BC V9P 2E1
Canada
250-248-7100
Fax: 250-248-7197 mail@frenchcreek.ca
www.frenchcreek.ca
Manufacturer and exporter of fresh and frozen seafood
President: Brad McLean
President: Brad McLean
Estimated Sales: $6,000,000
Number Employees: 15
Type of Packaging: Bulk

4698 **French Feast Inc.**
473 S Dean St
Englewood, NJ 07631
201-731-3102
Fax: 201-208-2923
Honey; gingerbread; baking mixes and ingredients; mustard; vinegar; hot chocolate powder; minds; confections; juice; snacks; jams and spreads; olives; salt;
Co-Owner: Phyllis Brooks
Year Founded: 1999
Estimated Sales: $423,431
Number Employees: 5
Number of Products: +700
Type of Packaging: Food Service, Private Label

4699 **French Gourmet Inc**
245 Coney Island Dr
Sparks, NV 89431-6303
775-525-2525
Fax: 775-525-2530 linda@frenchgourmet.com
www.frenchgourmet.com
Frozen dough, croissants, danish, puff pastry, breads, and muffin, cookie batters
Manager: Linda Coffman
lcoffman@frenchgourmet.com
Estimated Sales: $10-49,999,999
Number Employees: 5-9
Number of Brands: 2
Number of Products: 57
Square Footage: 50000
Type of Packaging: Food Service, Private Label, Bulk
Brands:
French Gourmet
Smart Gourmet

4700 **French Market Coffee**
640 Magazine Street
New Orleans, LA 70130
504-581-7234
Fax: 504-539-5427 800-535-1961
service@reilyproducts.com
www.frenchmarketcoffee.com
Manufacturer and packer of coffee
President: Fraser Bartlett
Year Founded: 1890
Estimated Sales: $2.5-5 Million
Number Employees: 20-49
Parent Co: Reily Foods Company
Type of Packaging: Consumer
Brands:
French Market

4701 **French Market Foods**
3935 Ryan St
Lake Charles, LA 70605-2817
337-477-9296
www.bigeasyfoods.com
Shrimp, frozen and fresh
President/CEO: Larry Avery
lavery@fmfoods.com
Estimated Sales: $5-9.9 Million
Number Employees: 50-99

4702 **French Meadow Bakery & Cafe**
2610 Lyndale Ave S
Minneapolis, MN 55408-1321
612-870-7855
Fax: 612-870-1196 www.frenchmeadowcafe.com
Organic and all-natural products including yeast-free, vegan, sprouted grain, gluten-free and Kosher Parve options.
Owner: Steve Shapiro
steve@frenchmeadowcafe.com
Estimated Sales: $5-9.9 Million
Number Employees: 20-49
Number of Brands: 4
Number of Products: 32
Square Footage: 48000
Type of Packaging: Consumer, Food Service, Private Label, Bulk
Other Locations:
French Meadow Bakery
Auburn WA
Brands:
Healthseed
Healthy Hemp
Mens Bread
Womens Bread

4703 **French Patisserie**
1090 Palmetto Ave
Pacifica, CA 94044
650-738-4990
Fax: 650-738-4995 800-300-2253
gateau@frenchpatisserie.com
www.frenchpatisserie.com
Frozen cakes, tarts, and dessert sauces
President: Marta Spasic
Contact: Frank Spasic
frank@frenchpatisserie.com
Estimated Sales: $5-10 Million
Number Employees: 20-49

4704 **French Quarter Seafood**
2933 Paris Road
Chalmette, LA 70043-3346
504-277-1679
Fax: 504-277-1679
Seafood
Owner: Philippe Despointes

4705 **French's Coffee**
1400 Central Rd
Walnut Creek, CA 94596-3794
925-932-5901
Coffee
Owner: Chet Parker
Estimated Sales: Under $500,000
Number Employees: 1-4

4706 **French's Flavor Ingredients**
4455 E Mustard Way
Springfield, MO 65803
800-841-1256
Provider of flavors to meat and poulty processors in the food manufacturing industry.
Technical Services: Cindy Bernskoetter
Parent Co: Reckitt Benckiser LLC

4707 **Fresca Mexican Foods LLC**
11193 W Emerald St
Boise, ID 83713-8932
208-376-6922
Fax: 208-375-2330 www.frescamex.com
Flour, corn tortillas and flavored wraps
President: Mike Allen
mallen@frescamex.com
Vice President, Sales/Marketing: Tom Nist
International Sales Manager: Keith Snyder
Estimated Sales: $25,600,000
Number Employees: 100-249
Number of Brands: 1
Number of Products: 60
Type of Packaging: Food Service, Private Label

4708 **Fresh Bellies**
PO Box 224
White Plains, NY 10605
866-888-0467
info@freshbellies.com freshbellies.com
Organic baby food
President/Owner: Saskia Sorrosa
Number of Brands: 1
Number of Products: 7
Type of Packaging: Consumer
Brands:
FRESH BELLIES

4709 **Fresh Express, Inc.**
P.O. Box 80599
Salinas, CA 93912
800-242-5472
www.freshexpress.com
Certified organic salads and lettuce, cole slaw & shreds, delicious kits, flavorful spinach, gourmet cafe salads, harvest originals, refreshing mixes, tasty greens mixes, and tender leaf mixes.
President: John Olivo
CEO: Kenneth Diveley
Year Founded: 1926
Estimated Sales: $368.3 Million
Number Employees: 5,000+
Square Footage: 20000
Parent Co: Chiquita Brands International, Inc
Type of Packaging: Bulk
Brands:
Fresh Express

4710 **Fresh Frozen Foods**
1814 Washington St
PO Box 215
Jefferson, GA 30549-2668
706-367-9851
Fax: 706-367-4646 800-277-9851
wecare@freshfrozenfoods.com
Strawberries, southern peas and beans, carrots, squash, zucchini, green beans, onions, potatoes, turnip roots.
President: Billy Griffin Jr
Year Founded: 1975
Estimated Sales: $40 Million
Number Employees: 50-99
Square Footage: 5600

4711 **Fresh Hemp Foods**
15.2166 Notre Dame Avenue
Winnipeg, NB R3H 0K1
Canada
800-665-4367
Fax: 204-956-5984
Hemp food products
President/CEO: Mike Fata
Type of Packaging: Bulk

4712 **Fresh Ideas**
8350 S Durango Dr
Suite 201
Las Vegas, NV 89113-4473
702-701-4272
freshideallc.com
Popcorn, side dishes and seasonings
Number of Brands: 1
Number of Products: 11
Type of Packaging: Consumer
Brands:
FRESH IDEAS

4713 **Fresh Island Fish**
312 Alamaha St
Unit G
Kahului, HI 96732-2430
808-871-1111
Fax: 808-871-6818 www.freshislandfish.com
Seafood
President: Mike Lee
Owner/Founder/C.E.O: Bruce Johnson
fif@maui.net
Estimated Sales: $10-20 Million
Number Employees: 50-99

4714 **Fresh Juice Delivery**
269 S Beverly Dr
Suite 1072
Beverly Hills, CA 90212-3851
310-271-7373
Manufacturer and exporter of fresh and fresh-frozen juices including citrus and blended
Estimated Sales: Less Than $500,000
Number Employees: 5-9
Parent Co: Saratoga Beverage
Type of Packaging: Consumer, Food Service
Brands:
Florida Pik't
Fresh Pik't
Just Pik't

4715 **Fresh Mark Inc.**
1888 Southway St. SW
Massillon, OH 44646
330-832-7491
Fax: 330-830-3174 www.freshmark.com
Bacon, ham, weiners, deli and luncheon meats, dry sausage and other specialty meat items.
CEO: Neil Genshaft
ngenshaft@freshmark.com
Year Founded: 1920
Estimated Sales: $219 Million
Number Employees: 500-999
Square Footage: 80000
Type of Packaging: Consumer, Food Service, Private Label
Brands:
Sugardale
Superior's Brand

4716 **Fresh Market Pasta Company**
43 Exchange Street
Portland, ME 04101-5009
207-773-7146
Fax: 207-871-7156
Pasta, noodles of all kinds, including ginger and squid's ink
President: Alex Gingrich
Estimated Sales: $500,000-$1,000,000
Number Employees: 10-19

4717 **Fresh Nature Foods**
8306 N Wall St
Spokane, WA 99208
509-368-7260
Fax: 509-290-6173 info@freshnaturefoods.com
freshnaturefoods.com
Green chickpeas, green hummus and veggie cakes
President/Owner: Ryan Davenport
VP, Food Service Sales: Brad Overberg
Number of Brands: 1
Number of Products: 7
Type of Packaging: Consumer, Food Service
Brands:
FRESH NATURE

4718 **Fresh Origins**
570 Quarry Rd
San Marcos, CA 92069-9744
760-736-4072
www.freshorigins.com

Manufacturer of microgreens.
Co-Founder: David Sasuga
Co-Founder: Kelly Sasuga
Contact: Philip Bosman
philip@freshorigins.com
Number Employees: 1-4
Brands:
MicroGreens
Micro Basil Nutmeg
Micro Cucumber
Micro Mustard Dijon
Micro Radish Ruby
Micro Tangerine Lace
Micro Wasabi
Micro Mint Lime
Petite Green Mixes
Herb Crystals
Flower Crystals
Fruit Crystals
Mini Herb Crystals
Mini Flower Crystals

4719 **Fresh Pack Seafood**
PO Box 1008
Waldoboro, ME 04572-1008
207-832-7720
Fax: 207-832-7795
Fresh seafood
President: Frank Minio
VP/General Manager: Roger Greene

4720 **Fresh Pasta Delights**
901 W Parker Rd # 135
Plano, TX 75023-7128
972-422-5907
Fax: 972-869-9937
Pasta and sauces
Owner: Jack Rayome
Director Research: Ray Etheridge
Estimated Sales: $5-9.9 000,000
Number Employees: 5-9
Square Footage: 12000
Type of Packaging: Consumer, Food Service, Private Label, Bulk

4721 **Fresh Roasted Almond Company**
24536 Gibson
Warren, MI 48089
586-619-2400
877-478-6887
warrenproduction@freshroastedalmondco.com
www.freshroastedalmondco.com
Dry roasted, sweetened and flavored kosher nut confections including almonds, pecans, cashews, peanuts and walnuts flavored in cinnamon, honey, maple, vanilla, cherry and spices
Owner: Dan Levy
Contact: Lin Bahni
freshroastedalmondco@freshroastedalmondco.com
Estimated Sales: $1-3 Million
Number Employees: 10-19
Square Footage: 9000
Type of Packaging: Consumer, Private Label, Bulk
Brands:
Kars
Ritter

4722 **Fresh Samantha**
84 Industrial Park Road
Saco, ME 04072-1840
207-284-0011
Fax: 207-284-8331 800-658-4635
Fresh juice
CEO: Doug Levin
Estimated Sales: Less than $500,000
Number Employees: 1-4
Type of Packaging: Consumer
Brands:
Fresh Samantha

4723 **Fresh Seafood Distrib**
9910 Milton Jones Rd
Daphne, AL 36526-6143
251-626-1106
Fax: 251-626-1109
Seafood
Co-Owner: Steve Miller
Estimated Sales: $3-5 Million
Number Employees: 5-9

4724 **Fresh Start Bakeries**
145 S. State College Blvd.
Suite 200
Brea, CA 92821-5806
714-256-8900
Fax: 714-256-8916
Baked goods including hamburger buns and English muffins.
CEO: Russ Doll
info@freshstartbakeries.com
Year Founded: 1962
Estimated Sales: $118 Million
Number Employees: 100-249
Square Footage: 180000
Parent Co: FSB Global Holdings, Inc.
Type of Packaging: Food Service

4725 **Fresh Tofu Inc**
1101 Harrison St
Allentown, PA 18103-3132
610-433-4711
Fax: 610-433-5611 info@freshtofu.com
www.freshtofu.com
Organic tofu and other soyfood products.
Owner/President: Gary Abramowitz
info@freshtofu.com
Estimated Sales: $2 Million
Number Employees: 20-49
Square Footage: 18000

4726 **Freshwater Farms Of Ohio**
2624 N US Highway 68
Urbana, OH 43078-9537
937-652-3701
Fax: 937-652-3481 800-634-7434
www.fwfarms.com
Visit our retail store to take home fresh rainbow trout fillets, smoked fillets, marinated fillets, seasoned trout patties, smoked trout spreads and a selection of Ohio foods. We also carry pond supplies and stocking fish, locally-madepottery and garden d,cor. Visit our sturgeon petting zoo, tour Ohio's largest indoor hatchery, & feed our trout by hand. We're open year round!
Owner/President: Dave Smith
drdaveffo@aol.com
Estimated Sales: Less Than $500,000
Number Employees: 5-9

4727 **Freshwater Fish Market**
1199 Plessis Road
Winnipeg, MB R2C 3L4
Canada
780-413-5370
Fax: 780-495-5384 800-345-3113
edmonton@freshwaterfish.com
www.freshwaterfish.com
Freshwater fish, whitefish and northern pike
President: Tom Dunn
Sales Manager: Doug Clayton
Human Resources: Wendy Matheson
Plant Manager: Dragon Vuksa
Type of Packaging: Consumer, Food Service

4728 **Frey Vineyards**
14000 Tomki Rd
Redwood Valley, CA 95470-6135
707-485-5177
Fax: 707-485-7875 800-760-3739
info@freywine.com www.freywine.com
Producer of organic wine with no sulfites added. They specialize in Organic Wine, Biodynamic Wine, No Sulfites Added Wine, and GMO Free Wine.
President: Paul Frey
CEO: Katrina Frey
cathie@freywine.com
Vice President, Sales: Jon Frey
Estimated Sales: $5-10,000,000
Number Employees: 10-19
Type of Packaging: Consumer

4729 **Freybe Gourmet Foods Ltd**
9525-201 St
Suite 203
Langley, BC V1M 4A5
Canada
604-607-7426
Fax: 604-607-7461 800-879-3739
to_freybe@freybe.com www.freybe.com
Manufacturers of sausages including bacon, deli meats, liver sausage & pate, all natural, dry cured, salami, smokies, weiners, and snack foods.
President & CEO: Sven Freybe
Director, Office Services: Karen Hunt
VP, Operations: Angela Doro
Year Founded: 1844
Estimated Sales: $57.52 Million
Number Employees: 350
Square Footage: 110255
Type of Packaging: Consumer, Food Service, Bulk

4730 **Frick Winery**
23072 Walling Rd
Geyserville, CA 95441-9548
707-857-1980
Fax: 707-857-1980 Frick@frickwinery.com
www.frickwinestore.com
Winery; Alcoholic beverages
Owner: Bill Frick
b.frick@frickwinery.com
Estimated Sales: Less Than $500,000
Number Employees: 1-4

4731 **Frick's Quality Meats**
360 M E Frick Dr
Washington, MO 63090-1050
636-239-2200
Fax: 636-239-7003 800-241-2209
www.frickmeats.com
Cured and smoked meats including sausage and ham
President: David Frick
Owner: Cindy Frick
cfrick@frickmeats.com
Marketing: Tom Schmiederer
Sales Director: David King
Operations Executive: Rob Rousch
Estimated Sales: $10-20 Million
Number Employees: 100-249

4732 **Fried Provisions Company**
141 N Washington St Apartment 1
Evans City, PA 16033-2001
724-538-3160
Fax: 724-538-3262
Cheese, luncheon meats, chopped ham, poultry and sausage
President: James Deily
Sales Manager: Tim Deily
Estimated Sales: $1.40 Million
Number Employees: 5
Parent Co: Fort Pitt Brand Meats
Type of Packaging: Consumer, Food Service, Private Label, Bulk
Brands:
Fort Pitt
Harmony

4733 **Frieda's Inc**
4465 Corporate Center Dr
Los Alamitos, CA 90720-2561
714-826-6100
Fax: 714-816-0277 mail@friedas.com
Exotic fruits and vegetables
President: Ann Hawkins
Chief Executive Officer: Karen Caplan
karenc@friedas.com
Vice President: Jackie Caplan
Regional Sales Manager: Dina Boyce
Chief Operating Officer: Jackie Wiggins
Purchasing Manager: Gloria Cardenas
Estimated Sales: $30,000,000
Number Employees: 100-249

4734 **Friendship Dairies LLC**
6701 County Rd 20
Friendship, NY 14739
585-973-3031
800-854-3243
www.friendshipdairies.com
Dairy products including cottage cheese and whey and whey powders including acid and neutralized; also, calcium lactate powder and sodium lactate
Director of Quality Control: Karen Martin
Director of Marketing: Paige Pistone
Vice President of Sales: Paul Dussault
Year Founded: 1917
Estimated Sales: $60 Million
Number Employees: 100-249
Square Footage: 15000
Parent Co: Saputo Dairy Foods USA, LLC
Type of Packaging: Consumer, Food Service

4735 Friendship International
21 Merrill Drive
Rockland, ME 04841-2142
207-594-1111
Fax: 207-236-6103
Manufacturer and exporter of live sea urchins
President: Jim Wadsworth
Contact: Rino Safrizal
safrizal@friends-international.org

4736 FrieslandCampina Ingredients North America, Inc.
61 S Paramus Rd
Suite 535
Paramus, NJ 07652
551-497-7300
www.frieslandcampina.com
Food additives including hydrolized proteins, bioactive peptides and protein fractions.
CEO: Rudy Dieperink
Inside Sales & Marketing: Rae Anne Popjes
Estimated Sales: $17.5 Million
Number Employees: 74
Number of Brands: 11
Parent Co: Royal FrieslandCampina
Other Locations:
DFE Pharma
Paramus NJ
FrieslandCampina Creamy Creation US
Paramus NJ
FrieslandCampina Ingredients Plant
Delhi NY
Brands:
Aerion
Esprion
Glutamine
Lactoperoxidase
Lactoval
Peptide Fm
Pharmatose
Primellose
Primojel
Respitose
Textrion

4737 Frio Foods
8600 Wurzbach Road
Suite 500
San Antonio, TX 78240-4331
210-278-4525
Fax: 210-278-1094
Processes frozen foods
President: Ron Trine
Brands:
Frio

4738 Frisco Baking Co Inc
621 W Avenue 26
Los Angeles, CA 90065-1095
323-225-6111
Fax: 323-225-3554
Sourdough products including par-baked dinner rolls and loaves, full baked rounds and baguettes, double baked loaf, french bread dinner rolls, loaves, party sandwiches, Italian twists and a variety of sandwich rolls from 4-12inches.
Owner: Damon Perata
Owner: Ronald Perata
Sales Manager: Rick Vanzutphen
Estimated Sales: $16.3 Million
Number Employees: 20-49

4739 Frisinger Cellars
2275 Dry Creek Rd
Napa, CA 94558
707-255-3749
Fax: 707-963-7867
Wines
President: Raymond Reyes
Contact: Jim Frisinger
jfrisinger@frisinger.net
Estimated Sales: Under $500,000
Number Employees: 1-4
Parent Co: Consolation Brand

4740 Frisson Normand
2200 Fletcher Avenue
3rd Floor
Fort Lee, NJ 07024
201-585-2179
Fax: 201-585-8575
Fruits
Marketing: Nicolas Lecuqu

4741 Frito-Lay Inc.
7701 Legacy Dr.
Plano, TX 75024-4099
800-352-4477
www.fritolay.com
Corn chips, potato chips, and other snack foods.
CEO, PepsiCo Foods North America: Steven Williams
Senior VP/CFO: Jamie Caulfield
Senior VP/General Counsel: Leanne Oliver
Senior VP/Foods & Global R&D: Denise Lefebvre
Senior VP/Chief Marketing Officer: Rachel Ferdinando
Senior VP, Sales: John Dean
Senior VP/Chief Customer Officer: Mike Del Pozzo
Estimated Sales: $15.79 Billion
Number Employees: 10000+
Number of Brands: 28
Parent Co: PepsiCo
Type of Packaging: Consumer, Food Service
Brands:
Lay's
Doritos
Cheetos
Tostitos
Ruffles
Fritos
Sun Chips
Stacy's
Smartfood
Rold Gold
Top N Go
Simply
Frito-Lay2GO
Cracker Jack
Baken-ets
Chester's
Funyun's
Grandma's
Matador
Miss Vickie's
Munchies
Munchos
Sabritones
Santitas
Maui Style
El Isleno

4742 Froehlich Alex Packing Co
77 D Street Ext
Johnstown, PA 15906-2908
814-535-7694
Fax: 814-535-7695
Livestock processor
President: David Froehlich
Estimated Sales: $5-10 Million
Number Employees: 10-19
Type of Packaging: Bulk
Other Locations:
Alex Froelich Packing Company
Johnstown PA

4743 Frog City Cheese
PO Box 94
106 Messer Hill Road
Plymouth Notch, VT 5056
802-672-3650
Fax: 802-672-1629
Granular curd (whole milk) cheese
Co-Owner: Jackie McCuin
Co-Owner: Tom Gilbert
Estimated Sales: $3-5 Million
Number Employees: 10-19
Type of Packaging: Consumer

4744 Frog Ranch Foods
5 S High St
Glouster, OH 45732-1051
740-767-3705
Fax: 740-767-3944 800-742-2488
info@frogranch.com www.frogranch.com
Traditional style salsas, pickles, peppers, tortilla chips
Owner: Craig Cornett
craig@frogranch.com
Estimated Sales: $2.5-5,000,000
Number Employees: 10-19
Type of Packaging: Private Label

4745 Frog's Leap Winery
8815 Conn Creek Rd
Rutherford, CA 94573
707-963-4704
Fax: 707-963-0242 800-959-4704
ribbit@frogsleap.com www.frogsleap.com
Producer of wines such as Cabernet Sauvignon, Sauvignon Blanc, Chardonnay, Zinfandel, Merlot, Petite Sirah, Heritage Blend and Pink.
Owner & Winemaker: John Williams
Chief Financial Officer: Doug Demerritt
Social Media & Marketing Manager: Natalie Barnard
Sales Manager: Michelle Watkins
Hospitality Director: Jami Castro
Vice President, Vineyard Operations: Frank Leeds
General Manager: Jonah Beer
Estimated Sales: $5-10,000,000
Number Employees: 20-49
Brands:
Cabernet Sauvignon
Chardonnay
Merlot
Sauvignon Blanc
Zinfandel

4746 From Oregon
2787 Olympic Street
Suite 4
Springfield, OR 97477-7809
541-747-4222
Fax: 541-747-5456
Jams, marmalades and berries
President: Bonnie Koenig
Estimated Sales: $1-4.9,000,000
Number Employees: 1-4

4747 From the Ground Up
Fairfield, NJ 07004
www.fromthegroundupsnacks.com
Cauliflower-based pretzels and crackers

4748 Froma-Dar
378 rue Principale
St. Boniface, QC G0X 2L0
Canada
819-535-3946
Fax: 819-535-7010
Dairy products including cheddar, curd and partly skim cheeses
President: Michel Veillette
Number Employees: 50-99
Square Footage: 40000
Type of Packaging: Consumer, Food Service, Private Label, Bulk
Brands:
Des Coteaux
Froma-Dar
Juneau

4749 (HQ)Front Range Snacks Inc
6547 S Racine Cir # 1800
Centennial, CO 80111-6463
303-744-8850
Fax: 303-389-6859
Processor and exporter of ready-to-eat popcorn
Owner: Tim Bradley
tim@openroadsnacks.com
Estimated Sales: Less Than $500,000
Number Employees: 1-4
Number of Brands: 1
Number of Products: 10
Square Footage: 80000
Type of Packaging: Consumer, Food Service, Private Label, Bulk
Brands:
Rocky Mountain Popcorn

4750 Frontenac Point Vineyard
9501 State Route 89
Trumansburg, NY 14886-9211
607-387-9619
contactus@frontenacpoint.com
www.frontenacpoint.com
wines. Varieties include Pinot Noir, Chambourcin, Frontenac Red, Chardonnay, Riesling and more.
Co-Owner: Jim Doolittle
Co-Owner: Carol Doolittle
Assistant Manager: Lawrence Doolittle
Estimated Sales: Under $500,000
Number Employees: 1-4
Type of Packaging: Consumer, Food Service, Private Label, Bulk

4751 **Frontera Foods**
449 N Clark St
Chicago, IL 60654
312-595-1624
Fax: 312-595-1625 800-509-4441
info@fronterafoods.com
Producer of Mexican food. Products include tortilla chips, sauces, spices and salsas.
Owner: Manny Valdes
Founder, Owner & Chef: Rick Bayless
Director of Sales: Joseph Valdes
Culinary Director: Jean Marie Brownson
Estimated Sales: $5-10,000,000
Number Employees: 11-50
Type of Packaging: Food Service
Brands:
Frontera Foods
Salpica

4752 **Frontier Co-op**
P.O. Box 299
3021 78th St.
Norway, IA 52318-9520
319-227-7996
Fax: 800-717-4372 844-550-6200
customercare@frontiercoop.com
www.frontiercoop.com
Sustainably sourced and organic herbs, spices, seasonings, teas, sauces, mixes, dips, dressings, dried fruits and vegetables, indgredients, flavors and extracts.
CEO: Tony Bedard
VP Finance: Nicole Erickson
VP Technical Services: Ravin Donald
VP Marketing: Dave Karpick
SVP Business Development: Clint Landis
VP Human Resources: Megan Schulte
EVP Operations: Cole Daily
Year Founded: 1976
Estimated Sales: $100-499.9 Million
Number Employees: 100-249
Type of Packaging: Consumer, Private Label
Brands:
Frontier
Aura Cacia
Simply Organic

4753 **Frontier Soups**
895 Northpoint Blvd
Waukegan, IL 60085
847-688-1200
Fax: 847-688-1206 800-300-7867
info@frontiersoups.com www.frontiersoups.com
Dried soup and pasta salad mixes
President: Trisha Anderson
Contact: Jane Murphy
jane@frontiersoups.com
Production: Eva Pantoja
Estimated Sales: $2.5-5 Million
Number Employees: 10-19
Square Footage: 16000
Type of Packaging: Consumer
Brands:
Frontier
Hearty Originals
Homemade In Minutes
I'Ll Bring the Saladd
Illinois Prairie
Minnesota Heartland
New Line Homemade
Wisconsin Lakeshore

4754 **Froozer**
1127 Auraria Pkwy
Suite 17
Denver, CO 80204-1896
720-446-0145
hello@froozer.com
www.froozer.com
Frozen whole food fruit snacks
President/Owner: Rich Naha
CEO: Des Hague
Number of Brands: 1
Number of Products: 6
Type of Packaging: Consumer
Brands:
FROOZER

4755 **Frostproof Sunkist Groves**
7307 US Highway
27thNorth
Frostproof, FL 33843
863-635-4873
Fax: 863-635-3447 www.frostproofgroves.com
Citrus fruits and juices
Owner: John Stephens
Estimated Sales: $1-3,000,000
Number Employees: 1-4

4756 **Frozen Specialties Inc**
8600 S Wilkinson Way
Suite G
Perrysburg, OH 43551
419-867-2005
www.frozenspecialties.com
Private label pizza and pizza bites, a multi-line supplier
President & CEO: Rich Alvarez
rich.alvarez@frc.com
Controller: Paul Nungester
Director of Marketing: Lori Hamilton
Vice President, Sales: Dan Burdick
Year Founded: 1969
Estimated Sales: $49.99 Million
Number Employees: 10-19
Number of Brands: 1
Number of Products: 6
Square Footage: 13395
Type of Packaging: Consumer, Private Label, Bulk
Brands:
Mr. P'S

4757 **Frozfruit Corporation**
14805 S San Pedro Street
Gardena, CA 90248-2030
310-217-1034
Fax: 310-715-6943
Manufacturer and exporter of frozen ice cream novelties and fruit bars
President: Tom Guinan
Estimated Sales: $500,000-$1 Million
Number Employees: 5-9
Square Footage: 150000
Type of Packaging: Consumer, Food Service, Private Label, Bulk
Brands:
Frozfruit
Frozfruit All Natural Fruit Bars
Summer Naturals

4758 **Fru-V**
Stouffville, ON
Canada
info@fruvsmoothie.com
www.fruvsmoothie.com
Frozen smoothie blends
Year Founded: 2016
Parent Co: Health Addict Inc

4759 **Fruigees**
Los Angeles, CA 91423
fruigees.com
Organic fruit snack
CEO: David Czinn
COO: Josh Kahn
Number of Brands: 1
Number of Products: 3
Type of Packaging: Consumer
Brands:
FRUIGEES

4760 **Fruit Acres Farm Marketand U-Pick**
3390 Friday Rd
Coloma, MI 49038
269-208-3591
fruitacres@iserv.net
www.fruitacresfarms.com
230 acre fruit farm growing sweet cherries, apples, sweet corn and peaches. Also sells gourmet jams, jellies, honey, sauces, pickles and country gifts.
Co-Owner: Annette Bjorge
Co-Owner: Randy Bjorge
Estimated Sales: $5-10 Million
Number Employees: 10-19

4761 **Fruit Belt Canning Inc**
54168 60th Ave
P.O. Box 81
Lawrence, MI 49064-9525
269-674-3939
Fax: 269-674-8354 office@fruitbeltfoods.com
www.fruitbeltfoods.com
Manufacturer, wholesaler/distributor of fruits and vegetables such as; asparagus, red tart cherries and strawberries
President: David Frank
davf@fruitbeltfoods.com
Vice President: Warren Frank
Sales Manager: Jim Armstrong
Estimated Sales: $5-9.9 Million
Number Employees: 100-249
Type of Packaging: Food Service, Private Label, Bulk
Brands:
Fruit Belt
Solar

4762 **Fruit Bliss**
1007 Sheffield Ave
Brooklyn, NY 11207
Fax: 718-398-2005 info@fruitbliss.com
Dried fruit infused with water
President/Owner: Susan Leone
Number of Brands: 1
Number of Products: 10
Type of Packaging: Consumer
Brands:
FRUIT BLISS

4763 **Fruit Fillings Inc**
2531 E Edgar Ave
Fresno, CA 93706-5410
559-237-4715
Fax: 559-237-0728 800-995-4514
www.fruitfillings.com
Pie and pastry filling, fruit glazes, pectin based jams, fresh California fruit
President: Stephen Norcross
Contact: Bill Barr
bbill@fruitfillings.com
Estimated Sales: $2.5-5 000,000
Number Employees: 20-49

4764 **Fruit Growers Supply Company**
27770 N Entertainment Drive
Valencia, CA 91355
888-997-4855
news@fruitgrowers.com www.fruitgrowers.com
Cooperative group for agricultural supplies. They manufacture pallets, irrigation systems, and boxes, and they sell other agricultural supplies such as outer wear and pesticides.
President: Bill Dodd
Estimated Sales: $3-5 Million
Number Employees: 1-4
Square Footage: 4800
Type of Packaging: Consumer, Private Label, Bulk

4765 **Fruit Ranch Inc**
6301 W Bluemound Rd
Milwaukee, WI 53213-4146
414-476-9600
Fax: 414-258-9377 800-433-3289
info@fruitranch.com
Fruit gift baskets. Wholesaler of baskets and supplies
Owner/President: Tanya Gearheart
Estimated Sales: Less Than $500,000
Number Employees: 5-9
Square Footage: 20000
Type of Packaging: Consumer, Private Label, Bulk

4766 **Fruit d'Or**
306 Route 265
Villeroy, QC G0S 3K0
Canada
819-385-1126
Fax: 819-715-0059 info@fruit-dor.ca
www.fruit-dor.ca
Organic cranberries and blueberries in dried, pureed, concentrated, frozen, and powedered forms; neutraceuticals
Founder/President/CEO: Martin Le Moine
Year Founded: 1999
Estimated Sales: $20-50 Million
Number Employees: 50-99

4767 **Fruit of the Boot**
5728 NW 27th Pl
Gaineswillve, FL 32606
352-376-3643
Fax: 352-335-9172
Cakes and pastries; cookies; confections; dry pasta; olive oil; balsamic vinegar
Owner/President: Andrea Tosolini
Year Founded: 1999
Estimated Sales: Less than $500,000
Number Employees: 1-4
Type of Packaging: Private Label

4768 Fruit of the Land Products
1 Promenade Circle
PO Box 977
Thornhill, ON L4J 8G7
Canada
905-761-9611
Fax: 905-761-9617 877-311-5267
info@fruitoftheland.com www.fruitoftheland.com
Kosher olive oil, honey, jams, jellies, preserves, foodservice, private label.
Marketing: Michael Kurtz

4769 Fruitcrown Products Corp
250 Adams Blvd
Farmingdale, NY 11735-6615
631-694-5800
Fax: 631-694-6467 800-441-3210
info@fruitcrown.com www.fruitcrown.com
Aseptic fruit flavors and bases for beverage, dairy and baking industries
President: Robert Jagenburg
orjagenburg@fruitcrown.com
Number Employees: 50-99
Type of Packaging: Bulk
Brands:
Asp
Exquizita
Fruitcrown
Huntingcastle

4770 Fruithill Inc
6501 NE Highway 240
Yamhill, OR 97148-8507
503-662-3926
Fax: 503-662-4270 www.fruithillinc.com
Frozen cherries, plums and fruit purees
President: April Ateka
aprila@fruithillinc.com
EVP/Sales: Lee Schrepel
Office Manager: Zach Kanen
Estimated Sales: $10-20,000,000
Number Employees: 50-99
Type of Packaging: Food Service, Private Label

4771 Fruition Northwest LLC
29345 NW W Union Rd
PO Box 130
North Plains, OR 97133
503-880-5193
High-quality infused-dehydrated berry fruits to the wholesale market.
Owner: Alan Krassowski
Estimated Sales: $210 Thousand
Type of Packaging: Bulk

4772 (HQ)FrutStix
1525 State St
Suite 203
Santa Barbara, CA 93101
805-965-1656
Fax: 805-963-8288 info@frutstix.com
www.frutstix.com
Fresh frozen fruit bars, fudge bars
President: William McKinley
Director of Sales/Marketing: Ed Jones
Contact: Lynne Burton
lburton@frutstix.com
Director of Operations: Agustin Munoz
Plant Engineer: Daniel Gavela
Estimated Sales: $5-10 Million
Number Employees: 5-9
Type of Packaging: Food Service, Private Label
Other Locations:
FrutStix-Manufacturing Plant
San Diego CA

4773 Frutarom Meer Corporation
Manofim St. Herzeliya
P.O. Box 3088
Hertzeliya Pituach, 46104
Israel
www.iff.com/en/taste/frutarom
Botanicals, extracts, gums, stabilizers, oleoresins, natural colors, enzymes and hydrocolloids
President: Amos Anatot
Year Founded: 1933
Estimated Sales: $20-50 Million
Number Employees: 5600
Number of Products: 70K
Square Footage: 100000
Parent Co: International Flavors-Fragrances
Type of Packaging: Bulk
Brands:
Merecol
Meretec
Merezan
Stamere

4774 Frutech International Corp
180 S Lake Ave # 335
Suite 335
Pasadena, CA 91101-4735
626-844-0200
Fax: 626-844-0202 info.mx@frutech.com
www.frutech.com
Citrus oil production
Owner: Scott Alexander
scott.a@frutech.com
Treasurer: Gene Adams
VP Finance: Pat Breyer
Estimated Sales: $500,000
Number Employees: 1-4
Parent Co: Frutech International Corporation

4775 Fruvemex
233 Paulin Ave
Calexico, CA 92231
760-203-1896
Fax: 760-203-2389 fcaballero@fruvemex.com
www.fruvemex.com
Refrigerated and frozen fruit and vegetable products
President: Gustavo Caballero
VP Sales/Marketing: Yvonne Brewer
Year Founded: 1986
Number Employees: 85
Square Footage: 180000
Type of Packaging: Bulk

4776 Fry Foods Inc
P.O. Box 837
Tiffin, OH 44883
800-626-2294
orders@fryfoods.com www.fryfoods.com
Frozen, battered and breaded appetizers such as onion rings, cheese sticks, mushrooms, jalapeno poppers, zucchini sticks and breaded cauliflower
President: Norman Fry
Vice President: David Fry
Year Founded: 1961
Estimated Sales: $20-50 Million
Number Employees: 50-99
Number of Brands: 1
Square Footage: 45000
Type of Packaging: Consumer, Food Service
Brands:
Fry Foods

4777 Fry Krisp Food Products
3360 Spring Arbor Rd
Jackson, MI 49203-3636
517-784-8531
Fax: 517-784-6585 877-854-5440
www.frykrisp.com
Batter mixes for poultry and seafood, funnel cake, corn dogs and onion ring for fairs, and breakfst items such as pancakes, cornbread, biscuit mix and distributor of yellow corn grits.
President: Richard Neuenfeldt
Estimated Sales: $2.5-5 Million
Number Employees: 5-9
Number of Brands: 2
Number of Products: 15
Square Footage: 24000
Type of Packaging: Consumer, Food Service, Private Label, Bulk
Brands:
Fry Krisp
Fry Krisp Batter Mixes
Oven Krisp Coating Mixes

4778 Fuchs North America
3800 Hampstead Mexico Rd
Hampstead, MD 21074
410-363-1700
Fax: 410-363-6619 800-365-3229
Flavors and seasonings
CEO: Daniel Cooper
CFO: Christopher Rodski
Director of Research and Development: Helga Nelson
Director of Marketing: Shannon Cushen
Director of Operations: Derrick Epley
Type of Packaging: Consumer

4779 Fudge Farms
204 N Red Bud Trl
Buchanan, MI 49107-1366
269-695-2008
800-874-0261
Confectionery products including hard and soft, sugar-free, salt-free, caramels, nougats, taffy, fruit chews, coffee, boxed chocolates, candy bars, and sugar-free lollipops
President: Kenneth Harrington
Estimated Sales: $2-2.5 Million
Number Employees: 20-49
Square Footage: 43000
Brands:
Golden Farm Candies

4780 Fudge Fatale
11950 Ventura Blvd.
Suite 3
Studio City, CA 91604
310-287-0600
Fax: 949-240-3086 800-809-8298
Fudge
President: Alexander Black
Sales: Rich Pariseau
Estimated Sales: $3-5 Million
Number Employees: 5-9

4781 Fuji Foods Corp
6206 Corporate Park Dr
Browns Summit, NC 27214
336-375-3111
Fax: 336-375-3663 information@fujifoodsusa.com
www.fujifoodsusa.com
Chicken, pork and beef broths including concentrated pastes and powders; also, savory flavors, soup bases; and spray dried flavor powders; spray drying services available.
VP Operations & Chief Operating Officer: Michael Russell
Plant Manager: Terry Lawson
Estimated Sales: $20-50 Million
Number Employees: 20-49
Square Footage: 20000
Parent Co: Fuji Foods Corporation
Type of Packaging: Food Service, Bulk

4782 Fuji Health Science/Inc
3 Terri Ln # 12
Unit 12
Burlington, NJ 08016-4903
609-386-3030
Fax: 609-386-3033 contact@fujihealthscience.com
www.fujichemicalusa.com
Markets and manufacturers natural specialty food ingredient, AstaReal astaxanthin, a powerful anti-oxidant
National Sales Manager: Joe Kuncewitch
kuncewitch@fujihealthscience.com
Estimated Sales: Under $500,000
Number Employees: 10-19

4783 Fuji Vegetable Oil Inc
1 Barker Ave # 290
White Plains, NY 10601-1535
914-761-7900
Fax: 914-761-7919 www.fujioilusa.com
Vegetable and other oil
Manager: Andre Cormeau
jcalton@fvo-usa.com
Quality Control: Thomas McBrayer
Sales Exec: Gita Calton
Estimated Sales: $2.5-5 000,000
Number Employees: 5-9

4784 Ful-Flav-R Foods
P.O.Box 82
Alamo, CA 94507
925-838-0300
Fax: 925-838-0310 www.fulflavr.com
Premium Ground Garlic, Minced Garlic (in oil & water), Ground and Minced Ginger, Ground Roasted Garlic, Ground Onion, diced Sweet Bell Peppers, Ground and Diced Jalepeno's, Fire Roasted Anaheim chili's, Ground Chili-Garlic Blends andother unique custom formulated blends. All of our products are pasteurized and pH controlled.
President: Joseph Farrell
Chief Operations Officer: Glen Farrell
Director Sales/Marketing: Steve Linzmeyer
Plant Manager: John Small
Estimated Sales: $1-2.5 Million
Number Employees: 5-9
Type of Packaging: Food Service, Bulk

Brands:
Ful-Flav-R

4785 **Fulcher's Point Pride Seafood**
101 South Ave
Oriental, NC 28571-9682
252-249-0123
Fax: 252-249-2337 www.toojays.com
Seafood
Owner: Chris Fulchers
chris.fulcher@toojays.com
Owner: Garland Fulcher
Vice President: Deborah Fulcher
Purchasing: Ralph Bard
Estimated Sales: $4 Million
Number Employees: 50-99
Type of Packaging: Consumer, Food Service, Bulk

4786 **Full Sail Brewing Co**
506 Columbia St
Hood River, OR 97031-2000
541-386-2247
Fax: 541-386-7316 888-244-2337
www.fullsailbrewing.com
Beers, core brews, seasonal, brews, and special releases.
CEO: Irene Firmat
irenef@fullsailbrewing.com
CFO: Mark Moreland
Executive Brewmaster: Jamie Emmerson
Estimated Sales: $20-50 Million
Number Employees: 20-49
Number of Brands: 2
Brands:
Full Sail
Session

4787 **Fullbloom Baking Co**
6500 Overlake Pl
Newark, CA 94560-1083
510-494-1700
Fax: 510-803-4517 800-201-9909
www.aryzta.com
Fresh, fully-baked and packaged items- your brand or ours. With the latest in mixing, baking and freezing techniques, our goal is to create whatever you need. We manufacture multiple variations of muffins, scones, laminates, bars andbrownies, loaf breads, cookies, and granolas.
CEO and Founder: Karen Trilevsky
CFO: Audrey Heng
Research & Development Manager: Peter Conn
Quality Assurance Manager: Rowena Aquilizan
Sales Director: Laure Chatard
Industrial Engineer: Jagadeesh Dixit
Engineering & Maintenance Manager: Leo Carpio
Number Employees: 100-249
Square Footage: 95000
Type of Packaging: Consumer, Private Label

4788 **Fuller Foods**
5040 SE Milwaukie Ave
Portland, OR 97202
503-308-3814
fullerfoods.com
Cheesy puffs
President: Jack Kuo
Year Founded: 2012
Estimated Sales: $200,000
Number Employees: 5
Type of Packaging: Private Label

4789 **Fulton Fish Market**
New York, NY
718-842-8908
customerservice@fultonfishmarket.com
fultonfishmarket.com
Fish, shellfish, and other seafood including caviar, eel, octopus, sea urchin, and squid.
CEO: Mike Spindler
Year Founded: 1822
Type of Packaging: Consumer

4790 **Fulton Provision Co**
16123 NE Airport Way
Portland, OR 97230-4953
503-254-3000
Fax: 503-254-6328 800-333-6328
Processor of steaks and meats including beef, pork, veal, lamb and poultry.
President: Charlie Benton
SVP Sales: Tom Semke
VP Operations: Mark Vaughan
Business Development Manager: Chad Warneke
Estimated Sales: $20-50 Million
Number Employees: 50-99
Parent Co: Sysco
Type of Packaging: Food Service, Bulk

4791 **Fumoir Grizzly**
159 Amsterdam
St Augustin, QC G3A 2V5
Canada
418-878-8941
Fax: 418-878-8942 info@grizzly.qc.ca
www.grizzly.qc.ca
Manufacturer and exporter of smoked salmon, trout, halibut
President: Pierre Fontaine
CEO: Laura Boivin
Controller: Sebastian Legault
Director Quality Management: Michele Tessier
Marketing, R&D: Marie-Pier Grondin
Sales Representative-Quebec: Normand Richard
Director Human Resources: Connie Biladeau
Production Manager: Sergiu Parsikov
Estimated Sales: $6.3,000,000
Number Employees: 37
Type of Packaging: Consumer, Food Service, Private Label, Bulk

4792 **Fun City Popcorn**
3211 Sunrise Ave
Las Vegas, NV 89101
702-367-2676
Fax: 702-876-1099 800-423-1710
www.funcitypopcorn.com
Caramel, cheese and butter popcorn; manufacturer of popcorn processing machinery
President/CEO: Richard Falk
CFO: Maryann Talavera
Estimated Sales: $1-3 Million
Number Employees: 5-9
Square Footage: 40000
Type of Packaging: Consumer, Food Service, Private Label, Bulk

4793 **Fun Factory**
6223 W Forest Home Ave
Milwaukee, WI 53220
414-543-5887
Fax: 414-543-7850 877-894-6767
Gum, candy
President: Mike Dunlap
mike@funfactoryinc.com
Brands:
Face Twisters Sour Bubble Gum

4794 **Fun Foods**
99 Murray Hill Pkwy
Suite D
East Rutherford, NJ 07073-2143
201-896-4949
Fax: 201-896-4911 800-507-2782
funfoodspasta@yahoo.com
Bi- and tri-colored holiday shaped gourmet pasta including Christmas trees, hearts, bunnies, stars and stripes, Jack O'Lanterns, star of David, angels, etc
Manager: Sharon Nicklas
Estimated Sales: $5-10 Million
Number Employees: 5-9
Square Footage: 8000
Type of Packaging: Consumer, Food Service, Private Label, Bulk
Brands:
All-American Sports Pasta
Bunny Pasta
Funfoods Holiday Pasta
Funfoods Premium
Harvest Pasta
Holiday Pasta
I Love Pasta
Lucky Pasta
Pasta Della Festa
Patriotic Pasta
Star of David Pasta

4795 **Functional Foods**
15765 Sturgeon St
Roseville, MI 48066
586-445-0550
Fax: 586-445-1118 877-372-0550
Chocolate
President/CEO: Thomas Morley, Jr
Brands:
Smartchocolates

4796 **Functional Foods**
470 US Highway 9
Englishtown, NJ 07726-8239
732-972-2232
Fax: 732-536-9179 800-442-9524
Microcrystalline and hydroxypropyl cellulose, cellulose and psyllium fiber, gum arabic and guar, cellulose and vegetable gums
Marketing Manager: Alpa Nanavati
Manufacturing Manager: Yogi Shah
Estimated Sales: $2.5-5 Million
Number Employees: 20-49

4797 **Functional Products LLC**
1179 Atlantic Blvd
Atlantic Beach, FL 32233
904-249-8074
Fax: 514-853-6851 info@mueggenburg.com
www.paulmueggenburg.de
Vitamins and food supplements.
Owner: Dirk Mueggenburg
dm4@muepr.com
International Trade: Miguel Chacon
Estimated Sales: $199 Thousand
Number Employees: 2
Parent Co: Muggenburg Pflanzliche Rohstoffe GmbH & Co.
Type of Packaging: Consumer, Bulk

4798 **Fungi Perfecti**
PO Box 7634
Olympia, WA 98507-7634
360-427-5861
Fax: 360-426-9377 800-780-9126
info@fungi.com
Gourmet and medicinal mushrooms.
Owner: Paul Stamets
stamets1@aol.com
Estimated Sales: $3-5 Million
Number Employees: 20-49

4799 **Fungus Among Us**
2210 Lake Ave
Po Box 352
Snohomish, WA 98290-1028
360-568-3403
Fax: 360-563-2663 www.fungusamongus.com
Gourmet organic mushrooms
Owner: Lynn Monroe
shrooms@fungusamongus.com
Founder: Lynn Lynn
Estimated Sales: Less Than $500,000
Number Employees: 1-4

4800 **Funkychunky Inc.**
7452 W 78th St
Edina, MN 55439
952-938-6663
Fax: 952-938-2294 888-473-8659
tore@funkychunkyinc.com
www.funkychunkyinc.com
Chocolate covered pretzels, chocolate popcorn, caramel corn and bars
Marketing: Tore Villberg
Contact: Funkychunky Gracous
funkychunkyincg@funkychunkyinc.com

4801 **Funnibonz LLC**
3 Lake View Ct
Princeton Jct, NJ 08550-4915
609-915-3685
Fax: 609-845-1806 877-300-2669
info@funnibonz.com www.funnibonz.com
BBQ sauces, rubs and marinades
CEO: Jim Barbour
Co-CEO: Ryan Marrone
Manager: James Barbour
Estimated Sales: Less Than $500,000
Number Employees: 5-9

4802 **Furmano's Foods**
PO Box 500
Northumberland, PA 17857
570-473-3516
Fax: 570-473-7367 800-952-1111
www.furmanos.com

Furmano's heritage of excellence is evident in our stewardship of the land as well as the products we produce. Still guided by the original values that made the Furmano's name synonymous with the quality, the care and dedication withwhich our products are sourced and processed grows with each generation. Furmano's produces healthy, great tasting canned and pouch tomato and bean products for both the retail grocery and foodservice segments of the food industry.
President/CEO: Chad Geise
CEO/Chairman: David Geise
CFO: Ted Hancock
Quality Control: Craig Adams
VP Sales/Marketing: Bob Vanderhook
Contact: Kip Anspach
kip.anspach@furmanos.com
Operations Dir.: Daniel Severn
Purchasing Dir.: David Furman
Year Founded: 1923
Number Employees: 250
Square Footage: 1200000
Type of Packaging: Consumer

4803 Furukawa Potato Chip Factory
P.O.Box 1129
Captain Cook, HI 96704-1129
808-323-3785
Fax: 808- 32-3 37
Potato chips and snack foods
Owner: Jerome Furukawa
Estimated Sales: $1-3,000,000
Number Employees: 1-4

4804 Fusion Gourmet
14824 S Main St
Gardena, CA 90248
310-532-8938
Fax: 310-532-8991 www.fusiongourmet.com
Specializes in authentically prepared, fines quality and all-natural cooking sauces, marinades, and dips from Southeast Asia
President: Annie Chu
Chief Executive Officer: Stephen Liaw
Vice-President: Alexander Shkolnik
Sales: Sandra Liaw
Estimated Sales: $3-5 Million
Number Employees: 1-4
Brands:
Abc
Bali's Best
Fatal Attraction
Pearl Empress
Sweet Seduction

4805 Fusion Jerky
405 S Airport Blvd
South San Francisco, CA 94080-6909
USA
650-589-8899
Fax: 650-589-3157
Meat Jerky
Ceo/Founder: Kai Yen Mai
Sales & Marketing Manager: Shruti Dixit
Contact: Kaiyen Mai
kaiyen@fusionjerky.com

4806 Future Bakery & Cafe
483 Bloor Street West
Toronto, ON M8Z 2E2
Canada
416-231-1491
Fax: 416-231-1879 www.zomato.com
Specialty and artisan breads, European pastries and cheesecakes
President/Owner: Borys Wrzesnewskyj
Estimated Sales: $2.5-5 Million
Number Employees: 50-99
Square Footage: 44000
Type of Packaging: Consumer
Brands:
Future Bakery

4807 Futurebiotics LLC
70 Commerce Dr
Hauppauge, NY 11788-3936
631-273-6300
Fax: 631-273-1165 800-645-1721
customerservice@futurebiotics.com
Manufacturer and distributor of natural health food supplements and vitamins
Owner: Saisul Kibria
skibria@aol.com
Manager: Ed Keenan
Director Operations: Wendy L Kauffman
Estimated Sales: $10-20 Million
Number Employees: 20-49
Type of Packaging: Consumer, Private Label, Bulk
Brands:
Vital K

4808 Futureceuticals Inc
2692 N State Route 1 17
Momence, IL 60954-3475
815-507-1400
Fax: 815-472-3529 888-452-6853
Sales@futureceuticals.com
Primary processor of nutraceuticals, functional foods and cosmetic ingredients. Processing capabilities include: fermentation, refining, IQF freezing, freeze drying, drum drying, air drying, spray drying, vacuum evaporationextraction, synthesis, milling, grinding and blending.
President: Edward Van Drunen
Director New Business Development Europe: Zheko Kounev
Vice President Business Development: John Hunter
jhunter@futureceuticals.com
Vice President Research & Development: Zbigniew Pietrzkowski
jhunter@futureceuticals.com
Director Quality Control: Boris Nemzer
jhunter@futureceuticals.com
FutureCeuticals Technical Sales: Kit Kats
Number Employees: 5-9
Square Footage: 6000000

4809 Fuzz East Coast
140 Sylvan Avenue
3rd Floor
Englewood Cliffs, NJ 07632
866-438-3893
Fax: 201-461-1091 info@fuzebev.com
www.drinkfuze.com/
Manufacturers a variety of Fuze Health Infusions drinks including green tea and fruit juice flavored beverages.
Co-Founder: Lance Collins
Co-Founder: Joe Rosamilia
Co-Founder: Bruce Lewin
Co-Founder: Paula Grant
Contact: Ashley Nadeau
anadeau@fuzebev.com
Type of Packaging: Food Service

4810 Fuzziwig's Candy Factory
656 Main Ave
Durango, CO 81301-5438
970-247-2770
www.fuzziwigscandyfactory.com
Candy
President: Gordon Allen
gordona@fuzziwigscandyfactory.com
Estimated Sales: Less Than $500,000
Number Employees: 5-9

4811 Fuzzy's Wholesale Bar-B-Q
408 W End Blvd
Madison, NC 27025
336-548-2283
Fax: 336-548-2272
Frozen pork barbecue, brunswick stew, gourmet chicken pot pies, home replacement meals.
President: Fred Nelson
Estimated Sales: Less than $500,000
Number Employees: 1-4

4812 G & J Land & Marine Food Distr
506 Front St
Morgan City, LA 70380-3708
985-385-2251
Fax: 985-385-3614 800-256-9187
order@gjfood.com www.agbr.com
Full service food distributor dedicated to providing an extensive grocery and janitorial product line to the offshore oil and gas, commercial shipping and restaurant industry.
President/Owner: Mike Lind
mike@gjfood.com
Financial Coroller: Christine DeHart
Vice President: Erik Lind
Operations: Adam Mayon
Purchasing: Jarrod Leonard
Estimated Sales: $10-20 Million
Number Employees: 100-249

4813 G A Food Svc Inc
12200 32nd Ct N
St Petersburg, FL 33716-1847
727-573-2211
Fax: 727-572-8209 800-852-2211
www.sunmeadow.com
Manufacturer of frozen and shelf stable meals serving senior and child nutrition programs, emergency response and disaster relief services and the military.
President: Glenn Davenport
CEO: Ken Lobianco
Year Founded: 1973
Number Employees: 100-249
Type of Packaging: Consumer, Food Service, Private Label
Brands:
SunMeadow™

4814 G Cefalu & Brother Inc
8005 Rappahanock Ave
Jessup, MD 20794-9438
410-799-2910
Fax: 410-755-1446 jessup29@aol.com
www.gcefalu.com
Processor/repacker of tomatoes and all types of produce.
Owner: John Cefalu
gessup29@aol.com
Estimated Sales: $10-20 Million
Number Employees: 20-49
Type of Packaging: Consumer, Food Service, Bulk

4815 G Debbas Chocolatier
5877 E Brown Ave
Fresno, CA 93727-1364
559-294-2071
Fax: 559-348-2289 www.ownbrandchocolate.com
Truffles, wine-filled biscotti and chocolate bars with fruits and nut meat
Owner: Maria Gutierrez
maria@gdebbas.com
Estimated Sales: $10-20,000,000
Number Employees: 20-49
Type of Packaging: Consumer
Brands:
De Bas Vineyard
Incognito

4816 G M Allen & Son Inc
267 Front Ridge Rd
Orland, ME 4472
207-469-7060
Fax: 207-469-2308
Processing of frozen wild blueberries.
President/CEO: Wayne Allen
HR Executive: Kermit Allen
info@gmallenwildblueberries.com
VP Operations: Kermit Allen
Estimated Sales: $2,000,000
Number Employees: 20-49

4817 G M P Laboratories Of Amer Inc
2931 E LA Jolla St
Anaheim, CA 92806-1306
714-630-2467
Fax: 714-237-1374 info@gmplabs.com
www.gmplabs.com
Leading contract manufacturer of high quality vitamins and nutritional supplements. Our laboratories can assist you in formulating, manufacturing, packaging your products while always maintaining absolute confidentiality.
President/CEO: Suhail Ishaq
sishaq@gmplabs.com
Estimated Sales: $20-50 Million
Number Employees: 50-99

4818 G Scaccianoce & Co
1165 Burnett Pl
Bronx, NY 10474-5716
718-991-4462
Fax: 718-991-0154
Processor and exporter of confectionery items including Jordan almonds, French mints and licorice
President: Donald Beck
gscaccianoceinc@hotmail.com
Estimated Sales: $2.5-5 Million
Number Employees: 5-9
Type of Packaging: Consumer, Food Service, Private Label, Bulk

4819 **G. Banis Company**
2711 Centerville Road
Suite 400
Wilmington, DE 19808
617-516-9092
info@banistradition.com
Olive oil, dried fruit, olives, pickles & pickled vegetables, sun-dried tomatoes, foodservice, private label.
Marketing: George Banis

4820 **(HQ)G.E. Barbour**
165 Stewart Ave
Sussex, NB E4E 3H1
Canada
506-432-2300
Fax: 506-432-2323 www.barbours.ca
Family-owned business since 1867. Manufacturer of tea, nut butters, spices and extracts.
President: Sylvia MacVey
VP: Blair Hystom
Marketing Manager: Gordonna Hache
Director of Sales: Mike Trecartin
Number Employees: 100-249
Type of Packaging: Consumer, Food Service, Private Label
Other Locations:
G.E. Barbour
St. John NB
Brands:
King Cole Tea
Serious Kick
Humble Tea
Nuts About
Barbours

4821 **G.E.F. Gourmet Foods Inc**
35584 County Road 8
Mountain Lake, MN 56159-2106
507-427-2631
Fax: 507-427-2631 800-692-6762
greatsnack@frontiernet.net
Manufactures Glad Corn A-maizing Corn Snacks.
Founder/Co-Owner: Stan Friesen
Founder/Co-Owner: Gladys Friesen
greatsnack@frontiernet.net
Type of Packaging: Food Service

4822 **G.H. Cretors**
Richfield, OH 44286
www.ghcretors.com
Gourmet popcorn
President: Claire Cretors
Brands:
Vita

4823 **G.S. Dunn Limited**
80 Park Street N
Hamilton, ON L8R 2M9
Canada
905-522-0833
Fax: 905-522-4423 info@gsdunn.com
www.gsdunn.com
Dry mustard products
President: Don Henry
Estimated Sales: $4.3 Million
Number Employees: 30

4824 **GAF Seelig Inc**
5905 52nd Ave
Flushing, NY 11377-7480
718-899-5000
Fax: 718-803-1198
Wholesaler and distributor of juice, milk, cheese, yogurt, sour cream, purees, raviolis and pastas, oils and vinegars, chocolate and many more food service items.
President: Rodney Seelig
rseelig@gafseelig.com
Executive Vice President: Gary Lavery Sr.
Director of Sales: John Arena
Estimated Sales: $5-10 Million
Number Employees: 100-249

4825 **GB Ratto International Grocery**
821 Washington St
Oakland, CA 94607-4029
510-832-6503
Fax: 510-836-2250 800-325-3483
http://rattos.com/
Olives, oils and spices
Owner: Elena Voiron
elena@rattos.com
General Manager: Susan Nelson
Estimated Sales: $2.5-5,000,000
Number Employees: 10-19

4826 **GC Farms**
15500 Hill Rd
Morgan Hill, CA 95037
408-778-0562
Fax: 408-779-4034 lori.rollins@gcfarms.com
www.gcfarmsinc.com
Frozen vegetables
CFO: Alice Chiala
COO: Tim Chiala
Estimated Sales: $50-100 Million
Number of Brands: 1
Parent Co: George Chiala Farms, Inc.

4827 **GCI Nutrients**
1163 Chess Dr # H
Foster City, CA 94404-1119
650-376-3534
Fax: 650-697-6300 866-580-6549
mikec@gcinutrients.com www.gcinutrients.com
Processor, importer and exporter of vitamins and supplements including beta carotene, essential fatty acids, herbal products, botanical extracts, food supplements, bulk ingredients, premium raw materials for nutritional and beverageindustries with over 42 years of experience
Owner: Richard Merriam
rickm@gcinutrients.com
General Manager: Mike Cronin
Controller: Fransisca Cronin
R&D: William Forgach
Marketing: Michael Sevohon
Production: Derek Cronin
Plant Manager: Mike Cronin
Purchasing Manager: Catherine Sabbah
Estimated Sales: $10 Million
Number Employees: 10-19
Number of Brands: 10
Number of Products: 300
Square Footage: 20000
Brands:
Abg
Cm-22
Eleutherogen
Gamma-E
Ge-Oxy 132
Lipo-Serine
Olivir
Oxi-Gamma
Oxi-Grape

4828 **GEM Berry Products**
PO Box 709
Orofino, ID 83544
208-263-7503
Fax: 866-357-3505 888-231-1699
gifrep52@gmail.com www.gemberry.com
Processor and exporter of spreads, jams and syrups including raspberry and huckleberry; berry filled chocolates, berry barbecue sauce and many other berry products.
President: Jack O' Brien
CFO: Betty Menser
Marketing: Harry Menser
Contact: Cathy Miller
cathy.miller@gemberryproducts.com
Production: Elizabeth O Brien
Estimated Sales: $50,000-100,000
Number Employees: 1-4
Square Footage: 5000
Type of Packaging: Food Service, Bulk
Brands:
Gem Berry
Litehouse
Taste the Beauty of North Idaho
Taste the Beauty of the Rockies

4829 **GEM Cultures**
PO Box 39426
Lakewood, WA 98496
253-588-2922
gemculture@juno.com
www.gemcultures.com
Manufacturer and exporter of shelf stable starters for cultured vegeterian foods including tempeh, miso, shoyu, natto, sourdough, nonyogurt and dairy cultures; importer of koji and natto starters
Owner: Betty Stechmeyer
Public Relations: Gordon McBride
Estimated Sales: $70,000
Number Employees: 1
Square Footage: 2000
Type of Packaging: Private Label
Brands:
Gem

4830 **GF Harvest**
1030 E Washington St
Powell, WY 82435
888-941-9922
www.glutenfreeoats.com
Gluten-free oats, oatmeal and oat flour
President/Owner: Seaton Smith
Number of Brands: 1
Number of Products: 18
Type of Packaging: Consumer
Brands:
CANYON OATS
GF HARVEST

4831 **GFA Brands Inc**
115 W Century Rd # 260
Paramus, NJ 07652-1431
201-568-9300
Fax: 201-568-6374 www.smartbalance.com
Cheese, margarine, mayonnaise, cereals, salad dressings, pickles and oils
President: Robert Harris
CEO: Steve Hughes
sh@smartbalance.com
CEO: Steve Hughes
Estimated Sales: $1-3 Million
Number Employees: 10-19
Type of Packaging: Consumer
Brands:
Gfa
H-O
Mrs Fanings
Spin Blend

4832 **GH Bent Company**
7 Pleasant St
Milton, MA 02186
617-322-9287
Cookies, brownies and crackers.
Estimated Sales: $500,000-$1 Million
Number Employees: 10-19
Square Footage: 60000
Type of Packaging: Food Service
Brands:
Bent's

4833 **GH Ford Tea Company**
PO Box 683
Shokan, NY 12481
845-464-6755
info@ghfordtea.com
www.ghfordtea.com
Processor, importer and exporter of whole leaf teas in tea ball packaging. Offers 30 to 50 blends and flavors utilizing original blending formulas and all natural flavoring.
President: Keith Capolino
ghfordtea@gmail.com
Estimated Sales: $2.5-5 Million
Number Employees: 5-9
Type of Packaging: Consumer, Food Service, Private Label, Bulk
Brands:
G.H. Ford

4834 **GKI Foods**
7926 Lochlin Road
Brighton, MI 48116
248-486-0055
Fax: 248-486-9135 www.gkifoods.com
Milk chocolate, sugar free chocolate, yogurt and cards products, panned and enrobed, bulk or packaged. Also produces custom granola (all natural, highly nutritional, low in fat and fat free), trail mixes, etc. Custom formulation. Aidcertified, GMP and HACCP accreditation.
President: Sue Wilts
Contact: Nancy Fletcher
nancy.fletcher@gkifoods.com
General Manager: Jim Frazier
Number Employees: 20-49
Square Footage: 60000
Type of Packaging: Consumer, Private Label, Bulk

4835 **GLCC Co**
39149 W Red Arrow Hwy
PO Box 329
Paw Paw, MI 49079-9389
269-657-3167
Fax: 269-657-4552 glcc@glccflavors.com
www.glccflavors.com
Flavors, juice concentrates and blends; custom repackaging available
President: Johnathan Davis
Finance Executive: Johnathan Davis
Quality Assurance Manager: Nicole Charron
Sales Exec: Thomas Manion
Human Resources Executive: Lisa Lull
th@glccflavors.com
VP Operations/Plant Manager: Fred Jeffers
Purchasing: Maria Galvan
Estimated Sales: $2.5 Million
Number Employees: 20-49
Square Footage: 70000
Type of Packaging: Bulk

4836 **GLG Life Tech Corporation**
1050 West Pender Street
Suite 2168
Vancouver, BC V6E 3S7
Canada
604-669-2602
Fax: 604-662-8858 www.glglifetech.com
Supplier of Stevia, which is a natural, zero calorie sweetening additive used in the food and beverage industries.
President/CFO: Brian Meadows
Chairman & CEO: Dr. Luke Zhang
Vice President, Marketing: James Kempland
Vice President, Sales: Jack Tokarczyk

4837 **GLG Life Tech Corporation**
10271 Shellbridge Way
Suite 100
Richmond, BC V6X 2W8
Canada
604-669-2602
Fax: 604-285-2606 855-454-7587
info@glglifetech.com www.glglifetech.com
Manufactures all-natural sweeteners, stevia extract and monk fruit extract.
Chairman/Chief Executive Officer: Dr. Luke Zhang
Vice Chairman: Brian Palmieri
President/Chief Financial Officer: Brian Meadows
Estimated Sales: $20 Million
Number Employees: 299
Number of Brands: 10
Brands:
AnySweetPLUS™
BlendSure™
MonkGold™
MonkSweet™
Organipure™
P-ProPlus
PureSTV™
RebPure™
RebSweet™
TasteBoost™

4838 **(HQ)GLK Foods, LLC**
11 Clark Street
Shortsville, NY 14548
855-572-8800
www.greatlakeskraut.com
Sauerkraut, cabbage products
President: David Flanagan
Contact: David Ford
djford@greatlakeskraut.com
Estimated Sales: $10-20,000,000
Number Employees: 100-249
Type of Packaging: Bulk

4839 **GMB Specialty Foods**
32422 Alipaz St #G
San Juan Capistrano, CA 92675-4187
949-240-3053
Fax: 949-240-3086 800-809-8298
www.gmbfoods.com
Sauces, toppings, marinades, dressings, rubs and salsas
President: Greg Bloom
Marketing Director: Helen Bloom
Estimated Sales: $1,000,000
Number Employees: 1-4
Type of Packaging: Private Label
Brands:
Basitan's
Edelweiss Dressings
Norman Bishop
Sallie's
Scottsdale Mustard Co
D'Oni Specialty Sauces
Lean on Me Naturally

4840 **GNS Foods**
2109 E Division St
Arlington, TX 76011-7817
817-795-4671
Fax: 817-795-4673 sales@gnsfoods.com
www.greatnuts.com
Raw and roasted nuts, packaged pecan candy and dried fruits including raisins, mango, pineapple, apple, banana chips, apricots and mixed; wholesaler/distributor of specialty foods; serving the food service market
President: Kim Peacock
Marketing: Carissa Mark
Contact: Lee Eggleston
sales@gnsfoods.com
Estimated Sales: $5-10 Million
Number Employees: 50-99
Square Footage: 25192
Type of Packaging: Consumer, Food Service, Private Label, Bulk
Brands:
Grove on the Go
Grove, Jr
Pecan Street Sweets
The Grove

4841 **GNS Spices**
766 Trotter Ct
Walnut, CA 91789-1277
909-594-9505
Fax: 909-594-5455
Processor and exporter of red savina and orange habanero peppers including pods, flakes and ground
President: Frank Garcia Jr
VP: Mary Garcia
Operations Manager: Frank Garcia Sr
Estimated Sales: $150,000
Number Employees: 2
Type of Packaging: Bulk

4842 **GNT USA**
660 White Plains Rd
Tarrytown, NY 10591
914-524-0600
info@gntusa.com
exberry.com
Natural colors for the food and beverage industry

4843 **GPI USA LLC.**
10062 190th Place
Suite 107
Mokena, IL 60448
706-850-7826
Fax: 708-785-0608 800-929-4248
karen.haley@foodgums.com
Specialize in carageenan used for stabilization and as an additive for both dairy products and in the red meat and poultry industries.

4844 **GREEN Energy**
Kailua, HI 96734
808-396-9454
drinkgreenenergy.com
Organic energy drink

4845 **GS Dunn & Company**
80 Park Street N
Hamilton, ON L8R 2M9
Canada
905-522-0833
Fax: 905-522-4423 info@gsdunn.com
www.gsdunn.com
Global supplier and manufacturer of dry mustard products
President: Ron Kramer
Director Technical Services: Nancy Post
Estimated Sales: $5 Million
Number Employees: 20-49
Square Footage: 70000
Type of Packaging: Food Service, Private Label, Bulk

4846 **GS Gelato & Desserts Inc**
1785 Fim Blvd
Fort Walton Bch, FL 32547-1152
850-243-5455
Fax: 850-243-5443 888-435-2767
info@gsgelato.com www.gsgelato.com
Dairy-free, gluten-free, organic frozen desserts
Marketing: Simona Faroni
Manager: Melissa Thompson
melissa@gsgelato.com
Number Employees: 20-49

4847 **GS-AFI**
238 Saint Nicholas Avenue
South Plainfield, NJ 07080-1810
908-753-9100
Fax: 908-753-9635 800-345-4342
Specialty premixes, spices and seasonings
President: David Hiller
Contact: Dagmar Hiller
Number Employees: 250-499

4848 **GSB & Assoc**
3115 Cobb International Blvd N
Kennesaw, GA 30152-4354
770-424-1886
Fax: 770-422-1732 877-472-2776
sales@gsbflavorcreators.com
www.gsbflavorcreators.com
Natural and artificial, artificial, water or oil soluble, liquid and spray dried flavors. Flavors are Kosher Certified. We also offer a line of Certified Organic Flavors.
President: Eugene Buday
sales@gsbflavorcreators.com
Estimated Sales: $5-10 Million
Number Employees: 10-19
Type of Packaging: Bulk

4849 **GTC Nutrition**
5 Westbrook Corporate Ctr #500
Westchester, IL 60154-5795
708-551-2600
Fax: 303-216-2477 800-443-2746
www.ingredion.com
A leading provider of high-quality, science based nutritional ingredients for today's healthy lifestyles. Proudly takes a multi-disciplinary approach to it's business by offering customer support that reaches beyond standard needs.Areas of expertise include scientific and technical counsel, marketing and brand development, applications innovation, logistics and regulatory support and customer service.
CEO: Patrick Smith
Marketing: Trina O'Brien
Estimated Sales: $5-10 000,000
Number Employees: 20-49

4850 **GU Energy Labs**
1609 4th St
Berkeley, CA 94710
800-400-1995
guenergy.com
Energy gels, chews, capsules and drinks
President & COO: Blair Clark
Type of Packaging: Consumer
Brands:
GU

4851 **GURU Organic Energy**
1592 Union St
San Francisco, CA 94123
www.guruenergy.com
Organic energy drinks
Brew Master: Luc Martin-Privat
Type of Packaging: Consumer
Brands:
GURU

4852 **GWB Foods Corporation**
PO Box 228
Brooklyn, NY 11204-0228
718-686-6611
Fax: 718-686-6161 877-977-7610
info@gwbfoods.com www.gwbfoods.com
Processor, exporter, importer and wholesaler/distributor of specialty and frozen foods including cookies, candies, crackers, rice cakes, vegetables in jars, bottled water, pickles and pimiento peppers
President: Joshua Weinstein
Export Manager: S Williams
Sales Manager: Jack Yumens
Estimated Sales: $2.5-5 Million
Number Employees: 10-19
Square Footage: 80000
Parent Co: President Baking Company
Type of Packaging: Consumer, Food Service, Private Label, Bulk
Brands:
Presidor

4853 **Gabila's Knishes**
100 Wartburg Ave
Copiague, NY 11726
631-789-2220
gabilas.com
Processor and exporter of frozen knishes
President: Gloria Gabay
Partner: Sophie Levy
Controller: Linda Ghignone
Estimated Sales: $1-2.5 Million
Number Employees: 20-49
Type of Packaging: Consumer
Brands:
King of Potato Pies

4854 **Gabriella's Kitchen**
3249 Lenworth Dr
Mississauga, ON L4X 2G6
Canada
844-754-6690
www.gabriellas-kitchen.com
Organic pasta
President: Vincent Micallef
Founder & CEO: Margot Micallef
Chief Marketing Officer: Marc Whitehead
Sr VP of North American Sales: John Shaw
VP of Corporate Development: Christopher Fenn
Type of Packaging: Private Label
Brands:
gaby
TOP-The Oil Plant
Sonoma Pacific
Aunt Zelda's
Gabriella's Kitchen

4855 **Gad Cheese Retail Store**
2401 County Road C
Medford, WI 54451
715-748-4273
Fax: 715-748-4299
Cheddar cheese, cheese curds, monterey jack, specialty cheese and more than 30 varieties. Retail outlet and an observation window.
President: Bruce Albrecht
VP: Diane Albrecht
Estimated Sales: Less Than $500,000
Number Employees: 1-4
Type of Packaging: Consumer, Food Service, Private Label, Bulk

4856 **Gadoua Bakery**
150 Bd Industriel
Napierville, QC J0J 1L0
Canada
450-245-7542
Fax: 450-245-7609 800-661-7246
info@gadoua.qc.ca www.gadoua.qc.ca
Bread, buns, bagels, english muffins, and tortillas
President: Pascal Gadoua
Year Founded: 1911
Estimated Sales: $40-60 Million
Number Employees: 550
Square Footage: 150000
Parent Co: George Weston Ltd.
Type of Packaging: Food Service
Brands:
Gadoua

4857 **Gadsden Coffee/Caffe**
PO Box 460
16850 West Arivaca Rd.
Arivaca, AZ 85601-0460
520-398-3251
Fax: 520-398-2001 888-514-5282
Specialty coffees
Owner: Tom Shook
Estimated Sales: $2.5-5,000,000
Number Employees: 10-19

4858 **Gaea North America LLC**
1915 Hollywood Blvd
Suite 200
Hollywood, FL 33020
954-923-7723
Fax: 954-923-7732 info@gaeaus.com
gaeaus.com
Greek food, including vinegars and dressings; olive oils.
CEO: David Neuman
Marketing Director: Keli Roberson
Director of Operations: Jimmy Campos
Estimated Sales: $25 Million
Number Employees: 5-9
Type of Packaging: Private Label

4859 **Gaia Herbs Inc**
101 Gaia Herbs Rd
Brevard, NC 28712-8930
828-884-4242
Fax: 828-883-5960 888-917-8269
info@gaiaherbs.com www.gaiaherbs.com
Organic processor of herbal extracts
Owner: Ric Scalzo
CEO: Ric Scalzo
VP: Daniel Vickers
Quality Control Director: Jim Grant
VP Marketing: Ann Buchman
VP Sales: Angela Guerrant
Human Resources Manager: Cynthia Chandler
kod@gaiaherbs.com
Purchasing: Kate Daigle
Year Founded: 1987
Estimated Sales: $11.5 Million
Number Employees: 100-249
Square Footage: 60000
Brands:
Echinacea
Echinacea/Goldenseal Supreme
Ginseng Extract

4860 **Gainey Vineyard**
3950 E Highway 246
Santa Ynez, CA 93460
805-688-0558
Fax: 805-688-5864 www.gaineyvineyard.com
Producer of wines, including Pinot Noir, Chardonnay and Syrah.
President: Daniel Gainey
daniel@gaineyvineyard.com
General Manager & Director of Winemaking: John Falcone
Estimated Sales: $5-10 Million
Number Employees: 10-19

4861 **Gaiser's European Style**
2019 Morris Ave
Union, NJ 07083-6013
908-686-3421
Fax: 908-686-7131
Processor, exporter and wholesaler/distributor of sausage, liverwurst and smoked ham
Owner: Efem Rablov
gaisers@verizon.net
Estimated Sales: $500,000-$1 Million
Number Employees: 10-19
Brands:
Gaiser's

4862 **Galante Vineyards**
18181 Cachagua Rd
Carmel Valley, CA 93924-9313
831-659-7620
Fax: 831-659-9525 800-425-2683
wine@galantevineyards.com
www.galantevineyards.com
Cabernet Sauvignon
Owner: Jack Galante
jack@gallantv.com
Estimated Sales: Less than $500,000
Number Employees: 5-9
Type of Packaging: Private Label
Brands:
Blackjack Pasture Cabernet
Galante Wines
Rancho Galante Cabernet
Red Rose Hill Cabernet

4863 **Galassi Foods**
2042 Glen Oaks Drive
Coralville, IA 52241
319-339-7409
lisa@galassifoods.com
www.galassifoods.com
Manufacturer of different pasta sauces.
Founder: Blake Niemann
Contact: Lisa Galassi
lisa@galassifoods.com
Brands:
Galassi

4864 **Galasso's Bakery**
10820 San Sevaine Way
Mira Loma, CA 91752-1116
951-360-1211
Fax: 951-360-0427 customercare@galassos.com
www.galassos.com
Sourdough, French, specialty and sliced breads, hot dog and hamburger buns, and assorted rolls.
CEO: Jeanette Galasso
CFO: Mark Bailey
mbailey@galassos.com
Sales & Operations Manager: John Galasso
Estimated Sales: $34.9 Million
Number Employees: 250-499
Number of Brands: 1
Square Footage: 110000
Type of Packaging: Consumer, Food Service, Private Label, Bulk
Brands:
Galasso

4865 **Galaxy Dairy Products**
700 Lake St # E
Ramsey, NJ 07446-1246
201-818-2030
Fax: 201-818-1969 galxdairy@aol.com
Dairy products
President: Thomas Phiebig
VP: Carole Phiebig
Estimated Sales: $30 Million+
Number Employees: 5-9
Type of Packaging: Private Label

4866 **Galaxy Desserts**
1100 Marina Way
Suite D
Richmond, CA 94804-3727
510-439-3160
Fax: 415-439-3169 800-225-3523
info@galaxydesserts.com
www.galaxydesserts.com
Gourmet desserts
President/CEO/Co-Founder: Paul Levitan
Co-Founder/Master Pastry Chef: John-Yves Charon
Sales/Marketing: Lisa Weaver
Year Founded: 1998
Estimated Sales: $20-50 Million
Number Employees: 250-499
Square Footage: 20000
Type of Packaging: Consumer, Food Service
Brands:
Galaxy Desserts

4867 **Galaxy Nutritional Foods Inc**
66 Whitecap Dr
Suite 2
North Kingstown, RI 02852-7445
401-667-5000
Fax: 302-655-5049 800-441-9419
www.goveggiefoods.com
Leading producer of healthy diary products such as soy based dairy, low-fat, and cholestral-free. Category leader in both supermarkets and health food stores.
President, CEO, COO: Brian O'Farrell
CEO: Richard Antonelli
rantonelli@galaxyfoods.com
Executive VP: Jerry Schwartz
Marketing VP: Whitney Velasco-Aznar
VP of Contract Manufacturing: Thomas Perno
Estimated Sales: $25-49.9 Million
Number Employees: 20-49
Number of Brands: 1
Brands:
Go Veggie

4868 **Galena Canning Co**
107 S Main St
Galena, IL 61036-2224
815-777-9495
Fax: 773-477-5627 info@galenacanning.com
www.galenacanning.com
Specialties in salsas, pasta sauce, BBQ sauces, chili, relishes, pickles, hot sauces, mustard, jams and jellies, fruit butter, syrups, toppings, flavored oils and vinegar.
Owner: Ivo Puidak
Estimated Sales: Less Than $500,000
Number Employees: 5-9

4869 **Galena Cellars Winery**
515 S Main St
Galena, IL 61036-2352
815-777-3330
Fax: 815-777-3335 800-397-9463
wine@galenacellars.com www.galenacellars.com
Producers, bottles and cellars a variety of wines using grapes, juice and fruit from across the US. Classic dry wines such as Chardonay, Cabernet Sauvignon, White Zinfandel, semi-dry and semi-sweet wines, selection of fruit wines anddessert ports.

Owner/President: Scott Lawlor
scott@galenacellars.com
VP: Karen Lawlor
Winemaker: Chris L White
Vineyard Tasting Room Manager: Jan Falson
Estimated Sales: $1.8,000,000
Number Employees: 20-49
Number of Products: 32
Type of Packaging: Consumer, Bulk
Brands:
Galena Cellars

4870 **Galilean Seafood Inc**
16 Broadcommon Rd
Bristol, RI 02809-2722
401-253-3030
Fax: 401-253-9207
Hand shucked clam supplier. Frozen and refrigerated clams, hard shell clams, scallops, conch, and mussels and a full line of hand shucked breaded clam items.
President: Mark Montopoli
Estimated Sales: 1-4,999,999
Number Employees: 50-99
Number of Brands: 3
Brands:
Galilean
King Conch
Pure Brand Products

4871 **Galland's Institutional Food**
520 Kentucky St
PO Box 3007
Bakersfield, CA 93305-4344
661-631-5505
Fax: 661-631-5513
Distributors of a full service food line, exceptions produce and meat.
President: Joan Galland
Owner: Leonard Galland
CFO: Leonard Galland
Estimated Sales: $3-5 Million
Number Employees: 10-19

4872 **Galleano Winery**
4231 Wineville Ave
Mira Loma, CA 91752-1412
951-685-5376
Fax: 951-360-9180 info@galleanowinery.com
www.galleanowinery.com
Wines and wine grapes
President/CEO: Donald Galleano
EVP: Charlene Galleano
Human Resources Director: Debbie Kreinbring
Estimated Sales: $810 Million
Number Employees: 10-19
Square Footage: 270000
Type of Packaging: Consumer, Private Label, Bulk
Brands:
Galleano
Green Valley

4873 **(HQ)Galliker Dairy Co**
143 Donald Ln
Johnstown, PA 15907-0159
814-266-8702
800-477-6455
info@gallikers.com www.gallikers.com
Processor and distributor of milk, ice cream, orange juice, iced tea, dips, sour cream, cottage cheese.
President & CEO: Louis Galliker III
Year Founded: 1914
Estimated Sales: $33 Million
Number Employees: 250-499
Square Footage: 94000
Brands:
Galliker's
Potomac Farms
Quality Chekd
Slim 'n' Trim

4874 **Galloway Co**
601 S Commercial St
PO Box 609
Neenah, WI 54956-3392
920-722-7741
Fax: 920-722-1927 800-722-8903
www.gallowaycompany.com
Processor of sweetened condensed milk, beverage bases, and dessert mixes.
CEO and Chairman: Timothy Galloway
Sales Exec: Tim Galloway
tgalloway@gallowaycompany.com
Year Founded: 1932
Estimated Sales: $20-50 Million
Number Employees: 20-49
Type of Packaging: Food Service, Private Label, Bulk
Brands:
Golden Crest

4875 **Gallup Sales Company**
530 E Historic Highway 66
Gallup, NM 87301
505-863-5241
Fax: 505-863-4219
Distributors of beer and wine.
President: Reed Ferrari
Vice President: Cecil Ferrari
Treasurer: Elsie Bernabe
Estimated Sales: $1-2,500,000
Number Employees: 10-19

4876 **Galvinell Meat Co Inc**
461 Ragan Rd
Conowingo, MD 21918-1224
410-378-3032
galvinell@zoominternet.net
www.galvinell.com
Custom meat processor, also cooker services and products and private label, custom slaughtering, and party platters, salads, charcoal and ice also available. Beef, pork, goat, and lamb.
President: Dennis Welsh
dennis@galvinell.com
Estimated Sales: $730 Thousand
Number Employees: 5-9
Type of Packaging: Consumer, Food Service, Private Label, Bulk

4877 **Gama Products**
12200 NW 36th Ave
Miami, FL 33167-2415
786-235-1515
Fax: 786-398-4575 info@gamaproducts.com
www.gamaproducts.com
Processor, importer and exporter of oils including corn, soy, canola, vegetable, rice bran and cottonseed.
President: Jose Abrante
Operations Manager: Rick Samudio
Estimated Sales: $10 Million
Number Employees: 12
Type of Packaging: Consumer, Food Service, Private Label, Bulk
Brands:
Bekal
Real

4878 **Gamay Flavors**
2770 S 171st St
New Berlin, WI 53151-3510
262-785-5104
Fax: 262-789-5149 888-345-4560
caryg@gamayflavors.com
Supplier to the food industry with products such as heat stable cheese flavorings, complete flavor systems and thermostable fillings. Gamay flavors include enzyme modified cheeses, natural cheese flavors, lipolyzed butter oils andcreams, natural butter and cream flavors, starter distillate replacers, liquid flavors, sweet flavors, savory flavors, and food colors.
President: Dr. Aly Gamay
Director of Sales and Marketing: Cary Gammons
Contact: Noelle Todd
noellet@gamayflavors.com
Operations: Randy Cook
Estimated Sales: $1-5 000,000
Number Employees: 5-9
Parent Co: R&D Technical Center-Gamay Flavors

4879 **(HQ)Gambino's Bakeries Inc**
2308 Piedmont St
Kenner, LA 70062-7960
504-712-0809
Fax: 504-466-1507 www.gambinos.com
Distribution of confections, specialty cakes, Italian cookies and pastries, internet specialties, Mardi Gras packages, Doberge cakes and King Cake packaging. Every cake is baked fresh daily and we now ship overnight.
Owner: Sam Scelfo
email@gambinos.com
Estimated Sales: Less Than $500,000
Number Employees: 5-9

4880 **Gambino's Bakery**
4821 Veterans Memorial Blvd
Metairie, LA 70006-5209
504-885-7500
Fax: 504-887-7442 800-426-2466
kingcakes@gambinosbakery.com
www.gambinos.com
Cakes, cookies, pies and doughnuts
Owner: Sam P Scelfo
samscelfo@gambinos.com
Manager: Theresa Ursin
Estimated Sales: Less Than $500,000
Number Employees: 5-9
Parent Co: Gambino's

4881 **(HQ)Gambrinus Co**
14800 San Pedro Ave # 310
Third Floor
San Antonio, TX 78232-3735
210-490-9128
Fax: 210-490-9984 www.gambrinus.com
Best known as importer of the Grupo Modelo brand portfilio for the eastern US. Also imports Moosehead Lager from Canada.
President/CEO: Carlos Alvarez
c.alvarez@gambrinusco.com
CFO: James Bolz
Estimated Sales: Under $500,000
Number Employees: 50-99
Other Locations:
Spoetzel Brewery
Shiner TX
Bridgeport Brewery
Portland OR
Trumer Brewery
Berkeley CA
Brands:
Kosmos Lager
Lorunita Extra
Modelo Especial
Negra Modelo
Pacifico Clara
Shiner Bock
Shiner Premium
Corona Extra
Corona Light
Negro Modelo
Pacifico Clara
Modleo Especial

4882 **Gandy's Dairies LLC**
201 University Ave
Lubbock, TX 79415-3426
806-765-8833
Fax: 806-765-5192 800-338-6841
www.deanfoods.com
Milk, dairy products
Manager: Steve Gerrish
Cio/Cto: Lori Sexton
lori_sexton@deanfoods.com
VP Sales: Bill Murphy
Plant Manager: Larry Hendricks
Year Founded: 1924
Number Employees: 100-249
Parent Co: Dean Foods Company

4883 **Ganeden, Inc**
5800 Landerbrook Dr
Suite 300
Mayfield Hts, OH 44124
440-229-5200
Fax: 440-229-5240 info@ganedenprobiotics.com
www.ganedenprobiotics.com
Manufacturer and distributor probiotic ingredients.
Chairman of the Board: Andy Lefkowitz
CEO: Michael Bush
Director of Marketing: Erin Marshall

4884 **(HQ)Ganong Bros Ltd**
One Chocolate Dr
St. Stephen, NB E3L 2X5
Canada
506-465-5600
Fax: 506-465-5610 888-270-8222
feedback@ganong.com www.ganong.com
Confectionery products including bagged candy, boxed chocolate and fruit snacks. Many old fashion varieties such as rich milk caramel, sinful chacolate truffles, peanut butter cups, delicious double dipped cherries and the one andonly chicken bones.

President & CEO: Bryana Ganong
VP, Innovation & Contract Manufacturing: Nicholas Ganong
CFO: Joe Lacey
Executive Vice Chair: David Ganong
Director, National Sales: John Burgess
Director, Operations: Tim Byrne
Year Founded: 1873
Estimated Sales: $32 Million
Number Employees: 325
Type of Packaging: Consumer, Private Label, Bulk
Brands:
Between Friends Promotional Candy
Delecto Chocolates
Fun Fruits Fruit Snacks-Sunkist
Ganong Chicken Bones
Ganong Chocolates
Ganong Fruitfull
Ganong Sugar Confections
Pal-O-Mine Chocolate Bars
Sunkist Flavour Bursts
Sunkist Fruit First Fruit Snacks
Tiffany Bagged Candy
Wildfruit Fruit Snacks

4885 **Ganong Bros Ltd**
500 St. George St
Moncton, NB E1C 1Y3
Canada
506-389-7898
Fax: 506-854-5826 www.ganong.com
Confectionery products including bagged candy, boxed chocolate and fruit snacks. Many old fashion varieties such as rich milk caramel, sinful chocolate truffles, peanut butter cups, delicious double dipped cherries and the one and onlychicken bones.
Estimated Sales: $32 Million
Number Employees: 325
Type of Packaging: Consumer, Private Label, Bulk

4886 **Garber Farms**
3405 Descannes Hwy
Iota, LA 70543-3118
337-824-6328
Fax: 337-824-2676 800-824-2284
www.garberfarm.com
Processor and exporter of long grain white rice and yams
Owner: Wayne Garber
Partner: Wayne Garber
Sales/Marketing Partner: Wayne Garber
layamla@aol.com
Production Manager: Earl Garber
Estimated Sales: $1-2.5 Million
Number Employees: 10-19
Square Footage: 200000
Type of Packaging: Consumer, Food Service, Private Label, Bulk
Brands:
Creole Classic
Creole Delights
Creole Rose
Louisiana Mini

4887 **Garber Ice Cream Co Inc**
360 Front Royal Pike
Winchester, VA 22602-7314
540-662-5422
Fax: 540-722-5088 800-662-5422
www.garbersicecream.com
Manufacturing of ice cream and frozen desserts and yogurt.
President: Gary Bayliss
garybayliss@garbersicecream.com
Secretary/Treasurer: Arthur Parrish
Marketing Director: Brian Judy
VP, Sales: Brian Judy
Estimated Sales: $5-10 Million
Number Employees: 50-99
Type of Packaging: Consumer, Private Label

4888 **(HQ)Garcoa Laboratories Inc**
26135 Mureau Rd # 100
Calabasas, CA 91302-3184
818-225-0113
Fax: 818-225-9251 800-831-4247
info@garcoa.com www.garcoa.com
Processor and exporter of vitamins and supplements.
President: Richard Soriano
rsoriano@ci.banning.ca.us
CEO: Gregory Rubin
VP/Sales: Terry Williams
R&D: Moh Chizari
Quality Control: Juan Leal
Marketing: Donna Fedecki
Sales: Gregory Rubin
Operations/Purchasing: Jack Clark
Estimated Sales: & 125 Million
Number Employees: 10-19
Square Footage: 8000000
Type of Packaging: Consumer, Private Label
Brands:
Clean N' Natural
Nature's Beauty
Nature's Glory
Vitamin Classics

4889 **Gardein**
1046 Princeton Dr
Suite 101
Marina del Ray, CA 90292
310-862-8686
www.gardein.com
Meatless prepared foods, including chick'n tenders and meatless meatballs
President/Owner: Yves Potvin
Number of Brands: 1
Number of Products: 25
Type of Packaging: Consumer
Brands:
GARDEIN

4890 **Garden & Valley Isle Seafood**
225 N Nimitz Hwy # 3
Honolulu, HI 96817-5349
808-524-4847
Fax: 808-528-5590 800-689-2733
info@gvisfd.com www.gvisfd.com
Ahi, sashimi, swordfish and snapper; importer and exporter of fresh seafood; wholesaler/distributor of smoked fish and general merchandise
President: Robert Fram
info@gvisfd.com
CFO: Richard Jenks
Vice President: David Marabella
Operations: Cliff Yamauchi
Estimated Sales: $13,500,000
Number Employees: 20-49
Square Footage: 18000
Type of Packaging: Bulk

4891 **(HQ)Garden Complements Inc**
920 Cable Rd
Kansas City, MO 64116-4244
816-421-1090
Fax: 816-421-4220 800-966-1091
info@gardencomplements.com
www.gardencomplements.com
Sauces including barbecue, Mexican, Italian and Asian marinades, salsas, salad dressing, gourmet products
President: Don Blackman
Marketing Director: Jim Pirotte
Estimated Sales: $1-2.5 Million
Number Employees: 5-9
Square Footage: 45000
Type of Packaging: Consumer, Food Service, Private Label, Bulk
Brands:
Amigo
Aussie
Aussie Sauce
Best Choice
Campfire
Gaetano's
Heritage
Old Southern
Primo

4892 **Garden Fresh Gourmet**
1220 E 9 Mile Rd
Ferndale, MI 48220-1972
248-336-8486
Fax: 248-336-8487 866-725-7239
info@gardenfreshsalsa.com
www.gardenfreshgourmet.com
Family owned fresh made salsa company.
Owner/President: Jack Aronson
CFO: Angel Compatna
angel@gardenfreshsalsa.com
Customer Services: Carol Bahri
Estimated Sales: $5-10 Million
Number Employees: 500-999

4893 **Garden Protein International**
200-12751 Vulcan Way
Richmond, BC V6V 3C8
Canada
604-278-7300
Fax: 604-278-8238 877-305-6777
www.gardein.com
Frozen and fresh meals
President: Yves Potvin
Vice President: Ihab Leheta
VP Sales: Richard Bauman
Estimated Sales: $3 Million
Number Employees: 20-49
Type of Packaging: Food Service

4894 **Garden Row Foods**
411 Stone Drive
St Charles, IL 60174-3301
630-762-8880
Fax: 630-587-9388 800-505-9999
eathot.com
Manufacturer and distributor of hot sauces and other products, including Engorphin Rush, Pyromania, Brutal Bajan, and 350 more products.
President: George Kosten
Vice President: John Reeves
Contact: Ed Costen
ek@eathot.com
Number of Products: 15
Square Footage: 2500
Parent Co: Garden Row Foods
Brands:
Caribbean Marketplace
Great Grub Rubs
Tropical Chile Co

4895 **Garden Row Foods**
9150 Grand Avenue
Franklin Park, IL 60131-3038
847-455-2200
Fax: 847-455-9100 800-555-9798
Manufacturer and distribuor of hot sauces and other products, including Endorphin Rush, Pyromania, Brutal Bajan and 350 more products.
Owner: Gary Poppins
Principal: George Kosten
Estimated Sales: $2.5-5,000,000
Number Employees: 10-19
Type of Packaging: Consumer, Food Service, Bulk
Brands:
Brutal Bajan
Endorphin
Mongo
Pyromania

4896 **(HQ)Garden Spot Distributors**
191 Commerce Dr
New Holland, PA 17557-9114
717-354-4936
Fax: 717-354-4934 800-829-5100
Natural, organic and specialty foods. Whole grain flours, beans, raw nuts and dried fruits; frozen foods; cereals and granola; breads and baked goods; snack foods; free-range and natural meats and seafood; special-dietary foods andprepared meals including more than 400 gluten free products
President: John Clough
jclough@gardenspotfoods.com
Marketing Coordinator: Amanda Byrd
Sales Director: Jean O'Donnell
General Manager/Operations Director: Brad Crull
Purchasing Manager: Mark Drury
Estimated Sales: $8 Million
Number Employees: 20-49
Number of Brands: 100+
Square Footage: 40000
Type of Packaging: Consumer, Private Label, Bulk
Other Locations:
Garden Spot Distributors
Sulphur Springs AR

4897 **Garden Valley Corp**
850 Garden Valley Cir
Sutherlin, OR 97479-9860
541-459-9565
Fax: 541-459-1865 gvc@rosenet.net
www.gvcbeans.com
Dehydrated vegetables: peas, lentils and legumes
Owner: Mark M Sterner
President: Perry Sterner
gvc@rosenet.net

Estimated Sales: $2.5-5 000,000
Number Employees: 20-49

4898 **Garden of Flavor LLC**
7501 Carnegie Ave
Cleveland, OH 44103-4809
216-702-7991
www.gardenofflavor.com
Organic juices; concentrates; powders; coffee and tea.
Owner: Lisa Reed
Number Employees: 1-10
Type of Packaging: Private Label

4899 **Garden of the Gods Gourmet**
2528 W Cucharras St
Colorado Springs, CO 80904-3029
719-471-2799
Fax: 719-577-4896 877-229-1548
www.godsmarketandcafe.com
A multi-faceted gourmet company. A unique blend of seasonings and spices, plus a variety of fresh and frozen specialty foods.
President: Sandy Vanderstoup
Estimated Sales: Less than $500,000
Number Employees: 20-49

4900 **Gardner Pie Co**
191 Logan Pkwy
Akron, OH 44319-1188
330-245-2030
Fax: 330-245-2036 www.gardnerpie.com
Frozen pies
Owner: Robert Goff
rgoff@gardnerpie.com
CEO: Tom Gardner
EVP: Kevin Ray
Director, Quality Assurance: Bryan Reynolds
VP, Marketing/Sales: Tom Cavanaugh
Sales Director: Kevin Hickernell
rgoff@gardnerpie.com
Estimated Sales: $3-5 Million
Number Employees: 50-99
Square Footage: 54000
Type of Packaging: Consumer, Food Service, Private Label

4901 **Gardner's Gourmet**
45450 Industrial Pl # 3
Fremont, CA 94538-6474
510-490-6106
Fax: 510-490-4563 800-676-8558
info@greatdrink.com www.greatdrink.com
Processor and exporter of frosted caffe ghiaccio, granitas, iced cappuccino and smoothie mixes, our original fruit ices, concentrates, frozen cocktails, fruit purees and flavoring syrups.
Owner: Beverly Fritz
Estimated Sales: $3-5,000,000
Number Employees: 1-4
Brands:
Ghiaccio
X-Treme Freeze

4902 **Gardners Candies Inc**
2600 Adams Ave
PO Box E
Tyrone, PA 16686-8850
814-684-3925
Fax: 814-684-3928 800-242-2639
info@gardnerscandies.com
www.gardnerscandies.com
Original Peanut Butter Meltaways®, boxed chocolates, pretzels and popcorn, brittle and roasted nuts, sugar free candy.
President: Sam Phillips
Year Founded: 1897
Estimated Sales: $25-49.9 Million
Number Employees: 100-249
Square Footage: 6708
Type of Packaging: Consumer

4903 **Garelick Farms**
626 Lynnway
Lynn, MA 01905-3030
781-599-1300
Fax: 781-598-1377 garelickfarms.com
Dairy
Vice President: Phil Littlefield
Vice President: Nicholas Scangas
Marketing Director: C Scangas
Purchasing Manager: D David
Year Founded: 1931
Estimated Sales: $20-50 Million
Number Employees: 500-999
Parent Co: Suiza Foods

4904 **(HQ)Garelick Farms**
2711 North Haskell Avenue
Suite 3400
Dallas, TX 75204
214-303-3400
Fax: 214-303-2307 800-343-4982
diane_gilley@deanfoods.com
www.garelickfarms.com
Milk, juice, spring water, cider and eggnog
Chairman/CEO: Gregg Engles
Managing Partner: Ton Davis
EVP/CFO: Shaun Mara
SVP/Chief Information Officer: Barbara Carlini
EVP/General Counsel: Steven Kemps
EVP Research/Development: Kelly Duffin-Maxwell
Sales/Marketing: Chris Keyes
Contact: Stephanie Hayward
stephanie_hayward@deanfoods.com
Purchasing: Steve Stewart
Number Employees: 1,000-4,999
Parent Co: Suiza Dairy Group
Type of Packaging: Consumer, Food Service
Other Locations:
Garelick Farms 508 473-0550
Mendon MA
Garelick Farms 800 343-4982
Franklin MA
Garelick Farms 800 648-0135
Burlington NJ
Brands:
All Natural
Garelick

4905 **Garland Truffles, Inc.**
3020 Ode Turner Rd
Hillsborough, NC 27278
919-732-3041
Fax: 919-732-6037 sheila@garlandtruffles.com
www.garlandtruffles.com
Mushrooms including rare truffle mushrooms, also, truffle tree nursery
Estimated Sales: $1.6 Million
Number Employees: 11
Type of Packaging: Food Service

4906 **Garlic Co**
18602 Zerker Rd
Bakersfield, CA 93263
661-393-4212
Fax: 661-393-9340 www.thegarliccompany.com
Peeled and processed garlic, shallots, onions and ginger
CFO: Gordon Cook
gcook@thegarliccompany.com
Vice President, Sales: John Duffus
Year Founded: 1980
Estimated Sales: $50-100 Million
Number Employees: 100-249

4907 **Garlic Festival Foods**
PO Box 2309
Hollister, CA 95024
831-638-9556
Fax: 831-638-3505 888-427-5423
custserv@garlicfestival.com
www.garlicfestival.com
Garlic seasoning, sauce, mustard and dressing
President, Founder: Caryl Simpson
CFO: Tracy Taggart
Estimated Sales: $500,000-$1 Million
Number Employees: 5-9
Square Footage: 20600
Parent Co: Randan Corporation
Type of Packaging: Consumer, Bulk
Brands:
Garli Garni
Garlic Festival
Gourmet Gold

4908 **Garlic Valley Farms Inc**
624 Ruberta Ave
Glendale, CA 91201
818-247-9600
Fax: 818-247-9828 800-424-7990
Info@GarlicValleyFarms.com
www.garlicvalleyfarms.com
Processor, importer and exporter of liquid garlic products including juices and purees
President: William Anderson
CFO: Sonja Anderson
R&D: Bill Brock
Contact: Noli Leoncio
noli@garlicvalleyfarms.com
Estimated Sales: $1.2,000,000
Number Employees: 5-9
Number of Products: 2
Square Footage: 30000
Type of Packaging: Consumer
Brands:
Garlic Juices

4909 **Garman Routing Systems Inc**
1612 Barthel Road
PO Box 1126
Taylor, TX 76574
410-561-8085
Fax: 410-561-8086 512-535-0178
www.garmanrouting.com
Route accounting and distribution software for all route distribution applications including that of sales order entry; sales analysis; inventory control; full service vending; truck dispatch. Food industry uses include soft drinkbottlers, bottled water delivery, snack food distributors, dairy delivery, and coffee delivery services.
Sales Manager: Chip Sturm

4910 **Garon Foods**
900 Camarato Dr
Herrin, IL 62948-6457
618-942-4810
Fax: 618-942-4811 gus@garonfoods.com
www.garonfoods.com
Manufactures peppers including jalapenos, habaneros, and bell, vegetables, herbs and fruits. Value added blending, sauces, and purees
Owner: Gary Griesbach
Sales: Gloryel Griesbach
Estimated Sales: A
Number Employees: 10-19
Number of Brands: 1
Type of Packaging: Bulk
Brands:
El Gusto

4911 **Garrett Popcorn Shops**
PO Box 11342
Chicago, IL 60611
312-944-4730
Fax: 312-280-9611 888-476-7267
www.garrettpopcorn.com
Several varieties of popcorn caramel crisp, cheese corn, cashew caramel crisp, macadamia caramel crisp
President: Karen Galaba
Estimated Sales: $300,000-500,000
Number Employees: 1-4
Type of Packaging: Bulk

4912 **Garrison Brewing**
1149 Marginal Rd
Halifax, NS B3H 4P7
Canada
902-453-5343
Fax: 902-453-4672 beer@garrisonbrewing.com
www.garrisonbrewing.com
Beers
President: Brian Titus
Plant Accountant: Lorna MacPhee
Marketing Coordinator: Katie McDonald
Sales Manager: Todd Johns
Office Administrator: Shelly Simpson
VP Operations: Mark Obermaier
BrewMaster: Daniel Girard
Estimated Sales: $826.6 Thousand
Number Employees: 10

4913 **Gartner Studios Inc**
220 Myrtle St E
Stillwater, MN 55082-5033
651-351-7700
Fax: 651-351-1408 www.gartnerstudios.com
Cakes, pastries.
Owner: Gregory Gartner
gregory.gartner@gartner.com
Marketing: Steve Griffith
Number Employees: 100-249

4914 **Garuda International**
PO Box 159
Exeter, CA 93221-0159
559-594-4380
Fax: 559-594-4689 www.garudaint.com
Development and marketing of ingredients derived from natural sources
President/CEO: J Roger Matkin
Marketing/Sales: Bassam Faress
Contact: Liang Chen
lchen@garudaint.com
Estimated Sales: $500,000-$1 Million
Number Employees: 5-9
Square Footage: 30000
Type of Packaging: Private Label, Bulk
Brands:
Cowcium
Lesstanol
Milcal
Milcal-Fg
Milcal-Tg
Moo-Calcium
Octacosanol Gf
Vege-Coat

4915 **Gary Farrell Vineyards-Winery**
10701 Westside Rd
Healdsburg, CA 95448-8355
707-473-2909
Fax: 707-433-9060 866-277-9463
concierge@garyfarrellwinery.com
Producer of a 1982 Russian River Valley Pinot Noir. Also produces premium Chardonnay, Merlot, Cabernet Sauvignon and Zinfandel.
President: Gary Farrell
Contact: Tara Albertson
tara@garyfarrellwinery.com
Number Employees: 5-9

4916 **Gary's Frozen Foods**
2311 109th St
Lubbock, TX 79423-7256
806-745-1933
Fax: 806-745-3141
Barbecue beef, frozen smoked beef brisket, corn dogs and super dogs
President: Buddy Tidwell
Estimated Sales: Under $500,000
Number Employees: 20
Type of Packaging: Consumer, Food Service

4917 **Gaslamp Co Popcorn**
880 Columbia Ave
Suite 6
Riverside, CA 92507-2159
951-684-6767
Fax: 951-864-6762 877-237-8276
www.rudolphfoods.com
Popcorn and kettle corn
President: John Rudolph
CEO: Leslie Accuar
leslie@gaslamppopcorn.com
Senior VP: Hap Eliott
Estimated Sales: Less Than $500,000
Number Employees: 5-9
Parent Co: Rudolph Foods

4918 **Gaspar's Linguica Co Inc**
384 Faunce Corner Rd
North Dartmouth, MA 02747-1257
508-998-2012
Fax: 508-998-2015 800-542-2038
gaspars@linguica.com www.linguica.com
Portugese sausage, linguica, chourico, turkey linguica and chourico, andouille, kielbasa, salapicao, chourizos and morcela
President: Charles Gaspar
Sales Director: Randy Gaspar
IT: Annette Scrocca
gaspararap@linguica.com
Plant Manager: Charles Gaspar
Estimated Sales: $6 Million
Number Employees: 20-49
Square Footage: 102000
Type of Packaging: Consumer, Food Service, Private Label

4919 **Gaston Dupre**
1000 Italian Way
Suite 200
Excelsior Springs, MO 64024-8016
817-629-6275
Fax: 816-502-6722
Wheat products-pasta
President: Terri Webb McMillin
Co-owner: Michelle Muscat
Estimated Sales: $10-20,000,000
Number Employees: 20-49
Brands:
Eddie's
Michelle's

4920 **Gateway Food Products Co**
1728 N Main St
Dupo, IL 62239-1045
618-286-4844
Fax: 618-286-3444 877-220-1963
traines@gatewayfoodproducts.com
www.gatewayfoodproducts.com
Syrups, vegetable oils and shortenings; exporter of corn syrup; wholesaler/distributor of general line items; also shortening flakes, popcorn oils and butter toppings
President: John Crosley
jcrosley@gatewayfoodproducts.com
Vice President: Carroll Crosley
Quality Control: Jeremy Gray
Marketing Director: Teresa Raines
Sales Director: Teresa Raines
Operations Manager: Jeremy Gray
Production Manager: Jim Raines
Plant Manager: Jim Raines
Purchasing Manager: John Crosley
Estimated Sales: $10-20 Million
Number Employees: 10-19
Number of Products: 9
Square Footage: 75000
Type of Packaging: Food Service, Private Label, Bulk
Brands:
Du Crose
Du Glaze
Du Sweet
Gateway-Du Bake

4921 **Gator Hammock Corp**
25 S State Route 29
Felda, FL 33930
863-675-0687
Fax: 863-675-4938 800-664-2867
chilegator@msn.com www.gatorhammock.com
Sauces, dressings, mustard, cabbage, pickles, and jam
Owner: Gator Hammock
VP/Quality Control/Production: Larry Stewart
Sales Manager/Public Relations: Jenna Barket
chilegator@msn.com
Estimated Sales: Less Than $500,000
Number Employees: 1-4
Parent Co: Gator Hammock
Type of Packaging: Private Label

4922 **Gaucho Foods**
2516 Main Avenue
Fayetteville, IL 62258
877-677-2282
Fax: 618-677-2210 info@gauchofoods.com
www.gauchofoods.com
Beef
President: Jack Lachmann
Estimated Sales: $5-9.9 Million
Number Employees: 15
Square Footage: 12000
Type of Packaging: Consumer, Food Service, Private Label, Bulk
Brands:
Gaucho

4923 **Gaudet & Ouellette**
Chemin Bas-Cap-Pele
Cap-Pele, NB E4N 1L8
Canada
506-577-4016
Fax: 506-577-4006
Smoked herring
President: Normand Ouellette
Estimated Sales: $5,000,000
Number Employees: 30
Type of Packaging: Bulk

4924 **Gay's Wild Maine Blueberries**
PO Box 100
Old Town, ME 04468
207-570-3535
Fax: 207-581-3499 wildblueberries@gwi.net
www.wildblueberries.com
Blueberries
President: Paul Gay

4925 **Gayle's Sweet N' Sassy Foods**
269 S Beverly Dr
Suite 472
Beverly Hills, CA 90212-3851
310-246-1792
Fax: 310-246-1794 info@gaylesbbq.com
www.gaylesbbq.com
Barbecue sauce
Owner: Gayle Gannes
g.gannes@gaylesbbq.com
Estimated Sales: Under $500,000
Number Employees: 20-49

4926 **Gaytan Foods Inc**
15430 Proctor Ave
City Of Industry, CA 91745-1024
626-330-4553
Fax: 626-330-1224 800-242-9826
ryan@gaytanfoods.com www.gaytanfoods.com
Snacks, pork rinds, cheese puffs
Owner: Rudolph Gaytan
rudolph@gaytanfoods.com
Number Employees: 100-249

4927 **Gearharts Fine Chocolates**
416 W Main St
Suite C
Charlottesville, VA 22903-5557
434-972-9100
Fax: 434-972-9104 800-625-0595
info@gearhartschocolates.com
www.gearhartschocolates.com
Chocolate
Owner: Tim Gearhart
info@gearhartschocolates.com
Marketing: William Hamilton
Estimated Sales: Less Than $500,000
Number Employees: 1-4

4928 **Gedney Foods Co**
12243 Branford St
Sun Valley, CA 91352
952-448-2612
888-244-0653
info@gedneypickle.com www.gedneyfoods.com
Condiments, barbecue sauces, vinegars, syrups, pickles, relishes, sauerkraut, salsas, salad dressings, mayonnaise, mustard; cucumbers
CEO: Gary Ethan Kamins
VP, Operations: Rod Prochaska
Estimated Sales: $6-8 Million
Number Employees: 100-249
Parent Co: PMC Global, Inc.
Type of Packaging: Consumer, Food Service, Private Label, Bulk
Brands:
Devil's Fire
Gedney
Geraldo's
Hiawatha
Max's
Minnesaurus Dill Picklodon
Northland
Northwoods
Pep Fest
State Fair
Cains
DelMonte

4929 **GeeFree**
1046 Princeton Dr
Suite 101
Marina del Ray, CA 90292
310-862-8686
www.gardein.com
Gluten-free puff pastry and prepared foods
President/Owner: Susan Hougui
Number of Brands: 1
Number of Products: 25
Type of Packaging: Consumer
Brands:
GEEFREE

4930 **Gehl Foods, Inc.**
N116 W 15970 Main Street
PO Box 1004
Germantown, WI 53022
262-251-8572
Fax: 262-250-6847 800-521-2873
help@gehls.com www.gehls.com
Beverages, savory sauces, wholesome puddings, chips and jalapenos.

President: Frank Hughes
CEO: Katherine Gehl
VP: Michael Stewart
VP Marketing: John Slawny
VP Sales: Tracy Propst
Human Resources Manager: Keri Cannestra
VP Operations: John Shaughnessy
Purchasing: Ken St Clair
Number Employees: 220
Square Footage: 633000
Brands:
Gehl Mainstream Cafe
Gehl Gourmet

4931 **Gel Spice Co LLC**
48 Hook Rd
Bayonne, NJ 07002-5007
201-339-0700
Fax: 201-339-0024 800-922-0230
sales@gelspice.com www.gel-spice.com
Spices, seeds and bakery ingredients
President: Harry Blumenfeld
harry@gelspice.com
Vice President: Jacob Engel
Marketing Director: Sherman Engel
Purchasing Manager: Gershon Engel
Number Employees: 50-99
Square Footage: 250000
Type of Packaging: Consumer, Food Service, Private Label, Bulk

4932 **Gelateria Naia**
736 Alfred Nobel Dr
Hercules, CA 94547-1805
510-724-2479
www.gelaterianaia.com
Gelato and sorbetto
Co-Founder: Trevor Morris
Co-Founder: Chris Tan
Contact: Tiona Beamon
tbeamon@bargelato.com
Estimated Sales: Less Than $500,000
Number Employees: 5-9

4933 **Gelati Celesti**
612 Meyer Ln # 2
Redondo Beach, CA 90278-5274
310-372-2593
Fax: 310-798-0043 800-550-7550
sales@gelaticelesti.com www.gelaticelesti.com
Gelati, sorbets and gelato truffles
President: Steve Edmonds
sales@gelaticelesti.com
Estimated Sales: $2.5-5,000,000
Number Employees: 10-19
Type of Packaging: Consumer, Food Service, Private Label, Bulk
Brands:
Gelati Celesti

4934 **Gelato Fiasco**
74 Maine St
Brunswick, ME 04011-2015
207-607-4262
delicious@gelatofiasco.com
www.gelatofiasco.com
Gelato
Co-Founder and CEO: Joshua Davis
Co-Founder and President: Bruno Tropeano
Marketing Director: Bobby Guerette
Sales Director: Steve Smith
Number Employees: 10-19

4935 **Gelato Fresco**
60 Tycos Drive
Toronto, ON M6B 1V9
Canada
416-785-5415
Fax: 416-781-3133 info@gelatofresco.com
www.gelatofresco.com
Natural ice cream, sorbet and tartufo
President: Hart Melvin
Estimated Sales: $1.3 Million
Number Employees: 5
Square Footage: 20000
Type of Packaging: Consumer, Food Service
Brands:
Gelato Fresco

4936 **Gelato Giuliana**
240 Sargent Dr # 9
110 Terminal Plaza
New Haven, CT 06511-6108
203-772-0607
Fax: 203-772-0612 gelatogiuliana@sbcglobal.net
Gelatos and flavored gelatos
Owner: Deborah Cairo
Vice President: Deborah Cairo
Research & Development: Giuliana Maravalle
Quality Congrol & Marketing Director: Deborah Cairo
Sales & Operations Manager: Mike Desarbo
Public Relations & Production Manager: Jarett Casman
dcairo@gelatogiuliana.com
Plant Manager & Purchasing Director: Giuliana Maravalle
Number Employees: 50-99
Square Footage: 20000

4937 **Gelita North America**
2445 Port Neal Rd
Sergeant Bluff, IA 51054-7728
712-943-5516
Fax: 712-943-3372 800-223-9244
service.na@gelita.com
Gelatine
President: Jorg Siebert
CFO: Robert Mayberry
robert.mayberry@gelita.com
VP Communications: Michael Teppner
Research & Development: Dr J Michael Dunn
Director Edible Gelatine: Jeremy Kaufmann
National Accounts Manager: Michelle Shapkauski
Senior Sales Manager: Tonja Lipp
Number Employees: 250-499
Brands:
Gelita

4938 **Gelnex Gelatins**
30 North Michigan Ave
Suite 1111
Chicago, IL 60601
312-577-4275
Fax: 888-505-1771 www.gelnex.com
Gelatins
President: Alessandro Luize
CEO: Ross Priebbenow
Executive VP: Felipe Chaluppe
fchaluppe@gelnex.com
Estimated Sales: $500,000-1 Million
Number Employees: 4

4939 **Gelsinger Food Products**
2014 Montrose Avenue
Montrose, CA 91020-1605
818-248-7811
Fax: 818-957-2545
Frozen and refrigerated beef, game meats, lamb, pork, veal, smoked meats, poultry, cured meats, cooked meats
President: Ron Gelsinger
paul@azspinal.org
Sales/Marketing Manager: Kirk Gelsinger
Estimated Sales: $2.5-5,000,000
Number Employees: 20-49

4940 **Gem Berry Products**
733 Kaniksu Shores Rd
Sandpoint, ID 83864
208-790-2804
Fax: 866-357-3505 800-231-1699
gemberryproducts@gmail.com
www.gemberry.com
Jams, jellies, syrups, gift packs.
President and Owner: Harry Menser
Sales and Marketing: Sandy Dell
Estimated Sales: $500,000-$1,000,000
Type of Packaging: Consumer, Food Service, Bulk

4941 **Gem Meat Packing Co**
515 E 45th St
Garden City, ID 83714-4896
208-375-9424
Fax: 208-375-1568 gempackonline@live.com
Beef, pork and sausages
President: Tyler Compton
Estimated Sales: $7 Million
Number Employees: 10-19

4942 **Gemsa Oils**
14370 Gannet St
La Mirada, CA 90638
714-521-1736
www.gemsaoils.com
Olive oil importer
President: Angela Viscomi
Type of Packaging: Consumer, Food Service, Private Label, Bulk
Brands:
Vita
Albergo

4943 **Genarom International**
6 Santa Fe Way
Cranbury, NJ 08512-3288
609-409-6200
Fax: 609-409-6500
Processor and exporter of marinades, sauces and flavors including beef, chicken, turkey, pork, ham, cheese, seafood and creams
CEO: Gary Rodkin
President/Comercial Foods: Paul Maass
Number Employees: 20-49
Square Footage: 60000
Type of Packaging: Food Service, Bulk
Brands:
Dohlar
Genarom

4944 **Gene & Boots Candies Inc**
2939 Pittsburgh Rd
Perryopolis, PA 15473-1005
724-736-2701
800-864-4222
customerservice@geneandboots.com
www.geneandboots.com
Chocolates and old fashion ice cream
Owner: Jan Donati
j.donati@geneandboots.com
Estimated Sales: $5-9.9 Million
Number Employees: 10-19
Square Footage: 8196
Type of Packaging: Consumer

4945 **Gene Belk Briners**
10380 Alder Ave
Bloomington, CA 92316-2302
909-877-1819
Fax: 909-877-2460 info@genebelkbriners.com
www.genebelkbriners.com
Pickled vegetables
Manager: Curtis Belk
Estimated Sales: $20-50 Million
Number Employees: 20-49
Type of Packaging: Food Service

4946 **Gene's Citrus Ranch**
4805 Buckeye Road
Palmetto, FL 34221-7400
941-723-0504
Fax: 941-723-3620 888-723-2006
www.citrusranch.com
Oranges and grapefruit
President: Scott Mixon
Vice President: Emory Mixon
Estimated Sales: $10-20,000,000
Number Employees: 10-19
Type of Packaging: Consumer, Food Service

4947 **General Mills**
1 General Mills Blvd.
Minneapolis, MN 55426
800-248-7310
www.generalmills.com
Branded consumer foods such as snacks, soups, ice cream, baking products, cereals, pasta, spices, and more.
Chairman/CEO: Jeffrey Harmening
CFO: Kofi Bruce
General Counsel/Secretary: Richard Allendorf
Chief Marketing Officer: Ivan Pollard
Year Founded: 1856
Estimated Sales: $15.6 Billion
Number Employees: 38,000
Number of Brands: 42
Type of Packaging: Consumer, Food Service
Other Locations:
Production Facility
Albuquerque NM
Production Facility
Belvidere IL
Production Facility
Buffalo NY
Production Facility

Carlisle IL
Production Facility
Carson CA
Production Facility
Cedar Rapids IA
Production Facility
Covington GA
Production Facility
Golden Valley MN
Production Facility
Great Falls MT
Production Facility
Hannibal MO
Production Facilty
Kansas City MO
Production Facility
Lodi CA
Production Facility
Milwaukee WI
Brands:
Betty Crocker®
Bisquick®
Gold Medal®
Immaculate Baking®
Jus-Rol®
Knack & Back®
La Saltena®
Pillsbury®
Yoki®
Cascadian Farm®
Cheerios®
Chex®
Cinnamon Toast Crunch®
Fiber One®
Kix®
Lucky Charms®
Monsters®
Total®
Trix®
Wheaties®
Haagen-Dazs®
Annie's®
Green Giant®
Hamburger Helper®
Old El Paso®
V.Pearl®
Wanchai Ferry®
Food Should Taste Good®
Larabar®
Liberte®
Mountain High®
Muir Glen®
Latina®
Blue Buffalo®
Totino's®
Bugles®
Fruit by the Foot®
Gardetto's®
Nature Valley®
Progresso®
Parampara®
Yoplait®

4948 **Generation Tea**
PO Box 907
Monsey, NY 10952-0907
845-352-1216
Fax: 845-352-2973 866-742-5668
info@generationtea.com www.generationtea.com
Chinese tea
Owner: Michael Sanft
msanft@generationtea.com
Co-Owner: Marci Sanft
Estimated Sales: $300,000-500,000
Number Employees: 1-4

4949 **Generous Coffee**
Denver, CO
info@generousmovement.com
www.generousmovement.com
Roasted coffee beans and ground coffee
President/Co-Founder: Benjamin Higgins
Co-Founder: Riley Fuller
Year Founded: 2017

4950 **Genesee Brewing Company**
445 Saint Paul Street
Rochester, NY 14605
585-263-9200
Fax: 585-546-8928 www.geneseebeer.com
Beers
President: Johnhen Henderson
CEO: Ramon Sanchez
Marketing Brand Manager: Jennifer McCauley
Vice President, Sales: Donald Cotter
Contact: Michael Baker
mbaker@highfalls.com
Estimated Sales: $2 Million
Number Employees: 460+
Number of Brands: 12
Parent Co: Cerveceria Costa Rica S.A.
Type of Packaging: Consumer, Food Service
Brands:
Genesee Beer
Genesee Cream Ale
Genesee Ice
Genesee Light
Genesee N.A.
Helles Bock
IPA
JW Dundee's Honey Brown Lager
Koch's Golden Anniversary
Michael Shea's Irish Amber
Orange Honey Cream Ale
Scotch Ale

4951 **Genesis Today**
6800 Burleson Rd # 180
Austin, TX 78744-2325
512-858-1977
800-916-6642
www.genesistoday.com
Superfood supplements
CEO: Lindsey Duncan
lduncan@genesistoday.net
CEO: William Meissner
CFO: Andy Bergad
Vice President: Jeff Brucker
Number Employees: 100-249

4952 **Geneva Food Products**
2664 Jewett Ln
Sanford, FL 32771-1678
407-323-5518
Fax: 407-323-4394 800-240-2326
Lysanders@genevafoods.com
Dried beans, soups, marinades, dip mixes and seasoning blends
President: Tom Vandermar
tom@genevafoods.com
Senior Partner: Gary Clark
Partner: Angie Fontes
Estimated Sales: $10-20,000,000
Number Employees: 10-19

4953 **Genghis Grill Franchise Concepts**
18900 Dallas Pkwy # 125
Dallas, TX 75287-6922
214-774-4240
Fax: 214-774-4243 www.genghisgrill.com
Asian prepared foods
CEO: Carrie Waddill
cwaddill@decaturisd.us
Number Employees: 10-19

4954 **Genisoy**
790 Tennessee Street
San Francisco, CA 94107
866-606-3829
Fax: 415-401-0087 866-972-6879
genisoy@worldpantry.com www.genisoy.com
Powdered beverage mixes, protein bars, sports nutrition products and soy protein bars
President: Tim Bruer
Marketing: Rich Martin
Plant Manager: Jeff Amlin
Estimated Sales: $.5-1 million
Number Employees: 1-4

4955 **Genisoy**
555 Steeprock Drive
Suite 700
Downsview, OH M3J 2Z6
800-268-7950
Fax: 800-680-8288 866-972-6879
genisoy@worldpantry.com
Soy products
President/CEO: Doug Williamson
CFO: Al Larson
Director Of Marketing: Sharon Jacobson
VP Sales/Marketing: Duke Field
Estimated Sales: $.5-1 million
Number Employees: 350
Parent Co: Genisoy
Brands:
Genisoy Soy Products
Mlo Sports Nutrition

4956 **Genius Juice**
Torrance, CA 90503
800-682-7790
contact@geniusjuice.com geniusjuice.com
Organic coconut smoothie
CEO: Shawn Sugarman

4957 **Genki USA**
Torrance, CA
www.getskinnynoodles.com
Gluten-free, soy-free noodles and rice
President & COO: Susan Bucher
Year Founded: 2009
Number of Brands: 1
Number of Products: 10
Type of Packaging: Consumer
Brands:
SMARTCAKE
SKINNY

4958 **Gentile Brothers Company**
10310 Julian Dr
Cincinnati, OH 45215
513-531-6000
Fax: 513-771-5569 800-877-7954
Produce
President: Jeff Oaks
CEO: Glen Bryant
CFO, COO: Rick Schimpf
West Virginia Sales Director: Ernie Coe
Director Marketing: Tom Rettig
General Sales: Jim Costello
VP Of Operations & Logistics: Brannon Player
Specialist/Banana/Pineapple: Jim Flehmer
Type of Packaging: Consumer

4959 **Gentle Ben's Brewing Co**
865 E University Blvd
Tucson, AZ 85719-5046
520-624-4177
Fax: 520-884-9776 www.gentlebens.com
Beers
President: Dennis Arnold
dennis@gentlebens.com
Estimated Sales: $1-2,500,000
Number Employees: 50-99
Type of Packaging: Private Label
Brands:
Copperhead Pale Ale
Gentle Ben Winter Brau
Nolan Porter
Red Cat Amber
Taylor Jane's Raspberry Ale
Tucson Blonde

4960 **Gentry's Poultry**
262 Speigner Rd
Ward, SC 29166-9438
803-254-8724
Fax: 864-445-2331 800-926-2161
Poultry
President: Wesley Gentry Jr
VP: Wesley Gentry III
Estimated Sales: $5-10 Million
Number Employees: 100-249
Type of Packaging: Consumer, Food Service

4961 **George A Dickel & Company**
1950 Cascade Hollow Road
P.O. Box 1448
Tullahoma, TN 37388
931-857-4110
888-342-5352
GeorgeDickel@consumer-care.net
www.dickel.com
Whiskey
Master Distiller: John Lunn
Plant Manager: Jennings Backus
Estimated Sales: $10-20 Million
Number Employees: 20-49
Parent Co: Guiness PLC
Type of Packaging: Consumer

4962 **George A Jeffreys & Company**
504 Roanoke St
Salem, VA 24153-3552
540-389-8220
Fax: 540-387-7418 www.novozymes.com
Enzymes

Manager: Doug Acksel
dacksel@novozymes.com
Estimated Sales: $5-10 Million
Number Employees: 10-19
Square Footage: 100000

4963 George Chiala Farms Inc
15500 Hill Rd
Morgan Hill, CA 95037-9516
408-778-0562
Fax: 408-779-4034 www.gcfarmsinc.com
Tomatillos, garlic, peppers
President: Alice Chiala
Chief Operating Officer: Tim Chiala
Chief Financial Officer: Christi Becerra
Quality Assurance Manager: Bob See
Sales Director: Joe Trammell
Production Manager: Sam Garcia
Plant Engineer: Rusty McMillan
Estimated Sales: $20-50 Million
Number Employees: 100-249
Number of Products: 300
Square Footage: 40000
Type of Packaging: Food Service, Bulk

4964 George E De Lallo Co Inc
6390 State Route 30
Jeannette, PA 15644-3193
724-523-6577
Fax: 724-523-0981 877-335-2556
info@DeLallo.com www.delallo.com
Pasta, sauces, olives, oils
President: Fran Delallo
fran@delallo.com
Purchasing Agent: J Panichella
Estimated Sales: $500,000-$1 Million
Number Employees: 50-99
Type of Packaging: Consumer

4965 George F Brocke & Sons
223 W 8th Street
Moscow, ID 83843-2326
208-289-4231
Fax: 208-289-4242
Garbanzo beans, rapeseed
President: George Brocke
General Manager: Dean Brocke
Estimated Sales: $10-20,000,000
Number Employees: 20-49

4966 George Noroian
5700 Balboa Drive
Oakland, CA 94611-2315
510-591-7044
Fax: 661-858-2656
Canned and frozen peaches and orange slices
Proprietor: George Noroian
Estimated Sales: $1-2.5 Million
Number Employees: 5-9
Square Footage: 200000

4967 George Robberecht Seafood
440 Mcguires Wharf Road
Montross, VA 22520-3603
804-472-3556
Fax: 804-472-4800
Blue crab, soft-shell crab, oysters, eel, seafood
President/CEO: Maurice Bosse
President: Wilhemina Bosse
Estimated Sales: $2.5-5 Million
Number Employees: 1-4

4968 George W Saulpaugh & Son
1790 Route 9
Germantown, NY 12526-5512
518-537-6500
Fax: 518-537-5555 info@saulpaughapples.com
www.saulpaughapples.com
Apples, pears, grapes and prunes
Vice President: David Jones

Estimated Sales: $10-20 Million
Number Employees: 20-49
Type of Packaging: Consumer, Food Service, Bulk
Brands:
Clermont

4969 George's Candy Shop Inc
558 S Broad St
Mobile, AL 36603-1124
251-433-1689
Fax: 251-433-3364 800-633-1306
www.3georges.com
Pecans and baked goods
President: Scott Gonzales
scott@3georges.com
VP: Sibhan Gonzales
Estimated Sales: $1500000
Number Employees: 50-99
Square Footage: 120000
Type of Packaging: Consumer
Brands:
3 George
Azalea
Nuthouse

4970 George's Inc
402 W Robinson Ave
Springdale, AR 72764
479-927-7000
800-800-2449
www.georgesinc.com
Frozen chickens.
Chairman: Gary George
Co-CEO & President: Carl George
carl.george@georgesinc.com
Co-CEO & President: Charles George
CFO: Susan White
Chief Strategy & Commercial Officer: Devin Cole
SVP of Foodservice: Brian Coan
Estimated Sales: $410 Million
Number Employees: 1000-4999
Square Footage: 24455
Type of Packaging: Private Label
Brands:
George's
Taste O'Spriing

4971 Georgetown Bagelry
5227 River Rd
Bethesda, MD 20816-1415
301-657-4442
Fax: 301-657-5573 www.georgetownbagelry.com
Bagels
Owner: Mary Beall Adler
mary@georgetownbagelry.com
Estimated Sales: Less Than $500,000
Number Employees: 5-9

4972 Georgetown Cupcake
111 Mercer St
New York, NY 10012-5212
212-431-4504
Fax: 212-431-4360
soho@georgetowncupcake.com
www.georgetowncupcake.com
Cupcakes
Contact: Emily Feldstein
efeldstein@citicenter.org
Estimated Sales: Less Than $500,000
Number Employees: 5-9

4973 Georgetown Farm
P.O.Box 106
Free Union, VA 22940
434-973-6761
Fax: 434-973-7715 888-328-5326
www.eatlean.com
Beef and bison meat; sausage and jerky products
Production: Craig Gibson
Plant Manager: Matt Albert
Estimated Sales: $3-5,000,000
Number Employees: 5-9
Brands:
Georgetown Farm Bison
Georgetown Farm Piedmontese

4974 Georgia Fruitcake Co
5 S Duval St
Claxton, GA 30417-2027
912-739-2683
Fax: 912-739-3419
www.georgiafruitcakecompany.com
Fruitcakes
Owner: Ira Womble
i.womble@georgiafruitcakecompany.com
Estimated Sales: $5-10 Million
Number Employees: 5-9
Number of Brands: 2
Number of Products: 2
Square Footage: 30000
Type of Packaging: Consumer
Brands:
Georgia
Georgia Fruit Cake

4975 Georgia Grinders
301-3400 W Hospital Ave
Chamblee, GA 30341
www.georgiagrinders.com
All-natural nut butters
Founder & CEO: Jaime Foster
Number of Brands: 1
Number of Products: 10
Type of Packaging: Consumer
Brands:
NATURALMOND
GEORGIA GRINDERS

4976 Georgia Nut Co
7500 Linder Ave
Skokie, IL 60077-3270
847-324-3600
Fax: 847-674-1173 877-674-2993
web@georgianut.com www.georgianutcorp.com
Confections, snacks, and nuts
President: Rick Drehobl
CEO: Dave Drehobl
CFO: Jack Arends
Director of Sales & Marketing: John Drehobl
Year Founded: 1945
Estimated Sales: $20-50 Million
Number Employees: 100-249
Square Footage: 2000
Type of Packaging: Bulk
Brands:
Georgia's
Solo
Drizzls
Malt Teenies
Speckles
Teenies

4977 Georgia Seafood Wholesale
5634 New Peachtree Rd
Chamblee, GA 30341
770-936-0483
Fax: 770-936-9332
Scallops, frozen seafood, shrimp
President: Liz Wang
Owner: Jack Wong
Estimated Sales: $3-5 Million
Number Employees: 5-9

4978 Georgia Spice Company
3600 Atlanta Industrial Parkway
Atlanta, GA 30331
404-696-6200
Fax: 404-696-4546 800-453-9997
SShapiro@gaspiceco.com gaspiceco.com
Spices and seasonings
Owner/CEO/Plant Manager: Selma Shapiro
R&D Director: Brian Lusty
Human Resources Director: S Lafosse
Manufacturing Director: Bob Kupinsky
Estimated Sales: $5 Million
Number Employees: 19
Square Footage: 78000
Type of Packaging: Food Service, Private Label, Bulk

4979 Georgia Wines Inc
6469 Battlefield Pkwy
Ringgold, GA 30736-5161
706-937-2177
Fax: 706-937-9860 info@georgiawines.com
www.georgiawines.com
Wines
President: Martha Prouty
proutym@georgiawines.com
Estimated Sales: $5-10 Million
Number Employees: 20-49

4980 Georis Winery
4 Pilot Rd
Carmel Valley, CA 93924-9515
831-659-1050
Fax: 831-659-1054 www.georiswine.com
Wines
President: Walter Georis
Purchasing: Sylvia Georis
Estimated Sales: $500,000-$1,000,000
Number Employees: 5-9
Type of Packaging: Private Label
Brands:
Estate Cabernet Sauvignon
Estate Merlot

4981 Gerard & Dominique Seafoods
16372a Lower Harbor Rd
Harbor, OR 97415
541-469-9494
Fax: 541-469-0757 800-858-0449
www.gdseafoods.com
Canned and frozen seafood
Owner: Julie Tomlinson
Estimated Sales: $190,000
Number Employees: 2
Type of Packaging: Consumer, Food Service
Brands:
Dick & Casey's

4982 Gerber Products Co
1812 N Moore St
Arlington, VA 22209
800-284-9488
www.gerber.com
Infant and toddler food.
President & CEO: Bill Partyka
Year Founded: 1927
Estimated Sales: $477 Million
Number Employees: 5,000-9,999
Parent Co: Nestle
Type of Packaging: Food Service, Bulk
Other Locations:
Production Facility
Fremont MI
Production Facility
Florham Park NJ
Production Facility
Fort Smith NJ
Brands:
Gerber 1st Foods
Gerber 2nd Foods
Gerber 3rd Fodos
Gerber Graduates
Gerber Good Start
Gerber Cereal
Lil'entrees
Pasta Pick Ups
Lil'meals
Nature Select

4983 Gerber's Poultry Inc
5889 Kidron Rd
Kidron, OH 44636
800-362-7381
sales@gerbers.com www.gerbers.com
Poultry.
Owner: Mike Gerber
Year Founded: 1952
Estimated Sales: $20-50 Million
Number Employees: 250-499

4984 Gerhart Coffee Co
224 Wohlsen Way
Lancaster, PA 17603-4043
717-397-8788
Fax: 717-397-3677 800-536-4310
sales@gerhartcoffee.com www.gerhartcoffee.com
Coffee
Owner: Peter Bard
peter_bard@gerhartcoffee.com
Sales: Donald Platt
Estimated Sales: $1-2,500,000
Number Employees: 10-19
Type of Packaging: Private Label

4985 Germack Pistachio Co
2140 Wilkins St
Detroit, MI 48207-2123
313-393-2000
Fax: 313-393-0636 800-872-4006
wholesale@germack.com www.germack.com
Dried fruit, chocolate and nuts
Estimated Sales: $1,000,000-$5,000,000
Number Employees: 20-49
Type of Packaging: Consumer, Food Service

4986 German Bakery at Village Corner
6655 James B Rivers Dr
Stone Mountain, GA 30083
770-498-0329
Fax: 770-498-9863 866-476-6443
germanrestaurant@aol.com
www.germanrestaurant.com
Bakery products
Owner: Hilde Friese
Co-Owner: Clause Friese
Estimated Sales: $1-3,000,000
Number Employees: 10-19
Brands:
Bailey's Irish Cream

4987 Germanton Winery
3530 Hwy 8 & 65
Germanton, NC 27019
336-969-6121
Fax: 336-969-6559 800-322-2894
sales@germantongallery.com
www.germantongallery.com
Wines
President: David Simpson
Treasurer: Judy Simpson
Estimated Sales: Less than $500,000
Number Employees: 1-4

4988 Gertrude & Bronner's Magic Alpsnack
P.O.Box 1958
Vista, CA 92085
844-937-2551
Fax: 760-745-6675 877-786-3649
info@drbronner.com www.drbronner.com
Energy snack bars
President: David Bronner
VP: Ralph Bronner
Estimated Sales: $1-3 Million
Number Employees: 1-4
Type of Packaging: Consumer
Brands:
Dr. Bronner's

4989 Gertrude Hawk Chocolates
901 Keystone Industrial Park Rd
Dunmore, PA 18512
800-822-2032
www.gertrudehawkchocolates.com
Chocolate
President & CEO: Bill Aubrey
baubrey@gertrudehawk.com
Chief Information Officer: Bruce Cottle
Human Resources Director: David Garton
Purchasing Director: Scott Melesky
Year Founded: 1936
Estimated Sales: $100-500 Million
Number Employees: 550

4990 Gesco ENR
139 Rue De La Reine
Gaspe, QC G4X 2R8
Canada
418-368-1414
Fax: 418-368-1812 gesco@globetrotter.qc.ca
Fresh and frozen shrimp
President: Gaetan Denis
Number Employees: 20-49
Type of Packaging: Consumer, Food Service, Private Label, Bulk

4991 Getchell Brothers Inc
1 Union St
P.O. Box 8
Brewer, ME 04412-2040
207-989-7335
Fax: 207-989-7810 800-949-4423
info@getchellbros.com www.getchellbros.com
Wines
President: Doug Farnham
Operations Manager: Bob Morse
Estimated Sales: $2.5-5,000,000
Number Employees: 20-49

4992 Geyser Peak Winery
2306 Magnolia Dr
Healdsburg, CA 95448-9406
707-857-9463
Fax: 707-857-9401 800-255-9463
www.geyserpeakwinery.com
Wines
Winemaker: Ondine Chattan
Manager: Lisa Flohr
lisa.flohr@accoladewinesna.com
Number Employees: 50-99
Brands:
Canyon Road
Geyser Peak
Venezia

4993 Gharana Foods
111 Glendale Ave
Edison, NJ 08817-5280
732-985-9331
Fax: 815-377-3743 orderinfo@gharanafoods.com
www.gharanafoods.com
Indian snacks
Founder: Achyut Patel
Number Employees: 1-4

4994 Ghirardelli Chocolate Co
1111 139th Ave
San Leandro, CA 94578
510-483-6970
800-877-9338
customerservice@ghirardelli.com
www.ghirardelli.com
Chocolates
CEO: Joel Burrows
VP of Professional Products: Chris Eklem
VP of Sales: Rob Budowski
VP of Operations: Samuel Bernegger
Year Founded: 1852
Estimated Sales: $100-500 Million
Number Employees: 250-499
Number of Brands: 1
Type of Packaging: Private Label
Brands:
Ghirardelli

4995 Ghyslain Chocolatier
350 W Deerfield Rd
Union City, IN 47390-1039
765-964-7905
Fax: 765-964-9138 866-449-7524
info@ghyslain.com www.ghyslain.com
Artisan chocolates
President: Ghyslain Maurais
info@ghyslain.com
Estimated Sales: $2.5-5 Million
Number Employees: 20-49

4996 Gia Michaels Confections Inc
318 Meacham Ave
Elmont, NY 11003-3214
516-354-3905
Fax: 516-328-3311 www.giamichaels.com
Cake decorations and confections
Owner: Gia Michaels
g.michaels@giamichaels.com
Marketing: Nicky Juliano
Number Employees: 1-4

4997 Gia Russa
500 McClurg Road
Boardman, OH 44512
330-965-8455
Fax: 330-965-3864 800-527-8772
info@summergardenfood.com
www.summergardenfood.com
Pasta and sauces
Owner/CEO: Thomas R. Zidian
VP Sales/Marketing: Michael Maiello
Plant Operations Manager: Kenny Navoney
Square Footage: 50000
Parent Co: Summer Garden Foods
Other Locations:
Zidian Manufacturing Facility
Youngstown OH

4998 Giambri's Quality Sweets Inc
26 Brand Ave
Clementon, NJ 08021-4211
856-783-1099
Fax: 856-783-6377 866-238-0169
dave@giambris.com www.giambris.com
Hard candies, creamy fudge and chocolates
Owner: David Giambri
dave@giambris.com
Vice President: Josephine Giambri
Number Employees: 10-19

4999 Giant Food
6300 Sherriff Road
Landover, MD 20785
301-341-4100
Fax: 301-618-4967 888-469-4426
www.giantfood.com
Baked products including bread, rolls, cakes, pies, sweetgoods, doughnuts and cookies
Manager: Tarjani Shah
Executive VP/General Manager: Bill Holmes
VP Quality Control: David Richman
Contact: Jennifer Bates
jennifer.bates@usfood.com
Manufacturing Director: Walter Auman
Number Employees: 5,000-9,999
Type of Packaging: Consumer

5000 Gibbon Packing
East Hwy 30
Gibbon, NE 68840
308-468-5771
Fax: 308-468-5262
Boneless beef and offal products

Chairman: Rick Elsman
Estimated Sales: $7 Million
Number Employees: 52
Square Footage: 15083
Type of Packaging: Consumer

5001 **Gibbons Bee Farm**
314 Quinnmoor Dr
Ballwin, MO 63011
636-394-5395
Fax: 636-256-0303 877-736-8607
Honey, salad dressing and honey mustard
Owner: Sharon Gibbons
Sales Manager: John Gibbons
Estimated Sales: $1-3,000,000
Number Employees: 1-4
Type of Packaging: Consumer
Brands:
Gibbons

5002 **Gibbsville Cheese Company**
W2663 County Road 00
Sheboygan Falls, WI 53085
920-564-3242
Fax: 920-564-6129 sales@gibbsvillecheese.com
www.gibbsvillecheese.com
Cheeses
Owner: Phillip Van Tatenhove
Estimated Sales: $1-2.5 Million
Number Employees: 10-19
Square Footage: 15000
Type of Packaging: Consumer

5003 **Gielow Pickles Inc**
5260 Main St
Lexington, MI 48450
810-359-7680
marketing@gielowpickles.com
www.gielowpickles.com
Pickles, sweet relish & peppers
Vice President: Craig Gielow
Year Founded: 1970
Estimated Sales: $40-50 Million
Number Employees: 20-49
Square Footage: 330000
Type of Packaging: Food Service, Private Label
Brands:
Cool Crisp

5004 **Gifford's Ice Cream**
25 Hathaway St
Skowhegan, ME 04976
207-474-9821
Fax: 207-474-6120 800-950-2604
info@giffordsicecream.com
www.giffordsicecream.com
Ice cream, non-fat frozen yogurt, sherbet and sorbet
President/Owner: Roger Gifford
CEO: Lindsay Skilling
Treasurer: John Gifford
Contact: Teresa Clement
teresaclement@giffordsicecream.com
Estimated Sales: $10-20 Million
Number Employees: 40+
Type of Packaging: Consumer, Food Service, Private Label, Bulk
Brands:
Gifford's

5005 **Gifford's Ice Cream & Candy Co**
8810 Brookville Rd
Silver Spring, MA 02910
800-708-1938
info@giffords.com
Ice cream and candy
President/CEO: Marcelo Ramagem
VP: Neal Lieberman
Number Employees: 5

5006 **Gift Basket Supply World**
815 Haines Street
Jacksonville, FL 32206-6050
904-353-6278
Fax: 904-633-8764 800-786-4438
Gourmet foods
President: David Paulk
Estimated Sales: $2.5-5,000,000
Number Employees: 5-9

5007 **Gil's Gourmet Gallery**
577 Ortiz Ave
Seaside, CA 93955-3522
831-394-3305
Fax: 831-394-9144 800-438-7480
gil@gilsgourmet.com www.gilsgourmet.com
Condiments, salsa, pasta sauce, olives
President: Gil Tortolani
gil@gilsgourmet.com
VP: Dylan Tortolani
Marketing Manager: Dave Elgin
Estimated Sales: $1-2,500,000
Number Employees: 10-19
Type of Packaging: Private Label, Bulk

5008 **Gilda Industries Inc**
2525 W 4th Ave
Hialeah, FL 33010-1339
305-887-8286
Fax: 305-888-4064 www.gildaindustries.com
Crackers
President: Juan Blazquez
gilda@gape.net
Director: Carmen Blazquez
Estimated Sales: $16,000,000
Number Employees: 50-99
Type of Packaging: Private Label

5009 **Gile Cheese Store**
116 N Main St
Cuba City, WI 53807-1538
608-744-3456
Fax: 608-744-3457 www.gilecheese.com
Cheese, cheese products
Owner: John Gile
Co-Owner: Diane Gile
Marketing: Tim Gile
Estimated Sales: Less Than $500,000
Number Employees: 1-4

5010 **Gill's Onions LLC**
1051 Pacific Ave
Oxnard, CA 93030-7254
805-240-1931
Fax: 805-271-1932 800-348-2255
sales@gillsonions.com www.gillsonions.com
Onions
President: Steve Gill
Director Sales and Marketing: Nelia Alamo
Estimated Sales: $3.5 Million
Number Employees: 100-249
Square Footage: 160000
Type of Packaging: Food Service, Bulk

5011 **Gillians Foods**
82 Sanderson Ave # 122
Lynn, MA 01902-1900
781-586-0086
www.gilliansfoodsglutenfree.com
Gluten free foods
Owner: Bob Otolo
chefbob@gilliansfoods.com
Number Employees: 5-9

5012 **Gillies Coffee**
150 19th St
P.O. Box 320206
Brooklyn, NY 11232-1005
718-499-7766
Fax: 718-499-7771 800-344-5526
info@gilliescoffee.com www.gilliescoffee.com
Coffee
Owner: David Chabbott
davidhchabbott@gmail.com
Estimated Sales: $3.4 Million
Number Employees: 20-49
Square Footage: 28000
Type of Packaging: Food Service, Private Label, Bulk
Brands:
Brooklyn Java
Gillies
Long Island Iced Tea

5013 **Gilly's Hot Vanilla**
877 East S
PO Box 1991
Lenox, MA 1240
413-637-1515
Fax: 413-637-1515 www.usbizs.com
Hot vanilla drink mixes
Owner: Joanne Deutch
Production: Carl Deutch
Estimated Sales: Under $500,000
Number Employees: 1-4
Type of Packaging: Consumer, Food Service, Bulk
Brands:
Gilly's Hot Vanilla

5014 **Gilmore's Seafoods**
129 Court St
Bath, ME 04530-2054
207-443-5231
Fax: 207-386-3271 800-849-9667
gilmore@gilmoreseafood.com gilmoreslobster.com
Seafood
Co-Owner: Kevin Gilmore
Co-Owner: Ben Gilmore
Contact: Danny Gilmore
danny@gilmoreseafood.com
Estimated Sales: $300,000-500,000
Number Employees: 1-4

5015 **(HQ)Gilster-Mary Lee Corp**
1037 State St
PO Box 227
Chester, IL 62233
618-826-2361
Fax: 618-826-2973
webmaster@gilstermarylee.com
www.gilstermarylee.com
Cake & bread mixes, pancake mixes, drink mixes, cereal, potatoes, frostings, muffin mixes, popcorn, stuffing, chocolate items, brownie mixes, pie shell, baking soda, soups, sauces, and gravies, pastas, cookie mixes, marshmallow itemsmacaroni & cheese, coatings, biscuit mixes, puddings & gelatins, rice, dinners, and organic foods.
VP Sales/Marketing: Tom Welge
Number Employees: 1000-4999
Type of Packaging: Consumer, Food Service, Private Label, Bulk
Other Locations:
Baking Mix/Shredded Wheat Plants
Chester IL
Baking/Mac&Cheese & Pasta Plants
Steeleville IL
Cocoa Plant
Momence IL
Baking Mix Plant
Centralia IL
Popcorn/Cereal Plant Dist, Ctr
McBride MO
Corrugated Sheet Plant
McBride MO
Baking Mix & Cereal Plants
Perryville MO
Popcorn Plant
Jasper MO
Cereal Plant
Joplin MO
Drink Mix Plant
Wilson AR
Brands:
Duff's
Hospitality
Py-O-My

5016 **Gilt Edge Flour Mills**
1090 W 1200 N
Richmond, UT 84333-1413
435-258-2425
Fax: 435-258-2428
customerservice@giltedgeflour.com
www.giltedgeflour.com
Flour
President: Keith Giusto
Vice President: Evan Perry
evan@giltedgeflour.com
Operations Manager: Dave Baker
Estimated Sales: $14 Million
Number Employees: 20-49
Type of Packaging: Consumer, Food Service, Private Label, Bulk
Brands:
Gilt Edge

5017 **Gimbals Fine Candies**
250 Hillside Blvd
S San Francisco, CA 94080-1644
650-588-4844
Fax: 650-588-0150 800-344-6225
info@gimbals.net www.gimbalscandy.com
Confectionary
President/CEO: Lance Gimbal
sales@gimbals.net
VP Sales/Marketing: Estle Kominowski
Purchasing: Ward Sims

Estimated Sales: $5-10 Million
Number Employees: 20-49
Number of Brands: 1
Number of Products: 100
Square Footage: 90000
Type of Packaging: Consumer, Bulk
Brands:
Jelly Bean
Kleergum
Lowcoom
Soft Chews
Taffy Delight
Taffy Lite
Ultimate

5018 Gimme Coffee
228 Mott St # 2
New York, NY 10012-5704
212-226-4011
877-446-6325
info@gimmecoffee.com www.gimmecoffee.com
Coffee
Manager: Eva Havle
eva.havle@gimmecoffee.com
Number Employees: 5-9

5019 Gimme Health Foods
San Rafael, CA 94903
gimmesnacks.com
Seaweed products
Co-Founder: Annie Chun
Co-Founder: Steve Broad
Brands:
gimMe
gimMe Organic

5020 Ginco International
725 Cochran St
Unit C
Simi Valley, CA 93065-1974
805-520-7500
Fax: 805-520-7509 800-284-2598
sales@ginsengcompany.com
Ginseng
President: Gary Raskin
VP Marketing: Linda Raskin
Sales Exec: Rick Seibert
sales@gincointernational.com
Estimated Sales: Less Than $500,000
Number Employees: 1-4
Square Footage: 30000

5021 Ginger People, The
215 Reindollar Ave
Marina, CA 93933
831-582-2494
Fax: 831-582-2495 800-551-5284
info@gingerpeople.com www.gingerpeople.com
Ginger products
President: Bruce Leeson
VP: Diana Cumberland
Contact: Robert Ballard
rballard@gingerpeople.com
Estimated Sales: $9 000,000
Number Employees: 18
Parent Co: Royal Pacific Foods

5022 Ginger Shots
Huntington Beach, CA 92649
888-413-1487
info@gingershots.com gingershots.com
Organic ginger and fruit juice blends
President & CEO: Zeyad Moussa
Number of Brands: 1
Number of Products: 6
Type of Packaging: Consumer
Brands:
GINGER SHOTS

5023 Gingerhaus, LLC
7486 North Shore Rd
Norfolk, VA 23505
757-348-4274
Fax: 888-712-4493 lee@gingerhaus.com
www.gingerhaus.com
Baked goods
Contact: Lee Shepherd
lee@indigoart.net

5024 Gingras Vinegar
1132 Grand Caroline
Rougemont, QC J0L 1M0
Canada
514-293-4591
866-469-4954
dgare@pomdial.com www.cidervinegar.com
Vinegars
Founder: Pierre Gingras

5025 Gingro Corp
5103 Main Street
Manchester Center, VT 05255
802-362-0836
Fax: 802-362-0741 candeleros@gmail.com
www.candeleros.net
Ethnic cuisine and all-natural, gourmet sauces, salsas and snacks
Contact: Lindy Bowden
beth@gringojacks.com

5026 Ginny Bakes
3535 NW 60th St
Miami, FL 33142-2026
305-638-5103
Baked goods
Founder: Ginny Simon
Contact: Stephanie Borges
sborges@coach.com
Number Employees: 20-49

5027 Ginseng Up Corp
16 Plum St
Worcester, MA 01604-3600
508-799-6178
Fax: 508-799-0686 800-446-7364
info@ginsengup.com www.ginsengup.com
Natural soft drinks; contract packaging available
President: Sang Han
Manufacturing Executive: Courtney Craite
courtney@ginsengup.com
Estimated Sales: $3 5 Million
Number Employees: 10-19
Parent Co: One Up
Type of Packaging: Consumer
Brands:
Cold/Hot Pack Tunnel Pasterized
Flavor
Ginseng Up

5028 Giorgio Foods
1161 Park Rd
PO Box 96
Temple, PA 19560
610-926-2139
Fax: 610-926-7012 800-220-2139
lbortz@giorgiofoods.com www.giorgiofoods.com
Mushrooms, cheese sticks, pierogies and gravy
President & CFO: Peter Giorgi
Estimated Sales: $5.3 Million
Number Employees: 40
Type of Packaging: Consumer, Food Service, Private Label, Bulk
Brands:
Brandywine
Pennsylvania Dutchman
Giorgio

5029 Giovanni Food Co Inc
6050 Court Street Rd
Syracuse, NY 13206-1711
315-457-2373
sales@giovannifoods.com
www.giovannifoods.com
Sauces
CEO: Louis DeMent
Chief Financial Officer: David Monahan
Vice President of Operations: Tim Budd
Director of Research & Development: Eric Lynch
National Sales Director: Joe Barbara
Production/Purchasing Manager: Katie Weber
Estimated Sales: $20-50 Million
Number Employees: 20-49
Number of Brands: 5
Square Footage: 67000
Type of Packaging: Consumer, Food Service, Private Label
Brands:
DEMENT'S
LUIGI GIOVANNI
TUSCAN TRADITIONS ORGANIC
TUSCAN TRADITIONS PREMIUM
JOSE PEDRO

5030 Giovanni's Appetizing Food Co
37775 Division Road
Richmond, MI 48062
586-727-9355
Fax: 586-727-3433 philipjr@gioapp.com
www.gioapp.com
Gourmet foods including antipasto, pickled mushrooms, chopped chicken liver and pates
President: Philip Ricossa
ricossa@gioapp.com
Vice President: Giovanni Ricossa
Estimated Sales: $2.5-5 Million
Number Employees: 10-19
Square Footage: 16000
Type of Packaging: Consumer, Food Service
Brands:
Champagne Delight
Giovanni's

5031 Girard Spring Water
1100 Mineral Spring Ave
North Providence, RI 02904-4104
401-725-7298
Fax: 401-725-7913 800-477-9287
Spring water and water coolers
President: John Ponton
Estimated Sales: $500,000-$1 Million
Number Employees: 1 to 4
Square Footage: 7500
Type of Packaging: Consumer, Private Label, Bulk

5032 Girard's Food Service Dressings
145 Willow Avenue
City of Industry, CA 91746
888-327-8442
sales@girardsdressings.com
www.girardsdressings.com
Mayonnaise, salad dressings, sauces and marinades.
Quality Control/R&D Manager: Jeff Stalley
Year Founded: 1935
Estimated Sales: $24 Million
Number Employees: 60
Number of Brands: 3
Number of Products: 175
Square Footage: 25000
Parent Co: HACO
Type of Packaging: Consumer, Food Service, Bulk
Brands:
Girard's

5033 Girardet Wine Cellar
895 Reston Rd
Roseburg, OR 97471-8611
541-679-7252
Fax: 541-679-9502 wine@girardetwine.com
www.girardetwine.com
Wines
President: Marc Girardet
genuine@gerardetwine.com
CEO: Bonnie Girardet
Winemaker/General Manager: Marc Girardet
Estimated Sales: Under $500,000
Number Employees: 1-4
Type of Packaging: Private Label

5034 Giulia Speciality Food
10 Dell Glen Ave #4
Lodi, NJ 07644-1740
973-478-3111
Fax: 973-478-1133
Mineral water, balsamic vinegar, olive oil, coffee, Easter eggs, rice
Vice President: Carmelo Lamonto
giulia10@optima.net
Estimated Sales: $2.5-5,000,000
Number Employees: 1-4
Brands:
Basso
Lasanta Maria
Mako
Pasta Maltagliati

5035 Giuliano's Specialty Foods
12132 Knott St
Garden Grove, CA 92841-2801
714-895-9661
Fax: 714-373-6872 www.giulianopeppers.com
Pickled peppers and vegetables
Owner: Errol Guiliano
CEO: Becky Childs
becky@giulianopeppers.com
Estimated Sales: $3.3 Million
Number Employees: 10-19
Square Footage: 40000

Type of Packaging: Consumer, Food Service

5036 (HQ)Giumarra Companies
P.O. Box 861449
Los Angeles, CA 90086
213-627-2900
Fax: 213-628-4878 www.giumarra.com
Produce marketing
Senior VP, Strategic Development: Hillary Brick
Director of Quality Control: Jim Heil
Manager: Donald Corsaro

Number Employees: 50-99
Other Locations:
Brands:
Arra
Grapeking
Natuures Partner®
Agricom
Arjuan Berry Farm
Arracado
Bauza
Cal Harvest
Corpora Agricola
David Del Curto
Liano Farms
Luv'ya
Marthedal Berry Farms
Payne Family Farms
Salazar Farms
Santa Marta
Subsole
Vbm
Yummy Fruit Company
Zespri

5037 Giusto's Specialty Foods Inc
344 Littlefield Ave
S San Francisco, CA 94080-6103
650-873-6566
Fax: 650-873-2826 getinfo@giustos.com
www.giustos.com
General grocery
President: Craig Moore
craig@giustos.com
Estimated Sales: $24,000,000
Number Employees: 20-49

5038 Givaudan Fragrances Corp
245 Merry Ln.
East Hanover, NJ 07936
973-386-9800
Fax: 973-428-6312 www.givaudan.com
Flavors and fragrances.
CEO: Gilles Andrier
CFO: Tom Hallam
President, Fragrance Division: Maurizio Volpi
President, Flavor Division: Louie D'Amico
Estimated Sales: $4.66 Billion
Other Locations:
Flavour Production Plant
Cincinnati OH
Flavour Creation Plant
Cincinnati OH
Flavour Creation Plant
East Hanover NJ
Flavour Application Plant
Elgin IL

5039 Gl Mezzetta Inc
105 Mezzetta Ct
American Canyon, CA 94503-9604
707-648-1050
Fax: 707-648-1060 800-941-7044
www.mezzetta.com
Peppers, olives, pickled vegetables, and other assorted gourmet specialties.
President: Jeff Mezzetta
HR Executive: Maritza Monge
mmonge@mezzetta.com
Director of Product Development: Shea Rosen
Estimated Sales: $20-50 Million
Number Employees: 100-249
Number of Brands: 5
Square Footage: 200000
Type of Packaging: Consumer, Food Service, Private Label
Brands:
Kona Coast
Mezzetta
Napa Valley Homemade
Deli Sliced
Gourmet Deli

5040 Glacial Ridge Foods
800 Industrial Dr
Starbuck, MN 56381-9775
320-239-2215
Fax: 313-535-4466
Chips, popcorn and pretzels
President: Mark Shirkey
National Sales Manager: Roger Spagnola
Estimated Sales: $500,000 appx.
Number Employees: 1-4
Brands:
Country Grown Foods

5041 Glacier Fish Company
2320 West Commodore Way
Suite 200
Seattle, WA 98199
206-298-1200
Fax: 206-298-4750 info@glacierfish.com
www.glacierfish.com
Fish
President: Jim Johnson
CEO: Mike Breivik
CFO: Rob Wood
VP Sales/Marketing: Merle Knapp
Contact: Stephanie Gilbert
stephanie@glacierfish.com
Estimated Sales: $20 Million
Number Employees: 250
Type of Packaging: Food Service, Bulk
Brands:
Glacier Freeze

5042 Glacier Foods
11303 Antoine Drive
Houston, TX 77066
832-375-6300
Fax: 559-875-3179 www.glazierfoods.com
Frozen and fresh fruit and vegetables
Owner: Jack Mulvaney
Contact: Greg Bohnsack
gregbohnsack@glazierfoods.com
Manager: Alvin Avoy
Plant Manager: Alvin McAvoy
Assistant Plant Manager: Sheila Young
Estimated Sales: $10-20 Million
Number Employees: 50-99
Square Footage: 1496520
Parent Co: JR Wood
Type of Packaging: Consumer, Food Service, Private Label, Bulk

5043 Gladder's Gourmet Cookies
1403 E Mlk Jr Industrial Blvd
Lockhart, TX 78644-3701
512-398-4523
Fax: 512-398-6323 888-398-4523
Raw cookie dough and brownie mixes
Owner: Dusty Baker
dbaker@gladders.com
Marketing Director: Susan Glader
VP Sales/Marketing: Dave Foreman
Director Operations: Kevin Cobb
General Manager: Mark Brown
Estimated Sales: $1-2,500,000
Number Employees: 20-49
Square Footage: 80000
Type of Packaging: Food Service
Brands:
Gladder's Gourmet Cookie

5044 Gladstone Food ProductsCompany
607 NE 69th St
Kansas City, MO 64188
816-436-1255
Fax: 816-436-1255
Mexican foods
President: Joe Catalano
Vice President: Kim Catalano
Estimated Sales: $1-2,500,000 appx.
Number Employees: 1-4

5045 Glamorgan Bakery
3919 Richmond Rd SW
Building 19
Calgary, AB T3E 4P2
Canada
403-232-2800
glamorganbakery@gmail.com
www.glamorganbakery.com
Freshly baked goods

President/Owner: Douwe Nauta
General Manager: Don Nauta
Sales/Customer Service: Jeremy Nauta
Number Employees: 8

5046 (HQ)Glanbia Nutritionals
121 4th Ave S
Twin Falls, ID 83301-6223
208-733-7555
Fax: 208-733-9222 www.glanbianutritionals.com
Nutritional ingredients
Chief Commercial Officer: Wilf Costello
SVP, Innovation: Eric Bastian
SVP, Product Strategy: Niamh Kelly
SVP, Quality: Barney Krueger
SVP, Procurement & Dairy Economics: Daragh Maccabee
SVP, Global Supply: John Mutchler
Year Founded: 1997
Estimated Sales: $20-50 Million
Number Employees: 50-99
Number of Brands: 1
Parent Co: Glanbia Plc
Brands:
Glanbia Foods

5047 Glatech Productions LLC
325 2nd St
Lakewood, NJ 08701-3329
732-364-8700
Fax: 732-886-2131 info@kosherGELATIN.com
www.koshergelatin.com
Kolatin kosher gelatin and Elyon confectionery products
CEO: Moshe Eider
glatech@gmail.com
VP: Moshe Eider
Number Employees: 1-4
Type of Packaging: Consumer, Bulk

5048 Glazier Packing Co
3140 State Route 11
Malone, NY 12953-4708
518-483-4990
Fax: 518-483-8300
Sausage and frankfurters; importer of other meat products
President/Owner: John Glazier
jglazier@glazierfoodservice.com
Vice President: Shawn Glazier
General Manager: Lynn Raymond
Estimated Sales: $10-11 Million
Number Employees: 50-99
Square Footage: 90000
Type of Packaging: Consumer, Food Service
Brands:
Tast-T
Tast-T Tender

5049 Glean, LLC
Snow Hill, NC 27856
info@liveglean.com
liveglean.com
Vegetable flours
Co-Founder: Annie Chun
Co-Founder: Steve Broad

5050 Glee Gum
305 Dudley St
Providence, RI 02907-1003
401-351-6415
Fax: 401-272-1204 info@gleegum.com
www.gleegum.com
Chewing gum and candy making kits
Contact: Molly Lederer
molly@gleegum.com

5051 Glen Summit Springs Water Company
P.O.Box 129
Mountain Top, PA 18707
570-474-5861
Fax: 570-474-9840 800-621-7596
www.glensummitspringswater.com
Bottled spring water
President: John Tidball
President: Nancy Quin Davis
Estimated Sales: $2.5-5 Million
Number Employees: 20-49

5052 Glen's Packing Co
200 E 1st St
Hallettsville, TX 77964
361-798-2601
Fax: 361-798-1201 800-368-2333
www.glenspacking.com
Fresh meats
President: Harold Dolezal
hdolezal@glenspacking.com
VP: Glen Jr Dolezal
Estimated Sales: $5-10 Million
Number Employees: 10-19
Type of Packaging: Consumer

5053 Glendora Quiche Company
210 W Arrow Hwy
San Dimas, CA 91773
909-394-1777
Fax: 909-394-1780
Quiches
Owner: Todd Bilef
President: Brad Kovar
Estimated Sales: $1-3,000,000
Number Employees: 1-4
Square Footage: 3000
Parent Co: Kovar Companies
Type of Packaging: Consumer, Food Service, Private Label, Bulk
Brands:
Glendora Quiche Co.

5054 Glenn Sales Company
6425 Powers Ferry Rd NW
Suite 120
Atlanta, GA 30339
770-952-9292
Fax: 770-988-9325
Seafood
President: Bruce Pearlman
Estimated Sales: $1,600,000
Number Employees: 5-9

5055 Glennys
1081 East 48th Street
Brooklyn, NY 11234
516-377-1400
Fax: 516-377-9046 888-864-1243
Natural snacks
Manager: Rhonda Talbot
Estimated Sales: $5-10 Million
Number Employees: 20-49
Type of Packaging: Consumer, Food Service
Brands:
Glenny's

5056 Glenoaks Food Inc
11030 Randall St
Sun Valley, CA 91352-2621
818-768-9091
Fax: 818-767-0742 www.jcrivers.com
Meat snacks
Owner: John Fallon
jjwf3@braincloud.com
Estimated Sales: $1-3,000,000
Number Employees: 20-49
Square Footage: 26000
Type of Packaging: Consumer, Private Label, Bulk
Brands:
J.C. Rivers Gourmet Jerky

5057 Glenora Wine Cellars
5435 State Route 14
Dundee, NY 14837-8804
607-243-5511
Fax: 607-243-5514 800-243-5513
info@glenora.com www.glenora.com
Wines
President: Gene Pierce
gpierce@glenora.com
Principal: Ed Dalrymple
Principal: Scott Welliver
Director Marketing: Gail Fink
Winemaker: Steve diFrancesco
Estimated Sales: $5-10 Million
Number Employees: 20-49
Square Footage: 35000
Type of Packaging: Consumer, Food Service, Private Label
Brands:
Finger Lakes
Glenora
Peach Orchard Farms
Trestle Creek

5058 Glier's Meats Inc
533 Goetta Pl
Covington, KY 41011-2203
859-291-1800
Fax: 859-291-1846 800-446-3882
www.goetta.com
German breakfast sausages
Owner: Dan Glier
dan@goetta.com
Director Marketing: Mark Balasa
Plant Manager: Tom Rabe
Estimated Sales: $2.2 Million
Number Employees: 10-19
Square Footage: 24000
Type of Packaging: Food Service, Private Label
Brands:
Glier's

5059 Global Bakeries Inc
13336 Paxton St
Pacoima, CA 91331-2339
818-896-0525
Fax: 818-896-3237
Baked goods
President: Albert Boyajian
Estimated Sales: $19,762,359
Number Employees: 100-249
Number of Products: 5
Square Footage: 40000
Type of Packaging: Consumer, Food Service, Private Label, Bulk

5060 Global Beverage Company
130 Linden Oaks
Suite C
Rochester, NY 14625-2834
585-381-3560
Fax: 585-381-4025 webmaster@wetplanet.com
Drinks
President: Carl Rapp
COO and CFO: Lowell Patric
Number Employees: 20-49

5061 Global Botanical
545 Welham Road
Barrie, ON L4N 8Z6
Canada
705-733-2117
Fax: 705-733-2391 info@globalbotanical.com
Herbs, spices, oils
President: Sandra Thuna
Office Manager: Therese White
General Manager: Joel Thuna
Number Employees: 12
Square Footage: 40000
Type of Packaging: Private Label, Bulk
Brands:
Excalibur
Global Botanical
Kidz
Naturalvalves
Pure-Li Natural

5062 Global Egg Corporation
283 Horner Ave
Toronto, ON M8Z 4Y4
Canada
416-231-2309
Fax: 416-231-8991 info@globalegg.com
www.globalegg.com
Eggs
CEO: Aaron Kwinter
Estimated Sales: $13 Million
Number Employees: 70
Square Footage: 50000
Type of Packaging: Food Service, Bulk
Brands:
Egg King
Global

5063 Global Food Industries
307 Circle Dr
Townville, SC 29689
864-287-1212
Fax: 864-287-1335 800-225-4152
info@globalfoodindustries.com
Dairy, dehydrated foods, beverages, and vegetarian foods
President: Neal Pfeiffer
Vice President: Paulette Harary
Office Manager: Sandra Sanoh
Number Employees: 5-9
Number of Brands: 1
Number of Products: 30
Type of Packaging: Food Service, Bulk
Brands:
Global Food

5064 Global Gardens Group Inc.
10691 Shellbridge Way # 130
Richmond, BC
Canada
855-409-4365
hello@globalgardensgroup.com
Non-dairy, vegetable-based beverage in original, unsweetened and vanilla flavors
President/Chief Executive Officer: Rob Harrison
Chief Financial Officer: Paul Lott
Vice-President, Marketing: Wade Bayne
Number of Brands: 1
Number of Products: 3
Type of Packaging: Consumer, Private Label
Brands:
Veggemo

5065 Global Health Laboratories
9500 New Horizons Boulevard
Amityville, NY 11701
631-777-2134
Fax: 631-777-3348 www.globalhealthlabs.com
Vitamins and nutritional supplements
Administrator: Susan Mc Guckian
Sales Director: James Gibbons
Contact: Cheryl Manzione
cmanzione@globalhealthlabs.com
Type of Packaging: Consumer, Private Label
Brands:
Herb Actives
Nature's Plus
Source of Life
Spirutein
Thermo Tropic

5066 Global Organics
68 Moulton St
Cambridge, MA 02138-1119
781-648-8844
Fax: 781-648-0774 info@global-organics.com
www.global-organics.com
Organic ingredients
President: Dave Alexander
Vice President: Roland Hoch
Account Manager: Dino Scarsella
Sales and Marketing Coordinator: Ravi Arori
Estimated Sales: Under $500,000
Number Employees: 25

5067 Global Preservatives
1401 Hodges Street
Lake Charles, LA 70601
337-491-0816
Fax: 337-433-4291 866-491-0816
Preservatives
President: William Woodward
R&D: Damon Thibodeaux
Operations Director: Tim Vaughan
Plant Manager: Bryan Hymel
Estimated Sales: $2.5 -$5 Million
Number Employees: 1-4
Square Footage: 40000

5068 Globus Coffee LLC
426 Plandome Rd
Manhasset, NY 11030-1943
516-304-5780
Fax: 631-364-4558 www.globuscoffee.com
Coffee
Owner: Kurt Kappeli
public@globuscoffee.com
CFO: Salvatore Errico
Manager: Ronald Levy
Estimated Sales: $820,000
Number Employees: 1-4

5069 Gloria Ferrer Champagne
23555 Highway 121
Sonoma, CA 95476-1427
707-933-1917
Fax: 707-996-0720 info@gloriaferrer.com
www.gloriaferrer.com
White, red, and sparkling wines
President & CEO: Thomas Burnet
Executive Winemaker: Bob Iantosca
VP of Production: Mike Crumly
VP Marketing/Advertising: David Brown
Year Founded: 1986
Estimated Sales: $20-50 Million

Number Employees: 50-99
Parent Co: Freixenet America
Brands:
Freixenet Spanish Wines
Freixenet Wines

5070 Gloria Jean's Gourmet Coffees
17691 Mitchell N
Irvine, CA 92614-6827
949-589-5040
Fax: 949-589-5041 877-320-5282
www.gloriajeans.com
Coffee
CEO: Neil Gill
VP Marketing: Diane Hays-Hoag
Franchising Manager: Shereen Rai
Contact: James Harris
j.harris@gloriajeans.com
Customer Service: Patti Graves
Estimated Sales: $8 Million
Number Employees: 140
Square Footage: 240000
Parent Co: Diedrich Coffee

5071 Gloria Winery & Vineyard
1648 E 8th St N
Springfield, MO 65802
417-926-6263
Wines
President: Michael Dennis
Estimated Sales: $500,000-$1,000,000
Number Employees: 1-4

5072 Glory Foods
901 Oak St
Columbus, OH 43205
614-252-2042
Fax: 614-252-2043 800-414-5679
www.gloryfoods.com
Fresh and frozen vegetables
President: Jacqueline Neal
Founder: Iris Cooper
Founder/Plant Manager: Dan Charna
Founder: Garth Henley
Controller: Julie Eikenberry
Contact: Dino Allen
dino.allen@gloryfoods.com
Estimated Sales: $3,500,000
Number Employees: 25
Type of Packaging: Food Service, Bulk

5073 GloryBee
PO Box 2744
Eugene, OR 97402
541-689-0913
800-456-7923
sales@glorybee.com glorybee.com
Honey, sweeteners, spices, dried fruits, nuts, oils and ingredients.
President: Richard Turanski
richard.turanski@glorybee.com
Vice President: Alan Turanski
Director of Sales and Marketing: Roger Plant
Purchasing Manager: Randy Djonne
Number Employees: 10-19
Type of Packaging: Consumer, Bulk
Brands:
GloryBee
Aunt Patty's
Honeystix
Agavestix

5074 Glossop's Syrup
2337 Roscomare Rd
Suite 2173
Los Angeles, CA 90077
424-832-7266
glossops.com
All-natural cocktail syrups
President/Owner: Michael Kaz
Number of Brands: 1
Number of Products: 6
Type of Packaging: Consumer
Brands:
GLOSSOP'S

5075 Glover's Ice Cream Inc
705 W Clinton St
Frankfort, IN 46041-1824
765-654-6712
Fax: 765-654-7977 800-686-5163
gloversicecream@att.net
www.gloversicecream.com
Ice cream, frozen yogurt and frozen novelties
President: Stephen Glover
Estimated Sales: $3-5 Million
Number Employees: 5-9
Square Footage: 18000
Type of Packaging: Consumer, Private Label

5076 Glow Gluten Free
New York, NY
800-497-7434
info@glowglutenfree.com
www.glowglutenfree.com
Gluten-free cookies
Cookie Commander in Chief: Jill Brack

5077 Gluck Brands
12320 Cardinal Meadow
Suite 160
Sugar Land, TX 77478
281-903-7082
gluck@glucksnacks.com
www.gluckbrands.com
Veggie sticks, chips, popcorn and protein crisps
Founder: Gabriel Navarro

5078 Glucona America
114 E Conde Street
Janesville, WI 53546-3010
608-752-0449
Fax: 608-752-7643
Gluconates and other supplements
Development Manager: Charles King
Marketing Manager: Scott Wellington
General Manager: Sean Trac
Estimated Sales: $20-50 Million
Number Employees: 20-49
Parent Co: Avebe
Type of Packaging: Food Service
Brands:
Gluconal

5079 Glunz Family Winery & Cellars
888 E Belvidere Rd # 107
Suite 211
Grayslake, IL 60030-2569
847-548-9463
Fax: 847-548-8038 www.glunzfamilywinery.com
Wines
Owner: Matthew Glunz
VP/Winemaker: Joe Glunz
Cellarmaster: Cipriano Luvieanos
Estimated Sales: Less Than $500,000
Number Employees: 1-4

5080 Gluten Free Foods Mfg.
5010 Eucalyptus Ave
Chino, CA 91710
909-823-8230
glutenfreefoodsmfg.com
Gluten-free pastas
Plant Manager: Bruno Campo
Number of Brands: 1
Number of Products: 8
Type of Packaging: Consumer
Brands:
PASTARISO

5081 Gluten Free Nation
1014 Wirt Rd # 230
Houston, TX 77055-6857
713-784-7122
Gluten free baked goods
Manager: Randi Markowitz
randi.markowitz@gfhouston.com
Number Employees: 5-9

5082 Gluten Free Sensations
53238 N US Highway 131
Three Rivers, MI 49093-9764
269-273-4090
glutenfreesensations.com
Gluten free foods
Owner: Loretta Hamelink
loretta2@glutenfreesensations.com
Estimated Sales: Less Than $500,000
Number Employees: 1-4

5083 Gluten-Free Heaven
274 S 700 W
Pleasant Grove, UT 84062
801-380-6478
orders@glutenfreeheaven.com
www.glutenfreeheaven.com
Gluten-free baking mixes and flours
Founder & CEO: Andrea Custer
Type of Packaging: Consumer
Brands:
GLUTEN-FREE HEAVEN

5084 Glutenfreeda Foods Inc
200 E Washington Ave
Burlington, WA 98233-1729
360-755-1300
Karen@glutenfreeda.com
www.glutenfreeda.com
Gluten free foods
CEO: Yvonne Gifford
yvonne@glutenfreeda.com
Chief Marketing Officer: Jessica Hale
Conventional Retail Sales: Kristine Ganes
Number Employees: 20-49

5085 (HQ)Glutino
3750 Ave. Francis Hughes
Laval, QC H7L 5A9
Canada
Fax: 450-629-4781 800-363-3438
www.glutino.com
Gluten free foods
President: Steven Singer
EVP: David Miller

5086 Go Max Go Foods
info@gomaxgofoods.com
www.gomaxgofoods.com
Vegan candy bars free from dairy, eggs, hydrogenated oils, trans fats, artificial ingredients, and cholesterol; 6 gluten-free flavors available
Co-Owner: Scott Ostrander
Co-Owner: Jon Ostrander

5087 Go Raw
1885 Las Plumas Ave
San Jose, CA 95133
408-272-4722
www.goraw.com
Seeds, seed bars, protein bars, crisps, bites and granola
Type of Packaging: Consumer
Brands:
GO RAW

5088 GoAvo
24 Cheyenne Dr
Montville, NJ 07045-9703
973-534-9951
www.goavospread.com
Avocado-based mayonnaise
Sales: Aaron Glick
Number of Brands: 1
Number of Products: 3
Type of Packaging: Consumer
Brands:
GOAVO

5089 GoBio!
RR 1
Action, ON L7J 2L7
Canada
519-853-2958
Fax: 519-853-8654 info@gobiofood.com
www.gobiofood.com
Organic foods
President: Anke Kruse
Brands:
Anke Kruse Organics

5090 GoMacro
415 S Wagoner Ave
Viola, WI 54664
608-627-2310
800-788-9540
www.gomacro.com
Macrobiotic bars
Owner: Jolanta Sonkin
Type of Packaging: Consumer
Brands:
GOMACRO
THRIVE

5091 Goat Partners Intl.
1600 Golf Rd
Suite 1200
Rolling Meadows, IL 60008
833-872-4628
askus@greengoatmilk.com greengoatmilk.com
Whole goat milk and goat milk powder

5092 **Godiva Chocolatier**
560 Lexington Ave #A
New York, NY 10022-6828
212-980-9810
Fax: 212-980-9811 800-946-3482
letters@godiva.com www.godiva.com
Chocolate
President, Worldwide: James Goldman
SVP: David Marberger
tommorick@godiva.com
VP Marketing/Merchandising: Michael Simon
Director PR/Promotions: Erica Lapidus
Master Chocolatier: Thierry Muret
Site Manager: Tom Morick
Number Employees: 10-19
Parent Co: Campbell Soup
Type of Packaging: Consumer
Brands:
Godiva
Godiva Chocolate
Godiva Biscuits

5093 **Godshall's Quality Meats**
675 Mill Rd
Telford, PA 18969-2411
215-256-8867
Fax: 215-256-4965 888-463-7425
Beef, beef products
President: Mark Godshall
Vice President: Floyd Kratz
fkratz@godshalls.com
Number Employees: 50-99
Type of Packaging: Private Label
Brands:
Godshall's

5094 **Godwin Produce Co**
1 Yam St
PO Box 163
Dunn, NC 28334
910-892-4171
Fax: 910-892-2232 godwinproduce@aol.com
www.sweettater.com
Sweet potatoes, watermelons and cantaloupes
Owner: Anthony Godwin
Owner: David Godwin
sweettater@aol.com
Office Manager: Susan Moore
Estimated Sales: $5-10 Million
Number Employees: 5-9
Square Footage: 255000
Type of Packaging: Consumer, Food Service, Private Label, Bulk
Brands:
Dunn's Best
Godwin
Godwin Produce
Godwin's Blue Ribbon
Sweet Carolina

5095 **Goen Technologies Inc**
375 Stewart Rd.
Wilkes Barre, PA 18706
973-929-3700
Fax: 973-889-4340 800-467-3041
support@trimspa.com www.trimspa.com
Weight loss supplements
President: Alex Goen
Public Relations Specialist: Chrissy Kulig
Estimated Sales: $20-50 Million
Number Employees: 100-249
Brands:
Trimspa
Winsuel

5096 **Goetze's Candy Co**
3900 E Monument St
Baltimore, MD 21205
410-342-2010
Fax: 410-522-7681 marketing@goetzecandy.com
www.goetzecandy.com
Confectionary, specifically chewy caramel
President: Mitchell Goetze
CEO: Spaulding Goetze
CFO: Dave Long
EVP: Todd Goetze
Year Founded: 1895
Estimated Sales: $20-50 Million
Number Employees: 50-99
Type of Packaging: Consumer, Food Service, Bulk
Brands:
Caramel Creams®
Cow Tales®

5097 **(HQ)Gold Coast Bakeries**
1590 E Saint Gertrude Place
Santa Ana, CA 92705
714-545-2253
Fax: 714-751-2253 orders@goldcoastbakery.com
www.goldcoastbakery.com
Sourdough, buns and rolls, and sliced bread
CEO: Rick Anderson
COO: Paul Cannon
Number Employees: 100-249
Square Footage: 440000
Type of Packaging: Consumer, Food Service, Private Label
Brands:
Breads of Venice
Gold Coast Baking Company
Pioneer French Bakery

5098 **Gold Coast Baking Co Inc**
1590 E Saint Gertrude Pl
Santa Ana, CA 92705
714-545-2253
Fax: 714-751-2253 orders@goldcoastbakery.com
goldcoastbakery.com
Bakery products and breads
Production Supervisor: Armando Ramirez
Estimated Sales: $76 Million
Number Employees: 100-249
Type of Packaging: Private Label
Other Locations:
Addison IL
Brands:
Pioneer French Bakery
Breads of Venice
Gold Coast

5099 **Gold Coast Ingredients**
2429 Yates Ave
Commerce, CA 90040-1917
323-724-8935
Fax: 323-724-9354 800-352-8673
info@goldcoastinc.com goldcoastinc.com
Flavor and color manufacturer
President: Jim Sgro
jim@goldcoastinc.com
CEO: Chuck Brasher
Vice President: Laurie Goddard
Estimated Sales: $12 Million
Number Employees: 20-49
Type of Packaging: Private Label, Bulk

5100 **Gold Crust Baking Co Inc**
6200 Columbia Park Rd
Landover, MD 20785-3216
301-364-3320
Fax: 301-364-3340 info@goldcrust.com
Bakery goods
Contact: Paul Christou
paul@goldcrust.com
Number Employees: 20-49

5101 **Gold Digger Cellars**
PO Box 2550
Oroville, WA 98844
509-476-4887
Fax: 509-981-6556
Wines
Preident/Winemaker: Amy Jo Morris
Number Employees: 15

5102 **Gold Dollar Products**
6073 Mt Moriah Rd Ext Ste 12
Suite 12
Memphis, TN 38115
901-948-8694
Fax: 901-948-0309 800-971-8964
golddoll@bellsouth.net
Vinegar, mustard, hot sauce, lemon juice, bottled water
President/Treasurer: Sondra Abraham
Vice President/Sec: George Abraham
VP, Consultant: Herbert Abraham
VP Marketing: George Abraham
Estimated Sales: $2.5-5,000,000
Number Employees: 1-4
Brands:
Gold Dollar
Gold Dollar Lemon
Gold Dollar/Monedade'oro

5103 **Gold Medal Bakery Inc**
21 Penn St
Fall River, MA 02724
508-674-5766
www.goldmedalbakery.com
Bread and rolls.
Controller: Claudette Torres
ctorres@goldmedalbakery.com
Year Founded: 1912
Estimated Sales: $50 Million
Number Employees: 250-499
Number of Brands: 2
Square Footage: 410000
Type of Packaging: Private Label
Brands:
Gold Medal
Fiber One

5104 **Gold Mine Natural Food Company**
13200 Danielson St
Suite A-1
Poway, CA 92064
858-537-9830
Fax: 858-695-0811 800-475-3663
customerservice@goldminenaturalfoods.com
www.goldminenaturalfoods.com
Specialty foods
Founder/Owner: Jean Richardson
Contact: David Kirchner
david@goldminenaturalfoods.com

5105 **Gold Pure Food ProductsCo. Inc.**
1 Brooklyn Rd
Hempstead, NY 11550-6619
516-483-5600
Fax: 516-483-5798 800-422-4681
Kosher salad dressings, sauces, mustards, and vinegar; importer of horseradish roots, dried peaches and dried apricots
President: Steven Gold
Vice President: Herbert Gold
Vice President Sales: Marc Gold
marc@goldshorseradish.com
Estimated Sales: $5-10 Million
Number Employees: 50-99
Square Footage: 300000
Type of Packaging: Consumer, Food Service, Private Label, Bulk
Brands:
Baker
Baker's
Dip N' Joy
Gold's
Nathan's
Old World
Uncle Dave's

5106 **Gold Standard Baking Inc**
3700 S Kedzie Ave
Chicago, IL 60632-2768
773-523-2333
Fax: 773-523-7381 800-648-7904
info@gsbaking.com www.gsbaking.com
Bakery products
President: Yianny Caparos
ycaparos@gsbaking.com
VP: Joe Chiodo
Sales Representative: Connie Holston
VP Business Development: Charles Chiodo
Estimated Sales: $2.5-5 Million
Number Employees: 100-249
Square Footage: 100000
Type of Packaging: Consumer, Food Service, Private Label, Bulk
Brands:
Croissant De Paris
Gold Standard

5107 **Gold Star Seafoods**
2300 W 41st St
Chicago, IL 60609-2214
773-376-8080
Fax: 773-376-9879 Vang@goldstarseafood.com
www.goldstarseafood.com
Seafood
President: Van Giragosian
vang@goldstarseafood.com
Estimated Sales: $10-20 Million
Number Employees: 10-19

5108 **Gold Star Smoked Fish Inc**
570 Smith St
Brooklyn, NY 11231-3820
718-522-1545
Fax: 718-260-9194 info@goldstarusa.com
www.goldstarusa.com
Smoked fish and specialty foods
President: Robert Pinkow
Estimated Sales: $10-20 Million
Number Employees: 20-49
Brands:
Cuetara
Denmark: Officer
Germany: Wessergold
Gerolsteiner
Gold Star
Hargita
Heine's
Iceland: Armant
Latvia: Unda
Poland: Solidarnosc
Teaports
Ukraine: Chumak, Nektar

5109 **Gold Sweet Company**
331 Old Ice House Road
PO Box 247
Lake Wales, FL 33859
863-676-0963
Fax: 863-676-0968 www.goldsweetco.com
Honey
Owner/Manager: Richard Phillips
Estimated Sales: $500,000-$1 Million
Number Employees: 1-4
Square Footage: 9000
Type of Packaging: Consumer, Food Service, Bulk

5110 **GoldFoods**
10637 N Kendall Dr
Suite 7E
Miami, FL 33176
305-924-4825
info@goldfoodsusa.com
goldfoodsusa.com
Chia and quinoa seeds
Type of Packaging: Consumer

5111 **GoldRush Mustard**
9540 Garland Rd
Suite 381-298
Dallas, TX 75218
214-335-8345
info@goldrushmustard.com
goldrushmustard.com
Flavored mustards
Empress: Kerry Cole
kerrygoldrush@gmail.com
Type of Packaging: Private Label

5112 **Goldcoast Salads**
3600 Shaw Blvd.
Naples, FL 34117
239-513-0430
Fax: 239-304-2156
Maine lobster, blue crab and smoked salmon spreads
President: Peter Radno Jr
Co-Owner: Adam Radno
Plant Manager: Ruben Valenzuela

5113 **Golden 100**
1600 Essex Ave
Deland, FL 32724-2102
386-734-0113
Fax: 386-734-9718
Flavors
President & CEO: Ronald Edmundson
Manager: Jeffrey Ross
jeffreyr@jogue.com
Operations Executive: Mike Bowes
Estimated Sales: $1.7 Million
Number Employees: 10-19
Square Footage: 80000
Parent Co: Jogue Inc.
Type of Packaging: Bulk
Brands:
Golden 100

5114 **Golden Alaska Seafoods LLC**
2200 Alaskan Way # 420
Suite 420
Seattle, WA 98121-1684
206-441-1990
Fax: 206-441-8112 www.goldenalaska.com
Frozen seafood
President: Joseph Fleming
Manager: Chris McReynolds
CFO: Markna Franklyn
Sales Manager: Markna Franklyn
Estimated Sales: $1-2,500,000
Number Employees: 5-9

5115 **Golden Brown Bakery Inc**
421 Phoenix St
South Haven, MI 49090-1309
269-637-3418
Fax: 269-637-7822 www.goldenbrownbakery.com
Bakery products
Owner: David Braschi
dave@goldenbrownbakery.com
Estimated Sales: $1-1,500,000
Number Employees: 20-49
Type of Packaging: Consumer, Food Service, Private Label, Bulk

5116 **Golden Cannoli**
99 Crescent Ave
Chelsea, MA 02150
617-868-2826
Fax: 617-497-5836 goldencannoli.com
Gourmet cannolis; fillings; cannoli shells; chips
Chairman/CEO: Francesco Bono
Chairman/CEO: Angelo Bresciani
Assistant Vice President: Eric Bresciani
VP of Sales & Marketing: Valerie Bono
Operations Manager: Ed Bresciani
Year Founded: 1970
Estimated Sales: $500,000 To 1 Million
Number Employees: 100-249
Type of Packaging: Private Label

5117 **Golden City Brewery**
920-12th St
Golden, CO 80401
303-279-8092
Fax: 303-279-8092 info@gcbrewery.com
gcbrewery.com
Beer
President: Jennie Sturdavant
Wholesale Distribution Manager: Josh Norton
Contact: Calvin Cline
ccline@gcbrewery.com
Assistant Brewer & Mad Scientist: Derek Sturdavant
Estimated Sales: $5-9.9 Million
Number Employees: 2-10
Type of Packaging: Private Label

5118 **Golden Eagle Olive Products**
749 N Plano St
Porterville, CA 93257-6330
559-784-3468
Fax: 559-784-2186
Olive oil
Owner: Jerry Padula
Vice President: Traci Padula
Assistant Manager: Traci Padula
Estimated Sales: $5-10 Million
Number Employees: 1-4
Square Footage: 40000
Type of Packaging: Consumer
Brands:
Golden Eagle

5119 **Golden Eagle Syrup**
205 1st Ave SE
Fayette, AL 35555-2719
205-932-5294
Fax: 205-932-5296 info@goldeneaglesyrup.com
www.goldeneaglesyrup.com
Syrups
Co-Owner/President: Trent Mobley
Co-Owner/Plant Manager: Vic Herren
Manager: Jim Herren
Office Manager: Martha Kimbrell
geagle@fayette.net
Estimated Sales: $2.5-5 Million
Number Employees: 5-9
Type of Packaging: Consumer, Food Service, Bulk

5120 **Golden Edibles LLC**
10396 W State Road 84
Suite 103
Davie, FL 33324
Fax: 973-807-1637 866-779-7781
sales@goldenedibles.com www.goldenedibles.com
Snacks
Co-Owner/President/CEO: Steve Asbaty
Co-Owner: Jenene Carlon
Contact: Ruben Pinchanski
ruben@goldenedibles.com
Type of Packaging: Consumer, Private Label

5121 **Golden Eye Seafood**
17640 Clarke Rd
Tall Timbers, MD 20690-2055
301-994-2274
Fax: 301-994-9960
Seafood
President: Robert Lumpkins
Estimated Sales: $1.2 Million
Number Employees: 5-9

5122 **Golden Flake Snack Foods**
1 Golden Flake Dr
Birmingham, AL 35205
800-367-7629
www.goldenflake.com
Snacks
President & CEO: Mark McCutcheon
Estimated Sales: $100-500 Million
Number Employees: 500-999
Number of Brands: 3
Brands:
Golden Flake
Maizetos
Tostados

5123 **Golden Fluff Popcorn Co**
118 Monmouth Ave
Lakewood, NJ 08701-3347
732-367-5448
Fax: 732-367-5448 goldenfluff@gmail.com
www.goldenfluff.com
Popcorn and other snacks
President: Ephraim Schwinder
goldenfluff@gmail.com
Estimated Sales: Less than $500,000
Number Employees: 10-19
Type of Packaging: Consumer, Bulk
Brands:
Dontil
Elyon
Golden Fluff

5124 **Golden Gulf Coast Packing Co**
260 Maple St
Biloxi, MS 39530-4501
228-374-6121
Fax: 228-374-0599 wildshrimp@hotmail.com
Shrimp
President/Owner: Richard Gollott
goldengulf123@hotmail.com
Estimated Sales: $10-20 Million
Number Employees: 5-9
Square Footage: 16000

5125 **Golden Harvest Pecans**
348 Vereen Bell Road
Cairo, GA 39828-4910
229-377-5617
Fax: 229-762-3335 800-597-0968
Pecans and preserves, cookies and jellies
President/CEO: J Van Ponder
Estimated Sales: $250,000
Number Employees: 500-999
Square Footage: 6218
Type of Packaging: Consumer, Food Service, Private Label, Bulk

5126 **Golden Island Jerky Co.**
Rancho Cucamonga, CA 91730
844-362-3222
www.goldenislandjerky.com
Flavored jerkies
President: Anna Kan
VP, Human Resources: Micki Jack
Number of Brands: 1
Number of Products: 6
Type of Packaging: Consumer
Brands:
GOLDEN ISLAND

5127 **Golden Kernel Pecan Co**
5244 Cameron Rd
Cameron, SC 29030-8207
803-823-2311
Fax: 803-823-2080 info@goldenkernel.com
www.goldenkernel.com
Pecans and other snacks

Co-Owner: David K Summers
Co-Owner/Sales Executive: Bill Summers
bill@goldenkernel.com
Number Employees: 20-49
Type of Packaging: Consumer, Private Label, Bulk
Brands:
Golden Kernel

5128 **Golden Malted**
4101 William Richardson Drive
South Bend, IN 46628
888-596-4040
ncdcs@goldenmalted.com www.goldenmalted.com
Gourmet malted pancake and waffle flour mixes.
President/CEO: Rick McKeel
Sales Manager: Edward Frank
Estimated Sales: $10-20,000,000
Number Employees: 50-100

5129 **Golden Moon Tea**
PO Box 146
Bristow, VA 20136
425-820-2000
Fax: 425-821-9700 877-327-5473
service@goldenmoontea.com
www.goldenmoontea.com
Tea and chocolates
President: Cynthia Knotts
Owner: Marcus Stout
Number of Products: 30
Type of Packaging: Consumer, Food Service, Private Label, Bulk
Brands:
Golden Moon Tea

5130 **Golden Peanut and Tree Nuts**
100 North Point Center East
Suite 400
Alpharetta, GA 30022
770-752-8160
www.goldenpeanut.com
Peanuts and tree nuts.
President: Clint Piper
Year Founded: 2000
Estimated Sales: $500 Million-$1 Billion
Number Employees: 1000+
Parent Co: Archer Daniels Midland
Type of Packaging: Consumer

5131 **Golden Platter Foods**
37 Tompkins Point Rd
Newark, NJ 07114-2814
973-344-8770
Fax: 973-465-7580 contact@goldenplatter.com
goldenplatter.com
Poultry products
President: Eli Barr
sbarich@goldenplatter.com
Estimated Sales: $6.5 Million
Number Employees: 100-249
Type of Packaging: Consumer, Food Service

5132 **Golden River Fruit Company**
7150 20th Street #A
Vero Beach, FL 32966-8805
772-562-8610
Fax: 772-567-6008
Grapefruit
CEO: George Lamberth
glambeth@goldenriverfruit.com
VP: David Milwood
General Manager/Purchasing Director: Fred Antwerp
Estimated Sales: $2 Million
Number Employees: 25
Square Footage: 13474
Type of Packaging: Bulk
Brands:
Bland Farms
Golden Eagle
Golden One
Golden River
Golden Sun
National Gold
National One
Sundance

5133 **Golden Specialty Foods Inc**
14605 Best Ave
Norwalk, CA 90650-5258
562-802-2537
Fax: 562-926-4491
wayne@goldenspecialtyfoods.com
Canned dips, salad dressings, sauces, seasonings, chicken and beef bases
CEO: Phil Pisciotto
CFO: Derky Howard
Quality Assurance Director: Javed Atcha
Sales: Andrea Bouras
COO: Jeff Chan
Estimated Sales: $3.5 Million
Number Employees: 50-99
Square Footage: 62000
Type of Packaging: Consumer, Food Service, Private Label, Bulk

5134 **Golden State Foods Corp**
18301 Von Karman Ave
Suite 1100
Irvine, CA 92612
949-247-8000
www.goldenstatefoods.com
Sauces, dressings, syrups, jams/jellies, meat products, produce, rolls and buns.
CEO & Chairman: Mark Stephen Wetterau
mwetterau@goldenstatefoods.com
SVP & Chief Financial Officer: Joe Heffington
EVP & Chief Administrative Officer: Bill Sanderson
SVP & Chief Legal Officer: John Page
Chief Human Resources Officer: Ed Rodriguez
Year Founded: 1947
Estimated Sales: Over $1 Billion
Number Employees: 1000-4999
Other Locations:
Phoenix AZ
Portland OR
St. Peter MO
Schertz TX
Spokane Valley WA
Suffolk VA
Tampa FL
City of Industry CA
Conyers GA
Garner NC
Lemont IL
Rochester NY
Whitewater WI

5135 **Golden State Herbs**
60125 Polk St
P.O. Box 756
Thermal, CA 92274-8944
760-399-1133
Fax: 760-399-1555 800-730-3575
www.goldenstateherbs.com
Herbs
Estimated Sales: $3.4 Million
Number Employees: 5-9
Square Footage: 100000

5136 **Golden Town Apple Products**
755 Principale St
Rougemont, QC J0L 1M0
Canada
519-599-6300
Fax: 519-599-2103 866-552-7643
pierre.lheureux@lassonde.com www.lassonde.com
Apple processing
Chairman/CEO: Pierre-Paul Lassonde
President/CEO: Jean Gattuso
VP/CFO: Guy Blanchette
Business Manager: Gerry Williams
Technical Director: Doug Johnson
Office Administrator: Darlene Gardner
Maintenance/Engineering Manager: Ron McQuarrie
Juice Production Coordinator: Jennifer Rear
Plant Manager: Bryan Lowe
GM/Purchasing/Sales: Keith Cummings
Number Employees: 20-49
Square Footage: 80000
Parent Co: A. Lassonde, Inc
Type of Packaging: Consumer, Bulk

5137 **Golden Valley Dairy Products**
1025 E Bardsley Ave
Tulare, CA 93274-5752
559-687-1188
Fax: 559-685-6551 www.saputo.com
Cheese
Manager: Mike Kothbauer
CEO: John Prince
Contact: Eddie Alanis
ealanis@landolakes.com
Estimated Sales: $500,000-$1,000,000
Number Employees: 5-9
Parent Co: DCCA
Type of Packaging: Consumer
Brands:
Ben & Jerry
Breyers
Haagen Dazs
Klondike

5138 **Golden Valley Foods Ltd.**
3841 Vanderpol Court
Abbotsford, BC V2T 5W5
Canada
604-857-0704
Fax: 604-607-5504 888-299-8855
www.goldenvalley.com
Eggs and egg products.
Plant & Quality Assurance Manager: Frank Curtis
Regional Sales Manager: Craig Ansell
Year Founded: 1950
Estimated Sales: $24.9 Million
Number Employees: 100
Parent Co: Fresh Start Food Corp.
Type of Packaging: Consumer, Food Service, Private Label
Brands:
Goldegg
Canadian Harvest
Born 3
Country Golden Yolks
Freerun
Freerun Omega 3
Organic
Premium Brand
Golden Valley

5139 **Golden Valley Natural**
815 E 1400 N
Shelley, ID 83274
888-270-7147
sales@goldenvalleynatural.com
www.goldenvalleynatural.com
Beef, buffalo and turkey jerky; fruit snacks
CEO: Bryce Espline
brycc@goldenvalleynatural.com
Number Employees: 50-99
Type of Packaging: Consumer
Brands:
Hero Jerky
Meliora Organic
Ascend
Healthy Partner Pet Snacks
Intermountain Bison

5140 **Golden Walnut Specialty Foods**
18279 Minnetonka Blvd
Wayzata, MN 55391-3342
95 -76 -079
Fax: 847-731-6433 800-843-3645
sales@goldenwalnut.com
Specialty food products including cookies, cakes, cheesecakes, shortbread and candy
President: Mark Sigel
Estimated Sales: $5-10 Million
Number Employees: 20-49
Parent Co: EMAC International
Type of Packaging: Consumer, Private Label, Bulk
Brands:
Almond Ingot
Amelia's Sugar Free Shoppe
Buckley's
Golden Walnut
Ingot
Monica's
Razzlenuts
Sideboard Sweets & Savories
Thimble

5141 **Golden West Food Group**
4401 S Downey Rd
Vernon, CA 90058
888-807-3663
Fax: 323-585-8483 info@gwfg.com
www.gwfg.com
Beef, poultry and pork products
CEO: Erik Litmanovich
Chief Sales Officer: Tim White
Contact: Mak Abbasi
it@gwfg.com
Estimated Sales: $100-499 Million
Number Employees: 750
Number of Brands: 14
Type of Packaging: Consumer, Food Service, Private Label
Brands:
Jack Daniels
Jack Link's

Certified Angus Beef
American BBQ Company
Teva Foods
Calle Sabor
Red Moon
Premium Cuts
Royal Poultry
Culver City Meat
Simple Eats
Tabiah Halal

5142 Golden West Fruit Company
2151 Saybrook Ave
Commerce, CA 90040
323-726-9419
Fax: 323-726-9504
Fruits, toppings, syrups, fillings & bottled fruit & beverages
President: Donald Campolo
Estimated Sales: $280,000
Number Employees: 1-4
Square Footage: 20000
Type of Packaging: Private Label, Bulk

5143 Golden West Specialty Foods
300 Industrial Way
Brisbane, CA 94005
415-657-0123
Fax: 415-657-0110 800-584-4481
info@gwsfoods.com www.gwsfoods.com
Sauces, marinades
President: Lawrence Ames
lca@gwsfoods.com
Number Employees: 1-4
Type of Packaging: Private Label
Brands:
Chinese Chicken Salad Dressing
Thai Sauce
Traditional Stir Fry Sauce

5144 Goldenberg's Peanut Chews
1300 Stefko Blvd
Bethlehem, PA 18017
888-645-3453
www.peanutchews.com
Confectionary
President & COO: David Yale
Year Founded: 1917
Estimated Sales: $20-50 Million
Number Employees: 100-249
Square Footage: 100000
Parent Co: Just Born, Inc.
Type of Packaging: Consumer, Food Service, Bulk
Brands:
Chew-Ets
Peanut Chews

5145 Goldilocks USA
30865 San Clemente St
Hayward, CA 94544-7136
510-476-0700
Fax: 510-476-0707 www.goldilocks-usa.com
Bakery products
Owner: Rob Yee
Estimated Sales: $5-10,000,000
Number Employees: 20-49

5146 Golding Farms Foods
6061 Gun Club Rd
Winston Salem, NC 27103-9727
336-766-6161
Fax: 336-766-3131
www.mrscampbellschowchow.net
Condiments and sauces
Owner: Ernest Golding
VP/CFO: Violet Golding
EVP: Ron Foster
Technical Director: Daniel Sortwell
Director Sales: Tom Clayton
information@goldingfarmsfoods.com
Operations Manager: Preston Myers
Production Manager: Lawrence Logan
Estimated Sales: 2.5-5 Million
Number Employees: 50-99
Number of Products: 150
Square Footage: 80000
Type of Packaging: Consumer, Food Service, Private Label, Bulk
Brands:
Golding
Golding Farms
Golding Gourmand
Mrs. Campbells
Naturally Healthy
Old Laredo

5147 Goldstar Brands LLC
2121 Tucker Industrial Rd
Tucker, GA 30084-5017
770-938-9884
Fax: 770-938-8964 888-296-7191
info@hongarfarms.com www.hongarfarms.com
Gourmet seasoned oils and vinegars, marinades, bread dippers and specialty items.
President: Joe Oxman
Estimated Sales: $1-2.5 Million
Number Employees: 10-19
Brands:
Hongar Farms

5148 Goldthread
932 Stanford St
Santa Monica, CA 90403
413-325-8987
info@goldthreadherbs.com
goldthreadherbs.com
Plant-based tonics
Co-Owner: William Siff
Co-Owner: Edith Siff
Number of Brands: 1
Number of Products: 10
Type of Packaging: Consumer
Brands:
GOLDTHREAD

5149 Goldwater's Food's Of Arizona
Salsa Express
PO Box 9846
Fredericksburg, TX 78624
Fax: 830-990-9481 866-779-7241
www.goldwaters.com
Fruit salsa and bean dips, barbecue sauces and chili
President: Carolyn Ross
Estimated Sales: $1-2,500,000
Number Employees: 1-4
Type of Packaging: Consumer
Brands:
Goldwater's
Goldwater's Taste of the Southwest

5150 Goll's Bakery
234 N Washington St
Havre De Grace, MD 21078-2909
410-939-4321
Fax: 410-939-2556
German style bakery products
Owner: Robert Goll
gollsbakery@aol.com
Owner: Susie Goll
Estimated Sales: Less Than $500,000
Number Employees: 5-9

5151 Gonard Foods
3915 Edmonton Trail NE
Unit 7
Calgary, AB T2E 6T1
Canada
403-277-0991
Fax: 403-277-0664
Meat products
President/Owner: Munir Lakha
Estimated Sales: $975,000
Number Employees: 3

5152 Gonnella Baking Company
1117 E Willey Rt
Schamburg, IL 60173
312-733-2020
Fax: 312-733-7056 800-322-8829
www.gonnella.com
Frozen bread and baked goods
President: Nicholas Marcucci
Vice President: Tom Marcucci
Vice President, Food Safety, Compliance: Dan Herzog
General Manager: Kenneth Gonnella

5153 Good Citizens
Simi Valley, CA 93063
hello@goodcitizens.com
goodcitizens.com
Organic macaroni and cheese
Number of Products: 10

5154 Good Culture
1621 Alton Pkwy
Irvine, CA 92606
Fax: 949-545-9965 844-899-8884
www.goodculture.com
Sour cream and cottage cheeses
Co-Founder: Anders Eisner
Co-Founder & CEO: Jesse Merrill

5155 Good Earth Company
890 Mountain Ave
Suite 105
New Providence, NJ 07974
888-625-8227
sales@goodearthteas.com
Teas
President: Ben Zaricor
National Sales Manager: Randy Duarte
Contact: John Ochoa
johno@goodearth.com
Purchasing Agent: Bill Lambert
Estimated Sales: $7.6 Million
Number Employees: 70
Type of Packaging: Private Label
Brands:
China Collection Teas
Energy Supplements
Functional Teas
Good Earth Teas
Herbal Teas

5156 Good Food For Good
100 Amber St
Unit 12
Markham, ON L3R 3J8
Canada
647-449-4922
info@goodfoodforgood.ca
goodfoodforgood.ca
Organic condiments
President: Richa Gupta

5157 Good Food Inc
4960 Horseshoe Pike
P.O. Box 160
Honey Brook, PA 19344-1361
610-273-3776
Fax: 610-273-2087 800-327-4406
info@goldenbarrel.com
www.goldenbarrel.com/goodfoodinc
Molasses, syrups, shoofly pie and funnel cake mixes; vegetable, cotton seed, coconut, peanut, corn, olive, canola and blended cooking oils
President: Larry Martin
lmartin@goldenbarrell.com
CEO: Ean Johnson
Year Founded: 1934
Estimated Sales: $20-50 Million
Number Employees: 100-249
Parent Co: Zook Molasses Company
Brands:
Mrs Schlorers
Golden Barrel

5158 Good Food Made Simple
180 Linden St
Wellesley, MA 02482
800-535-3447
www.goodfoodmadesimple.com
Prepared foods, including entr,es, burritos, waffles, oatmeal and wraps
VP, Brand Management & Sales: Russ Williams
Type of Packaging: Consumer
Brands:
GOOD FOOD MADE SIMPLE

5159 (HQ)Good For You America
110 S Bismark St
Concordia, MO 64020-8110
660-463-2158
Fax: 660-463-2459 866-329-5969
www.foodtabs.com
Emergency and survival food tablets and canned freeze-dried foods; importer of bulk ingredients and freeze-dried foods
Manager: Rachel Goring
Manager: Craig Sallin
craig.sallin@frac.org
Wholesale Director: Juanita Haley
Estimated Sales: Less Than $500,000
Number Employees: 1-4
Square Footage: 10000
Type of Packaging: Consumer, Private Label, Bulk

Other Locations:
Food Reserves-Laboratory
Kansas City MO
Food Reserves
Syracuse NY
Brands:
Food Reserves
Storehouse Foods

5160 **Good Fortunes & Edible Art**
6754 Eton Ave
Canoga Park, CA 91303-2813
818-595-1555
Fax: 818-595-1550 800-644-9474
Chocolate-dipped fortune cookies and pretzels
Owner: Karen Staitman
Brands:
A Dose of Good Fortunes
Candy Art
Cookie Art
Fractured Fortunes
Good Fortunes
Pretzel Twisters
Pretzel Wands
Sugar Art

5161 **Good Groceries**
98 4th Street
Brooklyn, NY 11231
347-853-7462
Fax: 718-768-0932 www.goodgroceries.com
Specialty bread products
President/Owner: Martin Sokoloff
VP: Fred Sokoloff
Marketing: Marty Sokoloff
VP Sales/Marketing/Sales Staff: Lu Arcouet
Contact: Steve Cocco
steve@good-groceries.com
Estimated Sales: $1 Million
Number Employees: 6
Type of Packaging: Consumer
Brands:
SUZIE'S

5162 **Good Harbor Fillet Company**
40 Herman Melville Blvd
New Bedford, MA 2740
978-281-6360
Fax: 978-281-4166 800-343-8046
Processed seafood products
President: John Cummings
Chief Financial Officer: Robert Fregault
VP: Bill Stride
Southeast Regional Manager: Dave Galloway
Quality Control Manager: Alan Pothier
VP Sales/Marketing: Annette Chalmers
West Coast Sales Manager: Joel Bortz
Chief Operating Officer: Dave Nelson
Purchasing Manager: Alan Gilbert
Number Employees: 50-99
Type of Packaging: Consumer, Food Service

5163 **Good Harbor Vineyards &Winery**
34 S Manitou Trail
Lake Leelanau, MI 49653-9589
231-256-7165
Fax: 231-256-7378 winery@goodharbor.com
www.goodharbor.com
Wines
Winemaker/Owner: Bruce Simpson
Associate: Richard Flores
Associate: Rocky Flores
Retail Sales/Owner: Debbie Simpson
debbie@goodharbor.com
Operations: William Schaub
Operations: Gary Schaub
Assistant Winemaker: David Hooper
Growing/Management Workforce: Ovidio Chapa
Estimated Sales: Under $500,000
Number Employees: 5-9
Type of Packaging: Private Label

5164 **Good Health Natural Foods**
3400 West Wendover Avenue
Suite E
Greensboro, NC 27407
336-285-0735
www.goodhealthnaturalfoods.com
Health snacks
CEO: Mark Gillis
Vice President: Terry Meyer
Contact: Don Heon
don.heon@e-goodhealth.com
Estimated Sales: $2.5-5,000,000
Number Employees: 1-4

5165 **Good Humor-Breyers Ice Cream**
800 Sylvan Ave.
Englewood Cliffs, NJ 07632
800-931-2854
customer.services@unilever.com
www.breyers.com
Ice cream, gelato and frozen dairy desserts.
Estimated Sales: $11 Billion
Number Employees: 1000-4999
Parent Co: Unilever
Type of Packaging: Consumer, Food Service, Private Label, Bulk
Other Locations:
Breyer's Manufacturing
Philadelphia PA
Breyer's Manufacturing
Long Island NY
Breyer's Manufacturing
Brooklyn NY
Brands:
Breyers®
Good Humor®
Carb Smart®
Fat Free®
Pure Fruit®
Breyers Blasts®
Klondike®
Popsicle®

5166 **Good Karma Foods**
2465 Central Ave
Suite 100
Boulder, CO 80301
800-550-6731
goodkarmafoods.com
Flaxmilk and drinkable yogurts
CEO: Doug Radi
CFO: Matt Riegner
Marketing: Brianna Littlepage
VP, Sales: Edward McDonald
COO: Kevin O'Rell
Type of Packaging: Consumer
Brands:
GOOD KARMA

5167 **Good Lovin' Foods**
877-760-6833
www.goodlovinfoods.com
Organic, fresh fruit snack bars
CEO: Ryan Smith
VP: Porter Smith
Number of Brands: 1
Number of Products: 4
Type of Packaging: Consumer
Brands:
GOOD LOVIN' FOODS

5168 **Good Old Dad Food Products**
185 Industrial Court B
Sault Ste. Marie, ON P6B 5Z9
Canada
705-949-7337
Fax: 705-949-0871 800-267-7426
www.ricos.ca
Frozen and premade pastas
Owner: Richard Palarchio
Number Employees: 10-19
Square Footage: 22000
Type of Packaging: Consumer, Food Service
Brands:
Rico's

5169 **Good Old Days Foods**
3300 S Polk St
P.O. Box 191470
Little Rock, AR 72204-7823
501-565-1257
Fax: 501-562-7439 www.goodolddaysfoods.com
Frozen fruit cobblers, corn bread dressing, bread pudding, sweet potato casserole
President: L C Elder
lc@goodolddaysfood.com
CEO: Carroll Elder
CFO: John Zacharison
VP: Robert Cochran
Sales Director: Doyle Rice
Estimated Sales: $10-20 Million
Number Employees: 50-99
Square Footage: 128340
Type of Packaging: Consumer, Food Service, Private Label

5170 **Good PLANeT Foods**
1813 115th Ave NE
Bellevue, WA 98004
425-449-8134
info@goodplanetfoods.com
goodplanetfoods.com
Plant-based cheeses
CEO: David Israel
VP, Operations: Spencer Oberg
Brands:
Good PLANeT Foods

5171 **Good Rub**
PO Box 1088
Morrisville, NC 27560
919-371-0329
distribution@good-rub.com
www.good-rub.com
Natural seasonings
President: Myriam Batista

5172 **Good Spread**
311 Mapleton Ave
Suite 373
Boulder, CO 80304
www.helpgoodspread.com
Organic peanut butter
Co-Founder: Alex Cox
Co-Founder: Mark Slagle
CEO: Robbie Vitrano
Brand Manager: Lauren Beno
Community Engagement: Daniel Anderson

5173 **Good Stuff Cacao**
3562 South Lapeer Rd
Metamora, MI 48455
248-690-5114
info@goodstuffcacao.com
www.goodstuffcacao.com
Cacao
Type of Packaging: Consumer

5174 **Good Wives**
330 Ballardvale St
Wilmington, MA 01887-1012
781-596-0070
Fax: 781-596-1131 800-521-8160
Frozen hors d'oeuvres, pastries, tortilla wraps, and flatbreads
Owner/CEO: Chris Collias
President: Randell Knopf
CFO: Bruce Robertson
Marketing: Sandra Gamble
Manager: Christian Collias
Plant Manager: John Reardon
Estimated Sales: Under $500,000
Number Employees: 100-249
Square Footage: 20000
Type of Packaging: Consumer, Food Service, Private Label

5175 **Good Zebra**
512-698-7907
info@goodseedburger.com
goodseedburger.com
Honey-sweetened animal crackers
Founder & CEO: Erika Szychowski
Number of Brands: 1
Number of Products: 3
Type of Packaging: Consumer
Brands:
GOOD ZEBRA

5176 **Good! Snacks**
340 S Lemon Ave
Unit 8093N
Walnut, CA 91789
415-762-0600
info@goodsnacks.com
goodsnacks.com
Protein bars

5177 **Good-O-Beverages Inc**
1801 Boone Ave
Bronx, NY 10460-5101
718-328-6400
Fax: 718-328-7002 info@good-o.com
www.good-o.com
Soft drinks, juices, teas and energy drinks
Owner: George Deyarca
slperry8978@yahoo.com
Plant Manager: Irving Mendelson

Estimated Sales: $10-20 Million
Number Employees: 50-99
Square Footage: 159000
Type of Packaging: Consumer
Brands:
Coco Rico
Kola Champagne
Red Pop
West Indian Kola

5178 **GoodBelly Probiotics**
PO Box 17460
Boulder, CO 80308
303-443-3631
info@goodbelly.com
goodbelly.com
Probiotic fruit juices and bars
Co-Founder: Steve Demos
Co-Founder: Todd Beckman
Type of Packaging: Consumer
Brands:
GOODBELLY
GOODBELLY PLUSSHOT
GOODBELLY STRAIGHTSHOT

5179 **GoodBites Snacks**
Venice, CA 90291
friends@goodbitesgroup.com
goodbitessnacks.com
Organic superfood snack bites
Founder: Angelica Xavier
Type of Packaging: Consumer
Brands:
GoodBites
GoodBites CBD

5180 **GoodMark Foods**
7700 France Ave S # 200
Edina, MN 55435-5867
952-835-6900
Fax: 952-469-5550 www.slimjim.com
Fries, meat and other snack foods
Manager: David Dart
VP: Paul Brunswick
Marketing Director: Jeff Slater
Sales Director: Michael Ritchey
Merchandise Support Manager: Amy Carroll
Operations Manager: Al Blalock
Number Employees: 50-99
Parent Co: ConAgra Foods
Type of Packaging: Private Label

5181 **GoodPop**
500 E 4th Street
Suite 603
Austin, TX 78701
888-840-0188
www.goodpops.com
Natural frozen fruit bars
CEO/Founder: Daniel Goetz
Number Employees: 1-4

5182 **Goodart Candy Inc**
335 E 40th St
Lubbock, TX 79404-2811
806-747-2600
Fax: 806-747-8330
Peanut patties and peanut brittle
Vice President: Ron Harbuck
goodartcandy@yucca.net
Estimated Sales: $500,000-$1 Million
Number Employees: 10-19
Square Footage: 37500
Type of Packaging: Private Label, Bulk
Brands:
Goodart's

5183 **Goodheart Brand Specialty Food**
11122 Nacogdoches Rd
San Antonio, TX 78217-2314
210-637-1963
Fax: 210-637-1391 888-466-3992
amvillarreal@goodheart.com www.goodheart.com
Specialty meats: quail, venison, bison, wild boar, pheasant and Argentinian all-natural beef
Owner: Amalia Palmaz
apalmaz@goodheart.com
Director Sales: Chef Tim Kennedy
Plant Manager: Demetrio Molales
Estimated Sales: $5-10,000,000
Number Employees: 50-99
Square Footage: 30000
Parent Co: Bluebonnet Company
Type of Packaging: Consumer, Food Service
Brands:
Goodheart

5184 **Goodie Girl**
Ridgefield, NJ 07657
www.goodiegirlcookies.com
Gluten- and peanut-free cookies
Owner/Founder: Shira Berk
Branding & Packaging: Michelle Suazo
Product Manager: Lauren Growney

5185 **Goodness Knows**
goodnessknows.com
Fruit and nut snack squares
Number of Brands: 1
Number of Products: 12
Type of Packaging: Consumer
Brands:
GOODNESS KNOWS

5186 **Goodseed Burgers**
512-698-7907
info@goodseedburger.com
goodseedburger.com
Hemp seed veggie burgers
Owner: Oliver Ponce
Owner: Erin Shotwell
Number of Brands: 1
Number of Products: 4
Type of Packaging: Consumer
Brands:
GOODSEED

5187 **Goodson Brothers Coffee**
138 Sherlake Ln
Knoxville, TN 37922-2307
865-693-3572
Fax: 865-691-8578 800-737-1519
info@goodsonbros.com
Coffee and tea
President: Jeff Goodson
Sales Executive: Kelly Hall
khall@goodsonbros.com
Estimated Sales: $1.2,000,000
Number Employees: 20-49

5188 **Goose Island Beer Co**
1800 W Fulton St
Chicago, IL 60612-2512
312-226-1119
Fax: 312-733-1692 800-466-7363
info@gooseisland.com
Beers
COO: Tony Bowker
Director of Operations: Mark Kamarauskas
Vice President of Sale: Bob Kenney
Brew master: Greg Hall
General Manager: Tim Lane
Estimated Sales: $2.5-5,000,000
Number Employees: 50-99
Square Footage: 74000
Type of Packaging: Consumer, Food Service
Brands:
Hey Nut
Honkers
Ipa
Oatmeal

5189 **Goosecross Cellars Inc**
1119 State Ln
Yountville, CA 94599-9407
707-944-1986
Fax: 707-944-9551 800-276-9210
webmaster@goosecross.com www.goosecross.com
Wines
President/CEO: David Topper
david@goosecross.com
Vice President/Winemaker: Geoff Gorsuch
Hospitality/Public Relations: Colleen Topper
Business Development/Distribution: Pamela Topper
Estimated Sales: $2.5-5,000,000
Number Employees: 10-19
Type of Packaging: Private Label
Brands:
Aeros
Bernard Pradel Cabernet
Goosecross

5190 **Gopal's Healthfoods**
800 CR 125
Sidney, TX 76474
866-646-7257
customercare@gopalshealthfoods.com
www.gopalshealthfoods.com
Nut and seed mixes, nut and seed butters, vegan parmesan, nori-wrapped energy sticks, fruit and nut bars, brownies, crackers
Founder: Stefan Knueppel

5191 **Gopicnic Inc**
4011 N Ravenswood Ave # 101
Suite 12
Chicago, IL 60613-4837
773-328-2490
Fax: 773-345-0734 service@gopicnic.com
Gluten-free, organic, vegetarian meals; cured meats and other snacks.
President: Thomas Falduto
tom.falduto@gopicnic.com
Marketing: Carolyn Wiesemann
Number Employees: 5-9

5192 **Gorant Chocolatier**
8301 Market St
Youngstown, OH 44512-6257
330-726-8821
Fax: 330-726-0325 www.gorant.com
Chocolate-coated candies
Owner: Joseph Miller
jmiller@gorant.com
Director of Operations: Jack Peluse
Number Employees: 100-249
Type of Packaging: Consumer, Private Label
Other Locations:
PMG Chocolatier
Niles OH
Gorant Candies
Warren Plaza, Warren OH
Gorant Candies
Howland Plaze, Warren OH
Brands:
Gorant & Yum Yum Chocolates

5193 **Gordon Biersch Brewery Restaurant**
357 E Taylor St
San Jose, CA 95112-3148
408-278-1008
Fax: 408-294-4052 info@gordonbiersch.com
www.gordonbierschbrewing.com
Beer
Co-Founder/President: Dean Biersch
Co-Founder/Director of Operations: Dan Gordon
dgordon@gordonbiersch.com
CFO: Larry Nally
Sales Director: Mark Blecher
Operations Manager: Eddie Sipple
Estimated Sales: $2.5-5,000,000
Number Employees: 20-49
Square Footage: 114000
Brands:
Gordon Biersch
Maibock Hefeweizen
Winter Block
Braumeister Select IPB

5194 **Gorton's Inc.**
128 Rogers St.
Gloucester, MA 01930
800-222-6846
www.gortons.com
Seafood.
CEO: Judson Reis
judson.reis@gortons.com
Director Marketing: Mark Lamothe
Year Founded: 1849
Estimated Sales: $280 Million
Number Employees: 1,000-4,999
Parent Co: Nippon Suisan Kaisha
Type of Packaging: Consumer, Food Service
Other Locations:
Gorton's Seafood
Cleveland OH
Brands:
Gorton's Popcorn Shrimp
Gorton's Fish Sticks
Gorton's Beer Battered Fillets
Gorton's Natural Catch
Gorton's Grilled Tilapia
Gorton's Shrimp Bowl
Gorton's Seafood Appetizers
Gorton's Parmesean Crusted Cod
Gorton's Pub Style Cod
Gorton's Simply Bake Salmon

5195 Gossner Foods Inc.
1051 N. 1000 West
Logan, UT 84321-6852
435-227-2500
Fax: 435-227-2550 800-944-0454
www.gossner.com
Cheeses.
President/CEO: Dolores Gossner Wheeler
dolores@gossner.com
Vice President: Greg Rowley
Year Founded: 1966
Estimated Sales: $335 Million
Number Employees: 250-499
Number of Brands: 1
Type of Packaging: Consumer, Food Service, Private Label, Bulk
Brands:
Gossner Foods

5196 Gotliebs Guacamole
PO Box 1036
Sharon, CT 06069-1036
860-365-0842
Guacamole
President: Richard Gotlieb
VP Marketing: Leslie MacKenzie
Production Manager: Laura Mars
Estimated Sales: $500,000-$1,000,000
Number Employees: 5-9
Brands:
Gotliebs

5197 Gould's Maple Sugarhouse
570 Mohawk Trail
Shelburne Falls, MA 01370
413-625-6170
www.goulds-sugarhouse.com
Maple syrup; pies
Owner/President: Edgar Gould
Owner/President: Helen Gould
Estimated Sales: $1-2,500,000
Number Employees: 5-9

5198 Gouldsboro Enterprises
14 Factory Rd
Gouldsboro, ME 04607-4222
207-963-2203
Fax: 212-925-1913
Lobster
President/Owner: Leonard Bishko
Vice President: Joseph Boyd
Estimated Sales: $300,000-500,000
Number Employees: 1-4

5199 Gourmantra Foods
95 Silver Rose Crescent
Markham, ON L6C 1W6
Canada
416-225-6711
Fax: 416-225-6711
Spices
CEO: Rachna Prasad
VP R&D: Rekha Prasad
COO: Mona Prasad
Number Employees: 5

5200 Gourmedas Inc
2425 Avenue Watt
Dock 4
Quebec, QC G1P 3X2
Canada
418-210-3703
Fax: 418-948-4083
Chocolate
President/CEO: Christoph Klein
Director of Operations: Giordano Perini

5201 Gourmet Basics
67 35th Street
Suite 3
Brooklyn, NY 11232-2200
718-509-9366
Fax: 866-900-7833 info@GourmetBasics.com
www.gourmetbasics.com
Organic chips and snacks
Contact: Jack Benz
jackbenz@gourmetbasics.com

5202 Gourmet Conveniences Ltd
457 Bantam Road
Litchfield, CT 06759
860-567-3529
Fax: 860-631-1012 866-793-3801
sales@sweetsunshine.com
www.sweetsunshine.com
Sauces
Founder/CEO: Paul Sarris
Number Employees: 4

5203 Gourmet Croissant
320 36th St
Brooklyn, NY 11232-2504
718-499-4911
Fax: 718-499-6394
Fresh and frozen baked goods
Co-Owner: Dino Alatsas
Co-Owner: Teddy Alatsas
Principal: Marie Fabrizio
Estimated Sales: Less than $500,000
Number Employees: 10-19
Square Footage: 16000

5204 Gourmet Foods Inc
2910 E Harcourt St
Compton, CA 90221-5502
310-632-3300
Fax: 310-632-0303
Hors d'oeuvres and banquet items
President: Joann Annunziata
jannunziata@gourmetfoodsinc.com
Estimated Sales: $5-10,000,000
Number Employees: 250-499

5205 Gourmet Ghee
Lynbrook, NY 11563
516-744-0770
contact@gourmetghee.com
www.gourmetghee.com
Original and flavored ghee (clarified butter)
Founder & Owner: Nazia Aibani
Year Founded: 2016
Number Employees: 10-19

5206 Gourmet House
PO Box 90340
Allentown, PA 18109-0340
Fax: 888-708-4882 800-226-9522
www.gourmethouserice.com
Rice
Marketing Manager/Sales Executive: Julie Wraa
Operations/Branch Manager: Steve Wraa
Number Employees: 60
Square Footage: 14432
Parent Co: Riviana Foods
Type of Packaging: Consumer, Private Label

5207 Gourmet Kitchen, Inc.
1238 Corlies Avenue
Neptune, NJ 07753
732-775-5222
Fax: 732-775-5225 800-492-3663
kgrossman@gourmetkitcheninc.com
www.gourmetkitcheninc.com
Hors d'oeuvres
Founder: Ray Walsh
Marketing: Kathleen Grossman

5208 Gourmet Market
5107 Kingston Pike
Knoxville, TN 37919-5152
865-330-0123
Fax: 865-584-5661
Gourmet and specialty foods
CEO: Eric Nelson
Estimated Sales: Less Than $500,000
Number Employees: 5-9
Brands:
Gourmet Foods Market

5209 Gourmet Mondiale
6865 Route 132
Ste-Catherine, QC J5C 1B6
Canada
450-638-6380
Fax: 450-638-7049
nino.piazza@mostimondiale.com
www.gourmetmondiale.com
Cooking wine, olive oil, balsamic vinegar.
Marketing: Nino Piazza

5210 Gourmet Nut
3611 14th Ave
Suite 654
Brooklyn, NY 11218-3787
347-413-5180
info@gourmetnut.com
www.gourmetnut.com
Nuts, dried fruits, seeds, chocolates and salts
President: Morris Elbaz
morris@gourmetnut.com
Estimated Sales: Less Than $500,000
Number Employees: 1-4

5211 Gourmet Products
PO Box 387
Thomaston, CT 06787-0387
860-283-5147
Fax: 860-283-6912
Sauces, mustards, relishes, salsas
Owner: A Yurgelun
Marketing Director: W Yurgelun
VP Operations: David Yurgelun
Production Manager: T Del Gadio
Purchasing Manager: T Curnell
Number Employees: 10-19
Square Footage: 12000
Type of Packaging: Consumer, Private Label, Bulk
Brands:
Gourmet Products
New Classics
New England

5212 Gourmet Sorbet Corporation
159 W 53rd St
New York, NY
646-243-9868
www.sorbabes.com
Manufacturer of sorbet.
Co-Founder: Nicole Cardone
Co-Founder: Deborah Gorman

5213 Gourmet Treats
1860 W 220th St # 445
Torrance, CA 90501-3679
310-212-6975
Fax: 310-212-0709 800-444-9549
info@gourmettreats.com
www.gourmet-treats.myshopify.com
Gourmet regular and fat-free cakes and cookies
President: Shaffin Jinnah
Estimated Sales: Less than $500,000
Number Employees: 1-4
Square Footage: 6000
Type of Packaging: Consumer, Private Label
Brands:
Gourmet Lite
Gourmet Treats

5214 Gourmet du Village
539 Village Road
Morin-Heights, QC J0R 1H0
Canada
800-668-2314
www.gourmetduvillage.com
Gourmet dips, seasonings and confectionary
President: Mike Tott
VP Product Development: Rebecca MacDonald
Marketing Assistant: Linda Zechner
Number Employees: 45

5215 Gourmet's Finest
704 Garden Station Rd
PO Box 160
Avondale, PA 19311
610-268-6910
Fax: 610-268-2298 info@gourmetsfinest.com
Mushrooms
Owner: Richard Pia
Type of Packaging: Food Service, Private Label

5216 Gourmet's Fresh Pasta
950 N Fair Oaks Ave
Pasadena, CA 91103-3009
626-798-0841
Fax: 626-798-3591 mayagjian@aol.com
www.gourmetpasta.com
Refrigerated, frozen and precooked pasta
President/CEO: Michael Yagjian
mayagjian@aol.com
Estimated Sales: $2.5-5 Million
Number Employees: 20-49
Square Footage: 60000
Type of Packaging: Consumer, Food Service, Private Label, Bulk

Brands:
California Cuisine
Gourmet Fresh

5217 **Gourmet's Secret**
5304 Roseville Rd
Suite F
North Highlands, CA 95660-5049
916-334-6161
Fax: 916-334-6161 gourmetsec@aol.com
Marinades and sauces; vinegars and oils
Partner: Rita Nelson
Estimated Sales: $100,000
Number Employees: 1-4
Brands:
Bachelor's Brew
Java Jelly

5218 **Gourm, Mist**
16850 Collins Ave
Suite 112190
Sunny Isles Beach, FL 33160
954-608-6858
Fax: 954-252-2247 866-502-8472
Oil and vinegar misters
President/CoFounder: Paige Simona

5219 **Gouvea's & Purity Foods Inc**
3049 Ualena St # 415
Honolulu, HI 96819-1946
808-847-3717
Fax: 808-847-6877 www.regospurity.com
Sausages
President: Scott Stevenson
Vice President: Bill Atherton
Manager: Stanley Griffon
stanley@gouveaspurity.com
Estimated Sales: $4000000
Number Employees: 10-19
Type of Packaging: Consumer, Food Service

5220 **Gouw Quality Onions**
5801-54 Avenue
Taber, AB T1G 1X4
Canada
403-223-1440
Fax: 403-223-2036
onions@gouwqualityonions.com
www.gouwqualityonions.com
Onions, radishes and red beets
Chairman: Casey Gouw, Sr.
Sales Manager/Controller: Casey Gouw
Warehouse/Plant Operations: Ken Gouw
Farm Manager: Kyle Gouw
Estimated Sales: D
Number Employees: 20-49
Type of Packaging: Consumer

5221 **Govadinas Fitness Foods**
2651 Ariane Drive
San Diego, CA 92117-3422
858-270-0691
Fax: 858-270-0696 800-900-0108
Health food bars and natural snacks
CEO: Larry Gatpandan
Accountant: Alberto Hael
VP: Zenaida Gatpandan
Marketing: Michael Pugliese
Sales: Lisa Gatpandan
Production: Jose Marquez
Purchasing: Nila Morrill
Estimated Sales: $3 Million
Number Employees: 20-49
Number of Products: 25
Square Footage: 10000
Type of Packaging: Private Label
Brands:
Bliss Bar
Hemp Bar
Praline Pack
Raw Power

5222 **Govatos Chocolates**
4105 Concord Pike
Talleyville Shopping Center
Wilmington, DE 19803-1401
302-478-5324
Fax: 302-652-3418 888-799-5252
GVTSCANDY@AOL.COM
www.govatoschocolates.com
Chocolates
Owner: Nicholas Govatos
Estimated Sales: Less Than $500,000
Number Employees: 1-4
Type of Packaging: Consumer

5223 **Goya Foods Inc.**
350 County Rd.
Jersey City, NJ 07307
201-348-4900
Fax: 201-348-6609 www.goya.com
Latin American food and condiments.
President/CEO: Bob Unanue
Year Founded: 1936
Estimated Sales: $1.5 Billion
Number Employees: 4,000
Number of Products: 2500
Type of Packaging: Consumer, Food Service
Other Locations:
Goya Foods of South Jersey
Pedricktown NJ
Goya Foods of Great Lakes
Angola NY
Goya Foods of Long Island
Bethpage NY
Goya Foods of Massachusetts
Webster MA
Goya Foods of Miami
Miami FL
Goya Foods of Orlando
Orlando FL
Goya Foods of Virginia
Prince George VA
Goya Foods of Illinois
Bolingbrook IL
Goya Foods of Texas
Brookshire TX
Goya Foods of California
City of Industry CA
Goya Foods of Atlanta
McDonough GA
Goya Foods of Puerto Rico
Bayamon PR
Goya Foods of the Dom. Rep.
San Cristobal, Dom. Rep.
Brands:
Goya®

5224 **Grabill Country Meats**
13211 West St
P.O. Box 190
Grabill, IN 46741-2031
260-627-3691
Fax: 219-627-2106 866-333-6328
info@grabillmeats.com www.grabillmeats.com
Canned beef, pork, chicken, and turkey products
President: Pat Fonner
Secretary/Treasurer: Dennis Fonner
Estimated Sales: $5-10 Million
Number Employees: 10-19
Type of Packaging: Consumer

5225 **Grace & I**
Los Angeles, CA
800-584-1736
delight@graceandi.com
www.graceandi.com
Preserves, fruit and nut presses, granola, and roasted nuts
President: Mina Kolahi

5226 **Grace Baking Company**
3200 Regatta Blvd
Suite G
Richmond, CA 94804
510-231-7200
Fax: 510-231-7210 www.gracebaking.com
Baked goods
Founder/Co-Owner: Glenn Mitchell
Co-Owner: Cindy Mitchell
Public Relations and Marketing: Fred Doar
Contact: Tom Deadmore
tdeadmore@goprime.com
Plant Manager: Mike Cassie
Parent Co: Maple Leaf Foods Inc
Type of Packaging: Food Service

5227 **Grace Foods International**
39-36 32nd Street
Suite 1
Astoria, NY 11106
718-433-4789
Fax: 718-433-0384 www.gracefoods.com
Beverages, canned meats and fish, chips, coconut products, jams and jellies, ready mixes, rice combos, sauces and condiments, spices and seasoning, teas and veggie meals

5228 **Grace Tea Co**
14 Craig Rd
Acton, MA 01720-5405
978-635-9500
Fax: 978-635-9701
customerservice@gracetea.com
www.gracetea.com
Teas
Owner: Hartley Johnson
hejohnson1@gracetea.com
VP: Richard Verdery
Operations Director: Richard Sanders
Estimated Sales: $48,000
Number Employees: 5-9
Number of Brands: 1
Number of Products: 20
Square Footage: 4000
Brands:
China Yunnan Silver Tip Choice
Connoisseur Master Blend
Darjceling Superb 6000
Demitasse After Dinner Tea
Earl Grey Superior Mixture
Flowery Jasmine-Before the Rain
Formosa Oolong Champagne of Tea
Gun Powder Pearl Pinhead Green Tea
Lapsang Souchong Smoky #1 Blend
Mountain-Grown Fancy Ceylon
Owner's Blend Premium Congou
Pure Assam Irish Breakfast
Russian Caravan Original China
Winey Keemun English Breakfast

5229 **Graceland Fruit Inc**
1123 Main St
Frankfort, MI 49635-9341
231-352-7181
Fax: 231-352-4881 800-352-7181
info@gracelandfruit.com www.gracelandfruit.com
Infused dried fruits and vegetables
President & CEO: Alan DeVore
CFO: Troy Terwilliger
VP Research Development: Nirmal Sinha PhD
VP Sales/Marketing: Brent Bradley
VP Human Resources: Doug Rath
COO: Dan Engler
Manager/Grower/Processor Relations: Ben Evans
Year Founded: 1976
Estimated Sales: $40 Million
Number Employees: 100-249
Number of Brands: 1
Number of Products: 50
Type of Packaging: Food Service, Private Label, Bulk
Brands:
Graceland Fruit

5230 **Gracious Gourmet**
PO Box 218
Bridgewater, CT 06752
860-350-1213
Fax: 860-350-1214 info@thegraciousgourmet.com
www.thegraciousgourmet.com
Chutneys, glazes, pestos, spreads and tapenades
President: Nancy Wekselbaum
Marketing: Natalie Nablitt
Sales: Deborah Sherman
deborahs@thegraciousgourmet.com
Number Employees: 4

5231 **Grady's Cold Brew**
819 Garrison Ave
Bronx, NY 10474
718-860-1600
info@gradyscoldbrew.com
gradyscoldbrew.com
Iced coffee beans, grounds and concentrates
Co-Founder: Kyle Buckley
Co-Founder: Dave Sands
Year Founded: 2011
Number Employees: 8
Square Footage: 15000
Type of Packaging: Food Service, Private Label

5232 **Graeter's Mfg. Co.**
1175 Regina Graeter Way
Cincinnati, OH 45216
800-721-3323
www.graeters.com
Ice cream, gelato, sorbet, dessert sauces and confectionary

President and CEO: Richard Graeter
Chief of Retail Operations: Chip Graeter
Chief of Quality Assurance: Robert Graeter
VP of Sales and Marketing: George Denman
Contact: Frank Benkalowycz
frank.benkalowycz@key.com

5233 **Graf Creamery Co**
N4051 Creamery Rd
Bonduel, WI 54107-8441
715-758-2137
Fax: 715-758-8020 www.grafcreamery.com
Butter and condensed and powdered buttermilk
President/CEO: James Bleick
Manager: Jim Bleick
jimb@grafcreamery.com
Plant Manager: Dale Hodmiewicz
Purchasing Director: Jay Winter
Estimated Sales: $10-24.9 Million
Number Employees: 20-49
Square Footage: 168000
Type of Packaging: Private Label, Bulk
Brands:
Cloverdale
Gold Medal
Golden Glow

5234 **Graffam Brothers**
211 Union St
Rockport, ME 04856-6107
207-236-3396
Fax: 207-236-2569 800-535-5358
sales@lobsterstogo.com www.lobsterstogo.com
Lobsters and clams
Owner: Janice Graffam
sales@lobstertogo.com
Number Employees: 10-19

5235 **Graft Cider**
218 Ann St.
Newburgh, NY 12550
410-967-1926
www.graftcidery.com
Hard flavored ciders
Co-Owner: Kyle Sherrer
Co-Owner: Sae Kenney
Number of Brands: 1
Number of Products: 38
Type of Packaging: Consumer, Private Label
Brands:
Graft Cider

5236 **Grafton Village Cheese Co LLC**
400 Linden St
Brattleboro, VT 05301-4474
802-246-2221
Fax: 802-843-2210 800-472-3866
info@graftonvillagecheese.com
www.graftonvillagecheese.com
Specialty cheeses
President: Bob Allen
ed@graftonvillagecheese.com
CFO: Bob Donald
Communications/Marketing: Melissa Gullotti
Sales Exec: Ed Reeves
Master Cheesemaker: Dane Huebner
Production Manager: Ellyn Ladd
Facilities Manager: Greg Kathan
Estimated Sales: $10 Million
Number Employees: 50-99
Parent Co: Windham Foundation
Type of Packaging: Consumer, Food Service, Private Label, Bulk
Brands:
Classic Reserve
Classic Reserve Ext Sharp Cheddar
Grafton Gold
Grafton Gold-Ext Aged Cheddar

5237 **Graham & Rollins Inc**
19 Rudd Ln
Hampton, VA 23669-4029
757-723-3831
Fax: 757-722-3762 800-272-2728
johnny@grahamandrollins.com
www.grahamandrollins.com
Crab
President: John Graham
VP: Johnny Graham
Manager: Terri Wallace
twallace@grahamandrollins.com
Estimated Sales: $1-2,500,000
Number Employees: 100-249

5238 **Graham Cheese Corporation**
502 State Road 57 E
Elnora, IN 47529
812-692-5237
Fax: 812-692-5650 800-472-9178
www.grahamcheese.com
Cheese
Plant Manager: Jerry Sims
Estimated Sales: $2,000,000
Number Employees: 20
Type of Packaging: Consumer, Food Service, Private Label, Bulk

5239 **Graham Chemical Corporation**
1250 S Grove Avenue
Suite 206
Barrington, IL 60010
847-304-4400
Fax: 847-304-8752 www.grahamchemical.com
Specialty chemical intermediates, surfactants, and performance additives.
Owner/Human Resources Executive: Brad Graham
Sales/Marketing Manager: Terri Kent
Estimated Sales: $1 Million
Number Employees: 6
Square Footage: 2000

5240 **Graham Fisheries**
13890 Shell Belt Rd
Bayou La Batre, AL 36509-2304
251-824-7370
Fax: 251-824-7370 shrimp1951@aol.com
Seafood, shrimp
Owner: Darrell Graham
Estimated Sales: $.5-1 million
Number Employees: 1-4

5241 **Grain Belt**
1860 Schell Rd
New Ulm, MN 56073-0128
507-354-5528
Fax: 507-359-9119 800-770-5020
schells@schellsbrewery.com grainbelt.com
Craft beer.
Quality Control Manager: Tom Kaehler
Director of Operations: John Stensland
Year Founded: 1890
Estimated Sales: $20-50 Million
Type of Packaging: Consumer, Food Service, Private Label

5242 **Grain Craft**
201 West Main Street
Suite 203
Chattanooga, TN 37408
423-265-2313
sales@graincraft.com
www.graincraft.com
Flour and grain
President/CEO: Charles Stout
Vice President: Robert Grizzard
Contact: Vicky Heineman
vheineman@graincraft.com
Estimated Sales: $10-19 Million
Number Employees: 20-49

5243 **Grain Millers Inc**
10400 Viking Dr
Suite 301
Eden Prairie, MN 55344-7268
952-829-8821
Fax: 952-829-8819 800-232-6287
info@grainmillers.com www.grainmillers.com
Specialty grain products
President: Steven Eilertson
steven.eilertson@grainmillers.com
SVP: Rick Schwein
Sales/Marketing Manager: Kris Nelson
Estimated Sales: $20-50 Million
Number Employees: 20-49
Type of Packaging: Food Service, Private Label, Bulk
Brands:
Grain Millers

5244 **Grain Place Foods Inc**
1904 N Highway 14
Marquette, NE 68854-2516
402-854-3195
Fax: 402-854-2566 888-714-7246
www.grainplacefoods.com
Grains, cereals
President: David Vetter
dvetter@grainplacefoods.com
Estimated Sales: $1-2,500,000
Number Employees: 20-49
Type of Packaging: Consumer, Private Label, Bulk
Brands:
Grain Place

5245 **Grain Process Enterprises Ltd.**
115 Commander Blvd
Scarborough, ON M1S 3M7
Canada
416-291-3226
Fax: 416-291-2159 800-387-5292
gbjr@grainprocess.com
Flours, granola cereals, grain, bread and muffin mixes
President: George Birinyi
Number Employees: 10
Square Footage: 225000
Type of Packaging: Consumer, Private Label, Bulk
Brands:
Brimley Stone
Grain-Pro
Happy Home
Millbrook

5246 **Grain Processing Corp**
1600 Oregon St
Muscatine, IA 52761-1404
563-264-4265
Fax: 563-264-4289 800-448-4472
sales@grainprocessing.com
Corn-based products
CEO: Gage Kent
Vice President: David Abbott
d_abbott@grainprocessing.com
R&D: Frank Barresi
Quality Control: Rani Thomas
Marketing/Public Relations: Diane Rieke
Technical Sales: Charles Lambert
Operations: Ron Zitzow
Purchasing: Brian Hasser
Number Employees: 10-19
Square Footage: 300000
Parent Co: Kent Corporation
Brands:
Incosity
Instant Pure-Cote
Maltrin
Maltrin Qd
Pure-Bind
Pure-Cote
Pure-Dent
Pure-Gel

5247 **Grain-Free JK Gourmet, Inc.**
635 Petrolia Rd.
Toronto, ON M3J 2X8
Canada
416-782-0045
Fax: 416-785-0686 800-608-0465
info@jkgourmet.com www.jkgourmet.com
Gluten-free products
President/Owner: Jodi Bager
Vice President: Steven Bager
Number Employees: 5

5248 **Grainaissance**
1580 62nd St
Emeryville, CA 94608
510-922-8856
Fax: 510-547-0526 800-472-4697
Rice-based products
President: Tony Plotkin
amazake@grainaissance.com
Estimated Sales: $1.4 Million
Number Employees: 11
Type of Packaging: Consumer
Brands:
Amazake
Grainaissance
Mochi

5249 **Grainful**
950 Danby Rd
Suite 180
Ithaca, NY 14850
info@grainful.com
www.grainful.com
Whole-grain based frozen entr,es
President/Owner: Jan Pajerski
Number of Brands: 1
Number of Products: 8
Type of Packaging: Consumer

Brands:
GRAINFUL

5250 **Grains of Health LLC**
34303 Bodkin Ter
Fremont, CA 94555-2625
510-516-2556
www.laikicrackers.com
Black and red rice crackers
Contact: Pradeep Akkunoor
Number of Brands: 1
Number of Products: 2
Type of Packaging: Consumer

5251 **Graminex**
95 Midland Rd
Saginaw, MI 48638-5770
989-797-5502
Fax: 989-799-0020 877-472-6469
www.graminex.com
Flower pollen extract and fabales
President: Cynthia May
CEO: Cindy May
graminex@graminex.com
Vice President: Parampal Singh
Estimated Sales: $3-5 Million
Number Employees: 1-4

5252 **Grand Central Bakery**
4440 NE Fremont
Portland, OR 97213
508-808-9877
Fax: 503-808-9851
gcb.info@grandcentralbakery.com
grandcentralbakery.com
Baked goods

5253 **Grand Metropolitan**
8710 Central Ave NE # 100
Minneapolis, MN 55434-3305
763-792-3836
Fax: 763-792-3839
Breads
Manager: Deryl R Glaze
VP: Marlene Johnson
Estimated Sales: Less than $500,000
Number Employees: 5-9
Parent Co: Diageo United Distillers and Vinters

5254 **Grand River Cellars**
5750 S Madison Rd
Madison, OH 44057-9001
440-298-9838
Fax: 440-298-1861 www.grandrivercellars.com
Wines
Manager: Cindy Lindberg
grcinfo@grandrivercellars.com
Vice-President: William Worthy
Estimated Sales: $2.5-5,000,000
Number Employees: 20-49

5255 **Grand Teton Brewing Co**
430 Old Jackson Hwy
Victor, ID 83455-5500
208-538-0068
Fax: 208-787-4114 888-899-1656
beermail@GrandTetonBrewing.com
www.grandtetonbrewing.com
Beer
President/CEO: Charlie Otto
VP: Ernie Otto
Estimated Sales: $5-10,000,000
Number Employees: 10-19
Type of Packaging: Consumer, Food Service
Brands:
Grand Teton Brewing
Teton

5256 **Grand View Winery**
PO Box 91
East Calais, VT 05667
802-456-7012
Fax: 802-456-7012
Wines
Winemaker/Owner: Phil Tonks
Estimated Sales: $3-5 Million
Number Employees: 5-9

5257 **Grandcestors**
Golden, CO 80403
grandcestors.com
Frozen paleo diet-friendly prepared meals
Number of Products: 7

5258 **Grande Cheese Company**
250 Camelot Dr
Fond du Lac, WI 54935
800-678-3122
www.grandecheese.com
Cheese
President: Wayne Matzke
VP Marketing/Sales: Elio Camilotto
filippo.candela@grande.com
Contact: Filippo Candela
filippo.candela@grande.com
Type of Packaging: Consumer, Food Service

5259 **Grande Custom Ingredients Group**
250 Camelot Dr
Fond du Lac, WI 54935
920-952-7200
Fax: 920-922-2921 800-772-3210
gcig@grande.com www.grandecig.com
Processor and exporter of specialty whey products and lactose.
Group Vice President: Paul Graham
Research & Development: Rory McCarthy
Sales & Marketing: Brad Nielsen
Operations: Lary Turner
Purchasing Director: Chris Richards
Square Footage: 10000
Parent Co: Grande Cheese Company
Type of Packaging: Bulk
Brands:
Grande Bravo Whey Protein
Grande Gusto Natural Flavor
Grande Ultra Nutritional Whey Prot.

5260 **Grande River Vineyards**
787 Elberta Ave
Palisade, CO 81526-8805
970-464-5867
Fax: 970-464-5427 800-264-7696
info@www.granderiverwines.com
www.granderivervineyards.com
Wines
Founder/Owner/Winemaker: Stephen Smith
bookkeeping@granderiverswines.com
Vineyard Manager: Jim Mayrose
Manager: Javanne Pergola
Estimated Sales: $660,000
Number Employees: 10-19
Type of Packaging: Private Label
Brands:
Grande River Vineyards
Grande River Vineyards Everyday
Grande River Vineyards Meritage

5261 **Grande Tortilla Factory**
914 N Grande Ave
Tucson, AZ 85745-2404
520-622-8338
Flour and corn tortillas, and tamales
President: Frank Pesqueira Jr
Estimated Sales: $200,000
Number Employees: 5-9
Type of Packaging: Consumer

5262 **Grandma Beth's Cookies**
1221 Toluca Avenue
Alliance, NE 69301-2447
308-762-8433
Fax: 308-762-6165
Cookies
Owner: Beth Fetcher
Estimated Sales: $500,000-$1,000,000
Number Employees: 1-4
Type of Packaging: Private Label

5263 **Grandma Browns Beans Inc**
Scenic Ave
Mexico, NY 13114
315-963-7221
Fax: 315-963-4072
grandmabrownsbeans@verizon.net
Beans
President/CFO: Sandra Brown
Estimated Sales: $2.5-3 Million
Number Employees: 10-19
Number of Products: 4
Square Footage: 144000
Type of Packaging: Consumer, Food Service
Brands:
Grandma Brown's

5264 **Grandma Emily**
Montreal, QC H4V 2V9
Canada
514-343-3661
877-943-3661
service@grandmaemily.com
www.grandmaemily.com
Granola bars and cereals
President/Owner: Corey Eisenberg
General Manager: Mina Hanna
Controller: Tina D'Onofrio
Sales and Business Development: Awa Diarra
Type of Packaging: Food Service, Bulk

5265 **Grandma Hoerner's Inc**
31862 Thompson Rd
Alma, KS 66401-9091
785-765-2300
Fax: 785-765-2303 hoerner@kansas.net
www.grandmahoerners.com
Organic reduced sugar preserves, pie fillings, fruit butters, hamburger relish and red pepper jelly
Owner: Duane Mc Coy
dmccoy@grandmahoerners.com
VP: Regina McCoy
Estimated Sales: $7.9 Million
Number Employees: 20-49

5266 **Grandma Pat's Products**
PO Box 158
Albin, WY 82050-0158
307-631-0801
Fax: 307-673-5765
Soup, chili-bean mixes and popcorn
Co-Owner: Pat Palm
Co-Owner: Chuck Palm

5267 **Grandpa Ittel's Meats Inc**
704 6th St
Howard Lake, MN 55349-5645
320-543-2285
Fax: 320-543-2285
Beef jerky and summer sausage
Owner: Jim Ittel
Estimated Sales: Less Than $500,000
Number Employees: 1-4
Type of Packaging: Consumer, Food Service, Private Label, Bulk

5268 **Grandpa Po's Nutra Nuts**
4528 E Washington Blvd
Commerce, CA 90040
323-260-7457
Fax: 888-812-4234 gocorny@nutranuts.com
www.nutranuts.com
Popcorn and soybean snacks
President: Mark Porro
CFO: Michael Porro
Estimated Sales: $200,000
Number Employees: 5
Square Footage: 3300

5269 **Grandpops Lollipops**
2600 Burlington St # A
Kansas City, MO 64116-3019
816-421-5282
Fax: 816-421-5599 800-255-7873
Lollipops and candy
President: Josh Sitzer
Estimated Sales: Under $500,000
Number Employees: 5-9
Brands:
Grandpops Lollipops

5270 **Grandview Farms**
417353 10th Line RR 1
Thornbury, ON N0H 2PO
Canada
519-599-6368
Fax: 519-599-6971 www.grandviewfarms.ca
Meat
President: Desmond Von Teichman
Plant Manager: Bob Hutchinson
Estimated Sales: $100-350,000k
Number Employees: 25
Square Footage: 30000
Type of Packaging: Food Service, Private Label
Brands:
Grandview Farms

5271 **GrandyOats**
34 Schoolhouse Rd
Hiram, ME 04041
207-935-7415
Fax: 207-935-7416 info@grandyoats.com
www.grandyoats.com
Organic granola, muesli, trail mix, roasted nuts and hot cereals
Co-Owner: Nat Peirce
Co-Owner: Aaron Anker
Year Founded: 1979
Number of Brands: 1
Number of Products: 1
Type of Packaging: Consumer
Brands:
GRANDYOATS

5272 **Granello Bakery**
5045 W Mardon Ave
Las Vegas, NV 89139-5521
702-361-0311
Fax: 702-361-0415 orders@granellobakery.com
www.granellobakery.com
Specialty baked goods such as breads, pastry, cake, tarts, cookies and bar cookies.
Owner: Laurie Steed
laurie@granellobakery.com
Year Founded: 1966
Estimated Sales: $20-50 Million
Number Employees: 50-99
Square Footage: 42000

5273 **Granite Springs Winery**
2860 Omo Ranch Rd
Somerset, CA 95684
530-620-6395
Fax: 530-620-4884 800-638-6041
latcham@directcon.net www.latcham.com
Wines
President: Jon Latcham
Winemaker: Craig Boyd
Estimated Sales: $1 2,500,000
Number Employees: 5-9

5274 **Granny Blossom Specialty Foods**
Route 30
Wells, VT 05774
802-645-0507
Fax: 802-645-0860
Specialty condiments
Owner: Bob Kopp
Owner: Doris Kopp

5275 **Granny Roddy's LLC**
4226 Holborn Avenue
Annandale, VA 22003
703-503-3431
Baking mixes
Marketing: Joanne Buto
Type of Packaging: Private Label

5276 **Granny's Best Strawberry Products**
PO Box 9
Victoria, ON N0E 1W0
Canada
519-426-0705
Fax: 519-426-2573 519-426-0705
Frozen strawberry puree
President: Gary Cooper
Type of Packaging: Private Label

5277 **Granowska's**
175 Roncesvalles Avenue
Toronto, ON M6R 2L3
Canada
416-533-7755
Fax: 416-533-3261
Baked goods
President: Elizabeth Klodas
Estimated Sales: $813,000
Number Employees: 15
Square Footage: 14000
Brands:
Granowska's

5278 **Grant Park Packing**
842 W Lake St
Chicago, IL 60607-1720
312-421-4096
Fax: 312-421-1484 sales@grantparkpacking.com
www.grantparkpacking.com
Pork, beef, poultry, sausage and Italian sausage
Owner: Joseph Maffei
joe@grantparkpacking.com
General Manager/Partner: Vince Maffei
Estimated Sales: $10 Million
Number Employees: 20-49
Square Footage: 35000
Type of Packaging: Consumer

5279 **Granville Gates & Sons**
60 Fish Plant Rd
Hubbards, NS B0J 1T0
Canada
902-228-2559
Fax: 902-228-2368
Dried and salted seafood
Manager: Garry Harnish
Office Manager: Norma Young
Plant Manager: Ed Grant
Estimated Sales: 5,000,000-9,999,999
Number Employees: 32
Type of Packaging: Bulk

5280 **Grapevine Trading Company**
738 Wilson St
Santa Rosa, CA 95401
707-576-3950
Fax: 800-469-6808 800-469-6478
Mustards, fruit and balsamic vinegars, olive oils, tapenades, wild mushrooms, chili peppers, pine nuts, dried tomatoes, polenta mixes, vanilla extract
President: Sandra Voorhis
sandra.vanvoorhis@hotmail.com
Estimated Sales: $1.3,000,000
Number Employees: 10
Brands:
California Harvest
Gourmet Fare
Grapevine Trading Co.
Wine Gift Packaging

5281 **Grass Run Farms**
Greeley, CO 80631
800-727-2333
grassrunfarms.com
Grass-fed beef

5282 **Grassland Dairy Products Inc**
N8790 Fairground Ave
Greenwood, WI 54437-7668
715-267-6182
Fax: 715-267-6044 800-428-8837
email@grassland.com www.grassland.com
Butter products
President: Dallas Wuethrich
CFO: Leony Gregorich
Estimated Sales: $38.8 Million
Number Employees: 250-499
Square Footage: 60000
Type of Packaging: Consumer, Food Service, Private Label, Bulk
Brands:
Grassland
Wuthrich
Country Cream
Fall Creek
Golden Goodness

5283 **Grasso Foods Inc**
2111 Kings Hwy
Swedesboro, NJ 08085-3216
856-467-2222
Fax: 856-467-5474 info@grassofoods.com
Peppers
President: Janet Schumann
janet.schumann@grassofoods.com
Number Employees: 5-9
Type of Packaging: Consumer, Food Service, Private Label, Bulk

5284 **Gratify Gluten Free**
Englewood Cliffs, NJ
Fax: 201-871-8726 800-200-6736
www.gratifyfoods.com
Gluten-free foods
Parent Co: Osem USA, Inc.

5285 **Graves Mountain Lodge Inc.**
Route 670
Syria, VA 22743-9999
540-923-4231
Fax: 540-923-4312 info@gravesmountain.com
www.gravesmountain.com
Pepper and cucumber relish, fruit preserves, jellies, chutney, apple butter and apple sauce
President: James Graves
Plant Manager: Gail Ford
Estimated Sales: $300,000- $500,000
Number Employees: 6
Number of Brands: 1
Square Footage: 20000
Parent Co: Graves Mountain Lodge
Type of Packaging: Consumer, Private Label
Brands:
Colonial Williamsburg
Graves Mountain

5286 **Gravity Ciders, Inc.**
8 Winkler Rd.
Sydney, NY 13838
www.awestruckciders.com
Homemade hard flavored ciders
Co-Founder: Casey Vitti
Co-Founder: Patti Wilcox
Year Founded: 2014
Number of Brands: 1
Number of Products: 5
Type of Packaging: Private Label
Brands:
Awestruck Ciders

5287 **Gravymaster, Inc.**
101 Erie Blvd
Canajoharie, NY 13317
800-526-6872
Fax: 888-673-2451 800-839-8938
info@richardsonbrands.com www.gravy.com
Sauces
President: Stephen Besse
Sales Executive: Cathy Testa
Consultant: John Mills
Sales Coordinator: MaryLou Sweet
Promotional Products Representative: Laurie Bluitt
Supply Chain Manager: Rebecca Woodruff
Estimated Sales: $10-20 Million
Number Employees: 20-49
Parent Co: Richardson Brands
Type of Packaging: Consumer, Food Service
Brands:
Gravy Master
Gravymaster

5288 **Gray & Company**
3325 W Polk Rd
Hart, MI 49420-8149
231-873-5628
Fax: 231-873-0348 800-551-6009
sales@cherryman.com www.grayandcompany.us
Maraschino cherries, glace fruit and chocolate cherry cordials
Director of Finance: Kevin Schulz
Executive Vice President: Joshua Reynolds
Food Scientist: Jillian Clark
Sales: Rich Bertellotti
Director of Cherry Operations: Dirk Williams
Plant Engineer: Benjamin Kirwin
Purchasing Manager: Steve Schauer
Estimated Sales: $28.2 Million
Number Employees: 250-499
Square Footage: 5000
Type of Packaging: Consumer, Food Service, Private Label, Bulk
Other Locations:
Hart MI
Dayton OR
Brands:
Cherryman
Pennant
Queen Anne
Towie
White Swan

5289 **Gray Duck**
Minneapolis, MN 55417
www.grayduckchai.com
Organic chai
Co-Founder: Katey Niebur
Co-Founder: Jon Alden

5290 **Gray's Brewing Co**
2424 W Court St
Janesville, WI 53548-3307
608-752-3552
Fax: 608-752-0821 office@graybrewing.com
www.graybrewing.com
Beer
Owner: Marina Bowser
Sales: Robert Gray
marina@graybrewing.com

Estimated Sales: Under $500,000
Number Employees: 10-19
Type of Packaging: Consumer, Food Service

5291 **Grays Ice Cream**
16 East Rd
Tiverton, RI 02878-3599
401-624-4500
Fax: 401-624-4500 graysicecream@gmail.com
www.graysicecream.com
Homemade ice cream, frozen desserts
President: Marilyn Dennis
mdennis@graysicecream.com
Estimated Sales: $580,000-1,000,000
Number Employees: 20-49

5292 **Graysmarsh Berry Farm**
6187 Woodcock Rd
Sequim, WA 98382-8144
360-683-5563
Fax: 360-683-6509 800-683-4367
www.graysmarsh.com
Fruit preserves and lavender products; U-pick berries
General Manager: Arturo Flores
Estimated Sales: $20-50 Million
Number Employees: 20-49
Type of Packaging: Consumer, Food Service, Bulk

5293 **Grayson Naturla Farms**
5630 Wilson Hwy
Independence, VA 24348
276-773-3712
graysonnatural.com
Meat products; health bars and other snacks
Owner: Gary Mitchell
Director of Marketing: Chris Anderson
Manager of Operations: Jenna Heise
Year Founded: 2007
Estimated Sales: $1 Million
Number Employees: 1-10

5294 **Great American Appetizers**
216 8th St N
Nampa, ID 83687-3029
208-465-5111
Fax: 208-465-5059 800-282-4834
marco@appetizer.com www.appetizer.com
Appetizers
President: Tammy Mika
tammy.mika@westin.com
Marketing/Sales Coordinator: Debbie Lindley
VP Retail Sales: Frank Benso
COO: Marco Meyer
Purchasing Director: Tammy Mika
Year Founded: 1959
Estimated Sales: $26.6 Million
Number Employees: 250-499
Number of Products: 100
Square Footage: 60000
Parent Co: Westin Foods
Type of Packaging: Consumer, Food Service, Private Label, Bulk
Brands:
Big Red
Brew House
Questias
Wahoo! Appetizers

5295 **Great American Barbecue Company**
52 Gedney Way
White Plains, NY 10605
914-686-2277
Fax: 203-661-6162
www.thegreatamericanbbq.com
Frozen and refrigerated beef and chichken
Owner: Dave Mann
Owner: Dan Ferreira
VP Sales: Troy Gall
Contact: Kaye Jackson
kaye@nyhospitalitygroup.com
Brands:
Great American Barbecue

5296 **Great American Cookie Company**
1346 Oakbrook Drive
Suite 170
Norcross, GA 30093
877-639-2361
Fax: 404-505-2835
customerservice@gfgmanagement.com
www.greatamericancookies.com
Refrigerated and frozen cookie dough
Manager: Mike Curtis
VP: T Lynch
VP: James Squire
Operations Manager: Danny Breault
Production Manager: Michael Curtis
Number Employees: 1,000-4,999
Parent Co: Mrs. Fields' Original Cookies

5297 **(HQ)Great American Dessert Co**
5842 Maurice Ave
Flushing, NY 11378-2333
718-894-3494
Fax: 718-894-6105 800-458-6467
info@juniorscheesecake.com
www.juniorscheesecake.com
Gourmet desserts
President: Michael Goodman
michaelgoodman@mycheesecake.com
Public Relations: Theresa Kramer
Purchasing: Grace Pavlak
Estimated Sales: $1-5,000,000
Number Employees: 50-99
Type of Packaging: Private Label
Brands:
Granny Cheescakes
Rode Lee

5298 **Great American Foods Commissary**
3864 FM 161 North
Hughes Springs, TX 75656
903-639-1482
Fax: 903-968-4376 office@davidbeards.com
www.davidbeards.com
Catfish, tomato relish, hot sauce and hushpuppies
President/CEO: David Beard
Purchasing: Terry Simpler
Estimated Sales: $20-50 Million
Number Employees: 20-49
Brands:
David Beards
David Beards Texas Style

5299 **Great American Popcorn Works of Pennsylvania**
PO Box 214
Telford, PA 18969-0214
215-721-0414
Fax: 215-721-6082 855-542-2676
www.popcornworks.com
Gourmet popcorn
Manager: Alice Barnes
Vice President: Jack Egner
Sales Director: Rob Rosen
Public Relations: Giselle Wetzel
Estimated Sales: Less than $500,000
Number Employees: 1-4
Number of Products: 65
Square Footage: 12000
Type of Packaging: Consumer, Food Service, Private Label, Bulk

5300 **Great American Seafood Company**
1711 W Kirby Ave
Champaigne, IL 61821-55
217-352-0986
www.greatamericanseafood.com
Seafood
Estimated Sales: $300,000-500,000
Number Employees: 5-9

5301 **Great American Smokehouse & Seafood Company**
15657 Highway 101 S
Brookings, OR 97415-9556
541-469-6903
Fax: 541-469-9692 800-828-3474
Seafood
Owner: Lee D Myers Sr
Co-Owner: Nancy Myers
Co-Owner: Lee Myers
Estimated Sales: $500,000-$1,000,000
Number Employees: 10-19

5302 **Great Atlantic Trading Company**
1204 Longstreet Circle
Brentwood, TN 37027-6506
615-661-6678
Fax: 910-575-7978 888-268-8780
www.caviarstar.com
Fresh and frozen seafood, American and imported caviar
President: Dana Leavitt
Estimated Sales: $3.2 Million
Number Employees: 1-4
Square Footage: 5000
Parent Co: Great Atlantic Trading Company

5303 **Great Circles**
5 Canal Street
PO Box 495
Bellows Falls, VT 05101
802-463-2111
Fax: 802-463-2110 877-877-2120
gcircles@sover.net http://www.sover.net
Health foods
President: Dwane Kurisu
CEO: Rich Kendall
Estimated Sales: $2.5-5,000,000
Number Employees: 1-4

5304 **Great Divide Brewing Co**
2201 Arapahoe St
Denver, CO 80205-2512
303-296-9460
Fax: 303-296-9464 info@greatdivide.com
Beer and ale
President/Brew master: Brian Dunn
Vice President: Tara Dunn
Vice President Operations: Mason Thomas
Estimated Sales: $5-10 Million
Number Employees: 1-4
Brands:
Arapahoe
Bee Sting
Denver
Hibernation
Saint Brigid's
Wit
Whitewater
Wild Raspberry

5305 **Great Earth Chemical**
7007 SW Cardinal Ln # 135
Suite 135
Portland, OR 97224-7248
503-620-7130
Fax: 503-670-1737 sales@nawpi.com
www.greatearthchemical.com
Food additives, nutritional supplements, vitamins and preservatives
Owner: Ruth Yein
ruth@greatearthchemical.com
Director of Sales: Daniel Kruszka
Number Employees: 20-49
Parent Co: North American World Trade Group

5306 **Great Eastern Sun Trading Co**
92 Mcintosh Rd
Asheville, NC 28806-1406
828-665-7790
Fax: 828-667-8051 800-334-5809
weborders@great-eastern-sun.com
Asian organic and natural foods
Owner: Berry Evans
generalmgr@great-eastern-sun.com
Finance: Brett Martin
Sales Manager: Mary Griffin
VP Operations/Purchaser: Jan Paige
Assistant Production Manager: Wendy Young
Warehouse/Shipping: Joe Putnam
Estimated Sales: $5-10 Million
Number Employees: 20-49
Brands:
MISO MASTER ORGANIC
EMERALD COVE
EMPEROR'S KITCHEN
ORGANIC PLANET
SUSHI SONIC
HAIKU
ONE WORLD
SWEET CLOUD

5307 **Great Expectations Confectionery Gourmet Foods**
1911 W Warren Boulevard
Chicago, IL 60612
773-525-4865
Fax: 773-281-5506
Candy and confections
President: John Prescott
Estimated Sales: $110,000
Number Employees: 2
Type of Packaging: Consumer, Private Label
Brands:
Great Expectations

5308 **Great Garlic Foods**
709 5th Ave
Bradley Beach, NJ 07720-1004
732-775-3311
Fax: 732-774-9386
Garlic products
Owner: Joe DE Santis
ggarlfoods@aol.com
Estimated Sales: $1-3 Million
Number Employees: 5-9
Type of Packaging: Consumer, Food Service, Private Label, Bulk

5309 **Great Glacier Salmon**
PO Box 1137
Prince Rupert, BC V8J 4H6
Canada
250-627-4955
Fax: 250-627-7945 greatglacier@hotmail.com
Salmon
Accounting: Mary Allen
General Manager: Robert Gould
Estimated Sales: $250,000 To 1,000,000
Number Employees: 20-49
Number of Brands: 2
Square Footage: 6400
Type of Packaging: Private Label, Bulk
Brands:
Glacier Caviar
Glacier Salmon

5310 **Great Gourmet Inc**
5115 Clark Canning House Rd
Federalsburg, MD 21632-2615
410-754-8800
Fax: 410-754-5997 sales@thegreatgourmet.com
Seafood and shellfish
Owner: Kim Scott
kim@thegreatgourmet.com
Number Employees: 20-49

5311 **Great Grains Milling Company**
105 Four Buttes Railroad Ave W
Scobey, MT 59263
406-783-5581
Red spring wheat flour and bran, cracked wheat cereal, pancake and waffle mixes
President: Alvin Rustebakke
Estimated Sales: $500,000-$1 Million
Number Employees: 1-4
Square Footage: 1600
Type of Packaging: Consumer, Food Service, Private Label

5312 **Great Harvest Bread Co**
28 S Montana St
Dillon, MT 59725-2434
406-683-6842
Fax: 406-683-5537 800-442-0424
www.greatharvest.com
Bread
President & CEO: Mike Ferretti
mikef@greatharvest.com
Dir.of Bakery Support & Operations: Mark Peterson
Number Employees: 20-49

5313 **Great Hill Dairy Inc**
160 Delano Rd
Marion, MA 02738-2029
508-748-2208
Fax: 508-748-2282 888-748-2208
www.greathillblue.com
Milk and cheeses
President: Tim Stone
President: Nancy Weaver
Estimated Sales: $500,000-$1,000,000
Number Employees: 1-4
Brands:
Great Hill Blue

5314 **Great Lakes Brewing Co.**
2516 Market Ave
Cleveland, OH 44113-3434
216-771-4404
Fax: 216-771-2799
glbcinfo@greatlakesbrewing.com
www.greatlakesbrewing.com
Beers; not to be confused with Canadian "Great Lakes Brewery."
President/CEO: Patrick Conway
Co-Owner: Daniel Conway
Marketing Director: Carey Roberts
Vice President Sales & Marketing: Bridget Barrett
Controller: Kevin Cawneen
Type of Packaging: Consumer, Food Service
Brands:
Burning River Pale Ale
Edmund Fitzgerald Porter
Commodore Perry India Pale Ale
Conway's Irish Ale
Dopplerock
Holy Moses White Ale
The Wright Pils
Oktoberfest
Nosferatu
Christmas Ale
Blackout Stout

5315 **(HQ)Great Lakes Cheese Company, Inc.**
17825 Great Lakes Pkwy
PO Box 1806
Hiram, OH 44234-1806
440-834-2500
Fax: 440-834-1002 glcinfo@greatlakescheese.com
www.greatlakescheese.com
Cheese
Chairman: Hans Epprecht
CEO/President: Gary Vanic
CFO: Russell Mullins
VP Sales: William Andrews
VP Human Resources: Beth Wendell
VP/General Mgr: John W Epprecht
Manufacturing/Operations Director: Steve Scott
Plant Manager: Thomas Eastham
Purchasing Clerk: Shelley Williamson
Estimated Sales: Over $1 Billion
Number Employees: 1000-4999
Square Footage: 400000
Type of Packaging: Private Label
Other Locations:
Great Lakes Cheese of New York
Adams NY
Great Lakes Cheese of Utah
Fillmore UT
Great Lakes Cheese Company-HQ
Hiram OH
Great Lakes Cheese of La Crosse
La Crosse WI
Great Lakes Cheese of Wisconsin
Plymouth WI

5316 **Great Lakes Cheese Company**
101 DeVoe Street
Wausau, WI 54403
715-842-3214
Fax: 715-842-4452 www.greatlakescheese.com
Specialty cheese products
COO: Randy Lewis
President of Administration/Treasurer: Daniel E Zagzebski
Estimated Sales: Below $5 Million
Number Employees: 100-249
Parent Co: Great Lakes Cheese Company, Inc.
Brands:
Great Lakes

5317 **Great Lakes Foods**
1230 48th Ave
Menominee, MI 49858-1002
906-863-5503
Fax: 906-863-2102 800-800-7492
jvan@greatlakesfoods.com
Canned mushrooms; fruit and vegetable canning, pickling and drying
President: Tom Ireland
Owner: Jerry Vandelaarschot
CFO: Don Kressin
dkressin@greatlakefood.com
Vice President: Johanne Ubbels
Estimated Sales: $1-2.5 Million
Number Employees: 50-99
Parent Co: Ubbelea Farms
Type of Packaging: Consumer, Food Service, Private Label
Brands:
Chateau
Riviera

5318 **Great Lakes Packing Co**
6556 Quarterline Rd
Kewadin, MI 49648-8907
231-264-5561
Fax: 231-264-5594 glpc@greatlakespacking.com
www.greatlakespacking.com
Frozen cherries
President/ Hart Plant Manager: Jon Veliquette
jon@greatlakespacking.com
Vice President: Dean Veliquette
Quality Assurance Manager: Roger Veliquette
Human Resources Manager: Trudy Cullimore
Estimated Sales: $1.7,000,000
Number Employees: 250-499
Type of Packaging: Consumer, Private Label
Brands:
Great Lakes

5319 **Great Lakes Tea & Spice**
6610 Western Ave
PO Box 661
Glen Arbor, MI 49636-5103
231-334-6747
Fax: 231-326-2333 877-645-9363
www.teaandspice.com
Loose teas, flowering teas and spices
President/Owner: Chris Sack
CEO: Heather Sack
Estimated Sales: Less Than $500,000
Number Employees: 1-4

5320 **Great Lakes Wine & Spirits**
373 Victor St
Highland Park, MI 48203-3117
313-453-2200
Fax: 313-867-4039 www.glwas.com
Wines, spirits, and beers.
Co-CEO: Lew Cooper III
Co-CEO: Syd Ross
EVP, Finance: John Queen
EVP, Operations: Lou Grech-Cumbo
EVP, IT: Mike Arkison
VP, National Accounts: Heather Kerr
VP, Wine Sales: Jason Howard
EVP, Sales: Ernier Almeranti
VP, Sales Development: Rick Lopus
VP, Human Resources: Stephanie Lyons
Year Founded: 2008

5321 **Great Midwest Seafood Company**
5406 Sheridan St
Davenport, IA 52806-2260
563-388-4770
Fax: 563-388-4772
Seafood
Owner: Jeff Melchert
kingfish@gmail.com
Estimated Sales: $10-20 Million
Number Employees: 10-19

5322 **Great Northern Baking Company**
443 Hoover St NE
Minneapolis, MN 55413
612-331-1043
Fax: 612-331-1052 info@greatnorthernbaking.com
www.greatnorthernbaking.com
Muffins, cakes, cookie bars and pretzels
President: Fred Johnson
Estimated Sales: $5-9.9 000,000
Number Employees: 50-99
Brands:
Mrs Feldman's Desserts

5323 **Great Northern Brewing Co**
2 Central Ave
Suite 1
Whitefish, MT 59937-2547
406-863-1000
Fax: 406-863-1001
brewmaster@greatnorthernbrewing.com
www.greatnorthernbrewing.com
Beer and lager
Owner: Dennis Konopatzke
General Manager/ Partner: Marcus Duffey
Controller: Uwe Schaefer
Retail Marketing & Promotion Manager: Jessica Lucey
Head Sales: Orie Roberts
kono@woodtechdoor.com
Tasting Room/Customer Service: Jessica Stanhope
Head Operations: Thomas Sierra
Production Manager: Dan Rasmussen
Estimated Sales: $2.5-5,000,000
Number Employees: 5-9
Parent Co: McKenzie River Partners
Type of Packaging: Consumer, Food Service
Brands:
Black
Premium
Whitefish
Wild Huckleberry

5324 **Great Northern Maple Products**
331 Rue Principale
Saint Honor, De Shenley, QC G0M 1V0
Canada
418-485-7777
Fax: 418-485-6185 info@greatnorthernmaple.com
www.greatnorthernmaple.com
Organic maple and fruit syrups
Director General: Gary Coppola
International Marketing Manager: Luc Tardiff

5325 **Great Northern Products Inc**
2700 Plainfield Pike
Cranston, RI 02921-2070
401-490-4590
Fax: 401-633-6051 info@northernproducts.com
www.northernproducts.com
Seafood
President: George Nolan
george@northernproducts.com
Executive Vice President: Peter Bruno
Quality Control/ Compliance: Kyle Wilkens
Domestic Sales: Don Nolan
COO: Jose Pons
Estimated Sales: $10.1 Million
Number Employees: 20-49
Number of Brands: 4
Number of Products: 40
Square Footage: 24000
Brands:
Commonwealth
Fruits De Mer
Langlois
Sabana
Sealicious
Simmonds

5326 **Great Pacific Seafoods**
PO Box 81165
Seattle, WA 98108
206-764-7180
Fax: 206-764-7187
Fresh and frozen salmon
Manager: Roger Stiles
Estimated Sales: $10-20,000,000
Number Employees: 50-99
Type of Packaging: Consumer, Food Service
Brands:
Great Pacific

5327 **Great Plains Beef LLC**
PO Box 82545
Lincoln, NE 68501-2545
402-479-2115
Fax: 402-458-4531 info@piedmontese.com
Beef
President: Billy Swain
Number Employees: 1-4
Brands:
Lone Creek Cattle Company
Great Plains
Certified Piedmontese

5328 **Great Recipes**
PO Box 647
Beaverton, OR 97075-0647
503-590-1108
Fax: 800-585-2331 800-273-2331
contactus@great-recipes.com
www.great-recipes.com
Bread, cookie, cake, brownie and muffin mixes
President: Mark Bonebrake
markb@great-recipes.com
Estimated Sales: $1-2,500,000
Number Employees: 1-4
Type of Packaging: Private Label
Brands:
Firenza
Great Recipes

5329 **Great River Organic Milling**
W26001 Volds Lane
Arcadia, WI 54612
608-687-9580
Fax: 608-687-3014 contact@greatrivermilling.com
www.greatrivermilling.com
Organic grains, flours and mixes
Owner: Rick Halverson
rhalverson@greatrivermilling.com
Customer Service: Nadine Bayer
Estimated Sales: Less Than $500,000
Number Employees: 1-4
Type of Packaging: Bulk

5330 **Great Spice Company**
12101 Moya Blvd
Reno, NV 89506-2600
Fax: 760-744-0401 800-730-3575
www.greatspice.com
Dehydrated and fresh herbs
President: Jay Fishman
Inventory Manager: Steve Addison
s.addison@hqorganics.com
Quality Manager: Ja Attaphongse
VP Sales: Jim Slatic
Founder/VP Operations: Jerry Tenenberg
Operations Manager: Dan Sullivan
Shipping Manager: Michael Tenenberg
Global Purchasing Coordinator: Rommina Chavarria
Estimated Sales: $3-5,000,000
Number Employees: 20-49
Type of Packaging: Food Service, Private Label, Bulk

5331 **Great Valley Mills**
1774 A County Line Rd
Barto, PA 19504-8720
610-754-7800
Fax: 610-754-6490 800-688-6455
Stone ground flour, pancake, muffin, bread and specialty dry food mixes
Owner: Steve Kantoor
Estimated Sales: $690,000
Number Employees: 6
Square Footage: 45000
Type of Packaging: Consumer, Food Service, Private Label
Brands:
1710
Covered Bridge Mills
Flip It
Great Valley Mills
Great Valley Mixes

5332 **Great Western Brewing Company**
519 Second Avenue N
Saskatoon, SK S7K 2C6
Canada
306-653-4653
Fax: 306-653-2166 800-764-4492
info@greatwesternbrewing.com www.gwbc.ca
Beer
President/CEO: Michael Micovcin
Brew master: Garry Johnston
Number Employees: 50-99
Type of Packaging: Consumer, Food Service

5333 **Great Western Co LLC**
30290 US Highway 72
Hollywood, AL 35752-6134
256-259-3578
Fax: 256-259-7087 www.gwproducts.com
Processor and exporter of popcorn, popping corn oil, cotton candy, sno-cone syrup, candy apple coatings, funnel cakes, waffle cones, corn dog mix, and other consession items
Contact: Tim Ferguson
timf@gwproducts.com
Estimated Sales: Less Than $500,000
Number Employees: 1-4
Number of Brands: 6
Type of Packaging: Consumer, Food Service, Private Label, Bulk
Brands:
Chillee Snow Cones
Frostee Snow Cones
Great Western Products Company
Peter's Movie Time Products
Premium America
Sunglo

5334 **Great Western Juice Co**
16153 Libby Rd
Maple Heights, OH 44137-1298
216-475-5770
Fax: 216-475-5772 800-321-9180
gwjuice@sbcglobal.net
Beverages
President: Doreen Coons
dcoons@fibreglast.com
VP: Bill Overton
Marketing/Sales: Phil Leroy
Public Relations: Connie Rice
Operations Manager: John Stevens
Plant Manager: John Taziros
Purchasing Manager: Bill Overton
dcoons@fibreglast.com
Estimated Sales: $1.6 Million
Number Employees: 20-49
Square Footage: 60000
Type of Packaging: Food Service, Private Label
Brands:
Ice & Easy
Perfection
Sunny Morning

5335 **Great Western Malting Co**
1705 NW Harborside Dr
Vancouver, WA 98660
360-693-3661
www.graincorp.com.au
Processed malt
President & CEO: Greg Friberg
Group Chief Financial Officer: Alistair Bell
Chief Information Officer: Andrew Baker
Estimated Sales: $27 Million
Number Employees: 50-99
Square Footage: 13440
Type of Packaging: Bulk
Other Locations:
Malt Plant
Vancouver WA
Malt Plant
Pocatello ID
Bagged Malt Country Warehouse
Vancouver WA
Bagged Malt Country Warehouse
Aurora CO
Bagged Malt Country Warehouse
Hayward CA
Bagged Malt Country Warehouse
Champlain NY
Bagged Malt Country Warehouse
Chicago IL
Bagged Malt Country Warehouse
Hickory NC
Bagged Malt Country Warehouse
British Columbia Canada
Bagged Malt Country Warehouse
Alberta Canada

5336 **Great Western Tortilla**
1761 E 58th Avenue
Denver, CO 80216-1505
303-298-0705
Fax: 303-298-0216
Tortilla chips and other snacks
Director Sales/Marketing: John Amerman
Estimated Sales: $10-20 Million
Number Employees: 50-99

5337 **Greater Knead, The**
1690 Winchester Rd
Bensalem, PA 19020
267-522-8523
info@thegreaterknead.com
www.thegreaterknead.com
Gluten free bagels and bagel chips
Founder/CEO: Michelle Carfagno
CFO: Christina Cassetti
Product Investigator: Mengyi Hu
Account Manager: Maxie Walsh
Warehouse Manager: Joe Otto
Year Founded: 2012
Number Employees: 20-49

5338 **Greater Omaha Packing Co Inc.**
3001 L Street
Omaha, NE 68107
402-731-1700
800-747-5400
info@greateromaha.com www.greateromaha.com
Beef.
President/CEO: Henry Davis
Credit/Account Manager: Carol Mesenbrink
Vice President, Sales: Dan Jensen
Year Founded: 1920
Estimated Sales: $1+ Billion
Number Employees: 1,000
Number of Brands: 5
Square Footage: 60000
Type of Packaging: Consumer, Food Service, Private Label, Bulk
Brands:
Omaha Natural Angus
Certified Angus Beef
Greater Omaha
Hereford Beef
Omaha Hereford

5339 **Greaves Jams & Marmalades**
PO Box 26
Niagara-on-the-Lake, ON L0S 1J0
Canada
905-468-3608
Fax: 905-468-0071 800-515-9939
greaves@greavesjams.com www.greavesjams.com
Jams, jellies, marmalades and condiments
President: Lloyd Redekopp
Vice President: Angela Redekopp
Production: Rudy Doerwald
Estimated Sales: $1.4 Million
Number Employees: 15
Number of Products: 1
Square Footage: 20000
Type of Packaging: Consumer, Private Label
Brands:
Greaves

5340 **Grebe's Bakery**
5132 W Lincoln Ave
Milwaukee, WI 53219-1684
414-543-7001
Fax: 414-543-8863 800-833-3158
info@grebesbakery.com www.grebesbakeries.com
Bakery products
President: Jim Grebe Sr
Year Founded: 1937
Estimated Sales: $10-20 Million
Number Employees: 100-249
Square Footage: 93000
Type of Packaging: Consumer, Bulk
Brands:
Grebe's

5341 **Grecian Delight Foods Inc**
1201 Tonne Rd
Elk Grove Village, IL 60007-4925
847-364-2030
Fax: 847-364-1077 800-621-4387
www.gdfsalesportal.com
Frozen Greek baked goods, meat products, pita bread, gyros, entrees and desserts
Owner/Human Resources & Sales Manager: Peter Parthenis
pparthenis@greciandelight.com
VP/CFO: Bill Pierreakeas
Research/Development Manager: John Matchuk
Quality Control Manager: Mary Funteas
Marketing Director: Deme Katsulis
VP Operations: Tom Valnoha
Purchasing Director: George Georganas
Number Employees: 250-499
Type of Packaging: Consumer, Food Service, Private Label, Bulk
Brands:
Athenian
Chicago Style
Pita Folds

5342 **Green & Black's OrganicChocolate**
PO Box 259011
Plano, TX 75025
973-909-3900
Fax: 973-909-3930 877-299-1254
greenandblacks@cohnwolfe.com
www.greenandblacks.com/us
Organic choclate
President/Owner: Neil Turpin
CFO: James Reed
Contact: Newell Holt
newell@greenandblacks.com
Number Employees: 8

5343 **Green Bay Cheese**
1 Overlook Point
Suite 300
Lincolnshire, IL 60069
262-677-3407
Fax: 847-267-3280 800-824-3373
www.saputospecialty.com/en/our-cheeses/green-bay-cheese
Cheeses
Chairman & CEO: Lino Saputo Jr.
CFO: Maxime Therrien
COO, Cheese Division (USA): Terry Brockman
Year Founded: 1975
Estimated Sales: $20-50 Million
Number Employees: 100-249
Parent Co: Saputo Cheese USA

5344 **(HQ)Green Bay Packaging Inc.**
1700 Webster Ct.
Green Bay, WI 54302
920-433-5111
Fax: 920-433-5471 www.gbp.com
Corrugated shipping containers and labels including coated and stock.
President/CEO: William Kress
bkress@gbp.com
Senior VP/General Counsel: Scott Wochos
Year Founded: 1933
Estimated Sales: $850 Million
Number Employees: 3,200
Type of Packaging: Consumer, Food Service, Private Label, Bulk

5345 **Green Beans Coffee Co Inc**
4300 Redwood Hwy # 100
San Rafael, CA 94903-2103
415-461-4023
info@greenbeanscoffee.net
www.greenbeanscoffee.com
Coffee
President & Co Founder: Jon Araghi
CEO & Co-Founder: Jason Araghi
Number Employees: 250-499

5346 **Green County Foods**
PO BOX 2813
Monroe, WI 53566-1364
608-328-8800
Fax: 608-328-8648 800-233-3564
custserv@greencountyfoods.com
www.greencountyfoods.com
Desserts and baked goods
President: Gene Curran
Sales: Wally Wagner
Public Relations: Jim Mason
Operations: Sharee Marzolf
Estimated Sales: $2.5-5,000,000
Number Employees: 10-19
Parent Co: Swiss Colony
Type of Packaging: Consumer, Food Service, Private Label, Bulk
Brands:
Richly Deserved
Sweet Treasures

5347 **Green Dirt Farm**
19915 Mount Bethel Rd
PO Box 74
Weston, MO 64098-9070
816-386-2156
info@greendirtfarm.com
www.greendirtfarm.com
Dairy products
Co-Founder: Jacqueline Smith
Co-Founder: Sarah Hoffman
sarah@greendirtfarm.com
Estimated Sales: Less Than $500,000
Number Employees: 1-4

5348 **Green Earth Orchards**
1412 Laird Ave
Salt Lake City, UT 84105
801-888-7161
info@greenearthorchards.com
Dried fruits
Number of Brands: 1
Number of Products: 1
Type of Packaging: Consumer, Bulk
Brands:
GREEN EARTH ORCHARDS

5349 **Green Foods Corp.**
2220 Camino Del Sol
Oxnard, CA 93030-8905
800-777-4430
info@greenfoods.com greenfoods.com
Powdered protein shakes and juices
President: Takahiko Amano
Chief Administrative Officer: Deborah Pollack
deborah@greenfoods.com
Technical Service Manager: Bob Terry
Estimated Sales: $10-20 Million
Number Employees: 5-9
Square Footage: 19600
Type of Packaging: Consumer
Brands:
Green Essence

5350 **Green Garden Food Products**
100 Litehouse Dr.
PO Box 1969
Sandpoint, ID 83864
253-395-4460
Fax: 253-395-0408 800-669-3169
info@ggfoods.com www.ggfoods.com
Condiments
President: Mark Hockman
Director Technical Services: Kyle Anderson
Estimated Sales: $25,000,000
Number Employees: 50-99
Type of Packaging: Consumer, Food Service

5351 **Green Gold Group LLC**
13905 Stettin Dr
Marathon, WI 54448-9476
715-842-8546
Fax: 715-842-4614 888-533-7288
www.greengoldgroup.com
Ginseng, herbs, whole roots and other health products
Owner: Sam Chen
mail@greengoldgroup.com
CEO: Phouangmala Chen
Estimated Sales: $1-3,000,000
Number Employees: 10-19
Square Footage: 7200
Type of Packaging: Consumer, Bulk

5352 **Green Gorilla**
22809 Pacific Coast Hwy
Malibu, CA 90265
323-452-5919
ilovegreengorilla.com
CBD-infused extra virgin olive oil
Founder & CEO: Steven Saxton
Senior VP, Sales: Herb Lewis
COO: Steve De Forest

5353 **Green Grown Products Inc**
13600 Marina Pointe Dr
Suite 315
Marina Del Ray, CA 90292
310-828-1686
Fax: 310-822-6440
Herbs, royal jelly, propolis, bee pollen, chia and sesame seeds, apricot kernels and turbinado sugar
President: Teri Bernardi
CEO: Hal Neiman
Estimated Sales: $2,000,000
Number Employees: 1-4
Square Footage: 16000
Parent Co: Earth Commodities
Type of Packaging: Private Label, Bulk

5354 **Green Mountain Chocolate Inc**
835 W Central St # 1
Franklin, MA 02038-3189
508-520-7160
Fax: 508-520-7161
info@greenmountainchocolate.com
www.greenmountainchocolate.com
Chocolates
Owner: Betty Duncan
b.duncan@greenmountainchocolate.com
Estimated Sales: Less Than $500,000
Number Employees: 1-4
Brands:
Green Mountain Chocolate Truffle

5355 **Green Mountain Cidery**
153 Pond Lane
Middlebury, VT 05753
802-388-0700
Fax: 802-388-0600 www.woodchuck.com
Hard cider
President: Joseph Cerniglia
VP: Dan Rowell
Director Marketing: Alan MacDonald
General Manager: Rob Hyman
Estimated Sales: $2.5-5 Millioin
Number Employees: 20-49
Square Footage: 50
Type of Packaging: Private Label
Brands:
Woodchuck Draft Cider

5356 **Green Mountain Creamery**
PO Box 6212
Brattleboro, VT 05302
802-251-2300
855-996-4946
www.greenmountaincreamery.com

Greek and Icelandic style yogurts
Type of Packaging: Consumer
Brands:
GREEN MOUNTAIN CREAMERY
YOYUMMY

5357 **Green Mountain Gringo**
4045 Indiana Ave
Winston-Salem, NC 27115
Fax: 802-875-3140 888-875-3111
www.greenmountaingringo.com
Salsa
Co-Founder: Christine Hume
Co-Founder: Dave Hume
Parent Co: TW Garner Food Company

5358 **Green Options**
17 Paul Dr
Suite 104
San Rafael, CA 94903-2043
415-526-1450
Fax: 415-526-1453 888-473-3667
Health foods
Manager: Michael Madden
Sales Manager: Jill Koperweis
Estimated Sales: $1-3,000,000
Number Employees: 9
Brands:
Veggie-Deli®
Veggie-Deli Slices®
Veggie-Jerky™
Veggie-Deli®Quick Stick

5359 **Green River Chocolates**
PO Box 421
Hinesburg, VT 05461
802-482-6727
info@adagiochocolates.com
adagiochocolates.com
Maple syrup, chocolates and chocolate products, butter corn syrup, crepes and pancake mixes, ice cream and pepper sauces
Estimated Sales: $1-3 Million
Number Employees: 5-9

5360 **Green Roads CBD**
601 Fairway Dr
Deerfield Beach, FL 33441
833-462-8922
support@greenroadsworld.com
www.greenroadsworld.com
CBD-infused dietary supplements
President: Craig Fabel
Co-Founder: Laura Fuentes

5361 **Green Source Organics**
7290 Kea Lani Dr
Boynton Beach, FL 33437
561-740-8595
blitz@gsoextracts.com
gsoextracts.com
Organic, powdered fruit and vegetable extracts

5362 **Green Spot Packaging**
100 S Cambridge Ave
Claremont, CA 91711-4842
909-625-8771
Fax: 909-621-4634 800-456-3210
info@greenspotusa.com www.lagunaliquid.com
Beverages, flavors and fragrances; aseptic packaging services available
CEO: John Tsu
Finance Executive: Don Koury
Sales Executive: Greg Faust
Chief Operating Officer: Dana Staal
Plant Manager: Roy Cooley
Estimated Sales: $6.5 Million
Number Employees: 20-49
Square Footage: 200000
Type of Packaging: Consumer, Food Service, Private Label, Bulk
Brands:
Action Ade
Apple Delight
Apple Royal
Awesome Orange
Black Cherry Royal
Citrus Royal
Galactic Grape
Good Buddies
Green Spot
Peach Royal
Superstar Strawberry
Tropical Royal

5363 **Green Turtle Bay Vitamin Company**
PO Box 642
Summit, NJ 07902
908-277-2240
Fax: 908-273-9116 800-887-8535
mail@energywave.com www.energywave.com
Processor and exporter of vitamin supplement formulas including herbal antioxidants, oils and herbs
President: Karen Horbatt
CEO: Gloria Mckenna
Quality Control: Monica Harris
Marketing: Michele Murphy
Estimated Sales: $600,000
Number Employees: 5
Brands:
Diabetiks
Maple Melts
Powermate
Powersleep
Powervites
Primrose Oile
Signal 369
Sunnie

5364 **Green Turtle Cannery & Seafood**
PO Box 585
81219 Overseas Hwy
Islamorada, FL 33036
305-664-9595
Fax: 305-664-9564
Specialty seafood products
President: Henry Rosenthal Jr.
Estimated Sales: $1-2,500,000
Number Employees: 20-49
Brands:
Sid and Roxie's

5365 **Green Valley Food Corp**
1501 Market Center Blvd
Dallas, TX 75207-3913
214-939-3900
Fax: 214-939-3999 800-853-8399
www.greenvalleyfood.com
Importer and wholesaler/distributor of cheese, meats, pates, cookies, crackers, breads, jams, jellies, preserves, soups, snack foods, pasta and confections; custom packer of domestic and imported cheeses
Owner: George Chang
Estimated Sales: $2,100,000
Number Employees: 20-49
Square Footage: 120000

5366 **Green Valley Foods**
1105 Front St NE
Salem, OR 97301
844-588-3535
info@welcometogreenvalley.com
welcometogreenvalley.com
Organic beans, rice and vegetables
COO: Peri Nathen

5367 **Green Valley Pecan Company**
1525 W Sahuarita Rd
Sahuarita, AZ 85629-8001
520-791-2880
Fax: 520-629-0119 sales@greenvalleypecan.com
www.greenvalleypecan.com
Pecans, nuts
President/CEO: Richard Walden
Controller: Heather Merchant
Chief Marketing Officer: Bruce Caris
bcaris@greenvalleypecan.com
Estimated Sales: $190 Thousand
Number Employees: 250-499
Parent Co: Farmers Investment Company

5368 **Green-Go Cactus Water**
PO Box 334
Oakville, CA 94562
707-944-2039
cactus@drinkgreen-go.com
drinkgreen-go.com
Cactus water
Founder: Sarita Lopez
Type of Packaging: Consumer
Brands:
GREEN-GO

5369 **Greenberg Cheese Co**
5743 Smithway St
Suite 308
Commerce, CA 90040-1549
323-727-7735
Fax: 323-727-7941 800-301-4507
www.greenbergcheesecompany.com
Cheese, cheese products
President & COO: Mike Greenberg
mike@greenbergcheesecompany.com
Director of Administration: Richard Holly
CFO: Merilyn Greenberg
Estimated Sales: $30 Million
Number Employees: 20-49
Number of Products: 300
Square Footage: 20000
Parent Co: Dairy Commodities Corporation
Type of Packaging: Food Service, Bulk
Other Locations:
Commerce CA

5370 **Greene Brothers Specialty Coffee Roaster**
313 High Street
Hackettstown, NJ 07840-1908
908-979-0022
info@greenesbeans.com
http://www.greenesbeans.com/
Coffee
Co-President: David Greene
Co-Presidemt: Brian Greene
Estimated Sales: $1-3,000,000
Number Employees: 10-19
Square Footage: 1500

5371 **Greenfield Mills**
10505 East 750
North Howe, IN 46746
260-367-2394
www.newrinkelflour.com
Wheat and buckwheat flour; also, pancake mixes, Certified Organic whole wheat and white soft wheat flour
President: Howard Rinkel
Vice President: Joyce Rinkel
Contact: Dave Rinkel
mazdadoc@yahoo.com
Estimated Sales: $300,000-500,000
Number Employees: 1-4
Square Footage: 24000
Type of Packaging: Consumer, Food Service
Brands:
New Rinkel

5372 **Greenfield Noodle & Spec Co**
600 Custer St
Detroit, MI 48202-3128
313-873-2212
Fax: 313-873-0515
Noodles
Owner: Kevin Michaels
VP: Mary Michaels
Estimated Sales: $1.3 Million
Number Employees: 10-19
Square Footage: 26000
Type of Packaging: Consumer, Food Service, Private Label, Bulk
Brands:
Greenfield
Mrs. Asien

5373 **Greenfield Wine Company**
205 Jim Oswalt Way Ste B
Vallejo, CA 94503-9695
707-552-5199
Fax: 707-963-8537
Wines
Owner: Tony Cartlidge
VP/Partner: Robert Babbe
Vice President: Elijah Selby
Marketing Manager: Dan Waggerman
Contact: Robert Babbe
rgbabbe@aol.com
General Manager: Tony Cartlidge
Estimated Sales: $10-24.9,000,000
Number Employees: 48

5374 **Greenhills Irish Bakery**
780 Adams St
Dorchester Ctr, MA 02124-5104
617-825-8187
info@greenhillsbakery.com
www.greenhillsbakery.com
Bakery products

President: Dermot Quinn
Estimated Sales: $10-20,000,000
Number Employees: 10-19

5375 Greenjoy
Okatie, SC 29909
greenjoylife.com
Superfood dressings and salad mixers

5376 Greenwave Foods
Berkeley, CA
510-898-1973
edazen.com
Edamame snacks
Founder: Rachel Greenberger
Brands:
eda-zen(c)
toasta ma-me
cruncha ma-me(c)

5377 Greenwell Farms Inc
81-6581 Mamalahoa Hwy
Kealakekua, HI 96750
808-323-2862
Fax: 808-323-2584 888-592-5662
sales@greenwellfarms.com
www.greenwellfarms.com
Coffee, specialty confectionary
President: Thomas Greenwell
tom@greenwellfarms.com
CEO: Jennifer Greenwell
Estimated Sales: $1-2.5 Million
Number Employees: 100-249
Type of Packaging: Consumer, Food Service, Private Label, Bulk
Brands:
Greenwell Farms

5378 Greenwood Associates
6280 W Howard St
Niles, IL 60714-3433
847-579-5500
Fax: 847-579-5501
info@greenwoodassociates.com
www.greenwoodassociates.com
Fruit concentrates and purees
President: Ron Kaplan
Estimated Sales: $5-10 Million
Number Employees: 20-49
Square Footage: 1000
Type of Packaging: Bulk

5379 Greenwood Ice Cream Co
4829 Peachtree Rd
Atlanta, GA 30341-3113
770-455-6166
Fax: 770-455-4152 800-678-6166
orders@greenwoodicecream.com
www.greenwoodicecream.com
Ice cream, frozen desserts
President: Mitchell Williams
mitchell@greenwoodicecream.com
Director: Robert Street
Director: Tony Yen
Estimated Sales: $4,000,000
Number Employees: 20-49
Brands:
Greenwood

5380 Greenwood Ridge Vineyards
5501 Highway 128
Philo, CA 95466-9477
707-895-2002
Fax: 707-895-2001
everybody@greenwoodridge.com
www.greenwoodridge.com
Wines
Owner: Allan Green
allan@greenwoodridge.com
Estimated Sales: $1-2,500,000
Number Employees: 1-4

5381 Greg's Lobster Company
136 Factory Road
Units 1-3
Harwich Port, MA 02645-1675
508-432-8080
Fax: 508-432-2203
Lobster
President: Leslie Sykes
Estimated Sales: $2.75 Million
Number Employees: 20

5382 Gregory's Foods, Inc.
1301 Trapp Rd
St Paul, MN 55121-1247
651-454-0277
Fax: 651-454-2254 800-231-4734
www.gregorysfoods.com
Frozen baked goods, mixes and bases; bakery ingredients and supplies
President: Greg Helland
cburton@gregorysfoods.com
Quality Control: Tom Hoebbel
Sales/Marketing: Randy Clemons
Estimated Sales: $5.7 Million
Number Employees: 50-99
Square Footage: 44000
Type of Packaging: Food Service, Private Label, Bulk

5383 Gress Enterprises
992 N South Rd
Scranton, PA 18504-1412
570-561-0150
Fax: 570-341-1299 www.gresscold.com
Frozen chicken products
Owner: E Gress
VP/General Manager: Keith Gress
VP Marketing: Glenn Gress
Estimated Sales: $5-10 Million
Number Employees: 10-19
Type of Packaging: Food Service, Bulk

5384 Grey Ghost Bakery
1750 Signal Point Rd.
Suite 2A
Charleston, SC 29412
803-238-1123
www.greyghostbakery.com
Cookies
Founder: Katherine Frankstone

5385 Grey Owl Foods
510 11th St SE
Grand Rapids, MN 55744
218-327-2281
Fax: 218-327-2283 800-527-0172
Rice and rice products
Director Sales/Marketing: Jim McCool
Estimated Sales: $10-20 Million
Number Employees: 10-19
Square Footage: 12000
Parent Co: SIAP Marketing Company
Type of Packaging: Consumer, Food Service, Bulk

5386 Greyston Bakery Inc
21 Park Ave.
Yonkers, NY 10703
914-376-3900
Fax: 914-375-1514 800-289-2253
info@greystonbakery.com www.greyston.org
Baked goods
President/CEO: Mike Brady
Founder: Bernie Glassman
Year Founded: 1982
Estimated Sales: $20-50 Million
Number Employees: 100-249
Type of Packaging: Consumer, Food Service

5387 Griffin's Seafood
24225 Highway 1
Golden Meadow, LA 70357
985-396-2453
Fax: 985-396-2459
Seafood
Owner: Archie Dantin
Estimated Sales: Under $500,000
Number Employees: 1-4

5388 Griffith Foods Inc.
1 Griffith Center
Alsip, IL 60803
708-371-0900
Fax: 708-371-4783 www.griffithfoods.com
Protein, side-dish and snack seasonings; sauces, gravies, and soups mixes; salsa and condiments; and bakery and dough blends.
Chairman: Brian Griffith
CEO: TC Chatterjee
Executive VP/CFO: Matt West
Year Founded: 1919
Estimated Sales: $286.8 Million
Number Employees: 1,000-4,999
Square Footage: 250000
Type of Packaging: Food Service, Private Label, Bulk

5389 Grillo's Pickles
Needham Heights, MA 02494
www.grillospickles.com
Organic pickles
Founder: Travis Grillo
Type of Packaging: Consumer
Brands:
GRILLO'S PICKLES

5390 Grimaud Farms-California Inc
1320 S Aurora St # A
Stockton, CA 95206-1616
209-466-3200
Fax: 209-466-8910 800-466-9955
Duck and guinea fowl
Owner: Howard Chan
howard@grimaudfarms.com
Vice President: Lauren Bartels
Vice President Sales: Jim Galle
Production/Plant Manager: Diego Davalos
Purchasing Agent: Istvan Deli
Estimated Sales: $6.4 Million
Number Employees: 100-249
Square Footage: 168000
Parent Co: Groupe Grimaud
Type of Packaging: Consumer, Food Service, Private Label, Bulk
Brands:
Grimaud Farms
Grimaud Farms Muscovy Ducks
Sonoma Foie-Gras

5391 Grimm's Fine Food
#100-10991 Shellbridge Way
Richmond, BC V6X 3C6
Canada
780-415-4331
Fax: 780-477-5287 866-663-4746
www.grimmsfinefoods.com
Processed meats and sausages
President: Rick Grimm
Plant Manager: George McCorry
Number Employees: 50-99
Parent Co: Fletcher's Fine Foods
Type of Packaging: Consumer, Food Service, Private Label, Bulk
Brands:
Deli Flavor
Fletchers

5392 Grimm's Locker Service
PO Box 4524
Sherwood, OH 43556-0524
419-899-2655
Fax: 419-899-2655
Canned meat and poultry
Owner: Michael Oskey
Estimated Sales: Below $5,000,000
Number Employees: 1-4

5393 (HQ)Grimmway Farms
P.O. Box 81498
Bakersfield, CA 93380
800-301-3101
media@grimmway.com www.grimmway.com
Carrots, potatoes, organic produce and juice
President: Jeff Meger
jmeger@grimmway.com
CFO: Steve Barnes
Vice President: Jeff Huckaby
Quality Assurance: Rory Gonzales
Sales Manager Juice Division: Paul Verderber
Type of Packaging: Consumer, Food Service
Other Locations:
Grimmway Farms
Arvin CA
Cal-Organic Farms
Lamont CA
Brands:
Grimmway

5394 Gringo Jack's
5103 Main St
Manchester Ctr, VT 05255-9772
802-362-0836
Fax: 802-362-0741 www.gringojacks.com
Sauces, salsas and dips, chips and soups
Founder and CEO: Jack Gilbert
gringojack@gmail.com
Co-Founder: Michele Kropp
Number Employees: 20-49

5395 **Grippo Foods**
6750 Colerain Ave
Cincinnati, OH 45239-5542
513-923-1900
Fax: 513-923-3645 800-626-1824
info@grippos.com www.grippos.com
Potato chips, pretzels, dips and other snacks
President: Ralph W. Pagel
VP: Nancy Schreiber
Purchasing: Ralph Pagel
Estimated Sales: $7.2 Million
Number Employees: 10-19
Square Footage: 99000
Type of Packaging: Consumer

5396 **Groeb Farms**
10464 Bryan Hwy
Onsted, MI 49265-0269
517-467-2065
Fax: 517-467-2840 800-530-9969
Honey; UPC labeling, tamper-evident packaging, re-closable cap, easy pour handle and shatterproof containers
President & CEO: Ernest Groeb
VP & CFO: Jack Irvin Jr
VP/COO: Troy Groeb
Director Retail Sales: Jim McCoy
Chief Procurement Officer: Alison Tringale
Type of Packaging: Consumer, Food Service, Private Label, Bulk
Other Locations:
Belleview FL
Miller's American Honey
Colton CA
Brands:
Gourmet Jose
Groeb Farms

5397 **Groff's Meats**
33 N Market St
Elizabethtown, PA 17022-2087
717-367-1246
Fax: 717-367-1952 www.groffsmeats.com
Beef, pork, poultry, deli items and specialty foods
Owner: Nancy Groff
nsgroff@aol.com
VP: Virginia Groff
Estimated Sales: $4 Million
Number Employees: 20-49
Square Footage: 9000
Type of Packaging: Consumer, Food Service, Private Label

5398 **Groovy Candies**
6770 Brookpark Rd
Cleveland, OH 44129
216-472-0206
Fax: 216-274-9200 888-729-1960
www.groovycandies.com
Candy
President: Ed Kitchen
Chairman: Bert Hiddie
Estimated Sales: $5-9.9 Million
Number Employees: 20-49
Number of Brands: 1
Number of Products: 25
Square Footage: 30000
Type of Packaging: Consumer, Private Label, Bulk
Brands:
Gladstone Candies

5399 **Grossingers Home Bakery**
244 W 54th St
New York, NY 10019-5515
212-362-8672
Fax: 212-362-8627 800-479-6996
hrgrsin@aol.com
Ice cream cakes
Owner: Herb Grossinger
Estimated Sales: Less Than $500,000
Number Employees: 5-9
Brands:
Bombe Glaze

5400 **Grote & Weigel Inc**
76 Granby St
Bloomfield, CT 06002-3512
860-242-8528
Fax: 860-242-4162
Processed meats and specialty sausages
Owner: Mike Grenier
customerservice@groteandweigel.com
Vice President: John Shieding
Estimated Sales: $5-10 Million
Number Employees: 20-49
Square Footage: 30000
Brands:
Clearfield
Grote & Weigel
Jersey Boardwalk
Marcello
Meinel
Riley's Beef Sausage
Texan Wiener

5401 **Groth Vineyards & Winery**
750 Oakville Cross Road
Oakville, CA 94562
707-944-0290
Fax: 707-944-8932 info@grothwines.com
www.grothwines.com
Wines
President: Dennis Groth
CFO: Carl Ebbeson
Vice President: Judith Groth
Marketing Director: Suzanne Groth
Finance Manager: Dawn Selanders
Contact: Mike Ferrante
mferrante@grothwines.com
Winemaker: Michael Weis
Estimated Sales: $1,2,000,000
Number Employees: 20
Type of Packaging: Private Label

5402 **Grounds For Thought**
174 S Main St
Bowling Green, OH 43402-2909
419-354-3266
Fax: 419-354-7512 www.groundsforthought.com
Coffee
Owner: Kelly Wicks
kelly@groundsforthought.com
Estimated Sales: Under $500,000
Number Employees: 10-19
Square Footage: 3000
Type of Packaging: Consumer, Food Service, Private Label, Bulk
Brands:
Black Swamp
Bluegrass
Grounds For Thought
John Z'S Big City

5403 **Grounds for Change**
15773 George Ln NE
Suite 204
Poulsbo, WA 98370
Fax: 360-779-0402 800-796-6820
info@groundsforchange.com
www.groundsforchange.com
Fair trade organic coffee beans
President/Co-Founder: Kelsey Marshall
Co-Founder: Stacy Marshall
Year Founded: 2003

5404 **Groundwork Coffee Co.**
5457 Cleon Ave
North Hollywood, CA 91601
818-506-6020
Fax: 818-506-6035 www.groundworkcoffee.com
Organic coffees and teas
Principal: Jeff Chean
Type of Packaging: Consumer
Brands:
GROUNDWORK

5405 **Groupe Paul Masson**
110-50, Rue De La Barre
Longueuil, QC J4K 5G2
Canada
514-878-3050
Fax: 450-651-5453 www.bloomberg.com
Alcoholic beverages
President: Jean Denis Cote
VP Marketing Development: Alain Lecours
Number Employees: 100-249
Type of Packaging: Consumer
Brands:
Aperossimo
Bau Maniere
Castelet
De Lescot
Dubleuet
El Condor
Foret Noire
L'Ombrelle
Nobella
Pica
Robert De Serbie
Valentino

5406 **Grouse Hunt Farm Inc**
458 Fairview St
Tamaqua, PA 18252-4718
570-467-2850
Fax: 570-467-2850 www.woswit.com
Dressings, relishes, mustards, sauces, seasonings, jellies, preserves, butters, fruits, horseradish, etc
Owner: Christopher Thompson
chris@woswit.com
Estimated Sales: Less Than $500,000
Number Employees: 1-4
Number of Brands: 2
Number of Products: 108
Square Footage: 40000
Type of Packaging: Private Label
Brands:
Grouse Hunt Farms
Pennsylvania Dutch Foods
Wos-Wit

5407 **Grow Co**
55 Railroad Ave
Ridgefield, NJ 07657-2109
201-941-8777
Fax: 201-342-9127 info@growco.us
Vitamins, minerals and flavors
Vice President: Massoud Avanaghi
arvanaghi@growco.us
Estimated Sales: $1-2.5 Million
Number Employees: 10-19
Square Footage: 91200
Brands:
Re-Natured

5408 **Grow-Pac**
2220 SW Lafollett Rd
Cornelius, OR 97113
503-357-9691
Fax: 503-357-2155
Frozen blackberries, blueberries, strawberries, marion berries
President: Lloyd Duyck
Co-owner: Geraldine Duyck
Contact: Nick Duyck
nickduyck@valleybluefarms.com
Estimated Sales: Under $500,000
Number Employees: 5
Brands:
Grow-Pac

5409 **Grower Shipper Potato Company**
One Fourth Mile Hwy 285
Monte Vista, CO 81144
719-852-3569
Fax: 719-852-5917
Potatoes
Manager: Mark Lounsbury
Vice President: Ron Heersink
Manager: Ken Shepherd
Estimated Sales: $10-20 Million
Number Employees: 20-49
Square Footage: 120000
Type of Packaging: Consumer, Food Service, Bulk
Brands:
Big Ram
Colorado Gold
Diamond
Jackpot

5410 **Growers Cooperative Juice Co**
112 N Portage St
Westfield, NY 14787-1054
716-326-3161
Fax: 716-326-6566 www.concordgrapejuice.com
Grape juice and juice concentrate
President: Steve Baran
dmom@concordgrapejuice.com
Quality Assurance Manager: Jim Gillespie
Sales Exec: Dave Momberger
General Manager: David Momberger
Plant Manager: Todd Donato
Estimated Sales: $5-10 Million
Number Employees: 20-49
Type of Packaging: Bulk

5411 **Growing Roots Foods**
700 Sylvan Ave
Englewood Cliffs, NJ 07632
www.growingrootsfoods.com
Organic corn, coconut and seed bites and clusters

Parent Co: Unilever US
Type of Packaging: Consumer
Brands:
GROWING ROOTS

5412 Grown-up Soda
424 E 57th St
Suite 3C
New York, NY 10022
212-355-7454
Fax: 212-208-4444 info@drinkgus.com
www.drinkgus.com
Sodas
Founder: Steve Hersh
Founder: Jeannette Luoh
Contact: Samantha Garchik
samantha@drinkgus.com
Parent Co: Utmost Brands

5413 Gruet Winery
8400 Pan American Fwy NE
Albuquerque, NM 87113-1832
505-821-0055
Fax: 505-857-0066 888-857-9463
info@gruetwinery.com www.gruetwinery.com
Wines
President/Winemaker: Laurent Gruet
laurent@gruetwinery.com
Vice President: Farid Himeur
Estimated Sales: $1-2,500,000
Number Employees: 20-49
Type of Packaging: Private Label
Brands:
Domaine St. Vincent
Gruet Winery

5414 Grumpe's Specialties
140 Market St
Baird, TX 79504-6406
325-854-1106
Fax: 325-854-1107 866-854-1106
artwork@grumpes.com www.grumpes.com
Personalized lollipops
President: Warren Harkins
Number Employees: 10-19

5415 Guapo Spices Company
6200 E Slauson Avenue
Los Angeles, CA 90040-3012
213-322-8900
Fax: 213-627-0601
Seasonings, spices

Estimated Sales: $2.5-5,000,000
Number Employees: 20-49
Type of Packaging: Private Label

5416 Guayaki
6782 Sebastopol Ave # 100
Sebastopol, CA 95472-3880
707-824-6644
Fax: 707-824-6644 888-482-9254
info@guayaki.com www.guayaki.com
Organic rainforest herbs
Co-Founder: Alex Pryer
Chief Executive Officer: Chris Mann
info@guayaki.com
Co-Founder: David Karr
VP of Sales: Luke Gernandt
Sales Coordinator: Saskia Baur
Customer Care: Scott Turner
Vice President Operations: Richard Bruehl
Productions: Lucia Diaz
Estimated Sales: $3 Million
Number Employees: 20-49
Number of Brands: 1
Number of Products: 13
Square Footage: 15000
Type of Packaging: Consumer, Food Service, Bulk
Brands:
Organic Guayaki Yerba Mate

5417 Guenoc & Langtry Estate
21000 Butts Canyon Rd
Middletown, CA 95461-9606
707-995-7501
Fax: 707-987-9351 info@langtryestate.com
www.langtryestate.com
Wines
Owner: Bill Foley
President: Tim Matz
Winemaker: Walter Jorge
Director Marketing: Karen Melander-Magoon
National Sales Manager: Greg Brolin
Media Inquiries: Sarah Johnduff
Year Founded: 1888
Estimated Sales: $20-50 Million
Number Employees: 1
Square Footage: 72000
Brands:
Domaine Breton
Guenoc
Langtry

5418 Guerra Nut Shelling Co Inc
190 Hillcrest Rd
Hollister, CA 95023-4944
831-637-4471
Fax: 831-637-1358 walnut@guerranut.com
www.guerranut.com
Walnuts
President: Frank V Guerra
frank@guerranut.com
CEO: Jeff Guerra
Estimated Sales: $5-10 Million
Number Employees: 50-99
Square Footage: 150000
Type of Packaging: Bulk
Brands:
Cal Best
Hillcrest

5419 Guers Dairy
1268 Tumbling Run Rd
Tamaqua, PA 18252-3400
570-277-6611
Fax: 570-277-0135 www.guersdairy.com
Milk and milk products
President: Danelle Yaag
dyaag@yahoo.com
Treasurer: William Yaag
VP: Edward Guers
Purchasing Manager: Dwight Manbeck
Estimated Sales: $10-20,000,000
Number Employees: 50-99

5420 Guggisberg Cheese
5060 State Route 557
Millersburg, OH 44654-9266
330-893-2500
Fax: 330-893-3240 800-262-2505
info@babyswiss.com www.babyswiss.com
Cheese
President: Richard Guggisberg
Year Founded: 1950
Estimated Sales: G
Number Employees: 100-249
Square Footage: 10000
Type of Packaging: Consumer, Food Service, Bulk
Brands:
Amish Farm
Guggisberg
Original Baby

5421 Guglielmo Winery
1480 E Main Ave
Morgan Hill, CA 95037-3299
408-779-2145
Fax: 408-779-3166 info@guglielmowinery.com
Wines
Winemaker/ President: George E. Guglielmo
george@guglielmowinery.com
CFO: Julie Bradford
Director of Sales: Gene Guglielmo
Dir. Of Retail Operations: Cindy Adams
Estimated Sales: $10-20 Million
Number Employees: 20-49
Type of Packaging: Consumer, Private Label, Bulk
Brands:
Emile's
Guflielmo Reserve
Guglielmo
Guglielmo Vineyard Selection

5422 Guida's Dairy
433 Park St.
New Britain, CT 06051
800-832-8929
www.supercow.com
Dairy products.
President: Michael Young
Estimated Sales: $149 Million
Number Employees: 250-499
Square Footage: 75000
Type of Packaging: Consumer, Food Service, Private Label
Brands:
Guida's

5423 Guido's International Foods
1669 La Cresta Dr
Pasadena, CA 91103-1260
626-296-1427
Fax: 626-296-0306 877-994-8436
Seasonings and sauces
President: Guido Meindl
Estimated Sales: $20,000
Number Employees: 2
Number of Brands: 7
Type of Packaging: Consumer, Food Service, Private Label, Bulk
Brands:
Guido's Serious

5424 Guidry's Catfish Inc
1093 Henderson Hwy
Breaux Bridge, LA 70517-7728
337-228-7546
Fax: 337-228-7544
www.catfishmarketingassociation.com
Fresh catfish
Owner: Bobby Jules
CAO: Sandra Robertson
sandra@guidryscatfish.com
Operations: Sandra Guidry-Robertson
Administrative Executive: Sandra Robertson
Estimated Sales: $10-20 Million
Number Employees: 100-249

5425 Guilliams Winery
3851 Spring Mountain Rd
St Helena, CA 94574
707-963-9059
Fax: 707-963-9059
Wines
President: John Guilliams
Estimated Sales: Less than $500,000
Number Employees: 1-4

5426 Guiltless Gourmet
80 Avenue K
Newark, NJ 7105
201-553-1100
deborah.ross@manischewitz.com
www.guiltlessgourmet.com
Natural, low-fat baked snacks, dips and salsas
President: Michael Shaw
VP Finance: Bart Glaser
VP Sales/Marketing: Robert Greenberg
Number Employees: 20-49
Parent Co: The Manischewitz Company
Type of Packaging: Consumer, Food Service, Private Label, Bulk
Brands:
Guiltless Gourmet

5427 Guinness Import Co
6 Landmark Sq
Stamford, CT 06901-2704
203-323-3311
Fax: 203-359-7209 800-521-1591
guinness@consumer-care.net www.guiness.com
Beers, stout
President: Tim Kelly
Chief Information Officer: Lynda Gutman
Contact: Charles Ireland
guinness-storehouse@guinness.com
Vice President Operations: Colin Funnell
Number Employees: 5-9
Parent Co: Guiness PLC
Type of Packaging: Consumer
Brands:
Asahi
Bass Ale
Furstenberg
Guinness Stout
Harp Lager
Kaliber
Guinness®

5428 **Guittard Chocolate Co**
10 Guittard Rd
PO Box 4308
Burlingame, CA 94010-2203
650-697-4427
Fax: 650-692-2761 800-468-2462
sales@guittard.com www.guittard.com
Chocolate and chocolate products
President & CEO: Gary Guittard
gary@guittard.com
Director Sales/Marketing: Mark Spini
Estimated Sales: $20-50 Million
Number Employees: 100-249
Brands:
Chocolate Products
Dick Servaes
Melt-N-Mold
Smooth-N-Melty

5429 **Gulf Atlantic Freezers**
PO Box 2493
Gretna, LA 70054-2493
504-392-3590
Fax: 504-392-3443
Frozen seafood
Contact: Al Smith
gafltd@msn.com

5430 **Gulf Central Seafood**
PO Box 373
Biloxi, MS 39533-0373
228-436-6346
Fax: 228-374-1207
Seafood, fresh, live and frozen
President: Rock Sekul
Estimated Sales: $2.5-5,000,000
Number Employees: 20-49
Brands:
Gulf Central
Gulf Star
Treasure Bay

5431 **Gulf City Marine Supply**
14650 Shell Belt
Bayou La Batre, AL 36509
251-824-2516
Fax: 251-824-7980
Seafood
President: Charles Graham
Estimated Sales: $500,000-$1 Million
Number Employees: 5-9
Parent Co: Gulf City Seafood

5432 **Gulf Crown Seafood Co**
306 Jon Floyd Rd
Delcambre, LA 70528-4522
337-685-4722
Fax: 337-685-4241 gulfcrown@gulfcrown.us
www.gulfcrown.us
Shrimp
President: John Floyd
Manager: Bonnie Richard
Sales: Crystal Marcaux
Manager: Stephen Greene
gulfcrown@gulfcrown.us
Estimated Sales: $7 Million
Number Employees: 5-9
Brands:
Gulf Crown

5433 **(HQ)Gulf Food Products Co Inc**
509 Commerce Pt
New Orleans, LA 70123-3203
504-733-1516
Fax: 504-733-1517 roberthoy@worldnet.att.net
Seafood
Owner: Albert Lin
gulffoodproducts@aol.com
Estimated Sales: Less than $500,000
Number Employees: 1-4
Square Footage: 16000

5434 **Gulf Marine**
501 Louisiana St
Westwego, LA 70094-4141
504-436-2682
Fax: 504-436-1585 sales@gulfmarineproducts.com
www.lapack.com
Shrimp, crawfish and other seafood
President: David Lai
Number Employees: 20-49

5435 **Gulf Marine & Industrial Supplies Inc**
5801 Armour Dr.
Houston, TX 77020
713-514-8010
Fax: 504-525-4761 800-886-6252
service@gulfmarine.net www.gulfmarine.net
Seafood, pork, beef, poultry, canned and frozen foods, fresh vegetables, beer, wine and other general merchandise
President: John Cotsoradis
General Manager: Dimitris Karmoukos
Estimated Sales: $30-50 Million
Number Employees: 50-99
Square Footage: 250000
Type of Packaging: Food Service
Other Locations:
Houston TX
New Orleans LA
Tampa FL
Long Beach CA

5436 **Gulf Packing Company**
618 Commerce St
San Benito, TX 78586-4216
956-399-2631
Fax: 956-399-2675
Meat, including heifer calf and packaged meats
CEO: Charlie Booth
VP: Carlos Salinas
Quality Control Manager: Fred Frausto
Manager: Ace Delacerta
Mngr: Frank Esquivel
Estimated Sales: $10-20 Million
Number Employees: 50 to 99
Type of Packaging: Consumer
Brands:
Quality Minded

5437 **Gulf Pecan Company**
5456 Highway 90 W
Mobile, AL 36619-4212
251-661-2931
ulfpecanco@yahoo.com
Farm products and raw materials; dried fruits and vegetables
Owner & President: Danny Fritz
Estimated Sales: $5-9.9,000,000
Number Employees: 3

5438 **Gulf Pride Enterprises**
391 Bayview Ave
Biloxi, MS 39530-2502
228-432-2488
Fax: 228-374-7411 888-689-0560
www.gulfprideenterprises.com
Shrimp
President: Kathy Cruthirds
kathy@gulfprideshrimp.com
Vice President: Wally Gollott
Estimated Sales: $10 Million-$50 Million
Number Employees: 50-99
Type of Packaging: Consumer, Private Label
Brands:
Captain Pierre
Gulf Pride
Magnolia Bay

5439 **Gulf Shrimp, Inc.**
100 Shrimp Boat Lane
Fort Myers Beach, FL 33931-2925
239-463-8788
Fax: 239-463-3550
Shrimp
Owner: Dennis Henderson
Manager: Dan Schribner
Estimated Sales: $2.5-5,000,000
Number Employees: 20-49

5440 **Gulf States Canners Inc**
1006 Industrial Park Dr
Clinton, MS 39056
601-924-0511
Canned soft drinks
President & CIO: Albert Clark
Estimated Sales: $75-99 Million
Number Employees: 50-99
Square Footage: 300000
Type of Packaging: Consumer, Food Service

5441 **Gulf Stream Crab Company**
13871 Shell Belt Rd
Bayou La Batre, AL 36509
251-824-4717
Fax: 251-824-7416
Crabs
President: Bryan Cumbie
Estimated Sales: $.5-1 million
Number Employees: 1-4

5442 **Gum Technology Corporation**
10860 North Mavinee Drive
Tucson, AZ 85737
520-888-5500
Fax: 520-888-5585 800-369-4867
info@gumtech.com www.gumtech.com
Food gums, hydrocolloids and stabilizing systems
President/CEO: Allen Freed
R&D/Laboratory Director: Aida Prenzno
Marketing Director: Janelle Litel
VP/Sales: Joshua Brooks
Contact: Beth Woodley
beth@milehighingredients.com
Estimated Sales: $5-10 Million
Number Employees: 5-9
Square Footage: 12000
Type of Packaging: Bulk
Brands:
Coyote
Coyote Star

5443 **Gumix International Inc**
2160 N Central Rd # 202
Fort Lee, NJ 07024-7547
201-947-6300
Fax: 201-947-9265 800-248-6492
info@gumix.com
Foods gums
President: Sean Katir
info@gumix.com
Estimated Sales: D
Number Employees: 5-9

5444 **Gumpert's Canada**
2500 Tedlo Street
Mississauga, ON L5A 4A9
Canada
905-279-2600
Fax: 905-279-2797 800-387-9324
info@gumpert.com www.gumpert.com
Toppings, puddings, flavors & extracts, glazes, icings, cake bases, powder fillings, creme pie fillings, fruit pie fillings, and bavarians
President: George Johnson
R&D/QA Manager: Erica Tulloch
Estimated Sales: $5 Million
Number Employees: 40
Number of Products: 200
Square Footage: 106000
Type of Packaging: Bulk
Brands:
Gumpert's

5445 **Gundlach-Bundschu Winery**
2000 Denmark St
Sonoma, CA 95476-9615
707-939-3015
Fax: 707-938-9460 www.gunbun.com
Wines
Owner: Jim Bundschu
jimb@gunbun.com
Winemaker: Keith Emerson
Director of Viticulture: Jim Bundschu
Estimated Sales: $1-2,500,000
Number Employees: 50-99
Number of Brands: 3

5446 **Gunnoe Farms Sausage & Salad**
2115 Oakridge Dr
Charleston, WV 25311-1499
304-343-7686
Fax: 304-343-4748 gunnoefarm@aol.com
Meat including sausage
President: Nancy Gunnoe
gunnoefarm@aol.com
Vice President: Joy Gunnoe
Sales Executive: Joy Gunnoe
Estimated Sales: $15 Million
Number Employees: 20-49
Type of Packaging: Consumer

5447 **Gunther's Gourmet**
PO Box 18215
Richmond, VA 23226
804-240-1796
Fax: 540-982-2015
chefmike@gunthersgourmet.com
www.gunthersgourmet.com
Salad dressing, salsa/dips, grilling sauces, marinades.
Marketing: Mike Lampros

5448 **Gurley's Foods**
1118 Highway 12 E
Willmar, MN 56201-3741
320-235-0600
Fax: 320-235-0659 800-426-7845
www.gurleysfoods.com
Nuts, nut mixes, chocolate covered nuts, nut bark
President & General Manager: Tom Taunton
Year Founded: 1979
Estimated Sales: $20-50 Million
Number Employees: 50-99
Brands:
Gurley's Candy
Gurley's Golden Recipe Nuts
Gurley's Natures Harvest
Rocky Mountain

5449 **GuruNanda**
6645 Caballero Blvd
Buena Park, CA 90620
866-421-0309
www.gurunanda.com
Essential oils
CFO: David Richards
SVP, Sales & Marketing: Whitney Messens
Type of Packaging: Consumer
Brands:
GURUNANDA

5450 **Gus' Pretzel Shop**
1820 Arsenal St # 5
St Louis, MO 63118-2529
314-664-4010
Fax: 314-664-0000 guspretzels.com
Pretzels
Owner: August J Koebbe Jr
Number Employees: 10-19

5451 **Gust John Foods & Products**
1350 Paramount Pkwy
Batavia, IL 60510-1461
630-879-8700
Fax: 630-879-8708 800-756-5886
www.northern-pines.com
Pancake, waffle and muffin mixes; also, pancake and sugar-free syrups
Owner: Gust Koutselas
gustjohnfoods@aol.com
Estimated Sales: $1 Million
Number Employees: 5-9
Type of Packaging: Consumer, Food Service, Private Label, Bulk
Brands:
Northern Pines Gourmet

5452 **Gustus Vitae Condiments LLC**
3016 E Colorado Blvd
Unit 70819
Pasadena, CA 91117
424-229-2367
www.gustusvitae.com
Condiments
Marketing Director: James Evans
Operations Manager: Francis Scanlon

5453 **Gutheinz Meats Inc**
520 Cedar Ave
Scranton, PA 18505-1191
570-344-1191
Fax: 570-344-1193 www.gutheinz.com
Meat products
President: Allen Leach
Estimated Sales: $2.5-5 Million
Number Employees: 5-9
Type of Packaging: Consumer

5454 **Gutsii**
12655 W Jefferson Blvd
Level 4
Los Angeles, CA 90066
team@gutsii.com
gutsii.com
Prebiotic chocolate bars
Founder: Janine Zappini
Marketing: Tamara Loehr

5455 **Guttenplan's Frozen Dough**
100 Highway 36
Middletown, NJ 07748
Fax: 732-495-2415 888-422-4357
info@guttenplan.com www.guttenplan.com
Frozen rolls, bread, dough and bagels, sweet goods
Owner/President: Jack Guttenplan
Estimated Sales: $10-25 000,000
Number Employees: 50-99
Number of Products: 7
Square Footage: 70000
Type of Packaging: Private Label

5456 **Guy's Food**
7223 West 95th Street
Suite 230
Overland Park, KS 66212
913-871-3616
Fax: 913-383-8436 800-821-2405
Snacks
President: Ron Hirasawa
CEO: John Morris
CFO: Thomas Price
VP of Sales: Reid Bennett
Operations Manager: Thomas Anderson
Plant Manager: George Flughum
Number Employees: 500-999
Type of Packaging: Private Label
Brands:
Guy's

5457 **Guylian USA Inc.**
560 Sylvan Ave
Englewood Cliffs, NJ 07632
201-871-4144
guylian.com
Chocolates and confections
President: Michael Cobb
Director of Sales & Marketing: Nicholas Goh
Year Founded: 1994
Estimated Sales: $1 Million
Number Employees: 1-10
Type of Packaging: Private Label

5458 **Gwinn's Foods**
6190 Bermuda Dr
St Louis, MO 63135-3264
314-521-8792
Fax: 314-521-8792
Beef, beef products, hot tamales
Owner: Joseph Frisella
Estimated Sales: $1-2,500,000
Number Employees: 5-9

5459 **H & B Packing Co**
702 Forrest St
Waco, TX 76704-2730
254-752-2506
Fax: 254-752-1451 www.handrfoods.com
Sausages
President: Jake K Bauer
Vice President: David Bauer
Sales Executive: Rick Bauer
IT Executive: Johnny Arispe
jad_jad_007@yahoo.com
Estimated Sales: $20-50 Million
Number Employees: 100-249

5460 **H & H Products Co**
6600 Magnolia Homes Rd
Orlando, FL 32810-4285
407-299-5410
Fax: 407-298-6966 800-678-8448
info@hartleysbrand.com
www.hhproductscompany.com
Juices, drink bases, liquid teas and syrups
Owner: Morris Hartley
mhartley@hartleysbrand.com
Founder: Len Hartley
Secretary: Betty Hartly
QC Manager: Joy Corbin
Regional Sales Manager: Emily Cooper
Regional Sales Manager: David Lynch
mhartley@hartleysbrand.com
Production Manager: Derrick Abner
Plant Manager: Jason Browning
Purchasing Manager: Mike Bowes
Estimated Sales: $6 Million
Number Employees: 20-49
Square Footage: 120000
Type of Packaging: Food Service, Private Label
Brands:
Bloody Mary Juice Burst
Citrus Punch Sugar-Free
Flavor Burst Liquid Citrus Tea
Flavor Burst Liquid Sweet Tea
Flavor Burst Liquid Unsweet Tea
Flavorburst
Hartley's
Juiceburst
Lemon/Lime Thristaway
Neutral Slush
Orange Thirstaway

5461 **H & W Foods**
2029 Lauwiliwili St
Kapolei, HI 96707-1836
808-682-8300
Fax: 808-841-8687 www.hwfoodservice.com
Refrigerated, frozen and dry meat products
Owner/CEO: Bill Loose
Chief Financial Officer: Jeff Sakamoto
IT Manager: Shelle Andrade
Estimated Sales: $5-10 Million
Number Employees: 5-9
Square Footage: 90000

5462 **H B Taylor Co**
4830 S Christiana Ave
Chicago, IL 60632-3092
773-254-4805
Fax: 773-254-4563 www.hbtaylor.com
Flavors, colors and food essentials.
President: Leon Juskaitis
Owner/Human Resources Executive: Saul Juskaitis
sjuskaitis@hbtaylor.com
Research & Development Director: Joy Souders
Quality Control Manager: Larry King
Operations Manager: Edward Juskaitis
Purchasing Manager: Mary Power
Estimated Sales: $3 Million
Number Employees: 10-19
Square Footage: 50000
Type of Packaging: Private Label, Bulk
Brands:
Cocoa Replacers
Dark Roast
Golden Roast
Hyskor
Lipo Butter
Liquimul Black
Mahogany Black
Sesa-Krunch
Sesame Seed

5463 **H Cantin**
1910 Av Du Sanctuaire
Beauport, QC G1E 3L2
Canada
418-663-3523
Fax: 418-663-0717 800-463-5268
cantinh@microtec.ca
Jams, pie fillings, pudding mixes, maple syrup, soup bases, bakery products and candies; importer of frozen fruit; exporter of marshmallow cones and caramels
President/General Manager: Leonce Tremblay
Number Employees: 50-99
Square Footage: 60000
Parent Co: Bon Bons Associates
Type of Packaging: Consumer, Food Service, Private Label, Bulk

5464 **H Coturri & Sons Winery**
6725 Enterprise Rd
Glen Ellen, CA 95442
707-525-9126
Fax: 707-542-8039 866-268-8774
Wines
Manager: Tony Coturri
Marketing Director: Harry Coturo
Operations Manager: Tony Coturri
Estimated Sales: $500,000-$1,000,000
Number Employees: 1-4

5465 **H Fox & Co Inc**
416 Thatford Ave
Brooklyn, NY 11212-5895
718-385-4600
Fax: 718-345-4283
Chocolate and fruit flavored syrups, dessert toppings and juice mixes

President: David Fox
dfox@foxsyrups.com
Executive VP: Kelly Fox
IT: David Frankum
Estimated Sales: $10-20 Million
Number Employees: 20-49
Square Footage: 36000
Type of Packaging: Food Service
Brands:
Fox
Fox's U-Bet
No-Cal

5466 **H Nagel & Son Co**
2428 Central Pkwy
Cincinnati, OH 45214-1804
513-665-4550
Fax: 513-665-4570 www.brightonmills.com
Flour and flour based mixes
President: Edward Nagel
Estimated Sales: $20-50 Million
Number Employees: 20-49
Number of Brands: 1
Type of Packaging: Food Service, Private Label, Bulk
Brands:
Brighton Mills

5467 **H R Nicholson Co**
6320 Oakleaf Ave
Baltimore, MD 21215-2213
410-580-0975
Fax: 410-764-9125 800-638-3514
Fruit juices and tea concentrates
President: H Robert Nicholson
Secretary/Treasurer: Su Shaffer
VP Sales/Marketing: Bob Homewood
Number Employees: 20-49
Square Footage: 114000
Type of Packaging: Consumer, Food Service
Brands:
Bombay Gold 100
Nicholson's Bestea
Nicholson's Bottlers
Nicholson's Chok-Nick

5468 **H&A Health Products, Inc**
3-180 Brodie Drive
Richmond Hill, ON L4B 3K8
Canada
514-979-3589
Fax: 514-694-4543 sales@hacanada.com
www.hacanada.com
Flavor enhancers, preservatives, sweeteners, food gums/hydrocolloids, shrink bags and casings.

5469 **H&H Fisheries Limited**
PO Box 172
Eastern Passage, NS B3G 1M5
Canada
902-465-6330
Fax: 902-465-2572 866-773-4400
Fresh and frozen seafood
Contact: Regionald Hartlen
Estimated Sales: $13.8,000,000
Number Employees: 30
Type of Packaging: Consumer, Food Service, Private Label, Bulk

5470 **H&K Packers Company**
420 Turenne Street
Winnipeg, NB R2J 3W8
Canada
204-233-2354
Fax: 204-235-1258
Pork and beef
President: Albert Kelly
Production: Jake Penner
Plant Manager: Andy Van Patter
Number Employees: 20-49
Square Footage: 20000
Type of Packaging: Bulk
Brands:
H&K Packers
Kings Choice

5471 **H&S Bakery**
620 South Bond Street
Baltimore, MD 21231
410-276-7254
Fax: 410-522-5200 800-959-7655
ematta@hsbakery.com www.hsbakery.com
Bakery products
President: Bill Paterakis
Director of Sales: Charlie Alves
Plant Manager: Matthew Kimmel
Number Employees: 2000+
Square Footage: 336000
Other Locations:
Community Market
Baltimore MD
Crispy Bagel Company
Baltimore MD
Baltimore Distribution Center
Baltimore MD
Annapolis Junction Dist. Center
Annapolis Junction MD
Corporate Office
Baltimore MD
Automatic Rolls of Baltimore, Inc.
Baltimore MD
Automatic Rolls of North Carolina
Clayton NC
Automatic Rolls of New England
Dayville CT
Automatic Rolls of New Jersey
Edison NJ
Bake Rite Rolls, Inc.
Bensalem PA
Mid Atlantic Baking Company
Baltimore MD
Schmidt Baking Company
Baltimore MD

5472 **H&S Edible Products Corporation**
119 Fulton Lane
Mount Vernon, NY 10550-4697
914-664-4041
Fax: 914-664-8304 800-253-3364
Dry bread crumbs, nuts
President: Mari Rowan
Vice President: Peter Rowan
Estimated Sales: $2,000,000
Number Employees: 20-49
Number of Products: 1
Square Footage: 13000
Type of Packaging: Food Service, Private Label, Bulk
Brands:
H&S Bread Crumbs

5473 **H-E-B Grocery Co. LP**
PO Box 839999
San Antonio, TX 78283-3999
210-938-8357
800-432-3113
www.heb.com
Processes milk and bread products.
President: Craig Boyan
Chairman/CEO: Charles Butt
butt.charles@heb.com
COO: Martin Otto
Year Founded: 1905
Estimated Sales: $21 Billion
Number Employees: 100,000
Type of Packaging: Consumer
Other Locations:
Westgate Manufacturing Facility
Austin TX
Central Market Manufacturing
San Antonio TX
Dairy Manufacturing Facility
Plano TX
Brands:
H-E-B
H-E-Buddy
H-E-B Select Ingredients
H-E-B Organics
H-E-B Kitchen & Table
Central Market
Hill Country Products
Cocinaware
ChefStyle
Sear 'n Smoke
GTC
Mia's Mirror

5474 **H. Interdonati**
PO Box 262
Cold Spring Harbour, NY 11724
631-367-6611
Fax: 631-367-6626 800-367-6617
flavorplus@aol.com www.hinterdonati.com
Ingredients and additives
President: Robert Interdonati
Sales Manager: Andrew Interdonati
andrewinterdonati@hinterdonati.com
Estimated Sales: $3 Million
Number Employees: 3
Square Footage: 2000
Brands:
Alnose

5475 **H. Reisman Corporation**
377 Crane Street
Orange, NJ 7051
973-882-1670
Fax: 973-882-0323
Vitamins and herbal extracts
Owner/President: Frank Molinaro
Estimated Sales: $5-10 Million
Number Employees: 20-49
Square Footage: 300000
Parent Co: LycoRed Company
Type of Packaging: Bulk
Brands:
Bionova
Floraglow
Lycomato
Phyto Foods

5476 **H.B. Dawe**
PO Box 100
Cupids, NL A0A 2B0
Canada
709-528-4347
Fax: 709-528-3463
Groundfish and shellfish
General Manager: Philip Hillyard
Number Employees: 100-249
Type of Packaging: Consumer, Food Service, Private Label, Bulk

5477 **H.B. Trading**
10 Taft Road
Totowa, NJ 07512-1006
973-812-1022
Fax: 973-812-2191 nico@nideco.com
Cookies and candies
Brands:
Brent & Sam's
Cape Cod Cranberry C
Cow-Town and Rancher's

5478 **H.Gass Seafood**
38945 Jacqueline Street
Hollywood, MD 20636
301-373-6882
Fax: 301-884-8350
Fresh oysters and crabs
Owner: James Payne
Number Employees: 10-19
Square Footage: 2000

5479 **H.K. Canning**
130 N Garden St
P.O. BOX 729
Ventura, CA 93002-0729
805-652-1392
www.whereorg.com
Canned and dry beans, soup and mushrooms
President: Henry Knaust
CFO: Richard Hanson
Vice-President: Carol Knaust
Estimated Sales: $4 Million
Number Employees: 66
Type of Packaging: Consumer, Food Service, Private Label, Bulk
Brands:
Freshman
Henry's Kettle
Knaust Beans
Meridian Foods
Norteno
Sea Valley
Seaside

5480 **H2rOse, LLC**
Los Angeles, CA 90046
info@drinkh2rose.com
www.drinkh2rose.com
Rose water beverage
Co-Founder & President: Kia Illulian
Type of Packaging: Consumer
Brands:
H2rOse

5481 **H3O**
PO Box 482
Beckley, WV 25802-0482
304-256-0436
Fax: 304-256-0520 888-436-9287
Bottled water
President: Jamison Humphrey

Estimated Sales: Under $500,000
Number Employees: 1-4
Brands:
H3o

5482 **HC Brill Company**
1912 Montreal Rd
Tucker, GA 30084
770-938-3823
Fax: 770-939-2934 800-241-8526
www.hcbrill.com
Ingredients and mixes
President: Cefo Grteor
CEO: Bret Weaver
Estimated Sales: $5-10 000,000
Number Employees: 50-99
Brands:
Brill's

5483 **HFI Foods**
17515 Northeast 6th Court
Redmond, WA 98074
425-883-1320
Fax: 425-861-8341
Surimi products; frozen entrees, mousse desserts and pasta salads
President: Byron Kuroishi
CFO: Yoshinari Kuroishi
Vice President: Christina Gaimaytan
Quality Control: Jenel Lee
Marketing Director: Gwen McLellan
Sales Director: Nori Ishiwari
Public Relations: Cindy Fuller-Stephens
Production Manager: Kazue Yamada
Plant Manager: Kazuo Yamada
Purchasing Manager: Cindy Fuller-Stephens
Estimated Sales: $12 Million
Number Employees: 50-99
Square Footage: 80000
Type of Packaging: Consumer
Brands:
Fitness First
Kibun
King Core
King Cove
Seastix

5484 **HH Dobbins Inc**
99 West Ave
Lyndonville, NY 14098-9744
585-765-2271
Fax: 585-765-9710 877-362-2467
bbaker@wnyapples.com
www.unitedapplesales.com
Produce, including apples, cabbage, pears and prunes
President: Howard Dobbins
hdobbins@wnyapples.com
Estimated Sales: $3-5 Million
Number Employees: 20-49
Parent Co: United Apple Sales Inc.
Type of Packaging: Consumer, Food Service, Bulk
Brands:
Old Dobbin

5485 **HMC Farms**
13138 S Bethel Ave
Kingsburg, CA 93631-9216
559-897-1025
Fax: 559-897-1610 hmcinfo@hmcmarketing.com
www.hmcfarms.com
Table grapes, peaches, plums, nectarines, and other stone fruit
Owner: Harold McClarty
President: Jon McClarty
CFO: Sarah McClarty
Contact: Joel Booth
joelb@hmcfarms.com
Estimated Sales: $20-50 Million
Number Employees: 20-49

5486 **HP Hood LLC**
6 Kimball Ln.
Lynnfield, MA 01940
617-887-3000
800-343-6592
www.hood.com
Dairy products.
Chairman/CEO: John Kaneb
john.kaneb@hphood.com
President: Gary Kaneb
COO: Jeffrey Kaneb
Senior VP, Milk Procurement: Mike Suever
VP, QS & Regulatory Affairs: Jonathan Fischer
VP, Marketing: Christopher Ross
Executive VP, Sales: James Walsh
Senior VP, Operations: H. Scott Blake
Year Founded: 1846
Estimated Sales: $2 Billion
Number Employees: 3,000
Number of Brands: 4
Type of Packaging: Consumer, Food Service, Private Label, Bulk
Brands:
Hood®
Lactaid®
Hoodsies®
Simple Smart®

5487 **HP Schmid**
231 Sansome St
Suite 300
San Francisco, CA 94104-2322
415-765-5925
Fax: 415-765-5922
Edible seeds; dry peas, beans and lentils; dried fruits, nuts and organic products; dehydrated garlic and onions
President/International Sales: Hans Schmid
hans@hpschmid.com
Sales/Service/Quality Assurance: Brian Kim
Sales/Marketing Manager: Margot Tripier
Materials Manager: Uwe Parl
Year Founded: 1978
Estimated Sales: $20-50 Million
Number Employees: 5-9

5488 **HSR Associates Inc**
18829 Paseo Nuevo Dr
Tarzana, CA 91356-5136
818-757-7152
Fax: 818-757-7141
Salad dressings; frozen baked goods, desserts, hors d'oeuvres/appetizers; ready made meals; jams and preserves
President: Steve Goodman
steve@hsrassociates.net
Number Employees: 5-9

5489 **HV Food Products Co**
1221 Broadway
Oakland, CA 94612
877-853-7262
www.hiddenvalley.com
Salad dressings, dressing mixes, dips, and salad toppings
Chairman & CEO: Benno Dorer
VP & Chief Marketing Officer: Eric Reynolds
Year Founded: 1954
Estimated Sales: $100-500 Million
Number Employees: 250-499
Number of Brands: 68
Parent Co: Clorox Company
Type of Packaging: Private Label
Brands:
Farmhouse Originals Ceasar
Greek Yogurt Lemon Garlic
Buffalo Ranch(c)
Greek Yogurt Ranch
Original Ranch(c) Dips Mix
Greek Yogurt Salad Dressing Mix
Homestyle Italian Pasta Salad
Original Ranch(c) Pasta Salad
Garlic Parmesan Crouton Bites
Original Ranch(c) Homestyle
Three Herb Ranch
Cheddar & Bacon Flavored Ranch
Honey BBQ Ranch(c)
Roasted Garlic Ranch
Greek Yogurt Spinach & Feta
Greek Yogurt Creamy Ceasar
Simply Ranch Cucumber Basil
Simply Ranch Classic Ranch
The Original Ranch(c)
Sriracha Ranch(c)
Salad Crispins(c)
Easy Squeeze Bottle
Light
and many more

5490 **Haagen-Dazs**
PO Box 2178
Wilkes-Barre, PA 18703
800-767-0120
www.haagendazs.us
Dairy, Ice Cream
Owner: Rex Bunzalang
Sr. V.P./Managing Dir., Int'l Div.: John Riccitiello
Senior VP R&D: Ken Snider
Sales Director: Yves Coleon
Estimated Sales: Under $500,000
Number Employees: 1-4
Parent Co: Diageo United Distillers and Vinters

5491 **Habby Habanero's Food Products**
6475 Ferber Road
Jacksonville, FL 32277-1513
904-333-9758
http://www.habbys.net/
Barbecue sauces
Contact: Malcolm Quincy
Contact: Jerry Quincy

5492 **Habersham Vineyards & Winery**
7025 S Main St
Helen, GA 30545-3615
706-878-9463
Fax: 706-878-8466 info@habershamwinery.com
www.habershamwinery.com
Wines
Owner: Tom Slick
CEO/CFO: Steve Gibson
Wine Maker: Andrew Beaty
Vineyard Manager: Terri Haney
Estimated Sales: $1.5 Million
Number Employees: 10-19
Square Footage: 12000
Type of Packaging: Private Label
Brands:
Creekstone
Habersham Estates
Southern Harvest

5493 **Haby's Alsatian Bakery**
207 US Highway 90 E
Castroville, TX 78009-5222
830-538-2118
Fax: 830-931-2194 info@habysbakery.com
www.habysbakery.com
Cookies, pies, cakes, apple fritters, strudels, stollens, bread and coffeecakes.
President: Sammy Tschirhart
VP/Secretary/Treasurer: Yvonne Tschirhart
Estimated Sales: $500,000-$1 Million
Number Employees: 10-19
Square Footage: 16200
Type of Packaging: Consumer

5494 **Hadley's Date Gardens**
83555 Airport Blvd # 11
Thermal, CA 92274-9127
760-399-5191
Fax: 760-399-1311 www.hadleys.com
Dates
Owner: Melinda Dougherty
mdougherty@hadleys.com
CEO: John Keck
Vice President: Sean Dougherty
Number Employees: 50-99
Type of Packaging: Consumer, Food Service, Private Label, Bulk
Brands:
Hadley Date Gardens

5495 **Hafner USA**
4609 Lewis Rd
Stone Mountain, GA 30083
678-406-0101
Fax: 678-406-9222 888-725-4605
www.hafner.com
Pastry shells, cream puffs, puff pastries and cake kits
President: Xavier M De Goursac
Marketing: Maria Dziebakowski
Estimated Sales: $5-10 000,000
Number Employees: 5-9

5496 **Hafner Vineyard**
4280 Pine Flat Rd
Healdsburg, CA 95448
707-433-4606
Fax: 707-433-1240 info@hafnervineyard.com
www.hafnervineyard.com
Wines

Partner/Owner: Richard Hafner
Partner: Julianne Farrell
Partner: Elizabeth Hafner
Managing Partner: Scott Hafner
Winemaker: Sarah Hafner
Estimated Sales: $2,500,000
Number Employees: 10
Type of Packaging: Private Label
Brands:
Hafner

5497 **Hagensborg Chocolates LTD.**
3686 Bonneville Place
Unit #103
Burnaby, BC V3N 4T6
Canada
604-215-0234
Fax: 604-215-0235 877-554-7763
sales@hagensborg.com www.hagensborg.com
Canned pate, chocolate and confectionery items, olive oils, sherry vinegar; exporter of smoked salmon fillets
President: Shelley Miller
Marketing: Shelley Wallace
Estimated Sales: $10-20 Million
Number Employees: 10-19
Square Footage: 30000
Type of Packaging: Consumer, Food Service, Private Label
Brands:
Hagensborg Meltaways Truffles
Kiss Me Frog Truffles
Truffles To Go

5498 **Hagerty Foods**
987 N Enterprise St
Suite J
Orange, CA 92867
714-628-1230
Condiments
President: Francisco Esquivel
Estimated Sales: $220,000
Number Employees: 3
Square Footage: 20000
Type of Packaging: Consumer, Food Service, Private Label
Brands:
Hagerty Foods
La Napa
Winemaker's Choice

5499 **Hahn Family Wines**
37700 Foothill Rd
Soledad, CA 93960
831-678-4555
Fax: 831-678-0557 info@hahnfamilywines.com
www.hahnwines.com
Wines
President: Bill Leigon
Sr. Director, Marketing: Vince Berry
Regional Sales Manager: Brent Ferro
Director of Winemaking: Paul Clifton
Estimated Sales: $7,500,000
Number Employees: 50-99
Square Footage: 30
Type of Packaging: Private Label
Brands:
Smith & Hook Winery
Huntington
Copa
Cycles
Gladiator
Lucienne
Bin 36

5500 **Hahn's Old Fashioned Cake Co**
75 Allen Blvd
Farmingdale, NY 11735-5614
631-249-3456
Fax: 631-249-3492 www.crumbcake.net
Coffee cake
President: Regina Hahn
Chief Operating Officer: Andrew Hahn
Estimated Sales: $2.5-5 Million
Number Employees: 10-19
Type of Packaging: Consumer, Food Service

5501 **Haig's Delicacies**
25673 Nickel Pl
Hayward, CA 94545-3221
510-782-6285
Fax: 510-782-5428 www.haigsdelicacies.com
Hummus, dips, sauces
Owner/Founder: Haig Takvorian
Marketing: Rita Takvorian
Estimated Sales: Less Than $500,000
Number Employees: 5-9

5502 **Haight Brown Vineyard**
29 Chestnut Hill Rd
Litchfield, CT 06759-4101
860-567-4045
Fax: 860-818-3770 800-577-9463
haightvineyard@aol.com
www.haightvineyards.com
Wines
Owner: Amy Fenew
Co-Partner: Amy Brown
Manager: Natash Gouey-Guy
Cellar Master: Salvatore Cimino
Estimated Sales: $2.5-5,000,000
Number Employees: 1-4
Brands:
Haight Vineyard Wines

5503 **Hail Merry**
9755 Clifford Dr
Unit 150
Dallas, TX 75220
214-905-5005
customerservice@hailmerry.com
www.hailmerry.com
Cups, bites and tarts
Founder: Susan O'Brien
Type of Packaging: Consumer
Brands:
HAIL MERRY

5504 **Haile Resources**
2650 Freewood Dr
Dallas, TX 75220-2511
214-357-1471
Fax: 214-357-9381 800-357-1471
www.haileresources.com
Food and beverage ingredients
President: Chris Beninate
chris@haileresources.com
Vice President: Elaine Haile
Estimated Sales: $500,000
Number Employees: 5-9
Type of Packaging: Private Label

5505 **(HQ)Hain Celestial Group Inc**
1111 Marcus Ave
Suite 100
Lake Success, NY 11042
800-434-4246
www.hain.com
Organic health products.
President/CEO: Mark Schiller
Executive VP/CFO: Javier Idrovo
Senior VP, R&D: Jeff George
Senior VP, Sales: Kevin Lasher
Chief Supply Chain Officer: Jerry Wolfe
Estimated Sales: $2.6 Billion
Number Employees: 6,300
Number of Brands: 29
Brands:
alba BOTANICA
Arrowhead Mills
Avalon Organics
Bearitos
BluePrint Organic
Candle Cafe Vegan
Casbah
Celestial Seasonings
DeBoles
Dream
Earth's Best Organic
Ella's Kitchen
Empire Kosher
FreeBird
Garden of Eatin'
GG Unique Fiber
Hain Pure Foods
Health Valley
Hollywood
Imagine
Jason
live clean
MaraNatha
Nile Spice
plainville Farms
Queen Helene
Rudis
Sensible Portions
Spectrum
SunSpire
Terra
The Greek Gods
Tilda
Walnut Acres
Westbrae Natural
WESTSOY
Yves Veggie Cuisine

5506 **Hain Celestial Group Inc**
4600 Sleepytime Dr
Boulder, CO 80301-3284
800-434-4246
www.hainpurefoods.com
Natural and organic foods
Brands:
Haine Pure Foods
Celestial Seasonings

5507 **Haines City Citrus Growers**
8 Railroad Ave
P.O.Box 337
Haines City, FL 33844-4245
863-422-1174
Fax: 863-421-4003 800-327-6676
Citrus fruits
President: Bob Turner
bob@hilltopcitrus.com
Treasurer: Dennis P. Broadaway
Finance Executive: Rod Hamric
Sales Exec: Bob States
Director Field Operations: Charles Counter
Packing House Manager: John Soles
Estimated Sales: $10-20 Million
Number Employees: 100-249
Parent Co: Citrus World

5508 **Haines Packing Company**
5 Mile Mud Bay Rd.
PO Box 290
Haines, AK 99827
907-766-2883
harry@hainespacking.com
www.hainespacking.com
Salmon, crab, halibut, and shrimp.
President/CEO: William Weisfield
CFO/Controller: Bob Hall
Vice President /Owner: Jan Supler
Year Founded: 1917
Estimated Sales: 100 Million
Number Employees: 40
Square Footage: 5963
Type of Packaging: Consumer, Food Service, Bulk
Other Locations:
Ward Cove Packing Co.
Seattle WA
Brands:
Northern Pride
Pirate

5509 **Hair Of The Dog Brewing**
61 SE Yamhill St
Portland, OR 97214-2134
503-232-6585
Fax: 503-235-8743
German style beer
Owner: Denver Bon
denver@hairofthedog.com
Brewer: Pat Savage
Estimated Sales: $500,000-$1,000,000
Number Employees: 1-4

5510 **Hak's**
1203 S Spaulding Ave
Los Angeles, CA 90019
424-235-0516
support@haksbbq.com
haks.com
Barbecue sauce
Founder: Sharone Hakman

5511 **Hakuna Banana**
242 N Avenue 25
Los Angeles, CA 90031-1982
323-736-1630
www.hakunabanana.com
Banana-based, non-dairy frozen dessert
Co-Founder: Hannah Hong
Number of Brands: 1
Number of Products: 8
Type of Packaging: Consumer
Brands:
HAKUNA BANANA

5512 **Halal Fine Foods**
73 Galaxy Blvd
Units 11 & 12
Toronto, ON M9W 5T4
Canada
416-679-8000
info@halalfinefood.com
www.halalfinefood.com
Halal foods including mantu, ashak, sauces, ready meals, cookies, and soups
President: Matin Hakimi
CEO, Director: Mohammad Amin
Account Manager: Rita Raji
Office Manager: Iwona Hakimi
Production Manager: Yusif Zafar

5513 **Hale Indian River Groves**
1650 90th Ave
Vero Beach, FL 32966
772-581-9915
Fax: 877-329-4253 800-562-4502
customercare@halegroves.com
www.halegroves.com
Fruit juicees and fruit gift baskets
VP: Fred Kuester
Internet Marketing Manager: Sean Leis
Sales: Sheila McCue Andrews
Customer Service Lead: Sally Costantini
Estimated Sales: $20-50 Million
Number Employees: 50-99
Type of Packaging: Consumer, Bulk

5514 **Hale and Hearty Soups**
Chelsea Market
75-9th Ave
New York, NY 10011
212-255-2433
www.haleandhearty.com
Restaurant chain producing homemade soups, sandwiches and salads
CEO: Andy Taylor
Chief Financial Officer: Bob Hernon
Recruitment & Development Manager: David Stafford
Vice President, Sales: Paul Schwartz
Director of Operations: Robert Monti
Estimated Sales: $5-10,000,000
Number Employees: 500-1000

5515 **Hale's Brewery**
4301 Leary Way NW
Seattle, WA 98107-4538
206-782-0737
Fax: 360-706-1572 info@halesbrewery.com
www.halesbrewery.com
Beers
President/Founder: Michael Hale
Accountant: Brenda Rock
Sales Manager: Bill Preib
Special Events Manager: Dana Hurt
Head Brewer: Chris Sheehan
Year Founded: 1983
Estimated Sales: $20-50 Million
Number Employees: 50-99
Brands:
Hale's Celebration Porter
Hale's Pale American Ale
Hale's Special Bitter
Moss Bay Extra Ale
Moss Bay Stout
Hale's Cream
Wee Heavy Winter Ale
Irish Style Nut Brown Ale
O'Brien Harvest Ale
Pale American
Hale's Dublin Style Stout
German Style Kolsch

5516 **Half Moon Bay Trading Co**
210 Mayport Rd
Atlantic Beach, FL 32233-3332
904-246-9493
Fax: 904-246-9442 888-447-2823
info@halfmoonbaytrading.com
www.halfmoonbaytrading.com
Condiments, salsas, glaze toppings & mixers
President: Robin Shepherd
CFO: Jeff Hite
VP Sales, Marketing & Product Dev.: Tom Nuijens
Contact: Peggy Cornelius
pcornelius@halfmoonbaytrading.com
Office & Traffic Manager: Ellen Singleton
Year Founded: 1992
Estimated Sales: $1,000,000 +
Number Employees: 1-4
Number of Brands: 5
Number of Products: 21
Square Footage: 10000
Type of Packaging: Consumer, Food Service, Private Label
Brands:
Beesting
Caribbean Condiments
Iguana
Sweetsting
Tamarindo Bay

5517 **Half Moon Fruit & Produce Company**
14275 Cacheville Road
Yolo, CA 95697-3114
530-662-1727
Fax: 530-662-6072
Prunes, plums and melons
President: B E Giovannetti
Operations Manager: Richard Monford
Estimated Sales: $10-20 Million
Number Employees: 7
Brands:
Buster
Melo-Glow
Morning Cheer
Valley King

5518 **Halfpops Inc**
16413 N 91st St # 105
Suite 105
Scottsdale, AZ 85260-3052
480-494-5117
info@halfpops.com
www.halfpops.com
Popcorn
CEO: Mike Fitzgerald
Estimated Sales: Less Than $500,000
Number Employees: 1-4

5519 **Haliburton International Inc**
3855 Jurupa St
Ontario, CA 91761-1404
909-428-8520
Fax: 909-428-8521 877-980-4295
www.haliburton.net
Fire roasted vegetables, including peppers, tomatoes, tomatillos, onions, garlic, shallots, squash, zucchini
Owner: Ian Schenkel
schenkel@haliburton.net
Estimated Sales: $36 Million
Number Employees: 50-99
Type of Packaging: Food Service, Bulk

5520 **Halifax Group**
1133 Connecticut Avenue, NW
Suite 700
Washington, DC 20036
202-530-8300
Fax: 202-296-7133 jsauter@thehalifaxgroup.com
www.thehalifaxgroup.com
Gourmet sauces, dressings, salsa, condiments and beverages
Principal: Chris Cathcart
Chief Executive Officer: David W. Dupree
Chief Financial Officer: Michael T. Marshall
Vice President: Katherine Trainor
Estimated Sales: $5-10 Million
Number Employees: 10-19
Brands:
Hill Farms
Redneck Gourmet
Scorned Woman
Southern Sensations
Wild Man

5521 **Hall Brothers Meats**
27040 Cook Rd
Olmsted Twp, OH 44138-1111
440-235-3262
Fax: 440-235-6696 www.hallsqualitymeats.com
Fresh and frozen beef, pork, poultry, lamb and seafood
President: Richard Hall
hall@hallbros.com
Estimated Sales: $10-20 Million
Number Employees: 5-9
Type of Packaging: Consumer, Food Service, Bulk

5522 **Hall Grain Company**
502 E Railroad Avenue
Akron, CO 80720
970-345-2206
Fax: 970-345-6680
Grains
Manager: Tim Mayes
Controller: Kevin Hall
VP: Pat Hall
Estimated Sales: $10-20 Million
Number Employees: 50-99

5523 **Halladay's Harvest Barn**
6 Webb Ter
Bellows Falls, VT 05101-3157
802-463-3471
Fax: 802-460-1132 halladay@sover.net
www.halladays.com
Seasonings, dips, cheesecake mixes, dry soup mixes, garlic oil and vinegars
Owner: Rick Govotski
holladay@sover.net
Co-Owner: Kathleen Govotski
Estimated Sales: $1-3 Million
Number Employees: 10-19

5524 **Hallcrest Vineyards**
379 Felton Empire Rd
Felton, CA 95018-9167
831-335-4441
Fax: 831-335-4450 info@hallcrestvineyards.com
www.hallcrestvineyards.com
Wines
President: Yuka Lu
yuka.lu@arbitech.com
Lab Director: Paul Bouswa
Sales Manager: Will Warto
Co-Owner/Public Relations: Lorraine Schumacher
Cellar Master: Giovanni Jovel
Estimated Sales: $2.5-5,000,000
Number Employees: 10-19
Type of Packaging: Private Label
Brands:
Hallcrest Vineyards
The Organic Wine Work
Vinatopia

5525 **Hallmark Fisheries**
63276 Charleston Ave
P.O. Box 5390
Charleston, OR 97420
541-888-3253
Fax: 541-888-6814 info@hallmarkfisheries.com
www.hallmarkfisheries.com
Fresh, frozen and canned seafood.
Office Manager: Loretta Boyce
Plant Quality Controller: Karen Smith
Estimated Sales: $20-50 Million
Number Employees: 100-249
Parent Co: California Shellfish
Type of Packaging: Consumer, Food Service, Private Label, Bulk
Brands:
Hallmark
Peacock
Point St. George

5526 **Halmoni's Divine Marinade**
113 Anderson Ave
Demarest, NJ 07627-1318
917-913-8961
www.divinemarinade.com
Marinades; BBQ and grilling sauces; and relish.
Co-Owner: Sandra Rhow-Haik
Co-Owner: Wendy Hegglin
Year Founded: 2013
Type of Packaging: Private Label

5527 **Halperns' Purveyors of Steak & Seafood**
4685 Welcome All Road
Atlanta, GA 30349
404-767-9229
Fax: 404-767-2611 866-659-6090
info@halperns.com halperns.com
Steak and seafood
President & COO: Ray Hicks
CEO: Kirk Halpern
VP: Jody Hicks

5528 **Halsted Packing House**
445 N Halsted St
Chicago, IL 60642-6518
312-421-5147
Fax: 312-421-4511
Lamb, pork and goat meat
Owner: William Davos
Co-Owner: Ann Davos
Estimated Sales: Less than $500,000
Number Employees: 5-9
Square Footage: 12800
Type of Packaging: Consumer, Food Service

5529 **Ham I Am**
5505 Longview St
Dallas, TX 75206-5607
972-447-0440
Fax: 972-447-0460 800-742-6426
www.hamiam.com
Pork products, quail, duck, turkey, Texas BBQ, desserts, breakfast ideas, homemade tamales, hors d'oeuvres, and party foods
President: Sharon Meehan
Manager: Meghan Meehan
meghanameehan@gmail.com
Estimated Sales: Under $500,000
Number Employees: 5-9
Type of Packaging: Private Label, Bulk

5530 **Hama Hama Oyster® Company**
301 N Webb Rd
Lilliwaup, WA 98555
360-877-6938
Fax: 360-877-6942 888-877-5844
Seafood
Owner: David Robins
Sales, Wholesale: Adam James
Estimated Sales: $500,000-$1,000,000
Number Employees: 1-4
Type of Packaging: Private Label, Bulk

5531 **Hamersmith, Inc.**
3200 NW 125 Street
Miami, FL 33167
305-685-7451
Fax: 305-681-6093 office@hamersmith.com
www.hamersmith.com
Shortenings, margarines, oils, puff paste, pan releases and spices; packagaing services
President: Calvin Theobald
Sales Director: Gerald Delmonico
Estimated Sales: $2.5-5 Million
Number Employees: 10
Number of Brands: 20
Number of Products: 9
Square Footage: 60000
Type of Packaging: Food Service, Private Label, Bulk

5532 **Hamilos Bros Inspected Meat**
1117 Greenwood St
Madison, IL 62060-1234
618-876-3710
Fax: 618-876-3732
Meat and fresh and frozen fish; wholesaler/distributor of canned goods, paper products and pre-packaged meat
Owner: Mike Skinner
Owner: Jeff Skinner
Estimated Sales: $500,000-$1 Million
Number Employees: 5-9
Type of Packaging: Consumer

5533 **Hamilton Marine**
20 Park Dr
Rockland, ME 04841-3441
207-594-8181
Fax: 207-594-8161 www.hamiltonmarine.com
Seafood
President: Leni Gronros
COO: Steve Graebert
Manager: Dave Perry
Estimated Sales: $5-10 Million
Number Employees: 5-9

5534 **Hammond Pretzel Bakery Inc**
716 S West End Ave
Lancaster, PA 17603-5050
717-392-7532
Fax: 717-392-8085 info@hammondpretzels.com
www.hammondpretzels.com
Handmade pretzels and chocolate pretzels
President: Brian Nicklaus
bnicklaus@hammondpretzels.com
General Manager: Brian Nicklaus
Estimated Sales: $10-20 Million
Number Employees: 10-19
Type of Packaging: Consumer
Brands:
Hammond's

5535 **Hammond's Candies**
5735 Washington St
Denver, CO 80216-1321
303-333-5588
Fax: 303-333-5622 888-226-3999
www.hammondscandies.com
Chocolates and traditional hard candy and confections
Owner: Bob List
CIO: Ross Chism
Marketing: Andrew Whisler
Contact: Anna Abromovich
anna@hammondscandies.com
Manager: Karlyn Pulst
Master Candymaker: Ralph Nafziger
Estimated Sales: $850,000
Number Employees: 100-249

5536 **Hammons Black Walnuts**
105 Hammons Dr
PO Box 140
Stockton, MO 65785
Fax: 417-276-5187 888-429-6887
info@black-walnuts.com www.black-walnuts.com
Walnuts
President: Brian Hammons
Year Founded: 1946
Estimated Sales: $1 to 2.5 Million
Number Employees: 80
Type of Packaging: Food Service, Private Label, Bulk

5537 **Hammons Products Co**
105 Hammons Dr
PO Box 140
Stockton, MO 65785-7608
417-276-5181
Fax: 417-276-5187 888-429-6887
www.hammonsproducts.com
Walnuts
President: Brian Hammons
bhammons@black-walnuts.com
VP Marketing: David Hammons
VP Sales: David Steinmuller
Estimated Sales: $10-20 Million
Number Employees: 100-249
Square Footage: 687000
Type of Packaging: Consumer, Food Service, Bulk
Brands:
Hammons

5538 **Hamms Custom Meats**
307 W Louisiana St
Mckinney, TX 75069-4417
972-542-3359
info@hamsdelivered.com
www.hamsdelivered.com
Custom cut meats
Owner: Ken Uselton
Partner: Carrie Galyean
Year Founded: 1954
Estimated Sales: $.5-1 million
Number Employees: 1-4
Type of Packaging: Consumer, Food Service, Bulk

5539 **Hampton Associates & Sons**
12728 Dogwood Hills Lane
Fairfax, VA 22033-3244
703-968-5847
jamcola@hotmail.com
Soft drinks
CEO/Chairman: Hampton Brown
Estimated Sales: Under $500,000
Number Employees: 1-4
Type of Packaging: Consumer, Food Service
Brands:
Bahama
Deep Purple
Diet Clear Jazz
Falcon Orange Soda
Jazz Cola
Rustler Root Beer

5540 **Hampton Chutney Company**
6 Main Street
Amagansett, NY 11930
631-267-3131
Fax: 631-267-6169 info@hamptonchutney.com
www.hamptonchutney.com
Fresh chutneys
Owner: Gary MacGurn
Co-Owner: Isabel MacGurn
Chef: Patty Gentry
Estimated Sales: Less than $500,000
Number Employees: 5-9

5541 **Hampton Farms**
202 Peanut St
Severn, NC 27877
252-585-0916
Fax: 252-585-1242 800-313-2748
www.hamptonfarms.com
Peanuts and peanut products
President & CEO: Dallas Barnes
VP Sales/Marketing: Thomas Nolan
Operations: Dan Hutton
Estimated Sales: $25 Million
Number Employees: 50-99
Parent Co: Meherrin Chemical
Type of Packaging: Private Label, Bulk
Brands:
Hamptom Farms

5542 **Hanan Products Co**
196 Miller Pl
Hicksville, NY 11801-1826
516-938-1000
Fax: 516-938-1925 info@hananproducts.com
www.hananproducts.com
Kosher non-dairy products
President: John Bauer
jbauer@hananproducts.com
Estimated Sales: $2.5-5,000,000
Number Employees: 20-49
Type of Packaging: Consumer, Food Service

5543 **Hancock Gourmet LobsterCo**
46 Park Dr
Topsham, ME 04086-1737
207-725-1855
Fax: 207-725-1856
cal@hancockgourmetlobster.com
www.hancockgourmetlobster.com
Lobster and other specialty seafood products
Founder & President: Cal Hancock
cal@hancockgourmetlobster.com
VP: Jack Rosberg
Executive Chef: Kevin Messier
Wholesale Sales Manager: Laura Meier
Director of Operations & Marketing: Amber Pelletier
Estimated Sales: $1.3 Million
Number Employees: 20-49
Type of Packaging: Consumer, Food Service, Bulk

5544 **Hancock Peanut Company**
P.O. Box 100
Courtland, VA 23837
757-653-9351
Fax: 757-653-2147
Peanuts
President: J Matthew Pope
VP Sales: Robert Pope
Contact: Melissa Rose
Number Employees: 50-99
Type of Packaging: Consumer, Food Service

5545 **Hand Made Lollies**
465 S Orlando Avenue
Suite 205
Maitland, FL 32751
877-784-2724
Fax: 877-249-6419 info@handmadelollies.com
www.handmadelollies.com
Handmade and personalized lollipops
President: Timothy Lang

5546 **Handley Cellars**
3151 Highway 128
Philo, CA 95466
707-895-3876
Fax: 707-895-2603 800-733-3151
info@handleycellars.com www.handleycellars.com
Wines

Winemaker & Owner: Milla Handley
milla@handleycellars.com
Director, Sales & Marketing: Travis Scott
National Sales Manager: Lulu McClellan
Hospitality Lead: Chris Richard
Cellar Master: Efrain Garcia
Estate Vineyard Manager: Jos, Jimenez
Estimated Sales: $5-10,000,000
Number Employees: 11-50
Type of Packaging: Private Label

5547 **Handy International Inc**
700 E Main St # 101
Salisbury, MD 21804-5035
410-912-2000
Fax: 410-968-1592 800-426-3977
www.handycrab.com
Frozen seafood
President: Terry Conway
Senior VP: Rosario D Nero
VP: Todd Conway
Sales Executive: Todd Mcallister
Estimated Sales: $8,000,000
Number Employees: 100-249
Type of Packaging: Consumer, Food Service
Brands:
Handy

5548 **(HQ)Handy Pax**
53 York Ave
Randolph, MA 2368
781-963-8300
Snack foods
President: Jay Sussman
Sales Manager: David Sussman
Number Employees: 10-19
Type of Packaging: Consumer, Private Label

5549 **Hangzhou Sanhe USA Inc.**
20536 Carrey Rd
Walnut, CA 91789
909-869-6016
Fax: 909-869-6015 www.sanheinc.com
Food ingredients and additives.
President: Aili Chen
Contact: Yun Qian
yunqian@sanheinc.com
Estimated Sales: $1 Million
Type of Packaging: Bulk

5550 **Hanks Beverage Co**
4625 E Street Rd
Feasterville-Trevose, PA 19053-6630
215-396-2809
Fax: 215-396-8077 800-289-4722
info@hanksbeverages.com
www.hanksbeverages.com
Gourmet soda
Manager: Jennifer Brady
Estimated Sales: $5-10 Million
Number Employees: 10-19

5551 **Hanley's Foods Inc.**
149 Ingram Hall
Baton Rouge, LA 70803
225-366-0992
hanleysfoods.com
Dressings and croutons
CEO: Richard Hanley
COO: Kate Hanley
VP of Manufacturing: Katie Hanley Dunlap
VP of Marketing: Marshall Thompson
VP of Operations: Scott Hallett
Year Founded: 2012
Number Employees: 1-10
Type of Packaging: Private Label

5552 **Hanmi Inc**
5447 N Wolcott Ave
Chicago, IL 60640-1017
773-271-0730
Fax: 773-271-1756 www.wangfood.com
Korean foods
Owner: Young Kim
chihanmi@yahoo.com
Contact: Sung Sohn
CFO: Michael Winiarski
Vice President: John Kim
Estimated Sales: $10-20 Million
Number Employees: 5-9

5553 **Hanna's Honey**
4760 Thorman Ave Ne
Salem, OR 97303-4644
503-393-2945
Fax: 503-393-2945 www.hannashoney.com
Package and wholesale gourmet Oregon honey.
President: Jean Hunter
CEO: Claude Hunter
Estimated Sales: $100,000
Number Employees: 2
Type of Packaging: Consumer
Brands:
Hanna's

5554 **Hannah Max Baking**
14601 S Main St
Gardena, CA 90248-1916
310-324-9871
Fax: 310-324-9871
Cookies
CEO: Joanne Adirim
joanne@hannahmax.com
Number Employees: 50-99

5555 **Hanover Foods Corp**
1125 Wilson Ave
P.O. Box 334
Hanover, PA 17331
717-632-6000
Fax: 717-637-2890 www.hanoverfoods.com
Processor and importer of canned, frozen, freeze-dried and fresh vegetables, beans, mushrooms, potato chips, pretzels, juices, sauces, salads, entrees, soups, desserts, etc.; also, spaghetti and meat balls in tomato sauce.
Chief Executive Officer: John Warehime
john.warehime@hanoverfoods.com
Executive Vice President: Gary Knisely
VP, Canning Operations: Dave Still
VP, Sales: Dan Schuchart
Year Founded: 1924
Estimated Sales: $20 50 Million
Number Employees: 250-499
Square Footage: 5161
Type of Packaging: Consumer, Private Label, Bulk
Brands:
Alcosa
Aunt Kitty's
Bickel's
Casa Maid
Clayton Farms
Dawn Glo
Dutch Farms
Farmer Girl
Gibbs
Hanover
Hanover Farms
Lk Burman
Maryland Chef
Mitchell's
Myers
O & C
Phillips
Round the Clock
Spring Glen
Spring Glen Fresh Foods
Sunnyside
Sunwise
Super Fine
Superfine
Vegetable Cocktail

5556 **Hanover Potato Products Inc**
60 Black Rock Rd
Hanover, PA 17331-4106
717-632-0700
Fax: 717-632-0756
Potato products
Owner: Kendra Kauffman
office@hanoverchamber.com
Estimated Sales: $250,000
Number Employees: 10-19
Square Footage: 17400
Parent Co: Hanover Foods Corp
Type of Packaging: Food Service

5557 **Hans Kissle Co**
9 Creek Brook Dr
Haverhill, MA 01832-1548
978-556-4500
Fax: 978-556-4612 www.hanskissle.com
Refrigerated salads, quiches, stuffings, desserts, deli meats and prepared meals
President/CEO: Ken Venti
CFO: Tim Sousa
Sales Exec: Kymberley Feldman
kboyle@hanskissle.com
Plant Manager: Eric Lane
Estimated Sales: $20-50 Million
Number Employees: 50-99
Square Footage: 112000
Type of Packaging: Food Service, Private Label, Bulk

5558 **Hansen Caviar Company**
881 New York 28
Kingston, NY 12401
845-331-5622
Fax: 845-331-8075 800-735-0441
hcaviar@aol.com
Caviar, foie gras, truffles, smoked fish and other specialty food products
President: Michael Hansen-Sturm
Estimated Sales: $500,000-$1,000,000
Number Employees: 1-4
Type of Packaging: Private Label
Brands:
Hansen
Hansen-Norge
St. Etienne

5559 **Hansen Packing Co**
807 State Highway 16
Jerseyville, IL 62052-2813
618-498-3714
Fax: 618-498-5507 www.hansenmeatco.com
Meat
Owner: Dave Hansen
Customs Processor/Logistics Operations: Todd Pearse
Customs Processor/Logistics Operations: Jim Woelfel
Marketing/Sales Manager: Ryan Hansen
Retail Manager/Daily Operations: Shon Kennedy
Manager Administrative Operations: Terrie Perry
hansenpacking@gtec.com
Lead Meat Processor: Mike Pearse
Livestock Consultant/Cattle Buyer: Ronnie Hansen
Driver Wholesale Orders: Dan Monroe
Estimated Sales: $3-5 Million
Number Employees: 5-9
Type of Packaging: Bulk
Brands:
Hansen

5560 **Hanson Thompson Honey Farms**
P.O.Box 129
Redfield, SD 57469
605-472-0474
Honey
President: Bruce Hanson
Co-Owner: Adrian Thompson
Estimated Sales: Under $500,000
Number Employees: 1-4

5561 **Hanzell Vineyards**
18596 Lomita Ave
Sonoma, CA 95476-4619
707-996-3860
Fax: 707-996-3862 maildesk@hanzell.com
www.hanzell.com
Wines
President: Jason Jardine
jason@hanzell.com
Director, Vineyard Operations: Jose Ramos Esquivel
Director of Winemaking: Michael McNeill
Estimated Sales: $5-9.9,000,000
Number Employees: 11-50

5562 **Happy & Healthy Products Inc**
1600 S Dixie Hwy
Suite 200
Boca Raton, FL 33432-7463
561-367-0739
Fax: 561-368-5267 behappy@fruitfull.com
www.happyandhealthy.com
Frozen fruit bars and dessert bars, fruit smoothies, dips and healthy snacks
President: Linda Kamm
president@happyandhealthy.com
Marketing Director: Tabitha Locke
Customer Service Manager: Susan Scotts
Public Relations: Mary Galinat
Operations Manager: Len Murray
General Manager: Rosemary Harris

Estimated Sales: $4 Million
Number Employees: 10-19
Number of Brands: 5
Type of Packaging: Consumer, Food Service, Private Label, Bulk
Brands:
Be Happy 'n Healthy Snacks
Fruitfull
Happy Indulgence
Happy Indulgence Deladent Dips

5563 **Happy Acres Packing Company**
PO Box 444
Petal, MS 39465-0444
601-584-8301
Sausage
President: Helen Jernigan
Estimated Sales: $500-1,000,000 appx.
Number Employees: 1-4

5564 **Happy Campers**
Portland, OR 97223
www.happycampersgf.com
Gluten-free bread
Co-Founder: Lacy Gillham
Co-Founder: Jan Taborsky

5565 **Happy Cow Creamery**
332 Mckelvey Rd
Pelzer, SC 29669-9243
864-243-9699
Fax: 864-869-8687 info@happycowcreamery.com
www.happycowcreamery.com
Milk, dairy
Owner: Nancy Grubbs
nancy@happycowcreamery.com
Estimated Sales: Less Than $500,000
Number Employees: 1-4

5566 **Happy Egg Dealers**
3204 E 7th Ave
Tampa, FL 33605-4302
813-248-2362
Fax: 813-247-1754
Eggs
Owner: Frank Selph
Estimated Sales: $10-20 Million
Number Employees: 10 to 19
Type of Packaging: Consumer, Bulk
Brands:
Belle Mead

5567 **Happy Family**
40 Fulton St
17th Fl.
New York, NY 10038
212-374-2779
855-644-2779
www.happyfamilyorganics.com
Organic foods for babies, toddlers, kids, and adults.
Founder & CEO: Shazi Visram
VP of Marketing: Helen Bernstein
VP Sales: Bob Zimmerman
Contact: Amanda Albers
amanda@happyfamilybrands.com
Founding Partner & COO: Jessica Rolph

5568 **Happy Goat**
314 Shawmut Ave
Boston, MA 02118
617-549-2776
Fax: 415-762-5282
Dessert toppings
Founder/Chief Executive: Michael Winnike
Partner/Director of Marketing/Media & Br: Kyle Pickering
Partner/Director of Operations and Accou: Sharon Winnike
Marketing: Michael Winnike

5569 **Happy Herberts Food Co Inc**
444 Washington Blvd # 2524
Jersey City, NJ 07310-1916
201-386-0985
Fax: 201-386-0984 800-764-2779
info@HappyHerberts.com
Snacks
Owner: Gary Plutchok
Estimated Sales: Less Than $500,000
Number Employees: 1-4
Brands:
Happy Herberts

5570 **Happy Hive**
4476 Tulane St
Dearborn Heights, MI 48125
313-562-3707
Fax: 313-562-3707
Candy/confectionery
Owner: Stanley Kozlowicz
Estimated Sales: Less than $100,000
Number Employees: 1-4
Type of Packaging: Consumer, Food Service, Bulk
Brands:
Happy Hive

5571 **Happy Planet Foods**
601-4180 Lougheed Hwy
Burnaby, BC V5C 6A7
Canada
Fax: 604-291-0981 800-811-3213
happy@happyplanet.com happyplanet.com
Juices, smoothies, soups, dairy products and plant milks
Co-Founder: Gregor Robertson
Co-Founder: Randal Ius

5572 **Happy's Potato Chip Co**
3900 Chandler Dr NE
Minneapolis, MN 55421-4494
612-781-3121
Fax: 612-781-3125
Snack foods
President: Steve Aanenson
Finance Executive: Betty Kapsner
Human Resource Executive: Allen Dick
Manager: Finn Henrikssen
Plant Manager: Finn Henrikssen
Estimated Sales: $5 Million
Number Employees: 50-99
Square Footage: 92000
Parent Co: Old Dutch Foods
Type of Packaging: Consumer, Food Service

5573 **Harbar LLC**
320 Turnpike St
Canton, MA 02021-2703
781-828-0848
Fax: 781-828-0849 800-881-7040
Tortillas and specialty flatbreads
Owner: Ezequiel Montemayor
emontemayor@harbar.com
Estimated Sales: $3 Million
Number Employees: 100-249
Square Footage: 80000
Type of Packaging: Consumer, Food Service, Private Label, Bulk
Brands:
MAYAN FARM
MARIA AND RICARDO'S
WRAPPY

5574 **Harbison Wholesale Meats**
2115 County Road
Suite 401
Cullman, AL 35057
256-739-5105
Fax: 256-739-8123
Meat
Proprietor: Gary Harbison

5575 **Harbor Fish Market**
9 Custom House Wharf
Portland, ME 04101-4708
207-775-0251
Fax: 207-879-0611 800-370-1790
info@harborfish.com www.harborfish.com
Seafood
Owner: Benjamin Alfiero
ben@harborfish.com
Owner: Mike Alfiero
Owner/VP: Michael Alfiero
Estimated Sales: $6.2 Million
Number Employees: 20-49
Square Footage: 16058

5576 **Harbor Seafood**
969 Lakeville Rd
New Hyde Park, NY 11040-3000
516-775-2400
Fax: 516-775-3641 800-645-2211
Seafood

President & CEO: Pete Cardone
peteharbor@aol.com
Director Sales, Marketing & Purchasing: Enrique Oyaga
Sales & Marketing: Trish Albano
VP International Purchasing: Bogdan Swita
Estimated Sales: $6.4 Million
Number Employees: 20-49
Square Footage: 20000

5577 **Harbor Spice**
100 Industry Ln
Forest Hill, MD 21050-1663
410-893-9500
Fax: 410-893-9502 www.harborspice.com
Spices
Manager: Dan Sanchuck
Estimated Sales: $1-2.5 000,000
Number Employees: 10-19

5578 **Harbor Sweets**
85 Leavitt St
Palmer Cove
Salem, MA 01970-5599
978-745-7648
Fax: 978-741-7811 800-243-2115
info@harborsweets.com www.harborsweets.com
Gift chocolates including wedding favors, perennial sweets, classics, dark horse collection, hunt collection, sweet treats, easter and spring gifts, custom chocolates and sugar-free
Owner: Phyllis Le Blanc
phyllis@harborsweets.com
Estimated Sales: $5.6 Million
Number Employees: 100-249
Square Footage: 76000
Brands:
Dark Horse Chocolates
Marblehead Mints
Perennial Sweets
Sweet Shells
Sweet Sloops
Topiary Toffee

5579 **Harbor Winery**
610 Harbor Blvd
West Sacramento, CA 95691
916-371-6776
Wines
Owner: Charles Myers
Estimated Sales: Less than $100,000
Number Employees: 1-4
Brands:
Harbor

5580 **Harbour Lobster Ltd**
5583 Hwy 3
P.O. Box 69
Shag Harbour, NS B0W 3B0
Canada
902-723-2500
Fax: 902-723-2568
Lobster and salted groundfish
President: Wayne Banks
Year Founded: 1972
Number Employees: 5-9
Type of Packaging: Bulk

5581 **Hard Eight Nutrition LLC**
7511 Eastgate Rd
Henderson, NV 89011
702-425-7638
www.bulksupplements.com
Dietary supplements, food ingredients and botanical extracts
CEO: Kevin Baronowsky
Type of Packaging: Consumer, Bulk

5582 **Hard-E Foods**
3228 N Broadway
St Louis, MO 63147-3515
314-533-2211
Fax: 314-533-2656 www.hardefoods.com
Hard cooked and deviled egg products; fresh cut vegetables
President/CEO: Judy Rutz
jrutz@hardefoods.com
Plant Manager: Larry Rutz
Estimated Sales: $2 Million
Number Employees: 20-49
Square Footage: 100000
Type of Packaging: Consumer, Food Service, Private Label

Brands:
Hard-E Foods

5583 **Hardscrabble Enterprises**
PO Box 1124
Franklin, WV 26807-1124
304-358-2921
Mushrooms
President: Paul Goland
Estimated Sales: Under $500,000
Number Employees: 1-4
Square Footage: 7000
Type of Packaging: Consumer, Food Service, Bulk
Brands:
American Shiitake
Hen-Of-The-Woods

5584 **Hardy Farms**
1659 Eastman Hwy
Hawkinsville, GA 31036-5913
478-783-3044
Fax: 478-783-0606 888-368-6887
info@hardyfarmspeanuts.com
www.hardyfarmspeanuts.com
Fresh green and boiled peanuts
President: Alex Hardy
hardyfarms@cstel.net
Estimated Sales: $1,000,000
Number Employees: 10-19
Number of Brands: 1
Number of Products: 3
Square Footage: 100000
Type of Packaging: Consumer, Food Service, Bulk

5585 **Harford Glen Water**
PO Box 214
Harford, NY 00001-2838
607-844-8351
Fax: 607-844-8351 866-844-8351
www.harfordglenwater.com
Natural spring water
President/CEO: Edmund McHale
CFO/VP: Lura McHale
Number Employees: 6
Number of Brands: 2
Number of Products: 5
Square Footage: 6000
Type of Packaging: Food Service, Private Label

5586 **Hari Om Farms**
8416 Shelbyville Hwy
Eagleville, TN 37060-9603
615-368-7778
Fax: 615-368-7650
Herbs and lettuce
Manager: Pedro Lopez
Estimated Sales: $1-2,500,000
Number Employees: 1-4
Square Footage: 120000
Type of Packaging: Consumer, Food Service, Bulk
Brands:
H2o
Hari Om Farms

5587 **Haribo of America**
1825 Woodlawn Dr # 204
Baltimore, MD 21207-4045
847-260-0580
info-us@haribo.com
www.haribo.com
Gummi and licorice candy products.
Vice President, Customer Marketing: Scott Miller
Sales Finance Manager: Lacy Cortez
Human Resources Coordinator: Lourdes Vazquez
Supply Chain Manager: Robert Coffey
Estimated Sales: $5-10,000,000
Number Employees: 51-200
Brands:
Haribo

5588 **Haring Catfish**
681 Pete Haring Rd
Wisner, LA 71378
318-724-6133
800-467-3474
info@haringcatfish.com www.haringcatfish.com
Catfish products
President/CEO: Carl Haring
Financial Manager: Josie King
Contact: Andrea Haring
andrea@haringcatfish.com
Purchaser: Hannah Harring Sharp
Estimated Sales: $275-300,000,000
Number Employees: 275-499
Parent Co: Wisener Minnow Hatchery Inc.

5589 **Harker's Distribution**
801 6th St SW
Le Mars, IA 51031
712-546-8171
Fax: 712-536-3159 800-798-7700
Frozen foods, including meats, poultry and seafood
President: Ron Geiger
CEO: Jim Harker
Sr. VP Sales/Marketing: Stan Dickman
Contact: Dick Blackwell
dblackwell@harkers.com
Purchasing Agent: Kevin Regan
Number Employees: 100-249
Other Locations:
Harker's Distribution
Denver CO

5590 **Harlan Bakeries**
7597 E US Highway 36
Avon, IN 46123
317-272-3600
800-435-2738
www.harlanbakeries.com
Bagels and other bakery products
President & Founder: Hugh Harlan
CFO: John Menne
Executive VP, Sales & Marketing: Joseph Latouf
Year Founded: 1991
Estimated Sales: $92 Million
Number Employees: 1,000-4,999
Number of Brands: 5
Square Footage: 2224
Brands:
Bagel King
Bigger Better
Giant Gourmet
Harlan Bakeries
World's Best

5591 **Harlin Fruit Co**
602 N 17th St
Monett, MO 65708-9178
417-235-7370
Fax: 417-235-7316
Fresh fruits and vegetables
Owner: Jerry Sutton
President: Dennis Hughes
Estimated Sales: $1-2.5 Million
Number Employees: 10-19
Type of Packaging: Consumer, Bulk
Brands:
Harlin Fruit

5592 **Harlon's LA Fish**
606 Short St
Kenner, LA 70062-7157
504-467-3809
Fax: 504-466-1503 www.laseafood.com
Seafood
Owner: Harlon Pearce
nolrah@aol.com
Estimated Sales: $10-20 Million
Number Employees: 10-19

5593 **Harlow House Company**
PO Box 12018
Atlanta, GA 30355
404-325-1270
Fax: 678-560-8355
Confectionery
President: David Swain
Estimated Sales: Less than $500,000
Number Employees: 4
Type of Packaging: Consumer, Bulk

5594 **Harmless Harvest**
200 Green St
Suite 1
San Francisco, CA 94111
www.harmlessharvest.com
Coconut water and pro-biotics
Type of Packaging: Consumer
Brands:
HARMLESS HARVEST

5595 **Harmon's Original Clam Cakes**
PO Box 1113
Kennebunkport, ME 04046-1113
207-967-4100
Fax: 207-967-1008 steve@harmonsclamcakes.com
www.harmonsclamcakes.com
Clam Cakes
Owner: Steven Liautaud

5596 **Harmony Bay Coffee**
25 Commerce Way # 5
North Andover, MA 01845-1002
978-557-0131
Fax: 978-557-0131 800-514-3663
www.harmonybaycoffee.com
Coffee
President/CEO: Michael Sullivan
VP of Marketing: Stephan Liff
Operations Manager: John Sullivan
Estimated Sales: Less Than $500,000
Number Employees: 5-9
Type of Packaging: Private Label
Brands:
Benley's Irish Creme
Harmony Bay

5597 **Harmony Cellars**
3255 Harmony Valley Rd
Harmony, CA 93435-5000
805-927-1625
Fax: 805-927-0256 800-432-9239
Wines
Co-Owner/Winemaker: Charles Mulligan
info@harmonycellars.com
Co-Owner/Business Manager: Kim Mulligan
Estimated Sales: $500,000-$1,000,000
Number Employees: 10-19
Brands:
Harmony Cellars

5598 **Harner Farms**
2191 Whitehall Road
State College, PA 16801
814-237-7919
Produce, including apples, cherries, plums and vegetables
Owner: Daniel Harner
Co-Owner: Pam Harner
Estimated Sales: $220,000
Number Employees: 4
Type of Packaging: Consumer, Food Service

5599 **Harney & Sons Tea Co.**
5723 Route 22
Millerton, NY 12546-6500
518-789-2100
Fax: 518-789-2100 800-832-8463
ht@harneyteas.com www.harney.com
Teas
President: John Harney
masterteablender@harneyteas.com
Marketing: Lisa Prindle
Sales: Michael Harney
Manager: Paul Harney
Purchasing: Elvira Cardenos
Year Founded: 1983
Estimated Sales: $2.5-5 Million
Number Employees: 200
Square Footage: 90000
Type of Packaging: Consumer, Food Service, Private Label, Bulk
Brands:
Harney & Sons

5600 **Harold Food Company**
11949 Steele Creek Road
Charlotte, NC 28273
704-588-8061
Fax: 704-588-4636
Frozen fruit cobblers, salads, spreads, chili and barbecue products; Dry, paper, frozen, fresh and refrigerated products
Marketing Director: Tom Taylor
General Manager: Butch Summey
Estimated Sales: $20-50 Million
Number Employees: 50-99
Square Footage: 46500
Type of Packaging: Food Service, Private Label, Bulk
Brands:
Harold Food Co.

5601 **Harold L King & Co Inc**
1420 Stafford St # 2
Redwood City, CA 94063-1077
650-368-2233
Fax: 650-368-3547 888-368-2233
kingcoffee@aol.com www.king-coffee.com
Coffee

President & CEO: Robert King
Secretary/Treasurer, CFO: John King
Vice President: Tim Kallok
Traffic Manager: Chris King
Year Founded: 1958
Estimated Sales: $25 Million
Number Employees: 5-9
Type of Packaging: Consumer

5602 **Harper's Country Hams**
2955 US Highway 51 S
PO Box 122
Clinton, KY 42031-8644
270-653-2081
Fax: 270-653-2409 888-427-7377
Country hams, bacon, and sausage
President: Betty Ellegood
betty@hamtastic.com
Treasurer: Doris Harper
Vice President: Brian Harper
Plant Manager: John Mcauliffe
Purchasing Manager: Brant Dublin
Year Founded: 1952
Estimated Sales: $20-50 Million
Number Employees: 100-249

5603 **Harpers Seafood Market**
526 W Jackson St
Thomasville, GA 31792-5903
229-226-7525
Fax: 229-228-6446
Oysters
President: Junior Harper
Estimated Sales: $10-20,000,000
Number Employees: 50-99
Type of Packaging: Consumer, Food Service
Brands:
Harper Seafood

5604 **Harpersfield Vineyard**
6387 State Route 307 West
Geneva, OH 44041
440-466-4739
info2@harpersfield.com
www.harpersfield.com
Wines
Manager: Adolf Ribic
Co-Owner: Wesley Gerlosky
Contact: Patricia Ribic
zzelda98@aol.com
Estimated Sales: $1-4.9,000,000
Number Employees: 1-4
Type of Packaging: Private Label

5605 **Harpo's**
477 Kapahulu Avenue
Honolulu, HI 96815
808-735-6456
Fax: 808-735-6456 alohaharpos@hawaii.rr.com
www.harposdressings.com
Gourmet salad dressings, marinades, and pizza
Contact: Mike Trombetta
alohaharpos@hawaii.rr.com
Manager: Ingrid Larsson
Number Employees: 1-4

5606 **Harpoon Brewery**
306 Northern Ave # 2
Boston, MA 02210-2367
617-574-9551
800-427-7666
www.harpoonbrewery.com
Malt beverages
CEO: David Altrich
altrichanglers@gmail.com
Founder/CEO: Dan Kenary
Estimated Sales: $34 Million
Number Employees: 100-249
Number of Brands: 3
Brands:
Harpoon
Pickwick
U.F.O.

5607 **Harrington's of Vermont**
210 E Main Rd
PO Box 288
Richmond, VT 05477
Fax: 802-434-3166 info@harringtonham.com
www.harringtonham.com
Smoked meats, cheese, maple syrup, seafood, sweets & snacks, condiments and cakes and pastries.
Owner/Chairman: Peter Klinkenberg
Director: John Balczuk
balczuk@harringtonham.com
CFO: R Klinkenberg
Marketing: Carol Wiseley
Year Founded: 1873
Estimated Sales: $20-50 Million
Number Employees: 10

5608 **Harris Crab House**
433 Kent Narrow Way N
Grasonville, MD 21638-1307
410-827-9500
Fax: 410-827-9057 www.harrisseafoodco.com
Crabs and oysters
Chairman: William Jerry Harris
Vice President: Art Oertel
Estimated Sales: $5-10 Million
Number Employees: 50-99
Type of Packaging: Consumer
Brands:
Bay Shore

5609 **Harris Farms Inc**
27366 W Oakland Ave
Coalinga, CA 93210-9627
559-884-2859
Fax: 559-884-2855 800-311-6211
info@harrisfarms.com www.harrisfarms.com
Tomatoes, onions, melons, almonds, bell peppers and garlic
President & Chairman: John C. Harris
Senior VP: Donald Devine
Office Manager: Janie Davis
Estimated Sales: $5-10 Million
Number Employees: 5-9
Type of Packaging: Consumer, Food Service, Private Label, Bulk
Brands:
Harris Farms
Harris Fresh
Harris Ranch

5610 **Harris Moran Seed Co**
555 Codoni Ave
Modesto, CA 95357-0507
209-579-7333
Fax: 209-527-5312
Vegetable seeds
President: Matthew Johnston
m.johnston@hmclause.com
CEO: Bruno Carette
VP Research: Jeff McElroy
Marketing Director: Bernie Hamel
US/Canada Sales Director: Dan Bailey
VP Of Production & Operations: Dennis Choate
Purchasing Agent: Maxine Corbett
Estimated Sales: $10-20 Million
Number Employees: 100-249
Parent Co: Groupe Limagrain
Brands:
Niagra Seed

5611 **Harris Ranch Beef Co**
16277 S McCall Ave
Selma, CA 93662-9458
559-896-3081
Fax: 559-896-3095 800-742-1955
www.harrisranchbeef.com
Beef products
Chairman: David Wood
Chairman of the Board: John Harris
Chief Financial Officer: Doug Sariss
Estimated Sales: $85 Thousand
Number Employees: 500-999
Number of Brands: 1
Square Footage: 17190
Parent Co: Harris Farms, Inc.
Type of Packaging: Consumer, Food Service, Private Label, Bulk
Brands:
Harris Ranch

5612 **Harris Tea Company**
44 New Albany Road
Moorestown, NJ 08057
856-793-0290
info@HarrisTea.com
www.harristea.com
Teas.
President/CEO: Kevin Shah
Estimated Sales: $5-10 Million
Number Employees: 10-19
Parent Co: Harris Freeman Enterprise
Type of Packaging: Food Service, Private Label
Brands:
BIG TEA
Dorset Tea
Newman's Own Organic
Red Rose
Salada
Southern Breeze™
Tea India ®

5613 **Harrisburg Dairies Inc**
2001 Herr St
PO Box 2001
Harrisburg, PA 17103-1624
717-233-8701
Fax: 717-231-4584 800-692-7429
sales@harrisburgdairies.com
www.harrisburgdairies.com
Dairy products
President & CEO: Fred Dewey
CMO: Matt Zehring
mzehring@harrisburgdairies.com
VP & CFO: Betsy Albright
VP & COO: Matt Zehring
Quality Control Manager: Rob Madigan
Sales Director: Jim Okum
Plant Manager: Miles Zehring
Number Employees: 100-249
Type of Packaging: Consumer
Brands:
Harrisburg Dairies

5614 **Harrison Napa Valley**
1443 Silverado Trail
Saint Helena, CA 94574
707-963-8762
Fax: 707-963-8762 www.whwines.com
Wines
Owner/Winemaker: Lyndsey Harrison
Tasting Room & Wine Club: Shelly Zanoli
Manager: Rob Monaghan
Winemaker: Jim McMahon
Estimated Sales: Less than $500,000
Number Employees: 1-4
Type of Packaging: Private Label
Brands:
Harrison

5615 **Harry & David**
2500 S Pacific Hwy
Medford, OR 97501-8724
541-864-2121
Fax: 541-864-2194 877-322-1200
service@harryanddavid.com
Fruit; beef steaks, ham, turkey; frozen truffles, cakes, cheesecakes, cookies and cinnamon rolls
President/CEO: Bill Williams
CAO: Judy Gifford
jgifford@harryanddavid.com
EVP Sales/Marketing: Cathy Fultineer
EVP Operations: Peter Kratz
Number Employees: 500-999
Parent Co: Bear Creek Corporation
Type of Packaging: Consumer, Food Service
Brands:
Harry & David

5616 **Harry London Candies Inc**
2457 W. North Avenue
Melrose Park, IL 60160
800-333-3629
customerservice@fanniemay.com
www.fanniemay.com
Chocolate truffles
President: Terry Mitchell
Chief Financial Officer: Matthew Anderson
Contact: Randall Dominowski
randalld@harrylondon.com
Estimated Sales: $20-49.9 Million
Number Employees: 100-249
Parent Co: Fannie May
Brands:
Harry London Chocolates
Heartland Chocolates

5617 **Harry's Cafe**
3621 Route 103
Mount Holly, VT 05758
802-259-2996
www.harryscafe.com
Sauces
Owner/Chef: Trip Pearce
Estimated Sales: $300,000-500,000
Number Employees: 5-9

5618 **Hart Winery**
41300 Avenida Biona
Temecula, CA 92591-5014
951-676-6300
Fax: 951-676-6300 877-638-8788
www.vinhart.com
Wines
Owner/Winemaker: Joe Hart
Owner/CEO: Nancy Hart
Winemaker: Bill Hart
Estimated Sales: $1-2.5 Million
Number Employees: 5-9
Square Footage: 3
Type of Packaging: Private Label
Brands:
Hart Winery

5619 **Hartford Family Winery**
8075 Martinelli Rd
Forestville, CA 95436-9255
707-887-8030
Fax: 707-887-7785 www.hartfordwines.com
Wines
General Manager, Winemaker: Jeff Stewart
Consumer Direct Sales Manager: Becky Craig
Hospitality Director: Melissa Cook
Estimated Sales: $5-10,000,000
Number Employees: 5-9
Other Locations:
Healdsburg Tasting Room & Salon
Healdsburg CA
Brands:
Hartford
Hartford Court

5620 **Harting's Bakery**
1212 Readings Rd
Bowmansville, PA 17507-0220
717-445-5644
Fax: 717-445-4818
Doughnuts and buns
President/CEO: Jocelyn Heft
COO: Thomas Lester
Plant Manager: William Burkhart
Estimated Sales: $1-2,500,000
Number Employees: 20-49

5621 **Hartley's Potato Chip Co**
2157 Back Maitland Rd
Lewistown, PA 17044-7311
717-248-0526
Fax: 717-248-3512
hartleyspotatochips@gmail.com
www.hartleyspotatochips.com
Potato chips, pretzels, cheese curls
President: Dan Hartley
dhartley@harkers.com
Estimated Sales: $1 Million
Number Employees: 10-19
Square Footage: 13742
Type of Packaging: Consumer, Food Service

5622 **Hartog Rahal Foods**
35 Maple Street
Norwood, NJ 07648-2003
201-750-0500
Fax: 212-687-2659
Fruit juice concentrates, fruit purees, frozen fruits and flavoring ingredients
President: Jack Hartog Jr
VP: Randy Loewis
Estimated Sales: $10-20 000,000
Number Employees: 20-49
Parent Co: Hartog Rahal Foods

5623 **Hartselle Frozen Foods**
411 Main Street West
Hartselle, AL 35640-2421
256-773-7261
Fax: 709-722-1116
Frozen meats
President: Billy Wiley
Secretary/Treasurer: Sam Wiley
Vice President: Danny Wiley

5624 **Hartsville Oil Mill**
311 Washington St
Darlington, SC 29532-4755
843-393-1501
Fax: 843-395-2690
Cotton oil
President/ Owner: Edgar Lawton
cottonoil@aol.com
Year Founded: 1900
Estimated Sales: $20-50 Million
Number Employees: 50-99

5625 **Hartville Kitchen**
1015 Edison St NW # 2
Hartville, OH 44632-8510
330-877-9353
Fax: 330-877-2101 info@hartvillekitchen.com
www.hartvillekitchen.com
Salad dressings
President: Vernon Sommers
Vice President: Vernon Sommers Jr.
Marketing & Advertisement Assistant: Sylvia DeMarco
Estimated Sales: $5-10,000,000
Number Employees: 50-200

5626 **Hartville Locker Service**
119 Sunnyside St SW
Hartville, OH 44632-8933
330-877-9547
www.hartvilleoh.com
Beef processing
Owner: James Young
Estimated Sales: $2.5-5,000,000
Number Employees: 1-4

5627 **Harvard Seafood Company**
PO Box 208
Grand Bay, AL 36541-0208
251-865-0558
Fax: 251-865-2187
Seafood

5628 **Harvest Bakery**
101 Windsor Pl # A
Central Islip, NY 11722-3329
631-232-1709
Fax: 631-232-1711 info@harvestbakery.com
www.harvestbakery.com
Bread and pastries
President: Bob Marconti
info@harvestbakery.com
Estimated Sales: $1-2.5 Million appx.
Number Employees: 20-49
Type of Packaging: Consumer
Brands:
Harvest Bakery

5629 **Harvest Direct**
61Accord Park Drive
Norwell, MA 02061
865-539-6305
Fax: 865-523-3372 800-733-2106
info@harvestdirect.com www.harvestdirect.com
Meat and milk alternatives
President: Roger Kilburn
Marketing Director: Monty Kilburn
Contact: Simon George
simon@harvestdirect.com
Manager Wholesale Division: Mary Ellen Kilburn
Estimated Sales: $500,000-$1,000,000
Number Employees: 5-9
Type of Packaging: Private Label
Brands:
Protflan
Solait
Veggie Ribs

5630 **Harvest Food Products Co Inc**
710 Sandoval Way
Hayward, CA 94544-7111
510-675-0383
Fax: 510-675-0396
sales@harvestfoodproducts.com
Pot stickers, egg rolls, wontons, barbecue pork buns and tempura shrimp
President: Yvonne Cooks
yvonne@womenprisoners.org
Estimated Sales: $10-20 Million
Number Employees: 50-99
Square Footage: 34000
Type of Packaging: Consumer, Food Service, Private Label, Bulk
Brands:
Harvest Foods

5631 **Harvest Innovations**
1210 N 14th St
Indianola, IA 50125-1508
515-962-5063
info@harvest-innovations.com
www.harvest-innovations.com
Natural ingredients
President: Jim Boes
jim.boes@harvest-innovations.com
Director Of Research: Dr. Noel Rudie
Product Development & Quality Assurance: Regena Butler
VP Sales/Marketing: Nicole Tomba
Innovation and Sales: Giovanni Santi
Director Food Technology: Dr. Wilmot Wijeratne
Number Employees: 1-4

5632 **Harvest Manor Farms**
1475 US Hwy 62W
Princeton, KY 42445
319-841-4170
Fax: 319-841-4134 877-984-6639
www.hoodysnuts.com
Nuts and seeds
President & CEO: Joseph Patten
VP Finance & Administration: Kathy Davis
SVP Sales & Commodity Acquisition: John Runck
Industrial Sales Manager: Debbie Parenza
Number of Brands: 1
Parent Co: TreeHouse Foods, Inc.
Brands:
Hoody's

5633 **Harvest Select**
730 Energy Center Blvd.
Suite 1402-E
Northport, AL 35473
205-614-6400
Fax: 334-628-2122 800-816-7426
info@harvestselect.com www.harvestselect.com
Alabama catfish
President: Randy Rhodes
VP Operations: Bobby Collins
bobby@harvestselect.com
Quality Assurance Manager: Tammy Spencer
VP Sales: Joe Connor
VP Sales: Shane Gaut
Human Resources Manager: Brenda Cook
Production Manager: Robert Lee
Plant Manager: Chris Hill
Estimated Sales: $20-50 Million
Number Employees: 250-499

5634 **Harvest Time Foods**
3857 Emma Cannon Rd
Ayden, NC 28513-7413
252-746-6675
Fax: 252-746-3160 www.annesdumplings.com
Frozen dumplings
President: Bryan Grimes
VP: Wendy Grimes
Estimated Sales: $5-9.9 Million
Number Employees: 20-49
Square Footage: 34000
Type of Packaging: Consumer, Food Service
Brands:
Anne's Chicken Base
Anne's Dumpling Squares
Anne's Dumpling Strips
Anne's Flat Dumplings
Anne's Old Fashioned
Anne's Pot Pie Squares
Mac's Dumplings

5635 **Harvest Time Seafood Inc**
208 W Elina St
Abbeville, LA 70510-8239
337-893-9029
Fax: 337-898-0614
Fresh and frozen crabmeat
Owner: Kevin E Dartez
kevin@hts.glacoxmail.com
Estimated Sales: $5-10 Million
Number Employees: 20-49

5636 **Harvest Valley Bakery Inc**
348 Civic Rd
La Salle, IL 61301-9710
815-224-9030
Fax: 815-224-9033 www.harvestvalleybakery.com
Cookies, brownies and bar cookies
President: Nancy Norton
n.norton@harvestvalleybakery.com
Estimated Sales: $10-20,000,000
Number Employees: 20-49
Square Footage: 24000
Type of Packaging: Food Service, Private Label, Bulk

5637 **Harvest-Pac Products**
22131 Bloomfield Rd
Chatham, ON N7M 5J3
Canada
519-436-0446
Fax: 519-436-0319 sales@harvestpac.com
www.harvestpac.com
Canned pumpkin, dark red kidney beans, chick peas and crushed tomatoes
President: Dan O'Neill
Operations Manager: Roger Sterling
Type of Packaging: Food Service, Private Label
Brands:
Harvest-Pac
Mom's Choice

5638 **Harvin Choice Meats**
300 McCrays Mill Road
Sumter, SC 29151-0939
803-775-9367
Fax: 803-775-9369 800-849-6328
harvinmeats@ftc-i.net www.harvinmeats.com
Ham, turkey, sausage, bologna, and hotdogs
Owner: S A Harvin Jr
CEO: W Scott Harvin
Year Founded: 1933
Estimated Sales: $20-50 Million
Number Employees: 50-99

5639 **Has Beans Coffee & Tea Co**
1078 Humboldt Ave
Chico, CA 95928-5960
530-332-9645
Fax: 530-926-6503 800-427-2326
info@hasbeans.com www.hasbeans.com
Coffee and tea
President: William Vonk
wv@hasbeans.com
Estimated Sales: $1.62 Million
Number Employees: 1-4
Type of Packaging: Private Label

5640 **Hastings Co-Op Creamery-Dairy**
1701 Vermillion St
PO Box 217
Hastings, MN 55033-3164
651-437-9414
Fax: 651-437-3547 info@hastingscreamery.com
www.hastingscreamery.com
Milk
Manager: David Zwart
david@hastingscreamery.com
General Manager: John Cook
Year Founded: 1922
Estimated Sales: $20-50 Million
Number Employees: 20-49
Type of Packaging: Consumer, Private Label

5641 **Hastings Meat Supply**
202 W 12th St
PO Box 1167
Hastings, NE 68901-3967
402-463-9857
Fax: 402-463-7181
Meat
Owner: Gary Deal
gary@hastingsfoods.com
Director: Jeff Andreasen
Estimated Sales: $1-3 Million
Number Employees: 1-4
Type of Packaging: Consumer, Food Service, Bulk

5642 **Hatch Chile Company**
6300 Riverside Plaza Lane NW
Suite 100
Albuquerque, NM 87120
912-267-9909
www.hatchchileco.com
Chiles, chile powder and dip mix
Founder & President: Steve Dawson
Year Founded: 1987

5643 **Hatfield Quality Meats**
2700 Clemens Rd
P.O. Box 902
Hatfield, PA 19440
215-368-2500
Fax: 215-368-3018 800-743-1191
www.hatfieldqualitymeats.com
Fresh and frozen pork products.
President: Craig Edsill
CEO: Doug Clemens
SVP & CFO: Josh Rennells
Year Founded: 1895
Estimated Sales: $138.3 Million
Number Employees: 1,000-4,999
Square Footage: 850000
Parent Co: Clemens Food Group
Type of Packaging: Consumer, Food Service, Private Label
Other Locations:
Hatfield Quality Meats
Chester PA
Brands:
Beaver Falls
Butcher Wagon
Cvf
Chef Pleaser
Gold Ribbon
Hatfield
Medford
Olde Philadelphia
Prima Porta
Tender Plus

5644 **Hathaway Coffee Co Inc**
6210 S Archer Rd
Summit Argo, IL 60501-1721
708-458-7666
Fax: 708-458-7668 www.krinos.com
Coffee
President: Michael Corden
Secretary: Joyce Cordon
Number Employees: 1-4

5645 **Hausbeck Pickle Co**
1626 Hess Ave
Saginaw, MI 48601-3970
989-754-4721
Fax: 989-754-3105 866-754-4721
tim@hausbeck.com www.hausbeck.com
Relish and pickles
CEO: Tim Hausbeck
Treasurer: Richard Hausbeck
Sales Manager: John Schnepf
Estimated Sales: $17,500,000
Number Employees: 20-49
Square Footage: 90000
Type of Packaging: Consumer, Food Service

5646 **Hauser Chocolates**
59 Tom Harvey Rd
Westerly, RI 02891-3685
401-596-8866
Fax: 401-596-0020 888-599-8231
hauser@hauserchocolates.com
www.hauserchocolates.com
Chocolates
Owner: Ruedi Hauser
hauser@hauserchocolates.com
Estimated Sales: $2.5-5 Million
Number Employees: 10-19
Type of Packaging: Consumer

5647 **Hausman Foods LLC**
4261 Beacon St
Corpus Christi, TX 78405-3326
361-883-5521
Fax: 361-883-1003 www.hausmanfoods.com
Fresh and frozen beef
President/CEO: Steve R McClure, Sr.
CFO: Amy Seward
aseward@samhausman.com
Vice President/General Manager: Jerry Simpson
Quality Control Manager: Beryl Henry
Vice President/Cold Storage Manager: Amy Seward
Dry Purchasing: Paul des los Santos
Estimated Sales: $46 Million
Number Employees: 100-249
Type of Packaging: Consumer, Food Service, Bulk

5648 **Havana's Limited**
4420 Coquina Avenue
Titusville, FL 32780-6552
321-267-0513
Fax: 321-267-5340
Hot sauces, dry rubs, seasonings and BBQ sauces
President/CEO: Mark Webber
Vice President: Bruce Webber
Number of Brands: 1
Number of Products: 10
Square Footage: 5000
Type of Packaging: Consumer, Food Service, Private Label, Bulk
Brands:
Ace Bandito

5649 **Haven's Candies**
87 County Rd
Westbrook, ME 04092-3807
207-772-1557
Fax: 207-775-0086 800-639-6309
info@havenscandies.com www.havenscandies.com
Chocolates and other confectionary; custom chocolate molding available
Owner: Andy Charles
Marketing Director: Krista Viola
Production Manager: Arthur Dillon
Estimated Sales: $1-2.5 Million
Number Employees: 20-49
Square Footage: 24000
Type of Packaging: Consumer, Private Label, Bulk

5650 **Haven's Kitchen Sauces**
109 W 17th St
New York, NY 10011
212-929-7900
info@havenskitchen.com
havenskitchen.com
Sauces and dressings; honey; organic popcorn; granola; peanute butter; pancake mix; baking mixes
Owner: Alison Cayne
Operations Manager: Shell Hatke
Year Founded: 2012
Number Employees: 3
Type of Packaging: Food Service, Private Label

5651 **Havi Food Services Worldwide**
227 South Blvd
Oak Park, IL 60302-4711
708-445-1700
Fax: 630-351-9479
Breads, rolls, baked goods
CEO: Jeff Somers
Number Employees: 50-99

5652 **Havoc Maker Products**
121 Old Sachems Head Rd
Guilford, CT 06437-3120
203-453-4943
Fax: 203-453-4943 800-681-3909
Hot sauce, salsa, chili and hot sauce mixes, black bean dip, popcorn and bottled spices
Owner: Ernest Neri
Number Employees: 1-4
Square Footage: 500
Type of Packaging: Food Service, Private Label, Bulk
Other Locations:
Havoc Maker Products
Old Lyme CT
Brands:
Havoc Maker

5653 **Hawaii Candy Inc**
2928 Ualena St # 4
Honolulu, HI 96819-1937
808-836-8955
Fax: 808-839-4040 800-303-2507
website@hawaiicandy.com www.hawaiicandy.com
Confectionery items and snacks
President: Keith Ohta
info@hawaiicandy.com
Secretary: Richard Ohta
Marketing: Ron Vogel
Estimated Sales: $5-10 Million
Number Employees: 20-49
Square Footage: 33000
Type of Packaging: Consumer, Food Service, Private Label, Bulk
Brands:
Hawaiian Island Crisp
Hawaiian Island Crisp Cookies

5654 **Hawaii Coffee Company**
1555 Kalani St
Honolulu, HI 96817
808-847-3600
Fax: 800-972-0777 800-338-8353
www.hawaiicoffeecompany.com
Coffee
President: Jim Wayman
Chief Marketing Officer: Wenli Lin
National Sales Account Manager: Malia Delapenia
Estimated Sales: $9 000,000
Number Employees: 51-200
Number of Brands: 4
Brands:
Hawaii Coffee Company
Lion Coffee

Royal Kona Coffee
Tiger Tea

5655 **Hawaii International Seafood**
371 Aokea Place
PO Box 30486
Kailua, HI 96819-1828
808-839-5010
Fax: 808-833-0712 info@cryofresh.com
www.cryofresh.com
Fish and seafood
President: Bill Kowalski
Estimated Sales: $2,000,000
Number Employees: 5-9

5656 **Hawaii Star Bakery**
944 Akepo Ln
Suite 3
Honolulu, HI 96817
808-841-3602
Fax: 808-842-7941
Bakery products
Owner: Liane Small
Sales Executive: Kenneth Ticman
Estimated Sales: $10-20 Million
Number Employees: 20-49
Type of Packaging: Consumer, Food Service

5657 **Hawaiian Bagel**
753 Halekauwila Street
Honolulu, HI 96813-5318
808-596-0638
Fax: 808-593-2434 hibagel@gte.net
Bagels and breads
President: Steve Gelson
Estimated Sales: $5-9.9,000,000
Number Employees: 20-49
Parent Co: Fch Enterprises, Inc.

5658 **(HQ)Hawaiian Host Inc**
500 Alakawa St
Suite 111
Honolulu, HI 96817-4576
808-848-0500
Fax: 808-845-7466 888-414-4678
info@hawaiianhost.com www.hawaiianhost.com
Chocolates and specialty chocolate products; tea, cofee and cookies
President: Keith Sakamato
CEO: Dennis Teranishi
Vice President Sales: Tad Teraizumi
Year Founded: 1927
Estimated Sales: $20-50 Million
Number Employees: 100-249

5659 **Hawaiian Isles Kona Coffee Co**
2839 Mokumoa St
Honolulu, HI 96819-4402
808-833-2244
Fax: 808-839-0277 800-657-7716
mailorder@hawaiianisles.com
www.hawaiianisles.com
Coffee
President: Michael Boulware
Owner: Glenn Boulware
Marketing: Sean Gano
Estimated Sales: $27.1 Million
Number Employees: 100-249
Number of Brands: 2
Brands:
Hawaii Coffee Roasters
Kona

5660 **Hawaiian King Candies**
550 Paiea St # 501
Honolulu, HI 96819-1837
808-833-0041
Fax: 808-839-7141 800-570-1902
dniiro@lava.net
Macadamia nut snacks
President: David Niiro
Contact: Marvin Sialco
info@hawaiianking.com
Estimated Sales: $10-24.9,000,000
Number Employees: 50-99
Type of Packaging: Consumer, Food Service, Private Label
Brands:
America
Enjoying Las Vegas
Enjoying San Francisco
Favorites of Hawaii
Hawaiian Delight
Hawaiian Joys
Hawaiian King
Hawaiian Majesty
New York Club
Passport
San Francisco Bay Traders
That's Hollywood
Usa

5661 **Hawaiian Natural Water Company**
98-746 Kuahao Pl Ste F
Pearl City, HI 96782
808-483-0520
Fax: 808-483-0536 hisprings@aol.com
www.hawaiianspring.com
Bottled spring water
President/CEO: Marcus Bender
CFO: Willard D Irwin
CFO: David Leaha
CEO: Tom Van Dixhorn
Executive VP Marketing: Ray Riss
Contact: Joan Teraizumi
k.crumley@unm.edu
Operations Manager: Tony Persson
Number Employees: 5-9
Type of Packaging: Private Label
Brands:
Hawaiian Natural Water

5662 **Hawaiian Sun Products**
259 Sand Island Access Rd
Honolulu, HI 96819-2227
808-845-3211
Fax: 808-842-0532
customerservice@hawaiiansunproducts.com
www.hawaiiansunproducts.com
Tropical fruit juices; Macadamia nut candy and spreads
President: Burt K Okura
Vice President: Kent Kurihara
Year Founded: 1952
Estimated Sales: $20-50 Million
Number Employees: 50-99
Brands:
Hawaiian Sun
Pokka

5663 **(HQ)Hawkhaven Greenhouse International**
W9554 Blackhawk Ct.
Wautoma, WI 54982
920-540-3536
Fax: 920-787-4295 800-745-4295
verdegrass@gmail.com www.hawkhaven.com
Wheat grass
President/Owner: Timothy Paegelow
Estimated Sales: Under $300,000
Number Employees: 1-4
Square Footage: 10000
Type of Packaging: Consumer
Brands:
Grower's Pack
Hawkhaven
Verdegrass

5664 **Hawkins Farm**
20015 116th St
Bristol, WI 53104-9232
262-857-2616
Fax: 506-755-6241
Corn and soybeans
Owner: Steve Hawkins
hawkinss@ih.k12.oh.us
Estimated Sales: Less Than $500,000
Number Employees: 5-9

5665 **Hawkins Inc**
2381 Rosegate
Roseville, MN 55113
800-328-5460
customer.service@hawkinsinc.com
www.hawkinsinc.com
Ingredients for meat, poultry, seafood, dairy and beverage industries
President & CEO: Patrick Hawkins
patrick.hawkins@hawkinsinc.com
CFO, VP & Treasurer: Jeffrey Oldenkamp
General Counsel, VP & Secretary: Richard Erstad
VP of Operations: Drew Grahek
VP of Purchasing, Logistics, and Sales: Theresa Moran
Year Founded: 1938
Estimated Sales: $345 Million
Number Employees: 500-999
Number of Brands: 3
Type of Packaging: Private Label
Brands:
e(Lm)inate®
Ultralac
Ultra-Pure Bestate

5666 **Hawthorne Valley Farm**
327 County Route 21C
Ghent, NY 12075-1927
518-672-7500
Fax: 518-672-4887 info@hawthornevalleyfarm.org
Value-added products, including yogurt, cheese, sauerkraut and baked goods.
Executive Director: Martin Ping
Marketing: Karen Press
Farm Tours: Rachel Schneider
Manager: John Kidney
john@hawthornevalleyfarm.org
Estimated Sales: $2.5-5,000,000
Number Employees: 100-249
Type of Packaging: Private Label
Brands:
Hawthorne Valley Farm

5667 **Hayashibara International Inc.**
546 Fifth Avenue
16th Floor
New York, NY 10036-5000
212-703-1340
Fax: 212-398-0687
Carbohydrate-based ingredients
Director- North America: Tomonari Mozumi
VP: Alan Richards
Sales: Akihiro Hashino
Number Employees: 10
Type of Packaging: Bulk

5668 **Haydel's Bakery**
4037 Jefferson Hwy
New Orleans, LA 70121-1643
504-837-0190
Fax: 504-837-5512 800-442-1342
www.haydelbakery.com
Specialty cakes
Owner: David Haydel
david.haydel@haydelbakery.com
Estimated Sales: $1-2,500,000
Number Employees: 20-49

5669 **Haydenergy Health**
9 Riva Court
Valley Stream, NY 11581
212-888-1008
Fax: 212-246-9344 800-255-1660
www.naura.com
Health food products
President: Naura Hayden
Vice President: Nancy Leonard
Estimated Sales: $2.5-5 Million
Number Employees: 1-4
Number of Brands: 1
Number of Products: 3
Square Footage: 8000
Type of Packaging: Consumer
Brands:
Dynamite Energy Shake
Dynamite Vites

5670 **Hazel Creek Orchards**
227 Smiling Apple Dr
Mt Airy, GA 30563-2714
706-754-4899
Fax: 706-754-1524
Apples, apple juice and fruit ciders
Owner: Horace Yearwood
Estimated Sales: $1-2.5 Million
Number Employees: 1-4
Square Footage: 16800
Type of Packaging: Consumer, Bulk
Brands:
Hazel Creek

5671 **Hazelnut Growers Of Oregon**
401 N 26th Ave
Cornelius, OR 97113-8510
503-648-4176
Fax: 503-648-9515 800-273-4676
nutsales@hazelnut.com www.hazelnut.com
Hazelnuts

President & CEO: Tim Ramsey
Quality Control: Don Marshall
VP Sales & Marketing: Patrick Gabrish
Customer Service & Logistics Coordinator: Claudia Arreola
VP Operations: Dick Vanderschuere
Production Manager: Emilio Briones
Plant Manager: Ken Guinn
Purchasing Manager: Mike Sook
Estimated Sales: $32 Million
Number Employees: 50-99
Type of Packaging: Consumer, Bulk
Brands:
Oregan Orchard

5672 **Hazle Park Quality Meats**
260 Washington Ave
West Hazleton, PA 18202
570-455-7571
Fax: 570-455-6030 800-238-4331
www.hazlepark.com
Processed meats
CEO: Gary Kreisel
Type of Packaging: Consumer, Food Service, Private Label, Bulk
Brands:
Hazle

5673 **Hazlitt 1852 Vineyards**
5712 Route 414
Hector, NY 14841
607-546-9463
Fax: 607-546-5712 888-750-0494
info@hazlitt1852.com hazlitt1852.com
Wines
CEO & Owner: Doug Hazlitt
Marketing Manager: Stephanie Jarvis
Human Resources Manager: Justin Thomas
Estimated Sales: $5-10,000,000
Number Employees: 50-200
Number of Brands: 2
Other Locations:
Hazlitt's Red Cat Cellars
Naples NY
Brands:
Hazlitt

5674 **Hazy Grove Nuts**
PO Box 25753
Portland, OR 97298-0753
503-670-8344
Fax: 503-968-2111 800-574-6887
lobbok7@gte.net
Hazelnuts.
President: Karen Lobb
Number Employees: 5—9
Type of Packaging: Private Label

5675 **Head Country**
2116 N Ash St
Ponca City, OK 74601-1105
580-762-1227
Fax: 580-765-8867 888-762-1227
www.headcountry.com
BBQ sauces, seasonings and marinades.
President: Brian Brassfield
bbrassfield@headcountry.com
Vice President, Co-Owner: Paul Schatte
Quality Control: Alan Slater
Marketing: Paul Schatte
Sales: Paul Schatte
Office Manager, Accounting: Linda Groth
Estimated Sales: Less Than $500,000
Number Employees: 10-19
Number of Brands: 1
Number of Products: 6
Type of Packaging: Consumer, Food Service, Private Label, Bulk
Brands:
Head Country

5676 **Healing Home Foods**
73 Westchester Ave
P.O. Box 390
Pound Ridge, NY 10576
914-764-1303
info@healinghomefoods.com
www.healinghomefoods.com
Organic, vegan, gluten-free and GMO-free granolas, crackers, chips, nuts, treats, and other snacks
Founder: Shelley Schulz
Wholesale Inquiries: John Schulz

5677 **Healing Solutions**
4703 W Brill St
Suite 101
Phoenix, AZ 85043
800-819-4098
support@healingsolutions.com
healingsolutions.com
Essential oils
Exec. VP, Sales & Marketing: Jason Kern
Year Founded: 2014
Number Employees: 51-200

5678 **Health & Nutrition Systems International**
6615 Boyntn Bch Blvd
Suite 117
Boynton Beach, FL 33437-3526
561-433-0733
Fax: 888-478-8467 info@hnsglobal.com
Diet products
President: Christopher Tisi
Controller: Al Dugan
Marketing Director: Steven Sarafian
Product Development/Sales: Jamie Heithoff
Human Resources/Director Operations: Mona Lalia
Graphic Design: Derek Lopez
Graphic Design: Cathy Card
Shipping/Receiving: Tonya Davis
Number Employees: 10-19

5679 **Health & Wholeness Store**
104 N Main St
Fairfield, IA 52556-2802
641-472-6274
Fax: 719-260-7400 800-255-8332
www.healthandwholenessllc.com
Herbs and herbal products
President: Prakash Srivastava
Senior VP: Steven Barthe
Marketing Director: Russ Guest
Public Relations: Marsha Bonne
Operations Manager: Kevin Olson
Plant Manager: Kishore Nareundkar
Estimated Sales: Less Than $500,000
Number Employees: 1-4
Number of Brands: 4
Number of Products: 600
Square Footage: 188000
Type of Packaging: Consumer
Brands:
Ayurveda
Clarified Butter
Maharishi
Yata, Pilta, Kapha Teas

5680 **Health Concerns**
8001 Capwell Dr
Oakland, CA 94621-2107
510-957-5118
Fax: 510-639-9140 800-233-9355
info@healthconcerns.com
Chinese herbs, medicinal mushrooms and energy tonics
President: Laurie Dearborn
laurie@healthconcerns.com
Estimated Sales: $3-5 Million
Number Employees: 10-19
Square Footage: 12000
Type of Packaging: Consumer
Brands:
Health Concerns

5681 **Health Garden USA**
750 Chestnut Ridge Rd
Suite 225
Spring Valley, NY 10977
845-877-7090
Fax: 845-364-6713 info@healthgardenusa.com
www.healthgardenusa.com
Sugar substitutes
Founder: Joel Phillip

5682 **Health Plus**
13837 Magnolia Ave
Chino, CA 91710-7028
909-627-9393
Fax: 909-591-7659 800-822-6225
order_desk@healthplusinc.com
www.healthplusinc.com
Psyllium and nutritional herbs, tablets and capsules
President: Rita Mediratta
ritam@healthplusinc.com
President: Pat Mediratta
Estimated Sales: $1-2.5 Million
Number Employees: 20-49
Square Footage: 34000
Type of Packaging: Bulk
Brands:
Adrenal Cleanse
Astazanthin
Az-One
Blood Cleanse
Brain Vita
Colon Cleanse
Ener Jet
Fireball Fat Burner
Heart Cleanse
Joint Cleanse
Kidney Cleanse
Liver Cleanse
Ora-Plus
Pat's Psyllium Slim
Prostate Cleanse
Shelly's Hair Care
Super Fat Burner

5683 **Health Products Corp**
1060 Nepperhan Ave
Yonkers, NY 10703-1432
914-423-2900
Fax: 914-963-6001 www.hpc7.com
Psyllium and nutritional herbs, tablets and capsules; contract packager of blending and filling powders
President: Joseph Lewin
zurion2@aol.com
Number Employees: 50-99
Brands:
Aspi-Cor
Khg-7
Lactalins
Malpotane
Tick Stop

5684 **Health Valley Company**
16100 Foothill Boulevard
Irwindale, CA 91706
626-334-3241
Fax: 626-334-0220 800-334-3204
www.healthvalley.com
Natural foods
President: Ben Brecher
CFO/Sr VP: Diane Beardsley
Number Employees: 250-499
Parent Co: Intrepid Food Holdings
Type of Packaging: Consumer, Food Service, Private Label, Bulk
Brands:
Health Valley

5685 **Health Warrior**
Richmond, VA 23230
804-381-5305
www.healthwarrior.com
Chia snack bars and protein powders
Co-Founder & CEO: Shane Emmett
Co-Founder: Dan Gluck
Co-Founder: Nick Morris

5686 **Health from the Sun**
1 Clock Tower
Suite 100
Maynard, MA 01754
781-276-0505
Fax: 781-276-7335 800-447-2229
www.healthfromthesun.com
Fatty acids and phytonutrients
Parent Co: Arkopharma
Brands:
Lean For Less

5687 **Health is Wealth Foods**
140 W Commercial Ave
Moonachie, NJ 7024
201-933-7474
Fax: 856-629-0378
Boxed, frozen and all natural foods; vegetarian and vegan items
President: Val Vasilief
Vice President: Jerry Colt
Estimated Sales: $5-10 Million
Number Employees: 5-9
Square Footage: 20000
Type of Packaging: Food Service, Private Label
Brands:
Health Is Wealth

5688 **Health-Ade LLC**
3347 Motor Ave
Suite 200
Los Angeles, CA 90034-9711
844-337-6368
info@health-ade.com
www.health-ade.com
Kombucha
Co-Founder: Vanessa Dew
Co-Founder and CEO: Daina Trout
Co-Founder and COO: Justin Trout
Year Founded: 2012

5689 **HealthBest**
133 Mata Way
Suite 101
San Marcos, CA 92069
760-752-5230
Fax: 760-752-1322 www.globalkaizen.com
Natural and organic beans, dried fruits, snack foods, grains, herbs, spices, seasonings, nuts, seeds, bee pollen, pasta, sugar-free candy
President: Jamie Hickerson
President: Laurence Hickerson
Director of Operations: Eric Pena
Production Manager: Armando Ramos
Estimated Sales: $3 Million
Number Employees: 20-49
Number of Brands: 2
Number of Products: 300
Square Footage: 80000
Parent Co: Nature's Best
Type of Packaging: Consumer, Private Label, Bulk
Brands:
Healthbest

5690 **Healthco Canada Enterprises**
PO Box 8249
Victoria, BC V8W 3R9
Canada
250-382-8384
Fax: 250-868-2195 877-468-2875
www.therebarstore.com
Organic nutrition bars

5691 **Healthee**
118 E St. Joseph St
Arcadia, CA 91006
626-574-1719
www.healtheeusa.com
Organic brown rice, fruit juices and turmeric drinks
Type of Packaging: Consumer
Brands:
healthee

5692 **Healthmate Products**
1510 Old Deerfield Rd Ste 103
Highland Park, IL 60035
847-579-1051
Fax: 847-579-1059 www.healthmateproducts.com
Papaya concentrates
President: Tim Burke
treedburke@gmail.com
CEO/ Manager of Public Relations: Celeste Burke
Estimated Sales: $1 Million
Number Employees: 1-4
Type of Packaging: Consumer, Food Service

5693 **Healthy Beverage LLC**
200 S Clinton St
Suite 100
Doylestown, PA 18901
Fax: 866-642-9179 800-295-1388
info@steaz.com steaz.com
Organic green tea
Co-Founder: Steven Kessler
Co-Founder: Eric Schnell
Year Founded: 2002
Estimated Sales: $4.5 Million
Number Employees: 8
Type of Packaging: Private Label
Brands:
Steaz

5694 **Healthy Food Brands LLC**
992 Bedford Ave
Brooklyn, NY 11205-4502
212-444-9909
www.hfbcandy.com
Candies and chocolates.
President: Sal Asaro
EVP: Russ Asaro
Estimated Sales: $30.6 Million
Number Employees: 1-4
Number of Brands: 2
Type of Packaging: Private Label
Brands:
Welch's
Simply Lite

5695 **Healthy Food Ingredients**
4666 Amber Valley Pkwy
Fargo, ND 58104
844-275-3443
www.hfifamily.com
Wheat, millet, durum, barley, sorghum, oat, rye, triticale, flax and ancient grains
President & CEO: Brad Hennrich
Estimated Sales: $50-100 Million
Number Employees: 20-49
Square Footage: 15000
Type of Packaging: Bulk

5696 **Healthy Grain Foods LLC**
4125 Yorkshire Ln
Northbrook, IL 60062-2915
847-272-5576
Fax: 847-272-5576
Cereals; research and development
President: Harold Zukerman
haroldzukerman@gmail.com
Estimated Sales: $1-2,500,000
Number Employees: 5-9

5697 **Healthy Life Brands LLC**
PO Box 812428
Wellesley, MA 02482
508-401-7040
Fax: 508-401-7430 www.eatveggiefries.com
Specialty fries made with a blend of vegetables, legumes, and potatoes
Co-Founder and CEO: David Peters
Co-Founder: Crista Peters
Brands:
Veggie Fries

5698 **Healthy N Fit International**
435 Yorktown Rd
Croton On Hudson, NY 10520-3703
914-271-6040
Fax: 914-271-6042 800-338-5200
Info@behealthynfit.com
www.behealthynfit.com/default.asp
Vitamins, minerals and food supplements; importer of herbs, nutraceuticals, ascorbic acid and nutritional raw materials; exporter of food and dietary supplements
CEO: Robert J Sepe
VP/CFO: Irene Sepe
Public Relations: Denise O'Neill
Estimated Sales: $7 Million appx.
Number Employees: 10-19
Number of Products: 1000
Square Footage: 160000
Type of Packaging: Consumer, Food Service, Private Label, Bulk
Brands:
Doctor's Nutriceuticals
Healthy'n Fit Nutritionals

5699 **Healthy Skoop**
2438 30th Street
Boulder, CO 80301
720-545-1753
healthyskoop.com
Protein powders and cookies
President/Owner: Robert Bennett
Marketing: Lauren Langtim
Sales: Bobby Macauley
Operations: Ned Brown
Type of Packaging: Consumer
Brands:
HEALTHY SKOOP

5700 **Healthy Times Baby Food**
San Diego, CA 92101
858-513-1550
Fax: 858-513-1533 hello@healthytimes.com
healthytimes.com
Organic baby food, baby cereal and milk formula.
President: Rondi Prescott
Estimated Sales: $5-10,000,000 appx.
Number Employees: 2-10

5701 **Heart Foods Company**
2235 E 38th St
Minneapolis, MN 55407-3083
612-724-5266
Fax: 612-724-5516 800-229-3663
Herbal cayenne formulas
Owner: Dick Quinn
Contact: Dixie Davidson
dharley-davidson@heartofdixiehd.com
Estimated Sales: $1-2.5 Million
Number Employees: 1-4
Number of Brands: 1
Number of Products: 13
Square Footage: 5000
Type of Packaging: Consumer

5702 **Heart to Heart Foods**
142 W 3200 N
Hyde Park, UT 84318
435-753-9602
Fax: 435-753-9605
Ice cream products
Owner: Craig Earl
Contact: Kirk Earl
ekirk@healthyheartmarket.com
Estimated Sales: $2.5-5,000,000
Number Employees: 10-19

5703 **Heartbreaking Dawns Artisan Foods**
PO Box 10877
Glendale, AZ 85318
646-957-3484
heartbreakingdawns.com
Manufacturer of hot sauce.
Co-Founder: Johnny McLaughlin
Co-Founder: Nicole McLaughlin

5704 **Hearthside Food Solutions**
3500 Lacey Rd
Suite 300
Downers Grove, IL 60515
630-967-3600
info@hearthsidefoods.com
www.hearthsidefoods.com
Nutrition and energy bars, cookies, crackers, snack foods, cereal and granola, and food packaging.
Chairman/CEO & Co-Founder: Rich Scalise
Senior VP/CFO: Fred Jasser
Senior VP Human Resources: Steve England
Year Founded: 2009
Number Employees: 5000-9999
Type of Packaging: Consumer, Private Label

5705 **Hearthstone Whole Grain Bakery**
4717 Meadow Lane
Bozeman, MT 59715-9631
406-586-1227
Fax: 406-586-1227 800-757-7919
Bakery
President: Gwen Phillips
Manager: Mavis Mason

5706 **Hearthy Foods**
2043 Imperial St
Los Angeles, CA 90021
213-372-5093
info@hearthyfoods.com
www.hearthyfoods.com
Gluten free desserts & baking flours
President: Riaz Surti
Year Founded: 2012

5707 **Heartland Brewery**
1430 Broadway
Suite 1513
New York, NY 10018
212-400-2300
Fax: 212-645-8306 info@heartlandbrewery.com
www.heartlandbrewery.com
Beers
CEO: John Bloostein
Marketing Director: Bonnie Bernier
Estimated Sales: $2.5-5,000,000
Number Employees: 50-99
Type of Packaging: Consumer, Food Service
Brands:
Heartland

5708 **Heartland Farms Dairy & Food Products, LLC**
3668 South Geyer Road
Suite 205
St. Louis, MO 63127
314-965-1110
Fax: 314-965-1118 888-633-6455
info@heartlandfarmsdairy.com
www.heartlandfarmsdairy.com
Dairy products
President: Tom Jacoby
Marketing Assistant: Pat Hittmeier
Sales of Dry Products: Tim Fann
Contact: Christine Anderson
canderson@heartlandfarmsdairy.com
Weights and Tests: Jenn Jacoby
Type of Packaging: Consumer, Bulk

5709 **Heartland Flax**
849 14th St SW
P.O. Box 777
Valley City, ND 58072
Fax: 701-845-2276 866-599-3529
info@heartlandflax.com www.heartlandflax.com
Flax ingredients
Director of Sales: Bob Larson
Technical Director: Bruce Livingood

5710 **Heartland Food Products**
1900 W 47th Place
Suite 302
Westwood, KS 66205
913-831-4446
Fax: 913-831-4004 866-571-0222
www.heartlandfoodproducts.com
Mashed potatoes
President: Bill Steeb
Founder: Mary Steeb
Contact: Tom Gray
tom.gray@heartlandfpg.com
Estimated Sales: Less than $500,000
Number Employees: 10-19
Type of Packaging: Bulk

5711 **Heartland Gourmet LLC**
52205 19th Street
Lincoln, NE 68512
402-423-1234
Fax: 402-423-4586 800-735-6828
www.heartlandgourmet.com
Organic, all natural and gluten free baking mixes; gluten free and gourmet frozen doughs
Sales & Product Development Manager: Susan Zink
Business Development Manager: Mark Zink
Estimated Sales: $2.3 Million
Number Employees: 20-49
Square Footage: 54000
Type of Packaging: Consumer, Private Label
Brands:
Wanda's

5712 **Heartland Ingredients LLC**
802 West College Street
Troy, MO 63379
Fax: 877-841-2067 800-557-2621
contactus@heartlandingredients.net
www.heartlandingredients.net
Ingredients, food and technical grade chemicals and colors, dairy products, meat products, sugar, artifical sweeteners, close dated finished products.

5713 **Heartland Mills Shipping**
124 N Hwy 167
Marienthal, KS 67863-6368
620-379-4467
Fax: 620-379-4459 800-232-8533
info@heartlandmill.com www.heartlandmill.com
Organic grains, flour, oat products and sunflower seeds
President: Larry Decker
VP: Mark Nightengale
Sales Executive: Carl Rosenlund
Manager: Carl Rosenlund
seanc@ekisticsinc.net
Estimated Sales: Less Than $500,000
Number Employees: 1-4
Square Footage: 28000
Type of Packaging: Food Service, Private Label, Bulk
Brands:
Heartland Mill

5714 **Heartland Strawberry Farm**
5111 Osage Rd
Waterloo, IA 50703-9390
319-232-3779
Fax: 888-757-7423 888-747-7423
berrypumpkinfarm@earthlink.net
Fruits and vegetables
Owner: Dave Myers
Number Employees: 1-4

5715 **Heartland Sweeteners**
14390 Clay Terrace Blvd
Suite 250
Carmel, IN 46032
317-566-9750
www.heartlandfpg.com
Coffee, coffee creamers and low-calorie sweeteners
Type of Packaging: Food Service
Other Locations:
Distribution Center
Indianapolis IN
Manufacturing
Indianapolis IN

5716 **Heartland Vinyards**
24945 Detroit Rd # G
Westlake, OH 44145-2554
440-871-0701
jwdover@aol.com
www.heartlandvineyards.com
Wines
Owner: Jerome M Welliver
jwdover@aol.com
Estimated Sales: $500-1,000,000 appx.
Number Employees: 5-9

5717 **Heartline Foods**
PO. Box 454
Westport, CT 06881-0454
203-222-0381
Fax: 203-226-6445
Paprika, beans, noodles, sauces, seasonings, pasta, soups and tapiocas.
President: Henry Ellett
Estimated Sales: $.5-1 million
Number Employees: 1-4
Brands:
China Bowl
Dinny Robb
Sinatra
Wye River

5718 **Hearttea Inc.**
195 Montague St
Suite 14F
Brooklyn, NY 11201
917-725-3164
info@heartoftea.com
Iced tea
Founder and President: Messi Gerami
Brands:
Heart of Tea

5719 **Hearty Naturals**
P.O.Box 3871
West McLean, VA 22103
513-443-2789
contactus@heartynaturals.com
heartynaturals.com
Coconut oil, ghee, moringa powder and coconut sugar.
Director: Amila Abeyseker
Year Founded: 1980
Estimated Sales: $3 Million
Number Employees: 40-50
Brands:
Hearty Naturals

5720 **Heaven Hill Distilleries Inc.**
1311 Gilkey Run Rd.
Bardstown, KY 40004
502-337-1000
Fax: 502-348-0162 www.heavenhill.com
Distilled spirits.
President: Max Shapira
Executive Vice President: Harry Shapira
Vice President, Human Resources: Debbie Morris
COO: Allan Latts
Year Founded: 1935
Estimated Sales: $193 Million
Number Employees: 250-499
Number of Brands: 34
Number of Products: 51
Type of Packaging: Consumer, Private Label, Bulk
Brands:
Admiral Nelson's Spiced Rum
Ansac Cognac
Bernheim Original Wheat Whiskey
Blackheart Premium Spiced Rum
Burnett's London Dry Gin
Burnett's Vodkas
Carolans Irish Cream Liqueur
Christian Brothers Brandies
Cinerator Hot Cinnamon Whiskey
Copa De Oro Coffee Liqueur
Coronet VSQ Brandy
Deep Eddy Vodkas
Domaine de Canton
Du Bouchett Liqueurs & Cordials
Dubonnet Apperitifs
Elijah Craig Bourbons
Evan Williams Bourbons
Fighting Cock Bourbon
Fulton's Harvest Cream Liqueur
Georgia Moon Corn Whiskey
Hnery Mckenna Single Barrel
HPNOTIQ
Irish Mist Liqueur
Larceny Bourbon
Lunazul Tequilas
Mellow Corn Whiskey
O'Mara's Irish Country Cream
Old Fitzgerald Bourbon
PAMA Pomegranate Liqueur
Parker's Heritage Collection
Pikesville Straight Rye Whiskey
Rittenhouse Straight Rye Whiskey
Sacred Bond
Two Fingers Tequilas

5721 **Heavenly Hemp Foods**
PO Box 1794
Nederland, CO 80466
303-938-0195
Fax: 303-443-1869 888-328-4367
Health foods
President: David Almquist
Marketing Director: Tom White
Operations Manager: Kathleen Chippi
Number Employees: 1
Brands:
Heaven Scent
Heaven Scent Windmill Cakes
Heaven Scent Butter
Heaven Scent Croutons

5722 **Heavenly Organics, LLC**
14300 E 125 Frontage Rd
Longmont, CO 80504
641-636-2095
info@heavenlyorganics.com
heavenlyorganics.com
Honey, whole cane sugar, chocolate honey candies
President: Wj Christopher
heavenlyorganics@yahoo.com
Chief Executive Officer/Founder: Amit Hooda
Operations Director: Jaison Lynch
Estimated Sales: A
Number Employees: 1-4

5723 **Heavenscent Edibles**
402 E 90th Street
New York, NY 10128-5119
212-369-0310
Fax: 212-369-0310
Brownies and holiday cookies

5724 **Hebert Candies**
574 Hartford Turnpike
Shrewsbury, MA 01545
508-842-5583
Fax: 508-842-3065 866-609-6533
info@herbertcandies.com www.hebertcandies.com
Kosher chocolate candies and confectionery products
CEO: Tom O'Rourke
Chief Financial Officer: Jeff Goodman
Purchasing Manager: Bob Kerekon
Estimated Sales: $10-20,000,000
Number Employees: 50-99
Square Footage: 100000
Type of Packaging: Consumer

5725 **Heck Cellars**
15401 Bear Mountain Winery Rd
Arvin, CA 93203-9743
661-854-6120
Fax: 661-854-2876

Wines, brandy; also, juices and bottled water
Owner: Gary Heck
gheck@korbel.com
Plant Manager: Tim Holt
Estimated Sales: $10-20 Million
Number Employees: 20-49
Square Footage: 1200000
Parent Co: F. Korbel & Brothers
Type of Packaging: Private Label, Bulk

5726 Hecker Pass Winery
4605 Hecker Pass Rd
Gilroy, CA 95020-8808
408-842-8755
Fax: 408-842-9799 carlo@heckerpasswinery.com
Wines
Owner/President: Mario Fortino
VP/Operations/Marketing: Carlo Fortino
Owner: Frances Fortino
Estimated Sales: Less Than $500,000
Number Employees: 1-4
Type of Packaging: Private Label
Brands:
Hecker Pass

5727 Heffy's BBQ Co.
Kansas City Southern Rlwy
Kansas City, MO 66117
816-200-2271
Fax: 816-366-3920 www.heffys.com
Sauces and cooking enhancers
CEO: Mike Farag
CMO: Jason Drumright
COO: Jeff Ratzloff

5728 Hegy's South Hills Vineyard & Winery
PO Box 727
Twin Falls, ID 83303-0727
208-599-0074
Fax: 208-734-6369
Wines
Owner/Vineyard Manager: Frank Hegy
Estimated Sales: Under $500,000
Number Employees: 1-4
Brands:
South Hills

5729 Heidi's Gourmet Desserts
1651 Montreal Cir
Tucker, GA 30084
770-449-4900
Fax: 770-326-6157 800-241-4166
Frozen speciality desserts
President: Larry Obertfell
Operations Director: Brian Schendider
Estimated Sales: $10-20 Million
Number Employees: 100-249
Square Footage: 134000
Type of Packaging: Consumer, Food Service, Private Label
Other Locations:
Heidi's Gourmet
Atlanta GA
Heidi's Gourmet
Sun Valley CA
Heidi's Gourmet
Salt Lake City UT

5730 Heidi's Salsa
12615 Beatrice St
Los Angeles, CA 90066-7003
USA
310-821-0211
heidi@lukofoods.com
www.lukofoods.com
Salsa, dips, sauces, seasonings, cooking enhancers
Owner: Heidi Luko
Co-Owner: Nikki Dougherty
Contact: Heidi Withers
heidi@lukofoods.com

5731 Heineman Winery
978 Catawba Ave
PO Box 300
Put In Bay, OH 43456-5507
419-285-2811
Fax: 419-285-3412 info@HeinemansWinery.com
www.heinemanswinery.com
Fruit juices and wine.
Owner: Louis Heineman
Vice President: Louis Heineman
Assistant Manager: Michael Bianichi
Estimated Sales: $500,000-$1 Million
Number Employees: 1-4
Parent Co: Heineman Beverage
Other Locations:
Heineman Distributing
Port Clinton OH
Brands:
Catawba Grape Juice
Heineman's

5732 Heinke Family Farm
5365 Clark Rd
Paradise, CA 95969-6392
530-877-5264
Beef, beef products
Owner: Dave Heinke
Estimated Sales: Less Than $500,000
Number Employees: 1-4

5733 Heinkel's Packing Co
2005 N 22nd St
Decatur, IL 62526
217-428-4401
800-594-2738
sales@heinkelspacking.com
www.heinkelspacking.com
Smoked meats, lunch meats and fresh sausages; boxed beef and pork; venison processing
Owner: Miles Wright
President: Wes Wright
Head of Production: Tom McCarthy
Year Founded: 1912
Estimated Sales: $5-9.9 Million
Number Employees: 20-49
Type of Packaging: Consumer, Food Service, Bulk
Brands:
Heinkel's

5734 Heintz & Weber Co
150 Reading St
Buffalo, NY 14220-2156
716-852-7171
Fax: 716-852-7173 info@webersmustard.com
www.webersmustard.com
Condiments
President: Steven Desmond
sdesmond@webersmustard.com
Executive VP: Suzanne Desmond
CEO: Steven Desmond
Estimated Sales: $5-10 Million
Number Employees: 5-9
Square Footage: 72000
Type of Packaging: Consumer, Bulk
Brands:
Weber's Horseradish Mustard
Weber's Hot Garlic M
Weber's Hot Piocacic
Weber's Spicy Dill Pickles
Weber's Sweet Pickle

5735 Heinz Portion Control
7500 Forshee Dr
Jacksonville, FL 32219
904-695-1300
www.heinzfoodservice.com
Manufacturer and exporter of portion controlled sugar, pepper, salt, ketchup, mustard, sauces, dressings, jams, jellies, syrup, preserves, mayonnaise and artificial sweeteners
Parent Co: The Kraft Heinz Company
Type of Packaging: Food Service, Private Label
Other Locations:
Portion Pac
Stone Mountain GA
Brands:
Chatsworth
Madeira Farms
Pitch'r Pak
Salsa Del Sol
Squeezers
Sweet Pleasers Gourmet
Sweet Portion
Taste Pleasers Gourmet

5736 Heinz Quality Chef Foods Inc
5005 C St SW
Cedar Rapids, IA 52404-7601
319-362-9633
Fax: 319-362-3924 800-356-8307
www.heinz.com
Frozen soups, sauces and entrees
President: Shannon Ashby
Plant Manager: Steve Maddocks
Estimated Sales: $10-20 Million
Number Employees: 100-249
Parent Co: Heinz USA
Type of Packaging: Food Service
Brands:
Quality Chef Foods, Inc.

5737 Heirloom Organic Gardens
743 Shore Rd
Hollister, CA 95023-9427
831-637-8497
www.heirloom-organic.com
Organic vegetables
President: Grant Brians
Estimated Sales: $.5-1,000,000
Number Employees: 10-19

5738 Heise Wausau Farms
2805 Valley View Rd
Wausau, WI 54403-8799
715-675-3862
Fax: 715-675-3256 800-764-1010
heisewausaufarms@yahoo.com
Ginseng, bee pollen capsules
President/Owner: Lyn Heise
heisewausaufarms@yahoo.com
Sales: Dan Heise
Estimated Sales: Less Than $500,000
Number Employees: 1-4
Square Footage: 16000
Brands:
Heise's
Jar-Lu

5739 Heitz Wine Cellars
436 Saint Helena Hwy S
St Helena, CA 94574-2206
707-963-3542
Fax: 707-963-7454 www.heitzcellar.com
Wines
President: Asuncion Tolley
tasuncion@heitzcellar.com
Winemaker: David Heitz
Estimated Sales: $5-10 Million
Number Employees: 5-9
Square Footage: 18726
Type of Packaging: Consumer
Brands:
Heitz

5740 Hela Spice Company
119 Franklin St
PO Box 1479
Uxbridge, ON L9P 1J5
Canada
905-852-5100
Fax: 905-852-1113 877-435-2649
www.helacanada.com
Custom blends, spice mixtures and seasoning blends for the meat and bakery industry
President: Walter Knecht
Senior Vice President-Sales: Paul Hoogenboom
Information Technology Manager: Gary Leung
Quality Assurance Manager: Crista Dagnall
Director of Technical Applications: Uwe Thode
Customer Service/Administration: Rita Irwin
Vice President-Food Safety: Dr. Thomas Varga
Purchasing Manager: Lisa Gay
Estimated Sales: $7 Million
Number Employees: 40

5741 Helados Mexico
Chino, CA 91708
www.heladosmexico.com
Fruit and ice cream bars

5742 Helen's Pure Foods
301 Ryers Ave
Cheltenham, PA 19012
215-379-6433
Fax: 215-663-5340 info@helenspurefoods.com
helenspurefoods.com
Hummus, dips, dressings, spreads and sandwiches.
Owner: Richard Goldberg
rgoldberg@helenspurefoods.com
Estimated Sales: $5-9.9,000,000
Number Employees: 2-10

5743 Helena View/Johnston Vineyard
3500 Highway 128
Calistoga, CA 94515
707-942-4956
Fax: 707-942-4956
Wines

Owner/Winemaker: Charles Johnston
Manager Public Relations: Sarah Marie Johnston
Winary Chief: Tom Gary
VP Administration: Charles Johnston
Brands:
Helena View
Moon Mountain

5744 **Hell On The Red Inc**
13716 E Fm 273
Telephone, TX 75488-5450
903-664-2573
Fax: 903-664-2301
lisa.hamilton@hellontheredinc.com
www.hellontheredinc.com
Pickled fruits and vegetables, vegetable sauces and seasonings & salad dressings
President: Thomas Baugh
Vice President: Patricia Baugh
Estimated Sales: $575,395
Number Employees: 1-4
Type of Packaging: Consumer, Private Label
Brands:
Hell on the Red

5745 **Hella Cocktail**
23-23 Borden Ave
Long Island City, NY 11101
646-854-8004
hellacocktail.co
Cocktail mixes and bitters
Co-Founder: Jomaree Pinkard
Co-Founder: Tobin Ludwig
Co-Founder: Eddie Simeon

5746 **Heller Brothers Packing Corp**
306 9th St
Winter Garden, FL 34787-3683
407-656-4986
Fax: 407-656-1751 855-543-5537
ptanner@hellerbros.com www.hellerbros.com
Citrus fruits
Owner/President: Harvey Heller
Owner/CEO: Harry Falk
hfalk@hellerbros.com
CFO: Jeff McKinney
General Manager: Don Barwick
VP Sales/Marketing: Rob Brath
Human Resources/Finance Executive: Jeff McKinney
General Manager: Billy Howard
Production: Al Jefferson
Estimated Sales: $3 Million
Number Employees: 250-499
Square Footage: 1000000
Type of Packaging: Consumer

5747 **Heller Estates**
69 West Carmel Valley Road
PO Box 999
Carmel Valley, CA 93924
831-659-6220
Fax: 831-659-6226 800-625-8466
info@hellerestate.com www.hellerestate.com
Organic wines
President: Robert Freeman
Controller: Pat Verde
Contact: Mary Roos
info@hellerestate.com
General Manager: Rene Schober
Estimated Sales: $1-2.5 Million
Number Employees: 7
Type of Packaging: Consumer

5748 **Hello Water**
888-474-3556
sayhello@hellowater.com hellowater.com
Fiber-infused water
Number of Brands: 1
Number of Products: 5
Type of Packaging: Consumer
Brands:
HELLO WATER

5749 **Hells Canyon Winery**
18835 Symms Rd
Caldwell, ID 83607-9513
208-454-3300
800-318-7873
hellwine@yahoo.com
Wines
Owner: Stephen C Robertson
hellwine@yahoo.com
Estimated Sales: Less Than $500,000
Number Employees: 1-4
Brands:
Hells Canyon

5750 **Helm New York Chemical Corp**
1110 Centennial Ave # 2
Piscataway, NJ 08854-4146
732-981-0528
Fax: 732-981-0965 www.helmus.com
Ingredients, additives and flavors
President: Beverly Marsh
bmarsh@helmus.com
CFO: Bill Van Fossen
Senior Vice President: Arun Manalkar
Number Employees: 20-49
Parent Co: Helm AG

5751 **Helms Bakery**
8758 Venice Blvd.
Ste. 100
Los Angeles, CA 90034
helmsinfo@wnmrealty.com
helmsbakerydistrict.com
Baked goods

5752 **Helms Candy Co., Inc**
3001 Lee Hwy
P.O.Box 607
Bristol, VA 24202-5939
276-669-2612
Fax: 276-669-0150 276-669-2533
www.helmscandy.com
Candies
President: George Helms
george@helmscandy.com
CEO: Helen Helms
VP Candy Division: Buzz Helms
VP Pharmaceutical Division: Mark Helms
Accounting Department: Deborah Smith
Production Supervisor: Tony Hatcher
Estimated Sales: $5-10,000,000
Number Employees: 2-10
Square Footage: 65000
Brands:
Cool-E-Pops
Happy Day Pops
Helms
Hot-C-Pops
Hot-N-Coldpops
Mint Lumps
Mint Puffs
Thank You Pops
Virginia Beauty
Zippy Pop

5753 **Helmuth Country Bakery Inc**
6706 W Mills Ave
Hutchinson, KS 67501-8890
620-567-2301
Fax: 620-567-2036 800-567-6360
info@helmuthfoods.com www.helmuthfoods.com
Cookies, candies, noodles and cotton candy
Owner: Jim Rein
jrein@helmuthfoods.com
VP: Katie Helmuth
Estimated Sales: Less Than $500,000
Number Employees: 1-4
Square Footage: 12000
Type of Packaging: Consumer, Food Service
Brands:
Cortland Manor
Hatties
Helmuth

5754 **Helshiron Fisheries**
7 Norman Road
Grand Manan, NB E5G 2G5
Canada
506-662-3696
Fax: 506-662-3779 lobfish@nbnet.nb.ca
Seafood
President: Ronald Benson
VP/Marketing Director: Morton Benson
Estimated Sales: $1,500,000
Number Employees: 9
Type of Packaging: Bulk
Brands:
Helshiron

5755 **Helthe Brands**
Austin, TX 78746
888-311-2157
hello@helthebrands.com helthebrands.com
Ayurvedic juices
Co-Founder: Swaroopa Masten
Co-Founder: Mark Masten
Brands:
Geevani
Senor Cane

5756 **Heltzman Bakery**
4749 Dixie Hwy
Louisville, KY 40216-2653
502-447-3515
www.heitzmanbakery.net
Bakery products, custom cakes and deli trays
President: Paul Osting
Manager: Nancy Kasey
Estimated Sales: Less Than $500,000
Number Employees: 5-9
Type of Packaging: Consumer, Food Service
Brands:
Springerlies

5757 **Heluva Good Cheese**
6 Kimball Ln
Suite 400
Lynnfield, MA 01940
617-660-7400
800-644-5473
www.heluvagood.com
Cheese, dips, cocktail sauce and mustard.
Director, Production & Quality Assurance: Bob Fratangelo
Production Manager: Steve De Mass
Year Founded: 1925
Estimated Sales: $20-50 Million
Number Employees: 100-249
Number of Products: 31
Square Footage: 42000
Type of Packaging: Consumer, Food Service, Private Label, Bulk
Brands:
Heluva Good Cheese

5758 **Hemp Fusion**
11660 Alpharetta Hwy
Suite 120
Roswell, GA 30076
877-669-4367
info@hempfusion.com hempfusion.com
Hemp-based nutritional supplements
Co-Founder & President: Jason Mitchell
Number of Brands: 1
Number of Products: 5
Type of Packaging: Consumer
Brands:
HEMP FUSION

5759 **Hemp Oil Canada**
PO Box 300
100 Prairie Rd
Ste. Agathe, MB R0G 1Y0
Canada
204-882-2480
Fax: 204-882-2529 800-289-4367
info@hempoilcan.com hempoilcanada.com
Hemp food ingredients
Controller: Jodi Schreyer Cloutier
Asst. Mgr., Marketing: Timothy Bonnar
Year Founded: 1998
Number Employees: 51-200
Type of Packaging: Bulk

5760 **Hemp Production Services**
706 6th Ave N
Saskatoon, SK S7K 2S9
Canada
844-436-7477
customerservice@hempproductionservices.com
www.hempproductionservices.com
Hempseed oil and powders
President: Garry Meier
VP, Operations: Kevin Friesen
Type of Packaging: Bulk

5761 **Hemp2o**
1000 Beecher St
San Leandro, CA 94577-1250
510-382-1231
hemp2o.com
Organic hemp beverages
Contact: Jennifer Kleinfeld
Number of Brands: 1
Number of Products: 9
Type of Packaging: Consumer

Brands:
HEMP2O

5762 **HempNut**
1286 Winter Solstice Avenue
Henderson, NV 89014-8869
707-576-7050
Fax: 707-579-0940 steve@thehempnut.com
www.thehempnut.com
Hempnuts
Founder/President: Richard Rose

5763 **Hena Inc**
660 Berriman St
Brooklyn, NY 11208-5304
718-272-8237
Fax: 718-272-8391
Iced coffee, iced tea mix and liquid concentrates.
President: Lan Tauber
lanny@henacoffee.com
Estimated Sales: $5-10 000,000
Number Employees: 5-9
Type of Packaging: Food Service, Private Label

5764 **Henderson's Gardens**
P.O. Box 214
Berwyn, AB T0M 0E0
Canada
780-338-2128
Fax: 780-338-2128
Corn, cucumbers, potatoes, tomatoes, cabbage, peas, beans and peppers
President: Robert Henderson
Number Employees: 3
Type of Packaging: Consumer, Food Service
Brands:
Pride of Peace Vegetables

5765 **Hendon & David**
PO Box 836
Millbrook, NY 999
845-677-9696
Fax: 845-677-9699 hendonco@aol.com
Macadamia nuts, cranberry grand marnier, exotic meat sauces, honeys, latin specialties, relishes, mustards
Owner: Helen Hendon
Brands:
Bushman's Best Mazavaroo
Clove Valley Farms
Hendon

5766 **Hendricks Apiaries**
4001 S Elati Street
Englewood, CO 80110-4555
303-789-3209
Specialty honey
President: Paul Hendricks
Co-Owner: Linda Hendricks
Estimated Sales: Under $500,000
Number Employees: 1-4
Square Footage: 6800
Type of Packaging: Consumer, Food Service, Private Label, Bulk
Brands:
Colorado Sunshine Honey

5767 **Henggeler Packing Company**
6730 Elmore Road
Fruitland, ID 83619
208-452-4212
Fax: 208-452-5416
Apples, plums and prunes
President: Gerald Henggeler
Vice President: Anthony Henggeler
Estimated Sales: $4 Million
Number Employees: 12
Type of Packaging: Consumer, Bulk
Brands:
Fortress
Fruitland

5768 **Henning Cheese Factory**
20201 Point Creek Rd
Kiel, WI 53042-4299
920-894-3032
Fax: 920-894-3022 kay@henningscheese.com
www.henningscheese.com
Cheese
President: Kerry Henning
Estimated Sales: $10-20 Million
Number Employees: 10-19
Type of Packaging: Consumer, Food Service, Private Label, Bulk
Brands:
Henning's

5769 **Henningsen Foods Inc**
14334 Industrial Rd
Omaha, NE 68144-3398
402-330-2500
Fax: 402-330-0875 800-228-2769
davids@henningsenfoods.com
www.henningsenfoods.com
Dried meats and eggs; contract dehydration
President: Jerry Walker
CEO: Arnulfo Arevalo
arnulfoa@henningsenfoods.com
R&D: Jason Zhang
Vice President, Sales: Aaron Heironimus
Logistics Manager: Gina Blankenau
Estimated Sales: $10-49.9 Million
Number Employees: 100-249
Square Footage: 12000
Type of Packaging: Food Service, Private Label, Bulk

5770 **Henry Broch & Co**
3940 Porett Dr
Gurnee, IL 60031-1244
847-816-6225
Fax: 847-816-6238 sales@hbroch.com
www.hbroch.com
Tomatoes and tomato powder, spices and vegetables
Manager: Donald Swanson
Sales Manager: James Kuzma
Estimated Sales: $5-10 Million
Number Employees: 5-9

5771 **Henry Davis Company**
3405 W 15th Ave
Gary, IN 46404-1964
219-949-8555
Fax: 219-949-9764
Seafood
President: Henry Davis
Estimated Sales: $1-3 Million
Number Employees: 20-49

5772 **Henry Estate Winery**
687 Hubbard Creek Rd
Umpqua, OR 97486-9611
541-459-5120
Fax: 541-459-5146 800-782-2686
winery@henryestate.com www.henryestate.com
Wines
President: Scott Henry
Vice President, Marketing: Syndi Beavers
Sales & Marketing Specialist: Crystal Loftin
Estimated Sales: $5-10,000,000
Number Employees: 11-50
Brands:
Henry Estate

5773 **Henry H. Misner Ltd.**
469 Norfolk St. N
Simcoe, ON N3Y 3P8
Canada
519-426-5546
Fax: 519-583-1529
Frozen shellfish and groundfish
President: Donald Misner
CFO: Nancy Misner
General Manager: Donald Misner
Number Employees: 20-49
Type of Packaging: Consumer, Food Service

5774 **Henry Hill & Co**
459 Walnut St
Napa, CA 94559-3101
707-253-1663
Fax: 707-257-2990
Wines
Owner: Mark Koehn
Estimated Sales: Less Than $500,000
Number Employees: 1-4
Brands:
Broken Rock Cellars

5775 **Henry J's Meat Specialties**
4460 W Armitage Ave
Chicago, IL 60639-3574
773-227-5400
Fax: 773-227-0414 800-242-1314
www.henryjmeats.com
Prepared meats
CEO: Forrest C. Krisco
fkrisco@henryjmeats.com
Executive Corporate Chief, R&D: Faustino Rivera
Quality Assurance, Plant Operations: Lorenzo Jackson
Customer Service: Alicia Vega
Estimated Sales: $1,000,000-1,490,000
Number Employees: 10-19

5776 **Herb Bee's Products**
210 Mallard Drive
Colchester, VT 05446-7013
802-864-7387
sierrassong@aol.com
Jam, jelly, relish, quick breads, cheese spreads, and vinegars
Owner: Rhonda Tebeau

5777 **Herb Patch of Vermont**
30 Island Street
Bellows Falls, VT 05101-3122
802-463-1400
Fax: 802-463-1911 800-282-4372
Cocoas, dessert beverages, dips, teas and herb blends; exporter of cocoa
Owner: John Moisis
Estimated Sales: Less than $500,000
Number Employees: 1-4
Square Footage: 13000
Brands:
Country Cow
Country Cow Cocoa
Cowpuccino Toppers

5778 **Herb Pharm**
PO Box 116
Williams, OR 97544
541-846-6262
Fax: 800-545-7392 800-348-4372
info@herb-pharm.com www.herb-pharm.com
Health supplements and personal care products
Founder/Co-Owner: Ed Smith
Founder/Co-Owner: Sara Katz
Co-Owner: Sara Katz
Number Employees: 50-99

5779 **Herb Society Of America**
9019 Kirtland Chardon Rd
Willoughby, OH 44094-5156
440-256-0514
Fax: 440-256-0541 herbs@herbsociety.org
www.herbsociety.org
Seasonings, spices
Executive Director: Katrinka Morgan
director@herbsociety.org
Administrative Support: Olivia Yates
Office Administrator: Michelle Milks
Editor: Robert Walland
Horticulturist: Robin Siktberg
HSA Librarian: Tara Coulter
Estimated Sales: $500,000-$1 000,000
Number Employees: 5-9
Type of Packaging: Private Label
Brands:
Herb Society of America

5780 **Herb Tea Company**
P.O.Box 1962
Oxnard, CA 93032-1962
805-486-6477
Fax: 805-385-3216
Tea
Sales Coordinator: Robert Lessin
Plant Manager: William Ashwell
Estimated Sales: $2.5-5 000,000
Number Employees: 10-19
Type of Packaging: Consumer, Private Label

5781 **Herb's Seafood**
112 Schoolhouse Road
Westampton, NJ 08060-3774
609-267-0276
Fax: 609-261-1949 800-486-0276
Prepared fish and poultry
Owner: Nash Cohen
VP Sales: Gary Cannard
Sales Manager: Richard Applebam
Plant Manager: William Byrne
Estimated Sales: $10-20 000,000
Number Employees: 2
Type of Packaging: Private Label
Brands:
Herbs Seafood

5782 **HerbCo International**
16661 W Snoqualmie River Rd NE
Duvall, WA 98019-9202
425-788-7903
Fax: 425-844-9114 888-643-7226
herbco@msn.com www.herbco.net
Culinary herbs and edible flowers
Owner: Ted Andrews
tandrews@herbco.net
Estimated Sales: $5-10 Million
Number Employees: 50-99
Brands:
Herbco
Generation Farms
Michigan Fine Herbs

5783 **HerbNZest LLC**
135 S Barrow Pl
Princeton, NJ 08540
917-582-1191
info@herbnzest.com
Chutney, relish and a variety of sauces.
Founder and CEO: Deboleena Dutta

5784 **HerbaSway Laboratories**
101 N. Plains Industrial Rd
PO Box 6098
Wallingford, CT 06492-0089
203-269-6991
Fax: 203-269-9703 800-672-7322
www.herbasway.com
Liquid dietary health supplements
Owner: Dr. Franklin St John
Founder/Owner: Lorraine St. John
Estimated Sales: $10-20 Million
Number Employees: 20-49

5785 **Herbal Magic**
1867 Yonge Street
Suite 700
Toronto, ON M4S 1Y5
Canada
416-487-7009
Fax: 416-487-4569 877-237-7225
melren@aol.com www.herbalmagic.com
Herbs for alternative uses
Founder/Master Herbalist: Renee Ponder
Estimated Sales: $300,000-500,000
Number Employees: 1-4

5786 **Herbal Products & Development**
1200 Trout Gulch Rd
Aptos, CA 95003-3038
831-688-8706
herbprodinfo@gmail.com
www.herbprod.com
Food concentrates, digestive enzymes, antioxidants, probiotics, tinctures, oils and liquid vitamins and minerals
President: Paul Gaylon
herbprodinfo@gmail.com
Number Employees: 1-4
Square Footage: 2400
Type of Packaging: Consumer, Private Label
Brands:
Liquid Life Essential Day & Night
Liver Restore
Plant Power
Power Plus
Pro Plus
Supreme 7

5787 **Herbal Science LLC**
3301 Bonita Beach Rd SW
Suite 308
Bonita Springs, FL 34134
239-597-8822
info@herbalsciencegroup.com
herbalsciencegroup.com
Herbs
President: Robert Gow
Year Founded: 2002
Estimated Sales: $800,000
Number Employees: 5-9

5788 **Herbal Water, Inc.**
901 N. Walton Ave.
Yuba City, CA 95993
610-668-4000
info@herbalwater.com
www.herbalwater.com
Water infused with herbs
Founder: Ayala Cahana

5789 **Herbalist & Alchemist Inc**
51 S Wandling Ave
Washington, NJ 07882-2192
908-689-9020
Fax: 908-689-9071 herbalist@nac.net
www.herbalist-alchemist.com
Herbs
President: David Winston
CEO: Beth Lambert
herbworld@aol.com
Estimated Sales: $1-3 Million
Number Employees: 10-19
Brands:
5lung Re-Leaf

5790 **Herbs America**
PO Box 446
Murphy, OR 97533
541-846-6222
Fax: 541-846-9488 herbs-america.com
Amazonian herbs, therapeutic teas and herbal extracts
Co-Founder: Mila Lazo
Co-Founder: Jerry Black
COO: Kevin Driskell
Type of Packaging: Consumer, Bulk
Brands:
HERBS AMERICA
MACA MAGIC

5791 **Herbs Etc**
1345 Cerrillos Rd
Santa Fe, NM 87505-3508
505-820-0410
Fax: 505-984-9197 888-694-3727
mailorder@herbsetc.com www.herbsetc.com
Liquid herbal extracts and fast acting softgel herbal medicines
Owner: Daniel Gagnon
Manager: Lynn Childson
lynn.childson@herbsetc.com
Estimated Sales: Less Than $500,000
Number Employees: 5-9
Square Footage: 14000
Type of Packaging: Consumer
Brands:
Allertonic
Deep Chi Builder
Deep Sleep
Depiezac
Echinacea Triple Source
Herbs, Etc.
Kidalin
Lung Tonic
Lymphatonic
Singers Saving Grace

5792 **Heringer Meats Inc**
16 W 7th St
Covington, KY 41011-2302
859-291-2000
Fax: 859-291-0444
Fresh and frozen meats
President: Ray Niemeyer
Vice President: Robert Hoeweller
Estimated Sales: $2.3 Million
Number Employees: 5-9
Type of Packaging: Consumer, Food Service
Brands:
Kahns
Plue Grass
Sara Lee

5793 **Heritage Books & Gifts**
308 Laskin Rd
Virginia Beach, VA 23451-3020
757-428-0400
Fax: 757-428-3632 800-862-2923
www.heritagestore.com
Essential oils, health foods, food supplements, vitamins, herbal teas, herbal tonics and supplements
Owner: Tom Johnson
tom.johnson@heritagestore.com
Chief Financial Officer: Jean Baviera
Marketing Director: David Riblet
Estimated Sales: $9 Million
Number Employees: 50-99
Square Footage: 12000
Type of Packaging: Consumer, Private Label, Bulk

5794 **Heritage Coffee Co & Cafe**
174 S Franklin St
Juneau, AK 99801-1362
907-586-1087
Fax: 907-586-1892 800-478-5282
coffeeinfo@heritagecoffee.com
www.heritagecoffee.com
Coffee
Manager: Gordon Berry
gordon@heritage-coffee.com
Estimated Sales: Less Than $500,000
Number Employees: 5-9
Brands:
Black Wolf Blend
Heritage Coffee

5795 **Heritage Family Specialty Foods Inc**
901 Santerre St
Grand Prairie, TX 75050-1939
972-660-6511
Fax: 972-660-4567 800-648-2837
info@hfsfoods.com www.heritagefamilyfoods.com
Dressings, salsas, soups, beverage mixes, marinades, spreads, mayos, and bbq sauces
President/CEO: Daniel Brackeen
VP/CFO: Cheryl Brackeen
Vice President: Johnny Lee Stanley
VP Quality Assurance: Amy Brackeen
Year Founded: 1991
Estimated Sales: $20-50 Million
Number Employees: 50-99
Square Footage: 65000
Type of Packaging: Food Service, Private Label
Brands:
Heritage Chipotle Roasted Salsa
Heritage Fresh Salsa
Heritage Garlic Mayo

5796 **Heritage Fancy Foods Marketing**
1360 Jamike Dr
Erlanger, KY 41018-0310
859-282-3782
Fax: 859-282-3781
Gourmet foods
President: Robert Carl
Brands:
Heritage Fancy Foods

5797 **Heritage Farms Dairy**
1100 New Salem Hwy
Murfreesboro, TN 37129-6914
615-895-2790
Fax: 615-895-0570 www.kroger.com
Fresh apple and orange juices, dairy products
Manager: Bill Crabtree
Controller: Mike Hunter
Sales Executive: Charlene Duke
Human Resource Executive: Jeff Philips
General Manager: Robert Allard
Number Employees: 100-249
Parent Co: Kroger Company
Type of Packaging: Consumer, Private Label, Bulk
Brands:
Kroger

5798 **Heritage Foods USA**
217 West 18th St
New York, NY 10113
718-389-0985
Fax: 718-389-0547 info@heritagefoodsusa.com
www.heritagefoodsusa.com
Frozen cabbage rolls and pierogies.
Principal: Peter Martins
Contact: Laura Campo
laura@heritagefoodsusa.com
Type of Packaging: Consumer, Food Service, Private Label
Brands:
Cheemo

5799 **Heritage Health Food**
PO Box 626
Collegedale, TN 37315
888-237-0807
heritagehealthfood.com
Vegetarian, All-Natural and Organic lines of prepared foods
Founder, President & CEO: Don Otis
Marketing: Jon Fish
Sales: Jay Jones
Number of Brands: 3
Type of Packaging: Consumer

Brands:
WORTHINGTON
HERITAGE HEALTH FOODS
KIM'S SIMPLE MEALS

5800 **Heritage Salmon**
P.O.Box 263
Eastport, ME 04631
207-853-6081
Fax: 207-853-6056 877-407-5577
www.heritagesalmon.com
Salmon
President: Glen Cooke
gcooke@heritagesalmon.com
Marketing: Aian Craig
Number Employees: 100-249
Number of Products: 60
Brands:
Heritage Salmon

5801 **Heritage Salmon Company**
100-12051 Horseshoe Way
Richmond, BC V7A 4V4
Canada
604-277-3093
Fax: 604-275-8614
Salmon
President: Ken Hirtle
CFO: Rob Reisen
Type of Packaging: Bulk

5802 **Heritage Short Bread**
35 Hunter Rd
Suite F
Hilton Head Isle, SC 29926-3715
843-422-3458
Fax: 888-744-6697 info@heritageshortbread.com
www.heritageshortbread.com
Shortbread cookies
Contact: Tom Cole
tom.cole@heritageshortbread.com
Estimated Sales: Less Than $500,000
Number Employees: 1-4

5803 **Heritage Wine Cellars**
12160 E Main Rd
North East, PA 16428-3644
814-725-8015
Fax: 814-725-8654 800-747-0083
matt@heritagewine.biz www.heritagewine.biz
Wines
President: Cathy Hoitink
cathy@heritagewine.biz
CEO: Robert Bostwick
President: Josh Bostwick
General Manager: Bob Bostwick
Estimated Sales: $2.5-5 000,000
Number Employees: 5-9
Brands:
Heritage

5804 **Heritage's Dairy Stores**
376 Jessup Rd
West Deptford, NJ 08086-2130
856-845-2855
Fax: 856-845-8392
mstrockbine@heritagesdairy.com
www.heritages.com
Milk, dairy products
President: Mike St Rockbine
mstrockbine@heritagesdairy.com
Number Employees: 500-999

5805 **Herlocher Foods**
415 E Calder Way
State College, PA 16801-5663
814-237-0134
Fax: 814-237-1893 800-437-5625
info@herlocherfoods.com
www.herlocherfoods.com
Dipping mustard and salsa
President: Neil Herlocher
CEO: Chuck Herlocher
info@herlocherfoods.com
Estimated Sales: $1-2.5 Million
Number Employees: 5-9
Brands:
Herlocher's Dipping Mustard

5806 **Herman Falter Packing Co**
384 Greenlawn Ave
Columbus, OH 43223-2610
614-444-1141
Fax: 614-445-3915 800-325-6328
info@faltersmeats.com www.faltersmeats.com
Meat
President: James Falter
Sales Exec: Lana Smith
lana@faltersmeats.com
Estimated Sales: $10-20 Million
Number Employees: 100-249

5807 **Herman's Bakery**
130 Main St S
Cambridge, MN 55008-1621
763-689-1515
Fax: 763-689-9642
Bakery products
Owner: Herman Oeistriech
hermansbakery@yahoo.com
Estimated Sales: $1-2.5 000,000
Number Employees: 20-49

5808 **Hermann J. Wiemer Vineyard**
3962 Rte 14
P.O. Box 38
Dundee, NY 14837
607-243-7971
Fax: 607-348-1498 800-371-7971
wines@wiemer.com wiemer.com
Wines
Owner, Manager & Winemaker: Fred Merwarth
Estimated Sales: $5-10 000,000
Number Employees: 10-19
Brands:
Hermann J. Wiemer

5809 **Hermann Pickle Co**
11964 State Route 88
Garrettsville, OH 44231-9115
330-527-2696
Fax: 330-527-2327 800-245-2696
www.hermannpicklecompany.com
Dill and kosher pickles, dill tomatoes and peppers
President/CEO: Larry Hermann
larry_hermannpickle@yahoo.com
Treasurer: Ruth Hermann
Vice President: Don Hermann
Estimated Sales: $10-20 Million
Number Employees: 50-99
Type of Packaging: Consumer, Bulk
Brands:
Hermann Pickle

5810 **Hermannhof Vineyards**
330 E 1st St
Hermann, MO 65041
573-486-1452
Fax: 573-486-3415 800-393-0100
hermannhofinfo@hermannhof.com
www.hermannhof.com
Wines
President: James Dierberg
Secretary: Mary Dierberg
Contact: Paul Leroy
sales@hermannhof.com
Estimated Sales: $10-20 Million
Number Employees: 5-9

5811 **Hernan**
1525 South Main Street
Suite 400
Del Rio, TX 78840
646-263-3598
ihernandez@hernanllc.com
www.hernanllc.com
Hot chocolate, chocolate confectionary
Marketing: Isela Hernandez

5812 **Hero Nutritionals**
1900 Carnegie Ave
Bldg A
Santa Ana, CA 92705
Fax: 949-379-6041 800-500-4376
heronutritionals.com
Gummy vitamins
CEO: Jennifer Hodges

5813 **Herold's Salads**
17512 Miles Ave
Cleveland, OH 44128-3404
216-991-9565
Fax: 216-991-9565 800-427-2523
www.heroldssalads.com
Salads, side dish vegetables and desserts
President/Owner: Cathy Herold
heroldsalads@yahoo.com
Quality Control: Stephanie Hunt
Marketing: Greg Johns
Sales Manager: Todd Kaminoski
Plant Manager: Walt Doughty
Estimated Sales: $2 Million
Number Employees: 20-49
Square Footage: 72000
Type of Packaging: Consumer, Food Service, Private Label, Bulk

5814 **Heron Hill Winery**
9301 County Route 76
Hammondsport, NY 14840-9685
607-868-4241
Fax: 607-868-3435 800-441-4241
info@heronhill.com www.heronhill.com
Wines
Owner: Lisa Cannac
mtabla@onthehouse.com
Estimated Sales: $5-10 Million
Number Employees: 20-49
Type of Packaging: Private Label

5815 **Herr Foods Inc.**
20 Herr Dr.
PO Box 300
Nottingham, PA 19362
800-523-5030
www.herrfoods.com
Snack foods.
Founder: James Herr
james.herr@herrs.com
Chairman: J.M. Herr
President/CEO: Ed Herr
Year Founded: 1946
Estimated Sales: $100-500 Million
Number Employees: 1000-4999
Type of Packaging: Consumer
Other Locations:
Herr's
Seaford DE
Herr's
Elkridge MD
Herr's
Egg Harbor NJ
Herr's
Oakland NJ
Herr's
Somerset NJ
Herr's
Lakewood NJ
Herr's
Hainesport NJ
Herr's
Newburgh NY
Herr's
Chillicothe OH
Herr's
Allentown PA
Herr's
Philadelphia PA
Herr's
Edinburg PA
Herr's
Nottingham PA
Brands:
Herr's®

5816 **Herrell's Ice Cream**
8 Old South St
Northampton, MA 01060-3847
413-586-9700
Fax: 413-584-5320 www.herrells.com
Ice cream
CEO: Stephen Herrell
Site Manager: Judy Herrell
Number Employees: 20-49

5817 **Herring Brothers Meats**
350 Water St
Guilford, ME 4443
207-876-2631
Fax: 207-876-2631 herringbros@hotmail.com
www.herringbrothersmeats.com
Meats

Owner: Thomas Gilbert
Owner: Trey Gilbert
Owner: Ellie Patterson
Estimated Sales: $5-10 Million
Number Employees: 20-49
Type of Packaging: Consumer, Private Label

5818 Hershey Co.
19 E Chocolate Dr.
Hershey, PA 17033
800-468-1714
www.thehersheycompany.com
Chocolate, confectionery, snack, refreshment and grocery products.
Chairman/President/CEO: Michele Buck
Senior VP/CFO: Steve Voskuil
Senior VP/General Counsel: Damien Atkins
Year Founded: 1894
Estimated Sales: $7.8 Billion
Number Employees: 15,360
Number of Brands: 31
Type of Packaging: Consumer, Food Service, Private Label
Brands:
Hershey's
Reese's
Hershey's Kisses
Lancaster
Hershey's Bliss
Twizzlers
Almond Joy
Mounds
York
Kit Kat
Pieces
5th Avenue
Brookside
Cadbury
Heath
Whoppers
Mr.Goodbar
Krackel
Take 5
Whatchamacallit
Skor
Symphony
Allan
Good & Plenty
Jolly Rancher
breathsavers
Bubble Yum
Ice Breakers
Milk Duds
Payday
Rolo
Zagnut
Zero

5819 Hershey Creamery Co
301 S Cameron St
Harrisburg, PA 17101
888-240-1905
info@hersheyicecream.com
www.hersheyicecream.com
Ice cream.
Vice President Central Region: Mark Scharlau
mrscharlau@aol.com
Executive Brand Manager: Zach Waite
Year Founded: 1894
Estimated Sales: $45.5 Million
Number Employees: 100-249
Square Footage: 65000
Type of Packaging: Consumer, Food Service, Bulk
Brands:
Hershey®'s Ice Cream
Benevita
Classic Banjo
Tropi-Kool Smoothies
Blenjavas
Twisted Peaks

5820 Hess Collection
4411 Redwood Rd
Napa, CA 94558-9708
707-255-1144
Fax: 707-253-1682 info@hesscollection.com
www.hesscollection.com
Wines
Chief Executive Officer: Timothy Persson
tpersson@hesscollection.com
Director Of Winemaking: Dave Guffy
Estimated Sales: $10-19 Million
Number Employees: 100-249
Number of Brands: 4
Square Footage: 100000
Type of Packaging: Private Label
Brands:
Artezin
Hess Collection
Hess Estate
Hess Select

5821 Heterochemical Corp
111 E Hawthorne Ave
Valley Stream, NY 11580-6319
516-561-8225
Fax: 516-561-8413
Vitamin K
President: Lynne Galler
VP: Raymond Berruti
Estimated Sales: $990,000
Number Employees: 10-19
Square Footage: 80000

5822 Heyday Beverage Co.
701 East 6th St
Austin, TX 78701
512-443-9876
info@drinkheyday.com
drinkheyday.com
Canned, cold-brew coffee
Founder & CEO: Bart Smith
Number of Brands: 1
Number of Products: 4
Type of Packaging: Consumer
Brands:
HEYDAY

5823 Heyerly Bakery
107 N Jefferson St
Ossian, IN 46777-1103
260-622-4196
Baked goods
President: Ronald Heyerly
Owner: Stan Heyerly
Estimated Sales: $500,000-$1 Million
Number Employees: 10-19
Type of Packaging: Consumer

5824 Hi Country Snack Foods
PO Box 159
Lincoln, MT 59639-0159
406-362-4050
Fax: 406-362-4275 www.hicountry.com
Beef jerky and sausage
President: James Johnson
COO: Fred Shammel
Contact: Chris Castagne
chris.castagne@hicountry.com
Year Founded: 1976
Number Employees: 50-99
Type of Packaging: Consumer, Food Service

5825 Hi Seas
8345 Shrimpers Row
Dulac, LA 70353-2205
985-563-7155
Fax: 985-563-2536
Shrimp
Owner: Eric Authamant
Estimated Sales: $5-10 Million
Number Employees: 10-19

5826 Hi-Country Foods Corporation
P.O.Box 338
Selah, WA 98942
509-697-7292
Fax: 509-697-3498
Fruit juice concentrates, bottled water, teas and new age beverages
President/Owner: Otis Harlan
CFO: Richard Johnson
CEO: Pat Kelly
Quality Control: Judy Groves
VP/Operations/Marketing: Patrick Kelly
Estimated Sales: $10-20 Million
Number Employees: 50-99
Square Footage: 150000
Type of Packaging: Food Service, Private Label, Bulk
Brands:
Hi-Country
Wenatchee Valley

5827 HiBix Corporation
5860 W Las Positas Blvd
Suite 21
Pleasanton, CA 94588
925-225-0800
Fax: 925-225-0700
Hibuscus extract
President/CEO: John-David Enright
SMO: Janet DiGiovanna
VP Sales: James Curley

5828 Hialeah Products Co
2207 Hayes St
Hollywood, FL 33020-3437
954-923-3379
Fax: 954-923-4010 800-923-3379
richnuts@aol.com
Nuts, dried fruits, candy and snacks
Owner: Richard Lesser
richard@newurbanfarms.com
CEO: Kathy Lesser
Research & Development: Noah Lesser
Estimated Sales: $10-25 Million
Number Employees: 10-19
Number of Brands: 2
Number of Products: 200+
Square Footage: 120000
Type of Packaging: Consumer, Food Service, Private Label, Bulk
Brands:
Oh Nuts

5829 Hiball, Inc.
1862 Union St
San Francisco, CA 94123-4308
415-931-1096
Fax: 415-931-1096 833-442-2553
www.hiball.com
Sparkling energy waters
President: Dan Soffer
dsoffer@epicor.com
Director of Sales: Dan Craytor
Sales Director: Dan Craytor

5830 Hibiscus Aloha Corporation
826 Queen St
Suite 200
Honolulu, HI 96813-5286
808-591-8826
Chocolate macadamia nut candy and cookies
President: Elvira Lo
chocolat_email@yahoo.com
Estimated Sales: $1-3 Million
Number Employees: 5-9

5831 Hickey Foods
PO Box 2312
Sun Valley, ID 83353
208-788-9033
Fax: 208-788-8879 800-215-0646
www.smokedtrout.com
Vacuum-packed smoked trout
President: Thomas M Hickey
Estimated Sales: $1-3 Million
Number Employees: 5-9

5832 Hickory Baked Ham Co
3221 Commerce Ct
Castle Rock, CO 80109-9458
303-688-2633
Fax: 303-688-8431
Smoked and cured poultry and meats.
President: Robert Anderson
Purchasing Manager: Robert Anderson
Estimated Sales: Less Than $500,000
Number Employees: 5-9
Square Footage: 18000
Parent Co: Hickory Baked Food
Type of Packaging: Consumer, Food Service, Private Label, Bulk
Brands:
Hickory Baked
High Valley Farm

5833 Hickory Farms
P.O.Box 219
1505 Holland Road
Maumee, OH 43537
419-725-9247
Fax: 419-893-0164 800-753-8558
www.hickoryfarms.com
Gourmet sausage and cheese gift baskets.

President/CEO: Diane Pearse
CFO: Joe Herman
Chief Marketing Officer: Judy Ransford
Contact: Bryan Bouley
bouley@hickoryfarms.com
COO: Matt James
Year Founded: 1951
Estimated Sales: $37 Million
Number Employees: 500-999
Type of Packaging: Consumer, Food Service, Bulk
Brands:
Hickory Farms

5834 **Hickory Harvest Foods**
90 Logan Pkwy
Akron, OH 44319-1177
330-644-6266
Fax: 330-644-2501 800-448-6887
www.hickoryharvest.com
Snack foods
President: Joe Swiatkowski
joe@hickoryharvest.com
VP, Sales: Mike Swiatkowski
Plant Manager: Nicholas Hamilton
Number Employees: 20-49
Type of Packaging: Consumer, Food Service, Private Label, Bulk
Brands:
Hickory Harvest Foods
I.M. Good Snacks

5835 **Hidden Mountain Ranch Winery**
2740 Hidden Mountain Rd
Paso Robles, CA 93446-8712
805-226-9907
Fax: 805-238-4997
Wines
Owner: Richard Gumerman
Estimated Sales: $1-2.5 000,000
Number Employees: 5-9

5836 **Hidden Springs Maple**
162 Westminster Rd
Putney, VT 05346-8812
802-387-5200
Fax: 802-387-5200 info@hiddenspringsmaple.com
www.hiddenspringsmaple.com
Maple syrup and candy; baking mixes; jams and preserves; cheese; hot and BBQ sauces.
Owner: Peter Cooper-Ellis
Year Founded: 2009
Estimated Sales: Less than $500,000
Number Employees: 20-49
Type of Packaging: Private Label

5837 **Hidden Villa Ranch**
310 N Harbor Blvd
Suite 205
Fullerton, CA 92832
800-326-3220
info@hiddenvilla.com www.hiddenvilla.com
Cheese and cheese products, liquid eggs.
President: Tim Luberski
tluberski@hiddenvilla.com
EVP: Greg Schneider
EVP: Michael Sencer
LA Division General Manager: Richard Schmidt
Year Founded: 1945
Estimated Sales: $500 Million
Brands:
Arizona Ranch Fresh
California Ranch Fresh
California Sunshine Dairy Pproducts
Hidden Villa Ranch
Horizon Orangic
Gold Circle Farms
Nestfresh
Smart Balance

5838 **Higa Food Service**
225 N. Nimitz Hwy
Honolulu, HI 96817
808-531-3591
Fax: 808-521-4951 www.higafoodservice.com
Meats
President/CEO: Sheldon Wright
Vice President, Processing: Jerry Higa
VP of Sales & Marketing: Shane Wright
Contact: Clifford Suwa
clifford@higafoodservice.com
Chief Operations Officer: Shaun Wright
Estimated Sales: $10-19.9 Million
Number Employees: 20-49

5839 **Higgins Seafood**
2798 Jean Lafitte Blvd
Lafitte, LA 70067-5206
504-689-3577
www.higginscrabhouse.com
Frozen seafood including crabs and oysters
President: Denny Higgins
astrocreepxero@aol.com
Estimated Sales: Less Than $500,000
Number Employees: 1-4
Type of Packaging: Consumer

5840 **High Brew Coffee**
Austin, TX 78704
www.highbrewcoffee.com
Canned, cold-brew coffee
Founder & CEO: David Smith
Number of Brands: 1
Number of Products: 3
Type of Packaging: Consumer
Brands:
HIGH BREW

5841 **High Country Elevators Inc**
62784 Highway 491
Dove Creek, CO 81324-9616
970-677-2251
Fax: 970-677-2461 hceinc@gmail.com
Dried beans, wheat and oils
Plant Manager: Bruce Riddel
Estimated Sales: Less Than $500,000
Number Employees: 1-4
Type of Packaging: Consumer, Food Service, Bulk

5842 **High Country Gourmet**
225 Mountain Way Drive
Orem, UT 84058-5121
801-426-4383
Fax: 801-426-4385 hictrygrmt@aol.com
Dehydrated soup mixes
President: Rod Meldrum
Type of Packaging: Consumer, Food Service, Private Label, Bulk
Brands:
High Country Gourmet

5843 **High Grade Beverage**
891 Georges Rd
Monmouth Jct, NJ 08852-3057
732-821-7600
Fax: 732-821-2898 887-327-4277
info@hgbev.com www.highgradebeverage.com
Soft drinks
President: Anthony DeMarco
ademarco@hgbev.com
Chairman: Joseph DeMarco
Corporate Controller: Jeffery Epstein
Corporate Vice President: Guy Battaglia
Corporate Secretary/Treasurer: Elizabeth DeMarco
Sales Manager: John Benvenuto
Operations Manager: John Morra
Number Employees: 100-249

5844 **High Liner Foods Inc.**
100 Battery Point
PO Box 910
Lunenburg, NS B0J 2C0
Canada
902-634-8811
Fax: 902-634-6228 info@highlinerfoods.com
www.highlinerfoods.com
Prepared, value-added frozen seafood.
Chairman: Henry Demone
President/CEO: Rod Hepponstall
Executive VP/CFO: Paul Jewer
Executive VP/General Counsel: Tim Rorabeck
VP, Quality Assurance/Food Safety: Meggan Hodgson
Senior VP, Marketing/Innovation: Craig Murray
Senior VP, North American Sales: Chris Mulder
Year Founded: 1926
Estimated Sales: $943 Million
Number Employees: 1,652
Number of Brands: 10
Type of Packaging: Consumer, Food Service, Private Label, Bulk
Other Locations:
High Liner Foods
Secaucus NJ
Brands:
Mirabel®
Icelandic Seafood®
FPI ® Brand
Viking®
High Liner®
American Pride®
High Liner Culinary
Fisher Boy®
Sea Cuisine®
Catch of the Day®
40 Fathoms®

5845 **High Mowing Organic Seeds**
76 Quarry Rd
Wolcott, VT 05680
802-472-6174
Fax: 802-472-3201 866-735-4454
www.highmowingseeds.com
Organic vegetable seeds
President/Owner: Tom Stearns
Type of Packaging: Consumer

5846 **High Quality Organics**
12101 Moya Blvd.
Reno, NV 89506
775-971-8550
hqorganics.com
Offers organic ingredients, including spices & herbs, spice extracts, dried vegetables, baking ingredients, and select grains.
Founder & President: Raju Boligala
Founder: Jerry Tenenberg
Founder: Jay Fishman
CFO: Rick May
VP, Quality & Operations: Chad Flores
Director, Sales: Jonathan Raju
Director, Customer Services: Cynthia Acuna
Director, Supply Chain: Gina Pepple
Year Founded: 1977
Number Employees: 51-200
Type of Packaging: Consumer, Food Service, Private Label, Bulk

5847 **High Ridge Foods LLC**
424 Ridgeway
White Plains, NY 10605-4208
914-761-2900
Fax: 914-761-2901
Dairy products, sugars and flowers
President: Nestor Alzerez
Sales Manager: Nestor Alzerez, Jr
Estimated Sales: $2.5 000,000
Number Employees: 1-4
Type of Packaging: Private Label, Bulk

5848 **High Rise Coffee Roasters**
2421 W Cucharras St
Colorado Springs, CO 80904-3048
719-633-1833
Fax: 719-471-4815
www.highrisecoffeeroasters.com
Coffee
President: Toby Anderson
highrisecoffee@hotmail.com
Estimated Sales: $1-2.5 000,000
Number Employees: 1-4

5849 **High Road Craft Ice Cream, Inc.**
2241 Perimeter Park Drive
Suite 7
Atlanta, GA 30341-1309
678-701-7623
sales@highroadcraft.com
www.highroadcraft.com
Frozen desserts, ice cream/sorbet
Marketing: Hunter Thornton

5850 **High Tide Seafoods Inc**
808 Marine Dr
Port Angeles, WA 98363-2104
360-452-8488
Fax: 360-452-6710 www.hightideseafoods.com
Fresh and frozen salmon
Owner: Jim Shefler
President: Ernest Vail
ernie@hightideseafoodsinc.com
Estimated Sales: $2.5 Million
Number Employees: 50-99
Type of Packaging: Consumer, Food Service
Brands:
High Tide Seafoods

5851 **High Valley Farm**
3221 Commerce Court
Castle Rock, CO 80109-9458
303-634-2944
Fax: 303-688-8431 www.hickorybakedham.com

Sausages and other processed meats, soup mixes, elk meat, bison meat
President: Robert Anderson

5852 **Highland Dairies**
PO Box 2199
Wichita, KS 67201-2199
316-267-4221
Fax: 316-267-1050 800-336-0765
www.hilanddairy.com
Milk, dairy products
Manager: Jerald Grey
President: Gary Aggus
Marketing Director: Ted Barlows
Number Employees: 100-249
Brands:
Highland
Old Chester

5853 **Highland Family Farms**
57746 Hwy 30
Mapleton, MN 56065
507-524-3797
www.highlandfamilyfarmsmn.com
Grains, vegetables and meat.
Owner/Partner: Kim Duncanson
General Operations: Gabriel Duncanson
Year Founded: 2017

5854 **Highland Farm Foods**
118 Fairfield Ave
Rock Hill, SC 29732
803-396-1439
highlandfarmfoods.com
Quinoa
CEO: Jack Smith
jack@highlandfarmfoods.com
Type of Packaging: Private Label

5855 **Highland Fisheries**
1E Fareham Park Road
Glace Bay, NS B1A 6C9
Canada
902-849-6016
Fax: 902-849-7794 fish.n.chips@btinernet.com
Fresh and frozen finfish
President: Josh Wallenham
Plant Manager: Greg Mitchelitis
Number Employees: 100-249
Type of Packaging: Bulk

5856 **Highland Laboratories**
PO Box 199
Mount Angel, OR 97362
503-845-9223
Fax: 503-845-6364 888-717-4917
www.highlandvitamins.com
Vitamins, minerals and protein powders
Owner/President: Kenneth Scott
CEO: Candy Scott
CFO/Human Resources: Jolyn Rothgery
Quality & Compliance Manager: John Mills
Accounts Manager: Kim Lang
kim@highlandvitamins.com
Sales Manager: Brian Taschereau
COO: Michael Carlson
Manufacturing Supervisor: Vadim Osipovich
Purchasing Manager: Michelle Brumer
Estimated Sales: $5.4 Million
Number Employees: 41
Square Footage: 120000
Type of Packaging: Private Label

5857 **Highland Manor Winery**
2965 S York Hwy
Jamestown, TN 38556-5334
931-879-9519
Fax: 931-879-2907 www.highlandmanorwinery.net
Wines
Owner: Butch Campbell
Co-Owner: Gertie Campbell
Estimated Sales: $2.5-5 Million
Number Employees: 5-9

5858 **Highland Sugarworks**
49 Parker Rd
Wilson Industrial Park, P.O. Box 58
Websterville, VT 5678
802-479-1747
Fax: 802-479-1737 800-452-4012
jclose@highlandsugarworks.com
www.highlandsugarworks.com
Pure maple syrup and pancake mixes
President: Jim Mac Isaac
jim@highlandsugarworks.com
Sales/Marketing: Jim Close
Operations: Deb Frimodig
Estimated Sales: $500,000-$1 Million
Number Employees: 10-19
Square Footage: 60000
Type of Packaging: Consumer, Food Service, Private Label, Bulk
Brands:
Highland Sugarworks

5859 **Highlandville Packing**
PO Box 190
Highlandville, MO 65669
417-443-3365
Fax: 417-443-3365 www.goatworld.com
Meat products
Owner: Neva Smith
Estimated Sales: $1-2.5 Million
Number Employees: 1-4

5860 **Hightower's Packing**
1713 Highway 518
Minden, LA 71055-8001
318-377-5459
Fax: 318-377-5408
Meat products
President: Marvin Hightower
marvinhightower@hughes.net
Estimated Sales: $2.5-5 Million
Number Employees: 5-9
Type of Packaging: Consumer, Bulk

5861 **Highwood Distillers**
PO Box 5693
High River, AB T1V 1M7
Canada
403-652-3202
Fax: 403-652-4227 hrplant@telus.net
Whiskey, vodka, rum, tequila, liquers and pre-mixers
President/Sales: Barry Wilde
Chairman/CEO: W Miller
Number Employees: 20-49
Square Footage: 120000
Type of Packaging: Consumer, Private Label
Brands:
Buccaneer
China White
Colita
Highwood
Marushka
Old Mexico
Triple Sec
White Lightning

5862 **Hikari Miso Intl.**
Torrance, CA 90501
hikarimiso.com
Organic miso pastes
Parent Co: Hikari Miso Co., Ltd.

5863 **(HQ)Hiland Dairy Foods Co**
1133 E Kearney St
Springfield, MO 65803-3435
417-862-9311
Fax: 417-837-1106 800-492-4022
www.hilanddairy.com
Milk, juice, fruit-flavored drinks, lemonade, water, ice cream, creams/half and half, lactose-free milk, butter, cottage cheese, cheese, shredded cheese, yogurt, sour cream, dips, to-go drinks, egg substitute and egg nog.
President/COO: Gary Aggus
gaggus@hilanddairy.com
Estimated Sales: $20-50 Million
Number Employees: 500-999
Type of Packaging: Consumer, Food Service
Other Locations:
Omaha NE
Chandler OK
Fayetteville AR
Fort Smith AR
Norman OK
Kansas City MO
Wichita KS
Little Rock AR
Norfolk NE
Des Moines IA
Dallas TX
Houstan TX
Waco TX

5864 **Hilary's Eat Well**
2205 Haskell Ave
Lawrence, KS 66046
785-856-3399
www.hilaryseatwell.com
Vegetarian burgers, sausages, bites and salad dressings
President & CFO: Lydia Butler
VP, Marketing: Becky Harpstrite
SVP, Sales: Greg Easter
Number of Brands: 1
Number of Products: 27
Type of Packaging: Consumer
Brands:
HILARY'S

5865 **Hill Top Berry Farm & Winery**
2800 Berry Hill Rd
Nellysford, VA 22958-2034
434-361-1266
Fax: 434-361-1266 www.hilltopberrywine.com
Wines
Owner: Kimberly Pugh
hilltop1@ntelos.net
Estimated Sales: $3-5 Million
Number Employees: 1-4

5866 **Hillandale**
US Highway 41 North
Lake City, FL 32055
386-397-1300
Fax: 386-397-1130 www.hillandalefarms.com
Eggs
President: Gary Bethel
Vice President: Steve Vendemia
Estimated Sales: $10-20 Million
Number Employees: 100-249
Type of Packaging: Consumer, Food Service

5867 **Hillard Bloom Packing Co Inc**
2601 Ogden Ave
Port Norris, NJ 08349-3141
856-785-0120
Fax: 856-785-2341
Fresh and frozen clams and oysters
Vice President: Todd Reeves
VP: Todd Reeves
Human Resource Manager: Barbara Huggins
Estimated Sales: $7600000
Number Employees: 1-4
Square Footage: 20000
Parent Co: Tallmadge Brothers

5868 **Hillbilly Smokehouse**
1801 S 8th St
Rogers, AR 72756
479-636-1927
Fax: 479-636-4590
Smoked ham, bacon, sausage, turkey, chicken, pork and beef
President: Tom Baumgartner
Vice President: Drew Baumgartner
Estimated Sales: $1 Million
Number Employees: 10
Number of Brands: 1
Number of Products: 20
Square Footage: 20000
Type of Packaging: Consumer

5869 **Hillcrest Orchard**
101 Autumn Ter
Lake Placid, FL 33852-6275
865-397-5273
Fax: 865-397-5273 ftpresto@tnni.net
Apples and grapes; fruit preserves and grape juice
Co-Owner: Frank Preston
Co-Owner: Twylia Preston
Estimated Sales: Under $100,000
Number Employees: 1-4
Number of Brands: 1
Number of Products: 15
Square Footage: 368000
Type of Packaging: Consumer, Food Service, Bulk
Brands:
Hillcrest Orchard

5870 **Hillcrest Vineyards**
240 Vineyard Ln
Roseburg, OR 97471-9097
541-673-3709
dyson@hillcrestvineyard.com
www.hillcrestvineyard.com
Wines

Manager: Della Terra
Owner: Richard Sommer
Estimated Sales: Less Than $500,000
Number Employees: 1-4

5871 Hillestad Pharmaceuticals
178 US Highway 51 N
Woodruff, WI 54568-9501
715-358-9773
Fax: 715-358-7812 800-535-7742
info@hillestadlabs.com www.hillestadlabs.com
Nutritional products
Marketing: Dan Hillestad
Estimated Sales: $10-20 Million
Number Employees: 20-49
Type of Packaging: Consumer, Private Label

5872 Hillmans Shrimp & Oyster
915 Broadway St
Port Lavaca, TX 77979-2711
361-552-9415
Fax: 281-339-1509 800-582-4416
www.hillmanoysters.com
Oysters, clams and shirmp
Owner: Cliford Hillman
clifordhillman@hillmanoyster.com
VP Marketing: Chris Hillman
Marketing Director: Tricia Roberts
Sales: Dale Rymer
Public Relations: Wendy Taylor
COO: Steve Taylor
Estimated Sales: $15 Million
Number Employees: 250-499
Number of Brands: 1
Number of Products: 12
Square Footage: 29860
Type of Packaging: Consumer, Food Service, Bulk
Brands:
Hillman

5873 Hillsboro Coffee Company
3803 Corporex Park Dr
#200
Tampa, FL 33619-1184
813-877-2126
Fax: 813-879-0524
Coffee
President: Neil McTague
VP Sales: John Sakkis
Estimated Sales: $5-10 Million
Number Employees: 8

5874 Hillside Candy Co
35 Hillside Ave
Hillside, NJ 07205-1833
973-926-2300
Fax: 973-926-4440 800-524-1304
info@hillsidecandy.com www.hillsidecandy.com
Sugarfree candy
President: Ted Cohen
ted@hillsidecandy.com
Marketing/Export Sales: Sandy Gencarelli
Estimated Sales: $5-10 Million
Number Employees: 10-19
Type of Packaging: Consumer, Food Service, Private Label, Bulk
Brands:
Golightly Sugar Free Candy
Shaken Country Meadows Sweets

5875 Hillside Lane Farm
160 Hillside Ln
Randolph, VT 05060
802-728-0070
Fax: 802-728-0071 info@hillsidelane.com
www.hillsidelane.com
Organic maple pancake & baking mixes, infused vinegars and syrups
President: Cathy Bacon
info@hillsidelane.com
Estimated Sales: $1-3 Million
Number Employees: 1-4
Number of Brands: 4
Number of Products: 17
Type of Packaging: Consumer, Food Service, Private Label, Bulk

5876 Hillson Nut Co
3225 W 71st St
Cleveland, OH 44102-5288
216-961-4477
Fax: 216-961-4480 800-333-2818
nuts@hillsonnut.com
Roasted, raw salted nuts and peanut butter
Owner: Edward Hillson
nuts@hillsonnuts.com
Vice President: Troy Sawvel
Estimated Sales: $500,000-$1 Million
Number Employees: 5-9

5877 Hilltop Meat Co
27630 US Highway 29
Andalusia, AL 36421-9465
334-388-2393
Fax: 334-388-3131 800-781-0053
Meat products
Owner: Billy Green
hilltop@alaweb.com
Estimated Sales: $1-2.5 Million
Number Employees: 5-9
Type of Packaging: Consumer

5878 Hilmar Cheese Company
8901 N Lander Ave
P.O. Box 910
Hilmar, CA 95324
209-667-6076
800-577-5772
info@hilmarcheese.com www.hilmarcheese.com
Cheese.
President & CEO: David Ahlem
Chief Financial Officer: Jason Price
VP, Sales & Marketing: Phil Robnett
Operations Manager: Ted Dykzeul
Year Founded: 1984
Estimated Sales: $100-500 Million
Number Employees: 500-999
Type of Packaging: Consumer, Food Service, Private Label
Brands:
Gina Marie Cream Cheese

5879 (HQ)Hilmar Ingredients
8901 N Lander Ave
PO Box 910
Hilmar, CA 95324
209-667-6076
Fax: 209-656-2557 888-300-4465
info@hilmaringredients.com
www.hilmaringredients.com
Functional whey proteins, high purity lactose and nutritious milk powders
President: Art De Rooy
CEO: John Jeter
CFO: Jay Hicks
Director, New Business & Applications: Grace Harris
Milk Powders, Sales Manager: Emil Skaria
Contact: Mark Petersen
mpetersen@hilmaringredients.com
Number Employees: 600
Other Locations:
Manufacturing Site & Visitor Center
Hilmar CA
Turlock Manufacturing Site
Turlock CA
Texas Manufacturing Site
Dalhart TX

5880 Hilo Fish Company
55 Holomua St
Hilo, HI 96720-5142
808-961-0877
Fax: 808-935-1603 info@hilofish.com
www.hilofish.com
Fresh billfish, bottomfish, tuna, open ocean fish; Frozen tuna, grouper, hamachi, snapper, and other seafood
CEO: Charlie Umamoto
President & COO: Kerry Umamoto
General Manager: Jamiesen Batangan
Marketing: Helene Rousselle
National Sales Manager: Sabrina Vaughn
Operationas Manager: Keith Hayashi
Estimated Sales: $20-50 Million
Number Employees: 20-49

5881 HimalaSalt
Sheffield, MA 01257
413-528-5141
www.himalasalt.com
Organic Himalayan salt
Founder: Melissa Kushi
Type of Packaging: Consumer
Brands:
HIMALASALT

5882 Himalayan Chef
Sheffield, MA 01257
413-528-5141
www.himalasalt.com
Organic Himalayan salt and seasonings
CFO: Nafees Anjum
Type of Packaging: Consumer
Brands:
HIMALAYAN CHEF

5883 Himalayan Heritage
N5821 Fairway Dr
Fredonia, WI 53021-9742
608-274-9640
Fax: 262-692-6387 888-414-9500
web@aliveandhealthy.com
Herbal dietary supplements
Co-Owner: Blair Lewis
Co-Owner: Karen Lewis
Estimated Sales: $1-3 Million
Number Employees: 10-19
Type of Packaging: Consumer, Food Service, Private Label, Bulk
Brands:
Attnetion Span
Erjuv-Powder
Five Forces of Nature
Immuno Force
Joyful Mind

5884 Hinckley Springs Bottled Water
800-201-6218
www.hinckleysprings.com
Bottled water
President: Dave Muscato
CEO: Tom Harrington
CFO: Jerry Hoyle
General Manager: Mike Garrity
Estimated Sales: $500,000-$1 Million
Number Employees: 50-99
Square Footage: 6000
Parent Co: DS Services of America
Type of Packaging: Consumer, Food Service, Bulk
Brands:
FIJI Water ®
LaCroix Sparkling Water
Mountain Valley Spring Water ™
Nursery ®
Polar Sparkling Water
Sparkling Ice
VOSS ® Water

5885 Hingham Shellfish
25 Eldridge Ct
Hingham, MA 02043
781-749-1374
Fax: 405-631-8473
Shellfish
President/Treasure: Myrle Derbyshire
Estimated Sales: $.5-1 million
Number Employees: 1-4

5886 Hint Mint
2432 East 8th Street
Los Angeles, CA 90021
213-622-6468
Fax: 213-622-1780 800-991-6468
www.hintmint.com
Breathmints and peppermint
Owner: Cooper Bates
Marketing: Wendy Campbell
Contact: Sue Chiang
sue@hintmint.com
Estimated Sales: $.5-1 million
Number Employees: 5-9
Brands:
Hint Mint

5887 Hint Water
2124 Union Street
Suite D
San Francisco, CA 94123
415-513-4050
Fax: 415-276-1786 info@drinkhint.com
www.drinkhint.com
Naturally flavored water
CEO/Founder: Kara Goldin
Contact: Nancy Binder
nancy@drinkhint.com

5888 **Hinzerling Winery**
1520 Sheridan Ave
Prosser, WA 99350-1140
509-786-2163
Fax: 509-786-2163 800-727-6702
info@hinzerling.com www.hinzerling.com
Wine, vinegar
Owner: Mike Wallace
info@hinzerling.com
Cellarmaster: Stan Kelly
Estimated Sales: $1-2.5 Million
Number Employees: 1-4
Type of Packaging: Private Label
Brands:
Hinzerling
Wallace

5889 **Hip Chick Farms**
707-861-9010
hipchicks@hipchickfarms.com
hipchickfarms.com
Organic chicken fingers, chicken meatballs and turkey patties
Co-Founder: Jen Johnson
Co-Founder: Serafina Palandech
Number of Brands: 1
Number of Products: 13
Type of Packaging: Consumer
Brands:
HIP CHICK FARMS

5890 **Hippeas**
Plainview, NY 11803
hippeas.com
Organic chickpea puffs
Founder: Livio Bisterzo
CEO: Joe Serventi
Number of Brands: 1
Number of Products: 13
Type of Packaging: Consumer

5891 **Hippie Snacks**
4612 Dawson St
Burnaby, BC V5C 4C3
Canada
877-769-6887
hello@hippiesnacks.com www.hippiesnacks.com
Coconut clusters, veggie clusters, sesame snacks and granola
President/Owner: Ian Walker
Number of Brands: 1
Number of Products: 11
Type of Packaging: Consumer
Brands:
HIPPIE SNACKS

5892 **(HQ)Hiram Walker & Sons**
2072 Riverside Drive E
Windsor, ON N8Y 1A7
Canada
519-254-5171
Fax: 519-971-5732 www.hiramwalker.com
Processor and exporter of blended whiskey, gin, scotch, vodka, rum, liqueurs, etc schnapps flavors include...peah,peppermint,blackberry,pumpkin spice,melon,triple sec blend, there are 43 alltogether.
Chairman/CEO: Paul Duffy
CFO: Thibault Cuny
SVP/Operations: Dan Denisoff
General Counsel: Thomas Lalla
SVP/Spirit Sales: Marty Crane
Marketing Director: Matt Aeppli
Estimated Sales: $199.43million
Number Employees: 500
Parent Co: Pernod Ricard
Type of Packaging: Consumer, Food Service
Other Locations:
Manufacturing Facility
Fort Smith AR
Brands:
Ballantine's
Beefeater
Canadian Club
Courvoisier
Irish Mist
Kahlua
Maker's Mark
Malibu
Midori
Sauza
Stolichnaya

5893 **Hirzel Canning Co & Farms**
20790 Bradner Rd
Luckey, OH 43443
419-419-7525
www.hirzelfarms.com
Manufacturer and exporter of canned tomatoes and tomato products, sauerkraut, sauces, salsa, tomato juice, tomato soup and more.
President & CEO: Stephen Hirzel
Office Manager: Lynn Hirzel
Manager: William Hirzel
Director, Manufacturing: Karl Hirzel
Crop Production: Lou Kozma, Jr.
Year Founded: 1923
Estimated Sales: $20-50 Million
Number Employees: 50-99
Number of Brands: 4
Number of Products: 30
Square Footage: 500000
Type of Packaging: Consumer, Food Service, Private Label, Bulk
Brands:
Dei Fratelli
Silver Fleece
Starcross

5894 **Hirzel Canning Co.**
325 W Williamstown Rd
Ottawa, OH 45875
419-523-3225
Fax: 419-523-6145 800-837-1631
info@hirzel.com www.deifratelli.com
Canned tomato products including whole, sliced, crushed, puree and sauce
President: Karl Hirzel
Plant Manager: Carl Hirzel
Estimated Sales: $2.5-5 Million
Number Employees: 5-9
Parent Co: Hirzel Canning
Type of Packaging: Consumer, Food Service, Private Label
Brands:
Dei Fratelli
Silver Fleece
Star Cross

5895 **Hnina Gourmet**
Los Angeles, CA 90046
323-876-2609
hninagourmet.com
Raw chocolate bars, cacao spreads, seed crackers and cacao truffles
Founder: Vanessa Morgenstern-Kenan

5896 **Hobarama Corporation**
400 NW 26th St
Miami, FL 33127-4120
305-531-9708
Fax: 305-531-9709 880-439-2295
www.bawls.com
Beverages
President: Hobart Buppert
Vice President: Lisa Karell
Contact: Eric Pyszka
eric.pyszta@bawls.com
Estimated Sales: $2.5-5 Million
Number Employees: 10-19
Type of Packaging: Bulk

5897 **Hobe Laboratories Inc**
6479 S Ash Ave
Tempe, AZ 85283-3657
480-413-1950
Fax: 480-413-2005 800-528-4482
hobelabs@aol.com www.hobelabs.com
Processor and exporter of weight loss and herbal teas
President: Bill Robertson
brobertson@hobelabs.com
Marketing Director: Brenda Martin
Operations Manager: Peter Samuell
Estimated Sales: $1.4 Million
Number Employees: 10-19
Square Footage: 27940
Type of Packaging: Consumer, Private Label
Brands:
Slim
Thermo Slim
Ultra Slim

5898 **Hodgson Mill Inc**
1100 Stevens Ave
Effingham, IL 62401-4265
217-347-0105
Fax: 217-347-0198 800-347-0198
customerservice@hodgsonmill.com
www.hodgsonmill.com
All natural and organic foods-flours, cereals, baking mixes, whole wheat pastas, gluten free pastas, gluten free mixes, baking ingredients-producers and manufacturers of whole grain foods. Co-packing for private label available
Owner: Bob Goldstein
bjgoldstein@hodgsgonmill.com
Vice President: Cathy Goldstein
Estimated Sales: $25-30 Million
Number Employees: 100-249
Square Footage: 120000
Type of Packaging: Consumer
Brands:
Don's Chuck Wagon
Hodgson Mill
Kentucky Kernel

5899 **Hodo**
2923 Adeline St
Oakland, CA 94608
510-464-2977
www.hodofoods.com
Soy products, including soymilk, tofu, yuba and ready-to-eat tofu and yuba meals
Type of Packaging: Consumer, Food Service
Brands:
HODO

5900 **Hoff's Bakery**
1 Brainard Ave
Medford, MA 02155-5247
781-396-8384
Fax: 781-396-7918 888-871-5100
www.hoffsbakery.com
Cakes and tortes, cheesecakes, pies and tarts, 1/2 sheet tray, individual desserts, and trifle cups
Owner: Vinny Frattura
vfrattura@hoffsbakery.com
Estimated Sales: $1.5 Million
Number Employees: 20-49

5901 **Hoff's United Food**
617 Main St
P.O.Box 145
Brownsville, WI 53006
920-269-4798
Fax: 920-583-2194 800-852-9658
www.hoffsqualitymeats.com
Smoked sausage, bacon
Owner: Tim Hoff
Marketing: Tim Hoff
Estimated Sales: $1-2.5 000,000
Number Employees: 10-19
Type of Packaging: Private Label, Bulk

5902 **Hofmann Sausage Co Inc**
6196 Eastern Ave
Mattydale, NY 13211-2209
315-437-7257
Fax: 315-437-2391 800-724-8410
sales@hofmannsausage.com
www.hofmannbrands.com
German-style sausages, deli meats and mustards
President: Rusty Flook
rusty@hofmannsausage.com
CEO: Walter Flook
Estimated Sales: $5-10Million
Number Employees: 20-49
Type of Packaging: Consumer, Bulk
Brands:
German
Snappy's

5903 **Hog Haus Brewing Company**
430 W Dickson St
Fayetteville, AR 72701-5107
479-521-2739
Fax: 479-442-0077
Beers
Owner/Operator: Julie Sill
Front of House: Marueen Robertson
Estimated Sales: Below $5 Million
Number Employees: 50-99
Type of Packaging: Consumer, Food Service
Brands:
Hoghaus

Ploughman's Pils
Woodstock Wheat

5904 **Hogtown Brewing Company**
2351 Royal Windsor Drive
Unit 6
Mississauga, ON L5J 4S7
Canada
905-855-9065
Fax: 905-822-0990 www.hogtownbrewers.org
Beers; bottling services
President: Maria Lopez
General Manager: Peter Lazaro
Number Employees: 5-9
Type of Packaging: Consumer, Food Service

5905 **Hogtowne B-B-Q Sauce Company**
1712 W University Avenue
Gainesville, FL 32603
352-375-6969
Fax: 352-373-6969 www.saltydogsaloon.com
Wholesaler/distributor of hot sauces, BBQ sauces, marinades and other specialty food products
Manager: Keith Singleton
Vice President: Pam Taylor-Kinard
Estimated Sales: $500,000-$1 Million
Number Employees: 20-49
Square Footage: 8000
Parent Co: Original Alan's Cubana
Type of Packaging: Consumer, Food Service, Private Label, Bulk

5906 **Holey Moses Cheesecake**
115 Francis S Gabreski Airport
Westhampton Beach, NY 11978
631-288-8088
Fax: 631-288-0551 800-225-2253
Cheesecake
President: Christopher Weber
Estimated Sales: Less than $500,000
Number Employees: 1-4

5907 **Holistic Products Corporation**
10 W Forest Avenue
Englewood, NJ 07631-4020
201-569-1188
Fax: 201-569-3224 800-221-0308
Processor, wholesaler/distributor and importer of health food products including propolis lozenges
President: Arnold Gans
a.gans@mdnu.com
VP Sales: Myra Gans
Number Employees: 38
Square Footage: 16000
Parent Co: MNI Group

5908 **Holland American International Specialties**
10343 Artesia Blvd
Bellflower, CA 90706
562-925-6914
Fax: 562-925-4507 www.1dutchmall.com
European and domestic specialty gourmet foods.
Manager: Maria Cervantes
Estimated Sales: $.5-1 million
Number Employees: 1-4

5909 **Hollandia Bakeries Limited**
PO Box 100
Mt Brydges, ON N0L 1W0
Canada
519-264-1020
800-265-3480
www.hollandiacookies.com
Cookies
President: Joop De Voest Jr
Controller: Rick Bannister
Quality Control: Mike Hobley
VP Sales: Doug Smith
Brands:
Kerleens
Sugar Free Cookies
Hard Cookies
Soft Cookies
Gourmet Specialty Cookies
Mini Tubs
Red Label

5910 **Hollman Foods**
PO Box 41724
Des Moines, IA 50311
308-468-5635
Fax: 308-468-6141 888-926-2879
hollfamilyenterprises@gmail.com
Barbecue sauce, seasonings, spices, smoked turkey, breading mixes, gourmet jellies and fruit butters; also, gift box items, dip mixes, and honey
Owner: Byron Holl
CEO: Judith Holl
Estimated Sales: $3-5 Million
Number Employees: 5-9
Number of Brands: 2
Number of Products: 30
Square Footage: 12000
Type of Packaging: Consumer, Food Service, Private Label
Brands:
Eden Farms
Hollmans

5911 **Hollow Road Farms**
271 Hollow Rd
Stuyvesant, NY 12173-1910
518-758-1881
Fax: 518-758-1899
Yogurt.
President: Joan Snyder
Estimated Sales: $500,000-$1 000,000
Number Employees: 2-4

5912 **Holly Camp Springs Inc**
PO Box 69
Hudgins, VA 23076-0069
804-795-2096
Fax: 804-795-1280 info@campholly springs.com
www.camphollysprings.com
Bottled spring water, bulk spring water
Owner: Dusty Dowdy
CFO: Jeannie Pierce
Vice President and Genreal Manager: Roland Dowdy
Contact: Roland Dowdy
rdowdy@camphollysprings.com
Plant Manager: Brandon Clements
Estimated Sales: $1.1,000,000
Number Employees: 5-9

5913 **Holly Hill Locker Company**
8728 Old State Road
Holly Hill, SC 29059
803-496-3611
Manufactuer of beef and pork
Owner: L Kenneth Folse Jr
Estimated Sales: Less than $500,000
Number Employees: 1-4
Type of Packaging: Consumer, Bulk

5914 **Holly's Oatmeal Inc**
241 Northside Dr
19 Calhoun Street
Torrington, CT 06790-3315
860-618-0090
Fax: 860-618-3008 hdimauro@optonline.net
Specialty oatmeals
Owner: Holly Dimauro
Estimated Sales: Less Than $500,000
Number Employees: 1-4

5915 **Holmes Cheese Co**
9444 State Route 39
Millersburg, OH 44654-9764
330-674-6451
Fax: 330-674-6673 www.holmescheese.com
Cheese and whey
President/CEO: Robert Ramseyer
rramseyer@holmescheeseco.com
VP: Walter Ramseyer
Estimated Sales: $4 Million
Number Employees: 20-49
Square Footage: 168000
Type of Packaging: Consumer, Food Service, Private Label, Bulk

5916 **Holmes Foods**
101 S Liberty Ave
Nixon, TX 78140-2401
830-582-1551
Fax: 830-582-1090 www.holmesfoods.com
Processor of poultry, whole birds, cut up parts, breast meat, and livers and gizzards
President & CEO: Phillip Morris
Controller: Chris Kutac
Assistant Controller: Becky Morris
SVP/Sales Director: Phil Hartung
Director/Live Operations: Keith Staggs
Year Founded: 1925
Estimated Sales: $20-50 Million
Number Employees: 100-249

5917 **Holsum Bakery Inc**
2322 W Lincoln St
Phoenix, AZ 85009-5827
602-252-2351
Fax: 602-252-6505 www.holsum.com
Baked goods.
Year Founded: 1900
Estimated Sales: $20-50 Million
Number Employees: 500-999
Other Locations:
Holsum Manufacturing Plant
Tempe AZ
Holsum Manufacturing Plant
Tolleson AZ
Brands:
Aunt Hattie's
Aunt Hattie's Quality Breads
Bar S
Holsum
Lefrancias
Roman Meal
Smart Kids

5918 **Holt's Bakery Inc**
101 Sellers St
Douglas, GA 31533-4607
912-384-2202
Fax: 912-384-7467 www.bullsheet.com
Baked goods, pastries, cookies
Owner: Howard Holt
CEO/Manager: Cecil Holt, Jr
Purchasing Agent: Paul Spivey
Estimated Sales: $1-2.5 000,000
Number Employees: 20-49

5919 **Holton Food Products**
500 W Burlington Ave
La Grange, IL 60525-2227
708-352-5599
Fax: 708-352-3788 info@holtonfp.com
www.holtonfoodproducts.com
Ingredients for frozen pies, cakes and cookies including egg whites and stabilizers
President: Ross Holton
ross.holton@hfpglobal.com
CEO: Paul Holton
Executive VP: John Holton
Estimated Sales: $2.5-5 Million
Number Employees: 10-19
Type of Packaging: Bulk

5920 **Holton Meat Processing**
701 Arizona Ave
Holton, KS 66436-1247
785-364-2331
biggsbeef.com/meat-processing.html
Beef
Owner: Lynn Brinkes
holtonmeat@gmail.com
Estimated Sales: $1-3 Million
Number Employees: 5-9
Type of Packaging: Consumer

5921 **Holy Kombucha**
Dallas, TX 75220
469-828-1572
855-694-6595
hello@holykombucha.com holykombucha.com
Carbonated probiotic kombucha
President/Owner: Leo Bienati
Number of Brands: 1
Number of Products: 13
Type of Packaging: Consumer
Brands:
HOME KOMBUCHA

5922 **Holy Smoke LLC**
991 Summerall Rd
Johns Island, SC 39455-8935
843-343-5581
www.holysmokeoliveoil.com
Smoked olive oils
Co-Founder: Kyle Payne
Co-Founder: Max Blackman
holysmokeoliveoil@gmail.com
Year Founded: 2012
Estimated Sales: $200,000
Number Employees: 1-4
Type of Packaging: Private Label

5923 **Hol, Mol,**
421 Obispo Ave
Long Beach, CA 90814-1502
562-439-2555
Fax: 512-671-4766 877-310-8453
info@holymole.com www.holemole.com
Salsa
Owner: Scott Bascon
onebite@holemole.com
Estimated Sales: Less Than $500,000
Number Employees: 5-9

5924 **Homarus Inc**
12-20 36th Ave
Long Island City, NY 11106
917-832-0333
Fax: 347-808-9948 info@homarus.com
Seafood, primarily lobster
Co-Owner/President: Peter Heineman
CEO: Chris Harvey
VP Sales: Thomas Marshall
Type of Packaging: Consumer, Food Service
Brands:
Homarus
Riverbank

5925 **Home Bakery**
300 S Main St
Rochester, MI 48307-2030
248-651-4830
Fax: 248-651-3458 sweet@thehomebakery.com
www.thehomebakery.com
Baked goods and chocolate
President: Tiffany Bruno
home_bakery@att.net
Estimated Sales: $500,000-$1 Million
Number Employees: 20-49
Type of Packaging: Food Service

5926 **Home Delivery Food Service**
1814 Washington St.
PO Box 215
Jefferson, GA 30549
706-367-9551
Fax: 706-367-4646
Frozen foods, meats and chicken
President: William Griffin, Sr.

5927 **Home Maid Bakery**
1005 Lower Main St
Wailuku, HI 96793-2008
808-244-7015
Fax: 808-242-8458 www.homemaidbakery.com
Bakery products
President: Jeremy Kozuki
jeremy@homemaidbakery.com
Sales Director: Leighton Saito
Operations: Wayne Takaki
Estimated Sales: $4-5 Million
Number Employees: 50-99
Number of Brands: 1
Number of Products: 100+
Type of Packaging: Consumer, Private Label

5928 **Home Market Food Inc**
140 Morgan Dr # 100
Norwood, MA 02062-5076
781-948-1500
Fax: 781-702-6171 800-367-8325
info@homemarketfoods.com
www.burgerdogs.com
Cooked steak, cooked meatballs, sausage, Italian sausage, cooked sausage
President: Wesley Atamian
Manager: Andy Stone
VP: Steve Smith
Director Sales: Dana Geremonte
VP Sales: Mike Weirmiller
Estimated Sales: $1-3 Million
Number Employees: 5-9
Brands:
Chef's Choice

5929 **Home Market Foods Inc.**
140 Morgan Dr.
Norwood, MA 02062
781-948-1500
www.homemarketfoods.com
Frozen foods, meal entrees, appteizers and snacks.
Chairman/CEO/President: Douglas Atamian
Year Founded: 1957
Estimated Sales: I
Number of Brands: 4
Type of Packaging: Consumer, Food Service, Private Label, Bulk
Brands:
Cooked Perfect®
RollerBites®
Bahama Mama®
Eisenberg®

5930 **Home Roast Coffee**
25126 State Road 54
Lutz, FL 33559-6256
813-949-0807
Fax: 813-948-6998
Coffee
Owner/President: Marvis Wood
Owner: Jaime Wood
Estimated Sales: $500,000-$1 000,000
Number Employees: 2-4

5931 **Home Run Inn Frozen Foods**
1300 Internationale Pkwy
Woodridge, IL 60517-4928
630-783-9696
Fax: 630-783-0069 800-636-9696
gyarka@homeruninn.com
www.homeruninnpizza.com
Frozen pizza
President: Joe Perrino
jperrino@homeruninn.com
Marketing Director: Gina Bolger
Operations: Dan Costello
Estimated Sales: $10-24.9 Million
Number Employees: 500-999
Type of Packaging: Consumer, Food Service, Private Label
Brands:
Home Run Inn

5932 **Home Style Bakery Of Grand Junction**
924 N 7th St
Grand Junction, CO 81501-3108
970-243-1233
www.homestylebakerygj.com
Baked goods
President: Donald Wilke
jdnwilk@juno.com
Estimated Sales: $1-2.5 Million
Number Employees: 20-49
Square Footage: 6000
Type of Packaging: Consumer, Food Service

5933 **Home Style Foods Inc**
5163 Edwin St
Hamtramck, MI 48212-3388
313-874-3250
Fax: 313-874-1026
Fresh prepared salads
President: Mike Kadian
Estimated Sales: $10-20 Million
Number Employees: 20-49
Type of Packaging: Private Label, Bulk

5934 **HomePlate Peanut Butter**
PO Box 40794
Austin, TX 78704
512-580-9980
info@homeplatepb.com
homeplatepb.com
Peanut butter
CEO & Co-Founder: Clint Greenleaf
Founding Partner: Danny Peoples
Founding Partner: Josh Beckett
Year Founded: 2015
Estimated Sales: Less than $500,000
Number Employees: 1-4
Type of Packaging: Private Label

5935 **Homefree LLC**
PO Box 491
Windham, NH 03087-0491
603-898-0172
800-552-7172
sales@homefreetreats.com
www.homefreetreats.com
Peanut, tree nut, egg and dairy free cookies and cakes
Founder: Jill Robbins
info@homefreetreats.com
Vice President, Sales & Marketing: Gail Schnur
Number Employees: 20-49
Type of Packaging: Consumer

5936 **Homegrown Naturals**
564 Gateway Dr
Napa, CA 94558
707-254-3700
Fax: 707-259-0219 800-288-1089
erciborgstrom@fantasticfoods.com
Natural foods products
Chief Executive Officer: John Foraker
VP Research/Development: Bob Kaake
Brand Team: Kathryn Keslosky
Web Marketing Manager: Mark Berger
Human Resources Manager: Amy Barberi
Consumer Relations Associate: Corrie Aldous
Consumer Relations Manager: Sherrie Crespin
Number Employees: 20-49
Brands:
Annie's

5937 **Homegrown Organic Farms**
PO Box 712
Porterville, CA 93258
559-306-1750
info@hgofarms.com
www.hgofarms.com
Fresh and freeze-dried organic fruit
CEO: Scott Mabs
Type of Packaging: Consumer

5938 **Homemade By Dorothy Boise**
5150 N Montecito Pl
Boise, ID 83704-2355
208-375-3720
800-657-7449
shop@homemadebydorothy.com
www.homemadebydorothy.com
Jellies, syrups, toppings, pancake and baking mixes, soups, beverages, candy, gift crates and baskets, seasonal and holiday products.
Owner: Anna Baumhoff
dorothy@dorthys.cc
Estimated Sales: $1-2.5 Million
Number Employees: 5-9

5939 **Homemade Harvey**
PO Box 49346
Los Angeles, CA 90049
310-472-4410
Fax: 310-471-4191 info@homemadeharvey.com
homemadeharvey.com
Organic crushed fruit snack pouches
CEO: Lawrence Jackson
Type of Packaging: Consumer

5940 **Homer's Ice Cream**
1237 Green Bay Rd
Wilmette, IL 60091-1699
847-251-0477
Fax: 847-251-0495 info@homersicecream.com
www.homersicecream.com
Ice cream and sorbet
Owner: Dean Poulos
icdino@yahoo.com
Marketing Director: Tean Poulos
VP: John Poulos
CEO: Stephen Poulos
Estimated Sales: $10-20 Million
Number Employees: 20-49
Square Footage: 16000
Type of Packaging: Consumer, Food Service, Private Label, Bulk

5941 **Homer's Wharf Seafood Company**
22 S Water Street
New Bedford, MA 02744-2613
508-997-0766
Fax: 508-999-9666
Seafood
Manager: Bruce Fontes
Estimated Sales: $10-20 Million
Number Employees: 50-99
Type of Packaging: Consumer

5942 **Homestead Baking Co**
145 N Broadway
Rumford, RI 02916-2801
401-434-0551
Fax: 401-438-0542 800-556-7216
pvican@homesteadbaking.com
www.homesteadbaking.com
Bread products
President: Peter Vican
pvican@homesteadbaking.com
VP: Bill Vican
Sales Manager: Vinny Palmiotti

Estimated Sales: $7 Million
Number Employees: 50-99
Square Footage: 160000
Type of Packaging: Food Service, Private Label, Bulk
Brands:
Matthews All Natural
Mrs Kavanagh's
New England Premium

5943 **Homestead Dairy**
11505 13th Rd
Plymouth, IN 46563-9014
574-936-6126
Fax: 315-769-8975
Dairy products
President: Robert Squires
Number Employees: 20-49

5944 **Homestead Fine Foods**
315 South Maple Ave
Suite 106
S San Francisco, CA 94080
650-615-0750
Fax: 650-615-0764 info@homesteadpasta.com
www.homesteadpasta.com
Fresh and frozen pastas and sauces
President: Terry Hall
Estimated Sales: $.5-1 million
Number Employees: 10-19
Type of Packaging: Consumer, Food Service, Private Label
Brands:
Homestead

5945 **Homestead Meats**
741 W 5th St
Delta, CO 81416-1505
970-874-1145
Fax: 970-856-3517 www.homesteadmeats.com
Frozen sausage; custom cut meat available
Owner: Delwin Bates
General Manager: Randy Sunderland
Estimated Sales: $1-2.5 Million
Number Employees: 20-49
Type of Packaging: Consumer, Food Service, Private Label
Brands:
Colorado Classic

5946 **Homestead Mills**
221 N River St
Cook, MN 55723-9503
218-666-5233
Fax: 218-666-5236 800-652-5233
www.homesteadmills.com
Grain, wild rice, cereals, flours and pancake mixes
Owner/President: Keith Aho
aho@homesteadmills.com
Owner/Vice President: Carol Aho
Plant Manager: Anita Reinke
Estimated Sales: $1 Million
Number Employees: 5-9
Number of Brands: 2
Number of Products: 27
Square Footage: 52000
Type of Packaging: Consumer, Food Service, Private Label, Bulk
Brands:
Country Blend Cereal
Homestead Mills
Noprthern Lites Pancakes
Potato Pancake Mix
South of the Border Chili
Specialty Flour
Uncle Waynes Fish Batter

5947 **Homestead Ravioli Company**
315 South Maple Avenue
Suite 106
South San Francisco, CA 94080
650-615-0750
Fax: 650-615-0764 Info@HomesteadPasta.com
www.homesteadpasta.com
Italian frozen specialties
President: Terry Hall
Estimated Sales: $5-9.9 Million
Number Employees: 10-19

5948 **Homestyle Bread Bakery**
3305 E Broadway Rd
Phoenix, AZ 85040-2829
602-268-0676
Fax: 602-276-1468
Bread and bakery products
President: James Boots
Vice President, Sales: Robert Schurman
Estimated Sales: $5-9.9 000,000
Number Employees: 20-49

5949 **Hometown Bagel Inc**
12401 S Kedvale Ave
Alsip, IL 60803-1818
708-385-0002
info@hometownbagel.com
www.hometownbagel.com
Bagel crisps
Co-Founder: Mike Lally
Co-Founder: Dawn Lally
Vice President: Russ Follis
russ@hometownbagel.com
Number Employees: 10-19

5950 **Homewood Winery**
23120 Burndale Rd
Sonoma, CA 95476-9722
707-996-6353
Fax: 707-996-6935 www.homewoodwinery.com
Wines
President/Vineyard Manager: David Homewood
davidhomewood@vom.com
Estimated Sales: Under $500,000
Number Employees: 1-4
Type of Packaging: Private Label

5951 **Honee Bear Canning**
72100 M 40
Lawton, MI 49065-8444
269-624-4611
Fax: 269-624-6009 800-626-2327
hbsales@honeebear.com www.honeebear.com
Berries, cherries, plums, asparagus, blueberries; pie fillings
President: Robert Packer
CEO: Steve Packer
steve@honeebear.com
Sales Manager: Ronald Armstrong
Director: Toby Fields
Estimated Sales: $10-20 Million
Number Employees: 50-99
Square Footage: 450000
Type of Packaging: Consumer, Food Service
Brands:
Michigan Made

5952 **Honest Tea Inc**
1 Coca-Cola Plz NW
Atlanta, GA 30313
800-520-2653
honestPR@coca-cola.com www.honesttea.com
Organic tea, lemonade, juice, and soda
Co-Founder & CEO Emeritus: Seth Goldman
seth@honesttea.com
Co-Founder: Barry Nalebuff
Marketing Director: Matt O'Brien
Number Employees: 50-99
Parent Co: The Coca-Cola Company
Type of Packaging: Consumer, Bulk

5953 **Honey Acres**
N1557 Hwy 67
Neosho, WI 53059
920-474-4411
info@honeyacres.com
www.honeyacres.com
Honey and honey products, including honey chocolates, honey mustards, andhoney straws.
CEO: John Gabielian
Marketing Manager: Debra Champeau
Director of Inside Sales & Marketing: Tiarra Detert
Plant Manager: Eugene Brueggeman
eugene@honeyacres.com
Year Founded: 1852
Estimated Sales: $5-9.9 Million
Number Employees: 30
Number of Products: 50
Square Footage: 144000
Type of Packaging: Consumer, Food Service, Private Label, Bulk
Brands:
Honey Acres

5954 **Honey Bear Fruit Basket**
6321 Washington St # N
Denver, CO 80216-1100
303-297-3390
Fax: 303-297-3393 888-330-2327
Fine wine jelly, sauce, scone mix, lemon curd
Owner: Carol Kincler
General Manager: Linda Wenz
Contact: Mary Cucarola
honeybearbaskets@gmail.com
Estimated Sales: $500,000-$1 Million
Number Employees: 1-4
Brands:
Penelope's

5955 **Honey Bee Company**
3875 Mansell Road
Alpharetta, GA 30022
800-367-7720
Fax: 800-728-4426 800-572-8838
catalogservice@hbham.com
www.honeybakedonline.com
Flavored honey
Manager: Ray Grant
Estimated Sales: $2.5-5 Million
Number Employees: 1-4
Type of Packaging: Private Label, Bulk

5956 **Honey Blossom**
The Colony, TX 75056
469-582-7508
info@rawhoneyblossom.com
rawhoneyblossom.com
Raw honey

5957 **Honey Butter Products Co**
103 S Heintzelman St
Manheim, PA 17545-1723
717-665-9323
Fax: 717-665-4422 www.downeyshoneybutter.com
Honey butter
Owner: Kevin Sadd
Estimated Sales: $1 Million
Number Employees: 5-9
Square Footage: 40000
Type of Packaging: Consumer, Food Service
Brands:
Downey's

5958 **Honey Dew Donuts**
2 Taunton St # 3
Plainville, MA 02762-2137
508-699-3900
Fax: 508-699-3949 www.honeydewdonuts.com
Donuts
President: Richard Bowen
richard@honeydewdonuts.com
Number Employees: 10-19

5959 **Honey Hut**
7304 Chippewa Rd
Brecksville, OH 44141-2304
440-526-0606
Fax: 216-661-1883 HoneyHut@Adelphia.net
www.honeyhut.com
Ice cream, frozen desserts
President/Owner: Frank Page
Estimated Sales: Less Than $500,000
Number Employees: 5-9

5960 **Honey Mama's**
2030 N Williams Ave
Portland, OR 97227-1930
888-506-2627
honeymamas.com
Gluten and dairy free snack bars and fudge.
Owner: Christy Goldsby
Year Founded: 2014
Estimated Sales: $200,000
Number Employees: 2
Type of Packaging: Private Label

5961 **Honey Ridge Farms**
12310 NE 245th Ave
Brush Prairie, WA 98606-7740
360-256-0086
Fax: 360-883-2679 info@honeyridgefarms.com
www.honeyridgefarms.com
Honey and gourmet honey products
Owner: Leeanne Goetz
info@honeyridgefarms.com
Estimated Sales: Less Than $500,000
Number Employees: 1-4

5962 **Honey Run Winery**
2309 Park Ave
Chico, CA 95928-6706
530-345-6405
Fax: 530-894-6639 honeyrun@honeyrun.com
Berry wines

President: John Hasle
VP: Amy Hasle
Estimated Sales: $.5-1 million
Number Employees: 1-4

5963 Honey Stinger
PO Box 771162
Steamboat Sprints, CO 80477
866-464-6639
www.honeystinger.com
Organic waffles, honey, protein bars, energy chews and gels
Number of Brands: 1
Number of Products: 5
Type of Packaging: Consumer
Brands:
HONEY STINGER

5964 Honey Wafer Baking Co
13952 Kildare Ave
Crestwood, IL 60445-2357
708-388-9010
Fax: 708-388-9680 800-977-9012
info@honeywater.com www.anisihoneywafer.com
Gourmet honey wafers
Owner/President: Tony Lewandowski
Vice President: Adrienne Lewandowski
Estimated Sales: Under $500,000
Number Employees: 1-4
Type of Packaging: Consumer
Brands:
Anisi

5965 Honey World
165 N Main Avenue
Parker, SD 57053
605-297-4188
Fax: 605-297-4118 candles@iw.net
Honey
President: Glen Wollman
Estimated Sales: $5-10 Million
Number Employees: 1-4
Type of Packaging: Private Label, Bulk

5966 Honeybaked Ham
12170 Mason Montgomery Rd
Cincinnati, OH 45249-1336
513-583-8792
Fax: 513-583-4190 www.honeybaked.com
Baked hams, turkey, frozen desserts and party trays
President/CEO: Craig Kurz
z8407@hbham.com
Site Manager: Ericka Puckett
Estimated Sales: $5-10 Million
Number Employees: 5-9
Brands:
Honey Baked Ham

5967 Honeydrop Beverages
Houston, TX 77056
www.honeydrop.com
Organic lemonades sweetened with honey
Contact: Becky Byszewski
bbyszewski@honeydrop.com
Brands:
Obe Sauce
Obe Sauce Mix

5968 (HQ)Honeyville Grain Inc
1080 N Main St
Suite 100
Brigham City, UT 84302
435-494-4200
Fax: 435-734-9482 www.honeyville.com
Bakery mixes and ingredients
Founder: Lowell Sherratt
VP Finance: Robert Anderson
Executive VP: Trevor Christensen
Director Marketing/Sales: Don Mann
Sales Manager: Craig Dunford
Assistant Operations Manager: Garth Rollins
Estimated Sales: $10-20 Million
Number Employees: 10-19
Square Footage: 120000
Type of Packaging: Consumer, Food Service, Private Label, Bulk
Other Locations:
California Distribution
Rancho Cucamonga CA
Utah Tempsure & Wholesale
Salt Lake City UT
Arizona Wholsale Distribution
Tempe AZ
Honeyville Grain Mill
Honeyville UT
Ohio Distribution Center
West Chester OH

5969 Honeywood Winery
1350 Hines St SE
Salem, OR 97302-2521
503-362-4111
Fax: 503-362-4112 800-726-4101
info@honeywoodwinery.com
www.honeywoodwinery.com
Grape and fruit wines
President: Lesley Gallick
info@honeywoodwinery.com
VP: Marlene K Gallick
Estimated Sales: $1 Million+
Number Employees: 5-9
Number of Brands: 5
Number of Products: 45
Square Footage: 88000
Type of Packaging: Private Label
Brands:
Honeyman & Wood
Honeywood Grande
Honeywood North American Grape
Honeywood Premium

5970 Hong Kong Noodle Company
2350 S Wentworth Ave
Chicago, IL 60616
312-842-0480
Fax: 312-842-7069
Egg noodles
Manager: Glenn Jung
Vice President/Co-Owner: Harry Chung
Estimated Sales: $2.5-5 Million
Number Employees: 20-49
Type of Packaging: Food Service

5971 Hong Kong Supermarket
5495 Jimmy Carter Blvd # F113
Norcross, GA 30093-1537
770-582-6800
Fax: 404-325-3311 www.hongkongmarketga.com
Oriental food items, ethnic foods, full line seafood
Owner: Ly Tieu
Estimated Sales: $10-20 Million
Number Employees: 1-4

5972 Hong Tou Noodle Company
7059 N Figueroa St
Los Angeles, CA 90042
323-256-3843
Noodles
Owner: Peter Kwong
General Manager: Peter Kong
Estimated Sales: $500,000-$1 000,000
Number Employees: 1-4

5973 Hongar Farms Gourmet Foods
2121 Tucker Industrial Rd
Tucker, GA 30084-5017
770-938-9884
Fax: 770-938-8964 888-296-7191
info@hongarfarms.com www.hongarfarms.com
Oils and vinegars
President: Todd Hurst
todd@hungarfarm.com
Estimated Sales: $.5-1 million
Number Employees: 5-9

5974 HongryHawg of Louisiana
P.O. Box 787
Prairieville, LA 70769
225-622-4011
Fax: 225-622-0546 888-772-4294
answers@cajunsauce.com www.cajunsauce.com
Hot sauce, barbecue sauce, jambalaya mix, cajun seasoning and gift boxes.
Owner: Hiram Davis
Estimated Sales: $5-10 Million
Number Employees: 5-9

5975 Honickman Affiliates
8275 Route 130
Pennsauken, NJ 08110-1435
856-665-6200
Fax: 856-661-4684 800-573-7745
Soft drinks
Chairman: Harold Honickman
CEO: Jeffrey Honickman
Chief Financial Officer: Walt Wilkinson
Business Development Manager: Larry Linder
Production Manager: Phil Forte
Estimated Sales: $10-20 Million
Number Employees: 20-49
Parent Co: PepsiCo North America
Type of Packaging: Consumer, Food Service
Brands:
Cadbury Schweppes
Coors
Pepsi-Cola
Snapple
South Beach

5976 Honig Vineyard and Winery
850 Rutherford Road
Rutherford, CA 94573
707-963-5618
Fax: 707-963-5639 800-929-2217
www.honigwine.com
Wines
President: Michael Honig
COO: Tony Benedetti
Marketing Director: Regina Weinstein
Estimated Sales: $5-9.9 Million
Number Employees: 5-9
Type of Packaging: Private Label

5977 Honolulu Fish Company
824 Gulick Avenue
Honolulu, HI 96819-1998
808-833-1123
Fax: 808-836-1045 sales@honolulufish.com
www.honolulufish.com
Sashimi-grade fish
Founder, Chief Executive Officer: Wayne Samiere
Contact: William Grafton
william@honolulufish.com

5978 Honso USA
P.O.Box 6729
Chandler, AZ 85246
602-377-8787
Fax: 480-377-6649 888-461-5808
info@honso.com www.HonsoUSA.com
Chinese herbal products.
President: Dan Wen
Estimated Sales: $300,000-500,000
Number Employees: 1-4

5979 Hood Home Service
187 S Winooski Ave
Burlington, VT 05401-4537
802-864-0941
Ice cream, frozen desserts, milk, juices
Plant Manager: David Roberts
Estimated Sales: $500,000 appx.
Number Employees: 1-4
Parent Co: Hood Foods

5980 Hood River Coffee Co
1310 Tucker Rd
Hood River, OR 97031-8647
541-386-3908
Fax: 541-386-3998 800-336-2954
customerservice@hoodrivercoffeeco.com
Coffee
Owner: Mark Hudon
mark@hoodrivercoffeeco.com
Number Employees: 5-9

5981 Hood River Distillers Inc
660 Riverside Dr
Hood River, OR 97031-1177
541-386-1588
Fax: 541-386-2520 HRDsales@HRDspirits.com
www.findmonarch.com
Spirits, including whisky, rum, gin, vodka, schnapps, Irish cream whiskey, scotch and liqueurs
President: Olivia Barker
oliviab@hrdspirits.com
CFO: Gary Goatcher
VP & General Manager: Lynda Webber
Director of Marketing: Tia Bledsoe
VP Sales: Erik Svenson
Materials/Special Projects Manager: Brad Whiting
Estimated Sales: $4.6 Million
Number Employees: 50-99
Square Footage: 212000
Brands:
Pendleton Whisky
Pendleton1910™
Yazi Ginger Vodka
Broker's London Dry Gin
Sinfire™ Cinnamon Whisky
Ullr Nordic Libation
Knickers Irish Cream Whiskey

Broker's Whiskey
Monarch
Hrd

5982 **Hood River Vineyards and Winery**
4693 Westwood Drive
Hood River, OR 97031
541-386-3772
Fax: 541-386-5880 hoodriverwines@gmail.com
www.hoodrivervineyardsandwinery.com
Wines
President: Bernie Lerch
VP: Anne Lerch
Contact: Anne Lerch
hoodriverwines@gmail.com
Estimated Sales: $1-2.5 Million
Number Employees: 1-4

5983 **Hood Sterile Division**
P.O.Box 491
Oneida, NY 13421-0491
315-363-3870
Fax: 315-363-9534 www.hphood.com
Coffeemate, beverages
Plant Manager: Steve Pelkey
Estimated Sales: Under $500,000
Number Employees: 100-249
Parent Co: Hood Foods

5984 **Hoodsport Winery**
23501 N US Highway 101 # 3
Hoodsport, WA 98548-9605
360-877-9894
Fax: 360-877-9508 800-580-9894
www.hoodsport.com
Wines
President: Peggy Patterson
CEO: Ann Patterson
ann@hoodsport.com
Estimated Sales: $5-10 Million
Number Employees: 10-19
Type of Packaging: Private Label
Brands:
Hoodsport

5985 **Hook Line and Savor**
Gloucester, MA 01930
833-457-2867
hooklineandsavor.com
Frozen fish
Founder: Freddie Turner
Marketing: Sean Rogerson

5986 **Hooks Cheese Co**
320 Commerce St
Mineral Point, WI 53565-1240
608-987-3259
Fax: 608-987-2658 hookscheese@yahoo.com
www.hookscheese.com
Cheese
President: Tony Hook
jahduda@yahoo.com
Owner: Julie Hook
Estimated Sales: $1-2.5 000,000
Number Employees: 5-9

5987 **Hoopeston Foods Inc**
201 W Travelers Trail
Suite 202
Burnsville, MN 55337-2913
952-854-0903
Fax: 952-854-6874 www.hfinc3.qwestoffice.net
Canned dry beans, chili, stews, soups, sauces, tamales and meats
President: Eric Newman
CEO: Tad Ballentyne
SVP: Corey Hoerning
Sales Manager: Lori Kalahar
Plant Manager: Mel Lollar
Estimated Sales: $5-10 Million
Number Employees: 20-49
Type of Packaging: Food Service, Private Label
Brands:
Nature's Gold
Tio Franco

5988 **Hoople Country Kitchen Inc**
714 N 5th St
Rockport, IN 47635-1103
812-649-2351
Fax: 812-649-2836 877-466-7537
customerservice@hooplecountrykitchens.com
www.hooplecountrykitchens.com
Pork sausage, prepared salads, corn meal mush and horseradish
President: David Caskey
Treasurer: Franklin Caskey
VP: Denise Caskey
Estimated Sales: $5-10 Million
Number Employees: 10-19
Type of Packaging: Consumer

5989 **Hop Kiln Winery**
6050 Westside Rd
Healdsburg, CA 95448
707-433-6491
Fax: 707-433-6436 info@hkgwines.com
www.hopkilnwinery.com
Wines
CEO: David Di Loreto
Contact: Ellissa Anderson
eanderson@hkgwines.com
Plant Manager: Erich Bradley
Estimated Sales: $5-9.9 Million
Number Employees: 10-19
Brands:
Chardonnay Barrel Select
Late Harvest Zinfandel
Marty Griffin Big Red
Primivito Zinfandel
Sonoma County Zinfandel
Thousand Flowers
Valdiguie

5990 **Hope Creamery**
9043 SW 37th Ave
Hope, MN 56046-2003
507-451-2029
www.hopecreamery.com
Butter
President/Owner: Victor Mrotz
tim@hopecreamery.com
Operations: Gene Kruckeberg
Estimated Sales: $300,000-$500,000
Number Employees: 1-4
Square Footage: 12000
Type of Packaging: Consumer, Bulk
Brands:
Hope

5991 **Hope Foods**
PO Box 3744
Boulder, CO 80307-3744
USA
303-248-7019
info@hopefoods.com
www.hopefoods.com
Hummus, dips, chocolate
President: Robbie Rech
Marketing Director: Will Burger
VP Of Sales: Alek Ramoska
VP Of Operations: Ian Beert
Estimated Sales: 160,000
Number Employees: 20-49

5992 **Hopkins Inn Of Lake Waramaug**
22 Hopkins Rd
Warren, CT 06777-1016
860-868-7295
Fax: 860-868-9248 info@thehopkinsinn.com
www.thehopkinsinn.com
Gourmet salad dressings
President: Beth Schober
hopkins@gmail.com
Estimated Sales: $1-2.5 Million
Number Employees: 20-49
Brands:
Hopkins Inn Caesar Dressing
Hopkins Inn House Dressing

5993 **Hopkins Vineyard**
25 Hopkins Rd
Warren, CT 06777-1015
860-868-7954
Fax: 860-868-1768 www.hopkinsvineyard.com
Wines
Owner: Hilary Criollo
hopkinsvineyard@charter.net
Estimated Sales: $1-2.5 Million
Number Employees: 5-9
Type of Packaging: Private Label
Brands:
Highland Estates
Hopkins Vineyard
Hopkins Westwind

5994 **Hops Extract Corporation of America**
1 West Washington Ave.
Yakima, WA 98903
509-248-1530
Fax: 509-457-4638 800-339-8410
sales@hopsteiner.com www.hopsteiner.com
Hops
Manager: Dave Dunmham
ddunmham@hopsteiner.com
Operations: Paul Signorotti
Year Founded: 1845
Estimated Sales: $20-50 Million
Number Employees: 20-49
Parent Co: S. S. Steiner, Inc.

5995 **Horizon Cellars Winery**
466 Vineyard Ridge
Siler City, NC 27344
919-742-1404
Fax: 919-742-3885 www.horizoncellars.com
Wines
Owner: Guy Loeffler
Contact: Nicole Loeffler
nicole@horizoncellars.com
Estimated Sales: $100,000
Number Employees: 6

5996 **Horizon Organic Dairy**
12002 Airport Way
Broomfield, CO 80021-2546
303-635-4000
888-494-3020
info@horizonorganic.com
Organic dairy products
President: Mike Ferry
Communication Manager: Sara Loveday
Contact: Heidy Sowatzke
heidys@horizonorganic.com
VP Operations: Jule Taylor
Estimated Sales: $20-50 Million
Number Employees: 50-99
Type of Packaging: Consumer
Brands:
Organic Cow

5997 **Horizon Poultry**
92 Cartwright Avenue
Toronto, ON M6A 1V2
Canada
519-364-3200
Fax: 519-364-4692 cphilipp@schneiderfoods.ca
www.schneiderfoods.ca/
Chickens; eggs
Quality Assurance: Cynthia Philippe
Number Employees: 165
Parent Co: J.M. Schneider
Type of Packaging: Consumer, Food Service, Private Label, Bulk

5998 **Horizon Snack Foods**
7066 Las Positas Rd # G
Livermore, CA 94551-5134
925-373-7700
Fax: 925-373-8303 800-229-2552
customerservice@horizonfoodgroup.com
Pies
Owner: Bob Sharp
Controller: Brett Howell
Estimated Sales: $2.5-5,000,000
Number Employees: 10-19

5999 **Horlacher Meats**
30 W 700 N # B
Logan, UT 84321-3214
435-752-1287
Fresh and frozen ham, beef jerky and roast beef
Owner: Betty Horlacher
mombetty8@yahoo.com
Estimated Sales: Less Than $500,000
Number Employees: 1-4
Square Footage: 32000
Type of Packaging: Consumer, Bulk

6000 **Hormel Foods Corp.**
1 Hormel Pl.
Austin, MN 55912
507-437-5611
www.hormelfoods.com
Meat and grocery products.

Chairman/President/CEO: Jim Snee
Executive VP/CFO: Jim Sheehan
Senior VP/General Counsel: Lori Marco
Senior VP, R&D: Kevin Myers
Vice President, Quality Management: Richard Carlson
Year Founded: 1891
Estimated Sales: $9 Billion
Number Employees: 20,000
Number of Brands: 52
Type of Packaging: Consumer, Food Service, Private Label
Other Locations:
Manufacturing Facility
Austin MN
Manufacturing Facility
Algona IA
Manufacturing Facility
Alma KS
Manufacturing Facility
Atlanta GA
Manufacturing Facility
Aurora IL
Manufacturing Facility
Barron WI
Manufacturing Facility
Beloit WI
Manufacturing Facility
Bondurant IA
Manufacturing Facility
Bremin GA
Manufacturing Facility
Browerville MN
Manufacturing Facility
Dayton OH
Manufacturing Facility
Dubuque IA
Manufacturing Facility
Eldridge IA
Brands:
Applegate®
Hormel®
Jennie-O Turkey®
Austin Blues BBQ®
Bacon 1®
Real Bacon Toppings
Black Label Bacon®
Bufalo®
Burke®
Cafe H®
Chi-Chi's®
Premium Chicken Breast®
Hormel Chili®
Columbus®
Compleats®
Cure 81®
Dan's Prize®
Del Fuerte®
Deli Meats
DiLusso Deli Company®
Dinty Moore®
Don Miguel®
Doña María™
Embasa®
Evolve™
Fire Braised Meats®
Fontanini®
Fuse Burger™
Gatherings®
Herbox®
Herdez®
Hormel Health Labs
House of Tsang®
Justin's®
La Victoria®
Little Sizzlers®
Lloyds Barbeque Co®
Mary Kitchen®
Muscle Milk®
Natural Choice®
Not So Sloppy Joe®
Old Smokehouse®
Hormel Pepperoni®
Refrigerated Entre,s
Hormel Side Dishes
Skippy®
SPAM®
Stagg Chili®
Hormel Taco Meats®
Valley Fresh®
Vital Cuisine™
Wholly Guacamole®

6001 Hornell Brewing Company
5 Dakota Dr
New Hyde Park, NY 11042-1109
516-812-0300
Fax: 516-326-4988

Beers
President: John Ferolito
Contact: Ann Marie
agallager@arizonaicedt.com
Estimated Sales: F
Number Employees: 500-999

6002 Horner International
5304 Emerson Drive
Raleigh, NC 27609
919-787-3112
Fax: 919-787-4272 sales@hornerintl.com
www.hornerinternational.com
Natural extracts and flavors
Contact: Ladiner Blaylock
ladiner.blaylock@hornerintl.com
Parent Co: Horner International

6003 Horseshoe Brand
1179 Rte. 199
Milan, NY 12571
845-240-2390
info@horseshoebrand.com
www.horseshoebrand.com
Flavored hot sauces and barbecue sauces
Owner: Ryan Fleischhauer
Year Founded: 2008
Number of Brands: 1
Number of Products: 11
Type of Packaging: Consumer, Private Label
Brands:
Horseshoe Brand

6004 Horst Seafood
2315 Industrial Blvd
Juneau, AK 99801-8534
907-790-4300
Fax: 907-790-5534 877-518-4300
horsts@gci.net
Fresh and frozen seafood
President: Horst Schramm
horsts@gci.net
Estimated Sales: Less Than $500,000
Number Employees: 1-4
Type of Packaging: Consumer

6005 Horton Fruit Co Inc
4701 Jennings Ln
Louisville, KY 40218-2967
502-969-1375
Fax: 502-964-1515 800-626-2245
Tomatoes, onions, spinach, kale, coleslaw, bananas, avocados, pineapples and caramel apples
Chairman/CEO: Albert Horton
ahorton@hortonfruit.com
President/COO: Jackson Woodward
Treasurer: Steve Edelen
Vice President: Bill Benoit
Sales/Procurement: Tom Smith
Transportation Manager: Bobby Harlow
Number Employees: 100-249
Square Footage: 400000
Type of Packaging: Consumer, Food Service, Private Label
Other Locations:
Louisville Produce Terminal
Louisville KY

6006 Horton Vineyards
6399 Spotswood Trl
Gordonsville, VA 22942-7735
540-832-7440
Fax: 540-832-7187 800-829-4633
vawinee@aol.com www.hortonwine.com
Wines
President: Dennis Horton
vawinee@aol.com
Estimated Sales: $5-10 Million
Number Employees: 10-19

6007 Hosemen & Roche Vitamins & Fine Chemicals
340 Kingsland Street
Building 787
Nutley, NJ 07110-1199
973-235-5000
Fax: 973-235-7605 800-526-6367
Bulk vitamins, carotenoids and citric acids for food manufacturing
President: Dr Franz B Humer
Chief Executive Officer: Severin Schwan
Chief Operating Officer: Pascal Soriot
Estimated Sales: Less than $500,000
Number Employees: 1-4
Parent Co: Hoffman-La Roche
Type of Packaging: Bulk
Brands:
Roche

6008 Hosford & Wood Fresh Seafood Providers
2545 E 7th Street
Tucson, AZ 85716-4701
520-795-1920
Fax: 520-795-1010
Seafood
President: Anita Wood
Secretary: Bruce Hosford

6009 Hosmer Mountain Bottling Co
217 Mountain St
Willimantic, CT 06226-3211
860-423-1555
Fax: 860-423-2207 800-763-2445
www.hosmersoda.com
Soft drinks
President/CEO: Andrew Potvin
VP Marketing Manager: Bill Potvin
Estimated Sales: $2.5-5 Million
Number Employees: 5-9
Type of Packaging: Private Label
Brands:
Hosmer Mountain Soft Drinks

6010 Hospitality Mints LLC
213 Candy Ln
P.O. Drawer 3140
Boone, NC 28607
Fax: 828-264-6933 800-334-5181
mints@hospitalitymints.com
www.hospitalitymints.com
Mint candies
President/CEO: Patrick Viancourt
CFO/COO: Walter Kaudelka
VP of Marketing: Kathi Guy
Estimated Sales: $500,000-$1 Million
Number Employees: 10-19
Square Footage: 252000
Parent Co: Party Sweets
Type of Packaging: Consumer, Food Service, Private Label, Bulk
Brands:
Hospitality

6011 Hoss-S
12985 Dunnings Hwy
PO Box 219
Claysburg, PA 16625-8202
814-693-3453
Fax: 814-239-5922 800-438-7439
www.hosswares.com
Prepared foods
Owner: Bill Campbell
VP: Mark Spinazzola
Plant Manager: Rocky Rhodes
Estimated Sales: Less Than $500,000
Number Employees: 5-9

6012 Host Defense Mushrooms
800-780-9126
info@fungi.com hostdefense.com
Mushroom capsules, extracts and sprays
Founder: Paul Stamets
Type of Packaging: Consumer

6013 Hostess Brands
PO Box 419593
Kansas City, MO 64141
816-701-4600
www.hostessbrands.com
Prepackaged sweet baked goods.
President/CEO: Andrew Callahan
Executive VP/CFO: Thomas Peterson
Executive VP/Chief Admin. Officer: Andrew Jacobs
Senior VP, Quality/Food Safety/R&D: Darryl Riley
Year Founded: 2013
Estimated Sales: $776 Million
Type of Packaging: Consumer
Brands:
Twinkies®
Hostess CupCakes®
DingDongs®
Zingers®

Donettes®
Ho Hos®

6014 Hot Cakes-Molten Chocolate
5427 Ballard Ave NW
Seattle, WA 98107-4052
206-453-3792
kirsten@kirstengrahampr.com
www.getyourhotcakes.com
Hot cakes and sauces
Founder: Autumn Martin
Estimated Sales: Less Than $500,000
Number Employees: 10-19

6015 Hot Licks
2830 Via Orange Way
Suite A
Spring Valley, CA 91978
Fax: 619-660-7429 888-766-6468
orders@hotlickssauces.com
www.hotlickssauces.com
Hot sauces, salsas, mustards, condiments, snacks, mixes and seasonings, bbq sauces, marinades, and gifts.
Estimated Sales: Less than $500,000
Number Employees: 1-4
Brands:
Amazon Pepper Products
California Just Chile!
Death Valley Habanero
Hot! Hot! Hot!
Ottimo
Pepe's Sauce
Ring of Fire

6016 Hot Mama's Foods
134 Avocado St
Springfield, MA 01104
413-737-6572
Fax: 413-737-6793
Gourmet foods, including salsa, hummus, pesto, prepared salads, dips and ready-to-cook products; custom packaging and consulting
President: Matt Morse
Finance & Business Development: Herb Heller
Executive Chef: Josh Cooper
Director of Human Resources: Lisa Dufour
Director of Operations: Jim Boyle
Estimated Sales: $14.9 Million
Number Employees: 90
Square Footage: 13500

6017 Hot Springs Packing Co Inc
580 Mid America Blvd
Hot Springs, AR 71913-8412
501-767-2363
Fax: 501-767-9715 800-535-0449
hspc@hotspringspacking.com
www.hotspringspacking.com
Specialty sausages, deli meats and hams
President/CEO: John Stubblefield
hspc@hotspringspacking.com
Estimated Sales: $4.3 Million
Number Employees: 20-49
Type of Packaging: Consumer, Food Service

6018 Hot Wachula's
P.O.Box 2376
Lakeland, FL 33806-2376
863-602-0857
Fax: 863-665-0358 877-883-8700
www.hotwachulas.com
Gourmet dips and sauces, marinades
President: Matt Barber
Estimated Sales: $1 Million
Number Employees: 5-9
Brands:
Hot Wachula's Gourmet Dips & Sauces

6019 Houdini Inc
4225 N Palm St
Fullerton, CA 92835-1045
714-525-0325
Fax: 714-996-9605
www.winecountrygiftbaskets.com
Gourmet food, wine and gift baskets
Owner: Tim Dean
tdean@houdiniinc.com
Estimated Sales: $500,000-$1 Million
Number Employees: 10-19
Brands:
California Pantry
Wine Country

6020 Houlton Farms Dairy
25 Commonwealth Ave
Houlton, ME 04730-2347
207-532-3170
Fax: 207-532-3613
Dairy products
Owner: Alice Lincoln
Estimated Sales: $5-10 000,000
Number Employees: 10-19

6021 House Foods America Corp
7351 Orangewood Ave
Garden Grove, CA 92841-1411
714-901-4350
Fax: 714-901-4235 877-333-7077
www.house-foods.com
Tofu and tofu products; importer of curry, spices, ramen noodles and tea.
President: Shigeru Natake
shigeru@house-foods.com
Marketing Manager: Masahiko Kudo
Sales & Foodservice: Hirofumi Fujimura
Production & Supply Chain Management: Hajime Inoue
Purchasing, Cost Reduction, Admin: Keiji Matsumoto
Estimated Sales: $11.2 Million
Number Employees: 100-249
Square Footage: 60000
Parent Co: House Foods Corporation
Other Locations:
Somerset NJ
Garden Grove CA
NY
Brands:
Hinoichi
House Foods

6022 House of Coffee Beans
2348 Bissonnet St
Houston, TX 77005-1512
713-524-0057
Fax: 713-795-5410 800-422-1799
contact@houseofcoffeebeans.com
www.houseofcoffeebeans.com
Coffee
Owner: Roger Farber
Estimated Sales: Less than $500,000
Number Employees: 5-9
Square Footage: 56000
Type of Packaging: Consumer, Food Service, Private Label, Bulk

6023 House of Flavors Inc
110 N William St
Ludington, MI 49431-2092
231-845-7369
Fax: 616-845-7371 800-930-7740
www.houseofflavors.com
Kosher ice cream and frozen novelties
Owner: Pat Calder
hfpat@houseofflavors.com
Number Employees: 1-4
Type of Packaging: Consumer, Food Service

6024 House of Herbs LLC
38 Ann St
Passaic, NJ 07055-5889
973-779-2422
Fax: 973-779-6809
Pickles, sauces and salad dressings
Owner: Paul Fischer
Number Employees: 5-9

6025 House of Raeford Farms Inc.
PO Box 699
Rose Hill, NC 28458
910-289-3191
www.houseofraeford.com
Chickens and turkeys.
Chairman: Marvin Johnson
Chief Executive Officer/President: Robert Johnson
President, Cooked Products Group: Donald Taber
Chief Financial Officer: Ken Qualls
Year Founded: 1925
Estimated Sales: $705 Million
Number Employees: 5,500
Number of Brands: 3
Square Footage: 400000
Type of Packaging: Food Service
Other Locations:
Further Processing Plant/Distrib.
Raeford NC
Chicken Processing Plant
Arcadia LA
Columbia Farms Chicken Processing
Columbia SC
Breaded Chicken & Turkey Products
Hemingway SC
Columbia Farms Chicken Plant
Greenville SC
Brands:
House of Raeford®
Speedy Bird®
Filet Of Chicken®

6026 House of Spices
12740 Willets Point Blvd
Flushing, NY 11368-1506
718-507-4600
Fax: 718-507-4798
customerservice@hosindia.com
www.hosindia.com
Pickles, condiment pastes, chutney, snack foods, candy, ice cream and frozen foods; importer of Indian-Pakistani basmati rice, lentils, spices, oils and nuts; exporter of pickles, condiments and spices.
President: Candace Kuechler
ckuechler@rich.com
Estimated Sales: $5-10 Millio
Number Employees: 50-99
Number of Brands: 25
Number of Products: 2000
Square Footage: 1200000
Type of Packaging: Consumer, Food Service, Private Label, Bulk
Other Locations:
Manufacturing Facility
Stafford TX
Manufacturing Facility
Elk Grove IL
Manufacturing Facility
Forestville MD
Manufacturing Facility
Hayward CA
Manufacturing Facility
Orlando FL
Manufacturing Facility
Norcross GA
Manufacturing Facility
Worcester MA
Brands:
Laxmi
Bombay Bites
Masala Craft
Maazo
Garvi Gujarat
Shamiana
Amma's Kitchen
Chai Bites

6027 House of Thaller Inc
1600 Harris Rd
Knoxville, TN 37924-2215
865-689-5893
Fax: 865-689-7132 800-462-3365
sales@houseofthaller.com
www.houseofthaller.com
Sandwich spreads and prepared salads
President: John Thaller
sales@houseofthaller.com
Finance Executive/HR Manager: Stephanie Cooper
R&D Director: Beth Ann Disney
Marketing Manager/Sales Executive: John Thaller
Production Manager: Wes Curnutt
Purchasing Agent: Katherine Reed
Estimated Sales: $8 Million
Number Employees: 20-49
Square Footage: 32000
Type of Packaging: Consumer, Food Service, Private Label, Bulk

6028 House of Tsang
2345 3rd St
San Francisco, CA 94107-3108
415-282-9952
Fax: 415-243-0157 lgmarconi@hormel.com
Asian sauces, marinades, oils, vegetables and sauce combinations.
Owner: David Haase
Estimated Sales: $1 Million
Parent Co: Hormel Foods International Corporation

6029 House of Webster
1013 N 2nd St
P.O. Box 1988
Rogers, AR 72757
479-636-2974
Fax: 479-636-2974 800-369-4641
houseofwebster.com

Jams, jellies, preserves, spreads; relish; salsa; mustard; syrup; BBQ sauce; pickled products; cheese products; crackers; cured meats; nuts; baking mixes; soups; spices and seasonings; tea and coffee.
President: John Griffin
Year Founded: 1934
Estimated Sales: $13 Million
Number Employees: 65
Type of Packaging: Food Service, Private Label

6030 House-Autry Mills Inc
7000 US Highway 301 S
Four Oaks, NC 27524-7628
919-963-6458
Fax: 910-594-0739 800-849-0802
info@house-autry.com www.house-autry.com
Baking mixes
CEO: Roger Mortenson
Estimated Sales: $10-20 Million
Number Employees: 100-249
Type of Packaging: Private Label

6031 Houser Meats
RR 2 Box 180B
Rushville, IL 62681
217-322-4994
Fax: 217-322-4994 www.housermeats.com
Beef, pork, lamb and venison
Partner: Douglas Houser
Partner: Terri Houser
Estimated Sales: $500,000-$1 Million
Number Employees: 5-9
Square Footage: 10000
Type of Packaging: Bulk

6032 Houston Calco, Inc
2400 Dallas St
Houston, TX 77003-3604
713-236-8668
Fax: 713-236-1920
Bean sprouts
Owner: Alice Chang
Estimated Sales: $5-10 000,000
Number Employees: 20-49
Type of Packaging: Private Label
Brands:
Calco

6033 Houston Tea & Beverage
7703 Cannon Street
Houston, TX 77055
832-348-7780
Fax: 832-348-7760 800-585-4549
Teas
President: Linda Williams
Contact: Al Hernandez
al@houstonteaandbeverage.com
Estimated Sales: Less than $500,000
Number Employees: 1-4
Square Footage: 8500
Type of Packaging: Private Label

6034 Howard Foods Inc
5 Ray St
Danvers, MA 01923-3531
978-774-6207
Fax: 978-777-2384 info@howardfoods.com
www.howardfoods.com
Specialty condiments, syrups, seasoning juices and chopped and minced garlic
Estimated Sales: $1-3 Million
Number Employees: 5-9
Brands:
Howard's

6035 Howard Turner & Son
1659 Route 1 Highway 7
Marie Joseph, NS B0J 2G0
Canada
902-347-2616
Fax: 902-347-2714
Fresh and frozen lobster and groundfish
President: Randy Turner
Type of Packaging: Bulk

6036 Howjax
PO Box 246063
Pembroke Pines, FL 33024-0117
954-441-2491
Fax: 954-962-7258
Gourmet condiments, and Caribean style chutney

6037 Howson Mills
320 Blyth Rd
Blyth, ON N0M 1H0
Canada
519-523-4241
866-422-7522
howson@howsons.ca www.howsons.ca
Durum flour.
Sales Manager: Dan Greyerbighl
Year Founded: 1875
Estimated Sales: $35 Million
Number Employees: 65
Type of Packaging: Bulk

6038 Hoyt's Honey Farm
11711 Interstate 10 E
Baytown, TX 77523
281-576-5383
Fax: 281-576-2191 hoyts@imsday.com
Honey
President: Gordon Brown
Estimated Sales: $5-10 Million
Number Employees: 5-9
Square Footage: 30000
Type of Packaging: Consumer, Food Service, Private Label, Bulk
Brands:
Hoyt's Pure Honey
Hoyts

6039 Hsin Tung Yang Foods Inc
405 S Airport Blvd
S San Francisco, CA 94080-6909
650-589-6789
Fax: 650-589-3157 info@htyusa.com
www.htyusa.com
Asian meat products
President: Kailen Mai
Contact: Peter Hamilton
p.hamilton@cymi.com
Director Manufacturing: Pin Chong
Estimated Sales: $10-20 Million
Number Employees: 20-49

6040 Hsu's Ginseng Enterprises Inc
T6819 County Rd W
Wausau, WI 54403-9461
715-675-2325
Fax: 715-675-7832 800-826-1577
info@hsuginseng.com www.hsuginseng.com
Ginseng products, royal jelly, bee pollen, astragalus, dong quai and goldenseal
President: Paul Hsu
info@hsuginseng.com
Vice President: Sharon Hsu
Estimated Sales: $5-10 Million
Number Employees: 50-99
Brands:
Root To Health

6041 Hu Kitchen
78 Fifth Ave
New York, NY 10011
212-510-8919
hukitchen.com
Organic dark chocolate
CEO: Rita Hudetz
Type of Packaging: Bulk

6042 Hubbard Peanut Co Inc
30275 Sycamore Ave
PO Box 94
Sedley, VA 23878
757-562-4081
Fax: 757-562-2741 800-889-7688
hubs@hubspeanuts.com www.hubspeanuts.com
Cocktail peanuts
President: Lynne Rabil
lynne@hubspeanuts.com
Plant Manager: David Benton
Estimated Sales: $10-24.9 Million
Number Employees: 10-19
Square Footage: 90000
Type of Packaging: Consumer, Food Service, Private Label

6043 Hubble
Manhattan Beach, CA 90266
dave@drinkhubble.com
www.drinkhubble.com
Sparkling cold-pressed juice
Founder & President: Dave Burchianti

6044 Hubers Orchard Winery-Vineyards
19816 Huber Rd
Borden, IN 47106-8309
812-923-9813
Fax: 812-923-3013 800-345-9463
info@huberwinery.com www.huberwinery.com
Wines, fruits, berries and vegetables
President: Ted Huber
dana.huber@huberwinery.com
VP: Greg Huber
Estimated Sales: $5-10 Million
Number Employees: 20-49

6045 Hubert's Lemonade
Tustin, CA 92780
877-265-3286
www.hubertslemonade.com
Flavored lemonades
President/Owner: Daniel Barba

6046 Huck's Seafood
508 Cynwood Dr # D
Easton, MD 21601-3892
410-770-9211
Fax: 410-763-8811
Crabs, oysters and clams; fish
Owner/President: James Ford, Jr
Orders: Amber Ford
Estimated Sales: $.5-1 million
Number Employees: 50
Square Footage: 5000
Type of Packaging: Consumer, Food Service, Bulk
Brands:
Huck's

6047 Huckleberry Patch
8868 US Hwy 2 East
Hungry Horse, MT 59919
406-387-5000
Fax: 406-387-4444 800-527-7340
info@huckleberrypatch.com
www.huckleberrypatch.com
Wildberry jellies, syrups, jams, preserves
Manager: Laurie Carpy
Estimated Sales: $5-10 Million
Number Employees: 10-19

6048 Hudson Henry Baking Co.
221 Palmer Country Ln
Palmyra, VA 22963-5451
817-733-0709
www.hudsonhenrybakingco.com
Granola products
Founder: Hope Lawrence
hope@hudsonhenrybakingco.com
Year Founded: 2012
Estimated Sales: #350,000
Number Employees: 7
Type of Packaging: Food Service

6049 Hudson River Foods
P.O. Box 11
Castleton, NY 12033
888-417-9343
info@hudsonriverfoods.com
www.hudsonriverfoods.com
All natural foods including baking mixes, cakes, brownies, cookies, icings, puddings, muffins, hempmilk, hemp tofu, chia greek yogurt, drink mixes, and Kombucha
Co-Founder: Dan Ratner
Co-Founder: Donna Ratner
Manager: Winston Edmonds
Warehouse Manager: Rebecca Sagendorf
Year Founded: 2005
Number Employees: 50-99
Number of Brands: 6
Brands:
Cherrybrook Kitchen
Tempt Hemp
European Gourmet Bakery
The Epic Seed
High Country Kombucha
Healthy To Go

6050 Hudson Valley Brewery
7 East Main St.
Beacon, NY 12508
845-218-9156
contact@hvbrewery.com
www.hudsonvalleybrewery.com
Beer, ale, sour IPAs
Founder/President: John-Anthony Gargiulo

Year Founded: 2016
Number of Brands: 1
Number of Products: 13
Type of Packaging: Consumer, Private Label, Bulk
Brands:
Hudson Valley

6051 Hudson Valley Farmhouse Cider
Centre Rd.
Staatsburg, NY 12580
845-266-3979
www.hudsonvalleyfarmhousecider.com
Farm-based cider; barrel-aged cider; pub cider; sparkling cider
Owner: Elizabeth Ryan
Year Founded: 1984
Number of Brands: 1
Number of Products: 6
Type of Packaging: Consumer, Private Label, Bulk
Brands:
Hudson Valley

6052 Hudson Valley Foie Gras
80 Brooks Rd
Ferndale, NY 12734-5101
845-292-2500
Fax: 845-292-3009
www.hudsonvalleyfoiegras.com
Duck foie gras
Operations Manager: Marcus Henley
Vice President: Izzy Yanay
info@hudsonvalleyfoiegras.com
Estimated Sales: $190 Thousand
Number Employees: 100-249

6053 Hudson Valley Fruit Juice
33 White St
Highland, NY 12528-1621
845-691-8061
Fax: 845-691-9056
Fruit and vegetable juices and vinegar
President: Vincent Nemeth
Manager: Sam Campese
Estimated Sales: $1-2.5 000,000
Number Employees: 2-4

6054 Hudson Valley Homestead
102 Sheldon Ln
Craryville, NY 12521-5324
518-851-7336
Fax: 518-851-7553 john102@hughes.net
Gourmet condiments
President: John King
jbk102@gmail.com
Estimated Sales: Less Than $500,000
Number Employees: 1-4
Type of Packaging: Private Label
Brands:
BushwhacKer's Mustard
Blow Hard Mustard
Hudson Valley Homestead

6055 Hudson Valley Hops
PO Box 292
Beacon, NY 12508
845-202-2398
admin@hvhops.com
www.hvhops.com
Harvester, processor and distributor of hops to brewers in the Hudson Valley
Co-Founder: Justin Riccobono
Co-Founder: Shawn McLearen
Year Founded: 2013
Type of Packaging: Bulk

6056 Hudson Valley Malt
320 Co. Rte. 6
Germantown, NY 12526
845-489-3450
info@hudsonvalleymalt.net
www.hudsonvalleymalt.net
Artisan craft malt
Co-Owner: Dennis Nesel
Co-Owner: Jeanette Nesel
Number of Brands: 1
Type of Packaging: Consumer, Bulk
Brands:
Hudson Valley Malt

6057 Hudsonville Ice Cream
345 E 48th St # 200
Holland, MI 49423-5381
616-546-4005
Fax: 616-546-4020
hello@hudsonvilleicecream.com
www.hudsonvilleicecream.com
Ice cream, frozen yogurt and sherbet
Owner: Heidi Buttrey
heidibuttrey@hudsonvilleicecream.com
VP Marketing & Sales: Jon Vanderwoude
Estimated Sales: $12 Million
Number Employees: 20-49
Number of Brands: 2
Type of Packaging: Consumer, Bulk
Brands:
Hudsonville Ice Cream

6058 Hue's Seafood
105 S 14th Street
Baton Rouge, LA 70802-4753
225-383-0809
Fax: 225-383-0809
Seafood
President: Tu Nguyen

6059 Hughes Springs Frozen Food Center
105 Foster St
Hughes Springs, TX 75656
903-639-2941
Meat packer
Owner: Alvin Dannelley
Estimated Sales: $1-2.5 Million
Number Employees: 1 to 4
Type of Packaging: Consumer

6060 Hughson Meat Company
407 S Guadalupe St
San Marcos, TX 78666
512-392-3368
Fax: 512-392-4190 877-462-6328
http://www.hughson-meat.com/retail
Meat products; slaughtering also available
Owner: Marvin Rutkowski
Estimated Sales: $3-5 Million
Number Employees: 5-9
Type of Packaging: Consumer

6061 Hughson Nut Inc
1825 Verduga Rd
Hughson, CA 95326-9675
209-883-0403
Fax: 209-883-2973 info@hughsonnut.com
www.hughsonnut.com
Almonds and almond products
President: Martin Pohl
martin@hughsonnut.com
Estimated Sales: $2.5-5 Million
Number Employees: 250-499
Number of Brands: 1
Square Footage: 300000
Type of Packaging: Consumer, Private Label, Bulk

6062 Hulman & Co
900 Wabash Ave
Terre Haute, IN 47807-3208
812-232-9446
Fax: 812-478-7181 www.clabbergirl.com
Baking powder, tobacco, liquor
President: Tony George
CEO: Mark Miles
Estimated Sales: $20-50 Million
Number Employees: 1000-4999

6063 Humbly Hemp
11749 W Pico Blvd
Los Angeles, CA 90064
424-259-3521
Hemp snack bars
CEO: Daniel Crawford
Number of Brands: 1
Number of Products: 3
Type of Packaging: Consumer
Brands:
HUMBLY HEMP

6064 Humboldt Bay Coffee Co.
526 Opera Alley
Eureka, CA 95501
707-444-3969
info@humboldtcoffee.com
www.humboldtcoffee.com
Organic coffees
CFO: Luci Ramirez
Year Founded: 1991

6065 Humboldt Brews LLC
856 10th St
Arcata, CA 95521-6232
707-826-2739
Fax: 707-826-2045 robinhewitt@hotmail.com
www.humboldtbrews.com
Beers
President: Mario Celotto
humcitypodcast@gmail.com
Number Employees: 10-19
Type of Packaging: Consumer, Food Service, Bulk
Brands:
Gold Nectar
Red Nectar

6066 Humboldt Chocolate
PO Box 1206
Eureka, CA 95502
707-630-5355
Fax: 707-312-8235 info@humboldtchocolate.com
www.humboldtchocolate.com
All-natural chocolate bars

6067 Humboldt Creamery
Modesto, CA 95351
888-316-6064
info@humboldtcreamery.com
www.humboldtcreamery.com
Ice cream and milk products
CFO: Ralph Titus
National Sales & Marketing Manager: Rod Masters
Operations Manager: Mike Callihan
Purchasing Manager: Mark McCurtain
Number Employees: 100-249
Parent Co: Foster Dairy Farms
Type of Packaging: Consumer, Food Service, Bulk

6068 Humco Holding Group Inc
7400 Alumax Rd
Texarkana, TX 75501-0282
903-831-7808
Fax: 903-334-6300 www.nomoreitch.com
Liquid and powder herbal supplements
President/CEO: Greg Pulido
gpulido@humco.com
CFO: Steve Woolf
Vice President: Susan Hickey
VP Quality/Regulatory Affairs: Steve Bryant
VP Sales: Alan Fyke
Estimated Sales: $10-20 Million
Number Employees: 100-249

6069 Hume Specialties
291 Pleasant Street
Chester, VT 05143-9351
802-875-3117
Fax: 802-875-3140
www.greenmountaingringo.com
Salsa and tortilla chips
President: Christine Hume
Executive VP/Production Manager: Dave Hume
Estimated Sales: $2.5-5 Million
Number Employees: 20-49
Square Footage: 28000
Type of Packaging: Consumer
Brands:
Green Mountain Gringo

6070 Humeniuk's Meat Cutting
PO Box 11
Ranfurly, AB T0B 3T0
Canada
780-658-2381
Fax: 780-658-2389
Fresh and frozen beef, pork and venison
President: Nector Humeniuk
Owner/Manager: Gerald Humeniuk
Secretary: Oksana Humeniuk
Number Employees: 10-19
Square Footage: 320000
Type of Packaging: Consumer, Food Service, Private Label, Bulk
Brands:
Granny's

6071 Humm Kombucha
1125 NE 2nd Street
Bend, OR 97701
541-306-6329
hummkombucha.com
Kombucha

Co-Founder & CEO: Jamie Danek
Co-Founder: Michelle Mitchell
Marketing: Ren, Mitchell
Sales: Sally Taylor
Operations: Wade Nolte
Number of Brands: 1
Number of Products: 10
Square Footage: 5000
Type of Packaging: Consumer
Brands:
HUMM

6072 Hummel Brothers Inc
180 Sargent Dr
New Haven, CT 06511-5958
203-787-4113
Fax: 203-498-1755 800-828-8978
www.hummelbrothers.com
Cold cuts, frankfurters and sausage
President: Michael Czekaj
michael@hummelbros.com
Vice President: Robert Hummel
Estimated Sales: $8 Million
Number Employees: 50-99
Square Footage: 188000
Type of Packaging: Consumer, Private Label
Brands:
Hummel Meats

6073 Humming Hemp
PO Box 487
723 The Parkway
Richland, WA 99352
503-559-6476
thehumminggroup.com
Hemp good snacks
CEO: Hilary Kelsay
VP, Sales & Marketing: Ross Elkin
COO: Max Schneider

6074 Hummingbird Kitchens
P.O.Box 1286
Whitehouse, TX 75791
903-839-6244
800-921-9470
Gourmet food mixes
President: Janet Faulkner
CEO: William Faulkner
Estimated Sales: $1-2.5 Million
Number Employees: 5-9
Number of Products: 51
Type of Packaging: Consumer, Private Label, Bulk

6075 Hummustir
535 Fifth Ave
27th Floor
New York, NY 10017
info@stiritup.com
www.hummustir.com
Hummus
Managing Director: Alon Kruvi
Number of Brands: 1
Number of Products: 4
Type of Packaging: Consumer
Brands:
HUMMUSTIR

6076 Humphrey Co
20810 Miles Pkwy
Cleveland, OH 44128-5508
216-662-6629
Fax: 216-662-6619 800-486-3739
www.humphreycompany.com
Premium white popcorn
Vice President: Tom Dickerhoof
tdickerhoof@humphreycompany.com
VP: Betsy Humphrey
Estimated Sales: $500,000-$1 Million
Number Employees: 5-9
Number of Brands: 1
Number of Products: 10
Square Footage: 44000
Type of Packaging: Consumer, Private Label

6077 Humphrey's Market
1821 S 15th St
Springfield, IL 62703-3298
217-544-7445
Fax: 217-544-7518 800-747-6328
www.humphreysmarket.com
Specialty sausage and hams
President: T Humphrey
Sales Exec: Grant Bradley
gbradley@humphreysmarket.com
Chairman: E Humphrey
Estimated Sales: $10-20 Million
Number Employees: 20-49
Square Footage: 29200

6078 Humphry Slocombe
2790A Harrison St
San Francisco, CA 94110
415-550-6971
info@humphryslocombe.com
www.humphryslocombe.com
Ice cream, ice cream cakes and ice cream pies
Co-Founder: Jake Godby
Co-Founder: Sean Vahey

6079 Hung's Noodle House
25-1410 40th Avenue NE
Calgary, AB T2E 6L1
Canada
403-250-1663
Fax: 403-291-0632 rickhungkee@hotmail.com
Noodles and rice
President: Ricky Chung
Production: Cindy Chung
Parent Co: Hung Kee Holdings Company
Brands:
Hung's Noodle House

6080 Hungry Sultan
14 Rancho Circle
Lake Forest, CA 92630
949-215-0000
Fax: 949-215-0965 info@hungrysultan.com
Mediterranean gourmet snack foods, including hummus
Founder: Fouad El-Abd
felabd@hungrysultan.com
Communications: Christina Romeo
Estimated Sales: Less than $500,000
Number Employees: 10-19

6081 Hunt Brothers Cooperative
20205 US Highway 27 North
Lake Wales, FL 33853-0631
863-676-1411
Fax: 863-676-8362 www.floridasnatural.com
Citrus fruits
President: Frank Hunt
Estimated Sales: $20-50 Million
Number Employees: 250-499
Number of Brands: 2
Type of Packaging: Consumer, Food Service, Bulk
Brands:
Seald Sweet
Treasure Pak

6082 Hunt Country Foods Inc
4559 Achilles Ln
Marshall, VA 20115-3014
540-364-2622
Fax: 540-364-3112 www.send-best-of-luck.com
Specialty cookies, cakes and chocolates
Owner: Maggi Castelloe
best.of.luck@starpower.net
Estimated Sales: Less than $500,000
Number Employees: 10-19
Brands:
Best of Luck
Best of Luck Horseshoe Chocolates
Horseshoe Cake
Horseshoes and Nails

6083 Hunt Country Vineyards
4021 Italy Hill Rd
Country Road 32
Branchport, NY 14418-9615
315-595-2835
Fax: 315-595-2835 800-946-3289
info@HuntWines.com www.huntwines.com
Wines, sherry and port
Owner: Joyce Hunt
joycehunt@huntwines.com
CEO, Owner: Arthur Hunt
Owner, Winemaker: Jonathan Hunt
Owner: Caroline Boutard Hunt
Marketing Operations Manager: Andy Marshall
General Manager: Jim Alsina
joycehunt@huntwines.com
Vineyard Manager: Dave Mortensen
Estimated Sales: $500,000-$1 Million
Number Employees: 20-49
Square Footage: 32000
Type of Packaging: Consumer, Private Label
Brands:
Fingerlakes Wine Cellars
Foxy Lady
Hunt Country Vineyards

6084 Hunt-Wesson Foods
222 Merchandise Mart Plaza
Chicago, IL 60654
209-334-3616
Fax: 209-333-7428 877-266-2472
www.hunts.com
Tomato products including diced, whole, stewed, sauce, and ketchup
President & CEO: Sean Connolly
EVP/CFO: David Marberger
EVP/General Counsel: Colleen Batcheler
EVP/Chief Human Resources Officer: Charisse Brock
Estimated Sales: $25-49.9 Million
Number Employees: 100-249
Parent Co: ConAgra Foods
Type of Packaging: Food Service
Brands:
Hunts
La Choy
Rosarita
Orville Redenbacher
Swiss Miss
Wesson
Peter Pan

6085 Hunter Farms-High Point Division
1900 N Main St
High Point, NC 27262-2132
336-822-2300
Fax: 336-882-2341 800-446-8035
kcavanaugh@harristeeter.com
www.hunterfarms.com
Dairy products
VP: Dwight Moore
Quality Assurance Manager: Gale Walton
Sales Development: Karin Cavanaugh
Director Sales: Bob Cooke
General Manager: Dwight Moore
Estimated Sales: $10-24.9 Million
Number Employees: 100-249
Parent Co: Harris Teeter
Type of Packaging: Consumer

6086 Hunter Food Inc
3707 La Palma Ave
Anaheim, CA 92806-2122
714-666-1888
Fax: 714-666-1222 www.hunterfood.com
Fresh, frozen, marinated, and non-marinated poultry
CEO: Huan Hua Le
Year Founded: 1991
Estimated Sales: $20-50 Million
Number Employees: 20-49

6087 Huppen Bakery
8721 Santa Monica Boulevard
Suite 201
Los Angeles, CA 90069-4507
323-656-7501
Fax: 323-656-1090
Swiss chocolates and wafer rolls
President: Urs Brauchli
Type of Packaging: Consumer, Bulk

6088 Hurd Orchards
17260 Ridge Rd
Holley, NY 14470-9353
585-638-8838
Fax: 585-638-5175 market@hurdorchards.com
www.hurdorchards.com
Preserves, vinegars, pickles, chili sauce, jams, marmalades; canned, brandied and dried fruit
Owner: Susan Machamer
market@hurdorchards.com
VP: Amy Machamer
Estimated Sales: $.5-1 million
Number Employees: 20-49

6089 Husch Vineyards & Winery
4400 Highway 128
Philo, CA 95466-9476
707-895-3216
Fax: 707-895-2068 800-554-8724
www.huschvineyards.com

Wines
President: Zach Robinson
VP: Amanda Robinson Holstine
Contact: Vicky Giusti
vicky@huschvineyards.com
Operations Manager: Al White
Production Manager: Brad Holstine
Estimated Sales: $2.5-5 Million
Number Employees: 10-19

6090 Huse's Country Meats
3697 State Highway 171
Malone, TX 76660
254-533-2205
Fax: 254-533-2498 husecountrymeats@yahoo.com
www.husescountrymeats.com
Smoked beef and pork sausage
Owner: Randy Huse
Estimated Sales: $5-10 Million
Number Employees: 10-19

6091 Husman Snack Food Company
PO Box 3900
Peoria, IL 61612
859-282-7490
Fax: 513-562-2646
techsupport@pinnaclefoods.com
Potato and tortilla chips
President/CEO: David Ray
Quality Assurance Manager: John Barlage
Plant Manager: Leroy Pennekamp
Number Employees: 100-249
Square Footage: 280000
Parent Co: Birds Eye Foods
Type of Packaging: Consumer, Private Label, Bulk
Brands:
Husman's

6092 Huy Fong Foods Inc
4800 Azusa Canyon Rd
Irwindale, CA 91706-1938
626-286-8328
Fax: 626-286-8522 customerservice@huyfong.com
www.huyfong.com
Chili pepper sauces and pastes
CEO: David Tran
customerservice@huyfong.com
Number Employees: 20-49

6093 Hybco USA
363 S Mission Rd
Los Angeles, CA 90033-3752
323-269-3111
Fax: 323-269-3130 Customerservice@hybco.com
www.hybco.com
Oils, rice and rice flour
President: David Kashani
Manager: Orly Kashani
orlyk126@yahoo.com
Estimated Sales: $2.5-5 Million
Number Employees: 10-19

6094 Hybread
4712 Admiralty Way
Suite 914
Marina del Ray, CA 90292
310-312-1200
info@hybread.com
hybread.com
Vegetable and whole grain bread
Managing Director: Alon Kruvi
Number of Brands: 1
Number of Products: 3
Type of Packaging: Consumer
Brands:
HYBREAD

6095 Hyde & Hyde Inc
300 El Sobrante Rd
Corona, CA 92879-5757
951-279-5239
Fax: 951-270-3526 www.hydeandhyde.com
Condiments for the fresh-cut produce industry; custom packaging and co-packaging
President: Tim Hyde
Number Employees: 250-499
Type of Packaging: Consumer, Private Label

6096 Hyde Candy Company
1916 E Mercer Street
Seattle, WA 98112
206-322-5743
Candy
President: Alfred Hyde

6097 Hyde Park Brewing Company
4076 Albany Post Rd.
Hyde Park, NY 12538
845-229-8277
www.hydeparkbrewing.com
Lager, pilsner, ale, stout, porter
Owner: Angelo LoBianco-Barone
Year Founded: 1995
Number of Brands: 1
Number of Products: 7
Type of Packaging: Consumer, Private Label

6098 Hydroblend Limited
1801 N Elder St
Nampa, ID 83687-3079
208-467-7441
Fax: 208-318-1445
Coating for potatoes, appetizers, fish, chicken and vegetbles
President: Mike Guthrie
mguthrie@hbspecialtyfoods.com
CEO: Bill Cyr
VP Sales/Marketing: Randy Hobert
R&D: Henning Melvej
Quality Control: Joshua Bevan
Customer Service: Gay Tisdale
Purchasing Director: Matt Haines
Estimated Sales: $10-20 Million
Number Employees: 20-49
Square Footage: 110000
Type of Packaging: Bulk
Brands:
Hb Batters
Hb Breadings

6099 Hye Cuisine
4730 S Highland Ave
Del Rey, CA 93616-9716
559-834-3000
Fax: 559-834-5882 hyecuisine@gmail.com
www.hyecuisineinc.com
Grape leaves and roasted eggplant
President: Raffi Santikian
hyecuisine@gmail.com
Secretary: Hilda Santikian
Estimated Sales: $1 Million
Number Employees: 10-19
Square Footage: 32000
Type of Packaging: Food Service, Private Label

6100 Hye Quality Bakery
2222 Santa Clara St
Fresno, CA 93721-2921
559-445-1511
Fax: 559-445-1540 877-445-1778
info@hyequalitybakery.com
Cracker breads
President: Sammy Ganimian
sg@hyequalitybakery.com
Estimated Sales: $10-20 Million
Number Employees: 10-19
Number of Brands: 2
Type of Packaging: Food Service
Brands:
Hye DeLites
Hye Roller

6101 Hygeia Dairy Company
5330 Ayers St
Corpus Christi, TX 78415-2104
361-854-4561
Fax: 361-854-7267 www.deanfoods.com
Milk, chocolate milk and orange juice
Manager: Scott Mc Clarren
VP: Doug Purl
Human Resources Director: Robin Somsngyi
Year Founded: 1927
Estimated Sales: $20-50 Million
Number Employees: 45
Square Footage: 34002
Parent Co: Hygeia Dairy Company
Type of Packaging: Consumer, Food Service, Private Label, Bulk
Brands:
Hygeia
Super Good

6102 I Heart Keenwah
PO Box 180032
Chicago, IL 60618
www.iheartkeenwah.com
Quinoa puffs, clusters and cereal
Co-Founder & President: Sarah Chalos
Co-Founder & President: Ravi Jolly
Number of Brands: 1
Number of Products: 8
Type of Packaging: Consumer
Brands:
I HEART KEENWAH

6103 I Heart Olive Oil
1513 SE 2nd Court
Ft Lauderdale, FL 33301-3937
954-607-1539
Fax: 954-761-1166
Olive oils and balsamic vinegars
Marketing: Beth Haralson

6104 I P Callison & Sons
2400 Callison Rd NE
Lacey, WA 98516-3154
360-412-3340
Fax: 360-412-3344
Flavours, specifically mint
President: Jim Burgett
callisons@callisons.com
Chief Financial Officer: Rick Robinson
Vice President: Jeff Johnson
Vice President, Innovation & Technology: Greg Biza
VP, Director of Global Sales: Philippe Job
Vice President, Operations: Damon Smith
Vice President, Controller: Cena Latshaw
Vice President, Purchasing: Les Toews
Number Employees: 50-99

6105 I Rice & Co Inc
11500 Roosevelt Blvd
Building D
Philadelphia, PA 19116-3080
215-673-7423
Fax: 215-673-2616 800-232-6022
amarino@iriceco.com www.iriceco.com
Syrups, flavorings, sundae toppings, fudge, bakery fillings, bases, tea blends and stabilizers.
President/CEO: Steve Kuhl
skuhl@iriceco.com
Plant Engineer/Maintenance Manager: Ashly Marchese
Estimated Sales: $20-50 Million
Number Employees: 20-49
Number of Brands: 1
Number of Products: 1000
Square Footage: 85000
Type of Packaging: Food Service, Private Label, Bulk
Brands:
Rice's Products

6106 I'm Different Snacks
920 N Formosa Ave
Los Angeles, CA 90046
hello@imdifferentsnacks.com
imdifferentsnacks.com
Coconut clusters
CEO: Eytan Moldovan
Number of Brands: 1
Number of Products: 3
Type of Packaging: Consumer
Brands:
I'M DIFFERENT

6107 I-Health Inc
55 Sebethe Dr
Suite 102
Cromwell, CT 06416
800-990-3476
www.i-healthinc.com
Vitamins, supplements and health food. Formerly known as Amerifit Brands.
Estimated Sales: $463 Million
Number Employees: 50-99
Parent Co: DSM
Other Locations:
Amerifit/Strength Systems USA
Bloomfield CT
Brands:
Azo
Culturelle
Dhea
Estroven
Flex Able
Sootherbs
Vitaball
Brainstrong
I-Cool
I Flex
Ovega-3

6108 **I. Deveau Fisheries LTD**
PO Box 577
Barrington Passage, NS B0W 2J0
Canada
902-745-2877
Fax: 902-645-2211 www.ideveau.com
Live lobster.
President: Berton German
Director, Sales: Joel German
Estimated Sales: $7 Million
Number Employees: 15
Type of Packaging: Bulk

6109 **ICL Performance Products**
622 Emerson Road
Suite 500
St. Louis, MO 63141
800-244-6169
www.icl-perfproductslp.com
Food-grade phosphoric acid, phosphate salts and food additives
President/CEO: Charles Weidhas
VP Finance: Paul Schlessman
Contact: K Amy
amy.zuzack@icl-pplp.com
VP Operations: Terry Zerr
Number Employees: 500-999
Parent Co: ICL Holdings

6110 **ICONIC Protein**
San Clemente, CA 92673
www.drinkiconic.com
Protein drinks
Founder & CEO: Billy Bosch

6111 **IFC Solutions**
1601 E Linden Ave
Linden, NJ 07036
908-862-8810
800-875-9393
ifc-solutions.com
Specialty ingredients manufacturer
President: David Dukes
Year Founded: 1939

6112 **IFM**
20 West 20th Street
Suite 303
New York, NY 10011
212-229-1633
Fax: 212-898-9024 franck@ifm-usa.com
Gourmet products
Marketing: Frank Foulloy

6113 **IFive Brands**
P.O.Box 9134
Seattle, WA 98109-0134
206-783-2498
Fax: 206-789-1016 800-882-5615
www.peppermints.com
Fat-free and sugar free mints
Owner: Brett Canfield
Estimated Sales: $3-5 Million
Number Employees: 1-4
Brands:
Penguin

6114 **IGZU**
hello@igzulife.com
igzulife.com
Bamboo leaf tea
Co-Founder & CEO: Zachary Anderson
Co-Founder & CFO: Courtney McCoy
Number of Brands: 1
Number of Products: 3
Type of Packaging: Consumer
Brands:
IGZU

6115 **II Sisters**
850 Airport St Ste 9
Moss Beach, CA 94038
650-728-5613
Fax: 650-728-5611 800-282-7058
summin_t@yahoo.com
Seasoned oils, herbal vinegars
President/Owner: Sudi Taleghani
CFO: Simmin Taleghani
Estimated Sales: $1-2.5 000,000
Number Employees: 5-9
Brands:
Ii Sisters
Ii Sisters
Sorrell Flavours

6116 **ILHWA American Corporation**
91 Terry St
Belleville, NJ 07109
973-759-1996
Fax: 973-450-0562 800-446-7364
info@ilhwana.com www.ilhwa-usa.com
Korean ginseng
President: Sang Kil Han
Warehouse Manager: Edner Louis
Estimated Sales: $2.5-5 Million
Number Employees: 1-4
Brands:
Il Hwa

6117 **IMAC**
1702 N Sooner Rd
Oklahoma City, OK 73141-1222
405-424-8794
Fax: 405-424-4822 888-878-7827
Dried food, anti-caking agents, flavor extenders, soy milk and cheese cultures
President: Jim Baird
Mananager: Ed Price
Manager: Alvin Thompson
Plant Manager: Bill Armstrong
Estimated Sales: $3-5,000,000
Number Employees: 20-49
Square Footage: 80000
Parent Co: ADFAC
Type of Packaging: Private Label, Bulk

6118 **IMAG Organics**
1923 Record Crossing Ave
Dallas, TX 75235
817-703-2321
855-301-0400
customerservice@bluegreenagave.com
bluegreenagave.com
Organic agave and chia
Contact: Janis Lee

6119 **IMO Foods**
P.O.Box 236
Yarmouth, NS B5A 4B2
Canada
902-742-3519
Fax: 902-742-0908 imofoods@ns.sympatico.ca
www.imofoods.com
Canned fish
President: Sidney Hughes
Executive VP/General Manager: Phillip Le Blanc
Director Marketing: David Jollimore
Number Employees: 100-249
Parent Co: IMO Foods
Type of Packaging: Consumer, Food Service, Private Label
Other Locations:
Brands:
Golden Treasure
Kersen
West Island

6120 **IOE Atlanta**
P.O.Box 267
Galena, MD 21635-0267
410-755-6300
Fax: 410-755-6367
Shellfish, sushi
Chairman: Charles Cully
CFO: Denise For
Number Employees: 10-19

6121 **IOM Grain**
974 E 100 N
Portland, IN 47371
260-726-6224
Fax: 260-726-6225 877-283-8882
info@iomgrain.com www.iomgrain.com
Non-GMO soybeans
President: Ramon Loucks
Plant Manager: Kyle Laux
Year Founded: 2003
Type of Packaging: Food Service, Private Label, Bulk

6122 **IQ Juice**
PO Box 1352
Bayville, NY 11709
516-864-0034
iqjuice.com
All-natural juice blends
Number of Brands: 1
Number of Products: 9
Type of Packaging: Consumer
Brands:
iQ Juice

6123 **ISF Trading**
Hobson's Wharf
P.O Box 772
Portland, ME 04104
207-879-1575
Fax: 207-761-5877 isfco@aol.com
www.seaurchinmaine.com
Urchin, lobster, crab, whelk, salmon and shrimp products
Founder: Atchan Tamaki
Office Manager: Lan Gao
Estimated Sales: $20-49.9 Million
Number Employees: 120

6124 **IZZE Beverage**
Boulder, CO
877-476-7380
www.izze.com
Sparkling fruit juices
Co-Founder: Todd Woloson
Co-Founder: Greg Stroh
Number of Brands: 1
Number of Products: 13
Type of Packaging: Consumer
Brands:
IZZE

6125 **Ian's Natural Food**
190 Fountain St
Framingham, MA 01702
508-283-1174
customerservice@iansnaturalfoods.com
www.iansnaturalfoods.com
Allergy-friendly frozen foods and snacks
Manager: Terrence Dalton
VP Marketing: Jeff Canner
Contact: Bruce Franklin
bruce.franklin@iansnaturalfoods.com
Estimated Sales: Less Than $500,000
Number Employees: 1-4
Type of Packaging: Consumer

6126 **Icco Cheese Co**
1 Olympic Dr
Orangeburg, NY 10962-2514
845-680-2436
Fax: 845-398-1669 johna@iccocheese.com
www.iccocheese.com
Processor, importer and exporter of grated parmesan cheese in shaker canisters and glass pet containers; processor and exporter of bread crumbs
President: Joseph V Angiolillo
icco@aol.com
Vice President: John Angiolillo
Estimated Sales: $10-15 Million
Number Employees: 50-99
Type of Packaging: Consumer, Food Service, Private Label, Bulk
Brands:
America's Choice
American Beauty
Berkley & Jensen
D'Agostino
Dominick's
Food Club
Giant
Icco Brand
Luigi Vitelli
Pastene
Pathmark
Price Chopper
Reggano
Ronzoni
San Giorgio
Shop Rite
Splendido
Weis

6127 **Ice Chips Candy**
818A 79th Ave SE
Olympia, WA 98501
866-202-6623
www.icechips.com
Sugar-free hard candy
Co-Founder: Charlotte Clary
Co-Founder: Bev Vines-Haines
Number of Brands: 1
Number of Products: 18
Type of Packaging: Consumer
Brands:
ICE CHIPS

6128 **Ice Cream Bowl**
532 Mcintire Ave
Zanesville, OH 43701-3342
740-452-5267
Fax: 740-452-0931 www.tomsicecreambowl.com
Ice cream
Owner: William Sullivan
thebowl532@aol.com
Estimated Sales: $1-3 Million
Number Employees: 20-49
Type of Packaging: Consumer

6129 **Ice Cream Club Inc**
1580 High Ridge Rd
Boynton Beach, FL 33426-8724
561-731-3331
Fax: 561-731-0311 800-535-7711
info@icecreamclub.com www.icecreamclub.com
Ice cream; soft serve machines
Co-President: Marie Lawson
President, CEO: Rich Draper
SVP: Tom Jackson
Estimated Sales: D
Number Employees: 20-49
Type of Packaging: Consumer, Food Service, Private Label, Bulk

6130 **Ice Cream Specialties Inc**
8419 Hanley Industrial Ct
St Louis, MO 63144
314-962-2550
800-662-7550
info@northstarfrozentreats.com
www.northstarfrozentreats.com
Ice cream
Estimated Sales: $98 Million
Number Employees: 100-249
Square Footage: 250000
Parent Co: Prairie Farms Dairy
Type of Packaging: Consumer

6131 **Icelandic Milk and Skyr Corporation**
135 W 26th Street
2nd Floor
New York, NY 10001
212-966-6950
Fax: 646-536-8159 info@siggisdairy.com
www.siggisdairy.com
Icelandic-style yogurt
CEO: Vicky Hilmarsson
Contact: Erik Adamsen
erik.adamsen@siggisdairy.com
Number Employees: 4

6132 **Icelandic Provisions**
New York, NY 10017
866-991-7597
hello@icelandicprovisions.com
www.icelandicprovisions.com
Icelandic-style yogurt
President & COO: Nico Bevers
Number of Brands: 1
Number of Products: 11
Type of Packaging: Consumer
Brands:
ICELANDIC PROVISIONS

6133 **Icicle Seafoods Inc**
4019 21st Ave W
Seattle, WA 98199
206-282-0988
Fax: 206-282-7222
customerservice@icicleseafoods.com
www.icicleseafoods.com
Seafoods
Year Founded: 1965
Estimated Sales: $100+ Million
Number Employees: 500-999

6134 **Idaho Candy Co**
412 S 8th St
Boise, ID 83702-7105
208-342-5505
Fax: 208-384-5310 800-898-6986
info@idahospud.com www.idahospud.com
Candy
President: Bob Allen
bob@idahospud.com
Quality Control Manager: Bob Riter
Estimated Sales: $1-5 Million
Number Employees: 20-49
Square Footage: 84000
Type of Packaging: Consumer, Food Service, Bulk
Brands:
Idaho Spud
Old Faithful
Owyhee

6135 **Idaho Frank Association Inc**
391 Taylor Blvd # 180
Pleasant Hill, CA 94523-2282
925-609-8458
Fax: 925-609-9318 info@idahofrank.com
www.idahofrank.com
Dehydrated potato
President: Ednalyn Watts
ewatts@idahofrank.com
Sales Manager: Tom Paratore
Estimated Sales: $5-10 Million
Number Employees: 1-4
Type of Packaging: Food Service, Private Label, Bulk

6136 **Idaho Milk Products**
2249 S Tiger Dr
Jerome, ID 83338-5080
208-644-2882
Fax: 208-644-2899 www.idahomilkproducts.com
Milk cream derivatives
Number Employees: 10-19

6137 **Idaho Pacific Holdings Inc**
4723 E 100 N
Rigby, ID 83442-5811
208-538-6971
Fax: 208-538-5082 800-238-5503
ipc@idahopacific.com
Dehydrated potato
President/CEO: Wally Browning
wallybrowning@idahopacific.com
CFO: Baden Burt
Quality Control Manager: Paul Eatinger
VP/Sales & Marketing: Jon Schodde
VP/Operations: Todd Sutton
Plant Manager: Steve McLean
Purchasing: Brian Hart
Year Founded: 1987
Estimated Sales: $40-50 Million
Number Employees: 100-249
Type of Packaging: Food Service, Private Label, Bulk
Brands:
Idaho-Pacific

6138 **Idaho Supreme Potatoes Inc**
614 E 800 N
PO Box 246
Firth, ID 83236-1112
208-346-4100
Fax: 208-346-4104 www.idahosupreme.com
Potato products
President/General Manager: Wade Chapman
CFO: Steve Prescott
sprescott@idahosupreme.com
Estimated Sales: $37.60 Million
Number Employees: 100-249
Square Footage: 100000
Type of Packaging: Consumer, Food Service, Private Label
Brands:
Idaho Supreme

6139 **Idaho Trout Company**
PO Box 72
Buhl, ID 83316-0072
208-543-6444
Fax: 208-543-8476 866-878-7688
rainbowtrout@idahotrout.com
Trout
Manager: Harold Johnson
Vice President: Gregory Kaslo
Sales/Shipping: Janie Higgins
General Manager: Harold Johnson
Estimated Sales: $10-25 Million
Number Employees: 50-99
Type of Packaging: Food Service, Private Label, Bulk
Brands:
Cold River
Idaho's Best
Rainbow Springs

6140 **Idahoan Foods LLC**
357 Constitution Way
Idaho Falls, ID 83402
800-746-7999
www.idahoan.com
Dehydrated potato products
President & CEO: Drew Facer
Year Founded: 1960
Estimated Sales: $50-99 Million
Number Employees: 500-999
Type of Packaging: Food Service, Private Label
Brands:
Idahoan

6141 **Ideal Dairy Farms**
239 Vaughn Rd.
Hudson Falls, NY 12839
518-747-5059
Fax: 518-747-4869 idealdairy1@yahoo.com
www.idealdairyfarms.com
Dairy products
Owner: Kristie Sorsen
Estimated Sales: $10-20 Million
Number Employees: 20-49
Square Footage: 7500
Type of Packaging: Consumer, Food Service

6142 **Ideal Distributing Company**
23800 7th Place W
Bothell, WA 98021-8508
425-488-6121
Fax: 425-488-8159
Tea, coffee
Principal: John Erdman
Co-Ownr: Cathy Erdman

6143 **Ideal Snacks Corp**
89 Mill St
Liberty, NY 12754-2038
845-292-7000
Fax: 845-292-3100 www.idealsnacks.com
Snacks
President: Gunther Brinkman
gunther.brinkman@idealsnacks.com
Director of Operations: LJ Goldstock
Estimated Sales: $3-5 Million
Number Employees: 100-249

6144 **Il Gelato**
2451 46th Street
Astoria, NY 11103-1007
718-937-3033
Fax: 718-786-5543 800-899-9299
Baked goods, gelato and individual desserts
President: Dimitri Pauli
Estimated Sales: $142,000
Number Employees: 30

6145 **Il Giardino Del Dolce Inc**
2859 N Harlem Ave
Chicago, IL 60707-1638
773-889-2388
Fax: 773-889-5990 info@IlGiardinoDelDolce.com
www.ilgiardinodeldolce.com
Cannoli shells, mini pasteries, butter cookies and cakes
Owner: Maria Ventrella
ilgiardinodeldolce@gmail.com
Estimated Sales: Less than $500,000
Number Employees: 10-19
Type of Packaging: Consumer
Brands:
Giardino

6146 **Illes Seasonings & Flavors**
2200 Luna Rd
Suite 120
Carrollton, TX 75006-6559
214-689-1300
800-683-4553
info@illesfoods.com www.illesfoods.com
Dry and liquid flavor solutions
Owner: Cristin Kahale
cristin@illesseasonings.com
CEO: Rick Illes
Estimated Sales: $28 Million
Number Employees: 50-99
Type of Packaging: Consumer, Food Service, Private Label

6147 **Illy Espresso of the Americas**
15455 N Greenway Hayden Loop
Scottsdale, AZ 85260-1611
480-951-4074
Fax: 480-483-8631 877-469-4559
info@illyusa.com www.illyusa.com
Espresso pods
Contact: Stefano Ripamonti
sripamonti@illyusa.com

Estimated Sales: $20-50 Million
Number Employees: 20-49

6148 Illy caffe
800 Westchester Ave
Suite S440
Rye Brook, NY 10573
914-253-4500
Fax: 914-253-4580 www.illy.com
Coffee
President & CEO: Greg Fea
Year Founded: 1933

6149 Imaex Trading Company
65 Crestridge Drive
Suwanee, GA 30024
678-541-0234
Fax: 678-541-0422 info@imaextrading.com
www.imaexseafoods.com
Frozen seafood products
CEO: Seng Angkawijana
pmulyadi@adfoods.com

6150 Imagine Chocolate
2416 W. Victory Blvd.
Suite 225
Burnank, CA 91506
916-837-5772
www.imaginechocolate.net
Chocolates
Founder and CEO: Mitch Koulouris
VP of Marketing: Randy Gordon
Brands:
Imagine Chocolate

6151 Imagine Foods
4600 Sleepytime Drive
Boulder, CO 80301
800-434-4246
www.imaginefoods.com
Organic soups, broths, stocks, sauces and gravies.
President/CEO: Irwin Simon
EVP/CFO: Stephen Smith
COO: James Meiers
Estimated Sales: $20-50 Million
Number Employees: 130
Number of Brands: 1
Parent Co: Hain Celestial Group
Type of Packaging: Consumer, Food Service
Brands:
Imagine Natural Creations

6152 Imani Chimani Chocolate
74 Georgia Ave
Brooklyn, NY 11207-2402
718-484-1011
www.imanichocolatiers.com
Chocolate products and crackers
President and Founder: Ramin Imani
general@imanichocolateer.com
Estimated Sales: Less Than $500,000
Number Employees: 1-4

6153 Imlak'esh Organics
6336 Lindmar Dr
Goleta, CA 93117
805-689-2269
connect@imlakeshorganics.com
imlakeshorganics.com
Cacao nibs, powders, wafers and clusters
Number of Brands: 1
Number of Products: 12
Type of Packaging: Consumer
Brands:
IMLAK'ESH ORGANICS

6154 Immaculate Baking Company
333 North Avenue
Wakefield, MA 01880
828-696-1655
Fax: 828-696-1663 888-826-6567
info@immaculatebaking.com
www.immaculatebaking.com
Cookies
Owner: Scott Blackwell
blackwell@immaculatebaking.com

6155 Immaculate Consumption
933 Main Street
Columbia, SC 29201
803-799-9053
Fax: 828-696-1663 888-826-6567
Bakes goods, cookies, scones, biscotti, and mojos
President/CEO: Scott Blackwell
Vice President: Caroline Blackwell
VP Sales: Don Porter
Estimated Sales: Under $1 Million
Number Employees: 10-19
Number of Brands: 1
Number of Products: 29
Square Footage: 40000
Type of Packaging: Consumer, Food Service, Private Label
Brands:
Immaculate Consumption

6156 Immordl
San Clemente, CA 92673
844-466-6735
iam@immordl.com immordl.com
Coffee-based superfood energy drink
Co-Founder: Scott Holmes
Number of Brands: 1
Number of Products: 1
Type of Packaging: Consumer
Brands:
IMMORDL

6157 Immu Dyne Inc
7453 Empire Dr # 300
Florence, KY 41042-2944
859-746-8772
Fax: 859-746-8772 888-246-6839
info@immudyne.com www.immudyne.com
Natural dietary supplements
President & CEO: Mark McLaughlin
markmcl@immudyne.com
Chairman: Anthony Bruzzese
VP: Alfred Munoz
Estimated Sales: Less Than $500,000
Number Employees: 1-4
Type of Packaging: Consumer, Food Service, Bulk

6158 Impact Confections
4017 Whitney St.
Janesville, WI 53546
608-208-1100
800-535-4401
info@impactconfections.com
www.impactconfections.com
Confectionery products
Founder/President: Brad Baker
CEO: Gary Viljoen
CFO: Rick Weina
Quality Manager: Dave Batchelder
Director Marketing: Jenny Doan
Contact: Andy Telatnik
atelatnik@impactconfections.com
Chief Operating Officer: George Wilson
Year Founded: 1981
Estimated Sales: $25-49.9 Million
Number Employees: 20-49
Number of Products: 40
Type of Packaging: Consumer
Brands:
Alien Pop
Alien Poppin' Pops
Carousel Pop
Color Blaster
Glow Pop
Happy Heart Lollipops
Hoppin' Pops
Lilliday Pops
Lollipop Paint Shop
Pop-A-Bear
Soccer Pops

6159 Imperial Flavors Beverage Co
6300 W Douglas Ave
Milwaukee, WI 53218-1551
414-536-7788
Fax: 414-536-7730 info@imperialflavors.com
www.imperialflavors.com
Juice and soda concentrates
President: Jack Pettigrew
Manager: Don Kosak
kosak@imperialflavors.com
Estimated Sales: $10-20 Million
Number Employees: 10-19
Square Footage: 36000
Type of Packaging: Consumer, Food Service, Private Label, Bulk
Brands:
Captain Jack's
Fruit N' Juice
Juice Plus
Juicy Orange
Milwaukee Seltzer Company
Tropics

6160 Imperial Foods, Inc.
5014 39th St
Long Island City, NY 11104
718-784-3400
Fax: 718-361-7993
Dairy products
General Manager: Charles Mikhitarian
Estimated Sales: $2.5-5 Million
Number Employees: 10-19
Square Footage: 16000
Brands:
Greenfield
Victor's

6161 Imperial Nougat Co
12035 Slauson Ave # C
Santa Fe Springs, CA 90670-8537
562-693-8423
Fax: 562-945-8852
Candy
President: Al Maghsoudi
imperialnougat@yahoo.com
Estimated Sales: $2.5-5 000,000
Number Employees: 5-9

6162 Imperial Salmon House
1632 Franklin Street
Vancouver, BC V5L 1P4
Canada
604-251-1114
Fax: 604-251-3177
Smoked salmon
President: Robert Blair
Number Employees: 5-9
Type of Packaging: Consumer, Food Service, Bulk

6163 Imperial Sensus
PO Box 9
Sugar Land, TX 77487-0009
281-490-9522
Fax: 281-490-9615 www.imperialsugarland.com
Inulin natural extract
VP Sales/Marketing: Sally Brain
VP of Technical Affairs: Bryan Tungland
Parent Co: Johnson Development Group
Type of Packaging: Food Service, Bulk
Brands:
Frutafit
Nutralin

6164 Imperial Sugar Company
3 Sugar Creek Center Blvd.
Suite 500
Sugar Land, TX 77478
800-727-8427
www.imperialsugar.com
Sugar.
President/CEO: John Sheptor
Year Founded: 1843
Estimated Sales: $848 Million
Number Employees: 530
Number of Brands: 5
Parent Co: Louis Dreyfus Holding BV
Brands:
Dixie Crystals®
Imperial Sugar®
Holly Sugar®
Steviacane®
Savannah Gold®

6165 Impossible Foods
Redwood City, CA 94063
855-877-6365
hello@impossiblefoods.com impossiblefoods.com
Plant-based meat alternative
Founder & CEO: Patrick Brown
Year Founded: 2011
Type of Packaging: Food Service

6166 Impromtu Gourmet
10711 Red Run Blvd
Ste 113
Owings Mills, MD 21117
212-475-4640
Fax: 800-858-6547 877-632-5766
www.impromptugourmet.com
Fresh gourmet foods
Founder/CEO: Max Polaner
Contact: Laura Mcmanus
info@impromptugourmet.com

6167 **Improper Goods**
16313 NE Cameron Blvd
Portland, OR 97230
503-662-7147
impropergoods.com
Cocktail bitters and syrups
Founder & President: Dan Brazelton
VP: Dylan Myers
Founder & CMO: Genevieve Brazelton
Number of Brands: 2
Number of Products: 18
Type of Packaging: Consumer
Brands:
THE BITTER HOUSEWIFE
RAFT

6168 **Improved Nature**
101 Vandora Springs Rd
Gardner, NC 27529
www.improvednature.com
Plant-based meat substitute
Sales: Larry Yates
Number of Brands: 1
Number of Products: 2
Type of Packaging: Consumer
Brands:
IMPROVED MEAT
PRIME PRO TEX

6169 **Imuraya USA**
2502 Barranca Pkwy
Irvine, CA 92606
949-251-9205
info@imuraya-usa.com
www.imuraya-usa.com
Japanese-style desserts
VP: Shin Imura
Number of Brands: 1
Number of Products: 11
Type of Packaging: Consumer

6170 **Imus Ranch Foods**
16 West Ave
Darien, CT 06820-4401
505-892-0883
Fax: 631-758-8360 888-284-4687
service@imusranchfoods.com
www.imusranchfoods.com
Tortilla chips, salsa and coffee
President: Don Imus
Chief Financial Officer: John Imus
Number Employees: 2
Type of Packaging: Consumer, Food Service
Brands:
Fred Imus Southwest
Fred Imus Turquoise
Imus Brothers Coffee

6171 **In Harvest Inc**
1012 Paul Bunyan Dr SE
PO Box 428
Bemidji, MN 56601-3447
218-751-8500
Fax: 218-751-8519 800-346-7032
www.indianharvest.com
Beans, grains, pastas and specialty rice blends
CIO/CTO: Mary Dickey
m.dickey@inharvest.com
CFO: Jeffrey Buelow
Director, Sales: Jeff Lande
Director, Culinary Development: Michael Holleman
Estimated Sales: $20-50 Million
Number Employees: 10-19
Number of Brands: 2
Type of Packaging: Consumer, Food Service, Private Label, Bulk
Brands:
InHarvest
KAMUT®

6172 **In The Raw**
2 Cumberland St
Brooklyn, NY 11205
800-611-7434
www.intheraw.com
Sweeteners
Founder: Marvin Eisenstadt
Year Founded: 1956
Number of Brands: 1
Number of Products: 7
Type of Packaging: Consumer
Brands:
IN THE RAW

6173 **Inbalance Health**
739 S Main St
Wayland, MI 49348-1320
269-792-1977
Fax: 269-792-1988
Health bars and supplements
CFO and COO: Lowell Johnson
Marketing and PR Lead: Nichole Allen
nallen@inbalancehealthcorp.com
Number Employees: 5-9

6174 **Inca Gold Organics**
21 Muir Dr
Scarborough, ON M1M 3B5
Canada
416-264-4622
info@incagoldorganics.com
incagoldorganics.com
Organic quinoa seeds, flakes, flour and snacks; chia seeds; maca products
President/Owner: Juana Garcia
Operations: Henry Falcon

6175 **Incredible Cheesecake**
3161 Adams Ave
San Diego, CA 92116-1638
619-563-9722
Fax: 619-563-1022
theincrediblecheese@yahoo.com
Frozen cheesecakes
Owner: Heladio Santiego
hsantiego@incrediblecheesecake.net
Estimated Sales: Less Than $500,000
Number Employees: 1-4
Square Footage: 14000

6176 **Incredible Foods**
75 Sprague St
Boston, MA 02136
857-345-9870
www.perfectlyfree.com
Non-dairy frozen desserts
Founder: David Edwards
Brands:
perfectly free

6177 **Indel Food Products Inc**
9515 Plaza Cir
El Paso, TX 79927-2005
915-590-5914
Fax: 915-590-5913 800-472-0159
gustavo@indelfoods.net www.indelfoods.net
Jalapenos and salsa
President: Gustavo Deandar
Estimated Sales: $2.5-5 Million
Number Employees: 5-9
Parent Co: Agroindustrias Deandar
Type of Packaging: Consumer, Food Service, Private Label, Bulk
Brands:
Del Sol

6178 **Indena USA Inc**
811 1st Ave
Seattle, WA 98104-1457
206-340-0863
Fax: 206-340-0863 greg@indenausa.com
www.indena.com
Herbal extracts
President: Biagio D. Beffa
Managing Director: Luca Giorgetti
Marketing Director: Christian Artaria
VP Sales: Greg Ris
Contact: Carlo Aloni
carlo.aloni@indena.com
Director of Purchasing: Giulio Simoni
Estimated Sales: $1-2.5 Million
Number Employees: 1-4
Parent Co: Indena S.p.A.
Type of Packaging: Bulk

6179 **Independent Bakers Association**
1223 Potomac St NW
Washington, DC 20007-3212
202-333-8190
Fax: 202-337-3809
Baked goods
President: Robert Pyle
VP Sales: Nicholas Pyle

6180 **Independent Dairy Inc**
126 N Telegraph Rd
Monroe, MI 48162-3299
734-241-6016
Fax: 734-241-1251 independentdairy@yahoo.com
Ice cream products
President: Michael Cheney
independentdairy@yahoo.com
Estimated Sales: $5-9.9,000,000
Number Employees: 50-99

6181 **Independent Meat Co**
2072 Orchard Dr E
Twin Falls, ID 83301-7992
208-734-9702
Fax: 208-734-9702 800-284-4626
info@salmoncreekfarms.com
www.independentmeat.com
Pork, hotdogs, bacon, and other cooked and cured meat products
President: Rob Stephens
CEO: Patrick Florence
patrick@fallsbrand.com
Plant Operations Manager: Chris Schmahl
Purchasing Manager: Phillip Burgoyne
Year Founded: 1904
Estimated Sales: $43 Million
Number Employees: 250-499
Type of Packaging: Consumer

6182 **Independent Packers Corporation**
2001 W Garfield St
C102
Seattle, WA 98119
206-285-6000
Fax: 206-285-9236
Fresh and frozen seafood including crab, cod, halibut, salmon and tuna
President: Jeffery Buske
Contact: Tammy Findlay
tammy@bbaybrewery.com
Estimated Sales: $3-5 Million
Number Employees: 100-249
Square Footage: 60000
Type of Packaging: Food Service, Private Label

6183 **India's Rasoi**
25 N Euclid Ave
St Louis, MO 63108-1445
314-361-6911
Fax: 314-727-8331 harinder@rasoi.com
www.rasoi.com
Indian specialties
President: Harinder Singh
harinder@rasoi.com
Estimated Sales: Less Than $500,000
Number Employees: 5-9

6184 **Indian Bay Frozen Foods**
PO Box 160
Centreville, NL A0G 4P0
Canada
709-678-2844
Fax: 709-678-2447 ackermans@ibffinc.com
www.ibffinc.com
Blueberries, lingonberries, jams and pie fillings; fish
President: Calvin Ackerman
Estimated Sales: 2.5-5 Million
Number Employees: 20-49
Square Footage: 40000
Type of Packaging: Consumer, Private Label, Bulk
Brands:
Ackerman's Wild

6185 **Indian Foods Company, Inc.**
204 Central Avenue
Suite 1
Osseo, MN 55369-1257
763-593-3000
866-331-7684
www.indianfoodsco.com
Indian specialties
Owner & President: Kavita Mehta
Estimated Sales: $74,000
Number Employees: 2
Square Footage: 8984
Brands:
Ashoka

6186 **Indian Hollow Farms**
15321 Us Hwy 14
Richland Center, WI 53581
608-536-3499
800-236-3944

Apples and apple cider
Owner: John Symons
ihfarms@mwt.net
Estimated Sales: $1-2.5 Million
Number Employees: 5-9
Square Footage: 200000
Type of Packaging: Consumer, Food Service, Private Label, Bulk
Brands:
Country Road
Iddian Hollow

6187 **Indian Ridge Shrimp Co**
120 Doctor Hugh St Martin Dr
Chauvin, LA 70344-2723
985-594-5869
Fax: 985-594-2168 800-594-0920
chris@pearlbrandseafood.com
www.louisianashrimpers.com
Shrimp
Owner: Andrew Blanchard
andrew_blanchard@louisianashrimpers.com
COO: Richard Fakier
Sales Manager: Daniel Babin
Estimated Sales: Less Than $500,000
Number Employees: 1-4
Square Footage: 100000
Type of Packaging: Consumer, Food Service
Brands:
Pearl

6188 **Indian River Select® LLC**
7929 SW Jack James Drive
Stuart, FL 34997
772-595-0070
Fax: 772-287-9828 888-373-7426
www.indianriverjuice.com
Orange and grapefruit juice
President: J Patrick Shirard
CEO: Clifford Burg
Contact: Marty Eskenazi
meskenazi@indianriverselect.com
Estimated Sales: $13.80,000,000
Number Employees: 82
Type of Packaging: Consumer, Food Service, Private Label
Brands:
Indian River Select

6189 **Indian Rock Vineyards**
1154 Pennsylvania Gulch Rd
Murphys, CA 95247-9589
209-728-8514
Fax: 209-728-8338 info@indianrockvineyards.com
www.indianrockvineyards.com
Wines
President: Boyd Thompson
Contact: Ed Bauer
ed@indianrockvineyards.com
Estimated Sales: $3-5 Million
Number Employees: 1-4

6190 **Indian Springs Vineyards**
PO Box 1450
Penn Vally, CA 95946
530-432-3782
Fax: 530-478-0903 800-375-9311
Wines
President: David McCord
Production Manager: Julie Holmes
Estimated Sales: Under $500,000
Number Employees: 8
Type of Packaging: Private Label

6191 **Indian Valley Meats**
HC 52 Box 8809
Indian, AK 99540-9604
907-653-7511
Fax: 907-653-7694 ivm@alaska.net
www.indianvalleymeats.com
Poultry, venison and fish
President: Douglas Drum
Plant Manager: Renia Drum
Estimated Sales: $2.5-5 Million
Number Employees: 10-19
Square Footage: 68000

6192 **Indiana Botanic Gardens Inc**
3401 W 37th Ave
Hobart, IN 46342-1751
219-947-4040
Fax: 219-947-4148 877-909-1502
www.botanicchoice.com
Herbal products and vitamins
President: Tim Cleland
Vice President: Tammy Cleland
VP Marketing: Kelly Fuscoe
Sales Executive: Pauline Cleland
Operations Director: Cathy Bilderback
Purchasing: Greg Villaroman
Year Founded: 1910
Estimated Sales: $25 Million
Number Employees: 100-249
Square Footage: 50000

6193 **Indiana Grain Company**
1700 Beason St
Baltimore, MD 21230-5347
410-685-6410
Fax: 410-685-0233
Grain and flour
President: Patrick Turner
CEO: Tom Grisafi
Number Employees: 20-49
Type of Packaging: Bulk

6194 **Indiana Sugars**
1145 101st St
Lemont, IL 60439-9622
630-986-9150
Fax: 630-739-1030 john@buysugars.com
Sugar
President/COO: John Yonover
Vice President, Marketing: Scott Sievers
Contact: Tina Arteaga
tina@buysugars.com
Estimated Sales: $5-10 Million
Number Employees: 10-19

6195 **Indianola Pecan House Inc**
1013 Highway 82 E
Indianola, MS 38751-2327
662-887-5420
Fax: 662-887-2906 800-541-6252
pecan@pecanhouse.com www.pecanhouse.com
Gourmet pecans, cookies and candies
Owner: Wheeler Timbs
ttimbs@pecanhouse.com
Estimated Sales: $2.5-5 Million
Number Employees: 50-99
Number of Brands: 1
Number of Products: 30
Brands:
Wheeler's

6196 **Indias House**
1101 E Broadway
Columbia, MO 65201-4909
573-817-2009
harinder@rasoi.com
Indian specialties
Owner: Balvir Singh
Estimated Sales: Less Than $500,000
Number Employees: 1-4
Parent Co: India's Rasoa

6197 **Indigo Coffee Roasters**
660 Riverside Dr # 1
Florence, MA 01062-2763
413-586-4537
Fax: 413-280-0008 800-447-5450
info@indigocoffee.com www.indigocoffee.com
Coffee
President: Lourdes Tallet
Square Footage: 4000
Type of Packaging: Consumer, Food Service, Private Label, Bulk
Brands:
Indigo

6198 **Indulgent Foods**
PO Box 10
Farmington, UT 84025
801-939-9100
Fax: 801-939-9373
customerservice@indulgentfoods.com
www.indulgentfoods.com
Hot cocoa and cappuccino
Owner: David Cowley
Contact: Brad Brower
bbrower@indulgentfoods.com
Estimated Sales: $3-5 Million
Number Employees: 5-9
Type of Packaging: Consumer, Food Service
Brands:
Cafe Tiamo

6199 **Ineeka Inc**
2023 W Carroll Ave Ste C263
Chicago, IL 60612
312-733-8327
Fax: 312-277-2555
Organic teas
Contact: Sumita Goel
sumita.goel@ineeka.com
Number Employees: 5

6200 **InfraReady Products Ltd.**
1438 Fletcher Road
Saskatoon, SK S7M 5T2
Canada
306-242-4950
Fax: 306-242-4213 800-510-1828
info@infrareadyproducts.com
www.infrareadyproducts.com
Cereal grains, oilseeds, pulses, ancient grains, and blends
President: Mark Pickard
Estimated Sales: $4.5 Million
Number Employees: 25
Square Footage: 79052

6201 **Ingenuity Beverages**
2 Cumberland St
Brooklyn, NY 11205
800-611-7434
www.intheraw.com
Coffee products, tea products and powdered drinks
CEO: George Hou
Year Founded: 1956
Number of Brands: 1
Number of Products: 7
Type of Packaging: Consumer, Bulk

6202 **Ingleby Farms**
123 N Main Street
Dublin, PA 18917-2107
215-249-1118
Fax: 215-249-3722 877-728-7277
www.peppersauces.com
Chilies, hot sauce and specialty foods
President: Carin Froehlich
Vice President: Dietrich Froehlich
Plant Manager: Hans Froehlich
Estimated Sales: $1-2.5 Million
Number Employees: 1-4
Type of Packaging: Private Label

6203 **Inglenook**
1991 St Helena Hwy
Rutherford, CA 94573
707-968-1100
www.inglenook.com
Wines
Owner: Francis Ford Coppola
Owner: Eleanor Coppola
General Manager: Philippe Bascaules
Manager: Larry Stone
Estimated Sales: $10-20 Million
Number Employees: 100-249

6204 **Ingles Markets**
2913 US Highway 70 W
Black Mountain, NC 28711-9103
828-669-2941
Fax: 828-669-3678
customerservice@ingles-markets.com
www.ingles-markets.com
Cakes, cookies, and deli products
President & CEO: James Lanning
CFO/Director/VP Media Relations: Ronald Freeman
Estimated Sales: $31.7 Million
Number Employees: 16,000
Other Locations:
Dairy Manufacturing
Asheville NC
Brands:
Milko
Sealtest

6205 **Ingleside Vineyards**
5872 Leedstown Rd
Colonial Beach, VA 22443-5424
804-224-8687
Fax: 804-224-8573 www.inglesidevineyards.com
Wines
President: Doug Flemer
info@inglesidevineyards.com
Gift Shop Manager: Nancy Flemer
Executive Winemaker: Bill Swain
Assistant Winemaker: Maria Swain

Year Founded: 1980
Estimated Sales: $20-50 Million
Number Employees: 10-19

6206 **Ingomar Packing Co**
9950 S Ingomar Grade Rd
P.O. Box 1448
Los Banos, CA 93635
209-826-9494
Fax: 209-854-6292 ingomar-sales@ingomar.com
www.ingomarpacking.com
Diced tomatoes and tomato paste
President & CEO: Greg Pruett
gregp@ingomar.com
COO: Kent Rounds
VP of Sales: William Cahill
Director of Quality Systems: John Palombi
Director of Sales: Mark Stegeman
Plant Manager: David Waggoner
Estimated Sales: $20-50 Million
Number Employees: 50-99
Square Footage: 10000
Type of Packaging: Bulk

6207 **Ingredia Inc**
625 Commerce Rd
Wapakoneta, OH 45895-8265
419-738-4060
Fax: 419-738-4426
Dairy ingredients
CEO: Alain Thibault
Contact: Harmony Villemin
s.cedat@idi-ingredients.com
General Manager: Benot Leclercq
Number Employees: 50-99
Parent Co: Coop Laitiere Artois Flandre

6208 **Ingredient Innovations**
313 NW North Shore Dr
Kansas City, MO 64151-1455
816-587-1426
Fax: 816-587-4167
roxanne@ingredientinnovations.com
www.ingredientinnovations.com
Natural dairy, chemical, fruit and meat flavors and colors; cereal ingredients
President: Roxanne Armstrong
roxanne@ingredientinnovations.com
Estimated Sales: $1-3 Million
Number Employees: 1-4

6209 **Ingredient Specialties**
180 West Chestnut St
Exeter, CA 93221
559-594-4380
Fax: 559-594-4689 www.ingredientspecialties.com
Distributor of food and industrial ingredients; specializes in artificial sweetners
Director of Marketing and Sales: Bassam Faress
Estimated Sales: $1-2.5 Million
Number Employees: 9

6210 **Ingredients Corp Of America**
1270 Warford St
Memphis, TN 38108-3421
901-458-5003
Fax: 901-458-5009 888-242-2669
www.memphi.net
Dried beans and spices
Owner: Derenda Ica
dlandrum@memphi.net
Estimated Sales: $1 Million
Number Employees: 20-49
Square Footage: 22000
Brands:
Barzi

6211 **Ingredion Inc.**
5 Westbrook Corporate Ctr.
Westchester, IL 60154
708-551-2600
Fax: 708-551-2700 800-713-0208
www.ingredion.com
Sweeteners, starches, corn syrups, glucose, and oils used in food and beverage products.
CEO: James Zallie
Executive VP/CFO: James Gray
Senior VP/General Counsel/CCO: Janet Bawcom
Senior VP/Chief Innovation Officer: Anthony Delio
COO: Robert Stefansic
Year Founded: 1906
Estimated Sales: $5.8 Billion
Number Employees: 11,000
Type of Packaging: Bulk
Brands:
Abc Carrier
Brewer's Crystals
Buffalo
Cerelose
Enzose
Fiberbond
Globe
Globe Plus
Invertose Hfcs
Proferm
Royal
Royal-T
Stablebond
Surebond
Ultrabond
Unidex

6212 **Ingretec**
1500 Lehman St
Lebanon, PA 17046-3337
717-273-0711
Fax: 717-273-1364 www.ingretec.com
Dairy ingredients
President: Philippe Jallon
Vice President: Valerie Crouse
Quality Control: Annabel Ries
Estimated Sales: $5 Million
Number Employees: 11-50
Number of Products: 50
Square Footage: 30000
Type of Packaging: Food Service, Bulk

6213 **Initiative Foods**
1117 K Street
Sanger, CA 93657
559-875-3354
Fax: 559-875-1879 www.initfoods.com
Organic baby food
President/Marketing Director: John Ypma
National Sales Director: Bill Astin
Contact: Richard Aguirre
richard@initfoods.com
Production Manager of Materials: Marvin Canales
Plant Manager: Richard Aguirre
Estimated Sales: $830,000
Number Employees: 6
Square Footage: 9970
Type of Packaging: Consumer

6214 **Inka Crops**
7011 Sylvan Rd
Suite B
Citrus Heights, CA 95610
916-723-1450
Fax: 916-723-1098 www.inkacrops.com
Corn, plantain, veggie and potato chips
President/Owner: John Chaloux
Type of Packaging: Consumer
Brands:
INKA CORN
INKA CHIPS
INKA CROPS VEGGIE CHIPS
INKA CROPS KETTLE CHIPS
INKA CROPS SEEDS & NUTS

6215 **Inked Organics**
755 Baywood Dr
2nd Floor
Petaluma, CA 94954
info@inkedorganics.com
inkedorganics.com
Organic breads
CEO: Scott Seymour
Number of Brands: 1
Number of Products: 5
Type of Packaging: Consumer
Brands:
INKED ORGANICS

6216 **Inko's Tea**
650 Executive Dr
Willowbrook, IL 60517
inkostea.com
Flavored white iced tea
President/Owner: Andy Schamisso
Number Employees: 10-19

6217 **Inland Empire Foods**
5425 Wilson St
Riverside, CA 92509
951-682-8222
Fax: 951-682-6275 888-452-3267
janelle@inlandempirefoods.com
www.inlandempirefoods.com
Bean and pea products
President: Mark Sterner
Contact: Sharmila Baba
sharmila@inlandempirefoods.com
Year Founded: 1985
Estimated Sales: $20-50 Million
Number Employees: 20-49

6218 **Inland Products**
545 N Main St
Carthage, MO 64836
417-358-4048
Fax: 417-358-7196
Animal and marine fats and oils
Vice President: Jack Sweeny
Estimated Sales: $10-20 000,000
Number Employees: 20-49

6219 **(HQ)Inland Seafood Inc**
1651 Montreal Cir
Atlanta, GA 30084
404-350-5850
Fax: 404-601-5539 800-883-3474
marketing@inlandseafood.com
www.inlandseafood.com
Seafood
President: Chris Rosenberger
Founder, Chief Executive Officer: Joel Knox
Executive Vice President: Robert Novotny
Safety Manager: Patricia Washington
Pomp Agency: Rodney Fund
Vice President of Sales: Stephen Musser
Chief Operating Officer: Bill Demmond
Director of Purchasing: Richard Luff
Estimated Sales: $1-3 Million
Number Employees: 100-249
Other Locations:
Birmingham AL
New Orleans LA
Charlotte NC
Inland Lobster
S. Portland ME

6220 **Inlet Salmon**
PO Box 21426
Fort Lauderdale, FL 33335-1426
954-525-9777
Fish and seafood
Sales Manager: Jim Gonzalez
Parent Co: Inlet Salmon

6221 **Inn Foods Inc**
310 Walker St
Watsonville, CA 95076-4585
831-724-2026
Fax: 831-728-5708 800-708-7836
www.innfoods.com
Frozen vegetables, fruits, french fries, potatoes, custom blends
President & CEO: Byron Johnson
Estimated Sales: $14.2 Million
Number Employees: 100-249
Square Footage: 20000
Parent Co: VPS Companies, Inc.
Type of Packaging: Consumer, Food Service
Brands:
Freidel's Finest
Gold Premium
The Inn
Valley Pokt

6222 **Inn Maid Food**
PO Box 1972
Lenox, MA 01240-4972
413-637-2732
Fax: 413-499-3839
Natural foods, including multi-grain cereal, granola, sunflower seeds, trail mix, multi-grain pancake and waffle mix and sugar-free fruit syrups
President: Jane Peters
Estimated Sales: $1-2.5 Million appx.
Number Employees: 1-4
Square Footage: 8000
Type of Packaging: Consumer, Food Service, Private Label, Bulk
Brands:
Berrylicious

Colonial Jacks
New Granola

6223 **Inniskillin Wines**
1499 Line 3
Niagra Parway
Niagara-On-The-Lake, ON L0S 1J0
Canada
905-468-2187
Fax: 905-468-5355 888-466-4754
inniskil@inniskillin.com www.inniskillin.com
Wines
President: Donald Ziraldo
VP: Karl Kaiser
Estimated Sales: $650,000
Number Employees: 20
Square Footage: 64000
Type of Packaging: Consumer, Food Service
Brands:
Inniskillin

6224 **Innocent Chocolate**
4360 Oakes Rd
Davie, FL 33314
800-591-0219
www.innocentchocolate.com
Chocolate
Founder: Ty Cherry
Parent Co: EarthCorp Foundation

6225 **Innophos Holdings Inc.**
259 Prospect Plains Rd.
Cranbury, NJ 08512
609-495-2495
Fax: 609-860-0138 www.innophos.com
Specialty ingredient solutions for food, health, and industrial markets, including phosphates, minerals, botanicals, protiens and other nutrition ingredients.
Chairman/President/CEO: Kim Ann Mink
Senior VP/CFO: Mark Feuerbach
Senior VP/CMO/CTO: Sherry Duff
Year Founded: 2004
Estimated Sales: $785 Million
Number Employees: 1,400

6226 **Innova Flavors**
2505 S Finley Rd # 100
Lombard, IL 60148-4867
630-928-4800
Fax: 630-928-4830 www.innovaflavors.com
Meat flavors
General Manager: Enrique Medina
emedina@innovaflavors.com
Senior Food Scientist: Jennifer Ma
Manager: Enrique Medina
emedina@innovaflavors.com
Estimated Sales: $680,000
Number Employees: 50-99
Parent Co: Griffith Laboratories

6227 **Innovative Beverage Concepts**
9600 Research Dr
Irvine, CA 92618-4666
949-831-8656
Fax: 949-831-2390 web@ibevconcepts.com
www.ibevconcepts.com
Oats, teas and coffees
Founder: Rich Principale
Number Employees: 10-19

6228 **Innovative Fishery Products**
3569 Hwy 1 Saint-Bernard St
PO Box 125
Belliveau Cove, NS B0W 1J0
Canada
902-837-5163
Fax: 902-837-5165 ifp@eastlink.ca
Fresh, frozen and salted clams, scallops, groundfish and lobster
President: Marc Blinn
CEO: Doug Bertram
VP: Victor (Allan) McGuire
Number Employees: 20-49
Square Footage: 64000
Type of Packaging: Bulk

6229 **Inny's Wholesale**
1068 Puuwai St
Honolulu, HI 96819-4330
808-841-3172
Fax: 808-841-1410
Seafood
President: Stanley Lum
Treasurer: Jane Lum

Estimated Sales: $3-5 Million
Number Employees: 1-4

6230 **Inovata Foods**
95 Spruce Street
Tillsonburg, ON N4G 5C4
Canada
519-688-3256
Fax: 519-842-4521 800-265-5731
sales@inovatafoods.com
Frozen entrees
President: Steve Parsons
Chief Financial Officer: Jason Yohemas
Chief Operating Officer: Neil Brooks
Director of Culinary Innovation: Jonathan Smid
VP Business Development: Chad Parsons
Estimated Sales: $31 Million
Number Employees: 300
Type of Packaging: Consumer, Food Service, Private Label
Brands:
Otter Valley

6231 **Inshore Fisheries**
PO Box 118
Middle West Pubnico, NS B0W 2M0
Canada
902-762-2522
Fax: 902-762-3464 www.inshore.ca
Fresh and frozen fish
President: Claude d'Entremont
Number Employees: 50-99
Type of Packaging: Consumer, Food Service

6232 **Instant Products of America**
835 S Mapleton Street
Columbus, IN 47201-7359
812-372-9100
Fax: 812-372-9132
Instant beverages, dry mixes, syrups and toppings
President: Rolf Walendy
Vice President: George Moon
Contact: Tom Behrman
tbehrman@instantproductsinc.net
Plant Manager: Mike Brannan
Estimated Sales: $10-24.9 Million
Number Employees: 50
Square Footage: 70000
Parent Co: Kruger Gmbh & Company
Type of Packaging: Consumer, Food Service, Private Label, Bulk
Brands:
Impress
Kruger

6233 **(HQ)Instantwhip Foods Inc**
2200 Cardigan Ave
Columbus, OH 43215-1092
614-488-2536
Fax: 614-488-0307 800-544-9447
info@instantwhipfoods.com
www.instantwhip.com
Distributor of dairy and nondairy toppings, dairy products, eggs, baked goods and desserts.
General Manager: Jim Ring
Vice President: Tom Michaelides
Square Footage: 41674
Type of Packaging: Consumer, Food Service, Private Label, Bulk
Other Locations:
Instantwhip Akron
Stow OH
Instantwhip Baltimore
Landover MD
Instantwhip Buffalo
Buffalo NY
Instantwhip Chicago
Chicago IL
Instantwhip Columbus
Grove City OH
Instantwhip Connecticut
Wallingford CT
Instantwhip Eastern New York
Binghamton NY
Instantwhip Indianapolis
Indianapolis IN
Instantwhip Minneapolis
Minneapolis MN
Instantwhip Pennsylvania
Blandon PA
Instantwhip Rochester
Rochester NY
Brands:
Instantwhip

6234 **Integrative Flavors**
3501 W Dunes Hwy
Michigan City, IN 46360-6717
219-879-8236
800-837-7687
www.integrativeflavors.com
Soup bases
President: Georgeann Quealy
VP: Brian Quealy
Director of Research & Development: Peter Hargarten
phargarten@integrativeflavors.com
Director of Regulatory Compliance: John True
Customer Service: Taylor Holm
Estimated Sales: $1,100,000
Number Employees: 10-19
Type of Packaging: Consumer, Food Service, Private Label, Bulk
Brands:
Cooks Delight

6235 **Intense Milk**
25 Anderson Rd
Buffalo, NY 14225
716-892-3156
www.intensemilk.com
Milk
Chief Executive Officer: Larry Webster
Chief Operating Officer: Joe Duscher
Year Founded: 2009
Parent Co: Upstate Niagara Cooperative Inc.
Type of Packaging: Consumer, Private Label

6236 **Inter Health Nutraceuticals**
5451 Industrial Way
Benicia, CA 94510-1010
707-751-2800
Fax: 707-751-2801 800-783-4636
info.benicia@lonza.com www.interhealthusa.com
Nutritional and botanical ingredients
President/CEO: Paul Dijkstra
CEO: Connelly Ann
cann@disneyconsumerproducts.com
CFO: Mary Helen Lucero
VP, Information Technologies: Fredrick Zilz
VP, International Sales: Jay Martin
COO: Navpreet Singh
Estimated Sales: $10-20 Million
Number Employees: 20-49
Number of Brands: 16
Parent Co: Lonza Group Ltd.
Type of Packaging: Private Label
Brands:
7-Keto
Aller-7
Cardiaslim
ChromeMate
L-OptiZinc
Lowat
Meratrim
OptiBerry
Protykin
Relora
Seditol
SuperCitrimax
Sytrinol
UCII
ZMA
Zychrome

6237 **Inter-American Products**
1240 State Ave
Cincinnati, OH 45204
513-762-4900
Fax: 513-244-3668 800-645-2233
edi@inter-americanfoods.com
www.interamericanproducts.com
Gelatins and puddings, nuts, powdered beverages, natural processed cheese, tea, extracts, peanut butter, coffee, soy sauce, steak and Worcestershire sauce, coconut, syrup, salad dressing, mayonnaise, preserves, jellies andbeverages.
Senior Marketing Manager: Jeff Pahl
Contact: Sergio Balegno
sbalegno@interamericanproducts.com
Technical Director: Terry Shamblin
Estimated Sales: Under $500,000
Number Employees: 5-9
Parent Co: Kroger Company

6238 **Inter-Continental Imports Company**
149 Louis Street
Newington, CT 06111
860-665-1101
Fax: 860-665-1085 800-424-4422
www.icaffe.com
Coffee
President/CEO: Vincent Saccuzzo
Office Manager: Lucy Pluchino
Purchasing Manager: Vincent Saccuzzo
Estimated Sales: $5-10 Million
Number Employees: 5-9
Type of Packaging: Private Label
Brands:
Grande Italia
Miscela Bar
Miscela Napoli

6239 **Interbake Foods**
3951 Westerre Parkway
Suite 200
Richmond, VA 23233
800-221-1002
meoakley@interbake.com
Gourmet crackers and cookies.
President: Peter McLaughlin
Year Founded: 1929
Number Employees: 1000-4999
Parent Co: George Weston Ltd.
Type of Packaging: Consumer, Food Service, Private Label, Bulk
Other Locations:
Interbake Foods
Green Bay WI

6240 **Intercorp Excelle Foods**
90 Sheppard Avenue East
Suite 400
North York, ON M2N 7K5
Canada
416-226-5757
Fax: 416-226-7544 888-473-6337
Refrigerated and shelf stable sauces, marinades, dips and dressings
President: Peter Luik
Treasurer: David Sharpe
Year Founded: 1985
Estimated Sales: Under $500,000
Number Employees: 100
Square Footage: 340000
Parent Co: Heinz Canada
Type of Packaging: Consumer, Food Service
Brands:
Excelle
Renee's Gourmet

6241 **Interfood Ingredients**
777 Brickell Ave
Suite 210
Miami, FL 33131
786-953-8320
info@interfood.com
www.interfood.com
Dairy ingredients and products
Managing Director & VP: Reniers Geoffrey
Year Founded: 1970
Estimated Sales: $235 Million
Number Employees: 200
Parent Co: Interfood Holding

6242 **Interfrost**
349 W Commercial St
East Rochester, NY 14445-2407
585-381-0320
Fax: 585-381-1052
Frozen fruits and vegetables
VP/General Manager: Thomas Crandall
Estimated Sales: $5-10 Million
Number Employees: 5-9
Parent Co: Cobi Foods

6243 **Interior Alaska Fish Processors**
2400 Davis Rd
Fairbanks, AK 99701-5700
907-456-3885
Fax: 907-456-3889 800-478-3885
order@santassmokehouse.com
Salmon and salmon products
Owner: Janet McCormick
akhunt@ak.net
CEO/President: Virgil Humphenour
Vice President: Marie Mitchell
Marketing Director: Shelbie Umphenour
Estimated Sales: $2.5-5 Million
Number Employees: 10-19
Type of Packaging: Private Label, Bulk

6244 **Intermex Products USA LTD**
1375 Avenue S # 300
Grand Prairie, TX 75050-1293
972-660-2071
Fax: 972-660-5941 www.intermexproducts.com
Mexican dishes and sauces
President: Juan Carlos Lorenzo
j.carlos@intermexproducts.com
Treasurer: Sandy Eastep
Vice President: David Hagli
Plant Manager: Gonzalo Branch
Estimated Sales: $10-20 Million
Number Employees: 20-49
Number of Brands: 2
Brands:
La Torre
La Mexicanita

6245 **Intermountain Canola Cargill**
2300 N Yellowstone Hwy
PO Box 9300
Minneapolis, MN 55440-9300
208-522-4113
Fax: 208-522-0794 800-822-6652
www.cargill.com
Specialty canola oils
President: Erwin Kelm
Finance Executive: Joann Wages
General Manager: Ernie Unger
Manager: R Covington
Estimated Sales: $10-20 Million
Number Employees: 10-19
Parent Co: Cargill Foods
Type of Packaging: Consumer, Food Service, Bulk

6246 **Intermountain Specialty Food Group**
265 Plymouth Ave
Salt Lake City, UT 84115
801-977-9077
Fax: 801-977-8202 www.intermountainfood.com
Pasta, sauces, dessert mixes, dip mixes, baking mixes and soup mixes
President: Debbie Chidester
Co-Owner: Jody Chidester
Contact: Jim Hubbard
jimhubbard@intermountainfood.com
Estimated Sales: $700 Thousand
Number Employees: 13
Number of Brands: 4
Type of Packaging: Consumer, Food Service, Bulk
Other Locations:
Intermountain Foods
Meridian ID
Brands:
Plentiful Pantry
Pasta Partners
Chidester Farms
Zpasta

6247 **International Bakers Services, Inc.**
1902 N Sheridan Ave
South Bend, IN 46628-1592
574-287-7111
Fax: 574-287-7161 info@internationalbakers.com
Flavors and flavor blends
President & CEO: William Busse

6248 **International Brownie**
602 Middle St
East Weymouth, MA 02189
781-340-1588
Fax: 781-331-1900 800-230-1588
Gourmet brownies
President: Cindy Rice
Contact: Brownie Reese
rbrownie@internationalbrownie.com
Estimated Sales: Less than $500,000
Number Employees: 1-4
Square Footage: 6000
Brands:
International Brownie

6249 **International Casein Corporation**
111 Great Neck Rd
Suite 218
Great Neck, NY 11021-5402
516-466-4363
Fax: 516-466-4365
Casein
President: Marvin Match
Number Employees: 5-9

6250 **International Casings Group**
4420 S Wolcott Ave
Chicago, IL 60609-3159
773-294-8996
Fax: 773-376-9292 800-825-5151
sales@casings.com www.casings.com
Sausage casings
President: Serge Atohoun
satohoun@casings.com
CFO: Bryan Schultz
VP: Eric Svendsen
Director of Sales: Jim Dunbar
Operations Manager: Jim Wilt
Estimated Sales: $10-20 Million
Number Employees: 100-249
Square Footage: 104000
Type of Packaging: Food Service
Other Locations:
International Casings Group
Santa Fe Springs CA
Brands:
Nature's Best

6251 **International Cheese Company**
67 Mulock Avenue
Toronto, ON M6N 3C5
Canada
416-769-3547
Fax: 416-769-7153 info@internationalcheese.ca
www.internationalcheese.ca
Italian cheese
President: M Pelosi
Number Employees: 10-19
Square Footage: 39996
Type of Packaging: Consumer, Food Service

6252 **International Chemical Corp**
7654 Progress Cir
Melbourne, FL 32904-1655
321-952-6466
Fax: 321-952-9883 800-914-2436
95263@msn.com
www.internationalchemicalcorp.com
Processor, importer and exporter of acids including ascorbic, citric, sorbic and tartaric; also, sodium citrate, sodium ascorbate and vanillin
Owner: Bob Catroneo
rcatroneo@floridachem.com
Number Employees: 1-4
Square Footage: 200000
Type of Packaging: Private Label, Bulk
Brands:
Ici

6253 **International Coconut Corp**
225 W Grand St
PO Box 3326
Elizabeth, NJ 07202-1205
908-289-1555
Fax: 908-289-1556
sales@internationalcoconut.com
Coconut
Owner: A Kaye
Vice President: Richard Kesselhaut
richard@internationalcoconut.com
Estimated Sales: $2.5-5 Million
Number Employees: 5-9
Square Footage: 46000
Type of Packaging: Consumer, Food Service, Private Label, Bulk
Brands:
Sno-Top

6254 **International Dehydrated Foods**
3801 E Sunshine St
Springfield, MO 65809
417-881-7820
800-641-6509
realfood@idf.com www.idf.com
Processed meat and poultry ingredients
Founder: William Darr
CEO: Andrew Herr
Senior Director, Sales: Lou Croce
Credit Manager, Corporate Office: Debbie Thomas
Year Founded: 1982
Estimated Sales: $50 Million
Number Employees: 5-9
Number of Brands: 1
Square Footage: 6973
Type of Packaging: Bulk
Brands:
IDF

6255 **International Delicacies Inc**
2100 Atlas Rd
Suite F
San Pablo, CA 94806-1100
510-669-2444
Fax: 510-669-2446 844-974-1030
Info@intldelicacies.com www.intldelicacies.com
Olive oils, pasta, bastoncini, cookies, panettone, pickles, balsamic vinegar, honey, infused oils, mustard, dolma, dried figs, fruit preserves, artichokes
Founder/CEO: Hossein Banejad
CFO: Ruth Banejad
VP Sales/Marketing: Maxx Sherman
Manager: Amanda Lee
amandal@intldelicacies.com
COO: Dean Wilkinson
Brands:
Amir
Anna's
Audisio & Lori
Looza
Pan Ducale
Rubino & Vero
Vicenzi

6256 **International Enterprises**
PO Box 158
Herring Neck, NL A0G 2R0
Canada
709-628-7406
Fax: 709-628-7875
Mussels
President: Wayne Fudge
Estimated Sales: $975,000
Number Employees: 7
Type of Packaging: Consumer, Food Service, Bulk

6257 **International Farmers Market**
PO Box 81226
Chamblee, GA 30366-1226
770-455-1777
Fax: 770-451-7474
www.internationalfarmersmarket.com
Dairy, meats, seafood, general grocery items, poultry, blue crab, catfish, clams
Contact: Jacqui Chew
jacqui@ifusionmarketing.com

6258 **International Flavors &Fragrances Inc.**
521 W. 57th St.
New York, NY 10019
212-765-5500
Fax: 212-708-7132 www.iff.com
Scents and flavors.
Chairman/CEO: Andreas Fibig
Executive VP/Integration Officer: Richard O'Leary
Divisional CEO, Scent: Nicolas Mirzayantz
Divisional CEO, Taste: Matthias Haeni
Executive VP, Operations: Francisco Fortanet
Year Founded: 1889
Estimated Sales: $5.1 Billion
Number Employees: 13,600
Number of Products: 38K
Type of Packaging: Bulk

6259 **International Food Packers Corporation**
4691 SW 71st Avenue
Miami, FL 33155-4657
305-740-5847
Fax: 305-669-1447
Canned corned beef, frozen cooked beef and beef cuts; importer of canned fish and rice
President: Richard Spradling
Estimated Sales: $2.5-5 Million
Number Employees: 5-9
Square Footage: 12000

6260 **International Food Products**
150 Larkin Williams Industrial Ct
Fenton, MO 63026
800-227-8427
info@ifpc.com www.ifpc.com
Food ingredients and additives
Chairman: Fred Brown, Sr.
CEO: Clayton Brown
VP, Finance: Kathy Langan
VP, Sales & Marketing: Jamie Moritz
VP, Quality & Regulatory: Mary Ellen Rowland
VP, Manufacturing: Mark Warren
VP, Supply Chain: Jennifer Hoerchler
Year Founded: 1974
Estimated Sales: $150 Million
Number Employees: 50-200
Square Footage: 68000
Type of Packaging: Consumer, Food Service
Other Locations:
St. Louis MO
Joplin MO
Kansas City MO
Houston TX
Dallas TX
Laredo TX
San Antonio TX
Indianapolis IN
Cleveland OH
Denver CO
Atlanta GA
Spokane WA
Plant City FL
Brands:
Dairy House Chocolate Dairy Powder(c)
Dairy House(c) Milk Flavors
Dairy House(c) Stabalizers
Dairy House(c) Vitamins
Ingredion(c)

6261 **International Foodcraft Corp**
1601 E Linden Ave
Linden, NJ 07036-1508
908-862-8810
Fax: 908-862-8825 800-875-9393
info@intlfoodcraft.com www.ifc-solutions.com
Anti-stick lubricants, release agents and food color concentrates
Owner: David Dukes
ddukes@intlfoodcraft.com
Technical Director: Ted Palumbo
Estimated Sales: $2 Million
Number Employees: 10-19
Type of Packaging: Bulk
Brands:
Coloreze
Confecto
Eez-Out
Pano

6262 **International Foodservice Manufacturers' Association**
180 N Stetson Ave
Suite 850
Chicago, IL 60601-6766
312-540-4400
Fax: 312-540-4401 ifma@ifmaworld.com
www.ifmaworld.com
President & CEO: Larry Oberkfell
Chief Financial Officer: Jennifer Tarulis
VP, Member Value: Mike Schwartz
Marketing Director: Cassie Kupfer Norris
VP, Sales & Member Services: Anthony R DePaolo
VP, Communications: Janet Rustigan
Estimated Sales: $20-50 Million
Number Employees: 10-19

6263 **International Fruit Marketing**
1201 S Orlando Ave # 340
Winter Park, FL 32789-7107
407-628-1121
Fax: 407-628-1829 intlfruit@aol.com
Fruit drinks, pure concentrates and citrus purees
President/CEO: Gene Hays
CFO: Robert Keyes
Vice President: Leland Anderson
Estimated Sales: $13 Million+
Number Employees: 1-4
Parent Co: SECO & Golden 100

6264 **International Glace**
1616 East Lyons Avenue
Spokane, WA 99217
760-731-3220
Fax: 760-731-3221 800-884-5041
alan@internationalglace.com
Importer of ginger, brewers' yeast spread and glace fruits
Manager: Marilyn Guest
Vice President: Bill Davids
Sales Director: Alan Sipole
Estimated Sales: $1-2.5 Million
Number Employees: 1-4
Type of Packaging: Consumer, Bulk

6265 **International Glatt Kosher**
5600 1st Ave Ste 19
Brooklyn, NY 11220
718-630-5555
Fax: 718-921-1542
Kosher foods
President: Leib Chaimovitz
Estimated Sales: Less than $500,000
Number Employees: 1-4

6266 **International Harvest Inc**
606 Franklin Ave
Mt Vernon, NY 10550-4518
914-699-5600
Fax: 914-699-5626 800-277-4268
info@internationalharvest.com
www.internationalharvest.com
Dried fruits, nuts, and seeds
President: Dennis Avalos
dennis.avalos@bnymellon.com
Number Employees: 20-49

6267 **International Home Foods**
1633 Littleton Rd
Parsippany, NJ 07054
973-359-9920
Fax: 973-254-5473
Canned beans, peas, apples, pasta, chicken, tomato paste, chili, mustard, instant hot cereal, nonstick cooking spray and glazed popcorn
Chairman/CEO: C Dean Metropoulos
SVP/CFO: Craig Steeneck
President/COO: Lawrence Hathaway
Sales/Marketing Executive: Mike Larney
Number Employees: 100
Parent Co: ConAgra Foods
Type of Packaging: Consumer
Brands:
Bumble Bee
Campfire
Campfire Marshmallows
Captain Jac
Chef Boyardee
Chef Boyardee Pastas
Clover Leaf
Crunch 'n Munch
Crunch'n'munch Glazed Popcorn
Dennison
Dennison's
Fireside
Franklin Crunch 'n' Munch
Golden Touch
Gulden's
Iron Kettle
Jiffy Pop
Libby's
Louis Kemp
Luck's
Luck's Beans
Maypo
Orleans
Pam
Pam Cooking Spray
Paramount
Ranch Style
Ranch Style Brand Beans
Ro*Tel
Royal Reef
Seafest
Swiftwater
Tuxedo
Western Gold
Wheatena

6268 **International Meat Co**
7107 W Grand Ave
Chicago, IL 60707
773-622-1400
Fax: 773-622-6829
www.internationalmeatcompany.com
Meat products
Owner: Victor Bomprezzi
Estimated Sales: $5-10 Million
Number Employees: 10-19
Type of Packaging: Consumer, Food Service

6269 **International Noodle Co**
32811 Groveland St
Madison Heights, MI 48071-1330
248-583-2479
Fax: 248-583-3004
Chinese noodle, egg roll wrapper, pasta, perogi wrapper
President: Robert Ip
Estimated Sales: $1-2.5 000,000
Number Employees: 5-9

6270 International Seafoods-Alaska
517 Shelikof St
P.O.Box 2997
Kodiak, AK 99615-6049
907-486-4768
Fax: 907-486-4885 info@isa-ak.com
www.isa-ak.com
Fresh or frozen fish and seafoods
Administrator: Ted Kishimoto
Estimated Sales: $4,200,000
Number Employees: 100-249
Type of Packaging: Consumer, Food Service, Private Label
Brands:
Internation Seafood of Alaska
Kodiak Seafood

6271 International Seafoods of Chicago
1133 W Lake St
Chicago, IL 60607-1618
312-243-2330
Fax: 312-243-1923
Seafood
President: Inkie Hong
Estimated Sales: $1,800,000
Number Employees: 5-9

6272 International Service Group
4080 Mcginnis Ferry Rd # 1403
Alpharetta, GA 30005-1774
770-518-0988
Fax: 770-518-0299
Peanuts, popcorn
President: John Kopec
j.kopec@isgnuts.com
Estimated Sales: $3-5 Million
Number Employees: 1-4
Type of Packaging: Consumer, Private Label, Bulk

6273 International SpecialtySupply
1011 Volunteer Dr
Cookeville, TN 38506-5026
931-526-1106
Fax: 931-526-8338 www.sproutnet.com
Alfalfa and bean sprouts
Owner: Robert Rust
Contact: Raymond Jones
r_cjones@me.com
Estimated Sales: Less Than $500,000
Number Employees: 1-4
Parent Co: International Specialty Supply
Type of Packaging: Consumer, Food Service, Private Label, Bulk

6274 International Spice
501 Prospect St.
Suite 111
Lakewood, NJ 08701
609-838-1717
www.zingspices.com
Herbs, rubs and spices
CEO: Noah Gross
ngross@intspice.com
Type of Packaging: Food Service, Private Label

6275 International Tea Importers
8551 Loch Lomond Dr
Pico Rivera, CA 90660
562-801-9600
Fax: 323-722-6368 877-832-5263
iti@teavendor.com www.teavendor.com
Tea
Founder: DeVan Shah
Contact: Desiree Nelson
teaconsultantd@gmail.com
Estimated Sales: $2.5-5 Million
Number Employees: 1-4

6276 International Trade Impact Inc
30 Gordon Ave
Lawrenceville, NJ 08648-1033
609-987-0550
Fax: 609-987-0252 800-223-5484
info@ititropicals.com www.ititropicals.com
Tropical juices
Owner: Gerrit Van Manen
gert@ititropicals.com
Estimated Sales: $2.5-5 Million
Number Employees: 10-19
Brands:
Ititropicals

6277 International Trading Company
300 Portwall Street
Houston, TX 77029
713-224-5901
Fax: 713-678-1718
Importer of gourmet foods
Sales Manager: Lenny Yassie

6278 International Vitamin Corporation
500 Halls Mill Road
Freehold, NJ 07728
732-308-3000
Fax: 855-482-3291 800-666-8482
www.ivcinc.com/
Vitamin supplements, herbal products and antioxidants
Manager: Barb McCleer
Vice President, General Counsel, Secreta: Ellen Chiniara
Contact: Phillip Abbatiello
phillip.abbatiello@ivcinc.com
Number Employees: 250-499
Type of Packaging: Consumer

6279 Internatural Foods
1455 Broad Street
4th Floor
Bloomfield, NJ 07003
973-338-1499
Fax: 973-338-1485 800-225-1449
www.internaturalfoods.com
Organic and natural products
President: Peter Leiendecker
VP: Linda Palame
Contact: Linda Palame
info@internaturalfoods.com
Estimated Sales: $1-2.5 Million
Number Employees: 1-4
Type of Packaging: Private Label
Brands:
Bio-Familia
Bisca
Blanchard & Blanchard
Cafix
Clipper
Davinci
Drsoy
Eddie's
Helwa
Kavli
McCann's
Monari Federzoni
Mount Hagen
Mrs Leeper's
Pero
Pritikin
Ryvita
Vivani

6280 Intervest Trading Company Inc.
106 Chain Lake Drive
Halifax, NS B3S 1A8
Canada
902-425-2018
Fax: 902-420-0763 info@intervest.ca
Fresh and frozen groundfish and shellfish
President: Jeff Whitman
Year Founded: 1988
Estimated Sales: $5 Million
Number Employees: 1,000-4,999
Type of Packaging: Bulk

6281 Inverness Dairy
1631 Woiderski Rd
Cheboygan, MI 49721
231-627-4655
Fax: 231-627-4655
Milk and butter
President: David Woiderski
Estimated Sales: $5-10 000,000
Number Employees: 20-49

6282 Inviting Foods
Chicago, IL 60661
844-782-5374
makeroats.com
Overnight oatmeal
Number of Products: 3
Brands:
Maker Overnight Oats

6283 Ipswich Ale Brewery
2 Brewery Pl
Ipswich, MA 01938-1196
978-356-3329
Fax: 450-973-1957 info@mercurybrewing.com
www.ipswichalebrewery.com
Soda and beers
President: Rob Martin
Brand Manager: John Thebeau
Sales & Event Coordinator: Mary Gormley
Brewery Operations Manager: Jim Dorau
Production Manager: Dan Lipke
Inventory Manager: Paul Gentile
Estimated Sales: Below $5 Million
Number Employees: 10-19
Type of Packaging: Consumer, Food Service
Brands:
Blueberry Ale
Ipswich Ale
Stone Cat Ale

6284 Ipswich Maritime Product Company
43 Avery St
Ipswich, MA 01938
978-356-9866
Fax: 978-356-9894 www.ipswichmaritime.com
Seafood
President: Peter Maistrellis
Contact: George Delaney
gdelaney@ipswichmaritime.com
Estimated Sales: $10-20 Million
Number Employees: 10-19

6285 Ipswich Shellfish Co Inc
8 Hayward St
Ipswich, MA 01938-2012
978-356-4371
Fax: 978-356-9235 800-477-9424
www.ipswichshellfish.com
Seafood
Owner, President: Chrissi Pappas
CEO: Alexis Pappas
Controller: Lou Cellineri
VP: Alexander Pappas
Sales Manager: Michael Gagne
Director of Human Resources: Kathy Waymous
Operations Manager: Bob Butcher
General Manager: Michael Trupiano
Purchasing Director: Vito Finazzo
Estimated Sales: $22.2 Million
Number Employees: 250-499
Square Footage: 35000

6286 Ira Higdon Grocery Company
150 IGA Way
Cairo, GA 39828
229-377-1272
jdunn@irahigdongc.com
www.irahigdongc.com
Groceries and meat.
President & CEO: Larry Higdon
Vice President: Katie Higdon
Director of Sales & Marketing: Jim Dunn
Year Founded: 1909
Estimated Sales: $106.3 Million
Number Employees: 100
Square Footage: 170000

6287 Irene's Bakery & Gourmet
1746 Winchester Rd
Bensalem, PA 19020-4542
215-244-6200
www.irenesbakery.com
Baked goods
Owner: Irene Zelikovich
Estimated Sales: Less Than $500,000
Number Employees: 5-9

6288 Iris Brands
St. Louis Park, MN 55426
solero.com
Crushed fruit bars and pops
Co-Founder: Joshua Hochschuler
Brands:
Solero

6289 Iron Horse Vineyards
9786 Ross Station Rd
Sebastopol, CA 95472-2179
707-887-1507
Fax: 707-887-1337 www.ironhorsevineyards.com
Wines

Co-Founder: Barry Sterling
barrys@ironhorsevineyards.com
CEO: Joy Anne Sterling
Co-Founder: Audrey Sterling
Partner/Operations Director: Laurence Sterling
Estimated Sales: $10-20 Million
Number Employees: 50-99
Type of Packaging: Private Label

6290 **Ironstone Vineyards**
1894 6 Mile Rd
Murphys, CA 95247-9543
209-728-1251
Fax: 209-728-1275 info@ironstonevineyards.com
www.ironstonevineyards.com
Wines
President: Stephen Kautz
skautz@ironstonevineyards.com
CEO: John Kautz
CFO: Michael Porten
Vice President: Francis Millier
Director of Operations: Bruce Rohroer
Estimated Sales: $5 Million
Number Employees: 100-249
Type of Packaging: Private Label
Brands:
Angels Creek
Creekside
Delta Bay

6291 **Irresistible Cookie Jar**
PO Box 3230
Hayden Lake, ID 83835-3230
208-664-1261
Fax: 208-667-1347
service@irresistiblecookiejar.com
Cookie and muffin mixes, cookie cutters and decorations
President: Wanda Hall
Estimated Sales: $300,000-500,000
Number Employees: 10
Brands:
Boyds' Kissa Bearhugs
Mimi's Muffins
Susan Winget

6292 **Irwin Naturals**
5310 Beethoven St
Los Angeles, CA 90066
888-223-1548
customersupport@irwinnaturals.com
irwinnaturals.com
CBD-infused nutritional supplements
President/Owner: Rebecca Pearman
CEO: Marc Washington

6293 **Isaacson & Stein Fish Company**
800 W Fulton Market
Chicago, IL 60607-1375
312-421-2444
Fax: 312-421- 432
Sushi-grade fish
President: Ben Willner
Owner: Sherwin Willner
Estimated Sales: $5-10 Million
Number Employees: 20-49

6294 **Isadore A. Rapasadi & Son**
PO Box 66
800 North Peterboro Road
Canastota, NY 13032
315-697-2216
Fax: 315-697-3300 800-828-7277
datudman@twcny.com
Potatoes and onions
President/CEO: Izzy Rapasadi
Sales Manager: Bob Rapasadi
Estimated Sales: F
Number Employees: 50-99
Square Footage: 180000
Type of Packaging: Bulk
Brands:
Raps Blue Ribbon
Stars & Stripes

6295 **Ise America Inc**
33335 Galena Sassafras Rd
Galena, MD 21635-1919
410-755-6300
Fax: 410-755-6367 www.iseamerica.com
Fresh eggs
Chairman: Hikonobu Ise
Manager: Larry Beck
larry-beck@iseamerica.com
Estimated Sales: $14.5 Million
Number Employees: 10-19
Square Footage: 12000
Type of Packaging: Consumer, Food Service
Other Locations:
CMC Food, Inc
Clark NJ
ISE Newberry, Inc.
Newberry SC

6296 **Isernio Sausage Company**
5600 7th Ave S
Seattle, WA 98108-2644
206-762-5259
Fax: 206-762-6207 888-495-8674
info@isernio.com
Pork, beef and lamb sausages
President: Frank Isernio
Contact: Greg Arend
grega@isernio.com
Estimated Sales: $2.5-5 Million
Number Employees: 20-49
Type of Packaging: Consumer, Food Service

6297 **Island Aseptics**
100 Hope Ave
Byesville, OH 43723-9460
740-685-2548
Fax: 740-685-6550 www.kerry.com
Beverages, including fruit juices
Controller: Sandy Smith
Human Resources: Missy Miller
Operations: Grace Lippolis
Assistant Plant Manager: John Kasinecz
Estimated Sales: $45.4 Million
Number Employees: 50-99
Square Footage: 15254
Type of Packaging: Private Label, Bulk

6298 **Island Delights, Inc.**
5104 Greenwich Road
Seville, OH 44273
330-769-2800
Fax: 330-769-3935 866-877-4100
acrall@islanddelights.com
www.islanddelights.com
Coconut candies
Sales: Ann Crall
Sales: Greg Miller
Estimated Sales: $5-10 Million
Number Employees: 15

6299 **Island Farms Dairies Cooperative Association**
2220 Dowler Place
P.O. Box 38
Victoria, BC V8W 2M1
Canada
250-360-5200
Fax: 250-360-5220 www.islandfarms.com
Dairy products
President: George Aylard
CEO: David McMillan
CFO: Eric Erikson
Quality Control: Sam Arora
Marketing: Jona De Jesus
Sales: Art Paulo
Operations: Greg Martin
Plant Manager: Al Snedden
Purchasing Director: Steve Wainwright
Number Employees: 250-499
Number of Products: 500
Type of Packaging: Consumer, Food Service, Private Label, Bulk

6300 **Island Lobster**
PO Box 258
Matinicus, ME 04851-0258
207-366-3937
Fax: 207-366-3380
Lobster
Owner: Marc Ames

6301 **Island Marine Products**
2772 Main Road
P.O. Box 40
Clarks Harbour, NS B0W 1P0
Canada
902-745-2222
Fax: 902-745-3247 islandmarine@ss.eastlink.ca
Processor and exporter of haddock, lobster and lobster meat and tuna
President: Cyril Swim
Estimated Sales: $10-20 Million
Number Employees: 15
Type of Packaging: Food Service, Bulk

6302 **Island Oasis Frozen Cocktail**
3400 Millington Rd.
Beloit, WI 53511
508-660-1177
Fax: 508-660-1435 800-777-4752
www.kerryfoodservice.com
Non-alcoholic beverage mixes; ice shavers and blenders
President & CEO: Gerry Behan
Marketing Director: Abhishek Trivedi
VP of Global & Strategic Accounts: Michael Walsh
Estimated Sales: $20-50 Million
Number Employees: 100-249
Number of Products: 16
Square Footage: 25000
Parent Co: Kerry Food Services
Brands:
Sb-3x

6303 **Island Princess**
2846 Ualena Street
Honolulu, HI 96819
808-839-5222
Fax: 808-836-2019 866-872-8601
info@islandprincesshawaii.com
www.islandprincesshawaii.com
Gourmet snack products
President: Michael Purdy
VP: Owen Purdy
Estimated Sales: $8 Million
Number Employees: 50-99
Number of Brands: 10
Number of Products: 100
Square Footage: 48000
Type of Packaging: Consumer, Food Service, Private Label, Bulk
Brands:
Hawaiian Princess Smoke
Island Princess

6304 **Island Scallops**
5552 Island Highway W
Qualicum Beach, BC V9K 2C8
Canada
250-757-9811
Fax: 250-757-8370 www.islandscallops.com
Fresh and frozen scallops; marine research hatchery
President/CEO: Robert Saunders
R&D: Barb Bunting
Processing Manager: Lorraine Hopps
Estimated Sales: $1 Million
Number Employees: 10
Type of Packaging: Consumer, Food Service

6305 **Island Seafood**
32 Brook Rd
Eliot, ME 03903-1423
207-439-8508
Fax: 207-439-9945 www.islandseafoodlobster.com
Seafood
Owner: Randy Townsend
randyisf@comcast.net
Estimated Sales: $3-5 Million
Number Employees: 20-49

6306 **Island Seafoods**
317 Shelikof St
Kodiak, AK 99615
907-486-8575
Fax: 907-486-3007 800-355-8575
www.islandseafoods.com
Seafood
Owner: Frank Tulcich
Contact: Claudine Alokli
calokli@pacseafood.com
Estimated Sales: $5-10 Million
Number Employees: 20-49

6307 **Island Snacks**
7650 Stage Rd
Buena Park, CA 90621
714-994-1228
info@islandsnacksinc.com
islandsnack.com
Nuts, trail mixes, candies and Hispanic snacks
President/Owner: Alln Barak
Year Founded: 1982
Type of Packaging: Consumer

6308 Island Spice
1209 NW 93rd Ct
Doral, FL 33172-2838
786-473-3465
Fax: 305-207-9353 Sales@IslandSpice.com
www.islandspice.com
Dry spices and sauces
President: Lawrence Shadeed
lawrence@islandspice.com
Estimated Sales: Less Than $500,000
Number Employees: 1-4

6309 Island Spring Inc
18846 103rd Ave SW
Vashon, WA 98070
206-463-9848
Fax: 206-463-5670
Organic soy and tofu products
President: W Lukoskie
luke@islandspring.com
R&D: Suni Kim Lukoskie
Estimated Sales: $2.5-5 Million
Number Employees: 10-19
Square Footage: 16000
Type of Packaging: Consumer, Food Service, Private Label, Bulk
Brands:
Island Spring

6310 Island Sweetwater Beverage Company
825 Lafayette Road
Bryn Mawr, PA 19010-1816
610-525-7444
Fax: 610-525-7502 www.peacemountain.com
Soft drinks, bottled waters, energy drinks; exporter of beer
President: Michael Salaman
Square Footage: 40000
Parent Co: A/S Beverage Marketing
Type of Packaging: Private Label
Brands:
4th of July Cola
Absolutenergy
Activin Energy
Beverly Hills
Citrimax
Citrimax-French Diet Cola
French Paradox
Island Sweetwater
Jazz
Kiwi Kola
Nicola
Rebound
Sangria Cola
Santa-Claus
Slender
Stampede

6311 Island Treasures Gourmet
9413 Center Point Lane
Manassas, VA 20110
703-801-4671
Fax: 703-590-8796 kcraigcgc@yahoo.com
www.islandtreasuresgourmet.com
Gourmet rum cakes
Owner: Cassandra Craig

6312 Island of the Moon Apiaries
17560 Company Road
85-B
Esparto, CA 95627
530-787-3993
Fax: 530-787-3993
Bee pollen, honey
President: Jerry Kaplan
Estimated Sales: $2.5-5 000,000
Number Employees: 1-4

6313 Isodiol
Escondido, CA 92029
855-979-6751
isodiol.com
Hemp-based beverages

6314 Issimo Food Group
PO Box 1991
La Jolla, CA 92038-1991
619-260-1900
Fax: 619-260-8400 www.issimo-group.com
Specialty chocolate candies and desserts
President/Owner: Willing Howard
Sales Manager: Kathleen Hornbacher
Estimated Sales: $1-2.5 Million
Number Employees: 20-49
Brands:
Chef Howard's Williecake
Ecco!
Issimo Celebrations!
Issimo's Creme Br-L,
Lilycake

6315 It's It Ice Cream Co
865 Burlway Rd
Burlingame, CA 94010-1705
650-347-2122
Fax: 650-347-2703 800-345-1928
comments@itsiticecream.com
www.itsiticecream.com
Ice cream novelties
President: Charles Shamieh
comments@itsiticecream.com
Sales Executive: Charles Shamieh
Production Manager: Peter Zaru
Plant Manager: Alex McDow
Estimated Sales: $4 Million
Number Employees: 20-49
Square Footage: 68000
Brands:
It's It

6316 Italia Foods
2365 Hammond Drive
Schaumburg, IL 60173
847-397-4479
Fax: 847-397-6817 800-747-1109
italiainc@aol.com www.italiafoods.com
Frozen pasta and sauces
President: Filippo Carabetta
fillic@aol.com
Chairman: Arsenio Carabetta
Vice President / Operations: Peter Carabetta
Vice President / Sales: Maria Carabetta
Estimated Sales: $4 Million
Number Employees: 60
Square Footage: 24000
Brands:
Italia
Mama Lina

6317 Italian Bakery of Virginia
205 1st St S # 205
Virginia, MN 55792-2699
218-741-3464
Fax: 218-741-2531 www.potica.com
Fresh pies
Owner: Joe Prebonich
Estimated Sales: $1-2.5 Million
Number Employees: 20-49
Type of Packaging: Consumer

6318 Italian Connection
55b W Shore Ave
Dumont, NJ 07628-2332
201-385-2226
Fax: 201-385-9026 www.italian-connection.com
Italian specialty foods
Owner: John Stracquadanio
info@italian-connection.com
Estimated Sales: Less Than $500,000
Number Employees: 1-4

6319 Italian Foods Corporation
7330 Chapel Hill Rd
Suite 102
Raleigh, NC 27607
919-341-0605
Fax: 510-868-4522 888-516-7262
sales@italianfoods.com
Pasta, sauces, spreads & toppings, oil & vinegar, rice, risotto, gnocchi, snacks, grilled vegetables, pasta express
President/Owner: Elena Lapiana
Sales: Francesca Lapiana
francesca.lapiana@italianfoods.com
Operations: Kirk Newcross

6320 Italian Gourmet Foods Canada
101-1240 Kensington Road NW
Calgary, AB T2N 3P7
Canada
403-283-5350
Fax: 403-283-3882 sales@peppinogourmet.com
www.peppinogourmet.com
Fresh pasta
President: Peter Bellusci
Type of Packaging: Consumer, Food Service
Brands:
The Perfect Pasta

6321 Italian Peoples Bakery Inc
31 Scotch Rd
Ewing, NJ 08628-2512
609-771-1369
Fax: 609-771-1369 www.italianpeoplesbakery.com
Baked goods
Manager: Sandy Elmer
Secretary/Treasurer: Carmen Guagliardo
Manager: Carlos Camey
Estimated Sales: $.5-1 000,000
Number Employees: 10-19
Parent Co: Italian Peoples Bakery

6322 Italian Rose Garlic Products
1380 W 15th St
Suite A
Riviera Beach, FL 33404-5310
561-863-5556
Fax: 561-863-1462 800-338-8899
info@italian-rose.com www.italian-rose.com
Garlic products
President/Founder: Ken Berger
CEO: Angelo Fraggos
Marketing Director: Arthur Conlan
Estimated Sales: $30 Million
Number Employees: 100-249
Type of Packaging: Consumer, Food Service, Private Label
Brands:
Italian Rose

6323 Itarca
1864 E 22nd St
Los Angeles, CA 90058
310-419-6433
Fax: 310-677-2782 800-747-2782
Fresh and frozen Italian pasta
President: Yvonne Smulovitz
Manager: Jascha Smulovitz
Contact: Pat Brophy
pat.brophy@freshpasta.com
Estimated Sales: $1.60 Million
Number Employees: 17

6324 Itella Foods
1622 South Gaffey St.
Suite 201
San Pedro, CA 90731
310-732-5875
info@ittellafoods.com
www.ittellafoods.com
Comfort foods including burritos, wraps, pizza, pasta, flatbreads, risotto, tartufo, biscotti, panettone, and more. Also organic, gluten free, vegan, and vegetarian options.
Owner: Salveatore Gallatti
COO: Stephanie Dieckmann
Vice President: Frank Brigulio
Estimated Sales: $20-50 Million
Number Employees: 100-249

6325 Ithaca Craft Hummus
Escondido, CA 92029
855-979-6751
info@ithacacoldcrafted.com ithacacoldcrafted.com
Cold-pressed hummus
Founder & President: Chris Kirby
Number of Products: 6
Brands:
Ithaca Cold-Crafted

6326 Ito Cariani Sausage Company
3190 Corporate Place
Hayward, CA 94545-3916
510-887-0882
Fax: 510-887-8323 us.kompass.com/
Meat products
President: Tony Nakashima
VP Finance: Allen Shiroma
Executive VP/General Manager: Ken Kamata
VP Sales: Al Lera
Estimated Sales: $10-20 Million
Number Employees: 50-99
Square Footage: 170000
Type of Packaging: Consumer, Food Service, Private Label, Bulk
Other Locations:
Ito Cariani Sausage Co.
Nishinomiya
Brands:
Cariani Italian Dry Salami
Cariani Italian Specialty Loaves

6327 **Ito En USA Inc**
20 Jay St.
Suite 530
Brooklyn, NY 11201
808-847-4477
Fax: 808-841-4384 info@itoen-usa.com
www.itoen-usa.com
Fruit juices, sports drinks, iced tea, coffee and canned teas
President: Nadene Tomiyasu
ntomisawa@itoen.com
CEO: Yosuke Honjo
Marketing Director: Alan Pollock
Year Founded: 1987
Estimated Sales: $20-50 Million
Number Employees: 50-99
Type of Packaging: Consumer, Food Service
Brands:
Aloha Maid
Itoen

6328 **Ivanhoe Cheese Inc**
11301 Hwy 62 RR 5
Madoc, ON K0K 2K0
Canada
613-473-4269
Fax: 613-473-5016 www.ivanhoecheese.com
Cheeses
President: Bruce Kingston
Vice President: Larry Hook
Sales: Paul McKinlay
Plant Manager: Chris Spencer
Estimated Sales: $16.5 Million
Number Employees: 80
Type of Packaging: Consumer, Food Service, Private Label, Bulk
Brands:
Ivanhoe
Ivanhoe Classics
Ivanhoe Fresh

6329 **Iveta Gourmet Inc**
2125 Delaware Ave
Suite F
Santa Cruz, CA 95060-5758
831-423-5149
Fax: 831-423-5169 iveta@iveta.com
www.iveta.com
Baked goods; jams, curds and clotted cream
Owner: John Bilanko
iveta@iveta.com
Co-Owner: Yvette Bilanko
Estimated Sales: $2.5-5 Million
Number Employees: 5-9
Brands:
Iveta Gourmet

6330 **Ivy Cottage Scone Mixes**
530 Fremont Ln
S Pasadena, CA 91030
626-441-2761
Fax: 626-441-9657
Prepared mixes for scones
President: Elaine Osmond

6331 **Ivy Foods**
3851 E. Thunderhill Place
Phoenix, AZ 85044-6679
480-626-2025
Fax: 480-704-4116 877-223-5459
support@nutribase.com www.nutribase.com
Wheat based meat substitutes
President: Mira Blue Machlis
Estimated Sales: $2.5-5 Million
Number Employees: 1-4
Square Footage: 48000
Brands:
Meat of Wheat

6332 **Iwamoto Natto Factory**
143 Hana Hwy # C
Paia, HI 96779
808-579-9935
Fax: 808-579-9933
Natto and noodles
Owner: Daryl Yamashita
Estimated Sales: $110,000
Number Employees: 1-4
Type of Packaging: Consumer, Food Service

6333 **Iya Foods LLC**
North Aurora, IL 60542
630-854-7107
hello@iyafoods.com
www.iyafoods.com
Sauces, powders, spices, herbs and seasonings
President/Owner: Toyin Kolawole
Type of Packaging: Bulk

6334 **J & B Sausage Co Inc**
100 Main
PO Box 7
Waelder, TX 78959-5329
830-788-7511
Fax: 830-788-7279 contact@jbfoods.com
Smoked sausage, bacon, ham, jerky and barbecued meat
President: Danny Janecka
CEO: Ty Ahrens
tahrens@jbfoods.com
Year Founded: 1959
Estimated Sales: $42040000
Number Employees: 250-499
Type of Packaging: Consumer, Food Service, Private Label, Bulk
Brands:
J Bar B
Singletree Farms
Texas Smokehouse
Cajun Hollar
Chefs-In-A-Bag

6335 **J & B Seafood**
9301 Faith St
Coden, AL 36523-3057
251-824-4512
Fax: 251-824-1260 jbfood1979@aol.com
www.jandbseafood.com
Seafood
Owner: Raymond T. Barbour
Estimated Sales: $7.7 Million
Number Employees: 100-249

6336 **J & G Poultry & Seafood**
2360 Monroe Dr
Gainesville, GA 30507-7343
770-536-5540
Fax: 770-531-0829
Poultry
Manager: Bob Gregory
jgpoultry@aol.com
Manager: Bob Gregory
Estimated Sales: $10-20 Million
Number Employees: 10-19

6337 **J & J Processing**
2757 Lawrence 2225
Pierce City, MO 65723-8391
417-476-5451
Fax: 417-529-8273
Beef, pork and deer processing
Owner: James Etter
Number Employees: 1-4

6338 **J & J Snack Foods Corp**
6000 Central Hwy
Pennsauken, NJ 08109
856-665-9533
800-486-9533
consumerrelations@jjsnack.com www.jjsnack.com
Nutritional snack foods and beverages.
Chairman/CEO: Gerald Shreiber
gshreiber@jjsnack.com
President: Dan Fachner
CFO: Dennis Moore
COO: Robert Radano
Year Founded: 1971
Estimated Sales: $1.08 Billion
Number Employees: 4,200
Number of Brands: 35
Square Footage: 70000
Type of Packaging: Food Service, Private Label
Brands:
Superpretzel
ICEE
Luigi's
Tio Pepe's Churros
The Funnel Cake Factory
WholeFruit
Country Home Bakery
Slush Puppie
Hill & Valley
Superpretzel Bavarian
Dutch Waffle
Readi-Bake
California Churros
Mary B's
Pretzel Fillers
Minute Maid
Labriola
New Day
Brauhaus Pretzel
Arctic Blast
Auntie Annie's
PhillySwirl
Supreme Stuffers
Daddy Ray's
Sour Patch Kids
Dogsters
Sweet Stuffers
Federal Pretzel Baking Company
Parrot-Ice
Corazonas' Heartbar
Patio
Kim & Scott's Gourmet Pretzels
Barq's
Oreo Churros
Shape Ups

6339 **J & J Wall Bakery Co**
8806 Fruitridge Rd
Sacramento, CA 95826-9708
916-381-1410
Fax: 916-381-6008 www.jjwallbaking.com
Frozen bread and rolls
President: Janet Wall
Year Founded: 1979
Number Employees: 50-99
Type of Packaging: Consumer

6340 **J & K Ingrediants**
160 E 5th St
Paterson, NJ 07524-1603
973-340-8700
Fax: 973-340-4994 sales@jkingredients.net
www.jkingredients.net
Bakery ingredients
President: James Sausville
jkfoods1@aol.com
Vice President of Research & Development: Nigel Weston
Vice President of Sales & Marketing: Al Orr
Director of National Sales: Kurt Miller
Customer Service: Cheryl Tirri
General Manager: Fred Denman
Controller: Andrew Madacsi
Senior Bakery Technician: Jeremy Jones
Estimated Sales: $19.5 Million
Number Employees: 20-49
Number of Brands: 11
Brands:
Bred-Mate
Cake-Mate
Milk-Free
Vita-Ex
Restore
Soft Bake
Verdi Line
"10" Potato
Choc-Dip
Toptex
Enak

6341 **J & L Grain Processing**
12456 Addison Ave
Riceville, IA 50466-7096
641-985-4255
Fax: 641-985-4256 800-244-9211
Grains
President/CEO: Joel Yorgey
jlgrain@omnitelcom.com
Estimated Sales: Below $5 000,000
Number Employees: 5-9

6342 **J & L Seafood**
13991 Shell Belt Rd
Bayou La Batre, AL 36509-2365
251-824-2371
Fax: 251-824-2371
Seafood
President: Joshua Alderman
Estimated Sales: $3-5 Million
Number Employees: 10-19

6343 **J & M Foods Inc**
9100 Frazier Pike
PO Box 250080
Little Rock, AR 72206-3894
501-663-1991
Fax: 501-663-2822 800-264-2278
info@jm-foods.com www.jm-foods.com
Flavored straws.
President: Jamie Parham
VP: Scott Thibault
Quality Control: David Hill
Director Sales/Marketing: Greg Parham
Plant Manager: David Harkey
Purchasing: Bryan Toland
Estimated Sales: $10-20 Million
Number Employees: 20-49
Type of Packaging: Private Label

6344 **J & M Wholesale Meat Inc**
2300 Hoover Ave
Modesto, CA 95354-3908
Canada
209-522-1248
Fax: 209-522-8834 855-522-1248
Fresh and frozen pork
President: J McCullough
Administrator Quality Control: Kevin McCullough
Sales Manager: Nannette McCullough
Number Employees: 20-49
Square Footage: 72000
Type of Packaging: Consumer, Food Service, Bulk

6345 **J B & Son LTD**
564 Mile Square Rd
Yonkers, NY 10701-6333
914-963-5192
Fax: 914-963-5192 www.yonkersny.gov
Specialty cheeses and pastas
President: Steven Brunetto
Sales: Steven Brunetto
Estimated Sales: $5-10 Million
Number Employees: 5-9
Square Footage: 6000
Type of Packaging: Consumer, Food Service, Private Label, Bulk

6346 **J Bernard Seafood**
1142 Front St
Cottonport, LA 71327
318-876-2716
Fax: 318-876-2925 www.crawfish.org
Seafood
President: James Bernard
Estimated Sales: $3.2 Million
Number Employees: 1-4

6347 **J C Watson Co**
201 E Main St
Parma, ID 83660
208-722-5141
Fax: 208-722-6646 nancy@soobrand.com
www.soobrand.com
Produce, including onions, apples, potatoes and plums
Owner: Jon Watson
Sales Manager: Nancy Carter
jonw@soobrand.com
Transportation Manager: Melanie Steinhaus
Number Employees: 5-9
Type of Packaging: Consumer, Food Service
Brands:
Soo

6348 **J Deluca Fish Co Inc**
2204 Signal Pl
San Pedro, CA 90731-7227
310-684-5180
Fax: 310-833-5285 www.jdelucafishco.com
Seafood
President/CEO: John DeLuca
Estimated Sales: $10-20 Million
Number Employees: 5-9
Number of Brands: 0
Type of Packaging: Bulk

6349 **J F O'Neill & Packing Co**
3120 G St
Omaha, NE 68107-1447
402-733-1200
Fax: 402-733-1724
Beef
President: Ron O'Neill
General Production Manager: Brian O'Neill
Estimated Sales: $12.2 Million
Number Employees: 50-99
Type of Packaging: Consumer, Food Service, Private Label, Bulk

6350 **J Filippi Winery**
12467 Baseline Rd
Rancho Cucamonga, CA 91739-9522
909-899-5755
Fax: 909-899-9196
www.sacramentalaltarwine.com
Wines
President: Joseph Filippi
josephfilippiwinery@aol.com
Vice President: Jared Filippi
Estimated Sales: $10-20 Million
Number Employees: 20-49
Number of Brands: 1
Brands:
J. Filippi

6351 **J G Noble Cheese Company**
6021 Etiwanda Ave
Etiwanda, CA 91739
909-899-2603
Cheeses
Partner: Bruce McBride
Partner: Mathilda McBride
Estimated Sales: $2.8 Million
Number Employees: 16

6352 **J G Townsend Jr & Co**
316 N Race St
P.O.Box 430
Georgetown, DE 19947-1166
302-856-2525
Fax: 302-855-0922
Frozen vegetables, including beans and peas
President: Paul Townsend
VP: John Townsend
Plant Manager: Soloman Henry
Estimated Sales: $2.5-5,000,000
Number Employees: 20-49
Type of Packaging: Consumer, Food Service
Brands:
Country Fair
Townsend

6353 **J G Van Holten & Son Inc**
703 W Madison St
Waterloo, WI 53594-1365
920-478-2144
Fax: 920-478-2316 800-256-0619
info@vanholtenpickles.com
www.vanholtenpickles.com
Pre-packaged pickles and relish
President: Steve Byrnes
sbyrnes@vanholtenpickles.com
President: Steve Byrnes
VP of Sales: Stef Espiritu
Operations Manager: Bruce Dorn
Estimated Sales: $7000000
Number Employees: 50-99
Type of Packaging: Consumer, Private Label, Bulk
Brands:
Big Papa
Garlic Gus
Hot Mama
Lil' Pepe
Van Holten

6354 **J H Verbridge & Son Inc**
6700 Lake Ave
Williamson, NY 14589-9569
315-589-2366
Fax: 315-589-7478
Frozen cherries, pineapples and strawberries
President: James Verbridge
jverbridge@jhverbridge.com
Executive VP: Gerald Verbridge
Plant Manager: Lloyd Verbridge
Estimated Sales: $1 Million
Number Employees: 20-49
Type of Packaging: Consumer, Food Service
Brands:
Big V

6355 **J J Gandy's Pies Inc**
3725 Alt 19 # A
Palm Harbor, FL 34683-1477
727-938-7437
Fax: 727-937-0830 ILovePies@JJGandys.com
www.jjgandys.com
Bakery items
Owner: Jeff Schmidt
ilovepies@jjgandys.com
Estimated Sales: Less Than $500,000
Number Employees: 5-9
Type of Packaging: Food Service

6356 **J J Produce**
4003 Seminole Pratt Whitney Rd
Loxahatchee, FL 33470-3754
561-791-1796
Fax: 561-422-9778 winston@jjproduce.com
Produce: green bell peppers, cucumbers. eggplant, red bell peppers, zucchini squash, tomatoes, and yellow crooked neck squash.
Owner: John Madden
Chief Financial Officer: Mark Campbell
Vice President: Chris Erneston
VP of Food Safety: Michael Bentel
VP of Business Development & Marketing: Brian Rayfield
VP of Sales: Kohl Brown
VP of Operations: David Beecher
Estimated Sales: $5-10 Million
Number Employees: 1-4

6357 **J Lohr Vineyards & Wines**
1000 Lenzen Ave
San Jose, CA 95126-2739
408-288-5057
Fax: 408-993-2276 sjwinecenter@jlohr.com
www.jlohr.com
Wines
Founder/Proprietor: Jerry Lohr
CEO: Steve Lohr
stevel@jlohr.com
VP Marketing: Cynthia Lohr
SVP Sales: Ken Lee
VP Production/Plant Manager: David Mezynski
Year Founded: 1974
Estimated Sales: $30-50 Million
Number Employees: 50-99
Type of Packaging: Private Label

6358 **J M Clayton Co**
108 Commerce St
PO Box 321
Cambridge, MD 21613-1862
410-228-1661
Fax: 410-221-0216 800-652-6931
info@jmclayton.com www.jmclayton.com
Chesapeake Bay blue crabs
President: John C Brooks Jr
CEO: William Brooks
bill@jmclayton.com
Estimated Sales: $3000000
Number Employees: 5-9
Square Footage: 116000
Type of Packaging: Consumer, Food Service, Private Label, Bulk
Brands:
Epicure

6359 **J M Swank Co**
395 Herky St
North Liberty, IA 52317-8523
319-626-3683
Fax: 319-626-3662 800-593-6375
www.jmswank.com
Food ingredients for the dairy, beverage, meat, bakery, snack, confection, ethnic and prepared foods industries
CEO: Shawn Meaney
Chief Financial Officer: Philip Garton
Senior Vice President: Paul Hillen
Vice President, Sales & Customer Service: Linda Loucks
Vice President, Operations: Reggie Hastings
Estimated Sales: $6 Million
Number Employees: 100-249
Parent Co: Conagra Brands
Other Locations:
Swank Great Lakes
Carol Stream IL
Swank South
Dallas TX
Swank West
Denver CO
Tolleson AZ
Buena Park CA
Modesto CA
Atlanta CA
Cedar Rapids IA
Iowa IA
Kansas KS
Wichita KS

Louisville KY
Mansfield MA

6360 **J Moniz Co Inc**
91 Wordell St
Fall River, MA 02721-4307
508-674-8451
Fax: 508-673-6464 www.jmoniz.com
Seafood
President/Treasurer/Clerk: John Moniz
joaomoniz@hotmail.com
Estimated Sales: $1,000,000
Number Employees: 5-9

6361 **J Morgan's Confections**
2665 Lincoln Ave
Ogden, UT 84401-3461
USA
801-399-3007
Fax: 801-399-3009
Caramels. truffles, fudge
Owner: Brian Squire
brians@jmorgansconfections.com
Estimated Sales: Less Than $500,000
Number Employees: 1-4

6362 **J P Green Milling Co**
496 E Depot St
Mocksville, NC 27028-2419
336-751-2126
Fax: 336-751-1349
Grits, feed, flour and corn meal
President: Ralph Naylor
Estimated Sales: $5-10 Million
Number Employees: 10-19

6363 **J P's Shellfish Co**
414 Harold L Dow Hwy
Eliot, ME 3903
207-439-6018
Fax: 207-439-7794 jpinfo@jpshellfish.com
www.jpshellfish.com
Seafood
President: John Price
jshellfish@aol.com
Sales Exec: John Price
Estimated Sales: $10-20 Million
Number Employees: 20-49

6364 **J R Carlson Laboratories Inc**
600 W University Dr
Arlington Heights, IL 60004
847-255-1600
888-234-5656
carlson@carlsonlabs.com www.carlsonlabs.com
Norwegian fish oils, vitamins, minerals, amino acids, special formulations and nutritional supplements.
President: Carilyn Carlson Anderson
VP, Marketing & Corporate Relations: Kirsten Carlson Cecchin
Year Founded: 1965
Estimated Sales: $24.3 Million
Number Employees: 100-249
Number of Products: 200
Square Footage: 40000
Type of Packaging: Consumer, Private Label
Brands:
Aces
Carlson
E-Gems
Key-E
Niacin-Time
Super-1-Daily

6365 **J Rettenmaier USA LP**
16369 US Highway 131 S
Schoolcraft, MI 49087-9150
269-679-2340
Fax: 269-679-2364 877-895-4099
info@jrsusa.com www.jrs.de
Researcher, developer and processor of organic fibers derived from vegetable raw materials that are used as functional additives and pulps.
Director of Administration & Controlling: Gerhard Goss
CEO: Thorsten Willmann
Director of Business Development: Curtis Rath
Director of Sales, Food Division: Dia Panzer-Biddle
Manager: Katie Bush
eyeluvme1991@yahoo.com
Estimated Sales: $12 Million
Number Employees: 50-99
Parent Co: J. Rettenmaier & Sohne GmbH & Co KG

6366 **J Turner Seafood**
4 Smith St
Gloucester, MA 01930-2710
978-281-8535
Fax: 978-281-1710 www.turners-seafood.com
Seafood
Contact: Peter Stark
pete@turners-seafood.com
Estimated Sales: $2,000,000
Number Employees: 5-9

6367 **J W Treuth & Sons**
328 Oella Ave
Catonsville, MD 21228-5499
410-747-6281
Fax: 410-465-4867 info@jwtreuth.com
www.jwtreuth.com
Meat products, fresh beef, pork, and poultry.
Co-Owner: Jason Trippet
Co-Owner: Mike Trippet
Estimated Sales: $28.1 Million
Number Employees: 50-99
Type of Packaging: Consumer, Food Service

6368 **J&D's Foods**
8230 5th Ave South
Suite A-1
Seattle, WA 98108
866-692-3980
www.jdfoods.net
Bacon salt

6369 **J&M Food Products Co**
P.O. Box 334
Deerfield, IL 60015
847-948-1290
Fax: 847-948-0468 sales@halalcertified.com
www.halalcertified.com
Shelf stable halal meals
VP: Mary Anne Jackson
Year Founded: 1991

6370 **J&R Fisheries**
PO Box 3302
Seward, AK 99664-3302
907-224-5584
Fax: 907-224-5572 kruzof@ak.net
www.jrfisheries.com
Seafood
Estimated Sales: $300,000-500,000
Number Employees: 1-4

6371 **J. Crow Company**
PO Box 172
New Ipswich, NH 03071-0172
603-878-1965
Fax: 603-878-1965 800-878-1965
jcrow@jcrow.com www.jcrow.com
Herbs, spices, essential oils and teas
Owner: Jeff Krouk
Contact: Michael Hinson
michael@mcnear.com
Estimated Sales: Less than $500,000
Number Employees: 1-4
Square Footage: 200000
Type of Packaging: Consumer
Brands:
J. Crow's

6372 **J. Fritz Winery**
24691 Dutcher Creek Rd
Cloverdale, CA 95425
707-894-3389
Fax: 707-894-4781 800-418-9463
info@fritzwinery.com www.fritzwinery.com
Wines
President: Clayton Fritz
cfritz@fritzwinery.com
Winemaker: Christina Pallmann
Estimated Sales: $2.5-5 Million
Number Employees: 10-19
Brands:
Fritz

6373 **J. Matassini & Sons Fish Company**
2008 N Garcia Ave
Tampa, FL 33602
813-229-0829
Fax: 813-229-7327
Fresh and frozen seafood
President: Pasquale Matassini
Estimated Sales: $1-3 Million
Number Employees: 5-9
Type of Packaging: Consumer, Food Service
Brands:
Matassini Seafoods

6374 **(HQ)J. R. Simplot Co.**
PO Box 27
Boise, ID 83707-0027
208-336-2110
jrs_info@simplot.com
www.simplot.com
Food manufacturing, seed production, farming, fertilizer manufacturing and frozen-food processing.
Chairman: Scott Simplot
President/CEO: Garrett Lofto
CFO/Treasurer: Brent Moylan
VP, Manufacturing & Supply Chain: Michael Johnston
Estimated Sales: K
Number Employees: 11,000+
Number of Products: 1000
Type of Packaging: Consumer, Food Service, Private Label
Other Locations:
J.R. Simplot Potato Processing
Aberdeen ID
J.R. Simplot Potato Processing
Caldwell ID
J.R. Simplot Potato Processing
Grand Forks ND
J.R. Simplot Potato Processing
Moses Lake WA
J.R. Simplot Potato Processing
Nampa ID
J.R. Simplot Potato Processing
Othello WA
J.R. Simplot Vegetable Processing
West Memphis AR
Brands:
Bent Arm Ale®
Conquest®
Simplot Harvest Fresh Avocados™
RoastWorks®
Simplot Simple Goodness™
Simplot Classic®
Simplot Good Grains™
Farmhouse Originals®
Freezefridge®
Infinity®
Kitchen Craft™
Megacrunch®
NaturalCrisp®
Old Fashioned Way®
SeasonedCrisp®
Select Recipe®
SIDEWINDERS™
Simplot Sweets®
Simplot Thunder Crunch®
Simply Gold®
Skincredibles®
Spudsters®
Tater Pals®
Traditional
True Recipe®
Simplot Daily Pick™
Batter Bites®
JR Buffalos®
Krunchie Wedges®

6375 **J. Stonestreet & Sons Vineyard**
7111 Highway 128
Healdsburg, CA 95448
707-473-3307
Fax: 707-433-9469 800-355-8008
info@stonestreetwines.com
www.stonestreetwines.com
Wines
President: Jess Jackson
Sales Manager: Mick Unti
Estimated Sales: $2.5-5 Million
Number Employees: 10
Brands:
Alexander Valley
Christopher's
Legacy Red Wine

6376 **J.A.M.B. Low Carb Distributor**
4100 N Powerline Road
Suite W3
Pompano Beach, FL 33073-3065
954-917-9881
Fax: 954-917-2590 800-708-6738
Low carb and sugar free foods.
CEO: Alan Beyda

6377 **J.B. Peel Coffee Roasters**
7582 North Broadway
Red Hook, NY 12571
845-758-1792
Fax: 845-758-1814 800-231-7372
jbpeel@twcmetrobiz.com www.jbpeelcoffee.com
Gourmet coffee
President: Gil Klein
VP: Pat Klein
Estimated Sales: Less than $500,000
Number Employees: 4
Number of Products: 200
Type of Packaging: Consumer, Private Label, Bulk

6378 **J.G. British Imports**
15302 21st Ave E
Bradenton, FL 34212-8121
941-745-1474
Fax: 941-926-1701 888-965-1700
www.sarasotamilitaryacademy.com
Tea
President: David Grace
CEO: Grace Sern
Manager: Felisa Choi
Estimated Sales: $100,000
Number Employees: 2
Type of Packaging: Private Label
Brands:
Rather Jolly Tea

6379 **J.M. Schneider**
254 Rue Principale
Saint Anselme, QC G0R 2N0
Canada
418-885-4474
Fax: 418-885-9408 www.schneiders.ca
Beef and pork
Plant Manager: Narie Claude Lamontadne
Plant Manager: Cal Petraszko
Number Employees: 100-249
Parent Co: J.M. Schneider
Type of Packaging: Consumer, Food Service
Brands:
Schneider

6380 **J.M. Smucker Co.**
1 Strawberry Ln.
Orrville, OH 44667-0280
888-550-9555
www.jmsmucker.com
Fruit spreads, juices, ice cream toppings, syrups, peanut butter and coffee.
Executive Chairman: Richard Smucker
President/CEO: Mark Smucker
mark.smucker@jmsmucker.com
Chief Legal & Compliance Officer: Jeannette Knudson
Chief Marketing & Commercial Officer: Geoff Tanner
Year Founded: 1897
Estimated Sales: $7.3 Billion
Number Employees: 7,140
Number of Brands: 40
Type of Packaging: Consumer, Food Service
Brands:
Smucker's
Jif
Folgers
Rachel Ray Nutrish
Dunkin' Donuts
Adams
Caf, Bustelo
Crisco
Crosse & Blackwell
Dickinson's
Meow Mix
Kava
Knott's Berry Farm
Laura Scudder's
Milk Bone
Medaglia D'Oro
Natural Balance Pet Foods
Kibbles 'n Bits
9 Lives
Pilon
R.W. Knudsen
Sahale Snacks
Santa Cruz Organic
Smucker's Natural
Smucker's Toppings
Smucker's Uncrustables
truRoots
Pup-Peroni
Nature's Recipe
Canine Carry Outs
Gravy Train
Milo's Kitchen
Snausages
Dad's
Bick's
Carnation
Double Fruit
Five Roses
Golden Temple
Robin Hood

6381 **J.N. Bech**
214 Dexter St
Elk Rapids, MI 49629
231-264-5080
Fax: 231-264-5107 800-232-4583
Mustards and barbecue glazes
President: John Bech
Office Manager: Lynn Haveman
Estimated Sales: $600000
Number Employees: 7
Type of Packaging: Consumer, Food Service, Private Label
Brands:
Bech

6382 **J.P. Sunrise Bakery**
14728 119th Avenue NW
Edmonton, AB T5L 2P2
Canada
780-454-5797
Fax: 780-452-7696 office@sunrise-bakery.com
www.sunrisebakery.com
Baked goods
President: Gary Huising
Director: Tony Bron
Director: Hank Renzenbrink
Number Employees: 80
Square Footage: 120000
Type of Packaging: Consumer, Food Service

6383 **J.R. Fish Company**
224 Front St
Wrangell, AK 99929
907-874-2399
Fax: 907-874-2398
Seafood
President: Janell Privett
Secretary/Treasurer: William Privett

6384 **J.R. Poultry**
2924 Maus Road
Fults, IL 62244-1506
618-458-7194
Fax: 706-777-8690
Poultry

6385 **J.R. Short Canadian Mills**
70 Wickstead Avenue
Toronto, ON M4G 2B5
Canada
416-421-3463
Fax: 416-421-2876
Confectioners corn flakes, corn meal, stablized wheat bran, wheat germ and corn germ
Vice President: Alexa Norris
Parent Co: J.R. Short Milling Company

6386 **J.R.'s Seafood**
9908 Southwest Highway
Oak Lawn, IL 60453
708-422-4555
Fax: 914-624-0329
Seafood
President: Frank Cestro
Owner: Carlos Grijalva
Estimated Sales: $1-3 Million
Number Employees: 5-9

6387 **J.S. McMillan Fisheries**
12 Orwell St
North Vancouver, BC V7J 2G1
Canada
604-981-4000
Fax: 604-981-4001
Canned salmon and groundfish
President: Steve Parkhill
VP Sales: Guy Dean
Number Employees: 250-499
Parent Co: J.S. McMillan
Type of Packaging: Consumer, Food Service
Brands:
Hywave
J.S. McMillan
Pinnacle
Snow Cod

6388 **J.T. Pappy's Sauce**
1909 1/4 N Las Palmas Avenue
Los Angeles, CA 90068-3270
323-969-9605
Fax: 323-969-9659 saucecentral@aol.com
Sauces and marinades
Number Employees: 8
Number of Brands: 1
Number of Products: 12
Type of Packaging: Consumer, Food Service, Private Label

6389 **J.W. Haywood & Sons Dairy**
1449 Mccloskey Avenue
Louisville, KY 40210-1740
502-774-2311
Ice cream
Owner: Charles Haywood
Estimated Sales: $300,000-500,000
Number Employees: 9
Type of Packaging: Consumer, Food Service

6390 **JBS Packing Inc**
101 Houston Ave
PO Box 399
Port Arthur, TX 77640-6413
409-982-3216
Fax: 409-982-3549 jbspacking@aol.com
www.jbspackinginc.com
Fresh and frozen shellfish
CFO: Mark Leckich
National Sales Specialist: Mark Malkemus
Estimated Sales: $20-50 Million
Number Employees: 100-249
Type of Packaging: Consumer, Food Service
Brands:
Lucky Seas
Sea Market

6391 **JBS USA LLC**
1770 Promontory Cir.
Greeley, CO 80634
970-506-8000
www.jbssa.com
Beef, pork and chicken.
CEO: Andre Nogueira
CFO: Denilson Molina
Estimated Sales: $27.8 Billion
Number Employees: 78,000
Number of Brands: 17
Parent Co: JBS S.A.
Type of Packaging: Consumer
Brands:
5 Star®
1855®
Chef's Exclusive®
Aspen Ridge®
Cedar River Farms®
Blue Ribbon®
Swift®
La Herencia®
Clear River Farms®
Showcase®
Certified Angus Beef®
Pilgrim's®
Grass Run Farms®
Moyer®
Four Star Beef®
Swift Premium®

6392 **JC's Midnite Salsa**
PO Box 89451
Tucson, AZ 85752-9451
520-574-3993
Fax: 520-572-1151 800-817-2572
Salsa
Estimated Sales: $300,000-500,000
Number Employees: 1-4

6393 **JC's Pie Pops**
20436 Corisco St.
Chatsworth, CA 91311
818-349-1880
Specialty pie products
CEO: Jennifer Constantine
Brands:
JC's pie bites
JC's pie pops

6394 **JD Sweid Foods**
9696-199A Street
Langley, BC V1M 2X7
Canada
604-888-8662
Fax: 604-888-0074 800-665-4355
info@jdsweid.com www.jdsweid.com
Poultry and meat products
President & CEO: Blair Shier
Estimated Sales: $49.1 Million
Number Employees: 600+
Type of Packaging: Consumer, Food Service, Private Label, Bulk
Brands:
Hampton House
Sensations

6395 **JE Bergeron & Sons**
7 Rue St John Baptiste
Bromptonville, QC J0B 1H0
Canada
819-846-2761
Fax: 819-846-6217 800-567-2798
www.nuvel.ca
Shortening and margarine
President: Philippe Bergeron
Secretary: Berengere Bergeron
VP: Danielle Bergeron
Number Employees: 20-49
Square Footage: 120000
Parent Co: Margarine Thibault
Type of Packaging: Consumer, Food Service, Private Label, Bulk
Brands:
Banquet
Bergeron
Canolean
Chef Gaston
G Blanchet
Rexpo
Silver
Tradition
Wonder

6396 **JER Creative Food Concepts, Inc.**
5743 Smithway St
Suite 305
Commerce, CA 90040-1549
323-721-1882
Fax: 323-721-4526 800-350-2462
Confectionery products
President: Jonathan Freed
Secretary/Treasurer: Ezekiel Freed
VP: Rose Freed
Purchasing Manager: Kit Phillips
Estimated Sales: $3.5 Million
Number Employees: 5
Square Footage: 12000
Type of Packaging: Bulk
Brands:
Gelite
Pectose-Standard

6397 **JES Foods**
4703 Broadway Ave
Cleveland, OH 44127
216-883-8987
Fax: 216-883-8984 www.jesfoods.com
Produce, including carrots, onions, celery, peppers and melons
President: Elaine R Freed
Estimated Sales: $5-10 Million
Number Employees: 10-19

6398 **JF Braun & Sons Inc.**
P.O.Box 6061
Elizabeth, NJ 07207
908-393-7400
Fax: 908-393-7439 800-997-7177
steve@jfbny.com www.jfbny.com
Imported dried fruits and nuts
President: Stephen O'Mara
Number Employees: 20-49
Brands:
J.F. Braun

6399 **JFG Coffee**
400 Poydras Str
10th Floor
New Orleans, LA 70130
Fax: 504-539-5427 800-535-1961
service@reilyproducts.com www.jfgcoffee.com
Coffee
President & COO: Mark Reed
Estimated Sales: $100 Million
Parent Co: Reily Foods Company

6400 **JJ Martin Group**
Newark, NJ 07114
862-240-1813
Fax: 862-240-1812 saluttiusa.com
Aloe vera drinks
Founder & CEO: John Ra
Brands:
Aloevine
Salutti

6401 **JJ's Tamales & Barbacoa**
1611 Culebra Rd
San Antonio, TX 78201-5914
210-737-1300
Fax: 210-733-8133
Mexican foods
Manager: Gilbert Aparipio
Manager: M Rodriguez
Estimated Sales: Under $500,000
Number Employees: 1-4

6402 **JK Sucralose**
98-A Mayfield Avenue
Edison, NJ 08837
732-512-0889
jkusa@jksucralose.com
www.jksucralose.com
Sweetners, sucralose
General Manager: Hugh Zhang
Quality Control Director: Jianxin An
EVP of Sales & Marketing: Craig Zezima
Contact: Ye Florey
florey@jksucralose.com
Estimated Sales: $25 Million
Number Employees: 219
Number of Brands: 1
Number of Products: 1
Square Footage: 135000
Brands:
Jk Sweet

6403 **JM All Purpose Seasoning**
PO Box 22162
Lincoln, NE 68542-2162
402-421-8326
Seasonings herbs and spices
Owner: James Meeks
Number Employees: 1-4

6404 **JMAC Trading, Inc.**
369 Van Ness Way
Suite 707
Torrance, CA 90501
310-781-9734
Fax: 310-212-6768 877-566-4569
mizuhashi@crystalnoodle.com
www.crystalnoodle.com
Instant noodle soup
President/CEO: Masaki Mizuhashi
Contact: Anthony Brown
anthonybrown@yrcfreight.com

6405 **JMH International**
1389 Center Dr
Suite 340
Park City, UT 84098-7660
435-645-9100
Fax: 435-645-9109 888-741-4564
info@jmhpremium.com www.jmhpremium.com
Flavor bases
President: Kirk Mellecker
Vice President: Marc Allen
marc@jmhpremium.com
Sales Director: Michael Norman
Estimated Sales: $500,000-$1 Million
Number Employees: 10-19
Type of Packaging: Consumer, Food Service, Bulk
Brands:
Jmh Premium

6406 **JMS Specialty Foods**
126 Jefferson St
Ripon, WI 54971-1383
920-748-1317
Fax: 920-745-6150 800-535-5437
Bottled fruit, peanut butter, barbacue and meat sauces, dessert toppings, maple syrup, jams, jellies, preserves and condiments
Principal: David Brink
Marketing Manager: Carrie Hogan
General Manager: Ken Miller
Plant Manager: Tim Carr
Number Employees: 3
Square Footage: 240000
Parent Co: J.M. Smucker Company
Type of Packaging: Consumer, Food Service, Private Label

6407 **JNB Foods, LLC**
1971 Western Ave.
Suite 177
Albany, NY 12203
607-267-5874
www.jnbfoods.com
Manufacturer of chutney, relish, salsa, and pickled vegetables.
Owner: Barry Moore

6408 **JR Laboratories**
Smith Hill Rd
Honesdale, PA 18431
570-253-5826
www.jrlaboratories.com/
Chinese herbal products and fluids
President: Jainie Minogue
Estimated Sales: $300,000-500,000
Number Employees: 1-4

6409 **JSL Foods**
3550 Pasadena Ave
Los Angeles, CA 90031-1946
323-223-2484
Fax: 323-223-9882 800-745-3236
noodles@jslfoods.com www.jslfoods.com
Pre-made pastas and specialty Chinese products
Owner: Steven Aceves
President: Teiji Kawana
EVP: Koji Kawana
Research Manager: Swee Seet
Marketing Director: Brenda Oshita
VP Sales & Marketing: Wayne Nielsen
saceves@jslfoods.com
VP Operations: Jerry Kobayashi
Plant Manager: Julio Castaneda
Purchasing Manager: Gregory Yee
Estimated Sales: $22.3 Million
Number Employees: 100-249
Square Footage: 60000
Type of Packaging: Food Service, Private Label, Bulk
Brands:
Amber Farms
Fortune

6410 **JTM Food Group**
200 Sales Ave
Harrison, OH 45030
800-626-2308
www.jtmfoodgroup.com
Beef patties, buns, bread sticks, dinner rolls, French bread pizza, spaghetti and meatballs, chili, taco and barbecue sauce.
President & CEO: Tony Maas
tonymaas@jtmfoodgroup.com
Chairman: Jack Maas
CFO: Bill Meier
VP, Business Development: Jerry Maas
VP, Operations: Joseph Maas
Year Founded: 1960
Estimated Sales: $100-500 Million
Number Employees: 250-499
Square Footage: 96000
Type of Packaging: Consumer, Food Service
Brands:
Chef Vito Pasta Meals
Cincy Style
J.T.M. Food Group
Texas Jack's Tex-Mex
Vito's Bakery

6411 **JUST Inc**
2000 Folsom St
San Francisco, CA 94110-1318
415-829-2325
Fax: 415-520-2156 844-423-6637
wecare@justforall.com www.ju.st
Vegan egg substitute, mayonnaise, salad dressing, cookie dough, and lab-grown meat
CEO/Co-Founder: Josh Tetrick
Co-Founder: Josh Balk
COO/CFO: Erez Simha
CTO: Peter Licari

Year Founded: 2011
Estimated Sales: $30 Million
Number Employees: 10-19

6412 **JVM Sales Corp.**
3401 A Tremley Point Rd
Linden, NJ 07036
908-862-4866
Fax: 908-862-4867 anthony@jvmsalescorp.com
jvmsales.com
Italian grated cheeses; custom blends
President & CEO: Mary Beth Tomasino
VP of Sales & Marketing: Anthony Caliendo
Estimated Sales: $2-4 Million
Square Footage: 150000
Type of Packaging: Consumer, Food Service, Private Label, Bulk
Other Locations:
JVM Sales South
Delray Beach FL

6413 **Ja-Ca Seafood Products**
3 Center Plaza
Boston, MA 02108-2003
978-281-8848
Fax: 978-281-2247
Seafood
President: Kenichi Kawauchi

6414 **Jack & Jill Ice Cream**
101 Commerce Dr
Moorestown, NJ 08057-4212
856-813-2300
Fax: 856-813-2373 info@jjicc.com
www.jjicc.com
Ice cream and frozen yogurt; cakes and fancy desserts
President: Jay Schwartz
jschwartz@jjicc.com
Founder: Mickey Schwartz
Marketing Director: Shawn Brady
VP Sales: John Corral
General Manager: Ken Schwartz
Number Employees: 500-999
Type of Packaging: Consumer, Food Service

6415 **Jack Brown Produce**
8035 Fruit Ridge Ave NW
Sparta, MI 49345-9758
616-887-9568
Fax: 616-887-9765 800-348-0834
info@jackbrownproduce.com
www.jackbrownproduce.com
Produce
Owner: Steve Thome
Chairman/VP: Philip Succop
Sales Exec: Mitch Brinks
mitch@jackbrownproduce.com
Operations Manager: Pat Chase
Estimated Sales: $6.5 Million
Number Employees: 20-49
Square Footage: 2000000
Type of Packaging: Consumer, Food Service, Private Label, Bulk
Brands:
Apple Ridge
Peach Ridge

6416 **Jack Daniel Distillery**
280 Lynchburg Hwy.
Lynchburg, TN 37352
931-759-6357
888-551-5225
www.jackdaniels.com
Whiskey.
CEO, Brown-Forman Corp.: Lawson Whiting
Year Founded: 1866
Estimated Sales: $121,700,000
Number Employees: 500+
Parent Co: Brown-Forman Corporation
Type of Packaging: Consumer
Brands:
Jack Daniel's®
Jack Daniel's Old No. 7
Jack Daniel's Tennessee Rye
Jack Daniel's Single Barrel
Jack Daniel's Gentleman Jack
Jack Daniel's Tennessee Fire
Jack Daniel's Tennessee Honey

6417 **Jack Miller's Food Products**
646 Jack Miller Road
Ville Platte, LA 70586
337-363-1541
Fax: 337-363-4784 800-646-1541
jackmiller@jackmillers.com www.jackmillers.com
Cajun barbecue and cocktail sauces
President/CEO: Kermit Miller
Estimated Sales: Below $5 Million
Number Employees: 5-9
Square Footage: 28000
Type of Packaging: Food Service, Bulk
Brands:
Jack Miller

6418 **Jack's Bean Co LLC**
402 N Interocean Ave
Holyoke, CO 80734-1000
970-854-3702
Fax: 970-854-3707
Beans and popcorn
General Manager: Steve Brown
Human Resources Manager: Henry Moore
Manufacturing/Operations Director: Rick Daniel
Estimated Sales: $10.3 Million
Number Employees: 10-19
Square Footage: 110000
Parent Co: ConAgra Foods
Type of Packaging: Consumer, Food Service, Private Label, Bulk

6419 **Jack's Paleo Kitchen**
Ferndale, WA 98248
Fax: 800-263-1688 www.jackfrancisfoods.com
Allergy-friendly paleo cookies
Co-Owner: Josh Francis
Co-Owner: Karissa Francis
Number of Brands: 1
Number of Products: 13
Type of Packaging: Consumer

6420 **Jackfruit Company, The**
5723 Arapahoe Ave
Suite 1B
Boulder, CO 80303
877-433-4024
knowjack@thejackfruitcompany.com
thejackfruitcompany.com
Organic jackfruit products
Founder: Annie Ryu
Number of Brands: 1
Number of Products: 13
Type of Packaging: Consumer, Food Service, Bulk
Brands:
THE JACKFRUIT COMPANY

6421 **Jackson Brothers Food Locker**
121 S Avenue H
Post, TX 79356
806-495-3245
Fax: 806-495-3741
jacksonbrothersmeat@gmail.com
www.jacksonbrothersmeat.com
Beef, pork and deer meat; slaughtering services also available
Owner: Joe Rodriguez
Co-Owner: David Hernandez
Estimated Sales: $3-5 Million
Number Employees: 5-9
Type of Packaging: Consumer

6422 **Jackson Meat**
13 W 6th Ave
Hutchinson, KS 67501-4650
620-259-6066
Fax: 620-259-6066 jacksonmeat@live.com
www.jacksonmeat.com
Meat products
Owner: A Bryan
Estimated Sales: $10-20 Million
Number Employees: 5-9
Type of Packaging: Consumer, Bulk

6423 **Jackson's Honest**
Crested Butte, CO
info@jacksonshonest.com
jacksonshonest.com
Coconut oil chips, tortillas and grain puffs
Co-Founder & CEO: Megan Reamer
Co-Founder & CFO: Scott Reamer
Operations: David McCormick
Number of Brands: 1
Number of Products: 20
Type of Packaging: Consumer
Brands:
JACKSON'S HONEST

6424 **Jacob & Sons Wholesale Meats**
306 Center St
PO Box 217
Martins Ferry, OH 43935-1793
740-633-3091
Fax: 740-633-3106
www.jacobandsonsqualitymeats.com
Meats and sausages
President: Michael Jacob
Estimated Sales: $1.60 Million
Number Employees: 10-19

6425 **Jacob Leinenkugel Brewing Co**
1 Jefferson Ave
Chippewa Falls, WI 54729-1318
715-723-5557
Fax: 715-723-7158 leinielodge@leinenkugels.com
www.leinie.com
Beers
President: Thomas Jacob Leinenkugel
Estimated Sales: $10-19 Million
Number Employees: 10-19
Parent Co: Molson Coors Brewing Company

6426 **Jacob's Meats Inc**
8127 N State Route 66
Defiance, OH 43512-6724
419-782-7831
Fax: 419-782-8128 www.jacobsmeats.com
Beef, pork and poultry
President: Mike Stork
jacobsmeats@bright.net
Estimated Sales: $1-3 Million
Number Employees: 5-9
Type of Packaging: Consumer, Food Service, Private Label, Bulk

6427 **Jacobsen's Salt Co.**
602 SE Salmon St
Portland, OR 97214
503-719-4973
jacobsensalt.com
Cooking ingredients, including sea salt, seasonings and spice blends
VP, Sales: Jody Cook
Year Founded: 2011
Type of Packaging: Consumer

6428 **Jacobsmuhlen's Meats**
1415 NW Susbauer Rd
Cornelius, OR 97113-6331
503-359-0479
Fax: 503-359-0479
jacobsmuhlensllc@frontier.com
Pork and beef
Owner: Larry Jacobsmuhlen
jacobesmuhlenllc@verizon.net
Estimated Sales: $15 Million
Number Employees: 1-4
Type of Packaging: Consumer

6429 **Jacques Pastries**
128 Main St
Suncook, NH 03275
603-485-4035
Fax: 603-268-0699 www.jacquespastries.com
Bakery products
Founder: Jacques Despres

6430 **Jacquet Bakery**
401 Park Ave South
10th Fl.
New York, NY 10016
jacquetbakery.com
Breads, cakes, crepes and waffles
VP, Sales and Operations: James Shankin

6431 **Jada Foods LLC**
3126 John P. Curci Dr.
Bay 1
Hallandale Beach, FL 33009
855-936-3746
www.krunchymelts.com
Meringues
Owner: Daniel Ginsberg
Contact: Moises Mizrahi
mmizrahi@jadafoods.com

6432 **Jade Leaf Matcha**
San Francisco, CA 94123
support@jadeleafmatcha.com
www.jadeleafmatcha.com

Organic Japanese matcha
Type of Packaging: Consumer, Bulk

6433 Jager Foods
613 Birch St S
Sauk Centre, MN 56378
320-491-7249
Fax: 320-732-4047 800-358-7251
Dried soup mixes
President: Pete Jager
Brands:
Jager
Shitake Mushroom Soup Mixes (4)

6434 Jagger Cone Co Inc
304 Ellis St
Stryker, OH 43557-9329
419-682-1816
jaggercone@aol.com
Ice cream cones
Owner: Jeff Jaggers
jaggercone@aol.com
Owner: Sherry Jagger
Estimated Sales: Less Than $500,000
Number Employees: 10-19
Type of Packaging: Consumer, Food Service

6435 Jaguar Yerba Company
P.O.Box 1192
Ashland, OR 97520
541-482-7745
Fax: 541-482-6780 800-839-0775
ecoteas@worldpantry.com www.yerbamate.com
Yerba mate teas
Owner: Stefan Schachter
Co-Founder: Brendan Girardi
Partner: Joe Chermesino
Estimated Sales: $3-5 Million
Number Employees: 1-4

6436 Jagulana Herbal Products
PO Box 45
Badger, CA 93603
559-337-2200
Fax: 559-337-2354 888-465-3686
www.immortalityherb.com
Dedicated to researching, developing and marketing jiaogulan and jiaogulan-based herbal products of the highest quality
President: Chris Gleen
Research: Michael Blumert
Estimated Sales: $1-3 Million
Number Employees: 1-4

6437 Jain Americas Inc
1819 Walcutt Rd
Suite I
Columbus, OH 43228-9149
614-850-9400
Fax: 614-850-8600 888-473-7539
info@jainamericas.com www.jainamericas.com
Dehydrated vegetables, fruit purees, puree concentrates and clarified juices
CEO: Narinder Gupta
Executive Vice President: Murali Ramanathan
murali@jainamericas.com
Number Employees: 20-49

6438 Jaindl Farms
3150 Coffeetown Rd
Orefield, PA 18069-2599
610-395-3333
Fax: 610-395-8608 800-475-6654
jaindl.com
Turkey
Owner & President: David Jaindl
jaindl2@aol.com
Year Founded: 1935
Number Employees: 100-249
Type of Packaging: Consumer, Food Service, Private Label, Bulk
Brands:
Grand Champion

6439 Jake's Grillin
76 Loganberry Ct
Hopewell Jct, NY 12533-5378
845-226-4656
Fax: 845-226-4656 jake@jakesgrillin.com
www.jakesgrillin.com
Rubs, sauces and marinades
President: Joe Moran
Brands:
JAKE'S GRILLIN

6440 Jakeman's Maple Products
454414 Trillium Line
RR #1
Beachville, ON N0J 1A0
Canada
519-539-1366
Fax: 519-421-2469 800-382-9795
info@themaplestore.com www.themaplestore.com
Maple syrup, sugar, candy and yogurt; coffee, tea and cookies
President: Robert Jakeman
CFO: Jane Henderson
Quality Control: Melissa Martin
Sales: Mary Jakeman
Production: Heather Crane
Estimated Sales: $1 Million
Number Employees: 11
Number of Brands: 1
Number of Products: 78
Square Footage: 26480
Parent Co: Auvergne Farms
Type of Packaging: Consumer, Food Service, Private Label, Bulk

6441 Jakes Brothers Country Meats
6089 Clarksville Pike
Joelton, TN 37080-8997
615-876-2911
www.stjacobs.com
Cured meats
Owner: Johnny Jakes
Estimated Sales: Less Than $500,000
Number Employees: 1-4

6442 Jamae Natural Foods
PO Box 481096
Los Angeles, CA 90048
323-937-3670
Fax: 323-937-0849 800-343-0052
order@jamae.com www.jamae.com
Cookies, soy nut crunch bars
President: Crystal You
Estimated Sales: $300,000
Number Employees: 3
Type of Packaging: Private Label
Brands:
Health Cookie
Soynut Crunch Bar
Soynuts

6443 Jamaica John Inc
9140 Belden Ave
Franklin Park, IL 60131-3506
847-451-1730
Fax: 847-451-1590 sales@jamaicajohn.com
www.jamaicajohn.com
Sauces
President: John Capozzoli
Quality Control: John Capozzoli Jr
Estimated Sales: $5-10 Million
Number Employees: 10-19

6444 Jamaican Gourmet Coffee Company
250 South 18th Street
Suite 802
Philadelphia, PA 19103
800-261-2859
sales@coffeeforless.com
Coffee, tea
President: Lloyd Parchment
Estimated Sales: Below $5 Million
Number Employees: 20
Square Footage: 55200

6445 James Candy Company
1519 Boardwalk
Atlantic City, NJ 08401-7012
609-344-1519
Fax: 609-344-0246 800-441-1404
Confectionery products
President: Frank Glaser
EVP Sales/Marketing: Lisa Glaser Whitley
Contact: Barbara Aleo
baleo@jamescandy.com
VP Operations: Susan Saraceni
Estimated Sales: $2 Million
Number Employees: 50-99
Type of Packaging: Consumer, Bulk
Brands:
James Chocolate Seal Taffy
James Cream Mints
James Salt Water Taffy
Mumsey

6446 James Frasinetti & Sons
7395 Frasinetti Rd
Sacramento, CA 95828
916-383-2444
Fax: 916-383-5825
Wines
Partner: Howard Frasinetti
Partner: Gary Frasinetti
gary@frassinetti.com
Estimated Sales: $2.5-5 Million
Number Employees: 36

6447 James L. Mood Fisheries
Woods Harbour
Nova Scotia, NS B0W 2E0
Canada
902-723-2360
Fax: 902-723-2880 info@moodfisheries.com
www.moodfisheries.com
Fresh seafood
President: Corey Mood
Vice President: Almond Mood
Estimated Sales: $674,000
Number Employees: 10
Type of Packaging: Consumer, Food Service, Private Label, Bulk

6448 James Skinner Company
4657 G St
Omaha, NE 68117-1410
402-734-1672
Fax: 402-734-0516 800-358-7428
www.skinnerbaking.com
Frozen baked goods
President: James Skinner
Chief Executive Officer: Jim Skinner
VP Marketing: Doug Dinnin
Contact: Scott Barrows
sbarrows@skinnerbaking.com
Director of Operations: Dennis Nolan
Plant Manager: Tom Urzendowski
Estimated Sales: $7.6 Million
Number Employees: 100-249
Square Footage: 300000
Type of Packaging: Consumer, Food Service, Private Label, Bulk
Brands:
Skinner Bakery

6449 Jamieson Laboratories
4025 Rhodes Drive
Windsor, ON N8W 5B5
Canada
519-974-8482
Fax: 519-974-4742 800-265-5088
www.jamiesonvitamins.com
Kefir, yogurt, cod liver oil, vitamins, mineral supplements; water purifying systems and filters.
President/CEO: Mark Hornick
Year Founded: 1922
Estimated Sales: $42 Million
Number Employees: 400
Number of Brands: 22
Square Footage: 40000
Parent Co: CCMP Capital Advisors LLC
Type of Packaging: Consumer
Other Locations:
Toronto ON
Brands:
Arthrimin GS™
Baby-D™
BodyGUARD™
Digestive Care™
Effervescent
Exxtra-C™
FluShield™
Healthy SLEEP™
Mega Cal™
NEM®
Neurosome™
Nutrisentials™
Omega Complete™
Omega-3 Brain™
Omega-3 Calm™
Omega-3 Select™
Prostease™
ProVitamina™
Red Dragon™
Relax & Sleep™
Slimdown®
Stressease™

6450 Jane Bakes
40 S Main St
Pearl River, NY 10965
845-920-1100
Fax: 845-920-1101 jane@janebakes.com
www.janebakes.com
Cookies
Founder: Jane Carroll

6451 Janes Family Foods
3340 Orlando Drive
Mississauga, ON L4V 1C7
Canada
905-673-7145
Fax: 905-677-0607 800-565-2637
www.janesfamilyfoods.com
Frozen breaded and battered seafood, poultry, vegetable and cheese products
Plant Manager: Pat Palmer
Estimated Sales: $19 Million
Number Employees: 100
Square Footage: 300000
Type of Packaging: Consumer, Food Service, Private Label, Bulk
Brands:
Crisp & Delicious
Golden Gate
J&J Gourmet
Janes Family Favourites

6452 Janowski's Hamburgers Inc
15 S Long Beach Rd
Rockville Centre, NY 11570-5621
516-764-9591
Fax: 516-764-1908
www.janowskishamburgers.com
Hamburger meats
Owner: William Vogelsberg
Estimated Sales: $2,500-4,999,999 Million
Number Employees: 10-19

6453 Japan Gold USA
13200 Danielson St
Poway, CA 92064
858-486-1707
sales@japangoldusa.com
japangoldusa.com
Japanese snacks, ingredients and condiments
President/Owner: Seigo Okada

6454 Jaquelina's
515 S 32nd St
Camp Hill, PA 17011-5106
717-737-9452
Fax: 717-737-9452
Vinegars and oils
President: Jacqueline Magaro
Estimated Sales: Less than $500,000
Number Employees: 1-4

6455 Jarchem Industries
414 Wilson Ave
Newark, NJ 07105
973-578-4560
Fax: 973-344-5743 info@jarchem.com
www.jarchem.com
Ingredients and additives
CEO: Arnold Stern
Contact: Hein Arthur
hein.arthur@jarchem.com
Mngr.: Howard Honing
Estimated Sales: $.5-1 million
Number Employees: 1-4

6456 Jardine Foods
1 Chisholm Trail
Buda, TX 78610-3350
512-295-4600
Fax: 512-295-3020 800-544-1880
www.jardinefoods.com
Ketchup, chilies, sauces, dips, salsa, BBQ saucees and jellies
Manager: Scott Bolding
CEO: Bobby Mcgee
VP Sales/Mearketing: Garth Gardner
VP of Operations: Scott Jackson
Director: Craig Lieberman
Director: Brad Wallace
Estimated Sales: $5-10 Million
Number Employees: 20-49
Number of Brands: 20
Number of Products: 200
Type of Packaging: Consumer, Food Service, Private Label, Bulk
Brands:
D.J. Jardine

6457 Jardine Ranch
910 Nacimiento Lake Dr
Paso Robles, CA 93446-8713
805-238-2365
Fax: 805-239-4334 866-833-5050
order@jardineranch.com www.jardineranch.com
Gift baskets of nuts
Owner: Bill Jardine
Owner: Mary Jardine
jardine@jardineranch.com
Manager: Duane Jardine
Estimated Sales: Less Than $500,000
Number Employees: 5-9
Type of Packaging: Consumer, Food Service, Bulk

6458 Jarrow Industries Inc
12246 Hawkins St
Santa Fe Springs, CA 90670-3365
562-906-1919
Fax: 562-906-1979
customerservice@jarrowindustries.com
www.jarrow.com
Vitamins and supplements
President: Mohammed Khalid
Estimated Sales: $20-49 Million
Number Employees: 100-249

6459 Jasmine & Bread
4478 Howe Hill Rd
South Royalton, VT 05068
802-763-7115
Fax: 802-763-7115
Condiments
Owner: Sherrie Maurer
Estimated Sales: $500,000-$1 000,000
Number Employees: 1-4
Type of Packaging: Private Label, Bulk

6460 Jasmine Vineyards, Inc.
33319 Pond Road
Delano, CA 93215
661-792-2141
Fax: 661-792-6365 jvine@jasminevineyards.com
www.jasminevineyards.com
Grapes
Number of Brands: 4
Type of Packaging: Consumer, Food Service, Bulk
Brands:
Havren
Jasvine
M and V
Vinmar

6461 Jason & Son Specialty Foods
2590 Mercantile Dr Ste A
Rancho Cordova, CA 95742
916-635-9590
Fax: 916-635-9711 800-810-9093
Specialty confectionery items, including trail mixes, nut clusters and raisins
President: William Jason
VP: Margaret Jason
General Manager: Richard Antti
Estimated Sales: $1255895
Number Employees: 15
Type of Packaging: Consumer, Food Service, Private Label, Bulk
Brands:
Jason & Son

6462 Jason Pharmaceuticals
11445 Cronhill Dr
Owings Mills, MD 21117
410-581-2080
Fax: 410-581-8070 800-638-7867
Dietetic products
President: Margaret MacDonald-Sheetz
CEO: Michael C. MacDonald
CFO: Timothy G. Robinson
CMO: Brian Kagen
Contact: Deborah Carey
deborah@medifast.com
Number Employees: 100-249
Parent Co: Medifast Inc.
Brands:
Jason Pharmaceuticals

6463 Jasper Products Corp
3877 E 27th St
Joplin, MO 64804
417-206-3877
info@jasperproducts.com
www.jasperproducts.com
Dairy products, fruit beverages and prepared foods
President: Ken Haubein
ken.haubein@jasperproducts.com
Plant Manager: Larry Bearden
Year Founded: 2001
Estimated Sales: $100-499 Million
Number Employees: 750
Square Footage: 2000000
Parent Co: Stremicks Heritage Foods, LLC

6464 Jasper Wyman & Son
22 S Main St
Topsfield, MA 01983-1835
978-887-7472
Fax: 978-887-6881 tom@wymans.com
www.wymans.com
Bluberry juice, frozen treats
Contact: Lisa Francis
lfrancis@wymans.com
Estimated Sales: $10-20 Million
Number Employees: 1-4

6465 Java Beans and Joe Coffee
1331 Commerce St.
Petaluma, CA 94549
707-462-6333
800-624-7031
sales@javabeansandjoe.com
Coffee, flavored coffee, K-Cups
Owner: Lauren Mountanos
Parent Co: Mountanos Family Coffee & Tea Co.

6466 Java Cabana
PO Box 520845
Miami, FL 33152-0845
305-592-7302
Fax: 305-592-9471 www.javacabana.com
Coffee
Owner: Jose Souto
Marketing Director: Beatriz Vescovacci
Estimated Sales: $2.5-5 Million
Number Employees: 20-49
Type of Packaging: Food Service, Private Label

6467 Java Sun Coffee Roasters
35 Atlantic Ave
Marblehead, MA 01945-3139
781-631-7788
Coffee
Owner: Cheryl Burka
javasuncoffee@gmail.com
Estimated Sales: Less Than $500,000
Number Employees: 5-9

6468 Java-Gourmet/Keuka LakeCoffee Roaster
2792 Route 54A
Penn Yan, NY 14527
315-536-7843
888-478-2739
susan@java-gourmet.com www.java-gourmet.com
Coffee, rubs, sauces and marinades, and other gourmet items
President/Owner: Susan Atkisson

6469 Javalution Coffee Company
2400 Boswell Road
Chula Vista, CA 91914
619-934-3980
Fax: 619-934-3205 800-982-3197
customerservice@javalution.com
www.javalution.com/index.php
Coffee
President: Scott Pumper
CEO/Chairman of the Board: Steve Wallach
Vice President of Business Development: Brent Jensen
Chief Science Officer: Jose Antonio
Vice President of Operations: Mike Kolinski
Type of Packaging: Food Service

6470 Javed & Sons
6711 Hornwood Dr.
Suite 250
Houston, TX 77074
713-835-6850
javed_sons@hotmail.com
javednsons.webs.com

Halal chicken
Owner: Iqbal Javed
Year Founded: 1999

6471 Javo Beverage Co., Inc.
1311 Specialty Dr
Vista, CA 92081
760-330-1141
www.javobeverage.com
Coffee, tea and botanical extracts
Vice President, Ingredients & Flavours: Joanne Sheean

6472 Jaxon's Ice Cream Parlor
128 S Federal Hwy
Dania Beach, FL 33004-3623
954-923-4445
Fax: 954-922-8293 www.jaxsonsicecream.com
Frozen dairy desserts, low calorie ice cream and frozen yogurt
Owner: Monroe Udell
jaxsons@bellsouth.net
Plant Manager: M Day
Number Employees: 20-49
Parent Co: Dillon Corporation
Type of Packaging: Consumer, Food Service, Private Label
Other Locations:
Jackson Ice Cream Co.
Hutchinson KS

6473 Jay Shah Foods
1121 Meyerside Drive
Mississauga, ON L5T 1J6
Canada
905-696-0172
Fax: 905-696-0174
East Indian specialty snack foods and chutneys
President: Jayant Shah
Sales/Marketing Manager: Jay Shah
Purchasing Manager: Shushi Shah
Estimated Sales: $1 Million
Number Employees: 6
Square Footage: 40000

6474 JaynRoss Creations LLC
Whitmore Lake, MI
734-657-5852
Manufacturer of south indian spiced relish.
Co-Founder: Peter Johnston

6475 Jayone Foods Inc
7212 Alondra Blvd
Paramount, CA 90723-3902
562-633-7400
Fax: 562-633-7401 info@jayone.com
www.jayonefoods.com
Gluten-free, vegan, non-GMO, sugar-free specialty items; tea, juices, cider; condiments, yogurt, sauces; and other snacks
President: Seung Lee
info@jayone.com
Marketing Director: Jackie Choi
Estimated Sales: $30 Million
Number Employees: 20-49

6476 Jazz Fine Foods
5065 Ontario E Street
Montreal, QC H1V 3V2
Canada
514-255-0110
Fax: 514-259-1788
General grocery
President: Laurent Durot

6477 Jean Niel Inc
2444 Merchant Ave # 105
Suite 105-106
Odessa, FL 33556-3485
727-834-8855
Fax: 727-834-8832 info@nielaromes.com
www.jeanniel.com/niel_inc_en.php
Flavors and fragrances for beverages, dairy, bakery, savory and confectionary products.
President: Angoine Deboutiny
Executive Vice President: Michael Uzan
Contact: Marketa Agbanlog
magbanlog@nielaromes.com
Number Employees: 5-9
Parent Co: Jean Niel

6478 Jecky's Best
26450 Summit Cir
Santa Clarita, CA 91350
661-259-1313
Fax: 661-259-5855 888-532-5972
jeckysbest@yahoo.com www.jabfoods.com
Frozen dough and unbaked goods
President: Jecky Bicer
jeckysbest@yahoo.com
VP: Eitay Bicer
VP: Areila Bicer
Estimated Sales: $5-10 Million
Number Employees: 20-49
Type of Packaging: Private Label
Brands:
Jecky's Best

6479 Jed's Maple Products
259 Derby Pond Rd
Derby, VT 05829-9605
802-744-2095
Fax: 802-766-2702 802-766-2700
www.jedsmaple.com
Maple syrup, candy, cream, lollipops, salad dressings and sauces
Co-Owner: Stephen Wheeler
Co-Owner: Amy Wheeler
Estimated Sales: Less Than $500,000
Number Employees: 5-9

6480 Jedwards International Inc
141 Campanelli Dr
Braintree, MA 02184-5206
781-848-1473
Fax: 617-472-9359 sales@bulknaturaloils.com
www.bulknaturaloils.com
Organic specialty oils, essential oils, butters, waxes and botanicals
Contact: Jeremy Bamsch
jeremy@bulknaturaloils.com

6481 Jeff's Garden
105 Mezzetta Ct
American Canyon, CA 94503
707-266-7444
consumerinfo@jeffsgardenfoods.com
jeffsgardenfoods.com
All-natural olives, peppers, capers and sun-dried tomatoes
President/Owner: Jeff Mezzetta
Number of Brands: 1
Number of Products: 20
Type of Packaging: Consumer
Brands:
JEFF'S NATURALS

6482 Jefferson Vineyards
1353 Thomas Jefferson Parkway
Charlottesville, VA 22902
434-977-3042
Fax: 434-977-5459 800-272-3042
office@jeffersonvineyards.com
www.jeffersonvineyards.com
Wines
General Manager: Andy Reagan
Contact: Missy Stevens
tastingroom@jeffersonvineyards.com
Winemaker/Vineyard Manager: Frantz Ventre
Estimated Sales: $5-10 Million
Number Employees: 10-19

6483 Jel Sert
501 Conde St
West Chicago, IL 60185
630-876-4838
800-323-2592
www.jelsert.com
Frozen juice pops, juice beverages and mixes
President: Kenneth Wegner
Research & Development Director: John Dobrozsi
Senior Quality Engineer: Erika Scherer
Director of Human Resources: Juan Chavez
Engineer & Plant Manager: Simon Richards
Square Footage: 1600000
Type of Packaging: Consumer, Food Service, Bulk
Brands:
Dad's Old Fashioned®
Dove® Chocolate
Flavor Aid
Fla-Vor-Ice®
Hi-C®
Hostess®
Jolly Rancher
Juicy Juice®
Kool Pops
My T Fine®
Otter Pops®
Pop-ice®
PureKick®
Royal®
Royal Delights
Skittles®
Slush Puppie®
Sonic™
Sour Patch Kids
Starbursts®
Sunkist
Sunny D®
SuperC®
Warheads®
Welch's®
Wyler's®
Wyler's® Light

6484 Jelks Coffee Roasters
P.O.Box 8667
Shreveport, LA 71148-8667
318-636-6391
Fax: 318-635-1384 800-235-7361
www.jelks-coffee.com
Coffee
President: Harvey Jelks
Estimated Sales: $2.5-5 Million
Number Employees: 5-9
Brands:
Toddy

6485 (HQ)Jelly Belly Candy Co.
One Jelly Belly Lane
Fairfield, CA 94533-6741
707-428-2800
Fax: 707-428-2863 800-522-3267
www.jellybelly.com
Candy
President: Lisa Brasher
CEO: Herman Rowland
hrowland@jellybelly.com
Vice President, Specialty Sales: John Pola
Chief Sales and Marketing Officer: Ryan Schader
Vice President, Sales: Andrew Joffer
Plant Manager: Anthony Habib
hrowland@jellybelly.com
Purchasing Manager: Reg Nelson
Estimated Sales: $215 Million
Number Employees: 500-999
Number of Brands: 2
Number of Products: 150
Square Footage: 350000
Type of Packaging: Consumer, Private Label
Other Locations:
Distribution Center
Pleasant Prairie WI
Brands:
Goelitz
Jelly Belly

6486 Jemm Wholesale Meat Company
4649 W Armitage Ave
Chicago, IL 60639-3405
773-523-8161
Fax: 773-523-8890
Frozen portion-controlled steaks and ground beef
President: Daniel Goldman
VP: Thomas Nacht
Plant Manager: Dominic Pinto
Estimated Sales: $14,100,000
Number Employees: 20-49
Type of Packaging: Consumer, Food Service
Brands:
Seasoned Delux

6487 Jeni's Splendid Ice Creams
401 N Front St
Suite 300
Columbus, OH 43215
614-488-3224
contact@jenis.com
www.jenis.com
Ice cream
Founder & CCO: Jeni Bauer
CEO: John Lowe
Contact: Steve Boutros
steve.boutros@jenis.com

6488 **Jennie-O Turkey Store**
1126 Benson Ave SW
Willmar, MN 56201
320-235-6080
Fax: 320-231-0779 turkeyinfo@j-ots.com
www.jennieo.com
Turkey products
President: Michael Tolbert
CEO: Jerry Jerome
CFO: Dwight York
VP Marketing: Bob Tegt
Sales Director: Jime Splinter
Public Relations: Dave Suheke
Operations Manager: Bob Wood
Purchasing Agent: Larry Hammond
Number Employees: 250-499
Parent Co: Hormel Foods Corporation
Type of Packaging: Consumer, Food Service

6489 **Jennies Gluten-Free Bakery**
590 Rocky Glen Rd
Moosic, PA 18507
570-457-2400
Fax: 570-457-3626 lainiehamlin@outlook.com
jenniesmacaroons.com
Macaroons and cakes
President: Arnold Badner
Estimated Sales: $4,000,000
Number Employees: 20-49
Square Footage: 120000
Type of Packaging: Food Service
Brands:
Manhattan Gourmet

6490 **Jenny's Country Kitchen**
438 Main St S
Dover, MN 55929
507-932-3035
Fax: 507-932-4777 800-357-3497
info@jennyscountrykitchen.com
www.jennyscountrykitchen.com
Cocoa and coffee products
President: Jenny Wood
CEO: Dan Wood
Estimated Sales: Below $5 Million
Number Employees: 10
Brands:
Jenny's Country Kitchen

6491 **Jenny's Old Fashioned**
38727 Taylor Pkwy
North Ridgeville, OH 44039
440-327-0775
Fax: 440-327-9349 800-452-3235
popcorn@jennyspopcorn.com
www.jennyspopcorn.com
Popcorn
Owner: Becky Finnegan
becky.finnegan@bendix.com
CEO: Bob Shearer
Plant Manager: Jay McGuire
Estimated Sales: $5-10 Million
Number Employees: 20-49
Type of Packaging: Private Label
Brands:
Jenny's

6492 **Jensen Meat Company**
2550 Britannia Blvd
Suite 101
San Diego, CA 92154
619-754-6400
Fax: 619-754-6450 info@jensenmeat.com
www.jensenmeat.com
Ground beef hamburger patties
President: Robert Jensen
CEO: Abel Olivera
CFO: Sam Acuna
VP of Executive Accounts: Patricia Lavigne
VP of Production: Anthony Crivello
Year Founded: 1958
Estimated Sales: $26.9 Million
Number Employees: 1-4
Type of Packaging: Consumer, Food Service, Private Label, Bulk
Brands:
Jensen Solos™
Slater's 50/50 Bacon Burger™
UNCUT™ Before the Butcher®

6493 **Jensen's Bread and Bakeries**
3420 SE 21st Ave
Portland, OR 97202
503-208-3987
Fax: 503-208-3988 www.jensensbread.com
Bread products

6494 **Jensen's Old Fashioned Smokehouse**
10520 Greenwood Ave N
Seattle, WA 98133
206-364-5569
Fax: 206-364-0880
retail@jensenssmokehouse.com
www.jensenssmokehouse.com
Smoked seafood
President: Michael Jensen
Estimated Sales: Below $5 Million
Number Employees: 5-9
Type of Packaging: Consumer, Food Service
Brands:
Wild Keta Salmon
Wild Keta Salmon
Wild Red King Salmon
Wild White King Salmon

6495 **Jer's Chocolates**
437 S Highway 101
Suite 105
Solana Beach, CA 92075
800-540-7265
info@jers.com
www.jers.com
Chocolates
CEO: Jerry Swain

6496 **Jerabek's New Bohemian Coffee House**
63 Winifred St W
Saint Paul, MN 55107
651-228-1245
Fax: 651-228-3011 info@jerabeks.com
Baked goods, coffees, collectables
Manager: Russell Sprangler
Estimated Sales: $500,000 appx.
Number Employees: 10-19

6497 **Jeremiah's Pick Coffee Co**
1495 Evans Ave
San Francisco, CA 94124-1706
415-206-9900
Fax: 415-206-9542 877-537-3642
office@jeremiahspick.com
www.jeremiahspick.com
Coffee
Owner: Jermiah Pick
office@jermiahspick.com
Operations Manager: Jay Meltesen
Estimated Sales: Below $5 Million
Number Employees: 10-19
Square Footage: 56000
Type of Packaging: Consumer, Food Service, Private Label, Bulk
Brands:
Cafe Pick
Chocatal
Jeremiah's Pick

6498 **Jerrell Packaging**
802 Labarge Drive
Birmingham, AL 35022
205-426-8930
Fax: 205-426-8989 john@jerrellpackaging.com
www.jerrellpackaging.com
Popcorn
President: John Lyon
Contact: Barry Cornell
barry@jerrellpackaging.com
Estimated Sales: Below $5 Million
Number Employees: 10-19

6499 **Jerry Brothers Industries Inc**
4619 Glasgow St
Richmond, VA 23234
804-271-0689
Fax: 804-271-1258 JBI@MIR-belting.com
www.jerrybrothers.com
Wholesaler/distributor of conveyor belts including smooth, incline, weigh scale and feeder for many parts of the food industry, including bakery, meat processing, salad, tobacco, and boxes for packaging.
Operations Manager: Carras Sayre
Estimated Sales: $2.5-5 Million
Number Employees: 10-19
Type of Packaging: Food Service

6500 **Jerry's Nut House**
2101 N Humboldt St
Denver, CO 80205
303-861-2262
Fax: 303-861-1214 orders@jerrysnuthouse.com
www.jerrysnuthouse.com
Nuts and snacks
President: Claude Julia
Customer Service Representative: Zuzana Baumhardt
baumhardt@jerrysnuthouse.com
Estimated Sales: $2600000
Number Employees: 10-19
Square Footage: 80000
Type of Packaging: Consumer, Food Service, Private Label, Bulk
Brands:
Jerry's

6501 **Jersey Fruit Co-Op**
800 Ellis Mill Rd # B
Glassboro, NJ 08028-3204
856-863-9100
Fax: 856-863-9490 sales@jerseyfruit.com
www.jerseyfruit.com
Bluberries, peaches, nectarines, and cranberries.
Owner: Franscio Allende
Director Of Marketing: Bob Von Rohr
Estimated Sales: $10-20 Million
Number Employees: 10-19
Type of Packaging: Food Service

6502 **Jersey Italian Gravy**
16 Thornton Rd
Oakland, NJ 07436
201-620-2111
info@jerseyitaliangravy.com
www.jerseyitaliangravy.com
Pasta sauce
President: Carlos Vega

6503 **Jerusalem House**
2425 W 18th Ave
Eugene, OR 97402
541-485-1012
Fax: 541-687-6853
Middle eastern specialty products
President: Simon Oueis
Estimated Sales: Less than $500,000
Number Employees: 1-4

6504 **Jeryl's Jems**
43 Eagle Lane
Tappan, NY 10983-1810
201-236-8372
Fax: 845-359-7386 jeryls.jems@yahoo.com
Cake truffles, cookies, brownies
President: Jeryl Kipnis Kronish

6505 **Jesben**
PO Box 38113
Pittsburgh, PA 15238
info@jesben.com
www.jesben.com
Slow cooker sauces
Founder: Susie Schwartz
Number of Products: 4
Brands:
Jesben

6506 **Jess Jones Vineyard**
6496 Jones Ln
Dixon, CA 95620-9601
707-678-3839
Fax: 707-678-3898 www.jessjonesvineyard.com
Wines
President: Jess Jones
CEO: Mary Ellen Jones
Estimated Sales: $700,000
Number Employees: 1-4
Square Footage: 20000
Type of Packaging: Consumer, Bulk
Brands:
California Golden Pop
Customer's Bags
Jess Jones Farms

6507 **Jessica's Natural Foods**
PO Box 145
Birmingham, MI 48012-0145
248-723-7118
Fax: 248-723-7121 info@jessicasnaturalfoods.com
www.jessicasnaturalfoods.com

Gluten free products
Estimated Sales: Less Than $500,000
Number Employees: 1-4

6508 **Jessie's Ilwaco Fish Company**
45 Shed B
Unit 4
San Francisco, CA 94133
360-642-3773
Fax: 360-642-3362 don@alberseafoods.com
Fish and seafood
Owner: Pierre Marchand
VP: Doug Ross
Marketing: George Alexander
Production: Phil Marchand
Estimated Sales: $20-40 Million
Number Employees: 100-249
Square Footage: 25000
Type of Packaging: Consumer, Food Service, Private Label, Bulk
Brands:
Custom Lable
Seaside

6509 **Jets Le Frois Corp**
56 High St
Brockport, NY 14420-2058
585-637-5003
Fax: 585-637-2855
Barbeque sauces and vinegars
Owner: Duncan Tsay
Estimated Sales: $5-10 000,000
Number Employees: 5-9
Type of Packaging: Private Label

6510 **Jewel Bakery**
1955 W North Ave
Melrose Park, IL 60160-1131
708-531-6000
Fax: 708-343-9450
Breads
CEO: Stephen Bowater
Number Employees: 100-249

6511 **Jewel Date Co**
84675 60th Ave
Thermal, CA 92274-8780
760-399-4474
Fax: 760-399-4476
Natural and organic pecans, dates, raisins, nuts and dried fruits
President: Gregory Raumin
CEO: Greg Raumin
greg@jeweldate.com
Sales Manager: John Ortiz
Estimated Sales: $1,300,000
Number Employees: 20-49
Parent Co: Covalda
Type of Packaging: Consumer

6512 **JiMMY! Bars**
Chicago, IL 60661
888-676-7971
support@jimmybars.com jimmybars.com
Protein bars
Co-Founder: Annette Del Prete
Co-Founder & Co-CEO: Jim Simon
Co-CEO: Jason Wadler

6513 **Jiaherb**
1 Chapin Rd
Unit 1
Pine Brook, NJ 07058
973-439-6869
Fax: 973-439-6879 888-542-4372
info@jiaherbinc.com www.jiaherbinc.com
Natural ingredients
President: Scott Chen

6514 **Jianlibao America**
420 5th Avenue
26th Floor
New York, NY 10018-2729
212-354-8898
Fax: 212-354-8838 800-526-1688
Beverages, Asian foodstuffs
President: Qishu Lin
Estimated Sales: $3 Million
Number Employees: 20

6515 **Jillipepper**
PO Box 7546
Albuquerque, NM 87194
505-609-8409
Fax: 505-344-6633 jilli@jillipepper.com
www.jillipepper.com
Salsas, sauces, dips
Founder, Owner: Jill Levin
jilli@swcp.com
VP: Lowell Levin
Production Manager: Martin Dobyns
Estimated Sales: $1-3 Million
Number Employees: 1-4
Type of Packaging: Private Label

6516 **Jilz Gluten Free**
2155 Sunset Dr
Ventura, CA 93001
805-585-5297
jilzglutenfree.com
Crackers

6517 **Jim Foley Company**
1121 Chestnut Hill Cir SW
Marietta, GA 30064-4652
770-427-5102
Fax: 770-427-5102
Seafood
President: Jim Foley

6518 **Jim's Cheese Pantry**
410 Portland Rd
Waterloo, WI 53594-1200
920-478-3571
Fax: 920-478-2320 800-345-3571
Cheese; jams, jellies and crackers
President: James Peschel
CEO: Jim Peschel
VP: Judy Peschel
Estimated Sales: $9.5 Million
Number Employees: 50-99
Square Footage: 100000
Type of Packaging: Consumer, Food Service

6519 **Jimbo's Jumbos Inc**
185 Peanut Dr
Edenton, NC 27932-9604
252-482-2193
Fax: 252-482-7857 800-334-4771
Snacks and peanuts; custom formulation
Manager: Hal Burns
Manager: Debbie Miller
dmiller@jimbosjumbos.com
Number Employees: 100-249
Type of Packaging: Private Label

6520 **Jimmy Dean Foods**
PO Box 2020
Springdale, AR 72765
800-925-3326
www.jimmydean.com
Breakfast sandwiches and sausage.
SVP & General Manager: Jeff Caswell
Parent Co: Tyson Foods, Inc.
Type of Packaging: Consumer, Food Service, Private Label, Bulk
Brands:
Fresh Taste Fast!
Jimmy Dean

6521 **Jimmys Cookies**
125 Entin Rd
Clifton, NJ 07014-1424
973-779-8500
info@jimmyscookies.com
www.jimmyscookies.net
Cookies
President/Owner: Michael Pisani
CEO: Howard Hirsch
CFO: Debbie Kinzley
Estimated Sales: Less Than $500,000
Number Employees: 1-4
Square Footage: 90000
Type of Packaging: Consumer, Food Service, Private Label, Bulk

6522 **Jimtown Store**
6706 Highway 128
Healdsburg, CA 95448-9634
707-433-1212
Fax: 707-433-1252 jimtown@jimtown.com
www.jimtown.com
Vegetable spreads
Owner: Karrie Brown
karriebrown@jimtown.com
Marketing Director: Haley Callahan
Catering: Susan Schmid
Estimated Sales: Less than $500,000
Number Employees: 10-19
Brands:
Chickpea Chipotle
Fig & Olive Tapenade
Spicy Olive

6523 **Jin+Ja**
New York, NY
215-690-1470
www.drinkjinja.com
Fresh juices
Founder & CEO: Reuben Canada
Brands:
JINJA

6524 **Jo Mar Laboratories**
583 Division St # B
Campbell, CA 95008-6915
408-374-5920
Fax: 408-374-5922 800-538-4545
info@jomarlabs.com www.jomarlabs.com
Health products; contract packaging
President: Joanne Brown
joanne@jomarlabs.com
Estimated Sales: $1-3 Million
Number Employees: 10-19
Square Footage: 14000
Parent Co: Jo Mar Labs
Type of Packaging: Consumer, Private Label

6525 **Jo's Candies**
2560 W 237th St
Torrance, CA 90505-5217
310-257-0260
Fax: 310-257-0266 800-770-1946
sales@joscandies.com
Gourmet chocolates and confectionary
President: Tom King
Controller: Grant Philders
Plant Manager: Dave Good
Estimated Sales: Below $5 Million
Number Employees: 5-9
Type of Packaging: Private Label, Bulk
Brands:
Chocolate Covered Graham Crackers
Dr. Peter's Peppermint Crunch
Jo's Candies
Jo's Original

6526 **JoJo's Chocolate**
Mesa, AZ 85205
805-395-6567
jojoschocolate.com
Chocolate bars
Co-Founder: Sterling Jones

6527 **Jodar Vineyard & Winery**
3405 Carson Ct
Placerville, CA 95667-5104
530-644-3474
Fax: 530-621-0324 jodarwinery@foothill.net
www.jodarwinery.com
Wines
Owner: Vaughn Jodar
jodarwinery@foothill.net
Partner: Byron Joder
Partner: Sherril Jodar
Estimated Sales: $500,000-$1 Million
Number Employees: 1-4
Brands:
Jodar

6528 **Jodie's Kitchen**
6349 82nd Ave N
Pinellas Park, FL 33781
Fax: 727-934-9967 800-728-3704
info@jodieskitchen.com www.jodieskitchen.com
Gourmet herb and spice blends
President: Nobert Moore
VP: Vickey Auge
Estimated Sales: $300,000-500,000
Number Employees: 1-4
Square Footage: 9600
Type of Packaging: Consumer, Private Label, Bulk
Brands:
Country Classic
Dip-Idy-Dill
Galloping Garlic
Garlic Galore

Magically Mexican
Obviously Onion

6529 Jody Maroni's Sausage Kingdom
P.O.Box 1487
Burbank, CA 91507
818-760-2004
Fax: 818-760-8341 info@jodymaroni.com
www.jodymaroni.com
Sausages
Owner: Jordan Monkarsh
VP Marketing: Richard Leivenberg
Contact: Scotty Shadix
scotty@jodymaroni.com
Number Employees: 50-99
Type of Packaging: Consumer, Food Service
Brands:
Jody Maroni

6530 Jody's Gourmet Popcorn
1160 Millers Ln
Virginia Beach, VA 23451-5716
757-422-8646
customerservice@jodyspopcorn.com
www.jodyspopcorn.com
Popcorn and fudge
Founder: Jody Wagner
Number Employees: 20-49
Other Locations:
Retail Store , Laskin Road
Virginia Beach VA
Brands:
Jody's

6531 Jodyana Corporation
18367 NE 4th Ct
Miami, FL 33179-4531
305-651-0110
Fax: 305-651-4535 888-563-5282
Coffee
President: Corey Colaciello
Chairman: Joe Colaciello
Estimated Sales: $620,000
Number Employees: 5
Number of Brands: 115
Square Footage: 12000
Type of Packaging: Food Service, Private Label, Bulk

6532 Joe Bertman Foods
P.O. Box 6562
Cleveland, OH 44101-1562
216-431-4460
Fax: 216-561-2232
www.bertmanballparkmustard.com
Mustard and horseradish sauce
President: Pat Mazoh
Type of Packaging: Consumer, Bulk
Brands:
Bertman Raddish Sauce
Joe Bertman's Ballpark Mustard
Mustard
Original

6533 Joe Clark Fund Raising Candies
621 E 1st Ave
Tarentum, PA 15084-2005
724-226-0866
888-459-9520
www.clarkcandies.com
Chocolates
Owner: Bob Clark
bob@clarkcandies.com
Estimated Sales: $3-5 Million
Number Employees: 5-9
Type of Packaging: Consumer
Brands:
Joe Clark's Candies, Inc.

6534 Joe Corbis' Wholesale Pizza
14100 Darnestown Road
Suite E
Darnestown, MD 20874
888-526-7247
www.joecorbi.com
Pizza
President: Drew McManigle
Estimated Sales: $10-20 Million
Number Employees: 260
Number of Brands: 1
Brands:
Joe Corbi's

6535 Joe Fazio's Famous Italian
1008 Bullitt Street
Charleston, WV 25301
304-344-3071
http://www.fazios.net
Italian foods, seafoods, steaks, sandwiches
Owner: Joe Fazio
Quality Control: Nell Fazio
Marketing Manager: Joe Fazio
Manager: Nell Fazio
Estimated Sales: Below $5 Million
Number Employees: 20-49
Brands:
Fazio's

6536 Joe Hutson Foods
8331 Sanlando Avenue
Jacksonville, FL 32211-5135
904-731-9065
Fax: 904-731-9066 keithhutson@juno.com
Sauces
President: Teresa Foster
CEO: Keith Hutson
Chairman Board: Joe Hutson
Number Employees: 1-4
Square Footage: 1200
Parent Co: Joe Hutson Foods
Brands:
Put Me Hot

6537 Joe Jurgielwicz & Sons
189 Cheese Ln
Hamburg, PA 19526-8057
610-562-3825
Fax: 610-562-0219 800-543-8257
joey@tastyduck.com www.tastyduck.com
Frozen ducklings
Owner: Ian Shollenberger
ian@tastyduck.com
CEO: Joe Jurgielwicz
Partner: Tom Jurgielewicz
Marketing: Joseph Jurgielewicz III
Office Manager: Amy Grimminger
Estimated Sales: $860,000
Number Employees: 20-49
Type of Packaging: Consumer, Food Service
Brands:
South Shore
South Side
Twin Lake

6538 Joe Patti's Seafood Co
524 S B St
Pensacola, FL 32502-5422
850-432-3315
Fax: 850-435-7843 800-500-9929
www.joepattis.com
Seafood and seafood products.
President: Frank Patti
Year Founded: 1933
Estimated Sales: $20-50 Million
Number Employees: 100-249

6539 Joe Tea and Joe Chips
PO Box 43255
Upper Montclair, NJ 07043-0255
973-744-7502
www.joetea.com
Iced teas, juices and chips
CEO and Co-Founder: Joe Prato
Co-Founder: Ann Prato

6540 Joel Harvey Distributing
8800 Ditmas Avenue
Brooklyn, NY 11236
718-629-2690
Fax: 718-629-2172
Chocolate, cookies, crackers, jellies and juices
President: Mark Statfeld
Estimated Sales: $1-2.5 Million
Number Employees: 10-19
Brands:
Ferrara
Guylian
Hero
Hershey
Kedem
Perugina
Venus

6541 Joelle's Choice Specialty Foods LLC
1829 Highway 1
Fairfield, IA 52566
641-472-2414
Fax: 641-472-3774 800-880-2779
http://joelleschoice.com
Shelf-stable soy products
President: Larry Sutton
Type of Packaging: Food Service

6542 Joey's Fine Foods
135 Manchester Place
Newark, NJ 07104
973-482-1400
Fax: 973-482-1597 sales@joeysfinefoods.com
www.joeysfinefoods.com
Mixes and baked goods
President: Aaron Aihini
Vice President Sales: Anthony Romano
Contact: Joe Aihini
Estimated Sales: $5.5 Million
Number Employees: 40
Square Footage: 168000
Type of Packaging: Consumer, Food Service, Private Label, Bulk
Brands:
Cottage Bake
Joey's
New Englander

6543 Joey's Home Bakery-Gluten Free
1532 SW 8th St
Boynton Beach, FL 33426-5827
561-292-4004
joey.palmbeach@gmail.com
www.joeyshomebakeryglutenfree.com
Gluten free bakery
Estimated Sales: Less Than $500,000
Number Employees: 1-4

6544 Jogue Inc
One Vanilla Lane
Northville, MI 48167
248-349-1500
Fax: 248-349-1505 800-531-3888
info@jogue.com www.jogue.com
Flavoring extracts, essential oils, food colors, ice cream toppings, juices and syrups
President/Owner: Dattu Sastry
Technical Sales Manager: Gary Holtquist
Estimated Sales: $10-20 Million
Number Employees: 20-49
Type of Packaging: Food Service, Private Label, Bulk
Other Locations:
Jogue
Detroit MI
Western Syrup Company
Santa Fe Springs CA
High Mountain Manufacturing Company
Salt Lake City UT
Brands:
Gold Label

6545 Johanna Foods Inc.
1 Johanna Farms Rd.
PO Box 272
Flemington, NJ 08822
908-788-2200
800-727-6700
info@johannafoods.com www.johannafoods.com
Fruit juices, beverages and yogurt.
President/CEO: Robert Facchina
robertfacchina@johannafoods.com
Quality Systems Coordinator: Nicole Branstetter
Year Founded: 1995
Estimated Sales: $100 Million
Number Employees: 500-999
Number of Brands: 3
Square Footage: 500000
Type of Packaging: Consumer, Food Service, Private Label, Bulk
Brands:
La Yogurt
Ssips
Tree Ripe

6546 Johlin Century Winery
3935 Corduroy Rd
Oregon, OH 43616-1811
419-693-6288
Fax: 419-693-6429 www.wineweb.com
Wines

President/Owner: Bolan and Jay Muchewicz
Estimated Sales: $500,000-$1 000,000
Number Employees: 1-4
Type of Packaging: Private Label

6547 **John A Vassilaros & SonInc**
2905 120th St
Flushing, NY 11354-2505
718-886-4140
Fax: 718-463-5037 info@vassilaroscoffee.com
www.vassilaroscoffee.com
Coffee and tea
President/CEO: Stefanie Kasselakis Kyles
Estimated Sales: $10-20 Million
Number Employees: 20-49
Number of Brands: 4
Type of Packaging: Private Label
Brands:
Downtown Sumatra
Midtown Caff
Vassi Espresso
Vassilaros

6548 **(HQ)John B. Sanfilippo & Son**
1703 N Randall Rd
Elgin, IL 60123-7820
847-289-1800
Fax: 847-289-1843 info@jbssinc.com
jbssinc.com
Nuts, dried fruit, salad toppers
Chairman & CEO: Jeffrey Sanfilippo
jsanfilippo@jbssinc.com
Group President/Secretary & CFO: Michael Valentine
Year Founded: 1922
Estimated Sales: $520 Million
Number Employees: 1000-4999
Number of Brands: 2
Type of Packaging: Consumer, Food Service, Private Label, Bulk
Other Locations:
John B. Filippo & Son
Bainbridge GA
John B. Filippo & Son
Garysburg NC
John B. Filippo & Son
Gustine CA
John B. Filippo & Son
Walnut CA
Brands:
Orchard Valley Harvest
Fisher
Southern Style
Squirrel Brand

6549 **John B. Wright Fish Company**
427 Main St
Gloucester, MA 01930
978-283-4205
Fax: 978-281-5944
Seafood
President: Brian Wright
Contact: David Wright
david@johnbwright.com
Estimated Sales: $5-10 Million
Number Employees: 5-9

6550 **John Conti Coffee Co**
4406 Ole Brickyard Cir
Louisville, KY 40218-3066
859-253-9770
Fax: 502-499-2944 800-928-5282
info@johnconti.com www.johnconti.com
Coffee
President: John Conti
CFO: Sherry French
sfrench@johnconti.com
Human Resources: Debbie Redmon
Operations Director: Mark Nethery
Estimated Sales: Under $500,000
Number Employees: 50-99

6551 **John Copes Food Products**
P.O. Box 334
Hanover, PA 17331
717-632-6000
Fax: 717-367-7317 800-888-4646
www.johncopes.com
Canned corn and frozen vegetables
President & COO: Thomas Cope
Chairman & CEO: Larry Jones
CFO/Treasurer: Don Long
Controller: Stephen Gaukler
VP Sales & Marketing: Steve Davis
Estimated Sales: $30-50 Million
Number Employees: 130
Parent Co: Hanover Foods
Type of Packaging: Consumer, Private Label
Brands:
Copes
Dutch Delight

6552 **John Garner Meats**
2365 N Rudy Road
Van Buren, AR 72956-8702
479-474-6894
Fax: 479-474-6897 800-543-5473
Portion controlled pork, poultry and beef
President: Dewayne Garner
President: T D Garner
Marketing Director: Ralph Farrar
Sales Director: Gary Scott
Contact: John Garner
jgarner@peppersource.com
Operations Manager: Rusty Underwood
Production Manager: Rusty Polk
Estimated Sales: $5 Million
Number Employees: 30
Square Footage: 40000
Type of Packaging: Food Service, Private Label, Bulk

6553 **John Hofmeister & Son Inc**
2386 S Blue Island Ave
Chicago, IL 60608-4292
773-847-0700
Fax: 773-847-6707 800-923-4267
ehofmeis@hofhaus.com www.hofhaus.com
Smoked and boiled hams and turkeys
President: Ej Hofmeister
Vice President: Robert Bukala
Marketing Manager: Matt Hofmeister
Human Resources Manager: Bob Bukala
Production: Chris Chin
Estimated Sales: $32,000
Number Employees: 50-99
Square Footage: 240000
Type of Packaging: Consumer, Food Service, Private Label
Brands:
Hofmeister Haus

6554 **John I. Haas**
5185 Macarthur Blvd NW
Suite 300
Washington, DC 20016
info@johnihaas.com
www.barthhaasgroup.com
Hops and hop aroma extract and oils
CEO: Henry Von Eichel
Estimated Sales: $160 Million
Number Employees: 2,000
Number of Brands: 7
Type of Packaging: Food Service, Private Label, Bulk
Brands:
Aromahop
Beta Stab
Hepahop Gold
Isahop
Lacto Stab
Redihop
Tetrahop Gold

6555 **John J. Nissen Baking Company**
34 Abbott St
Brewer, ME 4412
207-989-7654
Fax: 207-989-7654 contact@twinkies.com
Baked goods
President: Michael D Kafoure
President, Chief Executive Officer: Gregory Rayburn
Executive Vice President, Chief Administ: John Stew
CFO: Ronald B Hutchison
Executive Vice President of Operations: Gary Wandschneider
Estimated Sales: $10-20 Million
Number Employees: 20-49
Brands:
Hostess
Wonder Bread

6556 **John Kelly Chocolates**
1506 N Sierra Bonita Ave
Los Angeles, CA 90046-2812
323-851-3269
Fax: 323-851-1789 800-609-4243
service@johnkellychocolates.com
www.johnkellychocolates.com
Chocolates
Owner: John Kelson
john@johnkellychocolates.com
Marketing: John Nelson
Number Employees: 10-19

6557 **John Koller & Son Inc**
1734 Perry Hwy
Fredonia, PA 16124-2720
724-475-4154
Fax: 724-475-4777 www.fairviewswisscheese.com
Cheese
President: Richard Koller
rkoller54@aol.com
Estimated Sales: $10-20 000,000
Number Employees: 10-19
Parent Co: Fairview Swiss Chesse
Brands:
Fairview Swiss Cheese

6558 **John N Wright Jr Inc**
402 Railroad Ave
Federalsburg, MD 21632-1413
410-754-9044
Fax: 410-754-9045
Canned tomatoes
President: Mary Harding
jmharding@dmv.com
Estimated Sales: Less Than $500,000
Number Employees: 1-4

6559 **John Paton Inc**
73 E State St
Doylestown, PA 18901-4359
215-348-7050
Fax: 215-348-8147
questions@goldenblossomhoney.com
www.goldenblossomhoney.com
Honey
President: Jon Paton
jp@goldenblossomhoney.com
Estimated Sales: $860,000
Number Employees: 1-4

6560 **John Volpi & Co**
5263 Northrup Ave
St Louis, MO 63110-2033
314-772-8550
Fax: 314-772-0411 800-288-3439
info@volpifoods.com www.volpifoods.com
Italian meat products
CEO: Lorenza Pasetti
lpassetti@volpifoods.com
Year Founded: 1902
Estimated Sales: $20-50 Million
Number Employees: 100-249
Type of Packaging: Consumer, Food Service, Private Label, Bulk
Brands:
Volpi Foods

6561 **John W Macy's Cheesesticks Inc**
80 Kipp Ave
Elmwood Park, NJ 07407-1036
201-791-8036
Fax: 201-797-5068 800-643-0573
timmacy@cheesesticks.com
www.johnwmmacys.com
Cheesesticks, cheesecrisps and bread sticks
CEO: John Macy
johnmacy@cheesesticks.com
VP/Sales Manager: Tim Macy
Marketing: Julia D'Arcy
Estimated Sales: $8 Million
Number Employees: 50-99
Square Footage: 180000
Type of Packaging: Consumer, Food Service, Private Label, Bulk
Brands:
John Wm. Macy's Cheesecrips
John Wm. Macy's Cheesesticks
John Wm. Macy's Sweetsticks

6562 **Johnny Harris Famous Barbecue Sauce**
1651 East Victory Drive
Savannah, GA 31404
912-354-7810
Fax: 912-354-6567 888-547-2823
ashley@johnnyharris.com www.johnnyharris.com
Barbecue sauce
President: Maude Donaldson
Chief Financial Officer: Yvonne Donaldson
Vice President: Norman Heidt
Estimated Sales: $5-10 Million
Number Employees: 5-9
Square Footage: 12000
Type of Packaging: Consumer

6563 **Johns Cove Fisheries**
RR 3
Yarmouth, NS B5A 4B1
Canada
902-742-8691
Fax: 902-742-3574
Lobster, herring roe and scallops
President: Don Cunningham
Number Employees: 60
Type of Packaging: Consumer, Food Service, Bulk

6564 **Johnson Brothers Produce Company**
Highway 44 E
Whitakers, NC 27891-0730
252-437-2111
Fax: 252-437-2121
Sweet potatoes
President: Hursel Johnson
VP: Lou Johnson
Estimated Sales: $10-20 Million
Number Employees: 20-49
Type of Packaging: Bulk
Brands:
Norma Lou

6565 **Johnson Estate Winery**
8419 West Main Road
Westfield, NY 14787
716-326-2191
Fax: 716-326-2131 800-374-6569
jwinery@cecomet.net www.johnsonwinery.com
Wines
Owner and Vineyard Manager: Frederick Johnson
Marketing Contact: Bob Dahl
Operations Manager: Mark Lancaster
Estimated Sales: $3-5 Million
Number Employees: 5-9
Square Footage: 60000
Type of Packaging: Consumer

6566 **(HQ)Johnson Foods, Inc.**
336 E Blaine Ave
P.O. Box 916
Sunnyside, WA 98944
509-837-4214
Fax: 509-837-4855 johnsonfoodsinc.blogspot.ca
Processed cherries, asparagus and pickled vegetables
President: Gary Johnson
gary@johnsonfoods.com
Estimated Sales: $10-20 Million
Number Employees: 250-499
Square Footage: 40000
Type of Packaging: Consumer, Food Service, Private Label, Bulk

6567 **Johnson Foods, Inc.-Cannery Plant**
300 Warehouse Ave
Sunnyside, WA 98944-1310
509-837-4188
Fax: 509-839-3243
Processed cherries, asparagus and pickled vegetables
Manager: Pete Krause
Estimated Sales: $5-10 Million
Number Employees: 20-49
Parent Co: Johnson Foods, Inc.
Type of Packaging: Consumer, Food Service, Private Label
Brands:
Princess
Sunnyside

6568 **Johnson Sea Products Inc**
251-824-2693
Seafood
Manager: Sean Johnson
Estimated Sales: $100+ Million
Number Employees: 50-99

6569 **Johnson's Alexander Valley Wines**
8333 Highway 128
Healdsburg, CA 95448-9639
707-433-2319
Fax: 707-433-5302 800-888-5532
Wines
President: Ellen Johnson
Estimated Sales: Less than $500,000
Number Employees: 1-4
Type of Packaging: Private Label
Brands:
Johnson's Alexander Valley

6570 **Johnson's Food Products**
1 Mount Vernon St
Dorchester, MA 02125-1604
617-265-3400
Fax: 617-265-1099
Baking mixes, bases, flavorings and whipped toppings
President: John Anton
john.anton@johnsonfoods.com
VP: Peter Anton
Estimated Sales: $5-10 Million
Number Employees: 10-19
Square Footage: 80000
Type of Packaging: Consumer, Food Service, Bulk

6571 **Johnson's Real Ice Cream**
2728 E Main St
Columbus, OH 43209-2534
614-231-0014
Fax: 614-231-5450
www.johnsonsrealicecream.com
Ice cream and sherbet
President: Jim Wilcoxon
sales@johnsonsrealicecream.com
Estimated Sales: $380000
Number Employees: 10-19
Square Footage: 9600
Type of Packaging: Consumer, Food Service

6572 **Johnson's Wholesale Meats**
161 N Sixth St
Opelousas, LA 70570-2105
337-948-4444
Fax: 337-948-4495
Meat packer
Manager: David Comoeuax
Sales Manager: Billy Baque
Estimated Sales: $1-3 Million
Number Employees: 1 to 4
Type of Packaging: Consumer, Bulk

6573 **Johnson, Nash & Sons Farms**
415 John Rich Rd
Warsaw, NC 28398
910-289-6842
Fax: 910-289-6917
Fresh poultry and eggs
President: Don Taber
Estimated Sales: $567.8 Million
Number Employees: 5-9
Type of Packaging: Consumer, Food Service, Bulk
Brands:
House of Raeford

6574 **Johnsonville Sausage LLC**
1222 Perry Way
Watertown, WI 53094-6052
920-261-1053
Fax: 920-261-1870 888-556-2728
www.summersausagestory.com
Sausage
President: Alice Stayer
Chief Marketing Officer: Duane Draeger
ddraeger@johnsonville.com
Number Employees: 100-249
Type of Packaging: Consumer
Brands:
Hot'n Zesty Links
Johnsonville Bratwur
Johnsonville Country
Sage'n Pepper
Table Two Entree

6575 **Johnston County Hams**
204 N Brightleaf Blvd
Smithfield, NC 27577-4670
919-934-8054
Fax: 919-934-1091 800-543-4267
service@countrycuredhams.com
www.countrycuredhams.com
Hams, bacon and turkey
Cure Master: Rufus Brown
rufus@countrycuredhams.com
Estimated Sales: Below $5 Million
Number Employees: 10-19

6576 **Johnston Farms**
13031 Packing House Rd
Bakersfield, CA 93307
661-366-3201
Fax: 661-366-6534 johnstongiftfruit@gmail.com
Navel oranges, peppers and potatoes
Owner: Dennis Johnston
Co-Prtnr.: Gerald Johnston
Commercial Sales Department: Derek Vaughn
dennisj@johnstonfarms.com
Packinghouse Operations: Steve Staker
Plant Manager: Steve Stacker
Number Employees: 100-249

6577 **Johnston's Home Style Products**
PO Box 1737
Charlottetown, PE C1A 7N4
Canada
902-629-1300
Fax: 902-368-1776
Canned cranberry sauce and stews
President: Harris Johnston
Type of Packaging: Food Service, Private Label

6578 **Johnston's Winery Inc**
5140 Bliss Rd
Ballston Spa, NY 12020-2044
518-882-6310
Fax: 518-882-5551
Wines
President: Kurt Johnston
Estimated Sales: Less Than $500,000
Number Employees: 1-4
Brands:
Johnston's Winery

6579 **Joia All Natural Soda**
3440 Belt Line Blvd.
Suite 206
Minneapolis, MN 55416
612-308-2056
www.joialife.com
Sodas
Founder and CEO: Bob Safford
Co-Founder: Carleton Johnson
carleton.johnson@bwbsoda.com
Brands:
JOIA ALL NATURAL SODA

6580 **Joj, Bar**
PO Box 232087
Encinitas, CA 92024
877-643-3575
info@jojebar.com jojebar.com
Energy bars
Co-Founder: John Abate
Co-Founder: Jess Cerra
Number of Brands: 1
Number of Products: 7
Type of Packaging: Consumer
Brands:
JOJ□

6581 **Jolly Llama**
11805 N 200 3
Richmond, UT 84333
thejollyllama.com
Whole fruit and non-dairy squeezable sorbet pops
President/Owner: Scott Jacobson
Number of Brands: 1
Number of Products: 9
Type of Packaging: Consumer
Brands:
JOLLY LLAMA

6582 **Jomart Chocolates**
2917 Avenue R
Brooklyn, NY 11229-2525
718-375-1277
Fax: 718-382-7144
michael@jomartchocolates.com
www.jomartchocolates.com
Manufacturer of different chocolates and confections.
Founder and CEO: Michael Rogak
michael@jomartchocolates.com
Number Employees: 10-19

6583 **Jon Donaire Desserts**
9511 Ann Street
Santa Fe Springs, CA 90670-2615
562-941-1856
Fax: 562-946-3781 877-366-2473
JDdesserts@rich.com
iloveicecreamcakes.com/cake-brand/jon-donaire
Ice cream cakes
President: Mickey Del Duca
Dessert Specialist: Lisa Tanner
Estimated Sales: $10-50 Million
Number Employees: 100-249
Parent Co: Rich Products Corp.
Brands:
Jon Donaire

6584 **Jonathan Lord Cheesecakes**
87 Carlough Rd # A
Bohemia, NY 11716-2921
631-517-1271
Fax: 631-563-8505 800-814-7517
info@jonathanlord.com
www.jonathanlordcheesecake.com
Bakery Products
Owner: Carole Kentrup
Sales Director: William Kentrup
jlcorp@optonline.net
Estimated Sales: Below $5 Million
Number Employees: 10-19
Type of Packaging: Consumer, Food Service, Private Label, Bulk

6585 **Jonathan's Sprouts**
384 Vaughan Hill Rd
Rochester, MA 02770-2035
508-763-2577
Fax: 508-763-3316 bob@jonathansorganic.com
www.jonathanssprouts.com
Alfalfa sprouts, mung bean sprouts, citrus fruits and vegetables
President: Bob Sanderson
Owner/President: Barbara Sanderson
barbara@jonathansorganic.com
CEO: John Musser
Sales Director: Cathy Rounseville
Estimated Sales: $4 Million
Number Employees: 20-49
Square Footage: 60000
Type of Packaging: Consumer
Brands:
Jonathan's Organics
Jonathan's Sprouts

6586 **Jones Brewing Company**
260 2nd St
Smithton, PA 15479
724-483-2400
Fax: 724-565-5743 info@stoneysbeer.com
www.stoneysbeer.com
Beers, including non-alchoholic beer
Owner: Jon King
Brewmaster: Greg King
Purchasing: Joyce Winkler
Type of Packaging: Consumer, Private Label
Brands:
Equire
Eureka
Stoney's
Stoney's Black & Tan
Stoney's Harvest Gold
Stoney's Light
Stoney's Non-Alcoholic Brew

6587 **Jones Dairy Farm**
800 Jones Ave
Fort Atkinson, WI 53538
800-563-6637
www.jonesdairyfarmfoodservice.com
Sausage, bacon, ham, and liverwurst products.
President & CEO: Philip Jones
pjones@jonesdairy.com
Marketing Director: Bridget Molthen
Executive Vice President: Richard Lowry
Manager of Human Resources: Katherine Bruns
SVP, Operations: Roger Borchardt
Manager of Purchasing: Joyce Lemke
Year Founded: 1832
Estimated Sales: $30.7 Million
Number Employees: 250-499
Square Footage: 215000
Type of Packaging: Consumer, Food Service, Bulk
Brands:
Jones Sausagest
Ralph & Paula Adams Scrapple

6588 **Jones Packing Co**
22701 Oak Grove Rd
Harvard, IL 60033-8205
815-943-4488
Beef, lamb, pork and goat
Owner: Ray Jones
rjones@jonespacking.com
Estimated Sales: $4 Million
Number Employees: 10-19
Type of Packaging: Consumer, Food Service, Private Label

6589 **Jones Potato Chip Co**
823 Bowman St
Mansfield, OH 44903-4107
419-529-9424
Fax: 419-529-6789 800-466-9424
chips@joneschips.com
Potato chips
President: Robert Jones
bobmartin@joneschips.com
Quality Assurance Manager: Susie Drushel
Sales Exec: Bob Martin
Office Manager: Jim Ford
Production Manager: Roy Kehl
Plant Manager: Rick Bartram
Estimated Sales: $6 Million
Number Employees: 50-99
Type of Packaging: Consumer, Food Service, Private Label
Brands:
Jones
Thomasson's
Thomasson's Potato Chips

6590 **Jones Soda Company**
1000 First Ave South
Suite 100
Seattle, WA 98109
206-624-3357
Fax: 206-624-6857 800-656-6050
info@jonessoda.com www.jonessoda.com
Sodas
CEO: Jennifer Cue
COO: Eric Chastain
CFO: Max Schroedl
Content Creator: Cassie Smith
EVP US Sales: Steve Gress
Operations Manager: Chris Milberger
Year Founded: 1987
Estimated Sales: $20-50 Million
Number Employees: 50-99
Type of Packaging: Consumer
Brands:
Berry White
Betty
Dave
Purple Carrot

6591 **Jonny Almond Nut Co**
G4254 Fenton Rd
Flint, MI 48507-3614
810-767-6887
Fax: 810-767-6889 rich@jonnyalmond.com
Nuts, popcorn and other snacks
General Manager: Bob Bossman
Marketing: Rich Krafsur
Manager: Alicia Handlin
alyssa@jonnyalmond.com
Number Employees: 20-49

6592 **JonnyPops**
3600 Alabama Ave S
Minneapolis, MN 55416
651-243-0705
info@jonnypops.com
www.jonnypops.com
Popsicles
CEO: Erik Brust
CFO: Connor Wray
Number of Brands: 1
Number of Products: 11
Type of Packaging: Consumer, Food Service
Brands:
JONNYPOPS

6593 **Joray Candy**
1258 Prospect Avenue
Brooklyn, NY 11218
718-871-6300
Fax: 718-871-6300 joraycandy@msn.com
www.joraycandy.com
Kosher candy, dried fruit and other snacks
Marketing: Ray Shalhoub

6594 **Jordahl Meats**
25585 State Highway 13
Manchester, MN 56007-5020
507-826-3418
Meat products
Owner: Brian Jordahl
Estimated Sales: Less Than $500,000
Number Employees: 1-4
Type of Packaging: Consumer, Food Service, Private Label, Bulk

6595 **Jordan's Meats & Deli**
375 St. Croix Trail S
Lakeland, MN 55043
651-337-2224
jordanmeatsdeli.com
Meat products; serving the retail and food service markets; also, portion cutting services available.
Founder & Owner: Tony Jordan
Estimated Sales: $20-50 Million

6596 **Josef Aaron Syrup Company**
16541 Redmond Way
Suite 206
Redmond, WA 98052-4492
425-820-7221
Fax: 425-702-9292
Tea and coffee flavors, syrups
President: Judy Toller
Number Employees: 5-9

6597 **Joseph Adams Corp**
5740 Grafton Rd
Valley City, OH 44280-9327
330-225-9135
Fax: 330-225-9105
Oleoresins, essential oils, natural flavors and colors
President: Patrick Adams
Sales: Kathy Adams
Estimated Sales: $3 Million
Number Employees: 10-19

6598 **Joseph Campione Inc**
2201 W South Branch Blvd
Oak Creek, WI 53154-4906
414-761-8944
Fax: 414-761-2005 www.josephcampione.com
Italian breads
President: Angelina Campione
acampione@josephcampione.com
Number Employees: 100-249

6599 **Joseph D Teachey Jr Produce Co**
1307 N Norwood St
Wallace, NC 28466-1331
910-285-4502
Fax: 910-285-5491
Sweet potatoes
Owner: Joseph Teachey
Estimated Sales: $10-20 Million
Number Employees: 1-4
Brands:
Mary Jo's Blueberries
Mary Jo's Fancy

6600 **Joseph Farms**
10561 State Highway 140
PO Box 775
Atwater, CA 95301
209-394-7984
Fax: 209-394-4988 jgfinfo@josephfarms.com
www.josephfarms.com
Cheese
CEO: Michael Gallo
Sales Manager, Latin America: Javier Alvarez
jalvarez@josephfarms.com
Type of Packaging: Consumer, Food Service

Brands:
Joseph Farms Cheese

6601 Joseph J. White
1 Pasadena Rd
Browns Mills, NJ 8015
609-893-2332
Fax: 609-893-2316
Cranberries
President: Joe Darlington
Chairman Board: Thomas Darlington
Estimated Sales: $500,000-$1 Million
Number Employees: 10 to 19
Type of Packaging: Bulk

6602 Joseph Kirschner & Company
193 Riverside Dr
Augusta, ME 04330
207-623-3544
Fax: 207-623-1557
Meats
President: Marco Desalle
Purchasing Manager: Daniel Poulin
Estimated Sales: $200,000
Number Employees: 2

6603 Joseph Phelps Vineyards
200 Taplin Rd
St Helena, CA 94574-9544
707-967-9153
Fax: 707-963-4831 800-707-5789
minglis@josephphelps.com
www.josephphelps.com
Wines
Owner: Bill Phelps
bphelps@jpbwines.com
Founder & Chairman Emeritus: Joe Phelps
VP, CFO: Robert Boyd
VP, Director of Winemaking: Damian Parker
Winemaker: Ashley Hepworth
VP, Director of Sales & Marketing: Mike McEvoy
Director of Vineyard Operations: Philippe Pessereau
Vice President, Director of Winemaking: Damian Parker
Estimated Sales: $5 Million
Number Employees: 50-99
Square Footage: 200000
Type of Packaging: Consumer
Brands:
Insignia
Backus Vineyard
Freestone Vineyards
Ovation
Estate Grown Olive Oil
Fogdog
Napa Syrah
Viognier
Eisrebe
Innisfree

6604 Joseph Swan Vineyards
2916 Laguna Rd
Forestville, CA 95436-3729
707-573-3747
Fax: 707-575-1605 rod@swanwinery.com
www.swanwinery.com
Wines
Owner: Rod Berglund
rod@swanwineries.com
CEO: Lynn Swan-Berglund
Estimated Sales: Less than $500,000
Number Employees: 1-4
Brands:
Swan Joseph

6605 Joseph's Gourmet Pasta
262 Primrose St
Haverhill, MA 01830-3930
978-521-1718
Fax: 978-374-7917 800-863-8998
www.josephsgourmetpasta.com
Gourmet pastas
President & CEO: David Zwartendijk
Number Employees: 250-499
Square Footage: 150000

6606 Joseph's Lite Cookies
3700 J Street SE
Deming, NM 88030
575-546-2839
Fax: 575-546-6951 800-373-3726
www.josephslitecookies.com
Sugar free cookies, fat free cookies, brownies, syrups
President: Joseph Semprevivo
Contact: Joe Arriaga
joe@josephslitecookies.com
Estimated Sales: $5-10 Million
Number Employees: 20-49
Square Footage: 208000
Type of Packaging: Consumer

6607 Josephine's Feast
30 5th Ave
Apt 8F
New York, NY 10011-8810
917-622-7428
www.josephinesfeast.com
Preserves and chutney
Founder: Laura O'Brien

6608 Josh & John's Ice Cream
111 E Pikes Peak Ave
Colorado Springs, CO 80903
719-632-0299
Fax: 719-632-2833 800-530-2855
hello@joshandjohns.com www.joshandjohns.com
Ice cream
President/CEO/CFO: John Krakauer
krakauer62@gmail.com
Year Founded: 1986
Estimated Sales: Less Than $500,000
Number Employees: 10-19
Brands:
Josh & John's Ice Cream

6609 Josh Early Candies
4640 W Tilghman St
Allentown, PA 18104
610-395-4321
Fax: 610-398-8502 www.joshearlycandies.com
Candy and confections
Marketing: Barry Bobil
bub@joshearlycandies.com
Estimated Sales: Below $5 000,000
Number Employees: 10

6610 Jost Chemical
8150 Lackland Rd
St Louis, MO 63114-4524
314-428-4300
Fax: 314-428-4366 www.jostchemical.com
Chemical ingredients
President/Owner: Jerry Jost
jerryj@jostchemical.com
CFO: Jeff Lenger
Vice President: Keith Wunderli
Estimated Sales: $15.5 Million
Number Employees: 100-249

6611 Josuma Coffee Co
PO Box 1115
Menlo Park, CA 94026-1115
650-366-5453
Fax: 650-366-5464 info@josuma.com
www.josuma.com
Coffee
President: Joseph John
josuma@aol.com
Vice President: Urmila John
Estimated Sales: Under $300,000
Number Employees: 1-4
Type of Packaging: Private Label
Brands:
Espresso Blend
Green Coffee
Malabar Gorld Premium
Monsooned Malabar

6612 Joullian Vineyards
2 Village Dr
Suite A
Carmel Valley, CA 93924-9766
831-659-8100
Fax: 831-659-8102 866-659-8101
info@joullian.com www.joullian.com
Wines
Manager: Raymond E Watson III
Owner: Jeannette Joullian Sias
CFO: Robert Fain
Retail Operations Manager: Hal Ellison
Cellar Master: Elisio Cabrera
Office Manager: Holly Huebner
Winemaker/General Manager: Ridge Watson
Assistant Winemaker: Katherine Chadwell
Estimated Sales: $2.5-5 000,000
Number Employees: 1-4
Brands:
Joullian Vineyards

6613 Jovial Foods
41 Norwich-Westerly Rd
North Stonington, CT 06359
877-642-0644
info@jovialfoods.com www.jovialfoods.com
Gluten free foods made with einkorn flour
Founder/President: Carla Bartolucci

6614 Joy Cone Co
3435 Lamor Rd
Hermitage, PA 16148
724-962-5747
joycone@joycone.com
www.joycone.com
Ice cream cones
President: David George
CFO: Scott Kalmanek
Year Founded: 1918
Estimated Sales: $99 Million
Number Employees: 250-499
Number of Brands: 2
Brands:
Joy
Scoopy

6615 Joy's Specialty Foods
300 N Willow St
Mancos, CO 81328
970-533-1500
Fax: 970-533-2011 800-831-5697
Specialty condiments
President: Joy Kyzer
Vice President: Dave Kyzer
Estimated Sales: $300,000-500,000
Number Employees: 5
Type of Packaging: Consumer, Bulk
Brands:
Joy's

6616 Joyce Farms
4787 Kinnamon Rd
Winston Salem, NC 27103-9605
336-766-9900
Fax: 336-766-9009 800-755-6923
www.joyce-farms.com
Poultry, beef and game products
President/CEO: Ron Joyce
ronaldjoyce@joycefoods.com
VP, Finance: Ryan Joyce
Quality Assurance Manager: Jimmy Mitchell
Sales Manager: Nate Morgan
VP, Operations: Stuart Joyce
Year Founded: 1962
Estimated Sales: $20-50 Million
Number Employees: 100-249
Type of Packaging: Private Label

6617 Joyfuls
100 Passaic Ave
Suite 100
Fairfield, NJ 07004
888-989-9050
info@joyfuls.com www.joyfuls.com
Dark chocolate snacks
VP, Sales: Barry Octigan
Number of Products: 3
Brands:
Joyfuls

6618 Joyva Corp
53 Varick Ave
Brooklyn, NY 11237-1523
718-497-0170
Fax: 718-366-8504 info@joyva.com
www.joyva.com
Confectionery products
President: Milton Radutzky
Director: Richard Radutzky
Vice President: Harry Radutzky
Estimated Sales: $10-20 Million
Number Employees: 50-99
Type of Packaging: Consumer

6619 Juanita's Foods
645 Eubank Ave
P.O. Box 847
Wilmington, CA 90748
310-834-5339
Fax: 310-834-5064 800-303-2965
consumercomments@juanitasfoods.com
www.juanitas.com

Mexican foods
President: George De La Torre
CEO: Aaron De La Torre
Director, Quality Assurance: Rasheedi Samira
VP, Sales: John Thompson
Director, Human Resources: Diana Rodriguez
Operations Manager: Mark De La Torre
General Manager: Gina Harpur
Plant Manager: Frank Andrade
Purchasing Manager: Leo Medina
Year Founded: 1946
Estimated Sales: $41500000
Number Employees: 100-249
Type of Packaging: Consumer, Food Service, Private Label, Bulk
Brands:
Juanita's
Pico Pica
Tia Anita

6620 Jubelt Variety Bakeries
303 North Old Route 66
Litchfield, IL 62056
217-324-5314
jubelts@jubelts.com
www.jubelts.com
Cakes, breads, doughnuts and cookies
President: Lance Jubelt
Contact: Becky Brown
becky.brown@jubelts.com
Estimated Sales: $1,200,000
Number Employees: 35
Number of Brands: 2
Square Footage: 16000
Type of Packaging: Food Service, Bulk

6621 Jubilations
950 Highway 45 South
West Point, MS 39773
662-328-9210
Fax: 662-329-1558 800-530-7808
cheesecakes@jubilations.com
www.jubilations.com
Cheesecakes.
President and Founder: Tammy Craddock
Sales and Marketing: George Purnell
Purchasing Manager: Ed Griffith
Estimated Sales: B
Number Employees: 5-9
Square Footage: 24000
Type of Packaging: Consumer, Food Service, Private Label
Brands:
Jubilations

6622 Jubilee Foods
13050 N Wintzell Ave
Bayou La Batre, AL 36509
251-824-2110
www.jubileeseafood.com
Fresh and frozen shrimp
President: Charles Walton Kraver
shannon@jubileeseafood.com
Vice President: Frank Kawana
Quality Control: Mike Williams
Estimated Sales: Below $5 Million
Number Employees: 15
Brands:
Buyer Label
Jubilee
Southern Supreme

6623 Jubilee Gourmet Creations
PO Box 6305-0318
Manchester, NH 03108
603-625-0654
Fax: 603-625-0654
Brandied cherries, peaches and berries
President: Joyce Davis
Type of Packaging: Consumer, Food Service, Bulk

6624 Judicial Flavors
11400 Atwood Road
Auburn, CA 95603-9017
530-885-1298
Fax: 530-888-0311
Sauces, dressings, oils, marinades, mustard, nuts, spices and coffee
Estimated Sales: $1-3 Million
Number Employees: 5-9

6625 Judy's Cream Caramels
19995 SW Chapman Rd
Sherwood, OR 97140
503-625-7161
Fax: 503-625-1602
Cream caramels
Owner: Debbie Judy
Number Employees: 5-9
Type of Packaging: Consumer

6626 Juice Mart
6758 Julie Ln
West Hills, CA 91307
818-992-4442
Fax: 818-992-4479 877-888-1011
Juice concentrates and nutripaks
President: Linda Renaud
Estimated Sales: $500,000-$1 Million
Number Employees: 1-4

6627 Juice Tyme, Inc.
4401 S Oakley Avenue
Chicago, IL 60609
773-579-1291
Fax: 773-579-1251 800-236-5823
www.juicetyme.com
Juices, teas, energy drinks and beverage concentrates
CEO: Sam Lteif
EVP, Sales & Field Service Operations: Jerry Desmond
Contact: Brian Andrade
brian.andrade@bevolutiongroup.com
Estimated Sales: $30 Million
Number Employees: 50
Square Footage: 30000
Type of Packaging: Food Service

6628 Juicy Whip Inc
1668 Curtiss Ct
La Verne, CA 91750-5848
909-392-7500
Fax: 626-814-8016 www.juicywhip.com
Hispanic beverage concentrates
President/CEO: Gus Stratton
Purchasing: Craig Allen
Estimated Sales: $4 Million
Number Employees: 5-9
Square Footage: 88000
Brands:
Juicy Whip

6629 Julian Bakery
624 Garrison St
Oceanside, CA 92054
760-721-5200
customerservice@julianbakery.com
julianbakery.com
Manufacturer of gluten-free, low-carb products
VP, Sales: Barry Octigan
Number of Products: 115
Brands:
D-Max
ProGranola
PrimalThin
PaleoThin

6630 Julian's Recipe
Brooklyn, NY 11222
Fax: 888-645-8030 888-640-8880
info@juliansrecipe.com www.juliansrecipe.com
Waffles, chips, artisanal breads
Owner: Alex Dzieduszycki
Brands:
Julian's Recipe

6631 Julie Anne's
10634 San Palatina Street
Las Vegas, NV 89141
702-767-4765
www.julieannes.com
Organic breakfast cereals, granola and other snacks
Marketing: Julie Hession

6632 Julie's Real
100 Crescent Ct
Suite 700
Dallas, TX 75201
877-659-4375
info@juliesreal.com www.juliesreal.com
Nut butters and grain-free granolas
Founder: Julie Fox
Number of Brands: 1
Number of Products: 11
Type of Packaging: Consumer
Brands:
JULIE'S REAL

6633 Julius Sturgis Pretzel Bakery
219 E Main St
Lititz, PA 17543-2011
717-626-4354
Fax: 717-627-2682 info@juliussturgis.com
www.juliussturgis.com
Pretzels
Owner: Timothy Snyder
General Manager: Kurt Van Gilder
Estimated Sales: B
Number Employees: 25

6634 Jungbunzlauer Inc
95 Wells Ave
Suite 150
Newton, MA 02459
617-969-0900
Fax: 617-964-2921 office-bos@jungbunzlauer.com
www.jungbunzlauer.com
Ingredients and additives
President: Michael Alexandrow
Chief Executive Officer: Tom Knutzen
Chief Financial Officer: Michael Klaproth
Vice President, Product Management: Achim Hergel
Estimated Sales: $3.3 Million
Number Employees: 20-49
Parent Co: Jungbunzlauer Suisse AG
Type of Packaging: Bulk

6635 Junior's Cheesecake
58-42 Maurice Avenue
PO Box 780-208
Maspeth, NY 11378
718-852-5257
Fax: 718-260-9849 800-458-6467
info@juniorscheesecake.com
www.juniorscheesecake.com
Cheesecakes

6636 Juno Chef's
1 6 1/2 Station Rd
Goshen, NY 10924-6723
845-294-5400
Frozen pre-made meals
President: Julius Spessot
Contact: John Augustinski
johna@milmarfood.com
General Manager: Vilma Falcon
Estimated Sales: $6-10 Million
Number Employees: 50-99
Square Footage: 100000
Type of Packaging: Food Service

6637 Junuis Food Products
800 E Northwest Hwy # 510
Palatine, IL 60074-6511
847-359-4300
Fax: 847-359-4364
Frozen and fresh horseradish
President: John Russell
Estimated Sales: Less than $500,000
Number Employees: 1 to 4
Type of Packaging: Consumer, Food Service

6638 Jus-Made
9761 Clifford Dr Ste 100
Dallas, TX 75220
972-241-5544
Fax: 972-241-3399 800-969-3746
info@jus-made.com
Beverages and beverage mixes; beverage equipment
President: Gene Barfield
VP Sales: Jim Tanner
Contact: Matt Cook
mcook@jus-made.com
Operations Manager: Mike Sayre
Estimated Sales: $1-3 Million
Number Employees: 50-99
Square Footage: 14000
Type of Packaging: Consumer, Food Service, Private Label, Bulk
Other Locations:
Jus-Made
Houston TX
Brands:
Floria Julep
Orogold

6639 **Just Bagels**
527 Casanova St
Bronx, NY 10474
718-328-9700
Fax: 718-328-9997 www.justbagels.com
Bagels
President: Cliff Nordquist

6640 **Just Bare**
1770 Promontory Circle
Greeley, CO 80634
877-328-2838
wecare@justbarechicken.com
www.justbarechicken.com
American Humane Certified chicken
President/Owner: Steve Jurek

6641 **Just Born Inc**
1300 Stefko Blvd
Bethlehem, PA 18017-6672
610-867-7568
Fax: 610-543-4981 800-445-5787
Confectionery products
Co-CEO: Ross Born
Co-CEO: David Shaffer
dshaffer@justborn.com
President/COO: David Yale
Year Founded: 1923
Estimated Sales: $20-50 Million
Number Employees: 500-999
Number of Brands: 6
Type of Packaging: Consumer
Brands:
Goldenberg's Peanut Chews®
Hot Tamales®
Just Born®
Mike and Ike®
Peeps®
Teenee Beanee®

6642 **Just Cook Foods**
158 22nd Ave
San Francisco, CA 94121-1217
USA
415-269-2705
Fax: 415-684-7806 www.justcookfoods.com
Rubs, spices
Owner: Scott Lucas
scott@justcookfoods.com
Co-Founder: Cathy Storfer
Creative Chef: Daniel Capra

6643 **Just Date Syrup**
1007 Howard Ave
San Mateo, CA 94401
www.justdatesyrup.com
Alternative sweetener made from organic dates
Founder & CEO: Sylvie Charles
Number of Brands: 1
Number of Products: 1
Type of Packaging: Consumer
Brands:
JUST DATE SYRUP

6644 **Just Delicious Gourmet Foods**
PO Box 2747
Seal Beach, CA 90740-1747
949-215-5341
Fax: 714-870-0332 800-871-6085
Dry soup, bread and dip mixes
President: Diana Ferguson
Estimated Sales: $500,000
Number Employees: 5-9
Square Footage: 40000
Type of Packaging: Consumer, Food Service, Bulk
Brands:
Just Delicious

6645 **Just Desserts**
5000 Fulton Dr
Fairfield, CA 94534
415-780-6860
Fax: 415-780-6861 info@justdesserts.com
www.justdesserts.com
Specialty cakes, pastries, cookies
CEO: Michael Mendes
VP, Sales: Dean Gold
Contact: Ana Speros
asperos@justdesserts.com
Estimated Sales: $.5-1 million
Number Employees: 100-249
Type of Packaging: Private Label

6646 **Just Jan's Inc.**
22287 Mulholland Hwy #90
Calabasas, CA 91302-5157
USA
818-282-6236
jan@justjans.com
www.justjansjam.com
Jams, spreads, syrups
Chief Executive Officer/Founder: Jan Hogrewe
Estimated Sales: A
Number Employees: 1-4

6647 **Just Off Melrose**
1196 Montalvo Way
Palm Springs, CA 92262
760-320-7414
Fax: 760-327-0331
inforequest@justoffmelrose.com
www.justoffmelrose.com
Gourmet snacks
CEO: Brandon Tesmer
Contact: Carol Cross
ccross@justoffmelrose.com
Estimated Sales: $10-20 Million
Number Employees: 50
Brands:
Just Chips
Just Crisps
Just Croutons
Just Flatbread

6648 **Just Panela**
6676 Gunpark Dr
Suite D
Boulder, CO 80301
720-600-0522
info@justpanela.com
www.justpanela.com
Organic, artisanal cane sugar
Type of Packaging: Consumer, Bulk
Brands:
JUST PANELA

6649 **Just Tomatoes**
2101 W Hamilton Rd Wiley CA
Westley, CA 95387
209-894-5371
Fax: 209-894-3146 800-537-1985
customerservice@justtomatoes.com
www.shopkarensnaturals.com
Dried fruits and vegetables
Co-Owner: Karen Cox
Co-Owner: Bill Cox
karen@justtomatoes.com
Estimated Sales: $1.9 Million
Number Employees: 50-99
Type of Packaging: Consumer, Food Service, Private Label, Bulk
Brands:
Just

6650 **Just Truffles**
1363 Grand Ave
St Paul, MN 55105-2204
651-690-0075
Fax: 651-690-2052 877-977-9177
justtruffles@cs.com www.justtruffles.com
Truffles
Co-Founder and Owner: Kathleen O'Hehir-Johnson
Co-Founder and Owner: Roger Johnson
Number Employees: 5-9

6651 **Justin Vineyards & Winery LLC**
11680 Chimney Rock Rd
Paso Robles, CA 93446-9792
805-227-1160
Fax: 805-237-4152 800-237-4152
info@justinwine.com www.justinwine.com
Wines
President: Justin Baldwin
VP/Director Sales/Marketing: Rich Richardson
Marketing Manager: Tracy Dauterman
Regional Sales Manager: Joseph Spellman
Vice President, Director of Production: Fred Holloway
Estimated Sales: $2.5-5 Million
Number Employees: 20-49
Type of Packaging: Private Label
Brands:
Justin

6652 **Justin's Nut Butter**
736 Pearl St
Boulder, CO 80302
844-448-0302
www.justins.com
Nut butters and candy
President: Lance Gentry
CEO/Founder: Justin Gold
CFO: Lonna Borden
Director of Marketing: Lauren Lortie
SVP Sales and Marketing: James Borteck
Contact: Aaron Lord
aaron@justinsnutbutter.com
Type of Packaging: Consumer

6653 **Jyoti Cuisine India**
816 Newtown Rd
Berwyn, PA 19312-2200
610-296-4620
Fax: 610-889-0492 jyoti@jyotifoods.com
Indian foods
Founder: Jyoti Gupta
VP: Vijai Gupta
Number Employees: 5
Type of Packaging: Consumer, Food Service, Private Label
Brands:
India House
Jyoti

6654 **K & F Select Fine Coffees**
2801 SE 14th Ave
Portland, OR 97202-2203
503-234-7788
Fax: 503-231-9827 800-558-7788
Coffee products, torami syrups and sauces, taza rica cocoas, powdered drink mixes, and liquid fruit smoothie products.
Founder: Don Dominguez
ddominguez@kfcoffee.com
Director Sales/Marketing: Sandy Jumonville
Sales: Steve O Brien
Estimated Sales: $3228000
Number Employees: 10-19
Type of Packaging: Consumer, Food Service, Private Label, Bulk
Brands:
K&F
Taza Rica Mexican Spiced Cocoa

6655 **K & K Gourmet Meats Inc**
300 Washington St
Leetsdale, PA 15056-1004
724-266-8400
Fax: 724-266-8402 www.kkgourmetmeats.com
Frozen chicken, philly, and chicken philly steaks.
Owner: Arthur Katz
kkmeats@verizon.net
Number Employees: 20-49
Type of Packaging: Consumer, Food Service

6656 **K & S Cakes**
13539 Eagles Rest Dr
Leesburg, VA 20176
910-265-6779
kandscakes@hotmail.com
www.kandscakes.com
Cakes, baked goods, and gift baskets.
Owner: Kim Arico
Year Founded: 1997
Estimated Sales: Less Than $500,000
Number Employees: 1-4
Type of Packaging: Consumer, Bulk
Brands:
K&S

6657 **K Horton Specialty Foods**
28 Monument Sq
Portland, ME 04101-6447
207-228-2056
Fax: 207-228-2059
Specialty cheeses, olives, dried cured meats and meat pates, smoked seafood.
President: Kris Horton
Number Employees: 1-4

6658 **K L Keller Imports**
5332 College Ave
Suite 201
Oakland, CA 94618-2805
510-839-7890
Fax: 510-839-7895 orders@klkeller.com
www.klkeller.com

Olive, nut and, truffle oils; vinegar; condiments; herbs; spices; sea salts, and confections.
Owner: Kitty Keller
Sales: Lauren Zaira
Number Employees: 1-4

6659 K&N Fisheries
130 Seal Point Rd 1
Upper Port La Tour, NS B0W 3N0
Canada
902-768-2478
Fax: 902-768-2385
Fresh and salted fish.
Owner/Manager: Kirk Nickerson
Vice President: Gregory Nickerson
Estimated Sales: $2.3 Million
Number Employees: 17
Type of Packaging: Bulk

6660 K'ul Chocolate
2211 E Franklin Ave
Minneapolis, MN 55404
612-344-4300
info@kul-chocolate.com
kul-chocolate.com
Chocolate bars
Founder: Peter Kelsey

6661 K+S Windsor Salt Ltd.
755 boul St. Jean
Pointe Claire, QC H9R 5M9
Canada
514-630-0900
Fax: 514-694-2451 www.windsorsalt.com
Salt including table, food processing, water conditioning and ice melting.
President/CEO: Wes Clark
Marketing Manager: Michel Prevost
Year Founded: 1893
Estimated Sales: $4.89 Million
Number Employees: 861
Parent Co: K+S
Type of Packaging: Consumer, Food Service, Bulk
Other Locations:
Canadian Salt Company
Pugwash, Nova Scoti
Canadian Salt Company
Mines Seleine, Quebec
Canadian Salt Company-Warehouse
Goderich, Ontario
Canadian Salt Company-Warehouse
Clarkson, Ontario
Canadian Salt Company-Warehouse
Anjou, Quebec
Canadian Salt Company
Ojibway, Ontario
Canadian Salt Company
Windsor, Ontario
Canadian Salt Company
Regina, Saskatchewan
Canadian Salt Company
Lindbergh, Alberta
Brands:
Windsor
Safe-T-Salt
Morton
Tender Quick®
Windsor® Half Salt™
Windsor Nature's Seasons®

6662 K-Mama Sauce
4301 Benjamin St NE
Minneapolis, MN 55421
612-460-5156
kmamasauce.com
Korean hot sauce
Founder: K.C. Kye

6663 K.B. Hall Ranch
11999 Ojai Santa Paula Road
Ojai, CA 93023-8323
805-525-5875
Harvasts apricots and persimmons.
owner: Thomas Hall

6664 K.S.M. Seafood Corporation
PO Box 3057
Baton Rouge, LA 70821-3057
225-383-1517
Fax: 225-387-6641
Seafood
President: Bo Wallenhom
Estimated Sales: $10-20 Million
Number Employees: 50-99

6665 KARI-Out Co
399 Knollwood Rd
Suite 309
White Plains, NY 10603-1941
914-580-3200
Fax: 914-580-3248 800-433-8799
info@kariout.com www.kariout.com
Sauces; cooking sherrt; vinegar and food colors. Also food containers, specialty bags, cleaning supplies, placemats, napkins, cutlerly, and chopsticks & skewers.
President: Epstein Paul
Estimated Sales: $361000
Number Employees: 100-249
Square Footage: 3197
Parent Co: Perk-Up Inc.
Brands:
China Pack
Chinese-Lady
Kari-Out

6666 KAS Spirits
46 Miller Rd.
Mahopac, NY 10541
845-750-6000
info@kasspirits.com
www.kasspirits.com
Krupnikas spiced honey liqueur
Founder/Owner: Kestutis (Kas) Katinas
Year Founded: 2013
Number of Brands: 1
Number of Products: 1
Brands:
KAS

6667 KAYS Processing LLC
100 1st Ave SE
Clara City, MN 56222-1151
320-847-3220
Fax: 320-847-3110 massoud@kaysprocess.com
www.kaysdiabeticfoods.com
High protein snacks and cereals.
Owner: Massound Kezemzadeh
sales@kaysnaturals.com
Number Employees: 10-19

6668 KC Innovations Inc
2900 W 43rd Ave
Kansas City, KS 66103-3129
816-506-9023
nina@kc-innovations.com
Sauces, dressing, and dips.
President: Antiona Ward
Marketing: Nina Ward
Number Employees: 1-4
Type of Packaging: Private Label, Bulk

6669 KD Canners Inc
4444 Eastgate Pkwy
Unit 9 & 10
Mississauga, ON L4W 4T6
Canada
905-602-1825
Fax: 905-602-1826 KD@kdcanners.com
www.kdcanners.com
Tropical fruit juices; jams; chutney; sauce; organic soups; and Indian curries.
President: Krishna Tripathi
Vice President: Raju Tripathi
Estimated Sales: $2.5 Million
Number Employees: 16
Type of Packaging: Private Label
Brands:
Sahara

6670 KERN Ridge Growers LLC
25429 Barbara St
Arvin, CA 93203-9748
661-854-3141
Fax: 661-854-7229 kernridge.com
Grower, packer, and shipper of carrots, bell and chile peppers and Sunkist navel oranges.
General Manager: Bob Giragosian
bob@kernridge.com
Sales Manager: Rob Giragosian
Operations Manager: Pete Smith
Number Employees: 250-499
Type of Packaging: Consumer, Bulk
Brands:
Kern Ridge
Morn'n Fresh

6671 (HQ)KERR Concentrates Inc
2340 Hyacinth St NE
Salem, OR 97301-7566
503-378-0493
Fax: 503-378-1123 800-910-5377
info@kerrconcentrates.com
www.kerrconcentrates.com
Frozen fruit and vegetable juice concentrates, purees and puree concentrates.
CFO: David Gatti
R&D Technician: Tim Cohan
QA Manager: Jose Guerrero
Director of Sales: Trevor Albee
Manager: Mike Alley
mike.alley@kerrconcentrates.com
Plant Manager: Bart Hoopman
Purchasing: Jerry Mink
Estimated Sales: $5-10 Million
Number Employees: 20-49
Square Footage: 192000
Parent Co: International Flavors & Fragrances
Type of Packaging: Bulk
Other Locations:
Kerr Concentrates Div.
Woodburn OR

6672 KMC Citrus Enterprises Inc
16425 SE Highway 42
Weirsdale, FL 32195-2618
352-821-3666
Fax: 352-821-1400 863-298-8270
info@kmccitrus.com
Fresh and frozen orange puree and dried citrus.
President: Maristela Ferrari
VP: Keith Bowen
Estimated Sales: $1-3,000,000
Number Employees: 10-19
Type of Packaging: Consumer, Bulk
Brands:
KMC Citrus

6673 KODA Farms Inc
22540 Russell Ave
PO Box 10
South Dos Palos, CA 93665
209-392-2191
Fax: 209-392-6558 inquiry@kodafarms.com
www.kodafarms.com
Rice and rice flour.
General Manager/Pub Relations/VP: Ross Koda
VP: Laura Koda
VP: Robin Koda
VP/Secretary: Tama Koda
Estimated Sales: $10.4 Million
Number Employees: 50-99
Number of Products: 9
Square Footage: 60000
Type of Packaging: Consumer
Brands:
Blue Star Mockiko
Diamond K
Kokuho Rose
Sho Chiku Bai

6674 KOE Organic Kombucha
Vernon, CA 90058
drinkkoe.com
Organic kombucha
Exec. VP: Armen Soghomonian

6675 KOOL Ice & Seafood Co
110 Washington St
Cambridge, MD 21613-2804
410-228-2300
Fax: 410-228-1027 800-437-2417
info@freshmarylandseafood.com
www.freshmarylandseafood.com
Seafood
Owner: Dave Nickerson
Sales Exec: Tom Collins
tom@freshmarylandseafood.com
Estimated Sales: $5-10 Million
Number Employees: 20-49

6676 KOZY Shack Enterprises Inc
P.O. Box 64050
St Paul, MN 55164-0050
855-716-1555
www.kozyshack.com
Ready-to-eat puddings.
Chairman/President/CEO: Robert Striano
Year Founded: 1967
Estimated Sales: $48.5 Million

Number Employees: 249-499
Square Footage: 70000
Type of Packaging: Consumer, Food Service, Bulk
Brands:
Kozy Shack
Ready Grains™
Cowrageous!™
Smartgels
Simplywell®

6677 KP USA Trading
500 S Anderson Street
Los Angeles, CA 90033-4222
323-881-9871
Fax: 323-268-3669
Soybean, corn, cottonseed, sesame and other vegetable oils; importer of oriental foods including jasmine, sweet rice, noodles, rice stick and candy
VP: Jerry Wong
Manager: Joe Beatly
Manager: Nancy Wong
Number Employees: 10-19
Square Footage: 100000
Type of Packaging: Consumer, Food Service, Private Label, Bulk
Brands:
King Products
Mama

6678 KRAVE Jerky
117 W Napa St
Suite C
Sonoma, CA 95476-6647
USA
707-935-1035
info@kravejerky.com
www.kravejerky.com
Beef jerky
Owner: Jon Sebastiani
CEO: Erica Agrodnia
erica@kravejerky.com
Chief Financial Officer: David Lacy
Partner: Jens Hoj
Director Of Marketing: Chelsea Bialla
Vice President Of Operations: Paul Hettler
Number Employees: 5-9

6679 KT's Kitchens
1065 E Walnut Street
Suite C
Carson, CA 90746-1384
310-764-0850
Fax: 310-764-0855 ktaggares@ktskitchens.com
www.ktskitchens.com
Frozen pizza and refrigerated salad dressings.
President: Kathy Taggares
Contact: Mario Ayon
mario@ktskitchens.com
Estimated Sales: $32 Million
Number Employees: 100-249
Number of Brands: 2
Square Footage: 120000
Type of Packaging: Private Label
Brands:
Bob's Big Boy
KT's Kitchens

6680 Ka-POP!
Erie, CO 80516
kapopsnacks.com
Ancient grain snacks
Founder: Dustin Finkel

6681 Kaari Foods
Brooklyn, NY 11201
kaarifoods.com
Plant-based salad dressings, marinades and sauces
Co-Founder: Kellie Shoten
Co-Founder: Amanda Johnston

6682 Kachemak Bay Seafood
4470 Homer Spit Rd
Homer, AK 99603-8003
907-235-2799
Fax: 907-235-2799
Various fishes and other seafoods
Owner: William Sullivan
Estimated Sales: $380,000
Number Employees: 5

6683 Kaffe Magnum Opus
412 S Wade Blvd Ste 2
Millville, NJ 08332-3534
856-327-9975
Fax: 856-794-8900 800-652-5282
support@1cafe.com www.kmocoffee.com
Regular, flavored and decaffeinated coffee
President: Robert Johnson
CEO: Robert Kraeuter
VP: Cathy Johnson
Marketing Director: Heidi McDonough
Sales Representative: Meghan Kurz
Contact: Ciara Stupp
ciara@kmocoffee.com
Operations Manager: Paul Johnsones
Production Manager: Terry Kolonich
Estimated Sales: $500,000-$1 Million
Number Employees: 5-9
Brands:
Coffee Time
Kaffe Magnum Opus

6684 Kagome USA Inc
333 Johnson Rd
Los Banos, CA 93635
209-826-8850
www.kagomeusa.com
Tomato based sauces, creamy Sauces, oil based sauces, and specialty sauces.
President & CEO: Luis De Oliveira
Senior Human Resource & Safety Manager: Nida Reams
Product Development: Jennifer Hannon
Senior Operations Manager: Jaime Sandoval
Year Founded: 1988
Estimated Sales: $190.9 Million
Number Employees: 200-499
Other Locations:
R&D Office
Foster City CA
Manufacturing
Los Banos CA
Manufacturing
Osceola AR
Brands:
Kagome

6685 Kahiki Foods Inc
1100 Morrison Rd
Columbus, OH 43230-6645
614-322-3180
Fax: 614-751-0039 855-524-4540
www.kahiki.com
Frozen Asian entrees and appetizers.
President: Martin Kelly
VP, Manufacturing & Logistics: Mark Novak
Director, Marketing/R&D: Scott Corey
Director, Finance & Accounting: Matthew Szerencsits
Director, Operations: Mike Williams
Estimated Sales: $29.1 Million
Number Employees: 100-249
Number of Brands: 5
Square Footage: 119000
Type of Packaging: Food Service
Brands:
Bowl & Roll™
Kahiki
Steam & Serve™
StirFresh
Yum Yum Stix™

6686 Kaiser Pickles
500 York St
Cincinnati, OH 45214
513-621-2053
Fax: 513-455-8284 888-291-0608
customerservice@kaiserpickles.com
www.kaiserpickles.com
Pickle and pepper products
President: Ted G Kaiser
Contact: Liz Gast
liz@kaiserpickles.com
Estimated Sales: $10-20 Million
Number Employees: 16
Square Footage: 24616
Type of Packaging: Consumer, Food Service, Private Label, Bulk

6687 Kajun Kettle Foods
698 Saint George Ave
New Orleans, LA 70121-1117
504-733-8800
Fax: 504-736-0517 800-331-9612
www.kajunkettle.com
Sauces, gumbo and corn shrimp soup.
President: Pierre Hilzim
VP & sales exec: Monica Davidson
mdavidson@kajunkettle.com
Estimated Sales: $4 Million
Number Employees: 20-49
Square Footage: 344000
Type of Packaging: Consumer, Food Service, Private Label, Bulk
Brands:
Crawfish Monica

6688 Kakookies
PO Box 27585
Minneapolis, MN 55427-0585
www.kakookies.com
Cookies
Founder: Sue Kakuk

6689 Kaladi Brothers
6921 Brayton Dr Ste 201
Anchorage, AK 99507
907-644-7400
Fax: 866-893-4708 sales@kaladi.com
www.kaladi.com
Coffee
President: Tim Gravel
Contact: Brad Bigelow
brad@kaladi.com
Estimated Sales: $2.5-5 Million
Number Employees: 20-49

6690 Kalamazoo Creamery
706 Lake Street
Kalamazoo, MI 49001-2201
616-343-2558
Fax: 616-343-1620
Dairy products
President: William Steers
Brands:
Kalamazoo

6691 Kalena
Chicago, IL 60614
info@kalenasparkling.com
www.kalenasparkling.com
Sparkling coconut water
Number of Brands: 1
Number of Products: 4
Type of Packaging: Consumer
Brands:
KALENA

6692 Kalifornia Keto
Villa Park, CA 92861
info@kaliforniaketo.com
kaliforniaketo.com
Keto baking mixes and energy bites
Co-Founder: Kellie Shoten
Co-Founder: Amanda Johnston

6693 Kalin Cellars
61 Galli Dr # F
Novato, CA 94949-5701
415-883-3543
Fax: 415-883-2909 www.kalincellars.com
Wines
President: Terrance Leighton
CFO: Frances Leighton
Estimated Sales: Under $500,000
Number Employees: 1-4
Brands:
Kalin Cellars

6694 Kalot Superfood
Denver, CO
561-757-6541
www.kalotsuperfood.com
Fruit & nut butters
Founder: Jessica Goldstein

6695 (HQ)Kalsec
3713 W Main St
Kalamazoo, MI 49006
269-349-9711
800-323-9320
www.kalsec.com
Natural flavors, colors, extracts; spice oleoresins and essential oils.
Executive Chairman: George Todd
Research & Development: Don Berdahl
Plant Manager: Harry Todd
Estimated Sales: $3-5 Million
Number Employees: 100-249
Parent Co: Kalamazoo Holdings

Type of Packaging: Food Service, Bulk
Brands:
Kalsec

6696 **Kalustyan**
123 Lexington Ave # 1
New York, NY 10016-8120
212-685-3451
Fax: 212-683-8458 800-352-3451
www.kalustyans.com
Herbs; spices; rice; nuts; dried fruits; beans; seeds; oils, etc.
Owner: Saedul Alam
alam@kalustyans.com
Estimated Sales: $3 Million
Square Footage: 400000
Type of Packaging: Food Service, Bulk

6697 **Kameda USA Inc.**
3868 W. Carson St.
Suite 312
Torrance, CA 90503
310-944-9639
Fax: 310-868-2555 info@kamedausa.com
www.kamedausa.com
Various rice snacks
Co-Founder and Owner: Kathleen O'Hehir-Johnson
Co-Founder and Owner: Roger Johnson
Contact: Christopher Mur
christophermur@kamedausa.com

6698 **Kamish Food Products**
5846 N Kolmar Ave
Chicago, IL 60646-5806
773-725-6959
Fax: 773-267-0400
Baking mixes, chocolate products, jams, jellies and dehydrated fruit nuggets
President: Ted Kamish
VP: Ronald Kamish
Estimated Sales: $5 Million
Number Employees: 20-49
Type of Packaging: Food Service, Private Label, Bulk

6699 **Kan-Pak**
1016 S Summit St
Arkansas City, KS 67005-3339
620-442-6820
Fax: 800-360-7492 800-378-1265
info@kanpak.us www.kanpak.us
Juices, creamers, dairy, ice creams.
President: Janelle Oxford
Vice President: Steven Soza
Contact: Amy Blackburn
amy.blackburn@kanpak.us
Estimated Sales: $10-20 Million
Number Employees: 500-999

6700 **Kana Organics**
5716 Corsa Ave
Suite 110
Westlake Village, CA 91362
213-603-0448
info@kanaorganics.com
www.kanaorganics.com
Organic cocoa, olive oil, date syrup and soybean pasta
Founder: Ricardo Favareto
Number of Brands: 1
Number of Products: 7
Type of Packaging: Consumer
Brands:
KANA ORGANICS

6701 **Kangaroo Brands**
PO Box 3768
Dept. KAN
Omaha, NE 68103-0768
414-355-9696
Fax: 414-355-4295 877-266-2472
sales@kangaroobrands.com
www.kangaroobrands.com
Various types of bread and tortillas.
President: John Kashou
Treasurer: Bill Podewils
VP: George Kashou
Marketing: Salem Kashou
VP Sales: Phillip Gass
Operations Manager: Kristina A Kashou
Estimated Sales: $5-10 Million
Number Employees: 50-99
Number of Brands: 1
Number of Products: 3
Type of Packaging: Private Label

6702 **(HQ)Kantner Group**
625 Commerce Drive
Wapakoneta, OH 45895
419-738-4060
Fax: 419-738-4426 877-738-3448
www.kantnergroup.com
Dairy proteins and ingredients; and cheese products.
President: Doug Kantner
General Manager: John Sadowsky
CFO: Mike Koon
Quality Control: Joe Chayka
Sales/Operations: Pam Jeffery
Contact: Douglas Kantner
douglaskantner@kantnergroup.com
Purchasing: Paul Sharp
Purchasing: Mark Howell
Estimated Sales: $3-5 Million
Number Employees: 20-49
Type of Packaging: Food Service, Private Label, Bulk
Other Locations:
Kantner Ingredients
Wapakoneta OH
Blue Valley Foods
Hebron NE
Chianti Cheese of New Jersey
Pemberton NJ
Brands:
Chianti Cheese
Kantner
Blue Valley

6703 **Kapaa Bakery**
Kinipopo Shopping Village
PO Box 688
Kapaa, HI 96746-0688
808-821-0060
Baked goods
President: Paul Nishijo
Estimated Sales: $500,000 appx.
Number Employees: 5-9

6704 **Kapaa Poi Factory**
1181 Kainahola Rd
Kapaa, HI 96746-8926
808-822-5426
Poi, tofu and kulolo
President: Kenneth Fujinaga
Estimated Sales: $500,000
Number Employees: 1-4
Type of Packaging: Consumer

6705 **Kaplan & Zubrin**
134 Kaighn Ave.
Camden, NJ 08101
856-964-1083
Fax: 856-964-0510 www.kzpickles.com
Pickles; condiments; relishes; and peppers.
Estimated Sales: $4773872
Number Employees: 20-49
Square Footage: 222000
Parent Co: Patriot Pickles
Type of Packaging: Food Service

6706 **Kapow Now!**
108-375 Lynn Ave
North Vancouver, BC V7J 2C5
Canada
604-726-6391
info@kapownow.com
kapownow.com
Spreads and crackers
President/Owner: Tiffany Shen

6707 **Kara Chocolates**
575 E University Pkwy
Suite B43
Orem, UT 84097-7567
801-224-9515
Fax: 801-224-9588 800-284-5272
Chocolates and candy
Manager: Susan Boren
Manager: Steve Peterson
Estimated Sales: $5-10 Million
Number Employees: 20-49
Brands:
Kara

6708 **Kargher Corp**
3131 Sandstone Dr
Hatfield, PA 19440-1939
215-822-1186
Fax: 215-822-9666 800-355-1247
Chocolate products; chocolate nonpareils; and confectionary coated pretzels
CEO: Douglas Kargher
dkargher@kerrygroup.com
Estimated Sales: $5-10 Million
Number Employees: 20-49
Type of Packaging: Consumer, Food Service, Private Label, Bulk
Brands:
Kargher Chocolate Chips

6709 **Karine & Jeff**
1800 Century Park East
Suite 600
Los Angeles, CA 90067
www.karinejeff.us
Grains, vegetables, soups and purees
Founder & Co-President: Karine Lepillez
Number of Brands: 1
Number of Products: 14
Type of Packaging: Consumer
Brands:
KARINE & JEFF

6710 **Karl Ehmer**
6335 Fresh Pond Rd
Flushing, NY 11385-2623
718-456-8100
Fax: 718-456-2270 800-487-5275
info@karlehmer.com www.karlehmer.com
Sausages; deli and smoked meats.
President: Mark Hanssler
Quality Control: Gary Durante
Production Manager/VP: Allen Hanssler
Marketing Director: Will Osanitsch
Contact: Paul Haglich
Purchasing Manager: Daniel Durante
Estimated Sales: $5-10 Million
Number Employees: 20-49

6711 **Karl Strauss Brewing Co**
5985 Santa Fe St
San Diego, CA 92109-1623
858-273-2739
jobs@karlstrauss.com
www.karlstrauss.com
Beer; amber lager; and pale ale.
Owner: Karl Strauss
CEO: Ashley Freeborn
afreeborn@yourglobalgroup.com
CFO: Matthew Rattner
Marketing Director: Brian Bolten
Sales: Paul Timm
PR Manager: Melody Daversa
Operations: Grant Gotteshon
Production: Paul Segura
Estimated Sales: $.5-1 million
Number Employees: 50-99
Number of Brands: 25
Number of Products: 2
Square Footage: 88000
Parent Co: Associated Micro Breweries
Brands:
Downtown After Dark
Endless Summer Gold
Karl Strauss
Red Trolley Ale
Stargazer
Windansea Wheat

6712 **Karla's Smokehouse**
P.O.Box 537
Rockaway Beach, OR 97136-0537
503-355-2362
Smoke fish
Owner: Karla Steinhauser
Estimated Sales: Less than $500,000
Number Employees: 1-4

6713 **Karlin Foods**
1845 Oak St
Suite 19
Northfield, IL 60093-3022
847-441-8330
Fax: 847-441-8640 info@karlinfoods.com
www.karlinfoods.com
Dehydrated soup mixes and sauces; breadcumbs; seasonings; and stuffing mixes.
President: Mitchell Karlin
mkarlin@karlinfoods.com
Quality Assurance Manager: Vince Klemm
Director, National Sales: Jack Hounsell
Director, Operations: Jacob Drew

Estimated Sales: $10-20 Million
Number Employees: 10-19
Type of Packaging: Private Label

6714 **Karlsburger Foods Inc**
3236 Chelsea Rd W
Monticello, MN 55362-4667
763-295-2273
Fax: 763-323-1745 800-383-6549
www.karlsburger.com
Soup, sauce and gravy bases; and seasonings.
Owner: Mike Maher
mike@karlsburger.com
Number Employees: 20-49
Type of Packaging: Food Service
Brands:
Karlsburger

6715 **Karma Candy**
356 Emerald St N
Hamilton, ON L8L 8K6
Canada
905-527-6222
Fax: 905-527-6223
Seasonal chocolate and hard candy
General Manager: Joe Castro
VP, Operations: Samuel Singh

6716 **Karma Nuts**
11501 Dublin Blvd
Suite 200
Dublin, CA 94568
925-961-5491
info@karmanuts.com
www.karmanuts.com
Wrapped and roasted cashews
Founder: Ganesh Nair
Number of Brands: 1
Number of Products: 6
Type of Packaging: Consumer
Brands:
KARMA

6717 **Karmalize.Me**
225 Long Ave
Bldg 15
Hillside, NJ 07205
862-955-3492
admin@karmalize.me
www.karmalize.me
Nuts, seeds and nut butters.
Co-Founder: Shubhra Haryani
Co-Founder: Amit Haryani

6718 **Karn Meats**
922 Taylor Avenue
Columbus, OH 43219
614-252-3712
Fax: 614-252-8273 800-221-9585
info@karnmeats.com www.karnmeats.com
IQF ground beef patties and cooked ground beef crumbles
Contact: Todd Crawford
tcrawford@karnmeats.com
VP Operations: Michael Furr
Production Supervisor: Tony Furr
Plant Manager: Richard Karn
Estimated Sales: $10 Million
Number Employees: 50
Square Footage: 150000
Type of Packaging: Food Service, Private Label, Bulk

6719 **Karoun Dairies Inc**
13023 Arroyo St
San Fernando, CA 91340
818-767-7000
Fax: 818-767-7024 888-767-0778
contact@karouncheese.com
www.karouncheese.com
Cheese and cultured dairy products.
President & Chairman: Ara Baghdassarian
CFO: Tsolak Khatcherian
COO: Rostom Baghdassarian
Year Founded: 1990
Estimated Sales: $62.5 Million
Number of Brands: 6
Parent Co: Parmalat Canada
Type of Packaging: Consumer, Food Service
Brands:
Karoun
Arz
Queso Del Valle
Gopi
Yanni
Central Valley Creamery

6720 **Kashi Company**
PO Box 649
Solana Beach, CA 92075
877-747-2467
info@kashi.com www.kashi.com
Various multi-grain products
President/Owner: Tony Chow
CEO: David Denholm
Estimated Sales: $5-10 Million
Number Employees: 20-49
Parent Co: Kellogg Company
Type of Packaging: Food Service, Private Label
Brands:
Go Lean
Good Friends
Heart To Heart
Kashi Cereals
Kashi Frozen Foods
Kashi Snacks

6721 **Kasilof Fish Company**
1930 Merrill Creek Pkwy
Everett, WA 98203-5897
360-658-7552
Fax: 360-653-3560 800-322-7552
smokedsales@tridentseafoods.com
Smoked salmon and smoked seafood
President: Drew Ellison
Finance Manager: Julie Lorig
VP Sales & Marketing: Patti Moore
Estimated Sales: $2.5 Million
Number Employees: 25
Parent Co: Trident Seafoods
Type of Packaging: Consumer, Food Service, Private Label, Bulk
Brands:
Eagle River Brand
Kasilof Fish

6722 **Kasira**
5620 Knott Ave
Buena Park, CA 90621
800-220-6131
www.kasiratea.com
Coffee fruit tea
Number of Brands: 1
Number of Products: 5
Type of Packaging: Consumer
Brands:
KASIRA

6723 **Kasseler Food Products Inc.**
1031 Brevik Place
Mississauga, ON L4W 3R7
Canada
905-629-2142
Fax: 905-629-1699 sales@kasselerfoods.com
www.kasselerfoods.com
Bread and biscuits.
President: Erich Lamshoeft

6724 **Kastner's Pastry Shop & Grocery**
9467 Harding Ave
Surfside, FL 33154-2803
305-866-6993
Pastries
Owner: Philip Cohen
Estimated Sales: Less than $500,000
Number Employees: 5-9

6725 **Kate Latter Candy Company**
937 Decatur St,
New Orleans, LA 70116
504-525-5359
Fax: 504-828-0045 800-825-5359
New Orleans pralines, Southern candies, Cajun and Creole food products.
CEO: Pam Randazza
Estimated Sales: Less than $5 Million
Number Employees: 12
Brands:
Chef Hans
Kate Latters Chocolates

6726 **Kate's Vineyard**
5211 Big Ranch Rd
Napa, CA 94558-1004
707-255-2644
Fax: 707-966-2813
information@katesvineyard.com
www.katesvineyard.com
Wine
President: William Bryant
VP: Sally Bryant
Marketing VP: Kate Bryant
Contact: Kate Brunnell
Kate@Katesvineyard.Com
Estimated Sales: Less than $5 Million
Number Employees: 1-4
Brands:
Kate's
Sedna

6727 **Kateri Foods**
5415 Opportunity Court
Hopkins, MN 55343
952-933-9732
Fax: 952-933-9942 800-330-8351
Gluten-free; chocolate; candy; nuts; popcorn; and gift baskets.
Marketing: Patrick Knight
Type of Packaging: Consumer, Private Label

6728 **Kathie's Kitchen**
50 Devine St
North Haven, CT 06473-2244
203-407-0546
www.superseedz.com
Gourmet pumpkin seeds.
Founder: Kathie Pelliccio
Estimated Sales: Less than $500,000
Number Employees: 1-4
Brands:
SUPERSEEDZ

6729 **Kathryn Kennedy Winery**
13180 Pierce Rd
Saratoga, CA 95070
408-867-4170
Fax: 408-867-9463
cabernet@kathrynkennedywinery.com
www.kathrynkennedywinery.com
Wine
President/Winegrower: Marty Mathis
Directorr of sales: Eric Fountain
Contact: Alison Von Breitenfeld
qb@kathrynkennedywinery.com
Estimated Sales: Less than $5 Million
Number Employees: 1-4
Brands:
Kathryn Kennedy

6730 **Kathy's Gourmet Specialties**
PO Box 1058
Mendocino, CA 95460-1058
707-937-1383
Fax: 707-937-1383 info@kathysgourmet.com
Specialty sauces, mustards and condiments.
Owner: Shelley Pittman
Estimated Sales: $81,000
Number Employees: 2
Number of Products: 8
Type of Packaging: Consumer, Food Service, Private Label, Bulk
Brands:
Kathy's Gourmet Specialties

6731 **Katies Korner Inc**
1105 Tibbetts Wick Rd
Girard, OH 44420-1137
330-539-4140
Fax: 330-534-1412 www.katieskorner.com
Homemade ice cream and yogurt
Owner/President: Katherine Martin
Secretary/Treasurer: Keith Martin
Estimated Sales: Less than $500,000
Number Employees: 1-4

6732 **Katrina's Tartufo**
585 Bicycle Path
Port Jeffrsn Sta, NY 11776-3431
516-476-0863
Fax: 516-331-1269 800-480-8836
Ice cream
Owner: Rob Dineon
Estimated Sales: Less than $500,000
Number Employees: 10-19
Square Footage: 6000

6733 **Katy's Smokehouse**
740 Edwards St
Trinidad, CA 95570
707-677-0151
Fax: 707-677-9328
service@katyssmokehouse.com
www.katyssmokehouse.com
various smoked fish.
Owner: Bob Lake
CEO: Judy Lake
Estimated Sales: Less Than $500,000
Number Employees: 1-4
Type of Packaging: Consumer, Food Service
Brands:
Katy's Smokehouse

6734 **Katysweet Confectioners Inc.**
4321 W State Highway 71
PO Box 1237
La Grange, TX 78945-5150
979-242-5172
Fax: 800-231-5934 info@katysweet.com
www.katysweet.com
Candy and confections
Founder: Kay Carlton
Estimated Sales: Less than $500,000
Number Employees: 5-9

6735 **(HQ)Kauai Coffee Co Inc**
1 Numila Rd
Kalaheo, HI 96741-6000
808-335-3237
Fax: 808-335-0036 800-545-8605
retail@kauaicoffee.com
Roasted and specialty coffees.
President: Darla Domingo
Accountant: Candi Akita
Institutional Sales Manager: Faith Soto
Manager: Fred Cowell
Chief Operating Officer: Joan Momohara
Estimated Sales: $28 Million
Number Employees: 20-49
Number of Brands: 1
Type of Packaging: Private Label
Brands:
Kauai Coffee

6736 **Kauai Kookie**
P.O. Box 503
Eleele, HI 96705
808-335-5003
Fax: 808-335-5186 800-361-1126
info@kauaikookie.com www.kauaikookie.com
Cookies and dressings.
Marketing/Director Of Sales: Ruth Hashisaka
Plant Manager: Ellen Albarado
Estimated Sales: $1 Million
Number Employees: 20-49
Number of Brands: 2
Type of Packaging: Consumer, Food Service
Brands:
Hawaiian Hula Dressing
Kauai Kookie

6737 **Kauai Organic Farms**
P O Box 86
Kilauea, HI 96754
808-651-8843
Fax: 808-828-0151 phil@kauaiorganicfarms.com
www.kauaiorganicfarms.com
Organic Hawaiian yellow ginger and other ginger based products.
Owner/President: Phil Green
Public Relations: Linda Green
Estimated Sales: $.5-1 million
Number Employees: 5
Number of Products: 4
Square Footage: 8000
Type of Packaging: Bulk

6738 **Kauai Producers**
4334 Rice St
Suite 101
Lihue, HI 96766
808-245-4044
Fax: 808-245-9061 800-262-1400
kauai@hvcb.org www.gohawaii.com
Wholesaler/distributor of produce and dairy, frozen, dry and refrigerated products
President: Scott Nonaka
Vice President: Pearl Nonaka
Marketing Manager: Merle Nonaka
Estimated Sales: $4.5 Million
Number Employees: 23

6739 **Kaurina's, LLC**
2750 Northaven Road
Suite 302
Dallas, TX 75229-7072
972-888-9990
Fax: 972-888-9991 info@kaurinas.com
www.kaurinas.com
Organic kulfi and ice cream.
Type of Packaging: Consumer

6740 **Kava King**
123 N Orchard Street
Suite A4
Ormond Beach, FL 32174
386-673-4247
Fax: 386-671-9500 800-638-0082
Instant kava drink mixes.
VP: William Darby
Marketing Director: Jared White
Sales: Richard Bahmann
Contact: Todd Hotaling
todd@kavakingproducts.com
Estimated Sales: $300,000-500,000
Number Employees: 1-4
Type of Packaging: Consumer
Brands:
Kava King Beverage Mixes
Kava King Chocolates

6741 **Kay Foods Co**
1352 Division St
Detroit, MI 48207-2604
313-393-1100
Fax: 313-393-1083
Pre-made cold salads; also, gourmet candies.
Owner/VP: Mark Kisel
Estimated Sales: $2 Million
Number Employees: 5-9
Square Footage: 80000
Type of Packaging: Consumer, Food Service, Private Label
Brands:
Kay Foods

6742 **Kay's Naturals, Inc.**
PO Box 669
100 First Ave SE
Clara City, MN 56222
320-847-3220
866-873-5499
www.kaysnaturals.com
Cereals; protein chips; cookies; and pretzels.
Co-Founder: Ann Kazemzadeh
ann@kaysnaturals.com
Co-Founder: Massoud Kazemzadeh

6743 **Kayco**
72 New Hook Rd
Bayonne, NJ 07002
718-369-4600
customercare@kayco.com
kayco.com
Kosher, all natural, gluten free, vegan, and fair trade products; also specializes in grape juice.
President: Ilan Ron
CEO: Mordy Herzog
Financial Manager: Dov Levi
Executive Vice President: Harold Weiss
Year Founded: 1948
Estimated Sales: $86 Million
Number Employees: 500-999
Number of Brands: 76
Type of Packaging: Consumer, Food Service, Bulk

6744 **Kayem Foods**
75 Arlington St.
Chelsea, MA 02150
617-889-1600
800-426-6100
www.kayem.com
Deli products and meats, gourmet chicken, sausage and buns.
President/Chief Executive Officer: Matt Monkiewicz
Year Founded: 1909
Estimated Sales: $129 Million
Number Employees: 500-999
Number of Brands: 8
Square Footage: 160000
Type of Packaging: Consumer, Food Service, Private Label, Bulk
Other Locations:
Genoa Sausage Company
Woburn MA
Brands:
Kayem®

6745 **KeVita**
Oxnard, CA 93030
888-310-6106
www.kevita.com
Fermented beverages
Co-Founder: Bill Moses
Co-Founder: Chakra Earthsong
Year Founded: 2009

6746 **Kedem**
72 New Hook Rd
Bayonne, NJ 07002
718-369-4600
customercare@kayco.com
www.kayco.com
Kosher, gluten free and all natural products. Kosher grape juice, non-alcoholic wines, jams and, cooking products and biscuits.
President: Ilan Ron
CEO: Mordy Herzog
Financial Manager: Dov Levi
Executive Vice President: Harold Weiss
Year Founded: 1948
Estimated Sales: $50-90 Million
Number of Brands: 23
Parent Co: Kayco
Type of Packaging: Consumer

6747 **Keebler Company**
PO Box CAMB
Battlecreek, MI 49016
630-956-9742
800-962-1413
www.keebler.com
Baked goods
President and CEO: David Mackay
Contact: Dana Haller
dana_haller@keebler.com
Year Founded: 1898
Estimated Sales: $622 Million
Number Employees: 400
Square Footage: 325000
Parent Co: Kellogg Company
Type of Packaging: Consumer
Brands:
Keebler
Ready Crust
Hollow Tree

6748 **Keegan Ales**
20 St. James St.
Kingston, NY 12401
845-331-2739
www.keeganales.com
Craft IPA, American ales and stout
Founder/Owner: Tommy Keegan
Year Founded: 2003
Number of Brands: 1
Number of Products: 6
Type of Packaging: Consumer, Private Label
Brands:
Keegan Ales

6749 **Keenan Farms**
31510 Plymouth Ave
Kettleman City, CA 93239-9721
559-945-1400
Fax: 559-945-1414 info@keenanpistachio.com
www.keenanpistachio.com
Pistachios
President: Robert Keenan
robert@keenanpistachio.com
VP: Charles Keenan
Estimated Sales: $4 Million
Number Employees: 50-99
Brands:
Keenan Farms

6750 **Keep Healthy**
1019 Fort Salonga Rd
Northport, NY 11768
631-651-9090
info@keephealthyinc.com
keephealthyinc.com
Date bars
Founder: Ron Sowa

6751 **Keep Moving Inc.**
PO Box 1823
New York, NY 10156
contact@gutzyorganic.com
www.gutzyorganic.com
Organic, prebiotic fruit snacks.
Founder: David Istier
david.istier@energyfruits.com
Brands:
Energyfruits

6752 **Keeter's Meat Company**
901 U.S. 87
Tulia, TX 79088
806-995-3413
Fax: 806-995-1087 800-456-5019
www.keetersmeatcompany.com
Meat products
Co-Owner: Jerry Keeter
jkeeter@keetersmeatcompany.com
Co-Owner: Kati Keeter
Estimated Sales: $3 Million
Number Employees: 5-9
Type of Packaging: Consumer

6753 **Kefiplant**
2120, Joseph-St-Cyr
Drummondville, QC J2C 6V8
Canada
819-477-2345
Fax: 819-477-7595 info@kefiplant.com
www.kefiplant.com
Extracts
President & Sales Director: Chantale Houle
General Director: Alain Lambert

6754 **Kegg's Candies**
4934 Beechnut St
Houston, TX 77096-1605
713-664-3100
Fax: 713-664-4888
Candy
Number Employees: 10-19

6755 **Kehr's candies**
3533 W Lisbon Ave
Milwaukee, WI 53208-1954
414-344-4305
Fax: 414-933-2985
Candy
Owner: Paul Martinka
Paul@Kehrs.com
Estimated Sales: Less than $500,000
Number Employees: 5-9
Brands:
Kehr's Kandy

6756 **Kelapo**
Tampa, FL 33634
800-230-5952
www.kelapo.com
Virgin coconut oil
Number of Brands: 1
Number of Products: 12
Type of Packaging: Consumer
Brands:
KELAPO

6757 **Kelble Brothers Inc**
9111 Reiger Rd
Berlin Heights, OH 44814-9644
419-588-2015
Fax: 419-588-3116 800-247-2333
kelblebrosinc@yahoo.com www.kelbebros.com
Beef and lamb
Owner: Bill Fox
kelblebrothersinc@yahoo.com
VP: William Fox
Purchasing Agent: Rose Austin
Estimated Sales: $4 Million
Number Employees: 10-19
Square Footage: 48000
Type of Packaging: Consumer, Food Service, Bulk

6758 **Kelchner's Horseradish**
7520 Morris Ct., Ste 115
PO Box 245
Allentown, PA 18106
610-674-4450
Fax: 215-249-1931 800-424-1952
www.kelchnershorseradish.com
Prepared horseradish, tartar sauce, cocktail sauce, horseradish mustard and horseradish with beets
President: John Slaymaker
Chairman of the Board: Walter Slaymaker
Production: Richard Rankin
Estimated Sales: $4,700,000
Number Employees: 10-19
Square Footage: 20000
Type of Packaging: Consumer, Food Service
Brands:
Kelchner's

6759 **Keller's Bakery**
1012 Jefferson St
Lafayette, LA 70501-7991
337-235-1568
Fax: 337-235-8817
kellersbakerydowntown@gmail.com
www.kellersdowntown.com
Baked products
Owner/Operator: Kenneth Keller
Year Founded: 1973
Estimated Sales: $1-3 Million
Number Employees: 10-19

6760 **Keller's Creamery**
10220 N. Ambassador Dr
Kansas City, MO 64153
800-535-5371
www.kellerscreamery.com
Butter, butter oil, powdered milk, cream cheese, cheese products, heavy cream.
Chief Executive Officer: Richard Smith
Year Founded: 1906
Estimated Sales: $48 Million
Number Employees: 210
Square Footage: 6500
Parent Co: Dairy Farmers of America
Type of Packaging: Consumer, Food Service, Private Label, Bulk
Other Locations:
Keller's Creamery
Winnsboro TX
Brands:
Borden
Breakstones
Falfurrias
Hotel Bar
Keller's
Plugra

6761 **Kelley Bean Co Inc**
2407 Circle Dr
Scottsbluff, NE 69361
308-635-6438
Fax: 308-635-7345 info@kelleybean.com
www.kelleybean.com
Dried beans.
President: Kevin Kelley
kkelley@kelleybean.com
Chairman: Robert Kelley, Jr.
EVP & Chief Financial Officer: G. Lee Glenn
Director, Finance: Jim Loveridge
Business Development: Bryce Kelley
Controller: Judy Osborn
Human Resources Manager: Kim Ferguson
Operations/Seed Director: Chris Kelley
Year Founded: 1927
Estimated Sales: $36.1 Million
Number Employees: 20-49
Square Footage: 190000
Brands:
Browns Best

6762 **(HQ)Kelley Foods**
1697 Lower Curtis Rd
PO Box 708
Elba, AL 36323-8847
334-897-5761
Fax: 334-897-2712 eddiek@kelleyfoods.com
www.kelleyfoods.com
Various meats
President: Erik Ennis
eennis@drinkarizona.com
CEO: Eddie Kelley
Controller: Alex Mount
Vice President: J Kelley
VP Marketing: C Kelley
VP Operations: Dwight Kelley
Plant Manager: Max Glisson
Estimated Sales: $10-20 Million
Number Employees: 100-249
Type of Packaging: Food Service
Brands:
Bryan
Excel
Hormel
Kelley's

6763 **Kelley's Island Wine Company**
418 Woodford Road
Kelleys Island, OH 43438
419-746-2678
kiwineco@aol.com
Wines
President: Kirt Zettler
Owner: Toby Zettler
Estimated Sales: $5-9.9 Million
Number Employees: 5-9
Brands:
Coyote White
Inscription White
Long Sweet Red
Sunset Pink

6764 **Kelley's Katch Caviar**
210 Washington St
Savannah, TN 38372-1777
731-925-7360
Fax: 731-925-5631 888-681-8565
www.kelleyskatch.com
Paddlefish and sturgeon caviar.
Owner: Vickie Kelley
Estimated Sales: Less than $500,000
Number Employees: 1-4

6765 **Kellogg Canada Inc.**
5350 Creekbank Rd.
Mississauga, ON L4W 5S1
Canada
888-876-3750
www.kelloggs.ca
Breakfast foods.
President/CEO: Tony Chow
Estimated Sales: $1 Billion
Number of Brands: 18
Parent Co: Kellogg Company
Type of Packaging: Consumer
Brands:
All-Bran®
Corn Pops®
Eggo®
Froot Loops®
Just Right®
Crispix®
Kellogg's Corn Flakes®
Kellogg's Frosted Flakes
Krave®
Mini-Wheats®
Muslix®
Nutri-Grain®
Pop-Tarts®
Raisin Bran®
Rice Krispies Squares®
Rice Krispies®
Special K®
Vector®

6766 **(HQ)Kellogg Co.**
1 Kellogg Sq.
PO Box 3599
Battle Creek, MI 49017-3599
269-961-2000
Fax: 269-961-2871 800-962-1413
www.kelloggcompany.com
Breakfast foods manufacturer
Chairman/CEO: Steven Cahillane
President, Kellogg North America: Chris Hood
Senior VP/CFO: Amit Banati
Estimated Sales: $13.5 Billion
Number Employees: 34,000
Number of Brands: 28
Type of Packaging: Consumer
Other Locations:
R&D
Battle Creek MI
Brands:
Kellogg's
Special K
Cheez-It
Pringles
Keebler
Austin
Mother's Cookies
Morning Star Farms
Carr's
Gardenburger
Murray Sugar Free Cookies
Famous Amos
Frosted Mini-Wheats
Rice Krispies

Pop-Tarts
Chips Deluxe
Eggo
All-Bran
Nutri-Grain
Frosted Flakes
Crunchy Nut
Krave
Coco Pops
Froot Loops
Corn Flakes
Corn Pops
Fiber Plus
Town House

6767 **Kelly Corned Beef Co**
3531 N Elston Ave
Chicago, IL 60618-5687
773-588-2882
Fax: 773-588-0810 800-624-5617
www.kellyeisenberg.com
Corn beef and other deli meat products.
President: Marvin Eisenberg
Year Founded: 1929
Estimated Sales: $510000
Number Employees: 10-19
Parent Co: Eisenberg Sausage Company
Brands:
Eisenberg
Kelly

6768 **(HQ)Kelly Flour Company**
1208 N Swift Rd
Addison, IL 60101-6104
630-678-5300
Fax: 630-678-5311
Dry milk replacers and dry egg extenders
Manager: Dan Hoberg
Executive VP: Donald Kelly, Jr.
Plant Manager: Samuel Vergara
Estimated Sales: $3-5 Million
Number Employees: 20-49
Square Footage: 60
Type of Packaging: Food Service, Private Label
Brands:
Chickadee Products
Hi-Bak
Kel-Yolk
Thel-Egg

6769 **Kelly Foods**
513 Airways Blvd
Jackson, TN 38301
731-424-2255
info@kellyfoods.com
www.kellyfoods.com
Canned meat products; importer of corned beef.
President: Ann Koch
Contact: Tony Jordan
tony_jordan@kellysfoods.com
VP Operations: Mark Koch
Plant Manager: Bob James
Purchasing Manager: Mike Rushing
Estimated Sales: $5700000
Number Employees: 50
Square Footage: 260000
Type of Packaging: Consumer
Brands:
Hypower
Kelly

6770 **Kelly Gourmet Foods Inc**
2095 Jerrold Ave
Suite 218
San Francisco, CA 94124-1628
415-648-9200
Fax: 415-648-6164
Cooked, smoked and raw meats.
President: Rina Kelly
VP: Chris Kelly
Sales Director: Ed Kelly
Estimated Sales: Less than $500,000
Number Employees: 1-4
Type of Packaging: Consumer, Food Service, Bulk
Brands:
Fulton Organic Free Range Chicken
Fulton Valley Farms
Sierra Sausage Co.

6771 **Kelly Packing Company**
P.O. Box 27
Torrington, WY 82240
307-532-2210
Fax: 307-532-8482
Meat products
President: David Kelly
Estimated Sales: $4 Million
Number Employees: 5-9
Type of Packaging: Consumer
Brands:
Kelly

6772 **Kelly's Candies**
7 Twin Oaks Place
Pooler, GA 31322
254-289-6154
Fax: 412-573-0044 800-523-3051
Homemade fudge and chocolate candies
Owner: Gina Broderick
Estimated Sales: $.5-1 million
Number Employees: 5-9
Type of Packaging: Consumer, Private Label, Bulk
Brands:
Kelly's

6773 **Kelly-Eisenberg Gourmet Deli Products**
3531 N Elston Ave
Chicago, IL 60618
773-588-2882
Fax: 773-588-0810 800-624-5617
sales@kellyeisenberg.com
www.kellyeisenberg.com
Corned beef, hot dogs, roast beef, pastrami, Polish sausage
President: Marvin Eisenberg
VP: Cliff Eisenberg
VP: Howard Eisenberg
Operations Manager: Greg Timm
Estimated Sales: Below $5 Million
Number Employees: 20-49
Type of Packaging: Private Label
Brands:
Eisenberg Beef Hot Dogs
Eisenberg Corned Bee
Eisenberg Pastrami
Kelly Corned Beef

6774 **Kelsen, Inc.**
40 Marcus Drive
Suite 101
Melville, NY 11747
631-694-8080
Fax: 631-694-8085 888-253-5736
sales.usa@kelsen.com www.kelsen.com
Danish butter cookies
President: Lars Norgaard
Marketing: Gilbert Quiles
Contact: Nicolaj Andersen
na@kelsen.com
Estimated Sales: $5-10 Million
Number Employees: 5-9
Number of Brands: 4
Brands:
Bisca
Karenvolf
Kjeldsens
Royal Dansk

6775 **Kelson Creek Winery**
19919 Shenandoah School Rd
Plymouth, CA 95669
209-245-4700
Fax: 209-245-4707
Wine
Manager: April Ysmael
CEO: Tim Tado
Estimated Sales: $500,000-$1 Million
Number Employees: 1-4
Type of Packaging: Private Label
Brands:
Kelson Creek

6776 **Kemach Food Products**
9920 Farragut Rd
Brooklyn, NY 11236-2302
718-272-5655
Fax: 718-272-6226 info@kemach.com
www.kemach.net
Drink mixes; soup mixes; crackers; flour; cereals; pasta; baked goods; candy, chocolates, health food, chocolate syrup, juices, pasta sauces, ices, cones, etc.
President: Samuel Salzman
CFO: Aaron Daum
VP: Nik Salzman
Estimated Sales: $2.5-5 Million
Number Employees: 10-19
Square Footage: 15000
Type of Packaging: Consumer, Food Service, Private Label, Bulk
Brands:
A'Guania
Kemach
Matzo Meal
Mekach

6777 **Kemin Industries Inc**
2100 Maury St
Des Moines, IA 50317-1100
515-559-5100
Fax: 515-559-5232 800-777-8307
info@kemin.com www.kemin.com
Vitamin and supplement ingredients, natural preservatives, FloraGLO lutein, natural antioxidant preservatives
Co- Founder: Mary Nelson
VP: Charles Brice
Marketing Director: Andy Martin
Sales Manager: Linda Fullmer
Customer Service: Lori Barker
Number Employees: 100-249
Brands:
Floraglo
Myco Curb
Naturox
Oro Glo
Palasurance
Paradigmox
Roseen
Satise
Zenipro

6778 **Kemps LLC**
1270 Energy Ln
St Paul, MN 55108
www.kemps.com
Frozen yogurt, ice cream, sherbert, milk, juices, cottage cheese, sour cream and dips, and yogurt.
President & CEO: Greg Kurr
CFO: Daniel Jones
SVP, Growth & Innovation: Rachel Kyllo
VP, Operations: Bob Williams
General Manager: Brad Cuthbert
Year Founded: 1914
Estimated Sales: $116.7 Million
Number Employees: 1,125
Square Footage: 40000
Parent Co: Dairy Farmers of America

6779 **Ken's Foods Inc**
1 D'Angelo Dr
Marlborough, MA 01752
508-229-1100
www.kensfoods.com
Salad dressings, mayonnaise and sauces.
Year Founded: 1958
Estimated Sales: $106.4 Million
Number Employees: 800
Square Footage: 340000
Other Locations:
Ken's Plant Facility
McDonough GA
Ken's Plant Facility
Las Vegas NV

6780 **Kencraft, Inc.**
119 East 200 N.
Alpine, UT 84004-1631
801-756-6916
Fax: 801-756-7791 800-377-4368
sales@kencraftcandy.com
www.kencraftcandy.com
Candy and other confectionery products
President & Chief Executive Officer: David Taiclet
Contact: Gil Bowles
gilb@kencraftcandy.com
Estimated Sales: $34 Million
Number Employees: 200
Number of Brands: 12
Square Footage: 95000
Parent Co: Alpine Confections
Brands:
Bubblegum Buddies
Candy Climbers
Choco Pals
Chummy Chums
Circus Sticks
Kencraft Classics
Kookie Kakes
Lil' Lollies

Lollipals
Puppet Pals
Twist Pops
Twistix

6781 **Kendall Frozen Fruits, Inc.**
9777 Wilshire Blvd
Suite 818
Beverly Hills, CA 90212-1908
310-288-9920
Fax: 310-288-9913 susan@kendallfruit.com
www.kendallfruit.com
Frozen fruits including dried, juice concentrates, purees, freeze dried fruit, fruit powders, vegetable products, chocolate covered dried fruit, and yogurt covered dried fruit
President: Susan Kendall
Manager/Berkeley: Deborah Kendall
Manager/Littleton: Larry Kendall
VP Finance: Debra Olk
VP: Mike Daems
VP: Frank Abarca
VP: Kelly Marks
Estimated Sales: $3.6 Million
Number Employees: 14

6782 **Kendall-Jackson**
5007 Fulton Rd
Fulton, CA 95439
866-287-9818
866-287-9818
kjwines@kj.com www.kj.com
Wines
Manager: Mike Ward
Estimated Sales: Less than $500,000
Number Employees: 1-4
Parent Co: Kendall-Jackson Wine

6783 **Kendon Candies Inc**
460 Perrymont Avenue
San Jose, CA 95125
408-297-6133
Fax: 408-297-4008 800-332-2639
Lollipops
President: Kate Glass
Contact: Holly Anderson
h.anderson@kendoncandies.com

6784 **Kendrick Gourmet Products**
302 Brown Ave
Columbus, GA 31903-1253
706-687-0161
Fax: 706-682-1528 800-356-1858
Pecan candies, cakes, and brownies.
President: Bryan Stone
Vice President: Liz Kendrick
Manager: Stacey Chambers
Sales Manager: Robbing Carr
Estimated Sales: $5-9.9 Million
Number Employees: 10-19
Square Footage: 240000
Parent Co: Columbus Gourmet

6785 **Kenko International**
6984 Bandini Blvd
Los Angeles, CA 90040
323-721-8300
Fax: 323-721-9600 ronu@kenko-intl.com
www.kenkoco.com
Sweeteners, food acidulants, antioxidants, preservatives and other food chemicals.
President: Satomi Tsuchibi
Contact: Juliet Cunningham
jcunningham@alere.com
Estimated Sales: $2.7 Million
Number Employees: 15

6786 **Kennebec Fruit Company**
2 Main St
Lisbon Falls, ME 04252
207-353-8173
Moxie; yellow gentian based soft drink
Owner: Frank Anicetti
Estimated Sales: Less than $500,000
Number Employees: 1-4

6787 **Kennedy Gourmet**
115 N. Brandon Drive
Glendale Heights, IL 60139
713-795-5500
Fax: 713-795-5534 800-729-8116
info@imperial-foods.com
www.imperial-foods.com
Gourmet candy and foods
President: J Read Boles
Plant Manager: Sandy Lewis
Purchasing Manager: Sue Williams
Estimated Sales: Below $5 Million
Number Employees: 50
Square Footage: 160
Type of Packaging: Private Label
Brands:
Brazos Legends
Choc-Quitos
Chocolate Covered Pretzels
Chocolate Flavored Coffee Spoons
Chocolate Fortune Cookies
Graham Dunks
Gram Dunks
Nostalgic Creations
Sir George Fudge
Stirring Sticks
Tea Sickles
Which Ends

6788 **Kennesaw Fruit & Juice**
1300 SW 1st Ct
Pompano Beach, FL 33069-3204
954-532-7938
Fax: 954-784-1222 800-949-0371
www.kennesawjuice.com
Citrus juices including orange, grapefruit, lemonade, etc.; also, cored and chunked pineapple, fresh orange and grapefruit slices and fruit salad available
President: Len Roseburg
V.P./Prtnr.: Ed Zukerman
Estimated Sales: $3-5 Million
Number Employees: 20-49
Square Footage: 152000
Type of Packaging: Consumer, Food Service

6789 **Kenny's Candy & Confections**
Perham, MN 56573
kennyscandy.com
Fruit snacks, gummies, licorice and popcorn
Founder: Ken Nelson
Year Founded: 1987
Type of Packaging: Private Label

6790 **(HQ)Kenosha Beef International LTD**
Kenosha, WI
www.bwfoods.com
Meat products including frozen boxed beef patties
President, Chief Executive Officer: Dennis Vignieri
CFO: Jerry King
jking@bwfoods.com
VP HR & Safety: Phyllis Murray
VP Sales & Marketing: Wayne Wehking
EVP Operations & Procurement: John Ruffolo
Number Employees: 500-999
Type of Packaging: Consumer, Food Service
Brands:
Birchwood Foods
Bistro 36

6791 **Kent Foods Inc**
2600 Church St
Gonzales, TX 78629
830-672-7993
Fax: 830-672-7223 www.kentfeeds.com
Frozen and liquid egg products
President: Daw Lu
daw.lu@kentfeeds.com
Sales Executive: Ging Lu
Estimated Sales: $1-3 Million
Number Employees: 20-49
Square Footage: 45000
Type of Packaging: Food Service, Bulk
Brands:
Kent Foods

6792 **Kent Precision Foods Group Inc**
2905 US-61
Muscatine, IA 52761
800-442-5242
www.precisionfoods.com
Pickle and tomato mixes, pectins, jams, jellies, fruit preservatives, blended spices and seasonings, dessert mixes; exporter of dry soft serve and dessert mixes.
Manager of Business Development: Kirk Kuiper
Vice President of Sales & Marketing: Connie Huck
Year Founded: 1992
Estimated Sales: $69.4 Million
Number Employees: 20-49
Number of Brands: 8
Square Footage: 200000
Parent Co: Kent Corporation
Type of Packaging: Consumer, Food Service, Private Label, Bulk
Other Locations:
Manufacturing Location
Bolingbrook IL
Brands:
Foothill Farms®
Frostline® Frozen Treats
DOLE® Soft Serve
LAND O'LAKES™
Mrs. Dash® Foodservice
Sugar Twin®
Baker's Joy®
Sqwincher®

6793 **Kent Quality Foods Inc**
703 Leonard St NW
Grand Rapids, MI 49504-4236
616-459-4595
Fax: 616-459-5802 800-748-0141
information@kqf.com kqf.com
Manufacturer of franks, sausages and specialty meats. Founded in 1967.
President: Steve Soet
Year Founded: 1967
Estimated Sales: $46 Million
Number Employees: 100-249
Type of Packaging: Consumer, Food Service, Private Label, Bulk

6794 **Kent's Wharf**
31 Steamboat Hl
Swans Island, ME 4685
207-526-4186
Fax: 207-526-4291
Seafood
Owner: David Niquette
kentswharf@aol.com
Estimated Sales: $300,000-500,000
Number Employees: 1-4

6795 **Kentucky Beer Cheese**
224 Industry Pkwy
Suite A
Nicholasville, KY 40356-8015
859-887-1645
Fax: 859-277-6075 info@kentuckybeercheese.com
www.kentuckybeercheese.com
Processor and wholesaler/distributor of cheese spread and dip including hot, garlic and beer flavored.
Owner, President: Diane Evans
VP, Owner: Chris Evans
Estimated Sales: Less Than $500,000
Number Employees: 1-4
Square Footage: 4000
Parent Co: Evans Gourmet Foods, LLC
Type of Packaging: Consumer, Food Service
Brands:
Kentucky Beer Cheese

6796 **Kentucky Bourbon**
925 S. 7th Street
Louisville, KY 40203
866-472-7797
Fax: 866-574-4269 tracy@bourbonQ.com
www.bourbonQ.com
Gourmet sauces & spices
President: Shane Best
Contact: Jennifer Nolte
jennifer@bourbonq.com
Estimated Sales: $300,000-500,000
Number Employees: 10-19
Brands:
Bear Claw
Cultured Red Neck T-Shirts
Fighting Cock
Kentucky Bourbonq
Lady In Red
Moonshine Madness
Pappy's Best Premimum Marinade
Pappy's XXX White Lightnin
Sauce For Sissies
Shrimp Butler
Smoky Mountain Trail Rub

6797 **Kentwood Springs**
200 Eagles Landing Blvd
Lakeland, FL 33810
800-728-5508
www.kentwoodsprings.com
Spring water
President: Don Woods

Year Founded: 1963
Estimated Sales: $367.9 Million
Number Employees: 5,350
Number of Brands: 5
Parent Co: Ds Waters Holdings, LLC
Brands:
Abita Golden
Abita Purple
Abita Root Beer
Abita Seasmals
Abita Turboday

6798 Kenwood Vineyards
9592 Sonoma Hwy
Kenwood, CA 95452
707-833-5891
Fax: 707-833-1146 info@kenwoodvineyards.com
www.kenwoodvineyards.com
Wines
Manager: Alan Jensen
ajensen@kenwoodvineyards.com
Sales/Marketing: Paul Young
Public Relations: Margie Healy
Winemaker: Mike Lee
Number Employees: 50-99
Square Footage: 200000
Parent Co: Korbel Champagne
Type of Packaging: Consumer
Brands:
Kenwood Vineyards

6799 Kerala Curry
2277 Otis Johnson Rd
Pittsboro, NC 27312
919-545-9401
Fax: 919-545-9402 rolls@keralacurry.com
www.keralacurry.com
Gluten-free, organic/natural, USDA, chutney/relish, hors d'oeuvres/appetizers, ready meals/pizza/soup, ethnic sauces (soy, curry, etc.), foodservice.
Marketing: Rollo Varkey

6800 Kern Meat Distributing
2711 Wagel Rd
Brooksville, KY 41004
606-756-2255
Fax: 606-756-2114 webberfarms.com
Meat
President: Ed Kern
Estimated Sales: $10-20 Million
Number Employees: 20-49

6801 Kernel Fabyan's Gourmet Popcorn
3722 Illinois Avenue
St Charles, IL 60174-2421
630-485-4680
Fax: 630-513-0396 847-483-1377
Popcorn
Marketing: Eddie Nusinow

6802 Kernel Seasons LLC
2401 E Devon Ave
Elk Grove Vlg, IL 60007-6213
847-350-6041
Fax: 773-326-0869 866-328-7672
www.chicagocustomfoods.com
Popcorn seasonings, machines and accessories.
Founder/Owner/President/CEO: Brian Taylor
Marketing: Jean Doyle
Contact: Andrew Abovitz
aabovitz@kernelseasons.com
Number Employees: 5-9

6803 Kerr Brothers
Toronto, ON M8Z 4P6
Canada
416-252-7341
Fax: 416-252-6054 hr@kerrs.com
www.kerrs.com
Confections, candy, and cough drops.
VP of Sales: Lyndon Brown
Year Founded: 1895
Brands:
Soda Pops®
Sour Pops®

6804 Kerr Jellies
PO Box 599
Dana, NC 28724-0599
828-685-8381
Fax: 828-685-8381 877-685-8381
Jellies
President: Kathy Thompson

Estimated Sales: $5-10 Million
Number Employees: 5-9

6805 Kerri Kreations
216 Fern St
Santa Cruz, CA 95060
831-429-5129
kerrikreations@hotmail.com
www.kerrikreations.com
Organic, vegan cookies; gluten-free options available
Founder: Kerri O'Neill
Number Employees: 5-9

6806 Kerry Foodservice
30 Paragon Pkwy
Mansfield, OH 44903-8074
419-522-2722
Fax: 419-522-1152 800-533-2722
slinfo@kerrygroup.com
Processor and exporter of Italian syrups, specialty sugars and powdered toppings for coffees; also, coffee and tea flavors and extracts; private labeling available
Business Director: Peter Dillane
Marketing Director: Corrie Byron
Manager: James Powers
jpowers@stearns-lehman.com
Estimated Sales: $7.9 Million
Number Employees: 20-49
Square Footage: 200000
Type of Packaging: Private Label
Brands:
Dinatura
Dolce
Flavor-Mate
Gift of Bran
My Hero
Paradise Bay
Select Origins
Senza
Stearns & Lehman

6807 Kerry Sweet Ingredients
202 Market Street
Gridley, IL 61744
309-747-3541
Food ingredients
President: Gary Ringger
gringger@kerrygroup.com
Parent Co: Kerry Inc.

6808 Kerry, Inc
Global Technology & Innovation Center
3400 Millington Rd
Beloit, WI 53511
608-363-1200
www.kerry.com
Food ingredients, encapsulation, ingredient sourcing, in-house testing and spray drying services.
CEO/Executive Director: Edmond Scanlon
President/CEO, Kerry Taste & Nutrition: Gerry Behan
CFO: Marguerite Larkin
President/CEO, North America: Michael O'Neill
Global COO: Alan Barrett
Year Founded: 1972
Estimated Sales: Over $1 Billion
Number Employees: 25,255
Parent Co: Kerry Group Plc
Type of Packaging: Food Service

6809 Kershenstine Beef Jerky
550 Industrial Park Rd
Eupora, MS 39744
662-258-2049
Fax: 662-258-2002 www.pappysjerky.com
Processor and exporter of beef jerky
President: Timothy Kershenstine
Estimated Sales: $710,000
Number Employees: 5 to 9
Type of Packaging: Consumer

6810 Kervan USA
52 E Union Blvd
Bethlehem, PA 18018
610-866-2300
kervanusa.com
Gummies, licorice and marshmallow
Number of Products: 200+
Type of Packaging: Consumer, Bulk
Brands:
Crayola
Bebeto
Yumy Yumy

6811 Keto Foods
56 Park Pl
Suite 2
Neptune, NJ 07753
732-922-0009
Fax: 732-643-6677 email@keto.com
Diet coffee, tea and creamer; low carbohydrate foods and snacks.
President: Arnie Bey
Quality Control: Allan Nargolies
VP Corporation Counsel: Dan Majollo
Sales/Marketing Executive: Arnie Bey
Purchasing Agent: Megan Holman
Estimated Sales: $2.5-5 Million
Number Employees: 30
Square Footage: 120000
Type of Packaging: Consumer, Food Service, Bulk
Brands:
Slim Diez

6812 Ketters Meat Market & Locker Plant
118 W Main Ave
Frazee, MN 56544
218-334-2351
Beef, pork, turtle and deer
President: Kenneth Ketter
Estimated Sales: $1-3 Million
Number Employees: 5-9
Type of Packaging: Consumer, Food Service

6813 Kettle & Fire
Austin, TX 78701
415-857-0024
www.kettleandfire.com
Bone broths and soups
Co-Founder: Justin Mares
Co-Founder: Nick Mares
Year Founded: 2015
Number of Brands: 1
Number of Products: 6
Type of Packaging: Consumer
Brands:
KETTLE & FIRE

6814 Kettle Brand
PO Box 32368
Charlotte, NC 28232
800-438-1880
kettlebrand.com
Kettle potato and vegetable chips
President/Owner: Cameron Healy
CFO: Marc Cramer
Year Founded: 1982
Number of Brands: 1
Number of Products: 31
Type of Packaging: Consumer
Brands:
KETTLE BRAND
KETTLE UPROOTED
KETTLE BRAND KRINKLE CUT

6815 Kettle Cuisine
330 Lynnway
Lynn, MA 01901
617-409-1100
Fax: 617-884-1341 877-302-7687
www.kettlecuisine.com
Fresh soups and chowders
President/Founder: Jerry Shafir
Chief Executive Officer: Liam McClennon
Chief Financial Officer: James Reed
EVP Sales, Marketing, R&D: Mike Illum
VP Sales: Bob Benson
EVP Human Resources: Nora McCarthy
Chief Operating Officer: Jeremy Kacuba
Estimated Sales: $20-50 Million
Number Employees: 100-249
Type of Packaging: Consumer, Food Service

6816 Kettle Foods Inc
3125 Kettle Ct SE
Salem, OR 97301-5572
503-364-0399
Fax: 503-371-1447 www.kettlebrand.com
Natural potato chips and healthy snacks
Number Employees: 500-999

6817 **Kettle Master**
497 Farmers Market Rd
Hillsville, VA 24343-5106
276-728-7571
sales@kettlemaster.com
www.kettlemaster.com
Jellies, jams, salsa and sauces
Manager: Rex Horton
Marketing Sales Director: Ben Web
Operations Manager: Fred Jones
Number Employees: 5-9
Type of Packaging: Consumer, Private Label
Other Locations:
Chesapeake Bay Gourmet
Baltimore MD

6818 **Keurig Dr Pepper**
5301 Legacy Dr.
Plano, TX 75024
800-696-5891
www.keurigdrpepper.com
Coffee, hot and cold beverage maker systems, flavored soft drinks, teas, waters, juices, juice drinks, and more.
CEO: Robert Gamgort
CFO: Ozan Dokmecioglu
Chief Legal Officer/General Counsel: Jim Baldwin
Chief Research & Development Officer: David Thomas
Chief Marketing Officer: Andrew Springate
Year Founded: 2018
Estimated Sales: $11 Billion
Number Employees: 25,000
Number of Brands: 81
Number of Products: 530+
Type of Packaging: Consumer, Food Service, Bulk
Other Locations:
Production
Castroville CA
R&D, Professional Services
Burlington MA
Production
Knoxville TN
Production
Windsor VA
Production
Sumner WA
Keurig Canada
Montreal, QC, Canada
Brands:
Green Mountain Coffee®
Caribou Coffee®
Laughing Man®
Peet's Coffee®
The Original Donut Shop®
Van Houtte®
Revv®
Tully's Coffe®
Krispy Kreme®
Newmann's Own Organics®
Barista Bros®
Barista Prima Coffeehouse®
Br-lerie Mont Royal®
Br-lerie St. Denis®
Caf, Escapes®
Caf, Punta del Cielo®
Cinnabon®
Coffee People®
Diedrich Coffee®
Donut House Collection®
Emeril®
Gloria Jean's Coffees®
Hollys Coffee®
Kahl£a®
Laura Secord®
Orient Express®
Timothy's®
Panera Bread®
High Brew Coffee®
Gila Caf,®
Forto®
Adagio®
Dr. Pepper®
7UP®
A&W Root Beer®
Canada Dry®
Schweppes®
Sunkist®
Crush®
Sun Drop®
IBC®
Diet Rite®
Squirt®
Vernors®
Royal Crown Cola®
Hires®
Stewart's®
Big Red®
Cplus®
Cactus Cooler®
Nehi Cola®
Tahitian Treat®
Bai®
Deja Blue®
Penafiel®
Snapple®
Straight Up Tea®
Evian®
Neuro®
Vita Coco®
Cora®
Clamato®
Hawaiian Punch®
Margritaville®
Mott's®
Nantucker Nectars®
Orangina®
Mott's®
Nantucker Nectars®
Orangina®
ReaLemon®
Rose's®
SunnyD®

6819 **Keurig, Inc**
55 Walkers Brook Drive
Reading, MA 01867
781-928-0162
866-901-2739
www.keurig.com
Single cup coffee and brewers. Also tea, hot cocoa and iced beverages.
President: Michelle Stacy
Chief Financial Officer: Frances Rathke
VP/General Counsel: Howard Malovany
Director of Research: Karl Winkler
Director of Quality: William Hartman
Contact: Christina Adams
christina.adams@keurig.com
VP Manufacturing/Operations: Dick Sweeney
Number Employees: 185
Type of Packaging: Consumer
Brands:
Donut Shop
Green Mountain Coffee
Newmans Own
Barista Prima
Cafe Escapes
Celestial Seasonings
Coffee People
Dunkin Donuts
Emerils
Ghiradelli
Gloria Jeans
Millstone
Donut House

6820 **Kevala**
PO Box 670692
Dallas, TX 75367
877-379-1179
info@kevala.net
kevala.net
Spreads, oil, sweeteners, herbs, and spices.
Operations Manager: Gerardo Rodriguez
gerardo@kevala.net

6821 **Kevton Gourmet Tea**
385 Fm 416
Streetman, TX 75859-3024
903-389-2905
Fax: 903-389-5607 888-538-8668
Honey, flavored mixes, sour cream, tea, cocoa
CEO: Tanya Miller
Brands:
Bee My Honey
Good Stuff Cocoa
Not Just Jam
Tea Tyme Cookies
Countrymixes
Joy
Tease

6822 **Key Colony Red Parrot Juice**
16300 103rd St
Lemont, IL 60439-9666
630-783-8572
Fax: 630-783-8791 844-783-8572
www.redparrotjuice.com
Bag-in-box juices
President: Guy Sisto
SVP: Rob Baker
Regional Sales Coordinator: Tom Ambutas
Manager: Janice Baisden
janice@redparrotjuice.com
Estimated Sales: Less Than $500,000
Number Employees: 1-4
Type of Packaging: Food Service
Brands:
Red Parrot

6823 **Key III Candies**
4211 Earth Dr
Fort Wayne, IN 46809
260-747-7514
Fax: 260-747-9898 800-752-2382
Milk chocolate confections, caramels and pretzels.
President: Todd Haines
VP/Co-Owner: Richard Dickmeyer
Manager: Gary Yarger
Estimated Sales: $3-5 Million
Number Employees: 10-19
Square Footage: 20000
Type of Packaging: Consumer, Bulk
Brands:
Key Iii

6824 **Key Largo Fisheries**
1313 Ocean Bay Dr
Key Largo, FL 33037-4213
305-451-3782
800-432-4358
www.keylargofisheries.com
Seafood
President & Co-Owner: Tom Hill
tomhill13@aol.com
Co-Owner: Rick Hill
Estimated Sales: $10 Million
Number Employees: 20-49
Square Footage: 6000
Type of Packaging: Consumer, Food Service, Private Label

6825 **Key West Key Lime Pie Co**
225 Key Deer Blvd
Big Pine Key, FL 33043
305-872-7400
Fax: 305-872-7600 877-882-7437
keywestkeylimepieco.com
Key lime products
President: James Brush
Vice President: Alison Sloat
Estimated Sales: $400,000
Number Employees: 5-9
Number of Brands: 4
Number of Products: 100+
Square Footage: 2400
Type of Packaging: Consumer, Food Service, Private Label
Brands:
Key Lime Pie Slices Dipped In Choco
Key Lime Pies Assorted Flavors
Package Bulk Key Lime Filling

6826 **Keynes Brothers Inc**
1 W Front St
Logan, OH 43138-1825
740-385-6824
Fax: 740-385-9076 800-282-5627
www.keynesbros.com
Soft and whole wheat flour
Executive: William Keynes
wkeynes@keynesbros.com
Executive: Charles Keynes
Estimated Sales: $20-30 Million
Number Employees: 20-49

6827 **Keys Fisheries Market &Marina**
3502 Gulfview Ave
Marathon, FL 33050-2362
305-743-4353
Fax: 305-743-3562 866-743-4353
keys.fisheries@comcast.net
www.keysfisheries.com
Processor and wholesaler of seafood products.
Owner: Gary Graves
keysfisheries@comcast.net
Vice President: Gary Graves
Estimated Sales: $1-2.5 Million
Number Employees: 20-49
Type of Packaging: Consumer, Food Service

6828 **Keyser Brothers**
1146 Honest Point Rd
Lottsburg, VA 22511-2521
804-529-6837
Fax: 804-529-5144
Fresh and frozen seafood including crabs and pasteurized crab meat
President/CEO: R Calvin Keyser
Executive VP: Norman Keyser
Estimated Sales: $350,000
Number Employees: 20-25
Number of Brands: 1
Square Footage: 52500
Type of Packaging: Private Label
Brands:
Potomac River
Potomac River Brand

6829 **Keystone Coffee Co**
2230 Will Wool Dr
Suite 100
San Jose, CA 95112-2605
408-998-2221
Fax: 408-998-5021 www.keystonecoffee.com
Processor and exporter of gourmet coffee
President: Tim Wright
CEO: Dan Mckenrick
mdan@keystonecoffee.com
Estimated Sales: $3000000
Number Employees: 10-19
Brands:
Keystone

6830 **Keystone Pretzel Bakery**
124 W Airport Rd
Lititz, PA 17543-9294
717-560-1882
Fax: 717-560-2241 888-572-4500
www.keystonepretzels.com
Pretzels
President: George Phillips
mschaller@keystonepretzels.com
Sales Exec: Mike Schaller
Estimated Sales: $12 Million
Number Employees: 50-99
Type of Packaging: Consumer, Food Service, Bulk

6831 **Khatsa & Company**
PO Box 50754
13805 Main St
Bellevue, WA 98005-3733
206-404-9000
Fax: 425-649-0774 888-234-6781
President: Dachs Kyaping
Vice President: Nanang Nornang
Public Relations: Dachen Kyaping
Estimated Sales: $500,000-$1 Million
Number Employees: 1-4
Brands:
Khatsa
Liberate Your Senses
Urban Nomad Food

6832 **KiZE Concepts**
Oklahoma City, OK 73106
kizeconcepts.com
Energy bars
Business Development Manager: Sam Wolfe
Chief Marketing Officer: Justin Lane

6833 **Kibun Foods**
2101 4th Ave
Suite 1170
Seattle, WA 98121-2319
206-467-6287
Fax: 206-467-6612 www.kibunusa.com
Beer
President: Kristine Goodman
kgoodman@starbucks.com
Estimated Sales: $7,500,000
Number Employees: 10-19

6834 **Kicking Horse Coffee**
491 Arrow Rd
Invermere, BC V0A 1K2
Canada
250-342-4489
Fax: 250-342-4450 888-287-5282
mia@kickinghorsecoffee.com
www.kickinghorsecoffee.com
Ground, whole bean and cold brew coffee
Co-Founder: Elana Rosenfeld
Co-Founder: Leo Johnson

6835 **Kidfresh**
315 Fifth Ave
Suite 401
New York, NY 10016
212-686-4303
Fax: 212-686-4306 info@kidfresh.com
www.kidfresh.com
Frozen kids' meals
Co-Founder: Matt Cohen
Co-Founder: Gilles Deloux
Number of Brands: 1
Number of Products: 21
Type of Packaging: Consumer
Brands:
KIDFRESH

6836 **Kids Kookie Company**
1000 Calle Negocio
San Clemente, CA 92673
949-661-7880
Fax: 949-498-5496 800-350-7577
www.kidscookies.com
Holiday, theme, decorated, specialty shaped and pre-baked cookies
Owner: Dennis Sellers
VP: Gay Sellers
Contact: Marcy Sellers
marcy@kidscookies.com
Estimated Sales: $5-10 Million
Number Employees: 5-9
Type of Packaging: Food Service
Brands:
Kids Cookie

6837 **KidsLuv**
San Francisco, CA 94131
855-543-7588
hello@kidsluv.com kidsluv.com
Juice-infused water
Consultant: Jenn Goodrum
Number of Products: 4

6838 **Kidsmania**
12332 Bell Ranch Dr
Santa Fe Springs, CA 90670
562-946-8822
Fax: 562-946-8802 www.candynovelties.com
Candy toys and novelties
Owner: Foreman Lam
Estimated Sales: $300,000-500,000
Number Employees: 1-4
Number of Products: 100

6839 **Kii Naturals Inc**
100 Ortona Court
Vaughan, ON L4K 0A5
Canada
905-738-8887
Fax: 905-738-8968 www.kiinaturals.com
Artisan crisps, cereals, grains and superfoods
Chief Executive Officer/Founder: Sujay Shah
Number Employees: 50-99

6840 **KiiTO, Inc.**
Los Angeles, CA 90017
hi@drinkkiito.com
drinkkiito.com
Plant-based protein drinks

6841 **Kiki's Gluten-Free**
350 S Northwest Hwy
Suite 300
Park Ridge, IL 60068
hello@kikisglutenfree.com
kikisglutenfree.com
Gluten-free pizzas, cake mixes and pastas
Founder & CEO: Kiki Michalakos

6842 **Kilgus Meats**
3346 W Laskey Rd
Toledo, OH 43623-4030
419-472-9721
Sausage products and lunch meats
President: William Vallongo
General Manager: Till Ballongo
Estimated Sales: $540,000
Number Employees: 1-4
Square Footage: 4800
Type of Packaging: Consumer, Food Service, Bulk

6843 **Kill Cliff**
3916-199 Armour Dr NE
Atlanta, GA 30324
855-552-5433
customerservice@killcliff.com www.killcliff.com
Sports drinks
Founder: Todd Ehrlich
Number of Brands: 2
Number of Products: 7
Type of Packaging: Consumer
Brands:
ENDURE
KILL CLIFF

6844 **Kill Sauce**
Pasadena, CA 91105
www.killsauce.com
Hot sauces

6845 **Killer Creamery**
Boise, ID 83703
info@killercreamery.com
killercreamery.com
Keto-friendly ice cream
Founder: Louis Armstrong
Co-Founder: Liz Armstrong
VP, Marketing: Tate Glasgow

6846 **Kilwons Foods**
PO Box 3088
Santa Cruz, CA 95060
831-426-9670
Fax: 831-426-2720 kilwon@kilwonsfoods.com
www.kilwonsfoods.com
Sauce, gravy, dressing & dip mixes.
Owner: Kilwon Poveromo
Estimated Sales: Less than $500,000
Number Employees: 5-9
Brands:
Kilwons Foods

6847 **Kim & Scott's Gourmet Pretzels**
2107 West Carroll Ave
Chicago, IL 60612
312-243-9971
800-578-9478
www.kimandscotts.com
Soft pretzels and other baked goods
President/Owner: Kimberly Oster-Holstein
CEO/Owner: Scott Holstein
CFO: Maura Finn
Contact: Mike Connors
mike@kimandscotts.com
Estimated Sales: $10 Million
Number Employees: 50-99

6848 **Kim and Jake's**
641 S Broadway
Boulder, CO 80305
303-499-9126
info@kimandjakes.com
kimandjakes.com
Gluten-free breads, buns, rolls and cookies
Co-Founder: Jake Rosenbarger
Co-Founder: Kim Rosenbarger

6849 **Kimball Enterprise International**
3129 S Hacienda Heights Blvd
Suite 410
Hacienda Heights, CA 91745
213-276-8898
Fax: 213-947-1888 sales@garlicpeeler.com
www.garlicpeeler.com
Processor and exporter of roasted, peeled and chopped garlic, peeled and chopped shallots and garlic juice
President: Jimmy Tani
Estimated Sales: $2 Million
Number Employees: 20
Square Footage: 60000
Type of Packaging: Consumer, Food Service, Private Label, Bulk
Brands:
Kimball

6850 **Kime's Cider Mill**
171 Church St
Bendersville, PA 17306
717-677-7539
Fax: 717-677-7151
Apple butter and cider
Owner: Rick Kime
kimescider@netzero.com
Partner: Randy Kimes

Estimated Sales: Below $5 Million
Number Employees: 10-19
Type of Packaging: Consumer
Brands:
Kimes

6851 Kimmie Candy Company
525 Reactor Way
Reno, NV 89502
775-284-9200
Fax: 775-284-9206 888-532-1325
sales@kimmiecandy.com www.kimmiecandy.com
Confections
President/CEO: Joseph Dutra
Accounting: Linda Joo
VP Sales/Marketing: Bernie Leas
Sales Manager: Mark Bedingfield
Contact: Alexis Cissell
alexis@kimmiecandy.com
Operations: John Dutra
Production: OoIn Jung
Estimated Sales: $1-5 Million
Number Employees: 20
Square Footage: 40000
Type of Packaging: Consumer, Food Service, Private Label, Bulk
Brands:
Baby Dino Eggs
Choco Rocks
Kandy Kookies
Peanut Crunchers
Raisin Royales
Sunbursts

6852 Kind Snacks
1372 Broadway
Suite 3
New York, NY 10018-6123
212-819-2480
Fax: 212-616-3005 855-884-5463
customerservice@kindsnacks.com
www.kindsnacks.com
Gluten-free snack bars
Marketing: Mariana Rittenhouse
Year Founded: 2004
Number Employees: 20-49

6853 Kinder's BBQ
245 Ygnacio Valley Rd
Suite 200
Walnut Creek, CA 94596
925-939-7242
www.kindersbbq.com
BBQ sauces, marinades and rubs
President: Dan Avery

6854 King & Prince Seafood
1 King & Prince Blvd.
Brunswick, GA 31520
888-391-5223
marketing@kpseafood.com www.kpseafood.com
Seafood
President/CEO: Michael Alexander
Director of Marketing: Michael Tigani
SVP Sales & Marketing: Mark Sutherland
VP Human Resources: Tom Norton
Procurement Manager: Jay M
Estimated Sales: $20-50 Million
Number Employees: 100-249

6855 King & Prince Seafood Corp
1 King And Prince Blvd
PO Box 899
Brunswick, GA 31520-8668
912-265-5155
Fax: 912-264-4812 800-841-0205
sales@kpseafood.com www.kpseafood.com
Shrimp; lobster tails and stuffed fish; importer of frozen shrimp.
CEO: Volker Kuntzsch
vkuntzsch@kpseafood.com
Estimated Sales: $570,000
Number Employees: 500-999
Parent Co: Nippon Suisan Kaisha, Ltd.
Brands:
King & Prince
Mrs. Friday's
Oceanway Seafood
Pride of Alaska

6856 King 888 Company
PO BOX 51360
Sparks, NV 89436
775-530-5718
Fax: 800-785-3674 800-785-3674
www.king888.com
Energy drinks
Sales Representative: Gary Larson
Type of Packaging: Food Service

6857 King Arthur Flour
135 US Route 5 S
Norwich, VT 05055-9430
802-649-3361
Fax: 802-649-3365 800-827-6836
www.kingarthurflour.com
Flours, specialty flours and mixes
Co-CEO: Suzanne McDowell
Co-CEO: Karen Colberg
Senior VP: Michael Bittel
mikebittel@kingarthurflowers.com
VP, Sales: Beth Kluge
Year Founded: 1790
Estimated Sales: $45 Million
Number Employees: 300+
Number of Brands: 1
Square Footage: 16600

6858 King B Meat Snacks
P.O. Box 397
Minong, WI 54859-0397
715-466-2234
Fax: 715-466-5151 800-346-6896
info@linksnacks.com
Manufacturer and exporter of jerky and meat snacks
President: Troy Link
CEO: John Link
CFO: John Hermeier
Executive Vice President of Supply Chain: Karl Paepke
Director of Marketing: Jeff LeFever
Estimated Sales: $10-20 Million
Number Employees: 250-499
Type of Packaging: Consumer, Food Service, Private Label, Bulk
Brands:
B. King
Taylor Country Farms

6859 King Brewing Company
895 Oakland Ave
Pontiac, MI 48340
248-745-5900
Fax: 248-745-0160 kingbrewco@hotmail.com
www.kingbrewing.info
Wines
Owner: Tom King
Operations Manager: Robert Egelhoff
Estimated Sales: Less than $500,000
Number Employees: 1-4
Square Footage: 18
Type of Packaging: Private Label

6860 King Cole Ducks Limited
15351 Warden Ave.
PO Box 185
Newmarket, ON L3Y 4W1
Canada
905-836-9461
Fax: 905-836-4440 800-363-3825
rgrant@kingcoleducks.com
www.kingcoleducks.com
Processor and exporter of fresh and frozen duck including parts, smoked, boneless breast, peppered, fully cooked, etc
President: James Murby
VP: Robert Murby
Square Footage: 4000
Type of Packaging: Consumer, Food Service, Private Label, Bulk
Brands:
King Cole

6861 King Cupboard
15 Pepsi Dr
Red Lodge, MT 59068-9104
406-446-3060
Fax: 406-446-3070 800-962-6555
www.kingscupboard.com
All natural dessert sauces and hot chocolate mixes
President: Lila Randolph
li@kingscupboard.com
Estimated Sales: $5-10 Million
Number Employees: 50-99

Type of Packaging: Consumer, Food Service, Private Label, Bulk
Brands:
Beartooth Kitchens

6862 King Estate Winery
80854 Territorial Hwy
Eugene, OR 97405-9715
541-942-9874
Fax: 541-942-9867 800-884-4441
info@kingestate.com
Wines
CEO: Ed King
edk@kingestate.com
Director of Finance: Artie Weiner
Executive Vice President: Steve Thomson
CFO: Doyal Eubank
VP National sales: Rick Durette
Estimated Sales: Less than $500,000
Number Employees: 100-249
Brands:
Oregon

6863 King Fish Restaurants
7400 New LA Grange Rd
Suite 405
Louisville, KY 40222-8821
502-339-0565
Fax: 502-339-0230 www.kingfishrestaurants.com
Seafood
Owner: Brown Nolte-Meyer
bnoltemeyer@kingfishrestaurants.com
CEO: Kyle Noltmeyer
Estimated Sales: $10,000,000
Number Employees: 5-9

6864 King Floyd's
102 Hamilton Dr
Unit H
Novato, CA 94949
415-475-7811
Fax: 415-488-1424 admin@kingfloyds.com
kingfloyds.com
Bar provisions, including bitters, syrups and salts
Number of Brands: 1
Number of Products: 11
Type of Packaging: Consumer
Brands:
KING FLOYD'S

6865 King Food Service
7810 42nd St W
Rock Island, IL 61201-7319
309-787-4488
Fax: 309-787-4501 www.kingfoodservice.com
Seafood, poultry & meat
President: Matthew Cutkomp
CEO/CFO: Mike Cutkomp
Director of Sales & Marketing: Kelly McDonald
VP Operations: Chad Gaul
Estimated Sales: $24 Million
Number Employees: 10-19
Number of Products: 1500

6866 King Henry's Inc
29124 Hancock Pkwy
Valencia, CA 91355-1066
661-295-5566
Fax: 661-295-5099 henry@kinghenrys.com
www.kinghenrys.com
Organic chocolate confections; gummies/jellies of fruits and nuts; pretzels, and dried fruit.
Owner: Henry Davidian
henry@kinghenrys.com
Marketing: Joseph DeFelice
Estimated Sales: Less Than $500,000
Number Employees: 1-4

6867 King Juice Co
851 W Grange Ave
Milwaukee, WI 53221-4425
414-482-0303
Fax: 414-482-0719 www.kingjuice.com
Juices
President: Jon Christophersen
kezman@kingjuice.com
Estimated Sales: $500,000-$1 Million
Number Employees: 20-49
Brands:
Calypso
King Juice
Villa Quenchers

6868 **King Kold Meats**
331-333 North Main Street
Englewood, OH 45322-1388
937-836-2731
Fax: 937-836-5919 800-836-2797
dougsmith@kingkoldinc.com
www.kingkoldinc.com
Fresh and frozen meat products and entrees.
President: Doug Smith
Distributor Sales: Mike DeFrancis
Estimated Sales: $10-20 Million
Number Employees: 20-49
Number of Brands: 3
Number of Products: 125
Square Footage: 30000
Type of Packaging: Consumer, Food Service, Private Label, Bulk
Brands:
Evelyn Sprague
Hearth & Kettle
Kingkold

6869 **King Milling Co Inc**
115 S Broadway St
PO Box 99
Lowell, MI 49331-1666
616-897-9264
Fax: 616-897-4350 jcantrell@kingflour.com
www.kingflour.com
Wheat and white flour
President: Brian Doyle
bdoyle@kingmilling.com
VP: Steve Doyle
SVP: James Doyle
Estimated Sales: $20-50 Million
Number Employees: 20-49
Number of Brands: 6
Type of Packaging: Food Service, Bulk
Brands:
Ceres®
Kimco
Pathfinder
Pure Gold
Sincerity
Super Kleaned Wheat

6870 **King Nut Co**
31900 Solon Rd
Solon, OH 44139-3536
440-248-8484
Fax: 440-248-0153 800-860-5464
info@kingnut.com www.kingnut.com
Snack mixes, chocolates, nuts, dried fruit, granola and pretzels; exporter of salted nuts.
Chairman: Michael Kanan
President/CEO: Martin Kanan
SVP/CFO: Joseph Valenza
EVP/CMO: Matthew Kanan
VP Quality Assurance/Product Development: Debra Smith
Manufacturing/Plant Operations: Michael Smith
Estimated Sales: $35 Million
Number Employees: 100-249
Number of Brands: 3
Square Footage: 250000
Parent Co: Kanan Enterprises
Type of Packaging: Consumer, Food Service, Private Label, Bulk
Brands:
King's Delicious®
Peterson's
Summer Harvest®

6871 **King Oscar**
3838 Camino Del Rio North
Unit 115
San Diego, CA 92108
global.kingoscar.com
Canned seafood
President/Owner: John Engle
Number of Brands: 1
Type of Packaging: Consumer
Brands:
KING OSCAR

6872 **King of Pops Inc**
337 Elizabeth St NE
Suite B
Atlanta, GA 30307-1969
678-732-9321
Ice pops
CEO and Co-Founder: Steven Carse
Co-Founder: Nick Carse
Contact: Matt Anderson
andersonm@kingofpops.net

6873 **King's Command Foods Inc**
500 S Washington St
Green Bay, WA 54301-4219
800-345-0293
info@americanfoodsgroup.com
www.americanfoodsgroup.com
Portion controlled, pre-cooked and ready-to-eat beef, chicken, pork and veal products.
President: Ron Baer
Director of Quality Assurance: Alan Whittington
Year Founded: 1966
Estimated Sales: $50-99 Million
Number Employees: 100-249
Parent Co: American Foods Group
Type of Packaging: Consumer, Food Service

6874 **King's Hawaiian Holding Co Inc.**
19161 Harborgate Way
Torrance, CA 90501-1316
310-533-3250
Fax: 310-533-8732 877-695-4227
khcares@kingshawaiian.com
www.kingshawaiian.com
Hawaiian sweet bread, rolls, sauces and stuffing.
CEO: Mark Taira
Estimated Sales: $10-20 Million
Number Employees: 250-499
Number of Brands: 1
Square Footage: 150000
Brands:
King's Hawaiian

6875 **Kingchem**
5 Pearl Ct
Allendale Park
Allendale, NJ 07401-1656
201-825-9988
Fax: 201-825-9148 800-211-4330
customer-service@kingchem.com
www.kingchem.com
Herbal supplements
Owner: Anne Agler
a.agler@kingchem.com
Chief Executive Officer: Stephen Wang
Vice President, Accounting/Planning: Catherine Penetra
Vice President, Business Development: Keith Drouet
Chief Executive Officer: Lillian Wu
Estimated Sales: $1-9 Million
Number Employees: 20-49
Number of Brands: 1
Square Footage: 2500
Brands:
Kingchem

6876 **Kingly Heirs**
PO Box 283
Elkhart, IN 46515
574-596-3763
Fax: 527-296-1188 www.kinglyheirs.com/
Gourmet cake mixes.
President: Kingly Heirs

6877 **Kings Canyon**
1750 S Buttonwillow Ave
Reedley, CA 93654-4400
559-638-3571
Fax: 559-638-6326
Peaches, apricots and other fruits
President: Steve Kenfield
VP Sales: Fred Berry

6878 **Kings Processing**
14 Freeman St
PO Box 1251
Middleton, NS B0S 1P0
Canada
902-825-2188
Fax: 902-825-2180
Fresh salads and vegetables
Owner: Bruce Rand
Controller: Krysta Hatt
Quality Control: Cynthia Kenneally
Production Manager: Karen Cole
Plant Manager: Frank Ford
Estimated Sales: $6.9 Million
Number Employees: 50
Type of Packaging: Consumer, Food Service

6879 **Kings Seafood Co**
3185 Airway Ave
Suite H
Costa Mesa, CA 92626-4601
714-432-0400
Fax: 714-432-0111 800-269-8425
samking@kingsseafood.com
www.kingsseafood.com
Seafood
Owner: Steve Rhee
CEO: Sam King
sking@kingsseafood.com
CFO: Roger Doan
Estimated Sales: $5 Million
Number Employees: 20-49
Square Footage: 60000
Type of Packaging: Food Service

6880 **Kingsburg Orchards**
10363 E Davis Ave
P.O. Box 38
Kingsburg, CA 93631
559-897-5132
Fax: 559-897-4532 info@kingsburgorchards.com
www.kingsburgorchards.com
A variety of fruits
Owner: George Jackson
Estimated Sales: $100+ Million
Number Employees: 100-249
Brands:
Season Opener
Dinosaur Brand
Sugar Tree
Flavor Farmer
Flying Saucer
Apple Pears

6881 **Kingsbury Country Market**
5001 S Us 35
La Porte, IN 46345
219-393-3016
Beef, hog, rabbit, ostrich and lamb; custom butchering available
President: Jerry Winter
Treasurer: Sandra Winter
Number Employees: 5-9
Brands:
Butcher Boy

6882 **Kingston Fresh**
477 Shoup Ave
Suite 207
Idaho Falls, ID 83402-3658
208-522-2365
Fax: 208-552-7488 www.kingstonfresh.com
Potatoes; onions; broccoli; sweet pineapples; and lettuce.
President: Mike Kingston
CEO: Dave Kingston
Number Employees: 5-9
Type of Packaging: Consumer, Food Service
Brands:
Awesome
Russetts

6883 **Kingsville Fisherman's Company**
PO Box 37
Kingsville Dock
Kingsville, ON N9Y 2E8
Canada
519-733-6534
Fax: 519-733-6959
Processor and exporter of fresh and frozen perch and pickerel
President: Carl Fraser
Sales Manager: John Murray
Number Employees: 50-99
Type of Packaging: Bulk

6884 **Kinnikinnick Foods**
10940-120 Street NW
Edmonton, AB T5H 3P7
Canada
780-424-2900
Fax: 780-421-0456 877-503-4466
info@kinnikinnick.com www.kinnikinnick.com
Gluten-free bakery products
President & CEO: Jerry Bigam
CFO: Lynne Bigam
VP, Operations: Jay Bigam
Number Employees: 60
Number of Products: 120
Square Footage: 120000
Type of Packaging: Consumer, Food Service

Brands:
Kinnikinnick Foods, Inc.

6885 **Kiolbassa Provision Co**
1325 S Brazos St
San Antonio, TX 78207-6931
210-226-8127
Fax: 210-226-7464 800-456-5465
info@kiolbassa.com www.kiolbassa.com
Sausage products
President: Michael Kiolbassa
CEO: Robert Kiolbassa
rak@kiolbassa.com
Vice President: Sandra Kiolbassa
Secretary/Treasurer: Barbara Kiolbassa
Year Founded: 1949
Estimated Sales: $21 Million
Number Employees: 100-249
Type of Packaging: Consumer

6886 **Kiona Vineyards Winery**
44612 N Sunset Rd
Benton City, WA 99320-7500
509-588-6716
Fax: 509-588-3219 info@kionawine.com
www.kionawine.com
Wines and wine grapes
Owner: John Williams
kiona1wine@aol.com
Owner: Ann Williams
National Sales Manager: J J Williams
Manager/Winemaker: Scott Williams
Estimated Sales: Below $5 Million
Number Employees: 5-9
Number of Brands: 1
Number of Products: 16
Type of Packaging: Private Label
Brands:
Kiona

6887 **Kirby Holloway Provision Co**
966 Jackson Ditch Rd
Harrington, DE 19952-2417
302-398-3705
Fax: 302-398-4088 800-995-4729
www.kirbyandhollowayinc.com
Sausage and scrapple; wholesaler/distributor of meat and cheese products
Owner: Russell Kirby
rkirby@kirbyandhollowayinc.com
Owner: Rudy Kirby
General Manager: Bill Moore
Estimated Sales: $7 Million
Number Employees: 20-49
Type of Packaging: Consumer, Food Service, Private Label, Bulk

6888 **Kirigin Cellars**
11550 Watsonville Rd
Gilroy, CA 95020-9434
408-847-8827
Fax: 408-847-3820 folks@kirigincellars.com
www.kirigincellars.com
Wines
Manager: Allen Kreutzer
folks@kirigincellars.com
Estimated Sales: Below $5 Million
Number Employees: 10-19
Brands:
Kirigin Cellars

6889 **Kirin Brewery**
5230 Pacific Concourse Dr
Suite 310
Los Angeles, CA 90045
310-381-3040
Fax: 310-320-5955
Beer
President: Satoru Shimura
VP, Marketing: Randy Higa
Estimated Sales: $5-10 Million
Number Employees: 5-9
Parent Co: Mitsubishi International
Brands:
Kirin Beer
Kirin Ichiban
Kirin Lager

6890 **Kiska Farms**
25056 Ice Harbor Dr
Burbank, WA 99323
509-547-7746
Fax: 509-547-7746 kathy@kiskafarms.com
www.kiskafarms.com
Potatos
Owner: Lonnie Blasdel
lonnie@kiskafarms.com
Co-Owner: Judy Johnston
Estimated Sales: Less Than $500,000
Number Employees: 1-4

6891 **Kiss My Keto**
8066 Melrose Ave
Suite 4
Los Angeles, CA 90046
310-765-1553
hello@kissmyketo.com
www.kissmyketo.com
Ketogenic snack bars, creamers, protein powder, drink mixes, chocolate bars, supplements, and MCT oil
Co-Founder: Michael Herscu
Co-Founder: Alex Bird
Dietician Expert: Sofia Norton
Digital Marketing Manager: Kate Geller
Customer Service Lead: Lyn Villanueva
Number Employees: 35

6892 **Kistler Vineyards**
4707 Vine Hill Rd
Sebastopol, CA 95472-2236
707-823-5603
Fax: 707-823-6709 info@kistlervineyards.com
www.kistlervineyards.com
Chardonnay and Pinot Noir
President/CEO: Stephen Kistler
Operations: Jason Kesner
Year Founded: 1978
Estimated Sales: $20-50 Million
Number Employees: 50-99
Brands:
Durell Vineyard
Dutton Ranch
Hyde Vineyard
McCrea Vineyard
Sonoma Coast

6893 **Kitchen Cooked Inc**
632 N Main St
Farmington, IL 61531-1076
309-245-2196
Fax: 540-886-0558 800-752-1535
sklasing@kitchencooked.net
Potato chips
President: George Raymond Curry
orders@kitchencooked.net
Sales Exec: Paul Blackhurst
Estimated Sales: $1100000
Number Employees: 20-49
Type of Packaging: Consumer

6894 **Kitchen Pride Mushrooms Farm**
1034 County Road 348
Gonzales, TX 78629-2774
830-540-4528
Fax: 830-540-4556 sales@kitchenpride.com
www.kitchenpride.com
Mushrooms
President & CEO: Darrell McLain
dmclain@kitchenpride.com
Estimated Sales: $3 Million
Number Employees: 100-249
Square Footage: 400000
Type of Packaging: Consumer, Food Service, Private Label, Bulk
Brands:
Kitchen Pride Farms

6895 **Kitchen Table**
41 Princeton Dr
Syosset, NY 11791-6741
516-931-5113
Fax: 516-932-5467 800-486-4582
info@kitchentablebakers.com
Gourmet, wheat, gluten and sugar free wafer crisps
President/Owner: Barry Novick
Contact: Michelle Beamon
manlemi@nyp.org
Estimated Sales: Less Than $500,000
Number Employees: 1-4

6896 **Kitchens Seafood**
1001 E Baker St
Suite 202
Plant City, FL 33566
813-750-1888
Fax: 813-750-1889 800-327-0132
sales@kitchensseafood.com
www.kitchensseafood.com
Manufacturer, packer and importer of frozen seafood including lobster, crab, shrimp, shrimp meat and langostinos
President: Dan La Fleur
Type of Packaging: Consumer, Food Service, Private Label, Bulk
Other Locations:
Kitchens Seafood-Production
Jacksonville FL

6897 **Kitchun Grainfree Food**
Austin, TX 78726
thekitchun.com
Grain-free granola and cookie mixes
Co-Founder: Gloriana Koll
Co-Founder: Keesha Waits

6898 **Kite Hill**
3180 Corporate Pl
Hayward, CA 94545
888-588-0994
info@kite-hill.com www.kite-hill.com
Almond milk foods, including plant-based yogurts, pastas and artisanal cheeses
Co-Founder: Tal Ronnen
Number of Brands: 1
Type of Packaging: Consumer
Brands:
KITE HILL

6899 **Kith Treats**
337 Lafayette St
New York, NY 10012
646 648-6285
kith.com
Snackbar, including ice cream and cereal.
Founder: Ronnie Fieg
Year Founded: 2011
Estimated Sales: Less than $500,000
Number Employees: 51-200
Type of Packaging: Consumer, Private Label

6900 **Kitt's Meat Processing**
506 S 4th Ave
Dedham, IA 51440-2000
712-683-5622
www.kittsmeat.com
Bologna
Owner: David Kitt
Partner: Shawn Kitt
Estimated Sales: Less Than $500,000
Number Employees: 5-9

6901 **Kittling Ridge Estate Wines & Spirits**
271 Chrislea Road
Vaughan, ON L4L 8N6
Canada
905-945-9225
Fax: 905-738-5551 800-461-9463
www.kittlingridge.com
Wine and spirits
President/CEO: Rossanna Magnotta
Year Founded: 1992
Estimated Sales: $20-50 Million
Number Employees: 100-249
Parent Co: Magnotta Winery Corporation
Brands:
Canadian
Kingsgate

6902 **Kittridge & Fredrickson LTD**
2801 SE 14th Ave
Portland, OR 97202-2203
503-234-7788
800-558-7788
www.kfcoffee.com
Coffee and spiced cocoa.
Founder: Don Dominguez
Founder: Bud Dominguez
Estimated Sales: $10-20 Million
Number Employees: 10-19
Number of Brands: 2
Type of Packaging: Private Label

Brands:
K&F
TazArriba

6903 **Kiwa**
Ontario, CA 91761
info@kiwalife.com
www.kiwalife.com
Vegetable chips
Founder: Martin Acosta
Brands:
Kiwa
Kiwa Kids

6904 **Kiwi Kiss**
150 NW 16th Street
Boca Raton, FL 33432
hello@freshkiwikiss.com
www.freshkiwikiss.com
Strawberry-kiwi fruit treats
Number of Brands: 1
Number of Products: 1
Type of Packaging: Consumer
Brands:
KIWI KISS

6905 **Klaire Laboratories**
10439 Double R Blvd
Reno, NV 89521-8905
775-850-8800
Fax: 775-850-8810 888-488-2488
www.klaire.com
Processor and exporter of allergen-free nutritional supplements
President: Cary Fereuson
Number Employees: 20-49
Parent Co: Kek Industries
Brands:
Vital Life

6906 **Klara's Gourmet Cookies**
18 Railroad St
Lee, MA 01238-1638
413-243-3370
contact@klarasgourmet.com
www.klarasgourmet.com
Cookies
Founder: Klara Sotonova
contact@klarasgourmetcookies.com
Estimated Sales: Less than $500,000
Number Employees: 5-9
Brands:
KLARA'S GOURMET

6907 **Klein Foods, Inc**
1501 E Lyon St
Marshall, MN 56258-3614
Fax: 507-537-1940 800-657-0174
www.kleinfoods.com
Gourmet honey cremes, sauces, syrups, preserves, and more.
Owner & President: Stephen Klein
kleinfoods@yahoo.com
Estimated Sales: $5-9.9 000,000
Number Employees: 5-9
Other Locations:
Walnut Grove Mercantile
Marshall MN

6908 **Klein's Kosher Pickles**
4118 W Whitton Ave
Phoenix, AZ 85019
602-269-2072
Fax: 602-269-2069 800-437-4255
sales@kleinpickles.com
Kosher pickles
President: Byron Arnold
VP: Mark Arnold
Manager Sales & Marketing: Gary Allison
Retail Sales Manager: Don Snider
VP Operations: Jeff Knapp
VP Merchandising: Susan Arnold Demura
Estimated Sales: $1-2.5 Million
Number Employees: 20-49
Square Footage: 1200000
Type of Packaging: Consumer, Food Service
Brands:
Mrs. Klein's

6909 **Kleinpeter Farms Dairy LLC**
14444 Airline Hwy
Baton Rouge, LA 70817-6899
225-753-2121
Fax: 225-752-8964 www.kleinpeterdairy.com
Dairy products such as milk, cream and cottage cheese.
President/CEO: Sue Anne Kleinpeter Cox
Year Founded: 1913
Estimated Sales: Less Than $500,000
Number Employees: 1-4
Number of Brands: 1
Type of Packaging: Consumer, Food Service
Brands:
Kleinpeter

6910 **Klement Sausage Co Inc**
1036 W Juneau Ave
Suite 400
Milwaukee, WI 53233-1447
414-744-2330
Fax: 414-744-2438 800-553-6368
www.klements.com
Meat products
CEO: Ray Booth
bducharme@klementsausageco.com
Site Manager: Bryan Ducharme
bducharme@klementsausageco.com
Estimated Sales: $42.3 Million
Number Employees: 100-249
Number of Brands: 1
Square Footage: 13000
Parent Co: Tall Tree Foods
Type of Packaging: Food Service, Private Label
Brands:
Klement's

6911 **Klingshirn Winery**
33050 Webber Rd
Avon Lake, OH 44012-2330
440-933-6666
Fax: 440-933-7896 contactus@klingshirnwine.com
www.klingshirnwine.com
Wines
President: Lee Klingshirn
info@klingshirnwine.com
Estimated Sales: Below $5 Million
Number Employees: 5-9
Brands:
Klingshirn Winery

6912 **Klinke Brothers Ice Cream Co**
2450 Scaper St
Memphis, TN 38114-6546
901-322-6640
Fax: 901-743-8254
Ice cream and frozen yogurt.
President and CEO: John Klinke
john.klinke@klinkebrothers.com
VP of Operations: Russell Klinke
Estimated Sales: $20-50 Million
Number Employees: 50-99
Type of Packaging: Consumer, Food Service, Private Label, Bulk
Brands:
Angel Food

6913 **Klondike Cheese Factory**
W7839 State Rd 81
Monroe, WI 53566
608-325-3021
Fax: 608-328-9237 cheese@klondikecheese.com
www.klondikecheese.com
Cheese
President: Ronald Buholzer
Financial Controller: Tammy Fetterolf
Treasurer: David Buholzer
Production Manager: Jon Brunner
Year Founded: 1972
Estimated Sales: $82 Million
Number Employees: 100-249
Square Footage: 90000
Type of Packaging: Consumer, Private Label

6914 **Kloss Manufacturing Co Inc**
7566 Morris Ct
Suite 310
Allentown, PA 18106-9247
610-391-3820
Fax: 610-391-3830 800-445-7100
Processor and exporter of flavoring extracts for Italian ices and slushes; also, concession equipment and supplies, fountain syrups, popcorn, cotton candy, nachos and waffles
Owner: Stephen Lloss
skloss@klossfunfood.com
Estimated Sales: $3-5 Million
Number Employees: 10-19
Square Footage: 120000
Type of Packaging: Food Service, Private Label, Bulk
Brands:
Kloss

6915 **Klosterman Baking Co.**
4760 Paddock Rd
Cincinnati, OH 45229-1047
877-301-1004
info@klostermanbakery.com
www.klostermanbakery.com
Breads, buns, hoagies, flat breads and rolls.
President: Chip Klosterman
CEO: Kim Klosterman
CFO: Ross Anderson
Marketing Manager: Mike Braun
Human Resources Manager: Tim McCoy
IT: Brian Fey
bfey@klostermanbakery.com
Year Founded: 1910
Estimated Sales: $47900000
Number Employees: 20-49
Number of Brands: 1
Type of Packaging: Consumer, Food Service
Brands:
Klosterman

6916 **Knapp Vineyards**
2770 Ernsberger Rd
Romulus, NY 14541
607-869-9271
Fax: 607-869-3212 800-869-9271
winery@knappwine.com www.knappwine.com
Wines
Owner: Gene Pierce
Vice President: Susanna Knapp
Contact: John Mcnabb
john@knappwine.com
Estimated Sales: Below $5 Million
Number Employees: 20-49
Type of Packaging: Private Label
Brands:
Knapp

6917 **Knappen Milling Co**
110 S Water St
P.O. Box 245
Augusta, MI 49012-9781
269-731-4141
Fax: 269-731-5441 800-562-7736
Knappen@knappen.com
Soft wheat, cereal bran, wheat and flour
President/CEO: Charles B. Knappen III
Treasurer: Darrell Roese
Vice President: John Shouse
jshouse@knappen.com
VP of Sales & Grain Purchasing: Todd C. Wright
Plant Manager: Bob Likens
Number Employees: 20-49
Type of Packaging: Private Label, Bulk
Brands:
100% Flaked Wheat
Arbutus Flour
Heavy Bran
Satin White Flour
Sotac

6918 **Knese Enterprise**
27 Huron Rd
Bellerose, NY 11426
516-354-9004
Fax: 516-354-9004
Spicy gourmet mustard, kettle potato chips, pretzels and pretzel dip
President: Brad Knese
VP: Nancy Knese
Estimated Sales: $400,000
Number Employees: 2
Type of Packaging: Consumer
Brands:
Brad's Pretzel Dip
Kettle Chips
Pretzels

6919 **(HQ)Knight Seed Company**
12550 W Frontage Road
Suite 203
Burnsville, MN 55337-2402
952-894-8080
Fax: 952-894-8095 800-328-2999
Processor, importer and exporter of soybeans, dried beans, peas and buckwheat; exporter of lentils

President/CEO: Dave Dornacker
Export Manager: Jeff Pricco
VP: Tom Kennelly
Marketing: Tim Kukowski
Sales: Dan Dahlquist
Estimated Sales: $3-5 Million
Number Employees: 16
Square Footage: 12000
Other Locations:
Knight Seed Co.
Vanscoy SK
Brands:
Knight
Ksc
Legacy

6920 **Knight's Appleden Fruit LTD**
11687 County Road 2
Colborne, ON K0K 1S0
Canada
905-349-2521
Fax: 905-349-3129 www.knights-appleden.ca
Processor, importer and exporter of apples
President: Roger Knight
Estimated Sales: 1-2.5 Million
Number Employees: 20-49

6921 **Knott's Berry Farms**
1 Strawberry Lane
Orrville, OH 44667-0280
866-828-5502
www.knottsberryfarmfoods.com
Jams, jellies and preserves
President/CEO: Mark Smucker
CFO: Mark Belgya
Chief Marketing and Commercial Officer: Geoff Tanner
Number Employees: 100-249
Square Footage: 1000000
Parent Co: J.M. Smucker Company
Type of Packaging: Consumer, Food Service

6922 **Knotts Fine Foods**
125 N Blakemore St
Paris, TN 38242-4197
731-642-1961
Fax: 731-644-1962 joshknott@knottsfoods.com
www.knottsfoods.com
Refrigerated sandwiches and sandwich spreads; wholesaler/distributor of specialty foods
Owner: Josh Knott
joshknott@knottsfoods.com
VP Sales: BJ Knott
Estimated Sales: $5000000
Number Employees: 20-49
Square Footage: 240000
Brands:
Knott's
Knott's Meat Snacks
Knott's Novelty Candy
Knott's Salads

6923 **Knouse Foods Co-Op Inc.**
800 Peach Glen Rd.-Idaville Rd.
Peach Glen, PA 17375
717-677-8181
www.knouse.com
Apples and apple products, vinegar, cherries, tomato juice, pie fillings, and more.
President/Chairman: Kenneth Guise
kguise@knouse.com
CEO: Charles Haberkorn
Vice President, Marketing: Robert Fisher
Vice President, Sales: Richard Esser
Year Founded: 1949
Estimated Sales: $290 Million
Number Employees: 1,500
Number of Brands: 5
Square Footage: 557450
Type of Packaging: Consumer, Food Service, Private Label, Bulk
Brands:
Apple Time
Lincoln
Lucky Leaf
Mussleman's
Knouse Food Service

6924 **Know Allergies**
Charleston, SC
www.knowallergies.com
Granola bars
Founder: Amos Bartlett

6925 **Know Brainer**
Lafayette, CO 80026
303-475-0456
shari@myknowbrainer.com
www.myknowbrainer.com
Ketogenic coffee creamers, instant coffee, chai tea, matcha tea, and instant hot chocolate
Founder/CEO: Shari Leidich
Year Founded: 2016

6926 **Knudsen Candy**
25067 Viking St
Hayward, CA 94545-2703
510-293-6887
Fax: 510-293-6890 800-736-6887
Gourmet chocolates including bon bons, creams, regular and caramel nut clusters, truffles, etc.; also, private labeling available
President: Gary Love
Chairman: David Knudsen
Treasurer/Secretary: Kathy Knudsen
Vice President: Tod Knudsen
Marketing Director: Tod Knudsen
Estimated Sales: $2.5-5 Million
Number Employees: 10-19
Square Footage: 72000
Type of Packaging: Consumer, Private Label
Brands:
Enjoymints
Tropical Wonders

6927 **Koala Moa**
755 N Nimitz Hwy
Honolulu, HI 96817-5035
808-523-6701
Fax: 808-671-3527 koalamoa@gmail.com
Broiled chicken
Owner: Christina Shimabukuro
VP: Kristana Speach
Estimated Sales: $1-2.5 Million
Number Employees: 10-19
Square Footage: 28

6928 **Kobricks Coffee Company**
693 Luis Marin Blvd
Jersey City, NJ 07310-1225
201-656-6313
Fax: 201-656-3665 800-562-7491
info@kobrickcoffee.com www.kobrickcoffee.com
Italian espresso, coffee and tea.
President: Lee Kobrick
Co-Owner: Steve Kobrick
Estimated Sales: $10-24.9 Million
Number Employees: 30-50
Type of Packaging: Private Label
Brands:
Kobricks
La San Marco
Leodoro Espresso
Numi Teas
Shearer
Steven Smith Teamaker Teas
Tazo Teas
Torani Syrups

6929 **Kobu Beverages, LLC**
233 Dean St.
Brooklyn, NY 11217-2202
718-566-2739
www.kombrewcha.com
Alcoholic kombucha
Co-Founder: Barry Nalebuff
Co-Founder: John Hillgen
Co-Founder: Ariel Glazer
Brands:
Kobu Beverages, LLC

6930 **Koch Foods Inc**
1300 Higgins Rd
Suite 100
Park Ridge, IL 60068-5766
847-384-5940
Fax: 847-384-5961 800-837-2778
info@kochfoods.com www.kochfoods.com
Fresh and frozen chicken
President & CEO: Joe Grendys
CFO: Lance Buckert
Plant Manager: Jim Dunbar
Foodservice Sales: John Marler
Commodity Sales: Hans Schmidt
Operations Manager: Fred Koch
Year Founded: 1985
Estimated Sales: $20-50 Million
Number Employees: 20-49
Type of Packaging: Consumer, Food Service

6931 **Koda Farms**
PO Box 10
22540 Russell Ave
South Dos Palos, CA 93665
209-392-2191
inquiry@kodafarms.com
www.kodafarms.com
Organic, heirloom, Japanese-style rice
Co-Principal: Robin Koda
Co-Principal: Ross Koda
Number of Brands: 1
Type of Packaging: Consumer
Brands:
KOKUHO ROSE

6932 **Kodiak Cakes**
PO Box 980992
Park City, UT 84098
801-328-4067
Fax: 801-328-4068 flapjacks@kodiakcakes.com
www.kodiakcakes.com
Baking mixes, granola and oatmeal
CEO: Joel Clark
Number of Brands: 1
Type of Packaging: Consumer
Brands:
KODIAK CAKES

6933 **Kodiak Salmon Packers**
PO Box 30
Larsen Bay, AK 99624-0038
907-847-2250
Fax: 907-847-2244
Frozen and canned wild Alaskan salmon
President: Alan Beardsley
Executive VP: Van Johnson
Plant Manager: Grant Mirick
Estimated Sales: $750000

6934 **Koegel Meats Inc**
3400 W Bristol Rd
Flint, MI 48507
810-238-3685
Fax: 810-238-2467 www.koegels.com
Sausage, natural casing and long frankfurters, bratwurst, bockwurst and smoked specialties.
Founder: Albert Koegel
Controller: Jonathon Jury
jjury@koegelmeats.com
Sales Director: Tom Lakies
Operations Manager: Jim Lay
Year Founded: 1916
Number Employees: 50-99
Number of Products: 35
Square Footage: 400000
Type of Packaging: Consumer, Food Service

6935 **Koeze Company**
PO Box 9470
Grand Rapids, MI 49509-2237
616-724-2620
Fax: 866-817-0147 800-555-9688
bdekker@koeze.com www.koeze.com
Nut candies
President: Scott Koeze
CEO: Jeff Koeze
Marketing: Beth Dekker
Sales Director: Tom Lakos
Contact: Martin Andree
mjandree@koeze.com
Purchasing Manager: John Feenstra
Estimated Sales: $9672287
Number Employees: 20-49
Square Footage: 320000
Type of Packaging: Consumer, Bulk

6936 **Koffee Kup Bakery**
436 Riverside Ave
Burlington, VT 05401-1452
802-863-2696
Fax: 802-860-0116 koffeekupbakery.com
Bakery products including breads, rolls and doughnuts.
Chief Executive Officer: Andy Matthews
CFO: Eddie Matthews
ematthews@koffeekupbakery.biz
EVP, Sales & Marketing: Brian Carpentier
Controller: Shirley Patrick
Human Resources Manager: Judy Schraven
Plant Manager: Ron Roberge Jr.
Purchasing Manager: Steve Hebert

Estimated Sales: $10-20 Million
Number Employees: 50-99
Number of Brands: 1
Type of Packaging: Private Label
Brands:
Koffee Kup

6937 **Koha Food**
500 Alakawa St
Suite 104
Honolulu, HI 96817-4576
808-845-4232
Fax: 808-841-5398
Oriental foods
President: Paul Kim
Estimated Sales: $5-10 Million
Number Employees: 20-49

6938 **Kohana Coffee**
1221 S Mopac Expressway
Suite 100
Austin, TX 78746
512-904-1174
Fax: 512-532-0581 info@kohanacoffee.com
www.kohanacoffee.com
Coffee, decaff and cold brew coffee.
Owner: Victoria Lynden
Sales: Nate Creasey
Contact: Joe Browne
joe@kohanacoffee.com
Operations: Piper Jones
Estimated Sales: Under $500,000
Number Employees: 2

6939 **Kohinoor Foods**
40 Northfield Avenue
Edison, NJ 08837
732-868-4400
Fax: 732-868-3143 888-440-7423
info@kohinoorfoods.com
www.kohinoorfoods.com
Rice
CEO: Ganesh Skandan
Marketing: Rajan Kapoor
Contact: Amber Munir
amber@kohinoorfoods.com
Estimated Sales: $2.5-5 Million
Number Employees: 10-19
Brands:
Kohinoor
Satman Overseas

6940 **Kohler Original Recipe Chocolates**
725 Woodlake Rd
Suite D
Kohler, WI 53044-1334
920-208-4930
kohlerchocolates@kohler.com
www.kohlerchocolates.com
Chocolate and nuts
CEO and Chairman: Herb Koehler
Manager: Ron Tremaroli
ronald.tremaroli@kohler.com
Number Employees: 10-19

6941 **Koia**
1920 Hillhurst Ave
Unit V911
Los Angeles, CA 90027
info@drinkkoia.com
drinkkoia.com
Plant protein-based drinks
CEO: Christopher Hunter
Number of Brands: 1
Number of Products: 5
Type of Packaging: Consumer
Brands:
KOIA

6942 **Kokopelli's Kitchen**
9116 N Cave Creek Rd
Phoenix, AZ 85020
602-943-8882
Fax: 602-943-8740 888-943-9802
www.kokopelliskitchen.com
Gourmet dry baking mixes; rice; salad dressings; salsas; enchilada sauce; cocoas; beans; and soups.
President: Cheryl Joseph
Estimated Sales: $.5-1 million
Number Employees: 1-4
Number of Products: 45
Square Footage: 12000
Type of Packaging: Consumer, Bulk
Brands:
Kokopelli's Kitchen

6943 **Kola**
215 W 64th St
New York, NY 10065-6662
212-688-1895
rincakola@aol.com
Processor and exporter of soft drinks
Principal: Louis Jardines
Estimated Sales: $2.5-5 Million
Number Employees: 5-9
Type of Packaging: Consumer, Food Service, Private Label
Brands:
Golden Kola
Inca Kola

6944 **Kolatin Real Kosher Gelatin**
325 Second Street
Lakewood, NJ 08701
732-364-8700
Fax: 732-370-0877 info@koshergelatin.com
www.koshergelatin.com
Kosher gelatin
Parent Co: Glatech Productions

6945 **Kolb-Lena Bresse Bleu Inc**
3990 N Sunnyside Rd
Lena, IL 61048-9613
815-369-4577
Fax: 815-369-4914
Cheese including camembert, baby and bay Swiss, brie, feta and soft.
Quality Manager: Leisa Hubb
Manager: Randy Jenny
randy.jenny@bcusa.net
Estimated Sales: $35.7 Million
Number Employees: 100-249
Number of Brands: 1
Parent Co: Alouette Cheese USA
Type of Packaging: Consumer, Food Service
Brands:
Delico

6946 **Kollar Cookies**
PO Box 535
Long Branch, NJ 07740
732-343-4217
Fax: 732-750-1960 kollarcookies@aol.com
www.kollarcookies.com
Cookies
Owner: Pam Kimble
Estimated Sales: $1-2.5 Million
Number Employees: 5
Brands:
Kollar

6947 **Koloa Rum Corp**
2-2741 Kaumualii Hwy
Suite C
Kalaheo, HI 96741-8346
808-332-9333
Fax: 808-332-7650 www.koloarum.com
Hawaiian rums
Owner: Bob Gunter
info@koloarum.com
Public Relations: Jeanne Toulon
Estimated Sales: $2.5-5 Million
Number Employees: 5-9

6948 **Kombucha Wonder Drink**
PO Box 4244
Portland, OR 97208-4244
503-224-7331
Fax: 503-224-2295 877-224-7331
www.wonderdrink.com
USDA-certified sparkling fermented tea.
Founder/Owner: Steve Lee
stephenlee@wonderdrink.com
CEO: Craig Decker
Research & Development: Koei Kudo
Sales Director: Todd Hager
Estimated Sales: $650,000
Number Employees: 5-9
Type of Packaging: Consumer
Brands:
Kombucha Wonder Drink
Tea Tibet

6949 **Kona Brewing**
74-5612 Pawai Place
Kailua Kona, HI 96740
808-334-1133
Fax: 808-329-8869 webmail@konabrewingco.com
www.konabrewingco.com
Beer including lager, ale, IPA, and wheat beer.
President & CEO: Mattson Davis
Quality Control: Rich Tucciarone
Marketing Director: Steve Cole
Contact: Keala Aiwohi
keala.aiwohi@konabrewingco.com
Estimated Sales: $30-50 Million
Number Employees: 50-99
Type of Packaging: Private Label
Brands:
Kona Brewing

6950 **Kona Coffee Council**
PO Box 2077
Kealakekua, HI 96750
808-323-2911
www.kona-coffee-council.com
Coffee
President: Donna Woolley
Chair of Finance and Budget Committee: Jonathan Sechrist
VP: Gary Strawn
Contact: Roger Dilts
customkona@hotmail.com
Estimated Sales: $.5-1 million
Number Employees: 1-4

6951 **Kona Cold Lobsters**
73-4460 Queen Kaahumanu
Suite 103
Kailua Kona, HI 96740-2637
808-329-4332
Fax: 808-326-2882 info@konacoldlobsters.com
www.konacoldlobsters.com
Lobsters
President: Joseph Wilson
Manager: Philip Wilson
phil@konacoldlobsters.com
Estimated Sales: Less than $300,000
Number Employees: 10-19

6952 **Kona Fish Co Inc**
73-4776 Kanalani St
Suite 8
Kailua Kona, HI 96740-2625
808-326-7708
Fax: 808-329-3669 www.hilofish.com
Fresh, frozen seafood
Owner: Kerry Umamoto
Estimated Sales: $5-10 Million
Number Employees: 20-49

6953 **Kona Premium Coffee Company**
78-1095 Bishop Rd.
Holualoa, HI 96725
808-322-4160
Fax: 808-322-9275 888-322-9550
coffeeorders@KonaPremium.com
www.konapremium.com
Commercial and retail coffee
Owner/President: Robert Millslagle
General Manager: Westley Cornwell
CFO: Jeff Woode
Vice President: Barb Millslagle
Estimated Sales: $20-50 Million
Number Employees: 20-49
Type of Packaging: Private Label
Brands:
Kona Coffee
Royal Konaccino

6954 **KonaRed Corp.**
2042 Corte Del Nogal
Suite C
Carlsbad, CA 92011
949-682-4700
Fax: 949-449-8338 sales@konared.com
www.konared.com
Hawaiian coffee and coffee fruit products
Founder: Shaun Roberts
Number of Brands: 1
Number of Products: 9
Type of Packaging: Consumer
Brands:
KONARED

6955 **Konetzko's Meat Market**
516 Main St S
Browerville, MN 56438-1200
320-594-2915
Smoked meat and sausage
Owner: Jim Becker
Estimated Sales: Less than $500,000
Number Employees: 5-9
Type of Packaging: Consumer

6956 **Konto's Foods**
P.O.Box 628
Patterson, NJ 07544
973-278-2800
Fax: 973-278-7943 info@kontos.com
www.kontos.com
Flat bread, dough; meat products; cheese; olives; and Greek specialties.
Founder, Partner: Evripides Kontos
Partner: Steve Kontos
Partner: Michael Vorkas
Number Employees: 150
Square Footage: 300000
Type of Packaging: Food Service
Brands:
Konto's

6957 **Konzelmann Estate Winery**
1096 Lakeshore Rd
Niagara on the Lake, ON L0S 1J0
Canada
905-935-2866
Fax: 905-935-2864 wine@konzelmann.ca
www.konzelmann.ca
Wines
Owner: Herbert Konzelmann
Owner: Gudrun Konzelmann
VP: Jim Reschke
VP: Bruno Reis
Media Relations & Marketing: Claudia Konzelmann
VP of Marketing: Jansin Ozkur
Events & Retail: Bev Ferrante
Estimated Sales: $1.79 Million
Number Employees: 7
Type of Packaging: Bulk

6958 **Kookaburra**
14497 Fryelands Blvd SE
Monroe, WA 98272-2941
360-805-6858
www.kookaburralicorice.com
Licorice
President/Owner: Donald Cook
CEO: Bradley Cook
Manager: Robin Faulds
rfkookaburra@aol.com
Number Employees: 5-9

6959 **Kopali Organics**
8101 Biscayne Blvd
Suite 609
Miami, FL 33138-4668
305-751-7341
Fax: 305-751-7344
Organic foods
Contact: Fernanda Sanchez
fernanda@kopali.com
COO: Norman Brooks

6960 **Kopper's Chocolate**
45 Jackson Dr
Cranford, NJ 07016
800-325-0026
info@kopperschocolate.com
kopperschocolate.com
Chocolate beans
Co-Owner: Leslye Alexander
Co-Owner: Jeff Alexander
Year Founded: 1937

6961 **(HQ)Koppers Chocolate**
45 Jackson Drive
Cranford, NJ 07016
212-243-0220
800-325-0026
info@kopperschocolate.com
www.kopperschocolate.com
Processor, importer and exporter of confectionery items including chocolate covered espresso beans, chocolate covered gummy bears and Danish mint lentils.
President: Jeff Alexander
jeff@kopperschocolate.com
Director of Sales: Ellen Silverman
Estimated Sales: $7800000
Number Employees: 51-200

6962 **Koppert Cress USA**
23423 Middle Road
Route 48.
Cutchogue, NY 11935
631-734-8500
Fax: 631-734- 849 info.usa@koppertcress.com
www.koppertcress.com
Micro-vegetables
Member: Janny Hendrikse

6963 **Kor Shots**
Malibu, CA
korshots.com
Cold-pressed juice shots
Founder: Jordan Retamar
Number of Brands: 1
Number of Products: 6
Type of Packaging: Consumer
Brands:
KOR SHOTS

6964 **Korbs Baking Company**
540 Pawtucket Avenue
Pawtucket, RI 02860-6098
401-726-4422
Fax: 401-726-4446
Baked goods
President: Edmund Korb
Estimated Sales: $1-2.5 000,000
Number Employees: 50

6965 **Korea Ginseng Corp.**
12750 Center Court Dr S
Cerritos, CA 90703
contact@kgcus.com
www.kgcus.com
Ginseng products
VP, Sales: Adam Goodman

6966 **Kornfections**
14516 Lee Rd # C
Chantilly, VA 20151-1638
703-378-0009
Fax: 703-817-9560 800-469-8886
kornfections@verizon.net
Gourmet popcorn and confections.
President: Gerald Lerner
Vice President: Helen Lerner
Marketing/Public Relations: Jerry Lerner
Estimated Sales: $3-5 Million
Number Employees: 6
Number of Brands: 1
Number of Products: 22
Square Footage: 4800
Type of Packaging: Consumer, Food Service, Private Label, Bulk

6967 **Korte Meat Processors Inc**
810 Deal St
Highland, IL 62249
618-654-3813
Fax: 618-654-8207 www.korte-meats.com
Old Style German sausages, party and deli trays, cheese, and cure meats.
Owner: Dave Korte
Owner: Therese Korte
Year Founded: 1969
Estimated Sales: $3-5 Million
Number Employees: 5-9

6968 **Koryo Winery Company**
13719 Alma Ave
Gardena, CA 90249
310-532-9616
Fax: 310-532-3240
Wines
President: Sarah Kym
Operations Manager: Roy Kym
Estimated Sales: Less than $500,000
Number Employees: 20-49
Type of Packaging: Private Label
Brands:
Dong Dong Joo Rice Wine
Mackoly Rice Wine
Sochu Distilled Rice

6969 **Kosher French Baguettes**
683 McDonald Ave
Brooklyn, NY 11218
718-633-4994
Baguettes
Owner: Paul Gima
Estimated Sales: $300,000-500,000
Number Employees: 5-9

6970 **Kossar's Bagels & Bialys**
367 Grand St
New York, NY 10002-3951
212-473-4810
Fax: 212-253-2146 877-424-2597
www.kossarsbialys.com
Bakery products
Owner: Danny Cohen
mail@kossarsbialys.com
Estimated Sales: Less Than $500,000
Number Employees: 5-9
Brands:
Bialy
Kashruth

6971 **Kosto Food Products Co**
1325 N Old Rand Rd
Wauconda, IL 60084-3302
847-487-2600
Fax: 847-487-2654 www.kostofoods.com
Processor and exporter of salad dressings, food colorings, pudding and ice cream mixes; importer of colorants, stabilizers, ice cream mixes, drink crystals, meat extenders and puddings
President: Donald F Colby
General Manager: Steve Colby
Sales Director: Richard Gray
Estimated Sales: $1300000
Number Employees: 10-19
Type of Packaging: Consumer, Food Service, Private Label, Bulk
Brands:
Dari Pride
Food Pak
Freezerta
Kosto
Mack's
Mrs Slaby's
Slushade

6972 **Koukla Delights**
4648 St Laurent Blvd
Montreal, QC H2T 1R3
Canada
646-318-9131
info@koukladelights.com
koukladelights.com
Macaroons and cookies
President: Evelyn Jerassy

6973 **Kowalski Sausage Co**
2270 Holbrook St
Hamtramck, MI 48212-3487
313-873-8200
Fax: 313-873-4220 800-482-2400
www.kowality.com
Sausage
President: Michael Kowalski
Estimated Sales: $32800000
Number Employees: 100-249
Number of Brands: 2
Number of Products: 75
Type of Packaging: Consumer, Food Service
Brands:
Hunter's Sausage
Kowalski

6974 **Kozlowski Farms**
5566 Hwy 116
Forestville, CA 95436-9697
707-887-1587
Fax: 707-887-9650 800-473-2767
koz@kozlowskifarms.com
www.kozlowskifarms.com
Fruit spreads; jams; mustards; preserves; chutneys; jellys; fruit butters; dessert sauces; steak and BBQ sauces; fruit vinegar; salad dressings and chipotle sauces; apples an Pinot Noir grapes.
Vice President: Carol Every
carol@kozlowskifarms.com
CEO: Perry Kozlowski
CFO: Cindy Kozlowski-Hayworth
Estimated Sales: $1,000,000
Number Employees: 20-49
Number of Brands: 1
Number of Products: 90
Square Footage: 80000
Type of Packaging: Consumer, Private Label
Brands:
Kozlowski Farms
Sonoma County Classics

6975 **Kraemer Wisconsin Cheese LTD**
1173 N 4th St
Watertown, WI 53098-3201
920-261-6363
Fax: 920-261-9606 800-236-8033
www.kraemercheese.com
Cheese
Owner: Michael Kraemer
kwcheese@execpc.com
Estimated Sales: Below $5 Million
Number Employees: 5-9

6976 **Kraft Heinz Canada**
95 Moatfield Dr.
North York, ON M3B 3L6
Canada
416-441-5000
www.kraftcanada.com
Condiments, peanut butter, salad dressings, cheeses, desserts, frozen meals, macaroni and cheese, coffee blends, drink mixes, sweeteners, BBQ sauces, and more.
President, Canada Zone: Bruno Keller
CMO: Dana Somerville
VP of Sales: Peter Hall
Estimated Sales: $3.5 Billion
Number Employees: 2,000
Number of Brands: 6
Parent Co: The Kraft Heinz Company
Type of Packaging: Consumer, Food Service
Brands:
Baker's
Jell-O
Certo
Cool Whip
Caramels
Jet-Puffed
Magic Baking Powder
Amooza
Cheez Whiz
Cracker Barrel
Philadelphia
Kraft 100% Parmesan
Kraft Singles
P'tit Qu•bec
Velveeta
Nabob
Maxwell House
Tassimo
Gevalia Kaffe
Kool-Aid
MiO
Crystal Light
Tang
Country Time
Kraft Salad Dressings
Ren,e's
Classico
Kraft Dinner
Shake 'n Bake
Stove Top
Kraft Peanut Butter
Miracle Whip
Kraft BBQ Sauce
Kraft Mayo
Claussen
Oscar Mayer
Heinz Ketchup
MAX Boost Coffee
Crave
Bagel Bites
Catelli
Bull's Eye
Diana Sauce
Lea & Perrins

6977 **(HQ)Kraft Heinz Co.**
200 E. Randolph St.
Suite 7600
Chicago, IL 60601
800-543-5335
www.kraftheinzcompany.com
Food and beverage company manufacturing pasta, snack foods, sauces, cream cheese, beverages, condiments, etc.
President, US Zone: Carlos Abrams-Rivera
CEO: Miguel Patricio
CFO: Paul Basilio
Chief Growth Officer: Nina Barton
Chief Procurement Officer: Marcos Eloi
Year Founded: 1869
Estimated Sales: $26.27 Billion
Number Employees: 38,000
Number of Brands: 54
Type of Packaging: Consumer, Food Service
Brands:
Oscar Mayer
Ore-Ida
Kraft Macaroni & Cheese
Classico
Claussen
Caprisun
Heinz ABC
Wattie's
Weight Watchers Smart Ones
Kool-Aid
Jello
Philadelphia
Golden Circle
Lunchables
Planters
Pudliszki
Maxwell House
Grey Poupon
Complan
Master
Honig
Plasmon
Quero
Velveeta

6978 **Kramarczuk's Sausage Co**
215 E Hennepin Ave
Minneapolis, MN 55414-1013
612-379-3018
Fax: 612-379-7693 info@kramarczuk.com
www.kramarczuk.com
Sausages
President: Orest Kramarczuk
andrew@arvisev.com
Estimated Sales: $500,000-$1 Million
Number Employees: 20-49

6979 **Kramer Vineyards**
26830 NW Olson Rd
Gaston, OR 97119-8039
503-662-4545
Fax: 503-662-4033 800-619-4637
info@kramerwine.com www.kramervineyards.com
Wines
President/CEO/Winemaker: Trudy Kramer
trudy@kramervineyards.com
CEO: Kramer
VP/Secretary/Vineyard Manager: Keith Kramer
Marketing VP: Trudy Kramer
Estimated Sales: Less than $500,000
Number Employees: 5-9
Brands:
Kramer

6980 **Kraus & Co**
19700 Fairchild # 270
Suite 270
Irvine, CA 92612-2520
949-250-2955
Fax: 949-250-2960 800-662-5871
krausco@krausco.com www.krausco.com
Flavors, extracts, food colors, fruit preps, variegating sauces, toppings
Owner: Tom Kraus
krausco@krausco.com
Co-Founder/CEO: Eva Kraus
CFO: Saad Alhir
Estimated Sales: Less Than $500,000
Number Employees: 1-4
Type of Packaging: Food Service, Bulk

6981 **Krave Pure Food**
117 W Napa St
Suite C
Sonoma, CA 95476
877-891-1481
info@kravejerky.com www.kravejerky.com
Beef jerky
General Manager: Shane Chambers
VP, Marketing: Rusti Porter
Director of Operations: Ben Berry

6982 **Kreher Family Farms**
5411 Davison Rd.
P.O. Box 410
Clarence, NY 14031-0410
716-759-6802
Fax: 716-759-8687 www.krehereggs.com
Eggs, corn, soy, and wheat.
Year Founded: 1924
Type of Packaging: Private Label

6983 **Krema Nut Co**
1000 Goodale Blvd
Columbus, OH 43212-3889
614-299-4131
Fax: 614-299-1636 800-222-4132
nuts@krema.com www.krema.com
Peanut butter and nuts including cashews
President: Mike Giunta
nuts@krema.com
Estimated Sales: Less than $500,000
Number Employees: 5-9
Type of Packaging: Consumer, Food Service, Private Label
Brands:
Krema

6984 **Krenik's Meat Processing**
10740 130th St W
Montgomery, MN 56069-1870
507-364-5154
www.kreniks.com
Meats including steaks, pork chops, ribs, wieners, beef, pork, lamb and poultry products. Also, heat & eat, hot beef, bbq pulled pork, pork & kraut, roast pork, cooked potato dumplings, turkey 'n gravy, smoked pork, sausages, bolognabacon swiss & tomato bratwurst, italian bratwurst, breakfast sausage, beef snack sticks, pork jerky, king crab legs, cod, smoked carp, and custom cuts.
Owner: Jim Krenik
jim@kreniks.com
Estimated Sales: Less Than $500,000
Number Employees: 1-4

6985 **Krier Foods**
520 Wolf Rd
Random Lake, WI 53075-1280
920-994-2469
Fax: 920-994-9898 www.krierfoods.com
Beverages including juice and soda
Chairman of the Board: B Bruce Krier
Executive VP: Thoma Bretza
Contact: Karen Fahrenkrug
karen@krierfoods.com
Estimated Sales: $740,000
Number Employees: 50-99
Square Footage: 16456
Type of Packaging: Consumer
Brands:
Fruitland
Jolly Good

6986 **Krinos Foods**
1750 Bathgate Ave
Bronx, NY 10457
718-729-9000
Fax: 718-361-9725 info@krinos.com
www.krinos.com
Greek olives, sauces, salsas, and oils.
Owner: Eric Moscahlaidis
Year Founded: 1850
Estimated Sales: $304 Million
Number Employees: 100
Type of Packaging: Consumer, Food Service, Bulk
Other Locations:
Krinos Manufacturing Facility
Long Island City NY
Krinos Manufacturing Facility
Toronto, Canada
Krinos Manufacturing Facility
Montreal, Canada
Brands:
Apollo
Athens
Attiki
Florina
Haitoglou
Hermes
Horio
Macedonian
Melissa
Mevgal
Minerva
Mythos
Sarantis
Stella
Vlaha
Yiotis
Zanae

6987 **Krispy Kernels**
2620 Watt Street
Quebec, QC G1P 3T5
Canada
418-658-1515
Fax: 418-657-5971 877-791-9986
www.krispykernels.com
Peanuts, popcorn, candy and dried fruits and nuts
Owner: Denis Jalbert
CEO: Pierce Rivard
Quality Control: Stephen Jackson
Marketing Director: Renee Maude Jalbert
Sales Director: Stephane Gravel
Plant Manager: Jacques Bieion
Purchasing Manager: Marc Parent
Square Footage: 200000
Brands:
Krispy Kernels

6988 **Krispy Kreme Doughnuts Inc**
2116 Hawkins St
Charlotte, NC 28203
www.krispykreme.com
Bakery items and coffee including; doughnuts.
CEO: Michael Tattersfield
Year Founded: 1937
Estimated Sales: $518.7 Million
Number Employees: 4,300
Parent Co: JAB Holding Company

6989 **Kristian Regale**
14 Birkmose Park Ln
Hudson, WI 54016-2286
715-386-8388
Fax: 715-386-9295 info@kristianregale.com
www.kristianregale.com
Manufacturer and Importer of Swedish nonalcoholic apple and pear sparkling ciders,there are six flavors including the following, ap-ple,peach.pear,poegranate-apple,lingonberry-ap-ple,black currant.
Owner: Nancy Bieraugel
CHR/CEO: Ed Doherty
CFO: Dave Baldwin
Evp: Bob Gillespie
Estimated Sales: $3.4 Million
Number Employees: 7
Type of Packaging: Consumer, Food Service
Brands:
Kristian Regale

6990 **Kristin Hill Winery**
3330 SE Amity Dayton Hwy
Amity, OR 97101
503-835-4012
Fax: 503-835-4012
Wine
Owner: Eric Aberag
kristinhill1@msn.com
Co-Owner: Eric Aberg
Estimated Sales: Under $300,000
Number Employees: 1-4
Type of Packaging: Private Label
Brands:
Kristin Hill

6991 **Kroger Bakery**
16253 SE 122nd Ave
Clackamas, OR 97015-9136
503-650-2000
Fax: 503-650-2128
Bread and bakery products
Principal: Earl Bliven
ebliven@fredmeyer.com
Estimated Sales: $621,874 Thousand
Number Employees: 100-249

6992 **Kronos**
1 Kronos Dr.
Glendale Heights, IL 60139
224-353-5353
Fax: 224-353-5400 800-621-0099
requests@kronosfoodscorp.com
www.kronosfoodscorp.com
Mediterranean foods including gyro, pita, flatbread, tzatziki sauce, spanakopita, falafel, and tyropita
Chairman: Michael Austin
CEO: Howard Eirinberg
CFO: Herman Brons
Director of Marketing: Karyn Andrew
SVP Sales: Bob Michaels
Year Founded: 1975
Number Employees: 250-499

6993 **Kruger Foods**
18362 E Highway 4
Stockton, CA 95215-9433
209-941-8518
www.krugerfoods.com
Processor and exporter of condiments including relish, pickles, peppers and sauerkraut.
Chief Executive Officer: Kara Kruger
Contact: Jessica Altamirano
j.altamirano@krugerfoods.com
Director, Operations: Erik Kruger
Director, Technical Services: Christine Ramsey
Year Founded: 1930
Estimated Sales: $22 Million
Number Employees: 100
Square Footage: 120000
Type of Packaging: Consumer, Food Service, Bulk

6994 **Krupka's Blueberries**
2647 68th St
Fennville, MI 49408
269-857-4278
Fax: 269-857-4018 www.bluestarblueberries.com
Blueberries
Partner: Harold Krupka
Partner: Carmen Krupka
Sales Manager: Connie Krupka
Estimated Sales: $3 000,000
Number Employees: 50-99
Type of Packaging: Consumer, Bulk

6995 **Kruse & Son**
235 Kruse Ave
Monrovia, CA 91016-4899
626-358-4536
Fax: 626-303-7349
Meats
Owner: David Kruse
stevek@aol.com
Estimated Sales: $3,200,000
Number Employees: 100-249
Type of Packaging: Consumer, Food Service

6996 **Kruse Meat Products**
2100 Kruse Loop
Alexander, AR 72002
501-316-2100
Fax: 501-794-0256
Meat products
President: Jeanne Hutchinson
Estimated Sales: $1.8 Million
Number Employees: 15
Type of Packaging: Consumer

6997 **Kubisch Sausage Mfg Co**
50400 Rizzo Dr
Shelby Twp, MI 48315-3275
586-566-4661
Fax: 586-566-8661 800-852-5019
info@kubischsausage.com
www.kubischsausage.com
Sausage and other prepared meats
Owner: Vasilj Markovich
Estimated Sales: Less than $300,000
Number Employees: 10-19

6998 **Kubla Khan Food Company**
3369 SE Raymond Street
Portland, OR 97202-4360
503-234-7494
Fax: 503-234-7716
Frozen fruits and vegetables
President: Percy Loy
Estimated Sales: $470,000
Number Employees: 5
Type of Packaging: Food Service, Bulk
Brands:
Kubla Khan

6999 **Kuhlmann's Market Gardens & Greenhouses**
1320-167 Avenue NW
Edmonton, AB T5Y 6L6
Canada
780-475-7500
Fax: 780-472-9923 info@kuhlmanns.com
www.kuhlmanns.com
Processor, exporter and packer of cabbage, carrots, broccoli, peas and potatoes
Pres.: Dietrich Kuhlmann
Estimated Sales: C
Number Employees: 20-49
Type of Packaging: Consumer, Food Service

7000 **Kuju Coffee**
San Francisco, CA
415-634-5858
info@kujucoffee.com
www.kujucoffee.com
Instant coffee
Co-Founder & CEO: Jeff Wiguna
Co-Founder & COO: Justin Wiguna
Number of Brands: 1
Type of Packaging: Consumer
Brands:
KUJU COFFEE

7001 **Kulana Foods LTD**
590 W Kawailani St # J
Hilo, HI 96720-3173
808-959-9144
Fax: 808-959-8484
www.tasteofthehawaiianrange.com
Beef and pork slaughtering and processing
President: Brady Yagi
Estimated Sales: Below $5 000,000
Number Employees: 10-19
Type of Packaging: Private Label
Brands:
Fresh Aland Beef and Pork
Kulana Foods

7002 **Kuli Kuli, Inc.**
600 Grand Ave
Suite 410b
Oakland, CA 94610
510-350-8325
info@kulikulifoods.com
www.kulikulifoods.com
Superfood bars, moringa power, mooring tea
Owner/Cmo: Valerie Popelka
Chief Executive Officer/Founder: Lisa Curtis
lisa@kulikulibar.com
Chief Creative & Design: Anne Tsuei
COO/CTO: Jordan Moncharmont
Number Employees: 5-9

7003 **Kunde Estate Winery**
9825 Sonoma Highway
PO Box 639
Kenwood, CA 95452
707-833-5501
Fax: 707-833-2204 wineinfo@kunde.com
www.kunde.com
Ultra premium, estate grown, and sustainably farmed wines.
Chairman: Jeff Kunde
Vice President: Fred Kunde
Marketing Director: Marcia Kunde Mickelson
Contact: Tim Bell
tbell@kunde.com
Operations Manager: Bill Kunde
Winemaker: Zach Long
Year Founded: 1879
Estimated Sales: $30-50 Million
Number Employees: 50-99
Type of Packaging: Private Label
Brands:
Estate Cabernet Sauvignon
Estate Chardonnay
Estate Merlot
Estate Syrah
Estate Viognier
Estate Zinfandel (Ce

7004 **Kupris Home Bakery**
23 Williams Road
Bolton, CT 06043-7235
860-649-4746
Breads and pastries
Owner: Juris Kupris
Number Employees: 4

7005 **Kura Nutrition**
670 N Commercial St
Suite 204
Manchester, NH 03101
603-217-2665
kuranutrition.com
Vegan and dairy protein smoothie mixes
CEO: Kelli Rooney Hanzalik
Number of Brands: 1
Number of Products: 6
Type of Packaging: Consumer
Brands:
KURA

7006 **Kurtz Orchards Farms**
16006 Niagra River Parkway
PO Box 457
Niagra-on-the-Lake, ON L0S 1J0
Canada
905-468-2937
info@kurtzorchards.com
www.kurtzorchards.com
Jams, jellies, fruit butters, fruit sauces, honey butters, and wine jellies.
Pres.: Wilf Kurtz
CEO: Brad Kurtz
VP: Brad Kurtz
Plant Manager: Darren Hedges
Number Employees: 18
Number of Brands: 3
Brands:
Bethune
Black Cat
Superior

7007 **Kusha Inc.**
11130 Warland Drive
Cypress, CA 90630
949-930-1400
Fax: 949-250-1520 800-550-7423
Rice, basmati, jasmine, tea, grape seed oil, cheese
Vice President: Jerry Taylor
Contact: Mukesh Agrawal
mukesh@ltfoodsamericas.com
Estimated Sales: Under $500,000
Number Employees: 30
Type of Packaging: Consumer, Food Service, Private Label, Bulk
Brands:
Nasim
Pari
Royal

7008 **Kusmi Tea**
26 W 23rd Street
6th Floor
New York, NY 10010
646-346-1756
Fax: 646-624-2893 info.us@kusmitea.com
Kosher hot beverages and teas
Marketing: Lauriane Penfornis

7009 **Kutiks Honey Farm**
285 Lyon Brook Rd
Norwich, NY 13815-3420
607-336-4105
Fax: 607-336-4199
Portion packed honey and honey sticks; also, custom gift packs available
Owner/President: Charles Kutik
Owner: Caryn Kutik
Estimated Sales: Less Than $500,000
Number Employees: 1-4
Square Footage: 18740
Type of Packaging: Consumer, Food Service, Private Label, Bulk
Brands:
Kutik's Honey

7010 **Kutztown Bologna Company**
1500 Oregon Rd # 100
Leola, PA 17540-9753
717-556-0901
Fax: 717-560-0680 800-723-8824
info@kutztownbologna.com
www.actionvideoinc.com
Frozen beef and pork products
President: Gordon Harrower
VP: Gary Landuy
Estimated Sales: $670000
Number Employees: 1-4
Type of Packaging: Consumer, Private Label
Brands:
Kutztown

7011 **Kwangdong USA**
10 Corporate Park
Suite 130
Irvine, CA 92606
949-501-4610
Vitamin C beverage
Year Founded: 1963

7012 **Kween Foods**
San Diego, CA 92075
401-343-0805
admin@kween.co
kween.co
Granola butter
Co-Founder: Ali Bonar
Co-Founder: Eric Katz

7013 **Kwikpak Fisheries**
1016 W 6th Avenue
Suite 301
Anchorage, AK 99501-1963
206-443-1565
Fax: 206-443-1912 800-509-3332
ruthc@ydfda.org www.kwikpakfisheries.com
Smoked seafood.
General Manager: Jack Schultheis
Marketing: Ruth Carter
Contact: Marilyn Charles
marilyn@kwikpakfisheries.com

7014 **Kyger Bakery Products**
3825 State Road 38 E
Lafayette, IN 47905-5212
765-447-1252
Fax: 765-447-7989 info@harlanbakeries.com
Frozen desserts including cream and meringue pies and angel food and sheet cakes; also, retail and institutional packaging available
President: Joseph Latoufe
Vice President: Doug Harlan
Type of Packaging: Consumer
Brands:
Kyger

7015 **Kyler's Catch Seafood Market**
2 Washburn St
New Bedford, MA 02740-7336
508-984-5150
Fax: 508-991-4664 888-859-5377
info@kylerseafood.com www.kylerscatch.com
Fresh and frozen cod and flounder
Owner: Jeff Manfelt
jeff@kylerseafood.com
Controller: Steve Souza
EVP: Billy Arruda
Plant Manager: Paul Poliquin
Estimated Sales: $14 Million
Number Employees: 100-249
Type of Packaging: Private Label

7016 **Kyong Hae Kim Company**
2330 Kalakaua Ave
Suite 85
Honolulu, HI 96815-5001
808-926-8720
Fax: 808-841-2178
Owner: Kyong Kim

7017 **Kyowa Hakko**
600 Third Avenue
19th Floor
New York, NY 10017-9023
212-319-5353
Fax: 212-421-1283 800-596-9252
info@kyowa-usa.com www.kyowa-usa.com
Amino, nuclei and organic acids; exporter of food ingredients
President & CEO: Leo Cullen
VP Sales: D Christopher Nolte
Contact: Maurice Kirch
kirch@kyowa-usa.com
Estimated Sales: $20-50 Million
Number Employees: 10-19
Parent Co: Kyowa Hakko Kogyo Company
Brands:
Cognizin
Lumistor
Pantesin
Setria
Sustamine

7018 **(HQ)L & L Packing Co**
527 W 41st St
Chicago, IL 60609-2708
773-285-5400
Fax: 773-285-0366 800-628-6328
www.worldsbeststeak.com
Established in 1955. Supplier of prime and choice aged beef, pork, veal and lamb.
President: Joel Lezak
Sales Manager: Phil Lombardi
Estimated Sales: $24000000
Number Employees: 20-49
Type of Packaging: Consumer, Private Label

7019 **L & M Bakery**
11 Saint Mihiel Dr
Riverside, NJ 08075-1017
856-461-1660
Fax: 856-461-8524 888-887-1335
sales@lmbakery.com www.lmbakery.com
Fruit squares, nut bread, regular and sour cream coffee cakes and macaroons
Owner: John Kahl
VP: Johanne La Plante
Sales Director: Rick Fermoyle
sales@lmbakery.com
Plant Manager: Andy Stoehrer
Estimated Sales: $10-20 Million
Number Employees: 20-49
Square Footage: 20000
Type of Packaging: Consumer, Food Service
Brands:
L & M Bakery

7020 **L & M Lockers**
15 Bridge St
Belt, MT 59412
406-277-3522
Fax: 406-277-3522
Meat and fish
Owner: Steve Serquina
Partner: Jerry Wojtala
Estimated Sales: $200,000+
Number Employees: 1-4
Type of Packaging: Consumer, Food Service

7021 **L & M Slaughterhouse**
903 Mill Rd
Georgetown, IL 61846-6341
217-662-6841
abitor@aol.com
Beef, veal, lamb and pork; slaughtering services available
Owner: Todd Green
Estimated Sales: $1-3 Million
Number Employees: 1-4
Type of Packaging: Consumer

7022 **(HQ)L & S Packing Co**
101 Central Ave
Farmingdale, NY 11735-6915
631-845-1717
Fax: 631-420-7309 800-286-6487
sales@paesana.com www.paesana.com
Importer of gourmet condiments such as olives, capers, pickles, cocktail onions, mushrooms, etc.; serving food service, industrial and private label markets. Also, high quality authentic pasta sauces and Chinese sauces, see our ad onthe back cover of Vol
President: Louis Scaramelli
lou@paesana.com
Estimated Sales: $3-5 Million
Number Employees: 20-49
Type of Packaging: Consumer, Food Service, Private Label, Bulk
Other Locations:
L&S Packing Co.
Flushing NY
Brands:
Mi-Kee
Paesana
Table Joy

7023 **L & S Packing Co**
101 Central Ave
PO Box 709
Farmingdale, NY 11735-6915
631-845-1717
Fax: 631-420-7309 877-879-6453
info@paesana.com www.paesana.com
Olives
President: Louis Scaramelli
lou@paesana.com
Estimated Sales: $3-5 Million
Number Employees: 20-49

7024 **L A Burdick Chocolate**
47 Main St
P.O. Box 593
Walpole, NH 03608-3300
603-756-3701
Fax: 603-756-4326 800-229-2419
sales@burdickchocolate.com
www.burdickchocolate.com
Chocolates
CEO: Genna Bromley
gbromley@burdickchocolate.com

Number Employees: 50-99

7025 **L C Good Candy Company**
1825 E Tremont St
Allentown, PA 18109-1615
610-432-3290
Fax: 610-432-7455 lcgoodcandy@gmail.com
Candy and confections
President: Roland R Mink Jr
Estimated Sales: Below $200,000
Number Employees: 1-4

7026 **L F Lambert Spawn Co**
1507 Valley Rd
Coatesville, PA 19320
610-384-5031
Fax: 610-384-0390 www.lambertbiologicals.com
Processor and exporter of mushroom spawns
President: Hugh Mcintyre
hugh@lambertspawn.com
Owner: Rick McIntyre
VP of Operations: Joseph Mascrangelo
Estimated Sales: $3300000
Number Employees: 50-99

7027 **L H Hayward & Co**
5401 Toler St
New Orleans, LA 70123-5222
504-733-8480
Fax: 504-733-8155 info@camelliabeans.com
www.camelliabrand.com
Packaging of beans
Owner: Gordon K Hayward
ken@hhco.com
CO-Owner: Rick Hayward
Estimated Sales: $5-10 Million
Number Employees: 20-49
Type of Packaging: Private Label
Brands:
Camellia

7028 **L K Bowman**
12 Old Forge Rd
Nottingham, PA 19362-9747
610-932-2240
Fax: 610-932-4186 800-853-1919
Mushrooms
President: Robert Shelton
Vice President: Jack Shelton
jack.shelton@hanoverfoods.com
Estimated Sales: $10-20 Million
Number Employees: 1-4
Square Footage: 54417
Parent Co: Hanover Foods Corporation
Type of Packaging: Food Service, Private Label, Bulk
Brands:
Garden Path
Mother Earth
Nottingham

7029 **L Mawby Vineyards**
4519 S Elm Valley Rd
Peshawbestown, MI 49682-9473
231-271-3522
Fax: 231-271-2927 info@lmawby.com
www.lmawby.com
Wines
Owner: Stu Laing
stulaing@gmail.com
Estimated Sales: Less Than $500,000
Number Employees: 1-4
Brands:
L.Mawby
M.Lawrence

7030 **L&C Fisheries**
French River
RR #2
Kensington, PE C0B 1MO
Canada
902-886-2770
Fax: 902-886-3003
calvin@greengablesmussels.com
www.greengablesmussels.com
Fresh mussels, oysters, and fresh and frozen lobsters
Owner: Calvin Jollimore
Number Employees: 10-19
Type of Packaging: Consumer, Food Service

7031 **L&M Bakers Supply Company**
2501 Steeles Avenue W
Unit # 1
Toronto, ON M3J 2P1
Canada
416-665-3005
Fax: 416-665-8975 800-465-7361
www.lmbakersupply.com
Manufacturer & wholesaler/distributor of cake decorations and baking tools and supplies; serving the food service market
General Manager: Sheba Grinhaus
Number Employees: 20-49
Square Footage: 44000

7032 **L&M Evans**
PO Box 367
Conyers, GA 30012
770-483-9373
Fax: 847-647-1509
Seafood, clams, fish, fillets
President: L W Bill Evans
Owner: Gene Burkett
Estimated Sales: $300,000-500,000
Number Employees: 1-4

7033 **L'Esprit De Campagne**
1247 Wrights Mill Rd
Berryville, VA 22611-2243
540-955-1014
Fax: 540-955-1018 800-692-8008
lespritfods@hotmail.com
www.lespritdecampagne.com
Dried tomatoes, apples, cherries, blueberries, cranberries
President: Joy Lokey
jlockey@lespritdecampagne.com
CEO: Carey Lokey
Estimated Sales: Below $5 Million
Number Employees: 50-99
Brands:
L'Esprit

7034 **L. A. Smoking & Curing Company**
PO Box 21938
Los Angeles, CA 90021-0938
213-624-2369
Smoked and cured products
President: Bill Terhar
Estimated Sales: $10-24.9 Million
Number Employees: 100-249
Parent Co: Obester Winery

7035 **L. Craelius & Company**
370 N Morgan St
Chicago, IL 60607-1321
312-666-7100
Fax: 312-666-9747
Fresh poultry
President: Lawrence Craelius
Estimated Sales: $20-50 Million
Number Employees: 20-49

7036 **L.A. Libations**
715-B N Douglas St
El Segundo, CA 90245
lalibations.com
Specialty beverages
President & Co-Founder: Pat Bolden
CEO & Co-Founder: Danny Stepper
Co-Founder: Dino Sarti
Director, Sales: Glenn Marin
Brands:
The Living Apothecary
Aloe Gloe
KonaRed
trimino

7037 **L.B. Maple Treat**
1037 Boul. Industriel
Granby, QC J2J 2B8
Canada
450-777-4464
Fax: 450-777-2867 888-775-1111
www.lbmapletreat.com
Maple syrup and maple syrup products
President/Owner: Daniel Cousineau
Number of Brands: 2
Parent Co: Lantic, Inc.
Type of Packaging: Consumer, Private Label, Bulk
Brands:
L.B. MAPLE TREAT
UNCLE LUKE'S

7038 **L.H. Rodriguez Wholesale Seafood**
3541 S 12th Ave
Tucson, AZ 85713-5914
520-623-1931
Fax: 520-623-0737
Seafood
President: Levi Rodriguez
Treasurer: Albert Rodriguez
Vice President: Joe Rodriguez
Estimated Sales: $3-5 Million
Number Employees: 5-9

7039 **LA Bou Bakery & Cafe**
1179 Grass Valley Hwy
Auburn, CA 95603-3411
530-823-2303
Fax: 530-823-0400 customerservice@labou.com
www.labou.com
Gourmet coffees, pastries, soups, sandwiches, salads, desserts
Owner: Arlene Be
Number Employees: 10-19

7040 **LA Boulangerie**
7740 Formula Pl
San Diego, CA 92121-2419
858-578-4040
Fax: 858-536-5911 www.franklynatural.com
Baked goods
Owner: Gerald Sarnoo
Estimated Sales: Below $5 000,000
Number Employees: 10-19
Brands:
La Boulangerie

7041 **LA Buena Vida Vineyards**
416 E College St
Grapevine, TX 76051-5468
817-481-9463
Fax: 817-421-3635
Wines
Manager: Adam Artho
Marketing Director: Camille McBee
Manager: John Meyer
jmeyer@labuenavida.com
Estimated Sales: $2.5-5 Million
Number Employees: 10-19
Number of Products: 15
Brands:
La Buena Vida Vineyards

7042 **LA Canasta Mexican Foods**
3101 W Jackson St
PO Box 6939
Phoenix, AZ 85009-4833
602-269-7721
Fax: 602-269-7725 855-269-7721
www.la-canasta.com
Mexican food products including tortillas, chips, sauces and salsas.
Founder: Carmen Abril
President: Josie Ippolito
jippolito@la-canasta.com
Controller: Roger Kelling
Plant Manager: Ben Garduno
Estimated Sales: $19.9 Million
Number Employees: 100-249
Number of Brands: 2
Square Footage: 72000
Type of Packaging: Food Service, Private Label
Brands:
La Canasta
My Nana's

7043 **LA Chapalita Inc**
9643 Remer St
South El Monte, CA 91733-3032
626-443-8556
Fax: 626-443-7554 www.lachapalita.com
Tortillas, Mexican food
President: Luis Moya
VP Operation: Luis Moya Jr.
Estimated Sales: Below $5 Million
Number Employees: 5-9

7044 **LA Chiripada Winery**
Highway 75 Dr # 1119
Dixon, NM 87527
505-579-4437
Fax: 505-579-4437 800-528-7801
chiripa@lachiripada.com www.lachiripada.com
Wine

VP: Michael Johnson
Tasting Room Manager: Minna Santos
Estimated Sales: Below $5 Million
Number Employees: 1-4
Brands:
La Chiripada

7045 **LA Colonial**
1700 Rogers Ave
San Jose, CA 95112-1107
408-436-5551
Fax: 408-441-0430
Flour tortillas
CEO: George Robles
Marketing Director: George Robles
Estimated Sales: Below $5 Million
Number Employees: 20-49

7046 **LA Costa Coffee Roasting Co**
6965 El Camino Real # 208
Carlsbad, CA 92009-4102
760-438-8160
Fax: 760-438-5314
Coffee
President: Doug Novak
roastmaster@lacostacoffeeroasting.com
Estimated Sales: $10-20 000,000
Number Employees: 10-19

7047 **LA Grander Hillside Dairy Inc**
W11299 Broek Rd
Stanley, WI 54768-8215
715-644-2275
Fax: 715-644-0720 info@lagranderscheese.com
www.lagranderscheese.com
Cheese and dairy products
Owner: Randy LA Grander
lagranderscheez@yahoo.com
Estimated Sales: $3,500,000
Number Employees: 20-49
Type of Packaging: Consumer

7048 **LA Jota Vineyard Co**
1102 Las Posadas Rd
Angwin, CA 94508-9607
707-948-2648
Fax: 707-965-0324 877-222-0292
info@lajotawines.com
Wines
Manager: Ed Farver
VP: Joan Smith
Sales Manager: John Smith
Estimated Sales: Less Than $500,000
Number Employees: 1-4

7049 **LA Lifestyle Nutritional Products**
2230 Cape Cod Way
Santa Ana, CA 92703-3582
714-835-6367
Fax: 714-835-4948 800-387-4786
Processor and wholesaler/distributor of teas and herbal products
Owner: Patricia J Logsdon
Estimated Sales: $10-20 Million
Type of Packaging: Consumer

7050 **LA Mar's Donuts**
6950 E Belleview Ave # 200
Suite 200
Greenwood Vlg, CO 80111-1626
303-771-9999
Fax: 303-771-9991 www.lamars.com
Donuts
Number Employees: 5-9

7051 **LA Mexicana Tortilla**
10020 14th Ave SW
Seattle, WA 98146-3703
206-763-1488
Fax: 206-768-1050 info@lamexicana.com
www.lamexicana.com
Mexican foods
Owner: Keith Bloxham
keith@lamexicana.com
General Manager: William Fry
Retail Sales Manager: Jos, Cifuentes
keith@lamexicana.com
Estimated Sales: Below $5 Million
Number Employees: 50-99
Type of Packaging: Private Label
Brands:
Habero
La Mexicana
Souena

7052 **LA Mexicana Tortilla Factory**
715 Skyline Dr
Duncanville, TX 75116-3923
214-943-7770
Fax: 214-943-7778 www.lamexicana.com
Manufacturer of tortillas, tostadas, and tortilla chips
President: Ricardo Garza
Manager: Rafael Perez
Treasurer: Rebecca Garza
Year Founded: 1997
Estimated Sales: $18 Million
Number Employees: 50-99
Square Footage: 20000
Type of Packaging: Consumer

7053 **LA Mexicana Tortilleria**
2703 S Kedzie Ave
Chicago, IL 60623-4735
773-247-5443
Fax: 773-247-9004
Tortillas and corn chips
President: Rodolfo Guerrero
Estimated Sales: $4600000
Number Employees: 20-49
Type of Packaging: Consumer

7054 **LA Monica Fine Foods**
PO Box 309
Millville, NJ 08332
info@lamonicafinefoods.com
www.lamonicafinefoods.com
Surf clams and ocean clams from US certified waters, serving the fresh, canned and frozen markets.
Founder: Peter LaMonica
Number Employees: 20-49
Square Footage: 360000
Type of Packaging: Consumer, Food Service, Private Label, Bulk
Brands:
Cape May
Lamonica

7055 **LA Pasta Inc**
2727 Pittman Dr
Silver Spring, MD 20910-1807
301-588-1111
Fax: 301-588-7243 info@lapastainc.com
Manufacture fresh, frozen, and shelf-life pasta
President: Alexis Konownitzine
alexis@lapastainc.com
Estimated Sales: $5-10 Million
Number Employees: 20-49

7056 **LA Patisserie Bakery**
19758 Stevens Creek Blvd
Cupertino, CA 95014-2456
408-446-4744
Fax: 602-253-7430 www.lapatisserie.net
Bakery products
Owner: Eduardo Teixidor
President: Ed Teixidor
Partner: Mojgan Damaghani
mdamaghani@comcast.net
Estimated Sales: Below $5 000,000
Number Employees: 10-19
Type of Packaging: Private Label
Brands:
La Patisserie

7057 **LA Paz Products Inc**
345 Oak Pl
Brea, CA 92821-4122
714-990-0982
Fax: 714-990-2246 info@lapazproducts.com
www.lapazproducts.com
Cocktail mixes
President: Tim Casey
tcasey@lapazproducts.com
Marketing & Sales Manager: Greg Diem
Operations, Production, Purchasing: Mike Casey
Plant Manager: Mike Casey
Estimated Sales: $10-20 Million
Number Employees: 10-19
Type of Packaging: Consumer, Food Service

7058 **LA Quercia LLC**
400 Hakes Dr
Norwalk, IA 50211-9644
USA
515-981-1625
Fax: 515-981-1628 prosciutto@laquercia.us
www.laquercia.us
Cured meats
Owner: Herbert Eckhouse
prosciutto@laquercia.us
Estimated Sales: F
Number Employees: 20-49

7059 **LA Reina Inc**
316 N Ford Blvd
Los Angeles, CA 90022-1182
323-268-2791
Fax: 323-265-4295 800-367-7522
sales@lareinainc.com www.lareinainc.com
Flour tortillas
President: Thomas Gonzalez
tomgon@pacbell.net
CEO: Mauro Robles
VP: Walt Boudreaux
Operations: Francisco Arellano
Purchasing: Luis Farfan
Estimated Sales: $16,000,000
Number Employees: 250-499
Type of Packaging: Consumer, Food Service, Private Label
Brands:
La Reina

7060 **LA Rocca Vineyards & Winery**
12360 Doe Mill Rd
Forest Ranch, CA 95942
530-899-9463
Fax: 530-894-7268 800-808-9463
wine@laroccavineyards.com
www.laroccavineyards.com
Wines
Owner: Philip LA Rocca
Marketing Director: Phaedre LaRocco Morril
Estimated Sales: Under $500,000
Number Employees: 5-9
Brands:
La Rocca Vineyards

7061 **LA Segunda Bakery**
2512 N 15th St
Tampa, FL 33605-3406
813-248-1531
Fax: 813-248-3354 lscbakery@hotmail.com
www.cubanbread.com
Cuban Bread and baked goods
Owner: Rogger Berrocal
rberrocal@lasegundabakery.com
Number Employees: 20-49

7062 **LA Tapatia Tortilleria Inc**
104 E Belmont Ave
Fresno, CA 93701-1403
559-441-1030
Fax: 559-441-1712 www.tortillas4u.com
Corn and flour tortillas, chips and tostadas.
Owner/President: Helen Chavez-Hansen
SVP: John Hansen
Controller: Jose Angulo
Export Director: Dan Soleno
Regional Sales Manager: Dennis Walsh
Regional Sales Manager: Vickie Maravel
Sales & Marketing: Linda Ghilarducci
Estimated Sales: $25 Million
Number Employees: 100-249
Number of Brands: 2
Type of Packaging: Private Label
Brands:
La Tapatia
Sol De Oro

7063 **LA Torilla Factory**
3300 Westwind Blvd
Santa Rosa, CA 95403-8273
707-586-4000
Fax: 707-586-4017 800-446-1516
info@latortillafactory.com
www.latortillafactory.com
Corn and flour tortillas and tortilla chips and masa
President: Carlos Tamayo
Owner/President/VP Sales/Marketing: Sam Tamayo
CFO: Stan Mead
R&D Manager: Luz Ana Osbun
Executive Director Sales/Marketing: Jan Remak
Human Resources Manager: Jonna Green
COO/VP/Plant Manager: Sam Tamayo
Estimated Sales: $8000000
Number Employees: 250-499
Square Footage: 18160
Type of Packaging: Consumer, Food Service, Private Label, Bulk
Brands:
La Tortilla Factory

Wrap Arounds
Wrappers

7064 **LA Vencedora Products Inc**
3322 Fowler St
Los Angeles, CA 90063-2594
323-269-7273
Fax: 323-269-8775 800-327-2572
www.elranchochips.com
Fresh salsa, tortilla chips, nacho chips, and specialty chips
Owner: Victor Gregory
gregv7@msn.com
CEO: Richard Victor
Estimated Sales: $500,000-1 Million
Number Employees: 5-9
Square Footage: 32000
Type of Packaging: Consumer, Food Service, Private Label, Bulk
Brands:
El Rancho
El Rancho Bean Chips
El Rancho Salsa Fresca
El Rancho Tortilla Chips
Pocos

7065 **LA Vina Winery**
4201 Highway 28
Anthony, NM 88021-8551
575-882-7632
Fax: 575-882-7632 stark@lavinawinery.com
www.lavina.wolfep.com
Wine
Owner: Ken Stark
stark@lavinawinery.com
Co-Owner/CEO: Denise Stark
Estimated Sales: Below $5 Million
Number Employees: 1-4
Brands:
La Vina

7066 **LA Wholesale Produce Market**
1601 E Olympic Boulevard
Los Angeles, CA 90021
Fax: 213-622-7075 888-454-6887
admin@lanuthouse.com www.lanuthouse.com
Manufacturer, importer and exporter of tree nuts and peanuts; also, processor of peanut butter and manufactured and coated materials
Estimated Sales: $3-5 Million
Number Employees: 5-9
Square Footage: 88000
Parent Co: Morven Partners
Type of Packaging: Consumer, Food Service, Private Label, Bulk

7067 **LAVVA**
Warwick, NY 10990
lovvelavva.com
Plant-based yogurts
Founder: Liz Fisher

7068 **LEF McLean Brothers International**
PO Box 128
20 Erie St South
Wheatley, ON N0P 2P0
Canada
519-825-4656
Fax: 519-825-7374
Processor and exporter of fresh and frozen lake fish and seafood
President: Robert Ricci
VP Business Development: Danny Ricci
Type of Packaging: Consumer, Food Service, Private Label, Bulk

7069 **LFI Inc**
271 US Highway 46 # C101
Fairfield, NJ 07004-2495
973-882-0550
Fax: 973-882-0554 lfiinc@aol.com
www.lfiincorporated.com
Imported foods
Owner: Anthony Lisanti
lfiantonio@aol.com
Marketing Director: Danielle Iannacconi
Public Relations: Carol Lisanti
Estimated Sales: Below $5 000,000
Number Employees: 5-9
Type of Packaging: Private Label
Brands:
Antonia
Casa Primo

7070 **LIVE Soda**
4020 S Industrial Dr
Suite 133
Austin, TX 78744
info@livesoda.com
livesoda.com
Kombucha, drinking vinegar and probiotic soda
Founder: Trevor Ross
Brands:
LIVE Soda
Raw LIVE Soda
Sparkling LIVE Drinking Vinegars

7071 **LLJ's Sea Products**
PO Box 296
Round Pond, ME 04564-0296
207-529-4224
Fax: 207-529-4223
Canned and cured fish and seafood.
Owner: Stephen J Brackett
Estimated Sales: $3,000,000
Number Employees: 5-9

7072 **LSK Smoked Turkey Products**
1575 Bronx River Ave
Bronx, NY 10460
718-792-1300
Fax: 718-792-8883
Smoked turkey products
President: Dan Salmon
CEO: Owen Grossblatt
Contact: Owen Grossblatt
lskdan@aol.com
Plant Manager: John Garvin
Estimated Sales: $9 Million
Number Employees: 10-19
Brands:
Lsk

7073 **LWC Brands Inc.**
151 Regal Row
Dallas, TX 75247
214-630-9101
Fax: 214-630-7360 800-552-8006
orders@ladywaltons.com ladywaltons.com
Cookies, snacks and sauces
President/Owner: Mary Alizon-Walton
Contact: Ron Kirk
rkirk@ladywaltons.com
Estimated Sales: $2.3 Million
Number Employees: 2
Brands:
Lady Walton's
B.Bob's Foods

7074 **LYNQ**
Montreal, QC H3P 2R2
Canada
lynqlife.com
Superfood powders

7075 **La Abra Farm & Winery**
1362 Fortunes Cove Ln
Lovingston, VA 22949
434-263-5392
Fax: 434-263-8540
www.mountaincovevineyards.com
Wines
President: Albert C Weed Ii
Estimated Sales: Less than $200,000
Number Employees: 1-4

7076 **La Bonita Ole Inc**
5804 E Columbus Dr
Tampa, FL 33619
813-319-2252
Fax: 813-319-2263 800-522-6648
Tortillas
Founder/Owner/President/CEO: Tammy Young
Executive Administrator: Melanie Bodiford
Contact: Patrick Gallagher
patrick@tamxicos.com
VP Operations: Dave Waters
Brands:
Tamxicos
Wrapitz

7077 **La Brasserie McAuslan Brewing**
5080 St-Ambroise
Montreal, QC H4C 2G1
Canada
514-939-3060
Fax: 514-939-2541 info@mcauslan.com
www.mcauslan.com
Processor and exporter of beer and ale including stout
President: Peter McAuslan
Master Brewer and VP, Production: Ellen Bounsall
Number Employees: 100-249
Type of Packaging: Consumer, Food Service

7078 **La Brea Bakery Inc**
14490 Catalina St
San Leandro, CA 94577
855-427-9982
www.labreabakery.com
Bread and rolls; also, par-baked and frozen available.
President: John Yamin
jyamin@labreabakery.com
Year Founded: 1989
Estimated Sales: $124.4 Million
Number Employees: 100-249
Parent Co: Aryzta AG
Other Locations:
Direct Store Delivery
Los Angeles CA
Store Baked Delivery Nationwide
Swedesboro NJ

7079 **La Buena Mexican Foods Products**
234 East 22nd Street
Tucson, AZ 85726-6626
520-624-1796
Fax: 520-624-1846
Mexican food products including corn and flour tortillas, tamales and taco and tostado shells
Owner: Carlos Portillo
Contact: William Garcia
williamgarcia@restaurant.com
Estimated Sales: $5-10 Million
Number Employees: 20-49
Type of Packaging: Consumer

7080 **La Caboose Specialties**
145 S Budd St
Sunset, LA 70584
337-662-5401
Fax: 337-662-5813
Canned fruits, vegetables, preserves, jams and jellies
Owner: Margaret Brinkhaus
Estimated Sales: Under $100,000
Number Employees: 1-4
Type of Packaging: Consumer
Brands:
La Caboose

7081 **La Chiquita Tortilla Manufacturing**
3451 Atlanta Industrial Parkway
Atlanta, GA 30331
404-351-9822
Fax: 404-351-4446 800-486-3942
custserv@lctortilla.com
www.lachiquitatortilla.com
Flour and corn tortillas, hand cut chips and wraps and flavored tortillas
Owner/President/CEO: Marcelino Solis
EVP/General Manager: Adam Oliaro
Marketing Manager: Jose Solis
Plant Manager: Henry Sanchez
Estimated Sales: $10.7 Million
Number Employees: 90
Square Footage: 22000
Type of Packaging: Food Service
Brands:
La Chiquita
Provecho

7082 **La Choy**
Conagra Brands
222 w. merchandise mart plz, suite 1300
Chicago, IL 60654
312-549-5000
Fax: 402-595-4709 www.lachoy.com
Chinese food and soups
Estimated Sales: $20-49.9 Million
Number Employees: 20,900
Parent Co: ConAgra Foods

7083 **La Cookie**
531-A N. Hollywood Way
Burbank, CA 91505
713-784-2722
Fax: 713-784-3415 818-495-5732
Frozen cookie, muffin and brownie dough
Manager: Brian Fung

Estimated Sales: $300,000-500,000
Number Employees: 10-19
Square Footage: 20000
Parent Co: Pilsner Group
Type of Packaging: Food Service
Brands:
Neal's

7084 La Cookie
5700 Savoy Dr
Houston, TX 77036
713-784-2722
Fax: 713-784-3415
Baked goods
Manager: Brian Fung
Vice President: Victor Young
Estimated Sales: $1-2.5 000,000
Number Employees: 1-4

7085 La Crema Coffee Company
9848 Crescent Park Dr
West Chester, OH 45069
513-779-6278
Fax: 513-779-1908
melissa@lacremacoffeecompany.com
www.lacremacoffeecompany.com
Coffee and tea
President/Owner: Melissa Flohn
m.flohn@lacremacoffeecompany.com
Operations Manager: Cheryl Windhorst

7086 La Crosse Milling Company
105 Hwy 35
P.O. Box 86
Cochrane, WI 54622
608-248-2222
Fax: 608-248-2221 800-441-5411
ghartzell@lacrossemilling.com
Whole grain, organic and Kosher grain ingredients including oats, barley and wheat, products include conventional and organic oat flakes, oat flour, oat bran, oat fiber, pearled barley, barley flakes, barley flour, rolled wheat andother specialty milled grains.
President: Dan Ward
Controller/Assistant Treasurer: Teresa Waters
Safety Manager: Bryan Hoch
Quality Control Manager: Lori Dahl
Food Sales Assistant: Michelle Kosidowski
VP Sales: Glen Hartzell
Maintenance Manager: Dale Peterson
Feed Coordinator: Cara Lee Wiersgalla
Estimated Sales: $48.56 Million
Number Employees: 95
Type of Packaging: Bulk

7087 La Cure Gourmande USA
225 Liberty St
New York, NY 10281-1008
646-935-9329
www.curegourmande.com
Biscuits; confections; chocolate; caramel
Managing Director: Antoine Vera Medina
Year Founded: 1989
Number Employees: 300
Type of Packaging: Private Label

7088 La Esquina Food Products
114 Kenmare
New York, NY 10012
646-710-3183
Fax: 973-278-7943 www.esquinanyc.com
Manufacturer of salsa and black bean dip.
Founder: Derek Sanders
Sales Manager: Sean Marrow

7089 La Ferme Martinette
1728, Martineau's road
Coaticook, QC J1A 2S5
Canada
819-849-7089
Fax: 819-849-4042 888-881-4561
lisa@finemapleproducts.com
www.lafermemartinette.com
Maple syrup.
Marketing: Lisa Nadeau

7090 La Flor Spices
25 Hoffman Avenue
Hauppaugue, NY 11788-4717
631-885-9601
Fax: 631-851-9606
Manufacturer, importer, exporter and contract packager of spices, herbs, blends, seasonings and ground peppers
President: Ruben La Torre
VP: Dan La Torre
Sales/Distribution Manager: Ruben La Torre
Estimated Sales: $5 Million
Number Employees: 45
Square Footage: 124000
Type of Packaging: Private Label

7091 La Flor Spices Company
25 Hoffman Ave
Hauppauge, NY 11788-4717
631-851-9601
Fax: 631-851-9606
Spices
President: Reuben Latorre
Estimated Sales: $7.4 Million
Number Employees: 20-49
Type of Packaging: Consumer, Food Service, Bulk
Brands:
La Flor

7092 La Have Seafoods
3371 Hwy 331
La Have, NS B0R 1C0
Canada
902-688-2773
Fax: 902-688-2766 lahaveseafoods@eastlink.ca
Processor and exporter of fresh and salted fish including pollack, cod, haddock and scallops
President: Dave Himmelman
Estimated Sales: $6.2 Million
Number Employees: 45
Type of Packaging: Bulk

7093 La Maison Le Grand
935 Chemin Principal
St-Joseph-du-Lac, QC J0N 1M0
Canada
450-623-3000
info@maisonlegrand.com
www.maisonlegrand.com
Pesto, savory tapenades and aromatic sauces
Owner: Bernard Le Grand

7094 La Moderna
Leandro Valle No. 404-200
Toluca, MX 50070
Mexico
www.lamoderna.com.mx
Cookies, flour, pasta (dry), soups/broths.
Marketing: Robert Flegnann

7095 La Morena
Av. Virgen De La Caridad Lote 20 Al 27
Ciudad Industrial Xicohtencatl 2
Huamantla, 90500
Mexico
222-211-0515
Fax: 222-237-2700 www.lamorena.com.mx
Mayo/ketchup, salsa/dips, beans, spices, canned of preserved vegetables/fruit.
Marketing: Roberto Romo Michaud

7096 La Newyorkina
61 Commerce St
Brooklyn, NY 11231
646-861-0727
info@lanewyorkina.com
lanewyorkina.com
Mexican-style ice pops
Founder: Fany Gerson

7097 La Nova Wings
371 W Ferry St
Buffalo, NY 14213
716-881-3355
Fax: 716-881-3366 800-652-6682
www.lanova.com
Frozen chicken wings and tenders
President/CEO: Joseph Todaro
Sales, Eastern: Ben Lamonte
Sales (Midwest): Sam Pantano
Contact: Dave Alessi
dalessi@lanova.com
Estimated Sales: $4.1 Million
Number Employees: 15
Type of Packaging: Consumer, Food Service
Brands:
La Nova

7098 La Panzanella
18300 Cascade Ave S
Suite 260
Tukwila, WA 98188
206-903-0500
info@lapanzanella.com
lapanzanella.com
Crackers, cookies and snacks.
Owner: Paul Pigott
Brands:
Croccantini(c)
La Panzanella(c)

7099 La Pasta, Inc.
715-B N Douglas St
El Segundo, CA 90245
lalibations.com
Specialty beverages
President & Co-Founder: Pat Bolden
CEO & Co-Founder: Danny Stepper
Co-Founder: Dino Sarti
Director, Sales: Glenn Marin

7100 La Piccolina
1075 N Hills Drive
Decatur, GA 30033-4220
406-636-1909
Fax: 404-296-2008 800-626-1624
Processor and exporter of breadsticks, dips, biscotti, gourmet coffee, cranberry pecan bread, pasta, pasta sauces, olive oil, etc.
President: Olympia Manning
VP: Denise Walsh-Bandini
National Sales Manager: Denise Walsh-Bandini
Estimated Sales: $270,000
Number Employees: 5
Square Footage: 14400

7101 La Preferida, Inc.
3400 W 35th St
Chicago, IL 60632
773-254-7200
info@lapreferida.com
www.lapreferida.com
Mexican and Latin American foods and ingredients.
Owner: Richard Steinbarth
Marketing Manager: Jaime Munoz
Midwest Sales Manager: Bill Nash
Year Founded: 1949
Estimated Sales: $11 Million
Number Employees: 50-99
Number of Products: 250
Square Footage: 50000
Type of Packaging: Consumer, Private Label
Brands:
La Preferida

7102 La Regina di San Marzano USA
757 Third Ave
20th Floor
New York, NY 10017
212-461-3699
info@laregina.com
www.lasanmarzano.com
Pasta sauces and canned tomatoes

7103 (HQ)La Rochelle Winery
5443 Tesla Rd
Livermore, CA 94550
925-243-6442
Fax: 408-270-5881 888-647-7768
www.lrwine.com
Vintaged varietal wine
Manager: Janice Fisher
Partner: James Mirassou
Partner: Peter Mirassou
Contact: Jennifer Fazio
jennifer@stevenkent.com
Square Footage: 480000
Other Locations:
Mirassou Vineyards
Los Gatos CA
Brands:
Mirassou

7104 La Romagnola
2215 Tradeport Drive
Orlando, FL 32824-7005
407-856-4343
Fax: 407-856-7555 800-843-8359
Fettucine, spaghetti, linguine, angel hair pasta, pasta sheets, tortelloni, ravioli, triangoli and gnocchi; also, noodles including tomato, spinach, black and egg
Ceo: Andreas Rieder

Estimated Sales: $190,000
Number Employees: 3
Square Footage: 136000
Brands:
La Romagnola
Le Patron

7105 La Rosa Azzurra
2318 27th St
Astoria, NY 11105
718-777-7119
Fax: 718-545-3233 larosaazzurra@msn.com
www.larosaazzurra.com
Pasta

7106 La Selva Beach Spice
453 McQuaide Dr
La Selva Beach, CA 95076
831-724-4500
www.laselvabeachspice.com
Organic sugars, salt and spice blends.
Type of Packaging: Private Label

7107 La Societe
1415 Rue De La Montagne
Montreal, QC H3G 1Z3
Canada
514-507-9223
Fax: 514-325-6398 www.lasociete.ca
Processor and exporter of aroma coffee; importer of green coffee beans and cocoa; custom blending available
President: M Claude Parent
Sales/Marketing Executive: Andre Richer
Purchasing Agent: Linda McGail
Number Employees: 12
Square Footage: 24000
Type of Packaging: Consumer, Food Service, Private Label, Bulk
Brands:
Altima
Aroma
Bourbon Excelso

7108 La Spiga D'Oro Fresh Pasta Co
75 Pelican Way
Suite J
Pacifica, CA 94901
650-359-9526
Fax: 650-359-0654 800-847-2782
Gourmet fresh and frozen pasta.
President: Robert Clifford
Estimated Sales: Below $5 Million
Number Employees: 10
Brands:
La Spiga Doro

7109 La Superior Food Products
4307 Merriam Dr
Shawnee Mission, KS 66203
913-432-4933
Fax: 913-432-0121
Nacho chips, taco shells, flour tortillas, corn tortillas
President: George Young
CFO: Larry O'Brian
R & D: Gordan Grahm
Estimated Sales: $2.5-5 Million
Number Employees: 20-49
Type of Packaging: Private Label, Bulk
Brands:
La Superior

7110 La Tang Cuisine Manufacturing
3824 Artdale St
Houston, TX 77063-5246
713-780-4876
Fax: 713-780-4296
Asian foods including egg rolls, wonton, crab rangoon, spring roll and burritos.
President: Virginia Limbo
CEO: Joey Limbo
Estimated Sales: $250,000-$1 Million
Number Employees: 20-49
Number of Brands: 2
Number of Products: 5
Square Footage: 20000
Type of Packaging: Food Service, Private Label, Bulk
Brands:
La Tang
La Vida

7111 La Tempesta
439 Littlefield Ave
S San Francisco, CA 94080-6106
650-873-8944
Fax: 650-873-1190 800-762-8330
ltwebinfo@latempesta.com www.latempesta.com
Biscotti candy and confectionary products
President: Robert Sharp
CFO: Lee Rucker
Vice President, sales: Sam deLucca
VP of Business Development: Rodney bigs
VP Marketing: Karen Hunt
Vice President of Sales: Bob Yurick
Contact: Sonia Azar
sazar@latempesta.com
Plant Manager: Sonia Azar
Estimated Sales: $9000000
Number Employees: 60
Type of Packaging: Consumer
Brands:
Amore Bianco
Biscotti Toscani
Panforte

7112 La Tortilla Factory
3300 Westwind Blvd
Santa Rosa, CA 95403
Fax: 707-586-4017 800-446-1516
info@latortillafactory.com
www.latortillafactory.com
Tortillas and wraps
President/CEO: Jeff Ahlers
CFO: David Trogdon
EVP: Willie Tamayo
Marketing Project Manager: Lori Chellies Friend
Sr. Director, National Sales: Tom Moore
Year Founded: 1977

7113 La Tourangelle
125 University Ave
Suite 202
Berkeley, CA 94710
510-970-9960
Fax: 510-970-9964 866-688-6457
contact@latourangelle.com latourangelle.com
Artisanal oils
President & CEO: Matthieu Kohlmeyer
CFO: Gwenn Goffin
VP, QA: Hanh Nguyen
Director of Marketing: Rosanne Kim
Contact: Melinda Bruskrud
mbruskrud@latourangelle.com
Director of Production & Engineering: Nick Heiser
Number Employees: 12
Other Locations:
Oil Mill
Woodland CA
Warehouse
Woodland CA

7114 La Vans Coffee Company
158 2nd St
Bordentown, NJ 00505
609-298-0688
Coffees
Manager: Kostas Halkiadakis
Estimated Sales: Less than $500,000
Number Employees: 1-4

7115 La Victoria Foods
1 Hormel Place
Austin, MN 55912
626-312-2925
Fax: 626-280-4416 800-725-7212
www.lavictoria.com
Salsa, taco sauce, enchilada sauce, chiles and peppers
CEO: R Tanklage
VP: Jon Tanklage
Estimated Sales: $5-$10 Million
Number Employees: 5-9
Type of Packaging: Private Label
Brands:
La Victoria
La Victoria Salsa Su

7116 La Vigne Enterprises
PO Box 2890
Fallbrook, CA 92088-2890
760-723-9997
Fax: 760-728-2710 info@lavignefruits.com
www.lavignefruits.com
Exotic organically grown fruits, packaged frozen in 2 lb. or 28 lb. pails. Also, dried fruits and gourmet condiments.
President: Helene Beck
Contact: Henry Bolden
hbolden@lavignefruits.com
Number of Products: 10
Type of Packaging: Food Service, Private Label
Brands:
La Vigns

7117 LaCroix
Ft. Lauderdale, FL 33324
954-581-0922
888-241-7360
www.lacroixwater.com
Sparkling water
Founder: Nick Caporella
Brands:
LaCroix

7118 LaCrosse Milling Company
105 Highway 35
P.O.Box 86
Cochrane, WI 54622-0086
608-248-2222
Fax: 608-248-2221 800-441-5411
jbackus@lacrossemilling.com
www.lacrossemilling.com
Oatmeal and rolled oat flakes; exporter of milled oat products
President: Dan Ward
Vice President, Sales: Glenn Hartzell
Plant Manager: Bill Brueger
Estimated Sales: $10-20 Million
Number Employees: 60
Number of Products: 50
Type of Packaging: Food Service, Private Label, Bulk
Brands:
Diamond

7119 LaMonde Wild Flavors
7315 Pacific Circle
Mississauga, CA L5T-1V1
905-670-1108
Fax: 905-670-0076 800-263-5286
www.wildflavors.com
Natural food and pharmaceutical coloring blends
Chief Operating Officer: Erik Donhowe
Estimated Sales: $1-5 Million
Number Employees: 1-4

7120 Labatt Breweries Alberta
10119-45 Ave NW
Edmonton, AB T6E 0G8
Canada
780-436-6060
www.labatt.com
Marketing Manager: Blaine Kulak
Number Employees: 100-249
Parent Co: Labatt Brewing Company
Type of Packaging: Consumer, Food Service

7121 Labatt Breweries Newfoundland
60 Leslie St.
St. John's, NL A1E 2V8
Canada
709-579-0121
Fax: 709-579-2018 www.labatt.com
Technical Services & Operations Manager: Rod Penney
Number Employees: 85
Parent Co: Labatt Brewing Company

7122 Labatt Brewery London
150 Simcoe St
London, ON N6A 4M3
Canada
519-850-8687
Fax: 519-667-7304 www.labatt.com
Director: Doug Higgin
Number Employees: 400+
Parent Co: Labatt Brewing Company
Type of Packaging: Consumer, Food Service

7123 Labatt Brewing Company
207 Queen's Quay W.
Suite 299
Toronto, ON M5J 1A7
Canada
416-361-5050
Fax: 416-361-5200 800-268-2337
www.labatt.com
Beer.

President, Labatt Canada: Kyle Norrington
VP, Legal & Corproate Affairs: Charlie Angelakos
Director, Marketing: Andrew Oosterhuis
Year Founded: 1847
Estimated Sales: $296.58 Million
Number Employees: 3,400
Number of Brands: 60
Number of Products: 60
Square Footage: 88587
Parent Co: AB InBev
Type of Packaging: Consumer, Food Service
Brands:
Alexander Keith's India Pale Ale
Labatt Blue
Budweiser
Bud Light
Rolling Rock
Genuine Lager
Ice Beer
Wildcat Strong
Busch
Guinness Extra Stout
Kokanee
Blue Light
Lakeport
Lucky Lager
Labatt 50
Brava
Labatt Crystal
Oland
Labatt Lite
Labatt Ice
Labatt Genuine Honey
Labatt Sterling
Kokanee Gold
Schooner
Blue Star
Stella Artois
Legere
Bud Light Lime
Beck's
Corona Extra
Hoegaarden
Leffe
Michelo Ultra
Boddingtons Pub Ale
Bass
Lowenbrau
Modelo

7124 **Lacas Coffee Co Inc**
7950 National Hwy # A
Pennsauken, NJ 08110-1412
856-910-8662
Fax: 856-910-8671 800-220-1133
info@lacascoffee.com www.lacascoffee.com
Coffee, cocoa and tea.
President: John Vastardis
CEO: Louis Abbato
labbato@lacascoffee.com
Chief Financial Officer: Michael Vlahos
Senior Advisor: Tony Chigounis
Estimated Sales: $10-20 Million
Number Employees: 20-49
Number of Brands: 3
Type of Packaging: Food Service, Private Label
Brands:
Bigelow
Lacas
Newman's Own

7125 **Lacey Milling Company**
217 West Fifth Street
Hanford, CA 93230
559-584-6634
Fax: 559-584-9165
Flour
Owner: Scott Lindrum
Plant Manager: Steve Verschelden
Estimated Sales: $10-20 Million
Number Employees: 10-19
Type of Packaging: Bulk
Brands:
California Special
Lacey

7126 **Lactalis American GroupInc**
2376 S Park Ave
Buffalo, NY 14220
877-522-8254
www.lactalisamericangroup.com
Processor, exporter and importer of cheeses including Brie, Swiss, Roquefort, feta, edam, Gouda, mozzarella, ricotta, fontina, Asiago, shredded/grated, Parmesan and romano, as well as snack and spreadable cheese.
CEO: Thierry Clement
SVP & Chief Legal Officer: Pierre Lorieau
Marketing Director: Karine Blake
VP of Sales: Yann Connan
Year Founded: 1992
Estimated Sales: $415 Million
Number Employees: 1,600
Number of Brands: 10
Square Footage: 16231
Parent Co: Groupe Lactalis
Type of Packaging: Consumer, Food Service, Private Label
Brands:
Galbani
iStara
Le Chatelain
Galbani Precious
President
Rondele
Societe
Galbani Sorrento
Valbreso Feta
Don Bernardo

7127 **Lactalis Ingredients Inc**
2376 S Park Ave
Buffalo, NY 14220
liusa@lactalis.us
www.liusa.com
Produces whey products, milk powders, caseins, industrial butters, nutritional and formulated products.
CEO: Frederick Bouisset
VP, Sales: Yann Connan
Estimated Sales: $50,000-99,000 Million
Number Employees: 1,300
Parent Co: Lactalis American Group, Inc.
Type of Packaging: Consumer, Food Service, Private Label, Bulk

7128 **Lactalis USA Inc**
218 S Park St
Belmont, WI 53510-9639
608-762-5136
Manufacturer of cheese and cheese products.
CEO: Frederick Bouisset
Plant Manager: Renaudeau Christophe
Estimated Sales: $23 Million
Number Employees: 100-249
Parent Co: Lactalis American Group, Inc.
Type of Packaging: Consumer, Food Service, Private Label

7129 **Lad's Smokehouse Catering**
3731 School St
Needville, TX 77461
979-793-6210
Fax: 979-793-4220
Sausage
President: Robert Case
Estimated Sales: $1-3 Million
Number Employees: 1-4
Type of Packaging: Consumer
Brands:
Lad's

7130 **Ladoga Frozen Food & Retail**
237 S Washington St
Ladoga, IN 47954-7019
765-942-2225
Frozen meat including beef and pork; wholesaler/distributor of fruit and vegetables
President: Harold Lowe
Number Employees: 5-9
Type of Packaging: Consumer, Food Service

7131 **Ladson Homemade Pasta Company**
700 Daniel Ellis Dr
Charleston, SC 29412
843-588-5088
Fax: 843-556-3950 brian@riobertolinispasta.com
www.riobertolinispasta.com
Pastas and noodles from scratch
Owner: Brian Bertolini

7132 **Lady Gale Seafood**
101 Charenton Rd
Baldwin, LA 70514-0058
337-923-2060
Fax: 337-923-6909
Fresh and frozen shrimp
Owner: Wayne Stevens
CFO: Jessica Burns
Estimated Sales: Below $5 Million
Number Employees: 4
Type of Packaging: Consumer, Food Service

7133 **Laetitia Vineyard & Winery**
453 Laetitia Vineyard Dr
Arroyo Grande, CA 93420-9701
805-481-1772
Fax: 805-481-6920 888-809-8463
info@laetitiawine.com www.laetitiawine.com
Wine
President & Head Winemaker: Eric Hickey
HR Executive: Jan Wilkinson
jan@laetitaiwine.com
Marketing Coordinator: Jackie Ross
Division Sales Manager: Tabitha Alger
Operations: Dave Hickey
President & Head Winemaker: Eric Hickey
Estimated Sales: Below $5 Million
Number Employees: 50-99
Brands:
Avila
Barnwood
Laetitia

7134 **Lafayette Brewing Co**
622 Main St
Lafayette, IN 47901-1451
765-742-2591
Fax: 765-742-3443 www.lafbrew.com
Ale
Owner: Greg Emig
greg@lafayettebrewingco.com
Brewer: Chris Johnson
Quality Control: Nancy Emig
Estimated Sales: Below $5 Million
Number Employees: 20-49
Type of Packaging: Consumer, Food Service

7135 **Lafaza Foods**
Oakland, CA
510-282-1138
www.lafaza.com
Manufacturer of vanilla beans. extracts, and pure ground vanilla.
Co-Founder and CEO: Nathaniel Delafield
Brands:
LAFAZA

7136 **Lafitte Frozen Foods Corp**
5165 Caroline St
Lafitte, LA 70067-5423
504-689-2041
Fax: 504-689-3270
Fresh and frozen shrimp processor.
President: Paul Poon
rayz1679@aol.com
Estimated Sales: $8.5 Million
Number Employees: 50-99

7137 **Lafleur Dairy Products**
617 Hill St
New Orleans, LA 70121-1000
504-729-3330
Fax: 504-461-8655
Milk and yogurt
President: Cedric Lafleur
VP: Tommy Baker
CFO: Monica Sosta
Estimated Sales: Below $5 Million
Number Employees: 40
Parent Co: Borden
Type of Packaging: Consumer, Food Service, Bulk
Brands:
Borden

7138 **Lafollette Vineyard & Winery**
180 Morris St
Suite 160
Sebastopol, CA 95472
707-395-3902
Fax: 707-395-3905 info@lafollettewines.com
www.lafollettewines.com
Wines

Owner: Miriam Summerskill
Direct Sales & Marketing Manager: Andrew Fegelman
National Sales & Distribution Manager: Vikki Tola
Events Manager: Jana Church
Estimated Sales: $68,000
Number Employees: 1
Type of Packaging: Private Label
Brands:
La Follette

7139 **Lafourche Sugar LLC**
141 Leighton Quarters Rd
Thibodaux, LA 70301-6489
985-447-3210
Fax: 985-447-8731
Sugar and blackstrap molasses
President/CEO: Greg Nolan
gn@lafourchesugars.com
Estimated Sales: $1-3 Million
Number Employees: 50-99
Type of Packaging: Consumer

7140 **Lago Tortillas International**
1700 E 4th St
Austin, TX 78702-4427
512-476-0945
Fax: 512-476-4931 800-369-9017
Tortillas
President, CEO: Luis Centeno
Estimated Sales: $5-10 Million appx.
Number Employees: 100-249

7141 **Lagomarcino's Confectionery**
1422 5th Ave # 1422
Moline, IL 61265-1334
309-764-1814
Fax: 309-736-5423 lagos@netexpress.net
www.lagomarcinos.com
Ice cream and confections
Owner: Marybeth Lagomarcino
lago1908@aol.com
Estimated Sales: Less Than $500,000
Number Employees: 10-19
Brands:
Lagomarcino's

7142 **Lagorio Enterprises**
2771 E French Camp Rd
Manteca, CA 95336-9689
209-982-5691
Fax: 209-982-0235 mail@lagorio.com
www.lagorio.com
Grower, packer and exporter of fresh tomatoes
President: Ed Beckman
Estimated Sales: $5-10 Million
Number Employees: 100-249
Square Footage: 635772
Brands:
Ace-Hi

7143 **Laguna Beach Brewing Company**
237 Ocean Avenue
Laguna Beach, CA 92651
949-497-3381
Fax: 949-497-0659 info@oceanbrewing.com
www.oceanbrewing.com
Ale, stout, lager and porter
President: Ross Bartlett
Number Employees: 30-50
Type of Packaging: Consumer, Food Service, Private Label, Bulk
Brands:
Diver's Hole Dunkelweizen
Festival Light Ale
Greeter's Pale Ale
Laguna Beach Blinde
Main Beach Brown
Renaissance Red
Salt Kriek Cherry Be
Thousand Steps Stout
Victoria E.S.B.
Wipe Out

7144 **Lahaha Tea Co**
135 E Santa Clara St # B
Suite B
Arcadia, CA 91006-3288
626-215-6960
lahahatea@yahoo.com
Natural teas imported from China
President: Angie Lin
angielin@lahahatea.com
Number Employees: 5-9

7145 **Lahtt Sauce**
Monterey Park, CA 91754
323-238-9398
www.lahttsauce.com
Chili oil sauce
CEO: Maxine Lau
Year Founded: 2015

7146 **Laird & Company**
One Laird Road
Scobeyville, NJ 07724
732-542-0312
Fax: 732-542-2244 877-438-5247
sales@lairdandcompany.com
www.lairdandcompany.com
Established in 1780. Processor of apple brandy, bourbon, vodka, gin, blended whiskey and other spirits; importer of wine and bulk alcoholic beverages; imported olive oils and balsamic vinegars.
President: Larrie Laird
EVP: John Laird III
VP: Lisa Laird Dunn
SVP of Sales/Marketing: Tom Alberico
Operations Manager: Raymond Murdock
General Manager: Lester Clements
Estimated Sales: $20-50 Million
Number Employees: 35
Number of Brands: 7
Type of Packaging: Consumer, Private Label, Bulk
Brands:
Bankers Club
Barrister
Captains
G & W
Kasser
Laird's
Senators Club

7147 **Laird Superfood**
PO Box 2270
Sisters, OR 97759
888-670-6796
support@lairdsuperfood.com lairdsuperfood.com
Organic coffee and superfood coffee creamers
Founder: Laird Hamilton
Type of Packaging: Consumer
Brands:
LAIRD SUPERFOOD

7148 **Lake Champlain Chocolates**
750 Pine St
Burlington, VT 05401-4923
802-864-1808
Fax: 802-864-1806 800-634-8105
sales@lakechamplainchocolates.com
www.lakechamplainchocolates.com
Specialty chocolate candies
Owner: Jim Lampman
Sales Manager: Allyson Meyers
jim@lakechamplainchocolates.com
Estimated Sales: Less than $500,000
Number Employees: 100-249
Square Footage: 96000
Type of Packaging: Consumer, Food Service, Private Label, Bulk
Brands:
Five Star Bars
Original Chocolates of Vermont

7149 **Lake Charles Poultry**
2808 Fruge St
Lake Charles, LA 70615-3699
337-433-6818
Fax: 318-433-7855
Poultry
President: Danny Bellard
Estimated Sales: $5-10 Million
Number Employees: 5-9

7150 **Lake City Foods**
5185 General Road
Mississauga, ON L4W 2K4
Canada
905-625-8244
Fax: 905-625-8244 hello@lakecityfoods.com
www.lakecityfoods.com
Processor and exporter of drink mixes, jelly powders, soup bases and mixes, army rations, nondairy coffee creamers and camping and trail foods
Proprietor: Eyal Adda
Number Employees: 10-19
Parent Co: Eden Manufacturing Company
Type of Packaging: Consumer, Food Service, Private Label, Bulk

Brands:
Anytime
Camp Rite
Gibbons
Quickset

7151 **Lake Country Foods Inc**
140 S Concord Rd
Oconomowoc, WI 53066-3555
262-567-5521
Fax: 262-567-5714
Malted milk, malt extract, dry blended foods, etc
President: Phil Kemppainen
pkemppainen@lcfoods.com
CFO: John Waltenberry
Vice President: Phillip Vanderhyden
VP Sales: Myron Jones
Estimated Sales: $25 Million
Number Employees: 50-99
Square Footage: 150000

7152 **Lake Erie Frozen Foods Co**
1830 Orange Rd
Ashland, OH 44805-1335
419-289-9204
Fax: 419-281-7624 800-766-8501
mbuckingham@leffco.net www.leffco.net
Breaded cheese and vegetables
President: Mike Buckingham
mbuckingham@leffco.net
Estimated Sales: $2.4 Million
Number Employees: 20-49
Type of Packaging: Consumer, Food Service, Private Label

7153 **Lake Packing Co Inc**
755 Lake Landing Dr
Lottsburg, VA 22511-2503
804-529-6101
Fax: 804-529-7374 800-324-2759
info@manningshominy.com
www.manningshominy.com
Frozen oysters and canned tomatoes, tomato juice and hominy
Owner: S L Cowart Jr
Estimated Sales: Under $1,000,000
Number Employees: 20-49
Parent Co: Cowart Seafood
Type of Packaging: Consumer, Food Service, Private Label

7154 **Lake Sonoma Winery**
777 Madrone Rd
Glen Ellen, CA 95442-9522
707-721-1979
Fax: 707-431-8356 877-586-2796
info@lswinery.com www.lakesonomawinery.com
Wines
CEO: Gary Heck
President: David Ready
Sales: Pat Paulson
Marketing Director: Gary Heck
Estimated Sales: $1-$2.5 Million
Number Employees: 5-9
Brands:
Lake Sonoma Winery

7155 **Lake States Yeast**
428 W Davenport St
Rhinelander, WI 54501-3325
715-369-4949
Fax: 715-369-4969 lgary@lallemand.com
www.lallemand.com
Manufacturer and exporter of yeasts including inactive dried, torula, autolyzed, formulated and specialty grades that inlcudes smoked, roasted, and grill flavors.
President/Manager: Antoine Chagnon
Quality Control: Joelle Provix
Customer Service Manager: Linda Gary
Plant Manager: Stuart Bacon
Production Manager: Rick Bishop
Plant Manager: Stuart Bacon
Number Employees: 5-9
Parent Co: Rhinelander Paper Company
Type of Packaging: Private Label, Bulk
Brands:
Lake States

7156 **Lakefront Brewery Inc**
1872 N Commerce St
Milwaukee, WI 53212-3701
414-372-8800
Fax: 414-430-4400 info@lakefrontbrewery.com
www.lakefrontbrewery.com
Beer
Owner: Russ Klich
rushelakefront@brewery.com
Marketing Director: Chris Johnson
Dir. Of Communications: Matt Krajnak
Operations Manager: Chris Ranson
Estimated Sales: Below $5 Million
Number Employees: 100-249
Type of Packaging: Private Label
Brands:
River West Stein

7157 **Lakeport Brewing Corporation**
180 Henri Dunant St
Moncton, NB E1E 1E6
Canada
905-523-4200
Fax: 905-523-6564 800-268-2337
Processor and exporter of beer, ale, lager and stout
President: Teresa Cascioli
Sales/Marketing Executive: Ian McDonald
Estimated Sales: F
Number Employees: 200
Type of Packaging: Consumer, Food Service
Brands:
Brava
Lakeport Honey Lager
Lakeport Ice
Lakeport Light
Lakeport Pilsener
Lakeport Strong
Mongoose
Steeler Lager
Wee Willy

7158 **Lakeridge Winery & Vineyards**
19239 US Highway 27
Clermont, FL 34715-9025
352-394-8627
Fax: 352-394-7490 800-768-9463
www.lakeridgewinery.com
Wines
President: Geary Cox
Finance Executive: Mandi Enix
Vice President: Mandi Enix
menix@lakeridgewinery.com
Sales Executive: Kyle Johnson
Estimated Sales: $30 Million
Number Employees: 20-49
Number of Brands: 1
Brands:
Lakeridge

7159 **Lakeshore Winery**
5132 State Route 89
Romulus, NY 14541-9779
315-549-7075
Fax: 315-549-7102 info@lakeshorewinery.com
www.lakeshorewinery.com
Farm winery
Owner: Annie Bachman
annie@lakeshorewinery.com
Estimated Sales: Less Than $500,000
Number Employees: 1-4
Brands:
Lakeshore

7160 **Lakeside Foods Inc.**
1055 W. Broadway
Plainview, MN 55964
507-534-3141
www.lakesidefoods.com
Frozen and canned vegetables, frozen appetizers and seafood, canned meats and pet food, canned beans, whipped toppings and sauces.
CEO: Glenn Tellock
Estimated Sales: $103 Million
Number Employees: 500-999
Type of Packaging: Consumer
Other Locations:
Lakeside Foods-Manufacturing
Manitowoc WI
Lakeside Foods-Manufacturing
Belgium WI
Lakeside Foods-Manufacturing
Random Lake WI
Lakeside Foods-Manufacturing
Reedsburg WI
Lakeside Foods-Manufacturing
Seymour WI
Lakeside Foods-Manufacturing
Plainview MN
Lakeside Foods-Manufacturing
Brooten MN
Lakeside Foods-Manufacturing
Owatoona MN
Lakeside Foods-Manufacturing
New Richmond WI
Lakeside Foods-Manufacturing
Eden WI
Lakeside Foods-Distribution
Manitowoc WI
Lakeside Foods-Distribution
Plainview MN
Lakeside Foods-Distribution
Belgium WI
Brands:
Eureka
Hobby
Lakeside

7161 **(HQ)Lakeside Foods Inc.**
PO Box 1327
Manitowoc, WI 54221-1327
920-684-3356
Fax: 920-686-4033 800-466-3834
www.lakesidefoods.com
Food manufacturing company for private label consumers, including canned and frozen vegetables, frozen seafood, canned meats, pet food, canned beans, whipped topping and sauces.
CEO: Glenn Tellock
General Manager: Janet De Pirro
CFO: Denise Kitzerow
Quality Assurance Manager: Alex Kiel
Vice President, Sales: Matt Brown
Vice President, Operations: Bruce Jacobson
Year Founded: 1887
Estimated Sales: $103.5 Million
Number Employees: 1,000-4,999
Square Footage: 28500
Type of Packaging: Consumer, Food Service, Private Label
Other Locations:
Lakeside Foods Processing Plant
Manitowoc WI
Lakeside Foods Processing Plant
Belgium WI
Lakeside Foods Processing Plant
Random Lake WI
Lakeside Foods Processing Plant
Reedsburg WI
Lakeside Foods Processing Plant
Seymour WI
Lakeside Foods Processing Plant
Plainview MN
Lakeside Foods Processing Plant
Brooten MN
Lakeside Foods Processing Plant
New Richmond WI
Lakeside Foods Processing Plant
Eden WI
Lakeside Foods Processing Plant
Owatonna MN
Lakeside Foods Processing Plant
Mondovi WI
Lakeside Foods Processing Plant
Poynette WI
Brands:
Festal
Read
Tendersweet

7162 **Lakeside Foods Inc.**
705 Main St.
PO Box B
Belgium, WI 53004
262-285-3299
www.lakesidefoods.com
Canned and frozen vegetables, frozen appetizers and seafood, canned meats and pet food, canned beans, whipped toppings and sauces.
CEO: Glenn Tellock
Estimated Sales: $50-100 Million
Number Employees: 250-499
Parent Co: Lakeside Foods

7163 **Lakeside Mills**
PO Box 230
Rutherfordton, NC 28139-0230
828-286-4866
Fax: 828-287-3361 www.lakesidemills.com
Corn meal, hush puppy mix and breadings; importer of peppers and spices
VP: Aaron King
Contact: Kim King
kimking@lakesidemills.com
Number Employees: 10-19
Parent Co: Lakeside Mills
Type of Packaging: Consumer, Food Service, Private Label, Bulk
Brands:
Blue Ribbon
Kings Old Fashion

7164 **Lakeside Packing Company**
667 County Road #50
Harrow, ON N0R 1G0
Canada
519-738-2314
Fax: 519-738-3684 info@lakesidepacking.com
www.lakesidepacking.com
Pickles, peppers, relish, salsa, tomatoes
President/Board Member: Donald Woodbridge
VP/Board Member: Alan Woodbridge
Estimated Sales: $813,000
Number Employees: 20
Type of Packaging: Consumer, Food Service

7165 **Lakeview Bakery**
6449 Crowchild Trail SW
Calgary, AB T2E 5R7
Canada
403-246-6127
Fax: 403-246-6609
members.shaw.ca/organicbaking/
Bread, buns and pastries
President: Maureen Hinton
Sales & Distribution Manager: David Hinton
Number Employees: 5-9
Type of Packaging: Consumer, Food Service

7166 **Lakeview Banquit Cheese**
1755 S Fremont Dr
Salt Lake City, UT 84104-4218
801-364-3607
Fax: 801-364-3600 www.banquetcheese.com
Cheese including cheddar, Monterey jack and mozzarella
President: Val Hardcastle
Chief Executive Officer: Calvin Nelson
CFO: Reagan Wood
Secretary: Jenille Tyler
Vice President of Operations: Kirk Mackert
Plant Manager of Distribution: Andrew Pettersson
Estimated Sales: $14 Million
Number Employees: 10-19
Square Footage: 90000
Type of Packaging: Food Service, Private Label, Bulk
Brands:
Banquet Better Foods
Banquet Butter
Banquet Cheese
Gold Nugget Butter
Gold Nugget Cheese
Grand Teton
Grand Teton Cheese

7167 **Lakeview Cheese**
3030 N Lamb Blvd # 114
Las Vegas, NV 89115-3496
702-233-2439
lakeviewcheese.com
Cheese products
Owner: Debbie Gaglio
Estimated Sales: Less Than $500,000
Number Employees: 5-9

7168 **Lakeview Farms**
229 East Second Street
PO Box 98
Delphos, OH 45833-0098
419-695-9925
Fax: 419-695-9900 800-755-9925
sales_mrkt@lakeviewfarms.com
www.lakeviewfarms.com
Sour cream, mousse, cheesecake, fruit gelatins, sour cream dip, soy oil dips, imitation sour cream and specialty products.
CEO: Tom Davis
Contact: Maria Adamiec
madamiec@lakeviewfarms.com
Estimated Sales: $30-50 Million
Number Employees: 100-249
Number of Brands: 6
Type of Packaging: Food Service, Private Label, Bulk

Brands:
Fresh Creations
Lakeview Farms
Luisa's
Salads of the Sea
Senor Rico
Winky Foods

7169 Lakewood Juice Co.
Miami, FL 33127
866-324-5900
info@floridabottling.com
www.lakewoodorganic.com
Organic juices bottled fresh, frozen concentrates, supplement juices, and culinary juices.
Manager: Lee Wilson
Sales Manager: Holly Newberry
Contact: Pamela Ford
pford@floridabottling.com
Estimated Sales: $20-50 Million
Number Employees: 20-49
Parent Co: Florida Bottling
Type of Packaging: Consumer

7170 Lakewood Juice Company
1035 NW 21st Ter
Miami, FL 33127
305-324-5932
Fax: 305-325-9573 866-324-5900
info@floridabottling.com
Manufacturer and exporter of glass-packed fruit juices
President: Vivian Calzadilla
CEO: R Fuhrman
VP, Sales: Joseph Letiz
Contact: Pamela Ford
pford@floridabottling.com
Estimated Sales: $7,000,000
Number Employees: 50
Parent Co: Florida Family Trust
Type of Packaging: Consumer, Food Service, Bulk
Brands:
Coconut Grove
Lakewood
Rainberry
Summer Song

7171 Lakewood Vineyards Inc
4024 State Route 14
Watkins Glen, NY 14891-9630
607-535-9252
Fax: 607-535-6656 877-535-9252
wines@lakewoodvineyards.com
www.lakewoodvineyards.com
Wines
Owner: Beverly Stamp
lwoodwine@aol.com
Estimated Sales: $2.5-5 Million
Number Employees: 10-19
Brands:
Lakewood Vineyards
Mystic Mead

7172 (HQ)Lallemand
1620 Rue Prefontaine
Montreal, QC H1W 2N8
Canada
514-522-2133
Fax: 514-522-2884 www.bio-lallemand.com
Manufacturer and exporter of food and dairy microbial cultures, lactobacilli and bifidobacteria; also, custom formulations available
President: Roland Chagnon
Vice President: Francois Leblanc
Estimated Sales: $10-20 Million
Number Employees: 50-99
Square Footage: 100000
Type of Packaging: Consumer, Private Label, Bulk
Brands:
Ferlac
Gastro-Ad
Polylacton
Probiotic-2000
Rosell
Rosellac
Standard Formulation
Vitanat

7173 Lallemand American Yeast
1417 W Jeffrey Dr
Addison, IL 60101-4331
630-932-1290
Fax: 630-932-1291 mlegel@lallemand.com
www.lallemand.com
Baking enzymes, baking ingredients, dough conditioners, such as bromate replacers, chocolate, cocoa, eggs, nuts, oils, oxidizers, raisins, spices, sweetners, yeast foods, yeast (fresh & dry), starter cultures, baking powder, moldinhibitors
President: Gary Edwards
VP: Merna Legel
Quality Control: Mike Hudson
Sales: Steven Marinella
Estimated Sales: Below $5 Million
Number Employees: 10-19
Parent Co: Lallemand, Inc.
Type of Packaging: Food Service, Bulk
Brands:
American Yeast
Eagle
Essential
Fermaid
Lallemand

7174 Lallemand Inc
8480 St Laurent Boulevard
Montreal, QC H2P 2M6
Canada
514-381-5631
Fax: 514-383-4493 800-452-4364
americas-hn@lallemand.com www.lallemand.com
Yeast-cultures are fermented before being high density concentrated and granulated. Yeasts are then fluid bed-dried and bacteria are freeze-dried. Certified yeast for many of the wine countries around the world.
Sales Director: Aldo Fuoco

7175 Lallemand/American Yeast
47-00 Northern Boulevard
Long Island City, NY 11101
773-267-2223
Fax: 773-267-4508 gedwards@lallemand.com
www.lallemand.com
Yeast
President: Joanie Joans
Estimated Sales: $300,000-500,000
Number Employees: 5-9
Parent Co: Lallemand, Inc.

7176 Lallemand/American Yeast
PO Box 5512
Petaluma, CA 94955-5512
707-795-1468
Fax: 661-835-4990 800-423-6625
info@lallemand.com www.lallemand.com
Wine industry yeasts
Director: William Pursley
Parent Co: Lallemand, Inc.
Brands:
Enoferm
Fermaid
Lalvin
Uvaferm

7177 Lam's Food Inc
9723 218th St
Queens Village, NY 11429-1251
718-217-0476
Fax: 718-217-0655 andrew@lamsnacks.com
www.lamsnacks.com
Plantain and yuca chips in different flavors.
President: Andrew Lam
andrew@lamsnacks.com
VP: Trevor Lam
Sales/Marketing: Melissa Gaviria
Estimated Sales: $520,000
Number Employees: 1-4
Square Footage: 9600

7178 Lamagna Cheese Co
1 Lamagna Dr
Verona, PA 15147-1137
412-828-6112
Fax: 412-828-6782
customer_service@lamagnacheese.com
www.lamagnacheese.com
Manufacturer of ricotta, feta, provolone and mozzarella cheeses.
Owner: Michael Lamagna
CEO: John Sottile
jsottile@lamagnacheese.com
Estimated Sales: $10-20 Million
Number Employees: 20-49
Number of Brands: 1
Type of Packaging: Private Label
Brands:
Lamagna

7179 Lamb Weston Holdings Inc.
599 S. Rivershore Ln.
Eagle, ID 83616
208-938-1047
800-766-7783
www.lambweston.com
Frozen potato products.
President/CEO: Tom Werner
Senior VP/CFO: Robert McNutt
Senior VP/General Counsel: Eryk Spytek
Year Founded: 1950
Estimated Sales: $3.4 Billion
Number Employees: 7,200
Number of Brands: 8
Type of Packaging: Consumer, Food Service
Other Locations:
Lamb Weston Manufacturing Plant
Weston OR
Lamb Weston Manufacturing Plant
Kennewick WA
Lamb Weston Manufacturing Plant
Prosser WA
Lamb Weston Manufacturing Plant
Boise ID
Lamb Weston Manufacturing Plant
Alberta, Canada
Brands:
Sweet Things
Colossal Crisp
CrispyCoat Fries
Lamb Weston
Lamb's Seasoned
Lamb's Supreme
LW Private Reserve
Stealth Fries
Tavern Traditions

7180 Lambent Technologies
7247 Central Park Ave
Skokie, IL 60076
847-675-3951
Fax: 847-675-3013 800-432-7187
www.lambenttech.com
Manufacturer and exporter of nonionic emulsifiers including polysorbates, sorbitan esters and glycerol esters; also, silicone and nonsilicone antifoams and defoamers
President: Michael Hayes
Marketing Manager: Randy Cobb
Sales Manager: Kevin Hrebenar
Estimated Sales: $9800000
Number Employees: 55
Square Footage: 40000
Parent Co: Petroferm
Brands:
Lambent

7181 Lambert Bridge Winery
4085 W Dry Creek Rd
Healdsburg, CA 95448-9117
707-431-9600
Fax: 707-433-3215 800-975-0555
wines@lambertbridge.com
www.lambertbridge.com
Wine
President: Dean Agostinelli
dean@lambertbridge.com
Winemaker: Jill Davis
Estimated Sales: $1.1 Million
Number Employees: 5-9
Type of Packaging: Private Label
Brands:
Lambert Bridge Winery

7182 Lamex Foods Inc.
8500 Normandale Lake Blvd.
Suite 1150
Bloomington, MN 55437
952-844-0585
Fax: 952-844-0083 info@lamexfoods.eu
www.lamexfoods.eu
Many types of foods including; beef, fruit, honey, juice, pork, poultry, seafood, and vegetables.
President: Steve Anderson
CEO: Phillip Wallace
Vice President: Mark Barrett
Year Founded: 1966
Estimated Sales: $1.75 Billion
Number Employees: 48
Square Footage: 6000
Parent Co: Lamex Foods

7183 **Lamitech West**
115 Post Street
Santa Cruz, CA 95060
831-425-6625
Fax: 831-425-6627 TPocock@lamitech.com
www.lamitech.com
Manufacturer of paperboard products for food packaging, printing products, custom laminating and other converting services.
Vice President, General Manager: Adam Reiser
Senior Sales Representative: Tim Pocok
Number Employees: 1-4

7184 **Lammes Candies**
1000 W 38th St
Austin, TX 78705-1003
512-458-1885
Fax: 512-458-1844 800-252-1885
www.lammes.com
Founded 1885. Candy
Manager: Crystal Bertrand
VP: Bryan Teich
Manager: Richard Butler
rbutler@lammes.com
Estimated Sales: Less Than $500,000
Number Employees: 1-4
Number of Products: 1000
Brands:
Cashew Critters
Choc-Adillos
Longhorns
Peanut Paws
Texas Chewie Pecan Praline

7185 **Lamonaca Bakery**
304 7th St
Windber, PA 15963-1343
814-467-4909
Bread products and pizza shells
President: Mary La Monaca
Estimated Sales: $5-10 Million
Number Employees: 10 to 19
Type of Packaging: Consumer, Food Service

7186 **Lamoreaux Landing Wine Cellars**
9224 State Route 414
Lodi, NY 14860-9641
607-582-6011
Fax: 607-582-6010 info@lamoreauxwine.com
www.lamoreauxwine.com
Wines
Owner: Mark J Wagner
Retail Sales Manager: Susan Whitaker
markw@lamoreauxwine.com
Estimated Sales: $5-10 Million
Number Employees: 10-19
Type of Packaging: Private Label

7187 **Lampost Meats**
805 Shawver Drive
Grimes, IA 50111-1118
515-288-6111
Fax: 515-288-5727 sglksl@aol.com
Pork and beef offals
President: Stanley Lammers
Number Employees: 2
Parent Co: Walking S Farms

7188 **Lanaetex Products Incorporated**
151 3rd St
Elizabeth, NJ 7206
908-351-9700
Fax: 908-351-8753
Processor and exporter of food grade waxes
President: Mike Gutowski
Estimated Sales: $10-20 Million
Number Employees: 10-19

7189 **Lancaster Colony Corporation**
380 Polaris Parkway
Suite 400
Westerville, OH 43082
614-224-7141
www.lancastercolony.com
Amenities including glassware, ice and food molds, iced tea dispensers, wood grain serving trays, ice buckets, aluminum cookware and commercial coffee urns, candles and matting. Foodservice products include frozen appetizers, dips, andsalad dressings.
Executive Chairman: John Gerlach
President & CEO: David Ciesinki
Vice President/CFO: Thomas Pigott
General Counsel/Chief Ethics Officer: Matthew Shurte
Vice President, Investor Relations: Dale Ganobsik
Year Founded: 1969
Estimated Sales: $1.13 Billion
Number Employees: 500-1000
Type of Packaging: Consumer, Food Service, Bulk
Brands:
Marzetti
Sister Schubert's
New York Bakery
Flatout

7190 **Lancaster County WineryLTD**
799 Rawlinsville Rd
Willow Street, PA 17584-8700
717-464-3555
www.lancastercountywinery.com
Wines
President: Suzanne Dickel
Manager: Todd Dickel
Estimated Sales: Below $5 Million
Number Employees: 5-9

7191 **Lancaster Fine Foods**
2320 Norman Rd
Lancaster, PA 17601-5930
717-397-9578
Fax: 717-397-0941 info@lancasterfinefoods.com
www.lancasterfinefoods.com
Sauces, dressings
Owner: Dave Esh
dave@beaniesoflancaster.com
CEO: Michael Thompson
Director of Quality: Christie Oliver
Estimated Sales: $5.8 Million
Number Employees: 20-49

7192 **Lancaster Fine Foods**
2320 Norman Rd
Lancaster, PA 17601-5930
717-397-9578
Fax: 717-397-0941 info@lancasterfinefoods.com
www.lancasterfinefoods.com
Pickeled fruits, sauces, dressings
Owner: Dave Esh
dave@beaniesoflancaster.com
Number Employees: 20-49

7193 **Lancaster Packing Company**
7615 Lancaster Avenue
PO Box 465
Myerstown, PA 17067
717-397-9727
Fax: 717-397-7744 www.jakeandamos.com
Pennsylvania Dutch-style pickles, preserves, relishes, syrups, pickled vegetables and fruits, chow chow and fruit butters packed in glass canning jars
President: David Doolittle
CEO: Sue Doolittle
Estimated Sales: $5-10 Million
Number Employees: 5-9
Square Footage: 40000
Type of Packaging: Consumer, Private Label
Brands:
Jake & Amos

7194 **Lance Private Brands**
8600 South Boulevard
Charlotte, NC 28273
704-557-8313
Fax: 704-556-5781 888-722-1163
Kosher, organic/natural, cookies, private label.
Marketing: Drew Snyder
Contact: Teri Edwards
tedwards@lance.com

7195 **Lanco**
350 Wireless Blvd Ste 200
Hauppauge, NY 11788
631-231-2300
Fax: 631-231-2731 800-938-4500
sales@lancopromo.com www.lancopromo.com
Chocolate candy including squares, circles and triangles
President: Brian Landow
Number Employees: 175
Type of Packaging: Consumer, Food Service

7196 **Land O'Frost Inc**
911 Hastings Ave
Searcy, AR 72143-7401
501-268-2473
Fax: 501-268-0357 800-643-5654
www.landofrost.com
Processor and importer of ham, beef, chicken and turkey; also, pre-sliced luncheon meats, pre-portioned julienne meat strips and diced meats
President & CEO: David Van Eekeren
COO: William Marion
wmarion@landofrost.com
Number Employees: 500-999
Square Footage: 1052000
Type of Packaging: Consumer, Food Service, Private Label, Bulk
Brands:
Perfect-O-Portion
Salad Toppers
Sandwich Shop

7197 **(HQ)Land O'Frost Inc.**
16850 Chicago Ave.
Lansing, IL 60438
708-474-7100
Fax: 708-474-9329 800-323-3308
www.landofrost.com
Lunch and deli meats such as; beef, chicken, turkey, ham and meat ingredients.
President: Charles Niementowski
Chairman/CEO: Donna Van Eekeren
Chief Financial Officer: George Smolar
Director of Quality Control: Dayna Nicholas
Estimated Sales: $103.6 Million
Number Employees: 500-999
Square Footage: 100000
Type of Packaging: Consumer, Food Service, Private Label
Brands:
Delishaved
Land O'Frost
Premium
Bistro Favorites

7198 **Land O'Lakes Inc**
4001 Lexington Ave. N.
Arden Hills, MN 55126-2998
651-375-2222
800-328-9680
www.landolakesinc.com
A global crop inputs, dairy foods and animal nutrition co-operative.
President/CEO: Beth Ford
Senior VP/CFO: Bill Pieper
Senior VP/General Counsel: Sheilah Stewart
Senior VP/Chief Marketing Officer: Tim Scott
Executive VP/COO: Jerry Kaminski
Chief Supply Chain Officer: Yone Dewberry
Year Founded: 1921
Estimated Sales: $14 Billion
Number Employees: 10,000
Number of Brands: 5
Type of Packaging: Consumer, Food Service, Private Label, Bulk
Brands:
Land O'Lakes
Kozy Shack
Alpine Lace
WinField
Purina

7199 **Land-O-Sun Dairies Inc**
610 E State St
O Fallon, IL 62269-1538
314-436-6820
Fax: 618-628-3309 www.deanfoods.com
Fruit drinks, milk, cottage cheese, sour cream and dips
Manager: Bill Schaefer
COO: Chuck McQuig
Manager: Jeff Powell
Estimated Sales: $10-20 Million
Number Employees: 10-19
Parent Co: Suiza Foods

7200 **Landies Candies Co**
2495 Main St # 350
Suite 350
Buffalo, NY 14214-2154
716-834-8212
Fax: 716-833-9113 800-955-2634
larrys@landiescandies.com
www.landiescandies.com

Boxed chocolates including pecan, peanut, cashew, no sugar, cherry cordials and nut clusters; also, divinity, toffee, taffy, fondant mints, dipped pretzels, peppermint kisses, caramels, truffles and pecan praline dessert topping
President, CEO & Founder: Larry Szrama
larrys@landiescandies.com
Comptroller: Bob Szrama
Vice President: Bryan Tiech
Health & Safety Director: Alan Nowak
Marketing & Sales: Dennis Hussak
Operations Director: Dennis Hussak
Prod Suprv: Jimmy Del Gaudio
Plant Manager: John Davis
Estimated Sales: $1670977
Number Employees: 10-19
Type of Packaging: Consumer, Private Label, Bulk
Brands:
Cashew Critters
Choc Adillos
Choc'adillos
Longhorns
Texas Chewie

7201 **Landis Peanut Butter**
641 E Cherry Ln
Souderton, PA 18964-1236
215-723-9366
landispeanutbutter@yahoo.com
www.landispeanutbutter.com
Peanut butter
Owner: Raymond Landis
Estimated Sales: $500-1 Million appx.
Number Employees: 1-4

7202 **Landlocked Seafoods**
219 E 3rd St
Carroll, IA 51401
712-792-9599
Fax: 712-792-9599
mebner@landlockedseafood.com
Seafood
President: Michael Ebner
Contact: Mike Ebner
mebner@landlockedseafood.com

7203 **Landmark Vineyards**
101 Adobe Canyon Rd
PO Box 340
Kenwood, CA 95452-9045
707-833-0053
Fax: 707-833-1164 info@landmarkwine.com
www.landmarkwine.com
Wines
Owner/CFO: Michael Colhoun
Winemaker: Eric Stern
Public Relations: Mary Colhoun
Estimated Sales: $5-10 Million
Number Employees: 20-49
Brands:
Landmark Damaris Chardonnay
Landmark Grand Detou
Landmark Kastania Pi
Landmark Overlook Ch

7204 **Landolfi's Food Products**
302 Cummings Avenue
Trenton, NJ 08611
609-392-1830
Fax: 609-396-6581 landolfis@gmail.com
Frozen pasta, garlic bread and pizza dough
President: Jack Fu
Sales Director: Lori Landolfi
Director Manufacturing: Paul Melovich
Estimated Sales: $2 Million
Number Employees: 16
Square Footage: 40000
Type of Packaging: Consumer, Food Service, Private Label, Bulk

7205 **Landreth Wild Rice**
2320 Industrial Blvd
Norman, OK 73069-8518
405-360-2333
Fax: 405-360-6644 800-333-3533
Processor and exporter of wild rice
Principal: George Landreth
Estimated Sales: $110,000
Number Employees: 2
Type of Packaging: Consumer, Food Service, Private Label

7206 **Landry's Pepper Co**
1606 Cypress Island Hwy
PO Box 127
St Martinville, LA 70582-6013
337-394-6097
Fax: 337-394-7629 landry6097@aol.com
Hot sauces.
President: Lamar Bertrand
VP: Toby Bertrand
Estimated Sales: $500,000
Number Employees: 5-9
Square Footage: 120000
Type of Packaging: Consumer, Food Service, Private Label, Bulk
Brands:
Cajun Gourmet Magic
Landry's
Premium

7207 **Lane Southern Orchards**
50 Lane Rd
Fort Valley, GA 31030-5212
478-825-3266
Fax: 478-825-7995 800-277-3224
www.lanesouthernorchards.com
Packer of peaches, oranges, grapefruit, and pecans
President: Duke Lane
CEO: Mark Sanchez
mark@lanepacking.com
Marketing Director: Wendy Barton
Wholesale: Duke Lanc
Purchasing: Lori Buzze
Estimated Sales: $950,000
Number Employees: 250-499
Square Footage: 43152
Type of Packaging: Bulk
Brands:
Diamond D

7208 **Lane's Dairy**
310 N Concepcion St
El Paso, TX 79905-1605
915-772-6700
Fax: 915-772-3097
Manufacturer and exporter of milk and canned and bottled fruit juice
President: John Lane
Owner: Hilda Lane
Production Manager: Chris Lane
Estimated Sales: $2 Million
Number Employees: 20-49
Square Footage: 60000
Type of Packaging: Consumer
Brands:
Lanes Dairy

7209 **Lang Creek Brewery**
655 Lang Creek Rd
Marion, MT 59925
406-858-2200
Fax: 406-858-2499
Beer and ale
Owner/Brewmaster: John Campbell
Estimated Sales: $2.5-5 Million
Number Employees: 5-9
Number of Brands: 1
Number of Products: 8
Brands:
Tri-Motor
Windsock

7210 **Lang Pharma Nutrition Inc**
20 Silva Ln
Middletown, RI 02842-5638
401-848-7700
Fax: 401-848-7701 customer.service@langpni.com
Dietary supplements and pharma nutrition products.
Owner: Judy Pattie
jpattie@langpni.com
Vice President: Bruce Lang
Estimated Sales: $10-20 Million
Number Employees: 20-49
Number of Products: 250
Type of Packaging: Consumer, Food Service, Private Label, Bulk
Brands:
Enerjuice
Mr. Spice
Tangy Bang

7211 **Lang's Chocolates**
350 Pine St.
Williamsport, PA 17701
570-323-6320
info@langschocolates.com
www.langschocolates.com
Gourmet handcrafted chocolates and confections
Master Chocolatier: William Lang

7212 **Lange Estate Winery & Vineyard**
18380 NE Buena Vista Dr
Dundee, OR 97115-9104
503-538-6476
Fax: 503-538-1938 don@langewinery.com
www.langewinery.com
Wines
Owner: Don Lange
donlange@europa.com
Owner/CEO: Wendy Lange
National Sales Manager: Michael Sanders
donlange@europa.com
Owner, Winemaker: Don Lange
General Manager, Winemaker: Jesse Lange
General Manager, Winemaker: Jesse Lange
Estimated Sales: $680,000
Number Employees: 5-9
Brands:
Lange Winery

7213 **Langer Juice Co Inc**
City of Industry, CA
626-336-3100
bruce@langers.com
www.langers.com
Juices.
CEO: Bruce Langer
Quality Assurance Manager: Amandeep Kaur
National Sales Manager: Tom Bottiaux
Year Founded: 1960
Estimated Sales: $160 Million
Number Employees: 100-249
Square Footage: 140000
Type of Packaging: Consumer, Food Service, Private Label
Brands:
Dole
Langers Juice
Packers Pride
Tropicana

7214 **Lantana Hummus**
PO Box 40639
Austin, TX 78704
844-907-7626
customerservice@lantanafoods.com
www.lantanafoods.com
Gourmet hummus
CEO: Matt Gase
VP, Marketing: Kristin Garro
Number of Brands: 1
Number of Products: 8
Type of Packaging: Consumer
Brands:
LANTANA

7215 **Lanthier Bakery**
PO Box 640
58 Dominion Street
Alexandria, ON K0C 1A0
Canada
613-525-2435
Fax: 613-525-2818 info@lanthierbakery.com
Bread and rolls
President/CEO: Marc Lanthier
Type of Packaging: Consumer, Food Service
Brands:
Lanthier

7216 **Lantic Sugar**
4026, Notre-Dame Street East
Montreal, QC H1W 2K3
Canada
514-527-8686
Fax: 514-527-1401 info@lantic.ca
www.lantic.ca
Sugar including liquid, bulk, soft, icing, granulated, coarse, medium, instant, etc
President and CEO: Edward Makin
Chairman, Chief Executive Officer: A. Stuart Belkin
Vice-President, finance and secretary: Manon Lacroix, CPA, auditor CA
Consultant: Daniel Lafrance
Vice President of Sales: Mike Walton
Vice President of Operations: Bob Copeland

Number Employees: 400
Type of Packaging: Consumer, Food Service, Bulk
Brands:
Lantic

7217 Lapierre Maple Farms
99 de l'Escale
St-Ludger de Beauce, QC G0M 1W0
Canada
819-548-5454
www.lapierremaple.com
Organic maple syrup
President: Donald Lapierre

7218 Larabar
Denver, CO 80218
800-543-2147
info@larabar.com www.larabar.com
All-natural fruit, nut and dessert bars
Founder: Lara Merriken
Marketing Director: Ashley Capobianco
Contact: Cynthia Abrahamson
abrahamson@larabar.com

7219 Laredo Tortilleria & Mexican
1616 Woodside Ave
Fort Wayne, IN 46816-3942
260-447-2576
Fax: 219-447-2577 800-252-7336
http://www.laredomexicanfoods.com
Processor and wholesaler/distributor of Mexican food products including salsa, tortillas and tortilla chips; serving the food service market
President: Benito Trevino
General Manager: Raul Trevino
VP: Reynol Trevino
Manager: Frank Trevino
Estimated Sales: Less Than $500,000
Number Employees: 1-4
Parent Co: Tregar
Type of Packaging: Consumer, Food Service, Private Label, Bulk
Brands:
Don Pedro

7220 Lark Fine Foods
8 Scotts Way
Essex, MA 01929-1120
978-768-0012
Fax: 978-890-7135 mamccormick@gmail.com
www.larkfinefoods.com
Cookies, crackers.
Marketing: Mary Ann McCormick
Estimated Sales: Less Than $500,000
Number Employees: 5-9

7221 Larkin Cold Storage
4755 27th St
Long Island City, NY 11101-4410
718-937-2007
Fax: 718-937-3250
Chocolate bars, butter, cheese, other dairy and eggs, yogurt, honey, pickles & pickled vegetables
Owner: Anne Cheneby
anne@larkin.com
Marketing: Adam Moskowitz
Number Employees: 10-19

7222 Laronga Bakery
599 Somerville Ave
Somerville, MA 02143-3296
617-625-8600
Fax: 617-625-1853
customerservice@larongabakery.com
www.larongabakery.com
Bakery goods
Owner: Michael Ronga
mronga@larongabakery.com
Owner: Louis Ronga
General Manager: Steve Weinstein
Estimated Sales: $20-50 Million
Number Employees: 50-99
Brands:
La Ronga Bakery

7223 Larosa Bakery Inc
79 Newman Springs Rd E
Shrewsbury, NJ 07702-4038
732-842-2592
Fax: 732-842-8029 800-527-6722
www.ecannoli.com
Cannolis, cannoli cream, gourmet butter, cookies and biscotti
Owner: George Delaney
VP: Peter LaRosa
Sales Manager: George Delaney
gdelaney@kingofcannoli.com
Estimated Sales: $1-3 Million
Number Employees: 20-49
Type of Packaging: Consumer, Food Service, Bulk

7224 Larosa Bakery Inc
79 Newman Springs Rd E
Shrewsbury, NJ 07702-4038
732-842-2592
Fax: 732-842-8029 800-527-6722
www.ecannoli.com
Cannoli, cannoli cream, biscotti, cookies
Owner: George Delaney
gdelaney@kingofcannoli.com
Owner/VP: Peter La Rosa
Estimated Sales: $1.3 Million
Number Employees: 20-49
Brands:
Larosa's Famous Biscotti
Larosa's Famous Cannoli
Larosa's Famous Cookies

7225 Larry J. Williams Company
2686 Savannah Hwy
Jesup, GA 31545-5511
912-427-7729
Fax: 912-427-0611
Shrimp, crab, oysters, scallps, flounder, etc.
President: Larry Williams
l.williams@larryjwilliams.com
General Manager: Joey Williams
Estimated Sales: $1-3 Million
Number Employees: 20-49

7226 Larry's Beans
1509 Gavin St
Raleigh, NC 27608-2613
919-828-1234
Fax: 919-833-4567 www.larryscoffee.com
Wholesale coffee roaster
Owner: Charles Nichols
CFO: Brad Lienhart
VP: Kevin Bobal
Marketing: Kyley Schmidt
Sales: Erik Iverson
charlesnichols@larrysbeans.com
Plant Manager: Neal England
Estimated Sales: $3.0 Million
Number Employees: 10-19

7227 Larry's Sausage Corporation
931 S Eastern Boulevard
Fayetteville, NC 28306-7365
910-483-5148
Fax: 910-483-2526 larryssausage.com
Sausage
Founder/Co-Owner: Larry Godwin
CEO/Co-Owner: Sheila Abe
Estimated Sales: $5-10 Million
Number Employees: 20 to 49
Type of Packaging: Consumer

7228 Larry's Vineyards & Winery
3001 Furbeck Road
Altamont, NY 12009
518-355-7365
v1945p@juno.com
Wine
President/Owner: Larry Brooks
Contact: Donna Pace
v1945p@juno.com
Estimated Sales: Under $500,000
Number Employees: 1-4
Brands:
Larry's Vineyards

7229 Larsen Farms
2650 N 2375 E
Hamer, ID 83425
208-374-5592
Fax: 208-374-5497 www.larsenfarms.com
Producer of dehydrated and prepared potatoes.
President: Blaine Larsen
Cio/Cto: Kuhn Hay
felipe@kuhnhay.com
VP, Dehydration Operations: Jan Nel
Estimated Sales: $39 Million
Number Employees: 250-499
Number of Brands: 1
Square Footage: 125000
Type of Packaging: Consumer, Private Label
Other Locations:
Dalhart TX
Brands:
Larsen Farms

7230 Lartigue Seafood
23043 Perdido Beach Blvd
Orange Beach, AL 36561
251-948-2644
Seafood. Founded in 1979
President: Paul Lartigue Jr
Vice President: Paul Lartigue
Number Employees: 5

7231 Las Cruces Brand Products
6860 El Paso Dr
El Paso, TX 79905-3336
915-779-5709
Fax: 915-779-4559 www.las-cruces.org
Taco shells, tostada chips and flour and corn tortillas; also, salsa including jalapeno, red chile and chile con queso
Owner: Armando Viescas
aviescas@las-cruces.org
General Manager: Enrique Galindo
Office Manager: Elvira Martinez
Estimated Sales: $5-10 Million
Number Employees: 10-19
Square Footage: 18000
Type of Packaging: Consumer, Private Label
Brands:
Las Cruces

7232 (HQ)Las Cruces Foods
3070 Harrelson Street
Las Cruces, NM 88005
575-526-2352
Fax: 575-523-5271
Mexican products including tortillas and taco shells
President: David Grijalva
CEO: Miguel Grijalva
VP: Miguel Grisalva
Estimated Sales: $461,369
Number Employees: 5 to 9
Other Locations:
Las Cruces Foods
Albuquerque NM

7233 Las Olas Confections
401 East Las Olas Blvd
Suite 800
Fort Lauderdale, FL 33301
954-940-4000
www.lasolasbrands.com
Confections and snacks, including chocolate, hard candies and taffy.

7234 Lasco Foods Inc
4553 Gustine Ave
St Louis, MO 63116
314-832-1906
Fax: 314-832-7566
customerservice@lascofoods.com
www.lascofoods.com
Mixes including beverage, sauce, gravy, dressing and dessert; also, sauces, mayonnaise and dressings.
Owner: Tom Ellinwood
tellinwood@lascofoods.com
Estimated Sales: $20-50 Million
Number Employees: 20-49
Square Footage: 100000
Parent Co: Allen Foods
Type of Packaging: Food Service

7235 Laska Stuff
132 Griggs Street
Rochester, MI 48307-1414
248-652-8473
Specialty and organic food.
President: Steve Sparks

7236 Lassonde Pappas & Company, Inc.
1 Collins Dr.
Suite 200
Carneys Point, NJ 08069
800-257-7019
info@lassondepappas.com lassondepappas.com
Juices including apple, blueberry, grape, papaya and cranberry sauce, flavored waters, and juice cocktails, lemonades, organic products, and ready to drink teas.
President, Lassonde Pappas: Seth French

Year Founded: 1942
Estimated Sales: $450 Million
Number Employees: 650
Number of Brands: 1
Square Footage: 600000
Parent Co: Lassonde Industries, Inc.
Type of Packaging: Consumer, Private Label, Bulk
Other Locations:
Clement Pappas Food Plant
Springdale AR
Clement Pappas Food Plant
Seabrook NJ
Clement Pappas Food Plant
Mountain Home NC
Clement Pappas Food Plant
Ontario CA
Brands:
Clement Pappas

7237 **Latah Creek Wine Cellar**
13030 E Indiana Ave
Spokane Valley, WA 99216-1118
509-926-0164
Fax: 509-926-0710 www.latahcreek.com
Wines
President: Mike Conway
info@latahcreek.com
VP: Ellena Conway
Estimated Sales: $340,000
Number Employees: 5-9
Type of Packaging: Private Label

7238 **Latcham Vineyards**
2860 Omo Ranch Rd
Somerset, CA 95684-9204
530-620-6642
Fax: 530-620-5578 800-750-5591
latcham@directcon.net www.latcham.com
Wines
Owner: Franklin Latcham
jonlatcham@directcon.net
Winemaker: Craig Boyd
Sales Manager: Margaret Latcham
jonlatcham@directcon.net
Estimated Sales: $500,000-$1 Million
Number Employees: 10-19
Brands:
Barbera
Port

7239 **Late July Snacks**
595 Westport Ave
Norwalk, CT 06851
888-857-6225
www.latejuly.com
Organic snacks
Owner: Nicole Dawes
Contact: Aimee Allen
aimee.allen@latejuly.com

7240 **Latitude, LTD**
37 West Shore Road
Huntington, NY 11743
631-659-3374
Fax: 631-659-3376 latitudeltd@aol.com
Food ingredients manufacturer; including: sweeteners, vitamins, antioxidants and preservatives
Director: Laurel Eastman
Office Manager: Elissa Farrugia

7241 **Latonia Bakery**
3612 Decoursey Ave
Covington, KY 41015-1438
859-491-8855
Fax: 859-431-4169
Baked goods
President: Bernie Holmer
Estimated Sales: Under $500,000
Number Employees: 5-9

7242 **Latta USA**
Fair Lawn, NJ
201-512-8400
www.lattausa.com
Manufacturer of kefir and kombucha.
Sales Manager: Katie Scully
Brands:
Latta

7243 **Laura Chenel's Chevre**
22085 Carneros Vineyard Way
Sonoma, CA 95476-2826
707-996-1252
Fax: 707-996-1816 www.laurachenel.com
Goat cheese
Founder: Laura Chenel
Manager: Brenda Crow
brenda@laurachenel.com
Estimated Sales: Less Than $500,000
Number Employees: 5-9
Number of Brands: 1
Brands:
Laura Chenel's

7244 **Laura Paige Candy Company**
13 Jeanne Drive
Newburgh, NY 12550-1702
845-566-4209
Fax: 845-566-4766 infobe@marshalls.com
www.marshalls.com
Lollipops including hand painted seasonal and regular assortment
President: Elissa Koenig
Chairman: Dr. Louis Korngold
Vice President: Tracey Chalupa
Contact: Ellissa Koenig
ekoenig@marshalls.com
Estimated Sales: Less than $500,000
Number Employees: 30
Square Footage: 32000
Type of Packaging: Consumer, Food Service

7245 **Laura's French Baking Co**
6721 S Alameda St
Los Angeles, CA 90001-2123
323-585-5144
Fax: 323-585-0591 888-353-5144
Bread, croissants, danish, cakes and pastries
President: Sterling Kim
Manager: Charlie Son
charlieson99@gmail.com
Estimated Sales: Below $5 Million
Number Employees: 20-49
Type of Packaging: Food Service
Brands:
Laura's

7246 **Laurel Foods**
31181 Southwest Laurel Rd
Hillsboro, OR 97123
503-692-3663
Fax: 503-692-3664 contact@laurelfoods.com
www.laurelfoods.com
Organic nuts, nut butters and oils
Managing Director: Troy Johnson

7247 **Laurel Glen Vineyard**
969 Carquinez Ave
Glen Ellen, CA 95442
707-933-9877
Fax: 707-526-9801 info@laurelglenvineyard.com
www.laurelglen.com
Wines
Proprietor: Patrick Campbell
Manager: Randall Watkins
randall@laurelglen.com
Winemaker: Patrick Campbell
Estimated Sales: $4 Million
Number Employees: 5-9
Number of Brands: 5
Type of Packaging: Private Label

7248 **Laurel Hill Foods**
39 Franklin McKay Road
Attleboro, MA 02703
877-759-8141
Fax: 508-226-7060 sales@laurelhillfoods.com
www.laurelhillfoods.com
Chips and other snacks
Marketing: Jen Huntley-Corbin

7249 **Laurent's Meat Market**
528 Avenue A
Marrero, LA 70072-2117
504-341-1771
Fax: 504-341-0299
Processor and meat packer of fresh and smoked sausages, hogshead cheese, andouille, hamburger and hot patties
Owner: Layton Laurent Sr
Estimated Sales: $500,000
Number Employees: 1-4
Type of Packaging: Consumer, Food Service, Bulk

7250 **Laurie & Sons**
1580 Park Avenue
New York, NY 10029
212-866-6600
laurie@laurieandsons.com
www.laurieandsons.com
Manufacturer of toffee.
Founder: Laurie Pauker
lpauker@laurieandsons.com

7251 **Lava Cap Winery**
2221 Fruitridge Rd
Placerville, CA 95667-3700
530-621-0175
Fax: 530-621-4399 800-475-0175
www.lavacap.com
Wines
President: David Jones
Accountant: Barbara Beacham
General Manager: Jeanne Jones
Sales Director: Tim Hogan
Tour Coordinator: Julia Rosenkrantz
Winemaker: Thomas Jones
Vineyard Manager: Charles Jones
Estimated Sales: Below $5 Million
Number Employees: 10-19
Number of Brands: 1
Number of Products: 1
Square Footage: 96000
Type of Packaging: Private Label

7252 **Lavash Corp**
2835 Newell St
Los Angeles, CA 90039-3817
323-663-5249
Fax: 323-663-8062
Flatbread
Manager: Edmund Hartounian
lavashcorp@att.net
Director Marketing: Arthur Minassian
National Sales Manager: Adam Cardenas
Cust./Technical Support Manager: Lori Akian
Estimated Sales: Below $5,000,000
Number Employees: 10-19
Brands:
Wrap'n Roll

7253 **Lavazza Premium Coffees**
3 Park Ave # 35
New York, NY 10016-5902
212-725-9196
Fax: 212-725-9475 800-466-3287
info@lavazzausa.com www.lavazza.com
Lavazza coffees
General Manager: Ennio Ranaboldo
Founder: Luigi Lavazza
Contact: Bidya Alie
balie@sovrana.com
Estimated Sales: Below $5 Million
Number Employees: 20-49
Brands:
Lavazza

7254 **Lavoi Corporation**
1749 Tullie Circle
Atlanta, GA 30329
404-325-1016
bdoan@epibreads.com
www.epibreads.com
Bread and baked goods
CEO Emeritus: Robert Gansel
VP, Business Development: Hugh Sullins
Director, Quality Assurance: Mike Heyburn
Manager, Marketing: Brooke Doan
Year Founded: 1985
Estimated Sales: $89.1 Million
Number Employees: 263
Number of Brands: 1
Square Footage: 61000
Parent Co: R.W. Bakers Co
Type of Packaging: Consumer, Food Service
Brands:
EPI

7255 **Lawler Foods LTD**
1219 Carpenter Rd
Humble, TX 77396-1535
281-446-0059
Fax: 281-446-3806 800-541-8285
desserts@lawlers.com www.lawlers.com
Frozen cheesecakes, pies, brownies and sheetcakes
President: Bill Lawler
blawler@lawlers.com
CEO: Carol Lawler

Estimated Sales: $10-20 Million
Number Employees: 100-249
Square Footage: 220000
Type of Packaging: Consumer, Food Service, Private Label, Bulk

7256 Lawrence Foods Inc
2200 Lunt Ave
Elk Grove Village, IL 60007
847-437-2400
Fax: 847-437-2567 info@lawrencefoods.com
www.lawrencefoods.com
Bakers' and confectioners' supplies including fruit and cream fillings, icings, glazes, preserves and jellies; available in boxes, cans, pails, drums, totes and flexible pouches.
President: Paul Ferenchick
Chairman: Lester Lawrence
Executive Chairman: Cecil Gregory
CEO & General Counsel: Marc Lawrence
Year Founded: 1890
Estimated Sales: $200 Million
Number Employees: 100-249
Square Footage: 293000
Type of Packaging: Food Service, Private Label, Bulk
Brands:
Lawrence

7257 Lawry's Foods
24 Schilling Rd.
Hunt Valley, MD 21031
800-952-9797
www.mccormick.com/lawrys
Prepared gravy and sauce mixes, marinades, seasoned salt and pepper, spices and breadings.
President/CEO: Lawrence Kurzius
Year Founded: 1922
Estimated Sales: $500 Million-$1 Billion
Number of Brands: 1
Parent Co: McCormick & Company
Type of Packaging: Consumer
Brands:
Lawry's

7258 Lax & Mandel Bakery
14439 Cedar Rd
South Euclid, OH 44121
216-382-8877
Fax: 216-382-8875 kosher@laxandmandel.com
Cakes, pastries
Co-Owner: Sheldon Weiser
Co-Owner: Helen Weiser
Co-Owner: Jeffrey Weiser
Estimated Sales: $500,000-$1 Million
Number Employees: 3

7259 Laxson Co
264 W Lachapelle
San Antonio, TX 78204-1853
210-226-8397
Fax: 210-226-0537 laxsonco@laxsonco.com
www.laxsonco.com
Sausages, bacon, ham, cheese, spices
President/Director: Gary Laxson
laxsonco@laxsonco.com
Vice President: Lawrence Laxson
Estimated Sales: $20-50 Million
Number Employees: 20-49

7260 Lay Packing Company
622 E Jackson Avenue
Knoxville, TN 37915-1107
865-522-1147
Fax: 865-922-4321
Beef, pork, lamb and veal
Owner: Ira Lay Jr
General Manager: Jerry Simons
Estimated Sales: $1-3 Million
Number Employees: 10 to 19
Parent Co: Lay Packing Company
Type of Packaging: Consumer, Food Service, Private Label, Bulk

7261 Layman Distributing
1630 W Main St
PO Box 1015
Salem, VA 24153
540-389-2000
Fax: 540-389-2062 800-237-1319
lcc@laymandistributing.com
www.laymandistributing.com
Processor and distributor of candy, including brittles, fudge, chocolate, chews, nut clusters and taffy; meat and dairy; and condiments.
Owner: Justin Keen
justin.keen@laymancandy.com
Vice President of Sales: Scott Thomasson
V.P. Customer Relations: Kenny Keen
Estimated Sales: $5-10 Million
Number Employees: 10-19
Number of Brands: 2028
Number of Products: 122
Square Footage: 172000
Brands:
Layman's

7262 Lazy Creek Vineyards
4741 Highway 128
Philo, CA 95466
707-895-3623
Fax: 707-895-9226 888-529-9275
chandler@lazycreek.com
www.lazycreekvineyards.com
Estate wines
President: Josh Chandler
VP Marketing: Mary Beth Chandler
Estimated Sales: $5-10 Million
Number Employees: 5-9
Brands:
Lazy Creek Vineyards

7263 Lazzaroni USA
299 Market St
Suite 160
Saddle Brook, NJ 07663-5312
201-368-1240
Fax: 201-368-1262 www.lazzaroni-ita.com
Manufacturer and distributor of chocolates and cookies
President: Stefano Tombetti
Executive VP: Kathy Ecoffey
Contact: Theresa Strunck
tstrunck@lazzaroniusa.com

7264 Le Bleu Corp
3134 Cornatzer Rd
Advance, NC 27006-7212
336-998-2894
Fax: 336-998-4167 800-854-4471
info@lebleu.com www.lebleu.com
Manufacturer and distributor of bottled water
President/CEO: Jerry Smith
CEO: Brock Agee
b.agee@lebleu.com
Owner/Finance/HR & Sales Executive: Andy Scotchie
Director of Public Relations: Debbie Pullen
Plant Manager: Ed Hauser
Estimated Sales: $17.7 Million
Number Employees: 100-249
Square Footage: 300000
Type of Packaging: Consumer
Brands:
Le Bleu Bottled Water
Nascar Bottled Water

7265 Le Caramel
8047 El Capitan Dr
La Mesa, CA 91942-5515
619-562-0713
Fax: 619-562-1604 www.le-caramel.com
Caramels, dessert toppings (i.e. fudge sauce, caramel sauce, whipped cream, etc.).
Marketing: Christine Kugener

7266 Le Chef Bakery
7547 Telegraph Rd
Montebello, CA 90640-6516
USA
323-888-2929
Fax: 323-888-2946 www.lechefbakery.com
Baked goods, bread, biscuits, cakes, pastries, cookies
CEO: Jonathan Lau
jonathanl@lechef.net
Number Employees: 50-99

7267 Le Chic French Bakery
1043 Washington Ave
Miami Beach, FL 33139-5017
305-673-5522
Fax: 305-673-5522
Bakery products including baguettes, buttery croissants, danishes; as well as European style cakes, pies, tarts and pastries
Owner: M Sanchez
Estimated Sales: $2.5-5 000,000
Number Employees: 5-9

7268 Le Donne Brothers Bakery
143 Chestnut St
Roseto, PA 18013-1311
610-588-0423
cbath@epix.net
Breads: anchiove, French, Italian, sweet and Viennese, also; tomato pies
Owner: Robert Bath
Co-Owner: Connie Bath
Estimated Sales: Less Than $500,000
Number Employees: 1-4
Type of Packaging: Consumer

7269 Le Frois Foods Corporation
56 High St
Brockport, NY 14420-2058
585-637-5003
Fax: 585-637-2855
Vinegar
President: Duncan Tsay
Estimated Sales: Under $500,000
Number Employees: 5-9

7270 Le Grand
69 □milien Marcoux
Blainville, QC J7C 0B4
Canada
450-623-3000
Fax: 450-623-2300 info@maisonlegrand.com
www.maisonlegrand.com
Soups, sauces, pestos and chilies
Co-Founder: Bernard Le Grand
Co-Founder: Tatiana Bossy

7271 Le Grand Confectionary
4527 Harlin Drive
Sacramento, CA 95826
888-361-2125
Fax: 916-361-2150
customerservice@legrandtruffles.com
www.legrandtruffles.com
Chocolate truffles, other chocolate and candy, gift packs
Marketing: Jack Shaw

7272 Le Macaron
382 Saint Armands Cir
Sarasota, FL 34236-1313
941-552-8872
lemacaronfranchise@gmail.com
Macaron, french pastries
Owner: Audrey Guillem Saba
guillemlia@aol.com
Estimated Sales: Less Than $500,000
Number Employees: 5-9

7273 Le Pique-Nique
5 Penn Plaza
New York, NY 10001
800-400-6454
Fax: 510-339-7141 800-699-9822
www.thomasnet.com
Sausage including chicken, turkey, chicken/apple, cranberries, orange, maple syrup, etc
President: Dennis Donegan
Estimated Sales: Under $500,000
Number Employees: 1-4
Type of Packaging: Consumer, Food Service
Brands:
Calypso Caribbean
Tandoori
Thai Chicken

7274 Le Roy Ren,
14 NE 1st Ave
Suite 501
Miami, FL 33132
786-558-9968
info@thecalisson.com
us.calisson.com
Calissons, nougats, biscuits, chocolates, creams and jams.
Founder: Olivier Baussan

7275 (HQ)Le Sueur Cheese Co
719 N Main St
Le Sueur, MN 56058-1404
507-665-3353
Fax: 507-665-2820 800-757-7611
info@daviscofoods.com www.daviscofoods.com

Variety of cheese including low-fat, no-fat, enzyme-modified cheeses and other customer specified varieties
President: Mark Davis
Vice President: Jim Ward
Manager: Mitch Davis
mitch.davis@daviscofoods.com
Production Manager: Roger Schroder
Purchasing Manager: Gregory Bush
Estimated Sales: $14.90
Number Employees: 100-249
Square Footage: 12000
Parent Co: Davisco Foods International, Inc.
Other Locations:
Le Sueur Cheese Plant
Jerome ID

7276 Le Vigne Winery
5115 Buena Vista Dr
Paso Robles, CA 93446-8558
805-227-4000
Fax: 805-227-6128 800-891-6055
info@levignewinery.com www.levignewinery.com
Wines
Co-Owner: Sylvia Filippini
info@sylvesterwinery.com
Accounting Manager: Scott Keller
Marketing Manager: Zina Miakinkova
Sales Manager: Michael Barreto
Estimated Sales: Below $5 Million
Number Employees: 20-49
Brands:
Sylvester

7277 Lea & Perrins
801 Waukegan Rd
Glenview, IL 60025
www.leaperrins.com
Sauces and condiments specializing in worcestershire sauces and marinades.
Year Founded: 1839
Estimated Sales: $50-100 Million
Number Employees: 100-249
Number of Brands: 1
Parent Co: H.J. Heinz Company
Type of Packaging: Consumer, Food Service
Brands:
Lea & Perrins

7278 Leach Farms Inc
W1102 Buttercup Ct
P.O. Box 192
Berlin, WI 54923-8327
920-361-1880
Fax: 920-361-4474
www.leachfoods.com/contact.html
Fresh and frozen spinach and celery
Owner: Tom Leach
General Manager: Jacqueline Oldenburg
Chief Financial Officer: John Zander
Personnel Manager: Sara Block
Quality Assurance Manager: Alecia Vermeen
Sales Manager: Marybeth Yonke
Plant Manager: Loreen Greer
Estimated Sales: $30-50 Million
Number Employees: 10-19
Square Footage: 10000
Type of Packaging: Bulk

7279 Leader Candies
132 Harrison Place
Brooklyn, NY 11237-1522
718-366-6900
Fax: 718-417-1723
Processor and exporter of candies including hard, caramels, jelly beans, novelties, lollypops, filled, fundraising, hard toffee, starch jellies, bagged and nonchocolate, and nonfrozen freeze pops
President: Howard Kastin
Sales: Helen Garfield
VP Manufacturing: Malcom Kastin
Number Employees: 155
Square Footage: 320000
Type of Packaging: Consumer, Food Service, Private Label, Bulk
Brands:
Beaver Pop
Freez-A-Pops
Kastin's
Leader
Lolly Lo's

7280 Leaf Cuisine
828 Pico Blvd
Unit 2
Santa Monica, CA 90405
leafcuisine.com
Dairy-free spreads, 'cream cheese' and vegan snack packs
Chef: Rod Rotondi
Year Founded: 2004
Number of Brands: 1
Number of Products: 12
Type of Packaging: Consumer
Brands:
LEAF CUISINE

7281 Leaf Jerky
PO Box CAMB
Battle Creek, MI 49016
800-962-1413
www.leafjerky.com
Plant-based jerky
Parent Co: Kellogg Company

7282 Leahy Orchards
1772 Route 209
Franklin Centre, QC J0S 1E0
Canada
450-827-2544
Fax: 450-827-2470 800-667-7380
www.applesnax.com
Apple sauce in cans, jars and portion packs; also, pie filling
President/CEO: Michael Leahy
CEO: Beahy
VP Finance/Administration: Guylaine Yelle
VP Sales/Marketing/R&D: Doug Anderson
Director of Purchasing: Philip Seguin
Number Employees: 50-99
Type of Packaging: Consumer
Brands:
Apple Snax

7283 Leams
906 Texas Court
Hutchinson, KS 67502-5136
316-662-4287
Fax: 620-662-4287
Sweet and savory flavors
President: Alice Grigrest
Number Employees: 1-4

7284 Leaner Creamer
Beverly Hills, CA 90210
866-739-2298
leanercreamer.com
Coconut-based coffee creamer and coffee capsules
CEO: Jonathan Kashani
Director of Marketing: Natasha Kashani

7285 Leatex Chemical Co
2722 N Hancock St
Philadelphia, PA 19133-3597
215-739-2000
Fax: 215-739-5910 www.nielsen.com
Sulphonated castor oils
President: Denniston Brown
dennistonbrown@nielsen.com
VP Marketing: L Kevin McChesney
Estimated Sales: $5,000,000
Number Employees: 10-19

7286 Leavenworth Coffee Roast
894 Highway 2
Leavenworth, WA 98826
509-548-3313
Fax: 509-548-4251 800-246-2761
java@alpinecoffeeroasters.com
www.alpinecoffeeroasters.com
Coffee including 25 blends
President: Dale Harrison
VP: Veronica Harrison
Estimated Sales: $1-2.5 Million
Number Employees: 10-19
Type of Packaging: Consumer, Food Service
Brands:
Chatter Creek

7287 Leaves Pure Teas
7435 E Tierra Buena Lane
Scottsdale, AZ 85260
480-998-8807
Fax: 650-583-1163 800-242-8807
info@chinamist.com www.chinamist.com
Teas
President & Chief Operations Officer: Rommie Flammer
Co Founder, Co Chairman, Co CEO: Dan Schweiker
Operations Manager: Jeff Morris
Number Employees: 5-9
Type of Packaging: Private Label
Brands:
Leaves Pure Tea

7288 (HQ)Leavitt Corp., The
100 Santilli Hwy
Everett, MA 02149-1938
617-389-2600
Fax: 617-387-9085 contact@teddie.com
teddie.com
Peanut butter, salted and unsalted cashews and peanuts; raw cashews
President: James T Hintlian
jameshint@teddie.com
Executive VP: Mark Hintlian
Quality Control: Christopher Hayes
Operations Manager: Joseph Saraceno
Production Manager: Jack Skamarakas
Purchasing Manager: Frank Ciampa
Estimated Sales: $10-24.9 Million
Number Employees: 50-99
Type of Packaging: Consumer, Food Service, Private Label, Bulk
Brands:
Teddie
River Queen

7289 Lebanon Cheese Co
3 Railroad Ave
PO Box 63
Lebanon, NJ 08833-2156
908-236-2611
Fax: 908-236-6870 www.lebanoncheese.com
Cheese
President: Joe Lotito
Estimated Sales: $3 000,000
Number Employees: 5-9
Brands:
Lebanon Cheese

7290 Lebermuth Company
4004 Technology Dr
South Bend, IN 46628
574-259-7000
Fax: 574-258-7450 800-648-1123
info@lebermuth.com www.lebermuth.com
Essential oils, fragrances and flavors
President & CEO: Rob Brown
Chief Strategic Officer: Alan Brown
VP, Ingredient Bus. Dev.: Mel Brown
VP, Fragrance Bus. Dev.: Craig Sroda
Chief Financial Officer: Rebecca Brown
Exec. VP, Sales: Craig Lupinacci
Director of Operations: Phil Forte
Year Founded: 1908
Estimated Sales: $10-19 Million
Number Employees: 50-99
Type of Packaging: Bulk

7291 (HQ)Lebermuth Company
14000 McKinley Highway
Mishawaka, IN 46545
574-259-7000
Fax: 574-258-7450 800-648-1123
info@lebermuth.com www.lebermuth.com
Fragrance and flavor company
President: Rob Brown
CEO: Irvin Brown
Vice President: Alan Brown
Contact: Jodi Aker
jaker@lebermuth.com
Production Manager: Mike Ryan
Plant Manager: Robert Hall
Purchasing Manager: Jim Gates
Estimated Sales: $5-10 Million
Number Employees: 50
Square Footage: 180000
Type of Packaging: Bulk

7292 Leblanc Seafood
PO Box 509
Lafitte, LA 70067-0509
504-689-2631
Fax: 504-689-4303
Seafood

7293 **Lecoq Cuisine Corp**
35 Union Ave # 1
Bridgeport, CT 06607-2335
203-334-1010
Fax: 203-334-1800 croissant@lecoqcuisine.com
www.lecoqcuisine.com
Cakes/pastries, frozen desserts, full-line frozen, hors d'oeuvres/appetizers, other frozen, puffed snacks.
Owner: Tami Corby
tami@lecoqcuisine.com
Marketing: Eric Lecoq
Number Employees: 100-249

7294 **Lee Andersons**
51392 Harrison Street
Coachella, CA 92236-1563
760-398-3441
Dates
Marketing Manager: Ann Jolly
Estimated Sales: Under $500,000
Number Employees: 1-4

7295 **Lee Kum Kee**
#350, 30-56 Whitestone Expy
Whitestone, NY 11354
718-821-2199
Fax: 718-821-2989 800-346-7562
contact@lkkusa.com www.lkk.com
Processor, importer and exporter of condiments and sauces including chili.
Estimated Sales: $190,000
Number Employees: 3
Square Footage: 80000
Parent Co: Lee Kum Kee Company
Type of Packaging: Consumer, Food Service, Private Label, Bulk
Brands:
Lee Kum Kee
Panda

7296 **(HQ)Lee Kum Kee USA Inc**
14841 Don Julian Rd
City Of Industry, CA 91746-3110
626-709-1888
Fax: 626-709-1899 800-654-5082
contact@lkkusa.com us.lkk.com
Producer of authentic Chinese sauces including oyster flavored sauces, soy sauces, chili sauces and cooking sauces for industrial manufacturers.
Chairman: David Lee
Vice President, Finance: Dickson Chan
Sales Director: Grace Chow
HR, Recruiting: David Lo
General Manager: Rob Berry
Estimated Sales: $9.7 Million
Number Employees: 20-49
Square Footage: 50000
Type of Packaging: Private Label
Brands:
Choy Sun
Full House
Kum Chun Brand
Lee Kum Kee
Lee Kum Kee Premium
Panda Brand

7297 **Lee Seed Co**
2242 Iowa 182 Ave
Inwood, IA 51240-7592
712-753-4403
Fax: 712-753-4542 800-736-6530
www.soynuts.com
Roasted soynuts in 16 flavors
Co-Owner: Paul Lee
Co-Owner: Joyce Lee
joycelee@soynuts.com
Marketing Director: Scott Lee
Estimated Sales: $3-5 Million
Number Employees: 10-19
Type of Packaging: Consumer, Private Label, Bulk
Brands:
Super Soynuts

7298 **Lee's Food Products**
1233 Queen Street E
Toronto, ON M4L 1C2
Canada
416-465-2407
Canned soy sauce and Chinese vegetables including bamboo shoots, water chestnuts and mushrooms; importer of mushrooms, instant noodles and mini corn
President: Marilyn Wong
Secretary/Treasurer: L Wong
Estimated Sales: $5-10 Million
Number Employees: 45
Type of Packaging: Consumer, Food Service

7299 **Lee's Ice Cream**
7137 E. Stetson Dr.
Scottsdale, AZ 85251
410-581-0234
Fax: 410-581-7044 888-669-5337
Makers of premium gourmet ice cream products available in a variety of flavors.
Founder: Leon Garfield
Co-Founder: Jaques Rubin
Co-Founder: Steven Rubin
CEO: Steve Rubin
Number Employees: 100-249

7300 **Lee's Sausage Co**
1054 Neeses Hwy
Orangeburg, SC 29115-8606
803-534-5517
Fax: 803-531-2809 leessausage@yahoo.com
Sausage, liver pudding, BBQ meat, BBQ hash, BBQ sauce, chili
President: Freddy Lee
leessausage@yahoo.com
Estimated Sales: $2 Million
Number Employees: 20-49
Type of Packaging: Consumer, Private Label

7301 **Leech Lake Wild Rice**
115 6th St NE
Cass Lake, MN 56633
218-335-8200
Fax: 218-335-8309
Natural lake and river wild rice
Manager: Cheryl Dunn
Number Employees: 1-4
Brands:
Leech Lake

7302 **(HQ)Leech Lake Wild Rice**
51664 County Road 137
Deer River, MN 56636
218-246-2746
Fax: 218-246-2748 877-246-0620
llwrice@paulbunyan.net
Natural lake and river wild rice
Prime Manager: George Donnell
CFO: Mike Ziemer
Quality Control: Christine Cummings
R & D: Steve Mortinson
Public Relations: Don June
Production Manager: George Donnell
Estimated Sales: Below $5 Million
Number Employees: 5
Type of Packaging: Private Label
Brands:
Leech Lake Wild Rice

7303 **Leelanau Cellars**
5019 North West Bay Shore Drive (M-22)
Omena, MI 49674
231-386-5201
Fax: 231-386-9797 800-782-8128
info@leelanaucellars.com
www.leelanaucellars.com
Wines
Owner: Michael Jacobson
Owner: Bob Jacobson
Vineyard Manager: Marcel Lenz
General Manager: Tony Lentych
Tasting Room Manager: Carrie Hanson
Sales Manager: Scott Vicary
Estimated Sales: $5-10 Million
Number Employees: 10-19
Brands:
Leelanau

7304 **Leelanau Fruit Co**
2900 S West Bay Shore Dr
Peshawbestown, MI 49682-9614
231-271-3514
Fax: 231-271-4367 info@leelanaufruit.com
www.leelanaufruit.com
Processer and exporter of frozen and brined cherries and strawberries
President: Glen Lacross
General Manager: Allen Steimel
Estimated Sales: $1-3 Million
Number Employees: 20-49
Type of Packaging: Consumer, Food Service, Private Label, Bulk

7305 **Leeward Resources**
401 E Pratt Street
Suite 354
Baltimore, MD 21202-3117
410-837-9003
Fax: 410-837-7527
Spices, herbal extracts, botantials, essential oils, fruit juices
President: William Brown
Estimated Sales: $3.5 Million
Number Employees: 3

7306 **Leeward Winery**
2511 Victoria Ave
Oxnard, CA 93035-2931
805-656-5054
Fax: 805-656-5092 www.leewardwinery.com
Processor and exporter of table wines
President: Charles Brigham
Co-Owner: Chuck Gardner
Estimated Sales: $260,000
Number Employees: 4
Square Footage: 34000
Type of Packaging: Consumer, Food Service
Brands:
Leeward

7307 **Lef Bleuges Marinor**
1015 Rg Double
St-Felicien, QC G8K 2M1
Canada
418-679-4577
Fax: 418-679-9602
Frozen blueberries
President: Jeanne-Pierre Senneville

7308 **Lefse House**
5210-51 Ave
Camrose, AB T4V 4N5
Canada
780-672-7555
Fax: 780-608-2377 info@thelefsehouse.ca
www.thelefsehouse.ca
Scandinavian all natural baked goods including potato lefse, flatbread and specialty items
President/CFO: Bernell Odegard
Purchasing Manager: Helen Lien
Estimated Sales: Under $300,000
Number Employees: 5-9
Square Footage: 6400
Type of Packaging: Consumer, Food Service
Brands:
Lefse House

7309 **Left Hand Brewing Co**
1265 Boston Ave
Longmont, CO 80501-5809
303-772-0258
Fax: 303-772-9572 brewer@lefthandbrewing.com
www.pourhard.com
Processor and wholesaler/distributor of English style ale, stout and porter; also, German style lager and weiss beer
Owner: John Lindberg
jlindberg@boss-cellular.com
Quality Control: Andy Brown
Marketing/Sales/Public Relations: Chris Lennert
Operations Manager: Joe Schiraldi
Estimated Sales: Below $5 Million
Number Employees: 50-99
Square Footage: 52000
Type of Packaging: Food Service, Bulk
Brands:
Deep Cover Brown
Imperial
Juju Ginger
Left Hand Black Jack
Sawtooth
Tabernash

7310 **Left Hand Brewing Co**
1265 Boston Ave
Longmont, CO 80501-5809
303-772-0258
Fax: 303-772-9572 www.pourhard.com
Seasonal beer and lager
Owner: John Lindberg
CEO; Eric Wallece
Sales Manager: George Barela
jlindberg@boss-cellular.com
Director Manufacturing: Mark Luca
Estimated Sales: $5-9.9 Million
Number Employees: 50-99
Type of Packaging: Consumer, Food Service

Brands:
Blackjack Porter
Brown Ale
Deep Cover
Ginger Ale
Haystack
Interial Stout
Jack Man
Juju
Milk Stout
Toleftar Pilfen
Weat
Weiss

7311 **Lefty Spices**
Crain Hwy. Waldorf
Waldorf, MD 20601
301-399-3145
Fax: 240-607-6721
Flour, full-line baking mixes and ingredients, other meat/game/pate, BBQ sauce, other sauces, seasonings and cooking enhancers, rubs, spices.
Marketing: Walter Nash

7312 **Legacy Bakehouse**
N8w22100 Johnson Dr
Waukesha, WI 53186-1866
262-547-2447
Fax: 262-547-2047 800-967-2447
www.legacybakehouse.com
Bread and corn based snack chips
Owner: Chris Pinahs
CEO: Michael Heyer
Director Finance: Bill Bruggink
Quality Assurance: Janet Schultz
Vice President of Sales: Tom Reuteman
COO, Sales: Peter Sardina
Plant Manager: Chris Evans
Purchasing & Logistics: Cathy Huspen
Estimated Sales: $3 Million
Number Employees: 20-49
Square Footage: 236000
Type of Packaging: Consumer, Food Service, Private Label, Bulk
Brands:
Pinah's

7313 **Legacy Juice Works**
382 Broadway
Saratoga Springs, NY 12866
518-583-1108
juice@saratogajuicebar.com
saratogajuicebar.com
Wellness shots, cleanses and cold pressed juices
Co-Owner: Colin MacLean
Type of Packaging: Consumer
Brands:
LEGACY JUICE WORKS

7314 **Legally Addictive Foods**
630 Flushing Ave
Brooklyn, NY 11206
legallyaddictivefoods.com
Cookies and crackers
Founder: Laura Shafferman

7315 **Legend Brewing Co**
321 W 7th St
Richmond, VA 23224-2307
804-232-8871
Fax: 804-231-3417 info56@legendbrewing.com
www.legendbrewing.com
Beer, ale, stout and lager
President: Thomas E Martin
dave@legendbrewing.com
Sales Exec: David Gott
Brewmaster: Brad Mortensen
Estimated Sales: Below $5 Million
Number Employees: 20-49
Type of Packaging: Consumer, Food Service
Brands:
Brown Ale
Legand Brown
Legand Pilsner
Porter

7316 **Legendary Foods**
530 South Lake Ave
Suite 161
Pasadena, CA 91101
888-698-1708
www.legendaryfoodsonline.com
Nut snacks and butters
Founder: Michael Veni
Number of Brands: 1
Number of Products: 9
Type of Packaging: Consumer
Brands:
LEGENDARY FOODS

7317 **Legumex Walker, Inc.**
1345 Kenaston Blvd
Winnipeg, MB R6W 4B3
Canada
204-808-0448
Grains
Investor & Media Relations: Marin Landis

7318 **Lehi Mills**
833 E Main St
Lehi, UT 84043-2286
801-768-4401
Fax: 801-768-4557 877-311-3566
customerservice@lehirollermills.com
lehirollermills.com
Processor of flour, feed and meal; also, pancake mixes, cookie mixes, brownie mixes, bread mixes and preserves.
President: Sherman Robinson
COO: Brock Knight
Sales Exec: Steve DE John
sdejohn@lehirollermills.com
Year Founded: 1906
Estimated Sales: $20-50 Million
Number Employees: 20-49
Number of Brands: 3
Type of Packaging: Food Service, Private Label
Brands:
Lehi Roller Mills
Peacock
Turkey

7319 **Lehi Valley Trading Company**
4955 E McKellips Rd
Mesa, AZ 85215
480-684-1402
Fax: 480-461-1804 info@lehivalley.com
www.lehivalley.com
Beans, candy, dried fruit, granola, ice cream mix-ins, nuts and seeds, popcorn and nuggets, snack items and trail mix
President/Owner: Lewis Freeman
Contact: Jason Burrell
jason.burrell@lehivalley.com
Estimated Sales: $7.7 Million
Number Employees: 50

7320 **Lehigh Valley Dairy Farms**
880 Allentown Rd
Lansdale, PA 19446-5298
215-855-8205
Fax: 215-855-9834 800-395-7004
www.lehighvalleydairyfarms.com
Dairy
Estimated Sales: $10-19.9 Million
Number Employees: 100-249
Number of Brands: 3
Parent Co: Dean Foods
Brands:
Dairy Pure
Trumoo
Orchardpure

7321 **Lehmann Farms**
21034 Heron Way
Lakeville, MN 55044-8093
651-247-3377
Fax: 715-247-2226 800-446-5276
www.lehmannfarms.com
Gourmet foods
President: Doug Oaks
Estimated Sales: Less Than $500,000
Number Employees: 1-4
Parent Co: Lehmann Farms

7322 **Lehmann Mills Inc**
11000 Youngstown Salem Rd
PO Box 1083
Salem, OH 44460-9654
330-332-9951
Fax: 330-332-2208 888-919-9494
info@lehmannmills.com www.lehmannmills.com
Three-roll horizontal mills, Three-roll vertical mills, Technical field service Installation start-up and supervision, Operator training and maintenance,Consultation services,In-house CAD engineering, Custom-designed upgrades, Problemsolving capabilities
Owner: David Hrovatic
info@lehmannmills.com
Estimated Sales: $5-10 Million
Number Employees: 20-49

7323 **Lehr Brothers**
12901 Packing House Road
Edison, CA 93220
661-366-3244
Fax: 661-366-1449 spudron1@aol.com
Processor and exporter of potatoes
President: Ronald Lehr
VP: Ronald Lehr Jr
Estimated Sales: $17,155,306
Number Employees: 50
Square Footage: 45000
Type of Packaging: Bulk

7324 **Leiby's Premium Ice Cream**
116 Mountain Rd
Tamaqua, PA 18252
570-668-2399
Fax: 570-668-6065 877-453-4297
sales.leibys@earthlink.net
www.leibysicecream.com
Ice cream including mixes
President: Keith Zimmerman
VP/Secretary: William Parks
Estimated Sales: $5-10 Million
Number Employees: 10-19
Square Footage: 120000
Type of Packaging: Consumer, Bulk

7325 **Leidenfrost Vineyards**
5677 Route 414
PO Box 221
Hector, NY 14841
607-546-2800
Wines
Owner: John Leidenfrost
Estimated Sales: $340,000
Number Employees: 4
Brands:
Leidenfrost Vineyards

7326 **Leidenheimer Baking Co**
1501 Simon Bolivar Ave
New Orleans, LA 70113-2329
504-525-1575
Fax: 504-525-1596 800-259-9099
info@leidenheimer.com www.leidenheimer.com
Manufacturer of fresh and frozen New Orleans style French breads and rolls
President: Robert Whann
Year Founded: 1896
Estimated Sales: $20 Million
Number Employees: 50-99
Square Footage: 40000
Type of Packaging: Consumer, Food Service

7327 **Leidy's**
382 Main Street
PO Box 2
Harleysville, PA 19438-0002
215-723-4606
Fax: 215-721-2003 800-222-2319
www.leidys.com
Pork processing.
President/CEO: Jim Van Stone
CFO: Sally Schukraft
General Manager: Todd Wood
Contact: Karen Brown
karen@leidys.com
Estimated Sales: $20-50 Million
Number Employees: 100-249
Number of Brands: 1
Type of Packaging: Consumer, Bulk
Brands:
Leidy's

7328 **Leigh Olivers**
PO Box 8346
Tyler, TX 75711
903-245-9183
Fax: 903-421-1669
customerservice@leigholivers.com
www.leigholivers.com
Dips/salsa and cheeses
CEO: Leigh Vickery
VP: Ron Vickery

7329 **(HQ)Leighton's Honey Inc**
1203 W Commerce Ave
Haines City, FL 33844-3271
863-422-1773
Fax: 863-421-2299 leightonshoney@verizon.net
www.leightonshoney.com
Manufacturer and packer of pure honey.
President: Paul McCord
VP: Janet McCord
Year Founded: 1950
Estimated Sales: $2.5-5 Million
Number Employees: 10-19
Number of Brands: 2
Type of Packaging: Consumer, Food Service, Private Label, Bulk
Brands:
Leighton's
Orange Blossom Special

7330 **Leinenkugel's**
124 E Elm St
Chippewa Falls, WI 54729
888-534-6437
leinielodge@leinenkugels.com www.leinie.com
Alcoholic malt beverages, beer
President: Bill Leinenkugel
CFO: Dave Kahn
VP Marketing: Richard Leininkugel
Point-of-Sale Manager: John Leininkugel
Operations Manager: Pete Dawson
Estimated Sales: $5-10 Million
Number Employees: 50-99
Brands:
Amber Light
Berry Weiss
Honey Weiss
Leinenkugel Original
Light
Northwoods
Oktoberfest
Red

7331 **Leiner Health Products**
901 E 233rd St
Carson, CA 90745
310-835-8400
Fax: 310-952-7760
Vitamins
President: Gale Bansussen
CEO: Bob Kaminski
CEO: Robert R Reynolds
Manager Sales/Marketing: Tom Bovich
Contact: Lucy Bartelson
lbartels@leiner.com
Number Employees: 500-999
Brands:
Beneflex
Bumble Bee
Cardio Discovery
Liquimax
Natural Life
Omega Care
Pharmacist Formula

7332 **Lejeune's Bakery Inc**
1510 Main St
Jeanerette, LA 70544-3528
337-276-5690
www.lejeunesbakery.com
Baked goods
Owner: Matthew Juene
Estimated Sales: Less Than $500,000
Number Employees: 1-4

7333 **Lekithos**
Palm Beach Gardens, FL 33403
lekithos.com
Plant protein powders

7334 **Lemate Of New England Inc**
11 Perry Dr # C
Unit C
Foxboro, MA 02035-1047
508-543-9035
Fax: 781-784-7369 sales@lematecocktailmix.com
www.lematecocktailmix.com
Sweetened cocktail mixes and flavored syrups. Founded in 1977.
President: Kevin Christman
kevin@lematecocktailmix.com
Vice President: Marianne Christman
Number Employees: 5-9
Type of Packaging: Consumer, Food Service, Private Label, Bulk

7335 **Lemke Wholesale**
1225 N 8th St
Rogers, AR 72756
479-751-4671
Fax: 501-751-4671
Variety of food products.
President: Arnold E Lemke
Secretary: Lorene Lemke
Vice-President: Ronald Lemke

7336 **Lemmes Company**
7 Alice Street
Coventry, RI 02816-7300
401-821-2575
Spaghetti sauce, grated cheese, BBQ sauce, relish, jam, mustard
President: Michael Lemme
Estimated Sales: $2.5-5 000,000
Number Employees: 1

7337 **Lemon & Vine**
1340 4th Street
Napa, CA 94559
707-926-6073
Fax: 707-927-3514 info@lemonandvine.com
www.lemonandvine.com
Greek appetizers

7338 **Lemon Creek Winery**
533 E Lemon Creek Rd
Berrien Springs, MI 49103-9714
269-471-1321
Fax: 269-471-1322 lemoncreekwinery@gmail.com
www.lemoncreekwinery.com
Wines
Owner: Jeff Lemon
lemoncreekwinery@gmail.com
Estimated Sales: $1.8 Million
Number Employees: 10-19
Brands:
Lemon Creek Winery

7339 **Lemon-X Corporation**
168 Railroad Street
Huntington Station, NY 11746
631-424-2850
Fax: 631-424-2852 800-220-1061
sales@lemon-x.com www.lemon-x.com
Juices and cocktail mixes.
President: James Grassi
Co-Founder: Sonja Grassi
Contact: Greg Aluise
galuise@lemon-x.com
Estimated Sales: $20-50 Million
Number Employees: 100-249
Number of Brands: 5
Type of Packaging: Consumer, Food Service, Private Label, Bulk
Brands:
CareTree
Growers Fancy Juice
Honey Bear Farms
Lemon-X
Moon Lake

7340 **LemonKind**
349 5th Avenue
New York, NY 10016
954-678-1700
info@drinklemonkind.com
drinklemonkind.com
Ready-to-drink teas and juice beverages
Founder: Irene Rojas
Number of Brands: 1
Number of Products: 8
Type of Packaging: Consumer
Brands:
LEMONKIND

7341 **Lemoncocco**
66 S Hanford St
Suite 150
Seattle, WA 98134
206-624-3357
info@drinklemoncocco.com
drinklemoncocco.com
Coconut and lemon beverage

7342 **Lemur International**
3701 Collins Ave
Suite 3N
Richmond, CA 94806
510-620-9708
Fax: 510-620-9965 www.lemurinc.com
Organic vanilla and essential oils

7343 **Len Libby Chocolatier-Maine**
419 Us Route 1
Scarborough, ME 04070
207-883-4897
Fax: 207-885-5824 lenlibby@lenlibby.com
www.lenlibby.com
Chocolates and candies
Owner: Len Libby
Vice President: Maureen Hemond
Estimated Sales: $500,000-$1 Million
Number Employees: 10-19

7344 **Lenchner Bakery**
50 Drumlin Circle
Concord, ON L4K 3G1
Canada
905-738-8811
Fax: 905-738-3822 www.lenchners.com
Processor and exporter of kosher frozen entrees and dessert pastries including chocolate, almond, cheese, apple, blueberry, cherry, prune, lemon, spinach feta cheese, potato onion, etc.; also, bagels; private labeling available
President: Zeev Lenchner
Estimated Sales: $1-2.5 Million
Number Employees: 20-49
Square Footage: 40000
Parent Co: Lechner's
Type of Packaging: Consumer, Food Service, Private Label, Bulk
Brands:
Boueka
Rrrogala

7345 **Lender's Bagels**
PO Box 971
Miami, FL 33152
800-768-6287
www.lendersbagels.com
Bagels

7346 **Lendy's Cafe Raw Bar**
1581 General Booth Blvd # 101
Virginia Beach, VA 23454-5106
757-491-3511
Fax: 757-491-8821
Sauces including buffalo wing, habanero hot and barbecue
Owner: Kent Von Fecht
lendys1@cox.net
Estimated Sales: Less than $500,000
Number Employees: 10-19
Square Footage: 5000
Type of Packaging: Consumer, Food Service, Private Label, Bulk
Brands:
Buckman's Best
Buckman's Best Snack

7347 **Lengacher's Cheese House**
5015 Lincoln Highway
Kinzers, PA 17535-9709
717-355-6490
Cheese
President: Arthur Lengacher
Estimated Sales: $500,000 appx.
Number Employees: 1-4

7348 **Lengerich Meats Inc**
3095 Van Horn
P.O. Box 411
Zanesville, IN 46799-9027
260-638-4123
lengerich@frontier.com
www.lengerichmeatsinc.us
Beef, pork and lunch meats
Owner: Amy Stephan
Sales Manager: Debbie Woods
lengerichmeats@frontier.com
Estimated Sales: $670,000
Number Employees: 10-19
Type of Packaging: Consumer, Food Service

7349 **Lennox Farm**
518024 County Rd 124/RR 2
Shelburne, ON L0N 1S6
Canada
519-925-6444
Fax: 519-925-3285
Fresh and frozen rhubarb
President: William French

Estimated Sales: $1.4 Million
Number Employees: 12
Type of Packaging: Consumer, Food Service
Brands:
Lennox

7350 **Lenny & Larry's**
14300 Arminta St
Panorama City, CA 91402
www.lennylarry.com
Cookies, muffins and brownies
CEO: Barry Turner
Number of Brands: 3
Type of Packaging: Consumer
Brands:
THE COMPLETE COOKIE
THE MUSCLE MUFFIN
THE MUSCLE BROWNIE

7351 **Lenny's Bee Productions**
403 Wittenberg Road
Bearsville, NY 12409-5635
845-679-4514
Smoked trout, bee pollen and honey products
President: Leonardo Busciguo
Vice President: Lynn Duvall
Contact: Lenny Bee
lennysbeeproductions@gmail.com
Type of Packaging: Consumer, Food Service, Private Label
Brands:
Lenny's Bee Productions

7352 **Lenox-Martell Inc**
89 Heath St
Boston, MA 02130-1402
617-442-7777
Fax: 617-522-9455 877-325-2489
www.lenoxmartell.com
Processor of colas and juices; wholesaler/distributor of refrigerators and ice and soda machines; serving the food service market; also, installation and maintenance of draft beer systems available
CEO/Sales Executive: Jim Lerner
jlerner@lenoxmartell.com
Controller: David Nitishin
VP Marketing: John Dixon
Sales/Marketing: Jessica Miller
Operations Director: Rick Freitas
Year Founded: 1950
Estimated Sales: $8 Million
Number Employees: 50-99
Square Footage: 120000

7353 **Lenson Coffee & Tea Company**
PO Box 1103
Pleasantville, NJ 08232-6103
609-646-3003
Fax: 609-646-8606
Coffee; wholesaler/distributor of tea; serving the food service market
Owner: Jimmie Anderson
Estimated Sales: $5-10 Million
Number Employees: 20-49
Type of Packaging: Consumer, Food Service, Private Label

7354 **Lentia Enterprises Ltd.**
17733-66th Ave
Surrey, BC V3S 7X1
Canada
604-576-8838
Fax: 604-576-1064 888-768-7368
Naturally fermented, dehydrated sourdoughs from both wheat and rye flours, specialty malted products such as whole malted rye kernels, aroma malts, colouring malts and clean label bread mixes.
President/Board Member: Karl Eibensteiner
Director: Gertrude Eibensteiner
Estimated Sales: $4.08 Million
Number Employees: 23

7355 **Leo G. Atkinson Fisheries**
89 Daniel Head Road
South Side
Clarks Harbor, NS B0W 1P0
Canada
902-745-3047
Fax: 902-745-1245
Processor and exporter of fresh, frozen and salted seafood including haddock, cod, halibut and lobster. Founded in 1983.
President: Leo Atkinson

Estimated Sales: $9.9 Million
Number Employees: 20
Type of Packaging: Consumer, Food Service, Private Label, Bulk

7356 **Leo G. Fraboni Sausage Company**
1202 13th Ave E
Hibbing, MN 55746-1218
218-263-5074
Fax: 218-263-5074 sales@frabonis.com
www.frabonis.com
Smoked Polish sausages and frozen beef patties
President: Mark Thune
VP: Wayne Thune
Plant Manager: Don Johnson
Estimated Sales: $.5-1 million
Number Employees: 5-9
Type of Packaging: Consumer, Private Label, Bulk

7357 **Leo's Bakery**
1179 Ocean St
Marshfield, MA 02050
781-837-3300
Fax: 781-837-8949
Bakery products
President: Robert Gagnon
Estimated Sales: $500,000-$1 000,000
Number Employees: 10-19

7358 **Leo's Bakery & Deli**
101 Despatch Dr
East Rochester, NY 14445-1447
585-249-1000
Fax: 585-249-9231 www.leoselite.com
Baked goods
Owner: Patrick Bernunzio
bakery@watermark101.com
Estimated Sales: $630,000
Number Employees: 20-49
Type of Packaging: Consumer, Food Service, Private Label, Bulk
Brands:
Elite Bakery

7359 **Leon's Bakery**
1000 Universal Dr N
North Haven, CT 06473-3151
203-234-0115
Fax: 203-234-7620 800-223-6844
Frozen dough; exporter of wheat and white rolls
President: Luis Alpizar
CEO: John Ruth
CFO: Eric Olson
Sales Manager: Terry Ginn
Plant Manager: Fred Macey
Estimated Sales: $5-10 Million
Number Employees: 5-9
Square Footage: 300000
Type of Packaging: Food Service, Private Label, Bulk

7360 **Leon's Texas Cuisine**
2100 Redbud Blvd
Mckinney, TX 75069-8215
972-529-5050
Fax: 972-529-2244 scott@texascuisine.com
www.texascuisine.com
Producer of corny dogs and stuffed jalapenos
Senior VP: John Vroman
john@texascuisine.com
Director of Sales: Nickolas Hancock
Human Resources: Michell Ramos
Sr. Vice President of Operations: John Vroman
Estimated Sales: $500,000-$1 Million
Number Employees: 100-249
Brands:
Leon's Texas Cuisine

7361 **Leona Meat Plant**
PO Box 156
Troy, PA 16947
570-297-3574
Fax: 570-297-3562 www.leonameatplant.com
Meat including ham, bacon and sausage
President: Charles Debach II
Estimated Sales: $1200000
Number Employees: 5-9
Type of Packaging: Consumer

7362 **Leona's Restaurante**
4 Medina Ln
Chimayo, NM 87522
505-351-4569
888-561-5569
Produces a wide range of unique New Mexican products, including ristras; salsas and sauces; ground and dried items; coffee and tea; and preserves and snacks.
Owner: Leona Tiede
leonas@cybermesa.com
Estimated Sales: Less Than $500,000
Number Employees: 1-4
Number of Brands: 1
Type of Packaging: Consumer
Brands:
LEONA'S

7363 **Leonard Fountain Specialties**
4601 Nancy Avenue
Detroit, MI 48212-1213
313-891-4141
Fax: 313-892-9200 www.leonardssyrups.com
Syrups, juices and frozen cocktails.
CEO: Leonard Bugajewski
CFO: Sherri Iskra
Product Development & Marketing: Stephen Bugajewski
Plant Manager: John Bamford
Estimated Sales: $5-10 Million
Number Employees: 100-249
Number of Brands: 9
Square Footage: 75
Type of Packaging: Food Service, Private Label
Brands:
Bar-Pak
Bulk Co2
Frosty Pak
Lemon Twist
Orange Mist
Polar Pak
Quali-Tea
Thrifty Pak
Tropical Mist

7364 **Leonard Mountain Inc**
17402 E 176th St S
Bixby, OK 74008-7527
918-366-2800
Fax: 918-366-0335 800-822-7700
office@leonardmountain.com
www.leonardmountain.com
Fruit and vegetable dips, pasta salads, bread mixes, rice mixes, olives, soups, chili and pickled vegetables.
President: Debbie Berckefeldt
Estimated Sales: $10-20 Million
Number Employees: 5-9
Number of Brands: 7
Type of Packaging: Private Label
Brands:
Boot Scootin'
Leonard Mountain
Mama Leone's
Miss Leone's
Pappy's
Purely American
Redneck

7365 **Leonardo's of Vermont, LLC**
1160 Williston Rd.
South Burlington, VT 05403
902-863-8404
Manufacturer of pizza sauces.
President and Co-Owner: Sara Byers
Co-Owner: Kelly Byers

7366 **Leonetti Cellar**
1875 Foothills Ln
Walla Walla, WA 99362-9052
509-525-1670
Fax: 509-525-4006 info@leonetticellar.com
www.leonetticellar.com
Wines
Owner: Nancy Figgins
nancy@leonetticellar.com
VP Operations: Chris Figgins
Marketing: Nancy Figgins
Vineyard Manager: Jason Magnaghi
Estimated Sales: $500,000-$1 Million
Number Employees: 10-19
Parent Co: FIGGINS FAMILY WINE ESTATES
Brands:
Leonetti Cellar

7367 **Leonetti's Frozen Food**
5935 Woodland Ave
Philadelphia, PA 19143-5919
215-729-4200
Fax: 215-729-7581 866-551-7168
leonettifrozenfo@aol.com www.beststromboli.com
Frozen stromboli and calzones
President: Beth Di Pietro
leonettifrozenfo@aol.com
Plant Manager: Leroy Douglas
Estimated Sales: $1500000
Number Employees: 20-49
Square Footage: 132000
Type of Packaging: Consumer, Food Service, Private Label, Bulk
Brands:
Leonetti's

7368 **Lepage Bakeries**
Country Kitchen Plaza
PO Box 1900
Auburn, ME 04211-1900
207-783-9161
lbck@lepagebakeries.com
Bread, rolls, English muffins and donuts
President/CEO: Andrew Barowsky
Chairman: Albert Lepage
VP: Thomas Mato
Contact: Betty Bartos
betty.bartos@lepagebakeries.com
Estimated Sales: $5-10 Million
Number Employees: 525
Type of Packaging: Consumer

7369 **Leprino Foods Co.**
1830 W. 38th Ave.
Denver, CO 80211
303-480-2600
Fax: 303-480-2605 800-537-7466
www.leprinofoods.com
Mozzarella cheese, cheese blends, and pizza cheese made especially for pizzeria and foodservice operators, frozen food manufacturers and private label cheese packagers.
Chairman/CEO: James Leprino
CFO/SVP, Operations: Lance FitzSimmons
Year Founded: 1950
Estimated Sales: Over $1 Billion
Number Employees: 4,000+
Square Footage: 60000
Type of Packaging: Food Service, Bulk
Other Locations:
Leprino Foods
Allendale MI
Leprino Foods
Fort Morgan CO
Leprino Foods
Ravenna NE
Leprino Foods
Remus MI
Leprino Foods
Roswell NM
Leprino Foods
Waverly NY

7370 **Leraysville Cheese Factory**
42 Chedder Ln
Le Raysville, PA 18829-7922
570-744-2554
Fax: 570-744-1050 800-595-5196
info@leraysvillecheese.com
www.leraysvillecheese.com
Cheese
President: Milton Repsher Jr.
m.repsher@leraysvillecheese.com
Estimated Sales: Less than $500,000
Number Employees: 5-9
Type of Packaging: Private Label

7371 **Leroux Creek**
9754 3100 Rd
Hotchkiss, CO 81419-6114
970-872-2256
Fax: 970-872-2250 877-970-5670
www.lerouxcreek.com
Organic apple sauce and fruit puree.
President: Edward Tuft
edward@lerouxcreek.com
Quality Control: Wende Michael
Marketing: Sarah Tuft
Operations: Amy Sanders
Plant Manager: Arturo Mendoza
Purchasing: Edward Tuft
Estimated Sales: $1500000
Number Employees: 20-49
Number of Products: 14
Type of Packaging: Consumer, Private Label
Brands:
Leroux Creek

7372 **Leroy Hill Coffee Co Inc**
3278 Halls Mill Rd
PO Box 6219
Mobile, AL 36606-2502
251-476-1234
Fax: 251-476-1296 800-866-5282
goodtasteiseverything@leroyhillcoffee.com
www.hillandbrooks.com
Coffee and tea.
President: Deborah Hill
CEO: Roger Burchett
rburchett@hillandbrooks.com
General Sales Manager: Greg King
Estimated Sales: $15-20 Million
Number Employees: 100-249
Number of Brands: 1
Type of Packaging: Private Label
Brands:
Leroy Hill

7373 **(HQ)Leroy Smith Inc**
4776 Old Dixie Hwy
Vero Beach, FL 32967-1239
772-569-2059
Fax: 772-567-8428 www.leroysmith.com
Manufacturer and exporter of citrus fruit including grapefruit and oranges.
CEO: Elson Smith
elson.smith@leroysmith.com
Year Founded: 1947
Number Employees: 100-249
Type of Packaging: Consumer
Brands:
Golden Magic
Island Fruit
Magic River
Mystic River

7374 **Lerro Candy Company**
P.O. Box 106
Darby, PA 19023
610-461-8886
sales@lerrocandyco.com
www.lerrocandyco.com
Confectionery products including chocolate cherries
Owner/Manager: John Lerro
Estimated Sales: $$2.5-5 Million
Number Employees: 10-19
Type of Packaging: Consumer

7375 **Les Aliments Livabec Foods**
95 Rang St Louis Rr 2
Sherrington, QC J0L 2N0
Canada
450-454-7971
Fax: 450-454-9100 info@livabec.ca
www.livabec.ca/accueil
Processor and exporter of marinated mixed and roasted vegetables and mushrooms in oil; processor of antipasto calabrese, basil and sun-dried tomato pesto; importer of sun-dried tomatoes
President: Lino Cimagila
VP: Lino Cimaglia, Jr.
Estimated Sales: $2 Million
Number Employees: 3
Square Footage: 50000
Brands:
Livabec
Livia

7376 **Les Aliments Ramico Foods**
8245 Rue Le Creusot
St. Leonard, QC HIP 2A2
Canada
514-329-1844
Fax: 514-329-5096
Beans, soups, sauces, chicken and meat with beans
Director: Rami Matta
VP: Galal Matta
Estimated Sales: G
Number Employees: 10-19
Square Footage: 12000
Type of Packaging: Private Label

7377 **Les Boulangers AssociesInc**
18842 13th Pl S
Seatac, WA 98148-2399
206-241-9343
Fax: 206-433-2844 800-522-1185
gsimeon@lba-inc.com www.lba-inc.com
Frozen dough, thaw and serve pastries
Owner: Michel Robert
michel@lba-inc.com
Owner: Lynne Andagan
Vice President: Randal Chicoine
Food & Beverage Operations Manager: Philippe Janicka
Estimated Sales: $5-10 Million
Number Employees: 20-49
Type of Packaging: Private Label
Brands:
French Does
Lba

7378 **Les Bourgeois Vineyards**
12847 W Highway Bb
Rocheport, MO 65279-9496
573-698-2300
Fax: 573-698-2170 800-690-1830
info@missouriwine.com www.missouriwine.com
Wines
Owner: Curtis Bourgeois
bistro@missouriwine.com
CEO: Rachel Mills
Marketing Specialist: Tia Stratman
Director of Sales: Tim Weiss
bistro@missouriwine.com
VP Winery Operations: Cory Bomgaars
Estimated Sales: Below $5 Million
Number Employees: 50-99
Type of Packaging: Private Label
Brands:
Les Bourgeois

7379 **Les Brasseurs Du Nord**
875 Michele Bohec Boulevard
Blainville, QC J7C 5J6
Canada
450-979-8400
Fax: 450-979-3733 800-378-3733
commentaires@boreale.com www.boreale.com/fr
Processor and distributor of beer, ale and stout
Marketing Manager: Bernard Morin
Vice President: Laura Urtinowski
CEO: Daniel Lampron
Estimated Sales: $5-10 Million
Number Employees: 50-99
Square Footage: 140000
Type of Packaging: Consumer, Food Service
Brands:
Ber Boreale

7380 **Les Brasseurs GMT**
5585 De La Rouche
Montreal, QC H2J 3K3
Canada
514-274-4941
Fax: 514-274-6138 888-253-8330
info@brasseursrj.com www.brasseursrj.com
Beer, ale, lager and stout
Manager: Alain Hudon
Partner: Brasserie Le Cheval Blanc
Pioneer: Les Brasseurs GMT
Number Employees: 100-249
Type of Packaging: Consumer, Food Service
Brands:
Belle Gueule

7381 **Les Chocolats Vadeboncoeur Inc.**
8350 Parkway D'Anjou
Montreal, QC H1K 4S3
Canada
514-493-8504
Fax: 514-483-3956 800-276-8504
www.chocolatvadeboncoeur.com
Chocolate

7382 **Les Industries Bernard et Fils**
104 Rue Industrielle Du Boise
Saint Victor, QC G0M 2B0
Canada
418-588-3590
Fax: 418-588-6836 martin@bernards.ca
www.bernards.ca
Processor and exporter of pure maple and fruit syrups
President: Yves Bernard
Marketing Director: Martin Bernard

Estimated Sales: $4.4 Million
Number Employees: 35
Type of Packaging: Consumer, Food Service, Private Label, Bulk

7383 **Les Mouts De P.O.M.**
169 Rang 2
Sain-Francois-Xavier, QC J0B 2V0
Canada
819-845-5555
Fax: 819-845-2555
Tea, juice/cider, non-alcoholic and cold non-carbonated beverages
Marketing: Guy Bergeron

7384 **Les Palais Des Thes**
1001 Ave Of The Americas
Suite 1117
New York, NY 10018
917-515-2887
Fax: 212-813-2883
wholesale@us.palaisdesthes.com
www.palaisdesthes.com
Functional (antioxidants), vegetarian, tea, soft drinks.
Marketing: Cyrille Bessiere

7385 **Les Salaisons Brochu**
183 Route Du President-Kennedy
St. Henri De Levis, QC G0R 3E0
Canada
418-882-2282
Fax: 418-882-5212
Fresh and frozen pork
Contact: Laurent Brochu
Number Employees: 250-499
Type of Packaging: Consumer, Food Service, Private Label

7386 **Les Trois Petits Cochons**
4223 1st Ave
2nd Floor
Brooklyn, NY 11232
212-219-1230
Fax: 212-941-9726 800-537-7283
info@3pigs.com 3pigs.com
Pates, mini terrines, mousses, vegetable and seafood terrines, charouterie and pork free products.
President: Alain Sinturel
CEO: Jean Pierre Pradie
Year Founded: 1975
Estimated Sales: $20-50 Million
Number Employees: 20-49

7387 **Les Viandes du Breton**
150 Ch Des Raymond
Riviere-Du-Lup, QC G5R 5X8
Canada
418-863-6711
Fax: 416-863-6767 service@dubreton.com
www.dubreton.com
Fresh and frozen pork; exporter of hams, spare ribs, bellies, etc.
President: Vincent Breton
VP, Administration & Finance: Marie Jos,e Landry
Year Founded: 1944
Estimated Sales: $169 Million
Number Employees: 550
Parent Co: Bose Corporation
Type of Packaging: Consumer, Food Service, Private Label, Bulk
Brands:
Dubreton Natural

7388 **Les Viandes or Fil**
2080 Rue Monterey
Laval, QC H7L 3S3
Canada
450-687-5664
Fax: 450-687-2733
Processor and exporter of fresh and frozen pork
President: Antonio Filice
Vice President: Bernard Paquette
Estimated Sales: $15 Million
Number Employees: 50
Type of Packaging: Bulk

7389 **Lesaffre Yeast Corporation**
7475 W Main St.
Milwaukee, WI 53214
414-615-4094
800-770-2714
www.lesaffreyeast.com
Yeast
President & CEO: John Riesch
Parent Co: Lesaffre Group

7390 **Lesley Elizabeth Inc**
877 Whitney Dr
Lapeer, MI 48446-2565
810-667-0706
Fax: 810-667-7287 800-684-3300
sales@lesleyelizabeth.com
Gourmet sauces, oils, vinegarettes, pestos and crisps
President: Lesley Mc Cowen
CFO: Sally Burrell
sally@lesleyelizabeth.com
Marketing: Gary Bates
Estimated Sales: $1-5 Million
Number Employees: 10-19
Type of Packaging: Private Label
Brands:
Lesley Elizabeth
Lesley Elizabeth's Crisps
Lesley Elizabeth's Dipping Oils
Lesley Elizabeth's Dips
Lesley Elizabeth's Pesto
Lesley Elizabeth's Vinegarettes
Lesley Marinara

7391 **Lesley Stowe Fine Foods**
Richmond, BC V6V 1J6
Canada
604-238-2180
www.lesleystowe.com
Crackers and crisps
Founder/Consultant: Lesley Stowe

7392 **Leslie Leger & Sons**
34 Chemin De La Cote
P.O.Box 1061
Cap-Pele, NB E4N 3B3
Canada
506-577-4730
Fax: 506-577-4960 sales@leslieandsons.com
http://www.leslieandsons.com
Processor and exporter of smoked herring and brined alewife
President: Leslie Leger
Estimated Sales: $4.8 Million
Number Employees: 35
Type of Packaging: Bulk

7393 **Lesserevil Brand Snack Co**
83 Newtown Rd
2nd Floor
Danbury, CT 06810-4118
203-529-3555
talk2us@lesserevil.com
lesserevil.com
All natural snacks
Contact: Corey Benson
corey@lesserevil.com
Number Employees: 1-4

7394 **Lesserevil Brand Snack Co**
83 Newtown Rd
Second Floor
Danbury, CT 06810-4118
203-529-3555
talk2us@lesserevil.com
lesserevil.com
Healthier snack foods, using black beans and organic popcorn
Contact: Corey Benson
corey@lesserevil.com
Number Employees: 1-4

7395 **Let Them Eat Cake**
3805 S West Shore Blvd # B
Tampa, FL 33611-1047
813-837-6888
Fax: 813-831-6741
www.chocolateismycrayon.com
Custom mini pastries
Owner: Michael Baugh
letthemeatcake@tampabay.rr.com
Chef of Icing and Decorating: Lori Maniscalo
Chef of Pastry: Jason Lucas
Marketing Manager: Michael Baugh
Estimated Sales: Less Than $500,000
Number Employees: 1-4

7396 **Letterman Enterprises Inc.**
109 Fairfield Dr
State College, PA 16801-8248
814-574-4339
Fax: 814-466-6820 david@lettermaninc.com
www.feeltheflavors.com
Ethnic sauces (soy, curry, etc.), grilling sauces, marinades, other sauces, seasonings and cooking enhancers, foodservice.
Marketing: David Letterman
Contact: David Letterman
d_letterman1919@hotmail.com

7397 **Levain**
167 W 74th St # A
New York, NY 10023-2216
212-874-6080
Fax: 212-874-6413 www.levainbakery.com
Baked goods, breads, cookie mix
Owner: Constance Mc Donald
connie@levainbakery.com
Estimated Sales: Less Than $500,000
Number Employees: 5-9

7398 **Levant Mediterranean Snack Foods LLC**
113 Neck Road
Unit 5
Haverhill, MA 01835
978-241-9986
Fax: 978-241-9566 www.levantsnacks.com
Manufacturer of falafel chips.
President: Joe Dunne

7399 **Levesque**
500 Beaumont St
Montreal, QC H3N 1T7
Canada
514-273-1702
Fax: 514-273-2325 877-539-1702
ventes@salaisonlevesque.qc.ca
www.salaisonlevesque.qc.ca
Ham products
President/Owner: M Regis Levesque
VP: Mme Annie Levesque
Estimated Sales: $7.1 Million
Number Employees: 30

7400 **Lew-Mark Baking Company**
Fl 10
1000 N West St
Wilmington, DE 19801-1059
269-962-6205
Fax: 716-237-2735
Baked goods
President/CEO: M Serventi
Marketing Director: John Wheeler
Number Employees: 20-49
Parent Co: Archway Cookies

7401 **Lewes Dairy Inc**
660 Pilottown Rd
Lewes, DE 19958-1299
302-645-6281
Fax: 302-645-6290 info@lewesdairy.com
www.lewesdairy.com
Dairy products
Owner: Chip Brittingham
lewesdairy@dmv.com
Vice President: Walter Brittingham
Estimated Sales: $2.3 Million
Number Employees: 20-49
Type of Packaging: Consumer

7402 **Lewis Bakeries Inc**
500 N Fulton Ave
Evansville, IN 47710-1571
812-425-4642
Fax: 812-425-7609 www.lewisbakeries.net
Large independent bakery in the Midwest.
CFO: Jeffery Sankovitch
jsankovitch@lewisbakeries.com
Number Employees: 1000-4999
Type of Packaging: Consumer, Food Service, Private Label, Bulk
Other Locations:
Headquarters
Evansville IN
Bakery
Murfreesboro TN
Bakery
Ft. Wayne IN
Bakery
LaPorte IN
Bakery
Vincennes IN
Brands:
Bunny
Chief Kahai
Hartford Farms
Healthy Life

Gateway
Indiana Spud
Lewis

7403 **Lewis Cellars**
4101 Big Ranch Rd
Napa, CA 94558-1406
707-255-3400
Fax: 707-255-3402 info@lewiscellars.com
www.lewiscellars.com
Wines
Owner: Randy Lewis
info@lewiscellars.com
CEO: John Lewis
CFO: Debbie Lewis
Estimated Sales: Less Than $500,000
Number Employees: 1-4

7404 **Lewis Laboratories International Ltd.**
P.O. Box 373
Southport, CT 06890
203-226-7343
Fax: 203-454-0329 800-243-6020
customerservice@lewis-labs.com
Nutritional suppliments
President: Diana Lewis
Vice President: Myron Lewis
Estimated Sales: $500,000-$1 Million
Number Employees: 5-9
Brands:
Brewer's
Fabulous Fiber
Famous Original Formula Staminex
Lewis Labs Rda
Super Fabulous Fiber
Weigh Down

7405 **Lewis Sausage Corporation**
1050 Old Savannah Road
Burgaw, NC 28425
910-259-2642
Fax: 910-259-9881
Smoked and mild sausage
President: Edgar Hardy
Estimated Sales: $3 Million
Number Employees: 25
Type of Packaging: Consumer

7406 **Lexington Coffee & Tea**
2571 Regency Rd
Lexington, KY 40503-2920
859-277-1102
Fax: 859-277-6490
contactus@lexingtoncoffeeandtea.com
lexingtoncoffeeandtea.com
roasted coffee and tea. Some of their varieties include African City Roast, Costa Rican Tarrazu, Gourmet Five Star, Mocha Java, Indonesian City Roast, French Roast, Chocolate Hazelnut, Hazelnut French Roast and more.
Owner: Terri Wood
accounts@lexingtoncoffeeandtea.com
Estimated Sales: $5-10 000,000
Number Employees: 2-10
Brands:
Lexington Coffee Tea

7407 **Li'l Guy Foods**
3631 N Kimball Dr
Kansas City, MO 64161-9474
816-241-2000
Fax: 816-241-2025 800-886-8226
www.lilguyfoods.com
Mexican foods including corn tortillas, flour tortillas, flavored tortilla wraps, taco shells, tortilla chips, spices, taco sauce and salsa picante, cheeses and chorizo and chicharones.
President: David Sloan
VP, Director of Sales: Christina Sloan
VP: Edward Sloan
Director of Sales: Roberto Vidal
Office Manager/Customer Service: Jennifer Hart
Plant Manager: Edward Sloan
Estimated Sales: $2000000
Number Employees: 20-49
Square Footage: 120000
Parent Co: Sloan Acquisition Corporation
Type of Packaging: Consumer, Food Service
Brands:
Li'l Guy
V&V Supremo Cheeses & Meats

7408 **LiDestri Food & Drink**
815 W Whitney Rd
Fairport, NY 14450
585-377-7700
lidestrifoodanddrink.com
Sauces, dips and beverages for contract manufacturing and private label
Co-President, Sales and Supply Chain: John LiDestri
CEO: Giovanni LiDestri
VP, Finance: Jennifer Shepker
Co-President and CMO: Stefani LiDestri
Contact: David Leifer
dleifer@bridgesinc.info
COO: Phil Viruso
Estimated Sales: $285 Million
Number Employees: 500
Number of Brands: 2
Square Footage: 260000
Type of Packaging: Consumer, Private Label, Bulk
Other Locations:
Rochester NY
Fresno CA
Pennsauken NJ
Lansdale PA
Brands:
Cantisano
Francesco Rinaldi

7409 **Liberty Natural Products Inc**
20949 S Harris Rd
Oregon City, OR 97045-9428
503-631-4488
Fax: 503-631-2424 800-289-8427
jim@libertynatural.com www.libertynatural.com
Processor and exporter of gourmet breath fresheners, natural flavors and oils; processor of vitamins; importer of essential oils and botanical extracts; wholesaler/distributor of gourmet breath fresheners
Owner: Jim Derking
Sales Manager: Tabor Helton
jim@libertynatural.com
Operations Manager: Shane Reaney
Purchasing Manager: Michelle Falls
Estimated Sales: $1-2.5 Million
Number Employees: 20-49
Square Footage: 68000
Type of Packaging: Consumer, Bulk
Brands:
Max
Natural Gourmet Flavor Oil
Tib

7410 **Liberty Orchards Co Inc**
117 Mission Ave
P.O. Box C
Cashmere, WA 98815-1007
509-782-2191
Fax: 509-782-1487 800-231-3242
sales@libertyorchards.com
www.libertyorchards.com
Processor and exporter of confectionery products including chocolate, holiday and boxed nonchocolate candy
President: Sue Meiner
sue@libertyorchards.com
VP Marketing & Sales: Michael Rainey Sr
Estimated Sales: $12,377,000
Number Employees: 50-99
Type of Packaging: Consumer, Food Service
Brands:
Aplets
Cotlets
Fruit Chocolates
Fruit Delights
Fruit Festives
Fruit Parfaits
Fruit Softees
Grapelets
Hawaiian Festives

7411 **Liberty Vegetable Oil Co**
15306 Carmenita Rd
Santa Fe Springs, CA 90670-5606
562-921-3567
Fax: 562-802-3476
liberty@libertyvegetableoil.com
www.libertyvegetableoil.com
Tree nut oils, organic and non-GMO oils.
President: Ronald Field
CEO: Irwin Field
rfield@libertyvegetableoil.com
VP: Edward Field
Quality Assurance: William Kelleghan
Sales & Purchasing: Ronald Field
VP Operations: Lee Hibma
Estimated Sales: $7.1 Million
Number Employees: 20-49
Brands:
Lvo

7412 **Life Extension Foundation**
3600 West Commercial Blvd
Fort Lauderdale, FL 33309
954-766-8144
Fax: 954-761-9199 888-895-4771
customerservice@lifeextension.com
www.lifeextension.com
Health and nutritional supplements.
President: Bill Faloon
Founder: Saul Kent
Chief Financial Officer: James Murray
Vice President, Sales & Marketing: Rey Searles
Vice President of Purchasing: Connie Richter
Estimated Sales: $25-50 Million
Number Employees: 200+
Type of Packaging: Consumer

7413 **Life Force Specialty Foods**
1055 Saddle Ridge Road
Moscow, ID 83843-8774
208-882-9158
Fax: 208-882-9158 877-657-9471
www.lifeforce-specialty-foods.com
Honey wine
President: Garrick Kruse
Estimated Sales: $5-9.9 Million
Number Employees: 8
Brands:
Life Force

7414 **Life Plus Style Gourmet**
65 Roosevelt Ave
Suite 107
Valley Stream, NY 11581
516-823-3001
Fax: 516-823-3003 www.coneyislandclassics.com
Kettle corn
Sales: Andy Appell
andyappell@gmail.com
Brands:
Coney Island Classics

7415 **Life Spice & Ingredients LLC**
216 W Chicago Ave # 2
Chicago, IL 60654-3100
312-274-9992
Fax: 312-274-2381 www.lifespiceingredients.com
Spices
President: Peter Garvy
pgarvy@lifespiceingredients.com
Vice President of Sales & Marketing: Lisa Stern
Vice President of Operations: Holland Schlutz
Estimated Sales: $25 Million
Number Employees: 5-9

7416 **LifeAID**
2833 Mission St
Santa Cruz, CA 95060
888-558-1113
www.lifeaidbevco.com
Sports drinks
Co-Founder: Orion Melehan
Co-Founder: Aaron Hinde

7417 **LifeIce**
129 W 20th St
Apt 4C
New York, NY 10011-3642
917-414-0309
855-543-3423
www.lifeice.com
Frozen snacks
Founder: Paulette Fox

7418 **LifeTime**
1967 N Glassell St
Orange, CA 92865-4320
714-634-9340
Fax: 714-634-9340 800-333-6168
Vitamins
President: Tom Pinkowski
Vice President of Sales/Marketing: Tom Pinkowski

7419 **Lifeline Food Company,Inc.**
426 Orange Avenue
Seaside, CA 93955
831-899-5040
Fax: 831-899-0285 www.lifetimecheese.com
Dairy and cheese
President: Jone Chappell
CEO: Greg Chappell
greg@lifetimecheese.com
CFO: Greg Chappell
Sales: Andres Borowiak
Estimated Sales: Below $5 Million
Number Employees: 5-9
Number of Brands: 2
Type of Packaging: Private Label
Brands:
Dairytime
Energy Bars
Lifetime
Lifetime Fat Free Cheese
Lifetime Lactose/Fat Free Cheese
Lifetime Low Fat Cheese
Lifetime Low Fat Rice Cheese
Soy Cheese

7420 **Lifem Spice Ingredients**
300 Cherry Lane
Palm Beach, FL 33480
561-844-6334
Fax: 561-844-6335 www.lifespiceingredients.com
Supplier of spice blends and flavor systems.
VP Operations: Howard Schultz
Contact: Bruce Armstrong
barmstrong@lifespiceingredients.com

7421 **Lifestar Millennium**
PO Box 3837
Sedona, AZ 86340
925-202-4302
Fax: 970-422-4739 877-422-4739
lsmail@lifestar.com
Processor and exporter of natural nutritional supplements; importer of grapeseed oil
President: J Bentley
Estimated Sales: $300,000-500,000
Number Employees: 1-4
Type of Packaging: Consumer, Food Service
Brands:
Living Food Concentrates
Multiplex

7422 **Lifestyle Health Guide**
1603 Capitol Ave
Suite 314
Cheyenne, WY 82001
307-529-1239
Fax: 805-650-0997 800-822-3712
Processor, exporter and importer of health products including nutritional supplements
Owner: Larry Permen
President: Jean Koven
VP: Larry Permen
Estimated Sales: $3-5,000,000
Number Employees: 1-4
Brands:
Bread, Rice & Pasta Lovers Diet
Dermagest
Natragest
Sound Sleep

7423 **Lifeway**
6431 W Oakton St
Morton Grove, IL 60053
847-967-1010
Fax: 847-967-6558 877-281-3874
lifewaykefir.com
Kefir, frozen kefir, specialty cheeses and probiotic beverages for kids
President and CEO: Julie Smolyansky
julies@lifeway.net
CFO: Eric Hanson
Sr. EVP, Sales: Amy Feldman
COO: Edward Smolyansky
Estimated Sales: $4 Million
Number Employees: 250-499
Square Footage: 240000
Type of Packaging: Consumer
Brands:
Basics Plus
Farmer's Cheese
Kefir
Kefir Starter
La Fruta
Soy Treat
Sweet Kiss

7424 **Lifewise Ingredients**
3540 N 126 St
Suite D
Brookfield, IL 53005
262-788-9141
Fax: 262-788-9143 info@lifewise1.com
www.lifewise1.com
Processor and exporter of healthy food ingredients including monosodium glutamate replacements, flavor enhancers, and flavor maskers
Founder: Richard Share
Sales Director: Richard Share
Contact: Dean Antczak
dantczak@lifewise1.com
Lab Manager: Millie Galey
General Manager: Carol Bender
Estimated Sales: Below $5 Million
Number Employees: 5-9
Square Footage: 14000
Brands:
Bitzels
Lifewise Ingredients
Potentiator Plus
Simply Rich

7425 **Light Rock Beverage Company**
9 Balmforth Ave
Danbury, CT 06810
203-743-3410
Fax: 203-792-7909
Bottled water, other beverages
President: George Antous
Vice President: Fred Antous
General Manager: Thomas Antous
Estimated Sales: Below $5 000,000
Number Employees: 18
Brands:
Light Rock

7426 **Light Vision Confections**
1776 Mentor Ave
Cincinnati, OH 45212-3554
513-351-9444
Fax: 253-981-0758 www.lightvision.com
Holographic confectionery items including lollypops, hard candy and chocolate
President: Eric Begleiter
CEO: Mike Wodke
CFO: Paul Graham
Contact: Wodke Krista
krista.wodke@lightvision.com
Estimated Sales: Below $5 Million
Number Employees: 20-30
Type of Packaging: Food Service, Private Label
Brands:
Holopop
Popart

7427 **Lightlife**
153 Industrial Blvd
Turners Falls, MA 01376
413-774-9000
Fax: 413-774-9080 800-769-3279
info@lightlife.com lightlife.com
Processor and exporter of soy-based products like chili, sausages, deli meats, ground meat, tempeh, chicken, burgers and bacon
President: Daniel Abrahamson
dabrahamson@lightlife.com
General Manager: Darcy Zbinovec
R&D: Ron Desautels
Human Resources Director: Bobby Riley
Product Manager: Dean Kuhlka
Year Founded: 1979
Estimated Sales: $20-50 Million
Number Employees: 100-249
Square Footage: 80000
Parent Co: Maple Leaf Foods
Brands:
Gimme Lean
Light Burgers
Organic Flax Tempeh
Organic Garden Veggie Tempeh
Organic Smoky Tempeh Strips
Organic Soy Tempeh
Organic Three Grain Tempeh
Organic Wild Rice Tempeh
Smart Bacon
Smart Bbq
Smart Chili
Smart Cutlets
Smart Deli
Smart Dogs
Smart Ground
Smart Links
Smart Sausage
Smart Tenders
Smart Wings
Tofu Pups

7428 **Liguria Foods Inc**
1515 15th St N
Humboldt, IA 50548-1017
515-332-4121
Fax: 515-332-2629 www.liguriafoods.com
Sausage and salami; exporter of hard and Genoa salami and pepperoni.
Owner: Roger Lawson
Estimated Sales: $25 Million
Number Employees: 50-99
Square Footage: 45000
Parent Co: SMG
Type of Packaging: Consumer, Food Service, Private Label, Bulk
Brands:
Aquila D'Ora
Beirmeister
Buon Giorno
Gratifica
Liguria

7429 **Lillie's Q**
1856 W North Ave
Chicago, IL 60622
773-772-5500
www.lilliesq.com
Sauces, rubs, spices, marmalades, chips
Owner: Charlie McKenna
info@lilliesq.com
Number Employees: 20-49

7430 **Lily of the Desert**
1887 Geesling Rd
Denton, TX 76208
940-566-9914
Fax: 940-566-9925 800-229-5459
contact@lilyofthedesert.com
www.lilyofthedesert.com
Organic aloe vera beverages, cold brew coffee and tea, and dietary supplements
President: Don Lovelace
dlovelace@lilyofthedesert.com
Year Founded: 1971
Estimated Sales: $1-3 Million
Number Employees: 20-49
Type of Packaging: Consumer, Food Service, Private Label, Bulk
Brands:
Lily of the Desert

7431 **Lily's Sweets**
4840 Pearl East Cir
Suite 201E
Boulder, CO 80301
877-587-0557
info@lilyssweets.com lilyssweets.com
Chocolate products sweetened with stevia
Co-Founder: Cynthia Tice
Co-Founder: Chuck Genuardi
Type of Packaging: Consumer
Brands:
LILY'S

7432 **Lilydale Foods**
100 Commerce Valley Dr W
Markham, ON L3T 0A1
Canada
800-661-5341
www.lilydale.com
Fresh and frozen meats, poultry, sausages and sandwiches; also, further processed poultry products including fully cooked, par cooked, breaded and unbreaded.
Executive Chairman, Sofina Foods: Michael Latifi
President/CEO: Robert Wilt
Year Founded: 1940
Estimated Sales: Over $1 Billion
Number Employees: 2700
Square Footage: 81978
Parent Co: Sofina Foods Incorporated
Type of Packaging: Consumer, Food Service, Bulk
Brands:
Lilydale

7433 Lima Grain Cereal Seeds LLC
2040 SE Frontage Rd
Fort Collins, CO 80525-9717
970-498-2200
Fax: 970-223-4302 LCS-info@limagrain.com
www.limagrain.com
Processor and distributor of breakfast cereals in boxes and bags
President: Bernie Blach
Secretary: Cindy Blach
CFO: Kelly Mundorf
Executive VP: Cedric Audebert
cedric.audebert@limagrain.com
Marketing/Technical Manager: Zach Gaines
Number Employees: 5-9
Square Footage: 80000
Type of Packaging: Consumer, Food Service, Private Label, Bulk
Brands:
Colorado's Kernels
Las Palomas Grandes
Pop'n Snak

7434 Limehouse Produce Co
4791 Trade St # G
North Charleston, SC 29418-2824
843-556-3400
Fax: 843-556-3950 info@limehouseproduce.com
www.limehouseproduce.com
Fresh fruits and vegetables
Owner: John F Limehouse
Vice President: Andrea Limehouse
Sales: Ken Strange
limehouseproduce@comcast.net
Number Employees: 20-49

7435 Limited Edition
3106 N Big Spring St Ste 101
Midland, TX 79705
432-686-2008
Fax: 432-686-2035
Flavored honey butter, dip mixes, jalapenos, pickles and vegetables
Owner: Beverly Vaughan
Controller: Ann Wimberly
Estimated Sales: $300-500,000
Number Employees: 1-4
Square Footage: 20000
Type of Packaging: Consumer, Food Service, Private Label, Bulk
Brands:
Limited Edition Presents
Udderly Delightful

7436 Limitless
1500 W Carroll Ave
Chicago, IL 60607
sales@limitlesscoffee.com
limitlesscoffee.com
Cold brew coffee, coffee beans, green tea and sparkling water
Founder: Matt Matros
Co-Founder: Chris Fanucchi
Co-Founder: Craig Alexander

7437 Limpert Bros Inc
202 N West Blvd
Vineland, NJ 8360
856-691-1353
Fax: 856-794-8968 800-691-1353
www.limpertbrothers.com
Processor, importer and exporter of marshmallow fluff, hot fudge, cherries, butterscotch, carmel, and other toppings, flavors and ingredients.
President: Pearl Giordano
limpertbr@aol.com
R&D: Jim Behringer
Quality Control: Donna Phrampus
Estimated Sales: $1 Million
Number Employees: 10-19
Number of Brands: 1
Number of Products: 400
Square Footage: 280000
Type of Packaging: Food Service, Bulk
Brands:
Limpert Brothers

7438 Lincourt Vineyards
1711 Alamo Pintado Rd
Solvang, CA 93463-9712
805-688-8554
Fax: 805-688-9327
customerservice@lincourtwines.com
www.lincourtwines.com
Red and white wines
Owner: Bill Foley
Number Employees: 10-19
Square Footage: 16000
Parent Co: Folly Estates
Type of Packaging: Consumer
Brands:
Lin Court Vineyards

7439 Linda's Gourmet Latkes
PO Box 491413
Los Angeles, CA 90049
818-453-8690
Fax: 818-453-8679 888-452-8537
www.lindasgourmetlatkes.com
Latkes
President/Owner: Linda Hausberg
linda@lindasgourmetlatkes.com

7440 Linda's Lollies Company
1 International Blvd
Ste 208
Mahwan, NJ 07495-002
20- 25- 876
Fax: 201-252-8768 800-347-1545
info@lindaslollies.com www.lindaslollies.com
Processor and exporter of gourmet lollypops and confectionery gifts
President: Linda Harkavy
Sales & Marketing: Tammy Demone
Customer Services: Connie Atticella
Estimated Sales: $1500000
Number Employees: 1-4
Type of Packaging: Consumer, Food Service, Bulk
Brands:
Linda's Little Lollies
Linda's Lollies

7441 Linden Cheese Factory
P.O.Box 439
Linden, WI 53553
608-623-2531
Fax: 608-623-2567 800-660-5051
Monterey jack, cheddar, colby, longhorn cheese
President: David Schroeder
Estimated Sales: $5-10 000,000
Number Employees: 15

7442 Linden Cookies Inc
25 Brenner Dr
Congers, NY 10920-1397
845-268-5050
Fax: 845-268-5055 sales@lindencookies.com
www.lindencookies.com
Producer of cookies.
President: Paul Sturz
VP: Suzanne Sturz
Assistant VP: Christian Sturz
Manager: Christian Sturz
csturz@lindencookies.com
Estimated Sales: $10-20 Million
Number Employees: 20-49
Number of Brands: 1
Brands:
Linden's

7443 Lindner Bison
Newhall
Apt 111
Northern, CA 91355-5139
530-254-6337
Fax: 661-254-0224 klindner@lindnerbison.com
www.lindnerbison.com
Bison/turkey burgers
President: Kathy Lindner
COO: Ken Lindner
Number Employees: 1-4
Brands:
Bison
Bisurkey

7444 Lindsay Farms
PO Box 640481
Pike Road, AL 36064
800-243-4608
info@lindsayfarms.com www.lindsayfarms.com
Gourmet and specialty salsas, nuts, and pickled foods
Owner: Jon Winton
Type of Packaging: Private Label
Brands:
Lindsay Farms

7445 Lindsay's Teas
1331 Commerce St.
Petaluma, CA 94549
707-462-6333
800-624-7031
info@lindsaysteas.com www.lindsaysteas.com
Organic specialty teas
Manager: Melanie Mountanos
Estimated Sales: $20-50 Million
Number Employees: 20-49
Parent Co: Mountanos Family Coffee & Tea Co.
Brands:
Lindsay's Tea

7446 Lindt & Sprungli USA
One Fine Chocolate Pl
Stratham, NH 03885-2592
603-778-8100
www.lindt-spruengli.com
Manufacturer of fine chocolates
CEO: Daniel Studer
Contact: Lisa Cloutier
lcloutier@lindt.com
Year Founded: 1845
Estimated Sales: $30-50 Million
Number Employees: 650
Brands:
American Classics
Lindor Truffles
Lindt Chocolate

7447 Lindy's Homemade Italian Ice
920-A Black Satchel Drive
Charlotte, NC 28216
704-391-7994
Fax: 704-391-9016 lindysitalianice.com
Italian Ice

7448 Lingle Brothers Coffee
6500 Garfield Ave
Bell Gardens, CA 90201-1897
562-927-3317
Fax: 562-928-1505
Coffee
Owner: James Lingle
Estimated Sales: $10-20 000,000
Number Employees: 20-49

7449 Link Snacks Inc.
1 Snack Food Ln.
PO Box 397
Minong, WI 54859
715-466-2234
Fax: 715-466-5151 www.jacklinks.com
Meat and protein snacks, including jerky, sausages, sticks and strips.
Chairman: Jack Link
President/CEO: Troy Link
Estimated Sales: $1 Billion
Number Employees: 250-499
Number of Brands: 1
Type of Packaging: Consumer
Brands:
Jack Link's

7450 Lion Brewery Inc
700 N Pennsylvania Ave
Wilkes Barre, PA 18705-2451
570-823-8801
Fax: 570-823-6686 888-295-2337
info@lionbrewery.com www.lionbrewery.com
Fifteenth-largest American-owned brewery.
President & CEO: Cliff Risell
CEO: Jb Brombacher
jbrombacher@lionbrewery.com
Number Employees: 100-249
Type of Packaging: Consumer, Bulk
Brands:
Lionshead Pilsner
Lionshead Light

7451 Lion Raisins Inc
9500 S DE Wolf Ave
Selma, CA 93662-9534
559-834-6677
Fax: 559-834-6622 www.lionraisins.com
Grower and processor of California raisins and raisin products.
CEO: Al Lion
alion@lionsraisins.com
Number Employees: 250-499
Square Footage: 130000
Type of Packaging: Consumer, Food Service, Private Label, Bulk

Brands:
California Grown
Lion
Sunshine California

7452 **Lionel Hitchen Essitional Oils**
1867 Porter Lake Drive
Sarasota, FL 34240
941-379-1400
Fax: 941-379-1433 www.lheo.co.uk
Natural flavors and oils
President: Alison Barnes
General Manager: Suzy Nolan
snolan@lhitchenusa.com
Estimated Sales: $700,000
Number Employees: 8

7453 **Lioni Latticini Inc**
555 Lehigh Ave
Union, NJ 07083-7976
908-624-9450
Fax: 908-686-3449 info@lionimozzarella.com
www.lionimozzarella.com
Fresh whole milk mozzarella products
Owner: Michael Virga
Owner/VP: Salvatore Salzarulo
Marketing: Guiseppe (Sal) Salzarulo
Sales Manager: Michelina Salzarulo
Manager: Lori Church
lori@lionimozzarella.com
Operations Director: Guiseppe (Sal) Salarulo
Production Supervisor: Salvatore Salzarulo
Plant Supervisor: Salvatore Salzarulo
Estimated Sales: $5,700,000
Number Employees: 10-19

7454 **Lipid Nutrition**
24708 W Durkee Road
Channahan, IL 60410
815-730-5208
Fax: 815-730-5202
Manufacturer natural lipid ingredients
Contact: Ramesh Gaga
ramesh.gaga@unilever.com

7455 **Lipsey Mountain Spring Water**
P.O.Box 1246
Norcross, GA 30091-1246
770-449-0001
Fax: 770-234-6948 www.lipseywater.com
Bottled water
President: Joseph Lipsey Iii
Estimated Sales: $1-2.5 Million
Number Employees: 20-49

7456 **Lisa Shively's Kitchen Helpers, LLC**
802 Clarkway Ave
Po Box 2123
Eden, NC 27289
336-623-7511
Fax: 336-623-7511 kitchenhelpers@earthlink.net
Gluten-free, organic/natural, meals, hot chocolate, other soups, stews, beans, rubs, spices, cookbooks.
Marketing: Lisa Shively

7457 **Lisa's Organics**
PO Box 987
Carnelian Bay, CA 96140
530-584-1958
877-584-5711
www.lisasorganics.com
Organic frozen vegetables and vegetable side dishes
Founder: Lisa Marie Boudreau
Type of Packaging: Consumer

7458 **Lisanatti Foods**
1815 Red Soils Ct
Oregon City, OR 97045-4139
503-652-1988
Fax: 503-653-1979 866-864-3922
www.lisanattifoods.com
Vegetarian and cheese alternatives including soy satin
President: Philip J Lisac
National Sales & Marketing: Teresa Lisac
Production manager: Andy Ingersoll
Estimated Sales: $5-10 Million
Number Employees: 5-9
Parent Co: P&J Lisac Associates
Type of Packaging: Consumer, Food Service
Brands:
Lisanatti
Soy-Sation

7459 **Lisbon Sausage Co Inc**
PO Box 2028
New Bedford, MA 02741-2028
508-994-0453
Fax: 508-994-0453 joan@amarals.com
www.amarals.com
Portuguese sausage
President: Antonio Rodrigues
Vice President: Joan Sparrow
Contact: Joan Sparrow
joan@amarals.com
Estimated Sales: Below $5 000,000
Number Employees: 10-19

7460 **Lisbon Seafood Co**
1428 S Main St
Fall River, MA 02724-2604
508-672-3617
Fax: 508-672-4698
Seafood
Owner: Victor Da Silva
vncc@aol.com
Estimated Sales: $1-3 Million
Number Employees: 10-19

7461 **Litehouse Foods**
1109 N Ella Ave
Sandpoint, ID 83864
800-669-3169
www.litehousefoods.com
Dips & dressings.
Estimated Sales: I
Type of Packaging: Consumer

7462 **(HQ)Litehouse Foods**
100 Litehouse Dr
Sandpoint, ID 83864
800-669-3169
www.litehousefoods.com
Dressings and dips; portion control and bulk available, including vinaigrette, bleu cheese, ranch, caesar, coleslaw dressing, french, cumin citrus, tartar sauce, burger spread, BBQ sauce, cocktail sauce, deli salsa, mayonaisehorseradish, raspberry, honey mustard, Italian, also low calorie, specialty, and gluten free sauces and dressings.
President & CEO: Kelly Prior
VP, Finance & Accounting: Matt Burrows
SVP, Sales & Marketing: Brent Carr
VP, Operations: Rob Tyrrell
VP, Information Technology: Derek Christensen
Year Founded: 1963
Estimated Sales: $100-500 Million
Number Employees: 250-499
Type of Packaging: Consumer, Food Service, Private Label, Bulk

7463 **Little Amana Winery**
4400 I St
Amana, IA 52203
319-668-9664
Fax: 319-668-2853
Wine
Owner: Bob Zuber
Brands:
Ackerman
Breezy Hills
Jasper
Little Swan Lake
Park Farm
Sugar Grove
Summerset
Village

7464 **Little Bird**
25 Fairchild Ave
Suite 200
Plainview, NY 11803
646-620-6395
littlebirdkitchen.com
Chocolate bark and simple syrup flavored with jalapenos.
Co-Owner: Sara Meyer
Co-Owner: Corey Meyer

7465 **Little Crow Foods**
PO Box 1038
Warsaw, IN 46581-1038
574-267-7141
Fax: 574-267-2370 800-288-2769
customerservice@littlecrowfoods.com
www.littlecrowfoods.com
Manufacturer and contract packager of dry blended products including flour, pancake mixes and breakfast cereals; exporter of flour, cereals and seasoned coating mixes
President: Dennis Fuller
EVP: Kimberly Fuller
VP Operations: Ron Shipley
Estimated Sales: $8 Million
Number Employees: 50-99
Square Footage: 360000
Type of Packaging: Consumer, Food Service, Private Label, Bulk
Brands:
Miracle Maize

7466 **Little Duck Organics**
New York, NY 10017
877-458-1321
hello@littleduckorganics.com
littleduckorganics.com
No-sugar snacks using natural ingredients. Organic, Kosher, and gluten free.
CEO: Arthur Pergament
Contact: Charlee-Ann Charron
charlee@littleduckorganics.com
Number Employees: 5
Square Footage: 3187
Type of Packaging: Consumer
Brands:
LITTLE DUCK ORGANICS

7467 **Little Hills Winery**
710 S Main St
St Charles, MO 63301-3443
636-946-6637
Fax: 636-724-1121 877-584-4557
Wines
Owner: David Campbell
david@little-hills.com
Co-Owner: Tammy Campbell
Estimated Sales: $8.5 Million
Number Employees: 5 9

7468 **Little I**
815 3rd Street
Blaine, WA 98230
360-332-3258
Fax: 360-332-3279 www.littlei.com
Gourmet mints, cold-pressed enery and vitamin gums and other confections
Owner: Sarah Dalrymple

7469 **Little Miss Muffin**
4014 N Rockwell St
Chicago, IL 60618
773-463-6328
Fax: 773-463-7101 800-456-9328
Fresh and frozen cakes and pastries
Owner: Staci Minic Mintz
Contact: Kenny Munic
kenny@littlemissmuffin.com
Estimated Sales: $1.8 Million
Number Employees: 40
Type of Packaging: Consumer, Food Service
Brands:
Little Miss Muffin
Wide Shoulders Bakin

7470 **Little Portion Bakery**
350 Co Rd 248
Berryville, AR 72616
479-253-7710
877-504-9865
www.littleportionbakery.org
Granola, snack bars, cookies
Founder: Viola Talbot

7471 **Little Red Dot Kitchen**
PO Box 2571
Sunnyvale, CA 94087
408-673-8227
reddotkitchen.com
Roasted meat snack
CEO: Ching Lee
VP, Sales: Bonnie Frese

7472 **Little Red Kitchen**
Brooklyn, NY
littleredkitchenbakeshop.com
Cookies and pies
Founder: Susan Palmer

7473 **Little Rhody Brand Frankfurts**
5 Day St
Johnston, RI 02919-4301
401-831-0815
sales@littlerhodyhotdogs.com
www.littlerhodyhotdogs.com
Sausage, frankfurters, meat products and fast foods
President: Ed Robal
Estimated Sales: $3 Million
Number Employees: 1-4
Square Footage: 40000
Type of Packaging: Consumer, Food Service
Brands:
Little Rhody Brand

7474 **Little River Lobster Company**
PO Box 507
East Boothbay, ME 04544-0507
207-633-2648
Fax: 604-276-8371
Whole fish/seafood
President: Mike Dalton
Estimated Sales: $810,000
Number Employees: 1-4

7475 **Little River Seafood Inc**
440 Rock Town Rd
Reedville, VA 22539-3017
804-453-3670
Fax: 804-453-5421 kelly@littleriverseafood.com
www.littleriverseafood.com
Quality crab products.
President: Steven Minor
steve@littleriverseafood.com
Marketing Executive: Kelly Minor
Estimated Sales: $10,026,306
Number Employees: 50-99
Type of Packaging: Consumer, Food Service, Private Label, Bulk
Brands:
Little River Seafood

7476 **Little's Cuisine**
49 Locust Ave
Suite 104
New Canaan, CT 06840
203-228-4440
www.littlescuisine.com
Seasoning mixes and blends
President & Owner: Angela Colabella
angela@littlecuisine.com

7477 **Liuzzi Angeloni Cheese**
86 Rossotto Drive
Hamden, CT 06514
203-287-8477
Fax: 203-287-9898
Manufacturer of different cheeses including ricotta, mozzarella, and fresh curd.
Founder: Pasquale Liuzzi

7478 **LivBar**
249 Liberty St. NE
Suite 232
Salem, OR 97301
971-239-1209
hello@livbar.com
www.livbar.com
Energy bars that are organic, gluten free, dairy free, soy free, corn free, and GMO-free
Co-Founder: Gabe Johansen
Co-Founder: Jan Johansen
Year Founded: 2012

7479 **Live A Little Gourmet Foods**
P.O. Box 10916
Oakland, CA 94610
510-744-3683
Fax: 510-744-3684 888-744-2300
www.livealittle.com
Fresh salads dressings and croutons
Executive Chef, Founder, CEO: Virginia Davis
virginia@livealittle.com
Estimated Sales: $1-3 Million
Number Employees: 1-4
Number of Brands: 2
Brands:
Live a Little Dressings
Perfect Croutons

7480 **Live Gourmet**
Carpinteria, CA
info@livegourmet.com
Greenhouse-grown vegetables.
Number Employees: 70
Brands:
Live Gourmet(c)
Grower Pete's Certified Organic(c)

7481 **Live Love Pop**
4385 Sunbelt Dr
Addison, TX 75001-5134
214-697-6370
Fax: 972-380-4234 info@livelovepop.com
livelovepop.com
Gourmet popcorn
CEO: Lauren Brundage
Operations: Molly Brundage
Number of Brands: 1
Number of Products: 6
Type of Packaging: Consumer
Brands:
LIVE LOVE POP

7482 **Live Oaks Winery**
3875 Hecker Pass Road
Gilroy, CA 95020
408-842-2401
Wines
President: Richard Blocher
Estimated Sales: $500-1 Million appx.
Number Employees: 20-49

7483 **Livermore Falls Baking Company**
49 Gilbert St
Livermore Falls, ME 04254-4238
207-897-3442
Fax: 207-897-6381
Baked goods including rolls and pizza crusts
President: Anthony Maxwell
Estimated Sales: $990,000
Number Employees: 5 to 9

7484 **Livermore Valley Cellars**
1193 Ava St
Livermore, CA 94550
925-454-9463
Fax: 925-454-9463
Producer of wine
President: Chris Lagiss
CEO: Tim Sauer
Marketing Director: Tim Sauer
Estimated Sales: $1-2.5 Million
Number Employees: 1-4
Brands:
Lvc

7485 **Living Farms**
352 3rd Street E
Tracy, MN 56175-1527
507-629-3517
Fax: 507-629-4258
Processors of grains and vegetables
Owner: Ardell Anderson
Vice President/CEO: Janet Anderson
Estimated Sales: Under $500,000
Number Employees: 3

7486 **Living Harvest Foods**
PO Box 4407
Portland, OR 97208
503-274-0755
888-690-3958
www.livingharvest.com
Non dairy hemp milk, ice cream bars, ice cream, hemp protein powder, hemp oil
President/CEO: Hans Faster
CFO/COO: Catherine Hearn
Marketing Manager: Christina Volgyesi
Estimated Sales: $5 Million
Number Employees: 10
Square Footage: 6400

7487 **Living Intentions**
250 S Garrard Blvd
Richmond, CA 94801
415-824-5483
www.livingintentions.com
Popcorn, cereal, nut blends, seeds and trail mix.
Founder: Joshua McHugh

7488 **Living Raw**
2422 Douglass Glen Ln
Franklin, TN 37064-6760
312-933-6543
Fax: 678-669-5801
Chocolate truffles
Co-Owner: T.J. Dunham
Co-Owner: Ginger Dunham

7489 **Livingston Farmers Assn**
641 6th St
PO Box 456
Livingston, CA 95334-1397
209-394-7941
Fax: 209-394-7952 jim@lfa-ca.com
www.lfa-ca.com
Processor and exporter of sweet potatoes, peaches and almonds
President: Steve Moler
General Manager/CEO: James Snyder
Manager: Jenny Allen
jenny@lfa-ca.com
Estimated Sales: $6 Million
Number Employees: 20-49
Square Footage: 95200
Brands:
Yamato Colony

7490 **Livingston Moffett Winery**
1895 Cabernet Ln
Saint Helena, CA 94574
707-965-3694
Fax: 707-965-2058 800-788-0370
www.livingstonwines.com
Winery
President: Diane Livingston
Production Manager: Mark Moffett
Estimated Sales: Below $5 Million
Number Employees: 4
Brands:
Gemstone Vineyard
Moffett
Stanley's
Starrey's Ion
Syrah

7491 **Livingston's Bulls Bay Seafood**
631 Morrison St
Mc Clellanville, SC 29458
843-887-3519
Fax: 843-887-3989
Shrimp and oysters
Owner: Bill Livingston
livbullbay@aol.com
Co-Owner/CEO: Kathy Livingston
Estimated Sales: $1,000,000
Number Employees: 5-9

7492 **Liz Lovely Inc**
167 Mad River Canoe Rd
Waitsfield, VT 05673-4433
802-496-6390
Fax: 802-329-2043
Gluten free, vegan and non-GMO cookies.
Owner: Liz Holtz
liz@lizlovely.com
CEO: Liz Scott
Operations Manager: Emily Potter
Number Employees: 5-9

7493 **Llano Estacado Winery**
3426 EAST F.M. 1585
Lubbock, TX 79452
806-745-2258
Fax: 806-748-1674 800-634-3854
info@llanowine.com www.llanowine.com
Wine
President: Mark Hyman
CFO: Mary McGill
Vice President: James Morris
Operations Manager: Greg Bruni
Estimated Sales: Below $5 Million
Number Employees: 20-49
Type of Packaging: Private Label

7494 **Lloyd's**
740 Springdale Drive
Ste. 206
Exton, PA 19341
610-647-3144
Fax: 610-594-8654 lloydsofpa@aol.com
www.lloydspa.com
Frozen dessert mixes
Technical Director: Barry Jones
President: Andy Jones
Estimated Sales: $5-10 Million
Number Employees: 1-4
Number of Brands: 1
Number of Products: 20
Type of Packaging: Food Service, Private Label, Bulk

7495 **Loacker USA**
90 Broad St
Suite 402A
New York, NY 10004
212-742-8510
Fax: 212-747-8752 www.loackerusa.com
Wafers and chocolate bars
VP, Marketing: Crystal Black Davis
Year Founded: 1925
Estimated Sales: $349 Million
Number Employees: 834

7496 **Loafin' Around**
555 Eastview Dr
Madison, AL 35758-7824
301-570-4513
Fax: 301-216-1575
Breads
President: Blake Daniel
Estimated Sales: $62 K
Number Employees: 1

7497 **Lobster 4 Dinner**
106 Wharf Rd
Cape Wolf, PE C0B 1V0
Canada
888-230-0707
www.lobster4dinner.com
Lobster meat

7498 **Lobster Gram**
4664 N Lowell Ave
Chicago, IL 60630-4263
773-777-8315
Fax: 773-777-5546 800-548-3562
customerservice@lobstergram.com
www.lobstergram.com
Lobster
President: Michael Robinson
michael@livelob.com
Estimated Sales: $1-3 Million
Number Employees: 10-19

7499 **Loc Maria Biscuits**
Philadelphia, PA 19123
www.locmaria.fr
French biscuits
Number Employees: 350
Brands:
Gavottes
Traou Mad

7500 **Local Roots Farms**
RT 18 W. Lake Rd.
Burt, NY 14028
716-946-3198
localrootsfarmrt18.com
Various produce including, but not limited to tomatoes, beets, carrots, and onions.
Co-Owner: Jerry Winsquist
Co-Owner: Kristi Winquist
Type of Packaging: Consumer

7501 **Lochhead Mfg. Co.**
527 Axminster Dr
Fenton, MO 63026
800-776-2088
sales@lochheadvanilla.com
www.lochheadvanilla.com
Processor and exporter of vanilla extracts including pure, natural and artificial blends.
Co-Owner: John Lochhead
sales@lochheadvanilla.com
Co-Owner: George Lochhead
Estimated Sales: $10-20 Million
Number Employees: 10-19
Type of Packaging: Consumer, Private Label, Bulk

7502 **Lockcoffee**
6 Kilmer Road
Larchmont, NY 10538-2636
914-273-7838
Fax: 212-827-0945
Coffee
President: B Brown Lock
Estimated Sales: Under $500,000
Number Employees: 1-4

7503 **Lockwood Vineyards**
849 Zinfandel Lane
St. Helena, CA 94574
707-963-6925
Fax: 831-644-7829 info@lockwoodvineyard.com
www.lockwoodvineyard.com
Wines
Owner: Paul Toeppen
Estimated Sales: $2.5-5 Million
Number Employees: 5-9
Type of Packaging: Private Label

7504 **Locustdale Meat Packing**
377 Lavelle Road
Locustdale, PA 17945
570-875-1270
Sausage, kielbasa, ring bologna and roast chicken and turkey
Owner: Jack Holderman
Estimated Sales: $1-3 Million
Number Employees: 1-4

7505 **Lodi Canning Co**
307 Nestles St
PO Box 315
Lodi, WI 53555
608-592-4236
Fax: 608-592-4742 bob@lodicanning.com
www.lodicanning.com
Canned peas and creamed corn
President: Bob Goeres
bob@lodicanning.com
Estimated Sales: $2-5 Million
Number Employees: 100-249
Type of Packaging: Private Label
Brands:
Day By Day
Idol
Lodi's

7506 **Lodi Nut Company**
1230 S Fairmont Ave
Lodi, CA 95240
209-334-2081
Fax: 209-369-6815 800-234-6887
Black walnut kernels and nut factory gourmet nuts; also, custom processor and co-packer of English walnut, almond and macadamia kernels
President/Sales & Marketing Director: Kelvin Suess
Executive VP: Virgil Suess
Contact: Harvey Borton
hdborton@lodiacademy.net
Plant Manager: Reuben Rodriguez
Estimated Sales: $7,001,000
Number Employees: 75
Square Footage: 160000
Type of Packaging: Consumer, Food Service, Private Label, Bulk

7507 **Loew Vineyards**
14001 Liberty Rd
Mt Airy, MD 21771-9524
301-831-5464
Fax: 301-831-5464 loewvineyards@comcast.net
www.loewvineyards.net
Wines
Owner: Lois Loew
l.loew@loewvineyards.net
Estimated Sales: $800,000
Number Employees: 1-4

7508 **Loffredo Produce**
500 46th St
Rock Island, IL 61201
309-786-0969
Fax: 309-786-0660 800-383-3367
lbeener@loffredo.com www.loffredo.com
Produce
President: Gene Loffredo
CFO: Mark Zimmerman
Operations Director: Jerry Moore
VP Sales: John Loffredo
VP, Purchase: Mike Loffredo
Estimated Sales: $5-10 Million appx.
Number Employees: 50-99
Parent Co: Lofredo Fresh Produce

7509 **Log 5 Corporation**
4 Glenberry Court
Phoenix, MD 21131
410-329-9580
Fax: 443-705-0223 www.log5.com
Food ingredients; pasteurization process
President: Joost De Koomen
Vice President: Jochem Dekker
Contact: Chaus Davids
cdavids@log5.com

7510 **Log House Foods**
700 Berkshire Lane N
Plymouth, MN 55441
763-546-8395
info@loghousefoods.com
www.loghousefoods.com
Ingredients manufacturer
Co-Founder: Mary Kosir
Exec. VP: Larry Phillips
Year Founded: 1947
Type of Packaging: Private Label

7511 **Loghouse Foods**
700 Berkshire Ln N
Minneapolis, MN 55441-5499
763-546-8395
Fax: 763-546-7339 info@loghousefoods.com
www.loghousefoods.com
Twice-baked cinnamon toast and biscotti, flaked coconut, European-style melting creams for dipping and coating desserts, chocolate chips, candy coatings, etc.
President: Alan Kasdan
akasdan@loghousefoods.com
VP Operations: Josh Kasdan
Estimated Sales: $17,000,000
Number Employees: 20-49
Type of Packaging: Consumer, Food Service, Private Label
Brands:
Bella Crema
Jacobsen's Toast
Log House
Log House Candiquik
Plymouth Pantry

7512 **Lola Granola Bar Corporation**
PO Box 63
Croton Falls, NY 10519
914-617-8833
info@lolagranolabar.com
www.lolagranolabar.com
Manufacturer of granola bars and water.
Founder: Mary Molina
Contact: Ernie Molina
ernie@lolagranolabar.com
Brands:
LOLA GRANOLA BAR

7513 **Lola Savannah**
1701 Commerce St.
Houston, TX 77002-2244
713-222-9800
Fax: 713-222-9802 888-663-9166
lola@lolasavannah.com lolacc.com
Roasted coffee and tea
Owner: Duke Furgh
Vice President: Michael Spencer
Contact: Michael Spencer
mcs@lolasavannah.com
Operations Manager: Hank Segelke
Estimated Sales: Less than $500,000
Number Employees: 5-9
Type of Packaging: Consumer, Food Service, Private Label, Bulk

7514 **Lolonis Winery**
1930 Tice Valley Blvd
Walnut Creek, CA 94595-2203
925-938-8066
Fax: 925-938-8069
Wines
President: Petros Lolonis
Contact: Doreen Scallan
doreenscallan@yahoo.com
Estimated Sales: $600,000
Number Employees: 5-9
Brands:
Ladybug White Old Vines

7515 **Lombardi Brothers Meat Packers**
1926 W Elk Pl
P.O. Box 11277
Denver, CO 80211
303-458-7441
lombardibrothers.com
Beef, pork, lamb and veal; importer of wild game.
President & Owner: Victoria Phillips
General Manager: Jeff Harvey
Year Founded: 1947
Estimated Sales: $30 Million
Number Employees: 60
Square Footage: 30000
Type of Packaging: Food Service

Other Locations:
Lombardi Brothers Meat
Fridley MN
Lombardi Brothers Meat
Le Mars IA

7516 **Lombardi's Bakery**
177 E Main St
Torrington, CT 06790-5432
860-489-4766
Fax: 860-489-4766
Baked goods
Owner: Camillo Lombardi
Estimated Sales: Less Than $500,000
Number Employees: 1-4
Brands:
Lombardi's

7517 **Lombardi's Seafood**
1152 Harmon Avenue
Winter Park, FL 32789
407-628-3474
Fax: 407-240-2562 800-879-8411
quality@lombardis.com www.lombardis.com
Processor, importer and wholesaler/distributor of fresh and frozen seafood; serving the food service market
Owner: Vince Lomabardi
VP: Vince Lombardi
Contact: James Carr
jamescarr@lombardis.com
Supervisor: Mike Lombardi
Estimated Sales: $10-20 Million
Number Employees: 100-249
Type of Packaging: Food Service

7518 **Lombardi's Seafood Inc**
1888 W Fairbanks Ave
Winter Park, FL 32789-4502
407-628-3474
Fax: 407-628-5165 quality@lombardis.com
www.lombardis.com
Fresh and frozen seafood and shellfish
President: Anthony Lomabardi
Vice President: Tony Lombardi
Estimated Sales: $1 Million
Number Employees: 10-19

7519 **Lone Pine Enterprise Inc**
121 Durkee St
Carlisle, AR 72024
870-552-3217
Processor and exporter rice and soybeans
President: Jason Smith
Estimated Sales: Less Than $500,000
Number Employees: 1-4
Type of Packaging: Consumer, Food Service, Bulk

7520 **Lone Star Bakery**
106 W Liberty St
Round Rock, TX 78664-5122
512-255-7268
Fax: 512-255-6405 www.roundrockdonuts.com
Processor and exporter of pre-baked and frozen buttermilk biscuits, muffins, cinnamon rolls, brownies, sheet cakes, fruit cobblers,pie shells, pecan and fruit pie, and portioned cookie and dough
Owner: Dale Cohrs
VP: Bill Scott
Sales: Rick Perrett
Operations: Damon Smith
Plant Manager: Fred Alexander
Purchasing: Clint Scott
Estimated Sales: $450000
Number Employees: 50-99
Square Footage: 600000
Type of Packaging: Food Service, Private Label, Bulk
Brands:
Lone Star

7521 **Lone Star Consolidated Foods Inc.**
1727 North Beckley Avenue
Dallas, TX 75203
214-946-2185
Fax: 214-946-2286 800-658-5637
Manufacturer of baked sweet rolls, doughnuts, cinnamon rolls, fritters and hushpuppies.
CEO/COO: Dolores Burdines
Contact: Kevin Murray
kevin@lonestarfunfoods.com
Year Founded: 1950
Estimated Sales: $20-50 Million
Number Employees: 100-249
Number of Brands: 2
Brands:
Babycakes
Lone Star

7522 **Lone Wolf Farms**
99 Ordway Avenue
PO Box 317
Minto, ND 58261
701-248-3482
Fax: 701-248-3508 www.lonewolffarms.com
Supplier of potatoes
President: Keith Bjorneby
VP: Dean Bjorneby
Sales Manager: Chris Bjorneby
Office Manager: Suzi Tibert
Production Manager: Chris Bjorneby
Estimated Sales: $10-20 Million
Number Employees: 16
Type of Packaging: Consumer, Bulk

7523 **Long Food Industries**
709 Rock Beauty Road
Fripp Island, SC 29920-7344
843-838-3205
Fax: 843-838-3918 www.longfoodindustries.com
Shrimp, cooked/diced chicken, clam (meat and broth), beef (diced/cooked), lobster, fish and pork
President: Leon Long
Estimated Sales: $10-20 Million
Number Employees: 1
Type of Packaging: Food Service

7524 **Long Grove Confectionary**
333 Lexington Dr
Buffalo Grove, IL 60089-6542
847-459-3100
Fax: 847-459-4871 800-373-3102
linda_gadas@longgrove.com www.longgrove.com
Confectionery items including chocolates, molded chocolate, apples, novelties, custom molded logos and holiday boxes.
President: John Mangel
maureen_herrington@longgrove.com
Vice President: David Mangel
Marketing: Linda Gadas
Site Manager: Maureen Herrington
maureen_herrington@longgrove.com
Estimated Sales: $5-10 Million
Number Employees: 50-99
Square Footage: 100000
Type of Packaging: Consumer, Food Service, Private Label, Bulk
Brands:
Chicago Mints
Long Grove Confections
Myrties
Myrtles
Ultimate Apple

7525 **Long Island CauliflowerAssn**
139 Marcy Ave
Riverhead, NY 11901-3099
631-727-2212
Fax: 631-727-4295 www.licassoc.com
Cauliflower
President/CEO: Carl Key
Estimated Sales: $5-10 Million
Number Employees: 10-19

7526 **Long Trail Brewing Co Inc**
5520 US Route 4
Bridgewater Cors, VT 05035-9600
802-672-5011
Fax: 802-672-5012 www.longtrail.com
Brewers of beer and ale.
Founder: Andy Pherson
Operations Manager: Matt Quinlan
Facility Manager: Billy Gault
Estimated Sales: $10-20 Million
Number Employees: 50-99
Number of Brands: 14
Brands:
Culmination
Cranberry Gose
Double Bag
Green Blaze IPA
Harvest
Imperial Pumpkin
India Pale Ale
Limbo IPA
Long Trail Ale
Mostly Cloudy
Sick Day
Stand Out
Summer Ale
Unearthed

7527 **Long Vineyards**
1535 Sage Canyon Rd
St Helena, CA 94574-9628
707-963-2496
Fax: 707-963-5016
Wines
Co-Owner/President: Robert Long
Co-Owner: Zelma Long
Marketing/PR Director: Pat Perini Long
Winemaking Operations Director: Sandi Belcher
Estimated Sales: $500,000-$1 Million
Number Employees: 1-4
Brands:
Johannisberg Riesling
Sangiovese

7528 **Longacres Modern Dairy Inc**
1445 Route 100
PO Box 69
Barto, PA 19504
610-845-7551
Fax: 610-845-2041 info@longacresdairy.com
Dairy
President: Daniel T Longacre Jr
longacre@longacresicecream.com
VP: Newton T Longacre
Treasurer: Kathryn Longacre
CFO: Timoty T Longacre
Sales Exec: Timothy Longacre
Plant Engineer: Daniel Longacre
Estimated Sales: Below $5 Million
Number Employees: 10-19
Brands:
Longacre

7529 **Longbottom Coffee & TeaInc**
4893 NW 235th Ave # 101
Hillsboro, OR 97124-5835
503-648-1271
Fax: 503-681-0944 800-288-1271
info@longbottomcoffee.com
www.longbottomcoffee.com
Processor and importer of specialty coffees including certified organics, espresso, flavored, regionals and blends; wholesaler/distributor of espresso machines and fine teas
Owner: Jody Baccelleri
Marketing Director: Lisa Walker
Sales Director: Gabrielle Paeson
jbaccelleri@medicalteams.org
Manufacturing/Operations Director: Tom Brandon
Estimated Sales: $8 Million
Number Employees: 50-99
Square Footage: 112000
Type of Packaging: Consumer, Food Service, Private Label, Bulk

7530 **Longford-Hamilton Company**
17885 SW Tualatin Valley Hwy
Beaverton, OR 97006
503-642-5661
Fax: 503-649-1321 oldmillrum.com
Imported specialty foods and confectionery products
President: Malarkey Wall
Sales Director: Jan Rudolph
Estimated Sales: Below $5 Million
Number Employees: 1-4
Number of Brands: 1
Number of Products: 20
Type of Packaging: Consumer
Brands:
Old Mill Brand

7531 **Longleaf Plantation**
78 Baker Rd
Purvis, MS 39475
601-794-6001
Fax: 601-794-5052 800-421-7370
reeceholford@longleafplantation.net
www.longleafplantation.net
Manufacturers of pecans
President: Warren Hood Jr
reeceholford@longleafplantation.net
Sales Exec: Reece Holford
Estimated Sales: $5-10 Million
Number Employees: 20-49
Brands:
Longleaf Plantation

7532 **Longmeadow Building Dept**
20 Williams St
Longmeadow, MA 01106-1950
413-565-4153
Fax: 413-565-4112 www.longmeadow.org
Specialty sauces
Manager: Mark Denver
General Manager: Suzie Barton
Manager: Paul Healy
Estimated Sales: $2.5-5 Million
Number Employees: 5-9

7533 **Longo's Bakery Inc**
138 W 21st St
Hazleton, PA 18201-1909
570-454-5825
Fax: 570-454-6246 www.longosbakery.com
Breads, rolls, pizza shells
President: James N Capriotti
Estimated Sales: $500,000-$1 000,000
Number Employees: 20-49

7534 **Longreen Corp.**
5077 Walnut Grove Ave
San Gabriel, CA 91776
626-287-4700
bd@lgreenhealth.com
www.lgreenhealth.com
Health product manufacturer
Year Founded: 2010
Type of Packaging: Private Label
Brands:
Longreen

7535 **Longview Meat & Merchandise Ltd**
PO Box 173
Longview, AB T0L 1H0
Canada
403-558-3706
Fax: 403-558-3708 866 355 3759
Beef jerky, wholesaler of bavarian style sausage and pepperonis
President/Owner: Peter Lawson
Plant Manager: Jacky Lau
Estimated Sales: $1 Million
Number Employees: 12
Square Footage: 26000
Type of Packaging: Consumer, Food Service, Private Label, Bulk

7536 **LonoLife**
1722 South Coast Hwy
Suite 4
Oceanside, CA 92054
855-843-8566
contact@lonolife.com www.lonolife.com
Bone broth, keto broth, snack broth, collagen, protein coffee, cleanse drink powder, plant based protein
Co-Founder: Jesse Koltes
Co-Founder: Craig Leslie

7537 **Look Lobster Co**
32 Old House Point Rd
Jonesport, ME 04649-3385
207-497-2353
Fax: 207-497-5559 looklobster@myfairpoint.net
www.lookslobster.com
Lobster
President: Bert Sid Look
Vice President, Sales & Logistics: William Look
Estimated Sales: $.5-1 million
Number Employees: 5-9

7538 **Lopez Foods**
6016 NW 120th Ct
Oklahoma City, OK 73162-1729
405-603-7500
Fax: 405-603-6120 sales@lopezfoods.com
www.lopezfoods.com
Manufacturer of frozen ground beef patties, partially cooked and fully-cooked sausage patties and sliced Canadian-style bacon.
President: John C Lopez
jlopez@lopezfoods.com
Co-Owner, Chairman: John Lopez
CEO: Ed Sanchez
Number Employees: 20-49
Square Footage: 460192
Type of Packaging: Food Service
Brands:
Carneco Foods
Lopez Foods

7539 **LorAnn Oils**
4518 Aurelius Rd
Lansing, MI 48910
517-882-0215
800-862-8620
www.lorannoils.com
Oils, flavors, colors and specialty ingredients.
CEO: John Grettenberger
National Sales Manager: Troy Sprague
COO: Carl Thelen

7540 **Lora Brody Products Inc**
91 Edgewater Dr
Waltham, MA 02453-2405
781-899-3910
Fax: 617-558-5383 lora@lorabrody.com
www.lorabrody.com
Bread dough enhancer
President: Lora Brody
lora@lorabrody.com
Estimated Sales: $160,000
Number Employees: 1-4
Brands:
Dough Relaxer
Lora Brody Bread Dou
Sourdough Bread Enha

7541 **Lord's Sausage & Country Ham**
310 S Line St
Dexter, GA 31019-3967
478-875-3101
Fax: 478-875-3039 800-342-6002
www.lordssausage.com
Fresh and smoked pork sausage and cured country ham
President: Roger Lord
wayne@lordsausage.com
VP: Britt Lord
Estimated Sales: $10-20 Million
Number Employees: 20-49
Square Footage: 60000
Type of Packaging: Consumer, Food Service, Private Label, Bulk
Brands:
Lord's

7542 **Loretta's Authentic Pralines**
1100 N Peters St # 9
Stall #9
New Orleans, LA 70116-2629
504-529-6170
Fax: 504-945-5912 lorettas@nocoxmail.com
www.lorettaspralines.com
Pralines and confections
Owner: Loretta Harrison
Estimated Sales: $1-2.5 Million
Number Employees: 1-4

7543 **Lorina, Inc.**
2655 S Le Jeune Rd
Suite 904
Coral Gables, FL 33134
305-779-3085
Fax: 305-779-4949 lorina.us@lorina.com
us.lorina.com
French lemonade
President: Jean-Pierre Barjon
Estimated Sales: $17 Million
Number Employees: 5-9

7544 **Lorissa's Kitchen**
110 N 5th St
Suite 700
Minneapolis, MN 55403-1618
715-466-2234
Fax: 715-466-5151 lorissaskitchen.com
Meat jerky

7545 **Loriva Culinary Oils**
1192 Illinois Street
San Francisco, CA 94107
415-401-0080
Fax: 415-401-0087 866-972-6879
www.worldpantry.com
Processor and exporter of specialty oils including roasted, infused and toasted sesame, peanut, safflower, walnut, garlic, olive, avocado, hazelnut, macadamia, etc.; also, kosher varieties available
President: Patrick Lee
CEO: David Miller
Consumer Relations: Liz Scatena
Number Employees: 10-19
Parent Co: NSpired Natural Foods
Type of Packaging: Consumer, Food Service, Private Label, Bulk
Brands:
Loriva
Loriva Jazz Roasted Oils
Loriva Supreme Flavored Oils
Loriva Supreme Oils

7546 **Los Altos Food Products**
450 N Baldwin Park Blvd.
City Of Industry, CA 91746
626-330-6555
Fax: 626-330-6755 www.losaltosfoods.com
Mexican and Swiss cheeses
President: Raul Andrade
Co-Founder, Vice President: Gloria Andrade
Quality Control Manager: Sergio Mares
Director Sales & Marketing: William Finicle
Contact: Alin Andrade
aandrade@losaltosfoods.com
VP Operations: Alin Andrade
Estimated Sales: $21.5 Million
Number Employees: 1-4
Square Footage: 38000
Type of Packaging: Consumer, Food Service

7547 **Los Amigo Tortilla Mfg Co**
251 Armour Dr NE
Atlanta, GA 30324-3979
404-876-8153
Fax: 404-876-8102 800-969-8226
ruben@losamigos.com
Corn and flour tortillas and chips
President: Ruben N. Rodriguez, Jr
tom@losamigo.com
General Manager: Ruben Rodriguez
Sales Exec: Tom Gibbs
Operations: Tom Gibb
Plant Supervisor: Carlos Perez
Estimated Sales: Below $5 Million
Number Employees: 50-99

7548 **(HQ)Los Angeles Nut House Brands**
1601 E Olympic Blvd
Los Angeles, CA 90021-1936
213-481-0134
Fax: 213-481-0084
Nuts
Executive Director: Azuka Uzoh
Sales Director: Terry McClean
Purchasing Manager: Jon Anderson
Estimated Sales: $.5-1 million
Number Employees: 6
Type of Packaging: Private Label

7549 **Los Angeles Smoking & Curing Company**
1100 West Ewing Street
Seattle, WA 98119
213-628-1246
Fax: 213-614-8857 info@oceanbeauty.com
www.oceanbeauty.com
Herring, kippers, lox, roe, cod, mackerel, salmon, shad, caviar and whitefish
President: Howard Klein
VP Sales/Marketing: Richard Schaeffer
Contact: Glen Stein
gstein@oceanbeauty.com
Number Employees: 100-249
Parent Co: Ocean Beauty
Type of Packaging: Consumer, Food Service
Brands:
Kodikook
Lascco

7550 **Los Chileros**
309 Industrial Ave NE
Albuquerque, NM 87107-2232
505-768-1100
Fax: 505-242-7513 www.sfgfoods.com
Chiles, corn products, salsa, rubs and mixes
Manager: Charles Waghorne
chuck@loschileros.com
Estimated Sales: $1 Million
Number Employees: 5-9

7551 **Los Gatos Brewing Company**
130 N Santa Cruz Ave.
Los Gatos, CA 95030
408-395-9929
Fax: 408-395-2769 www.lgbrewingco.com
Restaurant and brewing center

Owner: Andy Pavicich Jr
Director Manufacturing: Jeff Alexander
General Manager: Randall Bertho
Estimated Sales: $2.5-5 Million
Number Employees: 100-249
Brands:
Hefeweizen
Los Gatos Lager
Nut Brown Ale

7552 **Los Gatos Tomato Products**
PO Box 429
Huron, CA 93234
559-945-2700
Fax: 559-945-2661 info@losgatostomato.com
www.losgatostomato.com
Tomato concentrates
CEO: Reuben Peterson
Controller: Linda Labandeira
Manager, Customer Service/Field Ops: Lance Dami
Estimated Sales: $7 Million
Number Employees: 20
Square Footage: 35000
Type of Packaging: Bulk

7553 **Los Pericos Food Products**
2301 Valley Blvd.
Pomona, CA 91768
909-623-5625
Fax: 909-623-5486 sales@lospericosfood.com
www.lospericosfood.com
Mexican tostada shells
Partner: Marcelino Ortega
Owner: Guadalupe Ortega
Partner: Luis Ortega
Contact: Jesse Ortega
jesse@lospericosfood.com
Estimated Sales: $3.9 Million
Number Employees: 46
Brands:
Tostada

7554 **Lost Coast Brewery**
1600 Sunset Dr
Eureka, CA 95503
707-267-9651
www.lostcoast.com
Brewery
President: Barbara Groom
Sales Director: Briar Bush
Year Founded: 1986
Estimated Sales: $20-50 Million
Number Employees: 50-99
Number of Products: 14
Type of Packaging: Private Label
Brands:
8-Ball Stout
Alleycat Amber
Arrgh! Pale Ale
Downtown Brown
Fogcutter Double IPA
Great White
Indica India Pale Ale
Raspberry Brown
Sharkinator
Tangerine Wheat Ale
Winterbraun

7555 **Lost Coast Roast**
550 G Street
Unit 36
Arcata, CA 95521
lostcoastroast.com
Organic cold brew coffee
Co-Founder: Dusty Miller
Co-Founder: Lucas Miller
Co-Founder: Jonny Miller
Co-Founder: Dylan Miller

7556 **Lost Mountain Winery**
2958 Lost Mountain Rd
Sequim, WA 98382
360-683-5229
Fax: 360-683-7572 888-683-5229
www.lostmountain.com
Wine
Co-Owner/Winemaker: Steve Conca
Co-Owner/Winemaker: Sue Conca
Estimated Sales: Less than $500,000
Number Employees: 1-4
Brands:
Lost Mountain Winery

7557 **Lost Trail Root Beer**
PO Box 670
Louisburg, KS 66053-0670
913-837-5202
Fax: 913-837-5762 800-748-7765
lcmill@micoks.net www.louisburgcidermill.com
Processor, wholesaler/distributor and exporter of apple cider and root beer; also, apple butter
President/Owner: Tom Schierman
Estimated Sales: $500,000-$1 Million
Number Employees: 5-9
Square Footage: 40000
Type of Packaging: Consumer, Private Label
Brands:
Lost Trail
Louisburg

7558 **(HQ)Losurdo Creamery**
20 Owens Rd
Hackensack, NJ 07601-3297
201-343-6680
Fax: 201-343-8078 888-567-8736
info@losurdofoods.com www.losurdofoods.com
Cheeses, romano, parmesan, parmaroma, ricotta, mozzarella, provolone.
President: Michael Losurdo Sr
Marketing Head: Dincenva Tulibutz
VP: Mark Losurdo
Estimated Sales: $20-50 Million
Number Employees: 100-249
Type of Packaging: Consumer, Food Service
Other Locations:
Losurdo Creamery
Heuvelton NY
Brands:
Losurdo

7559 **Lotsa Pasta**
1762 Garnet Ave
San Diego, CA 92109
858-581-6777
Fax: 858-581-6783 chef@lotsapasta.com
Pasta
Owner: Carol Blomstrom
Estimated Sales: Below $5 Million
Number Employees: 20-49
Brands:
Lotsa Pasta

7560 **Lotte USA Inc**
5243 Wayne Rd
Battle Creek, MI 49037-7323
269-963-6664
Fax: 269-963-6695 lotteusa-inc@yahoo.com
Cream-filled cookies, throat drops and chewing gum
President: T Kaneko
Marketing Manager: Julie Fanning
Sales Manager: Frank Deleo
Manager: Robin Bailey
rbailey@lotteusainc.com
Operations Manager: Dick Thomason
Purchasing Manager: Ron Parsons
Estimated Sales: $15,000,000
Number Employees: 10-19
Type of Packaging: Consumer, Food Service
Brands:
Full Blast Gum
Koala No March Cookie

7561 **Lotus Bakery**
3336 Industrial Dr
Santa Rosa, CA 95403
707-526-1520
Fax: 415-526-6377 800-875-6887
sales@lotusbakery.com
Bread, cookies and energy bars
Owner: Mark Menning
Estimated Sales: $400,000
Number Employees: 10-19
Type of Packaging: Private Label
Brands:
Spirulina Bee Bar
Spirulina Trail Bar

7562 **Lotus Brands**
PO Box 325
Twin Lakes, WI 53181
262-889-8561
Fax: 262-889-2461 800-824-6396
lotusbrands@lotuspress.com
www.lotusbrands.com
Teas and herbal supplements
President: Santosh Krinsky
Year Founded: 1992
Estimated Sales: $1-2.5 Million
Number Employees: 50-99
Number of Brands: 16
Number of Products: 1000
Square Footage: 152000
Type of Packaging: Consumer, Private Label, Bulk
Brands:
Ancient Secrets
Blue Pearl Incense
Dragon Eggs
Eco-Dent
Fuchs Tooth Brushes
Life Tree Products
Light Mountain
Nature's Alchemy
Neem Aura
Nirvana
Paul Penders
Rainforest Remedies
Sai Baba Nag Champa
Smile Brite
Tifert Aromatherapy
Yakshi Fragrances

7563 **Lotus Foods**
5210 Wall Avenue
Richmond, CA 94804
510-525-3137
Fax: 510-525-4226 info@lotusfoods.com
www.lotusfoods.com
Rice products
President/Partner: Kenneth Lee
CEO: Caryl Levine
Partner/VP: Caryl Levine
Marketing Director: Caryl Levine
Contact: Vivian Baker
vivian.baker@lotusfoods.com
Year Founded: 1995
Estimated Sales: $170,000
Number Employees: 3
Type of Packaging: Consumer, Food Service, Bulk
Brands:
Forbidden Rice

7564 **Lotus Manufacturing Company**
529 San Pedro Avenue
San Antonio, TX 78212-5057
210-223-1421
Fax: 210-223-1273
Breads and other bakery products
President: Germino Trevino
Estimated Sales: $1-2.5 Million
Number Employees: 1

7565 **Lou Pizzo Produce**
9660 NW 67th Pl
Parkland, FL 33076
954-941-8830
Fax: 954-941-8870
Produce
President: Louis Pizzo
VP: Angelina Pizzo
Estimated Sales: Below $5 000,000
Number Employees: 1-4
Brands:
Lou Pizzo

7566 **Lou-Retta's Custom Chocolates**
3764 Harlem Rd
Buffalo, NY 14215
716-833-7111
Fax: 716-689-8113
Chocolate laced popcorn, chocolate pretzel nuggets dusted with gold dust and flavored with fresh ground coffee
President: Loretta Kaminsky
VP Marketing: Ellen Bradbury
Estimated Sales: Below $5 Million
Number Employees: 15
Type of Packaging: Private Label
Brands:
Buffalo Gold
Espresso Gold

7567 **Lougheed Fisheries**
539 2nd Avenue E
Owen Sound, ON N4K 2G5
Canada
519-376-1586
Fax: 519-376-1589
Fresh and frozen fish and seafood
President: Greg Lougheed
Number Employees: 10-19

Type of Packaging: Bulk

7568 **Louie's Finer Meats**
Highway 63 North
2025 Superior Avenue
Cumberland, WI 54829
715-822-4728
Fax: 715-822-3150 800-270-4297
lfm@louiesfinermeats.net
www.louiesfinermeats.com
Smoked sausages
Owner/President: Louie Muench Sr
VP: Louie Muench Jr
Number Employees: 4

7569 **Louis Dreyfus Company Citrus Inc**
355 9th St.
Winter Garden, FL 34787
407-656-1000
www.ldc.com
Frozen fruit juice concentrates, citrus oils, pulp and purees.
CEO: Ian McIntosh
Head, Juice Platform: Murilo Parada
Year Founded: 1851
Estimated Sales: G
Number Employees: 100-249
Type of Packaging: Consumer, Food Service, Private Label, Bulk
Brands:
Sunshine State
Whole Sun
Winter Gold

7570 **Louis Dreyfus Company LLC**
40 Danbury Rd.
Wilton, CT 06897
203-761-2000
www.ldc.com
International agribusiness spanning production, refining, transport and merchandizing.
CEO: Ian McIntosh
Head, North America Region: Adrian Isman
Year Founded: 1851
Estimated Sales: K
Number Employees: 500-999
Parent Co: Louis Dreyfus Company B.V.

7571 **(HQ)Louis Dreyfus Corporation**
Westblaak 92
3012
Rotterdam,
Netherlands
www.ldc.com
International agribusiness spanning production, refining, transport and merchandizing.
Non-Executive Chairperson: Margarita Louis-Dreyfus
CEO: Ian McIntosh
CFO: Patrick Treuer
COO: Michael Gelchie
Year Founded: 1851
Estimated Sales: $36.5 Billion
Number Employees: 22,000+
Type of Packaging: Food Service, Private Label, Bulk
Brands:
Delta Rose
Missouri's Finest
Showboat

7572 **Louis J Rheb Candy Co**
3352 Wilkens Ave
Baltimore, MD 21229-4678
410-644-4321
Fax: 410-646-0327 800-514-8293
www.rhebcandy.com
Chocolate candy
President: Wynn Harger
rhebcandycl@comcast.net
Estimated Sales: $5-10 Million
Number Employees: 20-49
Type of Packaging: Consumer

7573 **Louis M Martini Winery**
254 Saint Helena Hwy S
St Helena, CA 94574-2203
707-968-9403
Fax: 707-963-8750 800-321-9463
www.louismartini.com
Wines
President: Michael Martini
michael.martini@louismartini.com
Sales Director: Bob Matheny
VP Operations/Winemaker: Michael Martini
Plant Manager: Michael Mullen
Number Employees: 100-249
Parent Co: E&J Gallo Winery
Type of Packaging: Consumer

7574 **Louis Maull Co**
219 N Market St
St Louis, MO 63102-1523
314-241-8410
Fax: 314-241-9840 www.maulls.com
Sauces including barbeque, worcestershire and steak
President: David Ahner
maulliv@maull.com
Estimated Sales: $5-10 Million
Number Employees: 10-19
Brands:
Maull's Barbecue Sauce

7575 **Louis Sherry Premium Chocolate and Tins**
3537 W North Avenue
Chicago, IL 60647-4808
212-849-2862
www.louis-sherry.com
Ice cream and frozen desserts
Director Operations: Israel Gonzalez

7576 **Louis Swiss Pastry**
400 Aabc
Aspen, CO 81611-2545
970-925-8592
Fax: 970-925-1269
Bread and bakery products
Owner: Felix Tornare
Owner: Karse Simon
Estimated Sales: $10-20 000,000
Number Employees: 10-19

7577 **Louisa Food Products Inc**
1918 Switzer Ave
St Louis, MO 63136-3779
314-868-3000
Fax: 314-868-3014
Frozen Italian foods including ravioli, cannelloni, tortellini and sauces
Owner: Tom Baldetti
CEO: John Baldetti
Sales Executive: Rob Foskett
Human Resources Manager: Gerry Balassi
tom.baldetti@louisafoods.com
Operations Executive: Pete Baldetti
Head of Purchasing: Sarah Schaefer
Estimated Sales: $14.1 Million
Number Employees: 10-19
Square Footage: 80000
Type of Packaging: Consumer, Food Service, Private Label, Bulk
Brands:
Louisa Pastas

7578 **Louisburg Cider Mill**
14730 K68 Hwy
Louisburg, KS 66053-8223
913-837-2143
Fax: 913-837-5762 800-748-7765
info@louisburgcidermill.com
www.louisburgcidermill.com
Cider, beverages and a variety of gift items
President: Shelly Schierman
Vice President: Tom Schierman
Estimated Sales: Less Than $500,000
Number Employees: 10-19
Type of Packaging: Private Label
Brands:
Lost Trail Root Beer
Louisburg Cider
Louisburg Farms

7579 **Louise's**
1700 Isaac Shelby Drive
Shelbyville, KY 40065-9172
502-633-9700
Fax: 502-633-3543
Fat free potato chips and crisps
Quality Assurance Manager: John Lindle
Estimated Sales: $5-9.9 000,000
Number Employees: 40

7580 **Louisiana Fish Fry Products**
5267 Plank Rd
Baton Rouge, LA 70805-2700
225-356-2905
Fax: 225-356-8867 800-356-2905
www.louisianafishfry.com
Cajun food mixes, breadings, seasonings and sauces.
President: William Pizzolato
Founder: Tony Pizzolato
Partner: Cliff Pizzolato
cliff@louisianafishfry.com
VP, Sales & Marketing: John Deutschman
Quality Assurance Manager: Tana Pittman
Marketing Brand Manager: Richard Rees
National Sales Manager: Patrick Murray
Purchasing Manager: Lisa Fox
Estimated Sales: $10-20 Million
Number Employees: 100-249
Number of Brands: 2
Type of Packaging: Consumer
Brands:
Louisiana Fish Fry
Tony's Seafood

7581 **Louisiana Gourmet Enterprises**
222 S Hollywood Rd
Houma, LA 70360
985-783-2446
Fax: 985-783-6079 800-328-5586
www.mampapauls.com
Cajun/Creole sauces, gumbo, piquante, seasonings and mixes including rice, dinner, cake and frosting
President: Nancy Wilson
Number Employees: 5-9
Type of Packaging: Consumer, Private Label, Bulk
Brands:
Lemon Velvet
Mam Papaul's
Mama Papaul's
Mardi Gras King
Red Velvet

7582 **Louisiana Oyster Processors**
10557 Cherry Hill Ave
Baton Rouge, LA 70816-4115
225-291-6923
Fax: 626-571-0613
Fresh oysters
Owner: Chester Williams
Estimated Sales: $5-10 Million
Number Employees: 10-19
Type of Packaging: Consumer, Food Service

7583 **Louisiana Packing Company**
501 Louisiana St
Westwego, LA 70094
504-436-2682
Fax: 504-436-1585 800-666-1293
www.lapack.com
Processor, importer and exporter of breaded, cooked and IQF shrimp
President: David Lai
CEO: John Mao
Plant Manager: David Lai
Estimated Sales: $500,000-$1 Million
Number Employees: 1-4
Square Footage: 132000
Type of Packaging: Consumer, Food Service, Private Label, Bulk
Brands:
Bayou Segnette
Fresh Sea Taste
Sea Ray
White Premium

7584 **Louisiana Pride Seafood**
2021 Lakeshore Drive Suite 300
New Orleans, LA 70122
504-286-8736
Fax: 504-286-8738
http://www.louisianaseafood.com
Seafood
President: Anthony Lama

7585 **Louisiana Rice Mill**
4 S Avenue D
PO Box 490
Crowley, LA 70526-5657
337-783-9777
Fax: 337-783-3204 contact@laricemill.com
www.laricemill.com
Long grain milled rice
President: William A Dore
bill.dore@supremerice.com

Estimated Sales: $11.9 Million
Number Employees: 50-99
Square Footage: 39732
Brands:
Sofgrain
Supreme

7586 (HQ)Louisiana Seafood Exchange
428 Jefferson Highway
Jefferson, LA 70121
504-283-9393
Fax: 504-834-5633 800-969-9394
bmiller@louisianaseafoodexchange.net
www.louisianaseafoodexchange.net
Seafood including bass, garfish, catfish, trout, amberjack, crab, shark and snapper
Owner/General Manager: Benny Miller
Sales: Steve Shonkoff
Estimated Sales: $20-50 Million
Number Employees: 50-99
Type of Packaging: Consumer, Food Service, Private Label, Bulk

7587 Louisiana Seafood Exchange
3790-D I-55 South
Jackson, MS 39212
601-853-4554
Fax: 601-853-4554
ray@louisianaseafoodexchange.net
www.louisianaseafoodexchange.net
Seafood including bass, garfish, catfish, trout, amberjack, crab, shark and snapper
Sales: Ray Hopkins
Type of Packaging: Consumer, Food Service, Private Label, Bulk

7588 Louisiana Seafood Exchange
11975 Lake Park Blvd.
Baton Rouge, LA 70809
225-756-5225
Fax: 225-756-5237 800-314-5225
robwalker@louisianaseafoodexchange.net
www.louisianaseafoodexchange.net
Seafood including bass, garfish, catfish, trout, amberjack, crab, shark and snapper
Sales: Robert Walker
Type of Packaging: Consumer, Food Service, Private Label, Bulk

7589 Louisiana Seafood Promotion & Marketing Board
051 North Third Street
3rd Floor
Baton Rouge, LA 70802
225-342-0552
Fax: 504-286-8738 info@louisianaseafood.com
www.louisianaseafood.com
Shrimp
President: Gerard Thomassie
Executive Director: Ewell Smith

7590 Louisiana Seafoods
2021 Lakeshore Dr
Suite 310
New Orleans, LA 70122
504-286-8736
Fax: 504-286-8738 info@louisianaseafood.com
www.louisianaseafood.com
Frozen alligator meat, blue crabmeat, crawfish meat, cooked crawfish
President/CEO: Gregory Benhard
Executive Director: Ewell Smith
CFO: Jorge Benhard
Chairman: Harlon Pearce
Marketing Specialist: John Folse
Communications Manager: Ashley Roth
Administrative Assistant: Krystal Cox
Brands:
Louisiana Premium Seafoods

7591 Louisiana Sugar Cane Co-Op Inc
6092 Resweber Hwy
St Martinville, LA 70582-6804
337-394-3785
Fax: 337-394-3787
Manufacturer of raw sugar.
President: Mike Melancon
mike@lasuca.com
Estimated Sales: $20-50 Million
Number Employees: 100-249
Type of Packaging: Consumer

7592 Louisiana Sugar Cane Cooperative
6092 Resweber Hwy
St Martinville, LA 70582-6804
337-394-3785
Fax: 337-394-5692 www.lasuca.com
Raw cane sugar and black strap molasses
President/General Manager: Michael Melancon
Vice President: Ross Harper
Grower Relations: John Hebert
Purchasing Manager: John La Vasseur
Human Resources: Neil Melancon
Plant Manager: Glenn Judice
Estimated Sales: $30-50 Million
Number Employees: 50-99
Brands:
St. Martin

7593 Louisville Dairy
4420 Bishop Ln
Louisville, KY 40218-4598
502-451-9111
Fax: 502-459-7858 www.deanfoods.com
Milk, dairy products
Manager: Steve Gurley
Estimated Sales: $20-50 Million
Number Employees: 100-249
Parent Co: Dean Foods Company

7594 (HQ)Lounsbury Foods
11 Wiltshire Avenue
Toronto, ON M6N 2V7
Canada
416-656-6330
Fax: 416-656-6803 lounsbury@lounsbury.ca
Vinegar, beet relish, mustard and sauces including regular and extra hot horseradish, seafood cocktail, mint, tartar, hot and barbecue. Founded in 1962.
Manager: Tim Higgins
Vice President: David Higgins
Number Employees: 15
Type of Packaging: Consumer, Food Service, Private Label, Bulk
Brands:
Cedarvale

7595 Love Beets
3 Bala Plz W
Suite 116
Bala Cynwyd, PA 19004-3402
856-692-1740
abbie@lovebeets.com
www.lovebeets.com
Beets and beet products
General Manager: George Shropshire
Controller: Chris Lauersen
Marketing Director: Natasha Lichty
National Director of Sales: Chris Horrell

7596 Love Creek Orchards
13558 Highway 16 N
13495 State Hwy 16 North
Medina, TX 78055
830-589-2588
Fax: 830-589-2880 800-449-0882
adamsapples@lovecreekorchards.com
www.lovecreekorchards.com
Grower of apples; processor of apple cider, jams, jellies, butter, sauce and gourmet flavored coffee
Owner: Brian Hutzler
b.hutzler@apple.com
Estimated Sales: Less Than $500,000
Number Employees: 1-4
Square Footage: 8000
Type of Packaging: Consumer, Food Service, Private Label, Bulk
Brands:
Apple Strudel Coffee Beans
Love Creek Orchards

7597 Love Good Fats
8 Market St
Suite 600
Toronto, ON M5E 1M6
Canada
info@lovegoodfats.com
www.lovegoodfats.com
Snack bars
Founder & CEO: Suzie Yorke

7598 Love Grown Foods
3455 Ringsby Ct
Suite 94
Denver, CO 80216
855-328-5683
lovegrown.com
Cereals

7599 Love Quiches Desserts
178 Hanse Ave
Freeport, NY 11520-4698
516-623-8800
Fax: 516-623-8817 info@loveandquiches.com
www.loveandquiches.com
Frozen layer cakes, mousses, tarts, pies, cheesecakes and quiches; exporter of cakes, cheesecakes and brownies.
Chairwoman/Founder: Susan Axelrod
CEO: Andrew Axelrod
CFO: Jeffrey Appleman
VP: Bonnie Warstadt
VP, R&D: Michael Goldstein
Director of Quality Assurance: Ellen Lazzaro
EVP, Sales & Marketing: Karen Sullivan
Estimated Sales: $37 Million
Number Employees: 100-249
Number of Brands: 2
Square Footage: 40000
Brands:
Sweet Singles
Gourmet Grab & Go

7600 Love The Wild
4720 Table Mesa Dr
Suite E200
Boulder, CO 80305
844-424-9875
sayhello@lovethewild.com lovethewild.com
Seafood kits and microwaveable bowls
Principal: Jacqueline Claudia

7601 Love You Foods
1650 S Plaza Way
Suite 2
Flagstaff, AZ 86001
844-693-2662
support@fatbomb.com www.dropanfbomb.com
Snacks, cheese crisps, nut butters and oils
Co-Founder: Kara Taylor
Co-Founder: Ross Taylor

7602 Love'n Herbs
70 Deerwood Lane
Apt 8
Waterbury, CT 06704-1665
203-756-4932
Fax: 203-756-4932 lovenherbs@aol.com
Distributors of all natural salad dressings and marinades that contain Canola oil, vineger, herbs and spices. No salt, no sugar, no MSG or preservatives. Also pure canola oil
President: Maria Klanko
Treasurer: Donald Klanko
VP: Peter Klanko
Estimated Sales: Under $300,000
Number Employees: 1-4
Square Footage: 4000
Parent Co: DaSilva-Klanko
Type of Packaging: Consumer
Brands:
All Natural Herbal
Love'n Herbs

7603 Love's Bakery
P.O.Box 294
911 Middle St
Honolulu, HI 96819-2317
808-841-0397
Fax: 808-841-2646 www.lovesbakeryhawaii.com
Breads
President: Mike Walters
Vice President, Sales/Marketing: Byron Chone
Estimated Sales: $10-19 Million
Number Employees: 250-499

7604 Lovebiotics LLC
Los Osos, CA
wholesale@thecoconutcult.com
www.thecoconutcult.com
Dairy-free, probiotic-infused coconut yogurt in various flavors
Founder: Noah Simon-Wadell

Number Employees: 11-50
Number of Brands: 1
Number of Products: 3
Type of Packaging: Consumer, Private Label
Brands:
The Coconut Cult

7605 **Lovin Oven Cakery**
2207 N IL Route 83
Round Lake Beach, IL 60073-4907
847-231-4700
Fax: 847-231-4250 888-775-0099
www.lovinovencakery.com
Homemade gingerbread cookies
Owner: Ken Slove
lovinovencakery@gmail.com
Estimated Sales: Less than $500,000
Number Employees: 20-49

7606 **Low Country Produce**
1919 Trask Parkway
Lobeco, SC 29931
800-935-2792
Fax: 800-985-0405 800-935-2792
info@lowcountryproduce.com
www.lowcountryproduce.com
Pickles, chutneys & relishes, soups & sauces, salsas & dips, jellies & preserves
Contact: Maggie Radzwiller
maggie@lowcountryproduce.com
Estimated Sales: Under $500,000
Number Employees: 1-4

7607 **Lowcountry Produce**
Raleigh, NC
800-935-2792
www.lowcountryproduce.com
Manufacturer of granola, sundries, canned goods, and baked goods.
Owner: Noel Garrett

7608 **Lowcountry Shellfish Inc**
7195 Bryhawke Circle
Charleston, SC 29418
843-767-9600
Fax: 843-552-6560 800-999-2503
l.brooks@lowcountryshellfish.com
www.ipswichshellfish.com
Seafood
Sales Manager: Paul Filo
Number Employees: 300
Parent Co: Ipswich Shellfish Company, Inc.

7609 **Lowell Farms**
4 N Washington St
El Campo, TX 77437
979-543-4950
Fax: 979-541-5655 888-484-9213
www.lowellfarms.com
Organic jasmine rice
Owner: Linda Raun
VP: Linda Raun
Estimated Sales: Below $5 Million
Number Employees: 5-9
Type of Packaging: Consumer, Bulk
Brands:
Lowell Farms

7610 **Lowell-Paul Dairy**
14332 County Road 64
Greeley, CO 80631-9317
970-353-0278
Fax: 970-353-0338
Fluid milk, cream and related products
President: Margaret Paul
Estimated Sales: $5-10 Million
Number Employees: 20-49

7611 **Lower Foods, Inc.**
700 South 200 West
Richmond, UT 84333
435-258-2449
Fax: 800-395-5691 800-295-7898
charliejcms@aol.com www.llranch.com
Sliced & shredded meats, poultry, hispanic items, pork, pot roast, pickled raw corned beef, oven roasted corned beef, smoked pastrami, prime rib, roast beef, and Angus beef
President: Alan Lower
VP/Accounting: Lori Howells
Director of Sales & Marketing: Vicki Boilesen
Director of Foodservice Sales: Charles Johnson
Customer Service: Stacy Knight
Estimated Sales: $120,000

Type of Packaging: Consumer

7612 **Lowery's Home Made Candies**
6255 W Kilgore Ave
Muncie, IN 47304-4794
765-288-7300
Fax: 765-747-9662 800-541-3340
www.loweryscandies.com
Confectionery including caramel, taffy, chocolate, chocolate covered nuts and chocolate covered cherries
President: Michael Brown
Owner: Thelma Brown
Owner: Donald Brown
Contact: Vicki Good
orders@loweryscandies.com
Estimated Sales: $7 Million
Number Employees: 20-49
Type of Packaging: Consumer

7613 **Lowery's Premium Roast Gourmet Coffee**
P.O.Box 1858
Snohomish, WA 98291
360-668-4545
Fax: 360-863-9742 800-767-1783
www.loweryscoffee.com
Coffee and wholesale and custom roasters, espresso machines, espresso accessories
President: Donald Lowery
CFO: Jeanette Zimmerman
Marketing: Mike Lowery
Contact: Don Lowery
dlowery@lowerycoffee.com
Roast/Operations Manager: Jerry Lowery
Estimated Sales: Below $5 Million
Number Employees: 20-49
Number of Brands: 2
Number of Products: 100
Square Footage: 20000
Type of Packaging: Private Label
Brands:
Lowery's Coffee
Pasano's Syrups

7614 **Lowland Seafood**
569 Kelly Watson Rd
Lowland, NC 28552-9653
252-745-3751
Fax: 252-745-5040
Fish, shrimp, crabs and scallops
President: Carol Potter
Estimated Sales: $1,500,000
Number Employees: 25
Type of Packaging: Consumer, Food Service, Bulk

7615 **Lt Blender's Frozen Concoctions**
1202 Post Office St
Galveston, TX 77550-5041
409-765-5666
Fax: 409-966-1581 info@ltblender.com
www.ltblender.com
Frozen concoction drinks in a bag: margarita; strawberry daiquiri; pina colada; mudslide; hurricane; mojito; peach bellini wine freezer; sangria wine freezer; strawberry wine freezer; and margarita wine freezer.
Founder/President: Ralph McMorris
Vice President Marketing: Scott Treadaway

7616 **Luban International**
9900 NW 25th St
Doral, FL 33172
305-629-8730
Fax: 305-629-8740
Cereals
Owner: Luis Banegas
xbanegas@gmail.com

7617 **Lubbers Family Farm**
862 Luce Strett SW
Grand Rapids, MI 49534
616-453-4257
info@lubbersfarm.com
Pork, beef, dairy, eggs, and fresh breads
President: Andy Lubber

7618 **Lubrizol Corp**
29400 Lakeland Blvd
Wickliffe, OH 44092
440-943-4200
www.lubrizol.com
Synthetic food colors, natural food colors, secondary blends, lakes, solutions

Chairman, President & CEO: Eric Schnur
Treasurer, CVP & CFO: J Brian Pitts
CVP, Operations & Supply Chain: Mike Vaughn
Year Founded: 1928
Estimated Sales: Over $1 Billion
Number Employees: 5,000-9,999

7619 **Lucas Meyer**
765 E Pythian Ave
Decatur, IL 62526-2412
217-875-3660
Fax: 217-877-5046 800-769-3660
Lecithin and soy flour
President: Peter Rohde
VP: Scott Hagerman
Director Sales/Marketing: Scott Hagerman
Sales Manager: Jack Chenault
Estimated Sales: $600000
Number Employees: 10-19

7620 **Lucas Vineyards & Winery**
3862 County Road 150
Interlaken, NY 14847-9805
607-532-4825
Fax: 607-532-8580 800-682-9463
info@lucasvineyards.com
www.lucasvineyards.com
Wines
President, General Manager and Founder: Ruth Lucas
Vice President of Administration: Ruthie Crawford
Vice President of Retail Sales: Stephanie Lucas Houck
Office Manager: Jessica Siurano
Winemaker: Jeffrey Houck
Plant Manager: Ruthie Lucas
Estimated Sales: $5-10 Million
Number Employees: 10-19
Type of Packaging: Consumer, Food Service
Brands:
Lucas

7621 **Lucas Winery**
18196 N Davis Rd
Lodi, CA 95242-9280
209-368-2006
Fax: 209-368-4900 info@lucaswinery.com
www.lucaswinery.com
Fine wines
Owner: David Lucas
david@lucaswinery.com
Estimated Sales: Less than $500,000
Number Employees: 1-4
Type of Packaging: Private Label
Brands:
Lucas

7622 **Lucerne Foods**
5918 Stoneridge Mall Road
Pleasanton, CA 94588
Canada
Fax: 925-226-9510 877-232-4271
www.lucernefoods.com
Baked goods, crackers, carbonated beverages, ice cream, juices and waters.
President: Dan Gott
Number Employees: 100-249

7623 **Lucero Olive Oil Mfr**
2120 Loleta Ave
Corning, CA 96021-9696
530-824-2190
Fax: 530-824-1243 877-330-2190
mail@lucerooliveoil.com www.lucerooliveoil.com
Olive oils
Owner: Bpb Crane
mail@lucerooliveoil.com
Number Employees: 20-49

7624 **Lucero Olive Oil Mfr**
2120 Loleta Ave
Corning, CA 96021-9696
530-824-2190
Fax: 530-824-1243 mail@lucerooliveoil.com
www.lucerooliveoil.com
Olive oils
Owner: Bpb Crane
mail@lucerooliveoil.com
Vice President: Anthony Lucerno
Operations Manager: Pete Johnston
Number Employees: 20-49

7625 **Lucia's Pizza Co**
10989 Gravois Industrial Ct
St Louis, MO 63128-2032
314-843-2553
Fax: 314-843-3576
Processor and wholesaler/distributor of frozen pizza
President: Darrell Long
sean@luciaspizza.com
Sales Exec: Sean Lynch
Estimated Sales: $1,600,000
Number Employees: 20-49
Square Footage: 50000
Type of Packaging: Consumer, Private Label
Brands:
Lucia's

7626 **Lucich Santos Farms**
12631 Rogers Rd
Patterson, CA 95363-8511
209-892-6500
Fax: 209-892-2446 www.blossomhillapricots.com
Processor and exporter of table grapes
Owner: Pete Lucich
Owner/Partner: David Santos
Sales Manager: Jim Lucich
blossomhill@inreach.com
Estimated Sales: $10.6 Million
Number Employees: 100-249
Square Footage: 23064
Parent Co: Stevco Inc.
Type of Packaging: Consumer, Bulk
Brands:
Sall-N-Ann

7627 **Lucile's**
2124 14th St
Boulder, CO 80302-4804
303-442-4743
Fax: 303-939-9848 800-727-3653
info@luciles.com www.luciles.com
Creole seasonings and French roast blend coffee
Owner: Josh Mcillwain
Sales Manager: Jennifer Fowler
jmcillwain@lucilleslist.com
Estimated Sales: $500,000-$1 Million
Number Employees: 20-49
Square Footage: 16000
Type of Packaging: Consumer, Food Service, Bulk
Brands:
Lucile's

7628 **Lucille's Own Make Candies**
156 Route 72 E
Manahawkin, NJ 08050
609-597-7300
Fax: 609-597-7393 800-426-9168
Candy and confections
President: Nathaniel Eismann
VP Sales: Janice Eismann
Estimated Sales: $500,000-$1 Million
Number Employees: 5-9

7629 **Lucini Italia Company**
601 22nd Street
San Francisco, CA 94107
866-972-6879
Fax: 415-401-0087 888-558-2464
www.lucini.com
Extra virgin olive oil
President: Renee Frigo
Estimated Sales: Less than $500,000
Number Employees: 5-9

7630 **Lucky Foods**
11847 SW Itel Street
Tualatin, OR 97062
503-612-1300
info@luckyfood.com
www.luckyfood.com
Korean foods

7631 **Lucky Nutrition**
1801 N Military Trl
Suite 120
Boca Raton, FL 33431-1810
Fax: 561-405-3158 800-928-4882
pickyeatersrule.com
Protein bars
Founder: Jamie Oberweger
Brands:
Luckybars

7632 **Lucky Seafood Corporation**
6203 Jonesboro Road
Morrow, GA 30260-1723
770-960-9889
Fax: 770-968-9400
Seafood
President: David Ng

7633 **Lucky Spoon Bakery LLC**
32 Dartmoor Pl
Salt Lake City, UT 84103-2275
USA
801-824-0624
www.luckyspoon.com
Baked goods, cookies, cupcakes, muffins
Contact: Pam Schulte
pam.schulte@luckyspoon.com
Estimated Sales: 250,000
Number Employees: 10

7634 **Lucky You**
3167 Commercial Street
San Diego, CA 92113
619-450-6700
Fax: 619-450-6701 customerservice@yldinc.com
www.yldinc.com
Chocolates and other candy.
Marketing: Deborah Roberts
Contact: Deborah Roberts
droberts@yldinc.com

7635 **Lucy's Foods**
408 Longs Rd
Latrobe, PA 15650-3506
724-539-1430
Fax: 724-532-0525 nzappone@aol.com
www.lucyshealthfoods.com
Frozen Italian foods, pasta and sausage
President: Nicky Zappone
lucyfoods@aol.com
Estimated Sales: $6 Million
Number Employees: 1-4
Type of Packaging: Consumer
Brands:
Delgrosso
Denunzio
Lotito
Rizzo's
Rosie's

7636 **Lucy's Sweet Surrender**
20314 Chagrin Blvd
Beachwood, OH 44122-4973
216-752-0828
Fax: 216-767-0735 info@lucyssweetsurrender.com
www.lucyssweetsurrender.com
Hungarian pastries and custom European baked goods
President: Michael Feigenbaum
Estimated Sales: Less Than $500,000
Number Employees: 5-9

7637 **Ludfords**
3038 Pleasant St
Riverside, CA 92507-5554
951-823-0306
Fax: 909-948-0597 support@ludfordsinc.com
www.ludfordsinc.com
Processor, importer and exporter of fresh, frozen and canned fruit juices including orange, apple, grape, etc
President: Paul Ludford
Contact: Matt Real
matt@ludfordsinc.com
Estimated Sales: Below $5,000,000
Number Employees: 1-4
Square Footage: 40000
Type of Packaging: Consumer, Food Service, Private Label
Brands:
Ludford's

7638 **Ludo LLC**
5325 Naiman Pkwy Ste G
Solon, OH 44139
440-542-6000
Fax: 440-542-9555 info@ludollc.com
Candy
Manager: Stephanie Holmes
Estimated Sales: $300,000-500,000
Number Employees: 1-4
Brands:
Bubble Candy

7639 **Ludwick's Frozen Donuts**
3217 3 Mile Rd NW
Grand Rapids, MI 49534-1223
616-453-6880
Fax: 616-453-1930 800-366-8816
Frozen doughnuts, fresh cookies, and seafoam candy frozen pastries.pies,cakes.
President: Thomas Ludwick
CEO: Jack Brown
Director of Sales: Jim Glupker
Contact: Sarah Trocke
sarahjtrocke@gmail.com
Estimated Sales: $5-10 Million
Number Employees: 10-19
Type of Packaging: Consumer, Food Service, Private Label, Bulk
Brands:
Kneadin the Dough

7640 **Ludwig Dairy Product**
1270 Mark St
Elk Grove Vlg, IL 60007-6708
847-860-8646
Fax: 847-860-5657 info@ludwigdairy.com
www.ludwigfoods.com
Dairy products
Owner: Mirek Gebka
ludwigdairy@gmail.com
Assistant Plant Manager: Duane Hadaway
VP Manufacturing: Mario Jedwabrik
Maintenance Manager: Rich Majewiski
Plant Manager: Michael Imel/ Ed Tomasziewicz
Estimated Sales: $410 K
Number Employees: 5-9
Type of Packaging: Private Label

7641 **Ludwig Fish & Produce Company**
409 Michigan Ave
La Porte, IN 46350
219-362-2608
Fax: 219-325-8311 800-362-2608
www.ludwigfishproduce.com
Wholesaler/distributor of frozen food, general line products, produce, provisions/meats and seafood; serving the food service market
President: Harold Robinson
Estimated Sales: $3,800,000
Number Employees: 20-49

7642 **Luhr Jensen & Sons Inc**
400 Portway Ave
Hood River, OR 97031-1192
541-386-3811
Fax: 541-386-4917 info@luhrjensen.com
www.luhrjensen.com
Sausage and brine mixes and seasonings and spices; also, sausage making kits, electric smokers and wood flavor fuels
President: Philip Jensen
philipjensen@luhrjensen.com
Customer Service: Linda Gordon
Estimated Sales: $10-20 Million
Number Employees: 250-499
Square Footage: 100000

7643 **Lukas Confections**
231 W College Ave
York, PA 17401-2103
717-843-0921
Fax: 717-854-9743 sales@warrellcorp.com
www.classiccaramel.com
Processor and exporter of sugarless and regular caramel toffee, taffy nougat and caramel including liquid; also salt water taffy and nutraceuticals
President/CEO: Robert Lukas
angie@classiccaramel.com
CFO: G Mark Zelinski
angie@classiccaramel.com
Contact: Angela Smith
angie@classiccaramel.com
Operations Manager: Joseph Stuck
Estimated Sales: $4 Million
Number Employees: 50
Number of Brands: 4
Number of Products: 110
Square Footage: 208000
Type of Packaging: Consumer, Private Label, Bulk
Brands:
Caramel Milk Roll
Classic
Dark Fruit Chews
Dorks
Flipsticks

7644 **Luke's Organic**
Santa Cruz, CA 95060
www.lukesorganic.com
Organic potato chips and tortilla chips
Founder: Jaap Langenberg
VP, Sales and Marketing: Steve Kneepkens

7645 **Lumar Lobster**
297 Burnside Ave
Lawrence, NY 11559
516-371-0083
Live lobster
President: Stanley Jassem
Estimated Sales: Less than $500,000
Number Employees: 1-4
Type of Packaging: Food Service

7646 **Lumen**
Oakland, CA 94607
www.drinklumen.com
Hemp elixir
Founder & CEO: Jacob Freepons
Co-Founder: Kris Taylor
Co-Founder: Yasir Kashim

7647 **Luna & Larry's Coconut Bliss**
PO Box 288
Eugene, OR 97440
541-345-0020
www.coconutbliss.com
Manufacturer of non-dairy ice cream.
Co-Founder: Larry Kaplowitz
Co-Founder: Luna Marcus
Quality Assurance Manager: Kate Campbell
Director of Marketing: Kim Clark
Director of Sales: Marc Donofrio
Contact: Karen Campbell
kate@coconutbliss.com
Purchasing Agent: J Luna
Brands:
Coconut Bliss

7648 **Luna's Tortillas**
8524 Harry Hines Blvd
Dallas, TX 75235-3013
214-747-2661
Fax: 214-747-5862 info@lunastortillas.com
www.lunastortillas.com
Mexican food products including corn tortillas, flour tortillas, tostadas, taco shells, nacho chips, tamales, hot sauce, pico de gallo, beans, chorizo, masa and hojas.
President: Fernando Luna
fernando@lunastortillas.com
Sales/Marketing Executive: Fernando Luna
Purchasing Agent: J Luna
Estimated Sales: $1,200,000
Number Employees: 10-19
Square Footage: 30000
Type of Packaging: Consumer, Food Service
Brands:
Luna's

7649 **Lund's Fisheries**
997 Ocean Dr
Cape May, NJ 08204
609-884-7600
Fax: 609-884-0664 info@lundsfish.com
www.lundsfish.com
Frozen cod, flounder, mackerel, squid, sturgeon, tuna, herring and shad.
Owner & Chairman: Jeffery Reichle
Owner & President: Wayne Reichle
wreichle@lundsfish.com
Director, Compliance & Quality Assurance: Marty Martinez
Director, Sales & Marketing: Randy Spencer
Director, Government Affairs: Jeff Kaelin
Year Founded: 1954
Estimated Sales: $219 Million
Number Employees: 250-499
Type of Packaging: Consumer, Food Service

7650 **Lundberg Family Farms**
5311 Midway
PO Box 369
Richvale, CA 95974
530-538-3500
Fax: 530-882-4500 info@lundberg.com
www.lundberg.com
Rice products
CEO: Grant Lundberg
VP Sales: Tim O'Donnell
Regional Sales Manager: Benjamin Strazze
Estimated Sales: Less Than $500,000
Number Employees: 1-4
Type of Packaging: Consumer, Food Service, Private Label, Bulk
Brands:
Evergood
Lundberg

7651 **Lupi-Marchigiano Bakery**
169 Washington Ave
New Haven, CT 06519-1618
203-562-9491
Fax: 203-562-5456
Baked goods
President: Pete Lupi
pete_lupi@lupis.com
Estimated Sales: Below $5 000,000
Number Employees: 20-49

7652 **Lusty Lobster**
10 Portland Fish Pier
Suite A
Portland, ME 04101-4620
207-773-2829
Fax: 207-774-3956
Lobster
President: Doug Douty
Estimated Sales: $10-20 Million
Number Employees: 10-19

7653 **(HQ)Luv Yu Bakery**
3410 Bashford Avenue Ct # 1
Louisville, KY 40218-3182
502-451-4511
Fax: 502-451-5510 luvyubrand@aol.com
www.luvyu.com
Chocolate-dipped, buffet and organic cookies, unique snacks, rice crackers and shrimp chips
President: Abel Yu
luvyubrand@aol.com
Vice President: Serena Yu
Number Employees: 10-19
Square Footage: 100000

7654 **Luvo Inc.**
Blaine, WA 98230
844-880-5886
luvofoods.com
Frozen meals
CEO: Christine Day
Type of Packaging: Consumer
Brands:
LUVO STEAM IN POUCH
LUVO FLIPPED BOWL
LUVO BOWL
LUVO PLANTED

7655 **(HQ)Luxco Inc**
5050 Kemper Ave
St Louis, MO 63139-1106
314-772-2626
Fax: 314-772-6021 contactus@luxco.com
www.luxco.com
Manufacturer, bottler, importer and exporter of quality distilled spirits and wines.
Chairman/CEO: Donn Lux
President/COO: David Bratcher
VP Finance/CFO: Steve Soucy
Chief Marketing Officer: Steve Einig
Director, Corporate R&D: John Rempe
EVP Sales: Dan Streepy
Contact: Tina Aebi
t.aebi@luxco.com
Warehouse Manager: Douglas Finkeldey
Estimated Sales: $23.8 Million
Number Employees: 1-4
Square Footage: 200000
Type of Packaging: Private Label
Brands:
American
Andrew's Long Island Iced Tea
Arrow
Azteca
Baron's
Bellows
Black Duck
Boord's
Bourbon Supreme
Brookside Reserve
Burke & Barry
Cachaca 61
Caffe Lolita
Calvert
Canada House
Canadian Deluxe
Canadian Reserve
Canadian Springs
Carlos
Chapala
Colonial Club
Conway's
Coronado
Country Club
Crystal Clear
Dan Tucker
Dark Eyes
David Nicholson 1843
Daviess County
Delacour
Dimitri
Dos Gusanos
Dos Trianos
El Mayor
Everclear
Exotico
Expresso
Ezra Brooks
Fonda Blanca
Gavilan
Getreide
Glaros
Gold Award
Golden Grain
Governor's Club
Grand Muriel
Gusano Rojo
Hawkeye
Henri Philipe
Highland Light
Highland Piper
Hot Shot
Hound Dog
Juarez
Kentucky's Choice
Kiev
Korski
Lady Bligh
La Prima
La Salle
Lightning
Limonce
Lord Ansley
Macalister
Pearl
Piping Rock
Rebel Yell
Pearl
Piping Rock
Rebel Yell
Saint Brendan's
Salvador's
Yago Sant'Gria

7656 **Luxor California Exports Corp.**
3659 India Street
2nd Floor
San Diego, CA 92103-4767
619-465-7777
Fax: 619-692-4292 rkafaji@aol.com
Supplier and exporter of agricultural commodities closeouts including dry beans, grains, oils, yeast, dry milk, butter, etc
President: Ray Kafaji
Marketing Director: Holland Clem
Estimated Sales: $1000000
Number Employees: 5
Type of Packaging: Bulk

7657 **Luxury Crab**
64 Airport Rd
Unit 2
St John's, NL A1A 4Y3
Canada
709-739-6668
info@whitecapseafoods.com
www.luxurycrab.com
Frozen crab and crab claws.
Chief Executive Officer: Randolph Bishop
Technical Director: Brian Cuff
Project Manager: Brad Hookey
Estimated Sales: $40 Million
Number Employees: 25
Other Locations:
Toronto ON
Winnipeg MB
Calgary AB
Vancouver BC
Danvers MA
Seattle WA

Brands:
Atlantic Queen
Classic
Luxury

7658 **Luyties Pharmacal Company**
4200 Laclede Street
Saint Louis, MO 63108
314-533-9600
Fax: 314-535-9600 800-325-8080
info@1800homeopathy.com
Processor and exporter of vitamins and homeopathic products
Director Marketing: Michael Smith
Number Employees: 50-99
Parent Co: Manola Company
Brands:
Luyties

7659 **Lve & Raymond Vineyards**
849 Zinfandel Ln
St Helena, CA 94574-1645
707-963-0869
Fax: 707-963-8498 800-525-2659
customerservice@raymondvineyards.com
www.lvecollection.com
Wines
President/Owner: Jean Charles Boisset
Winemaking Director: Stephanie Putman
Vineyard Manager: Eric Pooler
Assistant Winemaker: Kathy George
Manager: Craig Raymond
craymond@raymondwine.com
Number Employees: 20-49
Type of Packaging: Private Label
Brands:
Raymond Vineyard

7660 **Lynard Company**
15 Maple Tree Ave
Stamford, CT 06906
203-323-0231
Fax: 203-323-0231 lynardco@aol.com
Chocolates, candies, pretzels, nuts, popcorn, cookies, dried fruits, honey package designing
President: Lillian Flaster
Vice President: Howard Flaster
Contact: Lilian Flaster
lynardco@aol.com
Estimated Sales: Less than $200,000
Number Employees: 5-9

7661 **Lynch Foods**
72 Railside Road
North York, ON M3A 1A3
Canada
416-449-5464
Fax: 416-449-9165 www.lynchfoods.ca
Dessert toppings, chocolate syrup, corn syrup, mincemeat, condiments, sauces, Asian sauces, marinades, drink mixes.
President/Board Member: Scott Lynch
Chairman: Walker Lynch
VP Marketing: Peter Henderson
VP Sales: Scott Lynch
Estimated Sales: $16 Million
Number Employees: 140
Square Footage: 240000
Type of Packaging: Consumer, Food Service, Private Label, Bulk

7662 **Lyndell's Bakery**
720 Broadway
Somerville, MA 2144
617-625-1793
lyndells.com
Baked goods
Founder: Birger Lindahl
Contact: Adam Bagarella
abagarella@lyndells.com

7663 **Lynden Meat Co**
1936 Front St
Lynden, WA 98264-1708
360-354-2449
Fax: 360-354-7687
Livestock slaughtering services, herd managemnt, livestock breeding and grooming, livestock management, livestock selection, ice cube makers, ice block makers, industrial freezers.
Owner: Rick Biesheuvel
Estimated Sales: $3-5 Million
Number Employees: 5-9
Type of Packaging: Consumer

7664 **Lynfred Winery Inc**
15 S Roselle Rd # 14
Roselle, IL 60172-2043
630-529-9463
Fax: 630-529-4971 wineinfo@lynfredwinery.com
www.lynfredwinery.com
Wines
President: Fred Koehler
Manager: Allen Adomite
wineinfo@lynfredwinery.com
Estimated Sales: $8-20 Million
Number Employees: 50-99
Number of Brands: 1
Number of Products: 50
Square Footage: 24000
Type of Packaging: Private Label
Brands:
Lynfred

7665 **Lynn Dairy Inc**
W1929 US Highway 10
Granton, WI 54436-8899
715-238-7129
Fax: 715-238-7130 info@lynndairy.com
www.lynndairy.com
Milk, cheese and other dairy products.
President: William L Schwantes
lynndairy@fibernetcc.com
Marketing Director: Rick Beilke
Estimated Sales: $5-10 Million
Number Employees: 100-249
Type of Packaging: Bulk
Brands:
Lynn Dairy
Lynn Protiens

7666 **Lynn Springs Water LLC**
4325 1st Ave # 562
Tucker, GA 30084-4498
770-572-5928
Water
President: Tandrias Thomas
CEO: Jocelyn Facen
CFO: Al Thomas
Vice President: Derrick Smith
Estimated Sales: $1-2 Million
Number Employees: 20-49
Number of Brands: 1
Number of Products: 1
Square Footage: 12000
Type of Packaging: Bulk

7667 **Lyo-San**
500 Boul De L Aeroparc
C P 598
Lachute, QC J8H 4G4
Canada
450-562-8525
Fax: 450-562-1433 800-363-3697
lyo-san@lyo-san.ca www.lyo-san.ca
Manufacturer and exporter of freeze-dried yogurt cultures and bifido-bacteria; custom freeze-drying available. Founded in 1983.
President/Owner: Celine St-Pierre
Number Employees: 10-19
Square Footage: 180000
Type of Packaging: Consumer, Food Service, Private Label, Bulk
Brands:
Yogourmet

7668 **Lyoferm & Vivolac Cultures**
3862 E Washington St
Indianapolis, IN 46201-4470
317-356-8460
www.iquest.net
Cultures including dairy, meat and bakery starter, freeze dried/lyophilized and food fermentation
President/Vice President: Ethel Sing
Vice President: Edmond Sing
Estimated Sales: $2 Million
Number Employees: 23
Brands:
Lyoferm
Vivolac

7669 **(HQ)Lyons Magnus**
3158 E Hamilton Ave
Fresno, CA 93702-4163
559-442-5077
Fax: 559-233-8249 800-344-7130
www.lyonsmagnus.com
Fruit and flavor preparations for use in frozen desserts, cultured or beverage products, as well as fountain syrups and toppings, aseptic juices, beverage bases, fruit fillings, and breakfast condiments
President: Robert Smittcamp
CEO: Edward Carolan
CFO: Nasrim Fletcher
Research & Development: Lisa Balesteri
VP Quality Assurance: Steve Tweet
SVP Marketing: Jim Davis
VP Sales: Vince Veneziano
Manager: Eddie Ogualo
Director of Operations: Ken Atkins
Operations/Production Assistant: Monica Romero
Plant Manager: Noa Nguyen
VP of Purchasing: Don Savino
Estimated Sales: $47.7 Million
Number Employees: 250-499
Type of Packaging: Food Service, Private Label, Bulk
Other Locations:
Lyons-Magnus Plant Facility
Walton KY

7670 **Lyons Magnus**
95 Richwood Rd.
Walton, KY 41094
Fax: 859-485-7546 859-485-7546
www.lyonsmagnus.com
Fruit and flavor preparations for use in frozen desserts, cultured or beverage products, as well as fountain syrups and toppings, aseptic juices, beverage bases, fruit fillings, and breakfast condiments
Type of Packaging: Food Service, Private Label, Bulk

7671 **M & B Fruit Juice Co**
955 Home Ave
Akron, OH 44310-4121
330-253-7465
Fax: 330-253-8401
Fruit drink concentrates including orange, lemonade, pink lemonade, grape, cherry, lime, loganberry, iced tea and punch; also, vanilla and strawberry syrups
President: James Stone
jimbbstone@aol.com
Estimated Sales: $1-3 Million
Number Employees: 1-4
Square Footage: 40000
Type of Packaging: Consumer, Food Service, Private Label, Bulk
Brands:
Magic-Mix
Party Punch
Super-Mix
Trim-Lite
Wiz

7672 **M & B Products Inc**
8601 Harney Rd
Tampa, FL 33637-6605
813-988-2211
Fax: 813-980-6596 800-899-7255
www.mbproducts.com
Juice including orange, apple, orange/pineapple, grape, etc.; also, milk, milkshakes and frozen fruit juice bars
President: Allyson Hostetler
allyson@tidewell.org
CFO: Howard Hutchinson
Estimated Sales: $10-20 Million
Number Employees: 10-19
Type of Packaging: Consumer

7673 **M & CP FARMS**
3986 County Road Nn
Orland, CA 95963-9810
530-865-9810
Fax: 530-865-9793 greatolives@greatolives.com
www.greatolives.com
Olive spreads, mixes, cured olives,olive oil, stuffed olives, in addition to spicy beans, and sweet/sour pickles.
President: Maurice Penna
maurice@greatolives.com
Secretary/Treasurer: Cynthia Penna
Estimated Sales: $5 Million
Number Employees: 10-19
Square Footage: 60000
Parent Co: D. Beccaris
Type of Packaging: Consumer, Food Service, Private Label, Bulk
Brands:
Loam Ridge
M&Cp Farms

7674 M & M Label Co
380 Pearl St
Malden, MA 02148-6607
781-321-2737
Fax: 781-322-9065 800-637-6628
info@mmlabel.com www.mmlabel.com
Packaging.
Owner: Linda Difiore
ldifiore@mmlabel.com
Estimated Sales: $1.2 Million
Number Employees: 10-19

7675 M & S Tomato Repacking Co Inc
1026 Bay St
Springfield, MA 01109-2427
413-737-1308
Fax: 413-736-6433
Packer of tomatoes
Owner: Laurie Chruscieo
Treasurer: Laurie Chruscieo
Estimated Sales: $4 Million
Number Employees: 10-19
Type of Packaging: Consumer

7676 M Buono Beef Co
3650 S 3rd St
Philadelphia, PA 19148-5398
215-463-3600
Fax: 215-463-3481
Frozen portion-controlled beef and pork
Owner: Mike Buono
Estimated Sales: $2.9 Million
Number Employees: 10-19
Brands:
Colonial Beef

7677 M J Barleyhoppers Sports Bar
621 21st St
Lewiston, ID 83501-3285
208-748-1008
Fax: 208-799-1000 800-232-6730
ewilson@redlionlewiston.com
www.mjbarleyhoppers.com
Ale, stout and lager
Principal: Lee Duncan
Estimated Sales: $230,000
Number Employees: 10-19
Parent Co: Impact Restaurants
Type of Packaging: Consumer, Food Service
Brands:
Oktoberfest

7678 M S Walker Inc
20 3rd Ave
Somerville, MA 02143-4404
617-776-6700
Fax: 617-776-5808
Processor and importer of brandy, liqueurs, wines and spirits
President: Harvey Allen
CEO: Richard Sandler
rsandler@mswalker.com
CEO: Richard Sandler
Estimated Sales: $1-3 Million
Number Employees: 100-249

7679 M&H Erickson Ranch
3916 County Road Mm
Orland, CA 95963-9702
530-865-9587
Fax: 530-865-8637
Co-Owner: Heidi Erickson
Co-Owner: Merritt Erickson

7680 M&L Gourmet Ice Cream
2524 E Monument St
Baltimore, MD 21205-2539
410-276-4880
Fax: 410-525-8320
Processor and exporter of kosher ice cream
Owner: Chris Napfel
Estimated Sales: Less than $500,000
Number Employees: 1-4
Type of Packaging: Consumer, Food Service

7681 M&L Ventures
1471 W. COMMERCE COURT
Tucson, AZ 85746-6016
520-884-8232
Fax: 520-770-9649 sales@meritfoods.net
www.meritfoods.net
Products include produce and groceries, eggs and cheese, deli meats and salad dressings.
President: Matt Sadowsky
Secretary/Treasurer: Lynn Sadowsky
Manager: Bob Richter
Manager: Paul Rosthenhausler

7682 M&M Food Distributors/Oriental Pride
3322 Virginia Beach Blvd
Virginia Beach, VA 23452-5608
757-499-5676
Fax: 757-499-0807
Ethnic foods
President: Joan Mallen

7683 M-CAP Technologies
3521 Silverside Rd
Wilmington, DE 19810-4900
302-695-5329
Fax: 302-695-5350 jdoncheck@lakefield.net
Processor and exporter of industrial ingredients including bromate replacers, additives and preservatives; also, temperature release vitamins and minerals
President: Ernie Porta
VP Technology: James Doncheck
Number Employees: 5
Parent Co: DuPont Chemical
Brands:
Baker's Label

7684 M. Licht & Son
PO Box 507
Knoxville, TN 37901
865-523-5593
Fax: 865-523-0270
Processor and exporter of liquid artificial sweeteners
President: Richard M Licht
VP: Karen McGuire
Estimated Sales: $5-10 Million
Number Employees: 5-9
Square Footage: 12800
Type of Packaging: Food Service
Brands:
Smoky Mountain

7685 M. Marion & Company
422 Larkfield Center
Suite 253
Santa Rosa, CA 95403-1408
707-836-0551
Wines
President: M Dennis Marion
Estimated Sales: $500,000-$1 Million
Number Employees: 1-4

7686 M.A. Hatt & Sons
405 Hwy 324
Lunenburg, NS B0J 2C0
Canada
902-634-8407
Fax: 902-634-8407
Sauerkraut
President: Ralph Hatt
VP: Gladys Hatt
Number Employees: 5-9
Type of Packaging: Consumer, Food Service, Bulk
Brands:
Tan Cook

7687 M.A. Johnson Frozen Foods
1912 E Monroe Pike
Marion, IN 46953-2610
317-664-8023
Frozen foods
President: S Allen Johnson
Estimated Sales: $5-10 Million
Number Employees: 10

7688 M.A. Patout & Son LTD
3512 J. Patout Burns Rd.
Jeanerette, LA 70394
337-276-4592
Fax: 337-276-4247 ggilmore@mapatout.com
Sugar cane ingredients such as raw sugar, cane syrup and blackstrap molasses.
President/CEO: Craig Caillier
CFO: Randall Romero
Year Founded: 1825
Estimated Sales: $184 Million
Number Employees: 250-499
Square Footage: 150000
Type of Packaging: Bulk

7689 M.E. Franks Inc.
175 Strafford Ave
#230
Wayne, PA 19087
610-989-9688
Manufacturer of milk products.
President: Don Street
Estimated Sales: $1-2.5 Million
Number Employees: 10-19

7690 M.E. Swing Company
612 S Pickett St # D
Alexandria, VA 22304-4620
703-370-5050
Fax: 703-370-7286 800-485-4019
www.swingscoffee.com
Roasted coffee
Owner: Mark Woarmuth
Executive Vice President: Dwayne Walker
VP Marketing: Dwayne Walker
Contact: Carl Dodge
roaster@swingscoffee.com
Director of Operations: Darren Dimisa
Estimated Sales: Less than $500,000
Number Employees: 5-9
Square Footage: 12000
Type of Packaging: Consumer, Food Service, Bulk

7691 M.H. Greenebaum
64 Campbell Avenue
Airmont, NY 10901-6407
973-538-9200
Fax: 973-538-3599
Cheese, cheese products
President: Rasmus Andersen
Estimated Sales: $10-20 000,000
Number Employees: 5-9

7692 M/S Smears
490 Old U.S. Highway 74
P.O. Box 467
Chadbourn, NC 28431-0467
910-654-5163
Fax: 910-654-4734 www.sweetpotatoes.com
Pies
CEO: George Wooten
CFO: Stuart Hill
Opeartion Manager: Adam Wooten
Production Scheduler: Nicky Herring

7693 (HQ)MAFCO Worldwide
300 Jefferson St
Camden, NJ 08104
856-986-4050
Fax: 856-964-6029
magnasweet@mafcolicorice.com
mafco.com
Licorice products and other ingredients, including sweeteners
President & COO: Lucas Bailey
Global Research & Development Director: Mark Hines
SVP Strategy & Business Development: Jeff Robinson
Year Founded: 1902
Estimated Sales: $36 Million
Number Employees: 230
Type of Packaging: Bulk
Brands:
Magnasweet

7694 MAK Enterprises
37315 26th Street E
Palmdale, CA 93550-6414
661-272-1867
makenterprisesllc.com
Salsa and hot sauces
President/Owner: Mike Klumpp
CEO: Mark Taylor
CFO: Renee Taylor
Underground Operations Mgr: Doug Nestle
Number Employees: 20-49
Brands:
Hell's Furry Fire Hot Sauce
The Salsa Addiction

7695 MAK Wood Inc
1235 Dakota Dr # E
Unit E
Grafton, WI 53024-9477
262-387-1200
Fax: 262-387-1400 info@makwood.com
www.makwood.com

Novelty sugars, cranberry, probiotics, lactobacillus and bifidobacterium. Supplier of L-arabinose, L-fucose, L-rhamnose, lactates, and of other probiotics.
Owner: Mark Brudnak
Secretary/Treasurer: Joseph Brudnak
Sr Executive VP: Mark Brudnak
Manager, Technical Sales Services: Eric Baer
mark@makwood.com
Estimated Sales: $380,000
Number Employees: 5-9
Type of Packaging: Private Label, Bulk

7696 **MALK Organics**
8211 Dunlap St
Houston, TX 77074
281-974-3251
malkorganics.com
Almond, pecan and cashew milks
Founder & CEO: August Vega
Co-Owner: Justin Brodnax
Co-Owner: Joel Canada
Number of Brands: 2
Number of Products: 5
Type of Packaging: Consumer
Brands:
MALK
MALK COFFEE

7697 **MATI Energy**
201 W Main St
Suite 103
Durham, NC 27701
866-924-8005
www.matienergy.com
Energy drinks
President/Owner: Tatiana Birgisson
Number of Brands: 1
Number of Products: 6
Type of Packaging: Consumer
Brands:
MATI

7698 **MFI Food Canada**
70 Irene Street
Winnipeg, MB R3T 4E1
Canada
204-992-8200
Fax: 204-475-7740 www.michaelfoods.com
Egg products including egg whites and yolks, scrambled egg mix, omelettes and egg patties.
Human Resources Manager: Darren Luke
Plant Manager: Mark Driedger
Estimated Sales: $37 Million
Number Employees: 200
Number of Brands: 1
Parent Co: Michael Foods, Inc.
Type of Packaging: Food Service
Brands:
Papetti's

7699 **MG Fisheries**
7 Norman Road
Grand Manan, NB E5G 2G5
Canada
506-662-3471
Fax: 506-662-3779
Products include sea urchin, scallops, shark, monkfish, flounder, pollock-dried, cod-dried, pollock-salted, hake-dried, hake-salted, lobster-live, and cod-salted.
President: Maurice Green
Number Employees: 10-19
Type of Packaging: Consumer, Food Service

7700 **MGP Ingredients Inc**
100 Commercial St
Atchison, KS 66002-2514
913-367-1480
Fax: 913-367-0192 800-255-0302
www.mgpingredients.com
Process starches and specialty wheat proteins for food and non-food applications.
President/CEO: Tim Newkirk
CEO: Augustus C Griffin
augustus.griffin@mgpingredients.com
Vice President of Technical Services: Clodualdo Maningat
Vice President of Sales and Marketing: David Dykstra
Number Employees: 250-499

7701 **MI-AL. Corp**
27 Carpenter St
Glen Cove, NY 11542-2398
516-759-0652
Fax: 516-759-5752
Pasta
President/CFO: O. Michael Zara
Estimated Sales: $120,000
Number Employees: 4
Type of Packaging: Food Service, Private Label, Bulk
Brands:
Papagallo

7702 **MIC Foods**
8701 SW 137th Avenue
#308
Miami, FL 33183
786-507-0540
Fax: 786-507-0545 800-788-9335
info@micfood.com www.micfood.com/
Processor and importer of frozen plaintains, yuca, cassava and frozen fruit products.
President: Alfredo Lardizabal
Sales VP: Maria Krogh
maria@micfood.com
Estimated Sales: $5-10 Million
Number Employees: 5-9
Brands:
Big Banana
Costa Clara
Tio Jorge

7703 **MKE Enterprises LTD**
375 5th Avenue
New York, NY 10016-3323
212-447-0051
Fax: 212-447-0068 mkegroupltd@gmail.com

7704 **MO Air International**
183 Madison Avenue
Suite 1202
New York, NY 10016
212-792-9400
Fax: 212-490-1763 800-247-3131
www.moair-usa.com
Manager: Sherry Kawabe
Parent Co: Mitsui & Co.

7705 **MODe Sports Nutrition**
1599 Superior Ave
Unit B-2
Costa Mesa, CA 92627
949-274-9948
info@myfitmode.com
myfitmode.com
Cold-pressed energy shots, energy bars, and protein and electrolyte powders
Co-Founder & CEO: Tammo Walter
VP, Sales: Beau Clark
Co-Founder & COO: Nikki Halbur
Type of Packaging: Consumer
Brands:
MODE

7706 **MSRF, Inc.**
2501 N Elston Ave
Chicago, IL 60618
773-227-1115
Fax: 773-227-2031 www.msrf.com
Gourmet food gifts
President: David Reich
National Sales Manager: Scott Nejman
Contact: Fred Beegun
fred@msrf.com
Operations: Claire Danieleski
Estimated Sales: $7-19 Million
Number Employees: 20-49
Brands:
Msrf

7707 **MUD**
247 Beach 136th St
Belle Harbor, NY 11694-1323
516-507-0212
hello@eatmud.co
www.eatmud.co
Non-dairy frozen desserts.
CEO: Sam Friedman
Brands:
MUD

7708 **MUSH Foods**
Vista, CA 92081
hello@eatmush.com
eatmush.com
Overnight oats
Co-Founder & CEO: Ashley Thompson
Co-Founder & COO: Katherine Thomas

7709 **MXO Global**
220 Appin Ave
Mount Royal, QC H3P 1V8
Canada
tolerantfoods.com
Legume pasta
Founder: Tom Friedmann
Brands:
Tolerant

7710 **MYNTZ!**
19016 72nd Ave S.
Kent, WA 98032
425-656-9076
Fax: 425-656-8059 800-800-9490
www.myntz.com
MYNTZ! is a confection company that manufactures, packages and distributes up-scale consumer breath mints in a variety of flavors that include vanillamyntblast sugar-free, tropical fruit and orchard fruit.
President/CEO: David Parker
National Sales Director: Robert Kingsley
Customer Service: Diana Klein
Number Employees: 50-99
Brands:
Dropz
Myntz! Breath Mints
Myntz! Instastripz
Myntz! Lip Balm
Sqyntz! Supersourz

7711 **Maat Nutritionals**
1875 Century Park East
6th Floor
Los Angeles, CA 90067
310-407-8608
Fax: 310-407-8618 888-818-6228
info@e-maat.com www.e-maat.com
Dietary supplements, vitamins and minerals
President: Rick Mandell

7712 **Maberry & Maberry BerryAssociates**
729 Loomis Trail Rd
Lynden, WA 98264
360-354-7708
Fax: 360-354-3906 www.maberrys.com
Fresh and frozen blueberries, strawberries and raspberries
President: Curt Maberry
Director, Sales: Carl Swartz
Contact: Marlys Lange
marlys@maberrys.com
Estimated Sales: $2.5-5 Million
Number Employees: 20-49
Type of Packaging: Private Label, Bulk

7713 **Mac Farms Of Hawaii Inc**
89-406 Mamalahoa Hwy
Captain Cook, HI 96704-8941
808-328-2435
Fax: 808-328-8081 sales@macfarms.com
www.macfarms.com
Macadamia nuts, flavored macadamia nuts, chocolate covered macadamia nuts and macadamia nut cookies
President: Nicole Knight
sales@macfarms.com
Executive Vice President: Scott Wallace
VP Sales: Brian Loader
Manager: Rick Vigden
Estimated Sales: $20-50 Million
Number Employees: 100-249
Parent Co: Blue Diamond Growers
Type of Packaging: Consumer, Private Label, Bulk
Brands:
Macfarms of Hawaii

7714 **Mac Knight Smoke House Inc**
550 NE 185th St
Miami, FL 33179-4513
305-651-3323
Fax: 305-655-0039 sales@macknight.com
www.macknight.com
Processor and importer of smoked and fresh fish

President: Jonathan Brown
General Manager: Alex McMorran
Estimated Sales: $10-20 Million
Number Employees: 20-49
Square Footage: 20000
Type of Packaging: Consumer, Food Service, Private Label, Bulk

7715 **Mac's Donut Shop**
2698 Brodhead Rd
Aliquippa, PA 15001-2768
724-375-6776
Fax: 724-378-2961
Baked goods including doughnuts, cakes, pastries, cookies, muffins, brownies
Owner: Twila Mc Kittrick
VP: Twila McKittrick
Estimated Sales: $1.1 Million
Number Employees: 20-49
Type of Packaging: Consumer

7716 **Mac's Farms Sausage Co Inc**
209 Raleigh St
Newton Grove, NC 28366
910-594-0095
Fax: 910-594-1812 macfarms@intrstar.net
Sausage
Owner: Scott Mc Lamb
CEO: Scott McLamb
Estimated Sales: $700,000
Number Employees: 5-9
Type of Packaging: Bulk
Brands:
Double D
Mac's

7717 **Mac's Meats Inc**
1761 W Hadley Ave
Las Cruces, NM 88005-4122
575-524-2751
Fax: 575-526-3826
Meat including pork and beef
President: Al Guerrero
Estimated Sales: $10-20 Million
Number Employees: 5-9
Type of Packaging: Consumer, Food Service

7718 **Mac's Oysters**
414 Emerton Rd
Fanny Bay, BC V0R 1W0
Canada
250-335-2233
Fax: 250-335-2065 gordy@macsoysters.com
www.macsoysters.com
Clams and fresh shucked oysters
Managing Director: Gordon McLellan
Office Manager: Sally Kew
Number Employees: 50-99
Type of Packaging: Consumer, Food Service, Private Label, Bulk

7719 **Mac's Snacks**
615 N Great Southwest Pkwy
Arlington, TX 76011-5465
817-640-5626
Fax: 817-649-7832
Manufacturer of pork skins and cracklings.
Manager: David Sparesus
Plant Manager: David Sparesus
Estimated Sales: $10-20 Million
Number Employees: 20-49
Parent Co: Evans Food Products
Type of Packaging: Private Label, Bulk

7720 **MacEwan's Meats**
9620 Elbow Drive SW
Calgary, AB T2V 1M2
Canada
403-228-9999
Fax: 403-228-9999 www.macewansmeats.com
Meat pies including chicken, steak and scotch
President: John Hopkins
VP: Lynne Hopkins
Number Employees: 1-4
Square Footage: 6000
Type of Packaging: Consumer, Food Service, Bulk
Brands:
Macewan's

7721 **MacGregors Meat & Seafood**
265 Garyray Drive
Toronto, ON M9L 1P2
Canada
416-746-5951
888-383-3663
www.macgregors.com
Poultry, seafood and meat products; importer of beef and seafood
CFO: Ed de Vries
Vice President: John Hercus
VP of Sales, National Accounts: Rob Simpson
Number Employees: 180
Square Footage: 184000
Brands:
44th Street
Center-of-the-Plate Specialists
Certified Angus Beef
Niman Ranch
North Country Meat & Seafood
Organic Ocean
The Store

7722 **MacKay's Cochrane Ice Cream**
220 1st Street W
Cochrane, AB T4C 1A5
Canada
403-932-2455
Fax: 403-932-2455
generalinfo@mackaysicecream.com
www.mackaysicecream.com
Ice cream, frozen yogurt, sherbet and sorbet
Manager: Robyn MacKay
Production Manager: Rhona Mackay
Number Employees: 1-4
Type of Packaging: Consumer, Food Service
Brands:
Mackay's

7723 **MacKinlay Teas**
1289 Waterways Dr
Ann Arbor, MI 48108-2783
734-846-0966
Fax: 734-747-9193
Teas
President: Davinder Singh
Estimated Sales: $2.9 Million
Number Employees: 1-4
Type of Packaging: Private Label
Brands:
Mackinlay Tea's
Queen Jasmine
White Tiger Rice
Wild Blend Rice

7724 **Macabee Foods**
250 West Nyack Road
West Nyack, NY 10994
845-623-1300
Fax: 845-623-7649 www.macabeefoods.com
Kosher frozen pizza
President: Marvin Kochansky
VP: Jeffery Schmelzer
Number Employees: 5-9
Square Footage: 16000
Type of Packaging: Consumer, Food Service, Private Label
Brands:
Macabee

7725 **Macaron Paris LLC**
750 Third Ave.
New York, NY 10017
212-465-0510
www.macaroncafe.com
Manufacturer of macarons.
Public Relations: Cecile Cannone
Brands:
Macaron Cafe

7726 **Macco Organiques**
100 rue Mc Arthur
Valleyfield, QC J6S 4M5
Canada
450-371-1066
Fax: 450-371-5519 macco@macco.ca
www.macco.ca
Processor and exporter of food preservatives including: calcium acetate; calcium chloride dihy; calcium propionate; potassium acetate; potassium benzoate; sodium acetate anh; sodium benzoate; sodium diacetate; and sodium propionate.

President: Robert Briscoe
VP: Jacques Rochon
General Manager: Simon Rinella
Estimated Sales: 9.27 Million
Number Employees: 60

7727 **Macfarlane Pheasants**
2821 S US Highway 51
Janesville, WI 53546-8945
608-757-7881
Fax: 608-757-7884 800-345-8348
info@pheasant.com www.pheasant.com
Producer of high quality, young, pheasants; available fresh, frozen, smoked as whole birds or cut down sized products.
Owner: Bill Mac Farlane
CFO: Brad Lillie
Sales: Sarah Pope
Shipping Manager: David Lennox
Plant Manager: Bryan Carter
Estimated Sales: $1-3 Million
Number Employees: 50-99
Square Footage: 20000
Type of Packaging: Food Service

7728 **Machias Bay Seafood**
503 Kennebec Rd
Machias, ME 04654
207-255-8671
Fax: 207-255-8243
Seafood
Owner: Randy Ramsdell
Estimated Sales: $1-3 Million
Number Employees: 1-4

7729 **Mack's Bill Ice Cream**
3890 Carlisle Rd
Dover, PA 17315-4418
717-292-1931
Ice cream including chocolate, vanilla, oreo cookie, peanut butter, raspberry, banana, caramel, strawberry, etc. Founded in 1993.
Owner: Todd Mc Daniel
Finance Executive: Amy McDaniel
Estimated Sales: $500,000-$1 Million
Number Employees: 20-49
Type of Packaging: Consumer
Brands:
Bill Mack's

7730 **Mack's Homemade Ice Cream**
2695 S. Queen St.
York, PA 17402
717-741-2027
Fax: 717-747-0065
Owner: Walt Bloss
walt@macksicecream.com
Estimated Sales: $1-2.5 Million
Number Employees: 20-49
Parent Co: Bill Macks Homemade Ice Cream

7731 **Mackenzie Creamery**
6722 Pioneer Trl
Hiram, OH 44234-9714
330-569-3368
Fax: 330-569-3387 info@mackenziecreamery.com
www.mackenziecreamery.com
Organic Artisan goat cheeses
Founder/President: Jean Mackenzie
jeanniegoat@yahoo.com
Estimated Sales: Less Than $500,000
Number Employees: 10-19

7732 **Mackie International, Inc.**
#719 Palmyrita Avenue
Riverside, CA 92507-1811
951-346-0530
Fax: 951-346-0541 800-733-9762
www.mackieinternational.net
Ice pops, fruit flavored drinks and jellies
President: Ernesto Dacay
Sales/Marketing: Carmel Canete
Contact: Amando Briones
a.briones@mackieinternational.net
Estimated Sales: $10 Million
Number Employees: 50-99
Square Footage: 240000
Type of Packaging: Private Label, Bulk
Brands:
Berry Cool
Snowtime

7733 **Macrie Brothers**
750 S 1st Rd
Hammonton, NJ 08037-8407
609-561-6822
Fax: 609-561-6296 bluebuck@bellatlantic.net
Blueberries
Owner/CEO: Paul Macrie III
Superviser: Al Macrie
Operations: Nicholas Macrie
Production: Michael Macrie
Estimated Sales: Below $5 Million
Number Employees: 5
Square Footage: 120000
Type of Packaging: Consumer, Food Service, Private Label, Bulk
Brands:
Blue Buck

7734 **Mad Chef Enterprise**
PO Box 321
Mentor, OH 44061-0321
440-951-0846
Fax: 440-269-2387 800-951-2433
Sauces, seasonings, rubs. Additional products include aprons, grilling mitts, basting brushes, grill lighters, spatulas, grilling baskets, salt & pepper mills, skewers, and mugs
President: Michael D'Amico

7735 **Mad River Farm Kitchen**
100 Ericson Ct # 140
Arcata, CA 95521-8940
707-822-0248
Fax: 707-822-4441 contact@mad-river-farm.com
www.mad-river-farm.com
Gourmet food products such as sunshine marmalade, lemon marmalade, plum orange jam with brandied raisins and wild huckleberry jam
Owner: Robin Bartlett
bartlettmrf@gmail.com
Vice President: Steven Ulrich
Administration: Marika Myrick
Production and Shipping: Mike Myrick
Estimated Sales: Below $5 Million
Number Employees: 1-4
Number of Brands: 1
Number of Products: 25
Square Footage: 4000
Type of Packaging: Consumer, Food Service, Private Label, Bulk
Brands:
Mad River Farm

7736 **Mad Scientist Nuts**
3303 Airline Blvd
Suite 3A
Portsmouth, VA 23701-2635
757-288-6539
www.pizootz.com
Peanuts
CEO: Bo Perry
Brands:
Pizootz

7737 **Mad Will's Food Company**
2043 Airpark Ct Ste 30
Auburn, CA 95602
530-823-8527
Fax: 530-823-1756 888-275-9455
www.madwills.com
Barbecue sauces, salsas, salad dressings, mustards, marinades, marinara sauces, hot sauces, other sauces and specialty food sauces; private label and contract packaging
President: Kim Sullivan
Marketing Director: Tim Sullivan
Operations Manager: Roy Ballard
VP Purchasing: Vanessa Johnson
Estimated Sales: $2.7 Million
Number Employees: 20
Number of Products: 70
Square Footage: 84672
Type of Packaging: Private Label

7738 **Mada'n Kosher Foods**
128 SW 3rd Ave
Dania, FL 33004
954-925-0077
Fax: 954-921-8739
Frozen kosher foods including beef, fish and poultry
President: Samuel Weiss
VP: Richard Marsico
Director Operations: Richard Anthony
Estimated Sales: $210000
Number Employees: 10-19
Square Footage: 14000
Parent Co: Mada'n Corporation
Type of Packaging: Consumer, Food Service

7739 **Madani Halal**
100-15 94th Ave
Ozone Park, NY 11416
718-323-9732
info@madanihalal.com
www.madanihalal.com
Halal goat, lamb, and poultry
President & CEO: Imran Uddin
Year Founded: 1996

7740 **Maddalena Restaurant-Sn**
737 Lamar St
Los Angeles, CA 90031-2514
323-223-1401
Fax: 323-221-7261 800-626-7722
info@sanantoniowinery.com
Wines
Owner/Manager: Anthony Riboli
anthony@sanantoniowinery.com
President/VP: Santo Riboli
Owner/President/Marketing Director: Steve Riboli
Sales Manager: Rick Rechetnick
HR & Finance Director/Purchasing Agent: Tony Tse
Estimated Sales: $12.7 Million
Number Employees: 100-249
Square Footage: 930000
Type of Packaging: Consumer, Food Service
Brands:
Bodega De San Antonio Sangria
Kinderwood
La Quinta
Maddalena
Opaque
Riobli Family Wine Estates
San Antonio California Champagne
San Antonio Dessert
San Antonio Sacramental
San Antonio Specialty
San Antonio Winery
San Simeon
Stella Rosa Moscato D'Asti
Windstream Windbreak

7741 **Maddy & Maize**
61 Winifred Street West
Saint Paul, MN 55107
612-405-9155
info@maddyandmaize.com
www.maddyandmaize.com
Popcorn
CEO & Founder: Brett Striker
Estimated Sales: $1 Million
Brands:
Maddy & Maize

7742 **Made In Nature**
2500 Pearl St
Suite 315
Boulder, CO 80302
800-906-7426
www.madeinnature.com
Organic dried and fresh fruits and vegetables as well as pizza.
Founder & CEO: Doug Brent
Estimated Sales: $2.6 Million
Number Employees: 16
Square Footage: 2200
Type of Packaging: Consumer
Brands:
Made In Nature

7743 **Made Rite Foods**
2229 Sunnybrook Dr
Burlington, NC 27215-4856
336-229-5728
Fax: 336-545-1880
Salads and sandwiches
President: Jerry McMasters
Plant Manager: Alan Harder
Number Employees: 100-249
Parent Co: Made Rite Foods
Type of Packaging: Consumer, Food Service, Private Label, Bulk
Brands:
Made Rite
Sedgefield

7744 **Made-Rite Sandwich Co**
5828 Main St
Ooltewah, TN 37363-8714
423-238-5492
Fax: 423-238-5844 800-343-1327
contact@greatamericandeli.com
www.greatamericandeli.com
Products include sandwiches, cakes, Hot 2 Go sandwiches, burritos, pocket sandwiches and rollergrill products.
President: Earl R Sullivan
Finance Controller: Randall Desha
Purchasing Manager: Daryl Marsh
Estimated Sales: $20-49 Million
Number Employees: 100-249

7745 **Madecasse**
Brooklyn, NY 11201
917-382-2020
info@madecasse.com
madecasse.com
Chocolate bars, vanilla beans and vanilla extract
VP: Perry Abbenante
Brands:
Mad,casse

7746 **Madelaine Chocolate Company**
9603 Beach Channel Dr
Rockaway Beach, NY 11693-1398
718-945-1500
800-322-1505
service@madelainechocolate.com
www.madelainechocolate.com
Chocolate in various colors, and shapes, such as butterflies, flowers, hearts, its a boy/girl, chocolate coins and cigars, seasonal and holiday chocolates and truffles.
President & CEO: Jorge Farber
jfarber@madelainechocolate.com
VP, Sales & Marketing: Joan Sweeting
VP, Production: Sam Farber
Year Founded: 1949
Estimated Sales: $49.8 Million
Number Employees: 100-249
Square Footage: 200000
Type of Packaging: Private Label, Bulk
Brands:
Madelaine
Duets
Hatchers
Love & Kisses
Gooey Ghouls
Fiesta
Penny Lanes
Grand Estate Collection

7747 **Madera Enterprises Inc**
32565 Avenue 9
Madera, CA 93636-8346
559-431-1444
Fax: 559-674-8214 800-507-9555
maderaent@aol.com
Processor and exporter of custom fruit juice concentrates and purees including grape, apple, strawberry, plum, prune, date, raisin, pomegranate, etc.; also, dried fruits and vinaigrettes
President: Susan Nury
maderaent@aol.com
Marketing: Rosanna Andrews-White
Estimated Sales: $3-5 Million
Number Employees: 5-9
Type of Packaging: Bulk
Brands:
Mina
Zary

7748 **(HQ)Madhava Natural Sweeteners**
4665 Nautilus Court S
Suite 301
Boulder, CO 80301
800-530-2900
madhavasweeteners.com
Organic sweeteners, including honey, agave nectar and coconut sugar
CEO: Colin Sankey
Estimated Sales: $710,000
Number Employees: 20-49
Square Footage: 8974
Type of Packaging: Consumer, Food Service, Private Label, Bulk
Other Locations:
Madhava Honey
Parachute CO

Brands:
Agave Nectar
Ambrosia Honey
Mountain Gold Honey

7749 **Madhouse Munchies**
20 San Remo Drive
South Burlington, VT 05403
802-655-6662
Fax: 802-655-7711 888-323-4687
info@madhousemunchies.com
www.madhousemunchies.com
Low-fat, hand-cooked potato chips
President: J Ehlen
Sales/Marketing Associate: Eric Bleckner
Contact: Brad Hall
bhall@madhousemunchies.com
Estimated Sales: $740,000
Number Employees: 10
Brands:
Madhouse Munchies

7750 **Madison Foods**
238 Chester St
Saint Paul, MN 55107
651-265-8212
Fax: 651-297-6286 madisonfoodsmt.com
Butter substitutes; also, contract packager of retail and food service sauces
President: Steve Anderson
Estimated Sales: $.5-1 million
Number Employees: 1-4
Type of Packaging: Consumer, Food Service, Private Label, Bulk
Brands:
Better

7751 **Madison Park Foods**
PO Box 320
Brookside, NJ 07926
800-963-3540
madisonparkfoods.com
Rubs, seasonings and heirloom popcorn.
President: Christine Myers

7752 **Madison Vineyard**
HC 72 Box 490
Ribera, NM 87560
575-421-8028
Fax: 575-421-8028 madison@plateautel.net
Wines
Owner: Bill Madison
william.madison@madison.lib.oh.us
Partner: Elise Madison
Director: Shirley Flint
Estimated Sales: $190,000
Number Employees: 3

7753 **Madonna Estate Winery**
5400 Old Sonoma Rd
Napa, CA 94559-9708
707-255-8864
Fax: 707-257-2778 866-724-2993
mail@madonnaestate.com
www.madonnaestate.com
Wines include Chardonnay, Pinot Noir, Due Ragazze, Pinot Noir Riserva, Merlot, Cabernet Sauvignon.
President: Andrea Bartolucci
mail@madonnaestate.com
Marketing: Ron Arata
Public Relations: Brette Bartolucci
Vineyard Manager: Andrea Bartolucci
Estimated Sales: $2.5-5 Million
Number Employees: 5-9
Brands:
Madonna Estate Mont St John
Poppy Hill

7754 **Madrange**
85 Division Avenue
PO Box 409
Millington, NJ 07946
908-647-6485
Fax: 908-646-8305 800-899-6689
mkessler@charter.net www.fromartharie.com
Products include cooked hams, goat cheese, dips, butter, and pates/mousse.
General Manager: Ron Schinbeckler
Vice President: Richard Kessler
Regional Manager: Jim Gregori
Number Employees: 10-19
Type of Packaging: Private Label, Bulk

7755 **Madrinas Coffee**
St. Louis, MO 63042
madrinascoffee.com
Fair trade organic coffee
President/Owner: Justin Davis

7756 **Madrona Specialty Foods LLC**
18300 Cascade Ave S # 260
Suite 260
Seattle, WA 98188-4746
425-656-2997
Fax: 206-577-3406 info@madronafoods.com
www.madronaspecialtyfoods.com
Chocolate almond toffee, chcolate shapes, caramels, holiday candies, cookies, and hot cocoa
Owner: Paul Piggott
antonio@lapanzanella.com
Marketing: Erin Cammarano
Estimated Sales: $3.4 Million
Number Employees: 20-49
Type of Packaging: Private Label, Bulk
Brands:
Elegant Sweets
Hannah's Delight
Kingsley's Caramels

7757 **Madrona Vineyards**
PO Box 454
2560 High Hill Road
Camino, CA 95709
530-644-5948
Fax: 530-644-7517
winery@madronavineyards.com
www.madronavineyards.com
Wines
President: Richard Bush
Contact: Leslie Bush
leslie@madronavineyards.com
Estimated Sales: Below $5 Million
Number Employees: 20
Type of Packaging: Consumer

7758 **Madys Company**
1555 Yosemite Ave
San Francisco, CA 94124-3268
415-822-2227
Fax: 415-822-3673
Herbal, medicinal and regular teas; also, vitamins, ginseng root
Owner: Sandy Su Wing
General Manager: Marian Hong
Number Employees: 10-19
Square Footage: 13600
Parent Co: Azeta Brands
Type of Packaging: Consumer, Food Service, Private Label, Bulk
Brands:
Butterfly
Evergreen
Madys
Weiloss

7759 **Madyson's Marshmallows**
2211 W 3000 S # D
Suite D
Heber City, UT 84032-4520
435-315-0045
info@madysonsmarshmallows.com
Manufacturer of chocolate dipped marshmallows, stuffed marshmallows, s'mores kits, and beverage toppers.
CEO & Founder: Breeze Wetzel

7760 **Maebo Noodle Factory Inc**
711 W Kawailani St
Hilo, HI 96720-3155
808-959-8763
Fax: 808-959-4404 877-663-8667
sales@one-ton.com www.one-ton.com
Chinese foods including noodles, wonton chips and saimin
President/Manager: Blane Maebo
VP: Rachel Maebo
Contact: Maxine Hao
maxine@one-ton.com
Estimated Sales: $550000
Number Employees: 10-19
Type of Packaging: Consumer, Bulk
Brands:
Maebo Noodle Factory, Inc.

7761 **Maggie Lyon Chocolatiers**
6000 Peachtree Industrial Blvd
Norcross, GA 30071
770-446-1299
Fax: 770-446-2191 800-969-3500
sales@maggielyon.com www.maggielyon.com
Products include gourmet chocolates, truffles, toffee, caramels, bark and nut clusters, toffee, special occassion and gift baskets, easter selections, bulk chocolates, and promotional products.
President: Jeffery Pollack
Cfo: Linda Pollack
VP: Michael Pollack
Estimated Sales: $1.8 Million
Number Employees: 15
Type of Packaging: Private Label
Brands:
Connie's Handmade Toffee

7762 **Maggie's Salsa**
1303 Turley Rd
Charleston, WV 25314
304-550-5460
Fax: 304-881-0289
Salsa
President/Owner: Maggie Cook

7763 **Maggiora Baking Co**
1900 Garden Tract Rd
Richmond, CA 94801-1219
510-235-0274
Fax: 510-235-2427 info@maggiorabaking.com
Products include sourdoughs, french breads, focaccia, bread sticks, pesto dinner roll clusters, garlic rounds, Hawaiian bread/dinner rolls, Greek rings, egg bread and dinner rolls, and various specialty breads.
President: Dennis Maggiora
Sales Director: Robert Maggiora
Contact: Don Jones
don@maggiorabaking.com
General Manager: Don Maggiora
Estimated Sales: Less Than $500,000
Number Employees: 5-9

7764 **Magic Gumball Intl**
9310 Mason Ave
Chatsworth, CA 91311-5201
818-716-1888
Fax: 818-341-4234 800-576-2020
info@magicgumball.com www.magicgumball.com
Candy
Owner: Guy Hart
Estimated Sales: $5-10 Million
Number Employees: 50-99

7765 **Magic Ice Products**
1326 Ethan Ave
Cincinnati, OH 45225-1810
513-541-2645
800-776-7923
magiciceproducts@gmail.com
www.magiciceproducts.com
Processor and exporter of gourmet coffee flavor, slush and ice syrups; importer of shave ice machines and equipment
President: Shirley Weist
Number Employees: 5-9
Type of Packaging: Consumer, Food Service, Private Label
Brands:
Flavor Magic
Magic Ice

7766 **Magic Seasoning Blends**
720 Distributors Row
Po Box 23342
New Orleans, LA 70123-3208
504-731-3590
Fax: 504-731-3576 800-457-2857
www.magicseasoningblends.com
Dry spices, rubs, bottled sauces and marinades.
Owner: Paul Prudhomme
pprudhomme@chefpaul.com
President/CEO: Shawn McBride
CFO: Paula LaCour
R&D Director: Sean O'Meara
VP Sales/Marketing: John McBride
Director of Sales and Marketing: Anna Zuniga
pprudhomme@chefpaul.com
Human Resources Director: Naomi Roundtree
Director of Operations: Joey Duplechain
Vice President of Manufacturing: David Hickey
Purchasing Director: Patricia Cantrelle

Estimated Sales: $9.6 Million
Number Employees: 50-99
Number of Brands: 3
Number of Products: 29
Square Footage: 260000
Type of Packaging: Consumer, Food Service, Private Label, Bulk
Brands:
Barbecue Magic
Blackened Redfish Magic
Blackened Steak Magic
Breading Magic
Gravy & Gumbo Magic
Magic Pepper Sauce
Magic Sauce & Marinades
Meat Magic
Pizza & Pasta Magic
Pork & Veal Magic
Poultry Magic
Salmon Magic
Seafood Magic
Shrimp Magic
Sweetfree Magic
Vegetable Magic

7767 **Magic Valley Growers**
375 W Avenue D
Wendell, ID 83355-5512
208-536-6693
Fax: 208-536-6695 www.magicvalleygrowers.com
Grower and packer of specialty onions including pearl, boiler, peeled pearl and sets; exporter of pearl and boiler onions
President: Robert Reitveld
onions@magicvalleygrowers.com
VP: James Kelly
Estimated Sales: $1.1 Million
Number Employees: 20-49
Square Footage: 212400
Type of Packaging: Consumer, Private Label, Bulk
Brands:
Dutch Boiler
Dutch Girl
Top Hat

7768 **Magic Valley Quality Milk**
1756 S Buchanan St
P.O. Box 507
Jerome, ID 83338-6146
208-324-7519
Fax: 208-324-7554 www.mvqmp.com
Cooperative selling raw milk to food processors
General Manager: Alan Stutzman
Estimated Sales: $.5-1 million
Number Employees: 20-49

7769 **Magna Foods Corporation**
16010 Phoenix Drive
City of Industry, CA 91745-1623
626-336-7500
Fax: 626-336-3999 800-995-4394
magnafoods@aol.com
Processor and exporter of confectionery, candy, cookies, crackers and cocoa products
President: Yogi Atmadja
VP: Peter Surjadinata
Estimated Sales: $1.5 Million
Number Employees: 25
Square Footage: 20000
Parent Co: IBIS
Brands:
Coffeego
Danisa
Roma Marie

7770 **Magnanini Farm Winery**
172 Strawridge Rd
Wallkill, NY 12589-3905
845-895-2767
Fax: 845-895-9458 www.magwine.com
Wines
Owner: Richard Magnanini
rickmagnanini@gmail.com
CEO: Galba Magnanini
Estimated Sales: $500,000-$1 Million
Number Employees: 1-4
Type of Packaging: Private Label

7771 **Magnetic Springs**
1917 Joyce Ave
Columbus, OH 43219-1029
614-421-1780
Fax: 614-421-1681 800-572-2990
contact@magneticsprings.com
www.magneticsprings.com
Drinking, distilled, spring, artesian and infant water
President: Jeff Allison
jeff@magneticsprings.com
Plant Manager: Tim VanSickle
Estimated Sales: $11.9 Million
Number Employees: 50-99
Square Footage: 200000
Type of Packaging: Consumer, Food Service, Private Label, Bulk
Brands:
Magnetic Springs

7772 **Magnificent Muffin**
64 Toledo St
Farmingdale, NY 11735-6628
631-454-8022
Fax: 631-454-8574
Muffins and baked goods
Owner: Jon Schreckinger
Estimated Sales: Below $150,000
Number Employees: 1-4
Type of Packaging: Consumer, Bulk

7773 **Magnolia Bakery**
New York, NY
855-622-5379
info@magnoliabakery.com
Baked cupcakes, cookies, brownies and bars.
Co-owner: Steve Abrams
Co-owner: Tyra Abrams

7774 **Magnolia Citrus Assn**
1014 E Teapot Dome Ave
Porterville, CA 93257-9766
559-784-4455
Fax: 559-781-9182 www.tcoe.org
Processor, packer and exporter of Valencia and navel oranges
Manager: Dominick Arcure
Manager: Larry Fultz
Manager: Dominick Arcure
Estimated Sales: $10-20 Million
Number Employees: 10-19
Type of Packaging: Private Label, Bulk
Brands:
Magnolia
Malta
Memory

7775 **Magnolia Meats**
2013 Dutch Valley Rd
Knoxville, TN 37918
865-546-7702
Beef, pork and chicken
President: E Dean
Contact: Rob Noyes
robnoyes8@yahoo.com
Estimated Sales: $3-5 Million
Number Employees: 5-9
Type of Packaging: Consumer, Food Service, Bulk

7776 **(HQ)Magnotta Winery Corporation**
271 Chrislea Road
Vaughan, ON L4L 8N6
Canada
905-738-9463
Fax: 905-738-5551 800-461-9463
mailbox@magnotta.com www.magnotta.com
Wines and wine baskets, ice wines, sparking wines, various beers, and liquors
President/Ceo: Rossana Magnotta
Chief Financial Officer: Fulvio De Angelis
Estimated Sales: $23 Million
Number Employees: 107
Square Footage: 60000
Type of Packaging: Consumer
Other Locations:
Magnotta Winery Corp.
Scarborough ON
Brands:
Magnotta

7777 **Magnum Coffee Roastery**
1 Java Blvd
Nunica, MI 49448-9462
616-837-0333
Fax: 616-837-0777 888-937-5282
4sales@magnumcoffee.com
www.magnumcoffee.com
Coffee roasting and quality packaging services
Owner: Kevin Kihnke
kevin@magnumcoffee.com
General Manager: Nick Andres
Estimated Sales: $2.5-5 Million
Number Employees: 20-49
Type of Packaging: Private Label
Brands:
Island Trader
Magnum Exotic

7778 **Magrabar Chemical Corp**
6100 Madison Ct
Morton Grove, IL 60053-3216
847-965-7550
Fax: 847-965-7553 www.magrabar.com
Manufactures additives, release agents and viscosity modifiers
President: Susan Jenkins
sjjenkins@magrabar.com
Chairman of the Board: Sandy Roy
Vice President: Dale Roy
Technical Director: Jeffrey Conrad
Estimated Sales: $3.4 Million
Number Employees: 10-19

7779 **Mah Chena Company**
1416 W Ohio St
Chicago, IL 60642-7156
312-226-5100
Fax: 312-277-7170
Chinese frozen foods
President: Heather Shadur
Sales Manager: Jeffrey Hoffman
Plant Manager: Willis Yee
Number Employees: 10-19

7780 **Mahantongo Game Farm**
559 Flying Eagle Rd
Dalmatia, PA 17017-7003
570-758-6284
Fax: 570-758-2095 800-982-9913
mgf@tds.net www.pagamebirds.com
Processor and exporter of game birds including pheasants and partridges
Owner: Troy Laudenslager
mgf@tds.net
Estimated Sales: $360,000
Number Employees: 20-49

7781 **Maher Marketing Services**
1616 Corporate Ct # 140
Irving, TX 75038-2209
972-751-7700
Fax: 972-751-7777 mmaher@mahermark.com
www.mahermark.com
Cheeses, dairy products, frozen entrees, specialty snacks, crackers and cookies
President: Dan Vines
CEO: Mike Maher
CFO: Anne Maher
Marketing Manager: April Tieken
Estimated Sales: $5-10 Million
Number Employees: 5-9
Type of Packaging: Bulk

7782 **Mahoning Swiss Cheese Cooperative**
24060 Route 954 Highway N
Smicksburg, PA 16256-3428
814-257-8884
Fax: 724-286-9259
Cheese and butter
President: John Schablach
Plant Manager: Ralph Juart
Estimated Sales: Below $1 Million
Number Employees: 10

7783 **Maid-Rite Steak Company**
105 Keystone Industrial Park
Dunmore, PA 18512
800-233-4259
sales@mr-specialty.com www.mr-specialty.com
Portioned controlled meat products, including quick frozen beef, ground beef, pork, veal, and lamb products.
Executive Vice President: Michael Bernstein

Estimated Sales: $41.5 Million
Number Employees: 255
Square Footage: 115000
Type of Packaging: Consumer, Food Service, Private Label, Bulk
Brands:
Chef Italia
Maid-Rite
Minit Chef
Polarized

7784 **Main Squeeze**
28 S 9th St
Columbia, MO 65201-4814
573-817-5616
goodfood@main-squeeze.com
www.main-squeeze.com
Juice concentrates and bar mixes
Owner: Leigh Lockhart
leigh@main-squeeze.com
Estimated Sales: $500,000-$1 Million
Number Employees: 20-49

7785 **Main Street Gourmet**
170 Muffin Ln
Cuyahoga Falls, OH 44223
330-929-0000
800-678-6246
www.mainstreetgourmet.com
Gourmet fresh and frozen bakery items including an extensive selection of muffins and muffin batter, cookies, brownies and bars, granola, loaf cakes, cakes and baked goods and toppings.
CEO: Harvey Nelson
Manager, Quality Assurance: Angela Stoughton
Estimated Sales: $69 Million
Number Employees: 100-249
Square Footage: 65000
Parent Co: Clover Capital Partners LLC
Type of Packaging: Consumer, Food Service, Private Label, Bulk

7786 **Main Street Ingredients**
2340 Enterprise Avenue
La Crosse, WI 54603-1713
608-781-2345
Fax: 608-781-4667 800-359-2345
ingredients@agropur.com
www.mainstreetingredients.com
Hydrocolloids, stabilizers, and dairy ingredients including whey proteins, milk proteins, and milk powders serving the dairy, bakery and nutrition industries; also a private-label contract manufacturer
President: Bill Schmitz
Founder: Dave Clark
VP/Sales: Aaron Macha
Contact: Ellen Lusk
ellen.l@msing.com
VP/Operations: Rudy Rott
Number Employees: 125
Square Footage: 320000
Parent Co: Agropur
Brands:
Keystone
Cornerstone
Capstone
Gemstone

7787 **Maine Coast Nordic**
133 Smalls Point Rd
Mahiasport, ME 04655-3231
207-255-6714
Fresh salmon
President: Glen Cooke
g.cooke@cookeaqua.com
VP: William Groom
Estimated Sales: $760,000
Number Employees: 10
Parent Co: Nordic Enterprises
Type of Packaging: Bulk

7788 **Maine Coast Sea Vegetables**
3 George's Pond Rd
Franklin, ME 4634
207-565-2907
Fax: 207-565-2144 info@seaveg.com
www.seaveg.com
Edible seaweed products including sea vegetables, seasonings, snack bars, and chips. Wholesaler/distributor of seaweed including whole and ground
President/CEO: Shepard Erhart
President/CEO: Linnette Erhart
Treasurer/CFO: Carl Karush
Contact: Aaron Brown
aaron@seaveg.com
Operations Manager: Mary Ellen Lasell
Production Manager: Hannah Russell
Estimated Sales: $2 Million
Number Employees: 20
Number of Products: 40
Square Footage: 18000
Type of Packaging: Consumer, Bulk
Brands:
Maine Coast Crunch
Maine Coast Sea Vegetables
Sea Cakes
Sea Chips
Sea Seasonings
Sea Vegetables
Wild Crafted Food From the Gulf Of

7789 **Maine Lobster Outlet**
360 US Route 1
York, ME 03909-1631
207-363-4449
Fax: 207-363-0613 info@mainelobsteroutlet.com
Lobster
Owner: Sheila Barnes
sbarnes@mainelobsteroutlet.com
Estimated Sales: $1-3 Million
Number Employees: 10-19

7790 **Maine Mahogony Shellfish**
8 Johnson Ln
Addison, ME 04606
207-483-2865
Fax: 207-483-4389
Wholesale and retail products include lobster, clams, crab, halibut, mussels, and a wide variety of shellfish.
Manager: Robert Johnson

7791 **Maine Seaweed Company**
P.O. Box 57
Steuben, ME 04680
207-546-2875
Fax: 207-546-2875 hanson.larch@gmail.com
www.theseaweedman.com
Dried seaweeds, including kelp, alaria, digitata, dulse, bladderwrack, irish moss & ascophyllum nodosum.
President: Larch Hanson
Type of Packaging: Consumer

7792 **Maine Wild Blueberry Company**
320 Ridge Rd.
Cherryfield, ME 04622-0128
207-546-7573
Fax: 207-546-2713 800-243-4005
www.oxfordfrozenfoods.com
Canned, dehydrated and frozen wild blueberries
President/CEO: John Bragg
Co-CEO: Dave Hoffman
Chief Operating Officer: Ragnar Kamp
Treasurer: Geoff Baldwin
VP, Sales: Matthew Bragg
Director/Manufacturing: Milton Wood
Year Founded: 1997
Estimated Sales: $27 Million
Number Employees: 20-49
Square Footage: 100000
Parent Co: Oxford Frozen Foods
Brands:
Maine Wild

7793 **Maisie Jane's California Sunshine**
3764 Hegan Ln
Chico, CA 95928
530-899-7909
Fax: 530-895-3949 nuts@maisiejanes.com
www.maisiejanes.com
Nuts and nut butters
Founder: Maisie Jane Hurtado
Grower: Isidro Hurtado
Number of Brands: 1
Type of Packaging: Consumer
Brands:
MAISIE JANE'S

7794 **Maison Riviera**
1625, boul Lionel-Boulet
Suite 203
Varennes, QC J3X 1P7
Canada
Fax: 450-746-0993 800-363-0092
info@riviera1920.com riviera1920.com
Yogurts, desserts, cheeses, butters and goat milk products
Executive Vice President: Alain Chalifoux

7795 **Majestic Coffee & Tea Inc**
2027 San Carlos Ave
San Carlos, CA 94070-1929
650-591-5678
Coffee, tea
President: Bob Gard
Contact: Robert Gard
bobgard@aol.com
Estimated Sales: Less Than $500,000
Number Employees: 1-4
Brands:
Majestic Coffee and Tea

7796 **Majestic Foods**
33 Walt Whitman Rd
Suite 304
Huntington, NY 11746
631-424-9444
Fax: 631-424-5874 majesticfoods@sbcglobal.net
www.majesticfoods.net
Fruit concentrates, blends, essences and purees, canned fruits and vegetables, frozen fruits, dried fruits, nuts, vegetables and natural colors
President: Phil Maguire
Estimated Sales: $20-50 Million
Number Employees: 10-19

7797 **Maju Superfoods**
1455 Frazee Rd
Suite 500
San Diego, CA 92108
619-736-0622
www.majusuperfoods.com
Superfoods and supplements including black seed oil, hemp extract, spirulina, mushrooms, and powders
Co-Founder: Ryan Rigney
Co-Founder: Gunawan Wiyono
Year Founded: 2014

7798 **Makana Beverages Inc.**
Oxnard, CA
www.thebukombucha.com
Organic, raw, non-GMO, gluten-free and vegan kombucha in various flavors
Founder: Gary Hawes
CEO: Ryan Mason
Number of Brands: 1
Number of Products: 5
Type of Packaging: Consumer, Private Label
Brands:
TheBu Kombucha

7799 **Make It Simple**
8362 Tamarack Village
Suite 119-444
Woodbury, MN 55129
connect@makeitsimpledrinks.com
www.drinkpeptalk.com
Caffeinated sparkling water
Brands:
Pep Talk

7800 **Maker Oats**
844-782-5374
www.makeroats.com
Overnight oatmeal
Co-Founder: Jess Price
Co-Founder: Barry Nalebuff
Number of Brands: 1
Number of Products: 3
Type of Packaging: Consumer
Brands:
MAKER OVERNIGHT OATS

7801 **Maker's Mark DistilleryInc**
3350 Burkes Spring Rd
Loretto, KY 40037-8027
270-865-2881
Fax: 270-865-2196 www.makersmark.com
Processor and exporter of whiskey
President/COO: Rob Samuels
Manager: Victoria Mc Rae-Samuels

Estimated Sales: $25-49 Million
Number Employees: 50-99
Parent Co: Beam Suntory Inc.
Type of Packaging: Consumer
Brands:
Makers Mark

7802 **Malabar Formulas**
28537 Nuevo Valley Dr
Nuevo, CA 92567
909-866-3678
Milk digestants and activated enzyme concentrate
Owner: Shirley Partito

7803 **Malcolm Meats Co**
2665 Tracy Rd
Northwood, OH 43619-1006
419-666-0702
Fax: 419-666-2619 800-822-6328
www.sysco.com
Fine portion cut meat products including pork, lamb, veal, and poultry
President: Andrew Malcolm
Executive Vice President: Jeff Savage
Senior Vice President: Jerry Pasquale
Year Founded: 1982
Estimated Sales: $20-50 Million
Number Employees: 100-249

7804 **Malibu Beach Beverage**
885 Woodstock Rd
Roswell, GA 30075-2277
770-998-7204
877-825-0655
info@malibubev.com
Nutritional fruit flavored drinks including malibu mango; sunset strawberry; redondo raspberry; oceanside orange; beach peach; and tropical tea.
Chief Financial Officer: William Wager
Vice President Corporate Development: Jeff Glattstein
Chief Operations Officer: Patrick Doran

7805 **Malie Kai Hawaiian Chocolates**
PO Box 1146
Honolulu, HI 96807
808-599-8600
Fax: 808-599-8600 info@maliekai.com
www.maliekai.com
Chocolate bars
President/Owner: Nathan Sato

7806 **Mallard's Food Products**
708 L Street
Modesto, CA 95354-2240
209-522-1018
Fax: 209-577-8364
Fully-cooked entrees and pasta products
President/CEO: Dan Costa
CFO: Scott Wheeler
VP Sales: Steven Lay
Contact: Danita Thomson
danita.thomson@tyson.com
Plant Manager: Douglas Louis
Number Employees: 100-249
Parent Co: Tyson Foods

7807 **Maloney Seafood Corporation**
PO Box 690109
Quincy, MA 02269-0109
617-472-1004
Fax: 617-472-7722 800-566-2837
info@maloneyseafood.com
www.maloneyseafood.com
Importers of frozen seafood.
President: Thomas Maloney
Contact: Frank Maloney
frank@maloneyseafood.com
Estimated Sales: $10-20 Million
Number Employees: 5-9
Type of Packaging: Consumer, Food Service

7808 **Malt Diastase Co**
141 Lanza Ave # 31
Bldg 31
Garfield, NJ 07026-3539
973-772-2103
Fax: 973-772-0623 800-772-0416
Processor and exporter of flavoring extracts and syrups
President: Art Levy
Contact: Barry Kirsch
b_kirsch@maltproducts.com
Estimated Sales: $10-20 Million
Number Employees: 1-4
Type of Packaging: Food Service, Bulk

7809 **Malt Diastase Co**
88 Market St
Saddle Brook, NJ 07663
Fax: 201-845-0028 800-526-0180
www.maltproducts.com
Malt, molasses, natural sweeteners
Owner/President: Amy Targan
VP of Sales: John Johansen
Number Employees: 20-49
Type of Packaging: Bulk
Brands:
MaltRite
Nuvert

7810 **Malteurop North America**
3830 W Grant St
Milwaukee, WI 53215
414-671-1166
www.malteurop.com
Processor and exporter of malt, also offers several modes of commercial collaboration, as well as consulting, engineering, and training services.
CEO: Olivier Parent
President, North America: Kevin Eikerman
Chief Commercial & Innovation Officer: Alain Caekaert
Year Founded: 1984
Estimated Sales: $31.5 Million
Number Employees: 100-249
Parent Co: Malteurop
Type of Packaging: Food Service, Bulk

7811 **Mama Amy's Quality Foods**
5715 Coopers Avenue
Mississauga, ON L4Z 2C7
Canada
905-456-0056
Fax: 905-456-1536
Pizza and broccoli and cheese sticks, calzones, jambalaya
Sales/Marketing Director: Aldon Reed
Number Employees: 30
Square Footage: 28000
Type of Packaging: Consumer, Food Service, Private Label, Bulk
Brands:
Mama Amy's

7812 **Mama Del's Macacroni**
420 Main St
East Haven, CT 06512-2838
203-469-6255
Fax: 203-469-6255
Homemade pasta
Owner: Edward Cole
Estimated Sales: Less than $200,000
Number Employees: 1-4
Type of Packaging: Consumer, Food Service, Bulk
Brands:
Mama Del's

7813 **Mama Lil's Peppers**
5331 SW Macadam Ave.
Portland, OR 97239
503-206-6746
Fax: 503-961-7486 mamalils@zipcon.net
www.mamalils.com
Peppers in oil
President/Owner: Howard Lev

7814 **Mama Maria's Tortillas**
125 W 7200 S
Midvale, UT 84047-1011
801-566-5150
Fax: 801-566-7116 mamamarias@mtcon.net
Tortillas and tamales
President: Norbert Martinez
VP: Kenny Martinez
Estimated Sales: Below $5 Million
Number Employees: 20

7815 **Mama Mary's**
Fairforest, SC 29336
800-813-7574
info@mamamarys.com www.mamamarys.com
Pizza crusts, packaged pepperoni slices and pizza sauces.
President: Ken Romanzi
EVP, Sales & Marketing: Vanessa Maskal
EVP, Operations: William Herbes
Estimated Sales: $51 Million
Number Employees: 204
Number of Brands: 1
Square Footage: 50000
Parent Co: B&G Foods
Type of Packaging: Consumer
Brands:
Mama Mary's

7816 **Mama O's Premium Kimchi**
630 Flushing Ave
Suite 810
Brooklyn, NY 11206-5026
917-326-1557
mamaos@kimchirules.com
www.kimchirules.com
Manufacturer of kimchi.
Founder: Kheedim Oh
Estimated Sales: Less Than $500,000
Number Employees: 1-4

7817 **Mama Rap's & Winery**
PO Box 247
Gilroy, CA 95020-8029
408-842-5649
Fax: 408-842-8353 800-842-6262
info@rapazziniwinery.com
www.rapazziniwinery.com
Wine
Owner: Charles Larson
Estimated Sales: $1-2.5 Million
Number Employees: 5-9

7818 **Mama Rose's Gourmet Foods**
P.O. Box 36852
Phoenix, AZ 85067
602-477-8333
Fax: 602-477-8338 855-809-2848
tonya@mamarosefoods.com
www.mamarosefoods.com
Sixteen years producing gourmet packaged foods ie.. salsa, hot sauce ,jams, jellies, marinara and pizza sauce, pickled olives, prickly pear products, importing italian pasta and olive oil. Private label and co-packaging specialists
President: Tonya Greenfield
VP: Al Greenfield
Sales/Marketing Manager: Al Greenfield
Estimated Sales: $5-9.9 Million
Number Employees: 6
Brands:
Mama Rose's

7819 **Mama Rosie's Ravioli**
10 Dorrance St
Charlestown, MA 02129-1027
617-242-4300
Fax: 617-242-4208 888-246-4300
www.mamarosies.com
Frozen pastas as well as filled pasta products including Cheese Ravioli, Tortellini, Cheese Manicotti, Stuffed Shells, and more.
President: Brian McNulty
CEO: Nicholas Sardo
Estimated Sales: $5-10 000,000
Number Employees: 50-99
Brands:
Mama Rosie's

7820 **Mama Tish's Italian Specialties**
4800 S Central Avenue
Chicago, IL 60638-1500
708-929-2023
Fax: 708-458-0027
Italian ice cream and frozen desserts
President/CEO: M Rudasil
Marketing Director: M Wenzell
VP Sales: Fergal Mulchrone
Plant Manager: I Bidiman
Estimated Sales: $5-10 Million
Number Employees: 5

7821 **Mama Vida's Inc**
9631 Liberty Rd # N
Ste N
Randallstown, MD 21133-2434
410-521-0742
Fax: 410-521-0785 877-521-0742
nila@mamavida.com www.mamavida.com
Vegetarian chili, eggplant spread, dressings, mustard, sauces, soups, black bean dip, marinade, salsas, tapenades

Owner: Toto Mechali
toto@mamavida.com
President: Albert Toto
Chief Financial Officer: Miki Mechali
Quality Control: Heidi Czakny
Director of Marketing: Nila Mechali
Estimated Sales: $1 Million
Number Employees: 1-4
Number of Brands: 30
Number of Products: 18
Type of Packaging: Consumer, Food Service, Private Label, Bulk
Brands:
Toto's Gourmet Products

7822 **Mamie's Pies**
3701 Sacramento St
PO Box 119
San Francisco, CA 94118
415-870-0390
kiki@mamiespies.com
mamiespies.com
Frozen pocket pies
CEO: Kara Romanik
Operations: Peter Scherr
Number of Products: 3

7823 **Mamma Chia**
5205 Avenida Encinas
Suite E
Carlsbad, CA 92008
855-588-2442
www.mammachia.com
Chia seeds and beverages
Founder & CEO: Janie Hoffman
janie@mammachia.com
Brands:
Mamma Chia

7824 **Mamma Lina Ravioli Company**
6491 Weathers Pl
San Diego, CA 92121-2935
858-535-0620
Fax: 858-535-5993
Pasta products including ravioli and frozen lasagna
President: Chick Massullo
Estimated Sales: Less than $500,000
Number Employees: 10-19
Type of Packaging: Consumer, Food Service

7825 **Mamma Lombardi's All Natural Sauces**
877 Main Street
Holbrook, NY 11741
631-471-6609
infovilla@villalombardis.com
Sauces

7826 **Mamma Says**
49 Lincoln Road
Butler, NJ 07405-1801
973-283-4463
Fax: 973-283-2799 877-283-6282
Gourmet biscotti in almond pistachio and chocolate macademia
VP: Jason Cohen
Brands:
Mamma Says

7827 **Mammoth Creameries**
Austin, TX 78732
info@mammothcreameries.com
www.mammothcreameries.com
Keto ice cream
Co-Founder: Tim Krauss
Co-Founder: Susan Krauss
Number of Products: 2

7828 **Manassero Farms**
5405 Alton Pkw.
Ste. A-622
Irvine, CA 92604
949-554-5103
Fax: 949-551-6784 info@manasserofarms.com
www.manasserofarms.com
Various fresh produce, canned veggies, specialty jams and spreads, olive oils, raw organic honey, and specialty sauces.
Owner & CEO: Dan Manassero
Owner & Farm Chef: Anne Manassero
Year Founded: 1922
Type of Packaging: Consumer, Private Label

7829 **Mancan Wine**
1455 W 29th St
Cleveland, OH 44113-2970
216-367-2928
Fax: 216-927-3772 mancanwine.com
Wine in a can
Ohio Sales Manager: Alexander Feighan

7830 **Manchac Seafood Market**
131 Bait Alley
Ponchatoula, LA 70454
985-370-7070
Fax: 985-386-2762
Seafood
President: Duke Robin

7831 **Manchester Farms**
8126 Garners Ferry Rd
Columbia, SC 29209-9402
803-783-9024
Fax: 803-227-3103 800-845-0421
customerservice@manchesterfarms.com
www.manchesterfarms.com
Quail and bacon wrapped chicken; Franks-in-a-blanket; mini stuffed potato skins.
President: Brittney Miller
VP: Steve Odom
Total Quality Manager: Liz Benson
Marketing Manager: Matt Miller
Sales: Heather Ivey
Sales: Angela Covington
Director of Operations: Michael Davis
Plant Manager: Jennifer Alexander
Estimated Sales: Less Than $500,000
Number Employees: 1-4
Square Footage: 88000
Type of Packaging: Consumer, Food Service, Private Label
Brands:
Manchester Farms

7832 **Mancini Packing Co**
3500 Mancini Pl
Zolfo Springs, FL 33890-4710
863-735-2000
Fax: 863-735-1172 800-741-1778
rmancini@mancinifoods.com
www.mancinifoods.com
Peppers and olive oil
Chairman/President: Frank Mancini
fmancini@mancinifoods.com
VP: Alan Mancini
Estimated Sales: $11 Million
Number Employees: 50-99
Type of Packaging: Consumer, Food Service, Private Label, Bulk
Brands:
Mancini

7833 **Mancuso Cheese Co**
612 Mills Rd # 1
Joliet, IL 60433-2897
815-722-2475
Fax: 815-722-1302 pfalbo@mancusocheese.com
www.mancusocheese.com
Cheese including ricotta, mozzarella, etc.; exporter of pizza supplies; importer of pasta, olive oil, olives and anchovies; wholesaler/distributor of frozen foods, produce, meats, baked goods, general merchandise, etc.
President: Dominic Mancuso
mberta@mancusocheese.com
VP: Philip Falbo
Sales Exec: Mike Berta
Estimated Sales: $6 Million
Number Employees: 20-49
Square Footage: 80000
Type of Packaging: Consumer, Food Service, Bulk
Brands:
Mancuso

7834 **(HQ)Manda Fine Meats Inc**
2445 Sorrel Ave
Baton Rouge, LA 70802-4252
225-344-7636
Fax: 225-344-7647 800-343-2642
kcambre@mandafinemeats.com
www.mandafinemeats.com
Processor of smoked sausages, cajun andouille, boudin, bacon, cracklins and deli meats, including cooked roast beef, spiced turkey breasts and smoked hams.

President: Tommy Yarborough
CEO: Bobby Yarborough
Sales Director: Steve Yarborough
Plant Manager: Ronny Webb
Year Founded: 1947
Estimated Sales: $20-50 Million
Number Employees: 250-499
Number of Brands: 1
Number of Products: 20
Type of Packaging: Consumer, Food Service, Private Label, Bulk
Brands:
Manda

7835 **Mandarin Noodle Manufacturing Company**
3715 D Edmonton Trail NE
Calgary, AB T2E 3P3
Canada
403-265-1383
Fax: 403-264-3038 info@mandarinnoodle.com
www.mandarinnoodle.com
Rice and wonton noodles, rice rolls and wonton and egg roll wraps
President: Hang Trinh
Estimated Sales: $1.7 Million
Number Employees: 20
Type of Packaging: Consumer, Food Service

7836 **Mandarin Soy Sauce Inc**
4 Sands Station Rd
Middletown, NY 10940-4415
845-343-1505
Fax: 845-343-0731 info@wanjashan.com
www.wanjashan.com
Soy sauce, asian sauce, rice and vinegar
President: Alvin Lam
alvin.c.lam@chase.com
VP: Mike Shapiro
Estimated Sales: $165 Million
Number Employees: 20-49
Square Footage: 170000
Brands:
Wan Ja Shan

7837 **Manderfield's Home Bakery**
811 Plank Rd
Menasha, WI 54952-2923
920-882-6500
Fax: 920-725-7958 www.manderfieldsbakery.com
Bakery products
President: Jerry Manderfield
manderfieldshb@aol.com
Estimated Sales: $1-2.5 Million
Number Employees: 20-49

7838 **Mando Inc**
16 Humphrey St
Englewood, NJ 07631-3445
201-568-9337
Fax: 201-568-9426
Dumplings
President: Kyo Lee
Contact: Kyn Lee
jameschoi21@hotmail.com
Estimated Sales: $2.5-5,000,000
Number Employees: 5-9
Type of Packaging: Consumer, Food Service, Bulk
Brands:
Mandoo

7839 **Mane Inc.**
2501 Henkle Dr.
Lebanon, OH 45036
513-248-9876
Fax: 513-248-8808 requests@mane.com
www.mane.com
Flavors and seasoning blends
President/CEO: Jean Mane
President: Michell Mane
Executive Vice President: Kent Hunter
Contact: James Abel
james.abel@mane.com
Year Founded: 1871
Estimated Sales: 20-50 Million
Number Employees: 50-99
Square Footage: 65000

7840 **Mange**
PO Box 311
Somerville, MA 02143-0009
917-880-2104
Service@FreshFruitVinegars.com
www.freshfruitvinegars.com

Manufacturer of fruit vinegars.
Mange: Christopher Spivak

7841 **Manger Packing Corp**
124 S Franklintown Rd
Baltimore, MD 21223-2036
410-233-0126
Fax: 410-362-8065 800-227-9262
Manufacturer and packer of meat including pork, beef, chicken, lamb, veal and smoked ham; exporter of beef sausage
Owner: A Manger
Estimated Sales: $9 Million
Number Employees: 10-19
Type of Packaging: Consumer, Bulk

7842 **Mangia Inc.**
23166 Los Alisos Blvd
Suite #228
Mission Viejo, CA 92691
949-581-1274
Fax: 949-581-2906 866-462-6442
info@mangiainc.com www.mangiainc.com
Canned San Marzano tomato products, originally produced in Italy, with no preservatives or added salt
President: Matt Maslowski
Manager: Morgan Patterson
VP: Bob Maruca
Contact: Rosa Borrelli
rosacinzia@mangiainc.com
Estimated Sales: $1.3 Million
Number Employees: 12
Number of Brands: 1
Number of Products: 7
Type of Packaging: Consumer, Food Service
Other Locations:
Conditalia
Nocera Superiore, Italy
Brands:
Carmelia

7843 **Manhattan Bagel Company**
246 Industrial Way W
Eatontown, NJ 07724-2206
732-544-0155
Fax: 732-544-1315
Frozen bagel dough
President/CEO: Jason Genussa
Chairman of the Board: Jack Grumet
Plant Manager: B Hanley
Estimated Sales: $25-49.9 Million
Number Employees: 100-249
Parent Co: New York Coffee & Bagels

7844 **Manhattan Beach BrewingCompany**
124 Manhattan Beach Blvd
Manhattan Beach, CA 90266
310-798-2744
Fax: 310-798-0365
Coffee
President: David Zislis
Director Manufacturing: Karol Kmeto
Estimated Sales: $1-2.5 Million
Number Employees: 20-49
Brands:
Dominator Wheat
Rat Beach Red
Strand Amber

7845 **Manhattan Food Brands, LLC**
31 Bridge Street
Metuchen, NJ 08840
732-906-2168
Fax: 630-628-0385
Organic snack foods including corn cheese puffs, chocolate covered butter toffee and tortilla, reduced-fat potato chips, kettle cooked potato chips, peller snacks and popcorn products
President: Michael Season
Sales Director: Kelly Garrigan
Operations Manager: Mark Ruchti
Estimated Sales: $1.3 Million
Number Employees: 5-9
Number of Brands: 2
Number of Products: 35
Square Footage: 48000
Type of Packaging: Consumer, Food Service, Private Label, Bulk
Brands:
Butter Toffee Covered Popcorn
Chocolate Covered Potato Chips
Chocolate Covered Toffee Popcorn
Michael Season's Cheese Curls
Michael Season's Cheese Puffs
Michael Season's Kettle Potatoes
Michael Season's Organically Grown
Michael Season's Sensations
Sweet Organics

7846 **Manhattan Special Bottling**
342 Manhattan Ave
Brooklyn, NY 11211-2404
718-388-4144
Fax: 718-384-0244 www.manhattanspecial.com
Pure Espresso, sodas and iced coffee drinks
President: Aurora Passaro
apassaro@manhattanspecial.com
Estimated Sales: $2.5-5 Million
Number Employees: 5-9

7847 **Manildra Milling Corporation**
4210 Shawnee Msn Pkwy Ste 312a
Fairway, KS 66205
913-362-0777
Fax: 913-362-0052 800-323-8435
info@manildrausa.com www.manildrausa.com
Processor, exporter and importer of wheat gluten; processor of wheat starch
President: Gerry Degnan
Vice President of Business Development: Tom McCurry
Engineering Manager: Deryl Hancock
Number Employees: 10-19
Parent Co: Manildra Group
Type of Packaging: Bulk
Brands:
Gembond
Gemstar

7848 **Manischewitz Co**
80 Avenue K
Newark, NJ 07105-3803
201-553-1100
Fax: 201-333-1809
deborah.ross@manischewitz.com
www.manischewitz.com
Manufacturer and exporter of kosher foods including matzoth, crackers, cereals, wine, bagel mixes, candy, pickles, gefilte fish, borscht, doughnut mixes, bagel mixes and egg noodles.
President & CEO: David Sugarman
Contact: Bankier Alain
bankier.alain@manischewitz.com
Number Employees: 400
Number of Brands: 12
Type of Packaging: Consumer, Food Service, Private Label
Brands:
Manischewitz
Guiltless Gourmet
Season Brand
Mishpacha
Rokeach
Goodman's
Mrs. Adler's
Mother's
Horowitz Margareten
Carmel
Croyden House
Jason

7849 **Manischewitz Wine Co.**
1740 E 13th Street
Brooklyn, NY 11229-1902
718-339-0547
Fax: 718-336-1904 www.manischewitzwine.com
Kosher wine.
President & CEO: Rob Sands
Parent Co: Constellation Brands
Brands:
Manischewitz

7850 **Manitoba Harvest Hemp**
100 S Fifth Street
Suite 1085
Minneapolis, MN 55402-1204
800-665-4367
manitobaharvest.com
Hemp products
Co-Founder: Mike Fata
Brands:
Manitoba Harvest

7851 **Manitok Food & Gifts**
PO Box 97
Highway 59 Main Street
Callaway, MN 56521-0097
218-375-3425
Fax: 218-375-4765 800-726-1863
Products include handmade jewelry, dolls, quilts, birch bark baskets, canoes, trays, corporate gift baskets filled with hand-harvested and handmade food products, wild rice, berry jellies and syrups.
Manager: Dave Reinke
Estimated Sales: $5-9.9 Million
Number Employees: 4

7852 **Manley Meats Inc**
302 S 400 E
Decatur, IN 46733-9095
260-592-7313
Fax: 260-592-6731 manleymeats@adamwells.com
www.manleymeats.com
Canned and frozen beef, pork and chicken
President: Amanda Ogg
aogg@manleymeats.com
Vice President: Ronald Manley
Estimated Sales: $10-20 Million
Number Employees: 20-49
Type of Packaging: Consumer, Food Service

7853 **Mann Packing Co**
1250 Hansen St
Salinas, CA 93901-4552
831-422-0270
Fax: 831-422-1131 800-285-1002
www.veggiesmadeeasy.com
Fresh vegetables supplier.
Owner: Jose Areas
jose.areas@mannpacking.com
Number Employees: 500-999
Type of Packaging: Consumer, Food Service, Bulk
Brands:
Broccoli Wokly
Sugar Valley
Sunny Shores
Sunny Shores Broccoli Wokly

7854 **Mannhardt Inc**
3209 S. 32nd Street
Sheboygan Falls, WI 53082
920-467-1027
Fax: 773-625-5639 800-423-2327
mannhardt1@aol.com mannhardtice.com
Ice storage dispensers and bagging equipment
President: John Williams
Sales: Lori Justinger
Number Employees: 10-19

7855 **Manns Sausage Company**
125 N Main Street
Suite 500 #109
Blacksburg, VA 24060
540-605-0867
Fax: 540-953-0032 info@mannssausage.com
www.mannssausage.com
Sausages
Contact: Nathaniel Haile
nathaniel@mannssausage.com

7856 **Mansmith's Barbeque**
600 Mission Vineyard Rd
P.O.Box 247
San Jn Bautista, CA 95045
831-623-4981
Fax: 831-623-2150 800-626-7648
info@mansmith.com www.mansmith.com
Barbecue products including sauces, seasonings, pastes and grilling spices
Owner/President: Jon Mansmith
Owner/Secretary/Treasurer: Juanita Mansmith
Estimated Sales: Less Than $500,000
Number Employees: 1-4
Parent Co: Mansmith Enterprises
Type of Packaging: Consumer, Food Service, Private Label
Brands:
Mansmith's Gourmet

7857 **Mantrose-Haeuser Co Inc**
1175 Post Rd E
Westport, CT 06880-5431
203-454-1800
Fax: 203-227-0558 800-344-4229
info@mantrose.com www.mantrose.com
Edible coatings and glazes.

President: William Barrie
wbarrie@mantrose.com
VP/Controller: Sue O'Rourke
SVP, Research & Development: Stephen Santos
Estimated Sales: $10-20 Million
Number Employees: 100-249
Number of Brands: 12
Type of Packaging: Private Label
Brands:
Certicoat
Certified
Certiseal
Crystalac
Mantrocel
Mantroclear
NatureSeal
Poly-Soleil
Poly-Tresse
Reducit
TEALAC
VerdeCoat

7858 **Manuel's Mexican-American Fine Foods**
2007 S 300 W
Salt Lake City, UT 84115-1808
801-484-1431
Fax: 801-484-1440 800-748-5072
Tortilla chips, taco shells, corn tortilla, tostada shells and pre-cut tortillas
President: Orlando Torres
VP: Mike Torres
VP/Sales Exec: Paul Torres
Estimated Sales: Below $5 Million
Number Employees: 40
Type of Packaging: Consumer, Food Service, Private Label, Bulk

7859 **Manuel's Odessa Tortilla**
1915 E 2nd St
Odessa, TX 79761-5311
432-332-6676
Fax: 432-332-6699 800-753-2445
www.manuelstamales.com
Mexican foods including tortillas, and tamales.
President: Manuel Gonzalez
mangoniii@aol.com
Vice President: Evelyn Gonzalez
Year Founded: 1946
Estimated Sales: $1.1 Million
Number Employees: 10-19
Square Footage: 24000
Type of Packaging: Consumer, Food Service, Bulk
Brands:
Manuel's
Mito's

7860 **Manzana Products Co.**
9141 Green Valley Rd
Sebastopol, CA 95472
707-823-5313
Fax: 707-823-5218 northcoast.organic
Apple sauce, apple juice, apple cider and apple cider vinegar
CEO: Jean-Jacques Ducom
Year Founded: 1922
Estimated Sales: $6.2 Million
Number Employees: 100-249
Square Footage: 364000
Type of Packaging: Consumer, Private Label, Bulk
Brands:
North Coast

7861 **Maola Milk & Ice Cream Co.**
844-287-1970
emailus@maolamilk.com www.maolamilk.com
Fluid milk, flavored milk, cream, and egg nog.
Year Founded: 1920
Estimated Sales: $100 Million
Number Employees: 250-499
Square Footage: 7
Parent Co: Maryland & Virginia Producers Cooperative Association, Inc.
Type of Packaging: Consumer, Food Service, Private Label, Bulk
Brands:
Maola

7862 **Maola Milk & Ice Cream Co**
305 Avenue C
New Bern, NC 28560-3113
252-638-1131
Fax: 252-638-2268 800-476-1021
consumerservice@maolamilk.com
www.maolamilk.com
Dairy, Ice Cream
Owner: G D Currin
Manager: Alan Bentley
alanb@securewave.com
Estimated Sales: $.5-1 million
Number Employees: 250-499
Parent Co: Maola Milk & Ice Cream Company

7863 **Maple Acres Inc**
13910 Campbell Rd
Kewadin, MI 49648-9148
231-264-9265
Fax: 231-264-8532
Pure Northern Michigan maple syrup in 1/2 pint to one gallon jugs; private label available
President: Michael Luchenbill
President: Leta Luchenbill
Number Employees: 10-19
Square Footage: 12000
Type of Packaging: Consumer, Food Service, Private Label, Bulk
Brands:
Maple Acres

7864 **Maple Donuts**
3455 E Market St
York, PA 17402-2696
717-757-7826
Fax: 717-755-8725 800-627-5348
www.mapledonuts.com
Yeast raised, cake style, fresh and frozen doughnuts, as well as unbaked pie shells, fritters, cinnamon buns and other pastries.
President: Charles Burnside
charliemaple@aol.com
CEO: Nathaniel Burnside
VP/General Manager: Ralph Wooten
VP, Sales & Marketing: Damian Burnside
Sales & Marketing Manager: Luke Burnside
Maintenance Manager: Frank Stefano
Plant Manager: Garry Rausch
Estimated Sales: $40-50 Million
Number Employees: 100-249
Square Footage: 80000
Parent Co: Maple Donuts LLC
Type of Packaging: Private Label

7865 **Maple Donuts Inc**
10307 Hall Ave
Lake City, PA 16423-1226
814-774-3131
Fax: 814-774-3136 877-774-3668
Frozen donuts, pie shells, unfinished donuts, waffles
Chairman: Bruce MacLeod
CEO: Nat Burnside
Vice President: Patrick Riha
Estimated Sales: $10-20 Million
Number Employees: 50-99

7866 **Maple Grove Farms Of Vermont**
1052 Portland St
St Johnsbury, VT 05819-2041
802-748-5141
Fax: 802-748-9647 www.maplegrove.com
Pure maple syrup, fruit flavored syrups, sugar free syrup, specialty salad dressings, pancake & waffle mixes, gluten free products, maple candies & spreads.
Owner: Jim Schiller
Director, Finance: Jeffrey Donley
Plant Manager: Mark Bigelow
Estimated Sales: $11 Million
Number Employees: 100-249
Number of Brands: 4
Square Footage: 250000
Parent Co: B&G Foods
Type of Packaging: Consumer, Food Service, Private Label, Bulk
Brands:
Cozy Cottage
Maple Grove Farms of Vermont
Up Country Naturals
Vermont Sugar Free

7867 **Maple Hill Creamery**
5 Hudson St
Kinderhook, NY 12106
518-758-7777
Fax: 315-266-1269 maplehillcreamery.com
Milk, cheese and yogurt.
Co-Founder: Laura Joseph
Co-Founder: Tim Joseph
Brands:
Maple Hill(c)

7868 **Maple Hill Farms**
12 Burr Rd
Bloomfield, CT 06002-2204
860-242-9689
Fax: 860-243-2490 800-842-7304
www.mhfct.com
Dairy products
President: William Miller
info@maplehillfarm.com
Marketing Director: Scott Miller
Estimated Sales: $5-10 Million
Number Employees: 10-19

7869 **Maple Hollow**
W1887 Robinson Dr
Merrill, WI 54452-9543
715-536-7251
Maple syrup and sugar; wholesaler/distibutor of maple syrup processing machinery
Owner: Joe Polak
Vice President: Barbara Polak
Estimated Sales: $1 Million
Number Employees: 5-9
Number of Brands: 5
Number of Products: 4
Square Footage: 40000
Type of Packaging: Consumer, Private Label
Brands:
Forest Country
Maple Gardens
Maple Hollow

7870 **Maple Island**
3497 Seventh Avenue E
Suite 105
Saint Paul, MN 55109-2907
651-773-1000
Fax: 651-773-2155 800-369-1022
info@maple-island.com www.maple-island.com
Processor and packager of food powders and dairy products; agglomerate, blend and package into pouches and canisters.
President: Greg Johnson
Founder: John Stoltze
Sales Manager: David Doebler
Director, Operations: Randy Biebl
Plant Manager: Scott Larson
Estimated Sales: $28.7 Million
Number Employees: 10-19
Type of Packaging: Consumer, Food Service, Private Label, Bulk
Brands:
Bounce
Diet Freeze
Maple Island
Shakequik

7871 **Maple Leaf Bakery**
PO Box 55021
Montreal, QC H3G 2W5
Canada
416-926-2020
Fax: 416-926-2018 800-268-3708
Mediahotline@mapleleaf.com www.mapleleaf.ca
Bakery products
President/CEO: Michael McCain
Corporate Director: Robert Stewart
Chief Financial Officer: Michael H. Vels
SVP, Finance: Debbie Simpson
VP, Corporate Engineering: Peter Smith
CFSO and SVP, Six Sigma and Quality: Randall Huffman
Chief Marketing Officer: Stephen Graham
SVP, Communications: Lynda Kuhn
Chief Operating Officer: Richard A. Lan
SVP, Logistics and Purchasing: Bill Kaldis
Estimated Sales: $4,406,000
Number Employees: 18,000
Brands:
California Goldminer
Eurofresh
Home Fresh
Maple Leaf

7872 **Maple Leaf Cheesemakers**
554 Frst Street
New Glarus, WI 53574
608-527-2000
Fax: 608-527-3050 888-624-1234
mapleleaf1@tds.net
www.mapleleafcheeseandchocolatehaus.com
Cheese including monterey jack and gouda, fudge and chocolates
Owner: Barbara Kummerfeldt
Estimated Sales: $500,000-$1 Million
Number Employees: 20-49
Type of Packaging: Consumer, Food Service, Private Label, Bulk
Brands:
Maple Leaf

7873 **Maple Leaf Consumer Foods**
7840 Madison Ave # 135
Fair Oaks, CA 95628-3591
916-967-1633
Fax: 916-967-1690 800-999-7603
www.mapleleaf.com
Ham and bacon
General Manager: Charles Brougher
Estimated Sales: $5-10 Million
Number Employees: 10-19
Parent Co: Maple Leaf Foods
Type of Packaging: Consumer, Food Service, Private Label, Bulk

7874 **Maple Leaf Farms**
101 E Church
P.O. Box 167
St Leesburg, IN 46538
574-453-4455
800-348-2812
cturk@mapleleaffarms.com
www.mapleleaffarms.com
Duck products.
Co-President: John Tucker
Co-President: Scott Tucker
Chief Executive Officer: Terry Tucker
CFO & COO: Scott Reinholt
Year Founded: 1958
Estimated Sales: $45.3 Million
Number Employees: 1100
Type of Packaging: Consumer, Food Service, Private Label, Bulk
Brands:
C&D
C&D
Chef Tang
Ech
Fch
Gold Label
Maple Leaf

7875 **Maple Leaf Foods**
1 Warman Drive
Winnipeg, NB R2J 4E5
Canada
204-231-4114
Fax: 204-231-2944 800-564-6253
www.mapleleaf.com
Pork
CEO: Michael H McCain
CFO: Michael H Vels
Plant Manager: Jeff Parsons
Number Employees: 250-499
Parent Co: Schneider's Dairy
Type of Packaging: Food Service
Brands:
Burns
California Goldminer
Hygrade
Maison-Cousin
Nutriwhip
Shopsy's
Tenderflake

7876 **(HQ)Maple Leaf Foods International**
5160 Yonge St
Suite 300
North York, ON M2N 6L9
Canada
416-480-8900
Fax: 416-480-8950 800-268-3708
www.mapleleaf.ca
Processor, importer and exporter of fresh and frozen meat, seafood, dairy products, produce, potato products and specialty grains
President: Michael Detlefsen
Senior Vice President, Transactions and: Rocco Cappuccitti
Executive VP/Chief Strategy Officer: Douglas Dodds
Chief Information Officer: Patrick Ressa
Chief Financial Officer: Michael Vels
Estimated Sales: $6.4 Million
Number Employees: 23,000
Square Footage: 42000
Type of Packaging: Consumer, Food Service, Private Label, Bulk
Other Locations:
Maple Leaf Foods Internationa
Chatham NJ
Brands:
Bittner's
California Goldminer
Dempster's
Hot & Crusty
Hudrage
Maison Cousin
Maple Leaf
Medallion Naturally
Nature's Gourmet
Olivieri
Prime Naturally
Prime Turkey
Ready Crisp
Shopsy's
Slo-Roast Deli
Tender Flake
Top Dogs

7877 **Maple Leaf Meats**
PO Box 55021
Motreal, QC H3G 2W5
Canada
204-233-2421
Fax: 204-233-5413 800-268-3708
www.mapleleaf.com
Meat products
Director Corporate: James F Hankinson
President: Chaviva M Hosek
Controller: John Main
CEO: Chaviva M Hosek
Number Employees: 400
Square Footage: 1036000
Parent Co: Maple Leaf Foods
Type of Packaging: Consumer, Food Service, Private Label, Bulk
Brands:
Maple Leaf
Royale

7878 **Maple Leaf Pork**
P.O.Box 55021
Montreal, QC H3G 2W5
Canada
403-328-1756
Fax: 403-327-9821 800-268-3708
www.mapleleaf.ca
Processor and exporter of fresh and frozen pork including carcass, boxed and by-products
President: Michael McCain
Sales: Wilf Fiebich
General Manager: Ralph Miller
Plant Manager: Dave Wood
Number Employees: 100-249
Parent Co: Maple Leaf Foods
Type of Packaging: Consumer, Bulk

7879 **Maple Products**
1500 Rue De Pacifique
Sherbrooke, QC J1H 2G7
Canada
819-569-5161
Fax: 819-569-5168
Processor and exporter of maple syrup and sugar; also, kosher grades available
Production Manager: Ghislain Pare
Number Employees: 10-19
Parent Co: Citadelle
Type of Packaging: Food Service, Bulk
Brands:
Pride of Canada

7880 **Maple Ridge Farms**
975 S Park View Cir
Mosinee, WI 54455
Canada
715-693-4346
www.mapleridge.com
Processor for the production and extraction of essential oils and their fractions. Including caraway seed, cilantro (coriander foliage), dill seed and foliage. One hundred tons annually. Serving the bio-organic industry and ingredientmanufacturers
President: Martin Gareau

7881 **Maple Valley Cooperative**
919 Front St
P.O. Box 153
Cashton, WI 54619
608-654-7319
Fax: 877-579-5073
customerservice@maplevalley.coop
www.maplevalleysyrup.coop
Organic maple syrup, maple candy, maple sugar, and maple cream
Founder/President: Cecil Wright
General Manager: Renee Miller
Year Founded: 2007

7882 **Maple's Organics**
881 Route
Yarmouth, ME 04096-6930
207-846-1000
Manufacturer of gelato.
Co-Founder: Rachel Williams
Co-Founder: David Williams
Estimated Sales: Less Than $500,000
Number Employees: 5-9

7883 **Maplebrook Farm**
PO Box 966
Bennington, VT 05201-8005
802-440-9950
Fax: 802-440-9956 meri@maplebrookvt.com
www.maplebrookvt.com
Cheese.
Owner: Mike Scheps
Marketing: Meri Spicer

7884 **Maplegrove Foods**
1261 W State St
Ontario, CA 91762
909-545-6075
info@omasownfoods.com
omasownfoods.com
Noodle cups and fruit chips
President/Owner: Raj Sukul
Brands:
Oma's Own

7885 **Maplehill Creamery**
285 Allendale Rd W
Stuyvesant, NY 12173-2611
USA
518-758-7777
contact@maplehillcreamery.com
Yogurt, cheese
President: Tim Joseph
Director Of Marketing & Communications: Sara Talcott
Contact: Glenn Haakonsen
ghaakonsen@lenel.com
Estimated Sales: Less Than $500,000
Number Employees: 5-9

7886 **Maplehurst Bakeries LLC**
50 Maplehurst Dr
Brownsburg, IN 46112
800-428-3200
info@maplehurstbakeries.com
www.maplehurstbakeries.com
Bread and other bakery products including; rolls, cakes, donuts, pies, and danishes.
President: Luc Mongeau
Supply Chain Director: Craig Myers
Year Founded: 1967
Estimated Sales: $107.2 Million
Number Employees: 1,000-4,999
Parent Co: George Weston Ltd.
Type of Packaging: Food Service, Private Label, Bulk
Brands:
Freed's Bakery
Granny's Kitchen
La Baguetterie
Plush Pippin

7887 **Maplehurst Farms**
936 S Moore Rd
Rochelle, IL 61068-9789
815-562-8723
Fax: 815-562-7543 www.maplehurstfarms.com

Milk and cottage cheese
General Manager: Jim Black
Vice President: Steve Garish
Year Founded: 1909
Estimated Sales: $100-400 Million
Number Employees: 50-99
Parent Co: Dean Foods Company

7888 **Mapleland Farm**
647 Bunker Hill Rd
Salem, NY 12865-1716
518-854-7669
www.maplelandfarms.com
Manufacturer of pure maple products.
Co-Founder: David Campbell
Co-Founder: Terry Campbell
Estimated Sales: Less Than $500,000
Number Employees: 1-4

7889 **Mar-Jac Poultry Inc.**
1020 Aviation Blvd.
Gainesville, GA 30501
770-531-5000
Fax: 770-531-5015 info@marjacpoultry.com
www.marjacpoultry.com
Fresh and frozen chicken; whole birds (with or without giblets), fast food (8, 9, or 6 pieces), splits, or quarters, boneless butterflies, tenders, filets, or thigh meat, and parts; split breasts, drums, thighs, whole legs, legquarters, whole wings, cut wings, gizzards, livers, paws.
CFO: Tanveer Papa
Vice President, Operations: Joel Williams
Year Founded: 1954
Estimated Sales: $284 Million
Number Employees: 1000-4999
Number of Brands: 2
Square Footage: 300000
Type of Packaging: Food Service, Private Label
Brands:
M-J
Mar-Jac Brands

7890 **Mar-Key Foods**
PO Box 603
Vidalia, GA 30475
912-537-4204
Fax: 912-537-2542
Soft drink concentrates, pre-sweetened drink mixes and freeze pops
President: Louie Powell
Secretary: Diane Collins
Estimated Sales: $110,000
Number Employees: 20-49
Type of Packaging: Consumer, Food Service, Bulk
Brands:
Jolly Aid
Jolly Pops

7891 **(HQ)Maramor Chocolates**
1855 E 17th Ave
Columbus, OH 43219
614-291-2244
Fax: 614-291-0966 800-843-7722
Processor and exporter of kosher boxed chocolates, chocolate covered bagel chips and mints; packaged for racks and fund raising purposes; contract manufacturing available
President: Michael Ryan
Sales: Scott Sher
Contact: Crystal Burchett
cburchett@maramor.com
Estimated Sales: $1.6 Million
Number Employees: 20-49
Square Footage: 120000
Type of Packaging: Consumer, Private Label, Bulk
Brands:
Maramor

7892 **(HQ)Maranatha Natural Foods**
1192 Illinois Street
San Francisco, CA 94107
415-401-0080
Fax: 415-401-0087 866-972-6879
customerservice@worldpantry.com
www.worldpantry.com
Organic and regular nut and seed butters, trail mixes and dry roasted nuts and seeds; importer of cashews and sesame seeds; exporter of organic and regular nut and seed butters and trail mixes
President: Patrick Lee
CEO: David Miller
Estimated Sales: $10-20 Million
Number Employees: 20-49
Square Footage: 28000
Type of Packaging: Consumer, Food Service, Private Label, Bulk
Other Locations:
Marantha Natural Foods
San Leandro CA
Brands:
Marantha
Nuttin' Butter

7893 **Marathon Cheese**
1000 Progressive Ave
Medford, WI 54451-1698
715-748-4500
Custom packager of cheese
Contact: Mike Mathias
mmccallum@mcheese.com
Plant Manager: John Wanish
Number Employees: 250-499
Type of Packaging: Consumer, Food Service, Private Label, Bulk

7894 **(HQ)Marathon Cheese Corp**
304 East St
PO Box 185
Marathon, WI 54448-9643
715-443-2211
Fax: 715-443-3843
Custom packager of cheese
President: Dan Zastoupil
CEO: John Skoug
jskoug@mcheese.com
Director: Gene Land
Director Sales/Marketing: Mike Mathias
Corporate Controller: Amy Janke
Systems Manager: Arlin Bradfish
Plant Manager: Lisa Trace
Number Employees: 500-999
Type of Packaging: Consumer, Food Service, Private Label, Bulk
Other Locations:
Marathon Cheese
Mountain Home ID
Marathon Cheese
Medford WI
Marathon Cheese
Booneville MS

7895 **Marathon Enterprises Inc**
9 Smith St
Englewood, NJ 07631-4607
201-569-2915
Fax: 201-935-5693 800-722-7388
info@sabrett.com www.sabretthotstuff.com
Hot dogs including; all beef natural casing, pork and beef natural casing, or all beef skinless, available in cocktail size up to foot long franks, and condiments such as sauerkraut, mustard, relish and onions in sauce
President: Boyd G Adelman
VP Sales: Mark Rosen
Plant Manager: Herb Tetens
Number Employees: 250-499
Type of Packaging: Consumer, Food Service, Private Label, Bulk
Brands:
Sabrett

7896 **Marathon Packing Corp**
1000 Montague St
San Leandro, CA 94577-4332
510-895-2000
Fax: 510-895-2022 www.marathonpacking.com
Cooking oils and shortening
Chief Executive Officer: Cecilia Chan
Contact: Brendan Chan
brendan.chan@marathonpacking.com
Plant Manager: Luis Salazar
Estimated Sales: $10-20 000,000
Number Employees: 10-19

7897 **Marburger Farm Dairy**
1506 Mars Evans City Road
Evans City, PA 16033
724-538-4800
Fax: 724-538-3250 800-331-1295
www.marburgerdairy.com
Bottled milk and dairy products.
President: James Marburger
VP: Craig Marburger
Maintenance Manager: Larry Byers
Plant Manager: Garrie Wearing
Estimated Sales: $10-20 Million
Number Employees: 50-99
Number of Brands: 1
Type of Packaging: Private Label
Brands:
Marburger

7898 **Marcel et Henri Charcuterie Francaise**
415 Browning Way
South San Francisco, CA 94080
650-871-4230
Fax: 650-871-5948 800-227-6436
marcelethenri@sbcglobal.net
French pate and sausage.
President: Henri Lapuyade
Estimated Sales: $3 Million
Number Employees: 10-19
Number of Brands: 1
Number of Products: 50
Square Footage: 60000
Type of Packaging: Consumer, Food Service, Bulk
Brands:
Marcel Et Henri

7899 **Marcho Farms Inc**
176 Orchard Ln
Harleysville, PA 19438-1681
215-721-7131
Fax: 215-721-9719 ltufft@marchofarms.com
Grower and packer of milk fed veal. Processing primal, fresh cuts, portion control, precooked meatballs, meat loaf, bacon and philly steaks
President: Wayne A Marcho
wmarcho@marchofarms.com
Number Employees: 100-249

7900 **Marconi Italian Specialty Foods**
710 W Grand Ave
Chicago, IL 60654-5574
312-421-0485
Fax: 312-421-1286 sales@marconi-foods.com
www.marconi-foods.com
Manufacturers a variety of specialty Italian foods including cheeses; coffees; salad dressings; meats; olive oils; pasta; salads; sauces; seafoods; spices, and vinegars.
President/CEO/Co-Owner: Robert Johnson
Co-Owner: Sue Formusa
Estimated Sales: $5-10 Million
Number Employees: 5-9
Parent Co: V Formusa Company

7901 **Mardale Specialty Foods**
1120 Glen Rock Avenue
Waukegan, IL 60085-5458
845-299-0285
Fax: 847-336-5030
Portion controlled condiments including salad dressing, syrup, jam and mayonnaise
President: Ronald Tarantino
Plant Manager: Jim Streiff
Number Employees: 20-49
Type of Packaging: Food Service

7902 **Mardi Gras**
150 Bloomfield Ave
Verona, NJ 07044-2711
973-857-3777
Fax: 973-857-8884 maria@mardigrasfoods.com
www.mardigrasfoods.com
Gourmet fresh and frozen foods
Manager: Maria Carrozza
VP: Kim Newman
Estimated Sales: Below $5 Million
Number Employees: 10-19
Square Footage: 9600
Type of Packaging: Consumer

7903 **Margarita Man**
10818 Gulfdale St
San Antonio, TX 78216-3607
210-979-7191
Fax: 210-979-0718 800-950-8149
info@margaritamansa.com
www.margaritamansa.com
Frozen drink mixes; wholesaler/distributor of frozen beverage machines
President: Chris Murphy
ncmargman@nc.rr.com
Plant Manager: Steve Snyder
Estimated Sales: $1 Million
Number Employees: 5-9
Number of Brands: 1

Number of Products: 15
Square Footage: 10000
Brands:
Go Bananas
Go Mango
Just Add Tequila
Razzmatazzberry
The Margarita Man

7904 Mari's Candy
2266 S Blue Island Ave
Chicago, IL 60608-4345
773-254-3351
Fax: 773-254-3581
Mexican-style coconut candy
Owner: Raul Hernandez
VP/CEO: Maris Elena
VP of Retail: Raul Hernandez Jr.
VP of General Market: Maria Hernandez
VP of Wholesale: Rodrigo Hernandez
Estimated Sales: Less Than $500,000
Number Employees: 1-4
Type of Packaging: Consumer

7905 Mari's New York
115 4th Ave Apt 8a
Suite C5
New York, NY 10003-4909
Fax: 615-622-0281 support@marisny.com
Brownies

7906 MariGold Foods
16693 Coaltown Rd
Willis, TX 77378
936-344-0444
www.marigoldbars.com
Gluten free, organic, non-GMO protein bars
Co-Owner: Mari Ann Lisenbe
Co-Owner: Steve Lisenbe
Year Founded: 2012

7907 Maria & Son
4201 Hereford St
St Louis, MO 63109-1798
314-481-9009
Fax: 314-481-9109 866-481-9009
Frozen Italian pastas and sauces
President: John Ard
Estimated Sales: $5-10 000,000
Number Employees: 10-19
Brands:
Maria & Son
Tita's

7908 Maria and Ricardo's
320 Turnpike St
Canton, MA 02021
800-881-7040
info@harbar.com www.mariaandricardos.com
Tortillas, wraps and tortilla crisps
VP, Sales: Tom Stacey
Number of Brands: 2
Number of Products: 20
Type of Packaging: Consumer
Brands:
MARIA AND RICARDO'S ARTESANO

7909 Maria's Premium
www.mariaspremium.com
Flavored popcorn
Number of Brands: 1
Number of Products: 3
Type of Packaging: Consumer
Brands:
MARIA'S PREMIUM

7910 Mariani Nut Co
28306 County Road 90a
Winters, CA 95694
530-795-1546
Fax: 530-795-2681 www.marianinut.com
Processor and exporter of walnuts and almonds
President & CEO: Jack Mariani
Co-Owner: Gus Mariani
Partner: Martin Mariani
Vice President: Dennis Mariani
VP Marketing & Ecommerce: Matt Mariani
Marketin Mgr, VP Operations/Sales: John Martin
Estimated Sales: $5.5 Million
Number Employees: 10-19
Square Footage: 120000
Type of Packaging: Consumer, Bulk
Brands:
Mariani

7911 Mariani Packing Co.
500 Crocker Dr.
Vacaville, CA 95688-8706
707-452-2800
Fax: 707-452-2973 productinfo@mariani.com
www.mariani.com
Fresh dried fruit including; plums, apricots, cranberries, raisins, cherries, apples, and sun dried tomatoes.
President: George Sousa
Chairman/CEO: Mark Mariani
CFO: Forrest Chandler
Director Internet Sales: Stephen Sousa
Year Founded: 1906
Estimated Sales: $150 Million
Number Employees: 250-499
Square Footage: 10773
Type of Packaging: Consumer, Private Label, Bulk
Brands:
Mariani

7912 Marich Confectionery
2101 Bert Dr
Hollister, CA 95023-2562
831-634-4700
Fax: 831-634-4705 800-624-7055
weborders@marich.com www.marich.com
Candy including chocolate cherries, apricots, blueberries, strawberries and nut mixes; also, mints, toffee and maltballs.
President: Bradley Van Dam
CEO: Steve Atwood
satwood@marich.com
Executive VP/COO: Troy Van Dam
VP Marketing/Sales: Michelle Van Dam
Sales Manager: Ellen Filberman
Plant Manager: Victor Moreno
Estimated Sales: Below $5 Million
Number Employees: 20-49
Type of Packaging: Consumer
Brands:
Holland Mints
Marich
Wallabeans

7913 Marie Brizard Wines & Spirits
849 Zinfandel Lane
St. Helena, CA 94574
800-878-1123
Fax: 415-979-0305 info@boisset.com
www.boissetamerica.com
Processor, importer and exporter of alcoholic beverages including vodka, bourbon, tequila, scotch, brandy, cognac, schnapps, gin, rum, cordials, wines and champagne
President: Jean-Charles Boisset
VP/Director Marketing: Michael Avitable
VP/Director Sales: Robert Bermudez
Director Operations: Hubert Surville
Number Employees: 20-49
Square Footage: 26000
Parent Co: Marie Brizard Wines & Spirits USA
Brands:
Marie Brizard

7914 Marie Callender's
27101 Puerta Real # 260
Suite 260
Mission Viejo, CA 92691-8538
949-448-5300
Fax: 949-582-7358 800-776-7437
www.mariecallenders.com
Cornbread mixes, desserts, pie glazes, muffin mixes and much more
CEO: Ron Bidinost
ron.bidinost@prkmc.com
Estimated Sales: $1-3 Million
Number Employees: 1000-4999

7915 Marie Callender's Gourmet Products/Goldrush Products
491 San Carlos Street
San Jose, CA 95110-2632
408-288-4090
Fax: 408-279-3742 800-729-5428
www.mccornbread.com
Kosher sourdough baking mixes including pancake, biscuit, cornbread, nine-grain and wholewheat bread, etc
President: Henry Down
Contact: Jim Musante
jim@commissary.com
Number Employees: 20-49
Parent Co: International Commissary Corporation
Type of Packaging: Consumer, Private Label, Bulk
Brands:
Goldrush

7916 Marie F
123 Denison Street
Markham, ON L3R 1B5
Canada
905-475-0093
Fax: 905-475-0038 800-365-4464
fmarie@ca.inter.net
Beef, butcher supplies and sausage and sheep casings; importer of sausage casings, butcher suppliers and cures; exporter of sausage casings
President: Sandra Marie Rundle
Plant Manager: Alaister Sears
Estimated Sales: $4 Million
Number Employees: 25
Square Footage: 60000
Type of Packaging: Food Service

7917 Marie's Quality Foods
PO Box 1105
Brea, CA 92822
800-339-1051
www.maries.com
Salad dressing
President: Richard D Orr
VP Sales/Marketing: Richard Orr
Operations Manager: Drew Orr
Number Employees: 20-49
Square Footage: 400000
Type of Packaging: Consumer, Food Service, Private Label

7918 MarieBelle
484 Broome St
New York, NY 10013
212-925-6999
mariebelle.com
Chocolate
President & Founder: Maribel Lieberman
Type of Packaging: Private Label

7919 Maries Candies
311 Zanesfield Rd
West Liberty, OH 43357-9563
937-465-3061
Fax: 937-465-3336 866-465-5781
info@mariescandies.com www.mariescandies.com
Candy including turkins, peanut brittle, toffee, butter creams, peppermint chews and melt-aways
Owner: Jay R King
info@mariescandies.com
Co-Owner: Kathy King
Estimated Sales: $1,200,000
Number Employees: 20-49
Type of Packaging: Consumer

7920 Marietta Cellars
22295 Chianti Rd
Geyservill, CA 95441
707-433-2747
Fax: 707-857-4910 www.mariettacellars.com
Producer of wines the list of which includes Angeli Cuvee, Petit Sirah, Cabernet Sauvignon and Zinfandel.
President/CEO: Chris Bilbro
Office Manager: Suzie Buchignani
Bookkeeper: Judy Summary
Marketing Manager: Jake Bilbro
Contact: Will Hunter
will@mariettacellars.com
Facilities Manager: Sarah Herrerra
Cellar/Bottling Manager: Roman Cisneros
Estimated Sales: $1.5 Million
Number Employees: 15

7921 Marika's Kitchen
106 Old Route 1
Hancock, ME 04640-3448
207-422-2300
Fax: 207-422-2300 800-694-9400
marika_gauchi@hotmail.com
Almond and walnut baklava and Greek biscota
Owner: Gloria Day
Vice President: Michael Savoy
Number Employees: 1-4
Square Footage: 5000

Type of Packaging: Food Service, Bulk

7922 **Marimar Torres Estates**
11400 Graton Rd
Sebastopol, CA 95472-8901
707-823-4365
Fax: 707-823-4496 info189@marimarestate.com
www.sanfranciscobayarealimo.com
Wines
Proprietor/Winegrower: Marimar Torres
marimar@marimarestate.com
National Sales Manager: Kyle Ray
Cellar Master: Tony Britton
Vineyard Manager: Venutra Albor
Estimated Sales: $850,000
Number Employees: 5-9
Type of Packaging: Private Label
Brands:
Marimar Torres Estate

7923 **Marin Brewing Co**
1809 Larkspur Landing Cir
Larkspur, CA 94939-1801
415-461-4677
Fax: 415-461-4688 brendan@marinbrewing.com
www.marinbrewing.com
Beer
Proprietor: Brendan Moylan
brendan@marinbrewing.com
Brew Master: Arne Johnson
Marketing Manager: Ryan Purtill
Sales Manager: Curtis Cassidy
Estimated Sales: Below $5 Million
Number Employees: 100-249
Brands:
Albion Amber Ale
Marin Weiss
Miwok Weizen Bock
Mt. Tom Pale Ale
Old Dipsea Barley Wine
Point Reyes Porter
Raspberry Trail Ale
San Quentin's Breakout Stout

7924 **Marin Food Specialties**
14800 Highway 4
Byron, CA 94505-2236
925-634-6126
Fax: 925-634-4647
Processor, importer and exporter of specialty foods including cookies, fig and fruit bars, pasta, trail mixes, marinated vegetables, almond butter, spices and candy; gift baskets available
President: Joseph Brucia
VP: Fred Vuylsteke
Estimated Sales: $1-3 Million
Number Employees: 50 to 99
Square Footage: 60000
Type of Packaging: Consumer, Private Label, Bulk
Brands:
Marin
Spanky's

7925 **Marin French Cheese Co**
7500 Red Hill Rd
Petaluma, CA 94952-9438
707-762-6001
Fax: 707-762-0430 800-292-6001
cheesefactory@marinfrenchcheese.com
www.marinfrenchcheese.com
Cheeses including camembert cheese, breakfast cheese, brie cheese, schloss cheese and specialty flavored bries; also gift boxes available.
Owner: Teresa Gordon
tgordon@santiagocorp.com
Finance Manager: Candice Millhouse
Marketing: Maxx Sherman
Estimated Sales: $1.6 Million
Number Employees: 20-49
Type of Packaging: Consumer, Bulk
Brands:
Rouge Et Noir

7926 **Marin Kombucha**
Novato, CA 94925
415-496-5441
info@marinkombucha.com
marinkombucha.com
Kombucha
CFO: Kevin Igersheim

7927 **Marina Foods**
11125 NW 124th Street
Medley, FL 33178-3173
786-888-0129
Fax: 786-888-0134 info@marinafoods.com
www.marinafoods.com
Packers of edible oils, shortenings and related products.
President: John Ioannou
Contact: George Ioannou
george@marinafoods.com
Estimated Sales: $20 Million
Number Employees: 20-49
Number of Brands: 3
Type of Packaging: Consumer, Food Service, Private Label, Bulk
Brands:
Chef's Recipe
DiMarco
Marina

7928 **Marine MacHines**
3 Strawberry Hill Road
Bar Harbor, ME 04609-1206
207-288-0107
Fax: 207-288-0462
Sea urchin procesing technology and equipment.
President: Mickey Kestner

7929 **Mariner Neptune Fish & Seafood Company**
472 Dufferin Avenue
Winnipeg, NB R2W 2X6
Canada
204-589-5341
Fax: 204-582-8135 800-668-8862
www.marinerneptune.com
Distributor of fish, seafood and protein food products
President: John Alexander
VP: Russell Page
Marketing: Evan Page
Sales: Doug Chandler
Plant Manager: Chris Juerson
Estimated Sales: $16 Million
Number Employees: 42
Number of Products: 2000
Type of Packaging: Consumer, Food Service
Brands:
King Neptune
Mariner-Neptune

7930 **Mariner Seafood LLC**
86 Macarthur Dr.
New Bedford, MA 02740-7221
774-202-4121
Fax: 714-202-6605 www.marinerseafood.com
Fresh and frozen cod, hake, flounder, lobster and crab
President & CEO: Jack Flynn
jackflynn@marinerseafood.com
Estimated Sales: Less Than $500,000
Number Employees: 1-4
Type of Packaging: Consumer, Food Service, Private Label, Bulk
Brands:
Mariner Seafoods

7931 **Mario Camancho Foods**
2502 Walden Woods Dr
Plant City, FL 33566-7167
813-305-4534
Fax: 813-305-4546 800-293-9783
info@mariocamachofoods.com
www.mariocamachofoods.com
A leading manufacturer and distributor of olives, olive oil and other specialty food products
President: Shawn Kaddoura
CEO: Michelle Andersen
andersenm@mariocamachofoods.com
CEO: Bret Milligan
Marketing: Jeff Hanneken
Sales: Jon Horoquist
Production: Bob Fidoelke
Estimated Sales: $10-20 Million
Number Employees: 20-49
Square Footage: 375000
Parent Co: Angel Camacho S.A.
Type of Packaging: Consumer, Food Service, Private Label, Bulk
Brands:
Christos
Fragata
Pride of Spain
The Jug

7932 **Mario's Gelati**
88 E 1st Avenue
Vancouver, BC V5T 1A1
Canada
604-879-9411
Fax: 604-879-0435 info@mariosgelati.com
www.mariosgelati.com
Processor, importer and exporter of ice cream
President: Mario Loscerbo
Vice President: Chris Loscerbo
Estimated Sales: $5.4 Million
Number Employees: 30
Square Footage: 120000
Brands:
Mario's Gelati

7933 **Marion's Smart Delights**
1515 North Harrison Street
Arlington, VA 22205
703-593-3450
Dairy-free, gluten-free, kosher, nut-free, organic/natural, vegetarian, baking mixes and ingredients.
Marketing Director: Marion Braswell

7934 **Marion-Kay Spice Co**
1351 W US Highway 50
Brownstown, IN 47220
812-358-3000
Fax: 812-358-3400 800-627-7423
info@marionkay.com www.marionkay.com
Spice blends and extracts
Estimated Sales: $2500000
Number Employees: 20-49
Type of Packaging: Consumer, Food Service, Bulk
Brands:
Claudia Sanders
Cream of Vanilla
The House of Flavors

7935 **Maritime Pacific Brewing Co**
1111 NW Ballard Way
Seattle, WA 98107-4639
206-782-6181
Fax: 206-782-0718 marpac@maritimebrewing.com
www.maritimebrewery.com
Micro-brewery
President: George Hancock
Estimated Sales: Below $5 Million
Number Employees: 20-49

7936 **Marjie's Plantain Foods, Inc.**
PO Box 1211
New York, NY 10002
908-627-5627
Fax: 718-383-3337
info@marjiesplantainfoods.com
www.marjiesplantainfoods.com
Gluten-free, other lifestyle, vegetarian, frozen baked goods, other snacks.
Marketing: Majorie Gaston

7937 **Marjon Specialty Foods Inc**
3508 Sydney Rd
Plant City, FL 33566-1185
813-752-3482
Fax: 813-754-4974
www.marjonspecialtyfoods.com
Sprouts (bean, alfalfa and others), salad dressings, fresh ginger stir-fry sauce, tofu
Vice President: Pedro Agenjo
pagenjo@pb-santander.com
VP: Marcia Miller
Director of R&D: Jim Martin
Human Resources Manager: Joe Miller
pagenjo@pb-santander.com
Operations Manager: Martha Clingenpeel
Office Manager, Director of Sales & Purc: Lisa Minnes
Estimated Sales: $11 Million
Number Employees: 100-249
Square Footage: 21000

7938 **Mark West Wines**
7000 Trenton-Healdsburg Rd
Forestville, CA 95436
707-544-4813
www.markwestwines.com
Pinot Noir

7939 **Market Fisheries**
7129 S State St
Chicago, IL 60619-1017
773-483-3233
Fax: 773-483-0724
Seafood
President: Haim Brody
haim@centerstagechicago.com
Estimated Sales: $3-5 Million
Number Employees: 10-19

7940 **Market Square Food Co.**
444 Old Skokie Rd
Park City, IL 60085
847-599-6070
Fax: 847-599-6512 800-232-2299
info@marketsquarefood.com
www.marketsquarefood.com
Specialty food gift items
Founder: James Lockhart
Founder: David Lockhart
Estimated Sales: $2.5-5 Million
Number Employees: 5-9
Brands:
Animal Crackers
Happy Snacks

7941 **Markham Vineyards**
2812 Saint Helena Hwy N
P.O.Box 636
St Helena, CA 94574-9655
707-963-5292
Fax: 707-963-4616 info@markhamvineyards.com
www.markhamvineyards.com
Processor and exporter of wines
President: Bryan Del Bondio
bdelbondio@markhamvineyards.com
Winemaker: Kimberlee Nicholls
Associate Winemaker: James Coughlin
General Manager: Kathryn Fowler
Estimated Sales: $5-10 Million
Number Employees: 20-49

7942 **Markko Vineyard**
4500 S Ridge Rd W
Conneaut, OH 44030-9712
440-593-3197
Fax: 440-599-7022 800-252-3197
markko@suite224.net www.markko.com
Wines
Owner: Arnulf Esterer
markko@suite224.net
Owner: Tim Hubbard
Estimated Sales: $500,000-$1 Million
Number Employees: 1-4

7943 **Marks Meat**
N6586 McCurdy Rd.
Holmen, WI 54636
608-526-6058
www.marksmeats.net
Beef, pork and lamb; custom slaughtering services available
President: Kristie Akin
Estimated Sales: $110,000
Number Employees: 5-9
Type of Packaging: Consumer

7944 **Marley Orchards Corporation**
2820 River Rd
Yakima, WA 98902
509-248-5231
Fax: 509-248-7358
Produce including apples
Chief Financial Officer: Stanley Bostrom
President/Sales & Marketing Staff: William Gammie
Sales Representative: Tony Bishop
Contact: Angela Deaton
adeaton@jackfrostfruit.com
Estimated Sales: $2.8 Million
Number Employees: 75
Type of Packaging: Consumer, Food Service, Bulk

7945 **Marlow Candy & Nut Co**
65 Honeck St
Englewood, NJ 07631-4125
201-569-3725
Fax: 201-569-9533 www.marlowcandy.net
Wholesaler of packaged candy and nuts
President: Eric Lowenthal
rickyl@marlowcandy.net
Office Manager: Alden Kirk
Estimated Sales: $10-20 Million
Number Employees: 20-49

7946 **Marlow Wine Cellars**
Highway 41a-64
Monteagle, TN 37356
931-924-2120
Fax: 931-924-2587
Manufactuer of fine wines
President/Wine Maker: Joe Marlow
Sales Manager: Gena Stevens
Estimated Sales: $1-2.5 Million
Number Employees: 1-4

7947 **Marlyn Nutraceuticals**
4404 E Elwood St
Phoenix, AZ 85040-1909
480-991-0200
Fax: 480-991-0551 800-899-4499
Processor and exporter of health foods and natural vitamins, minerals and food supplements including B-complex and C-combination formulas, fish oils, fiber blends, multi-vitamins and enzymes
Owner: Joe Lehmann
Export Sales Manager: Mark Wojick
VP Sales: Don Haygood
lehmannj@naturallyvitamins.com
Estimated Sales: $5-10 Million
Number Employees: 50-99
Square Footage: 80000
Type of Packaging: Food Service, Private Label, Bulk
Brands:
All B-100
All B-50
Body-Fuel
Fiber
Fiber-7
Ginsen-Rgy
Hi C-Plex
Little Vab
Max-C-Plex
Mega C-Bio
Special C-500
Super Epa
Super Stress
Super Vab
Supreme B 150
Un-Fad Diet Packs
Vit-A-Boost

7948 **Marnap Industries**
225 French Street
Buffalo, NY 14211
716-897-1220
Fax: 716-897-1306 www.flavorchem.com
Processor and exporter of essential oils, spice blends, seasonings, flavor compounds and oleoresins; importer of essential oils and oleoresins
President: Dennis J Napora
VP: Kevin Martin
Sales: Joanne Evans
Production: J Cogley
Estimated Sales: $3-5 Million
Number Employees: 5-9
Number of Products: 100+
Square Footage: 48000
Parent Co: Flavorchem Corp.
Type of Packaging: Bulk
Brands:
Marnap-Trap

7949 **Marquez Brothers International**
101 South 11th Ave
Hanford, CA 93230-5043
408-960-2700
Fax: 408-960-3213 800-858-1119
www.marquezbrothers.com
Gelatin, sweet and sour cream, Mexican cheese and liquid yogurt
CEO: Gustave Marquez
VP: Juan Marquez
Contact: Gloria Castillo
gcastillo@marquezbrothers.com
Plant Manager: Juan Luis De La Torre
Estimated Sales: $1 Million
Number Employees: 10-19
Parent Co: Marquez Brothers International
Type of Packaging: Consumer, Food Service

7950 **Marquis**
600 St. Paul Ave
Suite 102
Los Angeles, CA 90017-2038
213-250-7414
drinkmarquis.com
Organic energy drinks
President/Owner: Danny Huang
CEO: Christopher Lai
Number of Brands: 1
Number of Products: 3
Type of Packaging: Consumer
Brands:
MARQUIS

7951 **Marroquin Organic Intl.**
303 Potero St
Suite 18
Santa Cruz, CA 95060
831-423-3442
Fax: 831-423-3432 info@marroquin-organics.com
www.marroquin-organics.com
Organic and non-GMO ingredients
President: Grace Marroquin
Vice President: Mark Nelson
Organic Ingredient Specialist: Helen Hudson
Contact: Ciaran Cooney
ccooney@paypal.com
Estimated Sales: $4-5 Million
Number Employees: 5-9

7952 **Mars Inc.**
6885 Elm St.
McLean, VA 22101
703-821-4900
www.mars.com
Pet products, chocolate, chewing gum, beverages, food and health products.
CEO: Grant Reid
CFO: Claus Aagaard
Vice President/General Counsel: Stefanie Straub
President, Innovation: Jean-Christophe Flatin
Global President, Mars Food: Fiona Dawson
Mars Wrigley: Andrew Clarke
Year Founded: 1911
Estimated Sales: $35 Billion
Number Employees: 100,000
Number of Brands: 74
Type of Packaging: Consumer, Bulk
Brands:
API
AQUARIAN
Banfield
BluePearl
Cesar
DREAMIES
Eukanuba
IAMS
NUTRO
PEDIGREE
Pet Partners
Royal Canin
SHEBA
TEMPTATIONS
WALTHAM
WHISKAS
WHISTLE
WISDOM PANEL
M&M's
Wrigley's
SNICKERS
TWIX
Skittles
DOVE
3 MUSKETEERS
5 Gum
Altoids
AMERICAN HERITAGE
AMICELLI
BALISTO
Big Red
Bounty
CELEBRATIONS
COMBOS
Doublemint
Eclipse
Ethel M
GALAXY
goodnessKNOWS
Hubba Bubba
Juicy Fruit
Life Savers
Maltesers
MARS
MILKY WAY
Orbit
Extra
Freedent
Starburst
Winterfresh
Wrigley's Spearminti

Abu Siouf
DOLIMO
Ebly
KAN TONG
MASTERFOODS
MIRACOLI
PAMESELLO
RARIS
Royco
SEEDS OF CHANGE
Suzi Wan
Tasty Bite
UNCLE BENS
CocoVia
CocoVia

7953 Marsa Specialty Products

5511 Long Beach Ave
Vernon, CA 90058
323-587-2288
Fax: 323-587-6729 800-628-0500
Dietetic products including syrups and ketchup
President: Helga Hanlein
Secretary/Treasurer: Allen Brown
Sales Director: James Hanelin
Estimated Sales: $1 Million
Number Employees: 10-19
Type of Packaging: Food Service

7954 (HQ)Marsan Foods

106 Thermos Road
Toronto, ON M1L 4W2
Canada
416-755-9262
Fax: 416-755-6790 sean@marsanfoods.com
www.marsanfoods.com
Processor and exporter of single-series frozen entries and bowls, family size entries, control and private label. Processor and exporter of specialty meal components for healthcare settings
President: James Jewett
Director Sales/Marketing: Sean Lippay
Number Employees: 100
Number of Products: 160
Square Footage: 300000
Type of Packaging: Consumer, Food Service, Private Label
Brands:
Balanced Cuisine
Puree Marsan

7955 Marshall Durbin Companies

2830 Commerce Blvd
P.O. Box 100755
Birmingham, AL 35210
Fax: 205-380-3251 800-768-2456
sales@marshalldurbin.com
www.marshalldurbin.com
Chicken eggs, chicken hatchery, raising, slaughtering and processing of chickens, wholesale poultry.
President: Melissa Durbin
Plant Manager: Allen Butler
Year Founded: 1939
Estimated Sales: $121.5 Million
Number Employees: 1,900
Other Locations:
Feed Mill
Haleyville AL
Feed Mill
Waynesboro MS
Hatchery
Moulton AL
Hatchery
Waynesboro MS
Broiler Office
Delmar AL
Processing Plant
Hattiesburg MS
Processing Plant
Jasper AL
Laboratory
Jackson MS
Distribution Center
Tarrant AL

7956 Marshall Ingredients

5740 Limekiln Rd
Wolcott, NY 14590
800-796-9353
cbones@marshallingredients.com
Fruits and vegetables in different forms such as fiber, pellet, whole, diced, sliced, powder, seeds, pomace
National Sales Manager: Casey Koehnlein
Contact: Scott Edwards
sedwards@marshallingredients.com
Type of Packaging: Bulk

7957 Marshall's Biscuit Company

T. Marzetti Company
380 Polaris Parkway, Suite 400
Westerville, OH 43082
251-679-6226
www.sisterschuberts.com
Breads, rolls
Branch Manager: Harris Morrisette
Estimated Sales: $10-20 Million
Number Employees: 50-99
Parent Co: T. Marzetti

7958 Marshallville Packing Co

50 E Market St
Marshallville, OH 44645
330-855-2871
Fax: 330-855-7991 www.marshallville-meats.com
Beef, pork including sausage, luncheon meats, poultry and cheese
President: Frank Tucker
Assistant Manager: John Tucker
Estimated Sales: $3 Million
Number Employees: 20-49
Square Footage: 81000
Type of Packaging: Consumer, Food Service, Bulk

7959 Martens Fresh

1323 Towpath Rd
Port Byron, NY 13140
315-776-8821
Fax: 315-776-8201 www.spudsrus.com
Potatoes
Owner: Timothy Martens
tim@spudsrus.com
Estimated Sales: $5-10 Million
Number Employees: 20-49
Square Footage: 25000
Type of Packaging: Consumer, Food Service, Private Label, Bulk

7960 Martha Olson's Great Foo

PO Box 66.
Sutter Creek, CA 95685-0066
209-234-5935
Fax: 209-223-7071 800-973-3966
www.marthasallnatural.com
All natural baking mixes including pancake, muffin, waffle, bread, cake and scone; also, chocolate sauce
Owner: Martha Olson
CEO: Margaret Brown
Marketing/National Accounts: Roylene Brown
Production Manager: Harvey Archer
Estimated Sales: $2.5-5 Million
Number Employees: 1-4
Brands:
Martha's All Natural
Martha's All Natural Baking Mixes

7961 Martha's Garden

475 Horner Avenue
Toronto, ON M8W 4X7
Canada
416-251-6112
Fax: 416-251-8443 866-773-2887
Fresh onions, cabbage, lettuce, celery, broccoli, cucumbers, carrots, cauliflower, tomatoes, zucchini, eggplant
President: Gus Arrigo, Jr.
Quality Assurance Manager: Jefery Musumi
Sales Manager: Richard Sabourin
Number Employees: 20-49

7962 Martin & Weyrich Winery

P.O.Box 1330
Templeton, CA 93465
805-239-1640
Fax: 805-238-0887 sales@martinweyrich.com
This winery produces a wide selection including Pinot Grigio, Moscato Allegro, Nebbiolo, Nebbiolo Vecchio, Insieme, Zinfandel La Primitiva, Cabernet Etrusco, Vin Santo, in addition to having a fine coffee selection includingcappuccino, espresso, latte and mochas.
Manager: Katie Stemper
Marketing Director: Larry Persinger
Production Manager: Craig Reed
Purchasing Manager: Cynthia Reed
Estimated Sales: $5-10 Million
Number Employees: 20-49
Square Footage: 24

7963 Martin Bauer Group

300 Harmon Meadow Blvd
Suite 510
Sacaucus, NJ 07094
201-659-3100
Fax: 201-659-3180
welcome@martin-bauer-group.us
www.martin-bauer-group.us
Tea and botanical extracts, herbal and fruit infusions, powders, flavors, phytopharmaceutical ingredients and nutritional supplements.
President & CEO: Ennio Ranaboldo
Managing Director: Albert Ferstl
Chief Financial Officer: William Nicholas
Year Founded: 1980
Estimated Sales: $20 Million
Number Employees: 3
Type of Packaging: Consumer
Brands:
Life Savers
Planters

7964 Martin Brothers SeafoodCo

133 Westbank Expy
Westwego, LA 70094-4213
504-341-2251
Fax: 504-341-2251
Frozen crabmeat and gumbo crabs
President: William Martin
Owner: Donna Martin
Estimated Sales: Less Than $500,000
Number Employees: 1-4
Type of Packaging: Consumer, Food Service, Bulk

7965 Martin Coffee Co

1633 Marshall St
Jacksonville, FL 32206-6011
904-355-9661
Fax: 904-355-9673 info@martincoffee.com
www.martincoffee.com
Coffee
President: Ben Johnson
benjohnson@martincoffee.com
VP: Harold Johnson
VP Sales/Marketing: Ben Johnson
Estimated Sales: $15 Million
Number Employees: 5-9
Type of Packaging: Consumer, Food Service, Private Label
Brands:
Martin

7966 Martin Farms

4021 Redman Road
Brockport, NY 14420
585-637-3636
Fax: 585-637-6852 877-838-7369
info@martinfarms.com www.martinfarms.com
Sliced, diced and halved sun-dried tomatoes; available in bags and oil
Owner: Joseph Martin
Contact: David Martin
david@martinfarms.com
Estimated Sales: Less than $500,000
Number Employees: 1-4

7967 Martin Ray Winery

2191 Laguna Rd
Santa Rosa, CA 95401-3705
707-823-2404
Fax: 707-829-6151 tiffany@martinraywinery.com
www.martinraywinery.com
Wines
Owner: Courtney Benham
Director, Sales/Marketing: Tiffany Zolli
Vice President of Sales: Ken Mulligan
info@martinray-winery.com
Estimated Sales: $10-20 Million
Number Employees: 20-49
Square Footage: 360000
Type of Packaging: Consumer
Brands:
Fountain Grove
Martini & Prati

7968 Martin Rosols

45 Grove St
New Britain, CT 06053-4198
860-223-2707
Fax: 860-229-6690 orders@martinrosols.com
www.martinrosolsinc.com
Cold cuts, hot dogs and kielbasa

President: Karen Rosol
karen@martinrosolsinc.com
CEO: Eugene Rosol
Vice President: Sarah Rosol
Estimated Sales: $2 Million
Number Employees: 20-49
Type of Packaging: Consumer, Private Label

7969 Martin Seafood Company
7901 Oceano Avenue, Units 46, 48, 50 &
P.O.Box 220
Jessup, MD 20794
410-799-5822
Fax: 410-799-3545
Frozen breaded seafood products; wholesaler/distributor of raw frozen seafood products; serving the food service market
Owner: Billy Martin
Secretary: Shawn Isaac
Estimated Sales: $3 Million
Number Employees: 20-49
Square Footage: 100000
Type of Packaging: Consumer, Food Service

7970 Martin's Potato Chips
5847 Lincoln Hwy W
PO Box 28
Thomasville, PA 17364
717-792-3565
Fax: 717-792-4906 800-272-4477
info2@martinschips.com
Manufacturer of potato chips, popcorn and distributor of pretzels.
President & CEO: Ken Potter
Director of Sales & Marketing: David Potter
Contact: Derek Bennett
derek.bennett@martinschips.com
Year Founded: 1941
Estimated Sales: $34 Million
Number Employees: 200
Square Footage: 75000
Type of Packaging: Consumer, Food Service, Bulk

7971 Martino's Bakery
335 N Victory Blvd
Burbank, CA 91502-1841
818-842-0715
Fax: 818-842-5111 www.martinosbakery.com
Breads, cakes and related products
Owner: Mario Corradi
response@martinosbakery.com
CEO: Andy Horvatch
Controller: Kathy Prince
Purchasing Agent: Diana Wang
Estimated Sales: Less than $500,000
Number Employees: 10-19

7972 Martins Famous Pastry Shoppe
1000 Potato Roll Ln
Chambersburg, PA 17202-8897
717-263-9580
Fax: 717-263-6687 800-548-1200
info@potatorolls.com www.potatorolls.com
Bread and roll manufacturer in the heart of "Pennsylvania Dutch" country.
President: Jim Martin
Estimated Sales: G
Number Employees: 250-499
Type of Packaging: Consumer, Food Service, Private Label
Brands:
Mr. C'S
Mr. G'S
Nibble With Gibble's

7973 Marubeni America Corp.
375 Lexington Ave.
New York, NY 10017
212-450-0100
Fax: 212-450-0700 www.marubeniamerica.com
Marubeni exports grains, meat, sugar and other foodstuffs to Asia.
President/CEO: Fumiya Kokubu
Year Founded: 1951
Estimated Sales: $273,000
Parent Co: Marubeni Corporation

7974 Maruchan Inc
15800 Laguna Canyon Rd
Irvine, CA 92618
949-789-2300
www.maruchan.com
Asian foods including wonton soup and instant ramen noodles.
President & Chairman: Mutsuhiko Oda
muoda@maruchaninc.com
Year Founded: 1953
Estimated Sales: $33.2 Million
Number Employees: 500-999
Parent Co: Toyo Suisan Kaisha
Type of Packaging: Consumer

7975 Marukai Market
1740 W Artesia Blvd # 114
Gardena, CA 90248-3238
310-660-6300
Fax: 310-660-6301 info@marukai.com
Established in 1965. Manufacturer, importer, and exporter of Japanese food products.
President: Masataka Hattori
Estimated Sales: $41 Million
Number Employees: 100-249
Parent Co: Marukai Corporation
Other Locations:
Marukai Corporation
Honolulu HI

7976 Marukan Vinegar USA Inc.
16203 Vermont Ave
Paramount, CA 90723-5042
562-630-6060
Fax: 562-630-0330 www.marukan-usa.com
Natural rice vinegars
President: John Tanklage
jtanklage@marukan-usa.com
CEO: Junichi Oyama
VP Sales/Marketing: Jon Tanklage
Sales/Marketing: Tom McReynolds
Operations: Tosh Zamoto
Production: Toru Saito
Production: Michitsugu Ogawa
Estimated Sales: $7-10 Million
Number Employees: 20-49
Square Footage: 60000
Parent Co: Marukan Vinegar Co, Ltd
Type of Packaging: Consumer, Food Service, Private Label, Bulk
Brands:
Marukan

7977 Marukome USA Inc.
17132 Pullman Street
Irvine, CA 92614
949-863-0110
Fax: 949-863-9813 www.marukomeusa.com
Miso manufacturer
President: Shigeru Sharasaka
Secretary: Tetsuhiko Iijima
Marketing: (Fred) Teruo Yamanaka
Contact: Toshio Abe
tabe@marukomeusa.com
Number Employees: 17

7978 Marva Maid Dairy
5500 Chestnut Ave
Newport News, VA 23605-2118
757-245-3857
800-768-6243
dlovell@marvamaid.com
Milk and specialty food products, including; milk, buttermilk, egg nog and orange juice
President: David Grogan
Owner: Dennis Bailey
Finance Manager: Jan Pass
Chief Engineer/Vice President: W Gross
Procurement & Plan Supervisor: Peter Natale
Marketing Manager: Scott Garrett
Sales Mgr/Dir of Product Management: Ed Boyd
Human Resources Director: Ruby Jones
Operations Manager: Bruce Matson
Plant Manager: Walter Auman
Purchasing Agent: Andrea Lopez
Number Employees: 100-249
Square Footage: 406728
Parent Co: Maryland & Virginia Milk Producers Coop Assoc, Inc.
Type of Packaging: Consumer
Brands:
Harvest Fresh
Marva Maid
Slendo

7979 Marwood Sales, Inc
6901 Shawnee Mission Pkwy
Overland Park, KS 66202
913-722-1534
Fax: 913-262-9132 800-745-2881
info@marwoodsales.com www.marwoodsales.com
Producer of dairy products such as natural, processed, and imitation cheese.
President: Mark Woodard
Domestic & International Sales: Larry Johnson
Estimated Sales: $8.2 000,000
Number Employees: 11-50
Brands:
Marwood

7980 Marx Brothers Inc
3100 2nd Ave S
Birmingham, AL 35233-3097
205-251-3139
Fax: 205-324-6322 800-633-6376
www.marxbrothersinc.com
Sweetened coconut
President: Edgar Marx
emarx@marxbrothersinc.com
Sales Exec: Edgar B Marx
Estimated Sales: $3 Million
Number Employees: 20-49
Type of Packaging: Consumer, Food Service, Private Label, Bulk

7981 Mary Ann's Baking Co Inc
8371 Carbide Ct
Sacramento, CA 95828-5636
916-681-7444
Fax: 916-681-7470 www.maryannsbaking.com
Danish and pastries
President: George Demas
Manager: Robert Burzinski
bob@maryannsbaking.com
General Manager: Bob Burzinski
Plant Manager: Don Lavelle
Estimated Sales: $10-20 Million
Number Employees: 100-249
Type of Packaging: Consumer

7982 Mary of Puddin Hill
512 N John St
Palestine, TX 75801
903-455-2651
Fax: 903-723-2889 800-545-8889
customerservice@puddinhill.com
www.puddinhill.com
Pecan fruit cakes and chocolate candy.
Owner: Ken Bain
Year Founded: 1839
Estimated Sales: $1.3 Million
Number Employees: 10-50
Type of Packaging: Private Label

7983 Mary's Gone Crackers
100 Kentucky St
Gridley, CA 95948
888-258-1250
info@marysgonecrackers.com
www.marysgonecrackers.com
Organic, gluten-free and vegan crackers, pretzels and cookies
CEO: John Sheptor
Estimated Sales: $6.5 Million
Number Employees: 50-99
Type of Packaging: Consumer
Brands:
MARY'S GONE CRACKERS

7984 MarySue.com
2600 Georgetown Rd
Baltimore, MD 21230
800-662-2639
info@marysue.com www.marysue.com
Manufacturer and importer of gourmet chocolate candy. Founded in 1948
President: William Buppert
VP Production: Mark Berman
Estimated Sales: $10 Million
Number Employees: 5-9
Square Footage: 204000
Type of Packaging: Consumer, Private Label, Bulk

7985 Maryland & Virginia Milk Producers Cooperative
1985 Isaac Newton Square W.
Suite 200
Reston, VA 20190-5094
703-742-6800
Fax: 757-952-2370 info@mdvamilk.com
www.mdvamilk.com
Milk.
President: Dwayne Myers
Director, Milk Marketing: Cooper Troye
tcooper@mdvamilk.com

Year Founded: 1920
Estimated Sales: $1.4 Billion
Type of Packaging: Consumer
Brands:
Marva Maid
Maola

7986 Marzetti
PO Box 29163
Columbus, OH 43229-0163
614-846-2232
Fax: 614-848-8330 tmoje@marzetti.com
www.marzetti.com
Salad dressings
President: Bruce Rosa
CIO: Kevin Moran
EVP: Gary Thompson
Controller: Steve Evans
VP Sales: Tim Tate
SVP Operations: Doug Fell
Year Founded: 1896
Number Employees: 100-249
Parent Co: T. Marzetti Company
Type of Packaging: Consumer, Private Label
Brands:
Marzetti's
Pfeiffer's

7987 Marzetti Foodservice
380 Polaris Parkway
Suite 400
Westerville, OH 43082
515-967-4254
Fax: 515-967-4147 800-247-4194
info@marzetti.com www.marzettifoodservice.com
Noodles, pasta, flatbreads, breads, rolls, dressings, sauces, dips, croutons, and dairy products
President: Carl Stealey
CEO: David Ciesinski
Vice President: Steven Hill
Estimated Sales: $20-50 Million
Number Employees: 100-249
Type of Packaging: Bulk
Brands:
Marzetti
Marzetti Frozen Pasta
Sister Schuberts
New York Bakery
Flatout Flatbread
Cardini's

7988 Marzipan Specialties Inc
1513 Meridian St
Nashville, TN 37207-0861
615-226-4800
Fax: 615-226-4882
Marzipan candy
Owner: Karl Schoenperger
Contact: Merika Schoenenberger
arzipan@isdn.net
Estimated Sales: Below $5 Million
Number Employees: 5-9
Type of Packaging: Consumer

7989 Masala Chai Company
PO Box 8375
Santa Cruz, CA 95061-8375
831-475-8881
Fax: 831-475-5967 masala@masalachaico.com
www.masalachaico.com
Processor and importer of chai teas including bottled and ready-to-drink, Indian spiced, regular, decaf and energy tonics
Co-Owner: Raphael Reuben
Co-Owner: Susan Beardsley
Estimated Sales: $240000
Number Employees: 1-4
Square Footage: 6000
Type of Packaging: Consumer, Food Service, Private Label, Bulk
Brands:
Aphroteasiac Chai
Masala Chai

7990 Masienda
11515 W Pico Blvd
Los Angeles, CA 90064
www.masienda.com
Red, blue and heirloom corn tortillas
Founder & CEO: Jorge Gaviria
VP, Marketing & Brand: Jackie Rangel
Retail Sales Manager: Darien Brown
VP, Operations: Danielle Dahlin
Number of Brands: 1
Number of Products: 3
Type of Packaging: Consumer, Food Service
Brands:
MASIENDA BODEGA

7991 Mason County Fruit Packers Cooperative
409 Wood St
Hart, MI 49420-1351
231-873-7504
Apple juice, applesauce, cherries, flavored juices, frozen fruits, plums and slice apples.
President: Roy Hackert
CEO: Doyle Fenner
Plant Manager: Joe Bates
Estimated Sales: $1 Million
Square Footage: 4000000
Type of Packaging: Consumer, Bulk

7992 Mason Dixie Biscuit Co.
PO Box 26155
Washington, DC 20003
202-880-2315
info@masondixiebiscuits.com
www.masondixiebiscuits.com
Frozen biscuits
CEO: Ayesha Abuelhiga
Executive Chef: Jason Gehring
COO: Ross Perkins
Number of Brands: 1
Number of Products: 4
Type of Packaging: Consumer
Brands:
MASON DIXIE

7993 Mason Jar Cookie Company
2240 W Woolbright Rd
Suite 402
Boynton Beach, FL 33426-6367
Fax: 212-202-6437 855-968-2536
masonjarcookiecompany.com
Cookie, brownie, granola, muffin, pancake, scone and hot cocoa mixes.
VP, Operations: Rachel Scarrett

7994 Massel USA
898 Carol Ct
Carol Stream, IL 60188
704-573-2299
info@massel.com
massel.com
Bouillon and seasonings
National Sales Manager: Marc Migdal
Type of Packaging: Consumer
Brands:
MASSEL

7995 Massimo Zanetti Beverage USA
1370 Progress Rd
Suffolk, VA 23434
888-246-2598
www.mzb-usa.com
Coffee manufacturer
Founder: Massimo Zanetti
Estimated Sales: Less Than $500,000
Number Employees: 1-4
Type of Packaging: Food Service, Private Label
Brands:
KAUAI COFFEE
Chock full o' Nuts
HILLS BROS
HILLS BROS CAPPUCINO
MJB
CHASE & SANBORN COFFEE
Segafredo ZANETTI
BRODIES
SM La San Marco

7996 Mastantuono Winery
2720 Oakview Rd
Templeton, CA 93465-8798
805-238-0676
Fax: 805-238-9257
Wine
Owner: Pasquale Mastantuono
Operations Manager: Pasquale Mastantuono
Estimated Sales: Below $5 Million
Number Employees: 5-9
Brands:
Mastantuono Wines

7997 Master Brew
PO Box 1508
3550 Woodhead Dr
Northbrook, IL 60065
847-564-3600
Fax: 847-564-2317
Coffee and tea
President: Ronald Weber
CEO: Joseph Weber
Estimated Sales: $9 Million
Number Employees: 120

7998 Master Mix
181 W Orangethorpe Avenue
Placentia, CA 92870-6931
714-524-1698
Fax: 714-524-8540
Processor and exporter of powdered mixes including soft serve, shake and yogurt; also, syrups, toppings, water soluable ginseng extract and drink bases
President: Pat Lagraffe
VP: Jim LaGraffe
Estimated Sales: $1-3 Million
Number Employees: 1-4
Square Footage: 20000
Type of Packaging: Consumer, Food Service, Private Label, Bulk
Brands:
Chalet Gourmet
Dairy's Pride
Master Mix

7999 Masters Gallery Foods Inc
328 County Road Pp
Plymouth, WI 53073-4143
920-893-8431
Fax: 920-893-6075 800-236-8431
dmacphee@mastersgalleryfoods.com
www.mastersgalleryfoods.com
Cheese
President and CEO: Jeff Giffin
jgiffin@mastersgalleryfoods.com
CFO: Catherine Schwartz
Executive Vice-President: Jeff Jeff Gentine
Vice President of Retail Sales: Dan MacPhee
Estimated Sales: Less Than $500,000
Number Employees: 5-9

8000 Masterson Co Inc
4023 W National Ave
Milwaukee, WI 53215-1000
414-647-1132
Fax: 414-647-1170 www.mastersoncompany.com
Premium fudge and caramel toppings, fruit toppings, shake bases, fountain syrups, marshmallow creme toppings, ice cream cone dips and coatings.
President: Mike Masterson
CEO: Nancy Albro
nancy.albro@mastersoncompany.com
Year Founded: 1848
Number Employees: 100-249
Type of Packaging: Food Service, Bulk
Brands:
Masterson

8001 Matador Processors
1820 N Council Rd
Blanchard, OK 73010
405-485-2597
Fax: 405-485-2597 800-847-0797
matador@matadorprocessors.com
www.matadorprocessors.com
Frozen foods including chile rellenos (stuffed peppers), stuffed jalapenos and breaded hors d'oeuvres including cheese bites, mushrooms, desserts, etc.; exporter of chile rellenos, stuffed jalapenos and mozzarella sticks
Owner: Betty Wood
CFO: Richard Clark
VP: Ron W Diggs
R&D: Debbie Funderburk
Plant Manager: Debbie Funderburk
Estimated Sales: $3 Million
Number Employees: 50-99
Square Footage: 108000
Type of Packaging: Food Service, Private Label
Brands:
Clif's
Matador

8002 **Matangos Candies**
S 15th & Catherine St
Harrisburg, PA 17101
717-234-0882
www.matangoscandies.com
Candy and other confectionery products
Owner/President: Peter Matangos
Estimated Sales: $100,000
Number Employees: 1-4
Type of Packaging: Consumer
Brands:
Matangoes

8003 **Matanzas Creek Winery**
6097 Bennett Valley Rd
Santa Rosa, CA 95404-8570
707-528-6464
Fax: 707-571-0156 800-500-6464
info@matanzascreek.com
www.matanzascreek.com
Wine
General Manager: Patrick Connelly
Estimated Sales: $7-20 Million
Number Employees: 5-9
Number of Brands: 2
Square Footage: 20
Type of Packaging: Private Label
Brands:
Journey
Matanzas Creek Winery

8004 **MatchaBar**
256 W 15th St
New York, NY 10011
212-627-1058
matchabarnyc.com
Matcha
President & Co-Founder: Max Fortgang
CEO & Co-Founder: Graham Fortgang

8005 **Materne North America**
20 W 22nd St
12th Fl.
New York, NY 10010
212-675-7881
www.gogosqueez.com
Applesauce snacks
President/Owner: Ivan Giraud
CEO: Michel Larroche
CFO: Carole Larson
VP, Quality: Mark Baumgarten
CMO: Helene Caillate
COO: Stephane Jacquet
Plant Manager: Don Tomaszewski
Brands:
GoGo squeeZ

8006 **Mathews Packing**
950 Ramirez Rd
Marysville, CA 95901-9444
530-743-9000
Fax: 530-742-6625
Dried prunes, pitted prunes, rice
Owner: Ed Mathews
VP/Marketing: Mark Mathews
Estimated Sales: $1-$2.5 000,000
Number Employees: 1-4
Type of Packaging: Private Label

8007 **Matilija Water Company**
1026 Santa Barbara Street
Santa Barbara, CA 93101
805-963-7873
Fax: 805-966-9811 www.getpurewater.com
Bottled water; also, wholesaler/distributor of water purification systems; serving the food service market
Sales Manager: Eric Berumen
Estimated Sales: $1-3 Million
Number Employees: 10-19
Type of Packaging: Consumer, Food Service

8008 **Matouk International USA Inc**
3801 N University Dr
#32
Sunrise, FL 33351
954-742-2204
Fax: 954-742-2533
Chutney/relish, full-line condiments, other condiments, other soups, stews, beans, BBQ sauce, ethnic sauces (soy, curry, etc.), herbs.
Manager: Riad Boulos
Estimated Sales: $100,000
Number Employees: 2

8009 **Matrix Health Products**
9316 Wheatlands Road
Santee, CA 92071-5644
619-448-7550
Fax: 619-448-2995 888-736-5609
info@earthsbounty.com www.matrixhealth.com
Manufacturer, importer and exporter of nutritional and herbal supplements including tablets, liquids, powders and capsules-also kosher & organic products. Teas, coffee & vanilla and nonjuice
President: Steven Kravitz
Number Employees: 10-19
Type of Packaging: Consumer, Private Label, Bulk
Brands:
Colloidal Silver
Dhea
Earth's Bounty
Melatonin
Meno-Select
Noni
Oxy-Caps
Oxy-Cleanse
Oxy-Max
Oxy-Mist
Prosta-Forte
Woman's Select

8010 **Matson Fruit Co**
201 N Railroad Ave
Selah, WA 98942
509-697-7100
matsonfruit.com
Processor and exporter of apples and pears.
President & General Manager: Rod Matson
on@matsonfruit.com
Estimated Sales: $25 Million
Number Employees: 100-249
Square Footage: 18000
Type of Packaging: Consumer, Food Service

8011 **Matson Vineyards**
10584 Arapaho Dr
Redding, CA 96003-7638
530-222-2833
lynette@matsonvineyards.com
www.matsonvineyards.com
Wines
Owner/Winemaker: Oscar Matson
Analyst /Marketing Manager: Kdiko Goto
Owner: Roger Matson
Marketing Manager: Lynette Shaw
Estimated Sales: Under $500,000
Number Employees: 1-4

8012 **Matt's Cookies**
482 N Milwaukee Ave
Wheeling, IL 60090-3067
847-537-3888
www.mattscookies.com
Cookies and fig bars
Year Founded: 1979
Number of Brands: 1
Number of Products: 10
Type of Packaging: Consumer
Brands:
MATT'S COOKIES

8013 **Matthew's Bakery**
71 W Broad St
Stamford, CT 06902-3713
203-316-9392
info@matthewsbakery.com
Breads, cakes, pastries, pies and desserts.

8014 **Matthews 1812 House**
250 Kent Road
P.O.Box 15
Cornwall Bridge, CT 06754-0015
860-672-0230
Fax: 860-672-1812 800-662-1812
info@matthews1812house.com
www.matthews1812house.com
All-natural cakes including apple crumb torte, brandied apricot, chocolate raspberry liqueur, chocolate rum, country spice, fruit and nut, fudge brownie torte, lemon rum, cookies, bar cookies, chocolate explosion brownies
President: Deanna Matthews
dm@matthews1812house.com
Corporate Secretary: Blaine Matthews
Manager: Cheryl Cass
Estimated Sales: $1 Million
Number Employees: 10-19
Square Footage: 8000
Type of Packaging: Consumer, Food Service, Private Label
Brands:
Matthews 1812 House

8015 **Matthiesen's Deer & Custom**
3357 252nd St
De Witt, IA 52742-9223
563-659-8409
mikkie@365adventure.com
Meat products including, beef, lamb, venison, pork and mettwurst
President: Sandy Matthiesen
Estimated Sales: $500,000-$1 Million
Number Employees: 5-9
Type of Packaging: Consumer

8016 **Mattingly Foods Of Louisville**
2055 Nelson Miller Pkwy
Louisville, KY 40223-2185
502-253-2000
Fax: 502-253-2020
Prime choice steaks
President: Thomas M Dawson
Number Employees: 50-99
Parent Co: Mattingly Foods
Type of Packaging: Food Service

8017 **Maui Bagel**
200 Dairy Rd
Kahului, HI 96732-2978
808-270-7561
Fax: 808-270-7919 www.mauicounty.gov
Bread, rolls, bagels, donuts, sandwiches
Manager: Jeff Murray
Number Employees: 250-499

8018 **Maui Coffee Roasters Wholesale**
360 Papa Pl # D2
Kahului
Kahului, HI 96732-2464
808-877-7780
Fax: 808-871-2684 800-645-2877
info@hawaiiancoffee.com www.superpages.com
Roasted coffee
President: Nick Matichyn
mauideveloper@gmail.com
CFO: Mike Vaki
Marketing Manager: Cark Musto
VP Sales: Mike Okazaki
Purchasing Manager: Nicky Matichyn
Estimated Sales: $1-2.5 Million
Number Employees: 1-4
Type of Packaging: Private Label, Bulk

8019 **Maui Gold Pineapple Company**
PO Box 880190
Pukalani, HI 96788
808-877-3805
info@pineapplemaui.com
www.pineapplemaui.com
Whole fresh, canned and fresh-cut pineapple; also, pineapple juice and concentrates
President: Darren Strand
CFO: Michael Hotta
Estimated Sales: $78 Million
Number Employees: 1,000
Square Footage: 10000
Type of Packaging: Consumer, Food Service, Private Label, Bulk
Brands:
Hawaiian Gold
King of Hawaii

8020 **Maui Potato Chip Factory**
295 Lalo St
Kahului, HI 96732-2915
808-877-3652
Fax: 808-877-3652
Potato chips
President: Mark Kobayashi
Estimated Sales: $150,000
Number Employees: 1-4
Type of Packaging: Consumer
Brands:
Original Maui Kitch'n Cook'd

8021 **Maui Soda & Ice Works**
918 Lower Main St
Wailuku, HI 96793-2007
808-244-7951
Fax: 808-244-4108 mauisoda.com
Beverages, soda

President: Robyn Taylor
robyn.taylor@mauisoda.com
Chairman: David Nobriga
Number Employees: 50-99

8022 **Maui Wine**
14815 Pillani Hwy
HC 1 Box 953
Kula, HI 96790
808-878-6058
Fax: 808-876-0127 877-878-6058
info@mauiwine.com www.mauiwine.com
Specialty, grape, and pineapple wines
President: Paula Hegele
Winemaker: Mark Beaman
Winery & Vineyard Engineer: Bill Long
Marketing & Branding Manager: Joe Hegele
Sales & Analytics Manager: Henry Hegele
Operations Manager: Ian Baldridge
Cellar Master: Keone Labuanan
Year Founded: 1974
Estimated Sales: $20-50 Million
Number Employees: 32
Type of Packaging: Private Label
Brands:
Maui Blanc
Maui Blush
Maui Brut
Maui Splash
Maui Ulupalakua Red

8023 **Maurice Carrie Winery**
34225 Rancho California Rd
Temecula, CA 92591
951-676-1711
Fax: 951-676-8397 800-716-1711
info@mauricecarriewinery.com
www.mauricecarriewinery.com
Wines
Owner: Budd VanRoekel
Owner: Maurice VanRoekel
Sales: Jana Prais
Accounting Manager: LaDawn Allen
Winemaker: Gus Vizgirda
Type of Packaging: Consumer

8024 **Maurice French Pastries**
4949 W Napoleon Ave
Metairie, LA 70001-2249
504-455-0830
Fax: 504-885-1527 888-285-8261
sales@mauricefrenchpastries.com
www.mauricefrenchpastries.com
Mardi Gras cakes
Owner: John Luc
Estimated Sales: Less Than $500,000
Number Employees: 5-9
Brands:
Maurice French Pastries

8025 **Maverick Brands, LLC**
990 Commercial St.
Palo Alto, CA 94303
424-571-7230
info@cocolibre.com
www.cocolibre.com
Manufacturer of coconut water.
CEO: Candace Crawford
Founder: Mark Shaw
Contact: Frank Hudson
frank@maverickbrands.com
Brands:
Coco Libre

8026 **Mavuno Harvest**
Philadelphia, PA
www.mavunoharvest.com
Organic dried fruit and nuts
Number of Brands: 1
Number of Products: 9
Type of Packaging: Consumer
Brands:
MAVUNO HARVEST

8027 **Maxfield Candy**
1050 S 200 W
Salt Lake City, UT 84101
801-355-5321
Fax: 801-355-5546 800-288-8002
Boxed chocolates, nut logs, cream sticks, holiday novelties, salt water taffy, cordial cherries, mint sandwiches, etc.; exporter of boxed chocolates
President: Taz Murray
Contact: Judy Adams
jadams@maxfieldcandy.com
Estimated Sales: $5-10 Million
Number Employees: 5-9
Square Footage: 424000
Parent Co: Alpine Confections
Type of Packaging: Consumer
Brands:
Maxfield

8028 **(HQ)Maxim's Import Corporation**
2719 NW 24th Street
Miami, FL 33142-7005
915-577-9228
Fax: 91- 57- 921 800-331-6652
info@maximsimports.com maximsimports.com
Processor, importer and exporter of shrimp; processor of packaged fish; exporter of frozen chicken, duck, turkey, pork and beef; wholesaler/distributor of shrimp, pork, beef, poultry, fish, produce and frozen, specialty and healthfoods
President: Luis Chi
CEO: Jeo Chi
Contact: Joe Chi
luis.chi@hotmail.com
Estimated Sales: $4.1 Million
Number Employees: 22
Square Footage: 140000
Type of Packaging: Bulk
Other Locations:
Maxim's Import Corp.
Salvador
Brands:
Airex
Alpromar
Caribe
De La Marca
Fish House
Flodi Pesca
Golden Star
Golfo Mar
Gulf Garden
Inter Ocean
Ocean Pac
Pacific Pride
Pesaca
Stefan Mar

8029 **Maxin Marketing Corporation**
92 Argonaut, Suite #170
Aliso Viejo, CA 92656-5318
949-362-1177
Fax: 949-362-0449
Snack foods
President: Terry Kroll
Estimated Sales: Less than $500,000
Number Employees: 1-4
Number of Brands: 2
Number of Products: 10
Type of Packaging: Consumer, Private Label, Bulk
Brands:
Health Creation Caramel Pretzels
Health Creation Onion Pretzels
Pocket Pretzels

8030 **Maxine's Heavenly**
Los Angeles, CA 90035
info@maxinesheavenly.com
www.maxinesheavenly.com
Gluten-free cookies
Co-Founder & CEO: Robert Petrarca
Marketing: Rachel Carmichael
Sales: Jeff Resnick
Founder & VP, Operations: Tim Miller
Number of Brands: 1
Number of Products: 4
Type of Packaging: Consumer
Brands:
MAXINE'S HEAVENLY

8031 **Maxwell House & Post**
800 Westchester Ave
Rye Brook, NY 10573-1354
914-335-2500
Fax: 914-335-2706
Coffee and breakfast foods
President: Ann Fudge
Estimated Sales: Under $500,000
Number Employees: 1-4
Parent Co: Kraft Foods

8032 **Maxwell's Gourmet Food**
3208 Wellington Ct # L
Raleigh, NC 27615-4121
919-878-4321
Fax: 919-878-4325 800-952-6887
Peanuts, peanut brittle, chocolate dipped peanut brittle, pecans, chocolate-dipped pecans, pecan brittle, chocolate dipped pecan brittle, cashews
Owner: Paxton Kemps
CEO: Don Kempf
CFO: Shelia Kempf
Director Of Marketing: David Chapman
Director of Sales: Amy Kempf
Production Manager: Ana Arrendondo
Estimated Sales: $500,000-$1 Million
Number Employees: 5-9
Brands:
Maxwell's Extraordinary

8033 **Maya Kaimal**
PO Box 700
Rhinebeck, NY 12572
845-876-8200
Fax: 845-876-8212 info@mayakaimal.com
www.mayakaimal.com
Indian meals, snacks and sauces
Founder: Maya Kaimal
CEO: Meena Mansharamani
CFO: Sunil Surana
Co-Founder: Guy Lawson
VP, Marketing: Michael Krishnan
Director of Operations: Elaine Delsol

8034 **Mayacamas Fine Foods**
20590 Palmer Avenue
Suite A
Sonoma, CA 95476
707-291-3024
Fax: 707-938-8350 800-826-9621
info@mayacamasfinefoods.com
www.mayacamasfinefoods.com
Processor and exporter of dehydrated soups, salad dressings, pasta sauces, gravies and seasonings
President: Vicki Webber
VP: Walter Rahrau
Contact: Craig Parrott
craig@mayacamasfinefoods.com
Estimated Sales: $2.4 Million
Number Employees: 1-4
Square Footage: 72000
Type of Packaging: Consumer, Food Service, Private Label

8035 **Mayacamas Vineyards & Winery**
1155 Lokoya Rd
Napa, CA 94558-9566
707-224-4030
Fax: 707-224-3979 www.mayacamas.com
Processor and exporter of wines including cabernet sauvignon, chardonnay, sauvignon blanc and pinot noir
Owner: John Fisher
johnf@mayacamas.com
Marketing Director: Trina Vaught
Estimated Sales: $88000
Number Employees: 10-19
Brands:
Mayacamas Vineyards

8036 **Mayakaimal Fine Indian Foods**
6384 Mill St # 2
Rhinebeck, NY 12572-1497
845-876-8200
Fax: 845-876-8212 info@mayakaimal.com
www.mayakaimal.com
Simmer sauces and spicy ketchup
President/Owner: Maya Kaimal
maya@mayakaimal.com
Sales Manager: Erica Chapman
Number Employees: 5-9

8037 **Mayer Bros**
3300 Transit Rd
Buffalo, NY 14224-2525
716-668-1787
Fax: 716-668-2437 800-696-2928
info@mayerbrothers.com www.mayerbrothers.com
Bottled spring water, apple cider and juices including orange, grapefruit, grape and apple; also, concentrates including fruit punch, orange, grape, iced tea and lemonade
Owner: John Mayer
Controller: Linda Tryka
HR Manager: Deborah Schasel

Estimated Sales: $28 Million
Number Employees: 100-249
Number of Brands: 1
Type of Packaging: Consumer, Food Service, Private Label, Bulk
Brands:
Mayer Bros.

8038 Mayer's Cider Mill
PO Box 347
Webster, NY 14580-347
Fax: 585-671-5269 800-543-0043
Cider, apples and apple pies; also, beer, grape juice and wine-making supplies
Owner: David N Bower
Estimated Sales: Less than $500,000
Number Employees: 10-19
Parent Co: Mayer's Cider Mill
Type of Packaging: Consumer, Bulk

8039 Mayfield Dairy Farms LLC
806 E Madison Ave
Athens, TN 37303-3858
423-745-2151
Fax: 423-745-9118 800-362-9546
www.mayfielddairy.com
Dairy products such as; ice cream, sherbert, cottage cheese, dip, sour cream, milk, whip cream and juices
President: C S Mayfield Jr
Cmo: Robbie Roberts
rroberts@deanfoods.com
Number Employees: 1000-4999
Parent Co: Dean Foods
Type of Packaging: Consumer, Food Service
Other Locations:
Braselton GA

8040 Mayfield Farms and Nursery
257 Highway 307
Athens, TN 37303
423-746-9859
mayfieldfarmandnursery@hotmail.com
Apple products including processed slices, dices, dumplings, fibre powder and juice, strawberries, squash, potatoes, peppers, and pumpkins.
Founder: Jesse Mayfield
Number Employees: 5-9
Type of Packaging: Consumer, Food Service

8041 Mayorga Coffee
15151 Southlawn Ln
Rockville, MD 20850-1385
301-315-8093
Fax: 301-315-8094 877-526-3322
info@mayorgacoffee.com
Coffee
President: Martin Mayorga
martin@mayorgacoffee.com
VP Finance/Administration: Lorena Herrada
VP Sales/Marketing: Jennifer Rogers
Vice President of Operations: Roger Fransen
Estimated Sales: $8.4 Million
Number Employees: 10-19
Square Footage: 24000

8042 Maysville Milling Company
661 Martin Luther King Boulevard
Maysville, NC 41056-7510
606-759-8789
Feed and cornmeal
President: Edward Trott
General Manager: William Lamkin
Estimated Sales: $2 Million
Number Employees: 7
Brands:
Mayco

8043 Maytag Dairy Farms Inc
2282 E 8th St N
Newton, IA 50208-8775
641-792-1133
Fax: 641-792-1567 800-247-2458
www.maytagdairyfarms.com
Cheeses including blue, cheddar, Swiss, edam, brick and cold pack
President: Chase Ashby
chaseashby@maytagblue.com
VP Operations/Production Manager: Jim Stevens
Plant Supervisor: Robert Wrdzinski
Estimated Sales: $4.6 Million
Number Employees: 20-49
Type of Packaging: Consumer

8044 Mayway Corp
1338 Mandela Pkwy
Oakland, CA 94607-2055
510-208-3023
Fax: 510-208-3069 800-262-9929
info@mayway.com www.mayway.com
Herbal health foods
President: Eva Lau
Estimated Sales: Below $5 Million
Number Employees: 20-49

8045 Maywood International Sales
PO Box 9292
Sante Fe, NM 87504
505-982-2700
Fax: 505-982-9780 805-500-5500
Oilseed manufacturer
Sales: Jacques Brazy
Sales: Peter Connick

8046 Mazelle's Cheesecakes Concoctions Creations
9016 Garland Road
Dallas, TX 75218
214-328-9102
Fax: 214-328-5202 sales@mazelles.com
www.mazelles.com
Cheesecakes and cheesecake petit fours vanilla, chocolate decadence, raspberry cassis, chocolate marble, turtle-praline chocolate chip, pumpkin, strawberries nad cream, keylime margarita, amaretto
CEO: Gina Roidopoulos
Estimated Sales: $3-5 Million
Number Employees: 10-19
Type of Packaging: Consumer, Food Scrvice
Brands:
Mazelle's

8047 Mazzetta Company
P.O. Box 1126
Highland Park, IL 60035
847-433-1150
Fax: 847-433-8973 seamazz@mazzetta.com
www.mazzetta.com
Seafood and fish such as orange roughy fillets, whiting fillets, greenshell mussels, raw and cooked shrimp, lobster tails, Chilean sea bass fillets, squid and crab meat.
President: Thomas Mazzetta
Contact: Dominic Benedetto
dominic@mazzetta.com
Estimated Sales: $1-3 Million
Number Employees: 10-19

8048 Mazzocco Vineyards
1400 Lytton Springs Road
Healdsburg, CA 95448
707-433-3399
Fax: 707-431-2369 800-501-8466
vino@mazzocco.com www.mazzocco.com
Wines
President: Thomas Mazzocco
Sales/Marketing Manager: Ned Carton
Contact: Karen Clarke
karen@mazzocco.com
Winemaker, General Manager: Antoine Favero
Estimated Sales: $1-2.5 Million
Number Employees: 5-9

8049 Mc Glaughlin Oil Co
3750 E Livingston Ave
Columbus, OH 43227-2282
614-231-2518
Fax: 614-231-7431 teresa@mcglaughlinoil.com
www.faslube.com
Oils, flavored and pure
Owner: Steve Theodor
steve@faslube.com
Estimated Sales: $5-10 Million
Number Employees: 10-19
Brands:
Petrol

8050 Mc Lure's Honey & MapleProd
46 N Littleton Rd
Littleton, NH 03561-3814
603-444-6246
Fax: 603-444-6659 info@mclures.com
Pure honey and maple syrup
Founder: Ralph Gamber
Manager: Gordon Hartford
ghartford@mclures.com
Number Employees: 20-49
Parent Co: Dutch Gold Honey

8051 Mc Steven's Coca Factory Store
5600 NE 88th St
Vancouver, WA 98665-0971
360-944-5788
Fax: 360-944-1302 800-547-2803
sales@mcstevens.com
Beverage mixes including white chocolate, regular and sugar-free cocoa, lemonade, cappuccino, chai, and apple cider; exporter of cocoa mixes
Owner: Brent Houston
brent@mcstevens.com
VP Marketing: Dave Demsky
VP Operations: Brent Huston
Estimated Sales: $500,000-$1 Million
Number Employees: 20-49
Type of Packaging: Consumer, Food Service, Private Label, Bulk

8052 (HQ)McAnally Enterprises
32710 Reservoir Rd
Lakeview, CA 92567
951-928-1935
Fax: 951-928-1947 800-726-2002
Processor and exporter of cartoned, frozen and liquid eggs and egg products
President: Carlton Lofgren
Rep. (S.W.): Glenn Lemley
Vice President: Don Brown
Marketing Director: John Klien
Operations Manager: Tom McAnally
Number Employees: 100-249
Square Footage: 80000
Type of Packaging: Food Service
Other Locations:
McAnally Enterprises
Phoenix AZ

8053 McArthur Dairy LLC
6851 NE 2nd Ave.
Miami, FL 33401-7724
561-659-4811
Fax: 561-659-1763 www.mcarthurdairy.com
Dairy products including buttermilk, regular, chocolate, low-fat and skim milk.
Director/CEO, Dean Foods: Ralph Scozzafava
Executive VP/CFO, Dean Foods: Jody Macedonio
Year Founded: 1929
Estimated Sales: $150-199 Million
Number Employees: 100-249
Parent Co: Dean Foods Company
Type of Packaging: Consumer, Food Service, Private Label, Bulk

8054 (HQ)McCain Foods Ltd.
439 King St W
5th Floor
Toronto, ON M5V 1K4
Canada
416-955-1700
www.mccain.com
Frozen french fries, potato products, appetizers, pizzas, pizza products, and desserts
President/CEO: Max Koeune
Chief Financial Officer: Pierre Danet
Chief Human Resources Officer: Alison DeMille
Chief Research & Development Officer: David Stewart
Chief Legal Officer: David Chad Hutchison
Chief Agricultre Officer: Han Van Den Hoek
Chief Growth Officer: Mauro Pennella
Year Founded: 1957
Estimated Sales: $6.8 Billion
Number Employees: 19,000
Type of Packaging: Consumer, Food Service
Other Locations:
Corporate Executive Headquarters
Toronto, Ontario, Canada

8055 McCain Foods USA Inc.
One Tower Ln.
11th Floor
Oakbrook Terace, IL 60181
800-938-7799
communications.usa@mccain.com
www.mccainusafoodservice.com
Frozen potato products including French fries, slices, dices, formed and private label brands. Also manufacturer of breaded and battered appetizers
Regional President, The Americas: Paolo Picchi
Year Founded: 1952
Estimated Sales: $632 Million
Number Employees: 3,800
Number of Brands: 6
Square Footage: 100000
Parent Co: McCain Foods Limited

Type of Packaging: Private Label
Other Locations:
Othello WA
Burley ID
Rice Lake WI
Plover WI
Appleton WI
Fort Atkinson WI
Easton ME
Grand Island NE
Lisle IL
Lodi NJ
Colton CA
Brands:
Anchor
Brew City
Harvest Splendor
McCain
Moore's
Ore-Ida

8056 **McCain Produce Inc.**
8734 Main Street
Florenceville-Bristol, NB E7L 3G6
Canada
506-392-3036
www.mccainpotatoes.ca
Potato grower and processor
Parent Co: McCain Foods Ltd.
Type of Packaging: Consumer, Food Service

8057 **(HQ)McCleskey Mills**
197 Rhodes Street
PO Box 98
Smithville, GA 31787-0098
229-846-2003
Fax: 229-846-4805 mmi@mccleskeymills.com
www.mccleskeymills.com
Manufacturer and exporter of shelled peanuts, seed peanuts, and peanut hulls
President: Keith Chandler
Chairman & CEO: Jerry Chandler
Vice President & CFO: Billy Marshall
VP, MIS: Cleve McRee
Accounting Manager & Quality Assurance: Robert Hamlin
Executive Vice President Sales: Joe West
Contact: Tyler Carlisle
tcarlisle@mccleskeymills.com
Plant Manager: James Champion
Estimated Sales: $2 Million
Number Employees: 9
Square Footage: 72000
Type of Packaging: Consumer, Bulk

8058 **McClure's Pickles LLC**
8201 Saint Aubin St
Detroit, MI 48211-1330
USA
248-837-9323
Fax: 866-796-9679
picklehelp@mcclurespickles.com
www.mcclurespickles.com
Pickles, chips, chutney, relish
Owner: Bob McClure
Co-Owner: Joe McClure
Contact: Mike Daronco
mike@mcclurespickles.com

8059 **McConnell's Fine Ice Cream**
835 E Canon Perdido St
Santa Barbara, CA 93103
805-963-8813
Fax: 805-965-3764 info@mcconnells.com
mcconnells.com
Manufacturer and exporter of ice cream
Owner: Jimmy Young
Contact: Mike Vierra
mvierra@mcconnells.com
Year Founded: 1949
Estimated Sales: Below $5 Million
Number Employees: 5-9
Type of Packaging: Consumer, Food Service

8060 **McConnell's Fine Ice Creams**
The Old Dairy
835 East Canon Perdido St
Santa Barbara, CA 93103
805-963-8813
info@mcconnells.com
mcconnells.com
Ice cream

President: Charley Price
cprice@mcconnells.com
Owner: Michael Palmer
Owner: Eva Ein
Year Founded: 1949

8061 **McCormick & Company**
24 Schilling Rd
Hunt Valley, MD 21031
410-527-6189
www.mccormickcorporation.com
Dessert products, honey, flavors and sauces.
Chairman/President/CEO: Lawrence Kurzius
lawrence_kurzius@mccormick.com
CAO: Malcolm Swift
Executive VP/CFO: Mike Smith
VP/General Counsel: Jeffrey Schwartz
Year Founded: 1889
Estimated Sales: $5.3 Billion
Number Employees: 12,400
Number of Brands: 32
Type of Packaging: Consumer, Food Service, Private Label, Bulk
Brands:
Aeroplane
Billy Bee
Brand Aromatics
Cattlemen's BBQ Sauce
Club House
Drogheria & Alimentari
Ducros
El Guapo
Frank's RedHot
French's
Giotti
Gourmet Garden
Kamis
Kitchen Basics
Kohinoor
Lawry's
Margao
McCormick
Old Bay
Schwartz
Silvo
Simply Asia
Stubb's
Thai Kitchen
Vahine
Wuhan Asia-Pacific Condiments
Zatarain's

8062 **McCormick Distilling Co**
1 McCormick Ln
Weston, MO 64098-9558
816-640-2276
Fax: 816-640-3082 888-640-3082
www.mccormickdistilling.com
Distiller of vodkas, tequilas, whiskey, and irish creams
President: Mick Harris
CFO: Chris Fernandez
cfernandez@mccormickdistillingco.com
VP Marketing: Patrick Fee
VP Sales: Shawn Scott
Estimated Sales: $20-50 Million
Number Employees: 100-249
Type of Packaging: Consumer, Private Label
Brands:
Tequila Rose
Broker's Gin
360 Vodka
Hussong's Tequila
Platte Valley Corn Whiskey
Triple Crown Whiskey
Tarantula
Keke
Five Farms Irish Cream
McCormick
Viaka
Pancho Villa
Montego Bay Rum
Ron Rio
Prince Alexis Vodka

8063 **McCoy Matt Frontier International**
362 Capistrano Avenue
Pismo Beach, CA 93449-1907
805-773-2994
Fax: 805-773-0378
President: Mat McCoy
Estimated Sales: Under $500,000
Number Employees: 1-4

8064 **McCrea's Candies**
202 Neponset Valley Pkwy
Hyde Park, MA 02136
617-276-3388
Fax: 617-276-3380 www.mccreascandies.com
Caramels
Founder: Jason McCrea
Marketing & Product Development: Kate McCrea
Operations: Jim LaFond-Lewis

8065 **McDaniel Fruit**
965 E Mission Rd
Fallbrook, CA 92028
760-728-8438
Fax: 760-728-4898 www.mcdanielavocado.com
Processor, importer and exporter of avocados
Owner: Kay Ahrend
kay@mcdanielavocado.com
VP Sales/Marketing: Rankin McDaniel
General Sales Manager: Laurie Johnson
Secretary: Larry McDaniel
Estimated Sales: $9.3 Million
Number Employees: 20-49
Square Footage: 40000
Type of Packaging: Consumer, Food Service, Private Label, Bulk
Brands:
Linda-Vista

8066 **McDowell Valley Vineyards & Cellars**
PO Box 449
Hopland, CA 95449-0449
707-744-1774
Fax: 707-744-1826
Wine
Owner, Winemaker: Bill Crawford
CEO: Gary Leonard
Sales Director: Bernadette Byrne
Estimated Sales: $1-2.5 Million
Number Employees: 5-9
Brands:
McDowell

8067 **McDuffies Bakery**
9920 Main St
PO Box 427
Clarence, NY 14031-2043
716-759-8510
Fax: 716-759-6082 800-875-1598
info@mcduffies.com www.mcduffies.com
Shortbread cookies and biscotti
President: Dave Thomas
VP: Brian Thomas
Operations: Duston Peace
Estimated Sales: $2 Million
Number Employees: 20
Square Footage: 40000
Type of Packaging: Food Service, Private Label

8068 **McEvoy Ranch**
5935 Red Hill Rd
PO Box 341
Petaluma, CA 94952-9437
707-778-2307
Fax: 707-778-0128 866-617-6779
www.mcevoyranch.com
Extra virgin olive oil, tapenades, bruschettas, vinegars, jams & spreads, olives, wine
Owner, Chairman, CEO: Nion McEvoy
President: Samantha Dorsey
CFO: Dana Breaux
Winemaker: Byron Kosuge
Consulting Winemaker & Agronomist: Maurizio Castelli
Marketing Director: Christina Cavallaro
Orchard Manager: Shari DeJoseph
Farming Manager: Ria D'Aversa
Culinary Director: Jacquelyn Buchanan
Estimated Sales: $20-50 Million
Number Employees: 20-49

8069 **McFarland Foods**
PO Box 460
Riverton, UT 84065-0460
801-254-5009
Fax: 801-254-0432 800-441-9596
info@dsi1968.com
Chicken and turkey products
President: Stephen Mcfarland
CFO: Barbara McFarland
Quality Control: Justin McFarland
Sales Director: Thomas Mathias

Number Employees: 20-49
Number of Brands: 1
Number of Products: 25
Square Footage: 48000
Type of Packaging: Consumer, Food Service, Private Label, Bulk

8070 **McGraw Seafood**
3113 Main St
Tracadie Sheila, NB E1X 1G5
Canada
506-395-3374
Fax: 506-395-2821
Fresh and frozen crab, scallops, cod, smelt, mackerel, herring and lobster
General Manager: Paul Boudreau
Number Employees: 100-249
Type of Packaging: Consumer, Food Service, Private Label, Bulk
Brands:
Mc Graw

8071 **McHenry Vineyard**
330 11th Street
Davis, CA 95616
530-756-3202
Fax: 530-756-3202 lmchenry@dcn.org
Wines
Operations Manager: Henry McHenry
Vineyard Manager: Linda McHenry
Estimated Sales: $45,000
Number Employees: 2
Type of Packaging: Private Label

8072 **McIlhenny Company**
Hwy. 329
Avery Island, LA 70513
800-634-9599
www.tabasco.com
Pepper sauces.
President/CEO: Harold Osborn
Year Founded: 1868
Estimated Sales: $1 Billion
Number Employees: 200
Type of Packaging: Food Service, Bulk
Brands:
TABASCO

8073 **McIntosh's Ohio Valley Wines**
2033 Bethel New Hope Rd
Bethel, OH 45106-9691
937-379-1159
Fax: 973-379-1962
Wine
President: Edward Covert
Estimated Sales: $1-2.5 000,000
Number Employees: 1-4

8074 **McJak Candy Company LLC**
1087 Branch Road
Medina, OH 44256
330-722-3531
Fax: 330-723-4793 800-424-2942
ljohns@mcjakcandy.com www.mcjakcandy.com
Produces fudge and lollipops
President: Larry Johns
Contact: W David
dsmith@mcjakcandy.com
Estimated Sales: $3-5 Million
Number Employees: 10-19
Number of Products: 20
Type of Packaging: Consumer, Private Label, Bulk

8075 **McKaskle Family Farm**
PO Box 10
Braggadocio, MO 63826
573-752-5001
info@mckasklefamilyfarm.com
www.mckasklefamilyfarm.com
Organic rice and popcorn.
Owner: Steve McKaskle
Owner: Kaye McKaskle
Brands:
Braggadocio
Texas Best
Hard Bargain

8076 **McKee Foods Corp.**
10260 McKee Rd.
PO Box 750
Collegedale, TN 37315
423-238-7111
Fax: 423-238-7127 800-522-4499
www.mckeefoods.com
Cookies, crackers, snack and granola bars, snack cakes and cereal.
President/CEO: Michael McKee
mike_mckee@mckee.com
CFO: Andrew Lang
Chairman/Chief Administrative Officer: R. Ellsworth McKee
Corp. Communications/Public Relations: Mike Gloekler
Year Founded: 1934
Estimated Sales: $1 Billion
Number Employees: 5,800
Number of Brands: 4
Type of Packaging: Consumer, Food Service, Private Label
Other Locations:
McKee Foods
Gentry AR
Stuarts Draft VA
Kingman AZ
Chattanooga TN
Brands:
Fieldstone Bakery
Drake's
Little Debbie
Sunbelt

8077 **McKee Foods Corp.**
10260 McKee Road
Collegedale, TN 37315
800-522-4499
www.mckeefoods.com
Snack foods and desserts
President: Mike McKee
Year Founded: 1934
Number Employees: 6,300
Number of Brands: 5
Brands:
DRAKE'S
FIELDSTONE BAKERY
HEARTLAND BRANDS
LITTLE DEBBIE
SUNBELT BAKERY

8078 **McKinlay Vineyards**
7120 NE Earlwood Road
Newberg, OR 97132-7010
503-625-2534
Fax: 503-625-2534
Wines
Contact: Matt Kinne
mkinne@monroecounty.gov
Estimated Sales: $67,000
Number Employees: 1

8079 **McKnight Milling Company**
15 CR 138
Hickory Ridge, AR 72347
870-697-2504
Fax: 870-697-2525 800-287-2383
hessmilling@yahoo.com
www.mcknightmilling.com
Basmati rice
Owner: Deloss Mc Knight
Plant Manager: Walter Pierce
Estimated Sales: $2.5 Million
Number Employees: 1-4
Square Footage: 11520
Type of Packaging: Consumer, Food Service, Private Label, Bulk
Brands:
Cache River

8080 **McLane's Meats**
5710 56 Ave
Wetaskiwin, AB T9A 2Y9
Canada
780-352-4321
Fax: 780-352-8522
www.shop-alberta.com/wetaskiwin/mclanes-meats.htm
Beef and pork sausage and wild game including deer, elk and moose; custom slaughtering services available
Owner: Robin McLane
Number Employees: 10-19
Type of Packaging: Private Label

8081 **McNasby's Seafood Market**
723 2nd Street
Annapolis, MD 21403-3323
410-295-9022
Fax: 410-280-3707
Seafood

8082 **McNeil Nutritionals**
7050 Camp Hill Rd
Fort Washington, PA 19034
215-273-7000
Fax: 908-874-1120 www.splenda.com
Artificial sweetners
President: Peter Luther
Vice President: Sheila Bergey
Contact: Joan Anton
janton@mcnus.jnj.com
Estimated Sales: $10-20 Million
Parent Co: Johnson & Johnson

8083 **McNeil Specialty Products Company**
PO Box 2400
501 George St.
New Brunswick, NJ 08903-2400
732-524-3799
Fax: 732-524-3303
artifical sweetners.such as sucralose.
President: Stephen Fanning
Director Sales (North America): Jim Thornton
Director International Sales: Joseph Zannoni
Contact: Donna Fernandez
donna@sucralose.com
Estimated Sales: $10-25million
Number Employees: 20-49
Parent Co: Johnson & Johnson

8084 **McSteven's**
5600 NE 88th St
Vancouver, WA 98665
360-816-5259
Fax: 360-944-1302 800-838-1056
mcstevens.com
Cocoa, drink mixes and bulk tea.
Type of Packaging: Private Label, Bulk

8085 **Mccadam Cheese Co Inc**
39 Mccadam Ln
Chateaugay, NY 12920-4306
518-497-6644
Fax: 518-497-3297 800-639-4031
info@mccadam.com www.mccadam.coop
A variety of cheeses including aged and waxed cheddars; flavored and reduced fat cheddars; muenster cheese; monterey jack cheese, and extra sharp cheddar cheese in addition to smoked cheeses.
Chairman: Carl Peterson
Chief Executive Officer: Paul Johnston
EVP/Finance & Administration: Margaret Bertolino
SVP/Information Services: Ralph Viscomi
SVP/Economics & Legislative Affairs: Robert Wellington
Director International Sales: Peter Gutierrez
Communications Director: Douglas DiMento
EVP/Chief Operating Officer: Richard Wellington
Plant Manager: Ron Davis
Estimated Sales: $10-20 Million
Number Employees: 100-249
Parent Co: Agri-Mark Inc

8086 **Mccall Farms**
6615 S Irby St
Effingham, SC 29541-3577
843-662-2223
Fax: 843-665-5234 800-277-2012
customerservice@mccallfarms.com
www.margaretholmes.com
Canned garbanzo, green and lima beans, collard greens, kale, spinach, okra, tomatoes, corn, peas, squash, succotash and peanuts
Owner: Jimmy Kremidas
Regional Sales Manager: Woody Swink
Sales Manager: David Wold
Vice President of Sales: Mark Tarkenton
jimmykremidas@gmail.com
Director Engineering: Jerry Gulledge
Estimated Sales: $5-10 Million
Number Employees: 100-249
Type of Packaging: Consumer, Food Service
Brands:
Canned Southern Vegetables
Lord Chesterfield
Margret Holmes

8087 **Mccartney Produce Co**
211 S Fentress St
Paris, TN 38242-4032
731-642-2362
Fax: 731-642-6681 www.mccartneyproduce.com
Fruit and vegetables

Cio/Cto: Mccartney Pierce
mpierce@mccartneyproduce.com
Chief Financial Officer: Debbie Woodard
Director, Sales/General Manager: Raymon Randolph
Estimated Sales: $10-20 000,000
Number Employees: 100-249

8088 Mcclancy Seasonings Co
1 Spice Rd
Fort Mill, SC 29707-9501
803-548-2366
Fax: 803-548-6273 800-843-1968
info@mcclancy.com www.mcclancy.com
Processor and exporter of spices, seasonings and dry food mixes including salad dressing, dips, breadings, batters, gravies, soups, sauces and meat marinades, snack food seasonings, nut and pretzel coatings, whole and ground spices;custom blending available.
President: Reid Wilkerson
Estimated Sales: G
Number Employees: 100-249
Type of Packaging: Consumer, Food Service, Private Label, Bulk
Brands:
Southern Sweetener(c)
Continental Chef(c)
Spice Trader(c)

8089 Mccreas Candies
202 Neponset Valley Pkwy
Hyde Park, MA 02136-2410
617-276-3388
Fax: 617-276-3380 www.mccreascandies.com
Manufacturer of candy and caramel.
CEO and Founder: Jason McCrea
Operations Manager: Jim LaFond-Lewis
Number Employees: 5-9

8090 (HQ)Mccullagh Coffee Roasters
245 Swan St
Buffalo, NY 14204
800-753-3473
sales@mccullaghcoffee.com
www.mccullaghcoffee.com
Processor, importer and exporter of coffee, tea, non-dairy creamer and hot chocolate
President: Warren Emblidge
VP of Sales and Marketing: Paul Zanghi
Estimated Sales: $9 Million
Number Employees: 50-99
Brands:
Alterra Coffee Roasters
Bigelow
Ecoverde Coffee
Folgers
Harney & Sons
illy
Lavazza
Lipton
McCullagh Coffee Roasters
Mighty Leaf Tea
Nespresso
Seattle's Best Coffee
Starbucks

8091 Mccutcheon Apple Products
13 S Wisner St
P.O. Box 243
Frederick, MD 21701-5625
301-662-3261
Fax: 301-663-6217 800-888-7537
www.mccutcheons.com
Products include apple juice, apple cider, fruit butters, preserves, jellies, juice sweetened fruit spreads, salad dressings, relishes, hot sauces and more.
President: Robert J Mc Cutcheon
VP Sales: Vanessa Smith
Estimated Sales: $10-20 Million
Number Employees: 20-49
Square Footage: 189000
Type of Packaging: Consumer, Private Label
Brands:
McCutcheons

8092 Mcfadden Farm
16000 Powerhouse Rd
Potter Valley, CA 95469-8771
707-743-1122
Fax: 707-743-1126 800-544-8230
mcfaddenfarm@pacific.net
www.mcfaddenfarm.com
Processor and exporter of organic herbs including garlic braids and wild rice
Owner: Eugene Mc Fadden
mcfaddenfarm@pacific.net
Estimated Sales: $1.5 Million
Number Employees: 20-49
Square Footage: 4000
Type of Packaging: Consumer, Food Service, Bulk

8093 Mcfarling Foods Inc
333 W 14th St
Indianapolis, IN 46202-2204
317-635-2633
Fax: 317-687-6844 www.mcfarling.com
Wholesaler/distributor of groceries, provisions/meats, frozen foods, produce and seafood; serving the food service market
President: Len Mcfarling
lmcfarling@mcfarling.com
CFO: Frank Chandler
Vice President: Jeffery Hillis
Quality Control Manager: Christopher Davis
Director of Marketing: Sue Sorley
VP Sales & Marketing: Jerry Ward
Procurement Manager: Len McFarling
Estimated Sales: $48 Million
Number Employees: 100-249
Square Footage: 120000

8094 Mcgraths Seafood
1 Elizabeth Pl
Streator, IL 61364-1192
815-672-2654
Fax: 815-672-3474
Frozen food
Owner: Kevin Gaede
Estimated Sales: Less Than $500,000
Number Employees: 1-4

8095 (HQ)Mcgregor Vineyard Winery
5503 Dutch St
Dundee, NY 14837-9746
607-292-3999
Fax: 607-292-6929 800-272-0192
info@mcgregorwinery.com
www.mcgregorwinery.com
Premium vinifera wines
Owner: Dan Jimerson
djimerson@mcgregorwinery.com
Estimated Sales: $5-10 Million
Number Employees: 10-19
Type of Packaging: Consumer, Food Service

8096 Mckenzie Country Classic's
160 Flynn Ave
Burlington, VT 05401-5400
802-864-4585
Fax: 802-651-7335 800-426-6100
Meats and cheeses for the food service industry.
Manager: Greg Rouliie
greg.rouliie@mckenziecountryclassics.com
Number Employees: 10-19
Type of Packaging: Consumer, Food Service

8097 Mclaughlin Seafood
728 Main St
Bangor, ME 04401-6810
207-942-7811
Fax: 207-947-9176 800-222-9107
www.mclaughlinseafood.com
Products include seafood in addition to cookbooks, clothing and kitchenware.
Owner: Reid Mc Laughlin
reid@mclaughlinseafood.com
Estimated Sales: Less Than $500,000
Number Employees: 1-4

8098 Mclemores Abattoir Inc
1912 Center Dr
Vidalia, GA 30474-9317
912-537-4476
Beef and pork
President: Eugene Mc Lemore
Owner: Gene Mc Lemore
Estimated Sales: $1.3 Million
Number Employees: 10-19
Type of Packaging: Consumer

8099 (HQ)Mcredmond Brothers
919 Massman Dr
Nashville, TN 37217-1205
615-361-8997
Fax: 615-361-5645 800-251-5930
Meat and blood meal
President: Linda Mc Redmond
mcredmond@bellsouth.net
VP: Charlie Sheridan
Plant Manager: Josh Rice
Estimated Sales: $570,000
Number Employees: 5-9
Type of Packaging: Consumer, Bulk

8100 Mctavish Shortbread
10234 NE Glisan St
Portland, OR 97220-4061
503-253-9394
Fax: 503-254-6616 800-256-9844
info@McTavishShortBread.com
www.mctavishshortbread.com
Shortbread cookies
Owner: Denise Pratt
denise@mctavishshortbread.com
Co-Owner: Bill Pratt
Estimated Sales: Less than $500,000
Number Employees: 10-19
Type of Packaging: Consumer, Food Service, Bulk
Brands:
McTavish

8101 Me & the Bees Lemonade
PO Box 40098
Austin, TX 78704
www.meandthebees.com
Honey-sweetened lemonade
CEO: Mikaila Ulmer
Number of Brands: 1
Number of Products: 4
Type of Packaging: Consumer
Brands:
ME AND THE BEES LEMONADE

8102 Me At Corral
3695 Thompson Bridge Rd
Gainesville, GA 30506-1515
770-536-9188
Fax: 918-622-8003
Meats
President: Richard Webb
Estimated Sales: $3-5 Million
Number Employees: 5-9

8103 Mead Johnson Nutrition
225 North Canal St.
25th Floor
Chicago, IL 60606
312-466-5800
www.meadjohnson.com
Infant and child nutrition.
President/CEO: Peter Kasper Jakobsen
EVP/CFO: Michel Cup
EVP, Infant & Child Nutrition: Aditya Sehgal
Chief Scientific Officer: Dirk Hondmann
Year Founded: 1905
Estimated Sales: $4 Billion
Number Employees: 7,500
Number of Brands: 8
Parent Co: Reckitt Benckiser
Brands:
Enfamil
Enfagrow
Enfakid
Enfapro A+
Choco Milk
Nutramigen
Lactum
Sustagen

8104 Meadow Brook Dairy Co
2365 Buffalo Rd
Erie, PA 16510-1459
814-899-3191
Fax: 814-464-9152 800-352-4010
www.meadowbrookdairy.com
Milk including whole, skim, 1% and 2%
CAO: Myrna Heise
myrna_heise@deanfoods.com
Marketing Director: Marty Schwartz
VP Sales/Marketing: Joseph Martin
Plant Manager: Rhett Flanders
Number Employees: 100-249
Parent Co: Dean Foods Company
Type of Packaging: Consumer, Food Service
Brands:
Flavortight
Milk Chugs
Swiss Premium Drinks

8105 **(HQ)Meadow Gold**
www.meadowgold.com
Dairy products including milk, sour cream, cottage cheese, cream cheese, yogurt, butter solid & quarters, flavored ice cream, flavored sherbert and fruit drinks.
Year Founded: 1901
Estimated Sales: $62.8 Million
Number Employees: 100-249
Parent Co: Dean Foods
Type of Packaging: Consumer, Food Service, Private Label, Bulk
Brands:
Meadow Gold
Private Labels
Tampico
Viva

8106 **Meadowbrook Farm**
2338 Hermany Avenue
Bronx, NY 10473-1198
718-828-6400
Fax: 718-828-8110
Dairy products
Manager: Phil Carlson
Contact: Bill Schwartz
mbrkfarms@aol.com
Estimated Sales: $2.5-5 000,000
Number Employees: 50-99
Brands:
Meadowbrook

8107 **(HQ)Meadowbrook Meat Company**
2641 Meadowbrook Rd.
Rocky Mount, NC 27801
252-985-7200
Fax: 252-985-7247 www.mbmfoodservice.com
Manufacturer & distributor of frozen foods
Chairman, President & CEO: Jerry Wordsworth
CFO: Jeffrey Kowalk
Exective Vice President & COO: Jim Sabiston
Business Development Manager: Kristine Newton
Director of Quality Assurance: Samuel Richardson
Contact: Mike Amodeo
mamodeo@mbmfoodservice.com
Executive Director of Operations: Andy Blanton
Distribution Manager: Earl Smith
Director of Purchasing: Mitch Brantley
Number Employees: 3,000
Square Footage: 800000
Type of Packaging: Consumer, Food Service
Other Locations:
MBM Corp.
Fort Worth TX

8108 **Meadows Country Products**
811 Scotch Valley Road
Hollidaysburg, PA 16648-9693
814-693-9714
Fax: 814-693-4625 888-499-1001
Refrigerated desserts, deli salads
President: James Meadows
Owner: Margie Meadows
Secretary/Treasurer: Margie Meadows
Quality Assurance/Plant Manger: Todd Hill
General Manager: Jon Thayer
Sales Manager: Norm Tucker
Office Manager: Eileen Snyder
Operations Manager: Jeff Meadows
Purchasing Director: Mike Ricker
Estimated Sales: Below $5 Million
Number Employees: 15
Number of Brands: 1
Number of Products: 60
Square Footage: 48000
Type of Packaging: Food Service, Private Label, Bulk
Brands:
Meadows Country Products

8109 **Meadowvale Inc**
109 Beaver St
Yorkville, IL 60560-1797
630-553-0202
Fax: 630-553-0262 800-953-0201
Wlsn75@aol.com
Ice cream, shake and soft serve mixes
President: Steve Steinwart
ssteinwart@meadowvale-inc.com
Sales Executive: Jason Leslie
Plant Manager: Thomas Schuch
Estimated Sales: $3 Million
Number Employees: 10-19
Square Footage: 60000
Type of Packaging: Consumer
Brands:
Dairy Queen

8110 **Meals-In-A-Minute**
19751 E. Mainstreet, R2
Parker, CO 80138
303-601-5992
mealsinaminute.com
Sauces, dips, marinades, rubs, jams, spices

8111 **Meat & Fish Fellas**
5036 N 54th Ave # 7
Suite 7
Glendale, AZ 85301-7509
623-931-6190
Fax: 623-931-2960 www.meatandfishfellas.com
Meat and seafood
Owner: J T Tarbell
Partner: Marty Menter
Partner: Inyol Kim
Estimated Sales: $3-5 Million
Number Employees: 20-49

8112 **Meat & Supply Co**
New York, NY 10009
646-864-0967
info@harryandidas.com
www.harryandidas.com
Sandwich counter and general store carrying locally sourced and in-house prepared goods. Also, catering services available.
Co-Founder: Will Horowitz
Co-Founder: Julie Horowitz
Year Founded: 2015
Estimated Sales: Less than $500,000
Number Employees: 5-10
Type of Packaging: Consumer, Food Service

8113 **Meat Center**
3035 Fm 822
Edna, TX 77957-5033
361-782-3776
Meat packer
Owner: Eli Salinas
Estimated Sales: Less Than $500,000
Number Employees: 1-4
Type of Packaging: Consumer, Bulk

8114 **Meat-O-Mat Corp**
592 Pacific St # B
Suite B
Brooklyn, NY 11217-2077
718-965-7250
Fax: 718-832-1027 mickfat@aol.com
www.meatomat.com
Processor of frozen meats including hamburger, beef and turkey patties.
President/Owner: Ronald Fatato
General Manager: Tony Quaranta
Vice President: Michael Fatato
Estimated Sales: $20-50 Million
Number Employees: 10-19
Number of Brands: 4
Type of Packaging: Consumer, Food Service, Bulk
Brands:
El Sol
Meat-O-Mat
The Big O
Top Kut

8115 **Meatco Sales Ltd.**
5315 54th Street
Mirror, AB T0B 3L0
Canada
403-788-2292
Fax: 403-788-2294 www.meatcosales.com
Fresh and frozen beef, pork, wild game and sausage
Manager: Chris Pfisterer
Manager: Steven Pfisterer
Owner: Herman Pfisterer
Number Employees: 1-4
Type of Packaging: Consumer, Food Service, Private Label, Bulk

8116 **Meatcrafters**
3900 Ironwood Pl
Landover, MD 20785
240-764-7653
Fax: 240-764-7653 info@meatcrafters.com
www.meatcrafters.com
Sausages and salamis
Marketing: Debra Moser
Sales: Mitchell Berliner
Production: Stanley Feder

8117 **Meating Place**
185 Grant St
Buffalo, NY 14213-1607
716-885-3623
Fax: 716-885-6328 www.meatingplace.com
Meat products including pork sausage and beef patties
President: Mark Lefens
Chairman: Jim Franklin
Vice President of Information Systems: Annica Burns
Information Technology Manager: Benjamin Isidore
Director of Marketing: Laurie Hachmeister
Sales Support Manager: Dawn Batchelder
Office Manager: Robert Wilborn
Production Manager: Shirleen Kajiwara
Estimated Sales: $4 Million
Number Employees: 20-49
Type of Packaging: Consumer, Food Service

8118 **Meatland Packers**
3326 15th Avenue SW
Medicine Hat, AB T1B 3W5
Canada
403-528-4321
Fax: 403-529-5986
Fresh and frozen beef, pork, lamb and wild game including elk, moose and deer
President: Frank Noel
Number Employees: 3
Type of Packaging: Consumer, Food Service, Private Label, Bulk

8119 **Medallion InternationalInc**
233 W Parkway
Pompton Plains, NJ 07444-1028
973-616-3401
Fax: 973-616-3405 www.medallionint.com
Flavors: natural and artificial; edible and essential oils
President: Michael Boudjouk
VP Business Development: William Lulum
Director Sales/Marketing: Paula Boudjouk
Plant Manager: Gwen Kenyon
Estimated Sales: $2 Million
Number Employees: 10-19
Type of Packaging: Consumer, Food Service, Private Label, Bulk

8120 **Medeiros Farms**
4365 Papalina Rd
Kalaheo, HI 96741
808-332-8211
Fax: 808-332-8211
Grass fed, free range beef.
President: Bernard M Medeiros
VP/Secretary: Natalie Silve
Estimated Sales: $10-20 Million
Number Employees: 5-9
Type of Packaging: Consumer

8121 **Meditalia**
P.O.Box 1393
New York, NY 10113-1393
212-616-3006
Fax: 212-616-3005
Dairy and egg-free jarred sauces
Founder/CEO: Daniel Lubetzky
VP/New Product Development & Marketing: Sasha Hare
VP/Sales: Rami Leshem
VP/Operations: Doris Rivera
Parent Co: PeaceWorks

8122 **Mediterranean Gyro Products**
1102 38th Ave
Long Island City, NY 11101-6041
718-786-3399
Fax: 718-786-8518 yani@mediterraneanpita.com
www.mediterraneanpita.com
Wholesaler/distributor of Greek specialty items; processor of pita bread
President: Vasilios Memmos
Contact: Sophia Maroulis
smaroulis@corfufoods.com
Purchasing Agent: Sophia Maroulis
Estimated Sales: $24 Million
Number Employees: 20-49

8123 **Mediterranean Pita Bakery**
9046 132 Avenue NW
Edmonton, AB T5E 0Y2
Canada
780-476-6666
Pita bread
Manager: Ahmed Hagar
Number Employees: 5-9
Type of Packaging: Consumer, Food Service

8124 **Mediterranean Snack Food Co**
708 Main St
Boonton, NJ 07005-1450
973-402-2644
Healthy, non-GMO and gluten-free snacks such as chips and crackers
President: Vincent James
vincent@mediterraneansnackfoods.com
Vice President: Franck Le Berre
Estimated Sales: Less Than $500,000
Number Employees: 1-4

8125 **Medlee Foods**
319 S Jefferson St
Suite 300
Chicago, IL 60661-5616
312-442-0406
medleefoods.com
Seasoned butter
President & CEO: Alberto Valdes
Number of Brands: 1
Number of Products: 4
Type of Packaging: Consumer
Brands:
MEDLEE

8126 **Medterra CBD**
9801 Research Dr
Irvine, CA 92618
800-971-1288
support@medterracbd.com www.medterracbd.com
CBD gel capsules
CEO: Jay Hartenbach

8127 **Meduri Farms**
P.O. Box 866
Dallas, OR 97338
877-388-8800
Fax: 800-310-4270
customerservice@meduriworlddelights.com
www.meduriworlddelights.com
Dried cherries, blueberries and strawberries; also, infused cherries with raspberry juice
President: Joe Meduri
Sales: Mike Meduri
Year Founded: 1984
Estimated Sales: Less Than $500,000
Number Employees: 5-9
Parent Co: Meduri Farms
Type of Packaging: Food Service, Private Label, Bulk
Brands:
Razzcherries

8128 **Meelunie America**
26105 Orchard Lake Rd Ste 210
Farmington Hills, MI 48334
248-473-2100
Fax: 248-473-2114 www.meelunie.com
Starch products: potatos, corn and wheat
Owner: William Lauer
Contact: Renee Barlow
renee.barlow@meelunie.com
Estimated Sales: $3-5 Million
Number Employees: 1-4

8129 **Mega Pro Intl**
251 W Hilton Dr # 100
St George, UT 84770-2201
435-673-1001
Fax: 435-673-1007 800-541-9469
info@mega-pro.com www.mega-pro.com
Processor, importer and exporter of nutritional supplements including vitamins for weight gain and loss
President: Dave Smith
megapro@mega-pro.com
Estimated Sales: $1.8 Million
Number Employees: 20-49

8130 **MegaFood**
Manchester, NH 03108
800-848-2542
questions@megafood.com www.megafood.com
Dietary supplements
Chief Executive Officer: Robert Craven
Quality Assurance Manager: Dale Bates
Marketing Communications Manager: Jamila Lasante
Customer Exeprience Manager: Amy Keronen
Year Founded: 1973
Estimated Sales: $20-50 Million
Number Employees: 50-99
Type of Packaging: Consumer
Brands:
Daily Foods
Essentials
MegaFood
Nutritional Therapeutix

8131 **Megatoys Inc**
6443 E Slauson Ave
Commerce, CA 90040-3107
323-887-8138
Fax: 323-887-8135 888-999-9168
www.megatoys.info
Toy company
President: Peter Woo
peter@megatoys.com
CEO: Charlie Woo
Finance: Teresa Chun
VP: Dennis Paris
Sales: Jackie Chanemougam
Estimated Sales: Less Than $500,000
Number Employees: 1-4
Brands:
M&M Easter Baskets
Peeps Easter Baskets

8132 **Megpies**
53 7th Ave
4th Fl
Brooklyn, NY 11217-3607
347-218-2971
Fax: 347-338-2559 www.megpies.com
Tarts
Owner: Meghan Ritchie
Year Founded: 2012

8133 **Mehaffies Pies**
3013 Linden Ave
Dayton, OH 45410-3053
937-253-1163
Fax: 937-254-4977 800-289-7437
www.mehaffiespies.com
Cheesecake, fresh and frozen pies
President: Greg Hay
greghay@mehaffiespies.com
Co-Owner: Jim Columbus
Sales: Mark Berry
Estimated Sales: $500,000-$1 Million
Number Employees: 10-19
Square Footage: 16000
Type of Packaging: Consumer, Food Service, Private Label, Bulk

8134 **Mei Shun Tofu Products Company**
523 W 26th St
Chicago, IL 60616-1803
312-842-7000
Fax: 312-791-9429
Canner and exporter of tofu
Owner: Yim Sung
Estimated Sales: Less than $500,000
Number Employees: 5 to 9
Type of Packaging: Consumer, Food Service, Private Label, Bulk

8135 **Meier's Wine Cellars Inc**
6955 Plainfield Rd
Cincinnati, OH 45236-3793
513-891-2900
Fax: 513-891-6370 800-346-2941
www.meierswinecellars.com
Juice, jams, jellies
President: Ralph Belling
r.belling@drinkmeiers.com
CEO: Bob Szabo
Controller: Barbara Boyd
Chairman: Robert Gottesman
Quality Manager: Dan Schuchter
Marketing Director: Lyn Lubin
Retail marketing & PR/ Advertising: Heather Friebus
Operations Manager: Ralph Belling
Bottling Manager: Mike Dooley
Estimated Sales: $5-10 Million
Number Employees: 20-49
Brands:
Breckenridge Farm Sparkling Juices
Meier's
Meier's Sparkling Ju

8136 **Meier's Wine Cellars Inc**
6955 Plainfield Rd
Cincinnati, OH 45236
513-891-2900
Fax: 513-891-6370 800-346-2941
info@meierswinecellars.com
www.meierswinecellars.com
Fruit juices and wine
President: Paul Lux
Quality Manager: Dan Schuchter
Winemaker: Robert Distler
Estimated Sales: $4.1 Million
Number Employees: 20-49
Square Footage: 80000
Type of Packaging: Consumer

8137 **Meijer Inc**
2929 Walker Ave NW
Grand Rapids, MI 49544-9428
616-453-6711
Fax: 616-791-2572 www.meijer.com
Supermarket chain with 190 plus stores, half are in Michigan and the rest are spread across the states of Ohio, Kentucky, Illinois, and Indiana. Has two manufacturing facilities for their products listed below.
Co-Chairman/CEO: Hank Meijer
Co-Chairman: Doug Meijer
Vice Chairman: Paul Boyer
Estimated Sales: Over $1 Billion
Number Employees: 10000+
Square Footage: 400000
Other Locations:
Dairy Manufacturing
Holland MI
Dairy/Meat Manufacturing
Carlinville IL
Brands:
Meijer
Meijer Gold
Meijer Organic
Meijer Natural
Meijer Ecowise
Meijer Elements

8138 **Meister Cheese Company**
1050 E Industrial Dr
Muscoda, WI 53573
608-739-3134
Fax: 608-739-4348 800-634-7837
grandpa@meistercheese.com
www.meistercheese.com
Cheese
President: Scott Meister
Partner: Vicki Thingbold
Sales/Marketing: Dan Meister
Contact: Rt Hardy
rhardy@meistercheese.com
Estimated Sales: $5-10 Million
Number Employees: 20-49
Type of Packaging: Private Label

8139 **(HQ)Mel-O-Cream Donuts Intl**
5456 International Pkwy
Springfield, IL 62711-7086
217-483-7272
Fax: 217-483-7744
Doughnuts and doughnut holes; frozen pre-formed and frozen pre-fried dough.
President/CEO: David Waltrip
CEO: Dave Waltrip
dwaltrip@mel-o-cream.com
CFO: David Drendel
Director, Operations: Dan Alewelt
Estimated Sales: $10-20 Million
Number Employees: 50-99
Number of Brands: 1
Number of Products: 200+
Square Footage: 65000
Type of Packaging: Food Service, Bulk
Brands:
Mel-O-Cream

8140 **Mel-O-Cream Donuts Intl**
5456 International Pkwy
Springfield, IL 62711-7086
217-483-7272
Fax: 217-483-7744 800-500-5414
Donuts

Owner: Robert Stevenson
CEO: Dave Waltrip
dwaltrip@mel-o-cream.com
General Manager: Lois Stevenson
Operations Manager: David Waltrip
Production Manager: Dan Alewelt
Estimated Sales: $1-2.5 Million
Number Employees: 50-99
Parent Co: Mel-O-Cream Donuts International

8141 **Melba's Old School Po Boys**
1525 Elysian Fields Avenue
New Orleans, LA 70117
504-267-7765
eatatmelbas.com
Prepared meals including shrimp & catfish platters, BBQ ribs, red bean, cabbage, baked chicken, bell pepper, roasted beef, rice, pork chops, bourbon chicken teriyaki plates, hamburgers, ham, sausage, turkey, vegetables, chicken or fishfillet platters, corn bread, gumbo, soups, desserts, salads, and prepared snack trays.
Founder/President & CEO: Scott Wolfe Sr.
Year Founded: 2005
Number Employees: 18
Type of Packaging: Consumer, Food Service, Bulk

8142 **Melchers Flavors of America**
5600 W Raymond Street
Indianapolis, IN 46241-4343
513-858-6300
Fax: 513-858-3110 800-235-2867
Food flavorings; including kosher, extracts, syrups and drink mixes
President: Hellmuth Starnitzkey
COO/VP: Wolfgang Boehmer
Purchasing Agent: Claudia Slaughter
Purchasing Manager: Kellie Hall
Estimated Sales: $5-9.9 Million
Number Employees: 20
Type of Packaging: Food Service, Bulk

8143 **Mele-Koi Farms**
787 Alderwood Drive
Newport Beach, CA 92660-7157
949-660-9000
Fax: 949-660-9000
Manufacturer and exporter of powdered tropical drink mixes
Owner: Lloyd L Aubert Jr
Estimated Sales: $400,000
Number Employees: 1 to 4
Number of Brands: 1
Number of Products: 1
Type of Packaging: Consumer
Brands:
Mele-Koi Hawaiian Coconut Snow

8144 **Meleddy Cherry Plant**
1952 Shiloh Rd
Sturgeon Bay, WI 54235
920-743-2858
Frozen red tart cherries
President: Melvin Selvick
VP: Eddy Selvick
Estimated Sales: $5-10 000,000
Number Employees: 20-49

8145 **Meli's Monster Cookies**
Austin, TX 78746
www.meliscookies.com
Cookie mixes
Co-Founder: Melissa Blue
Co-Founder: Melissa Mehall
Number of Brands: 1
Number of Products: 4
Type of Packaging: Consumer

8146 **Melitta USA Inc**
13925 58th St N
Clearwater, FL 33760-3721
727-535-2111
Fax: 727-535-7376 888-635-4880
consumerrelations@melitta.com www.melitta.com
Processor, importer and exporter of coffee; also, coffee machines and filters
President & CEO: Martin Miller
CEO: Marty Miller
mmiller@melitta.com
Senior Product Manager: Kerrie Tobin
Quality Assurance Manager: Mark Kiczalis
Marketing Director: Chris Hillman
VP Sales: Edward Mitchell
National Sales Manager: Thomas Best
Plant Manager: Matthias Bloedorn
Estimated Sales: $27 Million
Number Employees: 100-249
Square Footage: 104000
Type of Packaging: Consumer, Food Service
Brands:
Melitta

8147 **Mellace Family Brands**
6195 El Camino Real
Carlsbad, CA 92009
760-448-1940
Fax: 760-448-1945 866-255-6887
mrunion@mfbrands.com
Functional (antioxidants), kosher, organic/natural, vegetarian, nuts, other snacks, dried fruit, private label.
Marketing: Mike Runion
Contact: Chuck Amoura
camoura@mfbrands.com

8148 **Mellos North End Mfr**
63 N Court St
Fall River, MA 02720-2701
508-673-2320
Fax: 508-675-0893 800-673-2320
info@melloschourico.com
www.melloschourico.com
Processor and exporter of sausage patties, links and pork
Owner: Eduardo Rego
Sales Manager: Diane Rego
Contact: Dan Rego
dan@melloschourico.com
Estimated Sales: $500,000-$1 Million
Number Employees: 1-4
Type of Packaging: Consumer, Food Service, Bulk

8149 **Meluka Honey**
Santa Clarita, CA 91350
salesusa@melukahoney.com
www.melukahoney.com
Australian honey
Brands:
Meluka

8150 **Melville Candy Corp**
70 Finnell Dr # 16
Unit 16
Weymouth, MA 02188-1153
781-331-2005
Fax: 800-466-0516 jmelville8878@aol.com
www.melvillecandycompany.com
Gourmet hard candy lollipops
Owner: Sarah Delory
sarah@melvillecandycompany.com
CFO: Debra Katz
Marketing: Joe Melville
Manufacturing Staff: Liz Mazzilli
Number Employees: 100-249

8151 **Mememe Inc**
1470 Birchmont Road
Toronto, ON M1P 2G1
Canada
416-972-0973
Fax: 416-972-9592
Organic/natural, other baked goods, other condiments, pudding.
Marketing: Marcy Mihalcheon

8152 **Memphis Meats**
Berkeley, CA
founders@memphismeats.com
www.memphismeats.com
Meat products including chicken, beef and duck.
Co-Founder: Uma Valeti
Co-Founder: Nicholas Genovese
Year Founded: 2015

8153 **Mendocino Brewing Co Inc**
1601 Airport Rd
Ukiah, CA 95482-6456
707-463-2627
Fax: 797-744-1910 questions@mendobrew.com
www.mendobrew.com
Beer, stout, ale and lager
President, Chief Executive Officer: Yashpal Singh
yashpal@mendobrew.com
CFO: Jerome Merchant
CEO: Vijay Mallya
Marketing Director: Michael Lovett
Estimated Sales: $4.3 Million
Number Employees: 50-99
Square Footage: 260000
Type of Packaging: Consumer, Food Service
Brands:
Black Hawk
Blackhawk Stout
Blue Heron
Blue Heron Pale Ale
Eye of the Hawk
Eye of the Hawk Select Ale
Peregrine Golden
Peregrine Pale Ale
Red Tail
Red Tail Ale
Springtide Ale
Yuletide Porter

8154 **Mendocino Mustard**
1260 North Main Street
Suite 11
Fort Bragg, CA 95437
707-964-2250
Fax: 707-964-0525 800-964-2270
info@mendocinomustard.com
mendocinomustard.com
Specialty mustards including hot/sweet and spicy seeded with ale. Foods available in fat-free and sodium-free
Founder: Devora Rossman
Production Manager: Kathy Silva
Estimated Sales: $255000
Number Employees: 1-4
Number of Brands: 1
Number of Products: 2
Square Footage: 6400
Type of Packaging: Consumer, Food Service
Brands:
Mendocino
Seeds & Suds

8155 **Menehune Mac**
707 Waiakamilo Rd
Honolulu, HI 96817-4312
808-841-3344
Fax: 808-841-3344 sales@menehunemac.com
www.menehunemac.com
chocolate-covered macadamia nuts. They are known for their Menehune Milk Chocolate.
President: Neal Arakaki
neala@menehunemac.com
Estimated Sales: $5-10,000,000
Number Employees: 20-50

8156 **Menemsha Fish Market**
54 Basin Rd
Chilmark, MA 2535
508-645-2282
Fax: 508-645-9783
menemshafishmarket@yahoo.com
www.menemshafishmarket.net
Fresh and prepared seafood; fish, crabs, scallops and shellfish
Owner: Stanley Larsen
menemshafishmarket@yahoo.com
Estimated Sales: Less Than $500,000
Number Employees: 1-4
Type of Packaging: Consumer, Food Service, Private Label, Bulk
Brands:
Menemsha Bites
Poole's

8157 **Menghini Winery**
1150 Julian Orchards Dr
Julian, CA 92036
760-765-2072
Fax: 760-765-2072
Wines
Owner: Toni Menghini
mmenghini@gmail.com
Estimated Sales: Less Than $500,000
Number Employees: 1-4
Type of Packaging: Private Label
Brands:
Menghini

8158 **Mennel Milling Company**
319 S Vine Street
Fostoria, OH 44830
419-435-8151
Fax: 419-436-5150 800-688-8151
info@mennel.com www.mennel.com
Processor of flour used in cake mixes, cookies, snack crackers, breadings, batters, gravies, soups, ice cream cones, pretzels and oriental noodles.
President: D. Ford Mennel
Controller: Lori Kitchen
Senior Technical Advisor: C J Lin
Vice President of Operations: David Marty
Corp Milling Engineer: Joel Hoffa
Year Founded: 1886
Estimated Sales: Below $5 Million
Number Employees: 100-249
Type of Packaging: Bulk

8159 **Meramec Vineyards**
600 State Route B
St James, MO 65559-1000
573-265-7847
Fax: 573-265-3453 877-216-9463
www.meramecvineyards.com
Natural grape juice
President: P Meagher
Manager: Phyllis Meagher
Estimated Sales: $3-5 Million
Number Employees: 5-9
Type of Packaging: Consumer, Food Service
Brands:
Meramec

8160 **Merb's Candies**
4000 S Grand Blvd
St Louis, MO 63118-3466
314-832-7117
Fax: 314-832-0146
Candy including chocolates and novelties
President: Teri Bearden
tbearden@merbscandy.com
Estimated Sales: $500,000-$1 Million
Number Employees: 10-19
Type of Packaging: Consumer

8161 **Mercado Latino**
245 Baldwin Park Blvd
City Of Industry, CA 91746-1404
626-333-6862
800-432-7266
www.mercadolatinoinc.com
Manufacturer, importer and distributor of authentic Latin products with nine distribution centers in the western United States.
Estimated Sales: Less Than $500,000
Number Employees: 1-4
Brands:
Brillasol
Faraon
Milpas
Ola Blanca
Payaso
Siesta
Sol-Mex
Sun Sun

8162 **Mercer Foods**
1836 Lapham Dr
Modesto, CA 95354
209-529-0150
Fax: 209-526-3406 www.mercerfoods.com
Freeze-dried fruits and vegetables
CEO: David Noland
Brands:
Natural Heaven

8163 **Mercer Processing**
1836 Lapham Drive
Modesto, CA 95354
209-529-0150
Fax: 209-526-3406 sales@mercerfoods.com
www.mercerfoods.com
Freeze dried fruits, vegetables, and dairy products.
CEO: David Noland
Quality Manager: Cynthia Apodaca
Contact: Hannah E Silva
hsilva@mercerfoods.com
Estimated Sales: $12.9 Million
Number Employees: 75
Number of Brands: 3
Square Footage: 160000
Type of Packaging: Private Label
Brands:
AquaFruit
Mercer
Truth in Snacks

8164 **Mercer's Dairy**
13584 NYS Rt 12
Boonville, NY 13309
315-942-2611
Fax: 315-942-5315 866-637-2377
mercersdairy@gmail.com www.mercersdairy.com
Gluten-free, kosher, organic/natural, milk, yogurt, ice cream/sorbet, co-packing, private label.
Marketing: Dalton Givens

8165 **Merci Spring Water**
11570 Rock Island Ct
Maryland Heights, MO 63043-3522
314-872-9323
Fax: 314-872-9544
Processor and exporter of water including spring, purified and distilled; also, concentrated juices
President: Don Schneeberger
Estimated Sales: Under $500,000
Number Employees: 1-4
Square Footage: 90000

8166 **Mercon Coffee Group.**
2333 Ponce de Leon Blvd.
Suite 600, Coral Gables
Miami, FL 33134
786-254-2300
Fax: 201-418-0306 traders@merconcoffee.com
www.merconcoffee.com
Green coffee
Founder: Duilio Baltodano
President: Andreas Enderlin
CFO/Treasurer: Salvador Rodriguez
Sales Manager: Richard Etkin
Number Employees: 20-49
Brands:
Mercon

8167 **Meredith & Meredith**
2343 Farm Creek Rd
Toddville, MD 21672
410-397-8151
Fax: 410-397-8130
Frozen soft shell crabs, refrigerated blue crabmeat, oysters
President: Jennings Tolley
VP: Morgan Tolley
Estimated Sales: Below $5 000,000
Number Employees: 20-49
Type of Packaging: Consumer
Brands:
Meredith's

8168 **Meredyth Vineyard**
RR 628
Route 626
Middleburg, VA 20118
540-687-6277
Fax: 540-687-6288
Wine
Partner: Archie Smith

8169 **Meridian Beverage Company**
2255 Button Gwinnett Dr
Atlanta, GA 30340
770-248-9315
Fax: 770-263-6960 800-728-1481
Naturally flavored noncarbonated spring water beverages
President: Steve Lovinger
Convenience Store Manager: Ralph Grasso
Sales Manager: Marilyn Hunter
Number Employees: 20-49

8170 **Meridian Foods New Inc**
201 W Babb Rd
Eaton, IN 47338
765-396-3344
Fax: 765-396-3430 info@edenfoods.com
www.edenfoods.com
Processor and canner of organic dry beans.
Manager: Terry Evans
Quality Assurance Manager: Katie Henry
Estimated Sales: $10-20 Million
Number Employees: 20-49
Number of Brands: 1
Square Footage: 45000
Parent Co: Eden Foods
Type of Packaging: Private Label
Brands:
Eden

8171 **Meridian Trading Co.**
1136 Pearl Street
Suite 201
Boulder, CO 80302
303-442-8683
Fax: 303-379-5199 info@meridiantrading.com
www.meridiantrading.com
Herbal products, spices, organics
President: David Black
Estimated Sales: $5 Million
Number Employees: 1

8172 **Meridian Vineyards**
555 Gateway Dr.
P.O. Box 4500
Napa, CA 94558
707-259-4500
Fax: 707-259-4542 800-226-7133
inquiries@meridianvineyards.com
Wine including Cabernet Sauvignon, Chardonnay, Merlot, Moscato, Pinot Grigio, Pinot Noir, Ros,, Santa Barbara Chardonnay, Sauvignon Blanc
Winemaker: Lee Miyamura
Estimated Sales: $20-50 Million
Number Employees: 120
Parent Co: Treasury Wine Estates
Type of Packaging: Private Label, Bulk

8173 **Merisant**
33 N Dearborn Street
Suite 200
Chicago, IL 60602
312-840-6000
Fax: 312-840-5541 www.merisant.com
Artifical sweeteners
Chief Executive Officer, President: Paul Block
CFO: Julie Wool
VP/General Counsel/Secretary: Jonathan Cole
Quality Assurance Manager: Lonnie Morgan
Contact: Dan Beck
dan.beck@merisant.com
VP/COO: Richard Mewborn
Number Employees: 437
Square Footage: 52600
Type of Packaging: Consumer, Food Service
Brands:
Canderel
Equal
Pure Via

8174 **Merkley & Sons Packing Co Inc**
3994 W 180n
Jasper, IN 47546-8498
812-482-7020
Fax: 812-482-7033
Meat products including beef and pork
President: Dave Merkley
Treasurer: Selma Merkley
VP: David Merkley
Estimated Sales: $10-20 Million
Number Employees: 20-49
Type of Packaging: Consumer, Bulk

8175 **Merlin Candies**
5635 Powell St
Harahan, LA 70123
504-733-5553
Fax: 504-733-5536 800-899-1549
Processor, importer and exporter of confectionery products including custom molded and sugar-free chocolates, seasonal candies and chocolate trolls
President: Jean La Hoste
VP: Mary Crowley
Contact: Raymond Brinson
rbrinson@merlincandies.com
Estimated Sales: $1 Million
Number Employees: 5-9
Type of Packaging: Consumer, Food Service, Private Label
Brands:
Merlin's

8176 **Merlino Italian Baking Company**
19016 72nd Avenue South
Kent, WA 98032
425-656-9076
Fax: 425-656-8059 800-800-9490
info@merlinobaking.com
www.merlinobaking.com
Italian bakery goods, specialty cookies, soy products, organic products, health foods, etc

President: Greg Merlino
Vice President: Basel Nassar
Marketing: Margaret Domer
Plant Manager: Aurelio Coria
Estimated Sales: $3 Million
Number Employees: 20-49
Number of Brands: 3
Number of Products: 50
Square Footage: 20000
Parent Co: Seattle Gourmet Foods
Type of Packaging: Consumer, Food Service, Private Label
Brands:
Merlino Signature Brands

8177 Merlinos
1330 Elm Ave
Canon City, CO 81212-4499
719-275-5558
Fax: 719-275-8980 www.den-air.com
Fruit juices including cider-apple, cherry, apple-strawberry, blackberry, red raspberry and grape
President: Michael A Merlino
Estimated Sales: $1,127,516
Number Employees: 50-99
Type of Packaging: Consumer, Food Service, Private Label, Bulk

8178 Mermaid Spice Corporation
5702 Corporation Cir
Fort Myers, FL 33905
239-693-1986
Fax: 239-693-2099
Processor and importer of herbs, spices, seasonings, salt substitutes, rices, soup bases and salad dressings; exporter of spices and soup bases; also, custom blending available
General Manager: Mike Asaad
Estimated Sales: $1-3 Million
Number Employees: 1-4
Square Footage: 72000
Type of Packaging: Food Service
Brands:
Mermaid Spice

8179 Merrill Meat Co
813 WY 230
Encampment, WY 82325
307-327-5345
Meat
Owner: Cade Merrill
Estimated Sales: $500,000-$1 000,000
Number Employees: 1-4

8180 Merrill Seafood Center
6213 Merrill Rd
Jacksonville, FL 32277
904-744-3132
Seafood
President: Agostinho Arco
Estimated Sales: $500,000-$1 000,000
Number Employees: 1-4

8181 Merrill's Blueberry Farms
176 High Street
PO Box 149
Ellsworth, ME 04640-3141
207-667-9750
Fax: 207-667-4052 800-711-6551
merrblue@merrillwildblueberries.com
www.merrillwildblueberries.com
Wild blueberries
Estimated Sales: $1-3 Million
Number Employees: 10-19
Number of Brands: 1
Number of Products: 1
Square Footage: 200000
Type of Packaging: Private Label, Bulk
Brands:
Merrill's

8182 Merrimack Valley Apiaries
96 Dudley Rd
Billerica, MA 01821-4131
978-667-2337
Fax: 978-318-0881 www.mvabeepunchers.com
Honey
President: Andy Card Jr
Number Employees: 1-4

8183 Merritt Estate Winery Inc
2264 King Rd
Forestville, NY 14062-9703
716-965-4800
Fax: 716-965-4800 888-965-4800
nywines@merrittestatewinery.com
www.merrittestatewinery.com
Processor and exporter of table wines including red, white, rose, dry, sweet and sparkling
President: William T Merritt
Director of Marketing, Branding & Events: Michael J. Ferguson
Wholesale Sales: Mike Burkland
Manager: Jason Merritt
nywine@merritwestatewinery.com
Estimated Sales: $$1-2.5 Million
Number Employees: 1-4
Square Footage: 28000
Type of Packaging: Consumer, Food Service, Private Label
Brands:
Merritt

8184 Merritt Pecan Co
Highway 520
Weston, GA 31832
229-828-6610
Fax: 229-828-2061 800-762-9152
merritt@merritt-pecan.com
Processor and exporter of shelled and in-shell pecans
Owner: Tammy Merritt
merritt@merritt-pecan.com
President: Richard Merritt
Estimated Sales: $2 Million
Number Employees: 20-49
Square Footage: 54000
Type of Packaging: Consumer, Bulk
Brands:
Merritt Pecan Co.

8185 Merryvale Vineyards
1000 Main St
St Helena, CA 94574-2011
707-963-7777
Fax: 707-963-1949 800-326-6069
info@merryvale.com www.merryvale.com
Wines
President: Rene Schlatter
rschlatter@merryvale.com
Proprietor/CEO: Ren, Schlatter
Estimated Sales: $10-20 Million
Number Employees: 50-99
Number of Brands: 1
Brands:
Merryvale

8186 Mertz Sausage Co
619 Cupples Rd
San Antonio, TX 78237-4329
210-433-3263
Fax: 210-433-3218
Smoked, fresh and Italian sausage; also, Mexican chorizo
President: Alejandro P Pena
Manager: Terri Millmeyer
tmillmeyer@sarodeo.com
Estimated Sales: $250,000-$290,000
Number Employees: 1-4
Type of Packaging: Consumer
Brands:
Mertz Sausage

8187 Mesa Salsa
Santa Barbara, CA 93109
805-448-3836
info@mesasalsa.com
www.mesasalsa.com
Salsas
Co-Founder: Anne Altamirano
Co-Founder: Ali Altamirano

8188 Mesquite Organic Beef LLC
13808 E Greenwood Dr
Aurora, CO 80014-3952
303-680-1028
888-480-2333
Certified organic grass-fed beef producer.
CEO: Steve Atchley
satchley@mesquiteorganicbeef.com
Estimated Sales: Less Than $500,000
Number Employees: 1-4

8189 Messina Hof Winery & Resort
4545 Old Reliance Rd
Bryan, TX 77808-8995
979-778-9463
Fax: 979-778-1729 marketing@messinahof.com
www.messinahof.com
Wines
President/CEO: Paul Bonarrigo
owners@messinahof.com
CFO: Merrill Bonarrigo
Estimated Sales: $10-20 Million
Number Employees: 20-49
Type of Packaging: Private Label, Bulk

8190 MetaBall
General Nathan Cooper House
401 Route 24
Chester, NJ 07930
908-879-0880
800-247-6580
www.metaballenergybites.com
Energy bites
Founder: Susie Abramson

8191 Metabolic Nutrition
10450 W McNab Rd
Tamarac, FL 33321
800-626-1022
info@metabolicnutrition.com
www.metabolicnutrition.com
Processor and exporter of general and sports nutritional supplements
President/CEO: Murray Cohen
VP Marketing/CFO: Brian Cohen
VP/Sales: Jay Cohen
jay@metabolicnutrition.com
Estimated Sales: $1-2.5 Million
Number Employees: 5-9
Number of Products: 15
Square Footage: 56000
Type of Packaging: Private Label
Brands:
Advantage
Cgp
Hydravax
Protizyme
Synedrex
Tag

8192 Metafoods LLC
2970 Clairmont Rd NE # 510
Brookhaven, GA 30329-4418
404-843-2400
Fax: 404-843-1119 www.metafoodsllc.net
Frozen foods, beef, pork, poultry, frozen seafood, canned goods
President: Joe Wright
sales@metafoodsllc.com
CFO: Patricia Smith
Estimated Sales: $5-10 Million
Number Employees: 20-49

8193 Metagenics, Inc.
25 Enterprise
Aliso Viejo, CA 92656
949-366-0818
Fax: 949-366-0853 800-692-9400
www.metagenics.com
Vitamins, supplements and sports nutrition products
Founder: Jeff Katke
President & CEO: Brent Eck
VP of Research & Development: Matthew Tripp
Chief Science Officer: Jeffrey Bland
VP of Sales: Tim Katke
Contact: Laura Ajera
lauranajera@metagenics.com
Estimated Sales: $22.4 Million
Number Employees: 500-999
Square Footage: 88000
Brands:
Ethical Nutrients
Metagenics
Unipro

8194 (HQ)Metarom Corporation
11 School Street
Newport, VT 05855
802-334-0117
Fax: 514-375-7953 888-882-5555
accuil@metarom.fr
Natural and artificial flavors and colors; natural extracts

President: Andre Bilodeau
General Manager: Pierre Miclette
CFO: Fernande Dubois
Vice President: John Murphy
Quality Control: Alain Gauther
Estimated Sales: Less than $500,000
Number Employees: 1-4
Parent Co: Metarom Canada
Other Locations:
Metarom Corporation
Granby PQ

8195 **Metompkin Bay Oyster Company, Inc**
101-105 Eleventh Street
P.O. Box 671
Crisfield, MD 21817
410-968-0662
Fax: 410-968-0670 metbay@verizon.net
www.metompkinseafood.com
Fresh and frozen seafood
President: Casey Todd
Co-Owner: Mike Todd
Executive VP: Michael Todd
Sales Manager of Purchasing: Brenda Thomas
Estimated Sales: $5-10 Million
Number Employees: 100-249
Type of Packaging: Private Label

8196 **Metro Mint**
PO Box 885462
San Francisco, CA 94188
415-979-0781
Fax: 415-543-2749 www.metromint.com
Pure water, real mint, no sweeteners
President/Owner: Rio Miura
Controller: Elena Korsakova
Sales Manager: David Kennedy
Operations Manager: Evan Campbell

8197 **Metrohm USA**
9250 Camden Field Parkway
Riverview, FL 33578-8653
281-810-4355
Fax: 813-316-4900 info@metrohmusa.com
www.metrohm.com
Laboratory and testing equipment for research and development and quality control for the food and beverage industry.
President & CEO: Edward Colihan
CFO: E.V. Bosque
VP Marketing: Michael Allen
VP Sales: Robert Harshbarger
Contact: Frank Allers
frankallers@verizon.net
Estimated Sales: $40 Million
Number Employees: 50-99

8198 **Metropolitan Bakery**
262 S 19th St
Philadelphia, PA 19103-5707
215-545-6655
Fax: 215-985-1605 877-412-7323
wsborn@gmail.com www.metropolitanbakery.com
Breads
President/Owner: Jim Lily
President: Wendy Born
mail@metropolitanbakery.com
Number Employees: 20-49

8199 **Metropolitan Baking Co**
8579 Lumpkin St
Hamtramck, MI 48212-3622
313-875-7246
Fax: 313-875-7792 www.metropolitanbaking.com
Producer of bread, buns and rolls.
General Manager: Michael Zrimec
Cmo: George Kordas
gkordas@metropolitanbaking.com
Estimated Sales: $10-20 Million
Number Employees: 50-99
Number of Brands: 1
Type of Packaging: Food Service
Brands:
Metropolitan

8200 **Metropolitan Gourmet**
2 Cranberry Rd
Unit A-1A
Parsippany, NJ 07054-1053
973-588-5858
Fax: 973-588-5857
info@metropolitan-gourmet.com
www.metropolitan-gourmet.com
Gourmet baked goods
International Sales: David Park
Number Employees: 5-9

8201 **Metropolitan Sausage Manufacturing Company**
2908 Alexander Cres
Flossmoor, IL 60422-1704
708-331-3232
Fax: 708-798-2929
Meat and sausage
President: Willard Payne
Estimated Sales: $1-2.5 000,000
Number Employees: 1-4

8202 **Metropolitan Tea Company**
60 Industrial Pkwy
Suite 776
Cheektowaga, NY 14227
416-588-0089
Fax: 416-588-7040 800-388-0351
sales@metrotea.com www.metrotea.com
Bagged teas, loose teas, gift boxes, tea pots and mugs, tea presses, tea infusers, spoons and squeezers
President: Gerry Vandergrift

8203 **Metzer Farms**
26000 Old Stage Rd
Gonzales, CA 93926-9480
831-679-2355
Fax: 831-679-2711 800-424-7755
metzinfo@metzerfarms.com
www.metzerfarms.com
Asian duck egg products including incubated, salted and fresh; also, whole Chinese geese
President: John Metzer
metzer@metzerfarms.com
Estimated Sales: $3-5 Million
Number Employees: 10-19
Number of Products: 45
Square Footage: 124000
Type of Packaging: Consumer, Private Label
Brands:
Balut Sa Puti

8204 **Metzger Popcorn Co**
24197 Road U20
Delphos, OH 45833-9343
419-692-2494
Fax: 419-692-0890 800-819-6072
mail@metzgerpopcorn.com
www.metzgerpopcorn.com
Processor and exporter of popcorn
Owner: Bob Metzger
b.metzger@metzgerpopcorn.com
Estimated Sales: Less Than $500,000
Number Employees: 1-4
Square Footage: 40000
Type of Packaging: Consumer, Food Service, Private Label, Bulk
Brands:
Indian Creek
Mello-Krisp
Metzger Popcorn Co.

8205 **Metzger Specialty Brands**
250 W 57th St
Suite 1005
New York, NY 10107
212-957-0055
Fax: 212-957-0918 info@tillenfarms.com
www.tillenfarms.com
Asparagus (spicy and white), crunchy carrots, dilly beans, hot and spicy beans, maraschino cherries, snappers (snap peas), sweet bells (bell peppers), sunnysides (tomatoes), v-packed green beans
President/Owner: Tim Metzger
t_metzger@tillenfarms.com
Human Resources Manager: Tony Palacios
Warehouse Manager: Robert Stuckey
Estimated Sales: $2 Million
Number Employees: 2

8206 **Mex America Foods LLC**
1037 Trout Run Rd
St Marys, PA 15857-3124
814-781-1447
Fax: 814-834-9042
Tortillas including flour, whole wheat and corn; also, tortilla chips including white, yellow, blue and red
CEO: Mike Renaud
dstrikler@honnen.com
President, Chief Executive Officer: Ray Gunn
Quality, Training, Food Safety Manager: Toni McGill
Sales Manager: Ed Jurgielewicz
Vice President of Plant Operations: Tom Kornacki
Purchasing, Inventory and Scheduling Mgr: Margaret Hanes
Estimated Sales: $5 Million
Number Employees: 20-49
Number of Brands: 3-4
Number of Products: 1
Square Footage: 80000
Type of Packaging: Consumer, Food Service, Private Label, Bulk
Brands:
Mexamerica

8207 **Mexi-Frost Specialties Company**
37 Grand Avenue
Brooklyn, NY 11205-1309
718-625-3324
Fax: 718-852-8699
Frozen West Indian, Mexican, Caribbean, Chinese and Italian foods including chicken, meat pies, tamales, burritos, egg rolls
President: Gonzalo Armendariz Jr
VP: Gonzalo Armendariz, Jr.
VP Sales: Mark Armendariz
Plant Manager: Gonzaol Armendariz, Jr.
Estimated Sales: $5-10 Million
Number Employees: 20-49
Type of Packaging: Consumer, Food Service, Private Label, Bulk
Brands:
Gonzo's Little Big Meat
La Jolla
La Joya
Mexi-Frost

8208 **Mexican Accent**
16675 W Glendale Dr
New Berlin, WI 53151
262-784-4422
Fax: 262-784-5810
Processor and exporter of flour and corn tortillas; processor of tortilla chips; private labeling available
President: Mike Maglio
Contact: Steve Carew
scarew@mexicanaccent.com
Estimated Sales: $13 Million
Number Employees: 150
Square Footage: 240000
Type of Packaging: Consumer, Food Service, Private Label, Bulk
Brands:
Manny's
Mexican Accent
Rio Real

8209 **Mexican Corn Products**
238 Corduroy Rd
Vars, ON K0A 3H0
Canada
613-274-2872
mexicancornproducts@gmail.com
mexicancornproducts.com
Tortilla chips
Founder: Gabriela Godinez-Laverty
Co-Founder: Jos, Godinez Del Toro
Co-Founder: Jos, Godinez Luna

8210 **Meyenberg Goat Milk**
PO Box 934
Turlock, CA 95381
800-891-4628
info@meyenberg.com meyenberg.com
Goat milk
President: Robert Jackson
CFO: Doug Buehrle
Vice President: Carol Jackson
COO/Marketing: Tracy Plante-Darrimon
Plant Manager: Frank Fillman
Estimated Sales: $18-20 Million
Number Employees: 50
Number of Products: 25
Type of Packaging: Consumer, Bulk
Brands:
Meyenberg
Professional Preference

8211 **Meyer Brothers Dairy**
5130 Industrial St Ste 400
Maple Plain, MN 55359
952-473-7343
Fax: 952-473-8522
Products include milk, breakfast items, yogurt, pizza, meat, juices, eggs and bacon, coffee, bottled water, appetizers, produce and vegetables, butter and margarine, cheese and bakery items.
Manager: Jim Otis
Quality Control Manager: Tom Janas
Contact: Greg Hanson
gregh@meyerbro.com
Estimated Sales: $2.5-5 Million
Number Employees: 20-49

8212 **Meyer's Bakeries**
10491 W Battaglia Dr
Casa Grande, AZ 85293-7715
520-466-5491
Fax: 520-466-5996 800-528-5770
http://www.meyersbakeries.com
English muffins
Manager: Eric Robinson
Contact: Kathy Adair
kathy.adair@freshstartbakeries.com
Plant Manager: Frank Benefiel
Estimated Sales: $10-20 Million
Number Employees: 50-99
Square Footage: 160000
Parent Co: Meyers Bakeries
Type of Packaging: Food Service, Private Label, Bulk

8213 **Mezza**
222 E Wisconsin Avenue
Suite 300
Lake Forest, IL 60045-1723
847-735-2516
Fax: 415-727-4471 888-206-6054
Suppliers to the finest kitchens in America with a worldwide selection of gourmet pantry items
Type of Packaging: Food Service, Private Label

8214 **Mi Mama's Tortilla Factory Inc**
828 S 17th St
Omaha, NE 68108-3115
402-345-2099
Fax: 402-345-1059 www.mimamas.com
Corn and flour tortillas.
General Manager: Paul Sharrar
Manager: Art Velasquez
pats@mimamas.com
Estimated Sales: $10-20 Million
Number Employees: 20-49
Number of Brands: 1
Type of Packaging: Food Service
Brands:
Mi Mama's

8215 **Mi Ranchito Foods**
P.O. Box 6008
Phoenix, AZ 88023
602-272-3949
Fax: 602-278-6415
Frozen tamales; also, tortillas, chili and chili con carne
President: Joe Ramirez
Contact: Delia Cabrera
dcabrera@mi-ranchito.com
Estimated Sales: $17 Million
Number Employees: 5 to 9
Type of Packaging: Consumer, Food Service, Private Label, Bulk
Brands:
Mi Ranchito

8216 **Mi Rancho**
425 Hester St
San Leandro, CA 94577
510-553-0444
www.mirancho.com
Organic tortillas
President/Owner: Manuel Berber

8217 **Mia Products**
1520 N Keyser Ave
Scranton, PA 18504-9737
570-207-5328
Fax: 570-457-0915
Frozen juice bars
General Manager: T Cousins
President: Gerald Shriber
VP: Ernest Fogle
Number Employees: 1-4
Parent Co: J&J Snack Foods Company
Type of Packaging: Food Service
Brands:
Mia

8218 **Miami Beef Co**
4870 NW 157th St
Miami Lakes, FL 33014-6486
305-621-3252
Fax: 305-620-4562 info@miamibeef.com
Steaks, hamburgers, meat, beef, chicken, lamb, pork, sausage, roast beef, veal, prime rib, patties, stew, sirlion, tenderloim, soy, ground beef, breaded, cooked, hoagie, palomolla, pepper, salisbury, t-bone, sliced sandwich sirloinskirt steak, cubed steak, filet mignon
President: Michael Young
miamibeef@bellsouth.net
Head Sales: Barry Dean
Plant Manager: Russ Milina
Estimated Sales: $10.8 Million
Number Employees: 50-99
Type of Packaging: Consumer, Food Service, Private Label, Bulk
Brands:
Miami Beef

8219 **Miami Crab Corporation**
10815 NW 33 Street
Miami, FL 33172
305-470-1500
Fax: 305-470-1502 800-269-8395
mail@miamicrab.com www.miamicrab.com
Crabmeat products
Estimated Sales: $5-10 Million
Number Employees: 5-9
Type of Packaging: Consumer, Food Service
Brands:
Flamingo
Jackpot
Windy Shoal

8220 **(HQ)Miami Purveyors Inc**
7350 NW 8th St
Miami, FL 33126-2922
305-262-6170
Fax: 305-262-6174 800-966-6328
www.miamipurveyors.com
Manuafacturer and exporter of frozen foods including beef, pork, ham, poultry, seafood, fruits and vegetables
Owner: Rick Rothenberg
rick@miamipurveyors.com
Chief Financial Officer: Kaly Rosenberg
Estimated Sales: $14.1 Million
Number Employees: 50-99
Type of Packaging: Food Service

8221 **Micalizzi Italian Ice**
712 Madison Ave
Bridgeport, CT 06606-5511
203-366-2353
JAYICE712@aol.com
www.micalizzis.com
Italian ice and ice cream
Owner: Lucille Piccirillo
Co-Owner: Jay Piccirillo
Estimated Sales: Less Than $500,000
Number Employees: 1-4
Type of Packaging: Consumer, Food Service, Bulk

8222 **Miceli Dairy Products Co**
2721 E 90th St
Cleveland, OH 44104-3396
216-791-6222
Fax: 216-231-2504 www.miceli-dairy.com
Maker of Italian cheeses.
CEO: Joe Miceli
Year Founded: 1923
Number Employees: 100-249
Brands:
Miceli's

8223 **Michael Angelo's Inc**
200 Michael Angelo Way
Austin, TX 78728
877-482-5426
customerservice@michaelangelos.com
www.michaelangelos.com
Frozen italian entrees, lasagnas, stuffed pasta, snacks and appetizers, protein dishes
President & CEO: Michael Pugliese
Estimated Sales: $100+ Million
Number Employees: 250-499
Number of Brands: 1
Number of Products: 100
Square Footage: 132000
Type of Packaging: Consumer, Food Service, Bulk
Brands:
Michael Angelo's

8224 **Michael David Winery**
4580 W Highway 12
Lodi, CA 95242-9529
209-368-7384
Fax: 209-368-5801 888-707-9463
vintage@michaeldavidwinery.com
www.lodired.com
Wines
Partner: Mike Phillips
Partner: Dave Phillips
Estimated Sales: Below $5 Million
Number Employees: 100-249
Brands:
Michael David Vineyards

8225 **Michael Foods, Inc.**
301 Carlson Pkwy.
Suite 400
Minnetonka, MN 55305
952-258-4000
info@michaelfoods.com
www.michaelfoods.com
Processed egg and potato products.
President: Mark Westphal
Year Founded: 1987
Estimated Sales: $1.5 Billion
Number Employees: 3,500
Number of Brands: 6
Type of Packaging: Consumer, Food Service, Private Label, Bulk
Other Locations:
Michael Foods
Minneapolis MN
Brands:
Papetti's
Simply Potatoes
Abbotsford Farms
Dakota Growers Pasta Co
Davidson's
Bob Evans Farms

8226 **Michael Granese & Company**
640 E Main Street
Norristown, PA 19401-5123
610-272-5099
Fax: 610-272-1995 elio.camilotto@grande.com
Italian cheeses including ricotta, mozzarella, scamorza and cream twist
President: John Carfagno
Estimated Sales: $2.9 Million
Number Employees: 10
Square Footage: 8000
Type of Packaging: Consumer, Bulk
Brands:
Michael Granese Co.

8227 **Michael Mootz Candies**
1246 Sans Souci Pkwy
Hanover Twp, PA 18706-5230
570-823-8272
Fax: 570-826-1045 michaelmootzcandies.com
Confectionery products including chocolate coated creams, caramels and nuts, chocolate and chocolate chunks
President: Michael Mootz
Estimated Sales: $3-5 Million
Number Employees: 10-19
Type of Packaging: Consumer, Private Label

8228 **Michael's Cookies**
2205 6th Ave. S
Clear Lake, IA 50428
641-454-5577
Fax: 641-954-5451 800-822-5384
info@michaelscookies.com
www.michaelscookies.com
Frozen pre-portioned cookie doughs
COO/CFO: Scott Summeril
Quality Assurance: Myrkantra Dorlean
SVP Sales: Don Smith
Estimated Sales: $20-50 Million
Number Employees: 20-49
Number of Brands: 1
Number of Products: 1
Square Footage: 30000

Type of Packaging: Food Service, Private Label, Bulk
Brands:
Bonzers

8229 **Michael's Finer Meats/Seafoods**
3775 Zane Trace Dr
Columbus, OH 43228
800-282-0518
www.michaelsmeats.com
Processor and wholesaler/distributor of meat including beef, pork, lamb, veal and wild game
President: Jonathan Bloch
Vice President of Sales: Jeff Goebel
Number Employees: 100-249
Square Footage: 240000
Type of Packaging: Consumer, Food Service, Bulk

8230 **Michael's Gourmet Coffee**
PO Box 350003
Ft. Lauderdale, FL 33335
954-567-4500
888-346-4646
neverstopmike@yahoo.com
www.michaelscoffee.com
Manufacturer of coffee.
Founder and CEO: Michael Mistretta

8231 **Michael's Naturopathic Prgms**
6003 Randolph Blvd
San Antonio, TX 78233-5719
210-661-8311
Fax: 210-661-8048 800-845-2730
www.michaelshealth.com
Vitamins, minerals and herbal supplements
Owner: Michael Schwartz
michael@michaelshealth.com
Director: Roxanne Llewellyn
Estimated Sales: $6.8 Million
Number Employees: 20-49
Square Footage: 44180
Brands:
Michael's Health Products

8232 **Michael's Provision Co**
317 Lindsey St
Fall River, MA 02720-1132
508-672-0982
Fax: 508-672-1307
michaelschourico@hotmail.com
Meat products including Portuguese sausage
President: Ronald Miranda
info@michaelschourico.com
Owner: Joseph Miranda
Estimated Sales: $3-5 Million
Number Employees: 5-9
Type of Packaging: Consumer, Food Service, Bulk

8233 **Michaelene's Gourmet Granola**
7415 Deer Forest Ct
Clarkston, MI 48348-2734
248-625-0156
Fax: 248-625-8521
michaelenes@gourmetgranola.com
www.gourmetgranola.com
Granola
President: Michaelene Hearn
michaelene@gourmetgranola.com
Estimated Sales: Below $5 Million
Number Employees: 5-9
Type of Packaging: Bulk
Brands:
Michaelene's Gourmet
Michaelene's Gourmet Granola
Michaelene's Granola

8234 **Michel de France**
2020 South Haven Ave
Ontario, CA 91761
909-923-5205
Fax: 909-923-7804 info@micheldefrance.com
www.micheldefrance.com
European-style crepes and wafers.
Founder: Michel de France

8235 **Michel et Augustin**
98 4th St
Brooklyn, NY 11231
646-820-0935
micheletaugustin.com
Cookies

8236 **Michel's Bakery**
5698 Rising Sun Ave
Philadelphia, PA 19120-1698
267-345-7914
Fax: 215-745-1058 info@michelsbakery.com
www.michelsbakery.com
Danishes, cinnamon rolls, muffins, cakes, brownies and pies.
President: Jon Liss
CFO: Alan Stack
VP/General Manager: Stan Walulek
Purchasing Manager: Flo Collington
Year Founded: 1898
Estimated Sales: $20-30 Million
Number Employees: 100-249
Number of Brands: 2
Type of Packaging: Food Service, Private Label
Brands:
Michel's Family Bakery
Sensible Options

8237 **Michel's Magnifique**
34 N Moorie St
New York, NY 10003-2437
212-431-1070
Pates, mousses and sausage including saucisson
President: Ken Blanchette
Operations Manager: Allan Moss
Number Employees: 5-9
Type of Packaging: Consumer, Food Service

8238 **Michel-Schlumberger Wine Est**
4155 Wine Creek Rd
Healdsburg, CA 95448-9112
707-433-7427
Fax: 707-433-0444 800-447-3060
www.michelschlumberger.com
Wine
President: Jacques Schlumberger
CEO: Jerry Craven
President: Jacques Schlumberger
General Manager: Gary Brown
Public Relations: Joy Henderson
VP Operations/Production: Fred Payne
Estimated Sales: Below $5 Million
Number Employees: 20-49
Type of Packaging: Private Label
Brands:
25 Imports From France
Domaine Michel
Michel-Schlumberger

8239 **Michele Foods**
16117 LA Salle St
South Holland, IL 60473-2064
708-331-7453
Fax: 708-862-5347 www.michelefoods.com
Honey-based syrups
Owner: Michelle Hoskins
michele@michelefoods.com
VP: Paul Walk
Estimated Sales: $1 Million
Number Employees: 10-19
Square Footage: 400
Type of Packaging: Consumer, Food Service
Brands:
Michele's Honey Creme

8240 **Michele's Chocolate Truffles**
14704 SE 82nd Dr
Clackamas, OR 97015-9607
503-656-0220
Fax: 503-656-0440 800-656-7112
Gourmet hand dipped chocolate truffles, chews, nut clusters, cordials, toffee and caramel
Owner: Todd Davis
Estimated Sales: $3-5 Million
Number Employees: 5-9
Number of Brands: 1
Number of Products: 50
Square Footage: 10000
Type of Packaging: Consumer, Food Service, Private Label, Bulk
Brands:
Michele's Chocolate Truffles
Vicki's Rocky Road

8241 **Michele's Family Bakery**
2731 S Queen St
York, PA 17402
717-741-2027
Fax: 717-747-0065 www.macksicecream.com
Ice cream

Owner: Walt Bloss
Manager: Bill Lenick
Estimated Sales: $5-9.9 Million
Number Employees: 20-49

8242 **Michelle Chocolatiers**
122 N Tejon Street
Colorado Springs, CO 80903-1406
719-633-5089
Fax: 719-633-8970 888-447-3654
Processor, importer and exporter of ice creams and candy including chocolates and gold coins
VP: Jim Michopoulos
Estimated Sales: $5-10 Million
Number Employees: 20-49
Type of Packaging: Consumer, Private Label
Brands:
Gremlin
Michelle

8243 **Michelle's RawFoodz**
319 S Jefferson St
Suite 300
Chicago, IL 60661-5616
312-442-0406
medleefoods.com
Seasoned butter
President & CEO: Alberto Valdes
Number of Brands: 1
Number of Products: 4
Type of Packaging: Consumer
Brands:
MICHELLE'S RAWFOODZ

8244 **Michelle's RawFoodz**
1111 Finch Ave W
Toronto, ON M3J 2E5
Canada
info@rawfoodz.com
michellesrawfoodz.com
Dressings and dips
Co Founder: Michelle Cass
Number of Brands: 1
Number of Products: 11
Type of Packaging: Consumer

8245 **Michigan Celery Cooperative**
PO Box 306
Hudsonville, MI 49426
616-669-1250
Fax: 616-669-2890 www.michigancelery.com
Fresh celery including sliced and diced
General Manager: Gary Wruble
gwruble@michigancelery.com
Year Founded: 1951
Estimated Sales: Less Than $500,000
Number Employees: 1-4
Type of Packaging: Bulk

8246 **Michigan Dairy LLC**
29601 Industrial Rd
Livonia, MI 48150-2012
734-367-5390
Fax: 734-367-5391 www.thekrogerco.com
Dairy products including pasteurized milk, ice cream, yogurt, cottage cheese and sour cream
Manager: Jack Housley
Manager: Willow Brown
willow.brown@kroger.com
Plant Manager: Art Shank
Number Employees: 250-499
Parent Co: Kroger Company
Type of Packaging: Consumer

8247 **Michigan Desserts**
10750 Capital St
Oak Park, MI 48237-3134
248-544-4574
Fax: 248-544-4384 800-328-8632
sales@midasfoods.com www.midasfoods.com
Sweet dry mix items
President: Richard Elias
relias@midasfoods.com
Sr VP Sales/Marketing: Gary Freeman
Estimated Sales: $7 Million
Number Employees: 20-49
Square Footage: 180000
Parent Co: Midas Foods India
Type of Packaging: Consumer, Food Service, Private Label, Bulk
Brands:
American Savory
Michigan Dessert
Sin Fill

8248 **Michigan Farm Cheese Dairy**
4295 E Millerton Rd
Fountain, MI 49410-9583
231-462-3301
Fax: 231-462-3805 877-624-3373
cheese@andrulischeese.com
www.andrulischeese.com
Cheese including feta and farmer
President: Lu Andrulis
Marketing Director: Amanda Andrulis-Preston
Production Manager: Jim Stankowski
Estimated Sales: $1 Million
Number Employees: 10-19
Type of Packaging: Consumer
Brands:
Andrulis Farmers Cheese

8249 **Michigan Freeze Pack**
835 S. Griswold
P.O.Box 30
Hart, MI 49420
231-873-2175
Fax: 231-873-3025
msutton@michiganfreezepack.com
www.michiganfreezepack.com
Processor and exporter of asparagus, zucchini squash, celery, broccoli, peppers, carrots and eggplant
President: Gary Dennert
VP Sales/Finance: John Ritche
Contact: Ray Drum
rdrum@michiganfreezepack.com
Production Manager: Ronald Clark
Estimated Sales: $1 Million
Number Employees: 10
Square Footage: 400000
Type of Packaging: Food Service, Bulk

8250 **Michigan Milk Producers Assn**
41310 Bridge St
PO Box 8002
Novi, MI 48376-1302
248-474-6672
Fax: 248-474-0924 Burkhardt@mimilk.com
www.mimilk.com
Milk products include standardized milks, condensed whole milk, condensed skim milk, sweet condensed milks, instant nonfat dry milk, dried buttermilk, sweet cream butter, standarized cream, ice cream mixes, nonfat dry milk and driedwhole milk
President: Kenneth Nobis
nobis@mimilk.com
CEO: Joe Diglio
CFO: Josep Barenys
Director Quality: Sudeep Jain
Sr. Director Sales: Jim Feeney
Member Relations/Public Affairs: Sheila Burkhardt
General Manager: Clayton Galarneau
Estimated Sales: $20-50 Million
Number Employees: 100-249

8251 **Michigan Sugar Company**
122 Uptown Drive
Suite 300
Bay City, MI 48706
989-686-0161
Fax: 989-671-3719 www.michigansugar.com
Beet sugar
President/CEO: Mark Flegenheimer
CFO: Brian Haraga
Executive Vice President: Jim Ruhlman
VP Sales & Marketing: Pedro Figueroa
Vice President of Operations: Jason Lowry
Number Employees: 10-19
Type of Packaging: Consumer, Food Service, Private Label, Bulk
Other Locations:
Michigan Sugar Factory
Bay City MI
Michigan Sugar Factory
Caro MI
Michigan Sugar Factory
Croswell MI
Michigan Sugar Factory
Sebewaing MI
Brands:
Big Chief
Pioneer Sugar

8252 **MicroSoy Corporation**
300 Microsoy Dr
Jefferson, IA 50129
515-386-2100
Fax: 515-386-3287
Processor and exporter of microsoy flakes used in soy milk, tofu and other soy based foods
President/CEO: Terry Tanaka
CFO: Mike Mumma
Estimated Sales: $3.5 Million
Number Employees: 15
Square Footage: 115200
Parent Co: Mycal Corporation
Type of Packaging: Bulk
Brands:
Microsoy Flakes

8253 **Mid Atlantic Vegetable Shortening Company**
125 Sanford Ave
Kearny, NJ 07032-5918
201-467-0200
Fax: 201-991-0765 800-966-1645
jhulihan@midatlanticveg.com
www.midatlanticveg.com
Shortenings, oils, margarines, pan releases, zero trans fat shortening and margarines, and specialty products such as lecithin, garlic spread and spice products
President: Calvin Theobald
CEO: Perry Theobald
VP Sales/Marketing: James Hulihan
Regional Sales Manager: Sara Theobald
Estimated Sales: $5-10 Million
Number Employees: 20-49

8254 **Mid Kansas Co-Op Assn**
117 N Edwards Ave
Moundridge, KS 67107-8826
620-345-6361
Fax: 620-345-8817 800-864-4428
webmaster@mkcoop.com www.mkcoop.com
Cooperative offering grains
President: Dave Christianson
Manager: Kelly Reed
kreed@mkcoop.com
Estimated Sales: Less Than $500,000
Number Employees: 1-4

8255 **Mid Valley Nut Co**
2065 Geer Rd
PO Box 987
Hughson, CA 95326-9614
209-883-4491
Fax: 209-883-2435 info@midvalleynut.com
www.midvalleynut.com
Processor and importer of walnuts
President: Regina Arnold
mheskin@belkorpag.com
Sales: Mary Valdez
Production Manager: Billy Casazza
Estimated Sales: $4.6 Million
Number Employees: 100-249
Type of Packaging: Consumer, Private Label, Bulk

8256 **Mid-Atlantic Foods Inc**
8978 Glebe Park Dr
Easton, MD 21601-7004
410-822-7500
Fax: 410-822-1266 800-922-4688
sales@seaclam.com www.seawatch.com
Canned and frozen clams and seafood chowders, sauces and soups, clam juice
President: Bob Brennan
CEO: Steve Gordon
Marketing Director: Brian Shea
Contact: Betty Bain
bbain@seaclam.com
Estimated Sales: Less Than $500,000
Number Employees: 10-19
Square Footage: 33000
Type of Packaging: Consumer, Food Service, Private Label
Brands:
Gordon's Chesapeake Classics
Mid-Atlantic
Pot O' Gold
Tucker's Cove
Worcester

8257 **Mid-Eastern Molasses Company**
701 Seafarer Cir
Jupiter, FL 33477-9042
561-624-2843
Fax: 561-624-7060 memcomolas@aol.com
Molasses

8258 **Mid-Pacific Hawaii Fishery**
Old Airport Road
Hilo, HI 96720
808-935-6110
Fax: 808-961-6859
Processor and exporter of fresh tuna, marlin and shark
Owner: John Romero
Estimated Sales: $2.5-5 Million
Number Employees: 7
Type of Packaging: Consumer, Food Service
Brands:
Mid Pacific

8259 **Mid-South Fish Company**
P.O.Box 185
Aubrey, AR 72311-0185
870-295-5600
Fax: 870-295-3559
Owner: Algie Jolly
Estimated Sales: $.5-1 million
Number Employees: 1-4

8260 **Midamar**
1105 60th Ave SW
Cedar Rapids, IA 52404-7212
319-362-3711
Fax: 319-362-4111 800-362-3711
info@midamar.com www.midamar.com
Halal food products including crescent chicken, ethnic sauces, beef, lamb, shawarma, turkey and pizzas.
President: Bill Aossey
baossey@midamar.com
Estimated Sales: $20-50 Million
Number Employees: 50-99

8261 **Midas Foods Intl**
10750 Capital St
Oak Park, MI 48237-3134
248-544-4574
Fax: 248-544-4384 877-728-2379
sales@midasfoods.com www.midasfoods.com
Dry mix foods and bases including gravies, sauces, cheese sauce, soup bases, batter products .They manufacturer dry powdered mixes for food processing and national restaurant chains.
Owner: Richard Elias
relias@midasfoods.com
Number Employees: 10-19
Square Footage: 180000
Parent Co: MiDAS Foods International
Type of Packaging: Food Service, Bulk
Brands:
American Saucery

8262 **Middlebury Cheese Company**
11275 W 250 N
Middlebury, IN 46540-7708
574-825-9511
Fax: 574-825-1102 800-262-2505
www.heritageridgecreamery.com
Cheeses including cheddar, colby, colby jack, monterey jack, pepper jack
President: Dick Bylsma
dbylsma@agropur.com
CEO: Richard Guggisber
CEO: Dick Bylsma
Plant Manager: David Gall
Year Founded: 1979
Estimated Sales: $20-50 Million
Number Employees: 50-99

8263 **Middlefield Cheese House**
15815 Nauvoo Rd
Middlefield, OH 44062-8501
440-632-5228
Fax: 440-632-5604 800-327-9477
shop@middlefieldcheese.com
www.rothenbuhlercheesemakers.com
Swiss cheese, cheese spreads, apple butters and jams, maple syrup and maple popcorn, beef sticks, summer sausage, beef jerky
President: Ann Rothenbuhler
Contact: Blake Andres
blake@ddcclinic.org
Plant Manager: Steve Ilg
Estimated Sales: $130,000
Number Employees: 10-19
Square Footage: 8000
Type of Packaging: Bulk
Brands:
Middlefield

8264 **Middleswarth Potato Chips**
181 E State St
Kingston, PA 18704-1097
570-288-2447
Fax: 570-288-1381 toddhestor@hotmail.com
www.middleswarthchips.com
Potato chips including regular, barbecue, waffle style, sour cream and onion and salt and vinegar
President: Bob Middleswarth
VP: Anna Middleswarth
Manager: Jim Cobern
Estimated Sales: $3.3 Million
Number Employees: 10-19
Square Footage: 240000
Type of Packaging: Consumer, Food Service, Bulk

8265 **Midwest Blueberry Farms**
13720 Tyler St
Holland, MI 49424-9418
616-399-2133
Fax: 616-399-2133
Blueberries
Owner: Richard Keil
Estimated Sales: Under $300,000
Number Employees: 5-9
Brands:
Midwest Blueberry Farms

8266 **Midwest Food**
3100 W 36th St
Chicago, IL 60632-2304
773-927-8870
Fax: 773-927-8715 admin@midwestfoods.com
Canned spaghetti dinners and stew including beef, chicken and meatball
President: Erin Fitzgerald
Number Employees: 100-249
Parent Co: Owatonna Canning Company
Type of Packaging: Food Service, Private Label

8267 **Midwest Foodservice News**
2736 Sawbury Boulevard
Columbus, OH 43235-4579
614-336-0710
Fax: 614-336-0713
A regional food service publication with more than 28,000 readers in Ohio, Michigan, Indiana, Kentucky, Pennsylvania, and West Virginia

8268 **Midwest Frozen Foods, Inc.**
2185 Leeward Ln
Hanover Park, IL 60133-6026
630-784-0123
Fax: 630-784-0424 866-784-0123
Midwest Frozen Foods provides in house and private label frozen fruits and vegetables to the retail, food services and industrial manufacturing sectors.
President: Zafar Iqbal
VP: Athar Siddiq
Operations: Rob Linchesky
Production: Jose Manjarrez
Estimated Sales: $5 Million
Number Employees: 18
Number of Brands: 2
Number of Products: 100+
Square Footage: 20000
Type of Packaging: Food Service, Private Label, Bulk

8269 **Midwest Nut Co**
3105 Columbia Ave NE
Minneapolis, MN 55418-1896
612-781-6596
Fax: 612-781-6728 800-328-5502
Snack foods including salty and trail mixes and roasted and raw seeds including pumpkin and sunflower; also, confections
President: Laure Rockman
laurerockman@qwestoffice.net
Plant Manager: Tim Fischer
Estimated Sales: $3 Million
Number Employees: 10-19
Square Footage: 160000
Type of Packaging: Consumer, Food Service, Private Label, Bulk
Brands:
Aristo Snacks
Dijon Crunch
Fun Foods
Giant Cashews
Hokey Pokey
Midwest

8270 **Midwest Seafood**
5500 Emerson Way
Suite A
Indianapolis, IN 46226-1477
317-466-1027
Fax: 317-466-1033
Estimated Sales: $1-3 Million
Number Employees: 5-9

8271 **Miesse Candies**
118 N Water St # 102
Lancaster, PA 17603-5597
717-392-6011
Fax: 717-392-3898 miessecandies@gmail.com
www.miessecandies.com
Hard, soft and chocolate candy
Owner: Tracy Artus
miessecandies@gmail.com
Estimated Sales: Below $5 Million
Number Employees: 10-19

8272 **Mighty Leaf Tea**
136 Mitchell Blvd
San Rafael, CA 94903
415-491-2650
Fax: 415-472-1780 877-698-5323
www.mightyleaf.com
Whole-leaf tea blends
CEO: Gary Shinner
Contact: Rafael Chacon
rafael@mightyleaf.com
Estimated Sales: Below $5 Million
Number Employees: 5-9

8273 **Mighty Soy Inc**
1227 S Eastern Ave
Los Angeles, CA 90022-4809
323-266 6969
Fax: 323-266-3844 www.mightysoy.com
Soy milk
President: Maung Myint
VP/Secretary: Gin Lee
Estimated Sales: $486,000
Number Employees: 10-19
Square Footage: 16000

8274 **Mignardise**
1963 Patrick Farrar
Suite 200
Chambly, QC J3L 4N7
Canada
450-447-0777
info@mignardise.ca
www.mignardise.ca
Cakes/pastries, cookies.
Marketing: Joan Cartier

8275 **Miguel's Stowe Away**
17 Town Farm Ln
Stowe, VT 05672
802-253-8900
Fax: 802-253-3946 800-448-6517
mexicanfoods@miguels.com
Processor and exporter of Mexican food products including salsa cruda, blue and white corn tortilla chips, red chili sauce, flavored salsa and smoked jalapeno
President: Christopher Pierson
Regional Sales Manager: Tim Couture
Estimated Sales: $3-5 Million
Number Employees: 1-4
Square Footage: 20000
Type of Packaging: Consumer, Food Service, Bulk
Brands:
Miguel's

8276 **Mikaela's Simply Divine**
288 Route 46
Dover, NJ 07801
Fax: 866-648-7530 866-659-1553
info@sdbiscotti.com mikaelassimplydivine.com
Gluten-free biscotti
President & CEO: Mikaela Rae
CFO: Mark Leone
Operations: Christine Gold
Number of Brands: 1
Number of Products: 6
Type of Packaging: Consumer
Brands:
MIKAELA'S SIMPLY DIVINE

8277 **Mikawaya LLC**
5563 Alcoa Ave
Vernon, CA 90058-3730
323-587-5504
Fax: 213-625-0943 Sales@mikawayausa.com
Japanese pastries and ice cream
President: Frances Hashimoto
CEO: Jerry Bucan
jerry@mikawayausa.com
CFO: Joel Friedman
Estimated Sales: $5-10 Million
Number Employees: 20-49
Type of Packaging: Private Label
Brands:
Mikawaya
Mochi Ice Cream

8278 **Mike & Jean's Berry Farm**
16234 Kamb Rd.
Mt Vernon, WA 98273-8865
360-424-7220
Fax: 360-424-7225 mike@mikeandjeans.com
www.mikeandjeans.com
Fresh cauliflower, strawberries and raspberries; also, frozen strawberries and raspberries
Owner: Michael Youngquist
Co-Owner: Jeanne Youngquist
Manager: Mike Youngquist
mike@mikeandjeans.com
Year Founded: 1889
Estimated Sales: $20-50 Million
Number Employees: 20-49
Type of Packaging: Food Service, Private Label

8279 **Mike's Beverage Company**
249 Dufferin St.
Toronto, ON M6K 1Z5
Canada
647-428-3123
Subsidiary of Labatt Breweries of Canada. The company also sells coolers, ciders and flavoured malt beverages, including Palm Bay, Mike's Hard, Okanagan Cider, American Vintage Hard Iced Teas and Bud Lime-a-Ritas
Director of Marketing: Sung Kang
Senior Sales Manager: Mark Haynes
Parent Co: Labatt Brewing Company
Brands:
American Vintage Hard Iced Teas
Bud Lime-a-Ritas
Mike's Hard
Okanagan Cider
Palm Bay

8280 **Mike's Hot Honey**
67 West St
Suite 202
Brooklyn, NY 11222
347-450-4722
mikeshothoney.com
Chili pepper-infused honey
Founder: Michael Kurtz
Year Founded: 2011

8281 **Mike's Mighty Good**
PO Box 2205
Woodland, CA 95776-2205
530-669-6870
Fax: 530-669-6875 www.rightfoods.com
Soups, prepared salads and hot cereals.
Brand Manager: Carolyn Vinnicombe
Brands:
Dr. McDougall's Right Foods(c)

8282 **Mikesell's Potato ChipCompany**
330 Leo Street
Po Box 115
Dayton, OH 45404
937-228-9400
Fax: 937-461-5707 www.mikesells.com
Mike-Sell's Potato Chips include original, groovy, old fashiioned, reduced fat, and assorted flavors including barbecue, cheddar and sour cream, sour cream, green onion, salt and vinegar and smoked bacon. Additional products includepretzels, regular and cheese puffcorn, cheese curls, corn chips, tortilla chips, pork rinds and salsa dip.
President & CEO: Charles Shive
CFO: Paul McNiel
Executive VP, Sales: Phil Kazar
Marketing Director: Luke Mapp
Estimated Sales: $25-49 Million
Number Employees: 270
Number of Brands: 1

Type of Packaging: Consumer, Food Service
Brands:
Mikesell's

8283 **Mikey's**
Scottsdale, AZ 85254
eatmikeys.com
English muffins, muffin tops, sliced bread, pizza crust, pockets and tortillas

8284 **Mikey's**
480-696-2483
info@mikeysmuffins.com
www.eatmikeys.com
Gluten-free, dairy-free, soy-free, and paleo English muffins, muffin tops, sliced bread, pizza crusts, tortillas, and pizza pockets
Founder/CEO: Michael Tierney
Year Founded: 2014

8285 **Miko Meat**
230 Kekuanaoa Street
Hilo, HI 96720-6427
808-935-0841
Fax: 808-935-2781
Sausages and hot dogs
President: Ernest Matsumura
General Manager: Matt Asano
Estimated Sales: $620 K
Number Employees: 5-9

8286 **Milan Provision Co**
10815 Roosevelt Ave
Corona, NY 11368-2538
718-899-7678
Fax: 718-335-3354
Mexican meat
Owner: Salvatore Laurita
milanprovisions@aol.com
Estimated Sales: $1-3 Million
Number Employees: 10-19
Type of Packaging: Consumer, Food Service, Private Label, Bulk

8287 **Milani**
2905 Highway 61 N
Muscatine, IA 52761
800-442-5242
www.precisionfoods.com
Seasonings, salad dressings, sugar replacements, salt substitutes and base mixes
CEO: Gage Kent
CFO: Mark Dunsmore
Manager of Milani Foods: Linda Fortino
Number Employees: 1-4
Parent Co: Kent Precision Foods Group
Type of Packaging: Consumer, Food Service, Bulk

8288 **Milano Bakery Inc**
433 S Chicago St
Joliet, IL 60436-2268
815-727-2253
Fax: 815-727-3116 milanobakery@comcast.net
www.milanobakery.com
Italian bread, buns and rolls, wedding cakes and other speciality cakes, fruit cakes, strudels and coffee.
President: Mario DeBenedetti
Vice President: Darin DeBenedetti
Estimated Sales: $1-10 Million
Number Employees: 50-99

8289 **Milano's Of New York City**
56 Little West 12th St.
New York, NY 10014
800-643-6328
info@milanosausage.com
www.milanosausage.com
Manufacturer of cured meats.
Founder and CEO: Michael Milano

8290 **Milat Vineyards Winery**
1091 Saint Helena Hwy S
St Helena, CA 94574-2268
707-963-0758
Fax: 707-963-0168 800-546-4528
Wines including Chenin Blanc, Chardonnay, Merlot, Cabernet Sauvignon, Zinfandel, Zivio and dessert wines.
Owner: Mike Milat
mike@milat.com
Estimated Sales: $1-2.5 Million
Number Employees: 1-4
Brands:
Milat Vineyards

8291 **Mild Bill's Spices**
PO Box 1303
Ennis, TX 75120
972-875-2975
http://www.mildbills.com/
Processor and exporter of chili powder, seasoning blends and barbecue spices, salsa, relish
Owner: Bill Dees
Co-Owner: Tamara Dees
Type of Packaging: Consumer, Food Service
Brands:
Big Bruce's Gunpowder Chili
Fire Marshall's Cajun

8292 **Milea Estate Vineyard**
40 Hollow Circle Rdl
Staatsburg, NY 12580
845-264-0403
Fax: 845-389-0313 info@mileaestatevineyard.com
www.mileaestatevineyard.com
Pinot Noir, Riesling, Chardonnay, Vignoles, Traminette, Ros, and sparkling wine
Co-Founder: Barry Milea
Co-Founder: Ed Evans
Co-Founder: Bruce Tripp
Year Founded: 2015
Number of Brands: 1
Number of Products: 10
Type of Packaging: Consumer, Private Label
Brands:
Milea Estate Vineyard

8293 **Miles of Chocolate**
Austin, TX
milesofchocolate.com
Baked chocolate dessert
Co-founder: Miles Compton
Co-founder: Ben Welch

8294 **Miljoco Corp**
200 Elizabeth St
Mt Clemens, MI 48043-1643
586-777-4280
Fax: 586-777-7891 888-888-1498
info@mijoco.com www.miljoco.com
Manufacturers standard and custom thermometers.
President: Howard M Trerice
htrerice@miljoco.com
Reaserch Development: Heath Trerice
Quality Control: Bruce Trerice
Marketing: Mike Mroz
Sales: Tom Adams
Public Relations: Mike Mroz
Plant Manager: Alex Jakob
Purchasing: Kimberly Trerice
Estimated Sales: $10-20 Million
Number Employees: 20-49
Square Footage: 94000
Brands:
Miljoco

8295 **Milk Specialties Global**
7500 Flying Cloud Dr
Suite 500
Eden Prairie, MN 55344
952-942-7310
Fax: 952-942-7611 www.milkspecialties.com
Dairy protein ingredients
President/Owner: Eddie Wells
CEO: Dave Lenzmeier
davelenzmeier@milkspecialties.com
Estimated Sales: $35 Million
Number Employees: 500-999

8296 **MilkBoy Swiss Chocolate**
605 Montgomery St
Brooklyn, NY 11225
www.milkboy.com
Swiss chocolate
Number of Brands: 1
Number of Products: 10
Type of Packaging: Consumer
Brands:
MILKBOY

8297 **Milkadamia**
8100 S Madison St
Burr Ridge, IL 60527
630-861-2105
hello@milkadamia.com
www.milkadamia.com
Macadamia milk

8298 **(HQ)Milky Way Jersey Farm Inc**
220 Hidden Hills Rd
Starr, SC 29684-8809
864-352-2014
www.scmilkywayfarm.com
Milk
Co-Owner: Sherrie Peeler
Co-Owner: Lloyd Peeler
Manager: Davis Peeler
Number Employees: 1-4

8299 **Milky Whey Inc**
910 Brooks St # 203
Suite 203
Missoula, MT 59801-5784
406-542-7373
Fax: 406-542-7377 800-379-6455
dairy@themilkywhey.com
www.themilkywhey.com
Whey proteins and dry dairy ingredients including nonfat dry milk, whole milk, whey powder, butter, buttermilk powder, caseinates, lactose, nondairy creamers, whey protein concentrates and isolates, and cheese powders
President: Curt Pijanowski
curt@themilkywhey.com
CFO: Steve Schmidt
Vice President: Dan Finch
Operations Manager: Carla Messerly
Reception: Tony Cavanaugh
Estimated Sales: $1.2 Million
Number Employees: 10-19
Type of Packaging: Consumer, Private Label, Bulk

8300 **Mill Cove Lobster Pound**
381 Barters Island Rd
Trevett, ME 4571
207-633-3340
Fax: 207-633-7206 www.millcovelobster.com
Processor and wholesaler/distributor of seafood including lobster, shrimp, frozen cod, ocean perch, pollack, clams and oysters
President: Jeff Lewis
mclobster@roadrunner.com
Estimated Sales: $4-$5 Million
Number Employees: 10-19
Type of Packaging: Consumer

8301 **Mill Creek Vineyards**
P.O.Box 758
Healdsburg, CA 95448
707-431-2121
Fax: 707-431-1714 877-349-2121
brian@mcvonline.com www.millcreekwinery.com
Wines
Proprietor: William Kreck
kreck@millcreekwinery.com
General Manager: Yvonne Kreck
Winemaker: Jeremy Kreck
Wholesale Sales: John Miller
Wine Club, Director of Retail Operations: Bruce Thomas
Bookkeeper: Julie Ricetti
IT: Brian Kreck
Estimated Sales: Below $5 Million
Number Employees: 10-19
Type of Packaging: Private Label
Brands:
Felta Springs
Mill Creek Vineyards
Reflections

8302 **Mill Haven Foods LLC**
211 Leer St
New Lisbon, WI 53950-1170
608-562-6455
brian@millhavenfoods.com
www.millhavenfoods.com
Dairy
President: Hollie Slater
Partner: Brian Slater
brian@millhavenfoods.com
Vice President: Bruce Ritchart
Quality Assurance Manager: Chris Faber
Owner/Sales: Brian Slater
International Sales: Chris Dart
Number Employees: 20-49

8303 Millbrook Vineyards
26 Wing Rd
Millbrook, NY 12545-5017
845-677-8383
Fax: 845-677-6186 800-662-9463
millbrookwinery@millwine.com
www.millbrookwine.com
Wine
Owner: John Dyson
millbrookwinery@millwine.com
CFO: Eric Grans
General Manager/Sales Manager: Gary Goddard
Director of Marketing: Stacy Hudson
Director of Sales: Scott Koster
Estimated Sales: $5-10 Million
Number Employees: 10-19
Type of Packaging: Private Label
Brands:
Millbrook

8304 Mille Lacs Gourmet Foods
P.O.Box 8919
Madison, WI 53590
608-837-8535
Fax: 608-825-6463 800-843-1381
wjones@millelacs.com www.millelacs.com
Gourmet cheeses and chocolates
President: Jay Singer
VP: John Manzer
President: Jay Singer
Sales Director: David Sandorn
Estimated Sales: $5-10 Million
Number Employees: 20-49
Brands:
Degeneve
Heart of Wisconsin
Mille Lacs

8305 Mille Lacs Wild Rice Corp
25300 Paddy Ave
PO Box 200
Aitkin, MN 56431
218-927-2740
800-626-3809
info@canoewildrice.com www.canoewildrice.com
Processor and exporter of kosher wild rice
President: Chris Ratuski
Estimated Sales: $2.5 Million
Number Employees: 10-19
Type of Packaging: Consumer, Food Service, Private Label, Bulk
Brands:
Canoe

8306 Millen Fish
PO Box 864
Millen, GA 30442-864
478-982-4988
Fax: 912-982-1746
Fish and fish products
President: David McMillian
Estimated Sales: $3-5 Million
Number Employees: 10-19

8307 Miller Baking
1415 North 5th St
Milwaukee, WI 53212
414-347-2300
www.pretzilla.com
Pretzel bread, buns and snacks
Owner: Brian Miller

8308 Miller Brothers PackingCompany
1118 Highway 82 East
Sylvester, GA 31791
229-776-2014
Fax: 229-776-4728
Beef, sausage, pork, lamb and ostrich including emu and rhea; slaughtering services available
President/Co-Owner: Otis Miller
VP/Co-Owner: Dan Miller
Estimated Sales: $5-10 Million
Number Employees: 10-19
Type of Packaging: Food Service, Bulk
Brands:
Daeab
Gold Nugget

8309 Miller Johnson Seafood
4310 Heron Bay Loop Road S
Coden, AL 36523-3714
251-873-4444
Fax: 252-729-1427
Seafood
Owner: Miller Johnson

8310 Miller's Cheese Corp
196 28th Street
Brooklyn, NY 11232
718-965-1840
Fax: 718-965-0979
customerservice@millerscheesecorp.com
Kosher cheese. Founded in 1898.
Owner: Meyer Thurm
Marketing Director: Yudi Sherer
Sales: Sruly Sherer
Estimated Sales: $5 Million
Number Employees: 1-4
Type of Packaging: Consumer

8311 Miller's Country Hams
7110 Highway 190
Dresden, TN 38225-2276
731-364-3940
Fax: 731-364-5338 800-622-0606
millersham@crunet.com http://www.crunet.com
Country ham
President: Jan Frick
Quality Control: Mark Mash
Vice President: Mark Mash
CFO: Sharon Burress
Production Manager: Linda Burcham
Plant Manager: Barry King
Estimated Sales: $5-10 Million
Number Employees: 20-49
Brands:
Miller's Country Ham

8312 Miller's Meat Market
1524 S Main St
Red Bud, IL 62278-1316
618-282-3334
Fax: 618-282-7799 meatman@htc.net
www.yahoo.com
Fresh and cured meats including beef, pork, elk, buffalo, sausage, etc.; also, slaughtering services available
Owner: Kevin Miller
meatman@htc.net
Estimated Sales: $300,000-500,000
Number Employees: 5-9
Square Footage: 20000
Type of Packaging: Consumer, Food Service, Private Label

8313 Miller's Mustard LLC
139 Golfview Dr.
Gibsonia, PA 15044
412-894-7172
Fax: 412-894-7143 info@millersmustard.com
www.millersmustard.com
Manufacturer of mustard.
Co-Founder: Robb Miller
miller2@zoominternet.net
Co-Founder: Carol Miller

8314 Millflow Spice Corp.
60 Davids Dr
Hauppauge, NY 11788
Fax: 631-231-5500 866-227-8355
info@castellaimports.com
www.millflowspicecorp.com
Food colors, flavoring extracts, spices, seasonings and sauces including pesto, Worcestershire, soy, barbecue, hot and smoke
President: Zane Moses
Estimated Sales: $2.6 Million
Number Employees: 21
Parent Co: Regal Extract Company
Type of Packaging: Consumer, Food Service, Private Label, Bulk
Brands:
Bonton
Growers Company
Millflow
Regal

8315 Milliaire Winery
276 Main St
Murphys, CA 95247-9564
209-728-1658
Fax: 209-736-1915 wines@milliairewinery.com
www.milliairewinery.com
Wines
Manager: Jana Nadler
Manager: Liz Millier
lmillier@goldrush.com
Estimated Sales: $160,000
Number Employees: 5-9
Brands:
Milliaire Winery

8316 Millie's Pierogi
129 Broadway
Chicopee Falls, MA 01020
413-594-4991
800-743-7641
ann@milliespierogi.com www.milliespierogi.com
Fully cooked pierogies including cabbage, potato and cheese, cheese, prune and blueberry.
President: Ann Kerigan
Estimated Sales: Less than $500,000
Number Employees: 5-9
Brands:
Millie's Pierogi

8317 Milligan & Higgins
PO Box 506
Johnstown, NY 12095
518-762-4638
Fax: 518-762-7039 info@milligan1868.com
www.milligan1868.com
Manufacturer, importer and exporter of kosher edible and technical gelatins.
Year Founded: 1868
Parent Co: Hudson Industries Corporation
Type of Packaging: Bulk

8318 Milling Sausage Inc
629 S 10th Street
Milwaukee, WI 53204
414-645-2677
www.millingsausage.com
Sausages and frankfurters
Owner: Kate Mikolic
kmikolic@milwaukc.org
Number Employees: 1-4
Number of Products: 10
Type of Packaging: Bulk

8319 Millrose Restaurant
45 S Barrington Rd
South Barrington, IL 60010-9508
847-382-7673
Fax: 847-382-7693 800-464-5576
manager@millroserestaurant.com
Beer
Owner: William Rose
COO: Mike Sheridan
Director Manufacturing: Thomas Sweeney
Estimated Sales: $5-10 Million
Number Employees: 100-249

8320 Mills Brothers Intl
16000 Christensen Rd
Suite 300
Seattle, WA 98188-2967
206-575-3000
Fax: 206-957-1362 mbi@millsbros.com
www.millsbros.com
Specialty and organic grains, dried peas, dried beans, lentils, millet rice and corn products including popcorn kernels, flour, grits, meal and starch
President: Eric Mills
Year Founded: 1982
Estimated Sales: $36306000
Number Employees: 50-99
Square Footage: 26000
Type of Packaging: Consumer, Food Service, Private Label, Bulk
Brands:
Cascade
Mills Brothers International

8321 Mills Coffee Roasting Co
1058 Broad St
Providence, RI 02905-1600
401-781-7860
Fax: 401-781-7978 888-781-5282
www.thequeenbean.com
Coffee
President: David Mills
millscoffee@aol.com
Plant Manager: Mike Candy
Estimated Sales: Below $5 Million
Number Employees: 10-19
Type of Packaging: Private Label

8322 **Mills Seafood Ltd.**
5 Mills Street
Bouctouche, NB E4S 3S3
Canada
506-743-2444
Fax: 506-743-8497 millsseafood.ca
Seafood processor
Owner: Steven Mills
Vice President: Marie Allain
Quality Control: George Robichaud
Plant Manager: Laurie Allain
Number Employees: 50-99
Type of Packaging: Food Service

8323 **Millstream Brewing Co**
835 48th Ave
Amana, IA 52203-8122
319-622-3672
Fax: 319-622-6516
Beers, ales and lagers
Owner: Chris Priebe
chris@millstreambrewing.com
Estimated Sales: Below $5 Million
Number Employees: 10-19
Type of Packaging: Consumer, Food Service
Brands:
Millstream

8324 **Milmar Food Group**
One 6 1/2 Station Road
Goshen, NY 10924
845-294-5400
Fax: 845-294-6687 www.milmarfoodgroup.com
Frozen foods including breakfast selections, vegetarian, chicken, burrito, and pre-plated meal products
President: Martin Hoffman
EVP: Dov Peikes
Marketing Director: Rita O'Connor
Sales Director: Cindy Cohen
Purchasing: Barry Werk
Year Founded: 2000
Estimated Sales: $30 Million
Number Employees: 250
Number of Brands: 3
Number of Products: 100
Square Footage: 60000
Type of Packaging: Consumer, Food Service, Private Label, Bulk
Brands:
Mrs. Veggies
No Forks Required
Spring Valley

8325 **Milne Fruit Products Inc**
804 Bennett Ave
P.O. Box 111
Prosser, WA 99350-1267
509-786-2611
Fax: 509-786-1724 selkins@milnefruit.com
www.milnefruit.com
Processes fruit juice, fruit juice concentrates, purees, custom blends and nutritional ingredients. Flavors include concord grape, strawberry, cranberry, raspberry, blueberry and cherry and others
President: Randy Hageman
rhageman@milnefruit.com
General Manager: Randall Hageman
Research & Development: Eric Johnson
Quality Control: Eric Johnson
Sales Director: Shannon Elkins
Number Employees: 20-49
Parent Co: Ocean Spray Cranberries
Type of Packaging: Bulk

8326 **Milnot Company**
120 W Saint John Street
Litchfield, IL 62056-2169
217-324-2146
800-877-6455
www.milnot.com
Dairy products.
President: Christoph Rudolph
Number Employees: 20-49
Parent Co: Milnot Company
Type of Packaging: Consumer, Private Label, Bulk

8327 **Milnot Company**
1 Strawberry Ln.
Orrville, OH 44667
888-656-3245
www.milnot.com
Milk and dairy products.
CEO, Eagle Family Foods: Bernard Kreilmann
Year Founded: 1912
Estimated Sales: $100-500 Million
Number Employees: 250-499
Number of Brands: 1
Parent Co: Eagle Family Foods Group LLC
Type of Packaging: Consumer, Private Label
Brands:
Milnot

8328 **Milone Brothers Coffee Co**
1413 Lone Palm Ave
Modesto, CA 95351-2860
209-526-0865
Fax: 209-526-1652 800-974-8500
mbc@milone.com www.milone.com
Fresh roasted whole bean highest grade coffees. Custom blending/roasting, espresso and coffee machine experts
Owner: Joe Milone
joe@milone.com
Estimated Sales: $1 Million
Number Employees: 5-9
Square Footage: 12000
Type of Packaging: Food Service, Bulk
Brands:
Milone Brothers

8329 **Milos**
125 West 55th Street
New York, NY 10019
212-245-7400
Fax: 212-245-4828 newyork@estiatoriomilos.com
www.milos.ca
Frozen potato cakes
Owner: Costas Spiliadis
Contact: Billy Mack
billy@firstcoastal.com
Estimated Sales: $2.5-5 Million
Number Employees: 10-19

8330 **Milos Whole World Gourmet**
94 Columbus Rd
Athens, OH 45701-1312
740-589-6456
Fax: 740-594-9151 866-589-6456
info@miloswholeworld.com
www.gourmetyourway.biz
Pasta sauces and salad dressings
President/Owner: Jonathan Milo
Wholesale Sales Manager: Maryjane Burch
Production Manager: Mark Temple
Estimated Sales: Less Than $500,000
Number Employees: 1-4

8331 **Milroy Canning Company**
100 South Railroad Street
PO Box 125
Milroy, IN 46156
765-629-2221
Fax: 765-629-2645
Canned tomatoes
President: Robert Tobian
Vice President: Andrew Tobian
Estimated Sales: $10-20 Million
Number Employees: 20-49
Type of Packaging: Consumer

8332 **Milsolv Corporation**
PO Box 444
Butler, WI 53007-0444
262-252-3550
Fax: 262-252-5250 800-558-8501
Beverages, confectionery, canned foods, processed cheese, bakery, meat, seafood, dairy
Chairman: Ed mills
Sales: Mark Hartung
Brands:
Milsolv

8333 **Milton A. Klein Company**
PO Box 363
New York, NY 10021-0006
516-829-3400
Fax: 516-829-3427 800-221-0248
President: Irene Klein
VP: Allen Klein
Number Employees: 15
Square Footage: 6800

8334 **Milton's Local**
PO Box 1293
Hopewell, VA 23860-1293
804-925-2644
info@miltonslocal.com
miltonslocal.com
Sausages and bacon
Marketing Coordinator: Kelsey Ducker

8335 **Milwhite Inc**
5487 Padre Island Hwy
Brownsville, TX 78521-8300
956-547-1970
Fax: 956-547-1999 800-442-0082
www.milwhite.com
Manufacturer and importer of clay, talcs, calcium carbonate, barium sulfate, attapulgite, bentonite and other nonmetallic minerals; exporter of aflatoxin binders.
President: Mike Hughes
mhughes@milwhite.com
Accounting & Financial Manager: Hector Guerrero
Director, Health Science Division: Dr Orlando Osuna
Quality Assurance: Steve Lopez
Customer Service: Paola Tella
Estimated Sales: $20-50 Million
Number Employees: 20-49
Number of Brands: 5
Type of Packaging: Private Label, Bulk
Brands:
Blanca
Gel B
Milsorb
Super Gel B
Tdm

8336 **Mimac Glaze**
271 Glidden Road
Unit 17
Brampton, ON L6W 1H9
Canada
905-457-7737
Fax: 905-457-9828 877-990-9975
dave@mimacglaze.com www.mimacglaze.com
Icing stabilizers and ready-to-use icings
President: W David Miles
Secretary/Treasurer: Marion Miles
Production Manager: Werner Barduhn
Estimated Sales: $975,000
Number Employees: 6
Square Footage: 26400
Type of Packaging: Consumer, Food Service
Brands:
Paragon
Supreme

8337 **Mimi's Mountain Mixes**
120 Chadwick Ave
Suite 16
Hendersonville, NC 28792
937-380-5600
info@mimismixes.com
www.mimismountainmixes.com
Bread, cake, candy, cookie, donut, pancake and soft pretzel mixes.
President: Lin Johnson-Carlson

8338 **Mims Meat Company**
12634 E Freeway
Houston, TX 77015-5614
713-453-0151
Fax: 713-453-6714
Meat products including beef, pork, poultry, lamb, veal and wild game meats.
President & CEO: Dan Mims
danmims@mimsmeatcompany.com
Treasurer & CFO: Mary Mims
Human Resources: James Mercer
Warehouse Operations Manager: Derek Woods
Estimated Sales: $43.36 Million
Number Employees: 110
Parent Co: Glazier Foods

8339 **Min Tong Herbs**
318 7th St
Oakland, CA 94607-4112
510-873-8677
Fax: 510-873-8671 800-562-5777
mintongherbs@hotmail.com www.mintong.com.tw
Processor and importer of Chinese herbal extracts

President: Charles Chang
mintongherbs@aol.com
Vice President: Susan Chang
Sales: Tiffany Zhon
Estimated Sales: $500,000-$1 Million
Number Employees: 10-19
Number of Brands: 1
Type of Packaging: Consumer, Private Label, Bulk
Brands:
Min Tong

8340 Minas Purely Divine
1355 Rock Mountain Blvd
Stone Mountain, GA 30083-1536
404-508-6222
www.minasgf.com
Allergy-free, gluten free baked goods
Owner: Moses Julbe
mosesjulbe@minasgf.com
Number Employees: 5-9

8341 Mincing Overseas Spice Company
K N Building
10 Tower Road
Dayton, NJ 08810
732-355-9944
Fax: 732-555-9964 mail@mincing.com
www.mincing.com
Importers, processor of spices, seeds and aromatic herbs
President: Manoj Rupaerlia
CFO: K Jobanputra
Quality Controol: Nagy Beskal
Sales: Dorothy Hollomay
Plant Manager: Charles Armgnti
Purchasing: H Ruparelia
Estimated Sales: $.5-1 million
Number Employees: 1-4
Square Footage: 200000
Parent Co: Mincing Trading Corporation

8342 MindFull, Inc.
Hutto, TX 78634
info@mindfull.com
mindfull.com
Organic and electrolyte teas
President/Owner: Grant Burgess
CEO: Matt Jimenez

8343 Mindo Chocolate Makers
11061 Trinkle Rd
Dexter, MI 48130-9443
734-660-5635
info@mindochocolate.com
www.mindochocolate.com
Chocolate
Co-founder: Jose Meza
Co-founder: Barbara Wilson
Number Employees: 1-4

8344 Minerva Cheese Factory
430 Radloff Avenue
PO Box 60
Minerva, OH 44657
330-868-4196
Fax: 330-868-7947 jackie@minervadairy.com
www.cheesehere.com
Dairy products including butter, whey and cheese
Owner: Phillip Muller
VP: Adam Muller
Contact: Venae Banner
vbanner@minervacheese.com
Estimated Sales: $6 Million
Number Employees: 40
Type of Packaging: Consumer, Food Service, Private Label, Bulk

8345 Minerva Dairy Inc
430 Radloff Ave
PO Box 60
Minerva, OH 44657-1400
330-868-4196
Fax: 330-868-7947 www.minervadairy.com
Producer of various cheeses, cheese gift boxes, spreads, butters, meats and condiments.
President: Adam Mueller
CEO: Phil Mueller
phil@minervadairy.com
Treasurer: Venae Watts
Operations Manager: Dave Saling
Purchasing Manager: Anthony Aslanes
Estimated Sales: $25-49.9 Million
Number Employees: 20-49
Number of Brands: 2
Type of Packaging: Consumer, Food Service, Private Label, Bulk
Brands:
Amish Gourmet
Minerva

8346 Mingo Bay Beverages
721 Seaboard Street
Myrtle Beach, SC 29577-6520
843-448-5320
Fax: 843-448-4162 mingomoe@aol.com
Processor and exporter of coffee, tea and fruit bases, mixes and concentrates
President: Larry Moses
Estimated Sales: $1-5 Million
Number Employees: 8
Square Footage: 320000
Type of Packaging: Consumer, Food Service, Private Label, Bulk
Brands:
Mingo Bay Beverages

8347 Mingo River Pecan Company
2005 Babar Ln
P.O. Box 2030
Florence, SC 29503
843-662-2452
Fax: 843-664-2338 800-440-6442
swise@youngplantations.com
www.mingoriverpecans.com
Flavored pecans
Executive Director: Chenen Harvey
Estimated Sales: $20-50 Million
Number Employees: 100-249

8348 Minh Food
1303 W Harris Ave
Pasadena, TX 77506
713-475-1970
Fax: 713-740-7272
Egg rolls
President: Chi Nguyen
COO: William Hirsch
Number Employees: 100-249
Parent Co: Schwann's Sales

8349 Minh Food Corporation
1251 Scarborough Ln
Pasadena, TX 77506
713-740-7200
Fax: 713-740-7205 800-344-7655
Frozen Asian foods
Manager: Cole Lewis
CEO: Ron Minist
Executive VP: Mike Minist
Number Employees: 10-19
Parent Co: Schwann's Sales
Type of Packaging: Consumer, Food Service, Private Label

8350 Mini Pops Inc
208 Tosca Dr
Stoughton, MA 02072-1506
781-436-5864
Fax: 781-533-9033 info@minipopsinc.com
Flavored gluten free, organic, popped sorghum snack
Contact: Chrissy Conti
chrissy.conti@myminipops.com
Number Employees: 1-4

8351 Minn-Dak Farmers Co-Op
7525 Red River Rd.
Wahpeton, ND 58075
701-642-8411
Fax: 701-642-6814 www.mdf.coop
Beet sugar manufacturer.
President/CEO: Kurt Wickstrom
Vice President, Agriculture: Tom Knudsen
Executive VP/CFO: Rick Kasper
Information Technology Director: John Wieser
Vice President, Human Resources/Safety: Sheila Klose
Vice President, Operations: Paul Fry
Year Founded: 1972
Estimated Sales: $214.31 Million
Number Employees: 766
Type of Packaging: Bulk
Other Locations:
Minn-Dak Farmers Coop.
Wahpeton ND

8352 Minn-Dak Growers LTD
4034 40th Ave N
PO Box 13276
Grand Forks, ND 58203-3818
701-746-7453
Fax: 701-780-9050 info@minndak.com
www.minndak.com
Buckwheat, mustard, safflower and sunflower
Owner/President/General Manager: Harris Peterson
harris.peterson@minndak.com
Principal/CFO: Mona Kozojed
R&D Director: Mohammad Badaruddin
Quality Control Manager: Liz Carruth
Marketing Director: Kristin Sharp
Sales: Harris Peterson
Public Relations Director: Jaci Pau
Manufacturing Supervisor: Bruce Sondreal
Estimated Sales: $11 Million
Number Employees: 20-49
Number of Brands: 3
Number of Products: 9
Square Footage: 180000
Type of Packaging: Consumer, Food Service, Bulk
Brands:
Mdgl
Mdm
Minn-Dak

8353 Minn-Dak Yeast Co Inc
18175 Red River Rd W
Wahpeton, ND 58075-9697
701-642-3300
Fax: 701-642-1908 www.dakotayeast.com
Fresh bakers' yeast
EVP: Scott Miller
Manager: Richard Ames
rames@mdf.coop
Plant Manager: Richard Ames
Purchasing Director: John Nyquist
Estimated Sales: $9.5 Million
Number Employees: 20-49
Square Footage: 88000
Parent Co: Minn-Dak Farmers Cooperative
Brands:
Dakota Yeast

8354 Minnehaha Spring Water Company
1906 E 40th Street
Cleveland, OH 44103-3557
216-431-0243
Bottled natural spring water
President: Michael Wright
Number Employees: 20-49
Type of Packaging: Consumer, Food Service, Private Label, Bulk

8355 Minnesota Dehydrated Veg Inc
915 Omland Ave N
PO Box 245
Fosston, MN 56542-1001
218-435-1997
Fax: 218-435-6770 info@mdvcorp.com
www.mdvcorp.com
Dehydrated vegetables
Manager: Jim Noise
Marketing Director: Jam Moyes
ic@mdvcorp.com
CFO: Jim Noyes
CFO: Jordy Alson
Site Manager: Karla Holm
ic@mdvcorp.com
Estimated Sales: $5-10 Million
Number Employees: 50-99
Brands:
Minnesota Dehydrated Vegetables

8356 Minnesota Hemp Farms
14530 90th St S
Hastings, MN 55033
877-205-4367
www.mnhempfarms.com
Hemp products
President/Owner: John Strohfus
Year Founded: 2016

8357 Minnestalgia Foods LLC
41640 State Highway 65
PO Box 86
Mcgregor, MN 55760-1407
218-768-4917
Fax: 218-768-2543 800-328-6731
minnestalgia.com

Wild berry syrups, jams, jellies and sauces, maple syrup, honey and whipped honey; also, wild rice pancake mix and organic wild, cultivated long grain and broken wild rice
Owner: Jay Erckenbrack
minnestalgiawinery@citilink.net
General Manager: Lori Gordon
Estimated Sales: $700,000
Number Employees: 1-4
Square Footage: 6400
Type of Packaging: Consumer, Food Service, Private Label, Bulk
Brands:
Minnesota Wild

8358 **Minnestalgia Foods LLC**
41640 State Highway 65
PO Box 86
Mcgregor, MN 55760-1407
218-768-4917
Fax: 218-768-2543 800-328-6731
minnestalgia@citlink.net www.minnestalgia.com
Wines, soup and pancake mixes, berry and maple syrups, honeys, gift baskets and more!
President: Jay Erckenbrack
minnestalgiawinery@citilink.net
Estimated Sales: $1-3 Million
Number Employees: 1-4

8359 **Minor Fisheries**
176 West Street
Port Colborne, ON L3K 4E2
Canada
905-834-9232
Fax: 905-834-5662 catch@minorfisheries.net
www.minorfisheries.net
Whole, dressed, filleted, fresh and frozen fresh water fish including yellow perch, yellow pickerel, white perch, whitefish, smelt, rock bass, silver bass and lingcod. Founded in 1974
President: Rod Minor
Director: Dan Minor
Estimated Sales: $2.8 Million
Number Employees: 7
Square Footage: 8400
Type of Packaging: Consumer, Bulk

8360 **Minsa Corp**
4401 82nd St
Suite 1150
Lubbock, TX 79424-3396
806-799-3757
Fax: 806-799-3783 800-852-8291
Specialty corn flour for mixes, available in while, yellow, blue, red and purple corn. Organic, Non-Gmo or Conventional Gluten Free Whole Fiber Certified.
CEO: Rodrigo Ariceaga
CFO: Hubert Torres
Quality Assurance Manager: Sergio Gonzalez
Sales: Ricky Rodriguez
Contact: Penny Blackerby
penny.blackerby@minsa.com
Plant Manager: Jesus Ayala
Estimated Sales: $20-40 Million
Number Employees: 855

8361 **Minsley, Inc.**
989 S Monterey Ave
Ontario, CA 91761
909-458-1100
Fax: 909-458-1101 info@minsley.com
www.minsley.com
Organic grain bowls and cups
Number of Brands: 1
Number of Products: 10
Type of Packaging: Consumer
Brands:
MINSLEY

8362 **Mint Savor**
PO Box 13009
Jersey City, NJ 07303
info@mintsavor.com
www.mintsavor.com
Mints
Sales: Christina Nitsa
Brands:
Mint Savor
TEAKS

8363 **Minterbrook Oyster Co**
12002 114th Street Court Kp N
PO Box 432
Gig Harbor, WA 98329-5058
253-857-5251
Fax: 253-857-5521 www.minterbrookoyster.com
Processor and exporter of fresh and frozen oysters, Manila clams and mussels
President: Harold E Wiksten
COO: Erica Wiksten
mntrerka@aol.com
Sales Manager: Mike Paul
Estimated Sales: $8.6 Million
Number Employees: 5-9
Square Footage: 280
Type of Packaging: Consumer, Food Service, Private Label
Brands:
Minterbrook

8364 **Minus the Moo**
196 Quincy St
Dorchester, MA 02121-1996
703-999-7183
minusthemoo.com
Lactose-free ice cream
Co-Founder: Gwen Burlingame

8365 **(HQ)Minute Maid Company**
PO Box 1734
Atlanta, GA 30301
800-520-2653
www.minutemaid.com
World's leading marketer of premium fruit juices and drinks. Processor of chilled, aseptic and frozen concentrated juices, punches and lemonades including orange, grape, grapefruit, tangerine, lemon, lime, etc.; also, citrus oils
President: Mike Saint John
CEO: E Neville Isdell
Number Employees: 500-999
Parent Co: Coca-Cola Company
Type of Packaging: Consumer, Food Service
Other Locations:
Minute Maid
Dinuba CA
Minute Maid
Apopka MI
Minute Maid
Northampton MA
Minute Maid
Paw Paw MI
Minute Maid
Waco TX
Minute Maid
Petersborough ON
Minute Maid
Mississauga ON
Brands:
Minute Maid
Minute Maid Juice to Go
Minute Maid Just 15
Minute Maid Sparkling

8366 **Mira International Foods**
1200 Tices Ln Ste 203
East Brunswick, NJ 08816
732-846-5410
Fax: 732-613-7206 800-818-6472
www.miramango.com
Tropical nectars
President: Ramses Awadalla
CEO: Mark Awadalla
Vice President: Pancy Awadalla
Marketing Director: Mariam Gandour
Sales Director: Joseph Awadalla
Public Relations: Mark Awadalla
Estimated Sales: $5-10 Million
Number Employees: 5-9
Square Footage: 96000
Type of Packaging: Private Label
Brands:
Mira Mango Nectar

8367 **Miracapo Pizza**
2323 Pratt Blvd
Elk Grove Village, IL 60007
847-631-3500
miracapopizza.com
Premium pizzas, gourmet sandwiches, wraps, paninis, grab-n-go items, breakfast items and desserts. Gluten-free options.
VP, Finance: Dan Hoffman
VP, R&D and Quality Assurance: Lynn Waldman
Year Founded: 1984
Estimated Sales: $200 Million
Number Employees: 200-500
Square Footage: 150000
Brands:
Bravissimo!
Connie's Pizza
Little Lady
Primerro
Tenaro

8368 **Miracle Noodle**
8606 Santa Monica Blvd.
Suite 6920
Los Angeles, CA 90069
800-948-4205
Fax: 310-496-0651 www.miraclenoodle.com
Manufacturer of noodles, rice, and matcha.
President: Jonathan Carp
Vice President: Jill Goldstein

8369 **Miracle Tree**
Miami, FL 33139
888-590-1555
info@miracletree.org www.miracletree.org
Moringa tea
CEO: Kunal Mirchandani

8370 **Miramar Fruit Trading Company**
2300 Nw 92nd Ave
Doral, FL 33172-4814
305-883-4774
Fax: 305-883-4773 miramarfruit.4t.com
Canned guava pulp, mango pulp, grated coconut, papaya chunks, guava shells, orange shells, pina colada mix, black beans, green pigeon peas
President: Carlos Unanue
Manager: Maria Miguel
Estimated Sales: $2.5-5 Million
Number Employees: 11
Brands:
Ancel

8371 **Miramar Pickles & Food Products**
200 NW 20th Avenue
Fort Lauderdale, FL 33311
954-463-0222
Sauerkraut, pickles, pickled tomatoes
Estimated Sales: $100 Thousand
Number Employees: 1-4
Number of Brands: 1
Brands:
Miramar

8372 **Mirasco**
900 Circle 75 Pkwy SE # 1660
Atlanta, GA 30339-3095
770-956-1945
Fax: 770-956-0308 atlanta@mirasco.com
www.mirasco.com
Supplier of meats, poultry and seafood
President: Sami Rizk
sami.rizk@mirasco.com
Estimated Sales: $4.5 Million
Number Employees: 20-49
Type of Packaging: Food Service, Private Label, Bulk

8373 **Misfit Juicery**
Washington, DC 20036
703-465-5355
Fax: 703-243-6410 misfitjuicery.com
Juices made from imperfect fruits and vegetables
Founder: Elyse Cohen
Number of Brands: 1
Number of Products: 7
Type of Packaging: Consumer
Brands:
MISFIT

8374 **Mishawaka Brewing Company**
408 W Cleveland Rd
Granger, IN 46530
574-256-9993
misbrew@aol.com
Seasonal beer, ale, stout, lager and porter
Owner: Thomas R Schmidt
Estimated Sales: $1-2.5 Million
Number Employees: 20-49
Type of Packaging: Consumer, Food Service
Brands:
Four Horsemen

8375 **Mishler Packing Co**
5680 W 100 N
Lagrange, IN 46761-8605
260-768-4156
Fax: 260-768-4354 800-860-4156
www.mishlersmeats.com
Established in 1947. Manufacturer of pork burger patties.
Co-Owner: Dennis Monson
Co-Owner: Jonathan Monson
Estimated Sales: $20 Million
Number Employees: 20-49
Type of Packaging: Consumer

8376 **Mishrun**
Edison, NJ 08820
347-495-4320
contactmishrun@gmail.com
www.mishrun.com
Chutneys and relishes
Founder: Rashmi Mehndroo

8377 **Miss Ginny's Orginal Vermont Pickle Works**
655 N Main Street
Northfield, VT 05663-6829
802-485-3057
Fax: 802-485-3057
Pickles

8378 **Miss Jenny's Pickles**
6104 Old Orchard Road
Kernersville, NC 27284-3296
336-978-0041
jenny@missjennyspickles.com
www.missjennyspickles.com

8379 **Miss Jones Baking Co.**
5900 Hollis St
Suite W
Emeryville, CA 94608
www.missjones.co
Clean-label baking mixes
Founder & CEO: Sarah Jones Garibaldi
Number of Brands: 1
Number of Products: 18
Type of Packaging: Consumer
Brands:
MISS JONES BAKING CO.

8380 **Miss Meringue**
1709 LA Costa Meadows Dr
San Marcos, CA 92078-5105
760-471-4978
Fax: 760-712-7814 800-561-6516
Meringues and cookies
Owner: Roland D'Abel
CFO: Rick Lamb
Quality Control: Rom William
Estimated Sales: $5-10 Million
Number Employees: 100-249
Brands:
Miss Meringue
Splenda(r)

8381 **Miss Scarlett's Flowers**
1845 Anka St
Juneau, AK 99801-7211
907-586-1766
Fax: 907-586-6545 800-345-6734
Pickled fruits, olives and vegetables; mushrooms, artichokes, asparagus, eggplant, baby corn, green beans, carrots, Brussel sprouts, snow peas, snap peas, zucchini pickles, sweet baby onions, pickled garlic, cocktail tomatoes, babyokra, cap
Owner: Samra Green
missscarletts@gci.net
Co-Owner: Ralph Luper
Estimated Sales: Less Than $500,000
Number Employees: 1-4
Type of Packaging: Private Label
Brands:
Miss Scarlett

8382 **Miss Tea Brooklyn Inc**
184 Eagle St
Suite 5A
Brooklyn, NY 11222-1570
718-389-9090
Manufacturer of a variety of teas.
Co-Founder: Nir Kahan
Contact: Revital Shoua
revital@miss-tea.com
Estimated Sales: Less Than $500,000
Number Employees: 1-4

8383 **Mission Foods**
5860 S Ash Ave
Tempe, AZ 85283-5100
480-491-2511
www.missionfoods.com
Mexican tortillas and tortilla chips
Estimated Sales: $50-100 Million
Number Employees: 250-499
Parent Co: Gruma Corporation
Type of Packaging: Consumer, Food Service, Private Label, Bulk

8384 **(HQ)Mission Foods Corp.**
1159 Cottonwood Ln.
Suite 200
Irving, TX 75038
214-583-5113
www.missionfoods.com
Authentic Mexican food products, such as tortillas, salas, tostadas, and more.
CEO: Craig Leonard
Year Founded: 1977
Estimated Sales: $1.7 Billion
Number Employees: 5,700
Parent Co: Gruma Corporation
Type of Packaging: Consumer, Food Service, Private Label, Bulk
Brands:
Diago's
Diane's
Guerrero
Mission

8385 **Mission Foods Corp.**
5601 Executive Dr.
Irving, TX 75038
972-232-5200
www.missionfoods.com
Corn chips, salsa, tortillas and barbecue sauce
Estimated Sales: $25-49.9 Million
Number Employees: 100-249
Parent Co: Gruma Corporation
Type of Packaging: Consumer, Food Service, Private Label, Bulk

8386 **Mission Foods Corp.**
5505 E Olympic Blvd
Commerce, CA 90022
323-803-1400
www.missionfoods.com
Mexican food products
Estimated Sales: $20-50 Million
Number Employees: 250-499
Parent Co: Gruma Corporation
Type of Packaging: Consumer, Food Service, Private Label, Bulk

8387 **Mission Foodservice**
PO Box 2008
Oldsmar, FL 34677-7008
800-443-7994
Fax: 800-272-5207 mission@answers-sys.com
Manufacturer and exporter of Mexican foods including flour and corn tortillas, tortilla chips, pastries, taco and tostada shells
SVP/GM: Robert Smith
Marketing Director: Robin Tobor
VP Sales: Tom Daley
Number Employees: 1,000-4,999
Square Footage: 1680000
Type of Packaging: Consumer, Food Service, Private Label, Bulk
Brands:
Diago
Dianes
Guerrero
Marias
Mission

8388 **Mission Mountain Winery**
82420 US Hwy 93
PO Box 100
Dayton, MT 59914
406-849-5524
Fax: 406-849-5524
info@missionmountainwinery.com
www.missionmountainwinery.com
Wines
President: Thomas Campbell
Estimated Sales: $690,000
Number Employees: 10-19
Brands:
Mission Mountain

8389 **Mission Pharmacal Company**
10999 Interstate Hwy. 10 W.
Suite 1000
San Antonio, TX 78230-1355
210-696-8400
Fax: 210-696-6010 www.missionpharmacal.com
Vitamins and nutritional supplements.
President/CEO: Neil Walsdorf
Chairman: Neil Walsdorf
Executive VP/COO: James Walsdorf
Year Founded: 1946
Estimated Sales: $157 Million
Number Employees: 461
Number of Brands: 17
Square Footage: 31000
Type of Packaging: Consumer
Other Locations:
Commercial Office
Doylestown PA
Manufacturing, Distribution & R&D
Boerne TX
Specialty Manufacturing & Printing
San Antonio TX
Brands:
Aquoral
Avar-e
Avar
Binosto
CitraNatal
Eletone
Ferralet
Glyderm
Hyophen
Liquid KI
Lithostat
Oncovite
Ovace
Texacort
Uribel
UROCKIT-K
Utira-C

8390 **Mission Valley Foods**
43032 Christy St
Fremont, CA 94538
408-254-9387
General grocery
Owner: Jayant Patel
Estimated Sales: $990,000
Number Employees: 25
Type of Packaging: Private Label
Brands:
Brickenridge
Chef Martin

8391 **Mississippi Cheese Straw**
741 E Eighth St
Yazoo City, MS 39194-3309
662-746-7171
Fax: 662-746-7162 800-530-7496
info@mscheesestraws.com
www.mscheesestraws.com
Cheese, lemon, and chopped pecan and cinnamon straws and Mississippi mud puppies, cookies, chocolate chip, oatmeal, pecan
President: Hunter Yerger
hyerger@mscheesestraws.com
VP: Robbie Yerger
Estimated Sales: $2.5 Million
Number Employees: 10-19
Square Footage: 40000
Type of Packaging: Consumer
Brands:
Mississippi Cheese Straws
Mississippi Mud Pupp
Original Lemon Straw

8392 **Missouri Wine & Gift**
2167 W Terra Ln
O Fallon, MO 63366-2366
636-639-9858
missouriwineandgift@centurytel.net
Distributor/wholesaler of wines and wine accessories
Owner: Judy Evans
missouriwineandgift@centurytel.net
Estimated Sales: $110,000
Number Employees: 1-4

8393 Mister Bee Potato ChipsCo
512 West Virginia Ave
Parkersburg, WV 26101-1647
304-428-6133
Fax: 304-428-1291 info@misterbee.com
www.misterbee.com
Established in 1951. Manufacturer of potato chips.
Co-Owner: Mary Anne Ketelsen
Co-Owner: Douglas Ketelsen
Co-Owner: James Barton
Co-Owner: Gregory Barton
Co-Owner: Gregory Reed
Sales Exec: Douglas Klein
info@misterbee.com
Estimated Sales: $20-50 Million
Number Employees: 20-49
Type of Packaging: Consumer, Food Service, Bulk
Brands:
Mister Bee

8394 Mister Cookie Face
One Ice Cream Drive
PO Box 1318
Dunkirk, NY 14048
732-370-5533
Fax: 732-370-4015 800-333-0305
webmaster@fieldbrookfoods.com
www.cookieface.com
Novelty ice cream
President/ CEO: Kenneth Johnson
Controller & VP: Ronald Odebralski
Director Quality: Jack Lockwood
SVP Marketing & Sales: James Masood
Contact: Jack Lindstrand
jack.lindstrand@cookieface.com
Director Operations: Kevin Grismore
VP Purchasing: Robert Griewisch
Estimated Sales: $12.2 Million
Number Employees: 100-249
Square Footage: 80000
Type of Packaging: Consumer, Private Label, Bulk
Brands:
Mr. Cookie Face

8395 Mister Fish Inc.
288 Rolling Mill Rd
Baltimore, MD 21224-2033
410-288-2722
Fax: 410-288-4757 ed@misterfishinc.com
www.misterfishinc.com
Seafood
Owner: Frank Petilo
Estimated Sales: $1-3 Million
Number Employees: 20-49

8396 Mister Pickle's Inc
540 Auburn Ravine Rd
Auburn, CA 95603-3954
530-885-1000
www.mrpickles.com
Pickles
Owner: Alan Neihaus
Vice President: Scott Wiseman
Estimated Sales: Below $5 Million
Number Employees: 10-19

8397 Mister Snacks Inc
500 Creekside Dr
Amherst, NY 14228-2109
716-691-1500
Fax: 716-210-1010 800-333-6393
www.mistersnacks.com
Snacks, trail mixes, yogurt, candy and chocolate coated items.
President: Michael Stern
VP, Sales: Stephen Stern
VP, Operations: Ed Lilly
Estimated Sales: $10-20 Million
Number Employees: 20-49
Number of Brands: 2
Square Footage: 14
Type of Packaging: Private Label, Bulk
Brands:
Stone Mountain Snacks
Sunbird Snacks

8398 Mister Spear
2900 E Harding Way
Stockton, CA 95205-3577
209-464-5365
Fax: 209-464-3846 800-677-7327
misterspear@misterspear.com
www.misterspear.com
Shiitake mushrooms, artichokes, asparagus, avocados, sugar snap peas, tomatoes, bi-color corn, bing cherries, Fuji apples
President: Chip Arnett Jr
Estimated Sales: Less Than $500,000
Number Employees: 1-4
Type of Packaging: Consumer, Food Service
Brands:
Msi
Mister Spear

8399 Misty Islands Seafoods
P. O. Box 201 Lepreau
Dipper Harbour, NB E5J 2T1
Canada
506-659-2781
Fax: 506-659-3113
www.mistyharbourseafood.com
Seafood
Manager: Robert Melovidov
Manager: Richard Tremaine
Estimated Sales: $3-5 Million
Number Employees: 1-3
Parent Co: Coastal Enterprises

8400 Misty's Restaurant & Lounge
6235 Havelock Ave
Lincoln, NE 68507-1279
402-466-7222
Fax: 402-466-7222 www.mistyslincoln.com
All-purpose seasonings and Bloody Mary mix
Owner: Reece Hummell
Sales Representative: Dave Walbrecht
Director Operations: Brian Tones
Estimated Sales: $3.8 Million
Number Employees: 50-99
Type of Packaging: Consumer, Food Service

8401 Mitch Chocolate
300 Spagnoli Rd
Melville, NY 11747-3507
631-777-2400
Fax: 631-777-1449 www.misschocolate.com
Hard candy lollypops; wholesaler/distributor of salt water taffy and fundraising boxed chocolates
President: Lawrence Hirsihheimer
VP Operations: Martin Bloomfield
Estimated Sales: $3-5 Million
Number Employees: 5-9
Square Footage: 16000
Type of Packaging: Consumer, Private Label
Brands:
Frolic

8402 Mitchel Dairies
1591 E 233rd Street
Bronx, NY 10466-3336
718-994-6655
Fax: 718-994-6113
Dairy products including fluid milk
President: Philip Tulotta
Treasurer: Linda Tulotta
Estimated Sales: $110 K
Number Employees: 1

8403 (HQ)Mitchell Foods
80 Mitchell Foods Ln
Barbourville, KY 40906-7683
606-545-6677
Fax: 606-546-4190 888-202-9745
sales@mitchellfoods.com
Fresh marinated boneless pork chops, rib eyes, chicken breast, meat loaf and barbecue products; also, chili and beer cheese
President: Greg Mitchell
sales@mitchellfoods.com
Owner: Jim Mitchell
VP Quality Control: Greg Mitchell
Estimated Sales: $1-3 Million
Number Employees: 10-19
Square Footage: 60000
Type of Packaging: Consumer, Food Service, Private Label, Bulk
Other Locations:
Mitchell Foods
Lexington KY
Brands:
Mitchell Foods

8404 Mitchum Potato Chips
P.O.Box 36639
Charlotte, NC 28236
704-372-6744
Fax: 704-339-0066
Potato chips
President: John Wilson
Marketing Director: Henry Pully
COO: Tommy Thompson
Contact: Randy Hardin
rhardin@mitchumchips.com
Estimated Sales: $10-20 000,000
Number Employees: 1-4
Type of Packaging: Bulk
Brands:
Mdi
Mitchum Rices
Savealot
Tiggly Wiggly
Ukrop

8405 Mitsubishi Chemical Holdings
655 3rd Ave # 15
New York, NY 10017-9135
212-672-9400
Fax: 914-761-0108 webapid@m-chem.com
www.mitsubishichemical.com
Bacteriostatic emulsifiers; also, calcium suspension, confectionery including chocolate, low-fat spreads, dairy product analogs and fruit coatings
President: Tats Iwai
ageless@mgc-a.com
Sales: Takazumi Kanekiyo
Number Employees: 1000-4999
Parent Co: Mitsubishi Chemical Coorporation
Type of Packaging: Bulk
Brands:
Ryoto Sugar Ester

8406 (HQ)Mitsubishi Intl. Corp.
520 Madison Avenue
Floor 18
New York, NY 10022-4327
212-759-5605
Fax: 212-605-1810 800-442-6266
Food commodities: coffee, cocoa, dairy products, fruits, vegetables and frozen juice concentrates. Food ingredients, enzymes, emulsifiers, baking agents.
President: James Brumm
CFO: Yasuyuki Sugiura
Executive VP/COO: Yoshihiko Kawamura
Sales/Purchasing Representative: Patrick Welch
Contact: Keigo Ando
keigo.ando@mitsubishicorp.com
Number Employees: 250-499
Other Locations:
Seattle WA

8407 Mix-A-Lota Stuff LLC
4828 N Kings Hwy
Suite 424
Fort Pierce, FL 34951
727-365-7328
brendassauces@aol.com
www.mixalotastuff.com
Sauce
President: Brenda Chinn

8408 Mixallogy
Ponte Vedra Beach, FL 32082
mixallogy.com
Cocktail mixes
Founder & CEO: Gwen Manto
Co-Founder: Monica Pina Alzugaray
VP, Sales: Steve Manto

8409 Mixerz All Natural Cocktail Mixers
100 Cummings Center
Suite 220B
Beverly, MA 01915
978-922-6497
All natural cocktail mixers
Marketing: Christina Pesente

8410 Mixes by Danielle
615 Pelvedere Street
Warren, OH 44483
330-856-5190
Fax: 330-856-3386 800-537-6499
Urban spices
President: Trissa McClerry

8411 Mixon Fruit Farms Inc
2525 27th St E
Bradenton, FL 34208-7467
941-748-5829
Fax: 941-748-1085 800-608-2525
info@mixon.com www.mixon.com

Manufacturer, packer and exporter of citrus fruits, vegetables, fudge, honey, jellies, marmalades and spreads, salsa, dips, pickles and nuts
President: Dean Mixon
Estimated Sales: $3.43 Million
Number Employees: 50-99
Square Footage: 360000
Brands:
Mixon

8412 Miyako Oriental Foods Inc
4287 Puente Ave
Baldwin Park, CA 91706-3420
626-962-9633
Fax: 626-814-4569 877-788-6476
joearai@coldmountainmiso.com
www.coldmountainmiso.com
Miso in different flavors and colors. Used in making sauces, soups, marinades, dressings, dips and main dishes.
Vice President: Teruo Shimizu
shimizu@coldmountainmiso.com
VP: Teruo Shimizu
Marketing/Sales/Quality Assurance Mgr: Joe Arai
Estimated Sales: $3 Million
Number Employees: 10-19
Square Footage: 72000
Type of Packaging: Consumer, Food Service, Private Label, Bulk
Brands:
Cold Mountain
Kanemasa
Yamaizumi
Yamajirushi

8413 Miyoko's Kitchen
2086 Marina Ave
Petaluma, CA 94954
415-521-5313
info@miyokoskitchen.com
miyokoskitchen.com
Vegan cheese
Founder & CEO: Miyoko Schinner
CFO: John Breen
COO: Billy Bramblett
Quality Assurance Manager: Matt Smith
Square Footage: 30000

8414 Mizkan Americas Inc
2400 Nicholson Ave
Kansas City, MO 64120
800-323-4358
info@mizkan.com www.mizkan.com
Flavored vinegars, mustards, and cooking wines.
Executive VP: Clarice Moore
Marketing Director: Tom Matthews
Operations Manager: Mike Cole
Plant Manager: Wayne Towe
Purchasing Manager: Phyllis Conover
Number Employees: 10-19
Type of Packaging: Consumer, Food Service, Private Label, Bulk
Brands:
Cushing
Lincoln
Ozark
Rogers
Speas
Springdale

8415 (HQ)Mizkan Americas Inc
1661 Feehanville Dr
Suite 300
Mount Prospect, IL 60056
800-323-4358
info@mizkan.com www.mizkan.com
Flavored vinegars, mustards, and cooking wines.
President & Chief Operating Officer: Kevin Ponticelli
Chief Executive Officer: Koichi Yuki
Chief Financial Officer: Tommy Isshiki
Director, Information Technology: Mohammad Adnan
VP, Quality & Food Safety: Shen-Youn Chang
EVP, Retail Sales & Marketing: Mike Smith
VP, Marketing: Dan O'Leary
SVP, Sales: Paul Callahan
VP, Operations: Kevin Culver
Director, Operations: Alan Schmoldt
Director, Procurement: Penny Philp
Year Founded: 1804
Estimated Sales: $20 Million
Number Employees: 50-99
Brands:
Nakano
Holland House
Mitsukan
Barengo
World Harbors
Angostura
El Diablo

8416 Mizkan Americas Inc
176 First Flight Dr
Auburn, ME 04210
800-323-4358
info@mizkan.com www.mizkan.com
Flavored vinegars, mustards, and cooking wines.

8417 Mizkan Americas Inc
247 West Ave
Lyndonville, NY 14098
800-323-4358
info@mizkan.com www.mizkan.com
Flavored vinegars, mustards, and cooking wines.

8418 Mizkan Americas Inc
7673 Sodus Center
Sodus, NY 14551
800-323-4358
info@mizkan.com www.mizkan.com
Flavored vinegars, mustards, and cooking wines.

8419 Mizkan Americas Inc
445 N Dakota
Lake Alfred, FL 33850
800-323-4358
info@mizkan.com www.mizkan.com
Flavored vinegars, mustards, and cooking wines.

8420 Mizkan Americas Inc
526 Interstate Dr
Crossville, TN 38555
800-323-4358
info@mizkan.com www.mizkan.com
Flavored vinegars, mustards, and cooking wines.

8421 Mizkan Americas Inc
3290 7th Street Rd
Shively, KY 40216
800-323-4358
info@mizkan.com www.mizkan.com
Flavored vinegars, mustards, and cooking wines.

8422 Mizkan Americas Inc
702 Kiddville Rd
Belding, MI 48809
800-323-4358
info@mizkan.com www.mizkan.com
Flavored vinegars, mustards, and cooking wines.

8423 Mizkan Americas Inc
410 Seymour Court
Green Bay, WI 54306
800-323-4358
info@mizkan.com www.mizkan.com
Flavored vinegars, mustards, and cooking wines.

8424 Mizkan Americas Inc
7331 Ben Frederick Rd
Abbeville, LA 70510
800-323-4358
info@mizkan.com www.mizkan.com
Flavored vinegars, mustards, and cooking wines.

8425 Mizkan Americas Inc
4647 Bronze Way
Dallas, TX 75236
800-323-4358
info@mizkan.com www.mizkan.com
Flavored vinegars, mustards, and cooking wines.

8426 Mizkan Americas Inc
9860 S Hwy 478
Vado, NM 88072
800-323-4358
info@mizkan.com www.mizkan.com
Flavored vinegars, mustards, and cooking wines.

8427 Mizkan Americas Inc
4065 J St SE
Deming, NM 88030
800-323-4358
info@mizkan.com www.mizkan.com
Flavored vinegars, mustards, and cooking wines.

8428 Mizkan Americas Inc
10037 E 8th St
Rancho Cucamonga, CA 91730
800-323-4358
info@mizkan.com www.mizkan.com
Flavored vinegars, mustards, and cooking wines.

8429 Mizkan Americas Inc
46 Walker St
Watsonville, CA 95076
800-323-4358
info@mizkan.com www.mizkan.com
Flavored vinegars, mustards, and cooking wines.

8430 Mizkan Americas Inc
1901 Ragu Dr
Owensboro, KY 42303
800-323-4358
info@mizkan.com www.mizkan.com
Flavored vinegars, mustards, and cooking wines.

8431 Mizkan Americas Inc
1400 Waterloo Rd
Stockton, CA 95205
800-323-4358
info@mizkan.com www.mizkan.com
Flavored vinegars, mustards, and cooking wines.

8432 Mj Kellner Co
5700 International Pkwy
Springfield, IL 62711-4052
217-483-1700
Fax: 217-483-1771 mjk@mjkellner.com
www.mjkellner.com
Wholesaler/distributor of groceries, meats, produce, frozen foods, baked goods, equipment and fixtures, general merchandise and seafood; serving the food service market
Owner: William Kellner
Founder: Maurice Kellner
CFO: Kathy Dierkes
kathyd@mjkellner.com
Sales Manager: Bill Barris
Director of Sales & Marketing: Gary Boston
Number Employees: 50-99

8433 Mo Hotta Mo Betta
2822 Limerick St
Savannah, GA 31404-4172
912-748-2766
Fax: 912-748-1364 www.mohotta.com
Processor and exporter of hot sauces
President: Jim Kelley
jimkelley@mohotta.com
Estimated Sales: $110,000
Number Employees: 20-49
Type of Packaging: Consumer, Food Service
Brands:
Hot Sauce For Cool Kids
Mo Hotta-Mo Betta

8434 Mobile Bay Seafood
11801 Old Shipyard Rd
Coden, AL 36523
251-973-0410
Fax: 706-538-6850
Seafood
President: Bob Omainsky

8435 Mobile Processing
PO Box 501187 Mobile Al 36605
2201 Perimeter Rd Ste A
Mobile, AL 36615-1130
251-438-6944
Fax: 251-438-6948
Fresh and frozen seafood including shrimp
Owner/President: James Higdon
Estimated Sales: $2 Million
Number Employees: 50-99

8436 Moceri South Western
4909 Pacific Hwy
San Diego, CA 92110-4005
619-297-7900
Fax: 619-297-8900
Beverages and bottling
President: Grace Moceri
Estimated Sales: $10-20 000,000
Number Employees: 10-19
Type of Packaging: Private Label

8437 **Mod Squad Martha**
1202 Gregorie Commons
Johns Island, SC 29455
615-476-3696
melissa@modsquadmartha.com
modsquadmartha.com
Marinades, dressings and sauces.
Founder: Melissa Ann Barton

8438 **Model Dairy LLC**
500 Gould St
Reno, NV 89502-1466
775-788-7900
Fax: 775-788-7951 800-433-2030
Processor and wholesaler/distributor of a full line of dairy products including ice cream
Cmo: Derrick Alby
derrick_@deanfoods.com
VP/General Manager: Jim Breslin
Controller: Peggy Baker
Manager: Jim Breslin
Number Employees: 100-249
Square Footage: 100000
Parent Co: Suiza Dairy Group
Type of Packaging: Food Service

8439 **Modena Fine Foods Inc**
158 River Rd
Clifton, NJ 07014-1571
973-470-8499
Fax: 201-842-9001 www.modenafinefoods.com
Balsamic products, including balsamic vinegar, specialty wine vinegars, and balsamic condiments
President: Fred Mortadi
Vice President: Michael Giaimo
michael@modenafinefoods.com
Estimated Sales: $720,000
Number Employees: 10-19

8440 **Modern Day Masala, LLC**
Po Box 682374
Marietta, GA 30068-0040
866-611-3757
Fax: 866-611-1596
Gluten-free, organic/natural, USDA, full-line spices, spices, foodservice, private label.
Owner: Vikas Khanna
Marketing: Kristin Sharma

8441 **Modern Gourmet Foods**
18011 Mitchell S
Suite B
Irvine, CA 92614-6007
949-250-3129
sales@shonfelds.com
Designs, produces and manufactures gourmet food products that are sold straight to retailers. Company originally began as Shonfeld's USA, Inc. and was located in New Jersey.
Founder/Chairman: Boaz Shonfeld
President: Mark Greenhall
Vice President Sales, National Accounts: Jason Hoffman
Product Development: Yaron Bart
Estimated Sales: $15.5 Million
Number Employees: 10-19
Type of Packaging: Private Label

8442 **Modern Italian Bakery of West Babylon**
301 Locust Ave
Oakdale, NY 11769-1652
631-589-7300
Fax: 631-589-7383
Italian baked goods
President/CEO: James Turco
Estimated Sales: $20-49 Million
Number Employees: 100-249
Square Footage: 60000

8443 **Modern Macaroni Co LTD**
1708 Mary St
Honolulu, HI 96819-3103
808-845-6841
Fax: 808-845-6841 www.modernmacaroni.net
Dry Asian noodles, shrimp flakes and soybean flour
Owner: Darrell Siu
Estimated Sales: $900,000-$1 Million
Number Employees: 10-19
Square Footage: 4800
Type of Packaging: Consumer, Food Service
Brands:
Hula

8444 **Modern Oats**
9600 Research Dr
Irvine, CA 92618
888-662-2334
support@modernoats.com modernoats.com
Instant oatmeal
President/Owner: Richard Principale
Year Founded: 2013
Number of Brands: 1
Number of Products: 10
Type of Packaging: Consumer
Brands:
MODERN OATS

8445 **Modern Packaging**
3245 N Berkeley Lake Rd NW
Duluth, GA 30096
770-622-1500
Fax: 770-814-0046
www.modernpackaginginc.com
Contract packager of condiments and liquid food items; warehouse providing dry, cooler and humidity-controlled storage of foodstuffs, liquid packaging products and seasonal sales items; also, pick and pack and rail siding available
President: Herb Sodel
VP: Nancy Sodel
Estimated Sales: $3.6 Million
Number Employees: 50-99
Square Footage: 400000

8446 **Modern Pod Co.**
63 Baker St
Providence, RI 02905
info@modpodco.com
www.modpodco.com
Hummus snacks
General Manager: Levon Kurkjian
Number of Brands: 1
Number of Products: 4
Type of Packaging: Consumer
Brands:
HUMMUS POD

8447 **Modern Pop**
Laguna Beach, CA 92651
themodernpop.com
Frozen fruit bars
CEO: Julie Podolec
Number of Brands: 1
Number of Products: 12
Type of Packaging: Consumer
Brands:
MODERN POP

8448 **Modern Products Inc**
6425 W Executive Dr
Mequon, WI 53092-4478
262-242-2400
Fax: 262-242-2751 800-877-8935
modernfearn@aol.com www.modernfearn.com
Seasonings, spices, bake mixes, natural products and soy products
President: Gaylord G Palermo
modernfearn@aol.com
CEO & Chairman: Anthony Palermo
Secretary: Petronella Palermo
Quality Control Manager: Jim Kohnke
Estimated Sales: $2.5 Million
Number Employees: 20-49
Type of Packaging: Consumer, Food Service
Brands:
Classique Fare
Rearn Naturefresh
Spice Garden
Spike
Swiss Kriss
Vegeful
Vegit

8449 **Modern Table**
Walnut Creek, CA 94597
www.moderntable.com
Plant-based pastas and prepared meals
Marketing: Jennifer Eiseman
National Sales Manager: Jeff Schonhoff
Number Employees: 1,000-4,999
Number of Brands: 1
Number of Products: 12
Type of Packaging: Consumer

8450 **Modern Tea Packers**
P.O.Box 370708
Brooklyn, NY 11237-0708
718-417-1060
Fax: 718-417-6405
Tea and tea bags
Owner: Julius Medwin
CEO: Julius Neumann
Estimated Sales: $5-9.9 000,000
Number Employees: 20-49

8451 **Modesto WholeSoy**
PO Box 1277
Ceres, CA 95301
209-523-5119
Fax: 209-523-5519
Produces the highest quality liquid soybase for use in soymilk, yogurt, smoothies, ice cream and other dairy-like products.
CEO: Ken Norquist
CFO: Henry Gloasser
Plant Manager: Frank Gasca
Estimated Sales: $290,000
Number Employees: 3
Square Footage: 7668

8452 **Moet Hennessy USA**
85 10th Ave
New York, NY 10011
212-251-8200
www.mhusa.com
Wines and spirits.
President & CEO: Jim Clerkin
Managing Director: Jo Thornton
Year Founded: 1980
Estimated Sales: $884.58 Million
Number Employees: 3,452
Other Locations:
New Jersey
Massachusetts
Illinois
Florida
Georgia
Texas
California
Brands:
10 Cane
Ardbeg
Belvedere
Cape Mentelle Vineyards
Capezzana
Chandon
Chateau Cheval Blanc
Chateau D'Yquem
Chateau De Sancerre
Chateau La Nerthe
Cheval Des Andes
Chopin
Cloudy Bay Vineyards
Dom Perignon
Esperto
Glenmorangie
Grand Marnier
Green Point
Hennessy
Krug
Lapostolle
Livio Felluga
Moet & Chandon
Monsanto
Navan
Newton Vineyard
Numanthia
Ruinart
Terrazas De Los Andes
Veuve Clicquot

8453 **Mogen David Wine Corp**
85 Bourne St
Westfield, NY 14787
716-326-3151
www.mogendavid.com
Kosher and nonkosher wines including white, rose and red.
President: E. Schwartz
Year Founded: 1933
Estimated Sales: $200-500 Million
Number Employees: 100-249
Parent Co: The Wine Group
Type of Packaging: Consumer

8454 **Mohn's Fisheries**
1144 Great River Rd
Harpers Ferry, IA 52146-7565
563-586-2269
Fax: 563-423-1579
Seafood
Owner: Diane Mohn
Estimated Sales: $300,000-500,000
Number Employees: 1-4

8455 **Mokk-a**
Oostmaaslaan 628
Rotterdam, 3063 DJ
Netherlands
info@mokk-a.com
mokk-a.com
Coffee
Owner: Karen Glavimans-Hawa
Estimated Sales: A
Number Employees: 1
Parent Co: Danish Koffie Connection

8456 **Moledina Commodities**
5501 Muirfield Court
Flower Mound, TX 75028
817-490-1101
Fax: 817-490-1105 mohamed@moledina.com
Manufacturer of quality green coffees from throughout the work, with a strong emphasis on East African Coffees.
President: Mohamed Moledina
VP: Fidahusein R Moledina
fidahusein@moledina.com
Brands:
Moledina

8457 **Molinaro's Fine Italian Foods Ltd.**
2345 Stanfield Rd
Unit 50
Mississauga, ON L4Y 3Y3
Canada
905-281-0352
www.molinaros.com
Processor, importer and exporter of pizza, fresh and frozen pizza shells, fresh pasta, flatbread, focaccia, pasta sauce, fresh and frozen pasta entrees, meat, vegetable and cheese lasagna, panzerottis and calzones
President: Vince Molinaro
CEO: Gino Molinaro
Sales/Marketing: Catherine Pyman
Purchasing Manager: Frank Molinaro
Number Employees: 140
Square Footage: 304000
Type of Packaging: Consumer, Food Service, Private Label, Bulk
Brands:
Famosa
Molinaro's
Supremo

8458 **Molli**
Dallas, TX
info@mollisauces.com
mollisauces.com
Mexican sauces and marinades.
Co-Founder: Rodrigo Salas
Co-Founder: Leticia Castellanos
Brands:
Molli(c)

8459 **(HQ)Molson Coors Beverage Company**
250 South Wacker Dr.
Chicago, IL 60606
800-645-5376
www.molsoncoors.com
Brews and beer.
President/CEO, Molson Coors: Gavin Hattersley
President, Molson Coors Canada: Frederic Landtmeters
CFO: Tracey Joubert
President, Emerging Growth: Pete Marino
Chief Strategy Officer: Rahul Goyal
Chief People & Diversity Officer: Dave Osswald
Chief Marketing Officer: Michelle St. Jacques
President, U.S. Sales: Kevin Doyle
Chief Communications Officer: Adam Collins
Chief Legal & Government Affairs Officer: E. Lee Reichert
Chief Supply Chain Officer: Brian Erhardt
Estimated Sales: $6.7 Billion
Number Employees: 17,000
Number of Brands: 100
Type of Packaging: Consumer
Other Locations:
Molson Coors Canada
Montreal QC
Molson Coors Europe
Prague, Czech Rep.
Molson Coors International
New Delhi, India
MillerCoors
Chicago IL
Brands:
Blue Moon
Carling
Coors
Molson
Molson Canadian
Apatinsko
Astika
Barmen
Bergenbier
Black Horse
Black Ice
Bohemian
Borsodi
Branik
Burgasko
Caffreys
Cobra
Colorado Native
Creemore Springs
Crispin
Extra Gold Lager
Franciscan Well
Granville Island Brewing
Henry Weinhard's
Herman Joseph's Private Reserve
Hop Valley
Icehouse
India Beer
Jelen
Kamenitza
Keystone
Laurentide
Leinenkugel's
Mad & Noisy
Mad Jack
Magnum
Mickey's
Miller
Milwaukee's Best
Niksicko
Noroc
Old Style Pilsner
Old Vienna
Olde English 800
Ostravar
Ozujsko
Red Dog
Revolver Brewing
Rickard's
Saint Archer
Sharp's
Smith and Forge
Sparks
Standard Lager
Staropramen
Steel Reserve
Terrapin
Tomislav
Vratislav
Wanderoot
Winterfest
Worthington's
Zima
Cool

8460 **Molson Coors North America**
250 South Wacker Dr.
Chicago, IL 60606
800-645-5376
www.molsoncoors.com
Brews and beer; North American operating division of Molson Coors Beverage Company.
President/CEO, Molson Coors: Gavin Hattersley
President, U.S. Sales: Kevin Doyle
Chief Supply Chain Officer: Brian Erhardt
Year Founded: 2008
Estimated Sales: K
Number Employees: 10,000+
Parent Co: Molson Coors Beverage Company
Type of Packaging: Consumer
Other Locations:
Brewery
Albany GA
Brewery
Eden NC
Brewery
Elkton VA
Brewery
Fort Worth TX
Brewery/Corporate Office
Golden CO
Brewery
Irwindale CA
Brewery/Corporate Office
Milwaukee WI
Brewery
Trenton OH
Corporate Headquarters
Chicago IL
Watertown Hops Company
Watertown WI
Brands:
Aguila
Arnold Palmer Spiked Half & Half
Barmen
Blue Moon
Colorado Native
Coors
Crispin Cider
Cristal
Cusquena
Extra Gold Lager
Foster's
George Killian's Irish Red
Grolsch Premium Lager
Hamm's
Hnery Weinhard's
Herman Jospeh's Private Reserve
Hop Valley
Icehouse
Keystone
Lech Premium
Leinenkugel's
Magnum
Mickey's
Miller
Milwaukee's Best
Molson Canadian
Old Vienna
Old English
Peroni
Pilsner Urquell
Red Dog
Redd's
Revovler
Saint Archer
Sharp's
Smith & Forge Hard Cider
Sol Cerveza
Sparks
Steel Reserve
Terrapin
Tyskie Gronie

8461 **Mom N' Pops Inc**
834 Brooks St
New Windsor, NY 12553
845-567-0640
Fax: 845-567-0652
Wholesale manufacturers of candy and lollipops.
President: Barbara Regenbaum
Sales Director: Stacy Zagon
Estimated Sales: $2.5-5 Million
Number Employees: 10-19
Number of Brands: 1
Type of Packaging: Bulk
Brands:
MOM 'N POPS

8462 **Mom's Bakery**
1703 N Woods St
Sherman, TX 75092-3629
903-893-7585
Fax: 404-969-1144 txginal@aol.com
www.momsbakerysherman.com
Buttermilk and yeast raised biscuits
Owner: Gina Adams
VP: Daniel Kay
Estimated Sales: Less Than $500,000
Number Employees: 5-9
Square Footage: 225000
Type of Packaging: Food Service, Bulk

8463 **Mom's Famous**
145 NW 20th St
Boca Raton, FL 33431
561-750-1903
Fax: 561-750-4105
Baked goods
President: Tony Danesh

Estimated Sales: $575,000
Number Employees: 10-19
Brands:
Mom's Famous

8464 **Mom's Food Company**
Post Office Box 97
Osterville, MA 02655
508-648-0188
800-969-6667
Frozen meatballs and sauce
President: Laurie Gardella
Estimated Sales: $1.1 Million
Number Employees: 23
Square Footage: 48000
Type of Packaging: Consumer, Food Service, Private Label, Bulk
Brands:
Mom's

8465 **Mom's Gourmet, LLC**
17594 Walnut Trail
Chagrin Falls, OH 44023-6428
440-564-9702
skoepke@momsgourmet.net
www.momsgourmet.net
Dairy-free, gluten-free, lactose-free, organic/natural, sugar-free, vegetarian, full-line spices, rubs.
Marketing: Sally Koepke

8466 **Momence Packing Company**
PO Box 906
Sheboygan Falls, WI 53085
815-472-6485
Fax: 815-472-2459 888-556-2728
Frozen sausage
President: Patrick Garinger
Contact: Kirsten Mueller
kmueller@johnsonville.com
Estimated Sales: Below $5,000,000
Number Employees: 250-499
Type of Packaging: Consumer, Private Label

8467 **Mon Ami Restaurant**
3845 E Wine Cellar Rd
Port Clinton, OH 43452-3704
419-797-4446
Fax: 419-797-9171 800-777-4266
info@monamiwinery.com
www.monamiwinery.com
Champagne
Owner: John Kronberg
info@monamiwinery.com
Estimated Sales: $500,000-$1 Million
Number Employees: 50-99
Brands:
Mon Ami

8468 **Mona Lisa Foods**
600 West Chicago Ave
Suite 860
Chicago, IL 60654
312-496-7300
Fax: 312-496-7399 866-443-0460
www.monalisadecorations.com
Gourmet chocolate products
CEO: Antoine de Saint-Affrique
CEO & President, Americas: Peter Boone
CFO: Remco Steenbergen
Year Founded: 1987
Estimated Sales: $20-50 Million
Number Employees: 20-49
Number of Products: 50
Square Footage: 32000
Parent Co: Barry Callebaut

8469 **Monaco Baking Company**
14700 Marquardt Avenue
Santa Fe Springs, CA 90670
562-404-5028
Fax: 562-229-0963 800-569-4640
Manufacturer of gingerbread and shortbread cookies, shortbread and gingerbread cookie mixes.
Executive Director: Philip Moreau
Contact: Sonia Orozco
sonia@monacobaking.com
Year Founded: 1994
Estimated Sales: $20-50 Million
Number Employees: 20-49
Type of Packaging: Private Label

8470 **Monarch Beverage Company**
3630 Peachtree Road NE
Suite 775
Atlanta, GA 30326
404-262-4040
Fax: 404-262-4001 800-241-3732
info@monarchbeverages.com
www.monarchbeverages.com
Manufacturer and exporter of concentrates including sports and energy drinks, healthy fruit beverages, enhanced waters, ready-to-drink beverages, ready-to-drink coffees and soft drinks. Beverage brand franchisor.
CEO: Jacques Bombal
COO: Didier Arnaud
Estimated Sales: $3.2 Million
Number Employees: 30
Type of Packaging: Bulk
Brands:
Acute Fruit
American Cola
Comotion
Kickapoo Joy Juice
Ntrinsic
Planet Cola
Reaktor
Rush! Energy

8471 **Monarch Seafoods Inc**
515 Kalihi St
Honolulu, HI 96819-3268
808-841-7877
Fax: 808-847-3930 www.monarchseafoods.com
Seafood and seafood products
President: Thomas Mukaigawa
Estimated Sales: $.5-1 million
Number Employees: 10-19

8472 **Monastary Mustard**
840 South Main Street
Angel, OR 97362
503-949-6321
Info@MonasteryMustard.com
monasterymustard.com
Mustard
Mustard Flavor Creator: Sister Terry Hall

8473 **Monastery Fruitcake**
130 N Queen St
Martinsburg, WV 25401
304-596-2024
Fax: 304-264-3698
orders@monasteryfruitcake.org
monasteryfruitcake.org
Trappist monks at Holy Cross Abbey produce fruitcake and creamed honey.

8474 **Mondelez International**
100 Deforest Ave
East Hanover, NJ 07936
855-535-5648
www.mondelezinternational.com
Snacks
Chairman & CEO: Dirk Van De Put
President, North America: Glen Walter
Executive VP & CFO: Luca Zaramella
Estimated Sales: $25.9 Billion
Number Employees: 83,000
Brands:
OREO
Ritz
Trident
Halls
Chips Ahoy!
Triscuit
Dentyne
Green & Black's
Toblerone
belVita

8475 **Mondial Foods Company**
P.O.Box 75036
Los Angeles, CA 90075-0036
213-383-3531
Processor and exporter of pineapple and other tropical juices
President: Ben Gattegno
Estimated Sales: $210000
Number Employees: 20-49
Type of Packaging: Food Service, Bulk

8476 **Mondiv/Division of Lassonde Inc**
3810 Alfred Laliberte
Boisbriand, QC J7H 1P8
Canada
450-979-0717
Fax: 450-979-0279 infomondiv@mondiv.com
www.mondiv.com
Tapenades, bruschetta, glass jar gravy, specialty sauces and dips, glass jar soups and stews, meat-based pasta sauce, pasta sauce (non-meat), organic pasta sauces, organic glass jar soups, glass jar (ready-to-serve) meals, pestos andchutneys
President/Owner: Vito Monopoli

8477 **Money's Mushrooms**
#800-1500 W Georgia Street
Vancouver, BC V6G 2Z6
Canada
604-669-3741
Fax: 604-669-9732 800-669-7992
www.calbur.com
Processor, grower and exporter of canned and pickled mushrooms
President: Keith Potter
CFO: Cliff Lillicrop
VP Sales/Marketing: Dean Fleming
Number Employees: 900
Type of Packaging: Consumer, Food Service, Private Label, Bulk
Brands:
Moneys

8478 **Monin Inc.**
Clearwater, FL
855-352-8671
www.monin.com
Manufacturer and exporter of flavored syrups, smoothie mixes and purees, sauces, cocktail mixes, and sweeteners.
CEO: Bill Lombardo
Owner: Olivier Monin
VP of Marketing: Suzanna Geel

8479 **Monini North America**
6 Armstrong Rd # 4
Shelton, CT 06484-4722
203-513-2685
Fax: 203-513-2863 info@monini.us
www.monini.us
Oils
Chairman: Marco Petrini
Manager: Elizabeth Brooks
e.donovan@silkroutestrategists.com
Estimated Sales: Less than $200,000
Number Employees: 5-9
Type of Packaging: Private Label
Brands:
Amabile Umbro
Granfruttato
Ii Monello
Il Poggiolo
Monini

8480 **Monkey Media**
78 East 2nd Avenue
Vancouver, BC V5T 1B1
Canada
604-215-2163
Fax: 604-708-8747 877-666-6539
mike@monkeymedia.net
Software for the food industry
CEO: Steve Izen
CFO: Erle Dardick
Sales Director: Mike Tyler
Operations Manager: Marrianne Zakure
Estimated Sales: $1.5 Million
Number Employees: 13
Number of Products: 4
Square Footage: 2400
Parent Co: Monkey Media Software
Brands:
Monkey Baking
Monkey Catering
Monkey Party

8481 **Monks' Specialty Bakery**
3258 River Rd
Piffard, NY 14533
monksbread@gmail.com
monksbread.com
Bread and specialty foods.

8482 **Monogram Food Solutions**
530 Oak Court Drive
Suite 400
Memphis, TN 38117
901-685-7167
Fax: 901-259-6671 www.monogramfoods.com
Bacon, smoked meats
Contact: Spencer Mcclure
spencer.mcclure@pilottravelcenters.com

8483 **Monsanto Co**
304 Center St
West Fargo, ND 58078-1209
701-282-7338
Fax: 701-282-8218 800-437-4120
info@interstateseed.com
Soybean seeds
President: Bruce Hovland
Cmo: Jim Johnson
jim.m.johnson@monsanto.com
Marketing Coordinator: Gerri Leach
Sales Director: Bill Webber
Operations Manager: Vic Nordstrom
Estimated Sales: $2.5-5 Million
Number Employees: 20-49

8484 **Monsoon Kitchens**
159 Memorial Dr
Suite G
Shrewsbury, MA 01545
508-842-0070
Fax: 617-629-0160 info@monsoonkitchens.com
monsoonkitchens.com
Indian foods
Co-Founder: Swati Elavia
Type of Packaging: Consumer, Food Service

8485 **Monster Beverage Corp.**
1 Monster Way
Corona, CA 92879
800-426-7367
info@monsterbevcorp.com
www.monsterbevcorp.com
Energy drinks.
President/Vice Chair/COO: Hilton Schlosberg
Chairman/CEO: Rodney Sacks
Year Founded: 2002
Estimated Sales: $3.3 Billion
Number Employees: 1,991
Number of Brands: 7
Parent Co: The Coca-Cola Company
Type of Packaging: Consumer, Food Service
Brands:
Monster Energy
Burn
NOS
Full Throttle
Relentless
Mother
Reign
Predator

8486 **Monster Cone**
8500 Delmeade
Montreal, QC H4T 1L6
Canada
541-636-2022
Fax: 514-342-0346 800-542-9801
info@monstercone.com
Processor and exporter of waffle bowls and cones including plain and chocolate dipped
President: Daniel Mardinger
Number Employees: 50-99
Square Footage: 80000
Type of Packaging: Consumer, Food Service, Private Label, Bulk
Brands:
Monster Cone

8487 **Mont Blanc Gourmet**
2925 E Colfax Ave
Denver, CO 80206
303-755-1100
Fax: 303-283-1100 800-877-3811
Chocolate syrup, cocoa powders, chai mixes, cappuccino, mocha mixes, and powdered hot cocoa mix. Flavoring: chocolate, white chocolate, caramel, kahlua
Chocolatier & Co-Founder: Michael Szyliowicz
Certified Executive Chef: Charles V Heaton
Senior Lab Technologist: Lauren Yoon
Contact: Rebecca Gelston
rebecca@montblancgourmet.com
Estimated Sales: $1-$3 Million
Number Employees: 8
Brands:
Mont Blanc Chocolate Syrups

8488 **(HQ)Montana Coffee Traders**
5810 US Highway 93 S
Whitefish, MT 59937-8414
406-862-7628
Fax: 406-862-7680 800-345-5282
www.coffeetraders.com
Fresh roasted coffee and tea.
Owner: R C Beall
Estimated Sales: Less Than $500,000
Number Employees: 1-4
Other Locations:
Whitefish Coffeehouse
Whitefish MT
Columbia Falls Cafe
Columbia Falls MT
Kalispell Cafe
Kalispell MT

8489 **Montana Flour & Grains**
2225 Montana Hwy 223
Fort Benton, MT 59442
406-622-5436
Fax: 406-622-5439 800-622-5790
info@montanaflour.com www.montanaflour.com
Manufactures flour and other grain mill products specializing in organic flours
President: Andre Giles
andre@montanaflour.com
Estimated Sales: Below $5 Million
Number Employees: 10-19
Number of Brands: 3
Number of Products: 15
Type of Packaging: Food Service, Private Label, Bulk

8490 **Montana Mex**
PO Box 11255
Bozeman, MT 59719
hello@montanamex.com
www.montanamex.com
BBQ sauces, seasonings and oils
Chef & Co-Founder: Eduardo Garcia
Type of Packaging: Consumer
Brands:
MONTANA MEX

8491 **Montana Monster Munchies**
PO Box 10711
Bozeman, MT 59719-0711
406-388-3077
Fax: 406-388-2063 info@mtmonstermunchies.com
www.montanacookiecompany.com
Gluten free baked goods, cookies
Owner: Rich Powell
Estimated Sales: Less Than $500,000
Number Employees: 10-19

8492 **Montana Mountain Smoked Fish**
10 Elkhorn View Dr
Montana City, MT 59634
800-649-2959
Fax: 406-449-4755 800-649-2959
smkfishqueen@aol.com
Smoked salmon, sockeye salmon, keta salmon, rainbow trout, halibut and salmon spread. All natural, no preservatives
President: Kim Waltee
Estimated Sales: Less than $500,000
Number Employees: 1-4
Type of Packaging: Private Label

8493 **Montana Naturals**
1400 Kearns Blvd
Park City, UT 84060-6725
800-650-9597
www.mtnaturals.com
Processor and exporter of dietary supplements
General Manager: Sterling Gabbitas
Number Employees: 50-99
Square Footage: 104000
Parent Co: HealthRite
Type of Packaging: Consumer, Private Label
Other Locations:
Montana Naturals by HealthRit
Arlee MT
Brands:
Pure Energy

8494 **Montana Ranch Brand**
PO Box 2036
Billings, MT 59103
406-294-2333
Fax: 406-294-2336 www.montanaranchbrand.com
Natural Piedmontese beef, ranch beef, pioneer pork, prairie lamb, and heritage bison
President/Owner: Ralph Peterson
Number Employees: 3

8495 **Montana Specialty Mills LLC**
701 2nd St S # 5
P.O.Box 2208
Great Falls, MT 59405-1852
406-761-2338
Fax: 406-761-7926 800-332-2024
www.mtspecialtymills.com
Primary agricultural processor providing contracting, origination, storage and processing of grain and oilseed-based products to secondary food manufacturers
President: Steve Chambers
steve@mtspecialtymills.com
Controller: Cecil Swensen
General Manager: Gordon Svenby
Operations: Robert Bender
Conrad Plant Manager: Gordon Mattern
Estimated Sales: Below $5 Million
Number Employees: 20-49
Square Footage: 80000

8496 **Montana Tea & Spice Trading**
2600 W Broadway St
Missoula, MT 59808-1624
406-721-4882
Fax: 406-543-1126 montanatea@msn.com
www.montanatea.com
Tea and herbal tea blending, spice blending. Wholesale, retial and mail order
Owner: Sherri Lee
Estimated Sales: $750,000
Number Employees. 5-9
Number of Brands: 2
Number of Products: 300+
Square Footage: 16000

8497 **Montchevre-Betin, Inc**
4030 Palos Verdes Drive North
Suite 201
Rolling Hills Estates, CA 90274
310-541-3520
Fax: 310-541-3760 www.montchevre.com
Goat cheese
Owner: Arnaud Solandt
Estimated Sales: $1-3 Million
Number Employees: 5-9

8498 **Monte Cristo Trading**
14 Harwood Ct
Scarsdale, NY 10583-4121
914-725-8025
Fax: 914-725-0869
General grocery
President: Anton Derosa
aderosa@montecristo.com.au
Estimated Sales: $530,000
Number Employees: 1-4
Type of Packaging: Consumer, Food Service, Bulk

8499 **Monte Vista Farming Co**
5043 N Montpelier Rd
Denair, CA 95316-9608
209-874-1866
Fax: 209-874-2024 www.montevistafarming.com
Processor and exporter of almonds
President: Jonathan Hoff
jhoff@montevistafarming.com
CFO: Bob McClain
VP Sales: Dan Whisenhunt
Operations Manager: Renee Crozier
Estimated Sales: $1.3 Million
Number Employees: 50-99
Square Footage: 8000

8500 **Montebello Kitchens**
PO Box 610
Gordonsville, VA 22942
800-743-7687
Fax: 270-209-1371
Spices and rubs, dressing and marinades, sauces, Virginia peanuts, coups and milled grains.
Owner: Steven Lynch
selynch@montebellokitchens.com

8501 **Montebello Packaging**
1036 Aberdeen St
Hawkesbury, ON K6A 1K5
Canada
613-632-7096
Fax: 613-632-9638 bpilon@montebellopkg.com
www.montebellopkg.com
Aluminum aerosol cans & aluminum/laminate tubes
President: Betty Pilon
Chief Financial Officer: Greg Labuschagne
Vice President, Sales: Tom Zopf
Director of Information Technology: Jean-Francois Leclerc
Director of Quality Operations: Fred Long
Director of Sales: John Iorii
Estimated Sales: $20-50 Million
Number Employees: 240
Parent Co: The Jim Pattison Group
Brands:
M-Bond
M-Purity Ring
M-Purity Seal

8502 **Montelle Winery**
201 Montelle Dr
PO Box 147
Augusta, MO 63332-1518
636-228-4464
Fax: 636-228-4754 888-595-9463
info@montelle.com www.montelle.com
In the late 1960s and early 1970s, a few pioneering souls began to refurbish the old vineyards and winery buildings of Missouri's premier wine-growing regions
Owner: Tony Kooyumjian
Founder: Clayton Byers
Vineyard Manager: Paul Hopen
Cellar Master: Mark Nienhueser
Manager: Brian Obermark
manager@montelle.com
Estimated Sales: Less Than $500,000
Number Employees: 1-4
Number of Products: 15

8503 **Montello Inc**
6106 E 32nd Pl # 100
Tulsa, OK 74135-5495
918-665-1170
Fax: 918-665-1480 800-331-4628
www.montelloinc.com
Importer and distributor of emulsifiers and gums
President: Allen Johnson
allenj@montelloinc.com
VP: Leo Wooldridge
Estimated Sales: $6 Million
Number Employees: 5-9

8504 **Monterey Fish Company**
950 S Sanborn Rd
Salinas, CA 93901
831-771-9221
Fax: 831-775-0156 mntyfish@redshift.com
www.montereyfishcompany.com
Canned and frozen herring, anchovies, herring roe, mackerel, sardines and squid
President: Carmelo J Trinqali
VP: Sal Trinquali
Contact: Mary Brand
mbrand@cityofslt.us
VP Operations: Anthony Trinqali
Plant Manager: Joseph Tringali
Estimated Sales: $1-$2.5 Million
Number Employees: 1-4
Type of Packaging: Consumer, Food Service, Private Label
Brands:
Bono
Seawave

8505 **Monterey Mushrooms Inc**
260 Westgate Dr
Watsonville, CA 95076
Fax: 831-763-2300 800-333-6874
www.montereymushrooms.com
Manufacturer and exporter of canned, frozen and refrigerated mushroom stems/pieces, slices and buttons
President & CEO: Shah Kazemi
shah.kazemi@montmush.com
VP of Sales & Marketing: Mike O'Brien
Number Employees: 1000-4999
Type of Packaging: Consumer, Food Service, Private Label, Bulk
Other Locations:
Multi Site Fresh Operation Farms
Orlando FL
Multi Site Fresh Operation Farms
Princeton IL
Multi Site Fresh Operation Farms
Royal Oaks CA
Multi Site Fresh Operation Farms
Las Lomas CA
Multi Site Fresh Operation Farms
Morgan Hill CA
Multi Site Fresh Operation Farms
San Miguel, Mexico
Multi Site Fresh Operation Farms
Vancouver, BC Canada
Multi Site Fresh Operation Farms
Arroyo Grande CA
Multi Site Fresh Operation Farms
Madisonville TX
Multi Site Fresh Operation Farms
Loudon TX
Multi Site Fresh Operation Farms
Temple PA
Monterey Processing Facility
Bonne Terre MO
Monterey Product Development
Royal Oaks CA
Brands:
Let's Blend

8506 **Monterey Vineyard**
800 S Alta St
Gonzales, CA 93926
831-675-4000
Fax: 831-675-4019
Wines
General Manager/President: Ken Greene
Operations Manager: Ken Greene
Winemaker: Chris Mallar
Production Manager: Noel Vofter
Estimated Sales: Less than $500,000
Number Employees: 5-9

8507 **Monterrey Products**
803 S Zarzamora St
San Antonio, TX 78207-5363
210-435-2872
Fax: 210-435-2877 monpro@sbcglobal.net
www.monterreyproducts.com
Mexican products including mole sauce, candy, spices, chili powder and dry chili mixes
Owner: Ernest DE Los Santos
Vice President: Sylvia De Los Santos
Estimated Sales: $2 Million
Number Employees: 10-19
Type of Packaging: Consumer, Food Service

8508 **Monterrey Products**
803 S Zarzamora St
San Antonio, TX 78207-5363
210-435-2872
Fax: 210-435-2877 800-872-1652
monpro@sbcglobal.net
www.monterreyproducts.com
Spices, salsa and praline candies
Owner: Ernest DE Los Santos
Estimated Sales: Below $5 Million
Number Employees: 10-19
Brands:
Monterrey

8509 **Montevina Winery**
20680 Shenandoah School Road
Plymouth, CA 95669
209-245-6942
Fax: 209-245-6617 info@montevina.com
www.montevina.com
Wine
CEO: Louis Trinchero
VP: Jeff Meyers
Estimated Sales: $2.5-5 Million
Number Employees: 10-19

8510 **Monticello Canning Company**
PO Box 3509
Crossville, TN 38557
monticello.c@usa.net
monticellocanning.tripod.com
Canned vegetables including sweet red and green peppers, pimientos
President: Earl Dean
Treasurer: Alton Tabor
Vice-President: Warren Dean
Qualtity Control: Kevin Dean
General Manager: Greg Barnwell
Estimated Sales: $3-5 Million
Number Employees: 5-9
Type of Packaging: Consumer, Food Service, Private Label, Bulk
Brands:
Betty Ann

8511 **Monticello Vineyards-Corley**
4242 Big Ranch Rd
Napa, CA 94558-1301
707-253-2802
Fax: 707-253-1019
Wine@CorleyFamilyNapaValley.com
www.corleyfamilynapavalley.com
Wine and champagne
President: John Corley
john@monticellovineyards.com
Chairman: Jay Corley
Trade and Direct-to-Consumer Marketing: Leslie McCain
Sales & Marketing and Administration: Stephen Corley
Winemaker: Chris Corley
Estimated Sales: $1.3 Million
Number Employees: 10-19
Type of Packaging: Consumer

8512 **Montione's Biscotti & Baked Goods**
215 South Worcester St
Norton, MA 02766
508-285-4777
Fax: 508-285-4465 800-559-1010
www.montionesbiscotti.com
Baked goods, biscotti
President: Mary Montione
CFO: Dan Mahoney
Estimated Sales: $1 Million
Number Employees: 5-9
Type of Packaging: Private Label

8513 **Montmorenci Vineyards**
2989 Charleston Hwy
Aiken, SC 29801
803-649-4870
Fax: 803-642-1834
Wine
Owner/Winemaker: Robert Scott
Owner: Elaine Scott
General Manager: Stephanie Scott
Estimated Sales: $500,000-$1 Million
Number Employees: 1-4
Type of Packaging: Private Label
Brands:
Blanc Du Bois
Chambourcin
De Caradeuc White
Melody
Savannah White
Vin Eclipser

8514 **Montreal Chop Suey Company**
2100 Moreau Street
Montreal, QC H1W 2M3
Canada
514-522-3134
Fax: 514-522-8074
Chinese food products including fresh bean and alfalfa sprouts, fresh & frozen egg roll and wonton paste, fresh fried noodles and soya sprouts.
President: Bill Lee
Vice President: David Lee
VP: Robert Lee
Production Manager: Marc Comtols
Number Employees: 20
Square Footage: 140000
Type of Packaging: Consumer, Bulk
Brands:
Montreal Chop Suey

8515 **Monument Farms Dairy**
2107 James Rd
Middlebury, VT 05753-9525
802-545-2119
Fax: 802-545-2117
Milk and other dairy products
President: Robert James
bj@gmavt.net
VP: Peter James
Secretary/Treasurer: Millicent Rooney
VP/Plant Manager: Jonathan Rooney
Estimated Sales: $3.7 Million
Number Employees: 20-49
Type of Packaging: Private Label

8516 **Monument Farms Dairy**
2107 James Rd
Middlebury, VT 05753-9525
802-545-2119
Fax: 802-545-2117
Milk products
President: Robert James
bj@gmavt.net
Co-Owner: Jon Rooney
Co-Owner: James Rooney
Estimated Sales: $10-24.9 000,000
Number Employees: 20-49
Brands:
Monument Dairy Farms

8517 **Moo Chocolate/Organic Children's Chocolate LLC**
PO Box 271
Cos Cob, CT 06807-0271
203-561-8864
Fax: 203-869-7040 jackie@moochocolates.com
www.moochocolates.com
Gluten-free, kosher, organic/natural, chocolate bars.
Marketing: Jackie Eckholm

8518 **Mooala**
2633 McKinney Ave
Suite 130
Dallas, TX 75204
214-206-1902
info@mooala.com
www.mooala.com
Almond and banana milks
CEO: Jeff Richards
Number of Brands: 1
Number of Products: 4
Type of Packaging: Consumer
Brands:
MOOALA

8519 **Moody Dunbar Inc**
2000 Waters Edge Dr # 21
Johnson City, TN 37604-8312
423-952-0100
Fax: 423-952-0289
customerservice@moodydunbar.com
www.moodydunbar.com
Processor of bell peppers, pimientos and sweet potatoes, products are certified Kosher
CEO: Stanley Dunbar
CFO: Christy Dunbar
R&D/Quality Assurance Manager: Katie Rohrbacher Nixa
Vice President of Sales & Marketing: Ed Simerly
Estimated Sales: $37,000,000
Number Employees: 20-49
Number of Brands: 11
Type of Packaging: Consumer, Food Service, Private Label
Other Locations:
Saticoy Foods Corporation
Santa Paula CA
Dunbar Foods Corporation
Dunn NC
Brands:
CAL-SUN
CANNON
DUNBARS MARINATED ROASTED PEPPERS
DUNBARS ROASTED PEPPERS
DUNBARS SWEET POTATOES
DROMEDARY
SUNSHINE
OSAGE
DUNBARS CANDIED YAMS
NATURE'S PRIDE SWEET POTATOES
DUNBARS

8520 **Moon Dance Baking**
625 Martin Ave Ste 5
Rohnert Park, CA 94928-7935
USA
707-588-0800
Fax: 707-588-0804 info@hollybaking.com
www.moondancebaking.com
Cookies, biscotti
President: Debby Dyar
ddyar@hollybaking.com
Estimated Sales: G
Number Employees: 10-19

8521 **Moon Rabbit Foods**
267 Route 89
Savannah, NY 13146
828-273-6649
www.moonrabbitfoods.com
Manufacturer of baked desserts.
CEO: Candace Crawford
Founder: Mark Shaw

8522 **Moon Shot Energy**
208-411 Brazos St
Austin, TX 78701-3635
512-387-4703
www.moonshotenergy.com
Energy drinks
President: John Lee

8523 **Moon's Seafood Company**
461 N.
Harbor City Blvd
Melbourne, FL 32935
321-775-0552
Fax: 321-259-5958 800-526-5624
info@moonseafood.com www.moonseafood.com
Shrimp, scallops, clams and crabs
President: Jay Moon
Vice President: Rick Madrigal
Estimated Sales: $1-3 Million
Number Employees: 1-4
Brands:
Moon's Seafood

8524 **Moonlight Brewing Company**
2218 Laughlin Road
PO Box 6
Windsor, CA 95492-8213
707-528-2537
www.moonlightbrewing.com
Beer
President: Brian Hunt
Estimated Sales: $1-3 Million
Number Employees: 1-4
Brands:
Death and Taxes Black Beer
Full Moon Light Ale
Moonlight Pale Lager
Santa's Tipple
Twist of Fate Bitter Ale

8525 **Moonlight Co**
17719 E Huntsman Ave
Reedley, CA 93654-9205
559-638-7799
Fax: 559-638-7199
sales@moonlightcompanies.com
www.moonlightcompanies.com
Grapes and other summer fruit
President: Russ Tavlan
russ.tavlan@moonlightcompanies.com
Estimated Sales: $3-5 Million
Number Employees: 100-249
Type of Packaging: Consumer, Food Service, Private Label, Bulk
Brands:
Caliente
California Collection
Moonlight
Royal
The Ripe Stuff

8526 **Moonlight Gourmet**
PO Box 9686
Tyler, TX 75711-2686
903-581-1228
Fax: 903-581-1098 victoria@txmoon.com
www.txmoon.com
Milk chocolate pecans

8527 **Moonlight Mixes LLC**
2321 Cantrell Rd
Little Rock, AR 72202-2111
501-374-2244
www.wickedmixes.com
Manufacturer of coconut water.
President: Stan Roberts
Founder & CEO: Brent Bumpers
brent@wickedmixes.com
Sales Manager: Alex Robinson
Number Employees: 5-9

8528 **Moonlite Bar-B-Q Inn**
2840 W Parrish Ave
Owensboro, KY 42301-2689
270-684-8143
Fax: 270-684-8105 800-322-8989
pbosley@moonlite.com www.moonlite.com
Barbecue meats including mutton, pork and beef; also, bean soup, sauces and chili
President: Fred Bosley
fbosley@moonlite.com
VP: Ken Bosley
Marketing Director: Pat Bosley
Estimated Sales: $3 Million
Number Employees: 100-249
Number of Brands: 1
Number of Products: 48
Type of Packaging: Private Label
Brands:
Moonlite Bbq Inn

8529 **Moonshine Sweet Tea**
PO Box 500188
Austin, TX 78750
888-793-3883
info@moonshinesweettea.com
moonshinesweettea.com
Ready-to-drink and concentrated sweet tea
Founder: Joele Porter
CEO: Remmy Castillo
Year Founded: 1946
Number of Brands: 1
Number of Products: 7
Type of Packaging: Consumer, Food Service
Brands:
MOONSHINE SWEET TEA

8530 **Moonstruck Chocolate Co**
6600 N Baltimore Ave
Portland, OR 97203-5403
503-247-3448
Fax: 503-247-3450 800-557-6666
www.moonstruckchocolate.com
Manufacturer of chocolate.
Co-Owner: Sally Bany
Co-Owner: Dave Bany
dbany@moonstruckchocolate.com
Number Employees: 50-99

8531 **Moore Organics**
9047 Sutton Place
Hamilton, OH 45011
513-881-7144
Fax: 513-881-7145 sdagnillo@amtodd.com
Creates and manufactures natural and certified organic specialty ingredients.
Inside Sales Representative: Susan D'Agnillo
Contact: Galliano Enrique
galliano.enrique@moorelab.com

8532 **Moore's Candies**
3004 Pinewood Avenue
Baltimore, MD 21214
410-836-8840
Fax: 410-426-7073
Handcrafted chocolates and candy including truffles, almond crunch, chocolate-covered potato chips and pretzels, holiday and wedding chocolate items and specialty items
Co-Owner: Jim Heyl Jr
Co-Owner: Lois Heyl
VP: Dana Heyl
Estimated Sales: $3 Million
Number Employees: 5-9
Square Footage: 5000
Type of Packaging: Consumer, Food Service, Private Label, Bulk
Brands:
Moores

8533 **(HQ)Mooresville Ice Cream Co**
172 N Broad St
PO Box 118
Mooresville, NC 28115-3182
704-664-5456
Fax: 503-370-8516 800-304-7172
www.delux.com
Ice cream, low fat & no sugar added, sherbet, and novelties including ice cream sandwiches, flavored bars, and the infamous nutty cone.

President: Bob Stamey
Accounting: Tracy Potts
Manager: Marcus Ireland
Sales: Don Ashley
Manager: Brett French
brett@deluxe1924.com
Number Employees: 10-19
Type of Packaging: Consumer, Food Service, Private Label, Bulk
Brands:
Deluxe
Snickers
Twix
M&M
Dove
Klondike
Rich's

8534 **Moorhead & Company**
PO Box 1799
Rocklin, CA 95677
818-787-2510
Fax: 916-624-1604 800-322-6325
order@moorAgar.com www.mooragar.com
Manufacturer and importer of stabilizers including agar
President: Deborah Nichols
Sales/Marketing: Brenda Franklin
Estimated Sales: $180000
Number Employees: 3
Type of Packaging: Bulk
Brands:
Agarich
Agarloid
Agarmoor

8535 **Moosehead Breweries Ltd.**
89 Main St W
St. John, NB E2M 3H2
Canada
www.moosehead.ca
Processor and exporter of beer.
President & CEO: Andrew Oland
Executive Chairman: Derek Oland
CFO: Patrick Oland
VP, Supply Chain: Matthew Oland
Quality Control Technician: Jeanann Fairweather
Director of Marketing & Communications: Karen Cousins
Retail Operations Manager: Stephen Buckley
Special Projects Manager: Mary Gardner
Year Founded: 1867
Estimated Sales: $263.8 Million
Number Employees: 400
Type of Packaging: Consumer, Food Service
Brands:
Moosehead Lager

8536 **Morabito Baking Co Inc**
757 Kohn St
Norristown, PA 19401-3739
610-275-5419
Fax: 610-275-0358 800-525-7747
www.morabitobaking.com
Sourdough breads and Spoletti rolls
President: Aaron Chanthakoune
aaron@morabito.com
Marketing Manager: Joanna Morabito
Director of Sales: Marc Knox
Director of Human Resources: Cassandra Morabito
Estimated Sales: $10 Million
Number Employees: 100-249
Square Footage: 140000
Type of Packaging: Consumer, Food Service, Private Label, Bulk
Brands:
Morabito

8537 **Moravian Cookies Shop**
224 S Cherry St
Winston Salem, NC 27101-5231
336-924-1278
Fax: 336-924-9470 800-274-2994
sales@salembaking.com
Cookies and baked goods
President/Owner: Dewey Wilkerson
Contact: Brooke Smith
b.smith@salembaking.com
Operations Manager: Vincent Pellegrino
Estimated Sales: $2.30 Million
Number Employees: 25

8538 **More Than Gourmet**
929 Home Ave
Akron, OH 44310-4107
330-762-6652
Fax: 330-762-4832 800-860-9385
info@morethangourmet.com
www.morethangourmet.com
Stocks and sauces
Owner: Brad Sacks
bsacks@morethangourmet.com
CFO: Scott Bonnette
Marketing: Todd Hohman
Estimated Sales: $500,000-$1 Million
Number Employees: 20-49
Type of Packaging: Consumer, Food Service
Brands:
Demi-Glace Veal Gold
Glace De Poulet Gold
Veggie Glace Gold

8539 **Morehouse Foods Inc**
760 Epperson Dr
City Of Industry, CA 91748-1336
626-854-1655
Fax: 626-854-1656 888-297-9800
info@morehousefoods.com
www.morehousefoods.com
Yellow mustard, dijon mustard, stoneground mustard, honey spice mustard, spicy brown mustard, horseradish mustard, distilled vinegar and horseradish.
President: David Latter
davesr@morehousefoods.com
Year Founded: 1898
Estimated Sales: $20-50 Million
Number Employees: 20-49
Square Footage: 80000
Type of Packaging: Consumer, Food Service, Private Label, Bulk
Brands:
Chalif
El Rey
Morehouse
Redwood Empire
Rhinegeld

8540 **Moretti's Poultry**
2124 Tremont Ctr
Columbus, OH 43221-3110
614-486-2333
Fax: 614-486-2333 www.morettisofarlington.com
Fresh chicken and turkey
Owner: Tim Moretti
Estimated Sales: $1-3 Million
Number Employees: 20-49
Type of Packaging: Food Service, Bulk

8541 **Morey's Seafood Intl LLC**
1218 Highway 10 S
Motley, MN 56466-8209
218-352-6345
Fax: 218-352-6523 800-808-3474
www.moreysmarkets.com
Processor, importer and exporter of fresh and frozen fish including marinated salmon, marinated tilapia and marinated smoked fish and other speciality products.
President: Jim Walstrom
CFO: Gary Ziolkowski
Plant Manager: Patti Zahler
VP of Purchasing: Greg Frank
Year Founded: 1937
Estimated Sales: $20-50 Million
Number Employees: 10-19
Square Footage: 52000
Parent Co: Morey's Seafood International
Brands:
Morey's

8542 **Morgan Foods Inc**
90 W Morgan St
Austin, IN 47102
812-794-1170
888-430-1780
mfi-web@morganfoods.com
www.morganfoods.com
Canned foods including condensed soups, baked and refried beans, gravies, condiments and sauces.
SVP & Chief Financial Officer: Dan Slattery
dan.slattery@morganfoods.com
CEO & Chairman: John Morgan
Vice Chairman: Kelly Morgan Maciejak
Regional Sales Manager: Monty Craig
VP, Sales & Marketing: Bryan Flowers
VP, Human Resources: Phillip Bundy
Production Manager: Richard Miller
Year Founded: 1899
Estimated Sales: $48.5 Million
Number Employees: 250-499
Square Footage: 1000000
Type of Packaging: Consumer, Food Service, Private Label
Brands:
American Beauty
Royal Gem
Scott Country

8543 **Morgan Mill**
P.O.Box 525
Cherokee, NC 28719-0525
828-497-9227
Fax: 828-497-4330
Rainbow trout
Owner: Dale Owen
Estimated Sales: Less than $200,000
Number Employees: 1-4

8544 **Morgan Winery**
590 Brunken Ave
Suite C
Salinas, CA 93901
831-751-7777
Fax: 831-751-7780 www.morganwinery.com
Wine
Propietors: Donna Lee
Propietors: Dan Lee
Wine Maker: Giane Abate
Marketing Coordinator: Jason Auxier
Director of Sales: Jim McAllister
Contact: Jason Auxier
jason.auxier@morganwinery.com
Production Team: Carmen Maldonado
Estimated Sales: $850000
Number Employees: 5-9

8545 **Morii Foods, Inc.**
8215 SW Tualatin Sherwood Rd.
Tualatin, OR 97062-8441
503-691-7007
Fax: 503-692-5388
Rice noodles, instant short rice pasta, organic non-fried wheat noodles, vermicelli noodles
Vice President: Hideki Ogino
Estimated Sales: $32.33 Million
Number Employees: 1-4
Type of Packaging: Private Label, Bulk

8546 **Morinaga Nutritional Foods, Inc.**
3838 Del Amo Blvd
Suite 201
Torrance, CA 90503
310-787-0200
Fax: 310-787-2727 info@morinu.com
www.morinu.com
Tofu products
President & CEO: Hiroyuki Imanishi
Estimated Sales: $3-5 Million
Number Employees: 10-19
Square Footage: 20000
Parent Co: Morinaga Milk Company
Type of Packaging: Consumer, Food Service, Private Label
Other Locations:
Morinaga Nutritional Foods
Tualatin OR
Brands:
Mori-Nu

8547 **Morning Glory Dairy**
3399 S Ridge Rd
De Pere, WI 54115-9522
920-336-4206
Fax: 920-336-7317 www.deanfoods.com
Dairy
Manager: Calvin Rose
Plant Manager: Wally Hel
Estimated Sales: $10-20 Million
Number Employees: 100-249
Parent Co: Dairy Farmers of America

8548 **Morning Star Foods**
8 Joanna Court
East Brunswick, NJ 08816-2108
800-237-5320
Fax: 732-432-3928
Manufacturer and marketer of consumer packaged goods
President/CEO: Herman Graffinder
CFO: Craig Miller
Sr. VP Marketing: Toby Purdy
Sr. VP Operations: Samuel Hillin
Parent Co: Dean Foods Company
Type of Packaging: Private Label, Bulk

8549 **MorningStar Coffee Company**
207-E, Carter Drive
West Chester, PA 19382
888-854-2233
Fax: 610-701-7032 888-854-2233
www.morningstarcoffee.us
Specialty coffee roasters
President: Charles Streitwieser
cmarks@citymission.org
Estimated Sales: $450,000
Number Employees: 5-9
Type of Packaging: Private Label, Bulk
Brands:
Morning Star
Numit

8550 **Morningland Dairy Cheese Company**
6248 County Road 2980
Mountain View, MO 65548
417-855-0588
Fax: 417-469-5086 morninglanddairy@gmail.com
Gourmet health and raw milk cheeses
President: James Reiners
Estimated Sales: $3-5 Million
Number Employees: 5-9
Type of Packaging: Consumer, Food Service, Private Label, Bulk
Brands:
Morningland Dairy
Ozark Hills

8551 **Morningstar Farms**
1675 Fairview Rd
Zanesville, OH 43701-8890
740-453-5501
Fax: 740-453-7789 800-535-5644
www.morningstarfarms.com
Canned and frozen vegetarian foods
CEO/President: Dale Twomley
VP Finance/CFO: William Kirkwood
HR Executive: Don Michalenko
don.michalenko@kellogg.com
Plant Manager: Gene Fluck
Estimated Sales: $5-10 Million
Number Employees: 250-499
Square Footage: 800000
Parent Co: Kellogg Company
Type of Packaging: Consumer, Food Service
Brands:
Loma Linda
Morningstar Farms
Worthington

8552 **Morningstar Foods**
13448 Volta Rd
Los Banos, CA 93635
209-826-8000
Fax: 209-826-8266 www.morningstarco.com
Tomatoes and tomato paste
President: Chris Rufer
Sales & Marketing: Jennifer Ingram
Year Founded: 1970
Estimated Sales: $200-249 Million
Number Employees: 100-249

8553 **Moroni Feed Company**
15 E. 1900 S. Feed Mill Rd.
Moroni, UT 84646
435-436-8202
Fax: 435-436-8101 norbest@norbest.com
Fresh and frozen turkeys.
President/CEO, Norbest: Matt Cook
mcook@norbest.com
Estimated Sales: $125 Million+
Number Employees: 850
Parent Co: Norbest, LLC
Type of Packaging: Private Label
Brands:
Norbest

8554 **Morre-Tec Ind Inc**
1 Gary Rd
Union, NJ 07083-5527
908-686-0307
Fax: 908-688-9005 sales@morretec.com
www.morretec.com
Manufacturer, importer and exporter of magnesium chloride, food grade and potassium bromate; importer and wholesaler/distributor of low sodium substitutes and licorice, spray, dried and powder
Owner: Rachel Abenilla
rachela@morretec.com
Marketing Director: Michael Fuchs
Operations Manager: Norm Cantoe
Estimated Sales: $10-20 Million
Number Employees: 20-49
Number of Products: 150
Square Footage: 50000
Type of Packaging: Consumer, Bulk

8555 **Morreale John R Inc**
216 N Peoria St
Chicago, IL 60607-1706
312-421-3664
Fax: 312-421-8928 morrealemeat@aol.com
www.jrmorreale.com
Distributor of beef and pork products. Provides custom trimmed beef cuts and fresh beef trimmings.
President: Mike Magrini
President: Steve Hurckes
President: Jerry Schomer
Sales: Bob Apato
General Manager: Steve Hurckes
tfrigo@jrmorreale.com
Production Manager: Ramiro Corral
Estimated Sales: $25,000,000
Number Employees: 50-99
Number of Products: 1
Square Footage: 100000
Type of Packaging: Bulk

8556 **Morris J Golombeck Inc**
960 Franklin Ave
Brooklyn, NY 11225-2403
718-284-3505
Fax: 718-693-1941 golspice@aol.com
www.golombeckspice.com
Processor, importer and exporter of herbs and spices including basil, cassia, cayenne, garlic, ginger, paprika, etc
Owner: Hy Golombeck
mail@golombeckspice.com
Vice President: Sheldon Golombeck
Estimated Sales: $5-10 Million
Number Employees: 10-19
Square Footage: 480000
Type of Packaging: Bulk

8557 **Morris Kitchen**
Brooklyn, NY
347-457-6994
info@morriskitchen.com
www.morriskitchen.com
Manufacturer of cocktail syrup and mixers.
Founder: Kari Morris

8558 **Morris National**
760 Mckeever Ave
Azusa, CA 91702
626-385-2000
Fax: 626-969-8670 info@morrisnational.com
www.morrisnational.com
Truffles, licorice, hard candy and liquor-filled chocolates.
VP, Manufacturing: Claude Douessin
Year Founded: 1974
Parent Co: Morris National Canada

8559 **Morrison Farms**
R.R. 1 Box 50A
Clearwater, NE 68726
402-887-5335
Fax: 402-887-4709
morrison@nebraskapopcorn.com
www.morrisonfarms.com
High quality popcorn and dry, edible bean products
President: Frank Morrison
Estimated Sales: $300,000-500,000
Number Employees: 1-4

8560 **Morrison Lamothe**
5240 Finch Avenue East
Unit 2
Toronto, ON M1S 5A2
Canada
416-291-6762
Fax: 416-291-5046 877-677-6533
info@morrisonlamothe.com
www.morrisonlamothe.com
Frozen prepared beef, chicken and turkey pot pies, empanadas, puff pastry appetizers, strudels and wellingtons. Also offers single serve pasta frozen meals, compartment dinners, breakfast products, and bowl entrees.
President/CEO: J.M. Pigott
Estimated Sales: $45 Million
Number Employees: 350
Number of Brands: 4
Square Footage: 38000
Type of Packaging: Consumer, Private Label
Brands:
Cliffside
Holiday Farms
Pub Pies
Savarin

8561 **Morrison Meat Packers**
738 NW 72nd St
Miami, FL 33150-3695
305-836-4461
Fax: 305-836-2750 800-330-4267
gilda@morrisonmeat.com www.morrisonmeat.com
Processor of ham, ham products, and sausages.
President: Claudio Rodriguez
Vice President: Gilda Rodriguez
Year Founded: 1966
Estimated Sales: $20-50 Million
Number Employees: 50-99
Type of Packaging: Consumer

8562 **Morrison Meat Pies**
3403 S 1400 W # C
West Valley, UT 84119-4050
801-977-0181
Fax: 801-977-0448 www.morrisonmeatpies.com
Meat pies and frozen meat pie crust
Owner: Eugene Tafoya
Vice President, Manager: Susan Tafoya
Contact: Susan Tafoya
tafoya@morrisonmeatpies.com
Production Manager: Richard Gunther
Estimated Sales: $3-5 Million
Number Employees: 1-4
Type of Packaging: Consumer

8563 **Morrison Milling Co**
319 E Prairie St
Denton, TX 76201-6109
940-387-6111
Fax: 940-566-5992 800-531-7912
humanresources@morrisonmilling.com
www.morrisonmilling.com
Flour, processed corn, cornmeal, frosting mixes, soups, and gravies
President & CEO: Dale Tremblay
Operations Director: James Williams
Estimated Sales: $20-50 Million
Number Employees: 100-249
Parent Co: CH Guenther & Son
Type of Packaging: Private Label
Brands:
Morrison Brand

8564 **Morse's Sauerkraut**
3856 Washington Rd
Waldoboro, ME 04572-5502
207-832-5569
Fax: 207-832-2297 866-832-5569
morses@roadrunner.com
www.morsessauerkraut.com
Salsa, beet relish, pickled beets and sauerkraut
Owner: James Gammon
james@morsessk.com
Estimated Sales: Below $5 Million
Number Employees: 10-19
Type of Packaging: Consumer, Food Service
Brands:
Morse's

8565 **Mortgage Apple Cake**
677 Ramapo Rd
Teaneck, NJ 07666-1807
201-692-9538
angela@maccakes.com
www.maccakes.com
Manufacturer of apple cakes.
Founder: Angela Logan
Contact: Brenda Allen
brendaa@maccakes.com
Estimated Sales: Less Than $500,000
Number Employees: 1-4

8566 **Mortillaro Lobster Company**
65 Commercial St
Gloucester, MA 01930-5047
978-282-4621
Fax: 978-281-0579
Lobster
President: Vincent Mortillaro
Estimated Sales: $5-10 Million
Number Employees: 20-49

8567 **Mortimer's Fine Foods**
5341 John Lucas Drive
Burlington, ON L7L 6A8
Canada
905-336-0000
Fax: 905-336-0909
customerservice@mortimers.com
www.mortimers.com
Processor and exporter of frozen beef, prepared and vegetarian entrees and meat pies
VP Sales: Karim Talakshi
Type of Packaging: Consumer, Food Service, Private Label, Bulk
Brands:
Mortimer Fine Foods

8568 **Morton & Bassett Spices**
1400 Valley House Dr
Suite 100
Rohnert Park, CA 94928
415-883-8530
Fax: 415-883-0813 www.mortonbassett.com
Spices and seasonings
Founder: Morton Gothelf
mgothelf@mortonbassett.com
Estimated Sales: Below $5 Million
Number Employees: 10-19
Number of Products: 70
Brands:
M B Spices

8569 **Morton Salt Inc.**
123 North Wacker Dr.
Chicago, IL 60606-1743
312-807-2000
Fax: 312-807-2899 800-725-8847
www.mortonsalt.com
Salt including food grade and rock salt.
Chief Executive Officer: Christian Herrmann
Vice President/CFO: Tim McKean
Vice President/General Counsel: Chad Walker
Vice President, Human Resources: Nicole Turner
Vice President, Operations: Jennifer McCormick
Year Founded: 1848
Estimated Sales: $429.7 Million
Number Employees: 2,900
Square Footage: 95838
Parent Co: K+S AG
Type of Packaging: Consumer, Food Service, Private Label, Bulk
Other Locations:
Morton Salt Distribution
Newark CA
Grantsville UT
Perth Amboy NJ
Port Canaveral FL
Brands:
Morton Salt
Morton Rock Salt
Morton Evaporation Salt
Morton Solar Salt

8570 **Mosby Winery**
9496 Santa Rosa Rd
Buellton, CA 93427-9482
800-706-6729
info@mosbywines.com mosbywines.com
Wines, oils and balsamics.
Estimated Sales: $2.5-5 Million
Number Employees: 4
Type of Packaging: Private Label

8571 **Mosher Products Inc**
4318 Hayes Ave
Cheyenne, WY 82001-2349
307-632-1492
Fax: 307-632-1492 info@wheatandgrain.com
www.wheatandgrain.com
Organic grain
President: Leonard O Mosher
leonard@wheatandgrain.com
Estimated Sales: Below $5 Million
Number Employees: 20-49
Square Footage: 240000
Other Locations:
Bushnell NE
Brands:
Mosher Products

8572 **Moss Creek Winery**
6015 Steele Canyon Rd
Napa, CA 94558-9634
707-252-1295
Fax: 707-254-9327 info@mosscreekwinery.com
www.mosscreekwinery.com
Wines
Owner: Ann Moskowite
Owner: George Moskowite
gmoskowite@mosscreekwinery.com
Winemaker: Nils Venge
Estimated Sales: Less Than $500,000
Number Employees: 1-4
Brands:
Moss Creek

8573 **Mossholder's Farm Cheese Factory**
4017 N Richmond Street
Appleton, WI 54913-9704
920-734-7575
Cheese
Co-Owner: Larry Mossholder
Co-Owner: Lois Mossholder
Estimated Sales: Less than $500,000
Number Employees: 1-4

8574 **Mosti Mondiale/Gourmet Mondiale**
6865 Route 132
Ste-Catherine, QC J5C 1B6
Canada
450-638-6380
Fax: 450-638-7049
nino.piazza@mostimondiale.com
www.gourmetmondiale.com
Wine, olive oil, balsamic vinegar
Marketing: Nino Piazza

8575 **Mother Earth Enterprises**
15 Irving Place
New York, NY 10003-2316
212-777-1250
Fax: 212-614-8132 866-436-7688
denis@hempnut.com
Wholesaler/distributor of hempnuts; hemp oil, meal and flour; and toasted, sterilized and roasted grain hemp (seed). Highly adaptable for baking and cooking needs
President: Denis Cicero
Type of Packaging: Food Service

8576 **Mother Murphy's**
2826 South Elm-Eugene Street
Greensboro, NC 27406
336-273-1737
Fax: 336-273-0858 800-849-1277
www.mothermurphys.com
Flavor manufacturer serving the baking, beverage and tobacco industries.
President: David Murphy
Contact: Yuhong Chen
ychen@mothermurphys.com
Year Founded: 1920
Number of Products: 500
Square Footage: 210000
Type of Packaging: Private Label, Bulk

8577 **Mother Nature's Goodies**
13378 California St
Yucaipa, CA 92399-5106
909-795-6018
Fax: 909-795-0748
www.mothernaturesgoodies.com
Granola, seven grain bread, frozen pies and candy sundrops
President: Albert G Goude
Manager: Ronn Neish
CFO: Learner Guode
Estimated Sales: $3-5 Million
Number Employees: 10-19
Square Footage: 16000
Type of Packaging: Private Label
Brands:
Mother Nature's Goodies

8578 **Mother Parker's Tea & Coffee**
2530 Stanfield Road
Mississauga, ON L4Y 1S4
Canada
905-279-9100
Fax: 905-279-9821 800-387-9398
www.mother-parkers.com
Processor and exporter of ground and whole bean coffees and teas including orange pekoe, regular, decaffeinated, black and herbal; importer of green coffee and teas
Co-CEO: Michael Higgins
Co-CEO: Paul Higgins, Jr.
Sr. VP/Finance/Administration: Brian Goard
Vice President: Chris Bklecki
Number Employees: 280
Type of Packaging: Consumer, Food Service, Private Label, Bulk
Brands:
Blue Ribbon
Higgins & Burke
Mother Parkers

8579 **Mother Raw**
Toronto, ON M3J 2E5
Canada
855-464-0117
info@motherraw.com motherraw.com
Plant-based dressings, dips and condiments
Founder: Michelle Kopman

8580 **Mother Shucker's Original Cocktail Sauce**
900 Gregg Street, 1A
Columbia, SC 29201-3913
803-261-3802
Fax: 803-779-3444
mothershuckersauce@gmail.com
www.mothershuckersauce.com
Other condiments, other sauces, seasonings and cooking enhancers.
Marketing: Mary Sparrow

8581 **Mother Teresa's**
700 W Plantation Dr
Clute, TX 77531-5248
979-265-7429
Fax: 979-297-0932 888-265-7429
motTfinefoods@cs.com
www.motherteresasfinefoods.com
Vegetables, sauces and dressings
Owner: Teresa Polimano
mottfinefoods@cs.com
Estimated Sales: Less Than $500,000
Number Employees: 5-9
Brands:
Mother Teresa's Fine Foods

8582 **Mother's Mountain Pantry**
2 Mustard Hollow
Falmouth, ME 04105
207-781-4658
Fax: 207-781-2121 800-440-9891
sales@mothersmountain.com
www.mothersmountain.com
Mustard, horseradish, ketchup, dill, chili sauce, creamy horseradish sauce and hot pepper sauce. Just added-jams and jellies!
President: Carrol Tanner
CFO: Dennis Proctor
Estimated Sales: Below $5 Million
Number Employees: 6

8583 **Mother-In-Law's Kimchi**
Long Island City, NY 11101
www.milkimchi.com
Manufacturer of kimchi and gochujang
Owner: Lauryn Chun

8584 **Motherland International Inc**
8822 Flower Road
Suite 202
Rancho Cucamonga, CA 91730
909-596-8882
Fax: 909-596-8870 800-590-5407
www.motherlandinc.org
Processor and exporter of herbs and vitamins in powder and extract forms used in nutritional supplements; contract manufacturing available
President: Jackson Wen
Marketing: Michael Pinson
Estimated Sales: $1-3 Million
Number Employees: 20-49
Square Footage: 100000
Parent Co: Motherland International
Type of Packaging: Consumer, Food Service, Private Label, Bulk

8585 **Mott's**
PO Box 869077
Plano, TX 75086-9077
972-673-8088
800-426-4891
www.motts.com
Apple products that include apple sauce and apple juice.
CEO, Keurig Dr Pepper: Robert Gamgort
Year Founded: 1842
Estimated Sales: $228 Million
Number Employees: 1000
Number of Brands: 2
Parent Co: Dr. Pepper Snapple Group
Type of Packaging: Consumer, Food Service
Brands:
Mott's
Mott's for Tots
Mott's Sensibles
Mott's Fruit Flavoured Snacks

8586 **(HQ)Mott's LLP**
P.O. Box 869077
Plano, TX 75086-9077
Fax: 914-612-4100 800-426-4891
www.motts.com
Applesauce, cooking wine, cocktail mixes, fruit drinks, lime juice, apple juice, tomato-clam cocktail, fruit drinks, apple juice, tomato-clam cocktail, molasses
President/Sales: Michael McGrath
CFO: Dave Gerics
CEO: Jack Belsito
Estimated Sales: $300,000-500,000
Number Employees: 1-4
Parent Co: Cadbury Schweppes PLC
Type of Packaging: Consumer, Food Service, Bulk
Brands:
Clamato
Grandma's Molasses
Hawaiian Punch
Holland House
Ibc
Mauna La'i
Mott's
Mott's Fruitsations
Mr & Mrs T
Realemon
Reallime
Rose's
Ypp-Hoo

8587 **Motto**
Milton, MA
617-848-9248
orders@milkimchi.com
www.drinkmotto.com
Manufacturer of sparkling matcha tea.
Co-Founder: Tom Olcott
Co-Founder: Henry Cosby

8588 **Mound City Shelled Nut Inc**
7831 Olive Blvd
St Louis, MO 63130-2039
314-725-9040
Fax: 314-725-9044 888-338-6887
sales@moundcity.com www.moundcity.com
Chocolate candy, nut meats, shelled nuts, peanuts
President: Byron Smyrniotis
byron.smyrniotis@nutsgifts.com
Vice President: Stacy Smyrniotis
Estimated Sales: $1.8 Million
Number Employees: 1-4
Type of Packaging: Private Label
Brands:
Jordan Almonds

8589 **Mount Franklin Foods**
1800 Northwestern Dr
El Paso, TX 79912
Fax: 888-880-9154 800-351-8178
www.mountfranklinfoods.com
Candy and fruit-flavored snack manufacturer and nut processor
President & CEO: Gary Ricco
COO: Jay David
Number of Brands: 1
Number of Products: 7
Type of Packaging: Consumer, Private Label

8590 **Mount Mansfield Maple Products**
450 Weaver St
Suite 18
Winooski, VT 05404
802-497-1671
www.vermontpuremaple.com
Maple syrup
Co-Owner: Chris White
Co-Owner: Lindsay White

8591 **Mount Olympus Waters**
800-782-5508
www.mountolympuswater.com
Manufacturer and supplier of bottler spring water, cups, water coolers and coffee brewers
President: Dave Muscato
CEO: Tom Harrington
CFO: Jerry Hoyle
General Manager: Mike Garrity
Estimated Sales: $5-10 Million
Number Employees: 50-99
Parent Co: DS Services of America
Type of Packaging: Consumer, Food Service, Private Label, Bulk

8592 **Mount Palomar Winery**
33820 Rancho California Road
Temecula, CA 92591
951-676-5047
Fax: 951-676-8928 800-854-5177
info@mountpalomar.com
www.mountpalomarwinery.com
Manufacturer of fine wines.
President: Peter Poole
General Manager: Carol Darwish
Accounting Manager: Tara Ruth
Director, Operations: Kris May
Year Founded: 1969
Estimated Sales: $20-50 Million
Number Employees: 50-99
Number of Brands: 2
Brands:
Castelletto
Mount Palomar

8593 **Mountain City Coffee Roasters**
285 Beaverdam Rd
Enka, NC 28728
828-667-0869
Fax: 828-667-0869 888-730-0869
roastmaster@mountaincity.com
www.mountaincity.com
Coffee
Owner: Randall Sluder
Co-Owner/President: Debra Furr Sluder
Estimated Sales: Less Than $500,000
Number Employees: 1-4
Type of Packaging: Consumer, Bulk
Brands:
Mountain City

8594 **Mountain Cove Vineyards**
1362 Fortunes Cove Ln
Lovingston, VA 22949-2226
434-263-5392
Fax: 434-263-8540 aweed1@juno.com
www.mountaincovevineyards.com
Wines
President: Albert C Weed II
Estimated Sales: $1-3 Million
Number Employees: 1-4

8595 **Mountain Fire Foods**
2850 Main Road
Huntington, VT 05462-9608
802-434-2685
Fax: 802-434-2685
Marinades and ketchup
Owner: Karyl Kent

8596 **Mountain High Organics**
9 South Main St
New Milford, CT 06776
860-210-7805
Fax: 860-210-7837 mountainhighorganics.com
Organic pastas and oils
Founder: Joanne Fellin
Type of Packaging: Bulk

8597 **Mountain High Yogurt**
PO Box 9452
Minneapolis, MN 55440
303-761-2210
Fax: 763-764-8330 866-964-4878
www.mountainhighyoghurt.com
Original and honey style yogurt
President: Greg Bngles
Plant Manager: Ralph Lee
Number Employees: 20-49
Parent Co: Borden
Type of Packaging: Consumer, Food Service, Private Label
Brands:
Mountain High

8598 **Mountain Organic Foods**
920 Country Club Dr, Suite 1A
Moraga, CA 94556
925-377-0119
www.morfoods.com
Organic fruit bars.
Co-Owner: Ken Newman
Co-Owner: Craig Gass
Estimated Sales: $180,000
Number Employees: 2
Type of Packaging: Consumer
Brands:
BEAR FRUIT BAR

8599 **Mountain Rose Herbs**
35859 Highway 58
Pleasant Hill, OR 97455-9651
541-741-7307
Fax: 510-217-4012 800-879-3337
customerservice@mountainroseherbs.com
www.mountainroseherbsmercantile.com
Organic herbal products.
Owner: Julie Baily
Vice President: Shawn Donnille
Laboratory/Quality Control Manager: Steven Yeager
Marketing Director: Irene Wolansky
Terms Department Manager: Ray Sammartano
julie@mountainroseherbs.com
Public And Media Relations: Kori Rodley
Operations Manager: Jennifer Gerrity
Production Manager: Julie DeBord
Warehouse Manager: Kim Christenson
Purchasing Manager: Peggy Hall
Estimated Sales: Less Than $500,000
Number Employees: 5-9
Type of Packaging: Consumer, Bulk

8600 **Mountain States Pecan**
2830 N. Sycamore St.
Roswell, NM 88201
575-623-2216
Fax: 505-625-0126 farm@pecan.com
www.pecan.com
Grower and processor of pecans; gift tins available
Owner: Bruce Haley
Operations Manager: Reba Haley
Estimated Sales: $2.5-5 Million
Number Employees: 5-9

8601 **(HQ)Mountain States Rosen**
355 Food Center Dr # C16
C-16
Bronx, NY 10474-7053
718-842-4447
Fax: 718-617-4096 800-872-5262
info@rosenlamb.com
www.mountainstatesrosen.com
Lamb and veal
CEO: Dennis Stiffler
EVP: David Gage
Number Employees: 100-249
Type of Packaging: Food Service
Other Locations:
Mountain States Rosen, LLC
Greeley CO
Brands:
Cedar Springs Lamb

Cedar Springs Natural Veal
Shepherd's Pride

8602 **Mountain Sun Pubs & Breweries**
1535 Pearl St
Boulder, CO 80302-5408
303-546-0886
Fax: 303-413-1312 jess@mountainsunpub.com
www.longspeakpub.com
Beer
Owner: Kevin Daly
General Manager: Jessica Candaleria
Estimated Sales: $500,000-$1 Million
Number Employees: 20-49
Brands:
Colorado Kind Ale
Quinn's Golden Ale
Thunderhead Stout

8603 **Mountain Valley Poultry**
631 S Kansas Avenue
PO Box 6967
Brandon, FL 72766-6967
813-689-2616
Fax: 479-751-0506 www.mvpmarketing.com
Further processed poultry products including de-boned, cooked, etc
Owner: Don Walker
Estimated Sales: $.5-1 million
Number Employees: 1-4

8604 **Mountain Valley Products Inc**
108 East Blaine Avenue
PO Box 246
Sunnyside, WA 98944-0246
509-837-8084
Fax: 509-837-3481 www.valleyprocessing.com
Processor and exporter of fruit juice concentrates including apple and grape; also, apple juice
President: Mary Ann Bliesner
VP Operation: Kelly Bliensner
Maintenance Manager: Jay Fanciullo
Sales Manager: Terry Bliesner
Maintenance Supervisor: Mark Mulford
Production/Personnel: David Perez
Estimated Sales: $1.2 Million
Number Employees: 20-49
Square Footage: 180000
Type of Packaging: Bulk

8605 **(HQ)Mountain Valley Spring Company**
150 Central Avenue
Hot Springs, AR 71901-3528
501-624-1635
Fax: 501-623-5135 800-643-1501
www.mountainvalleyspring.com
Spring water
Chief Executive Officer: Breck Speed
CFO: Brad Frieberg
Retail: Taylor Cronor
HOD Sales: John Speed
Contact: Melanie Breeding
mbreeding@mountainvalleyspring.com
Estimated Sales: $10-20 Million
Number Employees: 100-249
Type of Packaging: Consumer, Food Service, Private Label
Brands:
Carolina Mountain Spring Water
Diamond Spring Water
Mountain Valley Spring Water

8606 **Mountain Valley Spring Water**
299 Haywood Rd
Asheville, NC 28806-4545
828-254-9848
Fax: 828-252-1528 800-627-1062
springwater@mountainvalleywaterasheville.com
www.mountainvalleywaterasheville.com
Manufacturers of bottled water
President: Don Freeman
Estimated Sales: $1-3 Million
Number Employees: 10-19
Type of Packaging: Private Label, Bulk
Brands:
Natural Mountain Water

8607 **Mountain View Fruit Sales**
4275 Avenue 416
Reedley, CA 93654-9141
559-637-9933
Fax: 559-637-9733
rataide@mountainviewfruit.com
Necatrines, peaches and plums
Owner: Mike Thurlow
Sales Manager: Mike Thurlow
mthurlow@mountainviewfruit.com
Number Employees: 100-249

8608 **Mountainbrook of Vermont**
P.O.Box 39
Jeffersonville, VT 05464
802-644-1988
Fax: 802-644-6795
Dipping oils, fruit spreads, dressings, packaged dry mixes, mustards, and gift packs.
Owner: Lisa Bryan
Estimated Sales: $1-3 Million
Number Employees: 1-4
Type of Packaging: Consumer

8609 **Mountainside Farms Inc**
55724 State Highway 30
Roxbury, NY 12474-1324
607-326-4161
Produces hormone and antibiotic free milk and cage free eggs.
Manager: Stacy Palamtier
stacyp@msfdairy.com
Estimated Sales: $10-50 Million
Number Employees: 1-4
Number of Brands: 2
Parent Co: Elmhurst Dairy
Type of Packaging: Consumer
Brands:
Mountainside Farms

8610 **Mountaire Corporation**
P.O. Box 1320
Millsboro, DE 19966
302-934-1100
877-887-1490
www.mountaire.com
Poultry.
Chairman/CEO: Ronald Cameron
CFO: Craig Lair
Year Founded: 1914
Estimated Sales: $630 Million
Number Employees: 7,000
Brands:
Mountaire

8611 **Mountanos Family Coffee & Tea Co.**
1331 Commerce St.
Petaluma, CA 94549
707-462-6333
800-624-7031
info@mfct.com www.mfct.com
Coffee, tea, and accessories
Director of Operations: Erik Bianchi
Number Employees: 50-99

8612 **Moutanos Brothers Coffee Company**
380 Swift Ave
Suite 13
South San Francisco, CA 94080
650-952-5446
Fax: 650-871-4845 800-624-7031
info@mountanosbros.com
www.mountanosbros.com
Coffee
President: Michael Mountanos
Contact: Dora Gomez-Loeza
dora@mountanosbros.com
Estimated Sales: Less than $500,000
Number Employees: 20-49
Brands:
Lindsay's Teas
Shade Grown Organic
Straight Coffees

8613 **Movie Breads Food**
225 Industrial Blouevard
Chateauguay, QC J6J 4Z2
Canada
450-692-7606
Fax: 450-692-1810 trmblaykein05@hotmail.com
Grocery
Brands:
Shei Brand
Tradewinds

8614 **Moweaqua Packing Plant**
601 N Main St
Moweaqua, IL 62550-3695
217-768-4714
Meatpackers@frontiernet.net
www.mowpackingplant.com
Beef and pork
Owner: Terry Yoder
meatpackers@frontiernet.net
Co-Owner: Don Baker
Estimated Sales: Less Than $500,000
Number Employees: 1-4
Type of Packaging: Consumer

8615 **Moyer Packing Co.**
741 Souder Rd.
Elroy, PA 18964
Fax: 970-346-4611 800-967-8325
www.mopac.com
Boxed and ground beef, and fresh and frozen boxed beef.
Year Founded: 1877
Estimated Sales: Less Than $500,000
Parent Co: JBS USA
Type of Packaging: Consumer, Private Label, Bulk
Brands:
Mopac

8616 **Mozzarella Co**
2944 Elm St
Dallas, TX 75226-1509
214-741-4072
Fax: 214-741-4076 800-798-2954
mozzcomanager@aol.com www.mozzco.com
Manufacturer of cheese.
Founder: Paula Lambert
mozzco@aol.com
Number Employees: 10-19

8617 **Mozzicato De Pasquale Bakery**
329 Franklin Ave
Hartford, CT 06114-1890
860-296-0426
Fax: 860-296-8129 info@mozzicatobakery.com
www.mozzicatobakery.com
Bread, pizza, cakes, cookies and ice cream
Owner: Gisella Mozzicato
President: Luigi Mozzicato
COO: Gina Mozzicato
Estimated Sales: $1.5 Million
Number Employees: 20-49

8618 **Mr Dell Foods**
300 W Major St
Kearney, MO 64060-8550
816-628-4644
Fax: 816-628-4633 mrdells@mrdells.com
www.mrdells.com
Various styles of hash browns, shredded potatoes, O'Brien potatoes, and souther style potatoes.
President: Tommy Baker
tbaker@mrdells.com
VP: Kurt Johnsen
Marketing/Sales Director: Tom Sherrer
Operations Manager: Rick Wilkins
Plant Manager: John Duncan
Estimated Sales: $8445651
Number Employees: 20-49
Square Footage: 160000
Type of Packaging: Consumer, Food Service, Bulk
Brands:
Mr. Dell's I.Q.F. Country Potatoes
Mr. Dell's I.Q.F. Hash Browns
Mr. Dell's I.Q.F. Herb & Garlic
Mr. Dell's I.Q.F. Santa Fe

8619 **Mr Espresso**
696 3rd St
Oakland, CA 94607-3560
510-287-5200
Fax: 510-287-5204 info@mrespresso.com
www.mrespresso.com
Roasted coffee.
President/CEO: Carlo Di Ruocco
info@mrespresso.com
CFO: Marie-Francoise Di Ruocco
Quality Control Supervisor: John Di Ruocco
VP, Sales/Director, Marketing: Luigi Di Ruocco
Director, Warehouse Operations: Alex Zambrano
Estimated Sales: $10-20 Million
Number Employees: 20-49
Number of Brands: 2
Type of Packaging: Private Label

Brands:
Faema
Mr. Espresso

8620 **Mr Jay's Tamales & Chili**
11200 Alameda St
Lynwood, CA 90262-1725
310-537-3932
Fax: 310-537-3938
Chili and tamales
President: Patricia Lang
Owner: Pat Lang
Estimated Sales: Less than $500,000
Number Employees: 1-4
Type of Packaging: Consumer
Brands:
Chicken Link
Chilly

8621 **Mr. C's**
7021 South 220th St
Kent, WA 98032
253-867-6130
888-929-2378
info@calsonindustries.com
www.calsonindustries.com/mrC
Cocktail mixes
President: Sadru Kabani
Parent Co: Calson Industries

8622 **Mr. Green Tea Ice Cream**
42 E Front St
Keyport, NJ 07735
732-446-9800
www.mrgreentea.com
Ice cream
Purchasing: Lori Emanuele
Year Founded: 1968

8623 **Mr. Mak's**
32 East Broadway
Suite 501
New York, NY 10002
888-953-9209
hello@mrmaks.com mrmaks.com
Chinese ginger and ginseng tea
Number of Brands: 1
Number of Products: 3
Type of Packaging: Consumer
Brands:
GINBAO

8624 **Mrs Annie's Peanut Patch**
1019 B St
Floresville, TX 78114-1947
830-393-7845
Fax: 830-393-9605 www.mrsanniescandy.com
Home-made peanut brittle, jalapeno peanut brittle, pecan brittle, peanut patties, pecan chewies, pecan pralines, flavored peanuts, all natural peanut butter and raw peanuts
Vice President: Mary Ann Sanchez
VP: Mary Ann Sanchez
Estimated Sales: Less Than $500,000
Number Employees: 1-4

8625 **Mrs Auld's Gourmet Foods Inc**
572 Reactor Way # B4
Reno, NV 89502-4133
775-856-3350
Fax: 775-856-3351 800-322-8537
john@mrs-aulds.com
Gourmet foods including brandied cherries, sweet and spicy pickles, marmalades, preserves, pancake, scone and soda bread mix, salsa, pasta sauce and bean, red corn and barbeque chips, chili sauce, pesto sauce, chestnuts
Owner: John Auld
Sales Manager: Teresa West
Estimated Sales: $1-3 Million
Number Employees: 5-9
Square Footage: 12000

8626 **(HQ)Mrs Baird's**
PO Box 976
Horsham, PA 19044
800-984-0989
www.mrsbairds.com
Bread, buns, donuts, cinnamon rolls, honey buns, applie pie and chocolate cup cakes
President, Grupo Bimbo: Fred Penny
Parent Co: Bimbo Bakeries USA
Type of Packaging: Consumer, Food Service, Private Label, Bulk
Other Locations:
Mrs Baird's Bakeries
Abilene TX
Mrs Baird's Bakeries
Fort Worth TX
Mrs Baird's Bakeries
Lubbock TX
Mrs Baird's Bakeries
Waco TX
Mrs Baird's Bakeries
Houston TX
Mrs Baird's Bakeries
San Antonio TX
Brands:
Mrs Baird's(c)

8627 **(HQ)Mrs Clark's Foods**
740 SE Dalbey Dr
Ankeny, IA 50021-3908
515-964-8036
Fax: 515-964-8397 800-736-5674
info@mrsclarks.com www.mrsclarks.com
Shelf-stable beverages, sauces and dressings
President: Ron Kahrer
QC: Ned Williams
Sales: Julie Southwick
Plant Manager: John Weber
Purchasing: Ron Mathis
Estimated Sales: $450,000
Number Employees: 100-249
Number of Brands: 12
Number of Products: 50
Square Footage: 240000
Parent Co: AGRI Industries
Type of Packaging: Consumer, Food Service, Private Label
Brands:
Alljuice
Nature's Choice

8628 **Mrs Fisher's Potato Chips**
1231 Fulton Ave
Rockford, IL 61103-4025
815-964-9114
Fax: 815-964-3880 www.mrsfisherschips.com
Potato chips including barbecue and sour cream and onion
Owner: Marilyn Blume
mblume@aa.com
VP: Chuck Diventi
Estimated Sales: $780,000
Number Employees: 10-19
Square Footage: 40000
Type of Packaging: Consumer
Brands:
Mrs. Fisher
Vita-Sealed

8629 **Mrs Grissom's Salads Inc**
2500 Bransford Ave
Nashville, TN 37204-2810
615-255-4137
Fax: 615-251-9763 800-255-0571
www.mrsgrissoms.com
Prepared salad
President: Grace G Grissom
CEO: Kenneth Funger
kfunger@xspedius.net
CEO: Kenneth Funger
Plant Manager: Jack McGhee
Estimated Sales: $3.1 Million
Number Employees: 50-99
Square Footage: 160000
Type of Packaging: Consumer

8630 **Mrs Mazzula Food Products Inc**
240 Carter Dr
Edison, NJ 08817-2097
732-248-0555
Fax: 732-248-0442
Sun dried tomatoes, zucchini, salsa, peppers
President: Christopher Lotito
President: Christopher Lotito
Estimated Sales: Less than $500,000
Number Employees: 20-49
Type of Packaging: Bulk

8631 **Mrs Prindables**
6300 W Gross Point Rd
Niles, IL 60714-3916
847-588-2900
Fax: 847-588-0392 888-215-1100
customerservice@mrsprindables.com
www.mrsprindables.com
Gourmet caramel apples
President: Tami Gray
tgray@affytapple.com
Number Employees: 50-99

8632 **Mrs Rios Corn Products**
215 W Avenue N
San Angelo, TX 76903-8434
325-653-5640
Fax: 325-657-0825
Producer of flour and corn tortillas
President: Armando Martinez
mrsrios@zipnet.net
Estimated Sales: $20-50 Million
Number Employees: 20-49

8633 **Mrs Stratton's Salads Inc**
380 Industrial Ln
Birmingham, AL 35211-4462
205-940-9640
Fax: 205-940-9650 www.mrsstrattons.com
Fresh salads including pimiento, potato, cole slaw, chicken and tuna
President: George Bradford
gbradford@mrsstrattons.com
President: R Vance Fulkerson
Director: Martha Bradford
Estimated Sales: $19 Million
Number Employees: 50-99
Type of Packaging: Consumer, Food Service, Private Label
Brands:
Mrs. Stratton

8634 **Mrs Sullivan's Pies**
256 Preston St
Jackson, TN 38301-4967
731-427-2101
Fax: 731-422-1045 info@mrssullivans.com
www.mrssullivans.com
Brownies and pies including coconut, chocolate and pecan
Vice President: Rodney Myrick
rodney@mrssullivans.com
Vice President: Rodney Myrick
rodney@mrssullivans.com
Operations/Manufacturing Director: Melvin Coope
Estimated Sales: $10-20 Million
Number Employees: 20-49
Square Footage: 36000
Type of Packaging: Consumer
Brands:
Mrs. Sullivan's

8635 **Mrs. Denson's Cookie Company**
120 Brush St
Ukiah, CA 95482
707-462-2272
Fax: 707-462-2283 800-219-3199
Processor and exporter of fruit juice and honey sweetened cookies including energy, reduced fat, fat-free, vegan and organic
President/Owner: Mike Bielenberg
Vice President: Desi Ringor
Number Employees: 50-99
Square Footage: 100000
Type of Packaging: Consumer, Food Service, Private Label, Bulk
Brands:
Monster Cookies
Mrs. Denson's
Total Fit

8636 **Mrs. Dog's Products**
PO Box 6872
Grand Rapids, MI 49516-6872
616-970-2677
800-267-7364
mrsdogsorders@comcast.net www.mrsdogs.com
Processor and exporter of gourmet mustard, Jamaican jerk marinade and habanero pepper sauces; also, shelled green chile pistachio nuts
Owner: Julie Curtis Applegate
Estimated Sales: Less than $500,000
Number Employees: 1-4
Type of Packaging: Consumer
Brands:
Mrs. Dog's

8637 **Mrs. Field's Hot Cocoas**
PO Box 617
Farmington, UT 84025-0617
801-934-1000
Fax: 801-451-6118 800-845-2400
Hot cocoa

8638 **Mrs. Fields Original Cookies**
Bloomfield, CO
800-266-2547
www.mrsfields.com
Cookies and baked goods.
CEO: Dustin Lyman
Year Founded: 1977
Estimated Sales: $100-129 Million
Number Employees: 4,000
Parent Co: Z Capital Partners

8639 **Mrs. Fly's Bakery**
608 W Main St
Collegeville, PA 19426-1925
610-489-7288
Fax: 610-489-7488
Bakery products
President: Richard Landis
Estimated Sales: $1-2.5 000,000
Number Employees: 1-4

8640 **(HQ)Mrs. Kavanagh's EnglishMuffins**
145 North Broadway
Rumford, RI 02916-2801
401-434-0551
Fax: 401-438-0542 800-556-7216
bids@homesteadbaking.com
www.homesteadbaking.com
Breads, rolls and English muffins.
President: Peter Vican
Vice President: Bill Vican
Sales Manager: Vinny Palmiotti
vikramsimha@vitalimages.com
Transportation Director: Jimmy Amaral
Estimated Sales: $5-10 Million
Number Employees: 20-49
Number of Brands: 2
Square Footage: 40000
Type of Packaging: Food Service, Private Label, Bulk
Brands:
Matthew's All Natural
Mrs. Kavanagh's

8641 **Mrs. Lauralicious**
19363 Willamette Drive
Suite 234
West Linn, OR 97068
866-658-8267
Fax: 888-656-6839
Fruit treats
Contact: Laura Becker
mrslauralicious@gmail.com

8642 **Mrs. Leeper's Pasta**
1000 Italian Way
Excelsior Springs, MO 64024
816-502-6000
Fax: 816-502-6722 800-848-5266
Flavored dry pasta including shapes, fettucine, angel hair, wheat-free, gluten-free, bulk, organic, kosher and private label
President: Michelle Muscat
VP/Director,Sales and Marketing: Ed Muscat
Number Employees: 700
Number of Brands: 6
Type of Packaging: Consumer, Food Service, Private Label, Bulk
Brands:
Eddie's Spaghetti Organic
Fortune Macaroni
Michelle's Organic
Mrs Leeper's Wheat/Gluten Free

8643 **Mrs. Malibu Foods**
23852 Pacific Coast Highway
Suite 372
Malibu, CA 90265-4876
310-589-2777
Fax: 310-589-9898 800-677-6254
Food
President/Owner: Debra Root
Estimated Sales: $500,000-$1 Million
Number Employees: 5-9
Type of Packaging: Private Label
Brands:
Mrs Malibu

8644 **Mrs. May's Naturals**
860 E 238th Street
Carson, CA 90745-6212
310-830-3130
Fax: 310-830-3045 877-677-6297
Vegan, non-GMO, cholesterol free, dairy free, wheat free, gluten free, 0 trans fat and contain no artificial colors or flavors, nut crunches and bars
President/Owner: Augustine Kim
mrsmay@mrsmay.com
Estimated Sales: $18 Million
Number Employees: 6

8645 **Mrs. McGarrigle's Fine Foods**
311 St Lawrence Street
PO Box 163
Merrickville, ON K0G 1N0
Canada
613-269-3752
Fax: 613-269-2736 877-768-7827
info@mustard.ca www.mustard.ca
Gourmet mustards, chutneys, preserves and seasonings
Owner: Janet Campbell

8646 **Mrs. Miller's Homemade Noodles**
110 Crawford Street
Fredericksburg, OH 44627
330-695-2393
Fax: 330-695-6900 800-227-4487
jim@mrsmillersnoodles.com
www.mrsmillersnoodles.com
Dairy-free, kosher, organic/natural, pasta (dry).
Marketing: Jim Gray
Contact: Jennifer Wiles
jenniferwiles@mrsmillersnoodles.com

8647 **Mrs. Smiths Bakeries**
5055 S Royal Atlanta Dr
Tucker, GA 30084-3097
770-723-6180
Fax: 770-939-6632
Baked goods, pies
President: James Allen
Estimated Sales: $20-50 Million
Number Employees: 100-249
Parent Co: Mrs. Smiths Bakeries

8648 **Mrs. Ts Pierogies**
600 E Centre St
PO Box 606
Shenandoah, PA 17976-0606
570-462-2745
Fax: 570-462-3299 800-743-7649
consumercontact@pierogies.com
www.pierogies.com
Low-fat pierogies
President: Tom Twardzik
Vice President: Tim Twardzik
IT Manager: Ted Twardzik
VP Marketing: Gary Loverman
VP Sales: Ron Suchecki
Estimated Sales: $10-20 Million
Number Employees: 100-249
Type of Packaging: Consumer, Food Service
Brands:
Mrs. T'S

8649 **Mrs. Willman's Baking**
3732 Canada Way
Burnaby, BC V5G 1G4
Canada
604-434-0027
Fax: 403-250-8706 http://www.mrswillmans.com
Sandwiches, donuts, pastries and sausage rolls
CEO: Winston Haffat
President: Eric Olsen
Parent Co: Beaumont Select Corporation
Type of Packaging: Consumer, Food Service
Brands:
Abm
Coral Food
Golden Crust
Prestige

8650 **Mt Baker Vineyards**
4298 MT Baker Hwy
Everson, WA 98247-9422
360-592-2300
Fax: 360-592-2526
mountbakervineyards@frontier.com
www.mountbakervineyards.com
Produces red, white, sparkling, dessert and plum wines. As of late 2016, the owners were looking to sell the company.
President: Randy Finley
mountbakervineyards@frontier.com
Manager: Philippe Renaud
Vice President: Patricia Clark-Finley
Sales: Randy Finley
Estimated Sales: $280 Thousand
Number Employees: 10-19
Number of Brands: 1
Type of Packaging: Consumer, Food Service, Private Label
Brands:
Mount Baker Vineyards & Winery

8651 **Mt Bethel Winery**
5014 Mount Bethel Dr
Altus, AR 72821-8878
479-468-2444
Fax: 479-468-2444 sales@mountbethel.com
www.mountbethel.com
Wines
Owner: Eugene Post
Estimated Sales: $300,000
Number Employees: 5-9

8652 **(HQ)Mt Capra Products**
279 SW 9th St
Chehalis, WA 98532-3313
360-748-4224
Fax: 360-748-3099 800-574-1961
www.mtcapra.com
Processor and exporter of dehydrated powder whey product and cheese including cheddar, feta and raw goat milk with no salt
Owner: Frank Stout
frank@mtcapra.com
Key Account Manager: Arny Davis
Estimated Sales: $$1-2.5 Million
Number Employees: 20-49
Square Footage: 20000
Other Locations:
Mount Capra Cheese
Chehalis WA

8653 **Mt Claire Beverages**
160 Perkins St
Torrington, CT 06790-6846
860-489-3804
Fax: 860-496-9425 888-525-2473
Water and soft drinks
Owner/CEO: Timothy Flynn
Manager: Bob Cox
bcox@lccc.wy.edu
Estimated Sales: Less Than $500,000
Number Employees: 5-9

8654 **Mt Eden Vineyards**
22020 Mount Eden Rd
Saratoga, CA 95070-9729
408-867-9587
Fax: 408-867-4329 info@mounteden.com
www.mounteden.com
Wines
President: Jeffrey Patterson
info@mounteden.com
Co-Owner/President: Ellie Patterson
CEO: Neil Hagen
Business Manager: Eleanor Davis Patterson
Operations Manager: Andrea Kyle
Estimated Sales: Below $5 Million
Number Employees: 5-9
Type of Packaging: Private Label
Brands:
Mount Eden Vineyards

8655 **Mt Franklin Foods**
1800 Northwestern Dr
El Paso, TX 79912-1122
915-877-1173
Fax: 915-877-1198 800-685-1475
customerservice@mountfranklinfoods.com
www.azarnutco.com
Candies and nuts
Vice President: Barbara Powell
Chief Operating Officer: Gary Ricco
Chief Financial Officer: Richard Salazar
Vice President: Barbara Powell
Quality Control: Oscar Moreno
Sr Marketing Manager: Beth Podol
Sr Vice President/Sales/Marketing: Dave Barnett
Public Relations Manager: Beth Podol
Estimated Sales: A
Number Employees: 5-9

8656 Mt Nittany Vineyard & Winery
300 Houser Rd
Centre Hall, PA 16828-8002
814-466-6373
Fax: 814-466-2766 sales@mtnittanywinery.com
www.mtnittanywinery.com
Wines
Owner: Joe Carroll
sales@mtnittanywinery.com
VP: Betty Carroll
Estimated Sales: $1-2.5 Million
Number Employees: 5-9
Brands:
Mount Nittany

8657 Mt Olive Pickle Co
1 Cucumber Blvd
PO Box 609
Mt Olive, NC 28365-1210
919-581-4760
Fax: 919-658-6296 800-672-5041
mrcrisp@mtolivepickles.com
www.mtolivepickles.com
Pickles, relishes and peppers
President & CEO: Bobby Frye
Executive Chairman: William Hardy Bryan
CFO: Dan Bowen
Director of Marketing: Keith Britt
VP Operations: Doug Brock
Production Supervisor: Jolene Borst
Procurement Manager: Phil Denlinger
Estimated Sales: $46.7 Million
Number Employees: 500-999
Number of Products: 80
Square Footage: 400000
Brands:
Mt. Olive

8658 Mt Pleasant Winery
3125 Green Mountain Dr
Branson, MO 65616-3817
417-336-9463
Fax: 417-336-9167 800-467-9463
mailto@mountpleasant.com
www.mountpleasant.com
Wines
President: Phillip Dressel
Manager: Kay Driden
Estimated Sales: Below $5 Million
Number Employees: 5-9

8659 Mt Sterling Co-Op Creamery
505 Diagonal St
Highland, WI 53543
608-734-3151
Fax: 608-734-3810 866-289-4628
mtsterling@mwt.net buymtsterlinggoatcheese.com/
Raw goat's milk cheeses including cheddar, feta, pasteurized country jack and pasteurized no salt cheddar
Marketing Director: Patricia Lund
Manager: Shannon Adams
mtsterlingcoop@centurytel.net
Office Manager: Shannon Adams
Head Cheesemaker: Bjorn Unseth
Plant Manager: Al Bekkum
Estimated Sales: $2 Million
Number Employees: 10-19
Number of Brands: 1
Number of Products: 13
Square Footage: 9800
Type of Packaging: Consumer, Food Service, Private Label, Bulk
Brands:
Kickapoo of Wisconsin
Mt. Sterling Cheese Co.

8660 Mt. Konocti Growers
2550 Big Valley Road
Kelseyville, CA 95451
707-279-4213
Fax: 707-279-2251 www.mtkonoctiwines.com
Grower, packer and exporter of bartlett pears
Manager: Robert Gayaldo
Number Employees: 5-9
Square Footage: 170000
Type of Packaging: Bulk
Brands:
Lady of the Lake
Lake Cove
Mt. Konocti

8661 Mt. Olympus Specialty Foods
65 W Main St
Westminster, MD 21157
410-848-7080
Gourmet and specialty foods
President: Harry Sirinakis
VP: Rebecca Sirinakis
Contact: Jay Rutherford
jrutherford@mtolympustech.com
Estimated Sales: $1.3 Million
Number Employees: 35

8662 Mt. Olympus Specialty Foods
1601 Military Road
Buffalo, NY 14217-1205
716-874-0771
Fax: 716-839-4006
Processor and exporter of meat, poultry and fish marinades, Greek salad dressings, pasta sauces and appetizers, gourmet foods, salsa, hot sauce and seasonings
CEO/President: George Bechakas
Executive VP: Nick Bechakas
Estimated Sales: $1-3 Million
Number Employees: 20-49

8663 Mt. View Bakery
18 1319 Old Volcano Rd.
Mountain View, HI 96771
808-968-6353
Bread, cookies, pies, donuts, rolls, muffins
President: Robert Kotomori
Estimated Sales: Less than $500,000
Number Employees: 5-9
Type of Packaging: Consumer
Brands:
Mt. View Bakery

8664 Mucci Food Products LTD
7676 Ronda Dr
Canton, MI 48187-2430
734-453-4555
Fax: 734-453-1722 www.mamamuccispasta.com
Fresh, dry and frozen filled pastas.
President: Vince Mucci
Estimated Sales: $10-20 Million
Number Employees: 10-19
Number of Brands: 1
Type of Packaging: Private Label
Brands:
Mama Mucci

8665 Mucke's Meat Products
2326 Main St
Hartford, CT 06120
860-246-5609
Fax: 860-541-6403 800-726-5598
www.muckes.com
Meat products including sausage, kielbasa, frankfurters, salami and liverwurst
President: Ernest Mucke
Estimated Sales: $5-10 Million
Number Employees: 20-49
Type of Packaging: Consumer, Food Service, Private Label
Brands:
Circle M

8666 Mucky Duck Mustard Company
1505 Bonner St
PO Box 250441
Ferndale, MI 48220-1973
248-544-4610
Fax: 248-544-4610 zilkod@aol.com
Gourmet marinades, salad dressings, mustard, ketchup, and BBQ sauces
President: Dave Zilko
Estimated Sales: Less than $500,000
Number Employees: 1-4
Type of Packaging: Consumer, Food Service
Brands:
American Connoisseur Gourmet
American Moir's
American Mucky Duck
American Special Edition
Mucky Duck

8667 Muffin Revolution
1080 Marina Way South
Richmond, CA 94804
510-859-7655
info@muffinrevolution.com
muffinrevolution.com
Muffins
Co-Founder: Marirose Piciucco
Co-Founder: Christy Kovacs
Number of Brands: 1
Number of Products: 6
Type of Packaging: Consumer
Brands:
MUFFIN REVOLUTION

8668 Muir Copper Canyon Farms
951 S 3600 W
Salt Lake City, UT 84104-4587
801-908-6091
Fax: 801-908-6176 800-564-0949
ldehaan@coppercanyonfarms.com
www.coppercanyonfarms.com
Packer and exporter of potatoes, onions and frozen ready-to-process cherries; wholesaler/distributor of fresh fruits and vegetables; serving the food service market in the Salt Lake City metropolitan area
President/CEO: Phil Muir
VP/Chief Financial Officer: Chuck Madsen
Controller: Adam Jensen
Sales: John Marsh
Manager: Andy Salmon
asalmon@coopercanyonfarms.com
Operations Manager: Andy Salmon
Estimated Sales: $16.6 Million
Number Employees: 50-99
Square Footage: 400000
Type of Packaging: Food Service, Private Label, Bulk
Brands:
Big M

8669 Muirhead Canning Co
5267 Mill Creek Rd
The Dalles, OR 97058-8501
541-298-1660
Fax: 541-298-4158 www.muirheadcanning.com
Canned fruits including apricots, cherries, peaches, pears and plums
President: Jenny Loughmiller
jtloughmiller@gmail.com
Co-Owner: Dawn Barrett
President: Russell Loughmiller
Estimated Sales: $5-10 Million
Number Employees: 20-49
Square Footage: 48000
Type of Packaging: Consumer
Brands:
Hoodcrest

8670 Muirhead of Ringoes, NJ, Inc.
43 Highway 202/31
Ringoes, NJ 08551
908-782-7803
Fax: 908-788-4221 800-782-7803
info@muirheadfoods.com
www.muirheadfoods.com
Specialty foods
President: Edward Simpson
Vice President: Doris Simpson
Marketing Director: Barbara Simpson
Estimated Sales: $500,000 appx.
Number Employees: 5-9
Number of Brands: 1
Number of Products: 25
Square Footage: 6000
Type of Packaging: Consumer
Brands:
Dragon's Breath
Hazel's
Muirhead

8671 Mullens Dressing
211 S Main St
Palestine, IL 62451
618-586-2727
Fax: 618-586-2718 mullens11@frontier.com
www.mullensdressing.com
Salad dressings and BBQ sauces
Owner: Jeffrey Shaner
mullens11@frontier.com
Estimated Sales: $300,000-500,000
Number Employees: 1-4
Square Footage: 30000
Type of Packaging: Consumer, Food Service
Brands:
Mullen's

8672 **Muller-Pinehurst Dairy**
2110 Ogilby Rd
Rockford, IL 61102-3400
815-968-0441
Fax: 815-961-1625 www.xta.com
Dairy products
President: Neal Rosinsky
CEO: Raymond Bikulcius
mullers@xta.com
Marketing Executive: Renee Florent
Sales Executive: Tom Erb
General Manager: Neal L Rosinsky
Estimated Sales: Less than $500,000
Number Employees: 100-249
Parent Co: Prairie Farms Dairy
Type of Packaging: Consumer

8673 **Mulligan Sales**
14314 Lomitas Ave
City of Industry, CA 91746
626-968-9621
Fax: 626-369-8452 mulligansales@yahoo.com
Distributor and processor of dairy products.
President: Jeff Mulligan
VP: Susan Kukta
Safety Manager: Madalyn Hochenedel
Human Resources Manager: Pam Hartnett
Estimated Sales: $4 Million
Number Employees: 23

8674 **Mullins Cheese Inc**
598 Seagull Dr
Mosinee, WI 54455-9551
715-693-3205
Fax: 715-693-2682 jobs@mullinscheese.com
www.mullinswhey.com
Cheese
President: Donald Mullins
donald.mullins@paradisesolutions.net
Number Employees: 50-99

8675 **Mullins Food Products**
2200 S. 25th Ave.
Broadview, IL 60155
708-344-3224
Fax: 708-344-0153 www.mullinsfood.com
Sauces, including barbecue, sweet & sour, mustard, ketchup, dressings, mayonnaise, salsa & picantes, pizza sauces, marinara, cocktail, tartar, teriyaki, Asian, icings, horseradish, buffalo & hot sauces, tzatziki, cheese sauces, steaksauces, coleslaw base, specialty blends, syrups, and spoonable dressings.
Owner: Jeanne Gannon
jgannon@mullinsfoods.com
Year Founded: 1934
Estimated Sales: $105 Million
Number Employees: 250-499
Square Footage: 325000
Type of Packaging: Consumer, Food Service, Private Label

8676 **Multi Marques**
4650 Rue Notre-Dame O
Montreal, QC H4C 1S6
Canada
514-934-1866
Fax: 514-934-1866 www.multimarques.com
Manufacturer and distributor of bread, rolls, fruit cake and sponge cake
Regional Plant Director: Francine Henderson
Number Employees: 2
Square Footage: 14984
Parent Co: Canada Bread
Type of Packaging: Consumer, Food Service
Brands:
Bon Matin
Cuisine Nature
Diana
Durviage
Gailuron
Maison Cousin
Petite Donceur
Pom

8677 **(HQ)Multiflex Company**
18 Utter Ave
Hawthorne, NJ 07506-2127
973-636-9700
marzipanco@aol.com
Processor and exporter of confectionery items including marzipan, icing decorations, edible Easter eggs, chocolate dessert cups, chocolate liqueur cups, lollypops, sugar decorations and decorated chocolate covered sandwich cookies
President: Rita Keller
Vice President: Rozie Keller
VP Sales: Royce Keller
Estimated Sales: $120,000
Number Employees: 2
Square Footage: 30000
Type of Packaging: Food Service, Private Label, Bulk
Brands:
Biermann
Crescent Confections
Keller's
Panorama Easter Eggs
Swissart
Ultra Dark Rondo Kosher

8678 **Multigrains Bread Co**
117 Water St
Lawrence, MA 01841-4720
978-691-6100
Fax: 978-373-4801 www.multigrainsbakeries.com
Multigrain breads
President: Joseph Faro
joseph@multigrainsbakeries.com
EVP/Director R&D: Chuck Brandano
Director of Quality: Adam Gabour
Director of Purchasing: Darren Gaiero
Number Employees: 100-249

8679 **Mung Dynasty**
2200 Mary St
Pittsburgh, PA 15203-2160
412-381-1350
Asian foods, specialty products
Owner: Chris Wahlberg
Estimated Sales: $1-2.5 Million
Number Employees: 1-4
Square Footage: 20000
Brands:
Mori-Nu Tofu
Mung Dynasty

8680 **Munk Pack**
Greenwich, CT 06830
munkpack.com
Protein cookies and oatmeal fruit squeezes
Co-Founder: Tobias Glienke
VP, Sales: Joseph DiBenedetto
Number of Brands: 2
Number of Products: 9
Type of Packaging: Consumer
Brands:
MUNK PACK
OATMEAL FRUIT SQUEEZE

8681 **Munkijo**
Irvine, CA 92618
949-861-2798
www.munkijo.com
Coconut products
President/Owner: Sonny Sisante
Number of Brands: 1
Number of Products: 10
Type of Packaging: Consumer
Brands:
MUNKIJO

8682 **Munsee Meats**
1701 W Kilgore Ave
P.O. Box 2843
Muncie, IN 47304-4997
765-288-3645
Fax: 765-282-8076 800-662-8001
www.munseemeats.com
Fresh and frozen beef products
President: Allysan Luczak
big_ds_girl8986@yahoo.com
CEO: Steve Hendrixson
Chief Financial Officer: Jeannie Bates
Sales: Carey Clark
Sales: Rick Allred
Sales: Mike Grubbs
Production: Frank Pease
Foreman: Rick Walsh
Production: Jeff Wray
Production: Terry Miller
Estimated Sales: $2.73 Million
Number Employees: 20-49
Brands:
Munsee Meats

8683 **Munson's Chocolates**
174 Hopriver Rd
Bolton, CT 06043-7444
860-649-4332
Fax: 860-649-7209 888-686-7667
munsons@munsonschocolates.com
www.munsonschocolates.com
Chocolate candy
Owner: Robert Munson
munsons@munsonschocolates.com
CEO: Karen Munson
Estimated Sales: $10-20 Million
Number Employees: 20-49
Square Footage: 105000
Type of Packaging: Consumer, Food Service, Private Label, Bulk
Brands:
Munson's

8684 **Muntons Ingredients**
2018 156th Ave NE, Ste 230
Bellevue, WA 98007
425-372-3082
terry.mcneill@muntons.com
www.muntons.com
Manufacture of grain malts and related ingredients
Executive Chairman: Tom Wells
MMI Inc, Vice President Sales: Terry McNeill
Parent Co: Muntons Malt

8685 **Muqui Coffee Company**
3398 Grossmont Drive
San Jose, CA 95132-3010
408-272-8471
Coffee roasters
President: Clyde McMorrow

8686 **Murakami Farms**
1431 SE 1st St
PO Box 9
Ontario, OR 97914
541-889-3131
Fax: 541-889-2933 800-421-8814
murakamionions.com
Packer and exporter of dry fresh yellow, red and white onions
President: Grant Kitamura
VP: David Murakami
Plant Manager: Paul Hopper
Estimated Sales: $2.5 Million
Number Employees: 25
Square Footage: 12000
Type of Packaging: Consumer, Food Service, Private Label

8687 **Murdock Farm Dairy**
62 Elmwood Rd
Winchendon, MA 01475
978-297-2196
Dairy products
Estimated Sales: $500,000-$1 000,000
Number Employees: 1-4

8688 **Murphy Goode Estate Winery**
4001 Highway 128
Geyserville, CA 95441
707-431-7644
Fax: 707-431-8640
general@murphygoodewinery.com
www.murphygoodewinery.com
Wine
Vice President: David Ready
Estimated Sales: $10-20 Million
Number Employees: 10-19
Number of Brands: 2
Type of Packaging: Private Label
Brands:
Goode & Ready
Murphy Goode

8689 **Murray Cider Co Inc**
103 Murray Farm Rd
Roanoke, VA 24019-8102
540-977-9000
Fax: 540-977-1336 info@murraycider.com
Apple juice and cider, also cherry-flavored apple cider
President: Robert Murray
info@murraycider.com
VP: Joe Murray
Estimated Sales: $100,000
Number Employees: 10-19
Square Footage: 240000

Type of Packaging: Consumer, Food Service, Private Label, Bulk
Brands:
Murray's

8690 **Murray's Chickens**
5190 Main St
South Fallsburg, NY 12779
845-436-5001
Fax: 845-436-5001 800-588-5051
www.murrayschicken.com
All-natural chicken burgers and marinated chicken breasts
President/Owner: Murray Bresky
murrayb@murrayschicken.com
VP Operations: Dean Koplik
Number Employees: 250-499
Brands:
Nature's Kitchen

8691 **Murvest**
5390 NW 12th Ave
Fort Lauderdale, FL 33309-3153
954-772-6440
Fax: 954-772-7728 murvest@msn.com
Pate's and sausages
President: John Murphy
Estimated Sales: Below $5 Million
Number Employees: 10-19
Brands:
Murvest

8692 **Musco Family Olive Co**
17950 Via Nicolo
Tracy, CA 95377
866-965-4837
Fax: 209-836-0518 800-523-9828
sales@muscoolive.com www.olives.com
Processor and exporter of canned olives including California stuffed green, Sicilian-style, black ripe and deli, and specialty olives and frozen ripe olives
President: Nicholas Musco
nicholasm@olives.com
CEO: Felix Musco
Director of Brand and Product Management: Tracy Wood
Director of Operations: Janet Mitchell Edwards
Director of Technical Services: Ben Hall
Year Founded: 1922
Number Employees: 250-499
Number of Brands: 7
Type of Packaging: Consumer, Food Service, Private Label
Brands:
Early California
Pearl's

8693 **Mushroom Co**
902 Woods Rd
Cambridge, MD 21613
410-221-8971
Fax: 410-221-8952
custserv@themushroomcompany.com
www.themushroomcompany.com
Canned, refrigerated, froze, organic, Kosher, seasoned, sauteed and sauced quality mushrooms.
President: Dennis Newhard
dnewhard@mushroomcanning.com
National Sales Manager: Ruth Newhard
Sales Representative: Fred Lister
Year Founded: 1931
Estimated Sales: $20 Million
Number Employees: 50-99
Square Footage: 150000
Type of Packaging: Consumer, Food Service, Private Label, Bulk
Brands:
Mga
Mother Earth
Mushroom Canning Company
Snocap

8694 **Mushroom Harvest**
PO Box 584
Athens, OH 45701
740-448-7376
Fax: 740-448-8007 info@mushroomharvest.com
www.mushroomharvest.com
Organic mushroom powder and capsules.
Owner: George Vaughan

8695 **Mushroom Wisdom, Inc**
1 Madison St
Bldg F6
East Rutherford, NJ 07073
973-470-0010
Fax: 973-470-0017 800-747-7418
www.mushroomwisdom.com
Processor and exporter of nutritional mushroom supplements and teas
President & CEO: Mike Shirota
VP: Joe Carroll
R&D: Dr. Cun Shuang
VP Marketing: Donna Noonan
Contact: Martin Agurto
martin.a@mushroomwisdom.com
Production: Masashi Ohara
Estimated Sales: $3-5 Million
Number Employees: 10-19
Number of Brands: 2
Number of Products: 24
Square Footage: 18000
Type of Packaging: Consumer, Food Service, Private Label, Bulk
Other Locations:
Maitake Products
Ridgefield Park NJ
Brands:
Grifron
Grifron D-Fraction
Grifron Mushroom Emperors
Grifron Prost Mate
Mai Green Tea
Mai Tonic Tea
Mushroom Wisdom

8696 **(HQ)Music Mountain Water Company**
305 Stoner Avenue
Shreveport, LA 71101
Fax: 318-221-6650 800-349-6555
info@musicmountain.com
www.musicmountain.com
Bottled spring water
President: Marcus Wren
Plant Manager: Sean Mccaskill
Estimated Sales: $1-3 Million
Number Employees: 20
Other Locations:
Music Mountain Spring Water
Alexandria VA
Music Mountain Spring Water
Monroe VA
Music Mountain Spring Water
Lake Charles VA
Music Mountain Spring Water
Ruston VA
Music Mountain Spring Water
Lafayette VA
Music Mountain Spring Water
Natchitoches VA
Music Mountain Spring Water
Austin TX
Music Mountain Spring Water
Tyler TX
Music Mountain Spring Water
Longview TX
Music Mountain Spring Water
Marshall TX
Music Mountain Spring Water
Alto TX
Music Mountain Spring Water
Crockett TX
Music Mountain Spring Water
Glenwood AR

8697 **Musicon Deer Farm**
385 Scotchtown Rd
Goshen, NY 10924
845-294-6378
Fax: 516-239-8915
Glatt kosher and venison
President: Norman Schlaff
Estimated Sales: $500,000-$1 Million
Number Employees: 1-4
Type of Packaging: Private Label

8698 **Mustard Seed**
203 Sanders Road
Central, SC 29630-9349
864-639-1083
877-621-2591
sheltoncj@aol.com
Natural, organic, vegetarian, whole grain, high fiber, gourmet, heart healthy burger and protein replacement mixes, burger n' a bag
Owner: Jane Shelton
Brands:
Burgers N'A Bag

8699 **Mutchler's Dakota Gold Mustard**
511 W Jackson Blvd.
Spearfish, SD 57783
605-642-8166
Fax: 605-642-0708 info@blackhills.com
www.blackhills.com
Mustard
President: Kelly Hitson
CEO: Betty Lenners

8700 **Muth's Candy Store**
630 E Market St
Louisville, KY 40202-1117
502-582-2639
Fax: 502-582-2639 www.muthscandy.com
Candy including chocolate, caramel and peanut brittle
President: Martha Vories
shop@muthscandy.com
Assistant Manager: Kimberly Bennett
Estimated Sales: Under $500,000
Number Employees: 5-9
Type of Packaging: Consumer
Brands:
Kentucky Tavern
Mojeska's
Muth's Kentucky

8701 **Mutual Fish Co**
2335 Rainier Ave S
Seattle, WA 98144
206-322-4368
Fax: 206-328-5889 www.mutualfish.com
Fresh seafood including salmon, halibut, catfish, cod, sea bass, and oysters
Estimated Sales: $1.5 Million
Number Employees: 20-49
Square Footage: 60000

8702 **My Boy's Baking LLC**
1466 Hampton Rd
Allentown, PA 18104-2018
610-759-4552
Fax: 610-759-4525 robert@myboysbaking.com
www.myboysbaking.com
Biscotti, cookies and rugelach
Marketing: Robert Levine

8703 **My Brother Bobby's Salsa**
PO Box 3659
Poughkeepsie, NY 12603
845-462-6227
mbbsalsa@aol.com
www.mbbsalsa.com
Kosher, preservative-free salsas and ready-made bruschetta topping
Owner/CEO: Robert Gropper
Year Founded: 1993
Number of Brands: 1
Number of Products: 4
Type of Packaging: Consumer, Private Label
Brands:
My Brother Bobby's Salsa

8704 **My Brother's Salsa**
1003 Beau Terre Dr
Suite 200
Bentonville, AR 72712
479-271-9404
www.mybrotherssalsa.com
Salsas and tortilla chips
Founder: Helen Lampkin

8705 **My Cup of Cake**
32 Woodland Drive
Port Washington, NY 11050
516-767-5137
sales@mycupofcake.com
Individual servings of cakes served in mugs.
Founder: Sharon Tracy

8706 **My Daddy's Cheesecake**
265 S Broadview St
265 S. Broadview
Cape Girardeau, MO 63703-5756
573-335-6660
800-735-6765
sales@mydaddyscheesecake.com
www.mydaddyscheesecake.com
Processor and exporter of confectionery items, cheesecakes, desserts, wedding and birthday cakes and gourmet cookies

Owner: Susan Stanfield
Estimated Sales: Less Than $500,000
Number Employees: 10-19
Square Footage: 10000
Type of Packaging: Consumer, Food Service, Private Label
Brands:
Cookie Wedgies
My Daddy's Cheesecake

8707 My Favorite Jerky
2000 5th Street
Apt C
Boulder, CO 80302-4948
303-444-2846
Fax: 303-444-9049
Beef jerky
President: James David
Brands:
My Favorite Jerky

8708 My Grandma's Coffee Cake
1636 Hyde Park Ave
Hyde Park, MA 02136-2458
617-364-9900
Fax: 617-364-0505 800-847-2636
www.mygrandma.com
Coffeecakes in a variety of flavors including Granny Smith Apple, Golden Raspberry, Cappuccino, New England Blueberry, Chocolate, Banana Walnut and Cape Cod Cranberry
President: Robert Katz
bmills@mygrandma.com
Controller: Seth Anapolle
EVP: Bruce Willis
VP of Marketing and Operations: Bruce Mills
Distribution Sales Manager: Gail Molino
VP Operations: Will Weeks
Estimated Sales: $5-6 Million
Number Employees: 20-49
Square Footage: 35600
Brands:
My Grandma's of New England

8709 My Own Meals Inc
400 Lake Cook Rd # 107
5410 W Roosevelt Rd
Deerfield, IL 60015-4929
847-948-1118
Fax: 847-948-0468 sales@myownmeals.com
www.myownmeals.com
Certified, halal and dhabiha halal meals, rations and food products
President: Mary Jackson
mary.jackson@myownmeals.com
CEO: Mary Anne Jackson
Manager: Robert Barnes
Estimated Sales: $.5-1 million
Number Employees: 5-9
Type of Packaging: Private Label
Brands:
J&M

8710 My Sweet
57 Porter Ave
Brooklyn, NY 11237
347-689-4402
info@mysweet.com
mysweet.com
Brigadeiros
Founder: Paula Barbosa

8711 My/Mo Mochi Ice Cream
5563 Alcoa Ave
Vernon, CA 90058-3730
323-587-5504
Fax: 323-587-5355 www.mymomochi.com
Ice cream
CEO: Ralph Denisco
Chief Financial Officer: Craig Berger
Chief Marketing Officer: Russell Barnett
Vice President, Sales: Thomas Bulowski
Production Manager: Tama Letuli
Number Employees: 51-200
Brands:
my/mo Mochi Ice Cream

8712 MySuperfoods Company
Summit, NJ 07901
www.mysuperfoodscompany.com
Superfood snacks
Co-Founder: Silvia Gianni
Co-Founder: Katie Jesionowski

8713 Myers Frozen Food Provisions
405 W Dorsey St
St Paul, IN 47272-9569
765-525-6304
Fax: 765-525-9635 info.myers@aol.com
www.myersfrozenfood.com
Frozen foods
President: Tony Myers
Sales Manager: Dan Gindling
Production Manager: Mike Myers
Estimated Sales: $3-5 000,000
Number Employees: 5-9
Brands:
Myers Frozen Food

8714 Mylk Labs
City of Industry, CA 91748
info@mylklabs.com
www.mylklabs.com
Oatmeal cups
Founder: Grace Cheng
Number of Brands: 1
Number of Products: 3
Type of Packaging: Consumer
Brands:
MYLK LABS

8715 Myron's Fine Foods, Inc.
Rrenovator's Old Mill
One River Street
Millers Falls, MA 01349
413-659-0247
Fax: 413-659-0249 800-730-2820
www.chefmyrons.com
Natural and kosher cooking sauces including tsukeyaki, soy sauce, szechuan, teriyaki, yakitori, ponzu, wild game and fish
President: Myron Becker
CFO: Lisa Richardson
Vice President: Kathy Becker
Production Manager: Steve Gambino
Plant Manager: Dawn Kennaway
Estimated Sales: Below $5 Million
Number Employees: 5-9
Number of Products: 9
Type of Packaging: Consumer, Food Service, Private Label, Bulk
Brands:
Chef Myron's Original #1 Yakitori
Chef Myron's Ponzu
Chef Myron's Premium
Chef Myron's Tsukeya
Myron's 20 Gauge

8716 Mystic Coffee Roasters
8 Steamboat Wharf
Mystic, CT 06355-2544
860-536-2999
www.mysticcoffeeroaster.com
Coffee, tea
President/Treasurer: Bruce Carpenter
greenmarbleman@aol.com
Estimated Sales: Less Than $500,000
Number Employees: 1-4

8717 Mystic Lake Dairy
24200 NE 14th Street
Sammamish, WA 98074
425-868-2029
Fax: 425-868-0553
Organic dairy products including goats milk
President: Gary Wallace
CEO: Nellie Wallace
Number Employees: 2
Brands:
Mystic Lake Dairy

8718 N A P Engineering
10965 Harborside Dr
Largo, FL 33773-4428
727-544-3118
www.napengineering.com
Manufacturer of Rotary Fillers and Sealers, Inline Tray Fillers and Sealersand Specialty Parts.
President: Paul Desocio
glouli@tampabay.rr.com
Estimated Sales: Less Than $500,000
Number Employees: 1-4

8719 N D Labs
202 Merrick Rd
Lynbrook, NY 11563-2622
516-612-4900
Fax: 516-504-0289 888-263-5227
sales@ndlabs.com www.nutritionaldesignsinc.com
Nutritional supplements and foods, including fiber and soy products, soy proteins, high-fiber cookies, vegetarian entrees, etc
Vice President: Beth Beller
beth@ndlabs.com
Vice President: Beth Beller
Marketing/Sales: Michael Allen
Public Relations: Sherry Shah
Estimated Sales: Less Than $500,000
Number Employees: 1-4
Number of Brands: 10
Type of Packaging: Consumer, Food Service, Private Label, Bulk
Brands:
Fiber 7
Fiber Supreme
Life Savy
Nana Flakes
Soy-Liccous Meals
Soypro

8720 N.B.J. Enterprises
3950 Demetropolis Rd
Mobile, AL 36693
251-661-2285
Fax: 251-661-6198
Seafood
Owner: Toni Gulsby
Estimated Sales: $1-3 Million
Number Employees: 10-19

8721 N.Y.K. Line (North America)
377 E Butterfield Rd
Lombard, IL 60148-5615
630-435-7800
Fax: 630-435-3110 888-695-7447
Contact: Kathleen Sarullo
kathy.sarullo@na.nykline.com
Estimated Sales: $.5-1 million
Number Employees: 5-9

8722 NAR
75 Hawthorne Village Road
Nashua, NH 03062
603-888-5420
Fax: 603-888-5419 bahar@nargourmet.com
www.nargourmet.com
Condiments, olive oil, other vinegar, spices, canned or preserved vegetables/fruit, dried fruit
Marketing: Bahar Ayasli
Contact: Asli Aksoy
asli@nargourmet.com

8723 NOKA
Pacific Palisades, CA
hello@nokaorganics.com
www.nokaorganics.com
Superfood smoothies
Co-Founder: Ryan Werner
Co-Founder: Adam Steiner
Number of Products: 6

8724 NORPAC Foods Inc
3225 25th St SE
Salem, OR 97302
consumeraffairs@norpac.com
www.norpac.com
Frozen vegetables, fruits and juices.
President & CEO: Shawn Campbell
Research & Development Manager: Kim Claggett
Director of Marketing: Brad Burden
VP of Operations: Mark Croeni
Year Founded: 1924
Estimated Sales: $476.3 Million
Number Employees: 1,500
Type of Packaging: Consumer, Food Service, Private Label, Bulk
Other Locations:
Lake Oswego OR
Salem OR
Hermiston OR
Quincy WA
Brands:
Flav-R-Pac
Westpac
Santiam
Grande Classics Island Blends
Grande Classics
Connoisseur Collection

Soup Supreme
Chili Supreme
Pasta Perfect
Fruit Topping
Flame Roasted Vegetables
Norpac
Scratch Recipe

8725 NOW Foods
244 Knollwood Dr.
Bloomingdale, IL 60108
888-669-3663
www.nowfoods.com
Vitamins, healthy foods, natural personal care and sports nutrition products.
CEO: Jim Emme
CFO: Andy Kotlarz
General Counsel: Beverly Reid
VP, Quality/Regulatory Affiars: Aaron Secrist
VP, Global Sales/Marketing: Dan Richard
Vice President, Human Resources: Michelle Canada
COO: Ernest Shepard
Year Founded: 1968
Estimated Sales: $100 Million
Number Employees: 100-249
Number of Brands: 9
Number of Products: 1500
Square Footage: 203000
Type of Packaging: Consumer, Private Label, Bulk
Brands:
Better Stevia
Living Now
Now Real Tea
Now Real Food
Ellyndale Foods
Coconut Infusions
Nutty Infusions
Q Cups
Sugarless Sugar

8726 NPC Dehydrators
11761 Highway 770 E
Eden, NC 27288
336-635-5190
Fax: 336-635-5193
Dry brewers yeast
President: R Dean Fullmer
Executive: Max Selty
Sales Director: Mike Morales
Public Relations: Charles Setlif
Estimated Sales: $5-10 Million
Number Employees: 30
Type of Packaging: Private Label
Brands:
Sonic Dried Yeast

8727 NPC Dehydrators
P.O.Box B
Payette, ID 83661-0017
208-642-4471
Fax: 208-642-4473
Dry brewers yeast
Manager: Vicki Swank
Estimated Sales: Less than $500,000
Number Employees: 1-4

8728 NSG Transport Inc
115 W 16th St
Gothenburg, NE 69138-1302
308-537-7191
Fax: 308-537-7193 www.nsgco.com
Processor and exporter of corn
President: Norman Geiken
wade@nsgco.com
Sales Exec: Wade Geiken
Estimated Sales: $3-5 Million
Number Employees: 20-49
Type of Packaging: Bulk

8729 Nabisco
7 Campus Dr
Parsippany, NJ 07054-0311
973-682-5000
Fax: 973-503-2153 www.snackworks.com
Baked goods including cookies and crackers
President/CEO: James Kilts Jr.
EVP/CFO: James Healey
EVP/CIO: Doreen Wright
Contact: Lois Collum
lois.collum@mdlz.com
Plant Manager: Larry Campbell
Purchasing Manager: Mike Swift
Parent Co: Kraft Foods
Type of Packaging: Consumer, Food Service
Brands:
100 Calorie Packs
Belvita
Chips Ahoy!
Barnum's Animals Crackers
Cameo
Nabisco Classics
Kraft Handi-Snacks
Easy Cheese
Flavor Originals
Ginger Snaps
Honey Maid
Kraft Cheese Nips
Mixers
Mallomars
Newtons
Nabisco 12 Packs
Nutter Butter
Nilla Wafers
Premium
Oreo
Ritz Bits Sandwiches
Ritz
Snackwells
Red Oval Farms Stoned Wheat Thins
Toasted Chips
Teddy Grahams
Triscuit
Wheat Thins
Wheatsworth

8730 Nacan Products
60 West Drive
Brampton, ON L6T 4W7
Canada
905-454-4466
Fax: 905-454-5207
Modified starches derived from corn, waxy maize and tapioca
President: Roland Sirois
Vicce-Chairman: Jim Grieve
Business Director: Dill Ruderman
Executive VP: John Morrell
Parent Co: National Starch & Chemical Company
Brands:
Nacan

8731 NadaMoo
5555 N Lamar Blvd
Suite K111
Austin, TX 78751
nadamoo.com
Dairy-free frozen dessert
President & CEO: Daniel Nicholson
Number of Brands: 2
Number of Products: 18
Type of Packaging: Consumer
Brands:
NADAMOO
NADAMOO ORGANIC

8732 Nagasako Fish
800 Eha St
Suite 12
Wailuku, HI 96793
808-242-4073
Fax: 808-244-7020
Seafood
Owner: Darryl Flinton
Estimated Sales: $5-10 Million
Number Employees: 10-19

8733 Nagase America Corp.
546 Fifth Ave
16th Fl
New York, NY 10036
212-703-1343
nagaseamerica.com
Functional ingredients for the food and beverage industries.

8734 Nahmias et Fils
201 Saw Mill River Rd. #C
Yonkers, NY 10701
914-294-0055
www.nahmiasetfils.com
Whiskey, fig-flavored distilled spirits
Founder: Dorit Nahmias
Year Founded: 2010
Number of Brands: 1
Number of Products: 3s
Type of Packaging: Consumer, Private Label
Brands:
Nahmias et Fils

8735 Naji's Pita Gourmet Restaurant
166 W Valley Ave
Birmingham, AL 35209-3620
205-945-6001
Fax: 205-945-6021 www.pita.net
Plain and wheat pita bread
Owner; President: Naji Constantine
naji@pita.net
Estimated Sales: Less Than $500,000
Number Employees: 10-19
Square Footage: 24000
Brands:
Pito

8736 Najila's
PO Box 74
Binghamton, NY 13905-0074
607-722-4287
Fax: 607-773-9012
Gourmet cookies
President/CEO: Najla Aswad
Type of Packaging: Food Service, Bulk
Brands:
Najla Gone Chunky

8737 Najla's Specialty FoodsInc
8007 Vine Crest Ave # 3
Suite 3
Louisville, KY 40222-8607
502-412-4420
Fax: 502-412-4421 877-962-5527
cookies@najlas.com www.najlas.com
Kosher, cookies, toffee, frozen bars, nuts, gift packs.
Owner: Najla R Aswad
cookies@najlas.com
Marketing: Najla Aswad
Estimated Sales: Less Than $500,000
Number Employees: 5-9

8738 Nakano Foods
55 E Euclid Ave
Mt Prospect, IL 60056 1283
847-290-0730
Fax: 847-590-0482 800-323-4358
dan_baron@nakanofoods.com
Wine and organic vinegars
Number Employees: 50-99

8739 Naked Bacon
Ste. Genevieve, MO
nakedbaconco.com
Gluten-free bacon
Founder: John Kreilich
Number of Brands: 1
Number of Products: 6
Type of Packaging: Consumer
Brands:
NAKED BACON

8740 Naked Infusions LLC
23679 Calabasas Rd.
Calabasas, CA 91302
818-239-9058
info@nakedinfusions.com
www.nakedinfusions.com
Manufacturer of salsa.
Founder: Selene Kepila
selene@nakedinfusions.com

8741 Naked Juice Company
Monrovia, CA 91016
877-858-4237
www.nakedjuice.com
Fruit juices and smoothies
Parent Co: Pepsico

8742 Naked Mountain Winery Vineyard
2747 Leeds Manor Rd
Rt. 688
Markham, VA 22643-1715
540-364-1609
drinknaked@nakedmtnwinery.com
www.nakedmtnwinery.com
Wines
Owner: Randall Morgan
drinknaked@nakedmtnwinery.com
Co-Owner: Meagan Morgan
Office Manager: Sandy Coleman
Marketing/Sales Manager: Drew Hauser
Assistant Winemaker: Don Oldham
Office Manager: Darlene Call
Estimated Sales: Below $5 Million
Number Employees: 1-4

Type of Packaging: Private Label
Brands:
Naked Mountain

8743 **Naleway Foods**
233 Hutchings Street
Winnipeg, MB R2X 2R4
Canada
204-633-6535
Fax: 204-694-4310 800-665-7448
sales@naleway.com www.naleway.com
Processor and exporter of frozen foods including pierogies and panzarotti
Sales: W Halley
Number Employees: 100-249
Type of Packaging: Consumer, Food Service

8744 **Nalle Winery**
2385 Dry Creek Rd
Healdsburg, CA 95448-9796
707-433-1040
Fax: 707-433-6062 www.nallewinery.com
Wines
Co-Owner: Lee Nalle
Co-Owner: Doug Nalle
doug@nallewinery.com
Winemaker: Doug Nalle
Winemaker: Andrew Nalle
Number Employees: 1-4
Number of Brands: 1
Brands:
Nalle

8745 **Namaste Foods**
P.O. Box 3133
Coeur d'Alene, ID 83816
866-258-9493
admin@namastefoods.com
www.namastefoods.com
Gluten free foods
Owner: Daphne Taylor

8746 **Nan Sea Enterprises of Wisconsin**
900 Gale St
Waukesha, WI 53186-2515
262-542-8841
Fax: 262-542-4356
Manufacturer and distributor of fresh frozen king, dungeness, golden and snow crab; also, lobster and lobster claws
President: Eric Muehl
VP: Robert Nell
Estimated Sales: $10-20 Million
Number Employees: 5-9
Type of Packaging: Food Service, Private Label

8747 **Nana Mae's Organics**
708 Gravenstein Highway North, #174
Sebastopol, CA 95472
707-829-7359
Fax: 707-829-7356 www.nanamae.com
Organic apple juice and sauce and vinegar and honey
Owner: Paul Kolling
Sales: Kendra Kolling
Estimated Sales: $1,000,000
Number Employees: 15
Number of Brands: 1
Number of Products: 15
Square Footage: 1056000
Type of Packaging: Consumer, Food Service, Private Label, Bulk

8748 **Nana's Cookie Co.**
4901 Morena Blvd
San Diego, CA 92117
800-836-7534
www.nanascookiecompany.com
Gluten-free cookies
President/Owner: Miriam Diamond
Year Founded: 1992
Number of Brands: 3
Number of Products: 17
Type of Packaging: Consumer
Brands:
NANA'S
NANA'S NO GLUTEN
NANA'S COOKIE BARS

8749 **Nanci's Frozen Yogurt**
4722 E Ivy St #108
Mesa, AZ 85205
480-834-4290
Fax: 480-834-4271 800-788-0808
info@nancis.com www.nancis.com
Soft-serve dessert mixes including frozen yogurt, fruit freezer sorbet, non-dairy soft serve, no-sugar-added mixes, smoothie base mixes, granita mixes and more than 90 flavors
President/CEO: John Wudel
Spokesperson: Nanci Wudel
Estimated Sales: $1-3 Million
Number Employees: 10-19
Type of Packaging: Food Service, Bulk
Brands:
Nanci's

8750 **Nancy's Candy**
2684 Jeb Stuart Highway
PO Box 860
Meadows Of Dan, VA 24120
276-952-2112
Fax: 276-952-1042 800-328-3834
nancyscandy@embarqmail.com
www.nancyscandycompany.com
Fudge, chocolates, nut brittles and more
Marketing: Nancy Galli
Contact: Nancy Galli
ngfudge@yahoo.com

8751 **Nancy's Probiotic Foods**
Eugene, OR 97402
nancysyogurt.com
Organic yogurt, kefir, cottage cheese, and sour cream
General Manager & CFO: Sue Kesey
Number of Brands: 1
Number of Products: 11
Type of Packaging: Consumer
Brands:
NANCY'S

8752 **Nancy's Shellfish**
91 Falmouth Rd
Falmouth, ME 04105-1841
207-774-3411
Fax: 207-780-0044
Shellfish, seafood
President: Joe Scola
Estimated Sales: $1.4 Million
Number Employees: 5-9

8753 **Nancy's Specialty Foods**
6500 Overlake Pl
Newark, CA 94560
510-494-1100
Fax: 510-494-1140 www.nancys.com
Processor and exporter of frozen appetizers, entrees and desserts.
President: Bob Kroll
markus.bahr@wellsfargo.com
CFO: Adam Ferris
Marketing/Communications Director: Diane DiMartini
VP Sales: R L Booth
VP Operations: David Joiner
Plant Manager: Rick Shepherd
Estimated Sales: $19.8 Million
Number Employees: 325
Square Footage: 172000
Type of Packaging: Consumer, Food Service, Private Label, Bulk
Brands:
Nancy's

8754 **Nanka Seimen Company**
3030 Leonis Blvd
Vernon, CA 90058
323-585-9967
Fax: 323-585-9969
Japanese-style and egg noodles, chow mein, wontons, egg rolls and gyoza skins
President: Shoi Chi Sayano
VP: Toshiaki Yoshida
Estimated Sales: $5-10 Million
Number Employees: 18
Square Footage: 80000
Type of Packaging: Consumer, Food Service
Brands:
Golden Dragon
Nanka Udon

8755 **Nanocor**
1500 W Shure Dr
Arlington Hts, IL 60004-1443
847-851-1918
Fax: 847-851-1919 www.nanocor.com
Manager: Tie Lin
Contact: Tie Lan
tie.lan@amcol.com
Number Employees: 100-249
Parent Co: AMCOL International Corp.

8756 **Nantong Acetic Acid Chemical Co., Ltd.**
PO Box 1447
Hilliard, OH 43026
614-947-0249
Fax: 866-521-7624 gord@ntacf.com
www.ntacf.com
Food additives and dye and pigment intermediates, as well as organic chemical raw materials
Sales Manager: Gord Chu
gchu@ntacf.com
General Manager: Caifeng Ding
Vice-General Manager: Qing Jiu
Type of Packaging: Bulk

8757 **Nantucket Pasta Company, Inc.**
20 Young's Way
Nantucket, MA 02584-2272
508-494-5209
www.nantucketpastagoddess.com
Pasta (fresh).
Marketing: Liliana Dougan

8758 **Nantucket Tea Traders**
P.O.Box 179
Nantucket, MA 02554-0179
508-325-0203
Fax: 508-325-0203
Processors of teas
President: Judy Kales
Sales: Paul Kales
Estimated Sales: $120,000
Number Employees: 1
Brands:
Nantucket Tea Trader

8759 **Nantucket Vineyard**
5 Bartlett Farm Rd
Nantucket, MA 02554-4341
508-228-9235
Fax: 508-325-5209 jay@ciscobrewers.com
Wine
Owner: Randy Hudson
Founder/Co-Owner: Dean Long
Estimated Sales: $5-9.9 Million
Number Employees: 1-4
Parent Co: Cisco Brewers
Type of Packaging: Private Label
Brands:
Nantucket Vineyard

8760 **Nantze Springs Inc**
156 W Carroll St
Dothan, AL 36301-4316
334-794-4218
Fax: 334-712-2899 800-239-7873
www.nantzesprings.com
Water
President: Malone Garrett
mgarrett@nantzesprings.com
Estimated Sales: $3-5 Million
Number Employees: 10-19
Brands:
Nantze Springs

8761 **Napa Barrel Care**
1075 Golden Gate Dr
Napa, CA 94558-6187
707-254-1985
Fax: 707-254-2092 info@barrelcare.com
www.barrelcare.com
Manufacturing and storage of wine barrels
President/Winemaker: Mike Blom
mike@barrelcare.com
Warehouse Manager: Jorge Vargas
Estimated Sales: Less Than $500,000
Number Employees: 1-4

8762 **Napa Cellars**
7481 Saint Helena Hwy
Napa, CA 94558-9400
707-944-2565
Fax: 707-944-9749 800-535-6400
info@napacellars.com www.napawineco.com
Wines
Manager: Dean Slattery
Winemaker: Rob Lawson
General Manager: Sheldon Parker
Estimated Sales: $1.6 Million
Number Employees: 5-9
Type of Packaging: Private Label
Brands:
Napa Wine

8763 **Napa Hills**
Chicago, IL 60614
nick@napahills.com
napahills.com
Sparkling water
Founder & CEO: Ellona Jarvis

8764 **Napa Valley Kitchens**
564 Gateway Dr
Napa, CA 94558-7517
707-254-3700
Fax: 707-259-0219
Manufacturer and exporter of flavored oils, marinades, and dressings
Chairman: John Foraker
Cfo: Dale Eagle
Vice President of R&D: Bob Kaake
Senior Vice President of Marketing: Sarah Bird
Sales Director: Terry Dudley
Production Manager: Mark Osborne
Estimated Sales: $10 Million
Number Employees: 75
Type of Packaging: Consumer
Brands:
Consorzio
Napa Valley Mustard Co.

8765 **Napa Wine Company**
7830-40 St. Helena Hwy.
Oakville, CA 94562
707-944-8669
Fax: 707-944-9749 800-848-9630
moreinfo@napawineco.com www.napawineco.com
Custom crush wine production
Managing Partner: Andrew Hoxsey
General Manager: Sheldon Parker
Winemaker: Rob Lawson
Estimated Sales: $5 Million
Number Employees: 20-49
Type of Packaging: Consumer, Private Label
Brands:
Napa Wine Company

8766 **Napoleon Locker**
3536 W Napoleon Wilson Street
Napoleon, IN 47034
812-852-4333
Beef and pork; slaughtering services available
Owner: Matt Brancamp
Co-Owner: Kimberly Brancamp
Estimated Sales: $.5-1 million
Number Employees: 10-19
Type of Packaging: Private Label

8767 **Napoli Pasta Manufacturers**
9719 S Dixie Hwy # 8
Miami, FL 33156-2834
305-666-1942
Fax: 305-254-6139 npmgroup@aol.com
www.worldtrade.org
Pasta products
President: Charlotte Gallogly
Plant Manager: Patricia Matuk
Estimated Sales: $5-9.9 Million
Number Employees: 1-4

8768 **Naraghi Group**
20001 Mchenry Ave
Escalon, CA 95320-9614
209-579-5253
Fax: 209-551-4544
Processor and exporter of grapes, peaches, apples, walnuts, pistachios and almonds
Owner: Miguel Lizarraga
miguel@naraghifarms.com
Owner: Wendell Naraghi
Plant Manager: Isidro Vaca
Number Employees: 1-4

8769 **Nardi Breads**
45 Glendale Rd
South Windsor, CT 06074-2415
860-289-5458
Fax: 860-289-9012
Bread and rolls
Founder: Pasquale Nardi
President: Charles Nardi
Estimated Sales: $5-9.9 Million
Number Employees: 10-19

8770 **Nardone Brothers**
420 New Commerce Blvd
Hanover Twp, PA 18706-1445
570-823-0141
Fax: 570-823-2581 800-822-5320
vjn1@att.net nardonebros.com
Pizza manufacturer serving the school and institutional food service markets nationwide since 1942.
President: Vince Nardone
CFO: Louis Nardone
VP: Frank Nardone
Manufacturing/Operations Director: Mario Nardone
Estimated Sales: $24.4 Million
Number Employees: 100-249
Type of Packaging: Consumer, Food Service
Brands:
Nardone Bros.
Vincenzo's

8771 **Naron Mary Sue Candies**
2600 Georgetown Rd
Baltimore, MD 21230-1302
410-467-9932
Fax: 410-467-1649 800-662-2639
www.marysue.com
Chocolate and soft candy
Owner: Bill Buppert
CFO: Mike Wiss
R & D: Mark Berman
Estimated Sales: $5-10 Million
Number Employees: 5-9

8772 **Nash Produce**
6160 S NC Highway 58
Nashville, NC 27856-8642
252-443-6011
Fax: 252-443-6746 800-334-3032
info@nashproduce.com www.nashproduce.com
Sweet potatoes and cucumbers
President: Thomas Joyner
thomasjoyner@nashproduce.com
VP: Richard Joyner
Director of Marketing: Tami Long
Sales Director: Don Sparks
Director of Accounting and Business: Sarah Payne
Estimated Sales: $40 Million
Number Employees: 100+
Type of Packaging: Consumer, Food Service, Private Label, Bulk
Brands:
Mr. Yam
Cajan Gold
Nash's Pride
Nash's Gold
Oh So Sweet

8773 **Nashoba Valley Winery**
100 Wattaquadock Hill Rd
Bolton, MA 01740-1238
978-779-5521
Fax: 978-779-5523 nashoba.winery@gte.net
www.nashobawinery.com
Wines
President: Richard Pelletier
rpelletier@nashobavalleywinery.com
VP: Cindy Rowe Pelletier
Estimated Sales: Below $5 Million
Number Employees: 20-49
Type of Packaging: Private Label

8774 **Nasonville Dairy**
10898 Hwy
10 West
Marshfield, WI 54449
715-676-2177
Fax: 715-676-3636
mailorder@nasonvilledairy.com
www.nasonvilledairy.com
Cheese, cheese products
Owner: Kim Heiman
Estimated Sales: Below $5 Million
Number Employees: 20-49

8775 **Nasoya Foods**
1 New England Way
Ayer, MA 01432-1514
978-772-6880
Fax: 978-772-6881 800-848-2769
info@vitasoy-usa.com www.myvitasoy.com
All-natural organic and all-natural tofu, wraps, noobles, spreads
Vice President: Susan Rolnick
srolnick@vitasoyusa.com
Vice President: Susan Rolnick
srolnick@vitasoyusa.com
Number Employees: 100-249

8776 **(HQ)Nassau Candy Distributors**
530 W John St
Hicksville, NY 11801-1039
516-433-7100
Fax: 516-433-9010 sales@nassaucandy.com
www.nassaucandy.com
Manufacturer, importer and distributor of confectionery items and gourmet foods.
President: Barry Rosenbaum
Chairman & CEO: Lesley Stier
Vice President: Carol Baca
carol.baca@nassaucandy.com
Number Employees: 100-249
Other Locations:
Nassau Candy Co.
Deer Park NY

8777 **Natalie's Orchid IslandJuice Co.**
330 North U.S. Highway One
Ft. Pierce, FL 34950
772-465-1122
Fax: 772-465-4303 800-373-7444
www.oijc.com
Fresh-squeezed fruit juices
Owner/CEO: Marygrace Sexton
COO: Frank Tranchilla
EVP: John Martinelli
Quality Assurance/Food Safety Manager: Brian Christensen
Director of Marketing: Natalie Sexton
Director of Customer Service/Logistics: David Cortez
Contact: Keith Camara
kcamara@oijc.com
Director of Operations: Jim Zurbey
Senior Production Manager: Peter Binns
Estimated Sales: $20-50 Million
Number Employees: 50-99
Number of Brands: 1
Type of Packaging: Consumer, Food Service
Brands:
Natalie's Orchid Island

8778 **Natchez Pecan Shelling Company**
P.O.Box 100
Taylorsville, MS 39168-0100
601-785-4333
Pecans
Owner: Harold Bynum
Estimated Sales: Less than $500,000
Number Employees: 1-4

8779 **Natchitoches Crawfish Company**
1205 Texas Street
Natchitoches, LA 71457
318-352-2194
Fax: 318-379-2816 mcfctr@bellsouth.net
natchitochescrawfish.com
Owner: Jimmy Strickland

8780 **Natierra**
7535 Woodman Pl
Van Nuys, CA 91405-1545
310-559-0259
Fax: 310-559-0289 www.natierra.com
Seeds; dried berries; cacao powder; and beets.
President/CEO: Thierry Olivier
Media Relations: Holly Franklin

8781 **Nation Pizza & Foods**
601 E Algonquin Rd
Schaumburg, IL 60173-3803
847-397-3320
Fax: 847-397-9456 www.nationpizza.com
Pizza crusts, pizzas, sauces, sandwiches, appetizers, hispanic foods, sweets, packaging
President: Richard Auskalnis
CFO: Joe Giglio
SVP: Jack Campolo
Quality Assurance: Teresa Martinez

Estimated Sales: $20-50 Million
Number Employees: 50-99
Parent Co: OSI Group
Type of Packaging: Consumer
Brands:
Father & Son
My Father's Best
Nation

8782 Nation Wide Canning Ltd.
324 Essex County Road 34 East
PO Box 227
Cottam, ON N0R 1B0
Canada
519-839-4831
Fax: 519-839-4993 www.cottamgardens.com
Canned and crushed tomatoes, mushrooms, potatoes, pie fillings, kidney beans and spaghetti and pizza sauce; also, private labeling available
President and CFO: H Finaldi
Office Manager: Irene Finaldi
Number Employees: 55
Square Footage: 200000
Type of Packaging: Private Label
Brands:
Cottam Gardens

8783 National Beef Packing Co LLC
12200 N. Ambassador Dr.
Suite 500
Kansas City, MO 64163
800-449-2333
www.nationalbeef.com
Fresh, chilled and processed beef products.
CEO: Timothy Klein
tklein@nationalbeef.com
Year Founded: 1992
Estimated Sales: $7.3 Billion
Number Employees: 8,200
Number of Brands: 5
Type of Packaging: Consumer, Food Service, Private Label, Bulk
Other Locations:
HQ
Kansas City MO
Dodge City KS
Liberal KS
Hummels Wharf PA
Moultrie GA
National Beef Leathers
St. Joseph MO
International Office
Chicago IL
Brands:
Black Canyon Angus
Black Canyon Premium Reserve
Certified Angus Beef
Certified Hereford Beef
Natural Angus Beef
Certified Premium Beef
National Beef Prime
Corned Beef
Heritage Farms

8784 National Beverage Corporation
8100 SW 10th Streeet
Suite 4000
Fort Lauderdale, FL 33324
954-581-0922
Fax: 954-473-4710 877-622-3499
salesteam@nationalbeverage.com
www.nationalbeverage.com
Canned and bottled beverages including soft drinks, juice and spring water
President: Joseph Caporella
Chairman/CEO: Nick Caporella
SVP Finance: George Bracken
EVP/Procurement: Edward Knecht
Executive Director/IT: Raymond Notarantonio
SVP/Chief Accounting Officer: Dean McCoy
Senior Director/Consumer Marketing: Brent Bott
Director/Stragetic Brand Management: Vanessa Walker
Senior Director/Beverage Analyst: Gregory Kworderis
Type of Packaging: Consumer, Food Service
Other Locations:
National Beverage Corp.
Hayward CA
Brands:
Asante
Big Shot
Cascadia Only 2 Calories
Cascadia Sparkling Cider
Clearfruit
Crystal Bay
Everfresh
Faygo
Lacroix
Mr Pure
Mt. Shasta
Ohana
Rip It
Ritz
Shasta
St. Nick's

8785 National Fish & Oyster
5028 Meridian Rd NE
Olympia, WA 98516-2339
360-491-5550
Fax: 360-438-3681 www.nationaloyster.com
Processor and exporter of fresh and frozen oysters
President: James Bulldis
VP: George Bulldis
Plant Manager: Catherine Gylys
Estimated Sales: $5-10 Million
Number Employees: 20-49
Square Footage: 12000
Type of Packaging: Consumer
Brands:
Sea Pearl

8786 National Fish & SeafoodInc
11-15 Parker St # 4
Gloucester, MA 01930-3017
978-282-7880
Fax: 978-282-7882 800-229-1750
comments@nationalfish.com
www.nationalfish.com
Seafood
President: Jack Ventola
jventola@nationalfish.com
Number Employees: 20-49

8787 (HQ)National Fish & Seafood Inc
11-15 Parker St # 4
Gloucester, MA 01930-3017
978-282-7880
Fax: 978-282-7882 800-229-1750
manager@nationalfish.com www.nationalfish.com
Seafood and seafood products
President & COO: Todd Provost
CFO: Ana Crespo
VP: Rick Waltzer
Purchasing Manager: Jason Brown
Estimated Sales: $20-50 Million
Number Employees: 20-49
Square Footage: 3500
Type of Packaging: Consumer, Food Service, Private Label
Brands:
National Fisheries

8788 National Flavors
1206 E Crosstown Pkwy
Kalamazoo, MI 49001-2563
269-344-3640
Fax: 269-344-1037 800-525-2431
national@nationalflavors.com
www.nationalflavors.com
Manufacturer of syrups, flavoring extracts, processed fruits and oils. Purchased land in 2015 to expand manufacturing facilities, due to be opened in late 2017.
President: Dan Hinkle
national@nationalflavors.com
Director of Research & Development: Polly B
Director of Sales & Marketing: Tony Overmyer
Director of Human Resources: Ann Woolley
Production Coordinator: Michael Visser
Estimated Sales: $4.8 Million
Number Employees: 20-49

8789 National Food Co LTD
3109 Koapaka St # C
Unit C
Honolulu, HI 96819-1998
808-839-1118
Fax: 808-839-6866
Owner: Teresa Goo
teresa.goo@nfcegypt.com
Estimated Sales: $5-10 Million
Number Employees: 1-4

8790 National Food Corporation
728-134th St. SW
Suite 103
Everett, WA 98204
425-349-4257
Fax: 425-349-4336 www.natlfood.com
Eggs and egg products including; yolks only, whole eggs, whites, and whole egg blends
President: Brian Bookey
VP Marketing: Roger Deffner
Sales Director: Gerry Wigren
Estimated Sales: $23.2 Million
Number Employees: 500
Type of Packaging: Consumer, Food Service

8791 National Foods
1414 S West Street
Indianapolis, IN 46225-1548
317-634-5645
800-683-6565
Processor and exporter of portion cut meat and frankfurters
President: Steve Silk
Senior VP/General Manager: Martin Silver
Sales/Marketing Executive: Mark Kleinman
Number Employees: 600
Square Footage: 720000
Parent Co: ConAgra Refigerated Prepared Foods
Type of Packaging: Consumer, Food Service
Other Locations:
National Foods
Indianapolis IN

8792 National Foods
PO Box 20046
Kansas City, MO 64195-0046
620-624-1851
Fax: 800-449-1333 www.nationalbeef.com
General grocery
President: John Miller
Sales Manager: Mike Sheehan
Parent Co: ConAgra Refigerated Prepared Foods

8793 National Foods
600 Food Center Drive
Bronx, NY 10474-7037
718-842-5000
Fax: 718-842-5664 800-683-6565
Processed meats, frankfurters, condiments and relishes. Kosher
President: Steve Silk
CFO: Bob Cahill
Executive VP: Marty Silver
Senior Marketing Manager: Leigh Platte
Sales Director: Scott Jacobs
Operations Manager: Henry Morris
General Manager: Robert Lichtman
Number Employees: 150
Parent Co: ConAgra Refigerated Prepared Foods
Type of Packaging: Private Label

8794 National Frozen Foods Corp
1600 Fairview Ave E
Suite 200
Seattle, WA 98102
206-322-8900
Fax: 206-322-4458 sales@nffc.com
www.nffc.com
Frozen foods including fruit and vegetable purees, vegetable blends, peas, corn, carrots, cooked squash, creamed corn, beans, pearl onions.
President & CEO: Dick Grader
Director of Chain Accounts: Sunshine Sang
Year Founded: 1912
Estimated Sales: $178.08 Million
Number Employees: 1,000-4,999
Square Footage: 12000
Type of Packaging: Consumer, Food Service, Private Label, Bulk
Other Locations:
Albany OR
Chehalis WA
Moses Lake WA
Quincy WA
Brands:
Valamont

8795 National Fruit Flavor Co Inc
935 Edwards Ave
New Orleans, LA 70123-3124
504-733-6757
Fax: 504-736-0168 800-966-1123
admin@nationalfruitflavor.com
www.nationalfruitflavor.com

Beverage concentrates, syrups and mixes. Manufacturer since 1917.
President: Gene Gamble
admin@nationalfruitflavor.com
Controller: Anthony Fulco
Vice President: Peter Gambel
Research and Development/Quality Control: Sharon Prados
Sales Manager: Avery Stirratt
Customer Service: Chris Rooks
Operations: Peter Gambel
Plant Manager: Giovanni Galvan
Purchasing: Michelle Adams
Estimated Sales: $10-20 Million
Number Employees: 20-49
Number of Brands: 6
Number of Products: 700
Square Footage: 41000
Type of Packaging: Consumer, Food Service, Private Label, Bulk
Brands:
Gambelini
National
Old Comiskey
Sno-Ball
Tasty
Zodiac

8796 **National Fruit Product Co Inc**
956 Poorhouse Rd
Winchester, VA 22603-3868
540-723-9614
Manufacturer of fruit products.
CEO and President: David Gum
Contact: Rhonda Alsberry
ralsberry@nfpc.com
Number Employees: 1-4
Brands:
WHITEHOUSE FOODS

8797 **National Grape Co-Op**
2 S Portage St.
Westfield, NY 14787-1492
Fax: 716-326-5111 800-340-6870
www.welchs.com
Fruit and berry juices and jams.
President/CEO/Director: Bradley Irwin
Year Founded: 1952
Estimated Sales: $650 Million
Number Employees: 1000-4999
Brands:
Welch's Fruit Juices
Welch's Jams, Jellie & Spreads
Welch's Fruit Fizz
Welch's Sparkling
Welch's Essentials
Welch's Refrigerted Juice Cocktails
Welch's Light
Welch's Concentrates
Welch's Natural Spreads
Welch's Food & Snacks
Welch's Chillers

8798 **National Harvest**
PO Box 26455
Kansas City, MO 64196-6455
816-842-9600
Fax: 816-531-3032 sales@nationalharvest.com
Baked potato meals and toppings
President: John Mueller
Estimated Sales: $1-3 Million
Number Employees: 5-9
Type of Packaging: Food Service, Private Label, Bulk
Brands:
Super Stuffers

8799 **National Importers**
120-13100 Mitchell Road
Richmond, BC V6V 1M8
Canada
604-324-1551
Fax: 604-324-1553 888-894-6464
ussales@nationalimporters.com
www.nationalimporters.com
Importer of gourmet, Mexican, Chinese, Indian, Thai foods, candy and groceries
Owner: David Dueck
Marketing: Barbara Allen
Office Manager: Peggy Hunter

8800 **National Meat & Provision Company**
321 W 10th St
Reserve, LA 70084-6603
985-479-4200
Fax: 985-479-4205 www.natcofs.com
Beef, lamb, veal, pork, poultry, sausages, wild game, seafood, and dairy
President: Anne Babin
anne@natcofoodservice.com
Chairman: Leonard Lalla
CEO/Secretary: John Lalla
VP: Earline Lalla
Operations Manager: Joe Schwab
Manager: Sam Najm
Estimated Sales: $39.06 Million
Number Employees: 60
Square Footage: 85000

8801 **National Pretzel Company**
2060 Old Philadelphia Pike
Lancaster, PA 17602
800-732-0089
Pretzels

8802 **National Raisin Co.**
PO Box 219
Fowler, CA 93625
559-834-5981
Fax: 559-834-1055 info@nationalraisin.com
www.nationalraisin.com
Raisins, nuts and other dried fruits.
President/CEO: Lindakay Abdulian
Founder/Senior Advisor: Kenneth Bedrosian
kenneth.bedrosian@national-raisin.com
Accounts Payable Manager: Carlotta Bedrosian
Vice President: Bryan Bedrosian
Senior VP, Sales/Marketing: Jane Asmar
Vice President, Grower Relations: Michael Bedrosian
Year Founded: 1969
Estimated Sales: $140 Million
Number Employees: 500-999
Number of Brands: 1
Square Footage: 400000
Type of Packaging: Consumer, Food Service, Private Label, Bulk
Brands:
Champion

8803 **National Sign Corporation**
1255 Westlake Ave N
Seattle, WA 98109-3531
206-282-0700
Fax: 206-285-3091 info@nationalsigncorp.com
www.nationalsigncorp.com
Manufacturing, installation and servicing of interior and exterior signage, including ADA signs.
President: Timothy Zamberlin
Estimated Sales: $5-10 Million
Number Employees: 35
Square Footage: 60000

8804 **(HQ)National Starch Food Innovation**
10 Finderne Ave
Bridgewater, NJ 08807
908-575-0178
Fax: 908-685-5355 800-743-6343
www.foodinnovation.com
Specialty starches for the food industry.
President: James Zallie
Contact: Bob Bacigalupo
kzizlercohen@citi-habitats.com
Parent Co: Ingredion Incorporated
Brands:
Baka-Snack
Batter BindS
Capsul
Capsul Ta
Clearjel
Colflo 67
Crisp Coat Uc
Crisp Film
Crystal Gum
Crystal Tex 627m
Dry-Flo
Elastigel 1000j
Eliane
Firm-Tex
Frigex W
Gel N Melt
H-50
Hi Flo
Hi-Cap 100
Hi-Maize 260
Hi-Maize Whole Grain Flour
Hi-Set 322
Hi-Set C
Homecraft Create
Hylon Vii
Instant Clearjel
Instant Pure-Flo F
Instant Textra
K4484
National
N-Creamer 46
N-Dulge
N-Lok 1930
N-Oil
Novation
N-Tack
Nutriose
N-Zorbit
Paselli
Perfectagel Mpt
Perfectamyl
Precisa
Pure-Flo
Purity Gum
Purity
Q-Naturale
Textaid
Textra
Thermflo
Thermtex
Ultra Create
Ultra-Crisp
Ultra-Sperse
Ultra-Tex

8805 **National Steak & Poultry**
301 E. 5th Ave.
Owasso, OK 74055
918-274-8787
www.nationalsteak.com
Marinated pre-portioned beef and poultry both fully cooked and fresh frozen.
President/CEO: Mike Wilson
Year Founded: 1980
Estimated Sales: $500 Million-$1 Billion
Number Employees: 500-999
Brands:
National Steak

8806 **(HQ)National Vinegar Co**
1750 S Brentwood Blvd # 351
Suite 351
St Louis, MO 63144-1331
314-962-4111
Fax: 314-962-4115 www.natvin.com
Distilled vinegar, apple cider vinegar, corn surgar vinegar, colored distilled vinegar, apple-flavored distilled vinegar, burgundy cooking wine, and Sauterne cooking wine
President: John Placio
Vice President: David Wolff
Manager: Joan Weiner
Estimated Sales: $1-3 Million
Number Employees: 1-4
Type of Packaging: Consumer, Food Service, Private Label, Bulk
Other Locations:
National Vinegar Company Plant
Alton IL
National Vinegar Company Plant
Olney IL
Brands:
Alton
Garden Harvest
Hardin

8807 **National Wine & Spirits**
Indianapolis, IN 46225
www.nwscorp.com
Alcoholic beverages, wine and spirits
Chairman, President, CEO & CFO: James LaCrosse
Corporate Controller & Treasurer: Patrick Trefun
VP, Information Systems: Dwight Deming
EVP & COO: John Baker
Year Founded: 1934
Estimated Sales: $100-500 Million
Number Employees: 1,600
Type of Packaging: Private Label

8808 **National Wooden Pallet & Container Association**
1421 Prince Street
Suite 340
Alexandria, VA 22314-2805
703-519-6104
Fax: 703-519-4720 palletcomm@aol.com
www.palletcentral.com
Manufacture, repair and distribute pallets and wood packaging in unit-load solutions.
President/CEO: Brent J. McClendon, CAE
Vice President of Operations and Events: Isabel Sullivan
Sales Director: Joni Leonardo
Contact: Patrick Atagi
patrick@palletcentral.com
Number Employees: 10-19

8809 **Native American Herbal Tea**
421 S Lincoln St
Aberdeen, SD 57401-4320
605-226-2006
Fax: 605-226-2414 888-291-8517
www.nativeamericantea.com
Coffee, tea
Manager: J Almon
nativeamericantea@yahoo.com
Estimated Sales: Below $5 Million
Number Employees: 5-9
Brands:
Native American

8810 **Native American Natural Foods**
287 Water Tower Road
Kyle, SD 57752
800-416-7212
Fax: 605-455-2019 800-416-7212
mtilsen@tankabar.com
Dairy-free, gluten-free, lactose-free, nut-free, organic/natural, USDA, health, fitness and energy bars, food service

8811 **Native Kjalii Foods**
459 Fulton St Ste 205
San Francisco, CA 94102
415-522-5580
Fax: 510-686-1757
Fruit and vegetable salsas, vegetable hummus and tortilla chips
President/Co-Owner: Bret Jeremy
Marketing/Co-Owner: Julie Jeremy
Estimated Sales: $3-5 Million
Number Employees: 1-4
Square Footage: 16000
Type of Packaging: Consumer, Food Service, Bulk
Brands:
Native Kjalii

8812 **Native Scents**
1040 Dea Ln
Taos, NM 87571-6277
575-758-9656
Fax: 575-758-5802 800-645-3471
Processor, importer and exporter of herbal teas and aromatic products, honey and essential oils, incense, bath products
President: Marlene Payfoya
CEO: Alfred Savinelli
nativescents@gmail.com
CEO: Alfred Savinelli
Estimated Sales: Less Than $500,000
Number Employees: 1-4
Number of Products: 127
Square Footage: 24000
Brands:
Native Scents

8813 **Native State Foods**
201 Bicknell Ave
Suite 206
Santa Monica, CA 90405
866-647-2291
nativestatefoods.com
Cereals and snack cups
Co-Founder & Co-CEO: Claudio Ochoa
Co-Founder: Angela Palmieri
Year Founded: 2014
Type of Packaging: Consumer
Brands:
PURELY PINOLE

8814 **Natra US**
2535 Camino Dek Rio South
Suite 355
Chula Vista, CA 91910
619-397-4120
Fax: 619-397-4121 800-262-6216
www.natrus.com
Importer and exporter of cocoa powder, butter and extract; also, chocolate, caffeine, theobromine and nutraceuticals
Manager: Maria Dominguez
Vice President: Martin Brabenec
Key Account Manager: Juan Carlos Vinolo
Estimated Sales: $650000
Number Employees: 1-4
Number of Brands: 2
Number of Products: 30
Parent Co: Natra S.A.
Type of Packaging: Consumer, Food Service, Bulk
Brands:
Natra Cacao
Natra Us
Natraceutical

8815 **Natrel**
333 Lebeau Blvd
St. Laurent, QC H4N 1S3
Canada
800-501-1150
www.natrel.ca
Milk, butter, ice cream mix, chocolate milk and lemonade
President: Serge Serge Paquette
VP Marketing: Doug Kelly McGregor Gillespie
VP Finance/Administration: Eric Brunelle
Plant Manager: Gerry Verhoef
Number Employees: 100-249
Parent Co: Natrel
Type of Packaging: Consumer
Brands:
Naterl
Quebon
Sealtest
Silk Soy
Ultra'cream

8816 **Natren Inc**
3105 Willow Ln
Thousand Oaks, CA 91361-4919
805-371-4737
Fax: 805-371-4742 800-992-3323
CustomerService@Natren.com www.natren.com
Yogurt starter and probiotic products
President: Natasha Trenev
CEO: Yordan Trenev
Contact: Diane Bassett
dianeb1@natren.com
Estimated Sales: $1.4 Million
Number Employees: 50-99
Brands:
Bifido Factor
Bifido Nate
Bio-Nate
D.F.A.
Digesta-Lac
Life Start
Megadophilius
Yogurt Starter

8817 **(HQ)Natrium Products Inc**
58 Pendleton Street
Cortland, NY 13045-2702
607-753-9829
Fax: 607-753-0552 800-962-4203
info@natrium.com www.natrium.com
Baking Soda/Sodium Biocarbonate
President: Tim Herman
herman@natrium.com
Estimated Sales: $10-20 Million
Number Employees: 20-49
Square Footage: 70000
Type of Packaging: Bulk
Brands:
Natrium

8818 **Natur Sweeteners, Inc.**
11155 Massachusetts Avenue
Los Angeles, CA 90025
310-445-0020
Fax: 310-473-1086 stephenf@naturresearch.com
www.cweet.com
Natural intense sweetener; characteristics and other performance qualities similar to cane sugar

8819 **Naturade Inc**
1 City Blvd West
Suite 1440
Orange, CA 92868
714-535-9178
Fax: 714-935-9837 800-421-1830
customerservice@naturade.com
www.naturade.com
Soy protein powder shake mixes, herbal-based cough and cold formulas, and colostrum supplements
Founder: Nathan Schulman
Chief Executive Officer: Rick Robinette
Contact: Chuck Glona
cglona@naturade.com

8820 **(HQ)Natural Balance**
383 Inverness Pkwy # 390
Englewood, CO 80112-5864
303-688-6633
Fax: 303-688-1591 800-624-4260
service@naturalbalance.com
www.naturalbalance.com
Processor and wholesaler/distributor of natural nutrition supplements for energy, weight loss and sports
President: Mark Owens
Executive VP: Tim Hinricks
Sales Coordinator: Scott Smith
Contact: Steven Kahl
skahl@mai-architects.com
Plant Manager: John O'Brien
Purchasing Manager: Stephanie McArthur
Estimated Sales: $11.4 Million
Number Employees: 100-249
Square Footage: 50000
Other Locations:
Natural Balance
Castle Rock CO

8821 **Natural Bliss**
800-637-8534
www.coffee-mate.com
Cold-brew coffee and coffee creamer
Manager, RTD Coffee: Avantika Chakravorty
Number of Brands: 2
Number of Products: 15
Parent Co: Nestl,
Type of Packaging: Consumer
Brands:
NATURAL BLISS
NATURAL BLISS COLD BREW

8822 **Natural By Nature**
316 Markus Crt
Newark, DE 19713
302-455-1261
Fax: 302-455-1262 jayt@ndpc.net
www.naturalbynaturedairy.com
Milk, sour cream, yogurt and other dairy products.
President: Stephanie McVaugh
National Sales Manager: Jay Totman
Year Founded: 1994
Estimated Sales: $100-500 Million

8823 **Natural Choice Distribution**
5427 Telegraph Ave Ste U
Oakland, CA 94609
510-653-8212
Fax: 510-653-8163
info@naturalchoicedistribution.com
Salsa and sandwiches, distribution of natural food products
Owner: Steve Cutter
Contact: Douglas Gwosdz
douglasgwosdz@naturalchoicedistribution.com
Estimated Sales: Below $5 000,000
Number Employees: 18
Type of Packaging: Private Label

8824 **Natural Company**
8 W Hamilton St
Baltimore, MD 21201-5008
410-628-1262
Fax: 410-796-3977
info@thenaturalcompany.com.au
www.keeper.com.au
Health food, tofu
President: Joan Huang
Estimated Sales: Below $5 Million
Number Employees: 6
Brands:
Moon Pads
The Keeper

8825 **Natural Earth Products**
692 Thomas S. Boyland St
Brooklyn, NY 11212
718-552-2727
Fax: 718-552-2730 info@nepdistributors.com
nepdistributors.com
Olive oil, chia seeds, quinoa, kasha, turmeric and lollipops.
VP: Michael Gurevich

8826 **Natural Enrichment Industries**
1800 W Oak St
Herrin, IL 62948-2074
618-942-2112
Fax: 618-942-4112 lorip@neitcp.com
www.neitcp.com
Tricalcium phosphate from a domestically produced lime
Sales & Marketing Representative: Marci Swartz
Sales Manager: Mary Clark
Contact: Scott Fheeler
scotts@neitcp.com
Number Employees: 20-49

8827 **Natural Exotic Tropicals**
450 SW 12th Ave
Pompano Beach, FL 33069
954-783-4500
Fax: 954-783-8812 800-756-5267
Sugar-free fruit spreads, jellies, marmalades, butters and juices
President: Van Herrington
CFO: Jayne Herrington
Estimated Sales: $5-10 Million
Number Employees: 20-49
Brands:
Natural Exotic Tropicals

8828 **Natural Feast Corporation**
PO Box 36
28 Old Farm Road
Dover, MA 02030-0036
508-785-3322
Fax: 508-984-1496
Frozen foods
President: Alan Attridge
Estimated Sales: $1-2.5 Million
Number Employees: 10

8829 **Natural Flavors**
268 Doremus Ave
Newark, NJ 07105-4879
973-589-1230
Fax: 973-589-0016 Flavorinfo@flavor.com
www.flavor.com
Natural and certified organic flavors
President: Herb Stein
Secretary: Joanne Hoffman
EVP: Julie Eisman
Director Quality Assurance: Robert Maxwell
E Commerce Manager: Josh Richards
National Sales Manager: Jeff Rakity
Manager: Isabel Couto
Estimated Sales: $2 Million
Number Employees: 10-19

8830 **Natural Food Holdings**
4241 US 75 Ave.
Sioux Center, IA 51250
800-735-7765
www.siouxpreme.com
Manufacturer and exporter of pork products.
CEO, Perdue Farms: Randy Day
Year Founded: 1969
Estimated Sales: $113 Million
Number Employees: 250-499
Square Footage: 50000
Parent Co: Perdue Farms
Type of Packaging: Consumer, Private Label, Bulk

8831 **Natural Food Mill**
2991 Doherty St
2991 Doherty Street
Corona, CA 92879-5811
951-279-5090
Fax: 951-279-1784 800-797-5090
www.foodforlife.com
Baked goods including sprouted grain breads
President: Jim Torres
Vice President: Charles Torres
Estimated Sales: $20-49,000,000
Number Employees: 50-99
Type of Packaging: Consumer
Brands:
Ezekiel 4:9(c)
Genesis 1:29(c)

8832 **Natural Food Source**
52 E Union Blvd
Bethlehem, PA 18017
610-997-0500
Fax: 610-954-9959 www.nimeks.com
Dried fruits, frozen vegetables, concentrates and purees.
VP: Kadir Veziroglu

8833 **Natural Food Supplements Inc**
8725 Remmet Ave
Canoga Park, CA 91304-1519
818-341-3375
Fax: 818-341-3376
Processor and contract packager of vitamins
President: Elmer Walters
Estimated Sales: $600,000
Number Employees: 5-9
Type of Packaging: Bulk
Brands:
Sunshine Valley

8834 **Natural Food World**
6009 Washington Blvd
Culver City, CA 90232-7425
310-836-7770
Fax: 310-836-6454
Health and dietetic foods
President: Anne Stern
Estimated Sales: $5-10 000,000
Number Employees: 10

8835 **Natural Foods Inc**
3040 Hill Ave
Toledo, OH 43607-2983
419-537-1711
Fax: 419-531-6887 vip@bulkfoods.com
www.3qf.com
Wholesaler/distributor, importer and packer of food, candy, nuts, spices, fruit, and chocolates
Owner: Frank Dietrich
Estimated Sales: $5 Million
Number Employees: 20-49
Square Footage: 1800000
Type of Packaging: Food Service, Bulk

8836 **Natural Formulas**
2125 American Ave
Hayward, CA 94545-1803
510-372-1800
Fax: 510-782-9793 www.gnld.com
Powdered drink mixes
Founder: Jerry Brassfield
Quality Control: Ric Green
Executive Vice President of Product: Anjana Srivastava
Chief Operating Officer: Kevin Fox
Estimated Sales: $10-20 Million
Number Employees: 50-99

8837 **Natural Fruit Corp**
770 W 20th St
Hialeah, FL 33010-2430
305-887-7525
Fax: 305-888-8208 info@nfc-fruti.com
www.nfc-fruti.com
Processor and exporter of frozen fruit bars, cocktail mixes and ice cream novelties
Founder/President: Simon Bravo
Quality Assurance Director: Angelica Delia
EVP Operations/Founder: Jorge Bravo Sr
Plant Supervisor: Peter Infante
Estimated Sales: $14 Million
Number Employees: 20-49
Square Footage: 40000
Brands:
Allison Jayne
Chunks O'Fruit
Fruti

8838 **(HQ)Natural Group**
505 South A Street
Second Floor
Oxnard, CA 93030
805-485-3420
Fax: 805-983-1428 www.naturalgroup.org
Soft drinks
Owner: Kanishka Lal
Executive VP: Judith Keer
Estimated Sales: $440,000
Number Employees: 7
Type of Packaging: Private Label
Brands:
Ame
Ame Celebration
Apres
Hildon Water
Purdey's
Yellow Gold Shelf St

8839 **Natural Habitats USA**
948 North St
Unit 7
Boulder, CO 80304
888-958-1967
info@natural-habitats.com
www.natural-habitats.com
Organic palm oil products
Managing Director: Neil Blomquist
Type of Packaging: Bulk

8840 **Natural Ice Fruits**
524 Mid Florida Dr
Suite 209
Orlando, FL 32824
407-270-9194
www.sofruitty.com
Vegan frozen fruit bars
Brands:
So Fruitty

8841 **Natural Intentions, Inc.**
PO Box 6688
Folsom, CA 95763
www.thedailycrave.com
Veggie chips, organic veggie straws, quinia chips and lentil chips in various flavors
Number of Brands: 1
Type of Packaging: Consumer, Private Label
Brands:
The Daily Crave

8842 **Natural Nectar**
196 E Main Street
Huntington, NY 11743
631-367-7280
Fax: 631-367-7282 www.natural-nectar.com
Baguette bites, Chocodream Fair Trade cookies and spreads, Cracklebred, Cracksnax, Mediterranean crackers, Mediterranean Sea Salt, Nectar Nugget Peanut Butter cup, natural Lady Fingers and organic biowafers
Contact: Vincent De Sartre
vincent@natural-nectar.com

8843 **Natural Oils International**
2279 Ward Ave
Simi Valley, CA 93065-1863
805-433-0160
Fax: 805-433-0182 www.naturaloils.com
Processor, importer and exporter of vegetable oils
President: Brendon Bonnar
Sales: Barbara Hardy
Sales: Jack Phillips
Estimated Sales: $1-3 Million
Number Employees: 1-4
Square Footage: 120000

8844 **(HQ)Natural Ovens Bakery Inc**
4300 County Road Cr
Manitowoc, WI 54220-9263
920-758-2500
Fax: 920-758-2594 800-558-3535
info@naturalovens.com www.naturalovens.com
Processor of bread, cookies, rolls and bagels.
CEO: Matt Taylor
CEO: Jim Irvin
jim.irvin@naturalovens.com
Year Founded: 1976
Estimated Sales: $20-50 Million
Number Employees: 100-249
Square Footage: 28000
Brands:
100% Whole Grain
Flax N' Honey
Nutty All-Natural Wheat
Sunny Millet

8845 **Natural Products Inc**
2211 6th Ave
Grinnell, IA 50112-2276
641-236-0852
Fax: 641-236-4835 npi@npisoy.com
www.npisoy.com
Roast and mill soybean, flour and grits for food industry
General Manager: Paul Lang
Quality Control: Ray Lang
Marketing Director: Jon Stratford
Estimated Sales: Below $5 Million
Number Employees: 20-49

8846 **Natural Quick Foods**
3737 NE 135th Street
Seattle, WA 98125-3831
206-365-5757
Fax: 206-365-5434
Vegan, organic pocket sandwiches
President: Larry Brewer
Estimated Sales: $5-10 Million
Number Employees: 5-9

8847 **Natural Rush**
PO Box 421753
San Francisco, CA 94142-1753
415-863-2503
Fax: 415-431-5763
Candy, confectionery and honey
President: Gilles Desaulniers
Estimated Sales: Under $500,000
Number Employees: 1-4
Type of Packaging: Private Label

8848 **Natural Sins**
New York, NY
naturalsinsonline.com
Baked fruit and vegetable chips
Co-Founder: Andres Dominguez
Number of Products: 6
Brands:
Natural Sins

8849 **Natural Spring Water Company**
300 Boggs Ln
Johnson City, TN 37604
423-926-7905
Fax: 423-926-8210
Contract packager and bottler of noncarbonated mountain spring water
President: Bill Lizzio
Team Leader: John Gustke
Number Employees: 10-19
Square Footage: 24000
Type of Packaging: Consumer, Food Service, Private Label, Bulk
Brands:
Laure Pristine

8850 **Natural Value**
1511 Corporate Way
Suite 100
Sacramento, CA 95831
916-836-3561
Fax: 916-914-2446 gary@naturalvalue.com
naturalvalue.com
Organic beans, lentils, tomatoes and condiments
President/Owner: Gary Cohen
CEO: Jody Cohen
Estimated Sales: $1-3 Million
Number Employees: 1-4
Number of Brands: 1
Number of Products: 200
Type of Packaging: Consumer, Food Service, Bulk
Brands:
Natural Value

8851 **Natural Way Mills Inc**
24509 390th St NE
Middle River, MN 56737-9367
218-222-3677
Fax: 218-222-3408 naturalwaymills@wiktel.com
www.naturalwaymills.com
Organic wheat, seven-grain cereal, rye, flax seed, barley, millet, brown rice, flour and grits; custom milling available
Owner: Ray Juhl
rayjuhl@naturalwaymills.com
CEO: Helen Juhl
Quality Control: Aaron Pervis
Sales: Leigh Mott
rayjuhl@naturalwaymills.com
Plant Manager: Charles Knapp
Estimated Sales: $620,000
Number Employees: 5-9
Brands:
7 Grain Cereal
Gold N. White Bread Flour

8852 **Naturalife Laboratories**
20433 Earl St
Torrance, CA 90503-2414
310-370-1563
Fax: 310-370-7354 800-231-3670
info@ParagonLabsUSA.com
www.paragonlabsusa.com
Custom manufacturer of dietary supplements, vitamins, minerals, herbal products and nutritional supplements; available in tablets, capsules, powders and liquids
President: Jay Kaufman
President: Richard Kaufman
Estimated Sales: $10-20 Million
Number Employees: 50-99
Type of Packaging: Consumer, Private Label, Bulk

8853 **Naturally Clean Eats**
Manhattan Beach, CA
naturallycleaneats.com
All-natural snack bars
Founder: Jessica Luengo
Number of Brands: 1
Number of Products: 4
Type of Packaging: Consumer
Brands:
NATURALLY CLEAN EATS

8854 **Naturally Delicious Inc**
1811 NW 29th St
Oakland Park, FL 33311-2123
954-485-6730
Fax: 954-485-6730 888-221-7352
info@naturally-delicious.com
www.naturally-delicious.com
Snack, natural cakes, cookies and brownies.
Owner/President: Arthur Price
aprice8945@aol.com
Estimated Sales: $750,000- 1 Million
Number Employees: 5-9
Square Footage: 20000
Brands:
Naturally Delicious

8855 **Naturally Homegrown**
945 184 Street
Surrey, BC V3S 9R9
Canada
604-465-7751
Fax: 604-465-7727 info@hardbitechips.com
hardbitechips.com
Kettle chips and root vegetable chips
Number of Products: 18
Brands:
Hardbite

8856 **Naturally Nutty**
P.O. Box 3151
Traverse City, MI 49685
888-224-9988
customerservice@naturallynutty.com
www.naturallynutty.com
Nut and seed butters
President: Katie Kearney
Year Founded: 2007

8857 **Naturally Scientific**
600 Willow Tree Road
Leonia, NJ 07605-2211
201-585-7055
Fax: 973-244-0044 888-428-0700
Liquid nutritional supplements and food and beverage ingredients
President/CEO: Frank Berger
Executive VP: Marc Pozner
Marketing Director: Douglas Lynch
Sales/Group Publisher: Jon Benninger
Contact: Rick Krupa
rkrupa@nsilabs.com
Estimated Sales: $1-3 Million
Number Employees: 5-9
Number of Products: 200
Type of Packaging: Consumer, Private Label

8858 **Naturalmond Almond Butter**
3400 W. Hospital Ave.
Unit 103
Chamblee, GA 30341
866-327-9301
www.naturalmond.com
Manufacturer of almond butter.
Founder and Owner: Jaime Foster
Brands:
NaturAlmond

8859 **Nature Cure Northwest**
5271 NE Falcon Ridge Ln
Poulsbo, WA 98370-8923
360-697-8691
Fax: 360-697-7179 800-957-8048
Bottled bee pollen pills
Owner: Wasser Schmitt
Estimated Sales: 724,000
Number Employees: 1-4
Type of Packaging: Food Service
Brands:
Nature Cure

8860 **Nature Kist Snacks**
5560 E. Slauson Ave.
Commerce, CA 90040
323-278-9578
Fax: 323-278-9579
Nut and seed trail mixes; private labeling available
President: Ronald L Mozingo
Office Manager: Nancy Freitas
Plant Manager: Rick Dorotheo
Estimated Sales: $10-20 Million
Number Employees: 20-49
Type of Packaging: Consumer, Private Label
Brands:
Fresh Pak
Nature Kist
Holiday Bonus

8861 **Nature Most Laboratories**
Trigo Business Park
60 Trigo Drive
Middletown, CT 06457-6157
860-346-8991
Fax: 860-347-3312 800-234-2112
sales@naturemost.com
Manufacturer, importer and exporter of products, vitamins, oils, minerals, herbal supplements
President: Robert Trigo
Marketing: Sam Schwartz
Sales: Donna Platnum
Operations: Fred Wuschner
Estimated Sales: $5-10 Million
Number Employees: 20-49
Number of Brands: 3
Number of Products: 300
Square Footage: 80000
Type of Packaging: Consumer, Private Label
Brands:
Naturemost Labs
Trigo Labs

8862 **Nature Nate's**
2910 Nature Nate Farm
McKinney, TX 75071
469-452-4429
www.naturenates.com
Honey products
Founder: Nathan Sheets
Brands:
Nature Nate's(c)

8863 **Nature Quality**
13805 Llagas Ave
San Martin, CA 95046
408-683-2182
Fax: 408-683-4249 natqual@aol.com
naturequality.com
Processor and exporter of IQF cut celery, olives, onions, garlic and peppers
President: Karen Ash
kash@naturesquality.com
Food Safety & Quality Assurance Manager: Nicole Kamath
Sales Manager: Melissa Guevara
Estimated Sales: $7 Million
Number Employees: 100-249
Square Footage: 40000
Type of Packaging: Food Service, Bulk

8864 **Nature Soy Inc**
713 N 10th St
Philadelphia, PA 19123-1902
215-765-3289
Fax: 215-765-3266 support@naturesoy.com
Manufacturer/supplier of healthy soy and vegetarian products to the ethnic market
President: Yat Wen
CEO: Gene He
he@naturesoy.com
EVP: Fenjin He
Estimated Sales: $2.4 Million
Number Employees: 20-49
Square Footage: 35000

8865 **Nature Zen USA**
159 River Rd
Essex Junction, VT 05452
info@nature-zen.com
www.nature-zen.com
Protein bars and powders
Number of Brands: 1
Number of Products: 7
Brands:
NATURE ZEN

8866 **Nature's Apothecary**
244 Knollwood Drive
Suite 300
Bloomingdale, IL 60108
970-664-1600
Fax: 970-664-5106 888-669-3663
www.nowfoods.com
Processor and exporter of fresh organic, medicinal, botanical and herbal liquid extracts
President: Jim Emme
Engineering Manager: Dan Mirjanic
Sales Manager: Dan Richard
Type of Packaging: Consumer, Private Label, Bulk

8867 **Nature's Bakery**
425 Maestro Dr
Suite 101
Reno, NV 89511
naturesbakery.com
Fig bars and brownies
Co-Founder: Dave Marson
Co-Founder: Sam Marson
Year Founded: 2010
Estimated Sales: $100+ Million
Number of Brands: 1
Number of Products: 5
Other Locations:
Manufacturing Location
Hazelwood MO
Manufacturing Location
Carson City NV
Commercial Office
Pasadena CA
Brands:
NATURE'S BAKERY

8868 **Nature's Bandits**
PO Box 541
Riverside, CT 06878-0541
203-571-2040
www.naturesbandits.com
Dried fruit and vegetable snacks.
Co-Founder: Tony Carvalho
Brands:
Nature's Bandits(c)

8869 **Nature's Best Inc**
195 Engineers Rd
Hauppauge, NY 11788-4020
631-232-3355
Fax: 631-232-3320 800-345-2378
info@naturesbest.com
www.theisopurecompany.com
Processor and exporter of athletic supplements and sport drinks
President: Hal Katz
Estimated Sales: $1.5 Million
Number Employees: 5-9
Brands:
Decades
No Holds Bar
Perfect 1100
Perfect Aminos
Perfect Carbs
Perfect Rx

8870 **Nature's Best Inc**
195 Engineers Rd
Hauppauge, NY 11788-4020
631-232-3355
Fax: 631-232-3320 800-345-2378
info@naturesbest.com
www.theisopurecompany.com
Sport nutrition products
President: Hal Katz
Purchasing Manager: Ernie Geraci
Estimated Sales: $5-10 Million
Number Employees: 5-9
Number of Brands: 4
Number of Products: 150
Type of Packaging: Consumer
Brands:
Decades
Isopure
No Holds Bar
Perfect
Perfect 1100
Perfect Animos
Perfect Carbs
Perfect Rx
Solid Protein

8871 **Nature's Bounty Co.**
2100 Smithtown Ave.
Ronkonkoma, NY 11779
631-200-2000
877-774-3361
consumeraffairsmgmt@nbty.com
www.naturesbountyco.com
Nutritional supplements and vitamins.
President/CEO: Paul Sturman
CFO: Ted McCormick
General Counsel/Chief Compliance Officer: Stratis Philipps
Estimated Sales: $3 Billion
Number Employees: 10,000+
Number of Brands: 19
Number of Products: 22K
Parent Co: KKR
Type of Packaging: Consumer, Private Label, Bulk
Brands:
Pure Protien
Nature's Bounty
Sundown Naturals
Solgar
Body Fortress
MET-Rx
Puritan's Pride
Ester-C
Osteo Bi-Flex
Dr. Organic
Best Ever Bar
Balance
American Health
Home Health
Sisu

8872 **Nature's Candy**
632 Fm 2093
Fredericksburg, TX 78624-7149
830-997-3844
Fax: 830-997-6528 800-729-0085
Processor and wholesaler/distributor of natural and fruit-filled candy, maple-coated nuts and seasoned nuts and seeds
President: Michael Zygmunt
michael@beneficialfoods.com
Office Manager: Karen Gold
Estimated Sales: $482,000
Number Employees: 5-9
Type of Packaging: Consumer, Private Label, Bulk

8873 **Nature's Dairy**
5104 S Main St
Roswell, NM 88203-0822
575-623-9640
Fax: 575-622-1318 www.novabus.com
Milk, dairy products; noncheese
President: Edward Avitia
edward.avitia@volvo.com
Estimated Sales: $5-10 000,000
Number Employees: 20-49
Brands:
Nature's Dairy

8874 **Nature's Earthly Choice**
Eagle, ID
208-898-4004
Fax: 208-939-2626 info@earthlychoice.com
www.earthlychoice.com
Manufacturer of quinoa.
President and Co-Founder: Chuck Watson
Brands:
NATURE'S Earthly Choice

8875 **Nature's Finest Products**
PO Box 801326
Dallas, TX 75380-1326
773-489-2096
Fax: 972-960-8760 800-237-5205
Gourmet foods
President: Mike Griffin

8876 **Nature's First Inc**
58 Robinson Blvd # C
Orange, CT 06477-3647
203-795-8400
Fax: 203-795-8300 800-523-3752
sales@naturesfirst.com www.naturesfirst.com
Coffee, creamers, hot chocolates, cappuccinos and chai
Owner: Harjit Singh
sales@naturesfirst.com
Estimated Sales: Less Than $500,000
Number Employees: 1-4

8877 **Nature's Fusions**
1405 W 820 N
Provo, UT 84601
801-872-9500
www.naturesfusions.com
Essential oils and CBD
CEO: C.J. Peterson
Number of Brands: 1
Brands:
NATURE'S FUSIONS

8878 **Nature's Godfather**
405 Waltham St
Suite 168
Lexington, MA 02421
339-970 9888
sales@belleandbella.com
www.belleandbella.com
Non-dairy yogurt starter and probiotics.
Managing Director: Ada Wong
Brands:
belle + bella
Probiology

8879 **Nature's Guru**
19416 Amhurst Ct
Cerritos, CA 90703-6787
949-478-4878
info@naturesguru.com
www.naturesguru.com
Chai
Brands:
Nature's Guru(c)

8880 **Nature's Habit Brand. Inc.**
PO Box 522
Washago, ON
Canada
707-712-2826
www.natureshabit.com
Manufacturer of granola and granola trail mixes.

8881 **Nature's Hand Inc**
info@natureshand.com
www.natureshand.com
Manufacturer and exporter of drink mixes and puddings
Estimated Sales: $500,000-$1 Million
Number Employees: 5-9
Number of Brands: 1
Number of Products: 4
Type of Packaging: Consumer
Brands:
Nature's Hand

8882 **Nature's Herbs**
PO Box 970
Merritt, BC V1K 1B8
Canada
250-378-8822
Fax: 250-378-8753 800-437-2257
www.naturesherbs.net/p/contact_us
Processor and exporter of dietary supplements and encapsulated herbs
President/CEO: Ross Blechman
Executive VP Sales: Dean Blechman
Estimated Sales: $5-10 Million
Number Employees: 250

Square Footage: 200000
Parent Co: Twin Laboratories
Type of Packaging: Consumer
Brands:
Healthcare Naturals
Herb Masters' Original
Nature's Herbs
Power Herbs

8883 **Nature's Hilights**
1608 Chico River Rd
Suite A
Chico, CA 95928
530-342-6154
Fax: 530-342-3130 800-313-6454
Baked products including rice crusts, bread, bread sticks, rice pizzas and frozen gluten-free desserts
President/CEO: Gayle Luna
Estimated Sales: $5-9.9 Million
Number Employees: 10-19
Type of Packaging: Food Service, Bulk

8884 **Nature's Hollow**
Probst Farms
3290 West 3500 South
Charleston, UT 84032
Fax: 435-216-9829 www.natureshollow.com
Sugar-free sauces and spreads
Number of Brands: 1
Brands:
NATURE'S HOLLOW

8885 **Nature's Kitchen**
4651 Woodstock Rd
Suite 208-101
Roswell, GA 30075
678-845-6897
info@natureskitchn.com
www.thenatureskitchen.com
Rubs, marinade and saucinades.
Co-Founder: Rory Mitchell
Co-Founder: Archana Mitchell
Brands:
Nature's Kitchen

8886 **Nature's Legacy Inc.**
417 S. Meridian Road
Hudson, MI 49247
517-448-2050
Fax: 517-448-2070 info@purityfoods.com
www.natureslegacyforlife.com
Organic pasta, flours, spelt granola, pretzels, sesame sticks, beans, grains, and seeds.
Owner/President: Donald Stinchcomb
Estimated Sales: $5.8 Million
Number Employees: 11
Square Footage: 24000
Type of Packaging: Consumer, Bulk
Brands:
VITASPELT
NATURE'S LEGACY
PURITY FOODS

8887 **Nature's Love**
PO Box 745
Snyder, CO 80750
970-571-7959
info@natureslove.org
natureslove.org
Hemp extract
Number of Products: 18

8888 **Nature's Nutrition**
100 North Main St
Marysville, OH 43040
321-255-5505
Fax: 321-255-5881 800-242-1115
www.nothinbutherbs.com
Organic food and nutritional supplements including vitamins, amino acids, antioxidants and proteins; also, weight loss aids
President: Dee Corbitt
Estimated Sales: $500,000-$1 Million
Number Employees: 5-9
Square Footage: 20000
Brands:
Harida
The Capsule

8889 **(HQ)Nature's Path Foods**
205 H Street
Suite 275
Blaine, WA 98230
888-808-9505
naturespath@worldpantry.com
www.naturespath.com
Organic cereal products
President & Founder: Arran Stephens
Co-CEO & COO: Ratana Stephens
Executive VP Sales & Marketing: Arjan Stephens
Director of Human Resources: Jyoti Stephens
Year Founded: 1985
Estimated Sales: $145.87 Million
Number Employees: 60
Square Footage: 29999
Type of Packaging: Consumer, Private Label, Bulk
Other Locations:
Nature's Path Foods
Blaine WA
Brands:
Nature's Path Organic
Envirokidz Organic
Optimum

8890 **Nature's Plus**
548 Broadhollow Rd
Melville, NY 11747-3722
631-293-0013
Fax: 800-688-7239 800-645-9500
salesinfo@naturesplus.com www.naturesplus.com
Processor and exporter of health products including protein weight loss supplements, vitamins and herbs
Director Marketing: Gerard McIntee
Estimated Sales: $15.1 Million
Number Employees: 5-9
Parent Co: Natural Organics

8891 **(HQ)Nature's Products Inc**
1301 Sawgrass Corporate Pkwy
Sunrise, FL 33323-2813
954-233-3300
Fax: 954-233-3301 800-752-7873
info@natures-products.com
Manufacturer and supplier of raw materials specializing in gelatin, flavors, active pharmaceuticals, botanicals and pharmaceutical additives. Providing import/export services, warehousing and freight forwarding to and from the UnitedStates and worldwide
President: Jose Minski
josem@npi-gmi.com
Number Employees: 100-249
Type of Packaging: Private Label, Bulk
Brands:
Curt Georgi Flavors & Fragrances
Gmi Gelatin
Health Assure

8892 **Nature's Provision Company**
452 Krumville Rd
Olivebridge, NY 12461-5528
845-657-6020
Powdered health food supplements for circulatory improvement; wholesaler/distributor of pH balanced cleansers and lubricants
President: Clark Jung
Vice President: Ann Jung
Estimated Sales: $130,000
Number Employees: 2
Brands:
Dr. Rinse Vita Flo Formula

8893 **Nature's Select Inc**
555 Cascade West Pkwy SE # 200
Grand Rapids, MI 49546-2105
616-956-1105
Fax: 616-956-0998 888-715-4321
naturesselect@aol.com www.natureselect.com
Dry roasted soynuts
President/Owner: Peter Assaly
naturesselect@aol.com
Estimated Sales: $500,000
Number Employees: 1-4
Number of Brands: 1
Number of Products: 9
Square Footage: 60000
Brands:
Nature's Select

8894 **Nature's Sunshine Products Company**
2901 W. Blue Grass Blvd.
Lehi, UT 84043
800-223-8225
www.naturessunshine.com
Health products including vitamins, minerals and herbs.
CEO: Terrence Moorehead
Executive VP/CFO: Joseph Baty
Executive VP/General Counsel: Nathan Brower
Vice President, Human Resources: Tracee Comstock
Executive VP/COO: Sue Armstrong
Year Founded: 1972
Estimated Sales: $367.81 Million
Number Employees: 1,003
Square Footage: 63000
Type of Packaging: Consumer
Brands:
Nature's Sunshine

8895 **Nature's Touch**
5105M Fisher St
Saint-Laurent, QC H4T 1J8
Canada
www.naturestouchfrozenfoods.com
Frozen fruit
Founder: John Tentomas
Year Founded: 2004
Number of Products: 9
Type of Packaging: Consumer, Private Label
Other Locations:
Freezing and Packing Facility
Abbotsford BC
Packing Facility
Front Royal VA
Brands:
Nature's Touch

8896 **(HQ)Nature's Way**
825 Challenger Dr
Green Bay, WI 54311
Fax: 800-688-3303 800-962-8873
www.naturesway.com
Herbs, vitamins and minerals, oils and probiotics
CFO: Rich Jones
CEO: Randy Rose
Contact: Dustin Borneman
dustin.borneman@naturesway.com
Operations Manager: Brian Hufford
Production Manager: Greg Bone
Purchasing Manager: Dave Anderson
Estimated Sales: $100-500 Million
Number Employees: 100-249
Number of Brands: 8
Parent Co: Schwabe North America
Type of Packaging: Private Label
Brands:
Alive!
Boericke & Tafel
Coconut Oil
CranRx
fortify
Ginkgold
Joint Movement
MCT Oil
NutraVege
Primadophilus
Remifemin
sambucus
Umcka ColdCare

8897 **Naturel**
9339 Foothill Blvd # A
Rancho Cucamonga, CA 91730-3548
909-987-0520
Fax: 909-390-5453 877-242-8344
Organic agave syrup prepared for 100% agave juice; natural fructose sweetener/flavor enhancer
Owner: Jong Kee Kim
National Sales Manager: Oscar Guerrero Whaley
Estimated Sales: Less than $500,000
Number Employees: 1-4
Parent Co: Industrializadora Integral Del Agave, SA DeCV

8898 **Natures Sungrown Foods Inc**
700 Irwin St # 103
Suite 103
San Rafael, CA 94901-3300
415-491-4944
Fax: 415-532-2233 hal@naturessungrown.com
www.naturessungrown.com

Manufacturer and exporter of natural beef and pork, organic foods (dried fruit, coffee, juice, sauce, tortilla chips, guacamole, jalapeno peppers and Mexican foods
President: Hal Shenson
hal@naturessungrown.com
Estimated Sales: $5-10 Million
Number Employees: 1-4
Number of Brands: 2
Type of Packaging: Consumer, Food Service, Private Label, Bulk
Brands:
Nature's Sungrown Beef
Vera Cruz Mexican Foods
Tree of Life
Sun Ridge Farms
Spice Hunter
Swiss Valley
Joseph Farms
Bar S
Eberley
Francesco Rinaldi
La Victoria

8899 **Naturex Inc**
375 Huyler St
South Hackensack, NJ 07606
201-440-5000
www.naturex.com
Natural antioxidants, colors, herbs and spices oleoresins and essential oils, and botanical extracts for the food, flavor and nutracceutical industries.
Chief Procurement Officer: Serge Sabrier
Year Founded: 1992
Estimated Sales: $404.9 Million
Number Employees: 1,700
Square Footage: 14991
Parent Co: Naturex, France Avignon Headquarters
Type of Packaging: Bulk
Other Locations:
Naturex, Inc. USA Chicago
Chicago IL
Naturex USA Atlanta Sales Office
Marietta GA
Naturex USA Californaia Sales Offic
Costa Mesa CA
Brands:
Stabil
Arom
Color
Healthy
Textur
F&V
Taste
Colorenhance
Osr
Stabilenhance
Wsr

8900 **Naughty Noah's**
201E-3211 Holiday Court
La Jolla, CA 92037
info@naughtynoahs.com
www.naughtynoahs.com
Instant Vietnamese pho noodles
CEO: JimmyTay Trinh
Number of Brands: 1
Number of Products: 3
Brands:
NAUGHTY NOAH'S

8901 **Naumes, Inc.**
PO Box 996
Medford, OR 97501
541-772-6268
Grower of apples, plums, pears, pomegranates, persimmons, and Asian pears.
President and CEO: Michael Naumes
CFO: Annie Eadie
VP, Fresh Division Manager: Laura Naumes
Estimated Sales: $23.4 Million
Number Employees: 700
Square Footage: 8000
Type of Packaging: Consumer

8902 **Navarro Pecan Co**
2131 E State Highway 31
Corsicana, TX 75109
903-872-5641
Fax: 903-874-7143 800-333-9507
sales@navarropecan.com www.navarropecan.com
Processor and exporter of kosher certified shelled raw and roasted pecans used as ingredients.
Chief Information Officer: Linda Garza
lgarza@navarropecan.com
Year Founded: 1977
Estimated Sales: $20-50 Million
Number Employees: 250-499
Square Footage: 200000
Type of Packaging: Consumer, Bulk
Brands:
Navarro

8903 **Navarro Vineyards**
5601 Highway 128
Philo, CA 95466-9513
707-895-3516
Fax: 707-895-3647 707-895-3686
office@navarrowine.com www.navarrowine.com
Wines
Owner: Deborah Cahn
Estimated Sales: $7 Million
Number Employees: 50-99
Type of Packaging: Private Label, Bulk

8904 **Navas Instruments**
105 Wind Tree Ln
Conway, SC 29526
843-347-1379
Fax: 843-347-2527 info@navas-instruments.com
www.navas-instruments.com
Laboratory instruments for testing ash and moisture in food, pet and animal feed, fertilizers, soils and wastewater
Contact: Pam Bailey
pbailey@navas-instruments.com

8905 **Navitas Naturals**
15 Pamaron Way
Novato, CA 94949
415-883-8116
Fax: 888-645-4282 888-645-4282
www.navitasorganics.com
Superfood shots, hot drink mixes, superfood ingredients, snack bars, seeds, nuts, and berries
Founder/CEO: Zach Adelman
z.adelman@navitasnaturals.com
Year Founded: 2003

8906 **Naya**
2030-340 Pie IX
Montreal, QC H1V 2C8
Canada
450-562-7911
Fax: 450-562-3654 info@naya.com
www.naya.com
Processor and exporter of bottled spring water
President: Anita Jarjour
Executive VP/COO: Stu Levitan
Director Sales Marketing: Raynald Brisson
VP Operations: Sylvain Mayrand
Number Employees: 100-249
Square Footage: 240000
Type of Packaging: Consumer, Food Service, Private Label
Brands:
Naya

8907 **Naylor Association Solutions**
5950 NW 1st Pl
Gainesville, FL 32607-6060
352-332-1252
Fax: 352-331-3525 www.naylor.com
Publications
Manager: Jason Dolder
jdolder@naylor.com
Number Employees: 250-499

8908 **Naylor Candies Inc**
289 Chestnut St
Mt Wolf, PA 17347-9702
717-266-2706
Fax: 717-266-2706 www.naylorcandies.com
Processor and exporter of confectionery products including butter toffee peanuts, butter mints, cashew crunch, peanut crunch and honey roasted peanuts; importer of cashews and peanuts
Owner: Dennis Naylor
dennis@cannonfamily.4t.com
Estimated Sales: $750,000
Number Employees: 10-19
Square Footage: 32000
Type of Packaging: Consumer, Private Label, Bulk

8909 **Naylor Wine Cellars Inc**
4069 Vineyard Rd
Stewartstown, PA 17363-8478
717-993-2431
Fax: 717-993-9460 800-292-3370
info@naylorwine.com www.naylorwine.com
Wines
President: Richard Naylor
Winemaker: Ted Potted
Contact: Dick Naylor
dick@naylorwine.com
Estimated Sales: $2.5-5 Million
Number Employees: 10-19
Type of Packaging: Private Label, Bulk
Brands:
Golden Grenadine
Naylor

8910 **Ne-Mo's Bakery Inc**
416 N Hale Ave
Escondido, CA 92029-1496
760-741-5725
Fax: 760-741-0659 800-325-2692
customerservice@horizonfoodgroup.com
www.nemosbakery.com
Processor and exporter of baked goods including hand-wrapped cake squares, cake slices, cinnamon rolls, cookies, muffins, mini loaf cakes, danish, cake breads, coffee cakes, and specialty cakes
Cio/Cto: Darren Watson
dwatson@nemosbakery.com
Senior VP: Sam Delucca Jr
Estimated Sales: $10-20 Million
Number Employees: 100-249
Square Footage: 120000
Type of Packaging: Consumer, Food Service, Private Label, Bulk
Brands:
Ne-Mo's

8911 **Neal's Chocolates**
2520 Lynwood Drive
Salt Lake City, UT 84109-1607
801-521-6500
Fax: 801-521-6555
Boxed chocolates
President: Neal Maxfield
Estimated Sales: Less than $500,000
Number Employees: 1-4

8912 **Nealanders Food Ingredients**
6980 Creditview Rd
Mississauga, ON L5N 8E2
Canada
905-812-7300
Fax: 905-812-7308 800-263-1939
www.nealanders.com
Oilseed manufacturer
President: Robert Leonard
CEO: Olav C. Caldenborgh
CFO: Jill Wuthmann
Parent Co: Nealanders International

8913 **Near East Food Products**
797 Lancaster Street
Leominster, MA 01453-4551
978-534-3338
800-822-7423
Thirty different flavors and varieties of pilafs, couscous and grain dishes including tabouleh
General Manager: Philip Wiggin
Estimated Sales: $500,000
Number Employees: 50-99

8914 **Neat Foods**
244 North Queen St.
Lancaster, PA 17603
866-637-6328
www.eatneat.com
Manufacturer of plant-based meat alternatives.
Co-Founder and CEO: Phil Lapp
phillapp@eatneat.com
Brands:
neat

8915 **Nebraska Bean**
85824 519th Ave
Clearwater, NE 68726-5239
402-887-5335
Fax: 402-887-4709 800-253-6502
brett@nebraskabean.com www.nebraskabean.com

Experienced grower, processor and packager of quality popcorn. The fully integrated operation offers microwave, bulk, private label and poly bags of popcorn
President: Brett Morrison
brett@nebraskabean.com
VP: Brett Morrison
Sales: Michelle Steskal
Estimated Sales: $10-20 Million
Number Employees: 20-49
Number of Brands: 1
Square Footage: 10000
Type of Packaging: Consumer, Food Service, Private Label, Bulk
Brands:
Morrison Farms

8916 **Nebraska Beef Council**
1319 Central Ave
PO Box 2108
Kearney, NE 68847-6869
308-236-7551
Fax: 308-234-8701 800-421-5326
info@nebeef.org www.nebeef.org
Beef
CEO: Sallie Atkins
satkins@nebeef.org
CEO: Forrest Roberts
Director of Marketing: Adam Wegner
Director of Industry Relations: Doug Straight
Estimated Sales: $3.58 Million
Number Employees: 5-9

8917 **Necco**
135 American Legion Highway
Revere, MA 2151
800-225-5508
Confections, candy
Contact: Lena Florentino
lena@seeleycapital.com

8918 **Nectar Island**
56 5th Ave
St Paul, MN 55128
651-292-9963
Fax: 651-905-1958
Fruit drinks flavors which include: pommegranate; pommegranate blueberry; pommegranate raspberry; mango peach; tropical berries; and guava orange.
Owner: Scott Johnson

8919 **Nedlog Company**
92 Messner Dr
Wheeling, IL 60090
847-541-0924
Fax: 847-541-1046 800-323-6201
Manufactures and markets over 60 formulas of standard traditional and more exotic juice-based concentrates such as strawberry-apple. Also have an equipment program based on purchase of juice concentrates
CEO: Grant Golden
President/COO: Glenn Golden
CFO: Marilyn Dougal
Research & Development: Gennady Koyfman
Public Relations: Karyl Golden
Estimated Sales: $3-5 Million
Number Employees: 7
Type of Packaging: Food Service, Private Label
Brands:
Berry Good
Classic Blends
Fiesta
Hiline
Nedlog 100
Tropical Blends

8920 **Neenah Springs**
512 Fandrich Street
Oxford, WI 53952
608-586-5696
Fax: 608-586-4509
Bottler of artesian water
President: Thomas Rogers
VP: John McFarland
Marketing Director: Dan Revoy
Public Relations: Kathy Payter
Operations Manager: Chris Coates
Plant Manager: Barbara Ravenscroft
Purchasing Manager: Wendy Jankowski
Estimated Sales: $4.8 Million
Number Employees: 52
Square Footage: 80000
Type of Packaging: Consumer, Food Service, Private Label
Brands:
Glacier Ice
Great Glacier
Mountain Mist
Neenah Springs

8921 **Neese Country Sausage Inc**
1452 Alamance Church Rd
Greensboro, NC 27406-9430
336-275-9548
Fax: 336-275-0750 800-632-1010
info@neesesausage.com www.neesesausage.com
Processor and packager of country sausage, liver pudding, c-loaf, souse meat and scraple
President: Thomas Neese Jr
Plant Manager: Michael Garrett
Estimated Sales: $5-10 Million
Number Employees: 20-49
Type of Packaging: Consumer, Food Service

8922 **Nehalem Bay Winery**
34965 Highway 53
Nehalem, OR 97131-9329
503-368-9463
Fax: 503-368-5300 888-368-9463
nbwines@hotmail.com
www.nehalembaywinery.com
Wines including Niagara grape, rhubarb, apple, wildflower honey, Chardonnay, white table, Pinot Noir and Pinot Noir Blanc
Owner: Ray Schackelford
Estimated Sales: $3-5 Million
Number Employees: 5-9
Type of Packaging: Consumer

8923 **Neighbors Coffee**
3105 E Reno Ave
Oklahoma City, OK 73117
405-552-2100
Fax: 405-232-3729 800-299-9016
sales@neighborscoffee.com
www.neighborscoffee.com
Coffee; wholesaler/distributor of tea, cocoa and cappuccino
President: Steve Neighbors
Sales Manager: Phil Huggard
Contact: Todd Henson
thenson@executivecoffee.com
Estimated Sales: $100,000
Number Employees: 50-99
Type of Packaging: Consumer, Food Service, Private Label, Bulk
Brands:
Neighbors

8924 **Neil Jones Food Company**
1701 W 16th Street
Vancouver, WA 98660-1067
360-696-4356
Fax: 360-696-0050 800-291-3862
sales@nwpacking.com
www.neiljonesfoodcompany.com
Manufacturer of canned fruits and vegetables
President/Owner: Matt Jones
CEO: L. Neil Jones
Estimated Sales: $500,000-$1 Million
Number Employees: 250-499
Type of Packaging: Consumer, Food Service, Private Label

8925 **Neilly's Foods**
1569 W King St
York, PA 17404-5656
717-668-3722
Fax: 717-885-5141 www.neillys.com
Frozen meals, appetizers, sauces, rice mixes and beans.
VP, Sales and Marketing: Julie Ndjee

8926 **Nekta**
PO BOX 1355
Auckland, 1140
New Zealand
649-250-2789
Fax: 649-573-7988 www.nekta.com
All-natural fruit carbohydrate derived from kiwifruit
Director: Adriana Tong
Director: Jonathan Wood

8927 **Nell Baking Company**
114 County Road 254
Kenedy, TX 78119-4267
830-583-3251
Fax: 830-583-9593 800-215-9190
nellbaking@yahoo.com
Biscotti in ten flavors, gourmet cookies and wafers
President: Lasca Arnold
Estimated Sales: $500,000
Number Employees: 10
Brands:
Biscotti Di Lasca
Cookies By Lasca

8928 **Nello's Sauce**
PO Box 80441
Raleigh, NC 27623
919-428-4338
Manufacturer of pasta sauce.
Founder: Neal McTighe
Contact: Neal Mctighe
nealmctighe@nellossauce.com

8929 **Nellson Candies Inc**
5800 Ayala Ave
Irwindale, CA 91706-6215
626-334-4508
www.nellsonllc.com
Manufacturer and exporter of custom formulated snack, diet/weight loss, sport nutrition and medical food nutrition bars
Processor: Hoa Nguyen
Estimated Sales: Less Than $500,000
Number Employees: 1-4
Square Footage: 89864
Type of Packaging: Consumer, Food Service, Private Label, Bulk

8930 **(HQ)Nellson Nutraceutical LLC**
5115 E LA Palma Ave
Anaheim, CA 92807-2018
714-765-7000
Fax: 714-765-7055 844-635-5766
www.nellsonllc.com
Powdered drinks including diet, muscle building and fiber
Principal: Richard Marconi
CEO: Jamie Better
Estimated Sales: G
Number Employees: 500-999

8931 **Nelly's Organics**
9811 Owensmouth Ave
Chatsworth, CA 91311
310-756-0738
info@nellysorganics.com
nellysorganics.com
Refrigerated organic candy bars
Founder: Carla Spiropulo
Number of Brands: 1
Number of Products: 7
Brands:
NELLY'S ORGANICS

8932 **Nelson Crab Inc**
3088 Kindred Ave
Tokeland, WA 98590
360-267-2911
Fax: 360-267-2921 800-262-0069
Processor, importer and exporter of canned, fresh, smoked and frozen seafood including salmon steaks, shad, crabs, crab meat and shrimp
President: Kristi Nelson
kristi@nelsoncrab.com
Plant Manager: Les Candler
Estimated Sales: $10-20 Million
Number Employees: 50-99
Type of Packaging: Food Service, Private Label
Brands:
Nelson Seatreats

8933 **Nelson Ice Cream**
920 Olive St W
Stillwater, MN 55082-5634
651-430-1103
www.nelsonsicecream.biz
Ice cream
Owner: Dave Najarian
dnajarian@nelsonsicecream.biz
Estimated Sales: $300,000-500,000
Number Employees: 20-49
Type of Packaging: Private Label

Brands:
Nelson's
Nelson's Dutch Farms

8934 **Nema Food Distribution**
18 Commerce Rd.
Suite D
Fairfield, NJ 07004
973-256-4415
Fax: 973-256-4442 www.nemahalal.com
Halal deli meat, beef, poultry, gyro, cheese, bread, heat & serve
President: Beyhan Nakiboglu
Year Founded: 2002

8935 **Neo North America Inc.**
San Francisco, CA
800-604-7051
www.neosuperwater.com
Manufacturer of water.
CEO and Founder: Ben Behrouzi
Brands:
NEO WATER

8936 **Nepco Egg Of Ga**
469 Ronthor Dr SE
Social Circle, GA 30025
770-464-2652
Fax: 770-464-2998 www.goodegg.com
Processor and exporter of egg products including standard yolk, whole, whites and albumen
Manager: Brad Ginnane
Plant Manager: Terry Anglin
Estimated Sales: $1-3 Million
Number Employees: 1-4
Square Footage: 240000
Parent Co: Rose Acre Farms
Type of Packaging: Bulk

8937 **Neptune Fisheries**
802 Jefferson Ave
Newport News, VA 23607
757-245-3231
Fax: 757-893-9227 800-545-7474
Processor and importer of frozen, cooked, peeled and deveined shrimp and scallops; also, lobster tails
President: Robin West
CFO: Richard Costa
National Sales Manager: Aaron Cabral
Sales Director: Sam Weinstein
Plant Manager: Reuben Benkovitz
Number Employees: 5-9
Square Footage: 240000
Type of Packaging: Consumer, Food Service, Private Label, Bulk
Brands:
Neptune

8938 **Neptune Foods**
4510 S Alameda St
Vernon, CA 90058-2011
323-232-8300
Fax: 323-232-8833 info@neptunefoods.com
www.neptunefoods.com
Frozen cod, perch, pollack, fish sticks, clams, lobster, oysters, scallops and shrimp
President: Howard Choi
info@neptunefoods.com
Marketing Manager: Kelly Osterhout
Controller/VP Human Resources: Martin Tsai
COO/Plant Manager: Barbara Letourneau
Estimated Sales: $29.8 Million
Number Employees: 250-499
Square Footage: 150000
Type of Packaging: Consumer, Food Service, Private Label, Bulk
Brands:
Captain Neptune
Mermaid Princess
Neptune

8939 **Nesbitt Processing**
611 NE 7th Ave
Aledo, IL 61231-1061
309-582-5183
Processor and wholesaler/distributor of beef, pork, lamb, goat and deer; slaughtering services available
President/General Manager: Omar Deeds, Jr.
Secretary/Treasurer: Edith Nesbitt
Number Employees: 3
Type of Packaging: Consumer

8940 **Neshaminy Valley Natural Foods**
5 Louise Dr
Warminster, PA 18974-1542
215-443-5545
Fax: 215-443-7087 info@nvorganic.com
Gourmet foods
President: Philip S Margolis
info@nvorganic.com
COO/VP: Gene Margolis
VP: Gene Margolis
Estimated Sales: $4.5 Million
Number Employees: 20-49
Brands:
Neshaminy Valley Natural

8941 **Nest Eggs**
411 W Fullerton Pkwy #1402W
Chicago, IL 60614-2849
773-525-4952
Fax: 773-525-5226 www.fact.com
Gourmet foods
Executive Director: Richard Wood
VP: Robert Brown
Sales Manager: Steve Roach
Estimated Sales: Below $5 Million
Number Employees: 5-9

8942 **NestFresh**
4340 Glencoe St
Denver, CO 80216
877-241-8385
nestfresh.com
Cage-free eggs
VP, Marketing: Nick Jioras
Year Founded: 1991
Brands:
NESTFRESH

8943 **Nestelle's, Inc.**
3540 Brooks Ave NE
Salem, OR 97301
503-393-7056
Fax: 503-393-7091
Flavoring extracts and food colors
President: Kathi Jenks
Estimated Sales: $620,000
Number Employees: 5
Square Footage: 52000

8944 **Nestle USA**
150 Oak Grove Dr
Mt Sterling, KY 40353-9087
859-499-1100
Fax: 859-498-4363 www.nestleusa.com
Prepared frozen foods including stuffed sandwiches and croissants, pizza snacks and waffles
CEO: Paul Merage
CFO: Glenn Lee
VP: Larry Johnson
Research & Development: Phil Mason
V P Finance: Glenn Lee
Manufacturing Development Manager: John Spinner
Purchasing Director: George Turner
Purchasing Manager: Russ Shroyer
Plant Manager: Mike Crawford
Purchasing Manager: George Turner
Number Employees: 500-999
Type of Packaging: Consumer, Food Service

8945 **Nestle USA Inc**
800 N Brand Blvd
Glendale, CA 91203-3213
818-549-6210
Fax: 818-549-6952 800-225-2270
www.nestleusa.com
Baby foods, bottled water, cereals, chocolate & confectionery, coffee, culinary, chilled & frozen foods, dairy, drinks, foodservice, healthcare nutrition, ice cream, petcare, sports nutrition, and weight management
CEO: Paul Grimwood
paul.grimwood@us.nestle.com
CEO: Paul Bulcke
EVP & CFO: Wan Ling Martello
EVP, CTO, Head of Research & Development: Werner Bauer
EVP Marketing, Sales & Nespresso: Patrice Bula
Deputy EVP Human Resources & Admin.: Jean-Marc Duvoisin
EVP Operations, GLOBE: Jose Lopez
Estimated Sales: Over $1 Billion
Number Employees: 10000+
Square Footage: 1500000
Parent Co: Nestle S.A.
Type of Packaging: Consumer
Brands:
Cerelac
Gerber
Graduates Toddler Foods
Naturnes
Nestum
Nestle Pure Life Water
Perrier
Poland Spring
S. Pellegrino
Chocapic
Cini Minis
Cookie Crisp
Estrelitas
Fitness
Nesquik
Aero
Butterfinger
Cailler
Crunch Bar
Kitkat
Orion
Smarties
Nestle Toll House
Wonka
Nescafe
Nespresso
Buitoni
Digiorno
Herta
Hot Pockets
Lean Cuisine
Maggi
Stouffer's
Thomy
Tombstone
Carnation
Coffee-Mate
La Laitiere
Nido
Juicy Juice
Nestea
Milo
Chef
Chef-Mate
Minor's
Sjora
Stouffer's
Boost
Nutren Junior
Peptamen Af
Resource
Dreyer's
Extreme
Haagen-Dazs
Movenpick
Alpo
Bakers
Purina
Beneful
Cat Chow
Chef Michael's
Jenny Craig
Powerbar
Maggi Bouillion Cubes

8946 **Neto's Market & Grill**
1313 Franklin Street
Santa Clara, CA 95050
408-296-0818
Fax: 408-217-2603 888-482-6386
netosausage@msn.com netosmarketandgrill.com
Portuguese, Italian, Mexican, Spanish and chicken sausages
Owner: Deborah Costa
Estimated Sales: $2.5-5 Million
Number Employees: 10-19
Number of Brands: 3
Number of Products: 32
Square Footage: 64000
Type of Packaging: Consumer, Food Service, Private Label, Bulk
Brands:
La Granada
Neto
Zorro

8947 **Network Food Brokers**
355 Lancaster Avenue
Haverford, PA 19041-1547
610-649-7210
Fax: 610-649-0747
Cheese

President: Nate Ostroff
Estimated Sales: $2.5-5 Million
Number Employees: 10

8948 NeuRoast
45 Wall St Ct
New York, NY 10005
info@neuroast.com
www.neuroast.com
Mushroom-enhanced coffee and coffee creamers
Founder: Alex Curtis

8949 Neuchatel Chocolatier
461 Limestone Rd
Oxford, PA 19363-1235
610-932-2706
Fax: 610-932-9036 800-597-0759
web_sales@neuchatelchocolates.com
www.neuchatelchocolates.com
Chocolate confections
Owner: Al Lauber
info@neuchatelchocolates.com
Estimated Sales: $1-3 Million
Number Employees: 20-49

8950 Neuman Bakery Specialties
1405 W Jeffrey Dr
Addison, IL 60101-4331
630-916-8909
Fax: 630-916-8919 800-253-5298
Wholesale bakery
President: George Neuman
gneuman@neumansbakery.com
CFO: Dan Neuman
R&D: James Neuman
Plant Manager: Bob Barrera
Estimated Sales: Below $5 Million
Number Employees: 10-19
Square Footage: 100000
Brands:
Neuman

8951 Nevada Baking Company
299 West Charleston Blvd
Las Vegas, NV 89127-3911
702-384-8950
Bread and rolls
President: Jim Miller
COO: Robert Mayfield
Sales Manager: Scott Pollock
Estimated Sales: $10-25 Million
Number Employees: 50-99
Brands:
Gail's
Roman Meal
Wholesome

8952 Nevada City Brewing
75 Bost Avenue
Nevada City, CA 95959-3024
530-265-2446
Fax: 530-265-2576 www.beerme.com
Beer
Co-Owner: Andy Sawdon
Co-Owner: Hans Schillinger
Director Manufacturing: Keith Downing
Estimated Sales: Under $500,000
Number Employees: 1-4
Brands:
Broad St. Brown
Fools Gold Ale

8953 Nevada City Winery
321 Spring St
Nevada City, CA 95959-2420
530-265-9463
Fax: 530-265-6860 800-203-9463
www.ncwinery.com
Wine
President: Dave Iorns
nccg@internet49.com
Director of Marketing: Rod Byers
Winemaker: Mark Foster
Estimated Sales: $2.5-5 Million
Number Employees: 10-19
Brands:
Nevada City Winery

8954 Nevada County Wine Guild
11372 Winter Moon Way
Nevada City, CA 95959
530-265-3662
855-494-7025
reachus@ourdailyred.com
Wine
Owner: Tony Norskog
Contact: Donn Berdahl
donn@ourdailyred.com
Estimated Sales: Less than $500,000
Number Employees: 1-4
Brands:
Our Daily Red

8955 New Age Beverages
1700 East 68th Ave
Denver, CO 80229
303-289-8655
newagebev.com
Natural, functional beverages, including RTD tea, energy drinks and premium bottled water
CEO: Brent Willis
Year Founded: 2003
Number of Brands: 5
Brands:
COCO LIBRE
XING
BUCHA
MARLEY BEVERAGE CO.
ASPEN PURE

8956 New Bakery Company of Ohio
3005 E Pointe Dr
Zanesville, OH 43701
740-454-6876
Fax: 740-588-5860 800-848-9845
www.newbakerycompany.com
Hamburger buns
Manager: Sam McLaughlin
Contact: Tara Blackstone
tblackstone@newbakerycompany.com
Plant Manager: Doug Wendeler
Number Employees: 250-499
Square Footage: 100000
Parent Co: Wendy's International
Type of Packaging: Food Service
Brands:
Sta Fresh
Wendy

8957 New Barn
888-635-7102
hello@thenewbarn.com www.thenewbarn.com
Almond milk beverages and frozen dessert
CEO: Ted Robb
Chief Commercial Officer: Billie Thein
Number of Brands: 3
Brands:
ALMONDMILK
ALMONDCRÔME
BARISTA ALMONDMILK

8958 New Barn Organics
1400 Valley House Dr
Suite 210
Rohnert Park, CA 94928
707-665-6307
888-635-7102
admin@newbarnorganics.com
www.newbarnorganics.com
Organic almond milk, non-dairy creamer, almond creme, almond dip, non-dairy buttery spread, single-serve coffee
Co-Founder: Dan Conrad
Co-Founder/CEO: Ted Robb
COO/CFO: Louis Kanganis
VP Innovation & Marketing: Darleen Scherer
VP Sales: Richard Tidrow
Year Founded: 2015
Number Employees: 20-49

8959 New Belgium Brewing Co
500 Linden St
Fort Collins, CO 80524
970-221-0524
888-622-4044
www.newbelgium.com
Beer
Co-Founder: Kim Jordan
Co-Founder: Jeff Lebesch
CEO: Steve Fechheimer
Year Founded: 1991
Estimated Sales: $58 Million
Number Employees: 500-999
Number of Brands: 8
Square Footage: 180000
Brands:
CITRADELIC
FAT TIRE
HOF TEN DORMAAL
GLUTINY
SLOW RIDE IPA
LIPS OF FAITH
SNAPSHOT WHEAT
RANGER IPA

8960 New Braunfels Smokehouse
1090 N. IH 35
New Braunfels, TX 78130
830-625-2416
Fax: 830-626-3785 800-537-6932
Emilio@nbsmokehouse.com
www.nbsmokehouse.com
Smoked meats including beef, pork, turkey, ham, chicken and venison; also, jerky
President: Susan Dunbar Snyder
CEO: Dudley Snyder
Vice President: Mike Dietert
Manager: Emilio Rodriquez
Estimated Sales: $5-10 Million
Number Employees: 120
Type of Packaging: Consumer, Food Service, Private Label, Bulk
Brands:
Dunbar Ranch

8961 New Business Corp
444 Rutledge St
Gary, IN 46404-1011
219-885-1476
www.gourmetsupreme.com
Ketchup, barbecue, seafood and Worcestershire sauces
President: Ralph Shanabarger
ralph.shanabarger@student.ctuonline.edu
Secretary: Naomi Woods
Estimated Sales: Under $500,000
Number Employees: 5-9
Square Footage: 7200
Brands:
Gourmet Slim #7
Gourmet Slim Cuisine
Gourmet Supreme

8962 New Canaan Farms
5916 W Highway 290
Dripping Springs, TX 78620
512-858-7669
Fax: 512-858-7513 800-727-5267
info@shopncf.com www.newcanaanfarms.com
Gourmet products including jams, salsa, dips and jellies: lemon fig, plum, peach, raspberry, strawberry, blackberry, etc.; also, mustards including jalapeno, honey and German and sauces including jalapeno shrimp, peach picantehabanero
President: Cindy Figer
cindy@shopncf.com
Production Manager: Patti Thurman
Estimated Sales: $1.2 Million
Number Employees: 10-19
Type of Packaging: Private Label

8963 New Century Snacks
5560 East Slauson Ave
City of Commerce, CA 90040
323-278-9578
Fax: 323-837-4699 800-688-6887
orders@NewCenturySnacks.com
www.energyclub.com
Hispanic snacks, candy, nuts, stoys, trail mix extra large packages, salty snacks, beef jerky, accessories and supplies
Owner: Miron Aviv
CEO: Tim Snee
CFO: Steve Deerwester
VP: Vincent Guiliano
Purchasing: Craig Hayman
Estimated Sales: $5-10 Million
Number Employees: 80
Number of Products: 300
Square Footage: 200000
Type of Packaging: Consumer, Private Label

8964 New Chapter
90 Technology Dr
Brattleboro, VT 05301-9180
802-257-0018
Fax: 802-257-0652 800-543-7279
info@newchapter.com www.newchapter.com
Whole food vitamins, organic herbal supplements, fish oil

Owner: Paul Schulick
CEO: Larry Allgaier
CFO: Ruth Austin
Executive Vice President: Herb Lewis
Quality Control Manager: Judy Mins
VP Marketing: Bob Lierle
National Sales Manager: Disa Pratt
info@new-chapter.com
Purchasing: Russ Thompson
Year Founded: 1982
Estimated Sales: $33.5 Million
Number Employees: 50-99
Square Footage: 93406

8965 (HQ)New City Packing Company
2600 Church Rd
Aurora, IL 60502-8732
630-851-8800
Fax: 630-898-3030
Purveyor of fine meats
President: Marvin Fagel
Vice President: Dave Aardema
National Sales: David McClendon
Estimated Sales: $6.6 Million
Number Employees: 30
Square Footage: 240000
Type of Packaging: Consumer

8966 New Direction Foods
16321 Gothard St
Suite C
Huntington Beach, CA 92647
562-606-8511
888-393-5590
curious@thecuriouscreamery.com
www.thecuriouscreamery.com
Ice cream mixes
Founder & CEO: Jareer Abu-Ali
VP, Business Development: Ron Tan
Brands:
The Curious Creamery

8967 New Earth
565 Century Ct
Klamath Falls, OR 97601-7100
541-882-5406
Fax: 541-885-5458 www.newearth.com
Processor and exporter of blue green algae products
President: Jerry Anderson
COO: Justin Straus
VP Sales: Roger Martin
VP Marketing/Strategy: Victor Bond
Number Employees: 50-99
Square Footage: 1000000
Brands:
Alpha Gold
Elz Super Enzymes
Omega Gold
Omega Suro
Planet Food
Spectrabiotic
Super Blue Green Enzymes
Super Q10

8968 New England Country Bakers
15 Mountain View Rd
Watertown, CT 6795
860-945-9994
Fax: 860-945-9996 800-225-3779
Pound, no-sugar cheesecake and layer cakes, pies and tea breads including apple crumb, maple, banana, blueberry crumb, cranberry, pumpkin and zucchini nut
President: David Spivak
Director Marketing: Donna Spivak
General Manager: Gary Shields
Production: Andrew Kandefer
Estimated Sales: $2 Million
Number Employees: 20-49
Number of Brands: 1
Number of Products: 50
Square Footage: 48000
Type of Packaging: Food Service

8969 New England Cranberry
82 Sanderson Ave
Lynn, MA 01902-1974
781-596-0888
Fax: 781-596-0808 800-410-2892
info@newenglandcranberry.com
www.newenglandcranberry.com
Processor and exporter of naturally sweetened dried cranberries, premium suger sweetened dried cranberries, dried wild blueberries, dried cherries, frozen whole cranberries, cranberry jams and jellies, cranberry chutney and pepperjelly, and fine chocolates with sweet cranberries
President: Ted Stux
Sales: Arthur Stock
Estimated Sales: $530000
Number Employees: 10-19
Square Footage: 7400
Type of Packaging: Consumer, Food Service, Bulk
Brands:
Fresh Pond
New England Cranberry

8970 New England Muffin Co Inc
337 Pleasant St
Fall River, MA 02721-3000
508-675-2833
Fax: 508-675-2833
Fresh and frozen Portuguese muffins in various flavors
President: Filomena Botelho
Owner: Jose Martin
josemartin@island-candy.com
Estimated Sales: $980,000
Number Employees: 5-9
Type of Packaging: Food Service, Bulk

8971 New England Natural Bakers
74 Fairview St E
Greenfield, MA 01301
413-772-2239
Fax: 413-772-2936 800-910-2884
nenb@nenb.com www.nenb.com
Organic granola and trail mix
President & CEO: Pam Clark
pclark@nenb.com
CFO: Didi Foley
Quality Control: Dale Parda
Quality Assurance & IT Coordinator: Dale Prada
Brand Sales & Marketing Manager: Larry Cornick
Vice President Of Sales & Marketing: Pam Clark
Director Of Operations: Scott Johnson
Number Employees: 10-19
Number of Brands: 1
Number of Products: 50
Square Footage: 60000
Type of Packaging: Consumer, Food Service, Private Label, Bulk
Brands:
New England Naturals

8972 New England Tea & Coffee Co
100 Charles St
Malden, MA 02148-6704
781-324-8094
Fax: 781-397-7580 800-225-3537
consumerrelations@necoffeeco.com
www.newenglandcoffee.com
Product line includes a variety of coffee, whole bean and ground, flavored and regular in addition to decaffeinated blends. Also available is tea, both regular and decaffeinated, flavored and non-flavored and a selection of gift itemsand gift baskets.
President/COO: James Kaloyanides
VP/Finance/Treasurer: Jamie Dostou
Vice President: Russell Ain
russell.ain@necoffeeco.com
VP/Product & Business Development: Michael Kaloyanides
VP/Operations & Human Resources: John Kaloyanides
VP/Purchasing: Stephen Kaloyanides
russell.ain@necoffeeco.com
Number Employees: 100-249

8973 New Era Canning Company
4856 1st St
New Era, MI 49446
231-861-2151
Fax: 231-861-4068
Canned fruits and vegetables including beans, asparagus, apples, and apple sauce
President/CEO: Rick Ray
CFO: Rick McClouth
Sales: Patrick Alger
Contact: Mike Aebig
maebig@gloryfoods.com
Production: Jim Merrill
Purchasing: Ron Fekken
Estimated Sales: $33 Million
Number Employees: 250
Number of Brands: 3
Number of Products: 65
Square Footage: 200000
Type of Packaging: Consumer, Food Service, Private Label
Brands:
Good Taste
Necco
New Era

8974 New Generation Foods
7438 Elmonds Street
Burnaby, BC V 3N1A8
Canada
604-515-7438
Fax: 402-733-5755 danehodge@hotmail.com
Portion-controlled and breaded foods including beef, chicken, pork and turkey
CFO: Steve McCurdy
National Sales Manager: Dane Hodges
Plant Manager: John Schull
Number Employees: 15

8975 New Glarus Bakery & TeaRoom
534 1st St
PO Box 595
New Glarus, WI 53574-8908
608-527-2916
Fax: 608-527-5799 866-805-5536
Cookies, breads, pastries, donuts and desserts.
Owner: Casey Umhoefer
casey@beachbody.com
Co-Owner: Nancy Weber
Estimated Sales: $500,000-$1 Million
Number Employees: 10-19
Brands:
New Glarus Bakery

8976 New Glarus Brewing CompaNy
2400 State Hwy 69
New Glarus, WI 53574
608-527-5850
Fax: 608-527-5855 www.newglarusbrewing.com
Beer
President: Daniel Carey
VP: Deborah Carry
Estimated Sales: Below $5 Million
Number Employees: 20-49

8977 New Grass Bison
PO Box 860033
Shawnee, KS 66286
866-422-5888
Natural and grassfed bison products

8978 New Harbor Fisherman's Cooperative
PO Box 125
New Harbor, ME 04554-0125
207-677-2791
Fax: 207-677-3835 866-883-2922
Lobster, crab and other seafood
Manager: Linda Vannah
Operations Manager: Ken Tonneson
Estimated Sales: $1 million
Number Employees: 1-4
Type of Packaging: Consumer, Bulk

8979 New Harmony Coffee & Tea Co.
505 S Main
New Harmony, IN 47631
812-682-4563
Coffee
Owner: Mary Webber
Brands:
New Harmony

8980 New Harvest Foods
323 3rd Ave
PO Box 96503, #12998
Washington, DC 20090-6503
920-822-2578
info@new-harvest.org
www.new-harvest.org
Canned vegetables including peas, green beans, sweet corn, carrots, potatoes, sauerkraut and mixed vegetables
President: Timothy Grygield
Executive Director: Isha Datar
Production Manager: Tom Wojcik
Plant Manager: Robert Tetzlaff
Estimated Sales: $5-10 Million
Number Employees: 20-49
Square Footage: 140000

8981 **New Holland Brewing Co**
66 E 8th St
Holland, MI 49423-3504
616-355-6422
Fax: 616-355-2940 www.newhollandbrew.com
Beer
President: Elizabeth Aker
lizby1947@yahoo.com
Co-Owner/Head Brewer: John Haggerty
CFO/Co-Owner: Dave White
Owner/Partner: Jason Spaulding
Sales/Marketing Director: Fred Bueltmann
Estimated Sales: $3.3 Million
Number Employees: 50-99
Square Footage: 19486

8982 **New Hope Mills Mfg Inc**
181 York St
Auburn, NY 13021-9009
315-252-2676
Fax: 315-282-0720 store@newhopemills.com
www.newhopemills.com
Mixes including pancake, bread and cookie; also, milled flour including buckwheat, wheat and pancake
President/CEO: Dale Weed
sales@newhopemills.com
Sales Exec: Dale Weed
Estimated Sales: $1.3 Million
Number Employees: 20-49
Number of Products: 20
Square Footage: 90000
Type of Packaging: Consumer, Food Service, Private Label, Bulk

8983 **New Hope Natural Media**
1401 Pearl Street
Suite 200
Boulder, CO 80302
303-939-8440
Fax: 303-998-9020 info@newhope.com
Supplements and ingredients
Executive Director: Len Monheit
Sr Marketing Manager: Brad Mastrine
Sales: Kim Merselis
Contact: Nicole Aulik
naulik@newhope.com
Estimated Sales: $25 Million
Number Employees: 45
Square Footage: 60000

8984 **New Hope Winery**
6123 Lower York Rd
New Hope, PA 18938-9620
215-693-1568
Fax: 215-794-2341 800-592-9463
info@newhopewinery.com
www.newhopewinery.com
Red wine
Owner: Sandra Pizza
sandra@newhopewinery.com
Estimated Sales: $710,000
Number Employees: 5-9
Number of Products: 25

8985 **New Horizon Farms**
319 Hiawatha Ave.
P.O. Box 708
Pipestone, MN 56164
507-825-5462
Fax: 507-825-5877 800-906-7447
www.newhorizonfarms.com
Pork production.
Managing Partner: Bob Taubert
Partner & Production Manager: Jerry Bauman
CFO: Erin Musch
Year Founded: 1993
Number Employees: 100-249
Type of Packaging: Bulk

8986 **New Horizon Foods**
33440 Western Ave
Union City, CA 94587-3202
510-489-8600
Fax: 510-489-9797
Dough conditioners, bread bases, natural mixes, beverage, cake, muffin, pudding, meat spices, spice blends, snack and chip seasonings, custard, ice cream, waffle cone and sauce mixes and bases; exporter of dough conditioners and cakeand muffin mixes
Owner: Ken Crawford
kenc@newhorizonfoodsinc.com
Senior Vice President: Yael Melzer
Number Employees: 10-19
Parent Co: Tova Industries
Type of Packaging: Consumer, Food Service, Private Label, Bulk

8987 **New Horizons Baking Co**
700 W Water St
Fremont, IN 46737-2165
260-495-7055
Fax: 219-495-2307 www.newhorizonsbaking.com
Buns and English muffins
President: Tilmon Brown
Vice President: Bob Creighton
Quality Assurance Manager: Marsha Black
Vice President of Sales: Mike Porter
Manager: Mark Duke
VP/Director Operations: John Widman
Plant Manager: Aaron Brown
Estimated Sales: $3-5 Million
Number Employees: 50-99
Square Footage: 160000
Type of Packaging: Food Service, Private Label, Bulk
Other Locations:
New Horizons Baking Company
Norwalk OH

8988 **New Jamaican Gold**
3536 Arden Rd
Hayward, CA 94545
510-887-4653
Fax: 510-887-7466 800-672-9956
Ready-to-drink coffee/ice cappuccino
CEO: Kenneth Yeung
becky2snoop@gmail.com
Sales Director: Kimi Tom
Estimated Sales: $1+ Million
Number Employees: 10-19
Brands:
Jamaican Gold

8989 **New Land Vineyard**
577 Lerch Rd
Geneva, NY 14456-9238
315-585-4432
Fax: 315-585-9844
Wines
Owner: Dale Nagy
Estimated Sales: Less than $500,000
Number Employees: 1-4

8990 **New Mexico Green Chile Company**
1807 Don Lewis Drive
Artesia, NM 88210
505-503-0996
stacy@greenchileco.com
www.greenchileco.com
Chile peppers, roasted tomatillos, dehydrated guajillo, red chile peppers, poblanos, and tamales
Manager: Samantha Lewis
Manager: Stacy Lewis
stacy@greenchileco.com

8991 **New Nissi Corp.**
529 E 39th St
Paterson, NJ 07504
973-278-4400
info@newnissi.com
www.nuttycrunchers.com
Natural nut and seed brittles
Founder: Steve Kim
steve.kim@newnissi.com
Year Founded: 1986
Number Employees: 1-4
Brands:
Nutty Crunchers

8992 **New Ocean**
3077 Mccall Dr # 12
Suite 12
Doraville, GA 30340-2832
770-458-5235
Fax: 770-485-5235
Seafood, shrimp, scallops, king crab, lobster tails, snow crab
President: Mei Lin
Estimated Sales: Less Than $500,000
Number Employees: 5-9

8993 **New Organics**
600 Lawnwood Road
Kenwood, CA 95452
734-677-5570
Fax: 707-833-0105
Organic ingredient supplier-grains, sweetners, oils, soy powders
President: Jethren Phillips
Manager: Mathew Keegan
Estimated Sales: $17.5 Million
Number Employees: 74
Number of Brands: 3
Number of Products: 100
Square Footage: 25000
Type of Packaging: Bulk
Other Locations:
American Health & Nutrition
Eaton Rapids MI
Brands:
Organic Garden
Organic Harvest
Soy-N-Ergy Soy Powders

8994 **New Orleans Fish House II LLC**
921 S Dupre St
New Orleans, LA 70125-1343
504-821-9700
Fax: 504-821-9011 800-839-3474
info@nofh.com www.neworleansfishhouse.com
Fresh and frozen catfish, tilapia, crawfish, softshell crabs, tuna, shark, red snapper, pompano, wahoo, drum, escalor and sheephead
Owner: Craig Borges
craig_b@nofishhouse.com
Owner/President: Bill Borges
VP Sales: Cliff Hall
Estimated Sales: $20-50 Million
Number Employees: 50-99
Type of Packaging: Consumer, Food Service, Private Label, Bulk

8995 **New Orleans Food Co-op**
2372 St. Claude Avenue
Suite 110
New Orleans, LA 70117
504-264-5579
Fax: 504-734-7684 800-628-4900
cook@bumblebee.com www.nolafood.coop
Canned shrimp, crab meat, oysters, clams, sardines, tuna and mackerel; also, bottled clam juice; exporter of canned shrimp; importer of canned seafood
VP Sales/Marketing: David Cook
Estimated Sales: $5-10 Million
Number Employees: 5-9
Type of Packaging: Consumer, Food Service, Private Label
Brands:
Cutcher
Dejean
Gulf Belle
Harris
Marvelous
Orleans

8996 **New Orleans Gulf Seafood**
509 Commerce Pt
New Orleans, LA 70123-3203
504-733-1516
Fax: 504-733-1517
Seafood
President: Albert Lin

8997 **New Packing Company**
1249 W Lake St
Chicago, IL 60607-1519
312-666-1314
Fax: 312-666-8698
Sausage
President: Kurt Kreuger
Estimated Sales: $1.8 Million
Number Employees: 19
Type of Packaging: Consumer

8998 **New Salem Tea-Bread Company**
837 Daniel Shays Hwy
New Salem, MA 01355
978-544-0294
Fax: 978-544-5643 800-897-5910
info@teabread.com
All natural, kosher tea breads. Flavors: lemon, banana orange cranberry, blueberry vanilla, pumpkin, carrot raisin, almond, apple cinnamon

Co-Owner: Steve Verney
Co-Owner: Kay Verney
Contact: Curran Tea
sales@teabreads.com

8999 New Season Foods Inc
2329 Yew St # A1
P.O. Box 157
Forest Grove, OR 97116-4401
503-357-7124
Fax: 503-357-0419 www.newseasonfoods.com
Drum-dried vegetable powders and other custom ingredients
CEO: Bruce McVean
Estimated Sales: $5-10 Million
Number Employees: 20-49
Square Footage: 600000
Type of Packaging: Bulk
Brands:
Flavorland
New Season Foods

9000 New Wave Cuisine
112 Schoolhouse Road
Mount Holly, NJ 8060
609-267-0276
Fax: 609-261-1949 800-486-0276
www.kaptainsketch.com
Frozen value-added poultry and seafood
President: Nash Cohen
Estimated Sales: $10-20,000,000
Number Employees: 20-49
Type of Packaging: Consumer, Food Service, Private Label
Brands:
Herb's Five Star
Kaptain's Ketch
Westhampton Farms

9001 New World Pasta Co
85 Shannon Rd
Harrisburg, PA 17112-2787
717-526-2200
Fax: 717-526-2468 800-730-5957
mikehoar@nwpasta.com
Pasta
President: Bastian De Zeeuw
CEO: Peter Smith
CFO: Gregory Richardson
SVP and Sales Development: Shane Faucett
SVP Operatons: Brett Beckfield
Number Employees: 1000-4999
Square Footage: 1200000
Parent Co: New World Pasta
Type of Packaging: Bulk

9002 New York Apple Sales Inc
17 Languish Pl
Glenmont, NY 12077-4819
518-477-7200
Fax: 518-477-6770 888-477-6770
kaari@newyorkapplesales.com
www.newyorkapplesales.com
Apples and pears.
President: Kaari Stannard
kaari@newyorkapplesales.com
VP, Sales: John Cushing
Sales: Michael Harwood
Food Safety Coordinator: Colleen O'Brien
Production & Logistics Manager: Michael Shannon
Estimated Sales: $29 Million
Number Employees: 20-49
Type of Packaging: Consumer, Food Service, Bulk

9003 New York Bakeries Inc
261 W 22nd St
Hialeah, FL 33010-1521
305-883-0790
Fax: 305-883-0790
Manufacturer and exporter of bread, rolls, and cakes.
President: Sarah Zimmerman
Estimated Sales: $35 Million
Number Employees: 50-99
Parent Co: New York Bakeries
Type of Packaging: Consumer, Food Service, Private Label

9004 New York Bottling Co Inc
626 Whittier St
Bronx, NY 10474-6121
718-842-7416
Fax: 718-542-9004
Bottled and canned soft drinks, water, ice, alcohol free cocktails, drink mixes, sports drinks, spring/mineral water, powdered drink mixes, frozen juices, shelf stable juices, fresh juice, chocolate, malt and other hot beverages
Contact: Zvi Hold
info@naturale90.com
Estimated Sales: $5-10 Million
Number Employees: 1-4
Brands:
La Pri Cranberry Apple Drink
La Pri Grapefruit Dr
La Pri Orange Drink

9005 New York Frozen Foods Inc
25900 Fargo Ave
Bedford, OH 44146-1369
216-292-5655
Fax: 216-292-5978 www.marzetti.com
Bread and rolls
President: Bruce Rosa
Executive Director: Mike Mahon
Controller: Mike Juhasz
Human Resource Executive: Vicki Verlato
Operations: Brian Millikin
Number Employees: 250-499
Parent Co: T. Marzetti Company
Type of Packaging: Consumer, Food Service

9006 New York Intl Bread Co
1500 W Church St
Orlando, FL 32805-2408
407-843-9744
Fax: 407-648-2785
Bread and baked products
CEO: Laura Masella
CEO: Laura Masella
Estimated Sales: $5-10 000,000
Number Employees: 50-99

9007 New York Pizza
725 E Internatl Speedway Blvd
Daytona Beach, FL 32118-4555
386-257-2050
www.nypizza.ru
Pizza
Owner: Richard Squillante
Estimated Sales: Less than $500,000
Number Employees: 1-4
Brands:
New York Pizza

9008 New York Pretzel
200 Moore St
Brooklyn, NY 11206
718-366-9800
Fax: 718-821-4544 info@nypretzel.com
www.nypretzel.com
Soft pretzels
President: Themis Makkos
VP: Richard Berger
Contact: Ronald Orfinger
jack@nypretzel.com
Estimated Sales: $9.7 Million
Number Employees: 75
Brands:
New York Pretzel

9009 New York Ravioli
12 Denton Ave S
New Hyde Park, NY 11040-4904
516-270-2852
Fax: 516-741-5289 888-588-7287
www.nyravioli.com
Ravioli and other products
President/Co-Founder: David Creo
VP/Co-Founder: Paul Moncada
Contact: Paul Moncada
paul@nyravioli.com
Estimated Sales: Less Than $500,000
Number Employees: 1-4
Type of Packaging: Food Service, Private Label, Bulk

9010 NewGem Products
3600-A Industry Drive East
Fife, WA 98424
253-896-3089
info@newgemfoods.com
www.newgemfoods.com
Fruit- and vegetable-based alternatives to seaweed wraps
CEO: Matthew De Bord
Corporate Executive Chef: Tracy Griffith
Number of Brands: 2
Brands:
ORIGAMI WRAPS
GEMWRAPS

9011 Newburg Corners Cheese Factory
Highway 33
Route 2
Bangor, WI 54614
608-452-3636
Fax: 608-452-3636
Cheese
Owner: Lowell Kitzmann
Owner: Mike Everhart
Number Employees: 1-4

9012 Newburgh Brewing Company
88 South Colden St.
Newburgh, NY 12550
845-569-2337
info@newburghbrewing.com
www.newburghbrewing.com
IPAs, American ales, sour beers, Belgian-style beers, stout
Founding Partner/Co-Owner: Christopher Basso
Year Founded: 2012
Number of Brands: 1
Number of Products: 14
Type of Packaging: Consumer, Private Label
Brands:
Newburgh Brewing Company

9013 Newby Teas
333 Albert Ave
Suite 633
East Lansing, MI 48823
517-999-0590
www.newbyteas.us
Tea
Brand Ambassador: Raji Singh
Brands:
Newby

9014 Newell Lobsters
72 Water St
PO Box 99
Yarmouth, NS B5A 4B1
Canada
902-742-6272
Fax: 902-742-1542
Processor and exporter of fresh herring roe and lobster
President: Robert Newell
Estimated Sales: $7.4 Million
Number Employees: 15
Type of Packaging: Consumer, Food Service, Private Label

9015 Newfound Resources
90 O'Leary Ave
Suite 203
St Josephs, NL A1B 2C7
Canada
709-579-7676
Fax: 709-579-7668 shrimp@nfld.com
www.newfoundresources.com
Processor and exporter of frozen shrimp
President: Brian McNamara
Controller: Bill Coady
Operations Manager: Jeff Simms
Estimated Sales: $6.6 Million
Number Employees: 60
Type of Packaging: Bulk

9016 (HQ)Newly Weds Foods Inc
2501 N Keeler Ave
Chicago, IL 60639-2131
773-489-6224
Fax: 773-489-2799 800-621-7521
nwfnorthamerica@newlywedsfoods.com
www.newlywedsfoods.com
Processor and exporter of breadings, batters, seasoning blends, marinades, glazes and capsicum products
President: Charles T. Angell
CFO: Brian Johnson
SVP Sales & Marketing: Bruce Leshinski
R&D: Jim Klein
Sales Director: Jim Chin
Contact: Mary Adderhold
madderhold@newlywedsfoods.com
VP Manufacturing: Mike Hopp
Plant Manager: Leo Vogler
Director of Purchasing: Tom Lisack

Estimated Sales: $959 Million
Number Employees: 1-4
Square Footage: 1500000
Other Locations:
Newly Weds Foods
Bethleham PA
Newly Weds Foods
Chicago IL
Newly Weds Foods
Cleveland TN
Newly Weds Foods
Watertown MA
Newly Weds Foods
Yorkville IL
Newly Weds Foods
Horn Lake MS
Newly Weds Foods
Edmonton AB
Newly Weds Foods
Montreal QC
Newly Weds Foods
Toronto ON
Brands:
Batter Blends
Blended Breaders
Newly Weds

9017 Newly Weds Foods Inc
437 S Mcclure Rd
Modesto, CA 95357-0519
209-491-7777
Fax: 209-575-1609 800-487-7423
www.newlywedsfoods.com
Seasonings and spices
Sales Manager: Bill McGlynn
General Manager: Coe Barnard
Plant Manager: Allen Holzman
Estimated Sales: $5-10 Million
Number Employees: 20-49
Parent Co: Heller Seasonings

9018 (HQ)Newman's Own
246 Post Rd E # 308
Suite 308
Westport, CT 06880-3615
203-222-0136
Fax: 203-227-5630 www.newmansown.com
Exporter of pizzas, complete skillet meals, salad dressings, sauces, salsas, marinades, beverages, cereals, popcorn, and wine
President & COO: Tom Indoe
CEO: Clea Newman
Business Development Manager: Steve Ripson
VP Marketing: Michael Havard
Director of Sales: Mark Tilley
Contact: M Anita
anita@newmansown.com
VP Operations: Bill Lee
Estimated Sales: $4.9 Million
Number Employees: 28
Square Footage: 16800
Type of Packaging: Consumer, Food Service
Other Locations:
Newman's Own
Aptos CA
Brands:
Newman's Own
Newman's Own Lemonade
Newman's Own Pasta Sauces
Newman's Own Popcorn
Newman's Own Salad Dressing
Newman's Own Salsa

9019 Newmarket Foods
2210 Pine View Way
Petaluma, CA 94954-5687
707-778-3400
Fax: 707-778-3434 www.newmarketfoods.com
VP Sales/Marketing: Tom Mierzwinski
Vice President: Thomas Mierzwinski
Estimated Sales: $1-2.5 Million
Number Employees: 1
Type of Packaging: Private Label
Brands:
Butterscotch Bliss
Chocolate Ecstasy
Hot Fudge Fantasy

9020 Newmeadows Lobster Inc
60 Portland Pier
Portland, ME 04101-4713
207-775-1612
Fax: 207-874-2456 800-668-1612
Lobster
Owner: Patricia Burch
patriciaburch@newmeadowslobster.com

Estimated Sales: $5-10 Million
Number Employees: 10-19

9021 Newport Flavours & Fragrances
833 N Elm St
Orange, CA 92867-7909
714-744-3700
Fax: 714-771-3588 www.newportflavours.com
Flavor extracts, concentrates, fillings, icings, glazes, syrups, toppings, oils and fragrances; also, contract packaging available
President: Bill Sabo
customerservice@naturesflavors.com
VP: Jeanne Aragon
Estimated Sales: $3.6 Million
Number Employees: 10-19
Square Footage: 35200
Type of Packaging: Consumer, Food Service, Private Label, Bulk

9022 Newport Ingredients
5850 West 3rd St
Suite 142
Los Angeles, CA 90036
323-284-5959
Fax: 323-285-5352 sales@newportings.com
newportingredients.com
Natural ingredients
President/Owner: Israel Jaeger

9023 Newport Meat Co North
16691 Hale Ave.
Irvine, CA 92606
949-474-4040
info@newportmeat.com
www.newportmeat.com
Meats including; beef, poultry, pork, lamb, veal, seafood, foie gras, vegetables, potato products, and more
President: Pat Ansboury
pat@facciola.com
CEO: Robert Facciola
CFO: Robert Cruz
Vice President: Michael Nicholas
Quality Assurance Manager: Ambrosio Huasanoi
VP Human Resources: Krystal Martinez
Purchasing Manager: Bret Vanvoorhis
Estimated Sales: $30.3 Million
Number Employees: 100-249
Square Footage: 84000
Parent Co: Sysco

9024 Newport Vineyards & Winery
909 E. Main Rd (RT 138)
Middletown, RI 02842
401-848-5161
Fax: 401-848-5162 info@newportvineyards.com
www.newportvineyards.com
Wine
Owner, Vintner: John Nunes
Owner, Vineyard Manager: Paul Nunes
Winemaker: George Chelf
Estimated Sales: $5 Million
Number Employees: 19
Type of Packaging: Private Label
Brands:
Newport

9025 Newton Candy Company
4912 Airline Dr # G
Houston, TX 77022-3078
713-691-6969
Fax: 713-691-6979
Candy
Manager: Muhammed Nazim
Estimated Sales: $2.5-5 000,000
Number Employees: 10-19

9026 Newton Vineyard
2555 Madrona Ave
St Helena, CA 94574-2300
707-204-7423
Fax: 707-963-5408 winery@newtonvineyard.com
www.newtonvineyard.com
Fine wines
President: Dr Su Hua Newton
CEO: Jean-Baptiste Rivail
Controller: Tim Lin
Winemaker: Alberto Bianchi
Assistant Winemaker: Andrew Holve
Estimated Sales: $20-50 Million
Number Employees: 1-4
Type of Packaging: Private Label

Brands:
Newton Vineyard

9027 Newtown Foods USA Inc
6 Penns Trl # 215
Suite 215
Newtown, PA 18940-1889
215-579-2120
Fax: 215-579-2129 info@newtownfoods.com
www.newtownfoods.com
Cocoa ingredients, dehydrated fruit, natural extracts, banana puree, spray-dried ingredients
Owner: John Mc Donald
nfoodsusa@aol.com
Estimated Sales: Below $5 Million
Number Employees: 1-4
Brands:
Duas Rodas Industrial
Dutch Cocoa Bv
Kievit
Schoemaker

9028 Nexcel Natural Ingredients
PO Box 3483
2520 S Grand Ave East
Springfield, IL 62703
217-391-0091
Fax: 217-391-0096 www.nexcelfoods.com
Natural oils
President/Owner: Rob Kirby
VP, Sales & Business Development: Lynn Myers

9029 Nexira
15 Somerset St
Somerville, NJ 08876-2828
908-707-9400
Fax: 908-707-9405 800-872-1850
info-usa@nexira.com www.nexira.com
Nexira is a global leader in natural ingredients and botanical extracts for food nutrition and dietary supplements. Nexira built its reputation as the world leader in acacia gum and now manufactures a wide range of functional andnutritional ingredients, antioxidants, and active botanicals for weight management, sports nutrition, digestive and cardiovascular health. It manufactures the following ingredients for the food and health industry: acacia gun, botanical extracts andpowders.
President: Stephane Dondain
heese@cnius.com
VP: Teresa Yazbek
Marketing/Logistics Specialist: Nina Segura
Sales: Bob Bremer
Estimated Sales: $14 Million
Number Employees: 10-19
Number of Brands: 25
Number of Products: 100
Type of Packaging: Bulk
Brands:
FIBREGUM
VINITROX
EXOCYAN
CACTi-NEA
NEOPUNTIA
ID-ALG
INSTANTGUM
SPRAYGUM
EFICACIA
EQUACIA
THIXOGUM

9030 Nhs Labs Inc
11665 W State St
Star, ID 83669-5223
208-939-5100
Fax: 208-939-5100 888-546-8694
info@nutritionmanufacturer.com
www.nutritionmanufacturer.com
Private label sports drinks, supplements, and energy drinks
CEO: Larry Leach
Number Employees: 50-99
Square Footage: 74000

9031 Niagara Chocolates
3500 Genesee St
Buffalo, NY 14225-5015
716-634-0070
Fax: 716-634-4855 877-261-7887
info@sweetworks.net www.niagarachocolates.com
Chocolate novelties including bars, truffles and boxed

President: Schmassmann Christoph
CFO: Ralph Nicosia
Quality Assurance Manager: Marsha Koerner
Director of Marketing: Jeanne Palka
Director Sales: Jerry Tubbs
Plant Manager: Parha Paraj
Purchasing Manager: Bob Dunn
Estimated Sales: $36.5 Million
Number Employees: 100-249
Square Footage: 115000
Parent Co: SweetWorks, Inc.
Type of Packaging: Consumer
Other Locations:
Oak Leaf Plant
Toronto ON
Brands:
Mercken's
Mercken's Chocolate
Sweet Works

9032 Niagara Foods
10 Kelly Ave
Middleport, NY 14105-1210
716-735-7722
Fax: 716-735-9076 www.agvest.com
Processor, importer and exporter of frozen vegetable products and fruit and vegetable powders and flakes; also, frozen and dehydrated fruits including apples, cherries, strawberries, cranberries and wild and cultivated blueberries
President: Barry Schneider
Contact: Bradley Devey
bradley@valley.net
General Manager: Bob Neuman
Estimated Sales: $14.9 Million
Number Employees: 50
Square Footage: 140000
Parent Co: Agvest
Type of Packaging: Consumer, Food Service, Private Label, Bulk
Brands:
Agvest
Quality

9033 NibMor
PO Box 6
Kennebunk, ME 04043
207-502-7541
info@nibmor.com
www.nibmor.com
Chocolate snacks
CEO: Ralph Chauvin
Operations Manager: Marcia Bell

9034 Nicasio Vineyards
14300 Nicasio Way
Soquel, CA 95073
831-423-1073
Wine
President: Dan Wheeler

9035 (HQ)Niche Import Co
45 Horsehill Rd # 106
Suite 106A
Cedar Knolls, NJ 07927-2009
973-993-8450
Fax: 973-898-0183 800-548-6882
mpersson@ourniche.com www.ourniche.com
Gourmet foods and beverages
President: Terri Nelson
tnelson@ourniche.com
Area Sales Manager: Matthew Nelson
Media Relations: Barbara Miele
Estimated Sales: $2.5-5 Million
Number Employees: 10-19
Type of Packaging: Private Label
Brands:
Asbach Uralt
Stroh
Underberg Bitters

9036 Niche W&S
45 Horsehill Road
Suite 106A
Cedar Knolls, NJ 07927
973-993-8450
Fax: 973-898-0183 www.ourniche.com
Fine wines and spirits
President: Terri Nelson
Estimated Sales: $10-20 Million
Number Employees: 10-19
Parent Co: Niche Import Company

9037 Nichelini Family WineryInc
2950 Sage Canyon Rd
St Helena, CA 94574-9641
707-963-0717
Fax: 707-963-3262 mail@nicheliniwinery.com
www.nicheliniwinery.com
International wines and spirits
Manager: Toni Irwin
nichwine@nicheliniwinery.com
Treasurer: Richard Wainright
Wine Maker: Greg Boeger
Estimated Sales: Less Than $500,000
Number Employees: 1-4
Type of Packaging: Private Label

9038 Nichem Co
750 Frelinghuysen Ave
Newark, NJ 07114-2221
973-399-9810
Fax: 973-399-8818 sales@nichem.com
www.nichem.com
Processor and importer of ingredients including citric acid, vanillin and sodium citrate; exporter of citric acid
President: Peg Blue
sales@nichem.com
Estimated Sales: $700,000
Number Employees: 5-9
Square Footage: 80000
Type of Packaging: Consumer, Food Service

9039 Nichols Farms
Nichols Farms
13762 First Ave
Hanford, CA 93230
559-584-6811
Fax: 559-688-1603 info@nicholsfarms.com
www.nicholsfarms.com
Almonds, pistachios and mixes
President/Owner: Chuck Nichols
Brands:
NICHOLS FARMS

9040 Nick Sciabica & Sons
2150 Yosemite Blvd
Modesto, CA 95354-3931
209-577-5067
Fax: 209-524-5367 800-551-9612
www.baginfusti.com
Extra-virgin olive oil; importer of olive oil, pasta and tomato products; wholesaler/distributor of wine vinegar, olive oil, canned tomatoes, olives and pasta
Partner: Jonathan Sciabica
Controller: Susan Ochoa
VP: Gemma Sciabica
Marketing Manager: Dean Cohan
Production Manager: Daniel Sciabica
Estimated Sales: $2.5 Million
Number Employees: 20-49
Number of Brands: 6
Number of Products: 150
Square Footage: 274912
Type of Packaging: Consumer, Food Service, Private Label, Bulk
Brands:
Marsala
Sciabica's Oil of the Olive

9041 Nick's Sticks
Wenzel's Farm
500 E 29th Street
Marshfield, WI 54449
715-257-0636
www.nicks-sticks.com
Beef snack sticks and jerky
Founder: Nick Wallace
Brands:
NICK'S STICKS
NICK'S JERKY

9042 Nickabood's Inc
1401 Elwood St
Los Angeles, CA 90021-2812
213-746-1541
Fax: 213-746-1542 bob@nickaboods.com
Health food products including sauces, honey, salad dressings, condiments seafood sauces, baked potato products, miso mayo, and frozen stuffed potatoes.
Vice President: Robert Abood
Estimated Sales: $700,000
Number Employees: 5-9
Number of Brands: 4
Number of Products: 15

Square Footage: 60000
Parent Co: Fisherman Wharf Foods
Type of Packaging: Private Label
Brands:
Desert Gold
Fisherman's Wharf
So Good
Spud King

9043 Nicky USA Inc
223 SE 3rd Ave
Portland, OR 97214-1006
503-234-4263
Fax: 503-234-8268 800-469-4162
info@nickyusa.com www.nickyusa.com
Distributor of natural game birds and meats including pheasant, poussin, quail, venison, buffalo, rabbit, ostrich, alligator, ducks and wild boar; also, sausage, veal, free-range lamb
Owner, President: Geoff Latham
glatham@nickyusa.com
VP: Melody Latham
Sales Office Manager: Ursula McVittie
Production Manager: Jace Hentges
Estimated Sales: $4 Million
Number Employees: 20-49
Square Footage: 20000
Type of Packaging: Consumer, Food Service, Private Label, Bulk
Brands:
Cervera
Country Game
Nicky Usa

9044 Nicola International
4561 Colorado Blvd.
Los Angeles, CA 90039-0758
818-545-1515
Fax: 818-247-8585
Finest olives, olive oils and grape leaves for deli departments, bakeries and the pizza industry, salad manufacturers, custom marination and creative gourmet dishes
President: Nicola Khachatoorian
VP: Alice Toomanian
Contact: Adik Khachatoorian
adikk@nicolainternational.com
Purchasing Manager: Claudine Reyes
Estimated Sales: $1-10 Million
Number Employees: 25
Type of Packaging: Food Service, Private Label
Brands:
Aiello

9045 Nicola Pizza
8 N 1st St
Rehoboth Beach, DE 19971-2116
302-226-2654
Fax: 302-226-3721 nicolapizza@comcast.net
www.nicolapizza.com
Spaghetti sauce
Owner: Nick Caggiano
VP: Nicolas Caggiano
CFO: Joan Caggiano
Estimated Sales: $1.2 Million
Number Employees: 20-49
Type of Packaging: Consumer, Food Service
Brands:
Mama Nichola's Sago
Nic-O-Boli

9046 Nicola Valley Apiaries
PO Box 1995
Merritt, BC V1K 1B8
Canada
250-378-5208
www.nicolavalleyhoney.com
Processor and packer of liquid, creamed, chunk and comb honey; also, beeswax
Partner: Alan Paulson
Partner: Margaret Paulson
Estimated Sales: $203,000
Number Employees: 2

9047 Nicole's Divine Crackers
1505 N Kingsbury Street
Chicago, IL 60642-2533
312-640-8883
Fax: 312-640-0988 nicolescrackers@msn.com
Crackers
President: Nicole Bergere
Estimated Sales: Below $5 Million
Number Employees: 5-9

9048 **Niebaum-Coppola Estate Winery**
1991 St Helena Highway
Rutherford, CA 94573
707-968-1100
Fax: 707-963-9084 800-782-4266
www.niebaum-coppola.com
Wines
Chairman: Francis Coppola
CEO: Jay Shoemaker
Estimated Sales: $5-10 Million
Number Employees: 20-49

9049 **Nielsen Citrus ProductsInc**
15621 Computer Ln
Huntington Beach, CA 92649-1607
714-892-5586
Fax: 714-893-2161 info@nielsencitrus.com
www.nielsencitrus.com
Processor and exporter of frozen, concentrated lemon and lime juice, lemon puree, lime puree, orange puree
President: Chris Nielsen
greg.hogue@verizon.net
Vice President: Earl Nielsen
Number Employees: 10-19
Square Footage: 40000
Type of Packaging: Consumer, Food Service, Private Label, Bulk
Brands:
Ez
Nielsen
Suntree

9050 **Nielsen-Massey Vanillas Inc**
1550 Shields Dr
Waukegan, IL 60085-8307
847-578-1550
Fax: 847-578-1570 800-525-7873
info@nielsenmassey.com nielsenmassey.com
Manufacturer of vanilla extracts and pure flavors
CEO: Kirk Trofholz
VP, Global Sales: Brent Allen
Director of Sales: Dan Fox
Year Founded: 1907
Estimated Sales: $20-50 Million
Number Employees: 20-49
Number of Brands: 1
Square Footage: 100500
Type of Packaging: Consumer, Food Service, Bulk
Other Locations:
Nielsen-Massey Vanillas Inter. B.V.
Leeuwarden, Netherlands
Brands:
Nielsen-Massey

9051 **Niemuth's Steak & Chop Shop**
715 Redfield St
Waupaca, WI 54981-1353
715-258-2666
www.niemuthssteakandchop.com
Processors of meat products including ham, bacon and sausage
President: Roger Niemuth
Owner: Robert Niemuth
Estimated Sales: $950,000
Number Employees: 10-19
Square Footage: 27000
Type of Packaging: Consumer

9052 **Night Hawk Frozen FoodsInc**
100 Nighthawk Cir
PO Box 867
Buda, TX 78610-9100
512-312-0757
Fax: 512-295-3988 800-580-4166
www.nighthawkfoods.com
Processor of frozen entrees including steak, beef and meatloaf dinners.
CEO: Leanne Logan
COO: Scott Logan
VP/Controller: Dale Reistad
VP Operations: Terrell Windham
Purchasing Manager: John Benites
Year Founded: 1939
Estimated Sales: $20-50 Million
Number Employees: 50-99
Number of Brands: 1
Number of Products: 18
Square Footage: 30000
Type of Packaging: Consumer, Food Service
Brands:
Night Hawk

9053 **Nikken Foods**
4984 Manchester Ave
St Louis, MO 63110-2010
314-881-5818
Fax: 502-292-3283 nikken@lilar.com
www.nikkenfoods.com
Processor, importer and exporter of soy sauce, fermented soy sauce powders, extracted seafood powders and concentrates and dehydrated mushrooms and oriental vegetables
Manager: Beth James
bethj@nikkenfoods.com
General Manager: Herb Bench
Number Employees: 10-19
Parent Co: Nikkens Foods Company
Type of Packaging: Bulk

9054 **Nikki's Coconut Butter**
Hudson, WI
nikki@nikkiscoconutbutter.com
www.nikkiscoconutbutter.com
Coconut butter spreads and chocolate bars
Owner: Andrew Frezza
Owner/CEO: Nikki Frezza

9055 **Nikki's Cookies**
2018 South 1st St
Milwaukee, WI 53207
414-481-4899
Fax: 414-481-5222 800-776-7107
customerservice@nikkiscookies.com
www.nikkiscookies.com
Processor and exporter of shortbreads and cookies
President: Nikki Taylor
Contact: Bill Danner
billdanner@nikkiscookies.com
Estimated Sales: Less than $500,000
Number Employees: 5-9
Square Footage: 120000
Type of Packaging: Consumer, Food Service
Brands:
English Toffee
Ladybug
Nikki's

9056 **Nikola's Foods**
8301 Grand Ave S
#110
Bloomington, MN 55420
952-229-4183
Fax: 952-253-5995 888-645-6527
sales@nikolasbakery.com www.nikolasbakery.com
A manufacturing and baking company that offers a full line of bakery products including muffins, cakes, dessert breads, cookies, croissants and macaroons; produces gluten free, organic and kosher products.
Director of Development and Innovation: Michael Itskovich
Contact: Gregory Noah
gnoah@nikolasbakery.com
Estimated Sales: $3.5 Million
Number Employees: 12
Type of Packaging: Consumer, Food Service

9057 **Niman Ranch**
1350 S Loop Rd # 102
Suite 120
Alameda, CA 94502-7081
510-995-8041
www.nimanranch.com
Meats
CEO: Jeff Swain
jeff.swain@nimanranch.com
Number Employees: 5-9

9058 **Nimble Nectar**
951-775-9543
info@nimblenectar.com
nimblenectar.com
Cocktail mixers
Co-Founder: Jason Joe
Co-Founder: Julie Joe
Sales: Noelle Arnzen
Brands:
NIMBLE NECTAR

9059 **Nimeks Organics**
52 E Union Blvd
Bethlehem, PA 18017
610-997-0500
Fax: 610-954-9959 www.nimeks.com
Dried fruits and nuts, frozen fruits and vegetables and fruit concentrates and purees

9060 **Nina's Gourmet Dip**
6305 Dunaway Court
Mc Lean, VA 22101-2205
703-356-1667
Fax: 703-356-8488
Gourmet and specialty foods
President: Bill Pournaras

9061 **Ninety Six Canning Company**
109 S Cambridge St
Ninety Six, SC 29666
864-543-2700
Canned barbecued hash
President/Owner: Jerry Gantt
Estimated Sales: $2.6 Million
Number Employees: 4
Type of Packaging: Consumer

9062 **Ninth Avenue Foods**
626-364-8722
steveg@ninthavenuefoods.com
www.ninthavenuefoods.com
Package dairy and nondairy products including flavored milks, protein fortified milks and beverages, organic blends, soy blends, nondairy creamers, nut and flax milk blends.
Director of Operations: Steve Goldenstein
Type of Packaging: Consumer, Private Label

9063 **Nips Potato Chips**
806 Pohukaina St
Honolulu, HI 96813
808-593-8549
donnachang@hotmail.com
Potato chips
CEO: Norman Nip
Estimated Sales: Less than $500,000
Number Employees: 1-4
Brands:
Nip's Potato Chips

9064 **Nirvana Natural Spring Water**
1 Nirvana Plaza
Forestport, NY 13338
315-262-8192
888-463-5675
www.nirvanawater.com
Bottled water

9065 **Nirwana Foods**
778 Newark Ave
Jersey City, NJ 07306
201-659-2200
Fax: 201-659-1260 www.nirwanafoods.com
Spices, almonds, cashews and tea.
President: Jimmy Singh
Brands:
Nirwana

9066 **Nisbet Oyster Company**
7081 Niawaukum St Hwy 101
P.O. Box 338
Bay Center, WA 98527-0338
360-875-6629
Fax: 360-875-6684 888-875-6629
sales@goosepoint.com www.goosepoint.com
Processor and exporter of Pacific and farm oysters; Pacific oyster farm operations; retail and food service products fresh and frozen
President, Owner: David Nisbet
Owner: Maureene Nisbet
Sales Manager: Josh Valdiz
Plant Manager: Kathleen Nisbet
Purchasing: Geoff Clarine
Estimated Sales: $10 Million
Number Employees: 75
Number of Brands: 1
Number of Products: 3
Square Footage: 12800
Brands:
Goose Point Oysters

9067 **Nisshodo Candy Store**
1095 Dillingham Blvd # I-5-109
Bldg I-5
Honolulu, HI 96817-4507
808-847-1244
mhirao@hawaiiantel.net
nisshodomochicandy.com
Candy
Number Employees: 5-9

9068 Nissin Foods USA Co Inc
2001 W Rosecrans Ave
Gardena, CA 90249-2994
310-327-8478
Fax: 323-515-3751 export@nissinfoods.com
www.nissinfoods.com

Asian noodles and noodle soup
President & CEO: Michael Price
b-barrett@mb1.nissinfoods.co.jp
CFO: Roy Shoemaker
Quality Control Director: Melinda Levinsky
VP Marketing: Carla Hunter
VP Sales: Terry McMartin
Human Resources Manager: Katrina Joy
b-barrett@mb1.nissinfoods.co.jp
Manufacturing Director: Mike Kirchner
Plant Manager: Don Babcock
Purchasing Manager: Billie Jo Dangro
Year Founded: 1948
Estimated Sales: $33.2 Million
Number Employees: 500-999
Square Footage: 64391
Parent Co: Nissin Foods USA Company
Type of Packaging: Private Label
Other Locations:
Nissin Foods USA Company
Fort Lee NJ
Brands:
Cup O' Noodles
Oodles of Noodles
Top Ramen

9069 Nissley Vineyards & Winery
140 Vintage Dr
Bainbridge, PA 17502-9357
717-426-3514
Fax: 717-426-1391 800-522-2387
winery@nissley.com www.nissleywine.com

Wine
President: Judith Nissley
winery@nissleywine.com
Vice President: John Nissley
Winemaker: William Gulvin
Estimated Sales: $2.5-5 Million
Number Employees: 10-19
Type of Packaging: Private Label
Brands:
Holiday White
Niagara
Rhapsody In Blue
Topaz
Whisper White

9070 Nita Crisp Crackers LLC
454 S. Link Lane
Fort Collins, CO 80524
970-482-9090
Fax: 970-482-1043 866-493-4609
www.nitacrisp.com
Artisan flatbreats in small batches or in bulk to natural grocers, specialty food stores, and restaurants from coast to coast
Managing Partner: Steve Landry
CEO: Paul Pellegrino
Customer Service / Sales: Michele Hattman
Estimated Sales: $170,000
Number of Products: 1
Square Footage: 5614
Type of Packaging: Consumer, Food Service, Bulk
Brands:
Nita Crisp

9071 Nitta Casings Inc
141 Southside Ave
Bridgewater, NJ 08807-3256
908-218-4400
Fax: 908-725-2835 800-526-3970
info@nittacasings.com www.nittacasings.com
Meat and collagen casings
President & CEO: Rod Moore
Chief Financial Officer: Bruce Zacharias
Operations Manager: David Bensimon
Estimated Sales: $20-50 Million
Number Employees: 250-499

9072 Nitta Gelatin NA
598 Airport Blvd
Suite 900
Morrisville, NC 27560
919-238-3300
Fax: 919-238-3222 800-278-7680
www.nitta-gelatin.com

Gelatin
President: Guergen Gallert
Contact: Jeremy Anderson
j.anderson@nitta-gelatin.com
Office Manager: Tsutomu Takase
General Manager: Jurgen Gallert
Estimated Sales: $2.5-5 Million
Number Employees: 1-4
Parent Co: Nitta Gelatin
Type of Packaging: Bulk
Brands:
Nitta Gelatin

9073 Niutang Chemical, Inc.
5181 Edison Ave
Chino, CA 91710
909-631-2895
Fax: 909-631-2309 sales@niutang.us
www.niutang.com
High-quality food additives and pharmaceutial intermediates including sucralose, aspartame and folic acid
President: Licheng Wang
Owner: Feng Lu
Director Technical & Quality Support: Kerry Kenny
Quality Manager: Sharon Bosch
Contact: Mandy Chen
mandy@niutang.us
Manager/Director: Jie Lin

9074 Nk Hurst Co Inc
230 W Mccarty St
Indianapolis, IN 46225-1234
317-634-6425
Fax: 317-638-1396 800-426-2336
www.nkhurst.com

Processor of dried beans.
President: Rick Hurst
Year Founded: 1938
Estimated Sales: $20-50 Million
Number Employees: 50-99
Number of Brands: 3
Type of Packaging: Consumer, Food Service, Bulk
Brands:
Hurst Family Harvest
Hurst's Brand Dry Beans
Hurst's HamBeens

9075 No Cow
1526 Blake St
Suite 200
Denver, CO 80202
info@nocow.com
nocow.com
Non-dairy bars, butters and cookies
Founder: Daniel Katz
Number of Brands: 1
Number of Products: 3
Brands:
NO COW

9076 No Evil Foods
PO Box 47
Asheville, NC 28801
828-367-1536
preach@noevilfoods.com
www.noevilfoods.com

Vegan plant meats
Co-Founder: Sadrah Schadel
Co-Founder: Mike Woliansky
Number of Brands: 1
Number of Products: 5
Brands:
NO EVIL FOODS

9077 No Pudge! Foods
PO Box 387
Wolfeboro Falls, NH 03896-0387
603-230-9858
Fax: 504-539-5427 888-667-8343
customerservice@nopudge.com
www.nopudge.com

Fat-free brownie mix
Founder/President: Lindsay Frucci
Estimated Sales: $1-2.5 Million
Number Employees: 2
Type of Packaging: Food Service
Brands:
No Pudge

9078 No Whey Foods
170 Oberlin Ave N
Suite 9
Lakewood, NJ 08701-4548
732-806-5218
www.nowheychocolate.com

Nut-free chocolates
Contact: Yochy Miller
Brands:
No Whey Foods

9079 Noble Chocolates NV
Handelsstraat 5
Veurne, 8630
Belgium
contact@noble-chocolates.com
www.noble-chocolates.com

Chocolates, chocolate truffles
Number Employees: 20-49

9080 Noble Popcorn
401 N 13th St
PO Box 157
Sac City, IA 50583
712-662-4728
Fax: 712-662-4797 800-537-9554
info@noblepopcorn.com www.noblepopcorn.com
Popcorn including popped, unpopped and flavored
CFO: Rhonda Lines
Plant Manager: Dan Martin
Estimated Sales: $1-3 Million
Number Employees: 10-19
Square Footage: 32000
Type of Packaging: Consumer, Food Service, Private Label, Bulk
Brands:
Cedar Creek
Noble Popcorn

9081 Nobletree Coffee
499 Van Brunt St
Unit 3A
Brooklyn, NY 11231
718-643-6080
nobletreecoffee.com

Coffee
Managing Director: Eric Taylor
Operations Manager: Nina Nathel
Production Manager: Sky Swartout
Brands:
Nobletree

9082 Nodine's Smokehouse Inc
65 Fowler Ave
PO Box 1787
Torrington, CT 06790-6529
860-489-3309
Fax: 860-496-9787 800-222-2059
nodinesmoke@optonline.com
www.nodinesmokehouse.com
Smoked hams, bacons, chicken, duck, turkey, goose, sausages, fish and cheeses
Owner: Ronald Nodine
VP: Johanne Nodine
Estimated Sales: $3-5 Million
Number Employees: 5-9
Type of Packaging: Consumer, Food Service

9083 Noel Corp
1001 S 3rd St
Yakima, WA 98901-3403
509-248-1313
Fax: 509-248-2843 www.noelcorp.com
Bottled and canned carbonated and noncarbonated beverages; also, bag-in-box juices including orange and apple
President: Rodger Noel
Controller: Martha Barman
VP: Justin Noel
Marketing Executive: Mike Sutton
Manager Sales: William Dalton
IT: Martha Berman
martha@noelcorp.com
Estimated Sales: $42.8 Million
Number Employees: 10-19
Square Footage: 200000
Type of Packaging: Consumer, Food Service, Private Label
Brands:
Dr. Pepper
Noel
Pepsi
Seven-Up

Squirt
Tap Juices

9084 Nog Incorporated
PO Box 162
Dunkirk, NY 14048
716-366-3322
Fax: 716-366-8487 800-332-2664
Ice cream ingredients including coatings, variegates and background flavors
President: Bruce Ritenburg
R&D Director: Bob Habich
Plant Manager: Rick Musso
Estimated Sales: $1-3 Million
Number Employees: 10-19
Square Footage: 96000
Type of Packaging: Bulk

9085 Noh Foods Of Hawaii
2043 S Beretania St # C
Honolulu, HI 96826-1344
808-944-0655
Fax: 808-944-0830 nohfoods@nohfoods.com
www.nohfoods.com
Seasonings and sauces
President: Raymond Noh
nohfoods@nohfoods.com
Estimated Sales: $3.5 Million
Number Employees: 10-19

9086 Nolechek Meats Inc
104 N Washington St
P. O. Box 599
Thorp, WI 54771-9239
715-669-5580
Fax: 715-669-7360 800-454-5580
nolechek@nolechekmeats.com
www.nolechekmeats.com
Smoked meats
Owner: William Nolechek Jr
nolechek@nolechekmeats.com
VP: Kelly Nolechek
Production: Leo Hawkeg
Estimated Sales: $1-3 Million
Number Employees: 5-9

9087 Nomi Snacks
Minneapolis, MN
www.nomisnacks.com
Fresh fruit and oat bars
Co-Founder: Will Handke
Number of Products: 6

9088 Nomolas Corp
999 Central Ave
Woodmere, NY 11598
516-569-3093
Health food
Chairman: Jay Salomon
Number Employees: 2

9089 Nona Lim
3310 Peralta St
Oakland, CA 94608
415-513-5328
www.nonalim.com
Noodle bowls, bone broths and soups
Founder: Nona Lim
Brands:
NONA LIM

9090 Nona Vegan Foods
Toronto, ON
Canada
416-836-9387
info@nonavegan.com
www.nonavegan.com
Dairy free, gluten free, preservative free creamy pasta sauces including alfredo, cheesy, and carbonara styles
Founder: Kailey Gilchrist
Year Founded: 2013

9091 Nonna Pia's Gourmet Sauces
114-1330 Alpha Lake Rd
Whistler, BC V0N 1B1
Canada
604-938-8840
888-372-1534
info@nonnapias.com nonnapias.com
Sauces, seasonings, cooking enhancers, vinegar, salad dressing
President: Natasha Strim
Director Of Sales: Kurt Koegler

9092 Nonni's Foods LLC
3920 E Pine St
Tulsa, OK 74115
918-621-1200
Fax: 918-560-4159 877-295-9604
info@nonnis.com nonnis.com
Biscotti, crackers and cookies
Chief Executive Officer: Brian Hansberry
brianhansberry@nonnis.com
Estimated Sales: $150 Million
Number Employees: 100-249
Number of Brands: 2
Number of Products: 16
Type of Packaging: Private Label
Brands:
Nonni's
THINAddictives

9093 Nonpareil Farms
40 N 400 W
Blackfoot, ID 83221-5632
208-785-5880
Fax: 208-785-3656 800-522-2223
www.greenerfieldstogether.org
Grower of potatoes including potato flakes, hash browns, potato slices, diced potatoes, scalloped & au gratin, mashed potatoes, and flavored potatoes in casseroles and mashed.
CEO: Christopher Abend
Treasurer & Secretary: Ilene Abend
IT: Kent Nelson
knelson@gotspuds.com
Estimated Sales: $46.2 Million
Number Employees: 500-999
Type of Packaging: Consumer

9094 (HQ)Noon Hour Food ProductsInc
215 N Desplaines St # 1
Floor One
Chicago, IL 60661-1072
312-382-1177
Fax: 312-382-9420 800-621-6636
Processor and importer of salted, canned and pickled fish, cheese and groceries
President: Paul Buhl
Executive VP: P Scott Buhl
Marketing Manager: Tyler Swanberg
Operations Manager: William Buhl
Estimated Sales: $6.7 Million
Number Employees: 20-49
Square Footage: 620000
Type of Packaging: Food Service
Other Locations:
Noon Hour Food Products
Minneapolis MN
Brands:
Bond Ost
Briny Deep
De Mill
I Will
Lunds
Noon Hour
Swan
Swan Island
Viking

9095 Noosa Yoghurt
PO Box 403
Bellvue, CO 80512
844-800-4329
info@noosayoghurt.com www.noosayoghurt.com
Australian-style yoghurt
Co-Founder: Koel Thomae
Co-Founder: Rob Graves
Number of Brands: 1
Number of Products: 12
Type of Packaging: Food Service
Brands:
NOOSA

9096 Noosh Brands
4439 Ish Dr
Simi Valley, CA 93063
805-522-5744
nooshbrands.com
Almond protein powder, butter and oil
Brands:
NOOSH

9097 Nootra Life
nootra.com
Probiotic smoothies and juice shots
Number of Brands: 1
Number of Products: 6
Brands:
NOOTRA

9098 Noour Inc.
Huntington Beach, CA
Fax: 818-484-2202 800-621-1378
info@noour.com noour.com
Date sugar, syrup and paste
Number of Brands: 1
Number of Products: 6
Type of Packaging: Bulk
Brands:
ROYAL PALM

9099 Nor-Cliff Farms
888 Barrick Rd.
Port Colborne, ON L3K 6H2
Canada
905-835-0808
Fax: 905-892-4011 sales@norcliff.com
Processor and exporter of fresh, frozen and marinated fiddlehead greens; also, soup mix
President: Nick Secord
Vice President: Nina Dilorenzo Secord

9100 Nor-Tech Dairy Advisors
629 S Minnesota Ave
Sioux Falls, SD 57104-4874
605-338-2404
Fax: 605-338-0439 www.nortechdairy.com
Dairy products marketing and trading
President: Mike Hines
Estimated Sales: $6 Million
Number Employees: 1-4
Type of Packaging: Food Service, Private Label, Bulk
Brands:
Nor-Tech

9101 Nora Snacks
13767 Milroy Place
Santa Fe Springs, CA 90670
562-404-9888
sales@norasnacks.com
www.norasnacks.com
Seaweed snacks
Co-Founder: Itthipat Peeradechapan
Co-Founder: Tim Minges

9102 Nora's Candy Shop
321 N DOXTATOR
Rome, NY 13440
315-337-4530
Fax: 315-339-4054 888-544-8224
customerservice@turkeyjoints.com
www.turkeyjoints.com
Candy and other confectionery products; also chocolate & cocoa products.
Owner: Spero Haritatos
Co-Owner: Sharon Haritatos
Estimated Sales: Less than $500,000
Number Employees: 5-9

9103 Norac Technologies
9110-23 Avenue
Edmonton Research Park
Edmonton, AB T6N 1H9
Canada
780-414-9595
Fax: 780-450-1016
Processor and exporter of spice extracts, egg yolk powder and essential, wheat germ and oat bran oils
President: Tom Evans
VP: Uy Nguyen
Plant Manager: Dan Moser
Number Employees: 10-19
Type of Packaging: Private Label, Bulk
Brands:
Labex
Sc

9104 Norben Co
38052 Euclid Ave # 209
Willoughby, OH 44094-6146
440-951-2715
Fax: 440-951-1366 888-466-7236
sales@norbencompany.com
www.norbencompany.com

Established in 1974. Supplier of chemicals and essential raw materials to the food, pharmaceutical and nutraceutical industries. Distributor of pea protien, pea starch, pea fiber, bamboo fiber, natural and GMO-free ingredients, nautralfibers, micronized products, low carbohydrate formulations, low fat formulations, custom blends, nautral flavor enhancers, probiotic and prebiotic ingredients, and seasoning blends.
President: B J Kresnye
bjkresnye@norbencompany.com
Estimated Sales: $6 Million
Number Employees: 5-9

9105 **Norbest, LLC**
PO Box 890
Moroni, UT 84646
Fax: 888-597-5416 800-453-5327
norbest@norbest.com www.norbest.com
Raw and cooked processed turkey products including roasts and deli breasts, and luncheon meats including ham, pastrami, salami, etc.
President/CEO: Matthew Cook
Year Founded: 1923
Estimated Sales: $100+ Million
Number Employees: 20-49
Type of Packaging: Consumer, Food Service, Private Label, Bulk
Brands:
Norbest

9106 **Nordic Group Inc**
253 Summer St # 203
Boston, MA 02210-1114
617-423-3358
Fax: 617-423-2057 800-486-4002
Processor and importer of fresh and frozen Norwegian seafood including smoked salmon, cod, haddock and fillets
Owner: Salmon Bake
Finance/Administration VP: Joe Mara
Regional Sales Manager: Joe Scharon
sbake@nordicgroupusa.com
Estimated Sales: $500,000-$1 Million
Number Employees: 5-9
Parent Co: Nordic Group ASA
Type of Packaging: Food Service, Bulk
Brands:
Fjord Fresh
Troll

9107 **Nordman Of California**
4070 S Reed Ave
Sanger, CA 93657-9541
559-638-9923
Wines
President: James Hansen
Estimated Sales: $2 000,000
Number Employees: 5-9
Type of Packaging: Bulk
Brands:
Grape Alpho

9108 **Norfolk Hatchery**
1000 East Omaha Avenue
PO Box 132
Norfolk, NE 68702-0132
402-371-5710
Fax: 402-371-5711 800-345-2449
www.norfolkhatchery.com
Poultry. Founded in 1926.
Owner/President: Paula Rasmussen
Estimated Sales: Less than $125,000
Number Employees: 2
Type of Packaging: Bulk

9109 **Norfood Cherry Growers**
383 Consession Rd 14 E
Simcoe, ON M3Y 4K3
Canada
519-426-5784
Fax: 519-426-7838 info@choosecherries.com
www.cherryprocessor.com
Frozen red pitted cherries
President: Drew Schuyler
Director: Marshall Schuyler
Estimated Sales: $500,000-1 Million
Number Employees: 5-9

9110 **Norimoor Lic**
4223 235th St
Flushing, NY 11363-1526
718-423-6667
Fax: 718-423-6668 info@norimoor.com
www.petselixir.com
Nature-made products for health, vitamins and toothpaste.
Owner: Karl Krupka
Estimated Sales: $500,000-$1 Million
Number Employees: 5-9
Brands:
Norimoor
Norivital Vitamins

9111 **Norm's Farms**
200 Washington St
Purdy, MO 65734
417-522-1375
normsfarms.com
Elderberry syrups and extracts

9112 **Norpac Fisheries Inc**
3140 Ualena St # 205
Honolulu, HI 96819-1965
808-528-3474
Fax: 808-537-6880 mjbudke@aol.com
Seafood-Live, fresh, frozen, manufactured
Owner: Michael Budke
mjbudke@aol.com
Estimated Sales: 10-20 Million
Number Employees: 5-9
Brands:
Mikarla's Best

9113 **Norpaco Inc**
80 Bysiewicz Dr
Middletown, CT 06457-7564
860-632-2299
Fax: 860-632-2150 800-252-0222
www.norpaco.com
Manufacturer of Italian-style specialty food products.
Owner: Dean Spilka
dean@norpaco.com
CEO: Donald Spilka
Estimated Sales: F
Number Employees: 1-4
Type of Packaging: Consumer, Private Label, Bulk
Brands:
Norpaco

9114 **North Aire Market, Inc.**
1157 Valley Park Drive
Suite #130
Shakopee, MN 55379-1964
952-496-2887
Fax: 952-496-3444 800-662-3781
sales@northairemarket.com
www.northairemarket.com
Dry soup mixes
Owner: Maggie Mortensen
maggie@northairemarket.com
Estimated Sales: Below $5 Million
Number Employees: 10-19
Type of Packaging: Consumer, Food Service, Private Label
Brands:
North Aire Simmering Soups

9115 **North American BeverageCo**
901 Ocean Ave
Ocean City, NJ 08226-3540
609-399-1486
Fax: 609-399-1506
inquiry@northamericanbeverage.com
www.chocolatemoose.us
High energy, low fat premium chocolate dairy drinks
President: John Imbessi
jcimbesi@aol.com
Controller: Tom Repichi
Estimated Sales: $10-20 Million
Number Employees: 1-4
Brands:
Chocolate Moose
Chocolate Moose Energy
Havana Cappucino
Red Rose Ice
Royal Mandalay Chai
White Chocolate Moose

9116 **North American Blueberry Council**
80 Iron Point Circle
Folsom, CA 95630-8593
916-983-0111
Fax: 916-983-9370 800-824-6395
info@blueberry.org www.nabcblues.org
Blueberry products
Chairman: Dave Arena
Treasurer: Art Galletta
Vice President: Nell Moore
Secretary: Tom Bodtke
Contact: Whitney Mustin
wmustin@nabcblues.org
Executive Director: Mark Villata
Number Employees: 4
Brands:
Blueberry Barbeque Sauce
Harvest Bar
Trader Joe's

9117 **North American Breweries Inc.**
445 Saint Paul St.
Rochester, NY 14605
585-546-1030
www.fifcousa.com
Brewed beer and ale.
CEO: Adrian Lachowski
Year Founded: 2009
Estimated Sales: $120 Million
Number Employees: 1,000-4,999
Parent Co: Florida Ice & Farm Co.
Type of Packaging: Consumer
Other Locations:
Sales & Marketing
Buffalo NY
Brands:
Pura Still
Genesee Brewing
Labatt USA
Cream Ale
Friends Fun Wine
Seagram'S Escapades
Hemptails
Magic Hat Brewing
Pyramid Brewing
Portland Brewing
Honey Brown Lager
Imperial
GBH

9118 **North American Coffees**
1 Cattano Ave
Suite 2
Morriston, NJ 07960
973-359-0300
Fax: 973-359-0440
Coffee, tea
President: Michael Cahill
Estimated Sales: $1-10 Million
Number Employees: 25

9119 **North American Enterprises**
4330 N Campbell Ave Ste 256
Tucson, AZ 85718
520-885-0110
Fax: 520-298-9733 800-817-8666
www.capitanelli.com
Importer/distributor of olive oil, oil, balsamic vinegar, pasta sauces, salad dressings and biscotti; importer of Italian dry pasta and gourmet products
Owner: Joe Lovallo
VP Marketing: Grant Lovallo
National Sales Manager: Tim Champa
Contact: Joe Goodrich
jgoodrich@hazloc.net
Estimated Sales: $10-20 Million
Number Employees: 10-19
Square Footage: 4600
Type of Packaging: Consumer, Food Service
Brands:
Capitanelli Fine Foods
Capitanelli Specialty Foods
Capitanelli's
Loison Panetoni
Rummo Gourmet Imported Pasta

9120 **North American Reishi/Nammex**
PO Box 1780
Gibsons, BC V0N 1V0
Canada
604-886-7799
Fax: 604-648-8954 info@nammex.com
www.nammex.com

Processor and exporter of standardized and certified organic mushroom extracts; also, whole dried mushrooms and mushroom mycelia
President: Jeffrey Chilton
Estimated Sales: $1.2 Million
Number Employees: 6
Type of Packaging: Bulk

9121 North American Water Group
8300 College Boulevard
Overland Park, KS 66210-1841
913-469-1156
Fax: 913-451-9418
Bottled water
President: Roger Hood
COO: Lee Dancer
Estimated Sales: $5-10 000,000
Number Employees: 1

9122 North Atlantic Inc
12 Portland Fish Pier # A
Portland, ME 04101-4620
207-774-6025
Fax: 207-774-1614 www.northatlanticseafood.com
President: Jerry Knecht
jerry@northatlanticseafood.com
Estimated Sales: $10-20 Million
Number Employees: 10-19

9123 North Atlantic Products
232 Buttermilk Ln
South Thomaston, ME 04858-3003
207-596-0331
Fax: 207-596-0532
Seafood

9124 North Atlantic Seafood
12a Portland Fish Pier
PO Box 682
Portland, ME 4101
207-774-6025
800-774-6025
info@northatlanticseafood.com
www.northatlanticseafood.com
Seafood including, bass, flounder, clams, cod, emperor, grouper, haddock, hake, halibut, lobster, mahi mahi, monk, mussels, oysters, perch, pollack, salmon, scallops, seabass, shark, shrimp, snapper, swordfish, tilapia, tuna andsole
Owner and Founder: Gerald Knecht
Chief Executive Officer: Terry Harriman
CFO: Stewart Wooden
VP & General Manager: Michael Norton
Quality Assurance Specialist: Jon Greenberg
Senior Sales Team Leader: Chris Bowker
Shipping/Receiving & Production Lead: Patrick Malia
Director of Procurement: Kevin Bolduc
Number Employees: 10-19

9125 North Bay Fisherman's Cooperative
Wharf Road
RR 4
Ballantyne's Cove, NS B2G 2L2
Canada
902-863-4988
Fax: 902-863-1112
Fresh and frozen lobster, scallops and groundfish; exporter of tuna
Manager: Kim MacDonald
Number Employees: 5-9
Type of Packaging: Consumer, Food Service, Private Label, Bulk

9126 North Bay Produce Inc
1771 N US Highway 31 S
Traverse City, MI 49685-8748
231-946-1941
Fax: 231-946-1902
marketing@northbayproduce.com
www.northbayproduce.com
Cooperative, importer and exporter of fresh produce including apples, asparagus, blueberries, cherries, peaches, plums, snow peas, sugar snaps, mangos, raspberries, blackberries, red currants, etc.; also, apple cider.
President: Mark Girardin
National Marketing Manager: Sharon Robb
Facilities & Compliance Manager: Jonathan Wall
Estimated Sales: $73 Million
Number Employees: 20-49
Number of Brands: 1
Square Footage: 15000
Type of Packaging: Consumer, Food Service, Private Label, Bulk
Other Locations:
North Bay Produce Warehouse
Miami FL
North Bay Produce Warehouse
Mascoutah IL
Brands:
North Bay

9127 North Bay Trading Co
13904 E US Highway 2
Brule, WI 54820-9038
715-372-5031
800-348-0164
borg@cheqnet.net www.northbaytrading.com
Organic and Canadian wild rice, heirloom beans, dehydrated vegetables, dry soup mixes
Owner: Greggar Isaksen
greggar@northbaytrading.com
Estimated Sales: $160,000
Number Employees: 5-9
Number of Brands: 2
Number of Products: 6
Type of Packaging: Consumer, Food Service, Bulk
Brands:
Brule Valley
North Bay Trading Company

9128 North Coast Farms
340 Woodpecker Ridge
Santa Cruz, CA 95060
831-426-3733
Fax: 831-426-5666 www.northcoastfarms.com
Processors of dressings: rasberry vinaigrette, maple dijon vinaigrette and apricot viniagrette, pancake and waffle mixes, wild rice , spices, seasoning, muffins

9129 North Coast Processing
5451 Avenida Encinas
Suite D
Carlsbad, CA 92008
814-725-9617
Fax: 814-725-4374 760-931-6809
info@northcoastphoto.com
www.northcoastphoto.com
Processor and contract packager of salad dressings, sauces, marinades and dry seasonings
President: Richard H Shute
Operations Manager: Tom Barnes
Plant Manager: Wilson Haller
Estimated Sales: $13 Million
Number Employees: 10-19
Square Footage: 50000
Type of Packaging: Consumer, Food Service, Private Label, Bulk
Brands:
Den
Garden Goodness

9130 North Country Natural Spring Water
P.O.Box 123
Port Kent, NY 12911
518-834-9400
Fax: 518-834-9429
Processor and importer of natural spring water
President: Roger Jakubowski
Estimated Sales: $1-3 Million
Number Employees: 10-19
Square Footage: 44000
Type of Packaging: Consumer, Food Service, Private Label, Bulk
Brands:
Loyola Springs
North Country

9131 North Country Smokehouse
471 Sullivan St
Claremont, NH 03743-5147
603-543-0234
Fax: 603-543-3016 800-258-4304
mike@ncsmokehouse.com
www.ncsmokehouse.com
Smoked hams, appelwood bacon, smoked turkey, sausages, chicken and duck, brisket, cheeses and spreads and gifts
Owner: Mike Satzow
mike@ncsmokehouse.com
Estimated Sales: $6 Million
Number Employees: 20-49
Square Footage: 60000
Brands:
North Country Smokehouse

9132 North Dakota Mill & Elevator Assn.
1823 Mill Rd.
Grand Forks, ND 58208-3078
800-538-7721
ndm-store@ndmill.com www.ndmill.com
Flour including semolina, durum, wheat and high-gluten.
President/CEO: Vance Taylor
CFO: Ed Barchenger
Vice President, Grain Procurement: Jeff Bertsch
Vice President, Quality Assurance: Bob Sombke
Vice President, Sales: Russ Bischof
Vice President, Production Operations: Chris Lemoine
Year Founded: 1922
Estimated Sales: $262.66 Million
Number Employees: 100-249
Square Footage: 18000
Type of Packaging: Consumer, Food Service, Private Label, Bulk
Brands:
Dakota Maid

9133 North Lake Fish Cooperative
RR 1
Elmira, PE C0A 1KO
Canada
902-357-2572
Fax: 902-357-2386 www.gov.pe.ca/fard
Processor and exporter of fresh and frozen scallops, skate, silversides and lobster
President: Walter Bruce
CEO/General Manager: Mickey Rose
Number Employees: 100-249
Type of Packaging: Bulk

9134 North Pacific Seafoods Inc
4 Nickerson St
Suite 400
Seattle, WA 98109
206-726-9900
Fax: 206-352-7421
www.northpacificseafoods.com
Wild Alaska seafood products.
President: Hisashi Sugiyama

9135 North Peace Apiaries
RR1 Station Main
Fort St. John, BC V1J 4H5
Canada
250-785-4808
Fax: 250-785-2664
Processor and exporter of honey and bee pollen
President: Ernie Fuhr
Secretary/Treasurer: Rose Fuhr
Estimated Sales: $496,000
Number Employees: 3
Square Footage: 15120
Type of Packaging: Consumer

9136 North River Roasters
8 North Cherry St.
Poughkeepsie, NY 12601
845-418-2739
hello@northriverroasters.com
www.northriverroasters.com
Micro-roasted, small batch fair trade organic whole bean coffee; sourced from Mexico & Peru
Founder/Owner: Feza Oktay
Year Founded: 2015
Number of Brands: 1
Number of Products: 4
Type of Packaging: Consumer, Private Label
Brands:
North River Roasters

9137 North Shore Bottling Co
1900 Linden Blvd
Brooklyn, NY 11207-6806
718-272-8900
Fax: 718-649-2596 www.nsbottle.com
Soft drinks, juices, food, and household items
President: Eric Miller
eric@brooklynbottling.com
VP/General Manager: Tom Deluca
Marketing Director: Karen Miller
Estimated Sales: $20-50 Million
Number Employees: 50-99
Brands:
Ballantine Ale

Country Club Malt Liquor
Gold Crown Lager
Iberia Malt Liquor
Laser Malt Liquor
Pony Malta
Private Stock Malt Liquor
Tornado Malt Liquor

9138 North Taste Flavourings
71 Rte 320
Anse-Bleue, NB E8N 2B7
Canada
506-732-0010
Fax: 506-732-5370 joel.albert@northtaste.ca
www.northtaste.ca
All-natural seafood flavors for soups, bisques, chowders, spreads, dips, sauces, stuffings, and other seafood dishes
President: Julien Albert
Research & Production Manager: Dr. Eric Albert
Quality Control Supervisor: Johanne Doucet
VP Sales & Marketing: Joel Albert
VP US Sales & Product Development: Jerry Levine
Director of Asian Sales: K. Nunokawa
Square Footage: 56000

9139 North West Pharmanaturals Inc
1000 Beacon St
Brea, CA 92821-2938
714-529-0980
Fax: 714-577-0985
Dietary supplements and herbal products in tablet and capsule form; manufacturer of soft gelatin capsule machines and ancillary equipment; also, custom grinding and granulation available
President: Jack Brown
jack@northwestpn.com
Operations Manager: Margaret Haines
Estimated Sales: $$10-20 Million
Number Employees: 10-19
Square Footage: 40000
Type of Packaging: Private Label, Bulk

9140 North of the Border
PO Box 433
Tesuque, NM 87574
505-982-0681
Fax: 505-820-2108 800-860-0681
gaytherg@comcast.net
Salsa, chile sauce, chile seasoning, BBQ/Hot sauce, catchup, and soups
Owner: Gayther Gonzales
Estimated Sales: $.5-1 million
Number Employees: 1-4

9141 Northampton Brewing Company
11 Brewster Ct
Northampton, MA 01060
413-584-9903
Fax: 413-584-9972
info@northamptonbrewery.com
www.northamptonbrewery.com
Beer, ale, lager, stout and seasonal
Manager: Jessica Bellingham
Estimated Sales: Less than $500,000
Number Employees: 50-99
Type of Packaging: Consumer, Food Service
Brands:
Northampton

9142 (HQ)Northeast Foods Inc
601 S Caroline St
Baltimore, MD 21231
800-769-2867
www.nefoods.com
Baked goods
President & CEO: Bill Paterakis
Year Founded: 1965
Number Employees: 100-249

9143 Northeast Kingdom Mustard Company
259 Derby Pond Road
Derby, VT 05829
802-766-2700
Fax: 802-766-2702 866-478-7388
wheeler@jedsmaple.com www.jedsmaple.com
Mustard, chutneys, jalapeno pepper jelly
Co-Owner: Steve Wheeler
Co-Owner: Amy Wheeler
Parent Co: Jed's Maple Products
Type of Packaging: Bulk

9144 Northeastern Products Company
P.O.Box 40
S Plainfield, NJ 07080
908-561-1660
Fax: 908-769-9200
Food flavorings
President: Paul Schiavi
CEO: Doug Connant
Controller: Tom Mathern
Marketing Director: Tina Hatten
Estimated Sales: Below $5 000,000
Number Employees: 50
Brands:
Northeastern

9145 Northern Breweries
Sault Ste.
Marie, ON P3C 4P6
Canada
514-908-7545
Fax: 705-675-2926 info@northernbreweries.com
www.northernbreweries.com
Ale
President: William R Sharp
Manager: James Kaminski
Number Employees: 10-19
Parent Co: Northern Breweries
Type of Packaging: Consumer, Food Service
Brands:
Northern

9146 Northern Dairy
3600 River Rd
Franklin Park, IL 60131-2152
847-671-2697
Dairy
President: Dick Bailey
CEO/Chairman: Howard Dean
VP Finance/CFO: William McManaman
Director Marketing/Advertising: Dave Rotunno
Corporate Purchasing: Jim Merret
Packing Buyer: Marvin Byrd
VP Frozen Desserts: Gary Cates
Parent Co: Dean Foods Company

9147 Northern Discovery Seafoods
E 5051 Grapeview Lp Rd
Grapeview, WA 98546
360-275-7246
Fax: 360-275-7245 800-843-6921
Seafood
President: Natalie Schonberg
VP: Kristian Schonberg
Number Employees: 3

9148 Northern Falls
7667 Spring Point Ct Ne
Rockford, MI 49341-8658
616-915-0970
Bottled water including caffeinated drinking, spring and flavored
Owner: John Neall
Estimated Sales: $1 Million
Number Employees: 25
Type of Packaging: Consumer, Private Label

9149 Northern Farmhouse Pasta LLC
65 Rockland Rd.
Roscoe, NY 12776
607-290-4064
northernfarmhousepasta@gmail.com
www.northernfarmhousepasta.com
Manufacturer of pasta.
Co-Founder: Bob Eckert

9150 Northern Feed & Bean Company
33278 Us Highway 85
Lucerne, CO 80646
970-352-7875
Fax: 970-352-7833 800-316-2326
mail@nfbean.com www.northernfeedandbean.com
Manufacturer and exporter of dried pinto beans
Manager: Larry Lande
Estimated Sales: $4.6 Million
Number Employees: 14
Square Footage: 27048
Type of Packaging: Consumer, Food Service, Private Label
Brands:
Frontier

9151 Northern Flair Foods
3247 Gladstone Ln
Mound, MN 55364
952-472-2444
Fax: 952-472-7444 888-530-4453
markgoldberg@yahoo.com
Gourmet chocolate and candies
President: Mark Goldberg
CEO: Stacy Goldberg
Estimated Sales: $5-10 000,000
Number Employees: 5-9
Brands:
Heavenly Bees
Malto Bella

9152 Northern Keta Caviar
5720 Concrete Way
Juneau, AK 99801-7813
907-586-6095
Fax: 907-586-6094
Salmon caviar
President/CEO: Elisabeth Babich
VP: Sean Fansler
Production Manager: Sean Fansler
Plant Manager: Mark Hiermonymus
Estimated Sales: $1-10 Million
Number Employees: 25

9153 Northern Lights Brewing Company
1701 S Lawson
Airway Heights, WA 99001
509-242-2739
Beer
Owner: Mark Irvin
Head Chef: Lane Truesdell
Estimated Sales: $2.5-5 Million
Number Employees: 5-9
Brands:
Chocolate Dunkel
Crystal Bitter

9154 Northern Meats
163 E 54th Ave
Anchorage, AK 99518-1227
907-561-1729
Fax: 907-561-6848
Meats
President: Jerry Urling
Estimated Sales: $10-20 Million
Number Employees: 1-4

9155 Northern Neck
15725 Kings Highway
Montross, VA 22520
804-493-8051
Fax: 804-493-9109 804-493-8051
www.realgingerale.com
Soft drink bottling
President: John Adams
CEO: Gregory Purcell
Chief Marketing Officer: Charles B Fruit
Public Relations: Arthur Carver
Director Manufacturing: Richard Landon
Estimated Sales: $1-1.7 Million
Number Employees: 18
Brands:
Alive
Aquarious
Carvers Original
Diet Lift
Fanta
Finlay

9156 Northern Ocean Marine
7 Parker St
Gloucester, MA 01930-3025
978-283-0222
Fax: 978-283-5577
Seafood
Owner: Jim Lebouf
Sales & Marketing: Deke Fyrberg
Estimated Sales: $1.4 Million
Number Employees: 5-9

9157 Northern Orcharad Co Inc
537 Union Rd
Peru, NY 12972-4664
518-643-2367
Fax: 518-643-2751 northernorchard@verizon.net
www.northernorchard.com
Wholesaler/distributor, exporter and packer of macintosh apples and honey

President: Albert Mulbury
Contact: Samson Church
schurch@northernorchard.com
Estimated Sales: $1,950,266
Number Employees: 20-49
Type of Packaging: Consumer
Brands:
Champlain Valley

9158 **Northern Packing Company**
2522 Rr 37
Brier Hill, NY 13614
315-375-8801
Fax: 315-375-8273
Packer of fresh and frozen beef
President: John Perretta
Estimated Sales: $3,300,000
Number Employees: 20
Type of Packaging: Consumer

9159 **Northern Products Corporation**
1932 1st Ave
Suite 705
Seattle, WA 98101-1040
206-448-6677
Fax: 206-448-9664 888-599-6290
Processor and exporter of frozen salmon, cod, halibut, flounder, pollock, squid, and rockfish
President: William Dignon
Plant Manager: Terry Barry
Estimated Sales: $1-3 Million
Number Employees: 1-4
Type of Packaging: Private Label, Bulk

9160 **Northern Soy Inc**
345 Paul Rd
Rochester, NY 14624-4925
585-235-8970
Fax: 585-235-3753 info@soyboy.com
www.soyboy.com
All-natural organic tofu, organic tempeh and soy products
President: Norman Holland
norman@soyboy.com
Vice President: Andrew Schecter
Estimated Sales: $5-10 Million
Number Employees: 20-49
Number of Brands: 1
Number of Products: 24
Square Footage: 140000
Type of Packaging: Consumer, Food Service, Private Label, Bulk
Brands:
Leaner Wiener
Not Dogs
Soyboy
Tofu Lin

9161 **Northern Utah Manufacturing**
185 E 300 N
Wellsville, UT 84339
435-245-4542
Fax: 435-245-4542
Dry milk
Manager: David Bigelow
Estimated Sales: $2.5-5 Million
Number Employees: 20-49

9162 **Northern Valley Baking Co**
47 E Madison Ave
Dumont, NJ 07628-2417
201-338-2812
Fax: 201-338-2812 info@nvbaking.com
Manufacturer of macaroons and g'nache.
Co-Founder: Tricia Vanech
Co-Founder: Elyse Pressner
Co-Founder: Eve Megerle
Estimated Sales: Less Than $500,000
Number Employees: 1-4

9163 **Northern Vineyards Winery**
223 Main St N
Stillwater, MN 55082-5021
651-430-1032
Fax: 651-430-1331 info@northernvineyards.com
www.northernvineyards.com
Wines
Manager: Cassie Pittman
VP: Ray Kenow
Manager: Robin Partch
robin@northernvineyards.com
Estimated Sales: Less than $500,000
Number Employees: 5-9
Type of Packaging: Private Label
Brands:
Northern Vineyards

9164 **Northern WIS Produce Co**
1310 Clark St
Manitowoc, WI 54220-5109
920-684-4461
Fax: 920-684-4471
Cheese
Owner: Dave Litterman
Estimated Sales: $1-3 000,000
Number Employees: 10-19
Brands:
Northern Wisconsin Cheese

9165 **Northern Wind Inc**
16 Hassey St
New Bedford, MA 02740-7209
508-997-0727
Fax: 508-990-8792 888-525-2525
www.northernwind.com
Processor and exporter of fresh and frozen seafoods including; bay and sea scallops, farm-raised chilean mussels, farm-raised chilean atlantic salmon, hard shell north atlantic lobsters, monkfish, skate
Owner: Colleen Avila
CEO: Ken Melanson
VP: Betsy Borba
Sales Manager: Rick Moreno
sma1217@aol.com
Plant Manager: Michael Fernandes
Estimated Sales: $15.3 Million
Number Employees: 50-99
Number of Brands: 3
Number of Products: 3
Type of Packaging: Food Service, Private Label, Bulk
Brands:
Captain's Call
Mariner's Choice
Ocean Request
Sea Spray
Bon Cuisine

9166 **Northland Cranberries**
20701 Main Street
Jackson, WI 53037
262-677-2221
Fax: 262-677-3647 866-719-5215
www.northlandjuices.com
Fruit juices
Chairman/CEO: John Swendrowski
Plant Supervisor: Dave Carroll
Number Employees: 100-249
Square Footage: 768000
Type of Packaging: Consumer, Food Service, Private Label
Brands:
Northland

9167 **(HQ)Northland Juices**
2 Seaview Blvd.
Port Washington, NY 11050
608-252-4714
Fax: 715-422-6800 866-719-5215
www.northlandjuices.com
Fruit juice, juice concentrate, fresh and fozen
Chairman/CEO/Treasurer: John Swendrowski
President/COO: Ricke Kress
Number Employees: 218
Number of Brands: 5
Number of Products: 250
Type of Packaging: Consumer, Food Service, Bulk
Other Locations:
Northland Cranberries
Jackson WI
Northland Cranberries
Dundee NY
Northland Cranberries
Cornelius OR
Northland Cranberries
Wisconsin Rapids WI
Brands:
Awake
Meadow Valley
Northland
Seneca
Treesweet

9168 **Northridge Laboratories**
20832 Dearborn St
Chatsworth, CA 91311
818-882-5622
Fax: 818-998-2815
Processor and exporter of vitamins, herbal supplements and protein powders
President: Brett Richman
CEO: Jane Richman
CFO: Charles Wands
Contact: Angie Armendariz
nrlabs@aol.com
Estimated Sales: $6400000
Number Employees: 50
Square Footage: 120000
Type of Packaging: Private Label

9169 **Northside Bakery**
149 N 8th St
Brooklyn, NY 11249-2001
718-782-2700
Fax: 718-782-7146
Breads and other baked goods
Owner: Richard Podedworny
info@oldpolandfoods.com
Co-Owner: Michael Hatcher
Estimated Sales: $480,000
Number Employees: 10-19

9170 **Northumberland Dairy**
256 Lawlor Lane
Miramichi, NB E1V 3M3
Canada
506-627-7720
800-501-1150
info@northumberlanddairy.ca
www.northumberlanddairy.ca
Dairy products including milk and cream; wholesaler/distributor of bottled water, ice cream, ice milk mix, fruit drinks and butter; serving the food service market
Director, Sales & Marketing: Paul Chiasson
Year Founded: 1942
Estimated Sales: $50 Million
Number Employees: 273
Number of Brands: 5
Square Footage: 79416
Parent Co: Agropur Dairy Co-Operative
Type of Packaging: Consumer, Food Service, Private Label
Brands:
Frontier Water
Jumbo Minisips
Max Cranberry Cocktail
Northshore Butter
Northumberland

9171 **(HQ)Northville Winery & Brewing Co**
630 Baseline Rd
Northville, MI 48167-1265
248-320-6507
Fax: 248-349-1165 northvillewinery@gmail.com
www.northvillewinery.com
Producer of ciders, wines and beers.
President: Diane Jones
Vice President: Cheryl Nelson
Estimated Sales: $180 Thousand
Number Employees: 1-4
Number of Brands: 1
Parent Co: Parmenter's Northville Cider Mill
Type of Packaging: Consumer, Food Service
Brands:
Northville Winery

9172 **Northwest Chocolate Factory**
2162 Davcor Street SE
Salem, OR 97302-1510
503-362-1340
Fax: 503-362-0186 www.nwchocolate.com
Processor and exporter of chocolate covered hazelnuts
President: Sam Kaufman
General Manager: Dan Kaufman
Number Employees: 5-9
Square Footage: 40000
Type of Packaging: Consumer

9173 **Northwest Fisheries**
RR 1
Hubbards, NS B0J 1T0
Canada
902-228-2232
Fax: 902-228-2116
Processor and exporter of fresh lobster, cod and halibut
President: Olimpio Martins
Number Employees: 5-9

Type of Packaging: Consumer, Food Service, Private Label, Bulk

9174 Northwest Hazelnut Company
19748 Highway 99e
P.O.Box 276
Hubbard, OR 97032
503-982-8030
Fax: 503-982-8028
Vacuum-packed hazelnuts
President: Jeff Kenagy
Vice President: Lisa Pascoe
Contact: Verne Gingerich
verne.gingerich@nwhazelnut.com
Estimated Sales: $5-10 Million
Number Employees: 4
Type of Packaging: Consumer, Food Service, Private Label
Brands:
Springhill

9175 Northwest Meat Company
440 N Morgan St
Chicago, IL 60642
312-733-1418
Fax: 312-733-1737
andrew@chicagowholesalemeats.com
www.chicagowholesalemeats.com
Beef, poultry, pork, veal, and lamb.
Owner: Stan Neva
Co-Owner: Lori Neva
Assistant/Office Manager: Audrey Ciota
Number Employees: 10-19

9176 Northwest Natural Foods
3805 56th Ave Ne
Olympia, WA 98506
360-866-9661
Fax: 360-866-0734
www.northwestnaturalfoods.com
Fresh and frozen fish/seafood
Owner: Gene Maltziffs
President: Euegene Maltzess
Contact: Eugene Maltzeff
eugene.maltzeff@nwnatural.com
Estimated Sales: $300,000
Number Employees: 8
Square Footage: 20000
Type of Packaging: Private Label
Brands:
Medallions

9177 Northwest Naturals LLC
11805 N Creek Pkwy S # 104
Bothell, WA 98011-8803
425-881-2200
Fax: 425-881-3063 nwn@nwnaturals.com
www.nwnaturals.com
Processor, importer and exporter of concentrates including juice and iced coffee and fruit beverages and flavors
Vice President: Mike Marquand
mikem@nwnaturals.com
CEO: James
VP Sales and Administration: Mike Marquand
VP Operations: Danny Shaffer
Estimated Sales: $5-10 Million
Number Employees: 20-49
Number of Brands: 4
Number of Products: 50
Square Footage: 120000
Parent Co: Tree Top
Type of Packaging: Consumer, Food Service, Private Label, Bulk

9178 Northwest Packing Co
1701 W 16th St
PO Box 30
Vancouver, WA 98660-1067
360-696-4356
Fax: 831-637-7890 800-543-4356
www.neiljonesfoodcompany.com
Tomato products including ketchup, paste, sauce, stewed and cooked
President/COO: Matt Jones
CEO: L Neil Jones
Sales: David Watkins
Plant Manager: Mike Mullin
Estimated Sales: $20-50 Million
Number Employees: 100-249
Parent Co: Northwest Packing
Type of Packaging: Consumer, Food Service, Private Label, Bulk

Brands:
San Benito

9179 Northwest Pea & Bean Co
6109 E Desmet Ave
Spokane Valley, WA 99212-1254
509-534-3821
Fax: 509-534-4350
Processor of lentils and green and yellow peas.
Manager: Brett Stauffer
Logistics Coordinator: Tim Kochel
Estimated Sales: $32 Million
Number Employees: 10-19
Number of Brands: 2
Parent Co: Cooperative Agricultural Producers
Type of Packaging: Food Service, Private Label, Bulk
Brands:
Empire
Speedy Cook'n

9180 Northwest Wild Products
354 Industry St.
Astoria, OR 97103
503-791-1907
amanda@northwestwildproducts.com
www.northwestwildproducts.com
Seafood including oysters, Dungeness crab, live lobster, Manila clams, Chinook salmon, coho salmon, wild sturgeon, razor clams, albacore tuna, ling cod, black cod, halibut, crayfish, dover sole, shrimp, scallops, sardines, mackeralanchovies, squid, mussels, and red snapper; Also exotic meats
Co-Owner: Amanda Cordero
Co-Owner: Ron Neva
Number Employees: 1-4

9181 Northwestern Coffee Mills
20146 Soderlund Rd
Mason, WI 54856-6300
715-746-2100
Fax: 715 747 5405 800-243-5283
sales@northwesterncoffeemills.com
www.northwesterncoffeemills.com
Coffee, tea, spices
President: Harry Demorest
Estimated Sales: Less Than $500,000
Number Employees: 1-4
Type of Packaging: Private Label
Brands:
American Breakfast Blend
Apostle Islands Organic Coffee
Brazil Serra Negra
Ice Road Blend-Darkest
North Coast Tea & Sp
Northwestern Coffee

9182 Northwestern Coffee Mills
30950 Nevers Rd
Washburn, WI 54891
715-373-2122
Fax: 715-747-5405 800-243-5283
Processor, importer and exporter of coffee and tea
Owner: Harry Demorest
Estimated Sales: Under $300,000
Number Employees: 1-4
Square Footage: 8000
Type of Packaging: Consumer, Food Service
Brands:
American Breakfast Blend
Backsettler Blend
Badger Blend
Baker's Blend
Broadway Red
Fancy Dinner Blend
Ice Road
Island Blend
Morning Sun
North Coast
Orange Rose
Sleepeasy
Stapleton

9183 Northwestern Extract
W194n11250 Mccormick Dr # 1
Germantown, WI 53022-3049
262-345-6900
Fax: 262-781-0660 800-466-3034
flavors@nwextract.com
www.northwesternextract.com
Flavorings and extracts

President: William Peter
CEO: Megan Bruzan
megan@nwextract.com
Marketing Director: Patricia Hein
Purchasing Manager: Michael Peter
Estimated Sales: $5-10 Million
Number Employees: 10-19
Square Footage: 40000
Type of Packaging: Consumer, Food Service, Private Label, Bulk
Brands:
Northwestern
Sparkle

9184 Northwestern Foods
1260 Grey Fox Road
Arden Hills, MN 55112
651-644-8060
Fax: 651-644-8248 800-236-4937
northwestern.n2ocompanies.com
Mixes including cocoa, cake, pancake, cappuccino, iced tea, power drinks and pizza dough
President: Kurt Kiaser
CEO: Bob Schafer
Vice President: Mimie Pollard
Sales Manager: Bob Freemore
Contact: Linda Petersen
lpetersen@n2ocompanies.com
Purchasing Manager: Nadine Vandeventer
Estimated Sales: $10-20 Million
Number Employees: 20-49
Square Footage: 48000
Type of Packaging: Consumer, Food Service, Private Label, Bulk

9185 Northwoods Candy Emporium
103 Branson Landing Blvd
Branson, MO 65616-2097
417-332-1010
info@northwoodscandy.com
www.northwoodscandy.com
Gourmet candy and cookies
Owner: Dennis Anderson
Production Manager: Al Hyde
Number Employees: 5-9
Brands:
Espress-Umms
Grandma's Recipe
Northwest Espresso B

9186 Norwalk Dairy
13101 Rosecrans Ave
Santa Fe Springs, CA 90670
562-921-5712
Fax: 562-921-5573
Milk including whole, kosher, reduced, nonfat and chocolate
VP: Tanya Vanderham
President: John Vanderham
Estimated Sales: $500,000-$1,000,000
Number Employees: 5-9
Type of Packaging: Consumer, Food Service
Brands:
Norwalk Dairy

9187 Nossack Fine Meats
7240 Johnstone Dr
Suite 100
Red Deer, AB T4P 3Y6
Canada
403-346-5006
Fax: 403-343-8066 www.nossack.com
Roast and corned beef, pastrami, sausage and ham; also, garlic rings and pizza products
President: Karsten Nossack
Manager of Finance: Ingrid Nossack
Estimated Sales: $27 Million
Number Employees: 70
Square Footage: 22000
Type of Packaging: Consumer, Food Service
Brands:
Butcher's Pride
Nossack

9188 Nostalgic Specialty Foods
399 S Federal Hwy
Boca Raton, FL 33432
561-391-8600
Gourmet and specialty foods
Owner: Leonard Felberbaum
Estimated Sales: $330,000
Number Employees: 6

9189 **Nothin' But Foods**
9 Bourmar Place
Elmwood Park, NJ 07407
203-557-8637
info@nothinbutfoods.com
www.nothinbutfoods.com
Snack bars and granola cookies.
Founder: Jerri Graham

9190 **Nothing But The Fruit**
300 Baker Ave
Suite 101
Concord, MA 01742-2131
978-341-1221
Fruit bites and fruit jerky
Brand Assistant: Olivia Dynan
Number of Brands: 1
Number of Products: 10
Brands:
NOTHING BUT THE FRUIT

9191 **Notre Dame Bakery**
26 Wildwood Subdiv
Conception Harbour, NL A1X 7J8
Canada
709-535-2738
Fax: 709-535-3406
Bread products, pies, cookies and muffins
President: John Mullett
Owner: Larry Mullett
Owner/Sales: Paula Mullett
CEO: John Mullett
Estimated Sales: $531,000
Number Employees: 8
Brands:
Humpty Dumpty Chips
Nestle Chocolates

9192 **Notre Dame Seafoods Inc.**
PO Box 201
Comfort Cove, NL A0G 3K0
Canada
709-244-5511
Fax: 709-244-3451
jeveleigh@notredameseafoods.com
www.notredameseafoods.com
Processor and exporter of canned and frozen crab, cod, turbit, capelin, squid, mackerel, lumpfish, roe and lobster
President & COO: Jason Eveleigh
VP/General Manager: Rex Eveleigh
Number Employees: 250-499
Parent Co: Provincial Investments
Type of Packaging: Consumer, Food Service

9193 **Nourishtea**
222 Islington Ave
Suite 6C
Toronto, ON M8V 3W7
Canada
416-539-9299
info@nourishtea.ca
www.nourishtea.ca
Herbal tea, black tea, green tea
Year Founded: 2007

9194 **Nouveau Foods**
Mountain View, CA
www.lotuspops.com
Flavored, roasted lotus seeds
Number of Brands: 1
Number of Products: 6
Brands:
LOTUS POPS

9195 **Novozymes North America Inc**
77 Perrys Chapel Church Rd
Franklinton, NC 27525-9677
919-494-3000
Fax: 919-494-3450 800-879-6686
enzymesna@novozymes.com
www.novozymes.com
Enzymes
President: Adam Monroe
ad@novozymes.com
EVP & CFO: Benny Loft
EVP & CSO: Per Falholt
Director Purchasing: Percy Taylor
Estimated Sales: $40 Million
Number Employees: 1000-4999
Parent Co: Novozymes
Type of Packaging: Bulk

9196 **Now & Zen**
908 Main St
Suite 130
Louisville, CO 80027-1867
720-508-3945
Fax: 303-530-6945 800-779-6383
www.now-zen.com
Whipped toppings including dairy-free, gluten-free and chocolate; also, vegan cookies, cakes, vegetarian turkey, steak, chicken and barbecue ribs
Founder & President: Steve McIntosh
Sales Director: Judy Stoffel
Operations Manager: Eleese Longino
Number Employees: 1-4
Number of Brands: 1
Number of Products: 15
Type of Packaging: Consumer, Food Service, Bulk
Brands:
Bbq Unribs
Chocolate Mousse Hip
Hip Whip
Unsteak-Out
Unturkey

9197 **Noyes, P J**
89 Bridge St
Lancaster, NH 03584-3103
603-788-2848
Fax: 603-788-3873 800-522-2469
Liquids, tablets and capsules
President: David Hill
Quality Control Manager: Janet Christenson
Marketing Executive: Jim Hoverman
Sales/Marketing Manager: Jennifer Cusick
Contact: Alan Balog
alanb@pjnoyes.com
VP/COO: Dennis Wogaman
Production Manager: Steve Skinner
Estimated Sales: $10 Million
Number Employees: 5-9
Square Footage: 70000
Type of Packaging: Private Label, Bulk
Brands:
Fishin' Chips
Noyes Precision

9198 **Nspired Natural Foods**
4600 Sleepytime Dr
Boulder, CO 80301
800-434-4246
Dried fruits, nuts and trail mixes
Chairman: Charles Lynch
CEO: Gordon Chapple
Number Employees: 5-9
Square Footage: 40000
Other Locations:
Nspired Natural Foods
Melville NY

9199 **Ntc Marketing**
5680 Main St
Williamsville, NY 14221-5518
716-884-3345
Fax: 716-884-4680 800-333-1637
info@ntcmarketing.com
Processor and importer of canned products including pineapples, pineapple juice, tropical fruits, tropical fruit mix, mandarin orange
Owner/Principal: Michael Derose
mjderose@ntcmarketing.com
Human Resource Executive: Sue Godzala
Estimated Sales: $3.3 Million
Number Employees: 10-19
Square Footage: 40000
Type of Packaging: Consumer, Food Service, Private Label, Bulk
Brands:
Libby's
P/L
Queen's Pride

9200 **Nu Life Market**
PO Box 105
Scott City, KS 67871
620-872-5236
Fax: 620-872-5019 866-962-5236
nulifemarket.com
Gluten-free sorghum flours, brans and grains
President/Owner: Earl Roemer
CFO: Kelsey Baker
VP, Sales & Marketing: Joshua Deschenes
Number of Brands: 1
Number of Products: 39
Brands:
NU LIFE MARKET

9201 **Nu Naturals Inc**
2220 W 2nd Ave
Suite 1
Eugene, OR 97402-7112
541-344-9785
Fax: 541-343-0915 800-753-4372
info@nunaturals.com www.nunaturals.com
Health products including diet nutrients, odorless garlic, vitamins, minerals, amino acids, green tea, herbs, extracts, etc.
Owner & CEO: Warren Sablosky
warren@nunaturals.com
Estimated Sales: $6+ Million
Number of Brands: 17
Number of Products: 78
Square Footage: 32000
Type of Packaging: Consumer, Private Label, Bulk
Brands:
Alcohol Free Stevia
Brain Herbs
Brain Well
Calm Mind
Clear Stevia
Daily Energy
Daily Soy
Extra Energy
Fast Asleep
Gentle Change
Joint Well
Level Right
Losweet
Mellowmind
Mental Energy Formula
Preventin Green Tea
Sweet 'n Healthy
Sweet-X
Throat Control Spray
Travel Well
Wellness Drops
White Stevia

9202 **Nu Products Co Inc**
74 Louis Ct
South Hackensack, NJ 07606-1727
201-440-0065
Fax: 201-440-0096 800-836-7692
spice@aol.com www.nuproductsseasoning.com
Suppliers of food seasonings
Owner: Henry Goldstein
sirspice@aol.com
Marketing Director: Jim Sandler
CFO: Celia Hester
Estimated Sales: Below $5 Million
Number Employees: 20-49
Type of Packaging: Bulk
Brands:
Nu

9203 **Nu-Tek Food Science**
5400 Opportunity Ct
Suite 120
Minnetouka, MN 55343
952-683-7580
Fax: 952-933-1396 info@nu-tekfoodscience.com
www.nu-tekfoodscience.com
Potassium chloride based sodium reduction products used for meat, cheese, poultry, bakery, snack foods, soups, sauces, gravies and spice blends. Salt reductions of 25-50%
President: Tom Yezzi
Director of Accounts Receivable/Payable: Kent McCoy
Director of Quality & Technical: Dustin Grossbier
Sr Director of Sales: John Musselman
Sr VP of Sales & Marketing: Dave Hickey
Contact: Dan Hagebak
dhagebak@nu-tekfoodscience.com
Sales Coordinator: Rob Manuel

9204 **Nu-Way Potato Products**
25 Colville Road
North York, ON M6M 2Y2
Canada
416-241-9151
Fax: 416-241-8274 joe@nuwaypotato.com
www.nuwaypotato.com
Fresh potatoes
President: Mike Sangiorgio
Office Manager: Nelson Ardon
Marketing Manager: Joe Montalbano
Office Manager: Nelson Ardon

Estimated Sales: $15 Million
Number Employees: 35
Type of Packaging: Consumer, Food Service

9205 Nu-World Amaranth Inc
552 S Washington St # 120
Suite #107
Naperville, IL 60540-6669
630-369-6851
Fax: 630-369-6851
customerservice@nuworldfoods.com
Manufacturer and exporter of amaranth-based products including popped, flour, pre-baked flat bread, sancks and cereal. Offers foods that are allergy free and gluten free foods
Founder/Co-Owner: Larry Walters
President: Susan Walters-Flood
CFO: Jim Behling
Vice President: Terry Walters
t.walters@nuworldamaranthinc.com
Manager/Co-Owner: Diane Walters
VP Production: Terry Walters
Estimated Sales: Under $500,000
Number Employees: 10-19
Number of Brands: 2
Number of Products: 15
Square Footage: 10800
Type of Packaging: Consumer, Private Label, Bulk
Brands:
Nu-World Amaranth

9206 Nu-World Foods
552 S Washington Street
Suite 107
Naperville, IL 60540
630-369-6819
Fax: 630-369-6851 877-692-8899
Amaranth-based food products
Contact: Marissa Kopp
marissa@nuworldfoods.com

9207 NuGo Nutrition
520 Second St
Oakmont, PA 15139
412-828-4115
888-421-2032
www.nugonutrition.com
Dark chocolate-coated protein bars
President/Owner: David Levine
dlevine@nugonutrition.com
VP: Steven Smith
Director of Marketing: Alyssa Nard
Estimated Sales: $1.3 Million
Number Employees: 5-9
Type of Packaging: Consumer

9208 NuLeaf Naturals
1550 Larimer St
Suite 964
Denver, CO 80202
720-372-4842
contact@nuleafnaturals.com
nuleafnaturals.com
Organic CBD oil
President/Owner: Jaden Barnes
Year Founded: 2014

9209 NuNaturals
2220 West 2nd Ave
Eugene, OR 97402
Fax: 541-683-5268 800-753-4372
support@nunaturals.com www.nunaturals.com
Stevia sweeteners, baking goods and collagens
President/Owner: Jake Sablosky
Founder & CEO: Warren Sablosky
General Manager: Travis DeBacker
Number of Brands: 1
Brands:
NUNATURALS

9210 NuPasta
55 Valleywood Dr
Markham, ON L3R 5L9
Canada
855-910-8800
www.nupasta.com
Konjac-based, gluten-free pasta
President/Owner: Stephen Cheung
Number of Brands: 1
Number of Products: 6
Brands:
NUPASTA

9211 NuZee, Inc.
2865 Scott St
Suite 107
Vista, CA 92081
844-696-8933
coffeeblenders.com
Functional coffee beverages
President/Owner: Travis Gorney
Type of Packaging: Private Label
Brands:
Coffee Blenders

9212 Nuchief Sales Inc
2710 Euclid Ave
Wenatchee, WA 98801-5914
509-663-2625
Fax: 509-662-0299 888-269-4638
nuchief@nwi.net
Grower, packer and exporter of apples and pears
President: Randy Steensma
randy@honeybear-nuchief.com
VP: Dave Battis
Quality Control: Ray Vespier
Sales: Joe Defina
Estimated Sales: $279.000
Number Employees: 5-9
Number of Brands: 5
Number of Products: 10
Type of Packaging: Consumer, Food Service
Brands:
Big Check
Crane & Crane
Keystone

9213 Nueces Canyon Range
9501 Highway 290 W
Brenham, TX 77833-9138
979-289-5600
Fax: 979-289-2411 800-925-5058
nueces@nuecescanyon.com
www.nuecescanyon.com
Smoked meats including briskets, hams, quail, etc., also meat seasonings
Owner: Angele Caloudas
nueces@nuecescanyon.com
Estimated Sales: Less Than $500,000
Number Employees: 5-9
Square Footage: 40000
Parent Co: Nueces Canyon Ranch
Type of Packaging: Consumer, Food Service

9214 Nueske's Applewood Smoked Meat
203 N Genesee St
Wittenberg, WI 54499-9154
715-253-4000
Fax: 715-253-4021 800-720-1153
nueske@nueske.com www.nueskes.com
Smoked meats including bacon, ham, sausage and specialty items
President: Robert Nueske
Cmo: Gilbert Thompson
gthompson@nueske.com
VP: James Nueske
Marketing: Tanya Nueske
Number Employees: 100-249

9215 Nui Foods
112 E Orangethorpe Ave
Anaheim, CA 92801
support@eatnui.com
www.eatnui.com
Low carb, low sugar cookies
Co-Founder: Victor Macias
Co-Founder/CEO: Kristoffer Quiaoit
Research & Development Manager: Juan Altamirano
Marketing Manager: Valerie Bui
Year Founded: 2016

9216 Nulaid Foods Inc
200 W 5th St
Ripon, CA 95366-2793
209-599-2121
Fax: 209-599-5220 www.nulaid.com
Egg products
President: David Crockett
CEO: Christopher Barry
cbarry@bainbridge.com
CFO: Scott Hennecke
Number Employees: 50-99
Type of Packaging: Consumer, Food Service, Private Label, Bulk
Brands:
Nulaid

9217 Numi Organic Tea
PO Box 20420
Oakland, CA 94620
888-404-6864
info@numitea.com www.numitea.com
Tea
Co-Founder & Chief Brand Officer: Reem Rahim
Co-Founder & CEO: Ahmed Rahim
Brands:
Numi(c)

9218 Numo Broth
1630 Oakland Rd
Unit A110
San Jose, CA 95131
nulifemarket.com
Brew-it-yourself bone broth kits
Founder: Faye Luong
Number of Brands: 1
Number of Products: 2
Brands:
NUMO BROTH

9219 Nunes Co Inc
930 Johnson Ave
Salinas, CA 93901
831-751-7500
Fax: 831-424-4955 employment@foxy.com
www.foxy.com
Grower and exporter of vegetables
Owner: Susan Canales
CFO: Mike Scarr
VP: David Nunes
VP Marketing: Matt Seeley
VP Sales: Mark Crossgrove
scanales@foxyproduce.com
Production Manager: Jim Nunes
Estimated Sales: $11,100,000
Number Employees: 100-249
Type of Packaging: Consumer, Food Service, Bulk
Brands:
Foxy
Nunes
Tubby

9220 Nunes Farms Marketing
4012 Pete Miller Rd
Gustine, CA 95322-9507
209-862-3033
Fax: 209-862-1038 www.nunesfarms.com
Processor and exporter of roasted almonds, mixed nuts and pistachios. candies toffee caramel chews, chocolate almonds and toffee almonds
Owner: Maureen Nunes
maureen@nunesfarms.com
Estimated Sales: Under $500,000
Number Employees: 10-19
Brands:
Almond Chews
California Crunchies
Caramel Chews
Chocolate Toffee Almonds
Foxy Salads

9221 Nuovo Pasta ProductionsLTD
125 Bruce Ave
Stratford, CT 06615-6102
203-380-4090
Fax: 203-336-0656 800-803-0033
www.nuovopasta.com
Frozen and fresh ravioli, tortelloni, gnocchi, pasta, and pasta sauces
President: Carl Zuanelli
CFO: Santa Vega
Marketing: Larry Montuori
Contact: Franco Dibattista
franco@nuovopasta.com
Production: Joe Dubee
Estimated Sales: Less Than $500,000
Number Employees: 5-9
Type of Packaging: Consumer, Food Service

9222 Nurture
28 S Waterloo Rd
Devon, PA 19333-1574
610-293-0718
Fax: 610-989-0991 888-395-3300
Ingredients for nutritional products
President: H Griffith
Contact: Sarah Mazzone
sarah@happyfamilybrands.com

Estimated Sales: $1,800,000
Number Employees: 5-9
Brands:
Nurture

9223 **Nurture Ranch**
2770 Main St
Suite 234
Frisco, TX 75033
866-467-2624
www.nurtureranch.com
Grass-fed ground beef, sirloin and jerky
CEO: Rodney Mason

9224 **Nush Foods**
333 W Hope Ave
Salt Lake City, UT 84115
801-953-1370
contact@nushfoods.com
nushfoods.com
Keto-friendly snack cakes
Founder: Muffy Mead-Ferro
Number of Brands: 1
Number of Products: 3
Brands:
NUSH

9225 **Nustef Foods**
2440 Cawthra Road #101
Mississauga, ON L5A 2X1
Canada
905-896-3060
Fax: 905-896-4349 877-306-7562
info@pizzellecookies.com
Processor and exporter of pizzelle cookies and polenta
President: Cesidio Nucci
Estimated Sales: $4 Million
Number Employees: 60
Square Footage: 48000
Type of Packaging: Consumer, Food Service, Private Label, Bulk
Brands:
Gold'n Polenta
Gold'n Treats
Reko

9226 **Nut Factory**
PO Box 815
Spokane Valley, WA 99016-0815
509-926-6666
Fax: 509-926-3300 888-239-5288
nuts@TheNutFactory.com www.thenutfactory.com
Processor, packager and importer of nuts and dried fruits
President: Gene Cohen
gene_cohen@yahoo.com
Estimated Sales: $1700000
Number Employees: 5-9
Type of Packaging: Consumer
Brands:
Big Value
Old Fashioned
Party Pak
Sunburst

9227 **NutRaw Foods**
Delano, CA
info@nutrawbar.com
www.nutrawfarms.com
Pistachio nut bars, oils and butters
Number of Brands: 1
Number of Products: 14
Brands:
NUTRAWBAR
NUTRAW SNACKS
NUTRAW BUTTER
NUTRAW OIL

9228 **Nutfield Brewing Company**
P.O.Box 40
Derry, NH 03038
603-434-9678
Fax: 603-434-1042
Ale, lager and stout
President: Jim Killeen
Sales Manager: Geoff Tyson
Estimated Sales: Below $5 Million
Number Employees: 5-9
Type of Packaging: Consumer, Food Service
Brands:
Nutfield Auburn Ale
Nutfield's Classic Root Beer

9229 **Nutiva**
213 West Cutting Blvd
Richmond, CA 94804
800-993-4367
help@nutiva.com
nutiva.com
Oils, baking ingredients, seeds and spreads
Founder: John Roulac
CEO: Steven Naccarato
EVP, Global Sales: Chris Amsler
Contact: Diana Albus
Plant Manager: Dave Mehrer

9230 **Nutmeg Vineyard**
PO Box 146
Andover, CT 06232-0146
860-742-8402
Wines
Owner: Anthony Maulucci
Type of Packaging: Private Label

9231 **Nutorious LLC**
2057 Bellevue St
Green Bay, WI 54311-5619
920-288-0483
Fax: 866-703-6595
Nuts
President/Owner: Carrie Liebhauser
Contact: Carrie Leiderhouser
carrie@nutoriousnuts.com
Number Employees: 5-9

9232 **Nutpods**
15900 SE Eastgate Way
Building B, Suite 125
Bellevue, WA 98008
800-977-6094
customerservice@nutpods.com www.nutpods.com
Non-dairy creamer
Founder & CEO: Madeline Haydon
CFO: Geoff Haydon
Sales: Mark Nunn
Operations: Tara Foster
Number of Brands: 1
Number of Products: 4
Brands:
NUTPODS

9233 **Nutra Food Ingredients, LLC**
4683 50th Street SE
Kentwood, MI 49512
616-656-9928
Fax: 419-730-3685
sales@nutrafoodingredients.com
www.nutrafoodingredients.com
Functional and nutritional ingredients supplier to the food, beverage, nutraceutical and cosmetics industries
President: Bryon Yang
Director of Business Development: Tim Wolffis
Quality Control: Monica Mylet
monica.mylet@nutrafoodingredients.com
Director of Sales and Marketing: Clarence Harvey
Year Founded: 2004
Estimated Sales: Under $500,000
Number Employees: 1-4
Other Locations:
Distribution Center
Edison NJ
Distribution Center
Carson CA

9234 **Nutra Nuts**
4528 E Washington Blvd
Commerce, CA 90040
323-260-7457
Fax: 323-260-7459 gocorny@nutranuts.com
www.nutranuts.com
Snack mixture of organic popcorn and soybeans flavored with sea salt or natural spices or coated with organic sugar
President: Mark Porro
CFO: Michael Porro
Estimated Sales: $300,000-500,000
Number Employees: 1-4
Number of Brands: 1
Number of Products: 3
Square Footage: 13200
Type of Packaging: Consumer, Food Service, Bulk
Brands:
Grandpa Po's Slightly Spicy
Grandpa Po's Slightly Sweet
Grandpa Po's Slightly Unsalted
Nutra Nuts

9235 **NutraSun**
6201 E Primrose Green Dr
Regina, SK S4V 3L7
Canada
306-751-2040
Fax: 306-751-2047 info@nutrasunfoods.com
www.nutrasunfoods.com
Organic and conventional, non-GMO flour
Director of Business Development: Kelvin Maloney

9236 **NutraSweet Company**
222 Merchandise Mart Plaza
Suite 936
Chicago, IL 60606
312-873-5000
Fax: 312-873-5050 800-323-5321
ordernow@nutrasweet.com www.nutrasweet.com
Sweeteners
CEO: Craig Petray
President/COO: William DeFer
CFO: James Stanley
SVP/Sales & Marketing: Kevin Bauer
Director Nutritional Science: Maureen Mackey
Purchasing Manager: James Pumphrey
Estimated Sales: $8.80 Million
Number Employees: 417
Parent Co: JW Childs Associates
Brands:
Equal
Nutrasweet

9237 **Nutraceutical International**
1777 Sun Peak Dr.
Park City, UT 84098
435-655-6000
800-669-8877
info@nutraceutical.com www.nutraceutical.com
Supplements.
CEO: Chad Clawson
Vice President/CFO: Cory McQueen
Cheif Marketing Officer: John D'Alessandro
Senior VP, Sales: David Bunch
COO: Camilla Shumaker
Year Founded: 1993
Estimated Sales: $188.07 Million
Number Employees: 810
Square Footage: 6103
Type of Packaging: Consumer, Food Service, Bulk
Brands:
Solaray
KAL
Food Source
Sunny Green
VegLife
Veglife
Allvia
Complimed
bioAllers
Herbs for Kids
NatraBio
Homeopathy for Kids
NaturalCare
Nutra BioGenesis
Oakmont Labs
Pioneer
VAXA
Zand
Nature's Herbs
Natural Balance
Natural Sport
BuckPower
FunFresh Foods
Dowd & Rogers
Miztique
Paleo Planet
Refrigerator Fresh
Sweet Moose
Taste Waves
World Berries
The Real Food Trading Co.
Zylicious
Spring Drops
Honey Gardens
Montana Big Sky
Premier One

9238 **Nutraceutical International**
1400 Kearns Blvd # 2
2nd Floor
Park City, UT 84060-7228
435-655-6000
Fax: 435-647-3802 800-669-8877
info@nutraceutical.com www.nutraceutical.com

Manufacturer and exporter of vitamins, minerals and nutritional supplements
President: Bruce R Hough
bruce.hough@nutraceutical.com
CEO/Director/Chairman: Frank W. Gay II
CFO/ VP: Cory J. McQueen
bruce.hough@nutraceutical.com
Executive Vice President: Gary M. Hume
VP Marketing/Sales: Christopher B. Neuberger
Vice President, Operations: Darren Peterson
Estimated Sales: $500,000-$1 Million
Number Employees: 500-999
Type of Packaging: Consumer, Private Label, Bulk
Brands:
Fentinel
Keep
Natural Health
Un-Soap

9239 **Nutraceutical International**
6704 Ranger Ave
Corpus Christi, TX 78415-5908
361-854-0755
Fax: 361-855-8031 800-338-4788
www.nutraceutical.com
Sublingual/liquid vitamins
Owner: Jerry Clure
COO: Gracie Villarreal
gvillarreal@nutriceuticalsolutions.com
Estimated Sales: $1.5 Million
Number Employees: 10-19
Type of Packaging: Consumer

9240 **Nutraceutics Corp**
2900 Brannon Ave
St Louis, MO 63139-1440
314-664-6684
Fax: 314-664-4639 877-664-6684
info@nutraceutics.com www.nutraceutics.com
Nutraceutical tablets, capsules, effervescents, tropicals and powers
President: Jennifer Cherry
jcherry@nutraceutics.com
Estimated Sales: $500,000-$1 Million
Number Employees: 20-49
Number of Brands: 50
Number of Products: 1000
Type of Packaging: Consumer, Private Label, Bulk
Brands:
Dh3
Dhea Plus
Diet Dhea

9241 **Nutralliance**
23600 Via Del Rio
Suite B
Yorba Linda, CA 92887
714-694-1400
Fax: 714-694-1411 844-410-1400
info@nutralliance.com www.nutralliance.com
Manufacturer of ingredients for the food, nutritional, pet and pharmaceutical industries.
CEO: Brian Salerno
Executive Vice President: Michael Sodaro
Technical Director: Stephen O'Brien

9242 **Nutranique Labs**
398 Tesconi Court
Santa Rosa, CA 95401-4653
707-545-9017
Fax: 707-575-4611
Processor and exporter of broccoli sprouts and certified nutraceutical powders including spinach, wheat grass juice, tomato, broccoli, garlic, carrot, green tea, kale and cruciferous blends
General Manager: Mark Martindill
Director Sales/Marketing: Nancy Costa
Operations Manager: Tom Ikesaki
Number Employees: 1-4
Parent Co: FDP USA
Type of Packaging: Bulk
Brands:
Nutranique Labs

9243 **Nutraplex**
658 Douglas Ave
Suite 1102
Altamonte Springs, FL 32714
www.nutraplex.com
Nutrition bars
Founder: Brad Fowler
Number of Brands: 1
Number of Products: 4
Brands:
NUTRAPLEX

9244 **Nutrex Hawaii Inc**
73-4460 Queen Kaahumanu Hwy
Suite 102
Kailua Kona, HI 96740-2632
808-326-1353
Fax: 808-329-4533 800-453-1187
info@nutrex-hawaii.com www.nutrex-hawaii.com
Nutrient-rich dietary supplement
President: Gerald R Cysewski
CEO: Andrew Jacobson
ajacobson@cyanotech.com
Vice President: Glen Johnson
Vice President of Sales and Marketing: Bob Capelli
Sales: Agnes Prehn
Estimated Sales: $500-$1 Million
Number Employees: 50-99
Number of Brands: 2
Parent Co: Cyanotech Corporation
Type of Packaging: Consumer, Private Label, Bulk
Brands:
Bioastin
Spirulina Pacifica

9245 **Nutri Base**
3851 East Thunderhill Place
Phoenix, AZ 85044-6679
480-626-2025
Fax: 480-704-4116 877-223-5459
support@nutribase.com www.nutribase.com
Cereals
President: Sat Samtolch Khalsu
Owner: Guru Simran Singh Khalsa
Contact: Meredith Averill
maverill@nutritionsoftware.org
Type of Packaging: Private Label
Brands:
Golden Temple
Rainforest
Wha Guru Chew

9246 **Nutri Fruit**
7510 SE Altman Rd
Gresham, OR 97080-8808
503-663-2680
Fax: 503-663-7095 nutrifruit@scenicfruit.com
Fruit
Owner: Maridean Eisele
maridean@scenicfruit.com
Estimated Sales: $1-2.5 Million appx.
Number Employees: 5-9
Brands:
Nutri-Fruito

9247 **Nutri-Bake Inc**
1208 Rue Bergar
Laval, QC H7L 5A2
Canada
450-933-5936
Fax: 888-263-3208 info@nutri-bake.com
www.organic-baked-goods.com
Manufacturer and wholesaler of baked goods
President: Peter Tsatoumas

9248 **Nutri-Cell**
1915 Trade Center Way
Naples, FL 34109
866-953-2355
www.nutricell.com
Manufacturer and exporter of animal-free nutritional supplements
Medical Consultant: Dr Derrick De Silva
Medical Consultant: Dr William Judy
Medical Consultant: Dr Bruce Dooley
Number Employees: 1-4
Number of Brands: 2
Number of Products: 7
Square Footage: 12000
Type of Packaging: Consumer, Private Label
Brands:
Nutri-Cell

9249 **Nutri-Nation**
1560 Broadway
Unit 1110
Port Coquitlam, BC V3C 2M8
Canada
604-552-5549
Fax: 604-941-0135 info@nutri-nation.com
www.nutri-nation.com
Private label manufacturer of energy and nutrition bars
Director of Business Development: Allison Cienciala
Type of Packaging: Private Label

9250 **NutriFusion**
10641 Airport Pulling Rd N
Suite 31
Naples, FL 34109-7330
239-300-9702
Fax: 866-393-1680 nutrifusion.com
Manufacturer of fruit and vegetable ingredients
CEO: William Grand
Executive Vice President: Myra Mackey
Director of Marketing: Eric Dunn

9251 **Nutribiotic**
PO Box 238
Lakeport, CA 95453
707-263-0411
Fax: 707-263-7844 800-225-4345
info@nutribiotic.com www.nutribiotic.com
Manufacturer and exporter of vitamins and supplements
President: Patrick Fourteau
CFO: Wendy Sexton
Sales Director: Teri Whitestone
Contact: Pam Lausten
sales@nutribiotic.com
Operations Manager: Wendy Brossard
Purchasing/Manufacturing Director: Kenny Ridgeway
Estimated Sales: Less Than $500,000
Number Employees: 1-4
Square Footage: 80000
Brands:
Citricidal
Fruitsnax
Grapefruit Extract
Jungle Juice
Meta Boost
Meta Rest
Nutribiotic
Prozone
Spectrum Nutritional Shake

9252 **Nutricepts**
2208 E 117th St
Burnsville, MN 55337-1265
952-707-0207
Fax: 952-707-0210 800-949-9060
info@nutricepts.com www.nutricepts.com
Processor and exporter of calcium salts, oxygen consuming agents, oxygen scavengers, mold inhibitors, sodium lactate, humectants, flavor enhancers, etc
President: Mark Cater
mw.cater@nutricepts.com
Estimated Sales: $3-5 Million
Number Employees: 1-4
Type of Packaging: Bulk
Brands:
Ampliflave
Oxyvac
Prop Whey
Surface Guard

9253 **Nutrilabs**
1230 Market St
Suite 401
San Francisco, CA 94102-4801
415-235-6205
Fax: 415-707-2122 877-468-8745
www.nutrilabs.com
Private label manufacturer vitamins and supplements
Owner: Etty Motazedi
VP: Elsie Orell
Contact: Shahin Kashani
skashani@nutrilabs.com
Purchasing Director: Argee Davidovici
Estimated Sales: Less than $500,000
Square Footage: 11200
Type of Packaging: Consumer, Private Label, Bulk
Brands:
Chromemate
Citrimax
Geri-Med
Renuz-U
Super B-12 Sublingual
Valerian Extract
Virility Plus

9254 **Nutrilicious Natural Bakery**
5446 Dansher Road
Countryside, IL 60525-3126
708-354-7777
Fax: 708-354-4797 800-835-8097
Cookies and doughnuts including plain, old-fashioned, spelt, whole wheat, low-fat baked and wheat-free spelt
President: Steve Maril
Contact: Gurbax Singh
singh@nutrilicious.com
General Manager: Joe Augelli
Number Employees: 12
Square Footage: 40000
Type of Packaging: Consumer, Food Service, Private Label

9255 **Nutrisciences Labs**
70 Carolyn Boulevard
Farmingdale, NY 11735
631-247-0600
855-492-7388
info@nutricaplabs.com www.nutrasciencelabs.com
Nutritional supplements including vitamins, minerals, and sports supplements
President/Founder: Jason Provenzano
Chief Executive Officer: Jonathan Greenhut
VP Digital Marketing: Andrew Goldman
VP Sales: Blayney McEneaney
Operations Manager: Dana Roveto
Estimated Sales: $45 Million
Number Employees: 40
Parent Co: Twinlab Consolidation Corporation

9256 **Nutrisoya Foods**
4050 Av Pinard
Saint-Hyacinthe, QC J2S 8K4
Canada
450-796-4261
Fax: 450-796-1837 877-769-2645
www.nutrisoya.com
Processor and exporter of soy milk, rice milk and almond mil
President: Nicholas Feldman
Estimated Sales: $4.1 Million
Number Employees: 17
Square Footage: 40000
Type of Packaging: Consumer, Food Service, Private Label, Bulk
Brands:
Natura
Nutribio
Nutrisoy
Nutrisoya

9257 **Nutrisport Pharmacal**
200 North Church Rd
Franklin, NJ 07416
973-209-7200
Fax: 973-209-4422 833-403-2861
www.nutrisportpharmacal.com
Private labeler of nutritional supplements
President/Owner: Vincent Paternoster
VP, Operations: William DiBernard
Year Founded: 1997
Type of Packaging: Private Label

9258 **Nutritech Corporation**
719 E Haley St
Santa Barbara, CA 93103
805-963-9581
Fax: 805-963-0308 800-235-5727
www.all-one.com
All-in-one multi-vitamin and mineral amino acid powder including rice original and base, green phyto base, active seniors and fruit antioxidant formulas
President/CEO: Douglas Ingoldsby
VP Sales: Lori Herman
Contact: Ron Adams
ron.adams@nutritech.com
VP Operations: Carol Huerta
Estimated Sales: $1-3 Million
Number Employees: 5-9
Type of Packaging: Consumer
Brands:
All One

9259 **Nutrition 21 Inc**
1 Manhattanville Rd
Purchase, NY 10577-2119
914-701-4500
Fax: 914-696-0860 www.nutrition21.com
Organic mineral nutrition includes chromium picolinate, selenium yeast and Cardea salt alternative compound
President: Joseph Weiss
CEO: Michael Satow
CFO: Whit Stearns Jr
Chief Science Officer: James Homorowski
VP Marketing: Sonny Stafford
VP Sales: Todd Spear
VP Operations: William Levi
Estimated Sales: $20-50 Million
Number Employees: 10-19
Brands:
Chromax

9260 **Nutrition Center Inc**
PO Box 950
2132 E Richards St
Douglas, WY 82633-0950
307-358-5066
Fax: 307-358-9208 800-443-3333
info@nutriwest.com www.nutriwest.net
Nutritional supplements
President: Tony White
tony@nutri-west.net
Marketing Director: Marcia White
Vice President: Tiffany Moore
Plant Manager: Glenn Goodell
Purchasing Manager: Marc Moore
Estimated Sales: $2.5-5 Million
Number Employees: 50-99
Square Footage: 240
Type of Packaging: Private Label
Brands:
Nutri West

9261 **Nutrition Supply Corp**
317 Industrial Cir
Liberty, TX 77575-3447
936-334-0514
Fax: 800-671-3144 888-541-3997
nsc24@nsc24.com www.nsc24.com
Processor and exporter of nutritional supplements, vitamins and encapsulated herbs
CEO: Frank Jordan
fjordan@healthinspirationministry.com
National Sales VP: Mark Campbell
Estimated Sales: Less than $500,000
Number Employees: 10-19
Square Footage: 60000
Type of Packaging: Consumer, Food Service
Brands:
Nsc-100
Nsc-24

9262 **Nutritional Counselors of America**
1267 Archie Rhinehart Pkwy
Spencer, TN 38585-4612
931-946-3600
Fax: 931-946-3602
Vitamins, minerals, herbs, herbal teas, nutritional supplements, and colon cleaners, neutraceuticals and probiotics
President/CEO: June Wiles
Estimated Sales: $3-$5 Million
Number Employees: 5 to 9
Square Footage: 10000
Type of Packaging: Consumer, Private Label
Brands:
6-N-1
K-Min
Min-Col
Nca

9263 **(HQ)Nutritional Labs Intl**
1001 S 3rd St W
Missoula, MT 59801-2337
406-273-5493
Fax: 406-273-5498 info@nutritionallabs.com
Nutritional and herbal supplements and nutraceuticals including tablets, and capsules
President & CEO: Terry Benishek
CEO: Peter Malecha
pmalecha@nutritionallabs.com
VP of Research & Development: Titut Yokelson
Director of Quality Assurance: Jera'le Smith
Director of Sales & Marketing: Doug Lefler
Sales Manager: Tito Flores
Director of Operations: Steve Dybdal
Estimated Sales: $21.4 Million
Number Employees: 50-99
Square Footage: 18000
Type of Packaging: Consumer, Private Label, Bulk

9264 **(HQ)Nutritional Research Associates**
407 E Broad St
South Whitley, IN 46787
260-723-4931
Fax: 260-723-6297 800-456-4931
pookjg@usa.net
Processor and exporter of vitamins including carotene, A, D and E
Manager: Jonathan Pook
Acting Manager: Jonathan Pook
Estimated Sales: $979000
Number Employees: 5-9
Square Footage: 40000
Type of Packaging: Consumer, Bulk
Brands:
Carex
Quintrex

9265 **Nutritional Specialties**
1967 N Glassell St
Orange, CA 92865-4320
714-634-9340
Fax: 714-634-9347 800-333-6168
www.lifetimevitamins.com
Herbal formulas and nutritional supplements; importer of chlorella powder and tablets; exporter of dietary supplements
President: Tom Pinkowski
VP: Tom Krech
VP: Sale Stauch
Estimated Sales: $10-20 Million
Number Employees: 20-49
Type of Packaging: Private Label, Bulk
Brands:
Lifetime
Tung Hai

9266 **Nutriwest**
P.O. Box 950
2132 E Richards St
Douglas, WY 82633
307-358-5066
Fax: 307-358-9208 800-443-3333
www.nutriwest.com
Vitamin products and food and sports drink supplements.
Year Founded: 1982
Estimated Sales: $20-50 Million
Number Employees: 20-49
Square Footage: 60000
Type of Packaging: Consumer, Private Label
Other Locations:
Nutriwest
Alliance NE
Brands:
Nutriquest
Nutriwest

9267 **Nutro Laboratories**
650 Hadley Road
South Plainfield, NJ 07080
908-754-9300
Fax: 908-754-5640 800-446-8876
Vitamins and other dietary supplements.
President: Michael Slade
Contact: Donna Cirullo
dcirullo@nbty.com
Estimated Sales: $25600000
Number Employees: 250-499
Type of Packaging: Consumer

9268 **Nuts & Stems**
PO Box 39
Rosharon, TX 77583-0039
281-464-6887
Fax: 281-464-7493
Gourmet flavored pistachios and cashews

9269 **Nuts 'N More**
10 Almeida St E
Providence, RI 02914
844-413-2344
questions@nuts-n-more.com nuts-n-more.com
Almond and peanut butter spreads and powders
Founder & CEO: Peter Ferreira
Number of Brands: 1
Number of Products: 18

9270 **Nuts + Nuts**
68 Jay St
Greendesk Suite 201
Brooklyn, NY 11201-1189
347-513-9670
cyrilla@nutsplusnuts.com
www.nutsplusnuts.com
Owner: Cyrilla Suwarsa
Number Employees: 5-9

9271 **Nuts About Granola**
46 W Philadelphia St
York, PA 17401-5319
717-814-9648
orders@nutsaboutgranola.com
www.nutsaboutgranola.com
Manufacturer of granola.
Co-Founder: Sarah Lanphier
Co-Founder: Gayle Lanphier
gayle@nutsaboutgranola.com
Number Employees: 1-4

9272 **Nuts About You**
Los Angeles, CA 90036
hello@nutsaboutyoula.com
Flavored almonds
Brands:
NUTS ABOUT YOU

9273 **Nuts For Cheese**
London, ON
Canada
519-601-5070
info@nutsforcheese.com
www.nutsforcheese.com
Artisan cashew cheeses
Founder: Margaret Coons
Year Founded: 2015

9274 **Nutty Bavarian**
305 Hickman Dr
Sanford, FL 32771-6905
407-444-6322
Fax: 407-444-6335 800-382-4788
bruno@nuttyb.com www.nuttyb.com
Cinnamon nut glaze syrup and fresh roasted gourmet nuts; Manufacturer of nut roasting carts and warmers as well as paper and plastic cones and gift tins for nuts
Owner: David Brent
bruno@nuttyb.com
Customer Service Manager: Amber Stefanisko
Controller: Keya Morgan
Vice President of Sales: David Zangenberg
bruno@nuttyb.com
Production Manager: Ed Conrado
Estimated Sales: $500,000-$1 Million
Number Employees: 10-19
Square Footage: 28800
Type of Packaging: Consumer, Bulk
Brands:
Nbr 2000
Nutty Bavarian

9275 **Nutty Goodness**
1750 Signal Point Rd
Suite 2B
Charleston, SC 29412
info@nuttygoodness.com
nuttygoodness.com
Fruit and nut bites
Operations: Nathan Ouellette
Number of Brands: 1
Number of Products: 5
Brands:
NUTTY GOODNESS

9276 **Nuttzo**
3525 Del Mar Heights Rd
Unit 728
San Diego, CA 92130
888-325-0553
info@nuttzo.com
www.nuttzo.com
Nut and seed butters
Founder and President: Danielle Dietz-LiVolsi
Brands:
NuttZo

9277 **Nuun Active Hydration**
800 Maynard Ave S
Suite 102
Seattle, WA 98134
206-219-9237
Fax: 206-260-8732 855-426-6886
nuunlife.com
Hydration products
President & CEO: Kevin Rutherford
Year Founded: 2004
Number Employees: 51-200

9278 **Nysco Products Inc**
2350 Lafayette Ave
Bronx, NY 10473-1104
718-792-9000
Fax: 718-792-7732 Chuck@NYSCO.com
www.nysco.com
NYSCO Products LLC designs and manufactures custom and stock displays.
Owner: Barry Kramer
info@nysco.com
Senior Vice President: Chuck Levin
Number Employees: 50-99

9279 **Nyssa-Nampa Beet Growers**
525 Good Ave
Nyssa, OR 97913-3664
541-372-2904
Fax: 541-372-5063
Cooperative of sugar beet processors
President: Steve Martineau
Executive Director: Norma Burbank
VP: Tom Church
Executive Director: Rich Turner
Estimated Sales: $130,000
Number Employees: 1

9280 **O & H Danish Bakery Inc**
1841 Douglas Ave
Racine, WI 53402-4696
262-637-8895
Fax: 262-631-5395 www.ohdanishbakery.com
Danish and pastries
Owner: Mike Olesen
mike@ohdanishbakery.com
Founder: Christian Olesen
Co-Owner: Myrna Olesen
Estimated Sales: $2.5-5 Million
Number Employees: 50-99
Brands:
Kringle

9281 **O C Schulz & Sons**
401 4th St
P.O. Box 39
Crystal, ND 58222-4038
701-657-2152
Fax: 701-657-2425
Potatoes
Owner: David Moquist
Secretary/Treasurer: David Moquist
Sales: Dave Moquist
Plant Manager & Sales: Andy Moquist
Estimated Sales: $1 Million
Number Employees: 10-19
Square Footage: 150000
Type of Packaging: Consumer, Food Service

9282 **O Olive Oil**
1997 S McDowell Blvd
Petaluma, CA 94954
707-766-1755
Fax: 707-763-3782 888-827-7148
info@ooliveoil.com www.ooliveoil.com
Extra virgin citrus olive oils and oak-aged vinegars
President/Founder: Greg Hinson
National Director Sales/Marketing: Shelly Haygood
Estimated Sales: $2 Million
Number Employees: 4
Type of Packaging: Private Label
Brands:
O Olive Oil
O Vinegar

9283 **O'Boyle's Ice Cream Company**
6414 N Radcliffe St
Bristol, PA 19007
215-788-3882
Ice cream, frozen yogurt and frozen desserts
Componet: Beverly Boyle
Number Employees: 10-19
Type of Packaging: Consumer, Food Service, Bulk
Brands:
Country Creamery

9284 **O'Brian Brothers Food**
PO Box 42382
Cincinnati, OH 45242
513-791-9909
Fax: 513-791-9011
Barbecue sauce and salad dressings including French, Italian, honey mustard and ranch
President/CEO: John O'Brian
Estimated Sales: $500,000-$1 Million
Number Employees: 1-4
Type of Packaging: Consumer, Food Service, Private Label
Brands:
Beamons

9285 **O'Brines Pickling**
4103 E Mission Avenue
Spokane, WA 99202-4402
509-534-7255
Fax: 509-534-5564
Pickled products
President: James Moore
VP: Marsha Moore
Estimated Sales: $5-9 Million
Number Employees: 10-19

9286 **O'Danny Boy Ice Cream**
100 Prosperity Dr
Trotwood, OH 45426-2600
937-837-2100
Ice cream
Owner: Dannial Haas
Co-Owner: Kathleen Haas
Estimated Sales: $2.5-5 Million
Number Employees: 1-4

9287 **O'Donnell Formulas Inc**
1145 Linda Vista Dr # 110
San Marcos, CA 92078-3820
760-471-1182
Fax: 760-471-1878 800-736-1991
Health food supplements
President/CEO: Wanda O'Donnell
CFO: Angela Bongiorno
Estimated Sales: Less Than $500,000
Number Employees: 5-9
Type of Packaging: Food Service
Brands:
Flora-Balance
Latero-Flora

9288 **O'Donnell-Usen**
5024 Uceta Road
Tampa, FL 33619-3249
813-241-9200
Fax: 813-630-1200
Seafood
Estimated Sales: $480,000
Number Employees: 10-19
Parent Co: ConAgra Foods

9289 **O'Doughs**
320 Oakdale Rd
Toronto, ON M3N 1W5
Canada
416-342-5700
855-636-8447
eatwell@odoughs.com odoughs.com
Gluten-free baked goods
Owner: Ari Weinberg

9290 **O'Garvey Sauces**
1151 Madeline Street
New Braunfels, TX 78132-4725
830-620-6127
Fax: 830-620-6662
Hot and mild salsas
President: Norma Garvey
Estimated Sales: $150,000
Number Employees: 1-4
Type of Packaging: Consumer, Food Service, Private Label, Bulk
Brands:
Max's Salsa Sabrosa & Design

9291 **O'Hara Corp**
120 Tillson Ave # 1
Rockland, ME 04841-3450
207-594-4444
Fax: 207-594-0407 www.oharabait.com
Processor and exporter of seafood including frozen scallops

Owner: Frank O'Hara
foharajr@oharacooperative.com
Estimated Sales: $4100000
Number Employees: 50-99
Type of Packaging: Consumer, Food Service
Brands:
Cape Ann
Down East
Tip Top

9292 **O'Neal's Fresh Frozen Pizza Crust**
122 E College Ave
Springfield, OH 45504-2505
937-323-0050
redparot@iapdatacom.net
Pizza crust including whole wheat
Manager: Brian O'Neill
Estimated Sales: $1-3,000,000
Number Employees: 20-49

9293 **O'Neil's Distributors**
110 S Iroquois Street
Goodland, IN 47948-8004
219-297-4521
Fax: 219-297-4625
Teas
Owner: Steven O'Neil
Estimated Sales: $2.5-5 000,000
Number Employees: 1-4

9294 **O'Neill Coffee Co**
20 Main Street Ext
West Middlesex, PA 16159-3478
724-528-2244
Fax: 724-528-1566 www.oneillcoffee.com
Coffee; wholesaler/distributor of teas and spices
President: Joseph Walsh
jwalsh@oneillcoffee.com
Account Manager: Neil Ostheimer
Estimated Sales: $1-3 Million
Number Employees: 10-19

9295 **O'Sole Mio**
4600, boul. Ambroise-Lafortune
Boisbriand, QC J7H 0G1
Canada
844-696-8933
info@osolemio.ca osolemio.ca
Pasta, sauces and prepared meals
President/Owner: Alfredo Napolitano

9296 **O-At-Ka Milk Prods Co-Op Inc.**
700 Ellicott St.
Batavia, NY 14020
585-343-0536
Fax: 585-343-4473 800-828-8152
www.oatkamilk.com
Meal replacement beverages, pet milk replacers, dairy base liqueurs, RTD beverages, high protein products, infant formula, evaporated milk, milk powders, butter, bulk cream and skim milk concentrate.
General Manager: Larry Webster
CEO: Bill Schreiber
CFO: Michael Fuchs
Vice President, Human Resources: Donna Maxwell
Year Founded: 1959
Estimated Sales: $274.56 Million
Number Employees: 400+
Square Footage: 600000
Type of Packaging: Consumer, Food Service, Private Label, Bulk
Brands:
Gold Cow
Spring Farm

9297 **OB Macaroni Company**
844-837-6259
info@obmacaroni.com
www.obmacaroni.com
Manufacturer of pasta
President: Jackie Krantz
Estimated Sales: $10-20 Million
Number Employees: 20-49
Square Footage: 50000
Type of Packaging: Consumer, Food Service, Private Label, Bulk
Brands:
O.B.
Q&Q
Q&Q Fideo

9298 **OCG Cacao**
1 Plummers Cor
Whitinsville, MA 01588-2135
508-234-5107
Fax: 508-234-5495 888-482-2226
ocggroup@aol.com
Dairy, bakery, confectionery products
President: Jean Chenal
General Manager: Roberta White
Estimated Sales: Below $5 Million
Number Employees: 1

9299 **OH Chocolate**
3131 E Madison Street
Seattle, WA 98112
Canada
206-329-8777
www.ohchocolate.com
Baked desserts and Belgian chocolates
President: Laurie Climan
Sales Manager: Mark Climan
Number Employees: 10-19
Type of Packaging: Consumer
Brands:
L'Or Chocolatier
Ott Chocolate

9300 **OHi Food**
750 Wesleyan Bay
Costa Mesa, CA 92626-6919
808-281-7815
www.ohifoodco.com
Superfood snack bar
Marketing Manager: Kayla Bittner
Number of Brands: 1
Number of Products: 4
Brands:
OHI

9301 **OK International Group**
73 Bartlett Street
Marlborough, MA 01752
508-303-8286
Fax: 508-303-8207 sales@okcorp.com
www.okcorp.com
Integrated packaging automation systems
Contact: Marcela Barragan
mbarragan@okcorp.com

9302 **OLLI Salumeria Americana**
1301 Rocky Point Dr
Oceanside, CA 92056
877-655-4937
info@olli.com www.olli.com
Artisanal cured meats
Founder and President: Oliviero Colmignolli

9303 **OMG! Superfoods**
2373 E Pacifica Pl
Rancho Dominguez, CA 90220
855-664-3663
omgsuperfoods.com
Superfood powders, including fruits, mushrooms and seeds

9304 **OMGhee**
24 Cedar St
Cedar Grove, NJ 07009
973-931-3476
mitul@omghee.com
www.omghee.com
Ghee (clarified butter)
Owner: Mitul Parekh

9305 **OMYA, Inc.**
9987 Carver Rd
Suite 300
Cincinnatti, OH 45242
513-387-4600
800-749-6692
www.omya.com
Fillers and pigments from calcium carbonate and dolomite, and distributor of chemical products.
President: Anthony Colak
CFO: Michael Phillips
Secretary: Leonard Eisenberg
Asst Sec: Patricia Kirkendall
Manager Technology Services: Michael Roussel
Sales Manager: Maria Burt
Contact: Hilary Allard
hilary.allard@omya.com
Manager: Scott McCalla
Manager Projects Engineering: Scott Schaffner
Director of Engineering: Rob Tikoft
Director Purchasing: Derrell Riley
Estimated Sales: $4.3 Million
Other Locations:
Proctor VT
Cincinnati OH
Woodland WA
Kingsport TN
Lucerne Valley CA
Johnsonburg PA
Florence VT
Hawesville KY
Sylacauga AL
Superior AZ
Long Beach CA

9306 **ONE Brands**
5400 West W.T. Harris Blvd
Suite L
Charlotte, NC 28269
888-231-2684
one1brands.com
High protein snack bars
President & CEO: Peter Burns
Year Founded: 1999
Brands:
ONE
ONE BASIX

9307 **ORB Weaver Farm**
3406 Lime Kiln Road
New Haven, VT 05472
802-877-3755
marjorie@orbweaverfarm.com
www.orbweaverfarm.com
Fresh fruits and vegetables, and fine cheeses
President: Marjorie Susman
marjorie@orbweaverfarm.com

9308 **OSF Flavors Inc**
40 Baker Hollow Rd
Windsor, CT 06095-2133
860-298-8350
Fax: 860-298-8363 800-466-6015
sales@osfflavors.com www.osfflavors.com
Manufacturer of flavors for food and beverage products.
Marketing Director: Olivier de Botton
Financial Controller: Adam Feltman
Manager of Research & Development: Linda Faulkner
Sales: Susan Nasby
Manager: Doug Nasby
dnasby@osfflavors.com
Operations Manager: Doug Nasby
Production/Purchasing Manager: Vincent Lacocca
Estimated Sales: $12.5 Million
Number Employees: 10-19
Square Footage: 10000
Other Locations:
OSF Europe
Chambly, France
OSF Asia
Tangerang, Indonesia

9309 **OWYN**
100 Passaic Ave
Suite 100
Fairfield, NJ 07004
833-533-7061
liveowyn.com
Plant-based protein beverages
VP: Jeff Miller

9310 **Oak Creek Brewing Company**
2050 Yavapai Dr
Sedona, AZ 86336
928-204-1300
Fax: 520-204-1361 bestbrew@sedona.net
www.oakcreekbrew.com
Seasonal beer, ale and lager
General Manager: Rita Kraus
Estimated Sales: $500,000-$1Million
Number Employees: 5-9
Type of Packaging: Consumer, Food Service

Brands:
Oak Creek

9311 **(HQ)Oak Farm's Dairy**
1148 Faulkner Ln
Waco, TX 76704
254-756-5421
Fax: 254-756-6987 www.oakfarmsdairy.com
Milk
President: Mackey Willims
CEO: Mickey Williams
General Sales Manager: Jerry Przada
Human Resources: Brad Patten
Estimated Sales: Less than $500,000
Number Employees: 100-249
Other Locations:
Oak Farms Dairy
Wichita Falls TX
Oak Farms Dairy
Weatherford TX
Oak Farms Dairy
Denison TX
Oak Farms Dairy
Paris TX
Oak Farms Dairy
Houston TX
Oak Farms Dairy
Beaumont TX
Oak Farms Dairy
Brenham TX
Oak Farms Dairy
San Antonio TX
Oak Farms Dairy
McAllen TX
Oak Farms Dairy
Waco TX
Oak Farms Dairy
Austin TX
Oak Farms Dairy
Tyler TX
Brands:
Oak Farm's

9312 **Oak Farms**
PO Box 961447
El Paso, TX 79996
214-941-0302
Fax: 214-941-0309 800-395-7004
www.oakfarmsdairy.com
Processors of milk and cream
General Manager: Craig Roberts
General Sales Manager: Jerry Przada
General Manager: Micky Williams
Number Employees: 250-499
Parent Co: Suiza Dairy Group
Type of Packaging: Consumer, Food Service
Brands:
Oak Farms

9313 **Oak Grove Dairy**
W10198 Oak Grove Rd.
Clintonville, WI 54929
715-823-6226
oakgrove@oakgrovedairy.com
www.oakgrovedairy.com
Milk, sour creams, yogurt, novelties, and cottage cheese
President: David Kust
Estimated Sales: $20-50 Million
Number Employees: 1000

9314 **Oak Grove Orchards Winery**
6090 Crowley Rd
Rickreall, OR 97371
541-364-7052
Wines
President: Carl Stevens
Estimated Sales: Under $500,000
Number Employees: 1-4

9315 **Oak Grove Smoke House Inc**
17618 Old Jefferson Hwy
Prairieville, LA 70769-3931
225-673-6857
Fax: 225-673-5757 www.oakgrovemix.webs.com
Seasoned and Cajun/Creole rice mixes, speciality spice mixes, breading and smoked meats
President: Robert Schexnailder
Estimated Sales: $500,000-$1 Million
Number Employees: 5-9
Number of Brands: 2
Number of Products: 15+
Square Footage: 51000
Type of Packaging: Consumer, Food Service, Bulk
Brands:
Oak Grove Smokehouse
Swamp Fire Seafood Boil

9316 **Oak Hill Farm**
15101 Hwy 12
Glen Ellen, CA 95442
707-996-6643
Fax: 707-935-6612 800-878-7808
info@oakhillfarm.net www.oakhillfarm.net
Sustainably grows over 200 varieties of vegetables, fruit, herbs and flowers.
Owner: Anne Teller
info@oakhillfarm.net
Estimated Sales: $780 Thousand
Number Employees: 20-49
Type of Packaging: Consumer

9317 **Oak Island Seafood Company**
PO Box 947
Portland, ME 04104-0947
207-594-9250
Fax: 207-594-9281
Seafood
President: Jay Trenholm

9318 **Oak Knoll Dairy, Inc.**
PO Box 443
Windsor, VT 05089
802-674-5426
Fax: 802-674-9166 oakknoll@earthlink.net
www.oakknolldairy.com
100% goats milk, 2% fat goats milk, chocolate goats milk, and half and half goats milk
Owner: George Redick
Owner: Karen Lindbo
Number Employees: 5-9
Square Footage: 30000
Brands:
Oak Knoll

9319 **Oak Knoll Winery**
29700 SW Burkhalter Rd
Hillsboro, OR 97123-9245
503-648-8198
Fax: 503-648-3377 800-625-5665
info@oakknollwinery.com
www.oakknollwinery.com
Wines
President: William Ellsworth
william.ellsworth@adrian.k12.or.us
VP Sales/Marketing: John Vuylsteke
Sales Manager: Natalie Epler
Founder: Marj Vuylsteke
Cellar Master: Tom Vuylsteke
Office Manager: Martha Miller
Estimated Sales: Below $5 Million
Number Employees: 10-19
Number of Brands: 2
Number of Products: 8
Type of Packaging: Consumer, Private Label, Bulk
Brands:
Oak Knoll

9320 **Oak Leaf Confections**
416-751-0740
Fax: 416-751-3656 877-261-7887
info@sweetworks.net sweetworks.net/oakleaf
Processor and exporter of confectionery products including malt balls, gum balls, bubble gum, hard candies and freeze pops
Owner/President: Philip Terranova
Number Employees: 300
Square Footage: 560000
Parent Co: SweetWorks Confections LLC
Type of Packaging: Consumer, Private Label, Bulk
Brands:
Bubble King

9321 **Oak Ridge Winery LLC**
6100 E Victor Rd
Lodi, CA 95240-0804
209-369-4758
Fax: 209-369-0202 info@oakridgewinery.com
www.oakridgewinery.com
Produces a wide variety of wines.
President: Rudy Maggio
rmaggi@oakridgewinery.com
Vice President of Marketing and Sales: Stephen Bei
Director of International Sales: Stephen Merritt
Tasting Room Manager: Shelly Maggio-Woltkamp
Director of Winemaking/Production Manage: Chue Her
Estimated Sales: $10-20 Million
Number Employees: 50-99
Number of Brands: 8
Type of Packaging: Consumer, Food Service
Brands:
Oak Ridge Winery
OZW
Old Soul
3 Girls
Maggio
Helena Ranch
Moss Roxx
Lodi Estates

9322 **Oak Spring Winery**
2401 E Pleasant Valley Blvd
Altoona, PA 16601-8967
814-946-3799
Fax: 814-946-4245 oakspringwinery@verizon.net
www.oakspringwinery.com
Wines
Founder: Sylvia Schraff
President: Scott Schraff
oakspringwinery@keycon.net
Treasurer: John Schraff
Estimated Sales: $5-9 Million
Number Employees: 1-4
Brands:
Oak Spring Winery

9323 **Oak State Products Inc**
775 State Route 251
PO Box 549
Wenona, IL 61377-7587
815-853-4348
Fax: 815-853-4625
Producer of soft cookies, cookie crumbs and toppings
Chairman & CEO: Rich Scalise
CFO & SVP, Finance: Fred Jasser
SVP, CCO: Chuck Metzger
SVP, Human Resources: Steve England
Year Founded: 1956
Estimated Sales: $22.8 Million
Number Employees: 250-499
Square Footage: 160000
Parent Co: Hearthside Food Solutions
Type of Packaging: Consumer, Bulk
Brands:
Oak State Cookie Jar Delight

9324 **Oak Street Manufacturing**
255 Welter Dr
Monticello, IA 52310
319-465-4042
Fax: 877-465-4042 877-465-4344
www.oakstreetmfg.com
Manufacturer and distributor of restaurant furnishings
President/Owner: Cindy Bagge
Year Founded: 1995

9325 **Oakhurst Dairy**
364 Forest Ave.
Portland, ME 04101
207-772-7468
800-482-0718
info@oakhurstdairy.com www.oakhurstdairy.com
Milk and dairy products including fluid milk, cream, sour cream, cottage cheese, butter, ice cream mixes, juices, drinks and water.
President: John Bennett
Quality Control Assurance Manager: Jeff Connolly
Human Resources Manager: Darlene Cadorette-Levesque
Year Founded: 1921
Estimated Sales: $110 Million
Number Employees: 200
Type of Packaging: Consumer
Brands:
Oakhurst

9326 **Oakhurst Industries**
2050 Tubeway Ave.
Commerce, CA 90040
818-502-1400
Fax: 818-502-1338
Bread and other bakery products
President: James Freund
Estimated Sales: $43.2 Million
Number Employees: 400
Square Footage: 81000

9327 **Oakland Bean Cleaning & Storage**
42445 County Road 116
Knights Landing, CA 95645-0518
530-735-6203
Fax: 530-735-6207
Dry, edible beans including kidney and pink
Operations Manager: Frank Anastasi
Estimated Sales: Less than $500,000
Number Employees: 1-4

9328 **Oakland Noodle Co**
10 W Main St
Oakland, IL 61943
217-346-2322
Fax: 217-346-2324
oaklandnoodle_company@yahoo.com
www.oaklandnoodle.com
Noodles
Owner: Clarence Ethington
Marketing Director: Stephanie Ethington
Estimated Sales: Under $500,000
Number Employees: 5-9
Square Footage: 2000
Brands:
Oakland Noodle

9329 **Oakrun Farm Bakery**
58 Carluke Road West
PO Box 81070
Ancaster, ON L9G 3L1
Canada
905-648-1818
Fax: 905-648-8252 800-263-6422
customerservice@oakrun.com www.oakrun.com
Processor and exporter of English muffins, pastries, bagels, muffins, danish, tarts, crumpets, and cakes.
President: Roger Dickhout
COO: Tony Tristani
Research & Development: Maria Pais
Quality Control: Rita Fajardo
Marketing Director: Andra Zondervan
VP Sales: Dave MacPhail
Plant Manager: Chet Czerny
Purchasing: Christine Richer
Number Employees: 100-249
Square Footage: 1068000
Type of Packaging: Consumer, Food Service, Private Label

9330 **Oasis Breads**
440 Venture St
Escondido, CA 92029
760-747-7390
Fax: 760-747-4854 www.oasisbreads.com
Flourless sprouted whole grain breads and deli breads.
President: Jim Pickell
Estimated Sales: $1300000
Number Employees: 5-9
Square Footage: 40000
Type of Packaging: Consumer, Private Label
Brands:
Oasis

9331 **Oasis Coffee Co Inc**
327 Main Ave
Norwalk, CT 06851-6156
203-847-0554
Fax: 203-846-9835 www.oasiscoffeect.com
Roasting coffee
President: Ralph Sandolo
oasiscoffeeco@yahoo.com
CEO: Veronica Sandolo
Vice President: Joseph Sandolo
Marketing Consultant: Martin Blank
Estimated Sales: $5-10 000,000
Number Employees: 5-9
Brands:
Oasis Coffee

9332 **Oasis Food Co**
635 Ramsey Ave
Hillside, NJ 07205
908-964-0477
800-275-0477
foodservice.us@aak.com www.oasisfoodsco.com
Butter blends and substitutes, salad dressings, shortenings, margarine, edible oils, mayonnaise, sauces, pan and grill oils.
President: Anthony Alves
Year Founded: 1975
Estimated Sales: $100-500 Million
Square Footage: 300000
Type of Packaging: Consumer, Food Service, Private Label, Bulk
Brands:
Olioro
Ex-Seed
Alpine Valley
Golden Delicious
Kleckner's
Grill Blazin BBQ Sauce

9333 **Oasis Mediterranean Cuisine**
1520 W Laskey Rd
Toledo, OH 43612-2914
419-269-1516
Fax: 419-324-7777 info@omcfood.com
www.omcfood.com
Mediterranean vegetarian cuisine
Owner: Francois Hashem
Quality Control: Tonny Obid
Estimated Sales: $5-10 Million
Number Employees: 20-49
Brands:
Non-Dairy Baklava

9334 **Oasis Winery**
14141 Hume Rd
Hume, VA 22639
540-635-7627
Fax: 540-635-4653 800-304-7656
Info@oasiswine.com www.oasiswine.com
Wines
Co- Founder: Tareq Salahi
Public Relations: Ann Runyon
Estimated Sales: $5-10 Million
Number Employees: 100-249
Type of Packaging: Private Label
Brands:
Bleu Rock Vineyard Wines
Fiery Rum Cellars
Oasis Wines & Sparkling Wines

9335 **Oatly**
67 Irving Place
9th Floor
New York, NY 10003
info.us@oatly.com
us.oatly.com
Oat milk
General Manager, U.S.: Mike Messersmith
Number of Products: 4

9336 **Oats Overnight**
2420 W 14th St
Suite B
Tempe, AZ 85281
support@oatsovernight.com
www.oatsovernight.com
Flavored oatmeal
Number of Brands: 1
Number of Products: 3
Brands:
OATS OVERNIGHT

9337 **Oatworks**
411 W. 14th St.
New York, NY 10014
646-624-2400
www.oatworks.com
Manufacturer of oat-powered fruit smoothies.
Founder: David Peters
Brands:
oatworks

9338 **Oberto Brands**
7060 Oberto Dr.
Kent, WA 98032
877-453-7591
www.oberto.com
Beef & turkey jerky, beef sticks & beefsteak, tender cut and canister beef jerky, microwave pork rinds, and traditional beef jerky.
President, Premium Brands: George Paleologou
Year Founded: 1918
Estimated Sales: $75-99 Million
Number Employees: 500-999
Number of Brands: 3
Square Footage: 40000
Parent Co: Premium Brands
Type of Packaging: Consumer
Brands:
Gentleman's Cut
Oberto
Pacific Gold

9339 **Oberweis Dairy Inc**
951 Ice Cream Dr # 1
North Aurora, IL 60542-1475
630-801-6100
Fax: 630-897-0562 866-623-7934
www.oberweis.com
Fluid dairy products, premium ice cream, and ice cream cakes, juice, meat products, crackers, cookies, salsas
Chairman: Jim Oberweis
President, Chief Executive Officer: Joe Oberweis
CFO: Jeff Wilhelm
jeff.wilhelm@oberweis.com
Vice President of Marketing: Bruce Bedford
VP Marketing: Mark Vance
VP, Sales: Lino Carrillo
VP, Operations: Mike McCarthy
VP Retail Operations: Elizabeth Craig
Estimated Sales: $1-2 Million
Number Employees: 100-249
Type of Packaging: Food Service, Private Label, Bulk

9340 **(HQ)Obester Winery**
12341 San Mateo Road
Half Moon Bay, CA 94019
650-726-9463
Fax: 650-726-7074 info@obesterwinery.com
www.obesterwinery.com
Wines
Owner: Kendyl Kellogg
kendyl.kellogg@mendonet.com
Estimated Sales: $3 Million
Number Employees: 5-9

9341 **Obis One**
Virginia Tech Corporate Research Center
1872 Pratt Dr, Suite 1375
Blacksburg, VA 24060
609-202-9766
pat@obisone.com
www.obisone.com
Black garlic
Founder: Patrick Lloyd
Brands:
Obis One

9342 **Oc Lugo Co Inc**
15 Third St # 2
New City, NY 10956-4946
845-480-5121
Fax: 845-480-5122 info@oclugo.com
www.oclugo.com
Supplier of chemicals, vitamins, minerals, gelatins and food ingredients. OC Lugo's other division is Critical Filtration supplies
President: Richard Lugo
rlugo@oclugo.com
Estimated Sales: $830,000
Number Employees: 5-9

9343 **Ocean Approved**
PO Box 8129
Portland, ME 04104
www.oceanapproved.com
Fresh, frozen kelp
President/Owner: Paul Dobbins
Year Founded: 2006

9344 **Ocean Beauty Seafoods Inc**
1100 W Ewing St
Seattle, WA 98119
206-285-6800
800-365-8950
info@oceanbeauty.com www.oceanbeauty.com
Manufacturer and distributor of seafood.
President & CEO: Mark Palmer
CFO: Tony Ross
VP, Retail Sales: Ron Christianson
Year Founded: 1910
Estimated Sales: $409 Million
Number Employees: 1,000-4,000
Type of Packaging: Food Service
Other Locations:
Ocean Beauty Seafood Facility
Boston MA
Ocean Beauty Seafood Facility
Cordova AK
Ocean Beauty Seafood Facility
Alitak AK
Ocean Beauty Seafood Facility
Kodiak AK
Ocean Beauty Seafood Facility
Los Angeles CA
Ocean Beauty Seafood Facility

Monroe AK
Ocean Beauty Seafood Facility
Naknek AK
Ocean Beauty Seafood Facility
Petersburg AK
Ocean Beauty Seafood Facility
Seattle WA
Ocean Beauty Seafood Facility
Nikiski AK
Brands:
Pillar Rock
Pink Beauty
Icy Point
Lascco
Pirate
Bay Beauty
McGovern's Best
Searchlight
Nathan's Smoked Salmon
Smoke It All
Taste T Pacific Whithing
Man of War Crab
XIP-Salmon Cavier
Sea Choice
Port Clyde Sardines
Neptune
Echo Falls
Ocean Beauty Brand

9345 Ocean Cliff Corp

362 S Front St
New Bedford, MA 02740-5745
508-990-7900
Fax: 508-990-7950
gregwhite@oceancliffcorporation.com
www.oceancliffcorporation.com
Fish and seafood liquid and powder extracts and spices including shrimp, clam, crab, fish, lobster and mussel
Owner: G White
Sales: Peter Shephard
gwhite@oceancliffcorporation.com
Estimated Sales: $2.5-5,000,000
Number Employees: 5-9
Square Footage: 40000
Type of Packaging: Bulk
Brands:
Ocean Cliff

9346 Ocean Crest Seafoods

P.O. Box 1183
Gloucester, MA 01931
978-281-0232
Fax: 978-283-3211 800-259-4769
www.neptunesharvest.com
Seafood
President/CEO: Leonard Parco
Estimated Sales: $1-3 Million
Number Employees: 20-49

9347 Ocean Food Co. Ltd.

3 Turbina Ave
Toronto, ON M1V 5G3
Canada
416-285-6487
Fax: 416-285-4012 info@oceanfood.ca
www.oceanfood.ca
Fish cakes and imitation crab and lobster.
President: Joe Nishikaze
Estimated Sales: $1.4 Million
Number Employees: 10
Type of Packaging: Consumer, Food Service

9348 Ocean Fresh Seafoods

4241 21st Ave W # 306
Seattle, WA 98199-1250
206-285-2412
Fax: 206-283-3408
Fresh and frozen fish and seafood
President: Ted Otness
Contact: Nita Waller
nitaw@oceanfreshsea.com
Plant Manager: Bill Bryant
Estimated Sales: $1,100,000
Number Employees: 5-9
Type of Packaging: Food Service
Brands:
Alaska Fresh

9349 Ocean Harvest

PO Box 60
Dennysville, ME 04628-0060
207-726-0609
Fax: 207-726-9571
Fish and seafood
Owner: Larry Matthews
Estimated Sales: $1-3 Million
Number Employees: 1-4

9350 Ocean King International

1680 S Garfield Avenue
Suite 202
Alhambra, CA 91801-5413
626-289-9399
Fax: 626-300-8177
Seafood
President/CEO: Jimmie Dang
CFO: Miling Shua
Vice President: Richard Mendelson
Secretary: Jorge Pardinas

9351 Ocean Mist Farms

10855 Ocean Mist Parkway
Castroville, CA 95012
831-633-2144
contactus@oceanmist.com
www.oceanmist.com
Spinach, cauliflower, celery, lettuce, artichokes, broccoli, etc.
CEO: Joe Pezzini
Sales Director: Tom Botelho
President of Production: Paul Scheid
Plant Manager: Mark Rensons
Estimated Sales: $9,200,000
Number Employees: 50-99
Type of Packaging: Consumer
Brands:
Ocean Mist

9352 Ocean Pride Fisheries

136 Jacquard Rd
PO Box 402
Lower Wedgeport, NS B0W 2B0
Canada
902-663-4579
Fax: 902-663-2698 jules@oceanpridefisheries.com
www.oceanpridefisheries.com
Processor and exporter of smoked salmon, cod and haddock
President: Milton Leblanc
Chief Operating Officer: Jules Leblanc
Estimated Sales: $1.3 Million
Number Employees: 10
Type of Packaging: Consumer, Food Service, Bulk

9353 Ocean Pride Seafood

207 S Richard St
Delcambre, LA 70528
337-685-2336
Fax: 337-685-2339
Shrimp and crawfish
President: Denise Dooley
Contact: David Kunes
opbob@msn.com
Estimated Sales: $500,000-$1 Million
Number Employees: 1-4

9354 Ocean Select Seafood

10714 Highway 14
Delcambre, LA 70528
337-685-5315
Fax: 337-685-6079
Seafood
President: Mitch Polito
Estimated Sales: $5-$10 Million
Number Employees: 1-4

9355 Ocean Spray International

One Ocean Spray Dr.
Lakeville-Middleboro, MA 02349
800-662-3263
www.oceanspray.com
Manufacturer of bottled juices and fruit ingredient supplier.
Interim CEO: James White
Senior VP/CFO: Daniel Cunha
Global Chief Innovation Officer: Rizal Hamdallah
VP, Marketing Services: Yash Sikand
COO: Brian Schiegg
Year Founded: 1930
Estimated Sales: $2.2 Billion
Number Employees: 2,000
Number of Brands: 26
Square Footage: 99000
Type of Packaging: Consumer, Food Service
Other Locations:
Middleboro MA
Lehigh Valley PA
Wisconsin Rapids WI
Markham WA
Kenosha WI
Henderson NV
Sulphur Springs TX
Tomah WI
Lanco, Chile
Brands:
Craisins
Cranapple
Crancherry
Crangrape
Cranicot
Cranorange
Ocean Spray
Ocean Spray Apple Juice
Ocean Spray Cranberries
Ocean Spray Cranberry Cocktail
Ocean Spray Fruit Punch
Ocean Spray Fruit Punch Cooler
Ocean Spray Grapefruit Juice
Ocean Spray Jellied Cran. Sauce
Ocean Spray Juice Blends
Ocean Spray Kiwi Straq. Juice
Ocean Spray Lemonade
Ocean Spray Orange Juice
Ocean Spray Pineapple Grapefruit
Ocean Spray Pink Grapefruit Juice
Ocean Spray Ruby Red & Mango
Ocean Spray Ruby Red Grapefruit
Ocean Spray Whole Berry Cranberries
Wellfleet Farms
Wellfleet Farms Cranberry Sauce
Wellfleet Farms Specialty Foods

9356 Ocean Springs Seafood

608 Magnolia Ave
Ocean Springs, MS 39564
228-875-0104
Fax: 228-875-0117
Frozen, fresh, headless and peeled shrimp
President: Earl Sayard
VP: Ruby Fayard
Secretary: Linda Fayard
Estimated Sales: $1500000
Number Employees: 5-9
Square Footage: 6000000
Type of Packaging: Private Label
Brands:
Surf Spray
Tropic

9357 Ocean Union Company

2100 Riverside Pkwy
Suite 129
Lawrenceville, GA 30043-5927
770-995-1957
Fax: 770-513-8662
Seafood, snapper, grouper, lobster, crab, tuna, eel, mackerel
President: Jackie Tsai

9358 Ocean's Balance

343 Ocean House Rd
Cape Elizabeth, ME 04107
lscali@oceansbalance.com
www.oceansbalance.com
Seaweed products
President/Owner: Tollef Olson
CEO: Mitchell Lench
Director of Sales & Marketing: Lisa Scali

9359 Ocean's Halo

1424 Chapin Ave
Burlingame, CA 94010
650-642-5907
www.oceanshalo.com
Seaweed snacks, broths, sauces, noodles and noodle bowls
Co-Founder: Robert Mock
Co-Founder and President: Shin Rhee
Brands:
Ocean's Halo

9360 Oceanfood Sales

1909 East Hastings Street
Vancouver, BC V5L 1T5
Canada
604-255-1414
Fax: 604-255-1787 877-255-1414
sales@oceanfoods.com www.oceanfoodsales.com
Processor and exporter of smoked salmon
VP: Robert Graham
VP, Controller: Louise Graham
Sales And Marketing Manager: Dave Slade
Customer Service: Dorothy Chaves
Production Manager: John Makowhichuk

Estimated Sales: $7.9 Million
Number Employees: 16
Type of Packaging: Consumer, Food Service, Private Label, Bulk

9361 **Oceanledge Seafoods**
138 Rankin Street
Rockland, ME 04841-2318
207-594-4955
Fax: 626-968-0196
Seafood
President: Steve Jonasson
Estimated Sales: $330,000
Number Employees: 2

9362 **Oceans Prome Distributing**
1413 Waukegan Rd
Glenview, IL 60025
847-998-5813
Fax: 847-729-5228
President: Jeffrey Burhop
Estimated Sales: $5-10 Million
Number Employees: 5-9

9363 **Oceanside Knish Factory**
3445 Lawson Blvd.
Oceanside, NY 11572
516-766-4445
Fax: 516-766-2319
Knishes
President: Leonard Model
knish1@aol.com
Estimated Sales: Below $5 Million
Number Employees: 20-49

9364 **Ocena Wineary & Vineyards**
4980 S. 52nd Ave
New Era, MI 49446
231-861-4657
renae@oceanawinery.com
www.oceanawinery.com
A family-operated winery specializing in estate wines made from French hybrid grapes, with a range from dry reds and whites to sweet, late harvest styles
Owner: Renae Goralski
Winemaker: Greg Goralski
Estimated Sales: Less than $500,000
Number Employees: 1-4

9365 **Octavia Tea LLC**
38w061 Tanglewood Drive
Batavia, IL 60510
866-505-6387
elizabeth@octaviatea.com
www.octaviatea.com
Tea.
Marketing: Elizabeth Stephano

9366 **Odell Brewing Co**
800 E Lincoln Ave
Fort Collins, CO 80524-2507
970-498-9070
Fax: 970-498-0706 cheers@odellbrewing.com
www.odellbrewing.com
Brewery
Founder: Doug Odell
CEO: Wynne Odell
Chief Financial Officer: Chris Banks
Chief Operating Officer: Brenden McGivney
Head of Human Resources: Corkie Odell
Estimated Sales: $20-50 Million
Number Employees: 100-249
Number of Brands: 55
Type of Packaging: Consumer, Food Service
Brands:
90 Shilling
Cutthroat Pale Ale
Loose Leaf Session Ale
India Pale Ale
Myrcenary Double IPA

9367 **Odell's**
Reno, NV
800-635-0436
odellscustomerservice@venturafoods.com
www.popntop.com
Popping oils and popcorn toppings.
Co-owner: Arthur Anderson
Co-owner: Vikki Anderson

9368 **Odom's Tennessee Pride Sausage Company**
PO Box 1187
Madison, TN 37116-1187
615-868-1360
Fax: 615-860-4703 www.tnpride.com
Breakfast sausage including fresh and fully cooked, breakfast sandwiches, appetizers, and gravy.
President: Larry Odom
Chairman: Richard Odom
Year Founded: 1943
Estimated Sales: $185 Million
Number Employees: 700
Square Footage: 18000
Type of Packaging: Consumer, Food Service, Private Label, Bulk
Brands:
Tennessee Pride Country Sausage

9369 **(HQ)Odwalla**
Sugar Land, TX
800-639-2552
consumers@odwalla.com www.odwalla.com
Almond milk, smoothies, juices and protein drinks
President/Owner: Alison Lewis
CEO: D. Stephen Williamson
CFO: James Steichen
SVP, Sales and Operations: Michael Cote
Contact: Monica Burns
burnsm@odshp.com
Estimated Sales: $25-49 Million
Number Employees: 60
Number of Brands: 1
Type of Packaging: Consumer
Brands:
Odwalla

9370 **Office General des EauxMinerales**
5260 Avenue Notre-Dame-De-Grace
Montreal, QC H4A 1K9
Canada
514-482-7221
Fax: 514-482-7093 www.saintjustin.ca
Bottler and exporter of carbonated natural mineral water
President: Nicole Lelievre
Number Employees: 23
Type of Packaging: Food Service
Brands:
Saint Justin

9371 **Offshore Seafood Co**
2586 25th Ave N
St Petersburg, FL 33713-3919
727-329-8848
www.offshoreseafood.com
Seafood including red grouper, gag grouper, red snapper, spiny FL Keys lobsters, stone crab claws, local wild caught shrimp and tuna
Co-Owner: Kent Sahr
Number Employees: 5-9
Type of Packaging: Food Service, Bulk

9372 **Offshore Systems Inc**
Mile 4 Captains Bay Rd
Dutch Harbor, AK 99692
907-581-1827
Fax: 907-581-1630
nreed@offshoresystemsinc.com
www.offshoresystemsinc.com
President: Daniel Roseta
Executive VP: Joey Willis
Director of Marketing: Wayne Bouck
Business Development Manager: Rick Wilson
Manager: Nick Reed
nreed@offshoresystemsinc.com
Operations Manager: Mike Peek
Number Employees: 20-49

9373 **Ogeki Sake USA Inc**
249 Hillcrest Rd
Hollister, CA 95023-4921
831-637-9217
Fax: 831-637-0953 question@ozekisake.com
www.ozekisake.com
Sake
President: Yasuo Umehara
yumehara@ozekisake.com
COO: Katsuyoshi Yoshida
Estimated Sales: $5-10 Million
Number Employees: 20-49
Type of Packaging: Private Label

9374 **Oh Baby Foods, Inc.**
21 West Mountain St., Suite 120
Fayetteville, AR 72701
800-788-1451
www.ohbabyfoods.com
Oh Baby Foods are all certified organic and non-GMO project verified. All ingredients are 100% US-grown and many are regionally raised.
Founder: Fran Free
Type of Packaging: Consumer

9375 **Oh Yes! Foods**
11420 Santa Monica Blvd
Suite 25966
Los Angeles, CA 90025
855-696-4937
www.ohyesfoods.com
Fruit- and vegetable-infused cheese pizza
Brands:
OH YES!

9376 **Oh, Sugar! LLC**
1050 Northfield Ct
Suite 125
Roswell, GA 30076
678-393-6408
Fax: 678-393-6489 866-557-8427
info@namsbits.com
Cookies and candy
Marketing: Amanda Black

9377 **Ohana Seafood, LLC**
255 Sand Island Rd
Suite 2C
Honolulu, HI 96819-2292
808-843-1844
Fax: 808-843-1844
Seafood
President: Jeffrey Yee
Vice President: Jeffrey Yee
Estimated Sales: $570,000
Number Employees: 1-4

9378 **Ohio Association Of Meat**
6870 Licking Valley Rd
Frazeysburg, OH 43822-9563
740-828-9900
Fax: 740-828-2635 val@oamp.org
www.oamp.org
Meats
Executive Secretary: Valerie Parks Graham
Contact: Valerie Graham
val@oamp.org
Estimated Sales: $5-10 Million
Number Employees: 5-9
Square Footage: 88464
Parent Co: Instantwhip Foods
Type of Packaging: Food Service, Private Label
Brands:
Instant Whip

9379 **Ohio Mushroom Company**
1893 N Dixie Hwy
Lima, OH 45801-3255
419-221-1721
Mushrooms
President: Robert Komminsk

9380 **Ohta Wafer Factory**
931 Hauoli St
Honolulu, HI 96826
808-949-2775
Puffed rice cakes and fortune and Japanese tea cookies
President: Herb Ohta
bran28@hotmail.com
Estimated Sales: $500,000-$1 Million
Number Employees: 1-4
Square Footage: 9000
Type of Packaging: Consumer, Food Service
Brands:
Ohta's Senbei

9381 **Oil & Olives Company**
5975 Sunset Dr
Suite 603
Miami, FL 33143
305-670-0979
sales@oilandolives.es
www.oilandolives.es
Olives, olive oil and dried fruits.
President: Manuel Sala Lopez

9382 **Oils Of Aloha**
66-935 Kaukonahua Rd
Waialua, HI 96791-8706
808-637-5620
Fax: 808-637-6194 800-367-6010
info@oilsofaloha.com
Salad oils and cooking oils
Chairman/Owner: Dana Gray
President: Matthew Papania
Marketing: Barbara Gray
Plant Manager: Matthew Papania
Estimated Sales: $5-10 Million
Number Employees: 20-49
Number of Brands: 1
Square Footage: 60000
Type of Packaging: Consumer, Food Service
Brands:
Oils of Aloha Macadamia Nut Oil

9383 **Oilseeds International LTD**
8 Jackson St
San Francisco, CA 94111-2022
415-956-7251
Fax: 415-394-9023 www.oilseedssf.com
Processes safflower oil, rice bran oil, and cottonseed cooking oil
President: John Gyulay
Vice President: Kenjiro Kondo
Marketing Director: Mickey Clements
Marketing: Roy Adam
Estimated Sales: $1-5 Million
Number Employees: 10-19
Type of Packaging: Bulk

9384 **Oilseeds International LTD**
8 Jackson St
San Francisco, CA 94111-2022
415-956-7251
Fax: 415-394-9023 sales@ricebranoil.biz
www.oilseedssf.com
Rice bran oil. Non-GMO and non-hydrogenated vegetable oil, meaning it contains no trans fats.
CFO: Akio Takami
Executive Vice President: Fumi Sugawara
Sales & Marketing: Collin Amon
Marketing Manager: Mickey Clements
Estimated Sales: $3.3 Million
Number Employees: 10-19
Type of Packaging: Bulk

9385 **Ojai Cook**
149 S Barrington Avenue
Los Angeles, CA 90049-3310
310-646-5001
Fax: 310-839-5135 886-571-1551
Condiments, sauces and beverages
President/CEO/Marketing Director: Joan Vogel
Brands:
Cocktail Duet
Prickly Pecans
Puckers

9386 **Ojai Cook LLC**
1205 Maricopa Hwy
Ojai, CA 93023-3128
805-646-8020
Fax: 805-646-8020 888-657-1155
Condiments
Owner: Marty Folk
Estimated Sales: $300,000-500,000
Number Employees: 5-9

9387 **Ojai Vineyard**
10540 Encino Dr
Oak View, CA 93022-9257
805-649-1674
Fax: 805-649-4651 info@OjaiVineyard.com
www.ojaivineyard.com
Wine
Owner: John Anderson
johna@ojaivineyard.com
Estimated Sales: $590,000
Number Employees: 1-4
Brands:
Ojai

9388 **Ojeda USA**
460 Southport Commerce Blvd
Spartanburg, SC 29306
864-574-6004
Fax: 864-574-6005 www.ojedausa.com
Commercial refrigeration equipment, specializing in novelty freezers and open air display cases
VP: Mark Thompson
Year Founded: 2005

9389 **Ok Industries**
PO Box 1787
Fort Smith, AR 72902
479-783-4186
Fax: 479-784-1358 800-635-9441
www.tenderbird.com
Fresh and frozen chicken.
President/CEO: Trent Goins
CFO: Scott Hunter
SVP, Supply Chain: Russ Bragg
Contact: Randall Goins
fgoins@okfoods.com
Estimated Sales: $20-50 Million
Number Employees: 100-249
Number of Brands: 2
Parent Co: OK Industries
Type of Packaging: Consumer, Food Service, Private Label
Brands:
O.K. Foods
TenderBird

9390 **Okahara Saimin Factory LTD**
1804 Waiola St
Honolulu, HI 96826-2698
808-949-0588
Fax: 808-949-0375 okaharasf001@hawaii.rr.com
www.buyimporter.com
Noodles
President: Kiyoko Okahara
okaharasf001@hawaii.rr.com
Estimated Sales: $1500000
Number Employees: 20-49
Type of Packaging: Consumer, Food Service

9391 **Okanagan Spring Brewery**
2808-27 Avenue
Vernon, BC V1T 9K4
Canada
250-542-2337
Fax: 250-542-7780 800-652-0755
info@okspring.com www.okspring.com
Beer, ale and stout
COO: Richardson Knudson
CEO: John Sleeman
Marketing Director: Paul Meehan
Managing Director: Rick Knudson
Parent Co: Seeman Brewing & Malting Company
Type of Packaging: Consumer, Food Service
Brands:
Okanagan Spring
Shastebury
Sleeman
Strohs Canada

9392 **Oklahoma City Meat Co Inc**
300 S Klein Ave
Oklahoma City, OK 73108-1495
405-235-3308
Fax: 405-235-9989 www.okcmeat.com
Beef, lamb and pork; wholesaler/distributor of chicken. Founded in 1957.
President: Tommy Saunders
office@okcmeat.com
Estimated Sales: $10-20 Million
Number Employees: 20-49
Type of Packaging: Food Service

9393 **Okuhara Foods Inc**
881 N King St
Honolulu, HI 96817-4554
808-848-0581
Fax: 808-841-5367
Pre-packaged frozen fish including salted butterfish, salmon and shellfish
President: James N Okuhara
okufoods@aol.com
Vice President: Satoru Okuhara
Estimated Sales: $10-20 Million
Number Employees: 20-49
Type of Packaging: Consumer, Bulk

9394 **Ola Loa**
1555 Burke Ave
Unit K
San Francisco, CA 94124
800-800-9550
www.olaloa.com
Vitamin beverage
Co-Founder: Gregory Kunin
Brands:
OLA LOA

9395 **Olam Spices**
205 East River Park Pl
Suite 310
Fresno, CA 93720
559-447-1390
USA@olamnet.com
www.olamgroup.com
Edible nuts, cocoa, coffee, cotton and spices and vegetable ingredients
Co-Founder/Group CEO: Sunny Verghese
Year Founded: 2002
Estimated Sales: $13.9 Billion
Number Employees: 5,000+
Number of Products: 47
Parent Co: Olam International
Type of Packaging: Bulk
Other Locations:
USA Head Office
Fresno CA

9396 **Oland Breweries**
3055 Agricola Street
Halifax, NS B3K 4G2
Canada
902-453-1867
Fax: 902-453-3847 800-268-2337
www.olandbrewery.ca
Beer, ale, stout and lager
Marketing Director: Brent Qartermain
Number Employees: 100-249
Parent Co: Labatt Breweries
Type of Packaging: Consumer, Food Service
Brands:
Labatt
Oland

9397 **Old Cavendish Products**
93 Densmore Rd
Cavendish, VT 05142
802-226-7783
Fax: 802-226-7783 800-536-7899
fruitcakes@tds.net www.cavendishfruitcake.com
All natural fruitcake, mustard, herb vinegars
President: Mary Ormrod
COO: Andrew Leven
Estimated Sales: $200K
Number Employees: 2
Type of Packaging: Consumer, Food Service, Private Label, Bulk

9398 **Old Chatham Sheepherding Co**
155 Shaker Museum Rd
Old Chatham, NY 12136-2603
518-794-7733
Fax: 518-794-7641 888-743-3760
cheese@blacksheepcheese.com
Sheep's milk cheese
Owner: Stew Adams
stew@blacksheepcheese.com
Owner: Nancy Clark
Marketing/Sales: Lorie Appleby
Kleinpeter/Cheesemaker: Benoit Mailloil
Administrative Manager: Sandra Hoehneker
Estimated Sales: $5-10 Million
Number Employees: 20-49
Number of Brands: 1
Number of Products: 14

9399 **Old Colony Baking Co Inc**
PO Box 1111
Northbrook, IL 60065-1111
847-498-5434
Fax: 847-760-0707 info@ocolony.com
www.ocolony.com
Pastries and co-branded cookies
President/Owner: Jeffrey Kaufman
CEO: Ann Kaufman
Estimated Sales: $1-3 Million
Number Employees: 10-19
Type of Packaging: Private Label
Brands:
Andes Chocolate Mint Chip Cookies
Big Top Animal Cookies
Chiquita Banana Cookies
Diamond Walnut Shortbread Cookies
Musselman's Apple Sauce Cookies
Realemon Lemon Cookies

9400 **Old Country Bakery**
5350 Biloxi Avenue
North Hollywood, CA 91601-3531
818-838-2302
Fax: 818-838-2307
Cakes and pastry

General Manager: Chris Meyer

9401 **Old Country Cheese**
5510 Cty. Hwy. D
Cashton, WI 54619
608-654-5411
Fax: 608-654-5411 888-320-9469
info@oldcountrycheese.com
www.oldcountrycheese.com
Cheese and jams
President: Kevin Everhart
County Chief: Michael Everhart
Estimated Sales: $1-2.5 Million
Number Employees: 20-49
Type of Packaging: Consumer, Private Label, Bulk
Brands:
Old Country Cheese

9402 **Old Country Meat & Sausage Company**
811 W Washington St
San Diego, CA 92103-1894
619-297-4301
Sausages
CEO: Manfred Spenner
Marketing Manager: Manfred Spenner
Estimated Sales: Under $500,000
Number Employees: 5-9
Type of Packaging: Bulk
Brands:
Old Country

9403 **Old Country Packers**
318 River St
Duryea, PA 18642
570-655-9608
Fax: 570-457-1678
Horseradish including white and red beet, cocktail sauce, chicken wing sauce including mild, hot and honey, sauce and garlic in water and oil
President: Edwarded Orkwis
Estimated Sales: $1 million
Number Employees: 1-4
Square Footage: 8000
Type of Packaging: Consumer, Food Service, Private Label
Brands:
Old Country
Town Tavern

9404 **Old Credit Brewing Co. Ltd.**
1-75 Horner Ave
Toronto, ON M8Z 4X5
Canada
416-494-2766
Fax: 905-274-4154 info@ontariocraftbrewers.com
www.ontariocraftbrewers.com
Amber/red ale and pilsner
President: Aldo Lista
Brewer: Orrin Besko
Number Employees: 5-9
Square Footage: 24000
Type of Packaging: Consumer, Food Service
Brands:
Old Credit

9405 **Old Creek Ranch Winery**
10024 Old Creek Rd
Ventura, CA 93001-1002
805-649-4132
Fax: 805-649-9293 winery@oldcreekranch.com
www.oldcreekranch.com
Premium wines
President: John Whitman
jwhitman@oldcreekranch.com
Winemaker: Charles Branham
Estimated Sales: Below $5 Million
Number Employees: 5-9
Number of Products: 3
Square Footage: 16000
Type of Packaging: Private Label
Brands:
Old Creek Ranch Winery

9406 **Old Dominion Peanut Corp**
208 W 24th St
Norfolk, VA 23517-1355
757-622-1633
Fax: 757-624-9415 800-368-6887
sales@odpeanut.com
Candy including hard candies, fund raising, cashew and peanut brittle and chocolate covered and butter toffee peanuts
President/CEO: William Delchiaro
willd@odpeanut.com
Estimated Sales: $4500000
Number Employees: 50-99
Square Footage: 200000
Parent Co: The Virginia Food Group
Type of Packaging: Consumer, Food Service, Private Label, Bulk
Brands:
Old Dominion

9407 **Old Dominion Spice Company**
10990 Leadbetter Road
PO Box 249
Ashland, VA 23005
804-550-2780
Fax: 804-550-2868 www.olddominionspice.com
Dry blends used in condiments, marinades, seasonings, rubs, breaders, batters and other coating systems
President: Lindy Thackston
Founder/CEO: Milton Parma
Research & Development Manager: David Pauly
SVP Sales: H Guy Moyers
Contact: David Pauly
david@olddominionspice.com
Estimated Sales: $550,000
Number Employees: 8
Square Footage: 16600

9408 **Old Dutch Foods LTD**
Roseville, MN
customerservice@olddutchfoods.com
www.olddutch.com
Snack foods including potato chips, popcorn, pretzels, salsa and dips
President: Steve Aanenson
Year Founded: 1984
Estimated Sales: $107 Million
Number Employees: 500
Number of Brands: 10
Type of Packaging: Private Label
Brands:
Dutch Gourmet
Humpy Dumpty
Ringolos
Old Dutch
Ripples
Restaurant Style
Tiny Twists
Puffcorn
Bac'n Puffs

9409 **(HQ)Old Dutch Mustard Company**
98 Cuttermill Road
Suite 260 S
Great Neck, NY 11021-3010
516-466-0522
Fax: 516-466-0762
custservice@olddutchmustard.com
mustard flour, prepared mustard, vinegar, sauce and juice
President: Paul Santich
Sales Manager: Evan Dobkins
Contact: Susan Bruno
sbruno@pilgrimfoods.net
Number Employees: 70
Square Footage: 400000
Type of Packaging: Consumer, Food Service, Private Label, Bulk
Other Locations:
Brands:
Old Dutch

9410 **Old Europe Cheese Inc**
1330 E Empire Ave
Benton Harbor, MI 49022-2000
269-925-5003
Fax: 269-925-9560 mike@oldeuropecheese.com
www.oldeuropecheese.com
Producer of specialty cheeses, focusing on Brie, Camembert, Gouda, Edam, fontina and mantoro.
General Manager: Francois Capt
Manager: Mike Balane
mike@oldeuropecheese.com
Estimated Sales: $18 Million
Number Employees: 100-249
Number of Brands: 1
Square Footage: 50000
Parent Co: I.L.A.S.
Type of Packaging: Consumer, Food Service
Brands:
Remy Picot

9411 **Old Fashioned Foods**
650 Furnace St
Mayville, WI 53050-1248
920-387-7924
Fax: 920-387-7929 www.oldfash.com
Cheese spreads, cheese sauce, tex-mex, cheese dips, nacho cheese sauce, squeeze cheese, squeeze salsa, glass cheese spreads, cheese sticks, and aerosol and portion control pouches.
Owner/President: Bernard Youso
byouso@oldfash.com
Chairman: Gary Youso
Quality Control: Ben Lindstrom
Marketing: Bernie Youso
Sales: Jim Clark
Production/Maintenance: Cory Lenhardt
Purchasing: Kathy Emmer
Estimated Sales: $5-10 Million
Number Employees: 50-99
Brands:
Old Faishoned Foods

9412 **Old Fashioned Kitchen Inc**
1045 Towbin Ave
Lakewood, NJ 08701-5931
732-364-4100
Fax: 732-905-7352 info@oldfashionedkitchen.com
www.oldfashionedkitchen.com
Specialy frozen foods nationally
President: Jay Çonzen
jayc@oldfashionedkitchen.com
SVP: Sal Mangiapane
Plant Manager: John Kercher
Year Founded: 1951
Estimated Sales: $20-50 Million
Number Employees: 50-99
Square Footage: 30000

9413 **Old Fashioned Natural Products**
2230 Cape Cod Way
Santa Ana, CA 92703-3582
714-835-6367
Fax: 714-835-4948 800-552-9045
alisha@lalifestyle.com www.lalifestyle.com
Vitamins and herbal teas and supplements; also, custom formulations and private labeling available
President: Patricia Logsdon
ofnp2@aol.com
VP: John Brown
Estimated Sales: $10-20 Million
Number Employees: 10-19
Square Footage: 32000
Type of Packaging: Private Label

9414 **Old Firehouse Winery**
5499 Lake Rd E
Geneva, OH 44041-9425
440-466-9300
Fax: 440-466-8011 800-362-6751
info@oldfirehousewinery.com
www.oldfirehousewinery.com
Ohio wines
Owner: Don Woodward
dave@oldfirehousewinery.com
Estimated Sales: $1-$3 Million
Number Employees: 5-9
Type of Packaging: Consumer

9415 **Old Home Foods Inc**
550 County Road D W # 18
Suite 18
New Brighton, MN 55112-3517
651-312-8900
Fax: 651-312-8901 info@oldhomefoods.com
www.oldhomefoods.com
Cultured dairy products like cottage cheese, sour cream, yogurt, dips, and salsa
CEO: Geoff Murphy
Estimated Sales: $20-50 Million
Number Employees: 10-19
Brands:
Old Home

9416 **Old House Vineyards**
18351 Corkys Ln
Culpeper, VA 22701-4413
540-423-1032
Fax: 540-423-1320 info@oldhousevineyards.com
www.oldhousevineyards.com
Wines
Owner: Patrick J Kearney
Winemaker: Doug Fabbioli
Estimated Sales: $3-5 Million
Number Employees: 1-4

9417 **Old Kentucky Hams**
PO Box 443
Cynthiana, KY 41031-0443
859-234-5015
Fax: 859-234-5015
Country hams and bacon
President: Nancy Hisle
Plant Manager: Elizabeth Hunt
Estimated Sales: $1-4.9 000,000
Number Employees: 1-4
Square Footage: 1
Type of Packaging: Private Label
Brands:
Old Kentucky Hams
Traditional Kentucky

9418 **Old London Foods**
Yadkinville, NC
www.oldlondonfoods.com
Low calorie snacks
President & CEO, B&G Foods: Robert Cantwell
Number Employees: 250
Parent Co: B&G Foods, Inc.

9419 **Old Mansion Inc**
3811 Corporate Rd
PO Box 1839
Petersburg, VA 23805
804-862-9889
800-476-1877
www.oldmansion.com
Quality spices, seasonings, coffee and teas
Sales: Tom Mullen
Number Employees: 20-49
Type of Packaging: Consumer, Food Service, Private Label, Bulk

9420 **Old Mill Winery**
403 S Broadway
Geneva, OH 44041-1844
440-466-5560
Fax: 440-466-2099 www.theoldmillwinery.com
Gourmet foods, wines
Owner: Dave Froelich
info@oldmillwinery.com
Winemaker: Bill Turgeon
Marketing Director: Shirley Barnett
Estimated Sales: $810,000
Number Employees: 10-19

9421 **Old Monmouth Candies**
627 Park Ave
Freehold, NJ 07728-2397
732-462-1311
Fax: 732-462-6820
Sales@OldMonmouthCandies.com
www.oldmonmouthcandies.com
Candy and confections
President: Hal Gunther
Manager: Steve Gunther
sgunther@oldmonmouthcandies.com
Estimated Sales: Below $5 Million
Number Employees: 10-19
Brands:
Old Monmouth

9422 **Old Neighborhood**
37 Waterhill St
Lynn, MA 01905
781-595-1557
Fax: 781-595-7523
www.oldneighborhoodfoods.com
Meat including; hot dogs, sausage, fresh-cut deli, pre-cut deli, meat case, and shaved meat.
Chief Executive Officer: Tom Demakes
Year Founded: 1893
Estimated Sales: $45.1 Million
Number Employees: 250-499
Square Footage: 66000
Type of Packaging: Food Service
Brands:
Thin 'n Trim
Old Neighborhood

9423 **Old Orchard Brands, LLC**
1991 12 Mile Rd.
Sparta, MI 49345
800-330-2173
oldorchard.com
Bottled and frozen fruit juices.
President/Founder: Mark Saur
VP Sales: Craig Lampright
Year Founded: 1985
Estimated Sales: $103.3 Million
Number Employees: 50-99
Square Footage: 140000
Parent Co: Lassonde Industries
Type of Packaging: Consumer
Brands:
Old Orchard

9424 **Old Rip Van Winkle Distillery**
113 Great Buffalo Trace
Frankfort, KY 40601
502-897-9113
Fax: 502-896-9989
pvanwinkle@oldripvanwinkle.com
www.oldripvanwinkle.com
Bourbon whiskey
Owner: Julian Van Winkle
Estimated Sales: $1-2.5 Million
Number Employees: 1-4
Brands:
Old Rip Van Wrinkle

9425 **Old Sacramento Popcorn Company**
1011 St
Sacramento, CA 95814
916-446-1980
Fax: 916-442-2676 www.oslhp.net
Processor and exporter of popcorn
Owner: Jim Scott
Estimated Sales: Less than $150,000
Number Employees: 1-4

9426 **Old South Winery**
65 S Concord Ave
Natchez, MS 39120-6806
601-445-9924
Fax: 601-442-1215 mailus@newu.net
www.oldsouthwinery.com
Wines
Owner: Galbreath Edeen
edeeng@newu.net
Co-Owner: Edeen Galbreath
Winemaker: Scott Gallbreath
edeeng@newu.net
Estimated Sales: $500,000-$1 Million
Number Employees: 1-4
Type of Packaging: Private Label
Brands:
Old South Winery
Old South Muscadine

9427 **Old Tavern Food Products Inc**
230 S Prairie Ave
Waukesha, WI 53186-5937
262-542-5301
Fax: 262-542-5676 888-542-5317
Cheese, gift packs
President: Jill Strong
rdwgksgp@execpc.com
VP: Gail Strong
Estimated Sales: $500,000-$1 Million
Number Employees: 5-9
Type of Packaging: Private Label, Bulk
Brands:
Old Tavern Club Cheese

9428 **Old Time Candy Co**
350 Commerce Dr E
Lagrange, OH 44050-9316
440-355-4345
Fax: 775-908-1995 www.oldtimecandy.com
Chocolate candy
Owner: Theresa Brunslik
Sales Manager: Lynn White
Estimated Sales: Less Than $500,000
Number Employees: 1-4
Type of Packaging: Consumer

9429 **Old Tyme Mill Company**
1517-21 S Kolmar Ave
Chicago, IL 60623
773-521-9484
Fax: 773-521-9486
Waffle, pancake and breading mix
President: John Pontikes
Treasurer: Dorothy Pontikes
Estimated Sales: $280,000
Number Employees: 4

9430 **Old Wine Cellar**
4411 220th Trl
Amana, IA 52203
319-622-3116
Fax: 319-622-6162
Wines
President: Les Aackermin
Estimated Sales: $1-2.5 Million
Number Employees: 5-9
Brands:
Old Wine Cellar

9431 **Old Wisconsin Food Products**
950 West 175 Street
Homewood, IL 60430
708-798-0900
Fax: 708-798-3178 888-633-5684
www.buddig.com
Sausage
President: John Buddig
CFO: Roger Buddig
Plant Manager: Charles Belter
Estimated Sales: $200,000
Parent Co: Carl Buddig & Company
Brands:
Carl Budding
Old Wisconsin

9432 **Old Wisconsin Sausage Inc**
4036 Weeden Creek Rd.
Sheboygan, WI 53081
920-458-4304
Fax: 920-458-2716 877-451-7988
sales@oldwisconsin.com www.oldwisconsin.com
Smoked sausages
President: Tom Buddig
Manager: Bob Gielissen
Vice President: Tim Belter
belter@oldwisconsin.com
Plant Manager: Bob Gielissen
Year Founded: 1942
Estimated Sales: $20-50 Million
Number Employees: 100-249
Type of Packaging: Consumer
Brands:
Ends and Curls
Old Wisconsin Mug

9433 **Old World Bakery**
1933 W Galbraith Rd
Cincinnati, OH 45239-4767
513-931-1411
Fax: 513-931-3560 owb@fuse.net
www.oldworldbakery.com
Natural breads
Founder: Odette Skally
Public Relations: Cheryl Deleon
Number Employees: 50-99

9434 **Old World Spices Inc**
5320 College Blvd
Overland Park, KS 66211-1621
816-861-0400
Fax: 816-861-7073 800-241-0070
www.oldworldspices.com
Seasoning, spice and sauce packaging
Owner: John Junge
sales@oldworldspices.com
Marketing: Kathy Wheat
Estimated Sales: $1-5 Million
Number Employees: 20-49
Brands:
Old World Creations
Party Creations
Soups For One

9435 **Olde Colony Bakery**
519 Wando Ln
Mt Pleasant, SC 29464-8211
843-216-3232
Fax: 843-216-5553 800-722-9932
OCBenne@aol.com www.oldecolonybakery.com
Gourmet cookies and benne seed wafers
Owner: Peter Rix
Owner: Sheila Rix
ocbbenne@aol.com
Estimated Sales: Less than $500,000
Number Employees: 5-9
Brands:
Olde Colony

9436 **Olde Estate**
782 Ne Harbour Drive
Boca Raton, FL 33431-6927
561-400-7444
Fax: 561-392-2204 denzykatz@aol.com
Classic rum cakes
President: Denise Katz

9437 **Olde Heurich Brewing Company**
1307 New Hampshire Avenue NW
Washington, DC 20036
202-333-2313
Fax: 202-333-9198 www.foggybottom.com
Beer
President: Gary Heurich
Estimated Sales: Below $5 Million
Number Employees: 5
Brands:
Foggy Bottom Ale
Foggy Bottom Lager
Foggy Bottom Porter
Olde Georgetown Beer
Olde Heurich
Senate Beer

9438 **Olde Tyme Food Corporation**
775 Benton Drive
East Longmeadow, MA 01028-3215
413-525-4101
Fax: 413-525-3621 800-356-6533
Snack foods including candy apples, cotton candy, waffles, waffle cones, peanuts
President: David Baker
Sales Director: David Wedderspoon
Estimated Sales: $1.7 Million
Number Employees: 21
Square Footage: 100000
Parent Co: Hampton Farms
Type of Packaging: Consumer, Food Service, Private Label, Bulk
Brands:
Olde Tyme
Ole Style Peanut Butter

9439 **Olde Tyme Mercantile**
1127 Mesa View Drive
Arroyo Grande, CA 93420-6542
805-489-7991
Fax: 805-481-5578
Gourmet products including olives, pickles, salad dressings, mustards, mayonnaise and candies
President: Larry Williams
CEO: Kevin Keim
Propietor: Diane Keim
Number Employees: 10-19
Square Footage: 8000
Type of Packaging: Consumer, Private Label
Brands:
Scully
Wah Maker

9440 **Olds Products Co**
10700 88th Ave
Pleasant Prairie, WI 53158
262-947-3500
Orders@OldsFitz.com
www.oldsproducts.com
Prepared mustard, specialty mustard blends, and vinegar
Supply Chain Manager: Brian Schnuckel
bschnuckel@oldsfitz.com
Estimated Sales: $6500000
Number Employees: 50-99
Parent Co: Olds Products Company
Type of Packaging: Consumer, Food Service, Private Label, Bulk
Brands:
Koops' Mustard
Fitzpatrick Bros

9441 **Ole Salty's Potato Chips**
1920 E Riverside Blvd
Loves Park, IL 61111
815-637-2447
www.olesaltys.com
Potato chips
Manager: Troy Wedeikand
Estimated Sales: Below $5 Million
Number Employees: 1-4
Brands:
Ole Salty's

9442 **Ole Smoky Candy Kitchen**
642 Ski Mountain Rd
Gatlinburg, TN 37738
865-436-4716
Fax: 865-436-0268
Maggie@olesmokycandykitchen.com
www.olesmokycandykitchen.com
Candy
President: Esther J Dych
Manager: David Dych
Estimated Sales: Less Than $500,000
Number Employees: 5-9
Type of Packaging: Consumer

9443 **Oley Distributing Company**
PO Box 4660
Fort Worth, TX 76164-0660
817-625-8251
Fax: 817-626-7269
President: Patricia O'Neal
VP: Phil O'Neal, Jr.
General Manager: Bill Smith
Estimated Sales: $5-10 Million
Square Footage: 225000

9444 **Oliva Verde USA**
7413 Troy Avenue
Suite 157
Raleigh, NC 27615
919-846-9020
Fax: 919-844-1050
Olive oil

9445 **Olive & Sinclair Chocolate Co**
1628 Fatherland St
Nashville, TN 37206-2026
615-262-3007
info@oliveandsinclair.com
Manufacturer of chocolate and confections.
Founder: Scott Witherow
Production Manager: Jason Thompson
Number Employees: 1-4

9446 **Olive Growers Council**
4601 W School Ave
Visalia, CA 93291-5223
559-734-1710
Fax: 559-625-4847 olivecouncil@sbcglobal.net
www.olivecouncil.com
Bulk green olives
President: Adin A Hester
adin@goldstate.net
Estimated Sales: Less Than $500,000
Number Employees: 1-4
Type of Packaging: Private Label

9447 **Olive Oil Factor**
197 Huntingdon Ave
Waterbury, CT 06708-1413
475-235-2666
Fax: 860-945-8662 info@theoliveoilfactory.com
www.theoliveoilfactory.com
Oils including extra virgin olive, flavored and dipping, and balsamic vinegar
President: David Miller
david@theoliveoilfactory.com
Estimated Sales: $350,000
Number Employees: 20-49
Square Footage: 20000
Type of Packaging: Consumer, Food Service, Private Label

9448 **Olive Oil Source**
1833 Fletcher Way
Santa Ynez, CA 93460-9380
805-688-1014
sales@oliveoilsource.com
www.oliveoilsource.com
Olive oils
President: Shawn Addison
General Manager: Suzette Stahl
Accounting Manager: Joy Jonas
VP Operations: Antoinette Addison
Number Employees: 10-19

9449 **Oliveo LLC**
1717 Rice St
Rosenberg, TX 77471
281-633-9335
Fax: 713-334-9929 888-924-6687
Extra virgin olive oil
Estimated Sales: $300,000-500,000
Number Employees: 1-4

9450 **Oliver Egg Products**
9422 Hungarytown Road
Crewe, VA 23930-4125
804-645-9406
Fax: 804-645-7429 800-525-3447
www.jamieoliver.com
Frozen and refrigerated egg whites, whole eggs, yolks and scrambled egg mix
Owner: Bill Oliver
Type of Packaging: Food Service, Bulk

9451 **Oliver Packaging & Equipment Co.**
3236 Wilson Dr NW
Walker, MI 49534
616-356-2950
Fax: 616-233-1132 800-253-3893
oliver-info@oliverquality.com
www.oliverquality.com
Bakery and meal packaging equipment
President/Owner: Chadd Floria

9452 **Oliver Winery**
200 E Winery Rd
Bloomington, IN 47404-2400
812-876-5800
Fax: 812-876-9309 800-258-2783
admin@oliverwinery.com www.oliverwinery.com
Producer of wines, including semi-sweet, semi-dry, dry whites, dry reds, dessert and sparkling.
President: Julie Adams
CEO: Bill Oliver
boliver@oliverwinery.com
Executive Vice President: Kathleen Oliver
Vice President of Wholesale Sales: Chris Hibbert
Human Resources Director: Jessika Hane
VP of Operations, Director of Winemaking: Dennis Dunham
Vineyard Manager: Bernie Parker
Estimated Sales: $18.7 Million
Number Employees: 50-99
Number of Brands: 8
Type of Packaging: Consumer, Food Service, Bulk
Brands:
Oliver
Orchard Stand
Bubblecraft
Beanblossom Hard Cider
Camelot Mead
Creekbend
Pilot Project
Vine Series

9453 **Olivia's Croutons**
1423 North Street
New Haven, VT 05472
802-453-2222
Fax: 802-453-7722 888-425-3080
info@oliviascroutons.com
www.oliviascroutons.com
All natural specialty croutons: Butter and garlic, parmesan pepper, vermont cheddar and dill, multi grain with garlic, and gazapach lowfat croutons. Also roasted onion tostini and lemon parsley tostini
President: Francie Caccavo
info@oliviascroutons.com
Estimated Sales: Below $5 Million
Number Employees: 5-9
Type of Packaging: Consumer, Food Service, Private Label, Bulk

9454 **Olivia's Kitchen**
1580 Park Ave
New York, NY 10029-1853
917-374-0077
Baked goods
Founder: Olivia Marjoram
Brands:
Olivia's Kitchen

9455 **Olivier's Candies**
2828 54th Ave SE
Calgary, AB T2C 0A7
Canada
403-266-6028
Fax: 403-266-6029 info@oliviers.ca
www.oliviers.ca
Chocolate, hard candy, brittles, barks
President: Wally Marcolin
Secretary: Rick Jeffrey
Number Employees: 10-19
Type of Packaging: Consumer, Bulk

9456 **Olivina. LLC**
4555 Arroyo Road
Livermore, CA 94550
925-455-8710
charles@theolivina.com
www.theolivina.com
Olive oils
President/Owner/CEO: Charles Crohare
charles@theolivina.com
General Manager: Alice Crohare
Estimated Sales: $25 Million
Number Employees: 20

9457 **Olivio Premium Products**
867 Boylston Street
Boston, MA 2116
customerservice@olivioproducts.com
www.olivio.com
Olive oil products
Contact: Ben Blier
bblier@motu.com

9458 **Olomomo Nut Company**
4760 Walnut St.
Boulder, CO 80301
877-923-6888
info@olomomo.com www.olomomo.com
Roasted & flavored nuts
Chairman & Founder: Justin Perkins
CEO: Mark Owens
VP Sales & Marketing: Justin Desiderio
Sales & Marketing Coordinator: Sarah Dhanraj
Production: Brian Starkman

9459 **Olsen Fish Co**
2115 N 2nd St
Minneapolis, MN 55411-2204
612-287-0838
Fax: 612-287-8761 800-882-0212
lutefisk@olsenfish.com www.olsenfish.com
Lutfisk and pickled herring
President: Chris Dorff
lutefisk@olsenfish.com
Estimated Sales: $3-5 Million
Number Employees: 10-19
Type of Packaging: Bulk
Brands:
Olsen

9460 **Olson Livestock & Seed**
31921 Rd 711
Haigler, NE 69030-4006
308-297-3283
Fax: 308-297-3284
Popcorn
Owner: Jeff Olson
Owner: Scott Olson
Owner: Steve Olson
Estimated Sales: $3-5 Million
Number Employees: 5 to 9

9461 **Olson Locker**
917 Winnebago Ave
Fairmont, MN 56031-3614
507-238-2563
Fax: 507-238-2564
Meat and meat products
President: Mark Olson
mark@olsonfarms.com
Estimated Sales: $460,000
Number Employees: 1-4
Type of Packaging: Consumer

9462 **Olymel**
2200 Pratte Ave.
Suite 400
Saint-Hyacinthe, QC J2S 4B6
Canada
450-771-0400
Fax: 450-773-6436 www.olymel.com
Pork and poultry.
President/CEO: Rejean Nadeau
First VP: Paul Beauchamp
Senior VP, Sales/Marketing: Richard Davies
Year Founded: 1991
Estimated Sales: $3.6 Billion
Number Employees: 13,000
Number of Brands: 3
Type of Packaging: Private Label, Bulk
Brands:
Olymel
Flamingo
Lafleur

9463 **Olympia Candies**
11606 Pearl Rd
Strongsville, OH 44136-3320
440-572-7747
Fax: 440-572-1819 800-574-7747
www.olympiacandy.com
Candied popcorn
Owner: Robert Mc Grath
sales@olympiacandy.com
Estimated Sales: $1-3 Million
Number Employees: 10-19

9464 **Olympia International**
2166 Spring Creek Road
Belvidere, IL 61008-9507
815-547-5972
Fax: 815-547-5973
pickles, mushrooms, horseradish, marinated peppers, beets and salads
President: Greg Bodak
Contact: Arturo Gonzalez
arturo@olympiaintl.com
Estimated Sales: $260,000
Number Employees: 1

9465 **Olympia Oyster Co**
1042 SE Bloomfield Rd
Shelton, WA 98584
360-426-3354
877-427-3193
info@olympiaoyster.com www.olympiaoyster.com
Oysters, clams, oyster soup bases
Estimated Sales: $1500000
Number Employees: 20-49
Type of Packaging: Consumer, Food Service

9466 **Olympia Provisions**
123 SE 2nd Ave
Portland, OR 97214-1002
503-894-8275
Fax: 503-894-8635 info@olympiaprovisions.com
www.olympiaprovisions.com
Salami, sausages, pft,, deli meats and pickles.
Controller: Jim Rowe
Contact: Michelle Cairo
Brands:
Olympia Provisions

9467 **Olympic Cellars**
255410 Highway 101
Port Angeles, WA 98362-9200
360-452-0160
Fax: 360-452-3782 info@OlympicCellars.com
www.olympiccellars.com
Wines
Owner: Kathy Charlton
wines@olympiccellars.com
Co-Owner: Molly Rivard
Co-Owner: Libby Sweetser
Winemaker: Benoit Murat
Estimated Sales: Less Than $500,000
Number Employees: 1-4
Type of Packaging: Private Label
Brands:
Olympic Cellars

9468 **Olympic Coffee & Roasting**
4907 119th Ave SE
Bellevue, WA 98006
206-244-8305
Fax: 206-244-8323 888-244-8313
Coffee
Director: Robert Doxsie
Estimated Sales: $5-10 Million
Number Employees: 5-9
Brands:
Olympic Coffee

9469 **Olympic Foods**
5625 W Thorpe Rd
Spokane, WA 99224
509-455-8059
Fax: 509-455-8329
fruit juice
President: Doug Koffinke
CEO: Howard Chow
CFO: Richard Cook
Contact: Valerie Biladeau
jkskwilcox@msn.com
Estimated Sales: $1-2.5 Million
Number Employees: 12
Square Footage: 348000
Type of Packaging: Consumer, Food Service, Private Label
Brands:
Albertson's
Citrus Sunshine
Dairyworld
Minute Maid
Newman's Own
Tree Top
Washington Natural
Western Family

9470 **Olympic Provisions Northwest**
1632 NW Thurman St
Portland, OR 97209-2519
503-894-8136
info@olympiaprovisions.com
www.olympiaprovisions.com
cured and non-cured meats, pate, and pickles
Co-Owner: Elias Cairo
Co-Owner: Michelle Cairo
Manager: Travis Lewis
tlewis@olympiaprovisions.com
Number Employees: 20-49
Brands:
OLYMPIA PROVISIONS

9471 **Om Mushrooms**
5931 Priestly Dr
Suite 101
Carlsbad, CA 92008
Fax: 760-798-8025 866-740-6874
info@ommushrooms.com ommushrooms.com
Organic mushroom powders
Co-Founder: Steve Farrar
Co-Founder: Sandra Carter

9472 **Omaha Meat Processors**
6016 Grover St
Omaha, NE 68106-4358
402-554-1965
Fax: 402-554-0224 omahameats@aol.com
Beef, pork steaks, sausage
President: David Kousgaard
omahameats@aol.com
Estimated Sales: $30 Million
Number Employees: 20-49
Square Footage: 9000
Type of Packaging: Food Service

9473 **Omaha Steaks Inc**
800-960-8400
www.omahasteaks.com
sausage, steak, veal and poultry, also desserts and wine
President: Bruce Simon
basimon@aol.com
Senior VP: Todd Simon
Number Employees: 1000-4999
Type of Packaging: Consumer, Food Service
Brands:
Omaha Steaks International

9474 **Omanhene Cocoa Bean Co**
5441 S 9th St
Milwaukee, WI 53221-4417
414-744-8780
Fax: 414-744-8786 800-588-2462
www.omanhene.biz
Hot cocoa mixes, chocolate
President: Steven Wallace
Operations Manager: Mario Nissen
Number Employees: 20-49
Number of Brands: 1
Number of Products: 5
Type of Packaging: Consumer, Private Label, Bulk
Brands:
Omanhene Cocoa

9475 **Omar Coffee Co**
41 Commerce Ct
Newington, CT 06111-2246
860-667-8889
Fax: 860-667-8883 800-394-6627
www.omarcoffee.com
Coffee carts and roasted coffee and tea.
Owner: Steve Costas
President: Diane Bokron
Year Founded: 1937
Estimated Sales: $30,900,000
Number Employees: 20-49
Number of Brands: 1
Square Footage: 30000
Type of Packaging: Consumer, Food Service
Brands:
Omar Coffee

9476 **Omega Foods**
395 Pendant Drive
Unit 2
Mississauga, ON L5T 2W9
Canada
905-212-9252
Fax: 905-212-9484 877-212-9484
info@omega-foods.com www.omega-foods.com
Salmon, tuna, mahi mahi burgers

President/Owner: Patrick Sullivan
Director Marketing/Administration: Lisa Baker
Sales: Lori Johansen
Operations: Carl Nelson
Plant Manager: Dana Davis
Estimated Sales: $500,000
Number Employees: 9
Number of Brands: 1
Number of Products: 3
Type of Packaging: Consumer, Food Service, Bulk
Brands:
Omega Foods

9477 **(HQ)Omega Nutrition**
6515 Aldrich Rd
Bellingham, WA 98226
Fax: 604-253-4228 800-661-3529
info@omeganutrition.com
www.omeganutrition.com
Organic oils: borage, flax, hazelnut, sesame, safflower, sunflower, pistachio, almond and canola; hazelnut flours
Owner: Bob Walbert
Marketing Director: Robert Gaffney
Contact: Simon Hatton
graphics@omeganutrition.com
Estimated Sales: $6.5 Million
Number Employees: 20-49
Square Footage: 64000
Type of Packaging: Food Service, Private Label
Other Locations:
OMEGA Nutrition U.S.A.
Vancouver BC
Brands:
Efa Balanced
Essential Balance
Nutriflax
Omegaflo
Omegaplus Gla

9478 **Omega Produce Company**
PO Box 277
Nogales, AZ 85628
520-281-0410
Fax: 520-281-1010
cucumbers and bell peppers
President: George Gotsis
ggomega1@aol.com
Secretary/Treasurer, VP: Toru Fujiwara
Office Manager: Norah Romero
VP Sales: J Nick. Gotsis
Estimated Sales: $10-20 Million
Number Employees: 10-19

9479 **Omega Protein**
610 Menhaden Rd.
Reedville, VA 22539
804-453-6262
hq@omegaprotein.com
www.omegaprotein.com
Menhaden oil, red meat and fish.
President/CEO: Bret Scholtes
Executive VP/CFO: Andrew Johannesen
President, Animal Nutrition Division: Dr. Mark Griffin
Vice President, Operations: Montgomery Deihl
Year Founded: 1913
Estimated Sales: $168 Million
Number Employees: 546
Parent Co: Cooke Inc.

9480 **Omega Pure**
1851 Kaiser Avenue
Irvine, CA 92614
562-429-3335
Fax: 562-421-0920 jinman@omegapure.com
www.omegapure.com
Omega-3 fish oil
General Manager: Monty Deihl
Chairman: Blaine Altaffer
National Sales Manager: Julie Inman
Parent Co: Omega Protein

9481 **On The Verandah**
1536 Franklin Rd
Highlands, NC 28741-8557
828-526-2338
Fax: 828-526-4132 otv1@ontheverandah.com
Sauces
Executive Chef: Andrew Figel
Contact: A Figel
otv1@ontheverandah.com
General Manager: Marlene Figel
Estimated Sales: Less Than $500,000
Number Employees: 10-19
Type of Packaging: Food Service, Bulk
Brands:
Alan's Maniac Hot Sauce

9482 **(HQ)On-Cor Frozen Foods**
www.on-cor.com
Frozen foods: chicken and noodles, hamburgers, lasagna, meat balls, stuffed peppers, stew, turkey and dumplings
Controller: John Statis
VP of Operations: Jim Bowen
Estimated Sales: $5.20 Million
Number Employees: 10-19
Type of Packaging: Consumer, Food Service
Brands:
On-Cor Frozen Entrees

9483 **On-Cor Frozen Foods Redi-Serve**
1225 Corporate Blvd.
Aurora, IL 60505
920-563-6391
Fax: 920-563-3013 www.on-cor.com
Frozen prepared foods: meat balls, beef patties, chicken patties and breaded veal cutlets
VP, Operations: Jim Bowen

Estimated Sales: $49.5 Million
Number Employees: 250-499
Parent Co: Encore Frozen Foods
Type of Packaging: Consumer, Food Service, Private Label

9484 **Onalaska Brewing**
248 Burchett Road
Onalaska, WA 98570-9405
360-978-4253
Beer
Owner: David Moorehead
Estimated Sales: Under $500,000
Number Employees: 1-4

9485 **Once Again Nut Butter**
12 S State St
PO Box 429
Nunda, NY 14517
585-468-2535
Fax: 585-468-5995 888-800-8075
onceagainnutbutter.com
Organic peanut butter, nut and seed butters, roasted and raw nuts, honey
General Manager: Bob Gelser
rgelser@onceagainnutbutter.com
Chief Financial Officer: Bryan Fritz
VP: Bill Owen
Quality Assurance Manager: Jake Rawleigh
Director Of Sales: Lisa Blatz
Production Manager: Esther Hinrich
Director of Purchasing: Lloyd Kirwan
Estimated Sales: $1.5 Million
Number Employees: 50-99
Square Footage: 40000
Type of Packaging: Consumer, Food Service, Private Label, Bulk
Brands:
Dawes Hill
Once Again Nut Butter

9486 **Once Upon a Farm**
San Diego, CA
888-983-1606
care@uponafarm.com onceuponafarmorganics.com
Organic, cold-pressed baby foods
CEO: John Foraker

9487 **One Culture Foods**
1802 Santo Domingo Ave
Duarte, CA 91010-2933
646-650-2989
www.oneculturefoods.com
Noodle cups, saut,s, marinades and dip
Founder: Hansen Shieh
Brands:
One Culture Foods

9488 **One Degree Organic Foods**
PO Box 128
Stn A
Abbotsford, BC V2T 6Z5
Canada
855-834-2642
info@onedegreeorganics.com
onedegreeorganics.com
Cereal, granola, flour, bread, seeds and tortillas
President/Owner: Stan Smith
General Manager: Rickard Werner
Number of Brands: 1
Number of Products: 7
Brands:
ONE DEGREE ORGANIC FOODS

9489 **One Potato Two Potato**
Womelsdorf, PA 19567
610-589-6500
www.onepotatosnacks.com
Chips
Sales Manager: Lauren Sweitzer
Brands:
ONE POTATO TWO POTATO

9490 **One Source**
300 Baker Ave
Concord, MA 01742
978-318-4300
Fax: 978-318-4690 800-554-5501
www.onesource.com
Seasonings, spices
President: Philip J Garlick
Chief Executive Officer: Jonathan A. Flatow
Chief Financial Officer: Robert E. Bies
Chief Technology Officer: Hank Weghorst
Chief Marketing Officer: James Rogers
SVP, Global Sales and Services: Colleen Honan
Contact: Nicki Hunt
nicola_hunt@onesource.com
Estimated Sales: $1-2.5 Million
Number Employees: 100-249

9491 **One Vineyard and Winery**
3268 Ehlers Ln
Saint Helena, CA 94574
707-963-1123
Fax: 707-963-1123
Table wines
President: George Watson
Contact: Elaine Watson
ewatson@onewomanwines.com
Estimated Sales: Less than $500,000
Number Employees: 1-4
Type of Packaging: Private Label

9492 **One World Enterprises**
1401 Westwood Blvd
Suite 200
Los Angeles, CA 90024
310-802-4220
Fax: 310-477-7077 888-663-2626
www.onenaturalexperience.com
Nutritional beverages
Chief Executive Officer: Rodrigo Veloso

9493 **Oneonta Starr Ranch Growers**
One Oneonta Way
PO Box 549
Wenatchee, WA 98807
509-663-2191
Fax: 509-663-6333 www.oneonta.com
Apples, pears, cherries, stone fruit, grapes and citrus
President/Owner: Dalton Thomas
VP: Brad Thomas
Director of Food Safety: Mary Jo Gash
Marketing Director: Scott Marboe
Human Resources: Linda Edwards
General Manager: Brian Focht
Type of Packaging: Consumer

9494 **Oneonta Starr Ranch Growers**
One Oneonta Way
Wenatchee, WA 98801
509-663-2191
www.oneonta.com
Apples, pears, cherries, plums, nectarines, peaches, kiwifruit, potatoes, onions, citrus fruits, etc.
Director, Marketing: Scott Marboe
Chief Operating Officer: Shashin Ashraf
Year Founded: 1934
Estimated Sales: $9 Million
Number Employees: 37
Square Footage: 10000

9495 **Onnit Labs**
4401 Freidrich Ln
Suite 302
Austin, TX 78744
855-666-4899
help@onnit.com www.onnit.com
Health foods including supplements, protein powders, coffees and teas, and MCT oils, and snacks

Founder & CEO: Aubrey Marcus

9496 **Ono Cones of Hawaii LLC**
98-723 Kuahao Pl # B3
Pearl City, HI 96782-3103
808-487-8690
Fax: 808-486-5292
Ice cream cones
Owner: Wayne Howard
Marketing Manager: Colleen Howard
Operations Manager: Larry Howard
Estimated Sales: $500,000
Number Employees: 1-4
Brands:
Ono Cones

9497 **Onoway Custom Packers**
PO Box 509
Onoway, AB T0E 1V0
Canada
780-967-2727
Fax: 780-967-2727
Beef, pork, lamb, ostrich and bison
President: Court Skinner
General Manager: Dave Skinner
Number Employees: 25
Type of Packaging: Consumer, Food Service, Private Label, Bulk

9498 **Ontario Foods**
1 Stone Road West
Guelph, ON N1G 4Y2
Canada
519-826-3145
Fax: 519-826-3460 888-466-2372
ag.info.omafra@ontario.ca www.omaf.gov.on.ca
Dehydrated and packaged food mixes
President: David Clarke
Export Marketing Officer: Diana Campbell
Brands:
Ontario Foods

9499 **Ontario Pork**
655 Southgate Drive
Guelph, ON N1G 5G6
Canada
519-767-4600
Fax: 519-829-1769 877-668-7675
krobbins@ontariopork.on.ca
www.ontariopork.on.ca
Fresh pork
Executive Director: Jack Silbar
Director Financial/Operational Services: Lloyd Bauemhuber
Divisional Manager, Communications and C: Keith Robbins
Director Sales/Logistics: Andrew Marks
Estimated Sales: $10 Million
Number Employees: 45
Type of Packaging: Consumer, Food Service
Brands:
Ontario Pork

9500 **Ontario Produce Company**
PO Box 880
Ontario, OR 97914
541-889-6485
Fax: 541-889-7823
Red, yellow and white onions; dry storage for onions
President and CEO: Robert A Komoto
Office Manager & Transportation: Janet Komoto
Shed Foreman: Arturo Rodriguez
Inspector: Alan Lovitt
Estimated Sales: $5-10 Million
Number Employees: 20 to 49
Square Footage: 160000
Type of Packaging: Consumer, Food Service, Private Label, Bulk
Brands:
A Brand
Foppiano
Fox Mountain
Golden Bird
Real West
Riverside
Rodeo
Silver Spur
Wowie!

9501 **Oogie's Snack LLC**
1932 W 33rd Ave
Denver, CO 80211-3412
303-455-2107
Fax: 303-496-0153 comments@oogiesnacks.com
www.oogiesnacks.com
Flavored gourmet popcorn
Contact: Laurie Conklin
laurie@oogiesnacks.com
Number Employees: 1-4

9502 **Oogolow Enterprises**
2560 Dominic Drive
Suite A
Chico, CA 95928-7185
530-893-2646
Fax: 530-893-9344 800-816-6873
Chicken, turkey, beef, ham and vegetable flavored meat analogs, vegetarian tamales, vegan cookies and energy bars.
President: Michael Epperson
oogolow@gmail.com
Estimated Sales: Below $5 Million
Number Employees: 15
Square Footage: 16000
Type of Packaging: Consumer, Food Service, Private Label
Brands:
No Bones Wheat-Meat
Today's Tamales
Tofurky

9503 **Ooh La La Candy**
855-817-1896
Fax: 914-381-8068 www.oohlalacandy.com
Candies, candy cupcakes, cards, and candy tins
Marketing: Sara Stevens
Contact: Steven Zorowitz
sales@oohlalacandy.com

9504 **Oorganik**
PO Box 37305
Houston, TX 77237-7305
281-240-7992
Fax: 281-240-2304
Health and dietetic foods
President: N Peabody
Estimated Sales: Under $500,000
Number Employees: 1-4

9505 **Opa! Originals**
Po Box 25151
Rochester, NY 14625-0151
585-368-5623
anastasia@opaoriginals.com
Greek soda

9506 **Opa's Smoked Meats**
410 S Washington St
Fredericksburg, TX 78624-4637
830-997-3358
Fax: 830-997-9916 800-543-6750
www.opassmokedmeats.com
Smoked and fresh sausage, ham, beef jerky, beef, pork tenderloins and poultry products
President: Helen Wahl
COO: Michael Schandua
michael@fbg.com
Controller: Ken Wahl
Estimated Sales: $20-50 Million
Number Employees: 50-99
Type of Packaging: Consumer, Food Service
Brands:
Opa's

9507 **Optima Wine Cellars**
101 Grant Avenue
P.O. Box 1691
Healdsburg, CA 95448
707-431-8222
Fax: 707-431-7828 info@optimawinery.com
Wines
Owner/Winemaker: Mike Duffy
Owner: Nicol Duffy
Estimated Sales: Below $5 Million
Number Employees: 2
Brands:
Optima

9508 **Optimal Automatics**
120 Stanley St
Elk Grove Village, IL 60007
847-439-9110
Fax: 847-439-9115 www.autodoner.com
Vertical broiler manufacturer
President/Owner: John Georgis

9509 **Optimal Nutrients**
1163 Chess Dr Ste F
Foster City, CA 94404
707-528-1800
Fax: 707-349-1686
Vitamins and supplements: royal jelly, beta carotene, essential fatty acids
President: Tim Lally
Vice President: Darlene Angeli
darlenea@optinutri.com
Estimated Sales: $500,000-$1 Million
Number Employees: 5-9
Square Footage: 20000
Parent Co: Pegasus Corp

9510 **Optimum Nutrition**
Dept 75 Meridian Lake Drive
Aurora, IL 60504
630-236-0097
800-763-3444
consumer@optimumnutrition.com
www.optimumnutrition.com
Sports drinks, vitamins and supplements
Founder: Mike Costello
Co-Founder: Tony Costello
Estimated Sales: $1-2.5 Million
Number Employees: 1-4
Brands:
American Body Building
Optimum Nutrition
Science Foods

9511 **Opus One**
7900 St. Helena Highway
P.O. Box 6
Oakville, CA 94562
707-944-9442
Fax: 707-948-2496 800-292-6787
info@opusonewinery.com
www.opusonewinery.com
Wines
Manager: David Pearson
Director Sales/Marketing: Scotty Barbour
Contact: Aliye Melton
aliye.melton@opusonewinery.com
Winemaker: Timothy Mondavi
Estimated Sales: Below $5 Million
Number Employees: 20-49
Brands:
Opus One

9512 **Orange Bakery**
17751 Cowan
Irvine, CA 92614-6064
949-863-1377
Fax: 949-863-1932 orangebakery.com
Frozen pastries
Year Founded: 1978
Number Employees: 50-99
Type of Packaging: Consumer, Food Service, Private Label, Bulk

9513 **Orange Bang Inc**
13115 Telfair Ave
Sylmar, CA 91342-3574
818-833-1000
info@orangebang.com
www.orangebang.com
Fountain and fruit syrups and fruit beverage concentrates
President: David Fox
Finance Manager: Richard Stein
obang@aol.com
Estimated Sales: $4.9 Million
Number Employees: 20-49
Square Footage: 132000
Type of Packaging: Consumer, Food Service

9514 **Orange County Distillery**
19B Maloney Lane
Goshen, NY 10924
845-651-2929
info@orangecountydistillery.com
www.orangecountydistillery.com
Vodka, corn whiskey, flavored whiskey, single-malt whiskey, bourbon and gin
Founder/Co-Owner: John Glebocki
Founder/Co-Owner: Bryan Ensall
Number of Brands: 1
Number of Products: 12
Type of Packaging: Consumer, Private Label

Brands:
Orange County Distillery

9515 **Orange Cove-Sanger Citrus**
180 South Ave
Orange Cove, CA 93646-9447
559-626-4453
Fax: 559-626-7357 www.ocsca.com
Oranges
President: Lee Bailey
General Manager: Kevin Severns
kevin@orangecovesanger.com
Vice President: Shawn Stevenson
Sales Manager: Dave Christofferson
Plant Manager: Bob Johnson
Estimated Sales: $10 Million
Number Employees: 50-99
Type of Packaging: Consumer, Food Service

9516 **Orange Peel Enterprises**
2183 Ponce DE Leon Cir
Vero Beach, FL 32960-5337
772-562-2766
Fax: 772-562-9848 800-643-1210
info@greensplus.com www.greensplus.com
Protein powders, energy bars
President: Ryan Deauville
ryan@greensplus.com
Director National Sales/Marketing: Todd Westover
Estimated Sales: $3.5 Million
Number Employees: 10-19
Square Footage: 60000
Type of Packaging: Consumer, Private Label
Brands:
Fiber Greens
Greens
Pro-Relight
Protein Greens

9517 **Orangeburg Pecan Co**
761 Russell St
Orangeburg, SC 29115
803-534-4277
www.uspecans.com
Shelled pecans
Founder: Marion H Felder
Number Employees: 10-19
Type of Packaging: Consumer, Food Service, Bulk

9518 **Orca Bay Foods**
2729 6th Ave S
Suite 200
Seattle, WA 98134
425-204-9100
Fax: 425-204-9200 800-932-6722
info@orcabayfoods.com orcabayseafoods.com
Frozen fish and seafood
President/CEO: Ryan Mackey
rmackey@orcabayfoods.com
VP/Finance: Jay Olsen
Senior Marketing Manager: Richard Mullins
National Sales Manager: Mark Tupper
Warehouse Manager: Troy Roy
Estimated Sales: $160 million
Number Employees: 200
Number of Brands: 1
Number of Products: 20
Square Footage: 70000
Type of Packaging: Consumer, Food Service, Private Label, Bulk
Brands:
Orca Bay

9519 **Orchard Heights Winery**
6057 Orchard Heights Rd NW
Salem, OR 97304-9509
503-391-7308
Fax: 503-364-1715
www.orchardheightswinery.com
Wines
CEO: Carol Wyscaver
cwyscaver@orchardheightswinery.com
Estimated Sales: $1-$2 Million
Number Employees: 1-4
Type of Packaging: Private Label
Brands:
Island Princess
Orchard Heights

9520 **Orchard Pond**
400 Cedar Hill Rd
Tallahassee, FL 32312
850-894-0154
hello@orchardpond.com
www.orchardpond.com
Granola, honey and pesto
Brands:
ORCHARD POND
ORCHARD POND ORGANICS

9521 **Orchid Island Juice Co**
330 N US Highway 1
Fort Pierce, FL 34950-4207
772-465-1122
Fax: 772-465-4303 800-373-7444
www.orchidislandjuice.com
Kosher, organic, natural juice and cider, non-alcoholic beverages, and full-line frozen products
CEO: Marygrace Sexton
Marketing: John Martinelli
Number Employees: 100-249

9522 **(HQ)Ore-Cal Corp**
634 Crocker St
Los Angeles, CA 90021-1002
213-623-8493
Fax: 213-228-6557 800-827-7474
CustomerService@ore-cal.com www.ore-cal.com
Shrimp, pangasius, mahi mahi, swordfish, calamari, breaded shrimp, and ready mixed entree dishes such as; shrimp scampi, seafood gumbo, cioppino, shrimp pad thai, and shrimp tom kha soup.
President: William Shinbane
Human Resources: Josephine Davif
Controller/Vice President Finance: Mark Feldstein
Vice President: Mark Shinbane
Lab Director: Avito Moniz
Human Resources Compliance & Regulatory: Wendy Gomez
Manager of National Sales: Shelley Gee
Manufacturing Supervisor: Rick Kanase
Estimated Sales: $10.9 Million
Number Employees: 50-99
Number of Brands: 1
Number of Products: 11+
Square Footage: 240000
Type of Packaging: Consumer, Food Service, Private Label, Bulk
Brands:
Harvest of the Sea

9523 **Ore-Ida Foods**
PO Box 57
Pittsburgh, PA 15230
412-237-5700
800-255-5750
www.oreida.com
Frozen potato products
VP of Marketing: Fed Arreola
Estimated Sales: $20-50 Million
Number Employees: 400
Number of Brands: 12
Parent Co: H.J. Heinz Company
Type of Packaging: Consumer, Food Service
Brands:
Creative Classics
Crispers
Crispy Crowns
Crispy Crunchies
Golden Crinkles
Golden Fries
Golden Patties
Golden Twirls
Pixie Crinkles
Steam n' Mash
Tater Tots
Texas Crispers
Zesties

9524 **Oregon Bark**
1400 NE 37th Ave
Portland, OR 97232
mail@oregonbark.com
www.oregonbark.com
Vegan, gluten free candy including peanut butter flake candy and hazelnut rosemary crisp candy
Owner: Anne Smith
Year Founded: 2012

9525 **Oregon Chai**
1745 NW Marshall Street
Portland, OR 97209-2420
503-221-2424
Fax: 503-796-0980 888-874-2424
nirvana@oregonchai.com www.oregonchai.com
Chai lattes, blends of tea, honey, vanilla and spices.
President: Cory Comstock
VP Finance: Kurt Peterson
Senior VP Marketing: Sean Ryan
VP Marketing: Lori Woolfrey
Sales Director: Tom Carl
Contact: Jeff Card
jeff.card@oregonchai.com
Production Manager: Emile Gaiera
Estimated Sales: $2.5-5 Million
Number Employees: 30
Square Footage: 36000
Type of Packaging: Consumer, Food Service
Brands:
Oregon Chai

9526 **Oregon Cherry Growers Inc**
1520 Woodrow St NE
Salem, OR 97301
Fax: 503-585-7710 sales@pcoastp.com
www.oregoncherry.com
Fresh, maraschino, froze, brined, glance, ingredient and canned cherries.
Chief Executive Officer: Tim Ramsey
tramsey@orcherry.com
VP, Human Resources & Communications: Michele Halverson
VP, Operations: Steve Travis
Year Founded: 1932
Estimated Sales: $46.1 Million
Number Employees: 100-249
Square Footage: 20000
Type of Packaging: Consumer, Food Service, Private Label, Bulk
Other Locations:
The Dalles OR
Salem OR

9527 **Oregon Cherry Growers Inc**
1st and Madison
P.O. Box 1577
The Dalles, OR 97058
Fresh, maraschino, froze, brined, glance, ingredient and canned cherries.
Chief Executive Officer: Tim Ramsey
Year Founded: 1932
Estimated Sales: $46.1 Million
Number Employees: 100-249
Type of Packaging: Consumer, Food Service, Private Label, Bulk

9528 **Oregon Flavor Rack**
spice@spiceman.com
www.spiceman.com
Small, medium, large and extra large salt-free spice blends and gift sets.
President: David Johns
spice@spiceman.com
Year Founded: 1991
Estimated Sales: Less Than $500,000
Number Employees: 1-4
Brands:
Spiceman's

9529 **Oregon Freeze Dry, Inc.**
525 W. 25th Ave. SW
Albany, OR 97322
541-926-6001
Fax: 541-967-6527 customerservice@ofd.com
www.ofd.com
Kosher meats, poultry, seafood, sweetened fruits, vegetables, military rations, pet treats
President and COO: Jim Merryman
VP of Finance: Dale Bookwalter
VP: Fred Vetter
Manager, R&D: Norm Jager
VP Business & Technical Development: Walter Pebley
Contact: Kelvin Adams
kelvin.adams@ofd.com
Estimated Sales: $27.6 Million
Number Employees: 201-500
Square Footage: 29000
Type of Packaging: Consumer, Private Label
Other Locations:
Brands:
Mountain House
EasyMeal

9530 **Oregon Fruit Products Co**
150 Patterson St NW
PO Box 5283
Salem, OR 97304-4042
503-378-0255
Fax: 503-588-9519 800-394-9333
cooking@oregonfruit.com www.oregonfruit.com
Canned fruits and berries
President: Joe Peterson
joep@ofpc.com
Sales Director: Bryan Brown
Operations Manager: Patti Law
Estimated Sales: A
Number Employees: 100-249
Type of Packaging: Consumer, Food Service, Private Label, Bulk
Brands:
Oregon Fruit

9531 **Oregon Harvest**
9348 N Peninsular Ave
Portland, OR 97217
503-249-0092
lillysfoods.com
Flavored hummus and salsas
Co-Founder: Lilly Moscoe
Number of Brands: 1
Number of Products: 9
Square Footage: 80000
Type of Packaging: Consumer
Brands:
LILLY'S

9532 **Oregon Hill Farms**
32861 Pittsburg Rd
St Helens, OR 97051-9110
503-397-2791
Fax: 503-397-0091 800-243-4541
Specialty fruit jams, syrups, fruit butters and dessert toppings
President: Thomas Mcmahon
tom@oregonhill.com
Operations Manager: Carmen McMahon
Estimated Sales: $3-5 Million
Number Employees: 5-9
Square Footage: 68000
Type of Packaging: Consumer, Food Service, Private Label
Brands:
Oregon Hill
Swan's Touch

9533 **Oregon Ice Cream Co.**
13115 NE 4th St, Suite 220
Vancouver, WA 98684
360-713-6800
sales@oregonicecream.com
www.oregonicecream.com
Organic ice cream.
President: Tom Gleason
Brands:
JULIE'S ORGANIC
ALDEN'S ICE CREAM
CASCADE GLACIER

9534 **(HQ)Oregon Potato Co**
650 E Columbia Ave
PO Box 169
Boardman, OR 97818
541-481-2715
Fax: 541-481-3443 800-336-6311
Potato products: flakes, flour, frozen, diced and fresh potatoes
Manager: Steve White
Director QA/Technical Services: Nick Ross
Director Global Sales: Barry Stice
Manager: Frank Tiegs
frank@ftiegs.com
Number Employees: 100-249
Square Footage: 400000
Type of Packaging: Private Label
Other Locations:
Oregon Potato Co.
Warden WA
Brands:
Oergon Trail
Regal Crest

9535 **Oregon Potato Co**
P.O. Box 3110
Pasco, WA 99302
509-545-4545
Fax: 509-545-4804 800-987-2726
customerservice@raderfarms.com
www.oregonpotato.com
Potatoes
President: Frank Tiegs
Sales: Jon Jardine
Sales: Steven DiNoia
Sales: Frank Simmons
Estimated Sales: $20-50 Million
Number Employees: 5-9
Brands:
Brittany Acres
Cajun Country
Northland

9536 **Oregon Pride**
3400 Crates Way
The Dalles, OR 97058-3552
908-537-7539
Fax: 908-537-2582 888-697-4767
Gourmet kippered beefsteak and beef jerky
President: James Perkins
Estimated Sales: Below $5 Million
Number Employees: 10

9537 **Oregon Raspberry & Blackberry Commission**
4845 B SW Dresden Ave
Corvallis, OR 97333
541-758-4043
Fax: 541-758-4553 www.oregon-berries.com
Berries
Marketing Director: Darcy Kockis

9538 **Oregon Seafoods**
723 S 2nd St
Coos Bay, OR 97420-1502
USA
541-267-3474
www.seafarepacific.com
Seafood
President/Owner: Mike Babcock
mike@oregonseafoods.com
Number Employees: 10-19

9539 **Oregon Spice Co Inc**
13320 NE Jarrett St
Portland, OR 97230-1093
503-238-0664
Fax: 503-238-3872 800-565-1599
kevin@oregonspice.com www.oregonspice.com
Spices and seasoning blends
President: Patty Boday
patty@oregonspice.com
Chairman: Larry Black
Estimated Sales: Below $5 Million
Number Employees: 20-49
Brands:
Oregon Spice

9540 **Orfila Vineyards**
13455 San Pasqual Rd
Escondido, CA 92025-7833
760-738-6500
Fax: 760-745-3773 info@orfila.com
www.orfila.com
Wines
Owner: Tom Blankenbeker
tom@orfila.com
Vice President: Leon Santoro
Estimated Sales: Below $5 Million
Number Employees: 20-49
Type of Packaging: Private Label
Brands:
Mendoza Ridge
Orfila Vineyards
Quatre Lepages

9541 **Organic Amazon**
Key Biscayne, FL 33149
info@organicamazon.com
organicamazon.com
A‡ai sorbet snack
Co-Founder: Rodrigo Lima
Co-Founder: Jayson Fittipaldi
Brands:
A‡ai To-Go

9542 **Organic Gemini**
68 33rd Street
4th Floor
Brooklyn, NY 11232
347-662-2900
hello@organicgemini.com
organicgemini.com
Tigernut snacks and beverages
Co-Founder: George Papanastasatos
Co-Founder: Mariam Kinkladze
Type of Packaging: Bulk

9543 **Organic Germinal**
8616 La Tijera Blvd
Suite 512
Los Angeles, CA 90045
310-846-5901
info@germinalorganic.com
www.germinalorganic.com
Organic crackers, bars and cookies
Owner: Emanuele Zuanetti
Number of Brands: 1
Number of Products: 10
Type of Packaging: Consumer
Brands:
ORGANIC GERMINAL

9544 **Organic Girl Produce**
900 Work St
Salinas, CA 93901
831-758-7800
www.iloveorganicgirl.com
Organic salad greens, dressings and flavored teas and waters
Owner & Partner: Steve Taylor
Brands:
ORGANICGIRL

9545 **Organic Gourmet**
14431 Ventura Blvd #192
Sherman Oaks, CA 91423
800-400-7772
Fax: 818-906-7417 scenar@earthlink.net
www.organic-gourmet.com
Organic vegetarian soups and stocks, yeast extract spreads, bouillon cubes and miso pastes
Founder & CEO: Elke Heitmeyer
Estimated Sales: $1-3 Million
Number Employees: 1-4
Number of Brands: 1
Number of Products: 16
Type of Packaging: Consumer, Food Service
Brands:
Organic Gourmet

9546 **Organic India USA**
7088 Winchester Circle
Suite 100
Boulder, CO 80301
888-550-8332
organicindiausa.com
Herbal and organic teas
Contact: Marie Camille
marie@organicindiausa.com
Estimated Sales: $2.8 Million
Number Employees: 12

9547 **Organic Liaison, LLC**
1515 N University Dr #222
Coral Springs, FL 33071-6096
954-755-4405
Organic weight loss energy and vitamin pills
CEO: Peggy Crawford
Type of Packaging: Consumer

9548 **Organic Milling**
505 W Allen Ave
San Dimas, CA 91773
909-599-0961
Fax: 909-599-5180 info@organicmilling.com
www.organicmilling.com
Breakfast cereals and granola
President: Wolfgang Buehler
Vice President, Operations: Lupe Martinez
Year Founded: 1960
Number Employees: 100-249
Number of Products: 29
Type of Packaging: Private Label, Bulk
Other Locations:
Warehouse & Distribution
San Dimas CA
Brands:
Nutritious Living
StaySteady

Breakfast Choice
Vita-Crunch

9549 **Organic Nectars LLC**
PO Box 158
Malden On Hudson, NY 12453-0158
845-246-0506
info@organicnectars.com
www.organicnectars.com
Raw low-glycemic agave sweeteners and desert syrups, cashew creme gelato, extra virgin olive oil, gojiberries, and raw cocao products.
Co-Founder & President: Lisa Protter
Vice President: Steve Treccase
stevetrec@gmail.com
Number Employees: 1-4
Type of Packaging: Consumer

9550 **Organic Olive Juice**
2 Gold St
Suite 3612
New York, NY 10038-4860
info@organicolivejuice.com
www.organicolivejuice.com
Olive oil, spreads and sauces.
Owner: Giuseppe Damiani

9551 **Organic Partners Intl.**
2705 E Burnside St
Suite 210
Portland, OR 97214
503-445-1065
www.organic-partners.com
Organic ingredient supply company
Managing Partner: Jeff Vinson

9552 **Organic Pastures**
7221 S Jameson Ave
Fresno, CA 93706
877-729-6455
www.organicpastures.com
Raw milk and raw milk products, including cream, kefir, cheese and butter
President/Owner: Aaron McAfee
Brands:
ORGANIC PASTURES

9553 **Organic Planet**
231 Sansome St # 3
San Francisco, CA 94104-2304
415-765-5590
Fax: 415-765-5922 www.organic-planet.com
Certified organic ingredients; edible seeds, dried fruits, tropical fruit, nuts, pulses, sweeteners
President: Hans Schmid
Sales: Carrie Hueseman
Estimated Sales: $20 Million
Number Employees: 5-9
Number of Brands: 1
Number of Products: 50
Brands:
Organic Planet

9554 **Organic RealBar**
Diamond Bar, CA
888-622-8828
support@organicrealbar.com organicrealbar.com
Organic snack bars
Brands:
RealBar

9555 **Organic Wine Co Inc**
1592 Union St # 350
San Francisco, CA 94123-4505
415-256-8888
Fax: 415-256-8883 888-326-9463
info@theorganicwinecompany.com
Organic wines
Owner: Veronique Raskin
vr@theorganicwinecompany.com
VP: Mike Jinoulhac
Vice President: Michelle Ginoulhac
Estimated Sales: $500,000-$1 Million
Number Employees: 1-4
Number of Products: 45
Brands:
Bousquette
Veronique

9556 **Organically Grown Co**
1800 Prairie Rd # B
Eugene, OR 97402-9722
541-689-5320
Fax: 541-461-3014 800-937-9677
davidl@organicgrown.com
www.organicgrown.com
Fruits and vegetables, tropical produce and dried fruit
CEO: Christopher Anderson
christopher.anderson@marriott.com
CEO: Josh Hinerfeld
Marketing Manager: Stacy Kraker
VP of Sales & Marketing: David Lively
Operations Manager: Anthony Seran
Purchasing/Inventory Director: David Amorose
Number Employees: 50-99
Other Locations:
Clackamas OR
Kent WA

9557 **Organics Unlimited**
8587 Avenida Costa Norte
Suite 2
San Diego, CA 92154
619-710-0658
info@organicsunlimited.com
www.organicsunlimited.com
Organic bananas, plantains, and coconuts
President/CEO: Mayra Velazquez de Leon
Director Operations: Marco Garcia Ojeda
Year Founded: 2000
Number Employees: 10-19

9558 **Oriental Foods**
2550 W Main Street
Suite 210
Alhambra, CA 91801-7003
626-293-1994
Fax: 626-293-1983
Seafood
President: Dr Venku Reddy
Estimated Sales: $1,300,000
Number Employees: 5

9559 **Orientex Foods**
1101 Railroad Ave
Pittsburg, CA 94565-2641
925-439-9009
Fax: 925-439-9242 800-660-0962
primoj@ramarfoods.com www.ramarfoods.com
Juice, cider, hors d'oeuvres, appetizers, ice cream, sorbet
CEO: Susan Quesada
susieq@raimerfood.com
Marketing: PJ Quesada
Number Employees: 50-99

9560 **(HQ)Original American Beverage Company**
74 Chester Main Road
North Stonington, CT 06359-1303
860-535-4650
Fax: 860-535-8545 800-625-3767
Old-fashioned soda and hard apple cider
President: Donald Benoit
Number Employees: 1-4
Square Footage: 20000
Type of Packaging: Consumer
Brands:
Chester's
Mystic Seaport

9561 **Original Chili Bowl**
4200 East Concours Dr.
Ontario, CA 91764
800-548-6363
www.theoriginalchilibowlfoodservice.com
Smoked barbecue meats and chili
COO: Bryan Cather
Technical Director: Robert Hastings
Plant Controller: Lil Green
Plant Manager: John Powers
Estimated Sales: $28600000
Number Employees: 50-99
Parent Co: Ajinomoto Windsor
Type of Packaging: Consumer, Food Service, Bulk
Brands:
Cripple Creek
Hickory Hollow

9562 **Original Foods**
701 Broad St East
Dunnville, ON N1A 1H2
Canada
905-701-7010
Fax: 418-527-3017 888-440-8880
service@originalfoods.com
www.originalfoods.com
Confectionery, syrups, pastry fillings
Assistant General Manager: Phillipe Canac-Marquis
Marketing & Logistics Manager: Kevin Tremblay
National Sales Manager: Dahna Weber
Customer Service: Chantal Langevin
Number Employees: 120
Brands:
Original 1957

9563 **Original Gourmet Food Co**
52 Stiles Rd
Suite 201
Salem, NH 03079-4807
603-894-1200
Fax: 603-894-5400 www.ogfc.net
Lollipops and wafers
CEO: Richard Alimenti
EVP: Al Mosto
Estimated Sales: Less Than $500,000
Number Employees: 1-4
Brands:
Original Gourmet

9564 **Original Herkimer Cheese**
2745 State Route 51
Ilion, NY 13357
315-895-7428
Fax: 315-895-4664 herkimer@cnymail.com
www.originalherkimercheese.com
Aged NY cheddar cheese, cheese balls & logs, cheese spreads, chocolate cheese fudge & other specialties.
President/Director Marketing: Michael Basloe
Estimated Sales: $3-5 Million
Number Employees: 20-49
Type of Packaging: Consumer, Food Service, Private Label, Bulk
Brands:
Herkimer
Ida Mae

9565 **Original Juan**
111 Southwest Blvd
Kansas City, KS 66103
913-432-5228
Fax: 913-432-5880 800-568-8468
Sauces, salsas, dips and snacks.
President & CEO: Joe Polo
VP, Sales: Greg Dennis
VP, Operations: Tom Clark
Year Founded: 1998
Number of Brands: 13
Number of Products: 1700
Square Footage: 60000
Type of Packaging: Consumer, Private Label
Brands:
American Stockyard
Cowtown BBQ
Da'Bomb
Fiesta Juan's
Longhorn
Mama Capri
Original Juan's
Pain 100%
Pain Is Good
Pancheros

9566 **Original Tony Packo's**
1902 Front St
Toledo, OH 43605-1226
419-691-6054
Fax: 419-691-8358 866-472-2567
shop@tonypacko.com www.tonypacko.com
Pickles, relishes
Owner: Tony Packo
Estimated Sales: Less than $500,000
Number Employees: 50-99
Brands:
Tony Packo's

9567 **Orinoco Coffee & Tea**
8265 Patuxent Range Rd
Suite L
Jessup, MD 20794
410-312-5292
Fax: 240-636-5196 info@orinococoffeeandtea.com
www.orinococoffeeandtea.com
Coffe and tea
CEO: Pedro Ramirez
Master Roaster, R&D: Juan Carlos Ramirez

9568 **Orlando Baking Co**
7777 Grand Ave
Cleveland, OH 44104-3061
216-361-1872
Fax: 216-391-3469 800-362-5504
www.orlandobaking.com
Italian, French, Rye and Wheat breads, subs, hoagies, kaisers and hamburger buns, dinner rolls and Ciabatta bread
President: Chester Orlando
Marketing Director: Sharon Jones
VP Sales: Nick Orlando
sorlando@orlandobaking.com
Year Founded: 1872
Estimated Sales: G
Number Employees: 250-499
Number of Products: 250
Square Footage: 250000
Type of Packaging: Consumer, Food Service, Private Label
Brands:
Orlando

9569 **Orleans Packing Co**
1715 Hyde Park Ave
Hyde Park, MA 02136-2457
617-361-6611
Fax: 617-361-2638 George@orleanspacking.com
www.orleanspacking.com
Olives
President: George Gebelein
george@orleanspacking.com
Vice President: Suzanne Gebelein
Estimated Sales: $1 Million
Number Employees: 10-19
Type of Packaging: Consumer, Food Service, Private Label, Bulk

9570 **Orlinda Milling Company**
9145 Highway 49 E
Orlinda, TN 37141-2025
615-654-3633
Fax: 615-654-4902
All-purpose and self-rising flour
President: Ricky Stark
Vice President: Bryant Stark
Secretary/Treasurer: Ronnie Stark
Estimated Sales: $470,000
Number Employees: 1-4
Type of Packaging: Consumer, Food Service
Brands:
Crown Jewel
Kwik Rize

9571 **Ormand Peugeog Corporation**
PO Box 227155
Miami, FL 33122-7155
305-624-6834
Fax: 305-624-0911
www.ormandpeugeog@aol.com
Wine and wine products
President: Paul Mirengoff.
CFO: Laura Robledo
Marketing Director: Olga Robledo
Plant Manager: Jose Robledo
Estimated Sales: $3 Million
Number Employees: 4
Square Footage: 240
Type of Packaging: Private Label
Brands:
Cristal
Frescas
Gatomax
Tai Bueno
This Way Jose

9572 **Orr Mountain Winery**
355 Pumpkin Hollow rd.
Madisonville, TN 73754
423-442-5340
theorrs@usit.net
www.tnvacation.com
Wines
Manager: Susan Whitaker
Sales Director: Lee Curtis
Estimated Sales: $500,000-$1 Million
Number Employees: 1-4
Brands:
Orr Mountain Winery

9573 **Ortho-Molecular Products Inc**
3017 Business Park Dr
Stevens Point, WI 54482-8835
715-342-9881
Fax: 715-342-9866 800-332-2351
www.discoverourstory.com
Vitamin supplements
President: Gary Powers
g.powers@ompimail.com
VP Sales: Jack Radloff
VP Operations: Dean Kramer
Estimated Sales: $5-10 Million
Number Employees: 50-99
Square Footage: 64000
Parent Co: Ortho Molecular Products

9574 **Orto Foods**
59 S Route 303
Congers, NY 10920-2470
516-725-5422
info@jicachips.com
www.jicachips.com
Jicama chips
Founder: Xin Wang
Brands:
JicaChips(c)

9575 **Orwasher's Bakery**
308 E 78th St # 1
New York, NY 10075-2222
212-288-6569
Fax: 212-570-2706 www.orwashers.com
Breads and rolls: black pumpernickel, challah, cinnamon raisin, marble, potato, rye, sour dough, white, and whole wheat.
President: Aparm Orwasher
Owner: Keith Cohen
Estimated Sales: Less than $500,000
Number Employees: 20-49
Type of Packaging: Consumer, Food Service
Brands:
Orwasher's

9576 **Osage Pecan Co**
909 W Fort Scott St
Butler, MO 64730
800-748-8305
sales@osagepecans.com www.osagepecans.com
Pecans and other nuts; also dried fruits
Estimated Sales: Less Than $500,000
Number Employees: 1-4
Number of Products: 100
Square Footage: 80000
Type of Packaging: Consumer, Food Service, Private Label, Bulk

9577 **Oscar's Wholesale Meats**
250 W 31st St
Ogden, UT 84401-3899
801-621-5655
Fax: 801-394-8113 oscarsmeat@live.com
www.oscarsmeat.comcastbiz.net
Steak, beef patties, poultry, bacon and roasts
Owner/President: Darrell Gardner
Estimated Sales: $25.5 Million
Number Employees: 10-19
Type of Packaging: Consumer, Food Service

9578 **Osceola Farms Sugar Warehouse**
1810 Old Dixie Highway
Pahokee, FL 33476
561-924-7156
Ground sugar, sugar cane, refining chocolate, sweeteners and confectionary products.
President: Jose Fanjul
VP: John Fanjul
Estimated Sales: $29000000
Number Employees: 1-4
Parent Co: Florida Crystals
Type of Packaging: Consumer

9579 **Osem USA Inc**
333 Sylvan Ave
Englewood Cliffs, NJ 07632-2724
201-871-4433
Fax: 201-871-8726 800-200-6736
Snacks
President: Izzet Ozdogan
robert@osemusa.com
Sales Exec: Robert Gatto
Estimated Sales: Below $5 Million
Number Employees: 5-9
Brands:
Osem

9580 **Oshkosh Cold Storage**
1110 Industrial Ave
Oshkosh, WI 54901-1105
920-231-0610
Fax: 920-231-9441 800-580-4680
ocstg@vbe.com www.oshkoshcheese.com
Cheese, cheese products
Owner: Jordan Doemel
jordand@oshkoshcheese.com
Marketing Director: Stan Dietsche
Estimated Sales: $500,000-$1 Million
Number Employees: 5-9
Type of Packaging: Bulk

9581 **Oskaloosa Food Products**
543 9th Ave E
Oskaloosa, IA 52577-3901
641-673-3486
Fax: 641-673-8684 800-477-7239
info@oskyfoods.com www.oskyfoods.com
Dried, frozen and liquid egg products.
President: Blair Van Zetten
Controller: Brad Hodges
bhodges@oskyfoods.com
Sales/Purchasing Director: Jason Van Zetten
Human Resource Manager: Joyce Wilson
Estimated Sales: $10 Million
Number Employees: 50-99
Type of Packaging: Consumer, Food Service, Private Label, Bulk

9582 **Oskar Blues Brewery**
1800 Pike Road
Unit B
Longmont, CO 80501
303-776-1914
www.oskarblues.com
Beer
Owner: Dale Katichis
Marketing: Chad Melis
Contact: John Boetcher
jboetcher@bmhc.com
Estimated Sales: $1.2 Million
Number Employees: 47
Square Footage: 15352

9583 **Oskri Corporation**
528 E Tyranena Park Rd
Lake Mills, WI 53551
920-648-8300
info@oskri.com
www.oskri.com
Organic coffee, dried fruit and soup bases, teas and herbal products
Owner: Fekri Zainoba
Sales Director: Jen Fredrich
Contact: Tricia Blasing
tricia.kastrosky@gmail.com
Estimated Sales: $500,000-$1 Million
Number Employees: 5-9
Type of Packaging: Consumer, Private Label, Bulk

9584 **Osowski Farms**
33 Gillespie Ave
Minto, ND 58261
701-248-3341
Fax: 701-248-3341
Sugar beets, grain and dry beans
Owner: Dave Osowski
CEO: Rod Osowski
Marketing Director: Wayne Osowski
Estimated Sales: $1-3 Million
Number Employees: 1-4
Type of Packaging: Consumer, Food Service, Bulk
Brands:
Wayne

9585 **Ossian Smoked Meats**
PO Box 405
Ossian, IN 46777-0405
260-622-4191
Fax: 260-622-4194 800-535-8862
www.ossianpackingcompany.com
Beef, pork, pork chops, sausage, steak, hamburger and ham
President: Peter Sorg

Estimated Sales: $10-20 Million
Number Employees: 15
Type of Packaging: Consumer, Food Service, Private Label, Bulk
Brands:
Hoosier Pride
Ye Olde Farm Style

9586 Osso Good, LLC
San Rafael, CA
hello@ossogoodbones.com
www.ossogoodbones.com
GMO-free, hormone-free and organic bone broth soups in various flavors; bone broth cleanse packages; Paleo diet-friendly soups
Co-Founder/CEO: Jazz Hilmer
Co-Founder/CEO: Meredith Cochran
Co-Founder/CFO: Toran Hilmer
Number of Brands: 1
Number of Products: 19
Type of Packaging: Consumer, Private Label
Brands:
The Osso Good Co.

9587 (HQ)Ostrom Mushrooms
8322 Steilacoom Rd SE
Olympia, WA 98513
360-491-1410
info@ostromfarms.com
www.ostrommushrooms.com
Mushrooms
President: David Knudson
Type of Packaging: Consumer, Private Label, Bulk

9588 Ota Tofu
812 SE Stark St
Portland, OR 97214-1228
503-232-8947
Tofu
President: Eileen Ota
tofuupsidedowncake@integraonline.com
Estimated Sales: $770,000
Number Employees: 10-19
Type of Packaging: Consumer, Bulk

9589 Otafuku Foods
13117 Molette St
Santa Fe Springs, CA 90670
562-404-4700
info@otafukufoods.com
www.otajoy.com
Japanese sauces
President/Owner: Taka Ozawa
Type of Packaging: Private Label
Brands:
OTAJOY

9590 (HQ)Otis Spunkmeyer
260 State St
Brockport, NY 14420
855-427-9982
ana.customercare@aryzta.com
www.otisspunkmeyer.com
Frozen cookie dough, fresh baked muffins, baked goods
President & CEO: John Schiavo
Year Founded: 1977
Estimated Sales: $500 Million
Parent Co: Aryzta AG
Type of Packaging: Private Label
Brands:
Otis Spunkmeyer
ARYZTA

9591 Otis Spunkmeyer
5855 Oakbrook Parkway
Suite F
Norcross, GA 30093-1838
770-446-1860
Fax: 770-446-2205 855-427-9982
Cookies, muffins, bagels and brownies
General Manager: Buck Hamillton
Contact: Chris Tralka
ctralka@spunkmeyer.com
Estimated Sales: $1-2.5 Million
Number Employees: 20-49
Parent Co: Otis Spunkmeyer
Type of Packaging: Consumer, Food Service
Brands:
Otis Spunkmeyer

9592 Otsuka America Foods Inc
400 Oyster Point Blvd
Suite 534
San Francisco, CA 94080-1904
415-986-5300
Fax: 415-236-6341 www.otsuka-america.com
Frozen vegetables and purees
Number Employees: 5-9
Brands:
Wild Veggie

9593 Ott Food Products Co
705 W Fairview Ave
Carthage, MO 64836-3724
417-358-2585
Fax: 417-358-4553 800-866-2585
www.ottfoods.com
Barbecue sauce and salad dressing: French, Italian, ranch and poppy seed
President: Jack Crede
jackc@ottfoods.com
Estimated Sales: $10-20 Million
Number Employees: 20-49
Type of Packaging: Consumer, Food Service
Brands:
Louis Albert & Sons
Ott's

9594 Ottawa Valley Grain Products
558 Raglan St S
Renfrew, ON K7V 1R8
Canada
613-432-3614
Fax: 613-432-6148 www.ovgp.ca
Milled, pearled and pot barley, wheat and barley flow
President/CEO: Ronald Wilson
Estimated Sales: $6.7 Million
Number Employees: 11
Number of Products: 7
Type of Packaging: Food Service, Bulk
Brands:
Valley

9595 Ottenberg's Bakers
1413 Progress Way
Sykesville, MD 21784-6437
410-549-3362
Fax: 410-549-0383 800-334-7264
www.ottenbergs.com
Breads and rolls
Owner: Lee Ottenberg
President: Ray Ottenberg
Plant Manager: Shawn Wooleyhand
Estimated Sales: $20 Million
Number Employees: 5-9
Type of Packaging: Food Service

9596 Ottens Flavors
7800 Holstein Avenue
Philadelphia, PA 19153
215-365-7800
Fax: 215-365-7801 800-523-0767
www.ottensflavors.com
Spray dry flavorings, imitation and natural confectionery oils and spices
President: George Robinson
CEO: Richard Robinson
Eastern Manager: Sharon D'Alo
Contact: Philip Bafundo
philip@ottensflavors.com
COO: Rudy Dieperink
Estimated Sales: $11.5 Million
Number Employees: 50-99
Square Footage: 109500
Type of Packaging: Food Service, Private Label, Bulk

9597 Otto's Naturals
1802 St Rt 31N
Clinton, NJ 08833
732-654-6886
info@ottosnaturals.com
www.ottosnaturals.com
Cassava flour
COO: John Olsen
Brands:
Otto's Naturals

9598 Ouachita Lumber Co
139 Syrup Mill Rd
West Monroe, LA 71291-7780
318-396-1960
Fax: 318-396-2560 info@ouachitalumber.com
www.ouachitalumber.com
Cane syrup
Owner: Fred Norris
Contact: Barbara Norris
barbara@ouachitalumber.com
Estimated Sales: $1.4 Million
Number Employees: 5-9
Type of Packaging: Consumer, Food Service, Private Label

9599 Ouhlala Gourmet
2655 S Le Jeune Rd
Suite 1011
Coral Gables, FL 33134-5803
305-774-7332
www.buddyfruits.com
Squeezable fruit to go
Owner: Jerome Lesur
jlesur@buddyfruits.com
Number Employees: 1-4

9600 Our Best Foods
170 Main St
Suite 210
Tewksbury, MA 01876-1762
978-858-0077
Fax: 978-858-0052 www.ourbestfoods.com
Hamburger patties, portabella mushrooms, corned beef, roast beef, pastrami, vegan burgers, bulk sliced trukey, meatballs, meatloaf, veal patties, and pepper steaks.
President: Micheal Naddif
Contact: Leon Berns
leon@naddif.com
Estimated Sales: $20-50 Million
Number Employees: 1-4
Type of Packaging: Food Service, Private Label
Brands:
Our Best

9601 Our Cookie
13301 SW 132nd Avenue
Suite 109
Miami, FL 33186
305-238-1992
877-885-2715
Cookies

9602 Our Farms To You, LLC
7752 Middle Road
Middletown, VA 22645-6006
703-507-7604
ourfarmstoyou@gmail.com
Dairy-free, chocolate, breakfast cereals, granola
Marketing: Melinda Bremmer

9603 Our Lady of Guadalupe Trappist Abbey
9200 NE Abbey Rd
Carlton, OR 97111-9666
503-852-0103
Fax: 503-852-7748 dicklayton@trappistabbey.org
www.trappistabbey.org
Fruitcake, date-nut cake
Business Manager: Richard Laytlon
Estimated Sales: Under $500,000
Number Employees: 20

9604 Out of a Flower
657 Edgewood Dr
Lancaster, TX 75146
214-630-3136
Fax: 214-630-8797 800-743-4696
Edible flower based ice cream and sorbets
President: Jose Sanabria
Estimated Sales: $100,000
Number Employees: 1-4
Brands:
Chiqui
Out of a Flower
Swiss Alp Mineral Water

9605 Outback Kitchens LLC
PO Box 153
Huntington, VT 05462
802-434-5262
Fax: 502-434-5262
Chutney

Estimated Sales: $300,000-500,000
Number Employees: 1-4

9606 **Outer Aisle**
103 Santa Felicia Dr
Galeta, CA 93117
805-242-9265
www.outeraislegourmet.com
Cauliflower-based bread alternatives
Founder: Jeanne David
Brands:
Plantpower

9607 **Outstanding Foods**
Venice, CA
www.outeraislegourmet.com
Plant-based bacon alternative
Founder: Dave Anderson
Brands:
PigOut

9608 **Outta the Park Eats**
PO Box 3422
Cary, NC 27519
919-462-0012
Fax: 800-341-8511 scottg@outtatheparksauce.com
www.outtatheparksauce.com
Gluten-free, organic and natural BBQ sauce
Marketing: Scott Granai

9609 **Oven Arts**
200 S Newman St
Hackensack, NJ 07601
Fax: 973-556-4824 855-354-4070
www.ovenarts.com
Brownies, cookies and dessert bars.
President: Betty Osmanoglu
Director, Sales & Marketing: Meghna Kashyap

9610 **Oven Fresh Baking Company**
250 N Washtenaw Ave
Chicago, IL 60612
773-638-1234
Fax: 773-638-1237
Croissants and muffins
President: George Spanos
gspanos@ovenfreshbaking.com
Marketing Director: Steve Sarsitis
Estimated Sales: $5-10 000,000
Number Employees: 100-249
Brands:
Oven Fresh

9611 **Oven Head Salmon Smokers**
101 Oven Head Road
Bethel, NB E5C 1S3
Canada
506-755-2507
Fax: 506-755-8883 877-955-2507
ovenhead@xplornet.ca
www.ovenheadsmokers.com
Smoked Atlantic salmon, salmon pate and jerky
President: R Joseph Thorne
Vice President: Debra Thorne
Estimated Sales: $691,000
Number Employees: 5
Number of Brands: 1
Number of Products: 3
Brands:
Oven Head

9612 **Oven Poppers**
99 Faltin Dr
Manchester, NH 03103-5755
603-644-3773
Fax: 603-669-8646
Frozen seafood entrees
President: Stacy Kimball
COO: Andy Desmarais
Plant Manager: James Carigran
Estimated Sales: $5-10 Million
Number Employees: 50-99
Type of Packaging: Consumer, Food Service
Brands:
Oven Poppers

9613 **Oven Ready Products**
3-111 Watson Road
Guelph, ON N1E 6X7
Canada
519-767-2415
Fax: 519-823-2196
Frozen pastry food products, beef rolls, fruit turnovers
President: Jim Harrison
Number Employees: 1-4
Type of Packaging: Consumer, Food Service
Brands:
Oven Ready

9614 **Overhill Farms Inc**
2727 E Vernon Ave
Vernon, CA 90058
323-582-9977
Fax: 323-582-6122 800-859-6406
sales@overhillfarms.com www.overhillfarms.com
Poultry, meat and seafood specialties; pastas, soups, sauces, vegetarian.
Chairman, CEO & President: James Rudis
Year Founded: 1968
Estimated Sales: $169.22 Million
Number Employees: 500-999
Square Footage: 25000
Type of Packaging: Consumer, Food Service, Private Label, Bulk
Brands:
Overhill Farms

9615 **Overlake Foods**
PO Box 2631
Olympia, WA 98507-2631
360-352-7989
Fax: 360-352-8076 800-683-1078
Frozen blueberries, raspberries, strawberries, blackberries and peaches
COO: Rodney Cook
Sales: Paul Askier
Estimated Sales: $1 Million
Number Employees: 4
Square Footage: 5400
Parent Co: Producer Marketing Group
Type of Packaging: Bulk
Brands:
Overlake

9616 **Oversea Casing Co**
601 S Nevada St
Seattle, WA 98108-1713
206-682-6845
Fax: 206-382-0883 info@overseacasing.com
www.overseacasing.com
Sausage casings
President: Mike Mayo
info@overseacasing.com
Sales Executive: David Mayo
Estimated Sales: $5.6 Million
Number Employees: 20-49
Square Footage: 31666

9617 **Oversea Fishery & Investment**
2752 Woodlawn Dr
Suite 5-110
Honolulu, HI 96822-1855
808-847-2500
Fax: 808-836-3308
Seafood
President: Francis Tsang
Estimated Sales: $3-5 Million
Number Employees: 1-4

9618 **Owensboro Grain Co**
822 E 2nd St
Owensboro, KY 42303
270-926-2032
Fax: 270-686-6509 800-874-0305
www.owensborograin.com
Refined soybean oil
President & CEO: Helen Cornell
CFO: Jeff Erb
Executive Vice President: John Wright
john.wright@owensborocatholic.org
Year Founded: 1906
Estimated Sales: $400 Million
Number Employees: 100-249

9619 **Owl's Brew**
135 W 29th St
Suite 602
New York, NY 10001-5104
212-564-0218
hoot@theowlsbrew.com
www.theowlsbrew.com
Cocktail teas
Founder and CEO: Jennie Ripps
President: Maria Littlefield
Number Employees: 10-19
Brands:
Owl's Brew

9620 **Oxford Frozen Foods**
4881 Main Street
Po Box 220
Oxford, NS B0M 1P0
Canada
902-447-2100
Fax: 902-447-3245 sales@oxfordfrozenfoods.com
www.oxfordfrozenfoods.com
Frozen blueberries, carrots and onion rings
President and CEO: John Bragg
Co-CEO: David Hoffman
Vice President, Sales & Logistics: Matthew Bragg
Customer Service Coordinator: Kerri Baker
COO: Ragnar Kamp
Director of Manufacturing: Milton Wood
Number Employees: 250-499
Type of Packaging: Consumer

9621 **Ozark Empire**
2301 S 1st St
Rogers, AR 72758-6416
479-636-3313
Fax: 479-631-3895
Bread and buns
Manager: Mike Klingman
mike@harrisbaking.com
Estimated Sales: $21.1 Million
Number Employees: 100-249
Square Footage: 2000
Type of Packaging: Consumer
Brands:
Best Choice
Iga
Ozark
Tender Crust

9622 **Ozarka Drinking Water**
4718 Mountain Creek Pkwy
Dallas, TX 75236
817-354-9526
www.ozarkawater.com
Drinking water
Manager: Randy Payne
Estimated Sales: $20-50 Million
Number Employees: 100-249
Parent Co: Ozarka Houston Water Company

9623 **Ozery Bakery**
11 Director Ct
Vaughan, ON L4L 4S5
Canada
905-265-1143
888-556-5560
mail@ozerybakery.com ozerybakery.com
Pita breads and brioches
Co-President: Alon Ozery
Co-President: Guy Ozery
Estimated Sales: $18 Million
Number Employees: 110

9624 **Ozery Bakery Inc**
11 Director Court
Vaughan, ON L4L 4S5
Canada
905-265-1143
Fax: 905-265-1352
Kosher bread, biscuits, crackers
Marketing: Paul Vlahos

9625 **Ozone Confectioners & Bakers Supplies**
55 Bank St
Elmwood Park, NJ 07407-1146
201-791-4444
Fax: 201-791-2893
Licorice, almonds, nonpareil seeds
President: Patrick Lapone
VP: Louis Lapone
Estimated Sales: $3-5 Million
Number Employees: 10 to 19
Number of Brands: 1
Type of Packaging: Private Label
Brands:
Lapone's Jordan

9626 **Ozuna Food Products Corporation**
1260 Alderwood Ave
Sunnyvale, CA 94089
408-400-0495
Fax: 408-400-0497 info@ozunafoodproducts.com
www.ozunafoodproducts.com
Corn and flour tortillas, tortilla chips

Owner: Vito Ozuna
Contact: Michael Ozuna
info@ozunafoodproducts.com
Estimated Sales: $300,000-500,000
Number Employees: 1-4
Square Footage: 225000
Type of Packaging: Consumer, Food Service, Private Label, Bulk

9627 PDEQ
PO Box 28511
Fresno, CA 93729
559-490-4412
hello@pdeq.net
pdeq.net
Tapioca-based cheese bread
President/Owner: Flavia Takahashi-Flores
Brands:
PDEQ

9628 P & J Oyster Co
1039 Toulouse St
French Quarter
New Orleans, LA 70112-3425
504-523-2651
Fax: 504-522-4960 contact@oysterlover.com
www.oystercapitalofamerica.com
Oysters
President: Alfred Sunseri
asunseri@neworleansoysterfestival.org
Sales Manager: Sal Sunseri Jr
Office Manager: Merri Sunseri-Schneider
Estimated Sales: $1-2.5 Million appx.
Number Employees: 20-49
Brands:
Gold Band Products

9629 P & L Poultry
3821 S Bates Court
Spokane, WA 99206-6348
509-892-1242
Fax: 509-892-1244
Chicken and turkey, frankfurters
President: John Singleton
Number Employees: 1-4
Type of Packaging: Consumer, Food Service, Private Label, Bulk

9630 P & M Staiger Vineyard
1300 Hopkins Gulch Rd
Boulder Creek, CA 95006-8632
831-338-0172
pmstaiger@msn.com
Wine
Owner: Paul Staiger
Estimated Sales: Under $300,000
Number Employees: 1-4

9631 P & S Food & Liquor
4910 W Irving Park Rd
Chicago, IL 60641-2619
773-685-0088
Fax: 773-685-0088
Wines
Owner: Edmund Sammando
Estimated Sales: $1 million
Number Employees: 1-4

9632 P & S Ravioli Co
1722 W Oregon Ave
Philadelphia, PA 19145-4726
215-339-9929
Fax: 215-465-3559 support@psravioli.com
www.psravioli.com
Pasta
Owner: Primo Di Giacomo
support@psravioli.com
Co-Owner: Secondo Ravioli
Plant Manager: Mariano DiGiacomo
Estimated Sales: Less than $500,000
Number Employees: 1-4
Brands:
P&S Ravioli

9633 P & T Flannery Seafood Inc
45 Pier # B
San Francisco, CA 94133-1022
415-346-1303
Fax: 415-346-1304
Swordfish, tuna, seafoods
President/CEO: Terence Flannery
Vice President: Peter Flannery
Estimated Sales: $4,351,163
Number Employees: 5-9
Type of Packaging: Private Label

9634 P C Teas Co
882 Mahler Rd # 8
Burlingame, CA 94010-1604
650-697-8989
Fax: 650-697-9016 800-423-8728
teas4u@teastohealth.com www.teastohealth.com
Herbal tea
President: Sunny Wong
teas888@aol.com
Estimated Sales: Below $5 Million
Number Employees: 10-19
Type of Packaging: Private Label
Brands:
Natural Green Leaf Brand

9635 P G Molinari & Sons
1401 Yosemite Ave
San Francisco, CA 94124-3321
415-822-5555
Fax: 415-822-5834 sales@molinarisalame.com
www.molinarisalame.com
Dry salami, sausage
President: Frank Giorgi
fg@molinarisalame.com
Sales Manager: Lou Mascola
Estimated Sales: Below $5 Million
Number Employees: 20-49
Type of Packaging: Food Service
Brands:
Finocchiona
Toscano Style

9636 P R Farms Inc
2917 E Shepherd Ave
Clovis, CA 93619-9152
559-299-0201
Fax: 559-299-7292 info@prfarms.com
www.prfarms.com
Almonds, olive oil, citrus, tree fruit, wine and raisin grapes
President: Pat Ricchiuti
Number Employees: 100-249
Type of Packaging: Consumer, Food Service, Private Label, Bulk
Other Locations:
Headquarters
Clovis CA
Enzo Olive Oil Company
Madera CA
Almond Facility
Madera CA
Brands:
Bella Frutta
P-R Farms
Enzo

9637 P&E Foods
3077 Koapaka St
Suite 202
Honolulu, HI 96819-5105
808-839-9094
Fax: 808-834-8409
Frozen meats
President: Stephen S C Lee
Contact: Stephen Leong
sleong@avsupply.com
Manager: Harry Toywooka
Estimated Sales: $5-10 Million
Number Employees: 20-49

9638 P&H Milling Group
1060 Fountain Street North
Cambridge, ON N3E 0A1
Canada
519-650-6400
Fax: 519-650-6429 info@dovergrp.com
Baking ingredients and flours
President: Sheila LaLang

9639 P&L Seafood of Venice
401 Whitney Ave # 103
Gretna, LA 70056-2500
504-363-2744
Fax: 504-392-3334 www.chartwellsmenus.com
Seafood
Manager: John Duke

9640 P-Bee Products
31650 SR 20
Suite 3
Oak Harbor, WA 98277
949-586-6300
Fax: 649-586-6360 800-322-5572
www.pbeeproducts.com
Nutritional supplements
President: Raymond Guna
Founder: Steven Kramar
Vice President: Lacey Guna
Estimated Sales: $500,000-$1 Million
Number Employees: 1-4
Type of Packaging: Consumer, Bulk
Brands:
P-Bee

9641 P. Janes & Sons
PO Box 10
Hant's Harbor, NL A0B 1Y0
Canada
709-586-2252
Fax: 709-586-2870
Seafood
Sales Director: Jeff Galliford
Purchasing Agent: Blair Janes
Type of Packaging: Consumer, Food Service, Private Label, Bulk

9642 P.A. Braunger Institutional Foods
900 Clark St
Sioux City, IA 51101
712-258-4515
Fax: 712-258-1130 www.braungerfoods.com
Frozen meats, general line products
President: Tony Wald
General Manager: J David
Estimated Sales: $10-20 Million
Number Employees: 50-99

9643 P.D.I Cone-Dutch Treat
69 Leddy St
Buffalo, NY 14210-2134
716-821-0698
www.pdicone.com
Sugar cones, candies and cookies
President: Michael Lichtenthal
Chief Executive Officer: James Lichtenthal
Office Administrator: Chrisanne Lichtenthal
Contact: Patrick Illig
pdi@pdicone.com
Plant Manager: Brian McMahon
Estimated Sales: Less Than $500,000
Number Employees: 5-9

9644 P.J. Markos Seafood Company
Eight Topsfield Road
Ipswich, MA 01938-2132
978-356-4347
Fax: 978-356-9380
Seafood
Estimated Sales: $1-3 Million
Number Employees: 5-9

9645 P.J. Merrill Seafood Inc
681 Forest Ave
Portland, ME 04103-4101
207-773-1321
Fax: 207-775-4160 www.pjmerrillseafood.com
Seafood
Owner: Paul Merrill
fpjmerri@maine.rr.com
Estimated Sales: $3-5 Million
Number Employees: 10-19

9646 P.M. Innis Lobster Company
P.O.Box 85
18 Yates Street
Biddeford Pool, ME 04006
207-284-5000
Fax: 207-283-3308 help@poollobster.com
www.poollobster.com
Lobster
Owner: Beth Baskin
Estimated Sales: $3-5 Million
Number Employees: 10-19

9647 P.T. Fish
10b Portland Fish Pier
Portland, ME 04101-4620
207-772-0239
Fax: 907-874-2072
Seafood
Owner: Michael Twiss

9648 (HQ)PAR-Way Tryson Co
107 Bolte Ln
St Clair, MO 63077-3219
636-629-4545
Fax: 636-629-8341 moreinfo@parway.com
www.parwaytryson.com
Food release coatings, bakery and seasoning sprays
President: Keyna Lowrey Klabzuba
Owner & CEO: Mandy Hanson
Contact: Mike Abts
mike@parwaytryson.com
Year Founded: 1948
Number Employees: 20-49
Type of Packaging: Food Service, Private Label, Bulk
Brands:
Vegalene
Bak-klene
MallowCreme
Saragosa Olive Oil
PuriCit Odor Eliminator

9649 PB Leiner USA
PO Box 645
Plainview, NY 11803
516-822-4040
Fax: 516-465-0331 www.pbgelatins.com
Porcine gelatin
VP, Sales & Marketing: Cheryl Michaels
Contact: Kim Hildebrandt
kim.hildebrandt@pbleiner.com
Parent Co: Tessenderlo Group
Brands:
SOLUGEL
PEPTEIN

9650 PEI Mussel King
318 Red Head Road
P.O.Box 39 Prince Edward Island
Morrell, PE C0A 1S0
Canada
902-961-3300
Fax: 902-961-3366 800-673-2767
info@peimusselking.com www.peimusselking.com
Mussels, oysters and clams
President: Russell Dockendorff Sr
Co-Owner: Dorothy Dockendorff
Number Employees: 20-49
Type of Packaging: Consumer, Food Service, Private Label, Bulk
Brands:
Pei Mussel King

9651 PET Dairy
800 E 21st St
Winston Salem, NC 27105-5354
336-784-1800
Fax: 336-784-1844 800-735-2050
www.petdairy.com
Ice cream, milk
Manager: Dennis Riggs
Division Sales Manager: Don Roland
Manager: Chris Richmond
Operations Manager: Mike Reid
Estimated Sales: $1 Million
Number Employees: 20-49
Parent Co: Dean Foods Company
Type of Packaging: Consumer
Other Locations:
Spartanburg SC
Portsmouth VA
Florence SC

9652 PGP International
P.O. Box 2060
351 Hanson Way
Woodland, CA 95776
530-662-5056
Fax: 530-662-6074 800-233-0110
info@pgpint.com www.pgpint.com
Specialty ingredients: rice flour, breaders
CEO: Nicolas Hanson
Research & Development: Jennifer Eastman
Quality Control: Aman Das
Marketing Director: Cary Maigret-Saptiste
Operations Manager: Joe Holbrook
Number Employees: 100-249

9653 PJ's Coffee & Tea
109 New Camellia Blvd.
suite 201
Covington, LA 70433
985-792-5899
Fax: 985-792-1201 800-527-1055
www.pjscoffee.com
Coffee and tea
Manager: Tom Boudreaux
Owner: Phyllis Jordan
Accounts Manager: Tanya Mareno
Wholesale Manager: Felton Jones
Cafe Operations Manager: Mindy McKnight
Estimated Sales: $500,000-$1 Million
Number Employees: 5-9
Type of Packaging: Private Label
Brands:
PJ's Coffee

9654 PLT Health Solutions Inc
119 Headquarters Plz
Morristown, NJ 07960-6834
973-984-0900
Fax: 973-984-5666 www.plthomas.com
Extracts for food, supplements and cosmeceuticals.
President & CEO: Paul Flowerman
Executive Vice President: Seth Flowerman
Contact: Jenson Chang
jensonchang@hotmail.com
Number Employees: 50-99
Brands:
5-Loxin
Ceamgel 1313
Ecoguar
Fenopure
Glisodin
Glocal
Meganatural
Nutralease
Nutraveggie
Nutricran
Ultraguar

9655 PMC Specialties Group Inc
501 Murray Rd
Cincinnati, OH 45217-1014
513-242-3300
Fax: 513-482-7373 800-543-2466
davidsc@pmsg.com www.pmcsg.com
Saccharin, BHT, methyl anthranilate and benzonitrile
President: Michael Buchanan
Contact: Antaeus Kelly
antaeusk@pmcsg.com
Estimated Sales: $70 Milion
Number Employees: 250-499
Square Footage: 7500
Parent Co: PMC Global, Inc.

9656 PMP Fermentation Products
900 NE Adams St
Peoria, IL 61603-4200
309-637-0400
Fax: 309-637-9302 800-558-1031
info@pmpinc.com www.pmpinc.com
Sodium gluconate, erythorbate, calcium gluconate, gluconic acid, glucono-delta-lactone, sodium erythorbate, calcium potassium gluconate.
President/CEO: Randall Niedermeier
Director, Corporate Planning & Sales: Jim Zinkhon
Director, Administration: Dan Rudy
Year Founded: 1985
Estimated Sales: $25000000
Number Employees: 50-99
Parent Co: Fuso Chemical Company
Type of Packaging: Bulk
Brands:
Eribate

9657 POG
PO Box 699
Grand Bend, ON N0M 1T0
Canada
519-238-5704
Fax: 519-238-6800
Onions
President/CEO: Nelson J Desjardine
Type of Packaging: Bulk

9658 POM Wonderful LLC
11444 W. Olympic Blvd.
Los Angeles, CA 90064
866-976-6999
pr.pom@wonderful.com www.pomwonderful.com
Pomegranates, fruit juices, extracts and more.
Owner: Lynda Resnick
Chief Executive Officer: Stewart Resnick
Chief Financial Officer: Marc Washington
Marketing Director: Molly Flynn
Year Founded: 2002
Estimated Sales: $762 Million
Number Employees: 100-249
Parent Co: The Wonderful Company
Type of Packaging: Bulk
Brands:
POM

9659 POP Fishing & Marine
1133 N Nimitz Hwy
Honolulu, HI 96817
808-537-2905
Fax: 808-536-3225 sales@pop-hawaii.com
www.pop-hawaii.com
Seafood
President: Sean Martin
Owner: Jim Cook
Contact: Romeo Caban
romeo@pop-hawaii.com

9660 POPTime
200 Clifton Blvd
Clifton, NJ 07011
862-225-9549
www.poptimesnacks.com
Popcorn
CMO: Valentin Polyakov
Brands:
POPTime

9661 (HQ)PR Bar
2350 E Germann Rd
Suite 31
Chandler, AZ 85286
480-963-4064
Fax: 858-576-9152 800-397-5556
customercare@prbar.com www.prbar.com
Nutritional drink mixes
CEO: Frank W Busch III
CFO/CPA, Director: Roger L Butterwick
Senior Advisor: Al Springer
VP, Sports Marketing: Anne Marie Berte
VP, Sales: Travis Goodwin
Number Employees: 50
Parent Co: Twinlab Corporation

9662 PS Seasoning & Spices
216 W Pleasant St
Iron Ridge, WI 53035-9665
920-387-2204
Fax: 920-387-2204 www.psseasoning.com
Seasoning and spices
Founder: Harold Hanni
Number Employees: 20-49

9663 PYCO Industries Inc
2901 Avenue A
Lubbock, TX 79404
806-747-3434
www.pycoindustriesinc.com
Cottonseed oil, whole cottonseed, meal, hulls and linters.
President: Robert Lacy
Chairman: Burt Heinrich
Burtaheinrich@gmail.com
VP, Finance: Tony Morton
VP, Marketing: Jerrod Drinnon
VP, Operations: Lewis Harvill
General Manager/Superintendent: Walt Stokes
Estimated Sales: $309 Million
Other Locations:
Plainsman Switching Co.
Lubbock TX

9664 (HQ)Pabst Brewing Company
Consumer Affairs Department
PO Box 792627
San Antonio, TX 78279
210-226-0231
Fax: 210-226-2512 800-947-2278
products@pabst.com www.pabst.com
Beers
Chairman: Dean Metropoulos
Co-CEO: Evan Metropoulos
Co-cEO: Daren Metropoulos
President: John Coleman
Chief Financial Officer: Brent Zachary
SVP/General Counsel: Jim Vieceli
Chief Marketing Officer: Daniel McHugh
VP Sales/National Accounts: Mark Beatty
Number Employees: 100-249
Type of Packaging: Consumer
Other Locations:
Pabst Brewery Location
San Antonio TX
Pabst Brewery Location
Milawaukee WI

Brands:
Augsberger
Big Bear
Bull Ice
Champale
Clash Malt
Colt 45
Country Club
Falstaff
Goebel
Ice Man
Jacob Best
Laser
Old Milwaukee
Olympia
Pabst Blue Ribbon Beers
Piels
Piels Light
Private Stock
Red Bull Malt Liquor
Red River
Schaefer
Schlitz
Silver Thunder Malt Liquor
Special Brew
St. Ides Special Brew
Stroh's
White Mountain

9665 Paca Foods Inc
5212 Cone Rd
Tampa, FL 33610-5302
813-628-8228
Fax: 813-628-8426 800-388-7419
Spice blends, beverage mixes, flour based mixes, seasonings, industrial premixes, nutrition blends
President: Robert Cabral
Chief Executive Officer: Michael Shepardson
michael.shepardson@pacafoods.com
VP/CFO: Paul Pritchard
Quality Manager: Ken Crane
Chief Operating Officer: Matt Schneider
Estimated Sales: $5 Million
Number Employees: 20-49
Square Footage: 120000
Type of Packaging: Private Label

9666 Pacari Organic Chocolate
Boca Raton, FL
pacarichocolate.us
Organic Ecuadorian chocolate

9667 Pacheco Ranch Winery
235 Alameda Del Prado
Novato, CA 94949-6657
415-883-5583
Fax: 415-883-6992
contact@pachecoranchwinery.com
www.pachecoranchwinery.com
Wines
Owner: Herbert Rowland
contact@pachecorachwinery.com
CFO: Debra Rowland
Quality Control: Jamie Mezes
Winemaker: Jamie Meves
Estimated Sales: $2.5-5 Million
Number Employees: 5-9
Brands:
Pacheco Ranch

9668 Pacific American Fish Co Inc
5525 S Santa Fe Ave
Vernon, CA 90058-3523
323-587-3298
Fax: 323-319-1517 800-625-2525
pehuh@pafco.net www.pafco.net
Shrimp, fish fillets and calamari steaks, rings and strips
Chairman/CEO: Peter Huh
Vice Chairman/VP, Operations & Sales: Paul Huh
VP, New Venture Development: Jihee Huh
Estimated Sales: $37.8 Million
Number Employees: 50-99
Number of Brands: 4
Square Footage: 10600
Type of Packaging: Consumer, Food Service
Other Locations:
San Francisco CA
Boston MA
Brands:
Oceankist
Pacific Surf
Pete's Seafood
Snak N'Go

9669 Pacific Beach Peanut Butter
8691 LA Mesa Blvd
La Mesa, CA 91942-9503
USA
630-329-0792
info@pbpeanutbutter.com
www.pacificbeachpeanutbutter.com
Peanut Butter
President/Owner: Matthew Mulvihill
matthew@pbpeanutbutter.com
Number Employees: 1-4

9670 Pacific Chai
PO BOX 10
Farmington, UT 84025
801-939-9100
Fax: 801-939-9373 888-882-4248
customerservice@indulgentfoods.com
www.pacificchai.com
Chai Tea
Estimated Sales: $5-10 Million
Number Employees: 10-19

9671 Pacific Cheese Co
21090 Cabot Blvd
PO Box 56598
Hayward, CA 94545-1110
510-784-8800
Fax: 510-784-8846 info@pacificcheese.com
www.pacificcheese.com
Cheese
CEO: Stephen Gaddis
sgaddis@pacific-cheese.com
President & CEO: Steve Gaddis
Year Founded: 1973
Estimated Sales: $20-50 Million
Number Employees: 100-249
Square Footage: 45000
Other Locations:
Excelpro Manufacturing Corp.
Wellsville UT

9672 Pacific Choice Brands
4652 E. Date Ave.
Fresno, CA 93725
559-476-3581
Fax: 559-237-2096 sales@pacificchoice.com
www.pacificchoice.com
Maraschino cherries, garlic, grape leaves, peppers, olives, salsa, sauces, capers and sun dried tomotoes
President: Allan Andrews
CFO: Faith Buller
VP: Villalobos Boni
Plant Manager: Chris Rabago
Purchasing Manager: Mireille Akel
Estimated Sales: $39.5 Million
Number Employees: 275
Square Footage: 225000
Type of Packaging: Consumer, Food Service, Private Label
Brands:
Durango Gold
Orlando
Pacific Choice

9673 Pacific Coast Brewing
906 Washington St
Oakland, CA 94607-4032
510-836-2739
Fax: 510-836-1987
Beer, ale, stout and porter
Owner: Steve Wolff
info@pacificcoastbrewing.com
Owner/Brewmaster: Don Gortemiller
Estimated Sales: Below $500,000
Number Employees: 20-49
Type of Packaging: Consumer, Food Service
Brands:
Grey Whale
Imperial
Pacific Coast Brewing Co.

9674 Pacific Coast Fruit Co
201 NE 2nd Ave # 100
Portland, OR 97232-2993
503-234-6411
Fax: 503-234-0072 www.pcfruit.com
Frozen fruits, juice concentrates
President: Dave Nemarnik
Secretary/Treasurer: Ellen McIntyre
Accounting Manager: Jeff Rine
Vice President, Director: Don Daeges
Sales Manager: Bob Meikle
Vice President of Operations: Joe Santucci
Number Employees: 250-499
Type of Packaging: Bulk

9675 Pacific Coast Producers
631 N Cluff Ave
Lodi, CA 95240-0756
209-367-8800
Fax: 209-367-1084 877-618-4776
sales@pcoastp.com
Canned fruits and vegetables
President & CEO: Daniel Vincent
dvincent@pcoastp.com
Vice President, Finance & CFO: Matt Strong
Vice President, Sales & Marketing: Andrew Russick
Number Employees: 1000-4999
Type of Packaging: Consumer, Food Service

9676 Pacific Collier Fresh Company
925 New Harvest Rd
Immokalee, FL 34142
239-657-5283
Fax: 239-657-4924 800-226-7274
Beans, cabbage, cucumbers, potatoes, squash, tomatos
Manager: Jennifer Levy
Estimated Sales: $10-20 Million
Number Employees: 20-49
Parent Co: Heller Brothers
Brands:
Sunripe

9677 Pacific Echo Cellars
8501 Highway 128
Philo, CA 95466
707-895-2065
Fax: 707-895-2758
Wines
Business manager: Mineille Guiliano
Manager: Walter Sawitsky
Winery Manager/Winemaker: Tex Sawyer
Vineyard Operations Manager: Bob Nye
Vineyard Manager: Tony Hortlig
Estimated Sales: $1-10 Million
Number Employees: 25
Type of Packaging: Private Label
Brands:
Pacific Echo
Scharffenberger

9678 Pacific Ethanol Inc.
400 Capitol Mall
Suite 2060
Sacramento, CA 95814
916-403-2123
Fax: 916-446-3937 info@pacificethanol.com
www.pacificethanol.net
Beverage alcohol, food grade yeast.
Co-Founder/CEO: Neil Koehler
Director/COO: Mike Kandris
CFO: Bryon McGregor
Vice President/General Counsel: Christopher Wright
Year Founded: 2003
Estimated Sales: $888 Million

9679 Pacific Farms
222 Juana Avenue
San Leandro, CA 94577
877-722-3276
Fax: 510-618-1605 info@pacificfarms.com
www.pacificfarms.com
Dehydrated and frozen vegetables
President: Garry Offenberg
CEO: Nate Offenberg
National Sales Manager: Lorrie Pullman
Operations Manager: Erleen Lum

9680 Pacific Foods
21612 88th Ave S
Kent, WA 98031-1918
253-395-9400
Fax: 253-395-3330 800-347-9444
Flavoring extracts, seasoning mixes, soup bases, baking powder, nuts and spices
President: James Hughs
Plant Manager: Brandan Caile
Vice President: Richard Weaver
Plant Manager: Mark Hendrickson
Estimated Sales: $5-10 Million
Number Employees: 50-99
Type of Packaging: Food Service, Private Label, Bulk
Brands:
Chef Classic
Crescent

9681 Pacific Foods of Oregon
19480 SW 79th Ave
Tualatin, OR 97062
503-692-9666
Fax: 503-692-9610 www.pacificfoods.com
Broths, stocks, soups, sauces, purees and non-dairy beverages.
Business Development Manager: Michael Mysels
Brands:
Pacific(c)

9682 Pacific Fruit Processors
7301 Ohms Lane
Suite 600, CA 55439
952-820-2518
Fax: 952-939-8106 pfpsalesorders@sunopta.com
Fruit ingredients
Prsident/CEO: Steve Bromley
COO: Frank Gonzalez
Estimated Sales: $93,000
Number Employees: 1
Square Footage: 7384
Type of Packaging: Food Service
Other Locations:
Pacific Fruit Processors
Lapham Co
Brands:
Lapham

9683 Pacific Gold Marketing
2109 E Division Street
Arlington, TX 76011
817-795-4671
Fax: 817-795-4673
Nuts, dried fruit and dark chocolate
President: Patricia Locktov
Estimated Sales: Below $5 Million
Number Employees: 100-249
Parent Co: GNS Foods
Brands:
Pacific Gold

9684 Pacific Gold Snacks
7060 South 238th Street
Kent, WA 98032
253-854-7056
pacificgoldsnacks.com
Beef jerky
President/Owner: Tom Hernquist
Parent Co: Oberto Sausage Co.
Brands:
PACIFIC GOLD
PACIFIC GOLD RESERVE

9685 Pacific Gourmet Seafood
26 Stine Road
Bakersfield, CA 93309-2011
661-533-1260
Fax: 805-831-9740
Seafood
Partner: Kelly Bowman
Partner: Patsy Bowman

9686 Pacific Grain & Foods
4067 W Shaw Ave
Suite 116
Fresno, CA 93722-6214
559-276-2580
Fax: 559-276-2936
www.pacificgrainandfoods.com
Beans, spices, seeds, chilies, edible nuts, dried fruit, rice and wheat.
President: Lee Perkins
lperkins@lightspeed.net
Sales Manager: Jose Alvarado
Number Employees: 10-19
Type of Packaging: Food Service, Private Label

9687 Pacific Harvest Products
13405 SE 30th Street
Bellevue, WA 98005-4454
425-401-7990
Dry blends, sauces, dressings, bases
Contact: Nicholas Ade
n.ade@pnb.org
Number Employees: 20-49
Type of Packaging: Consumer, Food Service, Private Label, Bulk
Brands:
Firmenich

9688 Pacific Hop Exchange Brewing Company
158 Hamilton Drive
Novato, CA 94949-5630
415-884-2820
Fax: 415-884-2820
Beer
President: Tom Whelan
CFO: Robert Ankrum
Brewer: Warren Stief
Estimated Sales: Under $500,000
Number Employees: 5-9
Square Footage: 3
Type of Packaging: Private Label
Brands:
06 Stout
Barbary Coast Barley
Gaslight Pale Ale
Graintrader Wheat Al
Holly Hops Spiced Al
I.P.A.
Irish Stout
Ol' Spout
St. Briogets Strong
Warren's Wonderful W

9689 Pacific Nutritional
6317 NE 131st Ave # 103
Vancouver, WA 98682-5879
360-896-2297
Fax: 360-253-6543
Tablet, capsule, powder and liquid nutritional formulations
President: Michael Schaesser
CEO: Tiffany Swett
CFO: Ron Golden
VP, Sales/Marketing: Tina Mori
COO: Scott Haugen
Estimated Sales: $27 Million
Number Employees: 50-99
Square Footage: 35000
Type of Packaging: Private Label

9690 Pacific Ocean Produce
105 Pioneer St
Santa Cruz, CA 95060-2159
831-423-2654
Fax: 831-423-2654
Dried seaweed
Owner: Matthew Hodel
Estimated Sales: $150,000
Number Employees: 2
Type of Packaging: Consumer, Bulk

9691 Pacific Poultry Company
PO Box 15851
1818 Kanakanui
Honolulu, HI 96830-5851
808-841-2828
Fax: 808-872-0872
Portion controlled poultry, barbecue sauce
President: Jaren Hancock
Treasurer: J Cuarisma
VP of Operations: Brent Hancock
Estimated Sales: $5-10 Million
Number Employees: 50-99
Square Footage: 41400
Type of Packaging: Consumer, Food Service, Private Label
Brands:
Ewa
Hawaii's Famous Huli Huli

9692 Pacific Salmon Company
21630 98th Ave W
Edmonds, WA 98020-3923
425-774-1315
Fax: 425-774-6856
Black cod, halibut, salmon, shark, smelt, squid, kosher foods and fish patties
Owner: John Mc Callum
Contact: James Chapa
johnmccallum@msn.com
Estimated Sales: $5-10 Million
Number Employees: 10 to 19
Brands:
Pacific

9693 Pacific Seafoods International
PO Box 401
Port Hardy, BC V0N 2P0
Canada
250-949-8781
Fax: 250-949-8781
Salmon fillets
President: Hardy Fish
CEO: Todd Harmon
Number Employees: 20-49
Square Footage: 48000
Type of Packaging: Consumer, Food Service, Private Label, Bulk
Brands:
St. Laurent
Treasure Island

9694 Pacific Soybean & Grain
411 Borel Ave
Suite 235
San Mateo, CA 94402-3512
650-525-0500
Fax: 415-433-9494 info@pacificsoy.com
www.pacificsoy.com
Oilseed: corn, soybean and sunflower
Manager: Lina Mesa
Contact: Dan Burke
burke@pacificsoy.com
Number Employees: 1-4

9695 Pacific Spice Co
6430 E Slauson Ave
Commerce, CA 90040-3108
323-890-0895
Fax: 323-726-9442 www.pacspice.com
Spices and herbs
President: Akiba Schlussel
akiba@pacspice.com
Estimated Sales: G
Number Employees: 100-249
Square Footage: 150000
Type of Packaging: Consumer, Food Service, Private Label, Bulk
Brands:
Pacific Natural Spices

9696 Pacific Standard Distributors
38954 Proctor Blvd
Suite 388
Sandy, OR 97055
760-479-1460
Fax: 800-741-2164 sales@modifilan.com
www.modifilan.com
Seaweed supplement capsules
Owner: Vladimir Bajanov
Contact: Michelle Arakaki
marakaki@modifilan.com
Estimated Sales: $1-3 Million
Number Employees: 1-4
Number of Products: 1
Type of Packaging: Consumer, Food Service, Bulk
Brands:
Modifilan

9697 Pacific Sun Olive Oil
22889 Gerber Road
PO Box 955
Gerber, CA 96035
530-385-1475
www.pacificsunoliveoil.com
Olive oils
President/Owner: Jane Flynn
General Manager: Brendon Flynn
Sales Manager: Leslie Stone
Estimated Sales: $15 Million
Number Employees: 15

9698 Pacific Trellis
1500 W Manning Ave
Reedley, CA 93654-9211
559-638-5100
Fax: 559-638-5400 www.pacifictrellisfruit.com
Stone fruits and grapes
Manager: Earl Mc Menamin
Contact: Tim Dayka
t.dayka@pacifictrellisfruit.com
Estimated Sales: $10-20 Million
Number Employees: 10-19

9699 Pacific Valley Foods Inc
2700 Richards Rd # 101
Bellevue, WA 98005-4200
425-643-1805
Fax: 425-747-4221 sales@pacificvalleyfoods.com
www.pacificvalleyfoods.com
French fries, frozen vegetables, frozen berries, tortillas, dried peas, lentils, chickpeas

Co-Owner/Co-Director: Scott Hannah
scott@pacificvalleyfoods.com
Co-Owner/Co-Director: Lynn Hannah
Executive VP: John Hannah
Estimated Sales: $2.7 Million
Number Employees: 5-9
Square Footage: 40000
Parent Co: Pacific Valley Foods
Type of Packaging: Consumer, Food Service, Private Label, Bulk
Brands:
Basic Country Goodness
Cedar Farms
Great Gusto
Hi West
Lynden Farms
Pacific Valley

9700 **Pacific Westcoast Foods**
3880 Sw 102nd Ave
Beaverton, OR 97005-3244
503-641-4988
Fax: 755-665-8610 800-874-9333
gourmet@teleport.com
Salad dressings, preserves, fruit syrups and fillings
President: Mark Roth
President: Gloria Sample
Estimated Sales: $280,000
Number Employees: 4
Square Footage: 20000
Type of Packaging: Consumer, Food Service, Private Label, Bulk

9701 **Pacific Western Brewing Company**
641 N Nechako Road
Prince George, BC V2K 4M4
Canada
250-562-2424
Fax: 250-562-0799 mail@pwbrewing.com
www.pwbrewing.net
Beer, lager and ale
CEO: Kazuko Komatfu
Marketing Director: Bruce Clark
Office Manager: Denise Vlanchette
Manager: Thomas Leboe
Estimated Sales: $2 Million
Number Employees: 50-99
Type of Packaging: Consumer, Food Service
Brands:
Amberale
Iron Horse
Lager
Pacific Pilsner

9702 **Pacifica Culinaria**
PO Box 507
Vista, CA 92085
760-727-9883
Fax: 951-727-9886 800-622-8880
sales@pacificaculinaria.com
www.pacificaculinaria.com
Infused avacado oils, infused vinegars, agave syrups, wasabi mayonnaise, spiced olives, mayan pearl fresh avacados

9703 **Paciugo Distribution**
1215 Viceroy Dr
Dallas, TX 75247
214-631-2663
info@paciugo.com
paciugo.com
Gelato, ingredients and beverage pouches
Contact: James Ludwick
james.ludwick@westhoustonent.com
Estimated Sales: $15 Million
Number Employees: 25

9704 **Packaged Products Division**
12395 Belcher Road S
Suite 350
Largo, FL 33773-3096
727-787-3619
Fax: 727-787-3619 888-833-2247
Snack foods
President: Roger Hoover
Vice President: Jason Brooks
Marketing Director: R Barry Williams
Sales Director: Pat Champagne
Public Relations: Angie Strother
Production Manager: Jerry Adams
Purchasing Manager: Jason Brooks
Estimated Sales: $3 Million
Number Employees: 25

9705 **Pacsea Corporation**
PO Box 898
Aiea, HI 96701-0898
808-836-8888
Fax: 808-836-7888
Seafood
President: Michael Li
Treasurer/Bookkeeper: Wendy Puampi
Vice-President: Gladis Li

9706 **Paddack Enterprises**
27052 State Highway 120
Escalon, CA 95320-9502
209-838-1536
Fax: 209-838-8063
Almonds
President: Vernon Paddack
Estimated Sales: $500,000 appx.
Number Employees: 5-9

9707 **Paesana Products**
101 Central Avenue
PO Box 709
East Farmingdale, NY 11735
631-845-1717
Fax: 631-845-1788 info@paesana.com
www.paesana.com
Pasta sauces, stuffed olives, peppers, artichokes, balsamic vinegars, garlic, mushrooms, olive oils, tomatoes, tuna
Contact: Edna Maniaci
ej@paesana.com

9708 **Page Mill Winery**
1960 S Livermore Ave
Livermore, CA 94550-9003
925-456-7676
info@pagemillwinery.com
www.pagemillwinery.com
Wines
Founder: Dick Stark
President: Michael Gibbs
Propreitor: Dane Stark
Sales Director: Gary Brink
Manager: Debbie Cristino
debbie@pagemillwinery.com
Operations Manager: Sue Swartz
Vineyard Manager: Leopoldo Gonzalez
Estimated Sales: Less than $500,000
Number Employees: 1-4

9709 **Pahlmeyer Winery**
811 Saint Helena Hwy S
St Helena, CA 94574-2266
707-255-2321
Fax: 707-255-6786 info@pahlmeyer.com
www.pahlmeyer.com
Wines
Founder: Jayson Pahlmeyer
info@pahlmeyer.com
Vice President: Michael Haas
Sales Manager: Camille Cox
Communications Director: Cleo Pahlmeyer
Controller: Lynn Gentry
Director of Winemaking-Napa Valley: Kale Anderson
Estimated Sales: $4 Million
Number Employees: 10-19
Type of Packaging: Private Label
Brands:
Jayson
Pahlmeyer

9710 **Pahrump Valley Winery**
3810 Winery Rd # 1
Pahrump, NV 89048-4898
775-751-7800
Fax: 775-751-7818 800-368-9463
pvwine@hotmail.com www.pahrumpwinery.com
Wines
Manager: Bill Loken
Estimated Sales: $5-10 Million
Number Employees: 20-49
Brands:
Pahrump Valley Winery

9711 **Paisano Food Products**
261 King Street
Elk Grove Village, IL 60007-1112
773-237-3773
Fax: 773-237-8114 800-672-4726
Dried beans, chicken
President: Paul Williams
Number Employees: 5-9
Parent Co: Cousin Foods
Type of Packaging: Food Service

9712 **Paisley Farms Inc**
38180 Airport Pkwy
Willoughby, OH 44094-8021
440-269-3923
Fax: 440-269-3929 800-474-5688
www.paisleyfarminc.com
vegetables and relishes
President: Kenneth Anderson
Estimated Sales: $24 Million
Number Employees: 20-49
Number of Brands: 1
Square Footage: 30000
Type of Packaging: Consumer, Food Service, Private Label, Bulk
Brands:
Paisley Farm

9713 **Paklab Products**
1315 Gay-Lussac
Boucherville, QC J4B 7K1
Canada
450-449-1224
Fax: 450-449-3380 888-946-3233
Grape juice
President: Claudio Garuti
Finance Director: Assunta Marcone

9714 **Palacios & Sons**
1431 Greenway Dr
Suite 800
Irving, TX 75038-2574
469-449-2060
www.charras.com
Tostadas, tortilla chips and snacks.
General Manager: Raul Gonzalez
Brands:
Charras(c)

9715 **Paleo Powder Seasoning**
979-540-9137
sales@paleopowderseasoning.com
www.paleopowderseasoning.com
Paleo-friendly, organic seasonings
Founder & Owner: Dustin Gersch
Brands:
PALEO POWDER

9716 **Paleo Prime Foods**
PO Box 577451
Chicago, IL 60657
312-659-6596
hey@paleoprimefoods.com
www.paleoprimefoods.com
Grain-free protein cookies
Founder: Casey McMillin
Brands:
PALEO PRIME

9717 **Paleo Ranch**
Lakeway, TX
www.paleoranch.com
Paleo-friendly protein snacks

9718 **Palermo Bakery**
1620 Fremont Blvd
Seaside, CA 93955-3607
831-394-8212
Fax: 831-394-0184 www.palermobakeryco.com
Breads
Owner: Rosario Zito
rosario.zito@palermobakery.com
Estimated Sales: $1.2 000,000
Number Employees: 10-19
Type of Packaging: Consumer, Food Service, Bulk
Brands:
Palermo

9719 **Palermo's Pizza**
Villa Palermo
3301 Canal Rd
Milwaukee, WI 53208
414-643-0919
www.palermospizza.com
Frozen pizza
CEO: Giacomo Fallucca
Brands:
PALERMO'S
SCREAMIN' SICILIAN PIZZA CO.
URBAN PIE PIZZA CO.
CONNIE'S PIZZA

9720 **Palm Beach Foods**
352 Tall Pines Rd
Suite F
West Palm Beach, FL 33413-1737
561-242-9229
Fax: 561-584-5780 855-9GL-TEN

Cookies and snacks
Contact: Daniela Sujoy
dsujoy@palmbeachfoods.com
Estimated Sales: Less Than $500,000
Number Employees: 1-4

9721 **Palme d'Or**
228 Principale
Saint Louis de Gonzague, QC J0S 1T0
Canada
450-377-8766
www.palmedor.ca/en/

Duck foie gras

9722 **(HQ)Palmer Candy Co**
2600 N US Highway 75
Suite 1
Sioux City, IA 51105-2444
712-258-5543
Fax: 712-258-3224 800-831-0828
vicki@palmercandy.com
www.palmerspecialtyfoods.com

Bagged, multi-pack vending snacks
President: Martin Palmer
Director of Quality Control: Dawn Gorham
VP, Marketing: Bob O'Neill
VP, Operations: Bill Kennedy
Purchasing Manager: Jeff Wilkerson
Estimated Sales: $15.50 Million
Number Employees: 50-99
Square Footage: 420000
Type of Packaging: Consumer, Food Service, Private Label, Bulk
Other Locations:
Palmer Candy Company
Kansas City MO
Brands:
Favorites
King Bing
Peanut Butter Bing
Twin Bing

9723 **Palmer Meat Packing Co**
1315 S 100 E
Tremonton, UT 84337-8727
435-257-5329

Meat and jerky
Owner: George Palmer
Estimated Sales: $14 Million
Number Employees: 1-4
Type of Packaging: Consumer, Food Service

9724 **Palmer Vineyards Inc**
5120 Sound Ave
Riverhead, NY 11901-5533
631-722-5364
Fax: 631-722-5634 800-901-8783
palmervineyards@mail.com
www.palmervineyards.com

Wines
Owner: Alexandra Adams
alexandra@palmervineyards.com
Winemaker: Tom Drozd
Estimated Sales: $2.5-5 Million
Number Employees: 10-19
Type of Packaging: Private Label

9725 **Palmetto Brewing Co**
289 Huger St
Suite B
Charleston, SC 29403-4560
843-937-0903
Fax: 843-937-0092 www.palmettobrewery.com

Beer
President/Brewmaster: Louis Bruce
Brewer: Ed Falkenstein
Estimated Sales: Less than $500,000
Number Employees: 1-4
Brands:
Palmetto

9726 **Palmetto Canning**
3601 US Highway 41 N
Palmetto, FL 34221
941-722-1100
pcrbaggs@tampabay.rr.com
palmettocanning.com

Canning and packaging sauces and beverage
Estimated Sales: $5-10 Million
Number Employees: 1-4
Square Footage: 128000
Type of Packaging: Consumer, Private Label
Brands:
Palmalito

9727 **Palmetto Pigeon Plant**
335 Broad Street
Sumter, SC 29150
803-775-1204
Fax: 803-778-2896 www.palmettopigeonplant.com

Squab, chicken and poussin
President: Anthony Barwick
Office Manager: Sherry Cannon
Estimated Sales: $10-20 Million
Number Employees: 50-99
Square Footage: 32400
Type of Packaging: Consumer

9728 **Palmieri Food Products**
145 Hamilton St
New Haven, CT 06511-5837
203-624-0042
Fax: 203-782-6435 800-845-5447
sales@palmierifoods.com

Sauces
President: Mary Palmeri
sales@palmierifoods.com
Estimated Sales: $5-10 Million
Number Employees: 10-19
Type of Packaging: Consumer, Food Service, Private Label, Bulk
Brands:
Andrews
Palmieri
Pinders

9729 **Palmyra Bologna Co Inc**
230 N College St
Palmyra, PA 17078-1697
717-838-6336
Fax: 717-838-5345 800-282-6336
www.seltzerslebanonbologna.com

Smoked bologna
President: Craig Seltzer
craig.seltzer@seltzerslebanonbologna.com
CFO: Peter Stanilla
Vice President, Sales: Perry Smith
Estimated Sales: $10 Million
Number Employees: 50-99
Type of Packaging: Consumer, Food Service, Private Label, Bulk
Brands:
Penn Dutch
Seltzers

9730 **Pamela's Products**
1 Carousel Ln
Ukiah, CA 95482-9509
707-462-6605
Fax: 707-462-6642 info@pamelasproducts.com
www.pamelasproducts.com

Cookies, bars, flours and baking mixes
President/Owner: Pamela Giusto-Sorrells
Estimated Sales: $450,000
Number Employees: 100-249
Type of Packaging: Consumer, Bulk
Brands:
Pamela's
Wheat-Free

9731 **Pamlico Packing Company**
66 Cross Road
P.O. Box 336
Grantsboro, NC 28529
252-745-3688
Fax: 252-745-3272 800-682-1113
kingcrab1@hotmail.com www.bestseafood.com

Scallops, shrimp, crabs, crabmeat, flounder, oysters, whiting and trout
President: Ed Cross
General Manager: Doug Cross
doug@bestseafood.com
Estimated Sales: $12 Million
Number Employees: 70
Type of Packaging: Consumer, Food Service, Bulk
Brands:
Seafood People

9732 **Pan American Coffee Co**
500 16th St
Hoboken, NJ 07030-2336
201-963-2329
Fax: 201-659-1883 800-229-1883
www.panamericancoffee.com

Coffee
President: Roy Montes
Quality Control: Edili Jerridy
General Manager: Ruth Santuccio
ruth@panamericancoffee.com
Estimated Sales: $5-10 000,000
Number Employees: 20-49

9733 **Pan De Oro Tortilla Chip Co**
3478 Main St
Hartford, CT 06120-1138
860-724-7063
www.pandeoro.com

Tortilla chips
Co-Founder: Richard Stevens
Co-Founder: John Grikis
Vice President: Lief Dana
Contact: Beth Gabriele
gabrielebeth@severancefoods.com
Number Employees: 50-99

9734 **Pan Pepin**
PO Box 100
Bayamon, PR 00960-0100
787-787-1717
Fax: 787-740-2029 www.panpepin.com

Sandwiches, hamburgers, hot dog buns
CEO/President: Rafael Rovira
Marketing Director: Mario Somoza
VP Finance: Carolina Rodriguez
General Manager: Miguel Santiago
Number Employees: 300
Type of Packaging: Consumer
Brands:
Healthy Juice
Nature Zone
Pan Pepin

9735 **Pan's Mushroom Jerky**
Vancouver, WA
hello@mushroomjerky.com
www.mushroomjerky.com

Mushroom jerky
President/Owner: Michael Pan

9736 **Pan-O-Gold Baking Co.**
444 E. Saint Germain St.
St. Cloud, MN 56304
320-251-9361
800-444-7005
info@panogold.com www.panogold.com

White and variety bread and buns, bagels, muffins, donuts, and rolls.
President: Howard Alton
Senior VP/CFO: Dennis Leisten
Vice President, Sales: Brent Schmaltz
Year Founded: 1911
Estimated Sales: $159.89 Million
Number Employees: 1,000-4,999
Number of Brands: 13
Square Footage: 190000
Type of Packaging: Consumer
Brands:
Country Hearth
Village Hearth
Artisan Hearth
Lakeland
New England
Frescados
Holsum
Pan-O-Gold
Fiber Up
Papa Pita
Papa's Organic
Bubba's Bagels
Maya's Tortillas

9737 **(HQ)Pandol Brothers Inc**
33150 Pond Rd.
Delano, CA 93215-9598
661-725-3755
Fax: 661-725-4741 sales.domestic@pandol.com
www.pandol.com

Green, black, red and seeded grapes; persimmons, blueberries, cherries, apples, peaches, plums, nectarines

President & CEO: Cheri Diebel
Safety Manager: Andrew Pandol
Account Manager: Andrew Brown
Manager: Carlos Mendoza
Director, Global Operations: David Sudduth
Year Founded: 1923
Estimated Sales: $20-50 Million
Number Employees: 20-49

9738 **Pandol Brothers Inc**
1737 North Wenatche Ave.
Suite A
Wenatchee, WA 98801
509-662-3763
Fax: 509-663-8449 pandolWA@pandol.com
www.pandol.com
Green, black, red and seeded grapes; persimmons, blueberries, cherries, apples, peaches, plums, nectarines

9739 **Pandol Brothers Inc**
San Francisco de Asis
150 of 621
Santiago,
Chile
pandolCL@pandol.com
www.pandol.com
Green, black, red and seeded grapes; persimmons, blueberries, cherries, apples, peaches, plums, nectarines

9740 **Panera Bread**
3630 S. Geyer Rd.
Suite 100
Saint Louis, MO 63127
314-984-1000
www.panerabread.com
Breads, sandwiches, drinks, soups, salads, pastries.
President/CEO: Niren Chaudhary
Founder/Chairman: Ronald Shaich
Senior VP/Chief Financial Officer: Michael Bufano
SVP/Chief Legal & Francise Officer: Scott Blair
Senior Vice President, Marketing: Christopher Hollander
Executive VP/Chief Operating Officer: Charles Chapman III
Year Founded: 1987
Estimated Sales: $2.7 Billion
Number Employees: 50,000+
Brands:
Panera(c)
Saint Louis Bread Co.(c)
Paradise Bakery & Cafe(c)

9741 **Pangburn Candy Company**
2000 White Settlement Road
Fort Worth, TX 76107-1467
817-332-8856
Fax: 940-887-4578
Candy
President: R Phillips
Estimated Sales: $2.5-5 Million
Number Employees: 50

9742 **Panhandle Food Sales**
1980 Smith Township State Rd
Burgettstown, PA 15021-2433
724-947-2216
Fax: 724-947-4940 info@panhandlefoodsales.com
www.panhandlefoodsales.com
Frozen pizza
Owner: Bill Dugas
Number Employees: 20-49

9743 **Panhandle Milling**
4805 FM809
Dawn, TX 79025
800-897-5226
www.panhandlemilling.com
Organic flours, whole wheat products and specialty grains
Brands:
Panhandle Milling
Ingredient Integrity
Specialty Grains
Specialty Blends

9744 **Panoche Creek Packing**
3611 W Beechwood Ave
Suite 101
Fresno, CA 93711-0648
559-449-1721
Fax: 559-431-9970 inquiry@panochecreek.com
www.panochecreek.com
Almonds
Owner: Estelle Holland
estelle@panochecreek.com
Vice President: John Blackburn
Marketing Manager: Ross Blackburn
Plant Manager: Jason Baldwin
Estimated Sales: Less than $500,000
Number Employees: 5-9
Type of Packaging: Private Label, Bulk
Brands:
Golden

9745 **Panola Pepper Co**
1414 Holland Delta Rd
Lake Providence, LA 71254-5545
318-559-1774
Fax: 318-559-3003 800-256-3013
panola@bayou.com www.panolapepper.com
Spices, hot sauce
President: Grady W Brown
panola@bayou.com
CFO: Janne Brown
Vice President: John Bowers
Public Relations: Jim Byrant
Estimated Sales: Below $5 Million
Number Employees: 20-49
Type of Packaging: Private Label
Brands:
Gourmet Pepper Sauce
Panola
Panola & Private Lab
Pasta Salad
Red Pepper Sauce
Southern Spice
Steak Sauce

9746 **Panorama Foods Inc.**
100 Messina Drive
Suite P
Braintree, MA 02184
781-592-1069
info@panoramafoods.com
www.panoramafoods.com
Crackers, drink mixes, and spices
President: Ken Meyers
Contact: Jan Siplon
jan.siplon@panoramafoods.com

9747 **Panorama Meats**
4325 W. Shaw Ave
Suite A
Fresno, CA 93722
707-765-6756
lori.carrion@panoramameats.com
www.panoramameats.com
Organic beef
Chief Executive Officer: Lori Carrion
Senior Advisor: Mack Graves
Sales Representative: Brian Graves
Contact: Darrell Wood
dwood@panoramameats.com
Vice President, Production: Wayne Langston

9748 **Panos Brands**
395 West Passaic St
Suite 240
Rochelle Park, NJ 07662
201-843-8900
Fax: 201-368-3575
customer.services@panosbrands.com
www.panosbrands.com
Cheese, Asian food, crackers, cookies, pastes, soy and rice powders, cakes, seafood, salsa
Member President: Kevin McGahren-Clemens
VP Sales: Steve Warner
VP Finance: John Lennan
Marketing: Steven Warner
Contact: Roger Valkenburgh
roger.vanvalkenburgh@panosbrands.com
Purchasing: Kathy Burkowski
Estimated Sales: $2.2 Million
Number Employees: 16
Brands:
Amore(c)
Andrew & Everett(c)
Better Than Milk(c)
Chatfield's(c)
Downey's(c)
KA-ME(c)
MI-DEL(c)
Mr.Spinkles
Sesmark(c)
Tap'n Apple(c)
Yankee Clipper(c)
Zapata(c)

9749 **Panther Creek Cellars**
110 SW Hwy 99E
Dundee, OR 97128
503-472-8080
Fax: 503-472-5667 info@panthercreekcellars.com
www.panthercreekcellars.com
Wines
Co-Owner: Linda Kaplan
Marketing Manager: Bill Hanson
Sales Manager: Mark Eggiman
Winemaker: Michael Stevenson
Estimated Sales: $750,000
Number Employees: 1-4
Type of Packaging: Consumer, Private Label

9750 **Pantry Shelf/Mixxm**
PO Box 613
Hutchinson, KS 67504
626-629-342
Fax: 620-662-9306 800-968-3346
Cakes, pastries, baking mixes, cocoa, baking chocolate, hot chocolate, alcoholic beverages, gift packs

9751 **Papa Dean's Popcorn**
999 East Basse Rd.
Suite 184
San Antonio, TX 78209-3827
877-855-7272
Fax: 210-822-2140 deanneu@aol.com
Flavored popcorn
Owner: Tara Zaglif
Contact: Martha Istueta
papadeans@me.com
Estimated Sales: Less than $500,000
Number Employees: 1-4
Number of Products: 25
Square Footage: 4800
Type of Packaging: Consumer, Food Service, Private Label, Bulk
Brands:
Papa Dean's

9752 **Papa Leone Food Enterprises**
205 S Camden Dr
Beverly Hills, CA 90212-1660
310-552-1660
Italian and French sauces
President: Edmond Negari
Estimated Sales: $1 Million
Number Employees: 2
Square Footage: 8000
Type of Packaging: Consumer, Food Service, Private Label
Brands:
Chef Alberto Leone
Magic Gourmet

9753 **Papas Chris A & Son Co**
921 Baker St
Covington, KY 41011-2007
859-431-0499
Fax: 859-431-0499
Candy and confectionery
President: Carl Papas
cpapas@topiczinc.com
Vice President: Chris Papas
Estimated Sales: $1-2,500,000
Number Employees: 1-4
Number of Products: 15
Square Footage: 12000
Type of Packaging: Consumer, Private Label, Bulk
Brands:
Chocolate Marshmallow
It's a Boy
It's a Girl
Sugar Sticks

9754 **Paper City Brewery**
108 Cabot St
Holyoke, MA 01040
413-535-1588
Fax: 413-538-5774 info@papercity.com
www.papercity.com
Ale
President: Jay Hebert
Estimated Sales: Below $5 Million
Number Employees: 5-9
Brands:
Paper City

9755 **Papes Pecan House**
101 S Highway 123 Byp
Seguin, TX 78155-5156
830-379-7442
Fax: 830-379-9665 888-688-7273
mrpetski@aol.com www.papepecan.com
Pecans
Owner: Kenneth Pape
papepecan@aol.com
Sales: Harold Pape
Estimated Sales: $8 Million
Number Employees: 10-19
Square Footage: 60000
Type of Packaging: Food Service, Private Label

9756 **Pappardelle's Inc**
3970 Holly St
Denver, CO 80207-1216
303-321-4222
Fax: 303-321-8554 800-607-2782
info@pappardellespasta.com
www.pappardellespasta.com
Pasta, ravioli, sauces and pestos
Owner: Adam Steinberg
adam@pappardellespasta.com
Vice President: Paula Steinberg
Estimated Sales: Below $1 Million
Number Employees: 10-19
Brands:
Pappardelle's

9757 **Pappy Meat Company**
5663 E Fountain Way
Fresno, CA 93727-7813
559-291-0218
Fax: 559-291-5304 www.pappyschoice.com
Spices and seasonings
President: Marie Papulias
VP: Edward Papulias
Estimated Sales: $2 Million
Number Employees: 20-49
Type of Packaging: Consumer, Food Service, Private Label, Bulk
Brands:
Pappy's Choice

9758 **Pappy's Sassafras Tea**
10246 Road P
Columbus Grove, OH 45830-9733
419-659-5110
Fax: 419-659-5110 877-659-5110
pappy@q1.net www.sassafrastea.com
Sassafras tea, green tea, raspberry tea and tea concentrate
President: Sandy Nordhaus
pappy@q1.net
VP: Don Nordhaus
Marketing & Sales: Jeff Nordhaus
Estimated Sales: $360,000
Number Employees: 5-9
Number of Brands: 1
Number of Products: 2
Square Footage: 45000
Type of Packaging: Consumer, Food Service, Private Label, Bulk
Brands:
Pappy's

9759 **Papy's Foods Inc**
4131 W Albany St
Mchenry, IL 60050-8390
815-385-3313
Fax: 815-385-3367 www.papys.com
Spices, gravy mixes, seasoning mixes, noodles and sauce
President: Matt Gallimore
custservice@papys.com
Chairman: David Gallimore
Controller, VP Finance: Elizabeth Olson
Estimated Sales: $1.5 Million
Number Employees: 50-99
Square Footage: 260000
Type of Packaging: Consumer, Food Service

9760 **Paradigm Foodworks Inc**
5875 Lakeview Blvd
Suite 102
Lake Oswego, OR 97035-7047
503-595-4360
Fax: 503-595-4234 800-234-0250
sales@paradigmfoodworks.com
www.paradigmfoodworks.com
Sauces, salad dressings, bbq sauces, marinades, preserves, dessert sauces and mustards
President: Lynne Barra
lbarra@paradigmfoodworks.com
CFO: David Barra
Quality Control: Dr David Schultz
Marketing: Barb Reyer
Sales: Jud Barra
Operations: Sam Barra
Purchasing: Danette Cooper
Estimated Sales: $5-10 Million
Number Employees: 20-49
Square Footage: 80000

9761 **Paradis Honey**
PO Box 99
5023-50 Street
Girouxville, AB T0H 1S0
Canada
780-323-4283
Fax: 780-323-4238 info@paradishoney.com
www.paradishoney.com
Clover honey, beeswax and pollen
President/CEO: Michael Paradis
Marketing Manager: Jean Paradis
Secretary/Treasurer: Lisa Paradis
Number Employees: 10
Type of Packaging: Bulk
Brands:
Honey

9762 **Paradise Fruits NA**
1504 Providence Highway
Suite 7B
Norwood, MA 02062
781-769-4900
Fax: 781-769-4910
jbrownbill@paradise-fruits.com
www.paradise-fruits.com
Frozen fruit and fruit ingredients
Sales Director: Jon Brownbill

9763 **Paradise Inc**
1200 W Dr. Martin Luther King Jr. blvd.
Plant City, FL 33563-5155
813-752-1155
Fax: 941-754-3168 paradisefruitco@hotmail.com
www.paradisefruitco.com
Candied fruits
Chairman/CEO: Melvin Gordon
President/Director: Randy Gordon
rgordon@paradisefruitco.com
Senior Vice President, Sales: Tracy Schulis
Executive Vice President: Mark Gordon
VP/Corporate Sales: Ron Peterson
Estimated Sales: $21 Million
Number Employees: 100-249
Number of Brands: 6
Square Footage: 275000
Type of Packaging: Consumer, Food Service, Private Label, Bulk
Brands:
PARADISE
PENNANT
SUNRIPE
MOR-FRUIT
DIXIE BRAND
WHITE SWAN

9764 **(HQ)Paradise Island Foods**
6451 Portsmouth Road
Nanaimo, BC V9V 1A3
Canada
250-390-2644
Fax: 250-390-2117 800-889-3370
lthomson@paradise-foods.com
www.paradise-foods.com
Muffin mixes, cheeses, pasta, yogurt, juice, candy, salad dressings and ethnic foods
President: Len Thomson
Vice President: Kevin Thomson
Estimated Sales: $15 Million
Number Employees: 60
Square Footage: 72000
Type of Packaging: Consumer, Private Label, Bulk

9765 **Paradise Locker Inc.**
405 W. Birch Street
Trimble, MO 64492
816-370-6328
Fax: 816-357-1229 info@paradisemeats.com
www.paradisemeats.com
Beef, pork and lamb
Owner & CFO: Teresa Fantasma
VP & CEO: Mario Fantasma
Marketing/Sales Director: Nick Fantasma
Plant Manager: Louis Fantasma
Estimated Sales: $2 Million
Number Employees: 21

9766 **(HQ)Paradise Products Corporation**
17851 Deauville Ln
Boca Raton, FL 33496-2458
Fax: 718-378-3521 800-826-1235
Marinated foods, condiments, olives, artichokes, pimientos, capers, cauliflower, cherries, corn, kumquats, mushrooms, olive oil, pickled onions, salsa, sauces
President: David Lax
Estimated Sales: $10-20 Million
Number Employees: 60
Square Footage: 450000
Type of Packaging: Consumer, Food Service, Private Label, Bulk
Brands:
Juliana
Paradise
Three Star

9767 **Paradise Tomato Kitchens**
1500 S Brook St
Louisville, KY 40208-1950
502-637-1700
Fax: 502-637-8060 info@paradisetomato.com
www.paradisetomato.com
Pouched tomatoes, tomato paste, puree, sauce and pizza sauce
Owner: Diana Ammons
dammons@paradisetomato.com
Research & Development: Arlen Campbell
Quality Control: Justin Uhl
Purchasing Manager: Nathan Cosby
Estimated Sales: $10-20 Million
Number Employees: 100-249
Type of Packaging: Food Service, Private Label

9768 **Paradise Valley Vineyards**
4077 W Fairmount Avenue
Phoenix, AZ 85019-3620
602-233-8727
Fax: 602-233-8727
Wines
President: Mark William Stern
Vice President: Tom Dibecco
Sales Director: Jeff Cayton
Estimated Sales: $500-1 000,000 appx.
Number Employees: 1-4
Type of Packaging: Private Label
Brands:
Paradise Valley Vineyards
Paraiso Del Sol

9769 **Paragon Fruits**
8670 Monticello Lane N
Suite B
Maple Grove, MN 55369
763-559-0436
Fax: 763-447-3399 info@spectrumfruits.com
spectrumfruits.com
Fruit ingredients

9770 **Paraiso Vineyards**
38060 Paraiso Springs Rd
Soledad, CA 93960-9517
831-678-0300
Fax: 831-678-2584 info@paraisovineyards.com
www.smithfamilywines.com
Wines
Owner: Richard Smith
rrsmith@paraisovineyards.com
General Manager: Jason Smith
Marketing Director: Dave Muret
Hospitality Director: Jennifer Murphy-Smith
Production, Winemaker, Sales: David Fleming
Estimated Sales: $1-2.5 Million
Number Employees: 5-9
Number of Brands: 1
Number of Products: 10
Type of Packaging: Private Label
Brands:
Paraiso

9771 **Paramount Caviar**
3815 24th St
Long Island City, NY 11101-3619
718-786-7747
Fax: 718-786-5730 800-992-2842
ladyofcaviar@aol.com www.paramountcaviar.com
Caviar and smoked salmon
Owner: Hossein Aimami
info@paramountcaviar.com
Vice President: Amy Aimani
Marketing: Amy Arrow
Estimated Sales: $1.4 Million
Number Employees: 5-9
Type of Packaging: Bulk
Brands:
Canolla Truffles
Fossen Smoked Salmon
Manchurian Saffron
Plantin Dried Mushro

9772 **Paramount Coffee**
130 N Larch St
Lansing, MI 48912-1244
517-372-5500
Fax: 517-372-2870 800-968-1222
www.paramountcoffee.com
Coffee
President: Jeff Poyer
Chairman and CEO: Angelo Oricchio
VP: Robert Morgan
Manager: Chris King
cking@paramountroasters.com
Estimated Sales: $5-10 Million
Number Employees: 100-249
Parent Co: Interstate Foods

9773 **Paramount Distillers**
3116 Berea Rd
Cleveland, OH 44111-1596
216-671-6300
Fax: 216-671-2299 800-821-2989
www.paramountdistillers.com
Spirits and liquors
Chairman & CEO: Robert Manchick
CFO: Robert Szabo
Director of Marketing: Lynn Lubin
VP Sales: John Pallo
Plant Manager: Dennis Fratiani
Estimated Sales: $27.8 Million
Number Employees: 337
Square Footage: 100000
Other Locations:
Paramount Distillers
Cincinnati OH
Brands:
Korski
Paramount
La Prima
Canadian Bay
Gold Award
Thunder 101
Lightning 101
Creme De Cacao
Creme De Menthe
Peppermint
Triple Sec
Davinia
Sour Apple
Peach
Amaretto
Butterscotch
Lasalle
Colonial Club
Rock N Rye
Glaros Ouzo
Grand Muriel

9774 **Parducci Wine Cellars**
501 Parducci Rd
Ukiah, CA 95482-3015
707-463-5357
Fax: 707-462-7260 888-362-9463
info@mendocinowineco.com www.parducci.com
Wines
Manager: Tim Thornhill
timthornhill@mendocinowineco.com
Marketing: David Hance
Winemaker: Robert Swain
Estimated Sales: $2 Million
Number Employees: 20-49

9775 **(HQ)Paris Foods Corporation**
3965 Ocean Gateway
P.O. Box 121
Trappe, MD 21673
410-200-9595
sales@parisfoods.com
www.parisfoods.com
Fruits and vegetables
Sales Contact: Ward Cain
ward@parisfoods.com
Estimated Sales: $50 Million
Number Employees: 100
Square Footage: 67000
Type of Packaging: Consumer, Food Service
Other Locations:
Paris Foods Forwarding Warehouse
Walkerville MI
Paris Foods Distribution Center
Lexington NC
Paris Foods Distribution Center
Houston DE
Cresco IA
Pittsburgh PA
Pennsauken NJ
Hillsboro IL

9776 **Paris Pastry**
7008 Shoshone Ave
Van Nuys, CA 91406
310-474-8888
Fax: 310-470-2097 805-487-2227
Mousses, cookies
President: Raymond Lobjois
Executive Chef: Eric Westphal
Estimated Sales: $260,000
Number Employees: 10-19
Square Footage: 48000
Type of Packaging: Consumer, Food Service, Private Label, Bulk

9777 **(HQ)Parish Chemical Company**
P.O.Box 277
Orem, UT 84059-0277
801-226-2018
Fax: 801-226-8496
Nutritional food additives, acidulants and preservatives, ferulic acid, carboxyethylgermanium sesquioxide and indole-3-carbinol
President: W Wesley Parish
Marketing Director: Bill Ellenberger
Estimated Sales: $1 Million
Number Employees: 20-49
Square Footage: 100000
Type of Packaging: Bulk
Other Locations:
Parish Chemical Co.
Orem UT

9778 **(HQ)Park 100 Foods Inc**
326 E Adams St
Tipton, IN 46072-2001
765-675-3480
Fax: 765-675-3474 800-854-6504
www.park100foods.com
Soups, sauces, chili, side dishes, gravies, fruit toppings, dips, entrees, breaded meats, seafood, pasta and protein kits
Chairman: Jim Washburn
jwashburn@park100foods.com
President: Gary Meade
VP: David Alves
Project Manager/National Sales: Robert Orr
Sales: Mike Taft
Estimated Sales: $20-50 Million
Number Employees: 50-99
Square Footage: 100000
Other Locations:
Kettle Processed Foods
Morristown IN
Kettle Processed Foods
Kokomo IN
Brands:
Park 100 Foods

9779 **Park Avenue Bakery**
44 South Park Ave
Helena, MT 59601
406-449-8424
www.parkavenuebakery.net
Breads, pastries, rolls, pizzas

9780 **Park Cheese Company Inc**
168 Larsen Drive
Fond Du Lac, WI 54937-8519
Fax: 920-923-8485 800-752-7275
Italian cheeses: asiago, aged provolone, romano, parmesan, pepato, fontina, Italian sharp, kasseri, and milk provolone.
President & COO: Eric Liebetrau
CEO: Alfred Liebetrau
Secretary/Treasurer: Lylia Liebetrau
Manager: Jason Blank
Director Sales & Marketing: Linda Cizek
Contact: Sue Behling
sueb@belgioioso.com
Plant Manager/General Manager: Steve Heard
Number Employees: 70
Square Footage: 80000
Type of Packaging: Consumer, Food Service, Private Label, Bulk
Brands:
Casaro

9781 **Parker Farm**
9405 Holly Street
Suite B
Minneapolis, MN 55433
763-780-5100
Fax: 763-780-5104 800-869-6685
Cheese, peanut butter, cream cheese and salsa
President: Rick Etrheim
Estimated Sales: $5 Million
Number Employees: 20-49
Type of Packaging: Private Label

9782 **Parker Fish Company**
63 Cross Cedar Rd
PO Box 324
Wrightsville, GA 31096-5300
478-864-3406
Fax: 478-864-9417
Seafood
President: Jeff Powell
Manager: Dennis Moore
Estimated Sales: $5-10 Million
Number Employees: 10-19

9783 **Parker Flavors Inc**
1801 Portal Street
Baltimore, MD 21224
410-633-2230
Fax: 410-633-3530 800-336-9113
parkerflavors.com
Extracts, emulsions and flavors
CEO: Tim Parker
Type of Packaging: Consumer, Food Service, Private Label, Bulk
Brands:
Parker

9784 **Parker House Sausage Co**
4605 S State St
Chicago, IL 60609-4699
773-538-1112
Fax: 773-285-0903 www.parkerhousesausage.com
Sausage
CEO: Sherlyn Alhambra
salhambra@parkerhousesausage.com
Number Employees: 20-49

9785 **(HQ)Parker Products**
3020 W. Lancaster Avenue
Fort Worth, TX 76107
817-336-7441
Fax: 817-877-1261 info@parkerproducts.com
www.parkerproducts.com
Desserts, candy, confectionery, ice cream toppings, fudge and flavors
President: Greg Hodder
Contact: Kim Ballinger
kim@parkerproducts.com
Estimated Sales: $10-19 Million
Number Employees: 30
Square Footage: 58000
Type of Packaging: Private Label, Bulk
Other Locations:
Parker Products
Andrews TX

9786 **Parkers Farm**
9405 Holly St NW
Suite B
Coon Rapids, MN 55433-5976
763-780-5100
Fax: 763-780-5104 800-869-6685
info@parkersfarm.com
Cheeses and bagel spreads
President: Rick Etrheim
Estimated Sales: $10-20 Million
Number Employees: 20-49

Type of Packaging: Consumer, Food Service, Private Label, Bulk

9787 **(HQ)Parkside Candy Co**
3208 Main St
Suite 1
Buffalo, NY 14214-1379
716-833-7540
Fax: 716-833-7560 www.parksidecandy.com
Lollipops, chocolates, fudge, pretzels
President: Phil Buffamonte
sales@parksidecandy.com
Estimated Sales: $14 Million
Number Employees: 20-49
Type of Packaging: Consumer, Food Service, Private Label, Bulk
Brands:
Aunt Angies
Old Fashioned

9788 **Parma Sausage Products**
1734 Penn Ave
Pittsburgh, PA 15222-4385
412-391-4238
Fax: 412-391-7717 877-294-4207
www.parmasausage.com
Sausage, prosciutto, coppa secca and salami, capicollo, mortadella, salami rosa, kolbassie, andouille, chorizo
President: Rina Edwards
darren@parmasausage.com
Vice President: Rita Spinabelli
Sales Exec: Darren Schumacher
Purchasing Manager: John Edwards
Estimated Sales: $1300000
Number Employees: 20-49
Type of Packaging: Consumer, Food Service, Private Label, Bulk
Brands:
Gigi
Parma

9789 **Parmalat Canada**
405 The West Mall
10th Floor
Toronto, ON M9C 5J1
Canada
800-563-1515
parmalat.ca
Milk, cheeses, spreads and yogurt.
CEO: Mark Taylor
Year Founded: 1997
Estimated Sales: $1.9 Billion
Number Employees: 3,500
Number of Brands: 10
Parent Co: Lactalis
Type of Packaging: Consumer, Food Service, Private Label, Bulk
Brands:
Lactantia
Beatrice
Cracker Barrel
Black Diamond
Cheestrings
Balderson
Galbani
Astro
President
Siggi's
P'tit Quebec
aMOOza!

9790 **Parmela Creamery**
Torrance, CA
310-584-7541
contact@parmelacreamery.com
www.parmelacreamery.com
Nut-based cheeses
Co-Founder: Laurice Do
laurice@parmelacreamery.com

9791 **Parmenter's Northville Cider Mill**
714 Baseline Rd
Northville, MI 48167
248-349-3181
Fax: 248-349-1165 info@northvillecider.com
www.northvillecider.com
Apple cider, preserves, donuts, maple products, apple products, specialty organic
President: Diane Jones
d_jones@northvillecider.com
Vice President: Cheryl Nelson
Estimated Sales: $250 Thousand
Number Employees: 50
Number of Brands: 1
Type of Packaging: Consumer
Brands:
Parmenter's Northville Cider Mill

9792 **Parmx**
4117-16a Street SE
Calgary, AB T2G 3T7
Canada
403-237-0707
Fax: 403-264-2153
Parmesan cheese
President/CEO: Vincent Aiello
Production: Frank Aiello
Number Employees: 20-49
Type of Packaging: Consumer, Food Service
Brands:
Parmx Cheese

9793 **Parny Gourmet**
390 NE 59th Terrace
Miami, FL 33137
305-798-5177
parny.gourmet@gmail.com
Sugar biscuits, candied hot pepper, pepper jam and sauce
Chef: Irene Brizard De Parny

9794 **Parrish's Cake Decorating**
225 W 146th St
Gardena, CA 90248-1803
310-324-2253
Fax: 310-324-8277 800-736-8443
Aluminum cake pans, cookie cutters, artificial icing, candy molds, plates and pillars, pastry bags, food colors and flavorings
President: Bob Parrish
customerservice@parrishsmagicline.com
VP: Norma Parrish
Estimated Sales: $1-3 Million
Number Employees: 10-19
Number of Products: 4000
Square Footage: 180000
Type of Packaging: Consumer, Food Service, Private Label, Bulk
Brands:
Magic Line
Magic Mist
Magic Mold
Perma-Ice

9795 **Parthenon Food Products**
226 S Main St
Ann Arbor, MI 48104-2106
734-994-1012
Fax: 734-994-7073 www.parthenonfoods.com
Greek salad dressings and marinades
President/Owner: Steve Gavas
CFO: John Gavas
Estimated Sales: $500,000
Number Employees: 10-19
Square Footage: 4000
Type of Packaging: Consumer, Food Service, Private Label, Bulk
Brands:
Perthenon Greek Salad Dressing

9796 **Particle Control**
6062 Lambert Ave NE
Albertville, MN 55301-3919
763-497-3075
Fax: 763-497-1773 norm@particlecontrolinc.com
www.particlecontrolinc.com
Flavors, whey, oat flour, sugar
President: Bill Arns
bill@particlecontrolinc.com
Estimated Sales: $700,000
Number Employees: 5-9
Square Footage: 104000

9797 **Particle Dynamics**
2601 S Hanley Rd
Saint Louis, MO 63144
314-968-2376
Fax: 314-646-3761 800-452-4682
info@particledynamics.com
www.particledynamics.com
Vitamins, minerals, flavors, acidulants, colors, spices
President: Paul T Brady
Marketing: Andrea Keith
Sales VP: Richard Miller
Contact: Sonia Belotti
sonia.belotti@savannah.co.za
Purchasing: Jim Cronk
Estimated Sales: $3500000
Number Employees: 20-49
Square Footage: 180000
Parent Co: KV Pharmaceutical
Type of Packaging: Bulk
Brands:
Descote
Destab
Micromask

9798 **Partners Coffee LLC**
4225 Westfield Dr SW
Atlanta, GA 30336-2651
404-344-5282
Fax: 404-349-6442 800-341-5282
Coffee
President: James Gilson
CEO: Mike Bacco
mjbacco@partnerscoffee.com
Sales/Marketing: Bert Kelly
Operations Manager: Gerry Larue
Production Manager: Bob Frazier
Purchasing Manager: Anne Gilson
Estimated Sales: $2559650
Number Employees: 10-19
Number of Brands: 3
Number of Products: 200
Square Footage: 80000
Type of Packaging: Consumer, Food Service, Private Label, Bulk
Brands:
Casa Europa
H&C
Partners

9799 **Partners: A Tasteful Choice**
20232 72nd Avenue South
Kent, WA 98032
253-867-1580
Fax: 206-762-8424 800-632-7477
service@partnerscrackers.com
www.partnerscrackers.com
Crackers, granola, cookies
President & Owner: Marian Harris
Vice President, Sales, Owner: Cara Figgins
caraf@partnerscrackers.com
Estimated Sales: $500,000-$1 Million
Number Employees: 1-4
Square Footage: 48000
Brands:
Blue Star Farms
Cracker Snackers
Get Movin Snack Packss
Gourmet Granola
Partners
Wisecrackers

9800 **Pascal Coffee**
960 Nepperhan Ave
Yonkers, NY 10703-1726
914-969-7933
Fax: 914-969-8248 roaster@optonline.net
Coffee
Manager: Dean Peialteos
Estimated Sales: Below $5 Million
Number Employees: 20-49
Brands:
Pascal Coffee

9801 **Pascha Chocolate**
1920 Yonge St.
Suite 200
Toronto, Ontario, M4S 3E6
CAN
855-472-7242
info@paschachocolate.com
paschachocolate.com
Organic chocolate
President & CEO: Simon Lester
Year Founded: 2013
Number Employees: 1-10

9802 **Pascobel Inc**
2066 De La Province
Longueuil, QC J4G 1R7
Canada
450-677-2443
Fax: 450-677-2899

Combolak, coverblak, viseolak, culurelak, fractolak and nonfat milk solids
President: Jean Guy Lauziere
Sales Manager: Guy Bouthillier
Technical Director: Pierre Combeaud
Number Employees: 20-49
Square Footage: 60000
Type of Packaging: Private Label, Bulk
Brands:
Belcover
Comboliak
Coverlak
Culturelak
Fractolak
Nollibel
Viscolak

9803 **Pasolivo Willow Creek Olive Ranch**
8530 Vineyard Drive
Paso Robles, CA 93446
805-227-0186
Fax: 805-226-8809 info@pasolivo.com
www.pasolivo.com
Olive oils
General Manger: Jillian Pasolivo
Marketing: Joel Pasolivo

9804 **Pasqualichio Brothers Inc**
115 Franklin Ave
Scranton, PA 18503-1935
570-346-7115
Fax: 570-346-4610 800-232-6233
www.butchervangourmet.com
Beef, veal, lamb, turkey, chicken and pork
President: Michael Pasqualichio
Owner: Don Pasqualichio
VP: Patrick Pasqualichio
Plant Manager: William Pasqualichio
Estimated Sales: $10 Million
Number Employees: 10-19
Square Footage: 20000
Type of Packaging: Consumer
Brands:
Pasqualichio

9805 **Passage Foods LLC**
30 Depot Street
PO Box 245
Collinsville, CT 06022
800-860-1045
Fax: 860-256-4559 info@passageusa.com
www.passagefoods.com
Ethnic sauces (soy, curry), grilling sauces, seasonings
Marketing: Mark Mackenzie
Contact: Chris Doutre
chris.doutre@passagefoods.com

9806 **Passetti's Pride**
923 Hotel Avenue
Hayward, CA 94541-4001
510-728-4969
Fax: 510-886-6909 800-521-4659
Sauces and marinades
Co-Owner: Valentino Passetti
Brands:
Passetti's Pride

9807 **Passport Food Group**
2539 E Philadelphia St
Ontario, CA 91761
310-463-0954
customerservice@passportfood.com
www.passportfood.com
Noodles, appetizers, fortune cookies and tofu, egg roll, wonton and potsticker wrappers
Senior Vice President: Brian Dean
bdean@passportfood.com
VP, Sales & Marketing, Retail: Terry Girch
Broker Sales Manager: Rich Frankey
Territory Sales Manager: Jeffrey Tavares
Year Founded: 1978
Estimated Sales: $50 Million
Number Employees: 200-500
Number of Brands: 4
Type of Packaging: Consumer, Food Service, Private Label, Bulk
Brands:
Wing Hing Gold Coin
Wing Hing Panda

9808 **Pasta Del Mondo**
27 Seminary Hill Rd
Suite 27
Carmel, NY 10512-1928
845-225-8889
Fax: 845-225-0900 800-392-8887
Pasta
President: Frank Marrone
Production Manager: Brendan Conboy
Estimated Sales: $300,000-500,000
Number Employees: 9
Square Footage: 12000
Type of Packaging: Consumer, Food Service, Private Label, Bulk
Brands:
Del Mondo

9809 **Pasta Factory**
11225 W Grand Ave
Melrose Park, IL 60164
847-451-0005
Fax: 847-451-6563 800-615-6951
Pasta
President: Michael Sica
VP: Irene Sica
Sales Manager/Marketing: Thomas Lichon
Contact: Brenda Sica
bsica@nova.edu
Operations/Purchasing Director: Joseph Sica
Estimated Sales: $2700000
Number Employees: 20-49
Square Footage: 64000
Parent Co: MAS Sales
Type of Packaging: Consumer, Food Service, Private Label, Bulk
Brands:
Pasta Factory

9810 **Pasta International**
5715 Coopers Avenue
Mississauga, ON L4Z 2C7
Canada
905-890-5550
Fax: 905-890-8939
Pasta: linguine, fettuccine, spaghetti, ravioli, tortellini, lasagna and cannelloni
President: Massimo Liberatore
Number Employees: 5-9
Square Footage: 116000
Type of Packaging: Consumer, Food Service
Brands:
Pasta International

9811 **Pasta Mami**
1600 Roswell St SE
Suite 12
Smyrna, GA 30080
770-438-6022
Fax: 770-438-9810
Pasta
President: Mark Portwood
Estimated Sales: $2.5-5 000,000
Number Employees: 10-19
Type of Packaging: Private Label
Brands:
Pasta Mami

9812 **Pasta Mill**
12803 149th Street NW
Edmonton, AB T5L 2J7
Canada
780-454-8665
Fax: 780-454-8668
Pasta and pasta sauces
President: Steve Parsons
General Manager: Brien Plunkie
Estimated Sales: $284,000
Number Employees: 3
Type of Packaging: Consumer, Food Service
Brands:
The Pasta Mill

9813 **Pasta Montana**
1 Pasta Pl
Great Falls, MT 59401-1377
406-761-1516
Fax: 406-761-1403 www.pastamontana.com
Pasta
President: Yasuhiko Harada
yasuhiko@costapasta.com
General Manager: Randy Gilbertson
Number Employees: 100-249
Square Footage: 30000
Type of Packaging: Consumer, Food Service, Private Label, Bulk
Brands:
Pasta Montana
Costa Pasta
Amarone Pasta

9814 **Pasta Prima**
3909 Park Rd
Suite H
Benicia, CA 94510-1167
530-671-7200
www.pastaprima.com
Pasta
Contact: Aaron Garcia
agarcia@valleyfine.com
Estimated Sales: Less Than $500,000
Number Employees: 5-9

9815 **Pasta Quistini**
1700 Ormont Dr
Toronto, ON M9L 2V4
Canada
416-742-3222
Pasta
President: Elena Quistini
Vice President: Orlando Quistini
Estimated Sales: $3 Million
Number Employees: 18
Type of Packaging: Consumer, Food Service
Brands:
Pasta Al Dente
Pasta Quistini

9816 **Pasta Shoppe**
Nashville, TN
615-831-0016
Fax: 615-781-9335 800-247-0188
john@pastashoppe.com pastashoppe.com
Organic pastas and pasta sauce
President & Owner: John Aron
VP & Owner: Carey Aron
carey@pastashoppe.com
Estimated Sales: $2.7 Million
Number Employees: 25
Type of Packaging: Private Label, Bulk
Brands:
Pastabilities
Tailgate & Celebrate
Pasta with Personality
Divine Meringues

9817 **Pasta Sonoma**
640 Martin Ave
Suite 1
Rohnert Park, CA 94928-7994
707-584-0800
Fax: 707-584-2332 info@pastasonoma.com
www.pastasonoma.com
Pasta
President: Don Luber
luber@pastasonoma.com
Director of Sales: Dale Lucas
Manager: Cindy Riddle
Estimated Sales: $2 Million
Number Employees: 5-9
Type of Packaging: Private Label

9818 **Pasta Valente**
PO Box 2307
Charlottesville, VA 22902-2307
434-971-3717
Fax: 434-971-1511 888-575-7670
retail@pastavalente.com
Pasta and marinara sauces
President: Mary F Valente
Officer: Lois Pecavage
Estimated Sales: $370,000
Number Employees: 5

9819 **Pastene Co LTD**
330 Turnpike St
Suite 100
Canton, MA 02021-2703
781-298-3397
Fax: 781-830-8225 www.pastene.com
Cheese, sauces, oil and vinegar, vegetables, fish, olives, peppers, beans, bread sticks, pasta, rice and polenta
Owner: Mark Tosi
mtosi@pastene.com
Year Founded: 1848
Number Employees: 20-49
Type of Packaging: Consumer, Food Service

Brands:
Pastene

9820 **Pastor Chuck Orchards**
PO Box 1259
Portland, ME 04104
207-773-1314
Fax: 207-871-0117
Applesauce, salsa and apple butter
President: Charles Waite Maclin

9821 **Pastorelli Food Products**
162 N Sangamon St
Chicago, IL 60607-2210
312-666-2041
Fax: 312-666-2415 800-767-2829
www.pastorelli.com
Pizza sauces, crusts, pasta sauces, oils and vinegars
Owner: Richard Pastorelli
rpastorelli@pastorelli.com
Estimated Sales: $5-10 Million
Number Employees: 10-19
Square Footage: 244000
Type of Packaging: Consumer, Food Service, Private Label, Bulk
Brands:
Italian Chef

9822 **Pastori Winery**
23189 Geyserville Ave
Cloverdale, CA 95425-9724
707-857-3418
Wines
Owner: Frank Pastori
frank@pedroncelli.com
Estimated Sales: $230,000
Number Employees: 1-4
Brands:
Pastori

9823 **Pastry Chef**
112 Warren Avenue
Pawtucket, RI 02860-5604
401-722-1330
800-639-8606
Cakes and pies
President: Per Jensen
CEO: Paul Meunier
Number Employees: 20-49
Number of Brands: 3
Number of Products: 110
Square Footage: 80000
Parent Co: Pastry Chef
Type of Packaging: Food Service, Private Label
Brands:
The Pastry Chef

9824 **Pat LaFrieda Meat Purveyors**
3701 Tonnelle Ave
North Bergen, NJ 07047-2421
201-537-8210
Fax: 201-864-2014 888-523-7433
info@lafrieda.com www.lafrieda.com
Meats
President: Mark Pastore
CEO: Pat LaFrieda
Number Employees: 1-4

9825 **Pat's Meat Discounter**
702 S 6th Ave
Mills, WY 82604-2532
307-237-7549
Meat
Owner: Patrick Keating
Estimated Sales: $500,000-$1 000,000
Number Employees: 1-4

9826 **Patagonia Provisions**
1750 Bridgeway
A100
Sausalito, CA 94965
415-729-9956
888-221-8208
marketing@patagoniaprovisions.com
www.patagoniaprovisions.com
Beef jerky, mussels, salmon, soups, chilis, sides, breakfast grains, snack bars, seeds, and beer
Founder: Yvon Chouinard
Managing Director: Birgit Cameron
Director of Sales: Erik Eaton
Number Employees: 20-49

9827 **Path of Life**
30W260 Butterfield Rd
Warrenville, IL 60555
844-248-9997
www.pathoflifebrand.com
Frozen prepared meals
Co-Owner: Jason Eckert
Co-Owner: Scott Schmidt
Brand Manager: Ashley Collins
Brands:
Path of Life

9828 **Pati-Petite Cookies Inc**
1785 Mayview Rd
Bridgeville, PA 15017-1592
412-221-4033
Fax: 412-221-8711 800-253-5805
Cookies
President: Keith Graham
CEO: William Graham
william.graham@paychex.com
VP: Bruce Graham
Estimated Sales: $1,400,000
Number Employees: 20-49
Square Footage: 90000
Type of Packaging: Consumer, Food Service, Bulk

9829 **Patience Fruit & Co.**
Villeroy, QC
Canada
www.patiencefruitco.com
Trail mixes, dried berries, organic juices, fresh cranberries and snack bites
EVP & General Manager: Carl Blouin

9830 **Patisserie Wawel**
2543 Ontario East
Bureau A
Montreal, QC H2K 1W5
Canada
614-524-3348
Fax: 514-524-1266 patisseriewawel@videotron.ca
Sponge cake, butter strudel, breads, butter fillings
President: Peter Sowa
Manager: Alina Zych
Estimated Sales: $1.4 Million
Number Employees: 20
Square Footage: 14000

9831 **Patric Chocolate**
6601 Stephens Station Rd
Suite 109
Columbia, MO 65202-0011
573-814-7520
patric-chocolate.com
Chocolates
Head Chocolate Maker: Alan McClure
Estimated Sales: Less Than $500,000
Number Employees: 1-4

9832 **Patricia Quintana**
Los Angeles, CA
chefpatriciaquintana.com
Artisanal salsas and dressings
Chef: Patricia Quintana
Brands:
Patricia Quintana

9833 **Patrick Cudahy LLC**
1 Sweet Applewood Ln
Cudahy, WI 53110
800-486-6900
www.patrickcudahy.com
Bacon, hams, lard, shortening, pepperoni, salami, bologna and sausage
President: Ken Sullivan
Year Founded: 1888
Estimated Sales: $200-300 Million
Number Employees: 1,000-4,999
Square Footage: 1000000
Parent Co: Smithfield Foods
Type of Packaging: Food Service, Private Label
Brands:
Agar
Appleblossom
Danzig
Golden Crisp
Heat & Eat
La Fortuna
Patrick Cudahy
Patricks Pride
Pavone
Realean
Royalean

9834 **Patriot Pickel Inc**
20 Edison Dr
Wayne, NJ 07470-4713
973-709-9487
Fax: 973-709-0995
Pickles
Owner: Mc Bill
billmc@patriotpickle.com
Number Employees: 20-49

9835 **Patsy's Brands**
236 W 56 Street
New York, NY 10019
212-247-3491
Fax: 212-541-5071 www.patsys.com
Pasta sauces
Marketing: Russ Cahill

9836 **Patsy's Candy**
1540 S 21st St
Colorado Springs, CO 80904-4206
719-632-3733
Fax: 719-633-6970 866-372-8797
www.patsyscandies.com
Chocolates, mints, taffy, fudge, truffles, roasted nuts, candied popcorn and English toffee
Owner: Wes Niswonger
wes@patsyscandies.com
Estimated Sales: $5-10 Million
Number Employees: 20-49
Square Footage: 48000
Type of Packaging: Consumer, Food Service, Private Label, Bulk
Brands:
Colorado Peanut Butter Nugget
Preludes
Rosecup Mints

9837 **Patsy's Italian Restaurant**
236 W 56th St
New York, NY 10019-4306
212-247-3491
Fax: 212-541-5071 sapatsys@aol.com
www.patsys.com
Sauces, marinaras, vegetables, olive oils and vinegars
President: Joseph Scognamillo
sapatsys@aol.com
Estimated Sales: $1-3 Million
Number Employees: 20-49
Brands:
Patsy's

9838 **PatsyPie**
2496 rue Remembrance
Lachine, QC H8S 1X7
Canada
514-695-0707
Fax: 514-695-3191 877-695-0707
Pastries, breads
Founder: Pat Libling

9839 **Patterson Frozen Foods**
100 W. Las Palmas Avenue
Patterson, CA 95363-0114
209-892-2611
Fax: 209-892-2582
Vegetables, pasta, pesto sauces, blends, stir frys and fruits
CFO: Russell Kenerly
Information Technology Software: Gregg Skarmas
Sales Manager: Tom Ielmini
Contact: Vance Blade
vance.blade@pattersonfoods.com
Vice President of Operations: B Ingebretsen
Manager of Purchasing: Joe Ghisletta
Estimated Sales: $310,000
Square Footage: 10496
Type of Packaging: Consumer, Food Service, Bulk
Other Locations:
Patterson Frozen Foods Plant
Monte Alto TX
Patterson Frozen Foods Plant
Guatemala
Brands:
Fair Acres
Fresh Pact
Microfresh
Pat-Son
Pour & Save
Springtime
Thrift-T-Pak

9840 **Patterson Vegetable Company**
100 W Las Palmas Avenue
Patterson, CA 95363
209-892-2611
Apricots, almonds, broccoli, spinach, tomatoes and peaches
CEO: Ray Walker
COO: Paul Fanelli
Number Employees: 600
Square Footage: 31964

9841 **Patti's Plum Puddings**
15020 Hawthorne Blvd
Suite C
Lawndale, CA 90260-1543
310-376-1463
Fax: 310-372-4132
Plum pudding and sauce
President/CEO: Patti Garrity
Estimated Sales: $50,000
Number Employees: 1-4
Number of Brands: 1
Number of Products: 2
Square Footage: 5340
Type of Packaging: Consumer
Brands:
Patti's Plum Pudding

9842 **Patty Palace Foods**
595 Middlefield Road
Unit 16
Toronto, ON M1V 3S2
Canada
416-297-0510
Fax: 416-297-4024 info@pattypalace.net
www.pattypalace.net
Sandwiches
President: Michael Davidson
Estimated Sales: $3.6 Million
Number Employees: 30
Type of Packaging: Consumer, Food Service
Brands:
Palace Foods
Montego Bay
Pieman and Montego

9843 **Paul Piazza & Son Inc**
1552 Saint Louis St
New Orleans, LA 70112-3254
504-524-6011
Fax: 504-566-1322 800-969-6011
kbaumer@paulpiazza.com www.paulpiazza.com
Shrimp, cod, perch and lobster
Owner: Luca Governale
Vice President, Sales: Andy Neely
lgovernale@paulpiazza.com
VP, Operations: Kathy Cooper
Plant Manager: Don Schwab
Estimated Sales: $10-20 Million
Number Employees: 20-49
Square Footage: 150000
Type of Packaging: Consumer, Food Service, Private Label, Bulk

9844 **Paul Schafer Meat Products**
343 N Charles St
Suite 3
Baltimore, MD 21201-4326
410-528-1250
Fax: 410-528-1059 FSIS.Outreach@usda.gov
www.fsis.usda.gov
Meat
Owner: Paul Schaefer
Director of Operations: Robert Fasulo
Estimated Sales: $1-2.5 Million
Number Employees: 5-9

9845 **Paul Stevens Lobster**
349 Lincoln St
Suite 32
Hingham, MA 02043-1609
781-740-8001
Fax: 781-749-2240
Fish and seafood; lobsters
Owner: Paul Stevens
Estimated Sales: $870,000
Number Employees: 1-4

9846 **Paul's Candy Factory**
434 South 300 West
Salt Lake City, UT 84101
801-363-8869
Fax: 801-359-4707 800-825-9912
www.westernut.com
Candy
President: Michael Place
Estimated Sales: Below $5 Million
Number Employees: 5-9
Brands:
Paul's Candy

9847 **Paulaur Corp**
105 Melrich Rd
Cranbury, NJ 08512-3589
609-395-8844
Fax: 609-395-8850 sales@paulaur.com
www.paulaur.com
Confectionery toppings and inclusions, sweeteners, sugars, carbohydrates; custom blending, granulating, agglomerating, sizing and sieving services
CEO: Alex Martello
abiamonte@eldor.com
Number Employees: 100-249
Type of Packaging: Bulk

9848 **Pauline's Pastries**
50 Viceroy Road
Suite 7
Vaughan, ON L4K 3A7
Canada
905-738-5252
Fax: 905-738-0345 877-292-6826
www.paulinespastries.com
Pastries
President/CEO: Robyn Perlmutar
Marketing Director: Pauline Perlmutar
Estimated Sales: $5 Million
Number Employees: 25
Type of Packaging: Consumer, Food Service
Brands:
Pauline's

9849 **Paulsen Foods**
748 Donald Hollowell Parkway
Atlanta, GA 30318
404-873-1804
paulsenfoods.com
Wholesale frozen breakfast, apetizers, entrees, and desserts.
Owner: Russell Paulsen
National Sales Manager: Tom Unverferth
Director of Operations: Mayra Vagras
Estimated Sales: $1-2.5 Million
Number Employees: 6
Square Footage: 80000
Type of Packaging: Consumer, Food Service, Private Label

9850 **Paumanok Vineyards**
1074 Main Road (Route 25)
P.O. Box 741
Aquebogue, NY 11931
631-722-8800
Fax: 631-722-5110 info@paumanok.com
www.paumanok.com
Wine
President: Charles Massoud
Estimated Sales: $1,400,000
Number Employees: 20-49
Brands:
Paumanok Vineyards

9851 **Pavel's Yogurt**
14710 Wicks Blvd
San Leandro, CA 94577
510-352-1474
www.pavels.net
Russian-style artisanal yogurt
Owner: Donald Sortor
Director of Operations: Luke Sortor
Number of Products: 5
Brands:
Pavel's Yogurt

9852 **Pavero Cold Storage**
10 North Rd
Highland, NY 12528-1017
845-691-2992
Fax: 845-691-2955 800-435-2994
applz25@aol.com www.paverocoldstorage.com
Apples and pears
President: Joseph Pavero
Cmo: Frank Sicolo
paveroapple@aol.com
Operations Manager: Jody Pavero
Estimated Sales: $8300000
Number Employees: 50-99

9853 **Paw Paw Grape Juice Company**
706 S Kalamazoo Street
Paw Paw, MI 49079-1558
269-657-3165
Fax: 269-657-4154 800-756-5357
www.warnerwines.com
Juices
President/CEO: James Warner
Estimated Sales: Under $500,000
Number Employees: 1-4
Parent Co: Warner Vineyards

9854 **Pawelski Farm**
736 Pulaski Hwy.
Goshen, NY 10924
845-772-2600
Yellow and red hybrid long-term storage onions
Contact: Chris Pawelski

9855 **Payne Packing Co**
704 W Richey Ave
Artesia, NM 88210-3434
575-746-2779
Beef, game and pork
President: Bob Yates
Estimated Sales: $260,000
Number Employees: 5-9
Type of Packaging: Consumer

9856 **Pazdar Winery**
6 Laddie Road
Scotchtown Branch, NY 10941-1708
845-695-1903
Fax: 845-695-1903 pazdar@citlink.net
www.pazdarwinery.com
Wines
President/CEO: David Pazdar
VP Marketing: Tracy Davis-Pazdar
Number Employees: 5-9
Parent Co: Pazdar Beverage Company
Type of Packaging: Consumer, Food Service
Brands:
Pazdar Winery
Sugary Wine

9857 **Peaberry's Coffee & Tea**
5655 College Ave
Oakland, CA 94618-1583
510-653-0450
Fax: 510-420-0260
peaberrys@rockridgemarkethall.com
Coffee and tea
Owner: Lynn Mallard
lynnmariemallard@gmail.com
Estimated Sales: Over $1 Million
Number Employees: 20-49
Type of Packaging: Private Label

9858 **Peace Mountain Natural Beverages**
PO Box 1445
Springfield, MA 01101-1445
413-567-4942
Fax: 413-567-8161
Bottled water, juices, nutraceuticals
Owner: J David
VP R&D: John Alden
Number Employees: 5-9
Type of Packaging: Private Label
Brands:
Cardio Water
Give Your Heart a Healthy Start
Jana
Miracle Ade
Miracle Juice
Miracle Juice Energy Drink
Peace Mountain
Skinny Water
Sports Juice

9859 **Peace River Citrus Products**
582 Beachland Boulevard
Suite 300
Vero Beach, FL 32963
772-492-4050
Fax: 772-492-4056 www.peacerivercitrus.com
Citrus
President: Bill Becker
Contact: Dale Shaffer
dshaffer@google.com
Plant Manager: Romilio Herrera
Estimated Sales: $1 million
Number Employees: 100-249
Type of Packaging: Bulk

Other Locations:
Peach River Citrus Products Plant
Arcadia FL
Peach River Citrus Products Plant
Bartow FL

9860 Peace Village Organic Foods
76 Florida Avenue
Berkeley, CA 94707-1708
510-524-4420
info@peacevillage.net
www.peacevillage.net
Asian pasta and food ingredients
President: Joel Wollner
Type of Packaging: Consumer, Private Label

9861 Peaceful Bend Winery
1942 Highway T
Steelville, MO 65565-5067
573-775-3000
Fax: 573-775-3001 winery@peacefulbend.com
www.peacefulbendvineyard.com
Wine
Owner: Katherine Gill
CEO: Clyde Gill
vinic0com@gmail.com
Estimated Sales: $500,000-$1 Million
Number Employees: 1-4
Brands:
Peaceful Bend

9862 Peaceful Fruits
330-356-8515
www.peacefulfruits.com
Organic fruit snacks
Founder/CEO: Evan Delehanty

9863 Peaceworks
PO Box 1393
Old Chelsea Station
New York, NY 10113
212-897-3985
www.peaceworks.com
Pesto and pasta sauces; tomato, olive and eggplant spreads
Founder: Daniel Lubetzky
Vice President, Sales: Rami Leshem
Sales Manager: Leah Majchel
leah@peaceworks.com
Estimated Sales: $1.3 Million
Number Employees: 5
Type of Packaging: Consumer, Food Service
Brands:
Azteca Trading Co.
Mediterranean Sprate
Moshe & Ali's Sprat,
Smoked Eggplant Sprat,
Wafa

9864 Peak Foods
877 W Main St.
Suite 700
Boise, ID 83702
208-343-2602
800-727-9939
doug-oppenheimer@oppcos.com peakfoods.com
Ready to whip toppings
Contact: Larry Lipshultz
larry-lipshultz@golbon.com

9865 Peanut Butter & Co.
PO Box 2000
New York, NY 10101
212-677-3995
Fax: 212-677-6977 866-456-8372
info@ilovepeanutbutter.com
www.ilovepeanutbutter.com
Peanut butter, jams and jellies, snacks and fluff
Founder, President: Lee Zalben
info@ilovepeanutbutter.com
Marketing: Linda Grimard-Bender
Year Founded: 1998
Estimated Sales: $3 Million
Number Employees: 20-49

9866 (HQ)Peanut Corporation of America
2121 Wiggington Road
PO Box 10037
Lynchburg, VA 24506
434-384-7098
Fax: 434-384-9528 gbparnell@aol.com
www.peanutcorp.com
Peanuts
Owner/President: Stewart Parnell
Corporate Office Manager: Gloria Parnell
Sales Director: David Yoth
Estimated Sales: $3-$5 Million
Number Employees: 20-49
Type of Packaging: Consumer, Food Service, Bulk
Other Locations:
Blakely GA
Suffolk VA
Plainview TX
Brands:
Parnell's Pride

9867 Peanut Patch
4322 E County 13th St
Yuma, AZ 85365-4631
928-726-6292
Fax: 928-726-2433 800-872-7688
thepeanutpatch@thepeanutpatch.com
www.thepeanutpatch.com
Peanuts
Owner: Donna George
usapnut@peoplepc.com
Estimated Sales: $1-3 Million
Number Employees: 10-19

9868 Peanut Patch Gift Shop
27478 Southampton Pkwy
Courtland, VA 23837
757-653-2028
Fax: 757-653-9530 800-544-0896
customerservice@feridies.com
www.thepeanutpatchgiftshop.com
Peanuts and peanut candies
President: Jane Riddick-Fries
janerf@peanutpatch.com
CFO: Paul Sheffer
R&D: Ted Fries
Number Employees: 50-99
Type of Packaging: Consumer, Food Service, Private Label
Brands:
Peanut Patch

9869 Peanut Processors Inc
7329 Albert St
Dublin, NC 28332
910-862-2136
Fax: 910-862-8076 800-330-3141
www.peanutprocessors.com
Peanuts
CEO: Houston Brisson
VP: Nile Brisson
Year Founded: 1962
Estimated Sales: $20-50 Million
Number Employees: 20-49

9870 Peanut Roaster
394 Zeb Robinson Rd
Henderson, NC 27537-8760
252-431-0100
Fax: 252-431-0224 800-445-1404
info@peanut.com www.peanut.com
Peanuts
President: John Monahan
monahanj@peanut.com
Marketing Director: Charles Penick
Quality Control: John William
Founder: Larry Monahan Sr.
Estimated Sales: Below $5 Million
Number Employees: 20-49
Brands:
The Peanut Roaster

9871 Peanut Shop
8012 Hankins Industrial Park
Toano, VA 23168-9259
757-566-4030
Fax: 757-566-2992 800-637-3268
www.thepeanutshop.com
Peanuts
General Manager: Pete Booker
Operations Manager: Larry Winslow
Estimated Sales: Less Than $500,000
Number Employees: 1-4
Type of Packaging: Consumer, Food Service, Private Label, Bulk
Brands:
Peanut Shop of Williamsburg
Smithfield Tavern

9872 Pear's Coffee
901 Ft. Crook Rd., N.
Bellevue, NE 68005
402-934-8210
Fax: 402-934-8218 800-828-7688
rrb@hermansnuthouse.com
www.hermansnuthouse.com
Coffee, nuts
President: John Larsen
Operations Manager: Adam Gaines
Estimated Sales: Below $5 Million
Number Employees: 20-49
Type of Packaging: Bulk
Brands:
Pear's Coffee

9873 Pearl Coffee Co
675 S Broadway St
Akron, OH 44311-1099
330-253-7184
Fax: 330-253-7185 800-822-5282
dianacoffee@aol.com
Coffee
President: John Economou
Vice President, Marketing: Johnna Economou
Estimated Sales: $9 Million
Number Employees: 10-19
Square Footage: 80000
Type of Packaging: Consumer, Food Service, Private Label
Brands:
Diana

9874 Pearl Crop
1550 Industrial Dr
Stockton, CA 95206
209-808-7575
Fax: 209-254-9859 info@pearlcrop.com
pearlcrop.com
Walnut and almond processor
President/Owner: Gearry Davenport
CEO: Ulash Turkhan
Other Locations:
Processing Plant
Ripon CA
Processing Plant
Linden CA

9875 Pearl River Pastry & Chocolate
4 E Dexter Plz
Pearl River, NY 10965-2360
845-735-5100
Fax: 845-735-6434 800-632-2639
sales@prpastry.com www.prpastry.com
Chocolates, cakes and pastries
Owner: J Koffman
jkoffman@prpastries.com
Estimated Sales: $5-10 Million
Number Employees: 50-99

9876 Pearl Valley Cheese Inc
54775 Township Road 90
Fresno, OH 43824-9796
740-545-6002
Fax: 740-545-7703 www.pearlvalleycheese.com
Cheese
President: Charles Ellis
sellis@pearlvalleycheese.com
General Manager: Chuck Ellis
Number Employees: 20-49
Type of Packaging: Consumer, Food Service, Private Label, Bulk
Brands:
Pearl Valley

9877 Pearson Candy Co
2140 W 7th St
St Paul, MN 55116-3199
651-698-0356
Fax: 651-696-2222
Candy: chocolate, multi-packs, mints, holiday novelties, vending, nut rolls and bun bars.
President & CEO: Michael Keller
Year Founded: 1909
Number Employees: 100-249
Type of Packaging: Consumer
Brands:
Salted Nut Roll
Bit-O-Honey
Mint Patties
Nut Goodie
Bun Bar
Coconut Patties

9878 **Pearson's Berry Farm**
34463 Range Rd 40
Site 24
Bowden, AB T0M 0K0
Canada
403-224-3011
Fax: 403-224-2096 www.pearsonsberryfarm.ca
Jams, pie fillings and dessert toppings
President: E Leonard Pearson
Sales Manager: Joyce Park
Number Employees: 20-49
Type of Packaging: Consumer, Food Service
Brands:
Pearson's Berry Farm

9879 **Pearson's Homestyle**
Site 24 Box 1 RR 1
Bowden, AB T0M 0K0
Canada
403-224-3339
877-224-3339
Sauces, spices and seasonings, beverages
President: Duane Mertin
Production: Debbie Mertin
Number Employees: 10-19
Square Footage: 22000
Type of Packaging: Private Label
Brands:
Gordo's

9880 **Peas of Mind**
2339 3rd Street
Unit 53-3R
San Francisco, CA 94107
415-504-2556
www.peasofmind.com
Baby food
Contact: Ron Parish
ron@peasofmind.com

9881 **Pease's Candy**
1701 S State St
Springfield, IL 62704-4098
217-523-3721
Fax: 217-523-7581 ILINI83@aol.com
www.peasescandy.com
Chocolates and nuts
Owner: Robert Flesher
Estimated Sales: $500,000-$1 Million
Number Employees: 5-9
Brands:
Pease's

9882 **Pecan Deluxe Candy Co**
2570 Lone Star Dr
Dallas, TX 75212-6308
214-631-3669
Fax: 214-631-5833 800-733-3589
pdcc_info@pecandeluxe.com
www.pecandeluxe.com
Dessert and baked goods ingredients: toffees, nuts, chocolate coated items, flavor bases, sauces
President: Jay Brigham
Chairman of the Board: Bennie Brigham
bennie_brigham@pecandeluxe.com
Chief Financial Officer: Keith Hurd
Chief Operating Officer: Tim Markowicz
VP Quality Assurance: Rick Hintermeier
VP Operations: Mike Cavin
Inventory/Production Coordinator: Wayne Miller
Purchasing Manager: James Mitchell
Estimated Sales: $20-50 Million
Number Employees: 250-499
Number of Products: 2000
Square Footage: 63000
Type of Packaging: Bulk

9883 **Peco Foods Inc.**
1101 Greensoro Ave.
Tuscaloosa, AL 35401
205-345-4711
Fax: 205-366-4533 www.pecofoods.com
Deli and tray-pack chicken.
President/CEO: Mark Hickman
mhickman@pecofoods.com
Chairman: Denny Hickman
Chief Financial Officer: Patrick Noland
Director, Technical Services: Curtis Stell
Director, Human Resources: Bart Carter
Director, Sales & Marketing: Bobby Wilburn
Director, Live Operations: Roddy Sanders
Chief Operations Officer: Benny Bishop
Year Founded: 1937
Estimated Sales: $582.2 Million
Number Employees: 1000-4999
Square Footage: 6185
Type of Packaging: Consumer, Food Service
Other Locations:
Peco Foods, Inc. Processing Plant
Tuscaloosa AL
Peco Foods, Inc. Processing Plant
Bay Springs MS
Peco Foods, Inc. Processing Plant
Brooksville MS
Peco Foods, Inc. Processing Plant
Sebastopol MS
Peco Foods, Inc. Processing Plant
Canton MS
Peco Foods, Inc. Processing Plant
Batesville AR
Peco Foods, Inc. Live Operations
Gordo AL
Peco Foods, Inc. Live Operations
Bay Springs MS
Peco Farms of Mississippi, LLC
Sebastopol MS
Peco Foods, Inc. Live Operations
Piladelphia MS
Peco Foods, Inc. Live Operations
Batesville AR

9884 **Peconic Bay Winery**
P.O.Box 818
Cutchogue, NY 11935
631-734-7361
Fax: 631-734-5867
Wine
Manager: Matt Gillies
Co-Owner: Ursula Lowerre
Contact: James Silver
romina@martemultimedia.com
Winemaker: Gregory Gove
Estimated Sales: Below $5 Million
Number Employees: 20-49
Brands:
Peconic Bay

9885 **Pecoraro Dairy Products**
287 Leonard St
Brooklyn, NY 11211-3618
718-388-2379
Fax: 315-339-3008 pcr2c1@aol.com
Cheeses
Owner: Ceasre Pecoraro
Operations: Ralph Parlato
Estimated Sales: Less Than $500,000
Number Employees: 1-4
Number of Brands: 4
Number of Products: 12
Square Footage: 14400
Type of Packaging: Consumer, Food Service, Private Label
Brands:
Brown Cow Farm East
Sweet Cheese, Queso Blanco

9886 **Pecos Valley Spice Company**
P.O.Box 2162
Corrales, NM 87048
505-243-2622
info@janebutelcooking.com
www.janebutelcooking.com
Chile, herbs, spices, corn & masa, barbecue, beans and nuts
Founder: Jane Butel

9887 **Pede Brothers Italian Food**
582 Duanesburg Rd
Suite 1
Schenectady, NY 12306-1096
518-356-3042
Fax: 518-355-7472 www.pedebrothers.com
Ravioli, lasagna sheets, manicotti, gnocchi, cavatelli, tortellini, stuffed shells, and rigatoni.
Owner: Romolo Pede
r.pede@pedebrothers.com
Year Founded: 1967
Estimated Sales: $20-50 Million
Number Employees: 20-49
Square Footage: 32000
Type of Packaging: Consumer, Food Service, Private Label

9888 **Pederson's Natural Farms**
1207 S Rice Street
Hamilton, TX 76531
pedersonsfarms.com
Fresh and smoked meat products
President/Owner: Cody Lane
Controller: Mark Wilson
VP: Neil Dudley
Marketing Director: Stacy Dudley
National Sales Manager: Brittany Hayes

9889 **Pedrizzetti Winery**
1645 San Pedro Ave
Morgan Hill, CA 95037
408-779-7389
Fax: 408-779-9083 wines@pedwines.net
Wines
President: Michael Sampognaro
Estimated Sales: $500,000-$1 Million
Number Employees: 1-4
Type of Packaging: Consumer, Private Label, Bulk
Brands:
Barbera
Sirah

9890 **Pedroncelli J Winery**
1220 Canyon Rd
Geyserville, CA 95441-9639
707-857-3531
Fax: 707-857-3812 800-836-3894
service@pedroncelli.com www.pedroncelli.com
Wines
Owner: Jim Pedroncelli
VP Marketing: Julie Pedroncelli St. John
VP Sales: Richard Morehouse
jim@pedroncelli.com
Estimated Sales: $1,500,000
Number Employees: 20-49
Type of Packaging: Private Label
Brands:
Pedroncelli

9891 **Peekskill Brewery**
53 South Water St. # 57
Peekskill, N7 10566
914-734-2337
mail@peekskillbrewery.com
www.peekskillbrewery.com
IPAs, sour beer
Co-Owner: Kara Berardi
Co-Owner: Keith Berardi
Co-Owner: Morgan Berardi
Number of Brands: 1
Number of Products: 10
Type of Packaging: Consumer, Private Label
Brands:
Peekskill Brewery

9892 **Peeled Snacks**
30 Martin St
Suite 3B
Cumberland, RI 02864
401-437-4386
customerservice@peeledsnacks.com
peeledsnacks.com
Puffed pea and dried fruit snacks
Founder: Noha Waibsnaider
Contact: Beth Kennedy
beth@peeledsnacks.com
Year Founded: 2004
Number Employees: 10-19

9893 **Peeler's Jersey Farms**
110 Newton Bridge Road
Athens, GA 30607-1163
706-543-7383
Fax: 706-543-2569
Milk and orange juice
President/CEO: Harvey Peeler, Sr.
Plant Manager: Vlaude Lollis
Estimated Sales: $25-49.9 Million
Number Employees: 50-99
Parent Co: Peeler's Jersey Farms

9894 **Peer Foods Group Inc**
1200 W 35th St
Chicago, IL 60609-1305
773-927-1440
Fax: 773-927-9859 800-365-5644
www.peerfoods.com
Bacon, hams and butts, pigs' feet, sausage and corned beef, pickled hocks
President: Larry O'Connell
CFO: Gary Radville
Director of Marketing: Harold Dangler
Director of Marketing: Gary Racine
Director Manufacturing: Bill Froula
Purchasing Manager: Brian Tooley

Estimated Sales: $10-20 Million
Number Employees: 100-249
Type of Packaging: Consumer, Food Service

9895 Peerless Coffee & Tea
260 Oak St
Oakland, CA 94607-4512
510-763-1763
Fax: 510-763-5026 800-310-5662
specialty@peerlesscoffee.com
www.peerlesscoffee.com

Coffee
President: Sonja Vukasin
CEO: George Vukasin
VP Administration General Counsel: Kristina Brouhard
Consultant: Michelle Thomas
Product Integrity & Quality Assurance: Stephanie Muljadi
Vice President of Marketing: Chris Browning
Director of Sales: Ruben Morales
Estimated Sales: $9.6 Million
Number Employees: 50-99
Square Footage: 260000
Type of Packaging: Consumer, Food Service

9896 Peet's Coffee
Berkeley, CA
510-594-2100
Fax: 510-594-2180 800-999-2132
customerservice@peets.com www.peets.com

Coffees, teas and coffee roasting equipment
CEO: Casey Keller
CFO: John Coletta
COO: Shawn Conway
Year Founded: 1966
Estimated Sales: $800 Million
Number Employees: 5,000
Square Footage: 60000
Parent Co: JAB Holding Company

9897 Peg's Salt
8354 Brooksville Rd
Greenwood, VA 22943-1721
434-249-2495
pegssalt.com

Salt
Contact: Cass Cannon
Brands:
Peg's Salt(c)

9898 Peggy Lawton Kitchens
253 Washington St
East Walpole, MA 02032-1133
508-668-1215
Fax: 508-660-1636 800-843-7325

Brownies and cookies
President: William Wolf
bwolf@plkitchens.com
Office Manager: Robert Willis
Estimated Sales: $2-5 Million
Number Employees: 10-19
Number of Products: 10
Square Footage: 20000
Type of Packaging: Consumer, Food Service, Private Label, Bulk
Brands:
Peggy Lawton

9899 Peju Province Winery
8466 Saint Helena Hwy
Rutherford, CA 94573
707-963-3600
Fax: 707-963-8680 800-446-7358
info@peju.com www.peju.com

Wines
Owner: Herta Behensky
hpeju@peju.com
Estimated Sales: Below $5 Million
Number Employees: 50-99
Brands:
Peju

9900 Pekarna Meat Market
119 Water St
Jordan, MN 55352-1555
952-492-6101
info@pekarnameats.com
www.pekarnameats.com

Beef, pork, wild game and sausage
Owner: John Pekarna
CEO: Kenny Pekarna
Estimated Sales: $4 Million
Number Employees: 5-9
Type of Packaging: Consumer, Private Label

9901 Pekarski Sausage
293 Conway Rd
South Deerfield, MA 01373-9663
413-665-4537
www.pekarskis.com

Meat and poultry
Marketing Director: Mike Pekarskis
Estimated Sales: Less Than $500,000
Number Employees: 1-4
Brands:
Pekarskis

9902 Peking Noodle Co Inc
1518 N San Fernando Rd
Los Angeles, CA 90065-1225
323-223-0897
Fax: 323-223-3211 info@pekingnoodle.com
www.pekingnoodle.com

Noodles, egg rolls, wontons, potsticker wraps, suey gow skins, fortune cookies and snack foods
Owner: Tony Li
chieffrank@yahoo.com
Vice President: Frank Tong
Plant Manager: Maria Gonzalez
Estimated Sales: $2200000
Number Employees: 50-99
Square Footage: 120000
Type of Packaging: Consumer, Food Service, Private Label, Bulk

9903 Pelican Bay Ltd.
150 Douglas Ave
Dunedin, FL 34698-7908
727-733-3069
Fax: 727-734-5860 800-826-8982
sales@pelicanbayltd.com www.pelicanbayltd.com

Baking and drink mixes, spice blends and gifts
Owner: Char Pfaelzer
char@pelicanbayltd.com
CEO. Jim Hubbard
Executive VP: David Pfaelzer
Plant Manager: Justin Pfaelzer
Purchasing: Greg Kathan
Estimated Sales: $4.7 Million
Number Employees: 20-49
Number of Brands: 1
Number of Products: 200
Square Footage: 120000
Type of Packaging: Consumer, Private Label, Bulk
Brands:
Pelican Bay

9904 Pelican Seafoods
P.O.Box 110
Pelican, AK 99832-0110
907-735-2211
Fax: 907-735-2281

Seafood
Manager: Vance Ady'wirta
COO: Rusty Roessler
General Manager: Glen Woods
Plant Manager: Steve Pringle
Estimated Sales: $10-20 Million
Number Employees: 50-99
Parent Co: Kake Tribal Corporation

9905 Pellegrini Wine Co
4055 W Olivet Rd
Santa Rosa, CA 95401-3839
707-545-8680
Fax: 707-545-3709 800-891-0244
info@pellegrinisonoma.com
www.pellegrinisonoma.com

Wines
Financial Manager: Richard Pellegrini
Owner/manager: Robert Pellegrini
robert@pellegrinisonoma.com
Partner/Property Manager: Jeanne Pellegrini
Treasurer: Verna Rayala
Estimated Sales: $1 Million
Number Employees: 10-19
Type of Packaging: Private Label
Brands:
Cloverdale Ranch
Olivet Lane
Pellegrini

9906 Pellman Foods Inc
122 S Shirk Rd
P.O. Box 337
New Holland, PA 17557
717-354-8070
Fax: 717-355-9944 info@pellmanfoods.com
www.pellmanfoods.com

Cakes, pies and tortes.
Controller: Michael Herr
VP, Sales & Marketing: Deryl Denlinger
Year Founded: 1973
Estimated Sales: $20-50 Million
Number Employees: 20-49
Number of Brands: 1
Number of Products: 30
Square Footage: 50000
Type of Packaging: Consumer, Food Service
Brands:
Pellman

9907 Pemaquid Seafood
32 CO OP Rd
Pemaquid, ME 04558-4315
207-677-2801
Fax: 207-677-2818 866-864-2897
pemaquidcoop@yahoo.com

Seafood
Manager: Wayne Dighton
Manager: Tom Simmons
Estimated Sales: Less Than $500,000
Number Employees: 1-4

9908 Pemberton's Foods Inc
32 Lewiston Rd
Gray, ME 04039-7536
207-657-6446
Fax: 207-657-6453 800-255-8401
www.pembertonsgourmet.com

Sauces, mixes, pancake, scone, syrup, seasonings, salsa, relish, mustard, pickles, jams, jellies
Owner: David Fillinger
info@pembertonsgourmet.com
Estimated Sales: $1 million
Number Employees: 5-9
Square Footage: 14000

9909 Penauta Products
PO Box 155 RR2
4276 Betaesda Road
Stouffville, ON L4A 7Z5
Canada
905-640-1564
Fax: 905-640-7479

Jarred honey and bee pollen
President: Paul Nauta
General Manager: Henry Nauta
Production Manager: Martin Nauta
Estimated Sales: $130,000
Number Employees: 3
Square Footage: 24000
Type of Packaging: Consumer, Food Service, Private Label, Bulk
Brands:
Ambrosia
Meadowview

9910 Pender Packing Co Inc
4520 NC Highway 133
Rocky Point, NC 28457-9108
910-675-3311
Fax: 910-675-1625 penderpacking@aol.com
www.penderpacking.com

Smoked sausage, liver pudding, c-loaf, souse loaf, chitterling loaf, chorizo, fatback and pork barbecue
President: Danny L Baker
penderpacking@aol.com
Estimated Sales: $4,900,000
Number Employees: 20-49
Type of Packaging: Consumer

9911 Pendery's
1221 Manufacturing St
Dallas, TX 75207
800-533-1870
email@penderys.com www.penderys.com

Bay leaves, cinnamon, garlic, ginger, paprika, chile pepper and herb blends
Estimated Sales: $1-3 Million
Number Employees: 5-9
Square Footage: 92000
Type of Packaging: Consumer, Food Service, Private Label, Bulk
Brands:
Chiltomaline

9912 **Penguin Frozen Foods Inc**
555 Skokie Blvd
Suite 440
Northbrook, IL 60062-2835
847-291-9400
Fax: 847-291-1588 800-323-1485
www.penguinfrozenfoods.com
Seafood and fish: shrimp, sole, turbot, fillets, lobster, crab meat
President: Ellen Paton
ellen@penguinfrozenfoods.com
Estimated Sales: $2,700,000
Number Employees: 10-19
Type of Packaging: Consumer, Food Service
Brands:
Campeche Bay
Dimo
Texas Bay

9913 **Penguin Natural Food Inc**
4400 Alcoa Ave
Vernon, CA 90058-2412
323-727-7980
Fax: 323-727-7983 www.penguinfoods.com
Rice, baking mixes, potato mixes, cornbreads, pastas and rice blends.
President: Scott Nairne
Estimated Sales: $20-50 Million
Number Employees: 50-99
Type of Packaging: Consumer, Food Service, Private Label

9914 **Penn Cheese**
7199 County Line Rd
Winfield, PA 17889-9266
570-524-7700
Fax: 570-523-9691 jon.weber@penncheese.com
Swiss cheese
President: Michael Price
General Manager: Jonathan Weber
jonathan.weber@penncheese.com
Production Manager: Thomas P. Weber
Estimated Sales: $5 Million
Number Employees: 10-19
Number of Brands: 2
Number of Products: 2
Square Footage: 81200
Type of Packaging: Private Label, Bulk
Brands:
Market Place
Pennsylvania People

9915 **Penn Dutch Meat & Seafood Market**
3950 N 28th Ter
Hollywood, FL 33020-1179
954-921-7144
Fax: 954-921-7448 sueg@penn-dutch.com
www.penn-dutch.com
Meats and general groceries
President: Greg Salsburg
greg@penn-dutch.com
CEO: George Ronkin
Secretary/Treasurer: Paul Salsburg
Managing Director: Kara Boehly
Estimated Sales: $20-50 Million
Number Employees: 100-249

9916 **Penn Dutch Meat & Seafood Market**
3201 North State Road 7
Margate, FL 33063
954-974-3900
sueg@penn-dutch.com
www.penn-dutch.com
Meats and general groceries

9917 **Penn Dutch Meat & Seafood Market**
2301 North University Dr.
Sunrise, FL 33322
sueg@penn-dutch.com
www.penn-dutch.com
Meats and general groceries

9918 **Penn Herb Co**
10601 Decatur Rd
Suite 2
Philadelphia, PA 19154-3212
215-632-4430
Fax: 215-632-7945 800-523-9971
www.pennherb.com
Encapsulated herbs ginseng and golden seal root; vitamins and supplements
President: William Betz
wbetz@penton.com
President: Ronald Betz
Estimated Sales: $3500000
Number Employees: 20-49
Square Footage: 92000
Brands:
Nature's Wonderland

9919 **Penn Shore Winery Vineyards**
10225 Lake Rd
Route 5
North East, PA 16428-2894
814-725-8688
Fax: 814-725-8689 www.pennshore.com
Wines
President: Jeffrey Ore
Vice President: Cheryl Ore
Estimated Sales: Less Than $500,000
Number Employees: 1-4
Number of Brands: 23
Type of Packaging: Bulk

9920 **Penn Street Bakery**
900 Hynes S.W.
Grand Rapids, MI 49507
616-241-2583
Fax: 616-241-6332 800-84 -AKES
www.pennstreetbakery.com
Baked goods, cakes, cookies

9921 **Pennacook Peppers**
2207 Wake Forest St
Virginia Beach, VA 23451
757-663-8798
pennacookpeppers.com
Salsa, jelly and spice blends.
Operations: Kevin Oelhafen
Brands:
Pennacook Peppers

9922 **Pennfield Farms**
1074 East Main St
Mt Joy, PA 17552
717-865-2153
Fax: 717-865-2186 800-732-0009
Eggs and chicken
President: Mark Mckay
Plant Manager: Bill Rahn
Number Employees: 400
Parent Co: Pennfield Corporation
Type of Packaging: Consumer, Bulk
Brands:
Coleman

9923 **Pennsylvania Brewing Company**
800 Vinial St
Pittsburgh, PA 15212
412-237-9400
Fax: 412-237-9406 pennbrew@hotmail.com
www.pennbrew.com
Beer and ale
President: Tom Pastorius
Manager: Rick Brown
Contact: Sandy Cindrich
sandy@pennbrew.com
Estimated Sales: Below $5 Million
Number Employees: 20-49
Type of Packaging: Consumer, Food Service
Brands:
Penn Dark
Penn Gold
Penn Maibok
Penn Marzen
Penn Pilsner
Penn Weizen

9924 **Pennsylvania Dutch: Birch Beer**
5175 Cold Spring Creamert Rd
Suite 4
Doylestown, PA 18901
856-662-1869
dschwarz@daretogodutch.com
www.daretogodutch.com
Soft drinks
President: Michael Geehring
Chairman: Lincoln Warrell
VP Finance: L Lebo
VP: Dwayne Schwartz
Estimated Sales: $1-$2.5 Million
Number Employees: 2
Brands:
Pennsylvania Dutch

9925 **Pennsylvania Macaroni Company**
2010-12 Penn Avenue
Pittsburgh, PA 15222
412-471-8330
Fax: 412-201-4751 800-223-5928
info@pennmac.com www.pennmac.com
Pasta, cheeses, deli meats and gift boxes
President: David Sunseri
Estimated Sales: $10-24 Million
Number Employees: 90

9926 **Pennsylvania Renaissance Faire**
2775 Lebanon Rd
Manheim, PA 17545-8711
717-664-0476
Fax: 717-664-3466 www.parenfaire.com
Wine
Vice President: Candace Smith
candace@parenfaire.com
VP: Barbara Lacek
Number Employees: 20-49
Brands:
Mazza Vineyards

9927 **Penny Lick Ice Cream Company**
580 Warburton Ave.
Hastings, NY 10706
914-525-1580
www.pennylickicecream.com
Locally-sourced, natural ingredient small batch ice cream and sorbets in various fruit and seasonal flavors
Owner: Ellen Sledge
Year Founded: 2013
Number of Brands: 1
Number of Products: 27
Type of Packaging: Private Label
Brands:
Penny Lick

9928 **Penobscot Mccrum LLC**
28 Pierce St
PO Box 229
Belfast, ME 04915-6648
207-338-4360
Fax: 207-338-5742 800-435-4456
www.penobscotmccrum.com
Potato pancakes, mashers, skins, and wedges.
Managing Partner: Jay McCrum
Managing Partner: David McCrum
Manager, JDR Transport, Inc.: Wade McCrum
Financial Analysis & Marketing: Nick McCrum
Manager, North Maine Farm Operations: Darrell McCrum
Estimated Sales: $33 Million
Number Employees: 100-249
Type of Packaging: Consumer, Food Service

9929 **Penotti USA**
4 Maplegrove Avenue
Westport, CT 06880-4917
203-341-9494
Fax: 203-277-0006 877-720-0896
www.penotti.com
Chocolate and nut spreads
President: Marcell Peteers
Contact: Stanley Rottell
stan@regattagingerbeer.com
Estimated Sales: $1 million
Number Employees: 1
Type of Packaging: Bulk

9930 **Penta Manufacturing Company**
50 Okner Pkwy
Livingston, NJ 07039-1604
973-740-2300
Fax: 973-740-1839 sales@pentamfg.com
www.pentamfg.com
Fructose, rice starch, nutraceuticals, food and flavor compounds, chemicals, cooking and essential oils, extracts, spices
Owner: Mark Esposito
SVP: George Volpe
Sales Manager: Christine Tavares
Contact: Fatima Jasmins
fatimaj@pentamfg.com
Estimated Sales: $10-20 Million
Number Employees: 20-49
Number of Products: 7000
Square Footage: 700000
Parent Co: Penta International Corporation

Type of Packaging: Food Service, Private Label, Bulk

9931 Penta Water
1601 E Steel Rd
Colton, CA 92324
800-531-5088
pentawater.com
Drinking water
Contact: Bill Austin
baustin@pentawater.com
New Media Relations: Joe Lupica
Square Footage: 220000

9932 People's Sausage Co
1132 E Pico Blvd
Los Angeles, CA 90021-2224
213-627-8633
Fax: 213-627-7767
info@peopleschoicebeefjerky.com
www.peopleschoicebeefjerky.com
Beef jerky
Owner: Brian Bianchetti
brian@peopleschoicebeefjerky.com
Estimated Sales: $3000000
Number Employees: 10-19
Square Footage: 20000
Type of Packaging: Consumer, Food Service, Private Label, Bulk

9933 Pepe's Inc
1325 W 15th St
Chicago, IL 60608-2190
312-733-2500
Fax: 312-733-2564 www.pepes.com
Mexican food
President: Betty Wright
b.wright@adm.com
General Manager: Mario Dovalina Jr
Number Employees: 1000-4999
Square Footage: 260000
Type of Packaging: Private Label, Bulk
Brands:
Aventura Gourmet
Pepe's

9934 Pepe's Mexican Restaurant
2429 W Ball Rd
Anaheim, CA 92804-5210
Canada
714-952-9410
Fax: 416-674-2805 www.pepesmexicanfood.com
Tortilla chips, flour tortillas, multi-grain snacks, burritos, jalapeno peppers, salsa and beans
Owner: Nathan Russi
Vice President: Ronaldo Sardelitti
VP Sales: Tom Reynolds
National Sales Manager: Tony Kent
Estimated Sales: Less Than $500,000
Number Employees: 5-9
Square Footage: 132000
Parent Co: Signature Brands
Type of Packaging: Consumer, Food Service
Brands:
Casa Del Norte
Gringos
Pepes

9935 Pepper Creek Farms
1002 SW Ard St
Lawton, OK 73505-9660
580-536-1300
Fax: 580-536-4886 800-526-8132
info@peppercreekfarms.com
www.peppercreekfarms.com
Jellies, mustards, peppers, salsa, relish, syrup, mixes, and seasonings
Owner: Craig Weissman
craig@peppercreekfarms.com
Vice President: Marshall Weissman
Estimated Sales: $600,000
Number Employees: 10-19
Square Footage: 30000
Type of Packaging: Consumer, Food Service, Private Label
Brands:
Jalapeno
Jalapeno Tnt
Wildfire

9936 Pepper Island Beach
PO Box 484
Lawrence, PA 15055-0484
724-746-2401
Fax: 724-746-1679
Hot sauce
President: Karen Hasak

9937 Pepper Mill Imports
P.O.Box 775
Seaside, CA 93955
831-899-2983
Fax: 831-899-2996 800-928-1744
sales@peppermillimports.com
www.peppermillimports.com
Olive oil, pepper and spice mills
President: William Sterling
Marketing: Amy Paris
Sales: Angel Geil
Estimated Sales: Below $5 Million
Number Employees: 10
Number of Brands: 2
Number of Products: 112
Square Footage: 120000
Type of Packaging: Consumer, Food Service, Private Label
Brands:
Melina's

9938 (HQ)Pepper Source Inc
2720 Athania Pkwy
Metairie, LA 70002-5904
504-885-3223
Fax: 504-885-3187 www.peppersource.com
Sauces and glazes, dry blends, custome rubs and packaging services.
President: Joe Morse
Contact: Shannon Glover
sglover@peppersource.com
Vice President of Operations: Paul Liggio
Production Supervisor: Mike Bartels
Estimated Sales: $15 Million
Number Employees: 5-9
Type of Packaging: Food Service, Private Label, Bulk
Other Locations:
Pepper Source
Van Buren AR
Pepper Source
Rogers AR

9939 Pepper Source LTD
11103 N Old Wire Rd
Rogers, AR 72756-9871
479-246-1030
Fax: 479-246-1061 www.peppersource.com
Sauces, marinades and glazes
VP Marketing: John Bowerman
Manager: Mark Watson
mwatson@peppersource.com
Plant Manager: Brad Palmer
Estimated Sales: $5-10 Million
Number Employees: 50-99
Type of Packaging: Private Label

9940 Pepper Source, Rogers
5800 Alma Hwy
Van Buren, AR 72956-7202
479-474-5178
Fax: 479-474-4729 sales@peppersource.com
www.peppersource.com
Sauces, marinades and glazes.
President: Wanda Patton
w.patton@peppersource.com
Director Sales: Mark Watson
VP Operations: Paul Liggio
VP Purchasing: Steven Campbell
Estimated Sales: $5-10 Million
Number Employees: 100-249
Type of Packaging: Private Label

9941 Peppered Palette
PO Box 29003
Bellingham, WA 98228
919-468-7101
Fax: 360-306-5589 866-829-9151
Hot sauce
Owner: Todd Guiton
toadster@pepperedpalette.com
Estimated Sales: $300,000-500,000
Number Employees: 1-4
Brands:
Toad Sweat

9942 Pepperidge Farm Inc.
595 Westport Ave.
Norwalk, CT 06851
203-846-7000
888-737-7374
www.pepperidgefarm.com
Desserts, pastries, breads and rolls
VP, Finance: Chris Dayton
Year Founded: 1937
Estimated Sales: $1 Billion
Number Employees: 5000-9999
Parent Co: Campbell Soup
Brands:
Goldfish
Milano
Pepperidge Farm

9943 Pepperland Farms
41177 N. Thibodaux Rd.
Ponchatoula, LA 70454
985-956-6703
Fax: 877-296-8683 www.pepperlandfarms.com
Chili peppers
Owner: Dennis Hall

9944 Peppers
17601 Coastal Hwy
Unit 1
Lewes, DE 19958-6217
302-703-6355
Fax: 302-644-6901 800-998-3473
peppers@peppers.com www.peppers.com
Hot sauces, salsa, mustards & dips, marinades & cajun injectors, peppers, pickles & relishes, olives, bloody mary & mixers, chili, soups, pasta & coffee, seasoning & rubs, curry & chutney, nuts & snacks, jelly, preserves & peanutbutter
Owner: Luther Hearn
chip@peppers.com
Number Employees: 20-49
Type of Packaging: Consumer, Food Service, Private Label, Bulk

9945 PepsiCo.
700 Anderson Hill Rd.
Purchase, NY 10577
914-253-2000
www.pepsico.com
Global brands food, snack and beverage company.
Chairman/CEO: Ramon Laguarta
President, Global Foodservice: Anne Fink
Vice Chairman/CFO: Hugh Johnston
EVP/Chief Scientific Officer: Rene Lammers
Year Founded: 1898
Estimated Sales: $67.1 Billion
Number Employees: 263,000
Number of Brands: 54
Square Footage: 40000
Type of Packaging: Consumer
Brands:
Pepsi
Frito-Lay
Quaker
Tropicana
Gatorade
Pure Leaf
Mountain Dew
Bubly
Naked
Lipton
Starbucks Frappacino
Aquafina
Brisk
Kevita
Life WTR
Sierra Mist
Stubborn Soda
IZZE
Propel
O.N.E
AMP ENERGY Organic
SOBE
Mug Root Beer
Doritos
Stacy's Pita Chips
Bare
Sabra
Ruffles
Smartfood
Cheetos
Tostitos
Fritos
Near East
Maker

Imag!ne
Sun Chips
Off The Eaten Path
Rold Gold
Miss Vickies
Red Rock Deli
Cracker Jack
Nut Harvest
Life
Matador
Santitas
Funyuns
Cap'n Crunch
Pasta Roni
Rice A Roni
Maui Style
Sabritones
Munchos
Grandma's
Aunt Jemima

9946 **Perdue Farms Inc.**
31149 Old Ocean City Rd.
Salisbury, MD 21804
800-473-7383
www.perdue.com
Chicken, turkey and pork.
Chairman: Jim Perdue
CEO: Randy Day
Senior VP/CFO: Brenda Galgano
General Counsel: Herb Frerichs
Senior VP, Corporate Communications: Andrea Staub
Year Founded: 1920
Estimated Sales: $6.7 Billion
Number Employees: 21,000
Number of Brands: 8
Type of Packaging: Consumer, Food Service, Private Label, Bulk
Other Locations:
Perdue Farms
Monterey TN
Brands:
Perdue
Coleman Natural
Harvestland
Simply Smart Organics
Draper Valley Farms
Petaluma Poultry
Prarie Grove Farms
Niman Ranch
Spot Farms
Full Moon

9947 **Pereg Gourmet Spices**
6966 Main St
Flushing, NY 11367-1724
718-261-6767
Fax: 718-261-7688 gill@pereg-gourmet.com
www.pereg-gourmet.com
Spices, oils, salads and spreads, toppings, bread crumbs, quinoa, rice mixes, salt, basmati rice, couscous
Owner: Chim Pereg
pereg.usa@verizon.net
Marketing: Gill Schnieder
Estimated Sales: $1 Million
Number Employees: 10-19

9948 **Perez Food Products**
2826 Southwest Blvd
Kansas City, MO 64108-3613
816-931-8761
Fax: 816-931-2825 www.perfectoutput.com
Mexican food
Owner: Jesse Perez
Sales Manager: Daniel Perez
Estimated Sales: $2,500,000
Number Employees: 5-9
Type of Packaging: Consumer

9949 **Perfect Addition**
P.O.Box 8976
Newport Beach, CA 92658
949-640-0220
Fax: 949-640-0304 perfectadd@aol.com
Frozen foods
President: Constance Grigsby
CFO/VP: Jack Grigsby
CEO/VP Marketing: Connie Grigsby
Estimated Sales: Less than $200,000
Number Employees: 1-4
Type of Packaging: Consumer, Private Label
Brands:
Perfect Addition Beef Stock
Perfect Addition Chi
Perfect Addition Fis
Perfect Addition Veg

9950 **Perfect Bite Co**
747 W Wilson Ave
Glendale, CA 91203-2447
818-507-1527
Fax: 818-507-1376 joe@theperfectbiteco.com
www.theperfectbiteco.com
Appetizers: crisps, cookies.
President/CEO: Teri Valentine
CFO/Secretary: John Valentine
john@theperfectbiteco.com
Vice President: Joe Forristal
Estimated Sales: $300,000
Number Employees: 10-19

9951 **Perfect Foods Inc**
862 Pulaski Hwy
Goshen, NY 10924-6032
845-651-2012
Fax: 845-783-9683 800-933-3288
info@800wheatgrass.com
www.drsqueezejuicers.com
Wheat grass, sunflower, buckwheat greens, juice
President: Harley Matsil
harleymatsil@yahoo.com
Year Founded: 1982
Estimated Sales: $200,000
Number Employees: 10-19
Square Footage: 24000
Type of Packaging: Consumer
Brands:
Green Gold Wheatgrass
Perfect Foods Wheatgrass Juice

9952 **Perfect Life Nutrition**
380 Saint Cloud Ave
West Orange, NJ 07052
973-980-2298
pnuff.com
Vegan baked peanut puffs
Founder: Juan Salinas
Brands:
P-nuff Crunch

9953 **Perfect Puree of Napa Valley**
2700 Napa Valley Corporate Dr
Suite L
Napa, CA 94558-7557
707-261-5100
Fax: 707-261-5111 info@perfectpuree.com
www.perfectpuree.com
Flavored purees
President: Tracy Hayward
thayward@perfectpuree.com
Marketing: Michele Lex
Estimated Sales: $1-3 Million
Number Employees: 10-19
Type of Packaging: Consumer, Bulk

9954 **Perfect Snacks**
3931 Sorrento Valley Blvd
Suite 100
Sorrento Valley, CA 92120
866-628-8548
perfectbar.com
Nut butter-based meal bars
CEO: Bill Keith

9955 **Perfections by Allan**
3 Old Creek Ct
Owings Mills, MD 21117
410-581-8670
Fax: 410-581-0877 800-581-8670
Dipping cookies and snacks
President: Allan Taylor
ataylor@perfectionsbyallan.com
Estimated Sales: Under $500,000
Number Employees: 1-4
Type of Packaging: Consumer, Private Label
Brands:
Grandma Taylor's Gourmet Dip

9956 **Perfetti Van Melle USA Inc**
3645 Turfway Rd
Erlanger, KY 41018
859-283-1234
perfettivanmelleus.com
Candy and chewing gum.
President & CEO: Sylvia Buxton
CFO: Fred King
VP, Marketing: Rachel Chambers
VP, Sales: Dan Hamilton
VP, Manufacturing: Francisco Tello
VP, Supply Chain: James Biro
Estimated Sales: $50-100 Million
Number Employees: 100-249
Type of Packaging: Consumer
Brands:
Airheads
Alpenliebe
Big Babol
Center Fruit
Chupa Chups
Daygum
Frisk
Fruittella
Golia
Happydent
Klene
Look-O-Look
Meller
Mentos
Morositas
Smint
StopNot
Sula
Vigorsol
Vivident

9957 **Performance Labs**
5115 Douglas Fir Rd
Suite M
Calabasas, CA 91302-2597
818-591-9669
Fax: 818-591-2116 800-848-2537
Nutritional and herbal supplements, vitamins and garlic
Owner: Richard Burke
CEO: David Mercer, Jr.
Contact: Jon Ackland
cousteau@performancelab.co.nz
Purchasing Manager: Allan Suda
Estimated Sales: $3 Million
Number Employees: 20-49
Type of Packaging: Consumer
Brands:
Cardiomax
Garlimax
Guardmax
Immumax
Relaxmax
Vitalert

9958 **Peri & Sons Farms**
102 McLeod St.
Yerington, NV 89447
775-463-4444
Fax: 775-463-4028 www.periandsons.com
White, yellow, red, sweet and organic onions.
Owner: David Peri
Year Founded: 1979
Number Employees: 1000-5000
Type of Packaging: Private Label

9959 **Perino's Inc**
6850 Westbank Expy
Marrero, LA 70072-2523
504-347-5410
Fax: 504-341-2504 www.perinosseafood.com
Seafood
Manager: Mark Somme
Manager: Paul Ocrne
Estimated Sales: $3-5 Million
Number Employees: 10-19

9960 **Perky Jerky**
7400 E Crestline Cir
Suite 130
Greenwood Vlg, CO 80111-3655
720-389-7171
888-343-6113
perkyjerky.com
Meat jerkies
Founder: Brian Levin
Contact: Jessie Arellano
jessiearellano@perkyjerky.com
Number Employees: 10-19

9961 **Perky's Pizza**
4029 Tampa Rd
Oldsmar, FL 34677-3206
813-855-7700
Fax: 813-855-0014 800-473-7597
perky@perkys.com www.perkys.com
Pizza producer of Perky's pizza products, program and product sales
President: Jim Howell
CEO: Frank Rozel
R&D: Bill Sweet
Marketing Manager: Anne Reilley
Sales: Rick White
Contact: G Gable
g.gable@perkys.com
Estimated Sales: $2.5-5 Million
Number Employees: 10-19
Square Footage: 8000
Type of Packaging: Food Service, Private Label
Brands:
Perky's Fresh Bakery

9962 **Perlarom Technology**
9133 Red Branch Rd
Columbia, MD 21045-2029
410-997-5114
Fax: 410-964-9374 leif.kjargaard@danisco.com
Flavors and extracts
Executive VP: Soren Bjerre Nielsen
CEO: Tom Knutzen
Vice President: Philippe Lavielle
Executive VP: Mogens Granborg
Estimated Sales: $2.5-5 Million
Number Employees: 20-49

9963 **Pernicious Pickling**
350 Clinton St
Suite A
Costa Mesa, CA 92626-6028
714-794-9845
www.perniciouspickling.com
Pickled vegetables
Contact: Kendra Coggin

9964 **Pernod Ricard USA**
250 Park Ave.
New York, NY 10177
212-372-5400
Fax: 914-539-4550 www.pernod-ricard-usa.com
Spirits and wines.
Chairman/CEO: Paul Duffy
Chief Financial Officer: Guillaume Thomas
Senior Vice President: James Slack
Chief Marketing Officer: Jonas Tahlin
Chief Commercial Officer: Julien Hemard
Senior VP, Communications/Sustainability: Amandine Robin
Senior VP, New Brand Ventures: Jeff Agdern
Year Founded: 1980
Estimated Sales: $100+ Million
Number Employees: 1000-4999
Number of Brands: 30+
Parent Co: Pernod Ricard SA
Brands:
Aberlour Single Malt
Absolut(c)
Altos
Aura
Avion(c)
Azteca de Oro
Ballantine's
Beefeater(c)
Brancott Estate(c)
Campo Viejo
Chivas Regal(c)
Fris
G.H. Mumm
Graffigna & Jacob's Creek
Hiram Walker(c)
Jameson(c) Irish
Kahlua
Kenwood(c) Vineyards
Lillet(c)
Longmorn
Lot 40 and Pike Creek
Malibu(c)
Martell(c)
Midleton
Mumm Napa(c)
Pernod(c)
Perrier-Jouet(c)
Plymouth(c) Gin
Powers
Redbreast Irish
Ricard(c)
Seagram's Extra Dry Gin(c)
The Glenlivet(c) Single Malt
100 Pipers
Smithworks Vodka
Royal Salut
Green Spot
Vida
Monkey 47

9965 **Perona Farms**
350 Andover Sparta Rd
Andover, NJ 07821-5016
973-729-6161
Fax: 973-729-1097 800-750-6190
info@peronafarms.com www.peronafarms.com
Salmon, seafood
President: Tracey Giller
tracey@peronafarms.com
CFO: Mark Avondoglio
Executive Chef: Kirk Avondoglio
Estimated Sales: $2.5 Million
Number Employees: 100-249
Square Footage: 16400
Brands:
Perona Farms

9966 **Perricone Juices**
550 B St
Beaumont, CA 92223-2672
951-769-7171
Fax: 951-769-7176 www.perriconejuices.com
Juice: orange, tangerine, grapefruit, lemon, lime, lemonade, strawberry, pomegranate and apple
President: Bob Rovzar
CEO: Tom Carmody
tcarmody@perriconejuices.com
CFO: Joe Perricone
Director of Human Resources: Will Martin
Production Manager: Humberto Orellana
Estimated Sales: $15.8 Million
Number Employees: 50-99
Square Footage: 60000
Type of Packaging: Consumer, Food Service
Brands:
Perricone Farms

9967 **Perrigo Nutritionals LLC**
515 Eastern Ave
Allegan, MI 49010-9070
269-673-8451
www.perrigonutritionals.com
Infant formula
Vice President, Operations: Sean Walsh
Number Employees: 1-4

9968 **Perry Creek Winery**
7400 Perry Creek Rd
PO Box 350
Somerset, CA 95684-9207
530-620-5175
Fax: 215-699-8200 800-880-4026
www.perrycreek.com
Wines
Founder: Michael Chazen
Estimated Sales: $1-2.5 Million
Number Employees: 10-19

9969 **Perry's Ice Cream Co Inc**
1 Ice Cream Plz
Akron, NY 14001-1031
716-542-5492
Fax: 716-542-2544 800-873-7797
www.perrysicecream.com
Ice cream, custard, gelato, frozen yogurt, sherbet & sorbet
President: Michael Firth
CEO: Thomas Perry
EVP: Mike Calhoun
Quality Control Manager: Jim Marshall
VP Marketing: Diane Austin
VP Sales: Ken Kwarta
VP Operations: Michael Diem
Plant Manager: Tom Kowalski
Director Purchasing: Leigyh Menzel
Number Employees: 250-499
Type of Packaging: Consumer, Bulk
Brands:
Perry's
Perry's Deluxe
Perry's Free
Perry's Light
Perry's Pride

9970 **Personal Edge Nutrition**
275 White Tree Lane
Ballwin, MO 63011-3338
514-636-4512
Fax: 514-636-8356
Energy and protein bars, powdered soy beverages
Parent Co: DuPont Chemical
Brands:
Personal Edge Supro

9971 **Pervida**
PO Box 10175
Blacksburg, VA 24062
540-808-0800
www.pervida.net
Health drinks
Managing Partner: Debbie Custer
Brands:
Pervida(c)

9972 **Pestano Foods**
New Rochelle, NY 10801
info@drinktoma.com
www.drinktoma.com
Artisanal Bloody Mary cocktail mix
Founder/Owner: Alejandro Lopez
Number of Brands: 1
Number of Products: 1
Type of Packaging: Consumer, Private Label, Bulk
Brands:
Toma

9973 **Pestos with Panache**
176 Johnson Street
Suite 8E
Brooklyn, NY 11201
917-656-3082
Fax: 212-230-7404
Pesto
President/Owner: Lauren Stewart

9974 **Petaluma Poultry**
2700 Lakeville Hwy
Petaluma, CA 94954-5606
707-763-1904
Fax: 707-763-3924 800-556-6789
petalumareception@petalumapoultry.com
www.petalumapoultry.com
Organic chicken
President: Dick Krengal
CFO: Dave Martinelli
dmartinelli@petalumapoultry.com
Sales Manager: Brian Starr
Director of Manufacturing: Bob Wolfe
Estimated Sales: $20-50 Million
Number Employees: 100-249
Square Footage: 30000
Parent Co: Coleman Natural
Type of Packaging: Consumer
Brands:
Rocky Jr
Rocky the Range
Rosie Organic

9975 **Pete & Joy's Bakery**
121 E Broadway
Little Falls, MN 56345-3038
320-632-6388
Fax: 320-632-2740
Rolls, coffee, cake
Owner: Peter Kamrowski
petenjoy@charter.net
Estimated Sales: $8 Million
Number Employees: 10-19

9976 **Pete and Gerry's Organic Eggs**
140 Buffum Rd
Monroe, NH 03771
603-638-2827
800-210-6657
familyfarmteam@peteandgerrys.com
www.peteandgerrys.com
Organic free range eggs
Owner/CEO: Jesse Laflamme
CFO: Keith Fortier
COO: Erik Drake
VP Marketing: Paul Turbeville
Number Employees: 50-99

9977 **(HQ)Pete's Brewing Company**
14800 San Pedro Ave
San Antonio, TX 78232-3733
210-490-9128
Fax: 210-490-9984 800-877-7383

Beer
President: Scott Barnum
CEO: Jeffrey Atkins
CEO: Carlos Alvarez
VP Sales: Don Quigley
Contact: James Bolz
j.bolz@petes.com
Number Employees: 50-99
Parent Co: Miller Brewing Company
Brands:
Pete's Wicked Ale

9978 Peter Cremer North America
3117 Southside Ave
Cincinnati, OH 45204-1215
513-471-7200
Fax: 513-244-7775 877-901-7262
www.petercremerna.com
Oleochemicals: fatty alcohols, acids, biodiesel, esters, glycerin and care products
CEO: Robin Avedesian-Scol
ravedesianscol@petercremerna.com
Number Employees: 100-249
Parent Co: Cremer
Brands:
Cremer Cunter

9979 Peter Michael Winery
12400 Ida Clayton Rd
Calistoga, CA 94515-9507
707-942-4459
Fax: 707-942-0209 800-354-4459
retail@petermichaelwinery.com
Wines
Owner: Peter Michael
retail@petermichaelwinery.com
Vice President: Bill Vyenielo
Estimated Sales: $1-2.5 Million
Number Employees: 20-49
Brands:
Peter Michael Winery

9980 Peter Pan Seafoods Inc.
3015 112th Ave. NE
Suite 100
Bellevue, WA 98004
206-728-6000
Fax: 206-441-9090 sales@ppsf.com
www.ppsf.com
Seafood including crab, herring and surimi blends, canned salmon, swordfish, mahi mahi and tuna.
President/CEO: Barry Collier
barryc@ppsf.com
Controller/Treasurer: Adrian Yonke
Year Founded: 1912
Estimated Sales: $225 Million
Number Employees: 1,000-4,999
Number of Brands: 8
Parent Co: Maruha Capital Investment, Inc.
Type of Packaging: Consumer, Food Service, Private Label, Bulk
Brands:
Deming's
Double Q
Gill Netter's Best
Humpty Dumpty
Peter Pan
SeaBlends
SeaKist
Unica

9981 Peter Rabbit Farms
85810 Peter Rabbit Ln
Coachella, CA 92236
760-398-0136
Fax: 760-398-0972 sales@peterrabbitfarms.com
www.peterrabbitfarms.com
Peppers, grapes, eggplant, leafy greens and Medjool dates
President/CEO: John Powell Jr
Controller: Stephanie Sibotka
stephanies@peterrabbitfarms.com
VP & COO: Steve Powell
Manager, Sales: John Burton
Number Employees: 100-249
Square Footage: 400000
Type of Packaging: Consumer, Food Service, Private Label, Bulk

9982 Peter's Mustards
PO Box 1036
Sharon, CT 06069-1036
860-364-0842
Mustard
President: Richard Harris

9983 Petersen Ice Cream Company
1104 Chicago Ave
Suite 6
Oak Park, IL 60302
708-386-6130
Fax: 708-386-6162 www.petersenicecream.com
Ice cream and frozen yogurt
President and CFO: Robert Raniere
Treasurer: D Raniere
Estimated Sales: $1-3 Million
Number Employees: 20-49
Type of Packaging: Consumer, Food Service

9984 Peterson & Sons Winery
9375 E P Ave
Kalamazoo, MI 49048-9762
269-626-9755
Fax: 616-626-9755
Wine
Owner: Duane Peterson
Sales Manager: Tony Peterson
Estimated Sales: Less Than $500,000
Number Employees: 1-4

9985 Peterson Farms Inc
3104 W Baseline Rd
Shelby, MI 49455-9633
231-861-0119
Fax: 231-861-2274 sarah@petersonfarmsinc.com
www.petersonfarmsinc.com
Fruit
CEO: Aaron Peterson
aaron@petersonfarmsinc.com
Chief Sales & Marketing Officer: Sarah Schlukebir
Director of Sales: Larry Hicks
Number Employees: 500-999
Brands:
Peterson Farms

9986 Petit Pot
4221 Horton St
Emeryville, CA 94608
650-488-7432
petitpot.com
Pot de crŠme, rice pudding and cookies.
CEO: Maxime Pouvreau
Brands:
Petit Pot(c)

9987 Petra International
1260 Fewster Drive
Unit 1
Mississauga, ON L4W 1A5
Canada
905-629-9269
Fax: 905-542-2546 800-261-7226
petra@petradecor.com www.petradecor.com
Gum paste flowers
President: Ham Go
Parent Co: Indomex Foods
Type of Packaging: Consumer, Private Label, Bulk
Brands:
Petra

9988 Petrofsky's Bakery Products
16647 Annas Way
Chesterfield, MO 63005-4509
636-519-1613
Dough and bagels
President: Jerry Shapiro
Vice President: Robert Petrofsky
Estimated Sales: $10-20 Million
Number Employees: 20-49
Parent Co: Maplehurst Bakeries
Type of Packaging: Consumer, Food Service

9989 Petschl's Quality Meats
1150 Andover Park E
Tukwila, WA 98188-3903
206-575-4400
Fax: 206-575-4463 info@petschls.com
Beef, lamb, pork, veal and chicken
Owner: Shelley Greene
shelley@petschls.com
Vice President: Nancy Kvinge
Estimated Sales: $9 Million
Number Employees: 20-49
Type of Packaging: Consumer, Food Service, Private Label, Bulk

9990 Pett Spice Products Inc
4285 Wendell Dr SW
Atlanta, GA 30336-1632
404-691-5235
Fax: 404-691-5237 orders@pettspice.net
Seasonings for marinades, glazes, salad dressings, soups, sauces, snack foods and breading
Owner: Ben Calhoun
bcalhoun@pettspice.net
Plant Manager: Mike Foley
Estimated Sales: $500,000-$1 Million
Number Employees: 5-9
Brands:
Pett Spice

9991 Pez Candy Inc
35 Prindle Hill Rd
Orange, CT 06477-3616
203-795-0531
Fax: 203-799-1679
Candy and dispensers
President: Joseph Vittoria
CEO: Christian Jegen
jegen@pezcandyinc.com
CFO: Brian Fry
VP Marketing: Peter Vandall
VP Sales: Dan Silliman
VP Operations: Mark Morrissey
Estimated Sales: $3,100,000
Number Employees: 100-249
Type of Packaging: Consumer
Other Locations:
PEZ Candy
Orange CT
Brands:
Pez

9992 Pfanstiehl Inc
1219 Glen Rock Ave
Waukegan, IL 60085-6249
847-623-0370
Fax: 847-623-9173
Lactic acid
Chairman: Jim Breckenridge
President: Cynthia Kerker
VP, Sales & Marketing: Chris Wilcox
VP, Research & Development: Trevor Calkins
Quality Control Chemist: Jimmy Moshopoulos
Contact: Jessica Bakutis
jessica.bakutis@pfanstiehl.com
Year Founded: 1919
Estimated Sales: $23.9 Million
Number Employees: 10-19
Parent Co: Med Opportunity Partners
Type of Packaging: Bulk

9993 Pfefferkorn's Coffee Inc
1200 E Fort Ave
P.O. Box 27007
Baltimore, MD 21230-5105
410-727-3354
Fax: 410-547-1652 800-682-4665
www.pfefferkornscoffee.com
Coffee
President: Louis Pfefferkorn
pfefferkornscoffee@verizon.net
VP/Owner: Samuel Pfefferkorn
Operations Manager: Charles Pfefferkorn
Estimated Sales: $.5-1 million
Number Employees: 10-19
Type of Packaging: Consumer
Brands:
Pfefferkorn's

9994 Pfeil & Holding Inc
5815 Northern Blvd
Woodside, NY 11377-2297
718-545-4600
Fax: 718-932-7513 800-247-7955
info@cakedeco.com www.cakedeco.com
Bakers' equipment and utensils, cake decorations, pastry bags, pans, tubes, tier separators, flavors and ingredients
President: David Gordils
davidg@cakedeco.com
CEO: Sy Stricker
Sales Director: Jenn Covalluzzi
Estimated Sales: $5-10 Million
Number Employees: 20-49
Number of Products: 7000
Square Footage: 200000
Brands:
PFEIL

9995 **Pfizer**
235 E 42nd St
New York, NY 10017-5703
212-573-3115
Fax: 212-309-0896 800-879-3477
www.pfizer.com
Chewing gum and breath mints
Trade Development Manager: Larry Roche
CEO: Ian C. Read
CFO: Frank D'Amelio
EVP: Rady Johnson
President: Mikael Dolsten, M.D
Sales/Marketing Executive: Michael Soriano
Estimated Sales: $1-3 Million
Number Employees: 1-4
Parent Co: Pfizer
Type of Packaging: Consumer, Food Service
Brands:
Bubbilicious
Certs
Chiclets
Clorets
Cool Mint Drops
Dentyne Ice
Mint*A*Burst
Trident
Vichy

9996 **Phamous Phloyd's Barbecue**
2998 S Steele St
Denver, CO 80210-6948
303-757-3285
Fax: 303-757-3373 800-497-3281
phloyd@4edisp.net www.phloyds.com
Condiments, Bloody Mary mixes, marinades, sauces, mustards and dry rubs
President/Owner: Mary Ellen Baran
Estimated Sales: Under $500,000
Number Employees: 1-4
Type of Packaging: Consumer, Bulk
Brands:
Phamous Phloyd's

9997 **Pharmachem Laboratories**
265 Harrison Ave
Kearny, NJ 07032-4315
201-246-1000
Fax: 201-991-5674 800-526-0609
www.pharmachemlabs.com
Ingredients: proteins, extracts, acids
President: David Holmes
CEO: Andrea Bauer
andrea.bauer@pharmachem.com
Number Employees: 50-99
Brands:
Berry-Max
Celadrin(c)
Cran-Max(c)
Enderma
Lactium(c)
Phase 2(c)
Prenulin(c)
Reducol

9998 **Pharmavite LLC**
8510 Balboa Blvd
Suite 100
Northridge, CA 91325-3581
818-221-6200
Fax: 818-221-6618 800-276-2878
www.pharmavite.com
Vitamin tablets and ingredients
President: Brent Belly
CEO: Connie Barry
Executive VP Marketing: Catherine Mardesich
Estimated Sales: $300,000-500,000
Number Employees: 5-9
Parent Co: Pharmavite Corporation
Type of Packaging: Bulk
Brands:
Nature Made
Nature's Resources

9999 **Pharmco Aaper**
58 Vale Rd
Brookfield, CT 06804-3984
203-740-3471
Fax: 203-740-3481 www.pharmcoaaper.com
Ethanol, solvents & custom sterile blends
President: Paul Demarco
paul@pharmco-prod.com
Manager of Domestic Sales: Amanda Cedeno
Number Employees: 50-99
Parent Co: GreenField

10000 **Phat Fudge**
578 Washington Blvd
Marina del Rey, CA 90292
www.phatfudge.com
Performance food
Founder/CEO: Mary Shenouda
Year Founded: 2016

10001 **Pheasant Ridge Winery**
3507 E County Road 5700
Lubbock, TX 79403-6962
806-746-6033
Fax: 806-746-6750 billgipson@aol.com
www.pheasantridgewinery.com
Wines
Manager: Bill Blackman
Owner: William Gibson
Estimated Sales: Below $5 Million
Number Employees: 5-9
Brands:
Proprietor's Reserve

10002 **Phenomenal Fudge Inc**
4668 VT Route 74 W
Shoreham, VT 05770-9689
802-897-7300
Fax: 802-897-7300 800-430-5442
info@pfudge.com www.pfudge.com
Fudge
Owner/Fudgemaker: Steve Jackson
Estimated Sales: Less Than $500,000
Number Employees: 1-4

10003 **Philadelphia Baking Company**
2550 Grant Ave
Philadelphia, PA 19114
215-464-4242
Fax: 215-464-5701
Breads
Manager: Rich Toney
Estimated Sales: $25-49.9 Million
Number Employees: 100-249
Parent Co: North East Foods

10004 **Philadelphia Candies Inc**
1546 E State St
Hermitage, PA 16148-1823
724-981-6341
Fax: 724-981-6490 pc@phillyc.com
Confectionery: marshmallow, dietetic, mints, creams, nougats, nuts, fruits and chocolates
President: Spyros Macris
pc@phillyc.com
Vice President: Georgia Macris
Estimated Sales: $1,100,000
Number Employees: 50-99
Type of Packaging: Bulk
Brands:
Loving Bunny

10005 **Philadelphia Cheese Steak**
520 E Hunting Park Ave
Philadelphia, PA 19124-6009
215-423-3333
Fax: 215-423-3131 800-342-9771
marketinginfo@phillycheesesteak.com
www.phillycheesesteak.com
Cheese and chicken steaks
President & CEO: John Karamatsoukas
Director of Quality Control: Caitlin Anderson
Year Founded: 1981
Estimated Sales: Less Than $500,000
Number Employees: 1-4
Parent Co: Tyson Foods
Type of Packaging: Consumer, Food Service
Brands:
Philadelphia Cheese Steak

10006 **Philadelphia Macaroni Co**
760 S 11th St
Philadelphia, PA 19147-2614
215-923-3141
Fax: 215-925-4298 www.philamacaroni.com
Pasta and noodles.
Director of Sales/Marketing: Joe Viviano
EVP Sales: Bill Stabert
Customer Service: Fran Pickel
Estimated Sales: $20-50 Million
Number Employees: 10-19
Type of Packaging: Food Service, Private Label, Bulk

10007 **Philip R's Frozen Desserts**
750 Main Street
Winchester, MA 01890
781-721-6330
Fax: 781-721-4590
philipjr@icecream-desserts.com
www.icecream-desserts.com
Ice Cream
President: Phil Rotundo
Estimated Sales: $770,000
Number Employees: 10

10008 **Philip Togni Vineyard**
3780 Spring Mountain Rd
St Helena, CA 94574-9580
707-963-3731
Fax: 707-963-9186 tognivyd@wildblue.net
www.philiptognivineyard.com
Cabernet wine
Owner: Philip Togni
tognivyd@wildblue.net
Partner: Birgitta Togni
Partner/Winemaker: Lisa Togni
Estimated Sales: $500,000-$1 Million
Number Employees: 1-4
Brands:
Philip Togni

10009 **Phillip's Candy House**
818 William T Morrissey Blvd
Dorchester, MA 02122-3404
617-282-2090
Fax: 617-288-4280 info@phillipschocolate.com
www.phillipschocolate.com
Candy
Owner: Maryann Nagle
Estimated Sales: $2,600,000
Number Employees: 10-19
Type of Packaging: Consumer, Private Label

10010 **Phillips Beverage Company**
500 Washington Ave South
Suite 1000
Minneapolis, MN 55415
612-362-7500
Fax: 612-362-7501 www.phillipsdistilling.com
Cordials and liqueurs
President: Dean Phillips
CEO: Edward Phillips
Estimated Sales: $10-20 Million
Number Employees: 6
Type of Packaging: Consumer, Food Service

10011 **Phillips Candies**
217 Broadway St
Seaside, OR 97138-5805
503-738-5402
Fax: 503-738-8326 candy@seasurf.net
www.phillipscandies.com
Saltwater taffy, chocolates and fudge
President: Steven C Phillips
Estimated Sales: $1-2.5 000,000
Number Employees: 10-19
Brands:
Phillips Candies

10012 **Phillips Foods**
3761 Commerce Dr
Suite 413
Baltimore, MD 21227
888-234-2722
comments@phillipsfoods.com
www.phillipsfoods.com
Seafood
President & CEO: Steve Phillips
Senior Vice President: John Knorr
Director, Global Quality Control: Bobby Love
Vice President Sales: Scott Miller
Controller: Bob Banks
bbanks@phillipsfoods.com
Director, Restaurant Operations: Larry McAllister
Logistics Manager: Dave Ehly
Year Founded: 1914
Estimated Sales: $47.2 Million
Number Employees: 223
Square Footage: 270000
Type of Packaging: Consumer, Food Service, Bulk
Brands:
Phillips

10013 **Phillips Gourmet Inc**
1011 Kaolin Rd
PO Box 190
Kennett Square, PA 19348-2605
610-925-0520
Fax: 610-925-0527 info@phillipsgourmet.com
www.phillipsmushroomfarms.com
Mushrooms
President: Marshall Phillips
marshall@phillipsgourmet.com
Number Employees: 100-249
Parent Co: Phillips Mushroom Farms
Type of Packaging: Consumer, Food Service
Brands:
Bella

10014 **Phillips Seafood**
1418 Sapelo Ave NE
Townsend, GA 31331-5732
912-832-4423
Fax: 912-832-6228 www.sapeloseafarms.com
Seafood
President: Myron Phillips
Number Employees: 1-4

10015 **Phillips Syrup Corp**
28025 Ranney Pkwy
Cleveland, OH 44145-1159
440-835-8001
Fax: 440-835-1148 800-350-8443
info@PhillipsSyrup.com www.phillipssyrup.com
Chocolate, sugar-free, sno-cone, slush and maple syrups, sundae toppings, fountain drinks, bar mixes and concentrates
President: Maggie Gillanders
m.gillanders@phillipssyrup.com
Public Relations: Raisa Hawal
Production/Plant Manager: Joseph Mazak
Purchasing Manager: Susan Connerton
Estimated Sales: $7000000
Number Employees: 10-19
Number of Products: 200
Square Footage: 60000
Type of Packaging: Food Service, Private Label
Brands:
Fundae
Phillips

10016 **Phin & Phebes**
Brooklyn, NY
718-383-4300
yum@phinandphebes.com
Ice cream
Co-Founder: Jess Eddy
Co-Founder: Crista Freeman

10017 **Phipps Desserts**
1875 Leslie St
Unit 21
North York, ON M3B 2M5
Canada
416-391-5800
Fax: 416-391-0182 www.phippsdesserts.com
Desserts and pastries
Proprietor: Janet Schriber
Estimated Sales: $205,000
Number Employees: 3
Type of Packaging: Consumer, Food Service
Brands:
Phipps

10018 **Phivida Organics**
600 B Street
Level 3
San Diego, CA 92101
844-744-6646
enquiries@feeloki.com feeloki.com
Hemp-infused water, and hemp oil and capsules
CEO: James Bailey

10019 **Phoenicia Patisserie**
PO Box 13128
Arlington, TX 76094-0128
817-261-2898
Fax: 817-274-3942
Pastries
Owner: Amer Hamedi

10020 **Phoenician Herbals**
P.O.Box 28381
Scottsdale, AZ 85255
480-368-8144
Fax: 480-368-2912 800-966-8144
Vitamins, supplements and teas
Owner: Redgie Hansen
Estimated Sales: $440,000
Number Employees: 5-9
Brands:
Phoenician Herbals

10021 **Phoenix Agro-IndustrialCorporation**
521 Lowell St
Westbury, NY 11590
516-334-1194
Fax: 516-338-8647
Frozen foods and groceries
President: Tomipor Pasto
Marketing: Julianna Edlyn
Purchasing Director: Neone Din
Estimated Sales: $3-5 Million
Number Employees: 5-9
Square Footage: 40000
Type of Packaging: Consumer, Private Label, Bulk
Brands:
Citizen Foods

10022 **Phoenix Foods**
1030 Reserve Dr
Canton, TX 75103-4947
903-287-9166
food@phoenixfoodco.com
phoenixfoodco.com
Dry mixes for soups, desserts and dips
Founder: Kenneth Johnsen
kjohnsen@homemadegourmet.com
Number Employees: 100-249
Brands:
Homemade Gourmet
Just In Time
Modern Pantry

10023 **Phoenix Laboratories**
200 Adams Boulevard
Farmingdale, NY 11735-6615
516-822-1230
Fax: 516-822-1252 800-236-6583
Vitamins
President: Mel Rich
VP: Steven Stern
Contact: Cynthia Marshall
cmarshall@phoenixlaboratories.com
Number Employees: 50-99

10024 **Phranil Foods**
3900 E Main Avenue
Spokane, WA 99202-4737
509-534-7770
Fax: 509-534-4244
Pies
Owner: Fran Bessermin
Controller: Bob Clements
Estimated Sales: $1-2.5 000,000
Number Employees: 20-49

10025 **Phyter Foods**
245 W Roosevelt Rd
Bldg 14-143
West Chicago, IL 60185
630-206-3701
phyterfood.com
Organic plant-based snack bars
Owner and Partner: Gloria Athanis
Chef, Owner and Partner: David Choi
Owner and Partner: Jeff Adeszko

10026 **Phyto-Technologies**
107 Enterprise Dr
Woodbine, IA 51579
712-647-2755
Fax: 712-647-2885 877-809-3404
extracts@phyto-tech.com www.phyto-tech.com
Nutritional and herbal supplements, extracts and blends
Founder/President: Albert Leung
albert.leung@photo-tech.com
Sales/Marketing: Terry Jinks
Estimated Sales: Below $5 Million
Number Employees: 10-19
Square Footage: 80000
Parent Co: Earth Power
Type of Packaging: Consumer, Private Label
Brands:
Earth Power's All American
Earthpower's Phytochi

10027 **Phytotherapy Research Laboratory**
W Fourth S
PO Box 627
Lobelville, TN 37097-0627
931-593-3780
Fax: 931-593-3782 800-274-3727
Herb extracts
President: Brent Davis
Estimated Sales: $500,000-$1 Million
Number Employees: 1-4
Square Footage: 50000
Type of Packaging: Private Label
Brands:
Forest Center
Hahg
Prl

10028 **(HQ)Piantedosi Baking Co Inc**
240 Commercial St
Malden, MA 02148-6709
781-321-3400
Fax: 781-324-5647 800-339-0080
www.piantedosi.com
Bread
President: Michelle Dalton
michelle.dalton@nttdata.com
Executive Vice President & Co-Owner: Joe Piantedosi
Number Employees: 100-249
Type of Packaging: Consumer, Food Service, Private Label, Bulk
Other Locations:
Piantedosi Baking Co.
Malden MA
Brands:
Piantedosi

10029 **Piazza's Seafood World LLC**
205 James Dr W
St Rose, LA 70087-4036
504-602-5050
Fax: 504-602-1555 info@cajunboy.net
www.cajunboy.net
crawfish, alligator, catfish, shrimp, squid, crabmeat and softshell crabs
Manager: Jennifer Champagne
CFO: Mike Sabolyk
Manager: Jarrod Champagne
jarrod@cajunboy.net
Estimated Sales: $5-10 Million
Number Employees: 10-19
Number of Products: 20
Type of Packaging: Food Service, Private Label
Brands:
Cajun Boy

10030 **Picaflor**
4745 Walnut St
Suite D
Boulder, CO 80301
720-442-3816
aaron@picaflor.co
www.picaflor.co
Pepper sauces and flakes
Chef and Farmer: Marcus McCauley
Year Founded: 2015

10031 **(HQ)Picard Peanuts**
447 Dundas Street E
Waterdown, ON L0R 2H1
Canada
905-690-1888
Fax: 519-426-0571 888-244-7688
www.picardpeanuts.com
Potato chip covered peanuts
President: James Picard Sr
CFO: John Picard
R & D: Lincoln Reid
CFO: John David
Quality Control: Michael Newsome
Estimated Sales: $3.8 Million
Number Employees: 23
Square Footage: 128000
Type of Packaging: Consumer, Bulk
Other Locations:
Picard Peanuts Ltd.
Waterford ON
Brands:
Chipnuts

10032 Pickle Cottage
12989 Windy Road
Bucklin, KS 67834-8807
316-826-3502
Fax: 316-826-3866
Snack foods and pickles
President: Barry Stimpert
Estimated Sales: $500,000-$1 000,000
Number Employees: 10-19

10033 Pickled Pink
6649 Peachtree Industrial Blvd
Suite G
Norcross, GA 30092
770-998-1500
jim@pickledpinkfoods.com
pickledpinkfoods.com
Pickled fruits and vegetables
Contact: Jim Lawlor

10034 Pickled Planet
225 Water St
Ashland, OR 97520
541-201-2689
pickledplanet@gmail.com
pickledplanet.com
Organic fermented vegetables
Founder: Courtlandt Jennings

10035 Picklesmith Inc
300 Green Ave
Taft, TX 78390-2708
361-528-4953
Fax: 830-885-4560 800-499-3401
Pickles and olives
President: David Smith
Estimated Sales: $1-3 Million
Number Employees: 1-4
Square Footage: 10000
Type of Packaging: Consumer, Food Service
Brands:
A.P. Smith Canning Co.
Picklesmith

10036 Pickwick Catfish Farm
4155 Highway 57
Counce, TN 38326
731-689-3805
Smoked catfish
Owner: Betty Knussmann
Co-Owner: Quentin Knussman
Estimated Sales: Less than $500,000
Number Employees: 5-9
Brands:
Pickwick Catfish

10037 Picnik
Austin, TX
picnikaustin@gmail.com
picnikaustin.com
Butter coffee
Founder & CEO: Naomi Seifter
Co-Founder: Kevin Ward

10038 Pictsweet Co
10 Pictsweet Dr
Bells, TN 38006-4274
731-663-7600
Fax: 731-663-7639 mailbox@pictsweet.com
www.pictsweet.com
Asparagus, beans, broccoli, brussels sprouts, carrots, cauliflower, turnip, mustard and collard greens, okra, peas, spinach, squash, succotash
President: Billy Ennis
Chairman/Ceo: James Tankersley
jtankersley@pictsweet.com
Marketing Director: Julia Wells
Director Manufacturing: Frank Tankersley
Estimated Sales: $10-20 Million
Number Employees: 500-999
Number of Products: 100
Parent Co: Pictsweet
Type of Packaging: Consumer, Food Service, Private Label
Brands:
Dulany
Everfresh
Pictsweet
Prime Froz-N
Tennessee
Winter Garden

10039 Pidy Gourmet Pastry Shells
90 Inip Dr
Inwood, NY 11096-1011
516-239-6057
Fax: 516-239-9306 www.pidy.com
Tart shells, chocolate, desserts
CEO: Jerome Haussoullier
Parent Co: Biscuits Bouvard
Type of Packaging: Consumer, Food Service
Brands:
Aperi-Coeur
Aperiquiche
Barquette
Crescentgarniture
Croustade 4cm
Croustade 5cm
Croustade 7cm
Escarcoque
Fishka
Fleurette
Gaurmande
Mignardise
Mini-Croustade
Mini-Croustade Shell
Mini-Easre
Mini-Roulet
Mint Shell
Puff Pastry Tartlet
Quiche
Roulet
Zakouski

10040 Pie Piper Products
654 South Wheeling Road
Wheeling, IL 60090
847-459-3600
Fax: 630-595-1551 800-621-8183
www.distinctivefoods.com
Cheesecakes, brownies, quiche and beef frankfurters
President: Josh Harris
joshh@distinctivefoods.com
Chief Financial Officer: Ron Buck
Vice President: Daniel Mager
Quality Control: Jay Trujillo
Marketing/Sales/Public Relations: Stephanie Jacobs
Engineer: Jim Howard
Production Manager: Mike Lopardo
Purchasing: Araeeli Ocampo
Estimated Sales: $10-20 Million
Number Employees: 40
Square Footage: 32000
Parent Co: Vienna Manufacturing Company
Type of Packaging: Consumer, Food Service, Private Label
Brands:
Pie Piper
Vienna Bageldog
Wunderbar

10041 Pied-Mont/Dora
176 Saint-Joseph
Anne Des Plaines, QC J0N 1H0
Canada
450-478-0801
Fax: 450-478-6381 800-363-8003
info@piedmontdora.com www.piedmontdora.com
Vegetable and fruit dips, jams, jellies and marmalades; chocolate spreads, pie fillings, syrups and drink crystals
President/Board Member: Louis Limoges
Marketing: Justin Bart
Estimated Sales: $6.9 Million
Number Employees: 40
Brands:
Bensons
Clancy
Dora
Mondial
Pied-Mont

10042 Piedmont Candy Co
404 Market St
PO Box 1722
Lexington, NC 27292-1293
336-248-2477
Fax: 336-248-5841
customerservice@piedmontcandy.com
www.piedmontcandy.com
Candy
President: Kelly Dunn
kellydunn@piedmontcandy.com
VP: Chris Reid
Estimated Sales: $2,556,054
Number Employees: 50-99
Type of Packaging: Consumer

10043 Piedmont Vineyards & Winery
PO Box 286
Middleburg, VA 20118
540-687-5528
Fax: 540-687-5777
Wines
President: Gerhard Von Finck
Estimated Sales: Below $5 Million
Number Employees: 5-9
Type of Packaging: Private Label
Brands:
Piedmont

10044 Piedra Creek Winery
6425 Mira Cielo
San Luis Obispo, CA 93401-8395
805-541-1281
Fax: 805-782-0648 www.piedracreek.com
Wines
Co-Owner: Margaret Zuech
Owner/Winemaker: Romeo Zuech
info@piedracreek.com
Estimated Sales: Less Than $500,000
Number Employees: 1-4
Brands:
Piedra Creek Winery

10045 Piemonte Bakery Co
1122 Rock St
Rockford, IL 61101-1431
815-962-4833
Bread, dinner rolls and po-boys
Owner: Steve McKebebaer
Secretary: Irene McKeever
Estimated Sales: $2,600,000
Number Employees: 10-19
Type of Packaging: Private Label
Brands:
Piemonte

10046 Pierceton Foods Inc
127 N First St
Pierceton, IN 46562-9336
574-594-2344
Fax: 574-594-2344
Porkfritters, cheeseburgers, steaks, beef and tender loins
President: Jerry Wagoner
Plant Manager: Ben Bunyan
Estimated Sales: $1,040,000
Number Employees: 5-9
Number of Brands: 1
Square Footage: 12000
Type of Packaging: Food Service
Brands:
Paul's

10047 Pierino Frozen Foods
1695 Southfield Rd
Lincoln Park, MI 48146-2275
313-928-0950
Fax: 313-928-5410 info@pierinofrozenfoods.com
www.pierinofrozenfoods.com
Pasta, sauce and gnocchi
Founder: Pierino Guglielmetti
Operations Manager: Gianni Guglielmetti
Plant Manager: Silvana Gugliemetti
Estimated Sales: $1 Million
Number Employees: 20-49

10048 Pierre's French Bakery
PO Box 14280
Portland, OR 97293-0280
503-233-8871
Fax: 503-233-5060
Bakery products
President: Larry McDonald
Estimated Sales: $1-2 000,000
Number Employees: 50

10049 Pierre's French Ice Cream Inc
6200 Euclid Ave
Cleveland, OH 44103-3724
216-432-1144
Fax: 216-432-0001 800-837-7342
icecream@pierres.com www.pierres.com
Ice cream, yogurt, sherbet, sorbet and smoothies
President: Shelly Roth
sroth@pierres.com
Director Marketing: Laura Hindulak
Operations: John Pimpo

Year Founded: 1932
Estimated Sales: $20-50 Million
Number Employees: 100-249
Number of Products: 235
Square Footage: 30000
Type of Packaging: Consumer
Brands:
Pierre's

10050 Pierz Cooperative Association
315 Edward St S
Pierz, MN 56364
320-468-6655
Fax: 320-468-2773 www.pierzcoop.com
Animal feed
Manager: Randy Sullivan
Estimated Sales: $9,032,630
Number Employees: 10-19
Brands:
Farmer Seed

10051 (HQ)Piggie Park Enterprises
1600 Charleston Hwy
West Columbia, SC 29169-5050
803-791-5887
Fax: 803-791-8707 800-628-7423
mail@piggiepark.com www.piggiepark.com
Barbecue sauce and meat
President: Maurice Bessinger
mbessinger@piggie.com
Estimated Sales: $4.3 Million
Number Employees: 20-49
Type of Packaging: Consumer, Food Service, Bulk
Brands:
Maurice's

10052 Pike Brewing Co
1415 1st Ave
Seattle, WA 98101-2017
206-622-6044
Fax: 206-622-8730 info@mdv-beer.com
www.pikebrewing.com
Beer, ale, stout and porter
Owner: Rosann Finkel
rfinkel@pikebrewing.com
General manager: Kim Brusco
Director Manufacturing: Allen Fal
Estimated Sales: $2.5-5 Million
Number Employees: 50-99
Brands:
Pike

10053 Pikes Peak Vineyards
3901 Jenitell Road
Colorado Springs, CO 80917-5351
719-576-0075
Fax: 719-226-0639
Wine
President: Bruce McClaughlin
Vice President: Taffy McCloughlen
General Manager: Frankie Tuft
Estimated Sales: Less than $300,000
Number Employees: 1-4
Brands:
Pikes Peak Vineyards

10054 Piknik Products Company
3806 Day Street
P.O. Box 9388
Montgomery, AL 36108-1720
334-240-2218
Fax: 334-265-9490
Mayonnaise, mustard and salad dressing
President: Herman Loeb
Estimated Sales: $29 Million
Number Employees: 205
Type of Packaging: Consumer, Food Service, Private Label
Brands:
Ol' South
Piknik
Salad Queen
Stewart's

10055 Pilgrim Foods
98 Cuttermill Rd
Suite 260S
Great Neck, NY 11021-3036
516-466-0522
Fax: 516-466-0762
CustService@Olddutchmustard.com
Juice, vinegar, mustard
President: Mycala Blanchard
mblanchard@pilgrimfoods.net
Estimated Sales: $5-10 Million
Number Employees: 1-4
Type of Packaging: Bulk

10056 Pilgrim's Pride Corp.
1770 Promontory Cir.
Greeley, CO 80634
970-506-8000
www.pilgrims.com
Chicken.
Global CEO: Jayson Penn
Year Founded: 1946
Estimated Sales: $10 Billion
Number Employees: 35,700
Number of Brands: 11
Parent Co: JBS S.A.
Type of Packaging: Consumer, Food Service, Private Label, Bulk
Other Locations:
WLR Foods
Broadway VA
Brands:
Pilgrim's
Pierce Chicken
Gold Kist Farms
Country Pride
Savoro
Just BARE Chicken
Gold'n Plump
Moy Park
Del Dia
O'Kane
To-Rico's

10057 Piller Sausages & Delicatessens
443 Wismer Street
Waterloo, ON N2K 2K6
Canada
519-743-1412
Fax: 519-743-7111 800-265-2628
www.pillers.com
Sausage and processed meats
President: William Huber, Jr.
Number Employees: 100-249
Type of Packaging: Consumer, Food Service, Private Label, Bulk

10058 Piller's Fine Foods
443 Wismer Street
Waterloo, ON N2K 2K6
Canada
519-743-1412
800-265-2627
www.pillers.com
Pork, beef, poultry, chubs and sticks, hot dogs and franks, luncheon meat, sausages, pate and coils
CEO: Willy Huber
VP of Innovation & Business Development: Gerhart Huber
VP of Sales & Marketing: Sean Moriarty
Number Employees: 200
Type of Packaging: Private Label
Brands:
Piller's
Piller's Turkey Bites

10059 (HQ)Pillsbury
PO Box 9452
Minneapolis, MN 55440
800-775-4777
Fax: 763-764-8330
consumer.services-pillsburycs@genmills.com
www.pillsbury.com
Bakery mixes and cake flour
General Manager: Alan Rodrigues
Mix Plant Manager: Ray Beckman
Number Employees: 100-249
Parent Co: General Mills
Type of Packaging: Consumer, Food Service, Bulk

10060 Pilot Meat & Sea Food Company
405 N Pilot Knob Road
Galena, IL 61036-8803
319-556-0760
Fax: 319-556-4131
Meat and seafood
CEO: Randall Sirk
Accountant: Ted Kipper
Estimated Sales: $1.2 Million
Number Employees: 7

10061 Pindar Vineyards
37645 Main Road
Route 25
Peconic, NY 11958
631-734-6200
Fax: 631-734-6205 info@Pindar.net
www.pindar.net
Wines
Owner: Herodotus Damianos
Chief Executive Officer: Kathy Krejci
Sales Manager: Steve Ciuffo
Estimated Sales: $5-10 Million
Number Employees: 20-49
Brands:
Spring Splendor
Summer Blush

10062 Pine Point Seafood
350 Pine Point Rd
Scarborough, ME 04074-9236
207-883-4701
Fax: 207-883-4797 www.maine-lobster.com
Lobster, lobster tails, clams and steaks
President: B Michael Thurlow
Estimated Sales: $1-3 Million
Number Employees: 5-9

10063 Pine Ridge Vineyards
5901 Silverado Trail
Napa, CA 94558-9417
707-252-9777
Fax: 707-253-1493 800-575-9777
info@pineridgewine.com
www.pineridgevineyards.com
Wines
President & CEO: Erle Martin
Vineyard Manager: Gustavo Avina
General Manager/Winemaker: Michael Beaulac
Assistant Winemaker: Michael Conversano
Enologist: Colleen Fitzgerald
Year Founded: 1978
Estimated Sales: $20-50 Million
Number Employees: 50-99
Brands:
Pine Ridge Winery

10064 Pine River Cheese & Butter Company
RR 4
Ripley, ON N0G 2R0
Canada
519-395-2638
Fax: 519-395-4066 800-265-1175
info@pineriverchesse.com
www.pineriverchesse.com
Cheese
President: Ian Courtney
Number Employees: 30
Square Footage: 96000
Type of Packaging: Consumer, Bulk

10065 Pine River Pre-Pack Inc
10134 Pine River Rd
Newton, WI 53063-9613
920-726-4216
Cheese and cheese spreads, chocolate confections
CEO: Philip Lindemann
Marketing Associate: Mary Lindenann
Contact: Ian Behm
ian@pineriver.com
Estimated Sales: $3004699
Number Employees: 10-19
Square Footage: 94800
Type of Packaging: Consumer, Private Label
Brands:
Pine River

10066 Pineland Farms
15 Farm View Drive
New Gloucester, ME 04260
207-688-4539
Fax: 207-688-4531 www.pinelandfarms.org
Salsa, dips, cheese, spreads and syrup
Principal: Sarah Hunt
Marketing: Neal Kolterman
Contact: Matt Anderson
manderson@pinelandfarms.com
Estimated Sales: $69,000
Number Employees: 51-200

10067 **Pines International**
1992 E 1400 Rd
Lawrence, KS 66044-9303
785-841-6016
Fax: 785-841-1252 800-697-4637
pines@wheatgrass.com www.wheatgrass.com
Grass: wheat, barley, rye and oat; powders and tablets; alfalfa
President: Ron Seibold
rseibold@wheatgrass.com
CEO: Steve Malone
Sales/Marketing: Allen Levine
Purchasing Director: Jeff Richards
Year Founded: 1976
Estimated Sales: $3,635,158
Number Employees: 20-49
Square Footage: 160000
Type of Packaging: Consumer, Private Label, Bulk
Brands:
Mighty Greens
Pines

10068 **Pino's Pasta Veloce**
1903 Clove Road
Staten Island, NY 10304-1607
718-273-6660
Fax: 718-720-5906
Pasta sauce, pasta heaters
Manager Marketing: Joe Klaus
VP Operations: Al Cappillo
Estimated Sales: $2.5-5,000,000
Number Employees: 1-4
Parent Co: AEI
Type of Packaging: Consumer, Food Service
Brands:
Pino's Pasta Veloce

10069 **Pinocchio Italian Ice Cream Company**
12814 163 Street NW
Edmonton, AB T5V 1K6
Canada
780-455-1905
Fax: 780-455-1906
Ice cream and sorbets
President: Salvatore Ursino
VP: Tom Ursino
Number Employees: 1-4
Type of Packaging: Consumer, Food Service
Brands:
Pinocchio

10070 **Pinter's Packing Plant**
193 S Front St
Dorchester, WI 54425-9559
715-654-5444
Fax: 715-654-5522 www.pinterspackingplant.com
Steak, roast, sausage and buffalo
Owner: Al Pinter
Estimated Sales: $180000
Number Employees: 10-19
Square Footage: 25600
Type of Packaging: Consumer

10071 **Pinty's Premium Foods**
5063 North Service Rd
Burlington, ON L7L 5H6
Canada
905-319-5300
Fax: 905-688-1222 800-263-7223
Retailsales@pintys.com www.pintys.com
Chicken fryers, nuggets, burgers, meat balls, wings, breasts; pierogies and pizza fingers
Chairman: Fred Williamson
Vice-Chairman: Ken Thorpe
Director: Randy Kane
VP Marketing: Jon Pintwala
Sales Manager: W Greer
Estimated Sales: $4.8 Million
Number Employees: 49
Type of Packaging: Consumer, Food Service
Brands:
Pinty's

10072 **Pintys Delicious Foods**
5063 North Service Road
Suite 101
Burlington, ON L7L 5H6
Canada
905-835-8575
Fax: 905-834-5093 800-263-9710
humanresources@pintys.com www.pintys.com
Poultry
President/Owner: Phil Kudelka
CEO: Aba Vanderlaan
CFO: Patricia Bowman
VP Operations: Jack Vanderlaan
Sales: Greg Fox
General Manager: Doug Bowman
Number Employees: 100-249
Square Footage: 360000
Type of Packaging: Food Service, Bulk
Brands:
Pintys Delicious Foods

10073 **Pioneer Dairy**
214 Feeding Hills Rd
Southwick, MA 01077
413-569-6132
Fax: 413-569-3762
Milk, cream, and ice cream
President: A Colson
Vice President: Paul Colson
Estimated Sales: $5-10 000,000
Number Employees: 30
Number of Brands: 2
Type of Packaging: Food Service, Private Label, Bulk
Brands:
Meadowbrook Creamery
Pioneer Dairy

10074 **Pioneer Foods Industries**
P.O. Box 1248
Stuttgart, AR 72160
870-673-4444
Fax: 870-355-2507 www.producersrice.com
Soups
President/CEO: Keith Glover
Executive Assistant: Lana Flowers
VP, Finance and Administration: Kent Lockwood
Vice President Marketing: Gary Reifeiss
Senior VP, Rice Sales and Marketing: Marvin Baden
Vice President of Operations: Kenny Dryden
Estimated Sales: Under $500,000
Number Employees: 10-19

10075 **Pioneer Frozen Foods**
627 Big Stone Gap Rd
Duncanville, TX 75137
972-298-4281
www.chg.com
Biscuits
President & CEO: Dale Tremblay
SVP & CFO: Justin Grubbs
SVP & COO: Eric Stockl
Estimated Sales: $92 Million
Number Employees: 100-249
Number of Brands: 1
Parent Co: C.H Guenther & Son, Inc.
Brands:
Pioneer

10076 **Pioneer Growers**
227 NW Avenue L
Belle Glade, FL 33430-1935
229-243-9306
Fax: 561-996-5703 www.pioneergrowers.com
Chinese cabbage, carrots, celery, corn and radishes
Vice President, General Manager: Gene Duff
Vice President of Quality Assurance: James Jacks
Sales/ Marketing: Jon Browder
Sales Exec: J D Poole
Number Employees: 20-49
Type of Packaging: Consumer, Bulk
Brands:
Frontier
Team
Well's Ace

10077 **Pioneer Live Shrimp**
2801 Meyers Road
Oak Brook, IL 60523-1623
630-789-1133
Fax: 312-226-7376
Shrimp
President: David Wong
VP: Chun Wah
Secretary: Esther Wong
Estimated Sales: $2.8 Million
Number Employees: 14
Square Footage: 56000

10078 **Pioneer Marketing International**
188 Westhill Drive
Los Gatos, CA 95032-5032
408-356-4990
Fax: 408-356-2795 www.pioneer.com
Corn, soybeans, alfalfa, canola, wheat, sunflowers; marketing, sales and product promotion
Partner: Russ Tritomo
Director Sales: Ed DeSoto
Estimated Sales: $1-5 Million
Number Employees: 4
Brands:
Pioneer(c)
Encirca(c)
Nutrivail

10079 **Pioneer Nutritional Formula**
304 Shelburne Center Rd
Shelburne Falls, MA 01370-9779
413-625-8627
Fax: 413-625-9619 800-458-8483
customerservice@pioneernutritional.com
www.pioneernutritional.com
Nutritional supplements
Manager: Sara Rowan
CEO: Jim Lemkin
Manager: Sarah Rhone
Estimated Sales: Less Than $500,000
Number Employees: 5-9
Number of Brands: 1
Number of Products: 23
Brands:
Pioneer

10080 **Pioneer Packing Co**
510 Napoleon Rd
PO Box 171
Bowling Green, OH 43402-4821
419-352-5283
Fax: 419-352-7330 wcontris@aol.com
www.pioneerpacking.com
Bacon, smoked meats and pork sausage
President: Jason Blower
jasonb@pioneersantaana.net
Estimated Sales: $5 Million
Number Employees: 20-49
Square Footage: 150000
Type of Packaging: Consumer, Bulk
Brands:
Amish
Country
Pioneer

10081 **Pioneer Snacks**
30777 Northwestern Highway
Suite 300
Farmington Hills, MI 48334-2594
248-862-1990
Fax: 248-862-1991
Meat sticks, beef jerky, sausage, beef steak, meat & cheese and turkey jerky
Marketing Manager: Craig Thomas
Type of Packaging: Consumer
Brands:
Hog Wild Pork Jerky

10082 **Piper & Leaf**
2211 Seminole Dr SW
Suite 151
Huntsville, AL 35805
256-929-9404
info@piperandleaf.com
piperandleaf.com
Teas and tisanes.
Owner: Caleb Christopher

10083 **Piper Meat Processing**
430 N Main St
Andover, OH 44003-9665
440-293-7170
Beef and pork
Owner: Terry Orahood
Estimated Sales: Less Than $500,000
Number Employees: 1-4
Type of Packaging: Consumer, Bulk

10084 **Pippin Snack Pecans**
1332 Old Pretoria Rd
PO Box 3330
Albany, GA 31721-8696
229-432-9316
Fax: 229-435-0056 800-554-6887
treypippen@gmail.com
Pecans

Manager: Trey Pippin
Estimated Sales: $7 Million
Number Employees: 50
Square Footage: 80000
Type of Packaging: Consumer, Food Service, Private Label, Bulk
Brands:
Pippin Snack

10085 Pipsnacks
1580 Park Ave
Suite 2
New York, NY 10029-1802
973-723-4246
pipsnacks.com
Popcorn
Co-Founder: Jen Martin
Brands:
Pipcorn

10086 Piqua Pizza Supply Co Inc
1727 W High St
Piqua, OH 45356-9325
937-773-0699
Fax: 937-773-6096 800-521-4442
www.piquapizza.net
Pizza crust
President: Paul Creager
ppsi-paulc@onecalmmail.com
Production Manager: Tom Fahestrock
Estimated Sales: $10-20 Million
Number Employees: 20-49
Type of Packaging: Consumer, Food Service, Private Label, Bulk
Brands:
Diana's

10087 Pita King Bakery
2210 37th St
Everett, WA 98201-4509
425-258-4040
Fax: 425-258-3366
Pita bread
President: Hauss Alaeddine
j_alaeddine@hotmail.com
CEO: Jason Aladdine
Number Employees: 10-19
Square Footage: 40000
Brands:
Pita Products
PitaSnax

10088 Pita Pal
3100 Canal St
Houston, TX 77003-1602
713-777-7482
comments@pitapal.com
www.pitapal.com
Hummus, salsa, salads, falafels
Contact: James Grimes
jgrimes@pitapal.com
Estimated Sales: Less Than $500,000
Number Employees: 5-9

10089 Pita Products
30777 Northwestern Highway
Suite 3200
Farmington Hills, MI 48334-2549
734-367-2700
Fax: 734-367-2701 800-600-7482
Pita chips
Type of Packaging: Consumer

10090 Pitbull Energy Products
20600 Belshaw Ave
Carson, CA 90746-3508
310-604-9100
Fax: 818-686-6009 800-686-3697
Energy drinks
President/CEO: Mr Roscoe
Contact: Tamara Clark
tclark@hiphopbev.com
Number Employees: 5-9
Brands:
Pit Bull

10091 Pittsburgh Brewing Co
3340 Liberty Ave
Pittsburgh, PA 15201-1394
412-682-7400
Fax: 412-682-2379 www.pittsburghbrewing.com
Beer
President/CEO: Eddie Lozano
CEO: Brian G Walsh
bwalsh@pittsburghbrewingco.com
Director of Sales & Marketing: David Sykes
Operations Manager: Melissa O'Dell
Brew master: Michael Carota
Plant Manager: Bill St Leger
Estimated Sales: $13 Million
Number Employees: 100-249
Square Footage: 27000
Parent Co: ICB Holdings, LLC
Type of Packaging: Consumer
Brands:
IC Light Mango
Iron City
Iron City Light

10092 Pittsfield Rye Bakery
1010 South St
Pittsfield, MA 01201-8225
413-443-9141
Fax: 413-499-5331 info@pittsfieldrye.com
www.pittsfieldrye.com
Bread and rolls
President: Arnold Robbins
Owner: Rick Robbins
Estimated Sales: $5-10 Million
Number Employees: 10-19

10093 Piveg, Inc.
11760 Sorrento Valley Rd
Suite L
San Diego, CA 92121
858-688-3070
Fax: 858-436-3071 ruben.angulo@piveg.com
www.piveg.com
Mexican chili flavors, powders and flakes, mole paste blends, lutein esters, zeaxanthin, beta carotene
President: Roberto Espinoza
Estimated Sales: $12 Million
Number Employees: 220
Type of Packaging: Private Label, Bulk

10094 Pizza Products
38300 W 10 Mile Road
Farmington Hills, MI 48335-2804
248-474-1601
Fax: 248-474-1608 800-600-7482
www.pizzahut.com
Pizza
Manager: Dave Sabol
Marketing Director: Norman Wainwright
Estimated Sales: Below $5 Million
Number Employees: 1-4

10095 Pizzey's Milling & Baking Company
121 4th Ave. S.
Twin Falls, ID 83301
Canada
208-733-7555
Fax: 204-773-2317 www.glanbiafoods.com
Flaxseed
President: Linda Pizzey
Vice President: Glenn Pizzey
Vice President of Business Development: Dave Snyder
Business Development Manager: Shawn Harrison
Estimated Sales: $10-20 Million
Number Employees: 20-49
Square Footage: 80000
Parent Co: Glanbia Nutritionals
Type of Packaging: Consumer, Food Service, Private Label, Bulk

10096 Plaidberry Company
830 Mimosa Ave
Vista, CA 92081
760-727-5403
dennisdickson@cs.com
Jams, muffins, pie and cake fillings, juices, confections, yogurt bases
President/Owner: Dennis Dickson
plaidberry@yahoo.com
Estimated Sales: Below 5 Million
Number Employees: 4
Number of Products: 6
Square Footage: 74000
Type of Packaging: Consumer, Bulk

10097 Plainfield Winery & Tasting Rm
6291 Cambridge Way
Plainfield, IN 46168-7905
317-837-9463
Fax: 317-837-8464 888-761-9463
info@chateauthomas.com
www.chateauthomas.com
Wines
President: Charles Thomas
Manager: Sheila Cavanaugh
info@chateuathomas.com
Purchasing Manager: Tommy England
Estimated Sales: $5-10 Million
Number Employees: 20-49
Type of Packaging: Private Label
Brands:
Chateau Thomas

10098 Plains Dairy Products
300 N Taylor St
Amarillo, TX 79107
806-374-0385
800-365-5608
www.plainsdairy.com
Milk, buttermilk, cottage cheese and yogurt
President & CEO: Dub Garlington
Controller: James Wood
Marketing Manager: Michael Holliman
mholliman@plainsdairy.com
Year Founded: 1934
Estimated Sales: $173.2 Million
Number Employees: 100-249
Number of Brands: 2
Brands:
Plains Dairy
Shurfine

10099 (HQ)Plainview Milk Products
130 2nd St SW
Plainview, MN 55964-1394
507-534-3872
Fax: 507-534-3992 800-356-5606
www.plainviewmilk.com
Butter, whey and milk; custom agglomeration and spray drying
General Manager: Dallas Moe
dmoe@plainviewmilk.com
Controller: Janna Van Rooyen
Sales Manager: Darrell Hanson
Plant Manager: Donny Schreiber
Number Employees: 50-99
Square Footage: 18060
Type of Packaging: Consumer, Food Service, Private Label, Bulk
Brands:
Greenwood Prairie

10100 Plainville Farms
304 S Water St
PO Box 38
New Oxford, PA 17350-9688
717-624-2191
Fax: 717-624-5121 800-724-0206
mail@plainvillefarms.com
www.plainvillefarms.com
Turkeys and specialty dishes
Estimated Sales: $20-50 Million
Number Employees: 50-99
Brands:
Heart Liteo
Veggie Growno

10101 Plam Vineyards & Winery
80125 Miramonte Lane
La Quinta, CA 92253
760-972-4465
ken@plam.com
www.plam.com
Wine
Co-Owner: Ken Plam
Co-Owner: Shirley Plam
Estimated Sales: Below $5 Million
Number Employees: 2
Type of Packaging: Private Label
Brands:
Plam Vineyards

10102 Planet Oat
Lynnfield, MA
800-242-2423
planetoat.com
Oat milk
VP, Marketing: Christopher Ross

10103 **Plant Based Foods**
21011 St. Louis Rd.
PO Box 1841
Middleburg, VA 20117
540-687-8432
Fax: 540-687-8434 info@plantbasedfoods.com
www.plantbasedfoods.com
Dip mixes and seasonings
Co-Founder: Matt Webb
Co-Founder: Alecia Webb

10104 **Plantation Candies**
4224 Old Bethlehem Pike
Telford, PA 18969
215-723-6810
Fax: 215-723-6834 888-678-6468
chuck@plantationcandies.com
www.plantationcandies.com
Bulk hard candy
Owner/President: Charles Crawford
chuck@plantationcandies.com
Estimated Sales: $1500000
Number Employees: 5-9
Type of Packaging: Consumer, Food Service, Private Label, Bulk
Brands:
Chocolate Straws
Dainties
Golden Crunchies
Jinglebits
Misty Mints

10105 **Plantation Pecan & GiftCompany**
HC-62 Box 139
Waterproof, LA 71375
318-749-5188
Fax: 318-749-5535 800-477-3226
www.plantationpecan.com
Pecans, pies, pralines and fudges
President: Harrison Miller
Co Owner: Carol Miller
Estimated Sales: Less than $500,000
Number Employees: 1-4
Brands:
Plantation Pecan

10106 **Plantation Products Inc**
202 S Washington St
Norton, MA 02766
508-285-5800
www.plantationproducts.com
Vegetable seeds, seed packets
President & CEO: Michael Pietrasiewicz
Estimated Sales: $50-99.99 Million
Number Employees: 20-49
Number of Brands: 6
Square Footage: 200000
Other Locations:
Warehouse/Distribution
West Bridgewater MA
Livingston Seeds
Columbus OH
International Headquarters
Brandon, Canada MB
Brands:
American Seed(c)
Ferry-Morse(c)
Livingston Seed
McKenzie
NK Lawn & Garden(c)
Jiffy(c)

10107 **Platte Valley Creamery**
1005 E Overland
Scottsbluff, NE 69361-3702
308-632-4225
Ice cream and desserts
President: Ron Smith
Estimated Sales: $1-3 Million
Number Employees: 1-4
Type of Packaging: Consumer

10108 **Plaza House Coffee**
339 Lincoln Avenue
Staten Island, NY 10306-5001
718-979-9555
Fax: 718-667-4394 plazahouse@aol.com
Coffee
President: Salvatore Rosso
Estimated Sales: Less than $500,000
Number Employees: 1-4

10109 **Plaza Sweets Bakery**
521 Waverly Ave
Mamaroneck, NY 10543-2235
914-698-0233
Fax: 914-698-3712 800-816-8416
Cakes
Owner: James Ward
Pres/CEO: Rodney Holden
Manager: Kathy Dumas
Estimated Sales: $5.8 Million
Number Employees: 20-49
Square Footage: 60000
Type of Packaging: Consumer, Food Service
Brands:
Plaza Sweets

10110 **Plaza de Espana Gourmet**
100 Kings Point Drive
Apt 1004
Sunny Isles Beach, FL 33160-4729
305-971-3468
Fax: 305-971-5004
Spanish foods, olive oil, artichokes, asparagus, piquillo peppers, wine and ham
President: Jesus Metias, Sr.
Vice President: Serafina Atalaya
Estimated Sales: $2.5-5 Million
Number Employees: 5-9
Parent Co: Plaza De Espana Gourmet Foods
Type of Packaging: Consumer, Food Service, Private Label, Bulk
Brands:
Cielo Azul
Plaza De Espana
Vega Fina
Vega Metias

10111 **Pleasant Grove Farms**
PO Box 636
Pleasant Grove, CA 95668
916-655-3391
Fax: 916-655-3699 info@pleasantgrovefarms.com
www.pleasantgrovefarms.com
Almonds, wheat, beans, popcorn and rice
President: Thomas Sills
VP Sales: Edward Sills
Estimated Sales: $1,100,000
Number Employees: 5-9
Number of Products: 9
Square Footage: 20000
Parent Co: Sills Farms
Type of Packaging: Bulk

10112 **Pleasant Valley Wine Co**
8260 Pleasant Valley Rd
Hammondsport, NY 14840-9514
607-569-6111
Fax: 607-569-6135 info@pleasantvalleywine.com
www.pleasantvalleywine.com
Wines, champagnes, ports and sherries
President: Michael Doyle
Estimated Sales: $19 Million
Number Employees: 50-99
Square Footage: 1440000
Type of Packaging: Consumer, Food Service, Private Label, Bulk
Brands:
Great Western
Millennium
Pleasant Valley

10113 **Pleasant View Dairy**
2625 Highway Ave
P.O. Box 1949
Highland, IN 46322-1614
219-838-0155
Fax: 219-838-1801
Milk, buttermilk and sour cream
President: Kenneth Leep
kenneth@pleasantviewdairy.com
Estimated Sales: Less than $500,000
Number Employees: 20-49
Square Footage: 160000
Type of Packaging: Consumer

10114 **Pleasoning Gourmet Seasonings**
2418 South Avenue
PO Box 2701
La Crosse, WI 54601
608-787-1030
Fax: 608-787-1030 800-279-1614
pleason@pleasoning.com www.pleasoning.com
Seasoning
President: Paul Boarman
Vice President: Lenore Italiano
Marketing Director: Kathy Boarman
Estimated Sales: $500,000-$1 Million
Number Employees: 1-4
Number of Brands: 1
Number of Products: 30
Square Footage: 12000
Type of Packaging: Consumer, Food Service, Bulk
Brands:
Pleasoning Gourmet Seasoning

10115 **Plehn's Bakery Inc**
3940 Shelbyville Rd
Louisville, KY 40207-3170
502-896-4438
Fax: 502-897-9176 www.plehns.com
Breads, cookies, doughnuts, pastries, pies, cakes and ice cream
President: Nathan Hoy
nhoy@missionit.com
Vice President: Theodore Bowling
Estimated Sales: $1.5 Million
Number Employees: 20-49
Type of Packaging: Consumer

10116 **Plentiful Pantry**
265 West Plymouth Ave
Salt Lake City, UT 84115
801-977-9077
www.plentifulpantry.com
Prepared meals, soups, desserts and hot chocolate.
Co-Founder: Debbie Chidester
Co-Founder: Jody Chidester
Year Founded: 1992

10117 **Plenty**
570 Eccles Ave.
San Francisco, CA 94080
650-735-3737
plenty.ag
Leafy greens including baby arugula, kale, beets, tatsoi, and mizuna.
Founder & CEO: Matt Barnard
Year Founded: 2013
Number Employees: 250-500
Type of Packaging: Private Label

10118 **Plenus Group Inc**
101 Phoenix Ave
Lowell, MA 01852-4930
978-970-3832
Fax: 978-441-2528 info@plenus-group.com
www.pgifoods.com
Soups, sauces, chowders, bisques, seafood appetizers and entrees
President: Joseph Jolly
jhjolly@plenus-group.com
VP/CFO/VP Operations/Production: Jennifer Jolly
Sales Manager/Coordinator: Jamie Crane
Estimated Sales: $10.5 Million
Number Employees: 20-49
Brands:
Boston Chowda Co
East Coast Gourmet

10119 **Plochman Inc**
1333 N Boudreau Rd
Manteno, IL 60950
815-468-3434
800-843-4566
plochman@plochman.com www.plochman.com
Mustards
Estimated Sales: $6.9 Million
Number Employees: 50-99
Type of Packaging: Consumer, Food Service, Private Label, Bulk
Brands:
Kosciusko
Plochman's

10120 **Plocky's Fine Snacks**
15 Spinning Wheel Rd
Suite 314
Hinsdale, IL 60521
630-323-8888
Fax: 630-323-8988 info@plockys.com
www.plockys.com
Tortilla chips, hummus chips, hummus, kettle chips, dip strips, salsa, potato sticks and nut mixes
President: Paul Cipolla
Marketing: Diane Cipolla
Contact: Esther Neal
esther@plockys.com

Estimated Sales: $9.3 Million
Number Employees: 16
Brands:
Nature Star
Ploccy's Apple Chips

10121 Pluester Quality Meat Co
Batchtown Rd
Hardin, IL 62047
618-396-2224
Meat, slaughtering services
President: Irene Pluester
Manager: Suzanne Pluester
Estimated Sales: $1-3 Million
Number Employees: 1-4
Type of Packaging: Bulk

10122 Plum Creek Winery
3708 G Rd
Palisade, CO 81526-9603
970-464-7586
Fax: 970-464-0457 www.plumcreekwinery.com
Wines
Manager: Jenne Baldwin
Marketing Director: Sue Phillips
Manager: Jenne Eaton
info@plumcreekwinery.com
Estimated Sales: Below $5 Million
Number Employees: 5-9
Brands:
Plum Creek

10123 Plum Organics
1485 Park Ave
Emeryville, CA 94608
877-914-7586
www.plumorganics.com
Organic baby food, formula, and kids snacks
Founder/CEO: Neil Grimmer
Product Innovation Manager: Meg Verdeyen
SVP Brand Marketing & Innovation: Ben Mand
Year Founded: 2005
Number Employees: 100-249

10124 Plumrose USA
651 W. Washington Blvd.
Suite 302
Chicago, IL 60661
800-526-4909
consumer@plumroseusa.com
www.plumroseusa.com
Deli meats, bacon, BBQ products, food service, specialty.
CEO: Dave Schanzer
Year Founded: 1932
Estimated Sales: $580 Million
Number Employees: 1,160
Number of Brands: 4
Square Footage: 5282
Parent Co: JBS USA
Type of Packaging: Consumer, Food Service
Other Locations:
Sliced Deli Meats
Booneville MS
Bacon
Elkhard IN
Barbecue Items & Ribs
Swanton VT
Deli Meats & Bacon
Council Bluffs IA
Customer Service Dist. Center
Tupelo MS
Sales Office
Bentonville AR
Sales Office
Upland CA
Brands:
DAK
Naked Meats
Plumrose
Knockout Meats

10125 Plus CBD Oil
10070 Barnes Canyon Rd
Suite 100
San Diego, CA 92121
855-758-7223
help@pluscbdoil.com pluscbdoil.com
CBD oil
CEO: Joseph Dowling
CFO: Joerg Grasser
Operations: Michael Mona

10126 Plus Pharma
2460 Coral St
Vista, CA 92081-8430
760-597-0200
Fax: 760-597-0734 info@pluspharm.com
www.pluspharm.com
Herbs, gelatin and vegetarian capsules
President: Bill Roberts
Estimated Sales: Less Than $500,000
Number Employees: 1-4

10127 Plush Puffs Marshmallows
3811 W Magnolia Blvd
Burbank, CA 91505-2820
USA
818-784-2931
Fax: 818-474-7816 www.plushpuffs.com
Marshmallow dessert toppings
President: Ann Hickey
Quality Coordinator: Darien Camacho

10128 Plyley's Candy
909 S Poplar St
Lagrange, IN 46761-2412
260-463-3351
Fax: 260-463-7011 877-665-2778
plyley@kuntrynet.com
Candy
President: Jack Plyley
jplyley@yahoo.com
VP: Willard Plyley
Estimated Sales: Below $500,000
Number Employees: 5-9

10129 Plymouth Artisan Cheese
106 Messer Hill Rd.
Plymouth Notch, VT 05056
802-672-3650
www.plymouthartisancheese.com
Cheese
President: Jesse Werner

10130 Plymouth Beef Co.
3585 Food Center Drive
Bronx, NY 10474
718-589-8600
Fax: 718-860-8930 info@plymouthbeef.com
www.plymouthbeef.com
Beef
Chairman: Gerald Sussman
Ceo/President: Andrew Sussman
Estimated Sales: $5 Million
Number Employees: 25
Type of Packaging: Consumer, Food Service

10131 Plymouth Cheese Counter
PO Box 517
Plymouth, WI 53073-0517
920-892-8781
Fax: 920-893-5986 888-607-9477
plychzct@excel.com www.cheesecapital.com
Cheese and gift baskets
Owner: Kris Hummes
Estimated Sales: Less Than $500,000
Number Employees: 5-9
Type of Packaging: Consumer

10132 Plymouth Colony Winery
56 Pinewood Rd
Plymouth, MA 02360
508-747-3334
Fax: 508-747-4463
Wine
Owner: Charles Caranci
General Manager: Lydia Carey
Estimated Sales: $10,950,985
Number Employees: 1-4
Type of Packaging: Private Label
Brands:
Plymouth Colony Winery

10133 Plymouth Lollipop Company
P.O. Box 413
Westford, MA 1886
888-662-4948
Fax: 508-866-0822 800-777-0115
Lollipops and confection ingredients
President: Bill Johnson
Estimated Sales: Less than $500,000
Number Employees: 1-4
Brands:
Plimouth Lollipop

10134 Pocas International
19 Central Blvd
South Hackensack, NJ 07606
201-941-7900
Fax: 201-941-9707
contact@pocasinternational.com
www.pocasinternational.com
Coconut water and aloe vera drink.
Brands:
Pocas
Ramun,
Poca's Tacos
OKF
Pocasville
Splash
Pearl Royal
Toucan

10135 Poche's Smokehouse
3015 Main Hwy
Suite A
Breaux Bridge, LA 70517-6347
337-332-2108
Fax: 337-332-5051 800-376-2437
support@pochesmarket.com
www.pochesmarket.com
Meat
Owner: Floyd Poche
Owner: Karen Poche
Estimated Sales: $5-10 Million
Number Employees: 20-49

10136 Pocino Foods
14250 Lomitas Ave
City Of Industry, CA 91746-3096
626-968-8000
Fax: 626-330-8779 800-345-0150
onlythebest@pocinofoods.com
www.pocinofoods.com
Deli meats (Italian and Mexican style), pizza toppings
CEO: Jason Katsuki
Vice President: Jim Pierson
National Sales Director: Karen Barro
Regional Sales Manager: Ramona Shope
Estimated Sales: $32 Million
Number Employees: 100-249
Number of Brands: 1
Type of Packaging: Private Label
Brands:
Pocino

10137 Poco Dolce
2419 3rd St
San Francisco, CA 94107-3110
USA
415-255-1443
Fax: 415-255-1743 www.pocodolce.com
Chocolate bars, truffles, toffee
Owner: Kathy Wiley
Manager: James Amendolagine
james.amendolagine@roku.com
Number Employees: 1-4

10138 Pocono Cheesecake Factory
HC 1 Box 95
Swiftwater, PA 18370
570-839-6844
Fax: 570-839-6844
Cheesecakes
Manager: Alferd Johnson
Estimated Sales: $300,000
Number Employees: 10-19
Square Footage: 12000
Brands:
Pocono Cheesecake

10139 Pocono Mountain Bottling Company
57 W Chestnut Street
Wilkes Barre, PA 18705-1751
570-822-7695
Bottled water and carbonated beverages
President/Treasurer: Veronica Iskra
Estimated Sales: $580,000
Number Employees: 5
Brands:
Pocono Mountain

10140 **Pocono Spring Company**
1545 Industrial Park Drive
PO Box 787
Mt Pocono, PA 18344-0787
570-839-2837
Fax: 570-839-6705 800-634-4584
Bottled water
President/CEO: Michael Melnic
CFO: Bill Fraser
Operations Manager: Tim Fitzgerald
Estimated Sales: $1-2.5 000,000
Number Employees: 20-49
Brands:
Pocono Spring

10141 **(HQ)Point Group**
1790 Highway A1a
Suite 103
Satellite Beach, FL 32937-5446
321-777-7408
Fax: 321-777-9777 888-272-1249
Coffee, tea, fruit extracts and juices
President: Gary Trump
VP: Roger Koltermann
Type of Packaging: Consumer, Food Service, Private Label, Bulk
Brands:
Mingo Bay Beverages, Inc.

10142 **Point Judith Fisherman's Company**
P.O.Box 730
Narragansett, RI 02882-0730
401-782-1500
Fax: 401-782-1599
Fish
Manager: Larry Rainey
Sales Manager: John McLaughlin
Estimated Sales: $10-20 000,000
Number Employees: 50-99

10143 **Point Lobster Co**
1 St. Louis Ave
Point Pleasant Beach, NJ
732-892-1729
Fax: 732-892-3928 info@pointlobster.com
pointlobster.com
Lobster

10144 **Point Reyes Farmstead Cheese Co.**
14700 Hwy 1
Po Box 9
Point Reyes Station, CA 94956
415-663-8880
Fax: 415-663-8881 800-591-6787
lynn@pointreyescheese.com
www.pointreyescheese.com
Cheese
President: Bob Giacomini

10145 **Point Saint George Fisheries**
PO Box 1386
Santa Rosa, CA 95402-1386
707-542-9490
Seafood
General Manager: Rich Amundson
Estimated Sales: $1-2.5 000,000 appx.
Number Employees: 1

10146 **Poiret International**
7866 Exeter Boulevard E
Tamarac, FL 33321-8797
203-926-3700
Fax: 954-721-0110 800-237-9151
Preserves and organic jams
CEO/Purchasing: Ed Kerzner
CFO: Sheila Kerzner
Marketing Director: Stan Margulese
Plant Manager: Frank Bilisi
Number Employees: 20-49
Square Footage: 100000
Parent Co: Siroper/E. Meurens SA
Type of Packaging: Consumer, Food Service, Private Label, Bulk
Brands:
Delice
Meurens
Poiret

10147 **Poison Pepper Company**
7310 E Shadywoods Court
Floral City, FL 34436-5732
888-539-5540
Fax: 727-894-5540 888-539-5540
Sauces
President: Tom Dahl

10148 **Pok Pok Som**
1222 Se Gideon St
Portland, OR 97202-2417
USA
503-235-0004
Fax: 503-232-0293 www.pokpoksom.com
Drinking vinegar
Owner: Andy Ricker

10149 **Pokanoket Ostrich Farm**
177 Gulf Rd
South Dartmouth, MA 02748
508-992-6188
Fax: 508-993-5356 pokanokets@aol.com
Ostrich meat
President: Alan Weinshel
National Sales Manager: Mike Yokemick
Contact: Gail Weinshel
pokanokets@aol.com
Estimated Sales: Below $5 Million
Number Employees: 1-4
Type of Packaging: Consumer, Food Service, Private Label
Brands:
Pokanoket Farm

10150 **Pokonobe Industries**
2701 Ocean Park Blvd
Suite 208
Santa Monica, CA 90405-5247
310-392-1259
Fax: 310-392-3659 www.pokonobe.com
Oils: almond, grapeseed, soy, sunflower, sesame, walnut, corn, olive, linseed, wheat germ, safflower, rice bran, avocado, pumpkinseed, flaxseed, hazelnut, macademia nut, coconut, palm
President: David Nagley
General Manager: Larry Kronenberg
Contact. Robert Grebler
info@pokonobe.com
Estimated Sales: $5-10 Million
Number Employees: 5-9
Square Footage: 7948
Type of Packaging: Bulk
Other Locations:
Pokonobe Industries
Santa Monica CA
Brands:
Pokonobe

10151 **Polar Beverages Inc.**
1001 Southbridge St.
Worcester, MA 01610
800-734-9800
customerservice@polarbev.com
polarbeverages.com
Soft drinks and water.
President/CEO: Ralph Crowley
CFO/COO: Michael Mulrain
Executive Vice President: Christopher Crowley
ccrowley@polarbev.com
Year Founded: 1882
Estimated Sales: $120.3 Million
Number Employees: 500-999
Square Footage: 350000
Type of Packaging: Consumer, Food Service, Private Label
Brands:
A&W
Adirondack Beverages
Adirondack Clear N' Natural
Cape Cod Dry
Diet Rite3
Polar
Royal Crown
Seagrams
Seven-Up
Silver Spring
Squirt
Sunkist Country Time
Waist Watcher

10152 **Polar Water Company**
45 Noblestown Rd
Carnegie, PA 15106
412-429-5550
Fax: 770-739-1884
Bottled water
Manager: Woody Godby
Number Employees: 20-49
Parent Co: Sontory Water Group

10153 **Polarica USA, Inc.**
5702 Marsh Drive
Suite G
Pacheco, CA 94553
415-647-1300
Fax: 888-502-7650 800-426-3872
sales@polaricausa.com www.polaricausa.com
Beef and specialty products
President: Carlos Tabeira
Manager: Mitch Niayesh
Estimated Sales: $5-10 Million
Number Employees: 5-9
Brands:
Polarica

10154 **Polka Home Style Sausage**
8753 S Commercial Ave
Chicago, IL 60617
773-221-0395
Sausage
President: Paul Szczepkowski
Owner: Ed Szczepkowski
Estimated Sales: Less than $500,000
Number Employees: 1-4
Type of Packaging: Consumer, Food Service
Brands:
Polka

10155 **Pollio Dairy Products**
8596 Main St
Campbell, NY 14821-9636
607-527-3621
Fax: 607-527-8060
Cheese
Manager: Dee Gibbs
Manager: Brian Smith
Manager: Mike Gracia
mgracia@kraft.com
Number Employees: 250-499
Type of Packaging: Consumer, Food Service

10156 **Pollman's Bake Shop**
750 S Broad St
Mobile, AL 36603-1197
251-438-1511
Fax: 251-438-9461
Cakes, pies and breads
Co-Owner: Charles Pollman
Co-Owner: Fred Pollman
Estimated Sales: $1-3 Million
Number Employees: 20-49
Type of Packaging: Consumer
Other Locations:
Pollman's Bake Shops
Mobile AL

10157 **Polly's Gourmet Coffee**
4606 E 2nd St
Long Beach, CA 90803-5307
562-433-2996
Fax: 562-439-4119 www.pollys.com
Coffee and tea
Owner: Mike Sheldrake
pollys@pollys.com
Estimated Sales: Under $500,000
Number Employees: 10-19
Brands:
Celebes Kalosi
Colombian Excelso
Colombian Supremo
Ethiopian Moka
Jamaica Blue Mountain
Java Estate
Kenya Aa
Kona Hawaii
La Minita Tarrazu
Sumatra Mandheling
Tanzanian Peaberry

10158 **Polypro International Inc**
7300 Metro Blvd
Suite 570
Edina, MN 55439-2346
952-835-7717
Fax: 952-835-3811 800-765-9776
polypro@polyprointl.com www.polyprointl.com
Guar and cellulose gums
President: Mark Kieper
polypro@polyprointl.com
Controller: Jennifer Jansson
Senior Account Manager, Sales/Technical: Louise Polizzotto
Customer Service/Logistics: Janet Burger

Estimated Sales: $2.5-5 Million
Number Employees: 1-4
Type of Packaging: Bulk
Brands:
Procol
Progum
Viscol

10159 **Pommeraie Winery**
10541 Cherry Ridge Road
Sebastopol, CA 95472-9644
707-823-9463
Fax: 707-823-9106
Wine
President: Judith Johnson
Estimated Sales: $500-1 000,000 appx.
Number Employees: 1-4

10160 **Pomodoro Fresca Foods**
16 Bleeker Street
Millburn, NJ 07079
973-467-6609
Fax: 973-467-3070
Sauces
President: Nancy Battista
Estimated Sales: $71,000
Brands:
Fresca Foods

10161 **Pompeian Inc**
4201 Pulaski Hwy
Baltimore, MD 21224-1699
410-276-6900
Fax: 410-276-3764 800-766-7342
www.pompeian.com
Spanish olive oil, vinegar and cooking wines.
President: Frank Patton
sales@pompeian.com
Chief Executive Officer: David Bensadoun
Year Founded: 1906
Estimated Sales: $20-50 Million
Number Employees: 50-99
Number of Brands: 4
Type of Packaging: Consumer, Food Service, Bulk
Brands:
Avallo
Laco
Pompeian Olive Oil
Romanza

10162 **Pon Food Corp**
101 Industrial Park Blvd
Ponchatoula, LA 70454-8306
985-386-6941
Fax: 985-386-6755 info@ponfoodcorp.com
www.ponchatoula.com
Groceries, frozen foods, meats, dairy products and seafood
President: Pam Barado
pbarado@ponfoodcorp.com
Co-owner: Michael Berner
Estimated Sales: $7.7 Million
Number Employees: 20-49
Square Footage: 72000

10163 **Pond Brothers Peanut Company**
426 County Street
Suffolk, VA 23434-4704
757-539-2356
Fax: 757-539-3995
Raw peanuts
President: Richard L Pond Jr
CEO: Jeffrey G Pond
Controller: Ernest Wyatt
Estimated Sales: $5-10 000,000
Number Employees: 1-4

10164 **Pond Pure Catfish**
14429 Market St
Moulton, AL 35650
256-974-6698
Fax: 403-252-3918
Catfish
Owner: Bobby Norwood
Estimated Sales: $300,000-500,000
Number Employees: 1-4

10165 **Ponderosa Valley Vineyard**
3171 Highway 290
Ponderosa, NM 87044-9716
575-834-7487
Fax: 505-834-7073 800-946-3657
winemaker@ponderosawinery.com
www.ponderosawinery.com
Wines
Owner: Henry Street
Owner: Mary Street
Estimated Sales: $150,000
Number Employees: 1-4
Number of Products: 21
Square Footage: 4000
Type of Packaging: Consumer
Brands:
Chamisa Gold
Jemez Blush
Jemez Red
N.M. Riesling
Ponderosa Valley Vineyards
Summer Sage
Vino De Pata

10166 **Pondini Imports**
PO Box 5250
Somerset, NJ 08875-5250
732-545-1255
Fax: 732-246-7570 spond@pondini.com
www.pondini.com
Coffee, olive oil, vinegar, cheese, pasta and rice
President/Owner: Matteo Panini
CEO: Seymour Pond
spond@pondini.com
Number Employees: 1-4

10167 **Pontchartrain Blue Crab**
38327 Salt Bayou Rd
Slidell, LA 70461-1103
985-649-6645
Fax: 504-781-5064
pbcinfo@pontchartrainbluecrab.com
www.pontchartrainbluecrab.com
Seafood
President/CEO: Gary Bauer
garyb@pontchartrainbluecrab.com
Estimated Sales: $5,000,000
Number Employees: 5-9

10168 **Ponti USA**
5 West 19th St
New York, NY 10011
www.ponti.com
Vinegars, pasta sauces, pickled vegetables and olives.
Brands:
Ponti

10169 **Pontiac Coffee Break**
2252 Dixie Hwy
Waterford, MI 48328
248-332-6333
Fax: 248-335-0525 info@coffeebreakinc.com
www.coffeebreakinc.com
Coffee
President: Robert Smith
Estimated Sales: $500,000-$1 Million
Number Employees: 10-19

10170 **Pontiac Foods**
PO Box 25469
Columbia, SC 29224
803-699-1600
Fax: 803-699-1649
Coffee
Manager: John Masa
General Manager: Joe Girone
Purchasing Manager: Stan Wilson
Estimated Sales: Under $500,000
Number Employees: 100-249
Brands:
Kroger
Pontiac Foods

10171 **Pony Boy Ice Cream**
211 Middle Road
Acushnet, MA 02743-2017
508-994-4422
Fax: 508-995-9459
Ice cream and frozen yogurt
President: Raymond White
Estimated Sales: $10-20 000,000
Number Employees: 10-19
Brands:
Pony Boy

10172 **Ponzi Vineyards**
19500 SW Mountain Home Road
Sherwood, OR Sherwood
503-628-1227
Fax: 503-628-1808 info@ponziwines.com
www.ponziwines.com
Wines
President: Richard Ponzi
Accountant: Jeff Newlin
Marketing/Sales Director: Maria Ponzi Fogelstrom
President/Director of Sales and Marketin: Anna Ponzi
Chief Executive Officer: Michel Ponzi
Winemaker: Luisa Ponzi
Estimated Sales: $1-3 Million
Number Employees: 10-19
Type of Packaging: Private Label
Brands:
Ponzi's

10173 **Poore Brothers**
5415 E High St
Suite 350
Phoenix, AZ 85054
623-932-6200
Fax: 602-522-2690 www.inventurefoods.com
Chips
Vice President, Sales: Russell Law
Parent Co: Inventure Foods Inc
Brands:
Bob's Texas Style
Boulder Canyon
Cinnabon
Poore Brothers
Tgi Friday's
Tato Skins

10174 **Pop & Bottle Inc.**
San Francisco, CA
www.popandbottle.com
Plant-based lattes
Co-Founder: Blair Fletcher-Hardy
Co-Founder: Jash Mehta

10175 **Pop Art Snacks**
PO Box 9614
Salt Lake City, UT 84109
801-983-7470
info@popartsnacks.com
www.popartsnacks.com
Flavored organic popcorn
Owner: Venessa Dobson
Owner: Mike Dobson
mike@popartsnacks.com

10176 **Pop Gourmet LLC**
13400 Interurban Ave S
Tukwila, WA 98168-3330
206-397-3896
www.popgourmetpopcorn.com
Popcorn and chips
CEO: David Israel
Number Employees: 5-9
Brands:
POP

10177 **Pop Zero**
3528 W 200 S
Units 1 & 2
Salt Lake City, UT 84104
801-456-5757
info@popzeropopcorn.com
www.popzeropopcorn.com
Flavored popcorn
Co-Founder: Josh Brownlow

10178 **Popchips**
550 Montgomery St
Suite 925
San Francisco, CA 94111-6500
415-391-2211
Fax: 415-391-2779 866-217-9327
sales@popchips.com www.popchips.com
Popped potato chips
Ceo: Patrick Turpin
Ceo: Keith Belling
Vice President: Martin Basch
Contact: Kristen Abbott
kristen@popchips.com
Estimated Sales: $500,000
Number Employees: 50-99

10179 **Popcorn Connection**
7615 Fulton Avenue
North Hollywood, CA 91605-1805
818-764-3279
Fax: 818-765-0578 800-852-2676
Popcorn and nuts
Owner: Kevin Needle
VP: Ross Wallach
Estimated Sales: $300,000
Number Employees: 3
Number of Products: 20
Square Footage: 14000
Type of Packaging: Consumer, Food Service, Private Label, Bulk
Brands:
Corn Appetit
Corn Appetit Ultimate
Fruit Corn Appetit
Video Munchies

10180 **Popcorn Popper**
6323 N 150 E
Monon, IN 47959
219-253-6607
Fax: 219-253-8172 800-270-2705
www.popcornpopper.com
Popcorn and gift baskets
President: Dani Paluchniak
Vice President: Joe Dold
Sales Manager: Steve Dold
Estimated Sales: $4041306
Number Employees: 5-9
Parent Co: Felknor International
Type of Packaging: Consumer
Brands:
Theater Ii
Wasbash Valley Farm
Whirley Pop

10181 **Popcorn World**
520 S Ohio Ave
Sedalia, MO 65301-4450
660-826-9975
Fax: 660-359-4475 800-443-8226
Popcorn
Owner: Pam Kaduce
CEO: Keith Kaduce
Estimated Sales: $1-3 Million
Number Employees: 20
Type of Packaging: Consumer, Food Service, Private Label, Bulk

10182 **Popcorner**
1429 N Illinois Street
Swansea, IL 62226-4234
618-277-2676
Fax: 618-236-9420
Popcorn
Owner: Connie Kimble
Number Employees: 1-4
Square Footage: 1200
Type of Packaging: Consumer, Private Label, Bulk

10183 **Popcornopolis LLC**
3200 E. Slauson Ave
Vernon, CA 90058
310-414-6700
800-767-2489
customerservice@popcornopolis.com
www.popcornopolis.com
Popcorn and gift baskets
Co-Founder: Kathy Arnold
karnold@popcornopolis.com
Co-Founder: Wally Arnold
Number Employees: 100-249

10184 **Popkoff's**
18901 Railroad St.
City of Industry, CA 91748
844-767-5633
service@popkoffs.com
www.popkoffs.com
Pasta and pierogies
Founder: Peter Popkoff
Square Footage: 60000
Type of Packaging: Private Label

10185 **Poppa's Granola**
473 Grout Road
Perkinsville, VT 05151-9682
802-263-5342
Granola
Co-Owner: Angela Page
Co-Owner: Jacquelin Antonivich
Type of Packaging: Consumer, Food Service, Bulk

10186 **Poppers Supply Company**
PO Box 90187
Allentown, PA 18109
503-239-3792
Fax: 503-235-6221 800-457-9810
info@poppers.com www.poppers.com
Popcorn and fountain syrup
President: Vernon Ryles Jr
Sales Manager: Jody Riggs
Estimated Sales: $1.4 Million
Number Employees: 10
Type of Packaging: Consumer, Food Service
Brands:
Allans
Poppers

10187 **Poppie's Dough**
2600 W 35th St
Chicago, IL 60632-1602
312-949-0404
Fax: 312-949-0505 888-767-7431
info@poppiesbakeshop.com
www.poppiesdough.com
Cookies
President: Mark Cwiakala
mcwiakala@poppiesdough.com
President: Ronnie Himmel
Marketing: Yesenia Mendez
Estimated Sales: $2.4 Million
Number Employees: 5-9
Brands:
Poppie's

10188 **Poppies International**
6610 Corporation Pkwy
Battleboro, NC 27809
252-442-4309
www.poppies.com
Bakery products and frozen desserts.
Contact: Pieter-Jan Buydaert
Brands:
Poppies
Delizza
d'Haubry
Rita

10189 **Poppilu**
Chicago, IL 60611
info@poppilu.com
www.poppilu.com
Antioxidant lemonade
Founder: Melanie Kahn

10190 **Poppin Popcorn**
933 4th Avenue N
Naples, FL 34102-5814
941-262-1691
Fax: 941-262-1691
Popcorn and maize
President: Mark Webb
Estimated Sales: Less than $500,000
Number Employees: 1-4

10191 **Poppingfun Inc**
1344 Constitution Dr
Neenah, WI 54956-1647
920-486-7210
Fax: 920-273-6013 Sales@poppingfun.com
www.poppingfun.com
Carbonated crystals
CEO: Julie Hesson
Founder/President: Lynn Hesson
Key Accounts: Mike Rieth
Executive Vice President: David Hesson
Technical Manager: Krista Bauman
Manager Quality/Research & Development: Lori Cramer
Contact: Keith Gray
keith@poppingfun.com
Production Manager: Chris Roebke
Number Employees: 10-19
Type of Packaging: Private Label, Bulk

10192 **Poppy Hand-Crafted Popcorn**
640 Merrimon Ave
Suite 201
Asheville, NC 28804
828-552-3149
www.poppyhandcraftedpopcorn.com
Flavored popcorn
Owner: Ginger Frank
Brands:
Poppy Hand-Crafted Popcorn

10193 **Popsalot**
PO Box 7040
Beverly Hills, CA 90212-7040
USA
213-761-0156
Fax: 562-200-7910 www.popsalot.com
Popcorn
President/Owner: Noah Sheray
Estimated Sales: $2-5 Million
Number Employees: 10-19

10194 **Porinos Gourmet Food**
280 Rand St
Central Falls, RI 02863-2512
401-273-3000
Fax: 401-273-3232 800-826-3938
porinos@aol.com
Pasta and sauces, salad dressings, marinades and pickled pepper
Owner: Michael Dressler
VP Operations: Marshall Righter
Estimated Sales: $1.9 Million
Number Employees: 10-19
Square Footage: 120000
Type of Packaging: Consumer, Food Service, Private Label

10195 **Pork Shop of Vermont**
631 N Pasture Road
Charlotte, VT 05445-9254
802-482-3617
Fax: 802-482-2801 800-458-3441
Sausage and ham
President: Joseph Keenan
Estimated Sales: $5-9.9 000,000
Number Employees: 7

10196 **Porkie Company of Wisconsin**
3113 E Layton Ave
Cudahy, WI 53110-1309
414-483-6562
Fax: 414-483-6561 800-333-2588
www.porkiesofwisconsin.com
Pork rinds and cracklings, beef jerky, corn, peanuts, pistachios and cashews, olives, pickles, pretzels, potato chips and cheese curls, pigs' feet, pork hocks and Polish sausage
President: Richard Rydeski
porkieone@aol.com
Executive VP: Thomas Rydeski
Production: Dan Rydeski
Plant Manager: Mike Sodemann
Estimated Sales: $1600000
Number Employees: 20-49
Number of Products: 50
Square Footage: 200000
Brands:
Jack's All American
Porkies
Snak Sales
Vinegar Joe

10197 **Porky's Gourmet Foods**
644 Blythe Ave
Gallatin, TN 37066-2226
615-230-7000
Fax: 615-230-2800 800-767-5911
flavor@porkysgourmet.com
www.porkysgourmet.com
Sauces, seasonings, relishes and jellies
President: Ron Boyle
flavor@porkysgourmet.com
Estimated Sales: $5-10 Million
Number Employees: 10-19
Type of Packaging: Consumer, Food Service, Private Label

10198 **Port City Pretzels**
PO Box 631
Portsmouth, NH 03802
603-502-7946
info@portcitypretzels.com
www.portcitypretzels.com
Pretzels
Owner: Suzanne Foley

10199 Port Lobster Co Inc
122 Ocean Ave
Kennebunkport, ME 04046-6302
207-967-2081
Fax: 207-967-8419 800-486-7029
www.portlobster.com
Lobster
President: Kenneth Hutchins
portlob@gwi.net
Estimated Sales: $1-3 Million
Number Employees: 5-9
Type of Packaging: Consumer

10200 Port Royal Seafood
1948 Sea Island Pkwy
PO Box 1008
St. Helena, SC 29920
843-812-0257
Shrimp
Owner: William Gay
Estimated Sales: $210,000
Number Employees: 3
Brands:
Royal Seafood

10201 Porter Creek Vineyards
8735 Westside Rd
Healdsburg, CA 95448-8335
707-433-6321
Fax: 707-433-4245
info@portercreekvineyards.com
www.portercreekvineyards.com
Wine
President: George Davis
dijon1@sonic.net
Estimated Sales: Under $1 Million
Number Employees: 5-9
Brands:
Procter Creek

10202 Porter's Pick-A-Dilly
Stew Industrial Park
Stowe, VT 05672
802-253-6338
Fax: 802-253-6852
Produce
President: Lynn Porter
Estimated Sales: Under $500,000
Number Employees: 1-4

10203 Portier Fine Foods
436 Waverly Ave
Mamaroneck, NY 10543
914-899-9006
Fax: 914-381-4045 800-272-9463
portier.finefoods@verizon.net
Salmon, trout, scallops, shrimp, caviar, game, birds and Belgian chocolates
President: Sean Portier
Sales Director: Patrick Portier
Estimated Sales: Below $5 Million
Number Employees: 10-19
Parent Co: Chenoceaux, Inc
Type of Packaging: Consumer, Food Service

10204 Portland Creamery
PO Box 12071
Portland, OR 97212
503-616-4443
info@portlandcreamery.com
www.portlandcreamery.com
Goat cheese
Owner/Chessemaker: Liz Alvis

10205 Portland Shellfish Company
92 Waldron Way
Portland, ME 04103
207-799-9290
Fax: 207-799-7179 www.portlandshellfish.com
Crab and lobster
President: Jeff Holden
Human Resources: John Maloney
john@pshellfish.com
Estimated Sales: $9 Million
Number Employees: 100-249
Square Footage: 48000
Type of Packaging: Consumer, Food Service, Private Label, Bulk
Brands:
Portland Lighthouse

10206 Portland Specialty Seafoods
12 Portland Fish Pier
Suite A
Portland, ME 04101-4620
207-775-5765
Fax: 207-774-1614
Seafood
Manager: Ethan Court
ethan@northlanticseafood.com
Administrator: Jessica Burton
Estimated Sales: $10-20 Million
Number Employees: 20-49

10207 Portlandia Foods
12665 NE Marx St
Portland, OR 97230
833-739-3663
portlandiafoods.com
Organic condiments
Co-Owner & Founder: Jeff Bergadine
CEO: Rian Hanneman
Brands:
Portland

10208 Porto Rico Importing
201 Bleecker St
Suite A
New York, NY 10012-1446
212-477-5421
Fax: 212-979-2303 www.portorico.com
Coffee and tea
President: Peter Longo
Manager: Kate Reilly
kate@portorico.com
Estimated Sales: $5-10 Million
Number Employees: 10-19

10209 Portsmouth Chowder Co
124 Heritage Ave
Suite 1
Portsmouth, NH 03801-8655
603-431-3132
Fax: 603-431-3132 877-616-7631
info@portsmouthchowder.com
www.portsmouthchowder.com
Chowder and seafood
Owner: Rob Lincoln
rob@portsmithchowder.com
Estimated Sales: Below $5 000,000
Number Employees: 1-4
Brands:
Portsmouth Chowder Company

10210 Portuguese Baking Company
P.O.Box 5550
Newark, NJ 07105-0550
973-589-8875
Fax: 973-589-6510
Portuguese rolls
President: Marvin Everseyke
CFO/VP: Louis Pereira
CEO: Steve Latner
Estimated Sales: Under $500,000
Number Employees: 250-499
Type of Packaging: Private Label, Bulk
Brands:
Austin Company
Portuguese Baking Company

10211 Poseidon Enterprises
3516 Green Park Circle
Charlotte, NC 28217-2854
704-944-1164
Fax: 704-405-0018 800-863-7886
Seafood, salmon, tuna, swordfish, grouper, snapper, live lobster
President: Richard Lavecchia

10212 Positively 3rd St Bakery
1202 E 3rd St
Duluth, MN 55805-2319
218-724-8619
Fax: 218-724-4185 3rdstreetbakery@gmail.com
Cookies, bagels, granola and bread
Owner: Paul Steklin
Estimated Sales: Less than $500,000
Number Employees: 10-19
Type of Packaging: Consumer, Food Service, Bulk

10213 Post Consumer Brands
20802 Kensington Blvd.
Lakeville, MN 55044
800-431-7678
www.postconsumerbrands.com
Cereal and grain products.
CEO: William Stiritz
Year Founded: 2015
Estimated Sales: $750 Million
Number Employees: 3,500
Number of Brands: 24
Parent Co: Post Holdings
Type of Packaging: Consumer, Food Service, Private Label, Bulk
Other Locations:
Asheboro NC
Coppell TX
Grove City OH
Northfield MN
Salt Lake City UT
St. Ansgar IA
Tremonton UT
Brands:
Alpha-Bits
Better Oats
Bran Flakes
Chips Ahoy! Cereal
Coco Wheats
Farina Mills
Golden Crisp
Golden Oreo's
Grape Nuts
Great Grains
Honey Bunches of Oats
Honey Maid S'Mores
Honeycomb
Post Hostess Cereal
Malt-O-Meal
Nilla Banana Pudding
Nutter Butter Cereal
Oh's
Oreo O's
Pebbles
Post Shredded Wheat
Raisin Bran
Sour Patch Kids Cereal

10214 Post Familie Vineyards
1700 Saint Marys Mountain Rd
Altus, AR 72821-9001
479-468-2741
Fax: 479-468-2740 800-275-8423
info@postfamilie.com www.arkansaswine.com
Wines, grape juices, jellies, champagne and grapes
President: Mathew J Post
VP/Director Marketing: Paul Post
Number Employees: 10-19
Type of Packaging: Consumer, Private Label, Bulk
Brands:
Aesop's Fable
Ozark Mountain Vineyards
Post Familie Vineyards

10215 Postum
Charlotte, NC
704-221-5587
info@postum.com
postum.com
Coffee alternative
Senior VP: Peter Hwang
Brands:
Postum

10216 Poteet Seafood Co
107 Speedy Tostensen Blvd
Brunswick, GA 31520-3149
912-264-5340
Fax: 912-267-9695
Seafood
Owner: Speedy Tostensen
poteetseafood@bellsouth.net
Estimated Sales: $350,000
Number Employees: 1-4

10217 Potlicker Kitchen
192 Thomas Road
Stowe, VT 05672
802-760-6111
potlickerkitchen@gmail.com
potlickerkitchen.com
Beer jelly, wine jelly and artisan jam
Owner: Nancy Warner
Year Founded: 2009
Estimated Sales: $7.4 Million
Number Employees: 38
Brands:
Potlicker

10218 Potomac Farms Dairy Inc
300 W Industrial Blvd
Cumberland, MD 21502-4156
301-722-4410
Fax: 301-722-8433 www.galliker.com
Milk
President: David W Gilles
Estimated Sales: $10-20 000,000
Number Employees: 50-99

10219 Pots de Creme
4954 Paris Pike
Lexington, KY 40511-9400
859-299-2254
Fax: 859-299-4638 www.kyagr.com
Produce, herbs, prawns, trout and tilapia
President: Susan Harkins
Director of Operations: Benson Bell
Number Employees: 1-4
Parent Co: Duntreath Farm
Brands:
Dubbasue and Company

10220 Potter Siding Creamery Company
P.O.Box 494
Tripoli, IA 50676-0494
319-882-4444
Baked goods and creams
Owner: Kurt Kortbein
Estimated Sales: Less than $500,000
Number Employees: 1-4

10221 Powder Pure
250 Steelhead Way
The Dalles, OR 97058-3570
541-298-4800
Fax: 888-765-1720 info@powderpure.com
www.powderpure.com
Fruit and vegetable powders
CEO: Mark Savarese
Contact: Skip Benner
skip@powderpure.com
Number Employees: 100
Square Footage: 140000
Type of Packaging: Bulk

10222 Powell & Mahoney Ltd.
39 Norman St
Salem, MA 01970
978-745-4332
info@powellandmahoney.com
www.powellandmahoney.com
Cocktail mixers
Marketing: Mark Mahoney

10223 Power Crunch
Irvine, CA
powercrunch.com
Protein powders and bars
Founder: Kevin Lawrence

10224 Power of 3
P.O. Box 434
Tenants Harbor, ME 04860
888-211-7911
info@powerof3nutrition.com
powerof3nutrition.com
Health foods

10225 PowerBar
Premier Nutrition
P.O. Box 933
Kings Mountain, NC 28086
800-587-6937
www.powerbar.com
Energy bars and sports drinks
President & CEO: Rob Vitale
SVP & CFO: Jeff Zadoks
Estimated Sales: $175 Million
Number Employees: 50-99
Parent Co: Post Holdings Inc
Type of Packaging: Private Label
Brands:
PowerBar(c) 10-12g Protein Snack Bar
PowerBar(c) 20-30g Proteinplus
PowerBar(c) Clean Whey Protein Bar
PowerBar(c) Clean Whey Protein Drink
PowerBar(c) Energy Blasts
PowerBar(c) Energy Gels
PowerBar(c) Performance Energy Bar
PowerBar(c) Protein Plus
PowerBar(c) Protein Shakes
PowerBar(c) Variety Packs

10226 Powerful Foods
1828 Bay Rd
Suite 201
Miami, FL 33139
305-779-2449
info@powerful.co
powerful.co
Greek yogurt and yogurt drinks, oatmeal, smoothies and snack bites
Controller: Daniela Koch
Marketing Manager: Laura Peimer
Brands:
Powerful Yogurt

10227 Powers Baking Company
7771 W Oakland Park Blvd
Miami, FL 33167-3705
305-381-7000
Fax: 305-769-1185
Breads, rolls and buns, cakes, pies, doughs, biscuits, baking mixes, supplies and cookies
President: Dolphus Powers
Estimated Sales: $5 Million
Number Employees: 80

10228 Prager Winery & Port Works
1281 Lewelling Ln
St Helena, CA 94574-2235
707-963-3720
Fax: 707-963-7679 800-969-7678
ahport@pragerport.com www.pragerport.com
Wine
Owner: Jim Prager
ahport@pragerport.com
CFO: Katie Rooney
Estimated Sales: $1-4.9 Million
Number Employees: 5-9
Brands:
Prager Winery & Port

10229 Praim Co
92 Jackson St
Salem, MA 01970-3068
978-745-9100
Fax: 978-745-9150 800-970-9646
sales@praimgroup.com www.praimgroup.com
Chocolate, toffee and truffles
CEO: Paul Pruett
Estimated Sales: Less Than $500,000
Number Employees: 1-4
Square Footage: 60000
Brands:
ChoxCard
Seapoint Edamama
Friendlys
Warhol
Bloomsberry & Co.
Mary Phillips
Rescue Bar
Anne Taintor
Bosco
Bubble Chocolate
Eric Condren
PAN AM
The Mensch On a Bench
GK Communications
Zone
Praim Confections
Waldo
Garfield
French Bull
Build-A-Bear
Dreamworks
Boss Baby
Trolls
Happiness Sell Sheet

10230 Prairie Berries Inc.
PO Box 21
Keeler, SK S0H 2E0
Canada
306-788-2018
Fax: 306-788-4811 prairieberries@sasktel.net
www.prairieberries.com
Saskatoon berries
President: Sandra Purdy
Number Employees: 5-9
Type of Packaging: Consumer, Food Service

10231 Prairie Cajun Wholesale
5966 Highway 190
Eunice, LA 70535
337-546-6195
Seafood and exotic meats; alligator and nutria
President: Jeffery Derouen
Estimated Sales: $1-2 Million
Number Employees: 10-19
Type of Packaging: Consumer, Food Service

10232 Prairie City Bakery
100 N Fairway Dr
Suite 138
Vernon Hills, IL 60061-1859
847-573-9640
Fax: 847-573-9643 800-338-5122
customerservice@pcbakery.com
www.pcbakery.com
Danish, cookies, muffins and cakes
Owner: Bill Skeens
bskeens@pcbakery.com
Estimated Sales: $2,200,000
Number Employees: 5-9
Type of Packaging: Consumer, Food Service, Bulk
Brands:
Prairie City

10233 (HQ)Prairie Farms Dairy Inc.
3744 Staunton Rd.
Edwardsville, IL 62025
618-659-5700
info@prairiefarms.com
www.prairiefarms.com
Cottage cheese, milk, sour cream, yogurt, ice cream, orange juice and fruit drinks.
CEO: Edward Mullins
emullins@prairiefarms.com
VP/CFO: Jason Geminn
Year Founded: 1938
Estimated Sales: $3 Billion
Number Employees: 5,700
Type of Packaging: Consumer, Food Service, Private Label, Bulk
Brands:
Prairie Farms
Swiss Valley Farms

10234 Prairie Malt
PO Box 1150
Biggar, SK S0K 0M0
Canada
306-948-3500
Fax: 306-948-5038 david_klinger@cargill.com
www.prairiemaltltd.com
Barley malt
President: Doug Eden
Number Employees: 50-99
Parent Co: Cargill, Incorporated
Type of Packaging: Bulk

10235 Prairie Mills Products LLC
401 E 4th St
P.O. Box 97
Rochester, IN 46975-1105
574-223-3177
Fax: 574-223-3414 www.prairiemills.com
Flour and cereal
President: Erik Bruun
Managing Director, CEO: John Cory
jcory@prairiemills.com
National Sales Manager: Gary Swaim
Estimated Sales: Less Than $500,000
Number Employees: 1-4
Type of Packaging: Private Label
Brands:
Amaizen Crunch
Prairie Star

10236 Prairie Mushrooms
52557 Range Road 215
Ardrossan, AB T8E 2H6
Canada
780-467-3555
Fax: 780-467-3893 info@prairiemushrooms.com
www.prairiemushrooms.com
Mushrooms
President: George DeRuiter
Marketing Manager: John Kostelyk
Sales: Kevin Christman
General Manager: Terry Uppal
Production: Don Kostelyk
Estimated Sales: $5-10 Million
Number Employees: 100-249
Type of Packaging: Consumer, Food Service
Brands:
Prairie Mushrooms

10237 Prairie Thyme LTD
4363 Center Pl
Unit 3
Santa Fe, NM 87507-1823
505-473-1945
Fax: 505-473-0363 800-869-0009
prairiethyme@worldpantry.com
www.prairiethyme.com
Condiments; vinegars, cooking oils, fruit salsas and chutneys
President/Owner: Gary Hall
prairiethyme@aol.com
Estimated Sales: Less Than $500,000
Number Employees: 1-4
Number of Brands: 1
Number of Products: 4
Square Footage: 6400
Parent Co: WorldPantry.com Inc.
Type of Packaging: Consumer, Food Service, Private Label, Bulk
Brands:
Prairie Thyme

10238 Prana
1440 Blvd Jules Poitras
Ville St Laurent, QC H4N 1X7
Canada
Fax: 514-276-5858 844-447-7262
www.pranasnacks.com
Trail mixes, organic nuts, chocolate barks and chia seeds

10239 Prayon Inc.
1610 Marvin Griffin Rd.
Augusta, GA 30906
206-213-5572
www.prayon.com
Phosphates and phosphoric acid.
Chairman: Olivier Vanderijst
CEO: Y. Caprara
Director of Finance: P. Schils
Director, Research: A. Germeau
Director, Sales & Marketing: V. Renard
Year Founded: 1882
Estimated Sales: $786 Million
Number Employees: 1,115
Parent Co: Prayon
Type of Packaging: Bulk
Brands:
Prayphos
Kasomel
Carfosel
Praylev

10240 Precise Food Ingredients
1432 Wainwright Way
Suite 150
Carrollton, TX 75007
972-323-4951
garrett.miller@precisefood.com
www.precisefood.com
Dry packaging and blending of seasonings for custom, industrial clients
President: Scott Miller
salesinfo@precisefood.com
VP of Sales & Marketing: Kevin Loiselle
Purchasing Agent: Linda Ransom
Year Founded: 1997
Estimated Sales: $6 Million
Number Employees: 20-49
Type of Packaging: Bulk

10241 Precision Blends
13460 Brooks Drive
Baldwin Park, CA 91706-2292
626-960-9939
Fax: 626-962-2570 800-836-9979
Blend spices
President: Charles Angell
Sales Manager: David Alnamva
Purchasing Manager: Charles Nordell
Estimated Sales: Under $500,000
Number Employees: 20-49
Type of Packaging: Private Label

10242 Preferred Brands Inc
9 W Broad St
Suite 5
Stamford, CT 06902-3734
203-348-0030
Fax: 203-348-0029 800-827-8900
comments@tastybite.com www.tastybite.com
Indian, Thai, vegetarian, vegan, kosher and gluten free rice, noodles, and entrees.
President/Owner: Ravi Nigam
CEO: Ashok Vasudevan
CFO: Sohel Shikari
EVP Sales & Marketing: Meera Vasudevan
VP Sales & Marketings: Hans Taparia
Estimated Sales: $5.7 Million
Number Employees: 10-19

10243 Preferred Meal Systems Inc
4135 Birney Ave
Moosic, PA 18507-1397
570-457-8311
Fax: 570-457-9241 www.preferredmeals.com
Portion control lunches
Executive Director: Bob Keen
Director Technology Services: Richard Ludt
Estimated Sales: $4,800,000
Number Employees: 250-499
Square Footage: 200000
Type of Packaging: Food Service, Private Label

10244 (HQ)Preferred Popcorn
1132 9th Rd
Chapman, NE 68827-2753
308-986-2526
Fax: 308-986-2626 info@preferredpopcorn.com
www.preferredpopcorn.com
Popcorn, salts and oils
CEO: Norm Krug
Estimated Sales: $30 Million
Number Employees: 20-49
Type of Packaging: Consumer, Food Service, Private Label, Bulk
Brands:
Widman's Country

10245 Premier Beverages
5301 Legacy Drive
Plano, TX 75024-3109
972-547-6295
Beverages
COO: Robert O'Brien
VP Sales: Scott Corridean
Estimated Sales: Under $500,000
Number Employees: 1-4

10246 Premier Juices
19321 US Highway 19 N # 405
Suite 405
Clearwater, FL 33764-3142
727-533-8200
Fax: 727-533-8500 info@premierjuices.com
www.premierjuices.com
Fruit juices
President: Jody Marshburn
jody@premierjuices.com
Estimated Sales: $2.5-5 Million
Number Employees: 1-4

10247 Premier Malt Products Inc
25760 Groesbeck Hwy
Suite 103
Warren, MI 48089-1589
586-443-3355
Fax: 586-443-4580 800-521-1057
Malt extracts, fungal amylase and sequestrants
President: Pat Maison
pat@premiermalt.com
Estimated Sales: $1500000
Number Employees: 10-19
Type of Packaging: Consumer, Food Service, Bulk
Brands:
Diamalt
Premose

10248 Premier Meat Co
5030 Gifford Ave
PO Box 58183
Vernon, CA 90058-2726
323-277-5888
Fax: 323-277-9100 800-555-5539
www.premiermeats.com
Beef, veal and pork
Owner: Manuel Hernandez
manuel.hernandez@premiermeats.com
Controller: Richard Orosco
Vice President: Eldad Hadar
Operations Manager: Orner Greenberg
Production Supervisor: Maricela Romero
Number Employees: 50-99
Type of Packaging: Consumer, Food Service, Bulk

10249 Premier Organics
810 81st Avenue
Oakland, CA 94621
510-632-8612
Fax: 510-380-6942 866-237-8688
Raw nut and seed butters
Contact: Santiago Cuenca-Romero
santiago@premierorganics.org
Type of Packaging: Consumer, Bulk
Brands:
ARTISANA

10250 Premier Pacific Seafoods Inc
333 1st Ave W
Seattle, WA 98119-4103
206-286-8584
Fax: 206-286-8810 www.prempac.com
Fish
President: Tom Coryell
tom@prempac.com
Estimated Sales: Under $500,000
Number Employees: 10-19
Type of Packaging: Bulk
Brands:
Ocean Phoenix
Premiere Pacific

10251 Premier Protein
5905 Christie Ave
Emeryville, CA 94608-1925
415-442-4343
Fax: 415-442-4347 888-836-8977
info@premiernutrition.com
www.premierprotein.com
Nutritional shakes, drinks, powders and bars
Owner: Karry Law
CEO: David Ritterbush
david@jointjuice.com
CFO: David Cooper
VP of Innovation and R&D: Ron Osbourne
VP of Marketing: Darcy Horn
VP of Sales: Lee Partin
VP of Operations: Stewart Irving
Estimated Sales: $5-10 Million
Number Employees: 10-19
Type of Packaging: Consumer, Private Label, Bulk
Brands:
Odyssey
Premier Nutrition
Premier Shots
Rocket Shot
Twisted Brand

10252 Premier Smoked Fish Company
3185 Tucker Rd
Bensalem, PA 19020
215-639-4569
Fax: 305-625-5528 800-654-6682
Fish; salmon, cured and herring
Owner: J Purner
COO: David Donahue
Controller: John Cicero
Plant Manager: David Sperry
Estimated Sales: $5200000
Number Employees: 5-9
Square Footage: 96000
Parent Co: SeaSpecialties
Brands:
Mama's
Seaspecialties

10253 Premiere Packing Company
PO Box 815
Greenacres, WA 99016-0815
509-926-6666
Fax: 509-926-3300 888-239-5288
nuts@thenutfactory.com www.thenutfactory.com
Snack foods, nuts, chocolates
President: Gene Cohen
Estimated Sales: Below $5 Million
Number Employees: 5-9

10254 Premiere Seafood
257 Midland Avenue
Lexington, KY 40508-1978
606-259-3474
Fax: 606-389-9390
Seafood
President: Rex Webb

10255 **Premium Brands**
PO Box 785
Bardstown, KY 40004-0785
502-348-0081
Fax: 502-348-5539
kentuckybourbon@bardstown.com
www.kentuckybourbonwhiskey.com
Liquor, whiskeys
President: Even Kulsveen
Estimated Sales: Less than $1 Million
Number Employees: 10

10256 **Premium Chocolatiers LLC**
170 Oberlin Ave N
Suite 9
Lakewood, NJ 08701-4548
USA
732-806-5218
www.premiumchocolatiers.com
Chocolate
Owner: Yochonon Miller
Estimated Sales: 260,000
Number Employees: 5

10257 **Premium Gold Flax Products & Processing**
1321 12th Ave. NE
Denhoff, ND 58430-9611
866-570-1234
info@premiumgoldflax.com
www.premiumgoldflax.com
Flaxseed
Co-Owner: Deborah Miller
tupper1956@yahoo.com

10258 **Premium Ingredients International US, LLC**
285 E Fullerton Ave
Carol Stream, IL 60188-1886
630-868-0300
Fax: 630-868-0310 info@prinovausa.com
www.prinovausa.com
Food ingredients and aroma chemicals
President: Donald Thorp
CEO: Richard Thorp
CFO: Donald Cepican
VP: Daniel Thorp
Research/Development Director: Suzanne Johnson
VP Sales/Marketing: Richard Calabrese
Contact: Kim Sean
kim.sean@prinovausa.com
Estimated Sales: $30-35 Million
Number Employees: 100
Parent Co: AMC Chemicals
Other Locations:
Premium Ingredients International
Holladay UT
Premium Ingredients International
Ellisville MO
Premium Ingredients International
Cranford NJ
Premium Ingredients Int'l(UK)
London, England

10259 **Premium Meat Co**
1100 W 600 N
Brigham City, UT 84302-4423
435-723-5944
www.premiummeatcompany.com
Beef, pork and lamb
Owner: Doug Price
Sales Manager: David Wells
Estimated Sales: $3-5 Million
Number Employees: 5-9

10260 **Premium Water**
7810 N W 100th Street
Kansas City, MO 64153
816-801-6900
800-332-3332
www.premiumwaters.com
Bottled water
President: Peter Johnson
Contact: Dawn Andresen
dawn.andresen@premiumwaters.com
GM: Bob McBride
Estimated Sales: $5-10 Million
Number Employees: 50-99
Square Footage: 80000
Type of Packaging: Consumer, Food Service, Private Label
Brands:
Acappella

10261 **Prescott Brewing Co**
130 W Gurley St
Suite A
Prescott, AZ 86301-3603
928-771-2795
Fax: 928-771-1115 angpbc1@cableone.net
www.prescottbrewingcompany.com
Beer
President: John Nielsen
pbc1@frontiernet.net
CFO: Roxanne Nielsen
Sales Director: Dave Jacobson
Estimated Sales: $1-5 Million
Number Employees: 50-99
Brands:
Liquid Amber
Lodgepole Light
Petrified Porter

10262 **President's Choice**
1 President's Choice Circle
Brampton, ON L6Y 5S5
Canada
888-495-5111
www.presidentschoice.ca
Cookies, cola, biscuits, lasagna, turkey, pizza, coffee, poultry, ice cream and juice
President, Loblaw Companies Limited: Sarah Davis
Number Employees: 14
Square Footage: 20000

10263 **Presque Isle Wine Cellars**
9440 W Main Rd
North East, PA 16428-2699
814-725-1314
Fax: 814-725-2092 800-488-7492
info@piwine.com www.piwine.com
Wines and wine-making supplies
Owner: Doug Moorhead
doug@piwine.com
Co-Owner: Laury Bouttcher
Estimated Sales: Below $5 Million
Number Employees: 10-19
Type of Packaging: Private Label
Brands:
Presque Isle Wine

10264 **Pressery**
2401 W 6th Avenue
Denver, CO 80204
info@pressery.com
www.pressery.com
Ramen kits, bone broth and cold-pressed juices
Founder & CEO: Ian Lee
Year Founded: 2013

10265 **Prestige Proteins**
1101 South Rogers Circle
Suite 1
Boca Raton, FL 33487-2748
561-997-8770
Fax: 561-997-8786 casein@casein.com
www.casein.com
Caseinate: calcium, sodium and potassium
Owner: Hue Henly
Sales Manager: Tina Thimlar
Estimated Sales: $1-2.5 Million
Number Employees: 1-4
Square Footage: 200000
Type of Packaging: Consumer, Food Service, Private Label, Bulk
Brands:
Prestige Proteins

10266 **(HQ)Prestige Technology**
1101 S Rogers Cir
Suite 1
Boca Raton, FL 33487-2748
561-997-8770
Fax: 561-997-8786 888-697-4141
casein@casein.com
Sodium and calcium caseinates
President: Hugh Henley
casein@gate.net
Director of Sales: Tina Thimlar
Estimated Sales: $18 Million
Number Employees: 10-19
Square Footage: 20000
Other Locations:
Prestige Technology Corp.
Minsk
Brands:
Prestige Proteins
Qualcoat

10267 **Presto Avoset Group**
PO Box 1086
Claremont, CA 91711-1086
909-399-0062
Fax: 909-399-1162
Nondairy toppings and icings
Brands:
Pastry Pride
Pastry Pro
Pour N' Performance
Pour N' Whip
Pride
Qwip
Tres Cremas

10268 **Preston Farms Popcorn**
1000 Zane Street
Louisville, KY 40210
502-813-3207
Fax: 502-813-3219 866-767-7464
Hybrid popcorn
CEO: Raymond Preston
President: Leigh Anne Preston
Private Label Sales: Charles Shacklette
Contact: Kermit Highfield
kermit@prestonfarms.com
Estimated Sales: $300,000-500,000
Number Employees: 10-19
Number of Products: 60
Type of Packaging: Private Label
Brands:
America's Premium
Gettelfinger Select
Heartland U.S.A.
Ky Poppers
Spee-Dee Pop

10269 **Preston Premium Wines**
502 E Vineyard Dr
Pasco, WA 99301
509-545-1990
Fax: 509-545-1098 info@prestonwines.com
Wines
President: Brett Preston
Estimated Sales: $5-9.9 Million
Number Employees: 20-49
Brands:
Preston Premium Wines

10270 **Preston Vineyards & Winery**
9282 W Dry Creek Rd
Healdsburg, CA 95448-9134
707-433-3372
Fax: 707-433-5307 800-305-9707
Wine, olives, produce and baked goods
Owner: Lou Preston
mail@prestonvineyards.com
Co-Owner: Susan Preston
Winemaker: Matt Norelli
Vineyard Manager: Jesus Arzate
Estimated Sales: $5-10 Million
Number Employees: 10-19
Brands:
Kuchen

10271 **Pretzel Perfection**
215 E Reserve St
Suite 101
Vancouver, WA 98661
USA
360-635-3886
www.pretzelperfection.com
Pretzels, chocolates
Chief Executive Officer/Founder: Amy Holyk
Contact: Roysan Biscieglia
rbiscieglia@pretzelperfection.com

10272 **Pretzel Pete**
130 Domorah Dr.
Montgomeryville, PA 18936
877-857-1727
www.pretzelpete.com
Pretzels and other snacks
President: Karl Brown

10273 **Pretzelmaker**
1346 Oakbrook Drive
Suite 170
Norcross, GA 30093
470-388-6170
877-639-2361
customerservice@gfgmanagement.com
www.pretzelmaker.com
Soft pretzels

10274 **Pretzels Inc**
123 W Harvest Rd
Bluffton, IN 46714-9007
260-824-4838
Fax: 260-824-0895 800-456-4838
www.pretzels-inc.com
Pretzels, cheese curls, corn puffs and cheese balls
President: William Huggins
CEO: William Mann
Marketing Director: Chip Manneson
Sales Director: Marvin Sparks
Operations Manager: John Sommer
Purchasing Manager: Steve Huggins
Number Employees: 250-499
Square Footage: 800000
Type of Packaging: Consumer, Food Service, Private Label, Bulk
Brands:
Harvest Road
William's Corn

10275 **(HQ)Price Co**
370 Breaum Rd
Yakima, WA 98908-8931
509-966-4110
Fax: 509-966-2988 www.priceapples.com
Apples and pears
President: Bob Price
bob@priceapples.com
CFO: Adam Hill
Number Employees: 100-249
Type of Packaging: Consumer, Food Service, Private Label, Bulk
Brands:
Gold Medal
Moon
Naches
Panda
Price
Priceless

10276 **Price Seafood**
650 Water Street
Havre De Grace, MD 21078
410-939-2782
Shrimp and crabs
Owner: Norris Price
Principal: Susan Price
Estimated Sales: $500,000- 1Million
Number Employees: 15
Square Footage: 32800
Brands:
Louisiana
Louisiana Cajun
Ocean Blue

10277 **Price's Creameries**
600 N Piedras St
El Paso, TX 79903-4023
915-565-2711
Fax: 915-562-8232 www.pricescreameries.com
Milk, ice cream, sherbet, mellorine, cream and ice milk mixes.
Director of Export & ESL Expansion: Gene Carrejo
Cmo: Irene Pistella
irene.pistella@deanfoods.com
Year Founded: 1906
Number Employees: 100-249
Parent Co: Dean Foods Company
Type of Packaging: Consumer
Brands:
Price's

10278 **Pride Dairies**
517 Thompson St
Bottineau, ND 58318-1205
701-228-2216
Fax: 701-228-3426 pride@utma.com
www.pridedairy.com
Butter, milk and ice cream
President: Jeff Beyer
Vice President: Floyd Slaughbaugh
Marketing: Shelly Spang
Estimated Sales: $10-20 Million
Number Employees: 5-9
Type of Packaging: Consumer, Food Service, Bulk
Brands:
Pride

10279 **Pride Enterprises Glades**
500 Orange Avenue Cir
Belle Glade, FL 33430-5221
561-996-1091
Fax: 561-996-8559
Sugarcane
Facility Manager: Peter Venables
Estimated Sales: Under $500,000
Number Employees: 5-9

10280 **Pride of Dixie Syrup Company**
217 Co Op Drive
Bono, AR 72416-8181
870-935-2252
Fax: 870-935-9325 800-530-7654
Pancake syrups: maple, honey and crystal white flavors
President: Troy Coleman
Estimated Sales: $180,000
Number Employees: 4
Square Footage: 15000
Type of Packaging: Consumer, Food Service, Private Label
Brands:
Craft's
Pride of Dixie

10281 **Priester's Pecans**
208 Old Fort Rd E
Fort Deposit, AL 36032-4012
334-227-4301
Fax: 334-227-4294 866-477-4736
customerservice@priesters.com
www.priesters.com
Pecan candies, pies, cakes, brownies, chocolates and cheese straws.
President: Thomas Ellis
priesters@aol.com
Owner: Ellen Burkett
CFO: Faye Hood
Plant Manager: Robert Hunter
Year Founded: 1935
Estimated Sales: $20-50 Million
Number Employees: 50-99
Number of Brands: 2
Type of Packaging: Food Service, Private Label, Bulk
Brands:
Cloverland Sweets
Priester's Pecans

10282 **Prifti Candy Company**
106 Green St
Worcester, MA 01604
508-754-5143
Fax: 508-754-0325 800-447-7438
Candies
Owner: Nick Prifti
Estimated Sales: Less than $500,000
Number Employees: 1-4
Brands:
Prifti Candy

10283 **Prima Foods International**
PO Box 2208
Silver Springs, FL 34489
352-732-9148
Fax: 352-732-0625 800-774-8751
Syrup, cocktail mixes, fruit purees and concentrates, drink bases and milk replacers
President: Hector Viale
Vice President: Celeste Viale
VP Sales: Mary Lou Sharp
Estimated Sales: $1 Million
Number Employees: 8
Square Footage: 40000
Type of Packaging: Food Service, Private Label, Bulk
Brands:
Flat Wood Farm
Prima Naturals

10284 **Prima Kase**
W6117 County Road C
Monticello, WI 53570
608-938-4227
Fax: 608-938-1227 kase@madison.tds.net
Cheeses
CEO: Steve McKeon
Estimated Sales: $2.5-5 Million
Number Employees: 5-9
Type of Packaging: Consumer, Food Service, Private Label, Bulk
Brands:
Prima Kase

10285 **Prima Wawona**
7108 N Fresno St
Suite 450
Fresno, CA 93720
559-787-8780
prima.com
Tree fruits, including peaches, plums, nectarines and apricots.
President & CEO: Dan Gerawan
Retail Sales Manager: Ben Vived
Estimated Sales: Over $1 Billion
Number Employees: 500-999
Brands:
Sweet 2 Eat

10286 **Primal Essence**
1351 Maulhardt Ave
Oxnard, CA 93030-7963
805-981-2409
Fax: 805-981-2419 877-774-6253
sales@primalessence.com
www.primalessence.com
Botanical extracts
President And General Manager: Mark Smythe
mark.smyth@mac.com
Number Employees: 5-9
Type of Packaging: Consumer, Food Service, Bulk

10287 **Primal Kitchen**
Oxnard, CA
888-774-6259
info@primalkitchen.com www.primalkitchen.com
Condiments, dressings, marinades, oils and protein bars
Founder: Mark Sisson

10288 **Primal Nutrition**
23805 Stuart Ranch Rd
Suite 145
Malibu, CA 90265
310-317-4414
888-774-6259
info@primalkitchen.com www.primalkitchen.com
Drink mixes, bars, oils and salad dressings.
Owner: Mark Sisson
Brands:
Primal Kitchen

10289 **Prime Cut Meat & Seafood Company**
2601 N. 31st Ave.
Phoenix, AZ 85009-1522
602-455-8834
800-277-1054
www.primecutusa.com
Meat, seafood
President: David Poppen
dpoppen@primemalta.com
VP/Treasurer: Linda Poppen
Estimated Sales: $17 Million
Number Employees: 50-99

10290 **Prime Food Processing Corp**
300 Vandervoort Ave
Brooklyn, NY 11211-1715
718-963-2323
Chinese dumplings and egg rolls
President: Yee Chan
Quality Control Director: Laymont Dofon
Estimated Sales: $13 Million
Number Employees: 50-99
Number of Brands: 1
Square Footage: 10000
Type of Packaging: Consumer, Food Service, Private Label, Bulk
Brands:
Prime Food

10291 **Prime Ingredients Inc**
280 N Midland Ave
Saddle Brook, NJ 07663-5721
201-791-6655
Fax: 201-791-4244 888-791-6655
www.primeingredients.com
Dessert, dips and sauces, cheese, creamers, mixes, glazes, oils, margarines and olive oil
Director: Christopher Walsh
chris@primeingredients.com
Estimated Sales: Below $5 Million
Number Employees: 5-9
Square Footage: 80000
Type of Packaging: Bulk

10292 Prime Ostrich International
8702a 98th Street
Morinville, AB T8R 1K6
Canada
780-939-3804
Fax: 780-939-4888 800-340-2311
Ostrich meat and meat pies
President: James Danyluik
Marketing Director: Michelle Danyluik
Number Employees: 5-9
Type of Packaging: Consumer, Food Service, Private Label, Bulk

10293 Prime Pak Foods Inc
2076 Memorial Park Dr
Gainesville, GA 30504-5802
770-536-8708
Fax: 770-536-1638 info@primepakfoods.com
www.primepakfoods.com
Beef, pork, veal, poultry and barbecue meat products
President: Todd Robson
CFO: Christy Phillips
Vice President: Milton Robson
Year Founded: 1972
Estimated Sales: $23.5 Million
Number Employees: 100-249

10294 Prime Pastries
370 North Rivermed Road
Concord, ON L4K 3N2
Canada
905-669-5883
Fax: 905-669-8655 smuchnik@primus.ca
www.primepastries.ca
Pastries
President: Steven Muchnik
CFO: Ashley Berman
Brands:
Prime Pastries

10295 Prime Produce
350 N Cypress St
Orange, CA 92866-1028
714-771-0718
Fax: 714-771-0728
Avocados
President: Avi Crane
Business Development Manager: Yair Crane
Sales Manager: Gahl Crane
Operations/Ripening Manager: Miguel Guzman
Estimated Sales: $5-10 Million
Number Employees: 20-49
Type of Packaging: Consumer, Food Service, Private Label, Bulk

10296 Prime Smoked Meats Inc
220 Alice St
Oakland, CA 94607-4394
510-832-7167
Fax: 510-832-4830
Pork
Owner: Dave Andes
Sales Manager: Tina DeMello
dave.andes@primesmoked.com
Office Manager: Elsie Jorstad
Production Manager: Jose Garcia
Estimated Sales: $5897842
Number Employees: 20-49
Square Footage: 48000
Type of Packaging: Consumer, Food Service, Private Label, Bulk
Brands:
James
Prime

10297 (HQ)Primer Foods Corporation
612 South 8th Street
PO Box 373
Cameron, WI 54822-0373
715-458-4075
Fax: 715-458-4078 800-365-2409
tkunz@primerafoods.com www.primerafoods.com
Egg products
President/CEO: Ron Ashton
Chief Executive Officer: John Ashton
Quality Control: Kristen Zuzek
Contact: Barry Eisen
eisen@primerafoods.com
Estimated Sales: $100 Million
Number Employees: 118
Square Footage: 105000
Other Locations:
Primera Foods
Penham MN
Primera Foods
Stockton IL
Primera Foods
Hayfield MN
Primera Foods
Faribault MN
Primer Foods
Altura MN
Brands:
Eggstreme Bakery Mix 100
Eggstreme Options
Eggstreme Yolk
Eggstreme-We 300
Insta Thick
Malta Gran
Prime Cap
Rice Complete
Rice Pro 35
Rice Trin
Tapi
Tomato Max

10298 Primera Meat Service
21649 N Stuart Place Rd
Harlingen, TX 78552-1962
956-423-3721
Fax: 956-423-3085
Meat products
Owner: Javier Abundiz
primerameats@gmail.com
Estimated Sales: $3-5 Million
Number Employees: 5-9

10299 Primex International Trading
5777 W Century Blvd
Suite 1485
Los Angeles, CA 90045
310-410-7100
Fax: 310-568-3336 info@primex.us
www.primex-usa.com
Pistachios, dried fruits and nuts.
Owner & CEO: Ali Amin
Quality System Director: Tiffany Weldin
Grower Relations Representative: Bob Engleman
Plant Manager: Mike Vasilescu
Year Founded: 1989
Estimated Sales: $184.5 Million
Number Employees: 10-19

10300 Primitive Feast
11693 San Vicente Blvd
Suite 488
Los Angeles, CA 90049
844-807-7688
info@primitivefeast.com primitivefeast.com
Frozen entr,es
Co-Founder: Betty Morin
Co-Founder: Yin Goh
Co-Founder: Scott Fennel
Co-Founder: Rick Friedman

10301 Primo Foods
56 Huxley Rd
Toronto, ON M9M 1H2
Canada
416-741-9300
Fax: 416-741-3766 800-377-6945
website@primofoods.ca www.primofoods.ca
Primo pasta, tomatoes, beans, sauces
VP: Tony Gucciardi
Sales: Phil Ulias
Square Footage: 200000
Type of Packaging: Consumer, Food Service, Private Label

10302 Primo Foods
606 Morse Street
Oceanside, CA 92054
760-439-8711
Fax: 760-439-3664 www.primofoodsinc.com
Fish, meats, poultry, dairy, vegetables, spices, seasonings, baking supplies, rices, grains, cheese, kosher and organic foods
Plant Manager: Gabe Soffiaturo
Parent Co: Nabisco
Type of Packaging: Consumer, Food Service

10303 Primo Water Corporation
101 N Cherry St
Suite 501
Winston-Salem, NC 27101
844-237-7466
primowater.com
Water dispensers, purified bottled water, self-service refill drinking water.
Chief Executive Officer: Jerry Fowden
Chief Financial Officer: Jay Wells
Chief Accounting Officer: Jason Ausher
VP/General Counsel/Secretary: Marni Morgan-Poe
SVP/Global Human Resources: Steve Edman
Estimated Sales: K
Number Employees: 10,000+
Type of Packaging: Consumer, Food Service, Private Label, Bulk
Other Locations:
Cliffstar Manufacturing Plant
East Freetown MA
Cliffstar Manufacturing Plant
Fontana CA
Cliffstar Manufacturing Plant
Fredonia NY
Cliffstar Manufacturing Plant
Greer SC
Cliffstar Manufacturing Plant
Joplin MO
Cliffstar Manufacturing Plant
N East PA
Cliffstar Manufacturing Plant
Walla Walla WA
Cliffstar Manufacturing Plant
Warrens WI
Cott Beverage Manufacturing Plant
Calgary, Alberta, Canada
Cott Concentrate Manufacturing
Columbus GA
Brands:
ALHAMBRA
ATHENA
BELMONT SPRINGS
CRYSTAL SPRINGS
DEEP ROCK WATER
HINCKLEY SPRINGS
KENTWOOD SPRINGS
SIERRA SPRINGS
SPARKLETTS
CANADIAN SPRINGS
JAVARAMA
STANDARD COFFEE
TERRAZA
S&D COFFEE & TEA
AIMIA FOODS
RCCI

10304 Primos Northgate
2323 Lakeland Drive
Flowood, MS 39232-9514
601-936-3398
Fax: 601-936-3797 www.primoscafe.com
Baked goods: pies, tarts, cupcakes, brownies and cookies
Owner: Don Primos
President: Peter Primos
Estimated Sales: $500,000 appx.
Number Employees: 20-49
Type of Packaging: Consumer
Brands:
Primos

10305 Primrose Candy Co
4111 W Parker Ave
Chicago, IL 60639-2176
773-276-9522
Fax: 773-276-7411 800-268-9522
support@primrosecandy.com
www.primrosecandy.com
Salt water taffy, lollipops, popcorn, sugar-free candies, and hard and chewy confections.
President/CEO: Mark Puch
mvp@primrosecandy.com
VP Sales/Marketing: Richard Griseto
Estimated Sales: $27,800,000
Number Employees: 100-249
Number of Brands: 2
Square Footage: 95000
Type of Packaging: Consumer, Food Service, Private Label, Bulk
Brands:
Primrose
Rockin' Rods

10306 Prince Michel
154 Winery Ln
Leon, VA 22725-2511
540-547-3707
Fax: 540-547-3088 800-869-8242
www.princemichel.com
Wine
Owner: Kristin Holzman
kholzman@princemichel.com
Estimated Sales: $5-10 Million
Number Employees: 20-49

10307 **Prince of Peace**
3536 Arden Rd
Hayward, CA 94545-3908
510-887-1899
Fax: 510-887-1799 800-732-2328
popsf@popus.com www.princeofpeacecharity.org
Ginseng tea
Vice President: Lolita Lim
lolita@popus.com
VP Finance: Agnes Tsang
National Sales Manager: Mike Jarrett
Purchasing: Maria Wong
Estimated Sales: $11,200,000
Number Employees: 20-49
Square Footage: 145548
Brands:
Gx Power
Hazelnut
Jamaican Gold
Mocha
Nature Soothe
New Jamaican Gold Cappuccino
Prince of Peace
Prince of Peace Hawaiian
Tiger Balm Analgesic Oitments

10308 **Principe Foods USA**
3605 Long Beach Blvd
Suite 200
Long Beach, CA 90807
310-680-5500
Fax: 559-272-6183
Deli meats
Brands:
Principe

10309 **Prinova**
285 Fullerton Ave
Carol Stream, IL 60188-1886
630-868-0300
Fax: 630-868-0310 info@prinovausa.com
www.prinovausa.com
Ascorbic acid, B vitamins and amino acids
Owner: Donald Thorp
sales@premiumingredients.com
Number Employees: 10-19

10310 **(HQ)Printpack Inc.**
2800 Overlook Pkwy. NE
Atlanta, GA 30339
404-460-7000
info@printpack.com
www.printpack.com
Printed, coated, laminated and flexible film, rolls, sheets and heat sealing paper; also, candy bar and meat wrappers.
Chairman & CEO: Jimmy Love
Senior VP & CFO: Tripp Seitter
Year Founded: 1956
Estimated Sales: Over $1 Billion
Number Employees: 1000-4999

10311 **Private Harvest**
5009 Windplay Dr
Suite 2
El Dorado Hills, CA 95762-9316
916-933-7080
Sauces and spreads.
President: Lynn Lok
Manager: Bonnie Ewing
Estimated Sales: $5-10 Million
Number Employees: 10
Parent Co: Private Harvest
Type of Packaging: Private Label
Brands:
Bobby Flay
Private Harvest
Private Harvest Bobby Flay
Private Harvest Tuscan Hills
Tuscan Hills

10312 **Private Label Foods**
P.O.Box 60805
Rochester, NY 14606
585-254-9205
Fax: 585-254-0186 info@privatelabelfoods.com
www.privatelabelfoods.com
Sauces, salad dressings, salsa and marinades
President: Frank Lavorato
VP: Bonnie Lavorato
Estimated Sales: $4 Million
Number Employees: 10-19
Square Footage: 200000
Type of Packaging: Food Service, Private Label

10313 **Private Spring Water**
13240 Llagas Ave
San Martin, CA 95046-9562
408-681-1500
Fax: 408-686-2100 877-664-1500
info@privatespringwater.com
www.privatespringwater.com
Bottled water
Owner: Ken Churchill
ken@privatespringwater.com
Number Employees: 10-19

10314 **Pro Form Labs**
PO Box 626
Orinda, CA 94563
707-752-9010
Fax: 707-752-9014 info@proformlabs.com
www.proformlabs.com
Nutritional powders and vitamins; weight control and sports nutrition tablets, capsules and powders
President: Doug Gillespie
Customer Service: Kellie Henry
Purchasing Agent: Alex Gillespie
Estimated Sales: $3-5 Million
Number Employees: 1-4
Square Footage: 100000
Parent Co: Gillespie & Associates
Type of Packaging: Consumer, Food Service, Private Label, Bulk
Brands:
Healthbody
Juice-Mate
Naturslim

10315 **Pro Pac Labs**
P.O.Box 9691
Ogden, UT 84409
801-621-0900
Fax: 801-621-0930 888-277-6722
Herbs, vitamins and minerals
President: Lew Wheelwright
CEO: Kim Wheelwright
Contact: Lauri Christiansen
lchristiansen@propaclabs.com
Estimated Sales: $9 Million
Number Employees: 100
Type of Packaging: Consumer, Private Label, Bulk

10316 **Pro Portion Food**
217 N Main Street
Sayville, NY 11782-2512
631-567-4494
Fax: 631-567-1636
Health and dietetics foods
President: Rhoda Rubin
Estimated Sales: $5-10 000,000
Number Employees: 15

10317 **Pro-Source Performance Prods**
2231 Landmark Pl
Manasquan, NJ 08736-1026
732-528-3260
Fax: 320-763-7996 www.prosource.net
Bodybuilding and nutritional supplements
Director: Donald Crank
Contact: Tom Chinery
tomc@prosource.net
Estimated Sales: $2.5-5 Million
Number Employees: 5-9
Brands:
Prosource

10318 **ProFormance Foods**
99 Meserole St
Apt 1
Brooklyn, NY 11206-2014
703-869-3413
info@eatprotes.com
eatprotes.com
Chips
Contact: Ryan Wiltse
Brands:
Protes

10319 **Proacec USA**
1158 26th Street
Suite 509
Santa Monica, CA 90403-4621
310-996-7770
Fax: 310-996-7772 www.proacec.com
Olives and olive oil
President: Paul Short
Estimated Sales: Below $5 Million
Number Employees: 10
Number of Brands: 4
Number of Products: 30
Square Footage: 2000
Type of Packaging: Consumer, Food Service, Bulk
Brands:
Caroliva
Don Quixate
El Carmen
Plantio Del Condado

10320 **Probar**
190 N Apollo Rd.
Salt Lake City, UT 84116
Fax: 801-456-8880 800-921-2294
info@theprobar.com www.theprobar.com
Plant based food products includings snack bars, energy bites, and nut butters
President: Jules Lambert
Founder/CEO: Jeff Coleman

10321 **Procell Polymers**
PO Box 33
Baton Rouge, LA 70821-0033
225-978-8069
Fax: 866-860-1269
Cellulose gum, guar gum, xanthan gum and other specialty products.
Manager: David Hatcher
Manager: Harry Steeghs
Type of Packaging: Bulk

10322 **Produce Buyers Company**
7201 W Fort St
Suite 93
Detroit, MI 48209
313-843-0132
Produce
President: Salvatore Cipriano
Estimated Sales: $1-3 Million
Number Employees: 1-4

10323 **Producer Marketing Overlake**
700 N Capitol Way
Olympia, WA 98512
360-352-9096
Fax: 360-352-8076
info@olympiafarmersmarket.com
www.olympiafarmersmarket.com
Blueberries, strawberries, sliced peaches, Marion blackberries, raspberries
President: Rod Cook
Sales: Paul Askier
General Manager: Bill Whaley
Estimated Sales: $5-10 Million
Number Employees: 5-9
Parent Co: Overlake Farms
Type of Packaging: Consumer, Food Service, Private Label, Bulk
Brands:
Bee Sweet
Overlake

10324 **Producers Cooperative**
1800 N Texas Ave
Bryan, TX 77803-1831
979-778-6000
Fax: 979-778-0243
producers@producerscooperative.com
www.producerscooperative.com
Pinto beans
Manager: Bob Beyer
Manager: Martin Jackson
martin.jackson@nestle.com
General Manager: Eob Beyer
Number Employees: 5-9
Square Footage: 40000
Type of Packaging: Private Label
Brands:
Cowboy
Hub of the Uncompaghre

10325 **Producers Cooperative Oil Mill**
6 SE 4th St
Oklahoma City, OK 73129-1000
405-232-7555
Fax: 405-236-4887 www.producerscoop.net
Cottonseed
President/Chief Executive Officer: Gary Conkling
gary.conkling@producerscoop.net
Director, Health, Safety & Environment: Becky Mosshammer
Estimated Sales: $15 Million
Number Employees: 50-99
Number of Products: 1

10326 **Producers Dairy Foods Inc**
250 E Belmont Ave
Fresno, CA 93701
559-264-6583
Fax: 559-457-4683
customer.service@producersdairy.com
www.producersdairy.com
Milk, yogurt, cottage cheese, ice cream, eggs, butter, water and juice
President: Scott Shehadey
Director of Sales & Marketing: Richie Shehadey
Year Founded: 1932
Estimated Sales: $100 Million
Number Employees: 20-49

10327 **Producers Peanut Company**
PO Box 250
Suffolk, VA 23434
757-539-7496
Fax: 757-934-7730 800-847-5491
pntkid@producerspeanut.com
www.producerspeanut.com
Peanuts and peanut butter
CEO: James Pond
Estimated Sales: $800,000
Number Employees: 20-49
Square Footage: 144000
Type of Packaging: Food Service, Private Label, Bulk
Brands:
Peanut & Tree Nut
Peanut Kids Company Store

10328 **Producers Rice Mill Inc.**
PO Box 1248
Stuttgart, AR 72160
870-673-4444
Fax: 870-673-7394 info@producersrice.com
www.producersrice.com
Rice and soybeans.
President/CEO: Keith Glover
kglover@producersrice.com
Chairman: Jerry Hoskyn
Year Founded: 1943
Estimated Sales: $550 Million
Number Employees: 500-999
Square Footage: 30000
Type of Packaging: Consumer, Food Service

10329 **Productos Del Plata**
71st 8040 NW
Miami, FL 33166
786-357-8261
Fax: 786-331-7500 info@pdpgroup.us
www.pdpgroup.us
Cookies, tea, baked goods, pasta, sauces and dessert toppings
Marketing: Mauricio Montero

10330 **Produits Alimentaire**
1186 Rue Du Pont
St Lambert De Lauzon, QC G0S 2W0
Canada
418-889-8080
Fax: 418-889-9730 800-463-1787
Flour, food colors, confectionery and syrup
Director: Michel Blouin
Number Employees: 20-49
Square Footage: 32000
Type of Packaging: Consumer, Food Service, Private Label, Bulk
Brands:
Blouin
Maltee
Pacha
Supreme

10331 **(HQ)Produits Alimentaire**
1805 Berlier St
Laval, QC H7L 3S4
Canada
514-334-5503
Fax: 514-334-3584 800-361-9326
www.berthelet.com
Flavorings, seasonings, puddings, soup bases, sauces, jams, food colorings, jelly powder, pie fillings, beverage syrups, bouillon bases, concentrates, sundae toppings and beverage crystals
Special Advisor: Guy Berthelet
Sales Manager: Pierre Berthelet
Operations & Human Resources Director: Dany Miville
Planning & Purchasing Manager: Roger Tremblay
Type of Packaging: Consumer, Food Service, Private Label, Bulk
Other Locations:
Produits Alimentaires Berthel
Blainville PQ
Brands:
Berthelet
Juwong
Le Saucier
McLean
Pasta Fiesta
Privilege
St. Hubert
5 Fourchettes

10332 **Produits Belle Baie**
10 rue du Quai
Caraquet, NB E1W 1B6
Canada
506-727-4414
Fax: 506-727-7166 info@bellebaie.com
Herring, shrimp and crab
President: Alie Lebouthiller
Vice President: Valmond Chaison
Quality Control: Georges Boudreau
Marketing & Sales Director: Fernand Brideaux
Production Manager: Georges Foulem
Estimated Sales: $10 Million
Number Employees: 150
Type of Packaging: Consumer, Food Service

10333 **Produits Ronald**
200 St Joseph Street
St. Damase, QC J0H 1J0
Canada
450-797-3303
Fax: 450-797-2389 800-465-0118
Canned corn-on-the-cob, marinades, sauces, baked beans, bouillons and fondue
President: Jean Messier
Vice President/General Manager: Bernard Belanger
Quality Assurance Manager: Lucie Labbe
Plant Manager: Louis Richard
Purchasing Manager: David Lussier
Number Employees: 100-249
Square Footage: 160000
Parent Co: A. Lassonde
Type of Packaging: Consumer, Food Service
Brands:
Camino Del Sol
Canton
Madelaine
Mont-Rougr
Rougemont

10334 **Profood International**
670 W Fifth Ave
Suite 116
Naperville, IL 60563
630-428-2386
Fax: 630-527-9905 888-288-0081
support@profoodinternational.com
www.profoodinternational.com
Preservatives, emulsifiers, enzymes, texturizers and acids
Contact: Dave Shi
daves@profoodinternational.com

10335 **Progenix Corporation**
7566 N 72nd Ave
Wausau, WI 54401
715-675-7566
Fax: 715-675-4931 800-233-3356
Ginseng, whole root, fiber, prong, powder and extract; capsules, teas and gift packaging
President: Robert Duwe
Number Employees: 20-49
Square Footage: 26000
Type of Packaging: Consumer, Food Service, Bulk
Brands:
Ameriseng
Wiscon
Wisconsin American Ginseng

10336 **Progressive Flavors**
409 E. Main
Madison, WI 53703
608-257-4626
Fax: 805-383-2644 800-827-0555
Flavors
President: Norma Schwarz
Estimated Sales: $5-10 Million
Number Employees: 4
Type of Packaging: Food Service, Bulk

10337 **Progresso Quality Foods**
500 W Elmer Rd
Vineland, NJ 08360-6314
856-691-1565
Fax: 856-794-1574 www.generalmills.com
Canned soups, bread crumbs, cooking oils and spaghetti sauce
CEO: John Komer
Estimated Sales: $61 Thousand
Number Employees: 20-49
Number of Brands: 1
Square Footage: 600000
Parent Co: General Mills
Type of Packaging: Consumer
Brands:
Progresso

10338 **Prohibition Distillery, LLC**
10 Union St.
Roscoe, NY 12776
917-685-8989
www.prohibitiondistillery.com
Vodka, gin, whiskey
Co-Founder: Brian Facquet
Co-Founder: John Walsh
Number of Brands: 1
Number of Products: 3

10339 **Project 7**
302 N El Camino Real
Suite 216
San Clemente, CA 92672
949-891-0729
Fax: 949-613-7170 info@project7.com
project7.com
Specialty candy and gum
President: Tyler Merrick
Controller: Paul Luster
Contact: Anoush Alexanian
alexanian@project7.com
Year Founded: 2008
Number Employees: 6

10340 **Prolimer Foods**
104 Liberte Avenue
Candiac, QC J5R 6X1
Canada
450-635-4631
Fax: 450-635-4637 877-535-4631
Hors d'oeuvres, appetizers, ready meals, pizza, soup, seafood, vegetables, fruit and olives
Marketing: Nicolas Bergeron

10341 **Prolume**
163 W. White Mountain Blvd
Lakeside, AZ 85929-7004
928-367-1200
Fax: 928-367-1205 info@prolume.com
www.prolume.com
Bioluminescence ingredients
CEO: Bruce Bryan
Brands:
Prolume

10342 **(HQ)Promised Land Dairy**
Colorado Springs, CO 80907
877-520-2479
consumercare@promisedlanddairy.com
www.promisedlanddairy.com
Milk products
General Sales Managers: Gordon Kuenemann
Director of Operations: Dene Smith
Year Founded: 1987
Estimated Sales: $50-100 Million
Square Footage: 35167
Type of Packaging: Consumer

10343 **Prommus Brands**
Chicago, IL
www.prommus.com
Hummus
Founder: Anthony Brahimsha
Year Founded: 2014

10344 **(HQ)Promolux Lighting**
Box 40
Shawnigan Lake, BC V0R 2W0
Canada
250-743-1222
Fax: 250-743-1221 800-519-1222
info2@promolux.com www.promolux.com
Lighting for food display cases

President: Mark Granfar
Quality Control: Trevor Brien
Marketing: Lyn Rose
Sales: Scott Werhun
Purchasing: Michael Vankesteron
Estimated Sales: $10-20 Million
Number Employees: 20
Number of Products: 3
Square Footage: 4000
Parent Co: Samark SA
Type of Packaging: Private Label
Brands:
Econofrost
Lighting
Long Life
Mr16
Multichrome
Promolux

10345 **Promotion in Motion Companies**
PO Box 558
Closter, NJ 07624-0558
201-784-5800
Fax: 201-784-1010 800-369-7391
mail@promotioninmotion.com
www.promotioninmotion.com
Brand name confections, fruit snacks and other fine foods
President/CEO: Michael Rosenberg
mrosenberg@promotioninmotion.com
Executive Director: Frank McSorley
COO: Basant Dwivedi
Number Employees: 250-499
Type of Packaging: Private Label

10346 **Proper-Chem**
46 Arbor Ln
Dix Hills, NY 11746
631-420-8000
Fax: 631-420-8003
Vitamins and supplements
President: Emil Backstrom
Estimated Sales: $3-5 Million
Number Employees: 10-19
Square Footage: 40000
Type of Packaging: Consumer, Private Label
Brands:
Goubaud
Proper-Care

10347 **Prosperity Organic Foods**
475 West Main Street
Boise, ID 83702
208-429-9800
Fax: 208-854-0907 888-557-5741
www.meltbutteryspread.com
Organic butter and spread substitutes.
Founder: Cynthia Rapp
Consumer Products Leader: Meg Carlson
Contact: John Horne
john@meltorganic.com
Type of Packaging: Consumer
Brands:
MELT ORGANIC

10348 **Protano's Bakery**
2301 N 22nd Ave
Hollywood, FL 33020-2003
954-925-3474
Fax: 954-925-3488 guy@protano.com
www.protanosbakery.com
Bakery products
Owner: Guy Protano Jr
greg@underweb.com
Plant Manager: Bob Woodmancy
Estimated Sales: $5-10 Million
Number Employees: 100-249

10349 **Protein Research**
1852 Rutan Dr
Livermore, CA 94551-7635
925-243-6300
Fax: 925-243-6308 800-948-1991
info@proteinresearch.com
www.proteinresearch.com
Amino acid, vitamin and mineral supplements
Owner: Robert Matheson
robert@proteinresearch.com
Director: Theodore Aarons
VP Operations: Daniel Aarons
Estimated Sales: $5-10 Million
Number Employees: 50-99
Number of Products: 12
Square Footage: 132000
Type of Packaging: Private Label, Bulk

10350 **Protica Inc**
1002 MacArthur Rd
Whitehall, PA 18052-7052
610-832-2000
Fax: 978-975-4325 800-776-8422
www.protica.com
Hydrolyzed proteins and fish gelatin
President: Peter Noble
Sales: Chris Gorski
Contact: Bill Dillon
wdillon@protica.com
Type of Packaging: Bulk

10351 **Protient**
PO Box 64101
St Paul, MN 55164-0101
651-481-2068
Fax: 507-334-8695 800-328-9680
www.landolakesinc.com
Dry cream powders, margarine and spreads
President: Christopher Policinsky
Contact: Steve Fiedler
sfiedler@landolakes.com
Number Employees: 50-99
Parent Co: Land O'Lakes
Type of Packaging: Consumer

10352 **Protient**
351 Hanson Way
Woodland, CA 95776
651-638-2600
Fax: 651-697-0997
Whey and soy proteins, hydrolysates and blends.
President: K Kachadurian
Chief Executive Officer: Nicolas Hanson
CFO: Tent Macoy
CEO: Todd Watson
Quality Control: Tom Yezzi
Market Development Specialist: Cheryl Reid
Sr Sales Manager: Kris Hanson
Estimated Sales: $5-10 Million
Number Employees: 20-49
Brands:
Protient

10353 **Protos Inc**
449 Glenmeade Rd
Greensburg, PA 15601-1170
724-836-1802
Fax: 724-836-3895 protos@protos-inc.com
www.protos-inc.com
Ostrich meats
President: Logan Dickerson
Number Employees: 20-49
Type of Packaging: Food Service, Private Label, Bulk
Brands:
Ostrim #1 Sports Meat Snack
Ostrim Ostrich Saute

10354 **Prova**
100 Conifer Hill Drive
Suite 208
Danvers, MA 01923
978-739-9055
Fax: 978-739-4044 877-776-8287
contact@provaus.com www.prova.fr
Flavors: vanilla, cocoa, coffee and caramel.
Vice President of Sales, North America: M. William Graham
Contact: Muriel Acat-Vergnet
muriel.acat-vergnet@provaus.com
Parent Co: Prova SAS
Type of Packaging: Bulk

10355 **Providence Cheese**
49 Rotary Dr
Johnston, RI 02919
401-421-5653
Fax: 401-421-3870
Pasta, cheese
President/Owner: Wayne Wheatley
irwind@highlands.k12.fl.us
Estimated Sales: Less than $500,000
Number Employees: 1-4
Type of Packaging: Private Label

10356 **Provimi Foods**
W2103 County Road VV
Seymour, WI 54165
920-833-6861
Fax: 920-833-9850 800-833-8325
info@provimifoods.com www.provimifoods.com
Veal and sauces
President: Dan Schober
CFO: Rod Mackenzie
Contact: Bruce Achten
achten@provimifoods.com
Year Founded: 1982
Type of Packaging: Consumer, Food Service, Private Label, Bulk
Brands:
Provimi

10357 **Provitas LLC**
5204 Blackhawk Dr
Plano, TX 75093-4901
972-767-8867
Fax: 972-793-8639 www.provitasllc.com
Vitamin powders, emulsions and oils
President: Mac Weber
Manager: Jenny Weber
Number Employees: 10-19
Type of Packaging: Bulk

10358 **Provost Packers**
5340 49th Avenue
PO Box 570
Provost, AB TOB 3S0
Canada
780-753-2415
Fax: 780-753-2413
Beef, pork and sausage
President: Bernard Bouma
Sales Manager: Lyle Bouma
Estimated Sales: $1-2 Million
Number Employees: 10-19
Square Footage: 328000
Type of Packaging: Consumer, Food Service, Private Label, Bulk
Brands:
Dutch Brothers
Provost Packers

10359 **Pruden Packing Company**
1201 North Main Street
Suffolk, VA 23434-5814
757-539-8773
Fax: 757-925-4971
Ham and pork shoulder
President: Peter Pruden
General Manager: K Jones
Plant Superintendent: Terry McNitt
Estimated Sales: $3.0 Million
Number Employees: 5-9
Parent Co: Smithfield Companies
Brands:
Champon
Peanut City
Pruden

10360 **Psycho Donuts**
2006 Winchester Blvd
Suite C
Campbell, CA 95008-3400
408-378-4540
www.psychodonuts.com
Donuts
Owner: Web Granger
psychodonuts@gmail.com
Number Employees: 5-9

10361 **Psyllium Labs**
1701 E Woodfield Road
Suite 636
Schaumburg, IL 60173
888-851-6667
info@psyllium.com www.psylliumlabs.com
Psyllium, chia and quinoa
Operations Executive: Drew West
Other Locations:
Manufacturing Facility
North Gujarat, India
Manufacturing Facility
Santa Cruz, Bolivia

10362 **Publix Super Market**
PO Box 407
Lakeland, FL 33802-0407
800-242-1227
www.publix.com
Groceries, produce, meat, seafood, deli, floral, beer, wine and dairy.
President/CEO: Todd Jones
Chairman: William Crenshaw
CFO: David Phillips

Year Founded: 1930
Estimated Sales: $38.1 Billion
Number Employees: 197,000
Other Locations:
Bakery Manufacturing
Atlanta GA
Dairy/Fresh Foods Manufacturing
Deerfield Beach FL
Fresh Foods Manufacturing
Jacksonville FL
Bakery/Deli/Dairy Manufacturing
Lakeland FL
Dairy Manufacturing
Lawrenceville GA

10363 **Puebla Foods Inc**
75 Jefferson St
Passaic, NJ 07055-6551
973-473-0201
Fax: 973-473-3854 pueblafoods@aol.com
Mexican products: tortillas, chips and taco shells, jalapenos, hot sauces, dried peppers, tomatillos and sodas
President: Felix Sanchez
VP: Carmen Sanchez
Contact: Martha Acevedo
macevedo@pueblafoods.com
General Manager: Gabriela Molina
Estimated Sales: Less Than $500,000
Number Employees: 1-4
Square Footage: 30000
Brands:
El Ranchito
Mipueblito
Pueblafood

10364 **Pulakos 926 Chocolate**
2530 Parade St
Erie, PA 16503-2034
814-452-4026
Fax: 814-456-4876 www.pulakoschocolates.com
Chocolates
Owner: Michael Noel
mnoel@pulakoschocolates.com
VP/Treasurer: J Pulakos
Plant Manager: Pete Skelton
Estimated Sales: $1300000
Number Employees: 20-49
Square Footage: 64000
Type of Packaging: Consumer, Food Service, Private Label

10365 **Pulmuone Foods USA Inc.**
2315 Moore Ave.
Fullerton, CA 92833
800-588-7782
inquiry@pulmuone.com
www.pulmuonefoodsusa.com
Pastas, sauces, meat, chicken and vegetable patties, soybean products.
CEO: Hyo-Yul Lee
VP, Food Safety & Compliance: Jung Han
Manager, Product Excellence Insights: Faye Lee
Director, Marketing: Sean Kim
Director, Engineering & Technology: Brian Seong-Jun Kim
Year Founded: 1981
Estimated Sales: $1.5 Billion
Number Employees: 110
Number of Brands: 5
Parent Co: Pulmuone Co., Ltd.
Type of Packaging: Consumer, Food Service, Private Label, Bulk
Brands:
Monterey Gourmet Foods
Wildwood
Emerald Valley Kitchen
Pulmuone
Nasoya

10366 **Puratos Canada**
520 Slate Dr
Mississauga, ON L5T 0A1
Canada
905-362-3668
Fax: 905-362-0296 info@puratos.ca
www.puratos.com
Dough conditioners, bases and mixes, custards, fruit compounds and fillings, glazes, chocolate products and ganache
President: Eddy Van Belle
Number Employees: 20-49
Square Footage: 160000
Parent Co: Puratos NV

Type of Packaging: Food Service, Private Label, Bulk
Brands:
Biopur

10367 **Pure Batch**
Hillsborough, NJ
609-373-2015
info@pure-batch.com
www.pure-batch.com
Cookies
Year Founded: 2015

10368 **Pure Dark**
800 High Street
Hackettstown, NJ 07840
973-856-1899
dawn.gallagher@effem.com
www.puredark.com
Cocoa, baking chocolate, chocolate bars and gift packs.
Marketing: Dawn Gallagher

10369 **Pure Extracts Inc**
59 Remington Blvd
Suite D
Ronkonkoma, NY 11779-6991
631-588-9727
Fax: 631-588-9729
Herbs and oils
Chairman/President: Gurjeet Bajwa
Owner/Sales Exec: Joe Singh
Manager: Nat Patel
pureextracts@yahoo.com
Estimated Sales: $500,000
Number Employees: 1-4
Square Footage: 3000

10370 **Pure Flo Water Co**
7737 Mission Gorge Rd
Santee, CA 92071-3399
619-448-5120
Fax: 619-596-4154 800-787-3356
www.pureflo.com
Bottled water: purified, fluoridated and spring; water filtration system services
CEO: Brian Grant
bgrant@pureflo.com
General Manager: Leslie Alstad
Director of Marketing & Technology: Damon Grant
Accounting Manager: Bernadette Meyer
Estimated Sales: $13 Million
Number Employees: 100-249
Number of Brands: 1
Square Footage: 9000
Type of Packaging: Consumer, Bulk
Brands:
Pure Flo Water

10371 **Pure Food Ingredients**
514 Commerce Pkwy
Verona, WI 53593
608-845-9601
Fax: 608-845-9628 800-355-9601
stan@itis.com
Canned tomatoes, chiles, jalapenos and olives; beeswax and honey
President: Stanley Kanter
Estimated Sales: $1,000,000
Number Employees: 5-9
Square Footage: 40000
Type of Packaging: Consumer, Food Service, Private Label, Bulk

10372 **(HQ)Pure Foods**
32533 Cascade View Drive
Sultan, WA 98294-7733
360-793-2241
Fax: 360-793-2485
Molasses and honey
President: Michael Ingalls
CEO: Denice Ingalls
Contact: Brian Albans
balbans@purefoodsco.com
Plant Manager: Dan Johnson
Estimated Sales: $5,000,000
Number Employees: 20 to 49
Square Footage: 36000
Type of Packaging: Consumer, Food Service, Private Label, Bulk
Brands:
Bear Mountain
Heins
Miller's
Pure Gold

10373 **Pure Foods Meat**
10 Shorncliffe Rd
Unit 5, Suite 202
Toronto, ON M9B 3S3
Canada
416-236-1163
consumercare@purefoodsmeat.ca
purefoodsmeat.ca
Pork
President: David Schwartz
VP, Business Development & Marketing: Anita Gravelle
Production Manager: Sol Colacci
Purchasing & Inventory Manager: Carla Verissimo
Year Founded: 1927
Estimated Sales: $86.05 Million
Number Employees: 600
Number of Brands: 1
Square Footage: 154591
Type of Packaging: Consumer, Food Service, Private Label, Bulk
Brands:
Legacy Pork

10374 **Pure Gourmet**
719 Bridle Road
Glenside, PA 19038-2005
215-609-4219
Fax: 763-322-7035
kellymacleod@puregourmetfoods.com
Ice cream and sorbet
Manager: Kelly Macleod
kellymacleod@puregourmetfoods.com
Estimated Sales: $150,000
Number Employees: 2

10375 **Pure Ground Ingredients**
2535 Business Pkwy
Minden, NV 89423
775-297-4047
info@puregroundingredients.com
puregroundingredients.com
Organic herbal ingredients
Founder: Kevin Lindseth
Sales Manager: Stacy Kixmiller

10376 **Pure Indian**
PO Box 296
Princeton Jct., NJ 08550
609-785-9100
Fax: 302-371-3081 877-588-4433
info@pureindianfoods.com
www.pureindianfoods.com
Ghee, oils and spices
Co-Founder: Sandeep Agarwal
Co-Founder: Nalini Agarwal
Year Founded: 2008

10377 **Pure Inventions LLC**
64 Grant Pl
Suite 3H
Little Silver, NJ 07739-1042
732-842-5777
Fax: 732-842-8422 info@pureinventions.com
www.pureinventions.com
Nutritional extracts and supplements
Member: Lori Mulligan
Member: Lynne Gerhards
Manager: Debbie Potts
info@pureinventions.com
Manager: Johanna Cerliglione
Estimated Sales: $2 Million
Number Employees: 10-19

10378 **Pure Life Organic Foods**
6625 W Sahara Ave
Suite 1
Las Vegas, NV 89146
708-990-5817
info@purelifeorganicfoods.com
www.purelifeorganicfoods.com
Organic sugars, coconut milk and coconut oil
Managing Director: Pradeep Mathur
Sales and Marketing Head: Sayida Bano
Parent Co: Pure Diets Intl. Ltd.
Type of Packaging: Bulk

10379 Pure Milk & Ice Cream Company
1819 Rutland Dr
Austin, TX 78758-5423
512-837-2685
Fax: 512-339-0677 www.oakfarmsdairy.com
Dairy
Manager: Patrick Cummins
Production Manager: Terry Welty
Estimated Sales: $5-10 Million appx.
Number Employees: 50-99
Parent Co: Pure Milk Company

10380 Pure Planet
2610 Homestead Pl
Rancho Dominguez, CA 90220
Fax: 562-951-5040 800-695-2017
info@pureplanet.com pureplanet.com
Organic plant powders
CEO: David Sandoval
dsandoval@organicbynatureinc.com
President: Amy Sandoval
General Sales Manager: Gerry Wong
Estimated Sales: $5.6 Million
Number Employees: 50-99
Brands:
Organic By Nature

10381 Pure Sales
660 Baker St
Suite 367
Costa Mesa, CA 92626-4470
714-540-5455
Fax: 714-540-5974 puresales@aol.com
Pasta
President: James Silver
puresales@aol.com
Estimated Sales: Under $500,000
Number Employees: 1-4

10382 Pure Source LLC
9750 NW 17th St
Doral, FL 33172-2753
305-477-8111
Fax: 305-477-4002 800-324-6273
info@thepuresource.com www.thepuresource.com
Vitamins, antioxidants, raw materials and packaging services
Owner: Joel Meyer
sylvia@thepuresource.com
Estimated Sales: Below $5 Million
Number Employees: 100-249
Square Footage: 280000
Type of Packaging: Consumer, Food Service, Private Label, Bulk
Brands:
Pure Source

10383 Pure Sweet Honey Farms Inc
514 Commerce Pkwy
Verona, WI 53593-1841
608-845-9601
Fax: 608-845-9628 800-355-9601
map007@earthlink.net www.puresweethoney.com
Honey, maple syrup and molasses
President: Stanley Kanter
stan@chorus.net
Sales Director: Mark Pelka
Estimated Sales: $470000
Number Employees: 5-9
Square Footage: 80000
Type of Packaging: Consumer, Food Service, Private Label, Bulk
Brands:
Springhill

10384 Pure's Food Specialties
2929 S 25th Ave
Broadview, IL 60155-4529
708-344-8884
Fax: 708-344-8703 www.puresfood.com
Cookies
President: Elliot Pure
epure@puresfood.com
Estimated Sales: Below $5 Million
Number Employees: 20-49
Type of Packaging: Bulk

10385 Pure7 Chocolate
82 Sanderson Ave
Lynn, MA 01902
844-547-8737
info@pure7chocolate.com pure7chocolate.com
Chocolate
Founder & CEO: Julie MacQueen
COO: Dennis Mehiel
Brands:
Pure7

10386 PureCircle USA
200 W Jackson Blvd
8th Floor
Chicago, IL 60606
630-361-0374
info.usa@purecircle.com
purecircle.com
Stevia
CEO: Lai Hock Meng
CFO: Lim Kian Thong
Year Founded: 2001
Estimated Sales: $127 Million
Parent Co: PureCircle Limited
Type of Packaging: Bulk

10387 PureForm CBD
Los Angeles, CA
www.pureformglobal.com
Manufacturer of non-hemp-based CBD for consumer brands
President/Owner: Jake Cormier

10388 Purely American
5635 Raby Road
Suite H
Norfolk, VA 23502
757-466-1312
Fax: 757-466-3041 800-359-7873
www.purelyamerican.com
Mixes, sauces and marinades, and peanuts.
President: Ray Leard
Estimated Sales: $500,000
Number Employees: 5
Type of Packaging: Private Label
Brands:
Peter's Beach Sauces
Purely American

10389 Purely Elizabeth
3200 Carbon Pl
Suite 101
Boulder, CO 80301-6135
720-242-7525
Fax: 888-586-9485 support@purelyelizabeth.com
purelyelizabeth.com
Gluten-free baking mixes, granola, oatmeal and superfood bars
Founder & CEO: Elizabeth Stein
elizabeth@purelyelizabeth.com
Director of Finance: Tracy Baumann
Marketing: Paige Mitchum
Operations: Garrett McBride
Estimated Sales: Less Than $500,000
Number Employees: 10-19
Brands:
Purely Elizabeth

10390 Purely Pecans
Valdosta, GA
800-627-6630
purelypecans.com
Grain-free granola and nut butters
Founder: Jeff Worn

10391 Puritan/ATZ Ice Cream
301 E Wayne St
Kendallville, IN 46755-1457
260-347-2700
Fax: 260-347-2652
Ice cream
GM: Terry Atz
GM: Jeff Atz
Estimated Sales: $5-10 Million
Number Employees: 10-19
Type of Packaging: Consumer, Food Service

10392 Purity Candy Co
422 Market St
Lewisburg, PA 17837-1422
570-524-0823
Fax: 570-524-7793 800-821-4748
www.puritycandy.com
Candy and chocolates
Owner: Margaret Burfeindt
m.burfeindt@purity.com
President: Theodore Roosevelt
General Manager Production: Sharon Weiser
Estimated Sales: Less Than $500,000
Number Employees: 1-4
Brands:
Purity Candy

10393 Purity Dairies LLC
360 Murfreesboro Pike
Nashville, TN 37210-2816
615-244-1900
Fax: 615-242-8547 www.puritydairies.com
Milk, ice cream, yogurt, cottage cheese, juice, sour cream and heavy cream
President: Mark Ezell
Cmo: Tim White
tim_white@deanfoods.com
Sales Manager: Mike Payne
Number Employees: 500-999
Parent Co: Dean Foods Company
Type of Packaging: Consumer, Food Service

10394 Purity Factories
96 Blackmarsh Rd
St. John's, NL A1C 5M9
Canada
709-579-2035
Fax: 709-738-2426 800-563-3411
orderdesk@purity.nf.ca www.purity.nf.ca
Jams, fruit syrups and biscuits
General Manager: Doug Spurrell
Sales Manager: Gerry Power
Type of Packaging: Consumer, Food Service, Private Label, Bulk

10395 Purity Farms
One Organic Way
La Farge, WI 54639
303-647-2368
Fax: 303-647-9875 877-211-4819
purityfarmsorganic@gmail.com
Organic butter
President: Kathy Feldenkreis
Number Employees: 1-4
Type of Packaging: Consumer, Food Service, Private Label, Bulk
Brands:
Purity Farms Ghee

10396 Purity Foods Inc
417 S Meridian Rd
Hudson, MI 49247-9709
517-448-2050
Fax: 517-448-2070 800-997-7358
info@purityfoods.com
www.publishing.com
Beans, grains, seeds, cereals, cookbooks, flours, granola, pastas, pretzels and sesame sticks.
President: Donald Stinchcomb
Regional Sales Manager: Hezeden Graye
Manager: Gabby Williamson
gabby.williamson@purityfoods.com
Estimated Sales: Less Than $500,000
Number Employees: 1-4
Square Footage: 60000

10397 Purity Ice Cream Co
700 Cascadilla St
Suite A
Ithaca, NY 14850-3255
607-272-1545
Fax: 607-272-1546 purityice@aol.com
Ice cream
Owner: Heather Lane
blane@purityicecream.com
Estimated Sales: $1000000
Number Employees: 20-49
Type of Packaging: Consumer, Food Service

10398 Purity Organic
405 14th Street
Suite 1000
Oakland, CA 94612
415-440-7777
info@purityorganic.com
purityorganic.com
Ready-to-drink juice, tea and coconut water
CEO: Douglas Abrams
Contact: Demian Flores
demian@purityorganic.com

10399 Purity Products
200 Terminal Dr
Plainview, NY 11803-2312
516-767-1967
Fax: 516-767-1722 800-256-6102
customercare@purityproducts.com
www.puritypgoducts.com

Sauces, mayonnaise, vinegar, mustard, salad dressings, vegetable oils, jellies, pickles
President: William Schroeder
President, Chief Executive Officer: Jahn Levin
jahn@purityproducts.com
CFO: Bruce Morecroft
Vice President of Quality Assurance: Richard Conant
Marketing: Al Rodriquez
Operations: Ricky Montejo
Purchasing Director: Charles Menezes
Estimated Sales: Less Than $500,000
Number Employees: 20-49
Square Footage: 400000
Parent Co: Sea Specialties Company
Type of Packaging: Food Service, Private Label, Bulk
Brands:
Chef's Choice
Cheryl Lynn
Ideal
Purity

10400 Puroast Coffee Co Inc
1221 Commerce Ave
Woodland, CA 95776-5902
530-668-0976
Fax: 530-668-0989 877-569-2243
info@puroast.com www.puroast.com
Low acid coffee
President: Carrie Vannuci
CEO: Kerry Sachs
Public Relations: Beth Goldstene
Operations Manager: Victor Quero
Production Manager: Sally Lopez
Purchasing Manager: Wendy Dial
Estimated Sales: $5-10 Million
Number Employees: 10-19
Type of Packaging: Private Label
Brands:
Puroast

10401 Putney House Trading LLC
P.O. Box 2520
New London, NH 03257
603-526-2336
Fax: 603-526-2386 sales@cavedonibalsamic.com
cavedonibalsamic.com
Vinegar; balsamic condiments
President/Owner: Paolo Cavedoni
Year Founded: 1860
Type of Packaging: Private Label
Brands:
Cavedoni Balsamic

10402 Putney Pasta
28 Vernon St
Suite 434
Brattleboro, VT 05301-3668
802-257-4800
Fax: 802-875-3322 800-253-3683
Pastas: tortellini, ravioli, agnolotti, fettucine, linguine, angel hair and gnocchi; sauses.
President: Rick McKelzey
carol@putneypasta.com
Estimated Sales: $3 Million
Number Employees: 1-4
Number of Brands: 1
Number of Products: 35
Square Footage: 168000
Type of Packaging: Consumer, Food Service, Private Label
Brands:
Putney Pasta

10403 Puueo Poi Shop
265 Kekuanaoa St
Suite D
Hilo, HI 96720-4396
808-935-8435
Fax: 808-934-7762
Hawaiian food: poi, lau-lau and kalua
Owner: Gilbert Chang
VP: Okyo Chang
Business Manager: Shirlene Rayoan
Estimated Sales: $500,000
Number Employees: 1-4
Square Footage: 11000
Type of Packaging: Consumer, Food Service, Private Label, Bulk
Brands:
Puueo Poi

10404 Pyramid Alehouse-Seattle
1201 1st Ave S
Seattle, WA 98134-1238
206-682-3377
Fax: 206-621-8483 host@pyramidbrew.com
www.pyramidbrew.com
Beer and soda
Manager: Alex Krallis
CFO: Eric Peterson
j.schaller@pyramidbrew.com
CFO: Wayne Drury
Chairman: George Hancock
Chairman: Martin Kelly
Site Manager: Jack Schaller
j.schaller@pyramidbrew.com
Estimated Sales: Under $500,000
Number Employees: 100-249
Type of Packaging: Private Label
Brands:
Amber Wheat Beer
Best Brown Ale
Hart
Thomas Kemper

10405 Pyramid Juice Company
160 Helman Street
Ashland, OR 97520-1720
541-482-2292
Fax: 541-482-1002
Organic fruit and vegetable juices
President/CEO: Judd Pindell
VP: Kim Kemske
Estimated Sales: $5-9.9 Million
Number Employees: 8
Square Footage: 14000
Brands:
Mind's Eye Smart Drinks
Pyramid Juice

10406 Pyrenees French Bakery
717 E 21st St
Bakersfield, CA 93305-5240
661-322-7159
Fax: 661-322-6713 888-898-7159
www.pyreneesbakery.com
Bread and rolls: sour dough, French, nine-grain, squaw, rye and whole wheat.
Owner: Marianne Laxague
order@pyreneesbakery.com
CEO: Juanita Laxague
Estimated Sales: Below $5 Million
Number Employees: 20-49
Square Footage: 86000
Brands:
Pyrenees
Sara Lee

10407 Pyure Brands
5405 Taylor Rd
Suite 10
Naples, FL 34109
305-509-5096
pyureorganic.com
Organic sweeteners
Founder & CEO: Ben Fleischer
Year Founded: 2008
Type of Packaging: Consumer, Bulk

10408 Q Bell Foods
PO Box 652
Nyack, NY 10960
845-358-1475
Fax: 845-353-5680
Chocolate wafer rolls and bars
Marketing: Bahram Shirazi
bshirazi@qbelfoods.com
Estimated Sales: $130,000
Number Employees: 2

10409 Q Drinks
45 Main St.
Brooklyn, NY 39425
718-398-6642
info@qdrinks.com
www.qdrinks.com
Sodas
Founder: Jordan Silbert
Contact: Meryll Cawn
meryll@qdrinks.com

10410 Q Mixers
45 Main St
Brooklyn, NY 11201
718-398-6642
info@qmixers.com
www.qdrinks.com
Bar mixers
Co-Founder & President: Ben Karlin
Founder & CEO: Jordan Silbert
Executive Vice President: Ted Roman
VP, Marketing: Jaron Berkhemer

10411 Q's Nuts
349 Highland Ave.
Somerville, MA 02144
617-764-3741
www.qsnuts.com
Roasted nuts
Co-Founder: Brian Quinn
Co-Founder: Beth Quinn

10412 Q.E. Tea
533 Washington Ave
Suite 100
Bridgeville, PA 15017
412-221-4444
800-622-8327
qetea@aol.com
Coffees and teas
President: Paul Rankin
Marketing Manager: Peter Shaffalo
Estimated Sales: $500,000-$1 Million
Number Employees: 5-9
Square Footage: 24000
Brands:
Hedley's
Q.E.

10413 QBI
500 Metuchen Road
South Plainfield, NJ 07080-4810
908-668-0088
Fax: 908-561-9682
Bioflavonoids, botanical powders, herbs, nutraceuticals, antioxidants, diet and sports supplements, fruit and vegetable powders, extracts and bee pollen
President: Joseph Schortz
VP Finance: Carlos Mendez
Marketing: Joan Naso
Sales Director: Allen Lovitch
International Account Executive: Rena Strauss-Cohen
Plant Manager: Donald Andrejewski
Number Employees: 50-99
Number of Products: 500
Square Footage: 224000
Type of Packaging: Bulk
Brands:
Phytoflow Direct Compression Herbs

10414 QST Ingredients
9734-40 6th Street
Rancho Cucamonga, CA 91730
909-989-4343
Fax: 909-989-4334 www.qsting.com
Seasonings, ingredients and sausage casings
Office Manager: Jill Mauleon

10415 Quady Winery
13181 Road 24
Madera, CA 93637-9087
559-673-8068
Fax: 559-673-0744 800-733-8068
info@quadywinery.com www.quadywinery.com
Wines
President: Andrew Quady
Chief Financial Officer: Laurel Quady
Assistant Marketing Manager: Colin Hugh
Winemaker: Darin Peterson
Number of Products: 7
Brands:
Electra
Elysium
Essensia
Starbound
Sweet Dessert Wine

10416 Quail Ridge Cellars & Vineyards
1155 Mee Lane
Saint Helena, CA 94574-9792
707-963-9783
Fax: 707-963-3593 800-706-9463
retail@ruthbench.com

Wine
President and CEO: Phillip Wade
CFO: Anthony Bell
Marketing Director: Michael Stedman
Public Relations: Victoria Olson
Production Manager: Jenel Hageman
Estimated Sales: $2.5-5 Million
Number Employees: 10-19
Type of Packaging: Private Label
Brands:
Bell Cellars
Fox Brook
Quail Creek

10417 **Quaker Bonnet**
175 Allen St
Buffalo, NY 14201-1515
716-884-0435
Fax: 716-885-7245 800-283-2447
liz@quakerbonnet.com www.quakerbonnet.com
Cookies and pastries
President: Liz Kolken
Vice President: Benjamin Kolken
Estimated Sales: Less than $500,000
Number Employees: 5-9
Square Footage: 17200
Type of Packaging: Consumer, Food Service, Private Label
Brands:
Banana Moon Snack Line
Buffalo Chips
Quaker Bonnet

10418 **Quaker Maid Meats**
610 Morgantown Rd.
Reading, PA 19611
610-376-1500
Fax: 610-376-2678 www.quakermaidmeats.com
Beef steaks, hamburger and veal patties, veal steaks and meatballs.
President: Stanley Szortyka
CFO: Andrew Sims
VP: Nancy Rubin
Director of Marketing: Joey Piazza
VP Sales: Tom Robinson
Year Founded: 1960
Estimated Sales: $20-50 Million
Number Employees: 60
Type of Packaging: Consumer, Food Service, Private Label
Brands:
Gina Lina's
Mama Lucia's
Quaker Maid

10419 **(HQ)Quaker Oats Company**
555 W. Monroe St.
Suite 1
Chicago, IL 60661
312-821-1000
www.quakeroats.com
Cookies, oats, oatmeal, farina, granola bars, puffed wheat, puffed rice, barley, groats, shredded wheat, pancake syrups and mixes, flour, corn syrups, baking mixes, pasta and corn meal.
Senior VP/General Manager: Robbert Rietbroek
IT: Mike Lyons
mike.lyons@pepsi.com
Estimated Sales: Over $1 Billion
Number Employees: 10000+
Number of Products: 195
Parent Co: PepsiCo
Type of Packaging: Consumer, Food Service
Brands:
Quaker
Life

10420 **Quaker Oats Company**
14 Hunter Street E
Quaker Park
Peterborough, ON K9J 7B2
Canada
705-743-6330
Fax: 705-876-4125 800-267-6287
www.quakeroats.ca
Breakfast cereal
Business Unit Leader: Timothy McLaren
Number Employees: 500-999
Parent Co: PepsiCo Canada
Type of Packaging: Consumer, Food Service
Brands:
Quaker

10421 **Quaker Sugar Company**
432 Rodney St
Brooklyn, NY 11211-3482
718-387-6500
Fax: 718-963-2767 info@quakersugar.com
www.quakersugar.com
Sugar
Owner: Harriet Gelfas
Contact: Ralph Balsamo
rbalsamo@quakersugar.com
Operations Manager: Adam Wechsler
Production Manager: Harry Wechsler
Estimated Sales: $1500000
Number Employees: 20-49
Type of Packaging: Consumer, Bulk
Brands:
Diamond

10422 **Quali Tech Inc**
318 Lake Hazeltine Dr
Chaska, MN 55318-1093
952-448-5151
Fax: 952-448-3603 800-328-5870
qtfood@qualitechco.com www.qualitechco.com
Food particulates, inclusions and pellets
President: Mike Hodgens
mikeh@qualitechco.com
CFO: Tom Halverson
Vice President of Business Development: Kye Ploen
Number Employees: 100-249
Square Footage: 180000
Type of Packaging: Bulk
Brands:
Flav-R-Grain
Flavor-Ettes
Flavor-Lites
Pell-Ettes
Pepr
Season-Ettes

10423 **QualiGourmet**
3780 rue La Verendrye
Boisbriand, QC J7H 1R5
Canada
514-287-3530
Fax: 514-287-3510 info@qualigourmet.ca
www.qualigourmet.ca
Salmon, mackerel, foie gras, duck, trout, caviar, charcuterie, jellies, fruit and wild berries
General Manager: Cathy Sahut
Buyer: Steve Labonte
Number Employees: 5-9
Type of Packaging: Food Service

10424 **Qualicaps Inc**
6505 Franz Warner Pkwy
Whitsett, NC 27377-9215
336-449-7300
Fax: 336-449-3333 800-227-7853
info@qualicaps.com www.qualicaps.com
Gelatin capsules
President: Greg Bowers
Sales: Matt Schappert
CFO: Dennis Stella
CEO: Herb Hugill
Quality Control: Schuck Waldroup
Estimated Sales: $5-10 Million
Number Employees: 100-249
Parent Co: Shionogi
Type of Packaging: Bulk

10425 **Qualifresh Michel St. Arneault**
4605 Thibault Avenue
St. Hubert, QC J3Y 3S8
Canada
450-445-0550
Fax: 450-445-5687 800-565-0550
French fries
President: Michelle St. Arneaul
National Manager, Sales And Marketing: Marc Dumas
Number Employees: 50-99
Type of Packaging: Consumer, Food Service, Private Label
Brands:
Golden Crop
Qualifreeze
Qualifresh

10426 **Quality Bakery**
Box 519
1305-7th Ave
Invermere, BC V0A 1K0
Canada
Fax: 888-682-9977 888-681-9977
info@healthybread.com www.healthybread.com
Rye bread
President: Peter Banga
Estimated Sales: $1.1 Million
Number Employees: 6
Square Footage: 30000
Type of Packaging: Consumer, Food Service, Private Label, Bulk
Brands:
Invermere
Quality Bakery
Yukon Sourdough Recipe

10427 **Quality Bakery Products**
14330 Interdrive W
Houston, TX 77032-3316
281-449-4977
Fax: 281-449-7820 866-449-4977
www.qualitybakeryproducts.net
Bread crumbs, croutons and stuffings, cakes, fruit fillings, cake glazes, and cheese pies
Vice President: Mike Tills
mtills@qualitybakeryproducts.net
Purchasing Manager: Henry Wellborn
Estimated Sales: $2.5-5 Million
Number Employees: 20-49
Type of Packaging: Consumer, Food Service, Private Label, Bulk
Brands:
Quality Hearth

10428 **Quality Candy Company**
525 S Lemon Avenue
DFL Warehouse
Walnut, CA 91789
909-444-1025
Fax: 909-595-4181 customerservice@qcandy.com
www.qcandy.com
Candy
CEO: Pierre Redmond
Estimated Sales: $10-20 Million
Number Employees: 20-49
Brands:
Choco-Starlight
Spi-C-Mint

10429 **Quality Crab Co Inc**
177 Knobbs Creek Dr
Elizabeth City, NC 27909-7002
252-338-0808
Fax: 252-338-6290 www.qualityseafoodco.com
Seafood
Owner: Billy Barclift
info@qualityseafoodco.com
VP: Roy Martin III
R&D Director: Rick Durren
Estimated Sales: $11,400,000
Number Employees: 50-99
Square Footage: 48000
Type of Packaging: Private Label
Brands:
Jumbo Lump

10430 **Quality Croutons**
4031 S Racine Ave
Chicago, IL 60609
773-890-2343
Fax: 773-927-8228 800-334-2796
Croutons and packaging services
President: David M Moore
Marketing/Sales: Deadra Ashford
Contact: Brandon Beavers
bbeavers@infomatrix.com
Production Manager: Keith Taylor
Estimated Sales: $1900000
Number Employees: 20-49
Square Footage: 140000
Type of Packaging: Food Service, Private Label, Bulk

10431 **Quality Dairy Co**
947 Trowbridge Rd
East Lansing, MI 48823-5217
517-319-4114
www.qualitydairy.com
Milk, ice cream and fruit juices

Manager: Swadhyaya Bey
Director, Retail Operations & Marketing: Michael Kosloski
Estimated Sales: Below $5 Million
Number Employees: 5-9
Type of Packaging: Private Label

10432 Quality Fisheries
157 Arbor St
Niota, IL 62358-1005
217-448-4241
Fax: 217-448-4021 qualityfisheries@yahoo.com
www.niotafishmarket.com
Seafood
Owner: Kirby Marsden
k.marsden@mchsi.com
Estimated Sales: $1 Million
Number Employees: 5-9
Square Footage: 24000

10433 Quality Food Company
25 Bath Street
Providence, RI 2908
401-421-5668
Fax: 401-421-8570 877-233-3462
info@qualityfoodcompany.com
www.qualitybeefcompany.com
Ground beef and seafood
Secretary: William Catauro
billcatauro@qualityfoodcompany.com
Vice President: Vincent Catauro, III
Sales: Gary Flynn
Purchasing: Mark Engelhardt
Year Founded: 1931
Estimated Sales: $10-20 Million
Number Employees: 20-49
Type of Packaging: Food Service

10434 Quality Food Products Inc
172 N Peoria St
Chicago, IL 60607-2311
312-666-4559
Fax: 312-666-7133
Eggs
President: George Aralis
Owner: Jim Aralis
qfp@earthlink.net
Estimated Sales: $10-20 Million
Number Employees: 10-19

10435 Quality Foods
705 Memorial Avenue
Qualicum Beach, BC 90733-1385
Canada
250-752-9281
Fax: 310-833-5424 877-833-7890
www.qualityfoods.com
Ethnic cuisine, snacks, fried onions, spices, chutneys, teas, pastes, pickles, sauces, salsa, dressings, marinades, relishes, mustard and condiments
Director of Operations: Ken Schley
Estimated Sales: $1-2.5 Million
Number Employees: 5-9
Brands:
California Cuisine
Clara's Kitchen
Cummings & York
Hothothot
Jewel of India
Mariachi
Nara
Nonna D'S
Samos
Sarah's Garden
Simple Nevada
Simply
Skull & Bones
Tara Foods
Tomales Bay
Tombstone

10436 Quality Ingredients
14300 Rosemount Dr
Burnsville, MN 55306-6925
952-898-4002
Fax: 952-898-4421 info@qic.us
www.qic.us
Powders: shortening, cream, whip, cheese, lemon. Services: spray drying, chilling and product development.
Director, Strategy/Marketing: Valorie Klemz
Manager: Stewart Flanery
sflanery@qic.us
Chief of Operations: Robert St.Louis
Estimated Sales: 19 Million
Number Employees: 50-99
Number of Brands: 2
Square Footage: 50000
Type of Packaging: Consumer, Food Service, Private Label, Bulk
Brands:
QuIC-FLAVOR
QuIC-CHEESE

10437 Quality Instant Teas
PO Box 1967
Morristown, NJ 07962-1967
973-257-9450
Fax: 973-257-9370 888-283-8327
Tea mixes and concentrates
President: Gary Vorsheim
Estimated Sales: $1 Million
Number Employees: 3
Type of Packaging: Private Label

10438 Quality Kitchen Corporation
204 Southern Blvd
Wyoming, DE 19934-1028
302-697-3118
officemail@salame.com
Juices and concentrates: grapefruit and orange
Sales: Jerry McGuire
Estimated Sales: $5,000,000
Number Employees: 20 to 49
Type of Packaging: Consumer, Food Service

10439 Quality Meats & Seafood
3239 39 St S
West Fargo, ND 58078
701-282-0202
Fax: 701-282-0583 800-342-4250
admin@qualitymeats.com www.qualitymeats.com
Portion cut beef, chicken, pork, sausage and seafood
President: Ron Jansen
CEO: Lee McCleary
CFO: Blair Kemmer
Estimated Sales: $20-50 Million
Number Employees: 50-99
Parent Co: Quality Boneless Beef Company
Type of Packaging: Consumer, Food Service, Bulk
Brands:
Valley Maid

10440 Quality Naturally Foods
18830 San Jose Ave
City Of Industry, CA 91748-1325
626-854-6363
Fax: 626-965-0978 888-498-6986
www.qnfoods.com
Bakery mixes, icings, fillings, cappuccino and cocoa drinks
President: Frank Watase
fwatase@qnfoods.com
VP: Lincoln Watase
Sales Manager: Jerry Tuma
Number Employees: 1-4
Square Footage: 224000
Type of Packaging: Food Service, Private Label, Bulk

10441 Quality Nut Co
3006 Yosemite Blvd
PO Box 739
Modesto, CA 95354-4176
209-526-3590
Fax: 209-526-8110 www.qualitynut.com
Walnuts
Owner: George Allen
georgeallen@qualitynut.com
Year Founded: 1967
Estimated Sales: $1-3 Million
Number Employees: 50-99
Type of Packaging: Consumer, Food Service

10442 Quality Sausage Company
1925 Lone Star Dr
Dallas, TX 75212-6302
214-634-3400
Fax: 214-634-2296 www.qualitysausage.com
Meat products including meat balls, taco meat, patties, pizza toppings and pepperoni.
Chairman: Paul Birinyi
CEO: Skippers Adams
CFO: Steve O'Brien
Director of Food Safety: Mark Mar
VP Sales: Tim Burns
Year Founded: 1976
Estimated Sales: $41100000
Number Employees: 100-249
Square Footage: 100000
Parent Co: H.M. International
Type of Packaging: Food Service

10443 Quality Seafood
399 Market St
Apalachicola, FL 32320-1425
850-653-9696
Fax: 850-653-3375 staceki@yahoo.com
Shrimp
President: Robert B. Kirvin
Estimated Sales: $140,000
Number Employees: 1-4
Type of Packaging: Private Label
Brands:
Quality

10444 Quality Snack Foods Inc
3750 W 131st St
Alsip, IL 60803
708-377-7120
Fax: 708-377-7125 sales@qsfinc.com
www.qsfinc.com
Custom packaging and manufactering of pork rinds, and precooked bacon.
Owner: Gary Trepina
Plant Manager: Luis Esparza
Estimated Sales: $5600000
Number Employees: 5-9
Square Footage: 160000
Type of Packaging: Private Label
Brands:
Prairieland

10445 Quality Snacks
New York, NY
Popcorn
Brands:
New Pop(c)

10446 Quantum Energy Squares
Santa Monica, CA
quantumsquares.com
Coffee-infused energy bars

10447 Quebec Ministry of Agriculture
191 Peachtree Street N.E
Suite 3240
Atlanta, GE 30303
Canada
404-584-2995
Fax: 404-584-2089 www.foodsofquebec.com
Ice cider, berries, maple syrup, game, specialty, cheese, yogurt, pork, veal, baked goods and seafood

10448 Queen Ann Ravioli & Macaroni
7205 18th Ave
Brooklyn, NY 11204-5634
718-256-1061
Fax: 718-256-1189 queenannravioli@aol.com
www.queenannravioli.com
Italian pasta and ravioli
President: George Switzer
Estimated Sales: $5-10 Million
Number Employees: 5-9
Type of Packaging: Private Label

10449 Queen Anne Coffee Roaster
1908 Queen Anne Ave N
Seattle, WA 98109-3674
206-284-2530
info@metropolitan-market.com
www.metropolitan-market.com
Coffee
Manager: Jim Hill
Director: Eric Stone
Roaster: Susan Hamilton
Estimated Sales: Less than $500,000
Number Employees: 100-249
Brands:
Queen Anne

10450 Queen Bee Gardens
262 E Main St
Lovell, WY 82431-2102
307-548-7994
Fax: 307-548-6721 800-225-7553
queenbee@queenbeegardens.com
Confectionery: truffles, pralines, toffee, mints and turtles
President: Clarence Zeller
Partner: Von Zeller
Vice President: Gene Zeller
Executive Secretary: Bessie Zeller

Estimated Sales: $3-5 Million
Number Employees: 10-19
Square Footage: 80000
Type of Packaging: Consumer, Private Label, Bulk
Brands:
Honey Essence
Q-Bee

10451 Queen City Coffee Company
9267 Cincinnati Dayton Rd
West Chester, OH 45069-3839
513-755-1095
Fax: 513-777-5204 800-487-7460
qcccorb@aol.com
Coffee beans and gift items
President: Robert Badura
Estimated Sales: $2.5-5 Million
Number Employees: 1-4
Type of Packaging: Consumer, Food Service, Private Label

10452 Queen City Sausage & Provision
1136 Straight St
Cincinnati, OH 45214-1736
513-541-5581
Fax: 513-541-6182 877-544-5588
www.queencitysausage.com
Sausage and luncheon meats, bologna and Dutch loaves
President: Elmer Hensler
ejhensler@queencitysausage.com
Marketing Manager: Mark Balasa
Sales Manager: Patrick Miller
Estimated Sales: $5200000
Number Employees: 20-49
Type of Packaging: Consumer, Food Service, Bulk

10453 Queen International Foods
300 S Atlantic Blvd
Suite 201d
Monterey Park, CA 91754-3228
626-289-0828
Fax: 626-289-7283 800-423-4414
Mexican food: burritos, tacos, taquitos, enchiladas and chimichangas
Owner: Liza Tang
Controller: Patricia Thistlewhite
National Sales Manager: Douglas Werner
Estimated Sales: $11,100,000
Number Employees: 1-4
Parent Co: La Reina
Type of Packaging: Consumer, Private Label
Brands:
Anita's
Maria's

10454 Queen of America
3220 SE County Hwy 484
Belleview, FL 34420
352-245-3600
Fax: 877-402-9523 www.queenofamerica.com
Honey, spreads and energy drinks
Type of Packaging: Consumer, Food Service, Bulk
Brands:
BeeBad
Mr. Honey & Mrs. Fruit
Queen of America

10455 (HQ)Queensboro Farm Products
4 Rasbach St
PO Box 227
Canastota, NY 13032-1496
315-687-6133
Fax: 315-697-8267
Cottage cheese, ice cream mix, butter and sour cream, milk
President: Steven Miller
General Manager: Don Landry
Estimated Sales: $10-20 Million
Number Employees: 50-99
Square Footage: 27800
Type of Packaging: Consumer
Brands:
Queensboro

10456 Queensboro Farm Products
152-02 Liberty Avenue
Jamica, NY 11433
718-658-5000
Fax: 718-658-0408
www.queensborofarmproducts.com
Dairy
President/CEO: Allen Miller
Controller: Andrew Flitt

Estimated Sales: $33 Million
Number Employees: 80
Number of Products: 80
Type of Packaging: Consumer, Food Service

10457 Queensway Foods Company
1611 Adrian Rd
Burlingame, CA 94010
650-871-7770
Fax: 650-697-9966 info@qfco.com
www.qfco.com
Chicken powder, rice sticks, peanuts, sugar, vegetable oils, preserved fruits, candy
Owner: May Huang
Contact: Ashly Grzyb
ashly.grzyb@redtri.com
Manager: Tim Yuen
Estimated Sales: $5-10 Million
Number Employees: 5-9
Brands:
American Queen
Ameriqueen Brand
Auntie Liu's
Chic Jiang
San Gallio
Tang Hoi Kee
White Rabbit

10458 Quelle Quiche
814 Hanley Industrial Court
Brentwood, MO 63144-1403
314-961-6554
Quiches: lorraine, spinach, broccoli and crab meat
President: Eric Victor Cowle
VP: G Daniella Cowle
Number Employees: 10-19
Square Footage: 34000
Parent Co: Renaissance Foods
Type of Packaging: Consumer, Food Service, Private Label
Brands:
Les Petites
Quelle

10459 Quetzal Internet Cafe
1234 Polk St
San Francisco, CA 94109-5542
415-800-7167
Fax: 415-673-4182 888-673-8181
Coffee beans
Owner: Wayne Newman
Estimated Sales: Less Than $500,000
Number Employees: 5-9
Type of Packaging: Private Label

10460 Quibell Spring Water Beverage
328 E Church Street
Martinsville, VA 24112-2909
540-632-0100
Fax: 540-344-0311 ieanne@quibell.com
Bottled water
President/Chairman: John Franck
Marketing Director: Dave Vandergrift
VP: Will Pannill
Plant Manager: Jeanne Staley
Estimated Sales: $1-2.5 Million appx.
Number Employees: 5
Square Footage: 288
Type of Packaging: Private Label
Brands:
Quibell

10461 Quigley Industries Inc
38880 Grand River Ave
Farmington, MI 48335-1526
248-426-8600
Fax: 248-426-8607 800-367-2441
sales@quigleyind.com www.quigleyind.com
Confections and lozenges
Owner: Carol Quigley
VP: David Hess
Marketing: Libby Moyer
Plant Manager: Tom Nissley
Purchasing Director: William Latsha
Estimated Sales: $9500000
Number Employees: 20-49
Square Footage: 72000
Parent Co: Joel
Type of Packaging: Consumer, Private Label, Bulk
Brands:
Old Fashioned
Simon
Simons

10462 Quilceda Creek Vintners
11306 52nd St SE
Snohomish, WA 98290-5727
360-568-2389
Fax: 360-568-2389 info@quilcedacreek.com
www.quilcedacreek.com
Wine
Partner: Alexander Golitzin
Partner: Jeannette Golitzin
jeannette@quilcedacreek.com
Estimated Sales: $350,000
Number Employees: 5-9
Type of Packaging: Consumer
Brands:
Quilceda Creek Vintners

10463 Quillin Produce Co
3120 Fresh Way SW
PO Box 225
Huntsville, AL 35805-6720
256-883-7374
Fax: 256-883-7364
jimQuillin@quillinproduce.com
www.quillinproduce.com
Whole and freshly cut produce
President: Jim Quillin
jimquillin@quillinproduce.com
Vice President: Wanda Quillan
Office Manager: Amanda Quillan
Comptroller: Tricia Quillan Morris
Buyer: Andy Quillan
Customer Service Manager: Jamie Thomas
Estimated Sales: $5-10 Million
Number Employees: 10-19

10464 Quillisascut Cheese Co
2409 Pleasant Valley Rd
Rice, WA 99167-9706
509-738-2011
loraleal@centurytel.net
www.quillisascut.com
Goat cheese
Owner: Lora Misterly
loralea@quillisascut.com
Owner: Lore Lea
Number Employees: 20-49
Type of Packaging: Food Service
Brands:
Quillisascut Cheese

10465 Quinault Pride
100 W Quinault St
Taholah, WA 98587
360-276-4431
Fax: 360-276-4880
Salmon: precooked, canned and foil pouched
Manager: Alan Heather
sunderwood@quinault.org
CFO: William Parkshurst
Sales Exec: David Underwood
Estimated Sales: $5-10 Million
Number Employees: 20-49
Type of Packaging: Consumer, Food Service, Private Label, Bulk

10466 Quinn Snacks
Boulder, CO
303-927-6655
quinnpopcrew@quinnpopcorn.com
www.quinnsnacks.com
Popcorn and pretzels
Co-Founder: Kristy Lewis
Co-Founder: Coulter Lewis
Brands:
Quinn

10467 Quinoa Corporation
PO Box 279
Gardena, CA 90248
310-217-8125
Fax: 310-217-8140 quinoacorp@aol.com
Pasta and grains
President: Dave Schnorr
Contact: Tom Spielberger
toms@quinoa.net
Estimated Sales: Below $5 Million
Number Employees: 1-4
Type of Packaging: Bulk
Brands:
Ancient Harvest Quinoa
Supergrain Pasta

10468 Quintessential Chocolates
251 W Main St
PO Box 687
Fredericksburg, TX 78624-3709
830-990-9382
Fax: 830-997-0811 800-842-3382
www.liquidchocolates.com

Chocolates
President: Lecia Duke
lduke@chocolat-tx.us
Sales: Hib Shelton
Public Relations: Carolyn Debus
Operations: Aaron Beeman
Production: Kelly Sundheimer
Purchasing: Jo Baethge
Estimated Sales: Less than $500,000
Number Employees: 5-9
Brands:
Canadian Blended Whisky Chocolates
Cutty Sark(r) Scots Whisky Chocolates
Jack Daniels
Kentucky Bourbon Chocolates
McCallan
Sam Houston Bourbon(tm) Chocolates
Whidbey's

10469 Quinzani Bakery
380 Harrison Ave
Boston, MA 02118-2281
617-426-2114
Fax: 617-451-8075 800-999-1062
Sandwich rolls, dinner rolls, French and Italian breads
President: Steven Quinzani
Purchasing Manager: Larry Quinzani
larryquinzani@quinzanisbakery.com
Estimated Sales: $10 Million
Number Employees: 50-99
Type of Packaging: Consumer, Food Service
Brands:
Quinzani

10470 (HQ)Quirch Foods
2701 S Le Jeune Rd.
12th Fl.
Coral Gables, FL 33134
800-458-5252
info@quirchfoods.com www.quirchfoods.com
Beef, pork, poultry, seafood, and deli meats.
President: Frank Grande
Year Founded: 1967
Type of Packaging: Private Label

10471 Quivira Vineyards & Winery
4900 W Dry Creek Rd
Healdsburg, CA 95448-9721
707-431-8333
Fax: 707-431-1664 800-292-8339
quivira@quivirawine.com www.quivirawine.com
Wines
Manager: Kris Cuneo
Co-Founder: Henry Wendt
Vineyard Manager: Tony Castellanos
Winemaker/General Manager: Grady Wann
National Sales Manager: Bill Wiebalk
Direct Sales & Inventory: Denise Rose
Assistant Tasting Room Manager: Jana Aitken
Concierge Relations: Pam Jorgensen
Winemaker: Steven Canter
COO: Denise Sanders
Cellar Master: Adam Armstrong
Accounting Manager: Sheila Williams
Office Administrator: Lori-Jo Martin
Estimated Sales: Below $5 Million
Number Employees: 10-19
Type of Packaging: Private Label
Brands:
Quivira

10472 Quong Hop & Company
40 Airport Blvd
S San Francisco, CA 94080
650-553-9900
Fax: 650-952-3329
Soy deli tofu, tofu burgers, hummus and tempeh
President/CEO: Frank Stephens
Estimated Sales: $3.1 Million
Number Employees: 42
Square Footage: 40000
Type of Packaging: Consumer, Food Service, Private Label, Bulk
Brands:
Quong Hop
Raquel's
Soy Deli

10473 Quorn Foods
PO Box 10789
Chicago, IL 60610
customer.services@quornfoods.com
www.quorn.us
Vegetarian frozen meats
CEO: Kevin Brennan

10474 R & D Sausage Co
15714 Waterloo Rd
Cleveland, OH 44110-1660
216-692-1832
Sausage
Owner: Joseph Zuzak
Estimated Sales: Less Than $500,000
Number Employees: 1-4
Type of Packaging: Consumer, Bulk

10475 R & R Seafood
801 1st Ave
Tybee Island, GA 31328
912-786-5504
Fax: 912-786-5504
Seafood
Owner: Robbie Robertson
Estimated Sales: Less than $100,000
Number Employees: 1-4

10476 R & S Mexican Food
5818 W Maryland Ave
Glendale, AZ 85301-3909
602-272-2727
Fax: 623-435-1377 www.rsmexfoods.com
Mexican foods: fruits, vegetables, canned goods, spices, tacos, tamales and tortillas
President: Danny Franks
contact@rsmexfoods.com
Sales/Marketing Manager: Mila Cano
Plant Manager: Francisco Ramirez
Estimated Sales: $4415000
Number Employees: 50-99
Square Footage: 140000
Type of Packaging: Consumer, Food Service

10477 R C Fine Foods Inc
139 Stryker Ln
Hillsborough, NJ 08844-1930
908-359-5500
Fax: 908-359-6957 800-526-3953
cs@rcfinefoods.com www.rcfinefoods.com
Mixes: soup, gravy, specialty, salad dressing, dessert and sauce, spices, seasonings, extracts, colors; dietetic products
Owner: Gary Cohen
gcohen@rcfinefoods.com
CEO: Anthony Todaro
Director Sales: Robert Dixon
Estimated Sales: $5,500,000
Number Employees: 50-99
Square Footage: 96000
Type of Packaging: Food Service
Brands:
RC Fine Foods

10478 R D Laney Family Honey Co
25725 New Rd
North Liberty, IN 46554-9379
574-656-8701
Fax: 574-656-8603 info@laneyhoney.com
www.laneyhoney.com
Honey, nuts
President: Dave Laney
Co-Owner: Kay Laney
Estimated Sales: Below $500,000
Number Employees: 5-9
Type of Packaging: Consumer
Brands:
Apple Blossom
Autumn Wildflower
Basswood
Blueberry Blossom
Buckwheat
Clover
Cranberry Blossom
Michigan Star Thistle
Orange Blossom
Spring Blossom
Wild Blackberry
Wildflower

10479 R Four Meats
24 2nd St SW
Chatfield, MN 55923-1208
507-867-4180
Fax: 507-867-4180
Deer, beef, pork and lamb
Owner: Jeff Remme
connie.r4@myclearwave.net
Estimated Sales: $1-2.5 Million
Number Employees: 5-9
Type of Packaging: Consumer

10480 R I Provision Co
5 Day St
Johnston, RI 02919-4301
401-831-0815
Fax: 401-274-5508 sales@littlerhodyhotdogs.com
www.littlerhodyhotdogs.com
Sausages, franks and toppings
President: Ed Robal
sales@littlerhodyhotdogs.com
Estimated Sales: $1-2.5 Million
Number Employees: 1-4
Number of Brands: 1

10481 R L Schreiber Inc
2745 W Cypress Creek Rd
Suite B
Ft Lauderdale, FL 33309
954-972-7102
Fax: 954-972-4406 800-624-8777
www.rlschreiber.com
Soup bases, sauces, gravies, spices, spice blends, custom blending and specialty items
Chairman: Tom Schreiber
COO: Tina Michel
Estimated Sales: $5-10 Million
Number Employees: 100-249
Square Footage: 125000
Type of Packaging: Food Service, Private Label

10482 R M Felts' Packing Co
35497 General Mahone Blvd
Ivor, VA 23866-2859
757-859-6131
Fax: 757-859-6381
customerservice@feltspacking.com
www.shopvafinest.com
Smoked ham and picnic hams
President: Robert M Felts Jr
CEO: Charles Stallard
Vice President: Robbie Feuts
Estimated Sales: $3-5 Million
Number Employees: 20-49
Square Footage: 68000
Type of Packaging: Consumer, Food Service, Private Label
Brands:
Southampton

10483 R M Lawton Cranberries Inc
221 Thomas St
Middleboro, MA 02346-3321
508-947-7465
Fax: 508-947-0280
Cranberries
Manager: Mark Di Carlo
Estimated Sales: $300,000-$375,000
Number Employees: 1-4
Type of Packaging: Food Service, Bulk
Brands:
R.M. Lawton Cranberries

10484 R T Foods Inc
11333 N Scottsdale Rd
Suite 105
Scottsdale, AZ 85254-5186
480-596-1089
Fax: 480-596-3315 888-258-4437
www.rtfoods.com
Tempura and breaded shrimp
Owner: Jeff Krause
jeff@rtfoods.com
Number Employees: 1-4

10485 R Torre & Co
233 E Harris Ave
S San Francisco, CA 94080-6807
650-875-1200
Fax: 650-875-1600 800-775-1925
www.torani.com
Italian flavoring syrups and fruit bases

Principal & Owner: Paul Lucheta
CEO: Melanie Dulbecco
CFO: Scott Triou
VP Research, Development & Innovation: Don Birnbaum
VP Marketing: Julie Garlikov
Director of Human Resources: Ro Carbone
Estimated Sales: $19.7 Million
Number Employees: 100-249
Square Footage: 330000
Type of Packaging: Consumer, Food Service
Brands:
Torani

10486 **R Weaver Apiaries**
16495 County Road 319
Navasota, TX 77868-6513
936-825-2333
Fax: 936-825-3642 www.beeweaver.com
Honey
Owner: Richard Weaver
Office Manager: Risa Davis
Estimated Sales: Less Than $500,000
Number Employees: 5-9
Square Footage: 40000
Type of Packaging: Consumer, Food Service, Private Label, Bulk
Brands:
Weaver's

10487 **R&A Imports**
1439 El Bosque Ct
Pacific Palisades, CA 90272
310-454-2247
Fax: 310-459-3218 zonevdka@gte.net
Vodka
President: Veronica Pekarovic
Estimated Sales: $1-$2.5 Million
Number Employees: 1 to 4
Brands:
Zone

10488 **R&J Farms**
9800 West Pleasant Home Road
West Salem, OH 44287
419-846-3179
Fax: 419-846-9603 rjfarms@rjfarms.com
www.rjfarms.com
Soy beans, sesame and sunflower seeds, grains, flour, microwaveable popcorn, chips and pretzels, garbanzo beans
Owner: Todd Driscoll
Number Employees: 5-9
Square Footage: 80000
Type of Packaging: Consumer, Private Label, Bulk
Brands:
Country Grown
Whole Earth

10489 **R&J Seafoods**
16050 Sterling Hwy
Ninilchik, AK 99639
907-567-3222
Fax: 907-567-7400 www.rjseafoods.com
Seafood
Plant Manager: Glen Guffey

10490 **R&R Homestead Kitchen**
2399 Loxley Ct
Saumico, WI 54173
920-544-5221
Fax: 920-227-4147 888-779-8245
fudge@randrhomestead.com www.rnrfudge.com
Fudge toppings
Owner: Richard Roffers

10491 **R.C. McEntire & Company**
P.O.Box 5817
Columbia, SC 29250-5817
803-799-3388
Fax: 803-254-3540
Tomatoes, peppers, lettuce, onions, cabbage and salads
Owner: Buddy McEntire
Estimated Sales: $10-20 Million
Number Employees: 10-19
Square Footage: 150000
Type of Packaging: Consumer, Food Service, Private Label, Bulk
Brands:
Dinner Reddi
Micro Fast
Salad Pak
Veg Fresh

10492 **R.D. Offutt Farms**
15357 US-71
Park Rapids, MN 56470
218-732-1461
www.rdoffuttfarms.com
Potatoes
President: Keith McGovern
Number Employees: 500+

10493 **R.E. Meyer Company**
4611 W Adams Street
Lincoln, NE 68524-1444
402-474-8500
Fax: 402-470-4380 888-990-2333
onlineorders@meyerfoods.com
Beef and pork
Owner: Robert Meyer
Number Employees: 100-249
Parent Co: Meyer Holdings
Type of Packaging: Food Service, Private Label, Bulk

10494 **R.H. Phillips**
26836 County Rd 12A
Esparto, CA 95627
530-662-3504
Fax: 530-662-2880
Wines
Head Winemaker: Barry Bergman
Quality Control: David Keim
Public Relations: Lane Giguiere
Plant Manager: Ken Lazzaroni
Estimated Sales: 21,720,000
Number Employees: 100-249
Type of Packaging: Private Label
Brands:
R.H. Phillips

10495 **R.J. Corr Naturals**
14028 S McKinley Avenue
Posen, IL 60469
708-389-4200
Fax: 708-389-4294
Juice blends, sodas and mineral water
President: Robert Corr
General Manager: James Corr
VP Operations: Thomas Swan
Number Employees: 10-19
Square Footage: 64000
Brands:
Gear Up
Ginseng Rush
Natures Flavors
North Star
Rj Corr
Robert Corr

10496 **R.L. Albert & Son**
2001 W. Main Street
Suite 155
Stamford, CT 069020
203-622-8655
Fax: 203-622-7454 www.albertscandy.com
Candy
CEO: Robert Katz
Sales/Marketing Manager: Jorge La Sada
Estimated Sales: $7 Million
Number Employees: 12
Brands:
Big Baby
Big Bol
Fortune Bubble
Fun Fruit
Gum Time
Ice Cubes
Mint Balls
Moritz Ice Cubes
Neon Lasers
Pnut Jumbo
So Joao
Stardrops

10497 **R.L. Zeigler Company**
1 Plant St.
Selma, AL 36703
205-758-3621
Fax: 205-758-0185 800-392-6328
zeigler@zmeats.com www.zmeats.com
Lunch meats, bacon and frankfurters
Chairman/Director: James Hinton
CEO/Director: W Lackey
CFO: Ken Fitzgerald
Contact: Spencer Harris
spencerharris@zmeats.com
Year Founded: 1927
Estimated Sales: $35 Million
Number Employees: 20-49
Square Footage: 100000
Type of Packaging: Consumer, Food Service, Private Label
Brands:
Talmadge Farms
Zeigler

10498 **R.M. Palmer Co.**
77 S. 2nd Ave.
West Reading, PA 19611
610-372-8971
sales@rmpalmer.com
www.rmpalmer.com
Confectionery items, such as chocolates.
President: Richard Palmer
Treasurer/CFO: Charles Shearer
Year Founded: 1948
Estimated Sales: $150-200 Million
Number Employees: 850
Number of Products: 500
Square Footage: 330230
Type of Packaging: Consumer, Bulk
Brands:
R.M. Palmer

10499 **R.W. Frookies**
PO Box 1649
Sag Harbor, NY 11963-0060
800-913-3663
800-913-3663
Cookies and baked goods
President: Ned Parkhouse
Estimated Sales: Under $500,000
Number Employees: 1-4

10500 **R.W. Garcia**
100 Enterprise Way
Suite C230
Scotts Valley, CA 95066
408-287-4616
Fax: 408-287-7724 rwgarcia.com
Tortilla chips and crackers
Owner: Robert Garcia
Sales Manager: Jake Stenton
robert_garcia@bd.com
Estimated Sales: $10-20 Million
Number Employees: 100-249
Square Footage: 60000
Parent Co: R.W. Garcia Company
Type of Packaging: Private Label
Brands:
Santa Cruz

10501 **RAB Food Group**
80 Avenue K
Newark, NJ 07105-3803
201-553-1100
Fax: 201-333-1809
deborah.ross@manischewitz.com
www.rabfoodgroup.com
Kosher foods: baked goods, pastas, soups, gefilte fish, grape juice and borscht.
President/CEO: Jeremy Fingerman
Vice President Sales: Kevin O'Brien
Contact: Monica Ruiz
mruiz@rabfoodgroup.com
Administrator: Deborah Ross
Number Employees: 1-4

10502 **RAJB Hog Foods Inc**
60 Amity St
Jersey City, NJ 07304-3510
201-395-9400
Fax: 201-395-9409 suzymody@rajbhog.com
www.rajbhog.com
Hors d'oeuvres, appetizers, ice cream and sorbet
President: Sanjeev Modi
Vice President: Sachin Mody
Marketing & Sales Manager: Suzy Mody
Number Employees: 1-4
Square Footage: 72000

10503 **RC Bottling Company**
1100 Independence Ave
Evanasville, IN 47714
812-424-7978
www.rcbeverage.com
Processor of soft drinks.
Vending Manager: Chris Blake

Year Founded: 1950
Estimated Sales: $20-50 Million
Number Employees: 300
Type of Packaging: Consumer, Food Service
Other Locations:
Mayfield KY
Vincennes IN
Marion IL
Scott City MO
Beaver Dam KY
Bowling Green KY

10504 RE Botanicals
Boulder, CO
303-214-2118
www.rebotanicals.com
Hemp-infused coconut oil
Founder: John Roulac

10505 REBBL
5900 Hollis St
Suite L
Emeryville, CA 94608
855-732-2500
info@rebbl.co rebbl.co
Coconut milk-based herb beverages
Co-Founder: Palo Hawken
CEO: Sheryl O'Loughlin
Controller: Ryan McKillop
Operations: Janaye Pohl

10506 REDCLAY Gourmet
678 Blue Rock Ct
Winston-Salem, NC 27103
336-575-3360
lance@redclaygourmet.com
www.redclaygourmet.com
Pimento cheese spreads
Owner: Michele Sawyer
Estimated Sales: Under $500,000
Number Employees: 9
Brands:
REDCLAY Gourmet

10507 REED'S Inc
13000 S Spring St
Los Angeles, CA 90061-1634
310-217-9400
Fax: 310-217-9411 800-997-3337
info@reedsgingerbrew.com www.reedsinc.com
Ginger soft drinks, candy and ice cream
President & CEO: Christopher Reed
Estimated Sales: $10-15 million
Number Employees: 50-99
Type of Packaging: Consumer
Brands:
China Cola
Reed's
Virgil's Root Beers

10508 RENFRO Foods Inc
815 Stella St
Fort Worth, TX 76104-1495
817-336-3849
Fax: 817-336-7910 jc@interstargroup.com
www.renfrofoods.com
Relishes, sauces, peppers and salsas
President: Doug Renfro
CEO: Bill Renfro
bill.renfro@renfrofoods.com
Vice President: Becky Renfro
Marketing: Dan Fore
InterStar PR: Jane Cohen
VP Production: James Renfro
Estimated Sales: $3.3 Million
Number Employees: 50-99
Number of Products: 27
Type of Packaging: Consumer, Food Service, Private Label
Brands:
Mrs Renfro's

10509 REX Pure Foods
2121 Chartres St
New Orleans, LA 70116
504-525-7305
800-344-8314
info@rexfoods.com www.rexfoods.com
Seafood spices and seasonings, sauces, blends, vinegar and mustard; packaging services
President: J Geldart
CEO: Jenni Ratliff
VP, Chief Marketing Officer: Gene Ratliff
Estimated Sales: $2.5 Million
Number Employees: 1-4
Type of Packaging: Consumer, Food Service, Bulk
Brands:
Rex

10510 RFS Limited
576 Colonial Park Dr
Suite 130
Roswell, GA 30075-3794
770-993-0030
Fax: 770-993-0792
Frozen broccoli, carrots, cauliflower, zucchini and squash
CEO: Fred Everett
fred.everett@rfs.com
National Sales Manager: Rob Rickerby
Estimated Sales: $1-2,500,000
Number Employees: 5-9
Type of Packaging: Food Service, Private Label, Bulk
Brands:
Roca

10511 RFi Ingredients
300 Corporate Dr
Suite 14
Blauvelt, NY 10913-1162
845-358-8600
Fax: 845-358-9003 800-962-7663
trishad@rfiingredients.com
www.rfiingredients.com
Antioxidants, antimicrobials, preservatives, natural colors; fruit, vegetable and botanical extracts
President & CEO: Jeff Wuagneux
jeffw@rfiingredients.com
Vice President, R&D: Ginny Bank
Executive Vice President: Trisha Devine
Chief Operating Officer: Drew Luce
Estimated Sales: $4-5 Million
Number Employees: 50-99
Number of Brands: 5
Type of Packaging: Bulk
Brands:
Colorpure
Oxyphyte
Phytbac
Phytonutriance
Stabilenhance

10512 RISE Brewing Co.
Cos Cob, CT
hello@risebrewingco.com
risebrewingco.com
Cold brew coffee
Co-Founder & CEO: Grant Gyesky

10513 RJ Balson and Sons Inc
PO Box 8153
Asheville, NC 28814
321-281-9473
contact@balsonbutchers.com
www.balsonbutchers.com
Bangers and bacon
President/CEO: Oliver Balson
oliver.balson@balsonbutchers.com

10514 RM Heagy Foods
227 Granite Run Drive
Suite 200
Lancaster, PA 17601
717-569-1032
Cheese, ice cream and sorbets, butters, dips and sauces, charcuterie meats.
CEO: Chuck Kukic
Chief Financial Officer: Douglas Hilliard
Sales & Marketing Manager: Abigail Heagy
Production Manager: Auston Martzall
Estimated Sales: $20-50 Million
Number Employees: 5-9

10515 RP's Pasta Company
1133 East Wilson Street
Madison, WI 53703
608-257-7216
Fax: 608-257-7267 freshpasta@rpspasta.com
www.rpspasta.com
Pasta
CEO & Master Pasta Maker: Peter Robertson
VP, General Counsel: Stephen Ciurczak
Quality Assurance Manager: Margo King
Estimated Sales: $5 Million
Number Employees: 50+
Type of Packaging: Food Service, Private Label
Brands:
RPs PASTA

10516 RPM Total Vitality
18032 Lemon Drive
Suite C
Yorba Linda, CA 92886-3386
714-524-8864
Fax: 714-524-3247 800-234-3092
Antioxidants: pollen and dimethylaminoethanol
Owner: Pat McBride
pat@rpmtv.com
Co-Owner: Roger McBride
Number Employees: 1-4
Square Footage: 4000
Brands:
Letan

10517 RW Delights
50 Division Ave
Suite 44
Millington, NJ 07946
917-301-5231
866-892-1096
info@heavenlysouffle.com
www.heavenlysouffle.com
Souffle and creme brulee desserts
President: Roxanne Kam
CEO: Wendy Friedman

10518 RW Garcia
521 Parrott St.
San Jose, CA 95112
408-287-4616
rwgarcia.com
Tortilla chips and crackers
President: Bob Garcia
Sales & Marketing Coordinator: January Riss
Snack Food Manufacturing: Allan Perkins
Year Founded: 1982
Estimated Sales: $40 Million
Number Employees: 50-200
Brands:
RW Garcia

10519 RXBAR
225 W Ohio
Suite 500
Chicago, IL 60654
312-624-8200
support@rxbar.com
www.rxbar.com
Protein bars
CEO & Co-Founder: Peter Rahal
Chief Marketing Officer: Lindsay (Rubin) Levin
Chief Sales Officer: Sam McBride
Year Founded: 2013
Estimated Sales: $2.2 Million
Number Employees: 50-200
Brands:
RXBAR

10520 Raaka Chocolate
64 Seabring St
Brooklyn, NY 11231
855-255-3354
help@raakachocolate.com
www.raakachocolate.com
Unroasted dark chocolate
Founder & CEO: Ryan Cheney
Co-Founder: Nathan Hodge
Estimated Sales: $2.4 Million
Number Employees: 11-50
Number of Brands: 1
Number of Products: 14
Brands:
Raaka

10521 Rabbit Barn
630 W Clausen Rd
Turlock, CA 95380-9703
209-632-1123
Fax: 209-632-1123 www.littlerabbitbarn.com
Rabbit meat
Owner: Larry Sigafoos
CEO: Sherri Sigafoos
Estimated Sales: $1-3 Million
Number Employees: 1-4
Square Footage: 8000
Type of Packaging: Private Label
Brands:
Rabbit Barn

10522 **Rabbit Creek**
903 N Broadway St
Po Box 1059
Louisburg, KS 66053-3541
913-837-2757
Fax: 913-837-5760 800-837-3073
rcreek@mokancomm.net
www.rabbitcreekgourmet.com
Mixes: muffin, dip, soup, scone, bread, brownie and cookie
President: Donna Cook
rcreek@mokancomm.net
Estimated Sales: $1-2.5 Million
Number Employees: 10-19
Number of Brands: 1
Number of Products: 120
Type of Packaging: Consumer, Private Label
Brands:
Rabbit Creek

10523 **Rabbit Ridge Winery**
1172 San Marcos Rd
Paso Robles, CA 93446-7343
805-467-3331
Fax: 805-467-3339 rabbitridgewines@yahoo.com
www.rabbitridgewinery.com
Wines
Founder/Winemaker: Erich Russell
President: Joanne James Russell
Compliance/Operations Manager: Sandy James
Director Paso Vineyard Operations: Robert Pierce
Paso Robles Office Manager: Jacqueline Pierce
Paso Robles Assistant to the Director: Mike Sanford
Healdsburg Operations Director: Linda Garwood
Healdsburg Warehouse Manager: Craig Wisdom
Manager: Sandy James
jessica@rabbitridgewinery.com
Estimated Sales: Below $5 Million
Number Employees: 5-9
Brands:
Rabbit Ridge

10524 **Raber Packing Co**
1413 N Raber Rd
Peoria, IL 61604-4790
309-673-0721
Fax: 309-673-6308 800-331-0543
www.raberpacking.com
Meat
President: Carroll Wetterauer
raberpacking@comcast.net
Year Founded: 1954
Estimated Sales: $3 Million
Number Employees: 20-49
Square Footage: 60000
Type of Packaging: Consumer

10525 **Raceland Raw Sugar Corporation**
175 Mill St.
PO Box 159
Raceland, LA 70394
985-537-3533
Fax: 985-537-7779 www.racelandrawsugar.com
Raw sugar and molasses
President: Daniel Duplantis
Estimated Sales: $33 Million
Number Employees: 100-249
Parent Co: M.A. Patout & Son
Type of Packaging: Bulk

10526 **Rachael's Smoked Fish**
150 Switzer Ave
Springfield, MA 01109
800-327-3412
rachaelsfoodcorp.com
Kosher foods: cream cheese, pickled herring, smoked fish and whitefish, salmon and herring salads
Plant Manager: Alan Axler
Number Employees: 38275
Square Footage: 24000
Type of Packaging: Consumer, Food Service, Private Label, Bulk
Brands:
Axler's
Springfield

10527 **Racine Danish**
2529 Golf Ave
Racine, WI 53404-1657
262-633-1819
Fax: 262-633-3036 customerservice@kringle.com
www.kringle.com
Pastries: danish
Owner: Mike Heyer
mheyer@kringle.com
Number Employees: 20-49

10528 **Radanovich Vineyards & Winery**
3936 Ben Hur Road
Mariposa, CA 95338-9466
209-966-3187
Wines
President: George Radanovich
Estimated Sales: $500,000-$1 000,000
Number Employees: 1-4

10529 **Radlo Foods**
313 Pleasant St
Watertown, MA 02472
617-926-7070
Fax: 617-923-6440 800-370-1439
Eggs and egg products
President & CEO: David Radlo
Contact: Jim Leroy
jiml@radlo.com
Estimated Sales: $2-5 Million
Number Employees: 1-4
Type of Packaging: Consumer, Food Service, Private Label, Bulk
Brands:
Born Free
Grown Free

10530 **Raffield Fisheries Inc**
1624 Grouper Ave
Port St Joe, FL 32456-5144
850-229-8494
Fax: 850-229-8782 eugene@raffieldfisheries.com
www.raffieldfisheries.com
Atlantic herring, black drum, roe, bluefish, blue runner, Jack Crevalle, ladyfish, Spanish sardines, butterfish, goatfish, croakers and crawfish
President: Harold Raffield
harold@raffieldfisheries.com
Secretary/Treasurer: Danny Raffield
Estimated Sales: $10-20 Million
Number Employees: 50-99
Type of Packaging: Consumer, Food Service, Private Label, Bulk

10531 **Ragersville Swiss Cheese**
2199 Ragersville Rd SW
Sugarcreek, OH 44681
330-897-3055
Fax: 330-897-0415
Swiss cheese
President/Owner: Richard Hicks
Estimated Sales: $3-5 Million
Number Employees: 1-4
Square Footage: 40000
Type of Packaging: Consumer

10532 **Ragold Confections**
516 NW 20th St
Wilton Manors, FL 33311
954-566-9092
Fax: 954-427-0413 rs@ragold.com
www.ragold.com
Candy
Chairman of the Board: Rainer Schindler
CFO: Arthur Pauly
Estimated Sales: $1.5 Million
Number Employees: 10-19
Type of Packaging: Private Label
Brands:
Dilbert Mints&Gummies
Juicefuls Hard Candy

10533 **Ragozzino Foods Inc**
10 Ames Ave
Meriden, CT 06451-2912
203-238-2553
Fax: 203-235-5158 800-348-1240
nancy@ragozzino.com www.ragozzino.com
Soups, pastas, sauces, entrees, side dishes and dips.
President: Nancy Ragozzino
CEO: Gloria Ragozzino
gloria@ragozzino.com
VP: John Ragozzino
VP Product Development: Susan Ragozzino
VP Purchasing/Distribution: Ellen Ragozzino
Estimated Sales: $23 Million
Number Employees: 100-249
Number of Brands: 1
Square Footage: 65000
Type of Packaging: Consumer, Food Service, Private Label
Brands:
Sugo

10534 **Ragsdale-Overton Food Traditions**
PO Box 1626
Smithfield, NC 27577-1626
919-284-6700
Fax: 919-284-6706 888-424-8863
Condiments, chutneys, sauces
Partner: Sue Overton
Public Relations: Carolyn Ragsdale
Estimated Sales: Under $500,000
Number Employees: 1-4
Type of Packaging: Private Label
Brands:
B-17
Raggy-O

10535 **Rahr Malting Co**
800 1st Ave W
Shakopee, MN 55379-1148
952-445-1431
info@rahr.com
www.rahr.com
Malt and brewing supplies
CEO: Gary Lee
Contact: April Abbott
aabbott@rahr.com
Year Founded: 1847
Estimated Sales: $43.6 Million
Number Employees: 5-9
Type of Packaging: Bulk

10536 **Rainbow Hills Vineyards**
26349 Township Road 251
Newcomerstown, OH 43832-9631
740-545-9305
www.ravensglenn.com
Wines
Owner: Lee Wyse
rainbowhillsvineyards@gmail.com
Estimated Sales: Below $5 Million
Number Employees: 5-9
Brands:
Rainbow Hill Vineyards

10537 **Rainbow Light Nutritional Systems**
125 McPherson St
Santa Cruz, CA 95060-5818
831-429-9089
Fax: 831-429-0189 800-635-1233
www.rainbowlight.com
Supplements and herbal extracts
President: Linda Kahler
Senior Director of Research: Marci Clow
Director of Marketing: Tisha Brady
Vice President of Sales: Ray Petrick
Contact: Barbara Apps
barbaraa@rlns.com
Vice President of Operations: Sharon Minski
Production Manager: Mark Keller
Purchasing Manager: Dee Dee Barrios
Estimated Sales: $6000000
Number Employees: 20-49
Number of Products: 150
Type of Packaging: Consumer
Brands:
Just Once Natural Herbal Extras
Rainbow Light
Rainbow Light Herbal

10538 **Rainbow Pops**
45 Benbro Dr
Cheektowaga, NY 14225-4805
716-685-4340
Fax: 716-685-0810 800-879-7677
Lollipops
President: Roe Baran
Number Employees: 20-49
Brands:
Popstop
Premium Rainbow Drops
Premium Rainbow Pops
Rainbow Pops

10539 **Rainbow Seafood Market**
4303 Maine Ave
Suite 107
Baldwin Park, CA 91706-2395
626-962-6888
Fax: 626-962-3677
Seafood

Owner: David Tran
Estimated Sales: $800,000
Number Employees: 1-4
Type of Packaging: Consumer

10540 Rainbow Seafoods
422a Boston St
Topsfield, MA 01983
978-887-9121
Fax: 978-887-9125 www.rainbowseafood.com
Seafood
President: Frank Powell
Sales: Neil Murphy
Estimated Sales: $2,500,000
Number Employees: 9
Brands:
Alda
North Breeze
Rainbow

10541 Rainbow Valley Frozen Yogurt
9444 W Shady Grove Ct
White Lake, MI 48386
248-355-1095
Fax: 248-353-3466 800-979-8669
Frozen yogurt mix
President: William Boyda
VP/Treasurer: Laurel Boyda
Estimated Sales: $500,000-$1,000,000
Number Employees: 5-9
Square Footage: 48000
Type of Packaging: Consumer, Food Service, Private Label, Bulk

10542 Rainforest Company
141 Millwell Dr
Maryland Heights, MO 63043
314-344-1000
Fax: 314-344-3044
michaelm@the-rainforest-co.com
Snacks: cashew and Brazil nut bars, popcorn, salad dressings, salsas, marinades and hot sauces
President: Rick Drevet
Controller: Sherry Dawes
Number Employees: 35
Square Footage: 80000
Brands:
Jungle Munch
Rainforest Crunch
River Bank

10543 Rainsweet Inc
1460 Sunnyview Rd. NE
P.O. Box 7079
Salem, OR 97301
503-363-4293
Fax: 503-585-4657 800-363-4293
linda@rainsweet.com www.rainsweet.com
Frozen blackberries, blueberries, black and red raspberries, boysenberries, IQF and puree cane berries, mushrooms, peppers, onions and bean sprouts
CEO: Rich Brim
richb@rainsweet.com
Quality Assurance Manager: Ian Bennet
Fruit Sales & Customer Service: Linda Ervin
Vegetable Sales: Chantal Wright
Field Manager: Bill Dinger
Estimated Sales: $30.4 Million
Number Employees: 100-249
Square Footage: 130000
Type of Packaging: Consumer, Food Service, Private Label, Bulk
Brands:
Rainsweet

10544 Rallis Whole Foods
2886 Riviera Drive
Windsor, ON N9E 3A4
Canada
519-796-9712
theo@rallisoliveoil.com
www.icepressed.com
Olive oils
Marketing: Theo Rallis

10545 Ralph Sechler & Son Inc
5686 SR 1
St Joe, IN 46785-0152
260-337-5461
Fax: 260-337-5771 800-332-5461
showroom@sechlerspickles.com
www.sechlerspickles.com
Pickles and peppers
Owner: Max Troyer
VP Technical Services: Karen Sechler-Linn
Sales Manager: Mark Decker
Estimated Sales: $10-20 Million
Number Employees: 20-49
Square Footage: 180000
Type of Packaging: Consumer, Food Service, Bulk
Brands:
Sechler's

10546 Ralph's Famous Italian Ices
11 Cooper St
Babylon, NY 11702-2901
631-893-5646
info@ralphsices.com
www.ralphsices.com
Italian ices
Manager: Stephen Lazarra
Owner: Lawerence Silvestro
Owner: Michael Scolaro
Estimated Sales: $300,000-500,000
Number Employees: 10-19
Brands:
Ralph's Italian Ices

10547 Ralph's Packing Co
500 W Freeman Ave
Perkins, OK 74059
405-547-2464
Fax: 405-547-2364 800-522-3979
comments@ralphspacking.com
www.ralphspacking.com
Fresh and smoked meat products available to consumers and wholesalers.
President: Gary Crane
garycrane@ralphspacking.com
Year Founded: 1959
Estimated Sales: $4 Million
Number Employees: 20-49
Square Footage: 39200
Type of Packaging: Consumer, Food Service, Private Label
Brands:
Big Nasty
Lil' Momma Nasty

10548 Ramona's Mexican Foods
13633 S Western Ave
Gardena, CA 90249
310-323-1950
Fax: 310-323-4210 sales@ramonas.com
ramonas.com
Frozen tortillas, burritos, tamales and Mexican dinners
Co-Founder: Ramona Acosta Banuelos
Co-Founder: Alejandro Banuelos
President & CEO: Martin Accosta Torres
Type of Packaging: Consumer, Food Service, Bulk
Brands:
Ramona's

10549 Ramos Orchards
9192 Boyce Rd
Winters, CA 95694-9625
530-795-4748
Fax: 530-795-4148
Walnuts, prunes and almonds
Owner: Fred Ramos
Estimated Sales: $4 Million
Number Employees: 20-49
Type of Packaging: Bulk
Brands:
Ramos Orchards

10550 Ramsen Inc
17725 Juniper Path
Lakeville, MN 55044-9482
952-431-0400
Fax: 952-431-8470 dbreuer@ramsendairy.com
www.ramsendairy.com
Dry dairy
Owner: Tim Krieger
Partner: John Baetty
jbaetty@ramsendairy.com
Marketing Director: Kathy Stevens
Sales Manager: Dennis Breuer
Estimated Sales: $10-20 Million
Number Employees: 10-19
Square Footage: 3600
Type of Packaging: Consumer, Food Service

10551 Ramsey Popcorn Co Inc
5645 Clover Valley Rd NW
Ramsey, IN 47166-8252
812-347-2441
Fax: 812-347-3336 800-624-2060
info@ramseypopcorn.com www.cousinwillies.com
Microwaveable popcorn
President: Wilfred Sieg
will@ramseypopcorn.com
Controller: Pat Smith
VP Operations: Daniel Sieg
Estimated Sales: $5 Million
Number Employees: 20-49
Type of Packaging: Consumer, Food Service, Private Label, Bulk
Brands:
Cousin Willie's

10552 Ranaldi Bros. Frozen Food Products
960 Greenwich Ave
Warwick, RI 02886-4513
401-737-5130
Fax: 401-738-4446
Frozen dough, stuffed breads, kosher dairy pastries
President: Gary Ranaldi
Vice President: Raymond Ranaldi
Sales Director: Robin Capraro
Purchasing Manager: Joseph O'Neil
Estimated Sales: $2,500,000
Number Employees: 30
Number of Products: 100
Square Footage: 130000
Type of Packaging: Consumer, Food Service, Private Label, Bulk
Brands:
Puff Dough

10553 Ranch Oak Farm
3005 Bledsoe St
Fort Worth, TX 76107-2905
817-877-3330
Fax: 817-877-3742 800-888-0327
info@RanchOak.com www.ranchoak.com
Smoked meats
President: Tom Misfeldt
info@ranchoak.com
Estimated Sales: Below $5 Million
Number Employees: 1-4
Type of Packaging: Private Label
Brands:
Ranch Oak Farm

10554 Rancho De Philo Winery
10050 Wilson Ave
Rancho Cucamonga, CA 91737-2314
Fax: 909-987-4208 909-987-4208
Dessert wine
President: Alan Tibbetts
Co-Owner: Janine Tibbetts
janinetibbetts@earthlink.net
Estimated Sales: Less Than $500,000
Number Employees: 1-4
Type of Packaging: Private Label
Brands:
Rancho De Philo
Triple Cream Sherry

10555 Rancho Sierra
42 W Market St
Salinas, CA 93901-2653
831-422-3629
Fax: 831-422-3629 800-398-2929
Tortillas and Mexican food
President: Pamela Mills
Estimated Sales: $4 Million
Number Employees: 40
Square Footage: 140000
Type of Packaging: Consumer, Food Service, Private Label, Bulk
Brands:
El Aguilia

10556 Rancho Sisquoc Winery
6600 Foxen Canyon Rd
Santa Maria, CA 93454-9656
805-934-4332
Fax: 805-937-6601 sisquoc@ranchosisquoc.com
www.ranchosisquoc.net
Wines
Manager: Mary Holt
COO: Edward Holt
Estimated Sales: Below $5 Million
Number Employees: 10-19

Brands:
Rancho Sisquoc

10557 **Rancho's**
1910 Madison Ave
Suite 724
Memphis, TN 38104-2620
901-276-8820
Fax: 901-744-0514
Sauces
Owner: Deborah Reinach
Estimated Sales: Less than $500,000
Number Employees: 1-4

10558 **Randal Optimal Nutrients**
1595 Hampton Way
Santa Rosa, CA 95407-6844
707-528-1800
Fax: 650-349-1686 800-221-1697
info@randaloptimal.com www.randaloptimal.com
Vitamins, minerals and nutritional supplements
President: Dan Brinker
dan@randaloptimal.com
Director Marketing/Technical Services: Donald Burns
Estimated Sales: $3200000
Number Employees: 20-49
Square Footage: 88000
Type of Packaging: Consumer, Private Label, Bulk
Brands:
Nuturpractic
Vimco

10559 **Randall Food Products**
8050 Hosbrook Road
Cincinnati, OH 45236
513-793-6525
www.randallbeans.com
Dry beans
President: W Mashburn
Office Manager: John Alyward
Estimated Sales: $5 Million
Number Employees: 20
Type of Packaging: Consumer, Private Label
Brands:
Randall

10560 **Randall Foods Inc**
2905 E 50th St
Vernon, CA 90058-2919
323-585-2094
Fax: 323-586-1587 800-372-6581
CS@RandallFoods.com www.randallfarms.com
Beef, chicken and pork
Owner: Ron Totin
ron@ranchofoods.com
Director Human Resources: Donna Zuchowski
Number Employees: 100-249
Square Footage: 336000
Brands:
Randall Foods

10561 **Randazzo's Honest To Goodness Sauces**
P.O. Box 901
Glen Rock, NJ 07452
201-543-1195
rochelle@randazzossauces.com
www.randazzossauces.com
Sauces: marinara, plum tomato, basil, tomato and pesto
Founder: Rochelle Randazzo
Estimated Sales: $5-10 Million
Number Employees: 10-19
Brands:
Randazzo's Honest to Goodness

10562 **Randolph Packing Co**
403 W Balfour Ave
Asheboro, NC 27203-3247
336-672-1470
Fax: 336-672-6545 www.randolphpacking.com
Meat
Owner: Don Garner
Estimated Sales: $30 Million
Number Employees: 50-99
Type of Packaging: Consumer

10563 **Randy's Donuts**
805 W Manchester Blvd
Inglewood, CA 90301-1524
310-645-4707
Donuts
Owner: Larry Weintraub
randysdonuts@yahoo.com
Number Employees: 10-19

10564 **Randy's Frozen Meats**
1910 5th St NW
Faribault, MN 55021-4606
507-334-7177
Fax: 507-334-9210 www.randysfoods.com
Pizzas
Co-Owner: Randy Creasman
Number Employees: 20-49
Type of Packaging: Consumer, Food Service, Private Label, Bulk

10565 **Ranieri Fine Foods**
278 Metropolitan Ave
Brooklyn, NY 11211-4006
718-599-9520
Fax: 718-599-6457
Dairy, cheese, meat, sauces and seasonings, baked goods, candy, grains and cereal, pasta, soups and stews.
President: Steven Shlopak
Estimated Sales: Under $500,000
Number Employees: 2-10
Brands:
Berni
Campi del Sole
Capretta
FIDA
Facino
Fatina-Murano
Fattoria Italia
Frumage
Galbusera
HAG
La Vallata
Madre Sicilia
Mellin
Osella
P.L.A.C
Pasta Campo
Ranieri
and more

10566 **Rao's Specialty Foods Inc**
17 Battery Pl
Suite 610
New York, NY 10004-1190
212-269-0151
Fax: 212-344-1680 info@raos.com
www.raos.com
Pasta and sauces, roasted peppers, olive oil & vinegars, marindaes & dressings, canned tomatoes and coffee
Owner: Ruby Briscol
rbriscol@raos.com
Owner: Lynn Iovino
Vice President: Jay Kuder
Marketing Manager: Ron Straci
Sales Manager: Peter Ardigo
Estimated Sales: $3.3 Million
Number Employees: 10-19
Number of Brands: 1
Number of Products: 20
Type of Packaging: Private Label
Brands:
RAO'S

10567 **Rapazzini Winery**
4350 Monterey Rd
Gilroy, CA 95020-8029
408-842-5649
Fax: 408-842-8353 800-842-6262
info@rapazziniwinery.com
www.rapazziniwinery.com
Wine, cooking wines, garlic, jelly, mustard, mayonnaise, spices, salsas and chips
Owner: Charles Larson
info@rapazzini.com
Owner: Alex Larson
Estimated Sales: Less Than $1Million
Number Employees: 5-9
Brands:
Rapazzini Winery

10568 **Rapunzel Pure Organics**
1455 Broad Street
4th Floor
Bloomfield, NJ 07003
973-338-1499
Fax: 973-338-1485 800-225-1449
info@rapunzel.com www.rapunzel.com
Organic sugar, chocolate, soups and bouillons, salt, vegetable juices, cocoa powder and spreads
President: Eckhart Kiesel
Director Sales/Marketing: Dale Kamibayashi
Sales Director: Jim Douglas
Number Employees: 5-9
Square Footage: 20000
Type of Packaging: Consumer, Food Service, Bulk
Brands:
A. Vogel
Bambu Juices
Biotta Juices
Faqs
Herbamare Juices
Rapunzel Pure Organi

10569 **Raquelitas Tortillas**
3111 Larimer St
Denver, CO 80205-2312
303-296-1672
Fax: 303-296-3008 www.raquelitas.com
Tortillas
Owner: Rich Schneider
rschneider@raquelitas.com
Number Employees: 10-19

10570 **Rare Hawaiian Honey Company**
66-1250 Lalamilo Farm Rd
Kamuela, HI 96743
888-663-6639
info@rarehawaiianhoney.com
www.rarehawaiianhoney.com
Organic honey
Commercial Director: Amy Domeier
Year Founded: 1982
Estimated Sales: Under $500,000
Number Employees: 8
Brands:
Rare Hawaiian

10571 **Ratners Retail Foods**
138 Delancey St
New York, NY 10002-3325
212-677-5588
www.nycfoods.com/ratners
Dairy
President: Harold Zankel
VP: Robert Hirmatz
Estimated Sales: $2.5-5 Million
Number Employees: 50-99

10572 **Raven Creamery Company**
3303 NE M L King Boulevard
Portland, OR 97212-2057
503-288-5101
Fax: 503-288-5103
Butter
President: Henry Turner
Marketing Director: Tom Hughes
Estimated Sales: $5-10 000,000
Number Employees: 10-19

10573 **Ravenswood Winery**
18701 Gehricke Rd
Sonoma, CA 95476-4710
707-938-1960
Fax: 707-933-2383 866-568-3946
customerservice@ravenswoodwinery.com
www.preferredlimousineservice.com
Wines
Founder: Joel Peterson
Chairman & CEO: W. Reed Foster
Chief Financial Officer: Callie Konno
Executive Vice President: Justin Faggioli
Estimated Sales: $625 Thousand
Number Employees: 50-99
Number of Brands: 1
Parent Co: Constellation Brand, Inc.
Brands:
Ravenswood

10574 **Ravico USA**
PO BOX 19
Riderwood, MD 21139-0019
443-921-8025
Fax: 443-921-8030 ravicousa@comcast.net
www.ravico.com
Chocolates, pastry shells and desserts
Owner: Jamie Fineran
Retail Sales Director: Erin Murdock Clark
Estimated Sales: Under $500,000
Number Employees: 1-4
Brands:
Ravico

10575 Ravioli Store
4344 21st St
Long Island City, NY 11101-5002
212-925-1737
877-727-8269
www.raviolistore.com
Pasta and sauces
Owner: Donna Seeherman
donna@raviolistore.com
Estimated Sales: $300,000-500,000
Number Employees: 20-49
Number of Brands: 52
Type of Packaging: Consumer, Food Service

10576 Raw Bite
10 Technology Dr
Suite 40
Hudson, MA 01749
844-729-2483
Organic fruit and nut bars
Number of Brands: 1
Number of Products: 5
Type of Packaging: Consumer
Brands:
RAWBITE

10577 Raw Rev
PO Box 359
Hawthorne, NY 10532
914-326-4095
rawrev.com
Plant-based superfood bars
Founder & President: Alice Benedetto

10578 RawFusion
1650 E Gonzales Rd
Suite 282
Oxnard, CA 93030
888-852-3350
info@rawplantprotein.com rawplantprotein.com
Plant-based protein powder and bars

10579 Rawmantic Chocolate
12 West 57th Street
Suite 807
New York, NY 10019
212-247-2229
info@rawmanticchocolate.com
rawmantic-chocolate.myshopify.com
Chocolates, protein bars and nut butters
Founder: Kasia Bosne
Brands:
Rawmantic Chocolate

10580 Ray's Sausage Co
3146 E 123rd St
Cleveland, OH 44120-3179
216-921-8782
Fax: 216-921-4736 www.rayssausage.com
Pork and beef sausage and links, souse and cheese
President: Renee Cash
CFO: Leslie Cash Lester
Vice President: Raymond Cash, Jr.
Marketing/Sales: Raymond Hardin
Estimated Sales: $600000
Number Employees: 5-9
Square Footage: 2800
Type of Packaging: Consumer, Food Service
Brands:
Ray's Headcheese
Ray's Italian Links
Ray's Sausage
Ray's Souse

10581 Raye's Mustard
83 Washington Street
P.O. Box 2
Eastport, ME 04631
800-853-1903
mustards@rayesmustard.com
www.rayesmustard.com
Mustard and mustard sauces
Owner: Karen Raye
Estimated Sales: $5-10 Million
Number Employees: 5-9
Type of Packaging: Consumer, Food Service, Bulk

10582 Raye's Old Fashioned Gourmet Mustard
83 Washington St
PO Box 2
Eastport, ME 04631
800-853-1903
mustards@rayesmustard.com
www.rayesmustard.com
Mustards
Owner: Kevin Raye
Owner: Karen Raye
Estimated Sales: $410,000
Number Employees: 6

10583 Raymond-Hadley Corporation
89 Tompkins St
Spencer, NY 14883
607-589-4415
Fax: 607-589-6442 800-252-5220
www.raymondhadley.com
South and Central American and African foods: barley, beans, bran, flour, cereal, dried fruit, grains, rice, spices, starches, vegetables and corn meal
President: Lori Maratea
Founder: Arthur B. Raymond
Founder: Francis E. Hadley
Vice President of Sales: Tracy McCutcheon
President: Elliot Dutra
Number Employees: 20-49
Square Footage: 204000
Type of Packaging: Bulk

10584 Reading Coffee Roasters
316 W Main St
Birdsboro, PA 19508-1900
610-582-2243
Fax: 610-582-3615 800-331-6713
www.thecoffeegourmet.com
Coffee
Owner: Albert Van Maanen
Co-Owner: Rosemary Hartigan
rdgcofrstr@aol.com
Estimated Sales: $300,000-500,000
Number Employees: 5-9
Type of Packaging: Private Label
Brands:
Jazzy Java Custom Flavored Gourmet
Oscars Flavoring Syrups
Reading Coffee Roast

10585 Ready Foods Inc
2645 W 7th Ave
Denver, CO 80204-4112
303-892-5861
Fax: 303-629-6148 800-748-1218
info@readyfoods.biz www.readyfoods.biz
Mexican food
Owner: Marco Abarca
mabarca@readyfoods.biz
Estimated Sales: $.5-1 million
Number Employees: 10-19
Type of Packaging: Food Service, Private Label, Bulk
Brands:
Marcos

10586 Ready Pac Foods Inc
4401 Foxdale St
Irwindale, CA 91706
800-800-4088
info@bfa.bonduelle.com www.readypac.com
Bag salads and fruit, vegetables and bistro bowls.
CEO: Mary Thompson
Chief HR Officer: Katie Lopez
Chief Manufacturing Officer: Mike Gomes
Chief Supply Chain Officer: Scott McGuire
Chief Procurement Officer: Scott Wilkerson
Year Founded: 1969
Estimated Sales: $50-100 Million
Number Employees: 1,000-4,999
Number of Brands: 1
Other Locations:
Processing Facility
Florence NJ
Processing Facility
Swedesboro NJ
Processing Facility
Jackson GA
Brands:
Ready Pac

10587 Real Aloe Company
7470 Dean Martin Drive
Suite 102
Las Vegas, NV 89139
877-301-8296
Fax: 702-462-5880 800-541-7809
www.realaloeinc.com
Aloe vera gel, juice and beverages
Owner: Frank Mundell
VP: M Mundell
Operations Manager: Dan Mundell
Estimated Sales: $1,100,000
Number Employees: 5-9
Square Footage: 21000
Type of Packaging: Consumer, Food Service, Private Label, Bulk
Brands:
Cal-Aloe Co.
Real Aloe Co.

10588 Real Coconut Co. Inc., The
www.therealcoconut.com
Gluten-free and dairy-free coconut flour tortillas and snack chips
Founder/President: Daniella Hunter
Number of Brands: 1
Number of Products: 6
Type of Packaging: Consumer, Private Label
Brands:
The Real Coconut

10589 Real Cookies
3212 Hewlett Avenue
Merrick, NY 11566-5505
516-221-9300
Fax: 516-221-9561 800-822-5113
Cookie dough and mixes: oatmeal raisin, mocha almond, ginger, macadamia, white chocolate, pecan and chocolate chip
President: Ellyn Knigin
CFO: Leonard Knigin
Vice President: Marian Knigin
Estimated Sales: $500,000-$1 Million
Number Employees: 5-9
Type of Packaging: Consumer, Food Service, Private Label, Bulk
Brands:
Grandma's Cookie Mix
Real Cookies

10590 Real Food Marketing
201 Wyandotte St
Suite 402
Kansas City, MO 64105
816-221-4100
Fax: 913-671-8083
Desserts, breads, meat pastries, ethnic breads, brownies, cookies, muffins, cakes, dietetic foods and pies.
President: John Fallucca
CFO: Tara Cupps
R&D: Bob Deal
Operations: Bill Scott
Purchasing: Clint Scott
Estimated Sales: $1-3 Million
Number Employees: 1-4
Number of Products: 50
Square Footage: 3600
Type of Packaging: Consumer, Food Service, Private Label, Bulk

10591 Real Kosher Sausage Company
9 Euclid Ave
Newark, NJ 07105-4527
973-690-5394
Fax: 212-598-9011
Kosher meats, sausage and deli
President/CEO: Jacob Hill
Estimated Sales: $750,000
Number Employees: 10
Square Footage: 60000
Type of Packaging: Consumer, Food Service, Private Label, Bulk
Brands:
999
Real Kosher

10592 Real Sausage Co
2710 S Poplar Ave
Chicago, IL 60608-5909
312-842-5330
Fax: 312-842-5414 nmakowski@realsausage.com
www.realsausage.com
Sausage

President: Nicole Makowski
Estimated Sales: Below $5 000,000
Number Employees: 20-49
Brands:
Real Sausage

10593 Real Torino
PO Box 448
Brookside, NJ 07926-0448
973-895-5420
Fax: 973-895-8824 peteritaly@aol.com
www.pasta.com
Bread, biscuits, cakes, pastries, cookies, crackers and pasta.
Marketing: Peter Carolan
Estimated Sales: $1.4 Million
Number Employees: 10

10594 Realsalt
475 West 910 South
Heber City, UT 84032
Fax: 435-654-3329 800-367-7258
Darrylb@realsalt.com www.realsalt.com
Kosher, stocks, spices, sea salt and minerals.
Quality Control Manager: Tiffany Riding
Sales Manager: Darryl Bosshaedt
Contact: Rhett Roberts
rhettr@redmondinc.com
Plant Manager: Dennis Schindler
Purchasing Manager: Delvon Julonder
Number Employees: 250
Parent Co: Redmond Inc.

10595 Rebec Vineyards
2229 N Amherst Hwy
Amherst, VA 24521-4378
434-946-5168
Fax: 804-946-5168 winery@rebecwinery.com
www.rebecwinery.com
Wines
Manager: Svetlozar Kanev
winery@rebecwinery.com
Estimated Sales: Below $500,000
Number Employees: 1-4
Type of Packaging: Private Label

10596 Rebecca-Ruth Candy Factory
116 E 2nd St
Frankfort, KY 40601-2902
502-223-7475
Fax: 502-226-5854 800-444-3866
office@rebeccaruth.com
Candy
President: Charles Booe
booe@rebeccaruth.com
Estimated Sales: Less Than $500,000
Number Employees: 5-9
Type of Packaging: Consumer, Private Label, Bulk
Brands:
100 Bourbon Whiskey
Buffalo Trace
Butter Creams
Classic Liquor Cremes
Creme De Menthe
Rebecca-Ruth

10597 Rebound
1 Pepsi Way
Newburgh, NY 12550-3921
845-562-5400
Fax: 845-562-7840
Bottled water
Owner: Tim Tenney
Estimated Sales: $5-10 Million
Number Employees: 5-9

10598 Reckitt Benckiser LLC
399 Interpace Pkwy.
PO Box 225
Parsippany, NJ 07054
973-404-2600
Fax: 973-404-5700 www.rb.com
Household cleaning and specialty food products.
CEO: Laxman Narasimhan
CFO: Adrian Hennah
Senior VP/General Counsel: Rupert Bondy
Year Founded: 1999
Estimated Sales: $14 Billion
Number Employees: 40,000
Number of Brands: 18
Square Footage: 139500
Type of Packaging: Consumer, Food Service, Bulk
Brands:
Dettol
Durex
Mucinex
Nurofen
Scholl
Strepsils
Veet
Clearasil
Gaviscon
Lysol
Harpic
Air Wick
Cillit Bang
Mortein
Vanish
Woolite
Finish
Calgon

10599 Rector Foods
2280 N Park Drive
Brampton, ON L6S 6C6
Canada
905-789-9691
Fax: 905-789-0989 888-314-7834
Seasoning blends
President: Eoin Connell
VP Sales: Michael Parry
Number Employees: 50
Square Footage: 212000

10600 Red Arrow Products Co LLC
633 S 20th St
Manitowoc, WI 54220-3816
920-769-1100
Fax: 920-769-1281 www.redarrowusa.com
Smoke and grill flavors; specialty browning
President: Jerald Kowalski
jerald@redarrow.com
Marketing Coordinator: Kayla Sommer
Sales: Mark Crass
Number Employees: 50-99
Type of Packaging: Food Service, Private Label, Bulk
Other Locations:
Red Arrow Products Co.
Manitowoc WI
Brands:
Aro-Smoke
Char Dex
Char Oil
Char Sol
Char Zyme
Grillin'
Maillose
Toastin
True Gold

10601 Red Baron
115 W College Dr
Marshall, MN 56258-3799
507-532-3274
Fax: 507-537-8333 800-769-7980
Pizza
Owner: Greg Flack
Contact: Randy Brooks
r.brooks@redbaron.com
Director Manufacturing: Guy Hinton
Estimated Sales: Under $500,000
Number Employees: 5-9
Parent Co: Schwann's Sales

10602 Red Brick Brewing Company
2323 Defoor Hills Road
Atlanta, GA 30318
404-355-5558
Fax: 404-350-0127 800-475-5417
info@atlantabrewing.com
www.redbrickbrewing.com
Seasonal beer, ale, stout, lager and pilsner
President: Robet Budd
Sales: Robert Fowler
Contact: Tyler Cates
tylercates@atlantabrewing.com
Estimated Sales: $10-20 Million
Number Employees: 10-19
Type of Packaging: Consumer, Food Service
Brands:
Red Brick

10603 Red Chamber Co
1912 E Vernon Ave
Vernon, CA 90058
323-234-9000
Fax: 323-231-8888 info@redchamber.com
www.redchamber.com
Seafood
CEO: Ming Bin Kou
CFO: Ming Shin Kou
VP: Andro Chen
VP, Food Innovation and R&D: Wales Yu
Year Founded: 1973
Estimated Sales: $100-500 Million
Number Employees: 100-249
Brands:
Aqua Star
Kitchens of the Oceans
Mid-Pacific Seafoods
Neptune Foods
Singleton Seafoods
Tampa Bay Fisheries
and more

10604 Red Creek Marinade Company
P.O.Box 19875
Amarillo, TX 79114-1875
806-358-3531
Fax: 806-358-1587 800-687-9114
Mesquite-flavored marinades
Partner: Lawrence E New
Contact: Ginger New
redcreek@arn.net
Estimated Sales: $1-3 Million
Number Employees: 1-4
Number of Brands: 1
Number of Products: 3
Type of Packaging: Consumer, Food Service, Bulk
Brands:
Red Creek

10605 Red Deer Lake Meat Processing
226 Avenue West
Calgary, AB T2J 5G5
Canada
403-256-4925
Fax: 403-256-8882 rdlmeats@telus.net
www.rdlmeats.ab.ca
Beef, hamburgers, pork, bacon, lamb, goat and sausage
President/General Manager Sales: Brian Barrett
CEO: Georgina Walker
Estimated Sales: $2-5 Million
Number Employees: 20-49
Type of Packaging: Consumer, Food Service, Private Label, Bulk
Brands:
Rdl (Red Deer Lake)

10606 Red Diamond Coffee & Tea
400 Park Ave
Moody, AL 35004
800-292-4651
qcdept@reddiamond.com www.reddiamond.com
Coffee, tea pods and coffee brewers.
VP, Sales Development: John Padgett
VP, Manufacturing: Joe George
Year Founded: 1906
Estimated Sales: $45.9 Million
Number Employees: 100-249
Square Footage: 195000
Type of Packaging: Consumer, Food Service, Private Label, Bulk
Brands:
Red Diamond Coffee & Tea

10607 Red Duck Foods
1515 SE Water Ave
Suite 103
Portland, OR 97214
USA
530-219-0150
www.redduckfoods.com
Artisanal ketchup, and BBQ, seafood and taco sauces
Marketing/Co-Founder: Jessica Hilbert
Operations/Co-Founder: Shannon Oliver
shannon@redduckfoods.com
Business Development: Karen Bonner
Number Employees: 5-9

10608 Red Gold Inc.
PO Box 83
Elwood, IN 46036
765-557-5500
Fax: 765-557-5501 866-729-7187
www.redgold.com
Sauces: tomato, pizza, taco, barbecue, chili, seafood, marinara and spaghetti; tomatoes
President/CEO: Brian Reichart
Senior VP/CFO: Tim Ingle

Year Founded: 1942
Estimated Sales: $750 Million
Number Employees: 2,100
Number of Brands: 5
Square Footage: 1000000
Type of Packaging: Consumer, Food Service, Private Label, Bulk
Other Locations:
Red Gold
Orestes IN
Red Gold
Geneva IN
Brands:
Red Gold
Tuttorosso
Red Pack
Sacramento
Tuong Ot Sriracha

10609 Red Hat Cooperative
809 Broadway Avenue E
Redcliff, AB T0J 2P0
Canada
403-548-6208
Fax: 403-548-7255 sales@redhatco-op.com
www.redhatco-op.com
Vegetables
President: Albert Cramer
CEO: Lyle Aleman
Quality Control: Cassandra Cadrmin
Sales Manager: Blaine Andres
Operations: Tim Donnelly
Purchasing: Crystal McHargue
Number Employees: 180
Type of Packaging: Consumer, Food Service

10610 Red Hot Chicago
2501 N Damen Ave
Chicago, IL 60647-2101
312-829-3434
Fax: 312-829-2704 800-249-5226
info@redhotchicago.com www.redhotchicago.com
Chicago style hot dogs, buns and condiments.
President: Billy Ladany
billy@redhotchicago.com
Estimated Sales: $1-2 Million
Number Employees: 5-9
Type of Packaging: Food Service, Bulk
Brands:
Red Hot Chicago

10611 Red Hot Foods
820 E Railroad Avenue
Santa Paula, CA 93060
805-258-3650
Fax: 805-525-6000 redhotfoods2003@yahoo.com
Condiments, relishes, salsas, sauces, olive oil, pesto, bean and chowder mixes.
President: Butch Baselite
Type of Packaging: Consumer, Food Service, Private Label, Bulk

10612 Red Lion Spicy Foods Company
420 W Broadway
Red Lion, PA 17356
717-309-8303
Fax: 717-244-7348 chip@redlionspicyfoods.com
www.redlionspicyfoods.com
Chili mixes and powder, dry rub, salsa, hot sauce, pepper pickles and garlic dills
President: Chip Welsh
Type of Packaging: Consumer

10613 Red Monkey Foods
6751 W Kings St
Springfield, MO 65802
417-319-7300
Fax: 314-754-9755 www.redmonkeyfoods.com
Spices, herbs, sauces, seasonings, cooking enhancers and rubs
President/Owner: Jeff Brinkhoff
CEO: Scott Bolonda
Contact: Tom Casey
tom.casey@redmonkeyfoods.com
Square Footage: 80000
Type of Packaging: Private Label

10614 Red Pelican Food Products
5650 Saint Jean Street
Detroit, MI 48213-3415
313-881-4095
Mustard, horseradish, relish, sauerkraut, vinegar, cheese, Belgian chocolate and sauce
President: Bernard Cornillie
Sales Manager: D Cornillie
Number Employees: 5-9
Square Footage: 56000
Type of Packaging: Consumer, Food Service, Private Label, Bulk

10615 Red Plate Foods
Bend, OR
541-550-7676
redplatefoods.com
Gluten-free baked goods
Co-Founder: Becca Williams
Co-Founder: Chell Williams

10616 Red River Commodities Inc
501 42nd St N
Fargo, ND 58102-3952
800-437-5539
contact@redriv.com www.redriv.com
Sunflower seeds, beans, millet, flax, soybeans and organics.
President & CEO: Eric Christianson
VP, Finance: Randy Wigen
Estimated Sales: $105.6 Million
Number Employees: 100-249
Square Footage: 140000
Type of Packaging: Food Service, Private Label, Bulk
Brands:
Brown Flax
Confection Sunflower Seed
Goldtex

10617 Red River Foods Inc
9020 Stony Point Pkwy
Suite 380
Richmond, VA 23235-1944
804-320-1800
Fax: 804-320-1896 www.redriverfoods.net
Nuts, seeds, dried foods and snack foods
President: James Phipps
Controller: Keith Dickerson
Vice President: Jack Dousfield
Estimated Sales: $10-49.9 Million
Number Employees: 10-19
Number of Products: 30

10618 Red Rocker Candy
92B Industrial Drive
Suite 6
Troy, VA 22974
434-589-2011
Fax: 434-589-3649
sue.charney@redrockercandy.com
www.redrockercandy.com
Candy
Manager: Sue Charney
Estimated Sales: $250,000
Number Employees: 5

10619 Red Rose Trading Company
520 N Charlotte St
Lancaster, PA 17603
717-293-7833
Granola, pancake, baking and gluten-free mixes and blends
Owner: J Leichter
Estimated Sales: $3-5 Million
Number Employees: 10-19
Square Footage: 56000
Type of Packaging: Consumer, Food Service, Private Label, Bulk

10620 Red Smith Foods Inc
4145 SW 47th Ave
Davie, FL 33314-4006
954-581-1996
Fax: 954-581-6775 www.redsmithfoods.com
Pickled eggs, sausage and pigs' feet
President: Stephen Foster
bburton@redsmithfoods.com
COO: Jon Foster
CFO: Tim Foster
Executive VP: David Foster
Marketing & Sales Director: Brian Burton
Plant Manager: Michael Sandy
Estimated Sales: $8 Million
Number Employees: 20-49
Number of Brands: 2
Number of Products: 6
Square Footage: 48000
Parent Co: Red Smith of Florida, Inc.
Type of Packaging: Consumer
Brands:
Big John
Red Smith

10621 Red Star Yeast
P.O. Box 737
Milwaukee, WI 53201-0737
414-271-6755
Fax: 414-347-4795 800-445-4746
www.redstaryeast.com
Yeast, fermentation products
President & CEO: John Riesch
CFO: Geoff O'Connor
Director of Sales: Dean Modglin
Year Founded: 1882
Estimated Sales: $20-50 Million
Number Employees: 1,000-4,999
Brands:
Red Star

10622 Red Steer Meats
3812 W Clarendon Ave
Phoenix, AZ 85019-3718
602-272-6677
Fax: 602-484-7381
Meat
President: Richard Barton
Vice President: Judy Barton
Estimated Sales: $5-10 000,000
Number Employees: 5-9
Type of Packaging: Private Label

10623 Red V Foods
1665 Heraeus Blvd
Buford, GA 30518
770-729-8983
Fax: 770-729-9428 info@redvfoods.com
www.redvfoods.com
Coconut products
Square Footage: 110000

10624 Red White & Brew
223 Ashley Ct
Redding, CA 96001-3656
530-222-5891
www.rwbaz.com
Beer
President: Bill Ward
Estimated Sales: $120,000
Number Employees: 3
Brands:
Red White & Brew

10625 Red's All Natural
803 N Derby Ln
North Sioux City, SD 57049
605-956-7337
www.redsallnatural.com
Frozen burritos
Founder & CEO: Mike Adair

10626 Redd Superfood Energy Bars
R.e.d.d., Inc.
PO Box 15388
Portland, ME 04112
207-370-4433
www.reddbar.com
Energy bars
Founder & Chairman: Alden Blease
CEO: Peter Van Alstine
Marketing: Reed Allen
Number Employees: 2-10
Brands:
Redd

10627 (HQ)Reddy Ice
5720 LBJ Freeway
Suite 200
Dallas, TX 75240
214-526-6740
800-683-4423
information@reddyice.com www.reddyice.com
Packaged ice products including cubes, blocks, and dry; Cold storage warehouse
Chairman: Bill Corbin
CEO: Deborah Conklin
CFO: Steven Janusek
COO: Paul Smith
Contact: Karen Apperson
kapperson@reddyice.com
Year Founded: 1927
Estimated Sales: $300 Million
Number Employees: 1000-4999

10628 Redhawk Vineyard & Winery
2995 Michigan City Rd NW
Salem, OR 97304-9704
503-362-1596
Fax: 503-585-4657 www.redhawkwine.com
Wines
Owner: John Pataccoli
jpatwine@aol.com
Estimated Sales: $350,000
Number Employees: 1-4
Type of Packaging: Private Label
Brands:
Redhawk

10629 Redhook Brewery
929 North Russell St.
Portland, OR 97227
503-331-7270
redhook@redhook.com
www.redhook.com
Beer and ale
President: David Mickelson
redhook@redhook.com
CFO & Treasurer: Mark Moreland
Sales & Marketing Manager: Tim Oneill
Marketing Manager: Nelson Ray
Operations Manager: Naomi Graf
Estimated Sales: $20.4 Million
Number Employees: 10-19
Parent Co: Craft Brew Alliance
Type of Packaging: Consumer, Food Service
Brands:
Ballard Bitter
Black Hook
Double Black
Esb
Hefeweizen
Rye
Wheatbrook
Winterhook

10630 Redmond Minerals Inc
475 W 910 S
Heber City, UT 84032-2494
435-657-3600
Fax: 435-529-7486 866-312-7258
mail@redmondminerals.com
www.redmondinc.com
Sea salt
CEO: Rhett Roberts
Estimated Sales: $20-50 Million
Number Employees: 30
Type of Packaging: Consumer, Food Service, Private Label, Bulk

10631 Redondo Iglesias USA
67 New Hook Rd.
Suite 2E
Bayonne, NJ 11530-1631
201-455-5266
Fax: 201-455-5268 www.redondousa.com
Spanish hams: Serrano and Iberico
Sales & Marketing: Kate Whittum
Brands:
Redondo Iglesias

10632 Redondo's LLC
94-140 Leokane St
Waipahu, HI 96797-2280
808-671-5444
Fax: 808-676-7009 www.redondos.com
Sausages
President: Hitoshi Okada
hitoshi@redondos.com
VP/General Manager: Yoshi Shinanti
VP: Toshiyuki Murakane
Owner: Frank Redondo
Estimated Sales: $5-10 Million
Number Employees: 20-49
Brands:
Pipikaula

10633 Redwood Hill Farm
2064 Gravenstein Hwy N
Bldg. 1, Suite 130
Sebastopol, CA 95472
707-823-8250
Fax: 707-823-6976 877-238-3543
contact@redwoodhill.com redwoodhill.com
Goat milk yogurt, cheeses and kefir
Manager: Jennifer Bice
Marketing Director: Sharon Bice
Accounting Manager: Andrew Malmanis
Quality Control Manager: Ann Caswell
Owner: Jennifer Lynn Bice
Estimated Sales: $1-2.5 Million
Number Employees: 20-49
Type of Packaging: Private Label
Brands:
Redwood Hill Farm

10634 Reed Lang Farms
118 W Colorado Ave
Rio Hondo, TX 78583
956-748-2354
Fax: 956-748-2888
Ruby Red and Rio Red grapefruits, navel oranges, Lula avacados, pecans, almonds and citrus blossom honey
President/Owner: Violet Lang
Estimated Sales: $50,000
Number Employees: 16
Square Footage: 44100
Type of Packaging: Private Label

10635 Reed's, Inc.
Los Angeles, CA
www.drinkreeds.com
Ginger beer

10636 Reeve Wines
PO Box 380
Healdsburg, CA 95448
707-235-6345
kelly@reevewines.com
www.reevewines.com
Wines
Co-Founder: Noah Dorrance
Co-Founder: Kelly Dorrance

10637 Refresco Beverages US Inc.
Tampa, FL 33614
813-313-1800
888-260-3776
ConsumerAffairs.NA@refresco.com
www.refresco-na.com
Soft drinks, sports and energy drinks, tea, and sparkling and flavoured water.
CFO, North America: Bill McFarland
COO, North America: Brad Goist
Estimated Sales: Over $1 Billion
Number Employees: 3,600
Type of Packaging: Consumer, Food Service, Private Label, Bulk
Brands:
RC Cola
RC Q
Mulberry Farms
Ben Shaws
red rain
Vit20
Orient Emporium
Vess
Vintage
Stars & Stripes
So Clear
Clear Choice
Chadwick Bay
Harvest Classic
eXact

10638 Regal Crown Foods Inc
41 Mason St
Worcester, MA 01610-3203
508-752-2679
Fax: 508-831-0775
Vinegar pickles
Owner: William McEntee
regalcrownfoods@aol.com
Public Relations: Monica Freund Kaufman
Plant Manager: David Giorgio
Estimated Sales: $1-3 Million
Number Employees: 1-4
Number of Brands: 12
Number of Products: 6
Type of Packaging: Food Service, Private Label

10639 Regal Food Service
13206 Advance Dr
Houston, TX 77065-1102
281-477-3683
Fax: 713-222-2549
Sandwiches and spreads
Manager: Charles Smith
Estimated Sales: $10 Million
Number Employees: 50-99
Type of Packaging: Consumer, Food Service

10640 Regal Health Food
3705 W Grand Ave
Chicago, IL 60651-2236
773-252-1044
Fax: 773-252-0817 info@regalsnacks.com
www.regalsnacks.com
Dried fruits and nuts
President: Gregory Piatigorsky
regalgourmetfoods@gmail.com
VP Marketing/Sales: Igor Piatigorsky
Estimated Sales: $10-20 Million
Number Employees: 10-19
Square Footage: 54000
Type of Packaging: Consumer, Food Service, Private Label, Bulk
Brands:
Regal

10641 Regatta Craft Mixers
63 Forest Ave
Locust Valley, NY 11560
info@regattacraftmixers.com
www.regattacraftmixers.com
Craft bar mixers
Acting CMO: Doug Metchick
Year Founded: 2006
Number of Products: 5

10642 Regco
46 Rogers Rd
Haverhill, MA 01835-6957
978-521-4370
Fax: 978-372-4371
Pitas
President: Regina Ragonese
pitadiva@regenies.com
Broker Sales Representative: Sheryl Makaron
Public Relations Director: Peter Ash
Production Supervisor: Guy Minnick
Number Employees: 20-49
Brands:
Regenie's

10643 Regenie's Crunchy Pi
46 Rogers Rd
Haverhill, MA 01835-6957
978-521-4370
877-734-3643
info@regenies.com www.regenies.com
Pita chips
President/Owner: Regina Ragonese

10644 Regennas Candy Shop
10 Maple Lane
Myerstown, PA 17067
717-866-1873
www.clearcandy.com
Candy

10645 Regez Cheese & Paper Supply
N2603 Coplien Rd
Monroe, WI 53566
608-325-3417
Fax: 608-325-3499
Cheese
President: Michael Einbeck
Estimated Sales: $530,000
Number Employees: 1-4

10646 Reggie Balls Cajun Foods
501 Bunker Rd
Lake Charles, LA 70615-3875
337-436-0291
Fax: 337-433-9851 www.ballscajunfoods.com
Cajum seasonings and mixes; Contract packaging and private labeling
Owner/President: Reginald Ball
Estimated Sales: Less Than $500,000
Number Employees: 1-4
Type of Packaging: Private Label

10647 Reggie's Roast
1501 West Blancke Street
Linden, NJ 07036
908-862-3700
Fax: 908-862-3711 www.reggiesroast.com
Coffee.
President: Reggie Chungloy
Estimated Sales: $260,000
Number Employees: 4

10648 Reginald's Homemade LLC
Manakin Sabot, VA 23103
804-972-4040
www.reginaldshomemade.com
Nut butters
Owner: Andrew Broocker

10649 Register Meat Co
3160 Willow St
Cottondale, FL 32431-3334
850-352-4269
Fax: 850-352-2628
Pork and sausage
President: Al Kaempfer
Estimated Sales: $10 Million
Number Employees: 10-19
Type of Packaging: Consumer, Bulk

10650 Registry Steak & Seafood
7661 S 78th Ave
Unit B
Bridgeview, IL 60455-1271
708-458-3100
Fax: 708-458-3103
Meat, seafood
President: Tony Migacz
ynotshrimp@yahoo.com
Senior Vice President: Anthony S Migacz
Estimated Sales: $10 Million
Number Employees: 20-49
Square Footage: 5000
Type of Packaging: Food Service, Private Label, Bulk

10651 Rego Smoked Fish Company
6980 75th St
Flushing, NY 11379
718-894-1400
Fax: 718-894-9100
Smoked salmon, sturgeon, trout, sablefish and whitefish
President: Jason Spitz
Manager: Sheldon Spitz
Owner: Conrad Spitz
Estimated Sales: $500,000-$1 Million
Number Employees: 1-4
Square Footage: 28000
Type of Packaging: Consumer, Bulk
Brands:
Spibro

10652 Reheis Co
235 Snyder Ave
Berkeley Heights, NJ 07922-1150
908-464-1500
Fax: 908-464-7726 rduffy@reheis.com
www.reheis.com
Potassium chloride
VP R&D: J C Parekh
VP Sales: D Fondots
VP Operations: J Bogan
Plant Manager: Gerry Kirwan
Estimated Sales: Less Than $500,000
Number Employees: 1-4
Brands:
Kci

10653 Rehemond Farm Inc
232 Pottle Hill Rd
Minot, ME 04258-4802
207-345-5611
Fax: 207-345-5611
Poultry
Owner: Noella Hemond
Number Employees: 5-9
Brands:
Oak Hurst Dairy

10654 Reid Foods
PO Box 406
Gurnee, IL 60031
847-625-7912
Fax: 847-625-7913 888-295-8478
reidfoods@yahoo.com www.reidfoods.com
Jams, dessert toppings, salsas, soups, pasta, pasta sauces, dips and chili
President: Maria Reid
Estimated Sales: $190,000
Number Employees: 3

10655 (HQ)Reilly Dairy & Food Company
6603 S Trask Avenue
Tampa, FL 33616
813-839-8458
Fax: 813-839-0394
Cheese, dairy, butter
President: Gerald Reilly
rdfjerry@gmail.com
Human Resources Director: Brenda Reilly
Estimated Sales: $16,000,000
Number Employees: 70
Square Footage: 36000
Type of Packaging: Consumer, Food Service, Private Label, Bulk
Brands:
Dixie Fresh
Wisconsin Gold

10656 Reilly's Sea Products
PO Box 149
South Bristol, ME 04568-0149
207-644-1400
Fax: 207-644-8192
Seafood
President: Terry Reilly
Estimated Sales: $5-10 Million
Number Employees: 20-49

10657 Reily Foods Company
400 Poydras St
10th Floor
New Orleans, LA 70130
Fax: 504-539-5427 800-535-1961
service@reilyproducts.com
www.reilyproducts.com
Coffee, tea, cake flour, sauces, chili seasonings, salad dressings, bean soups and brownie mixes.
President & COO: Mark Reed
Plant Manager: Duane Montague
Year Founded: 1902
Estimated Sales: $101.7 Million
Number Employees: 500-999
Square Footage: 500000
Type of Packaging: Consumer, Food Service, Private Label, Bulk
Brands:
Blue Plate Mayonnaise
Carroll Shelby Chili Kits
Cdm Coffee & Chicory
French Market Coffee
Jfg Coffee and Tea
La Martinique
Luzianne
No Pudge! Brownie Mix
Old Dutch
Presto
Swans Down Cake Flour
Try Me Sauces/Seasonings
Wick Fowler Chili Kits

10658 Reimann Food Classics
1304 E Cooper Drive
Palatine, IL 60074-7284
847-991-1366
Fax: 847-359-7528
Pancake and waffle mixes
President: E Reimann
Number Employees: 5-9
Type of Packaging: Consumer

10659 Reinhart Foods
235 Yorkland Blvd
Suite 1101
Toronto, ON M2J 4Y8
Canada
416-645-4910
Fax: 888-519-0079 cs@reinhartfoods.com
www.reinhartfoods.com
Vinegar, maraschino cherries, glace fruit, dates, raisins, coconut, mince meat, pie fillings, apples and pineapples
President/CEO: Jeff King
Director of Sales/Bus. Dev./Marketing: Michael J.
Parent Co: Reinhart Vinegars
Type of Packaging: Consumer, Food Service, Private Label, Bulk
Brands:
Allen's
Daltons
Jaffa

10660 Reinhold Ice Cream Company
800 Fulton St
Pittsburgh, PA 15233-2119
412-321-7600
Fax: 412-321-8456
Ice cream and frozen yogurt
President: Robert Mandell
Vice President: Michael Mandell
Salesman: Diane Beckerman
Contact: Joseph Olsavsky
joseph.olsavsky@philips.com
Plant Manager: Craig Metzgar
Estimated Sales: $7,400,000
Number Employees: 190
Type of Packaging: Consumer, Food Service, Private Label, Bulk

10661 Reist Popcorn Co
113 Manheim St
Mt Joy, PA 17552-1317
717-653-8078
Fax: 717-653-4121 reistpopcorn.com
Popcorn
President: David Reist
dreist@reistpopcorn.com
Estimated Sales: Less Than $500,000
Number Employees: 5-9
Type of Packaging: Private Label, Bulk
Brands:
Dutch Country
Hi-Pop

10662 Reiter Affiliated Companies
730 S A St.
Oxnard, CA 93030
805-483-1000
info@berry.net
www.berry.net
Strawberries, raspberries, blueberries and blackberries
President & CEO: Hector Lujan Valladolid
Year Founded: 1900
Number Employees: 10,000+
Type of Packaging: Private Label

10663 Reiter Dairy
216 E 11th St
Newport, KY 41071
859-431-7553
Fax: 859-431-0349 800-544-6455
www.reiterdairy.com
Juice and dairy
General Manager: Bill Riley
Cmo: Dan Smith
dan_smith@deanfoods.com
Year Founded: 1933
Number Employees: 250-499
Square Footage: 100000
Parent Co: Suiza Foods
Type of Packaging: Consumer, Food Service, Private Label, Bulk

10664 Reiter Dairy LLC
1961 Commerce Circle
Springfield, OH 45504
937-323-5777
Fax: 937-323-2420
www.deanfoods.com/brands/reiter-dairy/
Orange juice, bottled water, dairy, cheese, ice cream and sour cream.
Sales Executive: Steve Paasch
General Manager: Mike Allen
mike_allen@deanfoods.com
Year Founded: 1933
Estimated Sales: $100-124.9 Million
Number Employees: 100-249
Number of Brands: 3
Square Footage: 25000
Parent Co: Dean Foods Company
Type of Packaging: Consumer, Food Service
Brands:
Jersey Farms
Louis Trauth
Reiter

10665 Rejuvila
PO Box 21447
Boulder, CO 80308
877-480-4402
info@rejuvila.com
Supplements
Founder: Myra Michelle Eby
Contact: Alene Bourcier
arlene@rejuvila.com

Type of Packaging: Consumer

10666 **Remarkable Liquids**
2 Van Buren Blvd, NE Industrial Park
Altamont, NY 12009
518-861-5351
www.remarkableliquids.com
Craft beers, ciders, and meads.
General Manager: Spencer Noakes
Partner: Matt Hartman
VP, Operations: Chad Farrington
Operations Manager: Jason Napoleon
Year Founded: 2012
Estimated Sales: $11 Million
Number Employees: 52
Number of Brands: 67
Brands:
12% IMPORTS
ABANDON BREWING CO.
AGAINST THE GRAIN BREWERY
ALMANAC BEER CO.
ANCHORAGE BREWING CO.
ARGUS CIDERY
B. NEKTAR MEADERY
BEAU'S ALL-NATURAL BREWING
BREWMASTER JACK
BROUWERIJ ST. BERNARDUS
BROUWERIJ VERHAEGHE
CLARDERA BREWING
CAPTAIN LAWRENCE BREWING CO.
CIDER CREEK HARD CIDER
COLONY MEADERY
COMMUNITY BEAR WORKS
CROOKED STAVE
DARK HORSE BREWING
EVIL TWIN
FINBACK BREWERY
FOLEY BROTHERS BREWING

10667 **Rembrandt Foods**
1521 18th Street
Spirit Lake, IA 51360
877-344-4055
contactus@rembrandtinc.com
www.rembrandtfoods.com
Egg
President: David Rettig
Number Employees: 50-99
Type of Packaging: Food Service

10668 **Renaissance Vineyard & Winery**
12585 Rices Crossing Rd
Oregon House, CA 95962
530-692-2248
Fax: 530-692-2497 800-655-3277
www.renaissancewinery.com
Wine
President: Greg Holman
Vice President: Hagit Raubach
Sales: John Brooks
Office Manager: Sharon Shelton
Estimated Sales: $5-10 Million
Number Employees: 10-19
Number of Brands: 1
Type of Packaging: Consumer, Food Service
Brands:
Renaissance

10669 **Renard's Cheese**
248 County Rd S
Algoma, WI 54201-9444
920-487-2825
Fax: 920-487-5042 orders@renardscheese.com
www.renards.com
Cheese
Owner: Tina Renard
renards@renards.com
Proprietor: Gary Renard
Vice President: Chris Renard
Estimated Sales: $5-9.9 Million
Number Employees: 10-19
Type of Packaging: Private Label

10670 **Renault Winery**
72 N Bremen Ave
Egg Harbor City, NJ 08215
609-965-2111
www.renaultwinery.com
Vermouth and wine
Estimated Sales: $3649539
Number Employees: 100-249
Type of Packaging: Consumer

10671 **Rendulic Meat Packing Corp**
800 Manning Ave
Mckeesport, PA 15132-3699
412-678-9541
Fax: 412-678-8891 info@nemahalal.com
www.nemahalal.com
Meat: bologna, suckling pig, veal and lamb
President: Beyhan Nakiboglo
Estimated Sales: $3300000
Number Employees: 10-19
Type of Packaging: Consumer

10672 **Rene Produce Dist**
895 E Frontage Rd
Rio Rico, AZ 85648-9675
520-281-0806
Fax: 520-281-2933 reneprod@dakotacom.net
www.reneproduce.com
Cucumbers, eggplant, squash, tomatoes and peppers
President: Rene Carrillo
carrillo@reneproduce.com
Sales Manager: David Kennedy
Sales: George Quintero
Estimated Sales: $3-5 Million
Number Employees: 10-19
Type of Packaging: Consumer, Food Service
Brands:
Rene

10673 **Rene Rey Chocolates Ltd**
1119 West 14th Street
North Vancouver, BC V7P 1J9
Canada
604-985-0949
Fax: 604-985-0395 888-985-0949
sales@renerey.com www.renerey.com
Chocolate, candy
President: Rene Rey
Director Of Marketing: Gerald Pinton
Square Footage: 40000
Brands:
Maple Nuts
Nature Canada
Sun Moon Stars

10674 **Renfro Foods**
PO Box 321
Fort Worth, TX 76101
800-332-2456
www.renfrofoods.com
Condiments and dips
President/Owner: Doug Renfro
CEO: Bill Renfro
COO: Jack Renfro
Brands:
Mrs. Renfro's

10675 **Renwood Mills**
P.O. Box 350
Newton, NC 28658
828-464-1611
info@renwoodmills.com
www.renwoodmills.com
Processor of flour, corn meal, biscuit flour and baking mixes.
CEO: Bill Mackin
Commercial Business Manager: Steve Arndt
Year Founded: 1935
Estimated Sales: $271 Million
Number Employees: 100-249
Type of Packaging: Consumer, Food Service, Private Label, Bulk
Brands:
Redimix
Southern Biscuit
Tenda Bake

10676 **Renwood Winery**
12225 Steiner Rd
Plymouth, CA 95669-9502
209-245-6979
Fax: 916-245-6013 800-348-8466
www.renwood.com
Wines
President: Robert Smerling
info@renwood.com
CFO: Bob Moore
VP Marketing: Joe Cusimano
Manager: Abby Bishop
Operations Manager: Bryan Wilkinson
Estimated Sales: $5-10 Million
Number Employees: 10-19
Square Footage: 72
Type of Packaging: Private Label
Brands:
Renwood Wines
Santino Wines

10677 **Republic of Tea**
5 Hamilton Landing
Suite 100
Novato, CA 94949-8703
415-382-3400
Fax: 415-382-3401 800-298-4832
info@republicoftea.com www.republicoftea.com
Tea and teaware
President: Ronald Rubin
CFO: Steve Lohmann
VP: Tod Rubin
Contact: Elizabeth Anderson
elizabeth@elizabeth-haley.com
Operations: Eva Wong
Estimated Sales: $2.5-5 Million
Number Employees: 25
Brands:
Daily Green Teas
Red Tea
Republic of Tea

10678 **Republica Del Cacao LLC**
3780 Kilroy Airport Way
Suite 200
Long Beach, CA 90806
932-256-1320
Fax: 562-256-7001
Cocoa & baking chocolate, baking mixes and ingredients; chocolate bars
Manager: Bernard Duclos
Member: Ganzano Chieiboga
Estimated Sales: $74,000
Number Employees: 3

10679 **Request Foods Inc**
3460 John F Donnelly Dr
Holland, MI 49424-9569
616-786-0900
Fax: 616-786-9180 800-786-0900
info@requestfoods.com www.requestfoods.com
Frozen entrees and dinners
President: Jack Dewitt
jacdew@requestfoods.com
CFO: Bill Rysdyk
R & D: Jurgen Becker
Quality Control: Tom Muntter
Operations Director: Merle DeWitt
Purchasing Agent: Larry Vanderkolk
Estimated Sales: $31 Million
Number Employees: 250-499
Square Footage: 350000
Type of Packaging: Consumer, Food Service, Private Label

10680 **Research Products Co**
1835 E North St
Salina, KS 67401-8567
785-825-2181
Fax: 785-825-8908 800-234-7174
www.researchprod.com
Flour bleaching and maturing premixers; vitamins and minerals
President: Monte White
montewhite@researchprod.com
Estimated Sales: $10-20 Million
Number Employees: 50-99
Parent Co: McShares
Brands:
Kurolite
Oxylite

10681 **Reser's Fine Foods Inc**
P.O. Box 8
Beaverton, OR 97075
503-643-6431
800-333-6431
www.resers.com
Frozen dinners: cold salads, tortillas, salsas, smoked meats
President & CEO: Mark Reser
CFO & Treasurer: Paul Leavy
EVP, Sales, Marketing and R&D: Peter Sirgy
VP, Supply Chain: Pete Shepard
Year Founded: 1950
Estimated Sales: $310 Million
Number Employees: 3,000
Parent Co: Belletieri Company
Brands:
Reser's American Classics
Reser's Sensational Sides

Baja Cafe
Stonemill Kitchens

10682 **Resource Trading Company**
72 Commercial Street
Portland, ME 04104-1698
207-772-2299
Fax: 207-772-4709
Lobster, scallops and shrimp
President: Spencer Fuller
Domestic Sales: Tom Keegan
International Sales: Irene Ketalaar-Moon
Type of Packaging: Bulk
Brands:
Arctic Pride
Claw Island
Northern Lights

10683 **Restaurant Data**
1 Bridge St
Irvington, NY 10533-1560
732-667-5885
Fax: 914-591-5494 800-346-9390
info@netsoftsolutions.com restaurantdata.com
Cashew and other nuts; Co-packing services
President: James Santo
R&D: Paul Mlynar
Contact: Jeff Kydd
jeff@foodservicereport.com
Purchasing Director: Joe Di Donato
Estimated Sales: $1-2 Million
Number Employees: 1-4
Number of Brands: 1
Number of Products: 12
Square Footage: 48000
Type of Packaging: Consumer, Private Label, Bulk
Brands:
Nutsco

10684 **Restaurant Lulu GourmetProducts**
816 Folsom Street
San Francisco, CA 94107
415-495-5775
Fax: 415-495-7810 888-693-5800
Olive tapenade, honey, vinegars, seasonings, sauces and tomato
Manager: Tom Ratcliff
Sales Director: Leslie Wilson
Estimated Sales: $2.5-5 Million
Number Employees: 1-4
Square Footage: 16000
Type of Packaging: Private Label

10685 **Restaurant Systems International**
1000 South Avenue
Staten Island, NY 10314-3430
718-494-8888
Fax: 718-494-8776
Frozen yogurt
CEO: Richard Nicotra
Contact: Joe Giannetti
jgiannetti@restsys.com
Number Employees: 20-49
Square Footage: 40000

10686 **Reter Fruit**
3100 S Pacific Hwy
Medford, OR 97501-8758
541-772-9560
Fax: 541-772-5258
Pears
President: F Baker
Estimated Sales: $380000
Number Employees: 50-99
Type of Packaging: Consumer
Brands:
Maltese Cross
Sun-Sugared

10687 **Rethemeyer Coffee Company**
1711 N Broadway
St Louis, MO 63102
314-231-0990
Coffee
President: A Rethemeyer
Estimated Sales: Less than $500,000
Number Employees: 1-4
Brands:
Rethemeyer

10688 **Retzlaff Vineyards**
1356 S Livermore Ave
Livermore, CA 94550-9505
925-447-8941
Fax: 925-447-9641 retzlaffwinery@gmail.com
www.retzlaffvineyards.com
Wines
Owner: Gloria Taylor
retzlaffwinery@gmail.com
Marketing Manager: Connie Vander Vouter
Estimated Sales: Below $5 Million
Number Employees: 10-19
Brands:
Retzlaff Estate Wines

10689 **Reutter Candy & Chocolates**
4665 Hollins Ferry Road
Baltimore, MD 21227-4601
800-392-0870
Fax: 410-510-1222
Candy, chocolate
International Sales: Karl Heigold
Brands:
Choco Berries
Fine Mints
The Mint

10690 **Reva Foods**
Saint Petersburg, FL 33732
727-692-1292
www.revafoods.com
Sauces, salsas, relish, ketchups, rubs, and seasonings.
President: Kathy Varricchio

10691 **Revel, Gelato**
Huntington Beach, CA
866-203-9145
www.revelegelato.com
Whipped gelato

10692 **Revive Kombucha**
101 2nd St
Suite 190
Petaluma, CA 94952
707-536-1193
thirsty@revivekombucha.com
www.revivekombucha.com
Kombucha beverages
Founder & CEO: Sean J. Lovett
Executive Assistant: Leah Burke
Director of Operations: Rebekah Lovett
Number Employees: 11-50
Brands:
Revive Kombucha

10693 **Revonah Pretzel LLC**
507 Baltimore St Rear
Hanover, PA 17331-3396
717-630-2883
Fax: 717-632-3328 www.revonahpretzel.com
Pretzels and potato chips
Owner: Kevin Bidelspach
kevinb@revonahpretzel.com
Estimated Sales: $3900000
Number Employees: 5-9
Square Footage: 96000
Type of Packaging: Consumer, Food Service, Private Label, Bulk
Brands:
Bickel
Sam & Nick's
Tom Sturgis

10694 **Reynolds Sugar Bush**
188572 W Maple Road
Aniwa, WI 54408
715-449-2057
Fax: 715-449-2879
Maple syrup
President: Juan Reynolds
Estimated Sales: Below $5 000,000
Number Employees: 4
Type of Packaging: Private Label

10695 **Rezolex LLC**
3 E Fort Selden Rd
Radium Springs, NM 88054
575-527-1730
Fax: 575-527-0221 www.rezolex.com
Seasonings
President: Louis Biad
rezolex.com@zianet.com
Plant Manager: Robert Stomp
Estimated Sales: Below $5 000,000
Number Employees: 20-49

10696 **Rhino Foods Inc**
79 Industrial Pkwy
Burlington, VT 05401-5435
802-862-0252
Fax: 802-865-4145 info@rhinofoods.com
www.rhinofoods.com
Ice cream, brownies, cookie dough batter, cakes, truffles, pie squares and baking inclusions.
President/Owner: Ted Castle
tcastle@rhinofoods.com
Director of Finance & Administration: Jayne Magnant
Research & Development Specialist: Rob Douglas
Quality Assurance Manager: Lauren Weber
Director of Marketing: Dan Kiniry
Marketing Manager/Demand Planner: Gillian Bell
Director of Operations: Gene Steinfeld
Year Founded: 1981
Estimated Sales: $25 Million
Number Employees: 100-249
Number of Brands: 2
Square Footage: 29000
Type of Packaging: Consumer, Food Service, Private Label, Bulk
Brands:
Chessters
Vermont Velvet

10697 **Rhodes Bean & Supply Co-Op**
24710 S Bird Rd
Tracy, CA 95304-9339
209-835-1284
Fax: 209-835-1304 ken@beanplant.com
www.beanplant.com
Dried beans
General Manager: Ken Kirsten
ken@beanplant.com
Estimated Sales: $500,000-$1 Million
Number Employees: 10 19
Type of Packaging: Bulk
Brands:
Rhodes-Stockton Bean

10698 **Rhodes International Inc**
5121 S Murray Blvd
Salt Lake City, UT 84123-4602
801-972-0122
Fax: 801-972-0286 800-876-7333
customersatisfaction@rhodesbread.com
www.rhodesbread.com
Bread rolls
President & CEO: Ken Farnworth
Year Founded: 1932
Estimated Sales: $20-50 Million
Number Employees: 50-99
Square Footage: 30000
Type of Packaging: Consumer, Food Service, Private Label
Brands:
Dakota Hearth
Rhodes

10699 **Rhythm Superfoods**
PO Box 41345
Austin, TX 78704
512-441-5667
rhythmsuperfoods.com
Kale, beet and sweet potato chips
Co-Founder/President & CEO: Scott Jensen
Co-Founder & Creative Director: Keith Wahrer
CFO: Jeff Tusa
Controller: Alison White
Marketing Director: Sarah Caddell
VP Of Sales: Calvin Daily
Contact: Sarah Alexander
salexander@rhythmsuperfoods.com
Operations Director: Becky Conces
Type of Packaging: Consumer
Brands:
Rhythm Superfoods

10700 **Rib Rack**
Birmingham, MI
www.theribrack.com
BBQ sauce
VP, Sales: Rich Gustafson

10701 **Riba Foods**
P.O.Box 630461
Houston, TX 77263-0461
713-975-7001
Fax: 713-975-7036 800-327-7422
info@ribafoods.com www.ribafoods.com
Salsas, pickles, jalapeno peppers, mustards, sauces and bean dips
President: Miguel Barrios
Manager Sales/Marketing: Richard Wall
Contact: Misael Avellaneda
misael@ribafoods.com
Estimated Sales: $5-10 Million
Number Employees: 10-19
Number of Brands: 3
Number of Products: 45
Square Footage: 80000
Type of Packaging: Consumer, Food Service, Private Label
Brands:
Arriba
NortenA
Texas Pepper Works

10702 **Ribble Production**
1601 Mearns Road
Warminster, PA 18974-1115
215-674-1706
Fax: 215-674-0123
Decorative toppings, nonpareils, jimmies and mixes; custom manufacturing and packaging
VP: Joseph Van Houten
Number Employees: 20-49
Type of Packaging: Consumer, Food Service, Private Label, Bulk

10703 **Ribus Inc.**
10900 Manchester Rd
Suite 206
St. Louis, MO 63122
314-727-4287
Fax: 314-727-1199 info@ribus.com
www.ribus.com
Rice-based food ingredients, emulsifiers and extrusion aids
President: Steve Pierce
steve@ribus.com
Finance Supervisor: Michelle Kyle
Technical Manager: Neal Hammond
Manager, Global Marketing: Laurie Wittenbrink
Sales: Jim Goodall
Director of Operations: Peggy Vorwald
Estimated Sales: $720000
Number Employees: 1-4
Square Footage: 40000
Type of Packaging: Food Service, Private Label, Bulk
Other Locations:
RIBUS
Sabetha KS
Brands:
Nu-RICE
Nu-MAG
Nu-FLOW
Nu-FLAC
Nu-BAKE
Nu-BIND

10704 **Rice Company**
11140 Fair Oaks Blvd
Suite 101
Fair Oaks, CA 95628
916-784-7745
Fax: 916-784-7681 jobs@riceco.com
www.riceco.com
Rice, popcorn, rice flour, sugar, beans, peas, lentils and ginger
Owner: Duane Kistner
President: J Kapila
Operations Manager: Vicki Manzoli
Estimated Sales: $4500000
Number Employees: 50-99
Type of Packaging: Consumer, Food Service, Private Label, Bulk

10705 **Rice Foods**
826 Harrington St.
Mount Vernon, IL 62864-3923
618-242-0026
Fax: 618-242-3109
Rice
CEO: Lynn Withworth

10706 **Rice Fruit Co**
2760 Carlisle Rd
Gardners, PA 17324-9684
717-677-9842
Fax: 717-677-9842 800-627-3359
info@ricefruit.com www.ricefruit.com
Apples, peaches and pears.
President: David Rice
david.rice@ricefruitcompany.com
Sales: John Rice
Number Employees: 50-99
Type of Packaging: Consumer, Food Service, Bulk

10707 **Rice Hull Specialty Products**
1304 Highway
Spur 146
Stuttgart, AR 72160
870-673-8507
Fax: 870-673-2116 www.ricehull.com
Parboiled rice hulls
President: John Moore
Sales Manager: Greg Crawford
Estimated Sales: $1600000
Number Employees: 10-19

10708 **Rice Innovations**
13112 Santa Ana Ave
Unit A2-A3
Fontana, CA 92337
Canada
909-823-8230
Fax: 909-823-2708
Rice, potato pastas, beverages
General Manager: Raj Sukul
R&D: Ly Hung
Customer Service: Sally Chee
Estimated Sales: $100,000
Number Employees: 1-4
Type of Packaging: Private Label
Brands:
Body Fuel
Cafe Bonjour
Celifibr
Herb Science
Macariz
Medicea
Pastariso
Pastato
Rice Reality
Ying Yang

10709 **RiceBran Technologies**
6720 N Scottsdale Road
Suite 390
Scottsdale, AZ 85253
602-522-3000
Fax: 602-522-3001 info@ricebrantech.com
www.ricebrantech.com
Rice bran and rice bran oil
CEO: W. John Short
CFO: J. Dale Belt
Sales & Marketing: Mark McKnight
Contact: Robert Smith
rsmith@ricebrantech.com
Manufacturing & Supply Chain: Robert DePaul
Estimated Sales: $40 Million
Number Employees: 278
Other Locations:
Arbuckle CA
Dillon MT
Irving TX
Mermentau LA
Corporate Headquarters
Phoenix AZ
West Sacramento CA
Pelotas, Brazil
Brands:
Proryza P-35
Proryza Platinum
Proryza PF-20/50
RiBran

10710 **Riceland Foods Inc.**
PO Box 927
Stuttgart, AR 72160
870-673-5500
855-742-3929
riceland@riceland.com www.riceland.com
Rice and rice bran oils.
CEO: Danny Kennedy
Estimated Sales: $1.3 Billion
Number Employees: 1,500
Type of Packaging: Consumer, Food Service, Private Label, Bulk
Other Locations:
Newport AR
Weiner AR
Knobel AR
Holly Grove AR
Tuckerman AR
Corning AR
Stuttgart AR
Des Arc AR
Hazen AR
Wheatley AR
Dumas AR
Griffithville AR
Brands:
Riceland

10711 **Rices Potato Chips**
9407 Boyette Rd
Biloxi, MS 39532-8143
228-396-5775
Fax: 228-396-5775
Potato chips
President: Martha Vergunst
Estimated Sales: Less than $250,000
Number Employees: 2
Type of Packaging: Private Label

10712 **Ricetec**
1925 Fm 2917 Rd
PO Box 1305
Alvin, TX 77512
281-756-3300
Fax: 281-393-3532 800-580-7423
CustomerService@ricetec.com www.ricetec.com
Rice: Indian-style, basmati and American jasmine; rice mixes
President: John Nelson
jnelson@ricetec.com
CEO: Mike Gumina
EVP Business Development: Ken Fearday
VP Research & Development: Jose Re
Director Quality: Tim Williamson
Director Sales & Technical Services: Van McNeely
Estimated Sales: $33.4 Million
Number Employees: 50-99
Type of Packaging: Consumer, Food Service, Private Label, Bulk
Brands:
Chefs Originals
Jasmati
Kasmati
Texmati

10713 **Ricex Company**
1241 Hawks Flight Court
El Dorado Hills, CA 95762-9648
916-933-3000
Fax: 916-933-3232
Rice bran and rice bran fiber
President: Terrence Barber
CEO: Bradley Edson
CFO: Todd Crow
Contact: Terry Leclair
terry@inquira.com
Estimated Sales: $3511295
Number Employees: 12
Square Footage: 80000
Type of Packaging: Bulk
Brands:
Ricex

10714 **(HQ)Rich Products Corp**
1 Robert Rich Way
Buffalo, NY 14213-1701
716-878-8000
Fax: 716-878-8266 800-828-2021
www.richs.com
Baked goods, dough, nondairy creamers, whipped toppings and Italian foods
President & CEO: Bill Gisel
Chief Financial Officer: Jim Deuschle
jdeuschle@rich.com
Chief Operating Officer: Richard Ferranti
Estimated Sales: Over $1 Billion
Number Employees: 5000-9999
Parent Co: Rich Products Corporation
Type of Packaging: Consumer, Food Service, Private Label, Bulk
Brands:
Allen
Avoset
Bahama Blast(tm)
Byron's Barbecue
Casa Dibertacchi
Coffee Rich

Farm Rich
Gold Label Plus Dairy
Jon Donaire
Mother's Kitchen
Presto
Rich's Eclairs
Seapak
Tres Riches

10715 **Rich Products Corp**
1910 Gallagher Dr
Vineland, NJ 08360-1545
856-696-5600
Fax: 856-696-3341 800-818-9261
info@richs.com www.richs.com
Italian meat balls, pasta and sausage
Estimated Sales: $20-50 Million
Number Employees: 100-249
Square Footage: 100000
Parent Co: Rich Products Corporation
Type of Packaging: Consumer, Food Service

10716 **Rich's Ice Cream Co Inc**
2915 S Dixie Hwy
West Palm Beach, FL 33405-1585
561-833-7585
Fax: 561-655-1952 www.richicecream.com
Ice cream, cream puffs, chocolate eclairs and cakes
CEO: Jhon Rich
Controller: Bob Thomas
Marketing Director: Randy Rich
randyice@bellsouth.net
Number Employees: 100-249
Type of Packaging: Consumer, Food Service
Brands:
Rich Ice Creams

10717 **Richard Bagdasarian Inc**
65500 Lincoln St
Mecca, CA 92254-6500
760-396-2168
Fax: 760-396-2801 CBriones@mrgrape.com
www.mrgrape.com
Table grapes, citrus and vegetables
Owner: Mike Bozick
mbozick@mrgrape.com
VP/Manager: Nick Bozick
VP/Manager: Franz DeKlotz
VP/Manager: Bill Spidell
Number Employees: 10-19
Type of Packaging: Food Service

10718 **Richard E. Colgin Company**
2230 Valdina St
Dallas, TX 75207-6106
214-951-8687
Fax: 214-951-8668 888-226-5446
sales@colgin.com www.colgin.com
Liquid smoke flavorings
CEO: Kerry Thornhill
President: Elizabeth Thornhill
CFO: Sarah Johnson
Contact: Elizabeth Gardner
elizabeth@colgin.com
Estimated Sales: $2 Million
Number Employees: 20
Type of Packaging: Private Label
Brands:
Chigarid
Colgin

10719 **Richard Green Company**
1827 South Meridian St.
Indianapolis, IN 46225
317-972-0941
Fax: 317-972-1201 www.thepeanutking.com
Popcorn and nuts
President: Richard Green
Contact: Richard Byrd
rick@thepeanutking.com
Estimated Sales: $500,000-$1 Million
Number Employees: 5-9
Square Footage: 96000
Type of Packaging: Consumer, Private Label

10720 **Richard L. Graeser Winery**
255 Petrified Forest Rd
Calistoga, CA 94515
707-942-4437
Fax: 707-942-4437 www.graeserwinery.com
Wines
Owner: Richard Graeser
Estimated Sales: $500,000-$1 Million
Number Employees: 5-9
Type of Packaging: Private Label
Brands:
Graeser

10721 **Richard's Gourmet Coffee**
124 Turnpike St
Suite 10
West Bridgewater, MA 02379
508-587-0800
Fax: 508-587-8139 800-370-2633
sales@richardsgourmet.com
www.richardsgourmet.com
Coffees and teas, lemonade, cappuccino, cocoa and spiced cider
President: Richard Salzman
sales@richardsgourmet.com
Estimated Sales: Below $5 Million
Number Employees: 10-19
Type of Packaging: Private Label
Brands:
Richard's Gourmet

10722 **Richards Maple Products**
545 Water St
Chardon, OH 44024-1142
440-286-4160
Fax: 440-286-7203 800-352-4052
sales@richardsmapleproducts.com
www.richardsmapleproducts.com
Maple candy and syrup
Marketing Director: Debbie Richards
CFO: Annette Polson
Estimated Sales: Under $1 Million
Number Employees: 5-9
Square Footage: 16640
Type of Packaging: Consumer, Private Label, Bulk
Brands:
Richards' Maple Candy
Richards' Maple Syrup

10723 **Richards Natural Foods**
15213 S Hinman Road
Eagle, MI 48822-9703
517-627-7965
Natural and organic foods
President: Richard Osterbeck
EVP: Janet Splicer
Sales/Marketing: George Waite
Estimated Sales: Under $500,000
Number Employees: 1-4

10724 **Richardson Brands Co**
101 Erie Blvd
Canajoharie, NY 13317-1148
518-673-3553
Fax: 518-673-2451 www.richardsonbrands.com
Confectionery
Owner: Richard P Anderson
Supply Chain Manager: Rebecca Woodruff
Sr Traffic Controller: Marion Darrach
Senior VP Sales & Marketing: Michael Smith
Estimated Sales: $20 Million
Number Employees: 100-249
Type of Packaging: Consumer, Food Service, Private Label, Bulk
Brands:
Dryden & Palmer
Bogdon's
Gravy Master
Beechies

10725 **Richardson International**
2800 One Lombard Pl.
Winnipeg, MB R3B 0X8
Canada
204-934-5961
866-217-6211
communications@richardson.ca
www.richardson.ca
Grains and oilseed.
President/CEO: Curt Vossen
Year Founded: 1857
Estimated Sales: $28.6 Billion
Number Employees: 2,500
Type of Packaging: Consumer, Food Service, Private Label, Bulk

10726 **Richardson Vineyards**
2711 Knob Hill Road
Sonoma, CA 95476-9560
707-938-2610
Wines
President/CEO: Dennis Richardson
Estimated Sales: Less than $100,000
Number Employees: 1

10727 **Richardson's Ice Cream**
156 S Main St
Middleton, MA 01949-2452
978-774-5450
Fax: 978-777-6863
info@richardsonsicecream.com
www.richardsonsicecream.com
Ice cream
President: Dave Daniels
Estimated Sales: $5 Million
Number Employees: 10-19
Number of Brands: 1
Number of Products: 1
Type of Packaging: Consumer, Bulk
Brands:
Richardson's Ice Cream

10728 **Richelieu Foods Inc**
222 Forbes Rd
Suite 4400
Braintree, MA 02184
781-786-6800
Fax: 781-843-1784 info@richelieufoods.com
www.richelieufoods.com
Pizzas, salad dressings, marinades, crusts and salsas
President & CEO: Ric Alverez
Chief Growth Officer: Chris Dugan
Year Founded: 1862
Estimated Sales: $100 Million
Number Employees: 500-999
Type of Packaging: Private Label
Brands:
Caterer's Collection
Chef Antonio
Grocer's Garden
Willow Farms

10729 **Richland Beverage Association**
2415 Midway Rd
Suite 115
Carrollton, TX 75006-2500
214-357-0248
Fax: 214-357-9581 sales@texasselectna.com
Nonalcoholic malt beverages and beer
President: Martha Zelzer
sales@hphardware.com
Sales: John Rule
Sales: Dana Verrill
Estimated Sales: Less than $500,000
Number Employees: 1-4
Square Footage: 22800
Parent Co: Richland Corporation
Type of Packaging: Consumer, Food Service, Private Label
Brands:
Texas Select

10730 **(HQ)Richmond Baking Co**
520 N 6th St
P.O. Box 698
Richmond, IN 47375
765-962-8535
Fax: 765-962-2253 www.richmondbaking.com
Cracker and cookie crumbs, cracker meal and cookies.
President: Bill Quigg
billq@richmondbaking.com
Treasurer: Rob Quigg
Vice President, Sales: Don Lindeman
Year Founded: 1855
Estimated Sales: $20.2 Million
Number Employees: 100-249
Type of Packaging: Consumer, Food Service, Private Label, Bulk
Other Locations:
McMinnville OR
Brands:
Butternut
Butternut Baked Goods

10731 **Richmond Baking Co**
135 Industrial Dr
P.O. Box 744
Alma, GA 31510
912-632-7213
Fax: 912-632-7215 www.richmondbaking.com
Cracker and cookie crumbs, cracker meal and cookies.
Square Footage: 340000
Type of Packaging: Consumer, Food Service, Private Label, Bulk

10732 Rick's Chips
524 San Anselmo Avenue
Suite 210
San Anselmo, CA 94960
415-420-8151
Fax: 415-532-1526 rick@rickschips.com
Chips
Owner: Rick Hirsch
Estimated Sales: $500,000-1,000,000
Number Employees: 1-4
Brands:
Rick's Chips

10733 Rick's Picks
117 Grattan Street
Suite 319
Brooklyn, NY 11237
212-358-0428
Fax: 212-358-0231 www.rickspicks.com
Pickles
Owner: Richard Field
info@rickspicksnyc.com
Marketing: Jin Kim
Estimated Sales: Less Than $500,000
Number Employees: 1-4

10734 Rico Foods Inc
578 E 19th St
Paterson, NJ 07514-2711
973-278-0589
Fax: 973-278-0378 info@expreco.com
www.ricofood.com
Hispanic foods
President: Emilio Hernandes
emilio@ricofood.com
Vice President: Madeline Fernandez
Production Manager: Christine Hernandez
Estimated Sales: Below $5 Million
Number Employees: 20-49
Square Footage: 40
Type of Packaging: Private Label
Brands:
Delicia
Rico

10735 Ricos Candy Snack & Bakery
740 W 28th St
Hialeah, FL 33010-1220
305-885-7392
Fax: 305-885-7376
Candy, pork rinds and fried dough
President: Albertina Padron
VP: Steven Laderman
Estimated Sales: Less Than $500,000
Number Employees: 1-4
Type of Packaging: Consumer

10736 Riddles' Sweet Impressions
6311 Wagner Road NW
Edmonton, AB T6E 4N4
Canada
780-465-8085
Fax: 780-468-5929 riddles@telusplanet.net
Candy
President: Bill Agnew
VP Sales: Dave Read
Production Manager: Wendy Agnew
Number Employees: 30-50
Square Footage: 48000
Type of Packaging: Consumer, Food Service, Private Label, Bulk
Brands:
Riddle's

10737 Ridge Vineyards Inc
17100 Montebello Rd
Cupertino, CA 95014-5435
408-867-3233
Fax: 408-868-1350 www.ridgewine.com
Wines
Chairman: Paul Draper
CEO: Mark Vernon
mvernon@ridgewine.com
Chief Operating Officer: Eric Baugher
Estimated Sales: $10-24.9 Million
Number Employees: 20-49
Number of Brands: 1
Parent Co: Otsuka America, Inc.
Type of Packaging: Private Label
Brands:
Ridge Vineyards

10738 Riega
3517 Enterprise Dr
Suite C
Kansas City, MO 64129
816-744-8260
Fax: 816-533-7099 riegafoods.com
Sauce, dip and seasoning mixes, and organic flatbreads
President/Owner: Brad Gampper
Brands:
Le Pain des Fleurs

10739 Rier Smoked Salmon
224 County Rd
Lubec, ME 04652-3611
207-733-8912
Fax: 207-733-8986 888-733-0807
Salmon, salmon pate and lox; chicken
Owner: Vinny Gartmayer
Sales/Marketing: Frank Rier
Estimated Sales: $450,000
Number Employees: 5-9
Square Footage: 14000

10740 Riffel's Coffee Company
10821 E 26th St N
Wichita, KS 67226-4524
316-269-4222
Fax: 316-269-1361 888-399-4567
Arabica beans, Italian syrup, coffee jellies
Administrator: Linda Price
General Manager: Paul Hawley
Plant Manager: Lewis Lusk
Purchasing Manager: Chuck Anderson
Estimated Sales: Below $5 Million
Number Employees: 10-19
Number of Products: 700
Square Footage: 20000
Type of Packaging: Consumer, Food Service, Private Label, Bulk
Brands:
Riffels Gourmet Coffees

10741 Righetti Specialties Inc
7476 Graciosa Rd
Santa Maria, CA 93455-6110
805-937-2402
Fax: 805-937-7243 800-268-1041
susieq@susieqbrand.com www.susieqbrand.com
Beans, seasonings, pie mix, sauces & salsas, beef jerky, grilling wood.
Founder: Susan Righetti
susan@susieqbrand.com
VP: Renee Fowler
Estimated Sales: Below $5 Million
Number Employees: 5-9
Brands:
Righetti Specialty

10742 Rigoni Di Asiago
3449 NE 1st Avenue
Suite L-32
Miami, FL 33137
305-470-7583
Fax: 800-887-9023 info@rigonidiasiago-usa.com
rigonidiasiago-usa.com
Chocolate, honey, jams and preserves.
Marketing: Alberto Carli
Contact: Giacomo Cera
giacomo.cera@rigonidiasiago.com

10743 Rill Specialty Foods
11442 N Thorp Hwy
Thorp, WA 98946-9505
509-964-2520
Fax: 509-964-2075 www.rillsonline.com
Soup mixes, corn bread, muffins
Owner: Ninon Wheatley

10744 Rinehart Meat Processing
133 Bell Road
Branson, MO 65616-9169
417-869-2041
Fax: 417-334-2059
Lean ground beef, bacon and ham, sausage and beef jerky
President: Jack Harris
Plant Manager: Tim Stewart
Estimated Sales: $10-20 Million
Number Employees: 20-49

10745 Rio Grande Valley SugarGrowers
P.O. Boz 459
Santa Rosa, TX 78593
956-636-1411
Fax: 956-636-1449 www.rgvsugar.com
Sugar cane, raw sugar and molasses.
President & CEO: Randy Rolando
AG Manager: Jerry Lara
Year Founded: 1913
Estimated Sales: $12 Million
Number Employees: 190
Type of Packaging: Bulk

10746 Rio Naturals
5050 Robert J. Mathews Pkwy
Suite 200
El Dorado Hills, CA 95762
916-719-4514
Fax: 916-941-3690
Sweeteners
President: Jack Mortelli
Brands:
Riosweet

10747 Rio Syrup Co
2311 Chestnut St
St Louis, MO 63103-2298
314-436-7700
Fax: 314-436-7707 800-325-7666
flavors@riosyrup.com www.riosyrup.com
Syrups, extracts and concentrates, slush flavors and bases, fountain syrups and liquid food colors
President: Phillip Tomber
phil@riosyrup.com
Estimated Sales: $500,000-$1 Million
Number Employees: 5-9
Number of Products: 1200
Square Footage: 92000
Type of Packaging: Consumer, Food Service, Bulk
Brands:
Rio

10748 Rio Trading Company
4924 Campbell Blvd
Suite 120
Baltimore, MD 21236-5909
443-384-2500
Fax: 443-384-2525
Owner: Michael Sruanis
Estimated Sales: $500,000-$1 Million
Number Employees: 1-4
Brands:
Rio Trading

10749 Rio Valley Canning Co
225 S 13th St
Donna, TX 78537-3304
956-464-7843
Fax: 956-464-2538
Canned beans, peas, tomatoes, peppers and picante sauce
President: Robert Ault
Estimated Sales: $5-10 Million
Number Employees: 50-99
Type of Packaging: Consumer, Food Service, Private Label
Brands:
Rio Valley

10750 Rip Van
Brooklyn, NY
415-529-5403
www.ripvan.com
Wafel cookies
Co-CEO: Rip Pruisken
Co-CEO: Marco De Leon

10751 Ripensa A/S
5781 Lee Boulevard
Unit 208
Lehigh Acres, FL 33971-6339
941-561-5882
Fax: 941-561-5885
Baked goods, cookies, biscuits, tray packs, containers and acrylic jars
President: Steen Thy Jensen
CEO: Richard Recchia
Estimated Sales: Less than $500,000
Number Employees: 1-4
Type of Packaging: Private Label
Brands:
Ripensa

10752 **Ripon Pickle Co Inc**
1039 Beier Rd
Ripon, WI 54971-9063
920-748-7110
Fax: 920-748-8092 rpi@riponpickle.com
www.riponpickle.com
Celery, chili peppers, egg plant, onions, sauerkraut, green and red peppers
President: Darwin Wiese
Site Manager: Troy Gustke
tgusky@riponpickleco.com
Estimated Sales: $6.6 Million
Number Employees: 50-99
Square Footage: 280000
Type of Packaging: Consumer, Food Service, Private Label, Bulk
Brands:
Pickle O'Pete
Wisconsin Pride

10753 **Ripple**
Berkeley, CA
info@ripplefoods.com
www.ripplefoods.com
Plant-based milk alternative
Founder: Neil Renninger
Founder: Adam Lowry

10754 **Ripple Brand Collective**
225 North Route 303
Suite 101
Congers, NY 10920
845-353-1251
Fax: 845-353-5276 hello@barkthins.com
www.barkthins.com
Dark chocolate covered snacks
Founder and CEO: Scott Semel
Brands:
barkTHINS

10755 **Rippons Seafood**
11911 Coastal Hwy
Suite 120
Ocean City, MD 21842-2621
410-723-0056
www.ripponsseafood.com
Oysters, crab and shrimp.
Owner: Chan Rippons
Estimated Sales: $21 Million
Number Employees: 5-9
Type of Packaging: Consumer, Food Service, Private Label

10756 **Rise Bar**
16752 Millikan Ave
Irvine, CA 92606
800-440-6476
cs2@risebar.com www.risebar.com
Protein bars
Founder & CEO: Peter Spenuzza
Year Founded: 2011
Number Employees: 20-49

10757 **Rishi Tea**
427 E Stewart St
Stop 5
Milwaukee, WI 53207-1200
414-747-4001
Fax: 414-747-4008 866-747-4483
inquiries@rishi-tea.com www.rishi-tea.com
Tea
Owner: Joshua Kaiser
joshua@rishi-tea.com
Estimated Sales: $1.3 Million
Number Employees: 20-49
Square Footage: 64000
Type of Packaging: Consumer, Food Service, Private Label, Bulk

10758 **Rising Dough Bakery**
8135 Elder Creek Rd
Sacramento, CA 95824
916-387-9700
Fax: 877-349-8900
Cakes, pies, muffins, croissants and strudels
Owner: Colette Jamet
cs@risingdough.com
Estimated Sales: Below $5 Million
Number Employees: 20-49
Brands:
Rising Dough

10759 **Rising Sun Farms**
5126 S Pacific Hwy
Phoenix, OR 97535-6606
541-535-8331
Fax: 541-535-8350 800-888-0795
elizabeth@risingsunfarms.com
www.risingsunfarms.com
Oils, mustard, pesto sauces, dried tomatoes, vinegars, salad vinaigrettes, cheese tortas and marinades
Owner: Kim Allen
Coo: Jeff Williams
VP: Richard Fujas
Sales: Jenn Woodward
kim@risingsunfarms.com
Public Relations: Jim Woodward
Operations: Chris Hanry
Plant Manager: Richard Fujas
Purchasing Director: Lynn Perkins
Estimated Sales: $3.2 Million
Number Employees: 20-49
Type of Packaging: Consumer, Food Service, Private Label, Bulk
Brands:
Rising Sun

10760 **Risvold's Inc.**
1234 W. El Segundo Blvd.
Gardena, CA 90247
323-770-2674
Fax: 323-770-0800 tbrandon@risvolds.com
risvolds.com
Prepared salads, pasta salads, desserts, speads and dips
President/Sales: Kristie Brandon-Brown
CEO: Tim Brandon
Quality Control/Research And Development: Wendy O'Neill
Sales/Customer Service: Mary DeNava
Production Manager: Brock O'Neill
VP, General Manager And Purchasing: Jon Lew
Year Founded: 1937
Type of Packaging: Consumer, Food Service, Bulk
Brands:
LA COCINA MEXICANA
FUN-N-SUN
SEDONA BAKING COMPANY

10761 **Rita's Italian Ice**
2929 N. Rock Road
Wichita, KS 67226
316-440-4896
www.ritasice.com
Ice snacks and frozen custards
Senior Director, Franchise Sales: Gina Moughty

10762 **Ritchey's Dairy**
2130 Cross Cove Rd
Martinsburg, PA 16662-7619
814-793-2157
Fax: 814-793-0099 800-296-2157
ritcheysdairy@hotmail.com
www.ritcheysdairy.com
Milk, fruit drinks and ice tea
President: Ray Ritchey
rayr@ritcheysdairy.com
Estimated Sales: Below $5 Million
Number Employees: 50-99
Type of Packaging: Private Label
Brands:
Ritchey

10763 **Ritchie Creek Vineyard**
4024 Spring Mountain Rd
St Helena, CA 94574-9773
707-963-4661
Fax: 707-963-4936 www.ritchiecreek.com
Wines
President: R Minor
Co-Owner: Peter Minor
Estimated Sales: Below $5 Million
Number Employees: 5-9

10764 **Rito Mints**
1055, rue Laverendrye
PO Box 312
Trois Rivieres, QC G9A 5GA
Canada
819-379-1449
Fax: 819-379-0344 info@ritomints.com
www.ritomints.com
Candy: mints, hearts and lozenges
President: Morris Masif
General Manager: Peter Nassif
Number Employees: 15
Square Footage: 64000
Type of Packaging: Consumer, Food Service, Private Label, Bulk
Brands:
Rito
Sweet Notes
Ghost Talk

10765 **Ritual Coffee Roasters**
1026 Valencia St
San Francisco, CA 94110-2406
415-641-1011
info@ritualroasters.com
www.ritualroasters.com
Coffee
Manager: Briana Rognlin
briana@ritualroasters.com
Estimated Sales: Less Than $500,000
Number Employees: 5-9

10766 **Rivard Popcorn Products**
2870 Yellow Goos Road
Lancaster, PA 17601-6705
717-898-7131
Fax: 171-898-7265
Flavored popcorn, extruded corn, rice curls and puffs
President: Robert Rivard
National Sales Manager: Joe Guasco
Number Employees: 50-99
Type of Packaging: Consumer

10767 **Rivella USA**
3100 NW Boca Raton Boulevard
Suite 410
Boca Raton, FL 33431
561-417-5810
Fax: 561-417-5811
Soft drink
President: Franz Rieder
Vice President: Christian Mom
Estimated Sales: $1.1 Million
Number Employees: 8
Type of Packaging: Food Service, Bulk

10768 **River Hills Harvest**
3520 E 33Rd St
Minneapolis, MN 55406-2160
573-326-9454
855-662-3779
info@riverhillsharvest.com riverhillsharvest.com
Elderberry juice
President & CEO: Christopher Patton
Brands:
River Hills

10769 **River Market Brewing Company**
P.O.Box 901898
Kansas City, MO 64190-1898
816-471-6300
Fax: 816-471-5562 www.rivermarketbrews.com
Beer, ale, lager, stout and seasonal
President: David Pecha
Estimated Sales: $1-2.5 Million
Number Employees: 20-49
Type of Packaging: Consumer, Food Service

10770 **River Road Coffee**
PO Box 252
Lake Clear, NY 12945-0252
315-769-9941
Fax: 315-769-7130
Coffee
President: David Copeland
General Manager: Michelle Yadon
Estimated Sales: $2.5-5 000,000
Number Employees: 20

10771 **River Run Vintners**
65 Rogge Ln
Watsonville, CA 95076-9418
831-726-3112
Fax: 831-726-3112 riverrun@cruzio.com
www.riverrunwine.com
Wines
Manager: J P Pawloski
Estimated Sales: Less Than $500,000
Number Employees: 1-4
Brands:
River Run

10772 River Town Foods Corp
4601 Mcree Ave
St Louis, MO 63110-2239
314-776-5646
Fax: 314-776-6468 800-844-3210
mona@rivertownfoods.com
www.rivertownfoods.com
Salsas & Mexican sauces, marinades, dressings and spice blends.
President: Jeff Endraske
jeff@rivertownfoods.com
CEO: John Schnoebelen
General Manager: Monica Holtgreven
Estimated Sales: $500,000-$1 Million
Number Employees: 5-9
Number of Products: 153
Type of Packaging: Consumer, Food Service, Private Label, Bulk
Brands:
River Town Foods Rib Rub
Super Smokers Barbecue Sauces
Taste of The Hill

10773 Riverdale Fine Foods
919 N Main St
Dayton, OH 45405-4694
937-743-4377
Fax: 937-223-9456 800-548-1304
info@daytonnut.com www.riverdalefinefoods.com
Chocolates, nuts, snack mixes, cookie mixes and candy
President: Stanley Maschino
Estimated Sales: $3-5 Million
Number Employees: 10-19
Number of Brands: 5
Brands:
Candy Farm
Dayton's
Friesinger's
Minute Fudge
Yuletide

10774 Riverside Natural Foods
2720 Steeles Ave West
Bldg 4
Vaughan, ON L4K 4N5
Canada
416-360-8200
info@riversidenaturals.com
riversidenaturalfoods.com
Granola snackers
President/Owner: Nima Fotovat
Marketing: Janice Harada
Operations: Sahba Fotovat
Brands:
MadeGood

10775 Riverton Packing
2515 E Monroe Ave
Riverton, WY 82501-6104
307-856-3838
Meat
Owner: Rod Baltes
Estimated Sales: Less than $500,000
Number Employees: 1-4
Type of Packaging: Consumer, Food Service

10776 Riverview Foods
1360 Bethleham Road
PO Box 765
Warsaw, KY 41095
859-567-5211
Fax: 859-567-5213
Smoked meats, barbecue and tomato sauces; research and development services
President: Bob Weldon
VP Sales/Marketing: Robert Schroeder
General Manager: Mike Benton
Number Employees: 50-99
Square Footage: 100000
Type of Packaging: Consumer, Food Service, Private Label, Bulk
Brands:
Riverview Foods Authentic

10777 Riviana Foods Inc.
PO Box 2636
Houston, TX 77252
713-529-3251
sales@riviana.com
www.riviana.com
Rice and pasta.
President/CEO: Bastiaan de Zeeuw
bdezeeuw@riviana.com
Senior VP/CFO: Michael Slavin
Senior VP, Operations: Brett Beckfield
Senior VP, Marketing: Sandra Kim
Senior VP, Human Resources: Gerard Ferguson
Year Founded: 1965
Estimated Sales: $500 Million
Number Employees: 1,000-4,999
Number of Brands: 28
Parent Co: Ebro Foods, S.A.
Type of Packaging: Consumer, Food Service, Private Label, Bulk
Other Locations:
Corporate Office
Houston TX
Plant
Brinkley AR
Plant
Carlisle AR
Plant
Clearbrook MN
Plant
Hazen AR
Plant
Memphis TN
Brands:
Mahatma
Carolina
Minute
Success
AA Brand
Adolphus
Blue Ribbon Rice
Colusa Rose
Comet Rice
Gourmet House
Pear Blossom
Rice Select
River Rice
Sello Rojo
Water Maid
Wonder
Ronzoni
American Beauty
No Yolks
Skinner
Creamette
Light 'n Fluffy
Mrs. Weiss'
New Mill
Prince
San Giorgio
Wacky Mac

10778 Riviera Ravioli Company
643 Morris Park Ave
Bronx, NY 10460
718-823-0260
Fax: 718-823-0344 rivrav@verizon.net
Macaroni and pasta
President: Joseph Giordano
Plant Manager: Michael Somereve
Estimated Sales: $10-20 Million
Number Employees: 10-19
Brands:
Riviera

10779 RoRo's Baking Company
2201 Tucker St.
Suite 107
Dallas, TX 75214
972-897-2315
www.rorosbakingcompany.com
Baked goods
Co-Owner: Amy Collins
Co-Owner: Lauren Collins

10780 Road's End Organics
2160 Mountain Road
Suite 5
Carpinteria, CA 93014
805-684-8500
Fax: 805-684-8220 877-247-3373
http://www.roadsendorganics.com
Dairy free pasta and dip
President: Matthew Koch
Estimated Sales: $3-5 Million
Number Employees: 1-4
Parent Co: Edward & Sons Trading Company, Inc.

10781 Roadrunner Seafood Inc
548 E Crawford St
Colquitt, GA 39837-5200
229-758-6098
Fax: 229-758-3991 rrsfd@surfsouth.com
Seafood: catfish, conch, croaker, flounder, mullet, oysters and shrimp
President: James Stovall
Finance Executive: Amy Stovall
Number Employees: 20-49

10782 Roanoke Apple Products
844 Union St
Salem, VA 24153-5121
540-375-3782
Fax: 540-375-3782
Vinegar, apple cider, white and red wine
President: Glenn Dunville
Marketing Director: Deborah Dunville
Plant Manager: Randy Kesler
Estimated Sales: $1,100,000
Number Employees: 11
Square Footage: 66000
Type of Packaging: Food Service, Private Label, Bulk
Brands:
Bandana
Heidecker
Old Kettle

10783 Roasterie Inc
1204 W 27th St
Kansas City, MO 64108-3555
816-931-4000
Fax: 816-931-4040 800-376-0245
info@theroasterie.com www.theroasterie.com
Coffee
Owner: Gwyneth Bowen
gwynethmaree@gmail.com
Customer Service Manager: Stacy Barter
Quality Control: Norm Killnorm
CFO: Bill Molini
CFO: Carla O'Neill
CFO: Chris Mikuls
Estimated Sales: $1-2.5 Million
Number Employees: 20-49
Brands:
Roasterie

10784 Rob Salamida Co Inc
71 Pratt Ave
Suite 1
Johnson City, NY 13790-2255
607-729-4868
Fax: 607-797-4721 800-545-5072
info@spiedie.com www.huntersprideusa.com
Marinades, barbecue sauces and spice blends.
President: Robert Alan Salamida
sweethavens@msn.com
Estimated Sales: $4.2 Million
Number Employees: 1-4
Type of Packaging: Consumer, Food Service, Private Label
Brands:
Pinch
Spiedie Sauce
State Fair

10785 Robbie's Natural Products
8002 NE Hwy 99
Suite 78
Vancouver, WA 98665
360-433-2325
Fax: 626-457-8705
Ketchup, salsa, fruit syrup and sauces
President: Robbie Roberts
Sales Manager: Roberta Fleischer
Estimated Sales: $3-5 Million
Number Employees: 1-4
Type of Packaging: Consumer, Food Service

10786 Robbins Packing Company
229 Stockyard Row
Statesboro, GA 30458-4375
912-764-7503
Fax: 912-489-2823
Pork, beef, sausage and smoked meats
President: Wayne Paulk
President/Managing Partner: Rodney Poole
Sales Executive: Tom Collins
Sales Manager: Glen Brown
Plant Manager: Jack Kasses

Estimated Sales: $1-3 Million
Number Employees: 1-4
Square Footage: 210000
Type of Packaging: Consumer, Food Service, Private Label, Bulk

10787 **Roberian Vineyards**
12614 King Rd
Forestville, NY 14062
716-679-1620
roberian@fairpoint.net
Wines
President: Bob Roach
Wine Maker: Maryann Roach
Estimated Sales: Under $500,000
Number Employees: 1-4

10788 **Robert & James Brands**
950 E Maple Road
Birmingham, MI 48009-6408
248-646-0578
Fax: 248-646-6040
Condiments and relishes
Owner: Robert Arnold
Estimated Sales: $1-2.5 000,000
Number Employees: 5

10789 **Robert F Pliska & Company Winery**
101 Cantwell Court
Purgitsville, WV 26852
304-289-3493
Fax: 304-289-3900 877-747-2737
VineyardHome@frontiernet.net
www.vineyardhome.org
Wines
Owner & Wine Maker: Robert F Pliska
Purchasing Manager: TC McGee
Estimated Sales: $1-3 Million
Number Employees: 1-4
Parent Co: Piterra Farms
Type of Packaging: Consumer
Brands:
101 Piterra Place
Assumption Wines
Mt. Betty
Mt. Mama

10790 **Robert Keenan Winery**
3660 Spring Mountain Rd
St Helena, CA 94574-9677
707-963-9177
Fax: 707-963-8209 rkw@keenanwinery.com
www.keenanwinery.com
Wines
Owner: Michael Keenan
rkw@keenanwinery.com
General Manager: Matt Gardner
Wine Maker: Niles Venge
Estimated Sales: $1-2.5 Million
Number Employees: 5-9
Brands:
Robert Keenan Winery

10791 **Robert Mondavi Winery**
7801 Saint Helena Highway
Oakville, CA 94562
707-226-1395
Fax: 707-251-4110 888-766-6328
www.robertmondaviwinery.com
Wines
CEO: Greg Evans
Winemaker: Genevieve Janssens
genevieve@robertsinskey.com
VP Marketing: Kevin Conner
Vice President, Operations: Karen Egan
Estimated Sales: $42 Million
Number Employees: 600
Number of Brands: 1
Square Footage: 5000
Other Locations:
Woodbridge Winery
Acampo CA
Brands:
Mondavi

10792 **Robert Mueller Cellars**
6301 Starr Rd
Windsor, CA 95492-9653
707-837-7399
Fax: 707-431-8365 www.muellerwine.com
Wines
President: Robert Mueller
CEO: Bruce E Ollodart
Estimated Sales: $1-2.5 Million
Number Employees: 1-4
Brands:
Mueller

10793 **Robert Pecota Winery**
P.O.Box 303
Calistoga, CA 94515
707-479-7770
Fax: 707-942-6671 www.robertpecotawinery.com
Wines
Co-Owner & Partner: Robert Pecota
Co-Owner & Partner: Kara Pecota Dunn
Co-Owner & Partner: Andrea Pecota White
Operations Director/Guest Services: Brenda Wild
Consulting Winemker: Marco DiGiulio
Estimated Sales: $1-2.5 Million
Number Employees: 5-9
Type of Packaging: Private Label
Brands:
Robert Pecota

10794 **Robert Rothschild Farm**
3015 E Kemper Rd
Cincinnati, OH 45241
Fax: 888-907-8090 800-222-9966
info@davidevansfoods.com
www.robertrothschild.com
Sauces, dips, condiments and preserves
Chairman: Robert Rothschild
CEO: Andrew Deister
Chief Financial Officer: Shara Vross
Director of Product Development: Bridget Sherman
Quality Manager: Mercedes Grome
Marketing Director: Ryan Husted
Vice President of Sales: Dan Carley
Director of Specialty Sales: Patti Walters
Vice President of Operations: Mike Maloy
Supply Chain Manager: John Eagle
Estimated Sales: $16.5 Million
Number Employees: 50-99
Number of Brands: 1
Square Footage: 45000
Type of Packaging: Consumer
Brands:
Robert Rothschild

10795 **Robert Sinskey Vineyards Inc**
6320 Silverado Trl
Napa, CA 94558-9747
707-944-9090
Fax: 707-944-9097 800-869-2030
rsv@robertsinskey.com www.robertsinskey.com
Wines
Owner & Founder: Robert Sinskey
Winemaker: Jeff Virnig
Culinary Director: Maria Helm Sinskey
Sales Manager: Meg Bartley
National Wholesale Manager: Eric Sother
Vineyard Manager: Kirk Grace
Sales Manager: Meg Goddess
rsv@robertsinskey.com
Estimated Sales: Below $5 Million
Number Employees: 10-19
Type of Packaging: Private Label
Brands:
Rsv

10796 **Robert's Bakery**
17516 Minnetonka Boulevard
Minnetonka, MN 55345-1000
612-473-9719
Fax: 612-473-1835
Baked goods
President: Robert Larson
Estimated Sales: $5-9.9 000,000
Number Employees: 20

10797 **Robertet Flavors**
10 Colonial Dr.
Piscataway, NJ 08854
732-981-8300
Fax: 732-981-1717
robertetFlavors@robertetUSA.com
www.robertet.com
Flavorings.
Chairman/CEO: Philippe Maubert
Head of the Flavourings Division: Olivier Maubert
CFO: Gilles Audoli
Managing Director, Flavourings Division: Antoine Kastler
Director, Industrial Operations: Herve Bellon
Year Founded: 1850
Estimated Sales: $524.9 Million
Number Employees: 1,800
Number of Brands: 5+
Square Footage: 16805
Parent Co: Robertet SA
Type of Packaging: Food Service
Other Locations:
Robertet Culinary
Schoten, Belgium
Brands:
Citra-Next
Natur-Cell
Flavour Sensations
Smart Flavours
Accord Flavours

10798 **Roberto A Cheese Factory**
7465 Lincoln Street SE
East Canton, OH 44730-9439
330-488-1551
Fax: 330-488-1552
Cheese
President: Angelo Roberto
Co-Owner: Armand Babbo
Estimated Sales: $500,000-$1 000,000
Number Employees: 10-19
Brands:
Roberto Cheese

10799 **Roberts Ferry Nut Co**
20493 Yosemite Blvd
Waterford, CA 95386-9506
209-874-3247
Fax: 209-874-3707
www.robertsferrynutcompany.com
Almonds and popcorn
Owner: Brigitte Hayat
brigitteh@pjcc.org
Partner: Dorothy Mallory
Estimated Sales: $3135592
Number Employees: 20-49
Type of Packaging: Consumer, Bulk
Brands:
Roberts Ferry

10800 **Roberts Seed**
982 22 Rd
Axtell, NE 68924-3618
308-743-2565
Fax: 308-743-2048 robertsseed@gtmc.net
www.robertsseed.com
Grain, soybeans, popcorn kernels, wheat, corn and beans
President: Joe Roberts
robertsseed@gtmc.net
Estimated Sales: $950,000
Number Employees: 1-4
Square Footage: 30000
Type of Packaging: Private Label, Bulk

10801 **Robertson's Country Meat Hams**
P.O.Box 56
Finchville, KY 40022-0056
502-834-7952
Fax: 502-834-7095 800-678-1521
www.finchvillefarms.com
Country ham
President: William Robertson
Chief Financial Officer: Margaret Davis
Marketing Director: Jim Robertson
Estimated Sales: Below $5 Million
Number Employees: 10-19
Type of Packaging: Private Label, Bulk
Brands:
Finchville Farms

10802 **Robin & Cohn Seafood Distributors**
3225 Palmisano Boulevard
Chalmette, LA 70043-3633
504-277-1679
Fax: 504-277-1679
Seafood
President: Fay Cohn

10803 **Robinson Distributing Co**
701 Robinson Rd
London, KY 40741-9018
606-864-2914
Fax: 606-864-3252 800-230-5131
www.robinsonmeats50.com
Meats: hog sausage and deli
President: Jimmy Robinson
robinson@mis.net

Estimated Sales: $5,500,000
Number Employees: 20-49
Square Footage: 40000
Type of Packaging: Private Label

10804 Robinson's No 1 Ribs
940 Madison St
Oak Park, IL 60302-4430
708-383-8452
Fax: 708-383-9486 800-836-6750
charlie@rib1.com www.rib1.com
Barbecue sauces
Owner: Charlie Robinson
sales@rib1.com
Vice President: Helen Robinson
Marketing Director: Cordell Robinson
Operations Manager: Bruce Swerdlow
Estimated Sales: $500,000-$1 Million
Number Employees: 20-49
Square Footage: 40000
Parent Co: Robinson's #1 Ribs Restaurants
Type of Packaging: Consumer, Food Service, Bulk
Brands:
Charlie Robinson's

10805 Robller Vineyard Winery
275 Robller Vineyard Rd
New Haven, MO 63068-2102
573-237-3986
Fax: 573-237-3985
Wine
Owner: Robert Miller
robller@fidnet.com
Owner: Lois Mueller
Estimated Sales: Less than $200,000
Number Employees: 1-4
Brands:
Robller Vineyard and Winery

10806 Rocca's Italian Foods Inc
520 S Mill St
New Castle, PA 16101-4007
724-654-3344
Fax: 724-654-4954 www.roccapasta.com
Pasta
President: Anthony Rocca
roccafoods@aol.com
Estimated Sales: Below $5 000,000
Number Employees: 10-19
Brands:
Roccas

10807 Roche Caneros Estate Winery
122 West Spain Street
Sonoma, CA 95476-9700
707-935-7115
Fax: 707-935-7846 800-825-9475
info@rochewinery.com www.rochewinery.com
Wines
President: Joseph Roche
CFO: Kerstin Kohlstrom
Account Manager: Carrie MacDonough
Contact: Jennifer Brons
brons@rochewinery.com
Estimated Sales: $5-9.9 Million
Number Employees: 10-19
Type of Packaging: Private Label
Brands:
Roche

10808 Roche Fruit LLC
601 N 1st Ave
Yakima, WA 98902-2127
509-248-7200
Fax: 509-453-3835 michaelroche@jewelapple.com
www.rochefruit.com
Apple slices
Owner/Sales Manager: Michael Roche
michaelroche@rochefruit.com
Quality Assurance Manager: Marina Britt
Customer Service: Janet McKay
Operation Manager, Sales: Mike Hanses
Estimated Sales: $19 Million
Number Employees: 250-499
Parent Co: Roche Fruit
Type of Packaging: Private Label

10809 Rochester Cheese
4219 N Frontage Rd.
Rochester, MN 55901-6672
507-288-6678
Fax: 507-288-6175 888-288-6678
tomf@rochestercheese.com
Cheese

Plant Financial & Operational Director: Tom Ferris
Year Founded: 1976
Estimated Sales: $20-50 Million
Number Employees: 10-19
Parent Co: Prairie Farms Dairy
Type of Packaging: Private Label

10810 Rock Bottom Restaurant & Brewery
1001 16th St
Suite 100
Denver, CO 80265-0100
303-534-7616
Fax: 303-534-2129
www.rockbottom.com/denver-downtown
Beer, ale and stout
Manager: Jim Maresca
Managing Partner: Bennett Ponder
Managing Partner: Jessica Buesing
Manager: John Clure
jmcclure@rockbottom.com
Estimated Sales: $10-20 Million
Number Employees: 100-249
Parent Co: CraftWorks Restaurants & Breweries
Type of Packaging: Consumer, Food Service, Bulk
Brands:
Falcon Pale
Red Rock

10811 Rock Point Oyster Company
1733 Dabob Post Office Rd
Quilcene, WA 98376
360-765-3765
Fax: 360-765-3676
Oysters
President: Marshall Hinton
CEO: Dick Steele
Estimated Sales: Less than $500,000
Number Employees: 5

10812 Rock-N-Roll Gourmet
15 Outrigger St
Apt 302
Marina Del Ray, CA 90292
424-228-4901
Fax: 310-751-6397 800-518-3891
Potato chips, cookies and popcorn
President/Owner: Jean Ehrlich
CEO: Dan Ehrlich
CFO: Peter Vermeulen
Number Employees: 10

10813 Rockbridge Vineyard
35 Hillview Ln
Raphine, VA 24472-2403
540-377-6204
Fax: 888-511-9463 rockbridgewines@gmail.com
www.rockbridgevineyard.com
Wines
Onwer: Shepherd Rouse
Estimated Sales: $1-3 Million
Number Employees: 1-4
Type of Packaging: Consumer
Brands:
Dechiel
Rockbridge Vineyard

10814 Rocket Fizz
2619 Ventura Blvd
PO Box 3663
Camarillo, CA 93010-6647
805-987-7632
info@rocketfizz.com
www.rocketfizz.com
Soda and candy
Manager: Angela Morgan
Number Employees: 5-9

10815 Rocket Products Company
PO Box 565
Fenton, MO 63026
636-343-9110
Fax: 636-343-0897 800-325-9567
betty@rocketproducts.com
www.rocketproducts.com
Fruit concentrates
President/Founder/CEO: Charles Lazier, Jr.
General Manager: Michael Martin
Operations Director: Betty Honaker
Purchasing Director: Patty Bunse
Estimated Sales: $5-10 Million
Number Employees: 9
Number of Brands: 3
Number of Products: 11
Square Footage: 15000
Brands:
Dair-E Lite
Apache
Wild Rocket

10816 Rockland Bakery
94 Demarest Mill Rd W
Nanuet, NY 10954-2989
845-623-5800
Fax: 845-623-6921 800-734-4376
contactus@rocklandbakery.com
www.rocklandbakery.com
Bread, rolls, bagels, cakes, pies and challah
President: Sal Battaglai
battaglais@rocklandbakery.com
Director of Sales: Mike Battaglia
COO: Anthony Battaglia
Estimated Sales: $27 Million
Number Employees: 250-499
Type of Packaging: Consumer, Food Service

10817 Rockport Lobster Co
54 Commercial St
Gloucester, MA 01930-5025
978-281-0225
Fax: 978-281-8578
Lobster
Owner: Craig Babinski
Estimated Sales: Less Than $500,000
Number Employees: 1-4

10818 Rockview Farms
7011 Stewart and Gray Rd
Downey, CA 90241
562-927-5511
Fax: 562-928-9765 800-423-2479
www.rockviewfarms.com
Milk, butter, other dairy products and juices
VP, Sales & Marketing: Curt DeGroot
VP, Operations: Joe Lunzer
Estimated Sales: $135 Million
Number Employees: 300
Type of Packaging: Bulk

10819 Rocky Mountain Chocolate Factory
Durango, CO
888-525-2462
www.rmcf.com
Chocolate
Square Footage: 53000

10820 Rocky Mountain Coffee Roasters
P.O. Box 2609
Jasper, Alberta T0E 1E0, AB
Canada
780-852-4280
Fax: 780-852-5910 800-666-3465
www.rockymountainroasters.com
Coffee retail/wholesale/roaster
General Manager of Sales: Les Chorley
CFO: Brad Woods
Vice President: Andy Johnsen
VP Marketing: Andy Johnsen
Operations Manager: Jonathan Kitchensa
Estimated Sales: Under $500,000
Number Employees: 5-9
Brands:
Clipper Foods
Whitney Distributing

10821 Rocky Mountain Honey Company
642 N Pugsley St
Salt Lake City, UT 84103-1329
801-355-2054
Fax: 801-355-2054
Beeswax and honey
President: Floyd Meyer
Partner: Melvin Meyer
Estimated Sales: $1-3 Million
Number Employees: 1-4
Parent Co: Meyer Honey Company
Type of Packaging: Consumer, Food Service, Private Label, Bulk

10822 Rocky Mountain Meats
4803 43rd St.
PO Box 459
Rocky Mountain House, AB T4T 1A4
Canada
403-845-3434
Fax: 780-845-7418

Fresh beef, pork and wild game including deer, elk, moose and bear
Owner: Rudi Koller
Co-Owner/Office Admin: Stefanie Koller
Sales & Administrative Manager: Hauke Theirfelder
Estimated Sales: C
Number Employees: 10-19
Type of Packaging: Consumer, Food Service, Private Label, Bulk
Brands:
Rocky Mountain

10823 **Rocky Mountain Natural Meats**
9757 Alton Way
Henderson, CO 80640-8496
303-287-7100
Fax: 303-287-7272 800-327-2706
bison@greatrangebison.com
Meat distributor solely focusing on bison products.
CEO: Bob Dineen
bob@greatrangebison.com
Chief Financial Officer: Sharon Novacek
Safe Quality Food Practitioner: Mattie Hummel
Vice President, Sales & Marketing: Paul Bernardo
Estimated Sales: $20-49 Million
Number Employees: 100-249
Number of Brands: 1
Square Footage: 50000
Type of Packaging: Consumer, Food Service
Brands:
Great Range Brand Bison

10824 **Rocky Mountain Packing Company**
500 1st Street
Havre, MT 59501
406-265-3401
Fax: 406-265-3401
Meat products
Owner/President: David Swallow
Owner/CEO: Linda Swallow
Estimated Sales: $100,000-$120,000
Number Employees: 1-4
Type of Packaging: Consumer

10825 **Rocky Point Shrimp Association**
429 West Madison Street
Phoenix, AZ 85003
602-254-8041
Fax: 602-523-9637
Shrimp
Estimated Sales: $3-5 Million
Number Employees: 5-9

10826 **Rocky Ridge Maple**
1258 Route 249
Middlebury Center, PA 16935
607-742-9566
sales@rockyridgemaple.com
rockyridgemaple.com
Maple syrup
Founder: Joshua C. Bronson
Estimated Sales: Under $500,000
Number Employees: 1-4
Type of Packaging: Private Label, Bulk
Brands:
Rocky Ridge Maple

10827 **Rocky Top Country Store**
4201 Wears Valley Rd
Sevierville, TN 37862-8153
865-428-7311
Fax: 865-428-7524 866-260-0670
Fudge
Owner: Robert Glenn
Manager: Marni Sotomayor
Estimated Sales: $300,000-500,000
Number Employees: 1-4
Type of Packaging: Consumer

10828 **Rocky Top Farms**
11486 Essex Rd
Ellsworth, MI 49729-9650
231-599-2251
Fax: 231-599-2352 800-862-9303
sales@rockytopfarms.com www.rockytopfarm.com
Processor and exporter of preserves including raspberry, cherry, strawberry, blackberry and black raspberry; also, butter toppings
President: Tom Cooper
tomcooper@rockytopfarm.com
Estimated Sales: $3-5 Million
Number Employees: 5-9
Type of Packaging: Consumer, Bulk

10829 **Rod Golden Hatchery Inc**
85 13th St. NE
Cullman, AL 35055
256-734-0941
Broiler, fryer, and roaster chickens.
President: Forrest Ingram
Estimated Sales: $34 Million
Number Employees: 1010
Square Footage: 2000
Parent Co: Ingram Farms
Type of Packaging: Consumer, Food Service, Private Label, Bulk

10830 **Rodda Coffee Company**
PO Box 290
Yachats, OR 97498-0290
541-547-4132
Fax: 888-919-2722
Coffee
President: Tom Rodda
Estimated Sales: Under $500,000
Number Employees: 10-19
Brands:
Rodda Coffee

10831 **Rodelle Inc**
3461 Precision Dr
Fort Collins, CO 80528-4545
970-482-8845
Fax: 970-482-4236 800-898-5457
www.customblendinginc.com
Vanilla, baking essential, herbs and spices
Owner: John Conway
jconway@customblendinginc.com
Number Employees: 20-49

10832 **Rodgers' Puddings**
1410 Poindexter Street
Chesapeake, VA 23324
757-543-9290
reggie@rodgerspuddings.com
www.rodgerspuddings.com
Puddings: banana, coconut, guava and blueberry.
Owner: Reggie Rodgers
Estimated Sales: Under $500,000
Number Employees: 1-4
Type of Packaging: Food Service
Brands:
Rodgers'

10833 **Rodney Strong Vineyards**
11455 Old Redwood Hwy
Healdsburg, CA 95448-9523
707-431-1533
Fax: 707-433-0939 800-474-9463
info@rodneystrong.com
Wines
Proptietor: Tom Klein
tklein@rodneystrong.com
VP, Director of Winemaking: Rick Sayre
Estimated Sales: $.5-1 million
Number Employees: 100-249
Type of Packaging: Private Label
Brands:
Rodney Strong

10834 **Roelli Cheese Co**
15982 State Road 11
Shullsburg, WI 53586-9748
608-965-3779
Fax: 608-965-4510 800-575-4372
www.roellicheese.com
Cheese
Owner: Paul Roelli
VP: Gary Roelli
Estimated Sales: $1-3 Million
Number Employees: 10-19
Brands:
Balderson
Bingham Hill Cheeses

10835 **Roger Wood Foods Inc**
7 Alfred St
Savannah, GA 31408
912-652-9600
800-849-9272
info@rogerwoodfoods.com
www.rogerwoodfoods.com
Sausage, franks, turkey and pork products.
President: David Solana
dsolana@rogerwoodfoods.com
Vice President: Mark Solana
Plant Manager: Matthew Lumley
Year Founded: 1936
Estimated Sales: $50 Million
Number Employees: 100-249
Square Footage: 100000

10836 **Roger's Recipe**
518 Perron Hl
Glover, VT 05839-9735
802-525-3050
Brittle made with maple syrup
Owner: Michael Rogers
Estimated Sales: $300,000-500,000
Number Employees: 1-4
Type of Packaging: Consumer

10837 **Rogers Sugar Inc.**
4026 Notre-Dame St. East
Montreal, QC H1W 2K3
Canada
514-527-8686
www.lanticrogers.com
Icing sugar, liquid sugar and soft sugar. Molasses is sold as a by-product of the refining operation.
President: John Holliday
Chief Financial Officer/VP/Secretary: Manon Lacroix
Year Founded: 2008
Estimated Sales: $805 Million
Number Employees: 487
Number of Brands: 1
Square Footage: 7050
Type of Packaging: Consumer, Food Service, Bulk
Other Locations:
Rogers Sugar Limited
Alberta, Canada
Brands:
Roger's

10838 **Rogers Sugar Inc.**
123 Rogers St.
Vancouver, BC V6B 3N2
Canada
604-253-1131
www.lanticrogers.com
Granulated sugar of various grist sizes, sugar cubes, icing sugar, liquid sugars, soft sugars.
President/CEO: John Holliday
VP, Finance/CFO: Manon Lacroix
Vice President, Sales/Marketing: Mike Walton
VP, Operations/Supply Chain: Patrick Dionne
Year Founded: 2008
Estimated Sales: $805.2 Million
Number Employees: 700
Type of Packaging: Consumer, Food Service, Bulk
Brands:
Rogers
Lantic

10839 **Rogers Sugar Inc.**
5405 64th St.
Taber, AB T1G 2C4
Canada
403-223-3535
www.lanticrogers.com
Granulated sugar of various grist sizes, icing sugar, and liquid sugar. Beet molasses and beet pulp are produced as by-products.
President/CEO: John Holliday
Estimated Sales: $805 Million
Number Employees: 205-499
Type of Packaging: Consumer, Food Service, Bulk

10840 **Rogers' Chocolates Ltd**
4253 Commerce Circle
Victoria, BC V8Z 4M2
Canada
250-727-6851
Fax: 250-384-5750 800-663-2220
info@rogerschocolates.com
www.rogerschocolates.com
Processor and exporter of confectionery products including boxed cream-filled and dark chocolates, chocolate mint wafers, almond brittles, caramel nutcorn, fudge, etc
President: Steve Parkhill
Estimated Sales: $10 Million
Number Employees: 130
Square Footage: 87000
Type of Packaging: Consumer, Private Label
Brands:
Rogers Imperials
Victoria Creams

10841 **Rogue Ales Brewery**
748 SW Bay Blvd
Newport, OR 97365-4836
541-265-3188
Fax: 541-265-7528 www.rogue.com
Processor and exporter of ale, lager and barley wine
President: Jack Joyce
CEO: Jack Choice
jack@rogue.com
CEO: Jack Choice
Estimated Sales: $5-10 Million
Number Employees: 50-99
Type of Packaging: Consumer, Food Service

10842 **Rogue Creamery**
311 N Front St
Central Point, OR 97502
541-665-1155
Fax: 541-665-1133 866-396-4704
wholesale@roguecreamery.com
www.roguecreamery.com
Handmade cheese
Owner: David Gremmels
david@roguecreamery.com
CEO/Cheesemaker: Cary Bryant
Controller: Tyler Bare
Quality Control: Emily Aldrich
Marketing: Marguerite Merritt
Sales: Chelsea Faris
Production Manager: Brian Moss
Year Founded: 1933
Estimated Sales: $16 Million
Number Employees: 20-49
Type of Packaging: Consumer, Food Service, Private Label, Bulk

10843 **Roha USA LTD**
5015 Manchester Ave
St Louis, MO 63110-2011
314-289-8300
Fax: 314-531-0461 888-533-7642
roha.usa@rohagroup.com www.roha.com
Global manufacturer of color ingredients for food, beverage, pet food, cosmetic and industrial applications.
Estimated Sales: $10-20 Million
Number Employees: 50-99
Parent Co: ROHA Dyechem Pvt. Ltd.

10844 **Rohrbach Brewing Co**
3859 Buffalo Rd
Rochester, NY 14624-1103
585-594-9800
Fax: 585-594-1960 info@rohrbachs.com
Seasonal beer, ale, stout and lager
Owner: John Urlaub
jurlaub@rohrbach.com
CFO: Sam Fletcher
Sales Manager: Larry Schultz
Estimated Sales: $1-2.5 Million
Number Employees: 20-49
Type of Packaging: Consumer, Food Service

10845 **Rokeach Food Corp**
80 Avenue K
Newark, NJ 07105-3803
973-589-1472
Fax: 973-589-5298
Ethnic foods
CEO: Victor Ostreicher
Estimated Sales: Less than $500,000
Number Employees: 10-19
Brands:
Jericho Canyon Red
Rokeach Food

10846 **Roland Machinery**
816 N Dirksen Pkwy
Springfield, IL 62702-6115
217-789-7711
Fax: 217-744-7314 800-325-1183
Breadings, batters, baking powder, fermentation additives, dough conditioners, sausage/meat binders, chocolate milk, baking and cake mixes, etc.; exporter of baking mixes
CEO: Ray Roland
rroland@rolandmachinery.com
COO: Ian MacEwan
Vice President: Terry McGuire
Plant Manager: Keith Gill
Purchasing Manager: Mary Gajewski
Number Employees: 20-49
Square Footage: 280000
Parent Co: Abitec Corporation
Type of Packaging: Private Label, Bulk
Brands:
Best O' the Wheat
Choice Foods
Gold N Good
Golden Meal
Heritage Hearth

10847 **Roland Seafood Co**
1790 Mayport Rd
Atlantic Beach, FL 32233-1931
904-246-9443
Fax: 904-241-0645
Fish and shrimp
President: Brad Roland
Estimated Sales: Less Than $500,000
Number Employees: 1-4
Type of Packaging: Consumer, Food Service, Bulk
Brands:
Roland Star

10848 **Rolet Food Products Company**
70 Scott Ave
Brooklyn, NY 11237
718-497-0476
Fax: 718-497-0137
Producer of meat snacks & potato chips.
President: Mark Turetsky
Executive Vice President: Charles Littman
Contact: Raul Candelaria
raul@rolets.com
Operations Manager: Miles Turetsky
Estimated Sales: $5-10 Million
Number Employees: 50-99
Type of Packaging: Consumer

10849 **Rolling Pin Bakery**
119 5th Avenue W
Bow Island, AB T0K 0G0
Canada
403-545-2434
Fax: 403-545-2167
Bread, doughnuts, cakes and pastries
Partner: John Sytsma
Partner: Ineke Sytsma
Proprietor: Russell Dueck
Estimated Sales: $149,000
Number Employees: 3
Square Footage: 5500
Type of Packaging: Consumer, Food Service

10850 **Rolling Pin Bakery**
2211 Washington Street
Great Bend, KS 67530-2454
620-793-5381
Baked goods
President: Dave Cooley
Estimated Sales: $500,000
Number Employees: 5

10851 **Rollingstone Chevre**
27349 Shelton Rd
Parma, ID 83660-6731
208-722-6460
Fax: 208-722-6460 chevre@mac.com
Goat cheese
Owner: Karen Evans
chevre@mac.com
Owner: Charles Evans
Estimated Sales: Less Than $500,000
Number Employees: 1-4
Type of Packaging: Consumer, Bulk

10852 **Roma & Ray's Italian Bakery**
45 Railroad Ave
Valley Stream, NY 11580-6030
516-825-7610
Fax: 516-887-6866
Italian baked goods
President: Dario DE-Giovanni
robertde-giovanni@crhamilton.com
Estimated Sales: $10-20 000,000
Number Employees: 10-19

10853 **Roma Bakeries**
523 Marchesano Dr
Rockford, IL 61102-3596
815-964-6737
Fax: 815-964-6057
Rolls, bread, danish and pies
President: John Bowler
CFO: Gene Bowler
Vice President: Marilyn Bowler
Estimated Sales: $500,000-$1 Million
Number Employees: 10-19
Type of Packaging: Consumer
Brands:
Roma Bakeries

10854 **Roma Packing Company**
2266 Pawtucket Avenue
East Providence, RI 02914-1710
401-228-7170
Fax: 401-228-7178
Sausage including Italian and Polish
President: Steven Lombardi
Owner: Marsha Caputo
Estimated Sales: $3-5 Million
Number Employees: 5-9
Type of Packaging: Consumer, Private Label, Bulk

10855 **Roman Packing Company**
2001 S 13th Street
Norfolk, NE 68701-6615
402-371-5990
Fax: 402-371-5639 800-373-5990
Meat products including dressed beef, pork, sausage and luncheon meats
President: Wendell Newcomb
Estimated Sales: $10-20 Million
Number Employees: 20-49
Type of Packaging: Consumer

10856 **Roman Sausage Company**
1810 Richard Avenue
Santa Clara, CA 95050-2818
408-988-1222
Fax: 408-988-0546 800-497-7462
Processor and importer of patties including sausage, salmon and tuna; also, salmon fillets
President: Amir Kanji
akanji@biomeddiagnostics.com
Estimated Sales: $1,100,000
Number Employees: 10
Square Footage: 32000
Brands:
Prima Brands

10857 **Romanian Kosher SausageCo**
7200 N Clark St
Chicago, IL 60626-2416
773-761-4141
Fax: 773-761-9506
www.romaniankoshersausage.com
Sausages
President: Arnold Loeb
romaniankosher@gmail.com
Estimated Sales: Below $5 000,000
Number Employees: 20-49

10858 **Rombauer Vineyards**
3522 Silverado Trl N
St Helena, CA 94574-9663
707-963-5170
Fax: 707-963-5752 800-622-2206
info@rombauer.com www.rombauer.com
Winery
President: Koerner Rombauer
Chief Financial Officer: Tory Sims
Director, Marketing & Consumer Relations: Brandye Alexander
National Sales Manager: Alan Cannon
Chief Operating Officer: Robert Knebel
Estimated Sales: $40.5 Million
Number Employees: 20-49
Number of Brands: 1
Type of Packaging: Consumer, Food Service
Brands:
Rombauer Vineyards

10859 **Romero's Food Products Inc**
15155 Valley View Ave
Santa Fe Springs, CA 90670-5323
562-802-1858
Fax: 562-921-7240 800-719-2690
orders@romerosfood.com www.romerosfood.com
Mexican sweet bread, tortillas, taco and tostada shells and tortilla chips
President: Leon Romero
CEO: Richard Scandalito
General Manager: Robert Romero
Vice President: Raul Romero
Sales: Sam Valenzuela
Operations Manager: Alfonso Valcarcel
Estimated Sales: $20-30 Million
Number Employees: 100-249

Type of Packaging: Consumer, Food Service, Private Label, Bulk
Brands:
Romero's

10860 (HQ)Ron Son Foods Inc
81 Locke Ave
PO Box 38
Swedesboro, NJ 08085-1059
856-241-7333
Fax: 856-241-7338 jim@ronsonfoods.com
www.ronsonfoods.com
Manufacturer, importer and importer of canned mushrooms, olives, olive oil, Italian pasta, anchovies, roasted peppers and artichokes
Owner: Ron Son
ron@ronsonfoods.com
CEO: James Bianco
CEO: James Bianco
Chief Marketing Officer: Peter Goldsberry
VP Sales: James Bianco
ron@ronsonfoods.com
Estimated Sales: $2-4 Million
Number Employees: 5-9
Square Footage: 200000
Type of Packaging: Consumer, Food Service, Private Label, Bulk
Brands:
Ghigi
Leone Bianco
Ron Son
Trifoglio

10861 Ron's Home Style Foods
4614 Perry St
Houston, TX 77021-3439
713-747-9666
Fax: 713-640-2085 800-856-3131
service@ronsfoods.com www.ronsfoods.com
Refrigerated prepared foods: salads, spreads, desserts and frozen entrees
Number Employees: 20-49

10862 Ron's Wisconsin Cheese LLC
124 Main St
Luxemburg, WI 54217-1102
920-845-5330
Fax: 920-845-9423 ronscheese@centurytel.net
www.ronscheese.com
Cheese spreads
Co-Owner: Ron Renard
Co-Owner: Terry Renard
ronscheese@centratel.net
Estimated Sales: Less Than $500,000
Number Employees: 10-19
Type of Packaging: Private Label, Bulk

10863 Rondo Specialty Foods LTD
118 Quigley Blvd
New Castle, DE 19720-4104
302-325-1145
Fax: 800-876-7971 800-724-6636
info@rondofoods.com
Bread, biscuits, cakes, pastries, cookies, baking mixes and ingredients, coffee, chocolate bars and other chocolate.
Marketing: Robert Dundas
Contact: Robert Dundas
robert.dundas@rondofoods.com
Number Employees: 1-4

10864 Ronnoco Coffee Co
618 S Boyle Ave
St Louis, MO 63110-1628
314-371-5050
Fax: 314-371-5056 800-428-2287
info@ronnoco.com www.ronnoco.com
Coffee
President: Frank Guyol
Estimated Sales: Below $5 Million
Number Employees: 100-249
Brands:
Ronnoco

10865 Ronny Brook Farm Dairy
310 Prospect Hill Rd
Ancramdale, NY 12503
518-398-6455
Fax: 518-398-6464 800-772-6455
info@ronnybrook.com www.ronnybrook.com
Milk, half & half, cream, chocolate milk, coffee milk, strawberry milk, drinkable yogurts, yogurt, ice cream and butter
Owner: Ronald Osofsky
info@ronnybrook.com
Estimated Sales: $1-2.5 Million
Number Employees: 10-19
Type of Packaging: Consumer, Private Label

10866 Ronzoni
PO Box 5400
Largo, FL 33779
800-730-5957
www.ronzoni.com
Pastas, including gluten free, vegetable based, and whole grain varieties
President/CEO: Bastiaan de Zeeuw
Senior VP/CFO: Michael Slavin
Senior VP/COO: Enrique Zaragoza
Number Employees: 75
Parent Co: Riviana Foods Inc.
Type of Packaging: Consumer, Food Service
Brands:
Ronzoni
Ronzoni Garden Delight
Ronzoni Gluten Free
Ronzoni Healthy Harvest
Ronzoni Homestyle
Ronzoni Organic
Ronzoni Smart Taste
Ronzoni SuperGreens
Ronzoni Thick and Hearty

10867 Roode Packing Company
P.O.Box 510
Fairbury, NE 68352
402-729-2253
Fax: 402-477-5743
Beef, sausage and pork including smoked and cured
President: Tom Roode
Plant Manager: Dwayne Hasselbring
Estimated Sales: $3,250,000
Number Employees: 33
Type of Packaging: Consumer, Food Service

10868 Rooibee Red Tea
1102 Lyndon Lane, Suite B
Louisville, KY 40222
502-749-0800
rooibee@rooibeeredtea.com
www.rooibeeredtea.com
Rooibee Red Tea, made from the South African rooibos bush and USDA-certified organic, offers all the benefits of red tea in five flavors: watermelon mint, peach, unsweetened, cranberry pomegranate, and vanilla chai. Naturally caffeinefree.
Chief Tea Officer: Heather Howell
Director Of Sales: Mike Fulkerson
Contact: Bryon Evans
bryon@rooibeeredtea.com
Logistics Coordinator: Gary Jacobs
Type of Packaging: Consumer

10869 Roos Foods
P.O.Box 310
Kenton, DE 19955
302-653-0600
Fax: 302-653-8458 800-343-3642
rcastillo@roosfoods.com
Cheese, sour cream, exotic drinks, drink mixes, soy base drinks, and BBQ snacks
President: Anna Roos
Controller: Tammy Benini
Operations Manager: Alex Martin
Plant Manager: Roque Lopez
Estimated Sales: $4,900,000
Number Employees: 20-49
Number of Brands: 8
Number of Products: 98
Type of Packaging: Consumer, Food Service, Private Label
Brands:
Amigo
Mexicana
Roos
Santarosa
Snyapa
Wally's

10870 Root Cellar Preserves
9 Avon Road
Wellesley, MA 02482
781-864-7440
Fax: 530-326-6104
info@RootCellarPreserves.com
Gluten-free, kosher, organic/natural, vegetarian, full-line condiments, salsa/dips, canned or preserved fruits/vegetables, pickles & pickled vegetables
Founder: Susan,Jones
Founder: Lorne Jones
info@rootcellarpreserves.com
Estimated Sales: $100,000
Number Employees: 2

10871 Roquette America Inc.
2211 Innovation Dr.
Geneva, IL 60134
630-463-9430
Fax: 319-526-2542 www.roquette.com
Corn, wheat and potato food ingredients including modified starches, proteins and high fructose and maltose syrups.
President/Chief Executive Officer: Dominique Baumann
CFO: Eric Loges
Year Founded: 1933
Estimated Sales: $100 Million
Number Employees: 8,400
Square Footage: 19107
Parent Co: Roquette Freres

10872 Rosa Brothers Milk Co Inc
10090 2nd Ave
Hanford, CA 93230-9370
559-685-8825
info@rosabrothers.com
www.rosabrothers.com
Milk and milk products
President: Noel Rosa
Director of Sales & Marketing: Kathleen Johnson
Year Founded: 1953
Estimated Sales: $20-50 Million
Number Employees: 1-4
Type of Packaging: Consumer, Food Service

10873 Rosa Food Products
2750 Grays Ferry Ave
Philadelphia, PA 19146-3801
215-467-2214
Fax: 215-467-6850 rosa@rosafoods.com
Manufacturer and wholesaler of pastas, sauces, cooking ingredients, condiments, etc.
President: Jack Foti
CEO: Giacomo Foti
mfoti@rosafoods.com
Chief Financial Officer: Leonardo Foti
Manager: Mary Foti
Estimated Sales: $11 Million
Number Employees: 10-19
Number of Brands: 9
Square Footage: 68000
Type of Packaging: Consumer, Food Service, Private Label, Bulk
Brands:
Rosa
Rita
Leonardo
Luna
Pavilion
Cassino
Angela
He Man
Keller's

10874 Rosa Mexicano
846 7th Ave
5th Floor
New York, NY 10019-5221
212-757-5447
Fax: 212-397-3003 mpolton@rosamexicano.com
Salsa/dips, soups/broths, other sauces, seasonings and cooking enhancers, chips.
President, Chief Executive Officer: Howard Greenstone
Vice President: Louis Alvarez
Contact: Amanda Morlock
amorlock@babylonbeachhouse.com
Vice President of Operations: Christian Plotczyk
Estimated Sales: $92,000
Number Employees: 10-19

10875 Rosa's Horchata, LLC
655 Deerfield Road
Suite 100
Deerfield, IL 60015
847-267-0570
Fax: 847-729-7231 www.rosashorchata.com

Produces a bottled version of a traditional Mexican beverage, horchata, with a shelf stable (refrigeration not required). Available flavors include original with the taste of cinnamon rice and a hint of vanilla, Strawberry/Fresa withthe taste of fresh berries, Melon with the taste of ripe cantaloupe & honeydew melons, and Chocolate Mexicano with the rich taste of Mexican chocolate and a hint of cinnamon.
Co-Founder: Marvin Berger
Co-Founder & Sales Representative: Edward Noeh

10876 **Rosalind Candy Castle Inc**
1301 5th Ave
New Brighton, PA 15066-2117
724-843-1144
Fax: 724-847-2008 www.rosalindcandy.com
Confectionery including chocolates
President: James Crudden
orders@rosalindcandy.com
Estimated Sales: Less Than $500,000
Number Employees: 1-4
Type of Packaging: Consumer

10877 **Rosanna Imports Warehouse**
6755 E Marginal Way S
Seattle, WA 98108-3406
206-329-1881
Fax: 206-264-7637 877-343-3779
info@rosannainc.com www.rosannainc.com
Manufacturer of food products.
Founder and President: Rosanna Bowles
info@rosannainc.com
Number Employees: 10-19

10878 **Rosati Italian Water Ice**
201 E Madison Ave
Clifton Heights, PA 19018-2690
610-626-1818
Fax: 610-626-0706 855-476-7284
srrosati@aol.com www.rosatiice.com
Italian water ice
President: Rich Trotter
VP: Al Everets
Estimated Sales: $700,000
Number Employees: 10-19
Type of Packaging: Consumer

10879 **Rose Acre Farms**
911 N 1200 W
Wolcott, IN 47995
765-258-4015
Fax: 812-497-3311 ajackson@goodegg.com
www.goodegg.com
Eggs
President: Lois Rust
Director of Sales: Amanda Jackson
Manager: Kim Allman
kallman@goodegg.com
Plant Manager: Nick Cary
Commodities Purchasing: Joe Easton
Estimated Sales: $5-10 Million
Number Employees: 50-99
Parent Co: Rose Acre Farms
Type of Packaging: Food Service, Bulk

10880 **Rose Acre Farms Inc**
6874 N Base Rd
Seymour, IN 47274-8934
812-497-2557
Fax: 812-497-3311 800-356-3447
info2003@goodegg.com www.goodegg.com
Producer of fresh shell eggs and egg products
President: Lois Rust
lrust@goodegg.com
VP: Mark Whintington
Marketing Manager: Greg Hinton
Production Manager: Victor Ritteink
Number Employees: 1000-4999
Type of Packaging: Consumer, Food Service, Private Label

10881 **Rose City Pepperheads**
16285 SW 85th Ave # 403
Suite 403
Tigard, OR 97224-5424
503-443-3873
Fax: 503-443-3873
susan@rosecitypepperheads.com
www.rosecitypepperheads.com
Flavored pepper jellies.
Owner: Susan Mc Cormick
rosecitypepperheads@gmail.com
Estimated Sales: $300,000-500,000
Number Employees: 1-4
Type of Packaging: Consumer

10882 **Rose Creek Vineyards**
226 East Ave N
Hagerman, ID 83332
208-837-4353
Fax: 208-837-6405
Wines
Manager: Katie Owsley
Treasurer: Susan Martin
Vice President: Stephanie Martin
Estimated Sales: $1-4.9 000,000
Number Employees: 1-4

10883 **Rose Frozen Shrimp**
741 Ceres Avenue
Los Angeles, CA 90021-1515
213-626-8251
Fax: 213-626-4802
Shrimp
President: Ken Takiguchi
Estimated Sales: $10-20 000,000
Number Employees: 20

10884 **Rose Hill Distributors**
81 Rose Hill Road
Branford, CT 06405-4015
203-488-7231
Fax: 203-488-2100
Poultry
President/CEO: Frank Vastola
Estimated Sales: $5-10 000,000
Number Employees: 20

10885 **Rose Hill Seafood**
2621 Hamilton Rd
Columbus, GA 31904
706-322-1269
Fax: 562-220-1575
Frozen foods, canned foods goods, dry goods, poultry, seafood, and produce
Owner: Jeff Lundsford
Estimated Sales: $1-3 Million
Number Employees: 20-49

10886 **(HQ)Rose Packing Co Inc**
65 S Barrington Rd
South Barrington, IL 60010-9589
847-381-5700
Fax: 847-381-9424 800-323-7363
postmaster@rosepacking.com
www.rosepacking.com
Meat products including; canadian bacon, hams, boneless turkey, pork loin, sausages, meatballs, pork shoulder, toppings, fresh/frozen meats, pizza toppers, and zip-packs.
President & CEO: Dwight Stiehl
williamrose@rosepacking.com
CFO: James O'Hara
Executive Vice President: Jim Vandenbergh
Director of Information Systems: Marty Strickler
Quality Assurance Manager: Sean R. Tuftedal
Dir of Marketing & Advertising: Erik W. Vandenbergh
Retail Sales Manager: Larry Null
Lab Director: Maria Maris
Director of Operations: Michael Reiter
Director of Product Development: Peter D. Rose
Plant Superintendent: Joseph Mihalov
Purchasing Manager: Bob Jones
Number Employees: 500-999
Type of Packaging: Consumer, Food Service
Other Locations:
Rose Packing Company Plant
Chicago IL

10887 **Rose Randolph Cookies, LLC**
PO Box 1117
Wappingers Falls, NY 12590-8117
917-834-2310
barbara@roserandolphcookies.com
Manufacturer of cookies and baking mixes.
Founder: Barbara Demosthene
bdemosthene@roserandolphcookies.com

10888 **Rosebrand Corp**
585 Berriman St
Brooklyn, NY 11208-5203
718-257-2058
Fax: 718-257-2058 800-854-5356
Batch ice cream flavoring, fruit sundae toppings and fountain syrups. Founded in 1926.
President: Elliot Keller
ekeller@rosebrand.com
Customer Development: Elliot Keller
Estimated Sales: $3-5 Million
Number Employees: 10-19
Type of Packaging: Food Service

10889 **Rosebud Creamery**
Route 3
354 Cornelia Street
Plattsburgh, NY 12901
518-561-5160
Fax: 518-561-6068
Dairy
President: Frederick Perras
Estimated Sales: $500-1 000,000 appx.
Number Employees: 1-4
Brands:
Rosebud Creamery

10890 **Roseland Manufacturing**
119 Harrison Ave
Roseland, NJ 07068
973-228-2500
www.dialpestcontrol.com
Jams, jellies and perserves
Chief Executive Officer: Jerry Smith
Chief Operating Officer: Steven Adams
Estimated Sales: $500,000-$1 Million
Number Employees: 5-9

10891 **Roselani Tropics Ice Cream**
PO Box 1170
Wailuku, HI 96793-6170
808-244-7951
Fax: 808-244-4108 info@roselani.com
www.roselani.com
Carbonated beverages and ice cream
Manager: Todd Assmann
Sales Manager: Mike Nobriga
Estimated Sales: $15,151,351
Number Employees: 50-99
Type of Packaging: Consumer, Food Service

10892 **Rosemark Bakery**
258 Snelling Ave S
St Paul, MN 55105-2045
651-698-3838
Fax: 651-698-0828
Baked goods
Owner: Carol Rosemark
General Manager: Irv Gertz
Estimated Sales: $5-10 Million
Number Employees: 10-19

10893 **Rosen's Diversified Inc.**
1120 Lake Ave.
PO Box 933
Fairmont, MN 56031
507-238-6001
Fax: 507-238-9966
ContactUs@RosensDiversified.com
www.rosensdiversifiedinc.com
Agribusiness, beef processing, pet foods and carrier services.
CEO: Tom Rosen
trosen@riw2000.com
Year Founded: 1946
Estimated Sales: $3.2 Billion
Number of Brands: 7
Brands:
Rosen's Inc.
America's Heartland Beef
Long Prairie Packing Company
Great American
Skylark
Big City Reds
Sheboygan Sausage Company

10894 **Rosenberger's Dairies**
847 Forty Foot Rd
PO Box 901
Hatfield, PA 19440-2870
800-355-9074
Fax: 215-855-6486 800-355-9074
info@rosenbergers.com
Dairy products including eggs, milk, cream, sour cream and cheese; also, beverages including apple juice, iced tea and fruit drinks
President: Marty Margherio
VP: Marcus Rosenberger
Production Manager: Jeffery Rosenberger
Plant Manager: Gerry Whiting
Number Employees: 250-499
Square Footage: 432268
Type of Packaging: Consumer

Brands:
Rosenbergers

10895 Rosenblum Cellars
2900 Main St Ste 1100
Alameda, CA 94501
510-865-7007
Fax: 510-865-9225 www.rosenblumcellars.com
Wines
President: Kent Rosenblum
CFO: Tim Allen
Quality Control: Les Horton
Marketing Director: Kathy Coi
Operations Manager: Ron Pieretti
Estimated Sales: $5-9.9 Million
Number Employees: 20-49
Number of Brands: 1
Number of Products: 40
Square Footage: 232000
Other Locations:
Rosenblum Cellars
Healdsburgh CA
Brands:
Rosenblum

10896 Roses Ravioli
219 E Walnut Street
Oglesby, IL 61348-1203
815-883-8011
Fax: 815-883-8409
Ravioli, tortellini and pasta sauce
President: Barbara Shields
Owner: Rose Causa
Estimated Sales: $2.5-5 000,000
Number Employees: 1-4

10897 Rosetti's Fine Foods Biscotti
3 Railroad Ave
Clovis, CA 93612-1219
559-323-6450
Fax: 559-323-2022 www.rosettis.com
Biscotti, bark confections
President: Diane Rosetti
rosetti@pacbell.net
Secretary/Treasurer: Dan Rosetti
Estimated Sales: $500,000-$1 Million
Number Employees: 5-9
Brands:
Rosetti Fine Foods

10898 Roseville Corporation
120 Plum Ct
Mountain View, CA 94043-4899
650-255-9278
Fax: 650-592-8966 888-247-9338
www.bigsmiley.com
Candy
President: Enrique Ganitsky
Brands:
Betty Twist & Match Chocolate Candy
Big Smiley

10899 Rosina Food Holdings Inc
170 French Rd
Buffalo, NY 14227-2777
716-668-0123
Fax: 716-668-1132 888-767-4621
gsetter@rosina.com www.rosina.com
Italian foods including; appetizers, pastas, pizza toppings, meatballs, eggplant, specialty sausages, and entrees for consumers, industrial, foodservice and international markets.
President & CEO: Russell Corigliano
rcorigliano@rosina.com
Chairman: James Corigliano
CFO/COO: Roger Palczewski
VP: Joseph Corigliano
Manager Product Development: Nicholas Arbore
Quality Assurance Manager: Dan Etzinger
VP Marketing: Frank Corigliano
Communications Director: Nick Lukasiewicz
VP Engineering: Viren Sitwala
Estimated Sales: $32.4 Million
Number Employees: 250-499
Square Footage: 60000
Type of Packaging: Food Service
Brands:
Rosina
Celentano
San Rallo Gourmet Italian
Italian Village
Floresta

10900 Rosmarino Foods/R.Z. Humbert Company
16216 Turnbury Oak Drive
Odessa, FL 33556-2870
813-926-9053
Fax: 813-920-0734 888-926-9053
Speciality award winning foods such as all natural salad dressings, hearty pasta sauces, flavorful marinades, great grilling sauces, tangy BBQ sauces, and fiery hot sauces
President: Rosemary Humbert
VP Marketing: Roger Humbert
Number Employees: 8
Number of Brands: 3
Number of Products: 50
Square Footage: 260000
Type of Packaging: Consumer, Food Service, Private Label, Bulk
Brands:
Bonnies
Luna Rossa
Rosmarino

10901 Ross Fine Candies
4642 Elizabeth Lake Rd
Waterford, MI 48328-2831
248-682-5640
Fax: 248-682-0457
Candy and other confectionery products
President: Janet Greaves
Estimated Sales: $300,000
Number Employees: 5-9
Type of Packaging: Consumer, Private Label
Brands:
Ross Fine

10902 Ross-Smith Pecan Company
107 Plantation Oak Dr
Thomasville, GA 31792-3540
229-859-2225
Fax: 229-859-2382 800-841-5503
Manufacturer and exporter of nuts including shelled pecans
President: Betty McDuffie
Estimated Sales: Less than $500,000
Number Employees: 23

10903 Rossi Pasta LTD
106 Front St
Marietta, OH 45750-3123
740-373-5155
Fax: 740-373-5310 800-227-6774
info@rossipasta.com www.rossipasta.com
Gourmet handmade pasta products and sauces
President: John Hammat
Chairman: Frank L Christy
Estimated Sales: Below $5 Million
Number Employees: 1-4
Type of Packaging: Private Label

10904 Rostov's Coffee & Tea Co
1618 W Main St
Richmond, VA 23220-4633
804-355-1955
Fax: 804-355-6963 800-637-6772
www.rostovs.com
Coffee and tea
Owner: Tammy Rostov
Founder: Jay Rostov
Estimated Sales: Below $5 Million
Number Employees: 10-19
Type of Packaging: Consumer
Brands:
Rostov's Coffee Tea

10905 Rotella's Italian Bakery Inc.
6949 S. 108th St.
La Vista, NE 68128
402-592-6600
Fax: 402-592-2989 info@rotellasbakery.com
Hamburger buns, hoagies, bread loaves, dinner rolls and bread sticks, hot dog buns and brat buns, and specialty breads.
Controller: Dean Jacobsen
Sales Executive: Jim Rotella
jrotella@rotellasbakery.com
Year Founded: 1921
Estimated Sales: $133 Million
Number Employees: 250-499
Square Footage: 65000
Type of Packaging: Consumer, Food Service
Brands:
Rotella's

10906 Roth Cheese USA
5525 Nobel Dr.
Suite 100
Fitchburg, WI 53711
608-285-9800
Fax: 608-328-2120 info@emmirothusa.com
www.rothcheese.com
Havarti, gouda, blue, muenster and commodity cheeses
President: Tim Omer
CEO: Stephen McKeon
Quality Manager: Alecia Vermeern
SVP Sales & Marketing: Anthony Salathe
SVP Supply Chain & Operations: Ty Brannen
Estimated Sales: $25-49.9 Million
Number Employees: 20-49
Type of Packaging: Consumer, Food Service, Bulk
Brands:
Grand Cru Raclette
Grand Crue
Kronenost
Pesto Havarti
Rofumo
Roth Kase
Roth Kase
Ustenborg
Vangogh

10907 Rothbury Farms
PO Box 202
Grand Rapids, MI 49501-0202
616-574-5757
877-684-2879
www.rothburyfarms.com
Dry wheat-based products, including croutons, stuffing, and bread crumbs.
President: Robert Roskam
Manager: Janet Lennon
Year Founded: 1923
Estimated Sales: $128 Million
Number Employees: 1,000
Number of Brands: 2
Type of Packaging: Food Service, Private Label, Bulk
Brands:
Rothbury Farms
Grandpa's Oven

10908 Rothman's Food Inc
4718 Delmar Blvd
St Louis, MO 63108-1706
314-367-5448
Ethnic foods
Owner: A Rothman
Estimated Sales: Below $5 000,000
Number Employees: 5-9

10909 Rotteveel Orchards
6183 Reddick Ln
Dixon, CA 95620-9731
707-678-1495
Fax: 707-678-1446
Processor and exporter of almonds
President: Neil Rotteveel
info@rotteveel.com
Estimated Sales: $500,000-$1 Million
Number Employees: 5-9
Type of Packaging: Bulk

10910 Roudon-Smith Vineyards
13809 Serra Oaks Court
Saratoga, CA 95070
831-438-1244
Fax: 831-438-4374 sales@roudonsmith.com
www.roudonsmith.com
Wines
Owner: Annette Hunt
Owner: David Hunt
Estimated Sales: $1-2.5 Million
Number Employees: 1-4
Brands:
Roudon Smith Vineyards

10911 Rougie Foie Gras
1661 Rue Marcoux
Marieville, QC J3M 1E8
Canada
450-460-2107
Fax: 450-460-2963 www.rougie.ca
Foie gras (duck) and lobster

CEO: Benoit Cuchet
Sales & Marketing Manager: Thomas Delannoy
Customer Service: Sandra Ratelle
sandra.ratelle@euralis.ca
Processing: C,dric Martineau
Brands:
Rougie

10912 Round Hill Vineyards
1680 Silverado Trl S
St Helena, CA 94574-9542
707-963-5252
Fax: 707-963-0834 800-778-0424
info@rutherfordwine.com
www.roundhillwines.com
Wines
Owner: Morgan Zaninovich
morganz@roundhillwines.com
VP: Mark Fedorchak
Chairman: Erne Van Asperen
President: Virginia Van Asperen
Public Relations: Bonnie Zimmerman
Production Manager: Keith Groves
Plant Manager: Bob Iacampo
Estimated Sales: Below $5 Million
Number Employees: 50-99
Type of Packaging: Private Label
Brands:
Round Hill Vineyards
Rutherford Ranch
Van Asperen Vineyard

10913 Round Rock Honey Co, LLC
1308 Chisholm Tr
Suite 107
Round Rock, TX 78681
512-828-5416
Fax: 512-828-5416 www.roundrockhoney.com
Honey

10914 Rousseau Farming Co
102 S 95th Ave
Phoenix, AZ 85043
623-936-7100
Fax: 623-936-7386 admin@rfcaz.com
www.rousseaufarming.com
Fruits and vegetables
President: David Rousseau
Partner: Jean Biggs
jeanb@rfcaz.com
Estimated Sales: $1-2,500,000
Number Employees: 250-499

10915 Rousselot Inc
1231 S Rochester St # 250
Suite 250
Mukwonago, WI 53149-9031
262-363-6050
888-455-3556
gelatin.usa@rousselot.com www.rousselot.com
Global gelatin and collagen manufacturer.
Contact: James Mcdermott
james.mcdermott@rousselot.com
Number Employees: 5-9
Number of Brands: 4
Parent Co: Darling Ingredients
Type of Packaging: Bulk
Other Locations:
Sales Office
Mukwonago WI
Production
Dubuque IA
Production
Peabody MA
Brands:
Rousselot
Synergy Systems
ProTake
Peptan

10916 Route 11 Potato Chips
11 Edwards Way
Mount Jackson, VA 22842-2037
540-477-9664
Fax: 540-869-0176 800-294-7783
sales@rt11.com www.rt11.com
Handcooked potato chips, sweet potato chips, mixed vegetable chips and potato chip cookies.
President/CEO: Sarah Cohen
sarah@rt11.com
Year Founded: 1992
Estimated Sales: $20-50 Million
Number Employees: 20-49
Brands:
Route 11 Potato Chips

10917 Routin America
955 NW 17th Avenue
Suite F
Delray Beach, FL 334452516
export@routin.com
www.1883.com
Flavored syrups and sauces.
President: Jean Clochet
Estimated Sales: $1.5 Million
Number Employees: 2
Number of Brands: 1
Parent Co: Routin SA
Type of Packaging: Private Label
Brands:
1883

10918 (HQ)Rovira Biscuit Corporation
619 La Ceiba Ave
Ponce, PR 00717-1901
787-844-8585
Fax: 787-848-7176
customerservice@rovirabiscuits.com
www.rovirabiscuits.com
Crackers and biscuits; exporter of crackers
President and Director: Rafael Rovira
President, Rovira Foods: Frances Rovira
Executive VP and General Manager: Carlos Rovira
Quality Control: Carla Traverso
Export Sales Manager: Roberto Ponce
Estimated Sales: $50 Million
Number Employees: 300
Square Footage: 180000
Other Locations:
Rovira Biscuit Corp.
Pueblo Viejo PR

10919 (HQ)Rowena
758 W 22nd St
Norfolk, VA 23517-1925
757-627-8699
Fax: 757-627-1505 800-627-8699
rowena@rowens.com www.rowenas.com
Processor and exporter of gourmet pound cakes, jams, curds, dry mixes and sauces
Founder, President: Rowena Fullinwider
General Manager: Joan Place
Sales: Ann Cole
Contact: Tamikka Doman
tamikka@rowenas.com
Production: Renee Satterfield
Warehouse Manager: Dom Tamikk
Estimated Sales: $620000
Number Employees: 20-49
Square Footage: 52000
Type of Packaging: Consumer, Food Service, Private Label, Bulk
Brands:
Rowena's
Rowena's Gourmet Sauces
Rowena's Jams & Jellies
Rowena's Pound Cake

10920 Rowland Coffee RoastersInc.
P.O.Box 520845
Miami, FL 33152-0845
305-592-7302
Fax: 305-592-9471 866-318-0422
www.javacabana.com
Processor, importer and exporter of coffee; importer and wholesaler/distributor of coffee equipment and supplies including filters
President: Jose Souto
General Manager of Sales: Angeo Soupo
Estimated Sales: $2.5-5 Million
Number Employees: 50-99
Square Footage: 50000
Parent Co: Tetley USA
Type of Packaging: Consumer, Food Service, Private Label
Brands:
Cafe Bustelo

10921 Roy Dick Company
152 Harris Street
Griffin, GA 30223-7017
770-227-3916
Fax: 770-227-3916
Catfish, shrimp, oysters, chicken
Owner: Roy Dick

10922 Royal Atlantic Seafood
2 Carrie Lane
Gloucester, MA 01930-2328
978-281-6373
Fax: 978-283-7185
Seafood
President: Anne Mortillaro

10923 Royal Baltic LTD
9829 Ditmas Ave
Brooklyn, NY 11236-1925
718-385-8300
Fax: 718-385-4757
Manufactures smoked fish products; distributes gourmet foods, such as seafood delicacies, cheese, juice, feta, coffee, chocolate candy and sauces.
President: Alex Kaganovsky
alexkaganovsky@royalbaltic.com
Finance Manager: Alex Kaganovsky
Estimated Sales: $10-20 Million
Number Employees: 50-99
Type of Packaging: Consumer

10924 (HQ)Royal Caribbean Bakery
620 S Fulton Ave
Mt Vernon, NY 10550-5012
914-668-6868
Fax: 914-668-5700 888-818-0971
info@royalcaribbeanbakery.com
www.royalcaribbeanbakery.com
Jamaican baked goods and specialty foods
President/CEO: Jeanette Hosang
CEO: Vincent Hosang
Estimated Sales: $5-10 Million
Number Employees: 50-99
Square Footage: 240000
Type of Packaging: Consumer, Food Service, Private Label, Bulk
Other Locations:
Royal Caribbean Bakery
Orlando FL

10925 Royal Caviar Inc
4551 San Fernando Rd # 110
Glendale, CA 91204-3234
818-546-5858
Fax: 818-546-5856 www.royalcaviar.com
Caviar
President: Robert Khatchatrian

10926 Royal Center Locker Plant
104 S Chicago St
Royal Center, IN 46978-7029
574-643-3275
Fax: 574-643-3031
Meat products including beef, pork and lamb
Owner: Steve Layer
Estimated Sales: $12 Million
Number Employees: 10-19
Type of Packaging: Consumer

10927 Royal Crest Dairy
350 S Pearl St
Denver, CO 80209-2098
303-777-3055
Fax: 303-744-9173 888-226-6455
hr@royalcrestdairy.com www.royalcrestdairy.com
Milks, cream, butter, eggs, juices, water, bread, cheese, cottage cheese, sour cream, dips, yogurt and various seasonal items.
President: Ryan Bontrager
Founder: Paul Miller
CFO: Howard Lutz
VP Operations: Grady Cleckler
Estimated Sales: $20-50 Million
Number Employees: 100-249
Brands:
Royal Crest

10928 Royal Cup Coffee
PO Box 170971
Birmingham, AL 35217-0971
800-366-5836
webjava@royalcupcoffee.com
www.royalcupcoffee.com
Coffee, tea, and coffee equipment.
CEO: Bill Smith
Chief Financial Officer: William Wann

Year Founded: 1896
Estimated Sales: $100-$500 Million
Number Employees: 859
Number of Brands: 4
Square Footage: 260000
Type of Packaging: Food Service

Other Locations:
Royal Cup
Birmingham AL
Brands:
Prideland
Royal Cup
ROAR
H.C. Valentine

10929 Royal Food Products
2322 E Minnesota St
Indianapolis, IN 46203
317-782-2660
Fax: 317-782-2680 sales@royalfp.com
www.royalfp.com
Salad dressings, mayonnaise, mustard and sauces
President: Brian King
CEO: John Heidt
Director: James Heidt
Contact: Nancy Davidian
nancydavidian@royalfoodproducts.com
Estimated Sales: $8.5 Million
Number Employees: 55
Type of Packaging: Food Service
Brands:
Royal

10930 Royal Foods & Flavor
2456 American Ln
Elk Grove Vlg, IL 60007-6204
847-595-9166
Fax: 847-595-9690
Flavors, seasonings, yeast extracts and hydrolyzed vegetable proteins
Owner: Harry Gadhvi
harry.gadhvi@royalgoldribbonfoods.com
Estimated Sales: $730,000
Number Employees: 10-19
Type of Packaging: Bulk

10931 Royal Foods Inc
215 Reindollar Ave
Marina, CA 93933-3804
831-582-2495
Fax: 831-582-2495 800-551-5284
info@gingerpeople.com www.gingerpeople.com
Ginger
President/Owner: Bruce Leeson
Marketing Coordinator: Nicole DeCarli
Contact: Abbie Leeson
abbiel@gingerpeople.com
Estimated Sales: $9.5 Million
Number Employees: 10-19

10932 Royal Gourmet Caviar
27 Blake Ave
Lynbrook, NY 11563-2505
516-612-7407
Fax: 516-612-7408
Caviar, nuts and dried fruits
Distribution Manager: Donna Powers Bowe
Year Founded: 2000
Estimated Sales: Under $500,000
Number Employees: 1-4
Brands:
Royal Gourmet Caviar

10933 Royal Harvest Foods Inc
90 Avocado St
Springfield, MA 01104-3304
413-737-8392
Fax: 413-731-9336 sales@royalharv.com
www.royalharv.com
Poutry processing facility.
President: Jim Vallides
Sales Manager: Frank McNamara
Estimated Sales: Less Than $500,000
Number Employees: 1-4
Number of Brands: 1
Square Footage: 40000
Type of Packaging: Consumer, Food Service, Private Label
Other Locations:
Royal Harvest Foods
Marion AL
Brands:
Royal Harvest

10934 Royal Hawaiian OrchardsLP
24901 Dana Point Harbor Dr
#A-210
Dana Point, CA 92629-2930
949-661-6304
Fax: 949-487-0242
www.royalhawaiianorchards.com
Nuts
President: Scott Wallace
Senior Vice President: Randolph Cabral
Estimated Sales: 2,000,000.00

10935 Royal Home Bakery
160 Pony Drive
Newmarket, ON L3Y 7B6
Canada
905-715-7044
Baked goods including bread, buns, biscuits, tarts, cakes and Jamaican patties
Owner: Harold Chin
Manager: Doris Chin
Sales Manager: Hope Chin
Estimated Sales: Under $300,000
Number Employees: 1-4
Square Footage: 16000

10936 Royal Ice Cream Co
27 Warren St
Manchester, CT 06040-6500
860-649-5358
Fax: 860-647-7376 800-246-2958
sales@royalicecream.com
www.royalicecream.com
Portion packed spumoni, nut roll, tartufo, fruit sorbet, tortoni, bombe, etc.; also, ice cream cakes and pies
President: J Orfitelli
jso@royalicecream.com
VP: Cindy Orfitelli
Estimated Sales: $2000000
Number Employees: 10-19
Square Footage: 60000
Type of Packaging: Food Service, Private Label

10937 Royal Lagoon Seafood Inc
5208 Mobile South St
Theodore, AL 36582-1604
251-653-1975
Fax: 251-653-1972 800-844-6972
john@royallagoonseafood.com
www.royallagoonseafood.com
Seafood
Owner: Valmon Hammond
Sales: Tanya Hammond
val@valssfd.com
Estimated Sales: $5,000,000
Number Employees: 5-9

10938 Royal Madera Vineyards
7770 Road 33
Madera, CA 93636-8307
559-486-6666
Fax: 559-661-1427
www.royalmaderavineyards.com
Frozen foods
President: Steve Volpe
rmv@onemain.com
Estimated Sales: $10-20 Million
Number Employees: 10-19

10939 Royal Medjool Date Gardens
1203 Perez Rd
Bard, CA 92222
760-572-0524
Fax: 760-572-2292
Grower and exporter of dates and date trees.
General Manager: David Nelson
Estimated Sales: $3 Million
Number Employees: 75
Brands:
Medjool
Royal

10940 Royal Oak Peanuts
13009 Cedar View Rd
Drewryville, VA 23844-2001
434-658-9500
Fax: 703-991-8922 800-608-4590
info@royaloakpeanuts.com
www.royaloakpeanuts.com
Peanut and peanut products
President: Stephanie Pope
royaloakpeanuts@royaloakpeanuts.com
Sales/Marketing: Stephanie Pope
Number Employees: 1-4

10941 Royal Pacific Coffee Co
PO Box 6277
Scottsdale, AZ 85261-6277
480-951-8251
Fax: 480-951-0092 royalpacific@syspac.com
www.royalpacificintl.com
Tea
CEO: Art Gartenberg
Manager: Grace Hatter
grace@royalpacificintl.com
Estimated Sales: Less Than $500,000
Number Employees: 5-9
Type of Packaging: Private Label
Brands:
Royal Pacific Coffee
Royal Pacific Tea

10942 Royal Pacific Fisheries
Mi 14.5 Kalifornsky Beach Rd
Kenai, AK 99611
907-283-9370
Fax: 907-283-5974
Fresh, frozen and canned seafood
President: Marvin Dragseth
Estimated Sales: $5-9.9 Million
Number Employees: 5-9

10943 Royal Palate Foods
960 E Hyde Park Blvd
Inglewood, CA 90302-1708
310-330-7701
Fax: 310-330-7710
Processor, exporter and wholesaler/distributor of kosher foods including chicken, beef, soups, sauces, frozen entrees, hors d'oeuvres, etc.; serving the food service market; importer of canned vegetables and fruits
President: William Pinkerson
Estimated Sales: $500,000-$1 Million
Number Employees: 10-19
Square Footage: 32000
Type of Packaging: Food Service, Bulk
Brands:
Royal Palate
Sierra Spring Foods

10944 Royal Palm Popcorn Company
100 McGaw Dr
Edison, NJ 08837-3725
732-225-0200
Fax: 732-225-6363 800-526-8865
Gourmet popcorn
President: Michael Spitz
Number Employees: 10-19
Brands:
Joons Chocolate Popcorn
Park Avenue Gourmet
Rainbow Popcorn

10945 Royal Products
P.O.Box 13628
Scottsdale, AZ 85267-3628
480-948-2509
Fax: 480-951-0835 www.royalprod.com
Health vitamins and supplements
President: Johnny Shannon
CEO: David Stuart
Estimated Sales: Less than $100,000
Number Employees: 1-4
Type of Packaging: Food Service

10946 Royal Resources
PO Box 24001
New Orleans, LA 70184-4001
504-283-9932
Fax: 504-283-2620 800-888-9932
rrbanfos@bellsouth.net
Salad dressing, jellies, salsas, dessert toppings, hot sauces and cake mix

10947 Royal Ridge Fruits
13215 Road F SW
Royal City, WA 99357
509-346-1520
Fax: 509-346-2098 info@stoneridgeorchards.com
www.stoneridgeorchards.com
Frozen and dried fruits
Estimated Sales: $5-10 Million
Number Employees: 20-49
Square Footage: 200000
Type of Packaging: Private Label

10948 Royal Rose Syrups, LLC
14 Maine St.
Brunswick, ME 04011
718-303-0750
info@royalroseny.com
www.royalrosesyrups.com
Manufacturer of syrup for cocktails.
Co-Founder: Emily Butters
Co-Founder: Forrest Butler

10949 Royal Seafood Inc
2257 E 16th St
Brooklyn, NY 11229-4424
718-769-1517
Fax: 831-373-8336 www.netcostmarket.com
Frozen and fresh fish including cod, flounder, herring, mackerel, perch, salmon, sole, squid and tuna
Owner: Edward Schneider
edward.schneider@netcostmarket.com
Owner/VP: Elaine Pennisi
Estimated Sales: $800,000
Number Employees: 1-4
Type of Packaging: Consumer, Food Service
Brands:
Black Cod (Sablefish
Ca Halibut
Channel Rockfish (Thornyheads
Dover Sole

10950 Royal Touch Foods
315 Humberline Drive
Etobicoke, ON M9W 5T6
Canada
416-213-1077
Fax: 416-213-1055
Pork and beef sandwiches
President: Domenic Ruso
Estimated Sales: $5.6 Million
Number Employees: 50
Parent Co: J.M. Schneider
Type of Packaging: Food Service
Brands:
Hamish & Enzo
Royal Touch

10951 Royal Vista Marketing Inc
126 W Center Ave
Visalia, CA 93291-6228
559-636-9198
Fax: 559-636-9637 info@royalvista.com
Grower and exporter of table grapes, kiwifruit, stone fruit and figs; importer of stone fruit, kiwifruit and table grapes
Owner: Todd Steele
Sales Manager: Patrick Allen
todd@royalvista.com
Estimated Sales: $84000
Number Employees: 10-19
Square Footage: 96000
Parent Co: Atalanta
Type of Packaging: Consumer, Food Service, Bulk
Other Locations:
Alkop Farms
Chico CA

10952 Royal Wine Corp
63 Lefante Dr
Bayonne, NJ 07002-5024
718-384-2400
Fax: 718-388-8444 info@royalwines.com
www.royalwine.com
Manufacturer, importer and distributer of premium kosher wines, spirits and liquors. Affiliate of Kedem Food Products International.
President: David Herzog
CEO: Mordy Herzog
Chief Financial Officer: Sheldon Ginsberg
Executive Vice President: Sheldon Ginsberg
SVP: Phillip Herzog
Executive Vice President of Sales: Nathan Herzog
Estimated Sales: $49.5 Million
Number Employees: 200
Number of Brands: 61
Square Footage: 184000
Parent Co: KayCo
Type of Packaging: Consumer, Food Service
Brands:
Alexander Winery
Alfasi
Barkan Winery
Bartenura Wines
Bazelet ha Golan Winery
Binyamina
Binyamina Winery
Carmel Winery
Casa De Corca
Cave Winery
Celler De Capcanes
Covenant Winery
Domaine du Castel
Domaine Netofa
Don Alfonso
Elvi Winery
French Wines
Gamla
Goose Bay Winery
Hagafen Winery
Bokobsa Wines
Herzog Selection
Herzog Wine Cellars
Jeunesse Wines
Kedem
Flam Winery
Baron Edmond De Rothschild
Laufer Winery
Legend of Kremlin
Los Arango
Morad Winery
Pacifica
Porto Cordovero
Psagot Winery
Ramon Cardova Winery
Rashi Winery
S'forno Winery
Segal Winery
Shiloh Winery
Teal Lake Winery
Tio Pepe Winery
Tomintoul
Tulip Winery
Tzuba Winery
Weinstock Wine Cellars
Yatir Winery
Zion
Zachlawi
(in)
1848 Winery
Altoona Hills
Chateau Rollan De By
Clos Mesorah
Matar by Pelter
Montefiore Winery
Or Haganuz Winery
Padis Vineyards
Teperberg Winery
Terra di Seta
Titora Winery
Villa Cape Winery

10953 Royale Brands
5315 Tremont Ave
Davenport, IA 52807
563-386-5222
Fax: 563-386-1352 royale@netexpress.net
royalebrands.com
Produce and market frozen beverage products and equipment
President: Joe Colombari
Estimated Sales: Less than $500,000
Number Employees: 10-19
Number of Brands: 13
Number of Products: 250
Type of Packaging: Food Service
Brands:
Cruisin Cool
Energy Ice
Royale Smoothie

10954 Royce C. Bone Farms
2913 Sandy Cross Road
Nashville, NC 27856-8633
252-443-3773
Fax: 252-937-4990 www.ncsweetpotatoes.com
Sweet potatoes, romaine, tomatoes and pickles
Director: David Godwin
Co-Owner: Fay Bone
Vice President: Dewey Scott
Number Employees: 10-19
Brands:
Jean Sweet Potatos

10955 Rpac LLC
21490 Ortigalita Rd
Los Banos, CA 93635-9793
209-826-0272
Fax: 209-826-3882 info@rpacalmonds.com
www.rpacalmonds.com
Processor and exporter of almonds
Owner: Dave Parreira
dave@arpacalmonds.com
Partner: David Parreira
Shipping Manager: Janet Martin
Plant Manager: James Smith
Estimated Sales: $4500000
Number Employees: 20-49
Type of Packaging: Bulk

10956 Ruark & Ashton
1548 Taylors Island Road
Woolford, MD 21677-1327
410-221-6076
Fax: 410-221-6076 800-725-5032
Seafood
President: Terry Vinson
Estimated Sales: Under $500,000
Number Employees: 1-4

10957 Rubashkin
4308 14th Ave
Brooklyn, NY 11219-1428
718-436-5511
Fax: 718-435-4295
Kosher butcher
President: AA Rubashkin
Estimated Sales: $1-3 000,000

10958 Rubicon Food Products
180 Brodie Drive
Suite 1
Richmond Hill, ON L4B 3K8
Canada
905-883-1112
feedback@rubiconexotic.ca
rubiconexotic.ca
Tropical fruit juice
Financial Analyst: Ocean Yang Jiang
Quality Assurance Executive: Mohammad Bashar
Operation Director: Yuan Robin
Year Founded: 1982
Brands:
Rubicon

10959 Rubino's Seafood Company
735 W Lake St
Chicago, IL 60661
312-258-0020
Fax: 312-258-0028
Seafood
President: James Rubino
Estimated Sales: $1-3 Million
Number Employees: 5-9
Type of Packaging: Food Service

10960 Rubschlager Baking Corp
800-661-7246
CCC@westonfoods.com
www.rubschlagerbaking.com
Processor and exporter of rye breads.
President: Luc Mongeau
CFO: Tina Murrin
Number Employees: 1-4
Number of Brands: 2
Number of Products: 45
Parent Co: Weston Foods
Type of Packaging: Consumer, Food Service
Brands:
Rubschlager

10961 Ruby Rockets
55 Broadway
3rd Floor
New York, NY 10036
855-543-7677
www.rubyrockets.com
Frozen fruit and veggie pops
Founder: Wendy Makkena

10962 Rubys Apiaries
711 5th Ave
Milnor, ND 58060-4113
701-427-5200
Condiments and relishes
President: Dick Ruby
CEO: Doug Ruby
Estimated Sales: Less than $500,000
Number Employees: 1-4

10963 Rudd Winery
500 Oakville Xrd
Oakville, CA 94562
707-944-8577
Fax: 707-968-3807 info@ruddwines.com
www.ruddwines.com

Wines
President: Leslie Rudd
leslie@ruddwines.com
COO: Stephen Girard Jr
Marketing Director: Ellen Hunt
Estimated Sales: $5-10 Million
Number Employees: 20-49
Brands:
Bacigalupi Chardonnay
Jericho Canyon Red
Library Wines
Oakville Estate Red

10964 **Rude Custom Butchering**
6194 W Pines Rd
Mt Morris, IL 61054-9755
815-946-3795
Fax: 815-946-2333
Meats
President: Kevin Rude
Estimated Sales: $10-20 000,000
Number Employees: 20-49

10965 **Rudi's Organic Bakery**
3300 Walnut St # C
Unit C
Boulder, CO 80301-2529
303-447-0495
Fax: 303-447-0516 877-293-0876
www.rudisbakery.com
Fresh and frozen certified organic baked bread, buns, english muffins, bagels, and soft pretzels.
CEO: Jane Miller
aartzer@charterbaking.com
CFO: Mile Aufiero
Senior Marketing Manager: Maggie Garner
VP Sales: Tom Nash
Director Human Resources: Connie Dietsch
Site Manager: Andy Artzer
Purchasing Manager: Suzie Murphy
Estimated Sales: $20.7 Million
Number Employees: 50-99
Square Footage: 40000
Parent Co: Charter Baking Co.
Type of Packaging: Consumer, Food Service, Bulk
Brands:
Certified Organic Breads
Certified Organic Buns
Certified Organic Rolls

10966 **(HQ)Rudolph Foods Co**
6575 Bellefontaine Rd
Lima, OH 45804
419-648-3611
www.rudolphfoods.com
Manufacturer and exporter of pork rinds and related snacks
President: Richard Rudolph
VP, Sales & Marketing: Mark Singleton
Year Founded: 1955
Estimated Sales: $50 Million
Number Employees: 400
Number of Brands: 4
Square Footage: 110000
Type of Packaging: Consumer, Private Label, Bulk
Brands:
Grandpa John's
Pepe's
Rudolph's
Southern Recipe

10967 **Rudolph's Market & Sausage**
2924 Elm St
Dallas, TX 75226-1509
214-741-1874
Fax: 214-761-2017 www.rudolphsmeatmarket.com
Smoked meats and sausage
President: Justine M Andreason
Estimated Sales: $5-10 Million
Number Employees: 10-19
Type of Packaging: Consumer

10968 **Rudolph's Specialty Bakery**
390 Alliance Avenue
Toronto, ON M6N 2H8
Canada
416-763-4315
Fax: 416-763-4317 800-268-1589
www.rudolphsbakeries.com
Processor and exporter of rye and flat breads, tortillas and flan cakes
President: George Paech
Type of Packaging: Consumer, Food Service, Private Label

Brands:
Casa Jorge
Masala Roti
Roti & Chapati
Rudolph's
Taj Mahal
Wwrapps

10969 **Rudy's Tortillas**
2115 E Belt Line Rd.
Carrollton, TX 75006
214-634-7839
Fax: 214-638-5317 800-878-2401
www.rudystortillas.com
Tortillas, chalupas, tostadas, tacos, flavored wraps, shells and blue, red, yellow and white chips
President: Nansi Acevedo
nacevedo@rudystortillas.com
CEO: Louis Guerra
Vice President: Joe Guerra
Estimated Sales: $30 Million
Number Employees: 250-499
Brands:
Rudy's Tortillas

10970 **Ruef's Meat Market**
538 1st St
PO Box 251
New Glarus, WI 53574-8908
608-527-2554
bruef@charter.net
www.ruefsmeatmarket.com
Smoked meats and cheese
Owner: Willy Ruef
bruef@charter.net
CEO: Annette Ruef
Estimated Sales: Less than $300,000
Number Employees: 1-4
Type of Packaging: Consumer, Food Service, Bulk
Brands:
Ruef's Meat Market

10971 **Ruffner's**
704 W Lancaster Ave
Wayne, PA 19087-2515
610-687-9800
Fax: 610-687-9800 hhtp://www.supercuts.com
Cocktail drink mixes, green tomato salsa
Manager: Steve Costa
Estimated Sales: $300,000-500,000
Number Employees: 1-4
Brands:
Supercuts

10972 **Rufus Teague**
13410 W 73rd St
Shawnee, KS 66216-4182
913-706-3814
Fax: 913-562-9980 www.rufusteague.com
BBQ sauce, grilling sauce, rubs, spices
Owner: John McCone
Contact: Tony Munson
tony@rufusteague.com
Estimated Sales: 500,000
Number Employees: 10-19

10973 **Ruger LLC**
Bethesda, MD 20814
301-675-2398
www.rugerwafers.com
Manufacturer of wafers and wrapped candies.
Founder: Amir Frydman

10974 **Ruggiero Seafood**
474 Wilson Ave
Po Box 5369
Newark, NJ 07105-4833
973-344-2282
Fax: 973-589-5690 866-225-2627
info@ruggieroseafood.com
www.ruggieroseafood.com
Processor, importer and exporter of fresh, frozen and breaded calamari and calamari entrees
President: Rocco Ruggiero
rocco@ruggieroseafood.com
Controller: Connie Dasaliva
Vice President: Frank Ruggiero
Sales Manager: Steve Clemente
Manager Operations: Anthon Trimarche
Plant Manager: Marcos Fontana
Estimated Sales: $387,000
Number Employees: 20-49
Square Footage: 100000
Type of Packaging: Consumer, Food Service, Bulk

Brands:
Atlantic Coast
Fisherman's Pride
Fruit of the Sea
Northwind
Ocean Tide

10975 **(HQ)Ruiz Flour Tortillas**
1200 Marlborough Ave
Riverside, CA 92507
909-947-7811
Fax: 909-947-2338 info@ruizflourtortillas.com
www.ruizflourtortillas.com
Traditional and specialty, ethnic and gourmet flour tortillas serving food manufacturers, foodservice industry, restaurant distributors, retail food brokers, and specialty retail outlets
Founder: Edward Ruiz
CFO: Uriel Maciaf
Vice President: Vickie Salgado
R&D: David Rodriguez
Manager: Maria Lopez
Contact: Oscar Figari
oscarfigari@ruizflourtortillas.com
Purchasing: Carmen Sandoval
Type of Packaging: Food Service, Private Label, Bulk

10976 **(HQ)Ruiz Food Products Inc.**
501 S. Alta Ave.
PO Box 37
Dinuba, CA 93618
800-477-6474
contactus@ruizfoods.com www.ruizfoods.com
Frozen Mexican foods including burritos, enchiladas, tamales, soft tacos, chili rellenos, flautas and taquitos.
President/CEO: Rachel Cullen
Senior VP/CFO: John Landis
Year Founded: 1964
Estimated Sales: $276.2 Million
Number Employees: 3,500+
Number of Brands: 4
Square Footage: 200000
Type of Packaging: Consumer, Food Service, Private Label, Bulk
Brands:
El Monterey
Tornados
Artisan Bistro
Three Bold Brothers

10977 **Rule Breaker**
291 Union ST
Suite Phb
Brooklyn, NY 11231-4477
646-820-8074
Fax: 718-228-8455 hello@rulebreakersnacks.com
www.rulebreakersnacks.com
Bean-based brownies
Founder & CEO: Nancy Kalish
Finance Director: Cassie Abrams
Director, Marketing & Regional Sales: Brittany Barton
Field Sales Manager: Tracy McKinney
Social Media Manager: Erin Smith
Operations Director: Dawn Techow
Number Employees: 2-10
Brands:
Rule Breaker

10978 **Rumi Spice**
1400 W 46th St
Chicago, IL 60609-3212
213-447-6112
info@rumispice.com
www.rumispice.com
Saffron and spice blends
Co-Founder: Emily Miller
Director of New Product Development: Laura Willis
Year Founded: 2014
Estimated Sales: $500,000-$1,000,000
Number Employees: 2-10
Brands:
RUMI SPICE

10979 **Rumiano Cheese Co.**
511 9th St
Crescent City, CA 95531-3408
707-465-1535
Fax: 707-465-4141 866-328-2433
www.rumianocheese.com
Cheese manufacturer

President: Baird Rumiano
joby@rumianocheese.com
Logistics: Gary Smits
Production & Markering: Joby Rumiano
Office Manager: Tana Bachmann
Chief Operating Officer: Kirk Olsen
Production Manager: Enrique Leal
Lab Technician: Juan Pablo Gonzalez
Estimated Sales: $12 Million
Number Employees: 20-49
Number of Brands: 1
Square Footage: 16000
Type of Packaging: Consumer, Food Service
Other Locations:
Distribution & Packaging
East Williows CA
Brands:
Rumiano

10980 **Rumiano Cheese Factory**
1629 County Road E
Willows, CA 95988-9642
530-934-5438
Fax: 530-934-5114 866-328-2433
www.rumianocheese.com
Cheese manufacturer specializing in Dry Montery Jack and Peppato; products are kosher and non-GMO certified. Provides slicing, packaging and labelling services.
President: Baird Rumiano
Cmo: Bill Rhinehart
bill@rumianocheese.com
Chief of Finances: Tony Rumiano
Vice President: John Rumiano
Sales & Purchasing: Bill Rinehart
Sales: Richard Moore
Human Resources: Georgia Cruz
Customer Relations: Cathy Thidsouvanh
Cut & Wrap Manager: John Permann
Purchasing: Holly Myers
Estimated Sales: $12 Million
Number Employees: 100-249
Parent Co: Rumiano Cheese Company
Type of Packaging: Consumer, Food Service, Private Label

10981 **(HQ)Run-A-Ton Group Inc**
401 State Route 24 # 2
Suite 2
Chester, NJ 07930-2923
908-879-0880
Fax: 973-984-2424 800-247-6580
www.whollywholesome.com
Conventional and natural baked goods
President: Doon Wintz
CEO/Chairman: Robert Wintz
CFO: Linda Hendricks
Vice President: Lynn Nelson
Director Sales Development/Marketing: Janeen Ortega
Estimated Sales: $10-20 Million
Number Employees: 10-19
Number of Brands: 5
Number of Products: 1000
Square Footage: 10000
Type of Packaging: Consumer, Food Service, Private Label
Brands:
Apple Valley Inn
Buttery Baker
Simple Elegance
Wholly Wholesome
Outrageoulsy Decadent Cookies
Unique Belgique
Patrina's Bake House

10982 **Runamok Maple**
293 Fletcher Dr
Fairfax, VT 05454
802-849-7943
info@runamokmaple.com
runamokmaple.com
Maple syrup
Co-Owner: Eric Sorkin
Co-Owner: Laura Sorkin
Operations Manager: Dean Parent
Brands:
Runamok

10983 **(HQ)Runk Candy Company**
5141 Fischer Place
Cincinnati, OH 45217
513-641-2345
Fax: 513-641-2557 800-641-8551
sales@runkcandy.com www.runkcandy.com
Marshmallow-filled ice cream cones and specialty candies
President: Dan Runk
Vice President: Pamela Arbino
Estimated Sales: $5-9.9 Million
Number Employees: 20-49
Brands:
Marpro

10984 **Rural Route 1 Popcorn Co**
105 E Tama St
Livingston, WI 53554-9537
608-943-8283
Fax: 608-943-8283 800-828-8115
www.prpopcornstore.com
Popcorn
President: Bradley Biddick
Marketing Director: Nick Solomon
nicks@ruralroute1.com
CFO: Bradley Biddick
Estimated Sales: Below $5 Million
Number Employees: 20-49
Brands:
Almonds
Creamy Medley of Popcorn
Ivory Almond K'Nuckle

10985 **Rus Dun Farms Inc**
2295 Highway 57
Collierville, TN 38017-5329
901-853-0931
Fax: 901-853-0387 www.lakesofgreenbrier.com
Eggs
Owner: Mike Russell
Estimated Sales: Less Than $500,000
Number Employees: 1-4

10986 **Ruskin Redneck Trading Company**
1203 1st Street SW
Ruskin, FL 33570-5345
813-645-7710
Fax: 813-641-1979
Sauces
President: Sandra Council
Estimated Sales: $240,000
Number Employees: 2

10987 **Russ & Daughters**
179 E Houston St # 1
New York, NY 10002-1024
212-475-4880
Fax: 212-475-0345 800-787-7229
info@russanddaughters.com
www.russanddaughters.com
Smoked fish, caviar and specialty foods
Owner: Mark Federman
info@russanddaughters.com
Estimated Sales: Less than $500,000
Number Employees: 10-19

10988 **Russell & Kohne Inc**
149 Riverside Ave # B
Suite B
Newport Beach, CA 92663-4067
949-645-8441
Baked goods and breads.
Owner: Paul Kohne
Estimated Sales: $2.04 Million
Number Employees: 20-49

10989 **Russell Breweries, Inc.**
202-13018 80th Avenue
Surrey, BC V3W 2B2
Canada
604-599-1190
Fax: 604-599-1048 cheers@russellbeer.com
www.russellbeer.com
Ale
President/COO: Andrew Harris
CEO: Brian Harris
Number Employees: 1-4
Type of Packaging: Consumer, Food Service
Brands:
Russell Cream Ale
Russell Honey Blonde Ale
Russell Lemon Wheat Ale
Russell Oager
Russell Pale Ale
Russell Winter Ale

10990 **Russell E. Womack, Inc.**
P.O. Box 3967
Lubbock, TX 79452
806-747-2581
Fax: 806-747-2583 877-787-3559
rewi@casserolebean.com www.casserolebean.com
Dry pinto beans packed in poly and burlap sacks
Owner: Mike Byrne
Product Management/Quality Control: Mike Bryne
Director of Sales: Richard Byrne
Consumer Affairs: Walter James
warehouse Manager: Albert Rodriguez
Estimated Sales: $3800000
Number Employees: 20-49
Number of Brands: 1
Number of Products: 1
Square Footage: 144000
Type of Packaging: Consumer, Food Service

10991 **Russell Stover Candies Inc.**
4900 Oak St.
Kansas City, MO 64112-2702
800-777-4004
customerservice@russellstover.com
www.russellstover.com
Chocolate candy.
CEO: Andrew Deister
CFO: Dick Masinton
Year Founded: 1923
Estimated Sales: $600 Million
Number Employees: 5000-9999
Parent Co: Lindt & Sprungli
Type of Packaging: Consumer
Brands:
Russell Stovers
Whitman's
Pangburn's

10992 **Russian Chef**
40 E 69th St
New York, NY 10021-5016
212-249-1550
Fax: 212-249-5451
Processor and packer of fresh and pasteurized kosher caviar including domestic salmon, whitefish, sturgeon, paddlefish, hackleback and lumpfish; also, Scottish smoked salmon, tuna and smoked trout; importer of caviar
President: Simon Kublanov
Vice President: Lenny Kuvykin
Estimated Sales: $1-3 Million
Number Employees: 5-9
Square Footage: 27000
Type of Packaging: Consumer, Food Service
Brands:
Ivan the Terrible
Poriloff
Purepak
Russian Chef's

10993 **Russo Farms**
1962 S East Ave
Vineland, NJ 08360-7198
856-692-5942
Fax: 856-692-8534 www.russofarms.com
Fruits and vegetables including green onions, cabbage, peppers, eggplant, cucumbers, leafy greens, etc
President: Damian Russo
Estimated Sales: $12046688
Number Employees: 20-49
Type of Packaging: Consumer
Brands:
Pat's Best

10994 **Russo's Seafood**
201 E 40th St
Savannah, GA 31401-9120
912-234-5196
Fax: 912-234-5703 866-234-5196
www.russoseafood.com
Seafood
Manager: Nolan Mell
Manager: Bryan Gray
bcgray35@aol.com
Estimated Sales: $3-5 Million
Number Employees: 10-19

10995 **Rustic Bakery Inc.**
4324 Redwood Hwy
San Rafael, CA 94903-2103
415-479-5600
Fax: 415-479-5700 www.rusticbakery.com

Baked goods: cereal, cheese coins, cookies, flatbread
Vice President Of Sales: Scott Frank
scott@rusticbakery.com

10996 Rustic Crust Inc
31 Barnstead Rd
Pittsfield, NH 03263-3101
603-435-5119
info@rusticcrust.com
www.rusticcrust.com
All natural and organic ready-made pizza crusts, pizza sauce, and ciabatta flatbread.
Founder/President: Brad Sterl
Process and Quality Manager: Lynn Karam
Sales/Marketing Coordinator: Kathleen Carroll
VP Sales: Alan Witcher
Contact: Tammy Blinn
tblinn@rusticcrust.com
Estimated Sales: $8 Million
Number Employees: 10-19
Square Footage: 4699
Type of Packaging: Consumer

10997 Ruth Ashbrook Bakery
6445 NE Martin Luther King Jr Blvd
Portland, OR 97211-3031
503-240-7437
Fax: 503-289-7264
Snack cakes, pies, doughnuts and other goods
President: Gerald Martinson
Estimated Sales: $250,000
Number Employees: 4

10998 (HQ)Ruth Hunt Candy Co
550 Maysville Rd
Mt Sterling, KY 40353
859-498-0676
800-927-0302
Info@Ruthhuntcandy.com
www.ruthhuntcandy.com
Confectionary products including pulled cream candy, bourbon balls, caramels, assorted soft creams, and sugar free chocolates.
President: Larry Kezele
larry@ruthhuntcandy.com
Estimated Sales: $790000
Number Employees: 10-19
Number of Products: 70
Square Footage: 18000
Parent Co: Kezele Corporation
Type of Packaging: Consumer
Brands:
Blue Monday
Woodford Reserve

10999 Rutherford Hill Winery
200 Rutherford Hill Rd
Rutherford, CA 94573
707-963-1871
Fax: 707-963-1878 info@rutherfordhill.com
www.rutherfordhill.com
Wines
President: Anthony Terlato
VP: Willis Blakewell
Estimated Sales: $4500000
Number Employees: 20-49

11000 Rutter's Dairy
2100 N George St
York, PA 17404-1898
717-848-9827
Fax: 717-845-8751 800-840-1664
www.rutters.com
Milk and dairy products
President: Todd Rutter
CFO: Tom Jonson
Treasurer: Stewart Hartman
CEO: Scott Hartman
VP: Rey Sendy
Operations Manager: Todd Rutter
Plant Manager: Brett Garner
Number Employees: 500-999
Type of Packaging: Private Label
Brands:
Rutter's

11001 Rv Industries
1665 Heraeus Boulevard
Buford, GA 30518
770-729-8983
Fax: 770-729-9428 sales@rvindustries.com
www.rvindustries.com
Processor, importer and exporter of desiccated, sweetened and toasted coconut, coconut milk powder, aseptic coconut milk and water
President: Andres E Siochi
General Manager: Bob Weschrek
CFO: Bharat Shah
Sales: Robert Santiago
Production Manager: Guillermo Pineiro
Estimated Sales: $14,000,000
Number Employees: 20-49
Square Footage: 120000
Parent Co: RV Industries
Type of Packaging: Consumer, Food Service, Private Label, Bulk
Brands:
Fiesta
Red V
Tropical

11002 Ryals Bakery
135 S Wayne St
Milledgeville, GA 31061-3439
478-452-0321
www.ryalsbakery.dinehere.us
Breads, rolls, cakes
Owner: Jacob Ryals
Estimated Sales: Less Than $500,000
Number Employees: 5-9
Brands:
Ryals Bakery

11003 Rye Fresh
147 Ethel Road West
Piscataway, NJ 08854
732-855-0008
Fax: 732-855-9436 office@mycupful.com
mycupful.com
Milk
President & CEO: Marek Pyrycz
Brands:
Cupful

11004 Rygmyr Foods
1030 County Road EW
Suite 100
South Saint Paul, MN 55126-8153
612-292-8777
800-545-3903
Molded popcorn novelties
President: Paul Lattate
Estimated Sales: $10-20 Million
Number Employees: 30
Square Footage: 26000
Type of Packaging: Consumer, Private Label
Brands:
Bumpy & Jumpy
Cutie Cupid
Itchy Witchy
Rookie Spookie
Santa Pop

11005 Ryke's Bakery
1788 Terrace St # 1
Muskegon, MI 49442-5699
231-726-2253
Fax: 231-728-2162 info@rykes.com
www.rykes.com
Cakes, cookies, pies, breads and pastries
President: Renee Rouwhorst
Co-Owner: Butch Rouwhorst
Estimated Sales: $720,000
Number Employees: 20-49
Square Footage: 24000
Type of Packaging: Consumer

11006 Rymer Foods
4600 S Packers Avenue
Suite 400
Chicago, IL 60609-3338
773-254-7530
Fax: 773-927-7278 800-247-9637
Hamburgers, steaks, pot roast and meat loaf; also, frozen chicken
CEO: P Edward Schenk
President: Edward Hebert
Marketing Director: John Bormann
Operations Manager: Jose Muguerza
Number Employees: 10-19
Type of Packaging: Food Service

11007 Rymer Seafood
125 S Wacker Drive
Chicago, IL 60606-4424
312-236-3266
Fax: 312-236-4169
Seafood
President: Mark Bailin
Estimated Sales: $.5-1 million
Number Employees: 1-4

11008 S & D Coffee Inc
300 Concord Pkwy S
Concord, NC 28027-6702
704-782-3121
Fax: 800-950-4378 800-933-2210
www.sndcoffee.com
S&D is a coffee, tea and extracts supplier to the foodservice industry.
Chairman, President & CEO: Ron Hinson
hinsonr@sndcoffee.com
Number Employees: 1000-4999
Type of Packaging: Food Service, Private Label

11009 S & E Organic Farms Inc
1716 Oak St # 4
Bakersfield, CA 93301-3040
661-325-2644
Fax: 661-325-2602 seorganic@aol.com
Grower of organic vegetables, dry beans, grains and alfalfa; processor of frozen purees
President: Ed Davis
CEO: Shelley Davis
Manager: Cali Cheek
Estimated Sales: $500,000-$1 Million
Number Employees: 10-19
Type of Packaging: Bulk

11010 S & L Produce Inc
601 Medlin Rd
Walnut Hill, IL 62893
618-532-8344
Fax: 618 533 0378 www.slproduce.com
Produce
President: Mark Palazzolo
markslproduce@hughes.net
Estimated Sales: $1.5 Million
Number Employees: 5-9
Square Footage: 6000
Type of Packaging: Consumer, Food Service, Bulk

11011 S & M Communion Bread Co
829 Gale Ln
Nashville, TN 37204-3011
615-292-1969
Fax: 877-762-7323 www.buycommunion.com
Communion bread
President: Barbara Reynolds
drmom6278@aol.com
Estimated Sales: $3-5 Million
Number Employees: 10-19
Type of Packaging: Consumer
Brands:
S&M

11012 S & M Fisheries Inc
1272 Portland Rd US Route 1
Kennebunkport, ME 4046
207-985-3456
Fax: 207-985-3038 www.thelobsterco.com
Wholesale distributor of shellfish
President: Stephanie Nadeau
dcowan@lobsters.org
Office Manager: Josh Smail
Vice President, Operational VP: Michael Marceau
Estimated Sales: $2.3 Million
Number Employees: 10-19

11013 S A Carlson Inc
160 Camfield Rd
Yakima, WA 98908-9684
509-965-8333
Fax: 509-965-8311 sherm@sacarlson.com
www.sacarlson.com
Processed fruit ingredients including apple, pear, peach, grapes, berry fruits, etc.
President: Sherman Carlson
russell@sacarlson.com
Customer Service: Ruffell Carlson
Vice President: Russell Carlson
Sales: Russell Carlson
Estimated Sales: $5-10 Million
Number Employees: 1-4
Square Footage: 500000
Type of Packaging: Food Service, Bulk

Brands:
Invertec
Tastee

11014 **S A L T Sisters**
2124 W Wilden Ave
Building B
Goshen, IN 46528-1146
574-971-8368
Fax: 800-950-3205
Manufacturer of sugar, salt, dips, and other all-natural flavors.
Founder and CEO: Charmane Skillen
Number Employees: 5-9

11015 **S B Global Foods Inc**
1330 N Broad St # 1
PO Box 1322
Lansdale, PA 19446-1143
215-361-9500
Fax: 215-361-9323 877-857-1727
info@sbglobalfoods.com www.sbglobalfoods.com
Seasoned filled pretzel nuggets, chocolate covered peanut butter filled pretzel nuggets, and mini marshmellows.
President: Karl Brown
kbrown@sbglobalfoods.com
Estimated Sales: Below $5 Million
Number Employees: 5-9
Type of Packaging: Private Label
Brands:
American Cookie Boy
Pretzel Pete
Rocky Mountain Marshmallows
Rocky Mountain Popcorn

11016 **S P Enterprises**
1889 E Maule Ave # E
Las Vegas, NV 89119-4603
702-736-4774
Fax: 702-736-6180 800-746-4774
spcandy@msn.com www.espeezcandy.com
Candy
Owner: Sam Popowcer
spcandy@msn.com
CEO: Alan Popowcer
Estimated Sales: $3-5 Million
Number Employees: 5-9
Brands:
Lillipos
Money Candy

11017 **S S Lobster LTD**
691 River St
Fitchburg, MA 01420-2910
978-342-6135
Fax: 978-345-7341
Seafood (lobster, clams, shrimp)
President: Mark Strazdas
Estimated Sales: $10-20 Million
Number Employees: 20-49

11018 **(HQ)S S Steiner Inc**
655 Madison Ave # 1700
New York, NY 10065-8078
212-838-8901
Fax: 212-593-4238 sales@hopsteiner.com
www.hopsteiner.com
Processor, importer and exporter of hops extracts, pellets and oils.
President/COO: Louis Gimbel
VP of Sales: Mike Sutton
Estimated Sales: $20-50 Million
Number Employees: 10-19
Number of Brands: 1
Type of Packaging: Food Service
Other Locations:
Salem OR
Yakima WA
Brands:
Hopsteiner

11019 **S T Specialty Foods Inc**
8700 Xylon Ave N
Brooklyn Park, MN 55445-1817
763-493-9600
Fax: 763-493-9606
contactus@stspecialtyfoods.com
www.stspecialtyfoods.com
Manufacturer of dry pasta products including macaroni & cheese dinners, microwavable pasta dishes, boxed pasta side dishes, rice & vermicelli mixes and pasta salads
President/CEO: Dale Schulz
dschulz@stspecialtyfoods.com
VP of Quality, Research & Development: Mark Welken
Senior Vice President Sales & Marketing: Kevin Kollock
Vice President of Operations: Steve Favro
Estimated Sales: $14.8 Million
Number Employees: 50-99
Parent Co: TreeHouse Foods, Inc.
Type of Packaging: Consumer, Private Label
Other Locations:
S.T. Specialty Foods
Kenosha WI

11020 **S Zitner Co**
3120 N 17th St
Philadelphia, PA 19132-2357
215-229-9828
Fax: 215-229-9828 www.zitners.com
Confectionery products including caramel coated apples and Easter candy
Owner: Mc Murphy
mmurphy@szitnerco.com
Estimated Sales: $10-20 Million
Number Employees: 20-49
Square Footage: 300000
Type of Packaging: Consumer

11021 **S&B International Corporation**
2815 Dalemead St
Torrance, CA 90505-7039
310-257-0177
Fax: 310-543-2168
Seasonings
President: Richard Jones
Estimated Sales: $5-10 000,000
Number Employees: 1-4

11022 **S&D Bait Company**
PO Box 3525
Morgan City, LA 70381-3525
504-252-3500
Fax: 504-385-5412
Live bait

11023 **S&N Food Company**
1321 Woodthorpe Drive
Mesquite, TX 75181-3519
972-222-1184
Fax: 972-222-1184 sweetpotatodesserts@msn.com
Dessert mixes such as sweet potato pie, sweet potato muffins, sweet potato brownies, chocolate brownies, coffee & chocolate, pumpkin pie, pumpkin brownies, lemon pound cake, chocolate muffin & bread mix, chocolate pound cake, lemonsupreme muffin & bread mix, pumpkin pound cake, pumpkin pancake & waffle mix, sweet potato pound cake, sweet potato pancake & waffle mix, and spiced cider mix.
President: Shirley Peters
Estimated Sales: Below $500,000
Number Employees: 2
Type of Packaging: Consumer, Private Label
Brands:
Shirley's

11024 **S&P Marketing, Inc.**
11100 86th Ave
Maple Grove, MN 55369
763-559-0436
Fax: 763-557-1318
Fruit ingredients including tropical and temperate fruit juices, purees, dried fruits, powders and more. Niche products include tamarind, coconut cream, alphonso mango puree, prickly pear juice, puree, powder, fiber and oil.
President: Chareonsri Srisangnam
Marketing/R&D: Vinod Padhye
om@snpmarketing.com
Contact: Om Padhye
om@snpmarketing.com
Type of Packaging: Food Service, Bulk

11025 **S. Wallace Edward & Sons**
PO Box 25
Surry, VA 23883-0025
800-290-9213
Fax: 757-294-5378 800-222-4267
www.virginiatraditions.com
Virginia hams, sweet hams, bacon & sausage, soups & stews, specialty meats, desserts, poultry, snacks, seafood
President: Sammuel Edwards
carla@edwardsvaham.com
CEO: Wallace Edwards
Vice President: Amy Edwards Harte
Sales Director: Bob Unterbrink
Contact: Carla Drewry
carla@edwardsvaham.com
Operations Manager: Al Kadons
Number Employees: 22
Number of Brands: 2
Type of Packaging: Consumer
Brands:
Colonial Williamsburg
Edwards
Surry

11026 **S.A.S. Foods**
3005 Center Pl
Suite 200
Norcross, GA 30093
770-263-9312
Fax: 770-446-9234
Oriental grocery items, seafood, fin fish, shellfish
President: Goro Iwami
Estimated Sales: $5-10 Million
Number Employees: 5-9

11027 **S.D. Mushrooms**
P.O.Box 687
Avondale, PA 19311-0687
610-268-8082
Fax: 610-268-8644
Processor and importer of mushrooms and mushroom sauce
President/Owner: John D'Amico
Estimated Sales: $450,000
Number Employees: 1-4
Type of Packaging: Consumer, Food Service, Private Label, Bulk

11028 **S.L. Kaye Company**
230 5th Ave
New York, NY 10001-7704
212-683-5600
Fax: 212-947-7664 kaye230@aol.com
www.slkaye.com
Candy
President/Owner: Mitchell Katzman
Sales Manager: S Handy
Estimated Sales: $1-2.5 Million
Number Employees: 1-4
Brands:
Eskimo Pie Coffeepeaks
Eskimo Pie Miniatures
Eskimo Pie Snowpeaks
Needlers Jersey English Toffee
Titanic Esm Mints

11029 **S.T. Jerrell Company**
802 Labarge Dr
Bessemer, AL 35022
205-426-8930
Fax: 205-426-8989 www.jerrellpackaging.com
Non-fat dry milk
CEO: John Lyon
Vice President: Barry Cornell
Estimated Sales: Below $5 Million
Number Employees: 10-19
Square Footage: 100000
Type of Packaging: Food Service, Private Label, Bulk
Brands:
Cloverleaf Farms Peanut Butter
S. T. Jerrell Nonfat

11030 **S.W. Meat & Provision Company**
2019 N 48th St
Phoenix, AZ 85008-3303
602-275-2000
Sausage, ground beef and patties, portion cut steaks and aged beef sides
President: W David Hart
Estimated Sales: $1-2.5 Million
Number Employees: 5-9
Type of Packaging: Food Service

11031 **(HQ)SADKHIN Complex**
2306 Avenue U
Brooklyn, NY 11229-4917
718-769-7771
Fax: 718-769-8087 800-723-5446
NYOffice@sadkhin.com
Seasonal herbal formulas and multi-vitamins

Owner: Daniel Radinsky
daniel@sadkhin.com
Estimated Sales: Less Than $500,000
Number Employees: 1-4
Square Footage: 8800
Type of Packaging: Consumer
Other Locations:
Los Angeles CA
San Francisco CA
Boston MA
Philadelphia PA
Detroit MI
Brands:
The Sadkhin Complex(r)

11032 SANGARIA USA
3142 Pacific Coast Hwy
Suite 208
Torrance, CA 90505-6796
310-530-2202
Fax: 310-530-5335 sangaria@msn.com
www.sangariausa.com
Manufacturer, importer and exporter of soft drinks: Ramune drink, green tea, oolong tea, iced coffee, energy drink, fruit juices, etc
Owner: Leona Singer
Estimated Sales: $300,000-500,000
Number Employees: 1-4
Square Footage: 500000
Parent Co: Japan Sangaria Beverage Company
Type of Packaging: Consumer, Food Service
Brands:
Sangaria

11033 SAPNA Foods
1154 Oakleigh Drive
Atlanta, GA 30344
404-589-0977
Fax: 404-589-9711 info@sapnafoods.com
www.sapnafoods.com
Beans, chocolate, dried chilies and fruits, mushrooms, extracts and flavors, puree, nuts and seeds, teas, ginger, oils, saffron, spices and herbs.
President & CEO: Rishi A. Nagrani
rishi@sapnafoods.com
Vice President, Business Development: Jack Dahlheimer
Sales Representative: Evan Sowers
Director of Operations: William Sowers
Director of Purchasing: Neil Renfroe
Year Founded: 1997
Estimated Sales: $20 Million
Number Employees: 11-50
Type of Packaging: Food Service
Brands:
SAPNA Foods

11034 SASIB Biscuits and Snacks Division
118 W Streetsboro Street
Suite 306
Hudson, OH 44236-2711
330-656-3317
Fax: 330-656-2822
Baked goods, biscuits, snacks

11035 SBK Preserves
1161 East 156th Street
Bronx, NY 10474-6226
718-589-2900
Fax: 718-589-8412 800-773-7378
info@sarabeth.com www.sarabeth.com
Processor and exporter of jams, preserves, fruit spreads, syrups and granola cereal
President: Charlie Apt
Finance Executive: Carlos Blanco
VP: Suzanne Levine
Estimated Sales: D
Number Employees: 10-19
Square Footage: 30000
Parent Co: Sarabeth's Kitchen
Other Locations:
SBK Preserves
New York NY
Brands:
Sarabeth's

11036 SBS Americas
616 Corporate Way
Suite 2-5615
Valley Cottage, NY 10989
844-727-0827
Fax: 845-503-2379 www.bee-and-you.com
Honey, royal jelly and propolis
Food Production: Mustafa Bayraktar
Brands:
Bee & You

11037 SC Enterprises
RR 5
Owen Sound, ON N4K 5N7
Canada
519-371-0456
Fax: 519-371-5944
Fresh and frozen fish and wild game and rainbow trout.
Manager: Winston Jones
Number Employees: 10-19
Square Footage: 36000

11038 SD Watersboten
119 Millcreek Rd
Ardmore, PA 19003
610-645-7572
contact@sdwatersboten.com
www.sdwatersboten.com
Mineral waters
President & CEO: Denise Shamro
Estimated Sales: Under $500,000
Number Employees: 1-4
Type of Packaging: Private Label
Brands:
WATERSBOTEN

11039 SEW Friel
100 Friels Pl
PO Box 10
Queenstown, MD 21658-1674
410-827-8841
Fax: 410-827-9472 www.sewfriel.com
Processor, importer and exporter of canned corn.
President: Michael Foster
Number Employees: 20-49
Type of Packaging: Consumer, Food Service, Private Label, Bulk
Brands:
Friel's
Hudson
Ole Wye

11040 SFP Food Products
348 Highway 64 E
Conway, AR 72032-9414
501-327-0744
Fax: 501-327-2808 800-654-5329
jballard@sfpfoods.com www.sfpfoods.com
Processor and exporter of waffle, pancake and cone mixes; manufacturer and exporter of waffle and cone irons
President: Jon Ballard
VP Marketing/Sales: Jon Ballard
VP Operations: Ray Ballard
Estimated Sales: $3-5 Million
Number Employees: 5-9
Square Footage: 60000
Type of Packaging: Food Service, Private Label

11041 SIGCO Sun Products
227 6th St N
Breckenridge, MN 56520
218-643-8467
Fax: 218-643-4555 800-654-4145
www.sunopta.com
Sunflower oil
Sales Manager: Nancy Nelson
Plant Manager: John Bontjes

11042 SJH Enterprises
2415 Parview Rd Ste 4
Middleton, WI 53562
608-831-3001
Fax: 608-831-3001 888-745-3845
Broker of organic grains and natural colors and flavors
Manager: Hank Zimmerman
Estimated Sales: $170,000
Number Employees: 1-4
Type of Packaging: Consumer, Food Service, Private Label, Bulk

11043 SJR Foods
49 Brook Street
New Bedford, MA 02746-1742
617-500-4516
Fax: 781-821-5666 info@sjrfoods.com
www.sjrfoods.com
Cream cheese filled bagels including plain, cinnamon raisin, sesame, poppy and onion
Owner: Larry Barras
Brands:
Unholey Bagel

11044 SKW Nature Products
2021 Cabot Boulevard W
Langhorne, PA 19047-1810
215-702-1000
Fax: 215-702-1015
Cultures, enzymes, edible and industrial gelatins, hydrocolloids, flavors, fragrance raw materials and fruit systems
VP/General Manager: Kenneth Hughes
VP/General Manager: George Masson
Number Employees: 500-999
Parent Co: SKW

11045 SKW Nature Products
2350 Kerper Blvd
Dubuque, IA 52001
563-588-6244
Fax: 563-588-9063 info@degussa.com
www.degussa.com
Enzymes and flavor ingredients for food, beverage, dairy and specialties industries
Head Corporate Communications: Ralph Driever
Press Relations Officer: Hannelore Gantzer
Internal Communications: Markus Langer
Sales Manager: Jorge Martinez
Number Employees: 100-249

11046 SLT Group
303 Ridge Rd
Dayton, NJ 08810
732-837-3096
www.sltgroup.com
Basmati rice, lentils, beans, flour & spice
CEO: Sandip Patel
Estimated Sales: $38.9 Million
Number Employees: 9
Brands:
Heritage Select Brand

11047 SONOCO
5450 W Main St
Houma, LA 70360-1282
985-851-0727
Fax: 985-872-2251 800-458-7012
www.sontheimeroffshore.com
Provide offshore catering for people on drilling rigs.
President: Kent Sontheimer
Vice President, Finance: Pam Toups
Safety Director: David Soileau
Vice President, Sales: Juan Cosenza
Personnel Manager: Al Robinson
Vice President, Operations: Mark Hepburn
Number Employees: 250-499

11048 SOPAKCO Foods
215 S Mullins St
Mullins, SC 29574-3207
843-464-0121
Fax: 423-639-7270 800-276-9678
www.sopakco.com
Pasta sauces; also, retortable pouch manufacturer, canner and contract packager of poultry, meat, fish, pasta, vegetable, bean, fruit and dessert products, flexible, semi-rigid and glass containers
CEO: Al Reitzer
CFO: Steve Keight
R&D: Jim Dukes
Quality Control: Phyllis Calhoun
General Manager: Wynn Pettibone
Plant Manager: Carl Whitmore
Purchasing Director: Beverly Stacey
Estimated Sales: $5-10 Million
Number Employees: 100
Square Footage: 400000
Parent Co: Unaka Corporation
Type of Packaging: Consumer, Food Service, Private Label

11049 SOPAKCO Packaging
118 S Cypress St
Mullins, SC 29574-3004
843-464-7851
Fax: 843-464-2096 www.sopakco.com
Sure pak emergency meals
President: Lonnie Thompson
VP: Bill McCreary
Plant Manager: Vera Hahn
Purchasing Manager: Stewart Clark
Estimated Sales: $20-50 Million
Number Employees: 250-499
Parent Co: Sopacko

Type of Packaging: Consumer, Food Service, Private Label
Brands:
Sopakco

11050 **SOUPerior Bean & Spice Company**
3801 NE 109th Ave
Suite C
Vancouver, WA 98682-7779
360-882-4500
Fax: 360-882-1152 800-878-7687
soupbean@aol.com
Spice blends and mixes including bean soup, pasta salad, bread and broth
Owner: Paul Dendy
VP: Duane Rough Jr
Estimated Sales: $5-10 Million
Number Employees: 5-9
Square Footage: 11400
Brands:
Our Counrtry

11051 **SP Enterprises, Inc.**
1889 E Maule Ave
Suite E
Las Vegas, NV 89119
702-736-4774
Fax: 702-736-6180 800-746-4774
spcandy@msn.com www.espeezcandy.com
Kid's novelty candy
President: Sam Popowcer
Estimated Sales: $3-5 Million
Number Employees: 5-9
Brands:
Aunt Flo's Country Fudge
Espeez
Eye of the Dragon
Gold Mine Gum
Kid Wizard
Money Mints
Usa Mints
Viper
Viper Blast
Viper Gum
Viper Venom
Viper Vials

11052 **SPI West Port, Inc**
377 Swift Ave
South San Fancisco, CA 94080
info@alodrink.com
Aloe vera beverages
Brands:
Alo

11053 **SRA Foods**
1608 10th Ave N
Birmingham, AL 35203
205-323-7447
www.srafoods.com
Wholesale/distributor of meats to restaurants and grocery stores.
President: Anthony Anselmo
anthonya@srafoods.com
Estimated Sales: $50-100 Million
Number Employees: 50-99
Number of Brands: 14
Brands:
Cargill
Wayne Farms
Tyson
Peco
National Beef
Mountaire Fresh Young Chicken
Key Farms
Hormel Foods
Smithfield
Southeastern Meats
Creekstone Farms
Heartland
Michigan Turkey Producers
Kent Quality Foods

11054 **STE Michelle Wine Estates**
14111 NE 145th St
PO Box 1976
Woodinville, WA 98072-6981
425-488-1133
Fax: 425-415-3657 800-267-6793
info@ste-michelle.com www.smwe.com
Processor, exporter and importer of wines
President/CEO: Ted Baseler
CEO: Melissa Cable
melissa.cable@colsolarevineyards.com
EVP/CFO: Sheila Newlands
SVP/General Counsel: Tom Rowland
SVP Marketing: Martin Johnson
EVP Sales: Glenn Yaffa
SVP Human Resources: Susan Reams
EVP Winemaking/Vineyards/Operations: Doug Gore
Estimated Sales: $10-20 Million
Number Employees: 250-499
Type of Packaging: Consumer, Food Service, Private Label, Bulk
Other Locations:
Stimson Lane Vineyards
Woodinville WA

11055 **SVB Food & Beverage Company**
717 Corning Way
Martinsburg, WV 25405
304-267-8500
Fax: 540-636-4470 cs@svbfoods.com
www.svbfoods.com
Processor and exporter of sparkling cider
President: Ben R Lacy III
Manager: Richard Wadkins
Sales Manager: Debra Hunter
Contact: Ken Bookmyer
kbookmyer@svbfoods.com
Estimated Sales: $944,000
Number Employees: 20-49
Square Footage: 100000
Type of Packaging: Consumer
Brands:
Alpenglow

11056 **SWELL Philadelphia Chewing Gum Corporation**
North Eagle & Lawrence
Havertown, PA 19083
610-449-1700
Fax: 610-449-2557
Manufacturer and exporter of chewing bubble gum and candy
President: Edward Fenimore
Estimated Sales: $14.5 Million
Number Employees: 100-249
Square Footage: 600000
Type of Packaging: Private Label, Bulk
Brands:
Swell

11057 **SYFO Beverage Company of Florida**
10033 Sawgrass Drive West
Suite 202
Ponte Vedra Beach, FL 32082
904-381-9002
Fax: 904-381-9004
customerservice@syfobeverages.com
http://www.syfobeverages.com
Beverages
President: Cydelle Mendius
Estimated Sales: $1-2.5 Million
Number Employees: 1

11058 **Saad Wholesale Meats**
2814 Orleans St.
Detroit, MI 48207
313-831-8126
saadmeats@yahoo.com
www.saadmeats.com
Halal meats including beef bologna, lunch meats, hot dogs, salami, chicken patties, hamburger patties, chicken nuggets, chicken strips, turkey bacon, beef bacon, hickory smoked bacon, beef snack sticks, and sausage
President: Aref Saad
CEO: Mohamed Saad
Year Founded: 1976
Estimated Sales: $5.8 Million
Number Employees: 48
Number of Brands: 1
Brands:
Sharifa Halal

11059 **Saag's Products LLC**
1799 Factor Ave
San Leandro, CA 94577-5617
510-352-8000
Fax: 510-352-4100 855-287-6562
www.saags.com
Sausages, condiments, frankfurters, luncheon meats and pates, roast beef, corned beef and pastrami, salamis and dry cured meats, smoked hams and pork products, turkey breasts
President: Timothy Dam
CEO/Owner: Kathi Mosle
kmosle@saags.com
CFO: Mike Tye
VP: Jerry Meyer
VP Marketing: Bernard Steinert
Estimated Sales: $11 Million
Number Employees: 50-99
Square Footage: 80000
Type of Packaging: Food Service, Private Label, Bulk
Brands:
Wurstmeister

11060 **Sabatino Truffles USA**
135 Front Avenue
West Haven, CT 06516
718-328- 412
Fax: 718-328- 412 888-444-9971
w.matos@sabatinostore.com
www.sabatinostore.com
Extra virgin olive oil, truffles, truffle butter, truffle oil, pasta, mushrooms, sauces and creams.
President: Frederico Balestra
Contact: Vincent Jeanseaume
vincent@sabatinostore.com
Estimated Sales: $1-3 Million
Number Employees: 7
Parent Co: SABATINO ITALIA SRL
Type of Packaging: Food Service, Private Label

11061 **Sabinsa Corp**
20 Lake Dr
East Windsor, NJ 08520-5321
732-777-1111
Fax: 732-777-1443 info@sabinsa.com
www.sabinsa.com
Botanical extracts
Founder & Chairman: Muhammed Majeed
CEO, Sabinsa USA: Asha Ramesh
President, Worldwide: Shaheen Majeed
EVP Global Operations: Madhu Subramanian
President Research Development: N Kalyanum
Marketing Director: Liz Smith
Estimated Sales: $20-50 Million
Number Employees: 20-49
Brands:
Ashwagandha
Boswellin
Citrin
Citrin K
Curlumin C3 Complex
Digezyme
Guguldid
Lactospore

11062 **Sable & Rosenfeld Foods**
12 Lawton Blvd
Toronto, ON M4V 1Z4
Canada
416-929-4214
Fax: 416-929-6727 info@sableandrosenfeld.com
www.sableandrosenfeld.com
Cocktail garnishes, appetizers/condiments and sauces.
President: Myra Sable
VP: Kathy Smith
Sales: Mary O'Neill

11063 **Sabor Mexicano**
Berkeley, CA 94704
www.sabormexicano.com
Tortilla chips and salsas
Marketing Specialist: Halliny Ferreira

11064 **Sabra Blue & White FoodProducts**
PO Box 66063
Dallas, TX 75266-0634
718-389-3800
888-957-2272
www.sabra.com
Mediterranean dips, spreads, appetizers and gourmet specialities. As of September 2005 Strauss-Elite LTD has acquired a 51% stake in Sabra Salads
CEO: Ronen Zohar
Estimated Sales: $20-50 Million
Type of Packaging: Consumer, Food Service
Brands:
Sabra

11065 Sabra Dipping Company,LL
649 Benet Rd
Oceanside, CA 92058-1208
760-757-2622
Fax: 760-721-2600 800-748-5523
info@sbsalsa.com
Refrigerated salsa, shelf stable foods and sauces. Co-packer of specialty foods.
President/Manager: Doug Pearson
Vice President/Upper Management: Jackie Watson
Quality Assurance Manager: Tatiana Miranda
Contact: Carlos Heras
cheras@sbsalsa.com
VP Purchasing: Patrick Hickey
Estimated Sales: $10-15 Million
Number Employees: 100
Square Footage: 38000
Type of Packaging: Consumer, Food Service
Brands:
Chachies
Con Gusto
San Diego Salsa
Santa Barbara Salsa
Tio Tio

11066 Sabra-Go Mediterranean
PO Box 660634
Dallas, TX 75266-0634
631-694-9500
888-957-2272
www.sabra.com
Mediterranean style refrigerated dips and spreads that iclude hummus, eggplant dips, babaganoush spreads, and Mediterranean salsa
CEO: Ronen Zohar
CFO: Amit Anand
Executive VP/General Manager: Meiky Tollman
Chief Marketing Officer: Rodrigo Troni
Executive VP Sales: John McGuckin
Human Resources Director: Angela King
Executive VP Operations: Guy Nir
Parent Co: Strauss Holdings LTD

11067 Sacramento Baking Co
9221 Beatty Dr
Sacramento, CA 95826-9702
916-361-2000
Fax: 916-361-0117
Bakery items including cakes
Owner: Sam Alajou
Marketing Director: Sam Alaclu
Quality Control: Sam Elajou
Estimated Sales: $20-50 Million
Number Employees: 20-49
Brands:
Sacramento Baking

11068 Sacramento Cookie Factory
3428 Auburn Blvd
Sacramento, CA 95821-1904
916-482-8222
Fax: 916-482-8222 877-877-2646
www.wafercookie.com
Wafer cookies
President: Jiri Knedlik
sacoksac@pacbell.net
Number Employees: 5-9

11069 Saddleback Cellars
7802 Money Rd.
Oakville, CA 94562
707-944-1305
Fax: 707-944-1325 info@saddlebackcellars.com
www.saddlebackcellars.com
Fine wines
Founder: Nils Venge
General Manager: Rick Wehman
Estimated Sales: $20-50 Million
Number Employees: 20-49

11070 Sadler's Smokehouse
1206 N Frisco St
PO Box 1088
Henderson, TX 75652-6924
903-657-5581
Fax: 903-655-8404 www.sadlerssmokehouse.com
Barbecued beef and pork, smoked poultry and barbecue sauce; wholesaler/distributor of meats/provisions
CFO: Wendy Frey
wendy.frey@sadlersbbq.com
Plant Manager: Saul Quintanilla
Purchasing: Jarrod Ferguson
Estimated Sales: $6.5 Million
Number Employees: 250-499
Square Footage: 720000
Type of Packaging: Consumer, Food Service, Private Label
Brands:
Double S
Sadler's Smokehouse

11071 Safe Catch
85 Liberty Ship Way
Suite 203
Sausalito, CA 94965
415-944-4442
888-568-4211
info@safecatch.com safecatch.com
Seasoned canned tuna and salmon
President & Founder: Sean Wittenberg
Vice President, Operations: Kevin McCay
Marketing Manager: Michelle Watson
National Sales Manager: Sarena Hines
Number Employees: 1-10
Brands:
SafeCatch

11072 Safely Delicious
P.O. Box 26446
Overland Park, KS 66225
913-963-5140
safelydelicious@gmail.com
safelydelicious.com
Allergen-free snacks.
Founder: Lisa Ragan
Number Employees: 1-4
Brands:
Safely Delicious

11073 (HQ)Safeway Inc.
5918 Stoneridge Mall Rd.
Pleasanton, CA 94588
877-723-3929
www.safeway.com
Supermarket products such as bakery items, dairy, deli meats, dry cleaning, frozen foods, fuel, grocery, pharmacy, produce, meants, snack foods, and more.
Executive Chairman/CEO: Robert Miller
robert.miller@safeway.com
Executive VP/CFO: Peter Bocian
Year Founded: 1915
Estimated Sales: Over $1 Billion
Number Employees: 10000+
Number of Brands: 12
Parent Co: Albertsons
Type of Packaging: Consumer
Brands:
O Organics
Open Nature
Lucerne Dairy Farms
Signature Cafe
Signature Select
Signature Farms
Signature Care
Primo Taglio
debi lilly design
waterfrontBISTRO
Signature RESERVE
Value Corner

11074 Safeway Milk Plant
1115 W Alameda Dr
Tempe, AZ 85282-3384
480-894-4391
Fax: 480-929-8025 www.safeway.com
Milk including half and half, skim, whole, 1% and 2%
Plant Manager: Jason Glober
Plant Manager: Jeff Fowler
Number Employees: 50-99
Parent Co: Safeway Stores
Type of Packaging: Consumer, Food Service, Private Label, Bulk

11075 Saffron Road
Stamford, CT 06905
203-961-1954
877-425-2587
info@saffronroad.com saffronroad.com
Frozen entr,es, bowls, hors d'oeuvres, sauces, broths, chips and chickpea snacks
CEO and Founder: Adnan Durrani
Executive Vice President: Jack Acree
Brands:
Saffron Road

11076 Safie Specialty Foods
Chesterfield, MI
586-598-8282
info@safiefoods.com
safiefoods.com
Pickled products
Founder: Mary Safie
Contact: Anthony Latalla
alatalla@safiespecialtyfoods.com
Year Founded: 1994

11077 Sagawa's Savory Sauces
8292 SW Nyberg St
Tualatin, OR 97062-9457
503-692-4334
Fax: 503-691-0661
Hawaiian-style sauces including teriyaki, sweet and sour and Polynesian barbecue; salad dressings, seasonings and mixes.
President: Linda Rider
Estimated Sales: $540,000
Number Employees: 7
Square Footage: 21732
Type of Packaging: Consumer, Food Service
Brands:
Baste & Glaze
Sweet & Sassy

11078 Sage V Foods
1470 Walnut St
Suite 202
Boulder, CO 80302
303-449-5626
sales@sagevfoods.com
sagevfoods.com
Rice products
Owner: Pete Vegas
Controller: Whilma Aleman
Estimated Sales: $5-10 Million
Number Employees: 50-99
Type of Packaging: Food Service, Private Label, Bulk
Brands:
RYZE
Grain Trust

11079 Sagely Naturals
1811 Centinela Ave
Santa Monica, CA 90049
424-262-6614
info@sagelynaturals.com
www.sagelynaturals.com
CBD creams and capsules
Co-Founder: Kerrigan Behrens
Co-Founder: Kaley Nichol
Year Founded: 2015

11080 Saguaro Food Products
1319 N Main Ave
Tucson, AZ 85705
520-884-8049
Fax: 520-884-9704 800-732-2447
Southwest gourmet foods, potato, dips and sauces, tortilla and corn chips
General Manager: Ralph Cortese
Finance Manager: Laurie Cowan
Marketing Manager: Sue Heems
Operations Manager: Raul Ruiz
Estimated Sales: Below $500,000
Number Employees: 8

11081 Sahadi Fine Foods Inc
4215 1st Ave
Brooklyn, NY 11232-3300
718-369-0100
Fax: 718-369-0800 800-724-2341
pwhelan@sahadifinefoods.com
www.sahadifinefoods.com
Maufacturer of nuts and seeds. Importer of dried fruit, beans, nuts, olives, Mediterranean foods
Owner: Robert Sahadi
VP: Pat Whelan
Sales: Ashraf Bakhoum
rsahadi@sahadifinefoods.com
Operations: Kristin Fernandez
Production: Brian Whelan
Estimated Sales: $11 Million
Number Employees: 20-49
Square Footage: 174000

11082 **Sahadi Importing Company**
187 Atlantic Ave
Brooklyn, NY 11201
718-624-4550
Fax: 718-643-4415 sahadis@aol.com
www.sahadis.com
Ethnic foods
President: Charles Sahadi
VP: Robert Sahadi
Contact: Audrey Sahadi
asahadi@sahadis.com
Estimated Sales: Below $5 Million
Number Employees: 20-49
Brands:
Sahadi

11083 **Sahagian & Associates**
124 Madison St
Oak Park, IL 60302
708-848-5552
Fax: 708-386-5959 800-327-9273
sales@sahagianinc.com www.sahagianinc.com
Bubble gum, licorice, taffy, candy-coated chocolate malted balls, chocolate bites, almonds, chocolate and caramel popcorn; also, multi-colored and tri-colored popcorn, candy coated licorice, and chocolate dips
President: Linda G. Sahagian
greg@sahagianinc.com
Estimated Sales: $630,000
Number Employees: 11
Type of Packaging: Consumer, Private Label, Bulk
Brands:
A Foot Of
A Yard Of
The Whole 9 Yards

11084 **Sahalee of Alaska**
PO Box 104174
Anchorage, AK 99510-4174
907-349-4151
Fax: 907-349-4161 800-349-4151
sahalee@aol.com
Seafood
President/CEO: Hank Lind
VP/Secretary/Treasurer: Christa Lind
Sales Director: Bill Haller

11085 **Sahara Coffee**
2081 Mountain Vista Way
Reno, NV 89519-6269
775-825-5033
Fax: 775-825-3190
Processor and packer of whole leaf loose teas, organic dates and specialty coffees
Owner: Charles Hubach
Estimated Sales: Less than $500,000
Number Employees: 1-4
Brands:
Sahara

11086 **Sahara Date Company**
8456A Tyco Road
Vienna, VA 22182
703-745-7463
info@saharadate.com
www.saharadate.com
Dates
Co-Founder: Maile Ramzi
Co-Founder: Jean Houpert
Estimated Sales: $6.9 Million
Number Employees: 34
Brands:
Sahara Date Company

11087 **Sahara Natural Foods**
14855 Wicks Blvd
San Leandro, CA 94577
510-352-5111
Fax: 510-532-3227
Rice products, soups and organic bulk products
National Manager: Al Caldwell

11088 **Sahlen's**
318 Howard St
Buffalo, NY 14206-2760
716-852-8677
Fax: 716-852-8684 800-466-8165
www.sahlen.com
Meat products that include sausage, ham, bacon, lard and hot dogs
President: Joseph Sahlen
jsahlen@sahlen.com
VP: Christopher Cauley
Estimated Sales: $18 Million
Number Employees: 50-99
Brands:
Sahlen's

11089 **Saint Albans Cooperative Creamery**
138 Federal St.
Saint Albans, VT 05478
802-524-6581
www.stalbanscooperative.com
Milk, cream, skim and skim condensed milk, and dry/powdered milk.
CEO: Leon Berthiaume
CEO: Harold Howrigan
Year Founded: 1919
Estimated Sales: $361.29 Million
Number Employees: 70
Type of Packaging: Private Label, Bulk
Brands:
Orbit

11090 **Saint Armands Baking Company**
2594 12th Street
Sarasota, FL 34237-2943
941-365-7377
Baked goods
Owner: Richard Tritschler
Estimated Sales: Under $500,000
Number Employees: 1-4
Parent Co: Suncoast Bakeries

11091 **Sainte Genevieve Winery**
6231 State Route C
Ste Genevieve, MO 63670
573-483-3500
Fax: 573-483-3526 800-398-1298
spcandy@msn.com
www.saintegenevievewinery.com
Wines
Manager: Elaine Mooney
CEO: Lineus Hoffmeister
Estimated Sales: $500,000-$1 Million
Number Employees: 1-4
Brands:
Sainte Genevieve

11092 **Saintsbury**
1500 Los Carneros Ave
Napa, CA 94559-9742
707-252-0592
Fax: 707-252-0595 info@saintsbury.com
Wines
Managing Partner: Richard Ward
drdick@saintsbury.com
Managing Partner: David Graves
Partner: Richard Ward
drdick@saintsbury.com
Estimated Sales: Below $6 Million
Number Employees: 10-19
Brands:
Saintsbury

11093 **Sakeone Corp**
820 Elm St
Forest Grove, OR 97116-3041
503-357-7056
Fax: 503-357-1014 800-550-7253
www.sakeone.com
Sake
Owner: Steve Vuilsteke
Tasting Room Manager: Jennifer Brownstein
Plant Manager: Scott Eagler
Sales Manager: Greg Lorenz
VP Sales: Jim Scalace
Director Marketing: Dewey Weddington
Estimated Sales: Below $5 Million
Number Employees: 20-49
Type of Packaging: Private Label
Brands:
G
Momokawa
Moonstone

11094 **Salad Depot**
51 Romeo St
Moonachie, NJ 07074
201-507-1980
Fax: 201-507-9001
Vegetables
President/Owner: Dan Zeigler
Marketing Director: John Zeigler
Buyer: Doreen Congo
Estimated Sales: Below $5 000,000
Number Employees: 1-4
Brands:
Salad Depot

11095 **Salad Girl Inc**
1165 Summit Ave
Mahtomedi, MN 55115-1511
651-653-9155
saladgirlinc@comcast.net
Artisan vinaigrettes made with organic ingredients: Curry & Fig, Crisp Apple Maple, Lemony Herb, Pomegranate Pear, Honey & Ginger, and Blueberry Basil.
Founder/CEO: Pamela Powell
Number Employees: 10-19
Type of Packaging: Consumer

11096 **Salad Oils Intl Corp**
5070 W Harrison St
Chicago, IL 60644-5141
773-261-0500
Fax: 773-261-7555 saladoiljohn@earthlink.net
www.saladoils.net
Edible oils
Vice President: John Pacente
saladoiljohn@earthlink.net
VP: John Pacente
Estimated Sales: $1.1 000,000
Number Employees: 5-9
Square Footage: 15000
Type of Packaging: Private Label
Brands:
Irilla Extra Virgin O.O.
Mi Best Soybean Oil
Onte Verde O.O.
Rgo Mace O.O.
Rosa Canola Oil
Rosa Corn Oil
Rosa Peanut Oil

11097 **Salamandre Wine Cellars**
108 Don Carlos Dr
Aptos, CA 95003-2912
831-685-0321
newt@cruzio.com
www.salamandrewine.com
Wines
General Partner: Will Shoemaker
Winemaker: Wells Shoemaker
Estimated Sales: $170,000
Number Employees: 1-4
Brands:
Salamandre Wine Cellars

11098 **Salamatof Seafoods**
Bridge Access Road Mp 1.5
PO Box 1450
Kenai, AK 99611-1450
907-283-7000
Fax: 907-283-8499
Fresh and frozen seafood including salmon, halibut, herring and cod
Chairman: Shane Morgan
Director Manufacturing: Roy Bertoglio
Estimated Sales: $20-50 Million
Number Employees: 100-249
Type of Packaging: Consumer, Food Service, Bulk

11099 **Salba Smart Natural Prod LLC**
6418 S Quebec St
Bldg 4
Centennial, CO 80111-4628
303-999-3996
info@salbasmart.com
www.salbasmart.com
Whole and ground chia seeds.
President: Rally Ralston
Partner: Judith Brooks
judith@organicfoodbrokers.com
National Sales Director: Staci Owens
Operations Manager: Kayleen Nichols
Number Employees: 5-9

11100 **Salem Baking Company**
224 S Cherry St
Winston Salem, NC 27101-5231
336-748-0230
Fax: 336-748-0501 800-274-2994
sales@salembaking.com www.salembaking.com
Cookies: moravian, spice, sugar, lemon, keylime, black walnut, tangerine-orange and double chocolate.

President: Guy Wilkerson
Contact: April Boone
april.boone@salembaking.com
Estimated Sales: $3.5 Million
Number Employees: 1-4
Parent Co: Dewey's Bakery
Type of Packaging: Consumer, Food Service
Brands:
Moravian Hearth

11101 (HQ)Salem Oil & Grease Company
60 Grove St
Salem, MA 01970-2245
978-745-0585
Fax: 978-741-4426
Processor and exporter of sulphonated castor oil
President: V Smith
VP Sales: J Donovan
VP Production: G Hanson
Estimated Sales: $10-20 Million
Number Employees: 20-49

11102 Salem Old Fashioned Candies
93 Canal St
Salem, MA 01970-4839
978-744-3242
Fax: 978-745-9459
Candy including bagged, hard, lollypops, mints, rock and taffy
President: Freeman Corkum
Estimated Sales: $950,000
Number Employees: 10-19
Type of Packaging: Consumer
Brands:
Chestnut Street
Gems
Jane Stewart
Noah's Treats
Sea Chest
Seabreeze
Spindrift

11103 Salemville Cheese
W4481 County Road Gg
Cambria, WI 53923-9304
920-394-3431
Cheese
President: Henry Miller
CFO: William Schrock
Manager: Nelson Schrock
Plant Manager: Lavern Miller
Estimated Sales: $5-10 000,000
Number Employees: 20-49

11104 Sales Associates Of Alaska
1900 Phillips Field Rd
Fairbanks, AK 99701-2707
907-452-2201
Fax: 907-452-2201 800-478-2371
service@qualitysales.net www.qualitysales.net
Wholesale grocers.
President: Gary Nance
don@qualitysales.net
Secretary/Treasurer: Carl Olson
Estimated Sales: $1 Million
Number Employees: 20-49

11105 Sales USA
220 Salado Creek Road
Salado, TX 76571-5783
254-947-3838
Fax: 254-947-3338 800-766-7344
pompeii1@aol.com
Fruit and vegetable juices.
President: Rusty Justus
CEO: Ronald Cox
Plant Manager: Lee Simpkins
Estimated Sales: $1 Million
Number Employees: 4
Square Footage: 60000
Type of Packaging: Consumer, Food Service, Private Label, Bulk

11106 Salishan Vineyards
35011 NE North Fork Ave
La Center, WA 98629
360-263-2713
Fax: 360-263-3675
Wine
President: Joan Wolverton
CFO: Lincoln Wolverton
Estimated Sales: Under $300,000
Number Employees: 1-4
Type of Packaging: Private Label
Brands:
Salishan

11107 Sally Lane's Candy Farm
2215 Gum Springs Rd
Paris, TN 38242-6362
731-642-5801
Candy including peanut and coconut brittle and hard and sugar-free candies
Owner: Bobby Freeman
bobf5801@hotmail.com
Co-Owner: Jean Peterson
Number Employees: 10-19
Square Footage: 12000
Type of Packaging: Consumer
Brands:
Sally Lane's

11108 Sally Sherman
300 N MacQuesten Pkwy
Mt Vernon, NY 10550-1093
914-664-6262
Fax: 914-664-2846 718-822-1100
www.sallyshermanfoods.com
Premium salads
Owner/Operator: Felix Endico
General Manager: Paul Cannillo
VP Operations: Marc Mazzarulli
Account Manager: Debra Gentile
Estimated Sales: $20-50 Million
Number Employees: 50-99
Brands:
Endico
Hellmans

11109 Salmans & Assoc
1126 W Chestnut St
Chicago, IL 60642-4111
312-226-1820
Fax: 312-226-6806 sales@salmans.com
Cheese
President: Van Salmans
van@salmans.com
Estimated Sales: $650,000
Number Employees: 5-9
Brands:
Salmans

11110 Salmolux Inc
34100 9th Ave S # A
Federal Way, WA 98003-7393
253-874-6570
Fax: 253-874-4042 seafood@salmolux.com
Smoked seafood products, pates, spreads, salmon burgers, herring, flavored butters and canned seafood salads
President: George Kuetgens
Cmo: John Randisi
seafood@salmolux.com
National Sales Director: Kira Kuetgens
Plant Manager: Ray Crockett
Year Founded: 1988
Estimated Sales: $20 Million
Number Employees: 50-99
Square Footage: 60000
Type of Packaging: Consumer, Food Service, Private Label, Bulk
Brands:
Salmolux Anti Pasta
Salmolux Gourmet Smoked Salmon
Salmolux Saute Butters

11111 Salmon River Smokehouse
PO Box 40
Gustavus, AK 99826-0040
907-697-2330
Fax: 907-456-3889
Smoke a variety of fish products.

11112 Salonika Imports Inc
3509 Smallman St
Pittsburgh, PA 15201-1936
412-682-2700
800-794-2256
www.salonika.net
Mediterranean culinary products
President/Owner: Chris Balouris
sales@salonika.net
Number Employees: 5-9

11113 Salsa God
447 W 56th St
Suite 1E
New York, NY 10019
646-359-0573
danny@thesalsagod.com
www.thesalsagod.com
Salsa
Co-Founder: Danny Mayans
Co-Founder: Bella Mayans
Number Employees: 2
Brands:
Salsa God

11114 Salt Lake Macaroni & Noodle Company
5405 W 4700 S
Salt Lake City, UT 84118-6352
801-969-9855
Fax: 801-969-9856
Pasta
Manager: Mike Stover
Estimated Sales: $5-10 000,000
Number Employees: 5-9

11115 Salt River Lobster Inc
72 Tidewater Dr
Boothbay, ME 04537-4242
207-633-5357
Fax: 207-633-5357 orders@salt-river-lobster.com
www.salt-river-lobster.com
Sells lobster, shrimp, fish, and various other shellfish.
Estimated Sales: Less Than $500,000
Number Employees: 1-4

11116 Salt of the Earth Bakery
630 Flushing Avenue
4th Floor
Brooklyn, NY 11206
646-330-5089
info@saltoftheearthbakery.com
saltoftheearthbakery.com
Sea salt cookies and brownies
President: Haskel Rabbani
Estimated Sales: $1,000,000
Number Employees: 2-10
Brands:
Salt of the Earth

11117 SaltWorks
16240 Wood-Red Rd NE
Woodinville, WA 98072
425-885-7258
800-353-7258
info@seasalt.com www.seasalt.com
Seasalt

11118 Salty Girl Seafood
P.O. Box 6557
Santa Barbara, CA 93160
805-699-5025
hello@saltygirlseafood.com
www.saltygirlseafood.com
Sustainable, traceable seafood
Co-Founder: Laura Johnson
Co-Founder: Norah Eddy

11119 Salty Road
Brooklyn, NY
929-250-2615
wholesale@thesaltyroad.com
www.thesaltyroad.com
Manufacturer of taffy.
Owner: Marisa Wu
Brands:
Salty Road

11120 Salty Wahine Gourmet Hawaiian Sea Salt
1-3529 Kaumualii Highway
Unit 2B
Hanapepe, HI 96716
808-378-4089
Fax: 808-442-1230 www.saltywahine.com
Hawaiian sea salt
Owner and Founder: Laura Andersland

11121 Salute Sante! Food & Wine
68 Coombs St # I-2
Napa, CA 94559-3966
707-251-3900
Fax: 707-251-3939 info@grapeseedoil.com
www.grapeseedoil.com

Flavored and regular grapeseed oil
Founder, President: Valentin Humer
Estimated Sales: $690,000
Number Employees: 5-9
Type of Packaging: Consumer
Brands:
Salute Sante! Grapeseed Oil

11122 Salvy Sousa Dealer Locator
11242 282nd Rd
Arkansas City, KS 67005-8300
620-442-2700
Fax: 620-446-1362 jscarroll@salvysousa.com
www.salvysousa.com
Manufacturer of sauces and marinades.
CEO: Janet Carroll
Number Employees: 5-9

11123 Salwa Foods
P.O. Box 490579
Lawrenceville, GA 30049
770-263-8207
salwa@salwafoods.com
www.salwafoods.com
Halal chicken and beef products
Owner: Mushtaq "Mike" Mistry
Year Founded: 2002

11124 Sam KANE Beef Processors Inc
9001 Leopard St
Corpus Christi, TX 78409
800-242-4142
www.kanebeef.com
Processor and exporter of fresh, frozen and boxed beef.
Owner: Sam Kane
CEO: Alfred Bausch
CAO & CMO: Chuck Jackson
Director of Regulatory Compliance: Brian Honigbaum
Operations Manager: Dwayne Hubenak
Year Founded: 1949
Estimated Sales: $100-500 Million
Number Employees: 500-999
Type of Packaging: Consumer, Food Service, Bulk

11125 Sam Mills USA
2400 High Ridge Rd
Suite 102
Boynton Beach, FL 33426-8710
561-572-0510
Fax: 561-572-0511 info@sammillsusallc.com
www.sammills.com
Granola bars, pasta, mac & cheese, cookies and pretzels
Director of Operations: Tom Lagomarsini
Estimated Sales: Under $500,000
Number Employees: 2-4
Parent Co: Sam Mills Srl.
Type of Packaging: Food Service
Brands:
SamMills(c)

11126 Sam's Leon Mexican Food
5014 S 20th St
Omaha, NE 68107-2925
402-733-3809
www.samsleon.com
Tortillas, taco shells and hot sauce
Owner: David Murillo
Estimated Sales: Less than $500,000
Number Employees: 1-4
Type of Packaging: Food Service

11127 Samadi Sweets Cafe
5916 Leesburg Pike
Falls Church, VA 22041
703-578-0606
Fax: 703- 57-8 17
Middle Eastern pastries
Owner: Nora Burgan
Estimated Sales: Less than $500,000
Number Employees: 5-9

11128 Sambazon
209 Avenida Fabricante
Suite 200
San Clemente, CA 92672
949-498-8618
877-726-2296
info@sambazon.com www.sambazon.com
Organic açaí products including frozen superfruit packs, frozen desserts, sorbet, fresh juices, and energy drinks
Co-Founder: Jeremy Black
Co-Founder/CEO: Ryan Black
CFO/COO: Ricardo Perdigao
CMO: Renee Junge
Year Founded: 2000
Number Employees: 150
Type of Packaging: Food Service

11129 Sambets Cajun Deli
8650 Spicewood Spgs Rd # 111
Austin, TX 78759-4323
512-258-6410
Fax: 512-258-6284 800-472-6238
Cajun hot sauces, salsas and spices
Owner: Doug Slocombe
Estimated Sales: $300,000-500,000
Number Employees: 1-4

11130 Sambol Meat Company
PO Box 13376
Overland Park, KS 66282
913-334-8404
Meat and meat products. Founded in 1929.
Owner: Don Sambol
CEO: Bill Kolich
Marketing Manager: Mark Fishman
Estimated Sales: $.5-1 million
Number Employees: 1-4
Type of Packaging: Consumer
Brands:
Sambol

11131 Sampac Enterprises
551 Railroad Ave
S San Francisco, CA 94080-3450
650-876-0808
Fax: 650-876-0338 sales@sampacent.com
www.sampacent.com
Teas; wholesaler/distributor of herbs, teas, honey, bee pollen, etc
Owner: Sammy MA
sales@sampacent.com
Estimated Sales: $2.3 Million
Number Employees: 10-19
Square Footage: 80000
Type of Packaging: Private Label, Bulk

11132 Sampco
651 W Washington Blvd # 300
Chicago, IL 60661-2138
312-346-1506
Fax: 312-346-8302 800-767-1689
www.sampcoinc.com
Cooked beef products
President/CEO: David Morrison
gmorrison@sampcoinc.com
Vice President: Verna Macintosh
VP Industrial Sales: Rod McNally
Estimated Sales: $5-10 Million
Number Employees: 20-49
Type of Packaging: Private Label
Brands:
Classico
Sampco

11133 San Angelo Packing
4238 Sunset Dr
San Angelo, TX 76904
325-949-9401
Fax: 325-658-7272
Packer of beef; slaughtering services available.
General Manager: Jarrod Stokes
Estimated Sales: Below $5,000,000
Number Employees: 250-499

11134 San Anselmo's Cookies & Biscotti
PO Box 2822
San Anselmo, CA 94979-2822
415-492-1220
Fax: 415-492-1282 800-229-1249
Cookies and biscotti
Co-Owner: Jane Cloth Richman
VP Marketing: Jane Cloth-Richman
Estimated Sales: Below $5 Million
Number Employees: 20
Brands:
San Anselmo's

11135 San Antonio Farms
1555 E Highway 151
Platteville, WI 53818
800-236-1119
www.sanantoniofarmsonline.com
Mexican fajita marinade, pico de gallo, salsa, enchilada and picante sauce and peppers including jalapeno, serrano and chile.
Parent Co: Bay Valley Foods, LLC
Type of Packaging: Consumer, Food Service, Bulk
Brands:
Van De Walle Farms

11136 San Antonio Packing Co
1922 S Laredo St
San Antonio, TX 78207-7093
210-224-5441
Fax: 210-224-6664 www.sanantoniopacking.com
Meats including beef, lamb and pork
President: Ollie Craft
ollie.craft@mrcglobal.com
Co-Owner: Jennifer Roe
Estimated Sales: $7.4 Million
Number Employees: 50-99
Square Footage: 120000

11137 San Bernardo Ice Cream
2805 N Commerce Pkwy
Miramar, FL 33025-3956
954-322-2668
Fax: 954-441-9577
www.sanbernardoicecream.com
Manufacturer of ice cream.
Founder: Bob Tammara
Estimated Sales: Less Than $500,000
Number Employees: 1-4

11138 San Diego Soy Dairy
1330 Hill St # B
El Cajon, CA 92020-5758
619-447-8638
Fax: 619-447-2068 soydairy@att.net
www.sandiegosoydairy.com
Soy products including milk, tofu, salads and salad dressings; also, herbal teas
Owner/CEO: Luke Yam
soydairy@aol.com
Estimated Sales: $500,000-$1 Million
Number Employees: 5-9
Square Footage: 13200
Type of Packaging: Consumer, Food Service
Brands:
San Diego Soy Dairy
Waterfall

11139 San Dominique Winery
I-17 & State Highway 169
Camp Verde, AZ 86322
480-945-8583
Wines
President: William Staltari
Estimated Sales: Less than $500,000
Number Employees: 1-4
Brands:
San Dominique

11140 San Francisco Bay Coffee
1731 Aviation Blvd
Lincoln, CA 95648
916-258-8000
800-829-1300
service@sfbcoffee.com sfbaycoffee.com
Roasted coffee
President: Jon Rogers
VP: Jim Rogers
VP: Barbra Rogers
VP, Sales & Marketing: Kristen Rogers
Operations Manager: Pete Rogers
Year Founded: 1979
Estimated Sales: $100-140 Million
Number Employees: 230
Number of Brands: 2
Type of Packaging: Private Label
Brands:
San Franciso Bay
Organic Coffee Company

11141 San Francisco Bay Coffee Company
1731 Aviation Blvd
Lincoln, CA 95648
510-638-1300
Fax: 510-632-0839 800-829-1300
service@sfbcoffee.com
www.sanfranciscobaycoffee.com
Coffee including ground, beans, decaffeinated and flavored; also, aromatic, herbal and flavored teas

President/CEO/Founder: Jon B Rogers
Vice President/Sales: Jim Rogers
Co-Founder: Barbara Rogers
Purchasing Manager: Tom Gerber
Estimated Sales: $20-50 Million
Number Employees: 100-249
Square Footage: 82000
Parent Co: JBR Gourmet Foods
Type of Packaging: Consumer, Food Service, Private Label, Bulk
Brands:
East India Coffee & Tea Co.
Pastarific Pasta Co.
San Francisco Coffee

11142 San Francisco Fine Bakery
2537 Middlefield Rd
Redwood City, CA 94063-2825
650-369-8573
Fax: 650-369-8382 order@sffinebakery.com
Bakery products
Owner: Clifford Chen
clifford@sffinebakery.com
President, Chief Executive Officer: Daniel Huang
Estimated Sales: Below $5 Million
Number Employees: 20-49
Brands:
San Francisco Fine Bakery

11143 San Francisco French Bread
580 Julie Ann Way
Oakland, CA 94621
510-729-6232
Processor and exporter of sourdough bread, rolls and croutons
President: Tom Hofmeister
National Sales Manager: Terry McDonough
Contact: Norm Andrews
norm@asapwinetags.com
Number Employees: 5-9
Parent Co: IBC
Type of Packaging: Consumer, Food Service

11144 San Francisco Popcorn Works
1028 Revere Ave
San Francisco, CA 94124
415-822-4744
Fax: 415-822-3376 800-777-2676
www.sanfranciscopopcornremoval.com
Popcorn
President: Joan Adler
Estimated Sales: Below $5 Million
Number Employees: 10
Square Footage: 8
Type of Packaging: Private Label
Brands:
Naturfood
San Francisco Popcorn
Somewhat Sinful

11145 San Francisco Salt
30984 Santana St
Hayward, CA 94544
510-477-9600
Fax: 510-477-9621 800-480-4540
customerservice@sfsalt.com sfsalt.com
Salts: Himalayan, bath, dead sea, Epsom, scented, flavored and gourmet
President: Lee Williamson
Director of Sales: Marilou Collins
Operations Manager: Siro Rivera
Year Founded: 2002
Estimated Sales: $46 Million
Number Employees: 11-50
Brands:
Epsoak(c)
Minera(c)
San Francisco Salt Company(c)
Sherpa Pink(c)

11146 San Francisco Spice Co.
1640 Tide Court
Woodland, CA 95776
530-669-6703
Fax: 650-583-6376 866-972-6879
drmcdougalls@worldpantry.com
www.rightfoods.com
Produces a variety of packaged foods including soups, oatmeals, and quinoa products; offer organic and gluten free products.
President: Mike Vinnicombe
Research & Development Manager: Maria Firmacion
Quality Assurance/Shippping Supervisor: Maresa Scofield
Estimated Sales: $6 Million
Number Employees: 25
Number of Brands: 1
Square Footage: 175000
Type of Packaging: Consumer
Brands:
Dr. McDougall's Right Foods

11147 San Franola Granola
2440 Geary Blvd # C
San Francisco, CA 94115-3375
415-506-9582
Manufacturer of granola bars.
Co-Founder: Matt Teichmann
Co-Founder: David Miskie

11148 San Gennaro Foods Inc
19255 80th Ave S
Kent, WA 98032-1135
253-872-1900
Fax: 253-872-1919 800-462-1916
mail@polenta.net www.polenta.net
Pre cooked polenta. Also mayonnaise, barbeque sauces and salad dressings
President: Julio Jimenez
julio@polenta.net
Estimated Sales: $1-2.5 Million
Number Employees: 5-9
Type of Packaging: Private Label
Brands:
Northwest Gourmet
San Gennaro

11149 San Joaquin Figs Inc
3564 N Hazel Ave
PO Box 9547
Fresno, CA 93722-4912
559-224-4963
Fax: 559-224-4926 info@nutrafig.com
www.nutrafig.com
Figs including dried, diced and paste; also, fig juice concentrate
President: Sara Guerrero-Martinez
saraguerrero-martinez@nutrafig.com
Estimated Sales: $5.6 Million
Number Employees: 20-49
Brands:
California Classic
San Joaquin Supreme
The Nutra Fig

11150 San Joaquin Vly Concentrates
5631 E Olive Ave
Fresno, CA 93727-2708
559-458-2500
Fax: 559-458-2564 800-557-0220
inquiries@sjvconc.com www.sjvconc.com
SJVC produces red and white juice concentrates, the grape seed extract ActiVin and is the world's largest supplier of anthocyanin colors.
Number Employees: 20-49
Brands:
ActiVin

11151 San Jose Apartments
1500 Cunningham Ave
San Jose, CA 95122-2308
408-347-8209
Fax: 408-272-7118
Coffee
Manager: Thomasa Alpha
sanjoseapts@dkdpmco.com
Estimated Sales: $690,000
Number Employees: 5-9

11152 San Juan Coffee Roasting Co
18 Cannery Lndg
Friday Harbor, WA 98250
360-378-4443
Fax: 360-378-6658 800-624-4119
www.rockisland.com/sjcoffee
Fresh coffee roasted daily
President: Irene Herring
Operations Manager: Steve Herring
Estimated Sales: Less Than $500,000
Number Employees: 5-9

11153 San Luis Valley Hemp Co.
570 Columbia Ave
PO Box 130
Del Norte, CO 81132
719-299-5000
slvhemp.com
Hemp products
Partner: Dion Oakes
Partner: Monte Robertson
Operations: Brandi Wright

11154 San Marco Coffee, Inc.
3120 Latrobe Dr
Suite 280
Charlotte, NC 28211-2186
704-366-0533
Fax: 704-366-0534 800-715-9298
www.sanmarcocoffee.com
American coffee, espresso, cappuccino
Chief Executive Officer: Marc Decaria
marc@sanmarcocoffee.com
Number Employees: 5-9
Type of Packaging: Consumer, Food Service, Private Label
Brands:
San Giorgio

11155 San Marzano Imports
116 West Fourth Street
Howell, NJ 07731
732-364-1724
Fax: 732-364-1724
Dried tomatoes and Turkish and Greek olives
Sales Manager: Nick Soccodato
Number Employees: 5-9
Square Footage: 40000

11156 San-Ei Gen FFI
630 5th Ave
Suite 3201
New York, NY 10111
212-315-7850
Fax: 212-974-2540 contact@saneigen.com
www.saneigen.com
Food ingredients including coloring extracts and antioxidants.
President: Takashige Shimizu
Contact: Osamu Enomoto
oenomoto@saneigen.com
Estimated Sales: $5 Million
Number Employees: 1-4
Square Footage: 17600
Parent Co: San-El Gen FFI
Type of Packaging: Bulk

11157 San-J International Inc
2880 Sprouse Dr
Henrico, VA 23231-6072
804-226-8333
Fax: 804-226-8383 800-446-5500
info@san-j.com www.san-j.com
Gluten free tamari, Asian cooking sauces and salad dressings, brown rice crackers, organic shoyu, and soups.
President: Ola Badaru
obaru@san-j.com
Quality Manager: Mark Mansfield
Maintenance Manager: Gary Dudley
Purchasing Manager: Ola Badaru
Estimated Sales: $5.3 Million
Number Employees: 20-49
Number of Brands: 1
Number of Products: 22
Square Footage: 88000
Parent Co: San Jirushi Corporation
Type of Packaging: Consumer, Food Service, Bulk
Brands:
San-J

11158 San-J International Inc
2880 Sprouse Dr
Henrico, VA 23231-6072
804-226-8333
Fax: 804-226-8383 800-446-5500
info@san-j.com www.san-j.com
Canned tomatoes, pasta, assorted olive oils, olives, beans, condiments, sauces, soy sauces and more
President: Ola Badaru
obaru@san-j.com
Number Employees: 20-49

11159 Sanarak Paper & PopcornSupplies
456 Hinman Ave
Buffalo, NY 14216
716-874-5662
Fax: 716-874-4737 sanarak001@yahoo.com
www.buffalofunfoods.com
Popcorn
President: Jim Rogers
Estimated Sales: $500,000-$1 000,000
Number Employees: 5-9

11160 Sanborn Sourdough Bakery
5230 S Valley View Blvd
Suite A
Las Vegas, NV 89118-1626
702-795-1030
Fax: 702-795-8518
Breads, rolls, and buns
President: Donald Sanborn
CFO: Brenda Portela
General Manager: Joe Lazi
Operations Manager: John Klessia
Estimated Sales: $20-50 Million
Number Employees: 50-99
Brands:
Sanborn Sourdough Bakery

11161 Sanchez Distributors
9711 Mid Walk Dr
San Antonio, TX 78230-4075
210-341-1682
Fax: 210-341-7470
Ethnic foods
President: Roberto Sanchez
Sales Manager: Fernando Sanchez
Estimated Sales: $5-10 000,000
Number Employees: 1-4

11162 Sand Castle Winery
755 River Rd
Erwinna, PA 18920
610-294-9181
Fax: 610-294-9174 800-722-9463
info@sandcastlewinery.com
Wines
President: Paul Maxian
CEO: Joseph Maxian
winesand@epix.net
Marketing/Sales Manager: Stephanie Driver
Estimated Sales: $5-10 Million
Number Employees: 10-19
Type of Packaging: Private Label
Brands:
Johannisberg Riesling
Sand Castle Winery

11163 Sand Hill Berries
304 Deerfield Rd
Mt Pleasant, PA 15666-9150
724-547-4760
Fax: 724-547-7319 www.sandhillberries.com
Raspberries, blackberries, gooseberries, currants, jostaberries, jams, jellies, vinaigrettes, fruit sauce and vinegar
Owner: Susan Lynn
shberries@aol.com
Estimated Sales: Less Than $500,000
Number Employees: 1-4
Type of Packaging: Consumer, Private Label

11164 Sand Springs
160 Sand Springs Rd
Williamstown, MA 01267-2248
413-458-8281
Spring waters
Owner: Jennifer Morin
Estimated Sales: $2.5-5 000,000
Number Employees: 5-9

11165 Sandbar Trading Corp
408 S Pierce Ave
Louisville, CO 80027-3018
303-499-7480
Fax: 303-527-1727 www.snatea.com
Herbs and spices
President: Barry Cowper
Manager: Karen Harbour
kharbour@snat.com
Manager: Dave Halford
Number Employees: 1-4
Brands:
Sandbar Trading

11166 Sandco International
151 Union Chapel Rd
Northport, AL 35473
205-339-0145
Fax: 205-339-8222 800-382-2075
Processor and exporter of vitamins and sports supplements, anti-aging
President: Linda Sandlin
sandco@uronramp.com
Research & Development: Richard Sandlin
Marketing: Linda Madison
Purchasing Manager: Linda Wells
Estimated Sales: $1,100,000
Number Employees: 5-9
Square Footage: 80000
Type of Packaging: Consumer, Private Label, Bulk

11167 Sanders Candy Inc
23770 Hall Rd
Clinton Twp, MI 48036-1275
586-468-4300
Fax: 586-468-9407 800-852-2253
www.sanderscandy.com
Cookies, bread & rolls, danishes, cakes and doughnuts
President/CEO: Judith Brock
CFO: Joseph Talmage
Marketing Specialist: Susan Leso
VP Sales/Marketing: John McGuckin
Plant Manager: Mike Koch
Estimated Sales: $500,000-$1 Million
Number Employees: 100-249
Parent Co: Country Home Bakers
Type of Packaging: Private Label
Brands:
Sanders Brand Candy

11168 Sanders Meat Packing Inc
237 S. Main St.
Custer, MI 49405-0128
231-757-4768
Fax: 231-757-4786 800-968-5035
info@sandersmeats.com www.sandersmeats.com
Beef and pork products
Owner: Dale Sanders
Estimated Sales: $5-10 Million
Number Employees: 10-19
Type of Packaging: Consumer

11169 Sanderson Farms
P.O. Box 988
Laurel, MS 39441
800-844-4030
www.sandersonfarms.com
Poultry.
President/COO: Lampkin Butts
Chairman/CEO: Joe Sanderson
Treasurer/CFO: Mike Cockrell
Secretary/Chief Accounting Officer: Tim Rigney
Year Founded: 1955
Estimated Sales: $3.4 Billion
Number Employees: 17,000+
Square Footage: 11418
Type of Packaging: Consumer, Food Service, Private Label, Bulk
Brands:
Sanderson Farms

11170 Sandia Shadows Vineyard & Winery
8740 4th Street NW
PO Box 92675
Albuquerque, NM 87199-2675
505-856-1006
Fax: 505-858-0859 sandiawine@aol.com
Wine
Owner: Phillippe Littot
Estimated Sales: Less than $500,000
Number Employees: 1-4
Brands:
Sandia Shadows Vineyard & Wine

11171 Sandors Bakeries
2245 W Flagler St
Miami, FL 33135-1522
305-642-8484
Fax: 305-643-9358
Breads and other bakery products, except cookies and crackers
President: Orlando Sanchez
Estimated Sales: $237,263
Number Employees: 5-9

11172 Sandridge Food Corp
133 Commerce Dr
Medina, OH 44256-1333
330-725-2348
Fax: 330-722-3998 800-627-2523
www.sandridge.com
Refrigerated deli salads, sides, soups, sauces, and specialty dishes
President: William Frantz
CEO: Mark Sandridge
VP Finance: Rick Sisko
VP of Business Development: Frank Sidari
Sr Director, Food Safety & Quality: Joel Riegelmayer
VP Sales/Marketing: John Becker
Sr Director/Food Service Sales: Michael Sandridge
Manager of Customer Service: Lori Kyle
Operations Director: Barry Pioske
Purchasing Manager: Rich Graziosi
Estimated Sales: $20-50 Million
Number Employees: 250-499
Square Footage: 130000
Type of Packaging: Consumer, Food Service, Private Label, Bulk
Brands:
Sandridge Salads Set Free

11173 Sandstone Winery
4505 220th Trl
Amana, IA 52203-8029
319-622-3081
sandwine@netins.net
Homemade wines
President: Elsie Mattes
Vice President: Thomas Mattes
Estimated Sales: $550,000
Number Employees: 1-4
Type of Packaging: Consumer, Food Service
Brands:
Sandstone Winery

11174 Sandt's Honey Co
714 Wagener Ln
Easton, PA 18040-8253
610-252-6511
Fax: 610-252-9069 800-935-3960
www.sandtshoney.com
Processor and packer of all-natural and kosher certified honey
President: Lee Sandt
Vice President: Linda Sandt
Estimated Sales: $12 Million
Number Employees: 1-4
Type of Packaging: Consumer, Food Service, Private Label, Bulk
Brands:
Sandt's

11175 Sandusky Filling & Brittle
1034 Hancock St
Sandusky, OH 44870-3616
419-626-8080
Fax: 419-626-8330 800-274-8853
Candy
Manager: Dennis Babb
Specialty Sales: John Cayten
Estimated Sales: $10-20 Million
Number Employees: 20-49

11176 Sandy Candy
77 Fairfield Lane
Chester Springs, PA 19425
610-321-7263
Fax: 610-524-5649 800-386-7263
info@sandycandy.com
Confectionary candy
Contact: Sally Solomon
sandcrafters@comcast.net

11177 Sanford Milling Co Inc
1310 Nicholas St
1310 S. Nicholas Street
Henderson, NC 27536-5329
252-438-4526
Fax: 252-492-3014 866-438-4526
Flour
President: Scott Hartness
sanfordmilling@nc.rr.com
Estimated Sales: $10-20 Million
Number Employees: 10-19
Type of Packaging: Food Service, Private Label, Bulk
Brands:
Hartness Choice

Packers Blend
Snow Flake

11178 Sanford Winery
5010 Santa Rosa Rd # 6
Lompoc, CA 93436-9551
805-735-5900
Fax: 805-688-7381 800-426-9463
info@sanfordwinery.com www.sanfordwinery.com
Wines
Partner: Richard Sanford
CFO: Stuart Fries
Marketing Manager: Tom Prendiville
Manager: Anthony Terlato
Operations: Sharon Blewis
Purchasing Manager: Sharon Blewis
Estimated Sales: Below $5 Million
Number Employees: 5-9
Type of Packaging: Private Label
Brands:
Sanford

11179 Sangudo Custom Meat Packers
4920 47 Avenue
Sangudo, AB T0E 2A0
Canada
780-785-3353
Fax: 780-785-3111 888-785-3353
Frozen beef and pork, pepperoni, bacon and sausage
Owner: Kevin Meier
Owner: Jeff Senger
Number Employees: 1-4

11180 Sanitary Bakery
126 E Ridge St
Nanticoke, PA 18634-2813
570-735-6630
Fax: 320-632-2740 www.sanitarybakery.com
Cookies
Owner: Edward Kowalski
Estimated Sales: Under $500,000
Number Employees: 10-19

11181 Sanitary Tortilla Manufacturing Company
623 Urban Loop
San Antonio, TX 78204
210-226-9209
Fax: 210-226-9424
sanitarytortillacompany@gmail.com
www.sanitarytortillacompany.com
Tortillas and other corn products
Owner: Louis Garcia
General Manager: Garcia Luis
Estimated Sales: $8 Million
Number Employees: 10 to 19
Square Footage: 18000
Type of Packaging: Food Service

11182 Santa Barbara Bar
233 E Gutierrez Street
Santa Barbara, CA 93101
855-722-2701
sbbar.co
Nutritional snack bars
Founder & CEO: Peter Gaum
Number Employees: 2-10
Brands:
santa barbara BAR(c)

11183 Santa Barbara Olive Company
12477 Calle Real
Santa Barbara, CA 93117
805-562-1456
Fax: 805-562-1464 800-624-4896
info@sbolive.com www.sbolive.com
Gourmet olives, extra virgin olive oils, sauces, vegetables, condiments, salsas
President: Craig Makela
Vice President: Cindy Makela
Contact: Jason Pace
jason@sbolive.com
Estimated Sales: $10 Million
Number Employees: 17
Square Footage: 14000
Type of Packaging: Consumer, Food Service, Private Label, Bulk

11184 Santa Barbara PistachioCo
3380 Highway 33
Maricopa, CA 93252-9688
661-766-2485
Fax: 661-766-2436 800-896-1044
info@sbpistachios.com
www.santabarbarapistachios.com
Grower and packager of naturally organic pistachios brined with organic, kosher-certified ingredients. Manufacturer of pistachio flour and pistachio oil.
Owner: Gene Zannon
zannon@sbpistachios.com
Owner: Gail Zannon
Vice President: Mark Purcell
Vice President: Steve Bertrand
Estimated Sales: Less Than $500,000
Number Employees: 1-4
Square Footage: 8000
Type of Packaging: Consumer, Bulk
Brands:
Santa Barbara Pistachio

11185 Santa Barbara Roasting Co
321 Motor Way
Santa Barbara, CA 93101-3436
805-898-3700
Fax: 805-962-2590 800-321-5282
www.sbcoffee.com
Coffee
President: Corey Russell
corey@sbcoffee.com
Executive Director: Jami Dunlop
Director Operations: Matthew Moore
Estimated Sales: Below $5 Million
Number Employees: 20-49
Type of Packaging: Private Label
Brands:
Santa Barbara

11186 Santa Barbara Salsa
649 Benet Rd
Oceanside, CA 92058-1208
760-757-2622
Fax: 760-721-2600 800-748-5523
info@sbsalsa.com
Salsa and sauces
President: Doug Pearson
Estimated Sales: $2.5 Million
Number Employees: 10-19
Parent Co: California Creative Foods
Type of Packaging: Consumer, Bulk
Brands:
Chacies
Con Gusto
San Diego Salsa
Santa Barbara Salsa
Tio Tio

11187 Santa Barbara Salsa/California Creative
649 Benet Rd
Oceanside, CA 92058-1208
760-757-2622
Fax: 760-721-2600 800-748-5523
info@sbsalsa.com
Salsa Flavors: artichoke, key lime, garlic; peach; roasted garlic; mango peach; roasted chili; black bean; corn; cheese and salsa; hot pepper and marinades
President: Doug Pearson
Estimated Sales: $300,000-500,000
Number Employees: 1-4
Brands:
Chachies
Congusto
San Diego Salsa
Santa Barbara Salsa
Tio Tio

11188 Santa Barbara Winery
202 Anacapa St
Santa Barbara, CA 93101-1887
805-963-3633
Fax: 805-962-4981 wine@sbwinery.com
www.sbwinery.com
Wines
President/Production Manager: Bruce McGuire
Owner: Pierre Lafond
wine@sbwinery.com
CFO: Marty-Pooe Winnen
Dir. of Research & Development: Suzanne Fitzgerald
Quality Control Manager: Dan Cerepanya
Marketing Director: Michelle Lafond
Sales Manager: George Fakinos
Dir. of Public Relations: Suzanne Fitzgerald
Operations Manager: Dan Cerepanya
Site Manager: Pierre Lafond
Estimated Sales: Below $5 Million
Number Employees: 10-19
Brands:
Lafond
Santa Barbara Winery

11189 Santa Clara Nut Co
1590 Little Orchard St
San Jose, CA 95110-3599
408-298-2425
Fax: 408-298-0101 santaclaranut@aol.com
Manufacturer and exporter of shelled and in-shell walnuts
Owner/President: Jim Pusateri
santaclaranut@aol.com
VP: Salvatore Pusateri
Estimated Sales: $15 Million
Number Employees: 5-9
Number of Brands: 1
Number of Products: 1
Square Footage: 150000
Type of Packaging: Consumer, Food Service, Bulk
Brands:
Santa Clara

11190 Santa Cruz Chili & Spice
1868 E Frontage Rd
1868 E. Frontage Rd.
Tumacacori, AZ 85640
520-398-2591
Fax: 520-398-2592 sales@santacruzchili.com
www.santacruzchili.com
Chile paste, powder, sauces and spices
President: Jean Neubauer
santacruzchili@theriver.com
Sales Manager: Armida Castro
Estimated Sales: $500000
Number Employees: 1-4
Type of Packaging: Consumer

11191 Santa Cruz Mountain Brewing
402 Ingalls St # 27
Santa Cruz, CA 95060-5869
831-425-4900
Fax: 831-429-8915 anthony@scmbrew.com
www.scmbrew.com
Seasonal beer and lager
Owner/Brewer: Emily Thomas
Owner/Brewer: Chad Brill
chad@santacruzmountainbrewing.com
Brewhouse Operations/Brewer: Thomas Mills
Taproom Operations: Jenny Price
Sales and Distribution: Anthony Carlson
Number Employees: 1-4
Type of Packaging: Consumer, Food Service
Brands:
Pacific
Santa Cruz

11192 Santa Cruz Mountain Vineyard
P.O.Box 1592
Felton, CA 95018
831-426-6209
Fax: 831-335-4242
info@santacruzmountainvineyard.com
www.scmountainvineyard.com
Wines
Proprietor: Jeff Emery
Contact: Cynthia Bournellis
cynthia@santacruzmountainvineyard.com
Estimated Sales: Below $5 Million
Number Employees: 5-9
Brands:
Santa Cruz Mountain Vineyard

11193 Santa Elena Coffee Company
550 S Fm 1660
Suite
Hutto, TX 78634-4362
512-846-2908
Fax: 512-846-2710
Coffee

Owner: Linda Truong
VP/Plant Manager: Astrid Bernstorff
Marketing Director: Lissette Bernstorff
Purchasing Manager: Everardo Bernstorff
Number Employees: 5-9
Square Footage: 12000
Type of Packaging: Private Label
Brands:
Santa-Elena Coffee

11194 **Santa Fe Brewing Co**
35 Fire Place # Tasting
Santa Fe, NM 87508-4493
505-424-3333
Fax: 505-474-5573 info@santafebrewing.com
www.santafebrewing.com
Beer
Owner: Scott Biram
scott@santafebrewing.com
Estimated Sales: $275,000
Number Employees: 1-4
Brands:
Santa Fe Brewing

11195 **Santa Fe Seasons**
34 Uss Thresher Ln
Belen, NM 87002
505-988-1515
Fax: 505-988-1300 800-866-4695
www.santafeseasons.com
Salsa and seasonings
President: Greg Deneen
Vice President: Edith Deneen
Sales Director: Lisa Duck
Estimated Sales: Below $5 Million
Number Employees: 20
Brands:
De Santa Fe
Santa Fe Seasons

11196 **Santa Fe Vineyards**
18348 Us 84/285
Espanola, NM 87532
505-753-8100
Fax: 505-753-8100
www.estrelladelnortevineyard.com
Wines
Manager: Dan Doughtery
Estimated Sales: $500,000
Number Employees: 1-4
Brands:
Santa Fe Vineyards

11197 **Santa Maria Foods**
10 Armthorpe Rd
Branpton, ON L6T 5M4
Canada
905-790-1991
Fax: 416-675-7466
Prosciutto and mortadella, salami and cured meats, hams and specialty meats
President: Eddie Zilli
CEO: Frederick Jaques
CFO: Andrew Linley

11198 **Santa Monica Seafood Co.**
18531 S. Broadwick St.
Rancho Dominguez, CA 90220
310-886-7900
Fax: 310-886-3333 800-969-8862
info@smseafood.com
www.santamonicaseafood.com
Fresh and frozen fish including halibut, salmon, sea bass and swordfish.
President: Anthony Cigliano
anthony@smseafood.com
Controlling Partner: Marisa Cigliano
Controlling Partner: John Cigliano
Executive VP/Co-Owner: Michael Cigliano
Year Founded: 1939
Estimated Sales: $400 Million
Number Employees: 20-49
Type of Packaging: Consumer, Food Service, Private Label, Bulk
Other Locations:
Long Beach Seafoods
Del Mar CA
Brands:
Fan-Sea
Stars Pride
Stilwell's

11199 **Santa Ynez Wine Corp**
2922 Grand Ave
Los Olivos, CA 93441
805-688-9665
Fax: 805-686-1690 800-824-8584
www.arthurearl.com
Wines
Owner: Athuur White
Estimated Sales: $1-2.5 000,000
Number Employees: 5-9
Type of Packaging: Private Label
Brands:
Los Olivos Vintners

11200 **Santa's Smokehouse**
2400 Davis Rd
Fairbanks, AK 99701-5700
907-456-3885
Fax: 907-456-3889 800-478-3885
order@santassmokehouse.com
Reindeer and buffalo meat and sausages
Owner: Janet Mc Cormick
Estimated Sales: $300,000-500,000
Number Employees: 5-9
Parent Co: Interior Alaska Fish Processors

11201 **Santanna Banana Company**
12 Kelker Street
Harrisburg, PA 17113
717-238-8321
Fax: 717-238-4480
Bananas
President: Raymond Santanna
Vice President: David Santanna
Vice President: Richard Santanna
Estimated Sales: $16 Million
Number Employees: 41
Square Footage: 75000

11202 **Sante Specialty Foods**
491 Laurelwood Rd
Santa Clara, CA 95054-2416
408-451-9585
Fax: 408-451-9485 www.santenuts.com
Nuts
Owner: Sara Tidhar
Director Of Sales: Navot Tidhar
Number Employees: 1-4

11203 **Santini Foods**
16505 Worthley Dr
San Lorenzo, CA 94580
510-317-8888
Fax: 510-317-8343 800-835-6888
www.santinifoods.com
Milk products, syrups, sauces, and ethnic and specialty foods
President/Owner: Vikram Chand
CFO: Tyler Abbott
Vice President: Christopher Quie
Quality Control: Hal Burgan
Operations: Roger Tan
Year Founded: 1987
Estimated Sales: $11 Million
Number Employees: 50-99
Square Footage: 400000
Type of Packaging: Consumer, Food Service, Private Label, Bulk
Brands:
California Farms
La Vava Blanca
Lotus Bloom

11204 **Santini Foods**
16505 Worthley Dr
San Lorenzo, CA 94580-1811
510-317-7755
Fax: 510-317-8343 800-835-6888
www.santinifoods.com
Condensed milk, salad dressing, olive oil, syrup, jarred vegetables, mushrooms, pesto
Owner: Anna Liu
anna@santinifoods.com
Estimated Sales: $10-20 Million
Number Employees: 50-99
Parent Co: Corticella USA Organic Farms

11205 **Sapore della Vita**
West Country Club Drive N
Sarasota, FL 34243-3513
941-914-4256
kristine@saporedellavita.com
www.saporedellavita.com
Italian products: caramels, jams, marmalades, nut butter, biscotti, oils, sauces and confectionery.
Co-Owner: Kristine Insalaco-Gaioni
Year Founded: 2009
Estimated Sales: Under $500,000
Number Employees: 11-50
Type of Packaging: Food Service, Private Label
Brands:
Crema di Miele
Lick My Spoon
Marchesi
Sapore Del Tartufo
Villa Lan Franca

11206 **Sapp Birch Water**
40 E Chicago Ave
Suite 407
Chicago, IL 60611-2026
708-351-7777
info@sapplife.co
www.sapplife.co
Birch water
Co-Founder & Director: John Kavchak
Brands:
Sapp Birch Water

11207 **Sappore Coffee Co Of Alaska**
6436 Homer Dr # A
PO Box 221187
Anchorage, AK 99518-1900
907-333-3626
Fax: 907-333-3690
www.alaskacoffeecompany.com
Coffee
Owner: Lori Brewer
coffeequeen1@aol.com
Estimated Sales: $280,000
Number Employees: 10-19

11208 **Sapporo USA, Inc.**
11 E 44th St
Suite 705
New York, NY 10017
212-922-9165
Fax: 212-922-9576 info@sapporousa.com
Processor and importer of beer. They also prepare dishes using beer as an ingredient.
President: Tsukasa Orui
Contact: Saori Potts
saori@sapporousa.com
Estimated Sales: G
Number Employees: 30
Square Footage: 2000
Type of Packaging: Consumer, Food Service

11209 **Saputo Cheese USA Inc.**
One Overlook Point
Suite 300
Lincolnshire, IL 60069
847-267-1100
Fax: 847-267-1110 www.saputocheeseusa.com
Natural cheese products and exporter of whey.
President/COO: Terry Brockman
Year Founded: 1954
Estimated Sales: $430 Million
Number Employees: 250-499
Number of Brands: 15
Number of Products: 12
Square Footage: 270000
Parent Co: Saputo, Inc.
Type of Packaging: Consumer, Food Service, Bulk
Brands:
Black Creek
DCI Cheese
Dragone
Frigo Cheese
Great Midwest
Lorraine
Organic Creamery
Salemville
Saputo
Stella
Treasure Cave
Woolwich Dairy
Joan of Arc
Montchevre
Nikos

11210 **Saputo Dairy Division (Canada)**
2365, Chemin de la CoTe-de-Liesse
Saint-Laurent, QC H4N 2M7
Canada
514-328-6663
800-672-8866
www.saputo.com
Dairy products.
President/COO: Frank Guido
Parent Co: Saputo, Inc.
Other Locations:
Cheese Division
Lincolnshire IL
Dairy Division
Dallas TX

11211 **(HQ)Saputo Inc.**
6869, Metropolitain Est
Montreal, QC H1P 1X8
Canada
514-328-6662
800-672-8866
www.saputo.com
Dairy products.
Chair of the Board/CEO: Lino Saputo
President/COO: Kai Bockmann
Chief Financial Officer: Maxime Therrien
Chief Human Resources Officer: Ga,tane Wagner
Year Founded: 1954
Estimated Sales: $11.2 Billion
Number Employees: 16,800
Number of Brands: 45
Brands:
Alexis de Portneuf
Armstrong
Bari
Baxter
Baileys
Cheese Heads
Chevrai
Cracker Barrel
Dairyland
Cogruet
DuVillage 1860
International Delight
JOYYA
Kingsey
Milk2Go
Mornington Dairy
Neilson
Nutrilait
Saputo
Scotsburn
Stella
Wholesome Goat
Woolwich Dairy
Black Creek
DCI Cheese
Dragone
Frigo
Stella
Great Middwest
Lorraine
Organic Creamery
Salemville
Treasure Cave
DairYStar
Friendship Dairies
La Paulina
Molfino
Ricrem
Coon
Devondale
Great Ocead Road
Liddells
Mil Lel
Sungold
Warrnambool Cheese and Butter

11212 **Sara Lee Coffee & Tea**
1370 Progress Rd
Suffolk, VA 23434
757-538-8083
Fax: 757-215-7447
Roasts and packs coffee
CEO: Massino Zanetti
Manager: Chuck Gosstrom
Contact: Felix Venezuela
fvenezuela@saraleecoffee.com
Plant Manager: Buddy McGuire
Number Employees: 200
Brands:
Chase & Sanborn
Chock Full O'Nuts
Hills Bros
Mjb
Segafredo Espresso

11213 **Sara Lee Foodservice**
PO Box 3901
Peoria, IL 61612
800-261-4754
800-641-4025
www.saraleefoodservice.com
Roasted coffee
President/CEO: Sean Connolly
Contact: Brenda Barnes
bbarnes@saraleefoodservice.com
Regional Manager: Stephen Flwoer
Purchasing Manager Assoc.: Steve McCreary
Estimated Sales: $500,000-$1 Million
Number Employees: 5-9
Type of Packaging: Consumer, Food Service
Brands:
Cains
Superior

11214 **Sara Lee Frozen Bakery**
PO Box 708
Kings Mountain, NC 28086
800-323-7117
saraleefrozenbakery@casupport.com
www.saraleefrozenbakery.com
Bakery items, including pies, cakes, muffins, cornbread, donoughts
CEO: Craig Bahner
Sales Administrator/Contact: Tara Washington
twashington@saraleefoodservice.com
Parent Co: Tyson Foods Inc.
Type of Packaging: Food Service
Brands:
Bistro
Chef Pierre
Sara Lee

11215 **Sara Snacker Cookie Company**
41 Purdy Ave.
Suite 505
Rye, NY 10580
914-305-6363
Fax: 914-206-3635
Manufacturer of cookies.
CEO and Founder: Sara Leand

11216 **Sarabeth's Office**
1161 E 156th St
Bronx, NY 10474-6226
718-589-2900
Fax: 718-589-8412 800-773-7378
info@sarabeth.com www.sarabeth.com
Muffins, cakes, cookies, pastries, puddings, pies, croissants, brownies, tarts and frozen blintzes
Chief Executive Officer: William Levine
Executive VP: Jennifer Firestone
Vice President: David Case
david.case@sarabeth.com
Co-Owner: David Case
Estimated Sales: Below $5 Million
Number Employees: 10-19
Square Footage: 17200
Parent Co: Sarabeth's Kitchen
Type of Packaging: Consumer, Food Service
Other Locations:
Sarabeth's Bakery Ltd.
New York NY
Brands:
Sarabeth's

11217 **Sarah's Vineyard**
4005 Hecker Pass Rd
Gilroy, CA 95020-8843
408-842-4278
Fax: 408-842-3252 sales@sarahsvineyard.com
www.sarahs-vineyard.com
Wines
Proprietor: Tim Slater
Estimated Sales: $500,000-$1 Million
Number Employees: 5-9
Brands:
Sarah's Vineyard

11218 **Saranac Brewery**
830 Varick St
Utica, NY 13502
800-765-6288
www.saranac.com
Manufacturer, brewer and exporter of beer, ale, stout, lager and malt; also, soft drinks and juices
President: Fred Matt
Chairman & CEO: Nicholas Matt
Director of Operations: Jim Kuhr
Estimated Sales: $21 Million
Number Employees: 150
Number of Brands: 12
Square Footage: 360000
Type of Packaging: Consumer, Food Service, Private Label, Bulk
Brands:
Adirondack Amber
American Plsener
Black and Tan
Black Forest
English Pale Ale
Light
Mountain Berry
Saranac Diet Root Beer
Saranac Ginger Beer
Saranac Orange Cream
Saranac Root Beer
Traditional Lager

11219 **Sarant International Cmmdts**
213 Hallock Rd # 3b
PO Box 659
Stony Brook, NY 11790-3000
631-675-2875
Fax: 631-246-5257 psarant@aol.com
Processor and importer of dehydrated vegetables including tomatoes, celery, carrots and red and green bell peppers
President: Peter Sarant
Co-Secretary: Pamela Sarant
Number Employees: 1-4
Type of Packaging: Bulk

11220 **Saratoga Food Specialties**
771 W Crossroads Pkwy
Bolingbrook, IL 60490
800-451-0407
info@saratogafs.com www.saratogafs.com
Whole and ground spices, custom seasoning blends, seasoned rice, stuffing and gravy mixes.
President: Michael Marks
CFO: Ed Herbert
Vice President: Wade McGeorge
Research & Development: Paul Maki
Quality Control: Mark Beattie
Marketing Director: Kristi Freitager
Sales Director: George Rackos
Contact: Alan Ainsley
aainsley@saratogafs.com
Operations Manager: Jim Benja
Purchasing Manager: Ron Batzer
Estimated Sales: $30-40 Million
Number Employees: 100-249
Square Footage: 110000
Type of Packaging: Consumer, Food Service, Private Label, Bulk
Other Locations:
Saratoga Specialties Co.
Northlake IL

11221 **Saratoga Peanut Butter Company**
P.O. Box 5111
Saratoga Springs, NY 12866
888-967-3268
customerservice@saratogapb.com
www.yopeanut.com
Almond butter, peanut butter, and nut butter blends
Owner: Jessica Arceri
Marketing: Senia Fleming

11222 **Saratoga Salad Dressing**
5 Whitman Rd
Canton, MA 02021-2707
781-821-1010
Fax: 781-821-4303 www.saratogadressings.com
Pickled fruits and vegetables, vegetable sauces and seasonings, and salad dressings
Owner: Judy Pearlstein
jpearlstein@saratogadressings.com
Estimated Sales: $3,100,000
Number Employees: 20-49
Type of Packaging: Food Service, Private Label, Bulk
Brands:
Saratoga

11223 **(HQ)Saratoga Spring Water Co**
11 Geyser Rd
Saratoga Springs, NY 12866-9048
518-584-6363
Fax: 518-584-0380 888-426-8642
www.sswc.com
Spring water, orange and grapefruit juice and smoothies
President: Robin Prever
rprever@saratogaspringwater.com
CFO: Robert Braks
Vice President: Andrew Cook
Production Manager: Mike Lawson
Estimated Sales: $300,000-500,000
Number Employees: 50-99
Type of Packaging: Consumer, Food Service, Private Label
Other Locations:
Saratoga Beverage Group
Azusa CA
Brands:
Saratoga
Saratoga Splash
Saratoga Vichy

11224 **Sardinha's Sausage**
177 Lepes Rd
Somerset, MA 02726-2635
508-674-2511
Fax: 508-674-2511 800-678-0178
www.sardinhas.com
Gourmet smoked and fresh sausages including chourico, linguica, turkey dogs and kielbasa, breakfast and Italian sausage
President: Ed Sardinha
esardinha@sardinhas.com
Estimated Sales: Less Than $500,000
Number Employees: 1-4
Square Footage: 14400
Type of Packaging: Consumer, Food Service, Private Label, Bulk
Brands:
Francisco's
Portuguese Sausages
Sardinha's
Vincenza's

11225 **Sardinia Cheese**
312 Roosevelt Drive
Seymour, CT 06483-2128
203-735-3374
Fax: 203-732-3959 tmavuli@aol.com
Cheese
CEO/VP: Tony Mavuli
Estimated Sales: $5 000,000
Number Employees: 3
Type of Packaging: Private Label

11226 **Sargent and Greenleaf**
PO Box 930
Nicholasville, KY 40340-930
859-885-9411
Fax: 859-885-3063 800-826-7652
www.sglocks.com
Bottled and glass and plastic-packed pickled products including beets, cauliflower, onions, olives, pickles, peppers, gherkins, etc.; also, vinegar
Co-Owner: James Sargent
Co-Owner: Halbert Greenleaf
CEO: Jerry A Morgan
Director Sales: Richard Greenberg
Type of Packaging: Consumer, Food Service
Brands:
Lion
Supreme

11227 **Sargent's Bear Necessities**
321 Guay Farm Road
North Troy, VT 05859-9207
802-988-2903
Jams, jellies, pickles and relishes
Owner: Michelle Sargent
Number Employees: 1

11228 **(HQ)Sargento Foods Inc**
1 Persnickety Pl
Plymouth, WI 53073-3544
920-893-8484
Fax: 920-893-8399 800-243-3737
www.sargento.com
Natural and processed cheese manufacturer.
CEO: Louis Gentine
Executive VP: Karri Neils
karri.neils@sargentocheese.com
Estimated Sales: Over $1 Billion
Number Employees: 1000-4999
Type of Packaging: Consumer, Food Service, Private Label, Bulk
Brands:
Sargento
Snack Bites
Chef Blends
Artisan Blends
Natural Blends
Ultra Thin
Balanced Breaks

11229 **Sarliz LLC**
7000 Fordland Drive
Raleigh, NC 27606-4499
860-355-9697
Fax: 860-210-1999
Flavored soup stocks
President: Robert Greene
Type of Packaging: Consumer, Food Service, Private Label, Bulk
Brands:
Savory Basics

11230 **Sarris Candies Inc**
511 Adams Ave
Canonsburg, PA 15317-2103
724-745-4042
Fax: 724-745-5642 800-255-7771
www.sarriscandies.com
Candies
CEO: Josh Cas
jlucas@sarriscandies.com
Number Employees: 250-499

11231 **Sartori Co**
107 N Pleasant View Rd
PO Box 258
Plymouth, WI 53073-4948
920-893-6061
Fax: 920-892-2732
customercare@sartoricheese.com
www.sartoricheese.com
Cheese
Founder: Paolo Sartori
CEO: James C Sartori
info@sartorifoods.com
Sales Manager: Jim Tassielli
Number Employees: 20-49

11232 **Sarum Tea Company**
332 Main St
Lakeville, CT 06039
860-435-2086
Fax: 860-435-9304
Tea
President/CEO: W Harris
Manager: E Lloyd-Harris
Estimated Sales: Less than $500,000
Number Employees: 1-4
Brands:
Sarum Tea

11233 **Sassafras Enterprises Inc**
1622 W Carroll Ave
Chicago, IL 60612-2502
312-226-2000
Fax: 312-226-0873 800-537-4941
info@sassafrasenterprises.com
www.sassafras-wholesale.com
Gourmet gift baskets, natural pizza and pasta sauces, spices, oils, spreads, bruschettas, mixes, pastas and bread mixes
Owner: Rob Joslyn
rob.joslyn@marriott.com
VP: Nancy Schwab
Operations Manager: Ron Cahill
Estimated Sales: $10 Million
Number Employees: 5-9
Type of Packaging: Private Label
Brands:
Superstone

11234 **Saticoy Foods Corp**
554 Todd Rd
Santa Paula, CA 93060-9725
805-647-5266
Fax: 805-933-1523 www.moodydunbar.com
Processor of bell peppers, pimientos and sweet potatoes; products are certified kosher.
President: Jerry Hensley
CEO: Stanley Dunbar
Estimated Sales: $10-20 Million
Number Employees: 20-49
Parent Co: Moody Dunbar, Inc.

11235 **Satiety Winery & Cafe**
1027 Maple Ln
Davis, CA 95616-1720
530-757-2699
Fax: 530-668-9263
Wines, wine vinegars, table grapes, wine grapes
Owner: Sterling Chaykin
Estimated Sales: $270,000
Number Employees: 5-9
Brands:
Ambrosia
Satiety

11236 **Satin Fine Foods**
32 Leone Lane
Chester, NY 10918
contact@satinfinefoods.com
www.satinice.com
Gluten-free, dairy-free, nut-free, vegan, Kosher fondant and gum paste in various colors
Founder/CEO: Kevin O'Reilly
Year Founded: 2001
Number of Brands: 1
Number of Products: 4
Type of Packaging: Consumer, Private Label, Bulk
Brands:
Satin Ice

11237 **Sattwa Chai**
17900 NE Lewis Rogers Ln
Newberg, OR 97132-6521
503-538-4715
Fax: 503-538-5125 www.sattwachai.com
Tea, chai
Owner: Juanita Crampton
juanita@sattwa.com
Owner: David Fields
CFO/VP Operations: Juanita Crampton
Purchasing Manager: Jan Rhine
Estimated Sales: $2.5-5 Million
Number Employees: 1-4
Parent Co: Sattwa Chai
Type of Packaging: Food Service, Private Label, Bulk
Brands:
Black Tea Chai
Sattwa Sun Chai
Sattwa Chai Concentrate
Sattwa Kovalam Spice Chai
Sattwa Shanti Herbal Chai
Sattwa Sun Chai

11238 **Sau-Sea Foods**
303 S Broadway
Suite 224
Tarrytown, NY 10591
914-631-1717
Fax: 914-631-0865
Shrimp and sauces including cocktail, tartar and horseradish
President: Antonio Estadella
estadella@csi.com
National Sales Manager: Edward Cauley
Estimated Sales: $1,300,000
Number Employees: 5-9
Type of Packaging: Consumer, Food Service, Private Label, Bulk
Brands:
Sea Maid
Seagull Bay

11239 **Sauces N' Love**
86 Sanderson Ave
Suite 130
Lynn, MA 01902
781-595-7771
Fax: 781-595-7799 info@saucesnlove.com
saucesnlove.com
Homemade pasta sauces
Contact: Paolo Volpati-Kedra
paolo@saucesnlove.com
Estimated Sales: $5-10 Million
Number Employees: 10-19

11240 **Saucilito Canyon Vineyard**
3080 Biddle Ranch Rd
San Luis Obispo, CA 93401-8320
805-543-2111
Fax: 805-543-2111 info@saucelitocanyon.com
www.saucelitocanyon.com

Wines
Founder, Owner: Bill Greenough
Owner: Nancy Greenbough
nancy@saucelitocanyon.com
Marketing/Sales Manager: Nancy Greenbough
Winemaker: Amy Freeman
Estimated Sales: Less than $500,000
Number Employees: 1-4
Type of Packaging: Private Label
Brands:
Saucelito Canyon

11241 **Sauder's Eggs**
570 Furnace Hills Pike
Lititz, PA 17543-0427
717-626-2074
Fax: 717-626-0493 800-233-0413
info@saudereggs.com www.saudereggs.com
Eggs
President: Paul Sauder
CEO: Mark Sauder
Customer Sales Manager: Brian Chmiel
Director of Operations: Joe Brussell
Estimated Sales: Under $500,000
Number Employees: 1-4
Type of Packaging: Food Service, Private Label
Brands:
Sauder's

11242 **Saugy Inc.**
9 Sachemor Rd
Cranston, RI 02920-4514
401-640-1879
Fax: 401-383-9374 866-467-2849
saugy@cox.net www.saugys.com
Frankfurters
President & CEO: Mary O'Brien
Estimated Sales: $900,000
Number Employees: 3
Type of Packaging: Consumer, Food Service, Private Label, Bulk

11243 **Sausage Kitchen**
36 Main St
Lisbon Falls, ME 04252-1507
207-353-5503
Fax: 207-353-8707 888-453-5503
www.sausagekitchen.com
Sausages
President: Maurice Bonneau
info@sausagekitchen.com
Plant Manager: David Parker
Estimated Sales: $350,000
Number Employees: 1-4

11244 **Sausages by Amy**
1141 W Lake St
Chicago, IL 60607
312-829-2250
Fax: 312-829-2098
Sausages
President: Amy Kurzawski
VP: Chico Kurzawski
Estimated Sales: $5-10 Million
Number Employees: 50-99

11245 **Sausal Winery**
7370 Highway 128
Healdsburg, CA 95448
707-433-2285
Fax: 707-433-5136 800-500-2285
Wines
President: David Demostene
Estimated Sales: Below $5 Million
Number Employees: 10-19
Brands:
Sausal Wines

11246 **Saval Foods Corp**
6740 Dorsey Rd
PO Box 8630
Elkridge, MD 21075-6205
410-379-5100
Fax: 410-379-8068 800-527-2825
www.savalfoods.com
Meats & poultry, refrigerated products, non-foods, produce, frozen foods, general grocery items, and seafood products available to the commercial restaurant segment of the foodservice industry.
President: Dennis Barry
dennisbarry@savalfoods.com
Vice President: Richard Hatcher
Marketing Manager: Bryan Bernstein
Human Resources Manager: Paul Self
dennisbarry@savalfoods.com
Operations/ Quality Control Manager: Ron Tew
Production Manager: Joe Savage
Number Employees: 100-249
Type of Packaging: Food Service, Private Label, Bulk
Brands:
Elite
Saval

11247 **Savannah Bee Co.**
211 Johnny Mercer Blvd
Savannah, GA 31410-2119
912-234-0688
Fax: 912-234-0125 800-955-5080
info@savannahbee.com savannahbee.com
Honey
President/Owner: Ted Dennard
info@savannahbee.com
Estimated Sales: $1.1 Million
Number Employees: 20-49

11248 **Savannah Chanelle Vineyards**
23600 Big Basin Way
Saratoga, CA 95070-9755
408-741-2934
Fax: 408-867-4824 www.savannahchanelle.com
Wines
President: Michael Ballard
tastingroom@savannahchanelle.com
Co-Owner: Kellie Ballard
Winemaker: Tony Craig
Estimated Sales: $5-10 Million
Number Employees: 10-19
Brands:
Savannah Chanelle Vineyards

11249 **Savannah Cinnamon & Cookie Company**
P.O.Box 20251
Bradenton, FL 34204
Fax: 912-233-3004 800-288-0854
www.savannahcinnamon.com
Cinnamon and other liquid flavors for coffee, tea and juices
Owner: Brian Wiggins
Estimated Sales: $1-2.5 Million
Number Employees: 10-19
Type of Packaging: Consumer
Brands:
Savannah Cinnamon Mix
Savannah Squares

11250 **Savannah Food Co**
575 Industrial Rd
PO Box 1000
Savannah, TN 38372-5977
731-925-1155
Fax: 731-925-1855 800-795-2550
info@savannahclassics.com
www.savannahclassics.com
Manufacturer and marketer of homestyle hushpuppies and authentic southern side dishes.
President: John Bryan
VP, Sales & Marketing: Jim Sisco
VP, Operations: Paul Stodard
Direction of Production: Lynn Austin
Year Founded: 1970
Number Employees: 50-99
Type of Packaging: Consumer, Food Service, Private Label
Other Locations:
Savannah Foods & Industries
Breman GA
Brands:
Neokura
San Like
San Orange
San Red
San Yellow
San-Ei

11251 **Saveur Food Group**
101 Central Park west
Suite 3C
New york, NY 10023
212-595-5425
Fax: 732-730-9913 abankier@saveurfood.com
Beef, potato pancakes, vegetable pancakes, maztoh balls
Co-President & CEO: Paul Bensabat
Co-President & CFO: Alain Bankier
Estimated Sales: $5-10 Million
Number Employees: 50-99
Brands:
Ratner's

11252 **(HQ)Savino's Italian Ices**
1126 S Powerline Road
Deerfield Beach, FL 33442-8121
954-426-4119
Frozen Italian ice fruit desserts
CEO: Sal Savino
Number Employees: 1-4
Type of Packaging: Bulk

11253 **Savoia Foods**
402 W Lincon Hwy
Chicago Heights, IL 60411
708-756-7600
Fax: 708-754-2133 800-867-2782
www.savoiafoods.com
Pasta, brands spaghetti, spinach spaghetti, inguine, fettucine and lasagne
President/Owner: Rudolph Bamonti
Sales Executive: Julia Bamonti
Estimated Sales: $2.5-5million
Number Employees: 10-19
Type of Packaging: Consumer, Food Service
Brands:
Savoia

11254 **Savoie Industries**
351 Highway 999
Belle Rose, LA 70341
225-473-9293
Fax: 225-473-9294
Blackstrap molasses and sugar
President/GM: Patrick Cancienne
Vice President: Paul Cancienne
Estimated Sales: $10-20 Million
Number Employees: 50-99
Type of Packaging: Consumer

11255 **Savoie's Sausage and Food Products**
1742 Highway 742
Opelousas, LA 70570-0549
337-942-7241
Fax: 337-948-9571 info@savoiesfoods.com
www.savoiesfoods.com
Sausage including hog's headcheese, boudin, andouille and tasso; also, barbecue sauce, roux and dressing mix
President/Owner: Eula Savoie
Vice President: Frieda Hunt
frieda@savoiesfoods.com
Marketing Manager: Frederick Lafleur
Operations Manager: Gerald Boullion
Estimated Sales: $9 Million
Number Employees: 50-99
Square Footage: 100000
Type of Packaging: Consumer, Private Label
Brands:
Cajun House
Real Cajun
Savoie's

11256 **Savor Street**
159 Spring Valley Rd
Unit 101
Reading, PA 19605
800-523-8253
www.savorstreet.com
Baked snacks
Marketing Communications Coordinator: Laura Unger

11257 **Savory Foods**
900 Hynes Ave SW
Grand Rapids, MI 49507-1091
616-241-2583
Fax: 616-241-6332 800-878-2583
www.pennstreetbakery.com
Processor and exporter of pork rinds
Owner: Dan Abraham
Safety Manager: Adam Dengel
VP Sales/Production: K Sanderlin
dan.abraham@savoryfoods.com
Production Manager: Ed Thompson
Plant Manager: Rigel Olmos

Number Employees: 20-49
Square Footage: 120000
Type of Packaging: Food Service, Private Label
Brands:
Porkies
Savory
Southern Style

11258 **Savoury Systems Inc**
230 Industrial Pkwy # C
Branchburg, NJ 08876-3580
908-526-2524
888-534-6621
savourysystems.com
Savory flavors manufacturer.
President: David Adams
customerservice@savourysystems.com
Vice President, Marketing: Jackie Sun
Vice President & Director of Sales: Kevin McDermott
Director of Operations: Alex Carillo
Estimated Sales: $12.6 Million
Number Employees: 10-19
Brands:
Savorganic

11259 **Sawtooth Winery**
13750 Surrey Ln
Nampa, ID 83686-9128
208-467-1200
Fax: 208-468-7934 www.sawtoothwinery.com
Wines
Winemaker/General Manager: Brad Pintler
President: Ken McCabe
Partner: Charles Pintler
Retail Manager/Events Coordinator: Ina DeBoer
Manager: Ken Mccabe
kmccabe@sawtoothwinery.com
Estimated Sales: $1-2.5 Million
Number Employees: 5-9
Brands:
Sawtooth

11260 **Saxby Foods**
4120 98th Street NW
Edmonton, AB T6E 5A2
Canada
780-440-4179
Fax: 780-440-4480
Frozen desserts including cakes and cheesecakes
President: Jonathan Avis
Quality Control: Ana Avalos
Public Relations: Thea Avis
Plant Manager: Sean Gillis
Purchasing: Rhys Amatori
Estimated Sales: F
Number Employees: 120
Square Footage: 100000
Type of Packaging: Private Label
Brands:
Albertson's
Safeway
Walmart

11261 **Saxon Chocolates**
21 Coleville Rd
Toronto, ON M6M 2Y2
Canada
416-675-6363
Fax: 416-675-2777 sales@saxonchocolates.com
www.saxonchocolates.com
Belgian chocolates
President/Owner: Johan DeGrees
Estimated Sales: $2.3 Million
Number Employees: 20

11262 **Saxon Creamery**
855 Hickory Street
PO Box 206
Cleveland, WI 53015
920-693-8500
Fax: 920-693-8400 info@saxoncreamery.com
www.saxoncreamery.com
Cheeses
Plant Manager of Sales: Gerald Heimerl

11263 **Sazerac Co Inc**
101 Magazine St
5th Floor
New Orleans, LA 70130
504-831-9450
Fax: 504-831-9452 info@sazerac.com
www.sazerac.com
Distilled spirits
Marketing Services Director: Meredith Moody
PR Manager: Amy Preske
Year Founded: 1850
Estimated Sales: $50-100 Million
Number Employees: 14,800
Number of Brands: 36
Type of Packaging: Private Label
Brands:
1792
99 Brand
Ancient Age
Benchmark
Bentley's
Big House
Blantons
Bowman's
Bowman's Small Batch
Buckhorn
Buffalo Trace
Buffalo Trace Distillery Experiment
Colonel Lee
E.H. Taylor Jr.
Eagle Rare
Elmer T. Lee
Firefly
Flatboat
George T. Stagg
Hancock's
Kentucky Gentleman
Kentucky Tavern
Old Charter
Old Taylor
Rockhill Farms
SABI
Setter
Southern Comfort
Ten High
Tom Moore
Two Stars
Van Winkle
Very Old Barton
Virginia Gentlemen
W.L. Weller
Zackariah Harris

11264 **Sazerac Company, Inc.**
3850 N Causeway Blvd
Suite 1695
Metairie, LA 70002-3825
866-729-3722
info@sazerac.com
www.sazerac.com
Manufacturer and exporter of bourbon, scotch, whiskey, gin and vodka; importer of scotch
President & CEO: Mark Brown
mbrown@bourbonwhiskey.com
Owner: Chaolai Wu
Partner: Scott Newitt
Vice President of Human Resources: Kathy Thelen
Marketing Services Director: Meredith Moody
VP Sales & Marketing: Steve Wyant
PR Manager: Amy Preske
Plant Manager: Byron Du Bois
Number Employees: 350
Square Footage: 360000
Brands:
1792 Ridgemont Reserve Bourbon
99 Schnapps
Barton
Glenmore
Hartley Brandy
Highland Mist Scotch
House of Stuart Scotch
Imperial Blent
Inver House Scotch
Jacques Bonet Brandy
Kentucky Gentleman Bourbon-A-Blend
Kentucky Tavern Bourbon
Lauder's Scotch
Meukow Cognac
Monte Alban Mezcal
Montezuma Blue
Montezuma Tequila
Montezuma Triple Sec
Calypso Gold Rum
Calypso Light Rum
Canadian Host
Canadian Ltd
Canadian Supreme
Capitan Gold Tequila
Capitan Tequila & Triple Sec
Capitan White Tequila
Caravella
Chi-Chi's Appletini
Chi-Chi's Caribbean Mudslide
Mr. Boston
Northern Light Canadian
Old Thompson Blend
Pikeman Gin
Sabroso Di Cafe Liqueur
Amaretto De Sabroso
Colonel Lee Bourbon
Crystal Palace
Czarina
Di Amore
Skol
Ten High Bourbon
Tom Moore
Very Old Barton Bourbon
Wave Flavored Vodkas
Sambuca Di Amore
El Toro Tequila
Fleischmann's

11265 **Scala-Wisell International Inc.**
24 S Tyson Avenue
Suite 1
Floral Park, NY 11001
516-437-8600
Fax: 516-437-8686 info@scala-wisell.com
www.scala-wisellint.com
Manufacturer of candied fruit, sprinkles and toasted and sweetened coconut.
President: Carol Wisell
cwisell@scala-wisell.com
Type of Packaging: Bulk

11266 **Scally's Imperial Importing Company Inc**
4354 Victory Blvd
Staten Island, NY 10314-6733
718-983-1938
Fax: 718-259-2195 scallyimperial@aol.com
Manufacturer and marketer of Mission San Juan 100% fruit juices and smoothies in single serve and multiserve containers.
President/Sales/Plant Manager: Alex Scarselli
CEO: Alessandre Scarselli
VP/Purchasing Director: Christine Scarselli
Estimated Sales: $5 Million
Number Employees: 1-4
Number of Brands: 3
Number of Products: 20
Square Footage: 10000
Type of Packaging: Consumer, Food Service, Private Label
Brands:
Apple Brand Juices
Fruit Ole Smoothies
Mission San Juan Juices

11267 **Scandia Seafood Company**
130 Tillson Avenue
Rockland, ME 04841-3424
207-596-7102
Fax: 207-596-7105
Crabs, cold water shrimp, American lobster, Atlantic herring
President: Asger Jorgensen
Square Footage: 25000

11268 **(HQ)Scandinavian Formulas Inc**
140 E Church St
Sellersville, PA 18960-2402
215-453-2500
Fax: 215-453-2508 800-288-2844
www.scandinavianformulas.com
Manufacturer, importer and exporter of vitamins and supplements, chemicals and ingredients. Botanicals, extracts, oils, bulk tablets and soft gels.
President: Catherine Peklak
Marketing: Sylvie Millet
Sales/Purchasing: Mike Peklak
IT: Bob Blackledge
bob@scandinavianformulas.com
Estimated Sales: $1005000
Number Employees: 1-4
Number of Brands: 7
Number of Products: 7
Square Footage: 36000
Type of Packaging: Consumer, Private Label, Bulk
Other Locations:
Scandinavian Natural Health
Perkasie PA
Brands:
Alkyrol
Bilberry Extract
Dhea

Lycopene
Melatonin
Salix Sst
Sincera Skin Care Products

11269 Scandinavian Laboratories
316 Front Street
Belvidere, PA 07823-1510
908-475-4754
Fax: 908-469-4912 866-623-2650
scanlabs@epix.net www.oceanaproducts.com
Nutritional products including shark liver and fish oils, essential fatty acids, effervescent tablets and liquid emulsions; importer and exporter of nutritional supplements including shark liver oils
President: Olav Sandnes
Contact: Susan Battillo
susan@oceanaproducts.com
Estimated Sales: $500,000
Number Employees: 5-9
Type of Packaging: Private Label, Bulk
Brands:
Calcitrace
Ecomega
Glycomarine
Oceana
Pedia-Vit
Promega
Squalene

11270 Scenic Fruit Co
7510 SE Altman Rd
Gresham, OR 97080-8808
503-663-3434
Fax: 503-663-7095 877-927-3434
info@scenicfruit.com www.scenicfruit.com
Frozen berries
President: Judy England
CEO: Hugh Eisele
hugh.eisele@scenicfruit.com
Plant Manager: John Vasquez
Estimated Sales: $18 Million
Number Employees: 100-249
Type of Packaging: Food Service, Bulk

11271 Scenic Valley Winery
103 Coffee St
Lanesboro, MN 55949
507-259-4981
Fax: 507-467-2640
Wines
Owner: Karrie Ristau
Estimated Sales: $470,000
Number Employees: 5-9

11272 Schadel's Bakery
212 N Bullard Street
Silver City, NM 88061-5308
505-538-3031
Bakery
President/CEO: Dexter Seay
Estimated Sales: $500,000
Number Employees: 5-9

11273 Schaefers Market
411 Sinclair Lewis Ave
Sauk Centre, MN 56378-1350
320-352-6490
www.schaefersmarket.com
Frankfurters, bologna, sausage and poultry
Owner: Chris Lawinger
Estimated Sales: $17 Million
Number Employees: 10-19
Type of Packaging: Consumer

11274 Schaefers Market
411 Sinclair Lewis Ave
Sauk Centre, MN 56378-1350
320-352-6490
Fax: 320-352-2206 www.schaefersmarket.com
Meat packing and slaughtering
Owner: Chris Lawinger
Estimated Sales: Below $5,000,000
Number Employees: 10-19

11275 Schafer Fisheries Inc
2112 Sandridge Rd
Thomson, IL 61285-7709
815-259-4300
Fax: 815-259-4542 800-291-3474
Seafood
Owner: Mike Schafer
mike@schaferfish.com
Estimated Sales: $3-5 Million
Number Employees: 20-49

11276 Schaller & Weber Inc
2235 46th St
Astoria, NY 11105-1305
718-721-5480
Fax: 718-956-9157 800-847-4115
info@schallerweber.com www.winstonfarm.com
Ham and German-style sausage, poultry, cold cuts, cooked and smoked products, salami and cervelat and seafood
Owner: Ralph Schaller
jeremyschaller@gmail.com
Sales Exec: Jeremy Schaller
Estimated Sales: $12 Million
Number Employees: 50-99
Square Footage: 32000
Type of Packaging: Consumer

11277 Schaller's Bakery Inc
826 Highland Ave
Greensburg, PA 15601-4316
724-837-3660
Fax: 724-837-6764 800-241-1777
Baked goods
President: Warren Schaller
Contact: Weddell Schaller
donna.simmons@midohiodevelopment.com
Estimated Sales: $2 Million
Number Employees: 20-49
Square Footage: 63000
Type of Packaging: Consumer, Food Service, Private Label, Bulk

11278 Scharffen Berger Chocolate Maker
790 Tennessee St
San Francisco, CA 94107
866-608-6944
scharffenberger@worldpantry.com
www.scharffenberger.com
Dark chocolate
CEO: John Scharffenberger
CFO/COO: Jim Harris
Marketing: Norm Shea

11279 Schat's Dutch Bakeries
763 N Main St
Bishop, CA 93514-2427
760-873-7156
Fax: 760-872-4932 866-323-5854
schatsbakery@mindspring.com
Baked goods
Owner: Erick Schat
CFO: Mirika Marijke
Estimated Sales: Below $5 Million
Number Employees: 50-99
Brands:
Erick Schat

11280 Schenk Packing Co Inc
1321 S 6th St
Mt Vernon, WA 98273-4919
360-336-2128
Fax: 360-336-3092 info@schenkpacking.com
www.schenkpacking.com
Processor and exporter of meat products; custom slaughtering available.
Owner/President: Steve Lenz
stevel@schenkpacking.com
Operations Managerr: Marcie Lenz
Number Employees: 20-49
Square Footage: 84672
Type of Packaging: Consumer, Food Service

11281 Schepps Dairy
3114 S Haskell Ave
Dallas, TX 75223
214-824-8163
Fax: 214-824-1526 800-395-7004
Dairy products including; fluid milk, buttermilk, cream, half & half, lactose free milk, cottage cheese, sour cream, orange juice, fruit drink, yogurt, creamers, cream cheese, ice cream mix, cream topping, butter, eggs
Director: Debra Bowen
Vice President: Pat Boyle
Sales Director: Steve Schenkel
Contact: Debra Drinane
debra_drinane@deanfoods.com
Parent Co: Dean Foods
Type of Packaging: Consumer, Food Service, Private Label, Bulk
Other Locations:
Schepps Dairy
Houston TX
Brands:
Schepps Dairy
Silk
Horizon
International Delight
Oak Farms

11282 Schermer Pecan Co
811 S Veterans Blvd
Glennville, GA 30427-2800
912-654-2230
Fax: 912-654-2344 800-841-3403
losborne@leapfrogprco.com
www.schermerpecans.com
Manufacturer of pecans and pecan oil.
Owner: Putt Wetherbee
Manager: Melita Humphries
melita@schermerpecans.com
Number Employees: 100-249

11283 Schiavone's Casa Mia
1907 Tytus Avenue
Middletown, OH 45042-2367
513-422-8650
Fax: 513-422-8602
Sauces
President: Michael Schiavone
Estimated Sales: $500,000-$1 Million
Number Employees: 20-49

11284 Schiff Food Products CoInc
994 Riverview Dr
Totowa, NJ 07512-1129
973-237-1990
Fax: 973-237-1999 sales@schifffood.com
www.schifffoods.com
Manufacturer, importer and exporter of spices, seeds, herbs and dehydrated vegetables
President: David Deutscher
david.deutscher@schiffs.com
Estimated Sales: $15 Million
Number Employees: 20-49
Square Footage: 600000
Type of Packaging: Consumer, Private Label
Brands:
Schiff Food

11285 Schiff Nutrition International
P.O. Box 224
Parsippany, NJ 07054-0224
415-433-3777
800-526-6251
www.schiffnutrition.com
Vitamins and nutritional supplements.
President/CEO: Tarang Amin
EVP/CFO: Joseph Baty
VP/General Counsel: Scott Milstein
VP Research/Development: Shane Durkee
Contact: Webster Jarom
websterj@schiffnutrition.com
SVP of Operations: Jon Fieldman
Brands:
Move Free
Schiff
Megared
Digestive Advantage
Tiger's Milk
Sustenex

11286 Schillinger Genetics Inc
4401 Westown Pkwy # 225
Suite 225
West Des Moines, IA 50266-6721
515-225-1166
Fax: 515-225-1177 866-769-7200
heartland@heartlandfields.com
www.schillgen.com
Manufacturer and exporter of soybeans
President: John Schillinger
Marketing/Sales Director: Karen Labenz
Estimated Sales: $10-20 Million
Number Employees: 10-19
Parent Co: Monsanto
Type of Packaging: Consumer, Bulk
Brands:
Dekalb

11287 **Schiltz Foods Inc**
7 W Oak St
Sisseton, SD 57262-1440
605-698-7651
Fax: 605-698-7112 877-872-4458
jschiltz@schiltzfoods.com www.schiltzfoods.com
Processor and exporter of dressed geese and goose products
President: Richard Schiltz
richard.schiltz@schiltzfoods.com
VP/Director of Sales: James Schiltz
Estimated Sales: $2.1 Million
Number Employees: 100-249
Number of Brands: 4
Number of Products: 20
Square Footage: 136000
Type of Packaging: Consumer, Food Service, Private Label, Bulk
Brands:
All American Holiday Goose
Whetstone Valley

11288 **Schimpffs Confectionery LLC**
347 Spring St
Jeffersonville, IN 47130-3449
812-283-8367
Fax: 812-288-2229 info@schimpffs.com
www.schimpffs.com
Candy
Owner: Warren Schimpffs
info@schimpffs.com
Number Employees: 10-19

11289 **Schirf Brewing Company**
P.O.Box 459
250 Main Street
Park City, UT 84060-0459
435-649-0900
Fax: 435-649-4999 www.wasatchbeers.com
Beer
President: Greg Schirf
Contact: Paul Brown
paul@wasatchbeers.com
Estimated Sales: $20-50 Million
Number Employees: 50-99
Brands:
Wasatch

11290 **Schisa Brothers**
1 Commerce Blvd
Syracuse, NY 13211
315-463-0213
Fax: 315-463-0248
Processes and manufactures meat and meat products.
President: Bruce Dew
Number Employees: 47
Type of Packaging: Consumer, Food Service

11291 **Schlafly Tap Room**
2100 Locust St
St Louis, MO 63103-1616
314-241-2337
Fax: 314-241-8101 gimmes@schlafly.com
www.schlafly.com
Beer, ale, lager, stout and seasonal beers
President: Tom Schlafly
CEO: James Pendegraft
CFO/COO: Keith Moszczenski
Marketing Director: Mitch Turner
Estimated Sales: $20-50 Million
Number Employees: 100-249
Parent Co: Saint Louis Brewery
Type of Packaging: Consumer, Food Service
Brands:
Schlafly

11292 **Schleswig Specialty Meats**
Highway 59 South
Schleswig, IA 51461
712-676-3324
Fax: 712-676-3936
Manufacturer and packer of meats.
President: Richard Beatty
Plant Manager: Phil Smith
Estimated Sales: $5-10 Million
Number Employees: 25
Square Footage: 80000
Type of Packaging: Private Label

11293 **Schloss Doepken Winery**
9177 Old Route 20
Ripley, NY 14775-9510
716-326-3636
Wines
President: John Watso
schlossdoepkenwines@gmail.com
Estimated Sales: $500,000-$1 000,000
Number Employees: 1-4
Brands:
Schloss Doepken

11294 **Schlotterbeck & Foss Company**
117 Preble St
Portland, ME 04101
207-772-4666
Fax: 207-774-3449 800-777-4666
www.schlotterbeck-foss.com
Spicy salsas, grilling and stir-fry sauces.
President: Peter Foss
CEO: Richard Foss
Founder: Augustus G. Schlotterbeck
Marketing Manager: Charles Foss
Sales Director: Arthur Kyncos
Contact: Ron Badgett
rbadgett@schlotterbeck-foss.com
Plant Manager: Richard Raymond
Purchasing Manager: Annmarie Bruns
Estimated Sales: $5200000
Number Employees: 20-49
Square Footage: 120000
Type of Packaging: Consumer, Food Service, Private Label, Bulk
Brands:
Foss
Mos-Ness

11295 **Schlotzsky's**
11401 Century Oaks Terrace
Suite 400
Austin, TX 78758
512-236-3600
800-846-BUNS
www.schlotzskys.com
Catering, prepared foods

11296 **Schmidt Bros Inc**
2425 S Fulton Lucas Rd
Swanton, OH 43558-9658
419-826-3671
Fax: 419-826-8696 800-200-7318
lawrence@schmidtbrosinc.com
www.schmidtbrosinc.com
Grower of produce including pumpkins
President: Bob Schmidt
bob@schmidtbrosinc.com
VP: Robert Schmidt
Marketing Manager: Kathy Judge
Sales Director: Allen Schmidt
Estimated Sales: $3.5 Million
Number Employees: 50-99
Square Footage: 1500000
Type of Packaging: Bulk

11297 **Schneider Cheese**
N4085 County Road M
Waldo, WI 53093
920-467-3351
Fax: 920-467-6184
Cheese
President: John Schneider
CFO: Thomas Paul
Quality Control: Jane Gau
Estimated Sales: $10-20 000,000
Number Employees: 130

11298 **(HQ)Schneider Foods**
321 Courtland Ave East
Kitchener, ON N2G 3X8
Canada
519-741-5000
Fax: 519-749-7400 www.schneiders.ca
Processor and exporter of frozen and refrigerated frankfurters, meat pies, sausage, ham, bacon, deli meats and poultry; fat and calorie reduced products available
President: Douglas Dodds
President (Cust. Foods): Paul Lang
VP Business: John Howard
Quality Control: Judy Tetker
R & D: Tim Gorgon
Number Employees: 5,500
Square Footage: 2920000
Type of Packaging: Consumer, Food Service, Private Label, Bulk
Other Locations:
Schneider Corp.
Ayr ON
Brands:
Deli-Best
Lifestyle
Lunchmate
Mini-Sizzlers
Olde-Fashioned
Red Hots
Schneider's

11299 **Schneider Foods**
Perth County Road 139
Saint Marys, ON N4X 1C4
Canada
519-229-8900
Fax: 519-229-8953 800-567-1890
cwehniai@schneiderfoods.ca www.schneiders.ca
Frozen and fresh poultry
Founder: John Metz Schneider
Plant Manager: Cheryl Firby
Number Employees: 250-499
Parent Co: J.M. Schneider
Type of Packaging: Consumer, Food Service, Private Label

11300 **Schneider Foods**
550 Kipling Avenue S
Etobicoke, ON M8Z 5E9
Canada
416-252-5790
Fax: 416-252-6215 cwehniai@schneiderfoods.ca
www.schneiders.ca
Fresh and frozen beef
President/General Manager: Ron Flaury
CEO: Rick Young
Marketing Director: Doug Gingrich
Purchasing Agent: Carmela Cieri
Number Employees: 100-249
Parent Co: J.M. Schneider
Type of Packaging: Consumer, Food Service
Brands:
Schneider Foods

11301 **Schneider's Dairy Inc**
726 Frank St
Pittsburgh, PA 15227
412-881-3525
Fax: 412-881-7722 www.schneidersdairy.com
Milk, buttermilk, fruit drinks, 100% juice, iced tea, fresh creams, sour cream, dips, and ice cream mix. Wholesaler of; butter, margarine, eggs, yogurt, cheese, cream cheese, cottage cheese, ice cream mix, bottled water. Servingschools, healthcare facilities, supermarkets, convenience stores, restaurants, and foodservice companies.
President: William Schneider
CEO: David Schneider
dschneider@schneidersdairy.com
Director: Joe Pysola
Year Founded: 1935
Estimated Sales: $73 Million
Number Employees: 250-499
Square Footage: 60000
Other Locations:
Williamsport PA
Seneca PA
State College PA
Washington PA

11302 **Schneider-Valley Farms Inc**
1860 E 3rd St
Williamsport, PA 17701-3923
570-326-2021
Fax: 570-326-2736
Milk including whole, low-fat, flavored and skim, buttermilk, ice cream products, sherbet, ice cream mixes, sour cream, dips, fruit juices/drinks and iced teas; wholesaler/distributor of whipped topping, cottage cheese, yogurt, butteretc
President: William Schneider
Director: Clyde Mosteller
Vice President: Ed Schneider
edjr@schneidervfdairy.com
VP Sales: Edward Schneider
Number Employees: 20-49
Parent Co: Schneider's Dairy
Type of Packaging: Food Service

11303 **Schnuck Markets, Inc.**
11420 Lackland Rd.
PO Box 46928
St. Louis, MO 63146
314-994-9900
800-264-4400
nourish.schnucks.com
Grocery, bakery, deli, dairy, seafood, meat, frozen foods, produce, floral, liquor, and more.
Chairman/CEO: Todd Schnuck

Year Founded: 1939
Estimated Sales: $3.1 Billion
Number Employees: 14,500
Brands:
Valutime
Schnucks
Full Circle
Top Care
Schnucks
Culinaria

11304 Schobert's Cottage Cheese Corporation
586 Seiberling Street
Akron, OH 44306-3237
216-733-6876
Cottage cheese
President: Mike Barr
Estimated Sales: $2.5-5 000,000
Number Employees: 5

11305 Schoep's Ice Cream
514 Division St
Madison, WI 53704-5512
608-249-6411
Fax: 608-249-7900 800-236-4050
www.schoepsicecream.com
Ice cream, frozen yogurt, light ice cream, frozen custard, sherbet and novelties.
President: Paul Thomsen
CFO: Amy Mueller
amueller@schoeps.us
Number Employees: 100-249
Type of Packaging: Consumer, Food Service, Private Label, Bulk
Brands:
Schoep's

11306 Schoppaul Hill Winery atIvanhoe
301 S Locust Street
Denton, TX 76201-6055
940-380-9463
Fax: 940-387-5471
Wines
President: John Anderson
CFO: Gary Anderson
Estimated Sales: $5-9.9 000,000
Number Employees: 3

11307 (HQ)Schramsberg Vineyards
1400 Schramsberg Rd
Calistoga, CA 94515-9624
707-942-6668
Fax: 707-942-4336 800-877-3623
info1@schramsberg.com www.schramsberg.com
Sparkling wine
Owner: Sagir Ahmed
VP Sales & Marketing: Laurent Sarazin
Manager Public Relations: Matthew Levy
sahmed@phmhotels.com
Number Employees: 50-99
Number of Brands: 2
Number of Products: 7
Other Locations:
Schramsberg Vineyards
Alijo
Brands:
J. Schram
Mirabelle
Schramsberg

11308 Schreiber Foods Inc.
400 N. Washington St.
Green Bay, WI 54301
920-437-7601
Fax: 920-437-1617 contact@schreiberfoods.com
www.schreiberfoods.com
Dairy products such as cheese, yogurt, milk, milk powders and more.
President/CEO: Ron Dunford
SVP/CFO: Matt Mueller
SVP, U.S. Operations: Tony Nowak
SVP, Information Services: Tom Andreoli
SVP, Quality & Innovation: Vinith Poduval
SVP & Chief Commercial Officer: Trevor Farrell
Year Founded: 1945
Estimated Sales: Over $1 Billion
Number Employees: 8,000
Type of Packaging: Consumer, Food Service, Private Label, Bulk
Other Locations:
Tempe AZ
Gainesville GA
Carthage MO
Clinton MO
Monett MO
Mt Vernon MO
Ravenna NE
Shippensburg PA
Nashville TN
Stephenville TX
Logan UT
Smithfield UT
Wisconsin Rapids WI
Brands:
American Heritage
Clearfield
Cooper
Laferia
Lov-It
Menu
Raskas
Ready-Cut
School Chioce
Schreiber

11309 Schug Carneros Estate Winery
602 Bonneau Rd
Sonoma, CA 95476-9749
707-939-9363
Fax: 707-939-9364 800-966-9365
info@schugwinery.com www.schugwinery.com
Wines
President: Walter Schug
walter@schugwinery.com
Co-Owner: Gertrud Schug
Sales/Marketing Director: Alex Schug
Director of Retail Sales: David Cumming
Winery Chef: Kristine Schug
Winemaker: Michael Cox
Estimated Sales: $5-10 Million
Number Employees: 10-19
Brands:
Schug

11310 Schuil Coffee Co
3679 29th St SE
Grand Rapids, MI 49512-1811
616-956-6815
Fax: 616-956-7928 sales@schuilcoffee.com
www.schuilcoffee.com
Coffee
President: Lori Sytsma
lori@schuilcoffee.com
Estimated Sales: $500,000-$1 Million
Number Employees: 20-49
Type of Packaging: Private Label
Brands:
Coppets
Ibc
Schuil Coffee

11311 (HQ)Schulze & Burch BiscuitCo
1133 W 35th St
Chicago, IL 60609
773-927-6622
www.schulzeburch.com
Formed, baked, chewy and crunchy bars, toaster pastries, fruit bars, wire cut, laminated, extruded or rotary molded cookies and crackers, blended, coated or bases cereal and ingredients
VP of Sales: Steve Podracky
VP of Operations: Paul Salina
Production Supervisor: James Doubek
Year Founded: 1896
Estimated Sales: $96 Million
Number Employees: 100-249
Number of Brands: 3
Square Footage: 400000
Type of Packaging: Consumer, Food Service, Private Label, Bulk
Brands:
Pop Ups
Snackin Fruits
Toast'em

11312 (HQ)Schumacher Wholesale Meats
1114 Zane Ave N
Golden Valley, MN 55422-4679
763-546-3291
Fax: 763-546-0053 800-432-7020
Processor and wholesaler/distributor of meat
President: John F Schumacher
Sales/Marketing Manager: Matt Schumacher
Operations Manager: Bob Timm
Purchasing: Bob Timm
Estimated Sales: $6700000
Number Employees: 20-49
Type of Packaging: Consumer, Food Service, Private Label, Bulk
Brands:
Crown
Great Meats
Valley

11313 Schuman Cheese
40 New Dutch Ln
Fairfield, NJ 07004
800-888-2433
info@schumancheese.com
www.arthurschuman.com
Cheese
CEO: Neal Schuman
nschuman@arthurschuman.com
Strategy Analyst: Keith Schuman
National Account Manager: Allison Schuman
Business Manager: Ian Schuman
Year Founded: 1945
Estimated Sales: $20.9 Million
Number Employees: 100-249
Square Footage: 50400
Brands:
Cello(c)
Montforte

11314 Schuster Marketing Corporation
6251 W Forest Home Ave
Milwaukee, WI 53220-1916
414-543-2999
Fax: 414-543-5588 888-254-8948
Tablet pressed chewing gum with or without active ingredients such as nutraceuticals.
President: Stephen P Schuster
VP Sales: Heidi Schuster
Estimated Sales: $5-10 Million
Number Employees: 48
Brands:
Blitz Power Mints

11315 Schwab Meat Co
1111 Linwood Blvd
Oklahoma City, OK 73106-7039
405-235-2376
Fax: 405-236-4694 800-888-8668
websales@schwabmeat.com
www.schwabmeat.com
Fresh and frozen beef and pork
Owner: Scott Schwab
scott@schwabmeat.com
Marketing Director: Ron Walton
CFO: Gail Anderson
Estimated Sales: $10-20 Million
Number Employees: 20-49
Type of Packaging: Consumer, Food Service, Private Label, Bulk
Brands:
Schwab

11316 Schwan's Company
115 W. College Dr.
Marshall, MN 56258
507-532-3274
800-533-5290
questions@schwans.com
www.schwanscompany.com
Frozen foods including pizza, desserts and snacks. Serves restaurants and schools.
President, Schwan's Consumer Brands: Julie Francis
CEO: Dimitrios Smyrnios
Senior VP/Chief Information Officer: Kathy Persian
Senior VP, Product Innovation/Dvlp.: Stacey Fowler Meittunen
Year Founded: 1952
Estimated Sales: $3 Billion
Number Employees: 12,000
Number of Brands: 12
Number of Products: 300+
Type of Packaging: Consumer, Food Service, Private Label
Brands:
RED BARON
MAMA ROSA'S
FRESCHETTA
TONY'S
SCHWAN'S
SCHWAN'S CHEF COLLECTION
MRS. SMITH'S
EDWARDS
PAGODA
MINH
BIG DADDY'S
VILLA PRIME PIZZERIA

11317 **Schwan's Food Service Inc.**
115 W. College Dr.
Marshall, MN 56258
877-302-7426
questions@schwans.com
www.schwansfoodservice.com
Asian food, frozen pizza and desserts.
President, Schwan's Consumer Brands: Julie Francis
CEO: Dimitrios Smyrnios
Estimated Sales: $3 Billion
Number Employees: 12,000
Number of Brands: 12
Parent Co: Schwan's Company
Type of Packaging: Consumer, Food Service, Private Label, Bulk
Other Locations:
Atlanta GA
Crossville TN
Montgomery AL
Pembroke NC
Brands:
Red Baron
Tony's
Freschetta
Big Daddy's
Mrs. Smith's
Edwards
Villa Prima
Minh
Coyote Grill
Beacon Street Cafe
Stilwell
Schwan's

11318 **Schwebel Baking Co.**
965 E. Midlothian Blvd.
P.O. Box 6018
Youngstown, OH 44502
330-783-2860
Fax: 330-782-1774 800-860-2867
www.schwebels.com
White, wheat, whole and multigrain breads; deli buns, rolls and subs; bagels, light breads, pitas, flat bread and tortillas; cinnamon, italian, sour dough, potato, high fiber and raisin breads.
President/CEO: Steven Cooper
VP Marketing & Corporate Communications: Lee Schwebel
Senior VP, Sales: Alyson Winick
Year Founded: 1906
Estimated Sales: $130 Million
Number Employees: 1000-4999
Number of Brands: 6
Square Footage: 125000
Type of Packaging: Consumer, Food Service, Private Label, Bulk
Other Locations:
Akron OH
Saybrook OH
Austintown OH
Canton OH
Cleveland OH
Hilliard OH
Reynoldsburg OH
Mansfield OH
Solon OH
Struthers OH
Euclid OH
Erie PA
Reno PA
Brands:
Schwebel's
Cinnabon
Schwebel's Organic
Schwebel's Selects
Sun-Maid
'taliano

11319 **Scialo Brothers Bakery**
257 Atwells Ave
Providence, RI 02903-1521
401-421-0986
Fax: 401-274-6117 877-421-0986
www.scialobakery.com
Italian bread, bakery products, pastries, cakes, pies, cookies and wedding cakes
Co-Owner: Lois Ellis
scialobakery@scialobakery.com
Co-Owner: Carol Gaeta
Estimated Sales: Less Than $500,000
Number Employees: 10-19

11320 **Sconza Candy Co**
1 Sconza Candy Ln
Oakdale, CA 95361-7899
209-845-3700
Fax: 510-638-5792 877-568-8137
customerservice@sconzacandy.com
www.sconza.com
Candy including brittles, panned, butterscotch, hard, filled, mints, butter toffee nuts and seasonal
President: James Sconza
jrsconza@sconzacandy.com
Executive Vice President: Ron Sconza
Estimated Sales: $6 Million
Number Employees: 100-249
Square Footage: 200000
Type of Packaging: Consumer, Food Service, Private Label, Bulk
Brands:
Bean Heads
Bruiser
Fruit Breaker
Jordanettes
Meteorites
Pip Squeaks
Sconza
Screamer
Wizbanger
Zoygs

11321 **Scooty's Wholesome Foods**
PO Box 18898
Boulder, CO 80308-1898
303-440-4025
Fax: 970-663-6013
Gourmet and specialty foods
President: Scott Silverman
Estimated Sales: Under $500,000
Number Employees: 1-4

11322 **Scotian Gold**
2900 Lovett Road
Coldbrook, NS B4R 1A6
Canada
902-679-2191
Fax: 902-679-4540 888-726-8426
scotiangold.com
Tree fruit cooperative with 30 grower members.
CEO: David Parrish
Director of Sales: Dennis MacPherson
Estimated Sales: $21 Million
Type of Packaging: Consumer, Private Label
Brands:
Scotian Gold

11323 **Scotsburn Ice Cream Co.**
4600 Armand-Frappier St.
Saint-Hubert, QC J3Z 1G5
Canada
800-501-1150
www.scotsburn.com
By the scoop ice cream and frozen desserts.
Year Founded: 1900
Estimated Sales: $175 Million
Number Employees: 375
Number of Brands: 1
Number of Products: 5
Square Footage: 52786
Parent Co: Agropur Cooperative
Type of Packaging: Consumer, Food Service, Private Label

11324 **Scott Adams Foods**
288 Newton Sparta Rd
Newton, NJ 07860
973-300-2091
www.pdifoods.com
Vegan meat alternative and vegetarian wraps
President: Jack Parker
CEO: Scott Adams
Estimated Sales: $1-3 Million
Number Employees: 1-4
Parent Co: Parker Development, Inc
Type of Packaging: Private Label
Brands:
Dilberito
Protein Chef

11325 **Scott Farms Inc**
7965a Simpson Rd
Lucama, NC 27851-9371
919-284-4014
Fax: 919-284-4872 877-284-4030
info@scottfarms.com www.scottfarms.com
Grower and shipper of sweet potatoes
Owner: Linwood Scott
sales@scottfarms.com
Estimated Sales: Below $5 Million
Number Employees: 5-9
Brands:
Sonny's Pride

11326 **Scott Hams**
1301 Scott Rd
Greenville, KY 42345-4683
270-338-3402
Fax: 270-338-6643 800-318-1353
scotthams@att.net
Country cured and fully cooked hams, bacon, smoked sausage, turkey, jams and fruit butters, sorghum molasses, honey, dried apples, relish, bean soup mix, biscuits, pork cracklins and dog biscuits
Owner: June Scott
scotthams@att.net
Estimated Sales: Less Than $500,000
Number Employees: 1-4
Brands:
Scott's

11327 **Scott's Auburn Mills**
503 Dockins St
Russellville, KY 42276-2065
270-726-2080
mail@auburnkyusa.com
www.auburnkyusa.com
White and yellow corn meal and wheat flour
President: Ray Clark
Vice President: Dave Clark
Chief Miller: Joe Crain
Production: Robert Covington
Estimated Sales: $2 Million
Number Employees: 20-49
Square Footage: 80000
Type of Packaging: Consumer, Food Service, Private Label, Bulk

11328 **Scott's Candy**
819 South Veterans Blvd
Glennville, GA 30427
608-837-8020
Fax: 608-837-0763 800-356-2100
Processor and exporter of boxed and tinned chocolates
CEO: Gary Ricco
National Sales Manager: James Regan
Contact: Gary Ricco
gricco@wisconsincheeseman.com
Estimated Sales: $3-5 Million
Number Employees: 20-49
Parent Co: Wisconsin Cheeseman
Type of Packaging: Consumer, Private Label
Brands:
Classic Choice
Scott's

11329 **Scott's Sauce Co Inc**
1205 N William St
Goldsboro, NC 27530-2163
919-734-0711
800-734-7282
info@scottsbarbequesauce.com
www.scottsbarbecuesauce.com
Barbecue sauces
Owner: A Scott
ascott@scottsbarbecuesauce.com
Estimated Sales: Less Than $500,000
Number Employees: 5-9
Square Footage: 28000
Parent Co: Scott's Barbecue
Type of Packaging: Consumer
Brands:
Scott's Barbeque Sauce

11330 **Scott's of Wisconsin**
301 Broadway Dr
Sun Prairie, WI 53590
608-837-8020
Fax: 608-837-0763 800-693-0834
customerservice@wisconsincheeseman.com
www.wisconsincheeseman.com
Cheese spreads, chocolate candy
CEO: Holly Berkenstadt
President: Jay Singer
Marketing Director: Charlie Kesler
Sales Director: Jim Regan
Purchasing Manager: Mark Pelton
Estimated Sales: $1-2.5 Million
Number Employees: 20-49
Type of Packaging: Private Label

Brands:
Grace Rush
Nutty Pleasures
Pecanbacks
Scott's
Scott's of Wisconsin
Scottie
Trinkets

11331 **Scott-Bathgate**
149 Pioneer Avenue
Winnipeg, MB R3C 2M8
Canada
204-943-8525
Fax: 204-957-5902 800-216-2990
www.scottbathgate.com
Snack foods, food colorings, mustard, peanut butter, candy and shelled and in-shell sunflower seeds
National Director: Vic Homyshyn
Office/Credit Manager: D Sheridan
Production Manager: Jens Fieting
Type of Packaging: Food Service
Brands:
Food Club
Nutty Club

11332 **Scotty Wotty's Creamy Cheesecake**
216 Us Highway 206
Suite 14
Hillsborough, NJ 08844-4384
908-281-9720
Fax: 908-281-9720
Cheesecake
President: Scott Discount
Brands:
Scotty Wotty's

11333 **Scray's Cheese**
2082 Old Martin Rd
De Pere, WI 54115-8015
920-336-8359
Fax: 920-336-0553 ScrayCheese@yahoo.com
www.scraycheese.com
Cheese
President: Jim Scray
Estimated Sales: $500,000-$1 000,000
Number Employees: 10-19
Type of Packaging: Private Label
Brands:
Scray's Cheese

11334 **Screamin' Onionz**
399 Manchester Rd.
Poughkeepsie, NY 12603
www.loveonionz.com
Sliced, slow-cooked onions in flavoured sauces
Founder: Richard Romano
Year Founded: 2015
Number of Brands: 1
Number of Products: 3
Type of Packaging: Consumer, Private Label

11335 **Scripture Candy**
1350 Adamsville Industrial Pkw
Birmingham, AL 35224-3300
205-798-0701
Fax: 205-798-0702 888-317-7333
Info@scripturecandy.com
www.scripturecandy.com
Candy
Owner: Brian Adkins
badkins@scripturecandy.com
Number Employees: 10-19

11336 **Sculli Brothers**
622C Industrial Park Drive
Yeadon, PA 19050
215-336-1223
Fax: 215-336-1225 Scullibrothers@gmail.com
Ham, italian sausage, coteghino, and prosciuto
President: Robert Sculli
VP: Dawn Sculli
Estimated Sales: $150,000
Number Employees: 2
Square Footage: 11212
Type of Packaging: Private Label, Bulk
Brands:
Bari

11337 **Sea Bear Smokehouse**
605 30th St
Anacortes, WA 98221-2884
360-293-4661
Fax: 360-293-4097 800-645-3474
Processor and exporter of smoked fish and seafoods
President: Mike Mondello
CEO: Michael Mondello
mikem@seabear.com
VP Direct to Consumer: Patti Fisher
Marketing Manager: Barb Hoenselaar
Director Operations: Cathy Hayward-Hughes
Estimated Sales: $10.8 Million
Number Employees: 20-49
Type of Packaging: Consumer, Bulk

11338 **Sea Best Corporation**
PO Box 753
Ipswich, MA 01938-0753
978-768-7475
Fax: 314-241-1377
Seafood

11339 **Sea Breeze Fruit Flavors**
441 Main Road
Towaco, NJ 07082-1201
973-334-7777
Fax: 973-334-2617 800-732-2733
info@seabreezesyrups.com
www.seabreezesyrups.com
Syrups including chocolate, pancake and milkshake; sundae toppings, bar mixes, juice concentrates, soda, iced tea, lemonade, fruit juice, flavored water and beverage dispensing equipment.
President: Steve Sanders
Vice President: Josh Sanders
Technical Director: Frank Maranino
Contact: George Apostolopoulos
george@seabreezesyrups.com
Production Manager: Paul Maranino
Estimated Sales: $25-49.9 Million
Number Employees: 50-99
Number of Brands: 6
Type of Packaging: Consumer, Food Service, Private Label
Brands:
Bosco
Joshua Miguel
New York Bash
Sea Breeze
Toshimi
Tropic Beach

11340 **Sea Dog Brewing Company**
1 Bowdoin Mill Island
Suite 100
Topsham, ME 04086
207-725-0162
Fax: 207-947-8720 www.seadogbrewing.com
Beer
General Manager: Larry Killam
General Manager: Seth Hale
Contact: Jess Choate
jessc@seadogbrewing.com
Number Employees: 35
Type of Packaging: Consumer, Food Service
Brands:
Sea Dog

11341 **Sea Farm & Farm Fresh Importing Company**
855 Monterey Passage Road
Monterey Park, CA 91754
323-265-7075
Fax: 323-265-9578
Seafood products.
CEO: Hooi Eng Ooi
VP Operations: S Tan
Estimated Sales: $5-10 Million
Number Employees: 10-19

11342 **Sea Fresh USA Inc**
45 All American Way
PO Box 398
North Kingstown, RI 02852-2607
401-583-0200
Fax: 401-583-0222 mfox@seafreshusa.com
www.seafreshusa.com
Seafood including Rhode Island calamari, tuna, fluke, monkfish, skate, scup
Owner: James Fox
james@seafreshusa.com
Accounting: Cheryl Anyzaeski
Estimated Sales: $20-50 Million
Number Employees: 20-49

11343 **Sea Gold Seafood Products Inc**
38 Blackmer St
New Bedford, MA 02744-2614
508-993-3060
Fax: 508-993-3070 seagold01@msn.com
www.seagolddips.com
Dips including gourmet seafood and crab dip, buttered seafood and lobster dip, seafood and jalapeno crab dip, spicy shrimp dip, seafood and shrimp scampi dip, cajun seafood and crab dip, clams casino clam dip, and seafood newburgdip.
Owner: Micheal Trazzra
seagold1@aol.com
Operations Manager: Wendy Harwood
Estimated Sales: Below $5 Million
Number Employees: 10-19
Number of Brands: 1
Number of Products: 9
Square Footage: 20000
Type of Packaging: Consumer, Food Service
Brands:
Sea Gold

11344 **Sea Horse Wharf**
245 W Point Rd
Phippsburg, ME 04562-5127
207-389-2312
Fax: 207-389-1005
Seafood
Owner: Douglas Scott
Estimated Sales: $300,000-500,000
Number Employees: 1-4

11345 **Sea Lyons**
9093 Springway Ct
Spanish Fort, AL 36527-5522
251-626-2841
Fax: 251-626-2841
Seafood.
President: Martha Lyons
Vice President: Wade Lyons

11346 **Sea Pac Of Idaho Inc**
4074 N 2000 E
Filer, ID 83328-5033
208-326-3100
Fax: 208-326-5935
Trout and salmon jerky, smoked rainbow trout, and salmon sausages
President/General Manager: Ken Ashley
aken@seapacofidaho.com
Estimated Sales: $7.10 M
Number Employees: 20-49

11347 **Sea Pearl Seafood**
14120 Shell Belt Rd
Bayou La Batre, AL 36509-2308
251-824-2129
Fax: 251-650-1321 800-872-8804
www.sea-pearl.com
Frozen and breaded shrimp and oysters
Owner: Joseph G Ladnier
info@sea-pearl.com
Plant Manager: Allen Mayfield
Estimated Sales: $3.3 Million
Number Employees: 20-49
Type of Packaging: Consumer, Food Service, Bulk
Brands:
Neptune Delight
Sea Pearl Seafood Co., Inc.

11348 **Sea Ridge Winery**
13404 Dupont Road
Occidental, CA 95465
707-874-1707
800-692-5780
info@broncowine.com www.broncowine.com
Wines
President: Dan Wickham
Estimated Sales: $500-1 Million
Number Employees: 1-4

11349 **Sea Safari**
785 E Pantego St
Belhaven, NC 27810
252-943-3091
Fax: 252-943-3083 800-688-6174
seasafari@beaufortco.com
Processor and exporter of frozen crawfish and crab meat; also, canned blue crab meat

President/Finance & Sales Executive: Topper Bateman
General Manager: Guinn Leverett
Director Marketing: Christine Costley
Sales Manager: Frances Williams
Contact: Bateman Topper
tbateman@seasafari.com
Estimated Sales: $400,000
Number Employees: 4
Square Footage: 160000
Parent Co: Sea Safari
Type of Packaging: Consumer, Food Service
Brands:
Acadian Gourmet
Ecrevisse Acadienne
Louisianas Best

11350 **Sea Salt Superstore**
19004 Highway 99
Lynnwood, WA 98036
Fax: 425-640-2500 866-999-7258
customerservice@seasaltsuperstore.com
www.seasaltsuperstore.com
Gourmet foods, exotic spices and hand crafted natural sea salts to the gourmet food customers.
Contact: Jenny Mackie
jenny@seasaltsuperstore.com

11351 **Sea Salt Superstore**
11604 Airport Rd
Suite D300
Everett, WA 98204
425-249-2331
Fax: 425-249-2334
customerservice@seasaltsuperstore.com
www.seasaltsuperstore.com
Flavored sea salt
President: Scott Mackie
Customer Service & Sales: Jenny Mackie
Estimated Sales: $1 Million
Number Employees: 2-10
Brands:
Caravel Gourmet
Healthy Himalaya
Sealina Spa
Sea Salt Superstore

11352 **Sea Snack Foods Inc**
914 E 11th St
Los Angeles, CA 90021-2091
213-622-2204
Fax: 213-622-7845
Processor and exporter of cooked IQF shrimp and seafood cocktails
President/CEO: Fred Ockrim
fred@seasnack.com
VP: Jeffrey Kahn
Sales Director: Peter Peterson
Plant Manager: Alfred Dolor
Estimated Sales: $7 Million
Number Employees: 50-99
Square Footage: 8000
Type of Packaging: Consumer, Food Service
Brands:
O.K. Brand
Restaurant Row
Sea Snack
Twin Harbors

11353 **Sea Stars Goat Cheese**
1122 Soquel Ave
Santa Cruz, CA 95062-2106
831-423-7200
Fax: 831-454-0838
Cheese
Owner: Nancy Gassney
Estimated Sales: $2.5-5 000,000
Number Employees: 10-19
Type of Packaging: Private Label

11354 **Sea Veggies**
5801 S Malt Ave
Suite 220
Commerce, CA 90040
323-728-4762
Fax: 323-728-4761 info@sea-veggies.com
www.sea-veggies.com
Seaweed snacks
Number of Products: 10

11355 **Sea View Fillet Company**
15 Antonio Costa Ave
New Bedford, MA 02740-7347
508-984-1406
Fax: 508-984-1411
Seafood
Manager: Sandy Harbick
Estimated Sales: $10-24.9 000,000
Number Employees: 50-99

11356 **Sea Watch Intl**
8978 Glebe Park Dr
Easton, MD 21601-7004
410-822-7500
Fax: 410-822-1266 sales@seaclam.com
www.seawatch.com
Canned and frozen clams, crab cakes, extruded calamari rings, blue crab meat, squid, shrimp, soups and seafood chowders.
Vice President: Bernie Carr
bernie@seaclam.com
Controller: Betty Bain
Director, Quality Assurance: Larry Hughes
Senior Vice President of Sales: Michael Wyatt
Year Founded: 1978
Estimated Sales: $36.1 Million
Number Employees: 250-499
Number of Brands: 4
Square Footage: 15000
Type of Packaging: Food Service, Private Label
Brands:
American Original
Cap'ns Catch
Capt. Fred
Eastern Shore Foods, Llc
Mid-Atlantic Foods
Mr Frosty
Old Salt Seafood
Sailor's Choice
Seawatch
Tucker's Cove

11357 **Sea-Fresh Seafood Market**
1432 Hillcrest Rd
Mobile, AL 36695
251-634-8650
Fax: 714-897-4090
Seafood
President: Patrick Meacham
CFO: Rusty Brennan

11358 **SeaBear Wild Salmon**
605 30th Street
Anacortes, WA 98221
360-293-4661
Fax: 888-487-6427 800-645-3474
smokehouse@seabear.com www.seabear.com
Smoked seafood: salmon, cod, crab, scallops and rainbow trout.
President: Mike Mondello
mikem@seabear.com
Sales & Strategic Communication: Christine Bondick
Chief Operating Officer: Patti Fisher
Year Founded: 1957
Estimated Sales: $3 Million
Number Employees: 50-200
Type of Packaging: Food Service
Brands:
Gerard & Dominique
Pacific Alaska
SeaBear

11359 **SeaPak Shrimp**
1867 Demere Rd
Saint Simons Island, GA 31522
888-732-7251
seapak.com
Shrimp, seafood

11360 **SeaPerfect Atlantic Farms**
PO Box 12139
Charleston, SC 29422-2139
843-762-0022
Fax: 843-795-6672 800-728-0099
Scallops and clams
President: Carlos Celle
Sales Director: Michelle Black
General Manager: Knox Grant
Estimated Sales: $2.3 Million
Number Employees: 45
Square Footage: 136000
Brands:
Seaperfect

11361 **SeaSpecialties**
1111 NW 159th Dr
Miami, FL 33169-5807
305-625-5112
Fax: 305-625-5528 800-654-6682
Seafood
Quality Control: Irvin Norss
CFO: Michael Metzkes
Estimated Sales: $20-50 Million
Number Employees: 100-249

11362 **Seaberghs Frozen Foods**
200 Westchester Avenue
White Plains, NY 10601-4510
914-948-6377
Frozen foods
President: Harry Rich
Estimated Sales: $1-2.5 000,000
Number Employees: 1-4

11363 **Seaboard Foods**
9000 W. 67th St.
Suite 200
Shawnee Mission, KS 66202
800-262-7907
info@seaboardfoods.com seaboardfoods.com
Fresh, frozen and processed pork products.
President/CEO: Darwin Sand
Vice President, Marketing: Tom Blumhardt
Vice President, Plant Operations: Marty Hast
Year Founded: 1995
Estimated Sales: $38.8 Million
Number Employees: 4,986
Number of Brands: 5
Parent Co: Seaboard Corporation
Type of Packaging: Consumer, Food Service, Private Label, Bulk
Other Locations:
Processing Plant
Guymon OK
Ham Deboning Plant
Reynosa, MEXICO
Mount Dora Farms Management
Houston TX
Live Production Operations
Kansas
Daily's Premium Meats Bacon Plant
Salt Lake City UT
Daily's Premium Meats Bacon Plant
Missoula MT
Live Production Operations
Colorado
Live Production Operations
Texas
Brands:
Daily's Premium Meats
Prairie Fresh
Seaboard Farms
St. Joe Pork
67th Street BBQ
Quick Fire Premium Meats

11364 **Seabreeze Fish**
2311 R Street
Bakersfield, CA 93301-2986
661-323-7936
Fax: 805-323-7936
Seafood
Owner: Ben Kim
Estimated Sales: $300,000-500,000
Number Employees: 1-4

11365 **(HQ)Seabrook Brothers & Sons**
85 Finley Road
Seabrook, NJ 08302
856-455-8080
Fax: 856-455-9282 seabroc@seabrookfarms.com
www.seabrookfarms.com
Frozen vegetables
Procurement: Ivin Seabrook
Sales: Brian Seabrook
Customer Service: Keith Mount
Estimated Sales: $93 Million
Number Employees: 325
Number of Brands: 2
Number of Products: 150
Square Footage: 350000
Type of Packaging: Consumer, Food Service, Private Label, Bulk
Brands:
Seabrook Farms
Somerdale

11366 **Seafare Market Wholesale**
PO Box 671
Moody, ME 04054-0671
207-646-5160
Fax: 408-294-3948
Seafood
President: John Foye
Estimated Sales: $10-20 Million
Number Employees: 10-19

11367 **Seafood Connection**
841 Pohukaina St # I
Suite I
Honolulu, HI 96813-5332
808-591-8550
Fax: 808-591-8445 sales@seafood-connection.com
www.seafood-connection.com
Seafood and gourmet products
President: Stuart Simmons
Estimated Sales: $10-20 Million
Number Employees: 10-19

11368 **Seafood Dimensions Intl**
22343 LA Palma Ave # 106
Suite 106
Yorba Linda, CA 92887-3804
714-692-6464
Fax: 714-282-8997
Seafood
Owner: Christi Lang
Estimated Sales: $1.4 Million
Number Employees: 5-9
Number of Brands: 20
Number of Products: 50
Type of Packaging: Food Service
Brands:
20th Century Foods
Brooks Street Baking
Harvest Farm
Lil' Fisherman
Midship
Neptune
Schoner

11369 **Seafood Express**
179 Rossmore Rd
Brunswick, ME 04011
207-729-0887
Fax: 207-721-9146
Seafood
Contact: Thida Pov
tpov@seafoodexpress.in

11370 **Seafood Hawaii Inc**
875 Waimanu St # 634
Suite 634
Honolulu, HI 96813-5265
808-597-1971
Fax: 808-538-1973
Seafood
President: Jed J Inouye
Estimated Sales: $5-10 Million
Number Employees: 20-49

11371 **Seafood International**
1051 Old Henderson Hwy
Henderson, LA 70517-7805
337-228-7568
Fax: 337-228-7573 www.seafoodfromnorway.com
Seafood
Owner: Roy Robert
seafoodintl@cox-internet.com
Estimated Sales: $3,300,000
Number Employees: 5-9

11372 **Seafood Merchants LTD**
900 Forest Edge Dr
Vernon Hills, IL 60061-3105
847-634-0900
Fax: 847-634-1351
sales@theseafoodmerchants.com
Seafood
President: Roy Axelson
bonnie@theseafoodmerchants.com
CEO: Bonnie Axelson
bonnie@theseafoodmerchants.com
Sales Exec: Bonnie Axelson
Estimated Sales: $10-20 Million
Number Employees: 20-49
Square Footage: 23000
Type of Packaging: Consumer, Food Service, Bulk

11373 **Seafood Packaging Inc**
2120 Poydras St
New Orleans, LA 70112-1339
504-522-6677
Fax: 504-522-9008 800-949-9656
ksharp@seafoodpackaging.com
www.seafoodpackaging.com
Seafood
Owner: Kent Sharp
ksharp@seafoodpackaging.com
Estimated Sales: $5-10 Million
Number Employees: 5-9
Type of Packaging: Consumer

11374 **Seafood Plus Corporation**
10860 Bear Island Avenue
Orland Park, IL 60467-5397
708-795-4820
Fax: 708-795-7719
Seafood
President: Harry A Davros

11375 **Seafood Producers Co-Op**
2875 Roeder Ave
Suite 2
Bellingham, WA 98225
360-733-0120
Fax: 360-733-0513 jreynolds@spcsales.com
www.spcsales.com
Processor and exporter of salmon, halibut, sablefish and rockfish.
Chief Executive Officer: Joe Morelli
VP, Sales & Marketing: Jeff Reynolds
Sales Manager: Kurt Sigfusson
Traffic & Logistics: Jessie Koehler
Plant Manager: Craig Shoemaker
Year Founded: 1944
Estimated Sales: $45 Million
Number Employees: 5-9
Type of Packaging: Food Service, Bulk
Brands:
Alaska Gold
Longliner
Sitka Gold

11376 **Seafood Services**
49 Bromfield St
Newburyport, MA 01950-3003
508-999-6785
Fax: 508-993-4001
Seafood
President: David Horton
Contact: Dan Canavan
dcanavan@foodinno.com
Estimated Sales: $20-50 Million
Number Employees: 20-49

11377 **Seafood Specialties**
155 E Vienna St
Anna, IL 62906-1839
618-833-6083
Fax: 618-833-9433
www.seafoodspecialtiesonline.com
Seafoods
Owner: Al Bush
afishiebusiness@hotmail.com
Human Resources: Bridget Sprinkle
Estimated Sales: Under $500,000
Number Employees: 1-4

11378 **Seajoy**
6619 S Dixie Hwy
PO Box 344
Miami, FL 33143
305-669-0108
Fax: 302-663-0312 877-537-1717
www.seajoy.com
Shrimp including raw head-on whole shrimp, raw shell-on tails, raw shell-on E-Z peel meats, raw peeled & deveined tail on or off, uncut, raw peeled, butterfly meat, raw breaded shrimp meat, and raw peeled & deveined meat on skewers
Administrative President: Peder Jacobson
VP Sales & Operations: Brad Price
Estimated Sales: $220 Thousand
Brands:
Seajoy
Cjoy
Bluefield
Seabrook

11379 **Sealand Lobster Corporation**
PO Box 423
Tenants Harbor, ME 04860-0423
207-372-6247
Fax: 207-389-1819
Lobster

11380 **Sealaska Corp**
1 Sealaska Plz
Suite 400
Juneau, AK 99801
907-586-1512
Fax: 907-586-2304 corpcomm@sealaska.com
www.sealaska.com
Seafood
CEO: Anthony Mallott
CFO: Carrie Rorem
Vice President: David Aldrich
COO: Terry Downes
Year Founded: 1971
Estimated Sales: $100-200 Million
Number Employees: 20-49
Brands:
Ocean Beauty Seafoods

11381 **Seald Sweet**
1991 74th Ave
Vero Beach, FL 32966-5199
559-636-4400
Fax: 772-569-5110 www.sealdsweet.com
Grower, importer and exporter of citrus products including oranges, grapefruit, lemons, clementines, minneolas, tangerines and tangeros.
President: Jeff Baskovich
jbaskovich@sealdsweet.com
CFO: Christine Wallace
VP: David E Mixon
Marketing Manager: Kim Flores
Estimated Sales: $5-10 Million
Number Employees: 50-99
Square Footage: 60000
Type of Packaging: Food Service, Bulk
Brands:
Florigold
Seald Sweet

11382 **Seapoint Farms**
20042 Beach Blvd
Suite 102
Huntington Beach, CA 92648-3702
714-374-9831
info@seapointfarms.com
www.seapointfarms.com
Edamame and seaweed products
CEO: Kevin Cross
kcross@seapointfarms.com
National Sales Manager: Tim Boyer
COO: Phil Siegel
Estimated Sales: 1.6 Millin
Number Employees: 5-9

11383 **Seaside Ice Cream**
PO Box 734
Pelham, NY 10803-0734
914-636-2751
Fax: 631-728-1653
Ice cream
Owner: Arthur Haas

11384 **Season Brand**
80 Avenue K
Newark, NJ 07105
201-553-1100
contact@seasonproducts.com
www.seasonproducts.com
Canned fish and specialty vegetables
Brand Manager: Isabel Hill
Brands:
SEASON(c)

11385 **Season Harvest Foods**
4906 El Camino Real # 206
Suite 206
Los Altos, CA 94022-1444
650-968-2273
Fax: 877-413-3894 sales@seasonharvestfoods.com
www.seasonharvestfoods.com
Organic vegetable and spice supplier.

11386 **Seatech Corporation**
16825 48th Ave W Ste 222
Lynnwood, WA 98037
425-487-3231
Fax: 425-835-0367 johnw@seatechcorp.com
www.seatechcorp.com
Frozen shrimp, crab and scallops
President: John Wendt
j.wendt@seatech.com
CFO: Jim Schantz
ice President: Todd Wendt
Estimated Sales: $6 Million
Number Employees: 3
Number of Brands: 2
Square Footage: 4000
Type of Packaging: Consumer, Food Service, Private Label, Bulk
Brands:
Clean Kitchen
Chiquititos
Seatech

11387 **Seatrade Corporation**
P.O.Box 421
Hoboken, NJ 07030-0421
201-963-5700
Fax: 201-963-0577
Seafood
VP/Sales Manager: Richard Mendelson

11388 **Seattle Bar Company**
3302 Wallingford Avenue N
Seattle, WA 98103-9039
206-601-4301
Fax: 206-282-3548
Owner: Beth Campbell
Number Employees: 1-4
Brands:
Seattle Bar

11389 **Seattle Chocolates**
1180 Andover Park W
Tukwila, WA 98188-3909
425-264-2800
Fax: 425-264-2811 800-334-3600
info@seattlechocolates.com
www.seattlechocolates.com
Chocolate truffles and bars
President and CEO: Jean Thompson
VP Operations: Niel Campbell
Marketing Manager: Kirsty Ellison
Controller: Joe Slye
Estimated Sales: $10 Million
Number Employees: 10-19
Number of Brands: 1
Number of Products: 11
Type of Packaging: Consumer, Private Label, Bulk
Brands:
Chick Chocolates
Seattle Chocolates
Skinny Truffles

11390 **Seattle Gourmet Foods**
18200 Segale Park Dr B
Tukwila, WA 98188
425-656-9076
Fax: 425-656-8059 800-800-9490
sales@seattlegourmetfoods.com
www.seattlegourmetfoods.com
Chocolate meltaways, coffee spoons, molasses chews, thin mints, pecan delights, panned nuts, jams, jellies, fruit toppings, whipped taffy
General Manager: Tom Means
Controller: Mary Bides
marybides@seattlegourmetfoods.com
Distribution & Logistics Manager: Mike Harris
Year Founded: 1993
Estimated Sales: $63 Million
Number Employees: 275
Number of Brands: 11
Brands:
Anna's Honey
Buckeye Beans and Herbs
Biringer's Farm Fresh
Coffaro's Baking Company
Cucina Fresca
Dilettante Chocolates
FungusAmongUs
Maury Island Farm
Merlino Baking Co.
Myntz Breathmints
Quinn's

11391 **Seattle Seasonings**
3920 E Lidstrom Hill Rd
Port Orchard, WA 98366-4855
360-871-1511
Fax: 360-377-0642 contact@twosnootychefs.com
www.twosnootychefs.com
Seasonings, cooking enhancers, salts, rubs
Co-Owner: Gary Fuller
contact@twosnootychefs.com
Number Employees: 1-4

11392 **(HQ)Seattle's Best Coffee**
PO Box 3717
Seattle, WA 98124-8891
800-611-7793
customercare@seattlesbest.com
www.seattlesbest.com
Ground coffee and beans
Manager: James Strasbaugh
Contact: Donald Blankenship
don.blankenship@seattle.gov
Estimated Sales: $10.9 Million
Number Employees: 100-249
Type of Packaging: Consumer, Food Service

11393 **Seaver's Bakery**
719 East Center St
Kingsport, TN 37660
423-245-2441
Fax: 423-578-3434 www.seaversbakery.com
Baked goods
President: Ralph Coomer
President/CEO: Richard Seaver
Plant Manager: Richard McKinney
Estimated Sales: $250,000
Number Employees: 10-19
Type of Packaging: Consumer

11394 **Seavey Vineyard**
1310 Conn Valley Rd
St Helena, CA 94574-9610
707-963-8339
Fax: 707-963-0232 info@seaveyvineyard.com
www.seaveyvineyard.com
Wines
President: William Seavey
Director of Sales and Marketing: Alex Kajani
Manager: Dorie Seavey
dseavey@seaveyvineyard.com
Estimated Sales: $500,000-$1 Million
Number Employees: 5-9
Brands:
Seavey Cabernet Sauvignon
Seavey Chardonnay
Seavey Marlot

11395 **Seaview Lobster Co**
43 Government St
Kittery, ME 03904-1652
207-439-1599
Fax: 207-439-1476 800-245-4997
orders@seaviewlobster.com
www.seaviewlobster.com
Seafood
Owner: Tom Flanagan
seaviewlob@comcast.net
Estimated Sales: $.5-1 million
Number Employees: 10-19

11396 **Seawater Food & Beverage**
1212 Dolton Dr
Suite 301B
Dallas, TX 75207-2114
214-537-5070
info@seawatersolutions.com
mediterraneaseawater.com
Cooking seawater, zumo juice and potato chips
National Sales Manager: Jerald Morris
Purchasing & Logistics Manager: Lorena Pierce
Brands:
Mediterranea Seawater for Cooking
Seawater Soaked Potato Chips
Zumo Juices

11397 **Seaway Company**
PO Box 868
Fairhaven, MA 02719-0800
508-992-1221
Fax: 508-992-1253
Seafood
Owner: Steve Doonan
Estimated Sales: $1-3 Million
Number Employees: 1-4

11398 **Sebastiani Vineyards**
389 4th St E
Sonoma, CA 95476-5790
707-938-5532
Fax: 707-933-3390 855-232-2338
tastingroom@sebastiani.com
Wines
Proprietor: Bill Foley
President/CEO: Mary Ann Sebastiani Cuneo
COO: Emma Swain
Operations Manager: Paul Bergna
Sebastiani Vineyards & Winery Winemaker: Mark Lyon
Estimated Sales: $5-10 Million
Number Employees: 50-99
Type of Packaging: Consumer

11399 **Sebastiano's**
4448 Heatherdowns Blvd
Toledo, OH 43614-3113
419-382-0615
Fax: 419-382-0615
Ice cream, frozen desserts
Owner: Jonathan Sagaser
Vice President: Helane Stiebler
Estimated Sales: Less Than $500,000
Number Employees: 5-9

11400 **Sechler's Fine Pickles**
5685 State Road 1
Saint Joe, IN 46785
260-337-5461
Fax: 260-337-5771 800-332-5461
showroom@sechlerspickles.com
Pickles
Owner: David Sechler
General Manager: Max Troyer
Sales Executive: Mike Meyers
Estimated Sales: $4 Million
Number Employees: 32
Square Footage: 116000

11401 **Sechrist Brothers**
32 E Main St
Dallastown, PA 17313-2206
717-244-2975
Fax: 717-244-6532 sechristbrosmeats@gmail.com
www.sechristbros.com
Processor and packer of meat including bologna, smoked ham, frankfurters and sausage
President: George Sechrist
gssiii@earthlink.net
VP: Jacob Sechrist
Estimated Sales: $910,000
Number Employees: 5-9
Square Footage: 40000
Type of Packaging: Consumer

11402 **Secret Garden**
10989 County 14
PO Box 544
Park Rapids, MN 56470-2119
218-732-4866
Fax: 218-732-2007 800-950-4409
sgmorg@wcta.net www.secretgardengourmet.com
Gourmet wild rice, bread, entree and seasoning mixes
President: Anne Morgan
sgmorg@wcta.net
Sales/Marketing: Andrea Roberts
Estimated Sales: Less Than $500,000
Number Employees: 1-4
Square Footage: 24000
Type of Packaging: Consumer, Private Label
Brands:
Anne's Country Gourmet
Continental Cuisine
Creole Classics
Midhaven Farm Cafe
Midheaven Farm
Pastry Perfect
Secret Garden
Soup For Singles
Swany White
Swany White Certified Organic
The Secret Garden

11403 **Secret Tea Garden**
5559 West Boulevard
Vancouver, BC V6M 3W6
Canada
604-261-3070
Fax: 604-261-3075 info@secretgardentea.com
www.secretgardentea.com

Special varieties of tea
President: Erin McBeath
VP: With Kathy
Estimated Sales: Less than $500,000
Number Employees: 5

11404 Sedlock Farm
1557 Knoxville Road
Lynn Center, IL 61262-8504
309-521-8284
Fax: 309-521-8284
Fresh asparagus and asparagus products including fettucine; also, vinegars, hot pepper and jellies
Owner/CEO: John Sedlock
VP Manufacturing: Patricia Sedlock
Estimated Sales: Under $300,000
Number Employees: 6
Type of Packaging: Consumer, Food Service, Bulk

11405 Sedona Baking Company
c/o Risvold's Inc.
1234 W. El Segundo Blvd.
Gardena, CA 90247
323-770-2674
Fax: 323-770-0800 tbrandon@risvolds.com
risvolds.com
Cakes, particularly espresso
Founder: Sally McIntyre
CEO, Risvold's Inc.: Tim Brandon
Year Founded: 1991

11406 See Smell Taste
315 Sutter Street
5th Floor
San Francisco, CA 94108
415-986-4216
Fax: 415-986-4217 info@seesmelltaste.com
www.seesmelltaste.com
Herbs and spices

11407 See's Candies
20600 South Alameda Street
Carson, CA 90810
Fax: 800-275-4733 800-347-7337
qdordering@sees.com www.sees.com
Confectionary and chocolates
President & CEO: Charles Huggins
CFO: Ken Scott
General Manager: Jane Wellsplant
Estimated Sales: $.5-1 million
Number Employees: 5-9
Square Footage: 880000
Parent Co: See's Candies
Type of Packaging: Consumer
Brands:
See's Candies

11408 Seed Enterprises Inc
679 19th Rd
West Point, NE 68788-4510
402-372-3238
Fax: 402-372-2627 888-440-7333
Soybeans
President: Conrad Reeson
Estimated Sales: $1-3 Million
Number Employees: 5-9
Square Footage: 70000
Brands:
Sunrise

11409 Seeds of Change
P.O. Box 4908
Rancho Dominguez, CA 90220
888-762-7333
www.seedsofchange.com
Organic, non-GMO seeds of herbs and vegetables
Co-Founder: Alan Kapuler
CEO: Andrew Behar
Year Founded: 1989
Estimated Sales: $58 Million
Number Employees: 120
Parent Co: Mars, Inc.

11410 Seenergy Foods
121 Jevlan Drive
Woodbridge, ON L4L 8A8
Canada
905-850-2544
Fax: 905-850-2563 800-609-7674
info@seenergyfoods.com www.seenergyfoods.com
Processor and exporter of frozen vegetables including vegetable patties and IQF (individually quick frozen) beans
President/CEO: Shreyas Ajmera
Marketing/Sales: Carl McLaughlin
Estimated Sales: $3.2 Million
Number Employees: 80
Type of Packaging: Consumer, Food Service, Private Label, Bulk
Brands:
Presidents Choice

11411 Segall Nathan Co Inc
1667 Federal Dr # 12
Montgomery, AL 36107-1103
334-279-3174
Fax: 334-279-1751
Produce
Manager: Reid Barnes
nathansegallco@bellsouth.net
Estimated Sales: $3-5 Million
Number Employees: 5-9

11412 Seger Egg Corporation
P.O.Box 265
Farina, IL 62838-0265
618-245-3301
Fax: 618-245-3552
Eggs
President: Larry Seger
Sales/Marketing: Larry Pemberton
Estimated Sales: $10-20 000,000
Number Employees: 50-99

11413 Seghesio Family Vineyards
700 Grove St
Healdsburg, CA 95448-4753
707-433-0545
Fax: 707-433-0545 seghesio@seghesio.com
www.seghesio.com
Winery, specializing in zinfadel and Italian varietals.
CEO/President: Eric Martin
Chief Financial Officer: Pat Delong
Grower Relations & Viticulture Manager: Ned Neumiller
Ambassador: Pete Seghesio
Chief Operating Officer: Pat Delong
Production Manager/Winemaker: Ted Seghesio
Estimated Sales: $3.4 Million
Number Employees: 5-9
Number of Brands: 1
Parent Co: Crimson Wine Group
Type of Packaging: Consumer, Food Service
Brands:
Seghesio

11414 Seitenbacher America LLC
11505 Perpetual Drive
Odessa, FL 33556
727-376-3000
Fax: 727-376-4662
seitenbacheramerica@verizon.net
www.seitenbacher.com
Grain mix, berry mix, Honey Chia Muesli, cooking oils, nuts, cookies, cereals
President: Willi Pfannenschwarz
Manager: Harry Pfannenschwarz
Sales: Debbie Roberts
Contact: Harry Pfannenschwarz
harryp@seitenbacher.com
Estimated Sales: $600,000
Number Employees: 15
Square Footage: 11200

11415 Sejoyia Foods
195 Ctc Blvd
Louisville, CO 80027-3144
855-293-5577
customerservice@sejoyia.com sejoyia.com
Cookies and snacks
Founder & CEO: Sequoia Cheney
Brands:
Brussel Bytes
Cocoroons
Snips

11416 (HQ)Select Food Products
120 Sunrise Avenue
Toronto, ON M4A 1B4
Canada
416-759-9316
Fax: 416-759-9310 800-699-8016
www.selectfoodproducts.com
Manufacturers and exporter of salad dressings, sauces, salsas, relishes, mustard, gravies, canned dinners, etc; importer of tomatoes and tomato paste
President: Paul Fredricks
Number Employees: 150
Square Footage: 464000
Type of Packaging: Consumer, Food Service, Private Label, Bulk
Brands:
Duthie
Horne's
Laing's
Oxford Inn
Select

11417 Select Harvest USA
14827 W Harding Rd
Turlock, CA 95380
209-668-2471
Fax: 209-668-4988 info@selectharvestusa.com
selectharvestusa.com
Almonds
CEO: Robert Nunes

11418 Select Origins
PO Box 1748
Mansfield, OH 44901-1748
419-924-5447
General groceries
National Sales Manager: Noel Thompson
Estimated Sales: $5-10 000,000
Number Employees: 20

11419 Select Supplements Inc
5800 Newton Dr
Carlsbad, CA 92008-7311
760-431-7509
Fax: 760-804-8073
hectorg@selectsupplements.com
www.selectsupplements.com
Nutraceuticlas and other dietary supplement products.
Vice President: Hector Gudino
heg@select-ssi.com
Executive VP: Toshifumi Asada
QA/QC Manager: David Dean
Production Supervisor: James Morales
Purchasing Supervisor: Cheryl Moore
Estimated Sales: $990,000
Number Employees: 5-9

11420 Selecto Sausage Co
7120 Canal St
Houston, TX 77011-2754
713-926-1626
Mexican products including sausage, spices and tortillas
President: Carlos Gonzalez
Estimated Sales: $3-5 Million
Number Employees: 5-9
Type of Packaging: Consumer

11421 Selina Naturally
4 Celtic Dr
Arden, NC 28704-9157
828-299-9005
Fax: 828-654-0529 800-867-7258
info@selinanaturally.com
www.selinanaturally.com
Flavored Celtic sea salt
President/CEO: Selina Delangre
selina@celtic-seasalt.com
CFO: Theresa Imhoff
Estimated Sales: $4 Million
Number Employees: 20-49
Square Footage: 38000

11422 Sells Best
PO Box 428
Mishawaka, IN 46546-0428
574-255-1910
Fax: 574-258-6162 800-837-8368
www.coravent.com
Bakery mixes including breads, doughnuts, cakes and muffins including low fat, no cholesterol or preservatives and sugar free
President: Gary Sells
Office Manager: Kathy Campole
VP Sales: Coleman Caldwell
Director Manufacturing: Steven Surmay
Purchasing Manager: James Allen
Estimated Sales: $9 Million
Number Employees: 5-9
Square Footage: 80000

11423 **Selma Good Company**
PO Box 101
Selma, AL 36702
334-412-4214
robert@selmagood.com
gmommas.com
Cookies
Founder & Owner: Robert Armstrong
Estimated Sales: Under $500,000
Number Employees: 2-10
Brands:
G MOMMAS

11424 **Selma's Cookies**
2023 Apex Ct
Apopka, FL 32703-7720
407-884-9433
Fax: 407-884-6121 800-992-6654
www.selmas.com
Gourmet cookies, brownies and crispy rice treats.
President: Selma Sayin
selma@selmas.com
Estimated Sales: Less than $500,000
Number Employees: 50-99

11425 **Selwoods Farm Hunting Preserve**
706 Selwood Rd
Alpine, AL 35014-5431
256-362-7595
Fax: 256-362-3856 800-522-0403
www.selwoodfarm.com
Smoked turkey and hams, cakes, mustards, jams, cookkies, stone ground grits, and pancake mix
Owner: Dell Hill
Estimated Sales: $1-3 Million
Number Employees: 5-9
Type of Packaging: Consumer

11426 **Semifreddi's Bakery**
1980 N Loop Rd
Alameda, CA 94502-3540
510-596-9930
877-LOV-SEMI
www.semifreddis.com
Sourdough bakery
Contact: Michael Anderson
m.anderson@abbott.com
Number Employees: 50-99

11427 **Seminis Vegetable SeedsInc**
2700 Camino Del Sol
Oxnard, CA 93030-7967
805-485-7317
info@seminis.com
www.seminis.com
Hybrid vegetable seeds
VP Marketing: Jorge Christlieb
CEO: Bruno Ferrari
CFO: Gaspar Alvarez
IT: Erik Ackerman
erik.ackerman@seminis.com
Number Employees: 20-49
Parent Co: Seminis Vegetable Seeds
Brands:
Petoseed
Royal Sluis

11428 **Seminole Foods**
1966 Commerce Circle
P.O.Box 305
Springfield, OH 45501
Fax: 352-245-8534 800-881-1177
customerservice@seminolefoods.com
www.seminolefoods.com
Fresh ground horseradish and fine sauces
President: Robert Schneider
Contact: Mary Lerchen
marylerchen@seminoleFoods.com
Estimated Sales: Below $5 Million
Number Employees: 10
Square Footage: 76000
Type of Packaging: Consumer, Food Service, Private Label
Brands:
Seminole

11429 **Sempio Foods**
12928 Moore St.
Cerritos, CA 90703
562-207-9540
Fax: 562-207-5498 en.sempio.com
Soy sauce, noodles, seafood, yondu, Korean hot sauce, tea and vinegar.
President: Woong-kyu Lee
National Marketing Manager: Duffield Gary
HR Manager: Julie Lee
Year Founded: 1946
Estimated Sales: $2.5 Million
Number Employees: 5-9
Brands:
Sempio

11430 **Senape's Bakery Inc**
222 W 17th St
Hazleton, PA 18201-2426
570-454-0839
sfpayer@erols.com
Bread and pizza dough
President: Mary Lou Marchetti
Marketing: Mary Lou Marchetti
Estimated Sales: Below $5 000,000
Number Employees: 20-49

11431 **Senba USA**
23447 Cabot Blvd
Hayward, CA 94545
510-264-5850
Fax: 510-264-0938 888-922-5852
aoki@senbausa.com www.senbausa.com
Liquid sauces including teriyaki, beef and tempura; also, miso soup bases; importer of spray dried alcohol powder and tea extract; also, contract packaging and dry blending available
Sales: Hiro Aoki
Contact: Fernando Garcia
fgarcia@senbausa.com
Estimated Sales: $4.2 Million
Number Employees: 20-49
Square Footage: 52000
Parent Co: Senba Foods Company
Type of Packaging: Consumer, Food Service, Private Label, Bulk

11432 **Sencha Naturals**
912 E 3rd Street
Building 101
Los Angeles, CA 90013
213-346-9470
Fax: 213-947-1723 888-473-6242
inquiry@senchanaturals.com
www.senchanaturals.com
Green tea mints and green tea bars
President: David Kerdoon
Contact: Noe Claros
noe.claros@senchanaturals.com
Operations Manager: Desiree Thomas
Number Employees: 15

11433 **Seneca Foods Corp**
606 S Tremont St
Princeville, IL 61559-9468
309-385-4301
Fax: 309-385-2696 www.senecafoods.com
Canned vegetables including asparagus, pumpkins, green beans, corn and peas; also, salads including German potato, bean and garden salads
Manager: Wally Hochsprung
Vice President: Van Riper
Manager: L Dallinger
ldallinger@chiquita.com
Plant Manager: David Stoner
Estimated Sales: $10-20 Million
Number Employees: 100-249
Square Footage: 480000
Parent Co: Owatonna Canning Company
Type of Packaging: Consumer, Food Service, Private Label

11434 **(HQ)Seneca Foods Corp**
3736 S Main Steet
Marion, NY 14505
315-926-8100
webmaster@senecafoods.com
www.senecafoods.com
Largest processor of fruits and vegetables in North America
President & CEO: Kraig H. Kayser
kkayser@senecafoods.com
Chairman: Arthur Wolcott
SVP Technology and Planning: Carl Cichetti
Sr VP of Sales & Marketing: Dean Erstad
Sr. VP & Chief Administrative Officer: Cynthia Fohrd
Exec. VP & COO: Paul Palmby
Year Founded: 1949
Estimated Sales: Over $1 Billion
Number Employees: 1000-4999
Number of Brands: 6
Square Footage: 7000
Type of Packaging: Consumer, Food Service, Private Label
Other Locations:
Modesto CA
Geneva NY
Leicester NY
Marion NY
Buhl ID
Payette ID
Lebanon PA
Princeville IL
Dayton WA
Yakima WA
Arlington MN
Blue Earth MN
Glencoe MN
Brands:
Aunt Nellie's
Cherry Man
Green Valley
Libby's
Read
Seneca Snacks

11435 **Seneca Juice**
PO Box 997
Marion, NY 14505-0997
315-926-3228
Juice
President/CEO: Edward Lutten
Sales Manager: C Rothfuss
Sr. VP Operations: Ricke Kress
Estimated Sales: $5-10 Million
Number Employees: 50-99
Parent Co: Tree Top

11436 **Senomyx Inc**
4767 Nexus Center Dr
San Diego, CA 92121-3051
858-646-8300
Fax: 858-404-0752
Flavor ingredients.
President/CEO: John Poyhonen
john.poyhonen@senomyx.com
CFO/SVP: Tony Rogers
VP/General Counsel/Corporate Secretary: Catherine Lee
SVP/Chief Commercial Development Officer: Sharon Wicker
VP, Information Technology: Lorenzo Pena
Estimated Sales: $28 Million
Number Employees: 50-99
Number of Brands: 3
Brands:
Bittermyx
Savorymyx
Sweetmyx

11437 **Senor Felix's Gourmet Mexican**
4265 Maine Ave
Baldwin Park, CA 91706-3312
626-960-2800
Fax: 626-560-2855 senorfelix@ffci.us
Mexican fresh and frozen food, including enchiladas, burritos, taquitos, tamales, salsa, guacamole dip, etc
Owner: Lulu Juco
Controller: Sam Tabani
VP Sales/Marketing: Don O'Neill
Estimated Sales: $.5-1 million
Number Employees: 50-99
Type of Packaging: Private Label
Brands:
Delicioso
Pacifico
Senor Felix's

11438 **Senor Murphy Candymaker**
1904 Chamisa St
Santa Fe, NM 87505-3440
505-988-4311
Fax: 505-988-2050 877-988-4311
chocolate@senormurphy.com
www.senormurphy.com
Candy
Owner: Rand Levitt
chocolate@senormurphy.com
VP: Bob Murphy
Estimated Sales: $770000
Number Employees: 5-9
Type of Packaging: Consumer

11439 **Senor Pinos de Santa Fe**
2600 Camino Entrada
Santa Fe, NM 87507-0491
505-473-3437
Fax: 505-473-5808 senorpinos@aol.com
Blue-corn flour, southwestern specialties
Owner: Nate Pino
Estimated Sales: $1 Million
Number Employees: 30
Brands:
Josie's Best Blue Tortilla Chips

11440 **Sensational Sweets**
355 Sweets Ln
Lewisburg, PA 17837-7759
570-524-4361
Fax: 570-524-5360 info@sensationalsweets.com
www.sensationalsweets.com
Gourmet fudge, fudge bites, drizzled popcorn, dipped pretzels, and lollypops
Owner: Virginia Feitner
sweets@dejazzd.com
Estimated Sales: Less than $500,000
Number Employees: 10-19

11441 **Sensible Foods LLC**
PO Box 7345
Santa Rosa, CA 95407
707-569-0170
Fax: 707-762-1635 888-222-0170
Dried fruit and vegetable snacks. 100% natural, gluten free, and GMO free.
President/CEO: David Baxes
db@sensiblefoods.com
Vice President: Alan Christie
Type of Packaging: Consumer, Bulk

11442 **Sensible Portions**
4600 Sleepytime Drive
Boulder, CO 80301
973-283-9220
Fax: 973-283-2799 800-913-6637
www.sensibleportions.com
All natural and portion control snacks such as multi grain crisps, mini multi grain crisps, soy crisps, mini soy crisps, pita crackers, and pita chips.
President: Jason Cohen

11443 **Sensient Flavors and Fragrances**
2800 W Higgins Road
Suite 900
Hoffman Estates, IL 60169
847-755-5300
Fax: 847-755-5350
corporate.communications@sensient.com
www.sensientflavorsandfragrances.com
Flavoring extracts and syrups.
President, Flavors & Fragrances Group: E. Craig Mitchell
Estimated Sales: $100-200 Million
Number Employees: 1,000-4,999
Parent Co: Sensient Technologies Corporation

11444 **(HQ)Sensient Technologies Corp**
777 E Wisconsin Ave
Milwaukee, WI 53202-5304
414-271-6755
www.sensient.com
Colors, flavors and fragrances.
Chair/President/CEO: Paul Manning
paul.manning@sensient-tech.com
Senior VP/CFO: Stephen Rolfs
President, Colors Group: Michael Geraghty
President, Flavors & Fragrances Group: E. Craig Mitchell
Year Founded: 1882
Estimated Sales: $1.46 Billion
Number Employees: 4,000
Brands:
Sensient

11445 **Sensus America Inc**
100 Lenox Dr # 104
Suite 104
Lawrence Twp, NJ 08648-2332
646-452-6140
Fax: 646-452-6150 www.inspiredbyinulin.com
Supplier of ingredients to the food and beverage industries.
Sales Manager: Carol Malczan
Number Employees: 1-4
Parent Co: Sensus
Brands:
Frutafit
Frutalose

11446 **Sentry Seasonings**
928 N Church Rd
Elmhurst, IL 60126-1014
630-530-5370
Fax: 630-530-5385 wayne@sentryseasonings.com
www.sentryseasonings.com
Flavors and seasonings for food processing companies
President: Carla Staniec
carla@sentryseasonings.com
VP: Michael Staniec
Estimated Sales: $730000
Number Employees: 10-19
Square Footage: 120000
Type of Packaging: Consumer, Food Service, Private Label, Bulk

11447 **Seppic Inc**
30 Two Bridges Rd # 210
Fairfield, NJ 07004-1555
973-882-5597
Fax: 973-882-5178 877-737-7421
stephen.oneill@airliquide.com www.seppic.com
Ingredients, minerals and extracts
President: Jean Marc Giner
Marketing/Sales: Regis Cazes
Contact: Yves Bantec
y.bantec@seppic.com
Estimated Sales: $1-2.5 Million
Number Employees: 500-999
Parent Co: Seppic

11448 **Sequoia Brewing Co**
777 E Olive Ave
Fresno, CA 93728-3350
559-264-5521
Fax: 559-264-6033 scott@sequoiabrewing.com
Seasonal beer, ale, stout, lager and pilsner
President: Scott Kendall
scottk@sequoiabrewing.com
Operations Manager: Holly Bragg
Director Manufacturing: Kevin Cox
Estimated Sales: $1-2,500,000
Number Employees: 20-49
Type of Packaging: Consumer, Food Service
Brands:
Bridalveil Ale
San Joaquin Golden Ale
Tower Dark Ale

11449 **Sequoia Grove**
8338 Saint Helena Hwy
PO Box 449
Napa, CA 94558-9729
707-944-2945
Fax: 707-963-9411 800-851-7841
info@sequoiagrove.com www.sequoiagrove.com
Wines
Owner: Brett Adams
brett@sequoiagrove.com
CFO: Robert Aldridge
Vice President: Casandra Knox
Marketing Director: Anthony Ankers
Estimated Sales: $1-$2.5 Million
Number Employees: 10-19
Type of Packaging: Private Label
Brands:
Sequoia Grove

11450 **Sequoia Specialty Cheese Company**
7000 W Doe Ave # C
Visalia, CA 93291-8623
559-752-4106
Fax: 559-752-4108
Cheese
Administrator: Ray Chavez
Production Manager: Greg Moe
Estimated Sales: $1-23 000,000
Number Employees: 10-19
Number of Products: 10
Square Footage: 40000
Type of Packaging: Consumer, Food Service, Private Label
Brands:
Mt. Whitney

11451 **Serenade Foods**
9179 N 200 E
Milford, IN 46542
574-658-4121
Fax: 219-658-2246
Poultry
Communications Manager: Janelle Deatsman
Contact: Eric Essig
eessig@mapleleaffarms.com
Number Employees: 100-249
Parent Co: Maple Leaf Foods
Type of Packaging: Consumer, Food Service, Private Label, Bulk

11452 **Serendipitea**
73 Plandome Rd
Manhasset, NY 11030-2330
516-365-7711
Fax: 516-365-7733 888-832-5433
tea@serendipitea.com www.serendipitea.com
Tea; premium grade loose leaf
Principal: Linda Villano
tea@serendipitea.com
Estimated Sales: Less than $500,000
Number Employees: 5-9
Number of Brands: 1
Number of Products: 100+
Square Footage: 12000
Type of Packaging: Consumer, Food Service, Private Label, Bulk

11453 **Serendipity Cellars**
15275 Dunn Forest Rd
Monmouth, OR 97361
503-838-4284
Fax: 503-838-0067
Wines
Owner: Glen Longshore
Estimated Sales: $500,000-$1 000,000
Number Employees: 1-4

11454 **Serengeti Tea Co**
351 W Redondo Beach Blvd
Gardena, CA 90248-2101
310-527-5278
Fax: 310-527-2154 888-604-2040
tea@serengetitea.com www.serengetitea.com
Iced teas
Owner: David Massey
Estimated Sales: $690,000
Number Employees: 5-9
Brands:
Southern Breeze
Ticolino

11455 **Serious Foodie**
4754 Mainsail Dr
Bradenton, FL 34208-9409
844-736-6343
shop@serious-foodie.com
serious-foodie.com
Ingredients: sauces, rubs, vinaigrettes and marinades
President & CEO: James M. Pachence
Estimated Sales: $4 Million
Number Employees: 21
Brands:
Serious Foodie

11456 **Serranos Salsa**
632 Ralph Ablanedo Dr # 330
Austin, TX 78748-6619
512-328-9200
Fax: 512-328-3005 www.serranos.com
Soups, ensaladas, tortas
Owner: Adam Gonzales
Director: Eric Cross
Estimated Sales: $500-1 Million appx.
Number Employees: 5-9
Brands:
Serranos Salsa

11457 **Serro Foods LLC**
36 Koeppel Ave
Catskill, NY 12414-2018
518-943-9255
Pasta, grilling sauces, marinades and pasta sauce.
Founder and Owner: Charlie Serro
Estimated Sales: Less Than $500,000
Number Employees: 1-4
Brands:
Grandpa Pete's Sunday Sauce

11458 **(HQ)Serv-Agen Corporation**
1200 S Union Ave
Cherry Hill, NJ 8002
856-663-6966
Fax: 856-663-7016 cwslade1@msn.com
Food colors, flavorings, dehydrated vegetables, gravy and soup bases, spices, puddings and sauce mixes including soy and worcestershire
President: Barbara Pearlman
VP: Charles W Slade
Estimated Sales: $989,000
Number Employees: 5-9
Square Footage: 45000
Type of Packaging: Consumer, Food Service, Private Label, Bulk
Brands:
Bennetts
Clawson
Heinle
Key Lime
Lem
Lemon

11459 **Serv-Rite Meat Co Inc**
2515 N San Fernando Rd
Los Angeles, CA 90065-1325
323-227-1911
Fax: 323-227-9068 www.bar-m.com
Bacon, smoked ham and sausage
President: Nora Hizon
nhizon@bar-m.com
Marketing Manager: Anna Cornellius
Estimated Sales: $10-20 Million
Number Employees: 50-99
Square Footage: 160000

11460 **Service Foods**
4355 International Blvd
Suite 150
Norcross, GA 30093
770-446-3085
Fax: 770-446-3085 800-872-3484
Frozen food and freezer plans
Founder: Stan Sax
CEO: Keith Cantor
Assistant Marketing Manager: Deborah Zachary
Outside Sales Representative: Rene Elalouf
Customer Service: Stephanie Shaw
Estimated Sales: $5-10 Million
Number Employees: 20-49

11461 **Service Packing Company**
250 Southern Street
Vancouver, BC V6A 2P1
Canada
604-681-0264
Fax: 604-681-9309
Dates, currants, raisins, shredded coconut, chocolate chips, prunes and nuts including walnuts and almonds
President: Ron Huntington
Estimated Sales: $500,000-1,000,000
Number Employees: 1-4
Square Footage: 340000
Type of Packaging: Private Label
Brands:
Martins

11462 **Sesaco Corp**
6201 E Oltorf St # 100
Suite 100
Austin, TX 78741-7511
512-389-0790
Fax: 512-389-0790 800-737-2260
www.sesaco.com
Sesame seeds including white hulled
Executive Director: Ray Langham
Administration: Tina Smith
Director of Production: Jerry Riney
jriney@sesaco.com
Estimated Sales: $3-5 Million
Number Employees: 1-4
Type of Packaging: Consumer, Bulk
Brands:
Flour
Hp-White Hulled Sesame Seeds
Oil
T2p-Light
T4p-Medium Toasted Hulled Sesame
T5p-Dark
Tnp-Toasted Natural Sesame Seeds
Tahini
Wnp-Washed Natural Sesame Seeds

11463 **Sesinco Foods**
54 W 21st Street
New York, NY 10010-6908
212-243-1306
Fax: 212-243-2036
Frozen and canned foods, beverages, dairy products
President: Serbajit Singh
VP: Ann Gaudet
Estimated Sales: $1600000
Number Employees: 7
Type of Packaging: Consumer, Food Service

11464 **Sessions Co Inc**
801 N Main St
Enterprise, AL 36330-9108
334-393-0200
Fax: 334-393-0240
Peanut sheller and processor producing quality shelled peanuts and peanut seed. Also producers of crude peanut oil and peanut meal.
Principal: Mo Sessions
CFO: Jeff Outlaw
sesscom@frost.snowhill.com
Estimated Sales: $9.3 Million
Number Employees: 50-99
Square Footage: 40000
Type of Packaging: Consumer, Food Service, Private Label, Bulk

11465 **Seth Ellis Chocolatier**
5345 Arapahoe Ave Ste 5
Boulder, CO 80303
720-565-2462
Fax: 720-565-2462 hey@sethellischocolatier.com
Chocolate
President/Owner: Frederick Levine
Number Employees: 5

11466 **Sethness Caramel Color**
3422 W Touhy Avenue
Skokie, IL 60076
847-329-2080
Fax: 847-329-2090 mail@sethness.com
www.sethness.com
Producer of caramel color for beverage, bakery, nutritional, and other applications.
COO: Tom Schufreider
Type of Packaging: Food Service, Bulk
Other Locations:
Corporate Office
Skokie IL
Eastern Office
Avenel NJ
U.S. Plant & Research Center
Clinton IA
France Plant
Merville, France
China Plant
Lianyungang, China
India Plant
Ahmedabad, India

11467 **Setton Farms**
9370 Road 234
Terra Bella, CA 93270
559-535-6050
Fax: 559-535-6089 info@settonfarms.com
www.settonfarms.com
Pistachios, nuts, dried fruits and trail mixes
VP, Domestic Sales & Marketing: Joseph Setton
Other Locations:
Sales Office
New York NY
European Sales Office
The Netherlands
Brands:
Farmer Focus

11468 **Setton International Foods**
85 Austin Blvd
Commack, NY 11725
631-543-8090
Fax: 631-543-8070 800-227-4397
info@settonfarms.com
www.settoninternational.com
Pistachios, cashews, almonds, apricots, candy and snack foods
President: Joshua Setton
VP, Domestic Sales & Marketing: Joseph Setton
Human Resources Coordinator: Kellie Shepard
Logistics Manager: Patrick Braddock
Production Manager: Henry Scott
Plant Manager: Jeffrey Gibbons
Estimated Sales: $64 Million
Number Employees: 250-499
Square Footage: 55000
Type of Packaging: Consumer, Food Service, Private Label, Bulk
Other Locations:
Processing Facility
Terra Bella CA
European Sales Office
Zutphen, The Netherlands

11469 **Setton Pistachio**
9370 Road 234
Terra Bella, CA 93270
559-535-6050
Fax: 559-535-6089 info@settonfarms.com
www.settonfarms.com
Pistachios
President: Joshua Setton
settoninfo@settonfarms.com
VP, Domestic Sales & Marketing: Joseph Setton
Human Resources Coordinator: Kellie Shepard
Logistics Manager: Patrick Braddock
Project Manager: Henry Scott
Plant Manager: Jeffrey Gibbons
Estimated Sales: $64 Million
Number Employees: 100-249
Number of Brands: 2
Square Footage: 300000
Parent Co: Setton International Foods, Inc.
Type of Packaging: Consumer, Food Service, Bulk
Other Locations:
New York Sales Office
Commack NY
European Sales Office
Zutphen, The Netherlands
Brands:
Setton Farms
Setton Farms Chewy Bites

11470 **Seven Barrel Brewery**
5 Airport Rd # 16
West Lebanon, NH 03784-1658
603-298-5566
Fax: 603-298-5715 sevenbarrelbrew@gmail.com
Seasonal beer, ale, stout, lager and pilsner
President: Nancy Noonan
Manager: Earl Locke
Number Employees: 20-49
Type of Packaging: Food Service
Brands:
Seven Barrell

11471 **Seven Hills Coffee Co**
11094 Deerfield Rd
Blue Ash, OH 45242-4112
513-489-5220
Fax: 513-489-6888 www.sevenhillscoffee.com
Coffee
Owner: Michael Melzer
mmelzer@sevenhillscoffee.com
Operations Manager: Matthew Kasper
Estimated Sales: $2.5-5 000,000
Number Employees: 5-9

11472 **Seven Hills Winery**
212 N 3rd Ave
Walla Walla, WA 99362-1883
509-529-7198
Fax: 509-529-7918 877-777-7870
info@sevenhillswinery.com
www.sevenhillswinery.com
Wines
Founder/Winemaker: Casey McClellan
Estimated Sales: Below $5 Million
Number Employees: 5-9
Brands:
Seven Hills

11473 **Seven Keys Co Of Florida**
450 SW 12th Ave
Pompano Beach, FL 33069-3504
954-946-5010
Fax: 954-946-5012
Processor and exporter of tropical jams, jellies, marmalades and coconut toast spreads
President: Henry Stevens
Estimated Sales: $3-5 Million
Number Employees: 5-9
Square Footage: 45000
Type of Packaging: Consumer, Food Service, Private Label
Brands:
Lapham
Seven Keys

11474 Seven Lakes Vineyard & Winery
1111 Tinsman Rd
Fenton, MI 48430-1679
810-373-6081
Wines
President: Chris Guest
Manager: Karen Irwin
Estimated Sales: Less Than $500,000
Number Employees: 1-4

11475 Seven Seas Seafoods
901 S Fremont Ave Ste 168
Alhambra, CA 91803
626-570-9129
Fax: 626-570-0079
Seafood
President: Christopher Lin
VP: Sean Lin
Estimated Sales: $5-10 Million
Number Employees: 5-9

11476 Seven Sundays, LLC
PO Box 19294
Minneapolis, MN 19294
612-562-5316
www.sevensundays.com
Manufacturer of muesli.
Co-Founder: Hannah Bamstable
Co-Founder: Brady Bamstable
Contact: Hannah Barnstable
hannah@sevensundays.com

11477 Severance Foods Inc
3478 Main St
Hartford, CT 06120-1138
860-724-7063
Fax: 860-527-2045 www.severancefoods.com
Tortilla chips and tortillas including flour and corn
President: Richard Stevens
rstevens@severancefoods.com
Founder: John Grikis
Founder: Richard Dana
Estimated Sales: $3.35 Million
Number Employees: 50-99
Square Footage: 112000
Type of Packaging: Consumer, Food Service, Private Label, Bulk
Brands:
Pan De Oro

11478 Severino Pasta Mfg Co Inc
110 Haddon Ave
Westmont, NJ 08108-1000
856-854-3716
Fax: 856-854-6098 info@severinopasta.com
www.severinopasta.com
Pasta
Owner: Louis Severino
lseverino@severinopasta.com
VP/Partner: Louis Servino
Estimated Sales: Below $5 Million
Number Employees: 20-49

11479 Severn Peanut Co
413 Main St
Severn, NC 27877
252-585-1744
Fax: 252-585-1718 www.hamptonfarms.com
Peanuts
President: Dallas Barnes
Estimated Sales: $41.8 Million
Number Employees: 50-99
Square Footage: 10000
Parent Co: Meherrin Agriculture
Type of Packaging: Consumer, Bulk

11480 Seville Olive Company
663 S Anderson St
Los Angeles, CA 90023
323-261-2218
Fax: 323-261-1026
Olives, onions, cherries and peppers
President: Louis Pavlic Sr
loupav45@att.net
Estimated Sales: $10-20 000,000
Number Employees: 100-249

11481 Seviroli Foods
385 Oak St
Garden City, NY 11530
516-222-6220
Fax: 516-222-0534 www.seviroli.com
All natural frozen pasta products.
President: Anthony D'Orazio
adorazio@doraziofoods.com
CFO: Michael Romano
VP Sales/Marketing: Terry D'Ozario
VP Operations/COO: Frank D'Orazio
VP Production: Anthony D'Orazio
Estimated Sales: $8.4 Million
Number Employees: 50-99
Square Footage: 100000
Brands:
Dorazio

11482 Seviroli Foods Inc
601 Brook St
Garden City, NY 11530-6431
516-222-6220
Fax: 516-222-0534
Italian foods. Manufactures frozen pasta including ravioli, tortellini, manicotti, gnocchi, and stuffed shells
President: Joseph Seviroli Sr
Quality Assurance Manager: Nel Reformina
Estimated Sales: $5-10 Million
Number Employees: 250-499
Square Footage: 100

11483 Sewell's Seafood & Fish Market
1178 Lee St
Rogersville, AL 35652-7816
256-247-1378
Fax: 718-617-6851
Seafood
Owner: Tana Springer
tanaspringer@aol.com
Public Relations: Tana Springer
Estimated Sales: $1-3 Million
Number Employees: 1-4

11484 Sexy Pop LLC
100 Roslyn Ave.
Sea Cliff, NY 11579
516-671-4411
877-476-2755
info@robsbrands.com
Manufacturer of popcorn.
Founder and CEO: Robert Ehrlich
Contact: Rt Ehrlich
rob@sexypop.us
Brands:
Vegan Rob's
Crunchy Rob's

11485 Seydel Co
244 John B Brooks Rd
Pendergrass, GA 30567
706-693-2266
Fax: 706-693-2074 customerservice@seydel.com
www.seydel.com
Starch, dextrin and protein.
Chairman & CEO: Scott Seydel, Sr.
President & COO: Scott Seydel, Jr.
Chief Financial Officer: Graham Marsh
Estimated Sales: $43.5 Million
Number Employees: 50-99
Parent Co: Seydel Company
Type of Packaging: Food Service, Bulk
Brands:
Emdex
Emflo
Emgum
Emjel
Emox

11486 Seymour & Sons SeafoodsInc
3201 Saint Charles St
Diberville, MS 39540-5315
228-392-4020
Fax: 228-392-8028
Seafood including frozen catfish and lobster
President: Paul Seymour
Plant Manager: David Seymour
Estimated Sales: $1.2 Million
Number Employees: 5-9
Square Footage: 10000

11487 Sfoglia Fine Pastas & Gourmet
P.O.Box 921
Freeland, WA 98249
360-331-4080
Gourmet and specialty foods
President: Stephanie Jushinski
Estimated Sales: Less than $500,000
Number Employees: 1-4

11488 Sfoglini Pasta Shop
630 Flushing Avenue
2nd Floor
Brooklyn, NY 11206
917-338-5955
info@sfoglini.com
www.sfoglini.com
Pasta: durum semolina and grain
Co-Founder: Steve Gonzalez
Co-Founder, Marketing & Operations: Scott Ketchum
Estimated Sales: $4 Million
Number Employees: 35
Type of Packaging: Consumer, Private Label

11489 Shaanxi Jiahe PhytochemCo., Ltd.
140 Littleton Rd
Suite 200
Parsippany, NJ 07054
973-439-6869
Fax: 973-439-6879 info@jiaherbinc.com
jiaherb.com
Herbal extract and natural ingredients for the nutraceutical, pharmaceutical, cosmetic and food & beverage industries.
Vice President: Charlie Wang
Sales Manager: Scott Chen
Number Employees: 500

11490 Shabazz Fruit Cola Company
P.O. Box 835
Newark, NJ 07101
973-230-4641
Fax: 973-230-1651 info@shabazzfruitcola.com
Fruit flavored colas
CEO: Frank Shabazz

11491 Shady Grove Orchards
183 Shady Grove Road
Onalaska, WA 98570-9453
360-985-7033
Organic American chestnuts and chestnut flour, dried chestnut kernels and seedlings
Co-Owner: Annie Bhagwandin
Co-Owner: Omroa Bhagwandin
Brands:
Shady Grove Orchards

11492 Shady Maple Farm
2585 Skymark Ave
Mississauga, ON L4W 4L5
Canada
905-206-1455
Fax: 905-206-1477 www.shadymaple.ca
Processor and exporter of pure maple syrup products
President/CEO: Robert Swain
CFO: Darren Brash
Marketing Director: Marlene Jolicoeur
Sales Director: Daniel Neale
Number Employees: 10-19
Square Footage: 220000
Type of Packaging: Consumer, Food Service, Private Label, Bulk

11493 Shafer Lake Fruit Inc
60643 Red Arrow Hwy
Hartford, MI 49057-9703
269-621-3194
Fax: 269-621-4170
Packers of apples, peaches, plums and asparagus
President: Dale Drake
d_drake@frontier.com
Estimated Sales: $3-5 Million
Number Employees: 20-49
Type of Packaging: Consumer, Bulk

11494 Shafer Vineyards
6154 Silverado Trl
Napa, CA 94558-9748
707-944-2877
Fax: 707-944-9454 info@shafervineyards.com
Cabernet sauvignon, chardonnay, merlot, cabernet savignon, sangiovese
Owner: John Shafer
info@shafervineyards.com
President: Doug Shafer
Winemaker: Elias Fernandez
Estimated Sales: $5-10 Million
Number Employees: 10-19
Brands:
Firebreak
Hillside
Red Shoulder Ranch
Shafer Vineyards

11495 **Shafer-Haggart**
1055 West Hastings Street
Suite 1038
Vancouver, BC V6E 4E2
Canada
604-669-5512
Fax: 604-669-9554 info@shafer-haggart.com
www.shafer-haggart.com
Processor and importer of canned mushrooms, tomatoes, peaches, tuna and salmon; exporter of frozen poultry and canned corn and fish products
President: Clive Lonsdale
Sr. VP: Brian Dougall
Estimated Sales: $2.5-5 Million
Number Employees: 20-49
Type of Packaging: Consumer, Food Service, Private Label

11496 **Shah Trading Company**
3451 McNicoll Avenue
Scarborough, ON M1V 2V3
Canada
416-292-6927
Fax: 416-292-7932 info@shahtrading.com
www.shahtrading.com
Rice, spices, beans, peas, and lentils, specialty flours and nuts and dried fruits.
Other Locations:
Pulse and Canning Plant
Scarborough ON
Rice Plant
Scarborough ON
Brands:
Dunya Harvest

11497 **Shaker Country Meadowsweets**
35 Hillside Avenue
Hillside, NJ 07205
973-926-2300
Fax: 973-926-4440 800-524-1304
info@hillsidecandy.com www.hillsidecandy.com
Fruit flavored candy
Estimated Sales: $5-10 Million
Number Employees: 10-19

11498 **Shaker Museum**
707 Shaker Rd
New Gloucester, ME 04260-2652
207-926-4865
888-624-6345
usshakers@aol.com www.maineshakers.com
Herbal teas, culinary herbs, herb mixes
Executive Director: Leonard Brooks
Estimated Sales: Less than $200,000
Number Employees: 1-4
Type of Packaging: Consumer, Food Service, Bulk
Brands:
United Society of Shakers

11499 **Shaker Valley Foods**
3304 W 67th Pl
Cleveland, OH 44102-5243
216-961-8600
Fax: 216-961-8077 www.shakervalleyfoods.com
Deli meats and cheeses, fresh cut quality meats including steaks, chops, roasts, stews, cutlets, sausages, ground and pattied products.
President: Dean Comber
Human Resources Manager: Kim Andreas
Year Founded: 1984
Estimated Sales: $20-50 Million
Number Employees: 20-49

11500 **Shakespeare's**
3840 W River Dr
Davenport, IA 52802-2412
563-383-0150
Fax: 563-383-0151 800-664-4114
Specialty chocolates
Owner: Elisa Shakespeare
Contact: Michael Anglese
mikea@shopshakespeares.com
Estimated Sales: Less than $500,000
Number Employees: 10-19

11501 **(HQ)Shaklee Corp**
4747 Willow Rd
Pleasanton, CA 94588-2763
925-924-2000
Fax: 925-924-2862 800-742-5533
www.shaklee.com
Nutritional supplements
Chairman/CEO: Roger Barnett
CEO: Etta Adams
adams@shaklee.net
CFO: Mike Batesole
Sr EVP & COO: Luiz Cerqueira
Research & Development, Chief Scientist: Dr. Carsten Smidt
adams@shaklee.net
Chief Marketing Officer: Brad Harrington
SVP, Sales & Field Development: Laura Hughes
Number Employees: 1000-4999
Parent Co: Ripplewood Holdings
Type of Packaging: Consumer
Other Locations:
Shaklee Corporation
Norman OK
Brands:
Airsource
Perfect Pitcher
Shaklee Carotomax
Shaklee Flavomax

11502 **Shallon Winery**
1598 Duane St
Astoria, OR 97103-3707
503-325-5978
paul@shallon.com
www.shallon.com
Fine wines including whey wines and chocolate wines
President: Paul C Vanderveldt
paul@shallon.com
Estimated Sales: Less Than $500,000
Number Employees: 1-4
Brands:
Shallon Winery

11503 **Shallowford Farms Popcorn, Inc.**
3732 Hartman Road
Yadkinville, NC 27055-5638
336-463-5938
Fax: 336-463-2358 800-892-9539
amanda.booe@yahoo.com
Popcorn
President: Amanda Booe
Plant Manager: Caswell Booe
Estimated Sales: $500,000-$1 Million
Number Employees: 10-19
Square Footage: 84000
Type of Packaging: Consumer, Private Label, Bulk
Brands:
Dennis
Mr Snack

11504 **(HQ)Shamrock Foods Co**
3900 E. Camelback Rd.
Suite 300
Phoenix, AZ 85018
602-233-6400
800-289-3663
www.shamrockfoodservice.com
General line items, groceries, meats, produce, dairy products, frozen foods, baked goods, equipment and fixtures, general merchandise and seafood; serving the food service market.
President: Kent McClelland
CFO: Stephen Down
Year Founded: 1922
Estimated Sales: Over $1 Billion
Number Employees: 1000-4999
Number of Brands: 45
Type of Packaging: Food Service
Other Locations:
Phoenix AZ
Commerce City CO
Albuquerque NM
Eastvale CA
Brands:
Fair Meadow
Bountiful Harvest
Brickfire Bakery
Intros
Cobblestreet Market
Katy's Kitchen
Pier Port
Prarie Creek
ProClean
ProPak
ProSystem
ProWare
Rejuv
Trescerro
Villa Frizzoni
Vista Verde
Shamrock Farms
Gold Canyon Meat Co.
Markon
Jensen Foods
Coffee Roasters Ridgeline
Azar
B&G Foods, Inc.
Brown Paper Goods
Bueno
Cheese Merchants
Custom Culinary
Ecolab
Florida's Natural
Hormel Foods
Kellogg's
Kraft Heinz
Lamb Weston
Michael Foods Inc.
Mission Foodservice
NCCO
Nestl, Professional
Perdue
Rema Foods Imports
Rich's
Roland
Schreiber
Smithfield Farmland
Sugar Foods Corporation
Tysom

11505 **Shamrock Foods Co**
Boise Foods Branch
1495 N Hickory Ave
Meridian, ID 83642
208-884-8400
www.shamrockfoodservice.com
Serves Idaho, Oregon and Utah.
Parent Co: Shamrock Foods Co

11506 **Shamrock Foods Co**
Colorado Foods Branch
5199 Ivy St
Commerce City, CO 80022
800-289-3595
coinfo@shamrockfoods.com
www.shamrockfoods.com
Serves Colorado, Western Kansas, Western Nebraska and Wyoming.
Senior VP: Kent Mullison
kent_mullison@shamrockfoods.com
Number Employees: 500-999
Parent Co: Shamrock Foods Company

11507 **Shamrock Foods Co**
Arizona Foods Branch
2540 N 29th Ave
Phoenix, AZ 85009-1682
602-233-6400
Fax: 928-537-3428 800-289-3663
azinfo@shamrockfoods.com
www.shamrockfoodservice.com
Estimated Sales: $100+ Million
Number Employees: 10-19
Parent Co: Shamrock Foods Company

11508 **Shamrock Foods Co**
Southern California Foods Branch
12400 Riverside Dr
Eastvale, CA 91752
855-664-5166
cainfo@shamrockfoods.com
www.shamrockfoodservice.com
Parent Co: Shamrock Foods Company

11509 **Shamrock Foods Co**
New Mexico Foods Branch
2 Shamrock Way NW
Albuquerque, NM 87120
877-577-1155
nminfo@shamrockfoods.com
www.shamrockfoodservice.com
Serves New Mexico and West Texas.
Parent Co: Shamrock Foods Company

11510 **Shamrock Slaughter Plant**
6400 US Highway 83
Shamrock, TX 79079-4408
806-256-3241
Meat products
Owner: Larry Cook
Estimated Sales: $500,000-$1 Million
Number Employees: 1-4
Type of Packaging: Consumer

11511 **Shane Candy Co**
110 Market St
Philadelphia, PA 19106-3006
215-922-1048
Fax: 215-940-0003 www.shanecandies.com
Candy including chocolate, holiday and hard
Owner: Ryan Berley
ryan@franklinfountain.com
Estimated Sales: $5-10 Million
Number Employees: 20-49
Square Footage: 28800
Type of Packaging: Consumer

11512 **Shaner's Family Restaurant**
193 Main St
South Paris, ME 04281
207-743-6367
Ice cream, frozen desserts
President: John Shaner
Estimated Sales: $1-2.5 000,000
Number Employees: 20-49

11513 **Shanghai Co**
2800 SE Division St
Portland, OR 97202-1350
503-235-2525
Fax: 503-235-3842
Canned Chinese noodles
Owner: Brandon Wang
Estimated Sales: $1.1 Million
Number Employees: 10-19
Type of Packaging: Consumer

11514 **Shanghai Freemen**
2035 Route 27
Suite 08817
Edison, NJ 08817
732-981-1288
info@shanghaifreemen.com
shanghaifreemen.com
Dietary supplements and food and beverage ingredients, such as vitamins, stevia, natural beta carotene, energy beverage ingredients, amino acids and joint health products; their collection includes glucosamine, chondroitin, hyaluronicacid, fish gelatin, collagen, ascorbic acid, natural vitamin E, green tea extract, L-Glutamine, L-Valine, melatonin, probiotics, bromelain, vanillin, Sopure Stevia and many more.
President: Hanks Li
Director, Business Development Eastern: Paul Niemann
Director, Business Development Western: Lottie Siann
VP, Sales & Marketing: Christine Balediata
Year Founded: 1995
Estimated Sales: $100 Million
Number Employees: 51-200
Parent Co: Zhucheng Haotian Pharm Co.
Type of Packaging: Bulk
Other Locations:
Shanghai Freemen Europe B.V.
The Hague

11515 **Shank's Extracts Inc**
350 Richardson Dr
Lancaster, PA 17603-4034
717-393-4441
Fax: 717-393-3148 800-346-3135
www.shanks.com
Supplier of extracts, flavors, colors, syrups, emulsions and sauces to industrial, private label and grocery customers.
President: Jeff Lehman
Vice President, Sales: Mark Freeman
Estimated Sales: G
Number Employees: 50-99
Square Footage: 110000
Type of Packaging: Consumer, Food Service, Private Label, Bulk
Brands:
Gold Medal
Taste-T

11516 **Shanley Farms**
2448 Atascadero Road
Morro Bay, CA 93442
805-323-6525
hello@shanleyfarms.com
www.shanleyfarms.com
Finger limes and pearls; avocados and coffee trees.
Owner: Jim Shanley
Sales & Marketing: Megan Shanley
Operations Manager: Jessica Kamper
Estimated Sales: $4.9 Million
Number Employees: 11-50
Brands:
Citriburst Finger Limes

11517 **Shape Foods**
2001 Victoria Avenue E
Brandon, MB R7A 7L2
Canada
204-727-3529
Fax: 204-728-3529 info@shapefoods.com
Producer of conventional and organic flaxseed oil and meal.
Sales Manager: Dane Lindenberg
Square Footage: 70000
Type of Packaging: Private Label, Bulk
Brands:
Heart Shape
Royal Harvest
Flax Country

11518 **Shariann's Organics**
4600 Sleepytime Dr.
Boulder, CO 80301
63- 73- 220
Fax: 631-730-2550 800-434-4246
consumeraffairs@hain-celestial.com
http://www.hain-celestial.com/
Organic food products
President and CEO: Irwin Simon
CFO: Ira Lamel
Chief Marketing Officer: Maureen Putman
Estimated Sales: $900 Million
Number Employees: 130
Brands:
Shariann's Italian White Beans
Shariann's Refried Beans
Shariann's Spicy Vegetable

11519 **Sharkco's**
707 Jump Basin Rd
Venice, LA 70091-4351
504-534-9577
Fax: 504-534-2217
Seafood
Owner: Tuan Guyn
Estimated Sales: $5-10 Million
Number Employees: 10-19

11520 **Sharon Mill Winery**
5701 Sharon Hollow Rd
Manchester, MI 48158
734-971-6337
Fax: 734-971-6386 www.ewashtenaw.org
Wines
Director: Robert Tetens
Estimated Sales: $1-2.5 Million
Number Employees: 20-49

11521 **Sharp Rock Farm B & B**
5 Sharp Rock Rd
Sperryville, VA 22740-2333
540-987-8020
Fax: 540-987-9031 jeast@sharprockvineyards.com
www.sharprock.com
Wines
Owner: James East
Estimated Sales: $1-3 Million
Number Employees: 1-4

11522 **Shashi Foods**
55 Esandar Dr
Toronto, ON M4G 4H2
Canada
416-645-0611
Fax: 416-645-0612 866-748-7441
Spices, herbs, seasoning blends and specialty flours, also, custom grinding, blending, bottling, and bagging.
President: Sujay Shah
VP: Ajay Shah
Estimated Sales: $7.37 Million
Number Employees: 30
Brands:
Elephant Brand
Shashi
King of Spice
Patak's

11523 **Shashy's Bakery & Fine Foods**
1700 Mulberry St
Montgomery, AL 36106-1524
334-263-7341
Fax: 334-263-7343 www.shashysbakery.com
Baked goods
President: James Shashy
Owner: Jimmy Shashy
Estimated Sales: $500,000-$1 Million
Number Employees: 20-49
Type of Packaging: Consumer

11524 **Shasta Beverages Inc**
9750 Moravia Park Dr.
Baltimore, MS 21237-1090
510-783-3200
Fax: 510-783-8681 800-834-9980
www.shastapop.com
Flavored soft drinks including grape, cola, root beer, orange, kiwi/strawberry, black cherry, etc
Manager: Rick Reynolds
Controller: Charles Reisig
Executive VP: Miguel Abril
mabril@shastabeverages.com
Sales Executive: Michael Perez
Plant Manager: Dan Penrod
Estimated Sales: $20-50 Million
Number Employees: 1000-4999
Parent Co: National Beverage Company
Type of Packaging: Consumer, Food Service, Private Label
Brands:
Shasta

11525 **Shaw Baking Company**
240 S Algoma Street
Thunder Bay, ON P7B 3C2
Canada
807-345-7327
Fax: 807-345-7895 http://www.tbaytel.net
Rolls, doughnuts, muffins, danish pastries and bread including white and whole wheat
President/General Manager: G Shaw
Sales Manager: Joe Spina
Number Employees: 100-249
Type of Packaging: Consumer, Food Service
Brands:
Country Hearth
Holsum
Shaw

11526 **Shaw's Southern Belle Frozen, Inc.**
P.O. Box 28620
Jacksonville, FL 32226
904-768-1591
Fax: 904-766-3071 888-742-9772
info@shawsouthernbelle.com
www.shawsouthernbelle.com
Specialty seafood packer of full service deli & seafood, home meal replacement and frozen products.
Owner: Howard Shaw
CEO: John Shaw
Chief Financial Officer: Joanna Zimmerman
Executive Vice President: Sylvia Shaw
Restaurant Sales Executive: Howard "Bubba" Shaw
dgreer@shawsouthernbelle.com
Human Resources Executive: Leslie Faulk
Director of Systems & Processes: Heidi Bash
Purchasing Manager: John Shaw
dgreer@shawsouthernbelle.com
Estimated Sales: $10.5 Million
Number Employees: 100
Type of Packaging: Consumer, Food Service, Private Label
Other Locations:
Shaw's Cold Storage
Jacksonville FL

11527 **Shawmut Fishing Company**
PO Box 1986
Anchorage, AK 99508
709-334-2559
Fax: 709-596-7189
Frozen crabs
President: William Berry
VP: Thomas Caines
Type of Packaging: Consumer, Food Service, Bulk

11528 **(HQ)Shawnee Canning Co**
212 Cross Junction Rd
Cross Junction, VA 22625-2324
540-888-3429
Fax: 540-888-7963 800-713-1414
sales@shawneesprings.com
www.shawneesprings.com

Apple sauces, apples, peaches, ciders, preserves and jams, fruit butters, apple syrup, apple mixes, honey, pickles, salsa, dressings, relishes and fresh baked pies
President: William Whitacre
GM: Lisa Whitacre Johnson
Estimated Sales: $3 Million
Number Employees: 20-49
Square Footage: 39000
Type of Packaging: Consumer, Private Label
Brands:
Shawnee Springs

11529 (HQ)Shawnee Milling Co
201 S Broadway Ave
PO Box 1567
Shawnee, OK 74801-8427
405-273-7000
Fax: 405-273-7333 lspears@shawneemilling.com
www.shawneemilling.com
Flour, cornmeal, complete mixes, custom mixes
President: William Ford
bford@shawneemilling.com
CEo: Debra Howe
Vice President: Joe Lloyd Ford
Regional Sales Manager: James Smith
Plant Manager: Doug Myer
Purchasing Manager: Caleb Winsett
Number Employees: 250-499
Type of Packaging: Consumer, Food Service, Private Label, Bulk
Brands:
Shawnee Best
Shawnee Mills

11530 Shawnee Milling Co
PO Box 1567
Shawnee, OK 74802-1567
405-273-7000
Fax: 405-273-7333 800-654-2600
www.shawneemilling.com
Supplier of mixes and flours
President: Joe Ford
Director of Quality Control: Matthew Salter
Number Employees: 250-499
Parent Co: Shawnee Milling Company
Type of Packaging: Consumer, Food Service

11531 Shearer's Foods Inc
100 Lincoln Way E
Massillon, OH 44646-6634
330-767-4030
Fax: 330-767-3393 info@shearers.com
www.shearers.com
Regular, rippled, flavored and kettle-cooked potato chips
President: Robert Shearer
CEO: Christopher Fraleigh
CFO: Fritz Kohnmann
EVP: Montgomery Pooley
SVP Sales and Marketing: Bill McCabe
Public Relations: Melissa Shearer
VP Operations: Randy Whisler
VP Manufacturing: Joe McCarthy
Estimated Sales: $10-20 Million
Number Employees: 1000-4999
Square Footage: 150000
Type of Packaging: Consumer, Food Service, Private Label, Bulk
Brands:
Grandma Shearer's
Grandma Shearer's Snacks

11532 Shedd Food Products
4151 Gladewater Rd
Dallas, TX 75216-6435
214-374-4751
Fax: 214-761-4565
Margarine
Owner: Sherman Shead
Plant Manager: John Preacher
Estimated Sales: $300,000-500,000
Number Employees: 1-4
Parent Co: Unilever USA

11533 Sheffa Foods
P.O.Box 644
New York, NY 10028
484-494-1249
Fax: 484-497-5436 800-494-1956
contact@sheffafoods.com www.sheffafoods.com
Snack bars, granola bars, mixes and salad sprinkles.
Co-Founder & Owner: Leslie Angle
Co-Founder: Amotz Geshury
Type of Packaging: Food Service
Brands:
SHEFFA

11534 Sheila G Brands LLC
2253 Vista Parkway
Suite 8
West Palm Beach, FL 33411
561-688-1890
info@browniebrittle.com
www.browniebrittle.com
Manufacturer of brownie brittle snacks.
Founder and CEO: Sheila Mains
Contact: Justin Roberts
justinroberts@abssystems.net
Brands:
Brownie Brittle

11535 Sheila Gs Brownie Brittle Co
2253 Vista Pkwy
West Palm Beach, FL 33411-2722
USA
561-557-1178
Fax: 561-584-5881 www.browniebrittle.com
Cookies
CEO/Founder: Sheila Mains
Vice President Marketing: Nancy Eichler
Estimated Sales: Less Than $500,000
Number Employees: 1-4

11536 Sheila's Select Gourmet Recipe
325 W 600 S
Heber City, UT 84032-2230
435-654-6415
Fax: 435-654-5449 800-516-7286
www.bearcreekfoods.com
Soups(bagged and canned), culinary bases, freezies, and salsas.
President: Kevin Ruda
CFO: Al Van Leeuwen
VP of Operations: Kevin Kowalski
Marketing Director: Jeff Hanson
Sales Manager: Steve White
Brands:
Bear Creek Country Kitchens
Sheila's Select Gourmet Recipes

11537 Sheinman Provision Co
4192 Viola St
Suite 96
Philadelphia, PA 19104-1093
215-473-7065
Fax: 215-473-7038
Sausage, bologna and corned and roast beef
President: Stan Rultenberg
Estimated Sales: $3 Million
Number Employees: 1-4
Square Footage: 14000
Type of Packaging: Consumer, Food Service, Private Label, Bulk
Brands:
Philly Maid
Sheinman

11538 Shekou Chemicals
24 Crescent Street
Waltham, MA 02453-4358
781-893-6878
Fax: 781-893-6881
Processor, importer and exporter of ingredients including citric acid, ascorbic acid, sodium benzoate, sodium propionate, calcium propionate, ammonium bicarbonate, sodium erythrobate, sodium citrate, potassium citrate and potassiumsorbate
System Staff: Herb Kimiatek
Sales/Marketing Executive: Judith Roiva
Purchasing Manager: Simon Altstein
Estimated Sales: $1.1 Million
Number Employees: 7
Square Footage: 40000
Type of Packaging: Bulk

11539 Shelburne Falls Coffee Roaster
1335 Mohawk Trl
Shelburne Falls, MA 01370-9303
413-625-2123
Fax: 413-625-1083 shfallscoffee@cs.com
www.ibuycoffee.com
Coffee
Owner: Curtis Rich
curtrich@earthlink.net
Estimated Sales: $3-5 Million
Number Employees: 1-4

11540 Shell Ridge Jalapeno Project
1432 Highway 35 S
Rockport, TX 78382-3918
512-790-8028
Ethnic foods
President: Kay Segura Christian
Estimated Sales: $500,000
Number Employees: 1-4
Brands:
Kay's Hot Stuff

11541 Shelley's
700 Bergen Ave
Jersey City, NJ 07306-4890
201-433-2900
Fax: 201-433-4549
Provisions/meats including fresh and frozen beef, veal, lamb, pork and poultry
President: Shelley Geller
General Manager: Chuck Brennan
Estimated Sales: $11.3 Million
Number Employees: 20-49
Square Footage: 30000
Type of Packaging: Food Service

11542 Shelton's Poultry Inc
204 N Loranne Ave
Pomona, CA 91767
800-541-1833
www.sheltons.com
Free range poultry products; also, soups, chili, jerky, sausage, uncured frankfurters, meat balls, etc.
Chief Financial Officer: Lori Barragar
lbarrager@sheltons.com
Year Founded: 1924
Estimated Sales: $20-50 Million
Number Employees: 20-49
Type of Packaging: Consumer
Brands:
Shelton's

11543 Shemper Seafood Co
367 Bayview Ave
Biloxi, MS 39530-2502
228-435-2703
Fax: 228-432-2104
Seafood, seafood products
President: Gary Shemper
CEO: Jeffrey Shemper
camelot@datasync.com
Estimated Sales: Less Than $500,000
Number Employees: 1-4
Brands:
Shemper Seafood

11544 Shenandoah Mills
145 South Cumberland St
Lebanon, TN 37088-0369
615-444-0841
Fax: 615-444-0286 donya@shenandoahmills.com
www.shenandoahmills.com
Dry mixes including biscuit, pancake, corndog, apple fritters, corn meal, corn bread, gravy and hushpuppies; also, breadings including fish, chicken, pork, beef, etc
Founder, Owner, Chief Operating Officer: Dale Nunnery
VP: Danny Hodges
Plant Manager: Ike Sandy
Director Sales: George Stonesifer
Contact: Emily Drucker
emily@shenandoahmills.com
Estimated Sales: $4 Million
Number Employees: 25
Square Footage: 260000
Type of Packaging: Food Service
Brands:
Shenandoah

11545 Shenandoah Vineyards
12300 Steiner Rd
Plymouth, CA 95669-9503
209-245-4455
Fax: 209-245-5156 www.sobonwine.com
Wines
President: Leon Sobon
CEO: Shirley Sobon
Estimated Sales: Below $5 Million
Number Employees: 10-19

11546 **Shenk's Foods**
1980 New Danville Pike
Lancaster, PA 17603-9615
717-393-4240
Fax: 717-393-4240
Cheese, butter spreads, jellies, mustards, preserves, relishes and fruit spreads
President: Karl Achtermann
karl@shenks.com
Estimated Sales: $2 Million
Number Employees: 1-4
Square Footage: 36000
Type of Packaging: Consumer, Private Label
Brands:
Shenk's

11547 **(HQ)Shepherd Farms Inc**
9330 E 8th Rd
Hillsboro, IL 62049-3448
217-532-5268
Fax: 815-389-1997 800-383-2676
www.shepherdfarms.com
Processor and packer of popcorn including yellow, white and specialty hybrids packaged for microwave, air poppers and commercial poppers; also, soybeans and tofu; exporter of soybeans for tofu, miso, natto and shoyu, seed corn and seedsoybeans
Owner: Jim Shepherd
Estimated Sales: Less Than $500,000
Number Employees: 1-4
Square Footage: 80000
Type of Packaging: Consumer, Food Service, Private Label, Bulk
Other Locations:
Shepherd Farms
Beloit IL
Brands:
Boone County Supreme
Shepherd
Shepherd Supreme

11548 **Shepherdsfield Bakery**
777 Shepherdsfield Rd
Fulton, MO 65251-5974
573-642-0009
Fax: 573-642-1439
Frozen gourmet waffles, muffins, breads and whole wheat pancake mixes, pies, cookies and flour
Religious Leader: Thomas Mahaney
CEO: Vicki Staudenmyer
Estimated Sales: Less Than $500,000
Number Employees: 1-4
Square Footage: 80000
Type of Packaging: Consumer, Private Label

11549 **Sherbrooke OEM Ltd**
262 rue P,pin
Sherbrooke, QC J1L 2V8
Canada
819-563-7374
Fax: 819-563-7556 866-851-2579
info@sherbrooke-oem.com
www.sherbrooke-oem.com
President: Alain Brasseur
VP: Bryan Sinram
Marketing: Sylvie Hertrich
Sales: Ian Levasseus
Purchasing Director: Bernard Gilbert
Number Employees: 1-4
Number of Brands: 2
Number of Products: 3
Brands:
Jo Citrus
Jomints
M60 Energy Mints

11550 **Sherm Edwards Candies**
509 Cavitt Ave
Trafford, PA 15085-1060
412-372-4331
Fax: 412-373-8089 800-436-5424
Chocolate-covered candy
President: David Golembeski
Contact: Mark Edwards
mark@edwardmarc.com
Estimated Sales: $724000
Number Employees: 20-49
Type of Packaging: Consumer, Bulk

11551 **Sherrill Orchards**
3265 Valpredo Rd
Arvin, CA 93203
661-858-2035
Fax: 661-858-2035 soprus@aorldnet.att.com
Pomegranate juice, vinegar, apple cider and blends
President: Donna Sherril
Estimated Sales: $340,000
Number Employees: 5
Brands:
Sherrill

11552 **Sherwood Brands**
120 Jersey Ave
New Brunswick, NJ 08901
973-249-8200
info@sherwoodbrands.net
sherwoodbrands.net
Manufacturer of chocolates, truffles, cookies, snacks, tea and cappuccino.
Type of Packaging: Consumer, Private Label
Brands:
Candy Kaleidoscope
Cap'n Poptoy
Cherry & Berry Blast
Creative Gourmet
Tweety
Tweety Pops
Wan-Na-Bes

11553 **Sherwood Brands of Rhode Island Inc**
275 Ferris Avenue
Rumford, RI 02916-1033
401-726-4500
sherwoodbrands.net
Candy and candy novelties
Estimated Sales: $5-9.9 Million
Number Employees: 20-49
Parent Co: Sherwood Brands

11554 **Sheryl's Chocolate Creations**
11 Commercial St
Hicksville, NY 11801-5211
516-681-4060
Fax: 516-681-4189 888-882-2462
Hand-dipped chocolate chips, pretzel rods, pretzel twists, sourdough pretzels, mini pretzels, popcorn and assorted cookies
President: Sheryl Simon
Purchasing Manager: Ron Simon
Estimated Sales: $1-2.5 Million
Number Employees: 10-19
Square Footage: 16000
Type of Packaging: Consumer, Private Label, Bulk

11555 **Shields Date Garden**
80225 US Highway 111
Indio, CA 92201-6599
760-347-0996
Fax: 760-342-3288 800-414-2555
shieldate@aol.com
Nuts, dates and fruits including citrus and dried; also, mail order available
Owner: Greg Raumin
jeweldate@aol.com
Estimated Sales: $5-10 Million
Number Employees: 20-49
Type of Packaging: Consumer
Brands:
Date Crystals

11556 **Shiloh Farms**
191 Commerce Drive
New Holland, PA 17557
800-362-6832
info@shilohfarms.com www.shilohfarms.com
Grains, fruits, nuts, potatoes

11557 **Shine Companies**
4014 Evening Trail Drive
Spring, TX 77388-4936
281-353-8392
Fax: 281-353-8937
Processor and exporter of specialty seasonings, artichoke dips and toppings and marinades, salsas and condiments; importer of chile purees
President: Michael Shine
Executive VP: Janet Williams
Number Employees: 6
Square Footage: 5000
Brands:
Jazzie J
Semdiero

11558 **Shine Foods Inc**
21100 S Western Avenue
Torrance, CA 90501-1700
310-533-6010
Fax: 310-328-2608 www.shinefood.com
Dim sum, pot stickers, dumplings, gyoza, shumai and spring rolls
President: Stephen Y Lee
VP: John Freschi
Marketing Manager: Tracy Lee
Estimated Sales: $300,000-500,000
Number Employees: 1-4
Type of Packaging: Private Label, Bulk

11559 **Shining Ocean Inc**
1515 Puyallup St
Sumner, WA 98390-2234
253-826-3700
Fax: 206-283-7079 800-935-6464
email@kanimi.com www.kanimi.com
Frozen surimi, imitation crab and shrimp
President: Robert Bleu
CFO: Howard Frisk
R & D: Tim Taylor
Quality Control: Raymond McReaey
Sales Coordinator: Yuji Ishii
Year Founded: 1985
Estimated Sales: $30-50 Million
Number Employees: 100-249
Type of Packaging: Consumer, Food Service, Private Label
Brands:
Emerald Sea
Heathy 1
Kanimi-Tem
Pacific Choice
Sea Farer
Shining Choice

11560 **Shipley Do-Nut Franchise Co**
5200 N Main St
Houston, TX 77009-3665
713-869-4636
Fax: 713-863-9623
Donuts
President: Christopher Halsey
bodner.michael@gmail.com
Number Employees: 10-19

11561 **Shipyard Brewing Co**
86 Newbury St
Portland, ME 04101-4274
207 761 0807
Fax: 207-775-5567 800-789-0684
www.shipyard.com
Processor and exporter of beer, ale, stout and root beer
Owner: Fred Forsley
fforsley@shipyard.com
Master Brewer: Alan Pugsley
Director of Sales And Marketing: Bruce Forsley
fforsley@shipyard.com
Director Manufacturing: Paul Henry
Estimated Sales: Under $500,000
Number Employees: 50-99
Number of Brands: 17
Type of Packaging: Consumer, Food Service
Brands:
Blue Fin
Chamberlain
Goat Island Light
Longfellow Winter
Old Thumper Extra Special
Prelude Christmas

11562 **Shipyard Brewing Co**
86 Newbury St
Portland, ME 04101-4274
207-761-0807
Fax: 207-775-5567 www.shipyard.com
Beer
Owner: Fred Forsley
fforsley@shipyard.com
Estimated Sales: Under $500,000
Number Employees: 50-99
Parent Co: Philip Morris Companies

11563 **Shire City Herbals**
703 W. Housatonic Street
Suite 120
Pittsfield, MA 01201
413-213-6702
info@firecider.com
firecider.com

Cider
Co-Owner: Amy Huebner
Co-Founder & CEO: Dana St.Pierre
Sales & Customer Service: Brian Huebner
Wholesale & Customer Service: Bethany Geiger
Number Employees: 11-50
Type of Packaging: Food Service
Brands:
Fire Cider

11564 **Shirer Brothers Meats**
7805 Adamsville Otsego Rd
Adamsville, OH 43802-9732
740-796-3214
Beef, beef products
Owner: Jon Shirer
Estimated Sales: $1-2.5 000,000
Number Employees: 1-4

11565 **Shirley Foods**
505 Walnut St
Shirley, IN 47384-1229
765-738-6511
Fax: 765-738-6881 800-560-2908
www.shirleyfoods.com
Flour and corn tortillas
President: Gary Toth
gtoth@shirleyfoods.com
Estimated Sales: Less Than $500,000
Number Employees: 10-19
Brands:
Shirley Foods

11566 **Shirley J Ventures, LLC**
1464 W 40 South
Lindon, UT 84042
801-225-5073
Fax: 801-225-5616 www.shirleyj.com
Sauce, seasoning
President And CEO: Kelly Olsen
Contact: Joel Neilsen
joeln@shirleyj.com

11567 **Shoei Foods USA Inc**
1900 Feather River Blvd
Olivehurst, CA 95961
530-237-1295
www.shoeifoodsusa.com
Pine nuts, pumpkin seeds, sunflower seeds, walnut kernels.
President & CEO: Brian Dunning
briand@shoeiusa.com
Manager, Quality Control & Assurance: Tom Roach
Director, Global Sales & Marketing: John Gaffney
Director, Operations: Dwight Davis
Estimated Sales: $50-100 Million
Number Employees: 100-249
Number of Brands: 2
Number of Products: 5
Square Footage: 30000
Type of Packaging: Consumer, Food Service, Private Label, Bulk
Brands:
Shoei

11568 **Shonan USA Inc**
702 Wallace Way
Grandview, WA 98930-8844
509-882-5583
Fax: 509-882-5890 www.shonan-flv.co.jp
Refrigerated fruit juice concentrates including apple, cherry, grape, pear, carrot, strawberry and red raspberry
President: Akira Nozaka
Controller: Douglas Foth
Estimated Sales: $7 Million
Number Employees: 50-99
Type of Packaging: Bulk
Brands:
Shonan

11569 **Shonna's Gourmet Goodies**
320 W Center Street
West Bridgewater, MA 02379-1626
508-580-2033
Fax: 508-580-2044 888-312-7868
Frozen hors d'oeuvres
Owner/President: Howard Sherman
Estimated Sales: Less than $500,000
Square Footage: 12000
Type of Packaging: Private Label

11570 **Shooting Star Farms**
4000 Wright Rd.
Bartlesville, OK 74006
918-766-0800
Fax: 888-450-4004 888-850-8540
Dips, gourmet salsas, jellies
President: Jim Reali
Estimated Sales: $300,000-500,000
Number Employees: 1-4
Type of Packaging: Consumer

11571 **Shore Seafood Distr**
19424 Saxis Rd
Saxis, VA 23427
757-824-5517
Fax: 757-824-5662 www.shoreseafoodinc.com
Seafood
President: Greg Linton
mlinton@shoreseafoodinc.com
Vice President: Andy Drewer
Estimated Sales: $5-10 Million
Number Employees: 20-49
Type of Packaging: Private Label
Brands:
Chesapeake Bay Delight

11572 **Shore Trading Co**
665 Union Hill Rd
Alpharetta, GA 30004-5652
770-998-0566
Fax: 770-998-0571
Seafood
Owner: Ron Williams
ron@shoretrading.net
Owner: Marty Klausner
Estimated Sales: $1 Million
Number Employees: 1-4

11573 **Shoreline Chocolates**
212 W Shore Rd
Alburg, VT 05440
802-796-3730
Fax: 802-796-4725 800-310-3730
info@lakesendcheeses.com
Produces assorted homemade chocolates
Operator: Joanne James
Operator: Alton James
Estimated Sales: $300,000-500,000
Number Employees: 1-4

11574 **Shoreline Fruit**
10850 E Traverse Hwy
Suite 4460
Traverse City, MI 49684-1365
231-941-4336
Fax: 231-941-4525 800-836-3972
cs@shorelinefruit.com www.shorelinefruit.com
Dried fruits, fruit juice and fruit concentrate
CEO: John Sommavilla
cs@shorelinefruit.com
Marketing Manager: Kristen Moravcik
Director, Sales & Marketing: Brian Gerberding
Number Employees: 10-19
Other Locations:
Headquarters
Traverse City MI
Production & Storage
Williamsburg MI

11575 **Short's Brewing Co**
121 N Bridge St
Bellaire, MI 49615-9509
231-498-2300
www.shortsbrewing.com
Lagers and ales
Owner: Joseph Short
President: Leah Hannan
VP: Scott Bale
Estimated Sales: Less Than $500,000
Number Employees: 1-4
Square Footage: 56000

11576 **Shreve Meats Processing**
193 E Mcconkey Street
Shreve, OH 44676
330-567-2142
Beef and pork
Co-Owner: Ray Haas
Co-Owner: Tim Morris
Estimated Sales: $140,000
Number Employees: 4

11577 **Shrums Sausage & Meats**
4703 42 Ave
Box 1495
Stettler, AB T0C 2L0
Canada
403-742-1427
Fax: 403-742-1429
Fresh meats, processed meats, wild game, custom cutting & wrapping, pork, beef, and bison.
Manager: Randy Cherewko
Sales: Kelly Greenwood
Number Employees: 25
Type of Packaging: Consumer, Food Service

11578 **Shuckman's Fish Co & Smokery**
3001 W Main St
Louisville, KY 40212-1840
502-775-6478
Fax: 502-775-6373
shuckmans@kysmokedfish.com
www.kysmokedfish.com
Smokers of fish & seafood products.
President: Lewis Shuckman
lshuckman@kysmokefish.com
Estimated Sales: $3-5 Million
Number Employees: 10-19

11579 **Shuff's Meat Market**
12247 Baugher Rd
Thurmont, MD 21788-2333
301-271-2231
Fax: 301-271-1037
Meat products
Owner: Robin Shuff
Estimated Sales: $18 Million
Number Employees: 5-9

11580 **Shur-Good Biscuit Co.**
11677 Chesterdale Rd
Cincinnati, OH 45246-3917
513-458-6200
Fax: 513-458-6212
Cookies
CFO: Nicola Melillo
Marketing Director: William Klump
Sales Director: Mark O'Toole
Public Relations: Kathy Coggeshall
Operations Manager: Peter Lowes
Manager: Jerry Wallman
Estimated Sales: $5-10 Million
Number Employees: 100-249
Parent Co: Parmalat Bakery Group North America
Type of Packaging: Consumer

11581 **Sibu Sura Chocolates, LLC**
PO Box 215
Myersville, MD 21773
877-642-7872
www.sibusura.com
Manufacturer of chocolate, cocoa beans, and cocoa nib brew.
Owner: Julie McLean

11582 **Sidari's Italian Foods**
3820 Lakeside Ave E
Cleveland, OH 44114-3891
216-431-3344
Fax: 216-431-6227
Salad and pasta products.
President: Joseph Sidari
Controller: Marty Goellinitz
HR Executive: Marty Goellintz
siditalian@aol.com
Sales Manager: Joe Falsone
Estimated Sales: $8.7 Million
Number Employees: 50-99

11583 **Side Hill Farm**
74 Cotton Mill Hl # A110
Brattleboro, VT 05301-8602
802-254-2018
Fax: 802-254-3381 info@sidehillfarmjam.com
www.sidehillfarmjam.com
Manfacturer of jams
Owner: Kelt Naylor
Co-Owner: Caroline Naylor
Estimated Sales: $1-3 Million
Number Employees: 5-9
Number of Products: 14

11584 **Sidehill Farm**
PO Box 1558
Brattleboro, VT 05302
802-254-2018
Fax: 802-254-3381 info@sidehillfarmjam.com
Handmade jams, fruit butters and maple syrup.
Owner: Kelt Naylor
Year Founded: 1976
Estimated Sales: $1 Million
Number Employees: 2-10
Brands:
Maple Apple Drizzle
Sidehill Farm

11585 **Sieco USA Corporation**
9014 Ruland Rd
PO Box 55485
Houston, TX 77055-4612
713-464-1726
Olive oil, stuffed olives, vinegar and gift sets
President: Sherif Cheman
Marketing: Diann Fischer
Estimated Sales: B
Number Employees: 4
Number of Brands: 2
Number of Products: 11
Square Footage: 34400
Type of Packaging: Consumer, Food Service, Private Label, Bulk
Brands:
Amber
Sammy's

11586 **Siegel Egg Co**
90 Salem Rd # 3
North Billerica, MA 01862-2706
978-528-2010
Fax: 617-873-0824 info@siegelegg.com
www.siegelegg.com
Fresh and frozen eggs
Owner: Ken Siegel
kens@siegelegg.com
Office Manager: Amy Siegel
Plant Manager: Charlie Di Sciaca
Estimated Sales: $8.1 Million
Number Employees: 50-99
Square Footage: 36608
Type of Packaging: Consumer

11587 **(HQ)Siemer Milling Co**
111 W Main St
Teutopolis, IL 62467
217-857-3131
Fax: 217-857-3092 800-826-1065
www.siemermilling.com
Miller of wheat flours for applications from donuts to pretzels.
President: Richard Siemer
VP, Finance: Joyce Stock
VP, Grain Supply: Carl Schwinke
VP, Production: David Jansen
Year Founded: 1882
Estimated Sales: $75-99 Million
Number Employees: 170
Number of Brands: 3
Type of Packaging: Consumer, Food Service, Bulk
Other Locations:
Mill
Hopkinsville KY
Mill
Teutopolis IL
Mill
West Harrison IN
Brands:
Don's Chuck Wagon
Hodgson Mill
Kentucky Kernel

11588 **Siena Foods**
16 Newbridge Road
Toronto, ON M8Z 2L7
Canada
416-239-3967
Fax: 416-239-2084 800-465-0422
Processor, importer and exporter of Italian style meat including Genoa salami, mortadella, cappicola, prosciutto and hot and mild sausage
General Manager: Enzo DeLuca
Number Employees: 50-99
Type of Packaging: Consumer, Food Service

11589 **Sierra Cheese Mfg Co**
916 S Santa Fe Ave
Compton, CA 90221-4392
310-635-1216
Fax: 310-639-1096 800-266-4270
www.sierracheese.com
Italian cheese including mozzarella, ricotta, string, tuma, scamorze, requeson, feta, etc
President: John Curran
sierracheese@aol.com
Vice President: Charlene Franco
Sales Director: Carlos Rivera
General Manager: Charlene Franco
Purchasing Manager: Vince Inga
Number Employees: 20-49
Square Footage: 60000
Type of Packaging: Consumer, Private Label, Bulk
Brands:
Montebello
Sierra

11590 **Sierra Madre Coffee**
191 University Blvd
Denver, CO 80206-4613
303-446-0050
Fax: 303-393-8208
Coffee
President: Mena Moran

11591 **Sierra Nevada Cheese Co.**
6505 County Rd
Suite 39
Willows, CA 95988
530-934-8660
Fax: 530-934-8670 info@sierranevadacheese.com
www.sierranevadacheese.com
Cow's and goat's milk products
Co-Founder: Ben Gregersen
Co-Founder: John Dundon

11592 **Sierra Nevada Taproom &Rstrnt**
1075 E 20th St
Chico, CA 95928-6722
530-893-3520
Fax: 530-893-9358 info@sierranevada.com
Seasonal beer, ale, stout, lager and pilsner
President: Brittany Adams
blebeladams@sierranevada.com
President: Terence Sullivan
Quality Control: Rebecca Newman
Production Manager: Cory Ross
Estimated Sales: $32 Million
Number Employees: 500-999
Type of Packaging: Consumer, Food Service
Brands:
Porter & Stout
Sierra Nevada Bigfoo
Sierra Nevada Celebration
Sierra Nevada Pale Ale
Sierra Nevada Stout
Sierra Nevada Summer

11593 **Sierra Vista Winery**
4560 Cabernet Way
Placerville, CA 95667-8410
530-622-7221
Fax: 530-622-2413 800-946-3916
www.sierravistawinery.com
Wines
Owner: John Mac Cready
Owner/Winery Office VP: Barbara MacCready
Estimated Sales: Below $5 Million
Number Employees: 1-4
Type of Packaging: Private Label
Brands:
Sierra Vista

11594 **Siete Family Foods**
3571 Far West Blvd
Suite 200
Austin, TX 78731
sietefoods.com
Grain free tortillas and tortilla chips
Founder & President: Veronica Garza
Co-Founder & CEO: Miguel Garza
Brand Builder: Rebeca Palacios
Chief Operating Officer: Ben Ponder
Number Employees: 2-10
Brands:
Siete

11595 **Sifers Valomilk Candy Co**
5112 Merriam Dr
Shawnee, KS 66203-2118
913-722-0991
Fax: 913-722-5016 russ@valomilk.com
www.valomilk.com
Valomilk candy cups
President: Russell Sifers
russ@valomilk.com
Estimated Sales: $2.5-5 Million
Number Employees: 5-9
Number of Brands: 1
Number of Products: 1
Type of Packaging: Private Label
Brands:
Sifers Valomilk Candy Cups

11596 **Siggi's Dairy**
135 West 26th St
Suite 4C
New York, NY 10001
212-966-6950
www.siggisdairy.com
Icelandic-style yogurt
Founder and CEO: Siggi Hilmarsson
President: Bart Adlam
Contact: Virginia Wong
virginia.wong@skyr.com
Year Founded: 2004

11597 **Siggi's Dairy**
855-860-6683
siggis.com
A variety of yogurt products, uncluding cups, drinkables, and plant-based.
Founder: Siggi Hilmarsson
Year Founded: 2006
Parent Co: Lactalis
Type of Packaging: Private Label

11598 **Signature Beverage**
PO Box 695
Merrick, NY 11566-0695
516-867-8291
Fax: 516-377-1228 800-277-2755
signaturebeverage@gmail.com
signaturebeverage.net
Sparkling and spring water, root beer and black cherry and cream soda, diet root beer, diet black cherry, iced tea, lemonade, grape soda, raspberry lime rickey, orange soda
President: Mark Eisenberg
VP: Rebecca Scott
Sales Manager: Richard Stern
Estimated Sales: $1 Million
Number Employees: 5
Square Footage: 20000
Type of Packaging: Food Service, Private Label

11599 **Signature Brands LLC**
808 SW 12th St
Ocala, FL 34471-0540
352-622-3134
Fax: 352-402-9451 800-456-9573
info@signaturebrands.com
www.signaturebrands.com
Manufacturer, importer, and exporter of dessert decorating and specialty baking products. Importer of preserves.
Co-Founder: Louise Crawford
Co-Founder: Bobby Jones
Year Founded: 1951
Estimated Sales: $20-50 Million
Number Employees: 100-249
Square Footage: 80000
Parent Co: McCormick & Company
Type of Packaging: Consumer, Food Service, Private Label, Bulk
Brands:
Betty Crocker
Cake Mate
PAAS
Pumpkin Masters

11600 **Signature Foods**
73-D Enterprise Drive
Pendergrass, DR 30587
706-693-0098
Co-packer and support manufacturer for food companies
President: Oran B Talkington
Estimated Sales: $3.3 Million
Number Employees: 23

11601 Signature Fruit
1 Tiffany Point
Suite 206
Bloomingdale, IL 60108-2916
630-980-2481
Fax: 630-980-3211
Canned foods including fruits and vegetables
Director (Central Zone): Bruce Scheer
Business Manager (Midwest): Hank Gergovich
Estimated Sales: $3-5 Million
Number Employees: 1-4
Parent Co: Tri-Valley Growers
Type of Packaging: Consumer

11602 Signature Seafoods Inc
4257 24th Ave W
Seattle, WA 98199-1214
206-285-2815
Fax: 206-282-5938 www.signatureseafoods.com
Salmon
President: Gabriel Angelo
gangelo@signatureseafoods.com
Estimated Sales: $4,000,000
Number Employees: 5-9
Brands:
H&G Chum
King Salmon
Silver Salmon

11603 Signore Winery
153 White Church Road
Brooktondale, NY 14817-9769
607-539-7935
Wines
Owner: Daniel Signore
Estimated Sales: $1-4.9 000,000
Number Employees: 1-5

11604 Signorello Vineyards
4500 Silverado Trl
Napa, CA 94558-1100
707-255-5990
Fax: 707-255-5999 info@signorellovineyards.com
www.signorellovineyards.com
Wines
Owner: Ray Signorello
National Sales Director: Chris Carmichael
Director Marketing: Bruce Donsker
Contact: Jeff Adams
jadams@signorelloestate.com
Winemaker: Raymond Signorello
jadams@signorelloestate.com
Wine Maker / Vineyard Manager: Pierre Birebent
Estimated Sales: Below $5 Million
Number Employees: 5-9
Brands:
Signorello

11605 Sigona's
San Carlos, CA 94070
650-368-6992
helloFFT@sigonas.com
www.fruitforthought.com
Organic dried fruits
Brands:
Fruit for Thought

11606 Silani Sweet Cheese
10 Roybridge Gate
Suite 100
Woodbridge, ON L4H 3M8
Canada
905-792-3811
Fax: 905-792-7693 feedback@silani.ca
www.silanicheese.com
Processor and importer of cheese
President: Michael Talarico
CEO/VP: Joe Lanzino
Number Employees: 185
Square Footage: 100000

11607 Silesia Flavors
5250 Prairie Stone Pkwy
Hoffman Estates, IL 60192-3709
847-645-0270
Fax: 847-645-0266 info.us@silesia.com
www.silesia-aroma.com
Manufacturers of liquid, powder and granulated flavorings for the food and beverage industries.
Vice President: Richard Bartoszewski
richard@silesiafl.com
Vice President: Richard Bartoszewski
richard@silesiafl.com
Number Employees: 10-19
Brands:
Sil-A-Gran
Silarom
Silvanil

11608 Siljans Crispy Cup Company
23 Skyline Crest NE
Calgary, AB T2K 5X2
Canada
403-275-0135
Fax: 403-275-0061 4sale@siljanscrispycup.com
www.siljanscrispycup.com
Processor and exporter of edible cups for hors d'oeuvres and desserts
President: B Ersson
CEO: Christina Ersson
Estimated Sales: $500,000
Number Employees: 5
Number of Brands: 1
Number of Products: 1
Square Footage: 32000
Type of Packaging: Consumer, Food Service, Private Label, Bulk
Brands:
Salmolux
Siljans

11609 Sill Farm Market
50241 Red Arrow Hwy
Lawrence, MI 49064-8781
269-674-3755
Fax: 269-674-3756 www.sillfarms.com
Frozen and fresh sliced fruits
President: Lois Ross
lross@castleofspirits.com
Estimated Sales: $5-9.9 000,000
Number Employees: 20-49
Brands:
Plowshares
Sunshower

11610 Silva Farms
111 Alpine Dr
Gonzales, CA 93926
831-675-2428
Fax: 831-675-2375
Vegetables
Owner: Edward Skua Jr
Manager: Theresa Silva-Amaral
Estimated Sales: $500,000-$1 000,000
Number Employees: 100-249
Type of Packaging: Private Label, Bulk

11611 Silva International
523 N Ash St
Momence, IL 60954-1335
815-472-3535
Fax: 815-472-3536 silva-intl.com
Supplier of dehydrated vegetable, herb and fruit ingredients to the food industry.
President: Peter Schmidt
Vice President: Kent DeVries
Quality Assurance Manager: Ed Bove
General Manager: Steve DeYoung
Sales Manager: Darren VanEssen
Number Employees: 10-19
Other Locations:
Headquarters
Momence IL
South American Procurement
Santiago, Chile
South American Sales
Lima, Peru
European Procurement
Schwetzingen, Germany
Asian Quality & Procurement
Qingdao, China

11612 Silvan Ridge Winery
27012 Briggs Hill Rd
Eugene, OR 97405-9767
541-345-1945
Fax: 541-345-6174 info@silvanridge.com
Wines
Owner: Liz Chambers
CEO: Elizabeth Chambers
CFO: Jim Plumber
Quality Control: Bryan Wilson
Marketing: Phil Cowles
Sales: Ryan Shockley
liz@silvanridge.com
Public Relations: Angela Bennett
Operations: Haley Smith
Estimated Sales: Below $5 Million
Number Employees: 5-9
Number of Brands: 2
Brands:
Hinman Vineyards
Silvan Ridge

11613 Silvateam USA
3200 E Guasti Road
Suite 100
Ontario, CA 91761
909-635-2870
Fax: 909-635-2871 en.silvateam.com
Ingredient producers and manufacturers serving the food, beverage, feed and other industries.
Parent Co: Silvateam

11614 Silver Creek Distillers
134 North 3300 East
Rigby, ID 83442
208-754-0042
Fax: 208-754-4758
Beverage grade alcohol
Manager: Bill Scott
Contact: Gray Ottley
gray@waytogoidaho.com
Estimated Sales: $3.2 000,000
Number Employees: 5-9
Brands:
Teton Glacier Vodka

11615 Silver Creek Farms
450 Locust St S
Twin Falls, ID 83301-7848
208-736-0829
Fax: 208-736-0725
Smoked fruit and salmon

11616 Silver Creek Specialty Meats
153 W 28th Ave
Oshkosh, WI 54902-7202
920-232-3581
Fax: 920-232-3589 800-729-2849
office@silvercreekspecialtymeats.com
www.silvercreekspecialtymeats.com
Natural casing sausage
President: William Kramlich Sr
CEO: Bill Kramlich Jr
Estimated Sales: $4.5 Million
Number Employees: 10-19
Type of Packaging: Food Service, Private Label, Bulk

11617 Silver Fern Chemical Inc
2226 Queen Anne Ave N # C
Seattle, WA 98109-2372
206-282-3376
Fax: 206-282-0105 866-282-3384
info@silverfernchemical.com
www.silverfernchemical.com
Food chemicals and ingredients
President: Sam King
sam@silverfernchemical.com
Number Employees: 1-4

11618 Silver Fox Vineyards
4683 Morning Star Ln
Mariposa, CA 95338-9361
209-966-4800
Fax: 209-966-4369 enjoy@sti.net
Wines
Co-Owner/Co-Operator: Marvin Silver
Co-Owner/Co-Operator: Karen Silver
Estimated Sales: Below $5 Million
Number Employees: 1-4
Brands:
Silver Fox Vineyard

11619 Silver Lake Sausage Shop
80 Ethan St
Providence, RI 02909-5327
401-944-4081
Sausage
President: Erminia Santilli
Estimated Sales: Less Than $500,000
Number Employees: 1-4

11620 (HQ)Silver Lining Seafood
5303 Shilshole Ave. N.W.
PO Box 6092
Seattle, WA 98107-4000
206-783-3818
Fax: 206-782-7195 800-426-5490
www.tridentseafoods.com

Processor and exporter of fresh, smoked and canned seafood.
Plant Manager: Leigh Gerber
Estimated Sales: $500,000-$1 Million
Number Employees: 5-9
Type of Packaging: Consumer, Food Service, Bulk

11621 Silver Mountain Vineyards
PO Box 3636
Santa Cruz, CA 95063-3636
408-353-2278
Fax: 408-353-1898 info@silvermtn.com
www.silvermtn.com
Wine
President: Jerold O'Brien
info@silvermtn.com
Estimated Sales: Less Than $500,000
Number Employees: 1-4
Type of Packaging: Private Label
Brands:
Silver Mtn Vineyards

11622 Silver Oak
915 Oakville Cross Road
Oakville, CA 94562
707-944-8808
Fax: 707-944-2817 www.silveroak.com
Maker of Cabernet Sauvignon
President & CEO: David Duncan
CFO: Rickie Pina

11623 Silver Palate Kitchens
221 Knickerbocker Rd
Cresskill, NJ
201-568-0110
www.silverpalate.com
Vinegars, oils, chutneys, mustards, savories, sweet sauces, preserves, brandied fruits, salad dressings, pasta sauces, oatmeals and berry cereals.
President & CEO: Peter Harris
Estimated Sales: $20-50 Million
Number Employees: 20-49
Type of Packaging: Consumer, Food Service, Private Label, Bulk
Brands:
Silver Palate

11624 Silver Spoon
92 S Central Ave
Hartsdale, NY 10530-2301
914-328-1536
Fax: 914-694-5622
Manager: John Randall
Estimated Sales: Less than $500,000
Number Employees: 1-4
Parent Co: Armenia Coffee Corporation

11625 Silver Spring Foods
2424 Alpine Road
Eau Clair, MI 54703
Fax: 715-830-9702 800-826-7322
info@bredefoods.com silverspringfoods.com
Processor and exporter of horseradish and horseradish sauce, as well as other specialty sauces including mustards, siracha, tartar, and wasabi sauces.
Chairman/CEO: Nancy Bartusch
Distribution & Warehouse Manager: Allyssa Fradette
Estimated Sales: $630,000
Number Employees: 5-9
Square Footage: 36000
Parent Co: Hunstinger Farms, Inc.
Type of Packaging: Consumer, Food Service, Private Label, Bulk
Brands:
Brede Old Fashioned
Farmers
Hi Praize
Old Fashioned
Poznanski

11626 Silver Springs Citrus Inc
25411 Mare Ave
Howey-in-the-Hills, FL 34737
610-793-0266
800-940-2277
bhughes@aol.com www.healthysqueezejuices.com
Manufacturer, importer and exporter of juices.
Treasurer: Michael Hall
Human Resources: Debra Fontaine
Operations Manager: Patrick Falcone
Purchasing Director: Pat Patrick
Estimated Sales: $35.1 Million
Number Employees: 100-249
Square Footage: 1260
Type of Packaging: Consumer, Food Service, Private Label, Bulk

11627 Silver Star Meats Inc
1720 Middletown Rd
PO Box 393
Mc Kees Rocks, PA 15136-1602
412-771-4064
Fax: 412-771-2253 800-548-1321
info@silverstarmeats.com
www.silverstarmeats.com
Hams, sausages, hotdogs, kielbasa, lunch meats
President: Robert Geromoy
Plant Manager: Dominic Bovalina
Estimated Sales: $11 Million
Number Employees: 1-4
Square Footage: 110000
Type of Packaging: Consumer, Food Service, Private Label
Brands:
Rzaca

11628 Silver State Foods Inc
3725 Jason St
PO Box 11505
Denver, CO 80211-2624
303-433-3351
Fax: 303-433-2883 800-423-3351
tom@silverstatefoods.com
www.silverstatefoods.com
Canned and frozen foods including prepared, spaghetti sauce and egg noodles
Manager: Tom Ernst
Manager: Pasqual Aiello
pasqual.aiello@silverstatefoods.com
Estimated Sales: $600,000
Number Employees: 1-4
Number of Brands: 2
Number of Products: 2
Square Footage: 22400
Type of Packaging: Consumer, Food Service, Private Label, Bulk
Brands:
Aiellos
Salvatore's

11629 Silver Streak Bass Co
1205 Frank Stubbs Dr
PO Box 499
El Campo, TX 77437-6164
979-543-6343
Fax: 979-543-8988 info@silverstreakbass.com
www.silverstreakbass.com
Producer of farm-raised hybrid striped bass
Owner: James Ekstrom
jekstrom@silverstreakbass.com
Estimated Sales: Less Than $500,000
Number Employees: 1-4
Parent Co: Ekstrom Enterprises
Type of Packaging: Bulk
Brands:
Silver Streak

11630 Silver Sweet Candies
522 Essex St
Lawrence, MA 01840-1242
978-688-0474
Fax: 978-683-6636
Candy and confections
Owner: Robert Burkinshaw
candyman1806@aol.com
Estimated Sales: Below $5 000,000
Number Employees: 10-19

11631 Silver Tray Cookies
6861 SW 196th Avenue
Suite 203
Fort Lauderdale, FL 33332-1628
305-883-0800
Fax: 305-888-8438
Cookies, sugar free pound cake and fruit flavored cream cakes
President: Perry Burk
Estimated Sales: Below $5 Million
Number Employees: 2
Brands:
Silver Tray Cookies

11632 Silverado Vineyards Inc
6121 Silverado Trl
Napa, CA 94558-9415
707-257-1770
Fax: 707-257-1538 800-997-1770
neliason@silveradovineyards.com
Processors of wine
Owner: Ron Miller
rmiller@silveradovineyards.com
Owner: Diane Miller
General Manager: Russ Weis
Winemaker: Jon Emmerich
Number Employees: 20-49

11633 Silverbow Honey Company
1120 E Wheeler Rd
Moses Lake, WA 98837
509-765-6616
Fax: 509-765-6549 866-444-6639
Specialty honey, table honey, gourmet honey, sweet mustard, hot honey mustard, honey butter, gift sets, beeswax, beeswax candles and both colored and natural beeswax.
President: Gary Grigg
Office Manager: Eric Peters
Estimated Sales: $7.2 Million
Number Employees: 20-49
Square Footage: 152000
Type of Packaging: Consumer, Food Service, Private Label, Bulk
Brands:
Silverbow

11634 Silverland Bakery
439 Des Plaines Ave
Forest Park, IL 60130
708-488-0800
Fax: 708-488-0894 info@silverlandbakery.com
silverlandbakery.com
Brownies, bars, cookies and cakes.
Owner & President: Athena Uslander
Type of Packaging: Consumer, Food Service, Private Label
Brands:
Silverland Desserts

11635 Silverleaf International Corp
5050 Knight Rd
Suite 230 #218
Rosharon, TX 77583-2608
281-495-1250
Fax: 281-499-5505 800-442-7542
www.4garlic.net
Marinated garlic hors d'oeuvres, blue cheese and feta cheese stuffed olives, olive oils, dips and salsa, spices and seasonings, jams and jellies, sauces, Italian pasta.
President: Neal McWeeney
VP: Adriane McWeeney
Estimated Sales: Less Than $500,000
Number Employees: 1-4
Number of Brands: 1
Number of Products: 50
Type of Packaging: Consumer, Private Label

11636 Silverston Fisheries
1507 N 1st St
Superior, WI 54880-1146
715-392-5551
Fax: 715-392-5586
Fish
Owner: Stuart Siverston
Estimated Sales: $10-20 000,000
Number Employees: 20-49

11637 Simi Winery
16275 Healdsburg Ave
Healdsburg, CA 95448-9075
707-433-3686
Fax: 707-433-6253 www.simiwine.com
Wines
Owner: Peter Seghesio
VP Winemaker: Roger Coldschmidt
Executive VP: Steve Reeder
steve.reeder@simiwinery.com
Sales Director: Steve Messinger
Operations Manager: Jim Debonis
Estimated Sales: $20-50 Million
Number Employees: 50-99
Parent Co: Canandaigua Wine Company

11638 **Simit + Smith**
501 Broad Ave
Suite 6
Ridgefield, NJ 07657
201-699-0320
info@simitandsmith.com
simitandsmith.com
Simits, breads, pastries, breadsticks, biscotti and cookies
President & General Manager: Zulfikar Bekar

11639 **(HQ)Simmons Foods Inc**
601 N Hico St
Siloam Springs, AR 72761-2410
479-524-8151
Fax: 479-524-6562 888-831-7007
Chicken including; boneless skinless tenderloins and breasts, breaded tenderloins, chicken wings, fully cooked, ready to cook, frozen, fresh, marinated, glazed, grill marked, portioning and pack sizes
President: Tammy Bomar
tbomar@marykay.com
CFO: Mike Jones
Director Research & Development: Brian Davis
Marketing Manager: Joseph Meszaros
VP Sales: Chip Miller
Director of Public Relations: Mary Doyle
Plant Manager: Brian Burke
Number Employees: 100-249
Square Footage: 120000
Type of Packaging: Consumer, Food Service, Private Label, Bulk
Brands:
Manu Maker
Simmons
Town & Country
Water Valley Farms

11640 **Simmons Hot Gourmet Products Corp.**
22 Greenview Close
Lethbridge, AB T1H 4K8
Canada
403-327-9087
Fax: 403-328-9589 sales@firenbrimstone.com
www.firenbrimstone.com

11641 **Simon Hubig Company**
2417 Dauphine St
New Orleans, LA 70117
504-945-2181
Fax: 504-945-2328
Baked goods
President: Thomas Bowman
Owner: Otto Ramsey
Contact: Drew Ramsey
drew@hubigs.com
Production Manager: Mike Tricou
Estimated Sales: $2.3 Million
Number Employees: 40
Square Footage: 64000

11642 **Simon Levi Cellars**
9380 Sonoma Hwy
Kenwood, CA 95452-9032
707-833-5070
Fax: 707-833-1355 888-315-0040
info@slcellars.com www.slcellars.com
Wines
President: John Garaventa
j.garaventa@slcellars.com
Estimated Sales: $1-2.5 Million
Number Employees: 10-19
Brands:
Maboroshi
Slc

11643 **Simon's Specialty Cheese**
2735 Freedom Rd
Appleton, WI 54913-9315
920-788-6311
Fax: 920-788-1424 800-444-0374
www.simonscheese.com
Signature cheeses such as feta, extra sharp cheddar, and marbled cheeses.
President: Doug Simon
General Manager: David Sohrweide
Cheesemaker: Terry Lensmire
Operations/R&D: Chris Simon
Estimated Sales: $25-49.9 Million
Number Employees: 50-99
Type of Packaging: Private Label
Brands:
Simon's

11644 **Simpatica**
355 Lantana St.
Suite 725
Camarillo, CA 93010
310-286-2236
simpatica.ag
Avocados
Founder: Jamie Johnson
CEO & Partner: Scott Bauwens
Year Founded: 2013
Number Employees: 5-10
Type of Packaging: Private Label

11645 **Simple Foods**
116 Killewald Ave
Tonawanda, NY 14150
716-743-8850
800-234-8850
Nuts and nut butter
President: Karen Pease
Estimated Sales: Under $500,000
Number Employees: 1-4
Type of Packaging: Consumer, Bulk
Brands:
Annie's
Magic Munchie

11646 **Simple Mills**
435 N LaSalle St
2nd Floor
Chicago, IL 60654
312-600-6196
info@simplemills.com
www.simplemills.com
Natural baking mixes and crackers
Founder & CEO: Katlin Smith
Quality Assurance & Compliance: Ryan Johnson
Vice President, Marketing: Michelle Lorge
Vice President, Sales: Bobbie Turco
Operations Manager: Megan Huber
Estimated Sales: $500,000-$1,000,000
Number Employees: 100
Brands:
Simple Mills

11647 **Simplot Food Group**
PO Box 9386
Boise, ID 83707
208-336-2110
800-572-7783
jrs_info@simplot.com www.simplotfoods.com
Distributor of avocado pulp, frozen potatoes, frozen fruit, frozen vegetables and frozen cornados
Parent Co: J.R. Simplot Company
Type of Packaging: Food Service

11648 **Simply 7 Snacks**
PO Box 710543
Houston, TX 77271
877-682-2359
Fax: 877-682-2368
paul.albrecht@simply7snacks.com
www.simply7snacks.com
Hummus and Lentil chips
President: Rashim Oberoi
Contact: Paul Albrecht
palbrecht@simply7snacks.com

11649 **Simply Auri**
1111 Hope St.
Suite 8
Stamford, CT 06907
860-389-2265
info@simplyauri.com
simplyauri.com
Wood ear mushroom drink
Co-Founder: Wei Chien Liang
Number Employees: 2-10
Brands:
Mad,casse

11650 **Simply Delicious**
8411 Highway N Carolina 86 N
Cedar Grove, NC 27231
919-732-5294
Fax: 919-732-5180
Sauces, dressings
President: John Troy

11651 **Simply Divine**
334 Amsterdam Ave
New York, NY 10023-8205
212-541-7300
Fax: 917-553-7510 info@simplydivine.com
www.simplydivine.com
Kosher gourmet soups, sauces, entrees, salads and desserts
Owner/President: Judith Geller Marlow
jmarlow@simplydivine.com
Estimated Sales: $500,000-$1 Million
Number Employees: 20-49
Type of Packaging: Consumer, Food Service
Brands:
Simply Divine

11652 **Simply Gourmet Confections**
PO Box 50141
Irvine, CA 92619
714-505-3955
Fax: 714-505-3957 info@simplyscrumptious.com
www.simplyscrumptious.com
Gourmet confections and cookies
President/Owner: Debra Formaneck

11653 **Simply Gum**
270 Lafatette St
New York, NY 10012
info@simplygum.com
www.simplygum.com
All-natural chewing gum
Founder/CEO: Caron Proschan
Marketing: Kelsey Jones
Sales/Operations Coordinator: Elise Goree
Sr Operations Manager: Emanuel Storch
Year Founded: 2014

11654 **Simply Incredible Foods**
140 Market Ave
Port Edwards, WI 54469-1346
715-697-6232
Fax: 715-909-0060 www.cransations.com
Cranberry ingredients processor.
Contact: Christine Sohns
chrissohns@yahoo.com
Number Employees: 5-9
Brands:
Freeze Dried Cransations
Squozen Frozen
Cransations
RazzAronia

11655 **Simply Panache**
26 Towne Center Way
Suite 162
Hampton, VA 23666
800-313-5613
contact@amangoparty.com
www.amangoparty.com
Manufacturer of mango preserves.
Co-Founder: Tanecia Willis
Co-Founder: Lakesha Brown-Renfro
Co-Founder: Nzinga Teule-Hekima
Brands:
Mango Mango

11656 **Simply Scruptious Confections**
PO Box 50141
Irvine, CA 92619
714-505-3955
Fax: 714-505-3957 info@simplyscrumptious.com
www.simplyscrumptious.com
White bark candy falvors include peppermint, lemon, raspberry, cafe latte, key lime, cookies and cream and orange cremesicle. Also tea cake cookies

11657 **Simply Shari's Gluten Free**
890 Hampshire Rd
Suite S
Thousand Oaks, CA 91361-2875
805-241-5676
Fax: 602-218-8409 info@simplysharis.com
Cookies, pasta meals
Owner: Shari Cole
Co-Owner: Larry Schneider
Operations Manager: Lia Lang

11658 **SimplyFUEL, LLC**
Leawood, KS
913-269-1889
info@simplyfuel.com
simplyfuel.com
Protein balls
Founder: Mitzi Dulan

11659 **Simpson & Vail**
3 Quarry Rd
Brookfield, CT 06804-1053
203-775-0240
Fax: 203-775-0462 800-282-8327
info@svtea.com www.svtea.com
Processor, exporter and importer of coffee and gourmet tea
President: Jim Harron Jr
CEO: Joan Harron
Estimated Sales: $.5-1 million
Number Employees: 5-9
Square Footage: 32000
Type of Packaging: Food Service

11660 **Simpson Spring Co**
719 Washington St
South Easton, MA 02375-1139
508-238-4472
Fax: 508-238-5691 www.simpsonspring.com
Flavoring extracts for carbonated beverages
Owner: Jim Bertarelli
webmaster@simpsonspring.com
Estimated Sales: $2.9 Million
Number Employees: 10-19

11661 **Sims Wholesale**
540 River St
Batesville, AR 72501
870-793-1109
Fax: 870-793-2230
Wholesaler/distributor of general line products; serving the food service market
General Manager: Kenneth Thornton
Manager: Mike Hanson

11662 **Sinai Gourmet**
Montreal, QC
Canada
844-887-4624
info@sinaigourmet.com
sinaigourmet.com
Hot pepper coulis: ghost pepper, habanero and jalapeno.
Founder: Laurence Isaac
Number Employees: 2-10
Brands:
Sinai Gourmet

11663 **Sinbad Sweets**
2401 West Almond Avenue
Madera, CA 93637
559-298-3700
Fax: 559-298-9194 866-746-2232
www.sinbadsweets.com
Pastries including baklava, strudel, tarts and fillo; exporter of baklava
President: Michael Muhawir
CEO: Edwina Aquino Seidel
COO: Anita Reina
Vice President: John Seidel
Public Relations: Sascha Muhawi
Operations Manager: Larry Burrow
Production Manager: Klaus Gernet
Number Employees: 50-99
Square Footage: 120000
Type of Packaging: Consumer, Food Service, Private Label, Bulk
Brands:
Oliver Twist
Sinbad Sweets

11664 **Singer Extract Laboratory**
13301 Inkster Rd
Livonia, MI 48150-2226
313-345-5880
Fax: 313-345-8686
Extracts and flavorings, food colorings, bar specialties and syrups.
President: Mike Letourneau
Estimated Sales: Below $5 Million
Number Employees: 3
Number of Brands: 3
Number of Products: 50
Square Footage: 20000
Brands:
4%
Belmo
Seely

11665 **Singing Dog Vanilla**
255 Wallis St
Suite 1
Eugene, OR 97402
541-343-2746
Fax: 541-610-1868 888-343-0002
www.singingdogvanilla.com
Vanilla products

11666 **Singleton Seafood**
P.O.Box 2819
Tampa, FL 33601-2819
813-719-6626
Fax: 813-247-1782 800-732-3663
info@tbfish.com
Frozen shrimp, breaded fish and shrimp, peeled and deveined shrimp, cooked shrimp, shrimp specialties
President: Dennis Reeves
CFO: Andrew Hawaux
Vice President: Rob Sharpe
Research & Development: Nina Burt
Quality Control: Don Toloday
Marketing Director: Dan Davis
Sales Director: Doug Knudsen
Production Manager: Bill Jacks
Plant Manager: Mike Pent
Purchasing Manager: Bill Stone
Estimated Sales: $300,000-500,000
Number Employees: 1-4
Number of Brands: 8
Number of Products: 200
Square Footage: 800000
Parent Co: ConAgra Foods
Type of Packaging: Consumer, Food Service, Private Label, Bulk

11667 **Singleton Seafood Company**
1804 Turkey Creek Road
Plant City, FL
813-241-1500
Seafood
President: Robert Patterson
Human Resources Manager: Alan Lewis
Contact: Bob Bruno
bob.bruno@singletonseafood.com
Estimated Sales: $20-49.9 Million
Number Employees: 350
Type of Packaging: Private Label

11668 **Sini Fulvi U.S.A.**
136 Mohawk St
Newark, NJ 07114-3314
973-274-0822
Fax: 718-361-6999 sinifulvi@aol.com
Importer of Italian, Spanish and Portuguese cheeses and Italian cured meats
President: Agostino Sini
Vice President: Pierluigi Sini
Marketing Director: Michele Buster
Estimated Sales: $.5-1 million
Number Employees: 4
Parent Co: Sini Fulvi
Type of Packaging: Consumer, Food Service, Bulk
Brands:
Cacio De Roma
Cacio De Roma Cheese
Crotonese
Drunken Goat Cheese
Genuine
Genuine Fulvi Romano Cheese
I Buonatarula Sini
Pasture Sini
Rustico Cheese
Sfizio Crotonese
Sini Fulvi
Spizzico Pepato Aged
Triggi

11669 **Sioux Honey Assn.**
301 Lewis Blvd
Sioux City, IA 51101-2237
712-258-0638
Fax: 712-258-1332 www.suebee.com
Honey collective with more than 300 members.
President & CEO: David Allibone
CEO: Lisa Hansel
lhansel@suebeehoney.com
Year Founded: 1921
Number Employees: 100-249
Type of Packaging: Consumer, Food Service, Private Label, Bulk
Other Locations:
Processing Plant
Sioux City IA
Processing Plant
Anaheim CA
Processing Plant
Elizabethtown NC
Brands:
Aunt Sue's
Sue Bee

11670 **Sipp**
Stamford, CT
866-222-4735
hello@enjoysipp.com
www.enjoysipp.com
Sodas.
Year Founded: 2009
Brands:
Sipp

11671 **Sir Kensington's**
101 W 24th Street
Apartment 27H
New York, NY 10011
646-450-5735
Fax: 646-755-3765 hello@sirkensingtons.com
www.sirkensingtons.com
Condiments
Co-Founder: Mark Ramadan
Co-Founder: Scott Norton

11672 **Sir Real Foods**
50 Hazelton Drive
White Plains, NY 10605-3816
914-948-9342
Fax: 914-948-9342 www.sirreal.com
Juices, beverages
President: Michael Albert
Vice President: Douglas Albert
Estimated Sales: Under $500,000
Number Employees: 2
Brands:
Americus Natural Spring Water

11673 **Siren Snacks**
San Francisco, CA
hello@sirensnacks.com
www.sirensnacks.com
Protein bites
Co-Founder: Elizabeth Gianuzzi
Co-Founder: Abby Gianuzzi

11674 **Sirocco Enterprises Inc**
228 Industrial Ave
New Orleans, LA 70121-2904
504-834-1549
Fax: 504-837-7762 www.siroccoenterprises.com
Manufacturer and exporter of ready-to-use liquid cocktail mixers
Vice President: Anthony Muto
VP: Anthony Muto
Production: Benny Peel
Estimated Sales: $1 Million
Number Employees: 10-19
Number of Brands: 1
Number of Products: 10
Square Footage: 52000
Type of Packaging: Food Service
Brands:
Pat O'Brien's Cocktail Mixes

11675 **Sisler's Ice & Ice Cream**
102 South Grove Street
Ohio, IL 61349
815-376-2913
888-891-3856
sisler@sisler.com www.sislers.com
Ice, ice cream
Owner/Operator: Bill Sisler
Manager: Dan Thompson
Estimated Sales: $500,000-$1 Million
Number Employees: 5-9
Square Footage: 72000
Type of Packaging: Consumer, Food Service
Brands:
Sisler's Dairy

11676 **Sister River Foods**
PO Box 5563
Central Point, OR 97502
541-665-0348
www.eatparma.com
Vegan cheese manufacturer

11677 **Sister's Gourmet**
965 Patrick Industrial Ct
Winder, GA 30680-8336
770-338-1388
Fax: 770-338-1267 877-338-1388
www.sistersgourmet.com
Gourmet cookie mixes
Owner: Lisa Sorensen
Estimated Sales: $5-10 Million
Number Employees: 50-99

11678 **Sister's Gourmet**
965 Patrick Industrial Ct
Winder, GA 30680-8336
770-338-1388
Fax: 770-338-1267 www.sistersgourmet.com
Manufacturer of baking mixes.
President and Owner: Lisa Sorensen
Director of Sales and Marketing: Andy Dollar
Number Employees: 50-99
Type of Packaging: Consumer

11679 **Sisters' Gourmet**
PO Box 1550
Dacula, GA 30019-0027
216-292-7700
Fax: 216-292-7701 orders@brandcastle.com
www.sistersgourmet.com
Baking mixes: cookie and brownie
R&D Project Manager: Taylor Reagan
Marketing Services: Linda Bina
Number Employees: 11-50
Parent Co: Brand Castle
Type of Packaging: Consumer, Private Label
Brands:
Magical Reindeer Food
Sisters Gourmet

11680 **Sivetz Coffee**
349 SW 4th St
Corvallis, OR 97333-4622
541-753-9713
Fax: 541-757-7644
Roasted coffee beans, extracts, almond kernels, hazelnut kernels, and coffee roasting machines
President: Mike Sivetz
Number Employees: 1-4
Type of Packaging: Consumer, Bulk
Brands:
Sivetz Coffee Essence

11681 **Six Mile Creek Vineyard**
1551 Slaterville Rd
Ithaca, NY 14850-6335
607-272-9463
Fax: 607-277-7344 800-260-0612
info@sixmilecreek.com www.sixmilecreek.com
Wine
Owner: Amy Renodin
info@sixmilecreek.com
Co-Owner: Roger Battistella
Estimated Sales: Less Than $500,000
Number Employees: 1-4
Type of Packaging: Private Label
Brands:
Six Mile Creek

11682 **Sjaak's Organic Chocolates**
1340 Commerce St # D
Petaluma, CA 94954-8015
707-775-2434
www.sjaaks.com
Bite size chocolates available in small tubs, large tubs, and individually wrapped; box assortments; chocolate bars; corporate gifts; seasonal; and vegan. Organic, non-GMO ingredients.
Owner: Jacques Holten
Sales: Jessica Holten-Casper
Manager: Jessica Holten
jholten@sjaaks.com
Production: Leo Marrella
Number Employees: 1-4
Type of Packaging: Consumer, Private Label

11683 **Skedaddle Maple**
Florenceville-Bristol, NB
Canada
skedaddle-maple.com
Maple syrup
President: Adam Stone
Parent Co: Hilltop Farm Forestry Group
Brands:
Skedaddle

11684 **Skillet Street Food**
6100 4th Avenue S
Suite 155
Seattle, WA 98115
425-998-9817
www.skilletstreetfood.com
Bacon jam spread
Owner: Josh Henderson
Contact: Erik Abdelbari
erikabdelbari@skilletstreetfood.com
Square Footage: 5240

11685 **Skim Delux Mendenhall Laboratories**
715 Morton St
Paris, TN 38242-4296
731-642-9321
Fax: 731-644-3398 800-642-9321
Processor and exporter of dairy analogs, formulas and flavors for calcium-fortified milk, juice and fruit drink beverages; also, chocolate milkshake mixes
Owner: David Travis
Sales Assistant: Melissa Taylor
Estimated Sales: $500,000-$1 Million
Number Employees: 5-9
Type of Packaging: Bulk

11686 **Skimpy Cocktails LLC**
1000 E Belt Line Rd
Ste 242
Carrollton, TX 75006-6201
469-892-7988
Fax: 469-568-2617 www.skimpymixers.com
Juice, cider, non-alcoholic beverages
Owner: Krista LaMothe
CEO: Megan Toole
Founder: Summer Lamons
Contact: Krista Lamothe
krista@skimpymixers.com
Estimated Sales: 200,000
Number Employees: 4

11687 **Skinners' Dairy**
24741 Deer Trace Drive
Ponte Vedra Beach, FL 32082-2114
904-733-5440
Milk, dairy products
President: Denny Gaultney
Estimated Sales: $10-20 000,000
Number Employees: 100

11688 **Skinny Mixes LLC**
2849 Executive Dr
Suite 210
Clearwater, FL 33762-5329
727-826-0306
Fax: 727-800-9959
customerservice@skinnymixes.com
www.skinnymixes.com
Non-alcoholic cocktail mixes
Owner: Jordan Engelhardt
jordan@skinnymixes.com
Estimated Sales: 790,000
Number Employees: 1-4

11689 **Skinny Souping**
Chicago, IL
skinnysouping.com
Single-serving soups
Founder: Alison Velazquez

11690 **Skipping Stone Productions**
1335 Railroad Street
Paso Robles, CA 93446
805-226-2998
Wine infused cookies with Italian origins
Estimated Sales: $130,000
Number Employees: 3
Square Footage: 7736

11691 **Skjodt-Barrett Foods**
5 Precidio Ct
Brampton, ON L6S 6B7
Canada
905-671-2884
Fax: 905-671-2885 877-600-1200
www.sbfoods.com
Sauces, marinades, jams, spreads, toppings & fillings, icings & glazes and savoury fillings manufacturer.
President/Owner: Thomas Dreher
Estimated Sales: $49.8 Million
Number Employees: 172
Type of Packaging: Food Service, Private Label, Bulk
Other Locations:
Canadian Operation
Brampton ON
U.S. Operation
Lebanon IN
Brands:
Skjodt-Barrett

11692 **Skratch Labs**
2885 Wilderness Place
Unit B
Boulder, CO 80301
800-735-8904
info@skratchlabs.com www.skratchlabs.com
Sports nutrition products
Founder: Allen Lim

11693 **Sky Haven Farm**
4871 Shepherd Creek Rd
Cincinnati, OH 45223-1015
513-681-2303
Fax: 513-681-8305
Cured hams
Owner: Ed J Dreyer
skyhavenfarms@aol.com
Estimated Sales: $1-2.5 000,000
Number Employees: 1-4

11694 **Sky Valley Foods**
145 Cane Creek Blvd
Danville, VA 24540
lpayne@skyvalleyfoods.com
www.skyvalleyfoods.com
Condiments, sauces, salsas and sparkling beverages
Founder: Allen Lim
Brands:
Sky Valley
Organicville

11695 **Sky Vineyards**
4352 Cavedale Rd
Glen Ellen, CA 95442-9767
707-935-1391
Fax: 510-540-8442 www.skyvineyards.com
Wine
Owner: Lore Olds
COO: Linn Brinier
Manager of Sales: Matt Gerloff
Estimated Sales: $3-5 Million
Number Employees: 5-9
Brands:
Sky Vineyards

11696 **Skylark Meats**
4430 S 110th St
Omaha, NE 68137-1235
402-592-0300
Fax: 402-592-1414 800-759-5275
skysales@americanfoodsgroup.com
www.skylarkmeats.com
Corned beef and liver.
President: Paul Weiss
Chief Executive Officer: James Leonard
jamesleonard@skylarkmeats.com
Quality Assurance Manager: Jack Warner
Marketing Manager: Steve Giroux
VP Sales: John O'Brien
Human Resources Managers: Shane Keith
Operations Executive: Brayton Howard
Production Manager: Ray Marquez
Purchasing Manager: Barb Bevington
Year Founded: 1970
Estimated Sales: $41.1 Million
Number Employees: 250-499
Square Footage: 175000
Parent Co: Rosen's Diversified
Type of Packaging: Consumer, Food Service

11697 **Skyline Chili Inc**
4180 Thunderbird Ln
Fairfield, OH 45014-2235
513-874-1188
Fax: 513-874-3591 www.skylinechili.com
Chili
Vice President: Charlie Harnist
charnist@skylinechili.com
Number Employees: 500-999

11698 **SlantShack Jerky**
123 Butler St
Brooklyn, NY 11231
201-632-1035
www.slantshack.com

Beef jerky
President/Owner: Joshua Kace
CEO: David Koretz
Year Founded: 2009

11699 **Slap Ya Mama Cajun Seasoning**
1103 W Main Street
Ville Platte, LA 70586
337-363-6904
Fax: 337-363-6608 800-485-5217
sales@slapyamama.com www.slapyamama.com
Seasonings
General Manager: James Westerfield
Contact: Jack Walker
jack@slapyamama.com

11700 **Slate Quarry Winery**
460 Gower Road
Nazareth, PA 18064-9219
610-746-3900
Fax: 610-746-9684
Wine
General Manager: M Eleanor Butler
Production Manager: Sidney Butler
Estimated Sales: $1-2.5 Million
Number Employees: 5-9

11701 **Slathars Smokehouse**
RR 1
Box 52bb
Lake City, MN 55041-9312
507-753-2080
Beef
President: Khalil Robinson
Estimated Sales: $300,000-500,000
Number Employees: 1-4

11702 **Slather Brand Foods LLC**
28 Arabian Drive
Charleston, SC 29407
843-513-1750
Fax: 843-769-4876 info@slatheriton.com
Sauces
Founder: Robin Rhea
Contact: Brandy Bates
batesbl@gmail.com
Estimated Sales: $87,000
Number Employees: 2
Square Footage: 4374

11703 **Slawsa**
PO Box 272
Cramerton, NC 28032
comments@slawsa.com
www.slawsa.com
Salsa relish
CEO: Julie Busha
Estimated Sales: $6.4 Million
Number Employees: 54
Brands:
Slawsa

11704 **Sleeman Breweries, Ltd.**
551 Clair Rd W
Guelph, ON N1L 1E9
Canada
519-822-1834
800-268-8537
www.sleemanbreweries.ca
Beer, ale, & lager
President: Kenny Sadai
VP, Sales & Marketing: Greg Newbrough
Year Founded: 1834
Estimated Sales: $92.5 Million
Number Employees: 1,000
Square Footage: 98328
Parent Co: Sapporo Holdings Limited
Type of Packaging: Consumer, Food Service

11705 **Slide Ridge LLC**
PO Box 66
Mendon, UT 84325-0066
435-752-4956
www.honeywinevinegar.com
Honey, vinegar
Owner/Founder: Martin James
Sales And Marketing: Michael Morgan
Contact: Kelli Bess
kelli@slideridgehoney.com

11706 **Slim Jim**
Conagra Brands
222 W. Merchandise Mart Plz
Chicago, IL 60654
877-266-2472
www.slimjim.com
Meats and grain snack foods
EVP & CFO: David Marberger
EVP & Chief Customer Officer: Derek De La Mater
Estimated Sales: $50-100 Million
Number Employees: 20,900
Parent Co: ConAgra Foods

11707 **Slingshot Foods**
650 California St
7th Floor
San Francisco, CA 94108
415-423-2444
info@slingshotfoods.com
www.slingshotfoods.com
Breakfast granola
President/Owner: Will Hartley
Number of Products: 6

11708 **Slo Roasted Coffee**
1172 Los Olivos Ave
Los Osos, CA 93402-3231
805-528-7317
Fax: 805-528-1150 800-382-6837
www.sloroasted.com
Coffee
Owner: Chris Galloway
Owner: Joe Galloway
Estimated Sales: Less than $500,000
Number Employees: 10-19
Type of Packaging: Food Service

11709 **Small Axe Peppers**
514 51st Ave
Long Island City, NY 11101-5879
bronxhotsauce.com
Hot sauce
Co-Founder: John A. Crotty
Co-Founder: John Fitzgerald
Brands:
The Bronx Hot Sauce

11710 **Small Batch Organics**
53B Manchester Valley Road
Manchester Center, VT 05255-1054
802-367-1054
Fax: 802-367-1152 smallbatchvt@gmail.com
smallbatchgranola.com
Granola
President: Lindsay Martin
Brands:
Small Batch

11711 **Small Planet Foods**
PO Box 9452
Minneapolis, MN 55440
Fax: 763-764-8330 800-624-4123
Small Planet Foods, under the Cascadian Farm, Muir Glen, Larabar, and Small Planet brand labels, offers more than 100 products that are USDA-certified organic. Cascadian Farm products include breakfast cereals, frozen fruits andvegetables, fruit spreads, granola and granola bars. Muir Glen makes premium tomato products such as pasta sauces, soups, ketchup, salsa, and canned tomatoes. As part of its business, Small Planet Foods also makes and markets frozen smoothie mixkits.
CFO: Michael Shadrack
SVP: Daniel Lloyd
Director of Research & Development: Edward Greenheck
Quality and Regulatory Operations: Katrina Heinze
Marketing Manager: Matt McQuinn
Contact: Laura Arcieri
laura.arcieri@smallplanetfoods.com
VP Operations: Marv Shelby
Plant Manger: Barbara Nelson
Director of Purchasing: Peter Lecompte
Estimated Sales: $16.1 Million
Number Employees: 110
Parent Co: General Mills
Type of Packaging: Consumer
Brands:
Cascadian Farm
Muir Glen Organic
Larabar
Food Should Taste Good

11712 **Smart Baking Co.**
297 Power Ct
Sanford, FL 32771
407-915-5519
info@smartbakingco.com
smartbakingco.com
Gluten-free cakes and buns
COO: Joanne Walter

11713 **Smart Flour Foods, LLC**
4020 S Industrial Dr
Ste 110
Austin, TX 78744-1028
512-706-1775
Fax: 440-306-1775 www.smartflourfoods.com
Pizza, pizza crust, bread, pancake & waffle mix
CEO: Charlie Pace
Director Of Marketing: Sameer Shah
Sales Manager: Lauren Rohr
Estimated Sales: C

11714 **Smart Juice**
1139 Lehigh Ave
Suite 300
Whitehall, PA 18052
610-443-1506
Fax: 888-625-0295 smartjuice.us
Organic juices
Contact: Erdem Abdulhay
erdem@smartjuice.us

11715 **SmartSweets**
Vancouver, BC
Canada
hello@smartsweets.com
smartsweets.com
Sugar-free candy
CEO: Tara Bosch

11716 **Smarties**
1091 Lousons Rd
Union, NJ 07083-5029
908-964-0660
Fax: 908-964-0911 800-631-7968
www.smarties.com
Manufacturer of Smarties, the iconic Halloween candy.
Vice President, Management: Jessica Dee
Vice President, Communications: Liz Dee
Vice President, Operations: Sarah Dee
Estimated Sales: $10-20 Million
Number Employees: 100
Type of Packaging: Consumer
Brands:
Smarties

11717 **Smashmallow**
153 W Napa Street
Sonoma, CA 95476
707-512-0605
hello@smashmallow.com
smashmallow.com
Flavored marshmallows
Founder & CEO: Jonathan Sebastiani
Estimated Sales: $8 Million
Number Employees: 30
Parent Co: Sonoma Brands
Brands:
Smash Mallow

11718 **Smeltzer Orchard Co**
6032 Joyfield Rd
Frankfort, MI 49635-9163
231-882-4421
Fax: 231-882-4430 info@smeltzerorchards.com
www.smeltzerorchards.com
Processor and exporter of frozen apples, apple juice, asparagus and cherries; also, dried blueberries, cherries, apples, strawberries and cranberries
President: Tim Brian
info@smeltzerorchards.com
Plant Manager: Mike Henschell
Estimated Sales: $9.3 Million
Number Employees: 50-99
Type of Packaging: Food Service

11719 **Smiling Fox Pepper Company**
610 Cherrywood Drive
North Aurora, IL 60542-1032
972-754-2820
Fax: 630-337-3734 sfoxpepco@aol.com
Relishes and jellies
Co-Owner: Mary Patterson
Co-Owner: Scott Patterson

Type of Packaging: Consumer

11720 Smiling Hill Farm
781 County Rd
Westbrook, ME 04092-1910
207-775-4818
Fax: 207-775-3537 800-743-7463
Milk, dairy
Owner: David Knight
david.knight@hillsidelumber.com
Number Employees: 20-49

11721 Smirk's
17601 US Hwy 34
Fort Morgan, CO 80701
970-762-0202
Fax: 877-682-1065 www.smirksbrand.com
Dried fruits, nuts, grains, seeds, flour and bird food
President: Nicholas Erker
nerker@smirksbrand.com
Chief Financial Officer: Cindy Schmid
Director, Quality Assurance: Jesse Bellefeuille
Sales: Jason Strauch
Chief Operations Officer: Eric Nickell
Number Employees: 2-10
Type of Packaging: Bulk

11722 Smith & Salmon
110 Summit St
Burlington, VT 05401-3928
802-578-8242
sapmaplewater.com
Maple sap soda and seltzer
Co-Founder: Chas P. Smith
Brands:
Sap Maple

11723 Smith & Sons Seafood
1033 Mcintosh Industrial Blvd
Darien, GA 31305-6202
912-437-6471
Fax: 912-437-3553 shrimp@darientel.net
www.smithseafood.com
Shrimp
Owner: Gean Smith
shrimp@darientel.net
Number Employees: 20-49

11724 Smith & Truslow
3225 East 42nd Ave
Denver, CO 80216
303-339-6967
www.smithandtruslow.com
Smith & Truslow specializes in freshly ground organic spices & herbs.
Co-Founder/Co-Owner: Jean Gleason
jgleason@smithandtruslow.com
Co-Founder/Co-Owner: Jenny Ross
Type of Packaging: Consumer

11725 Smith Dairy
230 N Vine St
Orrville, OH 44667-1644
330-682-6230
Fax: 330-683-1079 800-776-7076
www.smithdairy.com
Dairy products including; milk, eggnog, ice cream, seasonal products, shake mixes, juices and drinks, water, cottage cheese, sour cream and dips.
President: Steve Schmid
Product Development Specialist: Mindy Mencl
Director of Marketin: Penny Baker
VP Sales & Marketing: Brian DeFelice
Contact: Alisha Bellmore
alishabellmore@smithdairy.com
VP Manufacturing Operations: Ron Them
Director of Purchasing: Ken Stuter
Number Employees: 1-4
Square Footage: 180000
Type of Packaging: Consumer, Food Service, Private Label
Brands:
Smith's
White Oak
Whale-Of-A-Pail
Ruggles

11726 Smith Frozen Foods Inc
101 Depot St
Weston, OR 97886
541-566-3515
Fax: 541-566-3707 www.smithfrozenfoods.com
Frozen vegetables including baby lima beans, diced and sliced carrots, kernel corn, corn-on-the-cob and peas
President & CFO: Gary Crowder
Co-Owner: Sharon Smith
Co-Owner: Gordon Smith
Corporate Controller: Rebecca Hatley
Director, Business Development: Ken Porter
Director, Quality Control & Assurance: John Humble
VP, Sales & Marketing: Kent Perkes
Sales Office Manager: Shelly Hall
VP, Logistics & Packaging: Aaron Ware
Warehouse Operations: Kelly Hahn
Director, Purchasing: Sandra Stewart
Year Founded: 1919
Estimated Sales: $85 Million
Number Employees: 250-499
Number of Brands: 1
Type of Packaging: Consumer, Food Service, Private Label, Bulk
Brands:
Smith

11727 Smith Meat Packing
2920 Riopelle
Detroit, MI 48207
313-833-1590
Fax: 313-832-0232 sales@lklpacking.com
www.smithmeatpacking.com
Packer of smoked and cured pork
President: Anthony Peters
Estimated Sales: $5-10 Million
Number Employees: 10-19
Square Footage: 60000
Type of Packaging: Bulk

11728 (HQ)Smith Packing Regional Meat
105-125 Washington Street
P.O. Box 520
Utica, NY 13503-0520
315-732-5125
Fax: 315-732-1166 sales@smithpacking.com
www.smithpacking.com
Meat: beef, pork, veal, lamb, chicken and turkey; eggs, ham, bacon, frankfurters, sausage, kielbasa and turkey breast
President: Wesley Smith
VP: Mark Smith
Estimated Sales: $12.6 Million
Number Employees: 1-4
Square Footage: 150000
Type of Packaging: Private Label
Brands:
Evergood
Honest John's

11729 Smith Provision Co Inc
1300 Cranberry St
Erie, PA 16501-1566
814-459-4974
Fax: 814-879-0998 800-334-9151
www.smithprovision.com
Smoked luncheon meats and ham, frankfurters, roast beef and sausage
Chairman of the Board: Magnus Weber
President: Michael Weber
mike.weber@smithhotdogs.com
VP: John Weber
Operations Manager: Travis Lindsay
Estimated Sales: $10 Million
Number Employees: 10-19
Square Footage: 51726
Type of Packaging: Consumer, Food Service, Private Label, Bulk
Brands:
Smith's

11730 Smith Vineyard & Winery
13577 Dog Bar Rd
Grass Valley, CA 95949
530-273-7032
Fax: 530-273-0229
Wines
Manager: Christina Smith
Estimated Sales: $1 Million
Number Employees: 5-9

11731 Smith's Bakery
P.O.Box 16389
Hattiesburg, MS 39404-6389
601-288-7000
Fax: 601-584-6487 www.forrestgeneral.com
Bakery
President: William C Oliver
Estimated Sales: $1.5 Million
Number Employees: 1-4

11732 Smith-Madrone Vineyards & Winery
4022 Spring Mountain Rd
PO Box 451
St Helena, CA 94574-9773
707-963-2283
Fax: 707-963-2291 contact@smithmadrone.com
www.smithmadrone.com
Wines
Manager: Stuart Smith
nvhigh@aol.com
Winemaker: Charles Smith
Estimated Sales: $1-2.5 Million
Number Employees: 5-9
Brands:
Smith-Madrone

11733 Smithfield Foods Inc.
200 Commerce St.
Smithfield, VA 23430
757-365-3000
www.smithfieldfoods.com
Pork processor and hog producer.
President/CEO: Kenneth Sullivan
kennethsullivan@smithfieldfoods.com
Executive VP/CFO: Glenn Nunziata
COO, U.S. Operations: Dennis Organ
Year Founded: 1936
Estimated Sales: Over $1 Billion
Number Employees: 54,000
Number of Brands: 14
Number of Products: 200
Parent Co: WH Group Limited
Type of Packaging: Consumer, Food Service, Private Label
Brands:
Smithfield
Eckrich
Farmland
Armour
Cook's
Gwaltney
John Morrell
Nathan's Famous
Kretschmar
Curly's
Carando
Margherita
Healthy Ones
Farmer John

11734 Smoak's Bakery & Catering Service
2058 Walton Way
Augusta, GA 30904-2302
706-738-1792
Fax: 706-733-8979 tomt3@bellsouth.com
Cakes, cookies and breads
President: Steve Pierce
General Manager: Audery Hawn
Owner: Dan Smoak
Estimated Sales: $1-2.5 Million
Number Employees: 20-49
Type of Packaging: Private Label

11735 Smoke & Fire Natural Food
35 Railroad Ave
Great Barrington, MA 01230-1510
413-528-8008
Fax: 413-528-7997
Smoked and flavored tofu
Owner: Robert Harvey
Co-Founder: Mona Young
Estimated Sales: Under $500,000
Number Employees: 5-9
Brands:
Smoke & Fire

11736 Smoke House
20 Smokehouse Rd
Sagle, ID 83860-8698
208-263-6312
Fax: 208-762-8979
Smoked meats
Owner: Dick Struntz
Estimated Sales: $.5-1 million
Number Employees: 1-4

11737 **Smoked Turkey Inc**
6608 E Marshville Blvd
Marshville, NC 28103-1198
704-624-6628
Fax: 704-624-2510
info@stegallsmokedturkey.com
www.stegallsmokedturkey.com
Frozen hickory-smoked turkey and honey-glazed ham
Estimated Sales: $500,000-$1 Million
Number Employees: 1-4
Square Footage: 440000
Type of Packaging: Private Label
Brands:
Stegall Smoked Turkey

11738 **Smokehouse Winery**
10 Ashby Rd
Sperryville, VA 22740-2243
540-987-3194
Fax: 540-987-8189
smokehousewinery@earthlink.net
Wines
Owner: John Hallberg
Estimated Sales: $300,000-500,000
Number Employees: 1-4

11739 **Smokey Denmark Sausage Co**
3505 E 5th St
Austin, TX 78702-4913
512-385-0718
Fax: 512-385-4843 info@smokeydenmark.com
www.smokeydenmark.com
Beef, pork and venison sausage
Owner: Jonathan Pace
jonathan@smokeydenmark.com
Quality Assurance Manager: Colby DeFriese
Estimated Sales: $2.5 Million
Number Employees: 20-49
Type of Packaging: Consumer

11740 **Smolich Bros. Home MadeSausage**
760 Theodore St
Crest Hill, IL 60403-2380
815-727-2144
www.smolichsausage.com
Sausage including hot, mild, smoked, pork and bratwurst
President: Rudy Smolich
Co-Owner: Joe Smolich
joe.smolich@smolichsausage.com
Estimated Sales: Less Than $500,000
Number Employees: 1-4
Type of Packaging: Consumer

11741 **Smothers Brothers Tasting Room**
1976 Warm Springs Rd
Glen Ellen, CA 95442-8717
707-833-1010
Fax: 707-833-2313 800-795-9463
www.smothersbrothers.com
Wines
President/Owner: Thomas Smothers
Owner: Marcy Smothers
Estimated Sales: Below $5 Million
Number Employees: 5-9
Brands:
Smothers/Remick Ridge

11742 **Smuggler's Kitchen**
PO Box 570
Dundee, FL 33838-0570
800-604-6793
Dehydrated foods including Irish potato soup, vegetable dips, Cajun and chili sauces, etc
Co-Owner: Tom Nischan
Co-Owner: Pat Nischan
Number Employees: 1-4

11743 **Smuttynose Brewing Co**
225 Heritage Ave # 2
Portsmouth, NH 03801-8642
603-436-4026
Fax: 603-433-1247 info@smuttynose.com
www.smuttynose.com
Beer
President: Peter Egelston
Executive Brewer: David Yarrington
CFO: Gale Merrigan
Head Brewer: Greg Blanchard
Sales Manager: Kevin Love
National Sales Manager: Anka Jacobs
Marketing: Jaime Pruzansky
Office Manager: Deb Fitt
Contact: Robby Brondolo
robby.brondolo@smuttynose.com
Estimated Sales: Below $5 Million
Number Employees: 20-49
Type of Packaging: Private Label
Brands:
Big Beer Series
Old Brown Bag
Portsmouth Lager
Smuttynose Belgian W
Smuttynose Robust Po

11744 **Snack Factory**
PO Box 3562
Princeton, NJ 08543-3562
609-683-5400
Fax: 609-683-9595 888-683-5400
info@pretzelcrisps.com www.pretzelcrisps.com
Pretzel crisps-all natural and fat free; available in garlic, original and everything flavors.
President: Warren Wilson
VP: Sara Wilson
Contact: Todd Grandt
todd@pretzelcrisps.com
Estimated Sales: $5 Million
Number Employees: 9
Square Footage: 800000
Type of Packaging: Consumer, Food Service, Private Label, Bulk
Brands:
Snack Factory

11745 **Snack Works/Metrovox Snacks**
612 N. Eckhoff St
Orange, CA 92868
714-634-3478
Fax: 714-634-4424 800-783-9870
questions@giftbasketsupplies.com
www.giftbasketsupplies.com
Popcorn, pretzels, chocolates
Owner: Paul Voxland
Estimated Sales: $500,000-$1 Million
Number Employees: 5-9

11746 **SnackMasters, LLC**
8332 Lander Ave
Hilmar, CA 95324
209-537-9770
Fax: 209-669-3240 800-597-9770
jerky@snackmasters.com www.snackmasters.com
Producer of meat snacks, including beef, beef heart, chicken, pork and turkey jerky.
President: James Rekoutis
Contact: Blanca Delhi
bdelhi@snackmasters.com
Estimated Sales: $10-20 Million
Number Employees: 50-99
Number of Brands: 2
Type of Packaging: Consumer
Brands:
Aubrey'S Jerky
SnackMasters

11747 **Snackerz**
6351 Chalet Dr
Commerce, CA 90040-3705
562-928-0023
Fax: 562-928-8923 888-576-2253
www.snackerz.com
Candy and nuts
Owner: Ron Emrani
ron@snackerz.com
Estimated Sales: $10-20 Million
Number Employees: 20-49
Type of Packaging: Consumer

11748 **(HQ)Snak King Corp**
16150 Stephens St
City Of Industry, CA 91745-1718
626-336-7711
Fax: 626-336-3777 info@snakking.com
www.snakking.com
Snack foods, caramel corn, tortilla and corn chips, popcorn, beef jerky, pork rinds, cheese and rice puffs, nut meats and candy.
Chairman/CEO: Barry Levin
jpapiri@snakking.com
VP Sales & Marketing: Joe Papiri
Sales Exec: Joe Papiri
Number Employees: 250-499
Type of Packaging: Consumer, Food Service, Private Label, Bulk
Other Locations:
Snak King Corp.
City Industry CA
Brands:
El Sabroso
Granny Goose
Jensen's Orchard
Snak King
The Whole Earth

11749 **Snake River Brewing Company**
265 S Millward St
Jackson, WY 83001-8582
307-739-2337
Fax: 307-739-2296
brewpub@snakeriverbrewing.com
www.snakeriverbrewing.com
seasonal beer, ale, stout, lager & pilsner.
Owner/President/CEO: Ted Staryk
Estimated Sales: $1.5 Million
Number Employees: 50-99
Type of Packaging: Consumer, Food Service
Brands:
Snake River

11750 **Snapdragon Foods**
PO Box 14103
Oakland, CA 94614
877-881-7627
info@snapdragonfood.com
www.snapdragonfood.com
Importer and manufacturer of Asian prepared meals
President: David Sakamoto
CEO: Seth Jacobson
Vice President of Sales: Ron Dallara
Estimated Sales: $1-2.5 Million
Number Employees: 5-9

11751 **Snappy Popcorn**
610 Main St
Breda, IA 51436-8719
712-673-2347
Fax: 712-673-2347 800-742-0228
jon@snappypopcorn.com
www.snappypopcorn.com
Manufacturer, wholesaler/distributor and exporter of popcorn and supplies
President: Alan Tiefenthaler
alan@itien.com
Office Manager: Lori Steinkamp
VP Sales: Jon Tiefenthaler
Estimated Sales: $1-2.5 Million
Number Employees: 20-49
Square Footage: 100000
Type of Packaging: Food Service, Bulk

11752 **Sneaky Chef Foods, The**
c/o Action Brand Management
851 Broken Sound Pkwy. # 155
Boca Raton, FL 33487
561-757-6541
Fax: 866-920-6487 info@thesneakychef.com
www.thesnackbrigade.com
No-nut butters, prepared spreads with vegetable purees to appeal to children
Founder/President: Missy Chase Lapine
Number of Brands: 1
Number of Products: 8
Type of Packaging: Consumer, Private Label
Brands:
The Sneaky Chef

11753 **Snelgrove Ice Cream Company**
850 E 2100 S
Salt Lake City, UT 84106-1832
801-486-4456
Fax: 801-486-3926 800-569-0005
www.dreyers.com
Processor, exporter and wholesaler/distributor of ice cream and ice cream novelties
President: David Mutzel
Contact: Troy Luckart
troy.luckart@dreyers.com
Estimated Sales: Less than $500,000
Number Employees: 50-99
Parent Co: MKD Distributing
Type of Packaging: Consumer, Food Service, Private Label, Bulk

11754 Snikiddy, LLC
2505 Walnut St.
Suite 100
Boulder, CO 80302
303-444-4405
www.snikiddy.com
Manufacturer of various types of snacks including veggie chips, popcorn, cheese puffs, and baked fries.
Founder: Mary Schulman
Contact: Erin Carrigan
erin.carrigan@snikiddy.com
Brands:
SmashPop
Baked Fries Sharing Packs
Cheese Puffs Sharing Packs
Eat Your Vegetables

11755 Sno Shack Inc
2774 N 4000 W
P.O. Box 1010
Rexburg, ID 83440-3106
208-359-0866
Fax: 208-359-1773 888-766-7425
sales@snoshack.com www.snoshack.com
Flavors, thickeners and sweeteners; also, shaved ice equipment including shavers, bottles, racks and yogurt flavoring, carts, concession trailers
Owner: Burt Hensley
Owner: Cheryl Lewis
Sales Director: Peter Orr
burt@snoshack.com
Manager: Bud Orr
Purchasing Manager: Brooke Anstine
Estimated Sales: Less Than $500,000
Number Employees: 1-4
Square Footage: 36000
Type of Packaging: Consumer, Food Service, Private Label
Brands:
Carts
Concessions
Kiosks

11756 Sno Wizard Inc
101 River Rd
New Orleans, LA 70121-4222
504-832-3901
Fax: 504-832-1646 800-366-9766
information@snowizard.com www.snowizard.com
Snowball, snowcone and shaved ice machines and flavorings
President: Ronnie Sciortino
Estimated Sales: $5-10 Million
Number Employees: 10-19
Square Footage: 20000
Type of Packaging: Consumer, Food Service, Bulk
Brands:
Ronald Reginald's
Snolite
Snowizard

11757 Sno-Co Berry Pak
1518 4th Street
Marysville, WA 98270-5012
360-659-3555
Fruit
President: Christie Monroe
Treasurer: Barbara Clark
Estimated Sales: $10-20 000,000
Number Employees: 20-49

11758 Sno-Pac Foods Inc
521 Enterprise Dr
Caledonia, MN 55921-1844
507-725-5281
Fax: 507-725-5285 800-533-2215
snopac@snopac.com www.snopac.com
Frozen organic vegetables including soy and eda mame beans, green peas, whole kernel corn, cut green and mixed
President: Peter Gengler
VP: Darlene Gengler
Estimated Sales: $3.5 Million
Number Employees: 50-99
Type of Packaging: Consumer, Food Service, Bulk
Brands:
Sno Pac

11759 Snokist Growers
10 W Mead Ave
Yakima, WA 98902-6026
509-453-5631
Fax: 509-453-9359 800-377-2857
Fresh apples, pears and cherries; also, canned apple rings and sauces, fruit purees, pears and plums
President: Jim Davis
CFO: Jim Davis
Sales Director: Rich Boldoz
Sales: Neil Galone
Purchasing Manager: Nancy Weaver
Estimated Sales: $100,000
Number Employees: 500-999
Number of Products: 10
Square Footage: 200000
Type of Packaging: Consumer, Food Service, Private Label, Bulk
Brands:
Blue Ribbon
Cohort
Dear Lady
Nu House
Red Ribbon
Snokist
Tri Our

11760 Snow Beverages
928 Broadway # 504
Suite 504
New York, NY 10010-8144
212-353-3270
Fax: 646-219-7559
Natural soda plus vitamins
CEO: Stuart Strumwasser
Contact: Melanie Randall
melanie@snowbeverages.com
Number Employees: 1-4

11761 Snow Dairy Inc
119 W 800 S
Springville, UT 84663-9416
801-489-6081
Fax: 801-489-6081 www.dairysnow.com
President: Mark Snow
Estimated Sales: Less Than $500,000
Number Employees: 1-4

11762 Snow Monkey
1223 Wilshire Blvd
Suite 1825
Santa Monica, CA 90403-5406
kingdom@snow-monkey.com
snow-monkey.com
Ice cream
Co-Founder: Rachel Geicke
Co-Founder: Mariana Ferreira
Director of Impact & Partnerships: Katie Krell
Number Employees: 2-10
Brands:
Snow Monkey

11763 Snow's Ice Cream Co Inc
80 School St
Greenfield, MA 01301-2410
413-774-7438
Fax: 413-774-5406 www.bartshomemade.com
Ice cream, sorbet and frozen yogurt: wholesaler/distributor of frozen food, candy, snack foods, sauces, mustards and salsa's
Owner: Gary Schaefer
gary@bartshomemade.com
Estimated Sales: Below $5 Million
Number Employees: 5-9
Square Footage: 64000
Parent Co: Another Roadside Attraction
Type of Packaging: Consumer, Food Service, Private Label, Bulk
Brands:
Bart's Homemade
Snow's Nice Cream

11764 SnowBird Corporation
379 Broadway
Bayonne, NJ 07002-3631
201-858-8300
Fax: 201-451-5000 800-576-1616
Bottled filtered, spring, and distilled water, coffee makers and hot foods; wholesaler/distributor of water fountains and bottled water coolers; repair services available
President: Diane Drey
Vice President: Gerald Giannangeli
Estimated Sales: $3-5 Million
Number Employees: 6
Square Footage: 264000
Brands:
Snowbird

11765 Snowbear Frozen Custard
328 E State St
W Lafayette, IN 47906
765-746-2930
www.snowbear.com
Retailers of frozen desserts
Partner: Richard Lodde
Partner: Kirk Lodde
Partner: William Lodde
Partner: Tom Lodde
Estimated Sales: $500,000-$1 Million
Number Employees: 10-19
Number of Products: 50

11766 Snowcrest Packer
1925 Riverside Road
Abbotsford, BC V2S 4J8
Canada
604-859-4881
Fax: 604-859-1426 800-265-3686
info@snowcrest.ca www.snowcrest.ca
Processor and importer of frozen apples, blueberries, cherries, cranberries, raspberries, strawberries, asparagus, beans, broccoli, brussels, sprouts, cauliflowers, corn, peas, peppers, rhubarb, spinach, squash and turnips
President: Tom Smith
Quality Control: Lim Lee
Sales: Pascal Countant
Operations Manager: Rob Christl
Number Employees: 120
Square Footage: 440000
Parent Co: Omstead Foods
Type of Packaging: Consumer, Food Service, Private Label, Bulk
Other Locations:
Snowcrest Packer Ltd.
Burnaby BC
Brands:
Bonniebrook
Brentwood
Delnor
Pennysaver
Snowcrest

11767 Snowizard Extracts
101 River Rd
New Orleans, LA 70121-4222
504-832-3901
Fax: 504-832-1646 800-366-9766
info@snowizard.com www.snowizard.com
Snoballs, snowcones and shaved ice
President: Ronnie Sciortino
Estimated Sales: $5-10 Million
Number Employees: 10-19
Type of Packaging: Private Label
Brands:
Snowizard

11768 Snyder Foods
15350 Old Simcoe Road
P.O Box 750
Port Perry, ON L9L 1A6
Canada
905-985-7373
Fax: 905-985-7289
Processor and exporter of meat and fruit pies, sausage rolls, quiche, stuffed sandwiches and pie and tart shells
General Manager: Dave Jackson
Number Employees: 125
Square Footage: 220000
Type of Packaging: Consumer, Food Service, Private Label
Brands:
J.M. Schneider
Maple Leaf
Marks & Spencer
Pillsbury
Red-L
Richs

11769 Snyder's of Hanover
PO Box 32368
Charlotte, NC 28232
800-233-7125
www.snydersofhanover.com
Snack foods including pretzels, flavored pretzel pieces and potato, tortilla and corn chips.
Chairman: Michael Warehime
Year Founded: 1909
Estimated Sales: $652 Million
Number Employees: 2,400

Number of Products: 45
Square Footage: 37800
Type of Packaging: Consumer

11770 Snyder's-Lance Inc.

13515 Ballantyne Corporate Pl.
Charlotte, NC 28277
800-438-1880
www.snyderslance.com
Sandwich crackers, nuts and seeds, captain's wafers, cookies, popcorn, pretzels, snack cakes, and 100 calorie packs.
President/CEO: Brian Driscoll
Year Founded: 2010
Estimated Sales: $1.62 Billion
Number Employees: 5,900
Number of Brands: 15
Parent Co: Campbell Soup Company
Type of Packaging: Consumer
Other Locations:
Lance
Hyannis MA
Brands:
Snyder's of Hanover
Lance
Cape Cod Potato Chips
Kettle Brand
Snack Factory Pretzel Chips
Late July Snacks
Emerald
Pop Secret
Tom's
Stella D'oro
O-Ke-Doke
Krunchers!
Jays
EatSmart Snacks
Archway

11771 So Delicious Dairy Free

1130 Shelley St
Springfield, OR 97477
541-338-9400
Fax: 541-338-9401 866-388-7853
info@turtlemountain.com
www.sodeliciousdairyfree.com
Processor and exporter of frozen nondairy desserts; also, fat-free
Founder, President, Chief Executive Offi: Mark Brawerman
Marketing: John Tucker
Contact: Michael Murray
mmurray@sodeliciousdairyfree.com
Director of Operations: Michael Dunteman
Estimated Sales: Under $500,000
Number Employees: 1-4
Type of Packaging: Consumer, Food Service, Private Label
Brands:
Carb Escapes
It's Soy Delicious
Organic Lil Buddies
Organic Soy Delicious
Soy Delicious Purely Decadent
Sweet Nothings

11772 SoBe Beverages

40 Richards Avenue
Norwalk, CT 06854-2327
203-899-7111
Fax: 914-253-2000 800-588-0548
www.sobebev.com
Healthy fruit and herb beverages with vitamins and minerals
General Manager: Scott Mossitt
Office Manager: Jessica Lee
Vice President, Marketing: Tom Smallhorn
Estimated Sales: $25-49.9 Million
Number Employees: 1,500
Number of Brands: 1
Parent Co: Pepsico
Brands:
SoBe

11773 Sobaya

201 Rue Miner
Cowansville, QC J2K 3Y5
Canada
450-266-8808
Fax: 450-266-4750 800-319-8808
info@sobaya.ca www.sobaya.ca
Natural pasta, organic pasta, Kamut organic pasta and Spelt organic pasta
President: Jacques Petit
Vice President: William Swaney
Marketing/Sales: Sandra Prevost
Number Employees: 7
Number of Brands: 1
Number of Products: 14
Square Footage: 20000
Parent Co: Eden Foods
Type of Packaging: Consumer, Private Label, Bulk
Brands:
Genmai Udon
Soba
Somen
Udon

11774 Sobon Estate

12300 Steiner Rd
Plymouth, CA 95669
209-333-6275
Fax: 209-245-5156 info@sobonwine.com
www.sobonwine.com
Wine
Co-Owner: Leon Sobon
Co-Owner: Shirley Sobon
Winemaker & Vineyard Operations Manager: Paul Sobon
Coordinator of Computer/Business Systems: Robert Sobon
Sales/Marketing: Tom Quinn
Estimated Sales: $5-10 Million
Number Employees: 10-19
Brands:
Shenandoah Vineyards
Sobon Estate

11775 Society Hill Snacks

8845 Torresdale Ave
Philadelphia, PA 19136-1510
215-708-8500
Fax: 215-288-4117 800-595-0050
contact@societyhillsnacks.com
www.societyhillsnacks.com
Gourmet sweet roasted nuts, snack mixes and great munchies.
President: Ronna Schultz
Estimated Sales: $1-3 Million
Number Employees: 10-19
Type of Packaging: Consumer, Food Service, Private Label, Bulk
Brands:
Afrique
Cinnful Coco
Cravin Asian
Hot Stuff
Loco Coco
Love That
Society Hill Gourmet Nut Company
Tres Toffee
Tropical Honey Glace

11776 Sofina Foods Inc

100 Commerce Valley Dr W
Markham, ON L3T 0A1
Canada
905-747-3333
855-763-4621
sales@sofinafoods.com www.sofinafoods.com
Pork, beef, turkey, chicken and fish
Executive Chairman: Michael Latifi
President/CEO: Robert Wilt
VP/Controller: Robert Andru
EVP/Chief Commercial Officer: Brent Quartermain
Estimated Sales: Over $1 Billion
Number of Brands: 9
Type of Packaging: Consumer, Food Service, Private Label
Brands:
Cuddy
Fletcher's
Janes
Lavazza
Lilydale
Mastro
Rio Mare
San Benedetto
San Daniele

11777 Sofo Foods

253 Waggoner Blvd
Toledo, OH 43612-1952
419-476-4211
Fax: 419-478-6104 800-447-4211
www.sofofoods.com
Appetizers, meat toppings and flour products such as doughs, pasta, cheese blends, and tomatoes.
CEO: Michael Sofo
Chief Operating Officer: Cos Figliomini
Chief Information Officer: Chuck Winters
Director, Corporate Accounting: Roger Bly
Director, Sales: Jeff Peer
VP, Operations: Gary Tolles
Director, Logistics: Jon Steinmetz
Director, Purchasing: Rob Kaufman
Estimated Sales: $20-50 Million
Number Employees: 250-499
Number of Brands: 6
Type of Packaging: Food Service
Other Locations:
New Albany IN
Suwanee GA
Houston TX
Brands:
A&M Cheese
Bellissimo
Spendida
Tolibia
Vantaggio
Vantaggio D'Oro

11778 Soft Cell Technology

6986 Bandini Blvd
Commerce, CA 90040-3326
323-726-7065
Fax: 323-726-7065 800-360-7484
sales@soft-gel.com www.soft-gel.com
Herbal and nutritional supplements
President: Ron Udell
ronu@soft-gel.com
VP Sales Administration: Diane Hembree
Number Employees: 10-19
Type of Packaging: Private Label, Bulk
Brands:
Coqsol
Sgti

11779 Soho Beverages

8075 Leesburg Pike
Suite 760
Vienna, VA 22182-2739
703-689-2800
Soft drinks
President: Tom Cox
Estimated Sales: $5-10 000,000
Number Employees: 5
Type of Packaging: Private Label
Brands:
Soho Natural Lemonades
Soho Natural Soda &

11780 Sokol Blosser Winery

5000 NE Sokol Blosser Ln
Dayton, OR 97114-7232
503-864-2282
Fax: 503-864-2710 800-582-6668
info@sokolblosser.com www.sokolblosser.com
Wine
President: Allison Sokol Blosser
Vice President: Michael Brown
michael@sokolblosser.com
Estimated Sales: Below $5 Million
Number Employees: 20-49
Number of Products: 7
Brands:
Evolution
Medetrina
Sokol Blosser

11781 Solana Beach Baking Company

5927 Farnsworth Court
Carlsbad, CA 92008-7303
760-444-9800
Fax: 760-444-9883
Breads and baked goods
President: David Wells
Quality Control: Kim Hogan
R & D: David Mears
Estimated Sales: $30-50 Million
Number Employees: 5-9

11782 Solana Gold Organics

1830 Gravenstein Hwy S
Sebastopol, CA 95472-4841
707-829-1121
Fax: 707-829-4715 800-459-1121
solanag@pacbell.net
Organic apples and apple products including kosher, dried, sauce, vinegar, juice, etc

Owner: John Kolling
jkolling@solanagold.com
Vice President: Cathy Gonzalez
Estimated Sales: $3 Million
Number Employees: 10-19
Type of Packaging: Consumer, Private Label, Bulk
Brands:
Solana Gold
Solana Gold Organics

11783 Solazyme Inc
225 Gateway Blvd
S San Francisco, CA 94080-7019
650-589-5883
Fax: 650-989-6700
Microalgae-based healthy food ingredients and oils. Microalgae-derived lipid, protein and fiber-based products for nutrition, taste, texture and functionality.
CEO: Jonathan Wolfson
CFO & COO: Tyler Painter
Contact: Annie Chang
achang@solazyme.com
Estimated Sales: Less Than $500,000
Number Employees: 1-4
Type of Packaging: Bulk
Other Locations:
Global Headquarters
San Francisco CA
Midwestern Operations
Peoria IL
South American Operations
Sao Paulo, Brazil

11784 Sole Grano LLC
16-00 Pollitt Dr
Suite 3
Fair Lawn, NJ 07410-2765
201-797-7100
info@solegrano.com
www.solegrano.com
Dried fruits, nuts, trail mixes, granolas, grains, beans, seeds, peas, lentils, and confections.
President: Harun Ekici
Number Employees: 1-4
Type of Packaging: Private Label

11785 Solgar Vitamin & Herbal
500 Willow Tree Rd
Leonia, NJ 07605
201-944-2311
Fax: 201-944-7351 877-765-4274
pr@www.solgar.com www.solgar.com
Natural dietary and nutritional supplements
President/CEO: Barry Skolnick
Year Founded: 1947
Estimated Sales: $100-500 Million
Number of Products: 400
Square Footage: 50000
Parent Co: NBTY
Type of Packaging: Consumer
Brands:
Kangavites
Natural Bouncin' Berry
Nature's Bounty
Solgar
Sundown

11786 Solis Winery
3920 Hecker Pass Rd
Gilroy, CA 95020-8805
408-847-6306
Fax: 408-847-5188 888-838-6427
www.soliswinery.com
Wines
President: David Vanni
VP/Owner: Valerie Vanni
Marketing Director: Steve Beck
Contact: Julie Vanni
julie@soliswinery.com
Plant Manager: Michael Vanni
Estimated Sales: $90,000 approx.
Number Employees: 5-9
Brands:
Solis

11787 Solnuts
711 7th St
Hudson, IA 50643
319-988-3221
Fax: 319-988-4647 800-648-3503
nnewton@kerrygroup.com
Dry roasted soy nuts and all natural full fat soy flour
Manager: Mike Patterson
Vice President: Michael Healy
Marketing Director: Jim Andrews
Sales/Marketing: Nancy Newton
Operations Manager: Dave Zanchetti
Production Manager: Mike Patterson
Plant Manager: Mike Devine
Estimated Sales: $3-5 Million
Number Employees: 5-9
Square Footage: 64000
Parent Co: B.V. Solnut
Type of Packaging: Food Service, Private Label, Bulk
Brands:
Solnuts

11788 Solo Foods
5315 Dansher Road
Countryside, IL 60525
800-328-7656
info@solofoods.com www.solofoods.com
Cake and pastry fillings, almond paste and marzipan, pie and dessery fillings, marshmallow and toasted marshmallow creme, fruit butters, Asian dipping sauces and marinades, seasoning mixes.
President: John Sokol Novak
COO: Ralph Pirritano
Contact: Sami Abdel-Malek
sabdel-malek@solofoods.com
Estimated Sales: $20-50 Million
Parent Co: Sokol and Company
Type of Packaging: Consumer, Food Service, Private Label
Brands:
Baker
Solo
Simon Fischer
Chun's

11789 Solo Worldwide Enterprises
5683 Columbia Pike Ste 100
Falls Church, VA 22041
703-845-7072
Fax: 703-560-5744 soloworld@aol.com
General grocery
President, US Division: Eyob Mamo
Estimated Sales: $500,000-$1 000,000
Number Employees: 5-9
Brands:
Solo

11790 Soloman Baking Company
3820 Revere St Ste A
Denver, CO 80239
303-371-2777
Fax: 303-375-9162
Pita bread, bagel and pita chips, snack mixes and tortillas greek pita
President: Sam Soloman
CEO: Andy Soloman
CFO: Malik Soloman
Estimated Sales: $3 Million
Number Employees: 12
Number of Products: 8
Square Footage: 48000
Type of Packaging: Consumer, Private Label

11791 Soloman Baking Company
3820 Revere St Ste A
Denver, CO 80239
303-371-2777
Fax: 303-375-9162
Bakery products
President: Sam Soloman
Marketing Director: Hian Soloman
CFO: Annas Soloman
Quality Control: Hiam Soloman
R & D: Max Soloman
Estimated Sales: $5-10 000,000
Number Employees: 5-9
Brands:
Soloman

11792 SoluBlend Technologies LLC
11487 Amherst Ct
Frankfort, IL 60423
815-534-5778
Fax: 815-463-5493
Dietary supplements and specialty ingredients.
Manager: Richard Staack
COO: Eric Kuhrts
Contact: Eric Kuhrts
ekuhrts@solublend.com

11793 Soluble Products Company
480 Oberlin Ave S
Lakewood, NJ 08701-6997
732-364-8855
Fax: 732-364-6689 Sales@associatedbrands.com
Manufacture of supplements for every lifestyle, including diet, bodybuilding, sports nutrition, nutraceutical and children's products
CEO: Stephen Hoffman
VP: Stewart Hoffman
Sales Manager: Thomas A Flora
Sales Manager: Thomas Flora
Estimated Sales: $2.5-5 Million
Number Employees: 20-49
Square Footage: 200000
Type of Packaging: Private Label
Brands:
Soluble Products

11794 Solvaira Specialties
50 Bridge St
North Tonawanda, NY 14120-6842
716-693-4040
Fax: 716-693-3528 888-698-1936
info@ifcfiber.com www.ifcfiber.com
A leading manufacturer of dietry fiber.
President/CEO: Dan Muth
Executive VP: Peter Vogt
pvogt@ifcfiber.com
R&D: Jit Ang
Exec VP of Operations: Brian Finn
Purchasing Manager: Steve Couladis
Year Founded: 2000
Number Employees: 50-99
Number of Brands: 10+
Type of Packaging: Bulk
Brands:
Just Fiber
Solkafloc
Fibrex
Nutrafiber
Keycel
Qualflo
Aplphacel
Floam
Vintnercel

11795 Somebody's Mother's Chocolate
5551 Cedar Creek Dr
Houston, TX 77056-2307
713-627-3055
info@somebodysmothers.com
www.somebodysmothers.com
Dessert toppings, chocolate
Owner: Lynn Lasher
Manager: Dino Bulsza
dbulsza@somebodysmothers.com
Estimated Sales: Less Than $500,000
Number Employees: 1-4

11796 Somerset Syrup & Concessions
100 Mcgaw Dr
Edison, NJ 08837-3725
732-225-0200
Fax: 732-225-6363 800-526-8865
www.eatfunfoods.com
Confection products
President: Robert Spitz
bspitz@somersetsyrup.com
Estimated Sales: Below $5 Million
Number Employees: 20-49

11797 Something Natural LLC
321 W. 2nd St.
Boston, MA 02127
617-315-7169
www.drinksomethingnatural.com
Manufacturer of carbonated water.
Founder: Randy Shefshick
sheffo14@gmail.com
Brands:
Something Natural

11798 Something Special Deli-Foods
224 Kaska Road
Sherwood Park, AB T8A 4G7
Canada
780-467-4448
Fax: 780-449-1238 800-461-5892
talktous@somethingspecialdeli.com
www.somethingspecialdeli.com
Salsa, dips, tapenades, pepper spreads and jellies.
President: Gordon Salamandick
Customer Care: Lori Martin

Estimated Sales: $20-50 Million
Number Employees: 10-19
Brands:
Something Special Gourmet Antipasto
Pepper Jellies

11799 **Sommer Maid Creamery Inc**
6069 Kellers Church Rd
PO Box 350
Pipersville, PA 18947-1019
215-345-6160
Fax: 215-345-4945 info@sommermaid.com
www.sommermaid.com
Cheese, eggs, butter and margarine
President: Brett Sexton
CFO: John T Poprick
VP/General Manager: Harry Mattern
Estimated Sales: $.5-1 million
Number Employees: 20-49
Type of Packaging: Consumer, Food Service, Private Label, Bulk
Brands:
State

11800 **Sommer's Food Products**
106 W 7th Street
Salisbury, MO 65281-1108
660-388-5511
Potato chips
President: Jack Richardson
Estimated Sales: $5-9.9 000,000
Number Employees: 7
Brands:
Sommer's Food

11801 **Sommers Organic**
339 Messner Drive
Wheeling, IL 60090
847-229-8192
Fax: 847-229-8264 877-377-9797
info@sommersorganic.com
Organic beef products, chicken products, turkey products, and pork products.
Chairman: Walter Sommers
Type of Packaging: Consumer

11802 **Sonne**
896 22nd Ave N
Wahpeton, ND 58075-3026
701-642-3068
Fax: 701-642-9403 800-727-6663
www.dakotagourmet.com
Roasted sunflower seeds, trail mixes and toasted corn and soybeans
President: Steven Bromley
Contact: Heather Budke
h.budke@sunopta.com
Estimated Sales: $3 Million
Number Employees: 20-49
Square Footage: 82200
Type of Packaging: Consumer, Food Service, Private Label, Bulk
Brands:
Dakota Gourmet
Dakota Gourmet Heart Smart
Dakota Gourmet Toasted Korn

11803 **Sonoita Vineyards**
290 Elgin Canelo Rd
Elgin, AZ 85611-8001
520-455-5893
Fax: 520-455-5893 winery@sonoitavineyards.com
www.sonoitavineyards.com
Wines
Founder: Gordon Dutt
General Manager: Mike Duppost
VP: Jack Strolline
Estimated Sales: $1-2.5 Million
Number Employees: 5-9

11804 **Sonoma Creamery**
21750 8th St E
Suite 1
Sonoma, CA 95476-9803
707-996-1000
Fax: 707-935-3535 info@sonomacreamery.com
sonomacreamery.com
Cheese crisps
President & CEO: John Crean
Vice President: Lou Biaggi
Year Founded: 1931
Number Employees: 10-19
Brands:
Mr. Cheese O's
Sonoma Creamery
Sonoma Jack
Sonoma Organics

11805 **Sonoma Flatbreads**
935 Taylor Station Rd
Columbus, OH 43230
info@sonomaflatbreads.com
sonomaflatbreads.com
Flatbread pizzas
Chairwoman: Jane Grote Abell

11806 **Sonoma Gourmet**
21787 8th St E Ste 7
Sonoma, CA 95476
707-939-3700
Fax: 707-939-3730
Specialty sauces and condiments
President and Owner: William Weber
Vice President: Roger Declercq
Contact: Pedro Andrade
pedro@sonomagourmet.com
Estimated Sales: $3.14 Million
Number Employees: 25
Number of Brands: 30
Number of Products: 200
Type of Packaging: Private Label
Brands:
Pometta's
Sonoma Gourmet

11807 **Sonoma Seafoods**
2 E Spain St
Sonoma, CA 95476-5729
707-996-1931
Fax: 707-935-8846 800-411-2123
Sonomaseafoods@sonomaseafoods.com
sonomaseafoods.com
Stuffed entree products include fish and stuffed seafood in addition to a recently introduced new product line including poultry, pork, beef and vegetables.
Owner: Pete Vivani
Partner: Scott Gray
Sales Manager: Georgine Drees
Estimated Sales: $5.9 Million
Number Employees: 20-49

11808 **Sonoma Syrup Co. Inc.**
PO Box 819
Sonoma, CA 95476-0819
707-996-4070
Fax: 707-935-6976 www.sonomasyrup.com
Dessert toppings, flavoring syrups
Owner: Karin Campion
Number Employees: 1-4

11809 **Sonoma Wine Services**
P.O.Box 207
Vineburg, CA 95487
707-996-9773
Fax: 707-996-0145
Wines: shipping, storage. Controlled environment bonded warehouse
President: Warren McCambridge
CFO: Denise McCambridge
Estimated Sales: Under $500,000
Number Employees: 1-4
Brands:
Sonoma Wine

11810 **Sonoma-Cutrer Vineyards**
4401 Slusser Rd
Windsor, CA 95492
707-528-1181
Fax: 707-528-1561 wineclub@sonomacutrer.com
www.sonomacutrer.com
wines. Some of their titles include Founders Reserve, Late Harvest Chardonnay, Sonoma Coast, Owsley Pinot Noir, Russian River Valley and more.
Winemaking Director: Mick Schroeter
Winemaker: Cara Morrison
General Manager: David Perata
david_perata@sonomacutrer.com
Estimated Sales: $1-2.5 Million
Number Employees: 50-99
Brands:
Alban Viognier
Chateau Montelena
Hartwell Cabernet
Louis Roederer
MacPhail Pinot
Oberschulte Syrah
Worthy Cabernet

11811 **Soozy's Grain-Free**
246 Fifth Ave, 3rd Floor
P.O. Box 20077
New York, NY 10001
hello@soozys.com
www.soozysgrainfree.com
Muffins that are paleo and free from grain, gluten, dairy, peanuts, and soy
President: Mason Sexton
CEO: Susan Chen
Year Founded: 2017
Parent Co: Mindful Foods

11812 **(HQ)Sopakco Foods**
118 South Cypress Street
Mullins, SC 29574-1047
843-464-7851
Fax: 843-464-2096 sfernald@sopakco.com
www.sopakco.com
Sauces, dressings
President/CEO: Lonnie Thompson
Contact: Phil Howard
phil.howard@precisioncolor.com
Manufacturing Director: William Pettibone
Plant Operations: Bill Jennings
Estimated Sales: $5-10 Million
Number Employees: 250-499

11813 **Sopako Foods**
P.O.Box 1047
Mullins, SC 29574-1047
843-464-7851
Fax: 843-464-2096
Military food rations
President: Lonnie Thompson
Estimated Sales: $5-10 Million
Number Employees: 250-499
Parent Co: Sopako Foods

11814 **Sophia Foods**
480 Wortman Ave
Brooklyn, NY 11208
718-272-1110
Fax: 718-272-1230 www.sophiafoods.com
Oil, vinegar, salt, vegetables, rice and grains, sauces and spreads, pasta, crackers, grissini, cakes and cookies, preserves and juices.
CEO: Candace Abitbul
candace@sophiafoods.com
Director of Sales & Business Development: Paul Berger
Year Founded: 1991
Estimated Sales: $2.4 Million
Number Employees: 11-50
Type of Packaging: Consumer, Food Service
Brands:
Sophia

11815 **Sophia's Sauce Works**
2533 N Carson Street
Carson City, NV 89706-0147
916-315-3584
Fax: 916-315-9372 800-718-7769
All natural sauces, spreads and dressings
Chairman: Sophia Fridas
President: Jim Fridas
Number Employees: 5-9
Square Footage: 8000
Parent Co: Sophia's Sauce Works
Type of Packaging: Consumer
Brands:
Sophia's Authentic
Sophia's Sauce Works

11816 **Sopralco**
6991 W Broward Blvd
Plantation, FL 33317-2907
954-584-2225
Fax: 954-584-3271 sopralco@aol.com
Ready-to-drink espresso
Owner: Peter Marciante
VP: Arcelia De Battisti
Marketing: Ana Ordaz
Estimated Sales: $1,500,000
Number Employees: 1-4
Square Footage: 1250
Parent Co: Sopralco
Type of Packaging: Consumer, Food Service
Brands:
Espre
Espre-Cart
Espre-Matic

11817 **(HQ)Sorbee Intl.**
9990 Global Rd.
Philadelphia, PA 19115
215-677-5200
Fax: 215-677-7736 800-654-3997
Confectionery items including sugar hard candy, low-fat candy bars and sugar-free items
CEO: Daniel Werther
CFO: Tom Keogh
VP Sales: Barry Sokol
Estimated Sales: $31 Million
Number Employees: 20-49
Other Locations:
Sorbee International Ltd.
Philadelphia PA
Brands:
Dream Candy
Global Brands
Sorbee

11818 **Sorrenti Family Farms**
14033 Steinegull Road
Escalon, CA 95320
209-838-1127
Fax: 209-838-7809 888-435-9490
Wild rice, blended rices, quick-cook rice mixes, pasta and wild rice mixes, soup mixes, muffin mixes, focaccia mix and pizza kits
President/CEO: Hita Sorenti
Estimated Sales: Less than $1 Million
Number Employees: 1-4
Brands:
Cucina Sorrenti
Mighty Wild
Rising Star Ranch
Sorrenti Family Farm
Urban Delights

11819 **Sorrento Lobster**
224 Ocean Ave
Sorrento, ME 04677
207-422-9082
Fax: 207-422-9033
Seafood.
Manager: Rick Freeman
Estimated Sales: $2,100,000
Number Employees: 5-9

11820 **Soteria**
180 Kite Lake Road
Fairburn, GA 30213-9608
404-768-5161
Fax: 404-768-3704
Natural and dry seasoning blends with no salt, MSG or calories
CEO: Lee Armstrong
Executive VP: Denise Armstrong
VP Operations: Keith Jackson
Number Employees: 1-4

11821 **Souperb LLC**
1350 Powell St
Emeryville, CA 94608-2506
415-685-8508
www.naturallysouperb.com
Soups, broths
Chef & Founder: Joanna Terry

11822 **Soupergirl**
314 Carroll St NW
Washington, DC 20012
202-609-7177
info@thesoupergirl.com
thesoupergirl.com
Vegan soups, salads, sandwiches, hummus, rolls and muffins, cookies and rice puddings.
Co-Founder: Sara Polon
Co-Founder: Marilyn Polon
Chief Operating Officer: Leslie Neviaser
Farmer: Georgia O'Neal
Estimated Sales: $3.6 Million
Number Employees: 41
Type of Packaging: Food Service
Brands:
Soupergirl

11823 **Source Food Technology**
2530 Meridian Parkway
#200
Durham, NC 27713
919-806-4545
Fax: 919-806-4842 866-277-3849
Cholesterol-free shortenings, fats and oils; also, cholesterol reduced egg and dairy products
CEO: Henry Cardello
VP Sales: Patrick Halliday
Estimated Sales: B
Number Employees: 5-9

11824 **Source Naturals**
23 Janis Way
Scotts Valley, CA 95066
831-438-1144
800-815-2333
www.sourcenaturals.com
Dietary supplements
President, CEO & Owner: Ira Goldberg
irag@thresholdent.com
Year Founded: 1982
Estimated Sales: $52.9 Million
Number Employees: 500-999
Square Footage: 100000
Parent Co: Threshold Enterprises
Brands:
Source

11825 **Souris Valley Processors**
641 Govt Road Allowance
Melita, MB R0M 1L0
Canada
204-522-8210
Fax: 204-522-8210
Beef and pork
President: Larry Danyluk
Estimated Sales: $1-2.5 Million
Number Employees: 5-9
Square Footage: 16000
Type of Packaging: Consumer, Food Service

11826 **South Beach Coffee Company**
PO Box 403003
Miami Beach, FL 33140
305-576-9696
Fax: 305-532-0409 info@discoverourtown.com
Coffee for wholesale and retail customers
President: Hagai Gringarten
Vice President: Droma Gringarten
Marketing Director: Karen Kong
Operations Manager: Ruben Meoqui
Estimated Sales: $1-5 Million
Number Employees: 13
Type of Packaging: Consumer, Private Label
Brands:
Lincoln Road Blend
Ocean Drive Blend
Ocean Road Blend

11827 **South Beach Novelties & Confectionery**
44 Robin Rd
Staten Island, NY 10305-4799
718-727-4500
Fax: 718-448-4108
Tobacco, tobacco products and confectionary.
Owner: John Lagana
Estimated Sales: $18 Million
Number Employees: 11
Square Footage: 6000

11828 **South Bend Chocolate Co**
3300 W Sample St
Suite 110
South Bend, IN 46619-3077
574-233-2577
Fax: 574-233-3150 800-301-4961
orders@sbchocolate.com www.sbchocolate.com
Distinctive chocolates, dried fruits, cherry treats, fudges, sugar free, creams, crunches, chocolates by the pound, gold boxes and gift baskets
Owner: Mark Tarner
orders@sbchocolate.com
Marketing Director: Kristina Pier
Year Founded: 1991
Estimated Sales: $20-50 Million
Number Employees: 100-249
Brands:
South Bend Chocolate

11829 **South Ceasar Dressing Company**
PO Box 612
Novato, CA 94948-0612
415-897-0605
Fax: 415-897-0605
Salad dressing
Partner: Shirley Lesley
Partner: Mark Lesley
Estimated Sales: Under $500,000
Number Employees: 1-4
Type of Packaging: Private Label
Brands:
South Ceasar Dressing Company

11830 **South County Creamery**
955 S. Main Street
Great Barrington, MA 01230
413-528-8400
Fax: 413-528-8402 socoreamery.com
Ice cream, sorbet and gelato
Co-Owner: Danny Mazursky
Estimated Sales: $300,000-500,000
Number Employees: 5-9
Brands:
Berkshire Ice Cream

11831 **South Georgia Pecan Co**
309 S Lee St
PO Box 5366
Valdosta, GA 31601-5723
229-244-1321
Fax: 229-247-6361 800-627-6630
info@georgiapecan.com www.georgiapecan.com
Esatblished in 1913. Manufacturer and exporter of shelled pecans and almonds.
Co-Owner: Jim Worn
Co-Owner: Ed Crane
Estimated Sales: $20-50 Million
Number Employees: 100-249
Type of Packaging: Consumer
Brands:
Dasher Pecan

11832 **(HQ)South Mill**
649 West South Street
Kennett Square, PA 19348
610-444-4800
Fax: 610-444-1338 info@southmill.com
www.southmill.com
National mushroom supplier.
Contact: Iris Ayala
iayala@southmill.com
Year Founded: 1978
Number Employees: 1,000
Type of Packaging: Consumer, Food Service, Private Label, Bulk
Other Locations:
Distribution
Atlanta GA
Distribution
New Orleans LA
Distribution
Houston TX
Distribution
Dallas TX
Brands:
Brown King
South Mill Mushroom Sales

11833 **South Shores Seafood**
1822 E Ball Rd
Anaheim, CA 92805-5936
714-956-2722
Fax: 714-956-0277
Seafood
President: Michael Armstrong
Estimated Sales: $2,000,000
Number Employees: 5-9

11834 **South Texas Spice Co LTD**
2106 Castroville Rd
San Antonio, TX 78237-3516
210-436-2280
Fax: 210-436-6658
Spices
President: Ida Faenz
Estimated Sales: $390,000
Number Employees: 5-9
Brands:
Menchaca
South Texas Spice
Yellow Rose

11835 **South Valley Farms**
15443 Beech Ave
Wasco, CA 93280-7604
661-391-9000
Fax: 661-391-9012 www.southvalleyfarms.com
Grower and exporter of almonds and pistachios; processor of hulled and shelled almonds
Vice President: Benjamin Barnes
ben.y.barnes@gmail.com
VP: Daryl Wilkendors
Processing Manager: Jonathan Meyer

Estimated Sales: $2.5-5 Million
Number Employees: 100-249
Square Footage: 320000
Parent Co: Farm Management Company
Type of Packaging: Bulk

11836 Southeast Dairy Processors Inc
3808 E Columbus Dr
Tampa, FL 33605-3221
813-620-1516
Fax: 813-626-1516
www.southeastdairyprocessors.com
Milk and dairy products
President: William Tiller
Estimated Sales: $5-10 Million
Number Employees: 5-9
Type of Packaging: Private Label

11837 Southeastern Fisheries Assn
1118 Thomasville Rd # B
Tallahassee, FL 32303-6238
850-224-0612
Fax: 850-222-3663 bobfish@aol.com
www.sfaonline.org
Hot sauces, fisheries
Executive Director: Robert P Jones
Chairman: Dennis Henderson
Executive Director: Robert Jones
Number Employees: 1-4

11838 Southeastern Grocers
8928 Prominence Parkway
Suite 200
Jacksonville, FL 32256
904-783-5000
800-967-9105
www.segrocers.com
Supermarket portfolio.
President/CEO: Anthony Hucker
Estimated Sales: $1.5 Billion
Number Employees: 45,000
Number of Brands: 4
Type of Packaging: Consumer, Food Service, Private Label
Brands:
Bi-Lo
Fresco y Mas
Harveys Supermarket
Winn-Dixie

11839 Southeastern Mills Inc
100 E 1st Ave
Rome, GA 30161
800-334-4468
www.semillsfoods.com
Flour, corn meal & grits, sauce & gravy mixes, specialty baking mixes, batters & breadings, seasonings & marinades.
Chief Executive Officer: Vernon Grizzard
vgrizzard@semills.com
Chief Financial Officer: Peter Hjort
VP, Business Development: George Manak
Director, Purchasing: Chris Wheeler
Year Founded: 1941
Estimated Sales: $37.5 Million
Number Employees: 100-249
Square Footage: 300000
Type of Packaging: Consumer, Food Service, Private Label, Bulk
Brands:
Four Roses
Good Loaf
Southeastern Mills
Stivers Best
Strong Boy

11840 Southern Art Company, LLC
PO Box 500398
Atlanta, GA 31150
800-257-6606
info@southernartco.com
www.southernartco.com
Manufacturer of dressings and sauces.
Founder: Kelly Woo

11841 Southern Baking
49 Batesville Ct
Greer, SC 29650-4800
864-627-1380
Fax: 864-627-1381 www.southern-baking.com
Bread
President: Mario Romano
Estimated Sales: $500,000-$1,000,000
Number Employees: 10-19

11842 Southern Bar-B-Que
PO Box 206
Jennings, LA 70546
337-824-3877
Fax: 337-824-6678 866-612-2586
Bbq sauce, basting sauce, crawfish, shrimp and crab boil, frying oil, grill-n-que rub, grill-n-que sauce, pepper sauce, roux, salsa, seasoning and spray basters
Contact: Mary Kojis
mkojis@southernco.com

11843 Southern Belle SandwichCompany
1969 N Lobdell Blvd
Baton Rouge, LA 70806
225-927-4670
Fax: 225-928-5661 800-344-4670
www.southernbellesandwich.com
Fresh sandwiches
President: Lloyd Bearden Jr
lbearden@southernbellesandwich.com
VP: Homer Miller
Sales Manager: Rick Bearden
Estimated Sales: $5-10 Million
Number Employees: 100-249
Square Footage: 40000
Parent Co: Bearden Sandwich Company
Type of Packaging: Consumer

11844 Southern Beverage Packers Inc
6341 Natures Way
Appling, GA 30802-5541
706-541-9222
Fax: 706-541-1730 800-326-2469
www.southernbev.com
Water and marketer of crystalline soft drink and fruit drinks
President: David Byrd
dbyrd@southernbev.com
Vice President: Stephen Byrd
Marketing Director: Jeff Millick
Production Manager: Lynn Hebbard
Plant Manager/Purchasing: Richard Maddox
Estimated Sales: $7 Million
Number Employees: 20-49
Number of Brands: 2
Number of Products: 50
Type of Packaging: Consumer, Bulk
Brands:
Carolina Choice
Flowing Wells
Flowing Wells Natural Water
Kist
Spingtime
Springtime Natural Artesian Water

11845 Southern Brown Rice
8553 Raybourn Rd
Weiner, AR 72479
870-684-2354
Fax: 870-684-2239 800-421-7423
Organically grown rice bran and flour; also, long, medium and short grain rice including basmati, brown, wild and wild blend
Manager: Bill Weeks
office@hoguefarms.com
Estimated Sales: $740000
Number Employees: 20-49
Square Footage: 56000

11846 Southern California Brewing Company
216 South Alameda Street
Los Angeles, CA
213-622-1261
Fax: 310-516-7989 www.angelcitybrewing.com
Seasonal beer, ale, stout, lager and pilsner
President/CEO: Michael Bowe
Vice President: Ray Mathys
Estimated Sales: $550,000
Number Employees: 3
Type of Packaging: Consumer, Food Service
Brands:
Bear Country Bavarian
Bock
California Light Blonde
Old Red Eye
Winter Wonder

11847 Southern Cotton Oil Co
2782 Chelsea Ave
Memphis, TN 38108-1705
901-452-3151
Fax: 901-452-8968 www.adm.com
Cottonseed oil mill
Contact: Gary Coleman
g_coleman@admworld.com
Number Employees: 100-249
Parent Co: Archer Daniels Midland Company
Type of Packaging: Bulk

11848 Southern Culture Foods
6400 Atlantic Blvd
Suite 135
Peachtree Corners, GA 30071
ebarrett@southernculturefoods.com
www.southernculturefoods.com
Pancake and waffle mix in flavors including banana pudding, birthday cake, gingerbread, lemon blueberry, red velvet, strawberry, sweet potato, vanilla, and bourbon salted pecan; Also stone ground grits, cornbread mix, fried chickenmix, and bacon rub
Founder & CEO: Erica Barrett
Year Founded: 2011

11849 Southern Delight Gourmet Foods
1621 Scottsville Rd
Bowling Green, KY 42104
270-782-9943
Fax: 270-843-7544 866-782-9943
Gourmet sauces, gourmet marinades, gourmet salsas, gourmet seasonings, gourmet gift sets
Owner: Bart Anderson
Estimated Sales: $3-5 Million
Number Employees: 1-4
Type of Packaging: Consumer

11850 Southern Farms Fish Processors
103 W 26th Avenue
Kansas City, MO 64116-3060
870-355-2594
Fax: 870-355-4024 800-264-2594
Frozen catfish fillets, nuggets, strips, tidbits and breaded
President: John Gentry
Type of Packaging: Consumer, Food Service
Brands:
Springwater Farms

11851 Southern Fish & Oyster Company
1 Eslava St
Mobile, AL 36603
251-438-2408
Fax: 251-432-7773
Seafood, oysters
Owner: Ralph Atkins
Estimated Sales: $1-3 Million
Number Employees: 10-19

11852 (HQ)Southern Flavoring Co
1330 Norfolk Ave
Bedford, VA 24523-2223
540-586-8565
Fax: 540-586-8568 800-765-8565
service@southernflavoring.com
www.southernflavoring.com
Liquid food flavorings
Owner: Thomas Thornton
tthornton@southernflavoring.com
Vice President: John Messier
VP Marketing: John Messier
Estimated Sales: $5 Million
Number Employees: 10-19
Square Footage: 140000
Parent Co: Southern Flavoring
Type of Packaging: Consumer, Private Label, Bulk
Brands:
Clapier Mill
Happy Home
Road Kill BBQ
Aunt Erma's Frugal Foods

11853 Southern Gardens Citrus
1820 County Road 833
Clewiston, FL 33440-9222
863-983-3030
Fax: 863-983-3060 www.ussugar.com
Citrus juices, concentrates, blends and ingredients
President: Robert Baker Jr
Finance Executive: Ginny Pena
VP Marketing: Charles Lucas
Contact: Dan Casper
dcasper@southerngardens.com
Number Employees: 100-249
Parent Co: US Sugar Corporation
Type of Packaging: Bulk

11854 **Southern Gold Honey Co**
3015 Brown Rd
Vidor, TX 77662-7902
409-768-1645
Fax: 409-768-1009 808-899-2494
Honey and specialty items including pecan cream honey and fruit flavored honeys
Owner: Gretchen Horn
Estimated Sales: Less than $500,000
Number Employees: 1-4
Type of Packaging: Consumer, Private Label
Brands:
Southern Gold Honey

11855 **Southern Heritage Coffee Company**
6555 E 30th St Ste F
Indianapolis, IN 46219
Fax: 317-543-0757 800-486-1198
kevin@heritage-coffee.com
www.coppermooncoffee.com
Processor, importer, exporter and contract roaster of coffee including house blends and gourmet, liquid concentrate, espresso, instant cappuccino, pads, hotel in-room filter packed coffees
Manager: Doug Bachman
CEO: Kevin Daw
Sales Director: Kevin Daw
Contact: Christophe Burt
cgutwein@coppermooncoffee.com
Operations Manager: Dick Middleton
Purchasing Manager: Tom Oldridge
Number Employees: 20-49
Square Footage: 208000
Type of Packaging: Consumer, Food Service, Private Label, Bulk
Brands:
Coffee Scapes
Espresso Caruso
Espresso Maria
Heritage Espresso Pods
Heritage Select
Mugshots
Sorengeti Coffees
Safari Blend Liquid Coffee
Santa's Favorite
Select Blend In-Room Coffee
Southern Heritage
World Coffee Safari Gourmet

11856 **Southern Ice Cream Specialties**
1058 King Industrial Dr
Marietta, GA 30062
770-428-0452
Fax: 770-426-5441
Ice cream novelties
Manager: Craig McDufie
Contact: William Boehm
wboehm@southernice.com
Plant Manager: Kevin Vondusaar
Number Employees: 100-249
Parent Co: Kroger Company
Type of Packaging: Consumer, Private Label
Brands:
Healthy Indulgence
Texas Gold

11857 **Southern Minnesota BeetSugar Cooperative**
83550 County Road 21
Renville, MN 56284
320-329-8305
Fax: 320-329-3252 info@smbsc.com
www.smbsc.com
Molasses, refined sugar, liquid sugar, granulated sugar, fruit sugar, liquid sucrose, baker's sugar.
President/CEO: Kelvin Thompsen
Chairman: Mark Arnold
Agricultural Research: Mark Bredehoeft
Year Founded: 1974
Estimated Sales: $474 Million
Number Employees: 850
Square Footage: 140000
Type of Packaging: Consumer, Bulk

11858 **Southern Okie**
PO Box 30261
Edmond, OK 73003-0005
405-657-7765
gina@southernokie.com
www.southernokie.com
Manufacturer of fruit spreads.
Founder and President: Gina Hollingsworth

11859 **Southern Packing Corp**
4004 Battlefield Blvd S
Chesapeake, VA 23322-2431
757-421-2131
Fax: 757-421-3633 sopaco@verizon.net
www.southernpacking.com
Processor and packer of beef, pork and veal
President/Senior Executive: Hyman Brooke
Secretary: Ronald Brooke
Treasurer: L.H. Brooke
Vice President/General Manager: B.B. Brooke
Estimated Sales: $4.1 Million
Number Employees: 20-49
Square Footage: 61200
Type of Packaging: Consumer, Food Service, Bulk
Brands:
Cavalier

11860 **Southern Peanut Co Inc**
7329 Albert St
Dublin, NC 28332
910-862-2136
Fax: 910-862-8076 800-330-3141
www.peanutprocessors.com
Peanuts including in shell, raw shelled, blanched redskins, peanut granules, oil & dry roasted peanuts and peanut butter
President: Nile Brisson
nbrisson@peanutprocessors.com
Plant Manager: Luke Clearman
Estimated Sales: $12 Million
Number Employees: 5-9
Square Footage: 540000
Parent Co: Peanut Processors
Type of Packaging: Consumer, Food Service, Bulk

11861 **Southern Popcorn Company**
3157 Norbrook Drive
Memphis, TN 38118-6608
901-362-5238
Fax: 901-888-0230
Popcorn, jellies, dessert toppings
President: Murrey Watkins
Estimated Sales: $5-10 Million
Number Employees: 10-19

11862 **Southern Pride Catfish Company**
2025 1st Ave Ste 900
Seattle, WA 98121
Fax: 334-624-8224 800-343-8046
Processor and exporter of farm-raised catfish
President: Joe Glover
Quality Control: Alice Moore
VP Sales: Randy Rhodes
Public Relations: Mary Hand
Operations Manager: Bobby Collins
Number Employees: 500-999
Type of Packaging: Consumer, Food Service, Private Label
Brands:
Southern Pride

11863 **Southern Roasted Nuts**
PO Box 508
Fitzgerald, GA 31750-0508
912-423-5616
Fax: 912-423-6550
Roasted nuts
President: Allen Conger
Estimated Sales: $10-24.9 000,000
Number Employees: 40

11864 **Southern Season**
201 S Estes Dr # 300
University Place
Chapel Hill, NC 27514-6118
919-929-7133
Fax: 919-942-9274 877-929-7133
customerservice@southernseason.com
www.southernseason.com
Chocolates, preserves, relishes, hams, cookware
President: Dave Herman
dherman@southernseason.com
VP Public Relations: Jay White
Year Founded: 1975
Estimated Sales: $25 Million
Number Employees: 250-499
Square Footage: 59000
Other Locations:
A Southern Season
Hillsborough NC
Brands:
A Southern Season
Alaska Smoked Salmon
Ashby's
Barbera Frantioia
California Harvest
Carolina Cupboard
Crook's
Frescobaldi Laudemio
Godiva
Johnston County Hams
Lindt
McEvoy Ranch
My Grandma's of New England
Nunez De Prado
Sparrow Lane
Terre D'Olivier

11865 **Southern Shell Fish Company**
501 Destrehan Avenue
Harvey, LA 70058-2737
504-341-5631
Fax: 504-341-5635
Processor, canner and exporter of crabmeat, oysters and shrimp
Manager: Dennis Skrmetta
Sales Manager: H Burke Jr
Plant Manager: Golden Boutte
Estimated Sales: $1,400,000
Number Employees: 1-4
Parent Co: Deepsouth Packing Company
Type of Packaging: Consumer, Food Service, Private Label
Brands:
Blue Plate
Dunbar
Gulf Kist
House of Windsor
Pride New Orleans

11866 **Southern Shellfish**
120 Johnny Mercer Boulevard
Savannah, GA 31410-2142
912-897-3650
Fax: 912-897-6036
Seafood, shellfish

11867 **Southern Snow**
103 W W St
Belle Chasse, LA 70037-1111
504-393-8967
Fax: 504-393-0112
Manufacturer and exporter of artificial concentrates including colors and flavors; also, ice block shavers
Owner: Milton Wendling
info@flavorsnow.com
Marketing: Danielle Havnen
Estimated Sales: $1500000
Number Employees: 20-49
Square Footage: 40000
Brands:
Southern Snow

11868 **Southern Style Nuts**
114 N Houston Ave
Denison, TX 75021-3013
903-463-3161
info@squirrelbrand.com
Roasted and blended nuts including snack mixes, hot and honey roasted peanuts, confectionery pecans and almonds and sweet and salty cashews
President: Michael Kurilecz
VP: Virgil Williamson
Estimated Sales: $54,000
Number Employees: 2
Type of Packaging: Consumer, Food Service, Private Label, Bulk
Brands:
Roann's Confections
Southern Style Nuts
Squirrel Brand

11869 **Southern Twist Cocktail**
PO Box 23
Folly Beach, SC 29439-0023
843-343-9577
info@southerntwistcocktails.com
southerntwistcocktails.com
Cocktail infusions
Owner: Rochelle Jones
Brands:
Southern Twist

11870 **Southside Seafood Inc**
1930 Pittston Ave # 1
Scranton, PA 18505-4497
570-969-9726
Fax: 570-961-5181 www.southsideseafood.net
Seafood
Owner: Carl Pazzaglia
Estimated Sales: $3-5 Million
Number Employees: 5-9

11871 **Southwest Cheese Company**
1141 Curry County Road
#4
Clovis, NM 88101
575-742-9200
bcochie@southwestcheese.com
www.southwestcheese.com
Cheese
Vice President, Sales: Dave Snyder
Cheese Sales Manager: Becky Pearson
Human Resources Director: Leah Jackson

11872 **Southwest Foods**
13157 US Highway 271
Tyler, TX 75708-2453
903-877-6800
Fax: 903-877-6903 888-937-3776
dennisprice@brookshires.com
www.brookshires.com
Baked goods
Manager: Sheila Vickery
Number Employees: 250-499
Brands:
South West

11873 **Southwest Specialty Food**
700 N Bullard Ave
Goodyear, AZ 85338-2506
623-931-3131
Fax: 623-931-9931 800-536-3131
southwest@asskickin.com www.asskickin.com
Makers of gourmet hot sauce and other fine products such as hot sauces, salsas, snacks, gift sets, marinades/sauces, chili mixes/spices, beverages and condiments.
Owner: Jeff Jacobs
southwest@asskickin.com
Estimated Sales: Below $5 Million
Number Employees: 10-19
Type of Packaging: Private Label
Brands:
Banditos Salsas
Candy Ass
Habanero Products From Hell
Seasonings From Hell
Spontaneous Combustion

11874 **Southwest Spirit**
701 Buford Drive
Socorro, NM 87801-4019
800-838-0773
Fax: 505-838-0177 info@swspirit.com
www.swspirit.com
Salsas
Co-Owner: Cynthia Fowler
Co-Owner: Jim Fowler
Type of Packaging: Consumer

11875 **Sovena USA Inc**
1 Olive Grove St
Rome, NY 13441-4815
315-797-7070
Fax: 315-797-6981
customerservice@sovenausa.com
www.sovenagroup.com
Domestic edible oils including olive, corn, soybean, peanut and salad; importer of olive oil
CEO: Steve Mandia
CFO: Dave Lofgren
VP: Bert Mandia
VP Sales/Marketing: Mark Mottit
Manager: Luis Gato
l.gato@sovenagroup.com
Estimated Sales: $12.7 Million
Number Employees: 1-4
Square Footage: 45000
Brands:
Clio Pomace
Clio Pure
Gem 100%
Gem Blended
Gem Extra

11876 **Sow's Ear Winery**
303 Coastal Rd
Brooksville, ME 04617-3705
207-326-4649
www.uniquemainefarms.com
Wines
Owner: Tom Hoey
Estimated Sales: Less Than $500,000
Number Employees: 1-4

11877 **Sowden Brothers Farm**
8888 Township Road
Live Oak, CA 95953
530-695-3750
Fax: 530-695-1395 www.organicprunes.com
Prune concentrate and dried prunes including Ashlock pitted and whole
President: Richard Taylor
VP: John Taylor
Estimated Sales: $20-50 Million
Number Employees: 50
Square Footage: 25000
Type of Packaging: Food Service, Private Label, Bulk
Brands:
Cal Gold
California Gold
Taylor Brothers Farms

11878 **Soy Vay Enterprises**
6223 Highway 9
Felton, CA 95018
831-335-3824
Fax: 831-335-3589 800-444-6369
support@soyvay.com www.soyvay.com
Teriyaki, salad dressing and marinade, hoisin and garlic-based sauce
President/Owner: Eddy Scher
Estimated Sales: $1-3 Million
Number Employees: 1-4
Type of Packaging: Consumer, Food Service, Private Label
Brands:
Cha-Cha Chinese Chicken Dressing
Chinese Marinade
Island Teriyaki
Soy Vay Veri-Veri Teriyaki

11879 **SoyLife Division**
3300 Edinborough Way # 712
Edina, MN 55435-5963
952-920-7700
Fax: 952-920-7704 www.soylife.com
Soy isoflavone, nutraceutical ingredients
President: Laurent Leduc
Chief Executive Officer: Ori Yehudai
Estimated Sales: Less than $500,000
Number Employees: 5-9

11880 **SoyTex**
609 Eagle Rock Ave
West Orange, NJ 07052-2903
973-243-1899
Fax: 973-243-0800 888-769-8391
soytex.com
Meat substitution products made from high quality soy protein concentrate using modern extrusion technology.
President: Joseph Nazarian
VP: Tirdad Zandieh

11881 **Soyfoods of America**
1050 17th Street NW
Washington, DC 20036
202-659-3520
Fax: 202-659-3522 www.soyfoods.org
Soy milk and yuba; also, regular and marinated tofu, cultured soy beverage, bulk soymilk
President/Owner: Kanin Lee
Estimated Sales: $3 Million
Number Employees: 27
Square Footage: 60000
Type of Packaging: Consumer, Food Service, Private Label, Bulk
Brands:
Furama
Soywise

11882 **Soylent**
555 Mateo St
Suite 227
Los Angeles, CA 90013
info@soylent.com
www.soylent.com
Meal replacement drinks and powders
CEO: Bryan Crowley
CFO: Demir Vangelov
VP Product Development & Innovation: Julie Daoust
VP Brand Marketing: Andrew Thomas
SVP Sales: Melody Conner
Year Founded: 2013
Number Employees: 50-99
Parent Co: Rosa Foods Inc.

11883 **Soylent Brand**
PO Box 165475
Irving, TX 75016-5475
972-255-4747
Salsa
President/CEO: Jack Veach
CFO: Fred Harper
Vice President: Morris Woodall
Research & Development: R Michael MacGregor
Quality Control: James Valikont, Jr.
Sales Director: Dana Davidson
Operations/Production: Lynne Wainman
Plant Manager: Robert Roggers
Number Employees: 10-19
Number of Brands: 1
Number of Products: 6
Square Footage: 22000
Parent Co: Solvent Interntional
Type of Packaging: Private Label
Brands:
Guacamole Salad
Salsa Picante
Tex-Mex
Verde

11884 **Soynut Butter Co**
4220 Commercial Way
Glenview, IL 60025-3597
847-635-9960
Fax: 847-635-6801
Peanut butter substitute, gluten, nut & peanut free snacks, gluten free corn crumbs.
President: Steve Grubb
s.grubb@soynutbutter.com
Number Employees: 5-9
Type of Packaging: Consumer, Food Service

11885 **(HQ)Spangler Candy Co**
400 N Portland St
PO Box 71
Bryan, OH 43506-1257
419-636-4221
Fax: 419-636-3695 888-636-4221
www.spanglercandy.com
Lollipops, candy canes and circus peanuts
President & CEO: Kirk Vashaw
Chairman: Dean Spangler
CFO: Bill Martin
VP Marketing: Jim Knight
VP Sales: Denny Gunter
VP Production: Steve Kerr
Number Employees: 500-999
Square Footage: 2000000
Other Locations:
Spangler Candy Co.
Bryan OH
Brands:
Astro Pops
Cane Classics
Dum Dum Pops
Picture Pops
Saf-T-Pops
Spangler Candy Canes
Spangler Chocolates
Spangler Circus Peanuts

11886 **Spangler Vineyards**
491 Winery Ln
Roseburg, OR 97471-9365
541-679-9654
Fax: 541-679-3888 info@spanglervineyards.com
www.spanglervineyards.com
Wine
Owner: Patrick Spangler
info@spanglervineyards.com
Co-Owner: Loree Spangler
Winemaker: Leonard Postles
Estimated Sales: Less than $500,000
Number Employees: 1-4
Type of Packaging: Private Label
Brands:
Spangler Wineyards

11887 Spanish Gardens Food Manufacturing
2301 Metropolitan Ave
Kansas City, KS 66106
913-831-4242
Taco shells, sauce, spices, tortilla chips and corn and flour tortillas
President: Norma Jean Miller
Estimated Sales: $1300000
Number Employees: 20-49
Square Footage: 160000
Type of Packaging: Consumer, Food Service, Bulk

11888 Sparboe Foods Corp
900 N Linn Ave
New Hampton, IA 50659-1204
641-394-3040
info@sparboe.com
www.sparboe.com
Fresh and frozen eggs
President: Bob Sparboe
Vice President: Beth Fechnell
Manager: Warren Miller
Estimated Sales: $20-50 Million
Number Employees: 100-249
Square Footage: 50000
Type of Packaging: Food Service, Private Label, Bulk
Brands:
Bes Tex
Except Mix

11889 Sparkletts
200 Eagles Landing Boulevard
Lakeland, FL 33810
800-728-5508
www.water.com
Bottled water for retail and businesses, as well as bottle water dispensers and break room supplies
President: David Muscato
Estimated Sales: $5200000
Number Employees: 50-99
Parent Co: DS Services of America
Type of Packaging: Consumer, Food Service
Brands:
Alhambra
Crystal Springs
Deep Rock Water
Hinckley Springs
Kentwood Springs
Mount Olympus
Sierra Springs

11890 Sparrow Lane
4110 Brew Master Dr
Ceres, CA 95307
209-538-7600
Fax: 209-538-7614 866-515-2477
sparrowlane.com
Wine and fruit vinegars
Chef: Jesse Layman

11891 Spaten North America Inc
4621 Little Neck Parkway
Little Neck, NY 11362
718-281-1912
Brewery
Number of Brands: 1
Parent Co: Spaten-Franziskaner-Brau
Brands:
Spaten

11892 Spaulding & Assoc
8700 N 2nd St # 202
Brighton, MI 48116-1296
810-229-4166
Fax: 810-227-4218
Cheese
President: Pat Spaulding
Estimated Sales: Less Than $500,000
Number Employees: 1-4

11893 SpecialTeas
2 Reynolds Street
Norwalk, CT 06855-1015
203-866-1522
Fax: 203-375-6820 888-365-6983
Gourmet tea
Managing Director: Juergen Link
Estimated Sales: $5-10 Million
Number Employees: 5-9

11894 Specialities Importers & Distributers
85 Division Avenue
PO Box 409
Millington, NJ 07946
908-647-6485
Fax: 908-647-8305 800-899-6689
www.specialitiesinc.com
Deli: cheeses, cured meats and hams.
President: Ron Schinbeckler
r.schinbeckler@specialitiesinc.com
Vice President, Sales & Marketing: Richard Kessler
Year Founded: 1991
Type of Packaging: Food Service
Brands:
Bellentani
Carpuela
Bayonne Ham
Ermitage
leBistro
Solera(c)

11895 (HQ)Specialty Bakers
450 S State Rd
Marysville, PA 17053-1009
717-957-2131
Fax: 717-957-0156 800-233-0778
CustomerService@SpecialtyBakers.com
www.specialtybakers.com
Manufacturer and exporter of sponge, snack and angel food cakes, lady fingers, dessert shells, French twirls and jelly rolls
President: John Piotrowski
CEO: Hamani Abdou
habdou@specialtybakers.com
Plant Manager: Richard Sychterz
Estimated Sales: $14 Million
Number Employees: 50-99
Square Footage: 150000
Type of Packaging: Consumer, Private Label
Other Locations:
Specialty Bakers
Marysville PA
Specialty Bakers
Lititz PA
Specialty Bakers
Dunkirk NY
Brands:
Specialty

11896 Specialty Cheese Co Inc
430 N Main St
Reeseville, WI 53579-9790
920-927-3888
Fax: 920-927-3200 800-367-1711
scci@specialcheese.com www.specialcheese.com
Cheese packaging
President: Paul Scharfman
CEO: Jacquelyn Austin
jacquelyn@specialcheese.com
Estimated Sales: $2.5-5 Million
Number Employees: 100-249
Type of Packaging: Private Label
Brands:
Hem
Lavacarica
Rich Cow

11897 Specialty Coffee Roasters
1300 SW 10th St
Suite 2
Delray Beach, FL 33444
Fax: 800-805-4422 800-253-9363
Processor, packer and importer of gourmet coffees; exporter of gourmet coffees
President: Gabriela Harvey
Estimated Sales: $300,000
Number Employees: 3
Square Footage: 20000
Parent Co: MGH Holdings Corporation
Type of Packaging: Consumer, Food Service, Private Label, Bulk
Brands:
Shalina

11898 Specialty Commodities Inc
1530 47th St N
Fargo, ND 58102-2858
701-282-8222
Fax: 701-264-5744
www.specialtycommodities.com
Manufacturer and importer of specialty ingredients for snack food, dairy, bakery, cereal, energy bar and confectionery. Products include dehydrated, dried fruit, legumes, nuts, seeds, spices and grains.
President: Ken Campbell
Vice President: Kevin Andreson
Number Employees: 10-19
Parent Co: Archer Daniels Midland Company
Type of Packaging: Private Label, Bulk
Other Locations:
Corporate Office
Fargo ND
Processing Plant
Lodi CA
Processing Plant
Stockton CA
Processing Plant
Modesto CA

11899 Specialty Food America Inc
5055 Huffman Mill Rd
Hopkinsville, KY 42240-9162
270-889-0017
888-881-1633
www.specialtyfoodamerica.com
Herbs and spices; cooking related supplies and contract packaging
Owner: Thomas L Marshall
specialtyfoodtom@gmail.com
Estimated Sales: Less Than $500,000
Number Employees: 1-4
Square Footage: 4800
Type of Packaging: Consumer, Private Label
Brands:
Lucini Honestete
Sonoma Syrups

11900 Specialty Food Association
136 Madison Ave
New York, NY 10016
646-878-0301
www.specialtyfood.com
Baby food, baked goods, baking mixes, beverages, condiments, confectionery, eggs, dairy, frozen food, meat and game, oils, snacks, seafood, soups, spreads and syrups, sauces, seasonings, grains and cereals, vegetables and fruits.
Contact: Equazia Cordero
equazia.cordero@xerox.com

11901 Specialty Food Magazine
136 Madison Ave
12th Floor
New York, NY 10016
212-482-6440
socialmedia@specialtyfood.com
www.specialtyfood.com
Food magazine
Sales Manager: Kathy Sackett
Publisher: Chris Crocker
ccrocker@specialtyfood.Com
Brands:
Specialty Food Magazine

11902 (HQ)Specialty Foods Group Inc
6 Dublin Ln
Owensboro, KY 42301
270-926-2324
800-238-0020
www.specialtyfoodsgroup.com
Spices, lunch meats, turkey, and pork products including bacon, ham, and sausage.
Year Founded: 1914
Estimated Sales: $234 Million
Number Employees: 250-499
Number of Brands: 7
Type of Packaging: Consumer, Food Service, Private Label, Bulk
Other Locations:
SFG Production Plant
Owensboro KY
SFG Production Plant
Humboldt IA
SFG Production Plant
Chicago IL
SFG Production Plant
Williamston NC
Brands:
Artisan Crafted Series
Field
Fischer's
Kentuckian Gold
Kentucky Legend
Mickelberry's
Scott Pete

11903 Specialty Foods South LLC
1023 Wappoo Rd # B37
Charleston, SC 29407-5960
843-766-2580
Fax: 843-766-2580 800-538-0003
Orders@foodforthesouthernsoul.com
www.foodforthesouthernsoul.com

Gourmet foods
Owner: James Hagood
jimmyhagood@foodforthesouthernsoul.com
Estimated Sales: Under $500,000
Number Employees: 5-9
Type of Packaging: Private Label, Bulk

11904 Specialty Ingredients
1130 W. Lake Cook Road
Suite 320
Buffalo Grove, IL 60089
847-419-9595
Fax: 847-419-9547 sales@ingredientsinc.com
www.ingredientsinc.com
Dehydrated/whole/starch potato products, soy based ingredients, dairy ingredients, food acids and salts, and frozen & dehydrated vegetables.
Chief Executive Officer, Owner: Debbie Stew
Sales: Jim Stewart

11905 Specialty Meats & Gourmet
1810 Webster St # 8
Hudson, WI 54016-9318
715-377-0734
Fax: 715-386-6613 800-310-2360
Marketer and processor of fresh and frozen farm raised game meat from alligator to yak; gourmet items, corporate gift boxes, etc.
Principal: Kent Phillips
Contact: Linda Janse
ljanse@smgfoods.com
Estimated Sales: Under $500,000
Number Employees: 1-4
Square Footage: 8000
Parent Co. Venison America
Type of Packaging: Consumer, Food Service

11906 Specialty Minerals Inc
35 Highland Ave
Bethlehem, PA 18017-9482
610-861-3496
Fax: 610-882-8726 800-801-1031
www.mineralstech.com
Manufacturer, sellers and exporters of food and pharmaceutical grades of precipitated calcium carbonate, ground limestone and talc
Chairman/CEO: Jospeh Muscari
CFO: Douglas Dietrich
Director: Gary Castagna
Sales: Jay Esty
Commercial Manager: Jay Esty
Number Employees: 50-99
Parent Co: Minerals Technologies Inc
Type of Packaging: Private Label
Other Locations:
SMI Mineral Plant
Adams MA
SMI Mineral Plant
Canann CT
SMI Mineral Plant
Barretts MT
SMI Mineral Plant
Lucerne Valley CA
Brands:
Albaglos
Jetcoat
Opacarb
Pcc

11907 Specialty Products
128 Rogers Street
Gloucester, MA 01930
216-362-1050
Fax: 216-362-6506 800-222-6846
luis.granja@gortons.com www.gortons.com
Processor and exporter of breading batter
Manager: Luis Granja
Controller: Sue Spisak
Plant Manager: Luis Granja
Estimated Sales: $10-20 Million
Number Employees: 20-49
Parent Co: Gorton's
Type of Packaging: Food Service, Private Label, Bulk

11908 Specialty Rice Inc
1000 W 1st St
Brinkley, AR 72021-9000
870-734-1235
Fax: 870-734-1237 800-467-1233
info@dellarice.com www.delroserice.com
Processor, miller and exporter of five types of rice
Manager: Ojus Ajmara
Manager: Glenda Hilsdon
glendah@dellarice.com
General Manager: Glenda Hilsdon
Estimated Sales: $800,000
Number Employees: 10-19
Square Footage: 32000
Brands:
Della
Della Gourmet Rice
Gourmet Basmati Rice
Jasmine

11909 Speco Inc
3946 Willow St
Schiller Park, IL 60176-2311
847-678-4240
Fax: 847-678-8037 800-541-5415
sales@speco.com www.speco.com
Manufacturer and exporter of meat cutting equipment including meat and mincer knives and bone collector systems
Vice President: Clarence Hoffman
clarence@speco.com
Office Manager: Sue Ryan
Sales Manager: Steve Jacob
Production Manager: Clarence Hoffman
Maintenance Supervisor: Ron Schulmeister
Estimated Sales: $7 Million
Number Employees: 50-99
Square Footage: 100000
Brands:
Superior
Triumph

11910 Spectrum Foods Inc
2520 South Grand Ave E
P.O. Box 3483
Springfield, IL 62703-5613
217-528-5301
Fax: 217-391-0096 lmyers@spectrum-foods.com
www.spectrum-foods.com
Offers natural and organic vegetable oil, organic soy products, and low sodium sea salt.
President: Rob Kirby
Chairman: Al Maiocco
VP Sales & Business Development: Lynn Myers
Manager: Karen Adamo
kglitter-adamo@spectrum-foods.com
Number Employees: 20-49
Type of Packaging: Bulk
Brands:
NEXCEL
NEXSOY

11911 Spelt Right Foods, LLC
961 Elton St.
Brooklyn, NY 11208
877-773-5801
Fax: 718-240-9041 info@speltright.com
www.speltright.com
Manufacturer of breads, doughs, and frozen baked goods made with spelt flour.
Co-Founder: Beth George
Co-Founder: Tim George
Contact: Menachem Delevkovitz
info@speltright.com

11912 Spence & Company
78 Campanelli Industrial drive
Brockton, MA 02301
508-427-5577
Fax: 508-427-5557 salmon@spenceltd.com
www.spenceltd.com
Smoked fish; importer of fish ingredients
President: Alan Spence
Estimated Sales: $4500000
Number Employees: 25
Type of Packaging: Consumer, Food Service

11913 Spencer Packing Company
PO Box 753
Washington, NC 27889-0753
252-946-4161
Fax: 252-946-4162
Processor and packer of pork
President: Harold Spencer
Estimated Sales: $1,250,000
Number Employees: 10-19

11914 Sperry Apiaries
15750 Highway 46
Kindred, ND 58051
701-428-3000
Honey
President: Mark Sperry
Estimated Sales: Under $500,000
Number Employees: 1-4
Number of Brands: 1
Number of Products: 1

11915 Spice & Spice
655 Deep Valley Drive
Ste 125
Rolling Hills Estates, CA 90274
310-265-2914
Fax: 310-265-2934 866-729-7742
info@spicenspice.com www.spicenspice.com
Bulk line of whole and ground spice products: black pepper, white pepper, cumin, cinnamon, crush chili, cinnamon stick, chili powder, granulated garlic, dry chili pods
Owner: Anthony Dirocco
CEO: Mukesh Thakker
R & D: Nitul Unekekett
Quality Control: Nina Lukamanje
Contact: Cindy Philips
cindy@calwind.com
Estimated Sales: $5-10 Million
Number Employees: 1-4
Number of Brands: 1
Number of Products: 25
Square Footage: 200000
Type of Packaging: Food Service, Bulk
Brands:
Boat Brand

11916 Spice Chain
6c Terminal Way
Avenel, NJ 07001-2228
732-499-9070
Fax: 732-499-9139
Spices including basil, bay leaves, garlic, oregano, paprika, pepper, etc
President: Andrew Barna
andrew.barna@spice-co.com
VP: James Peterkin
Estimated Sales: $11 Million
Number Employees: 50-99
Type of Packaging: Consumer, Food Service, Private Label, Bulk
Brands:
Pride of Malabar
Pride of Shandung
Pride of Szeged

11917 Spice Galleon
281 Commerce Street
Belgium, WI 53004-9408
262-285-4800
Fax: 262-285-4820 877-668-4800
Gourmet seasonings
President: Rick Boum
Estimated Sales: $1 Million
Number Employees: 25
Number of Brands: 5
Number of Products: 100
Square Footage: 40000
Type of Packaging: Consumer, Food Service, Private Label, Bulk

11918 Spice House International Specialties
47 Bloomingdale Road
Hicksville, NY 11801-1512
516-942-7248
Fax: 516-942-7249 www.spicehouseint.com
Spices and blends, specialty foods, hot sauces, dried fruits and nuts; serving the food service market from around the world
President: Anthony Provetto
Estimated Sales: $5-10 Million
Number Employees: 5-9
Square Footage: 18400
Type of Packaging: Consumer, Food Service, Private Label, Bulk

11919 **Spice Hunter Inc**
2000 W Broad St
Richmond, VA 23220-2006
804-359-5786
Fax: 805-544-9046 800-444-3061
www.spicehunter.com
Dried bean soups, entree seasonings, dips, salad seasonings, Asian soups, spices and drink mixes
President/CEO: Conrad Sauer
President: Lucia Cleveland
CFO: William Ulick
HR Executive: Karen Woodling
kwoodling@spicehunter.com
Estimated Sales: $17 Million
Number Employees: 50-99
Number of Products: 200
Square Footage: 226000
Parent Co: C.F. Sauer Company
Type of Packaging: Private Label, Bulk
Brands:
Oriental Noodle Soup
Quick & Natural Soup
Quick Pot Pasta
Savory Smoke
Simmer Kettle
Spice Hunter
Spice Hunter Spices & Herbs

11920 **Spice King Corporation**
438 El Camino Dr
Beverly Hills, CA 90212
310-836-7770
Fax: 310-836-6454
Processor, importer and exporter of custom formulated natural spices and seasonings; also, dehydrated vegetables and fruits
General Manager: James Stephens
VP: A Stern
Marketing Director: Anne Stern
Number Employees: 20-49
Square Footage: 100000

11921 **Spice Lab**
4000 N. Dixie Highway
Pompano Beach, FL 33064
954-275-4478
brett@thespicelab.com
www.thespicelab.com
Sea salts

11922 **Spice O' Life**
PO Box 70406
Seattle, WA 98127-0406
206-789-4195
Fax: 206-782-9339 www.spiceolife.com
Custom blended spices
Owner: Scotty McDonell
Account Manager: Judith Jager
Advertising Manager: David Barker
Number Employees: 1-4

11923 **Spice Of Life Co**
15445 Ventura Blvd # 115
Suite 115
Sherman Oaks, CA 91403-3005
818-909-0052
info@spice-of-life.com
www.spice-of-life.com
Meatless meats and jerky
Co-Founder: Spice Williams-Crosby
Contact: Crosby Gregory
spiceoflife@earthlink.net
Number Employees: 1-4

11924 **Spice Rack Chocolates**
10908 Courthouse Rd
Suite 102 #264
Fredericksburg, VA 22408
540-847-2063
Fax: 416-757-5183
Dark chocolates infused with hers and spices
President/Owner: Mary Schellhammer
CFO: Paul Schellhammer

11925 **Spice Time Foods**
940 Monroe Street
Hoboken, NJ 07030-6429
201-792-1200
Fax: 201-792-9796
Spices
President: John Stapleton
Director Manufacturing: John Hybner
Plant Manager: Jim Maurice
Parent Co: Gambrinus Company

11926 **Spice World Inc**
8101 Presidents Dr
Orlando, FL 32809
sworld@spiceworldinc.com
www.spiceworldinc.com
Processor and exporter of garlic, custom seasoning blends and garlic including minced, chopped and packed in olive oil or water
Year Founded: 1949
Estimated Sales: $5-10 Million
Number Employees: 100-249
Number of Brands: 1
Square Footage: 480000
Type of Packaging: Consumer, Food Service, Private Label, Bulk
Brands:
Spice World

11927 **Spiceland**
6604 W Irving Park Rd
Chicago, IL 60634-2435
773-736-1000
800-352-8671
Spices
Co-Owner: Doris Stockwell
Co-Owner: Jim Stockwell
Estimated Sales: Less than $500,000
Number Employees: 5-9
Brands:
Spiceland

11928 **Spicely**
4180 Business Center Dr.
Fremont, CA 94538
510-440-1044
Fax: 510-440-1008 customerservice@spicely.com
www.spicely.com
Organic and natural foods; planet friendly packaging; encourage certified fair trade.
Contact: Clara Bonner
clara@spicely.com
Parent Co: American Natural & Organic Spices
Type of Packaging: Consumer

11929 **(HQ)Spices of Life Gourmet Coffee**
4135 Dr Mlk Blvd
Fort Myers, FL 33916
239-334-8004
Fax: 941-549-9041
Coffee
Owner: Cheryl Dejonghe
Vice President: Edward Miller
Estimated Sales: $300,000-500,000
Number Employees: 1-4

11930 **(HQ)Spicetec Flavors & Seasonings**
11 Conagra Drive
Omaha, NE 68102-5003
402-595-4000
Fax: 402-595-4707 800-921-7502
www.conagrafoods.com
Savory flavors, seasonings, food bases, advanced flavoring systems
Vice President/General Manager: Amy Patterson
Senior Director, R&D: Joanne Ferrara
Senior Quality Specialist: Lachelle Petty
Director of Operations: Paul Werner
Estimated Sales: $20-49.9 Million
Number Employees: 295
Number of Brands: 1
Number of Products: 3000
Square Footage: 104000
Parent Co: Givaudan
Type of Packaging: Bulk
Other Locations:
Seasoning Blends Plant
Carol Stream IL
Seasoning/Culinary Bases Plant
Cranbury NJ
Brands:
Spicetec

11931 **Spicy Sense**
58 Jacobus Ave
Kearny, NJ 07032
718-790-0070
Coconut water
CEO: Sam Chawla

11932 **Spiech Farms Fruit & Floral**
61675 M 40
Paw Paw, MI 49079-9210
269-657-1980
Fax: 269-657-5023 www.spiechfarms.com
Concord grapes
President: Daniel Martinez
dmartinez@spiechfarms.com
Estimated Sales: $1 Million
Number Employees: 250-499
Square Footage: 36000

11933 **Spike Seasoning Magic**
6425 W Executive Dr
Mequon, WI 53092
262-242-2400
ModernFearn@aol.com
www.spike-it-up.com
Blended spices and seasonings.
Founder: Gayelord Hauser
Chairman/CEO: Anthony Palermo
Secretary: Petronella Palermo
Quality Assurance Manager: Jim Kohnke
Number Employees: 5-10
Parent Co: Modern Products
Type of Packaging: Consumer, Food Service

11934 **(HQ)Spilke's Baking Company**
590 Rocky Glen Rd.
Moosic, PA 18507
570-457-2400
Fax: 570-457-3626 arnold@macaroonking.com
www.macaroonking.com
Individually packaged macaroons and cakes including kosher
President: Arnold Badner
Estimated Sales: $10-20 Million
Number Employees: 10-19
Square Footage: 60000
Type of Packaging: Consumer, Food Service
Brands:
Jennie
Manhattan Gourmet
Red Mill Farms

11935 **Spinato's Fine Foods**
1920 E 5th Street
Tempe, AZ 85281-2905
480-275-4319
Fax: 480-275-7288 www.spinatosfinefoods.com
Gluten-free pizza and sauces
National Director of Sales: Todd Niezgodzki

11936 **Spindrift Beverage**
260 Charles St
Waltham, MA 02453
617-391-0356
www.spindriftfresh.com
Fruity sparkling water
Founder: Bill Creelman
Brands:
Spindrift Sparkling Water

11937 **Spinelli Coffee Company**
3100 Airport Way S
Seattle, WA 98134-2116
415-821-7100
Fax: 415-821-7199
Coffee
President: Christophe Calkins
Number Employees: 10

11938 **Spinney Creek Shellfish**
2 Howell Ln
Eliot, ME 3903
207-439-2719
Fax: 207-439-7643 877-778-6727
www.spinneycreek.com
Seafood
Owner: Tom Howell
Estimated Sales: $10-20 Million
Number Employees: 10-19

11939 **Spitz USA**
1775 Horseshoe Drive
Loveland, CO 80538-7201
970-613-9319
Fax: 970-613-9320
National Sales Manager: Roger Shantz

11940 **Splendid Specialties**
2198 South McDowell Blvd
Petaluma, CA 94954-5661
707-796-7800
Fax: 707-957-8022 info@tornranch.com
www.tornranch.com
Gourmet specialty foods that include the finest chocolates and baked goods, and famous dried fruit and nuts
President: Dean Morrow
CEO: Deana Kay
Estimated Sales: $20-50 Million
Number Employees: 50-99
Brands:
Cafe Time
Gigi Baking Company
Mashuga Nuts & Cookies
Splendid Specialties Chocolates

11941 **Splendid Spreads**
1483 Auburn Court
Eagan, MN 55122
877-632-1300
Fax: 651-688-7630 877-773-2374
http://splendidspreads.com
Gouret salmon spreads and toppings
President/Owner: Judy Tucker

11942 **Spoetzl Brewery**
603 E Brewery St
Shiner, TX 77984
361-594-3383
Fax: 361-594-4334 shiner@shiner.com
www.shiner.com
Brewery founded in Shiner, TX in 1909 producing the Shiner line of beers.
Manager: Carlos Alvarez
calvarez@shiner.com
Number Employees: 50-99
Parent Co: Gambrinus Company
Type of Packaging: Consumer
Brands:
Shiner Blonde
Shiner Bock
Shiner Dunkelweizen
Shiner Hefeweizen
Shiner Kolsch
Shiner Light

11943 **Spohrers Bakeries**
600 MacDade Boulevard
Collingdale, PA 19023-3804
610-532-9959
Fax: 610-532-8927
Pastries
Owner: David Olandi
Manager: Derek Everstyke
Brands:
Spohrers Bakeries

11944 **Spokandy**
1412 W 3rd Ave
Spokane, WA 99201-7024
509-624-1969
Fax: 509-624-2017 www.spokandy.com
Chocolates, wedding mints, brittles, barks, saltwater taffy
President: Todd Davis
spokandy@spokandy.com
Plant Manager: Mary Ellithorp
Estimated Sales: $5 Million
Number Employees: 10-19
Type of Packaging: Private Label

11945 **Spokane Seed Co**
6015 E Alki Ave
Spokane Valley, WA 99212-1019
509-535-3671
Fax: 509-535-0874 800-359-8478
spokseed@spokaneseed.com
www.spokaneseed.com
Processor and exporter of peas and lentils
President: Peter Johnstone
CFO: Jeff White
Sales: Nelson Fancher
Estimated Sales: $3900000
Number Employees: 20-49
Type of Packaging: Consumer, Food Service, Bulk
Brands:
Greenpod
Rumba

11946 **Spoonable**
345 Clinton Avenue
#4G
Brooklyn, NY 11238
718-974-0653
info@spoonablellc.com
www.spoonablellc.com
Salty caramel sauce, butterscotch sauce, chewy sesame caramel sauce, spicy chili caramel sauce, flowery lavender caramel sauce, peppered orange caramel sauce
President/Owner: Michelle Lewis
mnlewis@spoonablellc.com
Number Employees: 4
Number of Brands: 1
Number of Products: 7
Type of Packaging: Consumer, Food Service, Private Label, Bulk

11947 **Sportabs International**
PO Box 492118
Los Angeles, CA 90049-8118
310-451-2625
Fax: 310-207-8526 888-814-7767
Processor and exporter of multi-vitamin tablets
President: Richard Griswold
Estimated Sales: $500,000
Number Employees: 1-4
Type of Packaging: Consumer
Brands:
Spor Tabs

11948 **Sporting Colors LLC**
3630 S. Geyer Rd.
Suite 100
St. Louis, MO 63127
314-984-1000
Fax: 314-909-3300 888-394-2292
www.panerabread.com
President: William Moreton
CEO: S Jeff Schroeder
Senior Vice President: Liz Dunlap
Senior Vice President of Operations: Irene Cook
Estimated Sales: $1-3 Million
Number Employees: 20-49

11949 **Sportsman's Paradise Whites Ranch**
PO Box 129
Paradise, UT 84328
435-245-3053
Fax: 435-245-4603 www.whitesranch.com
Processor and canner of fresh rainbow trout
President: Grant White
Estimated Sales: $150000
Number Employees: 1-4
Type of Packaging: Consumer, Food Service

11950 **Sportsmen's Cannery**
381 Broadway
PO Box 1011
Winchester Bay, OR 97467-0800
541-271-3293
Fax: 541-271-9381 800-457-8048
orders@adventureinfood.com
www.sportsmenscannery.com
Gourmet canned seafood products including smokehouse and gift boxes
Manager: Brandy Roelle
Secretary: Mikyale Karcher
Estimated Sales: Below $1 Million
Number Employees: 10-19
Brands:
Sportsmen's Cannery

11951 **Sportsmen's Cannery & Smokehouse**
182 Bayfront Loop
Winchester Bay, OR 97467
541-271-3293
Fax: 541-271-9381 800-457-8048
karch@presys.com www.sportsmenscannery.com
Processor and canner of salmon, albacore tuna, sturgeon and shellfish
Manager: Brandy Roelle
Owner: Mikayle Karcher
Number Employees: 1-4
Type of Packaging: Consumer, Private Label
Brands:
Winchester

11952 **Sportsmens Seafoods**
1617 Quivira Rd
San Diego, CA 92109-7801
619-224-3551
Fax: 619-224-1646 www.sportsmensseafood.com
Canned fish including albacore, bonito, marlin, tuna and yellow tail
Owner: Joe Busalacchi
Estimated Sales: $300,000-500,000
Number Employees: 10-19

11953 **Spotted Tavern Winery &Dodd's Cider Mill**
PO Box 175
Hartwood, VA 22471-0175
540-752-4453
Fax: 540-752-4611
Wine, sparkling cider, Virginia hard cider and fresh apple cider in season.
Owner: Cathy Harris

11954 **Spottswoode**
1902 Madrona Ave
St Helena, CA 94574-2354
707-963-0134
Fax: 707-963-2886
spottswoode@spottswoode.com
www.spottswoode.com
Wine
President: Nicole Knoth
nicole@spottswoode.com
VP: Peah Armstrong
National Sales/Marketing: Lindy Novak Lahr
Consumer Sales/Tours: Shanyn McDaera
Winemaker: Rosemary Cakebread
Estimated Sales: Below $5 Million
Number Employees: 10-19

11955 **Sprague Foods**
385 College Street E
Belleville, ON K8N 5S7
Canada
613-966-1200
Fax: 613-962-8600 info@spraguefoods.com
Beans, soups, beans in sauce, pasta in tomato sauce, salad dressings
President: Roger Sprague
Number Employees: 20-49
Type of Packaging: Consumer, Food Service

11956 **Sprecher Brewing Co**
701 W Glendale Ave
Milwaukee, WI 53209-6509
414-964-7837
Fax: 414-964-2462 888-650-2739
beer@sprecherbrewery.com
www.sprecherbrewery.com
Hard sodas, ciders, and a wide variety of craft beers
President/Founder: Randal Sprecher
beer@sprecherbrewery.com
Brewmaster: Craig Burge
Production Manager: Tom Bosch
Year Founded: 1985
Estimated Sales: $20-50 Million
Number Employees: 50-99

11957 **(HQ)Spreda Group**
7410 New Lagrange Rd
PO Box 378
Louisville, KY 40222
502-426-9411
Fax: 502-423-7531
Fruit and vegetable powder, tomato paste, colors, spray and vacuum dried and dehydrated fruits and vegetables, apple pectin and apple juice concentrate
President: George Falk
VP: James Falk
Number Employees: 100-249
Type of Packaging: Food Service, Bulk
Brands:
Elmasu
Obi Pektin
Puccinelli
Spreda

11958 **Spring Acres Sales Company**
1280 Macedonia Rd
Spring Hope, NC 27882
252-478-5127
Fax: 252-478-5266 800-849-5436
Sweet potatoes including medium, large and jumbo

President: Cindy S Joyner
Quality Assurance: Jordan L Jackson
Domestic & Int'l Sales: Chris Thompson
Contact: Charlie Lewis
charlie@springacres.com
Estimated Sales: $500,000-$1,000,000
Number Employees: 1-4
Type of Packaging: Bulk
Brands:
Hernandez
Spring Acres
Tarheel

11959 Spring Creek Natural Foods
212 E Main St C
Spencer, WV 25276
518-436-7603
Fax: 518-436-9035
Tofu
President: Donald Carpenter
President: Mark Bossert
Estimated Sales: $2.5 Million
Number Employees: 15

11960 Spring Glen Fresh Foods
PO Box 518
Ephrata, PA 17522
717-733-2201
Fax: 717-721-6720 800-641-2853
www.springglen.com
Soup and stew including meat, poultry and seafood; also, potato, pasta and macaroni salad, coleslaw, entrees and desserts including cobblers, parfaits, cheese, puddings, gelatin and custards
President: John Warehime
VP General Manager: Steve Piechocki
Marketing Manager: Jeff Miller
Contact: David Karkosak
davidkarkosak@hanoverfoods.com
Plant Manager: Jeff Warehime
Purchasing Director: Rich Paulukow
Estimated Sales: $19 Million
Number Employees: 165
Square Footage: 90000
Parent Co: Hanover Foods Corporation
Type of Packaging: Consumer, Food Service, Private Label
Brands:
Deli Direct
Spring Glen

11961 Spring Grove Foods
312 S 3rd St
Miamisburg, OH 45342-2933
937-866-4311
Fax: 937-866-1410
Cheese, beef, pepperoni, ham, salami, sausage and bologna
President: Jerry Beale
Estimated Sales: $10 Million
Number Employees: 5 to 9
Square Footage: 30000
Type of Packaging: Food Service, Private Label, Bulk

11962 Spring Hill Meat Market
207 N Frank St
Spring Hill, KS 66083-8905
913-592-3501
Meat products
Owner: William Madison
Estimated Sales: Less Than $500,000
Number Employees: 1-4
Type of Packaging: Consumer

11963 Spring Hill Pure Water
136 Neck Rd
Haverhill, MA 01835-8028
978-373-3481
Fax: 978-521-0870 www.springhillwater.com
Dairy products
Owner: Harold Rogers
hrogers@springhillwater.com
Estimated Sales: Below $5 Million
Number Employees: 20-49

11964 Spring Kitchen
101 Chartres St
Houston, TX 77002-2307
713-222-0598
Fax: 713-222-0890 info@springkitchen.com
www.springkitchen.com
Spring rolls and eggrolls
Founder: Thu Do
Contact: Thu DO
thu@springkitchen.com
Number Employees: 5-9
Brands:
Spring Kitchen

11965 Spring Ledge Farm Stand
37 Main St
New London, NH 03257-7800
603-526-6253
Fax: 603-526-6679 info@springledgefarm.com
www.springledgefarm.com
Fresh grapes
President: Earl Andrews
Estimated Sales: $.5-1 million
Number Employees: 20-49

11966 Spring Mountain Vineyard
2805 Spring Mountain Rd
St Helena, CA 94574-1775
707-967-4188
Fax: 707-963-2753 877-769-4637
info@springmtn.com
www.springmountainvineyard.com
Wine
President: Don Yannias
Co-Owner: John Nickel
Director, Customer Relations & Events: Leah Smith
Estimated Sales: $3 Million
Number Employees: 50-99
Brands:
Chateau Chevalier

11967 Spring Street Bake Shop
400 Old Reading Pike
Pottstown, PA 19464
484-624-8201
Cookies and biscotti
General Operations Manager: Richard Zayaitz

11968 Springbank Cheese Company
201 Winniett St
Woodstock, ON N4S 6A1
Canada
519-539-7411
Fax: 519-539-0294 800-265-1973
spcheese@oxford.net www.springbankcheese.ca
Processor and packer of cheese
President: Tom Hemsworth
Estimated Sales: $2.6 Million
Number Employees: 10
Square Footage: 26000
Brands:
Gjetost Ekte
Wensleydale Blueberry

11969 Springdale Cheese Factory
19104 County Hwy Ee
Richland Center, WI 53581
608-538-3213
Fax: 608-538-3212 ltorkelson@aol.com
Muenster and brick cheese
President: Thomas Torkelson
Contact: Tom Torkelson
ltorkelson@aol.com
Estimated Sales: $6100000
Number Employees: 35
Type of Packaging: Consumer, Food Service

11970 Springdale Ice Cream & Bev
11801 Chesterdale Rd
Cincinnati, OH 45246-3407
513-671-2790
Fax: 513-671-2864 www.kroger.com
Ice cream
Human Resources: Stacey Rose
Plant Engineer: Mike Smith
Number Employees: 100-249

11971 Springfield Creamery Inc
29440 Airport Rd
Eugene, OR 97402-9537
541-689-2911
Fax: 541-689-2915 sue@nancysyogurt.com
www.nancysyogurt.com
Manufacturer of yogurt, cultured soy yogurt, cream cheese, cottage cheese, sour cream, and kefir.
Owner: Joe Kesey
esther@nancysyogurt.com
Owner: Sue Kesey
Marketing: Sheryl Kesey Thompson
Operations: Kit Kesey
Estimated Sales: $22 Million
Number Employees: 50-99
Number of Brands: 1
Number of Products: 13
Square Footage: 40000
Type of Packaging: Consumer, Food Service, Private Label, Bulk
Brands:
Nancy's

11972 Springhill Cellars
2920 NW Scenic Dr
Albany, OR 97321-9827
541-928-1009
Fax: 541-928-1009 springhill@proaxis.com
www.springhillcellarswinery.com
Wines
President: Michael Lain
Contact: Mervin Anthony
manthony@springhillcellars.com
Estimated Sales: Less Than $500,000
Number Employees: 1-4
Brands:
Springhill

11973 Springhill Farms
PO Box 10000
Neepawa, NB R0J 1H0
Canada
204-476-3393
Fax: 204-476-3791
Fresh and frozen pork
General Manager: William Teichroew
Number Employees: 400
Type of Packaging: Bulk
Brands:
Spring Hill Farms

11974 Springville Meat & ColdStorage
268 S 100 W
Springville, UT 84663-1804
801-489-6391
Fax: 801-491-3399
Domestic and game meats including ground beef and patties, beef, poultry, lamb and buffalo; also, custom processing available
President: David Cope
VP: Ray Cope
Estimated Sales: $810,000
Number Employees: 10-19
Square Footage: 100000
Type of Packaging: Consumer, Food Service

11975 Sprinkles Cupcakes
780 Lexington Ave
New York, NY 10065-8169
212-207-8375
888-220-2210
eat@sprinkles.com www.sprinkles.com
Cupcakes
Contact: Michael Lin
michael@sprinkles.com
Number Employees: 20-49

11976 Sprout Creek Farm
34 Lauer Rd.
Poughkeepsie, NY 12603
845-485-8432
info@sproutcreekfarm.org
www.sproutcreekfarm.org
Farm-made cow and goat milk cheese
President: Margot Morris
Year Founded: 1974
Number of Brands: 1
Number of Products: 7
Type of Packaging: Consumer, Private Label
Brands:
Sprout Creek Farm

11977 Sprout House
17267 Sundance Dr
Ramona, CA 92065
760-788-7979
Fax: 760-788-4800 800-777-6887
info@sprouthouse.com www.sprouthouse.com
Sprouting seeds
President: Richard Kohn
Marketing Director: Steve Meyerowitz
Estimated Sales: $500,000
Number Employees: 1-4
Type of Packaging: Private Label
Brands:
Hemp Sprout Bag

Sprout House & Salad
Sproutman's Organic

11978 **Sprout Nutrition**
50 Chestnut Ridge Rd
Montvale, NJ 07645
877-704-8777
info@sproutfoods.com
www.sproutorganicfoods.com
Organic baby food

11979 **Sprouts Farmers Market Inc.**
5455 E. High St.
Suite 111
Phoenix, AZ 85054
www.sprouts.com
National grocery store chain specializing in fresh foods and health foods.
Chief Executive Officer: Jack Sinclair
Chief Financial Officer: Denise Paulonis
Chief Operating Officer: Dan Sanders
Year Founded: 2002
Estimated Sales: $5.2 Billion
Number Employees: 30,000
Brands:
Country Kitchen Meals
Henry's Heritage Bread
Sprouts
Sunflower

11980 **Spruce Foods**
800 S El Camino Real
Suite 210
San Clemente, CA 92672-4274
949-366-9457
Fax: 800-708-9775 800-326-3612
bobbreen@sprucefoods.com
www.sprucefoods.com
Importer of organic grocery products
President: Bob Breen
Estimated Sales: $5-10 Million
Number Employees: 4
Number of Brands: 3
Number of Products: 160
Brands:
Lapas
Massetti
Montebello

11981 **Spruce Lane Investments**
37 Spruce Lane
Stratford, PE C1B 1M9
Canada
902-892-2600
Fax: 902-892-2620
Baked goods including danish, cinnamon rolls, bread, cookies, bagels, pies, rolls, etc
President/CEO: Robert DeBlois
Secretary/Treasurer: Elaine DeBlois
Estimated Sales: $1 Million
Number Employees: 20
Square Footage: 5200

11982 **Spruce Mountain Blueberries**
Mount Pleasant Road
PO Box 68
West Rockport, ME 04865-0068
207-236-3538
Fax: 207-236-8545
info@sprucemtnblueberries.com
Wild blueberry chutney, blueberry topping, cranberry chutney, conserves, jam, and blueberry vinegar
President: Molly Sholes
Estimated Sales: $75,000
Number Employees: 3
Number of Brands: 1
Number of Products: 7
Type of Packaging: Consumer, Food Service

11983 **Sprucewood Handmade Cookie Company**
PO Box 430
Warkworth, ON K0K 3K0
Canada
877-632-1300
Fax: 705-924-2626 info@sprucewoodbrands.com
www.sprucewoodbrands.com
Flavored shortbread cookies and nuts
President/Owner: Mark Pollard

11984 **Spurgeon Vineyards & Winery**
16008 Pine Tree Rd
Highland, WI 53543-9602
608-929-7692
Fax: 608-929-4810 800-236-5555
Wine in the following flavors; honey, cranberry, grape, sweet cherry, white and juice blend
Owner: Glen Spurgeon
spurgeon@mhtc.net
Co-Owner: Mary Spurgeon
Vice President: James Spurgeon
Estimated Sales: $1 Million
Number Employees: 1-4
Type of Packaging: Consumer, Private Label, Bulk
Brands:
Spurgeon Vinyards

11985 **Squab Producers of California**
409 Primo Way
Modesto, CA 95358-5721
209-537-4744
Fax: 209-537-2037 squabbob@aol.com
www.squab.com
Processor and exporter of fresh and frozen squab, pheasant, quail, poussin and partridge
President: Robert Shipley
squabbob@aol.com
Sales Exec: Robert Shipley
Estimated Sales: $5-10 Million
Number Employees: 50-99
Square Footage: 40000
Type of Packaging: Consumer, Food Service, Private Label, Bulk
Brands:
King-Cal
Mendes Farms
Sierra Gourmet

11986 **Squair Food Company**
1418 Newton Street
Los Angeles, CA 90021-2726
213-749-7041
Fax: 213-749-3591
http://www.sprucemtnblueberries.com
Mexican foods
President: Jerry Karrizer
Vice President: Morris Kharrazi
Estimated Sales: $5 Million
Number Employees: 1-4

11987 **Square One Organics**
PO Box 6549
River Forest, IL 60305
866-771-7138
info@squareoneorganics.com
www.squareoneorganics.com
Organic baby food.
Founder/Chief Executive Officer: Denise Henderson
Director of Accounting: Kathy Kruegger
Director of Communications: Mari Monaco Hynes
Director of Logistics: Jeffrey Henderson
Type of Packaging: Consumer

11988 **Square-H Brands Inc**
2731 S Soto St
Vernon, CA 90058-8026
323-267-4600
Fax: 323-261-7350 www.squarehbrands.com
Pork, sausage, ham and bacon
President/CEO: Henry Haskell
CEO: Edgar Borgja
edgar.borgja@sqhb.com
Quality Assurance Manager: Bill Parke
Sales Director: Kirk Kolden
Estimated Sales: $20-49.9 Million
Number Employees: 100-249
Number of Brands: 2
Number of Products: 200
Brands:
Hoffy
Bill Bailey's

11989 **Squire Boone Village**
406 Mount Tabor Rd
New Albany, IN 47150-2207
812-941-5900
Fax: 812-941-5920 888-934-1804
www.squireboone.com
Snacks
Owner: Rick Conway
ricksbv@aol.com
Number Employees: 100-249

11990 **Squirrel Brand Company**
113 Industrial Blvd Ste D
McKinney, TX 75069
214-585-0100
Fax: 214-585-0880 800-624-8242
info@squirrelbrand.com www.squirrelbrand.com
Nuts
President: Brent Meyer
Estimated Sales: $5-9.9 Million
Number Employees: 1-4
Square Footage: 160
Type of Packaging: Private Label
Brands:
Coconut Zipper
Squirrel
Squirrel Nut Caramel
Squirrel Nut Chew
Squirrel Nut Zippers

11991 **St Armands Baking Co**
2811 59th Avenue Dr E
Bradenton, FL 34203-5334
941-753-7494
Fax: 941-751-1417 sales@sabc.cc
www.starbake.com
Bread, rolls and sweet goods
President: Bernard Vroom
bernard@starbake.com
Estimated Sales: $1-3 Million
Number Employees: 5-9

11992 **St Arnold Brewing Co**
2000 Lyons Ave
Houston, TX 77020-2028
713-686-9494
Fax: 713-686-9474 800-801-6402
brewery@saintarnold.com www.saintarnold.com
Seasonal beer, ale, stout, lager and pilsner
President: Brock Wagner
brewery@saintarnold.com
Sales Rep: Frank Mancuso
Estimated Sales: Below $5 Million
Number Employees: 50-99
Type of Packaging: Consumer, Food Service
Brands:
Amber
Brown
Christmas
Elissa Ipa
Fancy Lawnmower
Kristall Weizen
Oktoberfest
Root Beer
Spring Bock
Summer Pils
Winter Stout

11993 **St Charles Trading Inc**
650 N Raddant Rd
Batavia, IL 60510-4207
630-377-0608
Fax: 630-406-1936
customerservice@stcharlestrading.com
Food ingredient distributor
President/VP Sales: Al Cicanci
CEO: William Manns
williammanns@stcharlestrading.com
Quality Assurance Officer: Dana Capes
Director of Operation: Janet Matthews
Estimated Sales: $15,000,000
Number Employees: 20-49
Square Footage: 40000

11994 **St Clair Ice Cream Co**
155 Woodward Ave # 7
Norwalk, CT 06854-4731
203-853-4774
Fax: 203-857-4099
Special occasion ice cream and sorbet molded into a variety of shapes.
Manager: Kay Gelsman
Estimated Sales: $5 Million
Number Employees: 5-9
Brands:
St. Clair Ice Cream

11995 **St Francis Winery & Vineyards**
100 Pythian Rd
Santa Rosa, CA 95409-6529
707-833-4668
Fax: 707-833-1394 info@stfranciswine.com
www.stfranciswinery.com
Wine

President: Christopher Silva
csilva@stfranciswine.com
CFO: Patti Smith
CEO: Lloyd Canton
Marketing Director: Nan Fontaine
Production Manager: Dennis Borell
Estimated Sales: Below $5 Million
Number Employees: 100-249
Brands:
Claret
Reserve Cabernet Sauvignon
Reserve Merlot
Reserve Zinfandel

11996 **St Innocent Winery**
5657 Zena Rd NW
Salem, OR 97304-9722
503-378-1526
Fax: 503-378-1041 www.stinnocentwine.com
Wine, still and sparkling
Owner: Mark Velossak
m_vlossak@stinnocentwine.com
Sales Manager: Felice Leonhardt
m_vlossak@stinnocentwine.com
Winemaker: Mark Vlossak
Estimated Sales: Below $5 Million
Number Employees: 10-19
Type of Packaging: Private Label
Brands:
St. Innocent

11997 **(HQ)St John's Botanicals**
7711 Hillmeade Rd
Bowie, MD 20720-4571
301-262-5302
Fax: 301-262-2489 www.stjohnsbotanicals.com
Spice blends, herb teas, essential oils, ginseng products, nutritional supplements
Owner: William Mussenden
Ceo: Sydney Vallentync
CFO: Patti Mussenden
Research/Dev: Diane Tolsen
Quality Control: Diane Tolsen
Marketing: Rayla Cuffey
Sales Manager: Rayla Cuffey
Pub Relations: Maria McCulvey
Operations Manager: Brandy Schwartz
Plant Manager: Diane Tolson
Purchasing: Sydney Vallentyne
Estimated Sales: Less Than $500,000
Number Employees: 5-9
Type of Packaging: Private Label, Bulk
Brands:
Rose Hill
Scent-O-Vac
The Prefume Garden

11998 **(HQ)St Julian Winery**
716 S Kalamazoo St
Paw Paw, MI 49079-1558
269-657-5568
Fax: 269-657-5743 800-732-6002
wines@stjulian.com www.stjulian.com
Processor and exporter of grape beverages including champagne, wine and juice
President: Kim Babcock
babcockk@stjulian.com
Executive VP: Charles Catherman
Marketing Director: Kim Babcock
VP Sales: Joe Zuiderueen
Wine Maker: David Miller, Ph.D.
Estimated Sales: $9 Million
Number Employees: 50-99
Type of Packaging: Consumer, Food Service

11999 **St Laurent Brothers**
1101 N Water St
Bay City, MI 48708-5625
989-893-7522
Fax: 989-893-6571 800-289-7688
Peanuts including salted, roasted and candy coated; also, peanut butter
Owner: Keith Whitney
Co-Owner: Steve Frye
Estimated Sales: $2 Million
Number Employees: 20-49
Type of Packaging: Consumer, Food Service, Bulk

12000 **St Mary Sugar Co-Op**
20056 Highway 182 W
Jeanerette, LA 70544-8532
337-276-6761
Fax: 337-276-4297 www.stmarysugar.com
Sugar and condiments

President: Raphael Rodriguez
Plant Manager: Ronald Guilotte Jr
Estimated Sales: $500,000-$1 000,000
Number Employees: 50-99

12001 **St-Germain Bakery**
1930 Dillingham Blvd
Honolulu, HI 96819-4021
808-847-5396
Fax: 808-842-7056 www.stghi.com
Breads, rolls, bakery products
Manager: Lorraine Yamada
Marketing Division Manager: Norikazu Miyata
Manager: Yukikazu Sato
sato@stghi.com
Estimated Sales: $8,065,258
Number Employees: 50-99
Number of Brands: 1
Brands:
Dee Lite

12002 **(HQ)St. Amour Inc/French Cookies**
2171 Grace Lane B
Costa Mesa, CA 92626
714-754-1900
infofrenchcookies@gmail.com
www.healthycookiesdirect.com
Cookies including madelines, croquants and teethers; also, snack foods
Owner: Daniel De St Amour
Number Employees: 5-9
Brands:
Rocks N' Rolls

12003 **St. Clair Industries**
3067 E Commercial Blvd
Ft Lauderdale, FL 33308
954-491-0400
Fax: 954-351-9082
Processor and exporter of catalyst altered water
President: Saul Rubinoff
CEO: Anne Rubinoff
Vice President: Anne Rubinoff
Estimated Sales: Less than $100,000
Number Employees: 2
Square Footage: 10000
Type of Packaging: Consumer, Bulk
Brands:
Briz
Willard

12004 **St. Croix Beer Company**
363 Webster St
Saint Paul, MN 55102
651-387-0708
Fax: 651-439-0221 info@stcroixbeer.com
www.stcroixbeer.com
Processor and wholesaler/distributor of lager and regular, maple and pepper ale
President: Tod Fyten
Estimated Sales: $86,000
Number Employees: 1-4
Type of Packaging: Consumer, Food Service
Brands:
Serrano
St. Croix

12005 **St. Jacobs Candy Co.**
180 Frobisher
Unit #2
Waterloo, ON N2J 4R8
Canada
519-884-3505
Fax: 519-884-9854 contactus@brittles-n-more.com
www.brittles-n-more.com
Candy manufacturer; brittles, fudges, beernuts, caramel, turkish delight, sponge toffee, hard candy drops &'shapes, hard candy suckers and batter crunch.
President: Michael McEachern
Operations: Deana Pfanner
Production: Rhys Carter
Estimated Sales: $750,000
Number Employees: 25
Number of Products: 9
Square Footage: 5000
Type of Packaging: Consumer, Private Label, Bulk

12006 **St. James Sugar Cooperative**
5354 Saint James Coop St
Saint James, LA 70086
225-265-4056
Fax: 225-265-4060
Blackstrap syrup and sugar

Sales Representative: Mr. Bourgeois
Estimated Sales: $10-20 Million
Number Employees: 50-99
Type of Packaging: Consumer

12007 **St. James Winery**
540 Sidney St
Saint James, MO 65559
573-265-7912
Fax: 573-265-6200 800-280-9463
info@stjameswinery.com www.stjameswinery.com
Wine and grape juice
President: Andrew Hofherr
Chairman of the Board: Patricia Hofherr
Vice President: John Hofherr
Vice President of Sales: Dean Chalem
Chief Executive Officer: Peter Hofherr
Estimated Sales: $5-10 Million
Number Employees: 20-49
Square Footage: 1200
Type of Packaging: Bulk
Brands:
St. James Winery

12008 **St. Julien Macaroons**
343 Main St.
Sandown, NH 03873-2101
603-887-2233
800-473-8869
www.macaroons.com
Manufacturer of macaroons.
Founder: James Price

12009 **St. Lawrence Starch**
141 Lakeshore Road E
Mississauga, ON L5G 1E8
Canada
905-271-8396
Fax: 905-271-1258
Starches and corn sweeteners including glucose and fructose
President: Ian Gray
CEO: Nick Lacivita
Sales Manager: Howard Low
Parent Co: Cargill Foods

12010 **St. Maurice Laurent**
735 6e Rang N Ss 1
St-Bruno-Lac-St-Jean, QC G0W 2L0
Canada
418-343-3655
Fax: 418-343-2996
Cheese and butter
President: Luc St Laurent
Number Employees: 25
Square Footage: 40000

12011 **St. Ours & Company**
1571 Commercial St
East Weymouth, MA 02189-3015
781-331-8520
Fax: 781-331-8628 email@saintours.com
www.saintours.com
Processor of frozen shellfish, including lobster, crab, dehydrated clam and seafood broths; wholesaler and distributor of seafood and specialty foods.
President: Fred St. Ours
Marketing Manager: Sharon St. Ours
Sales: John Christian
Director of Manufacturing: Richard St. Ours
Estimated Sales: $3-5 Million
Number Employees: 5-9
Type of Packaging: Consumer, Food Service, Bulk
Brands:
St. Ours

12012 **St. Simons Seafood**
130 Paradise Marsh Cir
Brunswick, GA 31525-2143
912-265-5225
Fax: 912-264-3181
Seafood and fish
President: Chuck Egeland
Estimated Sales: $1,500,000
Number Employees: 5-9

12013 **St. Stan's Brewing Company**
1028 11th St.
Modesto, CA 95354-0837
209-284-0170
Fax: 209-524-4827 info@ststans.com
www.ststans.com
Ales and lagers

President/CEO: Garith Helm
CFO: Romy Angle
VP, Co-Owner, COO: Richard Hodder
Plant Manager: Eric Kellner
Estimated Sales: $20-50 Million
Number Employees: 35
Type of Packaging: Private Label
Brands:
Red Sky Ale
St. Stan's Alt Beer

12014 Stacey's Famous Foods
10334 N Taryne Street
Hayden, ID 83835-9807
650-261-9912
800-782-2395
Frozen seafood, products such as; sauces, appetizers, quiches, pot pies, potatoe
Owner/President: Stacey James
Estimated Sales: Less than $500,000
Number Employees: 1-4
Brands:
Stacey's

12015 Stacy's Pita Chip Co
663 North St
Randolph, MA 02368-4317
781-961-7799
Fax: 781-961-2830 888-332-4477
www.stacyssnacks.com
Manufacturer and distributor of pita and soy-based chips.
President: Sheryl Carbone
sheryl.carbone@stacyssnacks.com
CEO: Mark Andrus
Estimated Sales: $5-10 Million
Number Employees: 10-19

12016 Stadelman Fruit LLC
111 Meade St
Zillah, WA 98953-9419
509-829-5145
Fax: 509-829-5164 www.stadelmanfruit.com
Processor and exporter of produce including apples, cherries, nectarines, pears, plums and prunes
President: Peter Stadelman
CEO: Rob Stewart
Manager: Rob Stewart
Number Employees: 500-999
Type of Packaging: Consumer, Food Service, Private Label, Bulk

12017 Staff Of Life Natural Foods
1266 Soquel Ave
Santa Cruz, CA 95062-2108
831-423-8632
Fax: 831-423-8065 staflife@pacbell.net
www.staffoflifemarket.com
Natural foods
Owner: Anthony Blanco
staffoflifemeats@gmail.com
VP: Gary Bascou
Estimated Sales: $5-10 Million
Number Employees: 100-249
Brands:
Beckmann
Imagine Foods
Natures Path
R.W.Knudsen

12018 Stafford County Flour Mills Company
PO Box 7
108 Church Street
Hudson, KS 67545
620-458-4121
Fax: 620-458-5121 800-530-5640
www.hudsoncream.com
Flour
President: Alvin A Brensing
Manager: Reuel Foote
Estimated Sales: $25-30 Million
Number Employees: 20-49
Type of Packaging: Consumer
Brands:
Hudson Cream Flour

12019 Stags' Leap Winery
6150 Silverado Trl
Napa, CA 94558-9748
707-944-1303
Fax: 707-944-9433 www.stagsleap.com
Winery
Manager: Robert Brittan
r.brittan@stagsleap.com
Winemaker: Christophe Paubert
Assistant Winemaker: Joanne Wing
Number Employees: 20-49
Number of Brands: 1
Parent Co: Treasury Wine Estates
Type of Packaging: Consumer, Food Service
Brands:
Stags' Leap

12020 Stahlbush Island Farms Inc
3122 SE Stahlbush Island Rd
Corvallis, OR 97333-2709
541-757-1497
Fax: 541-754-1847 sif@stahlbush.com
www.stahlbush.com
Frozen fruits, vegetables, grains and legumes.
Owners: Bill & Karla Chambers
Number Employees: 100-249

12021 Stahmann Farms
22500 S Highway 28
La Mesa, NM 88044-9531
575-526-2453
www.stahmannpecan.com
Pecans
Owner: Sally Stahmann-Solis
Vice-CEO: Deane Stahmann
Estimated Sales: Less Than $500,000
Number Employees: 5-9
Type of Packaging: Bulk

12022 Stallings Head Cheese Co
2314 Portsmouth St
Houston, TX 77098-3902
713-523-1751
Headcheese and boudin
Owner: Fred Chu
Estimated Sales: $1-3 Million
Number Employees: 1-4
Square Footage: 6000

12023 Stampede Meat, Inc.
7351 S 78th Ave
Bridgeview, IL 60455
Fax: 888-376-9349 800-353-0933
stampedemeat.com
Beef, pork and chicken products
CEO & President: Brock Furlong
CFO: Vito Giustino
COO: Jim Scott
VP, Technical Innovation & Development: Dennis Gruber
VP, Food Safety & Quality Assurance: Adam Miller
Sr. VP, Sales & Marketing: Ray McKiernan
Director, Human Resources: Christina Hackney
VP, Production: Krys Harbut
Estimated Sales: $45.5 Million
Number Employees: 250-499
Square Footage: 140000
Type of Packaging: Consumer, Food Service
Other Locations:
Cook Processing Facility
Oak Lawn IL
Brands:
Cro-Magnon
Cro-Man
Cro-Mag
Stampede
Mission Hill Bistro

12024 Stan-Mark Food Products Inc
1100 W 47th Pl
PO Box 09251
Chicago, IL 60609-4302
773-690-5086
Fax: 773-847-6253 800-651-0994
admin@Ingredients-USA.com
www.stanmarkfoods.com
Pickles, spices, grains and seeds, herring
General Manager: Mark Kongrecki
kongrecki@stanmark.biz
Estimated Sales: $20-50 Million
Number Employees: 20-49
Square Footage: 60000
Type of Packaging: Consumer, Private Label, Bulk

12025 Stanchfield Farms
73 Medford Rd
Milo, ME 04463
207-732-5173
Fax: 207-732-5173
Sweet and spicy pickles, pure fruit jams and jellies, bourbon barbeque sauce and marinades, fruit chutneys, and pickled vegetables
Type of Packaging: Consumer

12026 Standard Bakery Inc
79-7394 Mamalahoa Hwy # 79
Kealakekua, HI 96750-7910
808-322-3688
Fax: 808-322-2462 standardbakery@gmail.com
www.standardbakeryhawaii.com
Cakes, pies and pastries
President: Lloyd Fujino
standardbakery@gmail.com
Estimated Sales: $1 Million
Number Employees: 10-19
Type of Packaging: Consumer, Food Service

12027 Standard Functional Foods Grp
715 Massman Dr
Nashville, TN 37210
615-889-6360
Fax: 615-889-7775 800-226-4340
www.sffgi.com
Manufacturer, exporter and contract packager of candy including bars, boxed, log rolls and caramel corn.
President & COO: Tom Drummond
Chief Executive Officer: Jimmy Spradley
VP Administration & Corporate Secretary: Dennis Adcock
Vice President: Neil Spradley
Director of Business Development: Bryan Lewis
Director of Quality Assurance: Scott Sherry
Marketing Manager: Joanne Barthel
Director of Corporate Procurement: Brian Hillman
Director of Human Resources: Carol Cooper
Director of Operations: Bill Hardin
Year Founded: 1901
Estimated Sales: $41.2 Million
Number Employees: 500
Square Footage: 96500
Type of Packaging: Private Label, Bulk
Brands:
Coconut Waves
Cumberland Ridge
Goo Goo Cluster

12028 Standard Meat Co LP
5105 Investment Dr
Dallas, TX 75236-1420
972-283-8501
Fax: 214-561-0560 866-859-6313
www.standardmeat.com
Sausages and other prepared meats
Partner: Joseph Penshorn
Partner: William Rosenthal
Controller: Garry Custer
Food Safety & Research & Development: Scott Boleman
Quality Assurance: Jonathan Savell
Purchasing Manager: Sam Beede
Estimated Sales: $13.7 Million
Number Employees: 100-249
Square Footage: 195912

12029 Stangl's Bakery
572 Merchant St
Ambridge, PA 15003-2463
724-266-5675
stanglerbakery@yahoo.com
Baked goods
President: Lorianne Burgess
stanglsbakery@gmail.com
Estimated Sales: Less Than $500,000
Number Employees: 5-9

12030 Stanislaus Food Prod
1202 D St
Modesto, CA 95354-2407
209-548-3537
Fax: 209-527-0227 800-327-7201
freshpacktomato@stanislaus.com
Canned tomato paste and sauces
Owner: Tom Cortopassi
saintstanislaus@gmail.com
CFO: William Butler
VP Marketing: Cindy Brenon
SVP/Operations Executive: Mark Kimmel
Estimated Sales: $25 Million
Number Employees: 250-499
Square Footage: 50000
Type of Packaging: Food Service

Brands:
7/11
74-40
80-40
Al Dente
Alta Cucina
Full Red
Pizzaiolo
Pizzaletto
Pomarola
Saporito
Tomato Magic
Trattoria
Valoroso

12031 Stanley Orchards Sales,Inc.
2044 State Route 32
#6
Modena, NY 12548
845-883-7351
Fax: 845-883-5077 sales@stanleyorchards.com
www.stanleyorchards.com
Apple growing and storage/packing facility; importer of apples and pears; cold storage facility.
President/CEO: Ronald Cohn
Sales & Marketing: Jordan Cohn
Sales Manager: Anthony Maresca
Domestic Sales: Janine Skurnick
Controller: Susan Surprise
Import/Export Liason: Lorrie Hazzard
Estimated Sales: $293 Thousand
Number Employees: 8
Type of Packaging: Consumer, Food Service, Private Label, Bulk

12032 Stanley Provision Company
50 Batson Dr
Manchester, CT 6040
860-649-0656
888-688-6347
Sausage, kielbasa and ground beef
President: Stephen Wisniewski
Number Employees: 10-19
Square Footage: 30000
Type of Packaging: Consumer, Food Service

12033 Stanley's Best Seafood
7475 Patruski Road
Coden, AL 36523-3181
251-824-2801
Fax: 919-734-1201
Seafood
Owner: Robert Stanley

12034 Star Anise Foods
PO Box 591125
San Francisco, CA 94159
staranisefoods.com
Vietnamese food products
Co-Founder: Karen Cheng
Co-Founder: Thao Nguyen

12035 Star Fine Foods
2680 W Shaw Ln
Fresno, CA 93711
559-498-2900
Fax: 559-498-2910 starfinefoods.com
Olives, olive oil and vinegars
President & CEO: Jeff Freeman
jfreeman@borgesusa.com
Estimated Sales: $10-25,000,000
Number Employees: 20-49
Type of Packaging: Consumer, Food Service, Private Label, Bulk
Brands:
STAR
Cara Mia
Borges

12036 Star Kay White Inc
85 Brenner Dr
Congers, NY 10920-1307
845-268-6304
Fax: 845-268-3572 800-874-8518
inquiry@starkaywhite.com www.starkaywhite.com
Syrups, candies, panned-items and extracts and flavors
Owner/President/CEO/Plant Manager: Walter Katzenstein
walter@starkaywhite.com
General Manager: Don Heffner
R&D: Richard Sroka
Marketing: Stephen Platt
VP/Sales Executive: James Taft
Manufacuturing Supervisor: George Granada
Purchasing Manager: Judy Beaman
Estimated Sales: $8 Million
Number Employees: 50-99
Number of Brands: 1
Number of Products: 750
Square Footage: 180000
Type of Packaging: Bulk

12037 Star Ravioli Mfg Co
2 Anderson Ave # 2
Moonachie, NJ 07074-1678
201-933-6427
Fax: 201-933-0484 sales@starravioli.com
www.starravioli.com
Producers of more than thirty varieties of ravioli, as well as other italian specialties including manicotti, stuffed shells, gnocchi, cavatelli, tortellini, fettuccini and much more.
President: Laurence Piretra
CFO: Laurence Piretra
R&D: Rick Pisani
Quality Control: Rick Pisani
Estimated Sales: $3-5 Million
Number Employees: 10-19
Square Footage: 48000
Type of Packaging: Consumer, Food Service, Private Label, Bulk

12038 Star Route Farms
95 Olema Bolinas Rd
Bolinas, CA 94924-9710
415-868-1658
Fax: 415-868-9530 warrenweber@earthlink.net
www.starroutefarms.com
Produce
Owner: Warren Weber
warrenweber@earthlink.net
Estimated Sales: Below $5 Million
Number Employees: 20-49

12039 Star Seafood
14160 Shell Belt Road
Bayou La Batre, AL 36509
251-824-3110
Fax: 251-824-4199
Seafood

12040 Star Snacks
105 Harbor Dr
Jersey City, NJ 07305-4505
201-200-9820
Fax: 201-200-9827 888-782-7688
info@starsnacks.net www.starsnacks.net
Nuts and dried fruit.
Owner: Mendel Brachfeld
Year Founded: 1992
Number Employees: 50-99
Type of Packaging: Food Service, Private Label, Bulk

12041 Star of the West Milling Co.
121 E. Tuscola St.
Frankenmuth, MI 48734
989-652-9971
Fax: 989-652-6358 www.starofthewest.com
Flour, cereal bran and wheat germ.
Chairman: Art Loeffler
CEO: Jim Howe
Vice President, Grain Marketing: Gary Kaufman
Year Founded: 1870
Estimated Sales: $445 Million
Number Employees: 100-249
Square Footage: 45000
Type of Packaging: Private Label, Bulk

12042 Starbucks
2401 Utah Ave. S.
Seattle, WA 98134
206-749-5925
Fax: 206-447-0828 800-782-7282
www.starbucks.com
Whole bean coffees and espresso beverages, a variety of pastries and confections, coffee-related accessories and equipment. Also ice cream and coffee drinks including blended and flavored and dairy-free blended juiced teas.
President/CEO: Kevin Johnson
Executive Chairman: Myron Ullman
Systems Analyst: Kris Aamot
kaamot@starbucks.com
Year Founded: 1971
Estimated Sales: $24.71 Billion
Number Employees: 291,000
Number of Brands: 8
Type of Packaging: Consumer, Private Label, Bulk
Brands:
Starbucks Coffee
Seattle's Best Coffee
Teavana
Tazo
Evolution Fresh
La Boulange
Ethos Water
Torrefazione Italia Coffee

12043 Starich
248 Montclair Loop
Daphne, AL 36526-7150
251-626-5037
Seafood

12044 (HQ)Stark Candy Company
135 American Legion Highway
Revere, MA 02151-2405
985-446-1354
Fax: 985-448-1627 800-225-5508
www.necco.com
Manufacturer and exporter of candy. Founded in 1847.
President: Dominic Antonellis
General Manager: Bobby Folfe
VP Sales: Tom Drummond
Number Employees: 30
Type of Packaging: Consumer

12045 Starkel Poultry
10524 128th Street East
Puyallup, WA 98373
253-845-2876
Fax: 253-841-1004
Processor and exporter of bagged poultry including fresh and frozen
President: Elsie Starkel
Vice President: Leona Starkel
Estimated Sales: $4400000
Number Employees: 45
Type of Packaging: Consumer, Bulk

12046 Starkist Co
225 N Shore Dr # 400
Suite 400
Pittsburgh, PA 15212-5860
412-231-0361
Fax: 412-222-4050 www.starkist.com
Processor, canner and exporter of tuna
President, CEO: In-Soo Cho
Marketing: Barry Shepard
Vice President Sales: Stephen L Hodge
SVP of Corporate Affairs and Human Resou: Melissa Murphy
Estimated Sales: $5 million
Number Employees: 5-9
Parent Co: Del Monte Foods
Brands:
Chunk Light Tuna
Gourmet's Choice Tuna Fillets
Low Sodium Tuna
Solid White Albacore Tuna
Starkist Flavor Fresh Pouch
Starkist Lunch To-Go
Starkist Select
Starkist Tuna Creations

12047 Starport Foods
2655 Judah St
San Francisco, CA 94122
415-731-0663
Fax: 415-731-0663 866-206-9343
sales@starportfoods.com www.starportfoods.com
Ethnic specialty sauces, dressings and seasonings
Owner/VP: Cheryl Tsang
Estimated Sales: $500,000-$1 Million
Number Employees: 5-9
Number of Products: 40
Type of Packaging: Consumer, Food Service, Private Label, Bulk

12048 Starr & Brown
10610 NW Saint Helens Road
Portland, OR 97231-1048
503-287-1775
Wine
President: Eric Brown
Estimated Sales: Less than $500,000
Number Employees: 1-4

12049 Starr Hill Winery & Vineyard
861 Bailey Rd
Curwensville, PA 16833-7174
814-236-0910
Fax: 800-326-9618 www.groundhogwinetrail.com
Wines
Owner: Kenneth R Starr
info@starrhillwinery.com
Estimated Sales: Under $500,000
Number Employees: 10-19

12050 Startupcandy Co
534 S 100 W
Provo, UT 84601-4505
801-373-8673
Fax: 801-373-7312 www.startupcandy.com
Candy and confectionery products
Owner: Jon Startup
startupcandy@gmail.com
Vice President: Jon Startup
Estimated Sales: $2,000,000
Number Employees: 5-9
Type of Packaging: Consumer

12051 Starwest Botanicals Inc
161 Main Ave # A
Sacramento, CA 95838-2080
916-638-8100
Fax: 916-853-9673 800-800-4372
www.starwest-botanicals.com
Processor, importer and exporter of herbs and herbal extracts, spices and essential and vegetable oils; also, custom milling, blending and formulating available
Founder, President: Van Joerger
CEO: Shirley Abrahamson
shirleyabrahamson@starwestherb.com
VP Finance: Mark Wendley
SVP R&D/Production Manager: Dawn Bennett
Marketing/Product Development: Daniela Nelson
VP Sales: Richard Patterson
Purchasing: Bonnie Sadkowski
Estimated Sales: $9.8 Million
Number Employees: 50-99
Square Footage: 200000
Type of Packaging: Bulk
Brands:
Nature Actives
Starwest

12052 Stasero International
7021 South 220th Street
Kent, WA 98032
253-867-6130
Fax: 206-324-4586 888-929-2378
info@calsonindustries.com
www.calsonindustries.com/stasero
Drink mixes, syrups, sauces, toppings, frappes, accessories, and tea concentrates.
President: Sadru Kabani
Year Founded: 1918
Estimated Sales: $20-50 Million
Number Employees: 20-49
Parent Co: Calson Industries
Type of Packaging: Private Label
Brands:
Stasero

12053 Stash Tea Co
16655 SW 72nd Ave
Suite 200
Portland, OR 97224-7769
503-684-4482
Fax: 503-684-4424 800-547-1514
stash@stashtea.com www.stashtea.com
Tea: black, white, green, oolong, herbal, chais, Chinese & Japanese and iced teas.
President/CEO: Thomas Lisicki
CEO: Tom Lisicki
tom@stashtea.com
Quality Assurance Manager: Maria Lidiasari
VP Marketing: Dorothy Arnold
Sales Director: Kai Larsen
Human Resources Manager: Mitzi Bodine
Operations Manager: Jim Messina
Estimated Sales: $8,300,000
Number Employees: 50-99
Square Footage: 132000
Type of Packaging: Consumer, Food Service, Bulk
Brands:
Exotica
Stash
Stash Premium Organic Teas
Yamamotoyama 1690

12054 Stassen North America
408 S Pierce Ave
Louisville, CO 80027-3018
303-563-1016
Fax: 303-527-1702 sales@snatea.com
www.snatea.com
General grocery
President: Mike Fitzgerald
CEO: Barry Cooper
sales@snatea.com
Business Development Manager: Cecelia DesPortes
Estimated Sales: $2.5-5 Million
Number Employees: 10-19

12055 State Fish Distributors
39 S La Salle St.
Suite 1410
Chicago, IL 60603-1706
312-451-0800
Fax: 773-225-4660
Seafood
President: Donald Nathan

12056 State Garden Inc.
P.O. Box 6277
Chelsea, MA 02150
stategarden.com
Leafy greens, spinach, and celery.
Owner: Mark DeMichaelis
Year Founded: 1938
Number of Brands: 2
Type of Packaging: Private Label
Brands:
Olivia's Organics
Simple Beginnings

12057 State Of Maine Cheese Co
461 Commercial St
Rockport, ME 04856-4455
207-236-8895
Fax: 207-236-9591 800-762-8895
infoA@cheese-me.com www.cheese-me.com
Cheese
President: Cathe Morrill
c.morrill@cheese-me.com
Estimated Sales: $500,000-$1 Million
Number Employees: 5-9

12058 Statewide Meats & Poultry
211 Food Terminal Plz
New Haven, CT 06511
203-777-6669
Fax: 203-492-4073
Processor and wholesaler/distributor of meat
President: Stephen Falcigno
Estimated Sales: $7900000
Number Employees: 20-49

12059 Stauber Performance Ingrdients
4120 N Palm St
Fullerton, CA 92835-1026
714-441-3900
Fax: 714-441-3909 888-441-4233
customerservice@stauberusa.com
www.stauberusa.com
Leading supplier of bulk ingredients to the nutritional products, food, cosmetic and pet care industries.
President: Olivier Guiot
CEO: Sam Butler
sam.butler@viasat.com
COO & CFO: Steve Graham
Number Employees: 20-49
Type of Packaging: Bulk

12060 Stauffer Biscuit Co
P.O. Box 12002
York, PA 17402-0672
888-480-1988
www.stauffers.com
Cookies, crackers and snack products
President: Yujiro Kataoka
y.kataoka@stauffers.net
Vice President: Jim Biondolillo
Year Founded: 1871
Estimated Sales: $150 Million
Number Employees: 500-999
Parent Co: Meiji Co., Ltd.
Brands:
Stauffer's

12061 Stauffer's
8670 Farnsworth Rd
Cuba, NY 14727-9720
585-968-2700
Fax: 585-968-2722
Manufacturers of cookies.
Manager: John Fletcher
Estimated Sales: $2.5-5,000,000
Number Employees: 20-49
Brands:
Stauffer's

12062 Stavis Seafoods
212 Northern Ave
Suite 305
Boston, MA 02210-2090
617-897-1200
Fax: 617-897-1291 800-390-5103
fish@stavis.com www.stavis.com
Fresh and frozen seafood including cod, haddock, pollock, tuna, swordfish, mahi, snapper, grouper and seabass fillets, rockshrimp and baby scallops
President & CEO: Charles Marble
Chief Sustainability Officer: Richard Stavis
CFO: Mary Fleming
Executive Vice President: Stewart Altman
Director of Quality Assurance: Allison Roderick
VP Marketing: Michael Lynch
VP Sales: Stephen Young
VP Operations: Mohamad Fakira
Estimated Sales: $28.9 Million
Number Employees: 100-249
Square Footage: 10000
Type of Packaging: Food Service, Private Label, Bulk
Brands:
Bos'n
Boston Pride
Foods From the Sea
Prince Edward

12063 Stawnichy Holdings
PO Box 18
Mundare, AB T0B 3H0
Canada
780-764-3912
Fax: 780-764-3765 888-764-7646
shltd@telusplanet.net www.mundaresausage.com
Pepperoni, frankfurters, Ukrainian-style sausage, bologna, garlic rings, cooked and pressed ham, salami, ham and bacon loafs, macaroni and cheese loafs, corned beef, pastrami, beef jerky, bacon, veal cutlets, ground beef, pierogiesetc
VP/General Manager: E Stawnichy
Number Employees: 20-49
Square Footage: 46000
Brands:
Stawnichy's

12064 Ste Chapelle Winery
19348 Lowell Rd
Caldwell, ID 83607-9502
208-453-7840
Fax: 208-453-7831 877-783-2427
www.stechapelle.com
Wines
Manager: Mary Sloyer
mary.sloyer@ascentiawines.com
Estimated Sales: Below $5 Million
Number Employees: 20-49
Parent Co: Canandaigua Wine Company
Type of Packaging: Private Label

12065 Steak-Umm Company
P.O. Box 350
Shillington, PA 19607-0350
860-928-5900
Fax: 860-928-0351 http://www.steakumm.com
Quick and easy to prepare and delicious in an endless variety of recipes.
President: Dennis Newnham
Estimated Sales: $14 Million
Number Employees: 120
Square Footage: 352000
Brands:
Red.L
Spare-The-Ribs

Steak-Umm
Steak-Umm Sandwich To Go

12066 **Stearns Wharf Vintners**
217 Stearns Wharf # G
Santa Barbara, CA 93101-3582
805-966-6624
Fax: 805-966-6624 www.stearnswharf.org
Wines
President: Candy Scott
Estimated Sales: $2.5-5 Million
Number Employees: 5-9
Brands:
Stearns Wharf

12067 **Steckel Produce**
905 State Highway 16
Jerseyville, IL 62052-2834
618-498-4274
Fax: 618-498-4780
Fruits and vegetables
Owner: Robert Steckel
rsteckel@sincsurf.net
Estimated Sales: $3 Million
Number Employees: 5-9

12068 **Steel's Gourmet Foods,Ltd.**
55 E Front St # D175
Bridgeport, PA 19405-1489
610-277-1230
Fax: 610-277-1228 800-678-3357
Processor and exporter of gourmet, sugar free dessert toppings, jams, sweetners, syrups and condiments; also organic salad dressings, condiments, fruit spreads and low sugar fudge sauces.
President, Owner: Elizabeth Steel
Contact: Anna Steel
annasteel@steelsgourmet.com
Plant Manager: Carlos Short
Estimated Sales: $2.5 Million
Number Employees: 8
Number of Products: 60
Square Footage: 40000
Parent Co: Clack-Steel
Type of Packaging: Consumer, Private Label
Brands:
Charlie Trotter Foods
Daven Island Trade
Steel's Gourmet

12069 **Steep & Brew**
855 E Broadway
Monona, WI 53716-4012
608-223-0707
Fax: 608-223-0355 800-876-1986
coffee@steepnbrew.com
www.steepandbrewcoffee.com
Coffee
Owner: Mark Ballering
mb@steepnbrew.com
VP/Sales Manager: Mark Mullee
Estimated Sales: Below $5 Million
Number Employees: 10-19
Type of Packaging: Private Label
Brands:
Cafe Fair

12070 **Stefani Premium Foods**
1033 W Van Buren St # 5
Chicago, IL 60607-3288
312-275-9000
Fax: 312-275-9024
Produces a variety of Italian food products including sauces, relishes, pizza toppings, cheeses, and gift sets.
Founder/President/CEO: Phil Stefani
Executive Chef: Marcello Petrini

12071 **Stefano Foods**
4825 Hovis Rd
Charlotte, NC 28208-1510
704-399-3935
Fax: 704-399-3930 800-340-4019
www.stefanofoods.com
Frozen foods for supermarkets and the foodservice industry. pizza, calzones, tuscanni hand-held pizza, stromboli, stuffed pizza rings, italian paninis, quiche, quesadilla, flatbread melts, and breakfast sandwiches.
President: Enrico Piraino
Director Finance: Linda Wortman
VP: Stefano Piraino
VP Sales: Alan Hammer
Operations Executive: Todd Sanderhouse
General Manager Special Products: Al Silva
Purchasing Manager: Lynn Huss
Estimated Sales: $8.5 Million
Number Employees: 100-249
Square Footage: 124000
Parent Co: Smithfield Foods, Inc.
Type of Packaging: Consumer, Food Service, Bulk
Brands:
Take & Bake Deli Pizza
Stefano's

12072 **Stehlin & Sons Company**
10134 Colerain Ave
Cincinnati, OH 45251
513-385-6164
Fax: 513-385-6165 800-352-7396
www.stehlinsmeatmarket.com
Beef and pork
President: John Stehlin
Estimated Sales: $1,300,000
Number Employees: 10-19
Type of Packaging: Consumer, Bulk

12073 **Steiner Cheese**
201 Mill St
Baltic, OH 43804
330-897-5505
Fax: 330-897-6911 888-897-5505
Swiss cheese
President: James Sommers
VP: Dale Lendon
Estimated Sales: $5-10 Million
Number Employees: 5
Type of Packaging: Consumer, Bulk

12074 **Stella D'oro**
8600 South Boulevard
Charlotte, NC 28273
800-995-2623
www.stelladoro.com
Manufacturer of Italian baked goods.
Type of Packaging: Consumer

12075 **Stella Foods**
PO Box 99
Hinesburg, VT 05461-0099
802-482-2121
Fax: 802-482-2115
Feta cheese
President/CEO: Joseph Keenan
Marketing Director: Lynn Park
Estimated Sales: $10-24.9 Million
Number Employees: 50-99
Parent Co: Stella Foods

12076 **Stella Reedsburg**
1120 Commercial Ave
Reedsburg, WI 53959-2132
608-524-8244
Fax: 608-524-8091 www.saputo.com
Mozzarella cheese
Marketing Director: Cindy Zirngible
Plant Manager: Kelley Ford
Estimated Sales: $25-49.9 Million
Number Employees: 50-99
Parent Co: Stella Foods

12077 **Stellar Pasta Company**
955 Main Street
Great Barrington, MA 01230-2106
413-528-2150
Fax: 530-348-7081
Pasta

12078 **Stello Foods Inc**
551 Mahoning St
Punxsutawney, PA 15767
814-938-8764
Fax: 814-938-8769 800-849-4599
stellofoods@hotmail.com www.stellofoods.com
Peppers, mustards, sauces, salsas, BBQ sauces, spreads, spaghetti sauces, hot sauces, marinades & dressings
President: Nickki L Stello
Vice President: James Stello
Estimated Sales: $2.5 Million
Number Employees: 20-49
Square Footage: 240000
Type of Packaging: Consumer, Food Service, Private Label, Bulk
Brands:
Pinks
Rapes
Rosie's

12079 **Steltzner Vineyards**
5 Financial Plz # 104
Napa, CA 94558-6418
707-944-2486
Fax: 707-252-2079 800-707-9463
wines@steltzner.com www.steltzner.com
Winery, procuding red, white and dessert wines.
Owner/Proprietor: Dick Steltzner
National Sales Director: Allison Steltzner
Controller: Rebecca Rose
Estimated Sales: $1-2.5 Million
Number Employees: 1-4
Number of Brands: 1
Type of Packaging: Consumer
Brands:
Steltzner

12080 **Stengel Seed & Grain Co**
14698 SD Highway 15
Milbank, SD 57252-5452
605-432-6030
Fax: 605-432-6064 gstengel@tnics.com
www.tnics.com
Organic grains. Services include cleaning, dehulling, packaging, warehousing and shipping.
President: Doug Stengel
stengelseed@tnics.com
Estimated Sales: Less than $500,000
Number Employees: 5-9
Square Footage: 60000

12081 **Stepan Co.**
22 W. Frontage Rd.
Northfield, IL 60093
847-446-7500
Fax: 847-501-2100 www.stepan.com
Surfactants, polymers and specialty products for industries including nutrition, food and beverage, and personal care.
Chairman/President/CEO: F. Quinn Stepan
Vice President/CFO: Luis Rojo
Vice President/General Counsel: David Kabbes
Year Founded: 1932
Estimated Sales: $1.925 Billion
Number Employees: 2,096
Type of Packaging: Bulk
Brands:
Neobee 1053
Neobee 1095
Neobee 895
Neobee M-20
Neobee M-5
Wecobee Fs
Wecobee M
Wecobee S

12082 **Sterling Candy, Inc.**
27 Ludy Street
Hicksville, NY 11801
516-932-1104
Fax: 516-932-8392
Candy manufacturer and wholesaler.
President/CEO: Edward Greenberg

12083 **Sterling Caviar LLC**
9149 E Levee Rd
Elverta, CA 95626-9559
916-991-4420
Fax: 916-991-4334 800-525-0333
info@sterlingcaviar.com www.sterlingcaviar.com
White sturgeon including fresh, cold smoked and frozen
Manager: Peter Struffenegger
CFO: Joeseph Ruffo
R&D: Richard Helfrich
Manager: Carl Beckham
cbeckham@sterlingcaviar.com
Estimated Sales: $10-20 Million
Number Employees: 20-49
Square Footage: 110000
Parent Co: Stolt Sea Farm Group
Type of Packaging: Food Service

12084 Sterling Caviar LLC
Sterling Sturgeon
Sacramento, CA
916-991-4420
Fax: 916-991-4334 800-525-0333
info@sterlingcaviar.com www.sterlingcaviar.com
Caviar
Manager: Peter Struffenegger
Type of Packaging: Private Label

12085 Sterling Extract Co Inc
10929 Franklin Ave # V
Franklin Park, IL 60131-1430
847-451-9728
Fax: 847-451-9745
www.sterlingextractcompany.com
Pure and artifical vanilla flavoring extracts, flavors for ice cream, candy and bakery products.
President: Kitty Greenwood
kgreenwood@sterlingextractcompany.com
Vice President: Lynn Wakefield
Marketing Director: John Wakefield
Sales Director: Deborah Pavone
Estimated Sales: $1,500,000
Number Employees: 5-9
Type of Packaging: Bulk
Brands:
Bourbonil
Star-Van
Sterling Old Fashion Flavors
Vanaleigh 6b

12086 Sterling Foods LLC
1075 Arion Pkwy
San Antonio, TX 78216-2883
210-490-1669
Fax: 210-490-7964 www.sterlingfoodsusa.com
Gourmet cakes, biscuits, breads and rolls, cookies and brownies, loaf cakes and muffins
CEO: John D Likovich
jlikovich@sterling-fd.com
CEO: John Likovich
CFO: Mark Kuehl
SVP Sales/Marketing: Fred Friend
Human Resources Director: Jim Kuehl
SVP/COO: Nick Davis
Plant Manager: Hugo Salinas
Purchasing Manager: Barry Daley
Estimated Sales: $7900000
Number Employees: 100-249
Square Footage: 340000

12087 Sterling Vineyards
1111 Dunaweal Ln
Calistoga, CA 94515-9799
707-942-3344
Fax: 707-942-3463 servicedesk.na@diageo.com
www.sterlingvineyards.com
Wines
VP: Mike Westrick
Director, Operations: Vince Bonotto
Estimated Sales: $25 Million
Number Employees: 100-249
Parent Co: Diageo Chateau & Estate Wines

12088 Sterzing Food Co
1819 Charles St
Burlington, IA 52601-2201
319-754-8467
Fax: 319-752-7195 800-754-8467
www.sterzingchips.com
Potato chips, sour cream and dip
Owner: Craig Smith
craig@sterzingchips.com
Estimated Sales: $2 Million
Number Employees: 20-49
Type of Packaging: Consumer
Brands:
Sterzing's

12089 Steuk's Country Market &Winery
165 E Washington Row
Sandusky, OH 44870-2610
419-625-8324
Fax: 419-625-9007
Wines
President: Charles Sprigg
Estimated Sales: $2.5-5 000,000
Number Employees: 1-4

12090 Steve & Andy's Organics
630 Flushing Avenue
Brooklyn, NY 11206
718-499-7933
organic@steveandandys.com
steveandandys.com
Gluten-free cookies and candied orange peel.
Owner: Arjan Khiani
CEO: Michelle Schwartz
Business Development: Quinn Rhone
Estimated Sales: $2.2 Million
Number Employees: 51
Brands:
Steve & Andy's

12091 Steve Connolly Seafood Co Inc
34 Newmarket Sq
Boston, MA 02118-2601
617-427-7700
Fax: 617-427-7697 800-225-5595
retail@steveconnollyseafood.com
www.steveconnollyseafood.com
Fresh and frozen seafood, lobster, shellfish, smoked fish, prepared foods
Chairman & CEO: Stephen Connolly
Executive Vice President: David Coombs
Estimated Sales: $28 Million
Number Employees: 50-99
Type of Packaging: Bulk
Brands:
Steve Connolly

12092 Steve Mendez
16016 County Road 101
Woodland, CA 95776
530-662-0512
Fax: 530-662-9418
Condiments, beans and sprouts
President/Owner: Steve Mendez
Estimated Sales: $420,000
Number Employees: 10

12093 Steve's Authentic Key Lime Pies
204 Van Dyke Street
Brooklyn, NY 11231
770-333-0840
Fax: 770-436-4280 888-450-5463
inquiry@keylime.com www.keylime.com
Processor and exporter of key lime pies, pie filling, sorbet and novelty desserts
President: Kenneth Burts
Plt. Mgr.: K Michael Miller
Quality Control: Slorence Clay
Estimated Sales: $5-10 Million
Number Employees: 20-49
Square Footage: 48000
Type of Packaging: Food Service, Private Label
Brands:
Kenny's
Kenny's Island Style
Kenny's Key Lime Crunch

12094 Steve's Doughnut Shop
4 Winslow Ave
Somerset, MA 02726-2318
508-672-0865
Doughnuts
Owner: Mario Gulinello
Estimated Sales: $1-2.5 000,000
Number Employees: 10-19

12095 Steve's Ice Cream, Craft Collective
630 Flushing Ave.
4th Floor
Brooklyn, NY 11206
718-412-9393
888-782-7688
www.stevesicecream.com
Manufacturer of ice cream and sorbets.
Owner: David Stein
Contact: Forbes Fisher
ffisher@stevesicecream.com

12096 Steve's Mom
200 Food Center Dr
Bronx, NY 10474
718-842-8090
Fax: 718-832-6302 800-362-4545
ruggiebake@aol.com
Kosher dessert strudels, vegetable strudels, rugelach, coconut macaroons, brownies, and cheesecake
President: Suellen Schussel
Vice President: Erwin Schussel
Estimated Sales: $664696
Number Employees: 5-9
Square Footage: 10000
Type of Packaging: Consumer, Food Service, Private Label, Bulk
Brands:
Fudgeroons
Scotcheroons
Steve's Mom

12097 Steve's PaleoGoods
7800 Airport Hwy
Pennsauken, NJ 08109
856-356-2258
info@stevespaleogoods.com
www.stevespaleogoods.com
Paleo diet products
Founder: Steve Liberati

12098 Steven Roberts Originals
2780 Tower Rd
Aurora, CO 80011-3501
303-375-9925
info@originaldesserts.com
www.originaldesserts.com
Baked goods, cake pops, cake bars
President: Brian McGuire
CEO: Steven Fabos
Chairman: Charles Kosmont
HR Executive: Fran Adragna-Hayes
info@originalsdesserts.com
Number Employees: 500-999

12099 Stevenot Winery
458 Main St # B
PO Box 978
Murphys, CA 95247-9353
209-728-3485
info@stevenotwinery.com
www.stevenotwinery.com
Wines
Owner: David Oliveto
david@stevenotwinery.com
Winemaker: Chuck Hovey
Estimated Sales: $5-10 Million
Number Employees: 5-9
Type of Packaging: Bulk
Brands:
Shephard Ridge
Stevenot Winery

12100 Stevens Creative Enterprises, Inc.
New York, NY
646-558-6336
www.oohlalacandy.com
Manufacturer of coffee, tea, candy, baking mixes, and cocoa.
Founder: Sara Stevens
President: Rebecca Zorowitz
Brands:
Brew La La Coffee
Brew La La Tea
Ooh La La Candy
Chef Ooh La La Baking Mixes
Cocoa

12101 Stevens Point Brewery
2617 Water St
Stevens Point, WI 54481-5248
715-344-9310
Fax: 715-344-8897 800-369-4911
info@pointbeer.com www.pointbeer.com
Processor and exporter of beer and gourmet soda.
Founder: Frank Wahle
Founder: George Ruder
Co-Owner: Jim Wiechmann
Operating Partner: Joe Martino
Brewing: Gabe Hopkins
Director, Marketing: Julie Birrenkott
Year Founded: 1857
Estimated Sales: $20-50 Million
Number Employees: 20-49
Number of Brands: 2
Type of Packaging: Consumer, Private Label
Brands:
Point Premium
Point Special

12102 Stevens Sausage Co
3411 Stevens Sausage Rd
Smithfield, NC 27577-7539
919-934-3159
Fax: 919-934-2568 800-338-0561
tstev25536@aol.com www.stevens-sausage.com

Fresh ham, pork, frankfurters and sausage
President: Tim Stevens
tstev25536@aol.com
Marketing Executive: Tim Stevens
Estimated Sales: $11 Million
Number Employees: 50-99
Type of Packaging: Consumer, Food Service, Bulk

12103 Stevens Tropical Plantation
6550 Okeechobee Blvd
West Palm Beach, FL 33411-2798
561-683-4701
Fax: 561-683-4993
Processor and importer of syrups, fruit juices, nectar and beverage bases
President: Henry Stevens Jr
Estimated Sales: $1-3 Million
Number Employees: 5-9
Square Footage: 40000
Type of Packaging: Consumer, Food Service
Brands:
Parkway
Sunny Isle

12104 Stevenson-Cooper Inc
1039 W Venango St
PO Box 46345
Philadelphia, PA 19140-4391
215-223-2600
Fax: 215-223-3597 waxcooper@aol.com
Manufacturer and exporter of oils including cottonseed and palm oils; also, manufacturer of paraffin and sealing wax
President: Dennis Cooper
dcooper@stevensonseeley.com
R&D: Tammy Pullins
Estimated Sales: Below $5 Million
Number Employees: 5-9

12105 Stevison Ham Co
125 Stevison Ham Rd
PO Box 219
Portland, TN 37148-2037
615-325-7315
Fax: 615-325-5914 800-844-4267
sales@stevisonham.com
www.tennesseetraditions.com
Smoked ham, ribs, BBQ pork, beef, poultry
President: Michael Stevison
mstevison@stevisonham.com
VP Marketing: Sean Stevison
Vice President: John White
Customer Service: Lara Stevison
Estimated Sales: $20-30 Million
Number Employees: 50-99
Brands:
Stevison's

12106 Stevita Naturals
7650 U.S. 287 Frontage Rd
Arlington, TX 76001
214-556-5933
800-577-8409
stevitanaturals.com
Candy, gum and cocoa sweetened with stevia
President/Owner: Oscar Rodes

12107 Steviva Ingredients
725 NW Flanders Street
Suite 402
Portland, OR 97209
310-455-9876
Fax: 310-388-5393 800-851-6314
sales@steviva.com www.stevivaingredients.com
Manufacturer of sweeteners for the food and beverage industries.
President & CEO: Thom King

12108 Stewart Candies
600 Haines Ave
Waycross, GA 31501-2202
912-283-1970
Fax: 912-284-0354 candy.stewartdistribution.com
Candy and confections
President: Sam Stewart
sams@stewartcandy.com
CEO: Jimmy Stewart
CFO: Deen J Stewart
Estimated Sales: $20-50 Million
Number Employees: 10-19

12109 Stewart's Beverages
900 King Street
rye Brook, NY 10573
914-397-9200
800-762-7753
www.drinkstewarts.com
Soft drinks
President: Samuel M Simpson
CFO: Myron D Stadler
Number Employees: 10-19
Parent Co: Triarc Companies
Type of Packaging: Consumer, Food Service

12110 Stewart's Private Blend Foods
4110 W Wrightwood Ave
Chicago, IL 60639-2172
773-489-2500
Fax: 773-489-2148 800-654-2862
info@stewarts.com www.stewarts.com
Processor, importer and exporter of coffees including flavored, decaffeinated and roasted; also, flavored and blended teas
President: Donald Stewart
CEO: Robert Stewart
Vice President: William Stewart Jr
Contact: Steve Blair
steve.blair@stewarts.com
Production Manager: Elita Pagan
Plant Manager: Ed Fabro
Estimated Sales: $2,000,000
Number Employees: 20-49
Square Footage: 192000
Type of Packaging: Consumer, Food Service, Private Label, Bulk
Brands:
Stewarts

12111 Stewart's Shops Corp
2907 State Route 9
Ballston Spa, NY 12020-4201
518-581-1200
Fax: 518-581-1209 www.stewartsshops.com
Whole, 2% and skim milk; also, regular and low-fat ice cream
President: Gary Dake
gdake@stewartsshops.com
Estimated Sales: Over $1 Billion
Number Employees: 1000-4999
Type of Packaging: Consumer

12112 Stewarts Market
17821 State Route 507 SE
Yelm, WA 98597-9654
360-458-2091
Fax: 360-458-3150
Meat and homemade sausage
President: Dorthy Carlson
Vice President: Stewart Carlson
Estimated Sales: $3-5 000,000
Number Employees: 20-49

12113 Stewarts Seafood
8401 Highway 188
Coden, AL 36523-3059
251-824-7368
Fax: 251-824-7369
Seafood
President: Janice Stewart
Co-Owner: James O Stewart
Estimated Sales: $10-20 Million
Number Employees: 20-49

12114 Stichler Products Inc
1800 N 12th St
Suite 1
Reading, PA 19604-1545
610-921-0211
Fax: 610-921-0294 info@megacandyco.com
www.megabuttons.com
Confectionery products: candy, decorative and ornamental
President: Martin Deutschman
spicandy@aol.com
Vice President: Brad Deutschman
Public Relations: Rachel Buckholtz
Estimated Sales: $4700000
Number Employees: 20-49
Square Footage: 248000
Type of Packaging: Consumer, Food Service, Private Label, Bulk
Brands:
Candy Farms

12115 Stickney & Poor Company
12 Reynolds Dr
Peterborough, NH 03458-1611
603-924-2259
Processor and exporter of portion-controlled products including ketchup, relish, nondairy coffee creamers, honey, artificial sweeteners, jams, jellies, marmalades, preserves, mayonnaise, mustard, salt, pepper, vinegar, salad dressingsand dipping sauces
President: H Sandy Brown
VP: Chuck Lavery
Number Employees: 50-99
Type of Packaging: Food Service, Private Label, Bulk
Brands:
Harvest Selects
Stickney & Poor

12116 Stickney Hill Dairy Inc
15371 County Road 48
Kimball, MN 55353-9771
320-398-5360
Fax: 320-398-5361 sales@stickneydairy.com
www.stickneydairy.com
Goat cheeses
General Manager: Cheryl Willenbring
Quality Assurance Manager: Kathy Ratka
Manager: Frankie Lenzmeier
flenzmeier@stickneydairy.com
Estimated Sales: $2 Million
Number Employees: 10-19

12117 Sticky Fingers Bakeries
1839 W Summit Pkwy
Spokane, WA 99201-6027
509-922-1985
Fax: 509-922-7102 800-458-5826
sales@stickyfingersbakeries.com
www.stickyfingersbakeries.com
English scones
Site Manager: Ted Vogelman
ted@stickyfingersbakeries.com
Estimated Sales: Less Than $500,000
Number Employees: 5-9

12118 Sticky Toffee Pudding Company
1313 W. 9 1/2 St.
Austin, TX 78703
512-472-0039
tracyclaros@stickytoffeepuddingcompany.com
www.stickytoffeepuddingcompany.com
Cakes, puddings, bars, and dessert sauces.
Founder: Tracy Wilkinson-Claros

12119 Stiebs
11767 Road 27«
Madera, CA 93637
559-661-0031
Fax: 559-661-0032 info@stiebs.com
www.stiebs.com
Fruit and vegetable juices, concentrates, purees, powders and extracts
Owner: Heather Chavez
hchavez@stiebs.com
Partner: Brad Miller
Sales Manager: Brian Nova
Number Employees: 1-4

12120 Stimo-O-Stam, Ltd.
70593 Bravo St
Covington, LA 70433
Fax: 985-845-1489 800-562-7514
laurie_sre@yahoo.com www.stimostam.com
Processor and exporter Supplements, Nutritional: Energy Mixes
Manager: Alan Lafferty
Estimated Sales: $300,000-500,000
Number Employees: 1-4
Square Footage: 40000
Type of Packaging: Consumer
Brands:
Stim-O-Stam

12121 Stinking Rose, The
325 Columbus Ave
San Francisco, CA 94133-3907
415-781-7673
Fax: 415-781-2833 800-995-7674
sfcomments@thestinkingrose.com
www.thestinkingrose.com
Extra virgin olive oil, pickled garlic and garlic stuffed olives

Owner: Dante Serafini
comments@thestinkingrose.com
Owner: Jerry Dal Bozzo
Estimated Sales: $1-3 Million
Number Employees: 50-99

12122 Stirling Foods
P.O.Box 569
Renton, WA 98057
425-251-9293
Fax: 425-251-0251 800-332-1714
Processor and exporter of gourmet beverage flavors and syrups
President: Mark Greiner
CEO: Earl Greiner
Contact: Jeff Greiner
stirling@stirling.net
Estimated Sales: $1,300,000
Number Employees: 5-9
Type of Packaging: Consumer, Food Service, Private Label
Brands:
Stirling Gourmet Flavors

12123 Stirrings
376 Nash Rd
New Bedford, MA 2746
866-646-4266
customercare@stirringsshop.com stirrings.com
Cocktail mixers, bar ingredients and rimmers
Contact: Laura Camara
lcamara@stirrings.com
Year Founded: 1997

12124 Stock Popcorn Ind Inc
304 Vine St
Lake View, IA 51450
712-657-2811
Fax: 712-657-2550 stockpop@netins.net
Processor and exporter of yellow and white popcorn including processed unpopped and microwaveable; also, feed sack fashion packaging for popcorn
Owner: Jim Stock
stockpop@netins.net
Number Employees: 5-9
Type of Packaging: Consumer, Private Label, Bulk
Brands:
Lil' Chief
Lil' Chief Popcorn

12125 Stock Yards Packing Company
2457 W North Ave.
Melrose Park, IL 60160
312-733-6050
Fax: 708-223-1257 877-785-9273
customerservice@stockyardscustomerservice.com
www.stockyards.com
Processor and exporter of beef, pork, veal and lamb
President: Dan Pollack
Plant Manager: Oscar Moore
Estimated Sales: $10-20 Million
Number Employees: 100-249
Square Footage: 180000

12126 Stockton Graham & Co
4320 Delta Lake Dr
Suite 199
Raleigh, NC 27612-7000
919-881-0746
Fax: 919-881-0746 800-835-5943
info@stocktongraham.com
www.stocktongraham.com
Wholesale specialty beverages
President: Jeff Vojta
vojta@stocktongraham.com
Estimated Sales: $500,000-$1 Million
Number Employees: 10-19
Brands:
Stoktin Grahan

12127 Stokes Canning Company
18023 Peakview Place
Aurora, CO 80016-3152
303-292-4018
800-978-6537
www.stokeschile.com
Chile sauce
CEO: Jeffrey Nieder
Estimated Sales: $10-19 Million
Number Employees: 50-99
Parent Co: Centennial Specialty Food
Brands:
Strokes

12128 Stoller Fisheries
1301 18th St
PO Box B
Spirit Lake, IA 51360
712-336-1750
Fax: 712-336-4681 800-831-5174
stollerfisheries@mchsi.com
www.kreativekosherfoods.com
Processor and exporter of fresh fish including carp, buffalo, sheepheads and suckers- Asian Corp.
President: Larry Stoller
lstoller@stollerfisheries.com
Controller: Mark Salzwedel
VP: Thomas Opheim
Quality Control: LaRonna Opheum
Estimated Sales: $4 Million
Number Employees: 20-49
Square Footage: 140000
Parent Co: Progressive Companies
Type of Packaging: Bulk

12129 Stone Brewing
1999 Citracado Pkwy
Escondido, CA 92029-4158
760-294-7899
Fax: 760-471-7690 email@stonebrew.com
www.ubermary.com
Beer
President: Steve Wagner
stevew@stonebrew.com
Chairman/CEO: Greg Koch
Senior Vice President: Alan Eustace
VP Sales: Arlan Arnsten
HR Manager: Kathy Loven
stevew@stonebrew.com
Senior Vice President of Operations: Laszlo Bock
Production Manager/Head Brewer: Mitch Steele
Number Employees: 100-249
Brands:
Stone Pale Ale
Stone Smoked Porter
Stone Ipa
Stone Sublimely
Arrogant Bastard Ale

12130 Stone Crabs Inc
11 Washington Ave
Miami Beach, FL 33139-7395
305-534-8788
Fax: 305-532-2704 800-260-2722
Fresh and frozen stone crabs, whole lobsters and lobster tails
President: Stephen Sawitz
alopez@stonecrabsinc.com
CFO: Marc Fine
Marketing Director: Tracie Gordon
Operations Manager: James McClendon
Facilities: Alex Lopez
Plant Manager: Ron Pressley
Estimated Sales: $10-20 Million
Number Employees: 20-49
Type of Packaging: Consumer, Food Service
Brands:
Sci

12131 (HQ)Stone Hill Winery
1110 Stone Hill Hwy
Hermann, MO 65041-1280
573-486-2221
Fax: 573-486-3828
hermann-info@stonehillwinery.com
www.stonehillwinery.com
Grape juice, wine and champagne
Co-Owner: James Held
Co-Owner: Betty Held
Director of Sales & Advertising: Thomas Held
General Manager: Jon Held
Number Employees: 100-249
Other Locations:
Stone Hill Winery
New Florence MO
Stone Hill Winery
Branson MO
Brands:
Stone Hill Winery

12132 Stone Meat Processor
1485 Stonefield Way
Ogden, UT 84404
801-782-9825
Fax: 801-782-1109 Jared@stonemeats.com
www.stonemeats.com
Ground beef
President: Frank Stone
Marketing/Operations: Burke Stone
Estimated Sales: $10-20 Million
Number Employees: 20-49
Type of Packaging: Consumer, Food Service

12133 Stone Mountain Pecan Co
1781 Highway 78 NW
Monroe, GA 30655-5227
770-266-6659
Fax: 770-207-4403 800-633-6887
smpc1@mindspring.com
www.stonemountainpecan.com
Processors of pecans
President: Robby E Coker
smpc1@mindspring.com
Estimated Sales: $3200000
Number Employees: 10-19
Type of Packaging: Consumer, Food Service, Private Label, Bulk

12134 Stone Mountain Vineyards
1376 Wyatt Mountain Rd
Dyke, VA 22935-1371
434-990-9463
www.stonemountainvineyards.com
Wines
Founder: Alfred Breiner
General Manager & Assistant Winemaker: Kate Breiner
Estimated Sales: $3-5 Million
Number Employees: 1-4

12135 Stone's Home Made CandyShop
145 W Bridge St
Oswego, NY 13126-1495
315-343-8401
Fax: 315-343-8401 888-223-3928
Candy and confectionery products
Owner: Margaret Stachowicz
Estimated Sales: $300,000
Number Employees: 5-9
Square Footage: 9000
Type of Packaging: Consumer, Food Service

12136 StoneHammer Brewing
355 Elmira Rd N
Unit 135
Guelph, ON N1K 1S5
Canada
519-824-1194
Fax: 519-822-8201
Manufacturer and exporter of beer, lager and cask condition ale
CEO: Karen Cerniuk
General Manager: Brian Relly
Office Admin: Myriam Mullin
Sales & Service: Lee Ecclestone
Brewmaster: Charles MacLean
Brewery Manager: Brian Reilly
Estimated Sales: $382,000
Number Employees: 5
Type of Packaging: Consumer, Food Service
Brands:
Eramosa Honey Wheat
F and M Special Draft
Macleans Cask Conditioned
Macleans Pale
Oac Gold
Royal City
Saint Andre Vienna
Stone Hammer Pilsner

12137 Stonegate
2300 Lower Chiles Valley Rd
St Helena, CA 94574-9632
707-603-2203
Fax: 707-603-2209
Wines
President: Paul D Croft Croft
CFO: Cathy del Fava
Estimated Sales: $5-10 Million
Number Employees: 10-19

12138 Stoneridge Winery
13862 Ridge Rd
Sutter Creek, CA 95685
209-223-1761
Wines
Owner: Gary Porteous
gary.porteous@stoneridge.com
Estimated Sales: Below $5 000,000
Number Employees: 5-9

12139 (HQ)Stonewall Kitchen
2 Stonewall Ln
York, ME 03909-1665
207-351-2713
Fax: 207-351-2715 800-826-1752
info@stonewallkitchen.com
www.stonewallkitchen.com
Specialty foods
CFO: Laurie King
Executive VP: Natalie King
nking@stonewallkitchen.com
Estimated Sales: $10-50 Million
Number Employees: 100-249
Square Footage: 60000
Type of Packaging: Consumer
Brands:
Stonewall Kitchen

12140 Stonie's Sausage Shop
1507 Edgemont Blvd
Perryville, MO 63775-1230
573-547-2540
Fax: 573-547-1747 888-546-2540
contact@shopstonies.com www.shopstonies.com
Smoked meats and sausages
Owner: Roger Wibbenmeyer
contact@shopstonies.com
Co-Owner: Tyson Wibbenmeyer
Estimated Sales: $1-1.5 Million
Number Employees: 10-19
Square Footage: 60000
Type of Packaging: Food Service, Private Label

12141 Stonington Lobster Co-Op
Indian Point Rd
Stonington, ME 4681
207-367-2286
Fax: 207-367-2802
Lobster
Manager: Ronald Trundy
Manager: Steve Robins Iii
Estimated Sales: $5-10 Million
Number Employees: 5-9

12142 Stonington Vineyards
523 Taugwonk Rd
P.O. Box 463
Stonington, CT 06378-1805
860-535-1222
Fax: 860-535-2182 800-421-9463
info@stoningtonvineyards.com
www.stoningtonvineyards.com
Table wines including chardonnay, seaport white, fume vidal, white and bush, cabernet franc and gewurztraminer
Owner: Happy Smith
happy@stoningtonvineyards.com
General Manager/Winemaker: Mike McAndrew
Founder: Nick Smith
Founder: Happy Smith
Marketing Director: Nick Smith
Estimated Sales: $400000
Number Employees: 5-9
Square Footage: 40000
Type of Packaging: Consumer
Brands:
Seaport Blush
Seaport White
Seaport Wines
Stonington
Stonington Vineyards

12143 Stony Hill Vineyard
3331 Saint Helena Hwy N
St Helena, CA 94574-9660
707-963-2636
Fax: 707-963-1831 info@stonyhillvineyard.com
www.stonyhillvineyard.com
Wines
Owner: Peter Mccrea
Office Manager: Willinda McCrea
Vineyard and Winery Operations: Mike Chelini
Vineyard Foreman: Alejandro Salomon
Customer Relations: Mary Burklow
Estimated Sales: $500,000-$1 Million
Number Employees: 10-19
Brands:
Stony Hill Vineyard

12144 Stonybrook Mountain Winery
3835 State Highway 128
Calistoga, CA 94515-9739
707-942-5282
Fax: 707-942-5334 www.storybookwines.com
Wines
President: Jerry Seps
Contact: Norman Wu
nwu@apple.com
Estimated Sales: Less Than $500,000
Number Employees: 1-4
Brands:
Storybook Mountain Winery

12145 Stonyfield Organic
10 Burton Dr
Londonderry, NH 03053-7436
603-437-4040
Fax: 603-437-7594 800-776-2697
www.stonyfield.com
Natural organic yogurt, frozen yogurt, smoothies, snacks, milk, cream, and baby food
Chairman/Co-Founder: Gary Hirshberg
President/CEO: Esteve Torrens
Director Operations/Finance: Rick Burleigh
VP Research & Development: Paul Rosethal
VP Marketing: Christopher Malnar
Senior Director Sales: Mark Murphy
VP Human Resources: Sue Melvin
COO: Diane Carhart
VP Sourcing & Product Development: Rolf Carlson
Year Founded: 1983
Estimated Sales: $370 Million
Number Employees: 400
Brands:
Stonyfield Farm Frozen Yogurt
Stonyfield Farm Ice Cream
Stonyfield Farm Refrig Yogurt
Yo Baby Yogurt
Brown Cow

12146 Stop & Shop Manufacturing
104 Meadow Road
Readville, MA 02136-2349
508-977-5132
Processor and wholesaler/distributor of milk, juices and sodas
Marketing Director: William Sress
Estimated Sales: $3-5 Million
Number Employees: 20-49
Parent Co: Stop & Shop Supermarket Company
Type of Packaging: Consumer

12147 Storck Canada
100 City Centre Dr
PO Box 2103
Mississauga, ON L5B 3C6
Canada
905-272-4480
Fax: 905-272-6899 www.storck.com
Candy wholesaler
President & CEO: Ralph Hilpuesch
VP, Finance & Operations: Andrew Ruttgers
Brands:
Campino
Knoppers
Merci
Merci Crocant
Merci Pur
Mini Dickmann's
Super Dickmann's
Toffifee
Werther's Original

12148 Storck U.S.A.
Suite 400
Chicago, IL 60654
312-467-5700
Fax: 312-467-9722 800-852-5542
www.storck.us
Confectionary products
President & CEO: Ralph Hilpuesch
VP, Finance & Operations: Andrew Ruttgers
Year Founded: 1903
Estimated Sales: $87 Million
Number Employees: 7,000
Number of Brands: 5
Brands:
Werther's Original
Merci
Riesen
Toffifay
Mamba

12149 StoreHouse Foods
22431 Antonio Parkway
Suite B 160
Rancho Santa Margarita, CA 92688
www.storehousefoods.com
Gluten free portable meals
Founder: Yvonne Williams

12150 Storrs Winery
303 Potrero St # 35
Santa Cruz, CA 95060-2782
831-458-5030
Fax: 831-458-0464 salesmgr@storrswine.com
www.storrswine.com
Wines
President: Stephen Storrs
steves@storrswine.com
Owner/VP: Pamela Bianchini-Storrs
Operations Manager: Aaron Storrs
Production Manager: Morgan Storrs
Estimated Sales: $1-2.5 Million
Number Employees: 10-19
Brands:
Storrs

12151 Story Winery
10525 Bell Rd
Plymouth, CA 95669-9516
209-245-6208
Fax: 209-245-6619 800-712-6390
www.storywinery.com
Wines
Owner: Robert Campbell
rob@zin.com
CEO: Jan Tichenor
Marketing Director: Jan Tichenor
Estimated Sales: $500,000-$1 Million
Number Employees: 10-19
Brands:
Story Wine

12152 Story's Popcorn Company
P.O.Box 247
Charleston, MO 63834-0247
573-649-2727
Fax: 314-649-3374
Popcorn
President: A Story
Estimated Sales: $10-20 000,000
Number Employees: 1-4

12153 Stoudt Brewing Co
2800 N Reading Rd # 272
Adamstown, PA 19501
717-484-4386
Fax: 717-484-4182 jack@stoudtsbeer.com
www.stoudtsbeer.com
Seasonal beers, ale, stout, lager and pilsner
President: Carol Stoudt
CFO: Edward Stoudt
Estimated Sales: $6 Million
Number Employees: 50-99
Type of Packaging: Consumer, Food Service
Brands:
American Pale Ale
Stoudt Gold
Scarlet Lady Ale
Pilsener
Fat Dog Stout
Double India Pale Ale
Triple
Brewers Reserves
Old Abominable Barkey Wine

12154 Stoutridge Vineyard
10 Ann Kaley Lane
Marlboro, NY 12542
www.stoutridge.com
Gin, whiskey, brandy, vodka, natural wines
Co-Owner: Stephen Osborn
Co-Owner: Kimberly Wagner
Year Founded: 2001
Number of Brands: 1
Type of Packaging: Consumer, Private Label
Brands:
Stoutridge

12155 Strasburg Provision
1317 N Wooster Ave
Strasburg, OH 44680
330-878-5557
Fax: 330-878-5558 800-207-6009
Meat products and catering
President: Rudolf M Klapper
Sales: Herb Gritzan
Production: Frank H Klapper
Estimated Sales: $3000000
Number Employees: 20-49

Type of Packaging: Consumer, Food Service, Private Label, Bulk

12156 Strassburger Steaks
40 Broad St.
P.O. Box 465
Carlstadt, NJ 07072
201-842-8890
Fax: 201-842-8891 orders@strassburgersteaks.com
www.strassburgersteaks.com
Offers aged, cut and prime streaks, Berkshire pork, lamb, and veal.
CEO: Suzanne Strassburger Reidy
Type of Packaging: Consumer

12157 Strathroy Foods
PO Box 188
225 Lothian Avenue
Strathroy, ON N7G 3J2
Canada
519-245-4600
Fax: 519-245-3661
Processor and exporter of frozen vegetables including peas and carrots and other vegetable varieties
President: Craig Richardson
Estimated Sales: $20-50 Million
Number Employees: 200
Type of Packaging: Consumer, Food Service, Private Label
Brands:
Red Valley

12158 Straub Brewery Inc
303 Sorg St
St Marys, PA 15857-1592
814-834-2875
Fax: 814-834-7628 straub@straubbeer.com
www.straubbeer.com
Brewer
President & CEO: Bill Brock
Vice President, Sales, Marketing & PR: Cathy Lenze
Number Employees: 20-49
Brands:
Straub
Straub Light

12159 Straub's
8282 Forsyth Blvd
Clayton, MO 63105
314-725-2121
Fax: 314-725-2123 888-725-2121
straubs@anet-stl.com www.straubs.com
Steaks, seafood including lobster tails and gift baskets
President: Jack Straub
Founder: William A Straub
CEO: Jack W Straub Jr
Contact: Roger Mcelroy
roger@straubs.com
Number Employees: 100-249
Brands:
Straubs

12160 Straus Family Creamery
1105 Industrial Ave
Ste 200
Petaluma, CA 94952-1141
707-776-2887
Fax: 707-776-2888 800-572-7783
sfc@strausmilk.com
www.strausfamilycreamery.com
Producers of organic milk and dairy products.
President: Albert Straus
Quality Assurance Supervisor: Ian-Hero Serrano
Inside Sales Administrator: Carissa Biss
Director of People & Culture: Laurangelica Angel Lechon
Production Manager: Miguel Gonzales
Estimated Sales: Less Than $500,000
Number Employees: 5-9

12161 Strauss Bakery
5115 13th Ave
Brooklyn, NY 11219-3560
718-851-7728
Fax: 718-437-1882 tzvi@straussbakery.com
www.straussbakery.com
Bakery products
President: Elliot Berman
bakerellyb@aol.com
Sales Manager: John Macley
Estimated Sales: Less Than $500,000
Number Employees: 5-9

12162 Strauss Brands International
9775 S 60th St
Franklin, WI 53132
414-421-5250
info@straussbrands.com
straussbrands.com
Veal
CEO: Randy Strauss
VP, New Business Development: Lori Dunn
COO: Greg Martin
VP, International Operations: Steve Starnes
Estimated Sales: $50-100 Million
Number Employees: 200-500
Number of Brands: 5
Brands:
Free Raised
Strauss
Chiappetti
Musillami
Dos Mamacitas

12163 Strawberry Hill Grand Delights
1901 Revere Beach Pkwy
Suite 4
Everett, MA 02149-5904
617-319-3557
www.strawberryhillcandy.com
Lollipops, sweeteners, tea candies, chocolate, and marshmallows.
Founder: Henry Zunino
Number Employees: 10-19

12164 Strebin Farms
28245 SE Division Dr
Troutdale, OR 97060-9486
503-665-8328
Fax: 503-669-7783
Fresh and frozen red raspberries
CEO: William P Strebin
williams@strebin.com
Marketing Director: William P Strebin
Estimated Sales: $5-10 Million
Number Employees: 50-99
Type of Packaging: Food Service
Brands:
Strebin Farms

12165 Streblow Vineyards
PO Box 233
Saint Helena, CA 94574-0233
707-963-5892
Fax: 707-963-5835
Wine
President/Owner: Bruce Streblow
Co-Owner: Ana Canales
Brands:
Streblow Vineyards

12166 Streit Carl & Son Co
703 Atkins Ave
Neptune, NJ 07753-5169
732-775-0803
Fax: 732-775-2274 www.carlstreit.com
Processor and wholesaler/distributor of poultry, Italian sausage and special cuts of beef, lamb, veal and pork
Owner: Jim Robinson Jr
VP: Judith Robinson
Estimated Sales: $10-20 Million
Number Employees: 5-9
Square Footage: 12000
Brands:
Allen
Hatfield

12167 Streit's
171 Rt 303
Orangeburg, NY 10962
845-359-9203
Fax: 845-359-9208 info@StreitsMatzos.com
www.streitsmatzos.com
Matzos and other kosher foods.
Executive VP: Aron Yagoda
Executive VP: Aaron Gross
Executive VP: Alan Adler
Estimated Sales: $5-10 Million
Number Employees: 50-99
Brands:
Ethnic Delights
Streits

12168 Stremick's Heritage Foods
4002 Westminster Ave
Santa Ana, CA 92703-1310
714-775-5000
Fax: 714-775-7677 800-371-9010
info@heritage-foods.com
www.stremicksheritagefoods.com
Milk, cheese and cream, organic milk and soy milk
President/CEO: Louis Stremick
CFO: Mike Malone
VP Foodservice Sales: Tom Gustafson
VP Quality Assurance: Jin Jo
VP Sales & Marketing: Dan Nolan
Sales Manager: Tom Gustafson
Estimated Sales: $45.5 Million
Number Employees: 100-249
Type of Packaging: Consumer, Food Service
Other Locations:
Heritage Foods
Riverside CA

12169 Stretch Island Fruit
P.O. Box 649
Solana Beach, CA 92075
800-700-9687
www.stretchislandfruit.com
Fruit snacks
Year Founded: 1976
Estimated Sales: $20-50 Million
Number Employees: 50-99
Square Footage: 12000
Type of Packaging: Consumer, Food Service
Brands:
Stretch Island

12170 Stripling's General Store
1401 West Blvd
Moultrie, GA 31768-4223
229-985-4226
www.striplings.com
Beef and pork products including smoked sausage
President: Danny L Dunn
Number Employees: 5-9
Square Footage: 42000
Type of Packaging: Consumer
Other Locations:
Stripling's General Store
Cordele GA
Brands:
Dunn's

12171 Stroh Brewery
100 River Place Dr # 100
Detroit, MI 48207-4278
313-446-2000
Fax: 313-446-2880
Beer
President/CEO: J Stroh
CEO: William L Henry
Sr Director Corporate Communications/PR: Lacey Logan
VP International Sales: Jovan Jovanovski
Contact: Stephen Ewing
estephen@skillman.org
Estimated Sales: $1-2.5 Million
Number Employees: 250-499
Parent Co: Pabst
Type of Packaging: Private Label

12172 Stroh's Beer
Detroit, MI
strohs-beer.com
Pilsners
Chairman & CEO: Eugene Kashper
CFO: Eric Tis
Chief Sales Officer: Brian Smith
Year Founded: 1850
Parent Co: Pabst Brewing Company

12173 Strong Roots
The Rootstock, Rm 3103
109 S 5th Street
Brooklyn, NY 11249
929-466-1639
hello@strongroots.com
www.strongroots.com
Plant-based prepared foods
CEO: Sam Dennigan

12174 Strossner's Bakery & Cafe
21 Roper Mountain Rd
Greenville, SC 29607-4125
864-233-2990
Fax: 864-232-2819
www.strossnerspoundcakes.com

Prepared European bread mixes, cakes, tortes, fancy pastries, danish and baked/partially baked breads
Owner: Richard Strossner
HR Executive: Carol Martin
info@strossners.com
Sales Manager: Mary Michalsky
Production Manager: Connie Jud
Estimated Sales: $2,000,000
Number Employees: 50-99
Square Footage: 56000
Type of Packaging: Consumer, Food Service

12175 Strub Pickles
100 Roy Boulevard
Brantford, ON N3R 7K2
Canada
519-751-1717
Fax: 519-752-5540 info@strubpickles.com
www.strubpickles.com
Sauerkraut, hot peppers, sweet pimientos, horseradish, herring, jalapeno peppers, kosher dill pickles and relish; exporter of pickles, refrigerated and shelf stable foods, zucchini relish and chili sauce
President: Leo Strub
CEO: Martin Strub
CFO: Arnold Strub
Vice President: Anoy Strub
Number Employees: 100-249
Number of Brands: 2
Number of Products: 250
Square Footage: 424000
Type of Packaging: Consumer, Food Service, Private Label, Bulk
Brands:
Strub's
Willie's

12176 Strube Celery & Vegetable Co
2404 S Wolcott Ave # 16
Unit 16-20
Chicago, IL 60608-5341
773-446-4000
Fax: 312-226-7644 www.strube.com
Wholesale fresh fruits & vegetable
President: David Watson
Chief Executive Officer: Janet Fleming
Chief Financial Officer: Lisa Strube
Executive Vice President: Sue Strube
Chief Technology Officer: Tom Davidson
Director, Sales: Suzy Trott
Estimated Sales: $30 Million
Number Employees: 50-99
Square Footage: 70000

12177 Stryker Sonoma
5110 Highway 128
Geyserville, CA 95441-9422
707-433-1944
Fax: 707-433-1948 800-433-1944
Wine
Owner: Craig Mac Donald
Owner: Karen Naley
Owner: Kat Stryker
Estimated Sales: Below $5 Million
Number Employees: 10-19
Brands:
Stryker Sonoma Winery Vineyards

12178 Stuart & CO
12 Mcguinness Blvd S
Apt 2B
Brooklyn, NY 11222-4995
347-292-7456
Fax: 212-202-3868
BBQ sauce, potato chips, spice blends and beef jerky
Founder: Michael Steifman
Type of Packaging: Food Service
Brands:
A-Salted
Bitchin'
Brooklyn Bourbon
Cherry Bomb
Dark & Moody
Lakehouse Lime & Chili
Marshall's Curry
Mr. Fancy's
No.5
Smoky's House

12179 Stuart Hale Co
4350 W Ohio St
Chicago, IL 60624-1051
773-638-1800
Fax: 773-638-1888 info@grandwarehouse.com
www.grandwarehouse.com
Bakers' supplies including bakery pan grease and pan and white mineral oils
President: David Schulman
support@stuarthale.com
General Manager: Stuart Schulman
Estimated Sales: $170000
Number Employees: 10-19
Type of Packaging: Private Label, Bulk

12180 Stubb's Legendary BBQ
811 Barton Springs Rd
Austin, TX 78704-8702
512-480-0203
Fax: 512-476-3425 800-227-2283
www.stubbsbbq.com
Rubs, sauces and marinades
Year Founded: 1968
Estimated Sales: $30 Million
Brands:
Stubb's

12181 Stumptown Coffee Roasters Inc
100 SE Salmon St
Portland, OR 97214-3370
503-230-7797
Fax: 503-230-7125 www.stumptowncoffee.com
Coffee
Owner: Duane Sorenson
Number Employees: 50-99

12182 Sturm Foods Inc
215 Center St
Manawa, WI 54949-9277
920-596-2511
Fax: 920-596-3040 800-347-8876
www.sturmfoods.com
Healthy drink mixes and supplements
President & CEO: Michael Upchurch
Manager: Rob Rugger
rrugger@sturminc.com
Number Employees: 250-499
Parent Co: TreeHouse Foods
Type of Packaging: Consumer, Food Service, Private Label, Bulk
Brands:
Vita Splash
Fulfill Fitness
Power Edge
Morning Spark
Replenish
Moo Magic
Frappe Creme
Cider Drink Mix
Mixer Stix Drink Mix
McCann's Irish Oatmeal
For Pet's Sake

12183 Stutz Candy Company
7306 Frankford Avenue
Philadelphia, PA 19136-3827
215-333-7323
888-692-2639
Candy including boxed chocolates
President: John Glaser
Estimated Sales: $3,100,000
Number Employees: 5 to 9
Square Footage: 42000
Type of Packaging: Consumer

12184 Subco Foods Inc
4350 S Taylor Dr
Sheboygan, WI 53081-8479
920-457-7761
Fax: 920-457-3899 800-473-0757
mkhan@subcofoods.com www.subcofoods.com
Contract packager/ Private label manufacturer products include: drink mixes, iced tea mixes, hot chocolate, gelatins, puddings, cappuccino mixes, coffee creamers, instant gravies, soup bases, spice/spice blends, cake mixes andnutraceuticals
President: Masroor Khan
Year Founded: 1925
Estimated Sales: $13,100,000
Number Employees: 50-99
Square Footage: 375000
Type of Packaging: Food Service, Private Label
Other Locations:
Subco Foods Inc
West Chicago IL
Brands:
New Image

12185 Sucesores de Pedro Cortes
Manuel Camunas #205, Tres Monjitas
PO BOX 363626
Hato Rey, PR 00918-1485
787-754-7040
Fax: 787-754-2650 cortesco@tld.net
www.chocolatecortes.com
Chocolate and cocoa products; private labeling available; importer of chocolate, milk drinks and crackers; wholesaler/distributor of confectionery items, beverages and biscuits
President: Ignacio Cortes Del Valle
VP: Ignacio Cortes Gelpi
Number Employees: 50-99
Number of Brands: 11
Square Footage: 150000
Type of Packaging: Consumer, Private Label, Bulk
Brands:
Chocolate Cortes
Choki
Semi-Industrialized

12186 SuckerPunch Gourmet
7525 W 99th Place
Bridgeview, IL 60455
708-784-3000
contact@suckerpunchgourmet.com
suckerpunchgourmet.com
Pickles, Bloody Mary mix and salsa
President & COO: Todd Francisco
tfrancisco@suckerpunchgourmet.com
Director of Finance: Jennifer Martens
Founder & Exec. VP: David van Alphen
Brands:
SUCKERPUNCH

12187 Sucre
3930 Euphrosine St
New Orleans, LA 70125-1309
504-708-4366
Fax: 504-708-4367 855-557-8273
info@shopsucre.com
Macarons, dark chocolate and chocolate gifts
Founder: Joel Dondis
Executive Pastry Chef: Tariq Hanna
Manager: Michelle Kuehne
Number Employees: 10-19

12188 Sucre
3930 Euphrosine St
New Orleans, LA 70125-1309
504-708-4366
info@shopsucre.com
Manufacturer of macarons, chocolates, confections, and cakes.
Founder: Joel Dondis
Executive Pastry Chef: Tariq Hanna
Manager: Michelle Kuehne
Number Employees: 10-19

12189 Sudbury Soups and Salads
40 Walker Farm Rd
Sudbury, MA 01776-2442
978-443-7715
Fax: 978-443-7715 888-783-7687
sudsoup@ultranet.com
Natural foods, dry soup mixes, lentils
CEO: Susan Sullivan
Brands:
Sudbury

12190 Sudlersville Frozen Food Locker
PO Box 203
Sudlersville, MD 21668-0203
410-438-3106
Fax: 410-438-3121
Frozen meat products including beef and pork
President: William Faust
Chairman: Ronald Ford
Bookkeeper: Marge Messner
Estimated Sales: Less than $500,000
Number Employees: 5-9
Type of Packaging: Consumer
Brands:
Sudlersville

12191 **Sudwerk Privatbrauerei Hubsch**
2001 2nd St
Davis, CA 95618-5474
530-758-8700
Fax: 530-753-0590 www.sudwerk.com
Beer
Owner: Tim Mc Donald
VP: Dean Unger
Quality Assurance: Candace Whalin
Marketing Director: Dave Sipes
Contact: Kb Brandl
kb@sudwerkbrew.com
Plant Manager/Purchasing Director: Neil Jensen
Estimated Sales: Below $5 Million
Number Employees: 50-99
Brands:
Hubsch Doppel Bock
Hubsch Dunkel
Hubsch Lager
Hubsch Marzen
Hubsch Pilsener
Suderwerk Doppel
Suderwerk Dunkel
Suderwerk Lager
Suderwerk Mai Bock
Suderwerk Marzen
Suderwerk Pilsenser

12192 **Sugai Kona Coffee**
79-7098 Mamalahoa Hwy
Holualoa, HI 96725-8742
808-322-7717
Fax: 808-322-4008 kona@kona.net
www.sugaikonacoffee.com
Producers of Sugai Kona coffee
CEO: Lee Sugai
kona@kona.net
Estimated Sales: Less Than $500,000
Number Employees: 5-9
Number of Brands: 5
Number of Products: 30
Square Footage: 60000
Type of Packaging: Consumer, Food Service, Private Label, Bulk
Brands:
Sugai Kona Grove Coffee
Sugai Kona Coffee Emporium

12193 **Sugar & Plumm**
377 Amsterdam Ave
New York, NY 10024-6207
212-787-8778
Fax: 212-787-8780 info@sugarandplumm.com
www.sugarandplumm.com
Manufacturer of dark chocolate, truffles, boxed chocolate, macarons, and cookies.
Founder: Lamia Jacobs
CEO: Thierry Atlan
atlanthierry@sugarandplumm.com
Estimated Sales: Less Than $500,000
Number Employees: 1-4

12194 **Sugar Bob's Smoked Maple Syrup**
2564 Landgrove Rd
Londonderry, VT 05148
802-297-7665
sugarbobsfinestkind@gmail.com
www.sugarbobsfinestkind.com
Maple syrup
President & Sugarmaker: Robert F Hausslein
Estimated Sales: Under $500,000
Number Employees: 2-10
Brands:
Sugar Bob's Finest Kind

12195 **Sugar Bowl Bakery**
1963 Sabre St
Hayward, CA 94545-1021
510-782-2118
Fax: 510-782-2119 888-688-1380
info@sugarbowlbakery.com
www.sugarbowlbakery.com
Baked goods, gourmet cakes and pastries.
Chief Executive Officer: Andrew Ly
Director of Finance: Peter Vermeulen
General Manager/Vice President: Michael Ly
Assistant General Manager: Kristine Trieu
Buyer: Urmi Mukherjee
Buyer: Paul Rivas
Director of Sales & Strategy: Pete Thomsen
Human Resources Manager: Theresa Martinez
Director of Operations: Frank Kieffer
navision@sugarbowlbakery.com
Chef/Process Manufacturing Manager: Kevin Ly
Purchasing Agent: Kevin Ly
Estimated Sales: $30-60 Million
Number Employees: 250-499
Square Footage: 120000

12196 **Sugar Cane Growers Co-Op of Florida**
1500 George Wedgworth Way
Belle Glade, FL 33430
561-996-5556
info@scgc.org
www.scgc.org
Sugar and blackstrap molasses.
Founder/Chair: George Wedgworth
CEO: Antonio Contreras
CFO: Brian Lohmann
Year Founded: 1960
Estimated Sales: $100 Million
Number Employees: 550
Number of Brands: 6
Type of Packaging: Consumer
Brands:
Domino
C&H
Tate & Lyle
Lyles Golden Syrup
Sidul
Sores

12197 **Sugar Creek**
2101 Kenskill Ave
Washington Ct Hs, OH 43160-9404
740-335-7440
Fax: 740-335-7443 800-848-8205
www.sugarcreek.com
Manufacturer of bacon and turkey bacon.
Chairman/CEO: John Richardson
COO: Michael Richardson
CFO: Tom Bollinger
tbollinger@sugar-creek.com
VP of Quality Assurance: Rob Howe
VP of Sales: Jim Coughlin
Plant Manager: Dan Sileo
Estimated Sales: $20 Million
Number Employees: 1000-4999
Number of Brands: 1
Type of Packaging: Consumer, Food Service, Bulk
Other Locations:
Cincinnati OH
Hamilton OH
Frontenac KS
Cambridge City IN
Brands:
Sugar Creek

12198 **Sugar Creek Winery**
125 Boone Country Ln
Defiance, MO 63341-3103
636-987-2400
Fax: 636-987-2051 info@sugarcreekwines.com
www.sugarcreekwines.com
Wines
Owner: Ken Miller
kmiller@sugarcreekwines.com
President: Wesley Wissman
Estimated Sales: $5-10 Million
Number Employees: 20-49

12199 **Sugar Flowers Plus**
601 Vine St
Glendale, CA 91204
818-545-3592
Fax: 818-545-7459 800-972-2935
Cake decorations including gum paste flowers
Owner: Terry Becker
R&D: Anna Becker
Sales: Garrick Wright
Plant Manager: Gary Roundtree
Estimated Sales: $.5-1 million
Number Employees: 1-4
Type of Packaging: Consumer, Food Service
Brands:
Sugar Flowers

12200 **Sugar Foods Corp**
9500 El Dorado Ave
Sun Valley, CA 91352-1339
818-768-7900
Fax: 818-768-7619 info@sugarfoods.com
www.sugarfoods.com
Contract packager and exporter of dry entrees, side dishes, mixes including snack, nondairy creamer, sugar and sugar substitutes and croutons in bags, pouches, cups, cartons and canisters
President: Stephen O'Dell
sodell@sugarfoods.com
Operations Manager: Brian Thomson
Estimated Sales: $8500000
Number Employees: 250-499
Square Footage: 1400000
Parent Co: Sugar Foods Corporation

12201 **Sugar Foods Corp**
950 3rd Ave
12st Fl
New York, NY 10022
info@sugarfoods.com
www.sugarfoods.com
Sweetners, non dairy creamers, croutons, stuffing mixes, crumbs/cracker meal, snacks & snack mixes, specialty items, and almonds.
Chairman & CEO: Donald Tober
COO: James Walsh
jwalsh@sugarfoods.com
Year Founded: 1948
Number Employees: 500-999
Type of Packaging: Consumer, Food Service
Brands:
Almond Toppers
Blue Diamond
C&H
Crisp 'n Fresh
Fresh Gourmet
Natrataste
Non Diary Toppings
Sugar In the Raw
Supersnax
Sweet 'n Low
True Lemon

12202 **Sugar Plum**
88 Dilley St # 2
Kingston, PA 18704-3437
570-288-0559
Fax: 570-288-1710 800-447-8427
customerservice@sugar-plum.com
www.sugar-plum.com
Chocolate covered potato chips, chocolate covered pretzels and chocolate covered popcorn.
Owner: Frann Edley
frann@sugar-plum.com
Estimated Sales: Less Than $500,000
Number Employees: 1-4
Brands:
Dip Sticks
Get Popped
Supremes

12203 **Sugar Plum LLC**
5756 W Main St
Houma, LA 70360-1745
985-872-9524
Fax: 985-872-9664
Designer cakes, wedding cakes, holiday cakes, confectionary, and various other desserts
Owner: Cindy Dugas
thesugarplum1@comcast.net
Number Employees: 10-19
Square Footage: 10000

12204 **Sugar Sugar**
465 S. Orlando Ave
#205
Maitland, FL 32751
877-784-2724
Fax: 877-249-6419 info@handmadelollies.com
www.handmadelollies.com
Candy lollipops

12205 **SugarCreek**
12021 Sheraton Lane
Cincinnati, OH 45246
479-968-1005
Fax: 479-968-5651 800-445-2715
sales@sugarcreek.com www.sugarcreek.com
Pork bacon, turkey bacon, chicken bacon, sausage links and patties, flat surface proteins, large scale sous vide, meatballs

Chairman & CEO: John G Richardson
Chief Operating Officer: Michael Richardson
Chief Financial Officer: Thomas J Bollinger
VP, Sales & Business Development: Alan Riney
Director of Sales: Jennifer Hutcheson
EVP, Operations: Mike Rozzano
Estimated Sales: $20-50 Million
Number Employees: 700
Square Footage: 25000
Type of Packaging: Private Label

12206 Sugarbush Farm
591 Sugarbush Farm Rd
Woodstock, VT 05091-8089
802-457-1757
Fax: 802-457-3269 800-281-1757
contact@sugarbushfarm.com
www.sugarbushfarm.com
Waxed cheeses and Pure Vermont Maple Syrup
President: Elizabeth Luce
sugarbsh@sover.net
Vice President: Jeff Luce
Estimated Sales: $.5-1 million
Number Employees: 5-9

12207 Sugardale Foods Inc
800-860-6333
www.sugardale.com
Bacon, ham, hot dogs, lunch meats and weiners.
VP of Corporate Sales: Mark Slaughter
Estimated Sales: $100-500 Million
Number Employees: 500-999

12208 Sugarman of Vermont
P.O.Box 1060
Hardwick, VT 05843
802-472-9891
Fax: 802-472-8526 800-932-7700
sales@sugarmanofvermont.com
www.sugarmanofvermont.com
Processor and exporter of jams, jellies, marmalades and preserves; processor and exporter of maple syrup
President: Anthony Sedutto
Contact: Marilyn Rogerson
m.rogerson@sugarmanofvermont.com
Number Employees: 20-49
Square Footage: 160000
Type of Packaging: Consumer, Food Service, Private Label, Bulk
Brands:
Sugarman

12209 Sugarplum Desserts
20381 62nd Avenue
Building 5
Langley, BC V3A 5E6
Canada
604-534-2282
Fax: 604-534-2280 info@sugarplumdesserts.com
www.sugarplumdesserts.com
Thaw and serve cheesecakes and thaw and bake cookies
President: Leslie Goodman
Number Employees: 15
Square Footage: 32000

12210 Sugarright
Fairless Hills, PA
215-486-2105
sales@sugaright.com
www.sugaright.com
Various types of sugar and syrups.
President: Paul Farmer
Year Founded: 2016
Type of Packaging: Food Service, Bulk

12211 Suity Confections Co
8105 NW 77th St.
P.O. Box 558943
Miami, FL 33166
305-639-3300
Fax: 305-593-7070 info@suity.com
www.suity.com
Candy, gum, chocolates, and cookies
VP: Jose Garrido Jr
garridojr@waltonpost.com
Quality Control: Luis Perez
Estimated Sales: $20-50 Million
Number Employees: 20-49
Brands:
Bubble Gum
Fruiticas Lollipops
Fruity Ball
Party Snacks
Salty Snacks

12212 Suiza Dairy Corporation
131 Ave De Diego
San Juan, PR 00921
787-707-6500
earias@suizapr.com
www.suizapuertorico.com
Dairy Products
President: Carmen Marrero
Estimated Sales: $100-500 Million
Parent Co: Suiza Foods
Type of Packaging: Private Label

12213 Suja Juice
3831 Ocean Ranch Blvd
Oceanside, CA 92056
855-879-7852
info@sujajuice.com
www.sujajuice.com
Nutritious drinks
Co-Founder: Annie Lawless
CEO & Co-Founder: Jeff Church
Vice President, Sales: Jessica Pratt
Estimated Sales: $48.6 Million
Number Employees: 175
Brands:
Suja

12214 Suji's Korean Cuisine
71 Columbia St
Suite 125
Seattle, WA 98104
206-985-6640
www.sujiskorean.com
Korean BBQ, meals and sauces
Founder: Suji Park

12215 Sukhi's Gourmet Indian Food
23682 Clawiter Rd
Hayward, CA 94545-1329
510-264-9265
Fax: 510-264-1236 888-478-5447
info@sukhis.com www.sukhis.com
Gourmet indian food
President/Owner: Sukhi Singh
Number Employees: 50-99

12216 Sullivan Harbor Farm
1545 U.S.
Route 1
Hancock Village, ME 04640
207-422-2209
Fax: 207-422-8229 800-422-4014
sullivanharborfarm@verizon.net
www.sullivanharborfarm.com
Smoked salmon
Owner: Joel Franzman
Estimated Sales: $300,000-500,000
Number Employees: 1-4

12217 Sullivan Vineyards
1090 Galleron Rd
St Helena, CA 94574-9540
707-963-9646
Fax: 707-963-0377 877-244-7337
www.sullivanwine.com
Wines
CEO: Joanna C Sullivan
CFO: Sean Sullivan
VP Marketing: Kelleen Sullivan
Operations Manager: Ross Sullivan
Estimated Sales: Below $5 Million
Number Employees: 5-9
Type of Packaging: Private Label
Brands:
Sullivan Cabernet Sauvignon
Sullivan Chardonnay
Sullivan Coeur De Vigne
Sullivan Merlot

12218 Sulpice Chocolate
121 Barrington Commons Ct # A
Barrington, IL 60010-3256
630-301-2345
info@sulpicechocolat.com
www.sulpicechocolat.com
Manufacturer of dark chocolate bars.
Founder: Anne Shaeffer
anne.shaeffer@sulpicechocolat.com
Number Employees: 5-9
Brands:
Sulpice

12219 Summer Fresh
334 Rowntree Dairy Rd
Woodbridge, ON L4L 8H2
Canada
905-856-8816
Fax: 905-856-9298 877-472-5237
social@summerfresh.com www.summerfresh.com
Salads, dips, snacks and hummus
President: Susan Niczowski
CFO: Gilles Hamel
VP, Sales: Lynn Sandell
Director, Operations: Dane Adams
Senior Manager, Production: Predrag Knezevic
Estimated Sales: $100 Million
Number Employees: 51-200
Type of Packaging: Private Label
Brands:
Summer Fresh

12220 Summer Garden Food Manufacturing
500 McClurg Rd
Boardman, OH 44512
330-965-8455
Fax: 330-965-3864 info@summergardenfood.com
www.summergardenfood.com
Private label foods including Italian pasta sauces, cream based sauces, meat and fish sauces, specialty and finishing sauces, bbq and wing sauces, and salsas. Also, soups, simmer sauces, and marinades and dressings
Owner and CEO: Thomas R. Zidian
CFO: John Angelilli
VP: Anthony Larocca
Quality Control Manager: Sean Doering
Contact: John Angelilli
johna@summergardenfood.com
Manager: Rick Coradini
Estimated Sales: $1.3 Million
Number Employees: 20
Square Footage: 100000
Type of Packaging: Consumer, Private Label, Bulk

12221 Summer In Vermont Jams
686 Davis Rd
Hinesburg, VT 05461-9359
802-453-3793
Homegrown, homemade jams and jellies.
President: Norma Norris
Estimated Sales: $.5-1 million
Number Employees: 1-4

12222 Summerfield Farm Products
4206 Twymans Mill Rd
Orange, VA 22960-4850
540-547-9600
Fax: 540-547-9628 800-898-3276
www.summerfieldfarm.com
Free-range veal, venison, salmon and condiments
President: Jamie Nicoll
Marketing Manager: Mary Thornton
Financial Manager: Carolyn Mills
Accounts Receivable: Barbara Frazier
Estimated Sales: Below $5 Million
Number Employees: 10
Brands:
Summerfield Farms

12223 Summerfield Foods
335 Shiloh Valley Ct
Santa Rosa, CA 95403-8085
707-579-3938
Fax: 707-579-8442 sales@summerfieldfoods.com
Contract packager and exporter of canned vegetarian foods including refried beans, soups and chili; also, cookies and cakes; private labeling available
President: Roland Au
roland@summerfieldfoods.com
Executive VP: John Stanghellini
Estimated Sales: $2000000
Number Employees: 5-9
Type of Packaging: Consumer, Private Label
Brands:
Summerfield's

12224 Summerland Sweets
6206 Canyon View Road
Summerland, BC V0H 1Z7
Canada
250-494-0377
Fax: 250-494-7432 800-577-1277
summerlandsweets@telus.net
www.summerlandsweets.com

Canner of fruit candy/pectin jelly including apricot, cherry and apple; also, fruit leather, gourmet jam, fruit syrup and fruit pulp
President: Frances Beulah
Estimated Sales: $1,200,000
Number Employees: 10
Number of Brands: 2
Number of Products: 40
Type of Packaging: Food Service, Private Label

12225 Summit Brewing Company
910 Montreal Cir
Saint Paul, MN 55102
651-265-7800
Fax: 651-265-7801 info@summitbrewing.com
www.summitbrewing.com
Brewer of beer
President: Mark Stutrud
Contact: Derek Allmendinger
allmendinger.derek@summitbrewing.com
Operations Manager: Christopher Seitz
Production Manager: Jon Lindberg
Number Employees: 20-49
Square Footage: 232000
Brands:
Summit

12226 Summit Hill Flavors
21 Worlds Fair Drive
Somerset, NJ 08873
732-805-0335
Fax: 732-805-1994 www.summithillflavors.com
Natural flavorings for dry and liquid applications used for marinating meats and poultry. Flavorings for soups, gravies, sauces, food bases and pasta dishes.
Contact: Selvin Medina
medinaselvin@summithillflavors.com

12227 Summit Lake Vineyards
2000 Summit Lake Dr
Angwin, CA 94508-9778
707-965-2488
Fax: 707-965-2281
www.summitlakevineyards.securecheckout.com
Wines
Owner: Robert Brakesman
summitlake@summitlakevineyards.com
CEO: Heather Griffin
Marketing Director: Heather Griffin
Estimated Sales: $200,000-$300,000
Number Employees: 1-4
Number of Brands: 3
Number of Products: 3
Brands:
Clair Riley Zinfandel Port
Emily Kestral Cabern
Summit Lake Vinyards

12228 Sun Chlorella USA
3305 Kashiwa Street
Torrance, CA 90505-4022
310-891-0600
Fax: 310-891-0621 800-829-2828
www.sunchlorellausa.com
Ginseng and chlorella including tablets, liquid extract and green single cell algae with broken cell walls
President/CEO: Futoshi Nakayama
VP/Chief Financial Officer: Ellen Kubijanto
VP/Chief Operating Officer: Rose Straub
Marketing Manager: Susan Arboua
Public Relations: Janise Zantine
Estimated Sales: $24 Million
Number Employees: 61
Square Footage: 5000
Parent Co: YSK International Corporation
Brands:
Green Magician
Sun Chlorella
Sun Siberian Ginseng
Wakasa

12229 Sun Empire Foods
P.O.Box 376
Kerman, CA 93630-0376
559-846-8208
Fax: 559-846-9488 800-252-4786
Hand made coated delicacies
Co-Owner: Phil Dee
Co-Owner: Sandy Dee
Estimated Sales: $.5-1 million
Number Employees: 5-9
Number of Products: 100
Type of Packaging: Consumer

12230 Sun Garden Sprouts
1011 Volunteer Drive
Cookeville, TN 38506
931-400-2710
www.sproutnet.com
Bean sprouts
President: Robert Rust
Marketing: Kelly Warren
Estimated Sales: $5-10 Million
Number Employees: 20-49
Brands:
Sun Garden Sprouts

12231 Sun Glo Of Idaho
378 S 7th W
PO Box 300
Sugar City, ID 83448-5009
208-356-7346
Fax: 208-356-7351 bruce@sunglo-idaho.com
www.sungloidaho.com
Idaho potatoes
CEO: George M Crapo
george@sunglo-idaho.com
CEO: Ceorge Crapo
CFO: Bruce Crapo
VP Fresh Sales: Betty Miles
Human Resource Manager: Melissa Coles
Number Employees: 100-249
Type of Packaging: Consumer, Food Service, Private Label, Bulk
Brands:
Sun Supreme
Sun-Glo
Top Bakes

12232 Sun Grove Foods Inc
45 Tulip St
Passaic, NJ 07055-3133
973-574-1110
Fax: 973-574-1113 info@sungrovefoods.com
www.sungrovefoods.com
Olive oils.
Executive Vice President: Joanna Lacina
Contact: Ed Cekici
ecekici@sungrovefoods.com
Number Employees: 5-9

12233 Sun Groves Inc
3393 State Road 580
Safety Harbor, FL 34695-4931
727-726-8484
Fax: 727-726-7158 800-672-6438
www.sungroves.com
Citrus fruits, gift baskets, preserves, and fudge
Owner: Michelle Urbanski
Estimated Sales: $20-50 Million
Number Employees: 20-49
Brands:
Sun Groves

12234 Sun Harvest Foods Inc
6201 Progressive Dr # 400
Suite 400
San Diego, CA 92154-6651
619-661-0909
Fax: 619-690-1173 www.productosfrugo.com.mx
Processor, importer and exporter of IQF entrees, canned vegetables, jalapenos, tomatillo, sauces, salsa, broccoli, cauliflower, vegetable blends and fruit; kosher items available
President: Jorge Gonzalez
Sales & Marketing: Art Sanchez
Estimated Sales: $1.4 Million
Number Employees: 1-4
Square Footage: 640000
Parent Co: Productos Frugo S.A. de C.V.
Type of Packaging: Consumer, Food Service, Private Label, Bulk
Brands:
Secret Sun

12235 Sun Noodle
1933 Colburn St
Honolulu, HI 96819-3248
808-841-5808
Fax: 808-842-7622 info@sunnoodle.com
www.sunnoodle.com
Japanese style noodles
President: Hidehito Uki
Contact: Kenshiro Uki
kenshiro@sunnoodle.com
Estimated Sales: $2.5-5 Million
Number Employees: 5-9

12236 Sun Noodle New Jersey
40 Kero Road
Carlstadt, NJ 07072
201-530-1100
www.sunnoodle.com
Ramen noodles, yakisoba, udon, and soba noodles, ramen soup.
CEO: Hidehito Uki
Number Employees: 80
Square Footage: 10000

12237 Sun Olive Oil Company
4668 Town Crossing Drive
Suite 109
Jacksonville, FL 32246
904-645-6630
Fax: 805-434-0626 www.sunoliveoil.com
Olive oil
President: Rory Muniz
Brands:
Sun Olive Oil

12238 Sun Opta Inc.
2233 Argentia Rd.
Sutie 401
Mississauga, ON L5N 2X7
Canada
952-820-2518
info@sunopta.com
www.sunopta.com
Organic, non-GMO raw materials such as soy, corn, sunflower and coconut.
CEO: Joseph Ennen
CAO: Jill Barnett
CFO: Scott Huckins
Chief Information Officer: Rob Duchscher
Chief Quality Officer: David Largey
SVP, Supply Chain: Christopher Whitehair
Year Founded: 1973
Estimated Sales: $1.3 Billion
Number Employees: 1,300+
Type of Packaging: Consumer, Food Service, Bulk
Brands:
Sunrich Naturals
Nature's Finest
Pure Nature

12239 Sun Orchard INC
1200 S 30th St
Haines City, FL 33844-9099
863-422-5062
Fax: 863-422-5176 877-875-8423
www.sunorchard.com
Manufacturer of citrus fruits and juices.
President/CEO: Marc Isaacs
CFO: Thomas Spielberger
SVP, Strategy & Planning: Peter Maulbeck
Manager: Tom Winter
Estimated Sales: $20-50 Million
Number Employees: 100-249
Number of Brands: 4
Parent Co: Sun Orchard, Inc.
Type of Packaging: Food Service, Private Label
Brands:
EPIC
fOMZ
Fruit 66
Sun Orchard

12240 Sun Orchard Inc
2 South Biscayne Blvd.
Miami, FL 33131
786-646-9200
800-505-8423
info@sunorchard.com www.sunorchard.com
Juices including orange, grapefruit, lemon and lime; also, apple cider, lemonade, margarita mix and granita slushes
President/CEO: Marc Isaacs
CFO: Carl Colletti
SVP Sales: Bob Corlett
VP, Product Innovation: Tony Decastro
VP, Purchasing: Chris Hess
Estimated Sales: $20-50 Million
Number Employees: 50-99
Square Footage: 40000
Type of Packaging: Consumer, Food Service, Private Label, Bulk
Brands:
Sun Orchards Labels

12241 **(HQ)Sun Pac Foods**
10 Sun Pac Boulevard
Brampton, ON L6S 4R5
Canada
905-792-2700
Fax: 905-792-8490
Processor and contract packager of canned fruit juices, drinks and concentrates, bread crumbs, croutons and tortilla chips; importer of canned seafood and mandarin orange sections; exporter of juices and drinks
President: J Riddell
VP Finance: Vince McEwan
VP Imports/Exports: Cathy Knowles
Number Employees: 135
Square Footage: 1420000
Type of Packaging: Consumer, Food Service, Private Label, Bulk
Brands:
Featherweight
Fiesta
McDowell Ovens
Saico
Sun Crop
Sun Pac

12242 **Sun Pacific**
1095 E Green St
Pasadena, CA 91106
213-612-9957
customercare@sunpacific.com
www.sunpacific.com
Grower, exporter and shipper of produce
Founder: Berne Evans
berneevans@sunpacfic.com
Estimated Sales: $120,000
Number Employees: 20-49
Square Footage: 2310
Brands:
Cuties(c)
Mighties

12243 **Sun Ray International**
1260 Lake Blvd
Davis, CA 95616
530-297-1688
Fax: 530-758-0089 sales@sunraygroup.net
www.sunraygroup.net
Agricultural food ingredients such as dehydrated onion, garlic, tomato and other vegetable products.
Contact: Jihua Lui
jihua.lui@sunraygroup.net

12244 **Sun Rich Fresh Foods USA Inc**
515 E Rincon St
Corona, CA 92879-1391
951-735-3800
Fax: 951-735-3322 800-735-3801
customerservice@sun-rich.com www.sunrich.com
Fresh cut fruit
Vice President: Roxanne Emmerling
roxannee@sun-rich.com
EVP/CFO: Neville Israel
Vice President of Supply Chain: Jeff Pitchford
Quality Assurance Technician: Daysi Aleman
Sales/Marketing Coordinator: Lisa Ten Heggeler
Vice President of Sales and Marketing: Cam Haygarth
HR Manager: Sylvia Del Rio
roxannee@sun-rich.com
VP Operations: Dan O'Connell
Senior Production Manager: Javier Lopez
Number Employees: 100-249
Square Footage: 66000
Type of Packaging: Consumer, Food Service
Other Locations:
Vancouver, Canada
Los Angeles CA
Toronto, Canada
Reading PA

12245 **Sun State Beverage**
2442 Pleasant Hill Rd
Atlanta, GA 30349
770-451-3990
Fax: 770-813-0065
Beverages
President: John Son
Estimated Sales: $2.5-5 000,000
Number Employees: 1-4

12246 **Sun States**
PO Box 25965
Charlotte, NC 28229-5965
704-821-0615
Fax: 704-821-0616
Cheese
Marketing Director: Marty Crosby

12247 **Sun Sun Food Products**
14415 115th Avenue NW
Edmonton, AB T5M 3B8
Canada
780-454-4261
Fax: 780-453-1728
Oriental foods including bean sprouts, steamed noodles and wonton and egg roll wrappers
Manager: Ken Nhan
Type of Packaging: Food Service
Brands:
Sun Sun

12248 **Sun Tropics Inc**
2430 Camino Ramon
Suite 111
San Ramon, CA 94583-4214
925-380-6324
Fax: 925-202-2223 www.suntropics.net
Juice, cider, ice cream, sorbet
President: Sharon Sy
Contact: Rhonda Lowry
rlowry@suntropics.net
Estimated Sales: 2,200,000
Number Employees: 5-9

12249 **Sun Valley Mustard**
731 1st Ave N
Hailey, ID 83333-5024
208-578-0078
Fax: 208-785-0216 800-628-7124
bstuns@cs.com www.sunvalleymustard.com
Mustard
President: Latham Williams
General Manager: Barbara Stuns
Estimated Sales: Under $500,000
Number Employees: 1-4
Brands:
Sun Valley Mustard

12250 **Sun Valley Packing**
7381 Avenue 432
Reedley, CA 93654-9016
559-591-1515
Fax: 559-591-1616 sunvaly@mobynet.com
Plums, peaches and nectarines
Owner: Walter Jones
wjones@sunvalley.com
Number Employees: 250-499
Brands:
Kay Pak

12251 **Sun Valley Raisins Inc**
9595 S Hughes Ave
Fresno, CA 93706-9731
559-233-8070
Fax: 559-233-8075 info@sunvalleyraisins.com
www.sunvalleyraisins.com
Premium raisins from California's Central Valley for over 70 years.
Manager: Charles Degeneres
chuck@sunvalleyraisins.com
Number Employees: 5-9
Type of Packaging: Bulk
Brands:
Sun Valley

12252 **Sun West**
2281 W 205th Street
Torrance, CA 90501-1450
310-320-4000
Fax: 310-320-8444
Distributor of rice based sweetners and rice based proteins
President: Qasim Habib
Estimated Sales: $2.5-5 Million
Number Employees: 5

12253 **Sun West Foods**
1550 Drew Avenue
Suite 150
Davis, CA 95618-7852
530-758-8550
Fax: 530-758-8110 nor-calrice@saber.net
www.sunwestfoods.com
Grower/packer of processed wild rice; developer of proprietary wild rice varieties and specialty rices; processor of quick-cook wild and brown rice. Specializes in ingredient sales to packers and ingredient users
President: James Errecarte
Contact: Rebecca Baxter
rbaxter@sunwestfoods.com
Estimated Sales: $5-10 Million
Number Employees: 10-19
Square Footage: 92000
Type of Packaging: Food Service, Private Label, Bulk
Brands:
Nor-Cal

12254 **(HQ)Sun World Intl LLC**
73161 Fred Waring Dr
Suite 200
Palm Desert, CA 92260
760-398-9450
www.sun-world.com
Fresh fruits and vegetables ranging from apricots, peaches, nectarines and grapes to tangerines, grapefruit, lemons and oranges to sweet colored peppers and seedless watermelon. Also Medjool dates and Deglet Noor dates.
President: David Marguleas
EVP & CFO: Keith Mitchell
EVP, Business Development: Jeff Jackson
Marketing Manager: Dan, Joubert
Year Founded: 1976
Estimated Sales: $231.70 Million
Number Employees: 200-499
Type of Packaging: Private Label

12255 **Sun-Brite Canning**
1532 County Rd 34
Kingsville, ON N0P 2G0
Canada
519-326-9033
Fax: 519-326-8700 www.sun-brite.com
Tomato canners
President: Henry Iacobelli
Director of Sales: John Iacobelli
Plant Manager: Sam Lopez
Number Employees: 50-99
Type of Packaging: Consumer, Food Service, Private Label

12256 **Sun-Maid Growers of California**
13525 S Bethel Ave
Kingsburg, CA 93631-9232
559-896-8000
Fax: 559-897-2362 info@sunmaid.com
www.sunmaid.com
Sun-dried fruits including raisins, peaches, apricots and pears; raisin paste and juice concentrate
President & CEO: Harry Overly
Number Employees: 500-999
Type of Packaging: Consumer, Food Service, Private Label, Bulk
Brands:
Sun-Maid

12257 **Sun-Re Cheese Co**
178 Lenker Ave
Sunbury, PA 17801-2902
570-286-1511
Fax: 570-286-5123
Italian cheeses including pizza, mozzarella and ricotta
Owner: Thomas Aiello
thomas@strausmilk.com
Plant Manager: Gary Deates
Estimated Sales: $6.4 Million
Number Employees: 50-99
Square Footage: 224000
Type of Packaging: Consumer, Food Service, Private Label, Bulk

12258 **Sun-Rise**
3423 Casa Marina Road NW
Alexandria, MN 56308-9058
320-846-5720
Beverages
President: John Sherman
Brands:
Sun-Rise Beverages

12259 Sun-Rype Products
1165 Ethel St
Kelowna, BC V1Y 2W4
Canada
888-786-7973
www.sunrype.com
Juice and fruit snacks and also organic fruit snacks.
President & CEO: Lesli Bradley
Manager, Strategic Growth: Cindy Wilker
Year Founded: 1946
Estimated Sales: $148 Million
Number Employees: 335
Square Footage: 123602
Type of Packaging: Consumer, Food Service, Private Label, Bulk
Brands:
Energy-To-Go
Fruit-To-Go
Sun-Rype

12260 SunButter
PO Box 3022
Fargo, ND 58108
Fax: 701-282-5325 877-873-4501
sunbutter.com
Sunbutter, a nut spread made from sunflower seeds; whole sunflower seeds and trail mixes.
CEO: Rob Majkrzak
CFO: Randy Wigen
VP: Dan Hofland
VP Marketing: Dan Hofland
Contact: Nick Deutz
nickd@sunbutter.com
Operations Manager: Brad Newton
Number Employees: 200
Type of Packaging: Consumer, Food Service, Private Label, Bulk

12261 SunFed Ranch
203 Court St
Woodland, CA 95695
530-723-5373
sunfedranch.com
Beef products
President/Owner: Matt Byrne

12262 (HQ)SunWest Foods, Inc.
1550 Drew Avenue
Suite 150
Davis, CA 95618
530-758-8550
Fax: 530-758-8110 www.sunwestfoods.com
Processor and exporter of regular, organic and wild rice; also, walnuts, almonds, pistachios and pecans.
Contact: Jess Errecarte
jess@sunwestfoods.com
Year Founded: 1991
Brands:
Nutririte
Sunnuts
Sunwest

12263 SunWest Organics
1550 Drew Ave
Suite 150
Davis, CA 95618-7852
530-758-8550
Fax: 530-758-8110 www.sunwestfoods.com
Organic brown, pilaf, wild mix, wild and crisp rice
President: James Errecarte
Estimated Sales: $20-50 Million
Number Employees: 10-19
Square Footage: 30000

12264 Sunburst Foods
1002 Sunburst Dr
Goldsboro, NC 27534
919-778-2151
Fax: 919-778-9203
Processor and wholesaler/distributor of prepacked sandwiches
President: Ray Lewis
Chairman: B Darden
Vice President: Lori Moss
Maintenance Manager: Bill Sugg
Estimated Sales: $13 Million
Number Employees: 150
Square Footage: 150000
Type of Packaging: Consumer

12265 Sunburst Trout Farms
314 Industrial Park Drive
Waynesville, NC 28786
800-673-3051
www.sunbursttrout.com
Trout fillets, caviar and gift baskets
CEO: Sally Eason
Chief Financial Officer: Benjamin Eason
Marketing & HR Director: Anna Eason
Sales & Processing Manager: Wes Eason
Office Manager: Stephanie Strickland
Year Founded: 1948
Number Employees: 11-50
Type of Packaging: Food Service
Brands:
Sunburst Trout Farms

12266 Sunchef Farms
4722 Everett Avenue
Vernon, CA 90058-3133
323-588-5800
Fax: 323-588-2285
Portion-controlled chicken including marinated and flavored products
President: Steve Tsatas

12267 Sunco & Frenchie
489 Getty Avenue
Clifton, NJ 07011
Fax: 973-478-1063 973-478-1011
www.sunconatural.com
Dried fruits, nuts, granola, raw sugar, quick oats, corn meal, and juice.
Co-Owner: Joel Ammar
Year Founded: 2009
Estimated Sales: $1-5 Million
Number Employees: 15
Brands:
Frenchie(c)
Sunbest(c)
Sunco(c)

12268 Suncrest Farms
1336 Bethany Church Rd.
Princeton, KY 42445-5259
973-595-0214
Fax: 973-595-0214 www.suncrestfarms.com
Ham
Owner: E L Scott
Estimated Sales: Less than $500,000
Number Employees: 1-4
Brands:
Suncrest Farms

12269 Sundance Industries
P.O.Box 1446
Newburgh, NY 12551-1446
845-565-6065
Fax: 845-562-5699 sundanceind@verizon.net
www.sundanceind.com
Wheateena wheatgrass juicers.
President/CEO: Alden Link
Office Manager: Valerie Lynn
Estimated Sales: $1-3 Million
Number Employees: 1-4
Number of Brands: 1
Number of Products: 9
Square Footage: 56000
Type of Packaging: Consumer
Brands:
Wheateena

12270 Sunday House Foods
Sunco Avenue
Fredericksburg, TX 78624
830-997-2136
Fax: 830-997-6056
Smoked Turkey Products
President: Richard Dillow
CFO: Dan Mittel
Vice President: Steve Foucort
VP Sales: Michael Quint
Operations Manager: Larry Wray
Purchasing Manager: Ross Allen
Estimated Sales: $25-49.9 Million
Number Employees: 250-499
Parent Co: Granada Foods Corporation
Type of Packaging: Private Label
Brands:
Hill Country
Sunday House

12271 Sundia Corp
70 Washington St # 425
Suite 425
Oakland, CA 94607-3705
415-762-0600
sales@sundiacorp.com
www.sundiafruit.com
Fruit cups
Vice President: Mark Sherburne
mark@sundiacorp.com
CEO: Jim Watkins
VP Finance: Alex Auseklis
Founder/Chairman: Bradford Oberwager
VP Sales: Mark Sherburne
Chief Operating Officer: James Kairos
Estimated Sales: $7 Million
Number Employees: 10-19
Square Footage: 3200

12272 Sundial Herb Garden
59 Hidden Lake Rd
Higganum, CT 06441-4441
860-345-4290
Fax: 860-345-3462 sundial9@localnet.com
www.sundialgardens.com
Spices, herb blends, tea cake and scone mixes including hazelnut, pumpkin-ginger, cranberry and traditional; importer of rare and herbal teas
Owner: Ragna Goddard
VP: Thomas Goddard
Estimated Sales: Less Than $500,000
Number Employees: 1-4
Square Footage: 10000
Type of Packaging: Consumer
Brands:
Ceylon Teas
China Teas
Herbal Teas
India Teas
Mulling Cider
Sundial Blend Teas
Sundial Gardens

12273 Sunergia Soyfoods
1125 Little High St
Charlottesville, VA 22902
434-970-2798
Fax: 801-437-3484 800-693-5134
Seasoned tofu. Includes ten delicious flavors such as italian herb, savory portabella, peanut & ginger, indian masala, spicy thai, garlic shitake, porcini herb, spinach jalapeno, pesto and spicy indian.
President: Jon Kessler
Vice President: John Raphaelidis
Sales Manager: Marsha Burger
Operations Manager: Jon Kessler
Estimated Sales: $200,000
Number Employees: 3
Number of Brands: 2
Number of Products: 13
Type of Packaging: Consumer, Food Service, Private Label, Bulk
Brands:
More-Than-Tofu
Sunergia Breakfast Style Sausage
Sunergia More Than Tofu Garlic
Sunergia More Than Tofu Herbs
Sunergia More Than Tofu Porcinis
Sunergia More Than Tofu Savories
Sunergia More-Than-Tofu
Sunergia Organic Soy Sausage
Sunergia Smoked Portabella Sausage

12274 Sunfood
1830 Gillespie Way
Suite 101
El Cajon, CA 92020-0922
619-596-7979
Fax: 619-596-7997 888-729-3663
support@sunfood.com www.sunfood.com
Goji berries, raw cacao, goldenberries, and maqui.
President: Doug Harbison
CEO: Matt Alonso
matt.alonso@sunfood.com
CFO: Deion Stromenger
Chief Marketing Officer: Eric Cutler
Sales Executive: Sara Thompson
Operations Director: Jack Wortman
Facilities Manager: Jerome Fodor
Number Employees: 20-49
Type of Packaging: Consumer, Bulk

12275 Sunfresh Beverages Inc.
111 Oxmoor Road
Birmingham, AL 35209
706-324-0040
www.buffalorock.com
Producer of soft drinks and fruit beverages.
Chairman/CEO: James Lee
Estimated Sales: $5-9 Million
Number Employees: 50-99
Number of Brands: 1
Parent Co: Buffalo Rock Company
Type of Packaging: Consumer, Food Service
Brands:
Sunfresh

12276 Sunfresh Foods
125 S Kenyon St
Seattle, WA 98108-4207
206-764-0940
Fax: 206-764-0960 800-669-9625
www.sunfreshjams.com
Uncooked freezer jams and fruit sauces
President: David Allison
david.allison@schwab.com
VP Marketing: Jerry Brozowski
Estimated Sales: Below $5 Million
Number Employees: 5-9
Type of Packaging: Food Service, Private Label
Brands:
President's Choice
Sunfresh Freezerves
Western Classics

12277 Sunja's Oriental Foods
40 Foundry St # 1a
Waterbury, VT 05676-1554
802-244-7644
Fax: 802-244-6880 sunjas@madriver.com
www.sunjaskimchi.com
Oriental foods, kimchee, all natural sauces, frozen specialties, sushi
President: Sunja Hayden
sunjas@madriver.com
Estimated Sales: $5-10 Million
Number Employees: 5-9

12278 Sunland Inc/Peanut Better
PO Box 1059
Portales, NM 88130
575-356-6638
Fax: 575-356-6630
Peanuts, peanut butter and flavored infused peanut
President/CEO: Jimmie Shearer
Contact: Cheri Bostwick
cheri@sunlandinc.com

12279 Sunlike Juice
170 5th Avenue
Rougemont, QC J0L 1M0
Canada
416-297-1140
Fax: 416-297-5703 866-552-7643
www.alassonde.com
Processor and exporter of fruit juices and drinks including apple, apple/strawberry, cranberry cocktail, grapefruit, mango, orange juice, orange/pineapple, peach, pineapple, fruit punch, grape, papaya, pink lemonade, black cherry andiced tea
President/CEO: Jean Gattuso
EVP/General Manager of Sales: Pierre L Heureux
EVP/General Manager of Operations: Sylvain Mayrand
VP Marketing: Luc Prevost
VP Communications: Stefano Bertolli
Brands:
Sunlike

12280 Sunny Avocado
20872 Deerhorn Valley Road
Jamul, CA 91935-7937
619-479-3573
Fax: 619-479-2960 800-999-2862
Provides extra chunky avocado pulp, original mild qualcomole and spicy blends; guac, salsa and guacamaya drink
President: Enrique Bautista
VP: Ana Rosa Bautista
VP Sales/Marketing: Michael Spinner
Estimated Sales: $120000
Number Employees: 2
Type of Packaging: Food Service, Private Label, Bulk
Brands:
Sunny Avocado

12281 Sunny Delight Beverage Company
10300 Alliance Rd
Suite 500
Cincinnati, OH 45242
www.sunnyd.com
Fruit drinks
President: William Cyr
Year Founded: 1963
Estimated Sales: $341 Million
Number Employees: 800
Number of Brands: 3
Type of Packaging: Private Label
Brands:
Fruit 2o
Sunny D
Veryfine

12282 Sunny Dell Foods Inc
135 N 5th St
Oxford, PA 19363-1502
610-932-5164
Fax: 610-932-9479 bestshroom@aol.com
www.sunnydell.com
Mushrooms, IQF, refrigerated, canned, marinated, pouch packs, organic, roasted red peppers, pepperoncini's, garlic, salsa's, sauces and custom product development.
Cmo: Bobby Fella
bestshroom@aol.com
Finance Manager: Lori Caligiuri
Sales Manager: Bobby Fella
Purchasing Manager: Monica Philistine
Estimated Sales: $14.5 Million
Number Employees: 100-249

12283 Sunny Fresh Foods
206 W Fourth St
Monticello, MN 55362-8524
763-271-5600
Fax: 763-271-5711 800-872-3447
usaeggs@cargill.com www.sunnyfreshfoods.com
Eggs including fresh, liquid, mixes, omelets, diced, hard-cooked and pre-cooked
President: Michael Luker
Director Sales/Marketing: Dale Jenkins
Marketing Manager: Rebecca Hanf
Contact: Dennis Darnell
dennis_darnell@cargill.com
Number Employees: 250-499
Parent Co: Cargill Foods
Type of Packaging: Food Service, Private Label

12284 Sunny South Pecan Company
31 E Olliff Street
Statesboro, GA 30458
912-764-5337
Fax: 912-489-1391 800-764-3687
Processor and grower of pecans
Owner: Garland L Nessmith
VP: Steve Rushing
Estimated Sales: $500,000-$1 Million
Number Employees: 1-4
Square Footage: 46800
Type of Packaging: Consumer
Brands:
Savannah
Sunny South

12285 Sunnydale Meats Inc
165 Hyatt St
Gaffney, SC 29341-1558
864-489-6091
Fax: 864-489-6092
Beef, pork, chicken, turkey, bacon, sausage and wieners
President: Anthony Hopper Jr
Estimated Sales: $15 Million
Number Employees: 10-19

12286 Sunnyland Farms
P.O.Box 8200
Albany, GA 31706-8200
229-317-4979
Fax: 229-888-8332 800-999-2488
www.sunnylandfarms.com
Nuts, mixed nuts, pecans, dried fruits and specialty products.
Sales Manager: Beverly Willson
Purchasing: Larry Willson
Estimated Sales: $10-20 Million
Type of Packaging: Consumer, Bulk
Brands:
Sunnyland Farms

12287 Sunnyland Mills
4469 E Annadale Ave
Fresno, CA 93725-2221
559-233-4983
Fax: 559-233-6431 800-501-8017
mike@sunnylandmills.com
www.sunnylandmills.com
Leading manufacturer of premium quality organic and traditional bulgur wheat, pearled soft white wheat, and Grano
President: Steve Orlando
VP: Mike Orlando
Contact: Saso Danilovski
saso@sunnylandmills.com
Plant Manager: Steve Orlando
Number Employees: 10-19
Square Footage: 36000
Type of Packaging: Food Service, Bulk
Brands:
Sunnyland

12288 Sunnyrose Cheese
Hwy 25
Diamond City, AB T0K 0T0
Canada
403-381-4024
Fax: 403-381-3838 www.milkingredients.ca
Cheeses including cheddar, colby, mozzarella, Monterey jack, gouda, havarti, marble, parmesan and specialty
President Sales: Emanuela Leoni
Number Employees: 10-19
Parent Co: Agropur
Type of Packaging: Consumer, Food Service
Brands:
Sunnyrose Cheese

12289 Sunnyside Farms
PO Box 164
Neligh, NE 68756-0164
402-791-2210
Fax: 402-791-2210
Produce
President: James McNally
Estimated Sales: Under $500,000
Number Employees: 1-4

12290 Sunnyside Farms LLC
P.O.Box 478
Washington, VA 22747-0478
540-675-3669
Fax: 540-675-1135
Proceeor of beef
Owner: David Cole
Estimated Sales: $.5-1 million
Number Employees: 1-4

12291 Sunnyside Organics Seedlings
PO Box 478
Washington, VA 22747-0478
510-221-5050
Fax: 540-675-1135 sunnyside@organic.biz
www.organic.biz
Family owned farm that produces eggs, prime meats, and 200 kinds of fruits, vegetables and herbs.

12292 Sunnyside Vegetable Packing
730 Lebanon Road
Millville, NJ 08332-9773
856-451-5077
Fax: 856-451-4388
Vegetables
President: Vic Sammartano
Estimated Sales: Under $500,000
Number Employees: 50-99

12293 Sunray Food Products Corporation
3441 Kingsbridge Ave
Bronx, NY 10463-4003
718-548-2255
Fax: 718-548-2313
Nuts including cashews and pistachios; also, nut mixes, pumpkin and sunflower seeds
Manager: Agustine Morales
Manager: Dave Brechner
Estimated Sales: $423177
Number Employees: 10-19
Parent Co: Zenobia Company
Type of Packaging: Consumer, Food Service, Private Label, Bulk
Brands:
Private Stock
Zenobia

12294 **(HQ)Sunrich LLC**
3824 SW 93rd St
Hope, MN 56046-2010
507-451-4724
Fax: 507-451-2910 800-297-5997
sueklem@sunrich.com www.sunrich.com
Processor and exporter of soy products including milk, tofu powder and frozen green soybeans; also, corn products including grits and flour
President: Allan Routh
CFO: John Dietrich
Manager: Jon Meyer
john.meyer@sunopta.com
Estimated Sales: $9 Million
Number Employees: 20-49
Type of Packaging: Food Service, Private Label, Bulk
Other Locations:
SunRich
Cresco IA
Brands:
Soy Supreme
Sunrich
Sweet Beans

12295 **Sunridge Farms**
423 Salinas Rd
Royal Oaks, CA 95076-5232
831-786-7000
Fax: 831-786-8618 info@sunridgefarms.com
www.sunridgefarms.com
Organic and all natural nuts & seeds, dried fruit, candies, and snacks & tril mixes.
CFO: Phillip Adrian
Vice President: Larry Cox
Quality Assurance: Robert Yebra
Assistant Marketing Director: Vivian Guajardo
Sales: Eric Birckner
Director of Operations: Don Blodget
Production and Food Safety Supervisor: Pat Ryan
Estimated Sales: $900 Million
Number Employees: 20-49
Type of Packaging: Consumer, Bulk
Brands:
Sunridge Farms

12296 **Sunridge Farms Inc**
1582 Moffett St
Suite C
Salinas, CA 93905-3342
831-755-1530
Fax: 831-755-1429 info@coastlineproduce.com
www.coastlineproduce.com
Bulk and packaged organic and natural foods, snacks, dried fruits, nuts and trail mixes; natural candies; granolas and cereals; grain and bean blend; pastas
President/Owner: Steve Henderson
VP/Owner: Phil Adrians
phil@coastlinefamilyfarms.com
Owner: Larry Cox
Marketing Manager: Vivian Sotelo
Retail Sales Manager: Linda Kivlehan
Director of Operations: Don Blodget
Estimated Sales: $2.5-5 Million
Number Employees: 20-49
Type of Packaging: Consumer, Food Service, Bulk
Brands:
Coastline

12297 **(HQ)Sunrise Growers**
701 W Kimberly
Suite 210
Placentia, CA 92870
714-630-6292
Fax: 714-630-0920 website@sunrisegrowers.com
www.sunrisegrowers.com
Manufacturer, exporter and importer of frozen strawberries and purees
President: Ed Haft
CEO: Edward Haft
CFO: Tim Graven
VP: Carl Lindgren
Sales Executive: Steve Cjrcle
Contact: Doyal Andrews
dandrews@sunrisegrowers.com
Estimated Sales: $10-20 Million
Number Employees: 250-499
Square Footage: 1000000
Type of Packaging: Consumer, Food Service, Private Label, Bulk
Other Locations:
Frozsun Foods
Oxnard CA
Brands:
Frozsun

12298 **Sunrise Markets**
729 Powell St
Vancouver, BC V6A 1H5
Canada
604-253-2326
Fax: 604-251-1083 800-661-2326
www.sunrise-soya.com
Tofu and soy milk
President: Leslie Joe
Plant Manager: Jimmy Cuan
Estimated Sales: $16 Million
Number Employees: 160
Square Footage: 50000
Type of Packaging: Consumer, Food Service

12299 **Sunrise Winery**
1418 Shasta Avenue
San Jose, CA 95126-2531
408-741-1310
Wines
President: Rolayne Storz
Estimated Sales: $500-1 000,000 appx.
Number Employees: 1-4

12300 **Sunset Farm Foods Inc**
1201 Madison Hwy
Valdosta, GA 31601
Fax: 229-242-3389 800-882-1121
webinfo@sunsetfarmfoods.com
www.sunsetfarmfoods.com
Processor of smoked sausage, fresh sausage, smoked meats, cooked products (souse, chitterling loaf, liver pudding, chili).
Owner & President: Tom Carroll
t.carroll@sunsetfarmfoods.com
Plant Manager: Ricky Lightsey
Year Founded: 1918
Estimated Sales: $20-50 Million
Number Employees: 50-99
Number of Brands: 6
Number of Products: 250
Square Footage: 40000
Type of Packaging: Consumer, Food Service, Private Label, Bulk
Brands:
Flavority
George Maid
Georgia Reds
Georgia Special
Queen of Dixie
Southern Chef
Sunset Farm

12301 **Sunset Specialty Foods**
PO Box 50, PMB 145
Lake Arrowhead, CA 92352
909-337-7643
Fax: 909-337-0963
Processor and exporter of specialty frozen items including pizza, chocolate chip cookies, etc
President/CEO: James Tolliver
Estimated Sales: $5-10 Million
Number Employees: 11-50
Square Footage: 108000
Type of Packaging: Consumer, Food Service, Private Label, Bulk
Brands:
Amelia's
Deli
Dina
Maestro Giovanni

12302 **Sunshine Burger & Spec Food Co**
701 Jones Ave
Fort Atkinson, WI 53538-2118
920-568-1100
Fax: 920-568-1504 info@sunshineburger.com
www.sunshineburger.com
Vegan burgers made with non-GMO, organic whole food ingredients. Varieties include Orginal, Garden Herb, BBQ, Falafel, Mushroom, Southwest, and Hemp & Sage.
Owner: Carol Debberman
Owner: John Hiler
Manager: Ann Adkins
aadkins@sunshineburger.com
Estimated Sales: $500,000-$1 Million
Number Employees: 5-9
Square Footage: 14000
Type of Packaging: Consumer
Brands:
Organic Sunshine
Sunshine

12303 **Sunshine Dairy**
584 Coleman Rd
Middletown, CT 06457
860-346-6644
Fax: 860-346-5246
Milk, dairy products
President: Nancy A Guida
nguida@sunshinedairyfoods.com
Estimated Sales: $10-20 000,000
Number Employees: 20-49
Brands:
Guida

12304 **Sunshine Dairy Foods Inc**
801 NE 21st Ave
Portland, OR 97232-2280
503-234-7526
Fax: 503-233-9441 info@sunshinedairyfoods.com
Established in 1936. Processor of dairy products including ice cream, yogurt, fresh milk, and cultures.
President and CEO: Dirk Davis
CFO: Aaron Atkins
Chief Quality Officer: Michael Freudenthal
Sr. Manager of Sales: Chris Haines
Director of Operations: Scott Salisbury
West Plant Manager: Darin Quituqua
Estimated Sales: $20-50 Million
Number Employees: 100-249
Square Footage: 75000
Type of Packaging: Consumer, Food Service, Private Label, Bulk
Brands:
Albertson's
Quality Chekd
Tillamook
Western Family

12305 **Sunshine Farm & Garden**
696 Glicks Rd
Renick, WV 24966-6601
304-497-2208
Fax: 304-497-2698 barry@sunfarm.com
www.sunfarm.com
Processor, importer and exporter of organic fruits including apples and pawpaws; also, organic herbs and seeds
President: Barry Glick
barry@sunfarm.com
VP: Zak Glick
Estimated Sales: $400000
Number Employees: 20-49
Square Footage: 260000

12306 **Sunshine Farms**
N8873 Currie Rd
Portage, WI 53901-9218
608-742-2016
Fax: 608-742-1577 sunshine@jvlnet.com
www.jvlnet.com
Processor and wholesaler/distributor of cheese and goat milk; wholesaler/distributor of health foods
President: Daniel Considine
sunshine@jvl.net
Estimated Sales: $3-5 Million
Number Employees: 1-4
Type of Packaging: Consumer
Brands:
Sunshine Farms

12307 **Sunshine Food Sales**
2900 NW 75th St Ste 305
Miami, FL 33147
305-696-2885
Processor and importer of fresh and frozen fish including mackerel, kingfish, lobster and crabs
President: Carlos Sanchez
Co-Owner: David Dossi
Plant Manager: Jesus Alonsa
Number Employees: 1-4
Type of Packaging: Bulk

12308 **Sunshine Fresh**
4425 Vandenberg Dr
North Las Vegas, NV 89081-2716
702-838-4698
Fax: 702-838-4691 800-832-8081
info@sunshinefresh.com www.majorproducts.com
Pickles; wholesaler/distributor of deli products; serving the food service market,manufactures and packs liquid food products.

President: Michael Rosenblum
Estimated Sales: $8100000
Number Employees: 5-9
Type of Packaging: Consumer, Food Service, Bulk

12309 Sunshine International Foods
26 Spruce St
Methuen, MA 01844-4336
978-837-3209
Fax: 978-837-3161 info@sunshinefood.com
www.sunshinefood.com
All natural tahini paste.
Owner: Emile Maroun
info@sunshinefood.com
Managing Director: George Maroun
Estimated Sales: $500,000
Number Employees: 10-19
Square Footage: 6640

12310 Sunshine Nut Company
16192 Coastal Highway
Lewes, DE 19958
210-732-9460
info@sunshinenuts.com
www.sunshinenuts.com
Walnuts, almonds and pecans
Contact: Don Larson
don@sunshinenuts.com
Parent Co: John B. Sanfilippo & Son

12311 Sunshine Seafood
PO Box 136
Stonington, ME 04681
207-367-2955
Fax: 207-367-6394
Fish, seafood and shellfish.
President: James Eaton
Estimated Sales: $2,600,000
Number Employees: 10-19

12312 Sunstone Vineyards & Winery
125 N Refugio Rd
Santa Ynez, CA 93460-9303
805-688-9463
Fax: 805-686-1881 800-313-9463
www.sunstonewinery.com
Wines
President: Geoff Alexander
geoff@filmsantabarbara.com
CEO: Linda Rice
VP: Ashley Rice
Marketing Director: Anna Rice
Estimated Sales: Less Than $500,000
Number Employees: 1-4

12313 Sunsweet Growers Inc.
901 N. Walton Ave.
Yuba City, CA 95993
800-417-2253
sunsweet@casupport.com www.sunsweet.com
Dried fruits including prunes, apricots and mangos, as well as prune juice. nuts and more.
President/CEO: Dane Lance
Vice President/CFO: Ana Klein
VP, Global Sales/Marketing: Brad Schuler
Year Founded: 1917
Estimated Sales: $281 Million
Number Employees: 500-999
Type of Packaging: Consumer, Food Service, Private Label, Bulk
Brands:
Sunsweet

12314 Sunterra Meats
233 North Rd
P.O. Box 309
Trochu, AB T0M 2C0
Canada
403-442-4202
Fax: 403-442-2771 www.sunterrameats.ca
Fresh and frozen pork
President: Ray Price
VP Sales & Marketing: Tony Martinez
Plant Manager: Richard Johnson
Estimated Sales: $46 Million
Number Employees: 115
Type of Packaging: Food Service

12315 (HQ)Suntory International
7 Times Sq.
21st Floor
New York, NY 10036
212-891-6600
Fax: 212-891-6601 www.suntory.com
Bottled water, beverages, and alcoholic beverages.
President/CEO: Takeshi Niinami
Year Founded: 1967
Estimated Sales: $840 Million
Number Employees: 2,199
Parent Co: Suntory
Brands:
Nature's Twist
Orangina
Jim Beam
Maker's Mark
Suntory Whisky
Yamazaki
Hakushu
Hibiki
Toki
Sauza Tequila
Courvoisier
Bowmore Islay
Laphroaig
Canadian Club
Roku
Chateau Lagrange
Chateau Beychevelle
Robert Weil

12316 Sunup Green Coffee
New York, NY
212-842-9767
info@sunupgreencoffee.com
www.sunupgreencoffee.com
Green coffee beverage
Area Manager: Colin Fickes
Brands:
Sunup

12317 Sup Herb Farms
300 Dianne Dr
Turlock, CA 95380-9523
209-633-3600
Fax: 209-633-3644 800-787-4372
www.supherbfarms.com
Processors and marketers of culinary herbs and specialty products the selection of which includes fresh, frozen and freeze-dried varieties.
President: Mike Brem
EVP/Strategic Planning & CFO: Francis Contino
SVP/General Counsel & Secretary: Robert Skelton
VP/Human Relations: Cecile Perich
Number Employees: 100-249
Parent Co: McCormick & Company Inc

12318 SupHerb Farms
300 Dianne Dr
Turlock, CA 95380-9523
209-633-3600
Fax: 209-633-3644 800-787-4372
custserv@supherbfarms.com
www.supherbfarms.com
Frozen culinary herb and specialty vegetable ingredients
President & CEO: Matt Reid
VP Finance & Administration: Debbie Salcedo
Executive Corporate Chef: Scott Adair
VP Sales & Marketing: Don Douglas
National Account Manager: Stephanie Schutz
Human Resources Director: Patricia Silva
Plant Manager: Eduardo Luna
Estimated Sales: $3.4 Million
Number Employees: 100-249
Square Footage: 65190
Type of Packaging: Food Service, Bulk
Brands:
Supherb Farms

12319 Super Mom's LLC
625 2nd St
St Paul Park, MN 55071-1807
651-459-2253
Fax: 651-459-0804 800-944-7276
www.superamerica.com
Manufacturer of fresh and frozen bakery items (donuts, pastries, cookies, muffins, loaves. cupcakes, cakes, bread, and buns) and commissary items (pizza, hot meals, deli sandwiches, salads and wraps, vegetable trays, fruit cups andyogurt parfaits). Offers private label and co-packing services.
President: Doug Muchow
Estimated Sales: $14 Million
Number Employees: 250-499
Number of Brands: 1
Parent Co: Western Refining Inc.
Type of Packaging: Consumer, Private Label
Brands:
SuperMom's

12320 Super Nutrition Life Extension
1100 W Commercial Blvd # 100
Fort Lauderdale, FL 33309-3748
954-766-8433
Fax: 954-202-7745 800-678-8989
customerservice@lifeextension.com www.lef.org
Supplements including nutritional, anti-aging and sport supplements; also, vitamin formulas
Owner: William Flannon
Marketing/Design: Kathy Mooney
National Sales Manager: Michael Mooney

12321 Super Smokers Bar-B-Que
601 Stockell Dr
Eureka, MO 63025-1236
636-938-9742
Sauces
Number Employees: 10-19

12322 Super Snooty Sea Food Corporation
7 Fish Pier St E
Boston, MA 02210-2007
617-426-6390
Fax: 617-439-9144
Processor and wholesaler/distributor of frozen seafood including round and filleted flat fish
General Manager: Paul Sousa
Estimated Sales: $1-5 Million
Number Employees: 10-20
Type of Packaging: Consumer

12323 Super Stores Industries
2600 Spengler Rd
Turlock, CA 95380
209-668-2100
customersupport@savemart.com
www.ssica.com
Dairy products including milk, cottage cheese, yogurt and ice cream; orange juice.
President & CEO: Jay Simon
Year Founded: 1981
Estimated Sales: $50-100 Million
Number Employees: 100-249
Number of Brands: 3
Type of Packaging: Private Label
Brands:
Bayview Farms
Sunnyside Farms
Superstore

12324 SuperEats
205 West 10th St #GN
New York, NY 10014
802-760-7075
www.supereats.com
Chips
Co-Owner: Aaron Gailmor
Co-Owner: Charlie Ruehr
Brands:
SuperEats

12325 SuperFat
Beaverton, OR
hello@superfat.com
www.superfat.com
Nut butter snack pouches

12326 Superbrand Dairies
9 Wax Myrtle Ct
Montgomery, AL 36117-3770
334-277-6010
Fax: 334-279-6964
Frozen pizza
Owner: Dennis Houde
Plant Manager: J Parsons
Number Employees: 50-99
Parent Co: Winn Dixie
Type of Packaging: Private Label

12327 Superbrand Dairies
3000 NW 123rd Street
Miami, FL 33167-2517
305-769-6600
Fax: 305-783-2896
Milk and juice: orange, grapefruit and apple
Vice President: Pat Carraro
Number Employees: 50-99
Parent Co: Winn Dixie
Type of Packaging: Consumer

12328 **Superior Bakery Inc**
72 Main St
N Grosvenordale, CT 06255-1712
860-923-9555
Fax: 860-923-2087 www.superiorbakery.com
Italian bread and rolls-Italian sliced, vienna, grinder, pepper bisuits, torpedoes, round buns and pizza
VP Finance: Michael Faucher
General Manager: Victor Strama
Estimated Sales: $8.5 Million
Number Employees: 50-99
Square Footage: 120000
Type of Packaging: Consumer, Food Service, Private Label, Bulk
Brands:
Green-Freedman
Kasanofs's
Superior

12329 **Superior Baking Co**
176 N Warren Ave
Brockton, MA 02301-3431
508-586-6601
Fax: 508-580-4056 800-696-2253
sbaking1@comcast.net www.superiorbakery.com
Breads, rolls, bagels, pastries and wraps
President: Michael Debenedictis
sbaking1@comcast.net
VP Sales: Joseph Ferrini
Vice President: Robert DeBenedictis
Estimated Sales: Below $5 000,000
Number Employees: 20-49
Square Footage: 16000
Type of Packaging: Consumer, Food Service, Private Label, Bulk

12330 **Superior Bean & Spice Company**
PO Box 753
Brush Prairie, WA 98606-0753
360-694-0819
Fax: 360-883-6915
Vegetables, soup mixes
President: Duane Rough

12331 **Superior Cake Products**
105 Ashland Ave
Southbridge, MA 1550
508-764-3276
Fax: 508-765-5344 www.superiorcake.com
Cakes and snack cakes including carrot spice rolls, Boston cream pie, etc
President: Chris Smith
VP Finance: Michael Faucher
VP: Karo Mc Hugh
Contact: Sonia Carrasco
scarrasco@superiorcake.com
VP Operations: Raymond Faucher Jr
Type of Packaging: Consumer, Food Service, Private Label
Brands:
Superior Cake

12332 **Superior Dairy**
220 N Fulton St
Wauseon, OH 43567-1161
419-335-3553
Dairy products
President: Joseph Sorhnlen
President/COO: Daniel Sorhnlen
CEO: Joseph P Soehnlen
Sales Manager: Jeff Bouequin
Estimated Sales: $43,000
Number Employees: 2
Type of Packaging: Consumer, Private Label

12333 **Superior Farms**
2530 River Plaza Dr.
Sacramento, CA 95833
530-297-7299
Fax: 530-758-3152 800-228-5262
thiinc@superiorfarms.com
www.superiorfarms.com
Lamb, venison, buffalo and veal
CEO: Rick Stott
Chairman: Les Oesterreich
CFO: Jeff Evanson
VP Marketing & Brand Strategy: Bob Mariano
VP Sales: Kenneth Wilks
Human Resources Manager: Alfredo Saldivar
VP Operations: Shane MacKenzie
Plant Manager: Greg Ahart
Purchasing Manager: Brian Phelan
Estimated Sales: $34.5 Million
Number Employees: 250-499
Other Locations:
Boston MA
Chicago IL
Denver CO
Dixon CA
Hawarden IA
Vernon CA
Brands:
Superior Farms

12334 **Superior Foods**
275 Westgate Dr
Watsonville, CA 95076-2470
831-728-3691
Fax: 831-722-0926 info@superiorfoods.com
www.superiorfoods.com
Global supplier and manufacturer of frozen fruits, vegetables and grains for the consumer, foodservice, club and industrial markets.
President & CEO: R. Neil Happee
Number Employees: 50-99
Type of Packaging: Consumer, Food Service
Brands:
Asian Pride
Garden Fresh
Orchard Park
Superior Foods
Superior Pride

12335 **Superior Meat Co**
480 N 500 E
Vernal, UT 84078-1808
435-789-3274
www.superiormaintenanceservices.com
Meat products
Owner: D Reynolds
Sales Manager: D Reynolds
reynoldssno@msn.com
Estimated Sales: Less than $500,000
Number Employees: 1-4
Type of Packaging: Consumer, Food Service

12336 **Superior Mushroom Farms**
52557 Range Road
Suite 215
Ardrossan, AB T8E 2H6
Canada
780-922-2535
Fax: 780-922-2078 866-687-2242
Grower of fresh mushrooms
President/CEO: Brent Schwabe
Marketing/Sales Director: Wanda Ziober
Production Manager: Norman Schwabe
Estimated Sales: $5-10 Million
Number Employees: 76
Type of Packaging: Consumer, Food Service, Bulk

12337 **(HQ)Superior Nut & Candy**
1111 W 40th St
Chicago, IL 60609-2506
773-254-6000
Fax: 773-254-9171 800-843-2238
www.superiornutandcandy.com
Nuts including honey roasted, salted meats and trail mixes; also, fund raising programs available
Owner: Gary Chan
VP Finance: Ramona Mastrangelo
VP: Mona Mastrangelo
Director of Sales: Daniel Hathaway
gchan@superiornutandcandy.com
VP Operations: Richard Slayton
Purchasing: Leonard Shamoon
Estimated Sales: $16,068,865
Number Employees: 20-49
Square Footage: 102000

12338 **Superior Nut Company**
225 Monsignor Obrien Hwy
Cambridge, MA 02141
617-876-3808
Fax: 617-876-8225 800-251-6060
info@SuperiorNut.com www.superiornut.com
Nuts
President: Harry Hintlian
Estimated Sales: $1-2.5 Million
Number Employees: 1-4
Type of Packaging: Consumer, Food Service, Bulk
Brands:
Superior Nut Company

12339 **Superior Nutrition Corporation**
601 N Market Street
Wilmington, DE 19801-3006
302-655-5762
Fax: 302-655-5760 info@sncorp.com
www.sncorp.com
Baked onion pieces
Chief Executive Officer: Fatih Ozmen
Estimated Sales: $2.5-5 Million
Number Employees: 1-4

12340 **Superior Ocean Produce**
4423 N Elston Ave
Chicago, IL 60630
773-283-8400
Fax: 773-561-0139 bill@fishguy.com
www.fishguy.com
Seafood
Owner: William Dugan
bdugan@fishguy.com
Estimated Sales: $1-3 Million
Number Employees: 10-19

12341 **Superior Pasta Co**
905 Christian St
Philadelphia, PA 19147-3807
215-627-3306
Fax: 215-922-7114 www.superiorpasta.com
Pasta products
Owner: Joe Lonanno
fundraiser@superiorpasta.com
Estimated Sales: Less than $1 Million
Number Employees: 5-9
Type of Packaging: Private Label

12342 **Superior Pecans**
317 N Orange Ave
Eufaula, AL 36027-1623
334-687-2031
Fax: 334-687-2075 800-628-2350
www.superiorpecans.com
Pecans
Owner: Dee Kellogg
superiorpecans@gmail.com
Estimated Sales: Less Than $500,000
Number Employees: 1-4
Square Footage: 72000
Type of Packaging: Consumer

12343 **Superior Quality Foods**
2355 E Francis St
Ontario, CA 91761
909-923-4733
Fax: 909-947-7065 800-300-4210
Soup bases, beef extracts, dried seasonings and sauce mixes
President: Linda Owen
Vice President: Bob Grizzard
National Sales Manager: Paul Smalley
Contact: Cindy Deets
cdeets@superiortouch.com
Estimated Sales: $22.3 Million
Number Employees: 63
Parent Co: Southeastern Mills, Inc.
Type of Packaging: Food Service, Bulk

12344 **Superior Seafood**
4338 Saint Charles Ave
New Orleans, LA 70115-4742
504-293-3474
Fax: 504-293-0596 info@superiorseafoods.com
www.superiorseafoodnola.com
Seafood
President/Executive Chef: Justin Fergusen
Manager: John Michael
johnm.superiorseafood@gmail.com
Estimated Sales: Less than $500,000
Number Employees: 10-19

12345 **Superior Seafood & MeatCompany**
623 S Olive Street
South Bend, IN 46619-3309
574-289-0511
Fax: 574-289-0919
Seafood and meat
President: Joe Neary Sr

12346 **Superseedz**
50 Devine St
North Haven, CT 06473-2244
203-407-0546
Fax: 203-281-3407 www.superseedz.com
Flavored pumpkin seeds

Owner/Founder: Kathie Pelliccio
Contact: Joe Lupica
joe@superseedz.com
Estimated Sales: 823,000
Number Employees: 9

12347 **Suprema Specialties**
14253 S Airport Way
Manteca, CA 95336-8641
209-858-9696
Fax: 209-858-9599
Milk, cheese, cheeses include mozzarella, parmesan, ramano, Monterrey jack and chedder cheese
Owner: Ming Shin-Kou

12348 **Supreme Artisan Foods**
#308-124, 4653 Carmel Mountain Rd.
San Diego, CA 92130
844-278-3663
www.supremeartisanfoods.com
Producer of cheeses such as Baked Brie en croute and Torta Cheese spreads. Some of their products include Cantar, Traditional Olive Tapenade, Cantar, Feta Olive Tapenade and Cantar, Red Pepper Tuscan Tapenade.
CEO: Olivier Fischer-Morelle
Purchasing Executive: Scott Colling
Estimated Sales: $7.6,000,000
Number Employees: 60
Brands:
Cantar,

12349 **Supreme Chocolatier**
1150 South Ave
Suite 1
Staten Island, NY 10314-3404
718-761-9600
Fax: 718-761-5279 www.supremechocolatier.com
Chocolate novelties and gift baskets
Owner: George Biddle
george.biddle@supremechocolatier.com
VP Marketing: Wayne Stottmeister
Estimated Sales: $6,100,000
Number Employees: 50-99
Type of Packaging: Consumer
Brands:
Superior Chocolatier
Superior Confections, Inc.
The Chocolate Factory

12350 **Supreme Dairy Farms Co**
111 Kilvert St
Warwick, RI 02886-1006
401-739-8180
Fax: 401-739-8230 www.supremedairyfarms.com
Processor and importer of tomato products; also, mozzarella and ricotta cheese
President: Paul Areson
Director: Bill Toll
Contact: Vincent Bruzzese
vincent@supremedairyfarms.com
Estimated Sales: $1.8 Million
Number Employees: 1-4
Square Footage: 56000
Type of Packaging: Food Service, Private Label
Brands:
Avanti
Supreme Dairy Farms

12351 **Supreme Frozen Products**
5813 W Grand Ave
Chicago, IL 60639
773-622-3777
Fax: 773-622-3350 store@supremetamale.com
www.supremetamale.com
Mexican food including tamales, chili, fajitas and burritos
President: John Paklaian
Estimated Sales: $1.2 Million
Number Employees: 10
Square Footage: 24800

12352 **Supreme Frozen Products**
1495 Brummel Avenue
Elk Grove Village, IL 60007
847-979-8480
www.supremetamale.com
Beef tamales, been and bean burritos, beeh chili with beans, crispy pizza fluffs
Owner: John Pak
Estimated Sales: $5-10 Million
Number Employees: 10-19

12353 **Suram Trading Corporation**
2655 Le Jeune Road
Suite 1006
Coral Gables, FL 33134
305-448-7165
Fax: 305-445-7185
Frozen seafood shrimp
President and CEO: Guido Adler
Controller: Carmen Artime
Marketing: Kristina Adler
Sales: Michael del Aguila
Contact: Michael Aguila
mdelaguila@suram.com
Operations Manager: Kenji Kurenuma
Estimated Sales: $20-49.9 Million
Number Employees: 10
Number of Brands: 1
Brands:
Suram

12354 **Sure-Fresh Produce Inc**
1302 W Stowell Rd
Santa Maria, CA 93458-9730
805-349-2677
Fax: 805-349-2674 888-423-5379
www.surefreshproduce.com
Industrial frozen vegetable ingredient manufacturer of both conventional and organic bulk products
President: Robert Witt
robert@surefreshproduce.com
CFO: Renee Kolding
Quality Control: Corrie Landymore
Marketing Director: Matthew Johnson
Sales Representative: Armando Gonzalez
Estimated Sales: $10-20 Million
Number Employees: 50-99
Number of Products: 750
Square Footage: 100000
Type of Packaging: Food Service, Bulk
Brands:
Sure Fresh

12355 **Sure-Good Food Distributors**
6361 Thompson Rd
Syracuse, NY 13206-1448
315-422-1196
Fax: 315-478-5220
Fresh and frozen poultry
President: Jerry Savlov
Estimated Sales: $10-20 000,000
Number Employees: 10-19

12356 **Surface Banana Company**
1272 Gihon Road
Parkersburg, WV 26101
304-485-2400
Fax: 304-589-7252
Bananas and tomatoes; importer of bananas
Owner: David Surface
Estimated Sales: $300,000-500,000
Number Employees: 1-4

12357 **Surfing Goat Dairy**
3651 Omaopio Rd
Kula, HI 96790-8871
808-878-2870
Fax: 808-876-1826 info@surfinggoatdairy.com
Goat milk products: Milk, cheese, soaps
Number Employees: 1-4

12358 **Surgital America**
2805 North Commerce Parkway
Miramar, FL 33025
954-538-6891
customerservice@surgital.com
www.pastificiobacchini.com
Pasta
Marketing (Italy): Anna Baccarani
Type of Packaging: Food Service, Private Label
Brands:
Pastificio Bacchini

12359 **Surlean Foods**
1545 S San Marcos
San Antonio, TX 78207-7033
210-227-4370
Fax: 210-226-4208 800-999-4370
mcannon@surleanfoods.com
www.surleanfoods.net
Meats, soups, sauces, marinades and more
President: Daryl Scott
dscott@surleanfoods.com
Director of National Accounts: Bill McKenna
VP Sales & Marketing: Mike Cannon
Plant Manager: Ryan Scott
VP of Sales & Procurement: Chad Wilhite
Estimated Sales: $110,000
Number Employees: 250-499
Type of Packaging: Food Service

12360 **Susie's Smart Cookie**
333 Hook Rd.
Katonah, NY 10536
914-740-1007
susie@susiesmartcookie.com
www.susiesmartcookie.com
Manufacturer of healthy cookies.
President: Susan Allport
Contact: Susie Aliport
susie@susiesmartcookie.com
Brands:
Susie's Smart Cookie

12361 **Susie's South Forty Confection**
401 S Marienfeld St
Midland, TX 79701-5002
432-570-4040
Fax: 432-682-4040 800-221-4442
CustService@susiessouthforty.com
www.susiessouthforty.com
Toffee, pralines, fudge, gift baskets, gift tins
President/Owner: Susie Hitchcock-Hall
cust@susiessouthforty.com
Estimated Sales: $3-5 Million
Number Employees: 50-99
Type of Packaging: Consumer

12362 **Susquehanna Valley Winery**
802 Mount Zion Dr
Danville, PA 17821
570-275-2364
Fax: 570-275-5813
Wine
Owner: Miklos Latranyi
Partner: Mark Latranyi
Marketing Manager: Hildegard Latranyi
Estimated Sales: Below $5 000,000
Number Employees: 1-4
Brands:
Susquehanna Valley

12363 **Suss Sweets**
5 Columbia Ave
Nashua, NH 03064-1607
603-864-8563
Fax: 603-864-8621 www.susssweets.com
Candy caramels
Owner/Founder: Tammy Fahey
Number Employees: 1-4

12364 **Sustainable Sourcing**
PO Box 900
Great Barrington, MA 01230
413-528-5141
Fax: 413-528-5172 sales@himalasalt.com
www.himalasalt.com
Himalayan sea salt. Ethically Sourced, Kosher Certified, and Green-e Certified (made by 100% renewable wind and solar energy, sustainably packaged), with 5% of profits going to the environment and back to the source community.
Founder, CEO, President: Melissa Kushi
Estimated Sales: $1.5 Million
Number Employees: 10
Type of Packaging: Consumer

12365 **Suter Co Inc**
258 May St
Sycamore, IL 60178-1395
815-895-9186
Fax: 815-895-4814 800-435-6942
www.suterco.com
Processor of canned and refrigerated salads including tuna, chicken, ham, egg and seafood; also, shelf stable lunch kits, deviled egg kits.
President: Tim Suter
tsuter@suterco.com
Year Founded: 1925
Number Employees: 100-249
Type of Packaging: Consumer, Food Service, Private Label, Bulk
Brands:
Alaska Bay

Suter
Sycamore Farms

12366 Sutherland's Foodservice
16 Forest Pkwy
Building K
Forest Park, GA 30297-2015
404-366-8550
Fax: 404-366-8599 cservice@suthfood.com
www.suthfoodservice.com
Dairy, frozen foods, fresh and frozen meat, fresh and frozen poultry, fresh and frozen seafood, dry grocery, nonfood, and produce
CIO/CTO: Bonnie Wilson
bwilson@suthfood.com
Marketing Coordinator: Callie Crowe
Sales Manager: Drew Wilson
Estimated Sales: $20-50 Million
Number Employees: 100-249

12367 Sutter Buttes Olive Oil
2204 California St
Sutter, CA 95982-2445
530-763-7921
sales@sutterbuttesoliveoil.com
www.sutterbuttesoliveoil.com
Oils, spices, sauces, rubs, and salt.
Founder: Alka Kumar
Product Manager: Arek Kazimierczak
Number Employees: 20-49

12368 Sutter Foods LLC
1973 Barry Rd
Yuba City, CA 95993-9501
530-682-7776
Organic prunes. Wholesale only.
Estimated Sales: Less Than $500,000
Number Employees: 1-4

12369 Sutter Home Winery
277 Saint Helena Hwy S
St Helena, CA 94574-2202
707-963-3104
800-967-4663
info@sutterhome.com www.sutterhome.com
Processor and exporter of wines
President: Larry Dizmang
CEO: Sandra Barros
sbarros@tfewines.com
CFO: George Schofield
Public Relations Director: David Foster
Production Manager: Scott Harvey
Purchasing Agent: Marc Norwood
Number Employees: 100-249
Square Footage: 58624
Brands:
Sutter Home

12370 Sutton Honey Farms
285 Conns Ln
Lancaster, KY 40444-9706
859-792-4277
Fax: 859-792-4277 www.suttonhoneyfarm.com
Processor and packer of nonfiltered and creamed honey with fruit and cinnamon
President: Rick Sutton
VP: Dianne Sutton
Estimated Sales: A
Number Employees: 1-4
Square Footage: 16000
Type of Packaging: Consumer, Private Label, Bulk
Brands:
Sutton's

12371 Suzanna's Kitchen
4025 Buford Hwy
Peachtree Cor, GA 30096-4137
770-476-9900
Fax: 770-476-8899 www.suzannaskitchen.com
Foodservice partner manufacturing frozen heat-and-serve meat products including pork, veal, beef, turkey, barbecue, ribs, corn dogs and chicken breasts, breast strips, chicken patties and wings.
Founder: Barbara Howard
CEO: Brad Howard
bradh@suzannaskitchen.com
CFO: David Ashton
Director of Operations: Nelson Rodriguez
Number Employees: 100-249
Number of Products: 100+
Type of Packaging: Food Service, Private Label
Brands:
Suzanna's

12372 Suzanne's Specialties
411 Jersey Ave
New Brunswick, NJ 08901
732-828-8500
Fax: 732-828-8563 800-762-2135
info@suzannes-specialties.com
suzannes-specialties.com
Organic sweeteners and sugar alternatives including brown rice syrup, agave syrup and evaporated cane juice
President/Owner: Susan Morano
VP, Operations: Jim Morano
Number Employees: 20-49
Type of Packaging: Consumer, Food Service, Bulk
Brands:
Rice Nectar
Sunrice
Sunshine's
Suzanne's Conserves

12373 Suzanne's Sweets
9 Comanche Ct
Katonah, NY 10536-2917
Fax: 914-232-1291
Rugelach

12374 Suzhou-Chem Inc
396 Washington St
Suite 318
Wellesley, MA 02481
781-433-8618
Fax: 781-433-8619 info@suzhouchem.com
www.suzhouchem.com
Food and beverage ingredients including ascorbic acid, sodium ascorbate, calcium ascorbate, sodium saccharin granular, sodium saccharin dehydrate, sodium saccharin powder, calcium saccharin, insoluble saccharin, acesulfame-kaspartame, caffeine, potassium, sorbic acid, etc.
President: Joan Ni
Estimated Sales: $302 Million
Number Employees: 5 9
Type of Packaging: Bulk

12375 Svenhard's Swedish Bakery Inc
335 Adeline St
Oakland, CA 94607-2519
510-834-5035
Fax: 510-839-6797 800-705-3379
ccare@svenhards.com www.svenhards.com
Pastries such as; cinnamon rolls and danishes
President & CEO: Ronny Svenhard
CEO: Norman Andrews
norman@svenhards.com
Director of Manufacturing: Allen Herman
Estimated Sales: $19.2 Million
Number Employees: 250-499
Square Footage: 79768
Type of Packaging: Consumer, Food Service
Other Locations:
Svenhard's Swedish Bakery
Exeter CA
Brands:
Svenhards

12376 Svzusa Inc
1700 N Broadway Ave
Othello, WA 99344-8918
509-488-6563
Fax: 509-488-2631 info@svz-usa.com
www.svz.com
Liquid fruit and vegetable concentrates, proteins and blends.
President: Doug Granitz
doug.granitz@svz.com
CFO: Roger Wilson
Sales & Marketing Manager: Timothy Jaeger
Human Resources: Agatha Willis
Estimated Sales: $6.3 Million
Number Employees: 50-99
Parent Co: SVZ Industrial Products B.V.
Type of Packaging: Bulk

12377 Swagger Foods Corp
900 Corporate Woods Pkwy
Vernon Hills, IL 60061-3155
847-913-1200
Fax: 847-913-1263 info@swaggerfoods.com
Supplying the industrial, food service and retail markets as a manufacturer of seasonings, functional foods with vitamins, minerals, omega-3, other micronutrients/nutraceuticals, salt substitutes, soup mixes/bases, rubs, marinadesgravy/sauce mixes, dip/dressing mixes, drink mixes, side dish mixes and other dry blends including Ethnic.
President: Terry R Shin
terry.shin@swaggerfoods.com
Number Employees: 10-19
Type of Packaging: Consumer, Food Service, Private Label, Bulk
Brands:
Bits O' Butter
Fancy Pantry
Health-Fu'd
Spice So Rite
Swagger

12378 Swanson Vineyards & Winery
PO Box 459
Rutherford, CA 94573
707-944-0905
Fax: 707-967-3505 800-942-0809
www.swansonvineyards.com
Wines
Owner: W Clarke Swanson
Sales Manager: Michael Opdegraff
Contact: Chris Cutler
chris@chriscutler.com
Winemaker: Marco Capell
Estimated Sales: $5-9.9 Million
Number Employees: 20-49
Brands:
Swanson Vineyards & Winery

12379 Swany White Flour MillsLTD
206 2nd St SE
PO Box 214
Freeport, MN 56331-9036
320-836-2174
Fax: 320-836-2477 swanywhiteflour.com
White flours
President: Sharon Thelen
sa_thelen@hotmail.com
Number Employees: 1-4

12380 Swapples
Washington, DC
info@swapfoods.com
www.swapfoods.com
Paleo, vegan, and gluten free waffles in both sweet and savory flavors
Founder/CEO: Rebecca Peress
Year Founded: 2016

12381 Swatt Baking Co
222 Homer St
Olean, NY 14760-1132
716-372-9480
Fax: 716-373-6019 800-370-6656
www.lacinnamonbread.com
Rolls, regular and cinnamon bread and cinnamon bread sauce
President: Leonard Anzivine
VP: Lee Anzivine
lacinnamonbread@aol.com
Estimated Sales: $700000
Number Employees: 10-19
Square Footage: 37600
Type of Packaging: Food Service, Bulk
Brands:
L.A. Cinnamon

12382 Swedish Hill Vineyard &Winery
4565 State Route 414
Romulus, NY 14541-9769
607-403-0029
Fax: 315-549-8477 888-549-9463
info@swedishhill.com www.swedishhill.com
Winery, producing red, white, rose, sparkling and dessert wines.
President: Richard Peterson
CEO: Dave Peterson
info@swedishhill.com
Finance Manager: Amanda Fitzgerald
Director of Operations: Jean Peterson
Winemaker: Derek Wilber
Winemaker: Zach Pegram
Estimated Sales: $6 Million
Number Employees: 50-99
Number of Brands: 3
Type of Packaging: Consumer, Food Service
Other Locations:
Swedish Hill Lake Placid

Lake Placid NY
Swedish Hill Saratoga Springs
Saratoga Springs NY
Goose Watch Winery
Romulus NY
Goose Watch Lake Placid
Lake Placid NY
Penguin Bay
Hector NY
Brands:
Swedish Hill
Goose Watch
Penguin Bay

12383 **Sweeney's Gourmet Coffee Roast**
671 Middlegate Road
Suite C
Henderson, NV 89011-2628
702-558-0505
Fax: 702-558-3799
Coffee
President: Robert Sweeney
Estimated Sales: $2.5-5 Million
Number Employees: 1
Type of Packaging: Private Label, Bulk

12384 **Sweenors Chocolates**
21 Charles St
Wakefield, RI 02879-3621
401-783-4433
Fax: 401-783-9340 800-834-3123
www.sweenorschocolates.com
Chocolates, hard candies, fudge and mints
President: Brian Sweenor
Vice President: Brian Sweenor
Estimated Sales: $5-10 Million
Number Employees: 10-19
Type of Packaging: Consumer, Private Label, Bulk

12385 **Sweet & Sara**
4331 33rd St # 4
Suite 4
Long Island City, NY 11101-2316
718-707-2808
sara@sweetandsara.com
sweetandsara.com
Vegan treats
Owner: Sara Sohn
Number Employees: 10-19

12386 **Sweet & Saucy Inc**
5974 S Pennsylvania St
Centennial, CO 80121-2252
303-807-5132
Fax: 303-798-8258 jane@sweetandsaucy.net
www.sweetandsaucy.net
21 flavors of gourmet caramel and chocolate sauces.
President: Jane Jones
jane@sweetandsaucy.net
Vice President: Erin Jones
CMO: Robert Jones
COO: Brent Jones
Estimated Sales: Less Than $500,000
Number Employees: 1-4
Number of Brands: 1
Number of Products: 21
Type of Packaging: Consumer, Food Service
Brands:
Sweet & Saucy Caramel Sauces
Sweet & Saucy Chocolate Sauces

12387 **Sweet Additions**
4440 PGA Boulevard
Suite 600
Palm Beach Gardens, NY 33410
561-472-0178
Fax: 561-472-0548
customerservice@sweetadditions.com
sweetadditions.com
Manufacturer of organic sweeteners and sugar alternatives for the food and beverage industries.
President & CEO: Ken Valdivia
sweetadditions@gmail.com
Other Locations:
Corporate Headquarters
Palm Beach Gardens FL
Manufacturing Facility
Cameron WI
Brands:
CaneSweet
SweetDex
GrainSweet

12388 **Sweet Baby Ray's**
PO Box 31250
Chicago, IL 60631-0250
877-729-2229
service@sweetbabyrays.com
www.sweetbabyrays.com
Barbecue sauces, original, honey, hickory and brown sugar, sweet and spicy, chipotle, and sweet vidalia onion.
Founder: Dave Raymond
Operations Manager: Larry Duce Raymond
Estimated Sales: $20-50 Million
Number Employees: 5-9
Parent Co: Ken's Foods
Type of Packaging: Consumer, Food Service
Brands:
Sweet Baby Ray's

12389 **Sweet Blessings**
23805 Stuart Ranch Rd
Malibu, CA 90265-4856
310-317-1172
Fax: 310-317-1132
Chocolates
President: Dave Singelyn
CEO/Owner: B Wayne Hughes
VP Sales: Mark Bontempo
Estimated Sales: $3-5 Million
Number Employees: 5-9
Brands:
Noahs Buddies
Sweet Blessings

12390 **Sweet Breath**
950 3rd Ave
New York, NY 10022-2705
212-755-9300
Fax: 212-755-9305 877-673-9777
customercare@sweetbreath.com
www.sweetbreath.com
Breath fresheners, energy strips, vitamin strips and cough and cold strips instant energy for your body and mind
Founder/President: Jeffrey Hirschman
National Account Manager: David Hirschman
Vice President Marketing: Roger Mascall
Contact: Roger Mascall
roger.mascall@sweetbreath.com
Number Employees: 5-9
Brands:
Ice Chews
Ice Chips
Ice Chunks
Sweet Breath Xtreme Intense Breath

12391 **Sweet Candy Company**
3780 West Directors Row
Salt Lake City, UT 84104
801-886-1444
Fax: 801-886-1404 855-772-7720
mail@sweetcandy.com www.sweetcandy.com
Confectionery products including brittles, chocolates, holiday novelties, filled items, jellies, hard candies, jelly beans, marshmallows, mints, nougats, glazed nuts, taffy, etc.; also, in bags
Founder/President: Leon Sweet
Contact: Jacki Arevalo
arevaloj@sweetcandy.com
Type of Packaging: Consumer, Bulk

12392 **Sweet Christine's Bakery**
503 Orchard Avenue
Kennett Square, PA 19348
610-444-5542
www.sweetchristinesglutenfree.com
Gluten free baked goods
Contact: Kevin Mccann
kevin@sweetchristinesglutenfree.com

12393 **Sweet City Supply**
5820 Ward Ct
Virginia Beach, VA 23455
757-456-0800
Fax: 757-456-9980 888-793-3824
A contract manufacturer and national distributor of imported and domestic bulk and packaged candy, nuts, and confections.
President: Ronald Bublick
Type of Packaging: Food Service, Bulk

12394 **Sweet Corn Products Co**
124 N Broadway St
Bloomfield, NE 68718-4406
402-373-2211
Fax: 402-373-2219 877-628-6115
www.no-nobirdfeeder.com
Processor and exporter of sweet corn products including dry mature for tortilla chips and toasted nuts
General Manager: Raymon Lush
ray@sweetcornproducts.com
Estimated Sales: $2000000
Number Employees: 1-4
Square Footage: 92000
Type of Packaging: Consumer, Food Service, Private Label, Bulk
Brands:
Ugly Nut

12395 **Sweet Designs Chocolatier Inc**
16100 Detroit Ave
Lakewood, OH 44107-3715
216-226-4888
info@sweetdesigns.com
www.sweetdesigns.com
Manufacturer of assorted chocolates, truffles, and freshly dipped fruit.
Founder: Ines Rehmer
Estimated Sales: Less Than $500,000
Number Employees: 1-4

12396 **Sweet Earth Foods**
3080 Hilltop Rd
Moss Landing, CA 95039
831-375-8673
Fax: 831-375-3441 800-737-3311
zenfarmer@sweetearthfoods.com
www.sweetearthfoods.com
Vegetarian foods including soups, salads, burritos, salad dressings, salsa, hummus, vegeburgers, sweet bars, pies and seitan(wheat-meat)
Owner: Russell Hicks
sweetearth@pacbell.net
Co-Owner: Caren Hicks
Estimated Sales: $3-5 Million
Number Employees: 10-19
Square Footage: 8000
Type of Packaging: Consumer, Food Service, Bulk
Brands:
Awaken Foods
Fiesta Rice
Grand Life Seitan
Heat-N-Eat
Sweet Earth Natural Foods

12397 **Sweet Endings Inc**
1220 Okeechobee Rd
West Palm Beach, FL 33401-6947
561-655-0334
Fax: 561-209-1901 888-635-1177
swtend@aol.com www.sweetendingsdesserts.com
Processor and exporter of cakes, pies, tortes and crumbles including sugar and fat-free
Owner: Dalanna Browning
dalannabrowning@sweetendingsdesserts.com
Estimated Sales: $3-5 Million
Number Employees: 20-49
Square Footage: 12000
Type of Packaging: Food Service, Private Label

12398 **Sweet Fortunes of America**
783a Yerry Hill Road
Woodstock, NY 12498
845-679-7327
Fax: 845-679-7327
Gourmet and specialty foods
President: Carol Lieberman

12399 **Sweet Gallery Exclusive Pastry**
2312 Bloor St W
Toronto, ON M6S 1P2
Canada
416-766-0289
Fax: 416-766-7965
Processer of sponge cakes, butter cream tortes, pastries, croissants, wedding cakes, danishes and European cakes and pastries
President: Radi Jelenic
President: Lydia Jelenic
Number Employees: 10
Square Footage: 20000
Type of Packaging: Consumer

12400 **Sweet Grass Dairy**
19635 US Highway 19 N
Thomasville, GA 31792-9060
229-227-0752
Fax: 229-227-0752 sweetgrassdairy.com
Cow's milk cheese
Estimated Sales: Less Than $500,000
Number Employees: 1-4

12401 **Sweet Harvest Foods**
15100 Business Parkway
Rosemount, MN 55068
507-263-8599
Fax: 651-322-1229 info@sweetharvestfoods.com
www.sweetharvestfoods.com
Natural and organic honey and peanut butter.
President: Curt Riess
Quality Manager: Gary Stromley
COO: Brian McGregor
Plant Manager: Brian Pleschourt
Estimated Sales: $4.8 Million
Number Employees: 20-49
Type of Packaging: Consumer, Food Service, Private Label
Brands:
MEL-O HONEY
JOHN MOUNTAIN ORGANIC

12402 **Sweet Jubilee Gourmet**
273 Mulberry Drive
Suite 14
Mechanicsburg, PA 17050
717-691-9782
Fax: 717-691-0228 877-691-9732
diane@brittlebark.com
www.sweetjubileegourmet.com
Brittle candy made with assorted nuts, dried fruits and premium chocolate.
President/Owner: Diane Krulac
Estimated Sales: $750,000
Number Employees: 13
Square Footage: 10000

12403 **Sweet Lady Jane**
8360 Melrose Ave
Los Angeles, CA 90069
323-653-7145
Fax: 323-662-8950 www.sweetladyjane.com
Baked goods
Owner/Founder: Jane Lockhart
Contact: Oscar Gomez
ogomez@sweetladyjane.com
Estimated Sales: 500,000
Number Employees: 1-4

12404 **Sweet Leaf Tea Company**
515 S Congress Ave Ste 700
Austin, TX 78704
512-328-7775
Fax: 512-328-7725 www.sweetleaftea.com
Teas, lemonades, mixers and fixers
Founder/CEO: Clayton Christopher
CFO/COO: Brian Goldberg
Marketing Director: Adi Wilk
Co-Founder/VP of Sales: David Smith
Contact: Genevieve Court
vieve@sweetleaftea.com
VP Operations: Robert Walker
Production/Logistics Manager: Brian Selensky
Estimated Sales: $1.1 Million
Number Employees: 10

12405 **Sweet Life Enterprises**
2350 Pullman St.
Santa Ana, CA 92705
714-256-8900
Cinnamon rolls and cookies inluding chocolate chip, double fudge chocolate, oatmeal raisin, sugar, peanut butter, white chocolate, snickerdoodle, etc
President & CEO: Mike Gray
Quality Assurance Manager: Derek Osato
Marketing Manager: Stephanie Easterday
Vice President Sales: Lori Gray
Contact: Ryan Anita
ryan.anita@freshstartbakeries.com
VP Operations: Scott Fitzgerald
Estimated Sales: 20.9 Million
Number Employees: 115
Other Locations:
North America Support Offices
Santa Ana CA
Brands:
The Sweet Life

12406 **Sweet Loren's**
60 Broad Street
Floor 24
New York, NY 10004
646-257-5700
Fax: 646-930-5757 hello@sweetlorens.com
sweetlorens.com
Cookies
Founder & CEO: Loren Brill
Consumer Marketing Manager: Lindsey Tauer
Vice President, Sales: Yvette Baumgarten Borrack
Operations Manager: Melania Macko
Estimated Sales: $6.4 Million
Number Employees: 36
Brands:
Sweet Loren's

12407 **Sweet Mavens, LLC**
128B Addison Rd.
Glastonbury, CT 06033
860-490-1407
Fax: 860-568-6145 info@sweetmavens.com
www.sweetmavens.com
Manufacturer of biscotti, pecans, and almonds.
Founder: Anite Carpene
Contact: Anita Carpene
a.carpene@sweetmavens.com

12408 **Sweet Megan Baking Company**
234 Holland Rd.
Southampton, PA 18966
267-288-5080
www.glutenfreesweetmegan.com
No preservatives, all natural baked goods

12409 **Sweet Mountain Magic**
2131 N Larrabee Street
Apt 6205
Chicago, IL 60614-4422
773-755-4539
Fax: 703-437-1031
Ice cream
President: Stephen Kleiman
VP Marketing: Ehtel Hammer

12410 **Sweet Peas Floral Design**
6231 Pacific Ave # A2
Stockton, CA 95207-3700
209-472-9284
Fax: 209-472-9284
Marinades and barbecue sauces
Owner: Katie Wendland
Estimated Sales: $300,000-$500,000
Number Employees: 1-4
Square Footage: 7200
Type of Packaging: Consumer, Food Service
Brands:
Delta
Riverboat

12411 **Sweet Pillar**
Newport Beach, CA
310-913-7261
www.sweetpillar.com
Manufacturer of chocolate covered dates and mamool cookies.
Founder: Nadia Hubbi

12412 **Sweet Sams Baking Corp**
1261 Seabury Ave
Bronx, NY 10462-5526
718-822-0599
Fax: 718-409-0309 richardsklar@hotmail.com
www.sweetsams.com
Premium all butter bakery products
President: David Grogan
david.grogan@sweetsams.com
Estimated Sales: Less Than $500,000
Number Employees: 1-4

12413 **Sweet Sensations**
201 Humber Ave
Labrador City, NL A2V 2V3
Canada
709-944-2660
Fax: 709-944-2656
Chocolate and candies, also nuts and glazed nuts
Owner: Andrea Cormier
Estimated Sales: $1 Million

12414 **Sweet Shop USA**
1316 Industrial Rd
Mt Pleasant, TX 75455-2614
903-575-0033
Fax: 817-336-9169 888-957-9338
customercare@sweetshopusa.com
www.sweetshopusa.com
Chocolates, truffles, caramels and fudge.
President: Michael Moss
CEO: Jim Webb
jim@sweetshopusa.com
Chief Financial Officer: Matt Kelley
Lead Customer Service Representative: Sherry Bostick
Manager: Ashlyn Reynolds
Estimated Sales: $4.5 Million
Number Employees: 50-99
Number of Brands: 3
Square Footage: 66000
Type of Packaging: Consumer
Brands:
Mrs. Weinstein's Toffee
Price's Fine Chocolates
Sweet Shop USA

12415 **Sweet Street Desserts**
722 Hiesters Ln
Reading, PA 19605-3095
610-921-8113
Fax: 610-921-8195 800-793-3897
ussales@sweetstreet.com www.sweetstreet.com
Variety of coffee bar and desserts: hazelnut cappucino torte, apple crumb cake, chocolate chip crumb cake, sour cream coffee cake
President: Sandy Solmon
sandys@sweetstreet.com
Estimated Sales: $39400000
Number Employees: 500-999
Type of Packaging: Consumer, Food Service
Brands:
Sweet Street

12416 **Sweet Sue Kitchens**
106 Sweet Sue Drive
Athens, AL 35611-2181
256-216-0500
Fax: 256-216-0531
Processor and exporter of canned poultry products including chicken broth, chunks, stew and dumplings
Sales/Marketing Executive: Shirley Brown
Plant Manager: Bob Mahan
Purchasing Agent: Carol Moore
Parent Co: Sara Lee Corporation
Type of Packaging: Consumer, Food Service, Private Label

12417 **Sweet Swiss ConfectionsInc**
7821 W Electric Ave
Spokane, WA 99224-9000
509-838-1334
Fax: 509-456-0824 chocologos@sweetswiss.com
www.sweetswiss.com
Chocolate truffles, marzipan and personalized chocolate logos
President: Matt Phillipson
inquire@sweetswiss.com
Controller: Pam Martin
Vice President: Phina Phillipson
Estimated Sales: Below $5 Million
Number Employees: 5-9

12418 **Sweet Traders**
5362 Oceanus Dr # C
Suite C
Huntington Beach, CA 92649-1000
714-903-6800
Fax: 714-892-4345 info@sweettraders.com
www.sweettraders.com
Wine, chocolate, baked goods, and gift baskets; including chocolate wrapped wines and ciders, champagnes and nonalcoholic beverages
Owner: R Louw
rflouw@yahoo.com
Estimated Sales: Less Than $500,000
Number Employees: 1-4
Square Footage: 10000
Type of Packaging: Consumer, Private Label

12419 Sweet Water Brewing Co
195 Ottley Dr NE
Atlanta, GA 30324-3924
404-691-2537
Fax: 404-691-0936 Steve@sweetwaterbrew.com
www.sweetwaterbrew.com
Ale and stout
Owner: Fredrick Bensch
Sales: Dave Guender
Estimated Sales: $2.5-5 Million
Number Employees: 20-49
Type of Packaging: Consumer, Food Service
Brands:
Sweetwater
Sweetwater 42
Sweetwater Blue

12420 Sweet Water Seafood
369 Washington Ave
Carlstadt, NJ 07072-2805
201-939-6622
Fax: 201-939-4014 www.sweetwaterseafood.net
Frozen shellfish including squid, conch, clams and mussels
Manager: Teri Niece
Chairman: Robert Inglese
Manager: Theresa Niece
tniece@sweetwaterseafood.net
Estimated Sales: Less Than $500,000
Number Employees: 1-4
Square Footage: 132000
Type of Packaging: Consumer, Food Service, Private Label, Bulk
Brands:
Mussel King
Plumpy

12421 Sweet Whispers
6031 Crimson Ct
Mclean, VA 22101-0000
954-328-5079
info@sweetwhispers.store
sweetwhispers.store
Meringue filling
Co-Founder: Maria Umana
Co-Founder: Liliana Guerra
Year Founded: 2016
Brands:
Sweet Whispers

12422 Sweet'N Low
2 Cumberland St
Brooklyn, NY 11205
www.sweetnlow.com
Manufacturer of artificial sweeteners.
Chairman: Marvin Eisenstadt
President/CEO: Steven Eisenstadt
Estimated Sales: $100+ Million
Number Employees: 400
Number of Brands: 1
Parent Co: Cumberland Packing Corp.
Type of Packaging: Consumer
Brands:
Sweet'n Low

12423 SweetWorks Inc
3500 Genesee Street
Buffalo, NY 14225
716-634-0880
Fax: 716-634-4855 www.sweetworks.net
Chocolates, candy and gum products
Owner: Philip Terranova
CFO: Ralph Nicosia
Marketing Director: Jeanne Palka
Sales Director: Jerry Tubbs
Contact: Pascal Bieri
pbieri@sweetworks.net

12424 Sweetaly
Sweetaly Dolceria
Oceanside, CA 92056
760-539-2196
info@sweetaly.us
sweetaly.us
Italian desserts: mousse, tiramisu and panna cotta.
Co-Founder: Oliviero Colmignoli
Type of Packaging: Consumer, Private Label
Brands:
Sweetaly

12425 Sweetcraft Candies
PO Box 15
Timonium, MD 21094-0015
410-252-0684
Fax: 410-252-0352
Candy
President: George George

12426 Sweetener Supply Corp
9501 Southview Ave
Brookfield, IL 60513-1529
708-588-8400
Fax: 708-588-8460 888-784-2799
sweetenersupply.com
Manufacturer and distributor of sweeteners for the food, beverage and confectionery industries.
Number Employees: 20-49
Number of Brands: 5
Brands:
Delicious
Ridgeland
Ambersweet
Sur Sweet
Ultraclear

12427 Sweeteners Plus Inc
5768 Sweeteners Blvd
Lakeville, NY 14480-9741
585-346-3193
Fax: 585-346-2310 www.sweetenersplus.com
Manufacturer and distributor of liquid and dry sweeteners including white and brown sugar, organic and kosher products, fructose, maltitol, corn syrup, and invert syrups. Also bottling, custom blending, and liquid fondants. Shippedregionally long haul by rail and short haul by trucks and nationally by distribution products
President & CEO: Carlton Myers
Quality Assurance Manager: Mark Rudolph
VP Sales: Mark Whitford
Operation Manager: Bill Devine
Estimated Sales: $14.7 Million
Number Employees: 1-4
Type of Packaging: Food Service, Bulk

12428 Sweetery
1814 E Greenville St
Anderson, SC 29621-2035
864-224-8394
Fax: 864-224-8469 800-752-1188
www.thesweetery.net
Cakes, cheesecakes and pies
President: Jane Jarahian
jjarahian@sweetery.com
Estimated Sales: Under $500,000
Number Employees: 20-49
Type of Packaging: Consumer, Private Label
Brands:
Southern Special
Uggly Cake

12429 Sweetleaf Co
1203 W San Pedro St
Gilbert, AZ 85233-2406
480-921-2160
Fax: 480-966-3805 www.sweetleaf.com
Tea, extracts, sweetners
President: Carol May
cmay@wisdomnaturalbrands.com
Chief Executive Officer: James May
Number Employees: 20-49

12430 Sweetleaf Co
1203 W San Pedro St
Gilbert, AZ 85233-2406
480-921-2160
Fax: 480-966-3805 800-899-9908
info@wisdomnaturalbrands.com sweetleaf.com
Manufacturer of award-winning stevia sweetener.
President: Carol May
cmay@wisdomnaturalbrands.com
Number Employees: 20-49
Number of Brands: 5
Brands:
SweetLeaf Stevia
Sweet Drops
Water Drops
SugarLeaf
Organic SweetLeaf Stevia

12431 Sweetstacks LLC
PO Box 33227
San Diego, CA 92163-3227
619-997-1097
www.sweetstacks.com
Pancake mixes, baking mixes, fruit spreads, syrups
President: Elaine Babauta
Estimated Sales: C

12432 Sweetwater Spice Company
3800 N Lamar Blvd
Suite 730-155
Austin, TX 78756
800-531-6079
Fax: 512-857-0083 www.sweetwaterspice.com
Sauces and marinades
Contact: Scott Sapire
ssapire@mac.com

12433 Sweetwood Cattle Co
2670 Copper Ridge Cir
Suite 3
Steamboat Spgs, CO 80487-9492
970-879-7456
Fax: 970-870-7980 www.sweetwood.com
Meats
CEO: Ryan Wood
Vice President: Caitlin Colgan
Manager: Jeremiah Jackson
jeremiah@sweetwood.com
Operations Director: Rebecca Fix
Estimated Sales: Less Than $500,000
Number Employees: 5-9

12434 Sweety Novelty
633 Monterey Pass Rd
Monterey Park, CA 91754
626-282-4482
Fax: 626-282-2482
Frozen fruit bars and ice cream including red bean, mango, green tea, durian, peanut and taro; also, mocha ice cream including green tea, vanilla, strawberry, mango and taro
President: Tracy Lee
Manager: Patty Lee
Estimated Sales: $870,000
Number Employees: 10-19
Square Footage: 32000
Type of Packaging: Consumer, Food Service

12435 Swerseys Chocolate
63 Flushing Ave.
Brooklyn, NY 11205
718-497-8800
Fax: 718-497-8100 info@swerseys.com
www.swerseys.com
Manufacturer of chocolate, dried fruit and mixed nuts.
Owner: Jack Levy

12436 Swerve Sweetener
1000 S. Rendon
New Orleans, LA 70125
504-309-9280
Fax: 504-309-9287 888-979-3783
hello@swervesweetener.com
www.swervesweetener.com
Natural sweetener
President & CEO: Andress Blackwell
Marketing Manager: Natalia Matallana
Estimated Sales: $1-2 Million
Number Employees: 2-10
Brands:
Swerve

12437 (HQ)Swiss American Inc
4200 Papin St
St Louis, MO 63110-1736
314-533-2224
Fax: 314-533-0765 800-325-8150
Packer, importer and distributor of cheese and fine foods
President: Joseph Hoff
CEO: R Weil
VP: D Boyd
Contact: Chris Biscan
chris.biscan@swissamerican.com
Operations VP: David Boyd
Estimated Sales: Less Than $500,000
Number Employees: 1-4
Square Footage: 180000
Type of Packaging: Consumer, Bulk
Other Locations:
Swiss-American
North Charleston SC

Brands:
Capricorn
Dutch Garden
Dutch Garden Super Swiss
Epic
Fire Jack
Freshwrap Cuts
Freshwrap Slices
Mr. Sharp
Saint Louis
Verdaccio

12438 (HQ)Swiss Chalet Fine Foods
9455 NW 40th Street Rd
Doral, FL 33178-2941
305-592-0008
Fax: 305-592-1651 800-347-9477
info@scff.com www.scff.com
A wide range of quality gourmet products from sweets to savories
CFO: Donna Croup
donna@scff.com
Estimated Sales: $300,000-500,000
Number Employees: 5-9
Brands:
Felchlin-Swiss
Haco
Hero

12439 Swiss Dairy
12171 Madera Way
Riverside, CA 92503
951-898-9427
Fax: 951-734-3786
Milk
Office Manager: Lorry Olson
Contact: John Schneider
john_schneider@deanfoods.com
Estimated Sales: $.5-1,000,000
Number Employees: 5-9
Parent Co: Suiza Dairy Group
Type of Packaging: Consumer, Food Service

12440 Swiss Food Products
4333 W Division St
Chicago, IL 60651
312-829-0100
Fax: 773-394-6475 www.swissfoodproducts.com
Manufacturer and exporter of bases including soup, gravy, browning, seasoning and sauce; also, flavors
Estimated Sales: $5-10 Million
Number Employees: 10-19
Square Footage: 100000
Type of Packaging: Consumer, Food Service, Private Label, Bulk
Brands:
Swiss

12441 Swiss Heritage Cheese Inc
114 E Coates Ave
Monticello, WI 53570-9828
608-938-4455
Fax: 608-938-1325 www.tdsnet.com
Cheese
President/Treasurer: Paul Rufener
Estimated Sales: $1,600,000
Number Employees: 10-19
Brands:
Swiss Heritage Cheese

12442 Swiss Premium Dairy Inc
2401 Walnut St
Lebanon, PA 17042-9444
717-273-2658
Fax: 717-273-2794 800-222-2129
www.deanfoods.com
Milk including 2% and skim; also, chilled orange juice, iced tea and fruit drinks
General Manager: Mike Eiceman
mike_eiceman@deanfoods.com
Plant Manager: John Wengert
Year Founded: 1931
Estimated Sales: B
Number Employees: 100-249
Square Footage: 120000
Parent Co: Dean Foods
Type of Packaging: Consumer, Food Service, Private Label
Other Locations:
Wengert's Dairy
Camp Hill PA
Brands:
Swiss 2
Swiss Premium
Swiss Premium

12443 Swiss Way Cheese
1315 Us Highway 27 N
Berne, IN 46711-1031
260-589-3531
Fax: 219-589-3843 swoss@swissway.com
Cheese
President: Tim Ehlerding
Operations Manager: Russ Reimer
Estimated Sales: $2.5 Million appx.
Number Employees: 5-9
Type of Packaging: Private Label
Brands:
Berne Baby Swiss
Berne Swiss Lace

12444 Swiss-American Sausage Company
251 Darcy Pkwy
Lathrop, CA 95330
209-858-5555
Fax: 209-858-1102
Processor and exporter of meat pizza toppings including pepperoni, salami, ham, linguica and raw and cooked sausage
President/CEO: Theodore Arena
Human Resources: Heidi Moore
Sales Manager: Paul Sheehan
Estimated Sales: $300,000-500,000
Number Employees: 50-99
Square Footage: 360000
Type of Packaging: Food Service, Private Label
Brands:
Capo Di Monte

12445 Swisser Sweet Maple
6242 Swiss Road
Castorland, NY 13620-1244
315-346-1034
Fax: 315-346-1662
Pure NY maple syrup, pure maple cream spread, maple candies, maple lollipops, maple granulated sugar, gift arrangements, wedding party favors and corporate gifts. Retail, wholesale and bulk.
Co-Owner: Barbara Zehr
Co-Owner: Jason Zehr
Number Employees: 6
Type of Packaging: Consumer, Private Label, Bulk
Other Locations:
Swisser Sweet Maple
Casta-Land NY

12446 Swissland Milk
4310 South US Hwy 27
Berne, IN 46711
260-589-2761
Fax: 260-589-2761
Milk and yogurt
General Manager: Kirk Johnson
Estimated Sales: $1-2.5 Million
Number Employees: 10-19

12447 Switch Beverage
381 Post Rd
Darien, CT 06820
203-202-7383
Fax: 203-202-7386 www.switchbev.com
Juice
President/Owner: Mike Gilbert

12448 Switzer's Inc
209 S Belt E
Belleville, IL 62220
618-234-2225
Fax: 618-271-6339
bellevilleswitzerfoods@gmail.com
Frozen foods, groceries, provisions/meats and general merchandise; serving the food service market
President: Carolyn Hundley
switzerfoods@gmail.com
Estimated Sales: $20-50 Million
Number Employees: 20-49

12449 Sycamore Vineyards
PO Box 410
Saint Helena, CA 94574-0410
707-963-9694
Fax: 707-963-0554 800-963-9698
wineinfo@freemarkabbey.com
www.freemarkabbey.com
Wines
Director Winemaking: Ted Edwards
Winemaker: Tim Bell
Estimated Sales: $1.9 Million
Number Employees: 20

12450 Sylvin Farms Winery
24 N Vienna Ave
Egg Harbor City, NJ 08215-3245
609-965-1548
Sylvinfarms@comcast.net
www.sylvinfarmswinery.com
Wines
Proprieter: Frank Salek
Vineyard Manager: Franklin Salek
Estimated Sales: $500,000-$1 000,000
Number Employees: 1-4
Brands:
Sylvin Farms

12451 Symms Fruit Ranch Inc
14068 Sunny Slopes Rd
Caldwell, ID 83607
208-459-4821
Fax: 208-459-6932 www.symmsfruit.com
Produce including apples, cherries, peaches and plums, necatrines, pluots, pears, wine grapes, asparagus, onions and potatoes.
Partner: Jim Mertz
jim@symmsfruit.com
Year Founded: 1914
Estimated Sales: $20 Million
Number Employees: 100-249
Square Footage: 150000
Type of Packaging: Consumer, Food Service, Bulk
Brands:
Sss

12452 Symons Frozen Foods
619 Goodrich Rd
Centralia, WA 98531-9336
360-736-1321
Fax: 360-736-6328
Processor and exporter of frozen fruits and vegetables including blackberries, blueberries, red and black raspberries, corn, peas, peas/carrots and succotash
Owner: Bill James
bjames@symonsfrozenfoods.com
Production Manager: Howard McLoughlin
Estimated Sales: $18,200,000
Number Employees: 50-99
Type of Packaging: Consumer, Food Service, Private Label, Bulk

12453 Symphony Foods
1685 Short Street
Berkeley, CA 94702-1231
510-845-8275
Fax: 510-558-9255
General groceries
Owner: Alan Finkelstein
Number Employees: 1-4
Type of Packaging: Private Label

12454 Symrise Inc.
300 North St.
Teterboro, NJ 07608
201-288-3200
Fax: 201-462-2200 www.symrise.com
Global fragrance and flavorings company.
CEO: Dr. Heinz-J□rgen Bertram
CFO: Olaf Klinger
President, Scent & Care: Achim Daub
President, Nutrition: Dr. Jean-Yves Parisot
President, Flavor: Heinrich Schaper
Year Founded: 2003
Estimated Sales: $3.1 Billion
Number Employees: 9,649
Number of Products: 30K
Parent Co: Symrise AG
Other Locations:
Customer Service
Saddle Brook NJ
Engineering, Purchasing, Production
Branchburg NJ
Production
Elyria OH
Chemical Production
Goose Creek SC

12455 Synergy
2279 Resource Blvd
Moab, UT 84532-3406
435-259-5366
Fax: 435-259-2328 800-804-3211
customer-service@synergy-co.com
www.thesynergycompany.com
Organic nutritional supplements, vitamins, juice powder, and honey.

Founder/CEO: Mitchell May
CFO: Terry May
Quality Control Assurance: Tim Harkwright
Director of Sales: Sarah Muhlbradt
Contact: Steven Lattey
steven@synergyhc.com
Manager of Purchasing: Leslie Warren
Estimated Sales: Less Than $500,000
Number Employees: 1-4
Type of Packaging: Consumer

12456 **Synergy Flavors Inc**
1500 Synergy Dr
Wauconda, IL 60084-1073
847-487-1011
Fax: 847-487-1066
Global flavorings manufacturer.
Number Employees: 20-49
Type of Packaging: Consumer, Food Service, Bulk
Other Locations:
U.S. Headquarters
Wauconda IL
U.K. Headquarters
High Wycombe, UK
Hamilton OH
Rochester NY
Ballineen, Ireland
Sao Paulo, Brazil
Samut Prakan, Thailand

12457 **Synergy Plus**
500 Halls Mill Rd
Freehold, NJ 07728-8811
732-308-3000
Fax: 732-761-2878
Vitamins
Manager: Barb McCleer
Vice President, General Counsel, Secreta: Ellen Chiniara
Sales Coordinator: Arthur Edell
Estimated Sales: Under $500,000
Number Employees: 250-499

12458 **Synthite USA Inc.**
840 South Oak Park Avenue
Suite 212
Oak Park, IL 60304
708-446-1716
synthiteusa@synthite.com
www.synthite.com
Global premium ingredients company headquartered in India with operations in Sri Lanka, China, Brazil and the USA.
Contact: Joseph Jesus
josephj@synthite.com

12459 **Syracuse Casing Co**
528 Erie Blvd W
Syracuse, NY 13204-2423
315-475-0309
Fax: 315-475-8536 makincasin@aol.com
Natural sausage casings
President: Peter Frey Sr
Estimated Sales: $2200000
Number Employees: 5-9
Square Footage: 60000
Type of Packaging: Food Service, Private Label, Bulk

12460 **T G Lee Dairy**
315 N Bumby Ave
Orlando, FL 32803-6029
407-894-4941
Fax: 407-896-4757 800-432-4872
www.tgleedairy.com
Citrus juices and milk including low-fat, chocolate, whole, skim, 1% and 2%; also, cream and ice cream cones, sandwiches and dixies
Manager: Billy Giovanetti
billy_giovanetti@deanfoods.com
CEO: Howard Dean
VP Sales/Marketing: Bill Giovanetti
Manager: Billy Giovanetti
billy_giovanetti@deanfoods.com
Number Employees: 500-999
Parent Co: Dean Foods Company
Type of Packaging: Consumer, Food Service, Private Label, Bulk
Brands:
T.G. Lee Foods

12461 **T Hasegawa USA Inc**
14017 183rd St
Cerritos, CA 90703-7000
714-522-1900
Fax: 714-522-6800 www.thasegawa.com
Processor, importer and exporter of custom blended flavors and seasonings for beverages, cuisine, dairy, salad dressings, sauces and prepared foods
President: Mark Scott
mscott@thasegawa.com
President: Michiru Waku
Sales Manager (Western): Jeff Carlson
Sales Manager (Eastern): Robert Taylor
Estimated Sales: $8300000
Number Employees: 50-99
Square Footage: 216000
Parent Co: T. Hasegawa Company
Other Locations:
T. Hasegawa U.S.A.
Northbrook IL

12462 **T M Duche Nut Co**
1502 Railroad Ave
Orland, CA 95963-2035
530-865-5511
Fax: 530-865-7864 www.duchenut.com
Processor and exporter of almonds
President: Mosha Schwartz
CFO: Tim Gray
Manager: John Wilson
barbara.pruitt@pmi.org
Estimated Sales: $1-2.5 Million
Number Employees: 20-49
Type of Packaging: Consumer, Food Service, Private Label, Bulk

12463 **T O Williams Inc**
300 Wythe St
Portsmouth, VA 23704-5208
757-397-0771
Fax: 757-397-5702 towi@bellatlantic.net
Meat packer
Owner: Pete Chay
p.chay@towilliamsinc.com
CEO: Diane Chay
VP: Peter J Chay
President: Hyun J Chay
Marketing: Bridgette McClung
Estimated Sales: $1,600,000
Number Employees: 20-49
Square Footage: 39000
Type of Packaging: Food Service
Brands:
Blue Ribbon Hot Sausage
Diane's Italian Sausage
H.C. Smoked Sausage
Virginia Smoked Sausage

12464 **T Sterling Assoc**
121 W 4th St
Jamestown, NY 14701-5005
716-483-0769
Fax: 716-664-9508
Cheese marketing
Manager: Spring Martin
lakewoodcheeseny@windstream.net
Estimated Sales: $.5-1 000,000
Number Employees: 1-4
Type of Packaging: Private Label

12465 **T&T Seafood**
14550 Brown Rd
Baker, LA 70714
225-261-5438
Fax: 225-261-5260
Seafood
President: John Tourere
Estimated Sales: $2 Million
Number Employees: 1-4

12466 **T'Lish Dressings and Marinades**
904 5th Ave
Opelika, AL 36801-4133
205-503-8603
www.tlish.com
Salad dressings and marinades
Owner: Tiffany Denson
Brands:
T'Lish vinaigrette & marinade

12467 **T. Marzetti Company**
380 Polaris Pkwy.
Suite 400
Westerville, OH 43082
614-846-2232
Fax: 614-848-8330 800-999-1835
www.marzetti.com
Bread and rolls, caviar, croutons, dairy products, dips, dressings and sauces, noodles and pasta, and specialty products.
President: David Ciesinski
Director, Marketing: Irene Castle
Year Founded: 1896
Estimated Sales: $922.9 Million
Number Employees: 2,700
Number of Brands: 14
Square Footage: 28000
Type of Packaging: Food Service, Private Label, Bulk
Brands:
Marzetti
New York Brand
Sister Schubert's
Flatout
Girard's
Amish Kitchens
Chatham Village
Marshall's
Cardinis Salad Dressing
Reames
Inn Maid
Romanoff
Angelic Bakehouse
What's For Dinner?

12468 **T.B. Seafood**
450 Commercial St
Portland, ME 04101-4636
207-871-2420
Fax: 207-871-0906
Seafood
President: Roderick Wintle Jr

12469 **T.J. Blackburn Syrup Works**
108 East Lafayette
Jefferson, TX 75657
903-665-2541
Fax: 903-665-1128 800-657-5073
Established in 1972. Manufacturer of jams, jellies and syrups.
President: Jeffrey Fuquay
Chief Information Oficer: Sean Fuquay
Chief Operating Officer: Ronnie Bullard
Purchasing Executive: Troy Hunter
Estimated Sales: $40 Million
Number Employees: 50-99
Type of Packaging: Consumer, Bulk
Brands:
Blackburn's

12470 **T.J. Kraft**
1535 Colburn St
Honolulu, HI 96817-4905
808-842-3474
Fax: 808-842-3475 tkraft@norpacexport.com
Various types of fresh Hawaiian seafood
President: Thomas Kraft
Estimated Sales: $10-20 Million
Number Employees: 10-19

12471 **T.L. Herring & Company**
2101 Old Stantonsburg Road
P.O. Box 3186
Wilson, NC 27893
252-291-1141
Fax: 252-291-1142 TLHERRINGCO@yahoo.com
www.tlherring.com
Processor and packer of hot dog chili, fresh pork sausage, souse meat, cooked chitterlings, all with Southern flavorings
President: Thomas Mark
CFO: Jean Herring
Vice President: Mike Herring
Estimated Sales: $5-10 Million
Number Employees: 10 to 19
Square Footage: 44700

12472 **T.S. Smith & Sons**
8887 Redden Rd
Bridgeville, DE 19933
302-337-8271
Fax: 302-337-8417 www.tssmithandsonsfarm.com

Apples, peaches, nectarines, sweet corn, asparagus, strawberries, soybeans, wheat, barley and broiles; exporter of apples
President: Matthew Smith
Sales (Wholesale/Retail): Thomas Smith
Production Manager: Charles Smith
Estimated Sales: $3-5 Million
Number Employees: 20-49
Type of Packaging: Consumer, Bulk
Brands:
T.S. Smith & Sons

12473 T.W. Garner Food Company
614 W 4th St
Winston Salem, NC 27101-2730
336-661-1550
Fax: 336-661-1901 800-476-7383
www.twgarnerfoodservice.com
Manufacturer of hot sauces, wing sauces and sea-food sauces; sriracha sauces, salsa and tortilla strips.
CEO: Ann Garner Riddle
Chief Financial Officer: Matt Mccollum
Chief Marketing Officer: Glenn Garner
Chief Operating Officer: Heyward Garner
Estimated Sales: $17.7 Million
Number Employees: 27
Number of Brands: 3
Type of Packaging: Consumer, Food Service
Other Locations:
T.W. Garner Production Facility
Winston-Salem NC
Brands:
Garner Jams & Jellies
Green Mountain Gringo
Texas Pete

12474 T.W. Garner Food Company
4045 Indiana Ave
Winston-Salem, NC 27105
336-661-1550
www.texaspete.com
Manufacturer of hot sauces, wing sauces and sea-food sauces; sriracha sauces, salsa and tortilla strips.
CEO: Ann Garner Riddle
Chief Financial Officer: Matt Mccollum
Chief Marketing Officer: Glenn Garner
Chief Operating Officer: Heyward Garner
Number Employees: 65
Number of Brands: 3
Parent Co: T.W. Garner Food Company
Type of Packaging: Consumer, Food Service

12475 TBJ Gourmet
1554 Paoli Pike
Suite 254
West Chester, PA 19380
856-222-2000
info@tbjgourmet.com
tbjgourmet.com
Bacon jams
Managing Partner: Michael Oraschewsky
Estimated Sales: $1-2 Million
Type of Packaging: Food Service
Brands:
TBJ Gourmet

12476 TCHO Ventures
Pier 17
San Francisco, CA 94111
415-981-0189
Fax: 415-723-7497 info@tcho.com
www.tcho.com
Chocolate
President/Owner: Louis Rossetto
Director of Finance: Sam Christian
Contact: Chris Bell
c.bell@apple.com
Estimated Sales: $1.3 Million
Number Employees: 20

12477 TH Foods, Inc.
2134 Harlem Rd.
Loves Park, IL 61111
815-636-9500
Fax: 815-636-8400 sales@thfoods.com
www.thfoods.com
Manufacturer of crackers, snack crips and chips.
President: Ken Takao
Brands:
Crunchmaster
Harvest Stone

12478 TIC Gums
4609 Richlynn Drive
Belcamp, MD 21017
410-273-7300
Fax: 410-273-6469 800-899-3953
info@ticgums.com www.ticgums.com
Manufacturer of texture and stabilization ingredients for the food industry.
Contact: Philip Abecket
pabecket@ticgums.com
Number Employees: 50-100
Type of Packaging: Bulk

12479 TMI Trading Co
7 Bushwick Pl
Brooklyn, NY 11206-2815
718-821-5052
Fax: 718-821-6841 www.tmitrading.com
Asian-style beverages, snacks, and food.
Contact: Todd Abramson
todd@tmitrading.com
Number Employees: 5-9

12480 TNT Crust
P.O.Box 8929
Green Bay, WI 54308
920-431-7240
Fax: 920-431-7249 tntcrust@tyson.com
www.tntcrust.com
Processor and exporter of pre-made, partially baked pizza crusts including thin, thick and raised edge; also, fresh and frozen pizza dough.
President: Roger Lebreck
Vice President: Shreenivas Manthana
VP Sales/Marketing: Larry Kropp
Sales Director: Larry Kropp
VP Operations: Kent Reschke
VP Engineering: Phil Vangsnes
Number Employees: 100-249
Parent Co: FoodBrands America
Type of Packaging: Food Service

12481 TODDS Enterprises Inc
2450 White Rd
Irvine, CA 92614-6250
949-250-4080
Fax: 949-724-1338 800-568-6337
ed.stokes@us.hjheinz.com www.toddsfoods.com
Processor and exporter of soups, sauces, chili and salad dressings
Marketing Director: Ed Stokes
Contact: Carole Hoffman
Number Employees: 100-249
Type of Packaging: Food Service, Private Label
Brands:
Todd's

12482 TOST Beverages LLC
54 Elizabeth St. # 110
Red Hook, NY 12571
info@tostbeverages.com
www.tostbeverages.com
Sparkling, non-alcoholic fruit-flavored beverage
CEO: Brooks Addington
Number of Brands: 1
Number of Products: 1
Type of Packaging: Consumer, Private Label
Brands:
TOST

12483 TRC Corp
12320 E Skelly Dr
Tulsa, OK 74128-2414
918-437-7310
Fax: 918-492-9546 800-258-5028
customerservice@reachforlife.com
Super oxygenated drinking water
President: Rocky Heinrich
rockyh@trccorp.com
CEO: Elmer Heinrich
Vice President: Shirley Heinrich
Estimated Sales: $7.5 Million
Number Employees: 20-49
Type of Packaging: Consumer
Brands:
Liquidlise
Super Oxy-Pure

12484 Tabard Farm Potato Chips
PO Box 351
Middletown, VA 22645-0351
540-869-0104
Fax: 540-869-0176
Potato chips
Sales Manager: Sarah Cohen
Plant Manager: Chris Miller
Estimated Sales: $5-9.9 Million
Number Employees: 20-49
Parent Co: Tabard Corporation

12485 Tabatchinick Fine Foods
1230 Hamilton St
Somerset, NJ 08873-3343
732-247-6668
Fax: 732-247-6555 info@tabatchnick.com
www.tabatchnick.com
Homemade soups, sorbets, icepops and cheese
Owner: Ben Tabatchinick
ben@tabatchinick.com
CFO: Robert Ingebretsen
VP/National Food Service: Peter Hans
Institutional Sales: Marc Blake
Chief Engineer: Bud Barry
Retail Sales Coordinator: Claudia Davila
Commodities Coordinator: Barbara Slicner
Customer Relations: Michelle Kopitman
Plant Manager: Cezar Capalong
Estimated Sales: Below $5 Million
Number Employees: 20-49

12486 Tabco Enterprises
1906 W Holt Ave
Pomona, CA 91768-3351
909-623-4565
Fax: 909-623-2605
Processor and exporter of nutritional food supplements including deep sea fish oil, shark cartilage, multivitamins and minerals, grape seed extract, herbal products, spirulina, garlic, etc
President: Bruce Lin
Financial Officer: Rebecca Lin
Estimated Sales: $5-10 Million
Number Employees: 20-49
Square Footage: 80000
Parent Co: Essential Pharmaceutical
Brands:
Eden Life
Essential Elite
Wonderful Life

12487 Table De France
2020 S Haven Ave
Ontario, CA 91761-0735
909-923-5205
Fax: 909-923-7804 info@micheldefrance.com
www.micheldefrance.com
Authentic French-Style Crepes, soy wraps, fan wafers, butter wafer cookies, rolled wafers and filled rolled wafers, Paillette Feuilletine and Parisian cakes.
Owner: Ovi Constantine
Owner/CFO: Philip Bayon
Quality Control: Teresa Aguire
Sales Director: Erwan Le Bayon
ovi@micheldefrance.com
Plant Manager: Philippe Le Bayon
Estimated Sales: $820,000
Number Employees: 10-19
Number of Products: 4
Square Footage: 120000
Type of Packaging: Food Service, Private Label
Other Locations:
Table De France
Ontario CA
Brands:
Krazy
Michel De France
Table De France

12488 Table Talk Pies Inc
120 Washington St # 1
Worcester, MA 01610-2751
508-798-8811
Fax: 508-798-0848
customerservice@tabletalkpie.com
www.tabletalkpie.com
4, 6, 8, 9, and 10 inch pies in a variety of dessert and fruit flavors
Director of Sales/Marketing: Bob Littlefield
Inside Sales: Tara Tula
Sales/Marketing: Louise Lindberg
Logistics: Valdemar Siqueira
Estimated Sales: $40 Million
Number Employees: 50-99
Brands:
Table Talk

12489 **Tabor Hill Winery & Restaurant**
185 Mount Tabor Rd
Buchanan, MI 49107-8326
269-422-1161
Fax: 269-422-2787 800-283-3363
info@taborhill.com www.taborhill.com
Winery producing reds, whites, sparkling, dessert and non-alcoholic wines.
President: Linda Upton
CEO: Mike Merchant
Winemaker: Michael Merchant
Estimated Sales: $5.3 Million
Number Employees: 50-99
Number of Brands: 3
Type of Packaging: Consumer, Food Service
Other Locations:
Tabor Hill Champagne Celler
Bridgman MI
Tabor Hill Wine Port
Saugatuck MI
Brands:
Michael Merchant Winemaker
Tabor Hill
Grand Mark

12490 **Tadin Herb & Tea Co**
3345 E Slauson Ave
Vernon, CA 90058-3914
323-728-5100
Fax: 323-582-8687 800-838-2346
support@tadincorp.com
Tea bags and cellophane-packaged herbs and capsules and herbal remedies
Owner: Laura Alvarez
Sales Manager: Davor Hervas
lalvarezparra@tadin.com
Estimated Sales: $5-10 Million
Number Employees: 50-99
Brands:
Tadin

12491 **Taffy Town Inc**
55 W 800 S
Salt Lake City, UT 84101-2912
801-355-4637
Fax: 801-355-7664 800-765-4770
worlds_best_taffy@taffytown.com
www.taffytown.com
Salt water taffy
President: Jason Glade
worlds_best_taffy@taffytown.com
VP Marketing: Jason Glade
VP Manufacturing: Derek Glade
Estimated Sales: $1-2.5 Million
Number Employees: 20-49

12492 **Taft Street Winery**
2030 Barlow Ln
Sebastopol, CA 95472-2555
707-823-2049
Fax: 707-823-8622 www.taftstreetwinery.com
Wines consisting of Sauvignon Blancs, Chardonnays, Zinfadel, Russian river, PEKA Pinot Noir
President: Michael Tierney
miket@taftstreetwinery.com
General Manager/CEO: Mike Martini
Account Manager: Clayton SmithKey
Winemaker: Kent Barthman
Assistant Winemaker: Megan Baccitich
Cellar Master: Joel Rabune
Estimated Sales: $5-10 Million
Number Employees: 10-19
Type of Packaging: Private Label, Bulk

12493 **Taftsville Country Store**
2706 E Woodstock Rd
PO Box 2
Taftsville, VT 05073
802-457-1135
800-854-0013
clwilson@taftsville.com
Supplier of camembert, brie, stilton, gruyere and parmesan cheese, Vermont maple syrup, Vermont gourmet foods
President: Rebecca Loftus
Estimated Sales: $300,000-500,000
Number Employees: 1-4
Type of Packaging: Consumer
Brands:
Blythedale

12494 **Tahana Confections LLC**
PO Box 4314
Portsmouth, NH 03802-4314
603-498-6246
www.tahanaconfections.com
Candy: Caramel
Owner/Founder: Amanda Telford
amanda@tahanaconfections.com
Estimated Sales: 83,000
Number Employees: 5-9

12495 **Tahitian Gold**
23883 Madison St
Torrance, CA 90505-6008
310-465-0856
Fax: 310-465-0857 info@tahitianvanilla.com
www.tahitianvanilla.com
Dessert toppings, baking & mixing ingredients, extracts
Owner: Manu Martin
Sales Manager: Caryn Briedis
pacificislandimports@yahoo.com
Operations Manager: Eddie Kikuchi
Number Employees: 1-4

12496 **Taif Inc**
600 Kaiser Dr # A
Folcroft West Business Park
Folcroft, PA 19032-2122
610-522-0122
Fax: 610-522-5305 info@tallutos.com
www.tallutos.com
Frozen pasta and related items
President: Joseph A. M. Talluto
joseph_talluto@taifinc.com
VP: Gus De Nicola
Number Employees: 5-9
Square Footage: 54000
Type of Packaging: Food Service
Brands:
Talluto's

12497 **Tait Farm Foods**
179 Tait Rd
Centre Hall, PA 16828-7806
814-466-2386
Fax: 814-466-6561 800-787-2716
info@taitfarmfoods.com www.taitfarmfoods.com
Specialty jams, jellies, conserves, chutneys, scone and pan cake mixes, colonial fruit shrubs, international fruit sauces and herbal oils.
Wholesale Manager: Karen Myford
Estimated Sales: $80,000
Number Employees: 7
Type of Packaging: Private Label
Brands:
Raspberry Teriyaki
Tait Farm Foods

12498 **Taiyo International Inc.**
5960 Golden Hills Dr
Minneapolis, MN 55416-1040
763-398-3003
Fax: 763-398-3007 sales@taiyoint.com
www.taiyointernational.com
Manufacturer of functional ingredients for the food and pharmaceutical industries.
President: Nagahori Yamazaki
Executive Vice President: Yoshiki Yamazaki
Number Employees: 5-9
Brands:
Sunphenon
Organic Matcha Powder
Teavigo

12499 **Taj Gourmet Foods**
4600 Sleepytime Dr.
Boulder, CO 80301
610-692-2209
800-434-4246
www.ethnicgourmet.com
Processor and exporter of ethnic entrees including Thai, Indian and Italian
President: Paul Jaggi
VP: Sangeeta Jaggi
VP Operations: Harmeet Shanhu
Estimated Sales: $5-10 Million
Number Employees: 25
Square Footage: 120000
Brands:
Bravissimo
Taj
Thai Chef

12500 **Takara Sake USA Inc**
708 Addison St
Berkeley, CA 94710-1925
510-540-8250
Fax: 510-486-8758 info@takarasake.com
Manufacturer of sake, plum wine, mirin and sake kasu; importer of sake and shochu.
President: Yoshihiro Naka
yoshihiro@takarasake.com
Vice President: Hidetaka Iinuma
Regulations & Project Development: William Giddens
Senior Sake Tasting/Marketing Manager: Izumi Motai
Sales Manager: Samuel Geniella
Estimated Sales: $6.5 Million
Number Employees: 20-49
Number of Brands: 8
Square Footage: 15000
Parent Co: Takara Group
Type of Packaging: Consumer, Food Service
Other Locations:
Takara Sake USA New York (Sales)
Fort Lee NJ
Takara Sake USA Los Angeles (Sales)
Torrance CA
Brands:
Sho Chiku Bai
Hana
Yuki Nigori
Shirakabe Gura
Takara
Takara Plum
Kinsen Plum
Koshu Plum

12501 **(HQ)Takasago International Corp**
4 Volvo Dr
Rockleigh, NJ 07647-2508
201-767-9001
Fax: 201-784-7277 www.takasago.com
Flavors for soft drinks, desserts, confections, dairy products, and savory. Also food materials like fruit juices, coffee extracts, and tea extracts.
President & CEO: Satoshi Masumura
SVP, President USA Div.: Hisaya Fujiwara
VP Flavor Division: Takashi Matsuo
VP Research & Development Division: Takashi Miura
EVP Sales: Haruo Nakanishi
VP Public Relations: Hideki Saito
SVP Production: Kazuhiko Tokoro
Estimated Sales: $41.3 Million
Number Employees: 100-249
Square Footage: 50000
Other Locations:
Northvale NJ
Teterboro NJ
New York NY
Crystal Lake IL

12502 **Takeiya USA**
214 5th St # 204
Huntington Beach, CA 92648-8191
714-374-9900
Fax: 714-374-9925 www.takeyausa.com
Tea
CEO: John Lown
jlown@takeyausa.com
Vice President: Patrice Gerber
Customer Marketing Manager: Kristi Labrenz Galvan
Estimated Sales: D
Number Employees: 5-9

12503 **Taku Smokehouse**
550 S Franklin St
Juneau, AK 99801-1330
907-463-4617
Fax: 907-463-4644 800-582-5122
mailorder@takusmokeries.com
www.takustore.com
Processor and exporter of Alaskan salmon, halibut, crab and cod including frozen, portion cut, fillet, smoked, salted and packed
President: Sandro Lane
Smokehouse Manager: Jeremy LaPierre
General Manager: Eric Norman
CEO: Giovanni Gallizio
Contact: Laura Powers
lpowers@takusmokeries.com
Estimated Sales: Less than $500,000
Number Employees: 100-249
Square Footage: 200000

Type of Packaging: Consumer, Food Service, Private Label, Bulk
Brands:
Taku

12504 **Talbott Farms**
3800 F-1/4 Road
Palisade, CO 81526
970-464-5656
talbottfarms.com
Peach and wine grape grower.
Brands:
Mountain Gold
Talbott's

12505 **Talbott Teas**
6475 Christie Avenue,
Suite 150
Emeryville, CA 94608
Fax: 773-404-6420 855-850-6309
www.talbottteas.com
Teas, including gourmet, green, black, white, rooibos
CEO: Shane Talbott
Contact: Steven Nakisher
steven@talbottteas.com
Number Employees: 5

12506 **Talbott Vineyards**
1380 River Rd
Salinas, CA 93908
831-675-3000
Fax: 831-675-3120 www.talbottvineyards.com
Wines-specializing in Chardonnay and Pinot Noir
General Manager of Sales: Dan Karlsen
dan@talbottvineyards.com
VP Sales and Marketing: Matt Viotto
General Manager: Sam Balderas
Marketing Coordinator: Andy Abraham
Marketing Manager: Ross Allen
Manager: Dan Karlsen
dan@talbottvineyards.com
Estimated Sales: Below $5 Million
Number Employees: 10-19
Number of Brands: 3
Number of Products: 7
Parent Co: E&J Gallo Winery
Type of Packaging: Consumer
Other Locations:
Sleepy Hollow Vineyard
Gonzales CA
River Road Vineyard
Sant Lucia Highlands CA
Del Mar Vineyard
Dalinas Valley CA
Brands:
Kali Hart Chardonnay
Logan Chardonnay
Talbott Chardonnay
Talbott Diamond T Chardonnay

12507 **Talenti Gelato e Sorbetto**
Dallas, CA
www.talentigelato.com
Gelato and sorbetto.
Parent Co: Unilever

12508 **Talisman Foods**
3324 S 200 E
Salt Lake City, UT 84115
801-487-6409
Fax: 801-487-6409
Turkey
President: Chad Maddox
VP: Ben Maddox
Estimated Sales: $1-2,500,000
Number Employees: 5-9

12509 **Talk O'Texas Brands Inc**
1610 Roosevelt St
San Angelo, TX 76905-6235
325-655-6077
800-749-6572
customerservice@talkotexas.com
www.talkotexas.com
Pickled okra, liquid hickory smoked flavor
President/CEO: Larry Ricci
CEO: Russell Brown
VP: Lisa Ricci
VP Operations: Dan Herrington
Number Employees: 50-99
Square Footage: 180000
Type of Packaging: Consumer

12510 **Talking Rain Beverage Co**
30520 SE 84th St
Preston, WA 98050
425-222-4900
Fax: 425-222-4901 800-734-0748
events@talkingrain.com www.talkingrain.com
Spring water, oxygenated water, sparkling water, diet flavored non-carbonated water and flavored non-carbonated water, enhanced with fruit flavors, enriched with natural herbal supplements and infused with vitamins.
Owner: Doug Mac Lean
Technical Service: James Fecteau
VP Marketing/R & D: Nina Morrison
VP: Michael Fox
Quality Control: Sam Samia
VP Sales: Wayne King
National Accounts Manager: John Stevens
Plant Manager: Chuck Park
Purchasing Manager: Monica Runyon
Estimated Sales: $5-10 Million
Number Employees: 50-99
Brands:
Diet Ice Botanicals
Sparkling Ice
Talking Rain
Talking Rain Biotonical

12511 **Tall Grass Toffee Co**
14406 W 100th St
Lenexa, KS 66215-1155
913-599-2158
Fax: 913-599-2160 877-344-0442
www.tallgrasstoffee.com
Toffee and chocolate specialties
Owner: James Ladd
Estimated Sales: Less Than $500,000
Number Employees: 1-4

12512 **Tall Talk Dairy**
11961 S Emerson Road
Canby, OR 97013-9311
503-266-1644
Dairy products
Marketing Director: Harlent Peterson
Sales Director: Esther Peterson

12513 **Talley Farms**
2900 Lopez Dr
Arroyo Grande, CA 93420-4999
805-489-5400
Fax: 805-489-5201 www.talleyvineyards.com
Grower and exporter of produce including sugar peas, bell peppers, nappa, cabbage, romaine lettuce, zucchini, Blue Lake beans, spinach and cilantro
President: Brian Talley
btalley@talleyfarms.com
Sales: Todd Talley
Sales Director: Jeff Halfpenny
Operations Manager: Ryan Talley
Plant Manager: Arturo Ibarra
Estimated Sales: $10-20 Million
Number Employees: 250-499
Number of Brands: 2
Number of Products: 12
Type of Packaging: Consumer, Food Service, Bulk
Brands:
Arroyo Grande
Talley Farms

12514 **Talley Vineyards**
P.O.Box 360
Arroyo Grande, CA 93421-0360
805-489-2508
Fax: 805-489-5201 info@talleyvineyards.com
www.talleyfarms.com
Estate wines such as Chardonnay and Pinot Noir
President: Don Talley
Marketing Director: David Block
CFO: Brain Caley
Contact: Brian Fiorentino
brian@talleyvineyards.com
Estimated Sales: Below $5 Million
Number Employees: 10-19
Brands:
Talley Vineyards

12515 **Tallgrass Beef Company**
400 West Erie
Suite 500
Chicago, IL 60654
312-846-1361
tallgrassbeef.com
Beef

12516 **Tamarack Farms Dairy**
1701 Tamarack Rd
Newark, OH 43055-1390
740-522-8181
Fax: 740-522-9235 866-221-4141
investors@kroger.com www.kroger.com
Milk and juices including fruit and vegetable
Chairman/CEO: David B Dillon
VP Operations: Mark Prestidge
Plant Engineer: Tony Neely
Number Employees: 100-249
Parent Co: Kroger Company
Type of Packaging: Consumer, Food Service, Private Label, Bulk
Brands:
City Market
Dillons
Food4less
Gerbes
King Soopers
Owen's
Qfc
Ralphs
Smith's

12517 **Tamarind Tree**
518 Justin Way
Neshanic Station, NJ 8853
908-369-6300
800-432-8733
All-natural and preservative, wheat and gluten-free Indian vegetarian entrees, snack foods, condiments and spicy lentil crisps
President: Harshad Parekh
Number Employees: 1-4
Square Footage: 4000
Brands:
Pappadums
The Taste of India

12518 **Tamashiro Market Inc**
802 N King St
Honolulu, HI 96817-4513
808-841-8047
Fax: 808-845-2722 www.tamashiromarket.com
Japanese foods
President: Cyrus Tamashiro
Estimated Sales: $10-20 Million
Number Employees: 20-49

12519 **Tampa Bay Fisheries Inc**
3060 Gallagher Rd
Dover, FL 33527-4728
813-752-8883
Fax: 813-752-3168 800-732-3663
info@tbfish.com www.tbfish.com
Variety of fresh and frozen shrimp, crab, clams, scallops, lobster tails, squid, mussels, frog legs, oysters.
President: Robert Patterson
CFO: Tom Tao
VP Sales/Marketing: Robert Hatcher
Human Resources Director: Sandi Fail
Operations Manager: Fred Godbold
Plant Manager: Mary Brown
Purchasing Director: Brenda Newman
Estimated Sales: $25 Million
Number Employees: 500-999
Square Footage: 18562
Type of Packaging: Consumer, Food Service

12520 **Tampa Maid Foods Inc**
1600 Kathleen Rd
Lakeland, FL 33805-3435
863-687-4411
Fax: 863-683-8713 800-237-7637
info@tampamaid.com www.tampamaid.com
Processor, importer and exporter of frozen prepared seafood including breaded, peeled and deveined shrimp, stuffed flounder, oysters, scallops and appetizers
President/CEO: George Watkins
CFO: Dave Cordy
dcordy@tampamaid.com
Data Processing: Gene Gerstmeier
Production Manager: Kevin Stallworth
Purchasing Manager: Tim Moore
Number Employees: 250-499
Square Footage: 560000
Type of Packaging: Consumer, Food Service, Private Label, Bulk
Brands:
Beer'n Batter
Cap'n Joe
Dipt'n Dusted

Grand Bayou
Oven Ready
Shrimp Jammers
Tampa Maid
Tropic Isle
Shrimp Teazers
Crab Teazers

12521 Tampico Beverages Inc
3106 N Campbell Ave
Chicago, IL 60618-7921
773-296-0190
Fax: 773-296-0191 877-826-7426
comments@tampico.com www.tampico.com
Processor, exporter and importer of beverage bases and citrus blends
CEO: John Carson
CEO: Scott Miller
VP Marketing: Tracey Schroeder
Number Employees: 50-99
Type of Packaging: Bulk
Brands:
Tampico Punches

12522 Tampico Spice Co
5941 S Central Ave
Los Angeles, CA 90001-1128
323-235-3154
Fax: 323-232-8686 info@tampicospice.com
www.tampicospice.com
spices and seasoning blends.
Vice President: Gabriel Martinez
National Sales Manager: David Martinez
Operations: Eduardo Freiwald
Estimated Sales: $6 Million
Number Employees: 20-49
Type of Packaging: Consumer, Food Service, Private Label, Bulk
Brands:
Tampico

12523 Tamuzza Vineyards
111 Cemetry Road
Hope, NJ 07844
908-459-5878
Fax: 908-459-5560 856-896-0619
winemaker@tamuzzavineyards.com
www.tamuzzavineyards.com
Wines
President: Al Ivory
Owner: Paul Tamuzza
Winemaker: Paul Tamuzza
Estimated Sales: $5-9.9 Million
Number Employees: 10

12524 Tanglewood Farms
297 Riverdale Rd
Warsaw, VA 22572
804-394-4505
Fax: 804-333-0422
Produce products such as cantaloupe, squash, tomatoes
President: Earl Lewis
VP: John E Lewis
Marketing: Ken Taylor
Estimated Sales: $2.5-5 000,000
Number Employees: 5-9

12525 (HQ)Tanimura Antle Inc
1 Harris Rd
Salinas, CA 93908-8608
831-455-2950
Fax: 831-455-3913 800-772-4542
www.taproduce.com
Processor and exporter of cauliflower, broccoli, broccoflower, celery, lettuce, scallions, green onions and value-added products.
Executive Vice President: Gary Tanimura
CEO: Rick Antle
rick@taproduce.com
Executive Vice President: Mike Antle
Number Employees: 100-249
Type of Packaging: Consumer
Other Locations:
Tanimura & Antle
Salinas CA
Brands:
Brian
Salad Time
T & A
Tanbro

12526 Tank's Meats Inc
3355 S State Route 51
Elmore, OH 43416-9799
419-862-3312
www.tanksmeats.com
Beef and pork
President: Al Amstutz
al@tanksmeats.com
Estimated Sales: $5-10 Million
Number Employees: 10-19
Type of Packaging: Consumer, Food Service, Bulk

12527 Tantos Foods International
15 Josiah Court
Markham, ON L3R 9A1
Canada
905-943-9993
Fax: 905-943-9943 info@tantos.com
Processor, exporter and importer of hot sauce, frozen fruit pulp, plantain, cassava and taro chips, annatto seeds, powder norbixin and ackees
President: Sultanali Ajani
Manager: Konrad Lutz
Estimated Sales: $390,000
Number Employees: 3
Square Footage: 28000
Parent Co: Mejores Alimentos de Costa Rica/Alina Foods C.A.
Type of Packaging: Consumer, Food Service, Private Label, Bulk
Brands:
Banana Gold
Tantos

12528 Tanzamaji USA
5602 Hummingbird Lane
Fairview, TX 75069
info@tanzamaji.com
tanzamaji.com
Bottled water
Managing Director: Beda Ruefer
Brands:
Smart Harvest

12529 Taos Brewing Supply
20 ABC Mesa Road
El Prado, NM 87571
575-779-0449
info@taosmesabrewing.com
www.taosmesabrewing.com
Producer of beer
President: Jonathan Riebli
Number Employees: 5-9
Square Footage: 16000

12530 Taos Mesa Brewing Co
20 Abc Mesa Rd
El Prado
El Prado, NM 87529
575-758-1900
www.taosmesabrewing.com
Specialty beers
Owner: Dan Irion
dan@taosmesabrewing.com
Founder: Jayson Wylie
Founder: Peter Kolshom
Founder: Dan Irion
Number Employees: 5-9
Brands:
Taos

12531 Tapatio Hot Sauce
4685 District Blvd
Vernon, CA 90058-2731
323-587-8933
Fax: 323-587-5266 info@tapatiohotsauce.com
www.tapatiohotsauce.com
Processor and exporter of hot sauce
Owner/President: Luis Saavedra
Manager: Jose Saavedra
Estimated Sales: $2 Million
Number Employees: 20-49
Type of Packaging: Consumer, Food Service
Brands:
Tapatio

12532 Taqueria El Milagro
1927 S Blue Island Ave
Chicago, IL 60608-3014
773-579-2410
Fax: 773-650-4690 elmilagro@el-milagro.com
www.el-milagro.com
Mexican foods
President: Rafael Lopez
Marketing/Sales: Raulinda Fierria
Estimated Sales: Less Than $500,000
Number Employees: 5-9

12533 Tara Foods
801 Virginia Ave
Atlanta, GA 30354-1913
404-559-0605
Fax: 404-559-9090 www.tarafoodsindia.com
Peanut butter and flavoring extracts-nut spreads
Owner: Debra Theall
VP: Julie Davis
Plant Manager: Richard Barnhill
Estimated Sales: $300,000-500,000
Number Employees: 5-9
Parent Co: Kroger Company
Type of Packaging: Consumer, Food Service, Private Label
Brands:
Tara Foods

12534 Tarara Winery
13648 Tarara Ln
Leesburg, VA 20176-5236
703-771-7100
Fax: 703-771-8443 www.tarara.com
Wine specialties such as Chardonnay, Pinot Gris, Viognier, Cabernet Franc
Executive Director: Heather Akers
Manager: David Gwilliam
david.gwilliam@tarara.com
Operations Manager: Margaret Russell
Production Manager: Daniel Alcorso
Winemaker: Rob Warren
Estimated Sales: $5-10 Million
Number Employees: 20-49
Number of Products: 12
Brands:
Varietals
Viognier

12535 Tarazi Specialty Foods
13727 Seminole Dr
Chino, CA 91710-5515
909-628-3601
Fax: 909-590-4869 www.tarazifoods.com
Tahini and falafel dry mix
Owner: Ernest Busby
ernestbusby@tarazifoods.com
CFO: J Huleis
VP: J Huleis
Estimated Sales: $2-5 Million
Number Employees: 5-9
Square Footage: 47200
Type of Packaging: Consumer, Food Service, Private Label, Bulk
Brands:
Tarazi

12536 Tarazi Specialty Foods
13727 Seminole Dr
Chino, CA 91710-5515
909-628-3601
Fax: 909-590-4869 info@tarazifoods.com
www.tarazifoods.com
Sesame seeds-raw or roasted, Garbanzo beans, Tahini-a savory sesame paste, Falafel mix, and Tabouli
Owner: Rocco Fiore
rfiore@tarazifoods.com
CFO: Christine Huleis
Estimated Sales: $3 Million
Number Employees: 5-9
Brands:
Falafel Dry Mix
Tabouli
Tahini

12537 Target Flavors Inc
7 Del Mar Dr
Brookfield, CT 06804-2401
203-775-4727
Fax: 203-775-2147 800-538-3350
info@targetflavors.com www.targetflavors.com
Processor and exporter of flavorings and extracts
Owner: John Mac Lean
info@targetflavors.com
General Manager: Bill McLean
Estimated Sales: $2100000
Number Employees: 10-19
Square Footage: 100000

12538 **Tartine Bakery**
600 Guerrero St
San Francisco, CA 94110-1528
415-487-2600
Fax: 415-487-2605 info@tartinebakery.com
www.tartinebakery.com
Baked goods
Owner: Miranda Gomez
miranda.gomez@wellsfargo.com
General Manager: Suzanne Yacovetti
Estimated Sales: Less Than $500,000
Number Employees: 5-9

12539 **Tase-Rite Co**
1211 Kingstown Rd
Wakefield, RI 02879-2441
401-783-7300
Fax: 401-789-2889
General grocery and meats
President: Wesley Lessard
Marketing Director: Gary Lessard
Vice President: Gary Lessard
CFO: Wesley Lessard
Estimated Sales: $5-10 000,000
Number Employees: 5-9

12540 **Taste It Presents Inc**
200 Sumner Ave
Suite A
Kenilworth, NJ 07033-1319
908-241-0672
Fax: 908-241-9410 sales@tasteitpresents.com
www.tasteitpresents.com
Ethnic pastries
Vice President: Paula Perlis
andrew@tasteitpresents.com
Vice President: Larry Dimurro
Estimated Sales: $7.5 Million
Number Employees: 20-49
Type of Packaging: Consumer, Food Service, Private Label

12541 **Taste Maker Foods**
1415 E Mclemore Ave
Memphis, TN 38106-3470
901-274-4407
Fax: 901-272-1088 800-467-1407
custsvc@tastemakerfoods.com
Spcies, seasonings, bakery mixes and dry blends
Owner: Buford Tomlinson
stomlinson@tastemakerfoods.com
VP: Justin Reed
Quality Control: Stacey Castleman
Director Operations: Bill Tomlinson
Plant Manager: Justin Dukes
Estimated Sales: $5-10 Million
Number Employees: 20-49
Square Footage: 100000
Parent Co: Reed Food Technology
Type of Packaging: Consumer, Food Service, Private Label, Bulk
Brands:
Old Hickory
Taste Maker

12542 **Taste Teasers**
6910 Northwood Rd
Dallas, TX 75225
214-750-6334
Fax: 214-696-3316 800-526-1840
Processor and exporter of jalapeno based condiments and confections
President: Susanne Hilou
VP: Eddie Michel
Estimated Sales: $100,000
Number Employees: 1-4
Type of Packaging: Consumer, Food Service, Bulk
Brands:
Hot Chocolate-Fine Chocolate
Pepper Chicks

12543 **Taste Traditions Inc**
9097 F St
Omaha, NE 68127-1305
402-339-7000
Fax: 402-339-1579 800-228-2170
www.tastetraditions.com
Packer and exporter of precooked roast beef, pastrami, corned beef, smoked meats, frozen prepared soups, entrees, Mexican foods and home meal replacements
President: Harold Mann
CEO: Jeff Souba
jeffsouba@tastetraditions.com
VP: Linda Mann
VP Marketing: John Shipp
Sales Executive: Lewis Marshall
Plant Manager: Bruce Hamilton
Estimated Sales: $11.2 Million
Number Employees: 50-99
Brands:
El Hombre Hambre
Gourmet International
Mann's International

12544 **Taste Weavers**
PO Box 189
Urbana, OH 43078-0189
937-206-0388
Fax: 866-388-0784 888-810-8365
contact@tasteweavers.com www.tasteweavers.com
Manufacturer of dips, salsa, and grilling sauces.
Co-Founder: Robin Coffey
Co-Founder: Susan Neiswander

12545 **Taste Wine Co**
50 Third Ave
New York, NY 10003
212-461-1708
www.tastewineco.com
Winery
Year Founded: 2015
Estimated Sales: Less than $500,000
Number Employees: 2-10
Type of Packaging: Consumer, Private Label

12546 **Taste of Gourmet**
36 Sunflower Rd
Indianola, MS 38751
662-887-6760
Fax: 662-887-5547 800-833-7731
jennifer@tasteofgourmet.com
www.tasteofgourmet.com
Processor and exporter of catfish pate and capers; also, fudge and lemon pie mixes including fat-free
President: Evelyn Roughton
Estimated Sales: $885603
Number Employees: 20-49
Type of Packaging: Consumer
Brands:
Antique Crown Foods
Mississippi Delta Fudge
Mississippi Mousse
The Crown Restaurant Gourmet

12547 **Taste of Nature Inc.**
2828 Donald Douglas Loop North
Suite A
Santa Monica, CA 90405
310-396-4433
Fax: 310-396-4432 info@candyasap.com
www.candyasap.com
Candy
Manager: Scott Samet
Estimated Sales: $3-5 Million
Number Employees: 5-9
Brands:
Care Bears Gummi Bears
Cat In the Hat Cotton Candy
Cat In the Hat Sour Gummies
Cookie Dough Bites
Cotton Candy Swirl
Hulk Candies
Jolt Cola Energy Rush
Muddy Bears
Shari Candies
Sour Cotton Candy Swirl
Spiderman Cotton Candy
Spiderman Sour Gummi Mutant Spiders
Sqwiggles
Tiny Tarts

12548 **Tastebuds Popcorn**
208 N Main Street
Belmont, NC 28012
704-461-8755
mail@tastebudspopcorn.com
tastebudspopcorn.com
Popcorn
President: Jay Pithwa
General Manager: Jen Colangelo
Estimated Sales: $4 Million
Number Employees: 11-50
Brands:
Tastebuds Popcorn

12549 **Tastee Apple**
60810 County Road 9
Newcomerstown, OH 43832-9638
740-498-8316
Fax: 740-498-6108 800-262-7753
customerservice@tasteeapple.com
www.tasteeapple.com
Apple products including chocolate covered apples; caramel apples; apple cider; and apple powder, in addition to jelly apples, candy apples and wild apples.
President: Greg Hackenbracht
greg@tasteeapple.com
Number Employees: 250-499
Type of Packaging: Consumer, Food Service, Private Label, Bulk
Brands:
Tastee

12550 **Tastepoint**
10801 Decatur Rd
Philadelphia, PA 19154
215-632-3100
Fax: 215-637-3920 800-363-5286
customerrequest@tastepoint.com
www.tastepoint.com
Flavors including beef extract replacement, savory, nut, fruit, vanilla extract and raisin juice concentrate; also, stabilizers. Formerly known David Michael & Co.
Chairman & CEO: Andreas Fibig
EVP/General Counsel/Corp Secretary: Anne Chwat
EVP, Operations: Francisco Fortanet
Group President, Flavors: Matthias Haeni
Group President, Fragrances: Nicolas Mirzayantz
EVP/Global Scientific & Sustainability: Dr. Gregory Yep
EVP & Chief Financial Officer: Richard O'Leary
EVP & Chief Human Resources Officer: Dr. Susana Suarez Gonzalez
Year Founded: 1896
Estimated Sales: $22.2 Million
Number Employees: 100-249
Square Footage: 66000
Parent Co: International Flavors & Frangrances Inc.
Type of Packaging: Consumer, Private Label, Bulk
Brands:
Beefmate
Cocoamate
Dm Choice
Dm Ole
Fairway
Gorilla Vanilla
Honeymate
Michaelok
Michtex
Premier
Raisinmate
Super Supreme
Supervan
Supreme

12551 **Tasty Baking Company**
Navy Yard Corporate Center
#200, 3 Crescent Dr
Philadelphia, PA 19112
215-221-8500
800-248-2789
www.tastykake.com
Baked goods and snack cakes.
Research & Development: Shelley McDonnough
Year Founded: 1914
Estimated Sales: $250+ Million
Number Employees: 1,000-4,999
Parent Co: Flowers Foods
Brands:
Butterscotch Krimpets(c)
Chocolate Juniors(c)
Chocolate Kandy Kakes(c)
Cinnamon Mini Donuts
Coconut Juniors(c)
Creme Filled Butterscotch Krimpets(c)
Dreamies
Iced Fudge Cookies Bars
Jelly Krimpets(c)
Koffee Kake Juniors(c)
Peanut Butter Kandy Kakes(c)
Pretzel Rods
Rich Frosted Mini Donuts
Swirly Cups
and many more

12552 **Tasty Brand Inc**
24003 Ventura Blvd # A
Calabasas, CA 91302-3926
818-225-9000
Manufacturer of gummies, fruit snacks, and cookies.
CEO: Liane Weintraub
CEO: Candace Ciongoli
candace@tastybrand.com
Number Employees: 5-9

12553 **Tasty Mix Quality Foods**
88 Walworth St
Brooklyn, NY 11205-2808
718-855-7680
Fax: 718-855-7681 tastymx@aol.com
www.tastyblend.com
Dough conditioners and stabilizers for the pasta and bakery industries
President: Salvatore Ballarino
Manager: Sal Ballarino Jr
Estimated Sales: $500,000
Number Employees: 5-9
Square Footage: 20000
Type of Packaging: Consumer, Food Service, Private Label, Bulk
Brands:
Dough Stabilizer
Gold-Tex Flour
Shelf-Aid

12554 **Tasty Seeds Ltd**
130 Market Street
Winkler, NB R6W 4A3
Canada
204-331-3480
Fax: 204-325-6832 888-632-6906
Salted, seasoned and cajun sunflower seeds, and pumpkin seeds
Owner: Wayne Nestibo
Owner: Bryan Tyerman
Owner/Sales/Marketing Manger: Brad Edwards

12555 **Tasty Selections**
350 Creditston Road
Suite 102
Concord, ON L4K 3Z2
Canada
905-760-2353
Fax: 905-660-4585 www.tastyselections.com
Processor/manufacturers of frozen proportioned cookie dough, frozen muffin batters and a broad selection of thaw and serve cakes.
President: Alan Greenspoon
Owner: John Allenson
Estimated Sales: $2.3 Million
Number Employees: 60
Square Footage: 100000
Type of Packaging: Consumer, Food Service, Bulk

12556 **Tasty Tomato**
PO Box 6984
San Antonio, TX 78209-0984
210-822-2443
Fax: 210-822-2538 www.worldtrade.org
Spaghetti sauce
President: Charlotte Gallogly
Estimated Sales: $2.5-5 Million
Number Employees: 5

12557 **Tasty Toppings Inc**
2804 13th St
Columbus, NE 68601-4919
402-564-1347
Fax: 402-563-1469 800-228-4148
www.dorothylynch.com
Salad dressings
President: Gordon M Hull
Secretary: Joann Johnson
Number Employees: 20-49
Square Footage: 8000
Type of Packaging: Consumer, Food Service, Private Label
Brands:
Dorothy Lynch Home Style

12558 **Tastybaby**
26880 Pacific Coast Hwy
#748
Malibu, CA 90265
310-457-6040
Fax: 310-317-4404 866-588-8278
info@tastybaby.com
Frozen organic baby food
President/Co-Founder: Shannan Swanson
CEO/Co-Founder: Liane Weintraub

12559 **Tata Tea**
1001 Dr Martin L King Jr Blvd
Plant City, FL 33563-5150
813-754-2602
Fax: 813-754-2272 www.tata.com
Tea
President: Ashok Bhardwha
Chairman: Patrick McGoldrick
Quality Control: Ivey Campbell
Estimated Sales: $2.5-5 Million
Number Employees: 20-49
Brands:
Tata Tea

12560 **Tatangelo's Wholesale Fruit & Vegetables**
80 Hanlan Road
Unit 12
Woodbridge, ON L4L 3P6
Canada
905-850-0545
Fax: 905-850-2241 877-328-8503
Frozen fruit and vegetables
President: Rocco Tatangelo
Vice President: John Tatangelo
Estimated Sales: $6 Million
Number Employees: 14
Type of Packaging: Food Service
Brands:
Tatangelo

12561 **Tate & Lyle PLC**
5450 Prairie Stone Pkwy.
Hoffman Estates, IL 60192
847-396-7500
www.tateandlyle.com
Specialty and bulk ingredients manufacturer serving the food, beverage and animal feed industries.
Chairman: Dr. Gerry Murphy
Chief Executive: Nick Hampton
Chief Financial Officer: Imran Nawaz
Executive VP/General Counsel: Lindsay Beardsell
Estimated Sales: $3.9 Billion
Number Employees: 4,162
Type of Packaging: Bulk
Brands:
Avenacare Oat Beta Glucan
CLARIA Starches
DOLCIA PRIMA Allulose
PrOatein
PROMITOR Dietary Fiber
PromOat Beta Glucan
PUREFRUIT Monk Fruit Extract
SODA-LO Salt Microspheres
SPLENDA Sucralose
STA-LITE Polydextrose
TASTEVA Stevia Sweetener

12562 **Tate's Bake Shop**
43 North Sea Rd.
Southampton, NY 11968
631-283-9830
Fax: 631-283-9844 info@tatesbakeshop.com
www.tatesbakeshop.com
Cookies, bars, brownies, pies, cakes and gift baskets
Founder: Kathleen King
CEO: Maura Mottolese
Chief Financial Officer: Thomas Pawluk
Customer Service Manager: Jill Jenkins
Vice President, Operations: Ralph Palotta
Estimated Sales: $5 Million
Number Employees: 51-200
Brands:
Tate's Bake Shop

12563 **Tatra Herb Co**
222 Grove St
Morrisville, PA 19067-1235
215-295-5476
Fax: 215-736-3089 888-828-7248
www.tatraherb.com
Herbal teas
CEO: George Zofchak
Estimated Sales: Less Than $500,000
Number Employees: 1-4
Type of Packaging: Consumer

12564 **Tavalon Tea**
100 Louis Street
Unit G
South Hackensack, NJ 7606
800-282-5051
tavalon.com
Tea
Contact: John-Paul Lee
john-paul@tavalon.com

12565 **Taylor Cheese Corp**
508 N Mill St
Weyauwega, WI 54983-9046
920-867-2337
Fax: 920-867-2360
Custom cheese cut, slice and wrap services for private label or conversion needs. Shingled slice packaging gift box components.
President: Robert Ehrenberg
Marketing Director: Bob Ehrenberg
Estimated Sales: Below $5 000,000
Number Employees: 10-19

12566 **Taylor Farms**
911 Blanco Cir Ste B
Salinas, CA 93901
831-754-0471
Fax: 831-794-0473 www.taylorfarms.com
Fresh cut fruit and vegetables including cantaloupe, honeydew, pineapple, onions, lettuce, peppers, garlic, cabbage and tomatoes
Chairman/CEO: Bruce Taylor
CFO: Tom Brain
Food Safety Department: Marshall Braga
Harvest Operations: Carson Braga
VP Production: Vikki Chandley
Number Employees: 5,000-9,999
Square Footage: 200000
Type of Packaging: Consumer, Food Service, Private Label, Bulk

12567 **Taylor Farms Pacific**
1820 N Macarthur Dr # 200
Suite 200
Tracy, CA 95376-2831
209-830-1086
www.taylorfarms.com
Salads, fruits and vegetables.
Manager: Oneyda Garcia
Contact: Christina Larkin
clarkin@taylorfarms.com
Purchasing Manager: Christina Larkin
Estimated Sales: $20-49 Million
Number Employees: 10-19
Number of Brands: 1
Square Footage: 80000
Parent Co: Taylor Fresh Foods
Type of Packaging: Consumer
Brands:
Taylor Farms

12568 **Taylor Lobster Co**
32 Route 236
Kittery, ME 03904-5525
207-439-1350
Fax: 207-763-3861 info@taylorlobster.com
www.taylorlobster.com
Lobster
Owner: Bret Taylor
Estimated Sales: $1 Million
Number Employees: 10-19

12569 **Taylor Meat Co**
2211 W 2nd St
Taylor, TX 76574-2130
512-352-6357
Fax: 512-352-9426 info@taylormeat.com
www.taylormeat.com
Smoked meat company founded in 1947.
President: Ron Ivy
customerservice@taylormeat.com
Number Employees: 20-49
Type of Packaging: Consumer, Food Service, Bulk
Brands:
Tip Top

12570 **Taylor Orchards**
1665 E Fall Line Fwy
Highway 96 West
Reynolds, GA 31076-2707
478-847-5963
Fax: 478-847-4464 www.taylororchards.com
Processor, packer and exporter of peaches

Owner: Jeff Wainwright
gafruit@pstel.net
Owner/Sales Manager: Walter Wainwright
Estimated Sales: $7215000
Number Employees: 100-249
Square Footage: 16000
Type of Packaging: Consumer, Bulk

12571 Taylor Precision Products
2311 W 22nd St # 200
Oak Brook, IL 60523-5625
630-954-1250
Fax: 630-954-1275 866-843-3905
info@taylorusa.com www.taylorusa.com
Manufactures thermometers, scales and related measurement devices.
CFO: Donald Robinson
VP: Donald Robinson
Director Sales/Marketing: Kent Beaverson
Contact: Elvira Abate
eabate@taylorusa.com
Estimated Sales: $1-2,500,000
Number Employees: 10-19
Type of Packaging: Consumer, Food Service, Private Label, Bulk

12572 Taylor Provisions Company
63 Perrine Ave
Trenton, NJ 08638-5114
609-392-1113
Fax: 609-392-1354
Meat products. Founded in 1939.
President: John T Cumbler
VP: George Cumbler
Estimated Sales: $10 Million
Number Employees: 75

12573 (HQ)Taylor Shellfish Farms
130 SE Lynch Rd
Shelton, WA 98584-8615
360-426-6178
Fax: 360-427-0327 Marcelle@taylorshellfish.com
www.taylorshellfishfarms.com
Fresh and frozen oysters, clams, mussels, scallops and crabs
President: Jeff Pearson
Human Resources: John Fogo
Estimated Sales: $16 Million
Number Employees: 500-999
Type of Packaging: Consumer
Other Locations:
Taylor Shellfish Farms
Bow WA
Brands:
Taylor Shellfish

12574 Taylor Wine Company
10223 Middle Rd
Hammondsport, NY 14840-9582
607-868-3245
Fax: 607-868-3246
Wines
Manager: Matt Doyle
Estimated Sales: $1-3 Million
Number Employees: 10-19
Parent Co: Canandaigua Wine Company

12575 Taylor's Mexican Chili Co Inc
116 S West St
Carlinville, IL 62626-1758
217-854-8713
800-382-4454
www.taylorschili.com
Chili, sauce, beans
Owner: Joe Gugger
CEO: David Tucker
dave@taylorschili.com
Operations VP: Dave Tucker
Production VP: Dave Tucker
Estimated Sales: Less Than $500,000
Number Employees: 5-9
Brands:
Taylor's Mexican Chili

12576 Taylor's Poultry Place
4701 Augusta Rd
Lexington, SC 29073-9197
803-356-3431
www.taylorssteakhouse.com
Poultry
President: Luther Taylor
jwetzel@sumter-sc.com
Estimated Sales: Less than $500,000
Number Employees: 1-4

12577 Taylor's Sausage Co
1822 N Grand Blvd
St Louis, MO 63106-1299
314-652-3476
Sausages
President: John Taylor
Estimated Sales: Below $5 000,000
Number Employees: 5-9

12578 Tayse Meats
1979 W 25th St # C6
Cleveland, OH 44113-3435
216-664-1799
Beef
Owner: Keith Tayse
Estimated Sales: Less than $500,000
Number Employees: 1-4

12579 Taza Chocolate
561 Windsor St
Suite B206
Somerville, MA 02143-4189
617-623-0804
Fax: 617-716-2085 info@tazachocolate.com
www.tazachocolate.com
Chocolate, chocolate bars, cocoa, baking chocolate
Owner: Charles Braman
cbraman@aerotek.com
Founder: Kathleen Fulton
Estimated Sales: C
Number Employees: 50-99

12580 Taziki's Cafe
Birmingham, AL
www.tazikis.com
Greek and Mediterrian cuisine. Dishes include gyros, sandwiches, soups, and salads.
Founder: Keith Richards
CEO: Dan Simpson
CFO: Billy Magruder
VP, Marketing & Growth: Rachel Layton
COO: Mike Smith
Year Founded: 1998
Type of Packaging: Consumer

12581 Tazo Tea
Kent, WA
855-829-6832
www.tazo.com
Premium teas, bottled tea and juice, organic chai and full leaf teas.
CEO, Unilever: Alan Jope
Year Founded: 1994
Estimated Sales: $1 Billion+
Number Employees: 60
Parent Co: Unilever
Type of Packaging: Consumer, Food Service

12582 Tea Aura
234 Dunview Avenue
Toronto, ON M2N 4J2
Canada
416-225-8868
Shortbread cookies infused with tea
President: Susan Ho

12583 Tea Beyond
PO Box 1911
West Caldwell, NJ 07007
973-226-0327
Fax: 973-226-0327 info@teabeyond.com
www.teabeyond.com
Authentic teas

12584 Tea Forte
23 Bradford St # 8
Concord, MA 01742-2971
978-369-1598
Fax: 978-369-3427 info@teaforte.com
www.teaforte.com
Whole leaf teas with rough-cut herbs and flowers
President/Owner: Peter Hewitt
phewitt@teaforte.com
Estimated Sales: $10 Million
Number Employees: 20-49

12585 Tea Needs Inc
3000 Banyon Road
Boca Raton, FL 33432
561-237-5237
877-832-8289
mark@teaneeds.com
Disposable instant cup of tea with teabag inside each cup. Three lines are available: tea, fruit tea, and Chinese herb tea.
President & Owner: Mark Reiman
VP: Alla Kartel
Marketing: Ed Camargo
Operations: Joyce Liang
Estimated Sales: $10 Million
Number Employees: 20-49
Number of Brands: 6
Number of Products: 18
Square Footage: 10000
Type of Packaging: Consumer, Private Label, Bulk
Brands:
Happy Cup Tea

12586 Tea Room
130 Doolittle Dr
Units 2 and 13
San Leandro, CA 94577-1028
510-567-8868
Fax: 707-561-7081 info@thetearoom.biz
www.rimann.com
Loose leaf tea, drinking chocolate, macarons, truffles, and tea infused chocolate.
CEO and President: Heinz Rimann
Number Employees: 1-4
Brands:
TeaRoom

12587 Tea-n-Crumpets
252 Coleman Dr
San Rafael, CA 94901
415-457-2495
Fax: 415-457-1893
Organic crumpets, teas, jams, tea accessories and gift items from around the world.
President: Norman Barahona
CEO: Jena Rose
Estimated Sales: $1-3 Million
Number Employees: 1-4

12588 Teapigs
117 Grattan Street
Suite 320
Brooklyn, NY 11237
212-705-8723
info@teapigs.com
www.teapigs.com
Matcha green tea
Associate Marketing Manager: Emily Spring
General Manager: Matthew Wood
Number Employees: 11-50
Type of Packaging: Bulk
Brands:
teapigs

12589 Tearrific Ice Cream
480 Barnum Ave.
3rd Floor
Bridgeport, CT 06608
203-354-9805
info@tearrificicecream.com
www.tearrificicecream.com
Manufacturer of ice cream infused with tea.
Founder: Mario Leite
sleite@tearrificicecream.com

12590 Teasdale Quality Foods Inc
901 Packers St
PO Box 814
Atwater, CA 95301-4614
209-358-5616
Fax: 209-357-5239
customerservice@teasdalefoods.com
www.teasdalefoods.com
Mexican foods, beans and sauces.
CEO: Kenneth Ancalade
kennetha@teasdale.net
CEO: Alberto Bandera
Estimated Sales: $20-49 Million
Number Employees: 100-249
Number of Brands: 2
Square Footage: 250000
Type of Packaging: Consumer, Food Service, Private Label
Brands:
Aunt Penny's
Teasdale

12591 **Teawolf LLC**
25 Riverside Dr # 7
Pine Brook, NJ 07058-9391
973-575-4600
Fax: 973-575-4601 info@teawolf.com
www.teawolf.com
Manufacturer of coffee, tea, vanilla, chocolate, botanical and specialty products for the food, beverage and nutritional supplement industries.
Owner: Gambrell Bill
bgambrell@teawolf.com
Estimated Sales: $5-10 Million
Number Employees: 5-9
Type of Packaging: Private Label

12592 **Tebay Dairy Company**
Lubeck Road
Parkersburg, WV 26101-7761
304-863-3705
Fax: 304-863-8712
Dairy products including ice cream
Owner: Robert Kent Tebay
Owner: Bob Tebay
Estimated Sales: $3,200,000
Number Employees: 10-19
Type of Packaging: Consumer
Brands:
Tebay

12593 **Techno Food IngredientsCo., Ltd**
236 W Clary Ave
San Gabriel, CA 91776
626-288-8478
Fax: 626-288-8479 sales@techno-fi.com
www.techno-fi.com
Food ingredients specializing in sucralose.
Owner: Helena Xue
Number Employees: 200-500

12594 **Techno USA**
236 W Clary Avenue
San Gabriel, CA 91776
626-288-8478
Fax: 626-288-8479 sales@techno-fi.com
www.techno-fi.com
Sucralose
Owner: Helena Xue
Marketing Manager: Peter Zou
Estimated Sales: $370,000
Number Employees: 3
Parent Co: Techno Food Ingredients Co., Ltd.
Other Locations:
Headquarters
Guangzhou, China
Manufacturing Plant
Yongan, Fujian, China
San Gabriel CA
Vancouver, Canada
Hong Kong

12595 **Technology Flavors & Fragrances**
10 E Edison St
Amityville, NY 11701
631-789-8228
Fax: 631-842-8332
Natural and artificial flavors for the beverage and food industries
CFO: Joseph A Gemmo
Chairman/CEO: Phil Rosner
CEO: Philip Rosner
Marketing Director: Virginia Bonofligio
Sales Director: Gary Frumberg
Contact: Richard Cerniglia
cerniglia@tffi.com
Operations/Production: Ronald Dintemann
Plant Manager: Joseph Piazza
Purchasing Manager: Rose Marotta
Estimated Sales: $15,587,285
Number Employees: 50-99
Number of Products: 1200
Square Footage: 104000

12596 **Tecumseh Poultry, LLC**
13151 Dovers St.
Waverly, NE 68462
402-786-1000
www.smartchicken.com
Air-chilled chicken products including whole chickens, boneless skinless breasts, tenderloins, thin sliced breasts, boneless skinless thighs, drumsticks, thighs, and wings. Also, pre-cooked chicken sausage products includingfrankfurters; and chicken broth.
President: Kevin Siebert
Year Founded: 1998
Number Employees: 600
Number of Brands: 1
Type of Packaging: Private Label
Brands:
Smart Chiken

12597 **Ted Drewes Frozen Custard**
6726 Chippewa St
St Louis, MO 63109-2533
314-481-2652
Fax: 314-481-4241 www.teddrewes.com
Frozen custard
President: Ted Jr Drewes
Manager: Travis Dillion
tdrewes@teddrewes.com
Estimated Sales: Below $5 Million
Number Employees: 50-99

12598 **Ted Shear Assoc Inc**
1 West Ave # 210
Larchmont, NY 10538-2471
914-833-0017
Fax: 914-833-0233 ted.shear@verizon.net
Honey and vanilla extracts
President: Ted Shear
katestanley@avis.com
Estimated Sales: $1-3 000,000
Number Employees: 1-4
Type of Packaging: Private Label

12599 **Teddy's Tasty Meats**
6123 Mackay St
Anchorage, AK 99518-1739
907-562-2320
Fax: 907-562-1919
Meat
President: Ted Kouris
Secretary/Treasurer: Barbara Kouris
Vice President: Steven Kouris
Number Employees: 20-49

12600 **Tee Pee Olives, Inc.**
411 Theodore Fremd Avenue
Suite 120
Rye, NY 10580
914-925-0450
Fax: 914-925-0458 800-431-1529
lucy.teepeeolives@verizon.net
www.teepeeolives.com
Importer and packer of bulk Spanish green olives in the US.
Pres/CEO/Mktg/Purchasing: Lucy Landesman
CFO: William Barrett
VP/Quality Control: Robert Cory PhD
VP Sales: Deborah Eklund
COO: Joseph Fairchild
Plant Manager: Robert Roaden
Purchasing Manager: Emil Cairo
Estimated Sales: $10-20 Million
Number Employees: 50
Type of Packaging: Consumer, Food Service, Private Label, Bulk

12601 **Teeccino**
1015 Cindy Ln # A
Carpinteria, CA 93013-2905
805-966-0999
Fax: 805-966-0855 800-498-3434
info@teeccino.com www.teeccino.com
Herbal coffee, tea, and cereal.
President/Founder: Caroline MacDougall
CEO: Caroline Macdougall
caroline@teeccino.com
CFO: Jerry Isenberg
Marketing Communications: Danielle Edberg
Sales Manager: Devon Garnsey
Operations Manager: John Magee
Warehouse Manager: Eddie Bolvito
Estimated Sales: $1,000,800
Number Employees: 10-19
Number of Brands: 1
Number of Products: 7
Type of Packaging: Consumer, Food Service, Private Label, Bulk
Brands:
Balanced Coffee
Teeccino Caffeine-Fr

12602 **Teelee Popcorn**
101 W Badger St
Shannon, IL 61078-9020
815-864-2363
Fax: 815-864-2388 800-578-2363
Processor and exporter of microwaveable popcorn
Owner: Gary Armstrong
VP/Sales: Ken Weaver
garyarmstrong@teeleepopcorn.com
Estimated Sales: $2 Million
Number Employees: 20-49
Square Footage: 100000
Type of Packaging: Consumer, Private Label, Bulk
Brands:
Prime Time
Tee Lee

12603 **Teeny Foods Inc**
3434 NE 170th Pl
Portland, OR 97230-5072
503-252-3006
Fax: 503-254-3004 info@teenyfoods.com
www.teenyfoods.com
Producer of hand held entrees, filled breadmakers, pizza crust, flatbread.
President: Rick Teeny
rick.teeny@teenyfoods.com
General Manager: Darryl Abram
VP Finance: Don Parsons
VP: Debbi Teeny
Marketing Manager: Janna Woodgate
VP Sales: Darryl Abram
VP Operations: Michel Layonn
Plant Manager: Dave Hermanson
Purchasing: Ken Martin
Estimated Sales: $15-20 Million
Number Employees: 100-249
Square Footage: 116000
Brands:
Teeny Foods

12604 **Teeny Tiny Spice Company of Vermont LLC**
PO Box 1113
Shelburne, VT 05482
802-598-6800
Fax: 603-768-4247 info@teenytinyspice.com
www.teenytinyspice.com
Organic spice blends.
Owner: Thora Pomicter
Owner: Ed Pomicter

12605 **Teff Co**
7 9th Ave N
Nampa, ID 83687-3354
208-465-0987
Fax: 208-459-0481 888-822-2221
questions@teffco.com www.teffco.com
Whole grain and flour
President: Wayne Carlson
Marketing Director: Elizabeth Carlson
Manager: Gareth Carlson
Number Employees: 5-9
Brands:
Maskal Teff

12606 **Teixeira Farms, Inc.**
2600 Bonita Lateral
Santa Maria, CA 93458
805-928-3801
Fax: 805-928-9405 info@teixeirafarms.com
Grower of lettuce, broccoli, cabbage, and celery.
Co-Owner: Dean Teixeira
Co-Owner: Glenn Teixeira
Co-Owner: Marvin Teixeira
Co-Owner: Allan Teixeira
Co-Owner: Norman Teixeira
Contact: Dan Cooper
dan@teixeirafarms.com
Estimated Sales: $20-50 Million
Number Employees: 300
Type of Packaging: Consumer, Private Label, Bulk
Brands:
Teixeira

12607 **Tejon Ranch Co**
4436 Lebec Rd
Lebec, CA 93243-9705
661-248-3000
Fax: 661-248-6209 bzoeller@tejonranch.com
www.tejonranch.com
Processor and exporter of pistachios, walnuts, almonds and wine grapes

President/CEO: Robert Stine
CEO: Gregory S Bielli
bielli@tejonranch.com
CFO/VP/Corporate Secretary: Allen Lyda
Vice President, Controller: Abel Guzman
Vice President of Corporate Communicatio: Barry Zoeller
Vice President of Operations: Brian Grant
Estimated Sales: Less than $500,000
Number Employees: 100-249
Type of Packaging: Consumer, Private Label, Bulk

12608 **Tekita House Foods**
6848 El Paso Drive
El Paso, TX 79905-3336
915-779-2181
Fax: 915-775-1857
Mexican food products, including tortillas, tostadas, pico de gallo salsa, chorizo, tamales, chiles rellenos, taco roll, flautas and pork crackling
President: Nelson Guerra
Estimated Sales: $500,000 appx.
Number Employees: 10-19

12609 **Tell City Pretzel Company**
1315 Washington Street
Tell City, IN 47586
812-548-4499
Fax: 812-548-4434 www.tellcitypretzel.com
Hard pretzels
Owner: Craig Kendall
Plant Manager: Betty Beard
Estimated Sales: $110000
Number Employees: 3
Type of Packaging: Consumer, Bulk

12610 **Temo Candy**
495 W Exchange St
Akron, OH 44302-1403
330-376-7229
Confectionery products
President: Lawrence Temo
Estimated Sales: $344,051
Number Employees: 5-9
Square Footage: 30000
Parent Co: Temo's
Type of Packaging: Consumer
Brands:
Temo's

12611 **Tempest Fisheries LTD**
38 Hassey St
New Bedford, MA 02740-7209
508-997-0720
Fax: 508-990-2117
Fish and seafood
President: Timothy Mello
tempest01@rcn.com
Estimated Sales: $5-10 Million
Number Employees: 5-9

12612 **Templar Food Products**
571 Central Avenue
New Providence, NJ 7974
908-665-9511
Fax: 908-665-9122 800-883-6752
info@icedtea.com www.icedtea.com
Templar Food Products manufactures private-label tea using black, green, and oolong sourced from around the world. Tea mixture and flavor is customized according to customer preference.
President/Founder: Edward D Reeves
Manager of Laboratory: Trudy Genna
Sales Manager: Spencer Griffith
Contact: Michael Eagan
michael@icedtea.com
VP, Operations: Michael Murray
Estimated Sales: $870,000
Number Employees: 10-19
Type of Packaging: Private Label
Brands:
Perfect Choice

12613 **Temptee Specialty Foods**
2011 E 58th Ave
Denver, CO 80216
303-292-1577
Fax: 303-292-1701 800-842-1233
info@tempteeco.com tempteeco.com
Portion controlled deli meats including beef; also, specialty processing available
President: Jack Lowe
Sales Manager: Jim Mayworm
Estimated Sales: $3,616,653
Number Employees: 20-49
Square Footage: 40000

12614 **Ten Ren Tea & Ginseng Co Inc**
75 Mott St
New York, NY 10013-4812
212-349-2286
Fax: 212-349-2180 800-292-2049
tenrenusa@aol.com
Tea
President: Mark Lee
Founder: Ray Ho Lee
Estimated Sales: Below $5 Million
Number Employees: 10-19
Brands:
Ten Ren's Tea

12615 **Tenayo**
250 West Broadway
5th Floor
New York, NY 10013
917-677-7607
hello@tenayo.com
www.tenayo.com
Salsa
Founder: Arturo Cruz
Chief Marketing Officer: Andrew Bourke
Estimated Sales: $7 Million
Number Employees: 1-10
Brands:
Tenayo

12616 **Tennessee Bun Company**
2975 Armory Dr.
Nashville, TN 37204
615-256-6500
Fax: 615-256-2084 888-486-2867
www.buncompany.com
Hamburger buns
President: Joe Waters
Chief Executive Officer: Cordia Harrington
CFO: Tom Harrington
VP Operations: Dave Nemecheck
Contact: Katie Austin
katie.austin@buncompany.com
Estimated Sales: Below $5 Million
Number Employees: 50-99
Brands:
Tennessee Bun

12617 **Tennessee Valley Packing Co**
307 1/2 Carter St
Columbia, TN 38401-2925
931-388-2623
Fax: 931-388-2624
Meat products including sausages, frankfurters and bologna
President: Richard Jewell Jr
Estimated Sales: $3-5 Million
Number Employees: 5-9
Type of Packaging: Consumer

12618 **Tenth & M Seafoods**
1020 M St
Anchorage, AK 99501-3317
907-272-6013
Fax: 907-272-1685 800-770-2722
tenmsea@alaska.net www.10thandmseafoods.com
Processor, exporter and wholesaler/distributor of salmon, halibut, shrimp and king crab and scallops. Also operates under the name Alaska Sea Pack, Inc
President: Skip Winfree
tenmsea@alaska.net
Vice President: Rob Winfree
Sales Manager: Dannon Southall
Estimated Sales: $8 Million
Number Employees: 20-49
Type of Packaging: Consumer, Food Service

12619 **Terlato Kitchen**
2401 Waukegan Rd
Bannockburn, IL 60015-1505
855-805-7221
info@terlatokitchen.com
www.terlatokitchen.com
Pomodoro sauces, preserves and baking mixes
Sales Manager: Taylor Young
General Manager: Ann Kidd
Estimated Sales: Under $500,000
Number Employees: 2-10
Brands:
Terlato Kitchen

12620 **Terra Botanica Products**
92 Waycaster Circle
Dahlonega, GA 30533
Canada
770-718-9340
sales@terrabotanica.com
Homeopathics, botanical extracts, capsules, gels and vitamins
president: John Miller
CEO: Connie Miller
Marketing Director: John Miller
Sales Director: Paul Peterson
Contact: Greg Grabowski
ggrabowski@terrabotanica.com
Number Employees: 10,000+
Type of Packaging: Private Label

12621 **Terra Flavors & Fragrances**
45 W 34th Street
Suite 1103
New York, NY 10001
212-244-1181
Fax: 212-681-9813 info@terraflavors.com
www.terraflavors.com
Manufacturer of essential oils, natural flavors, synthetic aromas and botanical extracts.
Type of Packaging: Food Service

12622 **Terra Ingredients**
730 2nd Ave. S
Minneapolis, MN 55402
Fax: 612-486-3954 888-497-3308
hello@terraingredients.com
www.terraingredients.com
Beans, cereal, corn, flax, fonio, oilseeds including soybeans and chia, grains including quinoa and buckwheat, lintels, peas, and chickpeas.
Co-Founder & CEO: Rolf Peters
Co-Founder & COO: Tim Carlson
CFO: Bill Hren
Year Founded: 2000
Number Employees: 50-200
Type of Packaging: Private Label

12623 **Terra Ingredients LLC**
Minneapolis, MN
Fax: 612-486-3954 855-497-3308
hello@terraingredients.com
www.terraingredients.com
Whole organic ingredients for feed and consumer products, including flax, beans and lentils, corn, quinoa, millet, buckwheat, oats, rye, barley, wheat, soybeans, chia seeds and complete feed ingredient blends
Year Founded: 2000
Number of Brands: 1
Type of Packaging: Private Label, Bulk

12624 **Terra Origin, Inc.**
Hauppauge, NY 11788
631-300-2306
info@terraorigin.com
www.terraorigin.com
Health supplements and powders, including superfood powder blends, whey protein powder, bone broth protein, plant-based protein and antioxidant formula capsules
Year Founded: 2017
Number of Brands: 1
Number of Products: 21
Type of Packaging: Consumer, Private Label
Brands:
Terra Origin

12625 **Terra Sol Chile Company**
9415 Burnet Road 106
Austin, TX 78758
512-836-3525
Fax: 512-533-9388
Chili
Founder: Alexandra Weeks

12626 **Terra's**
PO Box 265
Perham, MN 56573-0265
218-346-4100
Beef
President: Rod Osvold
Estimated Sales: Under $500,000
Number Employees: 1-4

12627 **Terrace At J Vineyards**
11447 Old Redwood Hwy
Healdsburg, CA 95448-9523
707-431-5400
Fax: 707-431-5410 800-885-9463
info@jwine.com www.jwine.com
Wines
President: Judy Jordan
judy.jordan@jwine.com
Regional Sales Manager: Brandon Vorst
Public Relations: Robin Oden
Winemaker: Lisa Kashin
Estimated Sales: $5-9.9 Million
Number Employees: 50-99
Parent Co: E&J Gallo Winery
Type of Packaging: Private Label
Brands:
J Nicole Vineyard Pinot Noir
J Russian River Vall
J Sparkling Wine

12628 **Terranettis Italian Bakery**
844 W Trindle Rd
Mechanicsburg, PA 17055-4095
717-697-5434
Fax: 717-697-6815 www.terranettis.com
Baked goods manufacturer.
President: Terry McMahon
Number Employees: 20-49
Type of Packaging: Consumer, Food Service
Brands:
Terranetti's

12629 **Terrapin Ridge**
1208 S Myrtle Ave
Clearwater, FL 33756-3425
727-442-3663
800-999-4052
www.terrapinridge.com
Dips, dressings, extracts, jams, jellies, mustards, sauces, sweet toppings
Co-Owner: Brian Coughlin
Co-Owner: Mary O'Donnell
Co-Founder: Susan Furst
Number Employees: 5-9
Type of Packaging: Consumer, Private Label

12630 **Terrell Meats**
1211 E Main St
Delta, UT 84624
435-864-2600
Fax: 435-864-2600
Beef jerky, beef, pork and lamb
Partner: Clark Terrell
Estimated Sales: $1,200,000
Number Employees: 6
Type of Packaging: Consumer, Food Service

12631 **Terrell's Potato Chip Co**
218 Midler Park Dr
Syracuse, NY 13206-1819
315-437-2786
Fax: 315-437-2069 terrellschip@msn.com
Potato chips including regular, barbecue, onion and sour cream; also, salsa
President: Jack Terrell
terrellschip@msn.com
Estimated Sales: $6500000
Number Employees: 100-249
Type of Packaging: Consumer
Brands:
Bachman
Keystone

12632 **Terressentia Corp.**
3525 Iron Horse Rd # 104
Suite 104
Ladson, SC 29456-4331
843-225-3100
Fax: 843-225-3107 simon.burch@terressentia.com
www.terressentia.com
Distilled spirits
CEO: Joseph Bosco
joe@terressentia.com
CEO: Earl Hewlette
Number Employees: 10-19

12633 **(HQ)Terri Lynn Inc**
1450 Bowes Rd
Elgin, IL 60123-5539
847-741-1900
Fax: 847-741-7791 800-323-0775
sales@terrilynn.com www.terrilynn.com
Manufacturer and wholesaler of nuts, dried fruits and coated nuts.
President: Terri Graziano
Estimated Sales: $5-10 Million
Number Employees: 100-249
Number of Brands: 1
Number of Products: 600
Square Footage: 108000
Type of Packaging: Food Service, Private Label, Bulk
Other Locations:
Terri Lynn-Pecan Shelling Operation
Cordele GA

12634 **Terry Brothers, Inc**
5039 Willis Wharf Dr
Willis Wharf, VA 23486
757-442-6251
Fax: 757-824-3461 infoat@terrybrothers.com
www.terrybrothers.com
Clams and oysters
President: N Terry Jr
Estimated Sales: $2.5-5 Million
Number Employees: 5-9
Type of Packaging: Consumer, Food Service
Brands:
Sewansecott
Terry Brothers

12635 **Terry Foods**
Genesis Centre, 18 Innovation Way
North Staffs Business Park
Stoke-on-Trent, ST6 4BF
UK
enquiries@terryfoods.com
www.terryfoods.com
Ingredients wholesaler
CEO: John Gardiner
CFO: Nikolai Terry
Sales Manager: Larry Haws
Estimated Sales: $5-10 Million

12636 **Tessemae's All Natural**
8805 Kelso Dr.
Essex, MD 21221
855-698-3773
customerhappiness@tessemaes.com
www.tessemaes.com
Salad dressings, condiments, and marinades. Keto, vegan, and gluten free options available
Co-Founder: Brian Vetter
Co-Founder/CEO: Greg Vetter
Director Marketing: Keri Nwosu
EVP Sales & Strategy: Shawn McLaughlin
VP National Accounts: Mike Shields
Year Founded: 2009
Number Employees: 50-99

12637 **Tessenderlo Kerley Inc**
2255 N 44th St # 300
Phoenix, AZ 85008-3279
602-889-8300
Fax: 602-889-8430 800-669-0559
info-tki@tkinet.com www.tkinet.com
Producer of high quality gelatins for the food, pharmaceutical and photoghaphic industry, operating worldwide
Vice President: Larry Tryon
ltryon@tkinet.com
CEO: Jordan Burns
Estimated Sales: $3-5 Million
Number Employees: 50-99
Type of Packaging: Private Label
Brands:
Cryogel
Instagel
Solgel
Swiftgel

12638 **Test Laboratories Inc**
7121 Canby Ave
Reseda, CA 91335-4304
818-881-4251
Fax: 818-881-6370 rob@testlabinc.com
www.testlabinc.com
Processor and exporter of enzymes, flavors and ingredients.
President: Rob Brewster
Estimated Sales: $1,100,000
Number Employees: 20-49
Square Footage: 4000
Brands:
Brewster Nutrition
Testlab
Vitalfa

12639 **Testamints Sales-Distribution**
41 Lakeside Blvd
Hopatcong, NJ 07843-1339
226-946-3677
Fax: 973-895-3742 888-879-0400
orders@testamints.net www.testamints.net
Confections
President: Al Poe
Contact: Mark Bontempo
markbontempo@testamints.net
Estimated Sales: Less Than $500,000
Number Employees: 1-4
Brands:
Promise Pops
Testamints Chewing Gum
Testamints Fruit Flavored Candy
Testamints Sour Fruit Mints
Testamints Sugar Free Mints
Testamints Sugar Mints

12640 **Teti Bakery**
27 Signal Hill Avenue
Etobicoke, ON M9W 6V8
Canada
416-798-8777
Fax: 416-798-8749 800-465-0123
www.tetibakery.com
Pizza, pizza crusts and Italian flat bread; exporter of pizza crusts
President: Franco Teti
VP: Dino Teti
Sales Manager: Tony Saldutto
Estimated Sales: $2 Million
Number Employees: 50
Square Footage: 56000
Type of Packaging: Consumer, Food Service, Private Label, Bulk
Brands:
San Mario
Teti

12641 **(HQ)Tetley Tea**
890 Mountain Avenue
Suite 105
New Providence, NJ 07974
203-929-9200
Fax: 203-925-0512 800-728-0084
info@tetleyusa.com www.tetleyusa.com
Tea, coffee and tea bags
President: John Petrizzo
President: Glynne Jones
CFO: John Petrizzo
Sr. VP, Supply Chain: Dan Smith
Number Employees: 500-999
Parent Co: Tata Tea Ltd
Type of Packaging: Private Label
Brands:
Tetley Teas

12642 **Tetley USA**
1090 King Georges Post Road
Bldg 1
Edison, NJ 08837-3701
732-738-5599
Fax: 732-225-8469 800-728-0084
tetleyusa@worldpantry.com
Tea
VP Field Sales: Ann Rowe
Parent Co: Tetley Tea

12643 **Tetley USA**
1267 Cobb Industrial Dr
Marietta, GA 30066
770-428-5555
Fax: 770-427-7019 www.tetleyusa.com
Tea
President: Marty Kushner
CEO: Bruce Klodt
VP Sales: Elaine Meyers
Plant Manager: L Griffen
Estimated Sales: $20-50 Million
Number Employees: 100-249
Parent Co: Tetley Tea

12644 **Teton Waters Ranch LLC**
3301 Lawrence St. # 3
Denver, CO 80205
720-340-4590
www.tetonwatersranch.com
100% grass-fed and grass-finished beef frankfurters and sausages in various flavors
Founder: Jeff Russell
CEO: Walt Freese

Year Founded: 2008
Number of Brands: 1
Number of Products: 11
Type of Packaging: Consumer, Private Label
Brands:
Teton Waters Ranch

12645 **Tex-Mex Cold Storage**
6665 Padre Island Hwy
Brownsville, TX 78521-5218
956-831-9433
Fax: 956-831-9572
info@texmexcoldstorage.bzzp.net
www.texmexcoldstorage.bzzp.net
Seafood including shrimp; warehouse providing freezer and dry storage
President: Emilio Sanchez
VP: Norma Sanchez
Plant Manager: Nick Sato
Estimated Sales: $6,307,658
Number Employees: 225
Square Footage: 620000
Type of Packaging: Private Label, Bulk

12646 **Tex-Mex Gourmet**
201 W First Street
Brenham, TX 77833
979-836-4701
Fax: 713-784-7616 888-345-8467
info@texmexgourmet.com
www.texmexgourmet.com
Sauces
Number Employees: 10-19
Type of Packaging: Consumer, Private Label
Brands:
Los Tios
Tuldy's

12647 **TexaFrance**
525 Round Rock
Round Rock, TX 78681
512-246-2500
Fax: 512-246-2716 800-776-8937
info@texafrance.com www.texafrance.com
Processor and co-packer of natural pasta and pesto sauces, salad dressings, mustards, chutneys and jellies; private labeling available
President: Jean Parant
Vice President: David Griswold
VP Purchasing: David Griswold
Estimated Sales: $.2 Million
Number Employees: 7
Square Footage: 32000
Type of Packaging: Consumer, Private Label

12648 **Texas Beach**
Richmond, VA
757-403-3598
texasbeachllc@gmail.com
www.texasbeachbloodymary.com
Bloody Mary mix
President: Austin Green
CEO: Greg White
Number Employees: 2-10
Brands:
Texas Beach

12649 **Texas Chili Co**
3313 N Jones St
Fort Worth, TX 76106-4339
817-626-0983
Fax: 817-626-9105 800-507-0009
sales@texaschili.com www.texaschili.com
Frozen chili, taco filling and chili sauce
President: Danny Owens
sales@texaschilicompany.com
Plant Manager: Rebbca Marlvo
Estimated Sales: Below $10 Million
Number Employees: 5-9
Type of Packaging: Private Label
Brands:
Texas Chili

12650 **Texas Coffee Co**
3297 S M L King Jr Pkwy
Beaumont, TX 77705-2513
409-835-3434
Fax: 409-835-4248 800-259-3400
texjoy@texjoy.com www.texjoy.com
Tea, coffee, extracts, spices and seasonings; importer of coffee and tea
President/Operations: Carlo Busceme
cbusceme@texjoy.com
VP: Donald Fertitta
Estimated Sales: $10-20 Million
Number Employees: 20-49
Square Footage: 135000
Type of Packaging: Consumer, Food Service, Private Label, Bulk
Brands:
Seaport
Texjoy

12651 **Texas Coffee Traders Inc**
1400 E 4th St
Austin, TX 78702-3808
512-476-2279
Fax: 512-476-3617 800-343-4875
www.texascoffeetraders.com
Coffee, teas, candies, syrups, chocolate
President: Robert Beall
rc@texascoffeetraders.com
Marketing Director: Michael Gomez
Service Manager: Brad Nevens
Production Manager: Steven Kerner
Estimated Sales: Less than $500,000
Number Employees: 20-49
Parent Co: Montana Coffee Traders

12652 **Texas Crumb & Food Products**
3250 Towerwood Dr
Farmers Branch, TX 75234
972-243-8443
Fax: 972-484-9315 800-522-7862
info@dasbrot.com www.dasbrot.com
Bread crumbs, batters, breadings and stuffing and seasoning mixes
President: S Holtsclaw
Vice President: W Holtsclaw
Contact: Diana Podowski
dianapodowski@dasbrot.com
Estimated Sales: $900000
Number Employees: 5-9
Square Footage: 64000
Parent Co: Das Brot
Type of Packaging: Food Service, Private Label, Bulk

12653 **Texas Heat**
P.O.Box 33246
San Antonio, TX 78265
210-656-4328
Fax: 210-656-5916 800-656-5916
Picante sauce, chili mix and cheese dip
President: Robert Delgado
Estimated Sales: $1-3 Million
Number Employees: 1-4
Type of Packaging: Consumer, Food Service

12654 **Texas Reds Steak House**
400 E Main St
Red River, NM 87558-0111
575-754-2922
Fax: 575-754-2309 www.texasreds.com
Steak
President: William Gill
VP: Richard Gill
CFO: Deanna Tapia
Estimated Sales: $1-2.5 Million
Number Employees: 35
Brands:
Texas Red

12655 **Texas Sausage Co**
2915 E 12th St
Austin, TX 78702-2401
512-472-6707
Fax: 512-472-9360 www.texashotsausage.com
Processor and wholesaler/distributor of sausage; serving the food service market
President: Gary Tharp
hotlinks1@yahoo.com
Estimated Sales: $.5-1 million
Number Employees: 5-9
Type of Packaging: Consumer, Food Service

12656 **Texas Spice Co**
2709 Sam Bass Rd
Round Rock, TX 78681-1811
512-255-8816
Fax: 512-255-4189 800-880-8007
contact@texas-spice.net www.texas-spice.net
Wholesale and retail custom blending, spices, seasoning blends, bases, extracts, flavors, coffee & tea
Owner: Beckie Forsyth
Contact: Jason Spangler
spangler@texas-spice.net
Estimated Sales: Less Than $500,000
Number Employees: 1-4
Type of Packaging: Food Service
Brands:
Texas Spice

12657 **Texas Tamale Co**
9087 Knight Rd
Houston, TX 77054-4305
713-795-5500
Fax: 713-795-5534 info@texastamale.com
www.texastamale.com
Tamales, chili, and sauces.
COO and Co-Owner: Shirley Bailey
Number Employees: 10-19

12658 **Texas Tito's**
P.O. Box 12847
Austin, TX 78711
512-463-7476
Fax: 210-250-5055 877-99 -OTEX
www.gotexan.org
Texas regional food
President: Hiroshi Shimizu
State Marketing Coordinator: Susan Dunn
Coordinator for Marketing: Lindsay Dickens
Estimated Sales: $500,000-$1 Million
Number Employees: 250-499
Brands:
Go Texan

12659 **Texas Toffee**
5 Santa Fe Pl
Odessa, TX 79765
972-596-1031
Fax: 915-563-4105 800-599-2133
www.texastoffee.com
Processor and exporter of toffee including milk and white chocolate, bittersweet, peanut, butterscotch and sugar-free
President: Susan Leshnower
Number Employees: 1-4
Square Footage: 64
Type of Packaging: Consumer, Food Service, Private Label, Bulk
Brands:
Texas Toffee

12660 **Texas Traditions Gourmet**
PO Box 2705
Georgetown, TX 78627-2705
512-863-7291
Fax: 512-869-6212 800-547-7062
www.texastraditions.com
Processor and exporter of foods with Texas heritage, inlcuding mesquite smoke, jalapeno pepper, country-style German and black peppercorn mustard, jalapeno and red chile pepper, prickly pear cactus jelly, hot salt, seasoning blends anddry dip mixes
Founder, CEO: Dianna Howard
Estimated Sales: $300,000-500,000
Number Employees: 10-19
Brands:
Texas Hot Salt
Texas Traditions

12661 **Thackrey & Co**
660 Horseshoe Hill Rd
Bolinas, CA 94924
415-868-9543
Fax: 415-868-1781 www.wine-maker.net
Gourmet foods
President: Sean Thackery
Estimated Sales: Under $500,000
Number Employees: 1-4
Brands:
Thackrey

12662 **Thanasi Foods LLC**
PO Box 4307
4745 Walnut St Ste A
Boulder, CO 80306-4307
720-570-1065
Fax: 720-570-1064 866-558-7379
goneal@thanasi.com www.thanasifoods.com
Meats, nuts
Founder And CEO: Justin Havlick
Director of Marketing: Greg O'Neal
Sales Support Manager: Kimmee Helbak
Estimated Sales: C

12663 **The Thanksgiving Coffee Co**
19100 S Harbor Dr
Fort Bragg, CA 95437-5718
707-964-0118
Fax: 707-964-0351 800-462-1999
www.thanksgivingcoffee.com
Vacuum packed coffee including certified organic, shade grown, regular, decaffeinated and flavored
Owner: Susan Coy
kristina.robertson@va.gov
Secretary, Treasurer: Joan Katzeff
Plant Manager: David Gillette
Estimated Sales: $4741877
Number Employees: 20-49
Type of Packaging: Consumer, Food Service, Private Label, Bulk
Brands:
Aztec Harvest
Grand Slam
Inca Harvest
Mayan Harvest
Pony Express
Royal Garden Tea
Song Bird
Thanksgiving
Zip

12664 **That's How We Roll, LLC**
100 Passaic Ave. # 155
Fairfield, NJ 07004
973-602-3011
info@thwroll.com
www.thwroll.com
Snack crisps and cookies made with wholesome ingredients
Chief Operating Officer: Samuel Kestenbaum
Number of Brands: 3
Number of Products: 2
Type of Packaging: Consumer, Private Label
Brands:
Mrs. Thinsters
Kitchen Table Bakers
Party 'Tizers

12665 **That's It Nutrition**
834 S Broadway
8th Floor
Los Angeles, CA 90014-3501
213-892-1505
Fax: 888-782-8040 888-862-5235
support@thatsitfruit.com www.thatsitfruit.com
Fruit bars, truffles
Founder/CEO: Lior Lewensztain
Vice President, Sales: Rachelle Minteer
Chief Operating Officer: Miriam Lewensztain
Year Founded: 2012
Number Employees: 20-49
Type of Packaging: Bulk
Brands:
That's it(c)

12666 **Thatcher's Gourmet Specialties**
1201 Minnesota St
San Francisco, CA 94107-3407
415-643-9945
Fax: 415-643-9948 800-926-2676
sales@tgsp.com www.tgsp.com
Gourmet popcorn and snacks
President: Gus Ghassan
Vice President: Ghada Ghassan
Manager: Joe Eidson
Estimated Sales: Less Than $500,000
Number Employees: 1-4
Type of Packaging: Private Label
Brands:
Joy's Gourmet Snacks
Thatcher's
Thatcher's Special Popcorn

12667 **The Amazing Chickpea**
1600 Hwy. 100 South # 500A
St. Louis Park, MN 55416
612-548-1099
contact@theamazingchickpea.com
www.theamazingchickpea.com
Gluten-free chickpea butter spread in various flavors
Contact: Sunil Kumar
Year Founded: 2016
Number of Brands: 1
Number of Products: 4
Type of Packaging: Consumer, Private Label
Brands:
The Amazing Chickpea

12668 **The Ardent Homesteader**
PO Box 44
Arden, NY 10910
www.ardenthomesteader.com
Handmade, all-natural caramel sauce
Founder/Owner: Kristin Nelson
Year Founded: 2010
Number of Brands: 1
Number of Products: 1
Type of Packaging: Consumer, Private Label
Brands:
Cara-Sel

12669 **The Art of Broth, LLC**
818-715-9320
info@theartofbroth.com
www.theartofbroth.com
Sippable chicken, beef and vegan vegetable-flavored broth; broths are vegan, Kosher, non-GMO and gluten-free
Number of Brands: 1
Number of Products: 3
Type of Packaging: Consumer, Private Label
Brands:
The Art of Broth

12670 **The Bauman Family**
118 Hoffmansville Road
P.O. Box 210
Sassamansville, PA 19472-0210
610-754-7251
Fax: 610-754-7251 baumans@baumanfamily.com
www.baumanfamily.com
Apple butter

12671 **The Bites Company**
PO Box 122
Westport, CT 06881
203-296-2482
www.thebitescompany.com
Bite-size biscotti
Owner/Baker: Dina Upton

12672 **The Boisset Collection**
849 Zinfandel Ln
St. Helena, CA 94574
707-967-7667
customerservice@boisset.com
www.boissetcollection.com
Wines
President: Jean Charles Boisset
VP, Marketing & Communications: Patrick Egan
Director, Public Relations: Caroline de Laurens
caroline.delaurens@baccarat.fr
COO: Lisa Heisinger
Estimated Sales: $50-74,999,999
Number Employees: 40
Number of Brands: 17
Brands:
Bouchard Aine Fils
Boisset Classic
Boisset Mediterranee
Charles De Fere
Christophe Cellars
Evoluna Estate
Fog Mountain
J Moreau Fils
Jean-Claude Boisset
Joliesse Vineyards
Les Domaines Bernard
Lyeth Estate
Oceana Coastal
Ropiteall
Summerlake
Vienot
William Wheeler Winery

12673 **The Brooklyn Salsa Co LLC**
1717 Troutman Street
Suite 254
Ridgewood, NY 11385
347-470-5493
Fax: 347-435-2436 www.bksalsa.com
Salsa.
Co-founder: Matt Burns
matt@bksalsa.com
Co-founder/CEO: Rob Behnke
Operations Manager: Casey Gilbertson

12674 **The Bruss Company**
3548 N. Kostner Ave.
Chicago, IL 60641
773-282-2900
customer.bruss@tyson.com
www.bruss.com
Portion controlled steaks, pork, and veal.
Year Founded: 1937
Estimated Sales: $175 Million
Number Employees: 250-499
Number of Brands: 1
Square Footage: 52000
Parent Co: Tyson Foods
Type of Packaging: Consumer, Food Service
Brands:
Golden Trophy Steaks

12675 **The Chalet Market**
6410 Jackrabbit Lane
Belgrade, MT 59714
406-388-4687
800-752-1029
www.chaletmarket.com
Specialty deli, prepared foods

12676 **The Chili Lab**
Brooklyn, NY
info@thechililab.com
Manufacturer of chili salts and do-it-yourself hot sauce kits.
Founder: Thomas Kelly

12677 **The Coffee Bean & Tea Leaf**
1945 S La Cienega Blvd
Los Angeles, CA 90034
310-237-2326
877-653-1963
officecoffee@coffeebean.com
www.coffeebean.com
Coffee, tea and blended drinks
President and Chief Executive Officer: John Dawson
CEO: Sunny Sassoon
CFO: Karen Kate
VP of Store Development: William (Bill) Robards
Sr.Dir of Coffee Roasting&Manufacturing: Jay Isais
VP of Marketing: Diane Kuyoomjian
Sr.VP Sales & Supply Chain: Paul Balzer
Contact: Patrice Anderson
patricea@johnnycreates.com
Vice President of Operations: Jeff Schroeder
Estimated Sales: $300,000-500,000
Number Employees: 10-19

12678 **The Cookie Dough Cafe**
1701 E Empire St
Suite 360
Bloomington, IL 61704-7900
309-539-4585
Fax: 309-539-4585 www.thecookiedoughcafe.com
Cookie dough
Co-Owner: Joan Pacetti
Brands:
the cookie(c) dough cafe

12679 **The Coromega Company**
PO Box 131135
Carlsbad, CA 92013-1135
760-599-6088
Fax: 760-599-6089 877-275-3725
www.coromega.com
Flavored Omega-3 fish oil gel supplements and gummy supplements
Chief Operating Officer: Andrew Aussie
Year Founded: 1999
Number of Brands: 1
Number of Products: 6
Type of Packaging: Consumer, Private Label
Brands:
Coromega

12680 **The Crispery**
2728 Sterling Point Dr.
Portsmouth, VA 23703
501-224-8947
valerie@thecrispery.com
www.thecrispery.com
Marshmallow snacks.
Co-Owner: Judy Soldinger
Co-Owner: Steven Soldinger
Brands:
CRISPYCAKESTM

12681 **The Daphne Baking Company, LLC**
300 E 77th Street
Suite 21B
New York, NY 10075
212-517-7626
Fax: 646-349-4164
Frozen tarts, shells and cakes
Marketing: Bo Bartlett
Number Employees: 5

12682 **The Dow Chemical Company**
2211 H.H. Down Way
Midland, MI 48674
989-636-1000
Fax: 989-832-1456 800-331-6451
www.dow.com
Cooking oils and fat replacements
President & CFO: Howard Ungerleider
Chairman & CEO: Jim Fitterling
SVP of Operations & Manufacturing: Peter Holicki
Estimated Sales: $50-100 Million
Number Employees: 250-499
Type of Packaging: Private Label, Bulk

12683 **The Eli's Cheesecake Company**
6701 W. Forest Preserve Drive
Chicago, IL 60634
773-308-7000
Fax: 773-736-1169 800-999-8300
info@elicheesecake.com www.elicheesecake.com
Cheesecake
President: Marc S. Schulman

12684 **The Food Collective**
1882 McGraw Ave, Suite A
Irvine, CA 92614
949-797-0014
Fax: 949-797-0041 866-328-8638
Organic gourmet heat-n-serve frozen foods.
Owner: Stephen Moore
Type of Packaging: Consumer
Brands:
HELEN'S KITCHEN
ORGANIC BISTRO

12685 **The Good Bean**
2980 San Pablo Ave
Berkeley, CA 94702-2471
USA
561-243-7773
Fax: 510-295-2424 www.thegoodbean.com
Chips, chickpea snacks, fruitbars
Owner: Sarah Wallace
Owner: Suzanne Slatcher
Number Employees: 5-9

12686 **The Good Crisp Company**
www.thegoodcrispcompany.com
Gluten-free potato crisps in various flavors
Director, Sales/Marketing: Matt Parry
Number of Brands: 1
Number of Products: 3
Type of Packaging: Consumer, Private Label
Brands:
The Good Crisp Company

12687 **The Great San Saba River Pecan Company**
234 West Highway 190
San Saba, TX 76877
325-372-6078
Fax: 325-372-5852 800-621-8121
info@greatpecans.com www.greatpecans.com
Pecan preserves, pies, cakes, breads, candies, spreads, toppings and pecan praline popcorn
Co-Owner/President: Larry Newkirk
Type of Packaging: Consumer
Brands:
Great San Saba River Pecan

12688 **The Great Western Tortilla Co.**
1761 E 58th Ave.
P.O. Box 16346
Denver, CO 80216-0346
303-298-0705
Fax: 303-298-0216
Tortilla chips in a variety of stone-ground and natural flavors, salsa and hot sauce
President: William A Ralston
Estimated Sales: $20-50 Million
Number Employees: 50-99
Brands:
Buffalo Bill's
Wild West

12689 **The Hampton Popcorn Company**
999 S Oyster Bay Rd
Bethpage, NY 11714
888-947-6726
www.hamptonpopcorn.com
Popcorn
Chairman Of The Board: Robert Gutman
Estimated Sales: 82,000
Number Employees: 2

12690 **The Healthy Beverage Company**
329B S Main Street
Doylestown, PA 18901
215-321-8330
Fax: 866-642-9179 800-295-1388
info@steaz.com www.steaz.com
All-natural, organic and fair trade tea-based beveraged in product lines that include iced tea, sparkling green tea and energy drinks.
Owner: Eric Schnell
Director of Finance: Linda Flagler
VP Marketing: Lee Brody
Director of Operations: Carlos Valdes
Estimated Sales: $1-2.5 Million
Number Employees: 5-9
Type of Packaging: Consumer
Brands:
STEAZ

12691 **The Honest Stand**
PO Box 100742
Denver, CO 80250
chat@thehonestand.com
www.thehonestand.com
Plant-based, certified organic, dairy- and gluten-free cheese style dips in various flavors
Co-Founder: Alexandra Carone
Co-Founder: Jeremy Day
Year Founded: 2014
Number of Brands: 1
Number of Products: 5
Type of Packaging: Consumer, Private Label
Brands:
The Honest Stand

12692 **The Humphrey Co**
Po Box 832
Lockport, NY 14094
716-597-1974
Fax: 716-804-6881
Soft drinks, candy, full-line snacks, nuts, and popcorn.
President: Wendy Farnsworth
Marketing: Cyd Cehulik

12693 **The Invisible Chef**
1818 Hopple Ave SW
Canton, OH 44706-1909
USA
330-880-5223
Fax: 330-880-4749
contactus@theinvisiblechef.com
www.theinvisiblechef.com
Baking mixes
Co-Owner: Jill Mccauley
Estimated Sales: D
Number Employees: 10-19

12694 **The Jam Stand**
Brooklyn, NY
718-218-5194
info@thejamstand.com
thej.am
Jams.
Co-Founder: Jessica Quon
Co-Founder: Sabrina Valle

12695 **The Jersey Tomato Company**
38 Buff Ln
Suite 101
Hillsdale, NJ 07642-1101
dave@jerseytomatoco.com
jerseytomatoco.com
Tomato sauces
Marketing & Advertising: David Stoff
Brands:
The Jersey Tomato Co.

12696 **The Junket Folks**
One Hansen Island
Little Falls, NY 13365
877-248-2477
800-556-6674
info@junketdesserts.com www.junketdesserts.com
Desserts, custard, ice cream mix, tablets

12697 **The King's Kitchen**
129 W. Trade Street
Charlotte, NC 28202
704-375-1990
kingskitchen.org
Prepared foods

12698 **The Konery**
630 Flushing Ave
Suite 6N
Brooklyn, NY 11206-5026
917-750-4147
hello@thekonery.com
www.thekonery.com
Waffle cone
Cone Expert & Founder: Kristine Tonkonow
Number Employees: 1-50
Type of Packaging: Food Service
Brands:
Konery

12699 **The Kroger Co.**
300 N Lp Miller St
Murray, KY 42071
270-762-5100
Fax: 270-759-1919 800-632-6900
tcolson@kroger.com www.kroger.com
Hot chocolate mixes, breakfast drinks, instant teas and oatmeal; also, canned nuts
Manager: Bob Beuhler
bob.beuhler@kroger.com
Number Employees: 10,000
Parent Co: Kroger Company
Type of Packaging: Consumer, Private Label
Brands:
Kenlake Foods

12700 **The Lancaster Food Company**
Lancaster, PA
Certified organic and allergen-free breads and cookies
Co-Founder/CEO: Charlie Crystle
Co-Founder/Chief Product Officer: Craig Lauer
Vice-President, Operations: Polly Lauer
Year Founded: 2014
Number of Brands: 1
Number of Products: 7
Type of Packaging: Consumer, Private Label
Brands:
The Lancaster Food Company

12701 **The Little Kernel**
400 Madison Ave.
Manalapan, NJ 07726
732-607-3880
info@thelittlekernel.com
Olive-oil popped popcorn with no artificial ingredients, in various flavors
Co-Founder: Christopher Laurita
Co-Founder: Andy Epstein
Year Founded: 2016
Number of Brands: 1
Number of Products: 6
Type of Packaging: Consumer, Private Label
Brands:
The Little Kernel

12702 **The Lobster Place**
75 Ninth Avenue
Chelsea Market
New York, NY 10011
212-255-5672
info@lobsterplace.com
lobsterplace.com
Lobster, seafood
President: Brendan Hayes
CEO: Ian MacGregor
Lead Sales Executive: Joe Cooper
Contact: Renee Alevras
ralevras@lobsterplace.com
Operations Manager: Christian Quintana
Purchasing Manager: Mark Grobman

12703 **The Lollipop Tree, Inc**
181 York St
Auburn, NY 13021
315-252-2676
Fax: 315-282-0720 800-842-6691
www.lollipoptree.com
Baking mixes, pepper jellies, grilling sauces, hot chocolate mixes. Experienced in certified organic, sprouted wheat and spelt, low-carb, low/no sugar mixes and more.
President: Robert Lynch
CEO/Chairman/Founder: Laurie Lynch
CFO: Bob Lynch
Contact: Steve Wellauer
it@newhopemills.com
Estimated Sales: D
Number Employees: 20-49
Number of Products: 90
Square Footage: 237000
Type of Packaging: Consumer, Private Label
Brands:
Harborside
Lollipop Tree
Quick Loaf
The Lollipop Tree
Good Simple Food

12704 **The Long Life Beverage Company**
P.O.Box 7802
Mission Hills, CA 91346-7802
661-259-5575
800-848-7331
Processor, importer and exporter of organic herbal black and green teas, over 40 boxed varieties and 11 ready to drink bottled iced teas, and a variety of enhanced waters
Owner: Troy Long
Estimated Sales: $7.5 Million
Number Employees: 1-4
Number of Brands: 3
Number of Products: 52
Square Footage: 44000
Parent Co: Consac Industries
Type of Packaging: Consumer, Private Label
Brands:
Enhance Vitamin/Waters
Long Life Black Teas
Long Life Green Teas
Long Life Herbal Teas
Long Life Iced Teas

12705 **The Lovely Candy Company LLC**
1725 Kilkenny Ct
Woodstock, IL 60098-7437
USA
801-824-0624
www.lovelycandyco.com
Fruit chews, caramels, licorice, fudge rolls
CEO/Founders: Jackie & Mike Nakamura
Vice President Of Marketing: Brian Heiser
Contact: Brian Heiser
brianheiser@lovelycandyco.com

12706 **The Maple Guild**
One Sweet Tree Ln
Island Pond, VT 05846
802-723-6753
info@mapleguild.com
www.mapleguild.com
Maple syrup and maple syrup-infused tea and water
CEO: Mike Argyelan
Number of Brands: 2
Number of Products: 14
Type of Packaging: Consumer
Brands:
THE MAPLE GUILD
TAPT

12707 **The Mapled Nut Co.**
P.O. Box 303
Morrisville, VT 05661
802-888-9559
Fax: 80- 88- 955 800-726-4661
Gourmet maple sugar cashews, almonds, pecans and walnuts
Owner: Marsha Phillips
Estimated Sales: $.5-1 million
Number Employees: 1-4

12708 **The Matzo Project**
575 Union St
3rd Floor
Brooklyn, NY 11215-1024
929-276-2896
hello@matzoproject.com
www.matzoproject.com
Matzo
Co-Owner: Ashley Albert
Co-Owner: Kevin Rodriguez
Brands:
The Matzo Project

12709 **The Meeker Vineyard**
5377 Dry Creek Road
Healdsburg, CA 95448
707-431-2148
Fax: 707-431-2549 www.meekerwine.com
Wines the selection of which includes Chardonnay, Dry Rose, Zinfandel, Petite Sirah, Cabernet Sauvignon and Merlot, in addition to others.
President: Charles Meeker
VP Marketing/Operations: John Burtner
Contact: Julia Berman
julia@meekerwine.com
Estimated Sales: Less than $500,000
Number Employees: 1-4

12710 **The Murphs Famous Inc.**
395 Summit Point Drive
Suite One
Henrietta, NY 14467
888-281-6400
Fax: 585-321-9906 www.murphsfamous.com
Manufacturer of bloody mary mix.

12711 **The Naked Edge, LLC**
3020 Carbon Place #103
Boulder, CO 80301
888-297-9426
www.wildmadesnacks.com
Organic, non-GMO Veggie-Go's dried fruit & vegetable snack; available in strips or bites
Co-Founder: John McHugh
Co-Founder: Lisa McHugh
Number of Brands: 1
Type of Packaging: Consumer, Private Label
Brands:
Veggie-Go's

12712 **The New Primal**
3690 Old Charleston Hwy
Johns Island, SC 29455-7826
866-723-1386
meat@thenewprimal.com
thenewprimal.com
Beef and turkey jerky
Founder & CEO: Jason Burke
Senior Marketing Manager: Samantha Blatz
Director of Sales: David Paul Miller
Director of Operations: Ashley Zager
Estimated Sales: $9.6 Million
Number Employees: 10-50
Brands:
The New Primal

12713 **The Pantry Club**
2054 Weaver Park Dr.
Clearwater, FL 33765
877-335-8842
www.thepantryclub.com
Manufacturer of gourmet dip mixes and seasonings.
Co-Founder: Matt Webb
Co-Founder: Alecia Webb

12714 **The Peanut Butter Shop of Williamsburg**
8012 Hankins Industrial Park Road
Toano, VA 23168
757-566-0930
Fax: 757-566-1605 800-831-1828
info@thepeanutshop.com
www.thepeanutshop.com
Virginia peanuts and specialty nut meats, cocoa mixes including chocolate, raspberry, traditional and chocolate hazelnut
VP: Pete Booker
Marketing: Michael McDonald
Sales Director: Jeff Armbruster
Plant Manager: Larry Winslow
Number Employees: 20-49
Type of Packaging: Consumer
Brands:
Amber Brand Deviled Smithfield Ham
Colonial Williamsburg
King's Arms Tavern
Nut Case Collection
Peanut Shop of Williamsburg
Smithfield Tavern

12715 **The Perfect Pita**
7653 Fullerton Rd
Springfield, VA 22153
703-644-0004
info@theperfectpita.com
theperfectpita.com
Pita falafel, BLT sandwich, hummus, pizza, homemade soup, salads and desserts.
Director of Catering Sales: Michael Tam
Estimated Sales: $600,000
Number Employees: 10
Brands:
The Perfect Pita

12716 **The Pickle Juice Company**
206 S Town East Blvd
Mesquite, TX 75149
972-755-0289
sales@picklepower.com
www.picklepower.com
Sports drink
Owner: Brandon Brooks
VP, Global Sales & Marketing: Filip Keuppens
Year Founded: 2001
Estimated Sales: $10 Million
Number Employees: 11-50
Brands:
Extra Strength Pickle Juice Shots
Pickle Juice Sport Drink

12717 **The Pillsbury Company**
100 Justin Dr
Chelsea, MA 02150-4032
617-884-9800
Fax: 617-889-0281 800-370-7834
www.pillsbury.com
Frozen and par-baked goods including French bread
President: David Baker
Contact: Michael Blight
michael.blight@signaturebreads.com
Number Employees: 100-249
Square Footage: 400000
Parent Co: General Mills Inc
Type of Packaging: Food Service, Private Label

12718 **The Piping Gourmets**
786-233-8660
info@thepipinggourmets.com
www.thepipinggourmets.com
Gluten free and vegan whoopie pies
Co-Founder: Leslie Kaplan
Co-Founder: Carolyn Shulevitz
Number Employees: 5-9

12719 **The Poseidon Group**
300 Park Ave
12th Fl
New York, NY 10022-7412
646-926-0206
www.drinkcham.com
Chamomile tea
CEO & Co-Founder: Niko Nikolaou
Number Employees: 2-10
Brands:
cham cold brew tea

12720 **The Power of Fruit**
Po Box 456
Lebanon, NJ 08833-0456
908-450-9806
Fax: 908-566-3352
Dairy-free, gluten-free, kosher, nut-free, organic/natural, sugar-free, frozen desserts, foodservice.
Marketing: Ron Kazmierski
Contact: Scott Elser'
scott@poweroffruit.com

12721 **The Procter & Gamble Company**
1 P&G Plaza
Cincinnati, OH 45202
513-983-1100
Fax: 513-983-9369 800-692-0132
us.pg.com
Baby diapers, fabric care, feminine products, shampoos, paper towels, toilet paper, tissues, conditioners, dishwashing detergent, home cleaning products, razors, shaving gels, supplements, pregnancy tests, cough syrup, and more.

Chairman, President & CEO: David Taylor
CFO: Jon Moeller
Estimated Sales: $67.6 Billion
Number Employees: 97,000
Number of Brands: 57
Type of Packaging: Consumer
Brands:
Always
Ariel
Luvs
Pampers
Tide
Bounce
Cheer
Downy
Dreft
Era
Gain
Ace
Rindex 3en1
Bounty
Charmin
Puffs
Always Discreet
Tampax
Head & Shoulders
Aussie
Herbal Essences
Old Spice
Pantene
Cascade
Dawn
Febreeze
Joy
Mr. Clean
Swiffer
Salvo
Ambi Pur
Comet
Braun
Gillette
Venus
The Art of Shaving
Align
Clearblue
Meta
Pepto-Bismol
Prilosec OTC
Vicks
ZzzQuil
Crest
Fixodent
Oral-B
Scope
Ivory
Olay
Safeguard
Secret
Native
Snowberry
SK-II

12722 **The Pur Company**
23 Kodiak Crescent
Toronto, ON M3J 3E5
Canada
416-941-7557
info@thepurcompany.com
thepurcompany.com
Mints and gum
Founder & CEO: Jay Klein
Director of Sales & Marketing: John Kapralos
Sales Coordinator: Jenna Maislin
Director of People & Culture: Cerys Cook
Year Founded: 2010
Estimated Sales: $10-20 Million
Number Employees: 11-50
Brands:
pur

12723 **The Real Co**
3613F Kirkwood Hwy.
Wilmington, DE 19808
347-433-8945
info@thereal.co
www.thereal.co
Single-origin, non-GMO food products: quinoa, raw coconut sugar, raw cane sugar, pink Himalayan salt and white basmati rice
Founder: Colin Carter
Chief Executive Officer: Belal El-Banna
Chief Commercial Officer: Mo Elkateb
Number of Brands: 1
Number of Products: 6
Type of Packaging: Consumer, Food Service, Private Label
Brands:
The Real Co

12724 **The Really Great Food Company**
P.O. Box 2239
St. James, NY 11780
Fax: 631-382-8344 800-593-5377
orders@reallygreatfood.com reallygreatfood.com
Baking mixes

12725 **The Roscoe NY Beer Company, Inc.**
145 Rockland Rd.
Roscoe, NY 12776
607-290-5002
inquiries@roscoebeercompany.com
www.roscoebeercompany.com
IPAs, flavoured ale, rye beer, stout
Operations Manager: Josh Hughes
Director, Marketing and Events: Shannon Feeney
Year Founded: 2013
Number of Brands: 1
Number of Products: 11
Brands:
Trout Town

12726 **The Rubin Family of Wines**
5220 Ross Rd
Sebastopol, CA 95472-2158
707-887-8130
Fax: 707-887-8160 wine@rubinfamilyofwines.com
rubinfamilyofwines.com
Wines
Founder: Ron Rubin
Winemaker: Joe Freeman
Estimated Sales: Under $500,000
Number Employees: 1-4
Type of Packaging: Private Label
Brands:
River Road Vineyards

12727 **The Safe + Fair Food Company**
1 N LaSalle St.
Chicago, IL 60602
www.safeandfair.com
Allergy-safe snacks with allergen-free, gluten-free, and vegan options. Products include granola mix, popcorn, graham crackers, and chips.
Co-Founder: Dave Leyrer
Co-Founder: Pete Najarian
Number Employees: 10-50
Type of Packaging: Private Label

12728 **The Saucey Sauce CompanyInc.**
196 Court St.
Suite 2
Brooklyn, NY 11201
646-648-0159
www.getsauceynow.com
Manufacturer of Vietnamese homestyle sauces.
Co-Founder: Toan Huynh
Co-Founder: Ken Huynh
Contact: Sarah Briguglio
briguglios@getsauceynow.com

12729 **The Shed Saucery**
7501 Hwy 57
Ocean Springs, MS 39565
228-875-9590
contact@theshedbbq.com
theshedbbq.com
Barbeque sauces and meats
Co-Founder & Owner: Brad Orrison
Co-Founder & Owner: Brooke Lewis
Co-Founder: Brad Orrison
Estimated Sales: $1.2 Million
Number Employees: 3
Brands:
The Shed Barbeque & Blues Joint
The Shed BBQ Sauces & Marinades

12730 **The Sola Company**
4203 Montrose Blvd. # 490
Houston, TX 77006
800-277-1486
hello@solasweet.com
www.solasweet.com
Low-carb and low-glycemic index yogurt, ice cream, granola, bread, nut bars and sweetener
Co-Founder: Ed Bosarge
Co-Founder: Ryan Turner
Year Founded: 2012
Number of Brands: 1
Number of Products: 6
Type of Packaging: Consumer, Private Label
Brands:
Sola

12731 **The Soulfull Project**
Camden, NJ
megan@thesoulfullproject.com
www.thesoulfullproject.com
Vegan hot cereals; gluten free options available
Co-Founder: Megan Shea
Co-Founder: Chip Heim

12732 **The Sprout House**
874 Neighborhood Rd
Lake Katrine, NY 12499
800-777-6887
info@sprouthouse.com sprouthouse.com
Organic sprouting seeds, sprouters and wheatgrass juice supplies.
Brands:
Vermont Sprout

12733 **The Stephan Company**
4829 East 7th Avenue
Tampa, FL 33605
954-971-0600
Fax: 954-971-2633 www.thestephanco.com
Flavoring extracts and over-the-counter pharmaceuticals
Office Manager: Rita Chlau
Plant Manager: Mike Henry
Number Employees: 50-99

12734 **The Stroopie**
105 Old Dorwart St
Lancaster, PA 17603-3677
717-875-3426
sales@stroopies.com
www.stroopies.com
Stroopwafel
Co-Founder: Ed McManness
Co-Founder: Dan Perryman
Type of Packaging: Bulk
Brands:
Stroopies

12735 **The Sunshine Tomato Company**
149 Geary Avenue
New Cumberland, PA 17070
717 909 0844
www.sunshinepastasauce.com
Pasta sauce
President: Carla Noss
Brands:
Sunshine Pasta Sauce

12736 **The Swiss Bakery**
Burke Town Plaza
9536 Old Keene Mill Rd
Burke, VA 22015
703-569-3670
Fax: 703-321-3673 info@theswissbakery.com
www.theswissbakery.com
Fresh baked goods, cakes, pastries, tarts

12737 **The Tao of Tea**
3430 SE Belmont St.
Portland, OR 97214
503-736-0119
Fax: 503-736-9232 info@taooftea.com
taooftea.com
Tea and tea ware
Owner: Veerinder Chawla
Year Founded: 1997
Estimated Sales: $7.3 Million
Number Employees: 11-50
Type of Packaging: Consumer, Food Service, Private Label

12738 **The Tea Spot, Inc.**
4699 Nautilus Ct. South # 504
Boulder, CO 80301
303-444-8324
www.theteaspot.com
A variety of white, green, oolong, black, pu'erh, mate, herbal and organic teas in various flavors and sampler packs
CEO: Maria Upenski
Number of Brands: 1
Type of Packaging: Consumer, Private Label
Brands:
The Tea Spot

12739 **The Toasted Oat Bakehouse**
Columbus, OH
www.thetoastedoat.com
Gluten- and preservative-free all natural granola blends in various flavors
Founder: Erika Boll
Chief Financial Officer: Tom Kelley
Year Founded: 2013
Number of Brands: 1
Number of Products: 4
Type of Packaging: Consumer, Private Label
Brands:
The Toasted Oat

12740 **The Truffleist**
3146 45th St
Apt Basment
Astoria, NY 11103-1651
917-325-3374
jkunz@truffleist.com
www.truffleist.com
Truffle based oils, butters and mustards
President: Jimmy Kunz
Estimated Sales: Under $500,000
Number Employees: 1-4
Type of Packaging: Food Service
Brands:
The Truffliest

12741 **The Valpo Velvet Shoppe**
Downtown Valparaiso
55-57 W Monroe Street
Valparaiso, IN 46383
219-464-4141
Fax: 219-462-9785 www.valpovelvet.com
Ice cream, frozen yogurt and sherbet
President: Mike Brown
Treasurer: Elizabeth Brown
VP: Mark Brown
Secretary: Sue Cain
Estimated Sales: $810,000
Number Employees: 15
Square Footage: 6000
Parent Co: Valpo Velvet Ice Cream Company
Type of Packaging: Consumer, Food Service
Brands:
Valpo Velvet

12742 **The Van Cleve Seafood Company**
6910 Fox Ridge Rd.
Spotsylvania, VA 22551
800-628-5202
vancleveseafood.com
Crab pie
President & CEO: Monica Van Cleve-Talbert
Chief Financial Officer: Allie Cushing
Estimated Sales: $4-5 Million
Number Employees: 44
Type of Packaging: Food Service
Brands:
Girls With Crabs
Seafood Sisters
The Van Cleve Seafood Co.

12743 **The Veri Soda Company**
71 Fifth Ave.
4th Floor
New York, NY 10003-3004
203-409-3995
Manufacturer of organic sodas.
Founder: Leonard Freeke
Contact: Zeger Van Hcbvell
zeger@verisoda.com
Number Employees: 1-10

12744 **The Vine**
240 Main Street
PO Box 56
Manhasset, NY 11030-3928
516-365-8463
Fax: 516-869-0460 www.foodsofthevine.com
Marinara and salsa
Owner: Eve Durante
Co-Founder: Richard Mangione
Number Employees: 2-10
Brands:
The Vine

12745 **The Water Kefir People**
Bend, OR
www.thewaterkefirpeople.com
Small-batch crafted non-GMO and non-dairy water kefir beverages in various flavors
President/Owner: Crystal Bossola
Year Founded: 2014
Number of Brands: 1
Number of Products: 6
Type of Packaging: Consumer, Private Label
Brands:
The Water Kefir People

12746 **The Wine RayZyn Company**
3390 Mt Veeder Rd
Napa, CA 94558
707-251-1600
info@rayzyn.com
rayzyn.com
Wine grapes
Co-Founder: Andrew Cates
Estimated Sales: Under $500,000
Number Employees: 2-10
Brands:
CabernayZyn
ChardonayZyn
MerlayZyn

12747 **The Worlds Best Cheese**
111 Business Park Dr
Armonk, NY 10504
914-273-1400
Fax: 914-273-2052 800-922-4337
sales@wbcheese.com www.cheezwhse.com
Cheeses
Owner/President: Joseph Gellert
CEO: George Gellert
Marketing Director: Ellen Gellert
Sales Manager: Richard Rosenberg
Estimated Sales: $6.2 Million
Number Employees: 30
Other Locations:
Manufacturing Facility
Hauppauge NY

12748 **Theo Chocolate**
3400 Phinney Ave N
Seattle, WA 98103-8624
206-632-5100
Fax: 206-632-0413 info@theochocolate.com
www.theochocolate.com
Organic and Fair Trade bean-to-bar chocolate factory.
CEO: Joseph Whinney
jwhinney@theochocolate.com
CFO: Charles Horne
Vice President Sales and Marketing: Deborah Music
Number Employees: 50-99

12749 **Theriault's Abattoir Inc**
314 Hamlin Rd
Hamlin, ME 4785
207-868-3344
Fax: 207-868-2866
Meat products and hydrogenated fats
President: Reynold A Theriault
Estimated Sales: $36,000
Number Employees: 1-4
Type of Packaging: Consumer

12750 **Thermice Company**
1445 E Putnam Avenue
Old Greenwich, CT 06870-1379
203-637-4500
General grocery
President: Dave Herman
Estimated Sales: $.5-1 000,000
Number Employees: 5-9

12751 **Thermo Pac LLC**
1609 Stone Ridge Dr
Stone Mountain, GA 30083-1109
770-934-3200
www.thermopacllc.com
Wide range of thin-to-thick viscosity liquids including processed cheese sauces, tomato-based sauces and other savory or sweet sauces. Also peanut butter, in pouches, single serve cups and dried powder sticks.
Manager: Dave Barnes
Controller/Director: Leticia Simbach
IS Manager: Glenn Corbin
Administrative Assistant: Jean Williams
Plant Manager: John Stevens
Purchasing Manager: Buddy Wilson
Estimated Sales: $12.4 Million
Number Employees: 100-249
Square Footage: 120000
Parent Co: AmeriQual Group LLC
Type of Packaging: Consumer, Food Service, Private Label, Bulk

12752 **Thiel Cheese & Ingredients**
N7630 County Hwy BB
Attn: Kathy Pitzen
Hilbert, WI 54129
920-989-1440
Fax: 920-989-1288 kathyp@thielcheese.com
www.thielcheese.com
Manufacturer and custom formulator of processed cheeses that are used primarily as ingredients in other food products
President: Steven Thiel
Sales: Kathy Pitzen
Number Employees: 50-99
Type of Packaging: Consumer, Food Service, Private Label, Bulk
Brands:
Thiel

12753 **Think Jerky**
500 N Michigan Ave
Suite 600
Chicago, IL 60611-3754
312-380-0039
hello@thinkjerky.com
www.thinkjerky.com
Jerky: beef and turkey
Founder & CEO: Ricky Hirsch
Marketing Manager: S. Baer Lederman
Sales Manager: Lauren LeCoq
Chef: Gale Gand
Estimated Sales: $10 Million
Number Employees: 2-10
Brands:
Think Jerky(c)

12754 **Thinkthin, LLC**
Los Angeles, CA 90066
866-988-4465
customerservice@worldpantry.com
www.thinkproducts.com
Manufacturer of high protein snacks, smoothie mixes, and oatmeal.
Founder: Lizanne Falsetto
Brands:
thinkThin

12755 **Third Street Inc**
408 S Pierce Ave
Louisville, CO 80027-3018
303-527-1700
800-636-3790
info@3rdstreetchai.com www.thirdstreetchai.com
Bottled chai, lemonade, and iced tea.
Contact: Lisa Ginsberg
lisa@takethirdstreet.com
Number Employees: 5-9
Type of Packaging: Consumer

12756 **Thirs-Tea Corp**
4611 N Dixie Hwy
Boca Raton, FL 33431-5030
561-948-5600
info@thirs-tea.com
www.thirs-tea.com
Processor of tea beverages amd concentrates.
President: Ray Welch
Year Founded: 1977
Estimated Sales: $500,000-$1 Million
Number Employees: 11-50
Type of Packaging: Consumer, Food Service, Private Label, Bulk
Brands:
Thirs-Tea

12757 **This Bar Saves Lives, LLC**
Culver City, CA
310-730-5060
hello@thisbarsaveslives.com
www.thisbarsaveslives.com
Non-GMO, gluten-free healthy snack bar; with every purchase, the company gives food aid to a child in need from Haiti, the Democratic Republic of the Congo, Guatemala, South Sudan, the Philippines and/or Mexico
Co-Founder: Ryan Devlin
Co-Founder: Todd Grinnell
Co-Founder: Ravi Patel
Year Founded: 2013
Number of Brands: 1
Number of Products: 6
Type of Packaging: Consumer, Private Label
Brands:
This Bar Saves Lives

12758 **Thistledew Farm**
Rr 1 Box 122
Proctor, WV 26055-9608
304-455-1728
Fax: 304-455-1740 800-854-6639
www.thistledewfarm.com
Honey, hot pepper butter, hot honey mustard, wild wing and rib sauce, garden gourmet salad dressing, original honey mustard, red raspberry, and red raspberry honey vinegar, candles, cosmetics, gift boxes and crates, baskets, and othergreat products.
President: Ellie Conlon
CEO: S Conlon
Estimated Sales: $200,000
Number Employees: 1-4
Number of Brands: 2
Number of Products: 7
Square Footage: 20000
Type of Packaging: Consumer, Food Service, Private Label, Bulk
Brands:
Thistledew Farm's
West's Best

12759 **Tholstrup Cheese**
6366 Norton Center Dr
Muskegon, MI 49441-6032
231-798-4371
Fax: 231-798-4374 800-426-0938
Cheese
Manager: Torben Siggaard
VP: Hans Lund
Vice President: Vincent Staiger
Plant Manager: Ernst Siggaard
Estimated Sales: $500,000 appx.
Number Employees: 20-49
Brands:
Saga

12760 **Thoma Vineyards**
11975 Smithfield Rd
Dallas, OR 97338-9339
503-623-6420
Fax: 503-623-4310 800-884-1927
www.vanduzer.com
Wines
Manager: Jim Kakacek
Operations Manager: Marilynn Thoma
Estimated Sales: $300,000-500,000
Number Employees: 5-9

12761 **Thomas Brothers CountryHam**
1852 Gold Hill Rd
Asheboro, NC 27203-4291
336-672-0337
Fax: 336-672-1782 www.thomasbrothersham.com
Processor and packer of country hams; wholesaler/distributor of frozen and specialty foods and meats; serving the food service and retail markets in the southeast
President/CFO: Howard M Thomas
frank@thomasbrothersham.com
Quality Control: Don Thomas
Sales/Plant Manager: Don Thomas
Plant Manager: Don Thomas
Estimated Sales: $10-20 Million
Number Employees: 20-49
Number of Brands: 10
Number of Products: 300
Type of Packaging: Consumer, Private Label
Brands:
Farmer Dons Country Ham
Private Labels
Thomas Brothers Country Ham

12762 **Thomas Canning/Maidstone**
Rural Route 1
Maidstone, ON N0R-1K0
Canada
519-737-1531
Fax: 519-737-7003
Processor and canner of tomatoes and tomato juice
President: Bill Thomas
Type of Packaging: Food Service, Private Label
Brands:
Utopia

12763 **Thomas Dairy**
2096 US Route 7 N
Rutland, VT 05701-8701
802-773-6788
Fax: 802-747-7121 sales@thomasdairy.com
www.thomasdairy.com
Fluid milk
President: Richard Thomas
thomasdairy@aol.com
Founder: Orin Thomas
Marketing Director: John Thomas
Estimated Sales: $5-10 Million
Number Employees: 20-49
Brands:
Thomas

12764 **Thomas Fogarty Winery**
19501 Skyline Blvd
Woodside, CA 94062
650-851-6777
Fax: 650-851-5840 800-247-4163
info@fogartywinery.com www.fogartywinery.com
Wines
Director of Sales and Marketing: Anne Krolczyk
anne@fogartywinery.com
Winemaker: Michael Martella
Director of Sales and Marketing: Anne Krolczyk
Office Administrator: Melissa Baker
Tasting Room Manager: Rick Davis
Assistant Winemaker: Nathan Kandler
Accounting Manager: Carrie Larkin
Events Coordinator: Dana Miller
Events Coordinator: Becky Thatcher
Estimated Sales: Below $5 Million
Number Employees: 10-19
Brands:
Thomas Fogarty Winery

12765 **Thomas Gourmet Foods**
P.O.Box 8822
Greensboro, NC 27419-0822
336-299-6263
Fax: 336-299-7852 800-867-2823
info@thomasgourmetfoods.com
www.thomasgourmetfoods.com
Sauce, marinade, dressing, cocktail sauce, tartar sauce, Bloody Mary mix, marinara and pasta sauce
Owner: Dwight Thomas
CEO: Brian Thomas
Estimated Sales: $3-5 Million
Number Employees: 5-9
Number of Brands: 1
Type of Packaging: Consumer, Private Label, Bulk
Brands:
Thomas

12766 **Thomas Kemper Soda Company**
6500 River Place Boulevard Building 1
Suite 450
Austin, TX 78730
206-381-8712
host@tksoda.com
Beverages
President: Thomas Kemper
Chairman: Laura Bracken-Clough
President: T Maxwell Clough
Estimated Sales: $5-10 Million
Number Employees: 1
Brands:
Thomas Kemper Birch Soda
Thomas Kemper Cola
Thomas Kemper Cream

12767 **Thomas Kruse Winery**
3200 Dryden Avenue
Gilroy, CA 95020
408-842-7016
Fax: 408-842-7016 krusewine@aol.com
Manufacture of wine
President/CEO: Thomas Kruse
Marketing Director: Thomas Kruse
Contact: Karen Kruse
karenjkruse@aol.com
Estimated Sales: Below $5 Million
Number Employees: 1-4
Brands:
Thomas Kruse Winey

12768 **Thomas Lobster Co**
45 Bar Rd
Little Cranberry Island
Islesford, ME 4646
207-244-5876
Fax: 808-244-7020 David@thomaslobster.com
Lobster
President: David Thomas
david@thomaslobster.com
Number Employees: 1-4

12769 **Thomas Packing Company**
4643 Farley Dr
Columbus, GA 31907-6342
706-689-3513
Fax: 770-227-2166 800-729-0976
jon@crouch.com
Processor and packer of meat products including cured ham, bacon, smoked, andouille and frankfurters; also, smoked turkeys and hams for holiday gift boxes
President: Lee Thomas
CEO: Billy Thomas
Estimated Sales: $.5-1 million
Number Employees: 5-9
Square Footage: 104000
Type of Packaging: Consumer, Food Service, Bulk
Brands:
Thomas
Treasure

12770 **Thompson Packers**
550 Carnation St
Slidell, LA 70460-1899
985-641-6640
Fax: 985-645-2112 800-989-6328
Began in 1953. Manufacturer and exporter of frozen beef, pork, veal and lamb; processor of frozen ground beef and hamburger patties.
Owner: Mary Thompson
thompson@thompack.com
Estimated Sales: $21 Million
Number Employees: 10-19
Square Footage: 50000
Type of Packaging: Consumer, Food Service, Private Label

12771 **Thompson Seafood**
66 Franklin St
PO Box 1057
Darien, GA 31305
912-437-4649
Shrimp, trout and flounder
Owner: Glenn Young
Estimated Sales: $575,000
Number Employees: 1-4
Type of Packaging: Food Service, Bulk

12772 **Thompson's Fine Foods**
5973 Pheasant Dr
Shoreview, MN 55126
651-481-0374
Fax: 651-482-1944 800-807-0025
muclijoh@msn.com
Mild/sweet, medium/spicy, hot/spicy and hot/hot barbecue dipping sauces for meats, sandwiches and appetizers
Owner/President: John Thompson
muclijoh@msn.com
Estimated Sales: Under $500,000
Number Employees: 1-4
Type of Packaging: Consumer, Food Service, Private Label, Bulk
Brands:
Thompson's Black Tie

12773 **Thomson Meats**
618 Hamilton Avenue W
Melfort, SK S0E 1A0
Canada
306-752-2802
Fax: 306-752-4674
Value added meat products including fresh and frozen pork, beef and chicken
CEO: Paul Marciniak
CFO: Wendy Welsch
R&D: Daryl Durell
Marketing: Donna Walton
Sales: Ron Andrujek
Plant Manager: Gerard Kiefe
Number Employees: 42
Square Footage: 120000
Type of Packaging: Private Label, Bulk

12774 **Thor Inc**
1280 W 2550 S
Ogden, UT 84401-3238
801-393-3312
Fax: 801-621-3298 888-846-7462
Custom formulating and contract packaging for vitamins and supplements in liquids, capsules and powders
Owner: Whittle Allen
whittle.allen@thor.com

Estimated Sales: $10-20 Million
Number Employees: 10-19
Type of Packaging: Private Label

12775 **Thor-Shackel Horseradish Company**
Po Box 360
2424 Alpine Road
Eau Claire, WI 54702-0360
800-826-7322
Fax: 715-832-9915 www.silverspringfoods.com
Fresh grated horseradish and sauces including cocktail, horseradish, etc
General Manager: Michael Dogan
General Manager: Joe Dogan
Estimated Sales: $3-5 Million
Number Employees: 10-19
Square Footage: 120000
Type of Packaging: Consumer, Food Service, Private Label, Bulk
Brands:
Thor's

12776 **Thornton Foods Company**
8590 Magnolia Trail
Suite 121
Eden Prairie, MN 55344
952-944-1735
Fax: 952-944-2083 thorntonfoods@aol.com
Low-fat and fat-free dairy based food products including pasta and cheese sauces
President/CEO: Barbara Thornton
Partner: John Lindahl
Estimated Sales: Under $500,000
Number Employees: 1-4
Type of Packaging: Consumer, Food Service, Private Label, Bulk
Brands:
Living Light
Living Light Dairy Blend

12777 **Thornton Winery**
32575 Rancho California Road
Temecula, CA 92589-9008
951-699-0099
Fax: 951-699-5536 info@thorntonwine.com
www.thorntonwine.com
Wines, champagne
President: John Thornton
Co-Owner: Steve Thornton
CFO: Tim Kelly
Quality Control: Cheryl Rolph
Public Relations Manager: Jan Schneider
Production Manager: Jon McPherson
Estimated Sales: $5-10 Million
Number Employees: 50-99
Brands:
Thornton

12778 **Thorpe Vineyard**
8150 Chimney Heights Blvd
Wolcott, NY 14590-9201
315-594-2502
Fax: 315-594-2502 info@thorpevineyard.com
www.thorpevineyard.com
Wine
President: Fumie Thorpe
Estimated Sales: Less Than $500,000
Number Employees: 1-4
Type of Packaging: Private Label
Brands:
Thorpe Vineyard

12779 **Thoughtful Food**
Lafayette, CA
510-910-2581
www.thoughtfulfood.net
Organic, gluten-free, dairy-free and vegan snack mix and granola
Founder/CEO: Jennifer Bielawski
Year Founded: 2009
Number of Brands: 2
Number of Products: 7
Type of Packaging: Consumer, Private Label
Brands:
Nosh Organic
Giddy Up & Go

12780 **Three Acre Kitchen**
154 Farrington Corner Road
Hopkinton, NH 03229
603-223-5985
Fax: 603-223-5985
Balsamic salad dressing and sauces
Contact: Nancy Brown
nancyspecialtyfoods@comcast.net

12781 **Three Bakers Gluten Free Bakery**
360 J & J Road
Moscow, PA 18444
570-689-9694
contact@threebakers.net
threebakers.com
Gluten free products: breads, rolls, pizzas

12782 **Three Jerks Jerky**
515 Spoleto Dr
Pacific Palisades, CA 90272-4517
424-703-5375
info@threejerksjerky.com
www.threejerksjerky.com
Filet Mignon beef jerky
Co-Founder: Jordan Barrocas
Co-Founder: Daniel Fogelson
Estimated Sales: $4.5 Million
Number Employees: 52
Brands:
Three Jerks

12783 **Three Lakes Winery**
6971 Gogebic St
Three Lakes, WI 54562-9058
715-546-3080
Fax: 715-546-8148 800-944-5434
www.tlwinery.com
Wine including cranberry, apricot, cranberry/apple, cranberry/raspberry, blackberry, strawberry, wild plum, strawberry-rhubarb, red raspberry, rhubarb, Italian plum and kiwi
President: Mark Mc Cain
info@fruitwine.com
Advertising/Marketing: Marla Shane
Sales/Distribution: Mark McCain
Wine Maker: Scott McCain
Production Manager: Scott Foster
Estimated Sales: $720000
Number Employees: 5-9
Square Footage: 16000
Type of Packaging: Consumer
Brands:
Fruit of the Woods

12784 **Three Meadows Spirits LLC**
139 Coleman Station Rd.
Millerton, NY 12546
845-702-3903
peonyvodka@gmail.com
www.peonyvodka.com
Five-times distilled vodka infused with botanicals
Founder/Principal: Leslie Farhangi
Year Founded: 2016
Number of Brands: 1
Number of Products: 1
Type of Packaging: Consumer, Private Label
Brands:
Peony Vodka

12785 **Three Rivers Fish Company**
168 Riverfront Drive
Simmesport, LA 71369-0668
318-941-2467
Fax: 318-941-2467
Fresh and frozen seafood/fish
Owner: William Arnouville
Estimated Sales: $730,000
Number Employees: 1-4

12786 **Three Springs Farm**
1367 Highway 32A
Oaks, OK 74359
918-868-5450
Fax: 804-574-7248
Processor and contract packager of garlic seed and elephant garlic cloves
Owner: Garrett Doering
Number Employees: 5-9
Type of Packaging: Consumer, Private Label, Bulk

12787 **Three Trees Almondmilk**
San Mateo, CA
855-863-8733
contact@threetrees.com www.threetrees.com
Organic, additive-free almond milk in unsweetened and vanilla varieties
Co-Founder: Jenny Eu
Number of Brands: 1
Number of Products: 2
Type of Packaging: Consumer, Private Label
Brands:
Three Trees

12788 **Three Twins Ice Cream**
419 1st St.
Petaluma, CA 94952
707-763-8946
www.threetwinsicecream.com
Ice cream, ice cream cones, and ice cream sandwiches.
Founder and CEO: Neal Gottlieb
VP: Scott Sowry
Chief Sales and Marketing Officer: Sarah Bird
Director of Operations: Matt Grebil
Plant Manager: Todd Pimentel

12789 **ThreeWorks Snacks**
259 Niagara St., ON M6J 2L7
Canada
hello@threeworks.ca
www.threeworks.ca
Gluten-free, non-GMO, nut-free, no sugar added dehydrated apple chips in various flavors
Founder/CEO: Michael Petcherski
Year Founded: 2016
Number of Brands: 1
Number of Products: 6
Type of Packaging: Consumer, Private Label
Brands:
ThreeWorks

12790 **Thrive Farmers**
215 Hembree Park Drive
Suite 100
Roswell, GA 30076
855-553-2763
Fax: 855-872-8475 connect@thrivefarmers.com
www.thrivefarmers.com
Farmers of coffee beans and tea leafs
Founder & CEO: Michael Jones
Founder & Chief Sustainability Officer: Kenneth Lander
President: Tom Matthesen
Chief Operating Officer: Bart Newman
Chief Origin Officer: Edgar Cabrera Cozza
Year Founded: 2011
Number Employees: 11-50

12791 **(HQ)Thumann Inc.**
670 Dell Rd
Carlstadt, NJ 07072
201-935-3636
Fax: 201-935-2226
customer.service@thumanns.com
www.thumanns.com
Ham, roast beef, corned beef, pastrami, turkey, liverwurst, bologna, hot dogs, breakfast meats and sausages, cheeses, soups, salads, condiments and frozen products
Owner: Robert Burke
Product Manager: John Zelekowski
Year Founded: 1949
Estimated Sales: $50 Million
Number Employees: 200
Square Footage: 130000
Brands:
Thumann's

12792 **Thunderbird Real Food Bar**
1101-West 34th St. # 229
Austin, TX 78705
512-383-8334
support@thunderbirdbar.com
www.thunderbirdbar.com
Gluten-free, non-GMO, vegan, no-sugar-added fruit and nut snack bars in various flavors
Chief Executive Officer: Mike Elhaj
Number of Brands: 1
Number of Products: 14
Type of Packaging: Consumer, Private Label
Brands:
Thunderbird

12793 **Thyme & Truffles Hors d'Oeuvres**
51 Kesmark
Dollard-Des-Ormeaux, QC H9B 3J1
Canada
514-685-9955
Fax: 514-685-2602 877-785-9759
www.thymeandtruffles.com
Frozen oven-ready hors d'oeuvres with assorted fillings including canapes; also, frozen vegetarian entrees

President: Rhonda Richer
QA/QC Specialist: Santi Vicente
Sales Manager: Tim Lipa
Director of Operations: Gino Giansante
Production Manager: Alfred Meth
Number Employees: 50-99
Number of Products: 40
Square Footage: 50000
Type of Packaging: Food Service, Private Label, Bulk
Brands:
Thyme & Truffles

12794 **Thyme Garden Herb Co**
20546 Alsea Hwy
Alsea, OR 97324-9714
541-487-8671
Fax: 817-558-3570 800-482-4372
herbs@thymegarden.com www.thymegarden.com
Biscotti, teas and herbal vinegars and oils
Owner: Rolfe Hagen
herbs@thymegarden.com
CEO: Mary Doebbeling
Estimated Sales: Less Than $500,000
Number Employees: 1-4
Square Footage: 2000
Type of Packaging: Consumer, Food Service, Private Label, Bulk
Brands:
Our Thyme Garden

12795 **Thymly Products Inc**
1332 Colora Rd
Colora, MD 21917-1422
410-658-4826
Fax: 410-658-4824 877-710-2340
Manufacturer of dry food ingredients.
President: Trey Muller-Thym
CEO: Harry Muller-Thym
hmuller@thymlyproducts.com
Number Employees: 10-19
Type of Packaging: Private Label
Brands:
Baker's Cremes
Bread Glaze
Brew Buffers
Glalcto
Parve Plain Muffin

12796 **Tichon Sea Food Corp**
7 Conway St
New Bedford, MA 02740-7287
508-999-5607
Fax: 508-990-8271 info@tichonseafood.com
www.tichonseafood.com
Fresh and frozen fish including squid, scallops and fish sticks
President: Paul Saunders
paul@tichonseafood.com
VP: R Tichon
Executive VP: Ronald Tichon
Estimated Sales: $1,200,000
Number Employees: 20-49
Square Footage: 180000
Type of Packaging: Consumer
Brands:
Tichon

12797 **Tideland Seafood Company**
PO Box 99
Dulac, LA 70353
985-563-4516
Fax: 985-563-4296
Prepared fresh shrimp; fish & seafood canning and curing.
President: Judith Gibson
Estimated Sales: $5-10 Million
Number Employees: 5-9

12798 **(HQ)Tierra Farm**
2424 NY-203
Valatie, NY 12184
519-392-8300
Fax: 518-392-8304 info@tierrafarm.com
www.tierrafarm.com
Organic and gluten-free nut butters and nuts, raw and roasted seeds, dried fruit mixes, granolas, chocolate snacks and fair-trade coffee beans
Founder/President: Gunther Fishgold
Chief Executive Officer: Todd Kletter
Year Founded: 1999
Number of Brands: 1
Type of Packaging: Consumer, Private Label, Bulk
Brands:
Tierra Farm

12799 **Tiesta Tea**
213 West Institute Place # 310
Chicago, IL 60610
312-202-6800
customerservice@tiestatea.com
www.tiestatea.com
Loose leaf tea blends in various flavors; cold brew bottled tea
Co-Founder: Patrick Tannous
Co-Founder/Chief Executive Officer: Dan Klein
Year Founded: 2010
Number of Brands: 1
Number of Products: 50
Type of Packaging: Consumer, Private Label
Brands:
Tiesta Tea

12800 **Tiger Meat & Provisions**
1445 NW 22nd St
Miami, FL 33142-7741
305-324-0083
Fax: 305-324-1570
Packer of fresh pork
President: Jose Requejo
tiger_meat@bellsouth.net
Estimated Sales: $10-20 Million
Number Employees: 20-49
Type of Packaging: Food Service
Brands:
Tiger

12801 **Tiger Mushroom Farm**
PO Box 909
Nanton, AB T0L 1R0
Canada
403-646-2578
Fax: 403-646-2240
Mushrooms
President: Tiger Goto
Operations Manager: Jack Trinn
Estimated Sales: C
Number Employees: 20-49
Square Footage: 66000
Type of Packaging: Consumer, Food Service
Brands:
Tiger

12802 **Tigo+**
786-207-4772
info@tigosportsdrink.com
www.tigosportsdrink.com
Sports drink made with coconut water and amino acids, sweetened with Stevia; various flavors
Number of Brands: 1
Number of Products: 5
Type of Packaging: Consumer, Private Label
Brands:
Tigo+

12803 **Tillamook Country Smoker**
8335 North Hwy. 101
Bay City, OR 97107
www.tcsjerky.com
Beef jerky, steak cuts, nuggets, jerky sticks and other snacks
Co-Founder: Dick Crossley
Year Founded: 1975
Number of Brands: 1
Type of Packaging: Consumer, Private Label
Brands:
Tillamook Country Smoker

12804 **Tillamook County Creamery Association**
Tillamook, OR
503-842-4481
Fax: 503-842-6039 www.tillamook.com
Dairy butter, cheese, nonhygroscopic cheddar cheese whey powder and ice cream; exporter of dried whey, sour cream, yogurt, fluid milk.
Chief Executive Officer: Patrick Criteser
Chief Financial Officer: Linda Pearce
Director of R&D: Jill Allen
Vice President Sales & Marketing: Jay Allison
Plant & Facilities Manager: Rich Snyder
Year Founded: 1909
Estimated Sales: $49.4 Million
Number Employees: 250-499
Square Footage: 30000
Type of Packaging: Consumer, Food Service, Private Label, Bulk
Brands:
Tillamook

12805 **Tillamook Meat Inc**
405 Park Ave
Tillamook, OR 97141-2524
503-842-4802
Fax: 508-342-2330 www.tillamookmeat.com
Meat products including beef, lamb, pork and poultry, jerky
President/Co-Owner: Laurel Travis
VP/Co-Owner: Mark Travis
Estimated Sales: Less Than $500,000
Number Employees: 1-4
Type of Packaging: Consumer, Food Service, Bulk

12806 **(HQ)Tiller Foods Company**
967 Senate Dr
Dayton, OH 45459-4017
937-435-4601
Fax: 937-435-1408
Portion controlled dairy products including sour cream, half and half, nondairy creamers, whipped cream and toppings
President: Donald Tiller Jr
Sales Manager: David Yost
Estimated Sales: $5-10 Million
Number Employees: 5-9
Type of Packaging: Consumer, Food Service, Private Label, Bulk
Other Locations:
Tiller Foods Co.
Tampa FL

12807 **Tillie's Gourmet**
173 Ash Way
Doylestown, PA 18901
215-272-8326
Fax: 215-348-2192
Dressings, marinades and blue crab salsas

12808 **Tim's Cascade Snacks**
PO Box 2302
Auburn, WA 98071-2302
253-833-2986
Fax: 253-939-9411 800-533-8467
consumer_affairs@timschips.com
www.timschips.com
Snacks including original potato chips, jalapeno, sour cream and onion, cheddar. sea salt, dill picklie, onion ring chips, and popcorn.
President: Dennis M Mullen
COO: Jeff Leichleiter
Sales/Marketing Executive: George Masiello
Year Founded: 1986
Estimated Sales: $20-50 Million
Number Employees: 50-99
Square Footage: 130000
Parent Co: Agrilink Foods
Type of Packaging: Consumer, Food Service, Private Label

12809 **Timber Crest Farms**
4791 Dry Creek Rd
Healdsburg, CA 95448-9739
707-433-8251
Fax: 707-433-8255 888-766-4233
www.timbercrest.com
Organic and preservative free dried fruits, nuts, tomatoes and specialty food products
Co-Owner: Ronald Waltenspiel
Co-Owner: Ruth Waltenspiel
Public Relations: Ruth Waltenspiel
Estimated Sales: $4.5 Million
Number Employees: 250-499
Number of Brands: 2
Number of Products: 50
Square Footage: 120000
Type of Packaging: Consumer, Food Service, Private Label, Bulk
Brands:
Sonoma
Timber Crest Farm

12810 **Timber Lake Cheese Company**
PO Box A
Timber Lake, SD 57656
605-865-3605
Fax: 605-865-3605
Cheese
President: Virgil Johnson
Estimated Sales: Less than $500,000
Number Employees: 1-4

12811 Timber Peaks Gourmet
6180 Hollowview Ct
Parker, CO 80134-5808
303-841-8847
Fax: 303-805-0174 800-982-7687
www.timberpeaksgourmet.com
Cocoa, bean soups, dessert mixes, bread mixes, trail mixes, and dried salsa
President: Laurie Yankoski
laurie.yankoski@timberpeaksgourmet.com
Estimated Sales: Less Than $500,000
Number Employees: 1-4
Number of Brands: 1
Number of Products: 41
Square Footage: 6000
Type of Packaging: Consumer, Bulk
Brands:
Mud
Mountain House Kitchen

12812 Timeless Seeds
48 Ulm-Vaughn Rd
P.O. Box 331
Ulm, MT 59485
406-866-3340
Fax: 406-866-3341 orders@timelessfood.com
www.timelessfood.com
Organic lentils, peas, chickpeas, and heirloom grains
Founder/CEO: David Oien
Accounts: Heather Hadley
General Manager: Matthew Leardini
Year Founded: 1987
Number Employees: 10-19

12813 Tin Star Foods
Austin, TX
info@tinstarfoods.com
www.tinstarfoods.com
Grassfed cultured ghee; lactose- and casein-free
Founder/Chief Executive Officer: Hima Pal
Year Founded: 2014
Number Employees: 2-10
Number of Brands: 1
Number of Products: 1
Type of Packaging: Consumer, Private Label
Brands:
Tin Star Foods

12814 Tin Whistle Brewing Co
954 Eckhardt Ave W
Penticton, BC V2A 2C1
Canada
250-770-1122
Fax: 250-770-1122
Ale
President: Lorraine Nagy
Number Employees: 5-9
Type of Packaging: Consumer, Food Service
Brands:
Black Widow
Coyote
Ratle Snack

12815 Tincture Distillers
5521 27Th St N
Arlington, VA 22207-1773
888-658-6899
info@elementshrub.com
www.elementshrub.com
Shrub sodas
CEO & Founder: Charlie Berkinshaw
Estimated Sales: Under $500,000
Number Employees: 1-4
Brands:
Element Shrub

12816 Tinkyada
120 Melford Drive, Unit 8
Scarborough
Ontario, Ca M1B 2X5
416-609-0016
Fax: 416-609-1316 iris@tinkyada.com
www.tinkyada.com
Herbs

12817 Tiny But Mighty Popcorn
3282 62nd St
Shellsburg, IA 52332
800-330-4692
connect@tinybutmightyfoods.com
tinybutmightyfoods.com
Popcorn
Owner: Gene Mealhow
Chief Marketing Officer: Linda Rosenberg
Sales Manager: LeeAnn Stevens
Operations: Lynn Mealhow
Production Manager: Mark Kluber
Estimated Sales: $4.3 Million
Number Employees: 49
Brands:
Tiny But Mighty Popcorn

12818 Tiny Hero Foods
200 Kansas St. # 205
San Francisco, CA 94103
855-778-4662
www.tinyherofoods.com
Golden quinoa, quinoa and rice blends, quinoa side dishes, quinoa macaroni and cheese dish, quinoa breakfast packs
Chief Executive Officer: Aaron Jackson
Director, Marketing: Christine Lee
Year Founded: 2016
Number Employees: 2-10
Number of Brands: 1
Type of Packaging: Consumer, Private Label
Brands:
The Tiny Hero

12819 Tio Gazpacho
115 W 18th Street
2nd Fl
New York, NY 10011
917-946-1160
hola@tiogazpacho.com
www.tiogazpacho.com
Vegan soup
Founder: Austin Allan
Production Manager: Pearl Wong
Number Employees: 2-10
Brands:
tio gazpacho

12820 Tip Top Canning Co
505 S 2nd St
Tipp City, OH 45371-1753
937-667-3713
Fax: 937-667-3802 800-352-2635
info@tiptopcanning.com www.tiptopcanning.com
Producers of tomatoes and tomato products.
President: Randy Allen
rallen@tiptopcanning.com
Vice President: Scott Timmer
Sales Manager: Cynthia Timmer
Production Manager: Matt Timmer
Estimated Sales: $10-20 Million
Number Employees: 20-49
Number of Products: 60
Square Footage: 450000
Type of Packaging: Consumer, Food Service, Private Label, Bulk

12821 Tip Top Poultry Inc
327 Wallace Rd
Marietta, GA 30062-3573
770-973-8070
Fax: 770-973-6897 800-241-5230
www.tiptoppoultry.com
Processor and exporter of poultry
President: Evelyn Delong
evelyn.delong@regalpoultry.com
COO: Mike Brooks
CFO: Charlie Singleton
VP: Lee Bates
VP/Sales: Brian Tucker
Technical VP: Mitch Forstie
Production Manager: Steve Moore
Estimated Sales: $15 Million
Number Employees: 1000-4999
Type of Packaging: Consumer, Bulk

12822 Tipiak Inc
45 Church St
Suite 303
Stamford, CT 06906-1733
203-961-9117
Fax: 203-975-9081 sales@tipiak-e.com
www.tipiak.com
Specialty rices and beans, tapioca flour and pearls, frozen appetizers and desserts.
President: Laurent Chery
laurent.chery@tipiak-e.com
VP: Laurent Chery
Estimated Sales: Below $5 Million
Number Employees: 5-9

12823 Tipp Distributors Inc
500 W Overland Ave # 300
#300
El Paso, TX 79901-1086
915-594-1618
Fax: 915-590-1225 888-668-2639
Condiments and relishes
President: Ramon Carrasco
CEO: Luis Fernandez
consumer.relations@novamex.com
CFO: Thomas Deleon
Executive VP: Sanford Gross
Estimated Sales: $1-2.5 Million
Number Employees: 100-249
Brands:
Chata
Cholula
D'Gari
Ibarra
Jarritos
Mineragua
Rogelio Bueno
San Marcos
Sangria Seorial
Sidral Mundet
Tuny

12824 Tirawisu
13705 Ventura Blvd
Sherman Oaks, CA 91423-3023
818-906-2640
Fax: 516-599-6540
Exporter and processor of Italian desserts including chocolate mousse, tiramisu, gelato, tartufo, tortoni and spumoni; importer of Italian cakes and pasta
Owner/President: Aldo Antonoacci
Contact: Peter Kastelan
peter@il-tiramisu.com
Estimated Sales: Less Than $500,000
Number Employees: 5-9

12825 Titan Farms
5 RW DuBose Rd.
Ridge Spring, SC 29129
803-685-5381
Fax: 803-685-5885 www.titanfarms.com
Grower of peaches, bell peppers, and broccoli.
President & CEO: Chalmers Carr, III
VP & Administrative Manager: Lori Anne Carr
VP, Sales & Marketing: Daryl Johnston
VP, Operations: Jason Rodgers
Production Manager: Dwight Harmon
Year Founded: 1999
Type of Packaging: Consumer, Private Label

12826 Titusville Dairy Products Co
217 S Washington St
Titusville, PA 16354-1660
814-827-1833
Fax: 814-827-2510 800-352-0101
www.titusvilledairy.com
Ice cream mixes, dairy products, juices, fruit drinks and bottled water
President: Charles Turner Jr
VP: William Schneider Jr
Manager: Ralph Kerr
rktdpc@zoominternet.net
Plant Manager: Chester Anthony
Estimated Sales: $4 Million
Number Employees: 20-49
Square Footage: 120000
Type of Packaging: Consumer, Private Label
Brands:
Blossom Time
Natural Harvest
Titusville Dairy Products

12827 Tkc Vineyards
11001 Valley Dr
Plymouth, CA 95669
209-245-6428
Fax: 209-245-4006 888-627-2356
www.tkcvineyards.com
Family winery committed to the production of premium wines. Specialties include Zinfandel, Mourvedre and Cabernet
Owner/CEO: Harold Nuffer
VP/CFO: Monica Nuffer
Marketing Director: Monica Nuffer
Estimated Sales: Less Than $500,000
Number Employees: 1-4
Type of Packaging: Private Label
Brands:
Tkc Vineyards

12828 **To Market To Market**
200 12th St SW # 130
Suite 130
Loveland, CO 80537-6393
970-278-1000
Fax: 503-655-3390 kathy@tomarket-tomarket.com
tomarket-tomarket.com
Natural spice blends
President: Kent Heusinkveld
kent@tomarket-tomarket.com
Estimated Sales: Less Than $500,000
Number Employees: 5-9
Type of Packaging: Consumer, Food Service

12829 **To Your Health Sprouted Flour Co., Inc.**
PO Box 898
Floyd, VA 24091
540-283-9589
customerservice@bluemountainorganics.com
www.organicsproutedflour.com
Manufacturer of seeds and nuts, nut butters, frozen desserts, grains, dired fruits, and granola.
CEO: Jeff Sutton

12830 **Todd's**
PO Box 4821
Des Moines, IA 50305
515-266-2276
Fax: 515-266-1669 800-247-5363
Variety of food products, wet and dry, kosher and organic certified.
President/CEO: Alan Niedermeier
Quality Control: Diana Burzloff
Public Relations: Alissa Douglas
Operations: Duane Hettkamp
Production: Jeff Sullivan
Plant Manager: John Routh
Purchasing: Danielle Robinson
Estimated Sales: $1-3 Million
Number Employees: 30
Number of Brands: 40
Number of Products: 200
Square Footage: 320000
Type of Packaging: Consumer, Food Service, Private Label, Bulk
Brands:
Butcher's Friend
Papa Joe's Specialty Food

12831 **Todd's**
6055 Malburg Way
Vernon, CA 90058
323-585-5900
Fax: 323-585-5900 800-938-6337
Processor, importer and exporter of nuts and nut meats, dried fruit, trail mixes, candy, etc
President: Todd Levin
Estimated Sales: $5-10 Million
Number Employees: 5-9
Type of Packaging: Consumer, Food Service, Private Label, Bulk
Brands:
Dr Jerkyll & Mr Hide
Huckleberry's Farm
Just Snak-It
Lucy's Sweets
Todd's Treats

12832 **Todd's Salsa**
PO Box 7045
Bangor, ME 04402
844-328-7257
info@toddssalsa.com
www.toddsoriginalsalsa.com
Salsa
Owner: Todd Simcox
Type of Packaging: Food Service, Private Label
Brands:
Inner Beauty Hot Sauce
Todd's Salsa

12833 **(HQ)Toddy Products Inc**
803 W Kansas Ave
Midland, TX 79701-6121
713-225-2066
Fax: 713-225-2110 www.toddycafe.com
Processor and exporter of liquid concentrates including coffee, tea, mocha, chai, etc.; also, espresso pecan brittle; manufacturer of cold brew coffee makers
Owner: Strother Simpson
Vice President: Scott Schroer
Contact: Kathy Kat
kkat@toddycafe.com
Estimated Sales: $1500000
Number Employees: 5-9
Square Footage: 80000
Type of Packaging: Consumer, Food Service, Private Label, Bulk
Brands:
Toddy
Toddy Cappuccino
Toddy Coffee Crunch
Toddy Coffee Maker
Toddy Gourmet Iced Tea Concentrate
Toddy Mocha

12834 **Todhunter Foods**
222 Lakeview Avenue
Suite 1500
West Palm Beach, FL 33401-6174
561-655-8977
Fax: 561-655-9718 800-336-9463
www.todhunter.com
Cooking wines, powdered wine flavors, denatures spirits, vinegar and wine reductions.
President: Jay Maltby
CFO: Ezra Shashoua
Vice President: D Chris Mitchell
Sales Director: Jim Polansky
Plant Manager: Ousik Yu
Purchasing Manager: Frank Dibling
Number Employees: 410
Parent Co: Todhunter International
Type of Packaging: Consumer, Food Service, Private Label, Bulk

12835 **Todhunter Foods**
PO Box 1447
Lake Alfred, FL 33850-1447
863-956-1116
Fax: 863-956-3979 www.todhunter.com
Vinegar and cooking wine; contract packager of fruit juices and carbonated/flavored beverages; importer of alcoholic beverages and juice concentrates; exporter of alcoholic beverages and vinegar
President: Jay Maltby
Number Employees: 100-249
Square Footage: 1800000
Parent Co: Todhunter International
Type of Packaging: Consumer, Food Service, Private Label, Bulk

12836 **Toe-Food Chocolates and Candy**
2500 Milvia Street
Suite 216
Berkeley, CA 94704-2636
510-649-9250
Fax: 510-849-3810 888-863-3663
www.toefood.com
Chocolate and candy in the shape of feet.
Founder/CEO: Mark Wolpa
Estimated Sales: $300,000-500,000
Number Employees: 8
Brands:
Toe-Rific Candy

12837 **Toffee Boutique**
11353 Pyrites Way
Suite 16
Rancho Cordova, CA 95670-4454
916-638-8462
www.toffeeboutique.com
Manufacturer of toffee.
Founder: Lisa Ferrato
Estimated Sales: Less Than $500,000
Number Employees: 1-4

12838 **Toffee Co**
359 N Post Oak Ln # 126
#126
Houston, TX 77024-5942
713-688-5531
Fax: 713-688-7602 BBurk924@aol.com
www.toffeeco.com
Toffee, candy
Owner: Ben Burkholder
bburk924@aol.com
Estimated Sales: Less Than $500,000
Number Employees: 1-4

12839 **Tofield Packers Ltd**
5020 50th Avenue
Tofield, AB T0B 4J0
Canada
780-662-4842
Fax: 780-662-4842
Fresh and processed meats including sausage and wild game; also, custom slaughtering available
President: Dale Erickson
Estimated Sales: C
Number Employees: 10-19
Type of Packaging: Consumer, Bulk

12840 **Toft Dairy Inc**
3717 Venice Rd
Sandusky, OH 44870-1640
419-625-4376
Fax: 419-621-2010 800-521-4606
info@toftdairy.com www.toftdairy.com
Milk, ice cream, frozen yogurt, fruit drinks, orange juice, cottage cheese and sour cream
Owner: Thomas Meisler
tmeisler@toft.com
VP: Thomas Meisler
Plant Manager: Dan Meisler
Estimated Sales: $17.8 Million
Number Employees: 50-99
Square Footage: 188000
Type of Packaging: Consumer, Food Service, Private Label, Bulk

12841 **Tofu Shop Specialty Foods Inc**
65 Frank Martin Ct
Arcata, CA 95521-8930
707-822-7401
Fax: 707-822-7401 info@tofushop.com
www.tofushop.com
Fresh tofu, smoked tofu, fresh soymilks, international spiced tofu, seasoned and baked tofu
President: Matthew Schmit
info@tofushop.com
Estimated Sales: $500,000
Number Employees: 20-49
Number of Products: 22
Square Footage: 18000
Type of Packaging: Consumer, Bulk
Brands:
Snack Fu
Tofu Shop

12842 **Tofurky**
PO Box 176
Hood River, OR 97031
Fax: 541-386-7754 800-508-8100
www.tofurky.com
Tofu products, vegan meat alternatives
Contact: Jaime Athos
jathos@tofurkey.com

12843 **Tofutti Brands Inc**
50 Jackson Dr
Cranford, NJ 07016-3504
908-272-2400
Fax: 908-272-9492 info@tofutti.com
www.tofutti.com
Processor and exporter of nondairy food products including imitation cream cheese, no-cholesterol egg products made of egg whites and tofu with added vitamins and minerals and frozen tofu desserts
CEO: Shana Joseph
sjoseph@tofutti.com
CEO: David Mintz
CFO: Steven Kass
Director: Neal Axelrod
Estimated Sales: $10-20 Million
Number Employees: 5-9
Type of Packaging: Consumer, Food Service, Bulk
Brands:
Lite Lite Tofutti
Tofutti
Tofutti Better Than Cheesecake

12844 **Tokunaga Farms**
12019 S Highland Avenue
Selma, CA 93662-9003
559-896-0949
Farm products
President: George Tokunga

12845 **Tolteca Foodservice**
4305 Steve Reynolds Boulevard
Norcross, GA 30093
770-263-0490
800-541-6835
www.toltecafoods.com
A self-proclaimed one-stop shop for Mexican restaurants. A manufacturer of every kind of supplies a Mexican restaurant may need, including tortillas, spices, meats, dairy, oils, grains, fruit and vegetables, beverages, etc.

Estimated Sales: $1700000
Number Employees: 10-19
Number of Products: 2000
Square Footage: 50000
Type of Packaging: Consumer, Food Service, Private Label
Brands:
Mexican Bear

12846 **Tom & Dave's Coffee**
3095 Kerner Blvd # A
San Rafael, CA 94901-5420
415-454-3064
Fax: 415-454-3281 800-249-5050
orders@novarosti.com www.tomanddaves.com
Coffee
Owner: Christopher Rygg
customerservice@tomanddaves.com
Estimated Sales: Below $5 Million
Number Employees: 1-4
Type of Packaging: Private Label
Brands:
Columbian
House Blend
Moka-Java

12847 **Tom & Sally's Handmade Chocolates**
P.O.Box 600
Brattleboro, VT 05302-0600
802-254-4200
Fax: 802-254-5518 800-827-0800
Gourmet chocolate products including old-fashioned creams, foil-wrapped coins, spoons, nut patties, lollypops, almond bark, dessert toppings and molded
Chairman: Thomas E Fegley
Estimated Sales: $3-5 Million
Number Employees: 10-19
Square Footage: 46800
Type of Packaging: Consumer, Private Label
Brands:
Cowlicks
Dog-Gones
Reindeer Pies
Vermont Meadow Muffins
Vermont Pasture Patties

12848 **Tom Cat Bakery Inc**
43-05 10th St
Queens, NY 11101
718-786-7659
Fax: 718-786-9046
customerservice@tomcatbakery.com
www.tomcatbakery.com
French and Italian breads, rolls, baguettes
VP & General Manager: James Rath
jamesrath@tomcatbakery.com
EVP & General Manager: Peter Sonenstein
R&D Manager: Leonardo Duran
VP, Sales: John Martinez
Production Manager: Laurie Williams
Year Founded: 1987
Estimated Sales: $50-100 Million
Number Employees: 50-99
Number of Brands: 1
Brands:
Tom Cat Bakery

12849 **Tom Farms**
8542 N Harper Rd.
Leesburg, IN 46538
574-453-3300
Fax: 574-453-4787 www.tomfarms.com
Seed corn, corn and soybeans.
Co-Founder: Everett Tom
Co-Founder: Marie Tom
Managing Member: Kip Tom
CFO: Derrick Deardorff
Year Founded: 1952
Type of Packaging: Food Service, Bulk

12850 **Tom Ringhausen Orchards**
Route 16 & 100
PO Box 201
Hardin, IL 62047-0201
618-576-2311
800-258-6645
www.enjoycalhouncounty.com
Processor and grower of fruits and vegetables including apples, peaches, plums, pears, nectarines, blackberries, squash, pumpkins, melons and turnips. Also cider
President: Tom Ringhausen
Estimated Sales: Under $300,000
Number Employees: 400
Square Footage: 6000
Type of Packaging: Consumer
Brands:
Tom Ringhausen

12851 **Tom Sturgis Pretzels Inc**
2267 Lancaster Pike
Reading, PA 19607-2498
610-775-0335
Fax: 610-796-1418 800-817-3834
csr@tomsturgispretzels.com
www.tomsturgispretzels.com
Pretzels
President: Bruce Sturgis
Founder: Tom Sturgis
tsturgis@tomsturgispretzels.com
Vice President: Barbara Sturgis
Sales Director: Timothy Snyder
Operations Manager: Jean Harms
Production Manager: David Amour
Plant Manager: Mike Kappenstein
Estimated Sales: $5 Million
Number Employees: 20-49
Number of Brands: 3
Square Footage: 300000
Type of Packaging: Private Label
Brands:
Cousin Rachel Pretzels
Mr. C'S Pretzels
Tom Sturgis Pretzels

12852 **Tom Tom Tamale & BakeryCo**
4750 S Washtenaw Ave
Chicago, IL 60632-2096
773-523-5675
Tamales
President: Nick Petros
Estimated Sales: $500,000-$1 Million
Number Employees: 20-49
Type of Packaging: Consumer

12853 **Tom's Foods**
8600 South Blvd
Charlotte, NC 28273
877-309-6361
Snack foods including potato chips
Contact: Jack Warden
hr@tomsfoods.com
Plant Manager: John Rothenfluh
Parent Co: Snyders-Lance Inc.
Type of Packaging: Private Label

12854 **Tom's Snacks Company**
8600 S Boulevard
Charlotte, NC 28273
706-323-2721
Fax: 706-323-8231 800-995-2623
www.tomsfoods.com
Potato chips, thick and bold chips, thunder chips, cheezers, pork skins, rings, fries, corn and tortilla, bugles and mega twisters
Supply Chain VP, Lance Inc.: Blake Thompson
Contact: Marc Albers
malbers@tomsfoods.com
Estimated Sales: $.5-1 million
Number Employees: 50-99
Parent Co: Lance, Inc.
Type of Packaging: Consumer
Brands:
Tom's

12855 **Tomanetti Food ProductsInc**
625-631 Allegheny Avenue
Oakmont, PA 15139-2003
412-828-3040
Fax: 412-828-2282 800-875-3040
tomanetti@aol.com www.tomanetti.com
Gourmet pizza products including cheese analogs, crusts and focaccia; also, whole wheat pizzas
President: George Michel
Sales Manager: Christopher Presutti
Customer Service Representative: Jessica Piccolino
Operations: Jerry Drolz
Administrative Manager: Tammy Carroll
Estimated Sales: $10-20 Million
Number Employees: 20-49
Parent Co: Tomanetti Foods
Type of Packaging: Consumer, Food Service, Private Label, Bulk
Brands:
Graindance
Soydance

12856 **(HQ)Tomanetti Food Products**
631 Allegheny Avenue
Oakmont, PA 15139
412-828-3040
Fax: 412-828-2282 800-875-3040
tomanetti@aol.com www.tomanetti.com
Pizza shells, breadsticks and focaccia.
President: George Michel
COO: Robert Finlay
Sales Manager: Chris Presutti
Production Supervisor: Bill Vidra
Plant Manager: Paul Sypolt
Estimated Sales: Below $5 Million
Number Employees: 30

12857 **Tomanetti Food Products**
625 Allegheny Ave
Oakmont, PA 15139
412-828-3040
Fax: 412-828-2282 tomanetti@tomanetti.com
www.tomanetti.com
Manufacturer and distributor of pizza crusts and flatbreads.
President: Rodney Butcher
Estimated Sales: Under $500,000
Number Employees: 20-49
Parent Co: Hollymead Capital
Brands:
Graindance
Soydance

12858 **Tomaro's Bakery**
411 N 4th St
Clarksburg, WV 26301-2004
304-622-0691
www.tomarosbakery.com
Bread, rolls and pizza crusts
President: Janice Brunett
Manager: Steve Schartiger
tomarosbakery@aol.com
Estimated Sales: $6 Million
Number Employees: 20-49
Type of Packaging: Consumer

12859 **Tomasello Winery**
225 N White Horse Pike
Hammonton, NJ 08037-1868
609-561-0567
Fax: 609-561-8617 800-666-9463
wine@tomasellowinery.com
www.tomasellowinery.com
Wines
President: Chris Curry
ccurry@tomasellowinery.com
Owner: Jack Tomasello
Vice President: Jack Tomasello
Estimated Sales: Below $5 Million
Number Employees: 5-9
Brands:
Tomasello Winery

12860 **Tomasso Corporation**
20425 Clark Graham
Baie D'Urfe, QC H9X 3T5
Canada
514-325-3000
Fax: 514-457-5107 www.cordonbleu.ca
Frozen Italian entrees including meat lasagna, chicken lasagna, meat sauce, vegeatble lasagna, cannelloni, macaroni and cheese
Chairman/CEO: J-Rene Oumet
CFO/Treasurer: Peter Tasgal
Number Employees: 120
Square Footage: 212000
Type of Packaging: Food Service, Private Label
Brands:
Buona Cucina
Gusto Italia
Piazza Tomasso

12861 **Tomer Kosher Foods**
5340 Lincoln Avenue
Skokie, IL 60077
847-779-4870
matthew@rotemfoods.com
www.tomerkosher.com
Kosher beef and jerky
President: Justin Teten
justin@tomerkosher.com
Sales & Marketing: Matthew Sharos
Office Manager: Jennifer Morales
Brands:
TK Tomer Kosher

12862 **Tommy Tang's Thai Seasonings**
PO Box 46700
Los Angeles, CA 90046-7512
818-442-0219

Seasonings, spices
President: Sandi Tang
Owner: Tommy Tang
sandi.arabia@gmail.com
Estimated Sales: $1-2.5 Million
Number Employees: 10-19

12863 **Tommy's Jerky Outlet**
8640 Mentor Ave
Mentor, OH 44060-6140
440-255-3994
Fax: 305-723-7686 866-448-6942
info@tommysjerky.com www.tommysjerky.com
Beef jerky and jerky spices
President: Thomas Stabosz
Production: Joe Muscarella
Number Employees: 5-9
Number of Brands: 1
Number of Products: 9
Parent Co: TFS
Type of Packaging: Consumer, Food Service, Private Label, Bulk
Brands:
Gold Rush
Grandpa Vals
Toxic Tommy

12864 **Tomorrow Enterprise**
5918 Spanish Trl W
New Iberia, LA 70560
337-783-2666
Fax: 337-233-9514

Hot sauces
President: Tony Morrow

12865 **Toms Moms Foods, LLC**
5914 Grisby House Crt.
Centreville, VA 20120
614-716-9436

Manufacturer of homemade syrup.
Founder: Andy Humphries

12866 **Tone Products Inc**
2129 N 15th Ave
Melrose Park, IL 60160-1406
708-681-3660
Fax: 708-681-2368 800-536-8663
Processor and exporter of fountain beverages, energy drinks, fruit smoothies, pancake syrups, beverage concentrates, sauces and marinades.
President/CEO: Tim Evon
CEO: Timothy E Evon
timevon@toneproducts.com
Chief Financial Officer: William Hamen
Director, National Accounts: Tim Collins
VP, Sales: William Evon
Director, Operations: Greg Sperry
Director of Purchasing: Matt Claus
Estimated Sales: $12 Million
Number Employees: 50-99
Number of Brands: 9
Square Footage: 46000
Type of Packaging: Consumer, Private Label, Bulk
Brands:
Balboa Bay
Bonnie
Bonnie Maid
Evon's
Golden Kettle
Lost Lake
Rainbo-Rich
Sno-Bal
Timber Trails

12867 **Tonewood Maple**
301 Glen View Rd
Waitsfield, VT 05673-4401
802-496-5512
info@tonewoodmaple.com
www.tonewoodmaple.com
Manufacturer of solid and liquid maple products.
Founder: Dori Ross
info@tonewoodmaple.com
Number Employees: 1-4

12868 **Tonex**
27 Park Row
Wallington, NJ 07057-1629
973-773-5135
Fax: 973-916-1091 tonexinc@aol.com
Cappuccino, nondairy creamers, instant coffee and tea and chocolate covered nuts; importer and exporter of beer, vodka, candy, fresh and dried fruits, tea, instant cappuccino, juice and juice concentrates, etc
Owner: Bogdan Torbus
President: Grace Torbus
Marketing Director: Angela Torbus
Type of Packaging: Consumer, Food Service, Private Label, Bulk
Brands:
Chocolate Covered Nuts
Instant Cappuccino
Instant Tea

12869 **Tony Chachere's Creole Foods**
519 N Lombard St
Opelousas, LA 70570-6232
337-942-9303
Fax: 337-948-6854 800-551-9066
www.tonychachere.com
Seasonings and rice dinner mixes
President: Donald Chachere
Marketing Director: Christopher Roch
CFO: William Pollingue
CFO: Donald Chachere Jr
VP Sales: Mona Campbell Jr
Public Relations: Janice LeBlanc
Production Manager: Alex Chachere
Plant Manager: Carl Trahan
Estimated Sales: Below $1 Million
Number Employees: 50-99
Type of Packaging: Consumer, Food Service, Private Label, Bulk
Brands:
Instant Roux & Gravy
More Spice Seasoning
Tony Chachere's Orig

12870 **Tony Downs Foods**
54934 210th Ln
Mankato, MN 56001
507-387-3663
Fax: 507-388-6420 866-731-4561
mdowns@downsfoodgroup.com
www.tonydownsfoods.com
Poultry fully cooked, diced-frozen and commercial and retail canned chicken.
President: Mike Downs
mdowns@downsfoodsgroup.com
Vice President: Greg Cook
Director, Human Resources: David Ross
Year Founded: 1947
Estimated Sales: $22 Million
Number Employees: 20-49
Square Footage: 100000
Type of Packaging: Consumer, Food Service, Private Label, Bulk

12871 **Tony Vitrano Company**
7470 Conowingo Ave.
PO Box 2001
Jessup, MD 20794
410-799-7444
800-481-3784
dorothy@fruitiongifts.com
www.tonyvitranocompany.com
Established in 1934. Processor of apples, oranges, cucumbers, onions, lettuce, and squash.
President: Anthony Vitrano
Director of Marketing: Dorothy Vitrano
Contact: Dorothy Vitrano
dorothy@fruitiongifts.com
Estimated Sales: $20-50 Million
Number Employees: 51-200
Type of Packaging: Consumer, Food Service, Bulk
Brands:
Dole
Sunkist
Ocean Spray

12872 **Tony's Chocolonely**
1355 Nw Everett
Suite 100
Portland, OR 97209-2655
503-388-5990
mailme@tonyschocolonely.com
www.tonyschocolonely.com
Chocolate bars
American Brand Builder: Maudi Admiraal
US Sales Manager: Peter Zandee
Operations & Finance: Heather Bright
Office Manager: Meredith McEntee
Estimated Sales: $6.3 Million
Number Employees: 11-50
Brands:
Tony's Chocolonely

12873 **Tony's Ice Cream Co**
604 E Franklin Blvd
Gastonia, NC 28054-7111
704-867-7085
www.tonysicecream.com
Ice cream
President: Robert Coletta
Vice President: Louis Coletta
Manager: Cheryl Martin
Estimated Sales: Less Than $500,000
Number Employees: 5-9
Type of Packaging: Consumer

12874 **Tony's Pizza**
Marshall, MN
888-465-8324
Frozen pizza manufacturer.
Parent Co: Schwan's Company
Brands:
Tony's(c)

12875 **Tony's Seafood LTD**
5215 Plank Rd
Baton Rouge, LA 70805-2730
225-357-9669
Fax: 225-355-3530 800-356-2905
www.tonyseafood.com
Seafood
Owner: Darren Pizzolato
darren.pizzolato@tonyseafood.com
Year Founded: 1959
Estimated Sales: $20-50 Million
Number Employees: 1-4

12876 **Tonya's Gluten-Free Kitchen**
167 Sinclair Road
Newmanstown, PA 17073
717-949-4175
tonya@tonyasglutenfree.com
www.tonyasglutenfree.com
Gluten free soft pretzels
Contact: Ben Bernard
tonya@tonyasglutenfree.com

12877 **Too Cool Chix**
Too Cool Chix
New York, NY 10001
929-244-3022
orders@toocoolchix.com
Ice cream sandwich
President & CEO: Sharon Monahan
s.monahan@toocoolchix.com
Co-Founder: Michele Elmer
Number Employees: 1-4
Brands:
Too Cool Chix

12878 **Too Good Gourmet**
2380 Grant Ave
San Lorenzo, CA 94580-1806
510-317-8150
Fax: 510-317-8755 877-850-4663
info@toogoodgourmet.com
www.toogoodgourmet.com
Cookies
President: Jennifer Finley
jennifer@toogoodgourmet.com
Marketing/Sales: Katie Bidstrup
Estimated Sales: $5-10 Million
Number Employees: 50-99
Type of Packaging: Consumer, Food Service, Private Label, Bulk

12879 **Toom Dips**
Saint Paul, MN
651-447-8666
www.toomdips.com
Garlic dip made with all natural ingredients and based on Lebanese toum sauce, in various flavors
Founder/Chief Executive Officer: Matty Joyce
Number of Brands: 1
Number of Products: 4
Type of Packaging: Consumer, Private Label
Brands:
Toom

12880 **Tootsie Roll Industries Inc.**
7401 S. Cicero Ave.
Chicago, IL 60629
773-838-3400
Fax: 773-838-3435 866-972-6879
tootiseroll@worldpantry.com www.tootsie.com
Candy.
President/CEO/Director: Ellen Gordon
VP Finance/CFO: G. Howard Ember
VP: George Rost
Year Founded: 1896
Estimated Sales: $550 Million
Number Employees: 2,201
Number of Brands: 23
Square Footage: 2375000
Type of Packaging: Consumer, Food Service, Bulk
Brands:
Andes
Caramel Apple Pops
Candy Blox
Candy Carnival
Cella's Cherries
Charleston Chew
Charms
Child's Play
Cry Baby
DOTS
Dubble Bubble
Fluffy Stuff
Frooties
Fruit Chews
Junior Mints
Mini Bites
Nik-L-Nip
Razzles
Sugar Babies
Sugar Daddy
Tootsie Roll
Wack-O-Wax

12881 **Top Hat Co Inc**
2407 Birchwood Ln
Wilmette, IL 60091-2349
847-256-6565
Fax: 847-256-6579 info@tophatcompany.com
www.tophatcompany.com
Sauces including raspberry, hot, mocha and mint fudges, butterscotch, caramel, double chocolate fondue and bittersweet chocolate
President: Marla Murray
Contact: Brandon Chillingworth
chillingworthbrandon@tophat.com
Estimated Sales: Less than $1,000,000
Number Employees: 5-9
Type of Packaging: Consumer, Food Service, Private Label, Bulk
Brands:
Top Hat Dessert Sauces
Mayan Legacy
Prince of Orange
Southern Sin

12882 **Top Pot Doughnuts**
609 Summit Ave E
Seattle, WA 98102-4821
206-323-7841
www.toppotdoughnuts.com
Donuts
Contact: Adam Clark
aclark@toppotdoughnuts.com
Estimated Sales: Less Than $500,000
Number Employees: 5-9

12883 **Top Tier Foods Inc.**
3737 Oak St.
Vancouver, BC V6H SM4
Canada
778-628-0015
hello@toptierfoods.com
www.toptierfoods.com
Ready-to-serve quinoa pilafs in various flavors; sushi quinoa
President: Blair Bullus
Year Founded: 2013
Number of Brands: 1
Type of Packaging: Consumer, Private Label
Brands:
Quinoa Quickies

12884 **Topaz Farm**
17100 NW Sauvie Island Rd
Portland, OR 97231
503-708-0008
info@topazfarm.com
topazfarm.com
Pummpkins and berries
Owner: Kat Topaz
Estimated Sales: $3600000
Number Employees: 10-19

12885 **Topco Associates LLC**
150 Northwest Point Blvd.
Elk Grove Village, IL 60007
847-676-3030
Fax: 847-676-4949 consumerservices@topco.com
www.topco.com
Grocery, frozen, dairy, and bakery, branded meat, equipment and supplies, business services, world brands and diverting.
President/CEO: Randall Skoda
rskoda@topco.com
Executive VP/CFO: Thomas Frey
Senior VP & General Counsel: Andy Broccolo
Senior VP, Fresh: Scott Caro
Year Founded: 1944
Estimated Sales: $1 Billion
Number Employees: 250-499
Number of Brands: 21
Type of Packaging: Consumer, Food Service, Private Label
Other Locations:
Visalia CA
West Palm Beach FL
Miami FL
Quincy MA
Yakima WA
Brands:
Food Club
Shur Fine
Tippy Toes
Paws
Simply Done
@Ease
Sweet P's
Buckley Farms
Harvest Club
Over the Top
Cape Covelle
Papa Enzo's
CharKing
Culinary Tours
Top Care
Full Circle
Pure Harmony
Wide Awake Coffee Co.
Cow Belle Creamery's
Valu Time
Nostimo

12886 **Topo Chico Mineral Water**
5800 Granite Pkwy. # 900
Plano, TX 75024
888-456-4357
www.topochicousa.net
Sparkling mineral water in various flavors; bottled at source in Monterrey, Mexico
General Manager: Gerardo Galvan
Year Founded: 1895
Number of Brands: 1
Type of Packaging: Consumer, Private Label
Brands:
Topo Chico

12887 **Topolos at Russian River Vine**
5700 Gravenstein Highway North
Forestville, CA 95436-0358
707-887-3344
Fax: 707-887-1399
www.russianrivervineyards.com
Wine and gourmet foods
President: Michael Topolos
Estimated Sales: $1 Million
Number Employees: 25
Brands:
Topolos At Russian River Vine

12888 **Topor's Pickle & Food Svc Inc**
2800 Standish St
Detroit, MI 48216-1539
313-237-0288
Fax: 313-981-4249
Pickles, dill green tomatoes, hot pickles with red peppers, Hungarian hot banana peppers
President: Larry Topor
Estimated Sales: $3-5 000,000
Number Employees: 5-9

12889 **Torani**
233 East Harris Ave.
San Francisco, CA 94080
650-875-1200
855-972-0508
www.torani.com
Flavored syrups, sauces, and beverage bases.
CEO: Melanie Dulbecco
Contact: Christopher Bernardino
cbernardino@torani.com
Number Employees: 100

12890 **Torie & Howard LLC**
143 West St
Suite 121C
New Milford, CT 06776-3599
860-799-7772
www.torieandhoward.com
Candy.
Co-Founder: Torie Burke
info@torieandhoward.com
Co-Founder: Howard Slatkin
Number Employees: 1-4

12891 **Torke Coffee Co**
3455 Paine Ave
Sheboygan, WI 53081-8457
920-458-4114
Fax: 920-458-0488 800-242-7671
info@torkecoffee.com
www.torke-coffee.myshopify.com
Manufacturer of coffee and tea.
President: Jay Torke
Year Founded: 1941
Estimated Sales: $20-50 Million
Number Employees: 20-49
Brands:
Torke

12892 **Torkelson Cheese Co**
9453 W Louisa Rd
Lena, IL 61048
815-369-4265
info@torkelsoncheese.com
www.torkelsoncheese.com
Manufacturer and wholesaler of cheeses, specifically Muenster, brick, quesadilla and asadero cheeses; lactose manufacturer.
Owner: Lindsey White
Head Cheesemaker: Jamie White
Year Founded: 1985
Estimated Sales: $50-100 Million
Number Employees: 20-49
Number of Brands: 3
Type of Packaging: Consumer, Food Service, Bulk
Brands:
Torkelson Cheese Co.
El Ganador del Premio
Apple Jack Cheese

12893 **Torn & Glasser**
1769 Glendale Blvd
Los Angeles, CA 90026-1761
323-661-2332
Fax: 213-688-0941 800-282-6887
Nuts, dried fruit, seeds, granola, beans, rice, dry chili, candy, etc
Owner: Tony Tierno
VP: Greg Glasser
Purchasing Manager: Gus Gutmun
Estimated Sales: $300,000-500,000
Number Employees: 1-4
Type of Packaging: Consumer, Food Service, Private Label, Bulk

12894 **Torn Ranch**
23 Pimentel Ct
Suite B
Novato, CA 94949-5661
707-796-7800
Fax: 415-506-3002 info@tornranch.com
www.tornranch.com
Dried fruits, roasted nuts, snack foods and shortbreads.
President: Dean Morrow
Vice President: Sue Morrow
Quality Control: Robert Wagner
Contact: Rich Shaffer
shafcndy@aol.com
Estimated Sales: $5-10 Million
Number Employees: 50-99

Type of Packaging: Private Label
Brands:
Cafe Time
Gigi Baking Company
Mashuga Nuts & Cookies
Splendid Specialties Chocolate Co

12895 **Torre Products Co Inc**
479 Washington St
New York, NY 10013-1381
212-925-8989
Fax: 212-925-4627
Manufacturer, importer and exporter of flavoring extracts and essential oils
Owner: Liberty F Raho
Estimated Sales: $10-20 Million
Number Employees: 5-9
Square Footage: 33000
Brands:
Flambe Holiday
La Torinese
Rum-Ba
Soft Mac

12896 **Torrefazione Barzula & Import**
3117 Wharton Way
Mississauga, ON L4X 2B6
Canada
905-625-6082
Fax: 905-625-5741 866-358-5488
sales@barzula.com www.barzula.com
Processor, importer and exporter of coffee beans including green, espresso, Turkish and decaffeinated
President: Luigi Russignan
Treasurer: Gigliola Russignan
VP: Phil Cennova
Estimated Sales: $2.2 Million
Number Employees: 14
Number of Brands: 1
Number of Products: 12
Square Footage: 48000
Brands:
Barzula

12897 **Torrefazione Italia**
2401 Utah Avenue South
Seattle, WA 98134
206-624-5773
Fax: 206-624-3262 800-827-2333
Gourmet/ specialty coffee
President/COO: Dick Holbrook
VP Marketing: Kim Beerli
CFO: Chris December
Founder: Umberto Bizzarri
Sales Director: Tom Danowski
Operations Manager: Jane Albright
Estimated Sales: Below $500,000
Number Employees: 2
Type of Packaging: Private Label
Brands:
Torrefazione Italia

12898 **Torreo Coffee Company**
4950 Rhawn St
Philadelphia, PA 19136
215-333-1105
Fax: 215-333-6615 888-286-7736
torreo.com
Premium coffees
President: Eric Patrick
Vice President: H Patrick
Operations Manager: Howard Patrick
Estimated Sales: $500,000-$1 Million
Number Employees: 5-9
Square Footage: 38400
Parent Co: Torreo Coffee & Tea Company
Type of Packaging: Consumer, Private Label, Bulk
Brands:
Torreo

12899 **Tortillas Inc**
2912 Norht Commerce Street
North Las Vegas, NV 89030-3945
702-399-3300
Fax: 702-399-2507 gus@tortillasinc.com
www.tortillasinc.com
Tortillas
Owner: Gus Gutierrez
Partner: Jose Gutierrez
Owner: Salvo Gutierrez
Estimated Sales: $2.5-5 Million
Number Employees: 20-49

12900 **Totally Chocolate**
2025 Sweet Rd
Blaine, WA 98230-9198
360-332-3900
Fax: 360-332-1802 800-255-5506
sales@totallychocolate.com
www.totallychocolate.com
Chocolate
President: Ken Strong
kstrong@totallychocolate.com
VP Sales: Matt Roth
Plant Manager: Steve Hocker
Estimated Sales: $5-10 Millions
Number Employees: 50-99
Type of Packaging: Private Label
Brands:
Totally Chocolate

12901 **Totino's**
General Mills, Inc.
PO Box 9452
Minneapolis, MN 55440
800-248-7310
www.totinos.com
Pizza products and stuffed nachos.
President & COO, General Mills: Jeffrey Harmening
Chairperson & CEO, General Mills: Ken Powell
Estimated Sales: Under $500,000
Number Employees: 10-19

12902 **Toucan Chocolates**
RR 128
Box 72
Waban, MA 02468
617-964-8696
Fax: 800-816-8696
Chocolate
President: Michael Goldman

12903 **Touche Bakery**
384b Neptune Cr.
London, ON N6M 1A1
Canada
518-455-0044
Fax: 519-455-5843 aswartz@touchebakery.com
www.touchebakery.com
All natural, nut-free biscotti, cookies, and meringues
President: Peter Cuddy
President & CEO: Allan Swartz
Finance/Administration Manager: Pat Gauthier
Account Manager: Peggy Swartz
Administrative Assistant: Vickie Suter
Square Footage: 32000
Type of Packaging: Consumer, Food Service, Private Label

12904 **Touche Bakery**
384b Neptune Cr
London, ON N6M 1A1
Canada
519-455-0044
Fax: 519-455-5843 aswartz@touchebakery.com
www.touchebakery.com
Biscotti, meringues, cookies, brownies, frozen cookie dough, muffin and brownie batter
President/CEO: Allan Swartz
Estimated Sales: $1.2 Million
Number Employees: 20

12905 **Toufayan Bakeries**
175 Railroad Ave
Ridgefield, NJ 07657-2312
201-861-4131
Fax: 201-861-0392 msteve@toufayan.com
www.toufayan.com
Pita bread, flatbread, bagels, wraps, lavash, and bread sticks
Owner: Greg Toufayan
CFO, Controller: Kristine Toufayan
Vice President: Bob Thomas
VP & Treasurer: Suzanne Toufayan
VP Marketing: Karen Toufayan
VP Sales: Roy Peterson
Operations Manager: Chris Clark
Production Manager: Paul Steinbach
Purchasing Manager: James Bogosian
Estimated Sales: $26 Million
Number Employees: 20-49
Type of Packaging: Consumer, Food Service
Other Locations:
Orlando FL
Plant City FL

12906 **Tova Industries LLC**
P.O. Box 24410
Louisville, KY 40224
502-267-7333
Fax: 502-267-7119 888-532-8682
corporate@tovaindustries.com
www.tovaindustries.com
Dry mix food products, spices, table and beverage syrups
President: Zack Melzer
zackmelzer@tovaindustries.com
SVP: Yael Melzer
Year Founded: 1985
Estimated Sales: $100+ Million
Number Employees: 50-99
Number of Products: 1000
Type of Packaging: Consumer, Food Service, Private Label, Bulk
Other Locations:
New Horizon Foods
Union City CA
Brands:
Heritage-the Essence of Tradition
Lifesource Foods
Stoneground Mills
Superior Spices
Superior Syrups
Tova

12907 **Townsend Farms Inc**
23400 NE Townsend Way
Fairview, OR 97024-4626
503-666-1780
Fax: 503-618-8257 www.townsendfarms.com
Fresh and frozen blueberries, blackberries and strawberries; fresh black raspberries, mixed fruit, manoes, boysenberries, cherries, marionberries, red raspberries and pineapple; fresh raspberries
President: Tracy Casillas
tracyc@thecanbycenter.org
CEO: Jeff Townsend
CFO: Chris Valenti
Plant Manager: Reyes Pena
Purchasing: Mark Davis
Estimated Sales: $10-20 Million
Number Employees: 1000-4999
Square Footage: 4000
Type of Packaging: Consumer, Food Service, Private Label, Bulk

12908 **Trace Minerals Research**
1996 W 3300 S
West Haven, UT 84401-9774
801-731-6051
Fax: 801-731-3702 800-624-7145
info@traceminerals.com www.traceminerals.com
Dietary supplements
President: Matt Kilts
mattk@traceminerals.com
Chairman: George Harris
Sales Director: Ryan Fisher
Estimated Sales: $4972329
Number Employees: 50-99
Number of Products: 100
Square Footage: 52000
Type of Packaging: Consumer, Food Service, Private Label, Bulk

12909 **Tracy Luckey Pecans**
110 N Hicks St
PO Box 880
Harlem, GA 30814
706-556-6216
Fax: 706-556-6210 800-476-4796
Shelled pecans and pecan products
President: Francis Tracy
VP/CEO: Ruth Tracy
Controller: Ed Wicker
VP Marketing/Sales: Ruth Tracy
Contact: Nancy Studdard
nancy@tracy-luckey.com
Plant Manager: Homer Gay
Estimated Sales: $120,000
Number Employees: 50-99
Square Footage: 320000
Type of Packaging: Bulk
Brands:
Sunblet

12910 **Trade Marcs Group**
55 Nassau Ave
Brooklyn, NY 11222-3143
718-387-9696
Fax: 718-782-2471

General grocery
Manager: Andi Billow
Contact: Marc Greenberg
marc@cafelasemeuse.com
Estimated Sales: Less than $500,000
Number Employees: 1-4

12911 Trade Winds Pizza
1085 Parkview Road
Green Bay, WI 54304-5616
920-336-7810
Fax: 920-336-2942
Pizzas
Director Operations: Jim Peppich

12912 Trader Vic's Food Products
9 Anchor Dr
Emeryville, CA 94608
510-653-3400
Fax: 510-653-9384 877-762-4824
info@tradervics.com tradervics.com
Processor and exporter of nonalcoholic cocktail mixes, syrups, dry spices, sauces and salad dressings
CEO: Hans Richter
VP: Peter Seely
Estimated Sales: $540000
Number Employees: 6
Type of Packaging: Consumer
Brands:
Trader Vic's

12913 Tradeshare Corporation
207 Flushing Avenue
Brooklyn, NY 11205
718-237-2295
Food preparation and general grocery
President: Robert Krasnor
Estimated Sales: $2.5-5 000,000
Number Employees: 10-19

12914 Tradewinds
3601 South Congress Ave
Austin, TX 78704
www.tradewindstea.com
Brewed teas in nine flavors
President: Kenneth Lichtendahl
Marketing Director: Christy Lichtendahl
Estimated Sales: $5-10 Million
Number Employees: 5-9
Parent Co: Sweet Leaf Tea
Brands:
Concord Grape
Granny Smith Apple
Ice Tea
Lemon Tea

12915 Tradewinds Coffee Company
5500 Atlantic Springs Rd Ste 106
Raleigh, NC 27616
919-878-1111
Fax: 919-878-0041 800-457-0406
Coffee and coffee flavored candy
President: Art Watkins
Co-Owner: Elaine Watkins
Estimated Sales: Below $5 Million
Number Employees: 10-19
Brands:
Trade Winds Coffee

12916 Tradin Organics USA
100 Enterprise Way
Suite B 101
Scotts Valley, CA 95066
831-685-6565
info@tradinorganicsusa.com
tradinorganic.com
Fruits and berries.
VP, Sales & Procurement: Hendrik Rabbie
Contact: Jacqueline Chuang
jacqueline.chuang@tradinorganic.com
Parent Co: Tradin Organic

12917 Traditional Baking Inc
2575 S Willow Ave
Bloomington, CA 92316-3256
909-877-8471
Fax: 909-877-6728 admin@traditionalbaking.com
www.traditionalbaking.com
Cookies and sugar free cookies
CEO: Kathy Voortman
Research & Development Associate: Ruby Torres
Quality Assurance Manager: Trisha Winne
Account Manager: Mark Jordan
Human Resources Manager: Maria Prieto
Maintenance & Parts Manager: Fabian Galarza
Production Manager: Gerardo Perez
Warehouse Manager: Eli Valadez
Director of Procurement: Mike Shevette
Estimated Sales: Less Than $500,000
Number Employees: 1-4

12918 Traditional Medicinals Inc
4515 Ross Rd
Sebastopol, CA 95472-2250
707-823-8911
Fax: 707-823-1599 800-543-4372
www.traditionalmedicinals.com
Herb teas
Co- Founder, Chairman of the Board: Drake Sadler
Chief Executive Officer: Blair Kellison
President: Lynda Sadler
Vice President of Research and Developme: Josef Brinckmann
Vice President of Quality: Katie Huggins
Sales Coordinator: Brenda Hodges
Vice President of Sales: Darrick Blinoff
Contact: Liz Alber
lalber@tradmed.com
Estimated Sales: $3200000
Number Employees: 100-249
Brands:
Traditional Med Ginger Energy
Traditional Med Gypsy Cold Cure
Traditional Med Organics

12919 Trafalgar Brewing Company
1156 Speers Road
Oakville, ON L6L 2X4
Canada
905-337-0133
Fax: 905-845-2246 www.alesandmeads.com
Beer, ale, lager and stout
President: Mike Arnold
Estimated Sales: Under $500,000
Number Employees: 1-4
Type of Packaging: Consumer, Food Service
Brands:
Celtic
Elora Esb
Elora Grand Lager
Elora Irish Ale
Harbour Gold
Paddy's Irish Red
Port Side Amber
Trafalgar

12920 Trail's Best Snacks
930 S. White Station Road
Memphis, TN 38017
Fax: 507-677-2478 800-852-1863
www.trailsbest.com
Manufacturer of meat snacks.
Chairman/CEO: Karl Schledwitz
Estimated Sales: $10-20 Million
Number Employees: 5-9
Number of Brands: 3
Parent Co: Monogram Foods
Type of Packaging: Consumer, Bulk
Brands:
Happy Trails Meat Snack Sticks
Team Realtree
Trail's Best Snacks

12921 Trailblazer Foods
17900 NE San Rafael St
Portland, OR 97230-5930
503-666-5800
Fax: 503-666-6800 800-777-7179
customerserv@tbfoods.com
www.trailblazerfoods.com
Preserves, fruit products, quality foods, punches, marinades and syrups
President & CEO: Rob Miller
robm@tbfoods.com
CFO: Derek Lohrey
Quality Manager: Jeff Gleason
Marketing Director: Mike Miller
Director of Sales: Mike Post
VP Operations: Sebastian Pastore
Production Manager: Henry Catan
Estimated Sales: $20-50 Million
Number Employees: 20-49
Brands:
Walls Berry Farm Preserves
Walls Berry Farm Organic Preserves
Nalley Lumberjack Table Syrup
Portland Punch

12922 Traina Foods Inc
337 Lemon Ave
Patterson, CA 95363-9634
209-892-5472
Fax: 209-892-6231 info@traina.com
www.trainafoods.com
Sun dried fruit
President: Willie Traina
willie@traina.com
Number Employees: 100-249
Type of Packaging: Consumer, Food Service

12923 Tram Bar LLC
PO Box 1079
Victor, ID 83455
208-354-4790
www.katesrealfood.com
Organic energy bars.
Owner: Kate Schade
kate@katesrealfood.com
Marketing: Rachel Reich
Type of Packaging: Consumer

12924 Trans Pecos Foods
112 E Pecan St # 800
San Antonio, TX 78205-1578
210-228-0896
Fax: 210-228-0781 pjk@texas.net
www.transpecosfoods.com
Manufacturer, importer and exporter of frozen breaded vegetables
President: Patrick J Kennedy
Contact: Steven Skinner
steven.skinner@transpecosbanks.com
Plant Manager: Bruce Salcido
Estimated Sales: $3900000
Number Employees: 20-49
Parent Co: Anchor Food Products
Type of Packaging: Consumer, Food Service, Private Label, Bulk

12925 Trans-Ocean Products Inc
350 W Orchard Dr
Bellingham, WA 98225-1769
360-671-6886
Fax: 360-671-0354 800-290-2722
info@trans-ocean.com www.trans-ocean.com
Imitation crab, lobster and salmon meat
President: Robert Draper
robert.draper@deepwater.com
CFO: Allen Leaf
Research & Development Manager: Bill Ott
VP Sales & Marketing: Louis Shaheen
Procurement & Product Manager: Norio Yanagisawa
Number Employees: 100-249
Square Footage: 192000
Parent Co: Maruha Corporation
Type of Packaging: Consumer, Food Service, Private Label, Bulk
Other Locations:
Trans-Ocean Products
Williamsville NY
Southeast Sales
Chapel Hill NC
Northwest Office/Shrimp Sales
Lynnwood WA
Brands:
Classic
Pouch Pak
Transocean

12926 Trans-Packers Svc Corp
419 Vandervoort Ave
Brooklyn, NY 11222-5313
718-963-0900
Fax: 718-486-6344 877-787-8837
sales@transpackers.com www.transpackers.com
Contract packager of food and nonfood products including powders, granules, solids and liquids in glass jars and bottles, etc
Owner: Monica Weiss
monica@transpackers.com
Vice President: Daniel Weiss
Plant Manager: Nester Serrano
Estimated Sales: $4900000
Number Employees: 100-249
Square Footage: 400000
Type of Packaging: Consumer, Food Service

12927 **Transamerica Wine Corporation**
120 Brooklyn Navy Yard
Brooklyn, NY 11201
718-875-4017
Fax: 718-625-1180
Wines
Manager: Yeshiah Schwartz
Estimated Sales: $5-10 Million
Number Employees: 10-19

12928 **Transnational Foods**
1110 Brickell Ave # 808
Suite 808
Miami, FL 33131-3138
305-415-9970
www.transnationalfoods.com
Global manufacturer and distributor of hundreds of consumer products in categories such as beverages, cereals, dressings and soups.
President & CEO: Marcelo Young
myoung@transnationalfoods.com
CFO: Juan Iribarne
COO: Americo Preneste
Number Employees: 20-49
Number of Brands: 5
Number of Products: 500+
Type of Packaging: Consumer, Private Label
Brands:
Pampa(c)
So Natural
Ali's
della Natura(c)
TummyTreats

12929 **Transpacific Foods Inc**
2603 Main St # 730
Suite 730
Irvine, CA 92614-4264
949-975-9900
Fax: 949-975-9907 www.transpacificfoods.com
U.S. pineapple supplier
President: Septi Suwandi
Number Employees: 10-19
Type of Packaging: Consumer, Food Service

12930 **Trappey's Fine Foods Inc**
PO Box 13610
New Iberia, LA 70562-3610
337-365-8281
www.trappeys.com
Okra, pickled peppers, sauces and ethnic food
CEO: Edward Simmons
Estimated Sales: $10-20 Million
Number Employees: 50-100
Number of Brands: 1
Parent Co: B&G Foods
Brands:
Trappey's

12931 **Trappist Preserves**
540 East 105th Street #115
Cleveland, OH 44108
Fax: 216-249-3387 800-472-0425
info@monasterygreetings.com
www.monasterygreetings.com
Jellies, jams and marmalades including apricot, peach, strawberry, grape, etc
President: Damian Carr
Purchasing Manager: Henry Scarborough
Estimated Sales: $16 Million
Number Employees: 95
Type of Packaging: Consumer
Brands:
Trappist

12932 **Trappistine Quality Candy**
300 Arnold St
Wrentham, MA 02093
Fax: 215-922-1335 866-549-8929
info@trappistinecandy.com
www.trappistinecandy.com
Candy
Number Employees: 20-49

12933 **Trattore Farms**
7878 Dry Creek Road
Geyserville, CA 95441
707-431-7200
info@trattorefarms.com
www.trattorefarms.com
Wines, vinegars, and olive oils
President: Tim Boucher
CEO: Michelle Robson
Vice President: Mary Louise Bucher
Estimated Sales: $20 Million
Number Employees: 18
Other Locations:
Los Angeles CA
Lodi CA
South Kearney NJ
Chicago IL
Minneapolis MN
San Francisco CA
Portland OR
Seattle WA
Miami FL

12934 **Travel Chocolate**
PO BOX 4668 PMB59369
New York, NY 10163-4668
718-841-7030
Fax: 718-841-7030 info@travelchocolate.com
Organic chocolate bars

12935 **(HQ)Travis Meats Inc**
7210 Clinton Hwy
PO Box 670
Powell, TN 37849-5216
865-938-9051
Fax: 865-938-9211 800-247-7606
www.travismeats.com
Frozen veal and pork; also beef, including meat loaf, pot roast and hamburger patties.
CEO: W Travis
Vice President: Dale Travis
Customer Service: Margie McWhorter
Marketing: Jeanine Stanley
VP of Sales & Marketing: Larry King
Estimated Sales: $20-50 Million
Number Employees: 100-249
Square Footage: 110000
Type of Packaging: Consumer, Food Service
Other Locations:
Knoxville TN

12936 **Treasure Foods**
2500 S 2300 W # 11
West Valley, UT 84119-7676
801-974-0911
Fax: 801-975-0553 treasurefoods@hotmail.com
Processor and exporter of whipped honey butter, flavored fruit honey, scones; wholesaler/distributor of frozen foods and general line items; serving the food service market
Owner: Amin Motilla
CFO: Zarina Motiwala
Vice President: Mohamed Motiwala
Marketing Director: Amin Motiwala
Public Relations: Amin Motiwala
Production Manager: Fawad Motiwala
Plant Manager: Fawad Motiwala
Purchasing Manager: Amin Motiwala
Estimated Sales: $450,000
Number Employees: 5
Number of Brands: 3
Number of Products: 3
Square Footage: 14400
Parent Co: Algilani Food Import & Export
Type of Packaging: Food Service, Private Label, Bulk
Other Locations:
Treasure Foods
Salt Lake City UT
Brands:
Honey Butter Topping
Raspberry Honey Butter Topping
Scones

12937 **Treasury Wine Estates**
555 Gateway Dr.
P.O. Box 4500
Napa, CA 94558
707-259-4500
Fax: 707-259-4542 www.tweglobal.com
Wine
President-Americas: Victoria Snyder
Managing Director & CEO: Michael Clarke
CFO: Matt Young
Chief Marketing Officer: Michelle Terry
Chief People & Legal Officer: Linnsey Caya
COO: Tim Ford
Estimated Sales: $34.6 Million
Number Employees: 3400
Number of Brands: 44
Brands:
19 Crimes
Acacia Vineyard
Annie's Lane
Beaulieu Vineyard
Belcreme de Lys
Beringer Vineyards
Blossom Hill
Cavaliere d'Oro
Chateau St. Jean
Coldstream Hills
Devil's Lair
emBRAZEN
Etude
Fifth Leg
Greg Norman Estates
Heemskerk
Hewitt Vineyard
Ingoldby
Jamieson's Run
Killawarra
Leo Buring
Lindeman's
Maison de Grand Esprit
Matua
Meridian
Metala
Penfolds
Pepperjack
Provenance Vineyards
Rawson's Retreat
Samuel Wynn & Co.
Seppelt
Shingle Peak
Sledgehammer
Squealing Pig
St Huberts
Stags' Leap Winery
Stellina di Notte
Sterling Vineyards
T'Gallant
The Walking Dead Wine
Wolf Blass
Wynns Coonawarra Estate
Yellowglen

12938 **Treat Ice Cream Co**
11 S 19th St
San Jose, CA 95116-2202
408-292-9321
Fax: 408-298-5859 treat@treaticecream.com
Gourmet ice cream
Owner: Alfred Mauseth
treat@treaticecream.com
Vice President: Bob Mauseth
Estimated Sales: $3-5 Million
Number Employees: 5-9
Square Footage: 16000
Type of Packaging: Consumer, Private Label, Bulk
Brands:
Treat

12939 **Treats Island Fisheries**
PO Box 21
Scaly Mountain, NC 28775-0021
207-733-4580
Fax: 207-733-4880
Seafood
President: James English

12940 **Treatt USA Inc**
4900 Lakeland Commerce Pkwy
Lakeland, FL 33805
863-668-9500
www.treatt.com
Food additives including essential oils and aromatic chemicals.
Chairman: Tim Jones
CEO: Daemmon Reeve
CFO: Richard Hope
Year Founded: 1886
Estimated Sales: $116 Million
Number Employees: 370
Parent Co: Treatt PLC
Type of Packaging: Bulk
Brands:
Citreatt
Treattarome

12941 **Tree Ripe Products**
53 S Jefferson Rd
Whippany, NJ 07981-1082
973-463-0777
800-873-3747
www.1800treeripe.com
Processor and exporter of nonalcoholic cocktail mixes
President: Joel Fishman

Estimated Sales: $3,000,000
Number Employees: 20-49
Square Footage: 20000
Type of Packaging: Consumer, Food Service
Brands:
Frothee Creamy Head
Lem-N-Joy
Tree-Ripe

12942 Tree Top Inc
220 E Second St
Selah, WA 98942
509-697-7251
faq@treetop.com
www.treetop.com
Grape juice and concentrate, apple juice, apple sauce, apple concentrate and blended juices.
President & CEO: Tom Hurson
CFO: Craig Green
VP, Information Services & CIO: Dwaine Brown
VP, Fruit Procurement & Growth Services: Cris Hales
VP, Quality & Technical Service: Ken James
VP, Supply Chain: Monica Taylor
VP, Human Resources: Scott Washburn
VP, Operations: Gary Price
Year Founded: 1960
Estimated Sales: $399 Million
Number Employees: 1,008
Square Footage: 74000
Type of Packaging: Consumer, Food Service, Private Label, Bulk
Brands:
Tree Top

12943 TreeHouse Foods, Inc.
2021 Spring Rd.
Suite 600
Oak Brook, IL 60523
708-483-1300
info@treehousefoods.com
www.treehousefoods.com
Cereals, snack foods, condiments, frozen baked goods and frozen prepared meals.
President/CEO: Steven Oakland
Executive VP/CFO: William Kelley
Senior VP/COO: C. Shay Braun
Estimated Sales: $6.3 Billion
Number Employees: 13,489
Number of Brands: 4
Type of Packaging: Consumer, Private Label
Brands:
Bay Valley Foods
TreeHouse Private Brands
Flagstone Foods
E.D. Smith

12944 Treehouse Farms
116 Camino Agave
Elgin, AZ 85611
559-757-5020
Fax: 559-757-0510
Processor and exporter of almonds including natural, blanched, sliced, roasted, diced and slivered
President: David Fitzgerald
Executive Director: Jacob Carter
Sales Manager: Carol Coffey
Number Employees: 250-499
Square Footage: 400000
Parent Co: Yorkshire Foods
Type of Packaging: Private Label, Bulk
Brands:
Treehouse Farms

12945 Treesweet Products
16825 Northchase Drive
Suite 1600
Houston, TX 77060-6099
281-876-3759
Fax: 281-876-2643
Orange juice and products
President: Jeffrey Rosenberg
Estimated Sales: $500,000-$1 000,000
Number Employees: 5-9
Brands:
Awake
Orange Plus
Treesweet Products

12946 Trefethen Family Vineyards
1160 Oak Knoll Ave # 3
Napa, CA 94558-1398
707-255-7700
Fax: 707-255-0793 winery@trefethen.com
www.trefethen.com
Producer and exporter of wine
Owner: John Trefethen
VP Finance: Gerald Bush
VP: David C Whitehouse Jr
Marketing: Terry Hall
Sales Director: Betty Calvin
jtrefethen@trefethen.com
Public Relations: Terry Hall
Operations Manager: Richard De Garmo
Estimated Sales: $5 Million
Number Employees: 20-49
Square Footage: 16000
Brands:
Trefethen Vineyards

12947 Trega Foods
105 E 3rd Ave
Weyauwega, WI 54983
920-867-2137
Fax: 920-867-2249
Cheese such as cheddar, feta, mozzarella, mozzarella sticks, provolone and dairy ingredients
President: Doug Simon
VP: Richard Wagner
Contact: Kirsten Slocum
kirsten.slocum@agropur.com
Estimated Sales: $5-10 Million
Number Employees: 5-9
Type of Packaging: Consumer, Food Service
Other Locations:
Trega Foods Processing Plant
Little Chute WI
Trega Foods Processing Plant
Luxemburg WI
Brands:
Trega

12948 Treier Popcorn Farms
16793 County Line Rd
Bloomdale, OH 44817
419-454-2811
Fax: 419-454-3983 ptreier@wcnet.org
Popcorn including bagged, natural, buttered and microwaveable; wholesaler/distributor of commercial popcorn poppers and other concession supply equipment; serving the food service market
President: Don Treier
Secretary/Treasurer: Peggy Treier
Estimated Sales: $500,000-$1 Million
Number Employees: 15
Number of Brands: 2
Number of Products: 6
Square Footage: 12000
Parent Co: Treier Family Farms
Type of Packaging: Consumer, Food Service, Bulk
Brands:
Lake Plains
Pelton's Hybrid Popcorn

12949 Tremblay's Sweet Shop
10569 Main St
Hayward, WI 54843-6658
715-634-2785
Fax: 715-634-7830
Candy
President: Dennis Tremblay
Quality Control: Charles Tremblay
Manager: Charles Tremblay
Estimated Sales: Below $5 000,000
Number Employees: 20-49

12950 Trentadue Winery
19170 Geyserville Ave
Geyserville, CA 95441-9528
707-473-9338
Fax: 707-433-5825 888-332-3032
info@trentadue.com www.trentadue.com
Wines
Owner: Leo Trentadue
info@trentadue.com
Proprietor: Evelyn Trentadue
Proprietor, Vineyard Manager: Victor Trentadue
Winemaker: Miroslav Tcholakov
Estimated Sales: $5-10 Million
Number Employees: 10-19
Type of Packaging: Private Label
Brands:
Trentadue

12951 Trenton Bridge Lobster Pound
1237 Bar Harbor Rd
Trenton, ME 04605-6021
207-667-2977
Fax: 207-667-3412 www.trentonbridgelobster.com
Lobster
President: Anthony Pettegrow
info@trentonbridgelobster.com
Estimated Sales: $3-5 Million
Number Employees: 10-19

12952 Trenton Processing Ctr
120 W Broadway
Trenton, IL 62293-1306
618-224-7383
Fax: 618-224-9038 800-871-7675
tp1pork@sbcglobal.net
www.trentonprocessingcenter.com
Meat products
Owner: Gary Schwend
Founder: Calvin Schwend
Founder: Loretta Schwend
Purchasing Manager: Judy Kuhn
Estimated Sales: $5-10 Million
Number Employees: 10-19
Type of Packaging: Consumer

12953 Treo Brands
106 Calvert St
Harrison, NY 10528
914-341-1850
info@drinktreo.com
www.drinktreo.com
Flavored birch water
President: Brian O'Byrne
CEO: Bob Golden
Brand Manager: Zoe McElligott
Brands:
Treo

12954 TresOmega
9 S Main St
New Milford, CT 06776
860-210-7805
info@tresomega.com
www.tresomega.com
Coconut flour, pasta, chia seed, and coconut oil
Parent Co: Mountain High Organics, Inc.

12955 Tri State Beef Co
2124 Baymiller St
Cincinnati, OH 45214-2208
513-579-1722
Fax: 513-579-1739
CEO: Robert Runtz
Secretary/Treasurer: Betty Stout
Marketing Manager: Robert Runtz
Number Employees: 50-99
Parent Co: DaeKyung Oil and Transportation Co.
Type of Packaging: Consumer, Food Service, Bulk
Brands:
Soauthter

12956 Tri-Boro Fruit Co
2500 S Fowler Ave
Fresno, CA 93725-9308
559-486-4141
Fax: 559-486-7627
Grape grower
President: Chris Fazio
Executive: Tony Fazio
Estimated Sales: $5-10 000,000
Number Employees: 10-19

12957 Tri-Counties Packing Company
845 Vertin Ave
Salinas, CA 93901
831-422-7841
Fax: 831-422-7856
Celery and celery hearts
President/Owner: Jack Baillie
Sales: John Baillie
john@celeryhearts.com
Estimated Sales: $5 Million
Number Employees: 20-49
Number of Brands: 3
Number of Products: 1
Square Footage: 184000
Type of Packaging: Consumer
Other Locations:
Tri-Counties Packaging Coompany
Oxnard CA
Brands:
Candy Stick

Snappy
Tri-Sign

12958 Tri-State Dairy
120 West Jefferson Boulevard
Fort Wayne, IN 46802
256-534-8464
Fax: 256-534-6259 www.tristatedairy.osu.edu
Milk, dairy products
Marketing Director: D Fitch
Estimated Sales: Under $500,000
Number Employees: 100-249
Parent Co: Dean Foods Company

12959 Tri-State Ingredients
6147 Western Row Rd
Mason, OH 45040-2459
513-573-0057
Fax: 513-573-0870 800-622-1050
www.techfood.com
Herbal extracts
Owner: Lloyd Makstell
CEO: Edward Makstell
CFO: Nadine Whitsell
Estimated Sales: $5 Million
Number Employees: 10-19
Number of Products: 42
Square Footage: 203000
Parent Co: Technical Food Sales Inc
Type of Packaging: Bulk

12960 Tri-State Logistics Inc
3156 Spring Valley Road
Dubuque, IA 52001-1531
563-690-0926
Fax: 775-417-6709 866-331-7660
www.tri-statelogistics.com
Energy drink and power cool drink
President: Evan Fleisher
VP: Randy Sirk
Estimated Sales: C
Number Employees: 5-9
Square Footage: 3500
Type of Packaging: Private Label
Brands:
Rox Energy Drink

12961 Tri-Sum Potato Chip Company
80 Julian Dr
Leominster, MA 01453
978-697-2447
www.tri-sum.com
Potato chips, popcorn and cheese puffs
COO: Richard Gates
Contact: Richard Duchesneau
richard@tri-sum.com
Number Employees: 20-50
Type of Packaging: Consumer, Food Service, Private Label, Bulk
Brands:
Jp's
Suncrisp

12962 Triangle Seafood
212 Adams Street
Louisville, KY 40206-1862
502-561-0055
Fax: 502-561-0096
Seafood
President: J Shannon Bouchillon

12963 Tribali Foods
2275 Huntington Dr. # 342
San Marino, CA 91108
310-592-5420
hello@tribalifoods.com
www.tribalifoods.com
Organic, grass-fed Mediterranean style beef patties and Umami beef patties; organic, free-range chicken patties
Founder/Owner: Angela Bicos Mavridis
Year Founded: 2016
Number of Brands: 1
Number of Products: 3
Type of Packaging: Consumer, Private Label
Brands:
Tribali Foods

12964 Tribe 9 Foods
2901 Progress Rd
Madison, WI 53716
608-257-7216
www.tribe9foods.com
Fresh pasta, gluten free pasta, bars, cookies, and nut butters
Chairman & CEO: Brian Durst
President & CFO: Richard Ciurczak
Quality Assurance Manager: Margo King
VP Operations: William Ciurczak
Number Employees: 20-49
Brands:
Ona
RP's Pasta Company
Yumbutter
Taste Republic

12965 Tribe Mediterranean
110 Prince Henry Dr
Taunton, MA 02780-7385
774-961-0000
800-848-6687
info@tribehummus.com www.tribehummus.com
Processor and exporter of hummus dips/spreads
President/Ceo: Carlos Canals
Cfo: Charles Webster
Number Employees: 100-249
Square Footage: 240000
Type of Packaging: Consumer, Food Service, Private Label, Bulk
Brands:
Nathan's
Rite

12966 Tribeca Oven
447 Gotham Pkwy
Carlstadt, NJ 07072-2409
201-935-8800
Fax: 201-935-6685 www.tribecaoven.com
Breads including rye, white, wholewheat, etc
Manager: Jesse Kirsch
mcruz@tribecaoven.com
Facilities: Mario Cruz
Number Employees: 1-4
Type of Packaging: Consumer, Food Service

12967 Trickling Springs Creamery
2330 Molly Pitcher Hwy
Chambersburg, PA 17202-9299
717-709-0711
Fax: 717-709-0885
www.tricklingspringscreamery.com
Dairy
Co-Founder: Torie Burke
Co-Founder: Howard Slatkin
Sales Exec: Fred Rodes
tscmilkday@yahoo.com
Number Employees: 20-49

12968 (HQ)Trident Seafoods Corp
5303 Shilshole Ave NW
Seattle, WA 98107
206-783-3818
Fax: 206-782-7195 800-426-5490
humanresources@tridentseafoods.com
www.tridentseafoods.com
Seafood from Alaska and the Pacific Northwest.
Founder/Chairman: Chuck Bundrant
Chief Executive Officer: Joe Bundrant
Year Founded: 1973
Estimated Sales: $2.4 Billion
Number Employees: 1000-4999
Number of Brands: 3
Type of Packaging: Consumer, Food Service, Bulk
Brands:
Trident
Louis Kemp Crab Delights
Pure Alaska Omega

12969 Trident Seafoods Corp
P.O. Box 908
641 Shakes Street
Wrangell, AK 99929
907-874-3346
Fax: 907-874-3035
Processor and exporter of canned, fresh and frozen shrimp, crab, halibut, herring and salmon
Type of Packaging: Food Service, Bulk

12970 Trigo Corporation
PO Box 2369
Toa Baja, PR 00951-2369
787-794-1300
Fax: 787-794-3110
Rum, vodka, liquor and wine
Executive Director: Benigno Trigo
Marketing Director: Mariella Algarin
Marketing: Eunice Miranva
Number Employees: 20-49
Type of Packaging: Consumer
Brands:
Ponte Vecckio

12971 Triland Foods Inc
311 8th St
Sergeant Bluff, IA 51054-8516
712-943-7675
Fax: 712-943-6776 866-943-7675
www.trilandfoods.com
Pork products: pork rind pellets and pork crackling pellets
President: Joe Rieger
info@trilandfoods.com
Number Employees: 20-49

12972 Trinidad Benham Company
PO Box 427
Bridgeport, NE 69336
308-262-1361
Fax: 308-586-1058
Dry beans
President: Bill McCormack
Contact: Dale Eirich
deirich@trinidadbenham.com
Area Operations Manager: Dale Eirich
Estimated Sales: $3-5 Million
Number Employees: 25
Type of Packaging: Consumer, Food Service
Brands:
Benco Peak
Cookquick'
Evans
Jack Rabbit
Kings
Ranch Wagon
Royal Wrap
Shamrock

12973 Trinidad Benham Corporation
3650 S Yosemite, Suite 300
P.O. Box 378007
Denver, CO 80237
303-220-1400
Fax: 303-220-1490 info@trinidadbenham.com
www.trinidadbenham.com
Dry beans, rice, popcorn, and peas
Vice President: Steve Dipasquale
Estimated Sales: $36.3 Million
Number Employees: 500
Square Footage: 35000
Type of Packaging: Consumer, Food Service, Private Label, Bulk
Brands:
Jack Rabbit
Siler's
Green Earth Organics
Budget Buy
Everyday Chef
Wonder Foil
Peak
Master Wrap
Solfresco
Diamond
Cookquik Ranch Wagon
Sabor Del Campo

12974 Trinity Fruit Sale Co
7571 N Remington Ave # 104
Suite 104
Fresno, CA 93711-5799
559-433-3777
Fax: 559-433-3790 sales@trinityfruit.com
www.trinityfruit.com
Fresh cherries, apricots, peaches, plums, nectarines, kiwi, grapes, apples and pears
President: David White
Marketing Director: John Hein
Sales: Vance Uchiyama
Number Employees: 20-49

12975 Trinity Spice
901 W Florida Ave
Suite B
Midland, TX 79701
915-683-8333
Fax: 915-683-8333 800-460-1149
Gourmet Southern spice blends
President: S Floyd
Estimated Sales: $150,000
Number Employees: 1
Type of Packaging: Consumer, Food Service, Private Label, Bulk

Brands:
Southern Dynamite

12976 **Trio's Original ItalianPasta Co.**
32 Auburn Street
Chelsea, MA 02150-1825
617-884-5211
Fax: 617-884-2563 800-999-9603
Fresh and frozen pasta, sauces
President: Paul Stevens
Sales/Marketing: Kathy Burinskas
Director Operations: Steve Lagasse
Plant Manager: Jim Dee
Purchasing Manager: George Hachey
Estimated Sales: $5-9.9 Million
Number Employees: 35
Type of Packaging: Private Label

12977 **Triple D Orchards Inc**
8310 W Stormer Rd
Empire, MI 49630-9480
231-326-5174
Fax: 231-326-5480
Processor and exporter of canned and frozen sweet cherries
President: TJ Keyes
Year Founded: 1973
Estimated Sales: $20-50 Million
Number Employees: 100-249
Type of Packaging: Consumer, Food Service, Private Label, Bulk
Brands:
Glen Lake

12978 **Triple H Food Processors Inc**
5821 Wilderness Ave
Riverside, CA 92504-1004
951-352-5700
Fax: 951-352-5710 tharris3@triplehfoods.com
Barbecue sauces, bar mixes, oils, relishes, lemon juices, cajun sauces, citrus punches, spaghetti sauces, sno cone syrups, spices, dry rubs, preserves, hot sauces, salad dressings, jellies, oriental sauces, maple syrup, and salsas.
Vice President: Richard J Harris
rharris@triplehfoods.com
General Manager: Tommy Harris
Controller: Charles Richards
VP: Richard J Harris
Quality Assurance: Guillermo Loaiza-Aponte
Customer Service: Merilyn Ewart
Production Planner: Mike Elsman
Plant Manager: Ken Lujan
Purchasing: Greg Bourdon
Estimated Sales: $10-20 Million
Number Employees: 50-99
Type of Packaging: Private Label
Brands:
Triple H

12979 **(HQ)Triple K Manufacturing Company, Inc.**
4193 200 Street
PO Box 219
Shenandoah, IA 51601
712-246-4376
Fax: 712-246-4010 webmaster@x-tra-touch.com
www.xtratouch.com
Processor and exporter of baking flavorings; dry seasonings; salad dressings; sauces; dietary foods and cleaning products. Contract packaging and private label services also available.
President/Manager: Charles Maxine
Estimated Sales: $1.30 Million
Number Employees: 11
Square Footage: 15600
Type of Packaging: Consumer, Food Service, Private Label
Brands:
Drops O'Gold
X-Tra-Touch

12980 **Triple Leaf Tea Inc**
434 N Canal St # 5
S San Francisco, CA 94080-4667
650-588-8255
Fax: 650-588-8406 800-552-7448
triple@tripleleaf-tea.com
Processor and exporter of authentic, traditional Chinese medicinal teas including green, ginger, ginseng, diet and medicinal; also, American ginseng capsules
President: Johnson Lam
Estimated Sales: $450.00k
Number Employees: 5-9
Number of Brands: 1
Number of Products: 18
Square Footage: 20000
Type of Packaging: Consumer, Food Service, Private Label
Brands:
Triple Leaf Tea

12981 **Triple Rock Brewing Co Brkly**
1920 Shattuck Ave
Berkeley, CA 94704-1022
510-843-2739
Fax: 510-843-6920 reservations@triplerock.com
www.triplerock.com
Brewery
Co-Owner: Reid Martin
Co-Owner: John Martin
Manager: Jesse Sarinana
jessesarinana@triplerock.com
Head Brewer: Jeff Kimpe
Estimated Sales: $20-50 Million
Number Employees: 20-49
Type of Packaging: Consumer, Food Service

12982 **Triple Springs Spring Water Co**
199 Ives Ave # 1
Meriden, CT 06450-7179
203-235-8374
Fax: 203-686-0200
Natural spring water
President: George Kuchle
Estimated Sales: $9 Million
Number Employees: 10-19
Type of Packaging: Consumer, Bulk
Brands:
Triple Springs Spring Water

12983 **Triple U Enterprises**
26314 Tatanka Rd
Fort Pierre, SD 57532
605-567-3624
Fax: 605-567-3625 uuubuff@gwtc.net
Fresh, smoked, dried and frozen buffalo meat including portion cut
President: Kaye Ingle
CEO: Clint Amiotte
Estimated Sales: $700,000
Number Employees: 1-4
Type of Packaging: Consumer, Bulk

12984 **Triple XXX Root Beer Co.**
S.R. 26 W & Salisbury
West Lafayette, IN 47906
765-743-5373
Fax: 713-780-8764
contact@triplexxxrootbeer.com
www.triplexxxrootbeer.com
Soft drinks
President: Lee Lydick
Estimated Sales: Below $5 Million
Number Employees: 1-4
Brands:
Triple Xxx

12985 **Triple-C**
8 Burford Road
Hamilton, ON L8E 5B1
Canada
905-573-7900
Fax: 905-573-7867 800-263-9105
VP Sales/Marketing: Harry Scholtens
Brands:
Gummy Guy
Rachel's
Sour Simon

12986 **Tripoli Bakery Inc**
106 Common St
Lawrence, MA 01840-1633
978-682-7754
Fax: 978-687-8455 www.tripolibakery.com
Breads, rolls
President: Rosario Zappala
Estimated Sales: $1-2.5 000,000
Number Employees: 20-49

12987 **Tripper Inc**
PO Box 51440
Oxnard, CA 93031-1440
805-988-8851
Fax: 805-988-2992 www.tripper.com
Processor and importer of kosher & spices including pepper, nutmeg, cinnamon, and ginger; also, ingredients including vainilla beans and extracts; organic available
Owner: Francois Bervard
frab@tripper.com
Estimated Sales: $1-2.5 Million
Number Employees: 1-4
Square Footage: 60000
Type of Packaging: Food Service, Private Label, Bulk
Brands:
Alligator Pepper
Bullfrog Lavander
Chameleon Pepper
Cobra Vanilla
Dragon Cinnamon
Elephant Ginger
Flamingo Pepper
Gorilla Cloves
Leopard Cardamon
Orangutan Mace
Panther Pepper
Rhino Nutmeg
Tiger Pepper
Toro Safron
Tripper

12988 **Tristao Trading**
116 John St Rm 500
New York, NY 10038
212-285-8120
Fax: 212-964-1735 admin@tristaousa.com
Coffee
Manager: Liz Wagner
President: Ricardo Tristao
Contact: Joao Carollo
jcarollo@tristao.com
Estimated Sales: $5-10 000,000
Number Employees: 1-4

12989 **Triton Seafood Co**
7301 NW 77th St
Medley, FL 33166-2205
305-888-0051
Fax: 305-888-1485
All-natural conch chowder and conch fritters
CEO: Alfredo Alvarez
asa@tritonsfd.com
Marketing Director: Yvonne Conde
Estimated Sales: $1700000
Number Employees: 10-19
Type of Packaging: Food Service, Private Label
Brands:
Neptune's

12990 **Triumph Brewing Co**
138 Nassau St # A
Princeton, NJ 08542-7011
609-924-7855
Fax: 609-924-7857 www.triumphbrewing.com
Seasonal beer, ale, stout and pilsner
Manager: Doug Bork
General Manager: Eric Nutt
Estimated Sales: Below $5 Million
Number Employees: 50-99
Type of Packaging: Consumer, Food Service

12991 **Triumph Foods, LLC**
5302 Stockyards Espressway
St. Joseph, MO 64506
816-396-2700
800-262-7907
info@triumphfoods.com triumphfoods.com
Pork and pork products
Chief Executive Officer: Mark Campbell
SVP & Chief Financial Officer: Kevin Wedeking
VP, Finance & Accounting: Josh Kleinlein
VP, Human Resources & Communication: Kevin Neal
VP, Genetics & Livestock Procurement: Jerry Lehenbauer
EVP & Chief Operating Officer: Matt England
Year Founded: 2003
Estimated Sales: $1.6 Billion
Number Employees: 2,800
Square Footage: 11000
Type of Packaging: Consumer

12992 **Trophy Nut Co**
320 N 2nd St
Tipp City, OH 45371-1912
937-667-8478
Fax: 937-667-4656 800-219-9004
customercare@trophynut.com www.trophynut.com
Dry and oil roasted nuts
President: Mike Bhagmath
mbhagmath@loraincounty.us
CEO: Dave Henning
QA/QC Manager: Phyllis Nieter
VP Sales/Plant Manager: Bob Wilke
Operations Manager: Chrissy Wagner
Purchasing: Dawn Akers
Year Founded: 1968
Estimated Sales: $24 Million
Number Employees: 50-99
Square Footage: 110000
Type of Packaging: Consumer, Food Service, Private Label, Bulk
Brands:
Nut Barrel
Trophy Gold Nut Barrel
Trophy Nut
True Measures Baking Nuts

12993 **Tropic Fish Hawaii LLC**
2312 Kamehameha Hwy E-5
Honolulu, HI 96819
808-591-2936
Fax: 808-591-2934 sales@tropicfishhawaii.com
www.tropicfishhawaii.com
Tuna, billfish, bottomfish, open ocean fish
President & COO: Shawn Tanoue
CEO: Charles Umamoto
General Manager: Daryl Yamaguchi
VP Sales: Toby Arakawa
VP Operations: Shannon Tanoue
Estimated Sales: $20-50 Million
Number Employees: 100-249

12994 **Tropical Açaí LLC**
587 East Sample Rd. # 263
Pompano Beach, FL 33064
917-699-1923
855-550-2224
www.tropicalaçai.com
Organic a‡ai berry packs, a‡ai sorbets
General Manager: Renata Nogueria
Number of Brands: 1
Number of Products: 10
Type of Packaging: Consumer, Private Label
Brands:
Tropical A‡ai

12995 **Tropical Blossom Honey Co**
106 N Ridgewood Ave
Edgewater, FL 32132-1714
386-428-9027
Fax: 386-423-8469
Honey
Vice President: Michael Hauger
m.hauger@tropicbeehoney.com
VP: John Ginnis
Estimated Sales: $1.3 Million
Number Employees: 10-19

12996 **Tropical Cheese**
452 Fayette St
Perth Amboy, NJ 08861
732-442-4898
Fax: 732-442-8227 888-874-4928
admin@tropicalcheese.com
www.tropicalcheese.com
Hispanic specialty food products, including cheese products, tortillas, beverages, meat products, other dairy products and desserts.
President & Founder: Rafael Mendez
Vice President of Opertions: Alejandro Lopez
Production Manager: Alex Quiles
Year Founded: 1983
Number of Brands: 5
Type of Packaging: Consumer
Brands:
Authentic Latino Flavor
Flavor of Mexico
Flavor of Central America
Flavor of South America
Tropical

12997 **Tropical Commodities**
9230 Nw 12th Street
Miami, FL 33172
305-471-8120
Fax: 305-471-9825 tropicom@direcway.com
Fresh habanero chili peppers and mash as well as other varieties of chili peppers.
President: D Douglas Bernard
Vice President: Robert Kholer
Marketing: Alberto Beers
Estimated Sales: $1.3-1.5 Million
Number Employees: 5-9
Number of Products: 10
Square Footage: 60000
Type of Packaging: Private Label, Bulk
Brands:
Caribbean Hot Peppers

12998 **Tropical Foods**
350 Riverside Pkwy
Lithia Springs, GA 30122-3865
770-438-9950
Fax: 770-435-1371 800-544-3762
info@tropicalfoods.com www.tropicalfoods.com
Processor and importer of candy, dried fruits, nuts, seeds, Asian rice snacks and dessert toppings
President: David Williamson
President: John Bauer
Sales Director: Debbie Ponton
Manager: Peter Njuguna
njuguna@tropical.com
Operations Manager: William Stapleton
Estimated Sales: $10-20 Million
Number Employees: 10-19
Parent Co: Tropical
Type of Packaging: Food Service, Private Label, Bulk

12999 **(HQ)Tropical Foods**
1100 Continental Blvd
PO Box 7507
Charlotte, NC 28273-6380
704-588-0400
Fax: 704-588-3092 800-438-4470
info@tropicalfoods.com www.tropicalfoods.com
Snack mixes, dried fruits, roasted nuts, seeds, candy and confectionery, spices and specialty foods including oils, vinegars, mustards, artichoke hearts, roasted bell peppers and pasta
Owner/CEO: Angela Bauer
Chief Operating Officer: John Bauer
Director of Marketing: Chad Hartman
Director of Human Resources: Juan Gomez
Purchasing Manager: Bryan Keeton
Year Founded: 1977
Estimated Sales: $24600000
Number Employees: 100-249
Square Footage: 72000
Type of Packaging: Consumer, Food Service, BulkTropical Memphis
Memphis TN
Tropical Landover
Landover MD
Brands:
Christille Bay

13000 **Tropical Foods**
350 Riverside Pkwy.
Lithia Springs, GA 30122
800-544-3762
info@tropicalfoods.com www.tropicalfoods.com
Snack mixes, dried fruits, roasted nuts, seeds, candy and confectionery, spices and specialty foods including oils, vinegars, mustards, artichoke hearts, roasted bell peppers and pasta
Type of Packaging: Consumer, Food Service, Bulk

13001 **Tropical Foods**
1160 Mustang Dr.
Suite 400
DFW Airport, TX 75261
866-847-6887
info@tropicalfoods.com www.tropicalfoods.com
Snack mixes, dried fruits, roasted nuts, seeds, candy and confectionery, spices and specialty foods including oils, vinegars, mustards, artichoke hearts, roasted bell peppers and pasta
Type of Packaging: Consumer, Food Service, Bulk

13002 **Tropical Foods**
1650 Shelby Oaks Dr.
Suite 1
Memphis, TN 38134
800-223-8171
info@tropicalfoods.com www.tropicalfoods.com
Snack mixes, dried fruits, roasted nuts, seeds, candy and confectionery, spices and specialty foods including oils, vinegars, mustards, artichoke hearts, roasted bell peppers and pasta
Type of Packaging: Consumer, Food Service, Bulk

13003 **Tropical Foods**
3368 Bartlett Blvd.
Orlando, FL 32811
800-749-8869
info@tropicalfoods.com www.tropicalfoods.com
Snack mixes, dried fruits, roasted nuts, seeds, candy and confectionery, spices and specialty foods including oils, vinegars, mustards, artichoke hearts, roasted bell peppers and pasta
Type of Packaging: Consumer, Food Service, Bulk

13004 **Tropical Foods**
573-A Commerce Dr.
Upper Marlboro, MD 20774
800-220-0125
info@tropicalfoods.com www.tropicalfoods.com
Snack mixes, dried fruits, roasted nuts, seeds, candy and confectionery, spices and specialty foods including oils, vinegars, mustards, artichoke hearts, roasted bell peppers and pasta
Type of Packaging: Consumer, Food Service, Bulk

13005 **Tropical Illusions**
1436 Lulu Street
PO Box 338
Trenton, MO 64683-1819
660-359-5422
Fax: 660-359-5347 tropical@tropicalillusions.com
Processor and exporter of frozen drinks mixes including. cocktail, slush and granita, cream base, and smoothies.
President: Vance Cox
Vice President: Carrol Baugher
Estimated Sales: $590,000
Number Employees: 6
Square Footage: 200000
Type of Packaging: Food Service, Private Label
Brands:
Captain Space Freeze
Elmeco
Tropical Illusions

13006 **Tropical Link Canada Ltd.**
7668 Winston St.
Burnaby, BC
Canada
778-379-3510
Fax: 778-379-3511 www.tropicallinkcanada.ca
Organic cinnamon powder, cinnamon sticks, turmeric powder, coconut sugar, coconut oil, coconut vinegar, prepared fruit dips, rice blends, bulk dried fruit
Director: Sudhani Perera
Number of Brands: 2
Number of Products: 20
Type of Packaging: Consumer, Private Label, Bulk
Brands:
Snow Farms
Wild Tusker

13007 **Tropical Nut & Fruit Co**
3368 Bartlett Blvd
Orlando, FL 32811-6482
407-841-8273
Fax: 407-843-4340 800-749-8869
nutsnorl@aol.com
Custom snack mixes, freshly roasted nuts and seeds, baking items, candies, spices, dried fruit, grains and minibar items.
President: John Baller
david@tropicalnutandfruit.com
Estimated Sales: $6000000
Number Employees: 50-99
Type of Packaging: Consumer, Food Service, Private Label, Bulk

13008 **Tropical Nut Fruit & Bulk Cndy**
350 Riverside Pkwy
Lithia Springs, GA 30122-3865
770-438-9950
Fax: 770-435-1371 800-544-3762
info@tropicalfoods.com www.tropicalfoods.com

Nut candy, caramels, sesame sticks, soup mixes and dried fruits
President: David Williamson
Manager: Peter Njuguna
njuguna@tropical.com
Estimated Sales: $10-20 Million
Number Employees: 10-19
Square Footage: 56000
Type of Packaging: Consumer, Food Service, Bulk

13009 **Tropical Preserving Co Inc**
1711 E 15th St
Los Angeles, CA 90021-2715
213-748-5108
Fax: 213-748-4998 sales@tropicalpreserving.com
www.tropicalpreserving.com
Processor and exporter of jams, jellies and apple butter
President: Ronald Randall
Estimated Sales: $12,000,000
Number Employees: 20-49
Type of Packaging: Consumer, Private Label
Brands:
Market's Best

13010 **Tropical Treets**
130 Bermondsey Road
North York, ON M4A 1X5
Canada
416-759-8777
Fax: 416-759-7782 888-424-8229
www.tropicaltreets.com
Tropical ice cream; wholesaler/distributor of tropical food products, drinks and juices
CEO: Rumi Keshavjee
VP Sales/Marketing: Zahir Keshavjee
Estimated Sales: $471,000
Number Employees: 5
Square Footage: 24000

13011 **Tropical Valley Foods**
32 Powerdam Way
Dock 30
Plattsburgh, NY 12901
Fax: 518-478-8838 877-756-6831
www.nextchocolates.com
Chocolate coated fruits and nuts
President & Owner: Eric Bertheau
Quality Control: Darrell Clark
Marketing & HR Coordinator: Elizabeth LaRosa
elizabeth@tropical-valley-foods.com
Sales Consultant: Armand Langevin
Director of Operations: Amanda Gokey
Production Manager: Warren Caswell
Estimated Sales: $3.7 Million
Number Employees: 25
Brands:
next organics(c)

13012 **(HQ)Tropicana Products Inc.**
555 W. Monroe St.
Chicago, IL 60661
800-237-7799
www.tropicana.com
Orange and grapefruit juices, as well as frozen concentrates.
Chairman/CEO, PepsiCo: Ramon Laguarta
Year Founded: 1947
Estimated Sales: $431.9 Million
Number Employees: 1000-4999
Square Footage: 100000
Parent Co: PepsiCo
Type of Packaging: Consumer, Food Service
Brands:
Trop50
Tropicana
Tropicana Essentials
Tropicana Kids
Tropicana Twister

13013 **Troppers**
P.O.Box 50211
Santa Barbara, CA 93150-0211
805-969-4054
Baked goods
Manager: Diane Tourney
Estimated Sales: $.5-1 000,000
Number Employees: 1-4

13014 **Trotter Soft Pretzels**
1880 N Penn Road
Hatfield, PA 19440-1950
215-855-2197
Fax: 215-855-0725
Soft Pretzels, snack foods
Plant Manager: Wayne Childs
Estimated Sales: $10-20 Million
Number Employees: 20-49
Parent Co: J&J Snack Foods Company

13015 **Trout Lake Farm**
PO Box 181
Trout Lake, WA 98650
509-395-2025
Fax: 509-395-2749 800-655-6988
www.troutlakefarm.com
Processor, exporter and importer of certified organically grown medicinal and beverage tea herbs and spices including garlic, oregano, peppermint and spearmint
CEO: Lloyd Scott
Sales Manager: Martha-Jane Hylton
Contact: Sharon Frazey
sharon.frazey@troutlakefarm.com
Operations Manager: Gary Vollema
Estimated Sales: $3500000
Number Employees: 50
Square Footage: 160000
Type of Packaging: Bulk
Brands:
1st Sneeze Echinacea
Camus Prarie Tea
Florased Valerian
Trout Lake Farm

13016 **Troverco**
727 N 1st Street
St. Louis, MO 63102
Fax: 314-925-4099 800-468-3354
Manufacturer and distributor of prepared meals and snack foods.
CEO: Joseph Trover
Contact: Rodney Gordon
rodney.gordon@troverco.com
Type of Packaging: Consumer, Food Service, Private Label
Brands:
Deli Maid
Landshire

13017 **Troy Foods Inc**
404 E US Highway 40
Troy, IL 62294-2205
618-667-6332
www.troyfoodsinc.us
Meat including home cured ham and bacon, frankfurters, bologna and sausage
President: Don Nihiser
dnihiser@troyfoodsinc.com
Estimated Sales: $2,000,000
Number Employees: 5-9
Type of Packaging: Consumer

13018 **Troy Pork Store**
158 4th St
Troy, NY 12180
518-272-8291
Fax: 518-272-8291
Fresh, smoked and pickled pork and beef
Owner: Carmen Amedeo
Estimated Sales: $500,000-$1 Million
Number Employees: 1-4
Type of Packaging: Consumer

13019 **Troyer Foods Inc**
17141 State Road 4
PO Box 608
Goshen, IN 46528-6674
574-533-0302
Fax: 574-533-3851 800-876-9377
www.troyers.com
Brand Director/President: Paris Ball-Miller
Executive Director: Tony Swihart
CFO & Controller: Neal Yoder
Executive Director: Donald Hixenbaugh
Director of Marketing: Beth Rodick
Director of Sales: Terry Blythe
Operations Manager: Frank Herbes
Production Manager: Steve Gile
Number Employees: 100-249
Other Locations:
Central Warehouse Troyer Foods
Bloomington IN
South Warehouse Troyer Foods
Grandview IN

13020 **Tru Chocolate**
PO Box 317
Medford, MA 02155
855-878-2462
info@tru-chocolate.com
tru-chocolate.com
Dark chocolate covered almonds, raisins and pretzels
CEO: Michael F. Gilmore
Chief Financial Officer: David Dahn
Brands:
TRU Chocolate(c)

13021 **Tru Fru, LLC**
1546 S 4650 W # 200
Salt Lake City, UT 84104
888-437-2497
info@trufru.com www.trufru.com
Freeze-dried, dark chocolate-covered fruits
Co-Founder: Taz Murray
National Sales Director: Dion Rasmussen
Year Founded: 2015
Number of Brands: 1
Number of Products: 6
Type of Packaging: Consumer, Private Label
Brands:
TruFru

13022 **Tru-Blu Cooperative Associates**
PO Box 5
New Lisbon, NJ 08064-0005
609-894-8717
trublucoop@aol.com
Fresh and frozen blueberries
General Manager: Dennis Doyle
Number Employees: 1-4
Type of Packaging: Consumer

13023 **TruBrain**
Santa Monica, CA
650-241-8372
team@trubrain.com
www.trubrain.com
Drinks and bars to improve brain function; ketones
Founder/CEO: Chris Thompson
Finance & Strategy: Gary Epper
Lead Neuroscientist: Dr. Andrew Hill
Product Research & Development: Garrett Ruhland
Marketing: Bill Mackay
Analytics/Operations: Tomas Ferrari
Product Management: Celso Ferrari

13024 **TruMoo**
P.O. Box 961447
El Paso, TX 79996
800-395-7004
www.trumoo.com
Flavored milk and protein shakes.
CEO, Dean Foods Company: Ralph Scozzafava
Parent Co: Dean Foods Company
Type of Packaging: Consumer, Private Label

13025 **TruVibe Organics**
Santa Monica, CA
www.truvibeorganics.com
Organic superfood blends (raw cacao nibs, goji berries, chia seeds) and superfood meal replacement drinks
Co-Founder: Anand Dani
Co-Founder: Jason Dekker
Year Founded: 2013
Number of Brands: 1
Number of Products: 10
Type of Packaging: Consumer, Private Label
Brands:
Eat Clean Organic
TruVibe

13026 **Truan's Candies**
13716 Tireman St
Detroit, MI 48228
313-584-3400
800-584-3004
Chocolate
President: Mark Truan
Estimated Sales: $5-10 Million
Number Employees: 10-19
Type of Packaging: Private Label

13027 **Truchard Vineyards**
3234 Old Sonoma Rd
Napa, CA 94559-9701
707-253-7153
Fax: 707-253-7234

Wine
Owner: Anthony Truchard
truchard@aol.com
Estimated Sales: $5-10 Million
Number Employees: 20-49
Brands:
Truchard Vineyards

13028 **Truckee River Winery**
11467 Brockway Rd
Truckee, CA 96161-2115
530-587-4626
Fax: 530-550-8809 russ@truckeeriverwinery.com
www.truckeeriverwinery.com
Wines
Owner: Russ Jones
russ@truckeeriverwinery.com
Co-Owner: Joan Jones
Sales Manager: Kate Shaw-Outside
russ@truckeeriverwinery.com
Estimated Sales: Under $300,000
Number Employees: 1-4
Type of Packaging: Private Label
Brands:
Truckee River

13029 **Truco Enterprises**
2727 Realty Rd
Carrollton, TX 75006
972-869-4600
ontheborderproducts.com
Manufacturer of authentic Mexican-style chips, salsas and queso dips.
President & CEO: Jeff Partridge
CFO: Nicki Wolpmann
Contact: Kimberly Slone
kslone@pilgrims.com
Senior VP, Operations: Steve Slack
Brands:
On The Border(c)

13030 **True Beverages**
2001 East Terra Lane
O Fallon, MO 63366-4434
636-240-2400
Fax: 636-272-7546 800-325-6152
truefood@truemfg.com www.truemfg.com
Beverages
Owner: Bill Smith
Contact: Russel Gledstone
rgledstone@truemfg.com
Brands:
True Beverages

13031 **True Blue Farms**
9548 County Road 215
Grand Junction, MI 49056-9214
269-434-6112
Fax: 269-434-8192 877-654-2400
www.truebluefarms.com
Blueberries including fresh, frozen and puree
Owner: Shelly Hartmann
CEO: Myron Brady
Secretary: Evelyn Farmer
Marketing Manager: Juana Chavez
Sales: Ronald Benson
truebluefarms@btc-bci.com
Office Manager: Lee Erickson
Estimated Sales: Less Than $500,000
Number Employees: 5-9
Type of Packaging: Consumer, Food Service, Private Label, Bulk

13032 **True Jerky**
226 Union St
Suite A
San Francisco, CA 94123
858-336-2005
www.madebytrue.com
Flavored beef jerky, jerky snack mix and biltong
Chief Executive Officer: Jess Thomas
Year Founded: 2015
Number of Brands: 2
Number of Products: 12
Type of Packaging: Consumer, Private Label
Brands:
True Jerky
Made by True

13033 **True Nopal Cactus Water**
8255 East Raintree Dr. # 300
Scottsdale, AZ 85260
480-636-8044
info@truenopal.com
www.truenopal.com
All-natural cactus water
Number of Brands: 1
Number of Products: 1
Type of Packaging: Consumer, Private Label
Brands:
True Nopal

13034 **True Organic Product Inc**
20225 W Kamm Ave
Helm, CA 93627
559-866-3001
Fax: 559-866-3003 800-487-0379
info@trueorganicproducts.net
Processor and exporter of organic juices including orange, apple, pineapple, grape, tangerine, lime, watermelon, blackberry, soursop, lulo and pineapple blends
President/CEO: Jake Evan
CEO: Jake Evans
jevans@trueorganicproducts.net
Estimated Sales: $3-5 Million
Number Employees: 20-49
Square Footage: 48000
Brands:
True Organic

13035 **True Story Foods**
San Francisco, CA
888-277-1171
hi@truestoryfoods.com www.truestoryfoods.com
Organic, GMO-free deli meats, sausages, hot dogs and fresh pork
Founder/Chief Executive Officer: Phil Gatto
Number of Brands: 1
Number of Products: 34
Type of Packaging: Consumer, Private Label
Brands:
True Story Foods

13036 **True World Foods LLC**
24 Link Dr
Rockleigh, NJ 07647-2504
201-750-0024
Fax: 201-750-0025 info@trueworldfoods.com
www.trueworldfoods.com
Fresh seafood
President: Jackie Madsuka
CEO: Takeshi Yashiro
yashiro@trueworldfoods.com
Estimated Sales: $20-50 Million
Number Employees: 100-249

13037 **Truffle Treasures**
314 Richmond Road
Ottawa, ON K1Z 6X6
Canada
613-761-3859
www.truffletreasures.com
Handmade candies and chocolates including truffles, chocolate bars, brittle, dipped fruits, coffees & teas, cookies and other candies
Owner: Lara Vaarre

13038 **Truitt Bros Inc**
1105 Front St NE
PO Box 309
Salem, OR 97301-1034
503-362-3674
Fax: 503-581-5912 800-547-8712
truittbros@truittbros.com www.truittbros.com
Canned green beans, cherries, pears and plums; also, shelf stable entrees
Founder and CEO: David Truitt
davidt@truittbros.com
Estimated Sales: $20-50 Million
Number Employees: 500-999
Type of Packaging: Consumer, Food Service, Private Label
Brands:
Truitt Bros.

13039 **Trumark**
830 E Elizabeth Ave
Linden, NJ 7036
908-486-5900
Fax: 908-486-5900 800-752-7877
Processor and exporter of sodium and potassium lactate and lactate and acetate blends
President: Mark Satz
CEO: Jeff Wales
Contact: Kathy Moraglia
kathy@tru-mark.com
Estimated Sales: $780,000
Number Employees: 10-19

13040 **Trumps Food Interest**
646 Powell St
Vancouver, BC V6A 1H4
Canada
604-732-8473
Fax: 604-732-8433 info@trumpsfood.com
www.trumpsfood.com
Manufacturer of dessert products.
Managing Director: Heather Angel
Number of Products: 200+

13041 **Truth Bar LLC**
260 Charles St. # 210
Waltham, MA 02453
888-886-8959
www.truthbar.com
Various flavors of energy bars with prebiotics and probiotics
Co-Founder: Sean Fay
Co-Founder: Diana Stobo
Year Founded: 2014
Number of Brands: 1
Number of Products: 5
Type of Packaging: Consumer, Private Label
Brands:
Truth Bar

13042 **Tsar Nicoulai Caviar LLC**
60 Dorman Ave
San Francisco, CA 94124-1807
415-543-3007
Fax: 415-543-5172 800-952-2842
info@tsarnicoulai.com www.tsarnicoulai.com
Caviar and smoked fish
President/CEO: Mats Engstrom
Co-Owner: Dafne Engstrom
Manager: Marian Mahone
concierge@tsarnicoulai.com
Estimated Sales: $500,000-$1 Million
Number Employees: 20-49
Type of Packaging: Private Label
Brands:
Tsar Nicoulai Caviar

13043 **Tu Me Beverage Company**
818-237-5105
info@tumewater.com
www.drinktume.com
Turmeric-infused, naturally-sweetened flavored water
Co-Founder: Shaina Zaidi
Number of Brands: 1
Number of Products: 5
Type of Packaging: Consumer, Private Label
Brands:
Tu Me

13044 **Tualatin Estate Vineyards**
10850 NW Seavey Rd
Forest Grove, OR 97116-7703
503-357-5005
Fax: 503-357-1702 tualatinestate@yahoo.com
www.tualatinestate.com
Processor and exporter of table wines including chardonnay, pinot noir, pinot blanc, gewurtztraminer, riesling and semi-sparkling muscat
Founder: Jim Bernau
Vice President: William L Fuller
Operations Manager/Winegrower: Stirling Fox
Winemaker: Joe Dobbes
Estimated Sales: $600000
Number Employees: 10-19
Square Footage: 80000
Parent Co: Willamette Valley Vineyards
Type of Packaging: Consumer
Brands:
Tualatin Estate

13045 **Tucker Cellars**
70 Ray Rd
Sunnyside, WA 98944
509-837-8701
Fax: 509-837-8701 wineman@televar.com
www.tuckercellars.net
Wines and pickled vegetables
Co-Owner: Rose Tucker
Co-Owner: Randy Tucker

Estimated Sales: $1-2.5 Million
Number Employees: 5-9
Brands:
Tucker

13046 Tucker Packing Co
955 N Mill St
Orrville, OH 44667
330-683-3311
http://www.marshallville-meats.com/
Fresh and frozen beef, pork and lamb
President: John Tucker
Plant Manager: Leon Hilty
Estimated Sales: $1,600,000
Number Employees: 10-19
Type of Packaging: Consumer, Food Service, Bulk

13047 Tucker Pecan Co
350 N Mcdonough St
Montgomery, AL 36104-3652
334-262-4470
Fax: 334-262-4690 800-239-6540
sales@tuckerpecan.com www.tuckerpecan.com
Processor and wholesaler/distributor of pecans
President: David Little
sales@tuckerpecan.com
Operations Manager: David Little
Estimated Sales: $450,000
Number Employees: 10-19
Square Footage: 13436
Type of Packaging: Consumer, Food Service, Bulk

13048 Tucson Tamale Company
Tucson, AZ
520-398-6282
www.tucsontamale.com
Handmade tamales with various meat, cheese and bean fillings; organic hot sauce; oregano and seasoning mixes
Founder/Owner: Todd Martin
Year Founded: 2008
Number of Brands: 1
Type of Packaging: Consumer, Private Label
Brands:
Tucson Tamale

13049 Tudal Winery
1015 Big Tree Rd
St Helena, CA 94574-9711
707-963-3947
Fax: 707-968-9691 www.tudalwinery.com
Wines
Owner: Alma Tudal
matt@tudalwinery.com
Vice President: John Tudal
Marketing Director: Susan Greene
Estimated Sales: Less than $500,000
Number Employees: 1-4
Type of Packaging: Private Label
Brands:
2001 Estate Cabernet Sauvignon
Flat Bed Red
Tractor Shed Red

13050 Tufts Ranch
27260 State Highway 128
Winters, CA 95694-9066
530-795-4144
Fax: 530-795-3844
Grower and packer of apricots, prunes, kiwifruit and persimmons. Broker of walnuts and almonds
General Manager: Stan Tufts
Office Manager: Brad Graf
Estimated Sales: $5-10 Million
Number Employees: 50 to 99

13051 Tularosa Vineyards
23 Coyote Canyon Rd
Tularosa, NM 88352-9404
575-585-2260
Fax: 505-585-2260 800-687-4467
www.tularosavineyards.com
Wines
Owner: David Wickham
wine@nmex.com
Estimated Sales: $250,000
Number Employees: 5-9
Brands:
Tularosa Wines

13052 Tulkoff's Food ProductsInc
2229 Van Deman St
Baltimore, MD 21224-6604
410-327-6585
Fax: 443-524-0148 800-638-7343
www.tulkoff.com
Condiment, sauce and ingredient manufacturer.
Owner: Phil Tulkoff
dave@tulkoff.com
Number Employees: 50-99
Type of Packaging: Consumer, Food Service, Private Label, Bulk
Brands:
Snap-Back
Top
Tulkoff

13053 Tull Hill Farms Inc
2264 Hugo Rd
Kinston, NC 28501-7173
252-523-8052
Fax: 252-523-8052
Grower of sweet potatoes
Vice President: Michael Hill
the98@esn.net
Sales: Kendall Hill
Sales: Rob Hill
Estimated Sales: $1-2.5 Million
Number Employees: 20-49
Brands:
Hill's

13054 Tulocay Cemetery
411 Coombsville Rd
P.O.Box 7
Napa, CA 94558-3957
707-252-4727
Fax: 707-252-8375 888-627-2859
www.tulocaycemetery.org
Baking mixes, balsamic & champagne vinegars, dessert sauces, dipping and flavored oils, everyday classics, vinaigarettes & dressings, global herbed rubs, herbed rubs, marinades & glazes, mustards, savory sauces, tapenades & savorycondiments, gift sets, and fruit condiments
Manager: Peter Manasse
Director Manufacturing: William Cadman
Estimated Sales: Less than $500,000
Number Employees: 10-19

13055 Tumai Water
PO Box 1751
Martinsburg, WV 25402
304-264-1466
866-948-8624
Bottled spring water
Owner/President/CEO: Bob Downey
Estimated Sales: $32,000
Number Employees: 2
Square Footage: 4768
Parent Co: Spero Group
Type of Packaging: Consumer

13056 Tumbador Chocolate
34 34th St
Unit 6
Brooklyn, NY 11232-2020
718-788-0200
Fax: 718-788-3179 sales@tumbadorchocolate.com
www.tumbadorchocolate.com
Chocolates and spreads
CEO: Michael Altman
Sales Manager: Carolyn Barwicki
Estimated Sales: $2-5 Million
Number Employees: 11-50
Type of Packaging: Consumer, Food Service, Private Label
Brands:
Brooklyn Born Chocolate(c)
Tumbador(c) Chocolate

13057 Tumericalive Healing Enterprise
39 Broadway
Suite 1110
New York, NY 10006
347-559-6760
info@templeturmeric.com
www.templeturmeric.com
Manufacturer of turmeric-based beverages.
Founder and CEO: Daniel Sullivan
Contact: Michelle Tyler
michelle@tumericalive.com
Number Employees: 11-50

13058 Tuna Fresh
401 Whitney Ave # 103
Gretna, LA 70056-2500
504-363-2744
Fax: 504-392-3324 www.chartwellsmenus.com
Tuna
Manager: John Duke

13059 Tundra Wild Rice
PO Box 263
Pine Falls, NB R0E 1M0
Canada
204-367-8651
Fax: 204-367-8309
Processor and exporter of Canadian lake wild rice
President: Denis Pereux
Sales/Marketing: Ed Thibedeau
Number Employees: 4
Square Footage: 11360
Type of Packaging: Private Label, Bulk
Brands:
Tundra

13060 Turano Baking
6501 Roosevelt Rd
Berwyn, IL 60402-1100
708-788-9220
Fax: 708-788-3075 info@turano.com
www.turano.com
Fresh and frozen breads, rolls and pastries
President: Turano Co
aturano@turano.com
Chairman & CEO: Renato Turano
VP: Umberto Turano
EVP Sales & Marketing: Giancarlo Turano
EVP Production & Operations: Tony Turano
Estimated Sales: $6.76 Million
Number Employees: 250-499
Square Footage: 280000
Type of Packaging: Consumer, Food Service, Private Label
Brands:
Turano

13061 Turano Baking
6501 Roosevelt Rd
Berwyn, IL 60402-1100
708-788-9220
Fax: 708-788-3075 info@turano.com
www.turano.com
Baked goods, bread
Co-Owner/President: Turano Umberto
Co-Owner/Chief Executive Officer: Renato Turano
Vice President, Finance/Controller: Sandra Battersby
Executive VP Sales/Marketing: Giarcarto Turano
Estimated Sales: $46,000,000
Number Employees: 250-499
Type of Packaging: Private Label

13062 Turk Brothers Custom Meats Inc
1903 Orange Rd
Ashland, OH 44805-1399
419-289-1051
Fax: 419-281-8280 800-789-1051
www.turkbrothersmeats.com
Processor and wholesaler/distributor of beef, pork and lamb; wholesaler/distributor of frozen foods, equipment and fixtures and seafood; serving the food service market; also, slaughtering services available
Owner: Roy M Turk
VP: Kevin Turk
Estimated Sales: $5-10 Million
Number Employees: 10-19
Square Footage: 33684
Type of Packaging: Consumer, Food Service, Bulk

13063 Turkey Creeks Snacks Inc
1286 Thurston School Rd
Thomaston, GA 30286-7636
706-647-8841
Fax: 706-647-3978 800-329-8875
info@turkeycreeksnacks.com
www.turkeycreeksnacks.com
Pork rinds, hard cracklings and hot sauce
Owner: Laddie Fulcher
Estimated Sales: $3-5 Million
Number Employees: 20-49
Square Footage: 100000
Type of Packaging: Consumer, Food Service, Private Label, Bulk
Brands:
Deli Style

Sunrise Farms
Turkey Creek

13064 Turkey Hill Dairy Inc
2601 River Rd
Conestoga, PA 17516-9341
717-872-5461
Fax: 717-872-4130 800-693-2479
careers@turkeyhill.com www.turkeyhill.com
Ice cream, sherbet, frozen yogurt and drinks
President: Edison Abreu
edison.abreu@turkeyhill.com
Executive Vice President: John Cox
Number Employees: 500-999
Square Footage: 428000
Type of Packaging: Consumer, Private Label, Bulk
Brands:
Turkey Hill

13065 Turkey Hill Sugarbush
10 Waterloo Street
PO Box 160
Waterloo, QC J0E 2N0
Canada
450-539-4822
Fax: 450-539-1561 www.turkeyhill.ca
Processor and exporter of maple products including syrups, cookies, chocolates, coffee, tea, fudge, caramels, butter, soft and hard candies
President/Board Member: Michael Herman
Chairman: Brian Herman
Estimated Sales: $10-20 Million
Number Employees: 35
Number of Brands: 1
Number of Products: 85
Square Footage: 70000
Type of Packaging: Consumer, Private Label, Bulk
Brands:
Turkey Hill

13066 Turkey Store
116 4th Ave NW
Faribault, MN 55021
507-334-5555
Fax: 507-332-5349 www.jennieo.com
Fresh and frozen whole turkeys
Director Operations: Steve Williams
Manager Distribution: Pete Vikeras
Estimated Sales: Less Than $500,000
Number Employees: 1-4
Type of Packaging: Consumer, Private Label

13067 Turlock Fruit Co
500 S Tully Rd
Turlock, CA 95380-5121
209-634-7207
Fax: 209-632-4273 www.turlockfruit.com
Processor and exporter of honeydew melons
President: Donald Smith
Treasurer: Stephen Smith
Secretary: Stuart Smith
Estimated Sales: $500,000-$1 Million
Number Employees: 20-49
Type of Packaging: Consumer, Bulk
Brands:
King O' The-West
Oak Flat
Peacock
Sycamore

13068 Turnbull Bakeries
523 First Street
New Orleans, LA 70130-2004
504-581-5383
Fax: 504-581-6115 www.turnbullbakeries.com
Bread sticks, bread crumbs, and melba toast
Owner: Wayne Turnbull
Sales/Marketing: Steven Wolf
Sales/Marketing: Andrew Ford
Director of Sales: Frank LeCourt
Contact: Elizabeth Turnbull
turnbula@bellsouth.net
Chief Operating Officer: John Riddell
Plant Manager: Wes Stone
Number Employees: 10,000
Type of Packaging: Food Service, Private Label, Bulk

13069 Turnbull Cone Baking Company
PO Box 6248
Chattanooga, TN 37401-6248
423-265-4551
Fax: 423-624-8724
Ice cream cones and wafers; also, melba toast
President: Wayne W Turnbull
Director Sales: Deris Bagli
Number Employees: 100-249
Parent Co: Turnbull Bakeries
Type of Packaging: Private Label

13070 Turner & Pease Company
1519 Elliott Avenue W
Seattle, WA 98119-3129
206-282-9535
Fax: 206-282-9633
Butter
President: Milton Turner
National Sales: Bill Bowen
Number Employees: 25
Square Footage: 72000
Type of Packaging: Consumer, Food Service, Private Label, Bulk
Brands:
Creamerie Classique
Golden West
Meadowbrook

13071 Turner Dairy Farms Inc
1049 Jefferson Rd
Pittsburgh, PA 15235-4700
412-372-2211
Fax: 412-372-0651 800-892-1039
info@turnerdairy.net www.turnerdairy.net
Milk, premium ice teas, fruit drinks, juices, cultured dairy, cream, ice cream mixes, butter and eggs
President: Chuck Turner
Management: Jim Turner
Controller: Robin Turner
Year Founded: 1930
Estimated Sales: $20-50 Million
Number Employees: 100-249

13072 Turri's Italian Foods
16695 Common Rd
Roseville, MI 48066-1901
586-773-6010
Fax: 586-773-6851 www.turrisitalianfoods.com
A full line of Italian specialities including Ravioli, lasagna, manicotti, tortellini and other fine pastas
Vice President: John Turri
gail.turri@turrisitalianfoods.com
Secretary & Treasurer: Mary Derlicki
Executive Vice President: John Turri
Research & Development Manager: Jennifer Kaupp
Quality Assurance Manager: Andrea DeBusschere
VP National Sales & Marketing: Joe Morano
National Sales Manager: Joe Batayeh
Office Manager: Nora Allor
Plant Manager: Tom Dam
Purchasing Manager: Kevin Najor
Estimated Sales: $6.4 Million
Number Employees: 100-249
Square Footage: 140000
Type of Packaging: Consumer, Food Service, Private Label, Bulk
Brands:
Turris

13073 Turtle Island Foods
601 Industrial St
PO Box 176
Hood River, OR 97031-2006
541-386-7766
Fax: 541-386-7754 800-508-8100
info@tofurky.com
Processor, importer and exporter of soy meat analos including tempeh, tofurkey, deli slices, sausages, franks
President: Seth Tibbott
sue@tofurky.com
CFO: Sue Tibbott
VP: Bob Tibbott
Quality Assurance Manager: James Athos
Production Manager: Graciela Pulido
Plant Manager: Graciela Pulido
Estimated Sales: $2,398,946
Number Employees: 20-49
Number of Brands: 2
Number of Products: 25
Square Footage: 40000
Type of Packaging: Consumer, Food Service, Private Label, Bulk
Brands:
Super Burgers
Tofurky
Vegetaballs

13074 Turtle Island Foods
601 Industrial St
Hood River, OR 97031-2006
541-386-7766
Fax: 541-386-7754 800-508-8100
info@tofurky.com
Cheese and vegetable based soups
Founder: Seth Tibbott
sue@tofurky.com
CFO: Sue Tibbott
Production Manager: Graciela Pulido
Estimated Sales: Less than $500,000
Number Employees: 20-49
Brands:
Superburgers
Tempeh
Tofurky

13075 Turtle Island Herbs
4735 Walnut St # F
Boulder, CO 80301-2553
303-546-6362
Fax: 303-546-0625 800-684-4060
island@earthnet.net www.earthnet.net
Processor and wholesaler/distributor of organic herbal extracts and syrups
President: Feather Jones
CEO: Bahman Saless
VP Operations: Peter Danielson
Estimated Sales: $300,000-500,000
Number Employees: 1-4
Square Footage: 6000

13076 Turveda
www.turveda.com
Turmeric protein powder, turmeric capsules, turmeric tea K-cups, turmeric sparkling tonics in various flavors
Founder: Dev Chakrabarty
Number of Brands: 1
Number of Products: 12
Type of Packaging: Consumer, Private Label
Brands:
Turveda

13077 Tuscan Bakery
12831 NE Airport Way
Bldg 8
Portland, OR 97230-1030
503-256-2099
Fax: 503-256-1929 800-887-2261
Biscotti
Owner: Mike Lisac
VP: Wayne Winter
Estimated Sales: Less Than $500,000
Number Employees: 1-4
Square Footage: 12000
Type of Packaging: Consumer, Food Service
Brands:
Lawman's

13078 Tuscan Dairy Farms
117 Cumberland Blvd
Burlington, NJ 08016-9722
609-499-2600
800-648-0135
www.tuscandairy.com
Dairy, milk, Skinny cow, chocolate milk
Site Manager: Brian Kornfiend
brian_kornfiend@deanfoods.com
Number Employees: 20-49

13079 Tuscan Eat/Perdinci
3003 S Tamiami Trl
Sarasota, FL 34239-5108
941-565-7382
www.perdinci.com
Italian foods
Owner & President: Lorenzo Masolini
Estimated Sales: Under $500,000
Number Employees: 6
Brands:
Perdinci

13080 Tuscarora Organic Growers Cooperative
22275 Anderson Hollow Rd
Hustontown, PA 17229
814-448-2173
Fax: 814-448-2333 www.tog.coop
Cooperative providing fresh fruits and vegetables including certified organic

Bookkeeping/Sales: Sherry Meuser
Office Manager: Christine Treichler
Contact: Jeff Taylor
jeff@tog.coop
Operations Manager: Teresa Showalter
Number Employees: 1-4
Type of Packaging: Bulk
Brands:
Tuscarora Organic

13081 **Tusitala**
12400 Creel Rd
PO Box 189
Grand Bay, AL 36541
251-865-4353
Fax: 251-865-3763
Herbs and herbal supplements
President: George E. Spellmeyer
Secretary: Norma Jean Spellmeyer

13082 **Tuthilltown Spirits**
14 Grist Mill Lane
Gardiner, NY 12525
845-255-1527
distillery@tuthilltown.com
www.tuthilltown.com
Gin, vodka, flavored liqueur, corn whiskey, bourbon, rye, bitters
Co-Founder: Ralph Erenzo
Co-Founder: Brian Lee
Year Founded: 2005
Number of Brands: 5
Number of Products: 13
Type of Packaging: Consumer, Private Label
Brands:
Tuthilltown
Indigenous
Half Moon
Hudson New York
Basement Bitters

13083 **Tutti Gourmet**
76 Rue Cameron
Hudson, QC J0P 1H0
Canada
450-458-0911
inquiries@tuttigourmet.com
tuttigourmet.com
Biscotti, crackers and bites
President: Michael Kachani
tuttigourmet@hotmail.com
Brands:
Tutti Gourmet

13084 **Tuv-Taam Corp**
502 Flushing Ave
Brooklyn, NY 11205-1616
718-855-2207
Fax: 718-802-1872
Appetizers, entrees and dinners
President: Aaron Nutovics
hmaraldo@campusdirectory.com
Number Employees: 50-99

13085 **Twang Partners LTD**
6255 Wt Montgomery
San Antonio, TX 78252-2227
210-226-7008
Fax: 210-226-4040 800-950-8095
info@twang.com www.twang.com
Processor and importer of flavored salts including lemon-lime, traditional and colored margarita, beer, pickle and chili; also, Bloody Mary toppings
Owner: Roger Trevino Sr
VP Finance: Patrick Trevino
Sales/Marketing: Roger Trevino Jr
Estimated Sales: $10-20 Million
Number Employees: 20-49
Number of Brands: 10
Number of Products: 15
Square Footage: 24000
Type of Packaging: Consumer, Food Service, Private Label, Bulk
Brands:
Kid-Tastic
Texican
Twang

13086 **Twenty First Century Snacks**
921 S 2nd St
Ronkonkoma, NY 11779-7203
631-588-8000
Fax: 631-467-3995 800-975-2883
Assortment of nuts, candy and dried fruit
President: Eddie Bell
Estimated Sales: $1-2.5 000,000
Number Employees: 10-19
Type of Packaging: Consumer, Food Service, Private Label, Bulk

13087 **Twenty Rows**
880 Vallejo St
Napa, CA 94559-1823
707-265-7750
Fax: 707-944-0145 800-620-7697
tim@vinoce.com www.vinoce.com
Wines
President: Timothy Nuss
Manager: Tim Nuss
tim@vinoce.com
Number Employees: 5-9

13088 **Twenty-First Century Foods**
30 Germania St # 2
Jamaica Plain, MA 02130-2312
617-522-7595
Fax: 617-522-8772 www.21stcenturyfood.com
Soy products including tofu and tempeh; exporter of tempeh starter
Owner: Rudy Canale
rudy@cantinabostonia.com
Estimated Sales: $.5-1 million
Number Employees: 1-4
Square Footage: 3800
Brands:
Tofu Cream Chie
Tofu Pudding

13089 **Twenty-Two Desserts**
236 Livingston St
Apt 10F
Brooklyn, NY 11201
917-979-3438
info@malai.co
www.malai.co
Ice cream sorbet
Founder & CEO: Pooja Bavishi
Brands:
Malai

13090 **Twin City Bagels**
130 Hardman Ave South
South St Paul, MN 55075-2453
651-554-0200
Fax: 651-554-8383
Fresh and refrigerated bagels
Chief Financial Officer: Shimon Harosh
Chief Executive Officer: Michel Rouache
Vice President: Steve Hughes
Research & Development: Mark Heckel
Quality Control: Mark Heckel
Marketing Director: Steve Hughes
Sales Director: Steve Hughes
Contact: Josh Duncanson
duncansonj@cintas.com
Operations Manager: Steve Hughes
Production Manager: Jason Holt
Number Employees: 100-249
Type of Packaging: Consumer, Private Label

13091 **Twin City Foods Inc.**
10120 269th Pl. NW
PO Box 699
Stanwood, WA 98292
206-515-2400
Fax: 206-515-2499 www.twincityfoods.com
Frozen vegetables including; corn, peas, green beans, carrots, and baby lima beans.
President/COO: John Lervick
Chairman/CEO: Roger Lervick
rogerl@twincityfoods.com
Vice President, Finance: Thomas Hofbauer
Executive Vice President: Mark Levrick
Year Founded: 1943
Estimated Sales: $135 Million
Number Employees: 500-999
Square Footage: 10000
Type of Packaging: Consumer, Food Service, Private Label, Bulk
Other Locations:
Stanwood WA
Arlington WA
Ellensburg WA
Pasco WA
Kennewick WA
Lake Odessa MI

13092 **Twin County Dairy**
2206 540th Street SW
Kalona, IA 52247
319-656-2776
White cheddar cheese
President/Owner: John A Roetlin Jr
Estimated Sales: $9 Million
Number Employees: 5 to 9
Type of Packaging: Consumer, Private Label, Bulk

13093 **Twin Hens**
P.O.Box 439
Princeton, NJ 08542
908-925-9040
Fax: 908-281-9908
Chicken pot pies and gluten free beef pot pies
President/Owner: Linda Twining
VP: Kathy Herring

13094 **Twin Marquis**
7 Bushwick Place
Brooklyn, NY 11206-2802
718-386-6868
Fax: 718-821-6841 800-367-6868
info@twinmarquis.com www.twinmarquis.com
Processor and importer of Asian foods including buns, dumplings, sauces, soups, and noodles; also organic pasta and instant coffee and cappuccino
President: Joseph Tang
Executive Director: Terry Tang
Vice President: Alan But
Contact: Alan But
alan@twinmarquis.com
Estimated Sales: $3-4 Million
Number Employees: 50-99
Square Footage: 88000
Brands:
Chef One
Twin Marquis

13095 **Twin Oaks Community**
138 Twin Oaks Rd
Louisa, VA 23093-6337
540-894-5141
Fax: 540-894-4112 www.twinoaks.org
Tofu, soy milk, tofu salads, herbal spreads and vegetarian burgers
President: Sam Weinreb
Contact: Jeffrey Porter
mccune@twinoaks.org
Estimated Sales: Under $500,000
Number Employees: 50-99
Type of Packaging: Consumer

13096 **Twin Valley Developmental Services**
427 Commercial
P.O.Box 42
Greenleaf, KS 66943-0042
785-747-2251
Fax: 785-747-2278 800-748-7416
www.twinvalleythriftshop.com
Popped and flavored popcorn and related products
CEO: Ed Henry
VP Marketing: Nate Wirrick
Contact: Barbara Mccord
bmccord@tvds.org
Operations Manager: Carolyn Pinnick
Estimated Sales: $500-1 000,000 appx.
Number Employees: 20-49
Type of Packaging: Private Label

13097 **Twinlab Corporation**
4800 T-Rex Ave
Boca Raton, FL 33431
800-645-5626
product@twinlab.com www.twinlab.com
Processor and importer of vitamins and nutritional supplements.
Quality Assurance Manager: Mary Baum
mbaum@twinlab.com
Year Founded: 1968
Estimated Sales: $30 Million
Number Employees: 400
Type of Packaging: Consumer
Other Locations:
American Fork UT
Grand Rapids MI
Farmingdale NY
Brands:
Alvita
Metabolife
Nature's Herbs
Twinlab Bariatric Support

Twinlab Fuel
Twinlab Nutrition
Cheramino
Animal Friends
B-12 Dots
Allerdophilus Caps
Colon Care
Fibersol Capsules
Cal-Quick
Cellmins
Gaba Plus
Power Herbs

13098 (HQ)Two Chefs on a Roll
18201 Central Ave
Carson, CA 90746
310-436-1600
Fax: 310-436-1722 800-842-3025
www.twochefsonaroll.com
Dips, sauces, bakery, soups, pasta, salads and appetizers
President & CEO: Jeffrey Goh
Founder: Lori Daniel
CFO: Richard Tansley
Founder: Eliot Swartz
VP Research & Development/Quality Assur.: Kathy Ware
Director of Quality Assurance: Gerson Espindola
VP of Sales & Marketing: Dawn Rasmussen-Hickey
Contact: Joe Alonso
jalonso@twochefsonaroll.com
VP of Operations: Humberto Villagomez
Estimated Sales: $31.9 Million
Number Employees: 175
Square Footage: 100000
Parent Co: Bakkavor
Type of Packaging: Food Service, Private Label
Brands:
Two Chefs on a Roll

13099 Two Chefs on a Roll
46 Alberigi Dr.
Jessup, PA 18434
570-483-3000
Fax: 570-383-9806 www.twochefsonaroll.com
Dips, sauces, bakery, soups, pasta, salads and appetizers
Parent Co: Bakkavor
Type of Packaging: Food Service, Private Label

13100 Two Chicks and a Ladle
401 Second Avenue
14g
New York, NY 10010
212-251-0025
Fax: 914-631-1738 lisafood@aol.com
Fat-free cheesecakes
Co-owner: Cathy Golup
Co-owner: Lisa Adler

13101 Two Friends Chocolates
16 Depot Road
Boxborough, MA 01719
978-264-1949
contact@twofriendschocolates.com
www.twofriendschocolates.com
Chocolate truffles
Director: Neethu Viswanath
Type of Packaging: Private Label
Brands:
Two Friends

13102 Two Guys Spice Company
2404 Dennis Street
Jacksonville, FL 32204-1712
949-248-1269
Fax: 904-791-9330 800-874-5656
www.twoguysgrilling.net
Broker and wholesaler/distributor of dehydrated onions, garlic and vegetables; also, spices and industrial ingredients
President: Michael Simmons
Vice President: Guy Simmons
Estimated Sales: $2.4 Million
Number Employees: 1-4
Number of Brands: 1
Number of Products: 500
Square Footage: 20800
Type of Packaging: Food Service, Private Label, Bulk

13103 Two Leaves & A Bud Inc
23400 Two Rivers Rd
Suite 45
Basalt, CO 81621-9239
970-927-9911
Fax: 970-927-9917 866-631-7973
support@twoleavesandabud.net
www.twoleavestea.com
Teas
President/Owner: Richard Rosenfeld
richard@twoleavesandabud.net
Estimated Sales: $1 Million
Number Employees: 5-9

13104 Two Moms In The Raw
1200 S Fordham St # B
Longmont, CO 80503-7759
720-221-8555
Fax: 720-524-4094 info@twomomsintheraw.com
www.soulsprout.com
Manufacturer of raw snack foods like granolas bars, crackers, and nut bars.
Founder: Shari Leidich
Number Employees: 20-49

13105 TyRy Inc
4041 Alvis Court
Rocklin, CA 95677-7799
916-624-6050
Fax: 916-624-1604 800-322-6325
info@tyry.com
Manufacturer and exporter of health, backpacking, self-heating and emergency prepared foods, freeze-dried and no cooking required foods including; pre-packed beans, cereals, desserts, dried fruits and vegetables, grains and meatsubstitutes
President: Don Gearing
donald@tyry.com
Square Footage: 200000
Parent Co: TyRy, Inc
Type of Packaging: Consumer, Private Label, Bulk
Brands:
Alpineaire
Gourmet Reserves

13106 Tyee Wine Cellars
26335 Greenberry Rd
Corvallis, OR 97333-9534
541-753-8754
Fax: 541-753-0807 merrilee@storypages.com
www.tyeewine.com
Wine
Owner: Margaret Buchanan
tyeewine@peak.org
Co-Founder: Nola Moiser
Co-Founder: David Buchanan
Co-Founder: Margy Buchanan
Winemaker: Barney Watson
Estimated Sales: Less than $300,000
Number Employees: 1-4
Type of Packaging: Private Label
Brands:
Tyee

13107 Tyler Candy Co LLC
4337 DC Dr
Tyler, TX 75701-8416
903-561-3046
Fax: 903-581-8030 tylercandyco@aol.com
www.tylercandles.com
Hard candy
Manager: Ron Sumibek
ron@tylercandy.com
Estimated Sales: $5-10 000,000
Number Employees: 20-49
Type of Packaging: Consumer, Private Label
Brands:
Dickies

13108 Tyler Packing Co
2209 E Erwin St
Tyler, TX 75702-6420
903-593-9592
Fax: 903-593-1273
Beef, pork and veal
Owner: H C Buie
Estimated Sales: $3-5 Million
Number Employees: 5-9
Type of Packaging: Bulk

13109 (HQ)Tyson Foods Inc.
2200 W. Don Tyson Pkwy.
Springdale, AR 72762
479-290-4000
www.tysonfoods.com
Chicken, beef and pork products.
CEO: Noel White
President/Director: Dean Banks
Executive VP/CFO: Stewart Glendinning
Executive VP/General Counsel: Amy Tu
Executive VP/Chief Customer Officer: Scott Rouse
Estimated Sales: $40 Billion
Number Employees: 122,000
Number of Brands: 41
Type of Packaging: Consumer, Food Service, Bulk
Brands:
Tyson
Jimmy Dean
Hillshire Farm
Hillshire Snacking
Ball Park
Wright
Aidells
State Fair
Bonici
Bosco's Pizza Co.
The Bruss Company
Chairman's Reserve
Advance Pierre Foods
Gallo Salame
Barber Foods
IBP Trusted Excellence
Lady Aster
Mexican Original
Open Prairie Natural Angus
Russer
Star Ranch Angus
Supreme Tender
Big AZ
Fast Fixin'
Hot 'n' Ready
Wunderbar
Sara Lee
Golden Island
Nature Raised Farms
PB Jamwich
Landshire
Steakeze
Original Philly Cheesesteak Co.
Bryan
True Chews
Top Chews
Nudges
Reuben

13110 Tyson Foods Inc.
P.O. Box 2020
Springdale, AR 72765
800-233-6332
www.tyson.com
Meats including smoked, cured, pork, ham, beef, hot dogs and cold cuts
Group President, Poultry: Chad Martin
Group President, Prepared Foods: Noelle O'Mara
Year Founded: 1935
Type of Packaging: Consumer, Food Service, Private Label
Brands:
American Favorite
Black Forest
Fresh Cut
Wilson Continental D

13111 U Okada & Co LTD
1000 Queen St
Honolulu, HI 96814-4116
808-597-1102
Fax: 808-591-6634
Wholesaler/distributor of frozen foods, provisions/meats and seafood; serving the food service market
President: Dexter Okada
dexter@uokada.com
President: Saneo Okada
Estimated Sales: $10-20 Million
Number Employees: 20-49
Square Footage: 60000

13112 U Roast Em Inc
16778 W US Highway 63
Hayward, WI 54843-7214
715-634-6255
Fax: 715-934-3221 info@u-roast-em.com

Supplier of green coffee beans, bulk teas, home roasting supplies and coffee flavorings
Manager: Terry Wall
info@u-roast-em.com
Number Employees: 1-4
Type of Packaging: Consumer
Brands:
Bodum
Fresh Beans

13113 **U.S. Range**
1177 Kamato Rd
Mississauga, ON L4W IX4
Canada
905-624-0260
800-424-2411
www.garland-group.com
Manufacturer of cooking systems.

13114 **UBC Food Distributors**
12812 Prospect St
Dearborn, MI 48126-3652
877-846-8117
Fax: 313-846-8118 info@wellmadefood.com
www.wellmadefood.com
Honey, chocolates, cookies, juices, and snacks
Sales Manager: Hassan Houssami
Estimated Sales: $10-12 Million
Number Employees: 10
Other Locations:
East Coast NJ
West Coast CA
Brands:
Wellmade Honey

13115 **UBF Food Solutions**
2200 Cabot Dr Ste 200
Lisle, IL 60532
630-955-5394
www.unileverfoodsolutions.com
Sauces, dressings
Managing Director: Tracey Rogers
Estimated Sales: $25-49.9 Million
Number Employees: 250-499
Parent Co: Unilever

13116 **UFL Foods**
450 Superior Boulevard
Mississauga, ON L5T 2R9
Canada
905-670-7776
Fax: 905-670-7751
Processor and exporter of custom formulated and blended ingredients including milk replacers, mustard, seasonings, meat binders, curing preparations, etc.; also, pasta and rice sauce mixes, soup and sauce bases, batters andbreadings
VP: Jack Conway
Number Employees: 100-249
Square Footage: 440000
Parent Co: Newly Weds Foods
Type of Packaging: Food Service, Private Label, Bulk

13117 **ULDO USA**
10 Dewey Road
Lexington, MA 02420-1018
781-860-7800
Fax: 781-863-1973 productinfo@bakenjoy.com
Baked goods
Contact: Arlene Kolovson
imaginatemundo@hotmail.com
Brands:
Baken Joy

13118 **UNOI Grainmill**
Route 13-A
Seaford, DE 19973-5749
302-629-4083
Miller of whole wheat flour, white and yellow corn meal, buckwheat, etc
Owner: Janice Griffith
Manager: Charles Willoughby
Estimated Sales: Under $300,000
Number Employees: 3
Square Footage: 40000
Parent Co: United Nation of Islam
Type of Packaging: Private Label
Brands:
Hearn & Rawlins
White Dove

13119 **US Chocolate Corp**
4801 1st Ave
Brooklyn, NY 11232-4208
718-788-8555
Fax: 718-788-3311 uschoc@aol.com
Processor and exporter of kosher liquid marble chocolate and white parve coatings, fudge bases and flavors.
President: David Rosenberg
abe@uschoc.com
Estimated Sales: $10-20 Million
Number Employees: 10-19
Square Footage: 81000
Brands:
U.S. Brand

13120 **US Distilled Products Co**
1607 12th St S
Princeton, MN 55371-2311
763-389-4903
Fax: 763-389-2549 info@usdp.com
www.usdp.com
Alcoholic beverages
President: Bradley P Johnson
CFO: Pat Pelzer
Production Manager: Kevin Issendorf
Purchasing Manager: Todd Rhode
Year Founded: 1981
Estimated Sales: $20-30 Million
Number Employees: 250-499
Square Footage: 250000
Brands:
Athena Test
Black Eagle
Blanks
Cactus Bills
California Crest
California Ltd
English Guard
Gionelli
Karkov
Kingston
Marrone
McAdams
Mothers
Petri
The Antiquary
Tomatin
Trader Vics
Wakefield

13121 **US Durum Products LTD**
1812 William Penn Way
P.O.Box 10126
Lancaster, PA 17601-5831
717-293-8698
Fax: 717-293-8699 866-268-7268
wross@usdurum.com www.usdurum.com
Couscous
President: Wendy Ross
wross@usdurum.com
Estimated Sales: $2.5-5 Million
Number Employees: 10-19

13122 **US Foods & Pharmaceuticals Inc**
313 W Beltline Hwy # 182
Suite 182
Madison, WI 53713-2682
608-278-1293
Fax: 608-278-9042 800-362-8294
Milk minerals, dairy formulations, enhanced dairy products and formulations, nutritional products, nutraceuticals
President: Tammi Ceballos
tammi.ceballos@usfood.com
VP: James Henderson
Marketing Director: Richard Nelson
Public Relations: Kalle Smith
Operations Manager: Jay Zahom
Estimated Sales: $1,500,000
Number Employees: 5-9
Square Footage: 20000
Type of Packaging: Consumer
Brands:
Dari-Cal
Infalac
My-Baby

13123 **US Ingredients**
P.O.Box 9207
Naperville, IL 60567-0207
630-820-1711
Fax: 630-820-1883
Seasonings and food flavoring products

Owner: Eric Maul
Executive Vice President of Network Serv: Jim OBrien
Estimated Sales: $5-10 Million
Number Employees: 5-9

13124 **US Mills**
401 E City Ave Ste 220
Bala Cynwyd, PA 19004-1117
Fax: 781-444-3411 800-422-1125
Processor and exporter of natural/organic foods including ready-to-eat and hot cereals and graham crackers.
Executive VP: Cynthia Davis
Director of Marketing: Daniel Wiser
Sales: William Bunn
Number Employees: 6
Number of Brands: 5
Number of Products: 45
Type of Packaging: Consumer
Brands:
Erewhon
Farina Mills
New Morning
Skinner's
Uncle Sam Cereal

13125 **US Sugar Company**
111 Ponce de Leon Ave.
Clewiston, FL 33440
863-983-8121
info@ussugar.com
www.ussugar.com
Granulated, brown and powdered sugars; sugar and artificial sweetener packets; and orange juice.
President: William McDaniel
VP: Steve Ward
Contact: Sunil Abey
sabey@ussugar.com
VP Operations: Tom Moran
Plant Manager: Avery Foy
Estimated Sales: $25 Million
Number Employees: 20-49
Number of Brands: 30
Number of Products: 20
Square Footage: 300000
Type of Packaging: Consumer, Food Service, Private Label
Brands:
Private Label
Us Sugars

13126 **US Wellness Meats**
P.O. Box 249
Canton, MO 63435
877-383-0051
eathealthy@grasslandbeef.com
grasslandbeef.com
Meats
Owner: John Wood
Year Founded: 2000
Estimated Sales: $7,300,000
Number Employees: 9
Brands:
Grassland Beef

13127 **USA Beverage**
1410a E Old Us Highway 40
Warrenton, MO 63383-1316
636-456-5468
Fax: 636-456-3422
Wines
President: Hugh White
CFO: Thomas Nittler
Marketing Director: Darrell Wiss
Production Manager: Terre Novell
Plant Manager: Hugh White
Estimated Sales: $500,000
Number Employees: 20-49
Type of Packaging: Private Label
Brands:
Usa Beverages

13128 **USA Laboratories Inc**
1438 Highway 96
Burns, TN 37029-5030
615-441-1521
Fax: 615-446-3788 800-489-4872
usalabs@usalabs.com www.usalabs.com
Processor and exporter of vitamins, minerals, nutritional supplements and weight loss aids

President/Owner: Charles Stokes
CEO: Charles Stokes
R&D: David Bethshears
yumyum1969@live.com
Quality Control: Brad Stokes
Marketing Director: Erica White
Sales Director: Shelby Bethsheard
Contact: Suzzane Guire
yumyum1969@live.com
Operations: Ted Sanders
Estimated Sales: $4.7 Million
Number Employees: 1-4
Number of Brands: 5
Number of Products: 1000
Square Footage: 400000
Parent Co: USA Laboratories
Brands:
Burn Off
Jewel Laboratories
Nutrceuticals
Power Rangers Chewable Vitamins
Usa Best
Usa Laboratories Nutrients
Usa Sports Labs

13129 **UTZ Quality Foods Inc.**
900 High St.
Hanover, PA 17331
717-637-6644
Fax: 717-634-5890 800-367-7629
info@utzsnacks.com www.utzsnacks.com
Potato chips, pretzels, popcorn, tortilla chips, cheese curls, pub fries, pork rinds, etc.
President/COO: Tom Flocco
CEO: Dylan Lissette
Executive VP/CFO: Jay Thompson
Executive VP/Chief Customer Officer: Mark Schreiber
Year Founded: 1921
Estimated Sales: $215 Million
Number Employees: 2,500
Number of Brands: 9
Square Footage: 550000
Type of Packaging: Consumer, Food Service, Bulk
Other Locations:
Utz Distribution Centers
East Hartford CT
Patterson NY
Laurel DE
Newark DE
Auburn ME
West Springfield MA
North Easton MA
South Yarmouth MA
Wilmington MA
Shrewsbury MA
Cumberland MD
Waldorf MD
Hanover PA
Brands:
Bachman
Golden Flake
Dirty
Zapp's Potato Chips
Good Health
Snikiddy
Boulder Canyon
TGI Fridays Snacks
TORTIYAHS!

13130 **(HQ)Uas Laboratories**
9953 Valley View Rd
Eden Prairie, MN 55344
952-935-1707
Fax: 952-935-1650 800-422-3371
info@uaslabs.com
Manufacturer and exporter of nutritional supplements
President: S K Dash
Quality Control: Scot Elert
Marketing Director: Raj Dash
Operations Manager: Steven Shack
Estimated Sales: $3 Million
Number Employees: 10-19
Number of Products: 12
Square Footage: 21600
Type of Packaging: Consumer, Private Label, Bulk
Brands:
Dds
Dds Acidophilus
Dds Junior
Dds Plus
Uas Activin Plus
Uas Coenzyme Q10
Uas Joint Formula

13131 **Ubons Sauce LLC**
801 Jerry Clower Blvd.
Yazoo City, MS 39194
662-716-7100
info@ubons.net
ubonsbbq.com
Bloody mary mix and sauces.
Founder: Leslie Scott
Contact: David Rosen
david@ubons.net

13132 **Udi's Gluten-Free Foods**
1600 Pearl Street
Suite 300
Boulder, CO 80302
201-421-3970
udisglutenfree.com
Gluten free foods

13133 **Udi's Granola**
12000 E. 47th Avenue
Suite 400
Denver, CO 80239
303-657-6366
Fax: 303-657-5373 www.udisgranola.com
Flavored granola
Founder: Udi Baron

13134 **Ugo Di Lullo & Son**
1004 Edgewater Ave
Westville, NJ 08093-1246
856-456-3700
Fax: 856-456-7161
Canned goods
President: Ugo Di Lullo
Estimated Sales: $5-10 Million
Number Employees: 5-9

13135 **Uhlmann Co**
4801 Main St # 550
Suite 550
Kansas City, MO 64112 2544
816-221-8200
Fax: 816-221-5504 866-866-8627
www.heckersceresota.com
All-purpose unbleached and whole wheat flour
President: Judi Rasmussen
judi@heckersceresota.com
Retail Sales: Wesley Fehsenfeld
Estimated Sales: $10-20 Million
Number Employees: 10-19
Square Footage: 60000
Type of Packaging: Consumer, Food Service
Brands:
Ceresota
Heckers

13136 **Uinta Brewing Co**
1722 S Fremont Dr
Salt Lake City, UT 84104-4215
801-467-0909
Fax: 801-463-7151 info@uintabrewing.com
www.uintabrewing.com
Beer
President: William Hamill
Vice President: Steve Kuftinec
skuftinec@uintabrewing.com
Public Relations Officer: Steve Kustinec
Estimated Sales: $5-10 Million
Number Employees: 20-49
Square Footage: 104000
Type of Packaging: Private Label
Brands:
Uinta

13137 **Ultima Health Products Inc.**
3284 Niles-Cortland Rd.
Cortland, OH 44410
Fax: 330-638-5500 888-663-8584
www.ultimareplenisher.com
Electrolyte-balanced energy drink without sugar, carbs or calories
Vice-President, Sales: Skeet Freeman
Year Founded: 1996
Number of Brands: 1
Type of Packaging: Consumer, Private Label
Brands:
Ultima

13138 **Ultimate Bagel**
1226 State Street
Santa Barbara, CA 93101
805-845-2511
ultimatebagel@gmail.com
Bagels
President: Carol Kozak
Estimated Sales: $230,000
Number Employees: 6
Square Footage: 8000
Type of Packaging: Consumer, Food Service

13139 **Ultimate Biscotti**
1000 S Bertelsen Road
Suite 10
Eugene, OR 97402-5448
541-344-8220
Fax: 541-344-8357
Biscotti including ginger, hazelnut chocolate, citrus, etc.; also, wheat and gluten-free available
President: Heather Kent
Number Employees: 5-9
Square Footage: 24000
Type of Packaging: Consumer, Food Service, Bulk
Brands:
Ultimate Biscotti

13140 **Ultimate Foods**
P.O. Box 1008
Linden, NJ 07036
908-486-0800
Fax: 908-486-2999 www.ultimatefoodsservice.com
Offer a full line of fresh and frozen seafood, produce, meats, oils, pastas, canned tomatoes, and other grocery and specialty items.
General Manager: Scott Greisman
Seafood Buyer/Quality Control: John Parisi
Produce Buyer/Quality Control: Albert Sindoni
Road Sales Manager: Al Ferrentino
Operations Manager: Anthony Stropoli
Dry Goods Buyer: James Boniface
Estimated Sales: $3.6 Million
Number of Brands: 1
Type of Packaging: Food Service, Bulk
Brands:
ULTIMATE

13141 **Ultimate Gourmet**
12 Ilene Ct
Hillsborough, NJ 8844
908-359-4050
Fax: 908-359-2494
contact@ultimate-gourmet.com
www.ugbrands.com
Bar mixes, jellies, jams, sauces, brandied fruit, barbacue sauces, marinades and rubs
President: Tali Almagor
holly@altimate-gourmet.com
Estimated Sales: Less Than $500,000
Number Employees: 1-4
Type of Packaging: Consumer, Food Service, Private Label, Bulk
Brands:
Club Tahity
Cramore
Creamy Head
Firehouse
Giroux
Milem
Proud Mary
Raffetto
Tahiti

13142 **Ultimate Nut & Candy Company**
6333 West 3rd Street
Los Angeles, CA 90036
800-767-5259
Candy, nuts
President: Steve Turner
Quality Control: Theresa Malgonadio
Marketing Manager: Steve Turner
Number Employees: 20-49
Type of Packaging: Private Label
Brands:
Studio Confections
Ultimate Confections

13143 **Ultimate Nutrition**
161 Woodford Avenue
Farmington, CT 06034-0643
860-409-7100
Fax: 860-793-5006 www.ultimatenutrition.com
Food processor and exporter of food supplements including capsules, tablets, powders and protein bars
President: Victor Rubino
Advertising: Seth Darvick
VP Sales: Dean Caputo
Type of Packaging: Consumer

13144 Ultimate Salsa
PO Box 47343
Charlotte, NC 28247
704-847-4857
888-827-2572
Salsa
Co-Owner: Ellen Siegler
President: Tom Siegler
Brands:
Iguana Tom's

13145 Ultra Dairy
40236 State Highway 10
Delhi, NY 13753-3289
607-746-2141
Fax: 607-746-3725
Milk
Manager: Liz Van Buren
Senior VP: Fred Bruzzese
Estimated Sales: $10-24.9 Million
Number Employees: 100-249
Parent Co: Tuscan/Lehigh Valley Dairies
Brands:
Actic Splash
Lehigh Valley Dairies
Tuscan

13146 Ultra Enterprises
14108 Lambert Rd
Whittier, CA 90605-2427
562-945-4833
Fax: 562-698-7362 800-543-0627
b.kaliultra@verizon.net www.ultraent.com
Processor and sports nutrition of granulars
President/CEO: Bud Thompson
Vice President: Mary Thompson
Number of Products: 50
Type of Packaging: Consumer
Brands:
Sports Nutrition
Ultra Rain Glandulars

13147 Ultra Seal
521 Main St
New Paltz, NY 12561-1609
845-255-2490
Fax: 845-255-3553 info@ultra-seal.com
www.ultra-seal.com
Contract packager of portion controlled products including ketchup, mustard, powder lemonade, fruit juice, iced tea mix, etc
President: Dennis Borrello
dennisb@ultra-seal.com
Manager: Christine Downs
Executive: Terry Murphy
Estimated Sales: $5-10 Million
Number Employees: 100-249
Square Footage: 104000
Type of Packaging: Consumer, Food Service, Private Label, Bulk

13148 Umanoff & Parsons
1704 Boone Ave
Bronx, NY 10460-5400
212-219-2240
Fax: 718-684-7978 800-248-9993
Fresh and frozen all natural kosher dairy cakes, pies, quiches and tarts
President: Simon Seaton
Estimated Sales: $5,200,000
Number Employees: 20-49
Square Footage: 26000

13149 Umpqua Dairy
333 SE Sykes Ave
P.O. Box 1306
Roseburg, OR 97470
541-672-2638
Fax: 541-673-0256 888-672-6455
info@umpquadairy.com www.umpquadairy.com
Processor and exporter of ice cream, milk, cottage cheese, sour cream and butter
President: Douglas Feldkamp
Director, Sales & Marketing: Marty Weaver
COO: Steve Feldkemp
Year Founded: 1931
Estimated Sales: $50.2 Million
Number Employees: 100-249
Type of Packaging: Consumer, Food Service, Private Label

13150 Umpqua Oats
2980 Sunridge Heights Pkwy
Suite 130
Henderson, NV 89052
877-303-8107
brysonb@umpquaoats.com
umpquaoats.com
Oatmeal
Owner: Mandy Holborow
Co-Owner: Sheri Price
Sales & Marketing Manager: Bryson Buck
Co-Owner & Purchasing: Chris Holborow
Estimated Sales: $10-20 Million
Number Employees: 1-10
Brands:
Umpqua Oats

13151 UnReal Brands
Boston, MA
hi@getunreal.com
www.getunreal.com
Non-GMO, fair trade, gluten-free, artificial ingredient-free dark and milk chocolate peanut butter cups, chocolate-coated quinoa and chocolate-covered nuts
Co-Founder: Nicky Bronner
Co-Founder: Kristopher Bronner
Year Founded: 2010
Number of Brands: 1
Number of Products: 6
Type of Packaging: Consumer, Private Label
Brands:
UnReal

13152 Uncle Andy's Cafe
171 Ocean St
South Portland, ME 04106-3623
207-799-7199
Fax: 207- 79-9 34
Baked goods
Owner: Dennis Fogg
Estimated Sales: Less Than $500,000
Number Employees: 1-4

13153 Uncle Charley's Sausage
1135 Industrial Park Rd
Vandergrift, PA 15690-6050
724-845-3302
Fax: 724-845-3174 www.unclecharleys.com
Pork, pork products
President: Charles Armitage
CEO: Frances Armitage
charley@unclecharleyssausage.com
Vice President: Charles Armitage Jr
Estimated Sales: $5-10 Million
Number Employees: 20-49

13154 Uncle Dougie's
Chicago, IL
www.originaluncledougies.com
Preservative- and GMO-free barbecue sauces, marinades, seasonings, rubs, hot sauces and drink mixes in various flavors
Founder: Doug Tomek
Year Founded: 1989
Number of Brands: 1
Number of Products: 19
Type of Packaging: Consumer, Private Label
Brands:
Uncle Dougie's

13155 Uncle Fred's Fine Foods
209 N Doughty Street
Rockport, TX 78382-5322
361-729-8320
www.unclfred.com
Processor and importer of habanero ketchup, jelly, hot sweet mustard and chips, salsa, spices, meat rubs and sauces including cocktail, pepper and barbecue
President: Fred Franklin
VP/Co-Owner: Pat Marsh
Manager: Judith Jecmen-Fuhrman
Number Employees: 1-4
Square Footage: 6400
Parent Co: Island Enterprises
Type of Packaging: Consumer
Brands:
Uncle Fred's Fine Foods

13156 Uncle Lee's Tea Inc
11020 Rush St
South El Monte, CA 91733-3547
626-350-3309
Fax: 626-350-4364 800-732-8830
www.unclelee.com
Processor, exporter and importer of teas including herb, spiced, traditional and dieter's; co-packing and private label available
Vice President: Tim Carter
tim.carter@health.net
Chairman: Lee Rieho
Vice President: Jonason Lee
Sales Director: James O'Young
Public Relations: Patty Gillno
Plant Manager: Joe Villegas
Estimated Sales: $1400000
Number Employees: 20-49
Parent Co: Ten Ren Tea Company
Brands:
Uncle Lee's Tea

13157 Uncle Matt's Organic
PO Box 120187
Clermont, FL 34712
833-729-8625
Fax: 352-394-1003 media@unclematts.com
www.unclematts.com
Organic orange, grapefruit, apple juices; organic lemonade; organic probiotic waters in various flavors
Founder/Owner: Matt McLean
Year Founded: 1999
Number of Brands: 1
Number of Products: 11
Type of Packaging: Consumer, Private Label
Brands:
Uncle Matt's Organic

13158 Uncle Ralph's Cookies
801 N East St # 5
Frederick, MD 21701-4652
301-695-6224
Fax: 301-695-6327 800-422-0626
sales@uncleralphscookies.com
www.uncleralphscookies.com
Gourmet cookies, brownies, crumb cakes, pound cakes, and quick breads
Owner: Ed Riffle
Founder: Peggy Wight
Sales Director: Jamie Mater
eriffle@uncleralphscookies.com
Estimated Sales: $3-5 Million
Number Employees: 50-99
Square Footage: 120000
Type of Packaging: Consumer, Food Service, Private Label
Brands:
Uncle Ralph's

13159 Uncle Ray's Potato Chips
14245 Birwood St
Detroit, MI 48238
313-834-0800
Fax: 313-834-0443 800-800-3286
www.unclerays.com
Potato chips, nacho chips, popcorn, snack foods
President & COO: Brian Gaggin
CFO: Sandra Subotich
General Manager: Joseph Dilly
Year Founded: 1965
Estimated Sales: $20-30 Million
Number Employees: 200-499
Parent Co: AmeriFoods
Brands:
Unclerays

13160 Uncommon Grounds Coffee
2813 Seventh Street
Berkeley, CA 94710-2702
510-764-1211
Fax: 510-868-1841 800-567-9183
uncommon@uncommongrounds.net
www.uncommongrounds.net
Coffee
President/CEO: Kim Moore
CFO: Derek Lantner
Contact: Skip Blakely
skip.blakely@uncommongrounds.net
Operations Manager: Kim Moore
Production Manager: James Spottn
Estimated Sales: $2.3 Million
Number Employees: 14
Parent Co: Berkeley Coffee and Tea
Type of Packaging: Private Label
Brands:
Double Star Espresso
El Salvador Finca Las Nubes
Ethiopian Organic
Molta Roba

13161 **Une-Viandi**
505 Industriel Boulevard
St. Jean Sur Richelieu, NB J3B 5Y8
Canada
450-347-8406
Fax: 450-347-8142 800-363-1955
Processor, importer and exporter of meat products including bone-in and boneless beef, lamb and veal
President: Claude Berni
Export Manager: Lloyd Arshinoff
Number Employees: 50-99
Square Footage: 88000
Type of Packaging: Consumer, Food Service, Private Label, Bulk

13162 **Ungars Food**
9 Boumar Pl
Elmwood Park, NJ 07407-2615
201-773-6846
Fax: 201-703-9333 webquery@drpraegers.com
www.drpraegers.com
Veggie burgers, pancakes, breaded fish fillets, fillet fish sticks
Owner: Larry Praeger
larry@drpraegers.com
CFO: Jeff Coher
Estimated Sales: $2.5-5 Million
Number Employees: 50-99

13163 **(HQ)Ungerer & Co**
4 Bridgewater Ln
Lincoln Park, NJ 07035-1491
973-706-7381
Fax: 973-628-0251 www.ungererandcompany.com
Manufacturer, importer and exporter of natural and artificial fruit flavors and essential oils including lemon, orange, peppermint, spearmint, ginger, lime and dill
President: Cascy Annicchiarico
cannicchiarico@ungererandcompany.com
Estimated Sales: $10 Million
Number Employees: 100-249
Type of Packaging: Consumer, Private Label, Bulk
Other Locations:
Ungerer & Company Plant
Bethlehem PA
Ungerer & Company Plant
Oaxaca, Mexico

13164 **Unibroue/Unibrew**
80 Rue Des CarriŠres
Chambly, QC J3L 2H6
Canada
450-658-7658
Fax: 450-658-9195 info@unibroue.com
www.unibroue.com
Gourmet beer including black currant, apple, and chambly blonde
Brewing Supervisor: Martin Gagn,
Year Founded: 1990
Estimated Sales: $21million
Number Employees: 250
Parent Co: Sapporo
Type of Packaging: Consumer, Food Service
Brands:
Unibrew
Unibroue

13165 **Unica**
23w101 Kings Ct # 100
Glen Ellyn, IL 60137-7215
630-790-8107
Fax: 630-790-8117
Sugar free confectionary
President: Peter Zeuthen
Contact: Leif Pedersen
leif@unicable.com
Estimated Sales: $5-10 Million
Number Employees: 5-9
Brands:
Unica

13166 **Unified Food Ingredients**
145 Vallecitos DE Oro # 208
San Marcos, CA 92069-1459
760-744-7225
Fax: 760-744-7215
Processor, exporter and importer of dehydrated vegetables including bell peppers, carrots, celery, peas, corn, mushrooms, garlic, etc
Owner: Dan Stouder
VP: Dan Stouder
Sales Manager: Simone Grunewald
Customer Service: Kris Cannan
Operations Manager: Melissa Coetzee
Estimated Sales: $1-3,000,000
Number Employees: 1-4
Square Footage: 20000
Type of Packaging: Bulk

13167 **Unilever Canada**
160 Bloor St. East
Suite 1400
Toronto, ON M4W 3R2
Canada
416-415-3000
www.unilever.ca
Food products, personal care, and home products.
Director, Customer Development: Bruce Findlay
VP, Brand Strategy & Innovation: Margaret McKellar
Year Founded: 1949
Estimated Sales: $466 Million
Number Employees: 3,400
Square Footage: 80912
Parent Co: Unilever US
Type of Packaging: Consumer, Food Service
Brands:
Becel
Breyers
Hellmann's
Knorr
Lipton
Red Rose
Slim-Fast

13168 **Unilever Food Solutions**
800 Sylvan Ave
Englewood Cliffs, NJ 07632
foodsolutions@unilever.com
www.unileverfoodsolutions.us
Bases and bouillons, dressings and condiments, mayonnaise, sauces and gravies, seasonings, soups, teas and beverages.
President, Foods & Refreshment: Hanneke Faber
Number Employees: 250-499
Parent Co: Unilever USA
Type of Packaging: Consumer, Food Service, Private Label, Bulk
Brands:
Becel
Bertolli
Blue Band
Flora

13169 **Unilever US**
800 Sylvan Ave
Englewood Cliffs, NJ 07632
800-298-5018
www.unileverusa.com
Food products, personal care, and home products.
President, North America: Amanda Sourry
CEO: Alan Jope
CFO: Graeme Pitkethly
Chief R&D Officer: Richard Slater
VP, Human Resources, North America: Mike Clementi
Estimated Sales: $18 Billion
Number Employees: 5000-9999
Parent Co: Unilever N.V. & Unilever plc
Type of Packaging: Consumer, Food Service
Brands:
Hellmann's
Knorr
Lipton
Magnum
Talenti
Ben & Jerry's
Breyers
Good Humor
Klondike
Popsicle

13170 **Union**
14522 Myford Rd
Irvine, CA 92606-1000
714-734-2200
Fax: 714-734-2223 800-854-7292
Processor and exporter of Oriental ramen noodles
President: Sang Mook Lee
CEO: Victor Sim
Sales Manager: Bob Hicks
Estimated Sales: $10,900,000
Number Employees: 100-249
Square Footage: 200000
Type of Packaging: Consumer, Private Label
Brands:
Noodle Plus
Smack Cup-A-Ramen
Smack Ramen
Snoodles

13171 **Union Fisheries Corp**
6186 N Northwest Hwy
Chicago, IL 60631-2126
773-738-0448
Fax: 773-763-8775
Prepared fresh or frozen fish and seafood
Owner: Jim Gubrow
Estimated Sales: $3-5 Million
Number Employees: 5-9

13172 **Union Seafoods**
2100 W McDowell Rd
Phoenix, AZ 85009-3011
602-254-4114
Fax: 602-254-4117
Seafood
President: Ernest Linsenmeyer
Estimated Sales: $4,000,000
Number Employees: 1-4

13173 **Union Square Wines & Spirits**
140 Fourth Ave
New York, NY 10003
212-675-8100
Fax: 212-675-8663 info@unionsquarewines.com
www.unionsquarewines.com
wines and spirits
Sales Manager: David Hatzopoulos
Wine Director: Jesse Salazar
Sales General Manager: Katherine Moore
Year Founded: 1995
Estimated Sales: $500,000-$900,000
Type of Packaging: Consumer, Private Label

13174 **Union Wine Co**
19600 SW Cipole Rd
Tualatin, OR 97062
info@unionwinecompany.com
www.unionwinecompany.com
Wine
Founder & Owner: Ryan Harms
Director of Finance/Accounting: Eric Harms
VP Sales: Adam Coremin
Director of Winemaking: JP Caldcleugh
Year Founded: 2005
Number Employees: 20-49
Brands:
Underwood
Kings Ridge
Alchemist

13175 **Unique Beverage Company**
PO Box 2246
Everett, WA 98213-0246
425-267-0959
Fax: 425-353-5600
customerservice@cascadeicewater.com
www.cascadeicewater.com
Sodium-free, caffeine-free, sugar-free flavored sparkling water; organic varieties available
Chief Executive Officer: Mark Christensen
Number of Brands: 1
Type of Packaging: Consumer, Private Label

13176 **Unique Foods**
3221 Durham Dr # 107
Raleigh, NC 27603-3507
919-779-5600
Fax: 919-779-3766
Canned and exotic mushrooms
President: Louis J Deangelis Sr.
CEO: Louis De Angelis
VP: Louis J Deangelis Jr.
Marketing Head: Louis De Angelis
Contact: Gina Bissette
gina@uniquefoodcompany.com
Operations Manager: Bryan Parrish
Estimated Sales: $3,700,000
Number Employees: 20-49
Square Footage: 15000

13177 **Unique Ingredients LLC**
6460 S Mountainside Dr
Gold Canyon, AZ 85118-2900
480-983-2498
Fax: 509-653-1992 oly@werunique.com
www.werunique.com

Dried apples in a variety of cuts, styles and varieties; offering air dried, drum dried and upon request, freeze dried fruits and vegetables, specializing in apples, apricots, cherries, peaches, plums, raisins, bananas and all tropicalfruits
Founder: Dave Olsen
Finance and Accounting: Karen Bentz
Sales: Matt Gibbs
Contact: Delrae Blanchard
delrae@werunique.com
Operations: Becky Cornwall
Estimated Sales: $3 Million
Number Employees: 5-9
Number of Brands: 1
Number of Products: 100
Square Footage: 500
Type of Packaging: Private Label, Bulk
Brands:
Unique Ingredients

13178 **Unique Pretzel Bakery, Inc.**
215 East Bellevue Ave.
Reading, PA 19605
610-929-3172
Fax: 610-929-3444
Hard-baked pretzel "splits"; pretzel shells, chocolate-covered pretzels
Number of Brands: 1
Type of Packaging: Consumer, Private Label
Brands:
Unique

13179 **Unique Vitality Products**
29215 Hillrise Dr
Agoura Hills, CA 91301-1533
818-889-7739
Fax: 818-889-4895
Processor and exporter of vitamins
Owner: Pierre Van Wessel
uvppierre@extreme.com
CEO: Robert Van Wessel
CFO: Wendy Van Wessel
Quality Control: Ashwin Patel
Production: Hasmuck Patec
Estimated Sales: $.5-1 million
Number Employees: 1-4
Square Footage: 800000
Type of Packaging: Private Label, Bulk
Brands:
Hypo Form
Kidney Rinse
Liver Rinse
Unique Colonic Rinse
Vascustrem

13180 **Uniquely Together**
Apt 3
2000 W Estes Ave
Chicago, IL 60645-2452
847-675-1555
Fax: 847-675-4049 800-613-7276
Cocktail biscuit collection, line of chocolates, line of sandwich creme cookies; all natural
Owner: Mark Callahan
Owner: Anne Callahan
Number Employees: 5-9
Number of Brands: 1
Number of Products: 22
Square Footage: 22000
Type of Packaging: Consumer, Private Label
Brands:
Heavenly Cluster
Heavenly Clusters Collection
Martini Biscuit
Sweet Savory Cocktai

13181 **United Apple Sales**
124 Main St Ste 5
New Paltz, NY 12561
585-765-2460
Fax: 585-765-9710 uasales@aol.com
www.unitedapplesales.com
Grower, importer and exporter of apples
COO: Chuck Andola
Domestic/Export Sales: Dean Decker
Estimated Sales: $360,000
Number Employees: 1-4
Type of Packaging: Consumer, Food Service
Brands:
America's Fruit
Storm King

13182 **United Canadian Malt**
843 Park Street South
Peterborough, ON K9J 3V1
Canada
705-876-9110
Fax: 705-876-9118 800-461-6400
Processor, exporter and importer of dried and custom liquid brewing extracts, malt syrups and liquid malt
President/General Manager: Monte Smith
Estimated Sales: $500,000-999,999
Number Employees: 15
Square Footage: 499600
Type of Packaging: Bulk
Brands:
Bru-Mix
Canadian Grand
Master Baker
Master Brewer

13183 **United Canning Corporation**
12505 South Ave
North Lima, OH 44452
216-549-9807
Fax: 216-549-9809
Canned mushrooms
Owner: Andrew Dibacco
Plant Manager: Richard Innocenzi
Number Employees: 10-19
Square Footage: 135000
Type of Packaging: Consumer, Food Service, Private Label
Brands:
Frankies
Masterbrand
Sno-Top

13184 **United Citrus**
244 Vanderbilt Ave # 1
Norwood, MA 02062-5052
781-769-7300
Fax: 781-769-9492 800-229-7300
www.unitedcitrus.com
Bulk dry blends and liquid food products including: cocktail mixes, cocktail rimmers, beverage juices, energy drinks, hydration beverages, frozen carbonated beverages, superfruit beverages and dry blended specialty desserts
President: Richard Kates
rkates@unitedcitrus.net
VP/General Manager: Christopher Fernandes
R&D: Linda Halik
Quality Control: Cheryl Senato
Purchasing: Kristen Burbank
Estimated Sales: $5 Million
Number Employees: 10-19
Type of Packaging: Consumer, Food Service, Private Label, Bulk
Brands:
All-In-One
Best Way
Florida's Own
Good Spirits
Jollie Juan
Sir Citrus
The Last Word

13185 **United Dairy Farmers Inc.**
3955 Montgomery Rd.
Cincinnati, OH 45212
866-837-4833
consumerrelations@udfinc.com www.udfinc.com
Ice cream and dairy drinks.
President/CEO: Brad Lindner
blindner@udfinc.com
CFO: Marilyn Coleman
Year Founded: 1940
Estimated Sales: $500-$900 Million
Number Employees: 1000-4999
Number of Brands: 1
Brands:
UDF

13186 **United Dairy Inc.**
300 N. 5th St.
Martins Ferry, OH 43935
740-633-1451
800-252-1542
drinkunited.com
Full line of dairy products including fluid milk, low fat milks, chocolate, skim, half & half, buttermilk, dairy smart, ultra skim, juices and drinks. Also, cottage cheese, sour cream and dips, sterile products, yogurt and icecream.
CEO: Brad Lindner
Chief Financial Officer: George Wood
Year Founded: 1954
Estimated Sales: $145 Million
Number Employees: 250-499
Square Footage: 20000
Type of Packaging: Consumer
Other Locations:
Distribution Center
Lancaster OH
Distribution Center
Fairmont WV
United Dairy, Pennsylvania
Uniontown PA
United Dairy, West Virginia
Charleston WV
Distribution Center
West Portsmouth OH
Distribution Center
Paintsville KY
Distribution Center
Salem VA
Distribution Center
Beckley WV
Distribution Center
Galax VA

13187 **United Dairymen of Arizona**
2008 S. Hardy Dr.
Tempe, AZ 85282-1211
480-966-7211
www.uda.coop
Milk, butter and powdered dairy products.
Chief Executive Officer: Keith Murfield
CFO: Mark H.
VP, Quality Assurance: Heidi M.
VP, Operations: Steve B.
Year Founded: 1960
Estimated Sales: $780 Million
Number Employees: 300
Square Footage: 9000

13188 **United Fishing Agency LTD**
1131 N Nimitz Hwy # 38
Honolulu, HI 96817-4522
808-536-2148
Fax: 808-526-0137
Seafood
Manager: Frank Goto

Estimated Sales: $20-50 Million
Number Employees: 50-99

13189 **United Foods USA**
23447 Cabot Blvd
Hayward, CA 94545-1665
510-264-5850
Fax: 510-264-0938 www.ufiusa.com
Sauce, seasoning and dry mixes
Vice President: Hiro Aoki
aoki@sebbausa.com
Number Employees: 5-9

13190 **United Intertrade Corporation**
PO Box 821192
Houston, TX 77282-1192
713-827-7799
Fax: 713-827-7881 800-969-2233
info@mitalenacoffee.com
www.mitalenacoffee.com
Processor and canner of green and roasted coffee beans
President: Bob Ajouz
VP: Misako Ajouz
Number Employees: 5-9
Square Footage: 40000
Type of Packaging: Private Label, Bulk
Brands:
Bluebonnet
Cafe Dontedro
Cafe Orleans
Cafe Unico
Imperial Choice
Mediterranean

13191 **United Intratrade**
1139 Brittmoore Rd
Houston, TX 77043-5003
713-827-7799
Fax: 713-827-7881 713-827-7799
info@mitalenacoffee.com
www.mitalenacoffee.com

Coffee
President: Misako Ajouz
majouz@donpedrocoffee.com
VP/CFO: Misako Ajouz

Estimated Sales: $1 Million
Number Employees: 5-9
Type of Packaging: Private Label
Brands:
Bluebonnet Coffee
Cafe Don Pedro
Cafe Orleans-Coffee
Cafe Unico-Espresso
Divian Coffee
Diwan Coffee
Imperial Choice Coff
Mediterranean Coffee
Mitalena Coffee
Unico

13192 **United Juice Companies of America**
505 66th Ave. SW.
Vero Beach, FL 32968
772-562-5442
Fax: 888-562-9229 dan@unitedjuice.com
www.unitedjuice.com
Manufacturer of fresh squeezed and pasteurized juice.
President and CEO: Steve Bogen
COO: Marc Craen
VP of Food Service Sales: Dan Petry
Contact: Randy Plair
randy@lambethgroves.com
Type of Packaging: Private Label
Brands:
Lambeth Groves
Always Sweet
Froze-Fresh
Fresh Blendz

13193 **United Marketing Exchange**
215 Silver St
Delta, CO 81416-1517
970-874-3332
Fax: 970-874-9525
Processor and exporter of fresh fruits and onions
President: Harold Broughton
Sales Manager: Mike Gibson
mike@umefruit.com
Estimated Sales: $1089000
Number Employees: 1-4
Parent Co: Hi Quality Packing
Type of Packaging: Consumer
Brands:
Burrow
Owl
Tom-Tom

13194 **United Meat Company**
1040 Bryant St.
San Francisco, CA 94103
415-864-2118
Fax: 415-703-9061
Manufacturer, exporter, and importer of frozen portion controlled lamb, venison, veal and beef.
President: Phil Gee
Finance Executive: Bill Gee
Sales Executive: Leonard Gee
Contact: Philip Gee
philjr77@yahoo.com
Estimated Sales: $20-50 Million
Number Employees: 20-49
Square Footage: 19430
Type of Packaging: Food Service
Brands:
Umc

13195 **United Noodle Manufacturing Company**
3077 S 300 W
Salt Lake City, UT 84116-3414
801-485-0951
Chinese noodles and fortune cookies
Owner: Rufus Spraug
Estimated Sales: $$1-2.5 Million
Number Employees: 1-4
Type of Packaging: Consumer, Food Service

13196 **(HQ)United Pickles**
4366 Park Ave
Bronx, NY 10457-2494
718-933-6060
Fax: 718-367-8522 picklebiz@aol.com
www.unitedpickle.com
Pickle, sauerkraut and relish maker.
Owner: Steve Leibowitz
sleibowitz@unitedpickle.com
Number Employees: 1-4
Type of Packaging: Consumer, Food Service, Bulk
Other Locations:
United Pickle Products Corp.
Rosenhayn NJ
Brands:
Leibo
Leibowitz
Nathan's Famous
Teddy's
United
United Brand
Upco
Upzo

13197 **United Pies Of Elkhart Inc**
1016 Middlebury St
Elkhart, IN 46516-4510
574-294-3419
Baked products including pies
President: Blanche Nichols
VP of Sales: Kari Nichols
Estimated Sales: $10 Million
Number Employees: 5-9
Type of Packaging: Consumer

13198 **United Provision Meat Company**
156 S Ohio Ave
Columbus, OH 43205
614-252-1126
Fax: 614-252-1127 unitedmeats@cs.com
Portion control meats including cooked prime rib, meatballs, meatloaf, beef roasts, pork roasts, london broil, chicken, turkey, geese, duck, cornish hens, sloppy joes and corned beef and pastrami
President: Allen Scott
Estimated Sales: $5 Million
Number Employees: 5-9
Square Footage: 48000
Type of Packaging: Food Service

13199 **United Pulse Trading Inc**
1611 E Century Ave # 102
Suite 102
Bismarck, ND 58503-0780
701-751-1623
Fax: 701-751-1626 info@uspulses.com
www.agtfoods.com
Red split lentils, yellow split peas, green split peas, chickpeas, laird/eston/richlea lentils, whole red lentils, kabuli chickpeas and split desi chickpeas
President/Owner: Murad Katib
CFO: Lory Island
VP: Gaepan Bourassa
Manager: Eric Bartsch
agtfoods@agtfoods.com
Estimated Sales: Less Than $500,000
Number Employees: 1-4

13200 **United Salt Corp**
4800 San Felipe St
Houston, TX 77056-3908
713-877-2600
Fax: 713-877-2609 800-554-8658
uscinfo@tum.com www.unitedsalt.com
Processor and exporter of salt including plain, iodized, agricultural and water conditioning
President: Jim O'Donnell
VP: Theresa Feldman
Contact: Ashley Baker
abaker@aquasalt.com
Estimated Sales: $16,100,000
Number Employees: 10-19
Parent Co: Texas United Corporation
Type of Packaging: Consumer, Food Service, Private Label, Bulk
Brands:
Flavor House
Gulf
Ranch House

13201 **United Supermarkets**
2206 114th St
Lubbock, TX 79423-7235
806-745-9667
Fax: 806-745-9653 praterscontact@praters.com
www.praters.com
Smoked meats, breadings, frozen entrees, stuffings, gravies and casseroles
Owner: Chip Chenowetch
Sales Manager: Benny Cousatte
Purchasing Manager: Daryl Halsey
Estimated Sales: $10-20 Million
Number Employees: 20-49
Type of Packaging: Consumer

13202 **United Valley Bell Dairy**
508 Roane St
Charleston, WV 25302-2091
304-344-2511
Fax: 304-344-2518
Fluid milk
Manager: John Duty
Marketing Director: Halan Varley
Estimated Sales: Less than $500,000
Number Employees: 100-249
Type of Packaging: Private Label

13203 **United With Earth**
2833-7th St.
Berkeley, CA 94710
510-210-4359
Fax: 510-984-0538 www.unitedwithearth.com
Medjool dates, coconut and almond date rolls, pitted dates, California golden figs, Mission figs, Persian cucumbers
Number of Brands: 1
Type of Packaging: Consumer, Private Label, Bulk
Brands:
United With Earth

13204 **Universal Beef Products**
3511 Canal St
Houston, TX 77003-1835
713-224-6043
Fax: 713-224-0716 www.universalbeef.net
Beef products
President: Neil Brody
Estimated Sales: $2.5-5 000,000
Number Employees: 20-49

13205 **Universal Beverages Inc**
10033 Sawgrass Dr W # 202
Ponte Vedra Bch, FL 32082-3550
904-280-7795
Fax: 904-280-7794 ubisyfocorp@aol.com
www.syfobeverages.com
Processor and exporter of bottled water including purified and sodium free; also, regular and flavored seltzer and naturally sparkling water
CEO: Jonathan Moore
Plant Manager: Justin Jones
Estimated Sales: $$2.5-5 Million
Number Employees: 20-49
Square Footage: 400000
Parent Co: Universal Beverages Holding Corporation
Type of Packaging: Consumer, Food Service, Private Label
Brands:
Syfo

13206 **(HQ)Universal Beverages Inc**
3301 W Main St
Leesburg, FL 34748-9714
352-315-1010
Fax: 352-315-1009
Bottled water
Manager: Justin Jones
universalbeverages@yahoo.com
Site Manager: Justin Jones
Estimated Sales: $1.6 Million
Number Employees: 10-19
Type of Packaging: Private Label
Brands:
100% Purified Non Carbonated Water
Naturally Flavored S
Syfo Brand Original

13207 **Universal Formulas**
7136 E N Ave
Kalamazoo, MI 49048-9758
269-373-2930
Fax: 616-383-3449 800-342-6960
Enzymes, minerals and herbs. Founded in 1984.
President: Ralf Ostertag
CEO: Andrew Bruex
andrew@ilconline.com
Estimated Sales: $$2.5-5 Million
Number Employees: 5-9

13208 **Universal Impex Corporation**
780 Fenmar Drive
Toronto, ON M9L 2T9
Canada
416-743-7778
info@universalimpexcorp.com
www.universalimpexcorp.com

Seasonings and spices, sugars, baking products, flavors, fruit jams, condiments, sauces, marinades and dips, sweeteners, drinks (sodas, nectars, energy drink), coconut oil, coconut milk and plantain chips.
Operations Manager: Paul Bridgemohan
Estimated Sales: $5.7 Million
Number Employees: 15
Brands:
British Class
Cool Runnings
Mekong

13209 **Universal Nutrition**
3 Terminal Rd
New Brunswick, NJ 08901
732-545-3130
Fax: 732-509-0458 800-872-0101
info@universalusa.com
Bodybuilding supplements including aminos, bars, fat burners, joint support, proteins, vitamins, and minerals
President: Danny Keller
VP: Robert Gluckin
Chief Sales & Marketing Officer: Tim Tantum
Chief Creative & Strategy Officer: Phil K
Product Director: Jason Budsock
Year Founded: 1977
Number Employees: 250-499

13210 **Universal Poultry Company**
1769 Old West Broad Street
Athens, GA 30606-2867
706-546-6767
Fax: 706-546-6790
Poultry
Manager: Robert Harris
Estimated Sales: $500,000-$1 000,000
Number Employees: 5-9

13211 **Universal Preservachem Inc**
60 Jiffy Rd
Somerset, NJ 08873-3438
732-568-1266
Fax: 732-568-9040 mravitz@upichem.com
www.upichem.com
Wholesaler/distributor of chemicals and ingredients. Vitamins sweetners preservatives, antioxidants, acidulants, etc
Chairman of the Board: Herbert Ravitz
President: Dan Ravitz
Vice President: Michael Ravitz
Manager: Daniel Ravitz
dan@upichem.com
Estimated Sales: Less Than $500,000
Number Employees: 10-19
Square Footage: 240000
Type of Packaging: Private Label, Bulk

13212 **Unna Bakery**
1510 Lexington Ave
Apt 17E
New York, NY 10029-7171
917-543-8133
ulrika@unnabakery.com
www.unnabakery.com
Cookies
Founder & CEO: Ulrika Pettersson
Year Founded: 2015
Estimated Sales: Under $500,000
Number Employees: 1-4
Brands:
UNNA

13213 **Up Mountain Switchel**
295 Clinton Ave
Apt F14
Brooklyn, NY 11205-4747
315-939-3085
switcheldrink@gmail.com
drinkswitchel.com
Nutritious beverage
Co-Founder: Ely Key
Co-Founder: Garrett Riffle
Number Employees: 2-10
Brands:
Up Mountain Switchel

13214 **Upcountry Fisheries**
85 Kino Pl
Makawao, HI 96768-8891
808-871-8484
Fax: 808-871-6071
Seafood
Owner: Richard Samsing
Estimated Sales: $.5-1 million
Number Employees: 1-4

13215 **Upper Crust Bakery USA**
3655 W Washington St
Phoenix, AZ 85009-4759
602-255-0464
Fax: 602-255-0433 info@ucbakery.com
www.uppercrustbakeryusa.com
Baked goods including bread, rolls, pastries, cakes, croissants, muffins, and danishes
Chairman & CEO: Tab Navidi
Sales/Marketing: Pat Navidi
Year Founded: 1980
Estimated Sales: $20-50 Million
Number Employees: 100-249
Square Footage: 130000
Type of Packaging: Private Label

13216 **Upper Crust Biscotti**
P.O.Box 203
Pismo Beach, CA 93448-203
800-676-1691
Fax: 805-543-1284 866-972-6879
uppercrustbiscotti@worldpantry.com
Flavored regular and tiny biscotti, cookies and crostini
Owner: Terez Tyni
President: Tracey Amuiller
Estimated Sales: $500,000-$1Million
Number Employees: 11
Square Footage: 18000
Brands:
Itty-Bittie Biscotti
Itty-Bittie Cookies
Upper Crust Biscotti

13217 **Upstate Farms**
25 Anderson Rd
Buffalo, NY 14225
716-896-3156
foodservice@upstatefarms.com
upstatefarms.com
Dairy products, including yogurt and sour cream.
Chief Executive Officer: Larry Webster
Chief Operating Officer: Joe Duscher
Number Employees: 10-19
Parent Co: Upstate Niagara Cooperative Inc.
Type of Packaging: Consumer

13218 **Upstate Niagara Co-Op Inc.**
25 Anderson Rd.
Buffalo, NY 14225
716-892-3156
Fax: 716-892-3157 emailus@upstateniagara.com
www.upstateniagara.com
Dairy products including; milk, cream, flavored milks, butter, egg nog, yogurt, orange juice, iced tea, lemonade.
CEO: Larry Webster
CFO: Edward Luongo
Chief Operating Officer: Lawrence Webster
Year Founded: 1965
Estimated Sales: $719 Million
Number Employees: 500-999
Number of Brands: 5
Square Footage: 12468
Type of Packaging: Consumer, Food Service, Private Label, Bulk
Other Locations:
Fluid Milk Processing Plant
Buffalo NY
Fluid Milk Processing Plant
Rochester NY
Distribution Center
Syracuse NY
Cultured Product Processing Plant
Seneca NY
Cultured Product/North Country
North Lawrence NY
O-At-Ka Milk Products Coop
Batavia NY
Brands:
Upstate Farms
Intense Flavored Milks
Bison
Valley Farms
Milk For Life

13219 **Uptime Energy, Inc.**
7930 Alabama Ave.
Canoga Park, CA 91304
www.uptimeenergy.com
Energy drink with caffeine, coenzyme Q10, Ginkgo Biloba and ginseng; capsules also available
Chief Executive Officer: Benjamin Kim
Year Founded: 1985
Number Employees: 10-50
Number of Brands: 1
Type of Packaging: Consumer, Private Label
Brands:
Uptime

13220 **Upton's Naturals**
2054 West Grand Ave.
Chicago, IL 60612
info@uptonsnaturals.com
www.uptonsnaturals.com
Pre-packaged, marinated jackfruit and seitan; prepared vegan side dishes
Co-Founder: Nicole Sopko
Year Founded: 2006
Number of Brands: 1
Number of Products: 19
Type of Packaging: Consumer, Private Label
Brands:
Upton's Naturals

13221 **Uptown Bakers**
5335 Kilmer Pl
Hyattsville, MD 20781-1034
301-864-1500
Fax: 301-864-7744 info@uptownbakers.com
www.uptownbakers.com
European pastries and breads including scones, cinnamon bread, muffins, cookies, danish and cakes rolls
Owner: Michael Mc Cloud
orders@uptownbakers.com
CFO: Elliot Person
Estimated Sales: $13.4million
Number Employees: 100-249
Type of Packaging: Consumer, Food Service

13222 **Urban Accents**
4241 N Ravenswood Ave
Suite 1
Chicago, IL 60613-1199
773-528-9515
Fax: 773-528-9533 877-872-7742
mail@urbanaccents.com www.urbanaccents.com
Snack crackers and distinctive spices
President: Tom Knibbs
info@urbanaccents.com
Vice President: Jim Dygas
Estimated Sales: Below $5 Million
Number Employees: 5-9
Type of Packaging: Private Label
Brands:
Bloody Mary Blend

13223 **Urban Foods LLC**
PO Box 302
Sacramento, CA 95691
916-372-3663
info@urbanfoods.com
www.urbanfoods.com
All natural, gluten-free superfood snack bites and flavored seed blends
Co-Founder: Greg Durst
Co-Founder: Regan Durst
Year Founded: 2016
Number of Brands: 1
Number of Products: 8
Type of Packaging: Consumer, Private Label
Brands:
Urban Foods

13224 **Urban Moonshine**
Burlington, VT
802-428-4707
customerservice@urbanmoonshine.com
www.urbanmoonshine.com
Herbal supplements and bitters
Founder/Chief Executive Officer: Jovial King
Director, Sales: Megan Foster
Chief Operating Officer: Lexie Donovan
Year Founded: 2008
Number of Brands: 1
Type of Packaging: Consumer, Private Label
Brands:
Urban Moonshine

13225 Urban Oven
2431 N Arizona Ave
Suite 4
Chandler, AZ 85225-1391
480-921-2476
Fax: 480-921-2477 866-770-6836
gene@urbanoven.com www.urbanoven.com
Crackers
Owner: Gene Williams
gene@urbanoven.com
Director of Sales: Patty Clark
Number Employees: 10-19

13226 Urgasa
2655 S Le Jeune Rd.
Suite 810
Coral Gables, FL 33134
786-543-6693
sales@urgasa.us
urgasa.us
Quail meat and eggs
Director: David Lourenco
Brands:
URGASA

13227 Ursula's Island Farms Company
6321 Corgiat Drive S
Suite A
Seattle, WA 98108-2862
206-762-3113
Fax: 206-762-0658
Dried fruit
Owner: Ursula Blackburn

13228 Us Spice Mill Inc
4537 W Fulton St
Chicago, IL 60624-1609
773-378-6800
Fax: 773-378-0077 www.usspice.com
Manufacturer and importer of spices
President: Nick Patel
usspice@gmail.com
Estimated Sales: $600000
Number Employees: 5-9

13229 Utah Coffee Roasters
2375 S West Temple
South Salt Lake, UT 84115-2633
801-486-3334
Fax: 801-486-9714 888-486-3334
www.silverbeancoffee.com
The largest coffee roaster in Utah. We also produce; hot cocoa mixes, powder coffee creamers and powdered shake mixes
Owner: Dave Brog
dave@brog.com
Sales/Marketing Manager/EVP: Anton Broq
Estimated Sales: $500,000-$1 Million
Number Employees: 10-19

13230 Utzy, Inc.
PO Box 248
Lake Geneva, WI 53147
877-307-6142
care@utzy.com www.utzy.com
Herbal wellness supplements
Director, Digital Marketing: Daniel Powers
Year Founded: 2016
Number Employees: 2-10
Number of Brands: 1
Type of Packaging: Consumer, Private Label
Brands:
Utzy Naturals

13231 Uvalde Meat Processing
508 S Wood St
Uvalde, TX 78801-5653
830-278-6247
Fax: 830-278-6245
Sausage, venison, goat, beef, lamb and pork; also, game birds; slaughtering services available
Owner: Heather Mock
hmock@twu.edu
VP/Co-Owner: Gail Jackowski
Estimated Sales: $1-3 Million
Number Employees: 10-19

13232 V & E Kohnstamm Inc
882 3rd Ave # 7
Brooklyn, NY 11232-1902
718-788-1776
Fax: 718-768-3978 800-847-4500
flavorinfo@virginiadare.com
www.virginiadare.com
Flavors, masking agents, bases, extracts, vanilla, orange oils and colors
President: Howard Smith Jr
VP Finance: Bobby Corcoran
VP Research Dev/Quality Assurance: Michael Springsteen
VP Operations: Frederic Thor
Year Founded: 1835
Estimated Sales: $21100000
Number Employees: 100-249
Type of Packaging: Private Label, Bulk
Brands:
Veko

13233 V & V Supremo
2141 S Throop St
Chicago, IL 60608
Fax: 888-301-2244 888-887-8773
customerrelations@vvsupremo.com
www.vvsupremo.com
Cheddar cheeses
President: Gilberto Villase¤or II
VP of Marketing: Anne Marie Splitstone
Estimated Sales: $60 Million
Number Employees: 160
Number of Brands: 6
Parent Co: V & V Supremo Foods

13234 V Chocolates
440 Lawndale Dr
Salt Lake City, UT 84101
801-269-8444
Fax: 801-269-8449 vmail@vchocolates.com
www.vchocolates.com
Chocolates
Contact: Mark B Nelson
nelson@vchocolates.com
Number Employees: 12

13235 V L Foods
70 W Red Oak Lane
White Plains, NY 10604-3602
914-697-4851
Fax: 914-697-4888
President: Paul Pruzan
Brands:
Piccadeli

13236 V Sattui Winery
1111 White Ln
St Helena, CA 94574-1599
707-963-7774
Fax: 707-963-4324 info@vsattui.com
www.vsattui.com
Manufacturer of fine wines
President: Tom Davies
Director of Winemaking: Brooks Painter
Year Founded: 1882
Estimated Sales: G
Number Employees: 100-249
Type of Packaging: Consumer

13237 V.W. Joyner & Company
PO Box 387
Smithfield, VA 23431-0387
757-357-2161
Fax: 757-357-0184
Processor and exporter of smoked cured country hams, picnics and bacon for distribution to wholesale, retail and restaurant markets
VP/General Manager: Larry Santure
Plant Manager: R Howell
Number Employees: 10-19
Square Footage: 160000
Parent Co: Smithfield Companies
Type of Packaging: Consumer, Food Service, Private Label, Bulk
Brands:
Joyner's
Red Eye Country Picnic
V.W. Joyner Genuine Smithfield

13238 VCPB Transportation
600 Meadowlands Pkwy # 138
Secaucus, NJ 07094-1637
201-770-0070
Fax: 201-770-0102 info@vcpbtrans.com
www.vcpbtrans.com
Importers and distributors of a wide range of food ingredients, supplying food manufacturers, bakeries and food service companies throughout the USA
Owner: Fredric Israel
fisrael@vcpbtrans.com
Number Employees: 5-9
Type of Packaging: Food Service, Bulk

13239 VIP Food Svc
74 Hobron Ave
Kahului, HI 96732-2106
808-877-5055
Fax: 808-877-4960 www.vipfoodservice.com
Foodservice distributor on Hawaiian island of Maui with two stores that are also open to the public.
President: Nelson Okumura
Contact: Brian Tokeshi
btokeshi@vipfoodservice.com
Number Employees: 5-9
Type of Packaging: Consumer, Food Service

13240 (HQ)VIP Foods
1080 Wyckoff Ave
Flushing, NY 11385
718-821-5330
Fax: 718-497-7110 vipfoods@aol.com
Processor and exporter of soups, instant lunches, low-calorie sweeteners and mixes including dessert, pasta, tea, hot chocolate, pasta, pudding, cake and cake mixes, sauce and chicken coating
Owner: Mendel Freund
Sales Manager: Esther Freund
esther@vipfoodsinc.com
Estimated Sales: $10-20 Million
Number Employees: 20-49
Square Footage: 90000
Type of Packaging: Consumer, Food Service, Private Label, Bulk
Brands:
Kojel
Minute Lunch
Soup Bowl
Vip

13241 VIP Sales Company
2395 American Ave
Hayward, CA 94545
918-252-5791
Fax: 918-254-1667 866-536-8008
sbeck@vipfoods.com www.vipfoods.com
Packer and exporter of frozen fruits, vegetables and Chinese entrees and prepared foods; importer of raspberries, blueberries and broccoli
President: Guy Lewis
Sr. VP/COO: Lee Turman
VP Sales/Marketing: Steve Beck
Public Relations: Mick Lewis
Plant Manager: Don Avera
VP Purchasing: Fred Meyer
Estimated Sales: $5900000
Number Employees: 30
Number of Brands: 5
Number of Products: 180
Type of Packaging: Consumer, Food Service, Private Label, Bulk
Brands:
Basic Value
Food Pac
Food Trend
Tai Pan
Vip

13242 VLR Food Corporation
610 Oster Lane
Vaughan, ON L4K 2B9
Canada
905-669-0700
Fax: 905-669-9829 800-387-7437
Phylo dough, puff dough, vegetarian entrees, kosher products, hors doeuvres
General Manager: Jean-Marie Ouellette
Vice President: Rhys Quin
Estimated Sales: $21 Million
Number Employees: 250
Number of Brands: 3
Number of Products: 20
Type of Packaging: Food Service
Brands:
Jonathan T.
Tgf

13243 VOD Gourmet
3 Stormy Circle
PO Box 4922
Greenwich, CT 6830
203-531-5172
Fax: 203-532-4883 ulla@vodkacheese.com
Swedish cheese with peppercorn vodka, juniper berries, pre-cooked/frozen
Founder: Ulla Nylin

Estimated Sales: $130,000
Number Employees: 1-4
Type of Packaging: Private Label, Bulk
Brands:
Vod

13244 Vacaville Fruit Co
2055 Cessna Dr # 200
Vacaville, CA 95688-8838
707-447-1085
Fax: 707-447-1085 info@vacavillefruit.com
www.vacavillefruit.com
Processor importer and exporter of kosher dried fruit and fruit pastes; serving the food service market
President: Richard Nola
HR Executive: Nichole Nolz
info@vacavillefruit.com
Director Sales/Marketing: Nicole Nola
Plant Superintendent: Gary De La Rosa
Estimated Sales: $4200000
Number Employees: 50-99
Type of Packaging: Consumer, Food Service, Bulk

13245 Val Verde Winery
100 Qualia Dr
Del Rio, TX 78840-7697
830-775-9714
Fax: 830-775-5394 www.valverdewinery.com
Wines
Owner: Thomas Qualia
Operations Manager: Thomas Qualia
Estimated Sales: $300,000
Number Employees: 1-4
Type of Packaging: Private Label
Brands:
Val Verde Winery

13246 Val's Seafood
3437 Winford Drive
Mobile, AL 36619-4309
251-639-2570
Fax: 251-639-1198
Seafood
President: Val Hammond
Estimated Sales: $632,000
Number Employees: 1-4

13247 Valdez Food Inc
1815 N 2nd St
Philadelphia, PA 19122-2305
215-634-6106
Fax: 215-634-8645
Chinese food products including wonton soup, chow mein, fish cakes, shrim, egg & pizza rolls.
Owner: Perfecto Valdez
Treasurer: Juanito Valdez
Estimated Sales: $500,000-$1 Million
Number Employees: 10-19
Square Footage: 9000
Type of Packaging: Consumer

13248 Valentine Chemicals
129 Valentine Dr
Lockport, LA 70374-3969
985-532-2541
Fax: 985-532-6806 www.valentinechemicals.com
Sugar
President: Hugh Caffery
hugh@valentinechemicals.com
Estimated Sales: $500,000-$1 Million
Number Employees: 20-49
Type of Packaging: Consumer
Brands:
Valentine Sugars

13249 Valentine Enterprises Inc
1291 Progress Center Ave
Lawrenceville, GA 30043-4801
770-995-0661
Fax: 770-995-0725 info-sales@veiusa.com
www.veiusa.com
Powdered products including diet meal replacements, protein, fiber, sport fitness products, lecithin granules, etc
President & CEO: Alan Smith
Estimated Sales: $30 Million
Number Employees: 100-249
Square Footage: 50000

13250 Valhalla Winery
23785 Highway 126
Veneta, OR 97487-9101
541-935-9711
info@valhallawinery.com
www.valhallawinery.com
Winery; recently rebranded from Domaine Meriwether.
Owner: Eric Norman
Owner: Lori Norman
Estimated Sales: $160 Thousand
Number Employees: 1-4
Number of Brands: 1
Type of Packaging: Consumer, Food Service
Brands:
Valhalla Winery

13251 Valhrona
1801 Avenue of the Stars
Suite 600
Los Angeles, CA 90067-5908
310-277-0401
Fax: 310-277-7304
Candy and baking chocolate
President: Bernard Duclos
Founder: Monsieur Guironnet
Estimated Sales: $300,000-500,000
Number Employees: 1-4
Type of Packaging: Private Label
Brands:
Valrhona

13252 Valley Bakery
4058 Hastings Street
Burnaby, BC V5C 2H9
Canada
604-291-0674
valleybakery@shaw.ca
Cookies, breads, rolls and pastries
Owner: Ted Triezenberg
Estimated Sales: $150,000
Number Employees: 20-49
Type of Packaging: Consumer

13253 Valley Farms LLC
1860 E 3rd St
Williamsport, PA 17701
570-326-2021
Fax: 570-326-2736 www.valleyfarmsdairy.com
Milk
Chief Executive Officer: Larry Webster
Chief Operating Officer: Joe Duscher
Year Founded: 1962
Parent Co: Upstate Niagara Cooperative Inc
Type of Packaging: Consumer, Private Label

13254 Valley Fig Growers
2028 S 3rd St
Fresno, CA 93702-4156
559-237-3893
Fax: 559-237-3898 info@valleyfig.com
www.valleyfig.com
Fig growers cooperative exports dried figs worldwide.
President: Gary Jue
gjue@valleyfig.com
CFO: Jim Gargiulo
Operations Manager: Darin Ciotti
Number Employees: 50-99
Type of Packaging: Consumer, Food Service, Private Label, Bulk
Brands:
Blue Ribbon Orchard Choice
Sun-Maid

13255 Valley Grain Products
3599 W Menlo Avenue
Fresno, CA 93711-0854
559-675-3400
Fax: 559-675-0723
Corn flour, tortilla chips and taco shells
Manager: Barry Runyon
Number Employees: 2

13256 Valley Lahvosh
502 M St
Fresno, CA 93721-3013
559-485-0173
Fax: 559-485-0173 800-480-2704
customerservice@valleylahvosh.com
www.valleylahvosh.com
Crackerbreads, wraps and flatbreads
Owner: Rikki Aidoo
Vice President: Agnes Saghatelian
Marketing Coordinator: Jenni Bonsignore
Sales Director: Chip Muse
rikkia@valleylahvosh.com
Operations Manager: Danny Olosa
Production Manager: Brian Sperling
Estimated Sales: $3877239
Number Employees: 20-49
Number of Products: 33
Square Footage: 160000
Type of Packaging: Consumer, Food Service
Brands:
Calley Lahvosh
Hearts
Lahvosh
Round Lahvosh
Soft Square
Stone Street
Valley Bakery
Valley Lahvosh Crackerbread
Valley Lahvosh Flatbread
Valley Wraps

13257 Valley Meat Company
217 Daly Ave
Modesto, CA 95354
209-544-8950
Fax: 209-522-5892 800-222-6328
Hamburger patties and ground beef
Owner, Chief Executive Officer: Russell Heffner
Estimated Sales: $10 Million
Number Employees: 20-49
Type of Packaging: Consumer, Food Service, Bulk

13258 Valley Meats
2302 1st St
PO Box 69
Coal Valley, IL 61240-9408
309-517-6639
Fax: 309-799-7633 info@valleymeatsllc.com
www.valleymeatsllc.com
Fresh and frozen steaks, pork chops, beef patties, ground beef, pork and veal products; also, breaded beef, pork, chicken and veal
President: Sandy Belshouse
belshouse@valleymeatsllc.com
Regional Manager: Adam Jobe
Quality Assurance Manager: Sandy Belshause
VP Sales/Marketing: Randy Ehrlich
Regional Manager: Adam Jobe
Estimated Sales: $1.3 Million
Number Employees: 50-99
Type of Packaging: Consumer, Food Service

13259 Valley Milk Products
412 E King St
Strasburg, VA 22657
540-465-5113
Fax: 540-645-4042
Milk and specialty dried food ingredients
President: Don Utz
CFO: Jeff Mank
Estimated Sales: $10-24.9 000,000
Number Employees: 35

13260 Valley Queen Cheese Factory
200 E Railway Ave
Milbank, SD 57252-1813
605-432-4563
Fax: 605-432-9383 cheese@vqcheese.com
www.vqcheese.com
Whey and cheese
CEO: Mark Leddy
mleddy@vqcheese.com
Co-CEO: Dave Gonzenbach
Vice President: Max Gozenbach
Quality Control: Jody Kuper
Plant Engineer: Dave Gozenbach
Operations Manager: Lance Johnson
Estimated Sales: $10-20 Million
Number Employees: 100-249
Type of Packaging: Consumer
Brands:
Valley Queen

13261 Valley Sun Products Inc
3324 Orestimba Rd
Newman, CA 95360
Fax: 209-862-1100 800-426-5444
ranaya@valleysun.com www.valleysun.com
Sun-dried tomatoes, plain and in oil

Office Manager, HR & Administration: Rosie Anaya
ranaya@valleysun.com
Quality Assurance: Yolanda Padilla
Sales: Robert Young
Operations & Sales: Cesar Corona
Production Supervisor: Frank Lua
Estimated Sales: $11 Million
Number Employees: 250-499
Square Footage: 25000
Type of Packaging: Consumer, Food Service, Private Label, Bulk

13262 **Valley Tea & Coffee**
1101 W Valley Blvd Ste 103
Alhambra, CA 91803
626-281-5799
Fax: 626-281-5799
Tea and coffee
Manager: Ted Lee
CEO: Ted Lin
Estimated Sales: Under $300,000
Number Employees: 1-4
Type of Packaging: Food Service

13263 **Valley View Blueberries**
21717 NE 68th St
Vancouver, WA 98682-9060
360-892-2839
valley.view@comcast.net
Dried blueberries and strawberries, jams, syrups, glazes, honeys, trail mixes, pancake and corn bread mixes and chocolate covered blueberries; also, no-sugar products available
President: Vicki Duchesneau
valley.view@comcast.net
Estimated Sales: $86,000
Number Employees: 1-4
Square Footage: 8000
Type of Packaging: Consumer, Food Service, Private Label, Bulk
Brands:
Valley View Blueberries

13264 **Valley View Cheese Co Inc**
6028 Route 62
Conewango Valley, NY 14726-9730
716-296-5821
Fax: 716-296-5822 www.valleyviewcheese.com
Cheese
President: Rick Binder
Marketing Manager: Linda Bates
Plant Manager: Linda Bates
Estimated Sales: Less Than $500,000
Number Employees: 5-9
Brands:
Valley View Cheese

13265 **Valley View Packing Co**
7547 Sawtelle Ave
PO Box 3540
Yuba City, CA 95991-9514
530-673-7356
Fax: 530-673-9432 info@sacramentopacking.com
www.valleyviewfoods.com
Manufacturer and exporter of dried fruits and fruit juices and concentrates
Owner: Dennis Serger
serger@valleyviewpacking.com
Estimated Sales: $17 Million
Number Employees: 10-19
Type of Packaging: Consumer, Food Service, Private Label, Bulk

13266 **Valley View Winery**
1000 Upper Applegate Rd
Jacksonville, OR 97530-9175
541-899-8468
Fax: 541-899-8468 800-781-9463
www.valleyviewwinery.com
Wines
President: Mark Wisnovsky
CFO: Mark Wisnovsky
Vice President: Michael Wisnovsky
Estimated Sales: Less Than $500,000
Number Employees: 1-4
Type of Packaging: Private Label
Brands:
Anna Maria
Valley View

13267 **Valley of the Moon Winery**
P.O.Box 1951
Glen Ellen, CA 95442
707-996-6941
Fax: 707-996-5809
luna@valleyofthemoonwinery.com
www.valleyofthemoonwinery.com
Wines
Manager: Randy Meyer
Marketing Manager: Paul Young
President: Harold Duncan
Production Manager: Pat Henderson
Estimated Sales: $10-20 Million
Number Employees: 20-49
Brands:
Valley of the Moon

13268 **Vallos Baking Co**
1800 Broadway
Bethlehem, PA 18015-3802
610-866-1012
Fax: 610-866-1012
Bread, donuts and rolls
Owner: Tina Hanushack
Co-Owner: Gus Skoutelas
Estimated Sales: $10-20 000,000
Number Employees: 10-19
Type of Packaging: Consumer, Food Service

13269 **Van Der Heyden Vineyards**
4057 Silverado Trl
Napa, CA 94558-1113
707-257-0130
Fax: 707-257-3311 800-948-9463
Wine
Manager: Andrea Vander Heyede
Estimated Sales: $1-2.5 Million
Number Employees: 1-4
Type of Packaging: Private Label
Brands:
Van Der Heyden

13270 **Van Drunen Farms**
300 W 6th St
Momence, IL 60954-1136
815-472-3100
Fax: 815-472-3850 sales@vandrunen.com
www.vandrunenfarms.com
Manufacturer of fruit, vegetable and herb ingredients.
President: Edward Van Drunen
evandrunen@vandrunen.com
Sales Manager: Irv Dorn
Estimated Sales: $25-100 Million
Number Employees: 50-99
Type of Packaging: Consumer, Food Service, Private Label, Bulk
Brands:
Van Drunen Farms

13271 **Van Dyke Ice Cream**
145 Ackerman Ave
Ridgewood, NJ 07450-4205
201-444-1429
www.vandykes.com
Ice cream, frozen desserts and novelties
Owner: Demetrios Kotrokas
Estimated Sales: $2.5-5 000,000
Number Employees: 10-19

13272 **Van Eeghen International Inc**
750 Rue Gougeon
St Laurent, QC H4T 4L54
Canada
514-332-6455
Fax: 514-332-6475 www.vaneeghen.com
Dehydrated vegetables, culinary herbs and spices.
Director: Williem Van Eeghen
Account Manager: Tim Dias
Estimated Sales: $5 Million
Number Employees: 31
Square Footage: 20904

13273 **Van Hees Gmbh**
2500 Regency Pkwy
Cary, NC 27518-8549
919-654-6862
Fax: 919-654-6864 info@vanheesinc.com
www.van-hees.com
Premier manufacturer of functional ingredients tailored specifically to the meat industry.
President: W.D. (Dave) Pierce
Dir. of Technical Sales: Deanna Hofing
Contact: Frank Averta
faverta@vanheesinc.com
Parent Co: VAN HEES GmbH
Brands:
Bombal
Zartin
Sominus

13274 **Van Leer Chocolate Corporation**
600 W Chicago Ave.
Suite 860
Chicago, IL 60654
201-798-8080
Fax: 201-798-0138 800-225-1418
www.vanleerchocolate.com
Chocolate for baking, compounds, fountains, sugar-free, glazes and ice creams
Manager: Scott Applegate
CFO: Anthony Forns
Operations Manager: Robert Mohn
Plant Manager: Tom Jones
Year Founded: 1949
Estimated Sales: $25-49.9 Million
Number Employees: 100-249

13275 **Van Leeuwen**
56 Dobbin St
Brooklyn, NY 11222-3110
718-701-1630
hello@vanleeuwenicecream.com
www.vanleeuwenicecream.com
Ice cream and sobert
Co-Founder: Laura O'Neill
Co-Founder: Benjamin Van Leeuwen
Co-Founder: Peter Van Leeuwen
Wholesale Manager: Matt McKenna
Year Founded: 2008
Number Employees: 8
Type of Packaging: Consumer, Food Service

13276 **Van Oriental Food Inc**
4828 Reading St
Dallas, TX 75247-6705
214-630-0111
Fax: 214-630-0473 feedback@vaneggrolls.com
www.vaneggrolls.com
Frozen foods including regular and low-fat egg rolls, fried wontons, crab rangoon, enchiladas, burritos and spring rolls
President: Kimberly Nguyen
Co-Owner: Gretchen Perrenot
Corporate Treasurer: Theresa Motter
Sales Manager: Carl Motter
Contact: David Duval
david@vanfoods.com
Plant Engineer: Apollo Nguyen
Estimated Sales: $8.9 Million
Number Employees: 10-19
Square Footage: 224000
Type of Packaging: Consumer, Food Service, Private Label, Bulk

13277 **Van Otis Chocolates**
341 Elm St
Manchester, NH 03101-2708
603-668-1603
Fax: 603-627-0781 800-826-6847
www.vanotis.com
Chocolates
Owner: Mark Amiet
Co-Owner: Frank Bettencourt
Estimated Sales: Less Than $500,000
Number Employees: 1-4
Square Footage: 80000
Type of Packaging: Private Label
Brands:
Foiled Chocolate
Swiss Fudge Sampler Tier
Van Otis Swiss Fudge

13278 **Van Peenans Dairy**
978 Valley Rd
Wayne, NJ 07470-2997
973-694-2551
Fax: 973-696-3854
Dairy
Owner: Tunis Van Peenan
Estimated Sales: $5-10 000,000
Number Employees: 20-49

13279 **Van Roy Coffee Co**
4569 Spring Rd
Cleveland, OH 44131-1023
216-749-7069
Fax: 216-749-7039 877-826-7669
www.vanroycoffee.com
Roasted coffee and tea; also, spices
President: Jeff Miller
jeffm@vanroycoffee.com
Vice President: John Schanz
Estimated Sales: $1,400,000
Number Employees: 10-19
Square Footage: 152000
Type of Packaging: Food Service, Private Label, Bulk
Brands:
De-Kaffo
Van Roy

13280 **Van Tone Creative**
200 Metro Dr
Terrell, TX 75160-9169
972-563-2600
Fax: 972-563-2640 800-856-0802
Food, ice cream, bakers, dairy and beverage flavoring concentrates, food colors, slush concentrates and syrups including sno-cone, FCB, granita, smoothie, fruit drink and fountain
Vice President: Joe Gibbs
jgibbs@vantonecf.com
Vice President: Joe Gibbs
jgibbs@vantonecf.com
VP Marketing: Steve Myrlin
VP Sales: Joe Gibbs
Estimated Sales: $3494044
Number Employees: 20-49
Square Footage: 144000
Type of Packaging: Food Service, Private Label, Bulk
Brands:
Allez
Cyclone
Van Tone

13281 **Van Waters & Roger**
PO Box 446
Summit, IL 60501-0446
708-728-6830
Fax: 708-728-6801
Distributor of chemicals and food ingredients
President: Terry Irvine
President: James Lacey
Chief Marketing Department: Mark Buntin
Head Sales Department: Mike Clary
Number Employees: 250-499
Brands:
Van Waters & Roger

13282 **Van de Kamps**
Po Box 3900
Peoria, IL 61612
800-798-3318
www.vandekamps.com
Processor and exporter of pies, fish and vegetables
Plant Manager: James Frey
Number Employees: 100-249
Parent Co: Van de Kamps
Type of Packaging: Consumer, Food Service, Private Label
Brands:
Van De Kamp

13283 **Van's International Foods**
20318 Gramercy Pl
Torrance, CA 90501
310-320-8611
Fax: 310-320-8805 customerservice@vansintl.com
Round, square, toaster, mini and jumbo frozen waffles including original, whole grain, wheat-free, organic and gluten-free
President: James Kelly
Sales Director: Kim Fernandez
Contact: Gus Conde
gus.conde@vansintl.com
Operations Manager: Frank Copenhaver
Estimated Sales: $4600000
Number Employees: 40
Square Footage: 40000
Type of Packaging: Private Label
Brands:
Van's

13284 **Van-Lang Food Products**
5227 Dansher Rd
Countryside, IL 60525-3123
708-588-0800
Fax: 708-588-0801 info@vanlangfoods.com
Frozen hors d'oeuvres and appetizers
President: Hien Lam
Estimated Sales: Below $5 Million
Number Employees: 50-99
Type of Packaging: Food Service
Brands:
Van-Lang

13285 **Vana Life Foods**
Seattle, WA 98104-2205
347-446-6504
info@vanalifefoods.com
www.vanalifefoods.com
Green chickpea-based, pre-packaged superfood bowls in various flavors
Founder/Chief Executive Officer: Krishan Walia
Year Founded: 2015
Number of Brands: 1
Number of Products: 4
Type of Packaging: Consumer, Private Label
Brands:
Vana Life Foods

13286 **(HQ)Vance's Foods**
2129 Harrison St.
PO Box 627
San Francisco, CA 94110
800-497-4834
Fax: 800-497-4329 415-621-1171
info@vancesfoods.com
Processor and exporter of nondairy and fat-free potato-based milk substitutes including dry and liquid, and dry soy-based milk substitutes
President: Vance Abersold
VP: Glenn Abersold
Director Marketing: Frederick Mattos
Type of Packaging: Consumer, Food Service, Bulk
Brands:
Notmilk
Sno-E Tofu
Vance's Darifree

13287 **Vanco Trading Inc**
50 Old Kings Hwy N # 101
Suite 101
Darien, CT 06820-4609
203-656-2800
Fax: 203-655-8307 www.vancotrading.com
Food chemicals and ingredients
Owner: J Vaneck
janvaneck@vancotrading.com
Estimated Sales: $500,000-$1 Million
Number Employees: 1-4
Brands:
Quinine

13288 **Vancouver Island Brewing Company**
2330 Government Street
Victoria, BC V8T 5G5
Canada
250-361-0007
Fax: 250-360-0336 800-663-6383
www.vanislandbrewery.com
Brewer of lager and ale
President: Barry Fisher
General Manager: Jim Dodds
Number Employees: 20-49
Square Footage: 112000
Parent Co: Island Pacific Brewing Company
Type of Packaging: Consumer
Brands:
Blonde Ale
Hermann's Dark Lager
Hermannator Ice Bock
Piper's Pale Ale
Vancouver Islander Lager
Victoria Lager
Wolf's Scottish Cream Ale

13289 **Vande Walle's Candies Inc**
400 N Mall Dr
Appleton, WI 54913-8569
920-738-7799
Fax: 920-738-3280 800-738-1020
info@vandewallecandies.com
www.vandewallecandies.com
Candy including boxed, fund raising, Easter, Valentine, bars, brittles, caramels, chocolates, toffee, fudge, caramel corn and popcorn specialties
President: Steve Vande Walle
jaydv@aol.com
President: Thomas Walle
Vice President: Donald Walle
Estimated Sales: $3 Million
Number Employees: 20-49
Square Footage: 160000

13290 **Vanee Foods Co**
5418 Mcdermott Dr
Berkeley, IL 60163-1299
708-449-7300
Fax: 708-449-2558 jackridge@vaneefoods.com
www.vaneefoodscompany.com
Roasted gravies, broths, breakfast entrees, dinner entrees, chilis, meats, sauces and soups.
President: Al Van Eekeren
ronvanee@vaneefoods.com
CFO: Ron Van Eekeren
R&D Director: Robert Benson
Quality Assurance Director: Jack Ridge
VP Sales/Marketing Director: Michael Vanee
Human Resource Director: Beatrice Kemphel
President/Operations Director: Al Vanee
Purchasing Director: Dan Vanee
Estimated Sales: $17,000,000
Number Employees: 250-499
Square Footage: 850000
Type of Packaging: Food Service

13291 **Vanilla Corp Of America LLC**
2273 N Penn Rd
Hatfield, PA 19440-1952
215-996-1978
Fax: 215-996-9867
Grain and field bean merchant wholesalers
President: Doug Daugherty
vanillacorp@aol.com
Estimated Sales: $500,000-1 Million
Number Employees: 5-9
Type of Packaging: Food Service, Bulk

13292 **Vanlab Corporation**
86 White Street
Rochester, NY 14613
585-232-6647
Fax: 585-232-6168 bmarchetti@vanlab.com
Flavoring supplies, flavors
President: David A Patton
VP: Diane Merritt
R & D: Florent Montagne
VP: Jim Abraham
Marketing/Sales: Kim Kubach
Contact: Joette Astifan
jastifan@vanlab.com
Operations/Production: Jim Abraham
Plant Manager: Hank Rankowsky
Estimated Sales: $10-20 Million
Number Employees: 30-50
Square Footage: 35000
Type of Packaging: Food Service, Private Label, Bulk

13293 **Vanmark Equipment**
300 Industrial Pkwy
Creston, IA 50801-8102
641-782-6575
Fax: 641-782-9209 800-523-6261
www.vanmarkequipment.com
Manufacturer of industrial food processing for a wide range of produce products.
Manager: Tom Mathues
Sales: Tom Jones
Manager: Jason Davis
Operations: Rich Shafar
Estimated Sales: $5-10 Million
Number Employees: 20-49
Square Footage: 120000
Brands:
Vanmark

13294 **Vanns Spices LTD**
1716 Whitehead Rd
Suite A
Gwynn Oak, MD 21207-4029
410-944-3888
Fax: 410-944-3998 800-583-1693
sales@vannsspices.com www.vannsspices.com
Spices, seasonings and extracts

President: Meg Whitlock
meg@vannsspices.com
CEO: Erhan Kuran
Executive VP: Erhan Kurany
Estimated Sales: $3.6 Million
Number Employees: 1-4
Square Footage: 30000
Type of Packaging: Private Label, Bulk

13295 Vantage Foods
4000-4 St SE
Unit 225
Calgary, AB T2G 2W3
Canada
403-215-2820
Fax: 403-215-2830 info@vantagefoods.net
www.vantagefoods.net
Case-ready fresh meats including ground and sausage products
CEO: Gary Haley
President & COO: Leonal Kilgore
CFO: Don Finsstad
US Corporate Controller: Kelly Kuhn
Year Founded: 1997
Estimated Sales: $72 Million
Number Employees: 800

13296 Varco Brothers
1832 N Burling Street
Chicago, IL 60614-5104
312-642-4740
Noodles, spaghetti and macaroni
President: John Varco
Estimated Sales: $1-2.5 000,000
Number Employees: 1-5

13297 Varda Chocolatier
41 S Spring St
Elizabeth, NJ 07201-2608
908-354-9090
Fax: 908-354-9091 800-448-2732
www.vardachocolatier.com
Chocolate confectionery products including truffles, dessert cups, novelties and creative chocolate presentation
Owner: Varda Shandan
sales@vardachocolatier.com
Officer: Sue Hughes
Estimated Sales: $6.5 Million
Number Employees: 50-99

13298 Varet Street Market
89 Varet St
Brooklyn, NY 11206
718-302-0560
Fax: 718-302-0560
Tropical fruit
President: Alfonzo Estevez
CEO: Lely Estevez
Estimated Sales: Less than $400,000
Number Employees: 1-4
Type of Packaging: Food Service, Bulk
Brands:
Reyes Mares

13299 Varied Industries Corp
905 S Carolina Ave
Mason City, IA 50401-5813
641-423-1460
Fax: 641-423-0832 800-654-5617
www.vi-cor.com
Manufacturer and exporter of lactic acid fermentation and yucca extracts for food, feed and litter products
President: Mark Holt
VP/ Controller: Michael Lunning
Vice President: Gerry Keller
PD & Research Coordinator: Sangita Jalukar Ph. D.
Quality Manager: Julie Sanchez
VP/ Director of Marketing: Jodi Ames-Peterson
Exec. VP International BD: Roger Beers
Contact: Charlie Elrod
celrod@vicor.com
Vice President Operations: Henry Savoy
Production Supervisor Benjamin Facility: Robert Barber
Estimated Sales: $7.6 Million
Number Employees: 10-19
Square Footage: 60000
Parent Co: International Whey Technics
Brands:
Desert Gold Dry
Kulactic
Kulsar

13300 Varni Brothers/7-Up Bottling
400 Hosmer Avenue
Modesto, CA 95351-3920
209-521-1777
Fax: 209-521-0877 water@noahs7up.com
www.noahs7up.com
Manufacturer of soft drinks, spring water and other beverages.
President/CEO: Tony Varni
Contact: Deshawn Black
blackd@noahs7up.com
Estimated Sales: $17 Million
Number Employees: 60
Number of Brands: 4
Square Footage: 120000
Parent Co: Dr. Pepper/7-UP Bottling Companies
Type of Packaging: Food Service, Private Label
Brands:
Nella Bella
Noah's Water
Cock'n Bull
Cheerwine

13301 Vaughn Rue Produce
1217 Peachtree Rd NW
Wilson, NC 27896-2058
252-237-6710
Fax: 252-237-7662 800-388-8138
Sweet potatoes, butternut squash and pickles
President: Vaughn Rue
Estimated Sales: Below $5,000,000
Number Employees: 20-49
Brands:
Rue's Choice
Steakhouse

13302 Vaughn-Russell Candy Kitchen
401 Augusta Street
Greenville, SC 29601
864-271-7786
Fax: 704-484-8326 info@vaughnrussell.com
www.vaughnrussell.com
Confectionary manufacturer; original makers of "Incredible Edibles" and "Mint Pecans."
Owner: Chris Beard
Plant Manager: Ashton Beard
Estimated Sales: 500,000
Number Employees: 4
Type of Packaging: Consumer, Food Service, Bulk
Brands:
Vaughn Russell

13303 Vauxhall Foods
PO Box 430
Vauxhall, AB T0K 2K0
Canada
403-654-2771
Fax: 403-654-2211
Processor and exporter of dehydrated potato granules
President: Frank Gatto
CFO: Frank Inaba
Research & Development: Gordon Packer
General Manager: Ken Tamura
Production Manager: Ken Franz
Number Employees: 50-99
Square Footage: 200000
Type of Packaging: Food Service, Private Label, Bulk
Brands:
Chipper
Gourmet
V.G. Blue

13304 Vaxa International
4801 George Rd
Suite 190
Tampa, FL 33634
813-870-2904
Fax: 888-734-4154 877-622-8292
Customerservice@vaxa.com www.vaxa.com
Dietetic chocolate and vanilla powdered shake mixes
President: Bill Harper
VP: Chris Behan
Contact: Vicky Chaleff
vicky@vaxa.com
Estimated Sales: $1-3 Million
Number Employees: 20-49
Parent Co: Direct Access Network
Type of Packaging: Consumer, Private Label, Bulk
Brands:
Vaxa

13305 VegGuide.org
7122 S Jeffery Blvd
Chicago, IL 60649
773-363-3939
Fax: 773-363-7101
Frozen foods with soy products
General Manager: Cheryl Simms
Estimated Sales: Less than $500,000
Number Employees: 5-9
Type of Packaging: Private Label
Brands:
Natural Harvest
Vegetarian Cornmeal
Vegetarian Tamale

13306 Vega Food Industries Inc
80 Stamp Farm Rd
Cranston, RI 02921-3400
401-942-0620
Fax: 401-942-5760 800-973-7737
www.vegapeppers.com
Gourmet stuffed and sliced cherry peppers, olives, peppers and packed salads in oil and garlic
Owner: Dennis Christofaro
vegafoods@aol.com
VP: Anthony Cippola
Operations Manager: Frank Bisignano
Plant Manager: Carrie Zamborano
Estimated Sales: $1900000
Number Employees: 5-9
Square Footage: 20000
Type of Packaging: Consumer, Food Service, Private Label, Bulk
Brands:
Vega's Gourmet

13307 Vegan Metal FabricatorsCo
2045 State Route 339 E
Sedalia, KY 42079-9604
270-328-8980
Fax: 270-328-8983 veganmetal@wk.net
Metal Fabricators for food industry
Office Manager: Sherry Nelson
Estimated Sales: $.5-1 million
Number Employees: 1-4

13308 Vegan Rob's
100 Roslyn Ave
Sea Cliff, NY 11579-1274
516-671-4411
info@robsbrands.com
veganrobs.com
Vegan snacks
Founder & CEO: Robert Ehrlich
Eastern Regional Sales Manager: David Curtis
Number Employees: 11-50
Brands:
Rob's Brands

13309 Vegan Treats
1444 Linden St # 1
Bethlehem, PA 18018-2600
610-861-7660
info@vegantreats.com
www.vegantreats.com
Vegan baked goods
Manager: Laurence Koch
info@vegantreats.com
Number Employees: 20-49

13310 Vege USA
1425 S. Myrtle Avenue.
Monrovia, CA 91016
626-386-0800
Fax: 626-386-0900 888-772-8343
sales@vegeusa.com vegeusa.com
Vegetarian entrees; vegan protein, snacks and teas.
National Sales Director: Brian Schick
Office Manager: Hea-Jin Yoon
Year Founded: 1998
Estimated Sales: Under $500,000
Number Employees: 1-4
Type of Packaging: Food Service
Brands:
Vegetarian Plus(c)
VeriSoy(c)
Myrtle Greens

13311 **(HQ)Vege-Cool**
802 Inyo Ave
Newman, CA 95360
209-862-2360
Lima beans and peas
Owner: William Cerutti
Manager: Steve Lewis
Estimated Sales: $400,000
Number Employees: 3
Type of Packaging: Bulk

13312 **Vegetable Juices Inc**
7400 S Narragansett Ave
Chicago, IL 60638-6022
708-924-9500
Fax: 708-924-9510 888-776-9752
shvizdos@vegetablejuices.com
Natural and fresh ingredient products that deliver culinary and functional solutions to the food and beverage industry.
CEO: James Hurley
President, Chief Executive Officer: Elizabeth Doyle
Sr VP Sales/Marketing: Barry Horne
VP of Innovation and Research: Anthony Popielarz
Quality Control: Paul Bollinger
Director of Marketing: Dawn Molski
Vice President of National Sales: Mark Witowski
Operations: Mike O'Hara
Estimated Sales: $6 Million
Number Employees: 50-99
Square Footage: 700000
Type of Packaging: Food Service, Bulk

13313 **Vegetarian Traveler**
8362 Tamarack Village
Suite 119
Woodbury, MN 55125
vegetariantraveler.com
Salad toppers
Co-Founder: Chuck Krejci
Co-Founder & CEO: Christy Krejci

13314 **Veggie Grill**
Irvine, CA
www.veggiegrill.com
Vegetable based dishes. Gluten-free options. Available for catering.
CEO: Steve Heeley
Year Founded: 2006
Type of Packaging: Consumer

13315 **Veggie Land**
222 New Rd # 3
Parsippany, NJ 07054-5626
973-808-1540
Fax: 973-882-3030 888-808-5540
info@veggieland.com www.veggiburger.com
Processor and exporter of vegetarian foods including burgers, meat balls, frankfurters, sausage, sandwiches and chili
Executive VP: Len Torine
Estimated Sales: Below $5 Million
Number Employees: 20-49
Square Footage: 64000
Brands:
Veg-T-Balls
Veggieland

13316 **Vegi-Deli**
17 Paul Dr Ste 104
San Rafael, CA 94903
415-883-6100
Fax: 415-526-1453 888-473-3667
Vegetarian meat alternative deli products including pepperoni, cold cuts and pizza toppings and vegi-jerky, pepperoni snack sticks.
General Manager: Debra Ventura
Estimated Sales: $3-5 Million
Number Employees: 8
Square Footage: 24000
Type of Packaging: Consumer, Food Service, Private Label
Brands:
Quick Stix
Vegetarian Slice of Life

13317 **Vegy Vida**
1100 Sycamore Street
6th Floor
Cincinnati, OH 45202
513-659-0781
info@vegyvida.com
vegyvida.com
Salsa and dips for kids
Founder: Josh Young
Estimated Sales: Under $500,000
Number Employees: 17
Brands:
Vegy Vida

13318 **Velatis**
8408 Georgia Ave # B
Silver Spring, MD 20910-4442
301-578-8612
888-483-5284
www.velatis.com
Caramel
Owner: Tim Beyer
VP: Janet Beyer
Estimated Sales: $500,000-$1 Million
Number Employees: 5-9
Brands:
Vatore's

13319 **Velda Farms**
3634 South Vineland Road
Orlando, FL 32811
407-849-6202
Fax: 305-651-2766 800-795-4649
Processor of dairy products including milk, cream and ice cream
Principal: Janet Hill
CEO: Gregg Tanner
VP/CFO: Chris Bellairs
COO: Ralph Scozzafava
Year Founded: 1940
Estimated Sales: $10 Million
Number Employees: 35
Number of Brands: 2
Parent Co: Dean Foods
Type of Packaging: Consumer, Food Service, Private Label, Bulk
Brands:
Sunnydell
Velda

13320 **Vella Cheese Co**
315 2nd St E
Sonoma, CA 95476-5710
707-938-3232
Fax: 707-938-4307 800-848-0505
vella@vellacheese.com www.vellacheese.com
Cheese including Monterey jack, asiago, cheddar, dry jack and Italian-style table
President: Sarah Vella
Manager: Chicke Vella
Estimated Sales: $2,000,000
Number Employees: 10-19
Square Footage: 42960
Type of Packaging: Consumer
Brands:
Asiago
Bear Flag
Dry Sack
High Moisture Fresh Jack
Mezzo
Seasoned Cheddar Cheese
Seasoned Jack Cheese
Sello
Vella

13321 **Velvet Creme Popcorn Co**
4710 Belinder Rd
Westwood, KS 66205-1883
913-236-7742
Fax: 913-236-9631 888-553-6708
customerservice@velvetcremepopcorn.com
www.velvetcremepopcorn.com
Popcorn
President: Barbara Odle
staff@velvetcremepopcorn.com
Estimated Sales: $1 Million-1.5
Number Employees: 10-19
Square Footage: 120000
Type of Packaging: Consumer
Brands:
Velvet Creme

13322 **Velvet Ice Cream Co Inc**
11324 Mount Vernon Rd
Utica, OH 43080-7703
740-892-3921
Fax: 740-892-4339 800-589-5000
info@velveticecream.com
www.velveticecream.com
Ice cream and frozen desserts.
President: Kayla Allen
kallen@columbuscrewsc.com
CFO: Dave Elwell
VP: Mike Bearsohio
Foodservice Director: Joanne Dager
Treasurer: Tatla Dager
VP Marketing: Mike Dager
Marketing Assistant: Nathan Arnold
Plant Engineer: Jeff Belford
Number Employees: 100-249
Square Footage: 164000
Type of Packaging: Consumer

13323 **Vending Nut Co**
2222 Montgomery St
Fort Worth, TX 76107-4519
817-737-3071
Fax: 817-377-1316 800-429-9260
www.vendingnutco.com
Nuts wholesaler
President: Johnny Minshew
Estimated Sales: $4 Million
Number Employees: 10-19

13324 **Venice Baking Co**
134 Main St
El Segundo, CA 90245-3801
310-322-7357
contact@venicebakery.com
www.pizzaandiamo.com
Gluten free baked goods
Owner: James Desisto
jimmy@venicebakery.com
Number Employees: 20-49

13325 **Ventana Vineyards Winery**
2999 Monterey-Salinas Highway
Community Box #10
Monterey, CA 93940
831-372-7415
Fax: 831-375-0797 800-237-8846
Wines
Owner: Randy Pura
VP/Marketing Director: LuAnn Meador
Bookkeeper: Christy Florez
Vineyard Foreman: David Rodriguez
Production Manager: Reggie Hammond
Winemaker: Miguel Martinez
National Sales Manager: Terry Lannon
California Sales Manager: Sarah Robinson
Sales/Marketing: Gerre Calderon
Tasing Room Manager: Rosemary Hermans-Walls
Estimated Sales: $1-3 Million
Number Employees: 10-19
Type of Packaging: Private Label
Brands:
Ventana Wines

13326 **Ventre Packing Company**
P.O. Box 6487
Syracuse, NY 13217
315-463-2384
Fax: 315-463-5897
Manufacturer and packager of spaghetti sauces and salsas; prodution plant bought by Giovanni Food Company Inc in 2010.
Chairman: Marty Ventre
President/CEO: Martin Ventre
Number of Brands: 1
Parent Co: Giovanni Food Company Inc.
Type of Packaging: Consumer, Food Service, Private Label
Brands:
ENRICO'S

13327 **Ventura Coastal LLC**
2325 Vista Del Mar Dr
Ventura, CA 93001-3700
805-653-7000
Fax: 805-653-7777 sales@vcoastal.com
www.venturacoastal.com
Manufacturer and exporter of citrus concentrates and single strength juices; contract packager of frozen pectin products
President: William Borgers
borgens@vcoastal.com
EVP, Sales & Marketing: Rick Torres
Estimated Sales: $44 Million
Number Employees: 50-99
Type of Packaging: Consumer, Food Service, Private Label, Bulk
Other Locations:
Visalia CA
Tipton CA

13328 **Ventura Foods LLC**
40 Pointe Dr
Brea, CA 92821
714-257-3700
800-421-6257
www.venturafoods.com
Produces extensive line of branded and private label products, inlcuding: syrups, mayonnaise, salad dressings, oils, shortenings, and sauces. It also provides contract packaging services for a variety of products sold to retail andfoodservice customers.
President/CEO: Christopher Furman
cfurman@venturafoods.com
Executive VP & CFO: Erika Noonburg-Morgan
Executive VP, Sales & Marketing: John Buckles
Chief Administrative Officer: Andy Euser
Parent Co: CHS Inc
Type of Packaging: Consumer, Food Service, Private Label, Bulk
Brands:
Classic Gourmet
LouAna
Odell's
Hidden Valley
Marie's
Churn Spread
Grandioso
Pride
Smart Balance
Sunglow
Sauce Craft
Smokehouse 220
Extend
Mel-Fry
Phase
White Cap
Deans
Gold 'N Soft

13329 **Venture Vineyards**
8830 Upper Lake Rd
Lodi, NY 14860
607-582-6774
888-635-6277
venturev@capital.net
Grower of asparagus, raspberries and grapes including concord, Niagara, Catawaba, and Delaware. Also a processor of grape juice and importer and exporter of concord grapes
President: Melvin Nass
VP: Phyllis Nass
Operations Manager: Andrew Nass
Number Employees: 5-9
Square Footage: 40000
Brands:
Venture For the Best

13330 **Venus Wafers Inc**
100 Research Rd
Suite 3
Hingham, MA 02043-4345
781-740-1002
Fax: 781-740-0791 800-545-4538
www.venuswafers.com
Crackers
CFO: Edward Barmakian
Manager: James Anderko
jranderko@aol.com
Estimated Sales: $5-10 Million
Number Employees: 20-49
Type of Packaging: Consumer
Brands:
Deli-Catessen
Old Brussels
Venus Wafers

13331 **VerMints Inc.**
PO Box 850473
Braintree, VT 02184
781-340-4440
Fax: 617-765-4761 800-367-4442
wholesale@vermints.com www.vermints.com
All natural breath mints
Estimated Sales: $300,000-500,000
Number Employees: 1-4
Parent Co: Ohare Enterprises

13332 **Veramar Vineyard**
905 Quarry Rd
Berryville, VA 22611-4222
540-955-5510
Fax: 540-955-0404 jamesbogaty@veramar.com
www.veramar.com
Wines
Owner: Jim Bogaty
info@veramar.com
Co-Owner: Della Bogaty
Number Employees: 5-9

13333 **Verdant Kitchen**
1745 Corporate Drive
Suite 215
Norcross, GA 30093
912-349-2958
info@verdantkitchen.com
www.verdantkitchen.com
Ginger based products: baked goods, candies, cocktail syrups, infused honey and ginger ales
President & CEO: Ross Harding
Business Developer: Emma Evans
Estimated Sales: Under $500,000
Number Employees: 7
Brands:
Verdant Kitchen

13334 **Verday**
270 Lafayette St.
New York, NY 10012
hello@drinkverday.com
www.drinkverday.com
Flavored chlorophyll water
Founder/Chief Executive Officer: Randy Kohana
Number of Brands: 1
Number of Products: 4
Type of Packaging: Consumer, Private Label
Brands:
Verday

13335 **Verde Farms, LLC**
300 Trade Center # 3540
Woburn, MA 01801
617-221-8922
Fax: 617-221-8923 info@verdefarms.com
www.verdefarms.com
Organic, free range, hormone-free and grass-fed beef for retail, wholesale, foodservice and ingredient customers
Co-Founder/Chief Executive Officer: Dana Ehrlich
Vice-President, Marketing: Pete Lewis
Co-Founder/Director of Operations: Pablo Garbarino
Year Founded: 2005
Number of Brands: 1
Type of Packaging: Food Service, Bulk
Brands:
Verde Farms

13336 **Verdure Sciences**
1250 Conner St # 201
Suite 201
Noblesville, IN 46060-2900
317-776-3600
Fax: 317-776-3650 888-656-4364
info@vs-corp.com www.thymocid.com
Boswellia Serrata Extract
Owner/President/CEo: Ajay Patel
R&D: Dr Lal Hingorani
Marketing Director: Sonya Bucklew
Sales Director: Nipen Lavingia
Estimated Sales: $.5-1 million
Number Employees: 10-19
Number of Brands: 2
Number of Products: 30
Brands:
Wokvel

13337 **Verhoff Alfalfa Mill Inc**
1188 Sugar Mill Dr
Ottawa, OH 45875-8518
419-523-4767
Fax: 419-523-5715 800-834-8563
ags@alfagreen.us.com
www.alfagreensupreme.com
Dehydrated alfalfa
President: Constance Verhoff
verhoffalfalfa@embarqmail.com
Chief Executive Officer, Manager: Ken Vaupel
Vice President: Donald Verhoff
Operations Quality Control Manager: Michael Wood
Estimated Sales: $2274776
Number Employees: 20-49
Type of Packaging: Bulk

13338 **Verifine Dairy**
P.O.Box 879
Sheboygan, WI 53082-0879
920-457-7733
Fax: 920-457-5372 www.deanfoods.com
Milk
Manager: Steve Weinreich
Contact: Dale Aherns
dale_aherns@deanfoods.com
Plant Manager: Dale Ahrens
Estimated Sales: $10-24.9 Million
Number Employees: 50-99
Parent Co: Dean Foods Company

13339 **Veritas Chocolatier**
1816 Johns Drive
Glenview, IL 60025
847-729-8787
Fax: 847-729-8879 800-555-8331
Chocolate truffles
VP Marketing: Chris Samuel
VP Sales: Michael Gordon

13340 **Veritas Vineyard**
151 Veritas Ln
Afton, VA 22920-2342
540-456-8000
Fax: 540-456-8483 contact@veritaswines.com
www.veritaswines.com
Wines
Owner: Andrew Hodson
andrew.hodson@veritaswines.com
Estimated Sales: $3-5 Million
Number Employees: 10-19

13341 **Verlasso**
786-522-8418
www.verlasso.com
Farm-raised sustainable salmon
Year Founded: 2011
Number of Brands: 1
Number of Products: 1
Brands:
Verlasso

13342 **Vermilion Packers Ltd**
4825-47 Avenue
Vermilion, AB T9X 1J4
Canada
780-853-4622
Fax: 780-853-4623
vermillionpacker@hotmail.com
Fresh and cured meats including sausage
President: Rick Bozak
Estimated Sales: Below $5 Million
Number Employees: 14
Type of Packaging: Consumer, Food Service
Brands:
Vermilion

13343 **Vermont Bread Co**
80 Cotton Mill Hl
Brattleboro, VT 05301-8681
802-254-4600
Fax: 802-257-0165 info@vermontbread.com
All-natural, organic and premium bread
Ceo: Lisa Lorimer
Vice President: J Rogers
Plant Manager: Susan Vitelly
Estimated Sales: $10 Million
Number Employees: 50-99
Square Footage: 44000
Type of Packaging: Consumer, Food Service, Private Label
Brands:
Vermont
Windham Hearth

13344 **Vermont Chocolatiers**
9 East St
Northfield, VT 05663
802-485-5181
Fax: 802-485-5191 877-485-4226
Chocolate and shortbread
Co-Owner: Walter Delia
Co-Owner: Jane Delia
Estimated Sales: $300,000-500,000
Number Employees: 1-4

13345 **Vermont Coffee Co**
1197 Exchange St # 3
Suite 3
Middlebury, VT 05753-4463
802-398-2776
888-308-5099
friends@vermontcoffeecompany.com
www.vermontcoffeecompany.com
Manufacturer of coffee beans.
President: Paul Ralston
paul@vermontcoffeecompany.com
Number Employees: 10-19

13346 **Vermont Confectionery**
1541 West Rd (Rt 9)
Bennington, VT 05262-0380
80- 44- 261
Fax: 802-447-2610 800-545-9243
vtcandy@sover.net www.vermontcandy.com
Chocolate
Owner: George Mc Cain
Estimated Sales: $3-5 Million
Number Employees: 5-9

13347 **Vermont Country Naturals**
PO Box 238
Charlotte, VT 05445-0238
802-425-5445
Fax: 866-528-7091 800-528-7021
sales@vermontcountrynaturals.com
www.vermontspecialtyfoods.org
Kosher, wildcrafted maple sugar (powder and granules) and maple syrup
President: Joan Savoy
CEO: Jeffrey Madison
Estimated Sales: $300,000-500,000
Number Employees: 3
Square Footage: 14000
Parent Co: Vermont Country Maple Mixes
Brands:
Maple Sprinkles

13348 **Vermont Creamery**
40 Pitman Rd
Websterville, VT 5678
802-479-9371
Fax: 802-479-3674 info@vermontcreamery.com
www.vermontcreamery.com
Cheeses
Co-Founder: Allison Hooper
awolf@vermontcreamery.com
Co-Founder: Bob Reese
Accounting Manager: Matt Reese
General Manager: Adeline Druart
Quality Control Supervisor: Andrew Schmitt
Marketing Coordinator: Hilary Schwoegler
Sales Exec: Allison Wolf
Estimated Sales: $6.6 Million
Number Employees: 20-49

13349 **Vermont Creamery**
20 Pitman Rd.
PO Box 95
Websterville, VT 05678
802-479-9371
Fax: 802-479-3674 800-884-6287
www.vermontcreamery.com
Cream, butter, and cheese.
Co-Founder and CEO: Allison Hooper
Co-Founder and CEO: Bob Reese
President: Adeline Druart
Marketing Manager: FM Munoz
Director of Sales: Michele Haram

13350 **Vermont Food Experience**
PO Box 943
Shelburne, VT 05482-0943
802-985-8101
Fax: 802-885-2040
Gourmet and specialty foods
President: Richard Hurlburt
Estimated Sales: Under $500,000
Number Employees: 1-4

13351 **Vermont Harvest Spec Food LLC**
1799 Mountain Rd
Stowe, VT 05672-4389
802-253-7138
Fax: 802-253-7139 800-338-5354
info@vtharvest.com www.vtharvest.com
Jams, jellies, chutneys and breads
Owner: Whip Burks
whip@vtharvest.com
Estimated Sales: $1-3 Million
Number Employees: 1-4

13352 **Vermont Liberty Tea**
1 Derby Ln # 4
Waterbury, VT 05676-8926
802-244-6102
Fax: 802-244-6102
Herbal, green and black tea
Owner: John Mcconnell
vermontlibertytea@myfairpoint.net
Estimated Sales: $.5-1 million
Number Employees: 1-4

13353 **Vermont Made Richard's Sauces**
471 Bushey Rd
St Albans, VT 05478-9604
802-524-3196
Fax: 802-524-4224 sauce@vtmadebbqu.com
www.vtmadebbqu.com
BBQ sauce, game sauce and marinades, gift favors and hot sauce.
Owner: Steve Rocheleau
sauce@vtmadebbqu.com
Co-Owner: Martha Rocheleau
Estimated Sales: $150,000+
Number Employees: 1-4
Number of Products: 5
Type of Packaging: Consumer, Food Service, Private Label, Bulk

13354 **Vermont Natural Co**
201 VT Route 112
Jacksonville, VT 05342-9634
802-368-2231
Fax: 802-368-7556
www.vermontnaturalcoatings.com
Gourmet and specialty foods
Principal: Robert Moses
Manager: Annmary Block-Reed
ablock@vermontnaturalcoatings.com
Estimated Sales: $300,000-500,000
Number Employees: 12
Square Footage: 17
Type of Packaging: Private Label

13355 **Vermont Nut Free Chocolates**
10 Island Cir
Grand Isle, VT 05458-4408
802-372-4654
Fax: 802-372-4654 888-468-8373
customerservice@vermontnutfree.com
www.vermontnutfree.com
Nut free chocolates
Owner: Mark Elvidge
vtnutfree@aol.com
Estimated Sales: $1-3 Million
Number Employees: 20-49

13356 **Vermont Pretzel & Cookie Co.**
25 Rockingham Street
Bellows Falls, VT 05101
802-460-4600
Fax: 802-869-2837 888-671-4774
Stuffed and soft pretzels, cookies and bars
President: Christine Holtz

13357 **Vermont Signature Sauces**
PO Box 667
Saxtons River, VT 05154
802-869-5000
info@vermontsignaturesauces.com
Manufacturer of gourmet finishing sauces.
Founder: Karen Whitman

13358 **Vermont Smoke and Cure**
Hinesburg, VT
802-482-4666
www.vermontsmokeandcure.com
Smoked meats and meat snacks.
CEO: Chris Bailey

13359 **Vermont Specialty Food Association**
Freedom Foods
24 Pleasant Street
Randolph, VT 05060
802-728-0070
Fax: 802-728-0071
Fruit infused maple syrups, gift baskets, mustards, granola & mixes
Square Footage: 16000

13360 **Vermont Sweetwater Bottling Co**
1075 VT Route 30 N
Poultney, VT 05764-9633
802-287-9897
Fax: 802-287-9897 800-974-9877
york@sover.net
Soda
Co-Owner: Robert Munch
Co-Owner: Richard Munch
york@sover.net
Estimated Sales: $3-5 Million
Number Employees: 5-9

13361 **Vermont Tea & Trading Co Inc**
43 Court St
43 Court Street
Middlebury, VT 05753-1454
802-388-4005
Fax: 802-388-4005 888-255-9327
Loose leaf teas
Co-Owner: Curron Malhotra
Co-Owner: Bruce Malhotra
b.malhotra@vermonttea.com
Estimated Sales: $1-3 Million
Number Employees: 1-4

13362 **Vermont Tortilla Company**
22 Sage Court
Shelburne, VT 05482
802-999-4823
info@vttortillaco.com
www.vttortillaco.com
Tortillas
Co-Founder & Owner: April Moulaert
Chief Tortilla Officer: Azur Moulaert
Year Founded: 2015
Number Employees: 2-10
Brands:
Vermont Tortilla

13363 **Vermont Village**
698 South Barre Rd.
Barre, VT 05641
www.vermontvillage.com
Raw, organic apple cider sipping vinegar and vinegar shots; organic malt vinegar; organic flavored apple sauce; organic spiced apple butter
Owner: Joseph Shepherd
Number of Brands: 1
Type of Packaging: Consumer, Private Label

13364 **Vern's Cheese**
312 W Main St
Chilton, WI 53014-1312
920-849-7717
Fax: 920-849-7883 info@vernscheese.com
www.vernscheese.com
Cheeses
President: Vern Knoespel
info@vernscheese.com
Estimated Sales: $20-50 Million
Number Employees: 20-49

13365 **Veronica Foods Inc**
1991 Dennison St
Oakland, CA 94606-5225
510-535-6833
Fax: 510-532-2837 800-370-5554
info@evoliveoil.com www.evoliveoil.com
Olive oil manufacturers and importers
President: Michael Bradley
CEO: Mike Bradley
mbradley@evoliveoil.com
CFO: Leah Bradley
VP: Veronica Bradley
Marketing: Arnie Kaufman
VP Retail Sales: Arnie Kaufman
Operations: Fred Johnson
Production: Myron Manown
Plant Manager: Dave Fitzgerald
Purchasing: Fred Johnson
Estimated Sales: $16,200,000
Number Employees: 50-99
Square Footage: 684000
Brands:
Dainty Pak
Delizia
Italia
Panther
Purn Life

13366 **Veronica's Treats**
31 W Grove St # C
Middleboro, MA 02346-1859
508-946-4438
Fax: 508-946-4460 866-576-1122
info@veronicastreats.com
www.veronicastreats.com
Personalized cookies, brownies, and cupcakes
Owner: Hilary Souza
veronicastreats@gmail.com
Number Employees: 10-19
Square Footage: 24000
Type of Packaging: Private Label

13367 **Verve Coffee Roasters**
816 41st Ave
Santa Cruz, CA 95062-4421
831-475-7776
sarah.a@vervecoffeeroasters.com
www.vervecoffeeroasters.com
Coffee
Site Manager: Chris Baca
chrisb@vervecoffeeroasters.com
Number Employees: 10-19

13368 **Veryfine Products Inc**
3900 Aero Dr
Mason, OH 45040
service.fin@sunnyd.com
veryfine.com
Fruit juice drinks
President & CEO: Bill Cyr
Year Founded: 1865
Estimated Sales: $150 Million
Number Employees: 5-9
Square Footage: 350000
Parent Co: Sunny Delight Beverage Company
Type of Packaging: Private Label
Brands:
Veryfine Juices

13369 **Vessey & Co Inc**
1605 Zenos Rd
P.O. Box 28
Holtville, CA 92250-9603
760-356-0130
Fax: 760-356-0137 kevinolson@redshift.com
www.vessey.com
Grower of cabbage including red, green, bok choy and napa; also, red and yellow onions, red and yukon potatoes, sweet corn, cantaloupes and garlic including fresh, whole, peeled, minced and chopped; importer and exporter of garlic
President: Jon Vessey
Partner: Jack Vessey
jack@vessey.com
Sales Manager: David Grimes
Sales: Eric Pompa
Estimated Sales: $3100000
Number Employees: 10-19
Type of Packaging: Food Service, Bulk

13370 **Vestergaard Farms**
4408 S Wagner Rd.
Ann Arbor, MI 48103
734-929-2875
info@vestergaardfarms.com
www.vestergaardfarms.com
Various meat products including beef, pork, lamb, and poultry.
Owner: Michael Vestergaard
Year Founded: 2010
Type of Packaging: Private Label

13371 **Vetter Vineyards Winery**
8005 Prospect Station Rd
Westfield, NY 14787-9630
716-326-3100
Fax: 716-326-3100 wine@cecomet.net
Wines
Owner: Mark Lancaster
wine@fairpoint.net
Co-Owner: Barbara Lancaster
Estimated Sales: Less Than $500,000
Number Employees: 1-4
Type of Packaging: Private Label
Brands:
Vetter Vineyards

13372 **Via Della Chiesa Vineyards**
413 Church Street
Raynham, MA 02767-1008
508-822-7775
Fax: 508-880-0500
Wines
President: Robert DiCroce
CFO: Sharon Tweedy
Marketing Manager: Kate Desmond
Public Relations Officer: Lidm Piwa
Winery Manager: Dolly Tulsiani
Production Manager: Matyas Vogel
Estimated Sales: Below $5 Million
Number Employees: 10
Type of Packaging: Private Label
Brands:
Cranberry Blush Wine
Dry-Atlantic Coastal
Raspberry Rave Wine

13373 **Viader Vineyards & Winery**
1120 Deer Park Rd
Deer Park, CA 94576-9715
707-963-3816
Fax: 707-963-3817 www.viader.com
Wines
Owner: Delia Viader
delia@viader.com
Director of Operations: Alan Viader
Administrative Assistant: Valaree Martinez
Shipping Manager: Blanca Avina
Sales/Marketing Director: Janet Viader
Director of Operations: Alan Viader
Winemaker: Delia Viader
Number Employees: 5-9
Type of Packaging: Consumer, Food Service, Private Label
Brands:
Viader

13374 **Viano Vineyards**
150 Morello Ave
Martinez, CA 94553-3522
925-228-6465
Fax: 925-228-5670 info@vianovineyards.com
www.vianovineyards.com
Wines
Owner: John Viano
President: Paula Viano
Estimated Sales: Less than $400,000
Number Employees: 1-4
Brands:
Viano Winery

13375 **Viansa Winery**
25200 Arnold Dr
Sonoma, CA 95476-9222
707-939-0782
Fax: 707-935-5654 800-995-4740
ViansaService@viansa.com www.viansa.com
Wines
President: Austin Haynes
austinh@valleycom.org
CEO: Vicki Sebastiani
CFO: Russ Jay
Co. Founder: Sam Sebastiani
Winemaker: Michael Sebastiani
Estimated Sales: $5-10 Million
Number Employees: 50-99
Brands:
Nebbiolo
Vernaccia

13376 **Viau Foods**
6625 Ernest Cormier
Laval, QC H7C 2V2
Canada
450-665-6100
Fax: 450-665-7100 800-663-5492
www.viausila.com
Cooked or dry cured pepperoni, Italian cooked meats, sausages, pizza toppings and meatballs.

13377 **Vic's Corn Popper**
14935 Industrial Rd
Omaha, NE 68144-3232
402-932-0426
Fax: 402-331-2507 vic@vicspopcornomaha.com
www.vicspopcornomaha.com
Popcorn
President: Ken Nelson
Number Employees: 5-9
Brands:
Vic's

13378 **Vichy Springs Mineral Water**
2605 Vichy Springs Rd
Ukiah, CA 95482-3507
707-462-9515
Fax: 707-462-9516 vichy@vichysprings.com
www.vichysprings.com
Processor and exporter of naturally carbonated bottled mineral water
President: Gilbert Ashoff
VP: Marjorie Ashoff
Estimated Sales: $500,000 appx.
Number Employees: 10-19
Square Footage: 28000
Type of Packaging: Private Label
Brands:
Vichy Springs
Vichy Springs Mineral Water

13379 **Vickey's Vittles**
16420 Gledhill St
North Hills, CA 91343-2807
818-841-1944
Fax: 818-841-1191 vickeysvittles@msn.com
Specialty cookies, bundt cakes, brownies, dessert bars, pies and cobblers; also, gift baskets, fat-fee and low-fat items available
President: Vickey Conover
Estimated Sales: $300,000-500,000
Number Employees: 5-9
Brands:
Vickey's Vittles

13380 **Vicky's Artisan Bakery**
500 Alden Rd.
Unit 4
Markham, ON L3R 5H5
Canada
905-944-0940
info@artisanbakerycompany.com
artisanbakerycompany.com
Flatbreads
President: Richard Bedford
richard@artisanbakerycompany.com
Co-Founder: Vicky Min
Brands:
Vicky's All Natural

13381 **Victor Allen Coffee Company**
1401 12th St NW
Albuquerque, NM 87104-2117
505-856-5282
Fax: 505-856-5588 800-662-2575
email@avaloncoffee.com victorallen.com
Coffee and tea
Manager: Aaron Simpson
Marketing Specialist: Kathryn Utterback
VP Sales: Liz Kollar
Operations Manager: Andy Wieczorek
Estimated Sales: Below $5 Million
Number Employees: 5-9
Type of Packaging: Private Label
Brands:
Avalon Organic Coffee
Bosque Tea Co
High Desert Roasters
Rio Grande Roasters

13382 **Victor Allen's Coffee and Tea**
1101 Moasis Dr
PO Box 307
Little Chute, WI 54140
920-788-1252
800-394-5282
www.victorallen.com
Manufacturer of coffee and teas
Owner: Scott Dercks
Principal: Nathan Impola
Contact: Kate Bons
kjanssen@victorallen.com
Year Founded: 1979
Estimated Sales: $20-50 Million
Number Employees: 5-9
Type of Packaging: Private Label

13383 **Victor Ostrowski & Son**
524 S Washington St
Baltimore, MD 21231-3030
410-327-8935
Fax: 410-252-9372
Polish garlic bologna, liver sausage, stuffed cabbage and horseradishes
Owner/President: John Ostrowski
Estimated Sales: $1-3 Million
Number Employees: 5-9

Type of Packaging: Consumer

13384 **Victor Packing**
11687 Road 27 1/2
Madera, CA 93637-9440
559-673-5908
Fax: 559-673-4225 www.victorpacking.com
Manufacturer, and exporter of currants and raisins including organic, natural, golden and seedless; also, raisin juice concentrate and raisin paste available
Owner: Victor Sahatjian
victor@victorpacking.com
VP: Margaret Sahatjian
Domestic Sales: Kristina Surabian
International Sales: Richard Burright
Year Founded: 1928
Estimated Sales: $10 Million
Number Employees: 50-99
Square Footage: 150000
Type of Packaging: Consumer, Food Service, Private Label, Bulk
Brands:
Liberty Bell
Madera
Natural Thompson
Victor

13385 **Victor Preserving Company**
6318 Ontario Center Rd
Ontario, NY 14519-9324
315-524-2711
Fax: 315-524-7040 onedavid@aol.com
Sauerkraut
President/CEO: David Tobin
Estimated Sales: $3-5 Million
Number Employees: 10 to 19
Square Footage: 135000
Type of Packaging: Private Label

13386 **Victoria Amory & Co LLC**
440 Riversville Rd
Greenwich, CT 06831-3257
203-220-6454
shop@victoriaamory.com
Manufacturer of flatbread crisps, condiments, sauces, and mayonnaise.
Founder: Victoria Amory
vamory@victoriaamory.com

13387 **Victoria Fancy Sausage**
6506 118th Avenue NW
Edmonton, AB T5W 1G6
Canada
780-471-2283
Fax: 780-477-5381
Fresh beef, pork, chicken and wild game including venison, elk and moose
President: John Snyder
Vice President: Alan Snyder
Estimated Sales: A
Number Employees: 1-4
Square Footage: 14000
Type of Packaging: Bulk
Brands:
Victoria Fancy

13388 **(HQ)Victoria Fine Foods**
443 E 100th St
Brooklyn, NY 11236-2103
718-927-3000
Fax: 718-649-7069
victoria@victoriafinefoods.com
www.victoriafinefoods.com
Pasta and specialty sauces, condiments and gourmet spreads.
President: Brian Dean
CEO: Gerald Aquilina
Vice President, Finance: Robert Haberman
Executive VP, Sales: William Paskowski
Number Employees: 100-249
Type of Packaging: Consumer, Food Service, Private Label, Bulk
Brands:
Victoria

13389 **Victoria Gourmet Inc**
17 Gill St
Unit 4
Woburn, MA 01801-1768
781-935-2100
Fax: 781-935-9979 800-403-8981
info@vgourmet.com www.vgourmet.com
Blended seasonings
Founder, President: Victoria Taylor
vtaylor@vgourmet.com
Estimated Sales: $500,000-$1 Million
Number Employees: 10-19

13390 **Victoria's Catered Traditions**
1240 Eastridge Place
Manteca, CA 95336
209-823-9015
Fax: 208-823-8213 877-272-5208
Chocolate covered popcorn
Owner Principal: Victoria Costa

13391 **Victrola Coffee Roasters**
310 E Pike St
Seattle, WA 98122-3610
206-325-6080
info@victrolacoffee.com
www.victrolacoffee.com
Coffee
Contact: Joshua Boyt
joshua@victrolacoffee.com
Number Employees: 5-9

13392 **Vida Blend**
1430 State Highway 5s
Amsterdam, NY 12010-8184
518-620-6216
Fax: 866-243-6216 www.vida-blend.com
Organic nutrients and ingredients
Director: Freddy Luna
Formulator: Jessica Ruedisuelli
Marketing: Yasmin Pacia
Global Sales Associate: Linda Gibeault
Number Employees: 10-19

13393 **Vidalia Brands Inc**
PO Box 2120
Reidsville, GA 30453-2120
912-654-2726
Fax: 912-654-9135 800-752-0206
info@vidaliabrands.com www.vidaliabrands.com
Vidalia sweet onions, gourmet treats, peach salsa, blossom kit, salad dressings, relishes, BBQ sauce, chow-chow
President/CEO: Sandra Bland
Marketing Director: Wendy Moore
Vice President: Sandra Bland
Marketing & Communications Manager: Greg Smith
Public Relations: Susan Lynch
Plant Manager: Mike Gulbranson
Number Employees: 50-99
Type of Packaging: Private Label
Brands:
Vidalia

13394 **(HQ)Vidalia Sweets Brand**
818 Ga Highway 56 West
Lyons, GA 30436
912-565-8881
Fax: 912-565-0199
Fresh and pickled onions, onion relish, barbecue sauce, etc.; wholesaler/distributor of vidalia onions and specialty food products; serving the food service market
President: Jim P Cowart
Estimated Sales: $210000
Number Employees: 1-4
Type of Packaging: Consumer, Food Service
Brands:
Vidalia Sweets

13395 **Videri Chocolate Factory**
327 W. Davie Street
Suite 100
Raleigh, NC 27601
919-755-5053
hello@viderichocolatefactory.com
viderichocolatefactory.com
Chocolate bars
Co-Founder & Head Chocolate Maker: Sam Ratto
Co-Founder & Public Engagement: Starr Sink
Manager: Chris Heavener
Estimated Sales: $3.3 Million
Number Employees: 65
Brands:
Videri Chocolate Factory

13396 **Vie De France Yamazaki Inc**
2070 Chain Bridge Rd # 500
Suite 500
Vienna, VA 22182-2588
703-442-9205
Fax: 703-821-2695 800-446-4404
www.viedefrance.com
Baked goods including croissants, pastries, danish, breads and desserts.
President: Sadao Yasumura
Estimated Sales: $44.5 Million
Number Employees: 1000-4999
Square Footage: 30000
Type of Packaging: Consumer, Food Service, Bulk

13397 **Vie-Del Co**
11903 S Chestnut Ave
Fresno, CA 93725-9618
559-834-2525
Fax: 559-834-1348
Processor and exporter of fruit concentrates including grape; also, wine and brandy
President: Dianne Nury
dnury@vie-del.com
Vice President: Richard Watson
Customer Service: Janel Cook
Purchasing Manager: Robert Reiter
Estimated Sales: $18,800,000
Number Employees: 100-249

13398 **Vienna Bakery**
110 Maple Ave
Barrington, RI 02806-3520
401-245-2355
Fax: 401-247-5432 info@viennabakeryri.com
www.viennabakeryri.com
Gourmet bread and pastries
Owner: Joe Balasco
CEO: Bernie Jager
Marketing Manager: Bernie Jager
Number Employees: 20-49
Type of Packaging: Consumer, Food Service
Brands:
Vienna

13399 **Vienna Beef LTD**
6033 Malburg Way
Vernon, CA 90058-3947
323-583-8951
Fax: 323-585-7580 800-733-6063
www.viennabeef.com
Pickles, cured meat, soups, kosher specialties and desserts.
CEO: James Eisenberg
CFO: Richard Steele
Vice President of Marketing: Keith Smith
SVP/Sales & Marketing: Thomas McGlade
VP/Human Resources: Jane Lustig
VP/Purchasing: Richard Ewert
Number Employees: 10-19
Type of Packaging: Consumer, Food Service, Private Label

13400 **(HQ)Vienna Beef LTD**
2501 N Damen Ave
Chicago, IL 60647
773-278-7800
800-366-3647
info@viennabeef.com www.viennabeef.com
Meats including hot dogs, Italian beef, Polish sausage and condiments
President: Tim O'Brien
Finance Director: Richard Steele
Project Engineer: Jack Bodman
VP, Quality Assurance: Kim Brown
Production Director: Henry Stepniak
Year Founded: 1893
Estimated Sales: $86 Million
Number Employees: 500-999
Number of Brands: 4
Square Footage: 100000
Type of Packaging: Consumer, Food Service
Brands:
Bistro Soups and Chili
Chipico
Minaret
Vienna

13401 **Vienna Meat Products**
170 Nugget Avenue
Scarborough, ON M1S 3A7
Canada
416-297-1062
Fax: 416-297-0836 800-588-1931

Processor and importer of ham, sausage, cold cuts, turkey products, roast beef, corned beef and pastrami.
President: Michael Latifi
Director Retail Sales: Vince Romano
Estimated Sales: $9.5 Million
Number Employees: 100
Brands:
Austrian Crown
Grand Chef De Paris
Vienna

13402 **Vietti Foods Co Inc**
636 Southgate Ave
Nashville, TN 37203-5516
615-244-7864
Fax: 615-242-7055 www.viettichili.com
Processor and canner of pork and beef with barbecue sauce, chili spaghetti, regular chili and beef stew; also, sauces including hot dog, spaghetti and Creole.
President: Trent Baker
baker@viettifoodsinc.com
Vice President, R&D: Dee Folmar
Number Employees: 50-99
Parent Co: Zwanenberg Food Group BV
Type of Packaging: Consumer, Food Service, Private Label
Brands:
Vietti
Artisan Craft
Butcher's Cut
Southgate
Zwanenberg

13403 **Vigneri Chocolate Inc.**
810 Emerson St
Rochester, NY 14613-1804
585-254-6160
Fax: 585-254-6872 877-844-6374
info@vigneri.com www.vigneri.com
chocolate tablets, filled chocolates, chocolate dipped products, novelty chocolates, chocolate covered products, drinking chocolate and wellness chocolate in the gifting, snacking, entertaining and decorating categories for our VigneriChocolate bran
CEO: Alexander Vigneri
Number Employees: 10+
Square Footage: 60000
Type of Packaging: Consumer, Food Service, Private Label, Bulk
Brands:
Give Collection
By Nature By Hand
Surprizers!

13404 **Vigo Importing Co**
4701 W Comanche Ave
P.O. Box 15584
Tampa, FL 33614
800-282-4130
www.vigo-alessi.com
Processor and exporter of seasoned rice dinners, paella and bread crumbs; importer of olives, peppers, sundried tomatoes, olive oil, cheese, pasta, balsamic vinegar, bread sticks, pine nuts, coffee, vegetable pates, porcini mushroomsartichokes, etc.
General Manager: Sam Ciccarello
sam@vigo-alessi.com
Marketing Director: Laura De Lucia
VP, Sales: Alfred Alessi
Year Founded: 1947
Estimated Sales: $21.1 Million
Number Employees: 100-249
Square Footage: 165000
Type of Packaging: Consumer, Food Service, Private Label, Bulk
Brands:
Vigo
Alessi

13405 **Viki's Montana Classics**
801 Grand Dr
Bigfork, MT 59911-3532
406-837-5545
Fax: 406-837-5545 800-248-1222
Preserves and syrups
Owner: Viki Hoveland
Estimated Sales: $1-2.5 Million
Number Employees: 1-4
Parent Co: Canandaigua Wine Company

13406 **Viking Distillery**
1101 E Broad Ave
Albany, GA 31705-2872
229-436-0181
Fax: 229-434-1768 866-729-3722
info@sazerac.com www.sazerac.com
Bourbon blends, gin and vodka
President & CEO: Mark Brown
Vice President of Human Resources: Kathy Thelen
Marketing Services Director: Meredith Moody
Vice President of Sales & Marketing: Steve Wyant
PR Manager: Amy Preske
Plant Manager: Julius Drakes
Estimated Sales: $6 Million
Number Employees: 10-19
Parent Co: Barton Brands
Type of Packaging: Consumer

13407 **Viking Seafoods Inc**
50 Crystal St
Malden, MA 02148-5919
781-322-2000
Fax: 781-397-0527 800-225-3020
jcovelluzzi@vikingseafoods.com
Frozen seafood including fish cakes, fish and chips, cod, fish flake, halibut, perch, fish sticks, fish patties, scallops and shrimp; also, value-added products including Nordica and bake n'broil style.
President: Charles Gulino
CEO: James Covelluzzi
Sales Manager: Douglas Farrell
Contact: Leonard Abbene
abbene@vikingseafoods.com
Plant Manager: Joseph Novello
Estimated Sales: $8200000
Number Employees: 50-99
Type of Packaging: Consumer, Food Service
Brands:
Kitchens of the Sea
Viking

13408 **Viking Trading**
2375 John Glenn Dr
Suite 106
Atlanta, GA 30341
770-455-8630
Fax: 770-455-9632
Blue crab, caviar, conch, crab, crawfish, kingfish, lobster meat
President: Juan Vales
Principal: Frank Valdez

13409 **Vikis Foods**
999 South Oyster Bay Rd.
Suite 403
Bethpage, NY 11714
516-767-8700
Fax: 516-767-1300 info@vikisfoods.com
www.vikisfoods.com
Granola
President: Viktoria Sater
Vice President: Greg Gutsko
Director of Operations: Christine Busse
Estimated Sales: $1-5 Million
Number Employees: 11
Type of Packaging: Food Service
Brands:
Viki's Granola

13410 **Viktoria's Gourmet Foods, LLC**
Bethpage, NY 11714
516-767-8700
www.vikisfoods.com
Manufacturer of soft-baked granola.
Owner and Founder: Viki Sater

13411 **Villa Barone**
21825 Jerusalem Grade Road
Middletown, CA
707-987-8823
Fax: 707-235-8613 info@thevillabarone.com
www.thevillabarone.com
Olive oils and olive oil products
President: Robert Lipari

13412 **Villa Helena/Arger-Martucci Winery**
1455 Inglewood Ave
St Helena, CA 94574-2219
707-963-4334
Fax: 707-963-4748 www.arger-martucci.com
Wines
President: Carol Martucci
Marketing Director: Katarena Arger
Estimated Sales: $500,000-$1 Million
Number Employees: 1-4
Type of Packaging: Private Label
Brands:
Villa Helena

13413 **Villa Milan Vineyard**
7287 E County Road 50 N
Milan, IN 47031-8946
812-654-3419
Wines
President: John Garrett
CEO: Marc A McNeece
Estimated Sales: $2.5-5 Million
Number Employees: 10-19
Brands:
Villa Milan

13414 **Villa Mt. Eden Winery**
8711 Silverado Trl S
Saint Helena, CA 94574
866-931-1624
Fax: 707-963-7840
Processor and exporter of wines
Manager: Jeff Mc Bride
j.mcbride@villamteden.com
Estimated Sales: $10-20 Million
Number Employees: 10-19
Parent Co: Stimson Lane
Type of Packaging: Consumer

13415 **Village Roaster**
9255 W Alameda Avenue
Lakewood, CO 80226-2802
303-238-8718
Fax: 303-233-4370 800-237-3822
contact@villageroaster.com
www.villageroaster.com
Coffee
President: Jim Curtis
VP: Kathleen Curtis
CFO: Kathleen Curtis
Contact: Melissa Charles
charles@villageroaster.com
Estimated Sales: Under $500,000
Brands:
Village Roaster

13416 **Villar Vintners of Valdese**
4940 Villar Ln NE
Valdese, NC 28690
828-879-3202
Fax: 828-879-3202
Wines
President: Joel Talmas
CEO: Ernest Jahier
Estimated Sales: $3-5 000,000
Number Employees: 5-9
Brands:
Villar Vintners

13417 **Vilore Foods Co Inc**
8220 San Lorenzo Dr
Laredo, TX 78045-8704
956-722-7190
Fax: 956-728-8383 info@vilore.com
www.vilore.com
Jalapeno peppers
President: Suzanna Almanza
salmanza@vilore.com
Estimated Sales: $200 Million
Number Employees: 20-49

13418 **Vinalhaven Fishermens Co-op**
PO Box 366
Camden, ME 04843-0366
207-236-0092
Fax: 207-236-7733 janetvhcoop@hotmail.com
vinalhavencoop.com
Seafood
Owner: John R Long
Estimated Sales: $1-3 Million
Number Employees: 5-9

13419 **Vince's Seafoods**
1105 Lafayette St
Gretna, LA 70053-6345
504-368-1544
Fax: 504-368-1545
Processor and exporter of frozen and boiled seafood; shrimp, crabs, oysters, crawfish, catfish, tuna, trout, flounder and tilapia. Also gumbo and soups
President: Barbara Jimenez
vdesalvojr@yahoo.com

Estimated Sales: $500,000-$1 Million
Number Employees: 1-4
Square Footage: 32000

13420 **Vincent Arroyo Winery**
2361 Greenwood Ave
Calistoga, CA 94515-1031
707-942-6995
Fax: 707-942-0895 info@vincentarroyo.com
www.vincentarroyo.com
Wines
President: Vincent Arroyo
arroyo707@aol.com
Estimated Sales: Less than $1 Million
Number Employees: 5-9
Type of Packaging: Bulk

13421 **Vincent B Zaninovich & Sons**
20715 Avenue 8
Richgrove, CA 93261
661-725-2497
Fax: 661-725-5153 www.vbzgrapes.com
Processor and exporter of grapes
Owner: Antone Zaninovich
Owner/President: Vincent Zaninovich
vincentz@vbzgrapes.com
VP: Andrew Zaninovich
Sales Team Member: Joe Butkiewicz
Human Resources Director: Mark Boyer
Estimated Sales: $11 Million
Number Employees: 10-19
Square Footage: 30900
Type of Packaging: Bulk
Brands:
Mr Z
Richgrove King
Vbz

13422 **Vincent Formusa Company**
2150 Oxford Road
Des Plaines, IL 60018
847-813-6040
Fax: 312-421-1286 sales@marconi-foods.com
www.marconi-foods.com
Beans, salad dressings, giardiniera & peppers, olives, olive oils, pasta, Italian style salads, spices, tomatoes, vinegars
President: Robert Johnson
bob@marconi-foods.com
Estimated Sales: $830,000
Number Employees: 10
Square Footage: 100000
Type of Packaging: Consumer, Food Service, Bulk
Brands:
Digiovanni
Marconi

13423 **Vincent Piazza Jr & Sons**
5736 Heebe St
Harahan, LA 70123
504-734-0012
Fax: 504-734-8752 800-259-5016
packages@piazzaseafood.com
www.piazzaseafood.com
Shrimp; wholesaler/distributor of crab, crawfish, alligator, conch, octopus, clams, lobster, frog legs, scallops, turtle, gumbo, etc
Owner: Vincent Piazza Jr
Sales and Inventory Control: Nicholas Piazza
Contact: Bryan Piazza
bryanpiazza@piazzaseafood.com
Computer Systems and Purchasing: Bryan Piazza
Estimated Sales: $2.5-5 Million
Number Employees: 20-49
Square Footage: 24000
Type of Packaging: Food Service
Brands:
Lucky Star
Papa Piazza Brand
Papa's Fresh Catch
Tri Dragon

13424 **Vincent's Food Corporation**
179 Old Country Rd
Carle Place, NY 11514
516-481-3544
Fax: 516-742-4579
Sauces
President: Anthony Marisi
amarisi@vincentsclambar.com
Estimated Sales: $5-10 Million
Number Employees: 5-9

13425 **Vincor Canada**
441 Courtneypark Drive E
Mississauga, ON L5T 2V3
Canada
905-564-6900
Fax: 905-564-6909 800-265-9463
www.cbrands.com
Wine and vodka cooler importer, marketer and distributor.
President & CEO: Eric Morham
CFO: Don Dychuck
SVP Marketing, Canadian Portfolio: Steve Bolliger
Director Sales & Marketing, RJ Spagnols: Ellen Johnson
SVP Operations: Martin van der Merwe
Square Footage: 60655
Type of Packaging: Consumer, Food Service
Other Locations:
Vincor Quebec
Rougemont QC
Brands:
Camarad
Goundry Fine Wine
Hogue
Inniskillin
Jackson-Triggs
Kim Crawford Wines
Kumala
Loiseau Bleu
Pallenque
Toasted Head

13426 **Vine Village Day**
4059 Old Sonoma Rd
Napa, CA 94559-9702
707-255-4116
Fax: 707-255-8431 www.vinevillage.org
Wine
Executive Director: Michael Kerson
Estimated Sales: Below $5 Million
Number Employees: 20-49
Type of Packaging: Private Label
Brands:
Carneros Chardonnay

13427 **Vink & Beri**
140 Domorah Dr
Montgomeryville, PA 18936
215-654-5252
info@vinkandberi.com
www.vinkandberi.com
Aloe vera juices and syrup, coconut water, orange juice
Chairman: Cornelis Gerardus Vink
CEO: Vipul Chander Beri
Sr. Regional Sales Manager: Brandon Hawes
Estimated Sales: $1-2 Million
Number Employees: 11-50
Parent Co: Tropical General Investment (TGI) Group
Brands:
Alor
Bare Nature

13428 **Vino's Brew Pub**
923 W 7th St
Little Rock, AR 72201-4005
501-375-8466
Fax: 501-375-8468 www.vinosbrewpub.com
Beer
President: Henry Lee
CEO: Dan O'Byrne
Estimated Sales: Below $5 Million
Number Employees: 20-49
Type of Packaging: Private Label
Brands:
7th Street Pale
Big House Ale
Lazy Boy Stout

13429 **Vinoklet Winery**
11069 Colerain Rd
Cincinnati, OH 45252-1425
513-385-9309
Fax: 513-385-9379 vinokletwinery@fuse.net
www.vinokletwines.com
Wine manufacturer and restaurant service
Owner/Winemaker: Kreso Mikulic
vinokletwinery@fuse.net
Estimated Sales: $500,000 appx.
Number Employees: 10-19
Type of Packaging: Food Service
Brands:
Vinoklet

13430 **(HQ)Vinquiry Wine Analysis**
7795 Bell Rd
Windsor, CA 95492-8519
707-838-6312
Fax: 707-838-1765 info@vinquiry.com
Wine industry yeasts and supplements
President: Jose Santos
Founder: Marty Bannister
mbannister@vinquiry.com
Sales Manager, Winemaking Products: Max Buiani
Director of Operations: Michelle Bowen
Estimated Sales: $5-10 Million
Number Employees: 20-49
Square Footage: 41600
Type of Packaging: Private Label, Bulk
Other Locations:
Vinquiry Central Coast Office
Santa Maria CA
Vinquiry Napa Office
Napa CA

13431 **Vintage Bee Inc.**
4020 Stirrup Creek Dr.
Suite 109
Durham, NC 27703
919-699-6788
Manufacturer of honey.
Co-Founder: Van Tapp
Co-Founder: Laura Tapp

13432 **Vintage Italia**
513 Main St.
Windermere, FL 34786
407-217-5910
Fax: 407-217-5911 info@pastachips.com
www.pastachips.com
Pasta based chips
Founder: Jerry Bello

13433 **Vintage Plantations Chocolates**
461 Frelinghuysen Ave
Newark, NJ 07114-1426
908-354-9304
Fax: 973-242-1998 800-207-7058
Chocolate
President: Pierrick Chouard
Operations Manager: Bryan Sargent
Estimated Sales: Below $5 Million
Number Employees: 5-9
Type of Packaging: Private Label
Brands:
Dagoba Organic Chocolate
Fritz Knipschildt

13434 **Vintage Wine Estates**
205 Concourse Blvd
Santa Rosa, CA 95403
877-289-9463
www.vintagewineestates.com
Producer and retailer of wines and champagnes
Founding Partner & CEO: Pat Roney
President: Terry Wheatley
CFO: Katherine DeVillers
COO: Jeff Nicholson
Estimated Sales: $69 Million
Number Employees: 100-249
Number of Brands: 1
Number of Products: 42
Type of Packaging: Consumer
Brands:
Windsor Vineyards

13435 **Viobin USA**
226 W Livingston St
Monticello, IL 61856-1673
217-762-2561
Fax: 217-762-2489 888-473-9645
info@viobinusa.com www.viobinusa.com
Manufacturer of nutritional extract, defatted wheatgerm, and wheat germ oil.
CEO: Monte White
Marketing/Sales: Geni Heider
Manager: Bart Allen
sales@viobinusa.com
General Manager: Roger Mohr
Production: Kevin Stevens
Estimated Sales: $10-20 Million
Number Employees: 20-49
Number of Brands: 1
Parent Co: McShares, Inc.
Type of Packaging: Consumer, Bulk
Brands:
Viobin

13436 **Viola's Gourmet Goodies**
P.O.Box 351075
Los Angeles, CA 90035
323-731-5277
Fax: 323-731-6898 violasgg@pacbell.net
Gourmet relish, jelly, zinger and rim shot
Owner: Nancy Rowland
violasgg@pacbell.net
Estimated Sales: $.5-1 million
Number Employees: 1-4
Type of Packaging: Bulk
Brands:
Viola's

13437 **Violet Packing Holdings LLC**
123 Railroad Ave
Williamstown, NJ 08094-1699
856-629-7428
Fax: 856-629-6340 www.deiorios.com
Peppers, tomatoes and sauces including spaghetti and pizza
President: James Zhao
jamesz@genscript.com
VP Operations: Chip Sclafani
GM: Lou Sclafani
Estimated Sales: $10-20 Million
Number Employees: 50-99
Parent Co: Don Pepino Company
Type of Packaging: Consumer, Food Service
Brands:
Don Pepino
Sclafani
Violet

13438 **Violife**
Thessaloniki,
Greece
info@violifefoods.com
www.violifefoods.com
Vegan, lactose-free, non-GMO, gluten-free dairy and meat alternatives in various flavors
Number of Brands: 1
Number of Products: 43
Type of Packaging: Consumer, Private Label
Brands:
Violife

13439 **Virgil's Root Beer**
201 Merritt 7 Corporate Park
Norwalk, CT 06851
203-890-0557
Fax: 203-496-8883 800-997-3337
info@reedsinc.com www.virgils.com
Root beer in various flavors, including original, premium, extra, cherry, raspberry, spiced apple, plus ginger candy and ginger ice cream
CEO & Director: Val Stalowir
Chief Innovation Officer: Chris Reed
CFO: James Linesch
COO: Stefan Freeman
SVP Sales And Marketing: Neal Cohane
Contact: Peter Anton
panton@reedsgingerbrew.com
Estimated Sales: $20.38 Million
Number Employees: 20
Square Footage: 30000
Parent Co: Reed's Ginger Brew
Type of Packaging: Consumer, Food Service
Brands:
Virgil's

13440 **Virgin Raw Foods LLC**
11645 Wilshire Blvd.
Los Angeles, CA 90025
424-322-0535
800-830-7047
cs@virginrawfoods.com www.virginrawfoods.com
Royal honey infused with herbs and superfoods
Founder/Owner: Monika Kozdrowiecka
Number of Brands: 1
Number of Products: 1
Type of Packaging: Consumer, Private Label
Brands:
Bee Panacea

13441 **Virginia & Spanish Peanut Co**
260 Dexter St
Providence, RI 02907-2798
401-421-2543
Fax: 401-421-2557 800-673-3562
contact@vspnut.com www.vspnutco.com
Salted nuts, peanuts and peanut butter
President: Robert Kaloostian
vfpnutco@aol.com
VP/Treasurer: Candale Kaloostain
Estimated Sales: $10-20 Million
Number Employees: 5-9
Square Footage: 48000
Type of Packaging: Consumer, Food Service, Private Label, Bulk
Brands:
Anchor
Brown Bear

13442 **Virginia Artesian Bottling Company**
4300 Spring Run Rd
Mechanicsville, VA 23116-6639
804-779-7500
Fax: 866-291-9504 sales@virginiaartesian.com
virginiaartesian.com
Bottled water
Owner: Steven Brown
Sales Manager: Frank Atwood
Production Manager: Nick Brown
Year Founded: 2003
Estimated Sales: Under $500,000
Number Employees: 1-10
Type of Packaging: Food Service
Brands:
Virginia Artesian(c)

13443 **Virginia Chutney Company**
113A Aileen Rd.
Flint Hill
Washington, VA 22627
540-675-1984
Fax: 540-675-1985 sales@virginiachutney.com
www.virginiachutney.com
Chutneys
Contact: Oliver Turner
oliver@virginiachutney.com

13444 **Virginia Dare Extract Co**
882 3rd Ave # 2
Brooklyn, NY 11232-1902
718-788-1776
Fax: 718-768-3978 flavorinfo@virginiadare.com
www.virginiadare.com
Flavor and extract company founded in 1835.
President: Howard Smith
hsmith@virginiadare.com
Number Employees: 100-249
Type of Packaging: Bulk
Brands:
Contrasweet
G-Brew
Gourmet Brew
Prosweet
Superfex
Superfreeze
Tre Cafe
Vidarome

13445 **Virginia Diner Inc**
322 W Main St
Wakefield, VA 23888
888-823-4637
www.vadiner.net
Peanuts, cashews, almonds, peanut brittle, nutty candies, chocolates and snacks.
President: Christine Epperson
Year Founded: 1929
Estimated Sales: $100+ Million
Number Employees: 250-499
Number of Brands: 4
Brands:
Game Day Snacks
Norman Rockwell
Old Bay
Virginia Diner

13446 **Virginia Honey Company**
P.O.Box 1915
Inwood, WV 25428
304-267-8500
Fax: 304-263-0946
Honey, salad dressings, including Vidalia Onion Vinagarette salad dressing, sauces, jams and jellies, herring products, salmon products, condiments, horseradish, cream cheese, party platters
CEO: Terry Hess
Parent Co: Vita Food Products
Type of Packaging: Consumer, Food Service, Private Label, Bulk
Brands:
Virginia Brand
Vita Brand

13447 **Virginia Trout Co**
5480 Potomac River Rd
Monterey, VA 24465-2257
540-468-2280
Fax: 540-468-2279 info@virginiatroutfarms.com
Fresh and frozen mountain trout
Owner: Bryan Plemmons
b.plemmons@virginiatroutfarms.com
Estimated Sales: Less Than $500,000
Number Employees: 5-9
Type of Packaging: Food Service
Brands:
Allegheny
Mountain Trout

13448 **Visalia Citrus Packing Group**
19743 Avenue 344
Woodlake, CA 93286
559-564-3351
Fax: 559-564-3865 vcpg@vcpg.com
Golden State Citrus Packers is a licensed commercial shipper of citrus products for Sunkist Growers, Inc.
President: George Lambeth
Manager: John Kalendar
johnkalendar@vcpg.com
Office Manager: Judith Jenkins
Plant Manager: Raul Gamez
Number Employees: 100-249
Parent Co: Visalia Citrus Packing Group
Type of Packaging: Food Service

13449 **Visalia Produce Sales**
201 W Stroud Ave
Kingsburg, CA 93631-9531
559-897-6652
Fax: 559-897-6650 george@visaliaproduce.com
www.visaliaproduce.com
California fruits and vegetables
Owner: Stan Shamoon
Sales Representative: Stan Shamoon
Sales Representative: Aron Gularte
Sales Representative: George Matoian
Estimated Sales: $1-10 Million
Number Employees: 20-49

13450 **Vision Pack Brands**
531 Main Street
Suite 513
El Segundo, CA 90245
877-477-8500
Fax: 866-825-1808 877-477-8500
visionpack@verizon.net
www.visionpackbrands.com
Gourmet crackers, snacks and dip, candy, confections and beverages

13451 **Vision Seafood Partners**
41 Summer Street
Kingston, MA 02364-1418
781-585-2000
Fax: 773-561-0139
Seafood

13452 **Vista D'Oro Farms**
346-208th Street
Langley, BC V2Z 1T7
Canada
604-514-3539
Fax: 604-514-3599 855-514-3539
info@thepreservatory.com thepreservatory.com
Preserves, wines, jams and jellies
Owner: Lee Murphy
Estimated Sales: Under $500,000
Number Employees: 1-10
Type of Packaging: Food Service
Brands:
The Preservatory
Vista D'Oro

13453 **Vit-Best Nutrition**
2802 Dow Ave
Tustin, CA 92780
714-832-9700
info@vit-best.com
www.vit-best.com
Nutritional supplements and vitamins.

CEO: Tom Mooy
CFO: Stacey Kato
VP, Quality: Rick Beatty
VP, Sales: John Altenberg
VP, Operations: Juliun Brabon
Estimated Sales: $20-50 Million
Number Employees: 200
Square Footage: 140000
Parent Co: Xiamen Kingdomway Group Co.
Type of Packaging: Consumer, Bulk

13454 **Vita Food Products Inc**
2222 W Lake St
Chicago, IL 60612
800-989-8482
www.vitafoodproducts.com
Pickled herring, lox & nova salmon, cream cheese with salmon, horseradish, cocktail and tarter sauces; gourmet sauces, marinades, salad dressings, dessert toppers, syrups & honey, salsa, drinks.
President & CEO: Clifford Bolen
Chief Financial Officer: R. Anthony Nelson
Vice President: William Zaikos
Production Manager: Henry Williams
Purchasing Manager: Doug Clark
Estimated Sales: $32 Million
Number Employees: 100-249
Square Footage: 82200
Type of Packaging: Consumer, Food Service
Brands:
Vita
Elf
Jim Beam
Grand Isle
Virginia Brand
Oak Hill Farms
Biltmore
Scorned Woman
Sauza

13455 **Vita Plus Corp**
2514 Fish Hatchery Rd
P.O. Box 259126
Madison, WI 53713-2424
608-256-1988
Fax: 608-283-7990 608-256-1988
www.vitaplus.com
Dairy
Owner: Roop Rache
Co-Owner: Eddie Molina
CFO: Mike Miley
mmiley@vitaplus.com
Estimated Sales: $5-10 Million
Number Employees: 100-249
Brands:
Cortilite
Life Line Vita Plus
Vita-Plus

13456 **Vita-Pakt Citrus Products Co**
203 E Badillo St
Covina, CA 91723-2116
626-332-1101
Fax: 626-966-8196 888-684-8272
www.vita-pakt.com
Citrus and kiwi processor.
Chairman & CEO: James Boyles
james.boyle@vita-paktcitrus.com
Number Employees: 50-99
Type of Packaging: Consumer, Food Service, Bulk

13457 **Vita-Pure Inc**
410 W 1st Ave
Roselle, NJ 07203-1047
908-245-1212
Fax: 908-245-1999 www.vitapuretech.com
Food/dietary supplements, vitamins, nutritional supplements
President: Achyut Sahasra
vitapureinc@yahoo.com
Vice President: Jaqueline Schauffler
Marketing Director: Joseph Campis
Operations Manager: Sheldon Tannebaum
Production Manager: Angelo Padilla
Estimated Sales: $5-10 000,000
Number Employees: 20-49
Square Footage: 17500
Type of Packaging: Private Label

13458 **VitaThinQ Inc.**
Davie, FL
info@vitathinq.com
www.essentialmints.com
Caffeinated peppermints for weight loss; peppermints with melatonin for sleep aid
Number of Brands: 1
Number of Products: 3
Type of Packaging: Consumer, Private Label
Brands:
Essential Mints

13459 **Vitakem Neutraceutical Inc**
811 West Jericho Turnpike
Smithtown, NY 11787
855-837-0430
www.vitakem.com
Vitamins and supplements
President/CEO: Bret Hoyt Sr
Contact: Aaron Berkman
aaron@vitakem.com

13460 **Vital Choice**
P.O. Box 4121
Bellingham, WA 98227
800-608-4825
www.vitalchoice.com
Wild fish, shellfish, canned fish, meats, omega-3s, supplements, and organic foods
Year Founded: 2001

13461 **Vital Farms**
3913 Todd Lane
Suite 505
Austin, TX 78744
877-455-3063
info@vitalfarms.com
vitalfarms.com
Eggs and butter
President & Chief Operating Officer: Russell Diez-Canseco
CEO & Owner: Matt O'Hayer
Chief Financial Officer: Jason Dale
Director of Marketing: Kathryn McKeon
Senior Director of Human Resources: Jennifer A. Gregg
Year Founded: 2007
Estimated Sales: $5.4 Million
Number Employees: 50-200
Brands:
Certified Humane(c)
Vital Farms(c)

13462 **Vital Proteins LLC**
545 Busse Rd.
Elk Grove Village, IL 60007
224-544-9110
info@vitalproteins.com
www.vitalproteins.com
Collagen supplements in various flavors
Co-Founder/Chief Executive Officer: Kurt Seidensticker
Number of Brands: 1
Type of Packaging: Consumer, Private Label
Brands:
Vital Proteins

13463 **Vitale Poultry Company**
800 E Cooke Rd
Columbus, OH 43214
614-267-1874
Fax: 614-267-7824
Poultry processing
Co-Owner: Mark Cecutti
Co-Owner: Dan Cecutti
President: Rose Vitale
Estimated Sales: $5-9.9 000,000
Number Employees: 10-19

13464 **Vitalicious**
11 Broadway Ste 1155
New York, NY 10004
212-233-6030
Fax: 212-233-6031 877-848-2877
customerservice@vitalicious.com
www.vitalicious.com
100 calorie VitaTops, VitaMuffins, VitaBrownies, VitaMixes, VitaCakes
Contact: Ian Gillespie
ian.gillespie@vitalicious.com
Brands:
Vitatops
Vitamuffins
Vitabrownies
Vitamixes
Vitacakes

13465 **Vitality Life Choice**
5350 Capital Court, Suite #109
PO Box 21133
Carson City, NV 89721-1133
775-882-7186
Fax: 775-882-6686 800-423-8365
Health and nutritional supplements
President: Gary Paulsen

13466 **Vitality Works**
8500 Bluewater Rd. NW
Albuquerque, NM 87121
505-268-9950
Fax: 505-268-9952 www.vitalityworks.com
Herbal, vitamin and nutraceutical supplements
Chief Executive Officer: Mitch Coven
Production Manager: Jackie Keepers
Year Founded: 1982
Number of Brands: 1
Type of Packaging: Private Label
Brands:
Vitality Works

13467 **Vitamer Laboratories**
46 Corporate Park
Irvine, CA 92606
800-432-8355
customerservice@vitamer.com www.vitamer.com
Processor of dietary supplements and herbal products.
Year Founded: 1924
Estimated Sales: $20-50 Million
Number Employees: 100-249
Parent Co: Anabolic
Type of Packaging: Private Label

13468 **Vitamilk Dairy**
4141 Agate Road
Bellingham, WA 98226-8745
206-529-4128
Fax: 206-524-7070
Dairy products including milk, sour cream and ice cream
President: E Gerald Teel
VP Sales: Larry Burns
Plant Manager: Paul Nelson
Number Employees: 100-249
Type of Packaging: Consumer, Food Service, Private Label, Bulk

13469 **(HQ)Vitaminerals**
1815 Flower St
Glendale, CA 91201-2024
818-500-8718
Fax: 818-240-2785 800-432-1856
www.cryogel.tv
Processor and exporter of food supplements and vitamins
Owner: Michael Gorman
jgorman@vitamineralsinc.com
President: John Gorman
jgorman@vitamineralsinc.com
VP: Mike Gorman
National Sales Director: Charles DesVos
Estimated Sales: $5-10 Million
Number Employees: 20-49
Square Footage: 70000
Brands:
Hampshire Laboratories
Vitaminerals

13470 **Vitamins**
200 E Randolph Drive
Chicago, IL 60601-6436
312-861-0700
Fax: 312-861-0708
customerservice@vitamins-inc.com
www.vitamins-inc.com
Nutritional ingredients including defatted wheat germ, wheat germ oil and soluble vitamins
President: James Carozza
Vice President: Robert Lenburg
Contact: Bill Redwood
redwood@vitamins-inc.com
Number Employees: 1-4

13471 **Vitarich Ice Cream**
572 Highway 1
Fortuna, CA 95540-9711
707-725-6182
Fax: 707-725-6186 info@humboldtcreamery.com
www.humboldtcreamery.com
Ice cream, sherbet, frozen yogurt and ice cream mixes and novelties

President: Rich Ghilarducci
Number Employees: 20-49
Type of Packaging: Consumer, Food Service, Private Label, Bulk
Other Locations:
Vitarich Ice Cream Co.
Seattle WA
Brands:
Vitarich

13472 **(HQ)Vitarich Laboratories**
4365 Arnold Ave
Naples, FL 34104
239-430-2266
Fax: 239-430-4930 800-817-9999
Processor, importer and exporter of vitamins, nutraceuticals and food supplements including herbal, whole leaf wheat, barley and algae
President: Kevin Thomas
Marketing: Bill Foley
Sales Director: Frank Guzzo
Contact: Steve Colligan
colligans@vitarichlabs.com
Estimated Sales: $.5-1 million
Number Employees: 5-9
Square Footage: 80000
Type of Packaging: Consumer, Private Label, Bulk
Other Locations:
Vitarich Laboratories
Bainbridge GA
Brands:
Hydra-Green

13473 **Vitasoy USA**
57 Russell Street
Woburn, MA 01801
781-430-8988
Fax: 978-772-6881 800-848-2769
info@vitasoy-usa.com www.vitasoy-usa.com
Tofu, asian noodles, fresh pasta wraps, vegan sandwich spreads, soymilks, juices and teas
President/Chief Executive Officer: Walter Riglian
Contact: Terry Arkinstall
terry.arkinstall@vitasoy-usa.com
Chief Executive Officer: Tom Perry
Research & Development: Fred Jewett
Quality Assurance Manager: Rick Baum
Vice President, Marketing: Tim Kenny
Sales Executive: Eugene Lye
Public Relations: Stella Lung
Vice President, Operations: John Wareham
Production Supervisor: Edgar Bonilla
Facility Manager: Peter Breed
Purchasing Manager: Heidi Bonasoro
Estimated Sales: $20 Million
Number Employees: 160
Number of Brands: 4
Square Footage: 21227
Type of Packaging: Consumer, Food Service, Private Label
Brands:
Nasoya
Azumaya
San Sui
Vita

13474 **Vitatech Nutritional Sciences**
2802 Dow Ave
Tustin, CA 92780-7212
714-832-9700
Fax: 714-731-8482 info@vit-best.com
www.vit-best.com
Vitamins
CEO: Thomas Mooy
VP Supply Chain: Katie Watts
Director of Technical Services: David Jiang
Estimated Sales: $20-50 Million
Number Employees: 100-249
Type of Packaging: Private Label

13475 **Viterra, Inc**
2625 Victoria Ave.
Regina, SK S4T 7T9
Canada
306-569-4411
Fax: 306-569-4708 866-647-4090
www.viterra.com
Grain and oilseeds.
President/CEO: Kyle Jeworski
Estimated Sales: $2.4 Billion
Number Employees: 190,000
Parent Co: Glencore plc
Type of Packaging: Consumer, Food Service, Private Label, Bulk

Brands:
Dakota Growers Pasta
Pasta Sanita
Zia Briosa

13476 **Vity Meat & Provisions Company**
1418 N 27th Avenue
Phoenix, AZ 85009-3603
602-269-7768
Fax: 602-269-0044
Meats
President: Michael Brown
VP Finance: Gary Rasmussen
Estimated Sales: $.5-1 million
Number Employees: 1-4

13477 **Viva Tierra**
601 S 2nd St
Mt Vernon, WA 98273
360-855-0566
organic@vivatierra.com
www.vivatierra.com
Organic produce including apples, pears, peaches, and onions
President/CEO: Luis Acuna
EVP/CFO: Steve Mackey
Sales Manager: Matt Roberts
Organic Integrity & Logistics: Addie Pobst

13478 **Vive Organic**
2554 Lincoln Blvd. # 772
Venice, CA 90291
877-774-9291
contact@vive-organic.com www.vive-organic.com
Organic wellness shots in various flavors
Co-Founder/Chief Executive Officer: Wyatt Taubman
Co-Founder/Vice-President, Sales: J.R. Simich
Co-Founder/Chief Executive Officer: Kyle Withycombe
Number of Brands: 1
Number of Products: 3
Type of Packaging: Consumer, Private Label
Brands:
Vive Organic

13479 **Vivienne Dressings**
P.O.Box 16072
St Louis, MO 63105-0772
314-994-7549
Fax: 636-947-1123 800-827-0778
ttucker.vivienne@gmail.com www.vivienne.com
Gourmet dressings and marinades
President: Thomas A Tucker
Estimated Sales: Below $5 Million
Number Employees: 1-4
Brands:
Vivienne

13480 **Vivolac Cultures Corporation**
3862 E Washington St
Indianapolis, IN 46201
317-356-8460
Fax: 317-356-8450 sales@vivolac.com
www.vivolac.com
Manufacturer and exporter of dairy, meat and bread starter cultures in pelletized, frozen and freeze-dried form
President: Wesley Sing
Technical Sales Manager: Rossana Reyle
Chief Marketing Officer: Philip Reinhardt
Technical Sales: David Winters
Estimated Sales: $1.4 Million
Number Employees: 20-49
Type of Packaging: Private Label, Bulk
Brands:
Bioflora
Vivolac

13481 **Vivoo**
Via del Commercio 16
Verona, 37066
Italy
info@vivoo.it
www.vivoo-re-evolution.com
Organic raw chocolate bars, energy bites, energy bars; raw cacao powder, cacao butter and cacao beans
Founder: Giorgio Sergio
Number of Brands: 1
Type of Packaging: Consumer, Private Label
Brands:
Vivoo

13482 **Vivra Chocolate**
24 Walpole Park S
Walpole, MA 02081-2541
800-359-8950
info@vivrachocolate.com
vivrachocolate.com
Chocolate bars
Founder: Robert Leavitt
Director of Sales: Jordan Phillips
Number Employees: 2-10
Brands:
Vivra(c)

13483 **Vixen Kitchen**
Santa Cruz, CA
707-223-5627
info@vixenkitchen.co
www.vixenkitchen.co
Organic, natural, vegan- and paleo-friendly gelato in various flavors
Founder/Chief Executive Officer: Sundara Clark
Number of Brands: 1
Number of Products: 6
Type of Packaging: Consumer, Private Label
Brands:
Vixen Kitchen

13484 **Vocatura Bakery Inc**
695 Boswell Ave
Norwich, CT 06360-2826
860-887-2220
Breads
President: John Vocatura
Manager: David Vochtura
Estimated Sales: $500,000-$1 000,000
Number Employees: 10-19
Brands:
Vocatura

13485 **Vogel Popcorn**
21325 Hamburg Avenue
Lakeville, MN 55044
952-469-7482
Fax: 952-469-2152 www.vogelpopcorn.com
Popcorn
President: Gary Rodkin
EVP: Colleen Batcheler
Estimated Sales: $10-20 Million
Number Employees: 20-49
Parent Co: ConAgra Foods
Type of Packaging: Consumer, Private Label, Bulk

13486 **Voget Meats Inc**
2930 E St
Hubbard, OR 97032-9313
503-981-6271
Fax: 503-981-0220
Smoked meats, sausages
CEO: Merle Stutzman
Vice President: Grace Stuzman
Estimated Sales: $2.5-5 Million
Number Employees: 10-19
Type of Packaging: Private Label
Brands:
Voget Meats

13487 **Vogue Cuisine Foods**
PO Box 70608
Sunnyvale, CA 94086-0608
310-391-1053
Fax: 310-390-0883 888-236-4144
inquiry@voguecuisine.com
www.voguecuisine.com
Natural dehydrated low sodium and organic instant soup bases and mixes including chicken, beef, onion and vegetable vegetarian-chicken
President: Clinton Helvey
CEO: Carol Schlanger
Vice President: Clinton Helvey
Public Relations: Carol Helvey
Estimated Sales: Less Than $500,000
Number Employees: 5-9
Type of Packaging: Private Label
Brands:
Vogue Beef Base
Vogue Chicken Base
Vogue Onion Base
Vogue Vegebase
Vogue Vegetarian Chicken Base

13488 **Volcano Island Honey Company**
46-4013 Puaono Rd
Honokaa, HI 96727
808-775-1000
Fax: 808-775-0412 888-663-6639
www.volcanoislandhoney.com
Gourmet honey
Manager: Candice Choy
candice@volcanoislandhoney.com
Estimated Sales: Under $500,000
Number Employees: 5-9
Brands:
Rare Hawaiian

13489 **Vollwerth & Baroni Companies**
PO Box 239
Hancock, MI 49930-0239
906-482-1550
Fax: 906-482-0842 800-562-7620
topdog@vollwerth.com www.vollwerth.com
Sausage and meat products; wholesaler/distributor of hotel and restaurant supplies; serving the food service market
President: Robert Vollwerth
Vice President/General Manager: Jim Schaaf
Secretary/Treasurer: Mary Ann Berryman
Sales Representative: Richard Vollwerth
Contact: Mary Berryman
berryman@vollwerth.com
Packaging Manager: Don Hiltunen
Production Manager: Adam Manderfield
Estimated Sales: $3.5 Million
Number Employees: 35
Square Footage: 80000

13490 **Volpi Foods**
5263 Northrup Avenue
St Louis, MO 63110-3026
314-772-8550
Fax: 314-772-0411 800-288-3439
www.volpifoods.com
Italian specialty meats, salami, proscuitto ham, pancetta, coppa, rotola
President & CEO: Lorenza Pasetti
COO: Jim Fleming
Chief Marketing Officer: Tim Urban
Sales Director: Christine Illuminato
Estimated Sales: $20-50 Million
Number Employees: 100-349
Brands:
Volpi

13491 **Von Stiehl Winery**
115 Navarino St
Algoma, WI 54201-1246
920-487-5208
Fax: 920-487-5108 800-955-5208
vonstiehl@vonstiehl.com www.vonstiehl.com
Wine
President: William Schmiling
VP: Sandra Schmiling
Estimated Sales: $5 Million
Number Employees: 20-49
Type of Packaging: Consumer

13492 **Von Strasser**
1510 Diamond Mountain Rd
Calistoga, CA 94515-9669
707-942-0930
Fax: 707-942-0454 888-359-9463
wines@vonstrasser.com www.lvvsw.com
Wines
Owner: Rudy Von Strasser
rudy@vonstrasser.com
Director National Sales/Marketing: John Schulz
Vice President: Rita Von Strasser
Vineyard Manager: Gerardo Alfaro
Assistant Winemaker: Jason Bull
Vineyard Manager: Gerardo Alfaro
Estimated Sales: $2.5-5 Million
Number Employees: 5-9
Type of Packaging: Private Label
Brands:
Von Strasser
Von Strasser

13493 **Voodoo Doughnut**
22 SW 3rd Ave
Portland, OR 97204-2713
503-241-4704
www.voodoodoughnut.com
Donuts
Estimated Sales: Less Than $500,000
Number Employees: 5-9

13494 **Voortman Bakery**
4475 N Service Rd
Suite 600
Burlington, ON L7L 4X7
Canada
800-808-5950
info@voortman.com www.voortman.com
Manufacturers a variety of cookies including prepackaged family packs and seasonal cookies.
Co-Founder & President: Harry Voortman
VP, Sales: Stephane Musicka
Estimated Sales: $67 Million
Number Employees: 450
Number of Brands: 1
Square Footage: 23229
Type of Packaging: Consumer, Bulk
Brands:
Voortman

13495 **Vosges Haut-Chocolat**
2950 N Oakley Ave
Suite 203
Chicago, IL 60618-8010
773-388-5560
Fax: 773-772-7917 888-301-9866
www.vosgeschocolate.com
Chocolate truffles and gourmet gifts
Owner: Katrina Markoff
katrina@vosgeschocolate.com
Number Employees: 100-249

13496 **Vtopian Artisan Cheeses**
Portland, OR
contact@vtopiancheeses.com
www.vtopiancheeses.com
Artisan cashew cheeses including peppercorn brie, port cheddar, aged white cheddar, sharp cheddar, and camembert
Founder, Co-Owner: Imber Lingard

13497 **Vynecrest Winery**
172 Arrowhead Ln
Breinigsville, PA 18031-1462
610-398-7525
Fax: 610-398-7530 800-361-0725
wines@vynecrest.com www.vynecrest.com
Wines
Co-Owner: Janice Landis
Co-Owner: John Landis
john@vynecrest.com
Estimated Sales: Less than $200,000
Number Employees: 1-4
Type of Packaging: Private Label
Brands:
Vynecrest Vineyards

13498 **Vyse Gelatin Co**
5010 Rose St
Schiller Park, IL 60176-1023
847-678-4780
Fax: 847-678-0329 800-533-2152
sales@vyse.com www.vyse.com
Manufacturer, exporter and importer of food grade gelatins.
President: Gary Brunet
gbrunet@vyse.com
Estimated Sales: $2.5-5 Million
Number Employees: 10-19
Type of Packaging: Food Service, Private Label, Bulk
Brands:
150 Bloom
225 Bloom
610-D
710-D
Atlas
Celero
Economix
Finemix
Flour Fine
Hypowr
Pbc-210
Protector
Seeclear
Stabilo
Superclear
Superla
Supertex
Superwhip
Textura
Vee Gee
Velvatex
Viscomix
X-Fine

13499 **W & G Marketing Company**
413 Kellogg Avenue
PO Box 1742
Ames, IA 50010
515-233-4774
Fax: 515-233-4773 www.wgmarketing.com
Processor and exporter of roasting pigs including whole and frozen; also, meat and poultry by-products and fully cooked barbecue turkey, beef and pork
President/Sales and Marketing: Darren Dies
ddies@wgmarketing.com
VP Operations: Robert Olinger
Estimated Sales: $5-10 Million
Number Employees: 5
Square Footage: 21928
Type of Packaging: Consumer, Food Service, Private Label
Brands:
Hickory Grove
W&G's

13500 **W. Forrest Haywood Seafood Company**
431 Messick Rd
Poquoson, VA 23662-1815
757-868-6748
Fax: 757-868-1111
Fresh crabmeat
President: Laura Hornsby
forrestseafoodva@aol.com
VP: Delores Forrest
Estimated Sales: $2.5-5,000,000
Number Employees: 1-4

13501 **W.A. Beans & Sons**
229 Bomarc Road
Bangor, ME 04401
207-947-0364
Fax: 207-990-4211 800-649-1958
sales@beansmeats.com www.beansmeats.com
Processor and wholesaler of meats, including smoked poultry, gourmet sausages, pork chops, bacon, fish, and hams.
Estimated Sales: Under $5 Million
Number Employees: 20-49
Square Footage: 16
Type of Packaging: Consumer, Food Service, Private Label, Bulk

13502 **W.J. Stearns & Sons/Mountain Dairy**
50 Stearns Road
Storrs Mansfield, CT 06268-2701
860-423-9289
Fax: 860-423-3486 www.mountaindairy.com
Processor and wholesaler/distributor of dairy products including cream and milk
President: W Stearns
Vice President: James Stearns
Estimated Sales: $3 Million
Number Employees: 35
Type of Packaging: Consumer, Private Label

13503 **W.L. Petrey Wholesale Inc.**
10345 Petrey Hwy
Luverne, AL 36049
334-230-5674
Fax: 334-335-2422 mail@petrey.com
www.petrey.com
Wholesaler/distributor of frozen food, general merchandise, general line products, provisions/meats and seafood
President: Bill Jackson
CEO: James Jackson
Contact: Kevin Argo
kargo@petrey.com
Number Employees: 500-999

13504 **W.O. Sasser**
135 Johnny Mercer Blvd
Savannah, GA 31410-2118
912-897-1154
Fax: 912-897-0331
Seafood
Owner: William Sasser
Estimated Sales: $.5-1 million
Number Employees: 5-9

13505 **W.R. Delozier Sausage Company**
12350 Chapman Highway
Seymour, TN 37865-6231
865-577-5907
Sausages
President: W Delozier

Estimated Sales: Less than $500,000
Number Employees: 1-4

13506 **W.S. Wells & Sons**
P.O.Box 109
Wilton, ME 04294-0109
207-645-3393
Fax: 207- 64-5 33
Canned fiddleheads and dandelions, green beans, baked beans, soup mixes
Owner: Adrian Wells
Estimated Sales: $2.5-5 000,000
Number Employees: 10-19

13507 **W.T. Ruark & Company**
2543 Hoopers Island Rd.
Fishing Creek, MD 21634
410-397-3133
Established in 1948. Manufacturer of seafood including oysters, crabs and crabmeat.
President: William Ruark
Estimated Sales: $21 Million
Number Employees: 20-49
Type of Packaging: Consumer

13508 **W.T.I.**
281 Martin Luther King Jr Ave
Jefferson, GA 30549
417-767-4790
Fax: 706-387-5159 800-827-1727
kevon@wtiinc.com www.wtiinc.com
Marinades and flavorings for meat.
Owner: Wolf Ludwig
Sr. Vice President: Michael Crump
Quality Assurance Manager: Jenni Rench
Director of Sales and Marketing: Kevon Ledgerwood
Director of Operations: Stephan Georg
Production Manager: Ertan Hyuseinov
Square Footage: 140000

13509 **WACO Beef & Pork Processors**
523 Precision Dr
Waco, TX 76710-6972
254-772-4669
Fax: 254-772-4579 www.holysmokedsausage.com
Fresh portion controlled beef, chicken and pork including sausage, chorizo and bratwurst; importer of beef skirts; wholesaler/distributor of meat and general merchandise; serving the food service market
Manager: Sara Jones
Estimated Sales: $2.2 Million
Number Employees: 5-9
Square Footage: 28000
Type of Packaging: Food Service
Brands:
Precision

13510 **WBM International**
54 State Route 12
Flemington, NJ 08822-1540
973-350-8900
Fax: 973-350-8848 866-802-9366
support@wbminternational.com
wbminternational.com
Himalayan salt
Sales Representative: Juliana Mata
Director: Nafees Anjum
Estimated Sales: $7 Million
Number Employees: 35
Brands:
Himalayan Chef
Himalayan Glow
WBM

13511 **(HQ)WCC Honey Marketing**
636 Turnbull Canyon Rd # A
City Of Industry, CA 91745-1107
626-855-3086
Fax: 626-855-3087
Processor and exporter of natural sweeteners, syrups and nutritional supplements including honey, comb honey, molasses, blackstrap molasses, corn syrup, agave nectar and royal jelly; importer of honey, barley malt sweetener, rice syrupand juice concentrate
Owner: Anthony Li
info@wcchoney.com
General Manager: Chuck Burkholder
National Sales Manager: Norma Robinson
info@wcchoney.com
Purchasing Manager: James Littlejohn
Estimated Sales: $5-10 Million
Number Employees: 5-9
Square Footage: 118800
Type of Packaging: Consumer, Food Service, Private Label, Bulk
Other Locations:
Western Commerce Corp.
Kansas City MO
Brands:
Cucamonga
El Panal
Fruitsweet
Hawaiian Gold
Lo Han
Pot O' Gold
Powers

13512 **WEIS Markets Inc.**
1000 S. 2nd St.
PO Box 471
Sunbury, PA 17801
570-286-4571
866-999-9347
www.weismarkets.com
Grocery, bakery, deli, produce, floral, seafood, and more.
Chair/President/CEO: Jonathan Weis
jweis@weismarkets.com
Year Founded: 1912
Estimated Sales: $3.4 Billion
Number Employees: 18,000
Other Locations:
Manufacturing Facility-Market St
Sunbury PA
Manufacturing Facility-N 4th St
Sunbury PA
Brands:
Weis Five Star
Weis Quality
Full Circle

13513 **WG Thompson & Sons**
2 Hyland Dr.
Blenheim, ON N0P 1A0
Canada
519-676-5411
Fax: 519-676-3185 800-265-5225
Agricultural products including soybeans, edible beans, and commercial grains to domestic and export markets.
President: Wes Thompson
Estimated Sales: $100 Million
Number Employees: 350
Type of Packaging: Consumer, Food Service, Private Label, Bulk
Brands:
C&G
Hyland

13514 **WILD Flavors (Canada)**
7315 Pacific Circle
Mississauga, ON L5T 1V1
Canada
905-670-1108
Fax: 905-670-0076 800-263-5286
www.wildflavors.com
Flavors, colors, seasonings, spray-dried ingredients, sauces, batters, coatings, marinades; also, custom blending; exporter of cheese powders
Acting Director: Tim Husted
Director Finance: Tamara Robichaud
R & D: Allison Berridge
Chief Operating Officer: Erik Donhowe
Plant Manager: Dave Oldroyd
Purchasing Manager: Leigh Bailey
Number Employees: 30-50
Number of Products: 200
Square Footage: 240000
Parent Co: WILD Flavors
Type of Packaging: Food Service, Bulk

13515 **WK Eckerd & Sons**
107 Speedy Tostensen Blvd
Brunswick, GA 31520-3149
912-265-0332
Fax: 912-261-8460 eckerd@thebest.net
Seafood
President: William Eckerd
Owner: Bill Eckerd
Estimated Sales: Below $5 Million
Number Employees: 1-4

13516 **WSU Creamery**
Po Box 641122
Pullman, WA 99164-1122
800-457-5442
Fax: 509-335-7525 800-457-5442
salvadalena@wsu.edu www.wsu.edu/creamery
Cheddar cheese and ice cream
Creamery Manager: Russ Salvadalena
Assistant Manager: John Haugen
Contact: Lynn Chelgren
lynn@wsu.edu
Number Employees: 50
Square Footage: 80000
Type of Packaging: Consumer, Food Service
Brands:
Cougar Gold
Viking

13517 **Wabash Heritage Mfg LLC**
2525 N 6th St
Vincennes, IN 47591-2405
812-886-0147
Fax: 812-895-0064 info@knoxcountyarc.com
www.knoxcountyarc.com
Spices, powders
President: Michael Carney
Vice President: Bobby Harbison
bharbison@knoxcountyarc.com
Research & Development: John TRUE
Quality Control: John TRUE
Plant Manager: Leroy Douffron
Number Employees: 20-49
Number of Brands: 1
Number of Products: 90
Square Footage: 480000
Type of Packaging: Consumer, Food Service, Private Label, Bulk
Brands:
Wasbash Heritage

13518 **Wabash Seafood Co**
2249 W Hubbard St
Chicago, IL 60612-1613
312-733-5070
Fax: 312-733-2798 john@wabashseafood.net
www.wabashseafood.net
Seafood
President: John Rebello
john@wabashseafood.net
Estimated Sales: $10-20 Million
Number Employees: 20-49

13519 **Wabash Valley Farms**
6323 N 150 E
Monon, IN 47959-8010
219-232-4930
Fax: 219-253-1389 877-888-7077
Manufacturer of bagged popcorn, popcorn kernels, and popcorn makers.
President: Danielle Paluchniak
SVP of Sales: Tammy Luse
Contact: Trent Lehman
trent@intri-cut.com
Estimated Sales: Less Than $500,000
Number Employees: 1-4

13520 **Wabash Valley Produce Inc**
4886 E 450n
PO Box 127
Dubois, IN 47527-9660
812-678-3131
Fax: 812-678-5931
Bulk liquid egg products including pasteurized and raw whole eggs, egg whites and egg and salt yolks
President: Danielle Paluchniak
Chief Financial Officer/Sales: Andrew Seger
Vice President: Scott Seger
Human Resources Manager: Tom Seger
Purchasing Agent: Gene Bonifer
Estimated Sales: $24.5 Million
Number Employees: 100-249
Square Footage: 66000
Type of Packaging: Bulk

13521 **Wabi Fishing Company**
14608 Smokey Point Boulevard
Marysville, WA 98271-8946
360-659-9474
Fax: 360-659-9093 888-536-7696
Wild Pacific smoked salmon available in five flavors
President: Leo Palmer
Brands:
King Nova
Leo's
Sockeye Nova

13522 **Wachusett Brewing Co**
175 State Rd E
Westminster, MA 01473-1208
978-874-9965
Fax: 978-874-0784 info@wachusettbrew.com
www.wachusettbrew.com
Flavored ales.
Owner: Ned La Fortune
Office Manager: Megan Graves
Director, Administration: Lesa Bourgeios
Director, Marketing & Sales: TJ Morse
Sales Manager: Peter Quinn
Account & PR: Kim Slayton
Director, Operations: Brad Dufour
Plant Engineer: Kevin Buckler
Estimated Sales: Less Than $500,000
Number Employees: 1-4
Type of Packaging: Consumer, Food Service
Brands:
Wachusett

13523 **Wachusset Potato Chip Co Inc**
759 Water St
Fitchburg, MA 01420-6499
978-342-6038
Fax: 978-345-4894 800-551-5539
Potato chips, plain, salt and vinegar, rippled, barbeque, no salt added, ketchup, potato sticks, sour cream and onion, cheese twists, popcorn, cheese popcorn
President: Edward Krysiak
ed@wachusettchip.com
Estimated Sales: $10 Million
Number Employees: 50-99
Square Footage: 168000
Type of Packaging: Consumer, Food Service, Private Label
Brands:
Wachusett

13524 **Wackym's Kitchen**
PO Box 180871
Dallas, TX 75218
214-327-7667
info@wackymskitchen.com
www.wackymskitchen.com
Cookies
Founder: Paul Wackym

13525 **WaffleWaffle**
43 River Rd
Nutley, NJ 07110-3411
201-559-1286
info@mywafflewaffle.com
mywafflewaffle.com
Waffles: Belgian-style, cones, doughs, mixes, and waffle irons.
Co-Founder: Justin Samuels
Co-Founder: Samuel Rockwell
Vice President, Business Development: Brian Samuels
Chief Marketing Officer: David Song
Vice President, Sales: Bracken Abrams
Director of Operations: Grant Ramsey
Estimated Sales: $2 Million
Number Employees: 12
Type of Packaging: Consumer, Food Service, Private Label
Brands:
WaffleWaffle

13526 **Wagner Excello Food Products**
2625 Gardner Rd
Broadview, IL 60155
708-338-4488
Fax: 708-338-4495
Manufacturer of flavouring extracts and syrups.
Owner: Harry Berger

13527 **Wagner Gourmet Foods**
10618 Summit St
Lenexa, KS 66215
913-469-5411
Fax: 913-469-1367
customerservice@wagner-gourmet.com
www.hicks-ashby.com
Spices, preserves, jams, ice cream sauces, seasoned rice and gift pack assortments; importer of tea; wholesaler/distributor of snack foods including cookies
President: James T Baldwin
Estimated Sales: $3-5 Million
Number Employees: 5-9
Square Footage: 480000
Parent Co: Wagner Gourmet Foods
Type of Packaging: Consumer, Private Label

13528 **Wagner Seafood**
9626 S Pulaski Rd
Oak Lawn, IL 60453-3391
708-636-2646
Fax: 843-559-1156
www.wagnerseafood.dinehere.us
Seafood
Owner: Bob Wagner
Estimated Sales: Less Than $500,000
Number Employees: 1-4

13529 **Wagner Vineyards**
9322 State Route 414
Lodi, NY 14860-9641
607-582-6450
Fax: 607-582-6446 866-924-6378
d.wagner@wagnervineyards.com
www.wagnervineyards.com
Wines and beer; exporter of wines
President: Stanley A Wagner
s.wagner@wagnervineyards.com
Retail Manager: Carol Voorhees
COO: John Wagner
Director of PR & Marketing: Katie Roller
Operations: John Wagner
Estimated Sales: $2,762,368
Number Employees: 50-99
Square Footage: 144000
Type of Packaging: Consumer
Brands:
Wagner Brewing Co.
Wagner Vineyards

13530 **Wagshal's Imports**
4845 Massachusetts Ave NW
Washington, DC 20016-2065
202-363-5698
Fax: 202-363-0893 feedback@wagshals.com
www.wagshals.com
Beef, seafood, produce, sauces & condiments, dairy, wines, iberico pork
Principal: Aaron Fuchs
Director of Sales: Ann Sayre
Estimated Sales: Under $500,000
Number Employees: 1-4
Brands:
Wagshal's

13531 **Wah Yet Group**
28301 Industrial Blvd Ste C
Hayward, CA 94545-4429
510-887-3801
Fax: 510-887-3803 800-229-3392
Processor and exporter of diet and ginseng teas; importer of health drinks
President: Ying Lau
Manager: Judy Lau
Estimated Sales: $1-3 Million
Number Employees: 1 to 4
Square Footage: 4000
Type of Packaging: Consumer
Brands:
Chinese Ginseng
Green Leaf

13532 **Wai Lana Snacks**
5005 Raley Blvd.
Suite 1
Sacramento, CA 95838
888-924-5262
info@wailana.com www.wailana.com
Cassava chips, fruit and nut bars
Founder: Wai Lana
Number Employees: 11-50
Brands:
Wai Lana

13533 **Wainani Kai Seafood**
2126 Eluwene St
Suite A
Honolulu, HI 96819
808-847-7435
Fax: 808-841-7536 lpang00@yahoo.com
Seafood
President: Lance Pang
lpang00@yahoo.com
Estimated Sales: $3-5 Million
Number Employees: 5-9

13534 **Wainwright Dairy**
13607 161st Rd
Live Oak, FL 32060-6539
386-776-2001
info@wainwrightdairy.com
www.wainwrightdairy.com
Dairy products
Manager: James Wainwright
Number Employees: 5-9

13535 **Waken Meat Co**
1015 Boulevard SE
Atlanta, GA 30312-3809
404-627-3537
Fax: 404-624-3191
Beef, pork, chicken, frozen seafood
President: Charles Waken
Estimated Sales: $300,000-500,000
Number Employees: 5-9

13536 **Wakunaga Of America Co LTD**
23501 Madero
Mission Viejo, CA 92691-2764
949-855-2776
Fax: 949-458-2764 800-421-2998
info@wakunaga.com www.kyolic.com
Nutritional supplements
President: Kenro Nakamura
CEO: Kazuhiko Nomura
Research & Development Manager: Justin Oshima
Quality Control: Vithia Monica Lee
Manager: Jay Levy
jlevy@wakunaga.com
Estimated Sales: $24 Million
Number Employees: 50-99
Number of Brands: 5
Number of Products: 70
Square Footage: 42000
Parent Co: Wakunaga Pharmaceutical
Brands:
Besure
Estro Logic
Kyo-Chlorella
Kyo-Dophilus
Kyo-Green
Kyo-Green Harvest Blend
Kyolic
Moducare
Moduchol
Moduprost

13537 **Walcan Seafood**
PO Box 429
Heroit Bay, BC V0P 1H0
Canada
250-285-3361
Fax: 250-285-3313 www.walcan.com
Seafood processing
Manager: William Perez

13538 **Walden Farms**
1209 W Saint Georges Ave
Linden, NJ 07036-6117
908-925-6020
Fax: 908-925-9537 800-229-1706
info@waldenfarms.com www.waldenfarms.com
Processor and exporter of salad dressings, dips, bbq sauces, pancake syrups, fruit spread jams and jellies, fruit syrups, ketchup and seafood sauces, bruschetta and chocolate syrup.
President: Mitchell Berko
mitchellburko@waldenfarms.com
Vice President: Paul Berko
Operations: Brian Sherwood
mitchellburko@waldenfarms.com
Number Employees: 50-99
Square Footage: 64000
Type of Packaging: Consumer, Food Service
Brands:
Walden Farms

13539 **Walden Farms**
1209 W Saint Georges Ave
Linden, NJ 07036-6117
908-925-6020
Fax: 908-925-9537 800-229-1706
customerservice@waldenfarms.com
www.waldenfarms.com
Sauces
President: Mitchell Berko
mitchellburko@waldenfarms.com
Sales Director: Mitchell Berko
Operations Manager: V Naccarato

Estimated Sales: $500,000-$1 Million
Number Employees: 50-99
Type of Packaging: Private Label
Brands:
Walden Farms

13540 **Walden Foods**
660 N Loudoun St
Winchester, VA 22601-4986
540-622-2800
Fax: 540-253-9807 800-648-7688
All natural and gourmet applewood smoked seafood, poultry and meats
President: John P Good Jr
VP Marketing: Christine Hyre
Number Employees: 20
Square Footage: 50000
Parent Co: Walden Foods Inc.
Type of Packaging: Consumer, Food Service
Brands:
The Farm At Mt. Walden

13541 **Walker Foods**
237 N Mission Rd
Los Angeles, CA 90033-2103
323-268-5191
Fax: 323-268-7812 800-966-5199
info@walkerfoods.net www.walkerfoods.net
Producers of hot spicy tomato sauce and other tomato products
President: Robert Walker
Cmo: Fernando Montano
elpatowfi@aol.com
Director, Retail Sales: Andy Zahra
Production Manager: Alfred Heredia
Plant Manager: Fernando Montano
Estimated Sales: $10-20 Million
Number Employees: 50-99
Square Footage: 360000
Type of Packaging: Consumer, Food Service, Private Label, Bulk
Brands:
El Pato
Golden State

13542 **Walker Meats**
821 Tyus Carrollton Rd
Carrollton, GA 30117-9609
770-834-8171
Fax: 770-834-2208 800-741-3601
info@walkermeats.com www.walkermeats.com
Beef, pork, poultry, produce, seafood
President: Bill Walker
bill@walkermeats.com
Estimated Sales: $10-20 Million
Number Employees: 20-49

13543 **Walker's Seafood**
312 Southwest Sq
Jonesboro, AR 72401-5984
870-932-0375
Fax: 870-935-8697
Seafood
President: Darrell Walker
Secretary/Treasurer: Patricia Walker

13544 **Walkers Shortbread**
170 Commerce Dr
Hauppauge, NY 11788-3944
631-273-0014
Fax: 631-273-0438 800-521-0141
cs@walkersshortbread.com
us.walkersshortbread.com
Shortbread and cookies
President: Steve Dawson
CEO: Neil Apple
cs@walkersshortbread.com
CFO: Joseph Gadaleta
Marketing: Lisa Sherman
Estimated Sales: $2800000
Number Employees: 20-49
Parent Co: Walkers Shortbread
Type of Packaging: Consumer, Bulk
Brands:
Duchy Originals
Kambly
Walker's
Walkers

13545 **Wall Meat Processing**
21 N Creighton Rd
Wall, SD 57790
605-279-2348
Manufactures slab & sliced bacon and other meat products
Owner: Scott Carson
Estimated Sales: $1-3 Million
Number Employees: 1-4
Type of Packaging: Private Label

13546 **Wallaby Yogurt Co**
12002 Airport Way
Broomfield, CO 80021
707-553-1233
Fax: 707-553-1293 855-925-4636
info@wallabyyogurt.com www.wallabyyogurt.com
Organic yogurt, kefir, and sour cream
Founder: Jerry Chou
Marketing & Event Manager: Nicole Smith
Operations Manager: Tibi Molnar
Year Founded: 1995
Estimated Sales: $45 Million
Number Employees: 50-99
Parent Co: WhiteWave
Brands:
Wallaby

13547 **Wallace Edwards & Sons**
11455 Rolfe Highway
PO Box 25
Surry, VA 23883
757-294-3121
Fax: 757-294-5378 800-200-4267
info@edwardsvaham.com
www.edwardsvaham.com
Virginia hams, hickory smoked bacon, dry cured duck, sausage, turkey, and Virginia peanuts
President/CEO: Bob Anderson

13548 **Wallace Fisheries**
PO Box 2046
Gulf Shores, AL 36547-2046
251-986-7211
Fax: 251-987-5127
Seafood

13549 **Wallace Grain & Pea Company**
4932 State Route 27
Pullman, WA 99163
509-878-1561
Fax: 509-878-1671
Processor and exporter of chickpeas, barley, lentils and peas
President: Joe Hulett
Assistant Manager: Gary Heaton
Estimated Sales: $500,000-$1 Million
Number Employees: 1-4
Type of Packaging: Consumer, Food Service, Private Label, Bulk
Brands:
Palouse

13550 **Wallace Plant Company**
201 High St
Bath, ME 04530-1677
207-443-2640
Fax: 207-386-0268
Seafood
Owner: Wallace Plant
Estimated Sales: $1 Million
Number Employees: 5-9
Type of Packaging: Consumer

13551 **Wallingford Coffee Co Inc**
11401 Rockfield Ct
Cincinnati, OH 45241-1971
513-771-3131
Fax: 513-771-3138 800-533-3690
sales@wallingfordcoffee.com
www.wallingfordcoffee.com
Coffee, cappuccino and tea
President: Gary Weber
Controller: Michael Hoban
VP Operations: Gary Davis
Purchasing Manager: Brian Weber
Estimated Sales: $10-49 Million
Number Employees: 50-99
Number of Brands: 3
Brands:
Wallingford
White Castle
Aroma Valley

13552 **Wally Biscotti**
4850 E 39th Ave
Denver, CO 80207-1010
303-320-9969
Fax: 303-320-9966 866-659-2559
wallybicotti@aol.com
Biscotti
President: Wally Friedlander
Marketing Manager: Wally Biscotti
Operations Manager: Jamey Biscotti
Estimated Sales: $1-$1.3 Million
Number Employees: 20-49
Type of Packaging: Consumer, Food Service, Private Label, Bulk
Brands:
Wally Biscotti

13553 **Walnut Acres**
4600 Sleepytime Dr.
Boulder, CO 80301
800-434-4246
www.walnutacres.com
Soups, pasta sauces, salsas, juices and kid's snacks

13554 **Walsh's Coffee Roasters**
273 Baldwin Avenue
San Mateo, CA 94401-3914
650-347-5112
Fax: 650-347-0569
Coffee
Owner/President: John Walsh
Estimated Sales: Less than $500,000
Number Employees: 1-4

13555 **Walsh's Seafood**
RR 1
Gouldsboro, ME 04607
207-963-2578
Fax: 207-963-2578
Seafood
Owner: Craig Walsh

13556 **Walter P Rawl & Sons Inc**
824 Fairview Rd
Pelion, SC 29123
803-894-1900
www.rawl.net
Grower of peppers, beets, cilantro, collard, corn, green onion, jalapeno, kale, leeks, mustard, parsley, turnip, turnip root, yellow squash, zucchini.
President: Howard Rawl
Director, Accounting: Sue Elizabeth
Business Development Manager: Mark Haun
Senior Quality Assurance Manager: Nancy Shimabukuro
Marketing Manager: Christine Jackson
Director of Sales: Gary James
Director of Corp Strategy & HR: Tim Rabon
Operations Manager: Dale Clark
Director of Transportation: Jeff Pratt
Year Founded: 1920
Estimated Sales: Less than $500,000
Type of Packaging: Consumer, Food Service

13557 **Waltham Beef Company**
18 Food Mart Road
Boston, MA 02118-2802
617-269-2250
Fax: 617-269-8183
Processed beef, pork, poultry
President: Douglas Atamian
President: Wesley Atamian
Type of Packaging: Private Label

13558 **Waltkoch Limited**
1990 Lakeside Pkwy
Suite 240
Tucker, GA 30084
404-378-3666
Fax: 404-378-8492 www.waltkoch.com
Poultry frozen foods, meats, seafood.
Owner: Walter Koch
Partner: Sam Stanford
Chief Executive Officer: Keith Steinberg
Year Founded: 1950
Estimated Sales: $43 Million
Number Employees: 54
Type of Packaging: Consumer, Food Service

13559 Wampler's Farm Sausage Company
781 U.S. 70
Lenoir City, TN 37771
865-986-2056
Fax: 865-988-3280 800-728-7243
sales@wamplersfarm.com
www.wamplersfarm.com
Established in 1953. Processor, packer, and exporter of sausage.
Vice President: John Ed Wampler
Sales Manager: Doug Young
Operations Manager: Darrell Griffis
Plant Supervisor: Mike Marney
Plant Manager: Jim Wampler
Estimated Sales: $24000000
Number Employees: 100-249
Type of Packaging: Consumer, Food Service, Private Label, Bulk
Brands:
Wampler's Farm

13560 Wan Hua Foods
804 6th Avenue South
PO Box 14075
Seattle, WA 98134
206-622-8417
Fax: 206-622-7088 info@wanhuafoods.com
www.wanhuafoods.com
Fresh cooked noodles including udon, yaki soba, miki and chow mein
President: Sui-Ming Tam
Founder: Tony Tam
Founder: Judy Tam
Contact: Tai Chainarong
tai@wanhuafoods.com
Estimated Sales: C
Number Employees: 10-19
Square Footage: 48000
Brands:
Miki
Phillipino's
U-Don
Yakisoba

13561 Wanchese Fish Co Inc
2000 Northgate Commerce Pkwy
Suffolk, VA 23435-2142
757-673-4500
Fax: 757-653-4550 www.wanchese.com
Processor and exporter of fresh and frozen seafood including flounder, bass, scallops, tuna, scallops and shrimp.
President: Sam Daniels
sam@wanchese.com
CFO: Mark Palmer
VP: Kenny Daniels
Sales Manager: Gordon Craddock
Plant Manager: Chris Daniels
Estimated Sales: $6400000
Number Employees: 20-49
Square Footage: 1000000
Parent Co: Daniels Enterprises
Type of Packaging: Consumer, Food Service, Private Label, Bulk
Other Locations:
Wanchese Fish Co.
Hampton VA

13562 Wanda's Nature Farm
1700 Cushman Dr
Lincoln, NE 68512-1238
402-423-1234
Fax: 402-423-4586 800-735-6828
heartlandgourmet.com
Processor and exporter of natural mixes including bread, cake, muffin, pancake, pasta, pizza, bagels, etc
President: Susan Zink
Vice President: David Eisner
Marketing Director: Shari Rogge-Fidler
Estimated Sales: $2311332
Number Employees: 20-49
Type of Packaging: Consumer, Food Service

13563 Wandering Bear Coffee
162 W 13th St
Apt 42
New York, NY 10011-7813
929-251-3752
hello@wanderingbearcoffee.com
www.wanderingbearcoffee.com
Coffee
Co-Founder: Ben Gordon
Co-Founder: Matthew Bachmann
Number Employees: 2-10
Brands:
Wandering Bear Coffee

13564 Wapsie Creamery
300 10th St NE
Independence, IA 50644-1220
319-334-7193
Fax: 319-334-4914 markn@wapsievalley.com
www.wapsievalley.com
Monterey and marble pepper jack, cheddar and colby cheese; processor and exporter of kosher reduced lactose whey, edible dried delactose and lactose.
President: Mark Nielsen
VP: Wilbur Nielsen
Estimated Sales: $20-50 Million
Number Employees: 50-99
Square Footage: 78000
Type of Packaging: Consumer, Private Label, Bulk

13565 Wapsie Produce
702 E Water St
Decorah, IA 52101
563-382-4271
Fax: 563-382-8210 info@capons.com
www.capons.com
Processor and exporter of frozen capons and fowl
President: Marc Nichols
Vice President: Paul Nichols
paul.nichols@capons.com
Estimated Sales: $9 Million
Number Employees: 100
Type of Packaging: Consumer, Private Label
Brands:
Ioma
Minowa
Thrift

13566 War Eagle Mill
11045 War Eagle Rd
Rogers, AR 72756-7544
479-789-5343
Fax: 479-789-2972 866-492-7324
info@wareaglemill.com www.wareaglemill.com
Processor and miller of stone burr corn meal and wholewheat flour and mixes
President: Zoe Caywood
Contact: Barbara Allen
barbara@wareaglemill.com
Type of Packaging: Consumer

13567 Warbucks Seafood
1581 McDonald Avenue
Brooklyn, NY 11230
718-998-4900
Fax: 718-732-2884 info@warbucksseafood.com
www.blackdiamondcaviarnyc.com
Caviar
Co-Owner: Raymond Mizrahi
Estimated Sales: $1.5 Million
Number Employees: 6
Brands:
Black Diamond Caviar

13568 Warden Peanut Company
620 E Lime St
Portales, NM 88130
575-356-6691
Fax: 575-359-0072
Snack foods
VP: Sam Rigsey
General Manager: Bill Owen
Plant Manager: Leonard Stanton
Estimated Sales: Under $500,000
Number Employees: 20-49

13569 Warner Candy
Ste A
1240 Don Haskins Dr
El Paso, TX 79936-7887
847-928-7200
Fax: 847-928-2115
Candy
Estimated Sales: $10-20 Million
Number Employees: 20-49

13570 (HQ)Warner Vineyards
706 S Kalamazoo St
Paw Paw, MI 49079-1558
269-657-3165
Fax: 269-657-4154 800-756-5357
www.warnerwines.com
Wines
President: Patrick Warner
patrickwarner@verizon.net
Estimated Sales: $500,000
Number Employees: 5-9
Type of Packaging: Consumer, Private Label
Brands:
Warner Vineyards

13571 (HQ)Warner-Lambert Confections
810 Main St
Cambridge, MA 02139-3588
617-491-2500
Fax: 617-547-2381
Candy
President/CEO: J Craig
Plant Manager: Gerald Chesser
Estimated Sales: Under $500,000
Number Employees: 100-249

13572 Warrell Corp
1250 Slate Hill Rd
Camp Hill, PA 17011-8011
717-761-5440
Fax: 717-761-2206 844-234-3217
sales@warrellcorp.com www.warrellcorp.com
Processor, importer and exporter of confectionery products.
President: Kevin Silva
Executive VP, Sales & Marketing: Richard Warrell
Vice President, Operations: Robert Bard
Number Employees: 250-499
Type of Packaging: Consumer, Food Service, Private Label, Bulk
Brands:
Pennsylvania Dutch Candies
Bonomo Turkish Taffy
Katharine Beecher
Flipsticks
Classic Caramel

13573 Warrell Corp
1250 Slate Hill Rd
Camp Hill, PA 17011-8011
717-761-5440
Fax: 717-761-2206 800-233-7082
sales@warrellcorp.com www.warrellcorp.com
Candy
President: Patrick Huffman
patrickh@warrellcorp.com
Number Employees: 250-499

13574 (HQ)Warrell Corp
1250 Slate Hill Rd
Camp Hill, PA 17011-8011
717-761-5440
Fax: 717-761-5702 800-233-7082
sales@warrellcorp.com www.warrellcorp.com
Candies and chocolates
President & CEO: Matthew Caiazza
CFO: Patricia Zwergel
Executive Vice President: Richard Warrell
VP Sales & Marketing: Steve Sullivan
VP Operations: Robert Bard
VP Administration: Susan Tandle
Year Founded: 1965
Estimated Sales: $20-50 Million
Number Employees: 250-499
Number of Brands: 3
Square Footage: 200000
Type of Packaging: Private Label, Bulk
Brands:
Katherine Beecher
Melster
Pennsylvania Dutch Candies
Flipsticks
Classic Caramel
Nut N But Natural

13575 Warren & Son Meat Processing
7585 State Route 821
Whipple, OH 45788-5164
740-585-2421
Fax: 740-585-2073
Beef, pork, lamb, specialty meats and smoked sausage and ham

Owner/Sales: Danny Warren
Marketing Director: Kathryn Warren
Estimated Sales: $3-5 Million
Number Employees: 1 to 4
Type of Packaging: Consumer, Bulk

13576 Warren Laboratories LLC
1656 Ih 35 S
Abbott, TX 76621-3014
254-580-9990
Fax: 254-580-9944 800-421-2563
karenk@warrenlabsaloe.com
www.georgesaloe.com
Refined aloe vera beverages
Manager: Tony Tustejovsky
Contact: George Arren
georgew@warrenlabsaloe.com
Estimated Sales: $2100000
Number Employees: 10-19

13577 Warwick Ice Cream
743 Bald Hill Rd
Warwick, RI 02886-0713
401-821-8403
Fax: 401-821-8404 info@warwickicecreamco.com
www.warwickicecreamco.com
Ice cream cakes, pies and popsicles
Owner: Gerard Bucci Sr
Estimated Sales: $1-3 Million
Number Employees: 20-49
Type of Packaging: Consumer, Food Service, Bulk

13578 Warwick Valley Winery & Distillery
114 Little York Rd.
Warwick, NY 10990
845-258-4858
www.wvwinery.com
Fruit liqueurs, hard fruit ciders, gin, red and white wines
Owner: Jason Grizzanti
Year Founded: 2001
Number of Brands: 2
Number of Products: 23
Type of Packaging: Consumer, Private Label
Brands:
Warwick Winery
Doc's Draft Hard Cider
American Fruits
Warwick Distillery

13579 Wasatch Meats Inc
926 S Jefferson St
Salt Lake City, UT 84101-2983
801-363-5747
Fax: 801-799-5511 800-631-8294
www.wasatchmeats.com
Processors of meat including beef, pork and poultry.
President: Richard Broadbent
richb@wasatchmeats.com
VP: Scott Rich
VP Marketing: Mark Broadbent
VP Sales: Mark Broadbent
Operations Manager: Roger Rausch
Production Foreman: Dave Burke
Estimated Sales: $15,914,424
Number Employees: 20-49
Type of Packaging: Food Service

13580 Washington Fruit & Produce Company
401 N 1st Ave
P.O.Box 1588
Yakima, WA 98907-1588
509-457-6177
Fax: 509-452-8520 information@washfruit.com
www.washfruit.com
Processor and exporter of fresh fruits including apples, pears, and cherries.
Manager: Tom Hanses
Contact: Lorri Denison
ldenison@neptunesociety.com
Estimated Sales: Less than $500,000
Number Employees: 1-4
Type of Packaging: Consumer, Bulk

13581 Washington Potato Company
1900 1st Ave West
PO Box 3110
Pasco, WA 99302
509-545-4545
Fax: 509-545-4804 800-897-2726
customerservice@oregonpotato.com
www.oregonpotato.com
Processor and exporter of frozen and dehydrated potatoes
President/CEO: Frank Tiegs
Director of Sales: Barry Stice
Sales: Don Smith
Plant Manager: Bob Bernard
Estimated Sales: $16.6 Million
Number Employees: 100
Square Footage: 10000
Parent Co: Oregon Potato
Type of Packaging: Food Service, Bulk

13582 Washington Rhubarb Grower Assn
16623 88th St E
Sumner, WA 98390-8149
253-863-7333
Fax: 253-863-2775 800-435-9911
Cooperative of Washington rhubarb growers; also, manufacturer of IQF rhubarb
President: Stacey Ota
wa_rhubarb@yahoo.com
General Manager: Cindy Moore
Estimated Sales: Less Than $500,000
Number Employees: 1-4
Square Footage: 36000
Type of Packaging: Bulk
Brands:
First Pick
Sumner

13583 Washington State Juice
10725 Sutter Ave
Pacoima, CA 91331-2553
818-899-1195
Fax: 818-899-6042
Manufactures and processes fruit concentrates, blends and natural flavors. Custom blending is available
President: Fred Farago
Estimated Sales: $.5-1 million
Number Employees: 100-249
Type of Packaging: Food Service, Private Label, Bulk

13584 Wasson Brothers Winery
17020 Ruben Ln
Sandy, OR 97055
503-668-3124
Fax: 503-668-3124
Wines
Partner: James Wasson
Partner: John Wasson
Estimated Sales: $1-2.5 Million
Number Employees: 1-4
Brands:
Wasson

13585 (HQ)Water Concepts
561 Plate Drive
Suite 1
East Dundee, IL 60118
847-699-9797
Fax: 847-699-9889
Caffeine enchanced natural artesian water.
Owner: Steve Rodgers
Marketing: Joe Brumfield
Estimated Sales: $300,000-500,000
Number Employees: 1-4
Type of Packaging: Consumer, Food Service
Brands:
Water Joe

13586 Waterfield Farms
500 Sunderland Road
Amherst, MA 01002-1038
413-549-3558
Fax: 413-549-9945 bioshelter@aol.com
Tilapia fish, basil, tomatoes and pesto sauces
President: John Reid
Vice President: Tracy Hightower
Director of Aquaculture: Dr Jose Llobrera
Estimated Sales: $500-1 Million appx.
Number Employees: 20-49
Type of Packaging: Consumer, Food Service
Brands:
Hydroponic Sweet Basil
Tilapia
Waterfield Farms

13587 Waterfront Seafood
14358 Shell Belt Rd
Bayou La Batre, AL 36509-2330
251-824-2185
Fax: 251-824-4307
Seafood
Owner: Norowod Cain
Vice President: Nor Cain
Number Employees: 20-49

13588 Waterfront Seafood Market
2900 University Ave Ste A4
West Des Moines, IA 50266
515-223-5106
Fax: 515-224-9665 waterfrontseafood@msn.com
www.waterfrontseafoodmarket.com
Seafood
President: Ted Hanke
Estimated Sales: $3-5 Million
Number Employees: 50-99

13589 Watermark Innovation
400 Noyac Rd
Suite A-1
Southampton, NY 11968
631-259-2329
Fax: 631-259-2329
Flavored water
President: Patti Kelly

13590 Watershed Foods
202 N Ford St
Gridley, IL 61744-3902
309-747-3000
Fax: 309-747-4647
jill.legner@watershedfoods.com
Contract processor of yogurt, purees, fruits and other healthy snacks. Services include freeze drying and pumpable liquids and R&D test drying.
President & COO: Jeremy Zobrist
jeremy.zobrist@watershedfoods.com
CFO: Lynette Schick
Director of Food Quality & Safety: Craig Hammond
VP Sales & Marketing: Brandon Rinkenberger
VP & Director Operations: Marc Johnson
Manager: Jill Legner
Estimated Sales: $4.3 Million
Number Employees: 5-9

13591 (HQ)Watson Inc
301 Heffernan Dr
West Haven, CT 06516-4139
203-932-3000
Fax: 203-932-8266 800-388-3481
www.watson-inc.com
Ingredients manufacturer for the food and supplement industries.
President: James Watson
james.watson@watson-inc.com
Number Employees: 100-249
Type of Packaging: Bulk
Other Locations:
Watson Foods Co.
Rockville CT
Brands:
Oven Spring

13592 Watson Inc
301 Heffernan Dr
West Haven, CT 06516-4139
203-932-3000
Fax: 203-932-8266 800-388-3481
info@watson-inc.com www.watson-inc.com
Dietary supplements, gummy application, balery ingredients, nutrient premixe, spray dried nutrients, edible glitter, compressible sweeteners, hops
President: James Watson
james.watson@watson-inc.com
Estimated Sales: $20-50 Million
Number Employees: 100-249
Parent Co: Glanbia Nutritionals

13593 Watusee Foods
1368 Newton St NW
Apt A
Washington, DC 20010-3510
202-281-8245
hi@watuseefoods.com
watuseefoods.com
Chickpea snacks
Co-Founder & CEO: Jimmy Edgerton
Accountant: Miriam Discenza
Type of Packaging: Food Service
Brands:
Watusee Foods

13594 **Waugh Foods Inc**
701 Pinecrest Dr
East Peoria, IL 61611-4894
309-427-8000
Fax: 309-694-3115
Wholesaler/distributor of frozen and refrigerated food, fresh dairy and produce.
President: John Waugh
CEO: Joe Waugh
VP Sales: Jim Susin
Operations Manager: Norm Ralph
VP Purchasing: Tim Waugh
Year Founded: 1948
Estimated Sales: $20 Million
Number Employees: 50-99
Square Footage: 51550
Type of Packaging: Food Service

13595 **Wausau Paper Corp.**
100 Paper Pl.
Mosinee, WI 54455
715-693-4470
866-722-8675
torkusa@essity.com www.wausaupaper.com
Towels, tissue, soap, wipers and dispensing system.
President/CEO, Essity: Magnus Groth
Year Founded: 1899
Estimated Sales: $822 Million
Number Employees: 870
Number of Brands: 12
Parent Co: Essity
Type of Packaging: Food Service
Brands:
Artisan
DublSoft
DublNature
EcoSoft
Alliance
Wave'n Dry
Optiserv
Optiserv Hybrid
Optiserv accent
Revolution
DublServe
OptiSource Convertible
Silhouette
Dubl-tough

13596 **Waverly Crabs**
3400 Greenmount Ave
Baltimore, MD 21218-2823
410-243-1181
Fax: 410-243-0348
Crab
Owner: Jane Gordon
jgordon@bcps.org
Estimated Sales: $3-5 Million
Number Employees: 10-19

13597 **Wawa Inc**
Red Roof
260 W Baltimore Pike
Wawa, PA 19063
610-358-8000
800-444-9292
www.wawa.com
Milk and dairy products.
President & CEO: Chris Gheysens
chris.gheysens@wawa.com
Chief Financial Officer: Kevin Wiggins
Chief Operating Officer: Jim Morey
Year Founded: 1803
Estimated Sales: $10.6 Billion
Number Employees: 31,000

13598 **Wawona Frozen Foods Inc**
100 W Alluvial Ave
Clovis, CA 93611-9176
559-299-2901
Fax: 559-299-1921 info@wawona.com
www.wawona.com
Processor and exporter of IQF and syrup packed frozen fruits including peaches, strawberries and mixed fruit; also a variety of fruit-based portion controlled products; importer of frozen fruits including melons, grapes andpineapple
President: Jose Barajas
joseb@wawona.com
CFO: Julie Olsen
Director Quality Assurance: Duncan Donaldbe
VP Sales & Marketing: Willian Astin
Director of Sales: Toni Lindeleaf
VP Operations: Pete Peterson
Production Supervisor: Jose Valdez
Purchasing Manager: Ken Cole
Estimated Sales: $23.3 Million
Number Employees: 250-499
Square Footage: 125000
Type of Packaging: Consumer, Food Service, Private Label, Bulk
Brands:
Summer Prize
Wawona Frozen Foods

13599 **Wax Orchards**
P.O.Box 25448
Seattle, WA 98165-2348
206-463-9735
Fax: 206-463-9731 800-634-6132
customerservice@waxorchards.com
www.waxorchards.com
Fat-free, fruit-sweetened preserves and toppings
President: Anna Sestrap
Estimated Sales: $400,000
Number Employees: 5
Square Footage: 60
Brands:
Wax Orchards

13600 **Way Better Snacks**
800 Washington Ave N
Suite 207
Minneapolis, MN 55401-1148
612-314-2060
consumeraffairs@gowaybetter.com
gowaybetter.com
Crackers and tortilla chips
Founder & CEO: Jim Breen
Chief Financial Officer: Dan Wilkins
Vice President, Sales & Operations: Joe Lawer
Estimated Sales: $12-14 Million
Number Employees: 30
Brands:
Way Better Snacks

13601 **Wayco Ham Co**
506 N William St
Goldsboro, NC 27530-2804
919-735-3962
Fax: 919-734-4080 800-962-2614
tworrell@waycohams.com www.waycohams.com
Country ham and smoked turkey
President: Tony Worrell
tworrell@waycohams.com
VP: George Howell
Estimated Sales: $4300000
Number Employees: 20-49
Type of Packaging: Consumer, Food Service, Private Label

13602 **Wayfield Foods**
5145 Wellcome All Road
Atlanta, GA 30349
404-559-3200
Fax: 404-559-3206 www.wayfieldfoods.com
General grocery items, frozen foods, meats, dairy, deli items, seafood, produce
President: Ronald Edenfield
Estimated Sales: G
Number Employees: 500-999

13603 **Waymouth Farms Inc**
5300 Boone Ave N
Minneapolis, MN 55428-4034
763-533-5300
Fax: 763-533-9890 800-527-0094
www.goodsensesnacks.com
Dried fruit, nuts, seeds, trail mixes, and other snacks.
President: Gerard Knight
gknight@goodsensesnacks.com
Quality Manager: Dean Giroux
Marketing Manager: Kathleen Vargas
Regional Sales Manager: Bob Cosgrove
Purchasing Manager: Melissa Boeser
Estimated Sales: $32 Million
Number Employees: 100-249
Number of Brands: 7
Square Footage: 16240
Type of Packaging: Consumer, Food Service, Private Label, Bulk
Brands:
Good Sense
Goodniks
Kracker Nuts
Nutty Corn
Omega Munchies
Pea Poppers
Salad Pizazz!

13604 **Wayne Dairy Products Inc**
1590 NW 11th St
Richmond, IN 47374-1404
765-935-7521
Fax: 765-935-2184 www.smithdairy.com
Established in 1909. Processor of dairy products including milk, soft serve and hard ice cream, and shake mixes.
President: Steve Schmid
VP of Ice Cream: Pat Ruggles
VP of Sales: Brian DeFelice
Estimated Sales: $20-50 Million
Number Employees: 100-249
Parent Co: Smith Dairy
Type of Packaging: Consumer, Food Service, Private Label, Bulk
Brands:
Smith Dairy

13605 **Wayne E Bailey Produce Co Inc**
490 Old US Highway 74
P.O.Box 467
Chadbourn, NC 28431-9510
910-654-5163
Fax: 910-654-4734 800-845-6149
info@sweetpotatoes.com
Sweet potatoes
CEO/Owner: George Wooten
COO: Andy Pope
CFO: Stuart Hill
CEO: George Wooten
Sales: Ronnie Mercer
Estimated Sales: $3-5 Million
Number Employees: 50-99
Brands:
Girlwatcher
Playboy
Pride of Samspon

13606 **Wayne Estay Shrimp Company**
PO Box 946 Oak Street
Grand Isle, LA 70358-0946
504-787-2166
Fax: 504-787-3982 877-787-2166
Fish and seafood
President: Wayne Estay
Sales Manager: Wayne Estay
Estimated Sales: $300,000
Number Employees: 6

13607 **Wayne Farms LLC.**
4110 Continental Dr.
Oakwood, GA 30566
800-392-0844
www.waynefarms.com
Poultry producer.
President/CEO: J. Clinton Rivers
CFO/Treasurer: Courtney Fazekas
VP/General Manager, Prepared Foods: Tom Bell
VP, Quality Assurance & Food Safety: Bryan Miller
VP, Fresh Sales: Steve Clever
Year Founded: 1965
Estimated Sales: $2.2 Billion
Number Employees: 9,000
Number of Brands: 6
Parent Co: Continental Grain Company
Type of Packaging: Consumer, Food Service, Private Label
Other Locations:
Albertville AL
Danville AR
Decatur AL
Dobson NC
Dothan AL
Enterprise AL
Laurel MS
Pendergrass GA
Union Springs AL
Brands:
Wayne Farms
Platinum Harvest
Buffaloos
Chef's Craft
Crispy FlierS

Naked Truth
Ladybird
Quick Creations

13608 We Rub You
630 Flushing Ave
8th Fl.
Brooklyn, NY 11206
718-387-9797
eat@werubyou.com
www.werubyou.com
Korean BBQ marinades and sauces
Co-Founder: Ann Chung
Co-Founder: Janet Chung
Estimated Sales: $5.7 Million
Number Employees: 32
Type of Packaging: Food Service
Brands:
We Rub You

13609 Weaver Brothers
417 Dearborn Street
Berne, IN 46711-2012
219-589-2869
Fax: 219-589-3038
Cheese
Marketing Director: Wayne Amstutz

13610 Weaver Nut Co. Inc.
1925 W Main St
Ephrata, PA 17522-1112
717-738-3781
Fax: 717-733-2226 800-473-2688
info@weavernut.com www.weavergourmet.com
Processor importer and distributor of nuts, dried fruits, candies, confectionery items, snack mixes, gourmet coffees and teas, beans and spices; custom roasting and contract packaging available
President: E Paul Weaver III
Vice President: Michael Reis
Sales Director: Tom Flynn
Manager: Lisa Weaver
retail@weavernut.com
Estimated Sales: $18,000,000
Number Employees: 20-49
Number of Products: 3500
Square Footage: 116000
Type of Packaging: Consumer, Private Label, Bulk
Brands:
Arcor
Asher's
Hershey Chocolate
Jaret
Jelly Belly
Nabisco
Wilbur Chocolate

13611 Weaver Popcorn Co Inc
408 W Landess St
Van Buren, IN 46991
concessionsales@popweaver.com
www.popweaver.com
Regular and microwave popcorn; also, caramel popcorn specialties including caramel with almonds and pecans and fat-free
CFO: Brian Hamilton
National Sales Manager: Jim Labas
Year Founded: 1928
Estimated Sales: $20-50 Million
Number Employees: 100-249
Type of Packaging: Consumer, Food Service, Private Label, Bulk
Brands:
Bonnie Lee
Pop Weaver
Weaver Original

13612 Webb's Candy
38217 Highway 27
Davenport, FL 33837-7886
863-422-1051
Fax: 863-422-6214 800-289-9322
www.citruscandy.com
Mints, lemon drops, taffy, toffee, nougats, glazed and coated nuts, fudge, vanilla and chocolate candies, etc
President: John Webb
john@citruscandy.com
Estimated Sales: $1200000
Number Employees: 10-19
Type of Packaging: Consumer, Food Service, Bulk

13613 Webbpak Inc
110 Railroad Ave
Trussville, AL 35173
205-655-3500
Fax: 205-655-3500 800-655-3500
Vinegar, syrups, sauces, drink mixes and flavorings
President: Peter Calzone
Estimated Sales: Less Than $500,000
Number Employees: 1-4
Square Footage: 40000
Type of Packaging: Consumer, Food Service, Private Label
Brands:
Diamond Joe
Farmers Favorite
Flowing Gold
Formula 18
Johnny Boy Vanilla
Webb's

13614 Weber Flavors
549 Palwaukee Dr
PO Box 546
Wheeling, IL 60090
800-558-9078
www.weberflavors.com
Family-owned flavoring manufacturer founded in 1902.
Contact: Mary Marvan
marym@weberflavors.com
Number of Brands: 6
Brands:
Simply Natural
Simply Natural-Like
Whol-Bean
HoMaid
Waves
Petran

13615 Webster City Custom Meats Inc
1611 E 2nd St
PO Box 280
Webster City, IA 50595-1741
515-832-1130
Fax: 515-832-5515
www.webstercitycustommeats.com
Smoked ham, smoked bacon, smoked turkeys, fresh sausage products, boneless ham roasts, and smoked pork loins.
President: Dean Bowden
VP Sales & Marketing: Phil Voge
Operations Manager: Chip Abbott
Estimated Sales: $20 Million
Number Employees: 100-249
Square Footage: 57000
Type of Packaging: Food Service, Private Label

13616 Webster Farms
5859 Highway 1
Unit 1
Cambridge, NS B0P 1G0
Canada
902-538-9492
Fax: 902-538-7662 800-507-8844
webfarm@eastlink.ca www.websterfarms.ca
Frozen strawberries and rhubarb; also, dry beans
President: Greg Webster
Number Employees: 20-49
Type of Packaging: Consumer, Food Service

13617 Wechsler Coffee Corporation
250 Central Avenue
Teterboro, NJ 07608-1861
201-994-1861
800-800-2633
Gourmet coffee, tea and drink bases; importer of green coffee; wholesaler/distributor of general merchandise and groceries including coffee and tea; serving the food service market
President: Mike O'Donnell
VP Finance: Jim Pypen
Estimated Sales: $300,000-500,000
Number Employees: 10-19
Square Footage: 200000
Parent Co: Superior Coffee & Foods
Type of Packaging: Food Service, Private Label

13618 Wedding Cake Studio
7373 Stanhope Kell Road
Williamsfield, OH 44093
440-667-1765
Fax: 440-293-5573
Cakes and candy
President: Craig Harvey
Estimated Sales: Under $500,000
Number Employees: 1-4
Brands:
Ther Cake Loft

13619 Wedemeyer's Bakery
314 Harbor Way
S San Francisco, CA 94080-6900
650-873-1000
Fax: 650-873-3170
wedemeyer@wedemeyerbakery.com
www.wedemeyerbakery.com
Hearth bread, sliced bread and specialty rolls.
Owner/President: Laurence Strain
Estimated Sales: $1 Million
Number Employees: 20-49
Square Footage: 28636
Type of Packaging: Consumer, Food Service
Brands:
Better Way

13620 Weetabix Canada
751 D'Arcy St.
Cobourg, ON K9A 4B1
Canada
800-343-0590
Fax: 905-372-7261 888-933-8249
www.weetabix.com
Breakfast cereals and ingredients.
President/CEO, Post Consumer Brands: Howard Friedman
Year Founded: 1975
Estimated Sales: $300 Million
Number Employees: 250+
Number of Brands: 4
Parent Co: Post Holdings, Inc.
Type of Packaging: Consumer, Food Service, Private Label, Bulk
Other Locations:
Weetabix Food Company
Burton Latimer
Brands:
Alpen Dark Chocolate
Alpen No Added Sugar
Alpen Original Muesli
Barbara's Baked Original
Barbara's Baked White Cheddar
Barbara's Chocolate Chip
Barbara's Cinnamon
Barbara's Cinnamon Crunch
Barbara's Jalapeno
Barbara's Oatmeal
Barbara's Original
Barbara's Peanut Butter
Babara's Vanilla
Barbara's Vanilla Blast
Barbara's GrainShop
Barbara's Weetabix

13621 Weetabix Food Co.
500 Nickerson Road
Marlborough, MA 01752
800-343-0590
www.weetabixusa.com
UK-based cereal manufacturer with a plant in Cobourg, Ontario, Canada that serves the North American market.
CEO, Weetabix North America: Steve Van Tassel
Contact: James Gillespie
jgille@weetabixna.com
Parent Co: Bright Food (Group) Co., Ltd
Type of Packaging: Consumer, Food Service, Private Label, Bulk
Brands:
Weetabix
Alpen
Barbara's

13622 Wege Pretzel Company
PO Box 334
Hanover, PA 17331
717-843-0738
Fax: 717-633-3910 800-888-4646
info@wege.com www.wege.com
Producers of sourdough, whole wheat, organic, butter flavor and specialty pretzels.
President: Ike Laughman
Vice President: Edith Staub
VP Marketing: William Still
Estimated Sales: $8200000
Number Employees: 85
Square Footage: 440000
Parent Co: LDI
Type of Packaging: Consumer, Food Service, Private Label, Bulk

Brands:
Dutchie
Wege

13623 **Wege of Hanover**
PO Box 334
Hanover, PA 17331
717-843-0738
Fax: 717-633-3910 800-888-4646
info@wege.com www.wege.com
Pretzels
Manager: Carol Arentz
VP: Tony Laughman
Estimated Sales: $500-1 Million appx.
Number Employees: 50-99
Type of Packaging: Private Label
Brands:
Dutchie

13624 **Wegmans Food Markets Inc.**
1500 Brooks Ave.
PO Box 30844
Rochester, NY 14624-0844
800-934-6267
www.wegmans.com
Grocery, bakery, dairy, deli, floral, meat, produce, seafood, alcoholic beverages, and more.
President/CEO: Colleen Wegman
Chairman: Danny Wegman
daniel.wegman@wegmans.com
Senior VP: Nicole Wegman
Year Founded: 1916
Estimated Sales: $9.7 Billion
Number Employees: 50,000
Brands:
Wegmans Gluten Free
Wegmans Organic

13625 **Wei-Chuan USA Inc**
6655 Garfield Ave
Bell Gardens, CA 90201-1807
562-372-2020
Fax: 562-927-0780 info@weichuanusa.com
www.weichuanusa.com
Manufacturer and distributor of frozen Chinese foods.
President, Wei-Chuan USA: Steve Lin
stevel@weichuanusa.com
Year Founded: 1972
Number Employees: 250-499
Type of Packaging: Consumer, Food Service, Private Label
Other Locations:
Manufacturing Facility
Los Angeles CA
Manufacturing Facility
Murfreesboro TN
Brands:
Farmer King
Golden Foods
Ho-Tai
Lotus
Wei-Chaun
Wei-Chuan

13626 **Weibel Vineyards**
1 Winemaster Way # D
Suite D
Lodi, CA 95240-0860
209-365-9463
Fax: 209-365-9469 800-932-9463
www.weibel.com
Wines
President: Fred Weibel Jr
CFO: Bruce Baker
Sales: Douglas Richards
Manager: Liz West
liz@weibel.com
Operations Manager: Gary Habletzel
Estimated Sales: $4.5 Million
Number Employees: 20-49
Square Footage: 400
Type of Packaging: Private Label

13627 **Weil's Food Processing**
483 Erie Street N
PO Box 130
Wheatley, ON N0P 2P0
Canada
519-825-4572
Fax: 519-825-7437 email@weilsfood.ca
www.weilsfood.ca
Asparagus, canned tomatoes and potatoes
President: Henry Weil
Vice President/Board Member: Robert Weil
Sales: Mark Weil
Estimated Sales: $1-2.5 Million
Number Employees: 10-19
Type of Packaging: Consumer, Food Service, Private Label

13628 **Weinberg Foods**
11410 NE 124th Street
Suite 264
Kirkland, WA 98034-4305
800-866-3447
Fax: 310-230-9057 weinberg@weinbergfoods.com
www.bakingingredients.com
Kosher egg products, dry milk and vegetable powders; importer of kosher vegetable powders; exporter of kosher egg products
President: W Weinberg
Sales: Ashley Hester
Estimated Sales: $930,000
Number Employees: 4
Square Footage: 12000
Type of Packaging: Bulk

13629 **Weisenberger Mills**
2545 Weisenberger Mill Rd
Midway, KY 40347-9791
859-254-5282
Fax: 859-254-0294 800-643-8678
flourusa@te.net www.weisenberger.com
Processor and exporter of wheat flour, cornmeal and baking mixes including biscuit, pancake, pizza dough, cornbread and hush puppies; exporter of fish batter breading
President: Ernest Weisenberger
sales@weisenberger.com
Vice President: Philip Weisenberger
Estimated Sales: $900000
Number Employees: 5-9
Square Footage: 64000
Type of Packaging: Consumer, Food Service, Private Label

13630 **Weiser River Packing**
531 Unity Lane
Weiser, ID 83672-5372
208-549-0200
Fax: 208-549-0503
Processor and exporter of onions
President: Calvin Hickey
Estimated Sales: $1,000,000
Number Employees: 20
Type of Packaging: Consumer, Food Service, Private Label, Bulk
Brands:
Burger Buddies
Head of the Class
Sun Lovin
Weiser River Whoppers

13631 **Weiss Brothers Smoke House**
132 Norton Rd
Johnstown, PA 15906-2906
814-539-4085
Fax: 814-536-3951
Smoked and Italian sausage, bacon, frankfurters and bologna
President: Walter Grata
Quality Control: Joseph Miller
Estimated Sales: Below $5 000,000
Number Employees: 5-9

13632 **Weiss Homemade Kosher Bakery**
5011 13th Ave
Brooklyn, NY 11219
718-438-0407
Fax: 718-438-1872 800-498-3477
Kosher breads, cakes, pastries, rugulach and wedding cakes
President: Abe Weiss
Estimated Sales: $1-3 Million
Number Employees: 20-49

13633 **Weiss Noodle Company**
31313 Aurora Road
Cleveland, OH 44139-2705
440-248-4550
Dry Pasta
President: James Price
Estimated Sales: $5-10 Million appx.
Number Employees: 20-49
Parent Co: Ideal Macaroni Company

13634 **Welch Foods Inc**
300 Baker Ave # 101
Suite 101
Concord, MA 01742-2731
978-371-1000
Fax: 978-371-3855 800-340-6870
www.welchs.com
Juice, jellies and jams and frozen concentrates
President & CEO: Brad Irwin
birwin@welchs.com
CMO: Tom Dixon
Number Employees: 1000-4999
Square Footage: 2120000
Type of Packaging: Consumer, Food Service

13635 **Welch Foods Inc.**
300 Baker Ave.
Suite 101
Concord, MA 01742
978-371-1000
Fax: 978-371-3855 800-340-6870
www.welchs.com
Jams, jellies, marmalades, preserves, beverage and frozen dessert bases, juice concentrates, frozen dessert pops and juice including grape, tomato, apple cider, cranberry and cranberry blends.
President/CEO/Director: Bradley Irwin
Vice President/Chief Financial Officer: Michael Perda
Year Founded: 1869
Estimated Sales: $650 Million
Number Employees: 1000-4999
Parent Co: National Grape Cooperative
Type of Packaging: Consumer, Food Service
Brands:
Bama Fruit Spreads
Welch's

13636 **Welch's Global Ingredients Group**
300 Baker Avenue
Suite 101
Concord, MA 01742
978-371-3692
www.welchsgig.com
Manufacturer of grape juice, purees, FruitWorx real fruit pieces and powders.
General Sales Manager: Justin White
Contact: Kate Boze
kboze@welchs.com
Parent Co: Welch's Food

13637 **Welcome Dairy Inc**
H4489 Maple Rd
Colby, WI 54421-9519
715-223-2874
Fax: 715-223-3958 www.welcomedairy.com
Manufacturer of processed cheese products.
President: Tollefson Amanda
tollefson@welcomedairy.com
Number Employees: 50-99
Number of Brands: 1
Number of Products: 7
Brands:
Welcome

13638 **Weldon Ice Cream Co**
2887 Canal Dr
Millersport, OH 43046-9701
740-467-2400
mgmt@weldons.com
www.weldons.com
Ice cream including novelties, sandwiches, creamsicles and fudgecicles
Owner: David Pierce
david@weldons.com
Estimated Sales: $460000
Number Employees: 5-9
Type of Packaging: Consumer, Food Service, Bulk

13639 **Well Dressed Food Company**
96, Park Street
Tupper Lake, NY 12986
518-359-5280
Fax: 518-618-3147 sales@welldressedfoods.com
www.welldressedfoods.com
Breakfast mixes, sweet & savory jams, crunchy granola, dessert mixes, sauces/rubs and honey & toppings
President/Owner: David Tomberlin

13640 **Well-Pict Inc**
209 Riverside Rd
PO Box 973
Watsonville, CA 95076-3656
831-722-3871
Fax: 831-722-6041 sales@wellpict.com
www.wellpict.com
Strawberries, raspberries
Owner: Keith Bungo
kbungo@wellpict.com
CFO: George Schaaf
General Manager: Eric Miyasaka
Quality Control: Keith Bungo
Estimated Sales: $30-50 Million
Number Employees: 20-49

13641 **Wella Bar**
1403 MLK Jr. Industrial Blvd.
East Lockhart, TX 78644
877-725-7289
info@wellabar.com www.wellabar.com
Energy bars
Co-Founder: George Ghilarducci
Co-Founder: Deborah Nease
Brands:
Lockhart Fine Foods
Wella Bar

13642 **(HQ)Wellesse**
1441 W Smith Rd
Ferndale, WA 98248-8933
800-232-4005
Fax: 360-384-1140 800-232-4005
info@wellesse.com www.wellesse.com
Processor, exporter and contract packager of herbal and homeopathic food supplements in liquid form
President & CEO: Jim Thornton
COO & CFO: Shri Iyengar
Manager Research & Development: Mary Galloway
Quality Control Director: John Knight
VP Marketing/Product Management: Greg Andrews
VP Sales: Marc Kubota
Director Operations: Tim Schaafsma
Purchasing Manager: Scott Sticklin
Estimated Sales: $6 Million
Number Employees: 10-19
Square Footage: 181000
Type of Packaging: Consumer, Private Label
Brands:
Bioallers
Complimed
Natrabio
Nico-Rx
Symtec
Zand Hebs For Kids
Wellesse

13643 **Wellington Brewery**
950 Woodlawn Road West
Guelph, ON N1K 1B8
Canada
519-837-2337
Fax: 519-837-3142 800-576-3853
mail@wellingtonbrewery.ca
www.wellingtonbrewery.ca
Beer, ale, lager and stout
President: Doug Dawkins
VP: Brent Davies
General Manager: Sarah Dawkins
Marketing: Paul Aquilina
Sales Representative: Scotty Baugh
Operations Manager: Christopher Sheppard
Production Manager: Ian Meredith
Purchasing: Sarah Dawkins
Estimated Sales: $3,500,000
Number Employees: 30
Type of Packaging: Consumer, Food Service
Brands:
Beehive
Black Knight
Countryale
Iron Uke
Spa
Trailhead

13644 **Wellington Foods**
1930 California Avenu
Corona, CA 92881
951-547-7000
Fax: 562-989-9322 www.wellingtonfoods.com
Health foods and institutional foods
Owner: Anthony Harnack Sr
Contact: Hal Amick
hal.amick@colingordon.com
Estimated Sales: $2.5-5 Million
Number Employees: 20-49
Brands:
Wellington Foods

13645 **Wells Enterprises Inc.**
1 Blue Bunny Dr.
Le Mars, IA 51031
712-546-4000
Fax: 712-548-3800 www.wellsenterprisesinc.com
Ice cream and frozen novelty manufacturer.
President/CEO: Michael Wells
Executive VP/CFO: Jeremy Pinkerman
Senior VP/General Counsel: Erick Opsahl
Executive VP/COO: Liam Killeen
Year Founded: 1913
Estimated Sales: Over $1 Billion
Number Employees: 2,500+
Number of Brands: 4
Type of Packaging: Consumer, Food Service, Bulk
Other Locations:
Ice Cream Plant
St. George UT
Brands:
Blue Bunny
Blue Ribbon Classics
Bomb Pop
Chillycow

13646 **Welsh Farms**
1330 Main Ave
Clifton, NJ 07011-2215
973-772-2388
Fax: 973-403-0180
Ice cream and frozen yogurt
Owner: Atul Patel
anilkumar_290@msn.com
General Manager: Robert Pailillo
Plant Manager: Joe Marscovetta
Estimated Sales: Less Than $500,000
Number Employees: 1-4
Type of Packaging: Consumer, Food Service

13647 **Welsh Farms**
520 Main Avenue
Wallington, NJ 07057
973-777-2500
Fax: 973-249-3849 800-221-0663
wallington.questions@bordendairy.com
www.farmlanddairies.com
Powdered milk, buttermilk, ice cream and juice
President/CEO: Terri Webb
Estimated Sales: $1-2.5 Million
Number Employees: 20-49
Square Footage: 360000
Parent Co: Welsh Farms
Type of Packaging: Consumer, Food Service
Brands:
Welsh Farms-Ice Cream
Farmland Dairy
Clinton
Skim Plus
School Milk

13648 **Wenda America Inc**
1823 High Grove Ln
Suite 103
Naperville, IL 60540
844-999-3632
sales@wendaingredients.com
www.wendaingredients.com
Global meat and poultry ingredients manufacturer and processor.
President: Chad Boeckman
chadb@wendaingredients.com
Year Founded: 1995
Estimated Sales: $200 Million
Number Employees: 200-500
Number of Brands: 7
Type of Packaging: Bulk
Brands:
Wendaphos
Prosur
Novapro
NatureBind
Senor Paprika
Koolgel
SoyPura

13649 **Wendysue & Tobey's**
15530 Broadway Center St
Gardena, CA 90248-2137
310-516-9705
Fax: 310-516-0876
Bakery
President: John Roberts
info@wendysue-tobeys.com
Plant Manager: John Roberts
Estimated Sales: Below $5 Million
Number Employees: 20-49
Type of Packaging: Private Label

13650 **Wenger Spring Brook Cheese Inc**
12805 N Spring Brook Rd
Davis, IL 61019-9719
815-865-5612
Fax: 815-248-2450
Swiss and muenster cheeses
Owner: Fred S Wenger
wengers@state-isp.com
Vice President: John Wenger
Estimated Sales: $.5-1 million
Number Employees: 20-49
Type of Packaging: Consumer, Private Label, Bulk

13651 **Wenger's Bakery**
900 N 10th St
Reading, PA 19604-2302
610-372-6545
Buns, pies, cakes, breads, cookies and pastries
Owner: Javiar Martinez
Marketing Director: Peter Menicucci
Estimated Sales: Less Than $500,000
Number Employees: 1-4
Type of Packaging: Consumer

13652 **Wenk Foods Inc**
PO Box 368
Madison, SD 57042
605-256-4569
Fax: 605-256-3204 wfi@hcpd.com
Processor and exporter of frozen and dried egg products; also, frozen whole geese
President: William Wenk
Sales Director: Norbert Moldan
Number Employees: 50-99
Square Footage: 120000
Type of Packaging: Consumer, Food Service, Private Label, Bulk
Brands:
Wenk

13653 **Wenner Bakery**
33 Rajon Rd
Bayport, NY 11705
Fax: 631-563-6546 800-869-6262
sales@wennerbread.com www.wennerbakery.com
Frozen unbaked bread products including egg twist rolls, Italian bread, bagels, hard rolls, challah and specialty breads; also, par-baked breads and rolls.
CEO: Jeffrey Montie
Estimated Sales: G
Number Employees: 250-499
Square Footage: 72000
Type of Packaging: Food Service, Private Label, Bulk
Brands:
Npn
Swirl Onion
Steakhouse Style
Wenner
Rustica

13654 **Wente Family Estates**
5565 Tesla Rd
Livermore, CA 94550
925-456-2305
info@wentevineyards.com
www.wentevineyards.com
Wines
CEO: Carolyn Wente
Senior Brand Manager: Aly Wente O'Neal
Estimated Sales: $50-100 Million
Number of Brands: 5
Brands:
Wente
Murrieta's Well
entwine
Hayes Ranch
Double Decker

13655 **Wenzel's Bakery**
125 E Broad Street
Tamaqua, PA 18252-2007
570-668-2360
Baked goods
President: George Wenzel
Estimated Sales: $76,000
Number Employees: 3

Type of Packaging: Consumer

13656 Werling & Sons Slaughterhouse
100 S Plum Street
Burkettsville, OH 45310
937-338-3281
Fax: 419-375-0037 www.werlingandsons.com
Meat products and hydrogenated fats; custom slaughtering available
Owner/Marketing Manager: Edward Werling
VP Sales/Marketing: James Werling
Estimated Sales: $5-10 Million
Number Employees: 10
Square Footage: 17752
Type of Packaging: Consumer, Bulk

13657 Wermuth Winery
3942 Silverado Trl
Calistoga, CA 94515
707-942-5924
Cabernet sauvignon
Winemaker: Ralph Wermuth
Estimated Sales: A
Number Employees: 1-4

13658 Wessanan
420 W Broadway Avenue
Minneapolis, MN 55411
612-331-3775
Fax: 612-378-8398
Milk, dairy and non-cheese products
President: Tim Green
VP Sales: Pat Graiziger
Plant Manager: John Gronholm
Number Employees: 100-249
Brands:
Clover Leaf

13659 West Bay Fishing
RR 1
Box 752
Gouldsboro, ME 04607-9753
207-963-2392
Fax: 207-963-7403
Seafood
President: Richard Noble

13660 West Brothers Lobster
830 Pigeon Hill Rd
Steuben, ME 04680
207-546-3622
Fax: 207-255-3987
Lobster
Owner: Blair West
Estimated Sales: $300,000-500,000
Number Employees: 1-4

13661 West Coast Products
717 Tehama St
Orland, CA 95963-1248
530-865-3379
Fax: 530-865-1581 800-382-3072
www.westcoastproducts.net
Manufacturer and exporter of specialty olives and olive oil
President: Estelle Krackov
Manager: Dan Vecere
dan.vecere@westcoastproducts.net
Estimated Sales: $380,000
Number Employees: 10-19
Square Footage: 18608
Type of Packaging: Food Service, Bulk
Brands:
Olinda

13662 West Coast Seafood Processors Association
650 NE Holladay St
Suite 1600
Portland, OR 97232
503-227-5076
www.wcspa.com
Processor and exporter of frozen Pacific whiting
Manager: Tom Libby
Executive Director: Rod Moore
Contact: Rod Moore
tuna_1@charter.net
Estimated Sales: $10-20 Million
Number Employees: 100-249
Parent Co: California Shellfish
Type of Packaging: Bulk

13663 West Coast Specialty Coffee
71 Lost Lake Lane
Campbell, CA 95008
650-259-9308
Fax: 650-259-8024 rh@specialtycoffee.com
www.specialtycoffee.com
Coffee and coffee equipment and supplies
President: Robert Hensley
rh@specialtycoffee.com
Estimated Sales: $500,000
Number Employees: 2
Type of Packaging: Consumer, Food Service, Bulk

13664 West Liberty Foods LLC
207 W 2nd St
P.O. Box 318
West Liberty, IA 52776
888-511-4500
www.wlfoods.com
Ready-to-eat sliced processed meat, poultry and protein products.
CEO: Edward Garrett
President: Michael Quint
VP & CFO: Allen Hansen
VP & COO: Gerald Lessard
Quality Assurance: Chasity Abel
chasity.abel@wlfoods.com
Operations Manager: Chad Schnepper
Year Founded: 1996
Estimated Sales: $200-500 Million
Number Employees: 1,900
Square Footage: 175000
Parent Co: Iowa Turkey Growers Cooperative
Type of Packaging: Consumer, Food Service, Private Label
Other Locations:
West Liberty Foods Plant
Mt Pleasant IA
West Liberty Foods Plant
Sigourney IA

13665 West Pac
9671 N 5th E
Idaho Falls, ID 83401-5637
801-973-7400
Fax: 801-973-7436 800-973-7407
Cake mixes, barbecue sauces and spices; contract packager of liquid and dry mixes in cans, bottles and boxes
President: Hal Havens
Number Employees: 5-9
Square Footage: 80000
Type of Packaging: Consumer, Private Label
Brands:
Gourmet Spices

13666 West Pak Avocado Inc
38655 Sky Canyon Dr
Murrieta, CA 92563-2536
951-696-5845
Fax: 951-296-5744 800-266-4414
www.westpakavocado.com
Importer, exporter and packer of avocados; importer of Mexican and Chilean fruits; processor of persimmons and kumquats
President: Randy Shoup
randy.shoup@westpakavocado.com
Import Export Director: Dave Culpeper
VP/General Manager: Galen Newhouse
Estimated Sales: $3-5 Million
Number Employees: 50-99
Square Footage: 88000
Type of Packaging: Consumer, Food Service, Bulk
Brands:
Asian Star
West Pak

13667 West Park Wine Cellars
P.O.Box 280
West Park, NY 12493
845-384-6709
Fax: 845-384-6709
Wines
President: Louis Fiore
Estimated Sales: Under $300,000
Number Employees: 1-4
Type of Packaging: Private Label
Brands:
Full Service Caterin

13668 West Point Dairy Products
1715 East Road
West Point, NE 68788
402-372-5551
Fax: 402-372-5061 info@westpointdairy.com
www.westpointdairy.com
Dairy products including butter
Estimated Sales: $20-50 Million
Number Employees: 50-99
Type of Packaging: Private Label
Brands:
Country Cream Butter

13669 West Thomas Partners, LLC
4053 Brockton SE
Grand Rapids, MI 49512
616-755-8432
info@theglutenfreebar.com
www.theglutenfreebar.com
Gluten-free, non-GMO, soy-free and nut-free snack bars, energy bites and oats in various flavors
Co-Founder: Marshall Rader
Co-Founder: Elliott Rader
Year Founded: 2010
Number of Brands: 1
Number of Products: 17
Type of Packaging: Consumer, Private Label
Brands:
GFB: The Gluten Free Bar

13670 Westar Nutrition Corporation
350 Paularino Ave.
Costa Mesa, CA 92626
949-645-6100
Fax: 949-645-9131 800-645-1868
cs@vivalife.com www.vivalife.com
Nutraccuticals and nutritional supplements
President/CEO: David Fan
VP Sales & Business Development: May Chen
VP Regulatory/Buisiness Affairs: Cheryl Cartwright
Director/Production: Joe Ramos
Estimated Sales: $29800000
Number Employees: 20-49

13671 Westbend Vinyards
5394 Williams Road
Lewisville, NC 27023-8278
336-945-5032
Fax: 336-945-5294 866-901-5032
Wine
Owner: Jack Kroustalis
Manager: Steve Shepard
Estimated Sales: $500,000-$1 Million
Number Employees: 10-19

13672 (HQ)Westbrae Natural Foods
58 S Service Rd
Melville, NY 11747
631-730-2200
Fax: 631-730-2550 800-434-4246
www.westbrae.com
Processor, importer and exporter of natural and organic soy and rice beverages, tortilla and potato chips, soups, beans, chili, condiments, sauces, rice cakes, popcorn, pretzels, licorice, cookies, spreads and Asian foods
President/CEO: Irwin Simon
CFO/EVP: Ira Lamel
Number Employees: 1,000-4,999
Square Footage: 156000
Parent Co: The Hain Celestial Group, Inc.
Type of Packaging: Consumer, Private Label
Brands:
Bearitos
Little Bear Organic
Westbrae Natural
Westsoy

13673 Westbrae Natural Foods
4600 Sleepytime Dr.
Boulder, CO 80301
800-434-4246
www.westbrae.com
Natural and organic beans, pastas, vegetables, japanese misos and condiments.
President & CEO: Irwin Simon
Estimated Sales: $10-20 Million
Number Employees: 20-49

13674 **Westbrook Trading Company**
3410b Odgen Road SE
Calgary, AB T2G 4N5
Canada
403-290-0860
Fax: 403-264-3017 800-563-5785
Processor and exporter of fresh, frozen and boxed beef and pork
President: Michael Nutik
Sales Manager: Daren Uens
Number Employees: 100-249
Type of Packaging: Consumer, Food Service, Bulk

13675 **Westco-BakeMark**
7351 Crider Avenue
Pico Rivera, CA 90660-3705
562-949-1054
Fax: 562-948-5506 www.yourbakemark.com
Processor, importer and exporter of baking ingredients and supplies, including mixes, fillings, icings and frozen products.
Chief Supply Chain Officer: Jim Parker
CFO/VP of Finance: Refugio Reynoso
Marketing Director: David Roccio
EVP of Sales: William Day
VP of Human Resources: Kenneth Sparks
Estimated Sales: $20-50 Million
Number Employees: 500-999
Number of Brands: 1
Parent Co: CSM Bakery Solutions
Type of Packaging: Food Service, Bulk
Other Locations:
Union City CA
Reno NV
Phoenix AZ
Seattle WA
Brands:
Westco

13676 **Westdale Foods Company**
14541 S 88th Ave
Orland Park, IL 60462-2752
708-458-7774
Fax: 708-458-1298
Candy
Owner: Tom Vandervliet
Estimated Sales: $5-10 Million
Number Employees: 10-19
Brands:
Sachers
Schluckwerder
Schumann's
Schwarteau
Siljans
Simpkins
Smooth & Melty
Soldans

13677 **Western Bagel Baking Corp**
7814 Sepulveda Blvd
Van Nuys, CA 91405-1062
818-786-5847
Fax: 818-787-3221 wbinfo@westernbagel.com
www.westernbagel.com
Processor and exporter of fresh and frozen bagels.
President: Steve Ustin
Cmo: Corrie Ustin
custin@westernbagel.com
Vice President: Skip Scheidt
Operations Manager: Jim Schultz
Estimated Sales: $29280131
Number Employees: 250-499
Square Footage: 30000
Brands:
Western

13678 **Western Beef Jerky**
7209 B 101 Avenue NW
Edmonton, AB T6A 0H9
Canada
780-469-4817
Fax: 780-468-5006 info@westernbeefjerky.ca
www.westernbeefjerky.ca
Beef jerky
President: Danny Ljubsa
Estimated Sales: A
Number Employees: 1-4
Type of Packaging: Consumer

13679 **Western Buffalo Company**
1015 E St. Patrick Street
PO Box 4185
Rapid City, SD 57709
605-342-0322
Fax: 605-342-5375 800-247-3263
kenwbc@rushmore.com
www.westernbuffalocompany.com
Meat including beef and buffalo
President: Bruce Anderson
Secretary: Gail Hise
Plant Manager: Al Holzer
Estimated Sales: $10-20 Million
Number Employees: 20-49
Square Footage: 24000
Type of Packaging: Consumer, Food Service, Private Label, Bulk

13680 **Western Creamery**
91 Delta Park Blvd
Unit 2
Brampton, ON L6T 5E7
Canada
905-458-8696
Fax: 905-458-8717 800-265-3230
info@westerncreamery.com
www.westerncreamery.com
Dairy products including cotage cheese, cream cheese, sour cream, yogurt, baker's special, and maslanka
Director General, Libert,: Martin Valiquette
Parent Co: Libert, Natural Foods Inc.
Brands:
Western Creamery

13681 **Western Meat Co**
4101 Capitol Blvd SW
Tumwater, WA 98501-4069
360-357-6601
866-357-6601
info@westernmeats.comcastbiz.net
www.westernmeats.net
Beef and pork
President: Dennis Mydlar
Estimated Sales: $500,000-$1 Million
Number Employees: 5-9
Type of Packaging: Consumer, Food Service

13682 **Western New York Syrup Corporation**
3401 Rochester Road
Lakeville, NY 14480-0910
585-346-2311
Liquid sweeteners
Manager: Tim Calway
Assistant Manager: Lee Robinson
Estimated Sales: $5-10 Million
Number Employees: 1-4
Parent Co: Archer Daniels Midland Company
Type of Packaging: Bulk

13683 **Western Pacific Oils, Inc.**
201 S Anderson St
Los Angeles, CA 90033
213-232-5117
Fax: 213-232-5102 www.westpacoils.com
Palm oils and coconut oil.
Manager: Y Neman
Contact: Suraj Bhojwani
suraj@westpacoils.com
Estimated Sales: $900 Thousand
Type of Packaging: Food Service, Bulk
Brands:
Golden Palm Shortening
Golden Joma Palm Oil
Golden Palm Margarine
Golden Palm Cake & Icing
Golden Coconut Oil

13684 **Western Pacific Produce**
36 W Gutierrez
Santa Barbara, CA 93101
805-568-1550
Fax: 805-884-9181 800-963-4451
sales@western-pacific.com
www.western-pacific.com
Grower and packer of broccoli and other fresh produce.
President & CEO: Mark Vestal
mark@western-pacific.com
VP & Chief Financial Officer: Diana Vestal
Sales Manager: Steve Bellandi
Chief Operating Officer: Bob Cordova
Year Founded: 1990
Estimated Sales: $20-50 Million
Number Employees: 250-499
Type of Packaging: Consumer, Food Service, Private Label, Bulk

13685 **Western Sugar Cooperative**
7555 E. Hampden Ave.
Suite 520
Denver, CO 80231
303-830-3939
Fax: 303-695-1093 800-523-7497
www.westernsugar.com
Beet sugar, including fine granulated sugar, powdered sugar, and light and dark brown sugar for retail or industrial use. Also sugar beet pressed pulp, molasses beet pulp pellets, HE molasses, and molasses desugarized solubles.
President/CEO: Rodney Perry
Senior VP/CEO: Jason Bridges
Vice President/General Counsel: Heather Luther
Vice President, Operations: Parker Thilmony
Year Founded: 1901
Estimated Sales: $350 Million
Number Employees: 1,000+
Number of Brands: 1
Square Footage: 6321
Type of Packaging: Consumer, Private Label, Bulk
Brands:
GW

13686 **Western Syrup Company**
13766 Milroy Pl
Santa Fe Springs, CA 90670
562-921-4485
Fax: 562-921-5170
Processor and exporter of custom formulated beverage bases, concentrates, flavors and flavor emulsions for carbonated beverages, slushes, sno-cones, etc.; also, dessert toppings including chocolate syrup, fudge and fruit
President: Pushpa Sastry
Sales Director: Ken Molder
Plant Manager: Marlon King
Estimated Sales: $3-5 Million
Number Employees: 5-9
Square Footage: 110000
Parent Co: Western Syrup Company
Brands:
Bartenders Pride
High Mountains
Rooster
Western Syrup

13687 **Westfield Farm**
28 Worcester Rd
Hubbardston, MA 01452-1139
978-928-5110
Fax: 978-928-5745 877-777-3900
stetson222@verizon.net
www.westfield-farm.myshopify.com
Surface ripened and fresh goat cheese
Owner: Bob Stetson
Marketing Director: Debby Stetson
Sales Director: Bob Stetson\
stetson222@verizon.net
Estimated Sales: $500,000-$1 Million
Number Employees: 5-9
Square Footage: 12000
Type of Packaging: Consumer, Food Service
Brands:
Capri
Classic Blue
Hubbardson Blue

13688 **Westfield Foods**
19 Lark Industrial Pkwy # F
Greenville, RI 02828-3003
401-949-3558
Fax: 401-949-3738
Dry soup and rice mixes; also, chili
President: John Pezzillo
Estimated Sales: $130000
Number Employees: 1-4
Square Footage: 34000
Type of Packaging: Consumer, Food Service
Brands:
Millie's

13689 **(HQ)Westin Foods**
11808 W Center Rd # 1
Omaha, NE 68144-4435
402-691-8800
Fax: 402-691-7920 800-228-6098
jweese@westinfoods.com www.westinfoods.com
Bacon bits, imitation bacon bits, lecithin, onion rings, breaded cheese, sunflower seeds, soy products, corn starch, salad dressings, sauces, etc.; importer of olives; exporter of frozen breaded vegetables
Chairman/Ceo: Richard Westin Sr
CEO/President: Scott Carlson
scarlson@westinfoods.com
Number Employees: 250-499
Type of Packaging: Consumer, Food Service, Private Label, Bulk
Other Locations:
Westin
Wahoo NE
Brands:
Big Red
Fairbury
Feaster Foods
Great American

13690 **Westnut**
401 N 26th Ave
Cornelius, OR 97113-8510
800-382-5339
www.westnut.com
Nuts, hazelnuts
Estimated Sales: $5-10 Million
Number Employees: 20-49
Parent Co: Wilco Farm Stores

13691 **Weston Foods**
1425 The Queensway
Etobicoke, ON M8Z 1T3
Canada
416-252-7323
Fax: 416-252-5553 www.westonfoods.ca
Manufacturer of fresh and frozen baked goods.
President: Luc Mongeau
Number Employees: 5,000
Parent Co: George Weston Ltd.
Type of Packaging: Consumer, Food Service
Brands:
Weston
Ready Bake
Wonder
D'Italiano
Gadova
Gadova MultiGo
Country Harvest
All But Gluten
Fourn,e
Flat Oven
ACE
Colonial

13692 **Westport Locker LLC**
707 S West St
Westport, IN 47283-9116
812-591-3033
877-265-0551
www.westportnow.com
Meat products including beef, lamb and pork
Owner: Ben Davis
Estimated Sales: $3-5 Million
Number Employees: 5-9

13693 **Westport Rivers Vineyard**
417 Hixbridge Rd
Westport, MA 02790-1316
508-636-3423
Fax: 508-636-4133 800-993-9695
retail@westportrivers.com
www.westportrivers.com
Wine jellies, wine ketchup, wine mustards, wines, champagne
Owner: Bob Russell
Vice President: Carol Russell
Owner: Carol Russell
Sales Director: Jan Potts
bob@westportrivers.com
Estimated Sales: $1.5 Million
Number Employees: 10-19
Number of Brands: 2
Number of Products: 15
Square Footage: 10800
Type of Packaging: Private Label
Brands:
Westport Farms Sparkling
Westport Farms Specialty Foods
Westport Farms White & Rose
Westport Rivers Vine

13694 **Westtown Brew Works**
236 Schefflers Rd.
Westtown, NY 10998
www.westtownbrewworks.com
Farm-brewed wheat ales
Founder/Owner: Rich Coleman
Number of Brands: 1
Number of Products: 5
Type of Packaging: Consumer, Private Label

13695 **Westway Trading Corporation**
365 Canal Street
Suite 2900
New Orleans, LA 70130
701-282-5010
Fax: 701-281-2695 www.westway.com
Processor and exporter of molasses
CEO: Gene McClain
CFO: Thomas Masilla
Estimated Sales: $5-10 Million
Number Employees: 10-19
Type of Packaging: Bulk

13696 **Westwood Winery**
11 E Napa St # 3
Suite 3
Sonoma, CA 95476-6765
707-933-7837
Fax: 707-935-3286 info@westwoodwine.com
www.westwoodwine.com
Wines
Founder: Umbert Urch
Co-Owner: Betty Urch
Estimated Sales: $210,000
Number Employees: 5-9
Brands:
Stanley's
Westwood Winery

13697 **Wet Planet Beverage**
7 Purcell Court
Monachie, NJ 07074
201-288-1999
www.wetplanet.com
Root beer, spring water and colas; also, sports, guaranas and ginseng drinks
CEO: Robert Clamp
CFO: Katherine Butkevich
Number Employees: 5-9
Type of Packaging: Consumer, Food Service
Brands:
Blubotol
Blue Bottle
Cronk 2 O
First Tec
Jolt
Jolt-Cola
Pirate's Keg
Pirates Keg
Xtc

13698 **Wetherby Cranberry Company**
3365 Auger Rd
Warrens, WI 54666
608-378-4813
Fax: 608-378-3157 wetherby@mwt.net
www.freshcranberries.com
Cranberries
Owner: Nodji Van Wichen
Owner/CEO: James Van Wychen
Estimated Sales: $.5-1 million
Number Employees: 1-4
Type of Packaging: Consumer, Bulk
Brands:
Wetherby

13699 **Weyand's Fishery**
471 Biddle Ave
Wyandotte, MI 48192-2703
734-284-0400
Fax: 734-284-2671 800-521-9815
www.weyandfish.com
Fresh, frozen and batter-dipped fish
Owner: David Blume
david@weyandfish.com
Vice President: Carolyn Smith
Plant Manager: Richard Weyand
Estimated Sales: $5932554
Number Employees: 5-9
Square Footage: 64000
Type of Packaging: Consumer, Food Service, Private Label, Bulk

13700 **Weyauwega Star Dairy**
109 N Mill St
P.O. Box 658
Weyauwega, WI 54983
920-867-2870
888-813-9720
www.wegastardairy.com
Cheese manufacturer, specializing in Parmesan, Asiago and Romanao; sting cheeses and curds; meat products; spreadable cheeses. Provide private label, shredding and packing services.
President: James Knaus
Contact: Gerard Knaus
gknaus@wegastardairy.com
Estimated Sales: $12.5 Million
Number Employees: 75
Number of Brands: 7
Type of Packaging: Consumer, Food Service, Private Label, Bulk
Brands:
Weyauwega
Star Dairy
Alacreme
Scott's
Lakeside's
Rose Cottage
Fontina Cheese

13701 **Whaler Vineyard**
6201 Old River Rd
Ukiah, CA 95482-9657
707-462-6355
Fax: 707-462-6353 www.whalervineyard.com
Wines
President: Russ Nyborg
whalerzin@pacific.net
CFO: Tara Larwood
VP Marketing/VP Operations: Ann Nyborg
Estimated Sales: Less Than $500,000
Number Employees: 1-4
Type of Packaging: Private Label
Brands:
Flagship Shiraz
Flagship Zinfandel
Whaler Vineyard Flag

13702 **Whaley Pecan Co Inc**
1113 S Brundidge Blvd
Troy, AL 36081
334-566-3504
Fax: 334-566-9336 800-824-6827
info@whaleypecan.com www.whaleypecan.com
Processors of shelled pecans and some exports
Owner: Bob Whaley
whaleypecan@bellsouth.net
Estimated Sales: $5,000,000
Number Employees: 10-19
Square Footage: 160000
Type of Packaging: Consumer, Food Service, Bulk
Brands:
Whaley's
Whaley's Fancy Shelled

13703 **Wharton Seafood Sales**
43505 Belt Highway
PO Box 440
Paauilo, HI 96776-0440
808-776-1087
Fax: 877-591-8944 800-352-8507
Seafood
Owner/President: Bailey Wharton
wharton@aloha.net
Estimated Sales: Less than $100,000
Number Employees: 1-4

13704 **What's Brewing**
138 W Rhapsody Dr
San Antonio, TX 78216-3104
210-308-0062
Fax: 210-308-8883 877-262-7311
info@sacoffeeroasters.com
www.sacoffeeroasters.com
Coffee roasters
Owner: Tony Chbeir
tony@sacoffeeroasters.com
VP: Antoine Chebeir
Secretary/Treasurer: Pauline Chebeir
Estimated Sales: Less Than $500,000
Number Employees: 1-4

13705 Wheat Montana Farms Inc
10778 US Highway 287
Three Forks, MT 59752-9518
406-285-3614
Fax: 406-285-3749 800-535-2798
info@wheatmontana.com
www.wheatmontana.com

Grain, flour, bread
President: Dean Folkvord
Marketing Director: Rita DeAngelis-Kockl
National Sales Manager: Dan Scott
Estimated Sales: $5-10 Million
Number Employees: 100-249
Type of Packaging: Consumer, Food Service, Private Label, Bulk

13706 Wheeling Coffee & SpiceCo
13 14th St
Wheeling, WV 26003-2833
304-232-0141
Fax: 304-232-0162 800-500-0141
www.wheelingcoffeeco.com

Roast coffee and spices
President: Mary Martin
whgcoffee@wheelingcoffeeco.com
CEO: Stephanie Ann Lokmer
Estimated Sales: $5-9.9 Million
Number Employees: 10-19
Type of Packaging: Consumer, Food Service, Bulk
Brands:
Paramount Coffee

13707 Whetstone Candy Company
1 Dolphin Drive
St. Augustine, FL 32080
904-825-1700
Fax: 904-825-1750
sales@whetstonechocolates.com
www.whetstonechocolates.com

Candy and confectionery
President: Virginia Whetstone
Estimated Sales: $500,000 Thousand
Number Employees: 5
Number of Brands: 1
Brands:
Wheatstone

13708 Whetstone Chocolates
1 Dolphin Dr
St Augustine, FL 32080-4530
904-825-1700
Fax: 904-824-0436 877-261-7887
www.whetstonechocolates.com

Manufacturers, sells, and distributes chocolate, candy and gum products in the North American and worldwide confectionery markets.
Owner: Jose Lopez
CEO: Philip Terranova
VP Sales: Tom Fox
sales@whetstonechocolates.com
Number Employees: 10-19
Other Locations:
Sweetworks
Buffalo NY
Sweetworks
Toronto, Canada
Brands:
Niagara Chocolates
Oak Leaf Confections
Whetstone Candy

13709 Whipped Pastry Boutique
37 Richards Street
Brooklyn, NY 11231
718-858-8088
info@whippedpastryboutique.com
whippedpastryboutique.com

Tarts, pastries, breads, cakes and cookies
President & Founder: Michelle Tampakis
michelle@whippedpastryboutique.com
Estimated Sales: $1-3 Million
Number Employees: 10-20
Type of Packaging: Food Service, Private Label
Brands:
Whipped Pastry Boutique

13710 Whistler Brewing Company
1045 Miller Creek Road
Whistler, BC V0N 1B1
Canada
604-731-2900
Fax: 604-932-7293 tours@whistlerbeer.com
http://www.whistlerbeer.com

Processor and exporter of ale and lager
President: Trevor Khoe
Estimated Sales: F
Number Employees: 100-249
Type of Packaging: Consumer, Food Service

13711 Whistler Brewing Company
1045 Millar Creek Rd.
Whistler, BC V0N1B1
Canada
604-962-8889
www.whistlerbeer.com

Beer
President: David Beardsell
CFO: George Tetreau
Sales/Marketing: Brian Keast
General Manager: Eric Spence
Estimated Sales: $2.5 Million
Number Employees: 10-19
Number of Brands: 18
Number of Products: 18
Square Footage: 40000
Type of Packaging: Consumer, Food Service
Brands:
Albino Rhino Ale
Black Bear Ale
Brown Bear Ale
Brown Island Bitter
Hemp Cream Ale
Jow Stiff's Spiked Rootbeer
Polar Bear Ale
Rethink Beer

13712 Whitaker & Assoc Architects
1794 Charline Ave NE
Atlanta, GA 30306-3128
404-266-1265
Fax: 678-285-0547

Wholesale food manufacturing, dairy, beverage, bakery, meat, poultry, ingredients
Owner: Peggy Whitaker
Estimated Sales: Less Than $500,000
Number Employees: 1-4

13713 Whitcraft Winery
36 S Calle Cesar Chavez # A
Santa Barbara, CA 93103-3680
805-730-1086
Fax: 805-730-1086 info@whitcraftwinery.com
www.whitcraftwinery.com

Wines
Owner: Chris Whitcraft
cwhitcraft@whitcraftwinery.com
Estimated Sales: Less Than $500,000
Number Employees: 1-4
Number of Brands: 1
Number of Products: 12
Square Footage: 10000
Brands:
Whitcraft Winery

13714 White Camel Foods Group
333 16th St
Carlstadt, NJ 07072-1921
201-848-1215
info@whitecamelfoods.com
www.whitecamelhummus.com

Hummus
President: Glenn Rice
Number Employees: 2-10
Brands:
White Camel

13715 White Cap Fish Market
120 Main St # 1
Islip, NY 11751-3431
631-277-6577
Fax: 631-277-6578 info@whitecapfish.com
www.whitecapfish.com

Seafood including tuna
Owner: V Russo
Manager: Vinny Russo
info@whitecapfish.com
Estimated Sales: $1-3 Million
Number Employees: 20-49

13716 White Cloud Coffee
5089 Alworth St
Suite A
Boise, ID 83714
208-322-1166
Fax: 888-229-3249 888-229-3249
orders@whitecloudcoffee.com
www.whitecloudcoffee.com

Roasted coffee
CEO: Jerome Eberharter
Director Marketing: Ron Thompson
VP Sales/Operations: Roger Daub
Estimated Sales: $5-10 Million
Number Employees: 20-49
Brands:
Buckaroo
Cowboy
Kona Island

13717 White Coffee Corporation
18-35 38th Street
Long Island City, NY 11105
718-204-7900
Fax: 718-956-8504 800-221-0140
info@whitecoffee.com www.whitecoffee.com

Cocoa, coffee, tea, gelatin, soup mixes and bases
President: Carole White
Executive Vice President: Jonathan White
Vice President: Gregory White
Plant Manager: Tom Tolfree
Estimated Sales: $18,800,000
Number Employees: 100-249
Brands:
Melitta
Parker House
White House

13718 White Fence Farm
1376 Joliet Rd
Romeoville, IL 60446-4078
630-739-1720
Fax: 630-739-4466 wffchicago@yahoo.com

Poultry
President: Laura Hastert
wffchicago@yahoo.com
Estimated Sales: $5-10 Million
Number Employees: 250-499

13719 White Hall Vineyards
5282 Sugar Ridge Road
Crozet, VA 22932
434-823-8615
tastingroom@whitehallvineyards.com
www.whitehallvineyards.com

Wines
Co-Owner: Antony Champ
Co-Owner: Edith Champ
Contact: Michael Panczak
mpanczak@comclin.net
Estimated Sales: $3-5 Million
Number Employees: 5-9

13720 White House Foods
701 Fairmont Avenue
Winchester, VA 22601
540-662-3401
Fax: 540-665-4671 tbastas@nfpc.com
www.whitehousefoods.com

Apple products including apple juice, apple sauce, vinegar and apple slices.
Chairman & CEO: David Gum
VP of Food Service Div.: Mark Thomas
Brand Sales: Dave Durden
Director Private Label Retail: Charlie Wollbrinck
Type of Packaging: Consumer, Food Service, Private Label, Bulk
Other Locations:
National Fruit Product Plant
Winchester NC
National Fruit Product Plant
Lincolnton NC
Brands:
Orchard Boy
Shenandoah
Skyland
White House

13721 White Label Yerba Mate Soda
New York, NY
info@whitelabelmate.com
whitelabelmate.com

Soda
Co-Founder: Jesse Rudoy
Brands:
White Label Yerba Mate Soda

13722 White Oak Farm and Table
161 Cross Highway
Westport, CT 06880
203-716-1577
Fax: 877-236-4528
whiteoakfarmandtable@gmail.com
www.whiteoakfarmandtable.com

Pasta sauces, mustards, ketchups, fruit preserves, apple sauces, salad dressings, grilling sauces, salsas and tapenades.
President: Renee Hooper
Marketing Communications Manager: Bastien Huet
Estimated Sales: $1.4 Million
Number Employees: 33
Brands:
White Oak Farm and Table(c)

13723 White Oak Farms Inc
343 Main St
Sandown, NH 03873-2101
603-887-2233
Fax: 603-887-2880 800-473-8869
www.macaroons.com
Macaroons
President: James Price
info@macaroons.com
Estimated Sales: Below $5 Million
Number Employees: 5-9
Brands:
St. Julien Macaroons

13724 White Oak Pastures
101 Church St.
Bluffton, GA 39824
229-641-2081
www.whiteoakpastures.com
Grassfed beef, goat, and lamb; pastured beef, pork, turkey, chicken, duck, goose, guinea, and rabbit; organic vegetables including cabbage and kale.
Owner: Will Harris
Year Founded: 1866
Number Employees: 155+
Type of Packaging: Consumer, Private Label

13725 White Oak Vineyards & Winery
7505 Highway 128
Healdsburg, CA 95448-8020
707-433-8429
Fax: 707-433-8446
tastingroom@whiteoakwinery.com
www.whiteoakwinery.com
Wines
Owner: Bill Meyers
Marketing Director: Jerry Baker
CEO: Don Grogh
Public Relations: Denise Gill
Production Manager: Steve Ryan
Estimated Sales: $180,000
Number Employees: 10-19
Type of Packaging: Private Label
Brands:
White Oak Chardonnay
White Oak Merlot
White Oak Sauvignon

13726 White Oaks Frozen Foods
2525 Cooper Ave
Merced, CA 95348-4313
209-725-9492
Fax: 209-725-9441
www.whiteoakfrozenfoods.com
Reduced Moisture (RM) vegetable ingredients processor.
President: Jack Sollazzo
CEO: Suvan Sharma
Vice President, Sales: Dan Wilkinson
Number Employees: 1-4
Parent Co: Cascade Specialties, Inc.

13727 White Packing Company
1965 Jefferson Davis Highway
Fredericksburg, VA 22401
540-373-9883
Bacon producer.
President: Karl White
Year Founded: 1971
Estimated Sales: $21 Million
Number Employees: 150
Type of Packaging: Consumer

13728 White Rock Products Corp
14107 20th Ave # 403
Flushing, NY 11357-3045
718-746-3400
Fax: 718-767-0413 800-969-7625
info@whiterockbev.com
www.whiterockbeverages.com
Processor and exporter of carbonated and noncarbonated soft drinks; also, mixes, iced teas, fruit drinks and spring water
President: Larry Bodkin
lbodkin@whiterockbev.com
Marketing Director: Larry Bodkin
Estimated Sales: Less Than $500,000
Number Employees: 5-9
Number of Brands: 6
Type of Packaging: Consumer, Food Service
Brands:
Chocolate Delight
Delicious
Kentucky Nip
Kentucky Nip Cherry Julep
La Cascade Del Cielo
Lemon Licious Lemonade
Punch 'n Fruity
Pure Rock
Rock Pop Carbonated Beverages
Sarsaparilla
Sioux City
Sioux City Sarsaparilla
Southern Swirl
Tnt Chocolate
Tealicious Iced Tea
Western Style Soft Drinks
White Rock
White Rock Orchards
Workout Energy Drinks

13729 White Rock Vineyards
1115 Loma Vista Dr
Napa, CA 94558-9752
707-257-7922
Fax: 707-257-7922
caves@whiterockvineyards.com
www.whiterockvineyards.com
Wines
Owner: Terra Albee
terra@whiterockvineyards.com
Winemaker: Christopher Vandendriessche
Estimated Sales: $450,000
Number Employees: 5-9
Brands:
White Rock Vineyards
White Rock Vineyards

13730 White Stokes International
3615 South Jasper Place
Chicago, IL 60609
773-523-7540
Fax: 773-523-0767 800-978-6537
Quality ingredients for bakery, confectionary, and ice cream. Founded in 1906.
President: Nicholas Tzakis
Vice President: George Tzakis
Number Employees: 26

13731 White Toque
11 Enterprise Ave N
Secaucus, NJ 07094-2505
201-863-6699
Fax: 201-863-2886 800-237-6936
r.rullo@whitetoque.com www.whitetoque.com
Importer of IQF fruits and vegetables and specialty and broad-line food service distributors with a wide selection of imported European high quality frozen and dry goods
Owner: Didier Amiel
Sales Director: Graham Taylor
d.amiel@whitetoque.com
Number Employees: 10-19

13732 White's Meat Processing
23867 N 7 Mile Rd
Fort Gibson, OK 74434-6237
918-478-2347
Beef, pork and lamb
Owner: Brad White
Estimated Sales: $490,000
Number Employees: 1-4
Type of Packaging: Consumer, Bulk

13733 White-Stokes Company
1821 North Clybourn
Suite 3
Chicago, IL 60609-1399
773-254-5000
Fax: 773-523-7445 800-978-6537
www.whitestokes.com
Pie fillings; also, marshmallow, butterscotch and bittersweet hot fudge toppings, nougats, caramel creams, pectin, coconut paste, etc
President/CEO: Nicholas Tzakis
VP: George Tzakis
Customer Relations: Melissa Pagan
Estimated Sales: $1400000
Number Employees: 20-49
Type of Packaging: Bulk

13734 WhiteWave Foods
1225 Seventeenth Street
Suite 1000
Denver, CO 80202
303-635-4000
Fax: 303-443-3952 800-488-9283
www.whitewave.com
WhiteWave Foods Company makes and sells branded plant-based foods and beverages, coffee creamers and beverages, and premium products.
President: Blaine E. McPeak
Chief Executive Officer: Gregg L. Engles
Chief Financial Officer: Kelly J. Haecker
Contact: Katie Hofmann
khofmann@linkedin.com
Number of Products: 40
Square Footage: 60000
Type of Packaging: Consumer
Brands:
Silk
Alpro
International Delight
Mini Moo's
Land O'Lakes Half & Half
Horizon Organic

13735 Whitecliff Vineyard & Winery
331 McKinstry Rd.
Gardiner, NY 12525
845-255-4613
www.whitecliffwine.com
Chardonnay, Riesling, Merlot, Malbec, Traminette, Ros,, other wine blends
Co-Founder/Co-Owner: Michael Migliore
Co-Founder/Co-Owner: Yancey Stanforth-Migliore
Year Founded: 1979
Number of Brands: 1
Number of Products: 19
Type of Packaging: Consumer, Private Label
Brands:
Whitecliff

13736 Whitehall Lane Winery
1563 Saint Helena Hwy S
St Helena, CA 94574-9775
707-963-9454
Fax: 707-963-7035 greatwine@whitehalllane.com
www.whitehalllane.com
Wines
Owner: Thomas Leonardini
greatwine@whitehalllane.com
Winemaker: Dean Sylvester
Estimated Sales: Below $5 Million
Number Employees: 10-19
Brands:
Whitehall Lane

13737 Whitehall Specialties Inc
36120 Owens St
P.O. Box 677
Whitehall, WI 54773
715-538-2326
888-755-9900
www.whitehall-specialties.com
Imitation cheese, cheese food slices, blended cheese products, dried, grated
President & CEO: Steve Snyder
CFO: Mike Berg
Director, International Sales: Federico Noltenius
Year Founded: 1994
Estimated Sales: $50-100 Million
Number Employees: 100-249
Number of Brands: 2
Square Footage: 50
Type of Packaging: Food Service, Private Label, Bulk
Brands:
Ridgeview Farms
Whitehall

13738 Whitewave Foods Company
12002 Airport Way
Broomfield, CO 80021
303-635-4000
Fax: 303-635-5504 www.whitewave.com
Dairy products
President: Blaine McPeak
SVP: Roger Theodoredis
Contact: James Blumberg
melissa.gillespie@gsk.com

Number Employees: 350

13739 Whitey's Ice Cream Inc
2525 41st St
Moline, IL 61265-5017
309-762-2175
Fax: 309-762-0053 888-594-4839
whiteys@whiteysicecream.com
www.whiteysicecream.com
Ice cream, ice milk, frozen yogurt and novelties
CEO: Elizabeth Knoche
eknoche@whiteysicecream.com
Owner/CEO: Jon Tunberg
Owner/VP: Jeffrey Tunberg
Human Resources Director: Kirsten Runburg
Operations Director: Scott Larson
Plant Manager: Gary Neer
Purchasing Manager: Tom Hendrickx
Estimated Sales: $7500000
Number Employees: 250-499
Square Footage: 100000
Type of Packaging: Consumer, Private Label

13740 Whitfield Foods Inc
1101 N Court St
Montgomery, AL 36104
334-263-2541
800-633-8790
www.whitfieldfoods.com
Maple products including butter, syrup, and honey; juices; vitamin waters; greem teas.
President & CEO: Joe Friday
VP, Quality & Technical Services: Ed Watkins
Estimated Sales: $23.9 Million
Number Employees: 100-249
Square Footage: 225000
Type of Packaging: Consumer, Food Service, Private Label
Brands:
Alaga
Plow Boy
Yellow Label

13741 Whitford Cellars
4047 E 3rd Ave
Napa, CA 94558
707-942-0840
Fax: 707-942-0840 www.whitfordcellars.com
Winery of chardonnay, pinot noir and syrah
Co-Owner: Duncan Haynes
Co-Owner: Patricia Haynes
Contact: Patricia Haynes
whitford@napanet.net
Estimated Sales: $500-1 Million appx.
Number Employees: 1-4
Number of Brands: 2
Number of Products: 4
Square Footage: 10000
Type of Packaging: Private Label
Brands:
Old Vines
Whitford

13742 Whitley Peanut Factory Inc
2371 Hayes Rd
Hayes, VA 23072-3516
804-642-7688
Fax: 804-642-7658 800-470-2244
customercare@whitleyspeanut.com
www.whitleyspeanut.com
Peanuts, almonds, cashews, mixed nuts, pecans and honey-roasted, brazil nuts and filberts; Virginia hams.
President: Craig Smith
VP Sales: James Scannell
Estimated Sales: $590000
Number Employees: 20-49
Type of Packaging: Consumer, Food Service, Private Label, Bulk
Brands:
Flavor Crunch
The Peanut Factory

13743 Whitney & Sons Seafood
13326 US Highway 19
Hudson, FL 34667-1658
727-869-3728
Fax: 727-862-8283
www.whitneyandsonseafoods.com
Seafood
Owner: Mark Whitney
marksr@whitneyandsonseafoods.com
Vice President: Mark Whitney
Estimated Sales: $5-10 Million
Number Employees: 20-49

13744 Whitney Foods Inc
15504 Liberty Ave
Jamaica, NY 11433-1038
718-291-3333
Fax: 718-291-0560 www.steubenfoods.com
Dairy products
President: Mike Brown
mbrown@steubenfoods.com
Marketing Director: Bill Masterson
VP Sales: Robert Zak
Marketing: Brian Lee
Estimated Sales: $2.5-5 000,000
Number Employees: 20-49
Brands:
Whitney Yogurt

13745 Whole Earth Bakery
130 Saint Marks Pl
Suite 1009
New York, NY 10009-5843
212-677-7597
Fax: 212-677-7067
Baked goods
Owner: Peter Slyvestri
Estimated Sales: $110,000
Number Employees: 1-4

13746 Whole Herb Co
19800 8th St E
Sonoma, CA 95476-3805
707-935-1077
Fax: 707-935-3447 sales@wholeherbcompany.com
www.berjeinc.com
Raw material supplier of herbs, spices, botanicals, spice blends, extracts and essential oils.
Manager: Holly Sherwood
Number Employees: 20-49
Square Footage: 50000
Parent Co: Berj, Inc.
Type of Packaging: Food Service, Bulk
Brands:
Jasmine Green
Mango Sunrise Tea
Peach Ambrosia
Somaguard
Somaguard Premium Grape Extract
Summer Berry Delight

13747 Whole Life Nutritional Supplements
13340 Saticoy St Ste B
North Hollywood, CA 91605
818-255-5357
Fax: 818-255-5307 800-748-5841
wholelife2@aol.com
Wholesaler/distributor and contract packager of vitamins
Manager: Rajen Patel
Director Sales: Irma Arroyo
Contact: Zenit Simmons
wholelife2@aol.com
Estimated Sales: $1-3 Million
Number Employees: 5-9
Square Footage: 10000
Type of Packaging: Private Label

13748 Whole in the Wall
S. Washington St. Binghamton
Binghamton, NY 13903
607-722-5138
Fax: 607-722-4237 www.wholeinthewall.com
Premium quality natural pesto, whole wheat bread and bagels, mushroom soup.
President: Elliot Fiks
CFO: Stacey Gould
Estimated Sales: Less than $500,000
Number Employees: 10-19
Type of Packaging: Consumer, Food Service, Private Label, Bulk

13749 WholeMe
3255 Spring St NE
Suite 150
Minneapolis, MN 55413-4530
612-247-9728
hello@wholeme.com
www.wholeme.com
Granola snacks: coconut clusters, peanut chocolate clusters and more.
Co-Founder & CEO: Mary Kosir
Director of Sales: Dennis Lider
Co-Founder & Chief Operating Officer: Krista Steinbach
Year Founded: 2013
Estimated Sales: $500,000
Number Employees: 1-4
Brands:
WholeMe(c)

13750 Wholesome Bakery
299 Divisadero St
San Francisco, CA 94117
415-343-5414
info@wholesomebakery.com
www.wholesomebakery.com
Gluten-free, dairy free, egg free, soy free, trans fat free & low glycemic baked goods
Founder/CEO: Mandy Harper
Year Founded: 2009

13751 Wholesome!
14141 Southwest Freeway
Suite 160
Sugar Land, TX 77478
800-680-1896
wholesomesweet.com
Fair trade, organic sweeteners.
CEO: Nigel Willerton
Contact: Dawn Archer
dawn.archer@wholesomesweet.com
Number Employees: 50
Parent Co: Arlon Group
Type of Packaging: Food Service, Bulk
Brands:
Sucanat
Wholesome Foods

13752 Wholesum Family Farms
2811-3 N Palenque Ave
Nogales, AZ 85621
520-281-9233
Fax: 520-281-4366 marketing@wh.farm
www.wh.farm
Organic produce including tomatoes, cucumbers, peppers, eggplants, and squash
Chief Commercial Officer: Ricardo Crisantes
VP Business Development: Steve Lefevre
Quality Assurance: Rebeca Rabago
Marketing Specialist: Joanna Jaramillo
Sales Manager: Kristina Luna
Year Founded: 1928
Number Employees: 50-99

13753 Wholly Wholesome
General Nathan Cooper House
401 Route 24
Chester, NJ 07930
908-879-0880
800-247-6580
info@runaton.com www.whollywholesome.com
Organic and gluten-free pie shells, cakes, pies, and waffles
President/Owner: Doon Wintz
Contact: Lisa Colao
lisa.colao@runaton.com

13754 Wiards Orchards Inc
5565 Merritt Rd
Ypsilanti, MI 48197-9367
734-390-9211
Fax: 734-482-7753 www.wiards.com
Cider and apples
President: Jay Wiard
Vice President: Brandon Wiard
Events Coordinator: Rose Timbers
Estimated Sales: Less Than $500,000
Number Employees: 5-9

13755 Wiberg Corporation
931 Equestrian Court
Oakville, ON L6L 6L7
Canada
905-825-9900
Fax: 905-825-0070 info@wiberg.ca
Unitized ingredients, seasoning blends, natural spices, ASTA quality pepper, phosphates, casings and food additives.
President: Richard Welzel
Estimated Sales: $13 Million
Number Employees: 75
Square Footage: 91020

13756 **Wichita Fish Co**
1601 W Douglas Ave
Wichita, KS 67213-4022
316-265-3474
Fax: 316-262-7770 www.wichitafishcompany.com
Owner: Larry Towns
info@360wichita.com
Estimated Sales: Less Than $500,000
Number Employees: 5-9

13757 **Wichita Packing Co Inc**
340 N Oakley Blvd
Chicago, IL 60612-2216
312-763-3965
Fax: 312-421-0696
information@wichitapacking.com
www.wichitapacking.com
Incorporated in 1963. Manufacturer, packer and distributor of pork ribs.
Owner: Robert Golang
robertgolang@wichitapacking.com
Executive Vice President: Mark Guon
Number Employees: 20-49

13758 **(HQ)Wick's Pies Inc**
217 SE Greenville Ave
PO Box 268
Winchester, IN 47394-1714
765-584-8401
Fax: 765-584-3700 800-642-5880
www.wickspies.com
Frozen pies and pie shells
President: Mike Wickersham
wickspies@wickspies.com
VP: Clark Loney
Quality Control: Sue Bone
Marketing/Sales: Marsha Welch
Purchasing: Steve Burge
Estimated Sales: $9 Million
Number Employees: 50-99
Square Footage: 80000
Type of Packaging: Consumer, Food Service
Brands:
Wick's

13759 **Wicked Crisps**
209 Citation Ct
Greensboro, NC 27409-9026
www.wickedcrisps.com
Crisps
Founder: Phil Kosak
Brands:
Chad's Carolina Corn
Wicked Crisps

13760 **Wicked Mix**
2321 Cantrell Rd
Little Rock, AR 72202
501-374-2244
www.wickedmixes.com
Snack mix
President: Stan Roberts
stan@wickedmixes.com
Founder & CEO: Brent Bumpers
Sales Manager: Alex Newberry Robinson
Estimated Sales: $0.5-2 Million
Number Employees: 2-10
Brands:
Wicked Mix(c)

13761 **Wicked Whoopies**
621 Maine Ave
Farmingdale, ME 04344
Fax: 207-582-7007 877-447-2629
customerservice@wickedwhoopies.com
www.wickedwhoopies.com
Baked goods: whoopie pies, cake

13762 **Wickers Food Products Inc**
501 Main St
Hornersville, MO 63855-8501
573-737-2416
Fax: 573-737-2113 800-847-0032
wickers09@att.net www.wickersbbq.com
Marinades
Manager: Misty Edmonston
Estimated Sales: Less Than $500,000
Number Employees: 5-9
Brands:
Wicker

13763 **Wicklund Farms**
3959 Maple Island Farm Rd
Springfield, OR 97477
541-747-5998
Fax: 541-747-7299
Processor and exporter of spiced green beans and bean relish
President: Larry Wicklund
Estimated Sales: $1600000
Number Employees: 6
Type of Packaging: Consumer, Food Service, Private Label, Bulk

13764 **Widman's Candy Shop**
116 S Broadway
Crookston, MN 56716-1955
218-281-1487
Chocolate-covered potato chips, peanut butter candy, cow pies
President: George Widman
Estimated Sales: Less Than $500,000
Number Employees: 1-4

13765 **Widmer's Cheese CellarsInc**
214 W Henni St
P.O.Box 127
Theresa, WI 53091-9803
920-488-2503
Fax: 920-488-2130 888-878-1107
info@widmerscheese.com
www.widmerscheese.com
Brick, colby cheese and extra sharp cheddar
President: Joseph Widmer
joew@widmerscheese.com
Estimated Sales: Below $5 Million
Number Employees: 10-19
Number of Brands: 1
Number of Products: 10
Square Footage: 64000
Type of Packaging: Consumer, Bulk
Brands:
Widmer's Cheese

13766 **Widmers Wine Cellars**
116 Buffalo St
Canandaigua, NY 14424
585-374-6311
Fax: 585-374-3266
Wines
President: Clenn Curtiss
COO: Jake Makepeace
Director Engineering: Mack Baxter
Estimated Sales: $20-50 Million
Number Employees: 100-249
Parent Co: Canandaigua Wine Company

13767 **Widoffs Modern Bakery**
129 Water St
Worcester, MA 01604-5080
508-752-7200
Fax: 508-756-6365
Bakery products
President: Jerry Ducas
Contact: Daniel Ducas
danducas@gmail.com
Estimated Sales: Below $5 000,000
Number Employees: 20-49
Brands:
Hearth

13768 **Widow's Mite Vinegar Company**
1309 P Street NW
Apt 6
Washington, DC 20005-3750
202-462-3669
Fax: 202-462-3669 877-678-5854
Salad dressing mix and Creole vinegar
President: John Allen Franciscus
Vice President: James Franciscus
Type of Packaging: Consumer, Bulk

13769 **Wiederkehr Wine CellarsInc**
3324 Swiss Family Dr
Altus, AR 72821-9037
479-468-2611
Fax: 479-468-4791 800-622-9463
info@wiederkehrwines.com
www.wiederkehrwines.com
Winery, producing white, rose, red, dessert, sparkling and alcohol-free wines.
WineMaster: Al Wiederkehr
wiederkehr@centurytel.net
President: Gary Wiederkehr
Vice President & National Sales Manager: Dennis Wiederkehr
Chief Financial Officer: Beverly Morrow
Estimated Sales: $4 Million
Number Employees: 50-99
Number of Brands: 1
Brands:
Wiederkehr Wine

13770 **Wiegardt Brothers**
3215 273rd Street
Nahcotta, WA 98637
360-665-4111
Fax: 360-665-4950
Manufacturer and exporter of fresh oysters
President: Fritz Wiegardt
Estimated Sales: $10-20 Million
Number Employees: 50-99
Type of Packaging: Consumer
Brands:
Jolly Roger
Tidepoint

13771 **Wilbur Chocolate Candy**
48 N Broad St
Lititz, PA 17543-1005
717-626-3249
Fax: 717-626-3487 888-294-5287
www.360lancaster.com
Chocolate confectionery
President: W Shaughnessy
Sales Director: Mickey Radigan
Estimated Sales: Less Than $500,000
Number Employees: 1-4
Parent Co: Cargill Foods

13772 **Wilbur Chocolate Candy**
45 N Broad St
Lititz, PA 17543
888-294-5287
chocolate@cargill.com www.wilburbuds.com
Chocolate and cocoa products including cocoa powder, ice cream coatings, chocolate drops, cream coatings, confectionary coatings, chocolate coatings, sugar-free chocolate, chocolate chunks, compound drops, cocoa butter and chocolateliquor
President: Bryan Wurscher
Estimated Sales: Less Than $500,000
Parent Co: Cargill Incorporated
Brands:
Wilbur

13773 **Wilbur Packing Company**
PO Box 3598
Yuba City, CA 95992
530-671-4911
Fax: 530-671-4905 sales@wilburpacking.com
www.wilburpacking.com
California prunes and walnuts
Owner/President/Sales Manager: Richard Wilbur
VP: Randy Baucom
Plant Manager: Brad Meinen
Number Employees: 350
Square Footage: 121300
Type of Packaging: Consumer

13774 **Wilcox Farms**
40400 Harts Lake Valley Rd
Roy, WA 98580
360-458-7774
customerservice@wilcoxfarms.net
www.wilcoxfarms.com
Eggs and milk.
Co-Owner: Andy Wilcox
Co-Owner: Brent Wilcox
Co-Owner: Chris Wilcox
Year Founded: 1909
Estimated Sales: $100-500 Million
Number Employees: 100-249
Type of Packaging: Food Service, Bulk
Brands:
Wilcox

13775 **Wild Aseptics, LLC**
1261 Pacific Avenue
Erlanger, KY 41018
859-342-3600
Fax: 859-342-3610 877-787-7221
www.wildflavors.com

Bulk blending, ingredient processing and filling for the food and beverage industries, including high acid liquid ingredients for use in ready-to-use concentrates
Owner: Dr Hans Peter
CEO/President: Michael Ponder
CFO: Gary Massie
Quality Control: Karen Eberts
Sales: Kevin Farrell
Contact: Billie Davila
bdavila@wildflavors.com
Plant Manager: David Devine
Purchasing: Luke Seibert
Number Employees: 50-99
Square Footage: 130000
Parent Co: Rudolf Wild GmbH & Co. KG
Type of Packaging: Consumer, Food Service, Private Label, Bulk

13776 **Wild Bill's Foods**
200 Knauss Ave
Martinsville, VA 24112
276-656-3500
Fax: 717-295-9722 800-848-3236
www.wildbillsfoods.com
Beef jerky
General Manager/Public Relations: Michael Kane
CFO: Steve Woelkers
CEO: Phil Clemmens
R&D/Quality Control: Greg Rhinier
Marketing Director: John Connell
Sales Manager: Teresa Musser
Operations/Plant Manager: Steve Groff
Production Manager: Armando Torres
Estimated Sales: $10-15 Million
Number Employees: 20-49
Parent Co: Clemens Family Coporation
Type of Packaging: Consumer, Bulk

13777 **Wild Blueberries**
PO Box 100
Old Town, ME 04468
207-570-3535
Fax: 207-581-3499 wildblueberries@gwi.net
www.wildblueberries.com
Frozen wild blueberries.

13778 **Wild Fruitz Beverages**
270 Ridings Way
Ambler, PA 19002-5246
718-909-0819
Fax: 973-742-7634 888-688-7632
sales@wildfruitz.com www.wildfruitz.com
Carbonated natural fruit juices
President, CEO: Trev Warshauer
trev@wildfruitz.com
Chairwoman: Sally Watt
CFO: Jon Jensen
Estimated Sales: $3.3 Million
Number Employees: 6
Brands:
Wild Fruitz

13779 **Wild Hibiscus Flower Company**
PO Box 246
Richford, VT 05476-0246
800-499-8490
northamerica@wildhibiscus.com
www.wildhibiscus.com
Hibiscus, rose and butterfly pea flowers and extracts, teas and salts
Founder & Managing Director: Lee Etherington
Co-Owner: Jocelyn Etherington
Estimated Sales: $4.4 Million
Number Employees: 44
Type of Packaging: Food Service, Private Label
Brands:
b'Lure
Heart Tee
Wild Hibiscus Flowers

13780 **Wild Hog Vineyard**
30904 King Ridge Rd
Cazadero, CA 95421
707-847-3687
Fax: 707-847-3160 info@wildhogvineyard.com
www.wildhogvineyard.com
Wine
Owner: Daniel Schoenfeld
Co-Owner: Marion Schoenfeld
Estimated Sales: Less Than $500,000
Number Employees: 1-4
Square Footage: 8000
Brands:
Wild Hog Vineyard

13781 **Wild Horse Winery & Vineyards**
1437 Wild Horse Winery Ct
Templeton, CA 93465-8449
805-434-2541
Fax: 805-434-3516 info@wildhorsewinery.com
www.wildhorsewinery.com
Winery, producing red and white wines.
Senior Winemaker: Todd Ricard
Winemaker: Kip Lorenzetti
Estimated Sales: $10-20 Million
Number Employees: 20-49
Number of Brands: 1
Type of Packaging: Consumer, Food Service
Brands:
Wild Horse

13782 **Wild Leaf Active Tea**
Sparta, NJ 07871
888-605-7564
Tea
Founder: Susan Parnell
Year Founded: 2016
Estimated Sales: Under $500,000
Number Employees: 11-50
Type of Packaging: Food Service
Brands:
WildLeaf

13783 **Wild Planet Foods**
1585 Heartwood Drive
Suite F
McKinleyville, CA 95519
707-840-9116
Fax: 707-839-3260 800-998-9945
elizabeth@wildplanetfoods.com
www.wildplanetfoods.com
Seafood
President/Owner: Bill Carvalho
CEO: Terry Hunt
Vice President, Co- Founder: Bill McCarthy
Sales: Justin Desiderio
Contact: Suzie Blaney
suzie@wildplanetfoods.com

13784 **Wild Poppy**
2355 Westwood Blvd
Suite 413
Los Angeles, CA 90064-2109
310-384-1004
info@wildpoppyjuice.com
wildpoppy.life
Poppy juice and soda
Co-Founder & CEO: George Bryson
Director of Sales: Michael Thorne
Operations: Steve Altes
Estimated Sales: $4.5 Million
Number Employees: 30-60
Brands:
Wild Poppy

13785 **(HQ)Wild Rice Exchange**
1277 Santa Anita Ct
Woodland, CA 95776
530-669-0150
Fax: 530-668-9317 800-223-7423
thewildriceexch@aol.com www.wildrice.org
Processor, importer and exporter of wild rice, products and blends including basmati, arborio, red gourmet rices, organic, brown and polished white; also, quick-cook, frozen and pre-mixed pilaf; large line of specialty beans
Manager: Carlos Zambello
Sales: Carlos Zambello
Production: Golnar Emam
Type of Packaging: Consumer, Food Service, Private Label, Bulk
Brands:
Gourmet Valley
Gourmet Valley Foods
Great Valley

13786 **Wild Things Snacks**
115 N 36th St
Unit B
Seattle, WA 98103-8633
720-231-9196
getskinnydipped.com
Chocolate covered almonds
Co-Founder: Val Griffith
Co-Founder & CEO: Breezy Griffith
Chief Sales Officer: Chrissy Haller
Estimated Sales: Under $500,000
Number Employees: 1-4
Brands:
Skinny Dipped almonds

13787 **Wild Thyme Cottage Products**
127-B Donegani
Pointe Claire, QC H9R 5E9
Canada
514-695-3602
Fax: 514-695-3602
Processor and exporter of jams, jellies, marmalades, relishes and chutneys
President: David Ranlings
Number Employees: 1-4
Number of Brands: 1
Number of Products: 50
Square Footage: 2800
Type of Packaging: Consumer, Food Service
Brands:
Wild Thyme Cottage Products

13788 **Wild Thymes Farm Inc**
643 County Route 403
Greenville, NY 12083-1703
518-966-5990
Fax: 845-266-8395 845-266-8387
www.wildthymes.com
Chutneys, salad dressings, fruit spreads, sauces/marinades, mustards, balsamic vinegars
Owner: Enid Stettner
Owner: Ann Stettner
ann@wildthymes.com
Quality Control: Enid Stettner
Marketing Director: Ann Stettner
Estimated Sales: Less Than $500,000
Number Employees: 1-4
Number of Brands: 1
Number of Products: 50
Type of Packaging: Consumer, Food Service, Private Label, Bulk

13789 **Wild West Spices**
P.O.Box 471
Cody, WY 82414-0471
307-587-8800
Fax: 307-587-8800 888-587-8887
Western-style spice blends, grilling spices and rubs, all natural dry mixes and dips
President: Bonnie Dallinger
b.dallinger@wildwestspices.com
Estimated Sales: Less than $500,000
Number Employees: 1-4
Brands:
Wild West Spices, Inc.

13790 **Wild Zora Foods**
325 E 4th St.
Loveland, CO 80537
970-541-9672
support@wildzora.com
www.wildzora.com
Paelo foods including meat & veggie snack bars, soups, teas, and prepared meals
Founder/Owner: Zora Tabin
Content Marketing Manager: Hanna Jensen
Wholesale Manager: Lorenzo Moreno Jr
Project Manager: Michael Arden Conley
Year Founded: 2014
Number Employees: 20-49

13791 **Wildcat Produce**
PO Box 5224
McGrew, NE 69353
308-783-2438
Fax: 308-783-1054
Cucumbers, green beans, onions, potatoes and pumpkins
President: Mike Chrisman
CEO: Ruftin Rahmig
Brands:
Wildcat Produce Garden

13792 **Wilde Brands**
2705 Spruce St.
Boulder, CO 80302
720-328-0843
hello@wildebrands.com
www.wildebrands.com
Chips made from chicken
Founder/CEO: Jason Wright
EVP/CFO: Jerome Metivier
National Marketing Manager: Braden Bingham

Year Founded: 2014
Number Employees: 5-9

13793 **Wildhurst Vineyards**
3855 Main St
P.O.Box 1310
Kelseyville, CA 95451-7430
707-279-4302
Fax: 707-279-1913 800-595-9463
www.wildhurst.com
Wines
President: Myron Holdenried
info@wildhurst.com
Winemaker: Mark Burch
Estimated Sales: Below $5 Million
Number Employees: 5-9
Type of Packaging: Private Label
Brands:
Reserve Chardonnay
Reserve Fume Blanc
Wildhurst Cabernet F
Wildhurst Chardonnay
Wildhurst Merlot
Wildhurst Zinfandel

13794 **Wildlife Cookies Co**
2025 Forest Ridge Rd
St Charles, IL 60174-1482
630-377-6196
Fax: 630-377-6321 sales@wildlifecookie.com
www.wildlifecookie.com
Cookies
President: Kenneth Smith
Estimated Sales: Less Than $500,000
Number Employees: 1-4

13795 **Wildly Delicious**
114A Railside Rd
Toronto, ON M3A 1A3
Canada
416-444-2011
Fax: 416-444-0010 888-545-9995
feedback@wildlydelicious.com
www.wildlydelicious.com
Dip, mix and spread, seasoning, spices and salts, premium oils and vinegars, gourmet sauces, pastes and mustards.
COO: Austin Muscat
CEO: Michelle Muscat
Operations: Austin Muscat

13796 **Wildly Organic**
99 Edison Blvd
Silver Bay, MN 55614
218-220-5030
Fax: 218-220-5030 800-945-3801
help@wildlyorganic.com www.wildlyorganic.com
Coconut oil, cacao powders, nuts, sweeteners, herbs, dressings, popcorn, rice and grains, spices, seasonings and teas.
President: Fischer Annette
CEO: Chris Toal
Chief Financial Officer: Thomas Noll
Vice President, Sales & Marketing: Roxana C. Lopez
Director of Operations: Alex Bethke
Year Founded: 2000
Estimated Sales: $5 Million
Number Employees: 25
Brands:
Wilderness Family Naturals

13797 **Wildtime Foods**
1061 W 2nd Ave
Eugene, OR 97402-4947
541-747-1654
Fax: 541-747-5067 800-356-4458
info@wildtime.com
Bulk and packaged cereals
President: Genevieve Averill
Marketing Director: Whit Hemphill
Manager: Patrick Schoenherr
patrick@grizzliesbrand.com
Estimated Sales: Below $5 Million
Number Employees: 20-49
Square Footage: 18000
Brands:
Grizzliesh

13798 **Wildtree**
55 Jefferson Blvd.
Warwick, RI 2886
800-672-4050
Fax: 615-884-3359 rc@wildtree.com
Grapeseed oils, dressings and sauces

13799 **Wildway**
10203 Kotzebue St
Suite 101
San Antonio, TX 78217-4447
512-677-9965
info@wildwayoflife.com
www.wildwayoflife.com
Granola
Co-Founder: Kyle Koehler
Co-Founder: Kelli Koehler
Estimated Sales: Under $500,000
Number Employees: 1-10
Brands:
Wildway

13800 **Wileman Brothers & Elliott Inc**
40232 Road 128
Cutler, CA 93615-2104
559-528-4772
Fax: 559-528-2456 info@mr-sunshine.com
Offers a full line of California citrus products
President: Frank Elliott III
CEO: Tommy Elliott
CFO: Brian Johnson
brian@mr-sunshine.com
Research & Development: Brad McCord
Quality Control: Raul Lopez
Sales Manager: Andrew Felts
Public Relations: Truman McGuire
Operations Manager: Manuel Guillen
Production Manager: Mark Savage
Plant Manager: Jon Hornburg
Estimated Sales: $930,000
Number Employees: 100-249
Square Footage: 16110
Type of Packaging: Consumer, Food Service, Private Label, Bulk

13801 **Wilhelm Foods**
8951 NE Saint Paul Hwy
Newberg, OR 97132-7132
503-538-2929
Fax: 503-538-1992
Fruit syrups and toppings
President: Charles Cox
Estimated Sales: $5-10 Million
Number Employees: 10-19

13802 **Wilke International Inc**
14321 W 96th Ter
Lenexa, KS 66215-4709
913-438-5544
Fax: 913-438-5554 800-779-5545
whw@wilkeinternational.com
www.wilkeinternational.com
Processor, importer, exporter and wholesaler/distributor of lactic acid, lactates, sports nutrition and dietary supplements
President: Wayne Wilke
wwilke@wilkeinternational.com
Director Administration: John Veazey
General Manager: James France
Estimated Sales: $5-10 Million
Number Employees: 10-19
Type of Packaging: Bulk
Brands:
Createam
Nutrasense

13803 **(HQ)Wilkins Rogers Inc**
27 Frederick Rd
Ellicott City, MD 21043-4759
410-465-5800
Fax: 410-750-0163 consumer@wrmills.com
www.wrmills.com
Processor and exporter of flour, corn meal, baking mixes, breading and batters
President: Samuel Rogers
Joint CEO: Samuel Rogers
Joint CEO: Tom Rogers
black@wrmills.com
CEO: Sam Rogers Jr
General Manager: James Koehnlein
Director Sales/Marketing: Steve Friesner
Director/Operations: Aaron Black
Estimated Sales: $27,900,000
Number Employees: 100-249
Square Footage: 180000
Type of Packaging: Consumer, Food Service, Private Label, Bulk
Brands:
Crutchfield
Indian Head
Raga Muffins
Spanglers
Velvetx
Washington

13804 **Wilkinson-Spitz**
705 Bronx River Road
Suite 204
Yonkers, NY 10704-1752
914-237-5000
Fax: 914-237-7295
Candy
Manager: Joel Miller
VP: Jim Koehlein
Sales Director: Leon Gleaves
Estimated Sales: $1-2.5 000,000 appx.
Number Employees: 1

13805 **Will-Pak Foods**
3350 Shelby Street
Suite 200
Ontario, CA 91764-5556
909-945-4554
Fax: 909-899-7822 800-874-0883
taste_adv@earthlink.net www.tasteadventure.com
All-natural foods including soups, beans, chilies, and side dishes
President: Gary Morris
Estimated Sales: $990,000
Number Employees: 10
Square Footage: 40000
Type of Packaging: Food Service, Private Label, Bulk
Brands:
Taste Adventure

13806 **Willamette Valley Pie Co**
2994 82nd Ave NE
Salem, OR 97305
503-362-8857
info@wvpie.com
www.wvpie.com
Pies, cobblers, packaged fruit, jams, and syrups
CEO: Jeff Dunn
CFO/Controller: Michael Schelske
QA Manager: Scott Lemke
Warehouse Manager: Tom Parsons
Year Founded: 1999
Number Employees: 50-99

13807 **Willamette Valley Walnuts**
475 NE 17th Street
PO Box 1007
McMinnville, OR 97128-3326
503-472-3215
Fax: 503-472-3294
wine@walnutcitywineworks.com
www.walnutcitywineworks.com
Processor and exporter of shelled walnuts and English walnut meats
Owner: Zac Spence
VP: Todd Heidgerken
Brand Manager: Andrew Minor
General Manager: John Gilpin
Winemakers: John Davidson
Estimated Sales: $500,000-$1 Million
Number Employees: 1-4
Type of Packaging: Consumer, Food Service, Private Label, Bulk

13808 **Willcox Meat Packing House**
3266 N Fort Grant Rd
Willcox, AZ 85643-3020
520-384-2015
Meat products including beef, lamb and pork
Owner: David Harris
Manager: Scott Harris
Estimated Sales: $870,000
Number Employees: 5-9
Type of Packaging: Consumer, Food Service, Private Label, Bulk

13809 **William Bounds**
3737 W. 240th Street
Torrance, CA 90505-6003
310-375-0505
Fax: 310-375-0756 800-473-0504
support@wmbounds.com
Spices, flavored chocolate, colored sugars.
President: Helen Bounds
Contact: Bill Bounds
billb@wmboundsltd.com

Estimated Sales: Below $5 Million
Number Employees: 20-49

13810 **William E. Martin & Sons Company**
55 Bryant Avenue
Suite 300
Roslyn, NY 11576
516-605-2444
Fax: 516-605-2442 mail@martinspices.com
www.martinspices.com
Processor, wholesaler/distributor, exporter and importer of spices, seasonings, salts, herbs and herbal supplements, seeds, powders and raisins. Wholesaler/distributor of dehydrated onion and garlic products, full line of ground spicesand bakery seeds
Owner: William Martin Jr
Contact: Martin Spencer
spencer@martinspices.com
Estimated Sales: $10-20 Million
Number Employees: 22
Number of Brands: 1
Square Footage: 60000
Type of Packaging: Bulk
Brands:
W.E.M.

13811 **William Grant & Sons**
300 Spectrum Center St
Suite 1150
Irvine, CA 92618
www.williamgrant.com
Distiller
CEO: Simon Hunt
CFO: Jim Heaton
Regional Director: Michel Aboujawdeh
michel.aboujawdeh@wgrant.com
Year Founded: 1887
Estimated Sales: $120 Million
Number Employees: 2,800
Type of Packaging: Private Label
Brands:
Armida
Balvenie
Berentzen
Borgianni
Brolio
Castello Di Volpaia
Clan Macgregor
Colombo
Dry Sack
Fonterutoli
Frangelico Liqueur
Glenfiddich
Grant's
Licor 43
Luis Felipe Edwards
Marques De Murrieta
McDowell
Metaxa

13812 **William Harrison Winery LLC**
1443 Silverado Trl S
St Helena, CA 94574-9798
707-963-8762
Fax: 707-963-4552 800-913-9463
info@harrisonvineyards.com www.whwines.com
Garlic dill pickles
Manager: Bruce Bradley
CEO: Lyndsey Harrison
Manager: Scott Morrison
Hospitality Manager: Shelly Zanoli
Winemaker: Scott Morrison
Estimated Sales: Less than $500,000
Number Employees: 1-4
Type of Packaging: Consumer
Brands:
Aceto D'Oro
Kirk and Glotzer New
New York Deli

13813 **William Harrison Winery LLC**
1443 Silverado Trl S
St. Helena
St Helena, CA 94574-9798
707-963-8762
Fax: 707-963-8762 info@whwines.com
www.whwines.com
Wines
Owner: William Harrison
Marketing/Sales: Rob Monaghan
Manager: Scott Morrison
Winemaker/General Manager: Bruce Bradley
Number Employees: 1-4

Brands:
Mario Perelli-Minetti
Miriam

13814 **William Hill Estate Winery**
1761 Atlas Peak Rd
Napa, CA 94558-1251
707-224-4477
Fax: 707-224-4484 707-265-3024
www.williamhillwinery.com
Winery
Contact: Celina Marcus
celina.marcus@williamhill.com
Head Winemaker: Mark Williams
Estimated Sales: $2.2 Million
Number Employees: 20-49
Number of Brands: 1
Parent Co: E&J Gallo Winery
Type of Packaging: Consumer, Food Service
Brands:
William Hill

13815 **William Poll Inc**
1051 Lexington Ave
New York, NY 10021-3294
212-288-0501
Fax: 212-288-2844 800-993-7655
wpollny@aol.com www.williampoll.com
Baked potato thins, dips, sauces
President: Stanley Poll
wpollny@aol.com
Estimated Sales: Less than $500,000
Number Employees: 5-9
Type of Packaging: Consumer
Brands:
Baked Potato Thins
Dip Indulgence

13816 **Williams & Bennett**
1815 Cypress Lake Dr.
Orlando, FL 32837
561-276-9007
sales@williamsandbennett.com
www.williamsandbennett.com
Cookies, barks, toffees, brittles, pretzels, marshmallows and graham crackers
Co-Founder: Becky Gardner
Co-Founder: Bill Gardner
Year Founded: 1992
Estimated Sales: $10-20 Million
Number Employees: 2-10
Type of Packaging: Food Service, Private Label
Brands:
Nutter Butter
Oreo

13817 **Williams Candy Co**
1230 Perry St
Chesapeake, VA 23324-1334
757-545-9311
Candy
Owner: Lillie Williams
Estimated Sales: $220,000
Number Employees: 5-9

13818 **Williams Candy Company**
18 Main St
Somerville, MA 02145
617-776-0814
Fax: 617-776-0816
Chocolate candy
President: Ron Cataldo
Estimated Sales: Below $5 000,000
Number Employees: 5-9
Type of Packaging: Bulk

13819 **Williams Institutional Foods**
1325 Bowens Mill Rd SW
Douglas, GA 31533-3933
912-384-5270
Fax: 912-384-0533 info@williams-foods.com
www.williams-foods.com
Groceries, meat, frozen foods, bakery goods, equipment and general merchandise
President/Sales Manager: Craig McCrary
CEO/Purchasing: Bob Williams
bobwilliams@williams-foods.com
Marketing: Karen Williams
Sales: George Smith
Year Founded: 1951
Estimated Sales: $37000000
Number Employees: 50-99

13820 **Williams Pork**
551 Joe Brown Hwy N
Chadbourn, NC 28431-7202
910-654-0204
Fax: 910-628-0081 910-654-0204
www.williamsbluehut.com
Bacon, hams, sausages, pork chops, ribs

13821 **Williams Selyem Winery**
7227 Westside Rd
Healdsburg, CA 95448-8357
707-433-6425
Fax: 707-431-4862 contact@williamsselyem.com
www.williamsselyem.com
Wines
Manager: Bob Cabral
contact@williamsselyem.com
Proprietor: Kathe Dyson
Director of Marketing: Mark Malpiede
Director of Winemaking & General Manager: Bob Cabral
Winemaker: Lynn Krausmann
Assistant Winemaker: Mark Ray
Estimated Sales: $1-2.5 Million
Number Employees: 10-19
Brands:
Williams-Selym Winery

13822 **Williams-R J**
998 N Huron Rd
PO Box 249
Linwood, MI 48634-9219
989-697-5183
Fax: 989-697-4203 800-968-4492
dave@williamscheese.com
www.williamscheese.com
Cheese and cheese spreads
President, CEO, CFO: Michael Williams
mhw@williamscheese.com
Quality Assurance Manager: Toni Lorenz
Sales, Marketing & Public Relations: Pat Meehleder
Regional Head Of Sales: Dave Williams
Purchasing Director: Ladd Williams
Estimated Sales: $10-19 Million
Number Employees: 50-99
Number of Brands: 2
Square Footage: 16000
Brands:
Williams
Amish Country

13823 **Williams-R J**
998 N Huron Rd
Linwood, MI 48634-9219
989-697-5183
Fax: 989-697-4203 800-968-4462
mhw@williamscheese.com
www.williamscheese.com
Processed and flavored cheese
CEO: Michael H Williams
mhw@williamscheese.com
Marketing Manager: Jay Williams
Sales Director: Todd Williams
Operations Manager: Mike Williams Sr
Estimated Sales: $9 Million
Number Employees: 50-99
Square Footage: 80
Type of Packaging: Private Label
Brands:
Amish Country
Cheese Rounds and Bricks
Cheese Spreads
Williams

13824 **Williamsburg Chocolatier**
P.O.Box 1712
Williamsburg, VA 23187
757-253-1474
Fax: 804-966-9025 wmsbgchoc@aol.com
Confectionery products, pound cakes, chocolate lollypops, dessert toppings, fudge and seasonal chocolate specialties
Owner: Maryann Boho
Marketing: Lee Boho
Estimated Sales: Under 500,000
Number of Products: 50
Square Footage: 4800
Type of Packaging: Consumer

13825 **Williamsburg Winery LTD**
5800 Wessex Hundred
Williamsburg, VA 23185-8063
757-229-0999
Fax: 757-229-0911 wine@wmbgwine.com

Wines
President: Patrick Dufseler
pdufseler@wmbgwine.com
Estimated Sales: $3.7 Million
Number Employees: 50-99
Type of Packaging: Private Label
Brands:
Donmir Wine Cellars
La Donaings De Franc
Williamsburg Winery

13826 **Willie's Smoke House LLC**
562 S Main St
Harrisville, PA 16038-1626
724-735-4184
Fax: 724-735-4184 800-742-4184
www.smokedspecialtymeats.com
Hickory smoked meat products including ham, bacon, sausage, poultry, dried beef, jerky, pork loins, etc
Owner: John Mc Kee
williessmokehouse@gmail.com
Estimated Sales: $500,000 appx.
Number Employees: 5-9
Square Footage: 3800
Type of Packaging: Consumer

13827 **Willmar Cookie & Nut Company**
1118 U.S 12
Willmar, MN 56201-0088
320-235-0600
800-426-7845
www.gurleysfoods.com
Cookies and crackers. Salted and roasted nuts and seeds
Estimated Sales: $10-24.9 Million
Number Employees: 100-249
Number of Brands: 1
Square Footage: 140000
Type of Packaging: Private Label
Brands:
Gurley's

13828 **Willmark Sales Company**
33 Nassau Ave
Brooklyn, NY 11222-3132
718-388-7141
Fax: 718-963-3924
Processor and exporter of bakery ingredients
President: Robert Leibowitz
willmark01@aol.com
VP: Edward Leibowitz
Estimated Sales: $5-10 Million
Number Employees: 50-99

13829 **Willoughby's Coffee & Tea**
550 E Main St # 27
Branford, CT 06405-2948
203-481-1700
Fax: 203-481-1777 800-388-8400
www.willoughbyscoffee.com
Coffee
President: Barry Levine
CEO: Robert Williams
Manager: Merisa Mangano
merisa@willoughbyscoffee.com
Estimated Sales: $500,000-$1 Million
Number Employees: 10-19
Brands:
Willoughby's

13830 **Willow Foods**
7774 SW Nimbus Ave
Beaverton, OR 97008
503-641-6602
Fax: 503-641-6899 800-338-3609
info@luckyfood.com www.luckyfood.com
Chinese and Vietnamese cuisine, spring rolls, pot stickers and potato rolls.
Owner: Tammy Jo
CFO: Bonnie Tompkins
Sales Director: Peter Yu
Contact: Tanya Ramos
tammyjo@luckyfood.com
Estimated Sales: $1.35 Million
Number Employees: 20
Number of Brands: 1
Number of Products: 20
Square Footage: 40000
Type of Packaging: Consumer, Food Service, Private Label, Bulk
Brands:
Willow

13831 **Willow Tree Poultry Farm Inc**
997 S Main St # 2
Attleboro, MA 02703-6299
508-222-3621
Fax: 508-222-8258 info@willowtreefarm.com
www.willowtreefarm.com
Poultry products
President/CEO: Chester Cekala
CEO: Robert Arobian
rarobian@willowtreefarm.com
Estimated Sales: $14,500,000
Number Employees: 50-99

13832 **WillowOak Farms**
611 Hartless Road
Amherst, VA 24521
434-942-7104
Fax: 530-662-0907 888-963-2767
wiloakfarm@aol.com
www.willowoakfarmhorsetraining.com
All-natural hors d'oeuvre spreads, sauces and salad dressings
President: Kevin Sanchez
Research & Development: Massimo Di Sciullo
Director of Marketing: Kevin Sanchez
Contact: Willow Farm
millerfrm@gmail.com
Estimated Sales: $1-2.5 Million
Number Employees: 1-4
Number of Brands: 3
Number of Products: 30
Square Footage: 80000
Type of Packaging: Consumer, Food Service
Brands:
L'Ortolano
Willow Oak Farms

13833 **Willowcroft Farm Vineyards**
38906 Mount Gilead Rd
Leesburg, VA 20175-6721
703-777-8161
Fax: 703-777-8157 willowine@aol.com
www.willowcroftwine.com
Wine
Owner: Lewis Parker
willowwine@aol.com
Estimated Sales: Less Than $500,000
Number Employees: 1-4

13834 **Wilson Candy Co**
408 Harrison Ave
Jeannette, PA 15644-1997
724-523-3151
Fax: 724-523-5959 www.wilsoncandy.com
Boxed and bulk chocolates
President: Doug Wilson
VP: Kay Wilson
Production Manager: Rob Kane
Estimated Sales: $870,000
Number Employees: 10-19
Square Footage: 28800
Type of Packaging: Consumer, Private Label, Bulk
Brands:
Wunder Bar

13835 **Wilson's Fantastic Candy**
384 Greenway Rd
Memphis, TN 38117-4338
901-767-1900
Fax: 901-398-1375
Candy including caramels, chocolates, coconut, fudge, corn, bagged, fundraising, theater and vending; also, fat-free and sugar-free cookies and glazed nuts
Owner: Robert Wilson
VP/General Manager: Jerry Adams
Number Employees: 5-9
Square Footage: 60000
Parent Co: Kemmons Wilson Companies
Type of Packaging: Consumer, Bulk
Brands:
Wilson Foods

13836 **Wilsons Oysters**
1981 S Van Ave
Houma, LA 70363
985-857-8855
Fax: 985-857-8139 wilson@wilsonsoysters.com
Oysters
Owner: Toby Voisin
tobyvoisin@yahoo.com
Estimated Sales: $5-10 Million
Number Employees: 20-49

13837 **Wimberley Valley Winery**
2825 Lone Man Mountain Rd
Driftwood, TX 78619-9313
512-847-2592
Fax: 281-288-8298
Wines
Vice President: Dean Valentine
wimberleyvalleywinery@wvwtx.com
VP: Dean Valentine
Estimated Sales: $500,000-$1 Million
Number Employees: 5-9
Type of Packaging: Bulk
Brands:
Wimberley Valley

13838 **Winans Chocolates & Coffees**
121 West High Street
Piqua, OH 45356
937-381-0247
Fax: 937-773-2388 www.winanscandies.com
Candy
President: Joe Reiser
Estimated Sales: $10-20 Million
Number Employees: 20-49
Type of Packaging: Consumer

13839 **Winchell's Donut House**
18830 San Jose Ave
City Of Industry, CA 91748-1325
626-964-1478
Fax: 626-912-2779
wincustservdept@winchells.com
www.winchells.com
Donuts
IT Executive: Henry Lau
hlau@yumyumdonuts.com
Number Employees: 1000-4999

13840 **Winchester Cheese Company**
32605 Holland Rd
Winchester, CA 92596
951-926-4239
Fax: 951-926-3349
Gouda cheese
Manager: Jeff Floot
Estimated Sales: Less than $500,000
Number Employees: 5-9
Square Footage: 14600
Type of Packaging: Consumer, Food Service, Private Label, Bulk
Brands:
Cumin Gouda
Herb Gouda
Jalapeno Gouda
Mild Gouda
Sharp Gouda
Super Aged Gouda

13841 **Winchester Farms Dairy**
675 Rolling Hills Ln
Winchester, KY 40391-8102
859-745-5500
Fax: 859-745-5547 www.winchester.us
Milk including chocolate, 2%, whole and skim; also, buttermilk
President: Bill McCarthy
CFO: Mike McGuire
VP: Michael Schlotman
Manager: Bruce Abbot
bruce.abbot@kroger.com
Estimated Sales: $500,000-$1 Million
Number Employees: 100-249
Parent Co: Kroger Company
Type of Packaging: Consumer, Private Label
Brands:
Kroger

13842 **Windcrest Meat Packers**
1350 Scugog 3rd Line
Port Perry, ON L9L 1B3
Canada
905-985-7267
Fax: 905-985-9393 800-750-2542
Meat products including beef, pork, lamb, goat and veal
President: Victor Diminno
Estimated Sales: $1-2.5 Million
Number Employees: 10-19
Type of Packaging: Consumer, Private Label

13843 **Windmill Candies**
810 Prentice Street
Granite Falls, MN 56241
877-771-8892

Candy
President: Tom Aus
Vice President: Laurie Aus
Estimated Sales: Under $500,000
Number Employees: 6

13844 **Windmill Water Inc**
2042 Old US 66
P. O. Box 2174
Edgewood, NM 87015-6740
505-281-9287
Fax: 505-286-9669 Windmillwater@comcast.net
www.windmillwater.com
Bottled spring water
President: Leon Ricter
Plant Manager: Leon Ricter
Estimated Sales: Less Than $500,000
Number Employees: 5-9

13845 **Windsor Confections**
4632 Telegraph Ave
Oakland, CA 94609-2022
510-653-3703
Fax: 510-653-3755 800-860-0021
Chocolate confections including chocolate dipped strawberries and gift baskets
President: Jeff White
Estimated Sales: $5-10 Million
Number Employees: 10-19
Parent Co: California Autism Foundation
Brands:
Anytime Candy
Break Up
California Finest
Chewey Kisses
Chocolate Jollies
Hoopee Doops
My Selection
Old Fashioned
Patio Squares
Royal Gift
Smooth and Melties

13846 **Windwalker Vineyards & Winery**
7360 Perry Creek Rd
Somerset, CA 95684-9207
530-620-4054
Fax: 530-620-5224 windwalkerinfo@gotsky.com
www.windwalkervineyard.com
Wines
Owner: Jim Taff
windwalkervineyard@gotsky.com
Operations: Alanna Taff
Estimated Sales: More than $500,000
Number Employees: 5-9
Brands:
Windwalker

13847 **Windy City Organics**
3320 Commercial Ave.
Northbrook, IL 60062
800-925-0577
info@windycityorganics.com
www.windycityorganics.com
Chocolate, nut butters, snacks and supplements
CEO: Alex Malinsky
Social Marketing & Brand Communications: Anna Speaks
Sales & Account Management: Adam Fohrman
Estimated Sales: $3 Million
Number Employees: 25
Type of Packaging: Consumer, Private Label
Brands:
Sun Biotics
Rawmio
RawGuru
Dastony
Veggimins

13848 **Wine Country Chef LLC**
PO Box 1416
Hidden Valley Lake, CA 95461
707-322-0406
Fax: 800-306-2660
Organic spice blends and all natural marinades & sauces
President/Owner: Harold Imbrunetti
chef@winecountrychef.net
Estimated Sales: $250,000
Number Employees: 2
Number of Brands: 4
Number of Products: 4
Type of Packaging: Consumer, Food Service, Bulk
Brands:
Wine Country Chef Gourmet Marinade
Wine Country Chef Lemon Pepper Rub
Wine Country Chef Spiced Mustard
Wine Country Chief Spiced Bbq Rub

13849 **Wine Country Kitchens**
511 Alexis Ct
Napa, CA 94558-7526
707-252-9463
Fax: 707-252-9424 866-767-9463
info@winecountrykitchens.com
www.winecountrykitchens.com
Gourmet oils, wine vinegars, pasta suaces and salad dressings
Owner: Michele Channels
Controller: Debbie Azevedo
Vice President: D Mark Wilson
VP Business Development: Jack Harkins
Year Founded: 1995
Estimated Sales: $20-50 Million
Number Employees: 20-49
Type of Packaging: Private Label
Brands:
Napa Valley Barbeque Co.
Napa Valley Harvest
Wine Country Kitchens

13850 **Wine Country Pasta**
201 W Napa St
Sonoma, CA 95476-6643
707-935-1366
www.winecountry.com
Pasta
Owner: Zepe Devito
zdevito@winecountry.com
Estimated Sales: Below $5 000,000
Number Employees: 1-4

13851 **Wine Group**
315 Montgomery St
San Francisco, CA 94104
415-986-8700
Fax: 415-986-4305
Wines
Chairman: Arthur Ciocca
CEO: David Kent
Contact: Ashlee Bennick
ashlee.bennick@thewinegroup.com
Number Employees: 5-9
Type of Packaging: Consumer
Brands:
Franzia Wine
Glen Ellen
Mg Vallejo
Mogen David

13852 **Wine-A-Rita**
2011 Mall Drive
Suite 2
Texarkana, TX 75503
903-832-7309
Fax: 903-838-7803 info@wineglace.com
www.wineglace.com
Cocktail mixes
President: Donna Griffin
donna@wineglace.com
CEO: Judy Smith

13853 **Winfrey Fudge & Candy**
42 Newburyport Turnpike
Rowley, MA 01969-2106
978-948-7448
Fax: 978-948-7088 888-946-3739
info@winfreys.com www.winfreys.com
Chocolates and fudge
Owner: Chris Winfrey
Owner: Christine Winfrey
Estimated Sales: Below $5 Million
Number Employees: 10-19
Brands:
Winfrey's

13854 **Wing It Inc**
174 Queen St # 4f
Falmouth, MA 02540-3222
508-540-9860
Fax: 508-540-9861 Sales@Wingit.com
www.wingit.com
Buffalo wing sauce
President: Steven Robinson
sales@wingit.com
Estimated Sales: Less Than $500,000
Number Employees: 1-4
Type of Packaging: Consumer, Food Service, Private Label, Bulk
Brands:
Wing It

13855 **Wing Nien Food**
30560 San Antonio St
Hayward, CA 94544-7102
510-487-8877
Fax: 510-489-6666 ghall@wnfoods.com
www.wnfoods.com
Processor and packager of sauces, oils, salsa, mustard and syrups; exporter of organic oils and sauces; also, custom blending and packaging in portion packs, glass bottles and plastic containers available
Manager: Linda Lee
Manager: Margaret Liang
mliang@wnfoods.com
Plant Superintendent: Jon Choy
Estimated Sales: $10-20 Million
Number Employees: 20-49
Square Footage: 135000
Parent Co: US Enterprise Corporation
Type of Packaging: Consumer, Food Service, Private Label
Other Locations:
Wing Nien Co.
Vancouver BC

13856 **Wing Seafood Company**
1133 W Lake St
Chicago, IL 60607-1618
312-421-8686
Fax: 312-942-0391
Seafood
Owner: Wing Ng
Estimated Sales: $1.2 Million
Number Employees: 5-9

13857 **(HQ)Wing Sing Chong Company**
152 Utah Avenue
Suite 140
S San Francisco, CA 94080-6718
415-552-1234
Fax: 415-552-3812
Manufacturer, importer and wholesaler/distributor of Asian foods
Owner: Roberta Woo
Estimated Sales: $15 Million
Number Employees: 1-4
Square Footage: 150000
Brands:
Lantern

13858 **(HQ)Wing's Food Products**
50 Torlake Crescent
Toronto, ON M8Z 1B8
Canada
416-259-2662
Fax: 416-259-3414 custserv@wings.ca
www.wings.ca
Portioned controlled foods including ketchup, mustard, relish, vinegar, soy and plum sauce and steam cooked noodles; manufacturer of egg roll wrappers
President: Jennifer Chan
General Manager: Neal Lee
Finance Manager: Cynthia Lee
Number Employees: over 275
Parent Co: Wing's Food Products
Type of Packaging: Food Service, Private Label, Bulk
Other Locations:
Wing's Food Products
Edmonton AB
Brands:
Wing's

13859 **Wing-Time**
85 Exchange Street
Suite #330
Lynn, MA 01901
781-592-1069
Fax: 970-871-1215 info@wingtime.com
www.wingtime.com
Buffalo wing and barbecue sauces available in six varieties
President: Terence Brown
Estimated Sales: Below $5 Million
Number Employees: 1-4
Number of Brands: 1
Number of Products: 6
Type of Packaging: Consumer, Food Service, Private Label

13860 (HQ)Winger Cheese
P.O.Box 238
Towner, ND 58788
701-537-5463
Fax: 701-537-5854
Cheese
Owner: Pete Winger
Number Employees: 1-4
Type of Packaging: Food Service, Bulk
Brands:
Winger

13861 Wings Foods of Alberta Ltd
2959 Parsons Road
Edmonton, AB T6N 1A3
Canada
780-433-6406
Fax: 780-431-1026 www.wings.ca
Noodles, condiments and fortune cookies
President: Barry Lee
Sales Manager: Doug Petrie
Production Manager: Chris Hambley
Number Employees: 50-99
Square Footage: 340000
Type of Packaging: Private Label
Brands:
Pc
Wing's

13862 Wink Frozen Desserts
P.O. Box 111375
Stamford, CT 06911
516-323-5283
info@winkfrozendesserts.com
www.winkfrozendesserts.com
Fat free, sugar free ice cream
CEO: Gabriel Wolff
CMO: Jordan Pierson
Year Founded: 2012

13863 (HQ)Winmix/Natural Care Products
7466 Cape Girardeau Street
Englewood, FL 34224-8004
941-475-7432
Fax: 941-475-7432
Processor and exporter of soft serve ice cream and sorbets, meat analogs, fruit juice and beverage bases, low-fat replacers and nonfat mixes. Importer of juice and coffee bases.
Board of Directors: Winsor Eveland
Owner: Martha Efird
Estimated Sales: $100000
Number Employees: 2
Number of Products: 350
Square Footage: 8000
Type of Packaging: Consumer, Food Service, Private Label, Bulk
Brands:
Multy Grain Foods
Soy Flax 5000
Winmix

13864 Winn-Dixie Stores
5050 Edgewood Ct.
Jacksonville, FL 32254-3699
904-783-5000
800-967-9105
info@winndixie.com www.winndixie.com
Supermarket chain.
President/CEO, Southeastern Grocers: Anthony Hucker
Year Founded: 1925
Estimated Sales: $10 Billion
Number Employees: 41,000
Parent Co: Southeastern Grocers
Other Locations:
Manufacturing Facility
Baldwin FL
Manufacturing Facility
Jacksonville FL
Manufacturing Facility
Orlando FL
Manufacturing Facility
Miami FL
Manufacturing Facility
Hammond LA
Manufacturing Facility
Montgomery AL
Brands:
Astor
Thrifty Maid
Winn & Lovett
Winn-Dixie
Topcare
Paws
Fisherman's Wharf
Chex
Prestige
Valutime

13865 (HQ)Winning Solutions Inc
3810 Conflans Rd
Irving, TX 75061-3915
972-986-5355
Fax: 972-986-5337 800-899-2563
info@miracleofaloe.com www.miracleofaloe.com
Processor and exporter of aloe vera gel drinks, juice blends, etc
Owner: Jess Clarke
winninginc@aol.com
Estimated Sales: $500,000-$1 Million
Number Employees: 10-19
Square Footage: 8000
Type of Packaging: Consumer, Food Service
Other Locations:
Winning Solutions
Westport CT

13866 Winona Foods
1552 Lineville Road
Green Bay, WI 54313
920-662-2184
Fax: 920-662-2195 www.winonafoods.com
Cheese
President: Terry Steinmann
Marketing & Social Media: Nathan Meyer
Director of Human Resources: Chris Cohorst
Production Manager: Chad Koerten
Estimated Sales: $4-5 Million
Number Employees: 51-200
Type of Packaging: Consumer, Food Service

13867 Winona Packing Company
152 Highway 407
Winona, MS 38967
662-283-4317
Fax: 662-283-4799
Beef and pork; also, fresh and smoked sausage
President: Bill Graves Jr
Vice President: Vicky Stiemann
Estimated Sales: $10-20 000,000
Number Employees: 20-49
Type of Packaging: Consumer, Food Service

13868 Winsor SB Dairy
18 Clinton St
Johnston, RI 02919-4121
401-231-7832
Fax: 401-231-7832
Milk and dairy products
Owner: Albert Winsor
Estimated Sales: $2.5-5 000,000
Number Employees: 1-4

13869 Winter Harbor Co-Op Inc
23 Pendleton Rd
Winter Harbor, ME 04693-3233
207-963-5857
Fax: 207-963-7275
randy@winterharborlobster.com
www.winterharborlobstercoop.com
Whole fish and seafood
President: Michael Sargeant
Manager: Randy Johnson
Estimated Sales: $600,000
Number Employees: 5-9

13870 Winter Park Farm
4501 Howell Branch Rd
Winter Park, FL 32792-7359
407-671-5888
Cheese@WinterParkDairy.com
Dairy products
Estimated Sales: Less Than $500,000
Number Employees: 1-4

13871 Winter Sausage Manufacturing Company
22011 Gratiot Ave
Eastpointe, MI 48021
586-777-9080
Fax: 586-777-7996 800-321-2987
www.wintersausage.com
Sausages, premium deli meats and spiral hams. Proprietary and private label
President: Rosemary Wuerz
Founder: Eugene Winter
VP/Sales: Ron Eckert
R&D/Marketing: Dorianne Wuerz
Quality Control: Mary Ellen Menard
Sales Manager: Kevin McCauslin
Contact: Gary Taylor
wintersausage@aol.com
Production/Purchasing Director: Eugene Wuerz
Plant Manager: Greg Van Hazenbrouck
Estimated Sales: $4.7 Million
Number Employees: 40
Type of Packaging: Consumer, Private Label, Bulk
Brands:
Farmer Jack
Kroger
Lipary

13872 Winterbrook Beverage Group
2000 Schenley Place
Greendale, IN 47025-1593
812-537-7348
Bottled water
President: Raymond Smith
Brands:
Cascadia
Lacroix
Winterbrook

13873 Wintergreen Winery
462 Winery Lane
P.O. Box 648
Nellysford, VA 22958
434-361-2519
Fax: 434-361-1510 www.wintergreenwinery.com
Wine
Co-Owner: Jeff Stone
Co-Owner: Tamara Stone
Estimated Sales: $1-3 Million
Number Employees: 1-4

13874 Wisconsin Cheeseman
3650 Milwaukee Street
Madison, WI 53714-2399
608-837-5166
Fax: 608-837-5493 800-693-0834
customerservice@wisconsincheeseman.com
www.wisconsincheeseman.com
Food gifts company, products include; cheese, sausage, chocolates, fruitcakes, candy, nuts & snacks, sugar free items
CFO: Jay Singer
VP: Francis Cremer
VP Sales & Marketing: Bret Jenkin
Type of Packaging: Consumer, Food Service, Private Label, Bulk

13875 Wisconsin Dairyland Fudge Company
743 Superior Street
Wisconsin Dells, WI 53965
608-254-7771
Fax: 608-254-4859 www.dellsfudge.com
Dairy farm products
Manager: Roj Rosen
Estimated Sales: Below $5 Million
Number Employees: 20-49
Brands:
Dairyland
Swiss Made

13876 Wisconsin Farmers Union
117 W Spring St
Chippewa Falls, WI 54729-2391
715-723-5561
Fax: 608-943-6769 800-272-5531
info@wisconsinfarmersunion.com
www.midwestcsa.com
Aged, curd, fresh cheese; gift boxes are available
President: Sheri Reinhart
sheri.reinhart@alghs.k12.wi.us
Plant Manager/Production: Tim Tehl
Treasurer: Mark Liebaert
Vice President : Craig Myrhe
Estimated Sales: $500,000-$1 Million
Number Employees: 5-9
Brands:
Montforte

13877 **Wisconsin Milk Mktng Board Inc**
8418 Excelsior Dr
PO Box 182
Madison, WI 53717-1931
608-836-8820
Fax: 608-836-5822 800-589-5127
info@eatwisconsincheese.com
www.eatwisconsincheese.com
Cream cheese spreads; shredded mozzarella and cheddar cheeses
President: Jeff Laack
CEO: James Robson
VP: Mark Laack
Estimated Sales: $10-20 Million
Number Employees: 50-99
Square Footage: 50000
Type of Packaging: Consumer, Food Service, Private Label, Bulk
Brands:
Laack's Finest

13878 **Wisconsin Packaging Corp**
104 E Blackhawk Dr
PO Box 28
Fort Atkinson, WI 53538-1152
920-563-9363
Fax: 920-563-0222 www.wisconsinpackaging.com
Hamburger patties, chili and diced beef
President: Fred Negus
fnegus@wisconsinpackaging.com
VP Sales/Operations: Frank Vignieri
Plant Manager: Rick Chamber
Number Employees: 50-99
Square Footage: 280000
Type of Packaging: Consumer, Food Service, Private Label, Bulk

13879 **Wisconsin Specialty Protein**
222 West Washington Ave. # 250
Madison, WI 53703
info@teraswhey.com
Organic flavored whey protein powder; flavored fatty acid health oil
Founder: Tera Johnson
Number of Brands: 1
Type of Packaging: Consumer, Private Label
Brands:
tera's

13880 **Wisconsin Spice Inc**
478 S Industrial Park Rd
PO Box 190
Berlin, WI 54923-2241
920-361-3555
Fax: 920-361-0818 info@wisconsinspice.com
www.unclephilsmustard.com
Manufacturer and exporter of gourmet spices and herbs, seasoning blends, dry mustard products and prepared liquid mustards
President: Phillip Sass
wispice@wisconsinspice.com
VP Marketing: John Clausen
VP Sales: Phillips Sass
Estimated Sales: $7 Million
Number Employees: 20-49
Type of Packaging: Consumer, Food Service, Private Label, Bulk
Brands:
Uncle Phil's

13881 **Wisconsin Whey International**
N2689 County Road South
Juda, WI 53550-9714
608-233-5101
Fax: 608-934-1044
Processor and exporter of kosher and HALAL approved whey products including edible lactose and whey protein concentrate
President/CEO: Nicolas Hanson
Sales Manager: Doug Clairday
Number Employees: 50-99
Square Footage: 95600
Type of Packaging: Bulk
Brands:
Lactose Pharma
Wisconsin Whey International
Wpc 34
Xl 2000
Xl 440
Xl 480

13882 **Wisconsin Wilderness Food Products**
11 North Skoikie Hwy
Suite 207
Lake Bluff, IL 60044
847-735-8661
Fax: 847-735-8673 800-359-3039
Bread and dessert mixes including cranberry cinnamon, date nut and apple crisp; also, cranberry mustard and chutney, honey mustard and preserves
President: Margaret Gunn
Plant Manager: Christina Grohmann
Estimated Sales: $1000000
Number Employees: 10-19
Number of Brands: 2
Number of Products: 30
Square Footage: 84000
Type of Packaging: Consumer, Food Service, Private Label, Bulk

13883 **Wisdom Natural Brands-Uani**
1203 W San Pedro St
Gilbert, AZ 85233-2406
480-921-1373
Fax: 480-966-3805 800-899-9908
wisdom@wisdomnaturalbrands.com
www.wisdomnaturalbrands.com
Herbal teas
President: James May
jmay@wisdomnaturalbrands.com
Vice President: Steve May
Quality Control: Mike Small
Operations Manager: Mike Small
Estimated Sales: $1-3 Million
Number Employees: 20-49
Type of Packaging: Consumer, Private Label, Bulk
Brands:
La Merced Organic
Stevia Products
Sweet and Slender Natural Sweetener
Sweet Leaf
Wisdom Nutrition
Wisdom of the Ancients Herbal Teas

13884 **Wise Foods Inc**
228 Raseley St
Berwick, PA 18603
888-438-9473
www.wisesnacks.com
Pretzels, chips, cheese doodles, tortilla chips, dips, popcorn and pork rinds.
Controller & Director, Human Resources: Ken Krakosky
Year Founded: 1921
Estimated Sales: $20-50 Million
Number Employees: 500-999
Parent Co: Arca Continental
Type of Packaging: Consumer
Brands:
Bravos Tortilla Chips
Cheez Doodles
Cottage Cuts Potato Chips

13885 **Wise Mouth**
691 Main St
Warren, RI 02885
wisemouthtea.ma.us@gmail.com
www.wise-mouth.com
Tea
Owner & Founder: Lei Nichols
Brands:
Wise Mouth

13886 **Wish Farms**
P.O. Box 1839
Plant City, FL 33564
813-752-5111
info@wishfarms.com
wishfarms.com
An assortment of berries including strawberries, blueberries, backberries, and raspberries.
Owner: Gary Wishnatzki
VP, Marketing: Nick Wishnatzki
VP, Fresh Sales: James Peterson
VP, Accounting: Stephen Cramer
Year Founded: 1922
Type of Packaging: Private Label

13887 **Wishnev Wine Management**
2125 Oak Grove Rd Ste 120
Walnut Creek, CA 94598
925-930-6374
Fax: 925-930-6388
Wines
Owner: Sanford Wishnev
Estimated Sales: $300,000-500,000
Number Employees: 1-4
Type of Packaging: Private Label

13888 **Wisteria Candy Cottage**
39961 Old Highway 80
Boulevard, CA 91905
619-766-4453
800-458-8246
www.wisteriacandycottage.com
Candy
Owner: Dana Eascobellis
Co-Owner: LuzCelia Rankin
Estimated Sales: Less Than $500,000
Number Employees: 1-4
Type of Packaging: Private Label

13889 **Witness Tree Vineyard LTD**
7111 Spring Valley Rd NW
Salem, OR 97304-9777
503-585-7874
Fax: 503-362-9765 888-478-8766
info@witnesstreevineyard.com
www.witnesstreevineyard.com
Wines
CEO: Carolyn Devine
carolyn@witnesstreevineyard.com
Vice President: Dennis Devine
Marketing Manager: Carolyn Devine
Sales Director: William Rosser
Winemaker/Vineyard Manager: Steven Westby
Estimated Sales: $2.5-5 Million
Number Employees: 10-19
Type of Packaging: Private Label
Brands:
Witness Tree Vineyard

13890 **Wixon Inc.**
1390 E. Bolivar Ave.
St. Francis, WI 53235
414 769-3000
Fax: 414-769-3024 800-841-5304
service@wixon.com www.wixon.com
Manufacturer of food and beverage seasonings and flavor systems.
President: Peter Gottsacker
Chief Financial Officer: Peter Caputa
Year Founded: 1907
Estimated Sales: $100 Million
Number Employees: 100-249
Number of Brands: 3
Square Footage: 400000
Type of Packaging: Consumer, Food Service, Private Label, Bulk
Brands:
Wix-Fresh
Mag-nifique
Redi-Flow

13891 **Wixson Honey Inc**
4937 Lakemont Himrod Rd
Dundee, NY 14837-8820
607-243-7301
Fax: 607-243-7143 800-363-8209
www.wixsonhoney.com
Manufacturer and importer of honey including clover, buckwheat, orange, beeswax and fall flower
Owner: Jerald Howell
jerry@wixsonhoney.com
Estimated Sales: $3-5 Million
Number Employees: 5-9
Type of Packaging: Consumer, Food Service, Private Label, Bulk

13892 **Wizards Cauldron, LTD**
878 Firetower Road
Yanceyville, NC 27379
336-694-5665
Fax: 336-664-5284
Manufacturer and exporter of natural and organic salad dressing and sauces including barbecue, steak, soy, poultry, stir-fry, hot, table and vegetable
President: Sean Kearney
CEO: John Troy
Administration: Glenda Smith
Research & Development: Tina Toney
Quality Control: Jason Dawson
VP Sales and Marketing: Ron Rash
Contact: Steve Bailey
steve@wizardscauldron.com
Purchasing Manager: Sean Kearney

Number Employees: 5-9
Square Footage: 40000
Parent Co: Wizard's Cauldron
Type of Packaging: Consumer, Food Service, Private Label, Bulk
Brands:
Flavor of the Rainforest
Simply Delicious
Troys

13893 **Wockenfuss Candy Co**
6831 Harford Rd
Parkville, MD 21234-7716
410-483-4414
Fax: 410-485-6512 800-296-4414
info@WockenfussCandies.com
www.wockenfusscandies.com
Chocolate and old-fashioned candies
Manager: Wockenfuss Company
janice.wmotter@gmail.com
Number Employees: 100-249

13894 **Woeber Mustard Mfg Co**
1966 Commerce Cir
PO Box 388
Springfield, OH 45504-2012
937-323-6281
Fax: 937-323-1679 800-548-2929
raywoeber@woebermustard.com
www.woebermustard.com
Condiments and sauces including mustard, sandwich spreads, dips, vinegars, lemon juice, and garlic and horseradish products.
President: Ray Woeber
Vice President: Dick Woeber
Director, Quality Control: Randy Weyant
National Sales Manager: Wally Miller
Human Resources Manager: Judy Finnegan
Operations Manager: Christopher Woeber
Logistics Manager: Bob Sharp
Director, Purchasing: Nate Golden
Estimated Sales: $40 Million
Number Employees: 100-249
Number of Brands: 7
Type of Packaging: Consumer, Food Service, Private Label, Bulk
Brands:
Crowning Touch
Mayo Gourmet
Mister Mustard
Sandwich Pals
Simply Supreme Organic
Supreme Dips
Woeber's

13895 **Wohlt Cheese Corp**
1005 Orville Dr
P.O. Box 203
New London, WI 54961-9398
920-982-9000
Fax: 920-982-6288
Manufacturer of processed cheeses (including American cheese, cheese food, cheese spread and other cheese products); available in loaves and blocks, flavoured varities, custom blends and various melts. Offer shredding and dicingservices.
President: Marilyn Taylor
Quality Manager: Frederick Ladenburger
Production Manager: Mark Gelhausen
Estimated Sales: $19.6 Million
Number Employees: 50-99
Square Footage: 20000
Type of Packaging: Consumer, Food Service, Private Label, Bulk

13896 **Wohrles Foods**
1619 East St
Pittsfield, MA 01201-3857
413-442-1518
Fax: 413-442-6024 800-628-6114
jon@wohrlesfoods.com www.wohrlesfoods.com
Meat products, distribute food services
President: Walter Pickwell
info@wohrlesfoods.com
VP Marketing: Jon Pickwell
Sales Exec: John Pickwell
Estimated Sales: Less than $500,000
Number Employees: 20-49
Type of Packaging: Consumer, Private Label, Bulk

13897 **Wolf Canyon Foods**
27880 Dorris Dr Ste 200
Carmel, CA 93923
831-626-1323
Fax: 831-626-1325 info@wolfcanyon.com
www.wolfcanyon.com
Processor and exporter of freeze-dried fruits, vegetables, meat, seafood and dairy products
Founder: James Mercer
VP: Marybeth Frearson
Sales Manager: Carlos Forte
Estimated Sales: Under $500,000
Number Employees: 3
Square Footage: 320000
Type of Packaging: Bulk

13898 **Wolf Creek Winery**
2637 S Cleveland Massillon Rd
Barberton, OH 44203-6417
330-666-9285
Fax: 330-665-1445 800-436-0426
sara@wineryatwolfcreek.com
www.troutmanvineyards.com
Wine
Owner: Andy Troutman
andy@wineryatwolfcreek.com
Estimated Sales: $5-10 Million
Number Employees: 10-19
Number of Brands: 1
Number of Products: 15

13899 **Wolferman's**
2500 S Pacific Hwy
Medford, OR 97501-8724
800-798-6241
Fax: 800-999-7548 800-798-6241
service@wolfermans.com www.wolfermans.com
Fresh and frozen English muffins, crumpets and tea and toasting bread
President: Micheal Dubois
CFO: Shane Jarvis
CFO: Gary Strub
Contact: Sue Brown
sbrown@williamsfoods.com
Estimated Sales: $3-5 Million
Number Employees: 1-4
Square Footage: 440000
Parent Co: 1-800-Flowers.com
Type of Packaging: Consumer
Brands:
Charlie Trotter's
Wolferman's

13900 **Wolfgang Puck Food Company**
1250 4th Street
Suite 310
Santa Monica, CA 90401-1304
310-432-1350
Fax: 310-451-5595
Frozen California style pizzas, pastas, canned soups and gourmet specialities
President: Terry Hall
Number Employees: 1-4

13901 **Wolfies Roasted Nut Co**
1718 N Romick Parkway
Findlay, OH 45840
419-423-1355
info@wolfiesnuts.com
www.wolfiesnuts.com
Dry roasted and crisp-coated nuts including cashews, peanuts, almonds and mixes
President: Bill Wolf
Estimated Sales: Less Than $500,000
Number Employees: 11-50
Square Footage: 24000
Type of Packaging: Consumer, Food Service, Private Label

13902 **Wolfson Casing Corp**
700 S Fulton Ave
Mt Vernon, NY 10550-5014
914-668-5754
Fax: 914-668-6900 800-221-8042
Processor, exporter and importer of sausage casings.
CEO: Phiil Schartz
tschartz@dccasing.com
Executive VP: David Gordon
Estimated Sales: $26300000
Number Employees: 50-99
Square Footage: 40000

13903 **Wollersheim Winery**
7876 State Rd 188
Prairie Du Sac, WI 53578-0087
608-643-6515
Fax: 608-643-8149 800-847-9463
info@wollersheim.com www.wollersheim.com
Wines
President: Philippe Coquard
CFO: Jo Ann Wollersheim
Marketing Director: Julius Coquard
Operations Manager: Phil Coquard
Estimated Sales: Below $5 Million
Number Employees: 20-49
Type of Packaging: Private Label
Brands:
Wollersheim Winery

13904 **Wolverton Seafood**
PO Box 1721
Houlton, ME 04730-5721
506-276-4629
Fax: 506-276-1803
Seafood
Owner: Margaret Wolberton

13905 **Wonder Natural Foods Corp**
30 Blank Ln
Water Mill, NY 11976-2134
631-726-4433
Fax: 631-726-4433
Low fat, low calorie peanut butter spread
Owner: Stewart Lasdon
slx30@aol.com
Vice President: Stuart Lasdon
Estimated Sales: Under $500,000
Number Employees: 1-4
Type of Packaging: Private Label
Brands:
Peanut Wonder

13906 **Wonderful Citrus**
4000 E Goodwin Rd.
Mission, TX 78574
956-205-7300
contact.citrus@wonderful.com
www.wonderfulcitrus.com
Citrus fruit including grapefruit, manderins, lemons, limes, and oranges.
President: Zak Laffite
Number of Brands: 12
Type of Packaging: Private Label
Brands:
Wonderful Halos
Wonderful Sweet Scarletts
Paramount Citrus
Texas Grown Red Grapefuit
Ultimate
Kashu Gold Oranges
Gold Buckle Oranges
Satin Oranges
Blue Goose Minneolas
Belt Oranges

13907 **(HQ)Wonderful Pistachios & Almonds**
13646 Hwy 33
Lost Hills, CA 93249
661-797-6500
www.wonderfulpistachiosandalmonds.com
Grower and processor of almonds and pistachios.
President: Stewart Resnick
Co-Founder: Lynda Resnick
CFO: Mike Hohmann
VP, Domestic Sales: Michael Celani
Media Contact: Steven Bram
steven.bram@Wonderful.Com
Estimated Sales: $111 Million
Number Employees: 20-49
Square Footage: 15000
Other Locations:
Plant and Farming Facility
Lost Hills CA
Brands:
Everybody's Nuts
Paramount Farms
Sunkist

13908 **Wong Wing**
Florenceville-Bristol, NB E7L 1B2
Canada
866-622-2461
www.wongwing.ca
Frozen Chinese food

EVP: Peter Pope
Quality Assurance: Jeanette Sprague
Marketing/Sales: Shelly Bronnum
Number Employees: 100
Square Footage: 132000
Parent Co: McCain Foods Ltd.
Type of Packaging: Consumer, Food Service, Private Label, Bulk
Brands:
Belleisle

13909 **Wonton Food**
220-222 Moore St
Brooklyn, NY 11206-3744
718-628-6868
Fax: 718-628-1028 800-776-8889
goldenbowl@wontonfood.com
www.wontonfood.com
Producer of fortune cookies, eggroll and wonton skins, dry and fresh noodles including chow mein, lo mein, spinach and wonton; Importer of oriental canned and dry goods
President: Sing Lee
CEO: Norman Wong
CFO: Weilik Chan
Sales/Marketing Manager: Danny Zeng
Year Founded: 1984
Estimated Sales: $20-50 Million
Number Employees: 100-249
Type of Packaging: Consumer, Food Service, Private Label

13910 **Wonton Food**
1045 Firestone Parkway
La Vergne, TN 97086
615-501-8898
www.wontonfood.com
Producer of fortune cookies, eggroll and wonton skins, dry and fresh noodles including chow mein, lo mein, spinach and wonton; Importer of oriental canned and dry goods
Type of Packaging: Consumer, Food Service, Private Label

13911 **Wonton Food**
2902 Caroline St.
Houston, TX 77004
832-366-1280
www.wontonfood.com
Producer of fortune cookies, eggroll and wonton skins, dry and fresh noodles including chow mein, lo mein, spinach and wonton; Importer of oriental canned and dry goods
Type of Packaging: Consumer, Food Service, Private Label

13912 **Wood Brothers Inc**
3023 Augusta Rd
West Columbia, SC 29170-2864
803-796-5146
Fax: 803-796-5291 info@thewoodbrothers.com
www.woodbrothersfinefoods.com
Mayonnaise, barbecue and tartar sauces, mustard and salad dressings including Thousand Island, French, Italian, blue cheese and slaw
Vice President: Katrina Drew
kdrew@woodbrothersfinefoods.com
VP: Douglas Wood
Production Manager: James Wood
Estimated Sales: $110,000
Number Employees: 10-19
Type of Packaging: Food Service, Private Label, Bulk
Brands:
Capital
Cardinal
Carolina Chef
Glenwood
Holland

13913 **Wood Sugarbush**
N7845 170th St
Spring Valley, WI 54767-8101
715-772-4656
Fax: 715-772-4665 info@woodssugarbush.com
www.woodssugarbush.com
Certified organic maple syrup, cream and granulated sugar
President: Scott Wood
Partner: Scott Wood
Number Employees: 10-19
Number of Brands: 1
Number of Products: 4
Square Footage: 14000
Type of Packaging: Consumer, Food Service, Private Label, Bulk

13914 **Woodbine**
729 Pecan Point Rd
Norfolk, VA 23502-3416
757-461-2731
Fax: 757-461-4704
Beef and pork. Full distribution of food service items
President: Ray Lister
Production Manager: Aubrey Lister
Estimated Sales: $3-5 Million
Number Employees: 10-19
Type of Packaging: Food Service

13915 **Woodbury Vineyards**
3215 S Roberts Rd
Fredonia, NY 14063-9417
716-679-9463
Fax: 716-679-9464 866-691-9463
info@WoodburyVineyards.com
www.woodburyvineyards.com
Winery
President: Joseph Carney
Retail Sales Manager: Virginia Bragg
Manager: Lindsey Alfred
lindsey@woodburyvineyards.com
Estimated Sales: $1,700,000
Number Employees: 5-9
Brands:
Woodbury Vineyards

13916 **Wooden Valley Winery**
4756 Suisun Valley Rd
Fairfield, CA 94534-3114
707-864-0730
Fax: 707-864-6038 info@woodenvalley.com
www.woodenvalley.com
Wines
President: Adrienne Lanza
adrienne.lanza@woodenvalley.com
Vice President: Ron Lanza
Estimated Sales: $1-2.5 Million
Number Employees: 5-9
Brands:
Wooden Valley

13917 **Woodfield Fish & OysterCompany**
P.O.Box 259
Galesville, MD 20765-0259
410-897-1093
Fax: 410-867-3423
Packaged ice and oyster
Owner: Bill Woodfield
Treasurer: Shirley Day
Vice President: Bill Woddfield
Plant Manager: David Loftice
Purchasing Manager: Ray Hardesty
Estimated Sales: Less than $500,000
Number Employees: 1-4
Type of Packaging: Private Label
Brands:
Woodfield Fish & Oyster
Woodfield Ice

13918 **Woodie Pie Company**
110 S 13th Street
Artesia, NM 88210
575-746-2132
Baked goods including pies
President: D Balencia
Estimated Sales: $500,000-$1 Million
Number Employees: 1-4
Type of Packaging: Consumer
Brands:
Woodie Pie

13919 **Woodlake Ranch**
21730 Avenue 332
Woodlake, CA 93286
559-564-2161
Fax: 559-564-8120
Grower of olives
President: Everett Kracov
Manager: Randy Childrsh
Estimated Sales: Less than $300,000
Number Employees: 1-4
Type of Packaging: Food Service, Private Label, Bulk

13920 **Woods Smoked Meats Inc**
1501 Business Highway 54 W
Bowling Green, MO 63334-1030
573-324-2247
Fax: 573-324-2249 800-458-8426
Meats including ham, bacon, sausage, poulty, snack food, fresh sausage, exotic meats, game processing, cajun products, private labeling, federal inspection.
President: Ed Woods
wsmeats@yahoo.com
Co-Owner: Regina Woods
Estimated Sales: $5-10 Million
Number Employees: 10-19
Number of Brands: 2
Number of Products: 80
Square Footage: 64000
Type of Packaging: Consumer, Private Label, Bulk
Brands:
Sweet Betsy From Pike
Woods

13921 **Woodside Vineyards**
205 Constitution Dr
Menlo Park, CA 94025-1108
650-851-3144
Fax: 650-847-1490 info@woodsidevineyards.com
www.woodsidevineyards.com
Wines
Founder/President: Robert Mullen
bob@woodsidevineyards.com
Estimated Sales: $1,400,000
Number Employees: 5-9
Type of Packaging: Private Label
Brands:
Woodside Vineyards

13922 **Woodsmoke Provisions**
1240 Menlo Dr NW
Atlanta, GA 30318-4163
404-355-5125
Fax: 404-355-6850 www.woodsmoke.com
Salmon and trout
President: Mitchell Gallant
m.gallant@woodsmoke.com
Estimated Sales: $3-5 Million
Number Employees: 20-49

13923 **Woodstock Farms Manufacturing**
96 Executive Ave
Edison, NJ 08817
800-526-4349
www.woodstockfarmsmfg.com
Importer, processor, packager, and wholesale distributor of nuts, dried fruit, seeds, trail mixes, natural and organic products, and confections.
President: Bob Kaufman
VP, Sales & Customer Service: Matt Mellet
Square Footage: 100000
Parent Co: United Natural Foods
Type of Packaging: Consumer, Food Service, Private Label, Bulk
Brands:
Expressnacks
Woodfield Farms

13924 **Woodward Canyon**
11920 W Highway 12
Touchet, WA 99360-9710
509-525-4129
Fax: 509-522-0927 info@woodwardcanyon.com
www.woodwardcanyon.com
Wine
Owner: Rick Small
info@woodwardcanyon.com
Production Director: Rick Small
Estimated Sales: Below $5 Million
Number Employees: 5-9

13925 **Woodworth Honey & Bee Co**
8503 4th St SW
Halliday, ND 58636-9239
701-938-4647
Fax: 701-938-4657 bon@ndsupernet.com
www.ndsupernet.com
Processor and exporter of honey
Owner: Brent Woodworth
brentwoodworth@ndsupernet.com
Chief Executive Officer: Bruce Boynton
Estimated Sales: $10-20 Million
Number Employees: 10-19
Square Footage: 18000
Type of Packaging: Bulk

13926 **Woody's Bar-B-Q Sauce Company**
PO Box 66
Waldenburg, AR 72475-0066
870-579-2251
Fax: 870-579-2241 888-747-9229
Barbeque sauce
President: William Wood
CEO: Cecelia Wood
Estimated Sales: $300,000-500,000
Number Employees: 5-9
Number of Products: 7
Type of Packaging: Consumer, Food Service, Private Label, Bulk

13927 **Woolwich Dairy**
425 Richardson Road
Orangeville, ON L9W 4Z4
Canada
519-941-9206
Fax: 519-941-9349 877-438-3499
gerhard@woolwichnova.com
www.woolwichdairy.com
Goat's milk cheeses including cheddar, whole and crumbled feta, mozzarella, gouda, cream and brie
CEO: Tony Dutra
VP Marketing: Michael Domingues
VP Sales: Liz Long
Year Founded: 1983
Estimated Sales: $24 Million
Number Employees: 97
Number of Brands: 7
Number of Products: 109
Square Footage: 4000
Parent Co: Saputo
Type of Packaging: Consumer, Food Service, Private Label, Bulk
Brands:
Chevrai
Gourmet Goat
Madame Chevre

13928 **Worden**
7217 W Westbow Boulevard
Spokane, WA 99224-5668
509-455-7835
Fax: 509-838-4723 wordenwine@aol.com
Wine
President: Ken Barrett
CEO: Rebecca Chateaubriand
Estimated Sales: $1 000,000+
Number Employees: 10
Square Footage: 13000
Type of Packaging: Private Label, Bulk

13929 **World Art Foods**
702 S 53rd St
Temple, TX 76504-5113
254-774-8322
Fax: 254-773-7339 oneworld@vvm.com
Spreads, sauces, dressing and ketchup
President: Pat Guillen
Estimated Sales: $300,000-500,000
Number Employees: 5-9

13930 **World Casing Corp**
4706 Grand Ave
Maspeth, NY 11378-3007
718-628-3800
Fax: 718-628-5800 800-221-4887
casings@worldcasing.com www.worldcasing.com
Natural sausage casings
Owner: Irwin Feinstein
ifeinstein@wolfsoncasing.com
VP: Paul LoPiccolo
Estimated Sales: $2.5 Million
Number Employees: 20-49

13931 **World Cheese Inc**
178 28th St
Brooklyn, NY 11232-1604
718-965-1700
Fax: 718-965-0979
customerservice@worldcheeseco.com
www.worldcheeseco.com
World Cheese Company is the largest kosher cheese manufacturer in the United States.
Owner: Leo Thurm
lthurm@allkoshercheese.com
Year Founded: 1937
Number Employees: 20-49
Type of Packaging: Consumer, Food Service, Bulk
Brands:
Haolam
Ko-Sure
Migdal
Miller's
Schmerling
Taam Tov

13932 **World Citrus West**
130 W Santa Fe Avenue
Fullerton, CA 92832
714-870-6171
Fax: 714-871-4100
Processor and bottler of chilled citrus drinks and juices including orange and grapefruit
CEO: Stephen M Caruso
Sales Manager (Retail): Rod Adamson
Number Employees: 250-499
Parent Co: Florida's Natural Growers'
Type of Packaging: Consumer, Food Service, Private Label, Bulk
Brands:
Daily Sun
Donald Duck
Supersocco

13933 **World Confections Inc**
14 S Orange Ave # A
South Orange, NJ 07079-1754
718-768-8100
Fax: 718-499-4918 Info@worldconfections.com
www.worldconfections.com
Manufacturer and exporter of confectionery products including gum, bagged, bars, boxed chocolates, caramels, lollypops, jaw breakers, peppermint and lemon twists, seasonal, etc
President: Mathew Cohen
Contact: Devin Abbott
devina@worldconfections.com
Estimated Sales: $10 Million
Number Employees: 50-99
Type of Packaging: Consumer, Private Label, Bulk

13934 **World Cup Coffee & Tea**
1740 NW Glisan St
Portland, OR 97209-2225
503-228-5503
Fax: 503-228-3489 www.worldcupcoffee.com
Processor and exporter of coffee and teas; also, roasting and water filltration services available
Owner: Dan Welch
info@worldcupcoffee.com
Number Employees: 20-49
Square Footage: 50000
Type of Packaging: Consumer, Food Service, Bulk
Brands:
World Cup

13935 **World Famous Buffalo Wing Sauce**
PO Box 66
Buffalo, NY 14209-0066
716-912-9068
Fax: 716-853-2011 www.buffalowing.com
Produces buffalo wings, a variety of sauces, and gift novelty items.
Executive: Joanne Will
Estimated Sales: Below $5 Million
Number Employees: 6
Brands:
Frank & Teressa's Original Anchor
Frank & Teressa's Wing Sauce

13936 **World Flavors Inc**
76 Louise Dr
Warminster, PA 18974-1588
215-672-4400
Fax: 215-672-4405 www.worldflavors.com
Custom formulated, manufactured and packaged ingredients for food processors including liquid and ground spices, meat, poultry and seafood seasonings, flavors, breadings, salad dressings and meat binders, extenders and tenderizingcompounds
President: M Donna
donna_m@worldflavors.com
VP Sales: Thomas Holmquist
Estimated Sales: $4900000
Number Employees: 50-99
Type of Packaging: Food Service, Private Label, Bulk

13937 **World Ginseng Ctr Inc**
825 Kearny St
San Francisco, CA 94108-1303
415-362-2255
Fax: 415-362-0801 800-747-8808
info@worldginsengcenter.com
www.worldginsengcenter.com
Manufacturer and exporter of ginseng and frozen seafood
President: Raymond Chao
Manager: William Nghe
Treasurer: Jane Chao
Estimated Sales: Less Than $500,000
Number Employees: 1-4
Type of Packaging: Consumer, Food Service, Private Label, Bulk

13938 **World Harbors**
176 First Flight Dr
Auburn, ME 04210-9055
207-786-3900
Fax: 207-786-3900 800-355-6221
Gourmet specialty foods, sauces and marinades
President: Steven Arthurs
CFO: Karen Foust
Quality Control: Mike Murphy
Estimated Sales: $5-10 Million
Number Employees: 5-9
Parent Co: Angostura International
Type of Packaging: Consumer, Food Service
Brands:
Acadia Naturals
Angostura
World Harbors

13939 **World Herbs Gourmet**
165 Boston Post Rd
Old Saybrook, CT 06475
860-388-3781

13940 **World Nutrition, Inc.**
Scottsdale Seville
7001 N Scottsdale Rd
Scottsdale, AZ 85253-3666
480-921-1188
Fax: 480-921-1471 800-548-2710
customerservice@worldnutrition.info
www.worldnutrition.info
Processor and importer of vitamins, minerals, organic grains, fruits, vegetables and dehydrated fruits and vegetable juices
President: Ryuji Hirooka
CEO: Chuck Eberhardt
Marketing Manager: Robert Nisenfeld
Operations Executive: Andy Rodriguez
Plant Manager: Tony Negrete
Purchasing Agent: Rhonda Poe
Estimated Sales: $1.9 Million
Number Employees: 18
Square Footage: 34000

13941 **World Of Chantilly**
4302 Farragut Rd
Brooklyn, NY 11203-6520
718-859-1110
Fax: 718-859-1303 info@chantilly.com
www.chambordesserts.com
Kosher desserts including cakes, pies, brownies, tiramisu, tortes, etc
Owner: Daniel Faks
danny@chantilly.com
Owner/President: Alberto Faks
Estimated Sales: $1800000
Number Employees: 10-19
Square Footage: 40000

13942 **World Of Coffee**
328 Essex St
Stirling, NJ 07980-1302
908-647-1218
Fax: 908-647-7827 800-543-0062
www.worldofcoffee.biz
Coffee
Owner: Avi Greenfield
avigreenfield@worldofcoffee.biz
Estimated Sales: Less Than $500,000
Number Employees: 5-9

13943 **World Organics Corporation**
5242 Bolsa Ave Ste 3
Huntington Beach, CA 92649-1054
714-893-0017
Fax: 714-897-5677 plicata@prodigy.net

Vitamins, food supplements, herbal extracts and capsules and chlorophyll liquid and capsules
Owner: Paul Licata
CEO: Al Licata
Director of Sales: Bernie Lucich
Estimated Sales: Under $500,000
Number Employees: 12
Number of Brands: 4
Number of Products: 300
Square Footage: 16000
Type of Packaging: Private Label
Brands:
Natural's Concept
Nu-Vista
Poma Noni Berry
Seafood
Vita-Vista

13944 **World Spice**
223-235 Highland Parkway
Roselle, NJ 07203
908-245-0600
Fax: 908-245-0696 800-234-1060
sales@wsispice.com www.wsispice.com
Spices, seasonings, herbs and dehydrated vegetables
President: Bela Lowy
Vice President: J Lefbowitz
Estimated Sales: $2 Million
Number Employees: 5-9
Square Footage: 60000
Type of Packaging: Food Service, Bulk
Brands:
Wsi

13945 **World of Chia**
26310 Oakridge Dr
Suite 38
The Woodlands, TX 77380
800-251-6973
Fax: 281-609-0654 sales@worldofchia.com
www.worldofchia.com
Chia fruit spread
President: Fernando Ramirez Ocampo
Year Founded: 2009
Estimated Sales: $4-5 Million
Number Employees: 50
Parent Co: Space Enterprises
Brands:
World of Chia

13946 **World of Spices**
328 Essex St
Stirling, NJ 07980-1302
908-647-1218
Fax: 908-647-7827
Spices
President: Charles Newman
Estimated Sales: $2.5-5 000,000
Number Employees: 5-9

13947 **World's Best Donuts**
10 E Wisconsin St
P.O. Box 1272
Grand Marais, MN 55604
218-387-1345
bestdonuts@boreal.org
www.worldsbestdonutsmn.com
Donuts
Vice President: Stacey Hawkins
skizzle@boreal.org
Vice President: Stacey Hawkins
skizzle@boreal.org
Number Employees: 10-19

13948 **World's Finest Chocolate Inc**
4801 S Lawndale Ave
Chicago, IL 60632-3062
773-847-4600
Fax: 773-847-4006 888-821-8452
www.worldsfinestchocolate.com
Chocolate manufacturer serving the North American fundraising and promotional/gift markets.
Owner: Rodney Amison
rodney.amison@worldsfinestchocolates.com
CEO: Eddie Opler
Number Employees: 500-999
Type of Packaging: Consumer
Brands:
Queen Anne
World's Finest Chocolate

13949 **World's Greatest Ice Cream**
P.O.Box 190646
Miami Beach, FL 33119-0646
305-538-0207
Fax: 305-538-1026 info@thefrieze.com
www.thefrieze.com
Ice cream
President: Lisa Warren
Estimated Sales: $500,000-$1 Million
Number Employees: 10-19

13950 **Worldwide Specialties In**
2421 E 16th St Unit 1
Los Angeles, CA 90021
323-587-2200
Fax: 323-587-0050 800-437-2702
Gourmet specialty produce; importer and exporter of baby squash, French beans and fresh herbs
President: Horacio Belloflore
Treasurer: Nora Belloflore
Contact: Bruce Hoffman
bruce@californiaspecialtyfarms.com
Estimated Sales: $10,000,000
Number Employees: 126
Brands:
California Specialty Farms

13951 **Wornick Company**
4700 Creek Rd.
Cincinnati, OH 45242
800-860-4555
www.wornick.com
Convenience foods and military rations to restaurant chains, consumer product goods companies, and the U.S. government, including kids meals, sides, sauces, and breakfast.
President/Chief Executive Officer: John Kowalchik
VP Marketing/Business Development: Randy Newbold
Year Founded: 1970
Estimated Sales: $100-500 Million
Number Employees: 500-999
Square Footage: 600000
Type of Packaging: Food Service, Private Label
Other Locations:
Wornick Co.
McAllen TX

13952 **Worthington Foods**
P.O. Box CAMB
Battle Creek, MI 49016
614-885-9511
Fax: 614-885-2594 800-962-1413
Vegetarian foods
President/CEO: Dale Twomley
CFO: William Kirkwood
VP Sales: Jay Robertson
Merchandise Support Manager: Randy Wollert
Sales Director: David Schwantes
Public Relations: Veronica Peita
Estimated Sales: Less than $500,000
Number Employees: 1-4
Parent Co: Kellogg Company
Type of Packaging: Private Label

13953 **Worthmore Food ProductsCo**
1021 Ludlow Ave
Cincinnati, OH 45223-2687
513-559-1473
Fax: 513-559-0286 866-837-7687
worthmore@fuse.net www.worthmorefoods.com
Canner of food products including chili con carne, mock turtle soup, spaghetti sauce, pizza sauce and mushroom steak sauce
President: Phil Hock III
worthmore@fuse.net
Number Employees: 5-9
Type of Packaging: Consumer, Food Service, Private Label

13954 **Wow! Factor Desserts**
174 cree Road
Sherwood Park, AB T8A 3X8
Canada
780-464-0303
Fax: 780-467-3604 800-604-2253
www.wowfactordesserts.com
Baked goods including cheesecakes, cakes, tortes and pies for the food service sector
President: Bryan Yaakov
VP: Joanne Yaakov
Purchasing Manager: Dean McMullen
Estimated Sales: D
Number Employees: 50-99
Type of Packaging: Consumer, Food Service

13955 **Wrawp**
862 Towne Center Dr.
Suite A
Pomona, CA 91767
909-447-1800
855-972-9748
customerservice@wrawp.com www.wrawp.com
Organic, gluten-free veggie wraps, coconut wraps, and pizza crusts
Founder/CEO: Elena Semenova
Co-Founder: Kraig Dooman
Accounting: Iris Medina
Marketing & Brand Partnerships: Daniel Bauer
Operations Manager: Bioncia Martin
Production Manager: Anastasiia Lewis
Engineer: Vadim Kan
Year Founded: 2012
Number Employees: 20-49

13956 **Wrench Mints**
333 North Michigan Avenue
Suite 400
Chicago, IL 60601
312-496-3690
Fax: 312-496-3691
Mint candies
President: Angela Moran

13957 **Wright Brand Oysters**
9216 Faith St
Coden, AL 36523-3007
251-824-7880
Fax: 251-824-7880
Processor and distributor of oysters
President: Stanley Wright
Estimated Sales: $1-3 Million
Number Employees: 10-19

13958 **Wright Enrichment Inc**
6428 Airport Rd
PO Box 821
Crowley, LA 70526-1604
337-783-3096
Fax: 337-783-0724 800-201-3096
chris@wenrich.com www.thewrightgroup.net
Processor and exporter of custom vitamin, mineral and amino acid premixes, microencapsulates and direct compressed granulations
Owner: Grant Bergstrom
Marketing Manager: Chris Hebert
Regional Sales Manager: John Miller
grant@wenrich.com
Estimated Sales: $10-20 Million
Number Employees: 100-249
Type of Packaging: Bulk

13959 **Wright's Ice Cream Co**
3570 N State Road 63
Cayuga, IN 47928-8156
765-492-3454
Fax: 765-492-4915 800-686-9561
Ice cream and frozen desserts, dairy products, dried or canned, and candy and other confectionery products.
President: Ned Wright
Marketing Director: Ned Wright
Estimated Sales: Less Than $500,000
Number Employees: 1-4
Type of Packaging: Consumer
Brands:
Wright Delicious

13960 **Wrigley**
1132 W. Blackhawk St.
Chicago, IL 60642
312-794-6000
www.mars.com/made-by-mars/mars-wrigley
Gum, mints, hard and chewy candy and lollipops.
CEO: Martin Radvan
Year Founded: 1891
Estimated Sales: $5.3 Billion
Number Employees: 16,000
Number of Brands: 15
Parent Co: Mars, Incorporated
Brands:
Juicy Fruit
Wrigley's Spearmint
Altoids
Orbit
Extra
Starburst
Doublemint

Skittles
Freedent
5 Gum
Life Savers
Eclipse
Winterfresh
Big Red
Hubba Bubba

13961 Wunder Creamery
New York, NY
844-986-3371
www.wundercreamery.com
Yogurt made from low-fat curd cheese
Co-Founder: Kamilya Abilova
Number of Brands: 1
Number of Products: 6
Type of Packaging: Consumer
Brands:
WUNDER CREAMERY

13962 Wuollet Bakery
3608 W 50th St
Minneapolis, MN 55410-2014
612-922-4341
Fax: 612-922-4041 info@wuollet.com
www.wuolletbakery.com
Bakers of cakes, desserts, breads and pastries.
Owner: Jim Jurmu
info@woullet.com
CEO: Jim Jurmu
Operations Manager: Doug Wuollet
Estimated Sales: Less Than $500,000
Number Employees: 5-9

13963 Wurth Dairy
8805 Maple Avenue
Caseyville, IL 62232-2135
217-271-7580
Dairy
President: Albert Wurth
Estimated Sales: Under $500,000
Number Employees: 1-4

13964 (HQ)Wyandot Inc
135 Wyandot Ave
Marion, OH 43302-1595
740-383-4031
Fax: 740-382-5584 800-992-6368
www.wyandotsnacks.com
Private label snack foods including baked cheese puffs and chips including potato, tortilla, nacho and corn.
President & CEO: Rob Sarlls
CEO: Nick Chilton
nick.chilton@wyandotsnacks.com
CFO: Bob Wentz
Number Employees: 250-499
Type of Packaging: Consumer, Food Service, Private Label, Bulk
Brands:
Grandaddy's
Muchmates
Munchrights
Wyandot

13965 Wyandotte Winery LLC
4640 Wyandotte Dr
Gahanna, OH 43230-1258
614-476-3624
Fax: 614-934-5035 877-906-7464
info@wyandottewinery.com
www.wyandottewinery.com
Wines
Owner: Robin Coolidge
info@wyandottewinery.com
CEO: Joe Reardon
Marketing Director: Valerie Coolidge
Winemaker: Robin Coolidge
Estimated Sales: $500,000-$1 Million
Number Employees: 1-4
Brands:
Wyandotte Graystone Winery
Wyandotte Winery

13966 Wynnewood Pecan Company
301 S Washita Avenue
Wynnewood, OK 73098-7823
405-665-4102
Fax: 405-682-2503 800-892-4985
Pecans
President: Jeff Earles
Estimated Sales: Less than $500,000
Number Employees: 1-4

13967 Wysong Corp
7550 Eastman Ave
Midland, MI 48642-7809
989-631-0009
Fax: 989-631-8801 800-748-0188
wysong@wysong.net
www.grain-free-dog-food.com
Trail mixes, vitamins and potato chips; also, organic soy, wheat and rice baking items
Owner: Randy Wysong
wysong@wysong.net
Estimated Sales: $3100000
Number Employees: 20-49
Brands:
Wysong

13968 Xena International
910 S Division Avenue
Polo, IL 61064
815-946-2626
Fax: 815-946-2752
customerservice@xenainternational.com
www.xenainternational.com
Importer and manufacturer of dry and liquid ingredients.
President: Richard Sikorski
Contact: Nick Livingston
nick@xena.biz

13969 Ximena's Latin Flavors
21300 Hwy. 71 West
Suite 100
Spicewood, TX 78669
817-821-3246
ximena@latinflavors.net
Salsa, marinades, salad dressings and dips
Founder: Ximena Guerra
Brands:
Salsa Criolla

13970 Xochitl
17304 Preston Rd
Suite 1240
Dallas, TX 75252
214-800-3551
Fax: 214-800-3547 866-595-8917
info@salsaxochitl.com
Salsas, queso dips and corn chips
President: Carlos Salinas

13971 Xooz Gear
2831 El Dorado Parkway
Suite 103-139
Frisco, TX 75033
214-206-1222
info@sierramadrehoney.com
sierramadrehoney.com
Honey
General Manager: Alex Lopez
Type of Packaging: Food Service
Brands:
Sierra Madre Honey Co.

13972 Y & T Packing Co
1129 Taintor Rd
Springfield, IL 62702-1760
217-522-3345
Fax: 217-522-6395 www.turaskymeats.com
Packer/processor of meat
President: Joseph Turasky
Co-Owner: Joe Turasky
bradturasky@turaskymeats.com
Sales Manager: Tom Reilly
Estimated Sales: $1800000
Number Employees: 10-19
Type of Packaging: Consumer

13973 Y Not Foods
1322 SE 46th Lane
Suite 102
Cape Coral, FL 33904
608-222-2860
Fax: 239-205-6133 tony@ynotfoods.com
www.ynotfoods.com
Frozen sauce and smoothie chips for the prepared foods industry.
Contact: Aaron Steinmann
aarons@ynotfoods.com

13974 Y Z Enterprises Inc
1930 Indian Wood Cir # 100
Maumee, OH 43537-4001
419-893-8777
Fax: 419-893-8825 800-736-8779
info@almondina.com www.almondina.com
Processor and exporter of natural almond cookies including low-calorie, no-cholesterol, no-salt, kosher and parve
Owner: Yuval Zaliouk
CFO: Susan Zaliouk
Contact: Niwedita Bakshi
niwedita.bakshi@macys.com
Estimated Sales: Less Than $500,000
Number Employees: 5-9
Square Footage: 66000
Type of Packaging: Consumer
Brands:
Almondina

13975 Y Z Enterprises Inc
1930 Indian Wood Cir # 100
Maumee, OH 43537-4001
419-893-8777
Fax: 419-893-8825 800-736-8779
almondina@worldpantry.com
www.almondina.com
Cookies, biscuits. No artificial colors, flavors or preservatives.
Founder: Yuval Zaliouk
Contact: Mike Connors
mconnors@almondina.com
Estimated Sales: Less Than $500,000
Number Employees: 5-9
Type of Packaging: Consumer, Food Service, Private Label
Brands:
Almondina Biscuits

13976 Y&W Shellfish
8725 Us Highway 17
Woodbine, GA 31569
912-729-4814
Fax: 912-729-1143
Seafood
Owner: Richard Roberts

13977 Y.M.C. Corp.
481 W 26th St
Chicago, IL 60616
312-842-4900
Fax: 312-225-2262
Chinese foods and noodles
President: Harry Moy
harry.moy@ymcinc.com
Secretary: Tom Moy
Secretary: James Moy
Estimated Sales: $1,500,000
Number Employees: 17

13978 YB Meats of Wichita
798 N West St
Wichita, KS 67203
316-942-1213
Fax: 316-942-1419 www.yodermeatsks.com
Meat products
President: Ellsworth Kauffman
CEO: Erik Kaufmann
Marketing Director: Erik Kaufmann
Manager: Brad Warzeka
Estimated Sales: $500,000-$1 Million
Number Employees: 5-9
Type of Packaging: Consumer

13979 Ya-Hoo Baking Co
5302 Texoma Pkwy
Sherman, TX 75090-2112
903-893-8151
Fax: 903-893-5036 888-869-2466
customerservice@yahoocake.com
www.yahoocake.com
Dessert cakes, cobblers, cookies, cake and pie fillings, bread, frozen dough; custom work is our specialty
President: Chelsea Lanehart
clanehart@boongroup.com
R&D: Monette Wible
Director Sales/Marketing: David Millican
Sales Administrator: Tanda Wall
Purchasing Manager: Becky Roberts
Number Employees: 50-99
Square Footage: 180000
Type of Packaging: Consumer, Food Service, Private Label, Bulk

Brands:
Ya-Hoo!

13980 **Yai's Thai**
3047 Larimer St.
Suite 202
Denver, CO 80205
info@yaisthai.com
www.yaisthai.com
Thai curries, almond sauce, ginger lime sauce, garlic hot sauce, relish, and salsa. Products are paleo, vegan, and gluten free
Co-Founder/CEO: Leland Copenhagen
Co-Founder/COO: Sarah Hughes
VP Sales: Aaron Barnholt
Year Founded: 2016

13981 **Yakima Chief-Hopunion LLC**
306 Division St.
Yakima, WA 98902
509-453-4792
Fax: 509-453-1551 hops@ychhops.com
www.yakimachief.com
Processor and exporter of hops and hops products.
Contact: Stephen Carpenter
stephen.carpenter@hopunion.com
Year Founded: 1869
Estimated Sales: $140 Million
Number Employees: 20
Square Footage: 75000
Type of Packaging: Bulk

13982 **Yakima Craft Brewing Company**
2920 River Rd
Suite 6
Yakima, WA 98902-7332
509-654-7357
www.yakimacraftbrewing.com
Processor and exporter of ales, stout and porter
President: Jeff Winn
CEO/Founder: Chris McCoy
Director of Marketing: Sheldon Weddle
Contact: Chris Swedin
chris@yakimacraftbrewing.com
Estimated Sales: $500,000-999,999
Number Employees: 5-9
Square Footage: 162000
Type of Packaging: Consumer
Brands:
Bert Grant's

13983 **Yakima Fresh**
111 University Pkwy # 101
P.O. Box 1709
Yakima, WA 98901-1471
509-248-5770
Fax: 509-457-6137 steve.smith@yakimafresh.com
www.yakimafresh.com
Manufacturer and exporter of apples, cherries and pears
Quality Control Manager: Brian Mortimer
VP Marketing & Business Development: Tom Papke
Sales Manager: Randy Eckert
Manager: Steve Smith
steve.smith@yakimafresh.com
General Manager: Steve Smith
Estimated Sales: $2 Million
Number Employees: 20-49
Square Footage: 16452
Type of Packaging: Consumer, Food Service, Bulk
Other Locations:
Yakima Fresh Warehouse
Wapato WA
Yakima Fresh Warehouse
Zillah WA
Yakima Fresh Warehouse
Hood River OR

13984 **Yakima River Winery**
143302 West North River Road
Prosser, WA 99350-8228
509-786-2805
Fax: 509-786-3203
redwine@yakimariverwinery.com
Wine
Co-Owner: John Rauner
redwine@yakimariverwinery.com
Co-Owner: Louise Rauner
Winemaker: John Rauner
Estimated Sales: $500,000-$1 Million
Number Employees: 1-4
Type of Packaging: Private Label
Brands:
Yakima Valley

13985 **Yamamotoyama of America**
122 Voyager St
Pomona, CA 91768-3252
909-594-7356
Fax: 909-595-5849 info@yamamotoyama.com
www.yamamotoyama.com
Loose green, black, herbal, and flavored teas
Chairman: Kahei Yamamoto
Administration Manager/Purchasing: William Yu
Senior VP: Kazumi Ikeda
Contact: Kazuya Aburano
aburano@yamamotoyama.com
Estimated Sales: $20-50 Million
Number Employees: 100-249

13986 **Yamasa Corp USA**
3500 Fairview Industrial Dr SE
Salem, OR 97302-1154
503-363-8550
Fax: 503-363-8710 www.yamasausa.com
Soy sauce
President: Masura Ogura
Number Employees: 500-999
Square Footage: 83000
Parent Co: Yamasa Corporation
Type of Packaging: Consumer, Food Service, Bulk
Brands:
Yamasa

13987 **Yamasa Fish Cake Co**
515 Stanford Ave
Los Angeles, CA 90013-2189
213-626-2211
Fax: 213-627-9018 www.yamasafishcake.com
Fresh and frozen fish cakes
President: Frank Kawana
dwatanabe@yamasafishcake.com
Sales Exec: Doug Watanabe
Estimated Sales: $2,900,000
Number Employees: 20-49
Type of Packaging: Consumer, Food Service

13988 **Yamasho Inc**
750 Touhy Ave
Elk Grove Village, IL 60007-4916
847-981-9342
Fax: 847-981-9347 info@yamashoinc.com
www.yamashoinc.com
Japanese products
President: Kunio Iwadate
Estimated Sales: $20-50 Million
Number Employees: 5-9

13989 **Yamate Chocolatier**
320 Cleveland Ave
Highland Park, NJ 08904
732-249-4847
Fax: 732-545-4494 800-433-2462
Chocolate and confections
Co-Owner: Diane Yamate
Co-Owner: John Cunnell
Estimated Sales: $500,000-$1 Million
Number Employees: 1-4

13990 **Yamhill Valley Vineyards**
16250 SW Oldsville Rd
Mcminnville, OR 97128-8546
503-843-3100
Fax: 503-843-2450 800-825-4845
www.yamhill.com
Wines
President: Stephen Cary
info@yamhill.com
General Manager: David Anderson
Sales Exec: Sandi Kolb
Estimated Sales: $5-10 Million
Number Employees: 20-49
Brands:
Yamhill Wines

13991 **Yancey's Fancy**
857 Main Road
Corfu, NY 14036
www.yanceysfancy.com
Artisan cheese
Contact: Daniel Alidoust
dalidoust@yanceysfancy.com

13992 **Yankee Specialty Foods**
22 Fish Pier St W
Boston, MA 02210-2008
617-951-0740
Fax: 617-951-9907 800-688-9904
info@bayshorechowders.com
www.yankeespecialtyfoods.com
Processor and exporter of chili, soup, gumbo and chowder
Owner: Sara Giargiari
saragiargiari@yankeespecialtyfoods.com
Estimated Sales: $300000
Number Employees: 5-9
Type of Packaging: Consumer, Private Label
Brands:
Bay Shore

13993 **(HQ)Yarmer Boys Catfish International**
5192c Fannett Road
Beaumont, TX 77705-4202
409-842-1962
Fax: 409-842-1212 vsj42@aol.com
Shrimp
CEO: Glenda Jones
President: Vicky Jones
Sales Director: Trudy Verdine
Number Employees: 100-249
Type of Packaging: Private Label
Brands:
Fishermans Recs

13994 **Yaupon Tea**
143 Telfair Rd
Savannah, GA 31415-1604
912-596-1506
info@drinkasi.com
www.yaupontea.com
Tea
Founder: Lou Thomann
Accounting & Administration: Kelli Ventling
Lead Harvester: Elliott Day
Number Employees: 11-50
Brands:
ASI Yaupon Tea

13995 **Yaya's**
515 Acacia Avenue
Corona Del Mar, CA 92625-1906
949-675-7708
Organic and fat-free caramel popcorn
CEO/President: Bob George
VP: Patty George
Estimated Sales: Under $500,000
Number Employees: 1-4
Type of Packaging: Private Label

13996 **Yayin Corporation**
12725 Hatteras Street
Valley Village, CA 91607-1408
707-829-5686
Fax: 707-829-0993
Wines
President: Craig Winchell
Estimated Sales: $500,000-$1 000,000
Number Employees: 1-4

13997 **Ye Olde Pepper Co**
122 Derby St
Salem, MA 01970-5646
978-745-2744
Fax: 978-557-1017 866-526-2376
www.peppercandy.net
Hard and soft candy, chocolates
President: Robert Burkinshaw
candyman1806@aol.com
Estimated Sales: Below $5 Million
Number Employees: 20-49
Brands:
Black Jacks
Salem Gibralters

13998 **(HQ)Yellow Emperor Inc**
510 Conger St
Eugene, OR 97402-2718
541-485-6664
Fax: 541-485-0039 877-485-6664
office@yellowemperor.com
www.yellowemperor.com
Custom herbal extracts, ginseng, teas, tea concentrates and herbal honey
President: Andrew Levine
andy@yellowemperor.com

Estimated Sales: Less than $500,000
Number Employees: 1-4
Square Footage: 9600
Type of Packaging: Consumer, Private Label, Bulk
Brands:
Honeymoon
Inner Force
Oregon Natural Sportstonic
Phytotherapy
Wild American Herb Co.
Yellow Emperor

13999 **Yeomen Seafoods Inc**
30 Western Ave # 201
Gloucester, MA 01930-3664
978-283-7422
Fax: 978-283-7522
Whole frozen seafood
Owner: Tim Kennedy
yeomen@gis.net
Estimated Sales: $4.7 Million
Number Employees: 1-4

14000 **Yerba Prima**
740 Jefferson Ave
Ashland, OR 97520-3743
541-488-2228
Fax: 541-488-2443 800-488-4339
yerba@yerba.com www.yerbaprima.com
Processor and exporter of high quality dietary supplements, specializing in dietary fiber, internal cleansing aids and herbal products.
CEO: John Jung
yerba@yerba.com
Marketing Manager: Shelley Matteson
Estimated Sales: $5-10 Million
Number Employees: 10-19
Type of Packaging: Consumer, Private Label
Brands:
Aloe Falls
Yerba Prima

14001 **Yerba Santa Goat Dairy**
6850 Scotts Valley Rd
Lakeport, CA 95453
707-263-8131
Fax: 707-263-8131
Dairy products
Owner: Javier Salmon
Marketing Director: Chris Twohy
Contact: Christopher Twohy
yerbasanta44@hotmail.com
Estimated Sales: Below $5 000,000
Number Employees: 1-4

14002 **(HQ)Yergat Packing Co**
5451 W Mission Ave
Fresno, CA 93722-5074
559-276-9180
Fax: 559-276-2841 info@yergatpacking.com
www.yergatpacking.com
Processor and exporter of grapevine leaves
President: Kirk Yergat
Contact: Thao Duong
thaod@yergatpacking.com
Number Employees: 5-9
Parent Co: Yergat Packing Company
Type of Packaging: Consumer, Private Label

14003 **Yick Lung Company**
3015 Koapaka Street
Honolulu, HI 96819-1936
808-841-3611
Fax: 808-842-4763
Chips, candy and sunflower seeds
President: Patricia Ching
Chairman: Gertrude Lee
COO: Daniel King
Estimated Sales: $5-9.9 000,000
Number Employees: 20-49
Brands:
Yick Lung

14004 **Ying Leong Look Funn Factory**
1028 Kekaulike St
Honolulu, HI 96817-5007
808-537-4304
Ethnic foods
Owner: Fooying Chee
Estimated Sales: $2.5-5 000,000
Number Employees: 10-19

14005 **Ying's Kitchen**
485 Park Ave
Suite 1
Lake Villa, IL 60046-6547
847-403-7078
ying@yingskitchen.com
www.yingskitchen.com
Asian sauces, rubs and mixes
President & Owner: Ying Stoller
Estimated Sales: Under $500,000
Number Employees: 2-10
Type of Packaging: Food Service
Brands:
Ying's

14006 **Yo Mama's Foods**
9130 SW 51st Rd
Gainesville, FL 32608
support@yomamasfoods.com
www.yomamasfoods.com
Salad dressings, pasta sauces and marinades
Founder: David T. Habib
Year Founded: 2017
Estimated Sales: Under $500,000
Number Employees: 1-10
Type of Packaging: Food Service
Brands:
Yo Mama's

14007 **YoFiit**
167 Applewood Cr
Vaughan, ON L4K 4K7
Canada
647-997-7846
info@yofiit.com
yofiit.com
Fiber and energy bars; cereal; milk substitutes; quinoa; nutritional shakes.
Co-Founder: Marie Amazan
Year Founded: 2015
Number Employees: 5-9
Type of Packaging: Private Label

14008 **Yoakum Packing Co**
500 Front St
Yoakum, TX 77995-3009
361-293-3541
Fax: 361-293-2261 800-999-6997
www.farmpac.com
Smoked and cured pork, beef and poultry
President: Glen Kusak
glen@farmpac.com
Estimated Sales: $7,226,707
Number Employees: 50-99
Square Footage: 120000
Type of Packaging: Consumer, Food Service, Private Label, Bulk
Brands:
Farm Pac
Ranch Pac

14009 **Yoder Dairies**
1620 Mount Pleasant Rd
Chesapeake, VA 23322-1219
757-482-4068
Fax: 757-497-3510
Milk including standard homogenized, low-fat, skim, half/half and chocolate; also, cream buttermilk, whipping cream, eggs, eggnog, spring water and orange, grapefruit and apple juices, as well as ice cream.
President: Kenneth Miller
VP: L Miller
General Manager: Maria Dlah
Plant Manager: Lester Miller
Estimated Sales: $4.3 Million
Number Employees: 31
Type of Packaging: Consumer

14010 **Yogavive**
6 Beach Road #863
Tiburon, CA 94920
415-366-6226
Fax: 415-366-1750 info@yogavive.com
www.yogavive.com
Apple and mango chips in sweet and savory flavors. Certified Organic, Fair Trade, non-GMO, Gluten Free, Vegan, Kosher, and Halal.
President: Beau Giannini
beau@yogavive.com
VP Sales And Marketing: Michael Blicher
VP Operations: Richard Turner
Type of Packaging: Consumer

14011 **Yogi Tea**
950 International Way
Springfield, OR 97477
800-964-4832
yogitea.customerservice@yogiproducts.com
www.yogiproducts.com
Tea
Square Footage: 200000
Parent Co: Yogi Tea
Type of Packaging: Consumer, Food Service, Private Label, Bulk
Other Locations:
Tea Business Sales
Portland OR
Brands:
Ancient Healing Formulas
Golden Temple
Herb Technology
Rain Forest
Sweet Home Farm
Yogi Tea

14012 **Yogurtland Franchising Inc**
17801 Cartwright Rd
Irvine, CA 92614-6216
949-265-8000
Fax: 949-265-8000 www.yogurt-land.com
Yogurt
CEO: Phillip Chang
phillip.chang@yogurt-land.com
Number Employees: 20-49

14013 **(HQ)Yohay Baking Co**
146 Albany Ave
Lindenhurst, NY 11757-3628
631-225-0300
Fax: 631-225-4277
Processor, importer and exporter of wafer rolls, specialty cookies, biscotti, and fudge mix, kosher and all natural products. Retail packaging available
Owner: Michael Soloman
solomanyohay@aol.com
Number Employees: 20-49
Type of Packaging: Consumer, Food Service, Private Label, Bulk
Brands:
Fudge Gourmet
Gourmet Cookie Place
Sweetheart Fudge

14014 **Yokohl Packing Co**
125 S Mount Vernon Ave
Lindsay, CA 93247-2442
559-562-1327
Fax: 559-562-6732
Packer of oranges
Manager: Henry Howison
henry@yokohlvalley.com
Sales: Tim Bentley
Estimated Sales: $10-20 Million
Number Employees: 50-99
Type of Packaging: Bulk

14015 **Yonkers Brewing Company LLC**
92 Main St.
Yonkers, NY 10701
914-226-8327
info@yonkersbrewing.com
www.yonkersbrewing.com
Craft lagers, IPAs and ales
Co-Founder: John Rubbo
Co-Founder: Nick Califano
Number of Brands: 1
Number of Products: 12
Type of Packaging: Consumer, Private Label
Brands:
Yonkers Brewing Company

14016 **Yoo-Hoo Chocolate Beverage Company**
600 Commercial Ave
Carlstadt, NJ 7072
201-933-0070
Fax: 201-933-5360
consumer.relations@brandspeoplelove.com
www.drinkyoo-hoo.com
Chocolate drinks
President: Brian O'Byrne
Marketing Manager: Christine Karumpe
Contact: Brian O''Byrne
brian.obyrne@orangina.com
Plant Manager: Bill Pedeto

Estimated Sales: $16,500,000
Number Employees: 20-49
Parent Co: Yoo-Hoo Chocolate Beverage
Type of Packaging: Consumer

14017 Yoplait
5825 Explorer Drive
Mississauga, ON L4W 5P6
Canada
800-516-7780
www.yoplait.ca
Dairy products including regular and drinkable yogurt
Chairman/CEO: Jeffrey Harmening
CFO: Kofi Bruce
Chief Marketing Officer: Ivan Pollard
Number Employees: 4000
Parent Co: General Mills
Type of Packaging: Consumer
Brands:
Creamy
Minigo
Source
Tubes
Yop

14018 York Mountain Winery
7505 York Mountain Road
Templeton, CA 93465
805-237-7575
hreed@martinweyrich.com
Red and white wine, dry sherry, champagne and salad dressing
Owner: David Weyrich
Manager: Suzanne Redberg
Wine Maker: Steve Goldman
Estimated Sales: $920000
Number Employees: 5-9
Square Footage: 12000
Type of Packaging: Consumer
Brands:
Suzanne's Salad Splash
York Mountain

14019 Yorktown Baking Company
1500 Front St Ste 7
Yorktown Heights, NY 10598
914-245-9319
Fax: 914-243-7138 800-235-3961
Fresh and frozen batter including muffin, scone and cookie. Prepared flour mixes and doughs
Owner: Emil Gold
Estimated Sales: $2,600,000
Number Employees: 20-49
Type of Packaging: Consumer, Food Service
Brands:
Yorktown Baking Company

14020 Yoshida Food Products Co
8338 NE Alderwood Rd
Suite A
Portland, OR 97220-6809
503-284-1114
Fax: 503-284-0004 800-653-1114
info@yfintl.com www.yfintl.com
Non MSG, nonfat and cholesterol-free sauces, marinades, drippings and coatings
President: Matt Guthrie
CFO: Tim Sether
CEO: Junki Yoshida
Quality Control: John Hunter
VP Sales/Marketing: John Moran
Sales Director: Andy Moberg
Public Relations: Marti Lucich
Operations Manager: Eric Rinearson
Production Manager: Frank Heuschkel
Purchasing Manager: Ken Hamilton
Estimated Sales: $8 Million
Number Employees: 5-9
Square Footage: 260000
Parent Co: Heinz
Type of Packaging: Consumer, Food Service, Private Label, Bulk
Brands:
Benihana
Yoshida Foods International

14021 Yost Candy Co Inc
51 S Cochran St
Dalton, OH 44618-9602
330-828-2777
Fax: 330-828-8296 800-750-1976
info@yostcandy.com
Processor and exporter of lollypops and Halloween candy
President: Earl Yost
Vice President: Joe Yost
Sales Director: Earl Yost
Estimated Sales: $2000000
Number Employees: 10-19
Type of Packaging: Consumer, Private Label, Bulk
Brands:
Kiddi Pops
Licklers
Lil Kiddies

14022 Young Pecan
2455 Entrada Del Sol
Las Cruces, NM 88001
575-524-4321
Fax: 575-525-3432
Bagged and boxed pecans
Manager: Paul Koenig
Contact: Michael Cabezas
mcabezas@youngpecan.com
Purchasing Agent: Malcolm Burdett
Estimated Sales: $2.5-5 Million
Number Employees: 50-99
Parent Co: Young Pecan Company
Type of Packaging: Bulk

14023 (HQ)Young Pecan, Inc.
2005 Babar Ln
Florence, SC 29501
800-729-6003
www.youngplantations.com
Pecans
President & CEO: James Swink
Executive Vice President: Helen Watts
Estimated Sales: $75-99 Million
Number Employees: 183
Number of Brands: 3
Square Footage: 150000
Parent Co: King Ranch
Type of Packaging: Consumer, Food Service, Bulk
Other Locations:
Las Cruces NM
Los Angeles CA
Salem OR
Seattle WA
Detroit MI
Mason OH
Elizabeth NJ
Milwaukee WI
Brands:
Goodbee
Indian Creek
Schermer

14024 (HQ)Young Winfield
1700 Brampton Street
Hamilton, ON L8H 3S1
Canada
905-893-2536
Fax: 416-544-4390 youngwinfield.com
Onion oil, cajun spice, salt and vinegar seasonings
President/Contact: Amirali Sunderji
Estimated Sales: $3-5 Million
Number Employees: 12
Square Footage: 108000
Type of Packaging: Consumer, Food Service, Private Label, Bulk
Brands:
Simply Spice
You Win

14025 Young's Bakery
67 S Gallatin Ave
Uniontown, PA 15401-3540
724-437-6361
Cakes and cookies
President: Dino Palermo
Marketing Director: Ruth Palermo
Estimated Sales: Less than $500,000
Number Employees: 1 to 4
Type of Packaging: Food Service

14026 Young's Jersey Dairy
6880 Springfield Xenia Rd
Yellow Springs, OH 45387-9610
937-325-0629
Fax: 937-325-3226 cows@youngsdairy.com
www.youngsdairy.com
Milk, ice cream, rolls, bread and donuts
President: Robert Young
robertyoung@youngsdairy.com
Human Resource Manager: Ben Young
Sales Manager: Cathy Young
Estimated Sales: Below $5 Million
Number Employees: 100-249

14027 Young's Lobster Pound
4 Mitchell Street
Belfast, ME 04915
207-338-1160
Fax: 207-338-3498
Processor, exporter and importer of fresh and frozen seafood including crabs, lobster, live and shucked clams and mussels, scallops and shrimp; wholesaler/distributor of fresh and frozen seafood
Owner: Raymond Young
Co-Owner: Claire Young
Manager; Owner: Raymond Young
Estimated Sales: $3-5 Million
Number Employees: 20-49
Square Footage: 10944
Type of Packaging: Consumer, Food Service
Brands:
Young's Lobster Pound

14028 Young's Noodle Factory Inc
1635 Liliha St
Honolulu, HI 96817-3154
808-533-6478
Fax: 808-536-6533
Noodles
President/Treasurer: Erwin Young
Owner: Gordon Kwan
Estimated Sales: $1,000,000
Number Employees: 10-19
Type of Packaging: Food Service

14029 Your Bar Factory
7232 Coroner
LaSalle, QC H8N 2W8
Canada
514-364-0258
Fax: 514-364-2229 888-366-0258
info@yourbarfactory.com
www.yourbarfactory.com
Manufacturer rice crispy squares, and manufacturer of private label bars for various customers profiles including major retailers and smaller accounts
Chief Executive Officer: Martin Joyal
VP: Daniel Levesque
R&D: Melanie Carre
Quality Control: Celine Boiniere
Sales: Myrian Ang
Vice President of Operations: Chantal Glenisson
Purchasing: Anilcar Parraga
Estimated Sales: $10 Million
Number Employees: 60
Square Footage: 30000
Parent Co: Rapid Snack
Type of Packaging: Food Service, Private Label, Bulk

14030 Yum Yum Donut Shops Inc
18830 San Jose Ave
City Of Industry, CA 91748-1325
626-964-1478
Fax: 626-912-2779 www.yumyumdonuts.com
Donut shop chain on U.S. West Coast.
President: Lincoln Watase
Number Employees: 10-19

14031 Yum Yum Potato Chips
40 Du Moulin
Warwick, QC J0A 1M0
Canada
819-358-3600
Fax: 819-358-3687 800-567-5792
yumyum@yum-yum.com www.yum-yum.com
Snack foods including potato chips, cheese sticks, onion rings and fries
President: Pierre Riverd
Director Production: Guy Trudel
Number Employees: 200
Type of Packaging: Consumer, Private Label

14032 Yvonne's Gourmet Sensations
404 Berkshire Way
Marlton, NJ 08053-4222
856-985-7677
Fax: 856-810-3798
Gourmet chocolate pretzels, chocolate cookies, chocolate grahams, chocolate waffles
Marketing Manager: Gary Greenberg
Brands:
Yvonne's Gourmet

14033 **Z Foods Inc.**
9537 Road 29 1/2
Madera, CA 93637
559-673-6368
Fax: 559-673-7508 888-400-1015
Dried fruits
President: Daniel Villanueva
VP: Nina Zoria
Number Employees: 2

14034 **Z Specialty Food, LLC**
1250 Harter Ave # A
Woodland, CA 95776-6106
530-668-0660
Fax: 530-668-6061 800-678-1226
tasty@zspecialtyfood.com
www.ZSpecialtyfood.com
Processor and exporter of gourmet chocolate and vanilla nut butters cremes, honey and honey products including fruit spreads and honey straws, bee pollen, bees wax, royal jelly and propolis; also, gift packs
Co-Owner: Ishai Zeldner
Square Footage: 16000
Type of Packaging: Consumer, Food Service, Private Label, Bulk
Brands:
Chocolate & Vanilla Nut Spread
Gourmet Butters & Spreads
Gourmet Honey Collection
Honey Fruit Spreads
Honey In the Straw
Moonshine Trading

14035 **Z&S Distributing**
7090 N. Marks Avenue
Suite 104
Fresno, CA 93711
559-432-1777
Fax: 559-432-2888 800-467-0788
Fruits and vegetables.
President: Martin Zaninovich
Estimated Sales: $7,700,000
Number Employees: 10-19
Type of Packaging: Consumer
Brands:
Just-Ripe

14036 **Z-Trim Holdings, Inc**
1101 Campus Drive
Mundelein, IL 60060
847-549-6002
Fax: 847-549-6028 customerservice@ztrim.com
Ingredients
Sales Director: Rick Harris
VP Sales/Applications: Lynda Carroll
Applications Project Manager: Aili Young
Research Chef: Erin Ryan

14037 **Zabiha Halal Meat Processors**
1715 Cortland Ct
Addison, IL 60101
630-620-5000
Fax: 630-620-5013 info@fatimabrand.com
www.fatimabrand.com
Meats, poultry, and seafood
Co-Founder: Mohammed Yousuf Khan
Co-Founder: Laila Khan
Team Member: Sajid Khan
Year Founded: 1987
Number of Brands: 1
Brands:
Fatima

14038 **Zaca Mesa Winery**
6905 Foxen Canyon Rd
Los Olivos, CA 93441
805-688-9339
Fax: 805-688-8796 800-350-7972
info@zacamesa.com www.zacamesa.com
Wines
President/CEO: Brook Williams
CFO: Susan English
susan@zacamesa.com
VP Sales/Marketing: Jim Fiolek
Estimated Sales: $6.3 Million
Number Employees: 20-49
Brands:
Roussanne
Syrah
Z Gris Dry Rose
Zcuvee

14039 **Zachary Confections Inc**
2130 W State Road 28
Frankfort, IN 46041-8771
765-659-4751
Fax: 765-659-1491 800-445-4222
www.zacharyconfections.com
Processor and exporter of confectionery products including caramels, boxed chocolates, marshmallows, mints, nougats and holiday novelties.
President: Jack Zachary
Number Employees: 250-499
Type of Packaging: Consumer, Private Label, Bulk
Brands:
Zachary

14040 **Zachys Wine**
39 Westmoreland Ave
White Plains, NY 10606
914-448-3026
Fax: 914-313-2350 866-647-9075
cs@zachys.com www.zachys.com
wines & spirits
President: Jeff Zacharia
Year Founded: 1944
Number Employees: 51-200

14041 **(HQ)Zacky Farms**
2020 S East Ave
Fresno, CA 93721-3328
559-443-2700
Fax: 559-443-2778 800-888-0235
zfsales@zacky.com
Turkey
President: Richard Zacky
richardzacky@zacky.com
Estimated Sales: $500,000-$1 Million
Number Employees: 500-999
Type of Packaging: Consumer
Brands:
Culinary Classic Breast of Turkey N
Culinary Classic Slices Breast of T

14042 **Zarda Bar-B-Q & Catering Company**
214 N 7 Highway
Blue Springs, MO 64014
816-229-9999
Fax: 816-224-3171 800-776-7427
info@zarda.com www.zarda.com
Barbecue sauce and baked beans
President: Michael Zarda
Quality Control Manager: Brian Packer
Marketing Director: Terry Hyer
Plant Manager: Ron Dorris
Estimated Sales: $10-24.9 Million
Number Employees: 50-99
Brands:
Zarda

14043 **(HQ)Zartic Inc**
438 Lavender Dr NW
Rome, GA 30165
706-234-3000
Fax: 706-291-6068 800-241-0516
www.pierrefoods.com
Full service beef, poultry, veal and pork further processor
President: Anthony Schroder
CEO: James Mauer
jmauer@zetec.com
CFO: Robert Miles
Vice President of Technical Services: Bill Theis
Vice President of Research and Developme: Bernie Panchot
Sales VP: Mike Wilson
Senior Vice President of Operations: Mike Zelkind
Purchasing Agent: Ken Fries
Number Employees: 50-99
Type of Packaging: Consumer
Other Locations:
Zartic Inc (Beef Division)
Cedartown GA
Zartic Inc (Poultry Division)
West Rome GA
Zartic Inc (Pork Division)
Hamilton AL
Brands:
Circle Z
Crispy Steaks
Fryz
Jim's Country Mill Sausage
Shurtenda
Spicy Wings
Vittles
Z-Bird
Zartic
Zartic Beef Bakeables
Zartic Chicken Bakeables
Zartic Chicken Fried Beef Steaks
Zartic Chicken Fryz Flavorz
Zartic Chicken Tenderloins
Zartic Circle Z Beef Burgers
Zartic Crispy Steaks
Zartic Homestyle Meatloaf
Zartic Honey Hugged Chicken
Zartic Pork Bakeables
Zartic Pork Sausage Sampler
Zartic Rockin' Roasted Chicken
Zartic Veal Entree Legends
Zartic Veal Specialties

14044 **Zayante Vineyards**
420 Old Mount Rd
Felton, CA 95018-9054
831-335-7992
Fax: 831-335-5770
Wines
Owner: Prashant Kanhere
pkanhere@zayantevineyards.com
Co-Owner: Marion Nolten
Co-Owner: Kathleen Starkey-Nolten
Vineyard Manager: Greg Nolten
Estimated Sales: Less Than $500,000
Number Employees: 1-4
Type of Packaging: Private Label
Brands:
Zayante

14045 **Zazi Baking Company**
1360 Industrial Ave
Petaluma, CA 94952-6521
707-778-1635
Fax: 707-778-6991
Biscotti and cookies
President: Celeste Longo
VP: Debby Dyar
Estimated Sales: $5-10 Million
Number Employees: 10-19
Square Footage: 24000
Type of Packaging: Food Service, Private Label, Bulk
Brands:
Cookie Brittle
Mrs. Little's
Running Rabbit
Spendido Nuggets
Splendido Biscotti
Zazi Organics

14046 **Zazubean**
1529 W 6th Ave
Vancouver, BC V6J 1R1
Canada
604-801-5488
info@zazubean.com
www.zazubean.com
Organic fair trade chocolate
Co-Founder: Tiziana Ienna
Co-Founder: Tara Gilbert
Year Founded: 2007
Number Employees: 2-9

14047 **Zd Wines**
8383 Silverado Trl
Napa, CA 94558-9436
707-963-5188
Fax: 707-963-2640 800-487-7757
info@zdwines.com www.zdwines.com
Processor and exporter of wines including chardonnay, pinot noir and cabernet sauvignon
President/Partner: Brett DeLeuze
CEO/Partner: Robert DeLeuze
CFO: Julie De Leuze
Marketing Coordinator: Elyse Chambers
VP Sales: Teresa d'Aurizio
Winemaker: Chris Pisani
Estimated Sales: $5-10 Million
Number Employees: 20-49
Number of Brands: 2
Number of Products: 8
Square Footage: 90928
Type of Packaging: Consumer, Food Service
Brands:
Abacus
Z.D. Wines

14048 **Zebra Technologies Corporation**
3 Overlook Point
Lincolnshire, IL 60069
847-634-6700
Fax: 847-913-8766 866-230-9494
www.zebra.com
Bar code equipment including printers, supplies and software for point-of-application labeling and performance thermal transferring.
Chief Executive Officer: Anders Gustafsson
Chief Financial Officer: Olivier Leonetti
Senior VP, Corporate Development: Michael Cho
Senior VP/General Counsel/Secretary: Cristen Kogl
Chief Marketing Officer: Jeff Schmitz
Senior VP, Global Sales: Joachim Heel
Year Founded: 1969
Estimated Sales: $3.7 Billion
Number Employees: 7,400
Square Footage: 167600
Brands:
Zebra
Zebra Value-Line
Zebra Xii

14049 **Zego Foods**
912 Cole St.
Suite 294
San Francisco, CA 94117
415-706-8094
info@zegofoods.com
www.zegofoods.com
Seed & fruit snack bars, protein, oats, and muesli
Founder/CEO: Colleen Kavanagh
COO: Brian Jansen
Customer Relations: Danielle Schnake
Year Founded: 2013

14050 **Zeigler's**
1513 N Broad St
Lansdale, PA 19446-1111
215-855-5161
Fax: 215-855-4548 customerservice@zeiglers.com
Apple cider, lemonades, teas, juices and spices.
General Manager: Art Balzereit
a.balzereit@zeiglers.com
Estimated Sales: $20-50 Million
Number Employees: 50-99
Number of Brands: 1
Square Footage: 60000
Parent Co: LiDestri Food & Beverage
Type of Packaging: Consumer, Food Service, Private Label, Bulk
Brands:
Zeigler's

14051 **Zelda's Sweet Shoppe**
4113 Main St
Skokie, IL 60076-2753
847-679-0033
Fax: 847-679-0030 888-449-3532
www.zkgourmet.com
Baked goods, cakes, cookies
Owner: Linda Neiman
linda@zeldas.net
Number Employees: 10-19

14052 **Zemas Madhouse Foods Inc.**
P.O. Box 823
Highland Park, IL 60035-0823
847-910-4512
Fax: 847-780-3178 zemasfoods.com
Gluten-free cookies and baking mixes.
President: Jill Motew
Marketing Manager: Tricia Goldfarb
Year Founded: 2010
Estimated Sales: Less than $500,000
Number Employees: 2
Type of Packaging: Private Label

14053 **(HQ)Zenobia Co**
5774 Mosholu Ave # B
Bronx, NY 10471-2200
347-843-8080
Fax: 718-548-2313 866-936-6242
Processor, importer and exporter of pistachios, cashews, pumpkin and sunflower seeds, organic dried fruits, etc
President: Kenneth Bobker
National Sales Manager: Donald DiMatteo
Estimated Sales: $5-10 Million
Number Employees: 1-4
Square Footage: 100000
Type of Packaging: Consumer, Food Service, Private Label, Bulk
Other Locations:
Zenobia Co.
Bronx NY
Brands:
Indian
Zenobia

14054 **Zentis Sweet Ovations**
1741 Tomlinson Rd
Philadelphia, PA 19116-3847
215-676-3900
Fax: 215-613-2115 800-223-7073
Processor and exporter of fruit preparations
CEO: Kevin Daugherty
Plant Manager: Corey Arrick
Number Employees: 100-249
Parent Co: Systems Bio-Industries

14055 **(HQ)Zephyr Hills**
6403 Harney Rd
Tampa, FL 33610-9349
813-630-5763
Fax: 813-620-6862 800-950-9398
www.zephyrhillswater.com
Coffee and bottled spring and distilled water
President: Kim Jefferies
Quality Control Manager: Winnie Louie
Marketing/Sales Development Manager: Monica Kelley
Number Employees: 20-49
Parent Co: Nestl, Waters North America
Type of Packaging: Consumer
Brands:
Deer Park
Zephyrhillis

14056 **Zephyrhills Bottled Water Company**
6403 Harney Rd
Tampa, FL 33610-9349
813-630-5763
Fax: 813 620 6862 800 950 9398
Bottled water
President: Kim Jeffery
Marketing Director: John Bryan
Sales Manager: Monica Kelley
Operations Manager: Eddie Edmunds
Estimated Sales: $.5-1 million
Number Employees: 1-4
Parent Co: Perrier Group of America
Type of Packaging: Private Label

14057 **Zerna Packing**
2231 Highway 100
Labadie, MO 63055-2000
636-742-4190
Meat; smoking and curing available
Owner: Carl Zerna Sr
Estimated Sales: $1-3 Million
Number Employees: 1-4
Type of Packaging: Consumer, Food Service

14058 **Zeroodle**
Richmond Hill, ON L4B 1C9
Canada
905-889-9880
help@zeroodle.com
zeroodle.com
Bean pasta

14059 **Zest Tea LLC**
1100 Wicomico St
Suite 321
Baltimore, MD 21230-2063
636-579-1809
zesttea.com
Tea
Co-Founder: James Fayal
Co-Founder: Rickey Ishida
Chief Marketing Officer: Karyn Vilbig
Year Founded: 2013
Estimated Sales: Less than $500,000
Number Employees: 1-4
Type of Packaging: Food Service, Private Label

14060 **Zesty Z: The Za'atar Company**
630 Flushing Ave
Brooklyn, NY 11206
917-740-5241
zesty-z.com
Mediterranean inspired spreads and condiments.
Co-Founder: Alexander Harik
Co-Founder: Lorraine Harik
Year Founded: 2016
Number Employees: 1-4
Type of Packaging: Private Label

14061 **Zevia**
10200 Culver Blvd
Culver City, CA 90232
310-202-7000
855-469-3842
sales@zevia.com www.zevia.com
Soda
Principal Director: Derek Newman
Chief Executive Officer: Paddy Spence
VP Sales: Jeff Taylor
Contact: Nancy Aguilar
nancy@zevia.com
Operations Manager: Michael Spain
Estimated Sales: $500,000-1 Million
Number Employees: 10-19

14062 **Zhena's Gypsy Tea**
6041 Triangle Dr
Commerce, CA 90040-3642
323-767-0300
Fax: 805-646-4262 800-448-0803
info@gypsytea.com
Teas
Contact: Jeanne Cloutier
cloutier@gypsytea.com
Number Employees: 5-9

14063 **Ziegenfelder Ice Cream Co**
87 18th St
Wheeling, WV 26003-3756
304-232-6360
Fax: 304-232-6368 800-322-3642
info@twinpops.com www.budgetsaver.com
Manufacturer of ice cream pops.
President and CEO: Lisa Allen
budgetsaver@twinpops.com
Estimated Sales: $20-50 Million
Number Employees: 100 249
Type of Packaging: Consumer

14064 **Zimmerman Cheese Inc**
6853 State Road 78
South Wayne, WI 53587-9724
608-968-3414
Fax: 608-968-3425 paul@zimmermancheese.com
Cheese
President: Mark Witke
zimcheese@pcmli.com
Marketing Director: Linda Moe
Estimated Sales: $10-24.9 000,000
Number Employees: 5-9

14065 **Zinda Products**
104 avenue Libert,
Candiac, QC J5R 6X1
Canada
450-635-6664
Fax: 450-635-6632 888-867-6664
info@zindaproducts.com zindaproducts.com
Couscous
President & Founder: Majid Jamal Eddine
Quality and R&D Director: Marouane Abdellaoui
Estimated Sales: $9,721,564
Number Employees: 40
Type of Packaging: Private Label

14066 **Zink & Triest Company**
150 Domorah Dr
Montgomeryville, PA 18936-9633
215-469-1950
Fax: 215-628-8651 800-537-5070
Suppliers of vanilla beans, vanillin and ethyl vanillin
President: Henry Todd
Sales Manager: Amie Briethaupt
Contact: Tammy Adgalane
tadgalane@amtodd.com
Estimated Sales: $10-20 Million
Number Employees: 10-19

14067 **Zippy's Inc**
1765 S King St
Honolulu, HI 96826-2190
808-973-0880
Fax: 808-973-0888 customerservice@zippys.com
www.zippys.com
Chili manufacturing
President: Paul Yokota
pyokota@foodsolutionshi.com
Number Employees: 1000-4999

Brands:
Napolean's Bakery
Zippys

14068 **Zitos Specialty Foods**
129 Cousley Drive SE
Port Charlotte, FL 33952-9149
941-625-0806
Gourmet and specialty foods
Owner: David Smith
Co-owner: Christine Smith
Brands:
Zitos

14069 **Zoe's Meats**
2445 Bluebelle Dr
Santa Rosa, CA 95403-2548
707-545-9637
Fax: 707-542-9601 sales@zoemeats.com
www.zoemeats.com
Cured meats; cheese; eggs; spices; jams; canned vegetables; pickles and pickled vegetables.
Founder/CEO: George Gravros
Co-Founder/Partner: Charlie Hertz
Year Founded: 2006
Type of Packaging: Food Service, Private Label
Brands:
Daphne's Creamery
Emmy's Pickles & Jams
Yioryo
Zoe'S Meats

14070 **Zoelsmann's Bakery & Deli**
912 E Abriendo Ave
Pueblo, CO 81004
719-543-0407
Fax: 719-543-4083
Bread, cakes, pies and hard and sweet rolls
Owner: Ron Petkosek
Estimated Sales: $500,000-$1 Million
Number Employees: 5-9
Type of Packaging: Consumer, Food Service, Bulk

14071 **Zone Perfect Nutrition Company**
625 Cleveland Ave
Columbus, OH 43215
614-624-7485
Fax: 614-624-9001 800-390-6690
ansupport@abbott.com www.zoneperfect.com
Nutrition products, bars, meals, drinks and supplements
Chairman and Chief Executive Officer: Miles D. White
EVP, Finance and Chief Financial Officer: Thomas C. Freyman
EVP, Corporate Development: Richard W. Ashley
SVP, Chief Marketing Officer: Paul K. Magill
EVP, Human Resources: Stephen R. Fussell
Number Employees: 1,000-4,999
Parent Co: Abbott Laboratories

14072 **Zotter Chocolates**
10120 Ne Pine Island Rd
Suite 302
Cape Coral, FL 33909
239-214-7883
schokolade@zotter.at
zotter.at
Chocolate
Founder: Josef Zotter
Manager: Ulrike Zotter
Year Founded: 1987
Estimated Sales: Less than $500,000
Number Employees: 5-9

14073 **Zoup! Fresh Soup Co LLC**
28290 Franklin Rd
Southfield, MI 48034-1659
248-663-1111
support@zoup.com
www.zoup.com
Soup
CEO: Christine Bessert
christine@zoupco.com
Number Employees: 10-19

14074 **Zuccaro Produce**
455 37th Avenue NE
Columbia Heights, MN 55421
612-333-1122
Fax: 612-333-7511 zp@zuccarosproduce.net
zuccarosproduce.site123.me
Provides fruit, produce, dry and canned goods, paper and plastic products, and cleaning supplies to restaurants, food trucks, concession stands, and homes.
Year Founded: 1937
Estimated Sales: $2.5-5 Million
Number Employees: 20-49

14075 **Zummo Meat Co**
3705 Saint James Blvd
Beaumont, TX 77705-1143
409-842-1810
Fax: 409-842-5491 zummo@zummo.com
zummomeat.com
Meats including sausage and boudin
Owner: Frank Zummo
VP: Greg Zummo
Estimated Sales: $5-10 Million
Number Employees: 50-99
Type of Packaging: Consumer
Brands:
Zummo

14076 **Zuni Foods**
13838 Jones Maltsberger Road
San Antonio, TX 78247-3904
210-481-3600
Fax: 210-481-3603 800-906-3876
Mild table salsa
Owner: John Warlow
Brands:
Zuni Fire Roasted Salsa
Zuni Zalsa Verde

14077 **Zurheide Ice Cream Company**
816 Michigan Avenue
Sheboygan, WI 53081-3438
920-458-4581
Ice cream, ice milk, sherbert and frozen yogurt
President: John Zurheide
VP Sales: Wendy Kohl
Contact: Ralph Allen
wally@moosetracks.com
Plant Manager: Nate Dehne
Estimated Sales: $2.5-5 Million
Number Employees: 10-19

14078 **Zweigle's Inc**
651 Plymouth Ave N
Rochester, NY 14608-1689
585-546-1740
Fax: 585-546-8721 info@zweigles.com
www.zweigles.com
Processor of meat including sausages, pork, beef, chicken, deli meats and hot dogs.
President: Julie Camardo-Steron
Director, Marketing & Sales: Steve Vacanti
Sales Manager: Jim Vacanti
Year Founded: 1880
Estimated Sales: $20-50 Million
Number Employees: 50-99
Number of Brands: 1
Square Footage: 38500
Type of Packaging: Consumer, Food Service, Private Label, Bulk
Brands:
Zweigle's

Numeric

A

B

C

E

F

G

H

I

K

M

N

O

P

S

T

U

V

W

X

Y

Z

African

Arabic

Argentinean

Asian

Brazilian

Cajun

Chinese

Colombian

Creole

Cuban

Czech

Dutch

English/Scottish/Welsh

European

French

German

Greek

Hawaiian

Hispanic

Hungarian

Indian-Pakistani

Indonesian

Irish

Israeli/Jewish

Italian

Japanese

Korean

Kosher

Latin American

Lebanese

Mediterranean

Mexican

Middle Eastern

Moroccan

Polish

Portuguese

Puerto Rican

Romanian

Russian-Ukrainian

Scandinavian

Spanish

Swiss

Thai

Turkish

West Indian

Alabama

Alaska

Alberta

Arizona

Arkansas

British Columbia

California

Colorado

Connecticut

Delaware

District of Columbia

Florida

Georgia

Hawaii

Idaho

Illinois

Indiana

Iowa

Kansas

Kentucky

Louisiana

Maine

Manitoba

Maryland

Massachusetts

Michigan

Minnesota

Mississippi

Missouri

Montana

Nebraska

Nevada

New Brunswick

New Hampshire

New Jersey

New Mexico

New York

Newfoundland and Labrador

North Carolina

North Dakota

Nova Scotia

Ohio

Oklahoma

Ontario

Oregon

Pennsylvania

Prince Edward Island

Puerto Rico

Quebec

Rhode Island

Saskatchewan

South Carolina

South Dakota

Tennessee

Texas

Utah

Vermont

Virginia

Washington

West Virginia

Wisconsin

Wyoming

Numeric

A

B

C

D

L

M

S

T

U

V

W

X

Y

Z

2020 Title List

Visit www.GreyHouse.com for Product Information, Table of Contents, and Sample Pages.

Opinions Throughout History

Opinions Throughout History: Drug Use & Abuse
Opinions Throughout History: Gender: Roles & Rights
Opinions Throughout History: Globalization
Opinions Throughout History: Guns in America
Opinions Throughout History: Immigration
Opinions Throughout History: National Security vs. Civil & Privacy Rights
Opinions Throughout History: Presidential Authority
Opinions Throughout History: Robotics & Artificial Intelligence
Opinions Throughout History: Social Media Issues
Opinions Throughout History: The Death Penalty
Opinions Throughout History: The Environment
Opinions Throughout History: Voters' Rights

This is Who We Were

This is Who We Were: Colonial America (1492-1775)
This is Who We Were: 1880-1899
This is Who We Were: In the 1900s
This is Who We Were: In the 1910s
This is Who We Were: In the 1920s
This is Who We Were: A Companion to the 1940 Census
This is Who We Were: In the 1940s (1940-1949)
This is Who We Were: In the 1950s
This is Who We Were: In the 1960s
This is Who We Were: In the 1970s
This is Who We Were: In the 1980s
This is Who We Were: In the 1990s
This is Who We Were: In the 2000s
This is Who We Were: In the 2010s

Working Americans

Working Americans, 1880-2011 - Vol. 1 The Working Class
Working Americans, 1880-1999 - Vol. 2: The Middle Class
Working Americans, 1880-1999 - Vol. 3: The Upper Class
Working Americans, 1880-1999 - Vol. 4: Children
Working Americans, 1880-2015 - Vol. 5: At War
Working Americans, 1880-2015 - Vol. 6: Working Women
Working Americans, 1880-2016 - Vol. 7: Social Movements
Working Americans, 1880-2017 - Vol. 8: Immigrants
Working Americans, 1770-1869 - Vol. 9: From the Revolutionary War to the Civil War
Working Americans, 1880-2009 - Vol. 10: Sports & Recreation
Working Americans, 1880-2009 - Vol. 11: Inventors & Entrepreneurs
Working Americans, 1880-2011 - Vol. 12: Our History Through Music
Working Americans, 1880-2011 - Vol. 13: Education & Educators
Working Americans, 1880-2016 - Vol. 14: African Americans
Working Americans, 1880-2018: Vol. 15: Politics & Politicians
Working Americans, 1880-2020: Vol. 16: Farming & Ranching

Education

Complete Learning Disabilities Resource Guide
Educators Resource Guide
The Comparative Guide to Elem. & Secondary Schools
Charter School Movement
Special Education: A Reference Book for Policy & Curriculum Development

General Reference

African Biographical Dictionary
American Environmental Leaders
America's College Museums
Constitutional Amendments
Encyclopedia of African-American Writing
Encyclopedia of Historical Warrior Peoples & Modern Fighting Groups
Encyclopedia of Invasions & Conquests
Encyclopedia of Prisoners of War & Internment
Encyclopedia of Religion & the Law in America
Encyclopedia of Rural America
Encyclopedia of the Continental Congresses
Encyclopedia of the United States Cabinet
Encyclopedia of War Journalism
The Environmental Debate
The Evolution Wars: A Guide to the Debates
Financial Literacy Starter Kit
From Suffrage to the Senate
The Gun Debate: An Encyclopedia of Gun Rights & Gun Control in the US
History of Canada
Human Rights and the United States
Political Corruption in America
Privacy Rights in the Digital Age
Religious Right and American Politics
Speakers of the House of Representatives
The Value of a Dollar 1600-1865 Colonial to Civil War
The Value of a Dollar 1860-2019
US Land & Natural Resources Policy
World Cultural Leaders of the 20th Century

Business Information

Business Information Resources
The Complete Broadcasting Industry Guide: Television, Radio, Cable & Streaming
Directory of Mail Order Catalogs
Environmental Resource Handbook
Food & Beverage Market Place
The Grey House Homeland Security Resources
The Grey House Performing Arts Industry Guide
Guide to Healthcare Group Purchasing Organizations
Guide to U.S. HMOs and PPOs
Guide to Venture Capital & Private Equity Firms
Hudson's Washington News Media Contacts Guide
New York State Directory
Sports Market Place

Consumer Health

Comparative Guide to American Hospitals
Complete Mental Health Resource Guide
Complete Resource Guide for Pediatric Disorders
Complete Resource Guide for People with Chronic Illness
Complete Resource Guide for People with Disabilities
Dementia Handbook & Resource Guide
Older Americans Information Resource

SALEM PRESS

2020 Title List

SALEM PRESS

Visit www.SalemPress.com for Product Information, Table of Contents, and Sample Pages.

Critical Insights

Critical Insights: A Midsummer Night's Dream
Critical Insights: A Portrait of the Artist as a Young Man
Critical Insights: A Streetcar Named Desire
Critical Insights: Abraham Lincoln
Critical Insights: Absalom, Absalom!
Critical Insights: Adventures of Huckleberry Finn
Critical Insights: Aeneid
Critical Insights: Albert Camus
Critical Insights: Alice Munro
Critical Insights: Alice Walker
Critical Insights: All Quiet on the Western Front
Critical Insights: American Creative Non-Fiction
Critical Insights: American Multicultural Identity
Critical Insights: American Road Literature
Critical Insights: American Short Story
Critical Insights: American Sports Fiction
Critical Insights: American Writers in Exile
Critical Insights: Ancient Greek Literature
Critical Insights: Animal Farm
Critical Insights: Arthur Miller
Critical Insights: Barbara Kingsolver
Critical Insights: Beloved
Critical Insights: Benjamin Franklin
Critical Insights: Billy Budd, Sailor
Critical Insights: Brave New World
Critical Insights: Censored & Banned Literature
Critical Insights: Charles Dickens
Critical Insights: Civil Rights Literature, Past & Present
Critical Insights: Coming of Age
Critical Insights: Conspiracies
Critical Insights: Contemporary Canadian Fiction
Critical Insights: Contemporary Immigrant Short Fiction
Critical Insights: Contemporary Latin American Fiction
Critical Insights: Contemporary Speculative Fiction
Critical Insights: Cormac McCarthy
Critical Insights: Crime and Detective Fiction
Critical Insights: Crisis of Faith
Critical Insights: Cultural Encounters
Critical Insights: David Foster Wallace
Critical Insights: Death of a Salesman
Critical Insights: Dracula
Critical Insights: Dystopia
Critical Insights: Edith Wharton
Critical Insights: Emily Dickinson
Critical Insights: Ernest Hemingway
Critical Insights: Eugene O'Neill
Critical Insights: F. Scott Fitzgerald
Critical Insights: Fahrenheit 451
Critical Insights: Family
Critical Insights: Feminism
Critical Insights: Flannery O'Connor
Critical Insights: Flash Fiction
Critical Insights: Frederick Douglass
Critical Insights: Gabriel Garcia Marquez
Critical Insights: Gender, Sex and Sexuality
Critical Insights: Geoffrey Chaucer
Critical Insights: George Eliot
Critical Insights: George Orwell
Critical Insights: Good & Evil
Critical Insights: Great Expectations
Critical Insights: Greed
Critical Insights: Gustave Flaubert
Critical Insights: Gwendolyn Brooks
Critical Insights: Hamlet
Critical Insights: Harlan Ellison
Critical Insights: Harlem Renaissance
Critical Insights: Harry Potter Series
Critical Insights: Heart of Darkness
Critical Insights: Henry James
Critical Insights: Herman Melville
Critical Insights: Historical Fiction
Critical Insights: Holocaust Literature
Critical Insights: Horton Foote
Critical Insights: I Know Why the Caged Bird Sings
Critical Insights: In Cold Blood
Critical Insights: Inequality
Critical Insights: Invisible Man
Critical Insights: Isaac Asimov
Critical Insights: Isabel Allende
Critical Insights: Jack London
Critical Insights: James Baldwin
Critical Insights: James Joyce
Critical Insights: James McBride
Critical Insights: Jane Austen
Critical Insights: Jane Eyre
Critical Insights: John Cheever
Critical Insights: John Steinbeck
Critical Insights: John Updike
Critical Insights: Joseph Conrad
Critical Insights: King Lear
Critical Insights: Kurt Vonnegut
Critical Insights: Langston Hughes
Critical Insights: Leo Tolstoy
Critical Insights: LGBTQ Literature
Critical Insights: Life of Pi
Critical Insights: Lillian Hellman
Critical Insights: Literature of Protest
Critical Insights: Little Women
Critical Insights: Lolita
Critical Insights: Lord of the Flies
Critical Insights: Louisa May Alcott
Critical Insights: Louise Erdrich
Critical Insights: Macbeth
Critical Insights: Magical Realism
Critical Insights: Malcolm X
Critical Insights: Margaret Atwood
Critical Insights: Mario Vargas Llosa
Critical Insights: Mark Twain
Critical Insights: Martin Luther King, Jr.
Critical Insights: Mary Shelley
Critical Insights: Maya Angelou
Critical Insights: Midnight's Children
Critical Insights: Midwestern Literature
Critical Insights: Moby-Dick
Critical Insights: Modern Japanese Literature
Critical Insights: Mrs. Dalloway
Critical Insights: Nathaniel Hawthorne
Critical Insights: Nature & the Environment
Critical Insights: Neil Gaiman
Critical Insights: Nineteen Eighty-Four
Critical Insights: Of Mice and Men
Critical Insights: One Flew Over the Cuckoo's Nest
Critical Insights: One Hundred Years of Solitude
Critical Insights: Oscar Wilde
Critical Insights: Paradise Lost
Critical Insights: Paranoia, Fear & Alienation
Critical Insights: Philip Roth
Critical Insights: Political Fiction
Critical Insights: Post-Colonial Literature
Critical Insights: Pride and Prejudice
Critical Insights: Pulp Fiction of the '20s and '30s
Critical Insights: Ray Bradbury
Critical Insights: Raymond Carver
Critical Insights: Rebellion
Critical Insights: Richard Wright
Critical Insights: Robert A. Heinlein
Critical Insights: Robert Frost
Critical Insights: Roberto Bolano
Critical Insights: Romeo and Juliet
Critical Insights: Russia's Golden Age
Critical Insights: Salman Rushdie
Critical Insights: Satire
Critical Insights: Saul Bellow
Critical Insights: Sherman Alexie
Critical Insights: Short Fiction of Flannery O'Connor
Critical Insights: Slaughterhouse-Five
Critical Insights: Social Justice and American Literature
Critical Insights: Southern Gothic Literature
Critical Insights: Southwestern Literature
Critical Insights: Stephen King
Critical Insights: Survival
Critical Insights: Sylvia Plath
Critical Insights: T. S. Eliot

SALEM PRESS

2020 Title List

SALEM PRESS

Visit www.SalemPress.com for Product Information, Table of Contents, and Sample Pages.

Critical Insights (continued)

Critical Insights: Technology & Humanity
Critical Insights: Tennessee Williams
Critical Insights: The American Comic Book
Critical Insights: The American Dream
Critical Insights: The American Thriller
Critical Insights: The Awakening
Critical Insights: The Bell Jar
Critical Insights: The Canterbury Tales
Critical Insights: The Catcher in the Rye
Critical Insights: The Crucible
Critical Insights: The Diary of a Young Girl
Critical Insights: The Fantastic
Critical Insights: The Grapes of Wrath
Critical Insights: The Graphic Novel
Critical Insights: The Great Gatsby
Critical Insights: The Handmaid's Tale
Critical Insights: The Hero's Quest
Critical Insights: The Hobbit
Critical Insights: The House on Mango Street
Critical Insights: The Hunger Games Trilogy
Critical Insights: The Immigrant Experience
Critical Insights: The Inferno
Critical Insights: The Joy Luck Club
Critical Insights: The Kite Runner
Critical Insights: The Metamorphosis
Critical Insights: The Odyssey
Critical Insights: The Outsiders
Critical Insights: The Pearl
Critical Insights: The Poetry of Baudelaire
Critical Insights: The Poetry of Edgar Allan Poe
Critical Insights: The Red Badge of Courage
Critical Insights: The Scarlet Letter
Critical Insights: The Slave Narrative
Critical Insights: The Sound and the Fury
Critical Insights: The Sun Also Rises
Critical Insights: The Tales of Edgar Allan Poe
Critical Insights: The Woman Warrior
Critical Insights: Things Fall Apart
Critical Insights: Thomas Jefferson
Critical Insights: Tim O'Brien
Critical Insights: To Kill a Mockingbird
Critical Insights: Toni Morrison
Critical Insights: Violence in Literature
Critical Insights: Virginia Woolf & 20th Century Women Writers
Critical Insights: Walt Whitman
Critical Insights: War
Critical Insights: War and Peace
Critical Insights: Willa Cather
Critical Insights: William Faulkner
Critical Insights: Zora Neale Hurston
Critical Insights: Film - Alfred Hitchcock
Critical Insights: Film - Bonnie & Clyde
Critical Insights: Film - Casablanca
Critical Insights: Film - Stanley Kubrick

Literature

Critical Approaches to Literature: Feminist
Critical Approaches to Literature: Moral
Critical Approaches to Literature: Multicultural
Critical Approaches to Literature: Psychological
Critical Survey of American Literature
Critical Survey of Drama
Critical Survey of Graphic Novels: Heroes & Superheroes
Critical Survey of Graphic Novels: History, Theme, and Technique
Critical Survey of Graphic Novels: Independents and Underground Classics
Critical Survey of Graphic Novels: Manga
Critical Survey of Long Fiction
Critical Survey of Mystery and Detective Fiction
Critical Survey of Mythology & Folklore: Gods & Goddesses
Critical Survey of Mythology & Folklore: Heroes and Heroines
Critical Survey of Mythology & Folklore: Love, Sexuality, and Desire
Critical Survey of Mythology & Folklore: World Mythology
Critical Survey of Poetry
Critical Survey of Science Fiction & Fantasy Literature
Critical Survey of Shakespeare's Plays
Critical Survey of Shakespeare's Sonnets
Critical Survey of Short Fiction
Critical Survey of World Literature
Critical Survey of Young Adult Literature
Cyclopedia of Literary Characters
Cyclopedia of Literary Places
Introduction to Literary Context: American Poetry of the 20th Century
Introduction to Literary Context: American Post-Modernist Novels
Introduction to Literary Context: American Short Fiction
Introduction to Literary Context: English Literature
Introduction to Literary Context: Plays
Introduction to Literary Context: World Literature
Magill's Literary Annual
Masterplots
Masterplots, 2010-2018 Supplement
Notable African American Writers
Notable American Women Writers
Novels into Film: Adaptations & Interpretation
Recommended Reading: 600 Classics Reviewed

The Decades

The Sixties in America
The Fifties in America
The Seventies in America
The Eighties in America
The Nineties in America
The Forties in America
The Thirties in America
The Twenties in America
The 2000s in America
The 1910s in America

SALEM PRESS

2020 Title List

SALEM PRESS

Visit www.SalemPress.com for Product Information, Table of Contents, and Sample Pages.

Defining Documents in American History

Defining Documents: American West
Defining Documents: Business Ethics
Defining Documents: Capital Punishment
Defining Documents: Civil Rights
Defining Documents: Civil War
Defining Documents: Dissent & Protest
Defining Documents: Drug Policy
Defining Documents: Environment & Conservation
Defining Documents: Espionage & Intrigue
Defining Documents: Exploration and Colonial America
Defining Documents: Immigration & Immigrant Communities
Defining Documents: LGBTQ+
Defining Documents: Manifest Destiny and the New Nation
Defining Documents: Mental Health
Defining Documents: Native Americans
Defining Documents: Political Campaigns, Candidates & Discourse
Defining Documents: Postwar 1940s
Defining Documents: Prison Reform
Defining Documents: Secrets, Leaks & Scandals
Defining Documents: Slavery
Defining Documents: Supreme Court Decisions
Defining Documents: The 1900s
Defining Documents: The 1910s
Defining Documents: The 1920s
Defining Documents: The 1930s
Defining Documents: The 1950s
Defining Documents: The 1960s
Defining Documents: The 1970s
Defining Documents: The American Revolution
Defining Documents: The Cold War
Defining Documents: The Emergence of Modern America
Defining Documents: The Free Press
Defining Documents: The Gun Debate
Defining Documents: The Legacy of 9/11
Defining Documents: Reconstruction Era
Defining Documents: Vietnam War
Defining Documents: U.S. Involvement in the Middle East
Defining Documents: World War I
Defining Documents: World War II

Defining Documents in World History

Defining Documents: Asia
Defining Documents: Nationalism & Populism
Defining Documents: Renaissance & Early Modern Era
Defining Documents: The 17th Century
Defining Documents: The 18th Century
Defining Documents: The 19th Century
Defining Documents: The 20th Century (1900-1950)
Defining Documents: The Ancient World
Defining Documents: The Middle Ages
Defining Documents: The Middle East
Defining Documents: Women's Rights

Great Events from History

Great Events from History: The Ancient World
Great Events from History: The Middle Ages
Great Events from History: The Renaissance & Early Modern Era
Great Events from History: The 17th Century
Great Events from History: The 18th Century
Great Events from History: The 19th Century
Great Events from History: The 20th Century, 1901-1940
Great Events from History: The 20th Century, 1941-1970
Great Events from History: The 20th Century, 1971-2000
Great Events from History: Modern Scandals
Great Events from History: African American History
Great Events from History: The 21st Century, 2000-2016
Great Events from History: LGBTQ Events
Great Events from History: Human Rights

Great Lives from History

Computer Technology Innovators
Fashion Innovators
Great Athletes
Great Athletes of the Twenty-First Century
Great Lives from History: African Americans
Great Lives from History: American Heroes
Great Lives from History: American Women
Great Lives from History: Asian and Pacific Islander Americans
Great Lives from History: Inventors & Inventions
Great Lives from History: Jewish Americans
Great Lives from History: Latinos
Great Lives from History: Scientists and Science
Great Lives from History: The 17th Century
Great Lives from History: The 18th Century
Great Lives from History: The 19th Century
Great Lives from History: The 20th Century
Great Lives from History: The 21st Century, 2000-2017
Great Lives from History: The Ancient World
Great Lives from History: The Incredibly Wealthy
Great Lives from History: The Middle Ages
Great Lives from History: The Renaissance & Early Modern Era
Human Rights Innovators
Internet Innovators
Music Innovators
Musicians and Composers of the 20th Century
World Political Innovators

History & Government

American First Ladies
American Presidents
Civil Rights Movements: Past & Present
The 50 States
The Ancient World: Extraordinary People in Extraordinary Societies
The Bill of Rights
The Criminal Justice System
The U.S. Supreme Court

SALEM PRESS

2020 Title List

SALEM PRESS

Visit www.SalemPress.com for Product Information, Table of Contents, and Sample Pages.

Social Sciences

Countries, Peoples and Cultures
Countries: Their Wars & Conflicts: A World Survey
Education Today: Issues, Policies & Practices
Encyclopedia of American Immigration
Ethics: Questions & Morality of Human Actions
Issues in U.S. Immigration
Principles of Sociology: Group Relationships & Behavior
Principles of Sociology: Personal Relationships & Behavior
Principles of Sociology: Societal Issues & Behavior
Racial & Ethnic Relations in America
World Geography

Science

Ancient Creatures
Applied Science
Applied Science: Engineering & Mathematics
Applied Science: Science & Medicine
Applied Science: Technology
Biomes and Ecosystems
Earth Science: Earth Materials and Resources
Earth Science: Earth's Surface and History
Earth Science: Earth's Weather, Water and Atmosphere
Earth Science: Physics and Chemistry of the Earth
Encyclopedia of Climate Change
Encyclopedia of Energy
Encyclopedia of Environmental Issues
Encyclopedia of Global Resources
Encyclopedia of Mathematics and Society
Forensic Science
Notable Natural Disasters
The Solar System
USA in Space

Principles of Science

Principles of Anatomy
Principles of Astronomy
Principles of Biology
Principles of Biotechnology
Principles of Botany
Principles of Chemistry
Principles of Climatology
Principles of Communications Technology
Principles of Computer Science
Principles of Ecology
Principles of Mathematics
Principles of Modern Agriculture
Principles of Pharmacology
Principles of Physical Science
Principles of Physics
Principles of Programming & Coding
Principles of Robotics & Artificial Intelligence
Principles of Scientific Research
Principles of Sustainability
Principles of Zoology

Health

Addictions, Substance Abuse & Alcoholism
Adolescent Health & Wellness
Aging
Cancer
Community & Family Health Issues
Complementary & Alternative Medicine
Genetics and Inherited Conditions
Infectious Diseases and Conditions
Magill's Medical Guide
Nutrition
Principles of Health: Anxiety & Stress
Principles of Health: Diabetes
Principles of Health: Obesity
Principles of Health: Pain Management
Psychology & Behavioral Health
Women's Health

Careers

Careers in Building Construction
Careers in Business
Careers in Chemistry
Careers in Communications & Media
Careers in Education & Training
Careers in Environment & Conservation
Careers in Financial Services
Careers in Gaming
Careers in Green Energy
Careers in Healthcare
Careers in Hospitality & Tourism
Careers in Human Services
Careers in Information Technology
Careers in Law, Criminal Justice & Emergency Services
Careers in Manufacturing & Production
Careers in Nursing
Careers in Physics
Careers in Protective Services
Careers in Psychology & Behavioral Health
Careers in Public Administration
Careers in Sales, Insurance & Real Estate
Careers in Science & Engineering
Careers in Social Media
Careers in Sports & Fitness
Careers in Sports Medicine & Training
Careers in Technical Services & Equipment Repair
Careers in the Arts: Fine, Performing & Visual
Careers in Transportation
Careers in Writing & Editing
Careers Outdoors
Careers Overseas
Careers Working with Infants & Children

Business

Principles of Business: Accounting
Principles of Business: Economics
Principles of Business: Entrepreneurship
Principles of Business: Finance
Principles of Business: Globalization
Principles of Business: Leadership
Principles of Business: Management
Principles of Business: Marketing

2020 Title List

Visit www.HWWilsonInPrint.com for Product Information, Table of Contents, and Sample Pages.

The Reference Shelf

Affordable Housing
Aging in America
Alternative Facts, Post-Truth and the Information War
American Military Presence Overseas
Arab Spring
Artificial Intelligence
Business of Food, The
Campaign Trends & Election Law
Conspiracy Theories
Democracy Evolving
Dinosaurs
Embracing New Paradigms in Education
Faith & Science
Families - Traditional & New Structures
Future of U.S. Economic Relations: Mexico, Cuba, & Venezuela
Global Climate Change
Graphic Novels and Comic Books
Guns in America
Hate Crimes
Immigration
Immigration in the United States
Internet Abuses & Privacy Rights
Internet Law
Internet Safety
LGBTQ in the 21st Century
Marijuana Reform
National Debate Topic 2014/2015: The Ocean
National Debate Topic 2015/2016: Surveillance
National Debate Topic 2016/2017: US/China Relations
National Debate Topic 2017/2018: Education Reform
National Debate Topic 2018/2019: Immigration
National Debate Topic 2019/2020: Arms Sales
National Debate Topic 2020/2021: Criminal Justice Reform
New Frontiers in Space
The News and its Future
Paranormal, The
Politics of the Oceans
Pollution
Prescription Drug Abuse
Propaganda and Misinformation
Racial Tension in a Postracial Age
Reality Television
Representative American Speeches, Annual Edition
Rethinking Work
Revisiting Gender
Robotics
Russia
Social Networking
Social Services for the Poor
Space Exploration and Development
Sports in America
The American Dream
The Brain
The Digital Age
The South China Sea Conflict
The Supreme Court
The Transformation of American Cities
The Two Koreas
U.S. Infrastructure
Whistleblowers

Core Collections

Children's Core Collection
Fiction Core Collection
Graphic Novels Core Collection
Middle & Junior High School Core
Public Library Core Collection: Nonfiction
Senior High Core Collection
Young Adult Fiction Core Collection

Current Biography

Current Biography Cumulative Index 1946-2017
Current Biography Monthly Magazine
Current Biography Yearbook

Readers' Guide to Periodical Literature

Abridged Readers' Guide to Periodical Literature
Readers' Guide to Periodical Literature

Indexes

Index to Legal Periodicals & Books
Short Story Index
Book Review Digest

Sears List

Sears List of Subject Headings
Sears: Lista de Encabezamientos de Materia

History

Speeches of the American Presidents
American Reformers
American Game Changers: Invention, Innovation & Transformation

Facts About Series

Facts About American Immigration
Facts About China
Facts About the 20th Century
Facts About the Presidents
Facts About the World's Languages

Nobel Prize Winners

Nobel Prize Winners: 1901-1986
Nobel Prize Winners: 1987-1991
Nobel Prize Winners: 1992-1996
Nobel Prize Winners: 1997-2001
Nobel Prize Winners: 2002-2018

Famous First Facts

Famous First Facts
Famous First Facts About American Politics
Famous First Facts About Sports
Famous First Facts About the Environment
Famous First Facts: International Edition

American Book of Days

The American Book of Days
The International Book of Days

Grey House Publishing | Salem Press | H.W. Wilson | 4919 Route, 22 PO Box 56, Amenia NY 12501-0056